PATTERSON'S

# AMERICAN EDUCATION

## 2016 Edition

## VOLUME CXII

Editorial Staff

| | |
|---|---|
| Editor | Wayne Moody |
| Assistant Editor | Rita Ostdick |
| Assistant Editor | James Thiessen |



edi
EDUCATIONAL DIRECTORIES INC.

Educational Directories Inc.
PO Box 68097
Schaumburg IL 60168-0097
(847) 891-1250 or (800) 357-6183
www.ediusa.com



First edition published 1904. One Hundred Twelfth edition 2016

ISBN 978-0-9883500-6-9
ISSN 0079-0230
Library of Congress Catalog Card Number: 04-012953
Printed in the United States of America

# CONTENTS

# HOW TO USE THIS DIRECTORY

Patterson's AMERICAN EDUCATION (published annually since 1904) is THE standard directory to secondary schools and is the first in a series of school directories published by Educational Directories Inc. Patterson's ELEMENTARY EDUCATION (published annually since 1989) is identical in format to Patterson's AMERICAN EDUCATION but is a directory to elementary schools. The two volumes combined fulfill the need for a single, systematized, comprehensive directory to our nation's schools from kindergarten through post-graduate studies.

Patterson's AMERICAN EDUCATION contains 10,824 public school districts, 30,824 public secondary schools, 6,225 private and Catholic secondary schools and more than 7,000 post-secondary schools in an easy-to-use and consistent format. It is an invaluable resource for anyone involved in education or educational research. School registrars, guidance counselors, principals, superintendents, directors of admissions, financial aid officers, schools of education, public libraries, government agencies, armed forces, and business people find it a welcome replacement for the multitude of other directories required for national coverage of our nation's school systems with their variation in size, content, format and publishing date.

One of the primary objectives of this directory is to make available the latest, most comprehensive information about secondary and post-secondary schools in a condensed and easily accessible format. Its general organization is geographical. Entries are arranged alphabetically, by state, then by community (post office) and then by District and School name. Each state begins with a listing of the officials in its Department of Education followed by the head of the State Board of Education. If a state has intermediate superintendents (a level of superintendent between the state superintendent of schools and the superintendents who actually supervise the schools) they appear in a table preceding the community listings. Community listings follow and include the community name, county name, community population, district name, total district student enrollment, the superintendent's name, address, telephone, fax number and website where available followed by a listing of the district schools, showing their enrollment, grade range and the principal's name, address, telephone number and fax number. A district may be responsible for schools in more than one community. To achieve consistency, the district office is listed in the community in which it is located. A cross-reference is provided to and from the schools of the district located in other communities.

A short line may appear at the end of the listing of public secondary schools. This line separates the public secondary schools from the private and Catholic secondary schools and the post-secondary schools located in the community. Private and Catholic school listings include their enrollment, grade range and the principal's name, address, telephone number and fax number. Post-secondary school listings include their name, address and telephone number. Please refer to page vi, "Guide to Editorial Style," for an example of how these elements work together to provide an easy-to-use format.

## Schools Listed

Patterson's AMERICAN EDUCATION lists the following types of schools

- **Middle Schools** usually teach any combination of grades five through eight.
- **Junior High Schools** usually teach grades seven through nine.
- **Junior-Senior High Schools** usually teach any combination of grades five through eight and include nine through twelve.
- **High Schools** usually teach grades nine through twelve or ten through twelve.
- **K-12 Schools**
- **Vocational-Technical Schools**

The following are included:

- All graded state approved public secondary schools.
- All graded secondary schools belonging to the National Catholic Education Association.
- All graded, regionally accredited, private secondary schools.
- Private secondary schools belonging to the member associations of the Council of American Private Education.

Non graded, special education schools and other non-traditional secondary schools are not listed.

Patterson's ELEMENTARY EDUCATION lists Kindergarten Schools, Primary Schools, Elementary Schools, Middle Schools and K-12 Schools.

# ABBREVIATIONS

ALT . . . Alternative School
AVC. . . Area Vocational Center
AVTS . . Area Vocational Technical School
CCSD. . Community Consolidated School District
CDC . . Child Development Center
CESD. . Consolidated Elementary School District
CISD . . City Independent School District
CSD. . . City School District
CUSD. . Community Unit School District
ECC. . . Early Childhood Center
ECCSD . Elementary Community Consolidated School District
EHSD. . Elementary-High School District
ES . . . Elementary School
ESD. . . Elementary School District
EVD. . . Exempted Village District
HS . . . High School
HSD. . . High School District
IS. . . . Intermediate School
ISD . . . Independent School District
JESD . . Joint Elementary School District
JHS. . . Junior High School
JSD. . . Joint School District
JSHS . . Junior-Senior High School
JUESD . Joint Unified Elementary School District
JUHSD . Joint Unified High School District
JUNESD Joint Union Elementary School District
JUNHSD Joint Union High School District
JUSD . . Joint Unified School District
JVSD . . Joint Vocational School District
K . . . . Kindergarten
MS . . . Middle School
MSHS. . Middle School High School
PS . . . Primary School
RHSD. . Rural High School District
RISD . . Rural Independent School District
ROC . . Regional Occupational Center
ROP . . Regional Occupational Program
RSD. . . Reorganized School District
S . . . . School
SAD. . . School Administrative District
SC . . . School Corporation
SD . . . School District
SHS. . . Senior High School
SSD. . . Separate School District
UESD. . Unified Elementary School District
UFD. . . Union Free District
UHSD. . Unified High School District
UNESD . Union Elementary School District
UNHSD . Union High School District
UNSD. . Union School District
USD. . . Unified School District
Vo/Tech. Vocational/Technical

# GUIDE TO EDITORIAL STYLE

| | | |
|---|---|---|
| | **ALABAMA** [1] | **3** |
| [2] | Bessemer, Jefferson, Pop. 31,822 | |
| [3] | Bessemer CSD<br>PO Box 1230 35021<br>Ernest Nicholson, supt.<br>www.bessmeral.com | 4,900/K-12<br>205-481-9800<br>Fax 481-9859 [4] |
| | Bessemer Area Vo HS<br>50 High School Dr 35023<br>Theodore Jones, prin. | Vo/Tech<br>205-481-9842 |
| [5] | Davis MS<br>1224 Clarendon Ave 35020<br>Tolton Rosser, prin. | 700/7-8<br>205-481-9826 |
| | Lanier HS<br>100 High School Dr 35023<br>Michael Russell, prin. | 1,200/9-12<br>205-481-9836 |
| [6] | Jefferson County SD<br>Supt. — See Homewood | |
| | Gilmore/Bell Vo Ctr<br>4933 Bessemer Johns Rd 35023<br>J. Guyton, prin. | Vo/Tech<br>205-425-6172 |
| | Oak Grove S, 9180 Lock 17 Rd 35023<br>Jack Hazelrig, prin. | 1,000/K-12<br>205-491-1752 |
| [7] | Bessemer Academy<br>1705 4th Ave SW 35023<br>Glennwood Mathis, prin. | 300/K-12<br>205-428-6288 |
| [8] | Bessemer State Technical College<br>PO Box 308 35021 | Post-Sec.<br>205-428-6391 |

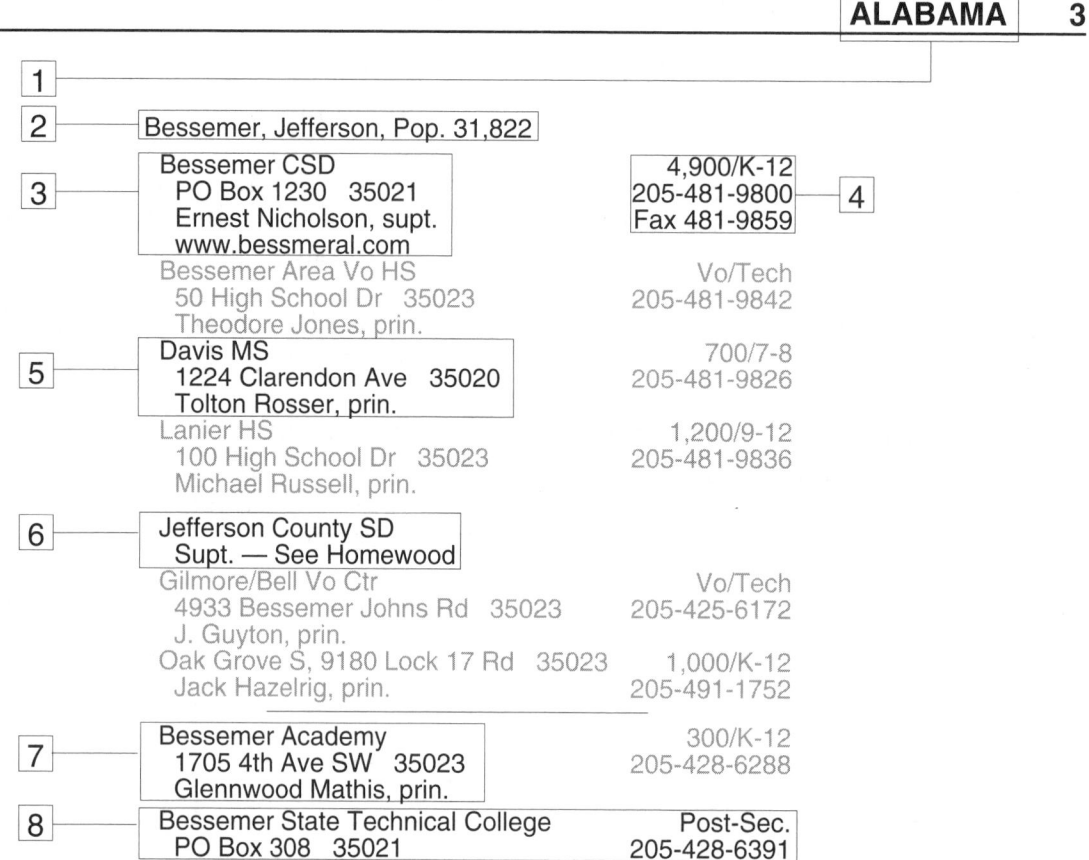

1. State.
2. City, county and city population.
3. Community school districts - school district name (refer to page v for abbreviations), address, superintendent's name and website (please enter as shown to access districts website).
4. Enrollment, grade range and phone number (fax number is included where available).
5. Community schools - school name, address and principal's name.
6. If the school district office is not located in this city, a cross-reference will show office location.
7. Private and Catholic secondary schools appear below a short line in the cities where they are located.
8. Post-secondary schools also appear below the line in the cities where they are located.

# SECONDARY SCHOOL COUNTS BY STATE

| State | Public | | | | | | Private | Catholic | Total |
|---|---|---|---|---|---|---|---|---|---|
| | Districts | 5-9 | 7-12 | 9-12 | 10-12 | K-12 | | | |
| Alabama | 137 | 232 | 71 | 213 | 7 | 71 | 105 | 10 | 846 |
| Alaska | 54 | 35 | 19 | 33 | 2 | 175 | 12 | 3 | 333 |
| Arizona | 112 | 186 | 13 | 190 | 1 | 5 | 45 | 13 | 565 |
| Arkansas | 233 | 150 | 121 | 107 | 36 | 1 | 40 | 6 | 694 |
| California | 468 | 1,223 | 63 | 1,004 | 8 | 11 | 481 | 125 | 3,383 |
| Colorado | 177 | 246 | 77 | 217 | 1 | 16 | 67 | 9 | 810 |
| Connecticut | 123 | 163 | 14 | 165 | 3 | 3 | 53 | 25 | 549 |
| Delaware | 16 | 33 | 2 | 24 | 0 | 0 | 22 | 10 | 107 |
| District Of Columbia | 1 | 13 | 2 | 13 | 0 | 0 | 12 | 8 | 49 |
| Florida | 67 | 505 | 47 | 392 | 10 | 13 | 405 | 37 | 1,476 |
| Georgia | 175 | 443 | 18 | 359 | 7 | 4 | 188 | 14 | 1,208 |
| Hawaii | 1 | 38 | 6 | 34 | 0 | 5 | 46 | 7 | 137 |
| Idaho | 109 | 92 | 37 | 77 | 7 | 16 | 23 | 1 | 362 |
| Illinois | 477 | 649 | 70 | 566 | 14 | 1 | 147 | 77 | 2,001 |
| Indiana | 290 | 295 | 106 | 240 | 7 | 3 | 79 | 25 | 1,045 |
| Iowa | 310 | 237 | 106 | 211 | 9 | 2 | 23 | 32 | 930 |
| Kansas | 281 | 208 | 114 | 208 | 1 | 3 | 28 | 16 | 859 |
| Kentucky | 168 | 211 | 31 | 192 | 6 | 8 | 48 | 29 | 693 |
| Louisiana | 70 | 198 | 62 | 159 | 5 | 57 | 81 | 52 | 684 |
| Maine | 107 | 85 | 19 | 86 | 2 | 10 | 29 | 4 | 342 |
| Maryland | 24 | 215 | 12 | 184 | 0 | 0 | 96 | 39 | 570 |
| Massachusetts | 226 | 273 | 54 | 224 | 1 | 1 | 107 | 52 | 938 |
| Michigan | 513 | 441 | 124 | 437 | 21 | 38 | 160 | 50 | 1,784 |
| Minnesota | 322 | 200 | 184 | 157 | 9 | 22 | 83 | 28 | 1,005 |
| Mississippi | 143 | 165 | 47 | 156 | 7 | 34 | 81 | 9 | 642 |
| Missouri | 446 | 324 | 199 | 295 | 9 | 5 | 65 | 44 | 1,387 |
| Montana | 160 | 209 | 3 | 164 | 0 | 1 | 13 | 9 | 559 |
| Nebraska | 245 | 110 | 160 | 101 | 1 | 5 | 16 | 28 | 666 |
| Nevada | 16 | 87 | 10 | 67 | 5 | 11 | 26 | 2 | 224 |
| New Hampshire | 77 | 80 | 4 | 74 | 0 | 2 | 41 | 8 | 286 |
| New Jersey | 267 | 373 | 36 | 305 | 9 | 0 | 106 | 61 | 1,157 |
| New Mexico | 89 | 129 | 28 | 99 | 5 | 0 | 36 | 3 | 389 |
| New York | 640 | 748 | 270 | 784 | 16 | 77 | 395 | 116 | 3,046 |
| North Carolina | 115 | 462 | 20 | 457 | 6 | 4 | 258 | 6 | 1,328 |
| North Dakota | 149 | 33 | 106 | 49 | 1 | 4 | 7 | 6 | 355 |
| Ohio | 610 | 543 | 164 | 554 | 11 | 9 | 112 | 81 | 2,084 |
| Oklahoma | 420 | 267 | 31 | 396 | 31 | 1 | 45 | 4 | 1,195 |
| Oregon | 166 | 191 | 40 | 170 | 2 | 15 | 63 | 11 | 658 |
| Pennsylvania | 496 | 446 | 164 | 403 | 23 | 1 | 226 | 84 | 1,843 |
| Rhode Island | 32 | 48 | 0 | 42 | 0 | 1 | 18 | 9 | 150 |
| South Carolina | 81 | 230 | 21 | 179 | 9 | 1 | 90 | 5 | 616 |
| South Dakota | 149 | 152 | 6 | 150 | 0 | 1 | 12 | 8 | 478 |
| Tennessee | 125 | 303 | 31 | 264 | 11 | 18 | 158 | 11 | 921 |
| Texas | 976 | 1,394 | 157 | 1,113 | 51 | 136 | 312 | 58 | 4,197 |
| Utah | 41 | 133 | 22 | 41 | 52 | 3 | 21 | 4 | 317 |
| Vermont | 51 | 28 | 22 | 26 | 0 | 11 | 23 | 2 | 163 |
| Virginia | 132 | 323 | 38 | 300 | 17 | 2 | 151 | 13 | 976 |
| Washington | 248 | 340 | 52 | 270 | 18 | 24 | 112 | 17 | 1,081 |
| West Virginia | 55 | 118 | 20 | 93 | 0 | 2 | 30 | 8 | 326 |
| Wisconsin | 376 | 331 | 79 | 322 | 5 | 12 | 95 | 52 | 1,272 |
| Wyoming | 48 | 57 | 8 | 53 | 2 | 7 | 2 | 0 | 177 |
| Total | 10,814 | 13,995 | 3,110 | 12,419 | 448 | 852 | 4,894 | 1,331 | 47,863 |

# SECONDARY SCHOOLS

# ALABAMA

## ALABAMA DEPARTMENT OF EDUCATION
**PO Box 302101, Montgomery 36130-2101**
**Telephone 334-242-9700**
**Fax 334-242-9708**
**Website http://www.alsde.edu**

State Superintendent of Education Dr. Thomas R. Bice

## ALABAMA BOARD OF EDUCATION
**PO Box 302101, Montgomery 36130-2101**

President Governor Robert Bentley

## PUBLIC, PRIVATE AND CATHOLIC SECONDARY SCHOOLS

**Abbeville, Henry, Pop. 2,658**
Henry County SD 2,800/PK-12
300 N Trawick St 36310 334-585-2206
Lesa Knowles, supt. Fax 585-2551
www.henrycountyboe.org
Abbeville JSHS 500/7-12
411 Graball Cutoff 36310 334-585-2065
Darryl Brooks, prin. Fax 585-6562
Other Schools – See Headland

Abbeville Christian Academy 200/K-12
PO Box 9 36310 334-585-5100
Ginger Webster, head sch Fax 585-5100

**Adamsville, Jefferson, Pop. 4,485**
Jefferson County SD
Supt. — See Birmingham
Bottenfield MS 800/6-8
400 Hillcrest Rd 35005 205-379-2550
Jonathan Shelby, prin. Fax 379-2553
Minor HS 1,000/9-12
2285 Minor Pkwy 35005 205-379-4750
Kalvin Eaton, prin. Fax 379-4795

**Addison, Winston, Pop. 756**
Winston County SD
Supt. — See Double Springs
Addison HS 300/7-12
PO Box 240 35540 256-747-2286
Micah Smothers, prin. Fax 747-6410

**Alabaster, Shelby, Pop. 29,944**
Alabaster CSD 6,200/K-12
1953 Municipal Way Ste 200 35007 205-663-8400
Dr. Wayne Vickers, supt. Fax 663-8408
www.alabasterschools.org
Thompson HS 1,800/9-12
100 Warrior Dr 35007 205-682-5700
Dr. Wesley Hester, prin. Fax 682-5705
Thompson MS 900/7-8
1509 Kent Dairy Rd 35007 205-682-5710
Neely Woodley, prin. Fax 682-5715

Kingwood Christian S 400/PK-12
1351 Royalty Dr 35007 205-663-3973
Ruth Gray, prin. Fax 663-7145

**Albertville, Marshall, Pop. 20,874**
Albertville CSD 4,100/PK-12
107 W Main St 35950 256-891-1183
Dr. Frederic Ayer, supt. Fax 891-6303
www.albertk12.org
Albertville HS 1,000/9-12
402 E Mccord Ave 35950 256-878-6580
Paul McAbee, prin. Fax 891-6305
Albertville MS 600/7-8
600 E Alabama Ave 35950 256-878-2341
Lance Kitchens, prin. Fax 891-6334

Marshall County SD
Supt. — See Guntersville
Asbury MSHS 400/6-12
1990 Asbury Rd 35951 256-878-4068
Amy Childress, prin. Fax 878-5233

Marshall Christian Academy 200/PK-12
1631 Brashers Chapel Rd 35951 256-279-0192
Fax 891-4160

**Alexander City, Tallapoosa, Pop. 14,759**
Alexander City SD 3,200/K-12
375 Lee St 35010 256-234-5074
Dr. J. Darrell Cooper, supt. Fax 329-6547
www.alexcityschools.net
Alexander City MS 500/7-8
359 State St 35010 256-234-8660
Reginald Clifton, prin. Fax 234-8659
Russell HS 1,000/9-12
225 Heard Blvd 35010 256-234-8611
Anthony Wilkinson, prin. Fax 234-8680

Central Alabama Community College Post-Sec.
1675 Cherokee Rd 35010 256-234-6346

**Alexandria, Calhoun, Pop. 3,872**
Calhoun County SD
Supt. — See Anniston
Alexandria HS 1,000/6-12
PO Box 180 36250 256-741-4400
Mack Holley, prin. Fax 820-7161

**Aliceville, Pickens, Pop. 2,445**
Pickens County SD
Supt. — See Carrollton
Aliceville HS 300/9-12
417 3rd St SE 35442 205-373-6378
Terry Sterling, prin. Fax 373-6730
Aliceville MS 300/5-8
1000 Columbus Rd NW 35442 205-373-6900
Fred Young, prin. Fax 373-8296

**Alpine, Talladega**
Talladega County SD
Supt. — See Talladega
Genesis Alternative Education Center Alt
22501 AL Highway 21 35014 256-315-5580
Joann Swain, prin. Fax 315-5585
Winterboro HS 300/5-12
22601 AL Highway 21 35014 256-315-5370
Emily Harris, prin. Fax 315-5380

**Andalusia, Covington, Pop. 8,865**
Andalusia CSD 1,700/K-12
1201 C C Baker Ave, 334-222-3186
Ted Watson, supt. Fax 222-8631
andalusia.schoolinsites.com
Andalusia HS 500/9-12
701 3rd St 36420 334-222-7569
Dr. Daniel Shakespeare, prin. Fax 222-5834
Andalusia JHS 400/7-8
1201 C C Baker Ave, 334-222-6542
Dr. Daniel Shakespeare, prin. Fax 222-3875

Covington County SD 2,900/PK-12
807 C C Baker Ave, 334-222-7571
Shannon Driver, supt. Fax 222-7573
www.cov.k12.al.us
Pleasant Home S 600/K-12
12548 Falco Rd 36420 334-222-1315
Craig Nichols, prin. Fax 222-4415
Straughn HS 400/9-12
29448 Straughn School Rd, 334-222-2511
John Evers, prin. Fax 222-4010
Straughn MS 300/6-8
29324 Straughn School Rd, 334-222-4090
Cassandra Scott, prin. Fax 222-4132
Other Schools – See Florala, Red Level

Lurleen B. Wallace Community College Post-Sec.
PO Box 1418 36420 334-222-6591

**Anniston, Calhoun, Pop. 22,755**
Anniston CSD 2,200/PK-12
PO Box 1500 36202 256-231-5000
Darren Douthitt, supt. Fax 231-5073
www.annistonschools.com/
Anniston HS 600/9-12
1301 Woodstock Ave 36207 256-231-5010
Dr. Sherron Jinadu, prin. Fax 231-5069
Anniston MS 500/6-8
4800 Mcclellan Blvd 36206 256-231-5020
Kimberly Garrick, prin. Fax 231-5024

Calhoun County SD 8,900/K-12
PO Box 2084 36202 256-741-7400
Joe Dyar, supt. Fax 237-5332
www.ccboe.us
Saks HS 500/8-12
4401 Saks Rd 36206 256-741-7000
Jody Whaley, prin. Fax 236-5121
Wellborn HS 500/7-12
135 Pinson Rd 36201 256-741-7600
Chris Hayes, prin. Fax 237-7071
White Plains HS 400/9-12
250 White Plains Rd 36207 256-741-7800
Andy Ward, prin. Fax 237-3301
White Plains MS 500/5-8
5800 AL Highway 9 36207 256-741-4700
Courtney Wilburn, prin. Fax 238-1715
Other Schools – See Alexandria, Jacksonville, Ohatchee, Weaver

Donoho S 400/PK-12
2501 Henry Rd 36207 256-237-5477
James Hutchins, head sch Fax 237-6474
Faith Christian S 300/PK-12
4100 Ronnaki Rd 36207 256-236-4499
Robert Phillips, hdmstr. Fax 236-4673
Sacred Heart S 200/PK-12
16 Morton Rd 36205 256-237-4231
Charlie Maniscalco, prin. Fax 237-2353

**Arab, Marshall, Pop. 7,960**
Arab CSD 2,500/PK-12
750 Arabian Dr NE 35016 256-586-6011
John Mullins, supt. Fax 586-6013
www.arabcityschools.org
Arab HS 800/9-12
511 Arabian Dr NE 35016 256-586-6026
Brad Cooper, prin. Fax 586-1948
Arab JHS 600/6-8
911 Old Cullman Rd SW 35016 256-586-6074
John Ingram, prin. Fax 586-1348

**Ardmore, Limestone, Pop. 1,178**
Limestone County SD
Supt. — See Athens
Ardmore JSHS 900/6-12
30285 Ardmore Ave 35739 256-423-2685
Randy Hamilton, prin. Fax 423-4991

**Ariton, Dale, Pop. 752**
Dale County SD
Supt. — See Ozark
Ariton S 700/K-12
PO Box 750 36311 334-445-5560
Ben Baker, prin. Fax 445-5561

**Arley, Winston, Pop. 344**
Winston County SD
Supt. — See Double Springs
Meek HS 200/7-12
6615 County Road 41 35541 205-384-5825
Marla Murrah, prin. Fax 384-6825

**Ashford, Houston, Pop. 2,133**
Houston County SD
Supt. — See Dothan
Ashford JSHS 700/7-12
607 Church St 36312 334-899-5411
James Odom, prin. Fax 899-7450
Houston County AVC Vo/Tech
PO Box 3005 36312 334-899-3308
Glenn Maloy, prin. Fax 899-8854

Ashford Academy 200/PK-12
1100 N Broadway St 36312 334-899-3286

**Ashland, Clay, Pop. 2,015**
Clay County SD 1,600/K-12
PO Box 278 36251 256-354-5414
William Walker, supt. Fax 354-5415
www.claycoboe.org
Other Schools – See Lineville

**Ashville, Saint Clair, Pop. 2,172**
Saint Clair County SD 8,100/PK-12
410 Roy Dr 35953 205-594-7131
Jenny Seals, supt. Fax 594-4441
www.sccboe.org
Ashville HS 400/9-12
33215 US Highway 231 35953 205-594-7943
Patti Johnson, prin. Fax 594-4349
Ashville MS 400/5-8
33221 US Highway 231 35953 205-594-7044
Rusty St. John, prin. Fax 594-2241
Eden Career-Technical Center Vo/Tech
45 County Road 33 35953 205-594-7055
Fax 594-4124
Yancy Alternative S Alt
466 10th St 35953 205-594-7492
David Gray, prin. Fax 594-3258
Other Schools – See Moody, Odenville, Ragland, Springville

**Athens, Limestone, Pop. 21,523**
Athens CSD 3,200/K-12
455 US Highway 31 N 35611 256-233-6600
William Holladay, supt. Fax 233-6640
www.acs-k12.org
Athens HS 900/9-12
PO Box 109 35612 256-233-6613
Christopher Bolen, prin. Fax 233-6617
Athens MS 500/7-8
601 S Clinton St 35611 256-233-6620
Melanie Barkley, prin. Fax 233-6623
Renaissance School 500/K-12
405 South St E 35611 256-614-3708
Joanna May, prin. Fax 233-6640

Limestone County SD 8,400/K-12
300 S Jefferson St 35611 256-232-5353
Dr. Tom Sisk, supt. Fax 233-6461
www.lcsk12.org
Clements MSHS 600/6-12
7730 US Highway 72 35611 256-729-6564
Keith Hairrell, prin. Fax 729-1029
East Limestone JSHS 1,300/6-12
15641 E Limestone Rd 35613 256-233-6660
Louis Berry, prin. Fax 230-9366
Limestone County Career Technical Center Vo/Tech
505 E Sanderfer Rd 35611 256-233-6463
Vince Green, prin. Fax 233-6667
Other Schools – See Ardmore, Elkmont, Lester, Tanner

---

Athens Bible S 300/K-12
507 Hoffman St 35611 256-232-3525
Athens State University Post-Sec.
300 N Beaty St 35611 256-233-8100
Lindsay Lane Christian Academy 300/PK-12
1300 Lindsay Ln S 35613 256-262-5323
Stephen Murr M.Ed., hdmstr. Fax 232-0425

**Atmore, Escambia, Pop. 10,046**
Escambia County SD
Supt. — See Brewton
Escambia County HS 500/9-12
1215 S Presley St 36502 251-368-9181
Dennis Fuqua, prin. Fax 368-0674
Escambia County MS 600/5-8
PO Box 1236 36504 251-368-9105
Anthony Morris, prin. Fax 368-0969

---

Escambia Academy 300/PK-12
268 Cowpen Creek Rd 36502 251-368-2080
Jefferson Davis Community College Post-Sec.
PO Box 1119 36504 251-368-8118

**Attalla, Etowah, Pop. 5,935**
Attalla CSD 1,500/PK-12
101 Case Ave SE 35954 256-538-8051
David Bowman, supt. Fax 538-8388
www.attalla.k12.al.us
Etowah HS 700/9-12
201 Case Ave SE 35954 256-538-8381
Ryan Barkley, prin. Fax 538-2136
Etowah MS 500/6-8
429 4th St SW 35954 256-538-3236
Wesley Gulledge, prin. Fax 538-3232

Etowah County SD
Supt. — See Gadsden
Career Technical Center Vo/Tech
105 Burke Ave SE 35954 256-538-3312
Mark Stancil, dir. Fax 538-1090
Etowah County Alternative S 200/Alt
106 Burke Ave SE 35954 256-538-8431
David Dixon, admin. Fax 538-8431

**Auburn, Lee, Pop. 52,538**
Auburn CSD 5,600/K-12
PO Box 3270 36831 334-887-2100
Dr. Karen T. DeLano, supt. Fax 887-2107
auburnschools.org
Auburn HS 1,400/10-12
405 Dean Rd 36830 334-887-4970
Dr. Shannon Pignato, prin. Fax 887-4177
Auburn JHS 1,100/8-9
332 E Samford Ave 36830 334-887-1960
Ross Reed, prin. Fax 887-4160

---

Auburn University 36849 Post-Sec.
334-844-4000
Lee-Scott Academy 600/PK-12
1601 Academy Dr 36830 334-821-2430
Dr. Don Roberts, hdmstr. Fax 821-0876

**Autaugaville, Autauga, Pop. 858**
Autauga County SD
Supt. — See Prattville
Autaugaville S 300/K-12
PO Box 99 36003 334-365-8329
Lesia Robinson, prin. Fax 365-8043

**Bay Minette, Baldwin, Pop. 7,923**
Baldwin County SD 28,300/PK-12
2600 Hand Ave 36507 251-937-0306
Hope Zeanah, supt. Fax 580-1856
www.bcbe.org
Baldwin County HS 1,100/9-12
1 Tiger Dr 36507 251-937-2341
Craig Smith, prin. Fax 937-2933
Bay Minette MS 600/7-8
1311 W 13th St 36507 251-580-2960
Kyle Nobles, prin. Fax 580-5120
North Baldwin Center for Tech Vo/Tech
505 W Hurricane Rd 36507 251-937-6751
Holly Resmondo, prin. Fax 937-4688
Other Schools – See Daphne, Elberta, Fairhope, Foley, Gulf Shores, Robertsdale, Spanish Fort

---

James H. Faulkner State Comm. College Post-Sec.
1900 S US Highway 31 36507 251-580-2100

**Bayou La Batre, Mobile, Pop. 2,494**
Mobile County SD
Supt. — See Mobile
Alba MS 700/6-8
14180 S Wintzell Ave 36509 251-824-4134
Rhonda Mayfield, prin. Fax 824-1324

**Bear Creek, Marion, Pop. 1,062**
Marion County SD
Supt. — See Hamilton
Phillips HS 200/7-12
142 School Ave 35543 205-486-3737
Keith Smith, prin. Fax 486-1716

**Beatrice, Monroe, Pop. 301**
Monroe County SD
Supt. — See Monroeville
Shields S 100/PK-12
17688 Highway 21 N 36425 251-789-2168
Duran Odoms, prin. Fax 789-2715

**Berry, Fayette, Pop. 1,134**
Fayette County SD
Supt. — See Fayette
Berry HS 300/7-12
18242 Highway 18 E 35546 205-689-4467
Trevor Kribbs, prin. Fax 689-8819

**Bessemer, Jefferson, Pop. 27,229**
Bessemer CSD 2,900/PK-12
PO Box 1230 35021 205-432-3000
Dr. Fred Primm, supt. Fax 432-3085
www.bessk12.org
Bessemer Center for Technology Vo/Tech
4940 Premiere Pkwy 35022 205-432-3805
Iverson Dudley, dir. Fax 432-0041
Bessemer City HS 9-12
4950 Premiere Pkwy 35022 205-432-3700
Reginald Ware, prin. Fax 434-2816
Bessemer City MS 700/6-8
100 High School Dr 35022 205-432-3600
Albert Soles, prin. Fax 432-3607
New Horizon S Alt
1701 6th Ave N 35020 205-432-3036
Edith Hunter, prin. Fax 432-3062

Jefferson County SD
Supt. — See Birmingham
Oak Grove HS 900/6-12
9494 Oak Grove Pkwy 35023 205-379-5000
Alan Pruden, prin. Fax 379-5045

---

Bessemer Academy 300/K-12
1705 4th Ave SW 35022 205-428-6288
ITT Technical Institute Post-Sec.
6270 Park South Dr 35022 205-497-5700

**Billingsley, Autauga, Pop. 144**
Autauga County SD
Supt. — See Prattville
Billingsley S 700/K-12
PO Box 118 36006 334-365-5516
Micheal Blair, prin. Fax 755-1633

**Birmingham, Jefferson, Pop. 210,274**
Alabama School of Fine Arts SD 400/7-12
1800 Rev Abraham Woods Blvd 35203 205-252-9241
Dr. Michael Meeks, supt. Fax 251-9541
www.asfa.k12.al.us
Alabama S of Fine Arts JSHS 400/7-12
1800 Rev Abraham Woods Blvd 35203 205-252-9241
Dr. Michael Meeks, supt. Fax 251-9541

Birmingham CSD 19,500/PK-12
PO Box 10007 35202 205-231-4600
Dr. Kelley Castlin-Gacutan, supt. Fax 231-4925
www.bhamcityschools.org
Arrington MS 300/6-8
2101 Jefferson Ave SW 35211 205-231-1130
Anthony Moss, prin. Fax 231-1133
Carver HS 900/9-12
3900 24th St N 35207 205-231-3900
Dr. Charles Willis, prin. Fax 231-3973
Dupuy Alternative S 100/Alt
4500 14th Ave N 35212 205-231-3250
Dr. Shirley Graham-Burrell, prin. Fax 231-3267
Green Acres MS 400/6-8
1220 67th St W 35228 205-231-1370
Dr. Willie Goldsmith, prin. Fax 231-1414
Huffman HS 1,100/9-12
950 Springville Rd 35215 205-231-5000
John Lyons, prin. Fax 231-5056
Huffman MS 300/6-8
517 Huffman Rd 35215 205-231-5370
WaShunda Gill, prin. Fax 231-5426
Jackson-Olin HS 1,200/9-12
510 12th Street Ensley 35218 205-231-6431
Dr. Janice Drake, prin. Fax 231-6527
Jones Valley MS 500/6-8
2000 31st St SW 35221 205-231-1040
Carolyn Denson, prin. Fax 231-1088
Mitchell MS 400/6-8
501 81st St S 35206 205-231-9400
Rameka Davis, prin. Fax 231-9464
Parker HS 900/9-12
400 Abraham Woods Jr Blvd 35204 205-231-2370
Darrell Hudson, prin. Fax 231-2916
Putnam MS 400/6-8
1757 Montclair Rd 35210 205-231-8680
Brenda Dial, prin. Fax 231-8685
Ramsay HS 700/Alt
1800 13th Ave S 35205 205-231-7000
Cassandra Fells, prin. Fax 231-7076
Smith MS 300/6-8
1124 Five Mile Rd 35215 205-231-5675
Dr. Demarcus Gates, prin. Fax 231-5899
Wenonah HS 900/9-12
2916 Wilson Rd SW 35221 205-231-1675
Regina Hope, prin. Fax 231-1655
Wilkerson MS 400/6-8
116 11th Ct W 35204 205-231-2740
Davida Hill-Johnson, prin. Fax 231-2790
Woodlawn HS 1,000/9-12
5620 1st Ave N 35212 205-231-8000
Jesse Daniel, prin. Fax 231-8084

Hoover CSD
Supt. — See Hoover
Berry MS 1,200/6-8
4500 Jaguar Dr 35242 205-439-2000
Christopher Robbins, prin. Fax 439-2001

Jefferson County SD 35,500/K-12
2100 18th St S 35209 205-379-2000
Dr. Craig Pouncey, supt. Fax 379-2311
www.jefcoed.com
Center Point HS 800/9-12
1000 Eagle Dr 35215 205-379-3400
Van Phillips, prin. Fax 379-3425
Erwin MS 6-8
532 23rd Ave NW 35215 205-379-3430
Serra Peterson, prin. Fax 856-6663
Fultondale JSHS 500/6-12
1450 Carson Rd N 35217 205-379-3500
Dr. Stephanie Robinson, prin. Fax 379-3545
Irondale MS 600/6-8
6200 Old Leeds Rd 35210 205-379-3800
Carita Venable, prin. Fax 379-3845
Jefferson Co. Counseling/Lrng Ctr-East Alt
50 Long St 35217 205-379-4250
Jason Wilson, prin. Fax 379-4295
Shades Valley Technical Academy Vo/Tech
5191 Pine Whispers Dr 35210 205-379-3300
Mary Beth Blankenship, prin. Fax 379-5397
Other Schools – See Adamsville, Bessemer, Dora, Gardendale, Hueytown, Irondale, Kimberly, Mc Calla, Pinson, Pleasant Grove, Trussville

Pelham CSD
Supt. — See Pelham
Riverchase MS 700/6-8
853 Willow Oak Dr 35244 205-682-5510
Susan Hyatt, prin. Fax 682-5515

Shelby County SD
Supt. — See Columbiana
Oak Mountain HS 1,700/9-12
5476 Caldwell Mill Rd 35242 205-682-5200
Kristi Sayers, prin. Fax 682-5205
Oak Mountain MS 1,200/6-8
5650 Cahaba Valley Rd 35242 205-682-5210
Larry Haynes, prin. Fax 682-5215

---

Altamont S 300/5-12
4801 Altamont Rd S 35222 205-879-2006
Sarah Whiteside, head sch Fax 871-5666
Birmingham-Southern College Post-Sec.
900 Arkadelphia Rd 35254 800-523-5793
Briarwood Christian S 1,900/PK-12
2204 Briarwood Way 35243 205-776-5800
Dr. Barrett Mosbacker, admin. Fax 776-5815
Brown Mackie College - Birmingham Post-Sec.
105 Vulcan Rd 35209 205-909-1500
Carroll HS 600/9-12
300 Lakeshore Pkwy 35209 205-940-2400
Charlie McGrath, prin. Fax 945-7429
Central Park Christian S 200/K-12
1900 43rd St W 35208 205-786-4811
Fortis Institute Post-Sec.
100 London Pkwy Ste 150 35211 205-940-7800
Herzing University Post-Sec.
280 W Valley Ave 35209 205-916-2800
Holy Family Catholic Academy 100/5-8
1916 19th Street Ensley 35218 205-780-5858
Sidney Moore, prin. Fax 785-2666
Holy Family Cristo Rey HS 200/9-12
2001 19th Street Ensley 35218 205-787-9937
Dr. Martha Barber, prin. Fax 787-8530
Hoover Christian S 100/PK-12
2113 Old Rocky Ridge Rd 35216 205-987-3376
Jefferson State Community College Post-Sec.
2601 Carson Rd 35215 205-853-1200
Lawson State Community College Post-Sec.
3060 Wilson Rd SW 35221 205-925-2515
Samford University Post-Sec.
800 Lakeshore Dr 35229 205-726-2011
Southeastern Bible College Post-Sec.
2545 Valleydale Rd 35244 205-970-9200
Southeastern School of Cosmetology Post-Sec.
849 Dennison Ave SW Ste 101 35211 205-925-0011
Strayer University Post-Sec.
3570 Grandview Pkwy Ste 200 35243 205-453-6300
University of Alabama at Birmingham Post-Sec.
1720 2nd Ave S 35294 205-934-4011
University of Alabama Hospital Post-Sec.
619 19th St S 35249 205-934-5490
Virginia College Post-Sec.
488 Palisades Blvd 35209 205-802-1200
Westminster S at Oak Mountain 200/7-12
5080 Cahaba Valley Tr 35242 205-995-9694

**Blountsville, Blount, Pop. 1,659**
Blount County SD
Supt. — See Oneonta
Moore HS 600/7-12
4040 Susan Moore Rd 35031 205-466-7663
Mike Stansberry, prin. Fax 466-7858
Pennington HS 600/7-12
81 College St 35031 205-429-4101
Brian Kirk, prin. Fax 429-4104

**Boaz, Marshall, Pop. 9,410**
Boaz CSD 2,200/PK-12
126 Newt Parker Dr 35957 256-593-8180
Dr. Mark Isley, supt. Fax 593-8181
www.boazk12.org/
Boaz HS 600/9-12
907 Brown St 35957 256-593-2401
Gary Minnick, prin. Fax 593-2403
Boaz MS 500/6-8
140 Newt Parker Dr 35957 256-593-0799
Dr. Richard Rutledge, prin. Fax 593-0729

Etowah County SD
Supt. — See Gadsden
Sardis MS, 1415 Sardis Dr 35956 400/6-8
Chris Royal, prin. 256-622-1120

---

Snead State Community College Post-Sec.
PO Box 734 35957 256-593-5120

**Brantley, Crenshaw, Pop. 786**
Crenshaw County SD
Supt. — See Luverne
Brantley S 600/PK-12
PO Box 86 36009 334-527-8879
Kris Odom, prin. Fax 527-3405

**Bremen, Cullman**
Cullman County SD
Supt. — See Cullman
Cold Springs HS 200/9-12
PO Box 130 35033 256-287-1787
Tim Burleson, prin. Fax 287-2841

**Brewton, Escambia, Pop. 5,355**
Brewton CSD 1,200/K-12
811 Belleville Ave 36426 251-867-8400
Dr. Kenneth Varner, supt. Fax 867-8403
www.brewtoncityschools.org/
Brewton MS 400/5-8
1384 Old Castleberry Rd 36426 251-867-8420
Madelyn Cave, prin. Fax 867-8422
Miller HS 400/9-12
1835 Douglas Ave 36426 251-867-8430
Mary Bell, prin. Fax 867-8407

Escambia County SD 4,300/K-12
PO Box 307 36427 251-867-6251
John J. Knott, supt. Fax 867-6252
www.escambiak12.net
Escambia Career Readiness Center Vo/Tech
2824 Pea Ridge Rd 36426 251-867-7829
David Lanier, dir. Fax 867-7064
Other Schools – See Atmore, East Brewton, Flomaton

---

Jefferson Davis Community College Post-Sec.
PO Box 958 36427 251-867-4832

**Bridgeport, Jackson, Pop. 2,317**
Jackson County SD
Supt. — See Scottsboro
Bridgeport MS 200/5-8
629 Dr Lee Ave 35740 256-495-2967
A.J. Buckner, prin. Fax 495-2850

**Brilliant, Marion, Pop. 893**
Marion County SD
Supt. — See Hamilton
Brilliant HS 200/7-12
PO Box 90 35548 205-465-2322
Jack Hayes, prin. Fax 465-2382

**Brookwood, Tuscaloosa, Pop. 1,803**
Tuscaloosa County SD
Supt. — See Tuscaloosa
Brookwood HS 1,000/9-12
12250 George Richmond Pkwy 35444 205-342-2777
Mark Franks, prin. Fax 247-4162

**Brundidge, Pike, Pop. 2,052**
Pike County SD
Supt. — See Troy
Pike County JSHS 500/7-12
552 S Main St 36010 334-735-2389
Willie Wright, prin. Fax 735-3176

**Bryant, Jackson**

---

Mountain View Christian Academy 100/PK-12
3665 AL Highway 73 35958 256-597-3467

**Buhl, Tuscaloosa**
Tuscaloosa County SD
Supt. — See Tuscaloosa
Sipsey Valley HS 400/9-12
15815 Romulus Rd 35446 205-342-2850
Dennis Alvarez, prin. Fax 342-2851
Sipsey Valley MS 6-8
15817 Romulus Rd 35446 205-342-2870
Frank Kelly, prin. Fax 342-2871

**Butler, Choctaw, Pop. 1,876**
Choctaw County SD 1,800/PK-12
107 Tom Orr Dr 36904 205-459-3031
Dorothy Banks, supt. Fax 459-3037
www.choctawal.org
Choctaw County HS 400/7-12
277 Tom Orr Dr 36904 205-459-2139
Celester Bolden, prin. Fax 459-2277
Other Schools – See Gilbertown

---

Patrician Academy 300/PK-12
901 S Mulberry Ave 36904 205-459-3605

**Calera, Shelby, Pop. 11,417**
Shelby County SD
Supt. — See Columbiana
Calera HS 600/9-12
100 Calera Eagle Dr 35040 205-682-6100
Joel Dixon, prin. Fax 682-6105

**Camden, Wilcox, Pop. 2,011**
Wilcox County SD 1,900/PK-12
PO Box 160 36726 334-682-4716
Andre Saulsberry, supt. Fax 682-4179
www.wilcox.k12.al.us
Camden S of Arts & Technology 300/7-8
PO Box 698 36726 334-682-4514
Andre Davis, prin. Fax 682-5934
Wilcox Central HS 600/9-12
PO Box 1089 36726 334-682-9239
Lenoise Richey, prin. Fax 682-5411
Wilcox County Alternative S Alt
PO Box 160 36726 334-682-5074
Robert Stallworth, admin. Fax 682-4769

---

Wilcox Academy 300/PK-12
PO Box 1149 36726 334-682-9619
Chris Burford, prin. Fax 682-2107

**Camp Hill, Tallapoosa, Pop. 1,004**
Tallapoosa County SD
Supt. — See Dadeville
Bell Career Tech Center Vo/Tech
251 M L King St 36850 256-896-0160
Gerry Moses, admin. Fax 896-0170
Tallapoosa County Alternative S 50/Alt
251 M L King St 36850 256-896-0160
John Wilcox, prin. Fax 896-0170

---

Lyman Ward Military Academy 100/6-12
PO Box 550 36850 256-798-9151

**Carbon Hill, Walker, Pop. 1,992**
Walker County SD
Supt. — See Jasper
Carbon Hill HS 400/9-12
217 Bulldog Blvd 35549 205-924-8821
Dr. Gypsy Stovall, prin. Fax 924-8877

**Carrollton, Pickens, Pop. 1,006**
Pickens County SD 2,800/K-12
377 Ladow Center Cir 35447 205-367-2082
Jamie Chapman, supt. Fax 367-8404
www.pickenscountyschools.net
Pickens County Career Center Vo/Tech
377 Ladow Center Cir 35447 205-367-2080
William Chan Mullenix, admin. Fax 367-8404
Other Schools – See Aliceville, Gordo, Reform

---

Pickens Academy 300/PK-12
225 Ray Bass Rd 35447 205-367-8144

**Cecil, Montgomery**

---

Macon East Academy 400/PK-12
15396 Vaughn Rd 36013 334-277-6566

**Cedar Bluff, Cherokee, Pop. 1,779**
Cherokee County SD
Supt. — See Centre
Cedar Bluff S 600/K-12
3655 Old Highway 9 35959 256-779-6211
Kevin Porter, prin. Fax 779-8328

**Centre, Cherokee, Pop. 3,423**
Cherokee County SD 4,100/PK-12
130 E Main St 35960 256-927-3362
William Guice, supt. Fax 927-3399
www.cherokeek12.org
Centre MS 500/5-8
1920 E Main St 35960 256-927-5656
Jennifer Mackey, prin. Fax 927-4656
Cherokee Co. Career & Technology Center Vo/Tech
600 Bay Springs Rd 35960 256-927-5351
Brett Keasler, prin. Fax 927-3501
Cherokee County HS 400/9-12
910 Warrior Dr 35960 256-927-3625
Wisdom Neyman, prin. Fax 927-6445
Other Schools – See Cedar Bluff, Gaylesville, Sand Rock, Spring Garden

**Centreville, Bibb, Pop. 2,751**
Bibb County SD 3,000/K-12
157 SW Davidson Dr 35042 205-926-9881
Duane McGee, supt. Fax 926-5075
www.bibbed.org/
Bibb County HS 600/9-12
220 Birmingham Rd 35042 205-926-9071
James Alston, prin. Fax 926-6848
Centreville MS 500/5-8
1621 Montgomery Hwy 35042 205-926-9861
Ernie Cutts, prin. Fax 926-3917
Other Schools – See West Blocton

---

Cahawba Christian Academy 100/PK-12
2415 Montevallo Rd 35042 205-926-4676

**Chatom, Washington, Pop. 1,283**
Washington County SD 3,300/K-12
PO Box 1359 36518 251-847-2401
Tim Savage, supt. Fax 847-3611
www.wcbek12.org
Washington County AVC Vo/Tech
PO Box 1298 36518 251-847-2040
David Wofford, prin. Fax 847-3489
Washington County JSHS 500/5-12
PO Box 1329 36518 251-847-2851
Rodney Smith, prin. Fax 847-2825
Other Schools – See Fruitdale, Leroy, Mc Intosh, Millry

**Chelsea, Shelby, Pop. 10,063**
Shelby County SD
Supt. — See Columbiana
Chelsea HS 1,000/9-12
PO Box 639 35043 205-682-7200
Kenneth Trucks, prin. Fax 682-7205
Chelsea MS 900/6-8
2321 Highway 39 35043 205-682-7210
Andrew Gunn, prin. Fax 682-7215

**Cherokee, Colbert, Pop. 1,027**
Colbert County SD
Supt. — See Tuscumbia
Cherokee HS 300/7-12
850 High School Dr 35616 256-359-4434
Pam Worsham, prin. Fax 359-4060

**Chickasaw, Mobile, Pop. 6,039**
Chickasaw CSD K-12
201 N Craft Way 36611 251-452-2256
Kyle Kallhoff, supt.
www.chickasawschools.com
Chickasaw HS 6-12
50 Chieftan Way 36611 251-380-8120
Jason Petro, prin. Fax 380-8115

**Childersburg, Talladega, Pop. 5,086**
Talladega County SD
Supt. — See Talladega
Childersburg HS 400/9-12
122 Faye S Perry Dr 35044 256-315-5475
Jesse Hooks, prin. Fax 315-5495
Childersburg MS 500/5-8
800 4th St SE 35044 256-315-5505
Jena Jones, prin. Fax 315-5520

**Citronelle, Mobile, Pop. 3,830**
Mobile County SD
Supt. — See Mobile
Citronelle HS 800/9-12
19325 Rowe St 36522 251-221-3444
Thomas Campbell, prin. Fax 221-3448
Lott MS 500/6-8
17740 Celeste Rd 36522 251-221-2240
Jason Golden, prin. Fax 221-2247

**Clanton, Chilton, Pop. 8,519**
Chilton County SD 7,700/PK-12
1705 Lay Dam Rd 35045 205-280-3000
Tommy Glasscock, supt. Fax 755-6549
www.chilton.k12.al.us
Chilton County HS 800/9-12
1214 7th St S 35045 205-280-2710
Dr. Cynthia Stewart, prin. Fax 755-0618
Clanton MS 600/6-8
835 Temple Rd 35045 205-280-2750
Kelvin Boulware, prin. Fax 755-2446
LeCroy Career Technical Center Vo/Tech
2829 4th Ave N 35045 205-280-2920
Dara Norman, prin. Fax 755-2035
Other Schools – See Jemison, Maplesville, Thorsby, Verbena

**Clayton, Barbour, Pop. 3,001**
Barbour County SD 900/PK-12
PO Box 429 36016 334-775-3453
David Hobdy, supt. Fax 775-7301
barbourschools.org
Barbour County JSHS 200/7-12
PO Box 339 36016 334-775-3545
Undrea Johnson, prin. Fax 775-8861

**Cleveland, Blount, Pop. 1,288**
Blount County SD
Supt. — See Oneonta
Blount County Career Technology Vo/Tech
PO Box 125 35049 205-625-3424
Johnny Pullen, dir. Fax 625-3427
Cleveland HS 500/7-12
71 High School St 35049 205-274-9915
Denise Martin, prin. Fax 274-0201

**Collinsville, DeKalb, Pop. 1,945**
De Kalb County SD
Supt. — See Rainsville
Collinsville S 800/K-12
PO Box 269 35961 256-524-2111
Donny Jones, prin. Fax 524-7526

**Columbia, Houston, Pop. 730**
Houston County SD
Supt. — See Dothan
Houston County JSHS 400/7-12
200 W Church St 36319 334-696-2221
Derrick Morris, prin. Fax 696-4677

**Columbiana, Shelby, Pop. 4,133**
Shelby County SD 21,200/K-12
PO Box 1910 35051 205-682-7000
Randy Fuller, supt. Fax 682-7005
www.shelbyed.k12.al.us
Columbiana MS 500/6-8
222 Joiner Town Rd 35051 205-682-6610
Dr. Kerry Rush, prin. Fax 682-6615
New Direction Alt
701 Highway 70 35051 205-682-5910
Russ Cofield, prin. Fax 682-5915
Shelby County College & Career Center Vo/Tech
701 Highway 70 35051 205-682-6650
Russ Cofield, prin. Fax 682-6655
Shelby County HS 700/9-12
101 Washington St 35051 205-682-6600
Gene Rogers, prin. Fax 682-6605
Other Schools – See Birmingham, Calera, Chelsea, Helena, Montevallo, Vincent

---

Cornerstone Christian S 200/PK-12
24975 Highway 25 35051 205-669-7777
Jay Adams, dir. Fax 395-8304

**Cordova, Walker, Pop. 2,077**
Walker County SD
Supt. — See Jasper
Bankhead MS 300/5-8
110 School Rd 35550 205-483-7245
Amber Freeman, prin. Fax 483-7244
Cordova HS 400/9-12
183 School Rd 35550 205-483-7404
Kathy Vintson, prin. Fax 483-1934

**Cottondale, Tuscaloosa**
Tuscaloosa CSD
Supt. — See Tuscaloosa
Bryant HS 900/9-12
6315 Mary Harmon Bryant Dr 35453 205-759-3538
Linda Harper, prin. Fax 759-8315
Eastwood MS 600/6-8
6314 Mary Harmon Bryant Dr 35453 205-759-3613
Portia Martin, prin. Fax 759-3798

Tuscaloosa County SD
Supt. — See Tuscaloosa
Davis - Emerson MS 400/6-8
1500 Bulldog Blvd 35453 205-342-2750
Marlon Murray, prin. Fax 247-4169

---

Tuscaloosa Christian S 300/PK-12
1601 Prude Mill Rd 35453 205-553-4303

**Cottonwood, Houston, Pop. 1,266**
Houston County SD
Supt. — See Dothan
Cottonwood S 700/K-12
663 Houston St 36320 334-691-2587
Judy Fowler, prin. Fax 691-4200

**Courtland, Lawrence, Pop. 595**
Lawrence County SD
Supt. — See Moulton
Hubbard HS 300/7-12
12905 Jessie Jackson Pkwy 35618 256-637-3010
Jewell Satchel, prin. Fax 637-3006

**Crossville, DeKalb, Pop. 1,821**
De Kalb County SD
Supt. — See Rainsville
Crossville HS 500/7-12
5405 County Road 28 35962 256-528-7858
David Uptain, prin. Fax 528-7840

**Cullman, Cullman, Pop. 14,641**
Cullman CSD 3,000/PK-12
301 1st St NE 35055 256-734-2233
Dr. Susan Patterson, supt. Fax 737-9621
www.cullmancats.net
Cullman City Career Tech S Vo/Tech
301 1st St NE 35055 256-734-2233
Dr. Susan Patterson, prin. Fax 737-9621
Cullman HS 900/9-12
510 13th St NE 35055 256-734-3923
Dr. Elton Bouldin, prin. Fax 734-9570
Cullman MS 500/7-8
800 2nd Ave NE 35055 256-734-7959
Patrick Hill, prin. Fax 734-7711

Cullman County SD 9,400/PK-12
PO Box 1590 35056 256-734-2933
Dr. Craig Ross, supt. Fax 736-2486
www.ccboe.org
CARE Alternative S Alt
192 County Road 940 35057 256-747-6371
Mike Grantham, coord. Fax 747-7376
Cullman Area Technology Academy Vo/Tech
17640 US Highway 31 35058 256-734-7740
Billy Troutman, prin. Fax 734-7464
Fairview HS 500/9-12
841 Welcome Rd 35058 256-796-5106
Dr. Chris Gambrill, prin. Fax 796-9025
Fairview MS 300/6-8
841 Welcome Rd 35058 256-796-0883
Trina Walker, prin. Fax 796-0885
Good Hope HS 400/9-12
210 Good Hope School Rd 35057 256-734-3807
Dr. Anita Kilpatrick, prin. Fax 734-3427
Good Hope MS 300/6-8
216 Good Hope School Rd 35057 256-734-9600
April Tucker, prin. Fax 734-9704
West Point HS 600/9-12
4314 County Road 1141 35057 256-734-5375
Heith Yearwood, prin. Fax 775-6047
Other Schools – See Bremen, Hanceville, Holly Pond, Vinemont

---

St. Bernard Prep HS 100/9-12
101 Saint Bernard Ave SE 35055 256-739-6682
Dan Baillargeon, hdmstr. Fax 734-2925

**Dadeville, Tallapoosa, Pop. 3,198**
Tallapoosa County SD 3,500/PK-12
679 E Columbus St 36853 256-825-0746
Joseph Windle, supt. Fax 825-8224
www.tallapoosak12.org
Councill MS 300/6-8
254 Leach St 36853 256-825-2846
Pam Langford, prin. Fax 825-7473
Dadeville HS 500/9-12
227 Weldon St 36853 256-825-7848
Chris Hand, prin. Fax 825-0697
Other Schools – See Camp Hill, New Site, Notasulga

**Daleville, Dale, Pop. 5,083**
Daleville CSD 1,200/PK-12
626 N Daleville Ave 36322 334-598-2456
Andrew Kelley, supt. Fax 598-9006
www.daleville.k12.al.us
Daleville JSHS 600/7-12
626 N Daleville Ave 36322 334-598-4461
Joshua Robertson, prin. Fax 598-3850

**Danville, Morgan**
Morgan County SD
Supt. — See Decatur
Danville HS 400/9-12
9235 Danville Rd 35619 256-773-9909
Marty Chambers, prin. Fax 773-5622
Danville MS 500/5-8
5933 Highway 36 W 35619 256-773-7723
Gary Walker, prin. Fax 773-7708

**Daphne, Baldwin, Pop. 21,279**
Baldwin County SD
Supt. — See Bay Minette
Daphne HS 1,200/9-12
9300 Lawson Rd 36526 251-626-8787
Dr. Meredith Foster, prin. Fax 626-3024
Daphne MS 600/7-8
1 Jody Davis Cir 36526 251-626-2845
Tiffany Irby, prin. Fax 626-0025

---

Bayside Academy 800/PK-12
303 Dryer Ave 36526 251-338-6300
United States Sports Academy Post-Sec.
1 Academy Dr 36526 251-626-3303

**Deatsville, Elmore, Pop. 1,131**
Autauga County SD
Supt. — See Prattville
Marbury HS 600/9-12
2360 US Highway 31 N 36022 334-387-1910
Donna Finch, prin. Fax 387-1920

Elmore County SD
Supt. — See Wetumpka
Holtville HS 500/9-12
10425 Holtville Rd 36022 334-569-3034
Tarica Lamar, prin. Fax 569-1013
Holtville MS 500/5-8
655 Bulldog Ln 36022 334-569-1596
Lee Jackson, prin. Fax 569-3258

---

J. F. Ingram State Technical College Post-Sec.
PO Box 220350 36022 334-285-5177

**Decatur, Morgan, Pop. 54,679**
Decatur CSD 8,700/PK-12
302 4th Ave NE 35601 256-552-3000
Dr. Edwin Nichols, supt. Fax 552-3981
www.dcs.edu
Austin HS 1,400/9-12
1625 Danville Rd SW 35601 256-552-3060
Dr. Donald Snow, prin. Fax 350-7802
Brookhaven MS 600/6-8
1302 5th Ave SW 35601 256-552-3045
Dr. Johnny Berry, prin. Fax 552-3047
Cedar Ridge MS 700/6-8
2715 Danville Rd SW 35603 256-552-4622
Johnnie Renick, prin. Fax 552-4623
Decatur HS 1,100/9-12
1011 Prospect Dr SE 35601 256-552-3011
Dr. Travis Schrimsher, prin. Fax 308-2535
Oak Park MS 600/6-8
1218 16th Ave SE 35601 256-552-3035
Wes Black, prin. Fax 552-3082

Morgan County SD 7,800/PK-12
1325 Point Mallard Pkwy SE 35601 256-353-6442
Bill Hopkins, supt. Fax 309-2187
www.morgank12.org
Priceville HS 400/9-12
317 Highway 67 S 35603 256-353-1950
Mark Mason, prin. Fax 353-2802
Priceville JHS 300/6-8
317 Highway 67 S 35603 256-355-5104
Mary Speegle, prin. Fax 355-5932
Other Schools – See Danville, Falkville, Hartselle, Somerville, Trinity

---

Calhoun Community College Post-Sec.
PO Box 2216 35609 256-306-2500
Decatur Heritage Christian Academy 400/K-12
PO Box 5659 35601 256-351-4275
Scott Mayo, hdmstr. Fax 355-4738

**Demopolis, Marengo, Pop. 7,436**
Demopolis CSD 2,300/PK-12
PO Box 759 36732 334-289-1670
Al Griffin, supt. Fax 289-1689
www.dcsedu.com
Demopolis HS 700/9-12
701 US Highway 80 W 36732 334-289-0294
Fax 289-8777
Demopolis MS 600/6-8
300 E Pettus St 36732 334-289-4242
Blaine Hathcock, prin. Fax 289-2670

**Dixons Mills, Marengo**
Marengo County SD
Supt. — See Linden
Marengo S 300/PK-12
212 Panther Dr 36736 334-992-2395
David Miller, prin. Fax 992-2197

**Dora, Walker, Pop. 1,996**
Jefferson County SD
Supt. — See Birmingham
Corner HS 500/9-12
4301 Warrior Jasper Rd 35062 205-379-3200
Ronald Cooper, prin. Fax 379-3245

Walker County SD
Supt. — See Jasper
Dora HS 500/9-12
330 Glenn C Gant Cir 35062 205-648-6863
Paige Skalnik, prin. Fax 648-4709

**Dothan, Houston, Pop. 64,426**
Dothan CSD 9,400/PK-12
500 Dusy St 36301 334-793-1397
Dr. Charles Ledbetter, supt. Fax 794-1499
www.dothan.k12.al.us
Beverlye Magnet MS 500/6-8
1025 S Beverlye Rd 36301 334-794-1432
Maria Johnson, prin. Fax 792-0886
Carver Magnet MS 500/6-8
1001 Webb Rd 36303 334-794-1440
Dr. Donnie Chambers, prin. Fax 794-1587
Dothan HS 1,200/9-12
1236 S Oates St 36301 334-794-1400
Stan Eldridge, prin. Fax 677-0099
Dothan Technology Center Vo/Tech
3165 Reeves St 36303 334-794-1436
Joey Meigs, prin. Fax 794-1439
Girard MS 500/6-8
600 Girard Ave 36303 334-794-1426
Darius McKay, prin. Fax 794-6373
Honeysuckle MS 600/6-8
1665 Honeysuckle Rd 36305 334-794-1420
LaTesha Weatherington, prin. Fax 678-6546
Northview HS 1,300/9-12
3209 Reeves St 36303 334-794-1410
Charles Corbitt, prin. Fax 702-4802
PASS Academy Alt
201 E Wilson St 36303 334-671-1474
Edward Fleming, prin. Fax 677-7480

Houston County SD 6,500/PK-12
404 W Washington St 36301 334-792-8331
Tim Pitchford, supt. Fax 792-1016
hcboe.us/
Houston County Alternative S Alt
315 N Foster St 36303 334-671-9295
Scott Stephens, prin. Fax 794-1016
Rehobeth HS 700/9-12
373 Malvern Rd 36301 334-677-7002
Bobby Boyd, prin. Fax 677-2699
Rehobeth MS 500/6-8
5631 County Road 203 36301 334-677-5153
John Dixon, prin. Fax 677-5947
Other Schools – See Ashford, Columbia, Cottonwood, Newton

---

Alabama College of Osteopathic Medicine Post-Sec.
445 Health Sciences Blvd 36303 334-699-2266
Emmanuel Christian S 500/PK-12
178 Earline Rd 36305 334-792-0935
Mark Redmond, admin. Fax 702-7410
Flowers Hospital Post-Sec.
PO Box 6907 36302 334-793-5000
Fortis College Post-Sec.
200 Vulcan Way 36303 334-677-2832
Houston Academy 600/PK-12
901 Buena Vista Dr 36303 334-794-4106
Dr. Scott Phillipps, hdmstr. Fax 793-4053
Northside Methodist Academy 400/PK-12
2600 Redmond Rd 36303 334-794-7273
Bill Reif, head sch Fax 702-8941
Providence Christian S 700/1-12
4847 Murphy Mill Rd 36303 334-702-8933
Emory Latta, head sch Fax 702-0700
Southeast Alabama Medical Center Post-Sec.
PO Box 6987 36302 334-793-8100
Wallace Community College Post-Sec.
1141 Wallace Dr 36303 334-983-3521

**Double Springs, Winston, Pop. 1,073**
Winston County SD 2,700/PK-12
PO Box 9 35553 205-489-5018
Gregory Pendley, supt. Fax 717-3391
www.winstonk12.org
Double Springs MS 300/5-8
PO Box 669 35553 205-489-3813
Ben Aderholt, prin. Fax 717-3392
Winston County HS 300/9-12
PO Box 549 35553 205-489-5593
Jeff Cole, prin. Fax 489-8204
Winston County Technical Center Vo/Tech
PO Box 1000 35553 205-489-2190
Barton Shannon, prin. Fax 717-3396
Other Schools – See Addison, Arley, Lynn

**Douglas, Marshall, Pop. 724**
Marshall County SD
Supt. — See Guntersville
Douglas HS 500/9-12
PO Box 300 35964 256-593-2810
Scott Bonds, prin. Fax 840-5489
Douglas MS 500/6-8
PO Box 269 35964 256-593-1240
Rita Walker, prin. Fax 593-1259

**Duncanville, Tuscaloosa**
Tuscaloosa County SD
Supt. — See Tuscaloosa
Duncanville MS 500/6-8
11205 Eagle Pkwy 35456 205-342-2830
Kaye Ridgway, prin. Fax 759-1998

**East Brewton, Escambia, Pop. 2,446**
Escambia County SD
Supt. — See Brewton
Neal HS 400/9-12
801 Andrew Jackson St 36426 251-867-4645
Patricia Frazier, prin. Fax 867-4642
Neal MS 400/5-8
703 Williamson St 36426 251-867-5035
Dennis Hadaway, prin. Fax 867-5051

**Eclectic, Elmore, Pop. 979**
Elmore County SD
Supt. — See Wetumpka
Eclectic MS 500/5-8
170 S Ann St 36024 334-541-2131
Blair Andress, prin. Fax 541-3556
Elmore County HS 500/9-12
155 N College Ave 36024 334-541-3662
Wes Rogers, prin. Fax 541-4441

**Eight Mile, See Prichard**
Mobile County SD
Supt. — See Mobile
Blount HS 1,200/9-12
5450 Lott Rd 36613 251-221-3070
Jerome Woods, prin. Fax 221-3075

**Elba, Coffee, Pop. 3,889**
Coffee County SD 2,000/PK-12
400 Reddoch Hill Rd 36323 334-897-5016
Terry Weeks, supt. Fax 897-6207
www.coffeecountyschools.org
Other Schools – See Jack, Kinston, New Brockton

Elba CSD 700/K-12
131 Tiger Dr 36323 334-897-2801
Chresal Threadgill, supt. Fax 897-5601
www.elbaed.com
Elba Area Vocational HS Vo/Tech
371 Tiger Dr 36323 334-897-2266
Fax 897-5106
Elba HS 400/7-12
371 Tiger Dr 36323 334-897-2266
Chris Moseley, prin. Fax 897-5106

**Elberta, Baldwin, Pop. 1,467**
Baldwin County SD
Supt. — See Bay Minette
Elberta MS 500/4-8
13355 Main St 36530 251-986-8127
Claude Eilert, prin. Fax 986-7472

**Elkmont, Limestone, Pop. 433**
Limestone County SD
Supt. — See Athens
Elkmont S 1,100/K-12
25630 Evans Ave 35620 256-732-4291
Garth Garris, prin. Fax 732-3418

**Elmore, Elmore**

---

Edgewood Academy PK-12
PO Box 160 36025 334-567-5102

**Enterprise, Coffee, Pop. 25,851**
Enterprise CSD 6,100/PK-12
PO Box 311790 36331 334-347-9531
Dr. Camille Wright, supt. Fax 347-5102
www.enterpriseschools.net/
Dauphin JHS 600/8-8
1271 Dauphin Street Ext 36330 334-347-1141
Judy Thomas, prin. Fax 347-0845
Enterprise HS 1,500/9-12
1801 Boll Weevil Cir 36330 334-347-2640
Matt Rodgers, prin. Fax 347-3144

---

Enterprise Preparatory Academy 100/PK-12
92 County Road 539 36330 334-308-0260
Enterprise State Community College Post-Sec.
PO Box 1300 36331 334-347-2623

**Eufaula, Barbour, Pop. 13,021**
Eufaula CSD 2,800/PK-12
333 State Docks Rd 36027 334-687-1100
Eddie Tyler, supt. Fax 687-1150
www.ecs.k12.al.us
Eufaula HS 700/9-12
530 Lake Dr 36027 334-687-1110
Steve Hawkins, prin. Fax 687-1121
Moorer MS 600/6-8
101 Saint Francis Rd 36027 334-687-1130
Penny Kinsey, prin. Fax 687-1138

---

Lakeside S 300/PK-12
1020 Lake Dr 36027 334-687-5748

**Eutaw, Greene, Pop. 2,918**
Greene County SD 1,300/PK-12
220 Main St 35462 205-372-3161
Dr. James Carter, supt. Fax 372-3247
www.greene.k12.al.us
Carver MS 300/4-8
PO Box 659 35462 205-372-4816
Barbara Martin, prin. Fax 372-4828
Greene County Career Center Vo/Tech
627 Mesopotamia St 35462 205-372-4636
Dr. Rhinnie Scott, prin. Fax 372-2358
Greene County HS 400/9-12
PO Box 658 35462 205-372-3789
Garry Rice, prin. Fax 372-3404

**Evergreen, Conecuh, Pop. 3,925**
Conecuh County SD 1,700/PK-12
100 Jackson St 36401 251-578-1752
Zickeyous Byrd Ed.D., supt. Fax 578-7061
www.conecuh.k12.al.us
Genesis S Alt
111 Perryman St 36401 251-578-5291
Susan Brewton-Coleman, prin. Fax 578-2377
Hillcrest HS 500/9-12
1989 Jaguar Dr 36401 251-578-1126
Rodney Drish, prin. Fax 578-7071
Marshall MS 200/6-8
428 Reynolds Ave 36401 251-578-2866
Geneva Lyons, prin. Fax 578-7067

---

Reid State Technical College Post-Sec.
PO Box 588 36401 251-578-1313
Sparta Academy 200/PK-12
300 Pierce St 36401 251-578-2852

**Excel, Monroe, Pop. 708**
Monroe County SD
Supt. — See Monroeville
Excel S 1,100/PK-12
PO Box 429 36439 251-765-2351
Marty Hanks, prin. Fax 765-9153

**Fairfield, Jefferson, Pop. 11,062**
Fairfield CSD 1,800/K-12
6405 Avenue D 35064 205-783-6850
Walter Gonsoulin Ph.D., supt. Fax 783-6805
Fairfield Alternative S Alt
6405 Avenue D 35064 205-264-9501
Dr. Gordon Fears, prin. Fax 783-6810
Fairfield Area Vocational HS Vo/Tech
610 Valley Rd 35064 205-785-5176
Valerie Holmes, prin. Fax 783-6748
Fairfield Preparatory HS 600/9-12
610 Valley Rd 35064 205-785-5176
Michelle Hayes, prin. Fax 783-6748
Forest Hills MS 300/7-8
7000 Grasselli Rd 35064 205-783-6841
Shun Williams, prin. Fax 783-6753

---

Miles College Post-Sec.
5500 Myron Massey Blvd 35064 205-929-1000
Restoration Academy 300/K-12
PO Box 30 35064 205-785-8805
Brian Goessling, prin. Fax 785-8809

**Fairhope, Baldwin, Pop. 15,206**
Baldwin County SD
Supt. — See Bay Minette
Fairhope HS 1,400/9-12
1 Pirate Dr 36532 251-928-8309
Jan Cardwell, prin. Fax 990-2053
Fairhope MS 700/7-8
2 Pirate Dr 36532 251-928-2573
Angie Hall, prin. Fax 990-0403

**Falkville, Morgan, Pop. 1,257**
Morgan County SD
Supt. — See Decatur
Falkville JSHS 400/6-12
43 Clark Dr 35622 256-784-5248
Glenn Lang, prin. Fax 784-9438

**Fayette, Fayette, Pop. 4,573**
Fayette County SD 2,400/PK-12
PO Box 686 35555 205-932-4611
Jim Burkhalter, supt. Fax 932-7246
www.fayette.k12.al.us
Fayette County HS 400/9-12
202 Tiger Dr 35555 205-932-6313
Dr. Jeremy Madden, prin. Fax 932-8361
Fayette MS 500/5-8
418 3rd Ave NE 35555 205-932-7660
Rodney Hannah, prin. Fax 932-7661
Hubbertville S 400/PK-12
7360 County Road 49 35555 205-487-2845
Tim Dunavant, prin. Fax 487-3375
Other Schools – See Berry

**Flomaton, Escambia, Pop. 1,423**
Escambia County SD
Supt. — See Brewton
Escambia County Alternative S Alt
21280 Highway 31 36441 251-296-4113
Hilda Rudolph Blakely, prin. Fax 296-4075
Flomaton HS 300/9-12
21200 Highway 31 36441 251-296-2627
Scott Hammond, prin. Fax 296-2625

**Florala, Covington, Pop. 1,935**
Covington County SD
Supt. — See Andalusia
Florala HS 200/7-12
22114 Begonia St 36442 334-858-3765
Brent Zessin, prin. Fax 858-6925

**Florence, Lauderdale, Pop. 38,649**
Florence CSD 4,300/K-12
PO Box 10 35631 256-768-3000
Dr. Janet Womack, supt. Fax 768-3006
www.florencek12.org/
Florence Career Technical Education Vo/Tech
PO Box 10 35631 256-768-3021
Darrin Lett, admin. Fax 768-3010
Florence Freshman Center 300/9-9
1203 Bradshaw Dr 35630 256-768-2400
Rod Sheppard, prin. Fax 768-2405
Florence HS 1,000/10-12
1201 Bradshaw Dr 35630 256-768-2200
Lynne Hice, prin. Fax 768-2205
Florence MS 700/7-8
648 N Cherry St 35630 256-768-3100
Aimee Rainey, prin. Fax 768-3105

Lauderdale County SD 8,500/PK-12
PO Box 278 35631 256-760-1300
Dr. Jennifer Gray, supt. Fax 766-5815
www.lcschools.org
Central S 1,400/PK-12
3000 County Road 200 35633 256-764-2903
Ryan Harrison, prin. Fax 764-5409
Rogers S 1,300/PK-12
300 Rogers Ln 35634 256-757-3106
David Matthews, prin. Fax 757-9625
Wilson S 1,300/PK-12
7601 Highway 17 35634 256-764-8470
Gary Horton, prin. Fax 764-1304
Other Schools – See Killen, Lexington, Rogersville, Waterloo

---

Heritage Christian University Post-Sec.
PO Box HCU 35630 256-766-6610
Mars Hill Bible S 600/PK-12
698 Cox Creek Pkwy 35630 256-767-1203
Shoals Christian S 200/PK-12
301 Heathrow Dr 35633 256-767-7070
Jim Koan M.A., hdmstr. Fax 766-5677
University of North Alabama Post-Sec.
1 Harrison Plz 35632 256-765-4100

**Foley, Baldwin, Pop. 14,389**
Baldwin County SD
Supt. — See Bay Minette
Foley HS 1,600/9-12
1 Pride Pl 36535 251-943-2221
Russ Moore, prin. Fax 943-3538
Foley MS 600/7-8
201 N Pine St 36535 251-943-1255
Danny McDuffie, prin. Fax 943-8221

---

Alabama Gulf Coast Christian Academy 100/PK-12
18930 County Road 28 36535 251-989-2333
Fortis College Post-Sec.
200 E Laurel Ave 36535 251-970-1460

**Fort Deposit, Lowndes, Pop. 1,336**
Lowndes County SD
Supt. — See Hayneville
Lowndes County MS 200/6-8
PO Box 393 36032 334-227-4206
Archie Curtis, prin. Fax 227-4125

**Fort Payne, DeKalb, Pop. 13,756**
Fort Payne CSD 3,100/PK-12
PO Box 681029 35968 256-845-0915
James Cunningham, supt. Fax 845-4962
www.ftpayk12.org
Fort Payne HS 800/9-12
201 45th St NE 35967 256-845-0535
Brian Jett, prin. Fax 845-7868
Fort Payne MS 900/5-8
4910 Martin Ave NE 35967 256-845-7501
Shane Byrd, prin. Fax 845-8292

**Fruitdale, Washington, Pop. 184**
Washington County SD
Supt. — See Chatom
Fruitdale S 400/K-12
PO Box 448 36539 251-827-6655
Curtis Stagner, prin. Fax 827-6573

**Fyffe, DeKalb, Pop. 992**
De Kalb County SD
Supt. — See Rainsville
Fyffe S 900/K-12
PO Box 7 35971 256-623-2116
Ricky Bryant, prin. Fax 623-4388

**Gadsden, Etowah, Pop. 36,211**
Etowah County SD 9,200/PK-12
3200 W Meighan Blvd 35904 256-549-7560
Dr. Alan Cosby, supt. Fax 549-7589
www.ecboe.org/
Gaston S 600/K-12
4550 US Highway 411 35901 256-547-8828
Tammy George, prin. Fax 543-7124
Hokes Bluff MS 300/6-8
3121 Appalachian Hwy 35903 256-492-1963
Greg Watkins, prin. Fax 492-1950
Other Schools – See Attalla, Boaz, Glencoe, Hokes Bluff, Rainbow City, Sardis City, Southside, Walnut Grove

Gadsden CSD 5,900/K-12
PO Box 184 35902 256-543-3512
Dr. Ed Miller, supt. Fax 549-2950
www.gcs.k12.al.us
Gadsden City HS 1,500/9-12
1917 Black Creek Pkwy 35904 256-543-3614
Jeffrey Colegrove, prin. Fax 543-4251
Gadsden MS 500/6-8
612 Tracy St 35901 256-547-6341
Joel Gulledge, prin. Fax 547-6323
Litchfield MS 300/6-8
1109 Hoke St 35903 256-492-6793
Dr. Charlie Parker, prin. Fax 492-4010
Sansom MS 500/6-8
2210 W Meighan Blvd 35904 256-546-4992
Russell Waits, prin. Fax 543-1060
Secondary Alternative S 600/Alt
607 S 12th St 35901 256-547-5446
Donna Smoots, prin. Fax 547-5448

---

Coosa Christian S 300/PK-12
2736 Wills Creek Rd 35904 256-547-1841
Gadsden State Community College Post-Sec.
PO Box 227 35902 256-549-8200
Holy Comforter Episcopal Day S 100/PK-12
156 S 9th St 35901 256-546-9071
Laura McCartney, hdmstr. Fax 546-7912

**Gardendale, Jefferson, Pop. 13,766**
Jefferson County SD
Supt. — See Birmingham
Bragg MS 900/6-8
840 Ash Ave 35071 205-379-2600
Larry Robertson, prin. Fax 379-2645
Gardendale HS 1,100/9-12
800 Main St 35071 205-379-3600
Jeff Caufield, prin. Fax 379-3645

---

Alabama State College of Barber Styling Post-Sec.
753 Main St 35071 205-631-8898

**Gaylesville, Cherokee, Pop. 143**
Cherokee County SD
Supt. — See Centre
Gaylesville S 400/PK-12
760 Trojan Way 35973 256-422-3401
Scott Hays, prin. Fax 422-3165

**Geneva, Geneva, Pop. 4,382**
Geneva CSD 1,200/K-12
511 Panther Dr 36340 334-684-1090
Rhonda Stringham, supt. Fax 684-3128
www.genevacity.schoolinsites.com
Geneva HS 400/9-12
505 Panther Dr 36340 334-684-9379
Mickey Bennett, prin. Fax 684-0303
Geneva MS 300/6-8
501 Panther Dr 36340 334-684-6431
Danny Bedsole, prin. Fax 684-0476

Geneva County SD 2,700/K-12
PO Box 250 36340 334-684-5690
Becky Birdsong, supt. Fax 684-5601
genevacounty.schoolinsites.com/
Other Schools – See Hartford, Samson, Slocomb

**Georgiana, Butler, Pop. 1,722**
Butler County SD
Supt. — See Greenville
Georgiana S 300/K-12
PO Box 680 36033 334-376-9130
Bryant Marlow, prin. Fax 376-2956

**Geraldine, DeKalb, Pop. 882**
De Kalb County SD
Supt. — See Rainsville
Geraldine S 1,200/K-12
13011 AL Highway 227 35974 256-659-2142
Steven Street, prin. Fax 659-4296

**Gilbertown, Choctaw, Pop. 214**
Choctaw County SD
Supt. — See Butler
Southern Choctaw HS 400/7-12
10941 Highway 17 36908 251-843-5645
Dr. Leo Leddon, prin. Fax 843-5649

**Glencoe, Etowah, Pop. 5,099**
Etowah County SD
Supt. — See Gadsden
Glencoe HS 300/9-12
803 Lonesome Bend Rd 35905 256-492-2250
Charlton Giles, prin. Fax 492-2265
Glencoe MS 300/5-8
809 Lonesome Bend Rd 35905 256-492-5627
Ginger Smith, prin. Fax 492-7076

**Gordo, Pickens, Pop. 1,715**
Pickens County SD
Supt. — See Carrollton
Gordo JSHS 600/7-12
630 4th St NW 35466 205-364-7353
Mark Capps, prin. Fax 364-6160

**Goshen, Pike, Pop. 265**
Pike County SD
Supt. — See Troy
Goshen JSHS 400/7-12
286 Eagle Cir 36035 334-484-3245
Major Lane, prin. Fax 484-3247

**Grady, Montgomery**

---

South Montgomery County Academy 100/PK-12
PO Box 10 36036 334-562-3235
Tim Davenport, head sch Fax 562-9059

**Grand Bay, Mobile, Pop. 3,617**
Mobile County SD
Supt. — See Mobile
Grand Bay MS 800/6-8
12800 Cunningham Rd 36541 251-865-6511
Wendell Ellis, prin. Fax 221-2405

**Grant, Marshall, Pop. 887**
Marshall County SD
Supt. — See Guntersville
Smith DAR HS 500/9-12
6077 Main St 35747 256-728-4238
Stacy Anderton, prin. Fax 728-8900
Smith DAR MS 500/5-8
6077 Main St 35747 256-728-5950
Tim Isbill, prin. Fax 728-8447

**Greensboro, Hale, Pop. 2,483**
Hale County SD 2,700/PK-12
1115 Powers St 36744 334-624-8836
Osie A. Pickens, supt. Fax 624-3415
www.halek12.org
College and Career Academy Vo/Tech
PO Box 517 36744 334-624-3691
James Essex, prin. Fax 624-1090
Greensboro HS 400/9-12
620 Carver St 36744 334-624-9156
Dr. Jessica Constant, prin. Fax 624-9157
Greensboro MS 300/6-8
620 Carver St 36744 334-624-4005
Anthony Sanders, prin. Fax 624-0308
Other Schools – See Moundville

---

Southern Academy 200/PK-12
407 College St 36744 334-624-8111
Marc Mickleboro, hdmstr. Fax 624-3778

**Greenville, Butler, Pop. 8,092**
Butler County SD 3,000/K-12
211 School Highlands Rd 36037 334-382-2665
Amy Bryan, supt. Fax 382-8607
www.butlerco.k12.al.us
Butler County Area Vocational HS Vo/Tech
100 Tiger Dr 36037 334-382-0266
Jennifer Burt, prin. Fax 382-8607
Greenville HS 700/9-12
100 Tiger Dr 36037 334-382-2608
Joseph Dean, prin. Fax 382-7202
Greenville MS 800/5-8
300 Overlook Rd 36037 334-382-3450
Catherine Tanner, prin. Fax 382-0686
Other Schools – See Georgiana, Mc Kenzie

---

Fort Dale Academy 400/K-12
1100 Gamble St 36037 334-382-2606

**Grove Hill, Clarke, Pop. 1,558**
Clarke County SD 3,300/PK-12
PO Box 936 36451 251-275-3255
Larry Bagley, supt. Fax 275-8061
www.clarkecountyschools.org/
Clarke County HS 400/9-12
PO Box 937 36451 251-275-3368
Debra Dennis, prin. Fax 275-4132
Wilson Hall MS 400/5-8
401 Carter Dr 36451 251-275-8993
Carolyn Taite, prin. Fax 275-4688
Other Schools – See Jackson

---

Clarke Preparatory S 300/PK-12
20100 Highway 43 36451 251-275-8576

**Guin, Marion, Pop. 2,339**
Marion County SD
Supt. — See Hamilton
Marion County HS 200/7-12
PO Box 549 35563 205-468-3377
Jason Bourland, prin. Fax 468-8047

**Gulf Shores, Baldwin, Pop. 9,533**
Baldwin County SD
Supt. — See Bay Minette
Gulf Shores HS 800/9-12
600 E 15th Ave 36542 251-968-4747
Dr. Ernie Rosado, prin. Fax 968-4770
Gulf Shores MS 400/7-8
450 E 15th Ave 36542 251-968-8719
Kyle McCartney, prin. Fax 967-1577

**Guntersville, Marshall, Pop. 8,040**
Guntersville CSD 1,900/PK-12
PO Box 129 35976 256-582-3159
Brett Stanton, supt. Fax 582-6158
www.guntersvilleboe.com
Guntersville HS 600/9-12
14227 US Highway 431 35976 256-582-2046
Roseanne Mabrey, prin. Fax 582-4742
Guntersville MS 400/6-8
901 Sunset Dr 35976 256-582-5182
Jeff Jones, prin. Fax 582-4477

Marshall County SD 5,000/PK-12
12380 US Highway 431 35976 256-582-3171
Dr. Cindy Wigley, supt. Fax 582-3178
www.marshallk12.org
Brindlee Mountain HS 400/9-12
994 Scant City Rd 35976 256-753-2800
Brian Pool, prin. Fax 753-2802
Brindlee Mountain MS 300/6-8
1050 Scant City Rd 35976 256-753-2820
Mike Little, prin. Fax 753-2822
Marshall Technical HS Vo/Tech
12312 US Highway 431 35976 256-582-5629
Sherman Leeth, prin. Fax 582-2580
Other Schools – See Albertville, Douglas, Grant

**Gurley, Madison, Pop. 783**
Madison County SD
Supt. — See Huntsville
Madison County HS 600/9-12
174 Brock Rd 35748 256-851-3270
Jeremy Lowry, prin. Fax 851-3272

**Hackleburg, Marion, Pop. 1,499**
Marion County SD
Supt. — See Hamilton
Hackleburg HS 200/7-12
PO Box 310 35564 205-935-3223
John Hardin, prin. Fax 935-8092

**Haleyville, Winston, Pop. 4,111**
Haleyville CSD 1,700/PK-12
2011 20th St 35565 205-486-9231
Alan Miller, supt. Fax 486-8833
haley-k12.us
Haleyville Center of Technology Vo/Tech
2007 20th St 35565 205-486-9481
William Bishop, prin. Fax 486-8735
Haleyville HS 500/9-12
2001 20th St 35565 205-486-3122
Holly Sutherland, prin. Fax 486-1660
Haleyville MS 400/6-8
2014 20th Ave 35565 205-486-9240
Richard Wilcoxson, prin. Fax 486-9244

**Hamilton, Marion, Pop. 6,817**
Marion County SD 3,500/PK-12
188 Winchester Dr 35570 205-921-3191
Ryan Hollingsworth, supt. Fax 921-7336
www.mcbe.net
Hamilton HS 500/9-12
211 Aggie Ave 35570 205-921-3281
Ronnie Miller, prin. Fax 921-2333
Hamilton MS 600/5-8
400 Military St S 35570 205-921-7030
Steven Deavours, prin. Fax 921-3821
Marion County Alternative S 50/Alt
188 Winchester Dr 35570 205-952-9083
Patrick Sutton, lead tchr. Fax 952-9083
Other Schools – See Bear Creek, Brilliant, Guin, Hackleburg

**Hampton Cove, Madison**
Huntsville CSD
Supt. — See Huntsville
Hampton Cove MS 600/6-8
261 Old Highway 431 Ste B 35763 256-428-8380
Dr. Debi Edwards, prin. Fax 428-8383

**Hanceville, Cullman, Pop. 2,928**
Cullman County SD
Supt. — See Cullman
Hanceville HS 400/9-12
801 Commercial St SE 35077 256-352-6111
Jimmy Collins, prin. Fax 352-6491
Hanceville MS 300/6-8
805 Commercial St SE 35077 256-352-6175
Cynthia Roden, prin. Fax 352-9741

---

Wallace State Community College Post-Sec.
PO Box 2000 35077 256-352-8000

**Harpersville, Shelby, Pop. 1,615**

---

Coosa Valley Academy 300/K-12
PO Box 250 35078 205-672-7326

**Hartford, Geneva, Pop. 2,582**
Geneva County SD
Supt. — See Geneva
Geneva County HS 200/9-12
301 Lily St 36344 334-588-2943
Max Whittaker, prin. Fax 588-3650
Geneva County MS 200/6-8
301 Lily St 36344 334-588-2943
Kevin LeSueur, prin. Fax 588-3650

**Hartselle, Morgan, Pop. 14,036**
Hartselle CSD 2,700/PK-12
305 College St NE 35640 256-773-5419
Dr. Vic Wilson, supt. Fax 773-5433
www.hartselletigers.org
Hartselle HS 1,000/9-12
1000 Bethel Rd NE 35640 256-751-5615
Jeff Hyche, prin. Fax 751-5638
Hartselle JHS 500/7-8
904 Sparkman St SW 35640 256-773-5426
Dr. Robbie Smith, prin. Fax 751-5658

Morgan County SD
Supt. — See Decatur
Morgan County Learning Center Alt
72 Plainview St 35640 256-773-6458
Layne Dillard, prin. Fax 309-2158

**Harvest, Madison, Pop. 5,123**
Madison County SD
Supt. — See Huntsville
Sparkman HS 1,800/10-12
2616 Jeff Rd 35749 256-837-0331
Chris Shaw, prin. Fax 837-7673
Sparkman Ninth Grade S 700/9-9
2680 Jeff Rd 35749 256-851-4560
Martin Hester, prin. Fax 851-4561

**Hayden, Blount, Pop. 432**
Blount County SD
Supt. — See Oneonta
Hayden HS 900/8-12
125 Atwood Rd 35079 205-647-0397
Allen Hargett, prin. Fax 647-8633

**Hayneville, Lowndes, Pop. 928**
Lowndes County SD 1,800/K-12
PO Box 755 36040 334-548-2131
Dr. Daniel Boyd, supt. Fax 548-2161
www.lowndesboe.org/
Central HS 300/9-12
145 Main St 36040 334-563-7311
Toriano Baker, prin. Fax 563-7299
Hayneville MS 300/6-8
PO Box 307 36040 334-548-2184
Keith Scissum, prin. Fax 548-5237
Project Success Learning Center Alt
147 Main St 36040 334-563-9869
Lorenza Smith, prin. Fax 563-9869
Other Schools – See Fort Deposit, Letohatchee

**Hazel Green, Madison, Pop. 3,538**
Madison County SD
Supt. — See Huntsville
Hazel Green HS 1,300/9-12
14380 Highway 231 431 N 35750 256-851-3220
Darrell Long, prin. Fax 851-3221
Meridianville MS 1,100/7-8
12975 Highway 231 431 N 35750 256-851-4550
Tom Highfield, prin. Fax 851-4551

**Headland, Henry, Pop. 4,460**
Henry County SD
Supt. — See Abbeville
Headland HS 300/10-12
8 Sporman St 36345 334-585-7086
Jason Bradford, prin. Fax 585-7088
Headland MS 600/6-9
1 Martin Luther King Dr 36345 334-585-7083
Kevin Sanders, prin. Fax 585-7085

**Heflin, Cleburne, Pop. 3,431**
Cleburne County SD 2,700/PK-12
141 Davenport Dr 36264 256-463-5624
Claire Dryden, supt. Fax 463-5709
www.cleburneschools.net
Cleburne County Career Technical S Vo/Tech
11200 Highway 46 36264 256-748-2961
Eric Lovvorn, prin. Fax 748-3904
Cleburne County HS 600/8-12
520 Evans Bridge Rd 36264 256-463-2012
Valrie Bain, prin. Fax 463-5504
Other Schools – See Ranburne

**Helena, Shelby, Pop. 16,576**
Shelby County SD
Supt. — See Columbiana
Helena HS 9-12
1310 Hillsboro Pkwy 35080 205-682-3650
April Brand, prin. Fax 682-3655
Helena MS 800/6-8
1299 Hillsboro Pkwy 35080 205-682-5300
Scott Knight, prin. Fax 682-5305

**Higdon, Jackson**
Jackson County SD
Supt. — See Scottsboro
North Sand Mountain S 700/K-12
PO Box 129 35979 256-597-2111
Chris Davis, prin. Fax 597-2505

**Highland Home, Crenshaw**
Crenshaw County SD
Supt. — See Luverne
Highland Home S 800/PK-12
18434 Montgomery Hwy 36041 334-537-4379
Cliff Maddox, prin. Fax 537-9805

**Hokes Bluff, Etowah, Pop. 4,266**
Etowah County SD
Supt. — See Gadsden

Hokes Bluff HS 400/9-12
1865 Appalachian Hwy 35903 256-492-1360
Scott Calhoun, prin. Fax 492-7502

**Holly Pond, Cullman, Pop. 794**
Cullman County SD
Supt. — See Cullman
Holly Pond HS 400/9-12
160 New Hope Rd 35083 256-796-5169
Kim Butler, prin. Fax 796-5199
Holly Pond MS 300/6-8
91 Buckner Rd 35083 256-796-5898
Dr. Chuck Gambrill, prin. Fax 796-0680

**Hollywood, Jackson, Pop. 967**
Jackson County SD
Supt. — See Scottsboro
Pruett Center of Technology Vo/Tech
29490 US Highway 72 35752 256-574-6079
Kerry Wright, prin. Fax 259-1644

**Homewood, Jefferson, Pop. 24,859**
Homewood CSD 3,600/K-12
450 Dale Ave 35209 205-870-4203
Dr. Bill Cleveland, supt. Fax 877-4544
www.homewood.k12.al.us
Homewood HS 1,000/9-12
1901 Lakeshore Dr S 35209 205-871-9663
Dr. Zack Barnes, prin. Fax 879-0879
Homewood MS 800/6-8
395 Mecca Ave 35209 205-870-0878
Jimmie Pearson, prin. Fax 877-4573

---

Islamic Academy of Alabama 200/PK-12
1810 25th Ct S 35209 205-870-0422

**Hoover, Jefferson, Pop. 80,440**
Hoover CSD 12,600/K-12
2810 Metropolitan Way 35243 205-439-1000
Dr. Kathy Murphy, supt. Fax 439-1003
www.hoover.k12.al.us
Bumpus MS 700/7-8
6055 Fleming Pkwy 35244 205-439-2200
Dr. Tamala Maddox, prin. Fax 439-2201
Crossroads S Alt
2826 Columbiana Rd 35216 205-439-1800
Anna Whitney, prin. Fax 439-1899
Hoover HS 2,600/9-12
1000 Buccaneer Dr 35244 205-439-1200
Don Hulin, prin. Fax 439-1201
Simmons MS 900/6-8
1575 Patton Chapel Rd 35226 205-439-2100
Brian Cain, prin. Fax 439-2101
Other Schools – See Birmingham, Vestavia Hills

---

Shades Mountain Christian S 400/PK-12
2290 Old Tyler Rd 35226 205-978-6001
Brian Willett, prin. Fax 978-9120

**Hope Hull, Montgomery**

---

Hooper Academy 400/PK-12
380 Fischer Rd 36043 334-288-5980

**Hueytown, Jefferson, Pop. 15,960**
Jefferson County SD
Supt. — See Birmingham
Hueytown HS 1,100/9-12
4881 15th Street Rd 35023 205-379-4150
Joseph Garner, prin. Fax 379-4195
Hueytown MS 800/6-8
701 Sunrise Blvd 35023 205-379-5150
Chris Anders, prin. Fax 379-5195
Jefferson Co. Counseling/Lrng Ctr-West Alt
131 Dabbs Ave 35023 205-379-4130
Jason Wilson, prin. Fax 379-4135

---

Valley Creek Academy 50/K-12
3253 Virginia Dr 35023 205-491-3330
Bill Short, prin.

**Huntsville, Madison, Pop. 175,870**
Huntsville CSD, PO Box 1256 35807 21,000/PK-12
Dr. E. Casey Wardynski, supt. 256-428-6800
www.huntsvillecityschools.org
Challenger MS 500/6-8
13555 Chaney Thompson Rd SE 35803
256-428-7620
Dianne Hasty, prin. Fax 428-7621
Columbia HS 700/9-12
300 Explorer Blvd NW 35806 256-428-7576
Greg Hicks, prin. Fax 428-7579
Grissom HS 2,000/9-12
7901 Bailey Cove Rd SE 35802 256-428-8000
Becky Balentine, prin. Fax 428-8001
Huntsville Center for Technology Vo/Tech
2800 Drake Ave SW 35805 256-428-7810
Shelton Cobb, prin. Fax 428-7811
Huntsville HS 1,700/9-12
2304 Billie Watkins St SW 35801 256-428-8050
Mark Mincher, prin. Fax 428-8051
Huntsville JHS 600/7-8
817 Adams St SE 35801 256-428-7700
Stephanie Wieseman, prin. Fax 428-7701
Johnson HS 600/9-12
6201 Pueblo Dr NW 35810 256-428-8100
Eric Jones, prin. Fax 428-8118
Lee HS 800/9-12
2500 Meridian St N 35811 256-428-8150
Anne Jobe, prin. Fax 428-8151
McNair JHS 400/7-8
3221 Mastin Lake Rd NW 35810 256-428-7660
Michael Morris, prin. Fax 428-7672
New Century Technology HS 300/9-12
2500 Meridian St N 35811 256-428-7800
Sheila Roby, prin. Fax 428-7801
Westlawn MS 500/6-8
4217 9th Ave SW 35805 256-428-7760
Paula Thompson, prin. Fax 428-7761
Williams MS 200/6-8
155A Barren Fork Blvd SW 35824 256-428-7330
Sanchella Graham, prin. Fax 428-7331
Other Schools – See Hampton Cove

Madison County SD 18,500/PK-12
PO Box 226 35804 256-852-2557
Matthew Massey, supt. Fax 852-2538
https://www.madison.k12.al.us
Madison County Career Technical Center Vo/Tech
1275 Jordan Rd 35811 256-852-2170
Michael Romine, prin. Fax 851-9790
Monrovia MS 1,100/6-8
1216 Jeff Rd NW 35806 256-851-4580
Derrell Brown, prin. Fax 851-4581
PACE Academy Alt
1275 Jordan Rd 35811 256-859-1148
Tandy Shumate, prin. Fax 859-1033
Other Schools – See Gurley, Harvest, Hazel Green, New Hope, New Market, Toney

---

Alabama A & M University Post-Sec.
4900 Meridian St N 35810 256-372-5000
Grace Lutheran S 100/PK-10
3405 Memorial Pkwy SW 35801 256-881-0553
Joshua Swartz, prin. Fax 881-0563
Huntsville Bible College Post-Sec.
904 Oakwood Ave NW 35811 256-539-0834
Huntsville Hospital Post-Sec.
101 Sivley Rd SW 35801 256-533-8123
J. F. Drake State Technical College Post-Sec.
3421 Meridian St N 35811 256-539-8161
Oakwood Adventist Academy 300/K-12
7000 Adventist Blvd NW 35896 256-726-7010
Oakwood University Post-Sec.
7000 Adventist Blvd NW 35896 256-726-7000
Providence Classical S 200/K-12
605 Clinton Ave E 35801 256-852-8884
Pattie Steward, admin. Fax 852-8884
Randolph S 1,000/K-12
1005 Drake Ave SE 35802 256-799-6100
Jay Rainey, hdmstr. Fax 881-1784
St. John Paul II Catholic HS 400/9-12
7301 Old Madison Pike NW 35806 256-430-1760
Vince Aquila, prin. Fax 430-1766
Union Chapel Christian Academy 200/K-12
315 Winchester Rd NE Ste B 35811 256-489-4728
Anita Weathers M.A., prin. Fax 489-9025
University of Alabama in Huntsville Post-Sec.
301 Sparkman Dr NW 35805 256-824-1000
Valley Fellowship Christian Academy 200/PK-12
3616 Holmes Ave NW 35816 256-533-5248
Patti Simon M.A., head sch Fax 533-5253
Virginia College Post-Sec.
2021 Drake Ave SW 35801 256-533-7387
Westminster Christian Academy 500/6-12
237 Johns Rd NW 35806 256-705-8000
Ron Klein, head sch Fax 705-8001
Whitesburg Christian Academy 400/PK-12
7290 Whitesburg Dr SW 35802 256-704-7373
Jerry Reeder, hdmstr. Fax 650-6115

**Ider, DeKalb, Pop. 708**
De Kalb County SD
Supt. — See Rainsville
Ider S 800/K-12
1064 Crabapple Ln 35981 256-632-2302
Jeff Watkins, prin. Fax 632-3481

**Indian Springs, Shelby, Pop. 2,352**

---

Indian Springs S 300/8-12
190 Woodward Dr 35124 205-988-3350
Gareth Vaughan, dir. Fax 988-3797

**Irondale, Jefferson, Pop. 12,191**
Jefferson County SD
Supt. — See Birmingham
Shades Valley HS 1,400/9-12
6100 Old Leeds Rd 35210 205-379-5350
Mary Beth Blankenship, prin. Fax 379-5395

---

Jefferson Christian Academy 200/PK-12
1500 Heritage Place Dr 35210 205-956-9111

**Irvington, Mobile**
Mobile County SD
Supt. — See Mobile
Bryant Career Technical S Vo/Tech
8950 Padgett Switch Rd 36544 251-957-2845
Thomas Reed, prin. Fax 221-5420
Bryant HS 1,600/9-12
14001 Hurricane Blvd 36544 251-824-3213
Doug Estle, prin. Fax 221-3605

**Jack, Coffee**
Coffee County SD
Supt. — See Elba
Zion Chapel S 800/K-12
29256 Highway 87 36346 334-897-6275
Kevin Killingsworth, prin. Fax 897-5136

**Jackson, Clarke, Pop. 5,191**
Clarke County SD
Supt. — See Grove Hill
Jackson HS 700/9-12
321 Stanley Dr 36545 251-246-2571
Stuart Etheredge, prin. Fax 246-3190
Jackson MS 500/6-8
235 College Ave 36545 251-246-3597
Adam Andrews, prin. Fax 246-6017

---

Jackson Academy 200/K-12
PO Box 838 36545 251-246-5552
Suzanne Bailey, head sch Fax 246-0202

**Jacksonville, Calhoun, Pop. 12,298**
Calhoun County SD
Supt. — See Anniston
Calhoun County Alternative S Alt
1200 Church Ave SE 36265 256-741-7900
Robin Kines, dir. Fax 435-0745
Calhoun County Career Technical Center Vo/Tech
1200 Church Ave SE 36265 256-741-4600
Kevin Lockridge, prin. Fax 435-4221
Pleasant Valley HS 500/7-12
4141 Pleasant Valley Rd 36265 256-741-6700
Mark Proper, prin. Fax 435-0171

Jacksonville CSD 1,600/PK-12
123 College St SW 36265 256-782-5682
Tim Nabors, supt. Fax 782-5685
www.jcsboe.org
Jacksonville HS 800/7-12
1000 George Douthit Dr SW 36265 256-782-8800
Rick Carter, prin. Fax 782-8801

---

Jacksonville Christian Academy 200/K-12
831 Alexandria Rd SW 36265 256-435-3333
Dr. Tommy Miller, prin. Fax 435-2059
Jacksonville State University Post-Sec.
700 Pelham Rd N 36265 256-782-5781

**Jasper, Walker, Pop. 14,147**
Jasper CSD 2,700/PK-12
PO Box 500 35502 205-384-6880
Dr. Ann Jackson, supt. Fax 387-5213
www.jasper.k12.al.us
Maddox MS 600/6-8
201 Panther Trl 35501 205-384-3235
Dr. Steven Hall, prin. Fax 387-5208
Walker HS 800/9-12
1601 Highland Ave 35501 205-221-9277
Gary Boling, prin. Fax 387-5228

Walker County SD 8,100/PK-12
PO Box 311 35502 205-387-0555
Dr. Jason Adkins, supt. Fax 221-5636
www.walkercountyschools.com
Curry HS 600/9-12
155 Yellow Jacket Dr 35503 205-384-3887
Rod Aaron, prin. Fax 221-7381
Curry MS 400/6-8
115 Yellow Jacket Dr 35503 205-384-3441
Barry Wilson, prin. Fax 384-1110
Walker County Alternative S Alt
1100 Viking Dr 35501 205-387-9984
Rickey Pate, prin. Fax 387-7239
Walker County Center for Tech Vo/Tech
1100 Viking Dr 35501 205-387-0561
Christopher McCullar, prin. Fax 384-5170
Other Schools – See Carbon Hill, Cordova, Dora, Oakman, Sumiton

---

Bevill State Community College Post-Sec.
1411 Indiana Ave 35501 205-387-0511

**Jemison, Chilton, Pop. 2,561**
Chilton County SD
Supt. — See Clanton
Jemison HS 700/8-12
25125 US Highway 31 35085 205-280-4860
Diane Calloway, prin. Fax 688-4761

**Killen, Lauderdale, Pop. 1,097**
Lauderdale County SD
Supt. — See Florence
Brooks JSHS 800/7-12
4300 Highway 72 35645 256-757-2115
Stephen Howard, prin. Fax 757-1136
Thornton Career Technical Center Vo/Tech
7275 Highway 72 35645 256-757-2101
Kelley Joiner, prin. Fax 757-8692

**Kimberly, Jefferson, Pop. 2,694**
Jefferson County SD
Supt. — See Birmingham
Jordan HS 800/9-12
1920 Blue Devil Dr 35091 205-379-4850
Clifton Kanaday, prin. Fax 379-4895
North Jefferson MS 600/6-8
8350 Warrior Kimberly Rd 35091 205-379-4000
Terry Henderson, prin. Fax 379-4045

**Kinston, Coffee, Pop. 531**
Coffee County SD
Supt. — See Elba
Kinston S 500/K-12
201 College St 36453 334-565-3016
Jennifer Lee, prin. Fax 565-3494

**Lafayette, Chambers, Pop. 2,991**
Chambers County SD 3,900/PK-12
PO Box 408 36862 334-864-9343
Kelli Hodge, supt. Fax 864-0119
www.chambersk12.org
Chambers County Career Tech Center Vo/Tech
PO Box 318 36862 334-864-8863
Ken Sealy, prin. Fax 864-9394
Lafayette HS 300/9-12
214 1st Ave SE 36862 334-864-9881
Don Turner, prin. Fax 864-0650
Powell MS 200/6-8
700 Martin Luther King Dr 36862 334-864-8876
Daron Brooks, prin. Fax 864-8169
Other Schools – See Valley

---

Chambers Academy 100/K-12
15048 US Highway 431 36862 334-864-9852

**Lanett, Chambers, Pop. 6,366**
Lanett CSD 800/K-12
105 N Lanier Ave 36863 334-644-5900
Phillip Johnson, supt. Fax 644-5910
www.lanettcityschools.org

Lanett HS 200/9-12
1301 S 8th Ave 36863 334-644-5965
Jennifer Boyd, prin. Fax 644-5979
Lanett JHS 100/7-8
1301 S 8th Ave 36863 334-644-5950
Joan Gilbert, prin. Fax 644-5964

---

Springwood S 300/PK-12
PO Box 1030 36863 334-644-2191

**Leeds, Jefferson, Pop. 11,579**
Leeds CSD 1,700/PK-12
PO Box 1029 35094 205-699-5437
John Moore, supt. Fax 699-6629
www.leedsk12.org/
Leeds HS 400/9-12
1500 Greenwave Dr 35094 205-699-4510
Brent Shaw, prin. Fax 699-4515
Leeds MS 500/5-8
1771 Whitmire St 35094 205-699-4505
Dr. Bobby Byrd, prin. Fax 699-4509

**Leighton, Colbert, Pop. 711**
Colbert County SD
Supt. — See Tuscumbia
Colbert County HS 500/7-12
2200 High School St 35646 256-446-8214
Melcha Satchel, prin. Fax 446-8951

**Leroy, Washington, Pop. 902**
Washington County SD
Supt. — See Chatom
Leroy S 800/K-12
PO Box 40 36548 251-246-2000
Danny Patterson, prin. Fax 246-2199

**Lester, Limestone, Pop. 111**
Limestone County SD
Supt. — See Athens
West Limestone S 1,000/K-12
10945 W School House Rd 35647 256-233-6687
Charlotte Craig, prin. Fax 233-8034

**Letohatchee, Lowndes**
Lowndes County SD
Supt. — See Hayneville
Calhoun HS 300/9-12
8213 County Road 33 36047 334-227-4515
Nicholas Townsend, prin. Fax 227-8335

**Lexington, Lauderdale, Pop. 728**
Lauderdale County SD
Supt. — See Florence
Lexington S 900/K-12
101 School St 35648 256-229-6622
Willie Joiner, prin. Fax 229-6636

**Lincoln, Talladega, Pop. 6,180**
Talladega County SD
Supt. — See Talladega
Drew MS 300/7-8
78975 AL Highway 21 35096 256-315-5280
Dr. Rhonda Lee, prin. Fax 315-5290
Lincoln HS 500/9-12
78989 AL Highway 77 35096 256-315-5295
Andy Keith, prin. Fax 315-5315

**Linden, Marengo, Pop. 2,103**
Linden CSD 500/PK-12
PO Box 480609 36748 334-295-8802
George Baldwin, supt. Fax 295-8801
www.lindencity.org
Austin JHS 100/6-8
PO Box 480699 36748 334-295-5378
Terry Gosa, prin. Fax 295-5376
Linden HS 200/9-12
PO Box 480729 36748 334-295-4287
Dr. Timothy Thurman, prin. Fax 295-0988

Marengo County SD 1,400/PK-12
PO Box 480339 36748 334-295-4123
Luke Hallmark, supt. Fax 295-2259
www.marengocounty.schoolinsites.com/
Other Schools – See Dixons Mills, Sweet Water, Thomaston

---

Marengo Academy 200/K-12
2103 S Main St 36748 334-295-4151

**Lineville, Clay, Pop. 2,331**
Clay County SD
Supt. — See Ashland
Central HS of Clay County 500/9-12
1 Bob Riley Dr 36266 256-396-1400
Steve Giddens, prin. Fax 396-2452
Central JHS of Clay County 7-8
1 Bob Riley Dr 36266 256-396-1401
Russell Hathcock, prin. Fax 396-2452

**Livingston, Sumter, Pop. 3,462**
Sumter County SD 1,800/PK-12
PO Box 10 35470 205-652-9605
Dr. Tyrone Yarbrough, supt. Fax 652-9641
www.sumter.k12.al.us
Bell-Brown Career Technical Center Vo/Tech
PO Box 1380 35470 205-652-9469
Fax 652-9487
Other Schools – See York

---

University of West Alabama Post-Sec.
UWA Station 04 35470 205-652-3400

**Loachapoka, Lee, Pop. 179**
Lee County SD
Supt. — See Opelika
Loachapoka HS 300/7-12
PO Box 187 36865 334-887-8038
Zelda Kitt, prin. Fax 887-5228

**Locust Fork, Blount, Pop. 1,182**
Blount County SD
Supt. — See Oneonta
Locust Fork HS 700/7-12
77 School Rd 35097 205-681-7846
Thomas Smitherman, prin. Fax 681-6175

**Lowndesboro, Lowndes, Pop. 112**

---

Lowndes Academy 200/K-12
PO Box 99 36752 334-278-3366

**Luverne, Crenshaw, Pop. 2,775**
Crenshaw County SD 2,200/PK-12
183 Votec Dr 36049 334-335-6519
Dr. Boyd English, supt. Fax 335-6510
crenshawcounty.schoolinsites.com
Crenshaw County AVTS Vo/Tech
183 Votec Dr 36049 334-335-6519
Ashley Catrett, prin. Fax 335-6510
Luverne S 900/PK-12
194 First Ave 36049 334-335-3331
Jamie Howard, prin. Fax 335-2246
Other Schools – See Brantley, Highland Home

---

Crenshaw Christian Academy 200/K-12
608 Country Club Dr 36049 334-335-5749

**Lynn, Winston, Pop. 651**
Winston County SD
Supt. — See Double Springs
Lynn HS 200/8-12
531 E Main St 35575 205-893-5471
Timothy Tittle, prin. Fax 893-2484

**Mc Calla, Jefferson**
Jefferson County SD
Supt. — See Birmingham
McAdory HS 900/9-12
4800 McAdory School Rd 35111 205-379-4700
Michael Humphries, prin. Fax 481-8037
McAdory MS 900/6-8
5450 Yellow Jacket Blvd 35111 205-379-4730
James McLeod, prin. Fax 379-4745

**Mc Intosh, Washington, Pop. 237**
Washington County SD
Supt. — See Chatom
McIntosh HS 300/6-12
PO Box 359 36553 251-944-2449
Jamelle Sauls, prin. Fax 944-8779

**Mc Kenzie, Butler, Pop. 519**
Butler County SD
Supt. — See Greenville
Mc Kenzie S 300/K-12
PO Box 158 36456 334-374-2711
Michael Gunter, prin. Fax 374-8108

**Madison, Madison, Pop. 41,860**
Madison CSD 8,200/PK-12
211 Celtic Dr 35758 256-464-8370
Dr. Dee Fowler, supt. Fax 464-8291
www.madisoncity.k12.al.us
Academy Alt
11306 County Line Rd 35756 256-216-5313
Dr. Treva Stewart, prin. Fax 216-5314
Clemens HS 9-12
11306 County Line Rd 35756 256-216-5313
Dr. Brian Clayton, prin. Fax 216-5314
Discovery MS 600/7-8
1304 Hughes Rd 35758 256-837-3735
Eric Terrell, prin. Fax 837-1573
Jones HS 2,300/9-12
650 Hughes Rd 35758 256-772-2547
Sylvia Lambert, prin. Fax 772-6698
Liberty MS 800/7-8
281 Dock Murphy Dr 35758 256-430-0001
Nelson Brown, prin. Fax 430-0282

---

ITT Technical Institute Post-Sec.
9238 Madison Blvd Ste 500 35758 256-542-2900
Madison Academy 900/PK-12
325 Slaughter Rd 35758 256-469-6400

**Maplesville, Chilton, Pop. 698**
Chilton County SD
Supt. — See Clanton
Isabella S 700/K-12
11338 County Road 15 36750 205-280-2770
Ricky Porter, prin. Fax 755-8549
Maplesville S 500/K-12
1256 AL Highway 139 36750 205-280-4900
Steven Hunter, prin. Fax 366-2531

**Marbury, Autauga, Pop. 1,390**
Autauga County SD
Supt. — See Prattville
Marbury MS 500/6-8
PO Box A 36051 334-365-3522
Jerome Barrington, prin. Fax 755-3168

**Marion, Perry, Pop. 3,671**
Perry County SD 1,800/PK-12
PO Box 900 36756 334-683-6528
John Heard, supt. Fax 683-8427
www.perrycountyal.org
Marion S 500/PK-12
PO Box 150 36756 334-683-6741
Fred Moore, prin. Fax 683-8838
Other Schools – See Uniontown

---

Judson College Post-Sec.
302 Bibb St 36756 800-447-9472
Marion Academy 100/PK-12
2002 Prier Dr 36756 334-683-8204
Marion Military Institute Post-Sec.
1101 Washington St 36756 800-664-1842

**Midfield, Jefferson, Pop. 5,311**
Midfield CSD 1,300/K-12
417 Parkwood St 35228 205-923-2262
Demica Sanders, supt. Fax 929-0585
www.midfield.k12.al.us/
Midfield Area Vocational HS Vo/Tech
1600 High School Dr 35228 205-923-2833
Marcus Harris, coord. Fax 929-0593
Midfield HS 400/9-12
1600 High School Dr 35228 205-923-2833
Shun Williams, prin. Fax 929-0593
Rutledge MS 400/5-8
1221 8th St 35228 205-780-8647
Marcus Harris, prin. Fax 780-3664

**Midland City, Dale, Pop. 2,267**
Dale County SD
Supt. — See Ozark
Dale County HS 400/9-12
PO Box 1140 36350 334-983-3541
Matthew Humphrey, prin. Fax 983-1549

**Millbrook, Elmore, Pop. 14,375**
Elmore County SD
Supt. — See Wetumpka
Millbrook MS 1,200/5-8
4228 Chapman Rd 36054 334-285-2100
Ayena Jackson, prin. Fax 285-2102
Stanhope Elmore HS 1,200/9-12
4300 Main St 36054 334-285-4263
Jamey McGowin, prin. Fax 285-4575

**Millport, Lamar, Pop. 1,035**
Lamar County SD
Supt. — See Vernon
South Lamar S 500/K-12
300 Sls Rd 35576 205-662-4411
Craig Henson, prin. Fax 662-4544

**Millry, Washington, Pop. 541**
Washington County SD
Supt. — See Chatom
Millry S 600/K-12
PO Box 65 36558 251-846-2987
John Carter, prin. Fax 846-2986

**Mobile, Mobile, Pop. 192,396**
Mobile County SD 58,200/PK-12
PO Box 180069 36618 251-221-4000
Martha Peek, supt. Fax 221-4399
www.mcpss.com
Baker HS 2,300/9-12
8901 Airport Blvd 36608 251-221-3000
Clem Richardson, prin. Fax 221-3004
Burns MS 1,000/6-8
6175 Girby Rd 36693 251-221-2025
John Adams, prin. Fax 221-2021
Calloway-Smith MS 800/6-8
350 N Lawrence St 36603 251-221-2042
D.H. Walton, prin. Fax 221-2041
Causey MS 1,400/6-8
2205 McFarland Rd 36695 251-221-2060
John Poiroux, prin. Fax 221-2062
Chastang MS 600/6-8
2800 Berkley Ave 36617 251-221-2081
Sonya Floyd, prin. Fax 221-2080
Clark-Shaw Magnet S 800/5-8
5960 Arlberg St 36608 251-221-2106
Joe Toomey, prin. Fax 221-2108
Davidson HS 1,600/9-12
3900 Pleasant Valley Rd 36609 251-221-3084
Lewis Copeland, prin. Fax 221-3083
Denton MS 800/6-8
3800 Pleasant Valley Rd 36609 251-221-2148
Clint Allen, prin. Fax 221-2152
Dunbar Magnet S 500/4-8
500 Saint Anthony St 36603 251-221-2160
Timesha Dumas, prin. Fax 221-2162
Eanes MS 400/6-8
1901 Hurtel St 36605 251-221-2189
Kirven Lang, prin. Fax 221-2191
LeFlore Magnet HS 900/9-12
700 Donald St 36617 251-221-3125
Alvin Dailey, prin. Fax 221-3667
Murphy HS 2,300/9-12
100 S Carlen St 36606 251-221-3184
William Smith, prin. Fax 221-3188
Pathway S Alt
100 N Florida St 36607 251-221-5010
Ronald Coleman, prin. Fax 221-6801
Phillips Preparatory S 800/6-8
3255 Old Shell Rd 36607 251-221-2286
Brenda Hartzog, prin. Fax 221-2285
Pillans MS 600/6-8
2051 Military Rd 36605 251-221-2300
Ed Sanderson, prin. Fax 221-2314
Rain HS 700/9-12
3125 Dauphin Island Pkwy 36605 251-221-3233
Marlon Firle, prin. Fax 221-3229
Scarborough MS 500/6-8
1800 Phillips Ln 36618 251-221-2323
Dr. Jason Laffitte, prin. Fax 221-2321
Washington MS 300/6-8
1961 Andrews St 36617 251-221-2361
Angie Brown, prin. Fax 221-2367
Williamson HS 800/9-12
1567 E Dublin St 36605 251-221-3411
Jeffery Tolbert, prin. Fax 221-3414
Continuous Learning Center Adult
1870 Pleasant Ave 36617 251-221-2122
Aithan Brewer, prin. Fax 221-2124
Other Schools – See Bayou La Batre, Citronelle, Eight Mile, Grand Bay, Irvington, Prichard, Semmes, Theodore

---

Bishop State Community College Post-Sec.
351 N Broad St 36603 251-405-7000
Blue Cliff Career College Post-Sec.
2970 Cottage Hill Rd # 175 36606 251-473-2220

Cottage Hill Christian Academy 200/9-12
7355 Creekwood Dr 36695 251-634-2513
Jim McMillan, head sch Fax 634-2566
Faith Academy 1,900/PK-12
8650 Tanner Williams Rd 36608 251-633-7267
Tim Skelton, hdmstr. Fax 633-9133
Fortis College Post-Sec.
3590 Pleasant Valley Rd 36609 251-344-1203
Fortis College Post-Sec.
300 Azalea Rd Ste F 36609 251-342-3230
ITT Technical Institute Post-Sec.
3100 Cottage Hill Rd Bldg 3 36606 251-472-4760
McGill-Toolen HS 1,100/9-12
1501 Old Shell Rd 36604 251-445-2900
Michelle Haas, prin. Fax 433-8356
Mobile Christian S 600/PK-12
5900 Cottage Hill Rd 36609 251-661-1613
Remington College Post-Sec.
828 Downtowner Loop W 36609 251-343-8200
St. Luke's Episcopal S 700/PK-12
1400 S University Blvd 36609 251-666-2991
St. Paul's Episcopal S 1,300/PK-12
161 Dogwood Ln 36608 251-342-6700
F. Martin Lester, hdmstr. Fax 342-1844
Spring Hill College Post-Sec.
4000 Dauphin St 36608 251-380-4000
UMS Wright Preparatory S 1,300/PK-12
65 Mobile St 36607 251-479-6551
Dr. Tony Havard, hdmstr. Fax 470-9010
University of Mobile Post-Sec.
5735 College Pkwy 36613 800-946-7267
University of South Alabama Post-Sec.
307 University Blvd N 36688 251-460-6101
Virginia College Post-Sec.
3725 Airport Blvd Ste 165 36608 251-343-7227

**Monroeville, Monroe, Pop. 6,440**
Monroe County SD 3,400/PK-12
109 Pickens St 36460 251-575-2168
Dr. James T. Jeffers, supt. Fax 575-9353
www.monroe.k12.al.us/
Carmichael Alternative S Alt
1323 Veterans Dr 36460 251-575-4189
Larry Woolfolk, prin. Fax 575-9648
Monroe County Career Technical Center Vo/Tech
230 Tiger Dr 36460 251-575-4381
Edna Richardson, prin. Fax 575-2017
Monroe County HS 600/9-12
212 Tiger Dr 36460 251-575-3258
Maurice Woody, prin. Fax 575-2019
Monroeville MS 400/5-8
201 York St 36460 251-575-4121
Valerie Stevens, prin. Fax 575-2934
Other Schools – See Beatrice, Excel, Uriah

Alabama Southern Community College Post-Sec.
PO Box 2000 36461 251-575-3156
Monroe Academy 500/PK-12
4096 S Alabama Ave 36460 251-743-3932

**Montevallo, Shelby, Pop. 6,221**
Shelby County SD
Supt. — See Columbiana
Calera MS 200/6-8
9178 Highway 22 35115 205-682-6140
Branden Vincent, prin. Fax 682-6145
Montevallo HS 400/9-12
980 Oak St 35115 205-682-6400
Jeremy Turner, prin. Fax 682-6405
Montevallo MS 300/6-8
235 Samford St 35115 205-682-6410
Sheila Lewis, prin. Fax 682-6415

University of Montevallo 35115 Post-Sec.
205-665-6000

**Montgomery, Montgomery, Pop. 203,255**
Montgomery County SD 32,100/K-12
PO Box 1991 36102 334-223-6700
Margaret Allen, supt. Fax 269-3076
www.mps.k12.al.us
Baldwin Arts & Academics Magnet S 600/6-8
410 S McDonough St 36104 334-269-3870
Jannette Wright, prin. Fax 269-3918
Bellingrath MS 700/6-8
3350 S Court St 36105 334-269-3623
Ibrahim Lee, prin. Fax 269-6173
Brewbaker MS 900/6-8
4425 Brewbaker Dr 36116 334-284-8008
Cameron Whitlow, prin. Fax 284-8052
Brewbaker Technology Magnet HS 600/9-12
4405 Brewbaker Dr 36116 334-284-7100
April Wise-Lee, prin. Fax 284-7110
Capitol Heights MS 800/6-8
116 Federal Dr 36107 334-260-1000
Jerone Torbert, prin. Fax 260-1049
Carr MS 800/6-8
1610 Ray Thorington Rd 36117 334-244-4005
Brittany Aarestad, prin. Fax 244-4009
Carver HS 1,300/9-12
2001 W Fairview Ave 36108 334-269-3636
Gary Hall, prin. Fax 269-3680
Davis HS 2,100/9-12
3420 Carter Hill Rd 36111 334-269-3712
Bobby Abrams, prin. Fax 269-3715
Fews Secondary Acceleration Academy 50/Alt
321 Early St 36104 334-269-3665
Charlesetta Robinson, prin. Fax 269-3743
Floyd MS for Math Science & Technology 500/6-8
3444 Le Bron Rd 36111 334-284-7130
Vince Johnson, prin. Fax 284-7125
Goodwyn MS 700/6-8
209 Perry Hill Rd 36109 334-260-1021
Curtis Black, prin. Fax 260-1079
Lanier HS 1,000/9-12
1756 S Court St 36104 334-269-3726
Antonio Williams, prin. Fax 269-6180
Lee HS 1,900/9-12
225 Ann St 36107 334-269-3742
Lorenza Pharrams, prin. Fax 269-3888
Loveless Academic Magnet HS 500/9-12
215 Hall St 36104 334-269-3839
Barbara Sankey, prin. Fax 269-3961
McKee MS 1,000/6-8
4017 McInnis Dr 36116 334-284-7528
Patrick Nelson, prin. Fax 241-5308
Montgomery Prep Acad Career Technologies Alt
1200 Hugh St 36108 334-241-5307
Marsha Baugh, prin. Fax 241-9604
Park Crossing HS 1,000/9-12
8000 Park Xing 36117 334-260-8121
Tracy Hubbert, prin. Fax 215-0706
Progressive Academy of Creative Ed 100/Alt
3315 Hayneville Rd 36108 334-269-3760
Rodrick James, prin. Fax 269-3989
Southlawn MS 700/6-8
5333 Mobile Hwy 36108 334-284-8086
Rafiq Vaughn, prin. Fax 284-8094
Washington Magnet HS 500/9-12
632 S Union St 36104 334-269-3617
Dr. Quesha Starks, prin. Fax 269-6140
Other Schools – See Pike Road

Alabama Christian Academy 1,000/PK-12
4700 Wares Ferry Rd 36109 334-277-1985
Alabama State University Post-Sec.
915 S Jackson St 36104 334-229-4100
Amridge University Post-Sec.
1200 Taylor Rd 36117 888-790-8080
Auburn University at Montgomery Post-Sec.
PO Box 244023 36124 334-244-3000
Baptist Medical Center Post-Sec.
301 Brown Springs Rd 36117 334-273-4400
Canterbury HS 100/6-12
3701 Atlanta Hwy 36109 334-834-2273
Community College of the Air Force Post-Sec.
100 S Turner Blvd 36114 334-649-5000
Eastwood Christian S 400/K-12
1701 E Trinity Blvd 36106 334-272-8195
Evangel Christian Academy 300/PK-12
3975 Vaughn Rd 36106 334-272-3882
Rev. Scott Matthes, admin. Fax 272-5662
Faulkner University Post-Sec.
5345 Atlanta Hwy 36109 334-272-5820
Fortis College Post-Sec.
3736 Atlanta Hwy 36109 334-272-3857
Huntingdon College Post-Sec.
1500 E Fairview Ave 36106 334-833-4222
Montgomery Academy 500/5-12
3240 Vaughn Rd 36106 334-272-8210
Vivian Barfoot, hdmstr. Fax 277-3240
Montgomery Catholic Prep HS 300/9-12
5350 Vaughn Rd 36116 334-272-7220
Chad Barwick, prin. Fax 272-2440
Montgomery Catholic Prep MS 200/7-8
5350 Vaughn Rd 36116 334-272-2465
Chad Barwick, prin. Fax 272-2330
Prince Institute - Southeast Post-Sec.
7735 Atlanta Hwy 36117 334-271-1670
St. James S 1,000/PK-12
6010 Vaughn Rd 36116 334-277-8033
Melba Richardson, head sch Fax 277-2542
South University Post-Sec.
5355 Vaughn Rd 36116 334-395-8800
Success Unlimited Academy 200/PK-12
2328 Fairlane Dr 36116 334-213-0803
The Hair Academy Post-Sec.
3150 McGeehee Rd 36111 334-281-0411
The Robert B. Adams/LabCorp CLS Program Post-Sec.
543 S Hull St 36104 334-263-5745
Trenholm State Technical College Post-Sec.
PO Box 10048 36108 334-420-4200
Trinity Presbyterian S 900/PK-12
1700 E Trinity Blvd 36106 334-213-2100
Kerry Palmer, head sch Fax 213-2171
Virginia College Post-Sec.
6200 Atlanta Hwy 36117 334-277-3390

**Moody, Saint Clair, Pop. 11,564**
Saint Clair County SD
Supt. — See Ashville
Moody HS 700/9-12
714 High School Dr 35004 205-640-5127
Cheryl Kuyk, prin. Fax 640-2300
Moody JHS 300/7-8
600 High School Dr 35004 205-640-2040
Cassandra Taylor, prin. Fax 640-3036

**Moulton, Lawrence, Pop. 3,330**
Lawrence County SD 5,000/PK-12
14131 Market St 35650 256-905-2400
Johnny Yates, supt. Fax 905-2406
www.lawrenceal.org
Jester Learning Center Alt
371 School St 35650 256-974-3252
Aaron Goode, prin. Fax 974-3296
Lawrence County Center of Technology Vo/Tech
179 College St 35650 256-974-3751
Robert Vinzant, prin. Fax 905-2482
Lawrence County JSHS 700/9-12
102 College St 35650 256-905-2440
Thomas Jones, prin. Fax 905-2444
Moulton MS 600/5-8
660 College St 35650 256-905-2460
Stacie Givens, prin. Fax 905-2481
Other Schools – See Courtland, Town Creek, Trinity

**Moundville, Hale, Pop. 2,391**
Hale County SD
Supt. — See Greensboro
Hale County HS 500/9-12
PO Box 188 35474 205-371-2514
Cathy Seale, prin. Fax 371-6800
Hale County MS 300/6-8
120 Wildcat Way 35474 205-371-7000
Eric Perry, prin. Fax 371-7099

**Mountain Brook, Jefferson, Pop. 20,299**
Mountain Brook CSD 4,500/K-12
32 Vine St, Birmingham AL 35213 205-871-4608
Dr. Richard Barlow, supt. Fax 802-1629
www.mtnbrook.k12.al.us
Mountain Brook HS 1,000/10-12
3650 Bethune Dr 35223 205-414-3800
Amanda Hood, prin. Fax 969-8113
Mountain Brook JHS 1,100/7-9
205 Overbrook Rd, Birmingham AL 35213
205-871-3516
Donald Clayton, prin. Fax 969-8113

**Munford, Talladega, Pop. 1,274**
Talladega County SD
Supt. — See Talladega
Mumford MS, 360 Cedars Rd 36268 6-8
Angel Carter, prin. 256-315-5235
Munford HS 500/9-12
300 Cedars Rd 36268 256-315-5220
Tim Young, prin. Fax 315-5240

**Muscle Shoals, Colbert, Pop. 12,952**
Muscle Shoals CSD 2,900/PK-12
PO Box 2610 35662 256-389-2600
Dr. Brian Lindsey, supt. Fax 389-2605
www.mscs.k12.al.us
Muscle Shoals Career Academy Vo/Tech
321 Broad St 35661 256-389-2660
Gary Williams, prin. Fax 389-2662
Muscle Shoals HS 900/9-12
1900 Avalon Ave 35661 256-389-2682
Chad Holden, prin. Fax 389-2689
Muscle Shoals MS 700/6-8
100 Trojan Dr 35661 256-389-2640
Dr. Matthew Carpenter, prin. Fax 389-2647

Northwest-Shoals Community College Post-Sec.
PO Box 2545 35662 256-331-5200

**New Brockton, Coffee, Pop. 1,118**
Coffee County SD
Supt. — See Elba
New Brockton HS 400/7-12
PO Box 399 36351 334-894-2350
Gray Harrison, prin. Fax 894-5204

**New Hope, Madison, Pop. 2,743**
Madison County SD
Supt. — See Huntsville
New Hope HS 400/9-12
5216 Main Dr 35760 256-851-3280
Lavell Everett, prin. Fax 851-3281

**New Market, Madison, Pop. 1,576**
Madison County SD
Supt. — See Huntsville
Buckhorn HS 1,300/9-12
4123 Winchester Rd 35761 256-851-3300
Todd Markham, prin. Fax 851-3301
Buckhorn MS 700/7-8
4185 Winchester Rd 35761 256-851-3230
William Markham, prin. Fax 851-3231

**New Site, Tallapoosa, Pop. 769**
Tallapoosa County SD
Supt. — See Dadeville
Horseshoe Bend S 800/K-12
10684 Highway 22 E 36256 256-329-9110
James Aulner, prin. Fax 329-9119

**Newton, Dale, Pop. 1,478**
Houston County SD
Supt. — See Dothan
Wicksburg S 1,000/K-12
1172 S State Highway 123 36352 334-692-5549
Cheryl Smith, prin. Fax 692-3184

**Northport, Tuscaloosa, Pop. 23,073**
Tuscaloosa County SD
Supt. — See Tuscaloosa
Collins-Riverside MS 500/6-8
1400 3rd St 35476 205-342-2680
Bryant Williams, prin. Fax 752-8024
Echols MS 700/6-8
2701 Echols Ave 35476 205-342-2884
Jason Stapp, prin. Fax 339-1064
Northside HS 400/9-12
19230 Northside Pkwy 35475 205-342-2755
Cynthia Long, prin. Fax 339-3437
Northside MS 400/6-8
19130 Northside Pkwy 35475 205-342-2740
Bobby Beasley, prin. Fax 247-4188
Tuscaloosa County HS 1,500/9-12
12500 Wildcat Dr 35475 205-342-2670
Cynthia Simpson, prin. Fax 333-3197

**Notasulga, Macon, Pop. 958**
Macon County SD
Supt. — See Tuskegee
Notasulga S 400/PK-12
500 E Main St 36866 334-724-1240
Brelinda Sullen, prin. Fax 257-4228

Tallapoosa County SD
Supt. — See Dadeville
Reeltown S 800/PK-12
4085 AL Highway 120 36866 334-257-1670
Thomas Cochran, prin. Fax 257-3978

**Oakman, Walker, Pop. 785**
Walker County SD
Supt. — See Jasper
Oakman HS 300/9-12
PO Box 286 35579 205-622-3381
Patrick Gann, prin. Fax 622-3542

**Odenville, Saint Clair, Pop. 3,535**
Saint Clair County SD
Supt. — See Ashville
Odenville MS 500/6-8
100 1st Ave 35120 205-629-2280
Walker Cook, prin. Fax 620-2282
St. Clair County HS 600/9-12
16700 US Highway 411 35120 205-629-6222
Brian Terry, prin. Fax 629-2228

**Ohatchee, Calhoun, Pop. 1,146**
Calhoun County SD
Supt. — See Anniston
Ohatchee HS 500/7-12
100 Cherokee Trl 36271 256-741-4900
Bobby Tittle, prin. Fax 892-9181

**Oneonta, Blount, Pop. 6,492**
Blount County SD, PO Box 578 35121 8,400/K-12
Rodney Green, supt. 205-625-4102
www.blountboe.net
Allgood Alternative S Alt
45 Community Rd 35121 205-274-9865
Jeff Dean, prin. Fax 274-9865
Appalachian S 600/K-12
350 County Highway 12 35121 205-274-9712
Jonathan Cleveland, prin. Fax 274-9706
Other Schools – See Blountsville, Cleveland, Hayden, Locust Fork, Remlap

Oneonta CSD 1,200/K-12
27605 State Highway 75 35121 205-625-4106
Dr. Michael Douglas, supt. Fax 274-2910
www.oneontacityschools.com
Oneonta HS 400/9-12
27605 State Highway 75 35121 205-625-3801
Lauren Wilson, prin. Fax 625-5015
Oneonta MS 6-8
27605 State Highway 75 35121 205-625-3018
Brad Newton, prin. Fax 625-3059

**Opelika, Lee, Pop. 26,170**
Lee County SD 8,700/K-12
2410 Society Hill Rd 36804 334-705-6000
James McCoy, supt. Fax 745-9822
www.lee.k12.al.us
Beauregard HS 600/9-12
7343 AL Highway 51 36804 334-745-5916
Richard Brown, prin. Fax 749-6421
Sanford MS 700/5-8
1500 Lee Road 11 36804 334-745-5023
Lura Reed, prin. Fax 745-5685
Other Schools – See Loachapoka, Smiths Station, Valley

Opelika CSD 4,300/PK-12
300 Simmons St 36801 334-745-9700
Dr. Mark Neighbors, supt. Fax 745-9706
www.opelikaschools.org
Opelika HS 1,300/9-12
1700 Lafayette Pkwy 36801 334-745-9715
Dr. Farrell Seymore, prin. Fax 745-9721
Opelika Learning Center 100/Alt
214 Jeter Ave 36801 334-741-5603
Steven Carson, prin. Fax 741-5604
Opelika MS 900/6-8
1206 Denson Dr 36801 334-745-9726
Keith York, prin. Fax 745-9730

---

Southern Union State Community College Post-Sec.
1701 Lafayette Pkwy 36801 334-745-6437
Trinity Christian S 300/K-12
PO Box 311 36803 334-745-2464

**Opp, Covington, Pop. 6,581**
Opp CSD 1,400/K-12
PO Box 840 36467 334-493-3173
Michael Smithart, supt. Fax 493-3060
www.oppcityschools.com
Opp HS 400/9-12
502 N Maloy St 36467 334-493-4561
Ron Snell, prin. Fax 493-2146
Opp MS 400/5-8
303 E Stewart Ave 36467 334-493-6332
Aaron Hightower, prin. Fax 493-1120

**Orange Beach, Baldwin, Pop. 5,326**

---

Columbia Southern University Post-Sec.
21982 University Ln 36561 251-981-3771

**Orrville, Dallas, Pop. 204**
Dallas County SD
Supt. — See Selma
Keith MSHS 300/6-12
1166 County Road 115 36767 334-996-8464
Frederick Hardy, prin. Fax 996-0918

**Oxford, Calhoun, Pop. 21,062**
Oxford CSD 4,100/K-12
PO Box 7670 36203 256-241-3140
Dr. Jeff Goodwin, supt. Fax 241-3938
www.oxfordcityschools.com
Oxford Area Vo HS Vo/Tech
1 Yellow Jacket Dr 36203 256-241-3166
Fax 241-3943
Oxford HS 1,200/9-12
1 Yellow Jacket Dr 36203 256-241-3166
Chris Cox, prin. Fax 241-3943
Oxford MS 700/7-8
1750 US Highway 78 W 36203 256-241-3816
Michael Maniscalco, prin. Fax 241-3831

**Ozark, Dale, Pop. 14,570**
Dale County SD 2,900/K-12
202 S Highway 123 Ste E 36360 334-774-2355
Donny Bynum, supt. Fax 774-3503
www.dalecountyboe.org/
Other Schools – See Ariton, Midland City, Pinckard, Skipperville

Ozark CSD 2,400/PK-12
1044 Andrews Ave 36360 334-774-5197
Dr. Richard McInturf, supt. Fax 774-2685
www.ozarkcityschools.net
Carroll HS 700/9-12
141 Eagle Way 36360 334-774-4915
Sean Clark, prin. Fax 774-1865
Carroll HS Career Center Vo/Tech
227 Faust Ave 36360 334-774-4949
Dana Griggs, prin. Fax 774-8314
Smith MS 500/6-8
994 Andrews Ave 36360 334-774-4913
Danelle Peterman, prin. Fax 774-0568

**Pelham, Shelby, Pop. 21,087**
Pelham CSD K-12
3113 Cummings St 35124 205-624-3700
Dr. Scott Coefield, supt. Fax 624-3980
www.pelhamcityschools.org
Pelham HS 1,700/9-12
2500 Panther Cir 35124 205-682-5500
Jason Yohn, prin. Fax 682-5505
Other Schools – See Birmingham

**Pell City, Saint Clair, Pop. 12,505**
Pell City CSD 4,200/PK-12
3105 15th Ave N 35125 205-884-4440
Dr. Michael Barber, supt. Fax 814-1010
www.pellcityschools.net
Duran JHS 300/8-8
309 Williamson Dr 35125 205-338-2825
Richard Garris, prin. Fax 884-6502
Pell City HS 1,300/9-12
1300 Cogswell Ave 35125 205-338-2250
Tony Dowdy, prin. Fax 338-2838

---

Victory Christian S 400/PK-12
PO Box 710 35125 205-338-2901

**Phenix City, Russell, Pop. 32,176**
Phenix City SD 6,400/PK-12
PO Box 460 36868 334-298-0534
Randy Wilkes, supt. Fax 298-2674
www.pcboe.net
Central HS 1,300/10-12
2400 Dobbs Dr 36870 334-298-3626
Tommy Vickers, prin. Fax 298-7690
Central HS Freshman Academy 400/9-9
2800 Dobbs Dr 36870 334-448-8880
Rachael Fowler, prin. Fax 448-8690
South Girard S 500/8-8
521 Fontaine Rd 36869 334-298-2527
Kerry McDonald, prin. Fax 297-8274
Success Academy Alt
1700 17th Ave 36867 334-298-9876

Russell County SD 3,200/PK-12
PO Box 400 36868 706-321-2224
Brenda Coley, supt. Fax 448-8314
rcsd-al.schoolloop.com/
Other Schools – See Seale

---

Chattahoochee Valley Community College Post-Sec.
2602 College Dr 36869 334-291-4900

**Phil Campbell, Franklin, Pop. 1,134**
Franklin County SD
Supt. — See Russellville
Phil Campbell HS 400/7-12
PO Box 849 35581 256-331-2150
Gary Odom, prin. Fax 331-2151

**Piedmont, Calhoun, Pop. 4,787**
Piedmont CSD 1,200/K-12
502 W Hood St 36272 256-447-8831
Matthew Akin, supt. Fax 447-6486
www.piedmont.k12.al.us/
Piedmont HS 300/9-12
750 Tom Bible Memorial Hwy 36272 256-447-2829
Adam Clemons, prin. Fax 447-8722
Piedmont MS 300/6-8
401 N Main St 36272 256-447-6165
Jerry Snow, prin. Fax 447-8070

**Pike Road, Montgomery, Pop. 5,366**
Montgomery County SD
Supt. — See Montgomery
Washington MS 600/6-8
696 Georgia Washington Rd 36064 334-215-8290
Orlando Ledyard, prin. Fax 215-1304

**Pinckard, Dale, Pop. 638**
Dale County SD
Supt. — See Ozark
South Dale MS 400/5-8
PO Box D 36371 334-983-3077
Bucky Sconyers, prin. Fax 983-5882

**Pinson, Jefferson, Pop. 7,099**
Jefferson County SD
Supt. — See Birmingham
Clay-Chalkville HS 1,300/9-12
6623 Roe Chandler Rd 35126 205-379-3050
Michael Lee, prin. Fax 680-8128
Pinson Valley HS 1,000/9-12
6895 Highway 75 35126 205-379-5100
Michael Turner, prin. Fax 379-5145
Rudd MS 900/6-8
4526 Rudd School Rd 35126 205-379-5300
Susan Slaney, prin. Fax 680-8124

**Pisgah, Jackson, Pop. 710**
Jackson County SD
Supt. — See Scottsboro
Pisgah S 600/K-12
60 Metcalf St 35765 256-451-3241
Rhonda Wheeler, prin. Fax 451-3457

**Plantersville, Dallas**
Dallas County SD
Supt. — See Selma

Dallas County HS 600/9-12
PO Box 145 36758 334-366-2232
Todd Reece, prin. Fax 366-4015

**Pleasant Grove, Jefferson, Pop. 10,034**
Jefferson County SD
Supt. — See Birmingham
Pleasant Grove HS 600/9-12
100 Spartan Dr 35127 205-379-5250
Wayne Byram, prin. Fax 379-5265
Pleasant Grove MS 500/6-8
805 7th Ave 35127 205-379-5280
Jarvis Watkins, prin. Fax 379-5295

**Prattville, Autauga, Pop. 33,381**
Autauga County SD 9,800/K-12
153 W 4th St 36067 334-365-5706
Spence Agee, supt. Fax 361-3828
www.acboe.net
Autauga County Tech Center Vo/Tech
1301 Upper Kingston Rd 36067 334-361-0258
Brock Dunn, admin. Fax 361-3839
Prattville HS 2,100/9-12
PO Box 680810 36068 334-365-8804
Richard Dennis, prin. Fax 358-0011
Prattville JHS 1,100/7-8
1089 Martin Luther King Dr 36067 334-365-6697
Janice Stockman, prin. Fax 361-3870
Second Chance Alternative S Alt
816 Cardinal Ln 36067 334-361-3834
Darryl Pickett, prin. Fax 361-3834
Other Schools – See Autaugaville, Billingsley, Deatsville, Marbury

---

Autauga Academy 300/PK-12
497 Golson Rd 36067 334-365-4343
Dr. Al Griffin, hdmstr. Fax 365-7713
East Memorial Christian Academy 300/K-12
1320 Old Ridge Rd E 36066 334-358-4085
Prattville Christian Academy 700/PK-12
322 Old Farm Ln N 36066 334-285-0077
Ron Mitchell, pres. Fax 285-1777

**Prichard, Mobile, Pop. 22,453**
Mobile County SD
Supt. — See Mobile
Faulkner Career Tech Center Vo/Tech
33 W Elm St 36610 251-221-5431
William White, prin. Fax 221-5433
Mobile County Training MS 200/6-8
800 Whitley St 36610 251-221-2267
Douglas July, prin. Fax 221-2269
Vigor HS 800/9-12
913 N Wilson Ave 36610 251-221-3045
Gerald Cunningham, prin. Fax 221-3378

**Princeton, Jackson**
Jackson County SD
Supt. — See Scottsboro
Paint Rock Valley S 100/K-12
PO Box 150 35766 256-776-2628
Clay Webber, prin. Fax 776-0042

**Ragland, Saint Clair, Pop. 1,613**
Saint Clair County SD
Supt. — See Ashville
Ragland S 600/K-12
1060 Main St 35131 205-472-2123
Roy Bliss, prin. Fax 472-0086

**Rainbow City, Etowah, Pop. 9,471**
Etowah County SD
Supt. — See Gadsden
Rainbow MS 700/6-8
454 Lumbley Rd 35906 256-442-1095
Tracy Cross, prin. Fax 442-1028

---

Westbrook Christian S 600/PK-12
100 Westminster Dr 35906 256-442-7457

**Rainsville, DeKalb, Pop. 4,882**
De Kalb County SD 8,700/K-12
PO Box 1668 35986 256-638-6921
Hugh Taylor, supt. Fax 638-6972
www.dekalbk12.org
De Kalb Vocational S Vo/Tech
PO Box 529 35986 256-638-4421
Gelane Nelson, prin. Fax 638-4420
Plainview S 1,100/K-12
PO Box 469 35986 256-638-3510
Tony Richards, prin. Fax 638-6811
Other Schools – See Collinsville, Crossville, Fyffe, Geraldine, Ider, Sylvania, Valley Head

---

Northeast Alabama Community College Post-Sec.
PO Box 159 35986 256-638-4418

**Ranburne, Cleburne, Pop. 406**
Cleburne County SD
Supt. — See Heflin
Ranburne MSHS 500/5-12
21045 Main St 36273 256-568-3402
Tim Ward, prin. Fax 568-2605

**Red Bay, Franklin, Pop. 3,100**
Franklin County SD
Supt. — See Russellville
Red Bay S 800/PK-12
PO Box 1518 35582 256-331-2270
Kenny Sparks, prin. Fax 331-2281

**Red Level, Covington, Pop. 487**
Covington County SD
Supt. — See Andalusia
Red Level HS 300/7-12
PO Box D 36474 334-469-5315
Randy McGlaun, prin. Fax 469-6192

**Reformi, Pickens, Pop. 1,691**
Pickens County SD
Supt. — See Carrollton
Pickens County JSHS 300/7-12
205 4th Ave SE 35481 205-375-2344
SheMia Wilson, prin. Fax 375-8151

**Remlap, Blount**
Blount County SD
Supt. — See Oneonta
Southeastern S 500/K-12
18770 State Highway 75 35133 205-681-3964
Billy Puckett, prin. Fax 681-3975

**Roanoke, Randolph, Pop. 6,021**
Roanoke CSD 1,600/PK-12
PO Box 1367 36274 334-863-2628
Chuck Marcum, supt. Fax 863-2849
www.roanokecityschools.org/
Handley HS 500/9-12
PO Box 1393 36274 334-863-6815
Greg Foster, prin. Fax 863-6284
Handley MS 600/4-8
PO Box 725 36274 334-863-4174
Lynn Robinson, prin. Fax 863-6129

**Robertsdale, Baldwin, Pop. 5,180**
Baldwin County SD
Supt. — See Bay Minette
Central Baldwin MS 700/7-8
PO Box 930 36567 251-947-2327
Phillip Fountain, prin. Fax 947-1949
Robertsdale HS 1,300/9-12
PO Box 69 36567 251-947-4154
Joseph Roh, prin. Fax 947-2666
South Baldwin Center for Tech Vo/Tech
19200 Carolina St 36567 251-947-5041
Kendall Mowdy, prin. Fax 947-4837
Taylor Alternative S 50/Alt
19150 Wilters St 36567 251-970-4415
Don Johnson, prin. Fax 970-4416

---

Central Christian S 300/PK-12
17395 State Highway 104 36567 251-947-5043
Tim Shelton, admin. Fax 947-2572

**Rockford, Coosa, Pop. 477**
Coosa County SD 1,200/K-12
PO Box 37 35136 256-377-4913
Dennis Sanford, supt. Fax 377-2385
www.coosaschools.k12.al.us
Central HS Coosa County 300/9-12
243 Coosa County Road 75 35136 256-377-4384
Delynn Bouldin, prin. Fax 377-4658
Central MS Coosa County 400/5-8
97 Coosa County Road 75 35136 256-377-1490
Fax 377-1493
Coosa County Science & Technology Ctr Vo/Tech
17768 US Highway 231 35136 256-377-4678
Jocelyn Marbury, dir. Fax 377-4589

**Rogersville, Lauderdale, Pop. 1,248**
Lauderdale County SD
Supt. — See Florence
Lauderdale County S 1,100/PK-12
PO Box 220 35652 256-247-3414
Eric Cornelius, prin. Fax 247-3444

**Russellville, Franklin, Pop. 9,705**
Franklin County SD 3,200/PK-12
PO Box 610 35653 256-332-1360
Gary Williams, supt. Fax 331-0069
www.franklin.k12.al.us/
Belgreen S 400/PK-12
14220 Highway 187 35653 256-332-1376
Myra Frederick, prin. Fax 332-7209
Franklin County Career Technical Center Vo/Tech
85 Jail Springs Rd 35653 256-332-2127
Scott Wiginton, dir. Fax 332-2219
Tharptown HS 300/7-12
255 Highway 80 35654 256-332-6485
Barry Laster, prin. Fax 332-2840
Other Schools – See Phil Campbell, Red Bay, Vina

Russellville CSD 2,500/K-12
1945 Waterloo Rd 35653 256-331-2000
Heath Grimes, supt. Fax 332-7323
www.rcs.k12.al.us
Russellville HS 700/9-12
1865 Waterloo Rd 35653 256-332-2110
Dr. Timothy Guinn, prin. Fax 332-8447
Russellville MS 600/6-8
765 Summit St 35653 256-331-2120
Dr. Karen Thorn, prin. Fax 332-8453

**Samson, Geneva, Pop. 1,902**
Geneva County SD
Supt. — See Geneva
Samson HS 200/9-12
209 N Broad St 36477 334-898-2371
R. DeWayne Hamilton, prin. Fax 898-7576
Samson MS 100/7-8
209 N Broad St 36477 334-898-2371
Ashley Sanders, prin. Fax 898-7576

**Sand Rock, Cherokee, Pop. 556**
Cherokee County SD
Supt. — See Centre
Sand Rock S 900/K-12
1950 Sand Rock Ave 35983 256-523-3564
John East, prin. Fax 523-3507

**Saraland, Mobile, Pop. 13,216**
Saraland CSD 2,100/K-12
943 Saraland Blvd S 36571 251-375-5420
Dr. Aaron Milner, supt. Fax 375-5430
www.saralandboe.org/
Saraland HS 700/9-12
1115 Industrial Pkwy 36571 251-602-8970
Beverly Spondike, prin. Fax 602-8994
Saraland MS - Nelson Adams Campus 600/5-8
401 Baldwin Rd 36571 251-679-9405
Alex Crane, prin. Fax 679-9456

**Sardis City, Etowah, Pop. 1,693**
Etowah County SD
Supt. — See Gadsden
Sardis HS 700/9-12
1420 Church St 35956 256-593-5221
Wendy Gibbs, prin. Fax 593-5223

**Satsuma, Mobile, Pop. 6,101**
Satsuma City SD 1,100/PK-12
PO Box 939 36572 251-380-8200
Joe Walters, supt. Fax 380-8201
satsumacity.schoolinsites.com/
Satsuma HS 700/7-12
1 Gator Cir 36572 251-380-8190
Joshua Verkouille, prin. Fax 380-8191

**Scottsboro, Jackson, Pop. 14,491**
Jackson County SD 5,700/PK-12
PO Box 490 35768 256-259-9500
Ken Harding, supt. Fax 259-0076
www.jackson.k12.al.us/
Jackson County Alternative S Alt
PO Box 490 35768 256-574-6446
Kerry Wright, prin. Fax 259-1392
Skyline S 500/K-12
897 County Road 25 35768 256-587-6561
Kevin Dukes, prin. Fax 587-6562
Other Schools – See Bridgeport, Higdon, Hollywood, Pisgah, Princeton, Section, Stevenson, Woodville

Scottsboro CSD 2,700/K-12
305 S Scott St 35768 256-218-2100
Dr. Sandra Spivey, supt. Fax 218-2190
www.scottsboroschools.net
Scottsboro HS 800/9-12
25053 John T Reid Pkwy 35768 256-218-2000
Kathy Hughes, prin. Fax 218-2090
Scottsboro JHS 400/7-8
1601 Jefferson St 35768 256-218-2300
Jason Hass, prin. Fax 218-2390

**Seale, Russell**
Russell County SD
Supt. — See Phenix City
Russell County HS 1,000/9-12
4699 Old Seale Hwy 36875 706-321-2246
Kendrick Britford, prin. Fax 855-4042
Russell County MS 600/7-8
4716 Old Seale Hwy 36875 706-321-2261
Barry Kirby, prin. Fax 855-4487

**Section, Jackson, Pop. 755**
Jackson County SD
Supt. — See Scottsboro
Section S 600/K-12
PO Box 10 35771 256-228-6718
Gene Roberts, prin. Fax 228-6252

**Selma, Dallas, Pop. 20,594**
Dallas County SD 3,300/K-12
PO Box 1056 36702 334-875-3440
Don Willingham, supt. Fax 876-4493
www.dallask12.org
Dallas County Alternative S Alt
Craig Industrial Bldg 37 36701 334-872-6761
Curtis Williams, prin. Fax 872-6761
Dallas County Career Technical Center Vo/Tech
1306 Roosevelt St 36701 334-872-8031
Jerolene Williams, dir. Fax 872-5697
Southside HS 400/9-12
7975 US Highway 80 E 36701 334-872-0518
Clarence Jackson, prin. Fax 872-0295
Tipton MS 200/7-8
2500 Tipton St 36701 334-872-8080
Jackie Averhart, prin. Fax 872-8008
Other Schools – See Orrville, Plantersville, Valley Grande

Selma CSD 4,100/PK-12
PO Box 350 36702 334-874-1600
Dr. Angela Mangum, supt. Fax 874-1604
www.selmacityschools.org
Hudson MS 500/7-8
1701 Summerfield Rd 36701 334-874-1675
LaShonda Moorer, prin. Fax 874-1679
Phoenix S 100/Alt
501 Plant St 36703 334-874-1718
Michael Bowers, prin. Fax 874-1649
Selma HS 1,000/9-12
2180 Broad St 36701 334-874-1680
Aubrey Larkin, prin. Fax 874-9450

---

Concordia College Alabama Post-Sec.
1712 Broad St 36701 334-874-5700
Ellwood Christian Academy 400/PK-12
1 Bell Rd 36701 334-877-1586
George C. Wallace State Comm College Post-Sec.
PO Box 2530 36702 334-876-9227
Meadowview Christian S 200/PK-12
1512 Old Orrville Rd 36701 334-872-8448
Morgan Academy 500/PK-12
2901 W Dallas Ave 36701 334-875-4464
Fred Williamson, hdmstr. Fax 875-4465
Selma University Post-Sec.
1501 Lapsley St 36701 334-872-2533

**Semmes, Mobile**
Mobile County SD
Supt. — See Mobile
Montgomery HS 1,900/9-12
4275 Snow Rd N 36575 251-221-3153
James Gill, prin. Fax 221-3150
Semmes MS 1,700/6-8
4566 Ed George Rd 36575 251-221-2344
Brenda Shenesey, prin. Fax 221-2347

**Sheffield, Colbert, Pop. 8,895**
Sheffield CSD 1,100/PK-12
300 W 6th St 35660 256-383-0400
Daniel Lankford, supt. Fax 386-5704
www.scs.k12.al.us
Sheffield HS 300/9-12
2800 E 19th Ave 35660 256-383-6052
Laura Kelly, prin. Fax 386-5707
Sheffield JHS 200/7-8
1803 E 30th St 35660 256-386-5735
Brezofski Anderson, prin. Fax 386-5706

**Skipperville, Dale**
Dale County SD
Supt. — See Ozark
Long HS 400/7-12
2565 County Road 60 36374 334-774-2380
Jason Steed, prin. Fax 774-3937

**Slocomb, Geneva, Pop. 1,949**
Geneva County SD
Supt. — See Geneva
Slocomb HS 300/9-12
591 S County Road 9 36375 334-886-2008
Harold Birge, prin. Fax 886-9889
Slocomb MS 300/6-8
591 S County Road 9 36375 334-886-2008
Zeb Brown, prin. Fax 886-9889

**Smiths, Lee, Pop. 3,456**

---

Glenwood S 400/PK-12
5801 Summerville Rd 36877 334-297-3614
Frankie Mitchum, hdmstr. Fax 214-9027

**Smiths Station, Lee, Pop. 4,838**
Lee County SD
Supt. — See Opelika
Smiths Station Freshman Center 9-9
1150 Lee Road 298 36877 334-664-4063
Dr. Brad Cook, prin.
Smiths Station HS 1,400/10-12
4228 Lee Road 430 36877 334-298-0969
Joaquin Richards, prin. Fax 298-1304
Smiths Station JHS 7-8
1100 Lee Road 298 36877 334-664-4070
Rick Harris, prin.

**Somerville, Morgan, Pop. 713**
Morgan County SD
Supt. — See Decatur
Brewer HS 900/9-12
59 Eva Rd 35670 256-778-8634
Jeremy Childers, prin. Fax 778-8012
Brewer Vocational HS Vo/Tech
59 Eva Rd 35670 256-309-2119
Christal Blevins, prin. Fax 309-2180

**Southside, Etowah, Pop. 8,359**
Etowah County SD
Supt. — See Gadsden
Southside HS 800/9-12
2361 School Dr 35907 256-442-2172
Chris Winningham, prin. Fax 442-2183

**Spanish Fort, Baldwin, Pop. 6,701**
Baldwin County SD
Supt. — See Bay Minette
Spanish Fort HS 1,000/9-12
1 Plaza De Toros Dr 36527 251-625-3259
Marty McRae, prin. Fax 615-5648
Spanish Fort MS 800/6-8
33899 Jimmy Faulkner Dr 36527 251-625-3271
Oliver Sinclair, prin. Fax 626-7201

**Spring Garden, Cherokee, Pop. 234**
Cherokee County SD
Supt. — See Centre
Spring Garden S 600/K-12
PO Box 31 36275 256-447-7045
Michael Welsh, prin. Fax 447-6947

**Springville, Saint Clair, Pop. 4,042**
Saint Clair County SD
Supt. — See Ashville
Springville HS 700/9-12
8295 US Highway 11 35146 205-467-7833
Virgil Winslett, prin. Fax 467-2734
Springville MS 500/6-8
6691 US Highway 11 35146 205-467-2740
Kimberly Brown, prin. Fax 467-2742

**Stevenson, Jackson, Pop. 1,968**
Jackson County SD
Supt. — See Scottsboro
North Jackson HS 500/9-12
45549 AL Highway 277 35772 256-437-2136
Sam Houston, prin. Fax 437-2400
Stevenson MS 300/5-8
701 Kentucky Ave 35772 256-437-2945
Dr. Rob Paradise, prin. Fax 437-2747

**Sulligent, Lamar, Pop. 1,890**
Lamar County SD
Supt. — See Vernon
Sulligent S 800/K-12
PO Box 909 35586 205-698-9254
Dr. Lisa Stamps, prin. Fax 698-8497

**Sumiton, Walker, Pop. 2,483**
Walker County SD
Supt. — See Jasper
Sumiton MS 400/5-8
275 1st St N 35148 205-648-2390
Chris Stephenson, prin. Fax 648-0183

---

Sumiton Christian S 400/K-12
155 Hosanna Dr 35148 205-648-6643
Cheryl Capps, prin. Fax 648-9893

**Sweet Water, Marengo, Pop. 258**
Marengo County SD
Supt. — See Linden
Sweet Water S 700/PK-12
PO Box 127 36782 334-994-4263
Phyllis Mabowitz, prin. Fax 994-4686

**Sylacauga, Talladega, Pop. 12,625**
Sylacauga CSD 2,400/PK-12
605 W 4th St 35150 256-245-5256
Michael Freeman, supt. Fax 245-6665
www.sylacauga.k12.al.us
Nichols-Lawson MS 600/6-8
1550 Talladega Hwy 35150 256-245-4376
Debbie Barnett, prin. Fax 245-4071
Sylacauga HS 700/9-12
701 N Broadway Ave 35150 256-249-0911
Jason Bryant, prin. Fax 245-1026

Talladega County SD
Supt. — See Talladega
Comer Memorial HS 500/7-12
801 Seminole Ave 35150 256-315-5400
Judson Warlick, prin. Fax 315-5420
Fayetteville S 600/K-12
170 WW Averitte Dr 35151 256-315-5550
Byron Brasher, prin. Fax 315-5575

**Sylvania, DeKalb, Pop. 1,781**
De Kalb County SD
Supt. — See Rainsville
Sylvania S 900/K-12
133 2nd St N 35988 256-638-2030
Westley King, prin. Fax 638-7839

**Talladega, Talladega, Pop. 15,505**
Talladega CSD 2,300/PK-12
PO Box 946 35161 256-315-5600
Douglas Campbell, supt. Fax 315-5606
www.talladega-cs.net
Ellis JHS 300/7-8
414 Elm St 35160 256-315-5700
Shari Dye, prin. Fax 315-5704
Talladega High Career Tech Vo/Tech
110 Picadilly Dr 35160 256-315-5688
Trisha Howell-Turner, dir. Fax 315-5690
Talladega HS 600/9-12
1177 McMillan St E 35160 256-315-5666
Darius Williams, admin. Fax 315-5670

Talladega County SD 7,200/K-12
PO Box 887 35161 256-315-5100
Dr. Suzanne Lacey, supt. Fax 315-5126
www.tcboe.org
Talladega County Central HS 200/7-12
5104 Howell Cove Rd 35160 256-315-5340
Quentin Lee, prin. Fax 315-5350
Other Schools – See Alpine, Childersburg, Lincoln, Munford, Sylacauga

---

Alabama Institute for the Deaf and Blind Post-Sec.
PO Box 698 35161 256-761-3207
Talladega College Post-Sec.
627 Battle St W 35160 256-362-0206

**Tallassee, Elmore, Pop. 4,755**
Tallassee CSD 1,900/K-12
308 King St 36078 334-283-6864
Wade Shipman, supt. Fax 283-4338
www.tcschools.com
Southside MS 600/5-8
901 EB Payne Sr Dr 36078 334-283-2151
Bruce Dean, prin. Fax 283-3577
Tallassee HS 500/9-12
502 Barnett Blvd 36078 334-283-2187
Matt Coker, prin. Fax 283-6210

**Tanner, Limestone**
Limestone County SD
Supt. — See Athens
Tanner S 900/K-12
12060 Sommers Rd 35671 256-233-6682
Billy Owens, prin. Fax 233-6449

**Tarrant, Jefferson, Pop. 6,300**
Tarrant CSD 800/PK-12
1318 Alabama St 35217 205-849-3700
Dr. Shelly Mize, supt. Fax 849-3728
www.tarrant.k12.al.us/
Tarrant HS 300/7-12
91 Black Creek Rd 35217 205-849-0172
Amy Banaszek, prin. Fax 849-3724

**Theodore, Mobile, Pop. 6,002**
Mobile County SD
Supt. — See Mobile
Hankins MS 1,000/6-8
5750 Katherine Hankins Dr 36582 251-221-2200
Cheryl Wittner, prin. Fax 221-2204
Theodore HS 1,800/9-12
6201 Swedetown Rd N 36582 251-221-3351
Ronald Rowell, prin. Fax 221-3355

**Thomaston, Marengo, Pop. 414**
Marengo County SD
Supt. — See Linden
Johnson S 200/K-12
PO Box 67 36783 334-627-3364
Lepolean Peterson, prin. Fax 627-3396

**Thomasville, Clarke, Pop. 4,190**
Thomasville CSD 1,500/PK-12
PO Box 458 36784 334-636-9955
Dr. Vic Adkison, supt. Fax 636-4096
www.thomasvilleschools.org/
Thomasville HS 500/9-12
777 Gates Dr 36784 334-636-4451
Chuck Alford, prin. Fax 636-0022
Thomasville MS 500/5-8
781 Gates Dr 36784 334-636-4928
Sandra Williams, prin. Fax 636-4924

**Thorsby, Chilton, Pop. 1,968**
Chilton County SD
Supt. — See Clanton
Thorsby S 900/K-12
54 Opportunity Dr 35171 205-280-4880
Russ Bryan, prin. Fax 646-2197

**Toney, Madison**
Madison County SD
Supt. — See Huntsville
Sparkman MS 800/6-8
2697 Carters Gin Rd 35773 256-851-4610
Ronnie Blair, prin. Fax 851-4611

**Town Creek, Lawrence, Pop. 1,049**
Lawrence County SD
Supt. — See Moulton
Hatton HS 400/7-12
6909 AL Highway 101 35672 256-685-4010
Brent Gillespie, prin. Fax 685-4007

**Toxey, Choctaw, Pop. 137**

---

South Choctaw Academy 300/PK-12
PO Box 160 36921 251-843-2426
Monteil Robinson, prin. Fax 843-2088

**Trinity, Morgan, Pop. 2,059**
Lawrence County SD
Supt. — See Moulton
East Lawrence HS 400/9-12
55 County Road 370 35673 256-905-2430
Jacki Hall, prin. Fax 905-2424
East Lawrence MS 500/5-8
99 County Road 370 35673 256-905-2420
Baine Garner, prin. Fax 905-2477

Morgan County SD
Supt. — See Decatur
West Morgan HS 400/9-12
261 S Greenway Dr 35673 256-353-5214
Keith Harris, prin. Fax 351-0161
West Morgan MS 400/5-8
261 S Greenway Dr 35673 256-353-5214
Jill Jones, prin. Fax 355-8713

**Troy, Pike, Pop. 17,799**
Pike County SD 2,200/K-12
101 W Love St 36081 334-566-1850
Dr. Mark Bazzell M.Ed., supt. Fax 566-2580
www.pikecountyschools.com
Troy-Pike Regional Center for Technology Vo/Tech
285 Gibbs St 36081 334-566-5395
Julie Simmons, prin. Fax 566-1690
Other Schools – See Brundidge, Goshen

Troy CSD 2,100/K-12
PO Box 529 36081 334-566-3741
Lee Hicks, supt. Fax 566-1425
www.troyschools.net
Henderson HS 600/9-12
PO Box 1006 36081 334-566-3510
Brent Harrison, prin. Fax 566-4940
Henderson MS 500/6-8
PO Box 925 36081 334-566-5770
Aaron Brown, prin. Fax 566-3071

---

Pike Liberal Arts S 400/PK-12
PO Box 329 36081 334-566-2023
Troy University 36082 Post-Sec.
334-670-3100

**Trussville, Jefferson, Pop. 19,764**
Jefferson County SD
Supt. — See Birmingham
Clay-Chalkville MS 1,100/6-8
6700 Trussville Clay Rd 35173 205-379-3100
Ron Tillman, prin. Fax 379-3145

Trussville City SD 4,200/K-12
113 N Chalkville Rd 35173 205-228-3018
Dr. Patricia Neill, supt. Fax 228-3001
trussvillecityschools.com/
Hewitt-Trussville HS 1,300/9-12
6450 Husky Pkwy 35173 205-228-4000
Timothy Salem, prin. Fax 228-4001
Hewitt-Trussville MS 1,000/6-8
5275 Trussville Clay Rd 35173 205-228-3700
Lisa Berry, prin. Fax 228-3701

**Tuscaloosa, Tuscaloosa, Pop. 89,545**
Tuscaloosa CSD 10,000/PK-12
PO Box 38991 35403 205-759-3700
Dr. Paul McKendrick, supt. Fax 759-3542
www.tusc.k12.al.us
Central HS 700/9-12
905 15th St 35401 205-759-3720
Clarence Sutton, prin. Fax 759-3756
Northridge HS 1,200/9-12
2901 Northridge Rd 35406 205-759-3590
Kyle Ferguson, prin. Fax 759-3605
Rock Quarry MS 500/6-8
2100 Rock Quarry Dr 35406 205-759-3578
Lynda Ingram, prin. Fax 759-3582
Southview MS 400/6-8
2605 Southview Dr 35405 205-752-1831
Tonya Crews, prin. Fax 554-7243
Tuscaloosa Career and Technology Academy Vo/Tech
2800 ML King Jr Blvd 35401 205-759-3649
Danielle Morton, prin. Fax 759-3767
Tuscaloosa Magnet MS 200/6-8
315 McFarland Blvd E 35404 205-759-3653
Kristi Thomson, prin. Fax 759-3784
University Place MS 200/6-8
2010 1st Ave 35401 205-759-3631
Tom Danner, prin. Fax 759-3635
Westlawn MS 400/6-8
1715 ML King Jr Blvd 35401 205-759-3673
Vertis Giles-Brown, prin. Fax 759-3770
Other Schools – See Cottondale

Tuscaloosa County SD 16,800/PK-12
PO Box 2568 35403 205-758-0411
Walter Davie, supt. Fax 758-2990
www.tcss.net
Hillcrest HS 1,300/9-12
300 Patriot Pkwy 35405 205-342-2800
Jeff Hinton, prin. Fax 247-4178
Hillcrest MS 600/6-8
401 Hillcrest School Rd 35405 205-342-2820
C'Kimba Hobbs, prin. Fax 247-4177
Holt HS 400/9-12
3801 Alabama Ave NE 35404 205-342-2768
Rachael McDaniel, prin. Fax 247-4179
Other Schools – See Brookwood, Buhl, Cottondale, Duncanville, Northport, Vance

---

American Christian Academy 900/PK-12
2300 Veterans Memorial Pkwy 35404 205-553-5963
Dr. Dan Carden, hdmstr. Fax 553-5942
Capitol S 100/PK-12
2828 6th St 35401 205-758-2828
DCH Regional Medical Center Post-Sec.
809 University Blvd E 35401 205-759-7111
Holy Spirit HS 200/7-12
601 James I Harrison Jr E 35405 205-553-5606
Scott Perry, prin. Fax 566-7103
North River Christian Academy 300/PK-12
1785 McFarland Blvd N 35406 205-349-4881
Dan Habrial, admin. Fax 349-3246
Shelton State Community College Post-Sec.
9500 Old Greensboro Rd 35405 205-391-2211
Stillman College Post-Sec.
PO Box 1430 35403 205-349-4240
Tuscaloosa Academy 400/PK-12
420 Rice Valley Rd N 35406 205-758-4462
Dr. Isaac Espy, hdmstr. Fax 758-4418
University of Alabama 35487 Post-Sec.
205-348-6010

**Tuscumbia, Colbert, Pop. 8,279**
Colbert County SD 2,800/PK-12
PO Box 538 35674 256-386-8565
Anthony Olivis, supt. Fax 381-9375
colbert.k12.al.us/
Colbert Heights HS 500/7-12
6825 Woodmont Dr 35674 256-383-7875
James Brudgie Davis, prin. Fax 389-8319
Other Schools – See Cherokee, Leighton

Tuscumbia CSD 1,500/K-12
303 N Commons St E 35674 256-389-2900
Darryl Aikerson, supt. Fax 389-2903
www.tuscumbia.k12.al.us
Deshler Career Technical Center Vo/Tech
200 N Commons St E 35674 256-389-2900
Vickey Moon, coord. Fax 389-2903
Deshler HS 400/9-12
200 N Commons St E 35674 256-389-2910
Russell Tate, prin. Fax 389-2915
Deshler MS 400/6-8
598 N High St 35674 256-389-2920
Bryan Murner, prin. Fax 389-2921
Tuscumbia City Alternative S Alt
303 N Commons St E 35674 256-389-2900
Paul Pickett, prin. Fax 389-2903

---

Covenant Christian S 200/PK-12
1900 Covenant Dr 35674 256-383-4436
Bill Deegan, admin. Fax 381-4437

**Tuskegee, Macon, Pop. 9,751**
Macon County SD 2,400/PK-12
PO Box 830090 36083 334-727-1600
Dr. Jacqueline Brooks, supt. Fax 724-9990
www.maconk12.org
Washington HS 700/9-12
3803 W Mrtn Luther King Hwy 36083 334-727-0073
Brelinda Sullen, prin. Fax 724-0222
Other Schools – See Notasulga, Tuskegee Institute

---

Tuskegee University Post-Sec.
1200 W Montgomery Rd 36088 334-727-8011

**Tuskegee Institute, See Tuskegee**
Macon County SD
Supt. — See Tuskegee
Macon County Area Vocational Center Vo/Tech
1902 Taylor St 36088 334-724-1236
Tuskegee Institute MS 400/7-8
1809 Franklin Rd 36088 334-727-2580
Rosemary Wright, prin. Fax 727-5089

**Union Springs, Bullock, Pop. 3,959**
Bullock County SD 1,300/K-12
PO Box 231 36089 334-738-2860
Elliott Harris, supt. Fax 738-2802
bullockcounty.schoolinsites.com
Bullock County Career Technical Ctr Vo/Tech
304 Blackmon Ave E 36089 334-738-4370
James Foulks, dir. Fax 738-4369
Bullock County HS 500/9-12
PO Box 5108 36089 334-738-2198
Derrick Harris, prin. Fax 738-2606
South Highlands MS 300/5-8
PO Box 111 36089 334-738-2896
Sean Dees, prin. Fax 738-5746

**Uniontown, Perry, Pop. 1,770**
Perry County SD
Supt. — See Marion
Hatch S 400/PK-12
PO Box 709 36786 334-628-4061
Leslie Turner, prin. Fax 683-4935

**Uriah, Monroe, Pop. 280**
Monroe County SD
Supt. — See Monroeville

Blacksher S 700/PK-12
PO Box 430 36480 251-862-2130
Donald Baggett, prin. Fax 862-2808

**Valley, Chambers, Pop. 9,430**
Chambers County SD
Supt. — See Lafayette
Burns MS 700/6-8
292 Johnson St 36854 334-756-3567
Dr. Frankie Bell, prin. Fax 756-7511
Valley HS 900/9-12
501 US Highway 29 36854 334-756-4105
James Davidson, prin. Fax 756-9602

Lee County SD
Supt. — See Opelika
Beulah HS 700/7-12
4848 Lee Road 270 36854 334-745-5010
Cincrystal Poythress, prin. Fax 749-1914

**Valley Grande, Dallas, Pop. 3,989**
Dallas County SD
Supt. — See Selma
Martin MS 300/7-8
2863 County Road 81, 334-872-6417
Paul Thomas, prin. Fax 875-4013

**Valley Head, DeKalb, Pop. 541**
De Kalb County SD
Supt. — See Rainsville
Valley Head S 500/K-12
PO Box 149 35989 256-635-6228
William Monroe, prin. Fax 635-6229

**Vance, Tuscaloosa, Pop. 1,508**
Tuscaloosa County SD
Supt. — See Tuscaloosa
Brookwood MS 800/6-8
17021 Brookwood Pkwy 35490 205-342-2748
Daniel Bray, prin. Fax 553-9910

**Verbena, Chilton**
Chilton County SD
Supt. — See Clanton
Verbena S 600/K-12
202 County Road 510 36091 205-280-2820
Carla White, prin. Fax 755-0393

**Vernon, Lamar, Pop. 1,977**
Lamar County SD 2,400/K-12
PO Box 1379 35592 205-695-7615
Garth Moss, supt. Fax 695-7678
www.lamarcountyschools.net
Lamar County S 700/4-12
8990 Highway 18 35592 205-695-7717
Vance Herron, prin. Fax 695-8218
Lamar County School of Technology Vo/Tech
43880 Highway 17 35592 205-695-7129
Ken Dawkins, prin. Fax 695-6153
Other Schools – See Millport, Sulligent

**Vestavia Hills, Jefferson, Pop. 33,714**
Hoover CSD
Supt. — See Hoover
Spain Park HS 1,500/9-12
4700 Jaguar Dr 35242 205-439-1400
Larry Giangrosso, prin. Fax 439-1401

Vestavia Hills CSD 6,400/K-12
PO Box 660826 35266 205-402-5100
Sheila Phillips, supt. Fax 402-5134
www.vestavia.k12.al.us
Liberty Park MS 500/6-8
17035 Liberty Pkwy 35242 205-402-5450
Kacy Pierce, prin. Fax 402-5450
Pizitz MS 1,100/6-8
2020 Pizitz Dr 35216 205-402-5350
Meredith Hanson, prin. Fax 402-5354
Vestavia Hills HS 1,800/9-12
2235 Lime Rock Rd 35216 205-402-5250
Dr. Tyler Burgess, prin. Fax 402-5262

**Vina, Franklin, Pop. 354**
Franklin County SD
Supt. — See Russellville
Vina S 300/PK-12
8250 Highway 23 35593 256-331-2260
James Pharr, prin. Fax 331-2292

**Vincent, Shelby, Pop. 1,969**
Shelby County SD
Supt. — See Columbiana
Vincent MSHS 500/6-12
42505 Highway 25 35178 205-682-7300
Michele Edwards, prin. Fax 682-7305

**Vinemont, Cullman**
Cullman County SD
Supt. — See Cullman
Vinemont HS 300/9-12
PO Box 189 35179 256-734-0571
Ferrell Runge, prin. Fax 739-8605
Vinemont MS 300/6-8
170 High School Rd 35179 256-739-1943
Dr. Vicky Spear, prin. Fax 737-1664
West Point MS 400/6-8
4545 County Road 1141 35179 256-734-5904
Clark Farley, prin. Fax 736-2354

**Wadley, Randolph, Pop. 735**
Randolph County SD
Supt. — See Wedowee
Wadley S 400/K-12
105 Bailey 36276 256-395-2286
Lori Carlisle, prin. Fax 395-4488

---

Southern Union State Community College Post-Sec.
PO Box 1000 36276 256-395-2211

**Walnut Grove, Etowah, Pop. 690**
Etowah County SD
Supt. — See Gadsden
West End HS 400/7-12
4515 Elm St 35990 205-589-6421
Craig Schoemaker, prin. Fax 589-4782

**Waterloo, Lauderdale, Pop. 203**
Lauderdale County SD
Supt. — See Florence
Waterloo S 300/PK-12
PO Box 68 35677 256-766-3100
Regina Adams, prin. Fax 766-3194

**Weaver, Calhoun, Pop. 2,963**
Calhoun County SD
Supt. — See Anniston
Weaver HS 500/7-12
917 Clairmont Dr 36277 256-741-7200
Michael Allison, prin. Fax 820-0811

**Wedowee, Randolph, Pop. 821**
Randolph County SD 2,100/K-12
182 Circle Dr 36278 256-357-4611
Rance Kirby, supt. Fax 357-4844
www.randolphboe.org
Randolph County HS 400/7-12
465 Woodland Ave W 36278 256-357-4751
Darren Anglin, prin. Fax 357-2310
Randolph-Roanoke Career Tech Vo/Tech
960 Main St S 36278 256-357-2839
Christy Fordham, prin. Fax 357-4580
Other Schools – See Wadley, Woodland

**West Blocton, Bibb, Pop. 1,231**
Bibb County SD
Supt. — See Centreville
Bibb County Career Academy Vo/Tech
17191 Highway 5 35184 205-938-7434
Wesley Lawley, prin. Fax 938-2037
West Blocton HS 500/9-12
4734 Truman Aldrich Pkwy 35184 205-938-9002
Terry Lawley, prin. Fax 938-9546
West Blocton MS 600/5-8
4721 Truman Aldrich Pkwy 35184 205-938-2451
Greg Blake, prin. Fax 938-3261

**Wetumpka, Elmore, Pop. 6,406**
Elmore County SD 11,100/PK-12
PO Box 817 36092 334-567-1200
Andre Harrison, supt. Fax 567-1405
www.elmoreco.com
Elmore County Technical Center Vo/Tech
800 Kelly Fitzpatrick Dr 36092 334-567-1218
Jimmy Hull, dir. Fax 567-1417
Wetumpka HS 1,100/9-12
1251 Coosa River Pkwy 36092 334-567-5158
Robert Slater, prin. Fax 567-1178
Wetumpka MS 900/5-8
1000 Micanopy St 36092 334-567-1413
Tremeca Jackson, prin. Fax 567-1408
Other Schools – See Deatsville, Eclectic, Millbrook

**Winfield, Marion, Pop. 4,666**
Winfield CSD 1,300/K-12
PO Box 70 35594 205-487-4255
Dr. Keith Davis, supt. Fax 487-4603
www.winfield.k12.al.us
Winfield HS 400/9-12
232 Pirate Cv 35594 205-487-6900
Benny Parrish, prin. Fax 487-4257
Winfield MS 400/5-8
481 Apple Ave 35594 205-487-6901
Wendell Goodwin, prin. Fax 487-6258

**Woodland, Randolph, Pop. 182**
Randolph County SD
Supt. — See Wedowee
Woodland S 800/K-12
24574 Highway 48 36280 256-449-2315
Jeffery Thompson, prin. Fax 449-2316

**Woodville, Jackson, Pop. 730**
Jackson County SD
Supt. — See Scottsboro
Woodville S 500/PK-12
290 County Road 63 35776 256-776-2874
Bruce Maples, prin. Fax 776-4718

**York, Sumter, Pop. 2,533**
Sumter County SD
Supt. — See Livingston
Sumter Central HS 600/9-12
13878 U S Highway 11 36925 205-652-1501
Stoney Pritchett, prin. Fax 652-1513

---

Sumter Academy 200/K-12
181 Sumter Academy Rd 36925 205-392-5238

# ALASKA

## ALASKA DEPARTMENT OF EDUCATION
**PO Box 110500, Juneau 99811-0500**
**Telephone 907-465-2800**
**Fax 907-465-4165**
**Website http://www.eed.state.ak.us/**

Commissioner of Education Mike Hanley

## ALASKA BOARD OF EDUCATION
**PO Box 110500, Juneau 99811-0500**

Chairperson Jim Merriner

## PUBLIC, PRIVATE AND CATHOLIC SECONDARY SCHOOLS

**Adak, Aleutians West, Pop. 290**
Aleutian Region SD
Supt. — See Anchorage
Adak S 50/PK-12
PO Box 2083 99546 907-592-3820
Julie Plummer, lead tchr. Fax 592-2249

**Akhiok, Kodiak Island, Pop. 51**
Kodiak Island Borough SD
Supt. — See Kodiak
Akhiok S 50/PK-12
PO Box 5049 99615 907-836-2223
Kendra Bartz, prin. Fax 836-2206

**Akiachak, Bethel, Pop. 621**
Yupiit SD 400/PK-12
PO Box 51190 99551 907-825-3600
Norma Holmgaard, supt. Fax 825-3655
www.yupiit.org/
Akiachak S 200/K-12
PO Box 51189 99551 907-825-3616
Chris Barr, prin. Fax 825-3640
Other Schools – See Akiak, Tuluksak

**Akiak, Bethel, Pop. 339**
Yupiit SD
Supt. — See Akiachak
Akiak S 100/PK-12
PO Box 49 99552 907-765-4600
Charles Burns, prin. Fax 765-4642

**Akutan, Aleutians East, Pop. 979**
Aleutian East Borough SD
Supt. — See Sand Point
Akutan S 50/PK-12
PO Box 25 99553 907-698-2205
Shiloh McManus, prin. Fax 698-2216

**Alakanuk, Wade Hampton, Pop. 660**
Lower Yukon SD
Supt. — See Mountain Village
Alakanuk S 200/PK-12
PO Box 9 99554 907-238-3312
Herbert Hooper, prin. Fax 238-3417

**Allakaket, Yukon-Koyukuk, Pop. 101**
Yukon-Koyukuk SD
Supt. — See Fairbanks
Allakaket S 50/PK-12
PO Box 69 99720 907-968-2205
Laurie Beam, prin. Fax 968-2250

**Ambler, Northwest Arctic, Pop. 248**
Northwest Arctic Borough SD
Supt. — See Kotzebue
Ambler S 100/PK-12
PO Box 109 99786 907-445-2154
Scott Lefebvre, prin. Fax 445-2159

**Anaktuvuk Pass, North Slope, Pop. 294**
North Slope Borough SD
Supt. — See Barrow
Nunamiut S 100/PK-12
PO Box 21029 99721 907-661-3226
Patrick Manning, prin. Fax 661-3402

**Anchorage, Anchorage, Pop. 265,438**
AVTEC SD
Supt. — See Seward
AVTEC Allied Health Dept Vo/Tech
1251 Muldoon Rd Ste 103 99504 907-334-2230
Ben Eveland, dir. Fax 334-2287

Aleutian Region SD 50/PK-12
PO Box 92230 99509 907-277-2648
Joe Beckford, supt. Fax 277-2649
www.aleutregion.org
Other Schools – See Adak, Atka

Anchorage SD 48,000/PK-12
5530 E Northern Lights Blvd 99504 907-742-4000
Ed Graff, supt. Fax 742-4318
www.asdk12.org
ACE / ACT Program Alt
3745 Community Park Loop 99508 907-742-3950
Robyn Harris, prin. Fax 742-3988
AVAIL S 100/Alt
425 C St 99501 907-742-4930
Nichelle Mauk, prin. Fax 742-4933
Bartlett HS 1,600/9-12
1101 Golden Bear Dr 99504 907-742-1800
Sean Prince, prin. Fax 742-1825
Begich MS 1,000/6-8
7440 Creekside Center Dr 99504 907-742-0500
Brian Singleton, prin. Fax 742-0510
Benson Secondary S 300/Alt
4515 Campbell Airstrip Rd 99507 907-742-2050
Frank Reuter, prin. Fax 742-2060
Central MS of Science 600/7-8
1405 E St 99501 907-742-5100
Joel Roylance, prin. Fax 742-5125
Clark MS 700/6-8
150 Bragaw St 99508 907-742-4700
Cessilye Williams, prin. Fax 742-4756
Dimond HS 1,700/9-12
2909 W 88th Ave 99502 907-742-7000
Tina Johnson-Harris, prin. Fax 742-7007
East Anchorage HS 2,200/9-12
4025 E Northern Lights Blvd 99508 907-742-2100
Sam Spinella, prin. Fax 742-2134
Goldenview MS 800/7-8
15800 Golden View Dr 99516 907-348-8626
Wendy Pondolfino, prin. Fax 742-8273
Hanshew MS 800/7-8
10121 Lake Otis Pkwy 99507 907-349-1561
Nancy Brain, prin. Fax 349-2835
King Career Center Vo/Tech
2650 E Northern Lights Blvd 99508 907-742-8900
Lou Pondolfino, prin. Fax 742-8907
Mears MS 800/7-8
2700 W 100th Ave 99515 907-742-6400
Michael Perkins, prin. Fax 742-6444
New Path HS Alt
1400 E 4th Ave 99501 907-742-4939
Nichelle Mauk, prin. Fax 742-4933
Polaris S 500/Alt
6200 Ashwood St 99507 907-742-8700
Carol Bartholomew, prin. Fax 742-8777
Romig MS 800/7-8
2500 Minnesota Dr 99503 907-742-5200
Sven Gustafson, prin. Fax 742-5252
SAVE HS 200/Alt
410 E 56th Ave 99518 907-742-1250
Karin Parker, prin. Fax 742-1266
Service HS 1,800/9-12
5577 Abbott Rd 99507 907-742-8100
John Gaskins, prin. Fax 742-6615
South Anchorage HS 1,500/9-12
13400 Elmore Rd 99516 907-742-6200
K. Johnson-Struempler, prin. Fax 742-6207
Steller JSHS 300/Alt
2508 Blueberry Rd 99503 907-742-4950
Reed Whitmore, prin. Fax 742-4966
Wendler MS 500/7-8
2905 Lake Otis Pkwy 99508 907-742-7300
Brendan Wilson, prin. Fax 742-7350
West Anchorage HS 1,800/9-12
1700 Hillcrest Dr 99517 907-742-2500
Rick Stone, prin. Fax 742-2525
Other Schools – See Chugiak, Eagle River

Chugach SD 100/PK-12
9312 Vanguard Dr Ste 100 99507 907-522-7400
Bob Crumley, supt. Fax 522-3399
www.chugachschools.com
Other Schools – See Chenega Bay, Tatitlek, Whittier

---

Alaska Career College Post-Sec.
1415 E Tudor Rd 99507 907-563-7575
Alaska Pacific University Post-Sec.
4101 University Dr 99508 800-252-7528
Anchorage Christian S 700/PK-12
6575 E Northern Lights Blvd 99504 907-337-9575
Thomas Cobaugh, admin. Fax 338-3903
Charter College Post-Sec.
2221 E Northern Lights #120 99508 907-277-1000
Grace Christian S 600/K-12
12407 Pintail St 99516 907-868-1203
Christopher Gionet, supt. Fax 644-2261
Holy Rosary Academy 100/K-12
1010 W Fireweed Ln 99503 907-276-5822
Catherine Neumayr, prin. Fax 258-1055
Lumen Christi JSHS 100/7-12
8110 Jewel Lake Rd Bldg D 99502 907-245-9231
John Harmon, prin. Fax 245-9232
University of Alaska Anchorage Post-Sec.
3211 Providence Dr 99508 907-786-1800

**Anderson, Denali, Pop. 234**
Denali Borough SD
Supt. — See Healy
Anderson S 50/K-12
PO Box 3120 99744 907-582-2700
Uwe Hoffmann, prin. Fax 582-2000

**Angoon, Skagway-Hoonah-Angoon, Pop. 409**
Chatham SD 100/K-12
PO Box 109 99820 907-788-3302
Bernie Grieve Ph.D., supt. Fax 788-3252
chathamsd.schoolwires.net
Angoon S 100/K-12
PO Box 209 99820 907-788-3811
Jim Parkin, prin. Fax 788-3812
Other Schools – See Gustavus, Haines, Tenakee Springs

**Aniak, Bethel, Pop. 452**
Kuspuk SD 400/PK-12
PO Box 49 99557 907-675-4250
Susan L. Johnson, supt. Fax 675-4305
www.kuspuk.org
Aniak JSHS 100/7-12
PO Box 29 99557 907-675-4330
Jami Allan Whedbee, prin. Fax 675-4256
Other Schools – See Chuathbaluk, Crooked Creek, Kalskag, Sleetmute, Stony River

**Anvik, Yukon-Koyukuk, Pop. 82**
Iditarod Area SD
Supt. — See Mc Grath
Blackwell S 50/PK-12
PO Box 90 99558 907-663-6348
Doug Goben, prin. Fax 663-6349

**Arctic Village, Yukon-Koyukuk, Pop. 142**
Yukon Flats SD
Supt. — See Fort Yukon
Arctic Village S 50/PK-12
PO Box 22049 99722 907-587-5211
Terry Reed, lead tchr. Fax 587-5210

**Atka, Aleutians West, Pop. 61**
Aleutian Region SD
Supt. — See Anchorage
Netsvetov S 50/K-12
PO Box 47050 99547 907-839-2210
Sally Swetzof, lead tchr. Fax 839-2212

**Atmautluak, Bethel, Pop. 277**
Lower Kuskokwim SD
Supt. — See Bethel
Alexie Memorial S 100/PK-12
PO Box ATT 99559 907-553-5112
Tania Erickson-Grant, prin. Fax 553-5129

**Atqasuk, North Slope, Pop. 231**
North Slope Borough SD
Supt. — See Barrow
Meade River S 100/PK-12
PO Box 91030 99791 907-633-6315
Debbe Lancaster, prin. Fax 633-6215

**Barrow, North Slope, Pop. 3,772**
North Slope Borough SD 1,900/PK-12
PO Box 169 99723 907-852-5311
Peggy Cowan, supt. Fax 852-9503
www.nsbsd.org/
Barrow HS 200/9-12
PO Box 960 99723 907-852-8950
Sherry McKenzie, prin. Fax 852-8969
Hopson Memorial MS 200/6-8
PO Box 509 99723 907-852-3880
Roger Wells, prin. Fax 852-7794
Kiita Learning Community 100/Alt
PO Box 169 99723 907-852-9677
Robert Johnson, prin. Fax 852-4334

Other Schools – See Anaktuvuk Pass, Atqasuk, Kaktovik, Nuiqsut, Point Hope, Point Lay, Wainwright

Ilisagvik College — Post-Sec.
PO Box 749 99723 — 907-852-3333

**Beaver, Yukon-Koyukuk, Pop. 83**
Yukon Flats SD
Supt. — See Fort Yukon
Cruikshank S — 50/PK-12
PO Box 24050 99724 — 907-628-6313
Clayton Ellsworth, lead tchr. — Fax 628-6615

**Bethel, Bethel, Pop. 5,648**
Lower Kuskokwim SD — 4,100/PK-12
PO Box 305 99559 — 907-543-4800
Jacob Jensen, supt. — Fax 543-4904
www.lksd.org
Bethel Regional HS — 500/7-12
PO Box 700 99559 — 907-543-3957
Elizabeth Balcerek, prin. — Fax 543-2327
Kuskokwim Learning Academy — 50/Alt
PO Box 1949 99559 — 907-543-5610
Doug Bower, prin. — Fax 543-5603
Other Schools – See Atmautluak, Chefornak, Eek, Goodnews Bay, Kasigluk, Kipnuk, Kongiganak, Kwethluk, Kwigillingok, Mekoryuk, Napakiak, Napaskiak, Newtok, Nightmute, Nunapitchuk, Platinum, Quinhagak, Toksook Bay, Tuntutuliak, Tununak

**Big Lake, Matanuska-Susitna, Pop. 3,191**
Matanuska-Susitna Borough SD
Supt. — See Palmer
Houston HS — 400/9-12
12501 W Hawk Rd, — 907-892-9400
William Johnson, prin. — Fax 892-9460
Houston MS — 400/6-8
PO Box 520920 99652 — 907-892-9500
Benjamin Howard, prin. — Fax 892-9560

**Brevig Mission, Nome, Pop. 377**
Bering Strait SD
Supt. — See Unalakleet
Brevig Mission S — 100/PK-12
General Delivery 99785 — 907-642-4021
Diane Crockett, prin. — Fax 642-4031

**Buckland, Northwest Arctic, Pop. 408**
Northwest Arctic Borough SD
Supt. — See Kotzebue
Buckland S — 200/PK-12
PO Box 91 99727 — 907-494-2127
Terri Walker, prin. — Fax 494-2106

**Cantwell, Denali, Pop. 205**
Denali Borough SD
Supt. — See Healy
Cantwell S — 50/K-12
PO Box 29 99729 — 907-768-2372
Caitlin Santos, prin. — Fax 768-2500

**Chalkyitsik, Yukon-Koyukuk, Pop. 69**
Yukon Flats SD
Supt. — See Fort Yukon
Tsuk Taih S — 50/PK-12
1 Marten Hill 99788 — 907-848-8113
Fax 848-8312

**Chefornak, Bethel, Pop. 415**
Lower Kuskokwim SD
Supt. — See Bethel
Chaptnquak S — 200/PK-12
PO Box 50 99561 — 907-867-8700
Andrea Engbretsen, prin. — Fax 867-8727

**Chenega Bay, Valdez-Cordova, Pop. 94**
Chugach SD
Supt. — See Anchorage
Chenega Bay Community S — 50/PK-12
PO Box 8030 99574 — 907-573-5123
Charley Rininger, prin. — Fax 573-5137

**Chevak, Wade Hampton, Pop. 915**
Kashunamiut SD — 300/PK-12
PO Box 345 99563 — 907-858-6195
Larry Parker, supt. — Fax 858-7328
www.chevakschool.org/
Chevak S — 300/PK-12
PO Box 345 99563 — 907-858-7712
Tariq Malek, prin. — Fax 858-6150

**Chignik, Lake and Peninsula, Pop. 87**
Lake & Peninsula SD
Supt. — See King Salmon
Chignik Bay S — 50/K-12
PO Box 9 99564 — 907-749-2213
Kitza Durlop, prin. — Fax 749-2261

**Chignik Lagoon, Lake and Peninsula, Pop. 69**
Lake & Peninsula SD
Supt. — See King Salmon
Chignik Lagoon S — 50/PK-12
PO Box 50 99565 — 907-840-2210
Joe Ward, prin. — Fax 840-2265

**Chignik Lake, Lake and Peninsula, Pop. 71**
Lake & Peninsula SD
Supt. — See King Salmon
Chignik Lake S — 50/K-12
General Delivery 99548 — 907-845-2210
Joe Ward, prin. — Fax 845-2254

**Chiniak, Kodiak Island, Pop. 45**
Kodiak Island Borough SD
Supt. — See Kodiak
Chiniak S — 50/K-10
Mile 49 99615 — 907-486-8323
Fax 486-3185

**Chuathbaluk, Bethel, Pop. 112**
Kuspuk SD
Supt. — See Aniak
Crow Village Sam S — 50/PK-12
PO Box CHU 99557 — 907-467-4229
Steven B. Porter, prin. — Fax 467-4122

**Chugiak, See Anchorage**
Anchorage SD
Supt. — See Anchorage
Chugiak HS — 1,200/9-12
16525 S Birchwood Loop Rd 99567 — 907-742-3050
David Legg, prin. — Fax 742-3148
Mirror Lake MS — 700/6-8
22901 Lake Hill Dr 99567 — 907-742-3500
Dr. Sherry Ellers, prin. — Fax 742-3545

Birchwood Christian S — 100/PK-12
22208 Birchwood Loop Rd 99567 — 907-688-2228
Todd Clark, prin. — Fax 688-2159

**Circle, Yukon-Koyukuk, Pop. 98**
Yukon Flats SD
Supt. — See Fort Yukon
Circle S — 50/PK-12
PO Box 49 99733 — 907-773-1250
Mathew Potter, lead tchr. — Fax 773-1259

**Coffman Cove, Prince of Wales-Outer Ketchikan, Pop. 173**
Southeast Island SD
Supt. — See Thorne Bay
Valentine S — 50/K-12
PO Box 18002 99918 — 907-329-2244
James Hughes, lead tchr. — Fax 329-2210

**Cooper Landing, Kenai Peninsula, Pop. 282**
Kenai Peninsula Borough SD
Supt. — See Soldotna
Cooper Landing S — 50/K-12
19030 Bean Creek Rd 99572 — 907-595-1244
Douglas Hayman, prin. — Fax 595-1461

**Copper Center, Valdez-Cordova, Pop. 312**
Copper River SD
Supt. — See Glennallen
Kenny Lake S — 100/1-12
HC 60 Box 224 99573 — 907-822-3870
Shaun Streyle, prin. — Fax 822-3794

**Cordova, Valdez-Cordova, Pop. 2,067**
Cordova CSD — 300/PK-12
PO Box 1330 99574 — 907-424-3265
Rich Carlson, supt. — Fax 424-3271
cordovasd.org
Cordova JSHS — 200/7-12
PO Box 1330 99574 — 907-424-3266
Tim Fraychinaud, prin. — Fax 424-5215

**Craig, Prince of Wales-Outer Ketchikan, Pop. 1,047**
Craig CSD — 400/PK-12
PO Box 800 99921 — 907-826-3274
Jack Walsh, supt. — Fax 826-3322
www.craigschools.com
Craig HS — 100/9-12
PO Box 800 99921 — 907-826-2274
Michael Silverman, prin. — Fax 826-3016
Craig MS — 100/6-8
PO Box 800 99921 — 907-826-3274
Jackie Hanson, prin. — Fax 826-3309

Southeast Island SD
Supt. — See Thorne Bay
Hollis S — 50/PK-12
PO Box 803 99921 — 907-530-7108
Julie Vasquez, lead tchr. — Fax 530-7111

**Crooked Creek, Bethel, Pop. 96**
Kuspuk SD
Supt. — See Aniak
John Sr. S — 50/PK-12
PO Box 20 99575 — 907-432-2205
Steven Porter, prin. — Fax 432-2206

**Deering, Northwest Arctic, Pop. 117**
Northwest Arctic Borough SD
Supt. — See Kotzebue
Deering S — 50/PK-12
PO Box 36009 99736 — 907-363-2121
Perrian Windhausen, prin. — Fax 363-2128

**Delta Junction, Southeast Fairbanks, Pop. 919**
Delta-Greely SD — 800/PK-12
PO Box 527 99737 — 907-895-4657
Laural Jackson, supt. — Fax 895-4781
www.dgsd.us
Delta Junction HS — 200/9-12
PO Box 647 99737 — 907-895-4460
Bob Burkhart, prin. — Fax 895-4049
Gerstle River S — 50/PK-12
PO Box 369 99737 — 907-895-1043
Jeff Lansing, prin. — Fax 895-5198
New Horizons HS — 50/Alt
PO Box 369 99737 — 907-895-4655
Laural Jackson, prin. — Fax 895-4246
Other Schools – See Fort Greely

**Dillingham, Dillingham, Pop. 2,086**
Dillingham CSD — 500/PK-12
PO Box 170 99576 — 907-842-5223
Danny Frazier, supt. — Fax 527-0565
www.dlgsd.org
Dillingham MSHS — 300/6-12
PO Box 170 99576 — 907-842-5221
William Schwan, prin. — Fax 842-4395

Southwest Region SD — 600/K-12
PO Box 90 99576 — 907-842-5287
David Piazza, supt. — Fax 842-5428
www.swrsd.org/
Other Schools – See Koliganek, Manokotak, New Stuyahok, Togiak

**Diomede, Nome, Pop. 111**
Bering Strait SD
Supt. — See Unalakleet
Diomede S — 50/PK-12
PO Box 7099 99762 — 907-686-3021
Pamela Potter, prin. — Fax 686-3022

**Dot Lake, Southeast Fairbanks, Pop. 12**
Alaska Gateway SD
Supt. — See Tok
Dot Lake S — 50/K-12
PO Box 2280 99737 — 907-882-2663
Jeff Rebitski, prin. — Fax 882-2112

**Eagle, Southeast Fairbanks, Pop. 85**
Alaska Gateway SD
Supt. — See Tok
Eagle Community S — 50/K-12
PO Box 168 99738 — 907-547-2210
Kristy Robbins, prin. — Fax 547-2302

**Eagle River, See Anchorage**
Anchorage SD
Supt. — See Anchorage
Eagle River HS — 800/9-12
8701 Yosemite Dr 99577 — 907-742-2700
Martin Lang, prin. — Fax 742-2710
Gruening MS — 600/7-8
9601 Lee St 99577 — 907-742-3600
Bobby Jefts, prin. — Fax 742-3666

Matanuska-Susitna Borough SD
Supt. — See Palmer
Alaska Middle College S — 100/11-12
10928 Eagle River Rd Ste 11 99577 — 907-746-8494
Kathy Moffitt, admin. — Fax 746-8485

Eagle River Christian S — 100/K-12
10336 E Eagle River Loop Rd 99577 — 907-694-4602
Denny Archer, admin. — Fax 694-4141

**Eek, Bethel, Pop. 296**
Lower Kuskokwim SD
Supt. — See Bethel
Eek S — 100/PK-12
PO Box 50 99578 — 907-536-5227
Brett Stirling, prin. — Fax 536-5628

**Egegik, Lake and Peninsula, Pop. 97**
Lake & Peninsula SD
Supt. — See King Salmon
Egegik S — 50/K-12
PO Box 10 99579 — 907-233-2210
April LeFevre, prin. — Fax 233-2254

**Eielson AFB, Fairbanks North Star, Pop. 2,496**
Fairbanks-North Star Borough SD
Supt. — See Fairbanks
Eielson JSHS — 400/7-12
675 Ravens Way 99702 — 907-372-3110
Mario Gatto, prin. — Fax 372-3202

**Elim, Nome, Pop. 322**
Bering Strait SD
Supt. — See Unalakleet
Aniguiin S — 100/PK-12
PO Box 29 99739 — 907-890-3021
Jack Kingsford, prin. — Fax 890-3031

**Emmonak, Wade Hampton, Pop. 759**
Lower Yukon SD
Supt. — See Mountain Village
Emmonak S — 200/PK-12
General Delivery 99581 — 907-949-1248
Thomas Gobeske, prin. — Fax 949-1148

**Fairbanks, Fairbanks North Star, Pop. 29,138**
Fairbanks-North Star Borough SD — 14,000/PK-12
520 5th Ave 99701 — 907-452-2000
Dr. Karen Gaborik Ed.D., supt. — Fax 451-0541
www.k12northstar.org
Fairbanks B.E.S.T. — 300/Alt
520 5th Ave 99701 — 907-452-2000
Kathy Hughes, dir. — Fax 451-1009
Hutchison HS — Vo/Tech
3750 Geist Rd 99709 — 907-479-2261
Tyrone Oates, prin. — Fax 479-8286
Lathrop HS — 1,200/9-12
901 Airport Way 99701 — 907-456-7794
Bob Meade, prin. — Fax 452-6735
Ryan MS — 400/7-8
951 Airport Way 99701 — 907-452-4751
Heather Stewart, prin. — Fax 451-8834
Smith MS — 300/7-8
1401 Bainbridge Blvd 99701 — 907-458-7600
Dave Dershin, prin. — Fax 458-7676
Tanana MS — 500/7-8
600 Trainor Gate Rd 99701 — 907-452-8145
Gregg Platt, prin. — Fax 456-2780
West Valley HS — 1,000/9-12
3800 Geist Rd 99709 — 907-479-4221
Dave Foshee, prin. — Fax 474-8901
Other Schools – See Eielson AFB, North Pole

Yukon-Koyukuk SD — 300/PK-12
4762 Old Airport Way 99709 — 907-374-9400
Kerry Boyd, supt. — Fax 374-9440
www.yksd.com
Other Schools – See Allakaket, Hughes, Huslia, Kaltag, Koyukuk, Manley Hot Springs, Minto, Nulato, Ruby

Aurora Tutoring S — 50/PK-12
201 Old Steese Hwy Ste 6 99701 — 907-374-8852
Baubi Jo Reid, prin. — Fax 374-8853
Fairhill Christian S — 100/PK-12
101 City Lights Blvd 99712 — 907-457-2167
Monroe Catholic JSHS — 200/7-12
615 Monroe St 99701 — 907-452-2044
Patrick Riggs, prin. — Fax 452-5978
University of Alaska Fairbanks — Post-Sec.
PO Box 757500 99775 — 907-474-7500

**False Pass, Aleutians East, Pop. 35**
Aleutian East Borough SD
Supt. — See Sand Point
False Pass S 50/PK-12
PO Box 30 99583 907-548-2224
Annette Barnett, prin. Fax 548-2304

**Fort Greely, Southeast Fairbanks, Pop. 513**
Delta-Greely SD
Supt. — See Delta Junction
Delta Junction MS 300/6-8
Building 725, 907-869-1043
Jeff Lansing, prin.

**Fort Yukon, Yukon-Koyukuk, Pop. 569**
Yukon Flats SD 300/PK-12
PO Box 350 99740 907-662-2515
Dr. Lance Bowie, supt. Fax 662-2519
www.yukonflats.net
Fort Yukon S 100/PK-12
PO Box 129 99740 907-662-2352
Debra Van Dyke, prin. Fax 662-2958
Other Schools – See Arctic Village, Beaver, Chalkyitsik, Circle, Venetie

**Fritz Creek, Kenai Peninsula, Pop. 1,832**
Kenai Peninsula Borough SD
Supt. — See Soldotna
Kachemak Selo S 100/PK-12
PO Box 15007 99603 907-235-5552
Tim Whip, prin. Fax 235-5644
Voznesenka S 100/PK-12
PO Box 15336 99603 907-235-8549
Michael Wojciak, prin. Fax 235-6086

**Galena, Yukon-Koyukuk, Pop. 441**
Galena CSD 300/PK-12
PO Box 299 99741 907-656-1205
Chris Reitan, supt. Fax 656-2238
www.galenaalaska.org
Galena Interior Learning Academy 200/9-12
PO Box 359 99741 907-656-2053
John Riddle, prin. Fax 656-2107
Huntington JSHS 50/7-12
PO Box 299 99741 907-656-1205
Beth Buchanan, prin. Fax 656-1368

**Gambell, Nome, Pop. 678**
Bering Strait SD
Supt. — See Unalakleet
Gambell S 200/PK-12
PO Box 169 99742 907-985-5515
Robert Cooper, prin. Fax 985-5435

**Glennallen, Valdez-Cordova, Pop. 422**
Copper River SD 400/K-12
PO Box 108 99588 907-822-3234
Dr. Michael Johnson, supt. Fax 822-3949
www.crsd.us
Glennallen JSHS 100/7-12
PO Box 108 99588 907-822-5286
Jack Von Thaer, prin. Fax 822-8501
Other Schools – See Copper Center, Slana

Alaska Bible College Post-Sec.
PO Box 289 99588 907-822-3201

**Golovin, Nome, Pop. 153**
Bering Strait SD
Supt. — See Unalakleet
Olson S 100/PK-12
PO Box 62040 99762 907-779-3021
Gay Jacobson, prin. Fax 779-3031

**Goodnews Bay, Bethel, Pop. 241**
Lower Kuskokwim SD
Supt. — See Bethel
Rocky Mountain S 50/PK-12
PO Box 153 99589 907-967-8213
Shannon Hutson, prin. Fax 967-8228

**Grayling, Yukon-Koyukuk, Pop. 182**
Iditarod Area SD
Supt. — See Mc Grath
David-Louis Memorial S 50/PK-12
PO Box 90 99590 907-453-5135
Michael Willyerd, prin. Fax 453-5165

**Gustavus, Skagway-Hoonah-Angoon, Pop. 422**
Chatham SD
Supt. — See Angoon
Gustavus S 100/K-12
PO Box 120 99826 907-697-2248
Dianne Sullivan, lead tchr. Fax 697-2378

**Haines, Haines, Pop. 1,608**
Chatham SD
Supt. — See Angoon
Klukwan S 50/K-12
HC 60 Box 2222 99827 907-767-5551
Katherine Carl, lead tchr. Fax 767-5573

Haines Borough SD 300/PK-12
PO Box 1289 99827 907-766-6700
Richard Carlson, supt. Fax 766-6794
www.hbsd.net
Haines HS 100/7-12
PO Box 1289 99827 907-766-6700
Rene Martin, prin. Fax 766-6791

**Healy, Denali, Pop. 980**
Denali Borough SD 700/PK-12
PO Box 280 99743 907-683-2278
Dan Polta, supt. Fax 683-2514
www.dbsd.org
Denali PEAK 500/Alt
PO Box 280 99743 907-683-7325
Garin Martin, prin. Fax 683-0329
Tri-Valley S 200/K-12
PO Box 400 99743 907-683-2267
Nathan Pitt, prin. Fax 683-2632
Other Schools – See Anderson, Cantwell

**Holy Cross, Yukon-Koyukuk, Pop. 171**
Iditarod Area SD
Supt. — See Mc Grath
Holy Cross S 50/PK-12
PO Box 210 99602 907-476-7131
Jeff Bader, prin. Fax 476-7161

**Homer, Kenai Peninsula, Pop. 4,783**
Kenai Peninsula Borough SD
Supt. — See Soldotna
Homer Flex S 50/Alt
4122 Ben Walters Ln 99603 907-235-5558
Christopher Brown, prin. Fax 235-5633
Homer HS 400/9-12
600 E Fairview Ave 99603 907-235-4600
Doug Waclawski, prin. Fax 235-8933
Homer MS 200/7-8
500 Sterling Hwy 99603 907-235-5700
Kari Dendurent, prin. Fax 235-2513
Razdolna S 100/PK-12
PO Box 15098 99603 907-235-6870
Timothy Whip, prin. Fax 235-6485

**Hoonah, Skagway-Hoonah-Angoon, Pop. 657**
Hoonah CSD 100/PK-12
PO Box 157 99829 907-945-3611
Dr. P.J. Ford Slack Ph.D., supt. Fax 945-3492
www.hoonahschools.org
Hoonah JSHS 100/6-12
PO Box 157 99829 907-945-3613
Lorrie Scoles, prin. Fax 945-3607

**Hooper Bay, Wade Hampton, Pop. 1,055**
Lower Yukon SD
Supt. — See Mountain Village
Hooper Bay S 400/PK-12
PO Box 249 99604 907-758-1200
Hammond Gracy, prin. Fax 758-1280

**Hope, Kenai Peninsula, Pop. 178**
Kenai Peninsula Borough SD
Supt. — See Soldotna
Hope S 50/K-12
PO Box 47 99605 907-782-3202
Michael Hanson, admin. Fax 782-3140

**Hughes, Yukon-Koyukuk, Pop. 77**
Yukon-Koyukuk SD
Supt. — See Fairbanks
Oldman S 50/K-12
PO Box 30 99745 907-889-2204
Patty White, admin. Fax 889-2220

**Huslia, Yukon-Koyukuk, Pop. 272**
Yukon-Koyukuk SD
Supt. — See Fairbanks
Huntington S 100/PK-12
PO Box 110 99746 907-829-2205
Casey Weter, prin. Fax 829-2270

**Hydaburg, Prince of Wales-Outer Ketchikan, Pop. 342**
Hydaburg CSD 50/K-12
PO Box 109 99922 907-285-3491
Lauren Burch, supt. Fax 285-3391
www.hydaburg.k12.ak.us
Hydaburg S 50/K-12
PO Box 109 99922 907-285-3591
Brad King, prin. Fax 285-3391

**Hyder, Prince of Wales-Outer Ketchikan, Pop. 82**
Southeast Island SD
Supt. — See Thorne Bay
Hyder S 50/K-12
PO Box 110 99923 250-636-2100
Fax 636-2112

**Igiugig, Lake and Peninsula, Pop. 34**
Lake & Peninsula SD
Supt. — See King Salmon
Igiugig S 50/K-12
PO Box 4010 99613 907-533-3220
Tate Gooden, lead tchr. Fax 533-3221

**Iliamna, Lake and Peninsula, Pop. 96**
Lake & Peninsula SD
Supt. — See King Salmon
Newhalen S 100/PK-12
PO Box 89 99606 907-571-1211
Ed Lester, prin. Fax 571-1466

**Juneau, Juneau, Pop. 28,325**
Juneau Borough SD 4,900/PK-12
10014 Crazy Horse Dr 99801 907-523-1700
Mark Miller, supt. Fax 523-1708
www.juneauschools.org
Dryden MS 600/6-8
10014 Crazy Horse Dr 99801 907-463-1850
Jim Thompson, prin. Fax 463-1828
Heeni MS 500/6-8
10014 Crazy Horse Dr 99801 907-463-1899
Molly Yerkes, prin. Fax 463-1877
Juneau-Douglas HS 700/9-12
10014 Crazy Horse Dr 99801 907-523-1500
Paula Casperson, prin. Fax 523-1616
Thunder Mountain HS 700/9-12
10014 Crazy Horse Dr 99801 907-780-1900
Dan Larson, prin. Fax 780-1909
YaaKoosge Daakahidi Alternative HS 100/Alt
10014 Crazy Horse Dr 99801 907-523-1800
Kristin Garot, prin. Fax 523-1819

University of Alaska Southeast Post-Sec.
11120 Glacier Hwy 99801 907-796-6000

**Kake, Wrangell-Petersburg, Pop. 485**
Kake CSD 100/PK-12
PO Box 450 99830 907-785-3741
Kevin Shipley, supt. Fax 785-6439
www.kakeschools.com
Kake S 100/PK-12
PO Box 450 99830 907-785-3741
Kevin Shipley, supt. Fax 785-6439

**Kaktovik, North Slope, Pop. 236**
North Slope Borough SD
Supt. — See Barrow
Kaveolook S 100/PK-12
PO Box 20 99747 907-640-6626
Todd Washburn, prin. Fax 640-6718

**Kalskag, Bethel, Pop. 186**
Kuspuk SD
Supt. — See Aniak
Morgan HS 100/7-12
PO Box 30 99607 907-471-2288
Severin Gardner, prin. Fax 471-2242

**Kaltag, Yukon-Koyukuk, Pop. 185**
Yukon-Koyukuk SD
Supt. — See Fairbanks
Kaltag S 50/PK-12
PO Box 30 99748 907-534-2204
Nancy Mason, prin. Fax 534-2227

**Karluk, Kodiak Island, Pop. 37**
Kodiak Island Borough SD
Supt. — See Kodiak
Karluk S 50/K-12
General Delivery 99608 907-241-2217
Kendra Bartz, prin. Fax 241-2207

**Kasaan, Prince of Wales-Outer Ketchikan, Pop. 44**
Southeast Island SD
Supt. — See Thorne Bay
Kasaan S 50/K-12
117 Kasaan Rd 99901 907-542-2217
Shane Scamahorn, lead tchr. Fax 542-2219

**Kasigluk, Bethel, Pop. 558**
Lower Kuskokwim SD
Supt. — See Bethel
Akiuk Memorial S 100/PK-12
General Delivery 99609 907-477-6829
Christina Powers, prin. Fax 477-6314
Akula Elitnaurvik S 100/PK-12
PO Box 79 99609 907-477-6615
Ross Bolding, prin. Fax 477-6715

**Kenai, Kenai Peninsula, Pop. 6,541**
Kenai Peninsula Borough SD
Supt. — See Soldotna
Kenai Alternative S 100/Alt
705 Frontage Rd Ste C 99611 907-335-2870
Loren Reese, prin. Fax 283-6463
Kenai Central HS 500/9-12
9583 Kenai Spur Hwy 99611 907-283-2100
Alan Fields, prin. Fax 283-3230
Kenai MS 400/6-8
201 N Tinker Ln 99611 907-283-1700
Vaughn Dosko, prin. Fax 283-3180
Marathon S 50/Alt
405 Marathon Rd 99611 907-335-3343
Dan Beck, admin. Fax 335-3342

**Ketchikan, Ketchikan Gateway, Pop. 7,299**
Ketchikan Gateway Borough SD 2,300/PK-12
333 Schoenbar Rd 99901 907-247-2109
Robert Boyle, supt. Fax 247-3822
www.kgbsd.org
Ketchikan HS 600/9-12
2610 4th Ave 99901 907-225-9815
Sam Nelson, prin. Fax 247-5761
Revilla HS 100/7-12
3131 Baranof Ave 99901 907-225-6681
Kurt Lindemann, prin. Fax 247-6681
Schoenbar MS 300/7-8
217 Schoenbar Rd 99901 907-225-5138
Casey Robinson, prin. Fax 225-5761

Southeast Island SD
Supt. — See Thorne Bay
Naukati S 50/PK-12
PO Box NKI 99950 907-629-4121
Ryan Nelson, lead tchr. Fax 629-4122
Port Protection S 50/PK-12
PO Box PPV 99950 907-489-2228
Jeff Theurer, lead tchr. Fax 489-2235
Whale Pass S 50/PK-12
126 Bayview Rd 99950 907-846-5320
Christine Cook, lead tchr. Fax 846-5319

**Kiana, Northwest Arctic, Pop. 351**
Northwest Arctic Borough SD
Supt. — See Kotzebue
Kiana S 100/PK-12
PO Box 190 99749 907-475-2115
Rex Kilburn, prin. Fax 475-2120

**King Cove, Aleutians East, Pop. 905**
Aleutian East Borough SD
Supt. — See Sand Point
King Cove S 100/PK-12
PO Box 69 99612 907-497-2354
Jason Martinez, prin. Fax 497-2408

**King Salmon, Bristol Bay, Pop. 341**
Lake & Peninsula SD 300/PK-12
PO Box 498 99613 907-246-4280
Ty Mase, supt. Fax 246-4473
www.lpsd.com
Other Schools – See Chignik, Chignik Lagoon, Chignik Lake, Egegik, Igiugig, Iliamna, Kokhanok, Levelock, Nondalton, Perryville, Pilot Point, Port Alsworth, Port Heiden

**Kipnuk, Bethel, Pop. 637**
Lower Kuskokwim SD
Supt. — See Bethel
Chief Paul Memorial S 200/PK-12
PO Box 19 99614 907-896-5011
LaDorothy Lightfoot, prin. Fax 896-5428

**Kivalina, Northwest Arctic, Pop. 368**
Northwest Arctic Borough SD
Supt. — See Kotzebue
McQueen S 100/PK-12
General Delivery 99750 907-645-2125
Dr. Zoe Theoharis, prin. Fax 645-2124

**Klawock, Prince of Wales-Outer Ketchikan, Pop. 670**
Klawock CSD 100/PK-12
PO Box 9 99925 907-755-2917
Jim Holien, supt. Fax 755-2320
www.klawockschool.com/
Klawock City S 100/PK-12
PO Box 9 99925 907-755-2220
Kelli Larson, prin. Fax 755-2913

**Kobuk, Northwest Arctic, Pop. 151**
Northwest Arctic Borough SD
Supt. — See Kotzebue
Kobuk S 50/PK-12
PO Box 40 99751 907-948-2231
Erin Meehan, lead tchr. Fax 948-2225

**Kodiak, Kodiak Island, Pop. 5,742**
Kodiak Island Borough SD 2,500/PK-12
722 Mill Bay Rd 99615 907-481-6200
Stewart McDonald, supt. Fax 481-6218
www.kibsd.org/
Kodiak HS 800/9-12
722 Mill Bay Rd 99615 907-481-2501
Phillip Johnson, prin. Fax 481-2505
Kodiak MS 500/6-8
722 Mill Bay Rd 99615 907-481-2200
Ron Bryant, prin. Fax 481-2201
Other Schools – See Akhiok, Chiniak, Karluk, Larsen Bay, Old Harbor, Ouzinkie, Port Lions

**Kokhanok, Lake and Peninsula, Pop. 153**
Lake & Peninsula SD
Supt. — See King Salmon
Kokhanok S 50/K-12
PO Box 1109 99606 907-282-2210
Nicole Metzgar, admin. Fax 282-2247

**Koliganek, Dillingham, Pop. 207**
Southwest Region SD
Supt. — See Dillingham
Koliganek S 100/K-12
PO Box 5052 99576 907-596-3444
Cody McCanna, prin. Fax 596-3484

**Kongiganak, Bethel, Pop. 430**
Lower Kuskokwim SD
Supt. — See Bethel
Ayagina'ar Elitnaurvik S 100/PK-12
PO Box 5109, 907-557-5551
Lewis Beaver, prin. Fax 557-5639

**Kotlik, Wade Hampton, Pop. 574**
Lower Yukon SD
Supt. — See Mountain Village
Kotlik S 200/PK-12
PO Box 20129 99620 907-899-4415
John Harris, prin. Fax 899-4515

**Kotzebue, Northwest Arctic, Pop. 2,953**
Northwest Arctic Borough SD 2,000/PK-12
PO Box 51 99752 907-442-1800
Dr. Annmarie O'Brien, supt. Fax 442-2246
www.nwarctic.org
Alaska Technical Center Vo/Tech
PO Box 51 99752 907-442-3733
Cheryl Edenshaw, dir. Fax 442-2764
Kotzebue MSHS 300/6-12
PO Box 264 99752 907-442-1876
Mike Lane, prin. Fax 442-2141
Star of the Northwest Magnet S Vo/Tech
PO Box 51 99752 907-442-1800
Paul Bartos, prin. Fax 442-2392
Other Schools – See Ambler, Buckland, Deering, Kiana, Kivalina, Kobuk, Noatak, Noorvik, Selawik, Shungnak

**Koyuk, Nome, Pop. 308**
Bering Strait SD
Supt. — See Unalakleet
Koyuk-Malemute S 100/PK-12
PO Box 53009 99753 907-963-3021
Mary Huntington, prin. Fax 963-2428

**Koyukuk, Yukon-Koyukuk, Pop. 94**
Yukon-Koyukuk SD
Supt. — See Fairbanks
Vernetti S 50/PK-10
PO Box 70 99754 907-927-2212
Patty White, prin. Fax 927-2251

**Kwethluk, Bethel, Pop. 696**
Lower Kuskokwim SD
Supt. — See Bethel
Ket'acik Aap'alluk Memorial S 200/PK-12
PO Box 150 99621 907-757-6014
Darrell Richard, prin. Fax 757-6013

**Kwigillingok, Bethel, Pop. 316**
Lower Kuskokwim SD
Supt. — See Bethel
Kwigillingok S 100/PK-12
PO Box 109 99622 907-588-8629
Megan Rosendall, prin. Fax 588-8613

**Larsen Bay, Kodiak Island, Pop. 83**
Kodiak Island Borough SD
Supt. — See Kodiak
Larsen Bay S 50/PK-12
PO Box 70 99624 907-847-2252
Kendra Bartz, prin. Fax 847-2260

**Levelock, Lake and Peninsula, Pop. 65**
Lake & Peninsula SD
Supt. — See King Salmon
Levelock S 50/K-12
PO Box 89 99625 907-287-3060
Cathy Pusch, admin. Fax 287-3021

**Mc Grath, Yukon-Koyukuk, Pop. 277**
Iditarod Area SD 300/PK-12
PO Box 90 99627 907-524-1200
Dr. Rodman Weston, supt. Fax 524-3217
www.iditarodsd.org
Mc Grath S 100/PK-12
PO Box 290 99627 907-524-3388
Fax 524-3751
Other Schools – See Anvik, Grayling, Holy Cross, Nikolai, Shageluk, Takotna

**Manley Hot Springs, Yukon-Koyukuk, Pop. 75**
Yukon-Koyukuk SD
Supt. — See Fairbanks
Manley Hart Springs Gladys Dart S 50/PK-12
PO Box 29 99756 907-672-3202
Fax 672-3201

**Manokotak, Dillingham, Pop. 440**
Southwest Region SD
Supt. — See Dillingham
Manokotak S 100/K-12
PO Box 30 99628 907-289-1013
Debra Forkner, prin. Fax 289-2050

**Marshall, Wade Hampton, Pop. 404**
Lower Yukon SD
Supt. — See Mountain Village
Marshall S 100/PK-12
PO Box 89 99585 907-679-6112
Joseph Gaylord, prin. Fax 679-6637

**Mekoryuk, Bethel, Pop. 184**
Lower Kuskokwim SD
Supt. — See Bethel
Nuniwarmiut S 50/PK-12
PO Box 49 99630 907-827-8415
Walt Betz, prin. Fax 827-8613

**Mentasta Lake, Southeast Fairbanks, Pop. 111**
Alaska Gateway SD
Supt. — See Tok
Mentasta Lake S 50/K-12
PO Box 6039 99780 907-291-2317
Craig Roach, prin. Fax 291-2327

**Metlakatla, Prince of Wales-Outer Ketchikan, Pop. 1,313**
Annette Islands SD 300/PK-12
PO Box 7 99926 907-886-6332
Eugene Avey M.A., supt. Fax 886-5130
aisdk12.org
Leask MS 100/6-8
PO Box 7 99926 907-886-6000
Jason Pipkin, admin. Fax 886-5119
Metlakatla HS 100/9-12
PO Box 7 99926 907-886-6000
Taw Lindsey M.A., prin. Fax 886-5120

**Minto, Yukon-Koyukuk, Pop. 200**
Yukon-Koyukuk SD
Supt. — See Fairbanks
Minto S 50/PK-12
PO Box 81 99758 907-798-7212
Vicky Charlie, prin. Fax 798-7282

**Mountain Village, Wade Hampton, Pop. 788**
Lower Yukon SD 2,000/PK-12
PO Box 32089 99632 907-591-2411
Jon Wehde, supt. Fax 591-2449
www.loweryukon.org
Beans S 200/PK-12
PO Box 32105 99632 907-591-2204
Diane Reed, prin. Fax 591-2819
Other Schools – See Alakanuk, Emmonak, Hooper Bay, Kotlik, Marshall, Pilot Station, Russian Mission, Scammon Bay, Sheldon Point

**Naknek, Bristol Bay, Pop. 421**
Bristol Bay Borough SD 200/PK-12
PO Box 169 99633 907-246-4225
Bill Hill, supt. Fax 246-6857
www.bbbsd.net
Bristol Bay MSHS 100/7-12
PO Box 169 99633 907-246-4265
James Dube, prin. Fax 246-4447

**Nanwalek, Kenai Peninsula, Pop. 231**
Kenai Peninsula Borough SD
Supt. — See Soldotna
Nanwalek S 100/K-12
PO Box 8007 99603 907-281-2210
Nancy Kleine, prin. Fax 281-2211

**Napakiak, Bethel, Pop. 354**
Lower Kuskokwim SD
Supt. — See Bethel
Miller Memorial S 100/PK-12
PO Box 34050 99634 907-589-2420
Linda Jennnings, prin. Fax 589-2515

**Napaskiak, Bethel, Pop. 403**
Lower Kuskokwim SD
Supt. — See Bethel
Qugcuun Memorial S 50/PK-12
PO Box 6199 99559 907-737-7214
Nick Straw, prin. Fax 737-7211
Williams Memorial S 100/K-12
PO Box 6089 99559 907-737-7212
Talbert Bentley, prin. Fax 737-7967

**Nenana, Yukon-Koyukuk, Pop. 357**
Nenana CSD 1,000/K-12
PO Box 10 99760 907-832-5464
Eric Gebhart, supt. Fax 832-5625
nenanalynx.org
Nenana City S 200/K-12
PO Box 10 99760 907-832-5464
Sherelyn Carrattini, prin. Fax 832-5625

**New Stuyahok, Dillingham, Pop. 495**
Southwest Region SD
Supt. — See Dillingham
Chief Blunka S 200/K-12
PO Box 29 99636 907-693-3144
Robin Jones, prin. Fax 693-3163

**Newtok, Bethel, Pop. 352**
Lower Kuskokwim SD
Supt. — See Bethel
Ayaprun S 100/PK-12
PO Box WWT 99559 907-237-2504
Grant Kashatok, prin. Fax 237-2506

**Nightmute, Bethel, Pop. 279**
Lower Kuskokwim SD
Supt. — See Bethel
Nightmute S 100/PK-12
General Delivery 99690 907-647-6313
Jerry White, prin. Fax 647-6227

**Nikiski, Kenai Peninsula, Pop. 4,284**
Kenai Peninsula Borough SD
Supt. — See Soldotna
Nikiski MSHS 400/6-12
PO Box 7112 99635 907-776-9400
Dan Carstens, prin. Fax 776-3486

**Nikolaevsk, Kenai Peninsula, Pop. 307**
Kenai Peninsula Borough SD
Supt. — See Soldotna
Nikolaevsk S 100/PK-12
PO Box 5129 99556 907-235-8972
Mike Sellers, prin. Fax 235-3617

**Nikolai, Yukon-Koyukuk, Pop. 83**
Iditarod Area SD
Supt. — See Mc Grath
Top of the Kuskokwim S 50/PK-12
PO Box 9190 99691 907-293-2427
Fax 293-2214

**Ninilchik, Kenai Peninsula, Pop. 836**
Kenai Peninsula Borough SD
Supt. — See Soldotna
Ninilchik S 200/K-12
15735 Sterling Hwy 99639 907-567-3301
Jeffrey Ambrosier, prin. Fax 567-3504

**Noatak, Northwest Arctic, Pop. 502**
Northwest Arctic Borough SD
Supt. — See Kotzebue
Napaaqtugmiut S 200/PK-12
PO Box 49 99761 907-485-2153
Stan VanAmburg, lead tchr. Fax 485-2150

**Nome, Nome, Pop. 3,196**
Nome SD 700/PK-12
PO Box 131 99762 907-443-2231
Shawn Arnold, supt. Fax 443-5144
www.nomeschools.com
Nome-Beltz JSHS 200/7-12
PO Box 131 99762 907-443-6151
Scott Handley, prin. Fax 443-3626

**Nondalton, Lake and Peninsula, Pop. 130**
Lake & Peninsula SD
Supt. — See King Salmon
Nondalton S 50/K-12
1000 School Rd 99640 907-294-2210
Ed Cox, prin. Fax 294-2265

**Noorvik, Northwest Arctic, Pop. 618**
Northwest Arctic Borough SD
Supt. — See Kotzebue
Aqqaluk / Noorvik S 200/PK-12
PO Box 165 99763 907-636-2178
Faith Jurs, prin. Fax 636-2160

**North Pole, Fairbanks North Star, Pop. 1,997**
Fairbanks-North Star Borough SD
Supt. — See Fairbanks
North Pole HS 700/9-12
601 NPHS Blvd 99705 907-488-3761
Annie Keep-Barnes, prin. Fax 488-1488
North Pole MS 700/6-8
300 E 8th Ave 99705 907-488-2271
Rich Smith, prin. Fax 488-9213

---

North Pole Christian S 100/PK-12
2936 Badger Rd 99705 907-488-0133
David Pearson, prin. Fax 488-8248

**Northway, Southeast Fairbanks, Pop. 65**
Alaska Gateway SD
Supt. — See Tok
Northway S 50/PK-12
PO Box 519 99764 907-778-2287
Scott Holmes, prin. Fax 778-2221

**Nuiqsut, North Slope, Pop. 391**
North Slope Borough SD
Supt. — See Barrow
Nuiqsut Trapper S 100/PK-12
PO Box 89167 99789 907-480-6712
John Lamont, prin. Fax 480-6621

**Nulato, Yukon-Koyukuk, Pop. 263**
Yukon-Koyukuk SD
Supt. — See Fairbanks
Demoski S 50/PK-12
PO Box 65029 99765 907-898-2204
John Brady, prin. Fax 898-2340

**Nunapitchuk, Bethel, Pop. 487**
Lower Kuskokwim SD
Supt. — See Bethel
Tobeluk Memorial S 200/K-12
PO Box 150 99641 907-527-5701
Edward Pekar, prin. Fax 527-5610

**Old Harbor, Kodiak Island, Pop. 215**
Kodiak Island Borough SD
Supt. — See Kodiak
Old Harbor S 50/K-12
PO Box 49 99643 907-286-2213
Kendra Bartz, prin. Fax 286-2222

**Ouzinkie, Kodiak Island, Pop. 146**
Kodiak Island Borough SD
Supt. — See Kodiak
Ouzinkie S 50/K-12
PO Box 49 99644 907-680-2204
Steve Doerksen, prin. Fax 680-2288

**Palmer, Matanuska-Susitna, Pop. 5,499**
Matanuska-Susitna Borough SD 16,900/PK-12
501 N Gulkana St 99645 907-746-9200
Dr. Deena Paramo, supt. Fax 746-4076
www.matsuk12.us
Beryozava S 50/K-12
501 N Gulkana St 99645 907-746-2500
Carl Chamblee, prin. Fax 495-2502
Colony HS 1,200/9-12
9550 E Colony Schools Dr 99645 907-861-5500
Cydney Duffin, prin. Fax 861-5509
Colony MS 600/6-8
9250 E Colony Schools Dr 99645 907-761-1500
Mary McMahon, prin. Fax 761-1592
Mat-Su Secondary S Alt
581 Outer Springer Loop Rd 99645 907-761-7238
Jeannie Roy, lead tchr. Fax 746-1647
Palmer HS 800/9-12
1170 W Arctic Ave 99645 907-746-8400
Reese Everett, prin. Fax 746-8481
Palmer MS 600/6-8
1159 S Chugach St 99645 907-761-4300
Thomas Lytle, prin. Fax 761-4372
Valley Pathways HS 200/7-12
PO Box 4897 99645 907-761-4650
James Wanser, prin. Fax 761-4680
Other Schools – See Big Lake, Eagle River, Sutton, Talkeetna, Wasilla

---

Amazing Grace Academy PK-12
2238 Inner Springer Loop 99645 907-745-2691

**Pelican, Skagway-Hoonah-Angoon, Pop. 82**
Pelican CSD 50/PK-12
PO Box 90 99832 907-735-2236
David R. Spence, supt. Fax 735-2263
Pelican S 50/PK-12
PO Box 90 99832 907-735-2236
David R. Spence, admin. Fax 735-2263

**Perryville, Lake and Peninsula, Pop. 111**
Lake & Peninsula SD
Supt. — See King Salmon
Perryville S 50/K-12
PO Box 103 99648 907-853-2210
Lindsey Moore, prin. Fax 853-2267

**Petersburg, Wrangell-Petersburg, Pop. 2,720**
Petersburg SD 400/K-12
PO Box 289 99833 907-772-4271
Erica Kludt-Painter, supt. Fax 772-4719
www.pcsd.us
Mitkof MS 100/6-8
PO Box 289 99833 907-772-3860
Rick Dormer, prin. Fax 772-3617
Petersburg HS 200/9-12
PO Box 289 99833 907-772-3861
Rick Dormer, prin. Fax 772-4168

**Pilot Point, Lake and Peninsula, Pop. 56**
Lake & Peninsula SD
Supt. — See King Salmon
Pilot Point S 50/PK-12
PO Box 467 99649 907-797-2210
Kitza Durlop, prin. Fax 797-2267

**Pilot Station, Wade Hampton, Pop. 567**
Lower Yukon SD
Supt. — See Mountain Village
Pilot Station S 200/PK-12
PO Box 5090 99650 907-549-3212
Cory Stringer, prin. Fax 549-3335

**Platinum, Bethel, Pop. 58**
Lower Kuskokwim SD
Supt. — See Bethel
Arviq S 50/PK-12
PO Box 28 99651 907-979-8111
Georgia Berry, prin. Fax 979-8308

**Point Hope, North Slope, Pop. 647**
North Slope Borough SD
Supt. — See Barrow
Tikigaq S 200/PK-12
PO Box 148 99766 907-368-2662
Gene Burke, prin. Fax 368-2770

**Point Lay, North Slope, Pop. 187**
North Slope Borough SD
Supt. — See Barrow
Kali S 100/PK-12
PO Box 59077 99759 907-833-2311
Glenn Cole, prin. Fax 833-2315

**Port Alexander, Wrangell-Petersburg, Pop. 51**
Southeast Island SD
Supt. — See Thorne Bay
Port Alexander S 50/PK-12
PO Box 8170 99836 907-568-2205
Kale Peacock, lead tchr. Fax 568-2261

**Port Alsworth, Lake and Peninsula, Pop. 150**
Lake & Peninsula SD
Supt. — See King Salmon
Tanalian S 50/PK-12
General Delivery 99653 907-781-2210
Nathan Davis, prin. Fax 781-2254

**Port Graham, Kenai Peninsula, Pop. 143**
Kenai Peninsula Borough SD
Supt. — See Soldotna
Port Graham S 50/PK-12
PO Box 5550 99603 907-284-2210
Nancy Klein, prin. Fax 284-2213

**Port Heiden, Lake and Peninsula, Pop. 100**
Lake & Peninsula SD
Supt. — See King Salmon
Meshik S 50/K-12
General Delivery 99549 907-837-2210
Derek Luke, prin. Fax 837-2265

**Port Lions, Kodiak Island, Pop. 189**
Kodiak Island Borough SD
Supt. — See Kodiak
Port Lions S 50/K-12
PO Box 109 99550 907-454-2237
Steve Doerksen, prin. Fax 454-2377

**Quinhagak, Bethel, Pop. 642**
Lower Kuskokwim SD
Supt. — See Bethel
Kuinerrarmiut Elitnaurviat S 200/PK-12
General Delivery 99655 907-556-8628
Peggie Price, prin. Fax 556-8228

**Ruby, Yukon-Koyukuk, Pop. 156**
Yukon-Koyukuk SD
Supt. — See Fairbanks
Kangas S 50/PK-12
PO Box 68110 99768 907-468-4465
Anne Titus, prin. Fax 468-4444

**Russian Mission, Wade Hampton, Pop. 309**
Lower Yukon SD
Supt. — See Mountain Village
Russian Mission S 100/PK-12
PO Box 90 99657 907-584-5126
Jason Moen, prin. Fax 584-5412

**Saint Marys, Wade Hampton, Pop. 483**
Saint Mary's SD 200/PK-12
PO Box 9 99658 907-438-2411
David Herbert, supt. Fax 438-2735
www.smcsd.us
Saint Mary's S 200/PK-12
PO Box 9 99658 907-438-2411
Dewayne Bahnsen, prin. Fax 438-2735

**Saint Michael, Nome, Pop. 392**
Bering Strait SD
Supt. — See Unalakleet
Andrews S 200/PK-12
100 Baker St 99659 907-923-3041
Craig Sherwood, prin. Fax 923-3031

**Saint Paul Island, Aleutians West, Pop. 459**
Pribilof SD 100/PK-12
PO Box 905 99660 907-546-3331
Connie A. Newman M.Ed., supt. Fax 546-2327
psd-k12.org
St. Paul S 100/PK-12
PO Box 905 99660 907-546-2221
Connie A. Newman M.Ed., prin. Fax 546-2356

**Sand Point, Aleutians East, Pop. 929**
Aleutian East Borough SD 200/PK-12
PO Box 429 99661 907-383-5222
Michael Seifert, supt. Fax 383-3496
www.aebsd.org
Sand Point S 100/PK-12
PO Box 269 99661 907-383-2393
Chris Bennett, prin. Fax 383-3833
Other Schools – See Akutan, False Pass, King Cove

**Savoonga, Nome, Pop. 668**
Bering Strait SD
Supt. — See Unalakleet
Kingeekuk Memorial S 200/PK-12
PO Box 200 99769 907-984-6811
Ralph Lindquist, prin. Fax 984-6413

**Scammon Bay, Wade Hampton, Pop. 473**
Lower Yukon SD
Supt. — See Mountain Village
Scammon Bay S 200/PK-12
103 Askinuk St 99662 907-558-5312
Melissa Rivers, prin. Fax 558-5320

**Selawik, Northwest Arctic, Pop. 742**
Northwest Arctic Borough SD
Supt. — See Kotzebue
Davis-Ramoth S 300/PK-12
PO Box 29 99770 907-484-2142
Lois Ballard, prin. Fax 484-2127

**Seldovia, Kenai Peninsula, Pop. 230**
Kenai Peninsula Borough SD
Supt. — See Soldotna
English S 50/K-12
PO Box 171 99663 907-234-7616
Alan Haskins, prin. Fax 234-7884

**Seward, Kenai Peninsula, Pop. 2,478**
AVTEC SD
PO Box 889 99664 907-224-6150
Ben Eveland, dir. Fax 224-4401
www.avtec.edu
AVTEC-Alaska's Institute of Technology Vo/Tech
PO Box 889 99664 907-224-6150
Ben Eveland, dir. Fax 224-4401
Other Schools – See Anchorage

Kenai Peninsula Borough SD
Supt. — See Soldotna
Seward HS 200/9-12
PO Box 1049 99664 907-224-3351
Trevan Walker, prin. Fax 224-3306
Seward MS 100/6-8
PO Box 1149 99664 907-224-9000
Andy Rothenberger, prin. Fax 224-9001

---

Alaska Vocational Technical School Post-Sec.
PO Box 889 99664 907-224-3322

**Shageluk, Yukon-Koyukuk, Pop. 78**
Iditarod Area SD
Supt. — See Mc Grath
Innoko River S 50/PK-12
PO Box 53 99665 907-473-8233
Joy Hamilton, prin. Fax 473-8268

**Shaktoolik, Nome, Pop. 250**
Bering Strait SD
Supt. — See Unalakleet
Shaktoolik S 100/PK-12
PO Box 40 99771 907-955-3021
Steven Sammons, prin. Fax 955-3031

**Sheldon Point, Wade Hampton, Pop. 121**
Lower Yukon SD
Supt. — See Mountain Village
Sheldon Point S 100/PK-12
PO Box 32, Nunam Iqua AK 99666 907-498-4112
James Van Sandt, prin. Fax 498-4111

**Shishmaref, Nome, Pop. 556**
Bering Strait SD
Supt. — See Unalakleet
Shishmaref S 200/PK-12
1 Seaview Ln 99772 907-649-3021
Ralph Watkins, prin. Fax 649-3031

**Shungnak, Northwest Arctic, Pop. 262**
Northwest Arctic Borough SD
Supt. — See Kotzebue
Shungnak S 100/PK-12
PO Box 79 99773 907-437-2151
Roger Franklin, prin. Fax 437-2177

**Sitka, Sitka, Pop. 8,072**
Mt. Edgecumbe HSD 400/9-12
1330 Seward Ave 99835 907-966-3200
Randy Hawk, supt. Fax 966-2442
www.mehs.us
Mt. Edgecumbe HS 400/9-12
1330 Seward Ave 99835 907-966-3200
Bernie Gurule, prin. Fax 966-2442

Sitka SD 1,300/PK-12
300 Kostrometinoff St 99835 907-747-8622
Dr. Mary Wegner, supt. Fax 966-1260
www.sitkaschools.org
Blatchley MS 300/6-8
601 Halibut Point Rd 99835 907-747-8672
Ben White, prin. Fax 966-1460
Pacific HS 50/Alt
509 Lincoln St 99835 907-747-0525
Mandy Summer, prin. Fax 747-7310
Sitka HS 300/9-12
1000 Lake St 99835 907-747-3263
Lyle Sparrowgrove, prin. Fax 747-3229

**Skagway, Skagway-Hoonah-Angoon, Pop. 884**
Skagway SD 100/PK-12
PO Box 497 99840 907-983-2960
Dr. Joshua Coughran, supt. Fax 983-2964
www.skagwayschool.org
Skagway S 100/PK-12
PO Box 497 99840 907-983-2960
Dr. Joshua Coughran, supt. Fax 983-2964

**Slana, Valdez-Cordova, Pop. 142**
Copper River SD
Supt. — See Glennallen
Slana S 50/1-12
PO Box 870 99586 907-822-5868
Linda Bates, prin. Fax 822-3850

**Sleetmute, Bethel, Pop. 86**
Kuspuk SD
Supt. — See Aniak
Egnaty Sr. S 50/K-12
PO Box 69 99668 907-449-4216
Steven B. Porter, prin. Fax 449-4217

**Soldotna, Kenai Peninsula, Pop. 3,894**
Kenai Peninsula Borough SD 9,000/PK-12
148 N Binkley St 99669 907-714-8888
Sean Dusek, supt. Fax 262-9645
www.kpbsd.k12.ak.us
Connections S 800/Alt
143 E Park Ave 99669 907-714-8880
Richard Bartolowits, prin. Fax 262-2859
River City Academy 100/7-12
426 W Redoubt Ave 99669 907-714-8945
Dawn Edwards-Smith, prin. Fax 714-8946
Skyview MS 400/7-8
46188 Sterling Hwy 99669 907-260-2500
Sarge Truesdell, prin. Fax 262-7036
Soldotna HS 500/10-12
425 W Marydale Ave 99669 907-260-7000
Tony Graham, prin. Fax 262-4288
Soldotna Prep S 9-9
426 W Redooubt Ave 99669 907-260-2300
Curtis Schmidt, prin. Fax 262-6555
Other Schools – See Cooper Landing, Fritz Creek, Homer, Hope, Kenai, Nanwalek, Nikiski, Nikolaevsk, Ninilchik, Port Graham, Seldovia, Seward, Tyonek

---

Alaska Christian College Post-Sec.
35109 Royal Pl 99669 907-260-7422
Cook Inlet Academy 100/PK-12
45872 Kalifornsky Beach Rd 99669 907-262-5101
Mary Rowley, admin. Fax 262-1541

**Stebbins, Nome, Pop. 556**
Bering Strait SD
Supt. — See Unalakleet
Tukurngailnguq S 200/K-12
General Delivery 99671 907-934-3021
John Juvinall, prin. Fax 934-3031

**Sterling, Kenai Peninsula, Pop. 5,392**

---

Academy of Higher Learning 50/K-12
32930 Fair Game Ave 99672 907-260-7741
Catherine Gibson, prin. Fax 260-7741

**Stony River, Bethel, Pop. 49**
Kuspuk SD
Supt. — See Aniak
Michael S, General Delivery 99557 50/K-12
Steven B. Porter, prin. 907-537-3225

**Sutton, Matanuska-Susitna, Pop. 308**
Matanuska-Susitna Borough SD
Supt. — See Palmer
Glacier View S 50/K-12
65975 S Wolverine Cir 99674 907-861-5650
Wendy Taylor, prin. Fax 861-5680

**Takotna, Yukon-Koyukuk, Pop. 38**
Iditarod Area SD
Supt. — See Mc Grath
Takotna S 50/PK-12
PO Box 90 99675 907-298-2115
Fax 298-2316

**Talkeetna, Matanuska-Susitna, Pop. 845**
Matanuska-Susitna Borough SD
Supt. — See Palmer
Susitna Valley JSHS 200/7-12
HC 89 Box 8580 99676 907-733-9300
Jason Mabry, prin. Fax 733-9380

**Tanana, Yukon-Koyukuk, Pop. 238**
Tanana CSD 50/K-12
PO Box 89 99777 907-366-7203
M. Therese Ashton, supt. Fax 366-7201
aktcsd.schoolwires.net
Sommer S 50/K-12
PO Box 89 99777 907-366-7203
M. Therese Ashton, supt. Fax 366-7201

**Tatitlek, Valdez-Cordova, Pop. 84**
Chugach SD
Supt. — See Anchorage
Tatitlek Community S 50/K-12
PO Box 167 99677 907-325-2252
Ted Palmer, prin. Fax 325-2299

**Teller, Nome, Pop. 229**
Bering Strait SD
Supt. — See Unalakleet
Isabell S 100/PK-12
100 Airport Ave 99778 907-642-3041
Susette Carroll, prin. Fax 642-3031

**Tenakee Springs, Skagway-Hoonah-Angoon, Pop. 127**
Chatham SD
Supt. — See Angoon
Tenakee Springs S 50/K-12
PO Box 62 99841 907-736-2204
Ann Coonnelly, lead tchr. Fax 736-2204

**Tetlin, Southeast Fairbanks, Pop. 122**
Alaska Gateway SD
Supt. — See Tok
Tetlin S 50/PK-12
100 Main St 99779 907-324-2104
Robert Litwack, prin. Fax 324-2120

**Thorne Bay, Prince of Wales-Outer Ketchikan, Pop. 450**
Southeast Island SD 200/PK-12
PO Box 19569 99919 907-828-8254
Lauren Burch, supt. Fax 828-8257
www.sisd.org/
Thorne Bay S 100/K-12
PO Box 19005 99919 907-828-3921
Rob O'Neal, prin. Fax 828-3901
Other Schools – See Coffman Cove, Craig, Hyder, Kasaan, Ketchikan, Port Alexander

**Togiak, Dillingham, Pop. 691**
Southwest Region SD
Supt. — See Dillingham
Togiak S 200/K-12
PO Box 50 99678 907-493-5829
Sam Gosuk, prin. Fax 493-5933

**Tok, Southeast Fairbanks, Pop. 1,157**
Alaska Gateway SD 400/PK-12
PO Box 226 99780 907-883-5151
Todd Poage, supt. Fax 883-5154
www.agsd.us/
Tok S 200/PK-12
PO Box 249 99780 907-883-5161
Jason Roslansky, prin. Fax 883-5165
Other Schools – See Dot Lake, Eagle, Mentasta Lake, Northway, Tetlin

**Toksook Bay, Bethel, Pop. 578**
Lower Kuskokwim SD
Supt. — See Bethel
Nelson Island Area S 200/PK-12
General Delivery 99637 907-427-7815
Daryl Daugaard, prin. Fax 427-7612

**Tuluksak, Bethel, Pop. 370**
Yupiit SD
Supt. — See Akiachak
Tuluksak S 200/PK-12
PO Box 115 99679 907-695-5600
Paul Thomas, prin. Fax 695-5645

**Tuntutuliak, Bethel, Pop. 403**
Lower Kuskokwim SD
Supt. — See Bethel
Angapak Memorial S 200/PK-12
General Delivery 99680 907-256-2415
Zachary Bastoky, prin. Fax 256-2527

**Tununak, Bethel, Pop. 322**
Lower Kuskokwim SD
Supt. — See Bethel
Albert Memorial S 100/PK-12
PO Box 49 99681 907-652-6827
Randy Heinrichs, prin. Fax 652-6028

**Tyonek, Kenai Peninsula, Pop. 165**
Kenai Peninsula Borough SD
Supt. — See Soldotna
Tebughna S 50/K-12
PO Box 82010 99682 907-583-2291
Richard Breske, prin. Fax 583-2692

**Unalakleet, Nome, Pop. 644**
Bering Strait SD 1,800/PK-12
PO Box 225 99684 907-624-4261
Dr. Bobby Bolen, supt. Fax 624-3099
www.bssd.org
Unalakleet S 200/PK-12
PO Box 130 99684 907-624-3444
Perry Corsetti, prin. Fax 624-3388
Other Schools – See Brevig Mission, Diomede, Elim, Gambell, Golovin, Koyuk, Saint Michael, Savoonga, Shaktoolik, Shishmaref, Stebbins, Teller, Wales, White Mountain

**Unalaska, Aleutians West, Pop. 4,083**
Unalaska CSD 400/PK-12
PO Box 570 99685 907-581-3151
John Conwell, supt. Fax 581-3152
www.ucsd.net
Unalaska City HS 200/7-12
PO Box 570 99685 907-581-1222
Jim Wilson, prin. Fax 581-2428

**Valdez, Valdez-Cordova, Pop. 3,714**
Valdez CSD 600/PK-12
PO Box 398 99686 907-835-4357
Jim Nygaard, supt. Fax 835-4964
www.valdezcityschools.org/
Gilson MS 100/6-8
PO Box 398 99686 907-835-2244
Rodney Morrison, prin. Fax 835-2540
Valdez HS 200/9-12
PO Box 398 99686 907-835-4767
Rodny Schug, prin. Fax 835-2596

---

Prince William Sound Community College Post-Sec.
PO Box 97 99686 907-834-1600

**Venetie, Yukon-Koyukuk, Pop. 159**
Yukon Flats SD
Supt. — See Fort Yukon
Fredson S 100/PK-12
PO Box 81089 99781 907-849-8415
Jake Kramer, lead tchr. Fax 849-8630

**Wainwright, North Slope, Pop. 547**
North Slope Borough SD
Supt. — See Barrow
Alak S 200/PK-12
PO Box 10 99782 907-763-2541
Bob Grimes, prin. Fax 763-2565

**Wales, Nome, Pop. 132**
Bering Strait SD
Supt. — See Unalakleet
Wales S 50/PK-12
PO Box 490 99783 907-664-3021
Roxanne Meneguin, prin. Fax 664-3031

**Wasilla, Matanuska-Susitna, Pop. 7,351**
Matanuska-Susitna Borough SD
Supt. — See Palmer
Burchell HS 300/Alt
1775 W Parks Hwy 99654 907-864-2600
Adam Mokelke, prin. Fax 864-2680
Mat-Su Career and Technical HS Vo/Tech
2472 N Seward Meridian Pkwy 99654 907-352-0400
Mark Okeson, prin. Fax 352-0480
Mat-Su Day S 100/Alt
2360 N Tait Dr 99654 907-864-6000
Wolfgang Winter, prin. Fax 864-6080
Teeland MS 700/6-8
2788 N Seward Meridian Pkwy 99654 907-352-7500
Katherine Ellsworth, prin. Fax 352-7585
Wasilla HS 1,300/9-12
701 E Bogard Rd 99654 907-352-8200
Amy Spargo, prin. Fax 352-8280
Wasilla MS 800/6-8
650 E Bogard Rd 99654 907-352-5300
Leigh Larson, prin. Fax 352-5380

---

Charter College Post-Sec.
721 W Parks Hwy Ste 5 99654 907-952-1000
Wasilla Lake Christian S 200/PK-12
2001 Palmer Wasilla Hwy 99654 907-373-6439
Dave Duncan, prin. Fax 373-6438

**White Mountain, Nome, Pop. 178**
Bering Strait SD
Supt. — See Unalakleet
White Mountain S 50/PK-12
PO Box 55 99784 907-638-3041
David Fair, prin. Fax 638-3031

**Whittier, Valdez-Cordova, Pop. 187**
Chugach SD
Supt. — See Anchorage
Whittier Community S 50/PK-12
PO Box 638 99693 907-472-2575
Melody Clifford, prin. Fax 472-2409

**Wrangell, Wrangell-Petersburg, Pop. 2,153**
Wrangell SD 300/K-12
PO Box 2319 99929 907-874-2347
Patrick Mayer, supt. Fax 874-3137
www.wrangellschools.org
Stikine MS 100/6-8
PO Box 1935 99929 907-874-3393
Kendall Benson, prin. Fax 874-3149
Wrangell HS 100/9-12
PO Box 651 99929 907-874-3395
Kendall Benson, prin. Fax 874-3143

**Yakutat, Yakutat, Pop. 549**
Yakutat SD 100/PK-12
PO Box 429 99689 907-784-3317
Robin Gray, supt. Fax 784-3446
www.yakutatschools.org
Yakutat S 100/PK-12
PO Box 429 99689 907-784-3317
Robin Gray, supt. Fax 784-3446

# ARIZONA

## ARIZONA DEPARTMENT OF EDUCATION
**1535 W Jefferson St, Phoenix 85007-3280**
**Telephone 602-542-5393**
**Fax 602-542-5440**
**Website http://www.azed.gov**

Superintendent of Public Instruction John Huppenthal

## ARIZONA BOARD OF EDUCATION
**1535 W Jefferson St, Phoenix 85007-3280**

Executive Director Vince Yanez

### COUNTY SUPERINTENDENTS OF SCHOOLS

Apache County Office of Education
R. Barry Williams, supt. 928-337-7539
PO Box 548, Saint Johns 85936 Fax 337-2033
schools.apachecounty.net

Cochise County Office of Education
Trudy Berry, supt. 520-432-8950
PO Box 208, Bisbee 85603 Fax 432-7136
www.cochise.az.gov/cochise_schools.aspx?id=462

Coconino County Office of Education
Risha VanderWey, supt. 928-679-8070
2384 N Steves Blvd Fax 679-8077
Flagstaff 86004
ccesa.az.gov

Gila County Office of Education
Dr. Linda O'Dell, supt. 928-425-3231
1400 E Ash St, Globe 85501 Fax 402-0038
www.gilacountyaz.gov

Graham County Office of Education
Donna McGaughey, supt. 928-428-2880
921 W Thatcher Blvd Fax 428-8824
Safford 85546
www.graham.az.gov/school-superintendent/

Greenlee County Office of Education
Tom Powers, supt. 928-865-2822
PO Box 1595, Clifton 85533 Fax 865-4417
www.co.greenlee.az.us/schools/

Lapaz County Office of Education
Jacquline Price, supt. 928-669-6183
1112 S Joshua Ave Ste 205 Fax 669-4406
Parker 85344
www.lapazschools.org

Maricopa County Education Service Agency
Dr. Don Covey, supt. 602-506-3866
4041 N Central Ave Ste 1200 Fax 506-3753
Phoenix 85012
education.maricopa.gov/

Mohave County Office of Education
Michael File, supt. 928-753-0747
PO Box 7000, Kingman 86402 Fax 718-4958
www.mohavecounty.us/ContentPage.aspx?id=130

Navajo County Office of Education
Linda Morrow, supt. 928-524-4204
PO Box 668, Holbrook 86025 Fax 524-4209
www.navajocountyaz.gov/schools/

Pima County Office of Education
Dr. Linda Arzoumanian, supt. 520-724-8451
200 N Stone Ave, Tucson 85701 Fax 770-4210
www.schools.pima.gov/

Pinal County Office of Education
Jill Broussard, supt. 520-866-6565
PO Box 769, Florence Fax 866-6973
www.ecrsc.org/pinalesa/

Santa Cruz County Office of Education
Alfredo Velasquez, supt. 520-375-7940
2150 N Congress Dr Fax 375-7958
Nogales 85621
www.co.santa-cruz.az.us/294/Superintendent-of-Schools

Yavapai County Office of Education
Tim Carter, supt. 928-771-3326
2970 Centerpointe East Dr Fax 771-3329
Prescott 86301
www.ycesa.com

Yuma County Office of Education
Thomas Tyree, supt. 928-373-1006
210 S 1st Ave, Yuma 85364 Fax 329-2008
www.yumasupt.org

### PUBLIC, PRIVATE AND CATHOLIC SECONDARY SCHOOLS

**Ajo, Pima, Pop. 3,253**
Ajo USD 15 400/PK-12
PO Box 68 85321 520-387-5618
Dr. Robert Dooley, supt. Fax 387-6545
www.ajoschools.org/
Ajo HS 100/9-12
PO Box 68 85321 520-387-7602
Dr. Lauren Carriere, prin. Fax 387-7603

**Anthem, Maricopa, Pop. 21,203**
Deer Valley USD 97
Supt. — See Phoenix
Boulder Creek HS 2,400/9-12
40404 N Gavilan Peak Pkwy 85086 623-445-8600
Lauren Sheahan, prin. Fax 445-8680

**Apache Junction, Pinal, Pop. 35,261**
Apache Junction USD 43 4,800/K-12
1575 W Southern Ave, 480-982-1110
Dr. Chad Wilson, supt. Fax 982-6474
www.ajusd.org
Apache Junction HS 1,500/9-12
2525 S Ironwood Dr, 480-982-1110
Larry LaPrise, prin. Fax 982-3787
Cactus Canyon JHS 800/7-8
801 W Southern Ave, 480-982-1110
Courtney Castelhano, prin. Fax 983-4913

---

Central Arizona College Post-Sec.
805 S Idaho Rd, 480-677-7700

**Ash Fork, Yavapai, Pop. 392**
Ash Fork JUSD 31 300/K-12
PO Box 247 86320 928-637-2561
Seth Staples, admin. Fax 637-2623
www.afjusd.org/
Ash Fork HS 100/9-12
PO Box 247 86320 928-637-2561
Seth Staples, prin. Fax 637-2623
Ash Fork MS 100/6-8
PO Box 247 86320 928-637-2561
Seth Staples, prin. Fax 637-2623

**Avondale, Maricopa, Pop. 74,219**
Agua Fria UNHSD 216 6,800/9-12
1481 N Eliseo Felix Jr Way 85323 623-932-7000
Dr. Dennis Runyan, supt. Fax 932-2796
www.aguafria.org
Agua Fria HS 1,600/9-12
530 E Riley Dr 85323 623-932-7300
Thom Luedemann, prin. Fax 932-0650
Other Schools – See Buckeye, Goodyear

Tolleson UNHSD 214
Supt. — See Tolleson
La Joya Community HS 1,800/9-12
11650 W Whyman Ave 85323 623-478-4400
Brandi Haskins, prin. Fax 478-7225
Westview HS 2,600/9-12
10850 W Garden Lakes Pkwy, 623-478-4600
Dr. Michele Wilson, prin. Fax 478-4669

---

Estrella Mountain Community College Post-Sec.
3000 N Dysart Rd, 623-935-8000
Maricopa Beauty College Post-Sec.
515 W Western Ave 85323 623-932-4414
Universal Technical Institute Post-Sec.
10695 W Pierce St 85323 623-245-4600

**Bagdad, Yavapai, Pop. 1,847**
Bagdad USD 20 400/PK-12
PO Box 427 86321 928-633-4101
Bryan Bullington, supt. Fax 633-4345
bagdadschools.org
Bagdad HS 100/9-12
PO Box 427 86321 928-633-2201
Tom Finnerty, prin. Fax 633-4345
Bagdad MS 100/6-8
PO Box 427 86321 928-633-2201
Tom Finnerty, prin. Fax 633-4345

**Beaver Dam, Mohave, Pop. 1,928**
Littlefield USD 9 500/PK-12
3490 E Rio Virgin Rd 86432 928-347-5486
Mark Coleman, supt. Fax 347-5967
www.lusd9.com/
Beaver Dam JSHS 100/7-12
3475 E Rio Virgin Rd 86432 928-347-5252
Mark Coleman, prin. Fax 347-5151

**Benson, Cochise, Pop. 5,014**
Benson USD 9 1,200/PK-12
360 S Patagonia St 85602 520-720-6700
Micah Mortensen, supt. Fax 720-6701
www.bensonsd.k12.az.us
Benson HS 400/9-12
360 S Patagonia St 85602 520-720-6840
Ben Rodriguez, prin. Fax 720-6710
Benson MS 400/5-8
360 S Patagonia St 85602 520-720-6801
Tammara Ragsdale, prin. Fax 720-6709

**Bisbee, Cochise, Pop. 5,464**
Bisbee USD 2 800/PK-12
100 Old Douglas Rd 85603 520-432-5381
James Phillips, supt. Fax 432-7622
www.busd.k12.az.us
Bisbee HS 400/9-12
100 Old Douglas Rd 85603 520-432-5714
Laura Miller, prin. Fax 432-6105
Lowell JHS 200/5-8
100 Old Douglas Rd 85603 520-432-5391
Tari Hardy, prin. Fax 432-6106

**Blue, Greenlee**
Blue ESD 22 50/PK-12
PO Box 80 85922 928-339-4346
Sally Hulsey, hdmstr. Fax 339-4116
Blue S 50/PK-12
PO Box 80 85922 928-339-4346
Sally Hulsey, prin. Fax 339-4116

**Bowie, Cochise, Pop. 442**
Bowie USD 14 100/K-12
PO Box 157 85605 520-847-2545
Jeff St. Clair, supt. Fax 847-2546
www.bowieschools.org
Bowie MSHS 50/6-12
PO Box 157 85605 520-847-2545
Jeff St. Clair, supt. Fax 847-2546

**Buckeye, Maricopa, Pop. 49,727**
Agua Fria UNHSD 216
Supt. — See Avondale
Verrado HS 1,500/9-12
20050 W Indian School Rd, 623-932-7400
Dr. Terry Maurer, prin. Fax 853-0369

Buckeye UNHSD 201 3,800/9-12
1000 E Narramore Ave 85326 623-386-9700
Eric Godfrey, supt. Fax 386-9923
www.buhsd.org
Buckeye Union HS 1,200/9-12
1000 E Narramore Ave 85326 623-386-4423
Tawn Argeris, prin. Fax 386-9711
Other Schools – See Goodyear

Litchfield ESD 79
Supt. — See Litchfield Park
Verrado MS 900/6-8
20880 W Main St, 623-547-1300
Karen Williams, prin. Fax 853-2358

**Bullhead City, Mohave, Pop. 38,810**
Bullhead City ESD 15 3,400/PK-8
1004 Hancock Rd 86442 928-758-3961
Riley Frei, supt. Fax 758-4996
www.bullheadschools.com
Bullhead City JHS 600/6-8
1062 Hancock Rd 86442 928-758-3921
Carolyn Stewart, prin. Fax 758-7428
Fox Creek JHS 600/6-8
3101 Desert Sky Blvd 86442 928-704-2500
Jon Jones, prin. Fax 704-2504

Colorado River UNHSD 2 2,300/9-12
PO Box 21479 86439 928-758-3961
Riley Frei, supt. Fax 219-3050
coloradoriverschools.org/
Mohave HS 1,500/9-12
2251 Highway 95 86442 928-758-3916
Steve Lawrence, prin. Fax 758-7145
Other Schools – See Mohave Valley

**Camp Verde, Yavapai, Pop. 10,552**
Camp Verde USD 28 1,400/PK-12
410 Camp Lincoln Rd 86322 928-567-8000
Dr. Amber Lee, admin. Fax 567-8004
www.campverdeschools.org
Camp Verde HS 500/9-12
1326 N Montezuma Castle Hwy 86322 928-567-8035
Robert Weir, prin. Fax 567-8045

Camp Verde MS 300/6-8
370 Camp Lincoln Rd 86322 928-567-8014
Danny Howe, prin. Fax 567-8022

**Casa Grande, Pinal, Pop. 47,575**
Casa Grande ESD 4 7,200/PK-8
220 W Kortsen Rd, 520-836-2111
Dr. Frank Davidson, supt. Fax 426-3712
www.cgesd.org
Cactus MS 900/6-8
1220 E Kortsen Rd, 520-421-3330
David Owen, prin. Fax 421-7425
Casa Grande MS 700/6-8
300 W McMurray Blvd, 520-836-7310
Jennifer Murrieta, prin. Fax 836-2399
Villago MS 800/6-8
574 E Lakeside Pkwy, 520-423-0176
Jeffrey Lavender, prin. Fax 423-0177

Casa Grande UNHSD 82 3,400/9-12
1362 N Casa Grande Ave, 520-316-3360
Dr. Shannon Goodsell, supt. Fax 316-3352
www.cguhsd.org
Casa Grande Union HS 1,400/9-12
2730 N Trekell Rd, 520-836-8500
Thomas Trigalet, prin. Fax 316-3353
Vista Grande HS 1,800/9-12
1556 N Arizola Rd, 520-876-9400
Glenda Sulley, prin. Fax 876-5348

**Chandler, Maricopa, Pop. 229,946**
Chandler USD 80 38,800/PK-12
1525 W Frye Rd 85224 480-812-7000
Dr. Camille Casteel, supt. Fax 224-9128
www.cusd80.com
Andersen JHS 900/6-8
1255 N Dobson Rd 85224 480-883-5300
Jim Anderson, prin. Fax 883-5320
Arizona College Prep - Erie 200/7-12
1150 W Erie St 85224 480-424-8000
Robert Bickes, prin. Fax 224-9268
Arizona College Prep - Oakland 400/6-8
191 W Oakland St 85225 480-224-3930
Jayson Phillips, prin. Fax 224-3940
Basha Accelerated MS 6-8
5990 S Val Vista Dr 85249 480-224-2100
David Loutzenheiser, prin. Fax 224-2120
Basha HS 2,400/9-12
5990 S Val Vista Dr 85249 480-224-2100
David Loutzenheiser, prin. Fax 224-2120
Bogle JHS 1,200/7-8
1600 W Queen Creek Rd 85248 480-883-5500
Susie Avey, prin. Fax 224-9141
Chandler Early College 9-12
2626 E Pecos Rd 85225 480-224-3060
Shawn Mitchell, head sch Fax 224-9345
Chandler HS 3,200/9-12
350 N Arizona Ave 85225 480-812-7700
Larry Rother, prin. Fax 812-7720
Elite Performance Academy 3-8
1825 S Alma School Rd, 480-812-2067
Thuy Padilla, admin.
Hamilton HS 3,500/9-12
3700 S Arizona Ave 85248 480-883-5000
Ken James, prin. Fax 883-5020
Hill Learning Academy 200/Alt
290 S Cooper Rd 85225 480-812-7150
Dave Constance, prin. Fax 224-9066
Santan JHS 1,200/7-8
1550 E Chandler Heights Rd 85249 480-883-4600
Barbara Kowalinski, prin. Fax 883-4620
Willis JHS 900/7-8
401 S McQueen Rd 85225 480-883-5700
Jeff Delp, prin. Fax 883-5720
Other Schools – See Gilbert, Queen Creek

Kyrene ESD 28
Supt. — See Tempe
Kyrene Aprende MS 1,000/6-8
777 N Desert Breeze Blvd E 85226 480-541-6200
Renee Kory, prin. Fax 541-6210
Kyrene Del Pueblo MS 1,000/6-8
360 S Twelve Oaks Blvd 85226 480-541-6800
Kelly Alexander, prin. Fax 541-6810

---

Chandler-Gilbert Community College Post-Sec.
2626 E Pecos Rd 85225 480-732-7000
Empire Beauty School Post-Sec.
2978 N Alma School Rd Ste 3 85224 480-855-7901
Golf Academy of America Post-Sec.
2031 N Arizona Ave Ste 2 85225 800-342-7342
International Baptist College Post-Sec.
2211 W Germann Rd, 480-245-7903
Quantum Helicopters Post-Sec.
2401 S Heliport Way, 480-814-8118
Seton Catholic Preparatory HS 600/9-12
1150 N Dobson Rd 85224 480-963-1900
Patricia Collins, prin. Fax 963-1974
Tri-City Christian Academy 300/PK-12
2211 W Germann Rd, 480-245-7902
Rev. Thad Todd, prin. Fax 245-7908
Valley Christian HS 400/9-12
6900 W Galveston St 85226 480-705-8888
Dan Kuiper, prin. Fax 705-8889

**Chinle, Apache, Pop. 4,452**
Chinle USD 24 2,800/K-12
PO Box 587 86503 928-674-9600
Quincy Natay, supt. Fax 674-9608
www.chinleusd.k12.az.us/
Chinle HS 1,000/9-12
PO Box 587 86503 928-674-9500
Douglas Clauschee, prin. Fax 674-9599
Chinle JHS 500/7-8
PO Box 587 86503 928-674-9400
Tammy Smith, prin. Fax 674-9499

**Chino Valley, Yavapai, Pop. 10,639**
Chino Valley USD 51 1,800/K-12
PO Box 225 86323 928-636-2458
Duane Howard, supt. Fax 636-1434
www.cvsd.k12.az.us
Chino Valley HS 800/9-12
PO Box 225 86323 928-636-2298
Wes Brownfield, prin. Fax 636-6219

Heritage MS 600/5-8
PO Box 225 86323 928-636-4464
Mardi Read, prin. Fax 636-6214

**Colorado City, Mohave, Pop. 4,817**
Colorado City USD 14 400/PK-12
PO Box 309 86021 928-875-9000
Carol Timpson, supt. Fax 875-8066
www.elcap.us
El Capitan S 400/4-12
PO Box 309 86021 928-875-9000
Shauna Hammon, prin. Fax 875-8068

**Coolidge, Pinal, Pop. 11,531**
Coolidge USD 21 3,700/PK-12
450 N Arizona Blvd, 520-723-2040
Charie Wallace, admin. Fax 723-2442
www.coolidgeschools.org/
Coolidge HS 800/9-12
684 W Northern Ave, 520-723-2305
Dawn Dee Hodge, prin. Fax 723-8249
Hohokam MS 500/6-8
684 W Northern Ave, 520-723-2304
Dawn Dee Hodge, prin.
Other Schools – See San Tan Valley

---

Central Arizona College Post-Sec.
8470 N Overfield Rd, 520-494-5444

**Corona, Pima, Pop. 5,546**
Vail USD 20
Supt. — See Vail
Corona Foothills MS 400/6-8
16705 S Houghton Rd 85641 520-879-3500
Margaret Steuer, prin. Fax 879-3501

**Cottonwood, Yavapai, Pop. 11,102**
Cottonwood-Oak Creek ESD 6 1,900/PK-8
1 N Willard St 86326 928-634-2288
Barbara U'Ren, supt. Fax 634-2309
www.cocsd.k12.az.us
Cottonwood MS 600/6-8
1 N Willard St 86326 928-634-2231
Denise Kennedy, prin. Fax 634-2874

Mingus UNHSD 4 1,200/9-12
1801 E Fir St 86326 928-634-8901
Dr. Paul Tighe, supt. Fax 649-4399
www.mingusunion.com
Mingus Union HS 1,200/9-12
1801 E Fir St 86326 928-634-7531
Jennifer Chilton, prin. Fax 639-4236

**Dewey, Yavapai, Pop. 3,640**
Humboldt USD 22
Supt. — See Prescott Valley
Bradshaw Mountain MS 300/7-8
12255 E Turquoise Cir 86327 928-759-4900
Jessica Bennett, prin. Fax 759-4920

**Dolan Springs, Mohave, Pop. 1,994**
Kingman USD 20
Supt. — See Kingman
Mt. Tipton S 300/K-12
16500 Pierce Ferry Rd 86441 928-767-3350
Deb Warren, prin. Fax 767-4330

**Douglas, Cochise, Pop. 17,315**
Douglas USD 27 4,100/PK-12
PO Box 1237 85608 520-364-2447
Ronald V. Aguallo, supt. Fax 224-2470
www.dusd.k12.az.us
Borane MS 400/6-8
PO Box 1237 85608 520-364-2461
Katie Walker, prin. Fax 364-5537
Douglas HS 1,400/9-12
PO Box 1237 85608 520-364-3462
Dr. Andrea Overman, prin. Fax 805-4171
Huber MS 500/6-8
PO Box 1237 85608 520-364-2840
Jeremy Long, prin. Fax 364-2421

---

Cochise College Post-Sec.
4190 W Highway 80 85607 800-966-7943

**Duncan, Greenlee, Pop. 683**
Duncan USD 2 300/K-12
PO Box 710 85534 928-359-2472
Eldon Merrell, supt. Fax 359-2807
dusdwildkats.org
Duncan ES 200/3-8
PO Box 710 85534 928-359-2471
Kent Baldwin, prin. Fax 359-1105
Duncan HS 100/9-12
PO Box 710 85534 928-359-2474
Toni Corona, dean Fax 359-1141

**Eagar, Apache, Pop. 4,784**
Round Valley USD 10
Supt. — See Springerville
Round Valley HS 400/9-12
550 N Butler St 85925 928-333-6800
Slade Morgan, prin. Fax 333-6819
Round Valley MS 300/5-8
126 W 2nd St 85925 928-333-6700
Marcie Udall, prin. Fax 333-5252
White Mountain Academy Alt
550 N Butler St 85925 928-333-6890
Chris Matthews, lead tchr.

**Elfrida, Cochise, Pop. 454**
Valley UNHSD 22 100/9-12
PO Box 158 85610 520-642-3492
Ron Aguallo, supt. Fax 642-3523
www.vuhs.net
Valley Union HS 100/9-12
PO Box 158 85610 520-642-3492
Ron Aguallo, admin. Fax 642-3523

**El Mirage, Maricopa, Pop. 30,983**
Dysart USD 89
Supt. — See Surprise
Dysart HS 1,700/9-12
11425 N Dysart Rd 85335 623-876-7500
Amy Hartjen, prin. Fax 876-7572

**Eloy, Pinal, Pop. 15,495**
Eloy ESD 11 1,000/PK-8
1011 N Sunshine Blvd, 520-466-2100
Ruby James, supt. Fax 466-2101
www.eloyesd.org
Eloy JHS 200/6-8
1011 N Sunshine Blvd, 520-466-2140
Kevin Oursler, prin. Fax 466-2150

Pinal County Office of Education
Supt. — See Florence
Villa Oasis Interscholastic Center 100/Alt
3740 N Toltec Rd, 520-450-4450
Justin DeMello, prin. Fax 450-4301

Santa Cruz Valley UNHSD 840 300/9-12
900 N Main St, 520-466-2220
Orlenda Roberts M.Ed., supt. Fax 466-2222
www.scvuhs.org/
Santa Cruz Valley Union HS 300/9-12
900 N Main St, 520-466-2200
Orante Jenkins, prin. Fax 466-2222

**Flagstaff, Coconino, Pop. 64,141**
Flagstaff USD 1 9,500/PK-12
3285 E Sparrow Ave 86004 928-527-6000
Barbara Hickman, supt. Fax 527-6015
www.fusd1.org
Coconino HS 1,400/9-12
2801 N Izabel St 86004 928-773-8200
Stacie Zanzucchi, prin. Fax 773-8247
Flagstaff HS 1,500/9-12
400 W Elm Ave 86001 928-773-8100
Tony Cullen, prin. Fax 773-8146
Mount Elden MS 800/6-8
3223 N 4th St 86004 928-773-8250
Steve Boadway, prin. Fax 773-8269
Sinagua MS 1,000/6-8
3950 E Butler Ave 86004 928-527-5500
Tari Popham, prin. Fax 527-5561
Summit HS TAPP Alternative S 100/Alt
4000 N Cummings St 86004 928-773-8198
Chris Koenker, prin. Fax 773-8427

---

Coconino Community College Post-Sec.
2800 S Lone Tree Rd, 928-527-1222
CollegeAmerica Post-Sec.
3012 E Route 66 86004 928-213-6060
Empire Beauty School Post-Sec.
1790 E Route 66 86004 928-774-7146
Northern Arizona University Post-Sec.
S San Francisco St 86011 928-523-9011

**Florence, Pinal, Pop. 25,223**
Florence USD 1 8,300/PK-12
PO Box 2850, 520-866-3500
Dr. Amy Fuller, supt. Fax 868-2302
www.fusdaz.com
Florence HS 700/9-12
PO Box 2850, 520-866-3560
Thad Gates, prin. Fax 868-2329
Other Schools – See San Tan Valley

Pinal County Office of Education 200/
PO Box 769 85132 520-866-6565
Jill Broussard, supt. Fax 866-6973
www.ecrsc.org/pinalesa/
Other Schools – See Eloy

**Fort Defiance, Apache, Pop. 3,530**
Window Rock USD 8 2,500/K-12
PO Box 559 86504 928-729-6705
Dr. Deborah Mayher, supt. Fax 729-5780
www.wrschool.net
Tsehootsooi MS 600/7-8
PO Box 559 86504 928-729-6803
David Moore, prin. Fax 729-6814
Window Rock HS 700/9-12
PO Box 559 86504 928-729-7004
Donna Manuelito, prin. Fax 729-7661

**Fort Huachuca, See Sierra Vista**
Fort Huachuca Accommodation SD 00 1,000/K-8
PO Box 12954 85670 520-458-5082
Bonnie Austin, supt. Fax 515-5972
www.fthuachuca.k12.az.us
Smith MS 300/6-8
PO Box 12954 85670 520-459-8892
Christa Jones, prin. Fax 335-6803

**Fort Thomas, Graham, Pop. 360**
Fort Thomas USD 7 500/K-12
PO Box 300 85536 928-485-9423
Shane Hawkins, supt. Fax 485-3019
www.ftusd.org/
Fort Thomas JSHS 200/7-12
PO Box 28 85536 928-485-2427
McKay DeSpain, prin. Fax 485-2834

**Fountain Hills, Maricopa, Pop. 22,214**
Fountain Hills USD 98 2,000/PK-12
16000 E Palisades Blvd 85268 480-664-5011
Tom Lawrence, supt. Fax 664-5099
www.fhusd.org
Fountain Hills HS 700/9-12
16100 E Palisades Blvd 85268 480-664-5500
Tom Brennan, prin. Fax 837-5699
Fountain Hills MS 500/6-8
15414 N McDowell Mountain R 85268 480-664-5400
Anita Gomez, prin. Fax 664-5499

---

American Institute of Interior Design Post-Sec.
13014 N Saguaro Blvd # 206 85268 480-946-9601

**Fredonia, Coconino, Pop. 1,295**
Fredonia-Moccasin USD 6 200/PK-12
PO Box 247 86022 928-643-7333
Joseph Wright, supt. Fax 643-7044
www.fredonia.org/
Fredonia-Moccasin HS 100/7-12
PO Box 247 86022 928-643-7333
Brett Waite, prin. Fax 643-7044

**Ganado, Apache, Pop. 1,188**
Ganado USD 20 1,400/K-12
PO Box 1757 86505 928-755-1000
William L. Allsbrooks, supt. Fax 755-1012
www.ganado.k12.az.us/
Ganado HS 500/9-12
PO Box 1757 86505 928-755-1500
William Stiver, prin. Fax 755-1502
Ganado MS 300/6-8
PO Box 1757 86505 928-755-1411
Steve Wyble, prin. Fax 755-1402

**Gila Bend, Maricopa, Pop. 1,896**
Gila Bend USD 24 400/PK-12
PO Box V 85337 928-683-2225
Dr. Anthony J. Perkins, supt. Fax 683-2671
www.gbusd.org
Gila Bend HS 100/9-12
PO Box V 85337 928-683-2225
Richard Moore, prin. Fax 683-2671

**Gilbert, Maricopa, Pop. 202,881**
Chandler USD 80
Supt. — See Chandler
Perry HS 2,300/9-12
1919 E Queen Creek Rd 85297 480-224-2800
Dan Serrano, prin. Fax 224-2820

Gilbert Unified SD 38,000/PK-12
140 S Gilbert Rd 85296 480-497-3300
Dr. Christina Kishimoto, supt. Fax 507-1320
www.gilbertschools.net
Campo Verde HS 1,800/9-12
3870 S Quartz St 85297 480-545-3100
Michael DeLaTorre, prin. Fax 545-3111
Gilbert Classical Academy 200/7-12
55 N Greenfield Rd 85234 480-497-4034
Dan Hood, prin. Fax 507-1645
Gilbert HS 2,700/9-12
1101 E Elliot Rd 85234 480-497-0177
Christopher Stroud, prin. Fax 497-5673
Gilbert JHS 700/7-8
1016 N Burk St 85234 480-892-6908
Kevin Rainey, prin. Fax 813-8240
Greenfield JHS 1,000/7-8
101 S Greenfield Rd 85296 480-813-1770
Brian Yee, prin. Fax 813-7279
Highland HS 2,900/9-12
4301 E Guadalupe Rd 85234 480-813-0051
Melinda Murphy, prin. Fax 813-0258
Mesquite HS 2,200/9-12
500 S McQueen Rd 85233 480-632-4750
Ken Fetter, prin. Fax 632-4777
Mesquite JHS 800/7-8
130 W Mesquite St 85233 480-926-1433
Dan Johnson, prin. Fax 813-9002
South Valley JHS 1,200/7-8
2034 S Lindsay Rd, 480-855-0015
Tim Cannon, prin. Fax 855-3542
Other Schools – See Mesa

Higley USD 60 10,400/PK-12
2935 S Recker Rd, 480-279-7000
Dr. Mike Thomason, supt. Fax 279-7500
www.husd.org
Higley HS 1,500/9-12
4068 E Pecos Rd, 480-279-7300
Roseyn Hood, prin. Fax 279-7305
Williams Field HS 1,500/9-12
2076 S Higley Rd, 480-279-8000
Dr. Terri Wattawa, prin. Fax 279-8005

---

Christ Our Saviour Academy K-12
202 S Gilbert Rd 85296 520-428-4631
Tim Ihms, prin.
Conservatory of Recording Arts/Sciences Post-Sec.
1205 N Fiesta Blvd 85233 480-858-9400
Gilbert Christian S 600/PK-12
3632 E Jasper Dr 85296 480-699-1215
Jim Desmarchais, supt. Fax 809-6677

**Glendale, Maricopa, Pop. 221,458**
Alhambra ESD 68
Supt. — See Phoenix
Barcelona MS 700/4-8
6530 N 44th Ave 85301 623-842-8616
Paige Brill, prin. Fax 842-1384

Deer Valley USD 97
Supt. — See Phoenix
Deer Valley HS 1,900/9-12
18424 N 51st Ave 85308 602-467-6700
Kim Crooks, prin. Fax 467-6780
Desert Sky MS 700/7-8
5130 W Grovers Ave 85308 602-467-6500
Patricia Resetar, prin. Fax 467-6580
Hillcrest MS 1,100/7-8
22833 N 71st Ave 85310 623-376-3300
Estela Hazelton, prin. Fax 376-3380
Mountain Ridge HS 2,300/9-12
22800 N 67th Ave 85310 623-376-3000
Shona Miranda, prin. Fax 376-3080

Glendale ESD 40 13,000/PK-8
7301 N 58th Ave 85301 623-237-7100
Dr. Joe Quintana, supt. Fax 237-7291
www.gesd40.org/
Bicentennial North S 800/4-8
7237 W Missouri Ave 85303 623-237-4009
Dr. Kenneth Fleming, prin. Fax 237-4915
Challenger MS 700/4-8
6905 W Maryland Ave 85303 623-237-4011
Tiffany Molina, prin. Fax 237-5115
Mensendick IS 900/4-8
5535 N 67th Ave 85301 623-237-4006
Jeff Vilardi, prin. Fax 237-4615

Glendale UNHSD 205 14,900/9-12
7650 N 43rd Ave 85301 623-435-6000
Brian Capistran, supt. Fax 435-6078
www.guhsdaz.org
Apollo HS 1,900/9-12
8045 N 47th Ave 85302 623-435-6300
Brooke Parsons, prin. Fax 435-6369
Glendale HS 1,700/9-12
6216 W Glendale Ave 85301 623-435-6200
Kevin Cashatt, prin. Fax 435-6270
Independence HS 1,900/9-12
6602 N 75th Ave 85303 623-435-6100
Rob Ambrose, prin. Fax 435-6157
Other Schools – See Phoenix

Peoria USD 11 36,100/PK-12
6330 W Thunderbird Rd 85306 623-486-6000
Dr. Denton Santarelli, supt. Fax 486-6009
www.peoriaud.k12.az.us
Cactus HS 1,400/9-12
6330 W Greenway Rd 85306 623-412-5000
Kristi Hammer, prin. Fax 412-5020
Ironwood HS 2,000/9-12
6051 W Sweetwater Ave 85304 623-486-6400
Vance Setka, prin. Fax 486-6424
Kellis HS 1,800/9-12
8990 W Orangewood Ave 85305 623-412-5425
Jeffrey Wooten, prin. Fax 412-5447
Other Schools – See Peoria

Tolleson UNHSD 214
Supt. — See Tolleson
Copper Canyon HS 1,700/9-12
9126 W Camelback Rd 85305 623-478-4800
Mindy Marsit, prin. Fax 478-4802

Washington ESD 6 22,100/PK-8
4650 W Sweetwater Ave 85304 602-347-2600
Dr. Paul Stanton, supt. Fax 347-2720
www.wesdschools.org
Other Schools – See Phoenix

---

Arizona College Post-Sec.
4425 W Olive Ave Ste 300 85302 602-222-9300
Arrowhead Christian Academy 100/K-12
4030 W Yorkshire Dr 85308 623-582-6871
Mark French, head sch Fax 581-9311
Glendale Community College Post-Sec.
6000 W Olive Ave 85302 623-845-3000
Herberger Young Scholars Academy 200/7-12
4701 W Thunderbird Rd 85306 623-543-8274
Joy Christian S 500/PK-12
21000 N 75th Ave 85308 623-561-2000
Kim Youngs, admin. Fax 362-3202
Midwestern University Post-Sec.
19555 N 59th Ave 85308 623-572-3200
Thunderbird School of Global Management Post-Sec.
1 Global Pl 85306 602-978-7100

**Globe, Gila, Pop. 7,446**
Globe USD 1 1,600/PK-12
460 N Willow St 85501 928-402-6000
Jerry Jennex, supt. Fax 425-8912
www.globeschools.org
Globe HS 500/9-12
460 N Willow St 85501 928-402-6000
Bobby Armenta, prin. Fax 425-8909
High Desert MS 500/5-8
460 N Willow St 85501 928-402-5900
Lori Rodriquez, prin. Fax 425-8710

**Goodyear, Maricopa, Pop. 63,699**
Agua Fria UNHSD 216
Supt. — See Avondale
Desert Edge HS 1,500/9-12
15778 W Yuma Rd 85338 623-932-7500
Julie Jones, prin. Fax 932-7502
Millennium HS 2,200/9-12
14802 W Wigwam Blvd, 623-932-7200
Tamee Gressett, prin. Fax 932-7204

Buckeye UNHSD 201
Supt. — See Buckeye
Estrella Foothills HS 1,000/9-12
13033 S Estrella Pkwy 85338 623-327-2400
Dr. Leslie Standerfer, prin. Fax 327-2499

Litchfield ESD 79
Supt. — See Litchfield Park
Western Sky MS 900/6-8
4905 N 144th Ave, 623-535-6300
Tami Garrett, prin. Fax 935-9536

**Grand Canyon, Coconino**
Grand Canyon USD 4 200/K-12
PO Box 519 86023 928-638-2461
Shonny Bria, supt. Fax 638-2045
www.grandcanyonschool.org
Grand Canyon S 200/K-12
PO Box 519 86023 928-638-2461
Steven Landes, prin. Fax 638-2045

**Heber, Navajo, Pop. 1,581**
Heber-Overgaard USD 6 400/PK-12
PO Box 547 85928 928-535-4622
Ron Tenney, supt. Fax 535-5146
www.heberovergaardschools.org
Mogollon JSHS 200/7-12
PO Box 279 85928 928-535-4238
Tim Slade, prin. Fax 535-3933

**Holbrook, Navajo, Pop. 4,904**
Holbrook USD 3 2,100/PK-12
PO Box 640 86025 928-524-6144
Dr. Robbie Koerperich, supt. Fax 524-3073
www.holbrook.k12.az.us
Holbrook HS 700/9-12
PO Box 640 86025 928-524-2815
Lance Phaturos, prin. Fax 524-3537
Holbrook JHS 400/6-8
PO Box 640 86025 928-524-3959
Tim Newton-Pender, prin. Fax 524-3766

---

Northland Pioneer College Post-Sec.
PO Box 610 86025 928-524-7311

**Joseph City, Navajo, Pop. 1,364**
Joseph City USD 2 400/PK-12
PO Box 8 86032 928-288-3307
Bryan Fields, supt. Fax 288-3309
www.josephcityschools.org
Joseph City JSHS 100/7-12
PO Box 8 86032 928-288-3361
Bryan Fields, prin. Fax 288-3825

**Kayenta, Navajo, Pop. 5,074**
Kayenta USD 27 1,800/PK-12
PO Box 337 86033 928-697-3251
Dr. Bryce Anderson, supt. Fax 697-2160
www.kayenta.k12.az.us
Kayenta MS 600/5-8
PO Box 337 86033 928-697-2303
David Hawley, prin. Fax 697-2308
Monument Valley HS 800/9-12
PO Box 337 86033 928-697-2175
Jack Gilmore, prin. Fax 697-2195

**Kearny, Pinal, Pop. 1,932**
Ray USD 3 400/PK-12
PO Box 427, 520-363-5515
Curt Cook, supt. Fax 363-5642
www.rayusd.org
Ray Jr-Sr HS 200/7-12
PO Box 427, 520-363-5515
Curt Cook, prin. Fax 363-5642

**Kingman, Mohave, Pop. 27,434**
Kingman USD 20 5,900/PK-12
3033 McDonald Ave 86401 928-753-5678
Roger Jacks, supt. Fax 753-6910
www.kusd.org
Kingman HS 1,500/10-12
4182 N Bank St, 928-692-6480
Janelle Victory, prin. Fax 692-6418
Kingman MS 700/6-8
1969 Detroit Ave 86401 928-753-3588
Don Burton, prin. Fax 753-1336
White Cliffs MS 700/6-8
3550 Prospector St 86401 928-753-6216
Cliff Angle, prin. Fax 753-4042
Williams HS 9-9
400 Grandview Ave 86401 928-718-6000
Gretchen Dorner, prin. Fax 718-1058
Other Schools – See Dolan Springs

---

Mohave Community College Post-Sec.
1971 E Jagerson Ave, 928-757-4331

**Lake Havasu City, Mohave, Pop. 51,709**
Lake Havasu USD 1 4,900/PK-12
2200 Havasupai Blvd 86403 928-505-6900
Fax 505-6999
www.havasu.k12.az.us/
Lake Havasu HS 1,900/9-12
2675 Palo Verde Blvd S 86403 928-854-5001
Scott Becker, prin. Fax 854-5499
Thunderbolt MS 900/7-8
695 Thunderbolt Ave 86406 928-854-7224
Marijo Mulligan, prin. Fax 854-7482

---

Charles of Italy Beauty College Post-Sec.
1987 McCulloch Blvd #205 86403 928-453-6666

**Lakeside, Navajo, Pop. 4,210**
Blue Ridge USD 32 2,400/PK-12
1200 W White Mountain Blvd 85929 928-368-6126
Michael Wright, supt. Fax 368-5570
www.brusd.k12.az.us
Blue Ridge HS 800/9-12
1200 W White Mountain Blvd 85929 928-368-6126
Jay Cox M.Ed., prin. Fax 368-9572
Blue Ridge JHS 400/7-8
1200 W White Mountain Blvd 85929 928-368-2350
Loren Webb M.Ed., prin. Fax 368-2399

**Laveen, Maricopa**
Phoenix UNHSD 210
Supt. — See Phoenix
Chavez HS 2,200/9-12
3921 W Baseline Rd 85339 602-764-4000
Dr. Shavon Waggoner, prin. Fax 764-4054
Fairfax HS, 8225 S 59th Ave 85339 1,900/9-12
Phillip Wooley, prin. 602-764-9000

**Litchfield Park, Maricopa, Pop. 5,366**
Litchfield ESD 79 8,900/PK-8
272 E Sagebrush St 85340 623-535-6000
Dr. Julianne Lein, supt. Fax 935-1448
www.lesd.k12.az.us
Heck MS 700/6-8
272 E Sagebrush St 85340 623-547-1700
Dr. Ron Sterr, prin. Fax 536-5955
Wigwam Creek MS 900/6-8
272 E Sagebrush St 85340 623-547-1100
John Scudder, prin. Fax 547-0873
Other Schools – See Buckeye, Goodyear

**Marana, Pima, Pop. 34,148**
Marana USD 6 12,400/PK-12
11279 W Grier Rd Ste 106 85653 520-682-4774
Dr. Doug Wilson, supt. Fax 682-2421
www.maranausd.org
ACE 50/Alt
13650 N McDuff Rd 85653 520-682-1014
Dave Liss, dir. Fax 682-1016
Marana Career and Technical HS 100/Alt
13650 N McDuff Rd 85653 520-682-4773
Denise Coronado, dir. Fax 682-4106
Marana MS 1,000/7-8
11279 W Grier Rd Ste 105 85653 520-682-4730
Kristin Reidy, prin. Fax 682-4790
Other Schools – See Tucson

**Maricopa, Pinal, Pop. 42,031**
Maricopa USD 20 5,200/PK-12
44150 W Maricopa Casa Grand,
520-568-5100
Steve Chestnut Ed.D., supt. Fax 568-5110
maricopausd.org/
Desert Wind MS 400/7-8
44150 W Maricopa Casa Grand,
520-568-7110
June Celaya, prin. Fax 568-7119
Maricopa HS 1,500/9-12
44150 W Maricopa Casa Grand,
520-568-8100
Renita Myers, prin. Fax 568-8119

**Mayer, Yavapai, Pop. 1,462**
Mayer USD 43 500/PK-12
PO Box 1059 86333 928-642-1000
Dean Slaga, supt. Fax 632-4005
www.mayerschools.org
Mayer HS 200/9-12
PO Box 1059 86333 928-642-1201
Jeff Duncan, prin. Fax 632-5714

---

Orme S 100/8-12
HC 63 Box 3040 86333 928-632-7601
Bruce Sanborn, head sch Fax 632-7605

**Mesa, Maricopa, Pop. 428,892**
East Valley Institute of Tech. SD 401
1601 W Main St 85201 480-461-4000
Dr. Sally Downey Ed.D., supt. Fax 461-4089
evit.com
East Valley Institute of Technology Vo/Tech
1601 W Main St 85201 480-461-4000
Dr. Sally Downey Ed.D., supt. Fax 461-4169
East Valley Institute of Technology East Vo/Tech
6625 S Power Rd 85212 480-308-4600
Craig Pearson, admin. Fax 308-4608

Gilbert Unified SD
Supt. — See Gilbert
Canyon Valley S 200/Alt
7007 E Guadalupe Rd 85212 480-507-0519
Chad Fitzgerald, prin. Fax 507-3978
Desert Ridge HS 2,500/9-12
10045 E Madero Ave, 480-984-8947
Mike Deignan, prin. Fax 354-5090
Desert Ridge JHS 1,300/7-8
10211 E Madero Ave, 480-635-2025
Jean Woods, prin. Fax 635-2044
Highland JHS 1,300/7-8
6915 E Guadalupe Rd 85212 480-632-4739
Marcie Taylor, prin. Fax 632-4729

Mesa USD 4 62,000/PK-12
63 E Main St 85201 480-472-0000
Dr. Michael Cowan, supt. Fax 472-0204
www.mpsaz.org
Carson JHS 800/7-8
525 N Westwood 85201 480-472-2900
Ray Chavez, prin. Fax 472-2899
Crossroads S 100/Alt
855 W 8th Ave 85210 480-308-7330
Patricia Goolsby, prin. Fax 472-9393
Dobson HS 2,900/9-12
1501 W Guadalupe Rd 85202 480-472-3000
Tamara Addis, prin. Fax 472-3075
East Valley Academy 200/Alt
855 W 8th Ave 85210 480-472-9350
Pat Goolsby, prin. Fax 472-9393
Franklin JHS 200/7-8
4949 E Southern Ave 85206 480-472-2600
Jeffrey Abrams, prin. Fax 472-2698
Fremont JHS 900/7-8
1001 N Power Rd 85205 480-472-8300
Todd Roberts, prin. Fax 472-8333
Kino JHS 700/7-8
848 N Horne 85203 480-472-2400
Keiko Dilbeck, prin. Fax 472-2549
Mesa Academy for Advanced Studies 400/4-8
6919 E Brown Rd 85207 480-308-7400
Bob Crispin, prin. Fax 308-7428
Mesa HS 3,400/9-12
1630 E Southern Ave 85204 480-472-5900
Lisa Creaser, prin. Fax 472-5995
Mountain View HS 3,200/9-12
2700 E Brown Rd 85213 480-472-6900
Greg Milbrandt, prin. Fax 472-6983
Poston JHS 900/7-8
2433 E Adobe St 85213 480-472-2100
Allen Flax, prin. Fax 472-2105
Red Mountain HS 3,200/9-12
7301 E Brown Rd 85207 480-472-8000
Jared Ryan, prin. Fax 472-8008
Rhodes JHS 1,000/7-8
1860 S Longmore 85202 480-472-2300
Kirk Thomas, prin. Fax 472-2299
Riverview HS 100/Alt
1731 N Country Club Dr 85201 480-472-5350
Raul Ruiz, prin. Fax 472-5355
Shepherd JHS 700/7-8
1407 N Alta Mesa Dr 85205 480-472-1800
Eileen Cahoon, prin. Fax 472-1888
Skyline HS 2,600/9-12
845 S Crismon Rd 85208 480-472-9400
Dr. Steve Green, prin. Fax 472-9406
Smith JHS 900/7-8
10100 E Adobe Rd 85207 480-472-9900
Casey Eagleburger, prin. Fax 472-9999
Stapley JHS 800/7-8
3250 E Hermosa Vista Dr 85213 480-472-2700
Ken Erickson, prin. Fax 472-2828
Superstition HS 50/Alt
10222 E Southern Ave, 480-472-9650
Lilia Gomez-Napier, prin. Fax 472-9660
Taylor JHS 900/7-8
705 S 32nd St 85204 480-472-1500
Gina Piraino, prin. Fax 472-1616
Westwood HS 2,900/9-12
945 W Rio Salado Pkwy 85201 480-472-4400
Shawn Lynch, prin. Fax 472-4509

---

Arizona Sch of Dentistry & Oral Health Post-Sec.
5850 E Still Cir 85206 866-626-2878
Arizona School of Health Sciences Post-Sec.
5850 E Still Cir 85206 866-626-2878
Avalon School of Cosmetology Post-Sec.
2111 S Alma School Rd #21 85210 480-897-1688
Carrington College Post-Sec.
1001 W Southern Ave Ste 130 85210 480-212-1600
DeVry University - Mesa Center Post-Sec.
1201 S Alma School Rd #5450 85210 480-827-1511
Everest College Post-Sec.
5416 E Baseline Rd Ste 200 85206 480-830-5151
Faith Christian S 100/PK-12
PO Box 9086 85214 480-833-1983
Dick Buckingham, admin. Fax 325-1096
International Academy of Hair Design Post-Sec.
1445 W Southern Ave # 2006 85202 480-820-9422
Mesa Community College Post-Sec.
1833 W Southern Ave 85202 480-461-7000
Pima Medical Institute Post-Sec.
957 S Dobson Rd 85202 480-644-0267
Redeemer Christian S 100/K-12
719 N Stapley Dr 85203 480-962-5003
Dr. Denise Monroe Ed.D., prin. Fax 833-7502
Sch of Osteopathic Medicine - AT Still U Post-Sec.
5850 E Still Cir 85206 866-626-2878

**Miami, Gila, Pop. 1,817**
Miami USD 40 700/K-12
PO Box 2070 85539 928-425-3271
Dr. Sherry Dorathy, supt. Fax 425-7419
www.miamiusd40.org
Miami JSHS 300/7-12
PO Box 2070 85539 928-425-3271
Glen Lineberry, prin. Fax 425-7027

**Mohave Valley, Mohave, Pop. 2,530**
Colorado River UNHSD 2
Supt. — See Bullhead City
River Valley HS 800/9-12
2250 E Laguna Rd 86440 928-768-2300
Dorn Wilcox, prin. Fax 768-6156

Mohave Valley ESD 16 1,700/PK-8
8450 S Olive Ave 86440 928-768-2507
Whitney Crow, supt. Fax 768-2510
www.mvesd16.org
Mohave Valley JHS 400/7-8
6565 S Girard Ave 86440 928-768-9196
Christina Stahl, prin. Fax 768-1129

**Morenci, Greenlee, Pop. 1,476**
Morenci USD 18 900/PK-12
PO Box 1060 85540 928-865-2081
Dr. David Woodall, supt. Fax 865-3130
www.morenci.k12.az.us/
Fairbanks MS 200/5-8
PO Box 1060 85540 928-865-3501
Anna VanZile, prin. Fax 865-5980
Morenci HS 400/9-12
PO Box 1060 85540 928-865-3631
Bryan Boling, prin. Fax 865-3614

**Nogales, Santa Cruz, Pop. 20,797**
Nogales USD 1 5,600/K-12
PO Box 5000 85628 520-287-0800
Fernando Parra, supt. Fax 287-3586
www.nusd.k12.az.us
Carpenter Middle Academy 600/6-8
595 W Kino St 85621 520-287-0820
Liza Montiel, prin. Fax 287-0817
Desert Shadows MS 800/6-8
340 Boulevard Del Rey David 85621 520-377-2646
Joan Molera, prin. Fax 377-2674
Nogales HS 1,700/9-12
1905 N Apache Blvd 85621 520-377-2021
Judith Mendoza-Jimenez, prin. Fax 281-4448
Pierson Vocational HS Vo/Tech
451 N Arroyo Blvd 85621 520-287-0915
Joel Kramer, lead tchr. Fax 287-0918

---

Lourdes HS 100/9-12
555 E Patagonia Hwy 85621 520-287-5659
Sandra Contreras, prin. Fax 287-2910

**Oro Valley, Pima, Pop. 40,283**
Amphitheater USD 10
Supt. — See Tucson
Canyon Del Oro HS 1,600/9-12
25 W Calle Concordia 85704 520-696-5560
Paul DeWeerdt, prin. Fax 696-5590
Ironwood Ridge HS 1,900/9-12
2475 W Naranja Dr, 520-696-3900
Natalie Burnett, prin. Fax 696-3999

**Page, Coconino, Pop. 6,933**
Page USD 8 2,100/K-12
PO Box 1927 86040 928-608-4100
Jim Walker, supt. Fax 645-2805
pageusd.org
Page HS 900/9-12
PO Box 1927 86040 928-608-4138
Paul Gagnon, prin. Fax 645-9243
Page MS 600/6-8
PO Box 1927 86040 928-608-4300
Christy Rodriguez, prin. Fax 645-9285

**Paradise Valley, Maricopa, Pop. 12,621**

---

Phoenix Country Day S 700/PK-12
3901 E Stanford Dr 85253 602-955-8200
Andrew Rodin, hdmstr. Fax 955-1286

**Parker, LaPaz, Pop. 2,994**
Parker USD 27 1,800/PK-12
PO Box 1090 85344 928-669-9244
James Lotts, supt. Fax 669-2515
www.parkerusd.org
Parker HS 400/9-12
PO Box 1090 85344 928-669-2202
Paul Olson, prin. Fax 669-2315
Wallace JHS 200/6-8
PO Box 1090 85344 928-669-2141
Amanda Maxwell, prin. Fax 669-2515

**Patagonia, Santa Cruz, Pop. 909**
Patagonia SD 100/PK-12
PO Box 254 85624 520-394-3000
Denise Blake, supt. Fax 394-3001
www.patagonia.k12.az.us
Patagonia Union HS 100/9-12
PO Box 254 85624 520-394-3050
Denise Blake, prin. Fax 394-3051

**Payson, Gila, Pop. 15,087**
Payson USD 10 2,500/K-12
PO Box 919 85547 928-474-2070
Greg Wyman, supt. Fax 472-2013
www.pusd.k12.az.us/
Payson Center for Success 50/Alt
PO Box 919 85547 928-472-2011
Linda Gibson, lead tchr. Fax 472-2039
Payson HS 700/9-12
PO Box 919 85547 928-474-2233
Brian Mabb, prin. Fax 472-2010
Rim Country MS 600/6-8
PO Box 919 85547 928-474-4511
Jennifer White, prin. Fax 472-2044

---

Payson Community Christian S 100/PK-12
1000 E Frontier St 85541 928-474-8050
David Callahan, admin. Fax 474-3252

**Peoria, Maricopa, Pop. 150,709**
Peoria USD 11
Supt. — See Glendale
Centennial HS 2,100/9-12
14388 N 79th Ave 85381 623-412-4400
Christine Lopezlira, prin. Fax 412-4420
Liberty HS 1,800/9-12
9621 W Speckled Gecko Dr 85383 623-773-6525
John Croteau, prin. Fax 773-6540
Peoria Flex Academy 100/Alt
11200 N 83rd Ave 85345 623-412-5475
Cybil Jacob, dir. Fax 486-6022
Peoria HS 1,700/9-12
11200 N 83rd Ave 85345 623-486-6300
Paul Bower, prin. Fax 486-6330
Sunrise Mountain HS 1,600/9-12
21200 N 83rd Ave 85382 623-487-5125
David Svorinic, prin. Fax 487-5140

**Phoenix, Maricopa, Pop. 1,416,459**
Alhambra ESD 68 13,800/PK-8
4510 N 37th Ave 85019 602-336-2920
Mark Yslas, supt. Fax 336-2270
www.alhambraesd.org/
Andalucia MS 1,100/4-8
4730 W Campbell Ave 85031 623-848-8646
Monique Martinez-Ortiz, prin. Fax 846-6044
Cordova MS 900/4-8
5631 N 35th Ave 85017 602-841-0704
Dr. Sharon Spearman, prin. Fax 973-8416
Granada East MS 1,200/4-8
3022 W Campbell Ave 85017 602-589-0110
Dr. Randy Martinez, prin. Fax 589-0140
Sevilla West S 1,100/4-8
3851 W Missouri Ave 85019 602-347-0232
Garry Glay, prin. Fax 347-9906
Simpson MS 900/4-8
5330 N 23rd Ave 85015 602-246-0699
Karen Stengel, prin. Fax 246-4305
Other Schools – See Glendale

Cartwright ESD 83 18,200/PK-8
5220 W Indian School Rd 85031 623-691-4000
Dr. Jacob A. Chavez, supt. Fax 691-5926
www.csd83.org
Atkinson MS 1,200/6-8
4315 N Maryvale Pkwy 85031 623-691-1700
Dr. Diana Romito, prin. Fax 691-1720
Castro MS 900/6-8
2730 N 79th Ave 85035 623-691-5300
Sarah Hernandez, prin. Fax 691-5320
Desert Sands MS 1,100/6-8
6308 W Campbell Ave 85033 623-691-4900
Michael Dellisanti, prin. Fax 691-4920
Estrella MS 1,300/6-8
3733 N 75th Ave 85033 623-691-5400
Ryan Anderson, prin. Fax 691-5420

Cave Creek USD 93
Supt. — See Scottsdale
Sonoran Trails MS 800/7-8
5555 E Pinnacle Vista Dr 85085 480-272-8600
Bill Dolezal, prin. Fax 272-8699

Deer Valley USD 97 34,400/PK-12
20402 N 15th Ave 85027 623-445-5000
Dr. James Veitenheimer, supt. Fax 445-5086
www.dvusd.org
Deer Valley MS 700/7-8
21100 N 27th Ave 85027 623-445-3300
Tamela Harris, prin. Fax 445-3380
Goldwater HS 1,900/9-12
2820 W Rose Garden Ln 85027 623-445-3000
Dr. Mike Andersen, prin. Fax 445-3080
O'Connor HS 2,500/9-12
25250 N 35th Ave, 623-445-7100
Dr. Lynn Miller, prin. Fax 445-7180
Vista Peak S Alt
19825 N 15th Ave 85027 623-445-3900
Brian Fineberg, prin. Fax 445-3980
Other Schools – See Anthem, Glendale

Fowler ESD 45 4,600/PK-8
1617 S 67th Ave 85043 623-707-4500
Dr. Marvene Lobato, supt. Fax 707-4560
www.fesd.org
Santa Maria MS 700/6-8
7250 W Lower Buckeye Rd 85043 623-707-1100
Dr. Desiree Castillo, prin. Fax 707-1110
Western Valley MS 800/6-8
6250 W Durango St 85043 623-707-2200
Trent Lyon, prin. Fax 707-2204

Glendale UNHSD 205
Supt. — See Glendale
Cortez HS 1,200/9-12
8828 N 31st Ave 85051 623-915-8200
Walter Sampson, prin. Fax 915-8244
Greenway HS 1,600/9-12
3930 W Greenway Rd 85053 623-915-8500
Edward Barnes, prin. Fax 915-8560
Moon Valley HS 1,500/9-12
3625 W Cactus Rd 85029 623-915-8000
Nathan Kleve, prin. Fax 915-8070
Sunnyslope HS 1,900/9-12
35 W Dunlap Ave 85021 623-915-8760
Steven Ducey, prin. Fax 915-8762
Thunderbird HS 1,600/9-12
1750 W Thunderbird Rd 85023 623-915-8900
Jeannie Paparella, prin. Fax 915-8971
Washington HS 1,700/9-12
2217 W Glendale Ave 85021 623-915-8400
Tami Strege, prin. Fax 915-8437

Isaac ESD 5 6,400/PK-8
3348 W McDowell Rd 85009 602-455-6700
Dr. Mario Ventura, supt. Fax 278-1693
www.isaacschools.org
Isaac MS 800/6-8
3402 W McDowell Rd 85009 602-455-6800
Bree Honeycutt, prin. Fax 455-6868
Pueblo Del Sol MS 600/6-8
3449 N 39th Ave 85019 602-455-6900
Armando Chavez, prin. Fax 484-4118

Kyrene ESD 28
Supt. — See Tempe
Kyrene Akimel A-al MS 1,100/6-8
2720 E Liberty Ln 85048 480-541-5800
Stephanie Phillips, prin. Fax 541-5810
Kyrene Altadena MS 1,100/6-8
14620 S Desert Fthills Pkwy 85048 480-541-6000
Nancy Corner, prin. Fax 541-6010
Kyrene Centennial MS 1,100/6-8
13808 S 36th St 85044 480-541-6400
Jocelyn Sims, prin. Fax 541-6410

Madison ESD 38 5,900/PK-11
5601 N 16th St 85016 602-664-7900
Quinn Kellis Ed.D., supt. Fax 664-7999
www.msd38.org
Madison # 1 MS 800/5-8
5525 N 16th St 85016 602-664-7100
Pam Warren, prin. Fax 664-7199
Madison Meadows MS 900/5-8
225 W Ocotillo Rd 85013 602-664-7600
Susan Doyle, prin. Fax 664-7699
Madison Park MS 500/5-8
1431 E Campbell Ave 85014 602-664-7500
Todd Stevens, prin. Fax 664-7599

Osborn ESD 8 3,000/PK-8
1226 W Osborn Rd 85013 602-707-2000
Patricia Tate, supt. Fax 707-2040
www.osbornnet.org
Osborn MS 600/7-8
1102 W Highland Ave 85013 602-707-2400
Marty Makar, prin. Fax 707-2440

Paradise Valley USD 31,600/PK-12
15002 N 32nd St 85032 602-449-2000
James Lee Ed.D., supt. Fax 449-2005
www.pvschools.net
Explorer MS 800/7-8
22401 N 40th St 85050 602-449-4200
Barbara Newman, prin. Fax 449-4205
Greenway MS 500/7-8
3002 E Nisbet Rd 85032 602-449-2400
Dr. Ibi Haghighat, prin. Fax 449-2405
Mountain Trail MS 800/7-8
2323 E Mountain Gate Pass 85024 602-449-4600
Craig Lahlum, prin. Fax 449-4605
North Canyon HS 2,200/9-12
1700 E Union Hills Dr 85024 602-449-5000
Elaine Jacobs, prin. Fax 449-5005
Paradise Valley HS 1,700/9-12
3950 E Bell Rd 85032 602-449-7000
Ian Deonise, prin. Fax 449-7005
Pinnacle HS 2,600/9-12
3535 E Mayo Blvd 85050 602-449-4000
Dr. Troy Bales, prin. Fax 449-4205
Shadow Mountain HS 1,600/9-12
2902 E Shea Blvd 85028 602-449-3000
David Appleman, prin. Fax 449-3005
Shea MS 700/7-8
2728 E Shea Blvd 85028 602-449-3500
Dan Knak, prin. Fax 449-3505
Star Tech Professional Center Vo/Tech
3950 E Bell Rd 85032 602-449-7036
Tony Maldonado, dir. Fax 449-2333
Sweetwater Community S Alt
4215 E Andora Dr 85032 602-449-2300
Jean Scharrer, prin. Fax 449-2305
Vista Verde MS 700/7-8
2826 E Grovers Ave 85032 602-449-5300
Andrea Hoffler, prin. Fax 449-5305
Other Schools – See Scottsdale

Phoenix UNHSD 210 25,800/9-12
4502 N Central Ave 85012 602-764-1100
Dr. Kent Scribner Ph.D., supt. Fax 271-3593
www.phoenixunion.org
Alhambra HS 2,800/9-12
3839 W Camelback Rd 85019 602-764-6022
Claudio Coria, prin. Fax 271-3497
Bostrom Alternative Center 300/Alt
3535 N 27th Ave 85017 602-764-1700
Alvin Watson, prin. Fax 271-2923
Browne HS 2,900/9-12
7402 W Catalina Dr 85033 602-764-8500
Dr. Gabriel Trujillo, prin. Fax 440-6803
Camelback HS 1,900/9-12
4612 N 28th St 85016 602-764-7000
Dr. Quintin Boyce, prin. Fax 271-2295
Central HS 2,300/9-12
4525 N Central Ave 85012 602-764-7500
John Biera, prin. Fax 271-2385
Franklin Police and Fire HS 300/9-12
1645 W McDowell Rd 85007 602-764-0200
Lorenzo Cabrera, prin. Fax 258-2868
Hayden Community HS 2,100/9-12
3333 W Roosevelt St 85009 602-764-3000
Ricardo Cordova, prin. Fax 229-8387
Maryvale HS 2,700/9-12
3415 N 59th Ave 85033 602-764-2000
Phillip Verdugo, prin. Fax 271-2597
Metro Tech HS Vo/Tech
1900 W Thomas Rd 85015 602-764-8000
Bryan Reynoso, prin. Fax 452-5302
North HS 2,600/9-12
1101 E Thomas Rd 85014 602-764-6500
Juan A. Nunez, prin. Fax 271-2765
Phoenix Union Bioscience HS 300/9-12
512 E Pierce St 85004 602-764-5600
Dr. Deedee Falls, prin. Fax 253-9013
South Mountain HS 1,800/9-12
5401 S 7th St 85040 602-764-5000
Kate McDonald, prin. Fax 271-2880

Suns-Diamondbacks Education Academy 200/Alt
2920 N 7th St 85014 602-764-0050
Rick Beck, prin. Fax 744-1221
Other Schools – See Laveen

Riverside ESD 2 800/PK-8
1414 S 51st Ave 85043 602-477-8900
Jaime Rivera Ed.D., supt. Fax 272-8378
resdonline.org/
Kings Ridge Preparatory Academy 400/5-8
3650 S 64th Ln 85043 602-477-8960
Talmadge Tanks, prin. Fax 936-5531

Roosevelt ESD 66 10,200/PK-8
6000 S 7th St 85042 602-243-4800
Dr. Jeanne Koba, supt. Fax 243-2637
www.rsd.k12.az.us
Greenfield MS 600/4-8
7009 S 10th St 85042 602-232-4240
Stuart Starky, prin. Fax 243-4973

Scottsdale USD 48 25,100/PK-12
3811 N 44th St 85018 480-484-6100
Dr. David Peterson, supt. Fax 484-6287
www.susd.org
Arcadia HS 1,700/9-12
4703 E Indian School Rd 85018 480-484-6300
Nathan Slater, prin. Fax 484-6301
Ingleside MS 800/6-8
5402 E Osborn Rd 85018 480-484-4900
Therese Tipton, prin. Fax 484-4901
Other Schools – See Scottsdale

Tempe UNHSD 213
Supt. — See Tempe
Desert Vista HS 3,000/9-12
16440 S 32nd St 85048 480-706-7900
Christine Barela, prin. Fax 706-7976
Mountain Pointe HS 2,600/9-12
4201 E Knox Rd 85044 480-759-8449
Bruce Kipper, prin. Fax 759-8458

Tolleson UNHSD 214
Supt. — See Tolleson
Sierra Linda HS 1,600/9-12
3434 S 67th Ave 85043 623-474-7700
Tim Madrid, prin. Fax 474-7790

Washington ESD 6
Supt. — See Glendale
Cholla MS 700/7-8
3120 W Cholla St 85029 602-896-5400
Phil Garitson, prin. Fax 896-5420
Desert Foothills JHS 700/7-8
3333 W Banff Ln 85053 602-896-5500
Susan Smith, prin. Fax 896-5520
Mountain Sky JHS 800/7-8
16225 N 7th Ave 85023 602-896-6100
Perry Mason, prin. Fax 896-6120
Palo Verde MS 900/7-8
7502 N 39th Ave 85051 602-347-2500
Jill Sarraino, prin. Fax 347-2520

Wilson ESD 7 1,300/PK-8
3025 E Fillmore St 85008 602-681-2200
Antonio Sanchez, supt. Fax 275-7517
www.wsd.k12.az.us
Wilson MS 600/4-8
2929 E Fillmore St 85008 602-683-2400
Cindy Campton, prin. Fax 275-8677

---

American Indian Coll of Assemblies/God Post-Sec.
10020 N 15th Ave 85021 602-944-3335
American Institute of Technology Post-Sec.
440 S 54th Ave 85043 602-457-3294
Anthem College Post-Sec.
1515 E Indian School Rd 85014 602-279-9700
Argosy University/Phoenix Post-Sec.
2233 W Dunlap Ave 85021 602-216-2600
Arizona Christian University Post-Sec.
2625 E Cactus Rd 85032 800-247-2697
Arizona Cultural Academy & College Prep 300/PK-12
7810 S 42nd Pl 85042 602-454-1222
Arizona Lutheran Academy 200/9-12
6036 S 27th Ave 85041 602-268-8686
Kurt Rosenbaum M.Ed., prin. Fax 243-1353
Arizona Summit Law School Post-Sec.
1 N Central Ave Ste 1400 85004 602-682-6800
Bourgade Catholic HS 400/9-12
4602 N 31st Ave 85017 602-973-4000
Kathy Rother, prin. Fax 973-5854
Brookline College Post-Sec.
2445 W Dunlap Ave Ste 100 85021 602-242-6265
Brophy College Prep HS 1,300/9-12
4701 N Central Ave 85012 602-264-5291
Bob Ryan, prin. Fax 234-1669
Brown Mackie College - Phoenix Post-Sec.
13430 N Black Canyon # 190 85029 602-337-3044
Bryman School Post-Sec.
2250 W Peoria Ave Ste A100 85029 602-274-4300
Carrington College Post-Sec.
8503 N 27th Ave 85051 877-206-2106
Carrington College - Westside Post-Sec.
2701 W Bethany Home Rd 85017 602-433-1333
Chamberlain College of Nursing Post-Sec.
2149 W Dunlap Ave 85021 602-331-2720
CollegeAmerica Post-Sec.
9801 N Metro Pkwy E 85051 602-257-7522
Collins College Post-Sec.
4750 S 44th Pl 85040 480-966-3000
DeVry University - Phoenix Campus Post-Sec.
2149 W Dunlap Ave 85021 602-870-9222
Dunlap-Stone University Post-Sec.
19820 N 7th St Ste 100 85024 800-474-8013
Empire Beauty School Post-Sec.
2727 W Glendale Ave Ste 200 85051 623-939-8364
Everest College Post-Sec.
10400 N 25th Ave Ste 190 85021 602-942-4141
Fortis College Post-Sec.
555 N 18th St Ste 110 85006 602-254-3099
Gateway Community College Post-Sec.
108 N 40th St 85034 602-286-8000
Grand Canyon University Post-Sec.
3300 W Camelback Rd 85017 602-639-7500
ITT Technical Institute Post-Sec.
10220 N 25th Ave Ste 100 85021 602-749-7900
ITT Technical Institute Post-Sec.
1840 N 95th Ave Ste 132 85037 623-474-7900
Motorcycle Mechanics Institute Post-Sec.
2844 W Deer Valley Rd 85027 623-869-9644
National Paralegal College Post-Sec.
717 E Maryland Ave 85014 800-371-6105
91st Psalm Christian S 100/PK-12
2020 E Baseline Rd 85042 602-243-1900
Rob Arthurs, prin. Fax 243-5919
North Valley Christian Academy 100/PK-12
42101 N 41st Dr 85086 623-551-3454
Nate Kretzmann M.Ed., dir. Fax 551-4067
Northwest Christian S 1,300/PK-12
16401 N 43rd Ave 85053 602-978-5134
Geoffrey Brown, supt. Fax 978-5804
Ottawa University Arizona Post-Sec.
10020 N 25th Ave 85021 602-371-1188
Paradise Valley Christian College Prep S 300/PK-12
11875 N 24th St 85028 602-992-8140
Sheryl Temple M.A., hdmstr. Fax 992-8152
Paradise Valley Community College Post-Sec.
18401 N 32nd St 85032 602-787-6500
Phoenix Christian Preparatory S 300/PK-12
1751 W Indian School Rd 85015 602-265-4707
Jeff Blake M.A., prin. Fax 277-7170
Phoenix College Post-Sec.
1202 W Thomas Rd 85013 602-285-7800
Phoenix Institute of Herbal Medicine Post-Sec.
301 E Bethany Home Rd #A100 85012
602-274-1885
Phoenix Seminary Post-Sec.
4222 E Thomas Rd Ste 400 85018 602-850-8000
Refrigeration School Post-Sec.
4210 E Washington St 85034 602-275-7133
Roberto-Venn School of Luthiery Post-Sec.
1012 Grand Ave 85007 602-243-1179
St. Marys Catholic HS 500/9-12
2525 N 3rd St 85004 602-251-2500
Suzanne Fessler, prin. Fax 251-2595
Scottsdale Christian Academy 800/PK-12
14400 N Tatum Blvd 85032 602-992-5100
Chet Crane, supt. Fax 992-0575
Shearim Torah HS for Girls 50/9-12
6516 N 7th St Ste 105 85014 602-324-3406
South Mountain Community College Post-Sec.
7050 S 24th St 85042 602-243-8000
The Art Institute of Phoenix Post-Sec.
2233 W Dunlap Ave 85021 602-331-7500
Valley Lutheran HS 200/9-12
5199 N 7th Ave 85013 602-230-1600
Robert Koehne M.A., prin. Fax 230-1602
West Coast Ultrasound Institute Post-Sec.
4250 E Camelback Rd 85018 602-954-3834
Xavier College Prep HS 1,200/9-12
4710 N 5th St 85012 602-277-3772
Sr. Joan Fitzgerald, prin. Fax 279-1346
Yeshiva HS of Arizona 50/9-12
727 E Glendale Ave 85020 623-266-1213
Rabbi Gavriel Goetz, head sch Fax 266-1237

**Pima, Graham, Pop. 2,335**

Pima USD 6 700/K-12
PO Box 429 85543 928-387-8000
Sean Rickert, supt. Fax 387-8020
www.pimaschools.org
Gila Valley Learning Center Alt
PO Box 429 85543 928-387-8015
Craig Lunt, dir. Fax 387-8020
Pima HS 200/9-12
PO Box 429 85543 928-387-8151
Crae Wilson, prin. Fax 387-8023
Pima JHS 100/7-8
PO Box 429 85543 928-387-8100
Mark Squires, prin. Fax 387-8021

**Pinon, Navajo, Pop. 897**

Pinon USD 4 1,300/PK-12
PO Box 839 86510 928-725-3450
Doug Vaughan, supt. Fax 725-2123
www.pusdatsa.org
Pinon HS 400/9-12
PO Box 839 86510 928-725-2400
Slade Morgan, prin. Fax 725-2470
Pinon MS 300/6-8
PO Box 839 86510 928-725-2300
Dr. Jasvir Sethi, prin. Fax 725-2370

**Prescott, Yavapai, Pop. 39,213**

Prescott USD 1 5,100/PK-12
146 S Granite St 86303 928-445-5400
Joe Howard, supt. Fax 776-0243
www.prescottschools.com
Prescott HS 1,700/9-12
1050 Ruth St 86301 928-445-2322
Stephanie Hillig, prin. Fax 778-6106
Prescott Mile High MS 700/7-8
300 S Granite St 86303 928-717-3241
Mark Goligoski, prin. Fax 717-3298

Yavapai Accommodation SD 200/7-12
2970 Centerpointe East Dr 86301 928-759-8126
Tim Carter, supt. Fax 759-8136
yasd99.com
Aspire JSHS 200/Alt
2970 Centerpointe East Dr 86301 928-759-8126
Dr. Kristen Rex, dir. Fax 759-8136
Other Schools – See Prescott Valley

---

Embry-Riddle Aeronautical University Post-Sec.
3700 Willow Creek Rd 86301 800-888-3728
Empire Beauty School Post-Sec.
410 W Goodwin St 86303 928-778-5064
Prescott College Post-Sec.
220 Grove Ave 86301 877-350-2100
Trinity Christian S 200/K-12
1077 Mogollon Rd 86301 928-445-6306
Kyle Maestri, hdmstr. Fax 445-7210
Yavapai College Post-Sec.
1100 E Sheldon St 86301 928-445-7300

**Prescott Valley, Yavapai, Pop. 38,121**

Humboldt USD 22 6,000/PK-12
6411 N Robert Rd 86314 928-759-4000
Dr. Paul Stanton, supt. Fax 759-4020
www.humboldtunified.com/

Bradshaw Mountain HS 1,700/9-12
6000 E Long Look Dr 86314 928-759-4100
Kort Miner, prin. Fax 759-4120
Other Schools – See Dewey

Yavapai Accommodation SD
Supt. — See Prescott
Yavapai County HS 100/Alt
6325 Baja Cir 86314 928-759-8126
Dr. Kristen Rex, dir. Fax 759-8136

---

Northcentral University Post-Sec.
10000 E University Dr 86314 928-541-7777

**Queen Creek, Maricopa, Pop. 25,755**
Chandler USD 80
Supt. — See Chandler
Casteel HS 7-9
24901 S Power Rd, 480-424-8100
Sandy Lundberg, prin. Fax 424-8120
Payne JHS 1,300/7-8
7655 S Higley Rd, 480-224-2400
Paul Bollard, prin. Fax 224-2420

Queen Creek USD 95 5,200/PK-12
20217 E Chandler Heights Rd, 480-987-5935
Dr. Perry Berry, supt. Fax 987-9714
www.qcusd.org/
Barney JHS 700/7-8
24937 S Sossaman Rd, 480-474-6700
Denise Johnson, prin. Fax 882-3181
Queen Creek HS 1,600/9-12
22149 E Ocotillo Rd, 480-987-5973
Dr. Joseph Farnsworth, prin. Fax 882-1276

---

Ambassador Christian Academy 50/K-12
19248 E San Tan Blvd, 480-387-0902
Amy Crislip, admin. Fax 452-0316
Freedom Christian Academy 100/PK-12
39731 N Kennedy Dr, 480-987-5488
Keather Healy, prin. Fax 987-9344

**Red Valley, Apache, Pop. 30**
Red Mesa USD 27
Supt. — See Teec Nos Pos
Red Valley/Cove HS 100/9-12
Navaho Route 13 86544 928-653-4200
Carena Begay, prin. Fax 653-4204

**Rio Rico, Santa Cruz, Pop. 18,904**
Santa Cruz Valley USD 35 3,400/PK-12
1374 W Frontage Rd 85648 520-375-8282
David Verdugo, supt. Fax 281-7093
www.santacruz.k12.az.us
Coatimundi MS 400/6-8
1374 W Frontage Rd 85648 520-375-8800
Lerona Dickson, prin. Fax 761-4669
Rio Rico HS 1,100/9-12
1374 W Frontage Rd 85648 520-375-8700
Shelly Vroegh, prin. Fax 377-9556

**Sacaton, Pinal, Pop. 2,641**
Sacaton ESD 18 400/PK-12
PO Box 98, 520-562-8600
Dr. Douglas Price, supt. Fax 763-4410
sacatonschools.org
Sacaton MS 200/5-8
PO Box 98, 520-562-8600
Philip Bonds, prin. Fax 763-4420

**Safford, Graham, Pop. 9,405**
Safford USD 1 3,200/PK-12
734 W 11th St 85546 928-348-7000
Dr. Mark Tregaskes, supt. Fax 348-7001
www.saffordusd.k12.az.us
Mt. Graham HS 100/Alt
300 W Discovery Park Blvd 85546 928-348-7060
Lori VanScyoc, prin. Fax 348-7061
Safford HS 800/9-12
1400 W 11th St 85546 928-348-7050
Rich DeRidder, prin. Fax 348-7057
Safford MS 500/7-8
612 W 11th St 85546 928-348-7040
Clay Emery, prin. Fax 348-7041

---

Safford College of Beauty Culture Post-Sec.
1550 W Thatcher Blvd 85546 928-428-0331

**Sahuarita, Pima, Pop. 24,638**
Sahuarita USD 30 6,000/PK-12
350 W Sahuarita Rd 85629 520-625-3502
Dr. Manuel Valenzuela, supt. Fax 625-5380
www.susd30.us
Sahuarita HS 1,200/9-12
350 W Sahuarita Rd 85629 520-625-3502
Kent Thompson, prin. Fax 399-1223
Sahuarita MS 700/6-8
350 W Sahuarita Rd 85629 520-625-3502
Stephanie Silman, prin. Fax 393-7043
Walden Grove HS 700/9-12
350 W Sahuarita Rd 85629 520-625-3502
Teresa Hill, prin. Fax 393-7048

**Saint David, Cochise, Pop. 1,668**
Saint David USD 21 400/PK-12
PO Box 70 85630 520-720-4781
Mark Goodman, supt. Fax 720-4783
www.stdavidschools.org/
Saint David HS 100/9-12
PO Box 70 85630 520-720-4781
Andrew Brogan, prin. Fax 720-4783

**Saint Johns, Apache, Pop. 3,399**
Saint Johns USD 1 900/K-12
PO Box 3030 85936 928-337-2255
Ed Burgoyne, supt. Fax 337-2263
www.sjusd.net
Saint Johns HS 300/9-12
PO Box 429 85936 928-337-2221
Roger Heap, prin. Fax 337-2867
Saint Johns Learning Center 50/Alt
PO Box 3030 85936 928-337-2221
Kim Fejes, dir. Fax 337-2263
Saint Johns MS 300/4-8
PO Box 3060 85936 928-337-2132
Tim Raban, prin. Fax 337-3147

**Saint Michaels, Apache, Pop. 1,404**

---

St. Michael Indian S 300/K-12
PO Box 650 86511 928-871-4636
Tracie Lee, prin. Fax 871-4443

**Salome, LaPaz, Pop. 1,511**
Bicentennial UNHSD 76 100/9-12
PO Box 519 85348 928-859-3453
Byron Maynes, supt. Fax 859-3875
www.salomehs.org
Salome HS 100/9-12
PO Box 519 85348 928-859-3453
Byron Maynes, supt. Fax 859-3875

**San Carlos, Gila, Pop. 4,011**
San Carlos USD 20 800/PK-12
PO Box 207 85550 928-475-2315
Catherine Steele, supt. Fax 475-2301
www.sancarlosbraves.org
San Carlos Alternative S Alt
PO Box 207 85550 928-475-5538
Delphine Rodriguez, prin. Fax 475-2301
San Carlos JSHS 300/7-12
PO Box 207 85550 928-475-2378
Carol Slim, prin. Fax 475-2697

**Sanders, Apache, Pop. 600**
Sanders USD 18 1,000/K-12
PO Box 250 86512 928-688-4750
Mike Murphy, supt. Fax 688-4723
www.sandersusd.net/
Sanders MS 200/6-8
PO Box 250 86512 928-688-4770
Josh Kervin, prin. Fax 688-4773
Valley HS 400/9-12
PO Box 250 86512 928-688-4200
Susan Clement, prin. Fax 688-4202

**San Luis, Yuma, Pop. 25,496**
Gadsden ESD 32 5,000/PK-8
PO Box 6870 85349 928-627-6540
Raymond Aguilera, supt. Fax 627-3635
www.gesd32.org/
San Luis MS 600/7-8
PO Box 6870 85349 928-627-6920
Rafael Sanchez, prin. Fax 627-9339
Southwest JHS 700/7-8
PO Box 6870 85349 928-627-6580
Richard West, prin. Fax 627-9266

Yuma UNHSD 70
Supt. — See Yuma
San Luis HS 2,700/9-12
PO Box 7380 85349 928-502-6100
Tom Safranek, prin. Fax 502-6222

**San Manuel, Pinal, Pop. 3,491**
Mammoth-San Manuel USD 8 800/PK-12
PO Box 406 85631 520-385-2337
John Ryan, supt. Fax 385-2621
www.msmusd.org
San Manuel JSHS 300/7-12
PO Box 406 85631 520-385-2336
John Ryan, prin. Fax 385-3035

**San Simon, Cochise, Pop. 160**
San Simon USD 18 100/K-12
PO Box 38 85632 520-845-2275
Jonathan Truschke, supt. Fax 845-2480
www.sansimon.k12.az.us
San Simon S 100/K-12
PO Box 38 85632 520-845-2275
Jonathan Truschke, admin. Fax 845-2480

**San Tan Valley, Pinal, Pop. 79,014**
Coolidge USD 21
Supt. — See Coolidge
Mountain Vista MS 300/6-8
33622 N Mountain Vista Blvd, 480-677-4400
Denise Taylor, prin. Fax 677-4406
San Tan Foothills HS 400/9-12
1255 W Silverdale Rd, 480-474-6800
Robert Edwards, prin. Fax 888-2611

Florence USD 1
Supt. — See Florence
Poston Butte HS 1,800/9-12
32375 N Gantzel Rd, 480-474-6100
Dr. Tim Richard, prin. Fax 888-0679

J.O. Combs USD 44 3,000/PK-12
301 E Combs Rd, 480-987-5300
Dr. Gayle A. Blanchard, supt. Fax 987-3487
www.jocombs.org
Combs HS 1,000/9-12
301 E Combs Rd, 480-882-3540
Brenda Mayberry, prin. Fax 987-0837
Combs MS 700/7-8
301 E Combs Rd, 480-882-3510
Mark Mauro, prin. Fax 888-8049

**Scottsdale, Maricopa, Pop. 213,310**
Cave Creek USD 93 5,700/PK-12
33616 N 60th St 85266 480-575-2000
Dr. Debbi Burdick, supt. Fax 488-7055
www.ccusd93.org
Cactus Shadows HS 1,700/9-12
5802 E Dove Valley Rd 85266 480-575-2400
Dr. Steve Bebee, prin. Fax 488-6701
Other Schools – See Phoenix

Paradise Valley USD
Supt. — See Phoenix
Desert Shadows MS 700/7-8
5858 E Sweetwater Ave 85254 602-449-6800
Patrick Clancy, prin. Fax 449-6805
Horizon HS 2,200/9-12
5601 E Greenway Rd 85254 602-449-6000
Linda Ihnat, prin. Fax 449-6005
Sunrise MS 700/7-8
4960 E Acoma Dr 85254 602-449-6100
Gregory Martin, prin. Fax 449-6105

Scottsdale USD 48
Supt. — See Phoenix
Chaparral HS 2,200/9-12
6935 E Gold Dust Ave 85253 480-484-6500
Gayle Holland, prin. Fax 484-6501
Cocopah MS 900/6-8
6615 E Cholla St 85254 480-484-4400
Lance Huffman, prin. Fax 484-4401
Coronado HS 1,300/9-12
7501 E Virginia Ave 85257 480-484-6800
Alyssa Tarkington, prin. Fax 484-6801
Desert Canyon MS 600/6-8
10203 E McDowell Mntn Ranch 85255 480-484-4600
Dale Link, prin. Fax 484-4601
Desert Mountain HS 2,300/9-12
12575 E Via Linda 85259 480-484-7000
Nicole Wilfert, prin. Fax 484-7001
Mohave MS 700/6-8
8490 E Jackrabbit Rd 85250 480-484-5200
Chris Asmussen, prin. Fax 484-5201
Mountainside MS 900/6-8
11256 N 128th St 85259 480-484-5500
Terri Kellen, prin. Fax 484-5501
Saguaro HS 1,300/9-12
6250 N 82nd St 85250 480-484-7100
Brian Corte, prin. Fax 484-7101
Supai MS 500/6-8
6720 E Continental Dr 85257 480-484-5800
Shelley Slick-Hummon, prin. Fax 484-5801

---

Arizona Culinary Institute Post-Sec.
10585 N 114th St Ste 401 85259 480-603-1066
Automotive Dealership Institute Post-Sec.
6613 N Scottsdale Rd 85250 480-998-7200
Bella Vista College Preparatory S 50/K-12
PO Box 28096 85255 480-575-6001
Brighton College Post-Sec.
7332 E Butherus Dr Ste 102 85260 800-354-1254
Cortiva Institute - Scottsdale Post-Sec.
8010 E McDowell Rd Ste 214 85257 480-684-1275
Devereux-Arizona Treatment Network Post-Sec.
11000 N Scottsville Rd #260 85254 480-998-2920
Empire Beauty School Post-Sec.
7730 E McDowell Rd 85257 480-949-7557
Frank Lloyd Wright Sch of Architecture Post-Sec.
PO Box 4430 85261 480-860-2700
Gateway Academy 50/K-12
9659 N Hayden Rd 85258 480-998-1071
Le Cordon Bleu College of Culinary Arts Post-Sec.
8100 E Camelback Rd # 1001 85251 480-990-3773
Notre Dame Preparatory HS 900/9-12
9701 E Bell Rd 85260 480-634-8200
James Gmelich, prin. Fax 634-8299
Penn Foster College Post-Sec.
14300 N Northsight Ste 120 85260 480-947-6644
Penrose Academy Post-Sec.
13402 N Scottsdale Rd #B160 85254 480-222-9540
Rancho Solano Preparatory S 600/PK-12
9180 E Via de Ventura 85258 480-646-8200
Dr. Audrey Menard, head sch
Scott Cole Academy Post-Sec.
7201 E Camelback Rd Ste 100 85251 480-994-4222
Scottsdale Community College Post-Sec.
9000 E Chaparral Rd 85256 480-423-6000
Sonoran Desert Institute Post-Sec.
10245 E Via Linda Ste 110 85258 480-314-2102
The Paralegal Institute Post-Sec.
7332 E Butherus Dr Ste 102 85260 800-354-1254
Thunderbird Adventist Academy 100/9-12
7410 E Sutton Dr 85260 480-948-3300

**Sedona, Coconino, Pop. 9,896**
Sedona-Oak Creek JUSD 9 1,300/K-12
221 Brewer Rd Ste 100 86336 928-204-6800
David Lykins, supt. Fax 282-0232
www.sedona.k12.az.us/
Sedona Red Rock HS 500/9-12
995 Upper Red Rock Loop Rd 86336 928-204-6700
Darrin Karuzas, prin. Fax 282-5992

---

Verde Valley S 100/9-12
3511 Verde Valley School Rd 86351 928-284-2272

**Seligman, Yavapai, Pop. 428**
Seligman USD 40 100/K-12
PO Box 650 86337 928-422-3233
Diane Pritchett, supt. Fax 422-3642
www.seligmanschools.org/
Seligman HS 100/9-12
PO Box 650 86337 928-216-4123
Marvin Baker, prin. Fax 422-3642

**Sells, Pima, Pop. 2,459**
Baboquivari USD 40 1,000/K-12
PO Box 248 85634 520-383-6746
Dr. Edna Morris, supt. Fax 383-5441
busd40.org
Baboquivari MS 200/6-8
PO Box 248 85634 520-383-6950
Yolanda Nunez, prin. Fax 383-5930
Indian Oasis JSHS 100/Alt
PO Box 248 85634 520-383-6746
Dawn Maddock, prin. Fax 383-5441
Other Schools – See Topawa

---

Tohono O'odham Community College Post-Sec.
PO Box 3129 85634 520-383-8401

**Show Low, Navajo, Pop. 10,473**
Show Low USD 10 2,400/PK-12
500 W Old Linden Rd 85901 928-537-6000
Kevin Brackney, supt. Fax 537-6009
www.show-low.k12.az.us
Show Low HS 800/9-12
500 W Old Linden Rd 85901 928-537-6200
Farrell Adams, prin. Fax 537-6299
Show Low JHS 600/6-8
500 W Old Linden Rd 85901 928-537-6100
Kevin Bortin, prin. Fax 537-6149
White Mountain Institute 50/Alt
500 W Old Linden Rd 85901 928-537-6201
Farrell Adams, prin. Fax 537-6299

**Sierra Vista, Cochise, Pop. 41,754**
Sierra Vista USD 68 5,000/PK-12
3555 E Fry Blvd 85635 520-515-2701
Kriss Hagerl, supt. Fax 515-2744
www.svusd68.org
Buena HS 2,200/9-12
3555 E Fry Blvd 85635 520-515-2800
Joe Farmer, prin. Fax 515-2877
Clark MS 800/7-8
3555 E Fry Blvd 85635 520-515-2930
Jim Sprigg, prin. Fax 515-2941

---

DeVoe College of Beauty Post-Sec.
PO Box 1571 85636 520-458-8660
Veritas Christian Community S 100/K-12
215 Taylor Dr 85635 520-417-1113
Jason Tinney, head sch Fax 417-0180

**Snowflake, Navajo, Pop. 5,508**
Snowflake USD 5 2,500/K-12
682 W School Bus Ln 85937 928-536-4156
Hollis Merrell, supt. Fax 536-2634
home.susd5.org
Snowflake HS 700/9-12
682 W School Bus Ln 85937 928-536-4156
Larry Titus, prin. Fax 536-4240
Snowflake JHS 400/7-8
682 W School Bus Ln 85937 928-536-4156
Brian Hoopes, prin. Fax 536-3007

**Somerton, Yuma, Pop. 14,249**
Somerton ESD 11 2,500/PK-8
PO Box 3200 85350 928-341-6000
Dr. Laura Noel, supt. Fax 341-6090
www.somerton.k12.az.us
Somerton MS 800/6-8
PO Box 3200 85350 928-341-6100
Elizabeth Garza, prin. Fax 341-6190

**Springerville, Apache, Pop. 1,931**
Round Valley USD 10 1,000/K-12
PO Box 610 85938 928-333-6580
Travis Udall, supt. Fax 333-2823
www.elks.net
Other Schools – See Eagar

**Sun City, Maricopa, Pop. 37,274**

---

Walter Boswell Memorial Hospital Post-Sec.
10401 W Thunderbird Blvd 85351 623-977-7211

**Sun Valley, Navajo, Pop. 299**

---

Native American Christian Academy 50/3-8
PO Box 4013 86029 928-524-6211
Kristopher Miller, admin. Fax 524-3230

**Superior, Pinal, Pop. 2,804**
Superior USD 15 400/PK-12
1500 W Sunset Dr Ste 101, 520-689-3000
Patrick O'Donnell, supt. Fax 689-3009
www.superiorusd.org
Superior HS 100/9-12
100 W Mary Dr, 520-689-3100
Billy Duarte, prin. Fax 689-3197
Superior JHS 100/7-8
100 W Mary Dr, 520-689-3100
Billy Duarte, prin. Fax 689-3197

**Surprise, Maricopa, Pop. 114,476**
Dysart USD 89 24,400/K-12
15802 N Parkview Pl 85374 623-876-7000
Dr. Gail Pletnick, supt. Fax 876-7042
www.dysart.org
Shadow Ridge HS 1,100/9-12
10909 N Perryville Rd, 623-523-5100
Michael Hawkins, prin. Fax 523-5111
Sundown Mountain Alternative Program Alt
23251 N 166th Dr 85387 623-876-7250
Anthony Capuano, prin. Fax 876-7261
Valley Vista HS 2,400/9-12
15550 N Parkview Pl 85374 623-523-8800
Roberta Lockhart, prin. Fax 523-8811
Willow Canyon HS 2,000/9-12
17901 W Lundberg St, 623-523-8000
Jayne Wieferich, prin. Fax 523-8097
Other Schools – See El Mirage

**Teec Nos Pos, Apache, Pop. 721**
Red Mesa USD 27 800/K-12
HC 61 Box 40 86514 928-656-4108
Dr. Tommie Yazzie, supt. Fax 656-4302
www.rmusd.net
Red Mesa HS 300/9-12
HC 61 Box 40 86514 928-656-4177
Blane Baker, prin. Fax 656-4178
Other Schools – See Red Valley

---

Immanuel Mission S 100/K-12
PO Box 1080 86514 830-200-0351
John Bloom, prin. Fax 435-7041

**Tempe, Maricopa, Pop. 156,729**
Kyrene ESD 28 17,700/PK-8
8700 S Kyrene Rd 85284 480-541-1000
David Schauer Ed.D., supt. Fax 541-1860
www.kyrene.org
Kyrene MS 1,200/6-8
1050 E Carver Rd 85284 480-541-6600
Jama Nacke, prin. Fax 541-6610
Other Schools – See Chandler, Phoenix

Tempe ESD 3 12,000/K-8
3205 S Rural Rd 85282 480-730-7100
Christine Busch, supt. Fax 730-7177
www.tempeschools.org
Connolly MS 1,100/6-8
2002 E Concorda Dr 85282 480-967-8933
Katherine Mullery, prin. Fax 929-9695
Fees College Preparatory Academy 900/6-8
1600 E Watson Dr 85283 480-897-6063
Kacy Baxter, prin. Fax 838-0853
Gililland MS 1,100/6-8
1025 S Beck Ave 85281 480-966-7114
JoLyn Gibbons, prin. Fax 829-6178

Tempe Academy of International Studies 6-8
2250 S College Ave 85282 480-459-5048
Marianne McMurrin, prin. Fax 621-6577

Tempe UNHSD 213 13,800/9-12
500 W Guadalupe Rd 85283 480-839-0292
Dr. Kenneth Baca, supt. Fax 413-0685
www.tuhsd.k12.az.us
Compadre Academy 600/Alt
500 W Guadalupe Rd 85283 480-752-3560
Ed Flores, prin. Fax 285-3252
Corona Del Sol HS 2,400/9-12
1001 E Knox Rd 85284 480-752-8888
Brent Brown, prin. Fax 820-3632
Marcos De Niza HS 1,900/9-12
6000 S Lakeshore Dr 85283 480-838-3200
Sean McDonald, prin. Fax 730-7665
McClintock HS 1,900/9-12
1830 E Del Rio Dr 85282 480-839-4222
Derek Hoffland, prin. Fax 752-8661
Tempe HS 1,400/9-12
1730 S Mill Ave 85281 480-967-1661
Mark Yslas, prin. Fax 736-4096
Other Schools – See Phoenix

---

Acacia University Post-Sec.
7665 S Research Dr 85284 480-428-6034
Arizona State University Post-Sec.
PO Box 870112 85287 480-965-2100
Brookline College Post-Sec.
1140 S Priest Dr 85281 480-545-8755
Bryan University Post-Sec.
350 W Washington St Ste 100 85281 602-384-2555
Carsten Aveda Institute Post-Sec.
3345 S Rural Rd 85282 480-491-0449
Conservatory of Recording Arts/Sciences Post-Sec.
2300 E Broadway Rd 85282 480-858-9400
Harrison Middleton University Post-Sec.
1105 E Broadway Rd 85282 877-248-6724
International Academy of Hair Post-Sec.
4812 S Mill Ave 85282 480-964-8675
ITT Technical Institute Post-Sec.
5005 S Wendler Dr 85282 602-437-7500
Rio Salado College Post-Sec.
2323 W 14th St 85281 480-517-8000
Sessions College of Professional Design Post-Sec.
398 S Mill Ave Ste 300 85281 480-212-1704
Southwest Coll of Naturopathic Medicine Post-Sec.
2140 E Broadway Rd 85282 480-858-9100
Southwest Institute of Healing Arts Post-Sec.
1100 E Apache Blvd 85281 480-994-9244
University of Advancing Technology Post-Sec.
2625 W Baseline Rd 85283 800-658-5744
University of Phoenix Post-Sec.
1625 W Fountainhead Pkwy 85282 602-557-2000
Western International University Post-Sec.
1601 W Fountainhead Pkwy 85282 602-943-2311

**Thatcher, Graham, Pop. 4,760**
Thatcher USD 4 1,300/K-12
PO Box 610 85552 928-348-7200
Paul Nelson, supt. Fax 348-7220
www.thatcherud.k12.az.us
Thatcher HS 400/9-12
601 N 3rd Ave 85552 928-348-7270
Carol McAtee, prin. Fax 348-7273
Thatcher MS 200/7-8
1130 N 4th Ave 85552 928-348-7262
Hal Mullenaux, prin. Fax 348-7263

---

Eastern Arizona College Post-Sec.
615 N Stadium Ave 85552 800-678-3808

**Tolleson, Maricopa, Pop. 6,455**
Tolleson UNHSD 214 8,200/9-12
9801 W Van Buren St 85353 623-478-4000
Dr. Lexi Cunningham, supt. Fax 936-5048
www.tuhsd.org
Tolleson Union HS 1,700/9-12
9419 W Van Buren St 85353 623-478-4200
Ernie Molina, prin. Fax 478-4226
University HS 500/9-12
9419 W Van Buren St 85353 623-478-4212
Susan Thompson, dean Fax 478-4226
Other Schools – See Avondale, Glendale, Phoenix

**Tombstone, Cochise, Pop. 1,359**
Tombstone USD 1 900/PK-12
PO Box 1000 85638 520-457-2217
Karl Uterhardt, supt. Fax 457-3270
www.tombstoneschools.org
Tombstone HS 400/9-12
PO Box 1000 85638 520-457-2215
Robert Devere, prin. Fax 457-3643

**Tonalea, Coconino, Pop. 542**
San Juan SD
Supt. — See Blanding, UT
Navajo Mountain HS 50/9-12
PO Box 10040 86044 435-678-1287
Gary Rock, admin. Fax 678-1289

**Tonopah, Maricopa, Pop. 60**
Saddle Mountain USD 90 1,700/K-12
38201 W Indian School Rd 85354 623-474-5115
Dr. Mark Joraanstad, supt. Fax 474-5190
www.smusd90.org
Tonopah Valley HS 400/9-12
38201 W Indian School Rd 85354 623-474-5201
Edgar Garcia, prin. Fax 474-5214

**Topawa, Pima, Pop. 298**
Baboquivari USD 40
Supt. — See Sells
Baboquivari HS 200/9-12
Indian Route 19 85639 520-383-6800
Dawn Maddock, prin. Fax 383-4852

**Tsaile, Apache, Pop. 1,179**

---

Din College Post-Sec.
1 Circle Dr 86556 928-724-6600

**Tuba City, Coconino, Pop. 8,486**
Tuba City USD 15 1,700/PK-12
PO Box 67 86045 928-283-1001
Dr. Harold Begay, supt. Fax 283-1201
www.tcusd.org
Nizhoni Accelerated Academy 50/Alt
PO Box 67 86045 928-283-1070
Charles Henderson, dir. Fax 283-1226
Tuba City HS 700/9-12
PO Box 67 86045 928-283-1050
Mary Begaye, prin. Fax 283-1204
Tuba City JHS 300/7-8
PO Box 67 86045 928-283-1040
Harriett Sloan-Carter, prin. Fax 283-1218

**Tucson, Pima, Pop. 507,980**
Altar Valley ESD 51 700/PK-8
10105 S Sasabe Rd 85736 520-822-1484
Dr. David Dumon, supt. Fax 822-1798
altarvalleyschools.org/
Altar Valley MS 300/5-8
10105 S Sasabe Rd 85736 520-822-9343
Josh Peebles, prin. Fax 822-5801

Amphitheater USD 10 14,500/PK-12
701 W Wetmore Rd 85705 520-696-5000
Patrick Nelson, supt. Fax 696-5015
www.amphi.com
Amphitheater HS 1,200/9-12
125 W Yavapai Rd 85705 520-696-5340
Jon Lansa, prin. Fax 696-5555
Amphitheater MS 600/6-8
315 E Prince Rd 85705 520-696-6230
Tassi Call, prin. Fax 696-6236
Cross MS 800/6-8
1000 W Chapala Dr 85704 520-696-5920
Andy Heinemann, prin. Fax 696-5996
La Cima MS 600/6-8
5600 N La Canada Dr 85704 520-696-6730
Christine Sullivan, prin. Fax 696-6792
Rillito Center 100/Alt
266 E Pastime Rd 85705 520-696-6420
Linda Haller, prin. Fax 696-6435
Other Schools – See Oro Valley

Catalina Foothills USD 16 5,000/PK-12
2101 E River Rd 85718 520-209-7500
Dr. Mary Kamerzell, supt. Fax 209-7570
www.cfsd16.org/
Catalina Foothills HS 1,700/9-12
4300 E Sunrise Dr 85718 520-209-8300
Dr. Angela Chomokos, prin. Fax 209-8520
Esperero Canyon MS 600/6-8
5801 N Sabino Canyon Rd 85750 520-209-8100
Mary Setliff, prin. Fax 209-8170
Orange Grove MS 600/6-8
1911 E Orange Grove Rd 85718 520-209-8200
Susan Rosenthal, prin. Fax 209-8275

Flowing Wells USD 8 5,500/PK-12
1556 W Prince Rd 85705 520-696-8800
Dr. David Baker, supt. Fax 690-2400
www.flowingwellsschools.org
Flowing Wells HS 1,700/9-12
3725 N Flowing Wells Rd 85705 520-696-8002
Jim Brunenkant, prin. Fax 690-2379
Flowing Wells JHS 800/7-8
4545 N La Cholla Blvd 85705 520-696-8550
Dr. Kimberley Parkinson, prin. Fax 690-2420
Sentinel Peak HS 50/Alt
4125 W Aerie 85705 520-696-8900
Alan Schmidt, prin. Fax 579-3773

Marana USD 6
Supt. — See Marana
Marana HS 1,900/9-12
12000 W Emigh Rd 85743 520-616-6400
Dr. Allison Murphy, prin. Fax 616-6426
Mountain View HS 1,900/9-12
3901 W Linda Vista Blvd 85742 520-579-4400
Patricia Cadigan, prin. Fax 579-4505
Tortolita MS 1,000/7-8
4101 W Hardy Rd 85742 520-579-4600
Rex Scott, prin. Fax 579-4646

Sunnyside USD 12 17,300/PK-12
2238 E Ginter Rd 85706 520-545-2000
Dr. Eugenia Favela, supt. Fax 545-2120
www.susd12.org
Apollo MS 800/6-8
265 W Nebraska St 85706 520-545-4500
Roy Massani, prin. Fax 545-4516
Challenger MS 1,000/6-8
100 E Elvira Rd, 520-545-4600
Roxana Rico, prin. Fax 545-4616
Desert View HS 2,100/9-12
4101 E Valencia Rd 85706 520-545-5100
Jose Gastelum, prin. Fax 545-5116
Lauffer MS 700/6-8
5385 E Littletown Rd, 520-545-4900
Robert Miranda, prin. Fax 545-4916
S.T.A.R. Academic Center 300/Alt
5093 S Liberty Ave 85706 520-545-2300
Art Menchaca, prin. Fax 545-2316
Sunnyside HS 2,300/9-12
1725 E Bilby Rd 85706 520-545-5300
Adriana Molina, prin. Fax 545-5316

Tanque Verde USD 13 1,700/PK-12
2300 N Tanque Verde Loop Rd 85749 520-749-5751
Kimberly Sharp M.Ed., supt. Fax 749-5400
www.tanqueverdeschools.org/
Gray JHS 300/7-8
11150 E Tanque Verde Rd 85749 520-749-3838
Greg Miller, prin. Fax 749-9668
Tanque Verde HS 400/9-12
4201 N Melpomene Way 85749 520-760-0801
A.J. Malis, prin. Fax 749-9668

Tucson USD 1 47,000/PK-12
1010 E 10th St 85719 520-225-6000
H.T. Sanchez Ed.D., supt. Fax 225-6174
www.tusd.k12.az.us
Catalina Magnet HS 1,200/9-12
3645 E Pima St 85716 520-232-8400
Kathryn Shaw, prin. Fax 232-8401

Cholla Magnet HS 1,600/9-12
2001 W Starr Pass Blvd 85713 520-225-4000
Frank Armenta, prin. Fax 225-4001
Dodge Magnet MS 400/6-8
5831 E Pima St 85712 520-731-4100
Daniel Schulter, prin. Fax 731-4101
Doolen MS 600/6-8
2400 N Country Club Rd 85716 520-232-6900
Venessa Morales, prin. Fax 232-6901
Gridley MS 700/6-8
350 S Harrison Rd 85748 520-731-4600
David Davies, prin. Fax 731-4601
Lawrence IS 300/3-8
4850 W Jeffrey Rd, 520-908-3900
Ann Kobritz, prin. Fax 908-3901
Life Skills/Core Plus 50/Alt
1010 E 10th St 85719 520-225-2600
Israel Macias-Reyes, coord. Fax 225-2601
Magee MS 700/6-8
8300 E Speedway Blvd 85710 520-731-5000
Daniel Erickson, prin. Fax 731-5001
Mansfeld MS 700/6-8
1300 E 6th St 85719 520-225-1800
Richard Sanchez, prin. Fax 225-1801
Palo Verde Magnet HS 1,000/9-12
1302 S Avenida Vega 85710 520-584-7400
Eric Brock, prin. Fax 584-7441
Pistor MS 1,000/6-8
5455 S Cardinal Ave 85746 520-908-5400
Angela Wichers, prin. Fax 908-5411
Project M.O.R.E. HS 100/Alt
440 S Park Ave 85719 520-225-2600
Israel Macias-Reyes, prin. Fax 225-2601
Pueblo Magnet HS 1,700/9-12
3500 S 12th Ave 85713 520-225-4300
Augustine Romero Ph.D., prin. Fax 225-4301
Rincon HS 1,100/9-12
421 N Arcadia Ave 85711 520-232-5600
Catherine Comstock, prin. Fax 232-5601
Sabino HS 1,200/9-12
5000 N Bowes Rd 85749 520-584-7700
Matt Munger, prin. Fax 584-7701
Sahuaro HS 1,800/9-12
545 N Camino Seco 85710 520-731-7100
Roberto Estrella, prin. Fax 731-7101
Santa Rita HS 1,100/9-12
3951 S Pantano Rd 85730 520-731-7500
James Palacios, prin. Fax 731-7501
Secrist MS 400/6-8
3400 S Houghton Rd 85730 520-731-5300
David Montano, prin. Fax 731-5301
Tucson Magnet HS 3,100/9-12
400 N 2nd Ave 85705 520-225-5000
Karyle Green, prin. Fax 225-5221
University HS 900/9-12
421 N Arcadia Ave 85711 520-232-5900
Amy Cislak, prin. Fax 232-5911
Utterback Magnet MS 800/6-8
3233 S Pinal Vis 85713 520-225-3500
Robin Dunbar, prin. Fax 225-3501
Vail MS 700/6-8
5350 E 16th St 85711 520-584-5400
Theresa Leal-Holmes, prin. Fax 584-5401
Valencia MS 700/6-8
4400 W Irvington Rd 85746 520-908-4500
Patricia Acosta, prin. Fax 908-4501

Vail USD 20
Supt. — See Vail
Andrada Polytechnic HS 600/9-12
12960 S Houghton Rd 85747 520-879-3300
Darcy Mentone, prin. Fax 879-3301
Desert Sky MS 700/6-8
9850 E Rankin Loop 85747 520-879-2700
Katie Dabney, prin. Fax 879-2701
Empire HS 800/9-12
10701 E Mary Ann Cleveland 85747 520-879-3000
Matt Donaldson, prin. Fax 879-3001
Pantano HS 100/Alt
13010 S Houghton Rd 85747 520-879-1200
Monica Wright, prin. Fax 879-1201

---

Arizona Academy of Beauty Post-Sec.
5631 E Speedway Blvd 85712 520-885-4120
Arizona Academy of Beauty - North Post-Sec.
4066 N Oracle Rd 85705 520-888-0170
AZ School of Acupuncture & Oriental Med Post-Sec.
4646 E Ft Lowell Rd Ste 103 85712 520-795-0787
AZ State School for the Deaf & Blind Post-Sec.
PO Box 85000 85754 520-770-3719
Brookline College Post-Sec.
5441 E 22nd St Ste 125 85711 520-748-9799
Brown Mackie College - Tucson Post-Sec.
4585 E Speedway Blvd # 204 85712 520-319-3300
Calvary Chapel Christian S 100/K-10
8725 E Speedway Blvd 85710 520-731-2100
Catherine Swearingen, admin.
Carondelet Saint Marys Hospital Post-Sec.
1601 W Saint Marys Rd 85745 520-622-5833
Carrington College Post-Sec.
3550 N Oracle Rd 85705 520-888-5885
Cortiva Institute - Tucson Post-Sec.
6390 E Broadway Blvd 85710 520-407-5160
Desert Christian HS 200/9-12
7525 E Speedway Blvd 85710 520-298-5817
John O'Hair, hdmstr. Fax 298-9312
Empire Beauty School Post-Sec.
3030 E Speedway Blvd 85716 520-327-6544
Fenster S 50/6-12
8505 E Ocotillo Dr 85750 520-749-3340
Tony Tsang M.S., hdmstr. Fax 749-3349
Green Fields Country Day S 200/K-12
6000 N Camino De La Tierra 85741 520-297-2288
Rebecca Cordier M.Ed., head sch Fax 618-2599
Gregory S 300/5-12
3231 N Craycroft Rd 85712 520-327-6395
Dr. Julie Sherrill, head sch Fax 327-8276
Han University of Traditional Medicine Post-Sec.
2856 E Fort Lowell Rd 85716 520-322-6330
HDS Truck Driving Institute Post-Sec.
PO Box 17600 85731 520-721-5825
Imago Dei MS, PO Box 3056 85702 100/5-8
Rev. Anne Sawyer, head sch 520-882-4008
Immaculate Heart HS 100/9-12
625 E Magee Rd 85704 520-297-2851
Dan Ethridge, prin. Fax 797-7374
ITT Technical Institute Post-Sec.
1455 W River Rd 85704 520-408-7488
Pima Community College Post-Sec.
4905 E Broadway Blvd 85709 520-206-4500
Pima Medical Institute Post-Sec.
3350 E Grant Rd 85716 520-326-1600
Pusch Ridge Christian Academy 500/6-12
9500 N Oracle Rd 85704 520-797-0107
Dr. Rodney Marshall, head sch Fax 797-0598
St. Augustine Catholic HS 100/9-12
8800 E 22nd St 85710 520-751-8300
Lynn Cuffari, prin. Fax 751-8304
Salpointe Catholic HS 1,100/9-12
1545 E Copper St 85719 520-327-6581
Sr. Helen Timothy, prin. Fax 327-8477
San Miguel HS 300/9-12
6601 S San Fernando Rd, 520-294-6403
John Omernik, prin. Fax 294-6417
San Pedro Valley Academy 50/9-12
6107 E Grant Rd 85712 877-304-3329
Southwest University of Visual Arts Post-Sec.
2525 N Country Club Rd 85716 520-325-0123
The Art Institute of Tucson Post-Sec.
5099 E Grant Rd Ste 100 85712 520-318-2700
Tucson College Post-Sec.
5151 E Broadway Blvd # 155 85711 800-915-2096
University of Arizona 85721 Post-Sec.
520-621-2211
Veritas Academy of Tucson 100/K-10
PO Box 35263 85740 520-576-0427
Brian McKinley, hdmstr.

**Vail, Pima, Pop. 9,882**
Vail USD 20 10,500/K-12
PO Box 800 85641 520-879-2000
Calvin Baker, supt. Fax 879-2001
www.vail.k12.az.us
Cienega HS 2,000/9-12
12775 Mary Ann Cleveland 85641 520-879-2800
Dr. Tricia Pena, prin. Fax 879-2801
Other Schools – See Corona, Tucson

**Wellton, Yuma, Pop. 2,851**
Antelope UNHSD 50 300/9-12
9168 S Avenue 36 E 85356 928-785-4041
Dr. Andrew Smith, supt. Fax 785-4588
www.antelopeunion.org/
Antelope Union HS 300/9-12
9168 S Avenue 36 E 85356 928-785-3344
Barton Rud, prin. Fax 785-9566

**Whiteriver, Navajo, Pop. 4,055**
Whiteriver USD 20 2,000/PK-12
PO Box 190 85941 928-358-5800
Dr. Rea Goklish, supt. Fax 358-5801
www.wusd.us
Alchesay HS 500/9-12
PO Box 190 85941 928-358-5690
Leeann Lacapa, prin. Fax 358-5691
Canyon Day JHS 200/6-8
PO Box 190 85941 928-358-5680
Vajra Miller, prin. Fax 358-5681

**Wickenburg, Maricopa, Pop. 6,301**
Wickenburg USD 9 1,600/PK-12
40 W Yavapai St 85390 928-668-5350
Dr. Howard Carlson, supt. Fax 668-5390
www.wickenburgschools.org/
Vulture Peak MS 200/6-8
920 S Vulture Mine Rd 85390 928-684-6700
Jennifer Teshka, prin. Fax 684-6746
Wickenburg HS 700/9-12
1090 S Vulture Mine Rd 85390 928-684-6600
Derek Streeter, prin. Fax 684-6628

---

Gospel Outreach Christian S 50/PK-12
515 W Wickenburg Way 85390 928-684-5227
Victor Bedoian, supt. Fax 684-2878

**Willcox, Cochise, Pop. 3,704**
Willcox USD 13 1,200/PK-12
480 N Bisbee Ave 85643 520-384-8600
Fax 384-4401
www.wusd13.org
Willcox HS 400/9-12
240 N Bisbee Ave 85643 520-384-8601
Jeff Thompson, prin. Fax 384-4006
Willcox MS 400/4-8
360 N Bisbee Ave 85643 520-384-8602
Mike Patterson, prin. Fax 384-6322

**Williams, Coconino, Pop. 2,960**
Williams USD 2 600/PK-12
PO Box 427 86046 928-635-4473
Rick Honsinger, supt. Fax 635-4767
www.wusd2.org
Williams HS 200/9-12
PO Box 427 86046 928-635-4474
Richard Van Nostrand, prin. Fax 635-2796

**Winkelman, Gila, Pop. 352**
Hayden-Winkelman USD 41 300/K-12
PO Box 409, 520-356-7876
Jeff Gregorich, supt. Fax 356-7303
www.hwusd.org
Hayden HS 100/9-12
PO Box 409, 520-356-7876
Jeff Gregorich, prin. Fax 356-7303

**Winslow, Navajo, Pop. 9,382**
Winslow USD 1 2,200/PK-12
PO Box 580 86047 928-288-8101
Lance Heister, supt. Fax 288-8292
www.wusd1.org
Winslow HS 800/9-12
PO Box 580 86047 928-288-8100
Chris Gilmore, prin. Fax 288-8290
Winslow JHS 400/7-8
PO Box 580 86047 928-288-8300
Darlene McCauley, prin. Fax 288-8393

**Young, Gila, Pop. 657**
Young ESD 5 50/PK-12
PO Box 390 85554 928-462-3244
Linda Cheney, supt. Fax 462-3283
www.youngschool.org/
Young S 50/PK-12
PO Box 390 85554 928-462-3244
Linda Cheney, prin. Fax 462-3283

**Yuma, Yuma, Pop. 91,424**
Crane ESD 13 6,300/PK-8
4250 W 16th St 85364 928-373-3400
Robert Klee, supt. Fax 782-6831
www.craneschools.org/
Centennial MS 700/7-8
2650 W 20th St 85364 928-373-3300
Helen Coffeen, prin. Fax 376-7742
Crane MS 700/7-8
4450 W 32nd St 85364 928-373-3200
Kari Neumann, prin. Fax 344-6821

Yuma ESD 1 9,100/PK-8
450 W 6th St 85364 928-502-4300
Darwin Stiffler, supt. Fax 502-4442
www.yuma.org
Castle Dome MS 800/6-8
2353 S Otondo Dr 85365 928-502-7300
Lori Sheffield, prin. Fax 341-1700
Fourth Avenue JHS 400/6-8
450 S 4th Ave 85364 928-502-7000
Jose Cazares, prin. Fax 783-2195
Gila Vista JHS 500/6-8
2245 S Arizona Ave 85364 928-502-7100
Rusty Tyndall, prin. Fax 782-1483
Watson MS 400/6-8
9851 E 28th St 85365 928-502-7400
Donna Franklin, prin. Fax 502-7403
Woodard JHS 800/6-8
2250 S 8th Ave 85364 928-502-7200
Andy Wait, prin. Fax 782-4596

Yuma UNHSD 70 11,000/9-12
3150 S Avenue A 85364 928-502-4600
Toni Badone, supt. Fax 344-9157
www.yumaunion.org/
Cibola HS 2,500/9-12
4100 W 20th St 85364 928-502-5700
Tim Brienza, prin. Fax 502-6046
Gila Ridge HS 1,800/9-12
7150 E 24th St 85365 928-502-6400
Shawn Wehrer, prin. Fax 502-6749
Kofa HS 2,200/9-12
3100 S Avenue A 85364 928-502-5400
Mike Sharp, prin. Fax 502-5693
Vista Alternative S 300/Alt
2350 S Virginia Dr 85364 928-343-2521
Tamara Ray, prin. Fax 343-2582
Yuma HS 1,500/9-12
400 S 6th Ave 85364 928-502-5000
Faith Klostreich, prin. Fax 502-5338
Other Schools – See San Luis

---

Arizona Western College Post-Sec.
PO Box 929 85366 928-317-6000
Yuma Catholic HS 300/9-12
2100 W 28th St 85364 928-317-7900
Armando Valenzuela, prin. Fax 317-8558

# ARKANSAS

## ARKANSAS DEPARTMENT OF EDUCATION
**4 State Capitol Rm 304A, Little Rock 72201**
**Telephone 501-682-4475**
**Fax 501-682-1079**
**Website http://www.arkansased.org/**

Commissioner of Education Dr. Tom Kimbrell

## ARKANSAS BOARD OF EDUCATION
**4 State Capitol, Little Rock 72201**

Chairperson Jim Cooper

## EDUCATION SERVICE COOPERATIVES (ESC)

Arch Ford ESC
Phillip Young, dir. 501-354-2269
101 Bulldog Dr, Plumerville 72127 Fax 354-0167
www.afsc.k12.ar.us/
Arkansas River ESC
Barbara Warren, dir. 870-534-6129
912 W 6th Ave, Pine Bluff 71601 Fax 534-2847
www.aresc.k12.ar.us/pages/ARESC
Crowley's Ridge ESC
John Manning, dir. 870-578-5426
1606 Pine Grove Ln Fax 578-5896
Harrisburg 72432
crowleys.crsc.k12.ar.us/
Dawson ESC
Ron Wright, dir. 870-246-3077
711 Clinton St Ste 201 Fax 246-5892
Arkadelphia 71923
www.dawson.dsc.k12.ar.us
De Queen/Mena ESC
John Ponder, dir. 870-386-2251
PO Box 110, Gillham 71841 Fax 386-7731
dmesc.org

Great Rivers ESC
Suzann McCommon, dir. 870-338-6461
PO Box 2837, West Helena 72390 Fax 338-7905
www.grsc.k12.ar.us/
Northcentral Arkansas ESC
Dr. Dennis Martin, dir. 870-368-7955
PO Box 739, Melbourne 72556 Fax 368-4920
naesc.k12.ar.us/
Northeast Arkansas ESC
Donna Harris, dir., 211 W Hickory St 870-886-7717
Walnut Ridge 72476 Fax 886-7719
nea.k12.ar.us
Northwest Arkansas ESC
Dr. Charles Cudney, dir. 479-267-7450
4 N Double Springs Rd Fax 267-7456
Farmington 72730
www.starfishnw.org
Ozarks Unlimited Resource Cooperative
Rick Nance, dir. 870-429-9100
5823 Resource Dr, Harrison 72601 Fax 429-9099
www.oursc.k12.ar.us

South Central ESC
Marsha Daniels, dir. 870-836-1600
2235 California Ave SW Fax 836-1629
Camden 71701
www.scsc.k12.ar.us
Southeast Arkansas ESC
Karen Eoff, dir. 870-367-6848
1022 Scogin Dr, Monticello 71655 Fax 367-9877
se.sesc.k12.ar.us/
Southwest Arkansas ESC
Phoebe Bailey, dir. 870-777-3076
2502 S Main St, Hope 71801 Fax 777-5793
www.swaec.org
Western Arkansas ESC
Guy Fenter, dir. 479-965-2191
3010 Highway 22 E Ste A Fax 965-2723
Branch 72928
sites.google.com/a/wscstarfish.com/waesc/home
Wilbur D. Mills ESC
Jeff Williams, dir. 501-882-5467
PO Box 850, Beebe 72012 Fax 882-2155
www.wilbur.k12.ar.us

## PUBLIC, PRIVATE AND CATHOLIC SECONDARY SCHOOLS

**Alexander, Saline, Pop. 2,843**
Bryant SD
Supt. — See Bryant
Bethel MS 900/6-8
5415 Northlake Rd 72002 501-316-0937
Todd Sellers, prin. Fax 653-5830

---

Avilla Christian Academy 100/PK-12
302 Avilla E 72002 501-408-4631
Rich Meyers, prin.

**Alma, Crawford, Pop. 5,279**
Alma SD 3,400/K-12
PO Box 2359 72921 479-632-4791
David Woolly, supt. Fax 632-4793
almasd.net
Alma HS 1,100/9-12
PO Box 2139 72921 479-632-2162
Jerry Valentine, prin. Fax 632-5070
Alma MS 800/6-8
PO Box 2229 72921 479-632-2168
Bob Wolfe, prin. Fax 632-2160

**Alpena, Boone, Pop. 380**
Alpena SD 500/K-12
PO Box 270 72611 870-437-2220
Andrea Martin, supt. Fax 437-2133
alpenaschools.k12.ar.us/
Alpena JSHS 200/7-12
PO Box 270 72611 870-437-2228
Steven Watkins, prin. Fax 437-5638

**Amity, Clark, Pop. 719**
Centerpoint SD 1,000/PK-12
755 Highway 8 E 71921 870-356-2912
Dan Breshears, supt. Fax 356-4637
www.goknights.us
Centerpoint HS 500/6-12
755 Highway 8 E 71921 870-356-3612
Nic Mounts, prin. Fax 356-4519

**Arkadelphia, Clark, Pop. 10,545**
Arkadelphia SD 2,000/K-12
235 N 11th St 71923 870-246-5564
Donnie Whitten, supt. Fax 246-1144
www.arkadelphiaschools.org
Arkadelphia HS 600/9-12
401 High School Rd 71923 870-246-7373
David Maxwell, prin. Fax 246-1154
Goza MS 500/6-8
1305 Caddo St 71923 870-246-4291
Angela Garner, prin. Fax 246-1153

---

Arkadelphia Beauty College Post-Sec.
203 S 26th St 71923 870-246-6726
Henderson State University Post-Sec.
1100 Henderson St 71999 870-230-5000
Ouachita Baptist University Post-Sec.
410 Ouachita St 71998 870-245-5000

**Armorel, Mississippi**
Armorel SD 400/PK-12
PO Box 99 72310 870-763-6639
Sally Bennett, supt. Fax 763-0028
armorel.k12.ar.us/
Armorel JSHS 200/7-12
PO Box 99 72310 870-763-7121
Teresa Lawrence, prin. Fax 763-7020

**Ashdown, Little River, Pop. 4,622**
Ashdown SD 1,500/K-12
511 N 2nd St 71822 870-898-3208
Jason Sanders, supt. Fax 898-3709
www.ashdownschools.org
Ashdown HS 500/9-12
171 S Locust St 71822 870-898-3562
Kay York, prin. Fax 898-4452
Ashdown JHS 300/6-8
600 S Ellen Dr 71822 870-898-5138
James Jones, prin. Fax 898-4472
Ashdown New Traditions S Alt
751 Rankin St 71822 870-898-4413
Susan Fleming, dir. Fax 898-4489

**Atkins, Pope, Pop. 2,978**
Atkins SD 1,000/K-12
307 N Church St 72823 479-641-7871
Mark Gotcher, supt. Fax 641-7569
atkinspublic.schoolinsites.com
Atkins HS 300/9-12
403 Avenue 3 NW 72823 479-641-7872
Margaret Robinson, prin. Fax 641-1306
Atkins MS 300/5-8
611 NW 4th St 72823 479-641-1008
Darrell Webb, prin. Fax 641-5504

**Augusta, Woodruff, Pop. 2,163**
Augusta SD 500/PK-12
1011 Carver S 72006 870-347-2241
Ray Nassar, supt. Fax 347-5423
www.augustasd.org/
Augusta HS 200/8-12
1011 Main St 72006 870-347-2515
Joseph Brown, prin. Fax 347-8113

**Bald Knob, White, Pop. 2,847**
Bald Knob SD 1,300/K-12
103 W Park Ave 72010 501-724-3273
Bradley Roberts, supt. Fax 724-6621
www.baldknobschools.org
Bald Knob HS 400/9-12
901 N Hickory St 72010 501-724-3843
Thomas Garner, prin. Fax 724-8323
Bald Knob MS 400/5-8
103 W Park Ave 72010 501-724-5652
Lori Finley, prin. Fax 724-2062

**Batesville, Independence, Pop. 10,067**
Batesville SD 2,900/K-12
955 Water St 72501 870-793-6831
Gary Anderson, supt. Fax 793-6760
www.batesvilleschools.com
Batesville HS 600/10-12
1 Pioneer Dr 72501 870-793-6846
David Campbell, prin. Fax 793-0607
Batesville JHS 700/7-9
2 Pioneer Dr 72501 870-793-7533
Matt Douglas, prin. Fax 793-0626
Other Schools – See Cushman

Southside SD 1,400/PK-12
70 Scott Dr 72501 870-251-2341
Roger Rich, supt. Fax 251-3316
southsideschools.org
Southside HS 500/9-12
70 Scott Dr 72501 870-251-2662
Roger Reid, prin. Fax 251-3316
Southside JHS 7-8
70 Scott Dr 72501 870-251-4003
George Sitkowski, prin. Fax 251-4011

---

Bee-Jay's Hairstyling Academy Post-Sec.
130 W Main St 72501 870-793-3898
Lyon College Post-Sec.
PO Box 2317 72503 870-307-7000
University of Arkansas Community College Post-Sec.
PO Box 3350 72503 870-612-2000

**Bauxite, Saline, Pop. 486**
Bauxite SD 1,100/PK-12
800 School St 72011 501-557-5453
Matt Donaghy, supt. Fax 557-2235
www.edline.net/pages/Bauxite_SD
Bauxite HS 500/9-12
800 School St 72011 501-557-5303
Ann Webb, prin. Fax 557-2274
Bauxite MS 500/6-8
6725 Benton Rd 72011 501-557-5491
Kim Arnold, prin. Fax 557-5509

---

Eaton Barber College Post-Sec.
8333 Sagebrush Cir 72011 501-375-0211

**Bay, Craighead, Pop. 1,780**
Bay SD 600/K-12
PO Box 39 72411 870-781-3296
Oliver Layne, supt. Fax 781-3712
www.edline.net/pages/bay

Bay JSHS 300/7-12
PO Box 39 72411 870-781-3297
Jodi Cobb, prin. Fax 781-3687

**Bearden, Ouachita, Pop. 942**
Bearden SD 600/K-12
100 Oak Ave 71720 870-687-2236
Denny Rozenberg, supt. Fax 687-3683
www.beardenschools.org/
Bearden JSHS 300/7-12
635 N Plum St 71720 870-687-2913
Charles Hudson, prin. Fax 687-2514

**Beebe, White, Pop. 7,140**
Beebe SD 3,300/PK-12
1201 W Center St 72012 501-882-5463
Dr. Belinda Shook, supt. Fax 882-5465
beebebadgers.org
Beebe HS 900/9-12
1201 W Center St 72012 501-882-5463
Scott Jennings, prin. Fax 882-8404
Beebe JHS 500/7-8
1201 W Center St 72012 501-882-5463
Chris Ellis, prin. Fax 882-8416

---

Arkansas State University - Beebe Post-Sec.
PO Box 1000 72012 501-882-3600

**Bee Branch, Van Buren**
South Side SD 500/K-12
334 Southside Rd 72013 501-654-2633
Billy Jackson, supt. Fax 654-2336
www.ssbb.k12.ar.us
South Side JSHS 200/7-12
334 Southside Rd 72013 501-654-2242
Tim Smith, prin. Fax 654-2331

**Benton, Saline, Pop. 30,248**
Benton SD 4,600/K-12
PO Box 939 72018 501-778-4861
Jeff Collum, supt. Fax 776-5777
ww2.bentonschools.org
Benton HS 1,000/10-12
211 N Border St 72015 501-778-3288
Lita Gattis, prin. Fax 776-5783
Benton JHS 800/8-9
411 N Border St 72015 501-778-7698
Curt Barger, prin. Fax 776-5744

Harmony Grove SD 1,100/K-12
2621 N Highway 229 72015 501-778-6271
Daniel Henley, supt. Fax 778-6271
www.harmonygrovesd.org
Harmony Grove HS 300/9-12
2621 N Highway 229 72015 501-776-2337
Chad Withers, prin. Fax 776-2337
Harmony Grove MS 400/5-8
2621 N Highway 229 72015 501-860-6796
Sarah Gober, prin. Fax 860-6796

**Bentonville, Benton, Pop. 34,453**
Bentonville SD 14,100/PK-12
500 Tiger Blvd 72712 479-254-5000
Michael Poore, supt. Fax 271-1159
bentonvillek12.org
Bentonville HS 3,600/9-12
1801 SE J St 72712 479-254-5100
Jack Loyd, prin. Fax 271-1184
Fulbright JHS 7-8
5303 SW Bright Rd 72712 479-802-7000
Bradley Webber, prin.
Lincoln JHS 1,100/7-8
1206 Leopard Ln 72712 479-254-5250
Don Hoover, prin. Fax 271-1128
Washington JHS 1,100/7-8
1501 NE Wildcat Way 72712 479-254-5345
Tim Sparacino, prin. Fax 271-1191

---

Ambassadors For Christ Academy 100/PK-12
PO Box 924 72712 479-273-5635
David Welshenbaugh, admin. Fax 273-0684
Northwest Arkansas Community College Post-Sec.
1 College Dr 72712 479-636-9222

**Bergman, Boone, Pop. 427**
Bergman SD 1,100/K-12
PO Box 1 72615 870-741-5213
Joe Couch, supt. Fax 741-6701
bergman.k12.ar.us
Bergman HS 300/9-12
PO Box 1 72615 870-741-1414
Tami Richey, prin. Fax 741-6701
Bergman MS 400/5-8
PO Box 1 72615 870-741-8557
Sarah Alexander, prin. Fax 741-3490

**Berryville, Carroll, Pop. 5,283**
Berryville SD 1,900/K-12
902 W Trimble Ave 72616 870-423-7065
Dr. Phil Clark, supt. Fax 423-6824
bobcat.k12.ar.us
Berryville HS 500/9-12
902 W Trimble Ave 72616 870-480-4632
Owen Powell, prin. Fax 480-4635
Berryville MS 500/6-8
902 W Trimble Ave 72616 870-480-4633
David Gilmore, prin. Fax 480-4634

**Bigelow, Perry, Pop. 315**
East End SD 600/K-12
114 W Panther Dr 72016 501-759-2808
Don Collins, supt. Fax 759-2667
eastendpanthers.com
Bigelow JSHS 300/7-12
114 W Panther Dr 72016 501-759-2602
Dr. Brad Gist, prin. Fax 759-3081

**Bismarck, Hot Spring**
Bismarck SD 1,000/K-12
11636 Highway 84 71929 501-865-4888
Susan Stewart, supt. Fax 865-3626
www.bismarcklions.net/
Bismarck HS 300/9-12
11636 Highway 84 71929 501-865-4541
Larry Newsom, prin. Fax 865-4542
Bismarck MS 300/5-8
11636 Highway 84 71929 501-865-4543
Michael Spraggins, prin. Fax 865-4505

**Blevins, Hempstead, Pop. 310**
Blevins SD 500/K-12
PO Box 98 71825 870-874-2801
Billy Lee, supt. Fax 874-2889
blevinshornets.weebly.com/
Blevins JSHS 300/7-12
PO Box 98 71825 870-874-2281
Jeffrey Steed, prin. Fax 874-2450

**Blytheville, Mississippi, Pop. 15,417**
Blytheville SD 2,000/PK-12
PO Box 1169 72316 870-762-2053
Richard Atwill, supt. Fax 762-0168
www.blythevilleschools.com
Blytheville HS - A New Tech S 700/9-12
600 N 10th St 72315 870-762-2772
Bobby Ashley, prin. Fax 762-0175
Blytheville MS 400/6-8
700 Chickasawba St 72315 870-762-2983
Mike Wallace, prin. Fax 762-0174

---

Arkansas Northeastern College Post-Sec.
2501 S Division St 72315 870-762-1020

**Bonnerdale, Hot Spring, Pop. 50**

---

Ewing Jr Academy 50/K-10
709 Adventist Church Rd 71933 870-356-2780

**Booneville, Logan, Pop. 3,888**
Booneville SD 1,300/K-12
381 W 7th St 72927 479-675-3504
John Parrish, supt. Fax 675-3186
www.booneville.k12.ar.us/
Booneville HS 300/10-12
945 N Plum St 72927 479-675-3277
Michael Johnson, prin. Fax 675-3214
Booneville JHS 300/7-9
835 E 8th St 72927 479-675-5247
Scotty Pierce, prin. Fax 675-0793

**Bradford, White, Pop. 744**
Bradford SD 500/K-12
PO Box 60 72020 501-344-2707
Arthur Dunn, supt. Fax 344-2706
bradford.k12.ar.us
Bradford JSHS 200/7-12
PO Box 60 72020 501-344-2607
Rick Wood, prin. Fax 344-2706

**Bradley, Lafayette, Pop. 627**
Emerson-Taylor-Bradley SD
Supt. — See Emerson
Bradley HS 200/7-12
521 School Dr 71826 870-894-3316
Mike Lyons, prin. Fax 894-3344

**Branch, Franklin, Pop. 358**
County Line SD 500/PK-12
12092 W State Highway 22 72928 479-635-2222
Taylor Gattis, supt. Fax 635-2087
indians.wsc.k12.ar.us/
County Line JSHS 200/7-12
12092 W State Highway 22 72928 479-635-2441
Eric Parsons, prin. Fax 635-2452

**Brinkley, Monroe, Pop. 3,151**
Brinkley SD 600/K-12
200 Tigers Dr 72021 870-734-5000
Dr. Arthur Tucker, supt. Fax 734-5187
www.brinkleyschools.com
Brinkley JSHS 300/7-12
100 Tigers Dr 72021 870-734-5005
Samuel White, prin. Fax 734-1354

**Brockwell, Izard**
Izard County Consolidated SD 500/K-12
PO Box 115 72517 870-258-7700
Fred Walker, supt. Fax 258-3140
icc.k12.ar.us/
Izard County Consolidated HS 200/9-12
PO Box 115 72517 870-258-7788
David Harmon, prin. Fax 258-3140
Izard County Consolidated MS 200/5-8
PO Box 115 72517 870-258-7788
William McBride, prin. Fax 258-3140

**Brookland, Craighead, Pop. 1,612**
Brookland SD 2,100/PK-12
200 W School St 72417 870-932-2080
Keith McDaniel, supt. Fax 932-2088
www.brooklandbearcats.org
Brookland HS 300/10-12
100 W School St 72417 870-932-2080
Steven Hovis, prin. Fax 932-1251
Brookland JHS 400/7-9
100 W School St 72417 870-932-8610
Bart Hyde, prin. Fax 974-9762

**Bryant, Saline, Pop. 16,446**
Bryant SD 8,300/PK-12
200 NW 4th St 72022 501-847-5600
Dr. Tom W. Kimbrell, supt. Fax 847-5695
www.bryantschools.org
Bryant HS 2,400/9-12
200 NW 4th St 72022 501-847-5605
Dr. Jay Pickering, prin. Fax 847-5612
Bryant MS 1,100/6-8
200 NW 4th St 72022 501-847-5651
Todd Sellers, prin. Fax 847-5654
Other Schools – See Alexander

---

Arkansas Christian Academy 200/PK-11
21815 Highway 30 West 72022 501-847-0112

**Burdette, Mississippi, Pop. 191**

---

Cotton Boll Technical Institute Post-Sec.
PO Box 36 72321 870-763-1486

**Cabot, Lonoke, Pop. 23,349**
Cabot SD 10,200/PK-12
602 N Lincoln St 72023 501-843-3363
Dr. Tony Thurman, supt. Fax 843-0576
cabot.k12.ar.us
Cabot Freshman Academy 9-9
18 Spirit Dr 72023 501-743-3576
Tanya Spillane, prin.
Cabot Freshman Academy 9-9
18 Spirit Dr 72023 501-743-3576
Tanya Spillane, prin. Fax 941-1505
Cabot HS 2,000/10-12
401 N Lincoln St 72023 501-843-3562
Henry Hawkins, prin. Fax 843-4231
Cabot JHS North 1,200/7-8
38 Spirit Dr 72023 501-743-3572
Michael Byrd, prin. Fax 605-8472
Cabot JHS South 1,100/7-8
39 Panther Trl 72023 501-743-3573
John West, prin. Fax 941-7746

**Calico Rock, Izard, Pop. 1,531**
Calico Rock SD 400/K-12
PO Box 220 72519 870-297-8339
Jerry Skidmore, supt. Fax 297-4233
pirates.k12.ar.us/
Calico Rock JSHS 200/7-12
PO Box 220 72519 870-297-3745
Anita Cook, prin. Fax 297-3168

**Camden, Ouachita, Pop. 11,970**
Camden Fairview SD 2,400/K-12
625 Clifton St 71701 870-836-4193
Mark Keith, supt. Fax 836-6039
cfsd.k12.ar.us/
Camden Fairview HS 700/9-12
1750 Cash Rd SW 71701 870-837-1300
Gary Steelman, prin. Fax 837-2330
Camden Fairview MS 500/6-8
647 J A Dooley Womack Dr 71701 870-836-9361
Andre Toney, prin. Fax 836-3717

Harmony Grove SD 1,000/K-12
401 Ouachita 88 71701 870-574-0971
Walton Pigott, supt. Fax 574-2765
www.hgsd1.com
Harmony Grove JSHS 400/7-12
401 Ouachita 88 71701 870-574-0867
Jeff Mock, prin. Fax 574-2765
Other Schools – See Sparkman

---

Camden Christian Academy 50/PK-12
1245 California Ave SW 71701 870-836-3716
Kathy Wells, admin. Fax 836-4511
Southern Arkansas University Tech Post-Sec.
100 Carr Rd 71701 870-574-4500

**Carlisle, Lonoke, Pop. 2,193**
Carlisle SD 800/PK-12
520 Center St 72024 870-552-3931
Jason Clark, supt. Fax 552-7967
bison.wmsc.k12.ar.us
Carlisle JSHS 400/7-12
520 Center St 72024 870-552-3931
Brad Horn, prin. Fax 552-3032

**Cave City, Sharp, Pop. 1,876**
Cave City SD 1,100/K-12
PO Box 600 72521 870-283-5391
Steven Green, supt. Fax 283-6887
www.cavecity.k12.ar.us
Cave City HS 400/9-12
PO Box 600 72521 870-283-3333
Marc Walling, prin. Fax 283-3322
Cave City MS 200/6-8
PO Box 600 72521 870-283-5392
Mark Smith, prin. Fax 266-3258

**Cedarville, Crawford, Pop. 1,339**
Cedarville SD 900/K-12
PO Box 97 72932 479-474-7220
Dr. Dan Foreman, supt. Fax 410-1804
www.cedarvilleschools.org
Cedarville HS 300/9-12
PO Box 97 72932 479-474-7021
Randal Betts, prin. Fax 410-1804
Cedarville MS 300/5-8
PO Box 97 72932 479-474-5847
Dr. Jim Cox, prin. Fax 471-7036

**Center Ridge, Conway, Pop. 385**
Nemo Vista SD 400/PK-12
5690 Highway 9 72027 501-893-2925
Cody Beene, supt. Fax 893-2367
socs.nemo.k12.ar.us
Nemo Vista HS 200/9-12
5690 Highway 9 72027 501-893-2811
Jeffery Andrews, prin. Fax 893-6472
Nemo Vista MS 6-8
5690 Highway 9 72027 501-893-6494
Tresa Virden, prin. Fax 893-6494

**Centerton, Benton, Pop. 9,305**

---

Life Way Christian S 500/PK-12
PO Box 220 72719 479-795-9322
Dr. Luke Bowers, admin. Fax 795-9399

**Charleston, Franklin, Pop. 2,451**
Charleston SD 700/PK-12
PO Box 188 72933 479-965-7160
Jeff Stubblefield, supt. Fax 965-9989
tigers.wsc.k12.ar.us/
Charleston HS 300/9-12
PO Box 188 72933 479-965-7150
Shane Storey, prin. Fax 965-9989
Charleston MS 100/5-8
PO Box 188 72933 479-965-7170
Melissa Moore, prin. Fax 965-9989

**Clarendon, Monroe, Pop. 1,643**
Clarendon SD 600/K-12
PO Box 248 72029 870-747-3351
Lee Vent, supt. Fax 747-5963
lions.grsc.k12.ar.us
Clarendon HS 300/7-12
PO Box 248 72029 870-747-3326
Cathy Tanne, prin. Fax 747-5444

**Clarksville, Johnson, Pop. 9,041**
Clarksville SD 2,600/K-12
1701 W Clark Rd 72830 479-705-3200
Dr. David Hopkins, supt. Fax 754-3748
www.csdar.org/
Clarksville JHS 600/7-9
1801 W Clark Rd 72830 479-705-3224
Paul Dean, prin. Fax 754-7431
Clarksville SHS 500/10-12
1703 W Clark Rd 72830 479-705-3212
John Burke, prin. Fax 754-2492

---

University of the Ozarks Post-Sec.
415 N College Ave 72830 479-979-1000

**Clinton, Van Buren, Pop. 2,548**
Clinton SD 1,400/K-12
765 Yellowjacket Ln 72031 501-745-6005
Andrew Vining, supt. Fax 745-2475
www.clintonsd.org
Clinton HS 300/10-12
489 Yellowjacket Ln 72031 501-745-6035
Frank McMurry, prin. Fax 745-2450
Clinton JHS 300/7-9
443 Yellowjacket Ln 72031 501-745-6079
Frank McMurry, prin. Fax 745-6065

**Concord, Cleburne, Pop. 243**
Concord SD 500/K-12
PO Box 10 72523 870-668-3844
Mike Davidson Ed.D., supt. Fax 668-3380
concord.k12.ar.us
Concord JSHS 200/7-12
PO Box 358 72523 870-668-3522
Scott Whillock, prin. Fax 668-3600

**Conway, Faulkner, Pop. 57,689**
Conway SD 8,200/PK-12
2220 Prince St 72034 501-450-4800
Dr. Greg Murry, supt. Fax 450-4898
www.conwayschools.org
Conway Area Career Center Vo/Tech
2300 Prince St 72034 501-450-4888
Jason Lawrence, prin. Fax 450-6658
Conway HS 1,200/10-12
2300 Prince St 72034 501-450-4880
Joel Linn, prin. Fax 450-4884
Conway JHS 700/8-9
1815 Prince St 72034 501-450-4860
Dr. Todd Edwards, prin. Fax 450-6651

---

Arkansas Beauty School - Conway Post-Sec.
1061 Markham St 72032 501-329-8303
Central Baptist College Post-Sec.
1501 College Ave 72034 501-329-6872
Conway Christian S 500/PK-12
500 E German Ln 72032 501-336-9067
Gloria Massey, head sch Fax 336-9251
Hendrix College Post-Sec.
1600 Washington Ave 72032 501-329-6811
St. Joseph S 500/K-12
502 Front St 72032 501-327-1204
Joe Mallett, prin. Fax 513-6805
University of Central Arkansas Post-Sec.
201 Donaghey Ave 72035 501-450-5000

**Corning, Clay, Pop. 3,348**
Corning SD 1,000/K-12
PO Box 479 72422 870-857-6818
Kellee Smith, supt. Fax 857-5086
www.corningschools.k12.ar.us/
Corning JSHS 500/7-12
PO Box 479 72422 870-857-3041
Andrew Eubanks, prin. Fax 857-6797

**Cotter, Baxter, Pop. 947**
Cotter SD 700/K-12
PO Box 70 72626 870-435-6171
Donald Sharp, supt. Fax 435-1300
www.cotterschools.net
Cotter JSHS 300/7-12
PO Box 70 72626 870-435-6323
Amanda Britt, prin. Fax 435-1300

**Cove, Polk, Pop. 372**
Cossatot River SD
Supt. — See Wickes
Cossatot River HS 500/7-12
6330 Highway 71 S 71937 870-387-4200
Ladonna White, prin. Fax 387-4250

**Crossett, Ashley, Pop. 5,460**
Crossett SD 2,000/PK-12
219 Main St 71635 870-364-3112
Dr. Barbara Wood, supt. Fax 304-2525
www.crossettschools.org
Crossett HS 600/9-12
301 W 9th Ave 71635 870-364-2625
Alicia Brown, prin. Fax 364-4792
Crossett MS 600/5-8
100 Petersburg Rd 71635 870-364-4712
Lou Gregorio, prin. Fax 364-3771

---

University of Arkansas - Monticello Post-Sec.
1326 Highway 52 W 71635 870-364-6414

**Cushman, Independence, Pop. 440**
Batesville SD
Supt. — See Batesville
White River Academy Alt
PO Box 370 72526 870-698-1145
Roger Head, dir. Fax 698-1455

**Danville, Yell, Pop. 2,373**
Danville SD 700/K-12
PO Box 939 72833 479-495-4800
Gregg Grant, supt. Fax 495-4803
www.dps-littlejohns.net
Danville HS 300/9-12
PO Box 939 72833 479-495-4810
Kim Foster, prin. Fax 495-4832
Danville MS 5-8
PO Box 939 72833 479-495-4827
Doug Sanders, prin. Fax 495-4831

**Dardanelle, Yell, Pop. 4,680**
Dardanelle SD 1,900/K-12
209 Cedar St 72834 479-229-4111
John Thompson, supt. Fax 229-1387
www.dardanellepublicschools.org
Dardanelle HS 500/9-12
1079 N State Highway 28 72834 479-229-4655
Marcia Lawrence, prin. Fax 229-4687
Dardanelle MS 300/7-8
2306 State Highway 7 N 72834 479-229-4550
John Keeling, prin. Fax 229-1697

**Decatur, Benton, Pop. 1,637**
Decatur SD 500/PK-12
1498 Stadium Ave 72722 479-752-3986
Jeff Gravette, supt. Fax 752-2490
www.decatursd.com
Decatur JSHS 200/7-12
1498 Stadium Ave 72722 479-752-3983
Toby Conrad, prin. Fax 752-2491

**Deer, Newton**
Deer / Mt. Judea SD 300/K-12
PO Box 56 72628 870-428-5433
Richard Denniston, supt. Fax 428-5901
deermtjudea.k12.ar.us
Deer JSHS 100/7-12
PO Box 56 72628 870-428-5288
Elvis Middleton, prin. Fax 428-5901
Other Schools – See Mount Judea

**De Queen, Sevier, Pop. 6,482**
De Queen SD 2,300/K-12
101 N 9th St 71832 870-584-4312
Bruce Hill, supt. Fax 642-8881
www.dequeenleopards.org
De Queen HS 500/10-12
1803 W Coulter Ave 71832 870-642-2426
Roger Busse, prin. Fax 642-4931
De Queen JHS 400/8-9
1803 W Coulter Ave 71832 870-642-3077
William Huddleston, prin. Fax 642-3355

---

Cossatot Community College Univ. of AR Post-Sec.
PO Box 960 71832 870-584-4471

**Dermott, Chicot, Pop. 2,294**
Dermott SD 400/K-12
525 E Speedway St 71638 870-538-1000
Maurice Smith, supt. Fax 538-1005
www.dermott.k12.ar.us
Dermott JSHS 200/7-12
525 E Speedway St 71638 870-538-1030
David Clinton, prin. Fax 538-1067

**Des Arc, Prairie, Pop. 1,696**
Des Arc SD 600/K-12
600 Main St 72040 870-256-4164
Ricky Burns, supt. Fax 256-3701
desarc.wmsc.k12.ar.us/
Des Arc JSHS 300/7-12
600 Main St 72040 870-256-4166
Nick Hill, prin. Fax 256-3701

**De Witt, Arkansas, Pop. 3,250**
De Witt SD 1,300/PK-12
PO Box 700 72042 870-946-3576
Lynne Dardenne, supt. Fax 946-1491
www.dewittschooldistrict.net
De Witt HS 400/9-12
1614 S Grandview Dr 72042 870-946-4661
Marty Weaver, prin. Fax 946-2746
De Witt MS 300/6-8
301 N Jackson St 72042 870-946-3708
Julie Blevins, prin. Fax 946-1301

**Dierks, Howard, Pop. 1,118**
Dierks SD 500/K-12
PO Box 124 71833 870-286-2191
Holly Cothren, supt. Fax 286-2450
www.dierksschools.org
Dierks JSHS 200/7-12
PO Box 124 71833 870-286-3234
Jody Cowart, prin. Fax 286-2450

**Donaldson, Hot Spring, Pop. 298**
Ouachita SD 500/K-12
166 Schoolhouse Rd 71941 501-384-2318
Ronnie Kissire, supt. Fax 384-5615
www.ouachita.dsc.k12.ar.us/
Ouachita JSHS 200/7-12
258 Schoolhouse Rd 71941 501-384-2323
Dr. David Thigpen, prin. Fax 384-5614

**Dover, Pope, Pop. 1,350**
Dover SD 1,400/K-12
PO Box 325 72837 479-331-2916
Jerry Owens, supt. Fax 331-2205
www.doverschools.net
Dover HS 400/9-12
PO Box 325 72837 479-331-2120
Jo Lynn Taverner, prin. Fax 331-3286
Dover MS 500/5-8
PO Box 325 72837 479-331-4814
Donald Forehand, prin. Fax 331-4965

**Dumas, Desha, Pop. 4,687**
Dumas SD 1,500/PK-12
213 Adams St 71639 870-382-4571
Kelvin Gragg, supt. Fax 382-4874
dpsd.k12.ar.us
Dumas HS 300/10-12
709 Dan Gill Dr 71639 870-382-4151
Lorrie Holt, prin. Fax 382-8904
Dumas JHS 300/7-9
315 S College St 71639 870-382-4476
Ronnieus Thompson, prin. Fax 382-2162

**Earle, Crittenden, Pop. 2,397**
Earle SD 700/K-12
PO Box 637 72331 870-792-8486
Rickey Nicks, supt. Fax 792-8897
www.earle.crsc.k12.ar.us/
Earle JSHS 300/7-12
PO Box 637 72331 870-792-8716
Juanita Bohannon, prin. Fax 792-1004

**Edmondson, Crittenden, Pop. 415**
West Memphis SD
Supt. — See West Memphis
West Memphis Learning Center 100/Alt
200 B J Taylor St 72332 870-735-5113
Larry Rooks, dir. Fax 732-8653

**El Dorado, Union, Pop. 18,658**
El Dorado SD 4,700/K-12
200 W Oak St 71730 870-864-5001
Jim Tucker, supt. Fax 864-5015
www.eldoradopublicschools.com
Barton JHS 700/7-8
400 W Faulkner St 71730 870-864-5051
Sherry Hill, prin. Fax 864-5064
El Dorado HS 1,300/9-12
2000 Wild Cat Dr 71730 870-864-5100
Alva Reibe, prin. Fax 863-3309
Murmil Heights Educational Center 200/Alt
2000 Ripley St 71730 870-864-5021
Jerry Langston, prin.

Parkers Chapel SD 700/K-12
401 Parkers Chapel Rd 71730 870-862-4641
Michael White, supt. Fax 881-5092
www.parkerschapelschool.com
Parkers Chapel JSHS 300/7-12
401 Parkers Chapel Rd 71730 870-862-2360
Michael LaRue, prin. Fax 881-5095

---

South Arkansas Community College Post-Sec.
PO Box 7010 71731 870-862-8131
West Side Christian S 100/PK-12
2400 W Hillsboro St 71730 870-863-5636
Jennifer Wylie, admin. Fax 863-3529

**Elkins, Washington, Pop. 2,568**
Elkins SD 1,100/K-12
349 N Center St 72727 479-643-2172
Dan Jordan, supt. Fax 643-3605
www.elkinsdistrict.org
Elkins HS 300/9-12
349 N Center St 72727 479-643-3381
Paula Wheeler, prin. Fax 643-2726
Elkins MS 200/6-8
349 N Center St 72727 479-643-2552
Steve Denzer, prin. Fax 643-4272

**Emerson, Columbia, Pop. 368**
Emerson-Taylor-Bradley SD 1,000/PK-12
PO Box 129 71740 870-547-2218
Gary Hines, supt. Fax 547-2077
www.emersontaylorbradley.org
Emerson HS 100/7-12
212 Grayson St 71740 870-547-2862
Jim Deloach, prin. Fax 547-2011
Other Schools – See Bradley, Taylor

**England, Lonoke, Pop. 2,789**
England SD 800/K-12
501 Pine Bluff Hwy 72046 501-842-2996
Eddie Johnson, supt. Fax 842-3698
england.k12.ar.us
England JSHS 300/7-12
501 Pine Bluff Hwy 72046 501-842-2031
Eddie Nally, prin. Fax 842-3263

**Eureka Springs, Carroll, Pop. 2,008**
Eureka Springs SD 600/K-12
147 Greenwood Hollow Rd 72632 479-253-5999
David Kellogg, supt. Fax 253-5955
eurekaspringsschools.k12.ar.us
Eureka Springs HS 200/9-12
2 Lake Lucern Rd 72632 479-253-8875
Fax 253-8390
Eureka Springs MS 200/5-8
142 Greenwood Hollow Rd 72632 479-253-7716
Cindy Holt, prin. Fax 253-7809

Clear Spring S 100/PK-12
PO Box 511 72632 479-253-7888
Charles Templeton, head sch Fax 253-0768

**Everton, Marion, Pop. 128**
Ozark Mountain SD
Supt. — See Saint Joe
Bruno-Pyatt JSHS 100/7-12
4754 Highway 125 S 72633 870-427-5227
Mitzi Cantrell, prin. Fax 427-5255

**Farmington, Washington, Pop. 5,772**
Farmington SD 2,000/K-12
42 S Double Springs Rd 72730 479-266-1800
Bryan Law, supt. Fax 267-6030
www.farmcards.org/
Farmington Freshman Academy 9-9
278 W Main St 72730 479-266-1861
Bob Echols, prin. Fax 267-6040
Lynch MS 500/6-8
359 Rheas Mill Rd 72730 479-266-1840
Terry Lakey, prin. Fax 267-6051

**Fayetteville, Washington, Pop. 71,413**
Fayetteville SD 9,000/K-12
1000 W Bulldog Blvd 72701 479-444-3000
Paul Hewitt, supt. Fax 973-8670
district.fayar.net/pages/Fayetteville_SD
Fayetteville SHS 1,800/10-12
994 W Martin Luther King Bl 72701 479-444-3050
John Jacoby, prin. Fax 444-3056
Ramay JHS 600/8-9
401 S Sang Ave 72701 479-444-3064
Lori Linam, prin. Fax 444-3013
Woodland JHS 700/8-9
1 E Poplar St 72703 479-444-3067
David McClure, prin. Fax 444-3039

Blue Cliff College Post-Sec.
3448 N College Ave 72703 479-521-2914
Fayetteville Christian S 200/PK-12
2006 E Mission Blvd 72703 479-442-2565
Brad Jones, supt. Fax 444-6156
Paul Mitchell The School Post-Sec.
2167 W 6th St 72701 479-442-5181
University of Arkansas at Fayetteville Post-Sec.
1 University of Arkansas 72701 479-575-2000

**Flippin, Marion, Pop. 1,337**
Flippin SD 800/K-12
210 Alford St 72634 870-453-2270
Dale Query, supt. Fax 453-5059
www.flippinschools.com
Flippin HS 300/9-12
103 Alford St 72634 870-453-2233
Cassie Gilley, prin. Fax 453-7380
Flippin MS 200/6-8
308 N 1st St 72634 870-453-6464
Norm Zielinski, prin. Fax 453-6465

**Fordyce, Dallas, Pop. 4,245**
Fordyce SD 600/PK-12
PO Box 706 71742 870-352-3005
Albert Snow, supt. Fax 352-7187
www.fordyceschools.org/
Fordyce HS 300/7-12
PO Box 706 71742 870-352-2126
Judy Hubbell, prin. Fax 352-3953

**Foreman, Little River, Pop. 984**
Foreman SD 600/K-12
PO Box 480 71836 870-542-7211
George Kennedy, supt. Fax 542-7225
www.foremanschools.org
Foreman JSHS 300/7-12
PO Box 480 71836 870-542-7212
Kim Cody, prin. Fax 542-7227

**Forrest City, Saint Francis, Pop. 15,183**
Forrest City SD 3,300/PK-12
625 Irving St 72335 870-633-1485
Tiffany Hardrick Ph.D., supt. Fax 633-1415
mustang.grsc.k12.ar.us/
Forrest City HS 900/9-12
467 Victoria St 72335 870-633-1464
Osceola Hicks, prin. Fax 261-1844
Forrest City JHS 500/7-8
1133 N Division St 72335 870-633-3230
Carlos Fuller, prin. Fax 633-6066

Calvary Christian S 100/PK-12
1611 N Washington St 72335 870-633-5333
Crowley's Ridge Technical Institute Post-Sec.
1620 New Castle Rd 72335 870-633-5411
East Arkansas Community College Post-Sec.
1700 New Castle Rd 72335 870-633-4480

**Fort Smith, Sebastian, Pop. 83,397**
Fort Smith SD 14,100/PK-12
PO Box 1948 72902 479-785-2501
Ben Gooden Ed.D., supt. Fax 785-1722
www.fortsmithschools.org
Belle Point Alternative Center 100/Alt
1501 Dodson Ave 72901 479-783-7034
Maria Arnold, dir. Fax 784-8161
Chaffin JHS 800/7-9
3025 Massard Rd 72903 479-452-2226
Todd Marshell, prin. Fax 478-3103
Darby JHS 600/7-9
616 N 14th St 72901 479-783-4159
Darren McKinney Ed.D., prin. Fax 784-8165
Kimmons JHS 900/7-9
2201 N 50th St 72904 479-785-2451
David Watkins, prin. Fax 784-8177
Northside SHS 1,400/10-12
2301 N B St 72901 479-783-1171
Ginni McDonald, prin. Fax 784-8144
Ramsey JHS 900/7-9
3201 Jenny Lind Rd 72901 479-783-5115
Dennis Siebenmorgen, prin. Fax 784-8178
Southside SHS 1,600/10-12
4100 Gary St 72903 479-646-7371
Wayne Haver, prin. Fax 648-8204
Adult Education Adult
501 S 20th St 72901 479-785-1232
Gary Udouj, dir. Fax 782-3401

Academy of Salon and Spa Post-Sec.
311 S 16th St 72901 479-782-5059
Trinity JHS 200/7-9
1205 S Albert Pike Ave 72903 479-782-2451
Dr. Jim Hattabaugh, prin. Fax 782-7263
Union Christian Academy 200/PK-12
4201 Windsor Dr 72904 479-783-7327
Paul Bridges, supt. Fax 783-9342
University of Arkansas at Fort Smith Post-Sec.
PO Box 3649 72913 479-788-7000

**Fouke, Miller, Pop. 849**
Fouke SD 1,100/PK-12
PO Box 20 71837 870-653-4311
Forrest Mulkey, supt. Fax 653-2856
fouke.schoolfusion.us
Fouke HS 300/9-12
PO Box 20 71837 870-653-4551
Ronnie Herron, prin. Fax 653-3313
Smith MS 300/6-8
PO Box 20 71837 870-653-2304
Amanda Whitehead, prin. Fax 653-7840

**Fox, Stone**
Mountain View SD
Supt. — See Mountain View
Rural Special HS 100/7-12
13237 Highway 263 72051 870-363-4365
Junior Barham, prin. Fax 363-4222

**Gentry, Benton, Pop. 3,064**
Gentry SD 1,400/K-12
201 S Giles Ave 72734 479-736-2253
Dr. Randy C. Barrett, supt. Fax 736-2245
www.gentrypioneers.com/
Gentry HS 400/9-12
201 S Giles Ave 72734 479-736-2666
Brae Harper, prin. Fax 736-5202
Gentry MS 400/6-8
201 S Giles Ave 72734 479-736-2251
Larry Cozens, prin. Fax 736-3414

Ozark Adventist Academy 100/9-12
20997 Dawn Hill East Rd 72734 479-736-2221

**Gosnell, Mississippi, Pop. 3,483**
Gosnell SD 1,400/K-12
600 N State Highway 181 72315 870-532-4000
Bonard Mace, supt. Fax 532-4002
www.gosnellschool.net
Gosnell JSHS 600/7-12
600 N State Highway 181 72315 870-532-4010
Len Whitehead, prin. Fax 532-4031

**Gravette, Benton, Pop. 2,243**
Gravette SD 1,800/PK-12
609 Birmingham St SE 72736 479-787-4100
Dr. Richard Page Ed.D., supt. Fax 787-4108
gravetteschools.net
Gravette HS 600/9-12
325 Lion Dr S 72736 479-787-4180
Jay Chalk, prin. Fax 787-4188
Gravette MS 400/6-8
607 Dallas St SE 72736 479-787-4160
Duane Thomas, prin. Fax 787-4178

**Greenbrier, Faulkner, Pop. 4,616**
Greenbrier SD 3,200/PK-12
4 School Dr 72058 501-679-4808
Scott Spainhour, supt. Fax 679-1024
www.greenbrierschools.org
Greenbrier HS 700/10-12
72 Green Valley Dr 72058 501-679-4236
Steve Landers, prin. Fax 679-5765
Greenbrier JHS 500/8-9
10 School Dr 72058 501-679-3433
Jason Miller, prin. Fax 679-3658

**Green Forest, Carroll, Pop. 2,720**
Green Forest SD 1,200/K-12
PO Box 1950 72638 870-438-5201
Matt Summers, supt. Fax 438-6214
www.gf.k12.ar.us
Green Forest HS 400/9-12
PO Box 1950 72638 870-438-5203
Terry Darnell, prin. Fax 438-4588
Green Forest MS 300/6-8
PO Box 1950 72638 870-438-5242
Josh Nation, prin. Fax 438-6343

**Greenland, Washington, Pop. 1,236**
Greenland SD 800/PK-12
PO Box 57 72737 479-521-2366
Dr. Larry Ben, supt. Fax 521-1480
www.greenlandsd.com
Greenland HS 300/9-12
PO Box 57 72737 479-521-2366
Gary Orr, prin. Fax 521-1350
Greenland MS 300/5-8
PO Box 57 72737 479-521-2366
Phil Costner, prin. Fax 251-1203

**Greenwood, Sebastian, Pop. 8,785**
Greenwood SD 3,400/K-12
420 N Main St 72936 479-996-4142
John Ciesla, supt. Fax 996-4143
www.greenwoodk12.com/
Greenwood HS 800/10-12
440 E Gary St 72936 479-996-4141
Jerry Efurd, prin. Fax 996-6548
Greenwood JHS 600/8-9
300 E Gary St 72936 479-996-7440
Cody Chatman, prin. Fax 996-7469

**Greers Ferry, Cleburne, Pop. 887**
West Side SD 500/K-12
7295 Greers Ferry Rd 72067 501-825-6258
Andy Chisum, supt. Fax 825-6258
www.westsideeagles.org
West Side JSHS 200/7-12
7295 Greers Ferry Rd 72067 501-825-7241
Gary Nipper, prin. Fax 825-7241

**Gurdon, Clark, Pop. 2,184**
Gurdon SD 800/K-12
1 Go Devil Dr 71743 870-353-4454
Allen Blackwell, supt. Fax 353-4455
www.go-devils.net
Cabe MS 200/5-8
7780 Highway 67 S 71743 870-353-4311
Amanda Jones, prin. Fax 353-5149
Gurdon HS 300/9-12
7777 Highway 67 S 71743 870-353-5123
Harvey Sellers, prin. Fax 353-5131

**Guy, Faulkner, Pop. 699**
Guy-Perkins SD 400/K-12
492 Highway 25 N 72061 501-679-7224
Brian Cossey, supt. Fax 679-3508
www.gptbirds.org
Guy-Perkins HS 200/7-12
492 Highway 25 N 72061 501-679-3507
Damon Teas, prin. Fax 679-3508

**Hackett, Sebastian, Pop. 782**
Hackett SD 600/PK-12
102 N Oak St 72937 479-638-8822
William Pittman, supt. Fax 638-7106
www.hackettschools.org
Hackett JSHS 300/7-12
102 N Oak St 72937 479-638-7003
Michael Freeman, prin. Fax 638-8210
Other Schools – See Hartford

**Hamburg, Ashley, Pop. 2,843**
Hamburg SD 1,600/PK-12
202 E Parker St 71646 870-853-9851
Max Dyson, supt. Fax 853-2842
www.hsdlions.org
Hamburg HS 500/9-12
1119 S Main St 71646 870-853-9856
Nick Adams, prin. Fax 853-2850
Hamburg MS 500/6-8
1109 Cub Dr 71646 870-853-2811
Tammy Streeter, prin. Fax 853-2835

**Hampton, Calhoun, Pop. 1,315**
Hampton SD 500/K-12
PO Box 1176 71744 870-798-2742
Jimmy Cunningham, supt. Fax 798-2239
www.edline.net/pages/Hampton_Public_Schools
Hampton JSHS 300/7-12
PO Box 1176 71744 870-798-2742
Bryan Sanders, prin. Fax 798-2090

**Harrisburg, Poinsett, Pop. 2,253**
Harrisburg SD 1,200/K-12
207 W Estes St 72432 870-578-2416
Danny Sample, supt. Fax 578-9366
www.hbgsd.org/
Harrisburg HS 300/9-12
401 W South St 72432 870-578-2417
Brandon Craig, prin. Fax 578-2338
Harrisburg MS 400/5-8
401 W South St 72432 870-578-2410
Cindy Armstrong, prin. Fax 578-6201

**Harrison, Boone, Pop. 12,739**
Harrison SD 2,800/PK-12
110 S Cherry St 72601 870-741-7600
Dr. Melinda Moss, supt. Fax 741-4520
harrison.k12.ar.us/
Harrison JHS 600/7-9
515 S Pine St 72601 870-741-3496
Mike Stokes, prin. Fax 741-0101
Harrison SHS 600/10-12
925 Goblin Dr 72601 870-741-8223
Bill Keaster, prin. Fax 741-2606

North Arkansas College Post-Sec.
1515 Pioneer Dr 72601 870-743-3000

**Hartford, Sebastian, Pop. 634**
Hackett SD
Supt. — See Hackett
Hartford HS 200/7-12
512 Ludlow St 72938 479-639-2239
David Lee, prin. Fax 639-2158

**Hartman, Johnson, Pop. 516**
Westside SD 600/K-12
1535 Rabbit Hill Rd 72840 479-497-1991
Shane Gordon, supt. Fax 497-9037
www.westsiderebels.net
Westside JSHS 300/7-12
400 Highway 164 72840 479-497-1171
Chase Carter, prin. Fax 497-1537

**Hattieville, Conway**
Wonderview SD 400/K-12
2436 Highway 95 72063 501-354-0211
J. Carroll Purtle, supt. Fax 354-6071
www.wonderviewschools.org
Wonderview JSHS 200/7-12
2436 Highway 95 72063 501-354-8668
Jason Reynolds, prin. Fax 354-8602

**Havana, Yell, Pop. 375**
Western Yell County SD 400/K-12
PO Box 214 72842 479-476-4116
Joe Staton, supt. Fax 476-4115
wolverines.k12.ar.us
Western Yell County JSHS 200/7-12
PO Box 214 72842 479-476-4100
Scott Smith, prin. Fax 476-4111

**Hazen, Prairie, Pop. 1,454**
Hazen SD 700/PK-12
305 N Hazen Ave 72064 870-255-4549
Nanette Belford, supt. Fax 255-4508
www.hazen.k12.ar.us
Hazen HS 200/9-12
305 N Hazen Ave 72064 870-255-4546
Roxanne Bradow, prin. Fax 255-4559

**Heber Springs, Cleburne, Pop. 7,068**
Heber Springs SD 1,700/K-12
1100 W Pine St 72543 501-362-6712
Dr. Alan Stauffacher, supt. Fax 362-0613
hssd.k12.ar.us
Heber Springs HS 500/9-12
1100 W Pine St 72543 501-362-3141
Bret Brown, prin. Fax 362-9931
Heber Springs MS 400/6-8
1100 W Pine St 72543 501-362-2488
Rita Watkins, prin. Fax 362-2193

**Hector, Pope, Pop. 441**
Hector SD 600/K-12
11520 SR 27 72843 479-284-2021
Walt Davis, supt. Fax 284-2350
wildcats.afsc.k12.ar.us/
Hector JSHS 300/7-12
11601 SR 27 72843 479-284-3536
Jordan Price, prin. Fax 284-5023

**Helena, Phillips, Pop. 5,687**
Helena/West Helena SD 1,100/PK-12
305 Valley Dr 72342 870-338-4425
John Hoy, supt. Fax 338-4434
hwh.grsc.k12.ar.us/
Other Schools – See West Helena

---

Phillips Comm. Coll. of the Univ. of AR Post-Sec.
PO Box 785 72342 870-338-6474

**Hermitage, Bradley, Pop. 823**
Hermitage SD 500/PK-12
PO Box 38 71647 870-463-2246
Tracy Tucker, supt. Fax 463-8520
hermitageschools.org
Hermitage HS 200/7-12
PO Box 190 71647 870-463-2235
Mark Price, prin. Fax 463-2122

**Highland, Sharp, Pop. 1,030**
Highland SD 1,600/K-12
1627 Highway 62 412, 870-856-3275
Tracy Webb, supt. Fax 856-2765
highlandrebels.k12.ar.us/
Highland JSHS 600/8-12
1627 Highway 62 412, 870-856-3273
Annette Scribner, prin. Fax 856-2768

**Hope, Hempstead, Pop. 9,935**
Hope SD 2,500/PK-12
117 E 2nd St 71801 870-722-2700
Bobby Hart, supt. Fax 777-4087
hpsdistrict.org
Garland Learning Center 50/Alt
601 W 6th St 71801 870-722-2705
Marilyn Hampton, dir. Fax 777-4315
Hope HS 600/9-12
1701 S Main St 71801 870-777-3451
Tommy Campbell, prin. Fax 722-2736
Yerger MS 400/7-8
400 E 9th St 71801 870-722-2770
Vanessa McCraw, prin. Fax 722-2707

Spring Hill SD 600/K-12
633 Highway 355 W 71801 870-777-8236
Angela Raney, supt. Fax 777-9200
sites.google.com/a/springhill.k12.ar.us/web/home
Spring Hill JSHS 300/7-12
633 Highway 355 W 71801 870-722-7430
Steve Britton, prin. Fax 722-7425

---

Garrett Memorial Christian S 200/PK-12
PO Box 223 71802 870-777-3256
University of Arkansas Community College Post-Sec.
PO Box 140 71802 870-777-5722

**Horatio, Sevier, Pop. 1,021**
Horatio SD 900/PK-12
204 Lawson Ln 71842 870-832-1940
Lee Smith, supt. Fax 832-4465
www.horatioschools.org
Horatio JSHS 400/7-12
PO Box 435 71842 870-832-1900
James Dobbins, prin. Fax 832-2174

**Hot Springs National Park, Garland, Pop. 34,276**
Cutter-Morning Star SD 600/K-12
2801 Spring St 71901 501-262-2414
Nancy Anderson, supt. Fax 262-0670
eaglesnest.dsc.k12.ar.us/
Cutter-Morning Star JSHS 300/7-12
2801 Spring St 71901 501-262-1220
Jonathan McAfee, prin. Fax 262-3757

Fountain Lake SD 800/K-12
4207 Park Ave 71901 501-701-1700
Darin Beckwith, supt. Fax 623-6447
www.flcobras.net
Fountain Lake HS 400/9-12
4207 Park Ave 71901 501-701-1706
Donald Westerman, prin. Fax 624-4053
Fountain Lake MS 400/5-8
4207 Park Ave 71901 501-701-1730
Frank Janaskie, prin. Fax 318-6922

Hot Springs SD 3,500/PK-12
400 Linwood Ave 71913 501-624-3372
Dr. Mike Hernandez Ed.D., supt. Fax 620-7829
www.hssd.net
Hot Springs HS 700/9-12
701 Emory St 71913 501-624-5286
Lloyd Jackson, prin. Fax 620-7820
Hot Springs MS 500/7-8
700 Main St 71913 501-624-5228
George Wilson, prin. Fax 620-7828
Summit S Alt
220 Tom Ellsworth Dr 71901 501-620-7830
Kelly Deardorff, dir. Fax 620-7833

Lakeside SD 3,100/PK-12
2837 Malvern Ave 71901 501-262-1880
Shawn Cook, supt. Fax 262-2732
lakesidesd.com
Lakeside HS 700/8-12
2871 Malvern Ave 71901 501-262-1530
Darin Landry, prin. Fax 262-6205

---

Christian Ministries Academy 100/K-12
PO Box 8500 71910 501-624-1952
David Pate, prin. Fax 318-2624
Hot Springs Beauty College Post-Sec.
100 Cones Rd 71901 501-624-0203
National Park Community College Post-Sec.
101 College Dr 71913 501-760-4222

**Hoxie, Lawrence, Pop. 2,716**
Hoxie SD 1,000/PK-12
PO Box 240 72433 870-886-2401
Radius Baker, supt. Fax 886-4252
hoxieschools.com
Hoxie HS 400/7-12
PO Box 240 72433 870-886-4254
Kelly Gillham, prin. Fax 886-4255

**Huntsville, Madison, Pop. 2,295**
Huntsville SD 2,300/K-12
PO Box F 72740 479-738-2011
Clint Jones, supt. Fax 738-2563
www.huntsvilleschooldistrict.org
Huntsville HS 600/9-12
PO Box 1377 72740 479-738-2500
Tricia DeWitt, prin. Fax 738-2849
Huntsville MS 500/6-8
PO Box G 72740 479-738-6520
Mike Cain, prin. Fax 738-6259
Other Schools – See Saint Paul

**Imboden, Lawrence, Pop. 668**
Sloan-Hendrix SD 600/K-12
PO Box 1080 72434 870-869-2384
Clifford Rorex, supt. Fax 869-2380
shsd.k12.ar.us
Sloan-Hendrix HS 300/8-12
PO Box 1080 72434 870-869-2361
Marty Moore, prin. Fax 869-2362

**Jacksonville, Pulaski, Pop. 27,377**
Pulaski County Special SD
Supt. — See Little Rock
Jacksonville HS 900/9-12
2400 Linda Ln 72076 501-982-2128
Dr. Jerry Bell, prin. Fax 982-1692
North Pulaski HS 800/9-12
718 Harris Rd 72076 501-982-9436
Jeff Senn, prin. Fax 241-2256

---

Arthur's Beauty College Post-Sec.
2600 John Harden Dr 72076 501-982-8987

**Jasper, Newton, Pop. 462**
Jasper SD 900/K-12
PO Box 446 72641 870-446-2223
Jeff Cantrell, supt. Fax 446-2305
jasper.k12.ar.us
Jasper JSHS 200/7-12
PO Box 446 72641 870-446-2223
Jeff Lewis, prin. Fax 446-5549
Other Schools – See Kingston, Oark

**Jessieville, Garland**
Jessieville SD 900/K-12
PO Box 4 71949 501-984-5381
Ron Looper, supt. Fax 984-4200
www.jsdlions.net
Jessieville HS 300/9-12
PO Box 4 71949 501-984-5011
Toby Packard, prin. Fax 984-4200
Jessieville MS 200/6-8
PO Box 4 71949 501-984-5610
Bob Pymn, prin. Fax 984-4200

**Jonesboro, Craighead, Pop. 66,085**
Jonesboro SD 5,600/PK-12
2506 Southwest Sq 72401 870-933-5800
Dr. Kim Wilbanks, supt. Fax 933-5838
www.jonesboroschools.net
Area Technical Center Vo/Tech
1727 S Main St 72401 870-933-5891
Eddie Crain, dir. Fax 933-5890
Camp JHS 600/7-9
1814 W Nettleton Ave 72401 870-933-5820
William Cheatham, prin. Fax 933-5837
Jonesboro SHS 1,100/10-12
301 Hurricane Dr 72401 870-933-5881
Leigh Ann Rainey, prin. Fax 933-5812
MacArthur JHS 600/7-9
1615 Wilkins Ave 72401 870-933-5840
Dr. Brad Faught, prin. Fax 933-5848
SUCCESS Alt
613 N Fisher St 72401 870-931-9647
Todd Rhoades, dir. Fax 934-3555

Nettleton SD 2,800/K-12
3300 One Pl 72404 870-910-7800
James Dunivan, supt. Fax 910-7854
nettleton.ar.schoolwebpages.com
Nettleton HS 600/9-12
4201 Chieftain Ln 72401 870-910-7805
Brian Carter, prin. Fax 910-7804
Nettleton JHS 500/7-8
4208 Chieftain Ln 72401 870-910-7819
David Shipman, prin. Fax 910-6984

Valley View SD 2,800/PK-12
2131 Valley View Dr 72404 870-935-6200
Bryan Russell, supt. Fax 972-0373
www.valleyviewschools.net
Valley View HS 700/10-12
5709 Kersey Ln 72404 870-935-4602
David Goodin, prin. Fax 935-6202
Valley View JHS 600/7-9
2118 Valley View Dr 72404 870-935-4602
Barry Jones, prin. Fax 932-2291
Adult Education Center Adult
2311 E Nettleton Ave 72401 870-935-6205
Steve Clayton, dir. Fax 935-6208

Westside Consolidated SD 1,700/K-12
1630 Highway 91 W 72404 870-935-7501
Dr. Bryan Duffie, supt. Fax 935-2123
www.westsideschools.org
Westside HS 600/8-12
1630 Highway 91 W 72404 870-935-7501
Michael Graham, prin. Fax 268-9119

---

Concordia Christian Academy 100/PK-12
1812 Rains St 72401 870-935-2273
Becky Bernau, prin. Fax 935-4717
Ridgefield Christian S 300/PK-12
3824 Casey Springs Rd 72404 870-932-7540
Marica Elder, admin. Fax 931-9711

**Judsonia, White, Pop. 1,987**
White County Central SD 700/K-12
3259 Highway 157 72081 501-729-3947
Sheila Whitlow, supt. Fax 729-3992
wccbears.org
White County Central JSHS 300/7-12
3259 Highway 157 72081 501-729-3947
Jackwlyn Underwood, prin. Fax 729-3947

**Junction City, Union, Pop. 576**
Junction City SD 500/K-12
PO Box 790 71749 870-924-4575
William Lowe, supt. Fax 924-4565
junctioncity.k12.ar.us/
Junction City JSHS 300/7-12
PO Box 790 71749 870-924-4576
Melanie Mason, prin. Fax 924-4565

**Kingston, Madison**
Jasper SD
Supt. — See Jasper
Kingston JSHS 100/7-12
PO Box 149 72742 479-665-2835
Marsha Shaver, prin. Fax 665-2577

**Kirby, Pike, Pop. 768**
Kirby SD 400/K-12
PO Box 9 71950 870-398-4212
Jeff Alexander, supt. Fax 398-4442
www.kirbytrojans.net/
Kirby HS 200/7-12
PO Box 9 71950 870-398-4211
Jarrod Bray, prin. Fax 398-5413

**Lake City, Craighead, Pop. 2,050**
Riverside SD 600/K-12
PO Box 178 72437 870-237-4329
Tommy Knight, supt. Fax 237-4867
riverside.k12.ar.us
Riverside HS 200/7-12
PO Box 178 72437 870-237-4328
Jeffery Priest, prin. Fax 237-9929

**Lake Village, Chicot, Pop. 2,553**
Lakeside SD 1,000/PK-12
1110 S Lakeshore Dr 71653 870-265-7300
Joyce Vaught, supt. Fax 265-5466
www.lsschool.org
Lakeside HS 400/9-12
1110 S Lakeshore Dr 71653 870-265-2232
Linda Armour, prin. Fax 265-7302
Lakeside MS 300/6-8
1110 S Lakeshore Dr 71653 870-265-2970
Arthur Gray, prin. Fax 265-7309

**Lamar, Johnson, Pop. 1,567**
Lamar SD 1,100/K-12
301 Elberta St 72846 479-885-3907
Jay Holland, supt. Fax 885-2380
lamarwarriors.org
Lamar HS 300/8-12
301 Elberta St 72846 479-885-3344
Charles Harris, prin. Fax 885-3842

**Lavaca, Sebastian, Pop. 2,248**
Lavaca SD 900/PK-12
PO Box 8 72941 479-674-5611
Steve Rose, supt. Fax 674-2271
www.lavacaschools.com
Lavaca HS 300/9-12
PO Box 8 72941 479-674-5612
Felicia Owen, prin. Fax 674-0087
Lavaca MS 300/5-8
PO Box 8 72941 479-674-5618
Kenny Holland, prin. Fax 674-2271

**Leachville, Mississippi, Pop. 1,967**
Buffalo Island Central SD
Supt. — See Monette

Buffalo Island Central JHS — 200/7-9
PO Box 110 72438 — 870-539-6883
Mark Hurst, prin. — Fax 539-6696

**Lead Hill, Boone, Pop. 266**
Lead Hill SD — 300/K-12
PO Box 20 72644 — 870-436-5249
Joe Hulsey, supt. — Fax 436-5946
leadhillschools.net
Lead Hill JSHS — 200/5-12
PO Box 20 72644 — 870-436-5677
Wanda Van Dyke, prin. — Fax 436-6827

**Lepanto, Poinsett, Pop. 1,866**
East Poinsett County SD — 700/PK-12
502 McClellan St 72354 — 870-475-2472
Gary Williams, supt. — Fax 475-3531
epc.k12.ar.us
East Poinsett County JSHS — 300/7-12
502 McClellan St 72354 — 870-475-2331
John Kelly, prin. — Fax 475-2206

**Leslie, Searcy, Pop. 431**
Searcy County SD
Supt. — See Marshall
North Central Career Center — Vo/Tech
402 Oak St 72645 — 870-447-6111
Tommy Welch, dir. — Fax 447-2872

**Lewisville, Lafayette, Pop. 1,260**
Lafayette County SD — 700/K-12
PO Box 950 71845 — 870-921-5500
Robert Edwards, supt. — Fax 921-4277
www.lcscougars.org
Other Schools – See Stamps

---

South Arkansas Christian S — 50/K-12
PO Box 990 71845 — 870-921-5050

**Lexa, Phillips, Pop. 285**
Barton-Lexa SD — 800/K-12
9546 Highway 85 72355 — 870-572-7294
David Tollett, supt. — Fax 572-4713
www.bartonsd.org
Barton JSHS — 400/7-12
9546 Highway 85 72355 — 870-572-6867
Christopher Goodin, prin. — Fax 572-4713

**Lincoln, Washington, Pop. 2,196**
Lincoln Consolidated SD 48 — 900/PK-12
107 E School St 72744 — 479-824-7310
Mary Ann Spears, supt. — Fax 824-3045
www.lincolncsd.com
Lincoln HS — 300/8-12
1392 E Pridemore Dr 72744 — 479-824-7451
Courtney Jones, prin. — Fax 824-3042

**Little Rock, Pulaski, Pop. 190,562**
Little Rock SD — 25,900/PK-12
810 W Markham St 72201 — 501-447-1000
Dr. Dexter Suggs, supt. — Fax 447-1159
www.lrsd.org
Accelerated Learning Center — 100/Alt
7701 Scott Hamilton Dr 72209 — 501-447-1370
Brenda Allen, prin. — Fax 447-1371
Central HS — 2,400/9-12
1500 S Park St 72202 — 501-447-1400
Nancy Rousseau, prin. — Fax 447-1401
Dunbar Magnet MS — 800/6-8
1100 Wright Ave 72206 — 501-447-2600
Eunice Thrasher, prin. — Fax 447-2601
Fair Magnet HS — 900/9-12
13420 David O Dodd Rd 72210 — 501-447-1700
Jeremy Owoh, prin. — Fax 447-1701
Hall HS — 1,200/9-12
6700 H St 72205 — 501-447-1900
Larry Schleicher, prin. — Fax 447-1901
Hamilton Learning Academy — 300/Alt
3301 S Bryant St 72204 — 501-447-3400
Willie Vinson, prin. — Fax 447-3401
Henderson Magnet MS — 700/6-8
401 John Barrow Rd 72205 — 501-447-2800
Frank Williams, prin. — Fax 447-2801
Mann Magnet MS — 800/6-8
1000 E Roosevelt Rd 72206 — 501-447-3100
Keith McGee, prin. — Fax 447-3101
McClellan Magnet HS — 900/9-12
9417 Geyer Springs Rd 72209 — 501-447-2100
Henry Anderson, prin. — Fax 447-2101
Metropolitan Career-Tech Center — Vo/Tech
7701 Scott Hamilton Dr 72209 — 501-447-1370
Cassandra Norm-McGhee, prin. — Fax 447-1371
Parkview Magnet HS — 1,100/9-12
2501 John Barrow Rd 72204 — 501-447-2300
Dr. Dexter Booth, prin. — Fax 447-2301
Pulaski Heights MS — 800/6-8
401 N Pine St 72205 — 501-447-3200
Dr. Suzanne Ross, prin. — Fax 447-3201
Adult Education Center — Adult
4800 W 26th St 72204 — 501-447-1850
Linda Kindy, coord. — Fax 447-1897
Other Schools – See Mabelvale

Pulaski County Special SD — 16,700/PK-12
925 E Dixon Rd 72206 — 501-234-2000
Dr. Jerry Guess, supt. — Fax 490-0483
www.pcssd.org
Fuller MS — 500/6-8
808 E Dixon Rd 72206 — 501-490-5730
Quynci Joyner, prin. — Fax 490-5736
Mills HS — 800/9-12
1205 E Dixon Rd 72206 — 501-490-5700
Duane Clayton, prin. — Fax 490-5709
Robinson HS — 500/9-12
21501 Highway 10 72223 — 501-868-2400
Mary Bailey, prin. — Fax 868-2405
Robinson MS — 400/6-8
21001 Highway 10 72223 — 501-868-2410
Kimala Forrest, prin. — Fax 868-2441

Other Schools – See Jacksonville, Maumelle, North Little Rock, Sherwood

---

Arkansas Baptist College — Post-Sec.
1621 Dr Martin Luther King 72202 — 501-370-4000
Arkansas Baptist S — 800/PK-12
62 Pleasant Valley Dr 72212 — 501-227-7077
Arthur Bennett, hdmstr. — Fax 227-0060
Arkansas Beauty School — Post-Sec.
5108 Baseline Rd 72209 — 501-562-5673
AR College of Barbering & Hair Design — Post-Sec.
2500 S State St 72206 — 501-376-9696
Arkansas School for the Blind — Post-Sec.
PO Box 668 72203 — 501-296-1810
Arkansas School for the Deaf — Post-Sec.
2400 W Markham St 72205 — 501-324-9506
Baptist Schools of Allied Health — Post-Sec.
11900 Colonel Glenn Rd 72210 — 501-202-6200
Catholic HS for Boys — 700/9-12
6300 Father Tribou St 72205 — 501-664-3939
Steve Straessle, prin. — Fax 664-6549
Central Arkansas Radiation Therapy Inst. — Post-Sec.
PO Box 55050 72215 — 501-664-8573
Eastern College of Health Vocations — Post-Sec.
200 S University Ave 72205 — 501-568-0211
Episcopal Collegiate S — 700/PK-12
1701 Cantrell Rd 72201 — 501-372-1194
Chris Tompkins, head sch — Fax 372-2160
Heritage College — Post-Sec.
1309 Old Forge Dr 72227 — 501-708-0909
ITT Technical Institute — Post-Sec.
12200 Westhaven Dr 72211 — 501-565-5550
Little Rock Adventist Academy — 50/K-10
8708 N Rodney Parham Rd 72205 — 501-225-6183
Little Rock Christian Academy — 1,300/K-12
19010 Cantrell Rd 72223 — 501-868-9822
Mt. St. Mary Academy — 500/9-12
3224 Kavanaugh Blvd 72205 — 501-664-8006
Angie Collins, prin. — Fax 666-4382
Philander Smith College — Post-Sec.
900 W Daisy L Gatson Bates 72202 — 501-375-9845
Pulaski Academy — 1,400/PK-12
12701 Hinson Rd 72212 — 501-604-1910
Matthew Walsh, pres. — Fax 225-1974
Remington College — Post-Sec.
19 Remington Dr 72204 — 501-312-0007
St. Vincent Infirmary Medical Center — Post-Sec.
2 Saint Vincent Cir 72205 — 501-660-3910
Southwest Christian Academy — 500/PK-12
11301 Geyer Springs Rd 72209 — 501-565-3276
University of Arkansas at Little Rock — Post-Sec.
2801 S University Ave 72204 — 501-569-3000
University of Arkansas/Medical Sciences — Post-Sec.
4301 W Markham St 72205 — 501-686-5000
Velvatex College of Beauty Culture — Post-Sec.
1520 Dr Martin Luther King 72202 — 501-372-9678
Washington Barber College — Post-Sec.
5300 W 65th St 72209 — 501-568-8800

**Lonoke, Lonoke, Pop. 4,204**
Lonoke SD — 1,800/K-12
401 W Holly St 72086 — 501-676-2042
Suzanne Bailey, supt. — Fax 676-7074
lonokeschools.org/
Lonoke HS — 600/9-12
405 W Academy St 72086 — 501-676-2476
Marc Sherrell, prin. — Fax 676-3716
Lonoke MS — 400/6-8
1100 W Palm St 72086 — 501-676-6670
Jeannie Holt, prin. — Fax 676-7013

**Mabelvale, Pulaski**
Little Rock SD
Supt. — See Little Rock
Mabelvale Magnet MS — 700/6-8
10811 Mabelvale West Rd 72103 — 501-447-3000
Rhonda Hall, prin. — Fax 447-3001

**Mc Crory, Woodruff, Pop. 1,707**
Mc Crory SD — 700/PK-12
PO Box 930 72101 — 870-731-2535
Bob Casteel, supt. — Fax 731-2536
mccrory.k12.ar.us/
Mc Crory JSHS — 300/7-12
PO Box 930 72101 — 870-731-2851
Aaron Wiggins, prin. — Fax 731-2574

**Mc Gehee, Desha, Pop. 4,181**
McGehee SD — 1,100/K-12
PO Box 767 71654 — 870-222-3670
Thomas Gathen, supt. — Fax 222-6957
www.mcgeheeschools.org
McGehee JSHS — 500/7-12
PO Box 767 71654 — 870-222-5026
Derrell Thompson, prin. — Fax 222-5838

---

Baptist School of Nursing-SE — Post-Sec.
Highway 1 NE 71654

**Magazine, Logan, Pop. 835**
Magazine SD — 600/PK-12
485 E Priddy St 72943 — 479-969-2566
Brett Bunch, supt. — Fax 969-8740
magazinerattlers.k12.ar.us
Leftwich HS — 300/7-12
292 E Priddy St 72943 — 479-969-2640
Randy Bryan, prin. — Fax 969-2610

**Magnolia, Columbia, Pop. 11,431**
Magnolia SD — 2,900/PK-12
PO Box 649 71754 — 870-234-4933
John D. Ward, supt. — Fax 901-2508
www.magnoliaschools.net
Magnolia JHS — 700/7-9
PO Box 649 71754 — 870-234-2206
Gwen Carter, prin. — Fax 234-1293
Magnolia SHS — 600/10-12
PO Box 649 71754 — 870-234-2610
Roger Loper, prin. — Fax 901-2509

---

Columbia Christian S — 300/PK-12
250 Warnock Springs Rd 71753 — 870-234-2831
Dr. Richard Britt, supt. — Fax 234-1497
Southern Arkansas University — Post-Sec.
100 E University 71753 — 870-235-4000

**Malvern, Hot Spring, Pop. 10,082**
Glen Rose SD — 1,000/PK-12
14334 Highway 67 72104 — 501-332-3694
Tim Holicer, supt. — Fax 332-3031
www.grbeavers.org
Glen Rose HS — 300/9-12
14334 Highway 67 72104 — 501-332-3694
Susan Blockburger, prin. — Fax 332-3902
Glen Rose MS — 300/5-8
14334 Highway 67 72104 — 501-332-3694
Shawn Pilgrim, prin. — Fax 332-3799

Magnet Cove SD — 600/K-12
472 Magnet School Rd 72104 — 501-332-5468
Danny Thomas, supt. — Fax 337-4119
magnetcove.k12.ar.us
Magnet Cove HS — 300/7-12
472 Magnet School Rd 72104 — 501-332-5466
Jeff Eskola, prin. — Fax 337-8711

Malvern SD — 2,100/K-12
1517 S Main St 72104 — 501-332-7500
Brian Golden, supt. — Fax 332-7501
malvernleopards.org
Malvern MS — 300/7-8
339 E Donnelly St 72104 — 501-332-7530
Velda Keeney, prin. — Fax 332-7532
Malvern SHS — 600/9-12
525 E Highland Ave 72104 — 501-332-6905
Jennifer Shnaekel, prin. — Fax 332-7523

---

College of the Ouachitas — Post-Sec.
1 College Cir 72104 — 501-337-5000

**Mammoth Spring, Fulton, Pop. 962**
Mammoth Spring SD — 500/K-12
410 Goldsmith Ave 72554 — 870-625-3612
David Turnbough, supt. — Fax 625-3609
www.mammothspringschools.com
Mammoth Spring HS — 200/7-12
410 Goldsmith Ave 72554 — 870-625-7212
Brian Davis, prin. — Fax 625-3609

**Manila, Mississippi, Pop. 3,321**
Manila SD — 1,000/PK-12
PO Box 670 72442 — 870-561-4419
Pamela Castor, supt. — Fax 561-4410
mps.crsc.k12.ar.us
Manila HS — 300/9-12
PO Box 670 72442 — 870-561-4417
Christopher Ferrell, prin. — Fax 561-4243
Manila MS — 300/5-8
PO Box 670 72442 — 870-561-4815
LeAnn Helms, prin. — Fax 561-4828

**Mansfield, Scott, Pop. 1,119**
Mansfield SD — 900/K-12
402 Grove St 72944 — 479-928-4006
Robert Ross, supt. — Fax 928-4482
mansfieldtigers.org
Mansfield HS — 300/9-12
2500 Highway 71 S 72944 — 479-928-1105
James Best, prin. — Fax 928-1108
Mansfield MS — 300/5-8
400 Grove St 72944 — 479-928-4451
Floyd Fisher, prin. — Fax 928-4323

**Marianna, Lee, Pop. 4,065**
Lee County SD — 1,000/PK-12
175 Walnut St 72360 — 870-295-7100
Willie Murdock, supt. — Fax 295-7125
lcsd1.grsc.k12.ar.us
Lee HS — 300/7-12
523 Forest Ave 72360 — 870-295-7130
Phylistia Stanley, prin. — Fax 295-7313

---

Lee Academy — 200/PK-12
973 Highway 243 72360 — 870-295-3444

**Marion, Crittenden, Pop. 12,214**
Marion SD — 4,200/K-12
200 Manor St 72364 — 870-739-5100
Don Johnston, supt. — Fax 739-5156
www.msd3.org/
Marion JHS — 700/8-9
801 Carter Dr 72364 — 870-739-5140
Elmer West, prin. — Fax 739-5142
Marion SHS — 900/10-12
1 Patriot Dr 72364 — 870-739-5130
Stephen Landers, prin. — Fax 739-5135

**Marked Tree, Poinsett, Pop. 2,530**
Marked Tree SD — 500/PK-12
406 Saint Francis St 72365 — 870-358-2913
Annesa Thompson, supt. — Fax 358-3953
mtree.k12.ar.us
Marked Tree JSHS — 200/7-12
406 Saint Francis St 72365 — 870-358-2891
Matt Wright, prin. — Fax 358-3953

---

Delta Technical Institute — Post-Sec.
PO Box 280 72365 — 870-358-2117

**Marmaduke, Greene, Pop. 1,093**
Marmaduke SD — 700/K-12
1010 Greyhound Dr 72443 — 870-597-2723
Tim Gardner, supt. — Fax 597-4693
www.mhs.nesc.k12.ar.us
Marmaduke JSHS — 300/7-12
1010 Greyhound Dr 72443 — 870-597-2723
Bill Muse, prin. — Fax 597-4693

**Marshall, Searcy, Pop. 1,315**
Searcy County SD 800/K-12
952 Highway 65 N 72650 870-448-3011
Alan Yarbrough, supt. Fax 448-3012
scsd.info
Marshall MSHS 400/7-12
950 Highway 65 N 72650 870-448-3331
Robin Morris, prin. Fax 448-5306
Other Schools – See Leslie

**Marvell, Phillips, Pop. 1,170**
Marvell-Elaine SD 400/PK-12
PO Box 1870 72366 870-829-2101
Dr. Joyce Cottoms Ph.D., supt. Fax 829-2044
marvell.grsc.k12.ar.us/
Marvell-Elaine HS 200/7-12
PO Box 1870 72366 870-829-1351
Sylvia Moore M.S., prin. Fax 829-3150

---

Marvell Academy 200/PK-12
PO Box 277 72366 870-829-2931
Herman Coats, hdmstr. Fax 829-3601

**Maumelle, Pulaski, Pop. 16,888**
Pulaski County Special SD
Supt. — See Little Rock
Maumelle HS 9-12
100 Victory Ln 72113 501-851-5350
Leslie Ireland, prin. Fax 851-5356
Maumelle MS 900/6-8
1000 Carnahan Dr 72113 501-851-8990
Ryan Burgess, prin. Fax 851-8988

**Mayflower, Faulkner, Pop. 2,195**
Mayflower SD 1,200/PK-12
7 Ashmore Dr 72106 501-470-0506
John Gray, supt. Fax 470-1343
www.mayflowerschools.org
Mayflower HS 300/9-12
10 Leslie King N 72106 501-470-0388
T.J. Slough, prin. Fax 470-2106
Mayflower MS 400/5-8
18 Eagle Circle 72106 501-470-2111
John Pipkins, prin. Fax 470-2116

**Maynard, Randolph, Pop. 421**
Maynard SD 500/K-12
74 Campus Dr 72444 870-647-3500
Patricia Rawlings, supt. Fax 647-2301
maynard.nesc.k12.ar.us/
Maynard JSHS 200/7-12
74 Campus Dr 72444 870-647-3500
Cindy Dauck, prin. Fax 647-2301

**Melbourne, Izard, Pop. 1,832**
Melbourne SD 900/K-12
PO Box 250 72556 870-368-7070
Gerald Cooper, supt. Fax 368-7071
bearkatz.k12.ar.us/
Melbourne JSHS 400/7-12
PO Box 250 72556 870-368-4345
Jim Carroll, prin. Fax 368-4349

---

Ozarka College Post-Sec.
PO Box 10 72556 870-368-7371

**Mena, Polk, Pop. 5,622**
Mena SD 1,900/K-12
501 Hickory Ave 71953 479-394-1710
Benny Weston, supt. Fax 394-1713
www.menaschools.org
Mena HS 600/9-12
PO Box 1810 71953 479-394-1144
Shane Torix, prin. Fax 394-1145
Mena MS 500/6-8
700 Morrow St S 71953 479-394-2572
Michael Hobson, prin. Fax 394-0258

Ouachita River SD 700/K-12
143 Polk Road 96 71953 479-394-2348
Jerrall Strasner, supt. Fax 394-6687
www.ouachitariversd.org
Acorn JSHS 200/7-12
143 Polk Road 96 71953 479-394-5544
Sean Couch, prin. Fax 394-1041
Other Schools – See Oden

---

Rich Mountain Community College Post-Sec.
1100 College Dr 71953 479-394-7622

**Mineral Springs, Howard, Pop. 1,190**
Mineral Springs SD 400/K-12
PO Box 189 71851 870-287-4748
Curtis Turner, supt. Fax 287-5301
mssd2.k12.ar.us/
Mineral Springs HS 200/7-12
PO Box 189 71851 870-287-4747
Stephanie Rowe, prin. Fax 287-5300

**Monette, Craighead, Pop. 1,489**
Buffalo Island Central SD 900/PK-12
PO Box 730 72447 870-486-5411
Gaylon Taylor, supt. Fax 486-2657
www.bicschools.net
Buffalo Island Central SHS 200/10-12
PO Box 730 72447 870-486-5512
Randy Rose, prin. Fax 486-2657
Other Schools – See Leachville

**Monticello, Drew, Pop. 9,357**
Drew Central SD 800/K-12
250 University Dr 71655 870-367-5369
Billy Williams, supt. Fax 367-1932
www.drewcentral.org/
Drew Central HS 300/9-12
250 University Dr 71655 870-367-6076
Melissia Vincent, prin. Fax 460-5501
Drew Central MS 100/5-8
250 University Dr 71655 870-367-5235
Joy Graham, prin. Fax 460-5502

Monticello SD 2,100/K-12
935 Scogin Dr 71655 870-367-4000
Sandra Lanehart, supt. Fax 367-1531
www.billies.org
Monticello HS 700/9-12
390 Clyde Ross Dr 71655 870-367-4050
Judy Holaway, prin. Fax 367-3699
Monticello MS 500/6-8
180 Clyde Ross Dr 71655 870-367-4040
Kevin Hancock, prin. Fax 367-5437
Occupational Education Center Vo/Tech
741 Scogin Dr 71655 870-367-4060
Randy Lay, dir. Fax 367-1385

---

University of Arkansas at Monticello Post-Sec.
346 University Dr 71656 870-460-1026

**Morrilton, Conway, Pop. 6,618**
South Conway County SD 2,200/K-12
100 Baramore St 72110 501-354-9400
Shawn Halbrook, supt. Fax 354-9464
www.sccsd.org
Morrilton HS 700/9-12
701 E Harding St 72110 501-354-9430
Danny Ketcherside, prin. Fax 354-9468
Morrilton JHS 300/7-8
1400 Poor Farm Rd 72110 501-354-9437
Robert Hogan, prin. Fax 354-9429

---

Sacred Heart S 200/PK-12
106 N Saint Joseph St 72110 501-354-8113
Buddy Greeson, prin. Fax 354-2001
University of Arkansas Community College Post-Sec.
1537 University Blvd 72110 501-354-2465

**Mountainburg, Crawford, Pop. 624**
Mountainburg SD 700/K-12
129 Highway 71 SW 72946 479-369-2121
Dennis Copeland, supt. Fax 369-2138
www.mountainburg.org
Mountainburg HS 200/9-12
129 Highway 71 SW 72946 479-369-2146
Jason Rutherford, prin. Fax 369-2845
Mountainburg MS 200/5-8
129 Highway 71 SW 72946 479-369-4506
Paul Roper, prin. Fax 369-4355

**Mountain Home, Baxter, Pop. 12,291**
Mountain Home SD 3,100/K-12
2465 Rodeo Dr 72653 870-425-1201
Dr. Jake Long, supt. Fax 425-1316
bombers.k12.ar.us
Mountain Home HS Career Academies 1,200/9-12
500 Bomber Blvd 72653 870-425-1215
Dana Brown, prin. Fax 508-6097
Mountain Home JHS 300/8-8
2301 Rodeo Dr 72653 870-425-1231
Ron Czanstkowski, prin. Fax 424-4797

---

Arkansas State University Mountain Home Post-Sec.
1600 S College St 72653 870-508-6100
Marsha Kay Beauty College Post-Sec.
408 Highway 201 N 72653 870-425-7575
Mountain Home Christian Academy 100/PK-12
1989 Glenbriar Dr 72653 870-424-6622
Lori Mathis, prin.

**Mountain Pine, Garland, Pop. 749**
Mountain Pine SD 600/PK-12
PO Box 1 71956 501-767-1540
Robert Gray, supt. Fax 767-1589
www.edline.net/pages/Mountain_Pine_SD
Mountain Pine JSHS 300/7-12
PO Box 1 71956 501-767-6917
Denise Taylor, prin. Fax 767-0170

**Mountain View, Stone, Pop. 2,714**
Mountain View SD 1,700/PK-12
210 High School Rd 72560 870-269-3443
Rowdy Ross, supt. Fax 269-3446
mountainviewschooldistrict.k12.ar.us/
Mountain View HS 400/9-12
210 High School Rd 72560 870-269-3943
Kim Cruce, prin. Fax 269-2372
Mountain View MS 300/6-8
210 High School Rd 72560 870-269-4335
Robert Ross, prin. Fax 269-4447
Other Schools – See Fox, Timbo

**Mount Ida, Montgomery, Pop. 1,049**
Mount Ida SD 500/K-12
PO Box 1230 71957 870-867-2771
Hal Landrith, supt. Fax 867-3734
www.mountidaschools.com
Mount Ida JSHS 300/7-12
PO Box 1230 71957 870-867-2771
Ron McGuire, prin. Fax 867-3734

**Mount Judea, Newton**
Deer / Mt. Judea SD
Supt. — See Deer
Mount Judea JSHS 100/7-12
PO Box 40 72655 870-434-5362
E.J. Freeman, prin. Fax 434-5359

**Mount Vernon, Faulkner, Pop. 139**
Mount Vernon-Enola SD 500/K-12
38 Garland Springs Rd 72111 501-849-2220
Larry Walters, supt. Fax 849-3076
mve.k12.ar.us/
Mount Vernon-Enola JSHS 200/7-12
38 Garland Springs Rd 72111 501-849-2221
Rudy Beavers, prin. Fax 849-3302

**Mulberry, Crawford, Pop. 1,638**
Mulberry/Pleasant View Bi-County SD 400/K-12
424 Alma Ave 72947 479-997-1715
Dana Higdon, supt. Fax 997-1897
www.mpvschools.com

Mulberry HS 100/10-12
424 Alma Ave 72947 479-997-1363
Melvin Williams, prin. Fax 997-1491
Other Schools – See Ozark

**Murfreesboro, Pike, Pop. 1,612**
South Pike County SD 800/K-12
PO Box 339 71958 870-285-2201
Roger Featherston, supt. Fax 285-2276
mboro.k12.ar.us/
Murfreesboro JSHS 300/7-12
PO Box 339 71958 870-285-2184
Kathaleen Cole, prin. Fax 285-2276

**Nashville, Howard, Pop. 4,566**
Nashville SD 1,900/K-12
600 N 4th St 71852 870-845-3425
Douglas Graham, supt. Fax 845-7344
www.nashvillesd.com
Nashville JHS 400/7-9
1000 N 8th St 71852 870-845-3418
Deb Tackett, prin. Fax 845-7334
Nashville SHS 400/10-12
1301 Mount Pleasant Dr 71852 870-845-3261
Tate Gordon, prin. Fax 845-7345

**Newark, Independence, Pop. 1,165**
Cedar Ridge SD 800/PK-12
1502 N Hill St 72562 870-799-8691
Andy Ashley, supt. Fax 799-8647
www.crsd.k12.ar.us/
Cedar Ridge JSHS 400/7-12
1500 N Hill St 72562 870-799-8691
Greg Thetford, prin. Fax 799-3225

**Newport, Jackson, Pop. 7,757**
Newport SD 700/PK-12
406 Wilkerson Dr 72112 870-523-1312
Dr. Larry Bennett, supt. Fax 523-1388
www.newportschools.org
Newport HS 400/7-12
406 Wilkerson Dr 72112 870-523-1321
Kenny Black, prin. Fax 523-1383

---

Arkansas State University - Newport Post-Sec.
7648 Victory Blvd 72112 870-512-7800

**Norfork, Baxter, Pop. 502**
Norfork SD 400/K-12
44 Fireball Ln 72658 870-499-5228
Mike Seay, supt. Fax 499-5109
norfork.k12.ar.us
Norfork JSHS 200/7-12
136 Mildred Simpson Dr 72658 870-499-7191
Bob Hulse, prin. Fax 499-5659

**Norman, Montgomery, Pop. 367**
Caddo Hills SD 600/PK-12
2268 Highway 8 E 71960 870-356-5700
Deric Owens, supt. Fax 356-3426
www.caddohills.org
Caddo Hills JSHS 300/7-12
2268 Highway 8 E 71960 870-356-5701
Todd Baxley, prin. Fax 356-3444

**Norphlet, Union, Pop. 829**
Smackover-Norphlet SD
Supt. — See Smackover
Norphlet JHS 200/6-8
PO Box 50 71759 870-546-2781
Raymond Coleman, prin. Fax 546-9554

**North Little Rock, Pulaski, Pop. 61,111**
North Little Rock SD 6,400/PK-12
PO Box 687 72115 501-771-8000
Kelly Rodgers, supt. Fax 771-8067
www.nlrsd.org
North Little Rock Academy 9-12
5500 Lynch Dr 72117 501-955-3600
Charles Jones, prin. Fax 955-3603
North Little Rock HS 1,400/9-12
101 W 22nd St 72114 501-771-8100
Randy Rutherford, prin. Fax 771-8123
North Little Rock MS 700/6-8
2400 Lakeview Rd 72116 501-771-8200
Lee Tackett, prin. Fax 771-8206

Pulaski County Special SD
Supt. — See Little Rock
Jacksonville MS 500/6-8
10200 Bamboo Ln 72120 501-833-1170
Mike Hudgeons, prin. Fax 833-1178

---

AR College of Barbering & Hair Design Post-Sec.
200 E Washington Ave 72114 501-376-9696
Central Arkansas Christian S 500/PK-12
1 Windsong Dr 72113 501-758-3160
Lee's School of Cosmetology Post-Sec.
2700 W Pershing Blvd 72114 501-758-2800
New Tyler Barber College Post-Sec.
1221 Bishop Lindsey Ave 72114 501-375-0377
Pulaski Technical College Post-Sec.
3000 W Scenic Dr 72118 501-812-2200
Shorter College Post-Sec.
604 N Locust St 72114 501-374-6305

**Oark, Johnson**
Jasper SD
Supt. — See Jasper
Oark JSHS 100/7-12
370 Highway 215 72852 479-292-3353
David Westenhover, prin. Fax 292-3435

**Oden, Montgomery, Pop. 227**
Ouachita River SD
Supt. — See Mena
Oden JSHS 100/7-12
135 School Dr 71961 870-326-4311
William Edwards, prin. Fax 326-5552

**Ola, Yell, Pop. 1,269**
Two Rivers SD 600/K-12
17727 E State Highway 28 72853 479-272-3113
Jimmy Loyd, supt. Fax 272-3125
www.trgators.org/
Two Rivers JSHS 400/5-12
17727 E State Highway 28 72853 479-272-3150
Barry Fisher, prin. Fax 272-3149

**Omaha, Boone, Pop. 159**
Omaha SD 400/K-12
522 College Rd 72662 870-426-3366
Jerry Parrett, supt. Fax 426-3355
omahaschool.weebly.com
Omaha JSHS 200/7-12
522 College Rd 72662 870-426-3373
Nathan White, prin. Fax 426-3360

**Osceola, Mississippi, Pop. 7,648**
Osceola SD 1,200/PK-12
2750 W Semmes Ave 72370 870-563-2561
Michael Cox, supt. Fax 563-2181
www.osd1.org/
Osceola HS 400/9-12
2800 W Semmes Ave 72370 870-563-2192
Tiffany Morgan, prin. Fax 622-1003

**Ozark, Franklin, Pop. 3,615**
Mulberry/Pleasant View Bi-County SD
Supt. — See Mulberry
Pleasant View JHS 100/7-9
5750 Hornet Ln 72949 479-997-8469
Dennis Fisher, prin. Fax 997-1667

Ozark SD 1,900/PK-12
PO Box 135 72949 479-667-4118
James Ford, supt. Fax 667-4092
www.ozarkhillbillies.org/
Ozark JHS 300/8-9
1301 Walden Dr 72949 479-667-4747
Michael Burns, prin. Fax 667-0898
Ozark SHS 400/10-12
1631 Hillbilly Dr 72949 479-667-4118
Jody Jenkins, prin. Fax 667-5921

---

Arkansas Technical University Ozark Cmps Post-Sec.
1700 Helberg Ln 72949 866-225-2884

**Palestine, Saint Francis, Pop. 671**
Palestine-Wheatley SD 700/PK-12
PO Box 790 72372 870-581-2646
Jon Estes, supt. Fax 581-4420
www.edline.net/pages/Palestine-Wheatley_School_Dist/
Palestine-Wheatley HS 200/9-12
PO Box 790 72372 870-581-2425
Randy Cannon, prin. Fax 581-4421
Palestine-Wheatley JHS 200/5-8
PO Box 790 72372 870-581-2246
Zenna Smith, prin.

**Pangburn, White, Pop. 587**
Pangburn SD 800/K-12
1100 Short St 72121 501-728-4511
Dr. Kathy Berryhill, supt. Fax 728-4514
www.pangburnschools.org
Pangburn MSHS 400/7-12
1100 Short St 72121 501-728-3513
David Rolland, prin. Fax 728-2212

**Paragould, Greene, Pop. 25,788**
Greene County Technical SD 3,200/PK-12
5413 W Kingshighway 72450 870-236-2762
Gene Weeks, supt. Fax 236-7333
www.gctsd.k12.ar.us/
Greene County Technical HS 700/10-12
4601 Linwood Dr 72450 870-215-4460
Chad Jordan, prin. Fax 239-6976
Greene County Technical JHS 500/8-9
5201 W Kingshighway 72450 870-215-4450
Michael Todd, prin. Fax 239-2148

Paragould SD 2,500/PK-12
1501 W Court St 72450 870-239-2105
Debbie Smith, supt. Fax 239-4697
paragould.k12.ar.us
Paragould HS 800/9-12
1701 W Court St 72450 870-236-7744
Jeremy Mangrum, prin. Fax 239-2934
Paragould JHS 500/7-8
1713 W Court St 72450 870-236-7744
Laurel Taylor, prin. Fax 239-0185

---

Crowleys Ridge Academy 300/PK-12
606 Academy Dr 72450 870-236-6909
Crowley's Ridge College Post-Sec.
100 College Dr 72450 870-236-6901

**Paris, Logan, Pop. 3,477**
Paris SD 1,200/PK-12
602 N 10th St 72855 844-963-3243
Wayne Fawcett, supt. Fax 208-7554
www.parisschools.org
Paris HS 300/9-12
2000 E Wood St 72855 479-963-2247
Bryan Hutson, prin. Fax 208-7564
Paris MS 400/5-8
602 N 10th St 72855 479-963-6995
Mike Nichols, prin. Fax 208-7482

**Pearcy, Garland**
Lake Hamilton SD 4,300/K-12
205 Wolf St 71964 501-767-2306
Steve Anderson, supt. Fax 767-5573
lhwolves.net
Lake Hamilton JHS 700/8-9
281 Wolf St 71964 501-767-2731
J.J. Humphries, prin. Fax 767-1711
Lake Hamilton SHS 1,000/10-12
280 Wolf St 71964 501-767-9311
Kirk Nance, prin. Fax 767-9318
New Horizon's Alternative S 100/Alt
382 Adam Brown Rd 71964 501-760-1720
Jodi Chalmers, dir. Fax 760-4857

**Pea Ridge, Benton, Pop. 4,709**
Pea Ridge SD 1,700/K-12
781 W Pickens Rd 72751 479-451-8181
Rick Neal, supt. Fax 451-8235
www.prs.k12.ar.us/
Pea Ridge HS 500/9-12
781 W Pickens Rd 72751 479-451-8182
Jon Laffoon, prin. Fax 451-0323
Pea Ridge MS 400/6-8
1391 Weston St 72751 479-451-0620
Matthew Wood, prin. Fax 451-0624

**Perryville, Perry, Pop. 1,437**
Perryville SD 1,000/K-12
614 S Fourche Ave 72126 501-889-2327
Dr. Ron Wilson, supt. Fax 889-5191
www.perryvilleschool.org
Perryville JSHS 500/7-12
325 Houston Ave 72126 501-889-2326
Kevin Campbell, prin. Fax 889-5006

**Piggott, Clay, Pop. 3,820**
Piggott SD 900/K-12
PO Box 387 72454 870-598-2572
Charnelsa Powell, supt. Fax 598-5283
www.piggottschools.net
Piggott HS 400/7-12
PO Box 387 72454 870-598-3815
Barry DeHart, prin. Fax 598-1560

**Pine Bluff, Jefferson, Pop. 48,534**
Dollarway SD 1,500/PK-12
4900 Dollarway Rd 71602 870-534-7003
Fax 534-7859
dollarway.k12.ar.us
Dollarway HS 500/9-12
4900 Dollarway Rd 71602 870-534-7003
Arnold Robertson, prin. Fax 534-1455
Morehead MS 300/6-8
2602 W Fluker Ave 71601 870-534-5243
Yolanda Prim, prin. Fax 535-1215

Pine Bluff SD 4,600/PK-12
PO Box 7678 71611 870-543-4200
Dr. Linda Watson, supt. Fax 543-4208
www.pinebluffschools.k12.ar.us/
Pine Bluff HS 900/9-12
711 W 11th Ave 71601 870-543-4300
Dr. Michael Nellums, prin. Fax 543-4302
Robey JHS 700/7-8
4101 S Olive St 71603 870-543-4290
Donald Booth, prin. Fax 850-2027

Watson Chapel SD 3,000/K-12
4100 Camden Rd 71603 870-879-0220
Danny Hazelwood, supt. Fax 879-0588
wc-web.k12.ar.us
Watson Chapel JHS 800/7-9
3900 Camden Rd 71603 870-879-4420
Henry Webb, prin. Fax 879-4426
Watson Chapel SHS 700/10-12
4000 Camden Rd 71603 870-879-3230
Leydel Willis, prin. Fax 879-1842

---

Jefferson Regional Medical Center Post-Sec.
1600 W 40th Ave 71603 870-541-7858
Ridgway Christian S 400/K-12
3201 Ridgway Rd 71603 870-879-6264
Southeast Arkansas College Post-Sec.
1900 S Hazel St 71603 870-543-5900
University of Arkansas at Pine Bluff Post-Sec.
1200 University Dr 71601 870-575-8000

**Pleasant Plains, Independence, Pop. 344**
Midland SD 500/K-12
PO Box 630 72568 501-345-8844
Dean Stanley, supt. Fax 345-2086
www.midland.k12.ar.us
Midland JSHS 200/7-12
PO Box 630 72568 501-345-2610
Donna Clark, prin. Fax 345-3355

**Pocahontas, Randolph, Pop. 6,538**
Pocahontas SD 1,900/K-12
2300 N Park St 72455 870-892-4573
Shannon Fish, supt. Fax 892-8857
www.pocahontaspsd.com
Pocahontas HS 400/10-12
2312 Stadium Dr 72455 870-892-4573
Ivy Pfeffer, prin. Fax 892-8857
Pocahontas JHS 500/7-9
2405 N Park St 72455 870-892-4573
Brent Miller, prin. Fax 892-8857

---

Black River Technical College Post-Sec.
PO Box 468 72455 870-248-4000

**Pottsville, Pope, Pop. 2,791**
Pottsville SD 1,600/K-12
7000 SR 247 72858 479-968-8101
Larry Dugger, supt. Fax 968-6339
www.pottsvilleschools.org
Pottsville HS 400/10-12
500 Apache Dr 72858 479-968-6334
Jonathan Bradley, prin. Fax 968-3442
Pottsville JHS 400/7-9
250 Apache Dr 72858 479-968-6574
Kenneth Bell, prin. Fax 498-2345

**Poyen, Grant, Pop. 289**
Poyen SD 600/PK-12
PO Box 209 72128 501-332-8884
Jerry Newton, supt. Fax 332-8886
www.poyenschool.com
Poyen JSHS 300/7-12
PO Box 209 72128 501-332-2939
Dennis Emerson, prin. Fax 332-7809

**Prairie Grove, Washington, Pop. 4,291**
Prairie Grove SD 1,800/K-12
110 School St 72753 479-846-4242
Dr. Allen Williams, supt. Fax 846-2015
pgtigers.org
Prairie Grove HS 500/9-12
500 Cole Dr 72753 479-846-4212
Ron Bond, prin. Fax 846-4207
Prairie Grove MS 600/5-8
806 N Mock St 72753 479-846-4221
Reba Holmes, prin. Fax 846-4275

**Prescott, Nevada, Pop. 3,248**
Prescott SD 1,000/K-12
762 Martin St 71857 870-887-3016
Robert Poole, supt. Fax 887-5021
www.curleywolves.org
Prescott HS 500/7-12
736 Martin St 71857 870-887-3123
Missy Walley, prin. Fax 887-3682

**Quitman, Cleburne, Pop. 754**
Quitman SD 600/PK-12
PO Box 178 72131 501-589-3156
Dennis Truxler, supt. Fax 589-3523
www.quitman.k12.ar.us
Quitman JSHS 300/7-12
PO Box 178 72131 501-589-2554
Michael Stacks, prin. Fax 589-3524

**Rector, Clay, Pop. 1,960**
Rector SD 600/K-12
PO Box 367 72461 870-595-3151
Johnny Fowler, supt. Fax 595-9067
www.rector.k12.ar.us
Rector HS 300/7-12
PO Box 367 72461 870-595-3553
Wade Williams, prin. Fax 595-3554

**Rison, Cleveland, Pop. 1,329**
Cleveland County SD 800/K-12
PO Box 600 71665 870-325-6344
Johnnie Johnson, supt. Fax 325-7094
www.rison.k12.ar.us
Rison JSHS 400/7-12
PO Box 600 71665 870-325-6241
Davy King, prin. Fax 325-6799

Woodlawn SD 600/K-12
6760 Highway 63 71665 870-357-8108
Dudley Hume, supt. Fax 357-8718
bears.k12.ar.us
Woodlawn JSHS 300/7-12
6760 Highway 63 71665 870-357-8171
Jeffery Wylie, prin. Fax 357-8022

**Rogers, Benton, Pop. 54,921**
Rogers SD 14,100/K-12
500 W Walnut St 72756 479-636-3910
Dr. Janie Darr, supt. Fax 631-3504
www.rogersschools.net/
Annex Alternative Center Alt
2922 S 1st St 72758 479-631-3690
Cindy Ford, prin. Fax 631-3612
Elmwood MS 800/6-8
1610 S 13th St 72758 479-631-3600
Bob White, prin. Fax 631-3603
Kirksey MS 900/6-8
2930 S 1st St 72758 479-631-3625
Mel Ahart, prin. Fax 631-3624
Lingle MS 700/6-8
901 N 13th St 72756 479-631-3590
Mary Elmore, prin. Fax 631-3594
Oakdale MS 700/6-8
511 N Dixieland Rd 72756 479-631-3615
Donna Charlton, prin. Fax 631-3617
Rogers Heritage HS 2,100/9-12
1114 S 5th St 72756 479-631-3579
Karen Steen, prin. Fax 631-3580
Rogers HS 2,100/9-12
2300 S Dixieland Rd 72758 479-636-2202
Charles Lee, prin. Fax 631-3554
Rogers New Technology HS 9-12
2922 S 1st St 72758 479-631-3621
Lance Arbuckle, prin.

---

Bryan University Post-Sec.
3704 W Walnut St 72756 479-899-6644
Providence Classical Christian Academy 200/K-12
4911 W Pleasant Grove Rd 72758 479-263-8861
Jason Ross M.Ed., hdmstr. Fax 439-8130

**Rose Bud, White, Pop. 462**
Rose Bud SD 800/PK-12
124 School Rd 72137 501-556-5815
Curtis Spann, supt. Fax 556-6000
rosebudschools.com
Rose Bud JSHS 400/7-12
124 School Rd 72137 501-556-5404
Danny Starkey, prin. Fax 556-6005

**Rosston, Nevada, Pop. 259**
Nevada SD 400/K-12
PO Box 50 71858 870-871-2418
Rick McAfee, supt. Fax 871-2419
www.nevadaschooldistrict.net/
Nevada JSHS 200/7-12
PO Box 50 71858 870-871-2478
Michael Odom, prin. Fax 871-2419

**Russellville, Pope, Pop. 27,404**
Russellville SD 5,100/PK-12
PO Box 928 72811 479-968-1306
Randall Williams, supt. Fax 968-6381
www.russellvilleschools.net/
Russellville HS 1,100/10-12
2203 S Knoxville Ave 72802 479-968-3151
Sheila Jacobs, prin. Fax 968-4264
Russellville JHS 800/8-9
2000 W Parkway Dr 72802 479-968-1599
Al Harpenau, prin. Fax 890-6419

Arkansas Beauty College Post-Sec.
109 N Commerce Ave 72801 479-968-3075
Arkansas Tech University Post-Sec.
1509 N Boulder Ave 72801 479-968-0389
Community Christian S 50/K-12
PO Box 1786 72811 479-968-1429
Rebecca Partain, admin. Fax 968-1436

**Saint Joe, Searcy, Pop. 132**
Ozark Mountain SD 700/K-12
250 S Highway 65 72675 870-439-2218
James Jones, supt. Fax 439-2604
www.omsd.k12.ar.us
Saint Joe JSHS 100/7-12
250 S Highway 65 72675 870-439-2213
Jess Knapp, prin. Fax 439-2604
Other Schools – See Everton, Western Grove

**Saint Paul, Madison, Pop. 113**
Huntsville SD
Supt. — See Huntsville
Saint Paul JSHS 100/7-12
PO Box 125 72760 479-677-2411
Audra Kimball, prin. Fax 677-2210

**Salem, Fulton, Pop. 1,613**
Salem SD 700/K-12
313 Highway 62 E Ste 1 72576 870-895-2516
Ken Rich, supt. Fax 895-4062
www.salemschools.net/
Salem JSHS 300/7-12
313 Highway 62 E Ste 2 72576 870-895-3293
Wayne Guiltner, prin. Fax 895-5937

**Scranton, Logan, Pop. 220**
Scranton SD 400/K-12
103 N 10th St 72863 479-938-7121
Dr. James Bridges, supt. Fax 938-7564
www.scrantonrockets.net
Scranton JSHS 200/7-12
103 N 10th St 72863 479-938-7121
Mark Siebenmorgen, prin. Fax 938-7564

**Searcy, White, Pop. 22,441**
Riverview SD 1,300/K-12
800 Raider Dr 72143 501-279-0540
Dr. Delena Gammill, supt. Fax 279-0737
riverview.k12.ar.us
Riverview HS 400/9-12
810 Raider Dr 72143 501-279-7700
George Lucas, prin. Fax 279-2848
Riverview JHS 200/7-8
820 Raider Dr 72143 501-279-7111
Stuart Hill, prin. Fax 279-7166

Searcy SD 3,700/K-12
801 N Elm St 72143 501-268-3517
Diane Barrett, supt. Fax 278-2220
www.searcyschools.org/
Ahlf JHS 600/7-8
308 W Vine Ave 72143 501-268-3158
Gene Hodges, prin. Fax 278-2212
Searcy HS 1,200/9-12
301 N Ella St 72143 501-268-8315
Claude Smith, prin. Fax 267-2249

Arkansas State University Searcy Campus Post-Sec.
PO Box 909 72145 501-207-4014
Harding Academy 700/PK-12
PO Box 10775 72149 501-279-7200
Harding University Post-Sec.
915 E Market Ave 72149 501-279-4000
Searcy Beauty College Post-Sec.
1004 S Main St 72143 501-268-6300

**Sheridan, Grant, Pop. 4,558**
Sheridan SD 4,100/K-12
400 N Rock St 72150 870-942-3135
Jerrod Williams, supt. Fax 942-2931
www.sheridanschools.org
Sheridan HS 1,200/10-12
700 W Vine St 72150 870-942-3137
Rodney Williams, prin. Fax 942-7546
Sheridan JHS 900/7-9
500 N Rock St 72150 870-942-3813
Jason Burks, prin. Fax 942-3034

**Sherwood, Pulaski, Pop. 28,899**
Pulaski County Special SD
Supt. — See Little Rock
Sylvan Hills HS 800/9-12
484 Bear Paw Rd 72120 501-833-1100
Tracy Allen, prin. Fax 833-1104
Sylvan Hills MS 800/6-8
10001 Johnson Dr 72120 501-833-1120
Jo Wilcox, prin. Fax 833-1137

Abundant Life S 300/K-12
9200 Highway 107 72120 501-835-3120
Justin Moseley, supt. Fax 835-4428

**Shirley, Van Buren, Pop. 283**
Shirley SD 400/K-12
199 School Dr 72153 501-723-8191
Betty McGruder, supt. Fax 723-4020
www.shirley.k12.ar.us/
Shirley JSHS 200/7-12
201 Blue Devil Dr 72153 501-723-8192
Randy Moore, prin. Fax 723-8114

**Siloam Springs, Benton, Pop. 14,431**
Siloam Springs SD 3,500/PK-12
PO Box 798 72761 479-524-3191
Kendall Ramey, supt. Fax 524-8002
www.siloamschools.com
Siloam Springs HS 1,200/9-12
700 N Progress Ave 72761 479-524-5134
Jason Jones, prin. Fax 524-8211
Siloam Springs MS 600/7-8
600 S Dogwood St 72761 479-524-6184
Teresa Morgan, prin. Fax 524-3228

John Brown University Post-Sec.
2000 W University St 72761 479-524-9500

**Smackover, Union, Pop. 1,823**
Smackover-Norphlet SD 800/K-12
112 E 8th St 71762 870-725-3132
Dave Wilcox, supt. Fax 725-1250
www.smackover.net
Smackover HS 400/9-12
1 Buckaroo Ln 71762 870-725-3101
Jan Henderson, prin. Fax 725-2540
Other Schools – See Norphlet

**Sparkman, Dallas, Pop. 421**
Harmony Grove SD
Supt. — See Camden
Sparkman HS 100/7-12
PO Box 37 71763 870-678-9312
Todd Lewis, prin. Fax 678-2917

**Springdale, Washington, Pop. 64,520**
Springdale SD 18,800/PK-12
PO Box 8 72765 479-750-8800
Dr. Jim Rollins, supt. Fax 750-8812
www.sdale.org
Archer Learning Center 400/Alt
500 E Meadow Ave 72764 479-750-8773
Dr. Kirk Freeman, prin. Fax 750-8778
Central JHS 900/8-9
2811 W Huntsville Ave 72762 479-750-8854
Paul Griep, prin. Fax 750-8700
George JHS 1,000/8-9
3200 Powell St 72764 479-750-8750
Don Hoover, prin. Fax 750-8756
Har-Ber HS 1,600/10-12
300 Jones Rd 72762 479-750-8777
Dr. Daniel Brackett, prin. Fax 306-4250
Lakeside JHS 8-9
3050 Hylton Rd 72764 479-750-8885
Dr. Michael Shepherd, prin. Fax 750-8701
Sonora MS 6-8
17051 E Highway 412 72764 479-750-8821
Dr. Shawna Lyons, prin. Fax 750-8823
Southwest JHS 900/8-9
1807 Princeton Ave 72762 479-750-8849
Shannon Tisher, prin. Fax 750-8704
Springdale HS 1,900/10-12
101 S Pleasant St 72764 479-750-8832
Peter Joenks, prin. Fax 750-8811

Baptist School of Nursing-NW Post-Sec.
610 E Emma Ave 72764 479-750-6200
Ecclesia College Post-Sec.
9653 Nations Dr 72762 479-248-7236
Northwest Technical Institute Post-Sec.
PO Box 2000 72765 479-751-8824
Shiloh Christian S 900/PK-12
1707 Johnson Rd 72762 479-756-1140
Ben Mayes, pres. Fax 756-7229

**Stamps, Columbia, Pop. 1,678**
Lafayette County SD
Supt. — See Lewisville
Lafayette County HS 300/7-12
1209 Alexander Ln 71860 870-533-4464
Opal Anderson, prin. Fax 533-2367

**Star City, Lincoln, Pop. 2,243**
Star City SD 1,700/K-12
400 E Arkansas Ave 71667 870-628-4237
Richard Montgomery, supt. Fax 628-4228
www.starcityschools.com
Star City HS 500/9-12
400 E Arkansas Ave 71667 870-628-4111
Mike Walker, prin. Fax 628-4165
Star City MS 400/6-8
400 E Arkansas Ave 71667 870-628-5125
Susan White, prin. Fax 628-1393

**State University, Craighead**

Arkansas State University Post-Sec.
PO Box 600 72467 870-972-2100

**Strawberry, Lawrence, Pop. 295**
Hillcrest SD 400/K-12
PO Box 50 72469 870-528-3856
Greg Crabtree, supt. Fax 528-3383
hillcrest.k12.ar.us
Hillcrest JSHS 200/7-12
PO Box 50 72469 870-528-3856
Mike Smith, prin. Fax 528-3383

**Strong, Union, Pop. 548**
Strong-Huttig SD 400/K-12
PO Box 735 71765 870-797-3040
Saul Lusk, supt. Fax 797-3012
strong.k12.ar.us
Strong HS 200/7-12
PO Box 735 71765 870-797-7322
Jeff Alphin, prin. Fax 797-2257

**Stuttgart, Arkansas, Pop. 9,196**
Stuttgart SD 1,800/K-12
2501 S Main St 72160 870-673-8701
Nathan Gills, supt. Fax 673-7337
www.stuttgartschools.org
Stuttgart HS 600/9-12
2501 S Main St 72160 870-674-1341
Donnie Boothe, prin. Fax 673-7337
Stuttgart JHS 300/7-8
2501 S Main St 72160 870-674-1368
Cedric Hawkins, prin. Fax 673-7337

Grand Prairie Evangelical Methodist S 100/K-12
PO Box 728 72160 870-830-0601
Thomas Bormann, prin. Fax 673-4718

**Subiaco, Logan, Pop. 567**

Subiaco Academy 200/7-12
405 N Subiaco Ave 72865 479-934-1005
Matt Stengel, hdmstr. Fax 934-1033

**Taylor, Columbia, Pop. 562**
Emerson-Taylor-Bradley SD
Supt. — See Emerson
Taylor HS 200/7-12
506 E Pine St 71861 870-694-2251
David Downs, prin. Fax 694-2901

**Texarkana, Miller, Pop. 29,379**
Genoa Central SD 1,100/PK-12
12472 Highway 196 71854 870-653-4343
Carl Waters, supt. Fax 653-2624
dragons1.k12.ar.us/dragons/
Cobb MS 300/5-8
11986 Highway 196 71854 870-653-2132
Deloris Coe, prin. Fax 653-6944
Genoa Central HS 300/9-12
12472 Highway 196 71854 870-653-2272
Debbie Huff, prin. Fax 653-6967

Texarkana Arkansas SD 4,300/K-12
3435 Jefferson Ave 71854 870-772-3371
Becky Kesler, supt. Fax 773-2602
www.tasd7.net
Arkansas Magnet HS 1,200/9-12
3512 Grand Ave 71854 870-774-7641
Eva Nadeau, prin. Fax 773-8408
North Heights Magnet JHS 600/7-8
3512 Grand Ave 71854 870-773-1091
Theresa Cowling, prin. Fax 772-2722
Texarkana Career & Technology Center Vo/Tech
3512 Grand Ave 71854 870-774-7641
Natasha Hampton, prin.

Trinity Christian S 300/PK-12
3107 Trinity Blvd 71854 870-779-1009

**Timbo, Stone**
Mountain View SD
Supt. — See Mountain View
Timbo S 100/K-12
23747 Highway 263 72680 870-746-4303
Jimmy Lowery, prin. Fax 746-4844

**Trumann, Poinsett, Pop. 7,174**
Trumann SD 1,300/K-12
221 N Pine Ave 72472 870-483-6444
Myra Graham, supt. Fax 483-2602
www.trumannwildcat.com
Trumann HS 400/9-12
1620 W Main St 72472 870-483-5301
Joshua Shepherd, prin. Fax 483-0227
Trumann IS 200/5-8
221 N Pine Ave 72472 870-483-5356
Bobby Benson, prin. Fax 483-2602

**Tuckerman, Jackson, Pop. 1,848**
Jackson County SD 800/PK-12
PO Box 1070 72473 870-349-2232
Chester Shannon, supt. Fax 349-2355
bulldogs.k12.ar.us/
Tuckerman HS 300/8-12
PO Box 1070 72473 870-349-2657
Michael Holland, prin. Fax 349-2294

**Umpire, Howard**
Cossatot River SD
Supt. — See Wickes
Umpire HS 50/7-12
PO Box 60 71971 870-583-2141
Carla Golden, prin. Fax 583-6364

**Valley Springs, Boone, Pop. 182**
Valley Springs SD 1,000/K-12
PO Box 640 72682 870-429-9200
Judith Green, supt. Fax 429-5551
valley.k12.ar.us
Valley Springs HS 300/9-12
PO Box 640 72682 870-429-9200
Ronnie Ruff, prin. Fax 429-8160
Valley Springs MS 300/5-8
PO Box 640 72682 870-429-9200
Tony Mincer, prin. Fax 429-8121

**Van Buren, Crawford, Pop. 22,172**
Van Buren SD 4,400/K-12
2221 E Pointer Trl 72956 479-474-7942
Dr. Harold Jeffcoat, supt. Fax 471-3146
www.vbsd.us
Butterfield Trail MS 500/6-8
310 N 11th St 72956 479-474-6838
Dr. Karen Endel, prin. Fax 471-3101
Northridge MS 200/6-8
120 Northridge Dr 72956 479-471-3126
Lonnie Mitchell, prin. Fax 471-3129
Van Buren Freshman Academy 200/9-9
821 E Pointer Trl 72956 479-471-3160
Lisa Miller, prin. Fax 471-0249

Van Buren HS 1,300/10-12
2001 E Pointer Trl 72956 479-474-6821
Eddie Tipton, prin. Fax 471-3199

**Vilonia, Faulkner, Pop. 3,760**
Vilonia SD 3,000/K-12
PO Box 160 72173 501-796-2113
David Stephens, supt. Fax 796-3134
www.viloniaschools.org
Vilonia Freshman Academy 500/9-9
1164 Main St Ste A 72173 501-796-2037
Ronnie Simmons, prin. Fax 796-4326
Vilonia MS 600/7-8
49 Eagle St 72173 501-796-2940
Lori Lombardi, prin. Fax 796-4697
Vilonia SHS 700/10-12
1164 Main St 72173 501-796-2111
Matt Sewell, prin. Fax 796-8895

**Viola, Fulton, Pop. 326**
Viola SD 400/K-12
PO Box 380 72583 870-458-2323
John May, supt. Fax 458-2214
violaschool.k12.ar.us
Viola JSHS 200/7-12
PO Box 380 72583 870-458-2213
Vicki Hurst, prin. Fax 458-4049

**Waldron, Scott, Pop. 3,541**
Waldron SD 1,600/PK-12
1560 W 6th St 72958 479-637-3179
Roy Wayman, supt. Fax 637-3177
waldron.k12.ar.us
Waldron HS 500/9-12
736 W Highway 80 72958 479-637-3405
Tammy Madden, prin. Fax 637-5624
Waldron MS 500/5-8
2075 Rice St 72958 479-637-4549
Kimberly Solomon, prin. Fax 637-3165

**Walnut Ridge, Lawrence, Pop. 4,854**
Lawrence County SD 800/K-12
508 E Free St 72476 870-886-6634
Terry Belcher, supt. Fax 886-6635
www.bobcats.k12.ar.us
Walnut Ridge JSHS 400/7-12
508 E Free St 72476 870-886-6623
Jacob Kersey, prin. Fax 819-0403

---

Williams Baptist College Post-Sec.
60 W Fulbright St 72476 870-886-6741

**Warren, Bradley, Pop. 5,957**
Warren SD 1,500/K-12
PO Box 1210 71671 870-226-8500
Marilyn Johnson, supt. Fax 226-8531
www.edline.net/pages/Warren_SD
Warren HS 400/9-12
PO Box 1210 71671 870-226-6736
Gary Jackson, prin. Fax 226-8527
Warren MS 400/6-8
PO Box 1210 71671 870-226-2484
Glenetta Burks, prin. Fax 226-8511

**Western Grove, Newton, Pop. 373**
Ozark Mountain SD
Supt. — See Saint Joe
Western Grove JSHS 100/7-12
300 School St 72685 870-429-5215
William Carter, prin. Fax 429-5276

**West Fork, Washington, Pop. 2,246**
West Fork SD 1,200/K-12
359 School Ave 72774 479-839-2231
John Karnes, supt. Fax 839-8412
www.westforkschools.org
West Fork HS 400/9-12
359 School Ave 72774 479-839-3131
John Crowder, prin. Fax 839-8412
West Fork MS 400/5-8
333 School Ave 72774 479-839-3342
Becky Ramsey, prin. Fax 839-8412

**West Helena, Phillips, Pop. 7,876**
Helena/West Helena SD
Supt. — See Helena
Central HS 600/7-12
103 School Rd 72390 870-572-6744
Earnest Simpson, prin. Fax 572-4502

---

De Soto S 300/K-12
PO Box 2807 72390 870-572-6717

**West Memphis, Crittenden, Pop. 26,012**
West Memphis SD 5,600/K-12
301 S Avalon St 72301 870-735-1915
Jon Collins, supt. Fax 732-8643
www.wmsd.net
Academies Of West Memphis Charter S 1,200/10-12
501 W Broadway St 72301 870-735-3660
Gary Jackson, prin. Fax 732-8510
East JHS 400/7-9
1151 Goodwin Ave 72301 870-735-2081
Arther Quarrels, prin. Fax 732-8583
West JHS 500/7-9
331 W Barton Ave 72301 870-735-3161
Charlie Tyler, prin. Fax 732-8566
Wonder JHS 400/7-9
1401 Madison Ave 72301 870-735-8522
Dr. Palmer Quarrels, prin. Fax 732-8584
Other Schools – See Edmondson

---

Mid-South Community College Post-Sec.
2000 W Broadway St 72301 870-733-6722
West Memphis Christian S 200/K-12
PO Box 996 72303 870-400-4000

**White Hall, Jefferson, Pop. 5,470**
White Hall SD 2,400/K-12
1020 W Holland Ave 71602 870-247-2002
Dr. Larry Smith, supt. Fax 247-3707
www.whitehallsd.org/
White Hall HS 700/9-12
700 Bulldog Dr 71602 870-247-3255
Don Stringer, prin. Fax 247-2756
White Hall MS 400/6-8
8106 Dollarway Rd 71602 870-247-2711
Douglas Dorris, prin. Fax 247-4879

**Wickes, Polk, Pop. 743**
Cossatot River SD 1,100/PK-12
130 School Dr 71973 870-385-7101
Donnie Davis, supt. Fax 385-2238
www.cossatot.us
Other Schools – See Cove, Umpire

**Wilson, Mississippi, Pop. 888**
Rivercrest SD 1,400/PK-12
22 N Jefferson St 72395 870-655-8633
Mike Smith, supt. Fax 655-8841
www.smccolts.com
Rivercrest HS 600/9-12
1700 W State Highway 14 72395 870-655-8111
Dr. Tom Bennett, prin. Fax 655-8507
Rivercrest JHS 200/7-8
1702 W State Highway 14 72395 870-655-8421
William Fortson, prin. Fax 655-9980

**Wynne, Cross, Pop. 8,285**
Wynne SD 2,800/K-12
PO Box 69 72396 870-238-5020
Carl Easley, supt. Fax 238-5011
wynne.k12.ar.us
Wynne HS 900/9-12
PO Box 69 72396 870-238-5070
Keith Watson, prin. Fax 238-5009
Wynne JHS 600/6-8
PO Box 69 72396 870-238-5040
David Stepp, prin. Fax 238-5043

**Yellville, Marion, Pop. 1,190**
Yellville-Summit SD 800/K-12
1124 N Panther Ave 72687 870-449-4061
Wes Henderson, supt. Fax 449-5003
yellvillesummitschools.com
Yellville-Summit HS 300/7-12
1124 N Panther Ave 72687 870-449-4066
David Wyatt, prin. Fax 449-4773

# CALIFORNIA

## CALIFORNIA DEPARTMENT OF EDUCATION
**1430 N St, Sacramento 95814-5901**
**Telephone 916-319-0800**
**Fax 916-319-0100**
**Website http://www.cde.ca.gov**

Superintendent of Public Instruction Tom Torlakson

## CALIFORNIA BOARD OF EDUCATION
**1430 N St, Sacramento 95814-5901**

President Dr. Michael Kirst

## COUNTY SUPERINTENDENTS OF SCHOOLS

Alameda County Office of Education
Karen Monroe, supt. 510-887-0152
313 W Winton Ave, Hayward 94544 Fax 670-4146
www.acoe.org

Alpine County Office of Education
Patrick Traynor, supt. 530-694-2230
43 Hawkside Dr Fax 694-2379
Markleeville 96120
www.alpinecoe.k12.ca.us

Amador County Office of Education
Dick Glock, supt. 209-257-5353
217 Rex Ave, Jackson 95642 Fax 257-5360
www.amadorcoe.org/

Butte County Office of Education
Tim Taylor, supt. 530-532-5650
1859 Bird St, Oroville 95965 Fax 532-5762
www.bcoe.org

Calaveras County Office of Education
Kathy Northington, supt. 209-736-4662
PO Box 760, Angels Camp 95221 Fax 736-2138
www.ccoe.k12.ca.us

Colusa County Office of Education
Michael West, supt. 530-458-0350
345 5th St Ste A, Colusa 95932 Fax 458-8054
www.ccoe.net

Contra Costa County Office of Education
Dr. Karen Sakata, supt. 925-942-3388
77 Santa Barbara Rd Fax 472-0875
Pleasant Hill 94523
www.cocoschools.org

Del Norte County Office of Education
Jeff Harris, supt. 707-464-0200
301 W Washington Blvd Fax 464-0238
Crescent City 95531
www.delnortecoe.org

El Dorado County Office of Education
Jeremy Meyers, supt. 530-622-7130
6767 Green Valley Rd Fax 621-2543
Placerville 95667
www.edcoe.org

Fresno County Office of Education
Jim Yovino, supt. 559-265-3000
1111 Van Ness Ave, Fresno 93721 Fax 265-4005
www.fcoe.org

Glenn County Office of Education
Tracey Quarne, supt. 530-934-6575
311 S Villa Ave, Willows 95988 Fax 934-6576
www.glenncoe.org

Humboldt County Office of Education
Garry Eagles Ph.D., supt. 707-445-7000
901 Myrtle Ave, Eureka 95501 Fax 445-7143
www.humboldt.k12.ca.us

Imperial County Office of Education
Jonathan Finnell, supt. 760-312-6464
1398 Sperber Rd, El Centro Fax 312-6568
www.icoe.org

Inyo County Office of Education
Dr. Terence McAteer, supt. 760-878-2426
PO Box G, Independence 93526 Fax 878-2279
www.inyo.k12.ca.us

Kern County Office of Education
Christine Frazier, supt. 661-636-4000
1300 17th St, Bakersfield 93301 Fax 636-4130
www.kern.org/

Kings County Office of Education
Tim Bowers, supt. 559-584-1441
1144 W Lacey Blvd, Hanford 93230 Fax 589-7000
www.kings.k12.ca.us

Lake County Office of Education
Brock Falkenberg, supt. 707-262-4100
1152 S Main St, Lakeport 95453 Fax 263-0197
www.lakecoe.org

Lassen County Office of Education
Patricia Gunderson, supt. 530-257-2196
472-013 Johnstonville Rd Fax 257-2518
Susanville 96130
www.lcoe.org

Los Angeles County Office of Education
Dr. Arturo Delgado, supt. 562-922-6111
9300 Imperial Hwy, Downey 90242 Fax 922-6768
www.lacoe.edu

Madera County Office of Education
Cecilia Massetti Ed.D., supt. 559-673-6051
1105 S Madera Ave, Madera 93637 Fax 673-5569
www.maderacoe.k12.ca.us

Marin County Office of Education
Mike Grant, supt. 415-472-4110
PO Box 4925, San Rafael 94913 Fax 491-6625
www.marinschools.org/

Mariposa County Office of Education
Robin Hopper, supt. 209-742-0250
PO Box 8, Mariposa 95338 Fax 966-4549
www.mariposa.k12.ca.us

Mendocino County Office of Education
Warren Galletti, supt. 707-467-5000
2240 Old River Rd, Ukiah 95482 Fax 462-0379
www.mcoe.us

Merced County Office of Education
Steven Gomes Ed.D., supt. 209-381-6600
632 W 13th St, Merced 95341 Fax 381-6767
www.mcoe.org

Modoc County Office of Education
Gary Jones, supt. 530-233-7100
139 Henderson St, Alturas 96101 Fax 233-5531
www.modoccoe.k12.ca.us

Mono County Office of Education
Stacey Adler, supt. 760-932-7311
PO Box 477, Bridgeport 93517 Fax 932-7278
www.monocoe.org

Monterey County Office of Education
Dr. Nancy Kotowski, supt. 831-755-0300
PO Box 80851, Salinas 93912 Fax 753-6473
www.monterey.k12.ca.us

Napa County Office of Education
Barbara Nemko, supt. 707-253-6800
2121 Imola Ave, Napa 94559 Fax 253-6841
www.napacoe.org

Nevada County Office of Education
Holly Hermansen, supt. 530-478-6400
112 Nevada City Hwy Fax 478-6410
Nevada City 95959
www.nevco.org/

Orange County Office of Education
Al Mijares, supt. 714-966-4000
PO Box 9050, Costa Mesa 92628 Fax 662-3570
www.ocde.us

Placer County Office of Education
Gayle Garbolino-Mojica, supt. 530-889-8020
360 Nevada St, Auburn 95603 Fax 888-1367
www.placercoe.k12.ca.us

Plumas County Office of Education
Terry Oestreich, admin. 530-283-6500
1446 E Main St, Quincy 95971 Fax 283-6530
www.pcoe.k12.ca.us

Riverside County Office of Education
Kenneth Young, supt. 951-826-6530
PO Box 868, Riverside 92502 Fax 826-6199
www.rcoe.us

Sacramento County Office of Education
David Gordon, supt. 916-228-2500
10474 Mather Blvd, Mather 95655 Fax 228-2403
www.scoe.net

San Benito County Office of Education
Lorna Gilbert, supt. 831-637-5393
460 5th St, Hollister 95023 Fax 637-0140
www.sbcoe.org

San Bernardino Co. Office of Education
Ted Alejandre, supt. 909-386-2704
601 N E St, San Bernardino 92415 Fax 386-2478
www.sbcss.k12.ca.us

San Diego County Office of Education
Randolph Ward, supt. 858-292-3500
6401 Linda Vista Rd Fax 292-3653
San Diego 92111
www.sdcoe.net

San Francisco County Office of Education
Richard Carranza, supt. 415-241-6000
555 Franklin St Fax 241-6012
San Francisco 94102
www.sfusd.edu

San Joaquin County Office of Education
Dr. James Mousalimas, supt. 209-468-4800
PO Box 213030, Stockton 95213 Fax 468-4819
www.sjcoe.org

San Luis Obispo Co. Office of Education
James Brescia, supt. 805-543-7732
3350 Education Dr Fax 541-1105
San Luis Obispo 93405
www.slocoe.org

San Mateo County Office of Education
Anne Campbell, supt. 650-802-5300
101 Twin Dolphin Dr Fax 802-5564
Redwood City 94065
www.smcoe.org

Santa Barbara County Office of Education
William Cirone, supt. 805-964-4711
PO Box 6307, Santa Barbara 93160 Fax 964-4712
www.sbceo.org

Santa Clara County Office of Education
Dr. Jon Gundry, supt. 408-453-6500
1290 Ridder Park Dr Fax 453-6601
San Jose 95131
www.sccoe.org

Santa Cruz County Office of Education
Michael Watkins, supt. 831-466-5600
400 Encinal St, Santa Cruz 95060 Fax 466-5607
www.santacruz.k12.ca.us

Shasta County Office of Education
Tom Armelino, supt. 530-225-0200
1644 Magnolia Ave Fax 225-0329
Redding 96001
www.shastacoe.org

Sierra County Office of Education
Merrill Grant, supt. 530-993-1660
PO Box 955, Loyalton 96118 Fax 993-0828
www.sierracountyofficeofeducation.org/

Siskiyou County Office of Education
Kermith Walters, dir. 530-842-8400
609 S Gold St, Yreka 96097 Fax 842-8436
www.siskiyoucoe.net/

Solano County Office of Education
Jay Speck, supt. 707-399-4400
5100 Business Center Dr Fax 863-4174
Fairfield
www.solanocoe.net/

Sonoma County Office of Education
Steven D. Herrington Ph.D., supt. 707-524-2600
5340 Skylane Blvd Fax 578-0220
Santa Rosa 95403
www.scoe.org/

Stanislaus County Office of Education
Tom Changnon, supt. 209-238-1700
1100 H St, Modesto 95354 Fax 238-4201
www.stancoe.org/

Sutter County Office of Education
Bill Cornelius, supt. 530-822-2900
970 Klamath Ln, Yuba City 95993 Fax 671-3422
www.sutter.k12.ca.us

Tehama County Department of Education
Charles Allen, supt. 530-527-5811
1135 Lincoln St, Red Bluff 96080 Fax 529-4120
www.tehamaschools.org/

Trinity County Office of Education
Bettina Blackwell, supt. 530-623-2861
PO Box 1256, Weaverville 96093 Fax 623-4489
www.tcoek12.org/

Tulare County Office of Education
Jim Vidak, supt. 559-733-6300
PO Box 5091, Visalia 93278 Fax 737-4378
www.tcoe.org/

Tuolumne County Office of Education
Marguerite Bulkin, supt. 209-536-2000
175 Fairview Ln, Sonora 95370 Fax 536-2003
www.tcsos.us

Ventura County Office of Education
Stan Mantooth, supt. 805-383-1900
5189 Verdugo Way Fax 383-1908
Camarillo 93012
www.vcoe.org

Yolo County Office of Education
Jesse Ortiz, supt. 530-668-6700
1280 Santa Anita Ct Ste 100 Fax 668-3848
Woodland 95776
www.ycoe.org

Yuba County Office of Education
Josh Harris, supt. 530-749-4900
935 14th St, Marysville 95901 Fax 741-6500
www.yuba.net/

## PUBLIC, PRIVATE AND CATHOLIC SECONDARY SCHOOLS

**Acton, Los Angeles, Pop. 7,398**
Acton-Agua Dulce USD 1,500/K-12
32248 Crown Valley Rd 93510 661-269-5999
Dr. Brent Woodard, supt. Fax 269-0849
aadusd.k12.ca.us/
High Desert MS 400/6-8
3620 Antelope Woods Rd 93510 661-269-0310
Lynn David, prin. Fax 269-9336
Vasquez HS 500/9-12
33630 Red Rover Mine Rd 93510 661-269-0410
Tyrone Devoe, prin. Fax 269-5325

**Adelanto, San Bernardino, Pop. 30,727**
Adelanto ESD 8,900/K-12
PO Box 70 92301 760-246-8691
Dr. Edwin Gomez, supt. Fax 246-8259
www.aesd.net
Columbia International Sci/Math/Tech S 600/7-8
PO Box 70 92301 760-530-1950
Mike McGirr, prin. Fax 530-1953
Other Schools – See Victorville

**Agoura Hills, Los Angeles, Pop. 19,692**
Las Virgenes USD
Supt. — See Calabasas
Agoura HS 2,200/9-12
28545 Driver Ave 91301 818-889-1262
Brian Mercer, prin. Fax 597-0816
Indian Hills Continuation HS - West 50/Alt
28545 Driver Ave 91301 818-889-1262
Brian Mercer, prin. Fax 597-0816
Lindero Canyon MS 1,000/6-8
5844 Larboard Ln 91301 818-889-2134
Dr. Abbe Irshay, prin. Fax 889-9432

**Alameda, Alameda, Pop. 69,145**
Alameda City USD 10,100/PK-12
2060 Challenger Dr 94501 510-337-7000
Barbara Adams Ed.D., supt. Fax 522-6926
www.alameda.k12.ca.us
Alameda HS 1,800/9-12
2201 Encinal Ave 94501 510-337-7022
Robert Ithurburn, prin. Fax 521-4740
Alameda Science & Technical Institute 200/9-12
2060 Challenger Dr 94501 510-337-7059
Tracy Corbally, dean Fax 337-7163
Encinal JSHS 1,100/6-12
210 Central Ave 94501 510-748-4023
Kirsten Zazo, prin. Fax 521-4956
Island Continuation HS 200/Alt
500 Pacific Ave 94501 510-748-4024
Ben Washofsky, prin. Fax 769-7417
Lincoln MS 1,000/6-8
1250 Fernside Blvd 94501 510-748-4018
Michael Hans, prin. Fax 523-6217
Wood MS 600/6-8
420 Grand St 94501 510-748-4015
Cammie Harris, prin. Fax 523-8829
Alameda Adult S Adult
500 Pacific Ave 94501 510-522-3858
Joy Chua, prin. Fax 522-0846

Regional Occupational Center & Program
Supt. — None
East Bay ROP Vo/Tech
1900 3rd St Rm 23 94501 510-879-3037
Brigitte Marshall, dir.

---

Alameda Beauty College Post-Sec.
2318 Central Ave 94501 510-523-1050
Argosy University San Francisco Campus Post-Sec.
1005 Atlantic Ave 94501 510-217-4700
California Crosspoint HS 200/9-12
1501 Harbor Bay Pkwy 94502 510-995-5333
Robin Hom, supt. Fax 995-5335
College of Alameda Post-Sec.
555 Ralph Appezzato Mem Pky 94501
510-522-7221
St. Joseph Notre Dame HS 400/9-12
1011 Chestnut St 94501 510-523-1526
Milt Werner, prin. Fax 523-2181

**Alamo, Contra Costa, Pop. 14,161**
San Ramon Valley USD
Supt. — See Danville
Stone Valley MS 700/6-8
3001 Miranda Ave 94507 925-855-5800
Jon Campopiano, prin. Fax 838-5680

**Albany, Alameda, Pop. 17,446**
Albany City USD 3,800/PK-12
1051 Monroe St 94706 510-558-3750
Valerie Williams, supt. Fax 559-6560
www.ausdk12.org
Albany HS 1,200/9-12
603 Key Route Blvd 94706 510-558-2500
Theodore Barone, prin. Fax 559-6584
Albany MS 900/6-8
1259 Brighton Ave 94706 510-558-3600
Deborah Brill, prin. Fax 559-6547
MacGregor Continuation HS 50/Alt
603 Key Route Blvd 94706 510-559-6570
Sabrina Greiten, prin. Fax 559-6572

---

Tilden Preparatory S 100/6-12
1231 Solano Ave 94706 510-525-5506
Dr. Shary Nunan, dir. Fax 525-5508

**Alhambra, Los Angeles, Pop. 81,736**
Alhambra USD 18,100/K-12
1515 W Mission Rd 91803 626-943-3000
Laura Tellez-Gagliano Ed.D., supt. Fax 943-8050
www.ausd.us
Alhambra HS 2,900/9-12
101 S 2nd St 91801 626-943-6910
Duane Russell, prin. Fax 308-2344
Century HS 200/Alt
20 S Marengo Ave 91801 626-943-6681
Phuong Nguyen, prin. Fax 308-2299
Independence HS Alt
20 S Marengo Ave 91801 626-943-6681
Phuong Nguyen, prin. Fax 308-2299
Keppel HS 2,500/9-12
501 E Hellman Ave 91801 626-943-6710
Jacinth Cisneros, prin. Fax 572-2217
Other Schools – See San Gabriel

---

Alhambra Beauty College Post-Sec.
200 W Main St 91801 626-282-6433
Alhambra Medical University Post-Sec.
25 S Raymond Ave Ste 201 91801 626-289-7719
Alliant International University Post-Sec.
1000 S Fremont Ave Unit 5 91803 626-270-3300
Everest College Post-Sec.
2215 W Mission Rd 91803 626-979-4940
Platt College Alhambra Post-Sec.
1000 S Fremont Ave Ste A9W 91803 626-300-5444
Ramona Convent Secondary S 300/9-12
1701 W Ramona Rd 91803 626-282-4151
Mary Mansell, prin. Fax 281-0797

**Aliso Viejo, Orange, Pop. 45,578**
Capistrano USD
Supt. — See San Juan Capistrano
Aliso Niguel HS 3,000/9-12
28000 Wolverine Way 92656 949-831-5590
Deni Christensen, prin. Fax 448-9854
Aliso Viejo MS 1,100/6-8
111 Park Ave 92656 949-831-2622
Cynthia Steinert, prin. Fax 643-2784
Avila MS 1,200/6-8
26278 Wood Canyon Dr 92656 949-362-0348
Josh Wellikson, prin. Fax 362-9076

---

Soka University of America Post-Sec.
1 University Dr 92656 949-480-4000

**Alpaugh, Tulare, Pop. 1,021**
Alpaugh USD 600/K-12
PO Box 9 93201 559-949-8413
Dr. Robert Hudson, supt. Fax 949-8173
www.tcoe.org/districts/alpaugh.shtm
Alpaugh JSHS 100/7-12
PO Box 9 93201 559-949-8413
Nancy Ruble, prin. Fax 949-8173
Tule Continuation HS 50/Alt
PO Box 9 93201 559-949-8644
Dr. Robert Hudson, dir. Fax 949-8173

**Alpine, San Diego, Pop. 13,892**
Alpine UNESD 2,000/PK-8
1323 Administration Way 91901 619-445-3236
Bruce Cochrane, supt. Fax 445-7045
www.alpineschools.net/
MacQueen MS 700/6-8
2001 Tavern Rd 91901 619-445-3245
Jon McEvoy, prin. Fax 445-6503

**Altadena, Los Angeles, Pop. 40,865**
Pasadena USD
Supt. — See Pasadena
Eliot MS 700/6-8
2184 Lake Ave 91001 626-396-5680
Lori Touloumian, prin. Fax 794-7238

---

Pasadena Waldorf S 200/PK-12
209 E Mariposa St 91001 626-794-9564
Douglas Garrett, admin. Fax 794-4704
Renaissance Academy 100/K-12
536 E Mendocino St 91001 626-765-9358
Sandra Staffer, dir. Fax 765-9360

**Alta Loma, San Bernardino**
Alta Loma ESD 6,300/K-8
9390 Baseline Rd 91701 909-484-5151
James Moore, supt. Fax 484-5155
www.alsd.k12.ca.us
Alta Loma JHS 800/7-8
9000 Lemon Ave 91701 909-484-5100
Susanne Melton, prin. Fax 484-5105
Vineyard JHS 800/7-8
6440 Mayberry Ave 91737 909-484-5120
Loren Thompson, prin. Fax 484-5125

Chaffey JUNHSD
Supt. — See Ontario
Alta Loma HS 2,700/9-12
8880 Baseline Rd 91701 909-989-5511
Jim Cronin, prin. Fax 987-8321

**Altaville, Calaveras**
Bret Harte UNHSD
Supt. — See Angels Camp
Vallecito Continuation HS 50/Alt
364 Murphys Grade Rd 95221 209-736-8327
Tracie Baughn, prin. Fax 736-0598

**Alturas, Modoc, Pop. 2,746**
Modoc JUSD 800/K-12
906 W 4th St 96101 530-233-7201
Tom O'Malley, supt. Fax 233-4362
www.modoc.k12.ca.us
High Desert Community Day S 50/Alt
802 N East St 96101 530-233-7201
Tom O'Malley, prin. Fax 233-5158
Modoc HS 300/9-12
900 N Main St 96101 530-233-7201
Tom O'Malley, prin. Fax 233-7306
Modoc MS 200/6-8
906 W 4th St 96101 530-233-7201
Noelle Knight, prin. Fax 233-7503
Warner Continuation HS 50/Alt
802 N East St 96101 530-233-7201
Tom O'Malley, prin. Fax 233-5158

Regional Occupational Center & Program
Supt. — None
Modoc County ROP Vo/Tech
139 Henderson St 96101 530-233-7102
Marian Hall, dir.

**American Canyon, Napa, Pop. 18,364**
Napa Valley USD
Supt. — See Napa
American Canyon HS 1,000/9-12
3000 Newell Dr 94503 707-267-2710
Damon Wright, prin. Fax 644-1139
American Canyon MS 1,000/6-8
300 Benton Way 94503 707-259-8592
Dan Scudero, prin. Fax 259-8800
Legacy HS, 3000 Newell Dr 94503 Alt
Damon Wright, prin. 707-265-2710

**Anaheim, Orange, Pop. 327,991**
Anaheim UNHSD 32,700/7-12
501 N Crescent Way 92801 714-999-3511
Michael B. Matsuda, supt. Fax 535-1706
www.auhsd.us
Anaheim HS 3,300/9-12
811 W Lincoln Ave 92805 714-999-3717
Dr. Anna Corral, prin. Fax 772-6537
Ball JHS 1,200/7-8
1500 W Ball Rd 92802 714-999-3663
Karen Dabney-Lieras, prin. Fax 563-9214
Brookhurst JHS 1,200/7-8
601 N Brookhurst St 92801 714-999-3613
Sam Joo, prin. Fax 999-1764
Dale JHS 1,300/7-8
900 S Dale Ave 92804 714-220-4210
Daphne Hammer, prin. Fax 220-4076
Gilbert HS 600/Alt
1800 W Ball Rd 92804 714-999-3738
Jei Garlitos, coord. Fax 999-5651
Katella HS 2,800/9-12
2200 E Wagner Ave 92806 714-999-3621
Dr. Ben Carpenter, prin. Fax 535-3991
Loara HS 2,700/9-12
1765 W Cerritos Ave 92804 714-999-3677
John Briquelet, prin. Fax 999-3703
Magnolia HS 1,900/9-12
2450 W Ball Rd 92804 714-220-4221
Robert Cunard Ed.D., prin. Fax 220-4233
Orangeview JHS 1,000/7-8
3715 W Orange Ave 92804 714-220-4205
Robert Saldivar, prin. Fax 220-3023
Polaris HS 200/Alt
1800 W Ball Rd 92804 714-999-3738
Jei Garlitos, coord. Fax 999-5651
Savanna HS 2,300/9-12
301 N Gilbert St 92801 714-220-4262
Carlos Hernandez, prin. Fax 995-2544
South JHS 1,600/7-8
2320 E South St 92806 714-999-3667
Benjamin Wolf Ed.D., prin. Fax 999-3721
Sycamore JHS 1,500/7-8
1801 E Sycamore St 92805 714-999-3616
Gary Brown, prin. Fax 776-3879
Western HS 2,300/9-12
501 S Western Ave 92804 714-220-4040
Joe Carmona, prin. Fax 220-4027
Other Schools – See Cypress, La Palma

Orange USD
Supt. — See Orange
Canyon HS 2,400/9-12
220 S Imperial Hwy 92807 714-532-8000
James Abercrombie, prin. Fax 921-0278

Placentia-Yorba Linda USD
Supt. — See Placentia
Esperanza HS 1,900/9-12
1830 N Kellogg Dr 92807 714-985-7540
Ken Fox, prin. Fax 693-7527

Regional Occupational Center & Program
Supt. — None
North Orange County ROP Vo/Tech
385 N Muller St 92801 714-502-5800
Dr. Michael Worley, supt. Fax 766-3880

---

Acaciawood S 100/1-12
2530 W La Palma Ave 92801 714-995-1800
Jim Miller, prin. Fax 876-0723
American Career College - Orange County Post-Sec.
1200 N Magnolia Ave 92801 714-763-9066
Anaheim University Post-Sec.
1240 S State College # 110 92806 714-772-3330
Bethesda University of California Post-Sec.
730 N Euclid St 92801 714-517-1945
Bristol University Post-Sec.
2390 E Orangewood Ave # 485 92806 714-542-8086
Brownson Technical School Post-Sec.
1110 S Technology Cir Ste D 92805 714-774-9443
California Career School Post-Sec.
1100 S Technology Cir 92805 714-635-6585
CA University of Management and Sciences Post-Sec.
721 N Euclid St 92801 714-533-3946
Connelly HS 200/9-12
2323 W Broadway 92804 714-776-1717
Sr. Francine Gunther, head sch Fax 776-2534
Evangelia University Post-Sec.
2660 W Woodland Dr Ste 200 92801 714-527-0691
Everest College Post-Sec.
511 N Brookhurst St Ste 300 92801 714-953-6500
Fairmont Preparatory Academy 700/9-12
2200 W Sequoia Ave 92801 714-999-5055
Robert Mendoza, hdmstr. Fax 999-0150

Integrity Christian S 100/1-12
4905 E La Palma Ave 92807 714-693-2022
Orange County Christian S 300/PK-12
641 S Western Ave 92804 714-821-6227
David Lewis, admin. Fax 952-8823
Saints of Glory S 50/K-12
1210 W Park Ave 92801 714-875-9387
I. Tsuruoka, pres. Fax 817-0612
Servite HS 1,000/9-12
1952 W La Palma Ave 92801 714-774-7575
Michael Brennan, prin. Fax 774-1404
South Baylo University Post-Sec.
1126 N Brookhurst St 92801 714-533-1495
Southern California Institute of Tech Post-Sec.
525 N Muller St 92801 714-300-0300
West Coast University Post-Sec.
1477 S Manchester Ave 92802 714-782-1700
Westwood College - Anaheim Post-Sec.
1551 S Douglass Rd 92806 714-704-2720

**Anderson, Shasta, Pop. 9,521**
Anderson UNHSD 2,000/9-12
1469 Ferry St 96007 530-378-0568
Tim Azevedo, supt. Fax 378-0834
www.auhsd.net
Anderson HS 600/9-12
1471 Ferry St 96007 530-365-2741
Brian Parker, prin. Fax 365-5446
North Valley HS 100/Alt
20083 Olinda Rd 96007 530-365-6054
Brandt Shriner, prin. Fax 378-1264
Oakview HS 100/Alt
20083 Olinda Rd 96007 530-378-6895
Brandt Shriner, prin. Fax 365-0801
Anderson Adult Education Adult
5250 W Anderson Dr 96007 530-365-3334
Brandt Shriner, prin. Fax 365-8440
Other Schools – See Cottonwood

Cascade UNESD 800/K-8
1645 Mill St 96007 530-378-7000
Baljinder Dhillon, supt. Fax 378-7001
www.cuesd.com/
Anderson MS 400/5-8
1646 Ferry St 96007 530-378-7060
Karin Cox, prin. Fax 378-7061

Happy Valley UNESD 500/K-8
17480 Palm Ave 96007 530-357-2134
Janet Tufts, supt. Fax 357-4143
www.hvesd.org
Happy Valley MS 200/5-8
17480 Palm Ave 96007 530-357-2111
Janet Tufts, prin. Fax 357-4193

**Angels Camp, Calaveras, Pop. 2,997**
Bret Harte UNHSD 800/9-12
PO Box 7000 95221 209-736-8340
Michael Chimente, supt. Fax 736-8367
www.bhuhsd.k12.ca.us
Bret Harte Union HS 700/9-12
364 Murphys Grade Rd 95222 209-736-2507
Tracie Baughn, prin. Fax 736-8383
Vierra HS 50/Alt
364 Murphys Grade Rd 95222 209-736-8327
Tracie Baughn, prin. Fax 736-0598
Other Schools – See Altaville

Calaveras County Office of Education 500/
PO Box 760 95221 209-736-4662
Kathy Northington, supt. Fax 736-2138
www.ccoe.k12.ca.us
Other Schools – See San Andreas

**Angwin, Napa, Pop. 2,912**

---

Pacific Union College Post-Sec.
1 Angwin Ave 94508 707-965-6311
Pacific Union College Prep S 100/9-12
1 Angwin Ave 94508 707-200-2648
Peter Fackenthall, prin. Fax 965-6689

**Antelope, Sacramento, Pop. 42,966**
Center JUSD 4,800/K-12
8408 Watt Ave 95843 916-338-6330
Scott Loehr, supt. Fax 338-6411
www.centerusd.k12.ca.us
Center HS 1,300/9-12
3111 Center Court Ln 95843 916-338-6420
Mike Jordan, prin. Fax 338-6370
McClellan Continuation HS 100/Alt
8725 Watt Ave 95843 916-338-6440
David French, prin. Fax 338-6535
Center Adult S Adult
3401 Scotland Dr 95843 916-338-6387
Fax 338-6386

Other Schools – See Roseville

Dry Creek JESD
Supt. — See Roseville
Antelope Crossing MS 900/6-8
9200 Palmerson Dr 95843 916-745-2100
Tracy Robinson, prin. Fax 745-2135

Roseville JUNHSD
Supt. — See Roseville
Antelope HS 1,800/9-12
7801 Titan Dr 95843 916-726-1400
John Becker, prin. Fax 726-0700

**Antioch, Contra Costa, Pop. 96,748**
Antioch USD 18,200/K-12
510 G St 94509 925-779-7500
Stephanie Anello Ed.D., supt. Fax 779-7509
www.antioch.k12.ca.us
Antioch HS 2,000/9-12
700 W 18th St 94509 925-779-7550
Louie Rocha, prin. Fax 779-7567
Antioch MS 800/6-8
1500 D St 94509 925-779-7400
Andy Cannon, prin. Fax 779-7414
Bidwell HS 200/Alt
800 Gary Ave 94509 925-779-7520
Carol Lowart, prin. Fax 779-7521
Black Diamond MS 800/6-8
4730 Sterling Hill Dr 94531 925-776-5500
Phyllis James, prin. Fax 779-2600
Dallas Ranch MS 1,400/6-8
1401 Mount Hamilton Dr 94531 925-779-7485
Ed Dacus, prin. Fax 706-1933
Deer Valley HS 2,700/9-12
4700 Lone Tree Way 94531 925-776-5555
Kenneth Gardner, prin. Fax 754-8094
Dozier-Libbey Medical HS 600/9-12
4900 Sand Creek Rd 94531 925-779-7540
Scott Bergerhouse, prin. Fax 779-7542
Live Oak Continuation HS 200/Alt
1708 F St 94509 925-779-7440
Mabel Rucker, prin. Fax 779-7441
Park MS 900/6-8
1 Spartan Way 94509 925-779-7420
John Jimno, prin. Fax 779-7421
Prospects HS 400/Alt
820 W 2nd St 94509 925-779-7490
Brian Clark, prin. Fax 779-7491
Antioch Adult S Adult
820 W 2nd St 94509 925-779-7490
Brian Clark, prin. Fax 775-7491

---

Cornerstone Christian S 500/PK-12
1745 E 18th St 94509 925-779-2010
Logan Heyer, prin. Fax 754-0769

**Anza, Riverside, Pop. 2,927**
Hemet USD
Supt. — See Hemet
Hamilton HS 400/9-12
57430 Mitchell Rd 92539 951-763-1865
Dave Farkas, prin. Fax 763-5420

**Apple Valley, San Bernardino, Pop. 66,794**
Apple Valley USD 13,900/PK-12
12555 Navajo Rd 92308 760-247-8001
Thomas Hoegerman, supt. Fax 247-4103
www.avusd.org
Apple Valley HS 2,100/9-12
11837 Navajo Rd 92308 760-247-7206
Dustin Conrad, prin. Fax 247-2092
Granite Hills HS 1,900/9-12
22900 Esaws Rd 92307 760-961-2290
Charles McCall, prin. Fax 961-8755

---

Apple Valley Christian S 200/PK-12
22230 Ottawa Rd 92308 760-995-3516
John Richart, admin. Fax 995-3524

**Aptos, Santa Cruz, Pop. 6,003**
Pajaro Valley USD
Supt. — See Watsonville
Aptos HS 1,400/9-12
100 Mariner Way 95003 831-688-6565
Casey O'Brien, prin. Fax 688-6430
Aptos JHS 700/7-8
1001 Huntington Dr 95003 831-688-3234
Rich Moran, prin. Fax 728-8139

---

Cabrillo College Post-Sec.
6500 Soquel Dr 95003 831-479-6100

**Arbuckle, Colusa, Pop. 2,990**
Pierce JUSD 1,300/K-12
PO Box 239 95912 530-476-2892
Carol Geyer, supt. Fax 476-2289
www.pierce.k12.ca.us
Arbuckle Alternative HS 50/Alt
960 Wildwood Rd 95912 530-476-2173
George Griffin, prin. Fax 476-2674
Johnson JHS 300/6-8
938 Wildwood Rd 95912 530-476-3261
Blake Kitchen, prin. Fax 476-2017
Pierce HS 400/9-12
960 Wildwood Rd 95912 530-476-2277
George Griffin, prin. Fax 476-3285

**Arcadia, Los Angeles, Pop. 55,191**
Arcadia USD 9,700/K-12
150 S 3rd Ave 91006 626-821-8300
David Vannasdall, supt. Fax 821-8647
site.ausd.net
Arcadia HS 3,700/9-12
180 Campus Dr 91007 626-821-8370
Dr. Brent Forsee, prin. Fax 821-1712
Dana MS 800/6-8
1401 S 1st Ave 91006 626-821-8361
Dr. Daniel Hacking, prin. Fax 447-1965
First Avenue MS 800/6-8
301 S 1st Ave 91006 626-821-8362
Tom Bruce, prin. Fax 446-1660
Foothills MS 800/6-8
171 E Sycamore Ave 91006 626-821-8363
Ben Acker, prin. Fax 303-7983
Rancho Learning Center 50/Alt
150 S 3rd Ave 91006 626-821-8371
Laurie McQuaid, admin. Fax 574-3806

---

Arroyo Pacific Academy 100/9-12
41 W Santa Clara St 91007 626-294-0661
Rio Hondo Preparatory S 200/6-12
PO Box 662080 91066 626-444-9531
Leslie Orsburn, prin. Fax 442-1113

**Arcata, Humboldt, Pop. 16,233**
Arcata ESD 900/K-8
1435 Buttermilk Ln 95521 707-822-0351
Barbara Short Ed.D., supt. Fax 822-6589
asd.humboldt.k12.ca.us/pages/Arcata_Elementary_District
Sunny Brae MS 200/6-8
1430 Buttermilk Ln 95521 707-822-5988
Lynda Yeoman, prin. Fax 822-7002

Northern Humboldt UNHSD
Supt. — See Mc Kinleyville
Arcata HS 800/9-12
1720 M St 95521 707-825-2400
Dave Navarre, prin. Fax 825-2407
Pacific Coast HS 50/Alt
1720 M St 95521 707-825-2443
Jon Larson, prin. Fax 825-2130

---

Humboldt State University Post-Sec.
1 Harpst St 95521 707-826-3011

**Arleta, See Los Angeles**
Los Angeles USD
Supt. — See Los Angeles
Arleta HS 1,700/9-12
14200 Van Nuys Blvd 91331 818-686-4100
Sandra Gephart, prin. Fax 890-1040

**Armona, Kings, Pop. 4,080**
Armona UNESD 1,200/PK-12
PO Box 368 93202 559-583-5000
Dr. Xavier Pena, supt. Fax 583-5004
www.auesd.com
Parkview MS 400/5-8
PO Box 368 93202 559-583-5020
Ernest Flores, prin. Fax 583-5030

---

Armona Union Academy 100/K-12
PO Box 397 93202 559-582-4468
Erik Borges, prin. Fax 582-6609

**Arroyo Grande, San Luis Obispo, Pop. 16,717**
Lucia Mar USD 10,600/K-12
602 Orchard Ave 93420 805-474-3000
Dr. Raynee Daley, supt. Fax 481-1398
www.lmusd.org
Arroyo Grande HS 2,200/9-12
495 Valley Rd 93420 805-474-3200
Conan Bowers, prin. Fax 473-4222
Lopez HS 100/Alt
1055 Mesa View Dr 93420 805-474-3750
Charlissa Skinner, prin. Fax 473-5518
Mesa MS 500/7-8
2555 S Halcyon Rd 93420 805-474-3400
Brett Gimlin, prin. Fax 473-4396
Paulding MS 700/7-8
600 Crown Hill St 93420 805-474-3500
Edward Arrigoni, prin. Fax 473-5525
Other Schools – See Nipomo, Pismo Beach

Regional Occupational Center & Program
Supt. — None
Santa Lucia ROP Vo/Tech
602 Orchard St 93420 805-474-3000
James Souza, dir. Fax 473-5593

---

Valley View Adventist Academy 100/K-10
230 Vernon St 93420 805-489-2687
Kris Phillips, prin. Fax 489-2704

**Artesia, Los Angeles, Pop. 16,099**
ABC USD
Supt. — See Cerritos
Ross MS 700/7-8
17707 Elaine Ave 90701 562-229-7785
Ricardo Brown, prin. Fax 402-6145

---

Angeles Institute Post-Sec.
11688 South St Ste 205 90701 562-531-4100

**Arvin, Kern, Pop. 19,155**
Arvin UNSD 3,000/PK-8
737 Bear Mountain Blvd 93203 661-854-6500
Michelle McLean Ed.D., supt. Fax 854-2362
www.arvinschools.com
Haven Drive MS 700/7-8
737 Bear Mountain Blvd 93203 661-854-6540
Aurora Moran Ed.D., prin. Fax 854-1440

Kern UNHSD
Supt. — See Bakersfield
Arvin HS 2,500/9-12
900 Varsity Rd 93203 661-854-5561
Carlos Sardo, prin. Fax 854-5943

**Atascadero, San Luis Obispo, Pop. 27,543**
Atascadero USD 4,900/K-12
5601 West Mall 93422 805-462-4200
Thomas Butler, supt. Fax 462-4421
www.atasusd.org/
Atascadero Fine Arts Academy 200/4-8
6100 Olmeda Ave 93422 805-460-2500
Kibbe Rubin, prin. Fax 460-2522
Atascadero HS 1,500/9-12
1 High School Hill Rd 93422 805-462-4300
Bill Neely, prin. Fax 462-4387
Atascadero JHS 600/6-8
6501 Lewis Ave 93422 805-462-4360
Jessica Lloyd, prin. Fax 462-4373
Del Rio Continuation HS 100/Alt
5601 West Mall 93422 805-462-4350
Chris Balogh, prin. Fax 462-0837
West Mall Alternative HS 50/Alt
5601 West Mall 93422 805-462-4238
Chris Balogh, prin. Fax 462-0837

---

Laurus College Post-Sec.
8693 El Camino Real 93422 805-267-1690

North County Christian S 200/PK-12
PO Box 6017 93423 805-466-4457
Danielle Boldt, admin. Fax 466-7948

**Atherton, San Mateo, Pop. 6,660**
Menlo Park City ESD 2,700/K-8
181 Encinal Ave 94027 650-321-7140
Maurice Ghysels Ed.D., supt. Fax 321-7184
www.mpcsd.org
Other Schools – See Menlo Park

Sequoia UNHSD
Supt. — See Redwood City
Menlo-Atherton HS 2,000/9-12
555 Middlefield Rd 94027 650-322-5311
Simone Kennel, prin. Fax 323-1411

---

Menlo College Post-Sec.
1000 El Camino Real 94027 650-543-3753
Menlo S 800/6-12
50 Valparaiso Ave 94027 650-330-2000
Than Healy, head sch Fax 330-2002
Sacred Heart Prep S 600/9-12
150 Valparaiso Ave 94027 650-322-1866
Dr. James Everitt, prin. Fax 322-7151

**Atwater, Merced, Pop. 27,459**
Atwater ESD 4,600/K-8
1401 Broadway Ave 95301 209-357-6100
Dr. Sandra Schiber, supt. Fax 357-6163
www.aesd.edu
Atwater Senior Academy Alt
1800 Juniper Ave 95301 209-357-6515
Aaron Delworth, prin.
Mitchell Senior ES 800/7-8
1753 5th St 95301 209-357-6124
Aaron Delworth, prin. Fax 357-6506

Merced County Office of Education
Supt. — See Merced
Valley Atwater Community Day S 100/Alt
1800 Matthews Ave 95301 209-381-4550
Carrie Harkreader, prin. Fax 385-5380

Merced UNHSD 10,300/9-12
3430 A St 95301 209-385-6413
Fax 385-6442
muhsd.k12.ca.us
Atwater HS 1,800/9-12
PO Box 835 95301 209-357-6000
Torrin Johnson, prin. Fax 357-6067
Buhach Colony HS 1,800/9-12
PO Box 753 95301 209-357-6600
Steve Hobbs, prin. Fax 357-6602
Other Schools – See Livingston, Merced

---

Sierra Academy of Aeronautics Post-Sec.
3515 Hardstand Ave Ste B 95301 209-722-7522

**Auburn, Placer, Pop. 12,869**
Placer UNHSD 4,400/9-12
13000 New Airport Rd 95603 530-886-4400
George Sziraki, supt. Fax 886-4439
sites.google.com/a/puhsd.k12.ca.us/puhsd-us/
Chana Continuation HS 200/Alt
3775 Richardson Dr 95602 530-885-8401
Stan Parker, prin. Fax 885-1657
Maidu HS 100/Alt
3775 Richardson Dr 95602 530-885-8401
Stanton Parker, prin. Fax 885-1657
Placer HS 1,300/9-12
275 Orange St 95603 530-885-4581
Peter Efstathiu, prin. Fax 823-5770
Placer S for Adults Adult
390 Finley St 95603 530-885-8585
Bill Bettencourt, prin. Fax 823-1406
Other Schools – See Colfax, Foresthill, Loomis

Regional Occupational Center & Program
Supt. — None
Forty-Niner ROP Vo/Tech
360 Nevada St 95603 530-889-5940
Ward Andrus, dir. Fax 887-1704

---

Forest Lake Christian S 400/K-12
12515 Combie Rd 95602 530-269-1535
Julie Moskus, dir. Fax 269-1541
Pine Hills Adventist Academy 100/K-12
13500 Richards Ln 95603 530-885-9447
Victor Anderson, prin. Fax 885-5237

**Avalon, Los Angeles, Pop. 3,671**
Long Beach USD
Supt. — See Long Beach
Avalon S 600/K-12
PO Box 557 90704 310-510-0790
Angelica Gonzalez, prin. Fax 510-2986

**Avenal, Kings, Pop. 15,241**
Reef-Sunset USD 2,600/PK-12
205 N Park Ave 93204 559-386-9083
Dr. David East, supt. Fax 386-5303
www.rsusd.net
Avenal HS 600/9-12
601 E Mariposa St 93204 559-386-5253
Juan Ruiz, prin. Fax 386-9413
Reef-Sunset MS 300/7-8
608 N 1st Ave 93204 559-386-4128
Fred Guerrero, prin. Fax 386-4918
Reef Sunset Sec Community Day S 50/Alt
205 N Park Ave 93204 559-386-0460
Juan Ruiz, prin. Fax 386-5303
Sunrise Continuation HS 50/Alt
209 N Park Ave 93204 559-386-4162
Juan Ruiz, prin. Fax 386-4937
Avenal Adult S Adult
205 N Park Ave 93204 559-386-9083
Susan VanDerMolen, prin. Fax 386-1752
Other Schools – See Kettleman City

**Avery, Calaveras, Pop. 622**
Vallecito UNSD 700/PK-8
PO Box 329 95224 209-795-8500
Don Ogden, supt. Fax 795-8005
vallecito-ca.schoolloop.com
Avery MS 200/6-8
PO Box 329 95224 209-795-8520
Jared Hungerford, prin. Fax 795-8539

**Azusa, Los Angeles, Pop. 45,586**
Azusa USD 10,000/PK-12
PO Box 500 91702 626-967-6211
Linda Kaminski, supt. Fax 858-6137
www.azusa.org
Azusa HS 1,300/9-12
PO Box 500 91702 626-815-3400
Ramiro Rubalcaba, prin. Fax 815-3430
Center MS 700/6-8
PO Box 500 91702 626-815-5184
Zepure Hacopian, prin. Fax 815-2601
Foothill MS 700/6-8
PO Box 500 91702 626-815-6600
Sam Perdomo, prin. Fax 815-1027
Slauson MS 900/6-8
PO Box 500 91702 626-815-5144
Dayna Mitchell, prin. Fax 815-5147
Other Schools – See Covina, Glendora

---

Azusa Pacific University Post-Sec.
PO Box 7000 91702 626-969-3434

**Baker, San Bernardino, Pop. 711**
Baker Valley USD 200/K-12
PO Box 460 92309 760-733-4567
Ronda Tremblay, supt. Fax 733-4605
www.baker.k12.ca.us
Baker HS 100/9-12
PO Box 460 92309 760-733-4567
Ronda Tremblay, supt. Fax 733-4605
Baker JHS 50/6-8
PO Box 460 92309 760-733-4567
Ronda Tremblay, supt. Fax 733-4605
Baker Valley Adult S Adult
PO Box 460 92309 760-733-4567
Ronda Tremblay, supt. Fax 733-4605

**Bakersfield, Kern, Pop. 338,954**
Bakersfield CSD 28,300/PK-8
1300 Baker St 93305 661-631-4600
Robert Arios Ed.D., supt. Fax 631-4623
www.bcsd.com
Cato MS, 4115 Vineland Rd 93306 6-8
Mike Havens, prin. 661-631-5245
Chipman JHS 900/7-8
2905 Eissler St 93306 661-631-5210
Russell Taylor, prin. Fax 631-3229
Compton JHS 600/7-8
3211 Pico Ave 93306 661-631-5230
Jennifer Payne, prin. Fax 631-3166
Curran MS 900/6-8
1116 Lymric Way 93309 661-631-5240
Jason Brannen, prin. Fax 631-4538
Emerson MS 800/6-8
801 4th St 93304 661-631-5260
Kempton Coman, prin. Fax 327-8505
Sequoia MS 900/6-8
900 Belle Ter 93304 661-631-5940
Gary McCloskey, prin. Fax 631-3236
Sierra MS 800/6-8
3017 Center St 93306 661-631-5470
Tomas Prieto, prin. Fax 631-4541
Stiern MS 1,400/6-8
2551 Morning Dr 93306 661-631-5480
Julie Short, prin. Fax 631-3241
Washington MS 600/6-8
1101 Noble Ave 93305 661-631-5810
Abraham Rivera, prin. Fax 631-3172

Beardsley ESD 1,700/K-8
1001 Roberts Ln 93308 661-393-8550
Paul Miller, supt. Fax 393-5965
www.beardsleyschool.org/
Beardsley JHS 300/7-8
1001 Roberts Ln 93308 661-392-9254
David Hilton, prin. Fax 399-3925

Edison ESD 1,100/K-8
11518 School St 93307 661-363-5394
Erica Andrews, supt. Fax 363-4631
www.edline.net/pages/Edison_Elementary
Edison MS 500/5-8
721 S Edison Rd 93307 661-366-8216
Loreda Clevenger, prin. Fax 366-0922

Fairfax ESD 2,300/K-8
1500 S Fairfax Rd 93307 661-366-7221
Michael Coleman, supt. Fax 366-1901
www.fairfax.k12.ca.us
Fairfax JHS 800/6-8
1500 S Fairfax Rd 93307 661-366-4461
Wendy Burkhead, prin. Fax 366-5831

Fruitvale SD 3,300/K-8
7311 Rosedale Hwy 93308 661-589-3830
Dr. Mary Westendorf, supt. Fax 589-3674
www.fruitvale.k12.ca.us
Fruitvale JHS 800/7-8
2114 Calloway Dr 93312 661-589-3933
Leslie Roberts, prin. Fax 588-3259

Greenfield UNESD 8,400/K-8
1624 Fairview Rd 93307 661-837-6000
Chris Crawford, supt. Fax 832-2873
www.gfusd.net
Greenfield Community S 100/Alt
725 Capitola Dr 93307 661-837-3717
Matt Earls, dir. Fax 837-3719
Greenfield MS 800/6-8
1109 Pacheco Rd 93307 661-837-6110
Sandra Welch, prin. Fax 832-7431

McKee MS 900/6-8
205 McKee Rd 93307 661-837-6060
Bethany Ferguson, prin. Fax 834-7566
Ollivier MS 800/6-8
7310 Monitor St 93307 661-837-6120
Sheila Johnson, prin. Fax 396-0963

Kern County Office of Education 3,700/
1300 17th St 93301 661-636-4000
Christine Frazier, supt. Fax 636-4130
www.kern.org/
Kern County Community S 1,500/Alt
1300 17th St 93301 661-636-4346
Warcester Williams, dir. Fax 636-4127

Kern UNHSD 36,300/9-12
5801 Sundale Ave 93309 661-827-3100
Dr. Bryon Schaefer, supt. Fax 827-3302
www.kernhigh.org
Bakersfield HS 2,800/9-12
1241 G St 93301 661-324-9841
David Reese, prin. Fax 324-3401
Centennial HS 1,800/9-12
8601 Hageman Rd 93312 661-588-8601
Dean Juola, prin. Fax 588-8608
East Bakersfield HS 2,200/9-12
2200 Quincy Dr 93306 661-871-7221
Librado Vasquez, prin. Fax 872-6980
Foothill HS 2,000/9-12
501 Park Dr 93306 661-366-4491
Gail Bentley, prin. Fax 363-6223
Frontier HS 2,500/9-12
6401 Allen Rd, 661-829-1107
Dan Shannon, prin. Fax 829-1185
Golden Valley HS 2,500/9-12
801 Hosking Ave 93307 661-827-0800
Paul Helman, prin. Fax 827-0480
Highland HS 1,900/9-12
2900 Royal Scots Way 93306 661-872-2777
Debra Vigstrom, prin. Fax 871-6052
Independence HS 1,800/9-12
8001 Old River Rd 93311 661-834-8001
Debbie Thompson, prin. Fax 398-0899
Liberty HS 1,800/9-12
925 Jewetta Ave 93312 661-587-0925
Libby Wyatt, prin. Fax 587-1299
Mira Monte HS 1,600/9-12
1800 S Fairfax Rd 93307 661-366-1800
William Sandoval, prin. Fax 363-6475
North HS 1,800/9-12
300 Galaxy Ave 93308 661-399-3351
Alan Paradise, prin. Fax 393-5918
Ridgeview HS 2,200/9-12
8501 Stine Rd 93313 661-398-3100
Steve Holmes, prin. Fax 398-9758
Ruggenberg Career Center Vo/Tech
610 Ansol Ln 93306 661-366-4401
John Eldridge, coord. Fax 363-0828
Schuetz Career Center Vo/Tech
8600 Shannon Dr 93307 661-827-4800
Misty Krugman, admin. Fax 827-4804
South HS 2,000/9-12
1101 Planz Rd 93304 661-831-3680
Connie Grumling, prin. Fax 837-2756
Stockdale HS 2,100/9-12
2800 Buena Vista Rd 93311 661-665-2800
Ramon Hendrix, prin. Fax 665-0914
Tierra Del Sol Continuation HS Alt
3700 E Belle Ter 93307 661-832-3700
Chris Dutton, admin. Fax 832-9807
Vista Continuation HS 300/Alt
200 P St 93304 661-327-8561
Tracey Lozano, admin. Fax 631-0558
Vista West Continuation HS 200/Alt
7115 Rosedale Hwy 93308 661-589-4242
Mike Mullings, admin. Fax 588-1627
West HS 2,100/9-12
1200 New Stine Rd 93309 661-832-2822
Terrie Bernardin, prin. Fax 831-5606
Bakersfield Adult HS Adult
501 S Mount Vernon Ave 93307 661-835-1855
Mark Wyatt, prin. Fax 835-9612
Other Schools – See Arvin, Lake Isabella, Lamont, Shafter

Lamont ESD
Supt. — See Lamont
Mountain View MS 500/7-8
8001 Weedpatch Hwy 93307 661-845-2291
Jonathan Martinez, prin. Fax 845-1839

Norris SD 3,700/K-8
6940 Calloway Dr 93312 661-387-7000
Kelly Miller, supt. Fax 399-9750
www.norris.k12.ca.us/
Norris MS 1,200/6-8
6940 Calloway Dr 93312 661-387-7060
Ryan Carr, prin. Fax 399-9356

Panama-Buena Vista UNSD 16,800/K-8
4200 Ashe Rd 93313 661-831-8331
Dr. Kevin Silberberg, supt. Fax 398-2141
www.pbvusd.k12.ca.us
Actis JHS 700/7-8
2400 Westholme Blvd 93309 661-833-1250
Patrick Spears, prin. Fax 833-9656
Stonecreek JHS 800/7-8
8000 Akers Rd 93313 661-834-4521
Matthew Kennedy, prin. Fax 834-6908
Tevis JHS 700/7-8
3901 Pin Oak Park Blvd 93311 661-664-7211
Paul Coon, prin. Fax 664-9659
Thompson JHS 700/7-8
4200 Planz Rd 93309 661-832-8011
Darryl Pope, prin. Fax 832-5165
Warren JHS 900/7-8
4615 Mountain Vista Dr 93311 661-665-9210
George Thornburgh, prin. Fax 665-9507

Regional Occupational Center & Program
Supt. — None
Kern HSD ROC Vo/Tech
501 S Mount Vernon Ave 93307 661-831-3327
Brian Miller, admin. Fax 398-8239

Rio Bravo-Greeley UNESD 1,000/K-8
6521 Enos Ln, 661-589-2696
Joost DeMoes, supt. Fax 589-2218
www.rbgusd.k12.ca.us
Rio Bravo-Greeley MS 500/5-8
6601 Enos Ln, 661-589-2505
Gary Bradshaw, prin. Fax 588-7204

Rosedale UNESD 5,400/K-8
2553 Old Farm Rd 93312 661-588-6000
John Mendiburu Ed.D., supt. Fax 588-6009
www.ruesd.net
Freedom MS 600/7-8
11445 Noriega Rd 93312 661-588-6044
Russell Sentes, prin. Fax 588-6048
Rosedale MS 700/7-8
12463 Rosedale Hwy 93312 661-588-6030
Becky Devahl, prin. Fax 588-6039

Standard ESD 2,900/K-8
1200 N Chester Ave 93308 661-392-2110
Paul Meyers Ed.D., supt. Fax 392-0681
district.standard.k12.ca.us
Standard MS 900/6-8
1222 N Chester Ave 93308 661-392-2130
Jason Hodgson, prin. Fax 392-2134

Vineland ESD 800/K-8
14713 Weedpatch Hwy 93307 661-845-3713
Matthew Ross, supt. Fax 845-8449
vineland.k12.ca.us
Sunset S 400/5-8
8301 Sunset Blvd 93307 661-845-1320
Charles Monaco, prin. Fax 845-3952

---

Bakersfield Adventist Academy 100/K-12
3333 Bernard St 93306 661-871-1591
Michael Schwartz, prin. Fax 871-1594
Bakersfield Christian HS 500/9-12
12775 Stockdale Hwy, 661-410-7000
Stephen Dinger, pres. Fax 410-7007
Bakersfield College Post-Sec.
1801 Panorama Dr 93305 661-395-4011
California State University-Bakersfield Post-Sec.
9001 Stockdale Hwy 93311 661-654-2782
DeVry University Post-Sec.
3000 Ming Ave 93304 661-833-7120
Garces Memorial HS 600/9-12
2800 Loma Linda Dr 93305 661-327-2578
Myka Peck, prin. Fax 327-5427
Kaplan College Post-Sec.
1914 Wible Rd 93304 661-836-6300
Lyle's College of Beauty Post-Sec.
2935 F St 93301 661-327-9784
Milan Institute Post-Sec.
2822 F St 93301 661-325-8900
San Joaquin Valley College Post-Sec.
201 New Stine Rd 93309 661-834-0126
Santa Barbara Business College Post-Sec.
5300 California Ave 93309 866-749-7222

**Baldwin Park, Los Angeles, Pop. 74,883**
Baldwin Park USD 15,200/PK-12
3699 Holly Ave 91706 626-962-3311
Paul Sevillano Ed.D., supt. Fax 856-4901
www.bpusd.net
Baldwin Park HS 2,300/9-12
3900 Puente Ave 91706 626-960-5431
Anthony Ippolito, prin. Fax 856-4059
Holland MS 600/6-8
4733 Landis Ave 91706 626-962-8412
James Michael Rust, prin. Fax 813-6148
Jones JHS 600/7-8
14250 Merced Ave 91706 626-962-8312
Elizabeth Cox, prin. Fax 856-4291
North Park Continuation HS 300/Alt
4600 Bogart Ave 91706 626-337-4407
Harris Vincent Pratt, prin. Fax 856-4402
Olive MS 500/6-8
13701 Olive St 91706 626-962-8416
Richard Noblett, prin. Fax 856-4568
Santa Fe S 400/3-8
4650 Baldwin Park Blvd 91706 626-856-1525
Margie Clark, prin. Fax 813-0614
Sierra Vista HS 2,000/9-12
3600 Frazier St 91706 626-960-7741
Jackie White, prin. Fax 856-4050
Sierra Vista JHS 800/7-8
13400 Foster Ave 91706 626-962-1300
Christine Simmons, prin. Fax 856-4577
Baldwin Park Adult & Community Education Adult
4640 Maine Ave 91706 626-939-4456
John Kerr Ed.D., prin. Fax 856-4384

**Ballico, Merced, Pop. 398**
Ballico-Cressey ESD 300/K-8
11818 Gregg Ave 95303 209-632-5371
Bryan Ballenger, supt. Fax 632-8929
www.ballicocressey.com
Ballico MS 200/3-8
11818 Gregg Ave 95303 209-632-5371
Bryan Ballenger, supt. Fax 632-8929

**Banning, Riverside, Pop. 28,937**
Banning USD 4,100/K-12
161 W Williams St 92220 951-922-0200
Robert Guillen, supt. Fax 922-0227
www.banning.k12.ca.us
Banning HS 1,100/9-12
100 W Westward Ave 92220 951-922-0285
Douglas Newton, prin. Fax 922-2137
Banning Independent Study Alt
1151 W Wilson St 92220 951-922-0268
David Sanchez, prin. Fax 922-2723
New Horizons Continuation HS 100/Alt
1151 W Wilson St 92220 951-922-0250
David Sanchez, prin. Fax 922-2750
Nicolet MS 700/6-8
101 E Nicolet St 92220 951-922-0280
Albert Evinger, prin. Fax 922-2748

**Barstow, San Bernardino, Pop. 21,497**
Barstow USD 6,000/K-12
551 S Avenue H 92311 760-255-6000
Jeff Malan, supt. Fax 255-8965
www.barstow.k12.ca.us
Barstow HS 1,400/9-12
551 S Avenue H 92311 760-255-6105
Derrick Delton, prin. Fax 256-4076
Barstow JHS 800/7-8
551 S Avenue H 92311 760-255-6200
Jose Rubio, prin. Fax 255-6205
Barstow STEM Academy 6-8
310 W Mountain View 92311 760-255-6150
Vinney Williams, prin. Fax 255-6104
Central Continuation HS 300/Alt
551 S Avenue H 92311 760-255-6063
Carolyn Norman, prin. Fax 256-2125

---

Barstow Community College Post-Sec.
2700 Barstow Rd 92311 760-252-2411

**Bay Point, Contra Costa, Pop. 20,582**
Mount Diablo USD
Supt. — See Concord
Gateway HS 50/Alt
235 Pacifica Ave 94565 925-458-1316
Rachelle Buckner, admin. Fax 458-1487
Riverview MS 700/6-8
205 Pacifica Ave 94565 925-458-3216
Eric Wood, prin. Fax 458-0875

**Beaumont, Riverside, Pop. 35,877**
Beaumont USD 8,700/K-12
PO Box 187 92223 951-845-1631
Maureen Latham Ed.D., supt. Fax 845-2039
www.beaumont-ca.schoolloop.com
Beaumont HS 2,400/9-12
PO Box 187 92223 951-845-3171
Christina Pierce, prin. Fax 769-9289
Glen View HS 100/Alt
PO Box 187 92223 951-845-6012
Matthew Russo, prin. Fax 769-8760
Mountain View MS 1,000/6-8
PO Box 187 92223 951-845-1627
Tyson Lingenfelter Ed.D., prin. Fax 845-8679
San Gorgonio MS 1,100/6-8
PO Box 187 92223 951-769-4391
Drew Scherrer, prin. Fax 769-8750
21st Century Learning Institute 100/Alt
PO Box 187 92223 951-845-1133
Matthew Russo, prin. Fax 845-1134
Beaumont Adult S Adult
PO Box 187 92223 951-845-6012
Anthony Hernandez, prin. Fax 769-8760

**Bell, Los Angeles, Pop. 35,263**
Los Angeles USD
Supt. — See Los Angeles
Bell HS 4,300/9-12
4328 Bell Ave 90201 323-832-4700
Rafael Balderas, prin. Fax 560-7874
Orchard Academy #2B 200/6-8
6411 Orchard Ave 90201 323-826-3951
David Manzo, prin. Fax 826-3951
Orchard Academy #2C 100/6-8
6411 Orchard Ave 90201 323-826-3975
Mirian Rubalcava, prin. Fax 826-3976

**Bellflower, Los Angeles, Pop. 74,379**
Bellflower USD 13,700/K-12
16703 Clark Ave 90706 562-866-9011
Brian Jacobs Ed.D., supt. Fax 866-7713
www.busd.k12.ca.us/
Bellflower MSHS 2,900/7-12
15301 Mcnab Ave 90706 562-920-1801
Michael Lundgren, prin. Fax 804-2387
Somerset Continuation HS 400/Alt
9242 Laurel St 90706 562-804-6548
Mark Kailiponi, prin. Fax 804-6587
Other Schools – See Lakewood

---

St. John Bosco HS 800/9-12
13640 Bellflower Blvd 90706 562-920-1734
Casey Yeazel, prin. Fax 867-5322

**Bell Gardens, Los Angeles, Pop. 41,928**
Montebello USD
Supt. — See Montebello
Bell Gardens HS 3,300/9-12
6119 Agra St 90201 323-826-5151
Juan Herrera, prin. Fax 887-7959
Bell Gardens IS 1,200/6-8
5841 Live Oak St 90201 562-927-1319
Ricardo Mendez, prin. Fax 806-5131
Suva IS 900/6-8
6660 Suva St 90201 562-927-2679
Dr. Teresa Alonzo Ed.D., prin. Fax 806-5132
Bell Gardens Adult Education Adult
6119 Agra St 90201 323-887-7955
Marcia Ugalde, prin. Fax 887-7958
Ford Park Adult S Adult
7800 Scout Ave 90201 562-927-7750
Fax 806-5133

---

InterAmerican Adult S 300/9-12
PO Box 541 90201 323-627-0704
Gladys Rendon, admin. Fax 386-4049

**Belmont, San Mateo, Pop. 24,354**
Belmont-Redwood Shores ESD 3,400/K-8
2960 Hallmark Dr 94002 650-637-4800
Michael Milliken Ph.D., supt. Fax 637-4811
www.brssd.org
Ralston IS 1,000/6-8
2675 Ralston Ave 94002 650-637-4880
Joe Funk, prin. Fax 637-4888

Sequoia UNHSD
Supt. — See Redwood City
Carlmont HS 2,100/9-12
1400 Alameda De Las Pulgas 94002 650-595-0210
Ralph Crame, prin. Fax 591-6067

---

Notre Dame de Namur University Post-Sec.
1500 Ralston Ave 94002 650-508-3500
Notre Dame HS 400/9-12
1540 Ralston Ave 94002 650-595-1913
Maryann Osmond, prin. Fax 593-9330

**Benicia, Solano, Pop. 25,504**
Benicia USD 4,900/K-12
350 E K St 94510 707-747-8300
Charles Young, supt. Fax 748-0146
www.beniciaunified.org
Benicia HS 1,700/9-12
1101 Military W 94510 707-747-8325
Damon Wright, prin. Fax 745-6769
Benicia MS 1,200/6-8
1100 Southampton Rd 94510 707-747-8340
Stephen Brady, prin. Fax 747-8349
Liberty Continuation HS 100/Alt
351 E J St 94510 707-747-8323
JoAnn Severson, prin. Fax 748-2684

**Ben Lomond, Santa Cruz, Pop. 6,022**
San Lorenzo Valley USD 4,300/K-12
325 Marion Ave 95005 831-336-5194
Dr. Laurie Bruton, supt. Fax 336-9531
www.slvusd.org
Other Schools – See Felton

**Berkeley, Alameda, Pop. 106,371**
Berkeley USD 9,300/PK-12
2020 Bonar St 94702 510-644-4500
Donald Evans, supt. Fax 540-5358
www.berkeleyschools.net
Berkeley HS 3,200/9-12
1980 Allston Way 94704 510-644-6120
Kristin Glenchur, prin. Fax 548-4221
Berkeley Technology Academy 100/Alt
2701 M L King Jr Way 94703 510-644-6159
Sheila Quintana, prin. Fax 644-4597
King MS 900/6-8
1781 Rose St 94703 510-644-6280
Janet Levenson, prin. Fax 644-8783
Longfellow Arts & Technology MS 500/6-8
1500 Derby St 94703 510-644-6360
Marcos Garcia, prin. Fax 644-8707
Willard MS 500/6-8
2425 Stuart St 94705 510-644-6330
Debbie Dean, prin. Fax 548-4219
Berkeley Adult S Adult
1701 San Pablo Ave 94701 510-644-6130
Burr Guthrie, prin. Fax 644-6784

---

Acupuncture & Integrative Medicine Coll. Post-Sec.
2550 Shattuck Ave 94704 510-666-8248
American Baptist Seminary of the West Post-Sec.
2606 Dwight Way 94704 510-841-1905
Bayhill HS, 1940 Virginia St 94709 100/9-12
Shelley Lobell, dir. 510-984-0599
Berkeley City College Post-Sec.
2050 Center St 94704 510-981-2800
Church Divinity School of the Pacific Post-Sec.
2451 Ridge Rd 94709 510-204-0700
Dominican School of Philosophy/Theology Post-Sec.
2301 Vine St 94708 510-849-2030
Franciscan School of Theology Post-Sec.
1712 Euclid Ave 94709 510-848-5232
Graduate Theological Union Post-Sec.
2400 Ridge Rd 94709 510-649-2400
Maybeck HS 100/9-12
2727 College Ave 94705 510-841-8489
William Webb, dir. Fax 704-0473
Pacific Lutheran Theological Seminary Post-Sec.
2770 Marin Ave 94708 510-524-5264
Pacific School of Religion Post-Sec.
1798 Scenic Ave 94709 510-849-8200
St. Marys College HS 600/9-12
1294 Albina Ave 94706 510-526-9242
Peter Imperial, prin. Fax 559-6277
Starr King School for the Ministry Post-Sec.
2441 Le Conte Ave 94709 510-845-6232
University of California Post-Sec.
110 Sproul Hall 94720 510-642-6000
Wright Institute Post-Sec.
2728 Durant Ave 94704 510-841-9230

**Bermuda Dunes, Riverside, Pop. 7,164**

---

Desert Christian Academy 500/PK-12
40700 Yucca Ln, 760-345-2848
Debbee Scott, head sch Fax 345-8173

**Beverly Hills, Los Angeles, Pop. 32,498**
Beverly Hills USD 4,500/PK-12
255 S Lasky Dr 90212 310-551-5100
Steve Kessler, supt. Fax 286-2138
www.bhusd.org/
Beverly Hills HS 2,000/9-12
241 S Moreno Dr 90212 310-229-3685
Dave Jackson, prin. Fax 286-7446

---

Academy of Couture Art Post-Sec.
8484 Wilshire Blvd Ste 730 90211 310-360-8888

West Coast Ultrasound Institute — Post-Sec.
291 S La Cienega Blvd # 500 90211 — 310-289-5123

**Bieber, Lassen, Pop. 307**
Big Valley JUSD — 200/K-12
PO Box 157 96009 — 530-294-5266
Paula Silva, supt. — Fax 294-5396
www.bigvalleyschool.org
Big Valley JSHS — 100/8-12
PO Box 157 96009 — 530-294-5231
Paula Silva, prin. — Fax 294-5100

**Big Bear Lake, San Bernardino, Pop. 4,883**
Bear Valley USD — 2,700/PK-12
PO Box 1529 92315 — 909-866-4631
Ron Peavy, supt. — Fax 866-2040
www.bearvalleyusd.org
Big Bear MS — 400/7-8
PO Box 1607 92315 — 909-866-4634
Dena Arbaugh, prin. — Fax 866-5679
Other Schools – See Sugarloaf

**Biggs, Butte, Pop. 1,654**
Biggs USD — 500/PK-12
300 B St 95917 — 530-868-1281
Doug Kaelin, supt. — Fax 868-1615
www.biggs.org/
Biggs HS, 3046 2nd St 95917 — 200/9-12
Doug Kaelin, prin. — 530-868-5825
Biggs Secondary Community Day S — 50/Alt
300 B St 95917 – Doug Kaelin, prin. — 530-868-1281

**Big Pine, Inyo, Pop. 1,716**
Big Pine USD — 200/K-12
PO Box 908 93513 — 760-938-2005
Pamela Jones, supt. — Fax 938-2310
www.bp.k12.ca.us
Big Pine HS — 50/9-12
PO Box 908 93513 — 760-938-2222
Katie Kolker, prin. — Fax 938-2310

Bishop USD
Supt. — See Bishop
Palisade Glacier Continuation HS — 50/Alt
PO Box 938 93513 — 760-938-2001
Randy Cook, prin. — Fax 938-2310

**Big Sur, Monterey**
Big Sur USD — 100/PK-12
69325 Highway 1 93920 — 805-927-4507
Gordon Piffero, supt. — Fax 927-8123
www.bigsurunified.org
Pacific Valley S — 50/PK-12
69325 Highway 1 93920 — 805-927-4507
Gordon Piffero, supt. — Fax 927-8123

**Bishop, Inyo, Pop. 3,811**
Bishop USD — 1,500/K-12
301 N Fowler St 93514 — 760-872-3680
Barry Simpson, supt. — Fax 872-6016
bishop-ca.schoolloop.com
Bishop Union HS — 700/9-12
301 N Fowler St 93514 — 760-873-4275
Allen Van Velzen, prin. — Fax 873-3065
Home Street MS — 400/6-8
201 Home St 93514 — 760-872-1381
Patrick Twomey, prin. — Fax 872-1877
Other Schools – See Big Pine

Inyo County Office of Education
Supt. — See Independence
Boothe S — 50/Alt
166 Grandview Dr 93514 — 760-873-3262
Dr. Terence McAteer, prin. — Fax 873-3324

Regional Occupational Center & Program
Supt. — None
Inyo County ROP — Vo/Tech
166 Grandview Dr 93514 — 760-873-3262
Sophie Kenn, dir. — Fax 873-3324

**Bloomington, San Bernardino, Pop. 23,603**
Colton JUSD
Supt. — See Colton
Baca MS — 800/7-8
1640 S Lilac Ave 92316 — 909-580-5014
Mike Williford, prin. — Fax 876-4195
Bloomington HS — 2,800/9-12
10750 Laurel Ave 92316 — 909-580-5004
Tina Petersen, prin. — Fax 876-6326
Harris MS — 900/7-8
11150 Alder Ave 92316 — 909-580-5020
Sandy Torres, prin. — Fax 820-2238
Slover Mountain Continuation HS — 300/Alt
18829 Orange St 92316 — 909-580-5013
Kristi Richardson, prin. — Fax 876-6363

---

Bloomington Christian S — 900/PK-12
955 Bloomington Ave 92316 — 909-877-1239
Stephane Bracken, prin. — Fax 873-3160

**Blue Jay, San Bernardino**
Rim of the World USD — 4,200/K-12
27315 N Bay Rd 92317 — 909-336-2031
Dr. Giovanni Annous, supt. — Fax 337-4527
www.rimsd.k12.ca.us
Other Schools – See Lake Arrowhead

**Blue Lake, Humboldt, Pop. 1,210**

---

Dell'Arte International School — Post-Sec.
PO Box 816 95525 — 707-668-5663

**Blythe, Riverside, Pop. 20,420**
Palo Verde USD — 3,500/K-12
295 N 1st St 92225 — 760-922-4164
Michael Davitt, supt. — Fax 922-5942
www.pvusd.us
Blythe MS — 500/7-8
825 N Lovekin Blvd 92225 — 760-922-1300
Douglas Ferber, prin. — Fax 922-3748
Palo Verde HS — 1,000/9-12
667 N Lovekin Blvd 92225 — 760-922-7148
Brandy Cox, prin. — Fax 922-8916
Palo Verde Valley Community Day S — Alt
811 W Chanslorway 92225 — 760-922-4884
Meliton Sanchez, prin. — Fax 922-1177
Twin Palms Continuation S — Adult
811 W Chanslor Way 92225 — 760-922-4884
Rachel Angel, prin. — Fax 922-1177

---

Palo Verde College — Post-Sec.
1 College Dr 92225 — 760-921-5500

**Bonsall, San Diego, Pop. 3,866**
Bonsall USD — 2,000/K-12
31505 Old River Rd 92003 — 760-631-5200
Justin Cunningham Ed.D., supt. — Fax 941-4409
www.bonsallusd.com
Bonsall HS, 7350 W Lilac Rd 92003 — 9-12
Lee Fleming, prin. — 760-631-5209
Sullivan MS — 500/6-8
7350 W Lilac Rd 92003 — 760-631-5210
Dr. Tim Heck, prin. — Fax 631-5230

**Boonville, Mendocino, Pop. 1,016**
Anderson Valley USD — 500/PK-12
PO Box 457 95415 — 707-895-3774
Michelle Hutchins, supt. — Fax 895-2665
www.avusd.k12.ca.us
Anderson Valley JSHS — 300/7-12
PO Box 130 95415 — 707-895-3496
Michelle Hutchins, prin. — Fax 895-3153
Rancheria Continuation S — 50/Alt
PO Box 457 95415 — 707-895-3151
Michelle Hutchins, lead tchr. — Fax 895-2665
Anderson Valley Adult S — Adult
PO Box 457 95415 — 707-895-2953
Michelle Hutchins, prin. — Fax 895-2665

**Boron, Kern, Pop. 2,180**
Muroc JUSD
Supt. — See North Edwards
Boron JSHS — 300/7-12
26831 Prospect St 93516 — 760-762-5121
Franklin Samples, prin. — Fax 762-5040

**Borrego Springs, San Diego, Pop. 3,399**
Borrego Springs USD — 500/PK-12
1315 Palm Canyon Dr 92004 — 760-767-5357
Martha Deichler, supt. — Fax 767-0494
www.bsusd.com
Borrego Springs HS — 200/9-12
1315 Palm Canyon Dr 92004 — 760-767-5335
Steve Dunn, prin. — Fax 767-5999
Borrego Springs MS — 100/6-8
1315 Palm Canyon Dr 92004 — 760-767-5335
Steve Dunn, prin. — Fax 767-5999

**Brawley, Imperial, Pop. 24,758**
Brawley ESD — 3,700/K-8
261 D St 92227 — 760-344-2330
Ronald Garcia, supt. — Fax 344-8928
www.besd.org
Worth JHS — 800/7-8
385 W D St 92227 — 760-344-2153
Terri Mason, prin. — Fax 351-5043

Brawley UNHSD — 1,800/9-12
480 N Imperial Ave 92227 — 760-312-6063
Simon Canalez, supt. — Fax 344-9520
www.brawleyhigh.org
Brawley HS — 1,600/9-12
480 N Imperial Ave 92227 — 760-312-6073
Jesse Sanchez, prin. — Fax 312-6064
BUHS Renaissance Community Day S — 50/Alt
480 N Imperial Ave 92227 — 760-312-5109
Antonio Munguia, admin. — Fax 344-7425
Desert Valley Continuation HS — 200/Alt
480 N Imperial Ave 92227 — 760-312-5110
Antonio Munguia, prin. — Fax 344-7425

**Brea, Orange, Pop. 38,164**
Brea-Olinda USD — 5,900/K-12
PO Box 300 92822 — 714-990-7800
Dr. Brad Mason, supt. — Fax 529-2137
www.bousd.us
Brea Canyon HS — 100/Alt
689 Wildcat Way 92821 — 714-990-7882
Carol Christman, prin. — Fax 990-7587
Brea JHS — 900/7-8
400 N Brea Blvd 92821 — 714-990-7500
Kelly Kennedy, prin. — Fax 990-7585
Brea-Olinda HS — 2,000/9-12
789 Wildcat Way 92821 — 714-990-7850
Jerry Halpin, prin. — Fax 990-7547

---

Brea School of Exceptional Children — Post-Sec.
875 N Brea Blvd 92821

**Brentwood, Contra Costa, Pop. 49,001**
Brentwood UNESD — 8,800/PK-8
255 Guthrie Ln 94513 — 925-513-6300
Dana Eaton, supt. — Fax 634-8583
www.brentwood.k12.ca.us
Adams MS — 1,000/6-8
401 American Ave 94513 — 925-513-6450
Mike Wood, prin. — Fax 513-3470
Bristow MS — 1,100/6-8
855 Minnesota Ave 94513 — 925-513-6460
Jon Ovick, prin. — Fax 516-8725
Hill MS — 900/6-8
140 Birch St 94513 — 925-513-6440
Kirsten Jobb, prin. — Fax 513-0696

Liberty UNHSD — 7,600/9-12
20 Oak St 94513 — 925-634-2166
Eric Volta, supt. — Fax 634-1687
libertyunion.schoolwires.net
Heritage HS — 2,200/9-12
101 American Ave 94513 — 925-634-0037
Larry Oshodi, prin. — Fax 240-0662
Independence HS — 500/Alt
929 2nd St 94513 — 925-634-2589
Guy Rognlien, dir. — Fax 634-5317
La Paloma Continuation HS — 200/Alt
400 Ghiggeri Dr 94513 — 925-634-2888
Chris Holland, prin. — Fax 634-6578
Liberty HS — 2,100/9-12
850 2nd St 94513 — 925-634-3521
Patrick Walsh, prin. — Fax 513-2739
Liberty Adult Education — Adult
929 2nd St 94513 — 925-634-2565
Guy Rognlien, dir. — Fax 634-5317
Other Schools – See Oakley

**Bridgeport, Mono, Pop. 560**
Eastern Sierra USD — 500/K-12
PO Box 575 93517 — 760-932-7443
Don Clark, supt. — Fax 932-7140
www.esusd.org
Other Schools – See Coleville, Lee Vining

Mono County Office of Education — 300/
PO Box 477 93517 — 760-932-7311
Stacey Adler, supt. — Fax 932-7278
www.monocoe.org
Other Schools – See Coleville, Lee Vining, Mammoth Lakes

Regional Occupational Center & Program
Supt. — None
Mono County ROP — Vo/Tech
PO Box 477 93517 — 760-932-7311
Rhea Kerby, dir. — Fax 932-7278

**Brisbane, San Mateo, Pop. 4,026**
Brisbane ESD — 500/K-8
1 Solano St 94005 — 415-467-0550
Toni Presta, supt. — Fax 467-2914
www.brisbanesd.org
Lipman MS — 200/6-8
1 Solano St 94005 — 415-467-9541
Jolene Heckerman, prin. — Fax 467-5073

**Buellton, Santa Barbara, Pop. 4,686**
Buellton UNESD — 700/PK-8
595 2nd St 93427 — 805-686-2767
Bryan McCabe, supt. — Fax 686-2719
www.buelltonusd.org
Jonata MS — 200/6-8
301 2nd St 93427 — 805-688-4222
Kathy Fayram, prin. — Fax 688-6611

**Buena Park, Orange, Pop. 78,169**
Buena Park ESD — 5,300/K-8
6885 Orangethorpe Ave 90620 — 714-522-8412
Greg Magnuson, supt. — Fax 994-1506
www.bpsd.k12.ca.us/
Buena Park JHS — 1,100/7-8
6931 Orangethorpe Ave 90620 — 714-522-8491
Erik Bagger, prin. — Fax 523-1602

Fullerton JUNHSD
Supt. — See Fullerton
Buena Park HS — 1,900/9-12
8833 Academy Dr 90621 — 714-992-8601
Jim Coombs, prin. — Fax 992-8619

---

Bethel Baptist Academy — 200/K-12
8251 La Palma 90620 — 714-521-5586
Dr. Dan Davidson, dir.

**Burbank, Los Angeles, Pop. 99,967**
Burbank USD — 15,300/K-12
1900 W Olive Ave 91506 — 818-729-4400
Matt Hill, supt. — Fax 729-4483
www.burbankusd.org
Burbank Community Day S — Alt
223 E Santa Anita Ave 91502 — 818-558-4693
Christine Krohn, prin. — Fax 846-3404
Burbank HS — 2,800/9-12
902 N 3rd St 91502 — 818-558-4700
Michael Bertram, prin. — Fax 845-6122
Burbank MS — 1,100/6-8
3700 W Jeffries Ave 91505 — 818-558-4646
Dr. Oscar Macias, prin. — Fax 842-3727
Burroughs HS — 2,700/9-12
1920 W Clark Ave 91506 — 818-558-4777
Deborah Madrigal, prin. — Fax 846-9268
Independent Learning Academy — Alt
3715 W Allan Ave 91505 — 818-558-5353
Emilio Urioste, prin.
Jordan MS — 1,100/6-8
420 S Mariposa St 91506 — 818-558-4622
Stacy Cashman, prin. — Fax 843-3509
Monterey Continuation HS — 200/Alt
1915 W Monterey Ave 91506 — 818-558-5455
Ann Brooks, prin. — Fax 841-2446
Muir MS — 1,300/6-8
1111 N Kenneth Rd 91504 — 818-558-5320
Dr. Greg Miller, prin. — Fax 841-4637
Burbank Adult S — Adult
3811 W Allan Ave 91505 — 818-558-4611
Emilio Urioste, dir. — Fax 558-4620

---

Bellarmine-Jefferson HS — 200/9-12
465 E Olive Ave 91501 — 818-972-1400
Michael Stumpf, prin. — Fax 559-6387
Brighton Hall S — 100/K-12
755 N Whitnall Hwy 91505 — 818-985-9485
Niranjala Peiris, dir. — Fax 861-7326
Elegante Beauty College — Post-Sec.
200 N San Fernando Blvd 91502 — 818-954-8894

Intercoast Colleges Post-Sec.
175 E Olive Ave Fl 3 91502 818-500-8400
Make-up Designory Post-Sec.
129 S San Fernando Blvd 91502 818-729-9420
New York Film Academy Post-Sec.
4444 W Lakeside Dr 91505 818-295-2020
Providence HS 400/9-12
511 S Buena Vista St 91505 818-846-8141
Joe Sciuto, head sch Fax 843-8421
Woodbury University Post-Sec.
7500 N Glenoaks Blvd 91504 818-767-0888

**Burlingame, San Mateo, Pop. 27,534**
Burlingame ESD 2,900/K-8
1825 Trousdale Dr 94010 650-259-3800
Maggie MacIsaac Ed.D., supt. Fax 259-3820
www.burlingameschools.org
Burlingame IS 900/6-8
1715 Quesada Way 94010 650-259-3830
Pamela Scott, prin. Fax 259-3843

San Mateo UNHSD
Supt. — See San Mateo
Burlingame HS 1,300/9-12
1 Mangini Way 94010 650-558-2899
Pyongduk Yim, prin. Fax 558-2852

---

Mercy HS 500/9-12
2750 Adeline Dr 94010 650-343-3631
Karen Hanrahan, prin. Fax 343-3358
Mills Peninsula Health Services Post-Sec.
1783 El Camino Real 94010 650-696-5678

**Burney, Shasta, Pop. 3,044**
Fall River JUSD 1,100/K-12
20375 Tamarack Ave 96013 530-335-4538
Greg Hawkins, supt. Fax 335-3115
www.frjusd.org
Burney Community Day S 50/Alt
20375 Tamarack Ave 96013 530-335-5189
Greg Hawkins, prin. Fax 335-3115
Burney JSHS 200/7-12
37571 Mountain View Rd 96013 530-335-4576
Ray Guerrero, prin. Fax 335-3554
Mountain View Continuation HS 50/Alt
20375 Tamarack Ave 96013 530-335-5189
Greg Hawkins, prin. Fax 335-3115
Other Schools – See Mc Arthur

**Byron, Contra Costa, Pop. 1,236**
Byron UNESD 1,700/PK-8
14301 Byron Hwy 94514 925-809-7500
Debbie Burnette Ed.D., supt. Fax 634-9421
www.byronusd.com
Excelsior MS 600/6-8
14301 Byron Hwy 94514 925-809-7530
Kelly Basmagian, prin. Fax 634-5120

**Calabasas, Los Angeles, Pop. 22,176**
Las Virgenes USD 11,300/PK-12
4111 Las Virgenes Rd 91302 818-880-4000
Dan Stepenosky Ed.D., supt. Fax 880-4200
www.lvusd.org
Calabasas HS 1,800/9-12
22855 Mulholland Hwy 91302 818-222-7177
C.J. Foss, prin. Fax 223-8477
Indian Hills Continuation HS - East 50/Alt
22855 Mulholland Hwy 91302 818-222-7177
C.J. Foss, prin. Fax 223-8477
Stelle MS 900/6-8
22450 Mulholland Hwy 91302 818-224-4107
Ryan Emery, prin. Fax 224-4989
Wright MS 800/6-8
4029 Las Virgenes Rd 91302 818-880-4614
Elias Miles, prin. Fax 878-0453
Other Schools – See Agoura Hills

---

Mesivta of Greater Los Angeles S 100/9-12
25115 Mureau Rd 91302 818-876-0550
Rabbi Shlomo Gottesman, dir. Fax 876-0537
MUSE MSHS 100/6-12
4345 N Las Virgenes Rd 91302 818-880-5437
Jeff King, head sch Fax 880-5430
Viewpoint S 1,200/K-12
23620 Mulholland Hwy 91302 818-591-6500
Mark McKee, head sch Fax 591-0834

**Calexico, Imperial, Pop. 38,495**
Calexico USD 8,100/K-12
901 Andrade Ave 92231 760-768-3888
Maria Ambriz, supt. Fax 768-3856
www.calexico.k12.ca.us/
Aurora HS 200/Alt
641 Rockwood Ave 92231 760-768-3940
John Moreno, prin. Fax 768-1459
Calexico HS 2,200/9-12
1030 Encinas Ave 92231 760-768-3980
Sergio Pesqueira, prin. Fax 357-9640
Camarena JHS 700/7-8
800 E Rivera Ave 92231 760-768-3808
Diego Romero, prin. Fax 768-3807
Moreno JHS 800/7-8
1202 Kloke Ave 92231 760-768-3960
Gabrielle Williams, prin. Fax 768-1905
Morales Adult Education Center Adult
1201 Kloke Ave 92231 760-768-3914
John Moreno, admin. Fax 768-3916

---

Calexico Mission S 300/K-12
601 E 1st St 92231 760-357-3711
Susan Smith, prin. Fax 357-3713
Vincent Memorial HS 300/9-12
525 Sheridan St 92231 760-357-3461
Sr. Guadalupe Hernandez, prin. Fax 357-0902

**California City, Kern, Pop. 13,467**
Mojave USD
Supt. — See Mojave
California City HS 400/9-12
8567 Raven Way 93505 760-373-5263
Michael Vogenthaler, prin. Fax 373-9028
California City MS 300/7-8
9736 Redwood Blvd 93505 760-373-3241
Ron Riley, prin. Fax 373-1355

**Calimesa, Riverside, Pop. 7,727**
Yucaipa-Calimesa JUSD
Supt. — See Yucaipa
Mesa View MS 600/6-8
800 Mustang Way 92320 909-790-8008
John Moore, prin. Fax 795-6810

---

Mesa Grande Academy 300/PK-12
975 Fremont St 92320 909-795-1112
Alfred Riddle, prin. Fax 795-1653

**Calipatria, Imperial, Pop. 7,613**
Calipatria USD 1,200/K-12
501 W Main St 92233 760-348-2892
Douglas Kline, supt. Fax 344-8926
www.calipatriahornets.org
Calipatria HS 300/9-12
601 W Main St 92233 760-348-2254
Joe Derma, prin. Fax 348-2431
Young MS 400/5-8
220 S International Blvd 92233 760-348-2842
Virginia Calsada-Medina, prin. Fax 348-2848

**Calistoga, Napa, Pop. 5,085**
Calistoga JUSD 800/K-12
1520 Lake St 94515 707-942-4703
Dr. Esmeralda Mondragon, supt. Fax 942-6589
www.calistoga.k12.ca.us
Calistoga JSHS 400/7-12
1608 Lake St 94515 707-942-6278
David Kumamoto, prin. Fax 942-6592
Palisades HS 50/Alt
1507 Grant St 94515 707-942-5255
David Kumamoto, prin. Fax 942-5255

**Camarillo, Ventura, Pop. 63,018**
Oxnard UNHSD
Supt. — See Oxnard
Camarillo HS 2,500/9-12
4660 Mission Oaks Blvd 93012 805-389-6407
Kimberly Stephenson, prin. Fax 484-8087
Frontier HS 400/Alt
545 Airport Way 93010 805-389-6450
Wayne Lamas, prin. Fax 389-6466
Rancho Campana HS 9-12
4235 Mar Vista Dr 93010 805-385-2500
Roger Adams, prin.

Pleasant Valley SD 7,100/PK-8
600 Temple Ave 93010 805-482-2763
RaeAnne Michael, supt. Fax 987-5511
www.pvsd.k12.ca.us
Las Colinas MS 1,000/6-8
5750 Fieldcrest Dr 93012 805-484-0461
Erik Goldman, prin. Fax 482-2443
Monte Vista MS 900/6-8
888 Lantana St 93010 805-482-8891
Joseph Herzog, prin. Fax 987-8951

Regional Occupational Center & Program
Supt. — None
Ventura County ROP Vo/Tech
465 Horizon Way 93010 805-388-4423
Peggy Velarde, dir. Fax 388-4428

Ventura County Office of Education 2,100/
5189 Verdugo Way 93012 805-383-1900
Stan Mantooth, supt. Fax 383-1908
www.vcoe.org
Gateway Community S Alt
200 Horizon Cir 93012 805-437-1460
James Koenig, prin. Fax 437-1493

---

California State University-Channel Isle Post-Sec.
1 University Dr 93012 805-437-8400
Saint John's Seminary Post-Sec.
5012 Seminary Rd 93012 805-482-2755

**Cambria, San Luis Obispo, Pop. 5,934**
Coast USD 700/K-12
1350 Main St 93428 805-927-3880
Victoria Schumacher, supt. Fax 927-0312
www.coastusd.org
Coast Union HS 200/9-12
2950 Santa Rosa Creek Rd 93428 805-927-3889
Jonathan Sison, prin. Fax 924-2933
Leffingwell Continuation HS 50/Alt
2820 Santa Rosa Creek Rd 93428 805-927-7148
Bob Watt, prin. Fax 927-6741
Santa Lucia MS 200/6-8
2850 Schoolhouse Ln 93428 805-927-3693
John Calandro, prin. Fax 927-4615

**Cameron Park, El Dorado, Pop. 17,664**
Buckeye UNSD
Supt. — See El Dorado Hills
Camerado Springs MS 600/6-8
2480 Merrychase Dr 95682 530-677-1658
Meg Enns, prin. Fax 677-9537

**Campbell, Santa Clara, Pop. 37,545**
Campbell UNESD 7,700/K-8
155 N 3rd St 95008 408-364-4200
Dr. Eric Andrew, supt. Fax 341-7280
www.campbellusd.org
Campbell MS 700/5-8
295 Cherry Ln 95008 408-364-4222
April Mouton, prin. Fax 341-7150
Other Schools – See Los Gatos, San Jose

Campbell UNHSD
Supt. — See San Jose
Westmont HS 1,600/9-12
4805 Westmont Ave 95008 408-626-3406
Abra Evanoff, prin. Fax 379-1720

---

The International Culinary Center Post-Sec.
700 W Hamilton Ave 95008 408-370-5555

**Canoga Park, See Los Angeles**
Los Angeles USD
Supt. — See Los Angeles
Canoga Park HS 1,700/9-12
6850 Topanga Canyon Blvd 91303 818-673-1300
Robert Garcia, prin. Fax 702-8942
Columbus MS 900/6-8
22250 Elkwood St 91304 818-702-1200
Debra McIntyre-Sciarrino, prin. Fax 348-2894
Owensmouth Continuation HS 100/Alt
6921 Jordan Ave 91303 818-340-7663
Allan Tamshen, prin. Fax 340-2947
Sutter MS 1,400/6-8
7330 Winnetka Ave 91306 818-773-5800
Kelly Welsh, prin. Fax 341-3039
El Camino Real Adult Education Adult
21213 Vanowen St 91303 818-610-5600
Andrea Rodriguez, prin.

---

AGBU Manoogian-Demirdjian S 800/PK-12
6844 Oakdale Ave 91306 818-883-2428
Faith Baptist S 1,200/PK-12
7644 Farralone Ave 91304 818-340-6131
Timothy Rasmussen, dir. Fax 592-0279
Valley College of Medical Careers Post-Sec.
8399 Topanga Canyon Ste 200 91304 888-271-1444

**Canyon Country, See Santa Clarita**
William S. Hart UNHSD
Supt. — See Santa Clarita
Canyon HS 2,500/9-12
19300 Nadal St 91351 661-252-6110
Jason d'Autremont, prin. Fax 251-1419
Sierra Vista JHS 1,200/7-8
19425 Stillmore St 91351 661-252-3113
Carolyn Hoffman, prin. Fax 250-8157

---

Charter College Canyon Country Post-Sec.
27125 Sierra Hwy Ste 329 91351 661-252-1864
Santa Clarita Christian S 500/K-12
27249 Luther Dr 91351 661-252-7371
Kirk Huckabone, admin. Fax 252-4354

**Capitola, Santa Cruz, Pop. 9,578**
Soquel UNESD 1,700/PK-8
620 Monterey Ave 95010 831-464-5633
Henry Castaniada, supt. Fax 475-5196
www.soqueldo.santacruz.k12.ca.us/
New Brighton MS 500/6-8
250 Washburn Ave 95010 831-464-5660
Craig Broadhurst, prin. Fax 475-8236

**Carlsbad, San Diego, Pop. 101,706**
Carlsbad USD 11,000/K-12
6225 El Camino Real 92009 760-331-5000
Suzette Lovely, supt. Fax 431-6707
www.carlsbadusd.k12.ca.us
Aviara Oaks MS 1,100/6-8
6225 El Camino Real 92009 760-331-6100
Bryan Brockett, prin. Fax 729-3040
Calavera Hills MS 600/6-8
6225 El Camino Real 92009 760-331-6400
Michael Ecker, prin. Fax 729-3040
Carlsbad HS 3,000/9-12
6225 El Camino Real 92009 760-331-5100
Joshua Porter, prin. Fax 729-6830
Carlsbad Seaside Academy 100/Alt
6225 El Camino Real 92009 760-331-5299
Jorge Espinoza, prin. Fax 729-1791
Carlsbad Village Academy 100/Alt
6225 El Camino Real 92009 760-331-5100
Jorge Espinoza, prin. Fax 729-1791
Sage Creek HS 9-12
6225 El Camino Real 92009 760-331-6600
Cesar Morales, prin. Fax 730-9698
Valley MS 1,000/6-8
6225 El Camino Real 92009 760-331-5300
Thomas Bloomquist, prin. Fax 720-2326

San Dieguito UNHSD
Supt. — See Encinitas
La Costa Canyon HS 2,300/9-12
1 Maverick Way 92009 760-436-6136
Bryan Marcus, prin. Fax 943-3539

---

APT College Post-Sec.
PO Box 131717 92013 800-431-8488
Army and Navy Academy 300/7-12
PO Box 3000 92018 760-729-2385
Arthur M. Bartell, pres. Fax 434-5948
Gemological Institute of America Post-Sec.
5345 Armada Dr 92008 760-603-4000
Golf Academy of America Post-Sec.
1950 Camino Vida Roble #125 92008 760-734-1208
Pacific Ridge S 400/7-12
6269 El Fuerte St 92009 760-448-9820
Dr. Bob Ogle, head sch Fax 683-6003

**Carmel, Monterey, Pop. 3,645**
Carmel USD 2,400/PK-12
PO Box 222700 93922 831-624-1546
Scott Laurence, supt. Fax 626-4052
www.carmelunified.org
Carmel HS 800/9-12
PO Box 222780 93922 831-624-1821
Rick Lopez, prin. Fax 626-4313
Carmel MS 600/6-8
PO Box 222740 93922 831-624-2785
Ken Griest, prin. Fax 624-0839

Carmel Valley HS 50/Alt
PO Box 222700 93922 831-624-4462
Tom Stewart, prin. Fax 624-4487
Carmel Adult Education Adult
PO Box 222700 93922 831-624-1714
Tom Stewart, prin. Fax 624-8747

**Carmichael, Sacramento, Pop. 58,920**
San Juan USD 44,800/PK-12
PO Box 477 95609 916-971-7700
Kent Kern, supt. Fax 971-7758
www.sanjuan.edu
Barrett MS 900/6-8
4243 Barrett Rd 95608 916-971-7842
Brent Givens, prin. Fax 971-7839
Churchill MS 1,000/6-8
4900 Whitney Ave 95608 916-971-7324
Michael Dolan, prin. Fax 971-7856
Other Schools – See Citrus Heights, Fair Oaks, Orangevale, Sacramento

---

Jesuit HS 1,100/9-12
1200 Jacob Ln 95608 916-482-6060
Michael Wood, prin. Fax 482-2310
Sacramento Adventist Academy 200/PK-12
5601 Winding Way 95608 916-481-2300
Matthew Jakobsons M.A., prin. Fax 481-7426
Victory Christian S 200/K-12
3045 Garfield Ave 95608 916-488-5601
John Huffman, prin. Fax 488-2589

**Carpinteria, Santa Barbara, Pop. 12,835**
Carpinteria USD 2,300/K-12
1400 Linden Ave 93013 805-684-4511
Micheline G. Miglis, supt. Fax 684-0218
www.cusd.net
Carpinteria HS 700/9-12
4810 Foothill Rd 93013 805-684-4107
Gerardo Cornejo, prin. Fax 566-5952
Carpinteria MS 500/6-8
5351 Carpinteria Ave 93013 805-684-4544
John Merritt, prin. Fax 566-3839
Foothill Alternative HS 50/Alt
4698 Foothill Rd 93013 805-684-3277
Barnaby Gloger, prin. Fax 566-9707
Rincon Continuation S 50/Alt
4698 Foothill Rd 93013 805-684-3277
Barnaby Gloger, prin. Fax 566-9707

---

Cate S 300/9-12
1960 Cate Mesa Rd 93014 805-684-4127
Benjamin Williams, hdmstr. Fax 684-8940
International Sports Sciences Post-Sec.
1015 Mark Ave 93013 805-745-8111
Pacifica Graduate Institute Post-Sec.
249 Lambert Rd 93013 805-969-3626

**Carson, Los Angeles, Pop. 87,081**
Long Beach USD
Supt. — See Long Beach
California Academy of Math & Science 700/9-12
1000 E Victoria St 90747 310-243-2025
Chris Brown, prin. Fax 516-4041

Los Angeles USD
Supt. — See Los Angeles
Academy of Education and Empowerment 9-12
22328 Main St 90745 310-847-6000
Michelle Bryant, prin.
Academy of Medical Arts at Carson HS 9-12
22328 Main St 90745 310-847-6000
Melinda Martes, prin.
Carnegie MS 1,000/6-8
21820 Bonita St 90745 310-952-5700
Cheryl Nakata, prin. Fax 830-9015
Carson HS 2,800/9-12
22328 Main St 90745 310-847-6000
Windy Warren, prin. Fax 518-5817
Curtiss MS 700/6-8
1254 E Helmick St 90746 310-661-4500
Gina Russell-Williams, prin. Fax 537-2115
Eagle Tree Continuation S 100/Alt
22628 Main St 90745 310-549-0970
Jaiyawanda Gant, prin. Fax 518-5746
White MS 1,900/6-8
22102 Figueroa St 90745 310-783-4900
Adaina Brown, prin. Fax 782-8954

---

California State Univ.-Dominguez Hills Post-Sec.
1000 E Victoria St 90747 310-243-3300

**Caruthers, Fresno, Pop. 2,460**
Caruthers USD 1,300/K-12
PO Box 127 93609 559-864-6500
Orin Hirschkorn, supt. Fax 864-8857
www.caruthers.k12.ca.us
Caruthers HS 500/9-12
PO Box 545 93609 559-864-6500
Mark Fowler, prin. Fax 864-8303
MARC HS, PO Box 545 93609 50/Alt
Tod Tompkins, dir. 559-495-6443

**Castaic, Los Angeles, Pop. 18,337**
Castaic UNSD
Supt. — See Valencia
Castaic MS 1,100/6-8
28900 Hillcrest Pkwy 91384 661-257-4550
Bob Brauneisen, prin. Fax 294-9714

**Castro Valley, Alameda, Pop. 58,286**
Castro Valley USD 9,000/PK-12
PO Box 2146 94546 510-537-3000
Parvin Ahmadi, supt. Fax 886-8962
www.cv.k12.ca.us
Canyon MS 1,400/6-8
19600 Cull Canyon Rd 94552 510-538-8833
Matthew Steinecke, prin. Fax 247-9439
Castro Valley HS 2,900/9-12
19400 Santa Maria Ave 94546 510-537-5910
Blaine Torpey, prin. Fax 582-3924
Creekside MS 800/6-8
19722 Center St 94546 510-247-0665
Mary Ann DeGrazia, prin. Fax 581-6617
Redwood HS 100/Alt
18400 Clifton Way 94546 510-537-3193
Erica Ehmann, prin. Fax 247-3397
Castro Valley Adult S Adult
4430 Alma Ave 94546 510-886-1000
Jerry Green, dir. Fax 537-8537

**Castroville, Monterey, Pop. 6,411**
North Monterey County USD
Supt. — See Moss Landing
North Monterey County HS 1,200/9-12
13990 Castroville Blvd 95012 831-633-5221
Antonio Vela, prin. Fax 633-2520
North Monterey County MS 600/7-8
10301 Seymour St 95012 831-633-3391
Marisa Martinez, prin. Fax 633-3680

**Cathedral City, Riverside, Pop. 50,401**
Palm Springs USD
Supt. — See Palm Springs
Cathedral City HS 2,700/9-12
69250 Dinah Shore Dr 92234 760-770-0100
Guillermo Chavez, prin. Fax 770-0149
Coffman MS 1,100/6-8
34603 Plumley Rd 92234 760-770-8617
Lucinda Killebrew, prin. Fax 770-8623
Mt. San Jacinto Continuation HS 500/Alt
30800 Landau Blvd 92234 760-770-8563
Milt Jones, prin. Fax 770-8568
Workman MS 1,500/6-8
69300 30th Ave 92234 760-770-8540
Brad Sauer, prin. Fax 770-8545

---

Mayfield College Post-Sec.
35325 Date Palm Dr Ste 101 92234 760-328-5554

**Cedarville, Modoc, Pop. 502**
Surprise Valley JUSD 100/K-12
PO Box 100 96104 530-279-6141
Janelle Anderson, supt. Fax 279-2210
www.svjusd.org
Surprise Valley HS 50/9-12
PO Box 100 96104 530-279-6141
Rikki-Lee Carey, prin. Fax 279-2210

**Ceres, Stanislaus, Pop. 43,964**
Ceres USD 11,600/PK-12
PO Box 307 95307 209-556-1500
Scott Siegel, supt. Fax 556-1090
www.ceres.k12.ca.us
Argus and Endeavor HS 300/Alt
PO Box 307 95307 209-556-1800
Jan Gordon, prin. Fax 538-1027
Blaker-Kinser JHS 700/7-8
PO Box 307 95307 209-556-1810
Kristi Britton, prin. Fax 541-0174
Central Valley HS 1,700/9-12
PO Box 307 95307 209-556-1900
Dan Pangrazio, prin. Fax 531-2748
Ceres HS 1,400/9-12
PO Box 307 95307 209-556-1920
Linda Stubbs, prin. Fax 538-8978
Chavez JHS 200/7-8
PO Box 307 95307 209-556-1830
Rosemarie Kloepfer, prin. Fax 538-3970
Hensley JHS 800/7-8
PO Box 307 95307 209-556-1820
Carol Lubinsky, prin. Fax 538-9428
Ceres Adult S Adult
2491 Lawrence St 95307 556-556-1557
Dustin Pack, prin.

Stanislaus County Office of Education
Supt. — See Modesto
Stanislaus County Institute of Learning Alt
3113 Mitchell Road 95307 209-238-8750
Marcelo Briones, prin. Fax 238-8774

---

Central Valley Christian Academy 200/PK-12
2020 Academy Pl 95307 209-537-4521
Benjie Maxson, prin. Fax 538-0706

**Cerritos, Los Angeles, Pop. 47,521**
ABC USD 20,500/K-12
16700 Norwalk Blvd 90703 562-926-5566
Mary Sieu, supt. Fax 404-1092
www.abcusd.k12.ca.us
Carmenita MS 700/7-8
13435 166th St 90703 562-229-7775
Kester Song, prin. Fax 404-7807
Cerritos HS 2,200/9-12
12500 183rd St 90703 562-228-7815
Patrick Walker, prin. Fax 924-3187
Gahr HS 2,000/9-12
11111 Artesia Blvd 90703 562-229-7730
Gina Zietlow, prin. Fax 924-8136
Haskell MS 500/6-8
11525 Del Amo Blvd 90703 562-229-7815
Camille Lewis, prin. Fax 809-7250
Tetzlaff MS 600/7-8
12351 Del Amo Blvd 90703 562-229-7795
Crechena Wise, prin. Fax 402-6412
Tracy Continuation HS 400/Alt
12222 Cuesta Dr 90703 562-229-7760
Jeff Green, prin. Fax 926-8740
Whitney JSHS 1,000/7-12
16800 Shoemaker Ave 90703 562-229-7745
Rhonda Buss Ed.D., prin. Fax 926-2751
ABC Adult HS Adult
12254 Cuesta Dr 90703 562-229-7960
Pao-Ling Guo, prin. Fax 921-9958
Other Schools – See Artesia, Hawaiian Gardens, Lakewood

---

Fremont College Post-Sec.
18000 Studebaker Rd # 900A 90703 800-373-6668
PCI College Post-Sec.
17215 Studebaker Rd Ste 310 90703 562-916-5055
Valley Christian HS 600/9-12
17700 Dumont Ave 90703 562-865-0281
Troy Stahl, prin. Fax 865-0082
Valley Christian MS 300/7-8
18100 Dumont Ave 90703 562-865-6519
Paul Theule, prin. Fax 403-3159

**Chatsworth, See Los Angeles**
Los Angeles USD
Supt. — See Los Angeles
Aggeler Community Day S 100/Alt
21050 Plummer St 91311 818-341-1232
Alex Placencio, prin. Fax 349-1404
Lawrence MS 1,600/6-8
10100 Variel Ave 91311 818-678-7900
Danford Schar, prin. Fax 349-4539
Stoney Point Continuation HS 100/Alt
10010 De Soto Ave 91311 818-678-3491
George Padgett, prin. Fax 773-1796

---

Chaminade College Prep MS 700/6-8
19800 Devonshire St 91311 818-363-8127
Michael Valentine, prin. Fax 363-1219
Phillips Graduate Institute Post-Sec.
19900 Plummer St 91311 818-386-5660
Sierra Canyon S 500/7-12
20801 Rinaldi St 91311 818-882-8121
James Skrumbis, hdmstr. Fax 534-2398
Univ of West Los Angeles School of Law Post-Sec.
9201 Oakdale Ave Ste 201 91311 818-775-4500

**Chester, Plumas, Pop. 2,075**
Plumas USD
Supt. — See Quincy
Almanor HS 50/Alt
PO Box 797 96020 530-258-2126
Terry Oestreich, prin. Fax 258-2306
Chester JSHS 200/7-12
PO Box 797 96020 530-258-2126
Jeff James, prin. Fax 258-2306

**Chico, Butte, Pop. 82,892**
Chico USD 12,800/K-12
1163 E 7th St 95928 530-891-3000
Kelly Staley, supt. Fax 891-3220
www.chicousd.org
Academy for Change 50/Alt
290 East Ave 95926 530-895-4047
Andrew Moll, prin. Fax 895-4048
Bidwell JHS 700/7-8
2376 North Ave 95926 530-891-3080
Judi Roth, prin. Fax 891-3082
Chico HS 1,700/9-12
901 Esplanade 95926 530-891-3026
Mark Beebe, prin. Fax 891-3284
Chico JHS 600/7-8
280 Memorial Way 95926 530-891-3066
Pedro Caldera, prin. Fax 891-3264
Fair View HS 200/Alt
290 East Ave 95926 530-891-3092
Andrew Moll, prin. Fax 891-3232
Marsh JHS 600/7-8
2253 Humboldt Rd 95928 530-895-4110
Jay Marchant, prin. Fax 895-4111
Pleasant Valley HS 1,900/9-12
1475 East Ave 95926 530-879-5100
John Shepherd, prin. Fax 879-5263

Regional Occupational Center & Program
Supt. — None
Butte County ROP Vo/Tech
2491 Carmichael Dr Ste 100 95928 530-879-7462
Susan Steward, dir. Fax 879-7458

---

California State University-Chico Post-Sec.
400 W 1st St 95929 530-898-6116
Champion Christian S 100/9-12
480 Rio Lindo Ave 95926 530-345-8008
Ken Petlock, prin. Fax 345-5405

**Chino, San Bernardino, Pop. 76,369**
Chino Valley USD 29,600/K-12
5130 Riverside Dr 91710 909-628-1201
Wayne Joseph, supt. Fax 548-6096
www.chino.k12.ca.us
Buena Vista Continuation HS 200/Alt
13509 Ramona Ave 91710 909-628-9903
Rigoberto Vasquez, prin. Fax 548-6027
Chino HS 2,600/9-12
5472 Park Pl 91710 909-627-7351
Felix Melendez, prin. Fax 548-6004
Lugo HS 2,200/9-12
13400 Pipeline Ave 91710 909-591-3902
Kimberly Cabrera, prin. Fax 548-6020
Magnolia JHS 900/7-8
13150 Mountain Ave 91710 909-627-9263
John Miller, prin. Fax 627-2165
Ramona JHS 700/7-8
4575 Walnut Ave 91710 909-627-9144
Kathy Nash, prin. Fax 548-6055
Chino Community Adult Adult
12970 3rd St 91710 909-628-1201
Carl Hampton, prin. Fax 548-6016
Other Schools – See Chino Hills, Ontario

---

Chino Valley Christian Academy 100/K-12
12205 Pipeline Ave 91710 909-464-8255
Gary Yamamoto, admin.

**Chino Hills, San Bernardino, Pop. 72,538**
Chino Valley USD
Supt. — See Chino

Ayala HS — 2,500/9-12
14255 Peyton Dr 91709 — 909-627-3584
Diana Yarboi, prin. — Fax 464-9239
Boy's Republic HS — 200/Alt
1907 Boys Republic Dr 91709 — 909-628-1217
Carl Hampton, prin. — Fax 628-9847
Canyon Hills JHS — 1,100/7-8
2500 Madrugada Dr 91709 — 909-464-9938
Shehzad Bhojani, prin. — Fax 548-6058
Chino Hills HS — 3,000/9-12
16150 Pomona Rincon Rd 91709 — 909-606-7540
Isabel Brenes, prin. — Fax 548-6041
Townsend JHS — 1,200/7-8
15359 Ilex Dr 91709 — 909-591-2161
Sharyn MacCharles, prin. — Fax 548-6057

**Chowchilla, Madera, Pop. 17,893**
Alview-Dairyland UNESD — 400/K-8
12861 Avenue 18 1/2 93610 — 559-665-2394
Loren York, supt. — Fax 665-7347
www.adusd.k12.ca.us
Dairyland MS — 200/4-8
12861 Avenue 18 1/2 93610 — 559-665-2394
Loren York, prin. — Fax 665-7347

Chowchilla ESD — 2,100/PK-8
PO Box 910 93610 — 559-665-8000
Dr. Charles Martin, supt. — Fax 665-5134
www.chowchillaelem.k12.ca.us
Wilson MS — 500/7-8
PO Box 910 93610 — 559-665-8070
Zach White, prin. — Fax 665-8004

Chowchilla UNHSD — 1,000/9-12
805 Humboldt Ave 93610 — 559-665-1331
Ronald Seals, supt. — Fax 665-4659
www.chowchillahigh.k12.ca.us
Chowchilla HS — 1,000/9-12
805 Humboldt Ave 93610 — 559-665-1331
Dr. Justin Miller, prin. — Fax 665-1074
Gateway Continuation HS — 50/Alt
805 Humboldt Ave 93610 — 559-665-1331
Michelle Irwin, prin. — Fax 665-2220

**Chula Vista, San Diego, Pop. 235,860**
Sweetwater UNHSD — 38,300/K-12
1130 5th Ave 91911 — 619-691-5500
Dr. Karen Janney, supt. — Fax 498-1997
www.sweetwaterschools.org
Bonita Vista HS — 2,300/9-12
751 Otay Lakes Rd 91913 — 619-397-2000
Bettina Batista, prin. — Fax 656-1203
Bonita Vista MS — 1,100/7-8
650 Otay Lakes Rd 91910 — 619-397-2200
Eduardo Reyes, prin. — Fax 482-9356
Castle Park HS — 1,700/9-12
1395 Hilltop Dr 91911 — 619-585-2000
Viky Mitrovich, prin. — Fax 427-5967
Castle Park MS — 1,000/7-8
160 Quintard St 91911 — 619-498-6000
Gina Galvez-Mallari, prin. — Fax 427-8045
Chula Vista HS — 2,700/9-12
820 4th Ave 91911 — 619-476-3300
Mary Rose Peralta, prin. — Fax 427-5824
Chula Vista MS — 1,100/7-8
415 5th Ave 91910 — 619-498-6800
Julissa Gracias, prin. — Fax 427-5723
Eastlake HS — 2,700/9-12
1120 Eastlake Pkwy 91915 — 619-397-3800
Maria Esther Lizarraga, prin. — Fax 656-9736
Eastlake MS — 1,600/7-8
900 Duncan Ranch Rd 91914 — 619-591-4000
Juan Ulloa, prin. — Fax 482-0553
Hilltop HS — 2,100/9-12
555 Claire Ave 91910 — 619-476-4200
Thomas Gray, prin. — Fax 425-3284
Hilltop MS — 1,100/7-8
44 E J St 91910 — 619-498-2700
Griselda Delgado, prin. — Fax 585-3576
Olympian HS — 1,700/9-12
1925 Magdalena Ave 91913 — 619-656-2400
Ernesto Zamudio, prin. — Fax 216-0650
Options Secondary S — 300/Alt
467 Moss St 91911 — 619-585-7896
Mercedes Lopez, prin. — Fax 420-5663
Otay Ranch HS — 2,700/9-12
1250 Olympic Pkwy 91913 — 619-591-5000
Jose Brosz, prin. — Fax 591-5010
Palomar Continuation HS — 400/Alt
480 Palomar St 91911 — 619-407-4800
Sarita Fuentes, prin. — Fax 585-6232
Rancho del Rey MS — 1,600/7-8
1174 E J St 91910 — 619-397-2500
Anna Pedroza, prin. — Fax 656-3810
Chula Vista Adult S — Adult
1034 4th Ave 91911 — 619-796-7000
Wes Braddock, prin. — Fax 425-5447
Other Schools – See Imperial Beach, National City, San Diego, San Ysidro

Calvary Christian Academy — 400/PK-12
1771 E Palomar St 91913 — 619-591-2260
Dr. Richard Andujo, hdmstr. — Fax 591-2261
Covenant Christian S — 100/K-12
505 E Naples St 91911 — 619-421-8822
Thomas McManus, admin. — Fax 216-9846
Kaplan College — Post-Sec.
555 Broadway Ste 144 91910 — 619-498-4100
Lutheran HS of San Diego — 100/9-12
810 Buena Vista Way 91910 — 619-262-4444
Scott Dufresne M.A., dir. — Fax 691-0424
Mater Dei Catholic HS — 700/9-12
PO Box 210760 91921 — 619-423-2121
George Milke, prin. — Fax 423-6910
Pima Medical Institute — Post-Sec.
780 Bay Blvd Ste 101 91910 — 619-425-3200
Southwestern College — Post-Sec.
900 Otay Lakes Rd 91910 — 619-421-6700
United States University — Post-Sec.
830 Bay Blvd 91911 — 619-477-6310

**Citrus Heights, Sacramento, Pop. 79,798**
San Juan USD
Supt. — See Carmichael
Mesa Verde HS — 1,000/9-12
7501 Carriage Dr 95621 — 916-971-5288
Colin Bross, prin. — Fax 971-5215
New San Juan HS — 700/9-12
7551 Greenback Ln 95610 — 916-971-5112
Vanessa Adolphson, prin. — Fax 971-5111
Sylvan MS — 500/7-8
7137 Auburn Blvd 95610 — 916-971-7873
Kristen Schnepp, prin. — Fax 971-7896
Sunrise Tech Center — Adult
7322 Sunrise Blvd 95610 — 916-971-7654
Bill Bettencourt, prin. — Fax 971-7695

Carrington College California — Post-Sec.
7301 Greenback Ln Bldg A 95621 — 916-722-8200

**City of Industry, Los Angeles, Pop. 217**
Bassett USD
Supt. — See La Puente
Torch MS — 800/6-8
904 N Willow Ave 91746 — 626-931-2700
Filiberto Lujan, prin. — Fax 931-2702

Hacienda La Puente USD — 20,600/K-12
PO Box 60002 91716 — 626-933-1000
Cynthia Parulan-Colfer, supt. — Fax 855-3505
www.hlpschools.org
Workman HS — 1,200/9-12
16303 Temple Ave 91744 — 626-933-8801
Ben Webster, prin. — Fax 855-3148
Other Schools – See Hacienda Heights, La Puente

Elegante Beauty College — Post-Sec.
1600 S Azusa Ave Unit 244 91748 — 626-965-2532
Everest College — Post-Sec.
12801 Crossroads Pkwy S 91746 — 562-908-2500

**Claremont, Los Angeles, Pop. 33,627**
Claremont USD — 6,900/K-12
170 W San Jose Ave 91711 — 909-398-0609
James Elsasser Ed.D., supt. — Fax 398-0690
www.cusd.claremont.edu
Claremont HS — 2,400/9-12
1601 N Indian Hill Blvd 91711 — 909-624-9053
Brett O'Connor, prin. — Fax 624-2128
Community Day S — 50/Alt
125 W San Jose Ave 91711 — 909-398-0316
Sean Delgado, prin. — Fax 398-0384
El Roble IS — 1,100/7-8
665 N Mountain Ave 91711 — 909-398-0343
Scott Martinez, prin. — Fax 398-0399
San Antonio HS — 100/Alt
125 W San Jose Ave 91711 — 909-398-0316
Sean Delgado, prin. — Fax 398-0384
Claremont Adult S — Adult
170 W San Jose Ave Ste 100 91711 — 909-398-0609
Felipe Delvasto, coord. — Fax 626-5109

Claremont Graduate University — Post-Sec.
150 E 10th St 91711 — 909-621-8000
Claremont McKenna College — Post-Sec.
500 E 9th St 91711 — 909-621-8000
Claremont School of Theology — Post-Sec.
1325 N College Ave 91711 — 909-447-2500
Harvey Mudd College — Post-Sec.
301 Platt Blvd 91711 — 909-621-8000
Keck Graduate Institute — Post-Sec.
535 Watson Dr 91711 — 909-607-7855
Pitzer College — Post-Sec.
1050 N Mills Ave 91711 — 909-621-8219
Pomona College — Post-Sec.
333 N College Way 91711 — 909-621-8000
Scripps College — Post-Sec.
1030 Columbia Ave 91711 — 909-621-8000
Webb S — 400/9-12
1175 W Baseline Rd 91711 — 909-626-3587
Taylor Stockdale, head sch — Fax 621-4582

**Clarksburg, Yolo, Pop. 410**
River Delta USD
Supt. — See Rio Vista
Clarksburg MS — 200/7-9
52870 Netherlands Ave 95612 — 916-744-1717
Laura Uslan, prin. — Fax 744-5704
Delta HS — 200/10-12
52810 Netherlands Ave 95612 — 916-744-1714
Laura Uslan, prin. — Fax 744-1673

**Clayton, Contra Costa, Pop. 10,503**
Mount Diablo USD
Supt. — See Concord
Diablo View MS — 700/6-8
300 Diablo View Ln 94517 — 925-672-0898
Patti Bannister, prin. — Fax 672-4327

**Clearlake, Lake, Pop. 14,540**
Konocti USD
Supt. — See Lower Lake
Highlands Academy — 100/Alt
13050 High Valley Rd, — 707-994-6447
Matthrew Strahl, prin. — Fax 994-5047
Konocti Education Center — Alt
15850A Dam Rd Ext, — 707-994-6447
Jeffrey Dixon, prin. — Fax 994-4121

**Cloverdale, Sonoma, Pop. 8,447**
Cloverdale USD — 1,400/PK-12
97 School St 95425 — 707-894-1920
Jeremy Decker, supt. — Fax 894-1922
www.cusd.org/
Cloverdale HS — 400/9-12
509 N Cloverdale Blvd 95425 — 707-894-1900
Kirsten Sanft, prin. — Fax 894-4804
Eagle Creek Community S — 50/Alt
322 N Washington St 95425 — 707-894-1900
Kirsten Sanft, prin. — Fax 894-1922
Echols-Hansen Continuation HS — 50/Alt
322 N Washington St 95425 — 707-894-1925
Kirsten Sanft, prin.
Washington MS — 400/5-8
129 S Washington St 95425 — 707-894-1940
Stefanie Schaeffer, prin. — Fax 894-1946

**Clovis, Fresno, Pop. 92,614**
Clovis USD — 37,000/K-12
1450 Herndon Ave 93611 — 559-327-9000
Janet Young Ed.D., supt. — Fax 327-9109
www.cusd.com
Alta Sierra IS — 1,400/7-8
380 W Teague Ave, — 559-327-3500
Steve Pagani, prin. — Fax 327-3590
Buchanan HS — 2,500/9-12
1560 N Minnewawa Ave, — 559-327-3000
Ricci Ulrich, prin. — Fax 327-3090
Clark IS — 1,500/7-8
902 5th St 93612 — 559-327-1500
Kevin Kerney, prin. — Fax 327-1556
Clovis Community Day Secondary S — 100/Alt
1715 David E Cook Way 93611 — 559-327-1980
Tom Judd, prin. — Fax 327-1989
Clovis HS — 2,800/9-12
1055 Fowler Ave 93611 — 559-327-1000
Denver Stairs, prin. — Fax 327-1010
Gateway HS / Enterprise — 300/Alt
1550 Herndon Ave 93611 — 559-327-1800
Rees Warne, prin. — Fax 327-1890
Reagan Educational Center — 2,200/7-12
2940 Leonard Ave, — 559-327-4000
Chuck Sandoval, prin. — Fax 327-4190
Clovis Adult S — Adult
1452 David E Cook Way 93611 — 559-327-2800
Kevin Cookingham, prin. — Fax 327-2889
Other Schools – See Fresno

Institute of Technology — Post-Sec.
564 W Herndon Ave 93612 — 559-297-4500
ITT Technical Institute — Post-Sec.
362 N Clovis Ave 93612 — 559-325-5400
Kaplan College — Post-Sec.
44 Shaw Ave 93612 — 559-325-5101
Milan Institute — Post-Sec.
731 W Shaw Ave 93612 — 559-323-2800
San Joaquin College of Law — Post-Sec.
901 5th St 93612 — 559-323-2100
Tower Christian S — 100/K-12
8753 Chickadee Ln, — 559-298-2772
Ann Raber, admin. — Fax 297-4348

**Coachella, Riverside, Pop. 40,549**
Coachella Valley USD
Supt. — See Thermal
Cahuilla Desert Academy — 800/7-8
82489 Avenue 52 92236 — 760-398-0097
Michael Reule, prin. — Fax 398-0088
Duke MS — 700/7-8
85358 Bagdad Ave 92236 — 760-398-0139
Encarnacion Becerra, prin. — Fax 398-5399
Coachella Valley Adult Education — Adult
1099 Orchard Ave 92236 — 760-398-6302
Jereme Weischedel, prin. — Fax 398-0436

**Coalinga, Fresno, Pop. 13,188**
Coalinga-Huron USD — 4,100/K-12
657 Sunset St 93210 — 559-935-7500
Dr. Helen Foster, supt. — Fax 935-5329
www.chusd.org
Cambridge HS — 50/Alt
516 Baker St 93210 — 559-935-7578
Jeff Hardig, prin. — Fax 935-1692
Coalinga HS — 1,100/9-12
750 Van Ness St 93210 — 559-935-7520
Margo Perkins, prin. — Fax 935-3571
Coalinga MS — 600/6-8
265 Cambridge Ave 93210 — 559-935-7550
Gary Miller, prin. — Fax 934-1311
Culwell Community Day S — 50/Alt
275 Cambridge Ave 93210 — 559-935-7660
Jeff Hardig, prin. — Fax 935-5601
Other Schools – See Huron

Faith Christian Academy — 100/PK-12
450 W Elm Ave 93210 — 559-935-9209
Tara Davis, prin. — Fax 935-0745
West Hills College Coalinga — Post-Sec.
300 W Cherry Ln 93210 — 559-935-2000

**Coarsegold, Madera, Pop. 1,773**
Yosemite USD
Supt. — See Oakhurst
Foothill HS — 50/Alt
43875 Patrick Ave 93614 — 559-658-8616
Dr. Randy Haggard, prin. — Fax 658-2034
Meadowbrook Community Day S — 50/Alt
45426 Road 415 93614 — 559-683-3533
Dr. Randy Haggard, prin. — Fax 683-3533
Yosemite Falls Education Center — 50/Alt
35572 Highway 41 93614 — 559-658-8801
Dr. Randy Haggard, prin. — Fax 658-2359

**Coleville, Mono, Pop. 479**
Eastern Sierra USD
Supt. — See Bridgeport
Coleville HS — 100/9-12
111591 US Highway 395 96107 — 530-495-2231
Steve Childs, prin. — Fax 495-2730

Mono County Office of Education
Supt. — See Bridgeport
Sawtooth Ridge Community S — 50/7-12
111591 Highway 395 96107 — 760-934-0031
Janet Hunt, prin.

**Colfax, Placer, Pop. 1,892**
Placer UNHSD
Supt. — See Auburn
Colfax HS 800/9-12
24995 Ben Taylor Rd 95713 530-346-2284
Paul Lundberg, prin. Fax 346-6476

**Colma, San Mateo, Pop. 1,713**
Jefferson ESD
Supt. — See Daly City
Franklin IS 500/7-8
700 Stewart Ave, Daly City CA 94015 650-991-1200
James Parrish, prin. Fax 756-5475

**Colton, San Bernardino, Pop. 51,046**
Colton JUSD 23,100/PK-12
1212 Valencia Dr 92324 909-580-5000
Jerry Almendarez, supt. Fax 433-9471
www.cjusd.net
Colton HS 3,300/9-12
777 W Valley Blvd 92324 909-580-5005
Joda Murphy, prin. Fax 876-4093
Colton MS 1,000/7-8
670 W Laurel St 92324 909-580-5009
John Abbott, prin. Fax 876-4095
Washington Alternative HS 200/Alt
900 E C St 92324 909-580-5011
Pete Tasaka, prin. Fax 876-6352
Other Schools – See Bloomington, Grand Terrace

Rialto USD
Supt. — See Rialto
Jehue MS 1,600/6-8
1500 N Eucalyptus Ave 92324 909-421-7377
Armando Urteaga, prin. Fax 421-7376

---

Coast Career Institute Post-Sec.
1250 E Cooley Dr 92324 877-277-7170
DeVry University Post-Sec.
1090 E Washington St Ste H 92324 909-514-1808
Four-D College Post-Sec.
1020 E Washington St 92324 909-783-9331

**Colusa, Colusa, Pop. 5,849**
Colusa County Office of Education 100/
345 5th St Ste A 95932 530-458-0350
Michael West, supt. Fax 458-8054
www.ccoe.net
Abel Community S, 146 7th St 95932 Alt
Maria Arvizu De Espinoza, prin. 530-473-1350

Colusa USD 1,300/K-12
745 10th St 95932 530-458-7791
Dwayne Newman, supt. Fax 458-4030
www.colusa.k12.ca.us
Colusa Alternative HS 50/Alt
901 Colus Ave 95932 530-458-2156
Darren Brown, prin. Fax 458-5783
Colusa HS 400/9-12
901 Colus Ave 95932 530-458-2156
Darren Brown, prin. Fax 458-5783
Egling MS 500/4-8
813 Webster St 95932 530-458-7631
Jody Johnston, prin. Fax 458-8107

**Commerce, Los Angeles, Pop. 12,764**

---

National Polytechnic College Post-Sec.
6630 Telegraph Rd 90040 323-728-9636

**Compton, Los Angeles, Pop. 94,840**
Compton USD 24,500/PK-12
501 S Santa Fe Ave 90221 310-639-4321
Dr. Carmella Franco, supt. Fax 632-3014
www.compton.k12.ca.us
Bunche MS 700/6-8
12338 S Mona Blvd 90222 310-898-6010
Frank Lozier, prin. Fax 638-4935
Centennial HS 1,100/9-12
2600 N Central Ave 90222 310-635-2715
Mattie Adams, prin. Fax 631-9164
Chavez Continuation HS 300/Alt
12501 S Wilmington Ave 90222 310-898-6340
Laura Henry, prin. Fax 763-4186
Community Day S 50/Alt
417 W Alondra Blvd 90220 310-898-6154
Yvonne Smith, prin. Fax 632-7304
Compton Early College HS 9-12
601 S Acacia St 90220 310-639-4321
Mattie Robertson, prin.
Compton HS 2,300/9-12
601 S Acacia Ave 90220 310-635-3881
Doi Johnson, prin. Fax 898-6402
Davis MS 1,100/6-8
621 W Poplar St 90220 310-898-6020
Lakeyshua Washington, prin. Fax 631-5725
Dominguez HS 2,400/9-12
15301 S San Jose Ave 90221 562-630-0142
Oscar Mendez, prin. Fax 408-2367
Enterprise MS 600/6-8
2600 W Compton Blvd 90220 310-898-6030
David Herrera, prin. Fax 632-4183
Marshall Alternative S 50/Alt
12501 S Wilmington Ave 90222 310-604-2780
Laura Henry, prin. Fax 223-0970
Middle Opportunity S Alt
2300 W Caldwell St Bldg A 90220 310-639-7329
Laura Henry, prin. Fax 632-7304
Roosevelt MS 1,100/6-8
1200 E Alondra Blvd 90221 310-898-6040
Dr. Rigoberto Roman, prin. Fax 631-3298
Tubman Continuation HS 50/Alt
12501 S Wilmington Ave 90222 310-898-6340
Laura Henry, prin. Fax 763-4186
Walton MS 600/6-8
900 W Greenleaf Dr 90220 310-898-6060
Dr. RoseMarie Hickman, prin. Fax 631-3409
Whaley MS 900/6-8
14401 S Gibson Ave 90221 310-898-6070
Dr. Candice Waters, prin. Fax 638-7079
Willowbrook MS 500/6-8
2601 N Wilmington Ave 90222 310-898-6080
Dennis Perry, prin. Fax 537-2932
Compton Adult S Adult
1104 E 148th St 90220 310-898-6490
Christopher Calvin, admin. Fax 898-6477
Other Schools – See Los Angeles

Regional Occupational Center & Program
Supt. — None
Compton Unified ROP Vo/Tech
1104 E 148th St 90220 310-898-6000
Ryan Whetstone, dir. Fax 763-3871

---

El Camino College Compton Center Post-Sec.
1111 E Artesia Blvd 90221 310-900-1600
St. Albert the Great MS 100/6-8
823 E Compton Blvd 90220 310-515-3891
Tina Johnson, prin. Fax 515-1413
Universal College of Beauty Post-Sec.
718 W Compton Blvd 90220 310-635-6969

**Concord, Contra Costa, Pop. 116,303**
Mount Diablo USD 31,900/PK-12
1936 Carlotta Dr 94519 925-682-8000
Dr. Nellie Meyer, supt. Fax 689-1649
www.mdusd.org
Concord HS 1,600/9-12
4200 Concord Blvd 94521 925-687-2030
Rianne Pfalsgraff, prin. Fax 682-4613
Crossroads HS 100/Alt
2701 Willow Pass Rd 94519 925-689-6852
Samantha Allen, admin. Fax 603-1771
Diablo Community Day S 50/Alt
1026 Mohr Ln 94518 925-676-6862
Thom Kwiatkowski, admin. Fax 682-9352
El Dorado MS 1,100/6-8
1750 West St 94521 925-682-5700
Robert Humphrey, prin. Fax 685-1460
Mount Diablo HS 1,500/9-12
2450 Grant St 94520 925-682-4030
Liane Cismowski, prin. Fax 687-9658
Nueva Vista HS / Summit/TLC 100/Alt
4200 Concord Blvd 94521 925-689-1487
Brook Penca, prin. Fax 689-2134
Oak Grove MS 700/6-8
2050 Minert Rd 94518 925-682-1843
Christina Filios, prin. Fax 682-2083
Olympic Continuation HS 400/Alt
2730 Salvio St 94519 925-687-0363
Lynsie Castellano, prin. Fax 798-6317
Pine Hollow MS 700/6-8
5522 Pine Hollow Rd 94521 925-672-5444
Shelley Bain, prin. Fax 672-9751
Summit HS 100/Alt
4200 Concord Blvd 94521 925-687-0991
Edward Penca, prin. Fax 603-1770
Ygnacio Valley HS 1,200/9-12
755 Oak Grove Rd 94518 925-685-8414
Efa Huckaby, prin. Fax 685-1435
Mount Diablo Adult Center Adult
1266 San Carlos Ave 94518 925-685-7340
Vittoria Abbate, dir. Fax 687-8217
Other Schools – See Bay Point, Clayton, Pleasant Hill, Walnut Creek

---

Carondelet HS 800/9-12
1133 Winton Dr 94518 925-686-5353
Kevin Cushing, prin. Fax 671-9429
De La Salle HS 1,000/9-12
1130 Winton Dr 94518 925-288-8100
Br. Robert Wickman, prin. Fax 686-3474
Heald College Post-Sec.
5130 Commercial Cir 94520 925-288-5800
ITT Technical Institute Post-Sec.
1140 Galaxy Way Ste 400 94520 925-674-8200
Paris Beauty College Post-Sec.
1655 Willow Pass Rd 94520 925-685-7600

**Corcoran, Kings, Pop. 24,292**
Corcoran JUSD 3,300/PK-12
1520 Patterson Ave 93212 559-992-8888
Rich Merlo, supt. Fax 992-3957
www.corcoranunified.com/
Corcoran HS 1,000/9-12
1520 Patterson Ave 93212 559-992-8884
Antonia Stone, prin. Fax 992-5066
Kings Lake Education Center 50/Alt
1520 Patterson Ave 93212 559-992-8885
Keith Airheart, admin. Fax 992-4858
Muir MS 700/6-8
1520 Patterson Ave 93212 559-992-8886
David Whitmore, prin. Fax 992-4423

**Corning, Tehama, Pop. 7,468**
Corning UNESD 1,700/K-8
1590 South St 96021 530-824-7700
Richard Fitzpatrick, supt. Fax 824-2493
www.corningelementary.org
Maywood MS 400/7-8
1666 Marguerite Ave 96021 530-824-7730
Dave Cory, prin. Fax 824-7742

Corning UNHSD 1,000/9-12
643 Blackburn Ave 96021 530-824-8000
John Burch, supt. Fax 824-8005
www.corninghs.org/
Centennial Continuation HS 100/Alt
250 E Fig Ln 96021 530-824-7400
Andrea Nilsen, prin. Fax 824-7405
Corning Community Day S 50/Alt
823 North St 96021 530-824-7140
Andrea Nilsen, prin. Fax 824-8005
Corning HS 1,000/9-12
643 Blackburn Ave 96021 530-824-8000
Charlie Troughton, prin. Fax 824-8005
Corning Adult S, 250 E Fig Ln 96021 Adult
Dr. Andrea Nilsen, prin. 530-824-7400

**Corona, Riverside, Pop. 147,939**
Corona-Norco USD
Supt. — See Norco
Auburndale IS 800/7-8
1255 River Rd 92880 951-736-3231
Ben Sanchez, prin. Fax 736-3360
Centennial HS 3,100/9-12
1820 Rimpau Ave 92881 951-739-5670
Dr. Ben Roberts, prin. Fax 739-5693
Citrus Hills IS 1,400/7-8
3211 S Main St 92882 951-736-4600
Andrew Roberts, prin. Fax 736-4623
Corona Fundamental IS 1,100/7-8
1230 S Main St 92882 951-736-3321
Kelli Jakubik, prin. Fax 736-3417
Corona HS 3,200/9-12
1150 W 10th St 92882 951-736-3211
Dr. Danny Kim, prin. Fax 736-3408
El Cerrito MS 1,200/6-8
7610 El Cerrito Rd 92881 951-736-3216
Dr. Shelly Yarbrough, prin. Fax 736-3286
Orange Grove HS 200/Alt
300 S Buena Vista Ave 92882 951-736-3339
Joe Almasy, prin. Fax 736-3435
Pollard HS 800/Alt
185 Magnolia Ave 92879 951-736-3367
Mike Ridgway, prin. Fax 736-7104
Raney IS 1,100/6-8
1010 W Citron St 92882 951-736-3221
John Sanchez, prin. Fax 736-3439
Santiago HS 3,800/9-12
1395 Foothill Pkwy 92881 951-739-5600
Dr. Ryan Lewis, prin. Fax 739-5639
Corona-Norco Adult Education Adult
300 S Buena Vista Ave 92882 951-736-3325
JoDee Slyter, prin. Fax 736-7159

---

Christian Heritage S 300/K-12
PO Box 1780 92878 951-736-3033
Arleen Morris, admin.
Crossroads Christian S 1,000/PK-12
2380 Fullerton Ave 92881 951-278-3199
Doug Husen, supt. Fax 493-2169
ITT Technical Institute Post-Sec.
4160 Temescal Canyon # 100 92883 951-277-5400
JEM College Post-Sec.
271 Ott St Ste 23 92882 951-549-0693

**Coronado, San Diego, Pop. 18,310**
Coronado USD 3,100/PK-12
201 6th St 92118 619-522-8900
Jeffrey Felix, supt. Fax 437-6570
coronadousd.net
Coronado HS 1,100/9-12
650 D Ave 92118 619-522-8907
Karl Mueller, prin. Fax 437-0236
Coronado MS 800/6-8
550 F Ave 92118 619-522-8921
Jay Marquand, prin. Fax 522-6948
Palm Academy, 555 D Ave 92118 50/Alt
Jennifer Moore, prin. 619-437-7256

**Costa Mesa, Orange, Pop. 106,497**
Newport - Mesa USD 21,800/K-12
2985 Bear St 92626 714-424-5000
Frederick Navarro Ed.D., supt. Fax 424-5018
www.nmusd.us
Back Bay HS 100/Alt
390 Monte Vista Ave 92627 949-515-6900
Debbie Lucker-Davis, prin. Fax 515-3380
Costa Mesa JSHS 1,700/7-12
2650 Fairview Rd 92626 714-424-8700
Jacob Haley, prin. Fax 424-8770
Early College HS 200/9-12
2990 Mesa Verde Dr E 92626 714-241-6108
David Martinez, prin. Fax 241-6185
Estancia HS 1,300/9-12
2323 Placentia Ave 92627 949-515-6500
Michael Halt, prin. Fax 515-6571
Monte Vista HS 100/Alt
390 Monte Vista Ave 92627 949-515-6900
Debbie Lucker-Davis, prin. Fax 515-3380
TeWinkle MS 700/7-8
3224 California St 92626 714-424-7965
Kira Hurst, prin. Fax 424-5680
Newport Mesa Adult Education Adult
2045 Meyer Pl 92627 949-515-6996
Becky Goegel, prin.
Other Schools – See Newport Beach

Regional Occupational Center & Program
Supt. — None
Coastline ROP Vo/Tech
1001 Presidio Sq 92626 714-979-1955
Carol Hume, supt. Fax 557-6812

---

James Albert School of Cosmetology Post-Sec.
1835 Newport Blvd 92627 949-642-0606
Orange Coast College Post-Sec.
PO Box 5005 92628 714-432-5072
Pacific College Post-Sec.
3160 Red Hill Ave 92626 714-662-4402
Paul Mitchell The School Post-Sec.
3309 Hyland Ave Ste J 92626 714-546-8786
Vanguard University of Southern CA Post-Sec.
55 Fair Dr 92626 714-556-3610
Waldorf S of Orange County 300/PK-12
2350 Canyon Dr 92627 949-574-7775
Kim Sava, dir. Fax 574-7740

**Cottonwood, Shasta, Pop. 3,202**
Anderson UNHSD
Supt. — See Anderson
West Valley HS 1,000/9-12
3805 Happy Valley Rd 96022 530-347-7171
Emmett Koerperich, prin. Fax 347-0481

Cottonwood UNESD 600/K-8
20512 1st St 96022 530-347-3165
David Alexander Ed.D., supt. Fax 347-0247
cwusd.com
West Cottonwood JHS 300/5-8
20512 1st St 96022 530-347-3123
Douglas Geren, prin. Fax 347-0247

Evergreen UESD 1,000/PK-12
19500 Learning Way 96022 530-347-3411
Brad Mendenhall, supt. Fax 347-7954
www.evergreenusd.org
Evergreen MS 400/5-8
19500 Learning Way 96022 530-347-3411
Felicia Ross, prin. Fax 347-7953

**Coulterville, Mariposa, Pop. 195**
Mariposa County USD
Supt. — See Mariposa
Coulterville HS 50/9-12
10326 Fiske Rd 95311 209-878-3028
Lydia Lower, prin. Fax 878-3067

**Courtland, Sacramento, Pop. 350**
River Delta USD
Supt. — See Rio Vista
Mokelumne HS 50/Alt
PO Box 574 95615 916-775-9160
Maria Elena Becerra, prin. Fax 775-1797
River Delta Community Day S 50/Alt
160 Courtland High School 95615 916-775-9160
Maria Elena Becerra, prin. Fax 775-1797

**Covelo, Mendocino, Pop. 1,175**
Round Valley USD 400/K-12
PO Box 276 95428 707-983-6171
Mike Gorman, supt. Fax 983-6655
www.roundvalleyschools.org/
Round Valley Continuation HS 50/Alt
PO Box 276 95428 707-983-6171
Mark Smith, prin. Fax 983-6179
Round Valley HS 100/9-12
PO Box 276 95428 707-983-6171
Mark Smith, prin. Fax 983-6179

**Covina, Los Angeles, Pop. 46,744**
Azusa USD
Supt. — See Azusa
Gladstone HS 1,400/9-12
1340 N Enid Ave 91722 626-815-3600
Scott Magnusson, prin. Fax 815-3655

Charter Oak USD 5,700/K-12
20240 E Cienega Ave 91724 626-966-8331
Michael Hendricks Ed.D., supt. Fax 967-9580
www.cousd.net
Charter Oak HS 1,900/9-12
1430 E Covina Blvd 91724 626-915-5841
Dr. Ivan Ayro, prin. Fax 915-3398
Royal Oak MS 900/7-8
303 S Glendora Ave 91724 626-967-6354
Maria Thompson, prin. Fax 331-2074
Other Schools – See Glendora

Covina-Valley USD 13,300/K-12
519 E Badillo St 91723 626-974-7000
Dr. Richard Sheehan, supt. Fax 974-7032
www.cvusd.k12.ca.us
Covina HS 1,400/9-12
463 S Hollenbeck Ave 91723 626-974-6020
Christiana Kraus, prin. Fax 974-6045
Fairvalley HS 200/Alt
758 W Grondahl St 91722 626-974-4800
Dana Craig, prin. Fax 974-4815
Las Palmas MS 1,000/6-8
641 N Lark Ellen Ave 91722 626-974-7200
Nicole Higuera, prin. Fax 974-7215
Northview HS 1,500/9-12
1016 W Cypress St 91722 626-974-6120
Dr. Julie Harrison, prin. Fax 974-6145
Sierra Vista MS 1,100/6-8
777 E Puente St 91723 626-974-7300
Danielle Travieso, prin. Fax 974-7315
Business Center Adult
342 S 4th Ave 91723 626-974-6800
Claudia Karnoski, prin. Fax 974-6814
Tri Community Adult Ed.-Griswold Center Adult
342 S 4th Ave 91723 626-472-7680
Dan Gribbon, prin. Fax 472-7681
Other Schools – See West Covina

---

American Graduate University Post-Sec.
733 N Dodsworth Ave 91724 626-966-4576
Firm Foundation Christian Academy 100/PK-12
541 S Aldenville Ave 91723 626-938-1199
Mary Carnighan, head sch

**Crescent City, Del Norte, Pop. 7,317**
Del Norte County Office of Education 500/
301 W Washington Blvd 95531 707-464-0200
Jeff Harris, supt. Fax 464-0238
www.delnortecoe.org
Del Norte Community Day S 50/Alt
400 W Harding Ave 95531 707-464-0750
Rob Parker, prin. Fax 464-5116
McCarthy Center 50/Alt
301 W Washington Blvd 95531 707-464-0399
Tony Fabricus, prin. Fax 465-5116

Del Norte County USD 4,000/K-12
301 W Washington Blvd 95531 707-464-6141
Jeff Harris, supt. Fax 464-0238
www.delnorte.k12.ca.us
Crescent Elk MS 600/6-8
994 G St 95531 707-464-0320
Paige Swan, prin. Fax 464-7920
Del Norte County HS 1,000/9-12
1301 El Dorado St 95531 707-464-0260
Randy Fugate, prin. Fax 464-0785
Educational Options Alt
400 W Harding Ave 95531 707-464-0750
Robert Parker, prin. Fax 465-5116
Sunset Continuation HS 100/Alt
2500 Elk Valley Cross Rd 95531 707-464-0380
Tony Fabricius, prin. Fax 465-5346

Regional Occupational Center & Program
Supt. — None
Del Norte County ROP Vo/Tech
1301 El Dorado St 95531 707-464-0274
Colleen Parker, dir. Fax 465-6923

---

Foursquare Christian S 100/PK-12
144 Butte St 95531 707-464-9501
Maria Guy, prin. Fax 465-3254

**Crockett, Contra Costa, Pop. 2,949**
John Swett USD
Supt. — See Rodeo
Carquinez MS 400/6-8
1099 Pomona St 94525 510-787-1081
Annie Flores-Aikey, prin. Fax 787-2359
Swett HS 500/9-12
1098 Pomona St 94525 510-787-1088
Jeff Brauning, prin. Fax 787-1930
Willow Continuation HS 50/Alt
1650 Crockett Blvd 94525 510-787-1286
Ken Nelson, prin. Fax 787-4770

**Crows Landing, Stanislaus, Pop. 352**
Chatom UNESD
Supt. — See Turlock
Mountain View MS 200/6-8
10001 Crows Landing Rd 95313 209-664-8515
Monica Schut, prin. Fax 669-1733

**Cudahy, Los Angeles, Pop. 23,704**
Los Angeles USD
Supt. — See Los Angeles
Elizabeth Learning Center 1,800/K-12
4811 Elizabeth St 90201 323-271-3600
Damian Lenon, prin. Fax 560-8412

**Culver City, Los Angeles, Pop. 36,982**
Culver City USD 6,800/K-12
4034 Irving Pl 90232 310-842-4220
David LaRose, supt. Fax 842-4205
www.ccusd.org
Culver City HS 2,300/9-12
4401 Elenda St 90230 310-842-4200
Lisa Cooper, prin. Fax 842-4303
Culver City MS 1,500/6-8
4601 Elenda St 90230 310-842-4200
Linsey Gotanda, prin. Fax 842-4304
Culver City USD Academy Alt
4601 Elenda St 90230 310-842-4200
Veronica Montes, prin.
Culver Park Continuation HS 100/Alt
4601 Elenda St 90230 310-390-8886
Veronica Montes, prin. Fax 390-3796
Culver City Adult S Adult
4909 Overland Ave 90230 310-842-4300
Veronica Montes, prin. Fax 842-4343

---

Antioch University Los Angeles Post-Sec.
400 Corporate Pointe 90230 310-578-1080
ITT Technical Institute Post-Sec.
6101 W Centinela Ave 90230 310-417-5800
West Los Angeles College Post-Sec.
9000 Overland Ave 90230 310-287-4200

**Cupertino, Santa Clara, Pop. 56,415**
Cupertino UNSD 18,600/PK-8
10301 Vista Dr 95014 408-252-3000
Dr. Wendy Gudalewicz, supt. Fax 343-2801
www.edline.net/pages/Cupertino_Union_SD
Hyde MS 1,000/6-8
19325 Bollinger Rd 95014 408-252-6290
Todd Shimada, prin. Fax 255-3288
Kennedy MS 1,300/6-8
821 Bubb Rd 95014 408-253-1525
Steven Hamm, prin. Fax 257-5777
Lawson MS 1,000/6-8
10401 Vista Dr 95014 408-255-7500
Jeff Bowman, prin. Fax 446-4987
Other Schools – See San Jose, Sunnyvale

Fremont UNHSD
Supt. — See Sunnyvale
Cupertino HS 1,900/9-12
10100 Finch Ave 95014 408-366-7300
Kami Tomberlain, prin. Fax 255-8466
Homestead HS 2,300/9-12
21370 Homestead Rd 95014 408-522-2500
Greg Giglio, prin. Fax 738-8631
Monta Vista HS 2,500/9-12
21840 McClellan Rd 95014 408-366-7600
April Scott, prin. Fax 252-1519

---

DeAnza College Post-Sec.
21250 Stevens Creek Blvd 95014 408-864-5678
Legend College Preparatory S 200/6-12
21050 McClellan Rd 95014 408-865-0366
Paul Chan, prin. Fax 253-6529

**Cutler, Tulare, Pop. 4,971**
Cutler-Orosi JUSD
Supt. — See Orosi

Lovell HS 100/Alt
12724 Avenue 392 93615 559-528-4703
Martha Calderon, prin. Fax 528-0102

**Cypress, Orange, Pop. 46,012**
Anaheim UNHSD
Supt. — See Anaheim
Cypress HS 2,600/9-12
9801 Valley View St 90630 714-220-4144
Jodie Wales Ed.D., prin. Fax 220-4174
Lexington JHS 1,200/7-8
4351 Orange Ave 90630 714-220-4201
Darrick Garcia, prin. Fax 761-4989
Oxford Academy 1,100/7-12
5172 Orange Ave 90630 714-220-3055
Ron Hoshi, prin. Fax 527-7128

---

Cypress College Post-Sec.
9200 Valley View St 90630 714-484-7000
Trident University International Post-Sec.
5757 Plaza Dr Ste 100 90630 800-579-3197

**Daggett, San Bernardino**
Silver Valley USD
Supt. — See Yermo
Calico Continuation HS 50/Alt
33525 Ponnay St 92327 760-254-2715
Michael Cox, prin. Fax 254-2194
Silver Valley Academy 50/Alt
33525 Ponnay St 92327 760-254-2715
Michael Cox, prin. Fax 254-2194
Silver Valley Community Day S 50/Alt
33525 Ponnay 92327 760-254-2715
Michael Cox, prin. Fax 254-2194
Silver Valley Adult S Adult
33525 Ponnay 92327 760-254-2715
Michael Cox, prin. Fax 254-2194

**Daly City, San Mateo, Pop. 97,070**
Bayshore ESD 400/K-8
1 Martin St 94014 415-467-5443
Dr. Audra Pittman, supt. Fax 467-1542
www.bayshore.k12.ca.us
Robertson IS 200/5-8
1 Martin St 94014 415-467-5443
Dr. Sergio Nesterov, prin. Fax 467-1542

Jefferson ESD 6,100/K-8
101 Lincoln Ave 94015 650-991-1000
Bernardo Vidales, supt. Fax 992-2265
www.jsd.k12.ca.us/
Pollicita MS 600/6-8
550 E Market St 94014 650-991-1216
Benjamin Turner, prin. Fax 755-2170
Rivera IS 500/7-8
1255 Southgate Ave 94015 650-991-1225
Dina Conti, prin. Fax 755-6273
Other Schools – See Colma

Jefferson UNHSD 5,000/9-12
699 Serramonte Blvd Ste 100 94015 650-550-7900
Thomas H. Minshew, supt. Fax 550-7888
www.juhsd.net
Jefferson HS 1,200/9-12
6996 Mission St 94014 650-550-7700
Jason Brockmeyer, prin. Fax 550-7790
Thornton HS 200/Alt
115 1st Ave 94014 650-550-7840
Monica Casey, prin. Fax 758-2092
Westmoor HS 1,700/9-12
131 Westmoor Ave 94015 650-550-7400
Allan Reyes, prin. Fax 550-7490
Adult Education Divison Adult
699 Serramonte Blvd Ste 111 94015 650-550-7890
Diana Rumney, prin. Fax 550-7889
Other Schools – See Pacifica

---

Bridgemont HS, PO Box 206 94016 50/9-12
Evan Anderson, prin. 415-685-5300
DeVry University Post-Sec.
2001 Junipero Serra Ste 161 94014 650-991-3520
Hilltop Beauty School Post-Sec.
6317 Mission St 94014 650-756-2720

**Dana Point, Orange, Pop. 32,532**
Capistrano USD
Supt. — See San Juan Capistrano
Dana Hills HS 2,800/9-12
33333 Golden Lantern St 92629 949-496-6666
Jason Allemann, prin. Fax 489-8317

**Danville, Contra Costa, Pop. 40,475**
San Ramon Valley USD 29,200/PK-12
699 Old Orchard Dr 94526 925-552-5500
Mary Shelton, supt. Fax 838-3147
www.srvusd.net/
Del Amigo Continuation HS 50/Alt
189 Del Amigo Rd 94526 925-855-2600
Amy Gillespie-Oss, prin. Fax 838-5372
Diablo Vista MS 900/6-8
4100 Camino Tassajara 94506 925-855-7600
Becky Ingram, prin. Fax 648-7167
Los Cerros MS 700/6-8
968 Blemer Rd 94526 925-855-6800
Evan Powell, prin. Fax 837-3512
Monte Vista HS 2,200/9-12
3131 Stone Valley Rd 94526 925-552-2800
Kevin Ahern, prin. Fax 743-1744
San Ramon Valley HS 2,100/9-12
501 Danville Blvd 94526 925-552-3000
Ruth Steele, prin. Fax 552-3060
Wood MS 1,000/6-8
600 El Capitan Dr 94526 925-855-4400
Christopher George, prin. Fax 820-1857
Other Schools – See Alamo, San Ramon

---

Athenian S 500/6-12
2100 Mount Diablo Scenic 94506 925-837-5375
Eric Niles, head sch Fax 362-7292

**Davis, Yolo, Pop. 62,607**
Davis JUSD 8,500/K-12
526 B St 95616 530-757-5300
Winfred Roberson, supt. Fax 757-5323
www.djusd.net
Davis S for Independent Study 100/Alt
526 B St 95616 530-757-5333
Karrie Hernandez, prin. Fax 757-5382
Davis SHS 1,700/10-12
315 W 14th St 95616 530-757-5400
William Brown, prin. Fax 757-5492
Emerson JHS 400/7-9
2121 Calaveras Ave 95616 530-757-5430
Stacy Desideri, prin. Fax 757-5434
Harper JHS 700/7-9
4000 E Covell Blvd 95618 530-757-5330
Kerin Kelleher, prin. Fax 757-5350
Holmes JHS 700/7-9
1220 Drexel Dr 95616 530-757-5445
Derek Brothers, prin. Fax 757-5435
King Continuation HS 100/Alt
635 B St 95616 530-757-5425
Michelle Flowers, prin. Fax 757-5440
Davis Adult S Adult
315 W 14th St 95616 530-757-5380
Grace Sauser, prin. Fax 757-5381

---

D-Q University Post-Sec.
PO Box 409 95617 530-758-0470
University of California Post-Sec.
1 Shields Ave 95616 530-752-1011

**Delano, Kern, Pop. 52,490**
Delano JUNHSD 4,200/9-12
1720 Norwalk St 93215 661-725-4000
Rosalina Rivera, supt. Fax 721-9390
www.djuhsd.org/
Chavez HS 1,400/9-12
1720 Norwalk St 93215 661-720-4502
Ben DeLeon, prin. Fax 725-8875
Delano HS 1,600/9-12
1720 Norwalk St 93215 661-720-4121
April Gregerson, prin. Fax 720-4119
Kennedy HS 800/9-12
1720 Norwalk St 93215 661-720-5102
Raudel Rojas, prin. Fax 721-0833
Valley HS 200/Alt
1720 Norwalk St 93215 661-720-4374
Chris Juarez, prin. Fax 725-7611
Delano Adult S Adult
1720 Norwalk St 93215 661-720-4173
Dr. Terri Nuckols, dir. Fax 725-5852

Delano UNESD 6,900/PK-8
1405 12th Ave 93215 661-721-5000
Rosalina Rivera, supt. Fax 725-2201
www.duesd.org
Almond Tree MS 700/6-8
200 W 15th Ave 93215 661-721-3641
Rodney Del Rio, prin. Fax 721-3649
La Vina MS 600/6-8
1331 Browning Rd 93215 661-721-3601
Jennifer Townson, prin. Fax 721-3662

**Delhi, Merced, Pop. 10,554**
Delhi USD 2,600/K-12
9716 Hinton Ave 95315 209-656-2000
Adolfo Melara, supt. Fax 668-6133
www.delhi.k12.ca.us
Delhi HS 700/9-12
9716 Hinton Ave 95315 209-656-2050
Vincent Gonzalez, prin. Fax 669-3168
Delhi MS 200/8-8
9716 Hinton Ave 95315 209-656-2050
Vincent Gonzalez, prin. Fax 669-3168
Shattuck Educational Park HS 50/Alt
9716 Hinton Ave 95315 209-656-2012
Francisca Briones, prin. Fax 669-6165
Delhi Adult S Adult
9716 Hinton Ave 95315 209-656-2012
Francisca Briones, prin. Fax 669-6165

**Del Mar, San Diego, Pop. 4,073**

---

Winston S of San Diego 100/4-12
215 9th St 92014 858-259-8155
Mike Peterson, hdmstr. Fax 259-8356

**Denair, Stanislaus, Pop. 4,321**
Denair USD 1,600/PK-12
3460 Lester Rd 95316 209-632-7514
Dr. Aaron Rosander, supt. Fax 632-9194
dusd.k12.ca.us
Denair HS 400/9-12
3460 Lester Rd 95316 209-632-9911
Alecia Myer, prin. Fax 632-8153
Denair MS 300/6-8
3460 Lester Rd 95316 209-632-2510
Travis Manley, prin. Fax 632-0269

**Desert Hot Springs, Riverside, Pop. 25,289**
Palm Springs USD
Supt. — See Palm Springs
Desert Hot Springs Alternative Center Alt
11695 Palm Dr 92240 760-329-3330
Milt Jones, prin. Fax 329-6677
Desert Hot Springs HS 1,900/9-12
65850 Pierson Blvd 92240 760-288-7000
George Bullis, prin. Fax 288-7010
Desert Springs MS 900/6-8
66755 Two Bunch Palms Trl 92240 760-251-7200
Kiela Snider, prin. Fax 251-7206
Painted Hills MS 800/6-8
9250 Sonora Dr 92240 760-251-1551
Michael Grainger, prin. Fax 251-5330

**Diamond Bar, Los Angeles, Pop. 54,094**
Pomona USD
Supt. — See Pomona
Lorbeer MS 700/7-8
501 S Diamond Bar Blvd 91765 909-397-4527
Angelique Butler, prin. Fax 396-9022

Walnut Valley USD
Supt. — See Walnut
Chaparral MS 1,300/6-8
1405 Spruce Tree Dr 91765 909-861-6227
Ronald Thibodeaux, prin. Fax 396-0749
Diamond Bar HS 3,000/9-12
21400 Pathfinder Rd 91765 909-594-1405
Denis Paul, prin. Fax 595-8301

---

California Intercontinental University Post-Sec.
1470 Valley Vista Dr # 150 91765 909-396-6090
Institute of Knowledge 200/K-12
1009 Via Sorella, 909-595-2401
Nagwa Amin, prin. Fax 594-1472

**Diamond Springs, El Dorado, Pop. 10,676**
El Dorado UNHSD
Supt. — See Placerville
Community Day S 50/Alt
385 Pleasant Valley Rd 95619 530-622-7090
Alison Gennai, prin. Fax 642-2291
Independence HS 100/Alt
385 Pleasant Valley Rd 95619 530-622-7090
Alison Gennai, prin. Fax 642-2291

**Dinuba, Tulare, Pop. 21,288**
Dinuba USD 6,200/K-12
1327 E El Monte Way 93618 559-595-7200
Joe Hernandez Ed.D., supt. Fax 591-3334
dusd.dinuba.k12.ca.us
Dinuba HS 1,800/9-12
1327 E El Monte Way 93618 559-595-7220
Michael Roberts, prin. Fax 591-3655
Reagan Academy 200/Alt
1327 E El Monte Way 93618 559-595-7295
Suzanne Rodriguez, prin. Fax 595-7248
Sierra Vista HS 100/Alt
1327 E El Monte Way 93618 559-595-7240
Suzanne Rodriguez, prin. Fax 595-8198
Washington IS 900/7-8
1327 E El Monte Way 93618 559-595-7252
Jonathan Torres, prin. Fax 595-8158
Dinuba Adult S Adult
1327 E El Monte Way 93618 559-595-7242
Suzanne Rodriguez, prin. Fax 595-7248

**Dixon, Solano, Pop. 17,699**
Dixon USD 3,600/K-12
180 S 1st St 95620 707-693-6300
Brian Dolan, supt. Fax 678-0726
www.dixonusd.org
Dixon Community Day S 50/Alt
180 S 1st St 95620 707-678-4061
Yvette Ramos, prin.
Dixon HS 1,200/9-12
555 College Way 95620 707-693-6330
Nick Girimonte, prin. Fax 678-9318
Jacobs IS 600/7-8
200 N Lincoln St 95620 707-678-9222
Dan Bledsoe, prin. Fax 678-1245
Maine Prairie HS 100/Alt
305 E C St 95620 707-678-4560
Yvette Ramos, prin. Fax 678-4892

**Dorris, Siskiyou, Pop. 895**
Butte Valley USD 300/K-12
PO Box 709 96023 530-397-4000
Edward Brown, supt. Fax 397-3999
www.bvalusd.org/
Butte Valley HS 100/9-12
PO Box 709 96023 530-397-3990
Jason Allen, lead tchr. Fax 397-3989
Butte Valley MS 50/7-8
PO Box 709 96023 530-397-3900
Edward Brown, admin. Fax 397-3899
Cascade Continuation HS 50/Alt
PO Box 709 96023 530-397-3363
Dennis Butler, lead tchr. Fax 397-3360
Butte Valley Adult S Adult
PO Box 709 96023 530-397-3363
Dennis Butler, lead tchr. Fax 397-3360

**Dos Palos, Merced, Pop. 4,873**
Dos Palos Oro Loma JUSD 2,400/K-12
2041 Almond St 93620 209-392-0200
Brian Walker, supt. Fax 392-3347
www.dpol.net
Bryant MS 500/6-8
16695 Bryant Ave 93620 209-392-0240
Laura Andrews, prin. Fax 392-2636
Dos Palos HS 700/9-12
1701 E Blossom St 93620 209-392-0300
Heather Ruiz, prin. Fax 392-2705
Other Schools – See South Dos Palos

**Downey, Los Angeles, Pop. 110,312**
Downey USD 22,700/K-12
PO Box 7017 90241 562-469-6500
Dr. John Garcia Ph.D., supt. Fax 469-6515
www.dusd.net
Columbus Continuation HS 400/Alt
12330 Woodruff Ave 90241 562-904-3552
Anthony Zegarra, prin. Fax 469-7320
Doty MS 1,400/6-8
10301 Woodruff Ave 90241 562-904-3586
Brent Shubin, prin. Fax 469-7240
Downey HS 4,200/9-12
11040 Brookshire Ave 90241 562-869-7301
Tom Houts, prin. Fax 469-7340
Griffiths MS 1,400/6-8
9633 Tweedy Ln 90240 562-904-3580
Dr. Rani Bertsch Ed.D., prin. Fax 469-7260
Stauffer MS 1,500/6-8
11985 Old River School Rd 90242 562-904-3565
Alyda Mir, prin. Fax 469-7300
Sussman MS 1,300/6-8
12500 Birchdale Ave 90242 562-904-3572
Dr. Robert Jagielski, prin. Fax 469-7280
Warren HS 3,700/9-12
8141 De Palma St 90241 562-869-7306
Laura Rivas, prin. Fax 469-7360
Downey Adult S Adult
12340 Woodruff Ave 90241 562-940-6200
Blanca Rochin, prin. Fax 940-6221

Los Angeles County Office of Education 6,800/
9300 Imperial Hwy 90242 562-922-6111
Dr. Arturo Delgado, supt. Fax 922-6768
www.lacoe.edu
Alternative Opportunity Programs 400/Alt
9300 Imperial Hwy 90242 562-803-8203
Mary Laihee, dir. Fax 401-5742
Other Schools – See Hawthorne, Los Angeles, Monterey Park, Pomona

Regional Occupational Center & Program
Supt. — None
Los Angeles County ROP Vo/Tech
9300 Imperial Hwy 90242 562-922-6850
Jimmy Benavides, dir. Fax 940-1672

---

Calvary Chapel Christian S 1,000/PK-12
12808 Woodruff Ave 90242 562-803-4076
Roger Stahlhut B.A., admin. Fax 803-4502
Los Amigos Research & Education Inst. Post-Sec.
PO Box 3500 90242 562-401-8111
St. Pius X / St. Matthias Academy 200/9-12
7851 Gardendale St 90242 562-861-2271
Erick Rubalcava, prin. Fax 869-8652

**Downieville, Sierra, Pop. 276**
Sierra-Plumas JUSD
Supt. — See Loyalton
Downieville JSHS 50/7-12
PO Box B 95936 530-289-3473
Merrill Grant Ed.D., supt. Fax 289-3693

**Duarte, Los Angeles, Pop. 20,755**
Duarte USD 3,900/K-12
1620 Huntington Dr 91010 626-599-5000
Dr. Allan Mucerino, supt. Fax 599-5069
www.duarte.k12.ca.us
Duarte HS 1,200/9-12
1565 Central Ave 91010 626-599-5700
Mark Sims, prin. Fax 599-5784
Mt. Olive Innovation and Technology S 100/Alt
1400 Mount Olive Dr 91010 626-599-5900
Luis Haro, prin. Fax 599-5984
Northview IS 600/7-8
1401 Highland Ave 91010 626-599-5600
Rick Crosby, prin. Fax 599-5684

---

Irell & Manella Grad Sch of Biological Post-Sec.
1500 Duarte Rd 91010 626-256-4673

**Dublin, Alameda, Pop. 43,591**
Dublin USD 6,300/K-12
7471 Larkdale Ave 94568 925-828-2551
Dr. Stephen Hanke, supt. Fax 829-6532
www.dublin.k12.ca.us
Dublin HS 1,700/9-12
8151 Village Pkwy 94568 925-833-3300
Carol Shimizu, prin. Fax 833-3322
Fallon MS 700/6-9
3601 Kohnen Way 94568 925-875-9376
Sheryl Sweeney, prin. Fax 829-6532
Valley Continuation HS 100/Alt
6901 York Dr 94568 925-829-4322
Thomas Orput, prin. Fax 833-7609
Wells MS 700/6-8
6800 Penn Dr 94568 925-828-6227
Kevin Grier, prin. Fax 829-8851
Dublin Adult Education Adult
6901 York Dr 94568 925-829-4322
Thomas Orput, prin. Fax 833-7609

---

Golden State College of Court Reporting Post-Sec.
6543 Regional St 94568 925-829-0115
Quarry Lane S 800/PK-12
6363 Tassajara Rd 94568 925-829-8000
Sabri Arac Ph.D., hdmstr. Fax 829-4928
Valley Christian S 800/PK-12
7500 Inspiration Dr 94568 925-560-6200
Dave Johnson, supt. Fax 828-5623

**Dunsmuir, Siskiyou, Pop. 1,565**
Dunsmuir JUNHSD 100/9-12
5805 High School Way 96025 530-235-4835
Ray Kellar, supt. Fax 235-2224
www.dunsmuirhigh.k12.ca.us/
Dunsmuir Community Day S 50/Alt
5805 High School Way 96025 530-235-2225
Ray Kellar, supt. Fax 235-2224
Dunsmuir HS 100/9-12
5805 High School Way 96025 530-235-4835
Ray Kellar, supt. Fax 235-2224

**Durham, Butte, Pop. 5,377**
Durham USD 1,000/K-12
PO Box 300 95938 530-895-4675
Len Foreman, supt. Fax 895-4692
www.durhamunified.org/
Durham HS 400/9-12
PO Box 600 95938 530-895-4685
Terry Bennett, prin. Fax 895-4688
Durham IS 200/6-8
PO Box 310 95938 530-895-4690
Jeff Kuhn, prin. Fax 895-4305

**Earlimart, Tulare, Pop. 8,499**
Earlimart ESD 1,900/K-8
PO Box 11970 93219 661-849-3386
Timothy Smith, supt. Fax 849-2352
www.earlimart.org

Earlimart Community Day S 50/Alt
PO Box 11970 93219 661-849-4841
Raylene Welch, lead tchr. Fax 849-2352
Earlimart MS 600/6-8
PO Box 11970 93219 661-849-2611
Phillip Nystrom, prin. Fax 849-4214

**East Palo Alto, San Mateo, Pop. 25,414**
Ravenswood City ESD 4,300/PK-12
2120 Euclid Ave 94303 650-329-2800
Dr. Gloria Hernandez-Goff, supt. Fax 323-1072
www.ravenswoodschools.org
Chavez Academy 300/6-8
2450 Ralmar Ave 94303 650-329-6700
Amika Guillaume, prin. Fax 326-8902
McNair Academy 300/6-8
2033 Pulgas Ave 94303 650-329-2888
Jennifer Gravem, prin. Fax 473-9247

---

Eastside College Preparatory S 300/6-12
1041 Myrtle St 94303 650-688-0850
Chris Bischof, prin. Fax 688-0859

**Eastvale, Riverside, Pop. 51,943**
Corona-Norco USD
Supt. — See Norco
Ramirez IS 800/7-8
6905 Harrison Ave, 951-736-8241
Kim Seheult, prin. Fax 273-3145
River Heights IS 1,100/7-8
7227 Scholar Way, 951-738-2155
Teri Dudley, prin. Fax 738-2175
Roosevelt HS 3,400/9-12
7447 Scholar Way, 951-738-2100
Jeremy Goins, prin. Fax 738-2104

**Edwards, Kern**
Muroc JUSD
Supt. — See North Edwards
Desert JSHS 600/7-12
1575 Payne Ave 93523 661-258-4411
Dr. David Ellms Ed.D., prin. Fax 258-5029

**El Cajon, San Diego, Pop. 94,267**
Cajon Valley UNESD 15,000/K-8
PO Box 1007 92022 619-588-3000
David Miyashiro Ed.D., supt. Fax 588-7653
www.cajonvalley.net
Cajon Valley Community Day S Alt
165 Roanoke Rd 92021 619-588-3265
Wendy Vaughn-Platt, prin. Fax 588-3168
Cajon Valley MS 800/6-8
550 E Park Ave 92020 619-588-3092
Greg Calvert, prin. Fax 579-4817
Emerald MS 700/6-8
1221 Emerald Ave 92020 619-588-3097
Steven Bailey, prin. Fax 588-3225
Greenfield MS 700/6-8
1495 Greenfield Dr 92021 619-588-3103
Karen Minshew, prin. Fax 588-3648
Hillsdale MS 1,400/6-8
1301 Brabham St 92019 619-441-6156
Marietta Minjares, prin. Fax 441-6185
Los Coches Creek MS 800/6-8
9669 Dunbar Ln 92021 619-441-5741
Dana Stevenson, prin. Fax 938-1850
Montgomery MS 800/6-8
1570 Melody Ln 92019 619-588-3107
Jacqueline Luzak, prin. Fax 441-6122

Grossmont UNHSD
Supt. — See La Mesa
Chaparral HS 300/Alt
1600 N Cuyamaca St 92020 619-956-4600
David Napoleon, prin. Fax 596-7815
El Cajon Valley HS 2,200/9-12
1035 E Madison Ave 92021 619-401-4700
Erin Richison Ed.D., prin. Fax 447-3943
Elite Academy 100/Alt
230 Jamacha Blvd 92019 619-588-3545
Barbara Schmidt, admin.
Granite Hills HS 2,800/9-12
1719 E Madison Ave 92019 619-593-5500
Mike Fowler, prin. Fax 588-9389
Grossmont HS 2,600/9-12
1100 Murray Dr 92020 619-668-6000
Daniel Barnes, prin. Fax 463-7108
Grossmont Middle College HS 100/11-12
8800 Grossmont College Dr 92020 619-644-7524
David Napoleon, prin. Fax 644-7011
IDEA Center 600/9-12
1600 N Cuyamaca St 92020 619-956-4332
David Napoleon, admin. Fax 596-7815
Phoenix Independent Study 50/Alt
1600 N Cuyamaca St 92020 619-956-4625
David Napoleon, prin. Fax 258-3750
Valhalla HS 2,100/9-12
1725 Hillsdale Rd 92019 619-593-5300
Mary Beth Kastan, prin. Fax 588-9713
Grossmont Adult S Adult
1550 Melody Ln 92019 619-588-3500
Robyn Wiggins, dir. Fax 579-9291

---

Advanced Training Associates Post-Sec.
1810 Gillespie Way Ste 104 92020 619-596-2766
Bellus Academy Post-Sec.
1073 E Main St 92021 619-442-3407
Christian JSHS 500/7-12
2100 Greenfield Dr 92019 619-201-8800
Tobin Wilkins, prin. Fax 201-8898
Cuyamaca College Post-Sec.
900 Rancho San Diego Pkwy 92019 619-660-4000
Foothills Christian HS 300/9-12
2321 Dryden Rd 92020 619-303-8035
Rev. Dan Deyling, prin. Fax 741-2648
Foothills Christian MS 100/6-8
350 Cypress Ln 92020 619-303-1641
Grossmont College Post-Sec.
8800 Grossmont College Dr 92020 619-644-7000
San Diego Christian College Post-Sec.
2100 Greenfield Dr 92019 619-201-8700
Southern California Seminary Post-Sec.
2075 E Madison Ave 92019 888-389-7244

**El Centro, Imperial, Pop. 42,253**
Central UNHSD 5,100/9-12
351 W Ross Ave, 760-336-4500
Renato Montano, supt. Fax 353-3606
www.cuhsd.net
Central Union HS 1,800/9-12
1001 W Brighton Ave, 760-336-4300
Craig Lyon, prin. Fax 353-3570
Desert Oasis HS 200/Alt
1302 S 3rd St, 760-336-4555
Fernando O'Campo, prin. Fax 337-3952
Southwest HS 2,100/9-12
2001 Ocotillo Dr, 760-336-4100
Dannette Morrell, prin. Fax 353-0467
Central Union Adult Education Adult
1302 S 3rd St, 760-336-4544
Fernando O'Campo, dir. Fax 336-4547

El Centro ESD 5,400/K-8
1256 Broadway St, 760-352-5712
Jon LeDoux, supt. Fax 312-9522
www.ecesd.com
Kennedy MS 400/7-8
900 N 6th St, 760-352-0444
Michael Castillo, prin. Fax 353-0325
Wilson JHS 700/7-8
600 S Wilson St, 760-352-5341
Rauna Fox, prin. Fax 337-3800

Regional Occupational Center & Program
Supt. — None
Imperial Valley ROP Vo/Tech
687 W State St, 760-482-2600
Mary Camacho, supt. Fax 482-2751

**El Cerrito, Contra Costa, Pop. 22,213**
West Contra Costa USD
Supt. — See Richmond
El Cerrito HS 1,300/9-12
540 Ashbury Ave 94530 510-231-1437
David Luongo, prin. Fax 525-1810
Korematsu MS 500/6-8
1021 Navellier St 94530 510-524-0405
Matthew Burnham, prin. Fax 559-8784

---

Prospect Sierra MS 300/5-8
960 Avis Dr 94530 510-528-5800
Katherine Dinh, head sch Fax 527-3728

**El Dorado, El Dorado**
El Dorado UNHSD
Supt. — See Placerville
Mountain View HS 50/Alt
6530 Koki Ln 95623 530-621-4003
Jennifer Myers, prin. Fax 622-6034
Union Mine HS 1,000/9-12
6530 Koki Ln 95623 530-621-4003
Paul Neville, prin. Fax 622-6034

**El Dorado Hills, El Dorado, Pop. 40,513**
Buckeye UNSD 4,600/PK-8
PO Box 4768 95762 916-985-2183
Dr. David Roth, supt. Fax 934-0920
www.buckeyeusd.org/
Rolling Hills MS 1,000/6-8
7141 Silva Valley Pkwy 95762 916-933-9290
Debra Bowers, prin. Fax 939-7454
Other Schools – See Cameron Park

El Dorado UNHSD
Supt. — See Placerville
Oak Ridge HS 2,300/9-12
1120 Harvard Way 95762 916-933-6980
Paul Burke, prin. Fax 933-6987

Rescue UNESD
Supt. — See Rescue
Marina Village MS 800/6-8
1901 Francisco Dr 95762 916-933-3993
George Tapanes, prin. Fax 933-3995

**Elk Creek, Glenn, Pop. 158**
Stony Creek JUSD 100/K-12
3430 County Road 309 95939 530-968-5361
Laurel Hill-Ward, supt. Fax 968-5102
www.scjusd.org
Bidwell Point HS 50/Alt
3430 County Road 309 95939 530-968-5361
Laurel Hill-Ward, prin. Fax 968-5535
Elk Creek JSHS 50/7-12
3430 County Road 309 95939 530-968-5361
Laurel Hill-Ward, prin. Fax 968-5102

**Elk Grove, Sacramento, Pop. 142,334**
Elk Grove USD 61,000/PK-12
9510 Elk Grove Florin Rd 95624 916-686-5085
Christopher Hoffman, supt. Fax 686-7787
www.egusd.net
Albiani MS 1,400/7-8
9140 Bradshaw Rd 95624 916-686-5210
Melanie Dopson, prin. Fax 686-5538
Cosumnes Oaks HS 1,700/9-12
8350 Lotz Pkwy, 916-683-7670
Maria Osborne, prin. Fax 683-4522
Eddy MS 800/7-8
9329 Soaring Oaks Dr 95758 916-683-1302
Mark Benson, prin. Fax 684-6142
Elk Grove HS 1,700/9-12
9800 Elk Grove Florin Rd 95624 916-686-7741
Catherine Guy, prin. Fax 685-5515
Franklin HS 2,800/9-12
6400 Whitelock Pkwy, 916-714-8150
Chantelle Albiani, prin. Fax 714-8155
Harris MS 1,200/7-8
8691 Power Inn Rd 95624 916-688-0080
Felicia Bessent, prin. Fax 688-0084
Johnson MS 1,500/7-8
10099 Franklin High Rd, 916-714-8181
Patrick McDougall, prin. Fax 714-8177
Kerr MS 900/7-8
8865 Elk Grove Blvd 95624 916-686-7728
Dawnelle Maffei, prin. Fax 685-2952
Laguna Creek HS 1,600/9-12
9050 Vicino Dr 95758 916-683-1339
Douglas Craig, prin. Fax 683-3128
Monterey Trail HS 2,200/9-12
8661 Power Inn Rd 95624 916-688-0050
Jana Durham, prin. Fax 688-0058
Pinkerton MS 900/7-8
8365 Whitelock Pkwy, 916-683-7680
Chandra Victor, prin. Fax 685-5703
Pleasant Grove HS 2,500/9-12
9531 Bond Rd 95624 916-686-0230
Hank Meyer, prin. Fax 686-0239
Other Schools – See Sacramento

---

DeVry University Post-Sec.
2216 Kausen Dr 95758 916-478-2847
Lutheran HS 100/9-12
9270 Bruceville Rd 95758 916-691-2277
James Maddock, prin. Fax 691-2292

**El Monte, Los Angeles, Pop. 112,772**
El Monte UNHSD 9,900/9-12
3537 Johnson Ave 91731 626-444-9005
Dr. Irella Perez, supt. Fax 350-1095
emuhsd.org
Arroyo HS 2,300/9-12
4921 Cedar Ave 91732 626-444-9201
Angelita Gonzales-Hernan, prin. Fax 443-1175
El Monte HS 1,900/9-12
3048 Tyler Ave 91731 626-444-7701
Robin Torres, prin. Fax 442-6594
Ledesma HS 400/Alt
12347 Ramona Blvd 91732 626-442-0481
Freddy Arteaga, prin. Fax 442-7260
Mountain View HS 1,800/9-12
2900 Parkway Dr 91732 626-443-6181
Larry Cecil, prin. Fax 442-7284
El Monte-Rosemead Adult Education Adult
10807 Ramona Blvd 91731 626-258-5800
Dr. Deborah Kerr, prin. Fax 258-5809
Other Schools – See Rosemead, South El Monte

Mountain View ESD 7,700/K-8
3320 Gilman Rd 91732 626-652-4000
Lillian Maldonado French, supt. Fax 652-4052
www.mtviewschools.com/
Kranz IS 900/7-8
12460 Fineview St 91732 626-652-4200
Sean Grycel, prin. Fax 652-4215
Madrid MS 900/6-8
3300 Gilman Rd 91732 626-652-4300
Cesar Flores, prin. Fax 652-4315
Magnolia Learning Center Alt
11919 Magnolia St 91732 626-652-4938
Terri Thomas, admin. Fax 652-4939

---

International Theological Seminary Post-Sec.
3225 Tyler Ave 91731 626-448-0023
Logos Evangelical Seminary Post-Sec.
9358 Telstar Ave 91731 626-571-5110
Palladium Technical Academy Post-Sec.
10503 Valley Blvd 91731 626-444-0880
Professional Institute of Beauty Post-Sec.
10801 Valley Mall 91731 626-443-9401

**El Segundo, Los Angeles, Pop. 15,912**
El Segundo USD 3,300/K-12
641 Sheldon St 90245 310-615-2650
Dr. Melissa Moore, supt. Fax 322-0231
www.elsegundousd.net
Arena HS 50/Alt
641 Sheldon St 90245 310-615-2650
Marisa Janicek, prin. Fax 322-7939
El Segundo HS 1,200/9-12
641 Sheldon St 90245 310-615-2662
Jaime Mancilla, prin. Fax 640-8079
El Segundo MS 800/6-8
641 Sheldon St 90245 310-615-2690
Dr. Jack Plotkin, prin. Fax 640-9634

---

Vistamar S 200/9-12
737 Hawaii St 90245 310-643-7377
Karen Eshoo, head sch Fax 643-7371

**El Sobrante, Contra Costa, Pop. 11,868**
West Contra Costa USD
Supt. — See Richmond
Crespi MS 600/7-8
1121 Allview Ave 94803 510-231-1447
Guthrie Fleischman, prin. Fax 243-2090

---

El Sobrante Christian JSHS 100/7-12
5070 Appian Way 94803 510-223-1966
Derrick Leonard, prin. Fax 223-5344

**Elverta, Sacramento, Pop. 5,268**
Elverta JESD 300/K-12
7900 Eloise Ave 95626 916-991-2244
Michael Borgaard, supt. Fax 991-0271
www.ejesd.net
Alpha Technology MS 100/6-8
7900 Eloise Ave 95626 916-991-4726
Michael Borgaard, prin.

**Emeryville, Alameda, Pop. 9,492**
Emery USD 700/K-12
1275 61st St 94608 510-601-4000
Dr. John Rubio, supt. Fax 601-4913
www.emeryusd.org/

Emery HS 200/9-12
915 54th St 94608 510-601-4000
Douglas Ferber, prin. Fax 601-4988

---

Expression College for Digital Arts Post-Sec.
6601 Shellmound St 94608 510-654-2934

**Encinitas, San Diego, Pop. 57,785**
San Dieguito UNHSD 12,400/7-12
710 Encinitas Blvd 92024 760-753-6491
Rick Schmitt, supt. Fax 943-3501
www.sduhsd.net
Diegueno MS 800/7-8
710 Encinitas Blvd 92024 760-944-1892
Jeffrey Copeland, prin. Fax 944-3717
Oak Crest MS 900/7-8
710 Encinitas Blvd 92024 760-753-6241
Ben Taylor, prin. Fax 942-0520
San Dieguito HS Academy 1,600/9-12
710 Encinitas Blvd 92024 760-753-1121
Bjorn Paige, prin. Fax 753-8142
Sunset HS 100/Alt
710 Encinitas Blvd 92024 760-753-3860
Rick Ayala, prin. Fax 753-8469
San Dieguito Adult HS Adult
710 Encinitas Blvd 92024 760-753-7073
Denise Stanley, prin. Fax 436-8376
Other Schools – See Carlsbad, San Diego, Solana Beach

---

Encinitas Country Day 300/K-12
3616 Manchester Ave 92024 760-942-1111
Graeg Lehmunn, prin.
Grauer S 100/7-12
1500 S El Camino Real 92024 760-944-6777
Dr. Stuart Grauer, head sch Fax 944-6784

**Encino, See Los Angeles**

---

Crespi Carmelite HS 600/9-12
5031 Alonzo Ave 91316 818-345-1672
Dr. Jonathan Schild, prin. Fax 705-0209
Ferrahian HS 300/6-12
5300 White Oak Ave 91316 818-784-6228
John Kossakian, prin. Fax 784-2457
Westmark S 200/1-12
5461 Louise Ave 91316 818-986-5045
Claudia Koochek, head sch Fax 986-2605

**Escalon, San Joaquin, Pop. 7,002**
Escalon USD 2,900/K-12
1520 Yosemite Ave 95320 209-838-3591
Ron Costa, supt. Fax 838-6703
www.escalonusd.org/
El Portal MS 700/6-8
805 1st St 95320 209-838-7095
Mark Vos, prin. Fax 838-3017
Escalon HS 900/9-12
1528 Yosemite Ave 95320 209-838-7073
David Lattig, prin. Fax 838-6127
Vista HS 100/Alt
1520 Yosemite Ave 95320 209-838-1450
David Lattig, admin. Fax 838-1922

**Escondido, San Diego, Pop. 140,582**
Escondido UNHSD 9,500/9-12
302 N Midway Dr 92027 760-291-3200
Steve Boyle, supt. Fax 480-3163
www.euhsd.org
Del Lago Academy Applied Science Campus 300/9-12
1740 Scenic Trails Way 92029 760-291-2500
Keith Nuthall, prin.
Escondido HS 2,700/9-12
1535 N Broadway 92026 760-291-4000
Richard Watkins, prin. Fax 739-7313
Orange Glen HS 2,300/9-12
2200 Glenridge Rd 92027 760-291-5000
Thomas Allison, prin. Fax 739-7314
San Pasqual HS 2,500/9-12
3300 Bear Valley Pkwy S 92025 760-291-6000
Tom McCoy Ed.D., prin. Fax 739-7315
Valley HS 400/Alt
410 Hidden Trails Rd 92027 760-291-2240
Dan Barajas, prin. Fax 741-7605
Escondido Adult S Adult
220 W Crest St 92025 760-739-7300
Dom Gagliardi, prin. Fax 739-7310

Escondido Union SD 19,000/PK-8
2310 Aldergrove Ave 92029 760-432-2400
Luis Rankins-Ibarra Ed.D., supt. Fax 735-2874
www.eusd.org
Bear Valley MS 1,100/6-8
3003 Bear Valley Pkwy S 92025 760-432-4060
Susan Freeman, prin. Fax 504-0158
Del Dios Academy of Arts and Sciences 800/6-8
1400 W 9th Ave 92029 760-432-2439
Albert Ngo, prin. Fax 432-0728
Hidden Valley MS 1,200/6-8
2700 Reed Rd 92027 760-432-2457
Trent Smith, prin. Fax 480-0845
Mission MS 1,000/6-8
939 E Mission Ave 92025 760-432-2452
Dr. Carlos Ulloa, prin. Fax 737-9085
Rincon MS 1,300/6-8
925 Lehner Ave 92026 760-432-2491
Beth Crooks, prin. Fax 743-6713

---

Calvin Christian S 300/6-12
2000 N Broadway 92026 760-489-6430
Frank Steidl, prin. Fax 489-7055
Escondido Adventist Academy 200/K-12
1301 Deodar Rd 92026 760-746-1800
Larry Rich, prin. Fax 743-3499
Westminster Seminary California Post-Sec.
1725 Bear Valley Pkwy 92027 760-480-8474

**Esparto, Yolo, Pop. 3,053**
Esparto USD 1,000/PK-12
26675 Plainfield St 95627 530-787-3446
Hortencia Phifer, supt. Fax 787-3033
www.espartok12.org
Esparto HS 300/9-12
26675 Plainfield St 95627 530-787-3405
Diego Ochoa, prin. Fax 787-4850
Esparto MS 200/6-8
26675 Plainfield St 95627 530-787-4151
Hortencia Phifer M.Ed., prin. Fax 787-3890
Other Schools – See Madison

**Etiwanda, See Rancho Cucamonga**
Chaffey JUNHSD
Supt. — See Ontario
Etiwanda HS 3,200/9-12
PO Box 447 91739 909-899-2531
Don Jaramillo, prin. Fax 899-3661

Etiwanda SD 13,000/K-8
6061 East Ave 91739 909-899-2451
Shawn Judson Ed.D., supt. Fax 899-1235
www.etiwanda.k12.ca.us
Day Creek IS 1,200/6-8
12345 Coyote Dr 91739 909-803-3300
Alicia Lyon, prin. Fax 803-3309
Etiwanda Community Day S 50/Alt
5959 East Ave 91739 909-899-1704
Jeff Sipos, dir. Fax 899-7596
Etiwanda IS 1,300/6-8
6925 Etiwanda Ave 91739 909-899-1701
Lori Arita, prin. Fax 899-5676
Summit IS 1,000/6-8
5959 East Ave 91739 909-899-1704
Ben Nakamura, prin. Fax 899-7596
Other Schools – See Fontana

**Etna, Siskiyou, Pop. 666**
Scott Valley USD
Supt. — See Fort Jones
Etna HS 200/9-12
PO Box 721 96027 530-467-3244
Mark Evans, prin. Fax 467-5763
Scott River HS 50/Alt
PO Box 59 96027 530-467-5279
Mark Evans, prin. Fax 467-3459
Adult S Adult
PO Box 721 96027 530-467-3244
Mark Evans, admin. Fax 467-5763

**Eureka, Humboldt, Pop. 25,748**
Eureka City SD 3,600/K-12
2100 J St 95501 707-441-2400
Fred Van Vleck Ed.D., supt. Fax 441-3326
www.eurekacityschools.org
Barnum Continuation HS 100/Alt
216 W Harris St 95503 707-441-2467
Rick Jordan, prin. Fax 441-0299
Eureka HS 1,300/9-12
1915 J St 95501 707-441-2508
Jennifer Johnson, prin. Fax 445-1956
Winship MS, 2500 Cypress Ave 95503 6-8
Shellye Horowitz, prin. 707-441-2488
Zane MS 600/6-8
2155 S St 95501 707-441-2470
Jan Schmidt, prin. Fax 441-0286
Eureka Adult Education Adult
2100 J St 95501 707-441-2448
Rick Jordan, prin. Fax 442-1403

Fortuna UNHSD
Supt. — See Fortuna
Academy of the Redwoods 200/Alt
7351 Tompkins Hill Rd 95501 707-476-4203
Luke Biesecker, prin. Fax 476-4439

Humboldt County Office of Education 300/
901 Myrtle Ave 95501 707-445-7000
Garry Eagles Ph.D., supt. Fax 445-7143
www.humboldt.k12.ca.us
Eureka Community S 100/Alt
1820 6th St 95501 707-445-7108
Jennifer Fairbanks, prin. Fax 445-7071
Other Schools – See Fortuna, Garberville

Regional Occupational Center & Program
Supt. — None
Humboldt County ROP Vo/Tech
901 Myrtle Ave 95501 707-445-7018
Lori Breyer, dir. Fax 445-7143

---

College of the Redwoods Post-Sec.
7351 Tompkins Hill Rd 95501 707-476-4100
Frederick and Charles Beauty College Post-Sec.
831 F St 95501 707-443-2733
Gospel Outreach S 50/K-12
2845 Saint James Pl 95503 707-445-2214
David Sczepanski, prin. Fax 445-2212
St. Bernard Academy 300/3-12
222 Dollison St 95501 707-443-2735
Paul Shanahan, dean Fax 443-4723

**Exeter, Tulare, Pop. 10,133**
Exeter USD 3,000/PK-12
215 N Crespi Ave 93221 559-592-9421
Tim Hire, supt. Fax 592-9445
www.exeter.k12.ca.us/
Exeter Union HS 1,000/9-12
505 Rocky Hill Dr 93221 559-592-2127
Robert Mayo, prin. Fax 592-3539
Kaweah Continuation HS 100/Alt
1107 Rocky Hill Dr 93221 559-592-4420
Darin Pace, prin. Fax 592-5246
Wilson MS 700/6-8
710 W Maple St 93221 559-592-2144
Sonia Wilson, prin. Fax 592-5536

---

Sierra View Junior Academy 100/K-10
19933 Avenue 256 93221 559-592-3689
Jeri Hoag, prin. Fax 592-5615

**Fairfax, Marin, Pop. 7,179**
Ross Valley ESD
Supt. — See San Anselmo
White Hill MS 600/6-8
101 Glen Dr 94930 415-454-8390
David Finnane, prin. Fax 454-3980

**Fairfield, Solano, Pop. 97,586**
Fairfield-Suisun USD 20,300/K-12
2490 Hilborn Rd, 707-399-5000
Kris Corey, supt. Fax 399-5160
www.fsusd.org
Armijo HS 2,200/9-12
824 Washington St 94533 707-422-7500
Eric Tretten, prin. Fax 438-3390
Fairfield HS 1,500/9-12
205 E Atlantic Ave 94533 707-438-3000
Kristen Witt, prin. Fax 422-0178
Garcia Career and College Academy 100/6-12
1100 Civic Center Dr 94533 707-424-9400
Cindy Lenners, prin.
Grange MS 800/6-8
1975 Blossom Ave 94533 707-421-4175
Christine Harrison, prin. Fax 422-4004
Green Valley MS 900/6-8
1350 Gold Hill Rd, 707-646-7000
Kristen Cherry, prin. Fax 864-1503
Public Safety Academy Vo/Tech
230 Atlantic Ave 94533 707-421-4100
Laurie Halcomb, prin.
Rodriguez HS 2,200/9-12
5000 Red Top Rd, 707-863-7950
Clarence Isadore, prin. Fax 863-7974
Sam Yeto Satellite Alt
824 Washington St 94533 707-438-3478
Sherry McCormick, prin.
Sem Yeto Continuation HS 500/Alt
205 E Alaska Ave 94533 707-438-3170
Sherry McCormick, prin.
Fairfield-Suisun Adult Education Adult
900 Travis Blvd 94533 707-421-4155
James Woods, prin. Fax 421-4158
Other Schools – See Suisun City

Regional Occupational Center & Program
Supt. — None
Solano County ROP Vo/Tech
2460 Clay Bank Rd 94533 707-399-4800
Janet Harden, dir. Fax 429-1360

Solano County Office of Education 300/
5100 Business Center Dr, 707-399-4400
Jay Speck, supt. Fax 863-4174
www.solanocoe.net/
Solano County Community S 100/Alt
2460 Clay Bank Rd, 707-399-4840
Rick Vaccaro, prin.

Travis USD 5,400/K-12
2751 De Ronde Dr 94533 707-437-4604
Kate Wren Gavlak, supt. Fax 437-8122
travisusd.org
Golden West MS 900/7-8
2651 De Ronde Dr 94533 707-437-8240
Jackie Tretten, prin. Fax 437-3416
Travis Community Day S 50/Alt
2785 De Ronde Dr 94533 707-437-8265
Allyson Rude Azevedo, prin.
Travis Education Center HS 100/Alt
2775 De Ronde Dr 94533 707-437-8265
Allyson Rude Azevedo, prin. Fax 437-0141
Vanden HS 1,600/9-12
2951 Markeley Ln 94533 707-437-7333
William Sarty, prin. Fax 437-7220

---

Fairfield Christian S 100/PK-12
PO Box 2172 94533 707-427-2665
Rev. Jason Yarbrough, supt. Fax 237-2307
Milan Institute of Cosmetology Post-Sec.
934 Missouri St 94533 707-425-2288
Solano Christian Academy 100/PK-12
2200 Fairfield Ave 94533 707-425-7715
John Reed, head sch Fax 429-2999
Solano Community College Post-Sec.
4000 Suisun Valley Rd, 707-864-7000

**Fair Oaks, Sacramento, Pop. 29,764**
San Juan USD
Supt. — See Carmichael
Bella Vista HS 2,000/9-12
8301 Madison Ave 95628 916-971-5052
Peggy Haskins, prin. Fax 971-5011
Del Campo HS 1,900/9-12
4925 Dewey Dr 95628 916-971-5664
Brett Wolfe, prin. Fax 971-5640
El Sereno Independent Study S 200/Alt
10700 Fair Oaks Blvd 95628 916-971-5060
Mia Funk, prin. Fax 971-5070
Rogers MS 600/6-8
4924 Dewey Dr 95628 916-971-7889
Gabriel Cooper, prin. Fax 971-7903

---

Freedom Christian S 100/K-12
7736 Sunset Ave 95628 916-962-3247
Annette Coller, admin. Fax 962-0783
Rudolf Steiner College Post-Sec.
9200 Fair Oaks Blvd 95628 916-961-8727
Sacramento Waldorf S 400/K-12
3750 Bannister Rd 95628 916-961-3900
Marcela Iglesias, admin. Fax 961-3970

**Fallbrook, San Diego, Pop. 29,874**
Fallbrook UNESD 5,800/K-8
321 Iowa St 92028 760-731-5420
Stephanie Weaver, supt. Fax 723-3895
www.fuesd.k12.ca.us
Potter IS 900/7-8
1743 Reche Rd 92028 760-731-4150
Leonard Rodriguez, prin. Fax 723-5740

Fallbrook UNHSD 2,900/9-12
2234 S Stage Coach Ln 92028 760-723-6332
Dr. Hugo A. Pedroza Ph.D., supt. Fax 723-1795
www.fuhsd.net
Fallbrook HS 2,600/9-12
2400 S Stage Coach Ln 92028 760-723-6300
Larry Boone, prin. Fax 723-6343
Ivy HS 100/Alt
1056 Winter Haven Rd 92028 760-723-6395
Melissa Marovich, prin. Fax 723-6392
Oasis Alternative HS 100/Alt
2208 S Stage Coach Ln 92028 760-723-1886
Melissa Marovich, prin. Fax 723-6411

**Farmersville, Tulare, Pop. 10,466**
Farmersville USD 2,400/K-12
571 E Citrus Dr 93223 559-592-2010
Ofelia Ceja-Lariviere, supt. Fax 592-2203
www.farmersville.k12.ca.us
Deep Creek Academy 100/Alt
281 S Farmersville Blvd 93223 559-747-6205
Lupe Perez, prin. Fax 747-0591
Farmersville HS 700/9-12
631 E Walnut Ave 93223 559-594-4567
Lisa Whitworth, prin. Fax 594-5287
Farmersville JHS 400/7-8
650 N Virginia Ave 93223 559-747-0764
Loretta Aragon, prin. Fax 747-2704

**Felton, Santa Cruz, Pop. 3,909**
San Lorenzo Valley USD
Supt. — See Ben Lomond
San Lorenzo Valley HS 700/9-12
7105 Highway 9 95018 831-335-4425
Karen van Putten, prin. Fax 335-1531
San Lorenzo Valley MS 500/6-8
7179 Hacienda Way 95018 831-335-4452
Jeff Calden, prin. Fax 335-3812

**Ferndale, Humboldt, Pop. 1,343**
Ferndale USD 500/PK-12
1231 Main St 95536 707-786-5900
Jack Lakin, supt. Fax 786-4865
www.ferndalek12.org/
Ferndale HS 100/9-12
1231 Main St 95536 707-786-5900
Jack Lakin, prin. Fax 786-4865

**Fillmore, Ventura, Pop. 14,823**
Fillmore USD 3,300/PK-12
PO Box 697 93016 805-524-6000
Adrian Palazuelos, supt. Fax 524-6060
www.fillmore.k12.ca.us
Fillmore HS 1,000/9-12
PO Box 697 93016 805-524-6100
Thomas Ito, prin. Fax 524-6121
Fillmore MS 800/6-8
PO Box 697 93016 805-524-6055
Scott Carroll, prin. Fax 524-6063
Sierra HS 100/Alt
PO Box 697 93016 805-524-8202
Cynthia Frutos, prin. Fax 524-6080

**Firebaugh, Fresno, Pop. 7,529**
Firebaugh-Las Deltas JUSD 2,200/PK-12
1976 Morris Kyle Dr 93622 559-659-1476
Russell Freitas, supt. Fax 659-2355
www.fldusd.org/
El Puente Continuation HS 50/Alt
1976 Morris Kyle Dr 93622 559-659-3899
Howard Yamagiwa, prin. Fax 659-1511
Firebaugh HS 700/9-12
1976 Morris Kyle Dr 93622 559-659-1415
Terry Anderson, prin. Fax 659-2636
Firebaugh MS 500/6-8
1976 Morris Kyle Dr 93622 559-659-1481
Marc Sosa, prin. Fax 659-7106
Firebaugh-Las Deltas Adult S Adult
1976 Morris Kyle Dr 93622 559-659-3899
Howard Yamagiwa, prin. Fax 659-1511

**Folsom, Sacramento, Pop. 69,359**
Folsom-Cordova USD
Supt. — See Rancho Cordova
Folsom HS 2,000/9-12
1655 Iron Point Rd 95630 916-294-2400
Howard Cadenhead, prin. Fax 355-1110
Folsom Lake HS 100/Alt
955 Riley St 95630 916-294-9809
Leane Linson, prin. Fax 294-9728
Folsom MS 1,200/6-8
500 Blue Ravine Rd 95630 916-983-4466
John Bliss, prin. Fax 983-3462
Sutter MS 1,300/6-8
715 Riley St 95630 916-985-3644
Keri Phillips, prin. Fax 985-7044
Vista Del Lago HS 1,400/9-12
1970 Broadstone Pkwy 95630 916-294-2410
John Dixon, prin. Fax 294-2411

---

Folsom Lake College Post-Sec.
10 College Pkwy 95630 916-608-6500

**Fontana, San Bernardino, Pop. 192,303**
Etiwanda SD
Supt. — See Etiwanda
Heritage IS 1,300/6-8
13766 S Heritage Cir 92336 909-357-1345
Laura Rowland, prin. Fax 357-8945

Fontana USD 39,000/PK-12
9680 Citrus Ave 92335 909-357-7600
Leslie A. Boozer Ph.D., supt. Fax 357-5012
www.fusd.net
Alder MS 1,300/6-8
7555 Alder Ave 92336 909-357-5330
Fax 357-5348
Almeria MS 1,000/6-8
7723 Almeria Ave 92336 909-357-5350
Letitia Bradley, prin. Fax 357-5360
Birch HS 400/Alt
7930 Locust Ave 92336 909-357-5310
Ed Campbell, prin. Fax 357-5319
Citrus Continuation HS 400/Alt
9820 Citrus Ave 92335 909-357-5300
Eric Groeber, prin. Fax 357-5302
Fontana HS 3,000/9-12
9453 Citrus Ave 92335 909-357-5500
Ofelia Hinojosa, prin. Fax 357-5629
Fontana MS 1,100/6-8
8425 Mango Ave 92335 909-357-5370
Sergio Chavez, prin. Fax 357-5391
Jurupa Hills HS 1,600/9-12
10700 Oleander Ave 92337 909-357-6300
Lorraine Trollinger, prin. Fax 357-7540
Kaiser HS 2,500/9-12
11155 Almond Ave 92337 909-357-5900
Terry Abernathy, prin. Fax 357-5997
Miller HS 2,700/9-12
6821 Oleander Ave 92336 909-357-5800
Moises Merlos, prin. Fax 357-7680
Ruble MS 1,200/6-8
6762 Juniper Ave 92336 909-357-5530
Caroline Labonte, prin. Fax 357-5539
Sequoia MS 1,200/7-8
9452 Hemlock Ave 92335 909-357-5400
Gorge Santiago, prin. Fax 357-5419
Southridge MS 1,200/6-8
14500 Live Oak Ave 92337 909-357-5420
Gerald Mullins, prin. Fax 822-4609
Summit HS 2,500/9-12
15551 Summit Ave 92336 909-357-5950
Raul Hernandez, prin. Fax 357-5959
Truman MS 1,300/6-8
16224 Mallory Dr 92335 909-357-5190
Kim Hall, prin. Fax 357-5199
Fontana Adult S Adult
10755 Oleander Ave 92337 909-357-5490
Cindy Gleason, prin. Fax 357-5556

**Foresthill, Placer, Pop. 1,441**
Placer UNHSD
Supt. — See Auburn
Foresthill HS 200/9-12
23319 Foresthill Rd 95631 530-367-5244
Randy Ittner, prin. Fax 367-4623

**Forestville, Sonoma, Pop. 3,212**
West Sonoma County UNHSD
Supt. — See Sebastopol
El Molino HS 800/9-12
7050 Covey Rd 95436 707-824-6570
Matt Dunkle, prin. Fax 887-0448

**Fort Bragg, Mendocino, Pop. 7,053**
Fort Bragg USD 1,800/PK-12
312 S Lincoln St 95437 707-961-2850
Dr. Charles Bush, supt. Fax 964-5002
www.fbusd.us
Fort Bragg HS 500/9-12
300 Dana St 95437 707-961-2880
Rebecca Walker, prin. Fax 961-2884
Fort Bragg MS 400/6-8
500 N Harold St 95437 707-961-2870
Johanna Jordan, prin. Fax 964-9416
Lighthouse Community Day S 50/Alt
250 S Sanderson Way 95437 707-964-1017
Coni Belli, prin.
Noyo HS 50/Alt
250 S Sanderson Way 95437 707-961-2889
Coni Belli, prin. Fax 964-1017
Shelter Cove S 50/Alt
310 S Lincoln St 95437 707-961-2889
Coni Belli, prin. Fax 964-1017
Coastal Adult S Adult
250 S Sanderson Way 95437 707-961-2889
Coni Belli, prin. Fax 964-1017

**Fort Irwin, San Bernardino, Pop. 8,282**
Silver Valley USD
Supt. — See Yermo
Fort Irwin MS 400/6-8
1700 Pork Chop Hill St 92310 760-386-1133
Colin Opseth, prin. Fax 386-2448

**Fort Jones, Siskiyou, Pop. 789**
Scott Valley USD 600/K-12
PO Box 687 96032 530-468-2727
Dr. Allan Carver, supt. Fax 468-2729
www.svusd.us/
Scott Valley Community Day S 50/Alt
11033 Quartz Valley Rd 96032 530-467-5279
Allan Carver, admin. Fax 467-3459
Scott Valley JHS 100/6-9
237 Butte St 96032 530-468-5565
Allan Carver, prin. Fax 468-5658
Other Schools – See Etna

**Fortuna, Humboldt, Pop. 11,506**
Fortuna ESD 1,100/K-8
500 9th St 95540 707-725-2293
Jeff Northern M.A., supt. Fax 725-2228
fesd-ca.schoolloop.com
Fortuna MS 200/5-8
843 L St 95540 707-725-3415
Vince Zinselmeir B.A., prin. Fax 725-6240
Thomas MS 300/5-8
2800 Thomas St 95540 707-725-5197
Julie Johansen M.A., prin. Fax 725-8637

Fortuna UNHSD 1,100/9-12
379 12th St 95540 707-725-4461
Glen Senestraro, supt. Fax 725-6085
www.fuhsdistrict.org
East HS 100/Alt
379 12th St 95540 707-725-4461
Danielle Carmesin, lead tchr. Fax 725-9746
Fortuna Union HS 800/9-12
379 12th St 95540 707-725-4461
Clint Duey, prin. Fax 725-5511
Other Schools – See Eureka

Humboldt County Office of Education
Supt. — See Eureka
Eel River Community S 100/Alt
2292 Newburg Rd 95540 707-725-0209
Jennifer Fairbanks, prin. Fax 725-0326

---

New Life Christian S 100/PK-12
1202 Ross Hill Rd 95540 707-725-9136
Karen Johnson, prin. Fax 725-1638

**Foster City, San Mateo, Pop. 29,077**
San Mateo-Foster City ESD 11,200/K-8
1170 Chess Dr 94404 650-312-7700
Dr. Joan Rosas Ph.D., supt. Fax 312-7348
www.smfcsd.net
Bowditch MS 900/6-8
1450 Tarpon St 94404 650-312-7680
Heather Gomez, prin. Fax 312-7639
Other Schools – See San Mateo

**Fountain Valley, Orange, Pop. 53,408**
Fountain Valley ESD 5,900/K-8
10055 Slater Ave 92708 714-843-3200
Mark Johnson Ed.D., supt. Fax 841-0356
www.fvsd.k12.ca.us
Fulton MS 900/6-8
8778 El Lago Cir 92708 714-375-2816
Kevin Johnson, prin. Fax 375-2825
Masuda MS 900/6-8
17415 Los Jardines W 92708 714-378-4250
Jay Adams, prin. Fax 378-4259
Other Schools – See Huntington Beach

Garden Grove USD
Supt. — See Garden Grove
Los Amigos HS 2,000/9-12
16566 Newhope St 92708 714-663-6288
Vicki Braddock, prin. Fax 663-6518

Huntington Beach UNHSD
Supt. — See Huntington Beach
Fountain Valley HS 3,500/9-12
17816 Bushard St 92708 714-962-3301
Morgan Smith, prin. Fax 964-0491
Valley Vista HS 300/Alt
9600 Dolphin St 92708 714-964-7766
Kerry Clitheroe, prin. Fax 964-3045

Ocean View SD
Supt. — See Huntington Beach
Vista View MS 700/6-8
16250 Hickory St 92708 714-842-0626
Fax 843-9156

---

Coastline Community College Post-Sec.
11460 Warner Ave 92708 714-546-7600
Modern Technology School Post-Sec.
16560 Harbor Blvd Ste K 92708 714-418-9100

**Fowler, Fresno, Pop. 5,491**
Fowler USD 2,300/K-12
658 E Adams Ave 93625 559-834-6080
Eric Cederquist, supt. Fax 834-3390
www.fowlerusd.org
Fowler HS 700/9-12
701 E Main St 93625 559-834-6160
Rick Romero, prin. Fax 834-3284
Fowler Unified Alternative Education 50/Alt
658 E Adams Ave 93625 559-834-6098
Jonathan Farley, prin. Fax 834-6721
Sutter MS 500/6-8
701 E Walter Ave 93625 559-834-6180
Gary Geringer, prin. Fax 834-4739

**Fremont, Alameda, Pop. 203,344**
Fremont USD 32,700/K-12
PO Box 5008 94537 510-657-2350
James Morris Ed.D., supt. Fax 659-2597
www.fremont.k12.ca.us
American HS 2,000/9-12
36300 Fremont Blvd 94536 510-796-1776
Steven Musto, prin. Fax 791-5331
Centerville JHS 900/7-8
37720 Fremont Blvd 94536 510-797-2072
Weste Petersen, prin. Fax 794-7588
Hopkins JHS 1,000/7-8
600 Driscoll Rd 94539 510-656-3500
Mary Miller, prin. Fax 656-3731
Horner JHS 1,000/7-8
41365 Chapel Way 94538 510-656-4000
Jana Holmes, prin. Fax 656-2793
Irvington HS 2,100/9-12
41800 Blacow Rd 94538 510-656-5711
Sarah Smoot, prin. Fax 623-9805
Kennedy HS 1,400/9-12
39999 Blacow Rd 94538 510-657-4070
Eddie Velez, prin. Fax 438-9287
Mission San Jose HS 2,200/9-12
41717 Palm Ave 94539 510-657-3600
Zachary Larsen, prin. Fax 657-2302
Robertson Continuation HS 300/Alt
4455 Seneca Park Ave 94538 510-657-9155
Sal Herrera, prin. Fax 657-5535
Thornton JHS 1,000/7-8
4357 Thornton Ave 94536 510-793-9090
Stan Hicks, prin. Fax 793-9756

Vista Alternative S 100/Alt
4455 Seneca Park Ave 94538 510-657-7028
Salvador Herrera, prin. Fax 657-0733
Walters JHS 700/7-8
39600 Logan Dr 94538 510-656-7211
Brian Weems, prin. Fax 656-4056
Washington HS 1,900/9-12
38442 Fremont Blvd 94536 510-505-7300
Rob Moran, prin. Fax 794-8437
Fremont Adult S Adult
4700 Calaveras Ave 94538 510-793-6465
Gladys Kiefer, prin. Fax 793-2271

Regional Occupational Center & Program
Supt. — None
Mission Valley ROP Vo/Tech
5019 Stevenson Blvd 94538 510-657-1865
Thomas Hanson, supt. Fax 438-0378

---

Alsion Montessori MSHS 100/7-12
PO Box 3296 94539 510-445-1127
California School for the Blind Post-Sec.
500 Walnut Ave 94536
California School for the Deaf Post-Sec.
39350 Gallaudet Dr 94538 510-794-3684
DeVry University Post-Sec.
6600 Dumbarton Cir 94555 510-574-1200
Fremont Christian S 800/PK-12
4760 Thornton Ave 94536 510-744-2249
Dr. Tricia Meyer, supt. Fax 744-2255
Northwestern Polytechnic University Post-Sec.
47671 Westinghouse Dr 94539 510-592-9688
Ohlone College Post-Sec.
43600 Mission Blvd 94539 510-659-6000
Queen of the Holy Rosary College Post-Sec.
43326 Mission Blvd 94539 510-657-2468
Unitek College Post-Sec.
4670 Auto Mall Pkwy 94538 888-735-4355
Wyotech Post-Sec.
420 Whitney Pl 94539 510-490-6900

**Fresno, Fresno, Pop. 482,604**
Central USD 14,000/K-12
4605 N Polk Ave 93722 559-274-4700
Michael A. Berg, supt. Fax 271-8200
www.centralunified.org/
Central HS East Campus 4,000/9-12
3535 N Cornelia Ave 93722 559-276-0280
Robert Perez, prin. Fax 276-5653
Central HS West Campus 9-12
2045 N Dickenson Ave, 559-276-5276
Robert Perez, prin. Fax 276-6380
Central Unified Alternative S 300/Alt
2698 N Brawley Ave 93722 559-276-5230
Jose Reyes, prin. Fax 276-8204
El Capitan MS 700/7-8
4443 W Weldon Ave 93722 559-276-5270
Jeff Wimp, prin. Fax 276-3121
Glacier Point MS 900/7-8
4055 N Bryan Ave, 559-276-3105
Heather Kuyper, prin. Fax 276-3105
Pathway Community Day School 50/Alt
11 S Teilman Ave 93706 559-487-1201
Nick Hustedde, prin. Fax 487-1204
Pershing Continuation HS 100/Alt
855 W Nielsen Ave 93706 559-268-2272
Nick Hustedde, prin. Fax 268-2279
Rio Vista MS 800/7-8
6240 W Palo Alto Ave 93722 559-276-3185
Joe Bracamonte, prin. Fax 276-3199
Central Unified Adult Education Adult
2698 N Brawley Ave 93722 559-276-5230
Jose Reyes, prin. Fax 276-8204

Clovis USD
Supt. — See Clovis
Clovis North Educational Center 1,900/7-12
2770 E International Ave, 559-327-5000
Scott Dille, prin. Fax 327-5290
Clovis West HS 2,200/9-12
1070 E Teague Ave 93720 559-327-2000
Marc Hammack, prin. Fax 327-2490
Kastner IS 1,100/7-8
7676 N 1st St 93720 559-327-2500
Ryan Eisele, prin. Fax 327-2790

Fresno County Office of Education 1,800/
1111 Van Ness Ave 93721 559-265-3000
Jim Yovino, supt. Fax 265-4005
www.fcoe.org
Heintz Education Academy 100/Alt
4939 E Yale Ave 93727 559-443-4863
Bill Johnson, prin. Fax 443-4856
Koontz Education Complex 100/Alt
1320 N Mariposa St 93703 559-443-4863
Bill Johnson, prin. Fax 264-6398

Fresno USD 74,000/PK-12
2309 Tulare St 93721 559-457-3000
Michael Hanson, supt. Fax 457-3786
www.fresnounified.org
Ahwahnee MS 700/7-8
1127 E Escalon Ave 93710 559-451-4300
Jose Guzman, prin. Fax 439-1808
Baird MS 600/5-8
5500 N Maroa Ave 93704 559-451-4310
Janetta McGensy, prin. Fax 432-4075
Bullard HS 2,500/9-12
5445 N Palm Ave 93704 559-451-4320
Carlos Castillo, prin. Fax 451-4339
Cambridge Continuation HS 400/Alt
1001 S Chestnut Ave 93702 559-253-6560
Pete Pulos, prin. Fax 266-9776
Computech MS 800/7-8
555 E Belgravia Ave 93706 559-457-2640
Andrew Scherrer, prin. Fax 457-2643
Cooper MS 500/7-8
2277 W Bellaire Way 93705 559-248-7050
Kristine Belcher, prin. Fax 224-7255

Design Science HS 300/9-12
2004 E Cambridge Ave 93703 559-248-7353
Roy Exum, prin.
Dewolf Continuation HS 300/Alt
2445 W Dakota Ave 93703 559-457-2990
Frank Duran, prin. Fax 224-2840
Duncan Polytechnical HS Vo/Tech
4330 E Garland Ave 93726 559-248-7080
Carol Hansen, prin. Fax 222-6186
Edison HS 2,200/9-12
540 E California Ave 93706 559-457-2650
Lindsay Sanders, prin. Fax 457-2742
Ft. Miller MS 900/7-8
1302 E Dakota Ave 93704 559-248-7100
Mike Jones, prin. Fax 221-7548
Fresno HS 2,400/9-12
1839 N Echo Ave 93704 559-457-2780
John Forbes, prin. Fax 457-2801
Gaston MS, 1100 E Church Ave 93706 6-8
Felicia Treadwell, prin. 559-457-3400
Hoover HS, 5550 N 1st St 93710 1,800/9-12
Rebecca Wheeler, prin. 559-451-4000
Kings Canyon MS 900/7-8
5117 E Tulare Ave 93727 559-253-6470
Clark Mello, prin. Fax 253-1005
McLane HS 2,400/9-12
2727 N Cedar Ave 93703 559-248-5100
Scott Lamm, prin. Fax 255-5253
Patino S of Entrepreneurship 10-12
2000 E Cambridge Ave 93703 559-248-7360
Dr. Brett Taylor, prin.
Phoenix Secondary Academy Alt
5090 E Church Ave 93705 559-253-6520
Brian Radtke, prin.
Roosevelt HS 2,200/9-12
4250 E Tulare St 93702 559-253-5200
Michael Allen, prin. Fax 253-5319
Scandinavian MS 600/7-8
3216 N Sierra Vista Ave 93726 559-253-6510
Julie Goorabian-Ellis, prin. Fax 252-7608
Sequoia MS 800/7-8
4050 E Hamilton Ave 93702 559-457-3210
Matt Ward, prin. Fax 497-1745
Sunnyside HS 3,200/9-12
1019 S Peach Ave 93727 559-253-6700
Tim Liles, prin. Fax 253-6799
Tehipite MS 500/7-8
630 N Augusta St 93701 559-457-3420
Yvonne Zysling, prin. Fax 457-3423
Tenaya MS 900/7-8
1239 W Mesa Ave 93711 559-451-4570
Heather Garcia, prin. Fax 431-0771
Terronez MS 800/7-8
2300 S Willow Ave 93725 559-253-6570
Virginia Mendez-Buelna, prin. Fax 253-6572
Tioga MS 800/7-8
3232 E Fairmont Ave 93726 559-248-7280
Kevin Evangilinos, prin. Fax 226-1296
Wawona MS 800/7-8
4524 N Thorne Ave 93704 559-248-7310
Kimberly Wong Villescaz, prin. Fax 227-5206
Yosemite MS 600/7-8
1292 N 9th St 93703 559-457-3450
Nichole Horn, prin. Fax 264-0933
Young Academic Center 1,400/Alt
822 N Abby St 93701 559-457-3190
Janice Trimble, prin. Fax 457-3193
Chavez Adult S Adult
2500 Stanislaus St 93721 559-457-6000
Sally Fowler, prin. Fax 457-6001

Regional Occupational Center & Program
Supt. — None
Fresno ROP Vo/Tech
1318 E Shaw Ave Ste 420 93710 559-497-3850
Valerie Vuicich, admin. Fax 497-3806

Washington USD 3,000/K-12
7950 S Elm Ave 93706 559-485-8805
John Pestorich, supt. Fax 485-4435
www.wusd.ws
Easton Community S 50/Alt
6041 S Elm Ave 93706 559-485-9350
Glen Freeman, prin. Fax 237-0270
Easton Continuation HS 50/Alt
5865 S Clara Ave 93706 559-485-9350
Glen Freeman, prin. Fax 237-0270
Washington Union HS 1,100/9-12
6041 S Elm Ave 93706 559-485-8805
Derek Cruz, prin. Fax 485-4435
West Fresno MS 300/6-8
2888 S Ivy Ave 93706 559-495-5607
Alan Macedo, prin. Fax 485-3006

---

Advanced Career Institute Post-Sec.
2953 S East Ave 93725 559-441-4345
Alliant International University Post-Sec.
5130 E Clinton Way 93727 559-253-2200
California Christian College Post-Sec.
4881 E University Ave 93703 559-251-4215
California State University-Fresno Post-Sec.
5241 N Maple Ave 93740 559-278-4240
DeVry University Post-Sec.
7575 N Fresno St 93720 559-439-8595
Fresno Adventist Academy 200/K-12
5397 E Olive Ave 93727 559-251-5548
Eric Johnson, prin. Fax 456-1735
Fresno Christian S 300/K-12
7280 N Cedar Ave 93720 559-299-1695
Jeremy Brown, supt. Fax 299-1051
Fresno City College Post-Sec.
1101 E University Ave 93741 559-442-4600
Fresno Pacific University Post-Sec.
1717 S Chestnut Ave 93702 559-453-2000
Heald College Post-Sec.
255 W Bullard Ave 93704 559-438-4222
Lyle's College of Beauty Post-Sec.
6735 N 1st St Ste 112 93710 559-431-6060

Manchester Beauty College Post-Sec.
3756 N Blackstone Ave 93726 559-224-4242
San Joaquin Memorial HS 600/9-12
1406 N Fresno St 93703 559-268-9251
Stephanie Nitchals, prin. Fax 268-1351
San Joaquin Valley College Post-Sec.
295 E Sierra Ave 93710 559-448-8282
San Joaquin Valley College Post-Sec.
4985 E Andersen Ave 93727 559-453-0123
Sierra Valley College of Court Reporting Post-Sec.
4747 N 1st St # D 93726 559-222-0947
United Education Institute Post-Sec.
2002 N Gateway Blvd 93727 559-456-0623

**Fullerton, Orange, Pop. 131,685**
Fullerton JUNHSD 14,800/9-12
1051 W Bastanchury Rd 92833 714-870-2800
Scott Scambray, supt. Fax 870-2807
www.fjuhsd.org
Fullerton Union HS 2,200/9-12
201 E Chapman Ave 92832 714-626-3801
Rani Goyal, prin. Fax 626-3839
La Sierra HS 700/Alt
951 N State College Blvd 92831 714-447-7820
Sandi Layana, prin.
La Vista HS 500/Alt
909 N State College Blvd 92831 714-447-5500
Sandi Layana, prin.
Sunny Hills HS 2,400/9-12
1801 Warburton Way 92833 714-626-4201
Allen Whitten, prin. Fax 738-3728
Troy HS 2,700/9-12
2200 Dorothy Ln 92831 714-626-4401
Will Mynster, prin. Fax 626-4492
Other Schools – See Buena Park, La Habra

Fullerton SD 13,600/K-8
1401 W Valencia Dr 92833 714-447-7400
Dr. Bob Pletka Ed.D., supt. Fax 447-7414
www.fullertonsd.org
Ladera Vista JHS 900/7-8
1700 E Wilshire Ave 92831 714-447-7765
Randa Schmalfeld, prin. Fax 447-7554
Nicolas JHS 800/7-8
1100 W Olive Ave 92833 714-447-7775
Rudy Torres, prin. Fax 447-7586
Parks JHS 1,000/7-8
1710 Rosecrans Ave 92833 714-447-7785
Sherry Dustin, prin. Fax 447-7753

---

California State University-Fullerton Post-Sec.
PO Box 34080 92834 657-278-2011
Eastside Christian S 200/K-12
1701 W Valencia Dr 92833 714-525-7200
Kim Van Geloof, head sch Fax 525-7200
Fullerton College Post-Sec.
321 E Chapman Ave 92832 714-992-7000
Grace Christian Academy 100/K-12
1619 W Louise Pl 92833 714-315-1619
Sydney Christy, admin.
Grace Mission University Post-Sec.
1645 W Valencia Dr 92833 714-525-0088
Hope International University Post-Sec.
2500 Nutwood Ave 92831 714-879-3901
Marshall B. Ketchum University Post-Sec.
2575 Yorba Linda Blvd 92831 714-449-7444
Rosary HS 600/9-12
1340 N Acacia Ave 92831 714-879-6302
Jen Almand, admin. Fax 879-0853
Western State University College of Law Post-Sec.
1111 N State College Blvd 92831 714-738-1000

**Galt, Sacramento, Pop. 22,880**
Galt JUNESD 3,900/K-8
1018 C St Ste 210 95632 209-744-4545
Karen Schauer, supt. Fax 744-4553
www.galt.k12.ca.us
McCaffrey MS 900/7-8
997 Park Terrace Dr 95632 209-745-5462
Julie Grandinetti, prin. Fax 745-5465

Galt JUNHSD 2,300/9-12
12945 Marengo Rd 95632 209-745-0249
Elizabeth Kaufman Ed.D., supt. Fax 745-0881
www.ghsd.k12.ca.us
Estrellita Continuation HS 200/Alt
12935 Marengo Rd 95632 209-745-2167
Maria Orr, prin. Fax 745-7026
Galt HS 1,000/9-12
145 N Lincoln Way 95632 209-745-3081
Bob Rappleye, prin. Fax 745-4786
Liberty Ranch HS 1,100/9-12
12945 Marengo Rd 95632 209-744-4250
Mike Tambini, prin. Fax 745-2601
Adult Education Adult
150 Camellia Way 95632 209-745-5852
Tony Lara, dir. Fax 745-7026

**Garberville, Humboldt, Pop. 894**
Humboldt County Office of Education
Supt. — See Eureka
Southern Humboldt Community S 50/Alt
286 Sprowl Creek Rd 95542 707-923-2550
Jennifer Fairbanks, prin.

**Gardena, Los Angeles, Pop. 56,918**
Los Angeles USD
Supt. — See Los Angeles
Gardena HS 1,900/9-12
1301 W 182nd St 90248 310-354-5000
Rosemarie Martinez, prin. Fax 366-6943
Moneta Continuation HS 100/Alt
1230 W 177th St 90248 310-354-4951
Antonio Morreale, prin. Fax 352-4027
Peary MS 1,800/6-8
1415 W Gardena Blvd 90247 310-225-4200
Marva Patton, prin. Fax 329-3957

Kiriyama Community Adult S — Adult
18120 S Normandie Ave 90248 — 310-354-4900
Wanda Chang, prin. — Fax 323-8981

---

Everest College — Post-Sec.
1045 W Rdnd Bch Blvd #275 90247 — 310-527-7105
Junipero Serra HS — 600/9-12
14830 Van Ness Ave 90249 — 310-324-6675
Jeff Guzman, prin. — Fax 352-4953
Pacific Lutheran HS — 100/9-12
2814 Manhattan Beach Blvd 90249 — 310-530-1231
Lucas Fitzgerald, prin. — Fax 530-1215
United Education Institute — Post-Sec.
661 W Redondo Beach Blvd 90247 — 424-246-3000

**Garden Grove, Orange, Pop. 166,793**

Garden Grove USD — 47,900/PK-12
10331 Stanford Ave 92840 — 714-663-6000
Gabriela Mafi, supt. — Fax 663-6100
www.ggusd.us/
Alamitos IS — 900/7-8
12381 Dale St 92841 — 714-663-6101
Christina Pflughoft, prin. — Fax 663-6277
Bell IS — 600/7-8
11852 Knott St 92841 — 714-663-6466
Matt Lambert, prin. — Fax 663-6238
Bolsa Grande HS — 2,100/9-12
9401 Westminster Ave 92844 — 714-663-6424
Louise Milner, prin. — Fax 663-6029
Doig IS — 900/7-8
12752 Trask Ave 92843 — 714-663-6241
Louie Gomez, prin. — Fax 663-6845
Garden Grove HS — 2,400/9-12
11271 Stanford Ave 92840 — 714-663-6115
Steve Osborne, prin. — Fax 663-6030
Hare HS — 500/Alt
12012 Magnolia St 92841 — 714-663-6508
Todd Nirk, prin. — Fax 663-6510
Irvine IS — 800/7-8
10552 Hazard Ave 92843 — 714-663-6551
Bill Gates, prin. — Fax 663-6013
Jordan IS — 700/7-8
9821 Woodbury Ave 92844 — 714-663-6124
Tracy Conway, prin. — Fax 663-6123
Lake IS — 600/7-8
10801 Orangewood Ave 92840 — 714-663-6506
Tahnee Phan, prin. — Fax 663-6065
Pacifica HS — 1,800/9-12
6851 Lampson Ave 92845 — 714-663-6515
Robin Patterson, prin. — Fax 663-6037
Ralston IS — 700/7-8
10851 Lampson Ave 92840 — 714-663-6366
Ruth Dietze, prin. — Fax 638-7155
Rancho Alamitos HS — 2,000/9-12
11351 Dale St 92841 — 714-663-6415
Mary Hibbard, prin. — Fax 663-6439
Santiago HS — 2,300/9-12
12342 Trask Ave 92843 — 714-663-6215
Michael Kennedy, prin. — Fax 530-0764
Walton IS — 700/7-8
12181 Buaro St 92840 — 714-663-6040
Janis Cody, prin. — Fax 534-4814
Lincoln Education Center — Adult
11262 Garden Grove Blvd 92843 — 714-663-6291
Connie Van Luit Ed.D., dir.
Other Schools – See Fountain Valley, Santa Ana, Westminster

---

Career Academy of Beauty — Post-Sec.
12471 Valley View St 92845 — 714-897-3010
Concorde Career Institute — Post-Sec.
12951 Euclid St Ste 101 92840 — 714-703-1900
Lola Beauty College — Post-Sec.
11883 Valley View St 92845 — 714-894-3366
Orangewood Academy — 200/PK-12
13732 Clinton St 92843 — 714-534-4694
Datha Tickner, prin. — Fax 534-5931
Shepherd's Grove S — 300/K-12
12901 Lewis St 92840 — 714-971-4159
Carole Barber, prin. — Fax 971-4106
Stanton University — Post-Sec.
12666 Brookhurst St 92840 — 714-539-6561
Thanh Le College School of Cosmetology — Post-Sec.
12875 Chapman Ave 92840 — 714-971-5844

**Garden Valley, El Dorado**

Black Oak Mine USD
Supt. — See Georgetown
Golden Sierra JSHS — 500/7-12
5101 Garden Valley Rd 95633 — 530-333-8330
Rebecca Evers, prin. — Fax 333-8333

**Georgetown, El Dorado, Pop. 2,308**

Black Oak Mine USD — 1,200/K-12
6540 Wentworth Springs Rd 95634 — 530-333-8300
Robert Williams Ed.D., supt. — Fax 333-8303
www.bomusd.org/
Other Schools – See Garden Valley, Greenwood

**Gerber, Tehama, Pop. 1,047**

Gerber UNESD — 400/K-8
23014 Chard Ave 96035 — 530-385-1041
Jenny Marr, supt. — Fax 385-1451
www.gerberschool.org
Gerber Community Day S — 50/Alt
23014 Chard Ave 96035 — 530-385-1041
Jenny Marr, prin. — Fax 385-1451

**Geyserville, Sonoma, Pop. 841**

Geyserville USD — 300/K-12
1300 Moody Ln 95441 — 707-857-3592
Jim Johnson, supt. — Fax 857-3071
www.gusd.com
Buena Vista HS — 50/Alt
1300 Moody Ln 95441 — 707-433-3207
Deborah Bertolucci, prin.
Geyersville New Tech Academy — 100/6-12
1300 Moody Ln 95441 — 707-857-3592
Deborah Bertolucci, prin. — Fax 857-3071

**Gilroy, Santa Clara, Pop. 47,703**

Gilroy USD — 11,100/PK-12
7810 Arroyo Cir 95020 — 408-847-2700
Barbara Brown Ph.D., supt. — Fax 847-4717
www.gilroyunified.org
Brownell MS — 800/6-8
7800 Carmel St 95020 — 408-847-3377
Greg Camacho-Light, prin. — Fax 846-7521
Christopher HS — 1,500/9-12
850 Day Rd 95020 — 408-848-7171
Greg Kapaku, prin. — Fax 847-7256
Gilroy HS — 1,500/9-12
750 W 10th St 95020 — 408-847-2424
Dr. Marco Sanchez, prin. — Fax 842-3311
Mt. Madonna HS — 300/Alt
8750 Hirasaki Ct 95020 — 408-842-4313
Jennifer Bowen, prin. — Fax 842-2918
Owens-Gilroy Early College Academy — 200/9-12
5055 Santa Teresa Blvd 95020 — 408-846-4909
Sonia Flores, prin. — Fax 848-4730
Solorsano MS — 1,100/6-8
7121 Grenache Way 95020 — 408-848-4121
Maria Walker, prin. — Fax 848-7121
South Valley MS — 700/6-8
385 I O O F Ave 95020 — 408-847-2828
Anisha Munshi, prin. — Fax 847-5708

Regional Occupational Center & Program
Supt. — None
Santa Clara County ROP South — Vo/Tech
700 W 6th St Ste L 95020 — 408-842-0361
Dr. David Matuszak, dir. — Fax 842-0653

---

Gavilan College — Post-Sec.
5055 Santa Teresa Blvd 95020 — 408-848-4800

**Glendale, Los Angeles, Pop. 184,933**

Glendale USD — 26,100/PK-12
223 N Jackson St 91206 — 818-241-3111
Dr. Donald Empey, supt. — Fax 548-9041
www.gusd.net/
Daily Continuation HS — 300/Alt
220 N Kenwood St 91206 — 818-247-4805
Dr. Rene Valdes Ed.D., prin. — Fax 547-3081
Glendale HS — 2,800/9-12
1440 E Broadway 91205 — 818-242-3161
Dr. Monica Makiewicz Ed.D., prin. — Fax 244-6309
Hoover HS — 1,900/9-12
651 Glenwood Rd 91202 — 818-242-6801
Dr. Jennifer Earl Ed.D., prin. — Fax 247-8825
Jewel City Community Day S — 50/Alt
223 N Jackson St 91206 — 818-241-3111
Dr. Rene Valdes Ed.D., dir. — Fax 547-0213
Roosevelt MS — 800/6-8
1017 S Glendale Ave 91205 — 818-242-6845
Dr. Mary Mason Ed.D., prin. — Fax 552-5188
Toll MS — 1,200/6-8
700 Glenwood Rd 91202 — 818-244-8414
Bill Card, prin. — Fax 500-1487
Wilson MS — 1,400/6-8
1221 Monterey Rd 91206 — 818-244-8145
Dr. Chris Coulter Ed.D., prin. — Fax 244-2050
Other Schools – See La Crescenta

---

Brand College — Post-Sec.
529 Hahn Ave Ste 101 91203 — 818-550-0770
Glendale Adventist Academy — 600/K-12
700 Kimlin Dr 91206 — 818-244-8671
Dr. Mario Negrete, prin. — Fax 546-1180
Glendale Community College — Post-Sec.
1500 N Verdugo Rd 91208 — 818-240-1000
Holy Family HS — 200/9-12
400 E Lomita Ave 91205 — 818-241-3178
Nancy O'Sullivan, prin. — Fax 241-7753
Integrated Digital Technologies — Post-Sec.
130 N Brand Blvd Ste 300 91203 — 818-396-3500
Moro Beauty College — Post-Sec.
124 N Brand Blvd 91203 — 818-246-7376
North-West College — Post-Sec.
221 N Brand Blvd 91203 — 818-242-0205
Uni Health America/Glendale Mem Hospital — Post-Sec.
1420 S Central Ave 91204 — 818-502-2334

**Glendora, Los Angeles, Pop. 48,747**

Azusa USD
Supt. — See Azusa
Sierra HS — 300/Alt
1134 S Barranca Ave 91740 — 626-852-8300
Mari Bordona, prin. — Fax 914-3797
Azusa Adult Educ Center — Adult
1134 S Barranca Ave 91740 — 626-852-8400
Mary Ketza, prin. — Fax 852-8407

Charter Oak USD
Supt. — See Covina
Arrow Continuation HS — 100/Alt
1505 Sunflower Ave 91740 — 626-914-3961
Lisa Raigosa, prin. — Fax 852-7685
Bridges Community Day S — 50/Alt
1507 Sunflower Ave 91740 — 626-914-3961
Lisa Raigosa, prin. — Fax 852-7685

Glendora USD — 7,500/PK-12
500 N Loraine Ave 91741 — 626-963-1611
Dr. Ann Keyes, supt. — Fax 335-2196
www.glendora.k12.ca.us
Glendora HS — 2,500/9-12
1600 E Foothill Blvd 91741 — 626-963-5731
Paul Lopez, prin. — Fax 963-2880
Goddard MS — 900/6-8
859 E Sierra Madre Ave 91741 — 626-852-4500
Brock Jacobsen, prin. — Fax 852-4520
Sandburg MS — 900/6-8
819 W Bennett Ave 91741 — 626-852-4530
Eric Osborne, prin. — Fax 852-4521
Whitcomb Continuation HS — 100/Alt
350 W Mauna Loa Ave 91740 — 626-852-4550
Ron Letourneau, prin. — Fax 852-4519
Glendora Adult S — Adult
350 W Mauna Loa Ave 91740 — 626-852-4550
Ron Letourneau, prin. — Fax 852-4519

---

Citrus College — Post-Sec.
1000 W Foothill Blvd 91741 — 626-963-0323
Grace Communion Seminary — Post-Sec.
PO Box 5005 91740 — 626-650-2306
St. Lucy's Priory HS — 700/9-12
655 W Sierra Madre Ave 91741 — 626-335-3322
Gina Giuliucci, prin. — Fax 335-4373

**Gold River, Sacramento, Pop. 7,625**

---

Bryan University — Post-Sec.
2317 Gold Meadow Way 95670 — 866-649-2400

**Goleta, Santa Barbara, Pop. 29,028**

Santa Barbara SD
Supt. — See Santa Barbara
Dos Pueblos HS — 2,300/9-12
7266 Alameda Ave 93117 — 805-968-2541
Shawn Carey, prin. — Fax 968-2891
Goleta Valley JHS — 800/7-8
6100 Stow Canyon Rd 93117 — 805-967-3486
Veronica Rogers, prin. — Fax 967-8176

**Gonzales, Monterey, Pop. 8,098**

Gonzales USD — 2,400/K-12
PO Box G 93926 — 831-675-0100
Candice McFarland, supt. — Fax 675-2763
www.gonzales.k12.ca.us
Fairview MS — 600/5-8
PO Box G 93926 — 831-675-3704
Al Velasquez, prin. — Fax 675-3274
Gonzales HS — 800/9-12
PO Box G 93926 — 831-675-2495
Cheryl Alves De Souza, prin. — Fax 675-8054
Somavia HS — 50/Alt
PO Box G 93926 — 831-675-1081
Patrick O'Donnell, admin. — Fax 675-1084

**Granada Hills, See Los Angeles**

Los Angeles USD
Supt. — See Los Angeles
Addams Continuation HS — 200/Alt
16341 Donmetz St 91344 — 818-271-2946
Paul Purkhiser, prin. — Fax 271-2569
Frost MS — 1,600/6-8
12314 Bradford Pl 91344 — 818-332-6900
Jose Ayala, prin. — Fax 360-9584
Henry MS — 1,100/6-8
17340 San Jose St 91344 — 818-832-3870
Sandra Cruz, prin. — Fax 368-7333
Kennedy HS — 2,500/9-12
11254 Gothic Ave 91344 — 818-271-2900
Richard Chavez, prin. — Fax 368-9527
Porter MS — 1,700/6-8
15960 Kingsbury St 91344 — 818-920-2050
Linda Ibach, prin. — Fax 891-7826
Valley Academy of Arts & Sciences — 900/9-12
10445 Balboa Blvd 91344 — 818-832-7750
Kelly Hanock, prin. — Fax 368-5140
Kennedy-San Fernando Adult Education — Adult
11254 Gothic Ave 91344 — 818-271-2550
Kathleen Javaheri, prin. — Fax 271-2559

---

Newberry School of Beauty — Post-Sec.
16852 Devonshire St 91344 — 818-366-3211

**Grand Terrace, San Bernardino, Pop. 11,712**

Colton JUSD
Supt. — See Colton
Grand Terrace HS — 9-12
21810 Main St 92313 — 909-580-5006
James Western, prin. — Fax 876-4001
Terrace Hills MS — 900/7-8
22579 De Berry St 92313 — 909-580-5022
Scott Boggs, prin. — Fax 783-3836

**Granite Bay, Placer, Pop. 19,714**

Eureka UNSD — 3,400/PK-8
5455 Eureka Rd 95746 — 916-791-4939
Tom Janis, supt. — Fax 791-5527
www.eureka-usd.k12.ca.us
Cavitt JHS — 400/7-8
7200 Fuller Dr 95746 — 916-791-4152
Jennifer Platt, prin. — Fax 791-7414
Other Schools – See Roseville

Roseville JUNHSD
Supt. — See Roseville
Granite Bay HS — 2,200/9-12
1 Grizzly Way 95746 — 916-786-8676
Jennifer Leighton, prin. — Fax 786-0766

**Grass Valley, Nevada, Pop. 12,474**

Grass Valley ESD — 1,400/PK-8
10840 Gilmore Way 95945 — 530-273-4483
Eric Fredrickson, supt. — Fax 273-0248
www.gvsd.us
Gilmore MS — 500/5-8
10837 Rough and Ready Hwy 95945 — 530-273-8479
Christopher Roberts, prin. — Fax 273-1675

Nevada County Office of Education
Supt. — See Nevada City
Jamieson HS — 50/Alt
12338 McCourtney Rd 95949 — 530-272-5464
Lisa Sanford, admin. — Fax 272-5870

Nevada JUNHSD 3,200/9-12
11645 Ridge Rd 95945 530-273-3351
Louise Johnson, supt. Fax 273-3372
www.njuhsd.com
Bear River HS 900/9-12
11130 Magnolia Rd 95949 530-268-3700
Amy Besler, prin. Fax 268-8372
Ghidotti HS 200/9-12
250 Sierra College Dr 95945 530-274-5270
Melissa Madigan, prin. Fax 274-5272
Nevada Union HS 2,100/9-12
11761 Ridge Rd 95945 530-273-4431
Dan Frisella, prin. Fax 477-9317
North Point Academy 100/Alt
11761 Ridge Rd 95945 530-477-1225
Melissa Madigan, prin. Fax 272-8564
NU Tech HS Vo/Tech
11761 Ridge Rd 95945 530-273-4431
Kelly Rhoden, admin. Fax 477-9317
Silver Springs HS 100/Alt
140 Park Ave 95945 530-272-2635
Marty Mathiesen, prin. Fax 272-2687
Nevada Adult Education Adult
12338 McCourtney Rd 95949 530-272-2643
Trisha Dellis, admin. Fax 272-3422

Pleasant Ridge UNESD 1,500/K-8
22580 Kingston Ln 95949 530-268-2800
Rusty Clark, supt. Fax 268-2804
www.prsd.k12.ca.us
Magnolia IS 600/6-8
22431 Kingston Ln 95949 530-268-2815
Gene Morgan, prin. Fax 268-2819

Union Hill ESD 500/K-8
10879 Bartlett Dr 95945 530-273-0647
David Curry, supt. Fax 273-5626
www.uhsd.k12.ca.us
Union Hill MS 7-8
11638 Colfax Hwy 95945 530-273-8456
Joe Limov, prin. Fax 273-0152

**Graton, Sonoma, Pop. 1,648**

Pacific Christian Academy 50/K-12
PO Box 369 95444 707-823-2880

**Greenfield, Monterey, Pop. 16,188**
Greenfield UNSD 2,600/K-8
493 El Camino Real 93927 831-674-2840
Doc Ervin, supt. Fax 674-3712
www.greenfield.k12.ca.us
Vista Verde MS 700/6-8
1199 Elm Ave 93927 831-674-1420
Traci Gholar, prin. Fax 674-1425

South Monterey JUNHSD
Supt. — See King City
Greenfield HS 900/9-12
225 S El Camino Real 93927 831-674-2751
Diana Jimenez, prin. Fax 674-2646

**Greenville, Plumas, Pop. 1,068**
Plumas USD
Supt. — See Quincy
Greenville JSHS 100/7-12
117 Grand St 95947 530-284-7197
Jerry Merica-Jones, prin. Fax 284-6710

**Greenwood, El Dorado**
Black Oak Mine USD
Supt. — See Georgetown
Divide HS 50/Alt
4405 State Highway 193 95635 530-333-8315
Rebecca Evers, admin. Fax 333-8317

**Gridley, Butte, Pop. 6,408**
Gridley USD 2,100/K-12
429 Magnolia St 95948 530-846-4721
Rick Rubino, supt. Fax 846-4595
www.gusd.org
Esperanza Continuation HS 50/Alt
581 Jackson St 95948 530-846-4383
Cindy Kershaw, prin. Fax 846-2435
Gridley HS 700/9-12
300 E Spruce St 95948 530-846-4791
Joey Adame, prin. Fax 846-3412
Gridley Unified Community Day S 50/Alt
581 Jackson St 95948 530-846-4721
Cindy Kershaw, prin. Fax 846-2435
Sycamore MS 400/6-8
1125 Sycamore St 95948 530-846-3636
Christine McCormick, prin. Fax 846-6796

**Groveland, Tuolumne, Pop. 585**
Big Oak Flat-Groveland USD 400/K-12
PO Box 1397 95321 209-962-5765
Dave Urquhart, supt. Fax 962-6108
www.bofg.k12.ca.us
Moccasin Community Day S 50/Alt
PO Box 1397 95321 209-962-7160
Wynette Hilton, prin. Fax 962-7160
Tioga HS 100/9-12
19304 Ferretti Rd 95321 209-962-4763
Ryan Dutton, prin. Fax 962-4507
Other Schools – See La Grange

**Guadalupe, Santa Barbara, Pop. 6,975**
Guadalupe UNESD 1,200/K-8
PO Box 788 93434 805-343-2114
Ed Cora, supt. Fax 343-6155
www.guadusd.org
McKenzie JHS 400/6-8
PO Box 788 93434 805-343-1951
Gabriel Solorio, prin. Fax 343-6931

**Gustine, Merced, Pop. 5,420**
Gustine USD 1,700/K-12
1500 Meredith Ave 95322 209-854-3784
Bill Morones, supt. Fax 854-9164
www.gustine.k12.ca.us
Gustine HS 500/9-12
501 North Ave 95322 209-854-6414
John Petrone, prin. Fax 854-1955
Gustine MS 400/6-8
28075 Sullivan Rd 95322 209-854-5030
Michael Bunch, prin. Fax 854-9592
Pioneer HS 50/Alt
501 North Ave 95322 209-854-6414
Adam Cano, prin. Fax 854-9581

**Hacienda Heights, Los Angeles, Pop. 53,234**
Hacienda La Puente USD
Supt. — See City of Industry
Los Altos HS 2,100/9-12
15325 Los Robles Ave 91745 626-934-5418
Cheli McReynolds, prin. Fax 855-3145
Newton MS 600/6-8
15616 Newton St 91745 626-933-2401
Dan Ma, prin. Fax 855-3832
Orange Grove MS 700/6-8
14505 Orange Grove Ave 91745 626-933-7001
Edna Moore, prin. Fax 855-3837
Puente Hills HS 100/Alt
15430 Shadybend Dr 91745 626-933-3400
Joaquin Martinez, prin. Fax 855-3719
Valley Alternative S 100/Alt
15430 Shadybend Dr 91745 626-933-3400
Joaquin Martinez, prin. Fax 855-3719
Wilson HS 1,700/9-12
16455 Wedgeworth Dr 91745 626-934-4410
Dr. Danielle Kenfield, prin. Fax 855-3792
Dibble Adult S Adult
1600 Pontenova Ave 91745 626-933-8301
Elbia Sarabia, dir. Fax 855-3528

**Half Moon Bay, San Mateo, Pop. 11,097**
Cabrillo USD 3,300/K-12
498 Kelly Ave 94019 650-712-7100
Jane Yuster Ed.D., supt. Fax 726-0279
www.cabrillo.k12.ca.us/
Cunha IS 800/6-8
498 Kelly Ave 94019 650-712-7190
Jarrett Dooley, prin. Fax 712-7195
Half Moon Bay HS 900/9-12
498 Kelly Ave 94019 650-712-7200
John Nazar, prin. Fax 712-7232
Pilarcitos Continuation HS 50/Alt
498 Kelly Ave 94019 650-712-7224
Rajan Bechar, prin. Fax 712-7225
Cabrillo Adult S Adult
498 Kelly Ave 94019 650-712-7224
Rajan Bechar, prin. Fax 712-7225

**Hamilton City, Glenn, Pop. 1,746**
Hamilton USD 800/K-12
PO Box 488 95951 530-826-3261
Charles Tracy, supt. Fax 826-0440
www.husdschools.org
Barkley HS 50/Alt
Hwy 32 & Los Robles St 95951 530-826-3331
Charles Tracy, prin. Fax 826-3929
Hamilton Community Day S 50/Alt
535 Sacramento Ave 95951 530-826-3261
Charles Tracy, prin. Fax 826-3929
Hamilton HS 300/9-12
620 Canal St 95951 530-826-3261
Cris Oseguera, prin. Fax 826-0440
Hamilton Adult S Adult
300 6th St 95951 530-826-3331
Sylvia Robles, dir. Fax 826-3929

**Hanford, Kings, Pop. 52,527**
Hanford ESD 6,100/K-8
PO Box 1067 93232 559-585-3601
Paul Terry, supt. Fax 584-7833
www.hesd.k12.ca.us/
Kennedy JHS 500/7-8
PO Box 1067 93232 559-585-3850
Jason Strickland, prin. Fax 585-2374
Wilson JHS 600/7-8
PO Box 1067 93232 559-585-3870
Kenneth Eggert, prin. Fax 585-2336

Hanford JUNHSD 4,400/9-12
823 W Lacey Blvd 93230 559-583-5901
William Fishbough, supt. Fax 589-9769
www.hjuhsd.k12.ca.us
Hanford Community Day S 50/Alt
120 E Grangeville Blvd 93230 559-583-5902
Scott Pickle, prin. Fax 582-5229
Hanford HS 1,500/9-12
120 E Grangeville Blvd 93230 559-583-5902
Scott Pickle, prin. Fax 582-5229
Hanford Night Continuation HS 100/Alt
1201 N Douty St 93230 559-583-5904
Heather Keran, prin. Fax 583-6580
Hanford West HS 1,300/9-12
1150 W Lacey Blvd 93230 559-583-5903
Darin Parson, prin. Fax 583-6708
Johnson HS 200/Alt
1201 N Douty St 93230 559-583-5904
Heather Keran, prin. Fax 583-6580
Sierra Pacific HS 700/9-12
1259 13th Ave 93230 559-583-5912
Greg Henry, prin. Fax 583-5914
Hanford Adult S Adult
905 Campus Dr 93230 559-583-5905
Heather Keran, prin. Fax 589-9564

Kings County Office of Education 300/
1144 W Lacey Blvd 93230 559-584-1441
Tim Bowers, supt. Fax 589-7000
www.kings.k12.ca.us
Kings County Community S 100/Alt
146 W Highland St 93230 559-589-2602
Rebecca Villa, prin. Fax 582-0731

Regional Occupational Center & Program
Supt. — None
Kings County ROP Vo/Tech
1144 W Lacey Blvd 93230 559-589-7026
Margie Newton, dir. Fax 589-7007

**Happy Camp, Siskiyou, Pop. 1,130**
Siskiyou UNHSD
Supt. — See Mount Shasta
Happy Camp HS 100/9-12
PO Box 437 96039 530-493-2697
Steve Van Ert, prin. Fax 493-2605

**Harbor City, See Los Angeles**
Los Angeles USD
Supt. — See Los Angeles
Humanities & Arts Academy of LA 9-12
24300 Western Ave 90710 310-257-7100
Gregory Fisher, prin. Fax 326-1805
Narbonne HS 3,300/9-12
24300 Western Ave 90710 310-257-7100
Gerald Kobata, prin. Fax 326-1805
Patton Continuation HS 100/Alt
24514 Western Ave 90710 310-257-4740
Reginald Obiamalu, prin. Fax 257-4742

**Hawaiian Gardens, Los Angeles, Pop. 14,073**
ABC USD
Supt. — See Cerritos
Fedde MS 400/7-8
21409 Elaine Ave 90716 562-229-7805
Ricardo Lois, prin. Fax 809-6895

**Hawthorne, Los Angeles, Pop. 81,457**
Centinela Valley UNHSD
Supt. — See Lawndale
Hawthorne HS 1,900/9-12
4859 W El Segundo Blvd 90250 310-263-4400
Dr. Mark Newell, prin. Fax 675-7017

Hawthorne SD 8,900/K-12
14120 Hawthorne Blvd 90250 310-676-2276
Dr. Helen Morgan Ed.D., supt. Fax 675-9464
www.hawthorne.k12.ca.us
Carson MS 800/6-8
13838 Yukon Ave 90250 310-676-1908
Mark Silva, prin. Fax 676-0634
Hawthorne MS 900/6-8
4366 W 129th St 90250 310-676-0167
Rudy Salas, prin. Fax 675-0924
Prairie Vista MS 1,000/6-8
13600 Prairie Ave 90250 310-679-1003
Dr. Patricia Ray, prin. Fax 679-1142

Los Angeles County Office of Education
Supt. — See Downey
Renaissance Community Day S 300/Alt
14600 Cerise Ave 90250 310-970-9914
Mark Nguyen, prin. Fax 679-8106

Wiseburn USD 3,600/K-12
13530 Aviation Blvd 90250 310-643-3025
Dr. Tom Johnstone, supt. Fax 643-7659
www.wiseburn.k12.ca.us
Dana MS 1,000/6-8
5504 W 135th St 90250 310-725-4700
Aileen Harbeck, prin. Fax 536-9091

**Hayfork, Trinity, Pop. 2,231**
Mountain Valley USD 300/PK-12
PO Box 339 96041 530-628-5265
Debbie Miller, supt. Fax 628-5267
www.mvusd.us
Hayfork HS 100/9-12
PO Box 10 96041 530-628-5261
Debbie Miller, prin. Fax 628-3091
Valley Continuation HS 50/Alt
PO Box 339 96041 530-628-5294
Wendy Platt, prin. Fax 628-5344
Mountain Valley Adult S Adult
231 Oak Ave 96041 530-628-5265
Debbie Miller, prin.

**Hayward, Alameda, Pop. 133,787**
Alameda County Office of Education 3,100/
313 W Winton Ave 94544 510-887-0152
Karen Monroe, supt. Fax 670-4146
www.acoe.org
Alameda County Community S 200/K-12
313 W Winton Ave 94544 510-670-6619
Carolyn Hobbs, prin. Fax 293-9201

Hayward USD 21,300/K-12
PO Box 5000 94540 510-784-2600
Stan Dobbs, supt. Fax 784-2641
www.husd.us
Brenkwitz Alternative HS 200/Alt
PO Box 5000 94540 510-723-3160
Shann Chu, prin. Fax 582-6376
Chavez MS 600/7-8
PO Box 5000 94540 510-723-3110
Sean Moffatt, prin. Fax 538-8478
Harte MS 600/7-8
PO Box 5000 94540 510-723-3100
Lisa Davies-Gomez, prin. Fax 886-5926
Hayward HS 1,600/9-12
PO Box 5000 94540 510-723-3170
George Bullis, prin. Fax 581-3145
King MS 600/7-8
PO Box 5000 94540 510-723-3120
Estella Santos, prin. Fax 781-6129
Mt. Eden HS 1,900/9-12
PO Box 5000 94540 510-723-3180
Greg Fobbs, prin. Fax 786-2269
Ochoa MS 600/7-8
PO Box 5000 94540 510-723-3130
Ariel Dolowich, prin. Fax 786-0559
Tennyson HS 1,300/9-12
PO Box 5000 94540 510-723-3190
Lori Villanueva, prin. Fax 582-0964

Winton MS 600/7-8
PO Box 5000 94540 510-723-3140
George Porter, prin. Fax 733-9043
Hayward Adult Education Center Adult
PO Box 5000 94540 510-293-8595
Guy Zakrevsky, prin. Fax 727-1139

New Haven USD
Supt. — See Union City
Conley-Caraballo HS 50/Alt
541 Blanche St 94544 510-471-5126
Ramon Camacho, prin. Fax 475-3949

Regional Occupational Center & Program
Supt. — None
Eden Area ROP Vo/Tech
26316 Hesperian Blvd 94545 510-293-2900
Linda Granger, dir. Fax 783-2955

San Lorenzo USD
Supt. — See San Lorenzo
East Bay Arts HS 300/9-12
20450 Royal Ave 94541 510-317-4471
Abigail Kotzin, prin. Fax 317-4495
Royal Sunset HS 200/Alt
20450 Royal Ave 94541 510-317-4400
Abigail Kotzin, prin. Fax 317-4495

---

California State University-East Bay Post-Sec.
25800 Carlos Bee Blvd 94542 510-885-3000
Chabot College Post-Sec.
25555 Hesperian Blvd 94545 510-723-6600
Heald College Post-Sec.
25500 Industrial Blvd 94545 510-783-2100
Life Chiropractic College West Post-Sec.
25001 Industrial Blvd 94545 800-788-4476
Moreau HS 900/9-12
27170 Mission Blvd 94544 510-881-4300
Lisa Tortorich, prin. Fax 581-5669
NCP College of Nursing Post-Sec.
21615 Hesperian Blvd Ste A 94541 510-785-0454

**Healdsburg, Sonoma, Pop. 11,079**
Healdsburg USD 2,500/K-12
1028 Prince Ave 95448 707-431-3488
Chris Vanden Heuvel, supt. Fax 433-8403
www.husd.com
Healdsburg HS 700/9-12
1024 Prince Ave 95448 707-431-3420
Dr. Lori Rhodes, prin. Fax 431-3467
Healdsburg JHS 500/6-8
315 Grant St 95448 707-431-3410
Bill Halliday, prin. Fax 431-3593
Marce Becerra Academy 50/Alt
1024 Prince Ave 95448 707-431-3449
Kestrel Montes, prin. Fax 431-3595

---

Rio Lindo Adventist Academy 200/9-12
3200 Rio Lindo Ave 95448 707-431-5100

**Heber, Imperial, Pop. 4,270**
Heber ESD 700/K-8
1052 Heber Ave 92249 760-337-6530
Jaime Silva, supt. Fax 353-3421
hesdk8.org
Heber ES 600/4-8
1052 Heber Ave 92249 760-337-6530
Patty Marcial, prin. Fax 353-3421

**Helendale, San Bernardino**
Helendale ESD 700/K-12
PO Box 249 92342 760-952-1180
Ross Swearingen, supt. Fax 952-1178
www.helendalesd.org
Riverview MS 100/7-8
PO Box 249 92342 760-952-1266
William Brown, prin. Fax 952-1178

**Helm, Fresno**
Golden Plains USD
Supt. — See San Joaquin
Rio Del Rey Continuation HS 50/Alt
PO Box 158 93627 559-866-5757
Aurora Guzman, prin.

**Hemet, Riverside, Pop. 76,330**
Hemet USD 21,500/K-12
1791 W Acacia Ave 92545 951-765-5100
Dr. Barry Kayrell, supt. Fax 765-5115
www.hemetusd.org
Acacia MS 900/6-8
1200 E Acacia Ave 92543 951-765-1620
Jeff Franks, prin. Fax 765-5149
Accelerated Core Education Alt
831 E Devonshire Ave 92543 951-925-2324
Frank Green, prin. Fax 765-5729
Alessandro HS 500/Alt
831 E Devonshire Ave 92543 951-765-5182
Tara O'Malley, prin. Fax 925-7548
ASPIRE Community Day S Alt
26866 San Jacinto St 92543 951-929-3071
Cristian Miley, prin.
Dartmouth MS 800/6-8
41535 Mayberry Ave 92544 951-765-2550
Eric Dahlstrom, prin. Fax 765-2559
Diamond Valley MS 1,200/6-8
291 W Chambers Ave 92543 951-925-2899
Robert Dominguez, prin. Fax 925-6297
Hemet HS 2,500/9-12
41701 Stetson Ave 92544 951-765-5150
Dr. Emily Shaw, prin. Fax 765-5177
Jackson College Prep HS 300/Alt
26400 Dartmouth St 92544 951-765-5193
Frank Green, prin. Fax 765-5195
Rancho Viejo MS 1,300/6-8
985 N Cawston Ave 92545 951-765-6287
Jon Workman, prin. Fax 925-5244

Tahquitz HS 1,500/9-12
4425 Titan Trl 92545 951-765-6300
Derek Jindra, prin. Fax 765-6344
West Valley HS 1,800/9-12
3401 Mustang Way 92545 951-765-1600
Alex Ballard, prin. Fax 765-1607
Hemet Adult Education Adult
831 E Devonshire Ave 92543 951-765-5190
Tara O'Malley, prin. Fax 925-7478
Other Schools – See Anza

---

Cornerstone Christian S 300/PK-12
26089 Girard St 92544 951-658-3203
Russell Schmidt, admin. Fax 658-0723

**Hercules, Contra Costa, Pop. 22,834**
West Contra Costa USD
Supt. — See Richmond
Hercules HS 1,000/9-12
1900 Refugio Valley Rd 94547 510-231-1429
Paul Mansingh, prin. Fax 245-1089
Hercules MS 700/6-8
1900 Refugio Valley Rd 94547 510-231-1429
Renee Lama, prin. Fax 245-1089

**Herlong, Lassen, Pop. 264**
Fort Sage USD 200/K-12
PO Box 35 96113 530-827-2129
Patrick Condon, supt. Fax 827-2019
www.fortsage.org
Fort Sage MS 50/7-8
PO Box 35 96113 530-827-2101
Patrick Condon, prin. Fax 827-3362
Herlong HS 100/9-12
PO Box 97 96113 530-827-2101
Patrick Condon, prin. Fax 827-3362

**Hermosa Beach, Los Angeles, Pop. 18,753**
Hermosa Beach City ESD 1,300/K-8
1645 Valley Dr 90254 310-937-5877
Patricia Escalante, supt. Fax 376-4974
www.hbcsd.org
Hermosa Valley ES 900/3-8
1645 Valley Dr 90254 310-937-5888
Kimberly Taylor, prin. Fax 798-4365

**Hesperia, San Bernardino, Pop. 88,087**
Hesperia USD 23,200/K-12
15576 Main St 92345 760-244-4411
David McLaughlin, supt. Fax 244-2806
www.hesperiausd.org
Canyon Ridge HS 200/Alt
12850 Muscatel St, 760-244-6530
Scott Ahlgren, prin. Fax 244-7210
Cedar MS 1,200/7-8
13565 Cedar St, 760-244-6093
Kelly Maxwell, prin. Fax 244-5439
Hesperia Community Day S 50/Alt
16527 1/2 Lemon St 92345 760-244-1771
Nate Lambdin, prin. Fax 948-0508
Hesperia HS 2,000/9-12
9898 Maple Ave 92345 760-244-9898
Michelle Estrada, prin. Fax 244-0939
Hesperia JHS 900/7-8
10275 Cypress Ave 92345 760-244-9386
Lisa Kelly, prin. Fax 244-0595
Mojave HS 300/Alt
16633 Lemon St 92345 760-948-3999
Nate Lambdin, prin. Fax 948-0508
Ranchero MS 1,100/7-8
17607 Ranchero Rd 92345 760-948-0175
Isaac Newman-Gomez, prin. Fax 948-0381
Shadow Ridge Alternative S Alt
12850 Muscatel St, 760-949-8267
Aiko Thomas, admin. Fax 948-7976
Sultana HS 2,200/9-12
17311 Sultana St 92345 760-947-6777
Lawrence Bird, prin. Fax 947-6788
Adult Education Center Adult
16527 Lemon St 92345 760-244-1771
Kim Walker, prin. Fax 948-3508
Other Schools – See Oak Hills

---

Hesperia Christian S 300/PK-12
16775 Olive St 92345 760-244-6164
Sharon Romero, admin. Fax 244-9756
San Joaquin Valley College Post-Sec.
9331 Mariposa Rd, 760-948-1947

**Highland, San Bernardino, Pop. 51,532**
Redlands USD
Supt. — See Redlands
Beattie MS 1,300/6-8
7800 Orange St 92346 909-307-2400
Angela Neuhaus, prin. Fax 307-2416

San Bernardino City USD
Supt. — See San Bernardino
San Andreas SHS 700/Alt
3232 Pacific St 92346 909-388-6521
Edward Hensley, prin. Fax 425-0523
San Bernadino Alternative Learning Ctr. 100/Alt
3236 Pacific St 92346 909-388-6221
Robyn Eberhardt, coord. Fax 388-6223
Serrano MS 800/7-8
3131 Piedmont Dr 92346 909-388-6530
Arwyn Wild, prin. Fax 864-6232

**Hillsborough, San Mateo, Pop. 10,401**
Hillsborough CSD 1,500/K-8
300 El Cerrito Ave 94010 650-342-5193
Anthony Ranii, supt. Fax 342-6964
www.hcsd.k12.ca.us
Crocker MS 500/6-8
2600 Ralston Ave 94010 650-342-6331
Jamie Adams, prin. Fax 579-5943

---

Crystal Springs Uplands S 400/6-12
400 Uplands Dr 94010 650-342-4175
Amy Richards, head sch Fax 342-7623
Nueva S 400/PK-12
6565 Skyline Blvd 94010 650-350-4600
Diane Rosenberg, dir. Fax 348-3642

**Hilmar, Merced, Pop. 3,392**
Hilmar USD 2,300/K-12
7807 Lander Ave 95324 209-667-5701
Isabel Cabral-Johnson, supt. Fax 667-1721
www.hilmar.k12.ca.us
Colony HS 50/Alt
7807 Lander Ave 95324 209-667-0276
Darlene Carvalho, prin. Fax 667-1532
Hilmar HS 700/9-12
7807 Lander Ave 95324 209-667-5903
Jeremy Nichols, prin. Fax 667-7628
Hilmar MS 500/6-8
7807 Lander Ave 95324 209-632-8847
Fax 667-7018
Irwin HS 50/Alt
7807 Lander Ave 95324 209-667-0276
Darlene Carvalho, prin. Fax 667-1532

**Hollister, San Benito, Pop. 34,317**
Hollister SD 5,100/PK-8
2690 Cienega Rd 95023 831-630-6300
Gary McIntire Ed.D., supt. Fax 634-2080
www.hesd.org
Accelerated Achievement Academy 100/4-8
1151 Buena Vista Rd 95023 831-636-4460
Joe Rivas, admin. Fax 634-4970
Maze MS 500/6-8
900 Meridian St 95023 831-636-4480
Diane Steele, prin. Fax 636-4488
Rancho San Justo MS 600/6-8
1201 Rancho Dr 95023 831-636-4450
Lisa Jelinek, prin. Fax 634-4952

San Benito County Office of Education 100/
460 5th St 95023 831-637-5393
Lorna Gilbert, supt. Fax 637-0140
www.sbcoe.org
Pinnacles Community S Alt
3230 Southside Rd 95023 831-636-2870
Colleen Grimes, prin. Fax 636-7885
San Benito County Opportunity S 100/Alt
460 5th St 95023 831-637-9269
Colleen Grimes, dir. Fax 636-7769

San Benito HSD 3,000/9-12
1220 Monterey St 95023 831-637-5831
John Perales, supt. Fax 637-6524
sbhsd-ca.schoolloop.com
San Andreas Continuation HS 200/Alt
191 Alvarado St 95023 831-637-9269
Colleen Grimes, prin. Fax 636-0376
San Benito HS 2,900/9-12
1220 Monterey St 95023 831-637-5831
Todd Dearden, prin. Fax 637-6524

**Hollywood, See Los Angeles**
Los Angeles USD
Supt. — See Los Angeles
Bernstein HS 1,000/9-12
1309 N Wilton Pl 90028 323-817-6400
Andre Spicer, prin. Fax 860-9711
Le Conte MS 900/6-8
1316 N Bronson Ave 90028 323-308-1700
Rosemary Hindinger, prin. Fax 856-3053

---

American Academy of Dramatic Arts Post-Sec.
1336 N La Brea Ave 90028 800-463-8990
Elegance International Post-Sec.
1622 N Highland Ave 90028 323-871-8318
Los Angeles Film School Post-Sec.
6363 W Sunset Blvd 90028 323-860-0789
Musicians Institute Post-Sec.
6752 Hollywood Blvd 90028 323-462-1384

**Holtville, Imperial, Pop. 5,905**
Holtville USD 1,600/PK-12
621 E 6th St 92250 760-356-2974
Celso Ruiz, supt. Fax 356-4936
www.holtville.k12.ca.us
Freedom Academy of the Imperial Valley Vo/Tech
524 W 8th St 92250 760-604-9252
Celso Ruiz, admin.
Holtville HS 500/9-12
755 Olive Ave 92250 760-356-2926
Jeff Magin, prin. Fax 356-1206
Holtville JHS 300/6-8
800 Beale Ave 92250 760-356-2811
Mario Garcia, prin. Fax 356-5741
Webb Continuation HS 50/Alt
522 W 8th St 92250 760-356-1304
Celso Ruiz, prin. Fax 356-5621

**Homeland, Riverside, Pop. 5,870**
Romoland ESD 2,100/K-8
25900 Leon Rd 92548 951-926-9244
Dr. Julie A. Vitale, supt. Fax 926-2170
www.romoland.net
Other Schools – See Menifee

**Hoopa, Humboldt**
Klamath-Trinity JUSD 1,100/PK-12
PO Box 1308 95546 530-625-5600
John Ray, supt. Fax 625-5611
www.ktjusd.k12.ca.us/
Hoopa Valley HS 200/9-12
PO Box 1308 95546 530-625-5600
Dustin Rossman, prin. Fax 625-5619
John Continuation HS 50/Alt
PO Box 1308 95546 530-625-5600
Jennifer Lane, prin. Fax 625-4840

Two Rivers Community Day S 50/Alt
PO Box 1308 95546 530-625-5600
Craig Kimball, prin. Fax 625-4840

**Hughson, Stanislaus, Pop. 6,490**
Hughson USD 2,100/K-12
PO Box 189 95326 209-883-4428
Brian Beck, supt. Fax 883-4639
www.hughson.k12.ca.us
Dickens HS 50/Alt
6937 Fox Rd 95326 209-883-4182
Debra Davis, admin. Fax 883-4726
Hughson HS 800/9-12
PO Box 99 95326 209-883-0469
Debra Davis, prin. Fax 883-0870
Ross MS 500/6-8
7448 Fox Rd 95326 209-883-4425
Ryan Smith, prin. Fax 883-2017
Valley Community Day S 50/Alt
PO Box 99 95326 209-883-0469
Andrew Reese, admin. Fax 883-0870

Keyes UNESD
Supt. — See Keyes
Spratling MS 200/6-8
5277 Washington Rd 95326 209-664-3833
John Stuart, prin. Fax 656-2384

**Huntington Beach, Orange, Pop. 183,010**
Fountain Valley ESD
Supt. — See Fountain Valley
Talbert MS 500/6-8
9101 Brabham Dr, 714-378-4220
Jennifer Morgan, prin. Fax 378-4229

Huntington Beach City ESD 7,200/PK-8
17011 Beach Blvd Ste 560, 714-964-8888
Gregg Haulk, supt. Fax 963-9565
www.hbcsd.us
Dwyer MS 1,200/6-8
1502 Palm Ave, 714-536-7507
Darrenn Platt, prin. Fax 960-0955
Sowers MS 1,300/6-8
9300 Indianapolis Ave, 714-962-7738
Dr. Cynthia Guerrero, prin. Fax 968-5580

Huntington Beach UNHSD 16,200/9-12
5832 Bolsa Ave 92649 714-903-7000
Greg Plutko, supt. Fax 892-5750
www.hbuhsd.edu
Coast HS, 17231 Gothard St, 100/Alt
Steve Curiel, prin. 714-842-4227
Edison HS 2,600/9-12
21400 Magnolia St, 714-962-1356
D'Liese Melendrez, prin. Fax 963-4280
Huntington Beach HS 2,800/9-12
1905 Main St, 714-536-2514
Daniel Morris, prin. Fax 960-7042
Marina HS 2,800/9-12
15871 Springdale St, 714-893-6571
Jessie Marion, prin. Fax 892-7855
Ocean View HS 1,500/9-12
17071 Gothard St, 714-848-0656
Courtney Robinson, prin. Fax 843-0541
Huntington Beach Adult Education Adult
17231 Gothard St, 714-901-8106
Steve Curiel, prin. Fax 373-5245
Other Schools – See Fountain Valley, Westminster

Ocean View SD 9,500/PK-8
17200 Pinehurst Ln 92647 714-847-2551
Dr. Carol Hansen, supt. Fax 847-1430
www.ovsd.org
Marine View MS 800/6-8
5682 Tilburg Dr, 714-846-0624
Bill Lynch, prin. Fax 846-2074
Mesa View MS 800/6-8
17601 Avilla Ln, 714-842-6608
Randy Lempert, prin. Fax 842-8798
Spring View MS 800/6-8
16662 Trudy Ln, 714-846-2891
Jason Blade, prin. Fax 377-9821
Other Schools – See Fountain Valley

Westminster SD
Supt. — See Westminster
Stacey MS 900/6-8
6311 Larchwood Dr, 714-894-7212
Heidi DeBritton, prin. Fax 373-0478

Apollos University Post-Sec.
17011 Beach Blvd Ste 900, 714-375-6697
Brethren Christian JSHS 300/6-12
21141 Strathmoor Ln, 714-962-6617
Rick Niswonger, prin. Fax 962-3171
Golden West College Post-Sec.
15744 Goldenwest St, 714-892-7711
Hebrew Academy 300/PK-12
14401 Willow Ln, 714-898-0051
Liberty Christian S 200/PK-12
7661 Warner Ave, 714-842-5992
David Whitmire, prin. Fax 848-7484

**Huntington Park, Los Angeles, Pop. 57,940**
Los Angeles USD
Supt. — See Los Angeles
Gage MS 2,500/6-8
2880 E Gage Ave 90255 323-826-1500
Cesar Quezada, prin. Fax 589-6925
Huntington Park HS 3,500/9-12
6020 Miles Ave 90255 323-826-2300
Lupe Hernandez, prin. Fax 583-0463
Marquez HPIAM HS 9-12
6361 Cottage St 90255 323-584-3800
Jonathan Chaikittirattan, prin. Fax 583-1305
Marquez LIBRA Academy 9-12
6361 Cottage St 90255 323-584-3800
Lisa Davis, prin. Fax 583-1305
Marquez School of Social Justice HS 9-12
6361 Cottage St 90255 323-584-3800
Kyle Boswell, prin. Fax 583-1305
Nimitz MS 2,000/6-8
6021 Carmelita Ave 90255 323-887-5400
Miguel Saenz, prin. Fax 773-5201
San Antonio Continuation HS 100/Alt
2911 Belgrave Ave 90255 323-826-2420
Allan Maciel, prin. Fax 826-2427
Huntington Park-Bell Community Adult S Adult
2945 Belgrave Ave 90255 323-826-2400
Clifton DeCordoba, prin. Fax 826-2413

ICDC College Post-Sec.
6812 Pacific Blvd 90255 323-277-0240
United Education Institute Post-Sec.
6055 Pacific Blvd 90255 323-319-9500

**Huron, Fresno, Pop. 6,708**
Coalinga-Huron USD
Supt. — See Coalinga
Huron MS 400/6-8
PO Box 99 93234 559-945-2926
Javier Gonzalez, prin. Fax 945-8482

**Idyllwild, Riverside, Pop. 2,853**

Idyllwild Arts Academy 300/9-12
PO Box 38 92549 951-659-2171
Dr. Doug Ashcraft, head sch Fax 659-2323

**Imperial, Imperial, Pop. 14,611**
Imperial USD 3,700/K-12
219 N E St 92251 760-355-3200
Bryan Thomason, supt. Fax 355-4511
www.imperialusd.org
Imperial Avenue Holbrook S 100/Alt
322 N Imperial Ave 92251 760-355-3207
Kerry Legarra, prin. Fax 355-3258
Imperial HS 1,000/9-12
517 W Barioni Blvd 92251 760-355-3220
Joe Apodaca, prin. Fax 355-0869
Wright MS 900/6-8
885 N Imperial Ave 92251 760-355-3240
Diego Lopez, prin. Fax 355-3256

Imperial Valley College Post-Sec.
380 E Aten Rd 92251 760-352-8320

**Imperial Beach, San Diego, Pop. 25,203**
Sweetwater UNHSD
Supt. — See Chula Vista
Mar Vista HS 1,600/9-12
505 Elm Ave 91932 619-628-5700
Juan Gonzalez, prin. Fax 424-6232
Sweetwater Community Day MS 50/Alt
505 1/2 Elm Ave 91932 619-628-3056
Fax 628-3060

**Independence, Inyo, Pop. 646**
Inyo County Office of Education 50/
PO Box G 93526 760-878-2426
Dr. Terence McAteer, supt. Fax 878-2279
www.inyo.k12.ca.us
Other Schools – See Bishop

Owens Valley USD 100/K-12
PO Box E 93526 760-878-2405
Dan Moore, supt. Fax 878-2626
www.ovusd.org
Owens Valley HS 50/9-12
PO Box E 93526 760-878-2405
Dan Moore, prin. Fax 878-2626

**Indio, Riverside, Pop. 75,249**
Desert Sands USD
Supt. — See La Quinta
Amistad Continuation HS 400/Alt
83501 Dillon Ave 92201 760-775-3570
David Gustafson, prin. Fax 775-3575
Desert Ridge Academy 1,100/6-8
79767 Avenue 39 92203 760-393-5500
Dan Borgen, prin. Fax 393-5502
Glenn MS of International Studies 1,300/6-8
79655 Miles Ave 92201 760-200-3700
Dr. Majid Salehi, prin. Fax 200-3709
Indio HS 2,100/9-12
81750 Avenue 46 92201 760-775-3550
Rudy Ramirez, prin. Fax 775-3565
Indio MS 900/6-8
81195 Miles Ave 92201 760-775-3800
Jesus Jimenez, prin. Fax 775-3807
Jefferson MS 600/6-8
83089 US Highway 111 92201 760-863-3660
Esther Lopez, prin. Fax 775-3597
Shadow Hills HS 1,200/9-12
39225 Jefferson St 92203 760-393-5400
Marcus Wood, prin. Fax 200-1967

Milan Institute Post-Sec.
45691 Monroe St Ste 2 92201 760-347-5000

**Inglewood, Los Angeles, Pop. 107,237**
Inglewood USD 12,600/K-12
401 S Inglewood Ave 90301 310-419-2700
Dr. Donald Brann, admin. Fax 680-5144
www.inglewood.k12.ca.us
Crozier MS 800/6-8
1210 W Regent St 90301 310-680-5280
Tanisha Taylor, prin. Fax 680-5299
Inglewood Continuation HS Alt
106 E Manchester Blvd 90301 310-330-5220
Debbie Tate, prin.
Inglewood HS 1,500/9-12
231 S Grevillea Ave 90301 310-680-5200
Jose Gallegos, prin. Fax 680-5201
Monroe MS 700/6-8
10711 S 10th Ave 90303 310-680-5310
Franklin Tilley, prin. Fax 680-5317
Morningside HS 1,100/9-12
10500 Yukon Ave 90303 310-680-5230
Reginald Sirls, prin. Fax 680-5257
ICAAS Adult
441 W Hillcrest Blvd 90301 310-330-5222
Debbie Tate, prin. Fax 330-5218

Crimson Technical College Post-Sec.
8911 Aviation Blvd 90301 866-451-0818
Daniel Freeman Mem. Hospital Post-Sec.
333 N Prairie Ave 90301 310-674-7050
Marinello School of Beauty Post-Sec.
240 S Market St 90301 310-674-8100
St. Marys Academy 300/9-12
701 Grace Ave 90301 310-674-8470
Nancy Portillo, prin. Fax 674-6255
Univ of West Los Angeles School of Law Post-Sec.
9800 S La Cienega Blvd 90301 310-342-5200

**Ione, Amador, Pop. 7,650**
Amador County USD
Supt. — See Jackson
Ione JHS 400/6-8
450 S Mill St 95640 209-257-5500
Dr. William Murray, prin. Fax 274-0671

**Irvine, Orange, Pop. 201,858**
Irvine USD 28,200/PK-12
5050 Barranca Pkwy 92604 949-936-5000
Terry L. Walker, supt. Fax 936-5259
www.iusd.org
Creekside HS 200/9-12
3387 Barranca Pkwy 92606 949-936-7400
Rebecca Roberts, prin. Fax 936-7409
Irvine HS 1,800/9-12
4321 Walnut Ave 92604 949-936-7000
Monica Colunga, prin. Fax 936-7009
Jeffrey Trail MS 7-8
155 Visions 92620 949-936-8700
Scott Bowman, prin. Fax 936-8709
Lakeside MS 700/7-8
3 Lemongrass 92604 949-559-1601
Gina Cuneo, prin. Fax 936-6109
Northwood HS 2,000/9-12
4515 Portola Pkwy 92620 949-936-7200
Leslie Roach, prin. Fax 936-7209
Rancho San Joaquin MS 900/7-8
4861 Michelson Dr 92612 949-936-6500
Mike Modeer, prin. Fax 936-6509
San Joaquin Alternative Education 100/Alt
3387 Barranca Pkwy 92606 949-936-7440
Rebecca Roberts, dir. Fax 936-7409
Sierra Vista MS 1,100/7-8
2 Liberty 92620 949-936-6600
Lynn Matassarin, prin. Fax 936-6609
South Lake MS 600/7-8
655 W Yale Loop 92614 949-936-6700
Belinda Averill, prin. Fax 936-6709
University HS 2,500/9-12
4771 Campus Dr 92612 949-936-7600
Kevin Astor, prin. Fax 936-7609
Venado MS 600/7-8
4 Deerfield Ave 92604 949-936-6800
Luis Torrez, prin. Fax 936-6809
Woodbridge HS 2,300/9-12
2 Meadowbrook 92604 949-786-1104
Christopher Krebs, prin.
Irvine Adult S Adult
3387 Barranca Pkwy 92606 949-936-7400
Linda O'Neal, dir. Fax 936-7459

Tustin USD
Supt. — See Tustin
Beckman HS 2,400/9-12
3588 Bryan 92602 714-734-2900
Adele Heuer, prin. Fax 505-9676

Alliant International University Post-Sec.
2855 Michelle Ste 300 92606 949-833-2651
Brandman University Post-Sec.
16355 Laguna Canyon Rd 92618 949-753-4774
California Southern University Post-Sec.
930 Roosevelt 92620 714-882-7800
Chicago Sch of Professional Psychology Post-Sec.
4199 Campus Dr 92612 949-737-5460
Concordia University Post-Sec.
1530 Concordia 92612 949-854-8002
Crean Lutheran South HS 500/9-12
12500 Sand Canyon Ave 92618 949-387-1199
Jeffrey Beavers, prin. Fax 387-1200
FIDM Fashion Institute of Design Post-Sec.
17590 Gillette Ave 92614 949-851-6200
Irvine Valley College Post-Sec.
5500 Irvine Center Dr 92618 949-451-5100
Stanbridge College Post-Sec.
2041 Business Center Dr 107 92612 949-794-9090
Tarbut V'Torah Day MSHS 300/6-12
5 Federation Way 92603 949-509-9500
Dr. Jeffrey Davis, head sch Fax 509-7866
University of California 92697 Post-Sec.
949-824-5011

**Irwindale, Los Angeles, Pop. 1,410**

Premiere Career College Post-Sec.
12901 Ramona Blvd Ste D 91706 626-814-2080
Public Health Foundation Enterprises Post-Sec.
12781 Schabarum Ave 91706 626-856-6376

**Jackson, Amador, Pop. 4,513**
Amador County Office of Education 300/
217 Rex Ave 95642 209-257-5353
Dick Glock, supt. Fax 257-5360
www.amadorcoe.org/
Other Schools – See Sutter Creek

Amador County USD 3,900/K-12
217 Rex Ave 95642 209-223-1750
Elizabeth Chapin-Pinotti, supt. Fax 296-3133
www.amadorcoe.org
Argonaut HS 600/9-12
501 Argonaut Ln 95642 209-257-7700
Kelly Hunkins, prin. Fax 223-3149
Jackson JHS 300/6-8
747 Sutter St 95642 209-257-5700
Janet DeLeo, prin. Fax 257-5757
Other Schools – See Ione, Sutter Creek

Regional Occupational Center & Program
Supt. — None
Amador County ROP Vo/Tech
217 Rex Ave 95642 209-259-5339
Elizabeth Chapin-Pinotti, dir.

**Jacumba, San Diego, Pop. 550**
Mountain Empire USD
Supt. — See Pine Valley
Jacumba MS 100/6-8
44343 Old Highway 80 91934 619-766-4464
Gary Brannon, prin. Fax 766-4532

**Jamul, San Diego, Pop. 5,990**
Jamul-Dulzura UNSD 1,200/K-12
14581 Lyons Valley Rd 91935 619-669-7700
Nadine Bennett, supt. Fax 669-0254
www.jdusd.net
Oak Grove MS 300/6-8
14344 Olive Vista Dr 91935 619-669-2700
Liz Bystedt, prin. Fax 669-7632

**Joshua Tree, San Bernardino, Pop. 7,144**

---

Copper Mountain College Post-Sec.
PO Box 1398 92252 760-366-3791

**Julian, San Diego, Pop. 1,474**
Julian UNESD 2,400/K-12
PO Box 337 92036 760-765-0661
Brian Duffy, supt. Fax 765-0220
www.juesd.net
Julian JHS 100/6-8
PO Box 337 92036 760-765-0575
Brian Duffy, prin. Fax 765-3340

Julian UNHSD 200/9-12
PO Box 417 92036 760-765-0606
David Schlottman, supt. Fax 765-2926
www.juhsd.org
Julian HS 200/9-12
PO Box 417 92036 760-765-0606
David Schlottman, supt. Fax 765-2926
Redding Continuation HS 50/Alt
PO Box 417 92036 760-765-0620
David Schlottman, supt. Fax 765-0889

**Jurupa Valley, Riverside**
Jurupa USD 19,900/K-12
4850 Pedley Rd, 951-360-4100
Elliott Duchon, supt. Fax 360-4194
www.jusd.k12.ca.us
Jurupa MS 1,200/7-8
8700 Galena St, 951-360-2846
Terri Stevens, prin. Fax 360-8928
Jurupa Valley HS 1,900/9-12
10551 Bellegrave Ave, 951-360-2600
Fax 360-2612
Mira Loma MS 900/7-8
5051 Steve Ave, 951-360-2883
Andrew Huben, prin. Fax 685-7405
Mission MS 900/7-8
5961 Mustang Ln, 951-222-7842
Monty Owens, prin. Fax 369-1407
Nueva Vista Continuation HS 300/Alt
6836 34th St, 951-360-2802
Michelle Markham, prin. Fax 360-0928
Patriot HS 2,400/9-12
4355 Camino Real, 951-361-6500
Roberta Pace, prin. Fax 361-6526
Rubidoux HS 1,700/9-12
4250 Opal St, 951-222-7700
Dr. Jose Araux, prin. Fax 275-0079
Steps Community Day S 100/Alt
4041 Pacific Ave, 951-222-7739
Michael Gray, prin. Fax 788-8689
Adult Education Adult
4041 Pacific Ave, 951-222-7739
Michael Gray, prin. Fax 788-8689

**Kelseyville, Lake, Pop. 3,286**
Kelseyville USD 1,700/K-12
4410 Konocti Rd 95451 707-279-1511
Dave McQueen, supt. Fax 279-9221
www.kvusd.org
Donaldson Continuation HS 50/Alt
4410 Konocti Rd 95451 707-279-8414
Heather Thomas, admin. Fax 279-4404
Kelseyville Community Day S 50/Alt
3980 Gard St 95451 707-279-2415
Heather Thomas, admin. Fax 279-4404
Kelseyville HS 600/9-12
5480 Main St 95451 707-279-4923
Matt Cockerton, prin. Fax 279-9173
Mountain Vista MS 400/6-8
5081 Konocti Rd 95451 707-279-4060
Heather Thomas, prin. Fax 279-8835

**Kentfield, Marin, Pop. 6,290**
Kentfield ESD 1,200/K-8
750 College Ave 94904 415-458-5130
Elizabeth Schott, supt. Fax 458-5137
www.kentfieldschools.org/
Kent MS 500/5-8
800 College Ave 94904 415-458-5970
Skip Kniesche, prin. Fax 458-5973

---

College of Marin Post-Sec.
835 College Ave 94904 415-457-8811
Marin Catholic HS 700/9-12
675 Sir Francis Drake Blvd 94904 415-464-3898
Chris Valdez, prin. Fax 461-6943

**Kerman, Fresno, Pop. 13,348**
Kerman USD 4,800/K-12
151 S 1st St 93630 559-846-5383
Robert Frausto, supt. Fax 840-4283
www.kermanusd.com
Enterprise HS 50/Alt
15405 W Sunset Ave 93630 559-842-3500
Rebecca Sanchez, prin. Fax 717-4233
Kerman HS 1,200/9-12
205 S 1st St 93630 559-842-2500
Pam Sellick, dir. Fax 840-4287
Kerman MS 700/7-8
601 S 1st St 93630 559-842-3000
Amanda Guizar, prin. Fax 840-4291

**Kettleman City, Kings, Pop. 1,426**
Reef-Sunset USD
Supt. — See Avenal
Adelante Continuation HS 50/Alt
PO Box 149 93239 559-386-9081
Juan Ruiz, prin. Fax 386-0207

**Keyes, Stanislaus, Pop. 5,468**
Keyes UNESD 1,100/PK-12
PO Box 310 95328 209-669-2921
Cynthia Schaefer, supt. Fax 669-2923
www.keyes.k12.ca.us/
Other Schools – See Hughson

**King City, Monterey, Pop. 12,778**
King City UNSD 2,500/K-8
435 Pearl St 93930 831-385-2940
Theresa Rouse, supt. Fax 386-0372
www.kcusd.org
Chalone Peaks MS 800/6-8
667 Meyer St 93930 831-385-4400
Mike Barbree, prin. Fax 385-4422

South Monterey JUNHSD 1,900/9-12
800 Broadway St 93930 831-385-0606
Daniel Moirao, supt. Fax 385-0695
www.smcjuhsd.org
King City HS 900/9-12
720 Broadway St 93930 831-385-5461
Janet Sanchez Matos, prin. Fax 385-0901
Portola-Butler Continuation HS 100/Alt
760 Broadway St 93930 831-385-4661
Michael Onderko, prin. Fax 385-0643
Other Schools – See Greenfield

**Kings Beach, Placer, Pop. 3,765**

---

Tahoe Expedition Academy 100/K-12
8651 Speckled Ave 96143 530-546-5253
Charles Clark, head sch

**Kingsburg, Fresno, Pop. 11,129**
Kingsburg JUNHSD 1,100/9-12
1900 18th Ave 93631 559-897-7721
Fred Cogan, supt. Fax 897-7759
www.khsvikings.com
Kingsburg HS 1,100/9-12
1900 18th Ave 93631 559-897-5156
Fred Cogan, prin. Fax 897-7759
Oasis Continuation HS 50/Alt
1900 18th Ave 93631 559-897-3880
Ryan Phelan, prin. Fax 897-0458

**La Canada Flintridge, Los Angeles, Pop. 19,647**
La Canada USD 4,000/K-12
4490 Cornishon Ave 91011 818-952-8300
Wendy Sinnette, supt. Fax 952-8309
www.lcusd.net
La Canada JSHS 2,100/7-12
4463 Oak Grove Dr 91011 818-952-4200
Ian McFeat, prin. Fax 952-4214

---

Flintridge Preparatory S 500/7-12
4543 Crown Ave 91011 818-790-1178
Peter Bachmann, hdmstr. Fax 952-6247
Flintridge Sacred Heart Academy 400/9-12
440 Saint Katherine Dr 91011 626-685-8500
Sr. Celeste Botello, prin. Fax 685-8555
St. Francis HS 700/9-12
200 Foothill Blvd 91011 818-790-0325
Thomas Moran, prin. Fax 790-5542

**La Crescenta, Los Angeles, Pop. 19,112**
Glendale USD
Supt. — See Glendale
Clark Magnet HS 1,100/9-12
4747 New York Ave 91214 818-248-8324
Douglas Dall, prin. Fax 957-2954
Crescenta Valley HS 2,900/9-12
2900 Community Ave 91214 818-249-5871
Dr. Linda Junge Ed.D., prin. Fax 541-9531
Rosemont MS 1,300/7-8
4725 Rosemont Ave 91214 818-248-4224
Dr. Cynthia Livingston Ed.D., prin. Fax 248-3790

**Ladera Ranch, Orange, Pop. 21,970**
Capistrano USD
Supt. — See San Juan Capistrano
Ladera Ranch MS 1,200/6-8
29551 Sienna Pkwy 92694 949-234-5922
George Duarte, prin. Fax 364-1149

**Lafayette, Contra Costa, Pop. 22,962**
Acalanes UNHSD 5,400/9-12
1212 Pleasant Hill Rd 94549 925-280-3900
John Nickerson, supt. Fax 932-2336
www.acalanes.k12.ca.us
Acalanes HS 1,400/9-12
1200 Pleasant Hill Rd 94549 925-280-3970
Allison Silvestri, prin. Fax 280-3971
Other Schools – See Moraga, Orinda, Walnut Creek

Lafayette SD 3,300/PK-8
3477 School St 94549 925-927-3500
Rachel Zinn, supt. Fax 284-1525
www.lafsd.k12.ca.us
Stanley MS 1,200/6-8
3455 School St 94549 925-927-3530
David Schrag, prin. Fax 283-1797

---

Bentley Upper S - Lafayette Campus 300/9-12
1000 Upper Happy Valley Rd 94549 925-283-2101
Arlene Hogan, head sch Fax 299-0469

**La Grange, Stanislaus**
Big Oak Flat-Groveland USD
Supt. — See Groveland
Pedro HS 50/9-12
3090 Merced Falls Rd 95329 209-852-2864
Dave Urquhart, prin. Fax 852-2125

**Laguna Beach, Orange, Pop. 22,111**
Laguna Beach USD 3,000/PK-12
550 Blumont St 92651 949-497-7700
Dr. Sherine Smith, supt. Fax 497-6021
www.lbusd.org
Laguna Beach HS 1,000/9-12
625 Park Ave 92651 949-497-7750
Dr. Christopher Herzfeld, prin. Fax 497-7766
Thurston MS 700/6-8
2100 Park Ave 92651 949-497-7785
Jennifer Salberg, prin. Fax 497-7798

---

Laguna College of Art and Design Post-Sec.
2222 Laguna Canyon Rd 92651 949-376-6000

**Laguna Hills, Orange, Pop. 29,183**
Saddleback Valley USD
Supt. — See Mission Viejo
Laguna Hills HS 1,800/9-12
25401 Paseo De Valencia 92653 949-770-5447
Bill Hinds, prin. Fax 830-0295

---

Allied American University Post-Sec.
22952 Alcalde Dr 92653 888-384-0849
Lake Forest Beauty College Post-Sec.
23565 Moulton Pkwy Ste A 92653 949-951-8883

**Laguna Niguel, Orange, Pop. 60,641**
Capistrano USD
Supt. — See San Juan Capistrano
Niguel Hills MS 1,300/6-8
29070 Paseo De La Escuela 92677 949-234-5360
Tim Reece, prin. Fax 249-2069

---

Laguna Niguel Jr. Academy 100/K-10
29702 Kensington Dr 92677 949-495-3428
David Tripp, prin. Fax 495-3438

**La Habra, Orange, Pop. 59,112**
Fullerton JUNHSD
Supt. — See Fullerton
La Habra HS 2,300/9-12
801 Highlander Ave 90631 562-266-5200
Karl Zener, prin. Fax 691-8280
Sonora HS 2,000/9-12
401 S Palm St 90631 562-266-2001
Adam Bailey Ph.D., prin. Fax 266-2040

La Habra City ESD 5,200/K-8
PO Box 307 90633 562-690-2305
Susan Belenardo Ed.D., supt. Fax 690-4154
www.lhcsd.k12.ca.us
Imperial MS 900/6-8
PO Box 307 90633 562-690-2344
Cathy Seighman, prin. Fax 526-3678
Washington MS 900/6-8
PO Box 307 90633 562-690-2374
Mario Carlos, prin. Fax 690-7834

---

Whittier Christian HS 700/9-12
501 N Beach Blvd 90631 562-694-3803
Carl Martinez M.A., head sch Fax 697-1673

**La Jolla, See San Diego**
San Diego USD
Supt. — See San Diego
La Jolla HS 1,600/9-12
750 Nautilus St 92037 858-454-3081
Chuck Podhorsky, prin. Fax 459-2188
Muirlands MS 1,100/6-8
1056 Nautilus St 92037 858-459-4211
Harlan Klein, prin. Fax 459-8075

---

Bishop's S 800/6-12
7607 La Jolla Blvd 92037 858-459-4021
Aimeclaire Roche, head sch Fax 459-3914
La Jolla Country Day S 1,200/PK-12
9490 Genesee Ave 92037 858-453-3440
Dr. Gary Krahn, head sch Fax 453-8210
National University Post-Sec.
11255 N Torrey Pines Rd 92037 858-642-8000
Sanford-Burnham Graduate School Post-Sec.
10901 N Torrey Pines Rd 92037 858-646-3100
Scripps Memorial Hospital Post-Sec.
9888 Genesee Ave 92037 858-457-6100
Scripps Research Institute Post-Sec.
10550 N Torrey Pines Rd 92037 858-784-8469
University of California Post-Sec.
9500 Gilman Dr 92093 858-534-2230

**Lake Arrowhead, San Bernardino, Pop. 12,063**
Rim of the World USD
Supt. — See Blue Jay

Henck IS 900/6-8
PO Box 430 92352 909-336-0360
Matthew Pollack, prin. Fax 336-3449
Rim of the World HS 1,300/9-12
PO Box 430 92352 909-336-2038
Derek Swem, prin. Fax 336-0254

**Lake Elsinore, Riverside, Pop. 50,250**
Lake Elsinore USD 21,500/K-12
545 Chaney St 92530 951-253-7000
Doug Kimberly Ed.D., supt. Fax 253-7084
www.leusd.k12.ca.us
Canyon Lake MS 1,200/6-8
33005 Canyon Hills Rd 92532 951-244-2123
Preston Perez Ed.D., prin. Fax 244-2103
Elsinore MS 700/6-8
1203 W Graham Ave 92530 951-674-2118
James Judziewicz, prin. Fax 674-6302
Lakeside HS 1,900/9-12
32593 Riverside Dr 92530 951-253-7300
Peter Hopping Ed.D., prin. Fax 253-7335
McCarthy Academy 200/Alt
1405 Education Way 92530 951-253-7777
Ryan Mulvanny, prin. Fax 245-1988
Ortega Continuation HS 200/Alt
520 Chaney St 92530 951-253-7065
Amy Campbell, prin. Fax 245-1988
Temescal Canyon HS 2,000/9-12
28755 El Toro Rd 92532 951-253-7250
Whitney D'Amico Ed.D., prin. Fax 253-7266
Terra Cotta MS 1,300/6-8
29291 Lake St 92530 951-253-7380
Sarah Arredondo, prin. Fax 674-5191
Valley Adult S Adult
520 Chaney St 92530 951-253-7093
Amy Campbell, prin. Fax 253-7039
Other Schools – See Wildomar

**Lake Forest, Orange, Pop. 74,539**
Saddleback Valley USD
Supt. — See Mission Viejo
El Toro HS 2,800/9-12
25255 Toledo Way 92630 949-586-6333
Terri Gusiff, prin. Fax 380-9874
Serrano IS 1,400/7-8
24642 Jeronimo Rd 92630 949-586-3221
Robert Sherlock, prin. Fax 586-3773

---

Elegante Beauty College Post-Sec.
23635 El Toro Rd Ste K 92630 949-586-4900

**Lake Isabella, Kern, Pop. 3,311**
Kern UNHSD
Supt. — See Bakersfield
Kern Valley HS 500/9-12
3340 Erskine Creek Rd 93240 760-379-2611
John Meyers, prin. Fax 379-8314

Kernville UNESD 800/K-8
3240 Erskine Creek Rd 93240 760-379-3651
Robin Shive, supt. Fax 379-3812
www.kernvilleusd.org
Rio Vista Community Day S 50/Alt
3240 Erskine Creek Rd 93240 760-379-4863
Jill Shaw, prin. Fax 379-1324
Wallace MS 300/5-8
3240 Erskine Creek Rd 93240 760-379-4646
Jill Shaw, prin. Fax 379-1322

**Lakeport, Lake, Pop. 4,650**
Lake County Office of Education 50/
1152 S Main St 95453 707-262-4100
Brock Falkenberg, supt. Fax 263-0197
www.lakecoe.org
Hance Community S 50/Alt
1510 Argonaut Rd 95453 707-263-5819
Lori LaBrie, lead tchr. Fax 263-6262

Lakeport USD 1,600/K-12
2508 Howard Ave 95453 707-262-3000
Erin Smith-Hagberg, supt. Fax 263-7332
www.lakeport.k12.ca.us
Clear Lake HS 500/9-12
2508 Howard Ave 95453 707-262-3010
Martin Wilkes, prin. Fax 262-3026
Lakeport Alternative S 50/Alt
2508 Howard Ave 95453 707-262-3013
Erin Smith-Hagberg, admin. Fax 263-6304
Lakeport Community Day S 50/Alt
2508 Howard Ave 95453 707-262-3013
Erin Smith-Hagberg, admin. Fax 263-6304
Natural Continuation HS 50/Alt
2508 Howard Ave 95453 707-262-3013
Erin Smith-Hagberg, admin. Fax 263-6304
Terrace MS 500/4-8
2508 Howard Ave 95453 707-262-3007
Jill Falconer, prin. Fax 262-5532

Regional Occupational Center & Program
Supt. — None
Lake County ROP Vo/Tech
1152 S Main St 95453 707-262-4162
Brock Falkenberg, dir. Fax 262-0197

**Lakeside, San Diego, Pop. 20,041**
Grossmont UNHSD
Supt. — See La Mesa
El Capitan HS 1,700/9-12
10410 Ashwood St 92040 619-938-9100
Laura Whitaker, prin. Fax 390-8503

Lakeside UNSD 4,500/PK-12
12335 Woodside Ave 92040 619-390-2600
David Lorden, supt. Fax 561-7929
www.lsusd.net
Lakeside MS 700/6-8
11833 Woodside Ave 92040 619-390-2636
Stephen Mull, prin. Fax 390-2643

Tierra Del Sol MS 600/6-8
9611 Petite Ln 92040 619-390-2670
Scott Goergens, prin. Fax 390-2518

**Lakewood, Los Angeles, Pop. 76,583**
ABC USD
Supt. — See Cerritos
Artesia HS 1,500/9-12
12108 Del Amo Blvd 90715 562-229-7700
Sergio Garcia, prin. Fax 809-5604

Bellflower USD
Supt. — See Bellflower
Mayfair MSHS 3,400/7-12
6000 Woodruff Ave 90713 562-925-9981
Matt Eeles, prin. Fax 804-1656

Long Beach USD
Supt. — See Long Beach
Hoover MS 1,000/6-8
3501 Country Club Dr 90712 562-421-1213
Stephanie Cooper, prin. Fax 421-8063
Lakewood HS 4,100/9-12
4400 Briercrest Ave 90713 562-425-1281
Shawn Abbate, prin. Fax 421-9616

Paramount USD
Supt. — See Paramount
Buena Vista HS Alt
3717 Michelson St 90712 562-602-8090
Dr. Andrea Aguilare-Nuno, prin. Fax 602-8091

---

St. Joseph HS 700/9-12
5825 Woodruff Ave 90713 562-925-5073
Dr. Teresa Mendoza, prin. Fax 925-3315

**La Mesa, San Diego, Pop. 54,494**
Grossmont UNHSD 23,100/7-12
PO Box 1043 91944 619-644-8000
Ralf Swenson, supt. Fax 465-1349
www.guhsd.net
Other Schools – See El Cajon, Lakeside, Santee, Spring Valley

La Mesa-Spring Valley SD 12,200/K-8
4750 Date Ave 91942 619-668-5700
Brian Marshall, supt. Fax 668-5809
www.lmsvsd.org
La Mesa Arts Academy 700/4-8
4200 Parks Ave 91941 619-668-5730
Beth Thomas, prin. Fax 668-8303
Parkway MS 800/7-8
9009 Park Plaza Dr 91942 619-668-5810
Mary Beason, prin. Fax 668-5779
Other Schools – See Spring Valley

---

California Hair Design Academy Post-Sec.
8011 University Ave Ste A2 91942 619-461-8600

**La Mirada, Los Angeles, Pop. 47,368**
Norwalk-La Mirada USD
Supt. — See Norwalk
Benton MS 600/6-8
15709 Olive Branch Dr 90638 562-943-1553
Michael Gotto, prin. Fax 947-3861
Hutchinson MS 600/6-8
13900 Estero Rd 90638 562-944-3268
Sara Siemens, prin. Fax 944-3269
La Mirada HS 2,200/9-12
13520 Adelfa Dr 90638 562-868-0431
Darryl Brown, prin. Fax 943-7872
Los Coyotes MS 600/6-8
14640 Mercado Ave 90638 714-523-2051
Christina Stanley, prin. Fax 739-2368
La Mirada Adult S Adult
15920 Barbata Rd 90638 562-670-9279
Sharon Todd, dir. Fax 670-1654

---

Biola University Post-Sec.
13800 Biola Ave 90639 562-903-6000
Heights Christian JHS 300/6-8
12900 Bluefield Ave 90638 562-947-3309
Rebecca Neal, prin. Fax 947-1001

**Lamont, Kern, Pop. 15,088**
Kern UNHSD
Supt. — See Bakersfield
Nueva Continuation HS 100/Alt
8600 Palm Ave 93241 661-845-1532
Mark Weir, admin. Fax 845-9523

Lamont ESD 2,800/K-8
7915 Burgundy Ave 93241 661-845-0751
Ricardo Robles, supt. Fax 845-0689
www.lamontschooldistrict.org
Other Schools – See Bakersfield

**Lancaster, Los Angeles, Pop. 151,168**
Antelope Valley UNHSD 25,500/7-12
44811 Sierra Hwy 93534 661-948-7655
David Vierra, supt. Fax 942-8744
www.avdistrict.org
Antelope Valley HS 1,800/9-12
44900 Division St 93535 661-948-8552
Jodie Radford, prin. Fax 945-8867
Desert Winds Continuation HS 1,200/Alt
45030 3rd St E 93535 661-948-7555
Will Laird, prin. Fax 948-5947
Eastside HS 2,400/9-12
3200 E Avenue J8 93535 661-946-3800
Kristen Tepper, prin. Fax 946-3850
Lancaster HS 2,400/9-12
44701 Eagle Way 93536 661-726-7649
Jose Barajas, prin. Fax 726-7694
SOAR HS 300/9-12
3041 W Avenue K 93536 661-722-6509
Chris Grado, prin. Fax 722-6583
Antelope Valley Adult HS Adult
45110 3rd St E 93535 661-942-3042
Steve Radford, prin. Fax 948-0846

Other Schools – See Littlerock, Palmdale, Quartz Hill

Eastside UNSD 3,400/K-8
45006 30th St E 93535 661-952-1200
Mark Marshall Ed.D., supt. Fax 952-1220
www.eastside.k12.ca.us
Cole MS 900/6-8
3126 E Avenue I 93535 661-946-1041
Francisco Pinto, prin. Fax 946-0166

Lancaster ESD 16,600/PK-8
44711 Cedar Ave 93534 661-948-4661
Dr. Michele Bowers Ed.D., supt. Fax 948-9398
www.lancsd.org
Amargosa Creek MS 1,000/6-8
44333 27th St W 93536 661-729-6064
Todd Coleman, prin. Fax 729-6858
Endeavour MS 800/6-8
43755 45th St W 93536 661-723-0351
Cheri Newlander, prin. Fax 723-1362
Lancaster Virtual Alternative Academy 100/Alt
44310 Hardwood Ave 93534 661-726-4354
Nesha Prather, coord. Fax 726-5457
New Vista MS 1,200/6-8
753 E Avenue K2 93535 661-726-4271
Kymberlee Cochran, prin. Fax 726-4278
Piute MS 1,300/6-8
425 E Avenue H11 93535 661-942-9508
Michael Davis, prin. Fax 940-6676

Westside UNESD
Supt. — See Quartz Hill
Westside Academy 50/Alt
5606 W Avenue L8 93536 661-206-3711
Debbie Rutkowski-Hines, prin. Fax 722-1046

Wilsona SD
Supt. — See Palmdale
Challenger MS 600/5-8
41725 170th St E 93535 661-264-1790
Janice Stowers, prin. Fax 264-1793
Wilsona Achievement Academy 50/Alt
41725 170th St E 93535 661-264-1790
Janice Stowers, prin. Fax 264-1793

---

Antelope Valley Christian S 300/PK-12
44514 20th St W 93534 661-943-0044
Douglas McKenzie, dir. Fax 943-6774
Antelope Valley College Post-Sec.
3041 W Avenue K 93536 661-722-6300
Bethel Christian S 400/PK-12
3100 W Avenue K 93536 661-943-2224
Matt Konnerth, prin. Fax 943-6574
Charter College Lancaster Post-Sec.
43141 Business Ctr Pkwy 102 93535 661-341-3500
Desert Christian HS 400/9-12
2340 W Avenue J8 93536 661-723-7441
Dr. Jan Spencer, prin. Fax 723-7437
Desert Christian MS 200/6-8
44662 15th St W 93534 661-723-0665
Brian Roseborough, dir. Fax 723-6774
Lancaster Baptist S 400/K-12
4020 E Lancaster Blvd 93535 661-946-4668
Jim Lee, admin. Fax 946-7374
Lancaster Beauty School Post-Sec.
44646 10th St W 93534 661-948-1672
Paraclete HS 700/9-12
42145 30th St W 93536 661-943-3255
John Anson, prin. Fax 722-9455
University of Antelope Valley Post-Sec.
44055 Sierra Hwy 93534 661-726-1911

**La Palma, Orange, Pop. 15,047**
Anaheim UNHSD
Supt. — See Anaheim
Kennedy HS 2,400/9-12
8281 Walker St 90623 714-220-4101
Russell Earnest, prin. Fax 995-1833
Walker JHS 1,100/7-8
8132 Walker St 90623 714-220-4051
Kirsten Levitin Ed.D., prin. Fax 220-2237

---

La Palma Christian S 100/PK-12
8082 Walker St 90623 714-527-3231
Karen Bland, dir. Fax 995-8046

**La Puente, Los Angeles, Pop. 39,527**
Bassett USD 4,300/K-12
904 N Willow Ave 91746 626-931-3000
Alex Rojas, supt. Fax 918-5105
www.bassettusd.org
Bassett HS 1,200/9-12
904 N Willow Ave 91746 626-931-2800
Gabriel Griego, prin. Fax 931-2850
Nueva Vista Continuation HS 100/Alt
904 N Willow Ave 91746 626-931-3177
William Avila, prin. Fax 931-3145
Bassett Adult S, 934 N Sunkist 91746 Adult
Albert Michel, prin. 626-931-3102
Other Schools – See City of Industry

Hacienda La Puente USD
Supt. — See City of Industry
La Puente HS 1,600/9-12
15615 Nelson Ave 91744 626-934-6797
Fernando Sanchez, prin. Fax 855-3798
Sierra Vista MS 400/7-8
15801 Sierra Vista Ct 91744 626-933-4001
Maria Ceja, prin. Fax 855-3817
Sparks MS 500/7-8
15100 Giordano St 91744 626-933-5001
Collin Miller, prin. Fax 855-3848
Hacienda La Puente Adult Education Adult
14101 Nelson Ave 91746 626-934-2987
Elena Paul, dir. Fax 934-2986
Willow Adult S Adult
14101 E Nelson St 91746 626-934-2801
Elena Paul, dir.

Regional Occupational Center & Program
Supt. — None
La Puente Valley ROP — Vo/Tech
341 La Seda Rd 91744 — 626-810-3300
Esperanza Fernandez, supt. — Fax 581-9108

Rowland USD
Supt. — See Rowland Heights
Nogales HS — 2,300/9-12
401 Nogales St 91744 — 626-965-3437
Kelly Godfrey, prin. — Fax 965-4587
Santana Alternative Education Center — 300/Alt
341 S La Seda Rd 91744 — 626-965-5971
Stephen Edmunds, prin. — Fax 854-2225

---

Bishop Amat HS — 1,400/9-12
14301 Fairgrove Ave 91746 — 626-962-2495
Dr. Richard Beck, prin. — Fax 960-0994
Hacienda LaPuente Valley Adult Education — Post-Sec.
14101 Nelson Ave 91746 — 626-934-2800

**La Quinta, Riverside, Pop. 36,785**
Desert Sands USD — 29,200/K-12
47950 Dune Palms Rd 92253 — 760-777-4200
Dr. Gary Rutherford, supt. — Fax 771-8505
www.dsusd.us
Horizon S — 400/Alt
43330 Palm Royale Dr 92253 — 760-238-9720
Rudy Wilson, prin. — Fax 360-2182
La Quinta HS — 3,000/9-12
79255 Blackhawk Way 92253 — 760-772-4150
Rebecca Cook, prin. — Fax 772-4166
La Quinta MS — 600/6-8
78900 Avenue 50 92253 — 760-777-4220
Janet Seto, prin. — Fax 777-4216
Paige MS — 1,000/6-8
43495 Palm Royale Dr 92253 — 760-238-9710
Derrick Lawson, prin. — Fax 345-1202
Summit HS — 300/Alt
43330 Palm Royale Dr 92253 — 760-238-9760
Rudy Wilson, prin. — Fax 238-9751
Other Schools – See Indio, Palm Desert

**Larkspur, Marin, Pop. 11,461**
Larkspur-Corte Madera SD — 1,400/K-8
230 Doherty Dr 94939 — 415-927-6960
Valerie Pitts, supt. — Fax 927-6964
www.lcmschools.org
Hall MS — 600/5-8
200 Doherty Dr 94939 — 415-927-6978
Tom Utic, prin. — Fax 927-6985

Tamalpais UNHSD — 3,800/9-12
PO Box 605 94977 — 415-945-3600
David Yoshihara, supt. — Fax 945-3719
www.tamdistrict.org
Redwood HS — 1,500/9-12
395 Doherty Dr 94939 — 415-924-6200
David Sondheim, prin. — Fax 945-3675
San Andreas HS — 100/Alt
599 William Ave 94939 — 415-945-3770
Corbett Elsen, prin. — Fax 945-3754
Tamiscal HS — 100/Alt
PO Box 605 94977 — 415-945-3750
Corbett Elsen, prin. — Fax 945-3752
Other Schools – See Mill Valley, San Anselmo

**La Selva Beach, Santa Cruz, Pop. 2,748**
Pajaro Valley USD
Supt. — See Watsonville
Renaissance HS — 200/Alt
11 Spring Valley Rd 95076 — 831-728-6344
Andrew Singleton, prin. — Fax 728-6419

---

Monterey Bay Academy — 200/9-12
783 San Andreas Rd 95076 — 831-728-1481
Rev. Jeff Deming, prin. — Fax 728-1485

**Lathrop, San Joaquin, Pop. 17,283**
Manteca USD
Supt. — See Manteca
Lathrop HS — 700/9-12
647 Spartan Way 95330 — 209-938-6350
Michael Horwood, prin. — Fax 938-6390

---

ITT Technical Institute — Post-Sec.
16916 S Harlan Rd 95330 — 209-858-0077

**Laton, Fresno, Pop. 1,814**
Laton USD — 600/K-12
PO Box 248 93242 — 559-922-4015
Larry Audet, supt. — Fax 923-4791
www.laton.k12.ca.us
Conejo MS — 100/6-8
PO Box 7 93242 — 559-922-4030
Dannette Bryson, prin. — Fax 923-9651
Laton HS — 200/9-12
PO Box 278 93242 — 559-922-4080
Jason Krikava, prin. — Fax 923-4072

**La Verne, Los Angeles, Pop. 30,232**
Bonita USD
Supt. — See San Dimas
Bonita HS — 2,000/9-12
3102 D St 91750 — 909-971-8220
Derek Bub, prin. — Fax 971-8229
Ramona MS — 1,300/6-8
3490 Ramona Ave 91750 — 909-971-8260
Anne Neal, prin. — Fax 971-8269

---

Calvary Baptist S — 100/PK-12
2990 Damien Ave 91750 — 909-593-4672
Taylora Dial, prin. — Fax 392-9533
Damien HS — 1,000/9-12
2280 Damien Ave 91750 — 909-596-1946
Dr. Merritt Hemenway, prin. — Fax 596-1946
Lutheran HS — 100/9-12
3960 Fruit St 91750 — 909-593-4494
Dr. Lance Ebel, prin. — Fax 596-3744

University of La Verne — Post-Sec.
1950 3rd St 91750 — 909-593-3511

**Lawndale, Los Angeles, Pop. 31,604**
Centinela Valley UNHSD — 5,900/9-12
14901 Inglewood Ave 90260 — 310-263-3200
Gregory O'Brien Ph.D., supt. — Fax 675-8286
www.centinela.k12.ca.us/
Centinela Valley Independent Study HS — 100/Alt
4409 Redondo Beach Blvd 90260 — 424-255-4066
Michael Martinez, prin. — Fax 978-3995
Lawndale HS — 2,200/9-12
14901 Inglewood Ave 90260 — 310-263-3100
Paula Hart Rodas, prin. — Fax 675-8174
Leuzinger HS — 1,500/9-12
4118 Rosecrans Ave 90260 — 310-263-2200
Dr. Pamela Brown, prin. — Fax 675-7023
Lloyde Continuation HS — 200/Alt
4951 Marine Ave 90260 — 310-263-3264
James Tarouilly, prin. — Fax 978-3995
Centinela Valley Adult S — Adult
4409 Redondo Beach Blvd 90260 — 424-255-4066
Paul Guzman, prin. — Fax 644-6142
Other Schools – See Hawthorne

Lawndale ESD — 6,300/K-12
4161 W 147th St 90260 — 310-973-1300
Ellen Dougherty Ed.D., supt. — Fax 675-6462
lesd-ca.schoolloop.com
Addams MS — 900/6-8
4161 W 147th St 90260 — 310-676-4806
Jennie Wright Ed.D., prin. — Fax 676-8621
Rogers MS — 900/6-8
4161 W 147th St 90260 — 310-676-1197
Maurita De La Torre Ed.D., prin. — Fax 675-0489

**Laytonville, Mendocino, Pop. 1,182**
Laytonville USD — 400/K-12
PO Box 868 95454 — 707-984-6414
Joan Potter, supt. — Fax 984-8223
layt.k12.ca.us
Laytonville Continuation HS — 50/Alt
PO Box 868 95454 — 707-984-6811
Tim Henry, prin. — Fax 984-8066
Laytonville HS — 100/9-12
PO Box 868 95454 — 707-984-6108
Tim Henry, prin. — Fax 984-8066

**Lebec, Kern, Pop. 1,432**
El Tejon USD — 900/K-12
PO Box 876 93243 — 661-248-6247
Rodney Wallace, supt. — Fax 248-6714
www.el-tejon.k12.ca.us
El Tejon MS — 200/5-8
PO Box 876 93243 — 661-248-6680
Rosalie Jimenez, prin. — Fax 248-5203
Frazier Mountain HS — 400/9-12
PO Box 876 93243 — 661-248-0310
Sara Haflich, prin. — Fax 248-0403

**Lee Vining, Mono, Pop. 220**
Eastern Sierra USD
Supt. — See Bridgeport
Lee Vining HS — 100/9-12
PO Box 268 93541 — 760-647-6366
Roger Yost, prin. — Fax 647-6695

Mono County Office of Education
Supt. — See Bridgeport
TIOGA Community S — Alt
132 Lee Vining Ave 93541 — 760-206-6014
Janet Hunt, prin. — Fax 934-1443

**Leggett, Mendocino, Pop. 105**
Leggett Valley USD — 100/K-12
PO Box 186 95585 — 707-925-6230
Anthony Loumena, supt. — Fax 925-6396
www.leggett.k12.ca.us
Leggett Valley HS — 50/9-12
PO Box 186 95585 — 707-925-6285
Anthony Loumena, prin. — Fax 925-6396
Other Schools – See Whitethorn

**Le Grand, Merced, Pop. 1,644**
Le Grand UNHSD — 500/9-12
12961 Le Grand Rd 95333 — 209-389-9403
Donna Alley M.A., supt. — Fax 389-9414
www.lghs.k12.ca.us/
Granada HS — 50/Alt
12961 E Le Grand Rd 95333 — 209-382-0202
Mike Magboo, prin. — Fax 382-1443
Le Grand Union HS — 500/9-12
12961 Le Grand Rd 95333 — 209-389-9400
Javier Martinez, prin. — Fax 389-4065

**Lemon Grove, San Diego, Pop. 24,153**
Lemon Grove SD — 3,800/PK-8
8025 Lincoln St 91945 — 619-825-5600
Ernest Anastos, supt. — Fax 462-7959
www.lgsd.k12.ca.us
Lemon Grove Academy MS — 700/7-8
7866 Lincoln St 91945 — 619-825-5628
Rick Oser, prin. — Fax 825-5781

**Lemoore, Kings, Pop. 23,462**
Lemoore ESD — 3,300/K-8
100 Vine St 93245 — 559-924-6800
Richard Rayburn, supt. — Fax 924-6809
www.luesd.k12.ca.us
Liberty MS — 700/7-8
100 Vine St 93245 — 559-924-6860
Ben Luis, prin. — Fax 924-6869

Lemoore UNHSD — 2,200/9-12
5 Powell Ave 93245 — 559-924-6610
Debbie Muro, supt. — Fax 924-9212
www.luhsd.k12.ca.us/
Jamison Alternative Education HS — 100/Alt
351 E Bush St 93245 — 559-924-6620
Sandi Lowe, prin. — Fax 924-6637

Lemoore HS — 1,900/9-12
101 E Bush St 93245 — 559-924-6600
Rodney Brumit, prin. — Fax 924-5086

---

Kings Christian S — 300/PK-12
900 E D St 93245 — 559-924-8301
Kevin Dalafu, admin. — Fax 924-0607
West Hills College Lemoore — Post-Sec.
555 College Dr 93245 — 559-925-3000

**Lennox, Los Angeles, Pop. 22,462**
Lennox ESD — 7,100/K-12
10319 Firmona Ave 90304 — 310-695-4000
Kent Taylor, supt. — Fax 695-4000
www.lennox.k12.ca.us
Lennox MS — 1,700/6-8
11033 Buford Ave 90304 — 310-419-1800
Debra Johnson, prin. — Fax 677-4635

**Lincoln, Placer, Pop. 41,451**
Western Placer USD — 8,000/PK-12
600 6th St Ste 400 95648 — 916-645-6350
Scott Leaman, supt. — Fax 645-6356
www.wpusd.k12.ca.us
Edwards MS — 700/6-8
204 L St 95648 — 916-645-6370
Stacey Brown, prin. — Fax 645-6379
Lincoln HS — 1,500/9-12
790 J St 95648 — 916-645-6360
Jay Berns, prin. — Fax 645-6349
Phoenix Continuation HS — 100/Alt
870 J St 95648 — 916-645-6395
Charles Whitecotton, prin. — Fax 645-6347
Twelve Bridges MS — 800/6-8
770 Westview Dr 95648 — 916-434-5270
Randy Woods, prin. — Fax 434-5240

**Linden, San Joaquin, Pop. 1,741**
Linden USD — 2,300/K-12
18527 E Highway 26 95236 — 209-887-3894
Wayne Brown, supt. — Fax 887-2250
www.lindenusd.com
Linden HS — 700/9-12
18527 E Front St 95236 — 209-887-3073
Richard Schmidig, prin. — Fax 887-3815
Other Schools – See Stockton

**Lindsay, Tulare, Pop. 11,716**
Lindsay USD — 4,200/PK-12
371 E Hermosa St 93247 — 559-562-5111
Thomas L. Rooney, supt. — Fax 562-4637
www.lindsay.k12.ca.us
Cairns Continuation HS — 100/Alt
467 E Honolulu St 93247 — 559-562-5913
Dennis Doane, prin. — Fax 562-1753
Lindsay Community Day S — Alt
270 N Harvard 93247 — 559-562-5913
Dennis Doane, prin.
Lindsay HS — 1,100/9-12
1849 E Tulare Rd 93247 — 559-562-5911
Heather Rocha, prin. — Fax 562-4291

**Littlerock, Los Angeles, Pop. 1,327**
Antelope Valley UNHSD
Supt. — See Lancaster
Littlerock HS — 1,700/9-12
10833 E Avenue R 93543 — 661-944-5209
Karen Parker, prin. — Fax 944-5191

Keppel UNESD
Supt. — See Pearblossom
Desert View Community Day S — 50/Alt
9330 E Avenue U 93543 — 661-944-2152
Ward Lunneborg, dir. — Fax 944-0694
Keppel Academy — 300/5-8
9330 E Avenue U 93543 — 661-944-2152
Gary Schatz, prin. — Fax 944-0694

**Live Oak, Sutter, Pop. 8,180**
Live Oak USD — 1,800/K-12
2201 Pennington Rd 95953 — 530-695-5400
Mathew Gulbrandsen, supt. — Fax 695-5460
www.lousd.k12.ca.us
Live Oak Alternative S — 50/Alt
2207 Pennington Rd 95953 — 530-695-5430
James VonBargen, prin. — Fax 695-5432
Live Oak HS — 500/9-12
2351 Pennington Rd 95953 — 530-695-5415
Tony Walton, prin. — Fax 695-5422
Live Oak MS — 500/5-8
2082 Pennington Rd 95953 — 530-695-5435
Parm Virk, prin. — Fax 695-5443

**Livermore, Alameda, Pop. 77,773**
Livermore Valley JUSD — 12,800/K-12
685 E Jack London Blvd 94551 — 925-606-3200
Kelly Bowers, supt. — Fax 606-3329
www.livermoreschools.com
Christensen MS — 600/6-8
5757 Haggin Oaks Ave 94551 — 925-606-4702
Pat Avilla, prin. — Fax 606-4705
Del Valle Continuation HS — 100/Alt
2253 5th St 94550 — 925-606-4709
Darrel Avilla, prin. — Fax 606-3371
East Avenue MS — 600/6-8
3951 East Ave 94550 — 925-606-4711
Helen Gladden, prin. — Fax 606-4763
Granada HS — 2,100/9-12
400 Wall St 94550 — 925-606-4800
Philomena Rambo, prin. — Fax 606-4808
Livermore HS — 1,900/9-12
600 Maple St 94550 — 925-606-4812
Vicki Scudder, prin. — Fax 606-4851
Mendenhall MS — 900/6-8
1701 El Padro Dr 94550 — 925-606-4731
Susan Sambuceti, prin. — Fax 606-4737
Vineyard Alternative S — 100/Alt
1401 Almond Ave 94550 — 925-606-4722
Bob See, prin. — Fax 606-4799

Livermore Adult Community Education Adult
1401 Almond Ave 94550 925-606-4722
Bob See, prin. Fax 606-3389

Regional Occupational Center & Program
Supt. — None
Tri-Valley ROP Vo/Tech
1040 Florence Rd 94550 925-455-4800
Julie Duncan, supt. Fax 449-9126

---

Las Positas College Post-Sec.
3000 Campus Hill Dr 94551 925-424-1000

**Livingston, Merced, Pop. 12,876**
Livingston UNSD 2,500/K-8
922 B St 95334 209-394-5400
Andres Zamora, supt. Fax 394-5401
www.livingstonusd.org
Livingston MS 800/6-8
101 F St 95334 209-394-5450
William Marroquin, prin. Fax 394-5451

Merced County Office of Education
Supt. — See Merced
Schelby S 50/Alt
6738 Sultana Dr 95334 209-394-1800
Lissa Mitchell, coord. Fax 394-7818

Merced UNHSD
Supt. — See Atwater
Livingston HS 1,200/9-12
1617 Main St 95334 209-394-7961
Mandy Ballenger, prin. Fax 358-1093

**Lodi, San Joaquin, Pop. 60,610**
Lodi USD 29,900/PK-12
1305 E Vine St 95240 209-331-7000
Dr. Cathy Nichols-Washer Ed.D., supt. Fax 331-7256
www.lodiusd.net/
Henderson S 100/Alt
13451 N Extension Rd 95242 209-331-7331
Dominee Muller-Kimball, prin. Fax 331-8274
Katnich Community Day S Alt
13451 N Extension Rd 95242 209-331-7331
Dominee Muller-Kimball, prin.
Liberty Continuation HS 100/Alt
660 W Walnut St 95240 209-331-7633
Tami Somera, prin. Fax 331-7624
Lincoln Technical Academy Vo/Tech
542 E Pine St 95240 209-331-7616
Deborah Chiene, prin. Fax 331-7526
Lodi HS 2,000/9-12
3 S Pacific Ave 95242 209-331-7819
Bob Lofsted, prin. Fax 331-7779
Lodi MS 900/7-8
945 S Ham Ln 95242 209-331-7540
Scott McGregor, prin. Fax 331-7550
Millswood MS 800/7-8
233 N Mills Ave 95242 209-331-8332
Erin Lenzi, prin. Fax 331-8347
Tokay HS 2,100/9-12
1111 W Century Blvd 95240 209-331-7990
Erik Sandstrom, prin. Fax 331-7168
Lodi Adult S Adult
542 E Pine St 95240 209-331-7605
Deborah Chiene, prin. Fax 331-7167
Other Schools – See Stockton

---

Elliot Christian HS 200/9-12
2695 W Vine St 95242 209-368-2800
Thomas Spadafore, admin. Fax 333-5208
Lodi Academy 100/9-12
1230 S Central Ave 95240 209-368-2781
Tim Kubrock, prin. Fax 368-6142
Vineyard Christian MS 100/6-8
2301 W Lodi Ave 95242 209-333-8300
Randal Oliver, prin. Fax 339-4327

**Loma Linda, San Bernardino, Pop. 22,264**

---

Loma Linda Academy 1,300/K-12
10656 Anderson St 92354 909-796-0161
Dr. Douglas Herrmann, hdmstr. Fax 478-6829
Loma Linda University 92350 Post-Sec.
909-558-1000

**Lomita, Los Angeles, Pop. 19,339**
Los Angeles USD
Supt. — See Los Angeles
Fleming MS 1,700/6-8
25425 Walnut St 90717 310-257-4500
Peter Hastings, prin. Fax 326-9071

**Lompoc, Santa Barbara, Pop. 41,015**
Lompoc USD 9,800/K-12
PO Box 8000 93438 805-742-3300
Trevor McDonald, supt. Fax 735-8452
www.lusd.org
Cabrillo HS 1,400/9-12
PO Box 8000 93438 805-742-2900
Jeff Wagonseller, prin. Fax 733-4156
Forinash Community Day S Alt
PO Box 8000 93438 805-742-3135
Brian Jaramillo, prin.
Lompoc HS 1,400/9-12
PO Box 8000 93438 805-742-3000
Paul Bommersbach, prin. Fax 742-3004
Lompoc Valley MS 600/7-8
PO Box 8000 93438 805-742-2600
Schel Brown, prin. Fax 737-9480
Maple HS 200/Alt
PO Box 8000 93438 805-742-3150
Brian Jaramillo, prin. Fax 742-3163
Lompoc Adult Education Adult
PO Box 8000 93438 805-742-3100
Mary Coggins, coord. Fax 742-3085
Other Schools – See Vandenberg AFB

**Lone Pine, Inyo, Pop. 1,990**
Lone Pine USD 400/K-12
PO Box 159 93545 760-876-5579
Dr. Sean Cianfarano, supt. Fax 876-5438
lpusd-ca.schoolloop.com
Lone Pine HS 100/9-12
PO Box 159 93545 760-876-5577
Sean Cianfarano, prin. Fax 876-1037
Sierra Alternative Learning Academy Alt
PO Box 159 93545 760-876-5577
Sean Cianfarano, prin.
Lone Pine Adult S Adult
PO Box 159 93545 760-876-5579
Sean Cianfarano, prin. Fax 876-5438

**Long Barn, Tuolumne, Pop. 153**
Summerville UNHSD
Supt. — See Tuolumne
Cold Springs HS 50/Alt
25910 Long Barn Rd 95335 209-586-3011
David Johnstone, prin. Fax 928-1422
Long Barn HS 50/Alt
25910 Long Barn Dr 95335 209-586-3011
Mitch Heldstab, prin. Fax 928-1422

**Long Beach, Los Angeles, Pop. 443,652**
Long Beach USD 80,100/PK-12
1515 Hughes Way 90810 562-997-8000
Christopher Steinhauser, supt. Fax 997-8280
www.lbschools.net
Bancroft MS 1,000/6-8
5301 E Centralia St 90808 562-425-7461
Kimberly Dalton, prin. Fax 425-9741
Beach HS, 3701 E Willow St 90815 Alt
Troy Bennett, prin. 562-595-8893
Cabrillo HS 3,200/9-12
2001 Santa Fe Ave 90810 562-951-7700
Cheryl Cornejo, prin. Fax 951-7797
Educational Partnership HS 800/Alt
1794 Cedar Ave 90813 562-218-0493
Gregory Mendoza, prin. Fax 218-1573
Franklin Classical MS 1,000/6-8
540 Cerritos Ave 90802 562-435-4952
Rosalind Morgan, prin. Fax 432-6308
Hamilton MS 1,000/6-8
1060 E 70th St 90805 562-602-0302
Kathleen Cruz, prin. Fax 602-1354
Hill Classical MS 1,000/6-8
1100 Iroquois Ave 90815 562-598-7611
Mona Merlo, prin. Fax 598-6329
Hughes MS 1,600/6-8
3846 California Ave 90807 562-595-0831
Sally Gregory, prin. Fax 595-9221
Jefferson Leadership Academies 900/6-8
750 Euclid Ave 90804 562-438-9904
Kevin Maddox, prin. Fax 439-3718
Jordan HS 3,600/9-12
6500 Atlantic Ave 90805 562-423-1471
Veronica Coleman, prin. Fax 422-9091
Keller Dual Immersion MS 6-8
7020 Brittain St 90808 562-421-8851
Thomas Espinoza, prin.
Lindbergh STEM Academy 700/6-8
1022 E Market St 90805 562-422-2845
Connie Magee, prin. Fax 423-8176
Lindsey Academy 900/6-8
5075 Daisy Ave 90805 562-423-6451
Lorena Moreno, prin. Fax 422-3800
Marshall Academy of the Arts 800/6-8
5870 E Wardlow Rd 90808 562-429-7013
Marie Hatwan, prin. Fax 429-6973
McBride HS 9-12
7025 E Parkcrest St 90808 562-425-3539
Steve Rockenbach, prin. Fax 420-9590
Millikan HS 4,100/9-12
2800 Snowden Ave 90815 562-425-7441
Michael Navia, prin. Fax 425-1151
Polytechnic HS Vo/Tech
1600 Atlantic Ave 90813 562-591-0581
Diane Prince, prin. Fax 591-0631
Reid Continuation HS 400/Alt
2153 W Hill St 90810 562-989-2098
Jeff Cornejo, prin. Fax 989-2097
Renaissance HS for the Arts 500/9-12
235 E 8th St 90813 562-901-0168
Quentin Brown, prin. Fax 435-7147
Rogers MS 900/6-8
365 Monrovia Ave 90803 562-434-7411
Kimberly Holland, prin. Fax 434-0581
Sato Academy of Mathematics and Science 9-12
1100 Iroquois Ave 90815 562-598-7611
Mona Merlo, prin.
Stanford MS 1,300/6-8
5871 E Los Arcos St 90815 562-594-9793
David Costa, prin. Fax 594-8591
Stephens MS 900/6-8
1830 W Columbia St 90810 562-595-0841
Salvador Madrigal, prin. Fax 426-5631
Washington MS 1,100/6-8
1450 Cedar Ave 90813 562-591-2434
Megan Traver, prin. Fax 591-6888
Wilson HS 4,100/9-12
4400 E 10th St 90804 562-433-0481
Sandy Blazer, prin. Fax 433-2731
Long Beach School for Adults Adult
3701 E Willow St 90815 562-595-8893
Peter Davis, prin. Fax 988-1486
Other Schools – See Avalon, Carson, Lakewood, Signal Hill

Los Angeles USD
Supt. — See Los Angeles
Rancho Dominguez Preparatory S 1,100/6-12
4110 Santa Fe Ave 90810 310-847-6400
Keri Lew, prin. Fax 518-1022

Regional Occupational Center & Program
Supt. — None
Long Beach USD ROP Vo/Tech
3701 E Willow St Ste B 90815 562-595-8893
Matt Saldana, dir. Fax 424-8976

---

California State University-Long Beach Post-Sec.
1250 N Bellflower Blvd 90840 562-985-4111
Charter College Long Beach Post-Sec.
100 W Broadway Ste 3000 90802 562-216-7500
DeVry University Post-Sec.
3880 Kilroy Airport Way 90806 562-427-0861
First Baptist Church S 200/K-12
1000 Pine Ave 90813 562-432-8447
Timothy Egge, prin. Fax 499-6847
John Wesley Intl. Barber/Beauty Coll Post-Sec.
717 Pine Ave 90813 562-435-7060
Long Beach City College Post-Sec.
4901 E Carson St 90808 562-938-4111
Pacific Baptist S 200/K-12
3332 Magnolia Ave 90806 562-426-5214
St. Anthony HS 400/9-12
620 Olive Ave 90802 562-435-4496
Mike Schabert, prin. Fax 437-3055
WyoTech Post-Sec.
2161 Technology Pl 90810 562-624-9530

**Loomis, Placer, Pop. 6,199**
Placer UNHSD
Supt. — See Auburn
Del Oro HS 1,700/9-12
3301 Taylor Rd 95650 916-652-7243
Dan Gayaldo, prin. Fax 652-3706

**Los Alamitos, Orange, Pop. 10,908**
Los Alamitos USD 9,700/PK-12
10293 Bloomfield St 90720 562-799-4700
Dr. Sherry Kropp Ed.D., supt. Fax 799-4730
www.losal.org
Laurel HS 100/Alt
3591 Cerritos Ave 90720 562-799-4820
Heidi Olshan, prin. Fax 799-4822
Los Alamitos HS 3,100/9-12
3591 Cerritos Ave 90720 562-799-4780
Dr. Brandon Martinez, prin. Fax 799-4798
McAuliffe MS 1,300/6-8
4112 Cerritos Ave 90720 714-816-3320
Ann Allen, prin. Fax 816-3362
Oak MS 1,100/6-8
10821 Oak St 90720 562-799-4740
Erin Kominsky, prin. Fax 799-4773

**Los Altos, Santa Clara, Pop. 27,727**
Los Altos ESD 4,500/K-8
201 Covington Rd 94024 650-947-1150
Jeffrey Baier, supt. Fax 947-0118
www.lasdschools.org/
Blach IS 500/7-8
1120 Covington Rd 94024 650-934-3800
Bhavna Narula, prin. Fax 968-3918
Egan IS 600/7-8
100 W Portola Ave 94022 650-917-2200
Keith Rocha, prin. Fax 949-3748

Mountain View-Los Altos UNHSD
Supt. — See Mountain View
Los Altos HS 1,600/9-12
201 Almond Ave 94022 650-960-8811
Wynne Satterwhite, prin. Fax 948-8672

**Los Altos Hills, Santa Clara, Pop. 7,599**

---

Foothill College Post-Sec.
12345 S El Monte Rd 94022 650-949-7777
Pinewood S - Upper Campus 300/7-12
26800 W Fremont Rd 94022 650-209-3010
Scott Riches, pres. Fax 209-3011

**Los Angeles, Los Angeles, Pop. 3,699,911**
Compton USD
Supt. — See Compton
Vanguard Learning Center 300/6-8
13305 S San Pedro St 90061 310-898-6050
Kevin Curry, prin. Fax 327-7180

Los Angeles County Office of Education
Supt. — See Downey
Los Angeles County HS for the Arts 600/Alt
5151 State University Dr 90032 323-343-2787
Lisa Sherman Cold, prin. Fax 343-2549

Los Angeles USD 619,300/PK-12
333 S Beaudry Ave 90017 213-241-1000
Ramon Cortines, supt. Fax 241-8442
www.lausd.net
Academic Leadership Community S 400/9-12
322 Lucas Ave 90017 213-240-3815
Tadeo Climaco, prin. Fax 482-0232
Academy for Multilingual Arts & Science 9-12
8800 S San Pedro St 90003 323-565-4600
Simone Charles, prin. Fax 750-1084
Academy of Environmental & Social Policy 9-12
3921 Selig Pl 90031 323-224-5991
Brendan Schallert, prin. Fax 224-5992
Adams MS 1,100/6-8
151 W 30th St 90007 213-745-3700
Evelyn Wesley, prin. Fax 749-8542
Alonzo Community Day S 200/7-12
5755 Fountain Ave 90028 323-817-6500
Joseph Zanki, prin. Fax 817-6599
Ambassador School of Global Leadership 100/6-12
701 S Catalina St 90005 213-480-4540
Gregory Jackson, prin. Fax 480-4599
Apex Academy 300/7-12
1309 N Wilton Pl 90028 323-817-6550
Cesar Lopez, prin. Fax 817-6555
Audubon MS 800/6-8
4120 11th Ave 90008 323-290-6300
Charmain Young, prin. Fax 296-2433

Bancroft MS 1,000/6-8
929 N Las Palmas Ave 90038 323-993-3400
Maria Rico, prin. Fax 461-8246
Belmont HS 1,200/9-12
1575 W 2nd St 90026 213-241-4300
Kristen McGregor, prin. Fax 250-9706
Belvedere MS 1,500/6-8
312 N Record Ave 90063 323-266-5400
Helen Carrillo, prin. Fax 269-6769
Berendo MS 1,200/6-8
1157 S Berendo St 90006 213-739-5600
Rosa Trujillo, prin. Fax 382-8599
Bethune MS 1,300/6-8
155 W 69th St 90003 323-541-1800
Carlos Gonzalez, prin. Fax 759-1271
Boyle Heights Continuation S 100/Alt
544 S Mathews St 90033 323-264-8070
Leigh Orr, prin. Fax 266-7177
Bravo Medical Magnet HS 1,900/9-12
1200 Cornwell St 90033 323-227-4400
Maria Flores, prin. Fax 342-9139
Burbank MS 800/6-8
6460 N Figueroa St 90042 323-340-4400
Christine Moore, prin. Fax 257-7420
Burroughs MS 2,000/6-8
600 S McCadden Pl 90005 323-549-5000
Steve Martinez, prin. Fax 934-9051
Business and Technology S 6-8
1420 E Adams Blvd 90011 323-846-2235
Maria Ozaeta, prin.
Carver MS 1,100/6-8
4410 McKinley Ave 90011 323-846-2900
Latasha Buck, prin. Fax 232-5344
Castro MS 6-8
1575 W 2nd St 90026 213-241-4415
Erick Mitchell, prin. Fax 241-4418
Central HS Tri-C 600/Alt
716 E 14th St 90021 213-745-1901
Helene Cameron, prin. Fax 748-3458
Cheviot Hills Continuation S 100/Alt
9200 Cattaraugus Ave 90034 310-838-8462
Rhea Turek, prin. Fax 839-4051
City of Angels Independent Study 1,700/Alt
221 S Eastman Ave 90063 323-415-8350
Vince Carbino, prin. Fax 261-0618
Clinton MS 1,000/6-8
3500 S Hill St 90007 323-235-7200
Brenda Pensamiento, prin. Fax 846-0054
Cochran MS 1,200/6-8
4066 W Johnnie Cochran Vst 90019 323-730-4300
Gilberto Samuel, prin. Fax 733-9106
Communication and Technology S 9-12
6100 S Central Ave 90001 323-846-2118
Cynthia Gonzalez, prin.
Cortines S of Visual & Performing Arts 1,500/9-12
450 N Grand Ave 90012 213-217-8600
Kenneth Martinez, prin. Fax 928-0933
Crenshaw STEM Magnet HS 1,500/9-12
5010 11th Ave 90043 323-290-7800
Lenalda Corley, prin. Fax 292-6712
Dorsey HS 1,400/9-12
3537 Farmdale Ave 90016 323-298-8400
Reginald Sample, prin. Fax 298-8501
Downtown Business HS 1,100/9-12
1081 W Temple St 90012 213-481-0371
Jared DuPree, prin. Fax 482-0792
Drew MS 1,200/6-8
8511 Compton Ave 90001 323-826-1700
Nnamdi Uzor, prin. Fax 583-6030
Eagle Rock JSHS 2,700/7-12
1750 Yosemite Dr 90041 323-340-3500
Mylene Keipp, prin. Fax 255-3398
Early College Academy 10-12
400 W Washington Blvd 90015 323-521-1200
Michael Dean, prin.
Edison MS 1,200/6-8
6500 Hooper Ave 90001 323-826-2500
Salvador Velasco, prin. Fax 581-8389
Ellington Continuation HS 100/Alt
1541 W 110th St 90047 323-418-4130
Cecil McLinn, prin. Fax 754-1281
El Sereno MS 1,400/6-8
2839 N Eastern Ave 90032 323-224-4700
Joyce Dara, prin. Fax 223-9024
Fairfax HS 2,400/9-12
7850 Melrose Ave 90046 323-370-1200
Carmina Nacorda, prin. Fax 651-5803
Fine and Performing Arts Academy 9-12
300 E 53rd St 90011 323-846-4700
Omar Del Cueto, prin. Fax 846-4714
Foshay Learning Center 2,000/Alt
3751 S Harvard Blvd 90018 323-373-2700
Yvonne Garrison, prin. Fax 733-2120
Franklin HS 1,900/9-12
820 N Avenue 54 90042 323-550-2000
Regina Marquez Martinez, prin. Fax 258-5940
Fremont HS 3,500/9-12
7676 S San Pedro St 90003 323-565-1200
Pedro Avalos, prin. Fax 971-5890
Garfield HS 2,500/9-12
5101 E 6th St 90022 323-981-5500
Mario Cantu, prin. Fax 268-4957
Gompers MS 1,100/6-8
234 E 112th St 90061 323-241-4000
Elizabeth Pratt, prin. Fax 418-0778
Green Design S 9-12
6100 S Central Ave 90001 323-846-2108
William Lupejkis, prin.
Griffith MS 1,400/6-8
4765 E 4th St 90022 323-266-7400
Rose Anne Ruiz, prin. Fax 268-6375
Hamilton HS 3,000/9-12
2955 S Robertson Blvd 90034 310-280-1400
Gary Garcia, prin. Fax 842-8663
Harte Prep MS 1,000/6-8
9301 S Hoover St 90044 323-242-5400
Luz Cortes, prin. Fax 757-0408

Hawkins Community Health Advocates S 9-12
825 W 60th St 90044 323-789-1282
Claudia Rojas, prin.
Hawkins Critical Design and Gaming S 9-12
825 W 60th St 90044 323-789-1282
Andre Hargunani, prin.
Hawkins RISE S, 825 W 60th St 90044 9-12
Anthony Terry, prin. 323-789-1282
Highland Park Continuation S 100/Alt
928 N Avenue 53 90042 323-254-3421
Irene Narvaez, prin. Fax 340-8132
Hollenbeck MS 1,400/6-8
2510 E 6th St 90023 323-780-3000
Randy Romero, prin. Fax 269-8137
Hollywood HS 1,700/9-12
1521 N Highland Ave 90028 323-993-1700
Alejandra Sanchez, prin. Fax 957-0238
Hope Continuation S 100/Alt
7840 Towne Ave 90003 323-565-1292
Tipawan McGee, prin. Fax 565-1319
Irving Magnet MS 700/6-8
3010 Estara Ave 90065 323-259-3700
Kirk Roskam, prin. Fax 254-6447
Jefferson HS 1,600/9-12
1319 E 41st St 90011 323-521-1200
Agustin Gonzalez, prin. Fax 231-4755
Kahlo Continuation HS 200/Alt
1924 S Los Angeles St 90011 213-763-1090
Sandra Washington, prin. Fax 763-1092
Kim Academy 900/6-8
615 Shatto Pl 90005 213-739-6500
Edward Colacion, prin. Fax 384-3083
King-Drew Medical Magnet HS 1,600/9-12
1601 E 120th St 90059 323-566-0420
Reginald Brookens, prin. Fax 567-1429
King MS 1,500/6-8
4201 Fountain Ave 90029 323-644-6700
Mark Naulls, prin. Fax 913-3594
LACES Magnet S 1,600/6-12
5931 W 18th St 90035 323-549-5900
Harold Boger, prin. Fax 938-8737
Leadership in Entertainment & Media Arts 9-12
3501 N Broadway 90031 323-441-7614
Gustavo Barientos, prin. Fax 441-7688
Liechty MS 1,300/6-8
650 S Union Ave 90017 213-989-1200
Adalberto Vega, prin. Fax 484-2700
Lincoln HS 2,000/9-12
3501 N Broadway 90031 323-441-4600
Jose Torres, prin. Fax 223-1291
Los Angeles Academy 1,800/6-8
644 E 56th St 90011 323-238-1800
Raul Correa, prin. Fax 231-0136
Los Angeles HS 1,900/9-12
4650 W Olympic Blvd 90019 323-900-2700
Helena Yoon-Fontamillas, prin. Fax 936-8455
Los Angeles HS For The Arts 400/9-12
701 S Catalina St 90005 213-480-4600
Susan Canjura, prin. Fax 480-4650
Los Angeles River S 9-12
2050 N San Fernando Rd 90065 323-276-5535
Kristine Puich, prin. Fax 276-5544
Los Angeles S of Global Studies 400/9-12
322 Lucas Ave 90017 213-240-3850
Christian Quintero, prin. Fax 240-3875
Los Angeles Teacher Prep Academy 200/9-12
1575 W 2nd St 90026 213-580-6430
Robert Lopez, prin. Fax 580-6499
Los Angeles Technology Center Vo/Tech
3721 W Washington Blvd 90018 323-732-0153
Juan Jimenez, prin. Fax 731-1568
Mann JHS 600/6-8
7001 S St Andrews Pl 90047 323-541-1900
Orlando Johnson, prin. Fax 758-8203
Manual Arts HS 3,100/9-12
4131 S Vermont Ave 90037 323-846-7300
Erica Thomas, prin. Fax 232-0837
Marina Del Rey MS 900/6-8
12500 Braddock Dr 90066 310-578-2700
Lorraine Machado, prin. Fax 821-3248
Markham MS 1,200/6-8
1650 E 104th St 90002 323-568-5500
Luis Montoya, prin. Fax 569-6066
Marlton S 300/Alt
4000 Santo Tomas Dr 90008 323-296-7680
Annick Draghi, prin. Fax 290-1794
Marshall HS 2,900/9-12
3939 Tracy St 90027 323-671-1400
Patricia Heideman, prin. Fax 665-8682
McAlister JSHS 200/Alt
611 S Carondelet St 90057 213-381-2823
Tara Thurston, prin. Fax 384-8947
Mendez HS 400/9-12
1200 Plaza Del Sol St 90033 323-981-5400
Mauro Bautista, prin. Fax 307-0788
Metropolitan Continuation S 200/Alt
727 Wilson St 90021 213-623-4272
Raul Aguilar, prin. Fax 629-1069
Middle College HS 400/9-12
1600 W Imperial Hwy Bldg 16 90047 323-418-4700
Betty Washington, prin. Fax 242-2449
Monterey Continuation HS 100/Alt
466 Fraser Ave 90022 323-269-0786
Janine Antoine, prin. Fax 526-0795
Muir MS 1,300/6-8
5929 S Vermont Ave 90044 323-565-2200
Aminika Readeux, prin. Fax 778-9824
Newmark Continuation HS 100/Alt
134 Witmer St 90026 213-250-9675
Justin Lauer, prin. Fax 482-3697
New Open World Academy 1,000/K-12
3201 W 8th St 90005 213-480-3700
Charles Smith, prin. Fax 389-1559
New Technology HS @ Jefferson 300/9-12
1319 E 41st St 90011 323-521-1290
Marvin Smith, prin. Fax 521-1294

Nightingale MS 1,100/6-8
3311 N Figueroa St 90065 323-224-4800
Musetta Malone, prin. Fax 222-4506
Obama Global Preparation Academy 1,200/6-8
1700 W 46th St 90062 323-421-1700
David Devereaux, prin. Fax 293-2003
Palms MS 1,700/6-8
10860 Woodbine St 90034 310-253-7600
Derek Moriuchi, prin. Fax 559-0397
Partnership Academy for the Arts 9-12
2265 E 103rd St 90002 323-568-4100
Carlos Montes, prin. Fax 249-4709
Performing Arts Community S 9-12
6100 S Central Ave 90001 323-846-2136
Sally Lopez, prin.
Phoenix Continuation HS 100/Alt
12971 Zanja St 90066 310-306-8775
Nancy Huerta, prin. Fax 827-3876
Pio Pico MS 700/6-8
1512 Arlington Ave 90019 323-733-8801
Miranda Conston-Ra, prin. Fax 735-2665
Public Service Community S 9-12
6100 S Central Ave 90001 323-846-2128
Karen Mercado, prin. Fax 846-2122
Pueblo de los Angeles Continuation HS 100/Alt
2506 Alta St 90031 323-223-3258
Michael Olivo, prin. Fax 223-4537
Ramona Opportunity HS 100/Alt
231 S Alma Ave 90063 323-266-7600
Anna Carrasco, prin. Fax 415-8077
Riley HS - Cyesis 200/Alt
1524 E 103rd St 90002 323-563-6692
Linda Roussel, prin. Fax 566-6379
Roosevelt Communication/Media/Tech HS 500/9-12
456 S Mathews St 90033 323-780-6500
Benjamin Gertner, prin. Fax 269-5473
Roybal Learning Center 300/9-12
1200 Colton St 90026 213-580-6430
Sarah Usmani, prin. Fax 580-6499
Santee Education Complex 2,200/9-12
1921 Maple Ave 90011 213-763-1000
Martin Gomez, prin. Fax 742-9883
School for Visual Arts & Humanities 9-12
701 S Catalina St 90005 213-480-4700
Eftihia Danellis, prin. Fax 480-4750
School of Arts and Culture 6-8
1420 E Adams Blvd 90011 323-846-2245
Anita Maxon, prin.
School of Business and Tourism 300/9-12
322 Lucas Ave 90017 213-240-3800
Nova Meza, prin. Fax 482-0232
School of History & Dramatic Arts 9-12
2050 N San Fernando Rd 90065 323-276-5500
Irene Narvaez, prin. Fax 276-5514
School of Sci/Tech/ Engineering/Math 9-12
456 S Mathews St 90033 323-780-6537
Jose Espinoza, prin. Fax 269-5473
School of Social Justice 9-12
322 Lucas Ave 90017 213-240-3800
Nova Meza, prin. Fax 482-0232
Solis Learning Academy 9-12
319 N Humphreys Ave 90022 323-729-1700
Jose Rodriguez, prin. Fax 264-2002
STEM @ Bernstein S 9-12
1309 N Wilton Pl 90028 323-817-6461
Paul Hirsch, prin. Fax 817-6465
STEM Academy of Boyle Heights 9-12
456 S Mathews Blvd 90033 323-268-1031
Adriana Trejo, prin. Fax 780-3069
Stevenson MS 1,900/6-8
725 S Indiana St 90023 323-780-6400
Leo Gonzalez, prin. Fax 265-3952
Studio S 6-8
2050 San Fernando Rd 90065 323-225-4542
Leah Raphael, prin. Fax 276-5444
32nd Street / USC MaST S 1,100/K-12
822 W 32nd St 90007 213-748-0126
Ezequiel Gonzalez, prin. Fax 744-1608
Torres Engineering and Technology Acad 100/9-12
4211 Dozier St 90063 323-265-6795
Alex Fuentes, prin. Fax 265-6796
Torres Humanitas Visual Arts & Tech 100/9-12
4211 Dozier St 90063 323-265-6830
Deborah Lowe, prin. Fax 265-6831
Torres Performing Arts Academy 200/9-11
4211 Dozier St 90063 323-265-6725
Carolyn McKnight, prin. Fax 265-6726
Torres Renaissance Academy 100/9-12
4211 Dozier St 90063 323-265-6760
Jose Gonzalez, prin. Fax 265-6761
Torres Social Justice Leadership Academy 100/9-12
4211 Dozier St 90063 323-265-6665
Roseann Cazares, prin. Fax 265-6866
Twain MS 700/6-8
2224 Walgrove Ave 90066 310-305-3100
Althea Ford, prin. Fax 398-1627
UCLA Community S 1,000/K-12
700 S Mariposa Ave 90005 213-480-3750
Leyda Garcia, prin. Fax 480-3759
University HS 2,000/9-12
11800 Texas Ave 90025 310-914-3500
Eric Davidson, prin. Fax 478-6535
USC Hybrid HS 9-12
350 S Figueroa St Ste 100 90071 213-929-1046
Mide Macaulay, prin. Fax 929-1047
Venice HS 2,300/9-12
13000 Venice Blvd 90066 310-577-4200
Oryla Wiedoeft, prin. Fax 306-3249
View Park Continuation HS 100/Alt
4701 Rodeo Rd 90016 323-292-0331
Victorio Gutierrez, prin. Fax 292-7920
Virgil MS 1,200/6-8
152 N Vermont Ave 90004 213-368-2800
Gerardo Loera, prin. Fax 383-8774
Washington Preparatory HS 1,700/9-12
10860 S Denker Ave 90047 323-418-4000
Dechele Byrd, prin. Fax 754-3517

Webster MS 700/6-8
11330 Graham Pl 90064 310-235-4600
Peter Benefiel, prin. Fax 477-0146
WESM Health/Sports Medicine HS 1,200/9-12
7400 W Manchester Ave 90045 310-338-2400
Debra Bryant, prin. Fax 410-1067
West Adams Preparatory HS 2,600/9-12
1500 W Washington Blvd 90007 323-373-2500
Erica Nava, prin. Fax 373-2518
West Hollywood Community Day School 100/Alt
1049 N Fairfax Ave 90046 323-654-4155
Karen Cheval, prin. Fax 654-5635
Whitman Continuation HS 100/Alt
7795 Rosewood Ave 90036 323-651-0645
Conrado Tiu, prin. Fax 653-9214
Widney JSHS 200/Alt
2302 S Gramercy Pl 90018 323-731-8633
Carrie Delisle, prin. Fax 734-8048
Wilson HS 2,000/9-12
4500 Multnomah St 90032 323-276-1600
Luis Lopez, prin. Fax 223-7936
Wright Magnet MS 800/6-8
6550 W 80th St 90045 310-258-6600
Christina Wantz, prin. Fax 568-8942
Young Continuation HS 100/Alt
3051 W 52nd St 90043 323-296-3258
Wanda Robinson, prin. Fax 292-6595
Belmont Community Adult Education Adult
1575 W 2nd St 90026 213-241-8500
Fax 241-8525
East Los Angeles Occupational Center Adult
2100 Marengo St 90033 323-276-7000
Andrea Rodriguez, prin. Fax 223-6365
East Los Angeles Skills Center Adult
3921 Selig Pl 90031 323-224-5970
Donna Brashear, prin. Fax 222-2351
Evans Community Adult Education Adult
717 N Figueroa St 90012 213-626-7151
Clifton DeCordoba, prin. Fax 626-4487
Franklin Community Adult S Adult
820 N Avenue 54 90042 323-550-2100
Karen Kuser, prin. Fax 550-2011
Fremont-Washington Community Adult S Adult
7676 S San Pedro St 90003 323-565-1300
Michael Wada, prin. Fax 565-1301
Friedman Occupational Center Adult
1646 S Olive St 90015 213-765-2400
Bernadine Gonzalez, prin. Fax 748-7406
Garfield Community Adult S Adult
4343 New York Ave 90022 323-262-9115
Penny Kunitani, prin. Fax 262-9765
Hollywood Community Adult Education Adult
1521 N Highland Ave 90028 323-993-1800
Fax 993-1801
Jefferson Community Adult S Adult
1319 E 41st St 90011 323-235-8120
Anna Carrasco, prin. Fax 233-9658
Los Angeles Adult Education Adult
4650 W Olympic Blvd 90019 323-900-3500
Celia Dominguez, prin. Fax 900-2796
Manual Arts-Crenshaw Community Adult S Adult
4131 S Vermont Ave 90037 323-846-3000
Joanna McConaghy, prin. Fax 234-1310
Metropolitan Skills Center Adult
2801 W 6th St 90057 213-386-7269
Candace Lee, prin. Fax 386-4554
Roosevelt Community Adult S Adult
456 S Mathews St 90033 323-780-6650
Penny Kunitani, prin. Fax 780-6668
Venice Community Adult S Adult
13000 Venice Blvd 90066 310-577-4230
Cynthia Tollette, prin. Fax 577-4238
Waters Employment Preparation Center Adult
10925 S Central Ave 90059 323-564-1431
Elsa Madrid, prin. Fax 566-0147
Westchester-Emerson Community Adult S Adult
8810 Emerson Ave 90045 310-258-2000
Cynthia Tollette, prin. Fax 645-8043
Westside Community Adult S Adult
7850 Melrose Ave 90046 323-370-1040
James Chacon, prin. Fax 370-1055
Wilson-Lincoln Community Adult S Adult
4500 Multnomah St 90032 323-276-1700
Fax 276-1710

Other Schools – See Arleta, Bell, Canoga Park, Carson, Chatsworth, Cudahy, Gardena, Granada Hills, Harbor City, Hollywood, Huntington Park, Lomita, Long Beach, Maywood, Mission Hills, North Hills, North Hollywood, Northridge, Pacoima, Panorama City, Rancho Palos Verdes, Reseda, San Fernando, San Pedro, Sherman Oaks, South Gate, Sunland, Sun Valley, Sylmar, Tarzana, Tujunga, Van Nuys, Venice, Walnut Park, Wilmington, Woodland Hills

Regional Occupational Center & Program
Supt. — None
Los Angeles USD ROC/P Vo/Tech
333 S Beaudry Ave 90017 213-241-3162
Isabel Vazquez, dir.

---

Abraham Lincoln University Post-Sec.
3530 Wilshire Blvd Ste 1430 90010 213-252-5100
Academy for Jewish Religion Post-Sec.
574 Hilgard Ave 90024 310-824-1586
Advanced Computing Institute Post-Sec.
3470 Wilshire Blvd Ste 1100 90010 213-383-8999
AMDA College and Conservatory Post-Sec.
6305 Yucca St 90028 323-469-3300
American Career College - Los Angeles Post-Sec.
4021 Rosewood Ave 90004 323-668-7555
American Evangelical University Post-Sec.
1818 S Western Ave Ste 409 90006 323-643-0301
American Film Institute Conservatory Post-Sec.
2021 N Western Ave 90027 323-856-7600
American Jewish University Post-Sec.
15600 Mulholland Dr 90077 310-476-9777
Angeles College Post-Sec.
3440 Wilshire Blvd Ste 310 90010 213-487-2211
Archer S for Girls 400/6-12
11725 W Sunset Blvd 90049 310-873-7000
Elizabeth English, hdmstr. Fax 873-7070
Arete Preparatory Academy 50/9-12
11500 W Olympic Blvd # 318 90064 310-478-9900
James Hahn, head sch Fax 478-9901
Argosy University Los Angeles Post-Sec.
5230 Pacific Concourse #200 90045 310-531-9700
Associated Technical College Post-Sec.
1670 Wilshire Blvd 90017 213-353-1845
Bais Yaakov S 300/9-12
7353 Beverly Blvd 90036 323-938-3231
Rabbi Jacob Friedman, dir. Fax 930-0477
Bishop Conaty-Our Lady Loretto HS 400/9-12
2900 W Pico Blvd 90006 323-737-0012
Richard Spicer, prin. Fax 737-1749
Bishop Mora Salesian HS 500/9-12
960 S Soto St 90023 323-261-7124
Sam Robles, prin. Fax 261-7600
Bnos Devorah HS 50/9-12
461 N La Brea Ave 90036 323-930-0047
Shulamith May, head sch Fax 930-1901
Bnos Esther HS 9-12
116 N La Brea Ave 90036 310-933-4171
Brentwood S 700/7-12
100 S Barrington Pl 90049 310-476-9633
Dr. Michael Riera, head sch Fax 476-4087
Bryan University Post-Sec.
3580 Wilshire Blvd Ste 400 90010 213-484-8850
California Healing Arts College Post-Sec.
12217 Santa Monica Blvd 90025 310-826-7622
California State University-Los Angeles Post-Sec.
5151 State University Dr 90032 323-343-3000
Cathedral HS 700/9-12
1253 Bishops Rd 90012 323-225-2438
Br. John Montgomery, prin. Fax 222-7223
CBD College Post-Sec.
3699 Wilshire Blvd Ste 400 90010 213-427-2200
Charles R. Drew Univ. of Med. & Science Post-Sec.
1731 E 120th St 90059 323-563-4800
Chicago Sch. of Professional Psychology Post-Sec.
617 W 7th St 90017 800-721-8072
Chicago Sch of Professional Psychology Post-Sec.
1145 Gayley Ave 90024 310-208-4240
Children's Hospital of Los Angeles Post-Sec.
4650 W Sunset Blvd 90027 323-669-2301
Coast Career Institute Post-Sec.
1354 S Hill St 90015 213-235-0606
Colburn School Post-Sec.
200 S Grand Ave 90012 213-621-2200
Concord Law School of Kaplan University Post-Sec.
10866 Wilshire Blvd # 1200 90024 310-689-3200
Dongguk University Post-Sec.
440 Shatto Pl 90020 213-487-0110
East Los Angeles Occupational Center Post-Sec.
2100 Marengo St 90033 323-223-1283
Episcopal S of Los Angeles 50/6-12
6325 Santa Monica Blvd 90038 323-462-3752
Rev. Maryetta Anschutz, head sch
Everest College Post-Sec.
3460 Wilshire Blvd Ste 500 90010 213-388-9950
Everest College Post-Sec.
3000 S Robertson Blvd # 300 90034 310-840-5777
FIDM Fashion Institute of Design Post-Sec.
919 S Grand Ave 90015 213-624-1200
Fremont College Post-Sec.
3440 Wilshire Blvd Fl 10 90010 800-373-6668
Gnomon School of Visual Effects Post-Sec.
1015 N Cahuenga Blvd 90038 323-466-6663
Harvard-Westlake MS 700/7-9
700 N Faring Rd 90077 310-274-7281
Jeanne Huybrechts, head sch Fax 288-3331
Hebrew Union College Post-Sec.
3077 University Ave 90007 213-749-3424
Holy Trinity S 100/5-8
3716 Boyce Ave 90039 323-663-2064
Karen Lloyd, prin. Fax 664-2581
ICDC College Post-Sec.
5422 W Sunset Blvd 90027 323-468-0404
Immaculate Heart MSHS 700/6-12
5515 Franklin Ave 90028 323-461-3651
Virginia Hurst, prin. Fax 462-0610
International Christian Education Coll. Post-Sec.
3807 Wilshire Blvd Ste 730 90010 213-368-0316
International Reformed University/Sem Post-Sec.
125 S Vermont Ave 90004 213-381-0081
John Tracy Clinic Post-Sec.
806 W Adams Blvd 90007 213-748-5481
Kabbaz HS 200/9-12
3261 Overland Ave 90034 310-836-3464
Learnet Academy Post-Sec.
3251 W 6th St 90020 213-387-4242
Los Angeles Adventist Academy 200/PK-12
846 E El Segundo Blvd 90059 323-321-2585
Carol Todd, prin. Fax 324-3207
Los Angeles City College Post-Sec.
855 N Vermont Ave 90029 323-953-4000
Los Angeles Co. Coll. Nursing/Alld Hlth Post-Sec.
1237 N Mission Rd 90033 323-226-4911
Los Angeles ORT College Post-Sec.
6435 Wilshire Blvd 90048 323-966-5444
Los Angeles Pacific College Post-Sec.
3550 Wilshire Blvd Ste 460 90010 213-384-2318
Los Angeles Southwest College Post-Sec.
1600 W Imperial Hwy 90047 323-241-5225
Los Angeles Trade-Technical College Post-Sec.
400 W Washington Blvd 90015 213-763-7000
Loyola HS 1,200/9-12
1901 Venice Blvd 90006 213-381-5121
Frank Kozakowski, prin. Fax 368-3819
Loyola Marymount University Post-Sec.
1 LMU Dr 90045 310-338-2700
Marinello School of Beauty Post-Sec.
1241 S Soto St Ste 101 90023 323-980-9253
Marinello School of Beauty Post-Sec.
6111 Wilshire Blvd 90048 323-938-2005
Marlborough S 500/7-12
250 S Rossmore Ave 90004 323-935-1147
Priscilla Sands, head sch Fax 933-0542
Marymount HS 400/9-12
10643 W Sunset Blvd 90077 310-472-1205
Jacqueline Landry, head sch Fax 476-0910
Mesivta Birkas Yitzchok 100/9-12
6022 W Pico Blvd 90035 323-937-4748
Rabbi Sholom Tendler, prin. Fax 937-4782
Methodist Theological Seminary Post-Sec.
2525 James M Wood Blvd 90006 213-386-0080
Milken Community S 700/7-12
15800 Zeldins Way 90049 310-440-3500
Gary Weisserman, head sch Fax 471-5139
Mt. St. Mary's College Post-Sec.
12001 Chalon Rd 90049 310-954-4000
Mt. St. Mary's College - Doheny Campus Post-Sec.
10 Chester Pl 90007 213-477-2500
New Covenant Academy 100/K-12
3119 W 6th St 90020 213-487-5437
Franklin Park, admin. Fax 487-5430
Notre Dame Academy for Girls 400/9-12
2851 Overland Ave 90064 310-839-5289
Lilliam Paetzold, prin. Fax 839-7957
Occidental College Post-Sec.
1600 Campus Rd 90041 323-259-2500
Otis College of Art and Design Post-Sec.
9045 Lincoln Blvd 90045 310-665-6800
Pacific States University Post-Sec.
3450 Wilshire Blvd Fl 5 90010 323-731-2383
Pacific Union College Post-Sec.
1720 E Cesar E Chavez Ave 90033 323-268-5000
Pilgrim S 300/PK-12
540 S Commonwealth Ave 90020 213-385-7351
Mark Brooks, head sch Fax 386-7264
Pilibos Armenian S 700/K-12
1615 N Alexandria Ave 90027 323-668-2661
Dr. Alina Dorian, prin. Fax 662-0332
Price S 200/PK-12
7901 S Vermont Ave 90044 323-565-4199
Dr. Feager Pertilla, supt. Fax 753-6770
Ribet Academy 400/PK-12
2911 N San Fernando Rd 90065 323-344-4330
Sacred Heart HS 200/9-12
2111 Griffin Ave 90031 323-225-2209
Raymond Saborio, prin. Fax 225-5046
SAE Institute of Technology Post-Sec.
6565 W Sunset Blvd Ste 100 90028 323-466-6323
St. Mary Magdalen S 100/5-8
1223 S Corning St 90035 310-652-4723
Nuria Gordillo, prin. Fax 933-7453
Shalhevet S 200/9-12
910 S Fairfax Ave 90036 323-930-9333
Rabbi Ari Segal, head sch Fax 930-9444
Shepherd University School of Theology Post-Sec.
3200 N San Fernando Rd 90065 323-550-8888
Southern California Inst. Architecture Post-Sec.
960 E 3rd St 90013 213-613-2200
Southern CA Univ School of Oriental Med. Post-Sec.
1541 Wilshire Blvd Fl 3 90017 213-413-9500
Southwestern Law School Post-Sec.
3050 Wilshire Blvd 90010 213-738-6700
Summit View S - Westside 100/1-12
12101 W Washington Blvd 90066 310-751-1100
Keri Borzello, head sch Fax 397-4417
SUTECH School of Voc/Tech Training Post-Sec.
3455 E Olympic Blvd 90023 323-262-3210
Theatre of Arts Post-Sec.
6755 Hollywood Blvd Fl 2 90028 323-463-2500
Union Institute & University Post-Sec.
6701 Center Dr W Ste 1200 90045 310-417-3500
Universal College of Beauty Post-Sec.
8619 S Vermont Ave 90044 323-750-5750
Universal College of Beauty Post-Sec.
3419 W 43rd Pl 90008 323-298-0045
University of California Post-Sec.
1147 Murphy Hall # 951436 90095 310-825-4321
University of Philosophical Research Post-Sec.
3910 Los Feliz Blvd 90027 323-663-2167
University of Southern California Post-Sec.
University Park 90089 213-740-2311
Verbum Dei HS 300/9-12
11100 S Central Ave 90059 323-564-6651
Rev. Michael Mandala, pres. Fax 564-9009
Village Glen S - Westside 300/K-12
4160 Grand View Blvd 90066 310-751-1101
Nata Preis, dir.
Virginia School Center Post-Sec.
1033 S Broadway 90015 213-747-8292
West Los Angeles VA Medical Center Post-Sec.
Wilshire & Sawtelle Blvds 90073 310-824-3132
Westwood College - Los Angeles Post-Sec.
3250 Wilshire Blvd Fl 400 90010 213-739-9999
Wildwood MSHS 400/6-12
11811 W Olympic Blvd 90064 310-478-7189
Landis Green, head sch Fax 478-6875
Windward S 500/7-12
11350 Palms Blvd 90066 310-391-7127
Thomas Gilder, head sch Fax 397-5655
World Mission University Post-Sec.
500 Shatto Pl Ste 600 90020 213-385-2322
Yeshiva Gedolah of Los Angeles HS 100/9-12
5444 W Olympic Blvd 90036 323-938-2071
Rabbi Yossi Gross, dir. Fax 938-4650
Yeshiva Ohr Elchonon Chabad Post-Sec.
7215 Waring Ave 90046 323-937-3763
Yeshiva Ohr Elchonon Chabad West Coast 100/9-12
7215 Waring Ave 90046 323-937-3763
Rabbi Ezra Schochet, dean Fax 937-9456
Yeshiva University Girls HS 200/9-12
1619 S Robertson Blvd 90035 310-203-0755
Rabbi Abraham Lieberman, head sch Fax 551-0312
Yeshiva University Los Angeles Boys HS 200/9-12
9760 W Pico Blvd 90035 310-203-3180
Yo San Univ. of Traditional Chinese Med. Post-Sec.
13315 W Washington Blvd 90066 310-577-3000

**Los Banos, Merced, Pop. 35,167**
Los Banos USD 8,300/K-12
1717 S 11th St 93635 209-826-3801
Dr. Steve Tietjen Ed.D., supt. Fax 826-6810
www.losbanosusd.k12.ca.us
Crossroads Alternative Education Center 100/Alt
265 Mercey Springs Rd Ste C 93635 209-826-4013
Barbara Severns Ed.D., prin. Fax 826-4104
Los Banos Community Day S 50/Alt
715 W H St 93635 209-827-5600
Janette Alvarado, prin.
Los Banos HS 1,400/9-12
1966 S 11th St 93635 209-826-6033
Veli Gurgen, prin. Fax 827-4156
Los Banos JHS 1,400/7-8
1750 San Luis St 93635 209-826-0867
Deo Brasil, prin. Fax 826-8532
Pacheco HS 1,200/9-12
200 Ward Rd 93635 209-827-4506
Daniel Sutton, prin. Fax 827-4715
San Luis HS 200/Alt
125 7th St 93635 209-826-8410
Chan Meas, prin. Fax 826-2252

Merced County Office of Education
Supt. — See Merced
Valley Los Banos Community S 100/Alt
715 W H St 93635 209-827-5600
Lori Gattuso, prin. Fax 827-1486

---

Merced College-Los Banos Campus Post-Sec.
22240 Highway 152 93635 209-826-3495

**Los Gatos, Santa Clara, Pop. 28,259**
Campbell UNESD
Supt. — See Campbell
Rolling Hills MS 900/5-8
1585 More Ave 95032 408-364-4235
Cynthia Dodd, prin. Fax 341-7070

Loma Prieta JUNESD 400/PK-8
23800 Summit Rd 95033 408-353-1101
Corey Kidwell, supt. Fax 353-8051
www.loma.k12.ca.us
English MS 100/6-8
23800 Summit Rd 95033 408-353-1123
Denee Signorelli, prin. Fax 353-5024

Los Gatos UNESD 3,100/K-8
17010 Roberts Rd 95032 408-335-2000
Diana Abbati, supt. Fax 395-6481
www.lgusd.org
Fisher MS 1,100/6-8
19195 Fisher Ave 95032 408-335-2300
Lisa Fraser, prin. Fax 356-7616

Los Gatos-Saratoga JUNHSD 3,200/9-12
17421 Farley Rd W 95030 408-354-2520
Bob Mistele, supt. Fax 354-4198
www.lgsuhsd.org
Los Gatos HS 1,800/9-12
20 High School Ct 95030 408-354-2730
Markus Autrey, prin. Fax 354-3742
Other Schools – See Saratoga

**Los Molinos, Tehama, Pop. 1,963**
Lassen View UNESD 300/K-8
10818 State Highway 99E 96055 530-527-5162
Gerard Walker, supt. Fax 527-2331
www.lassenview.org
Lassen View Community Day S 50/4-8
10818 State Highway 99E 96055 530-527-5162
Gerard Walker, admin. Fax 527-2331

Los Molinos USD 600/K-12
7851 State Highway 99E 96055 530-384-7826
Charles Ward, supt. Fax 384-7832
www.lmusd.net
Los Molinos Community Day S 50/Alt
7851 State Highway 99E 96055 530-384-7900
Cliff Curry, coord.
Los Molinos HS 200/9-12
PO Box 609 96055 530-384-7900
Cliff Curry, prin. Fax 384-1534

**Los Nietos, Los Angeles, Pop. 24,164**
Los Nietos ESD 1,900/PK-8
8324 Westman Ave 90606 562-692-0271
Jonathan Vasquez, supt. Fax 699-0082
www.losnietos.k12.ca.us
Los Nietos MS 400/7-8
11425 Rivera Rd 90606 562-695-0637
Shanonn Brann Zelaya, prin. Fax 695-3805

**Los Olivos, Santa Barbara, Pop. 1,116**

---

Dunn S 200/6-12
PO Box 98 93441 805-688-6471
Mike Beck, head sch Fax 686-2078
Midland S 100/9-12
PO Box 8 93441 805-688-5114
William Graham, head sch Fax 686-2470

**Los Osos, San Luis Obispo, Pop. 13,912**
San Luis Coastal USD
Supt. — See San Luis Obispo
Los Osos MS 400/6-8
1555 El Morro Ave 93402 805-534-2835
Andre Illig, prin. Fax 528-5133

**Lost Hills, Kern, Pop. 2,409**
Lost Hills Union ESD 600/K-8
20951 Pavilion Way 93249 661-797-2626
Harrison Favereaux, supt. Fax 797-2580
Thomas MS 200/6-8
20979 Lobos Ct 93249 661-797-2626
Veronica Sanchez-Gregory, prin. Fax 797-3015

**Lower Lake, Lake, Pop. 1,225**
Konocti USD 3,200/K-12
PO Box 759 95457 707-994-6475
Donna Becnel, supt. Fax 994-0210
www.konoctiusd.org
Carle Continuation HS 100/Alt
PO Box 309 95457 707-994-1033
Matthew Strahl, prin. Fax 994-4121
Lewis Alternative S 100/Alt
PO Box 5000 95457 707-994-2045
Jeffrey Dixon, prin. Fax 994-6807
Lower Lake HS 800/9-12
PO Box 799 95457 707-994-6471
Melissa Lambert, prin. Fax 994-4050
Other Schools – See Clearlake

**Loyalton, Sierra, Pop. 752**
Sierra-Plumas JUSD 400/K-12
PO Box 955 96118 530-993-1660
Merrill Grant Ed.D., supt. Fax 993-0828
www.sierracountyofficeofeducation.org
Loyalton HS 100/7-12
PO Box 37 96118 530-993-4454
Tom Jones, prin. Fax 993-4667
Sierra Pass HS, PO Box 37 96118 50/Alt
Tom Jones, prin. 530-993-1325
Other Schools – See Downieville

**Lucerne Valley, San Bernardino, Pop. 5,647**
Lucerne Valley USD 2,500/K-12
8560 Aliento Rd 92356 760-248-6108
Suzette Davis, supt. Fax 248-6677
lucernevalleyusd.org
Community Day S 50/Alt
8560 Aliento Rd 92356 760-248-2408
Suzette Davis, prin. Fax 248-6677
Lucerne Valley JSHS 300/7-12
8560 Aliento Rd 92356 760-248-2124
Patricia Countney, prin. Fax 248-2162
Mountain View HS 50/Alt
8560 Aliento Rd 92356 760-248-2408
Suzette Davis, prin. Fax 248-6677

**Lynwood, Los Angeles, Pop. 69,209**
Lynwood USD 15,700/K-12
11321 Bullis Rd 90262 310-886-1600
Paul Gothold, supt. Fax 763-0959
www.lynwood.k12.ca.us
Chavez MS 800/6-8
3898 Abbott Rd 90262 310-886-7300
Larry Reed, prin. Fax 603-2048
Firebaugh HS 1,400/10-12
5246 Martin Luther King Blv 90262 310-886-5200
Hector Preciado, prin. Fax 637-8041
Hosler MS 800/7-8
11300 Spruce St 90262 310-603-1447
Hector Marquez, prin. Fax 764-4124
Lynwood HS 4,100/9-12
4050 E Imperial Hwy 90262 310-603-1582
Carlos Zaragoza, prin. Fax 638-9253
Lynwood MS 1,000/7-9
12124 Bullis Rd 90262 310-603-1466
Luz Castillo, prin. Fax 638-2156
Vista Continuation HS 300/Alt
11300 Wright Rd 90262 310-603-1516
Maribel Martinez, prin. Fax 537-7295
Lynwood Adult S Adult
4050 E Imperial Hwy 90262 310-604-3096
Dr. Jean Jones, prin. Fax 635-9107

---

American Career College Post-Sec.
3680 E Imperial Hwy Ste 500 90262 310-900-8050

**Mc Arthur, Shasta, Pop. 335**
Fall River JUSD
Supt. — See Burney
Fall River Community Day HS 50/Alt
44144 A St 96056 530-336-7154
Greg Hawkins, prin. Fax 336-7071
Fall River JSHS 200/7-12
PO Box 340 96056 530-336-5515
Jeanne Utterback, prin. Fax 336-6256
Soldier Mountain Continuation HS 50/Alt
44144 A St 96056 530-336-7159
Greg Hawkins, prin. Fax 336-7071

**Mc Clellan, Sacramento**
Twin Rivers USD 31,300/PK-12
5115 Dudley Blvd Bay A 95652 916-566-1600
Dr. Steven Martinez, supt. Fax 566-1784
www.twinriversusd.org/
Keema HS 700/Alt
5201 Arnold Ave 95652 916-566-3410
Elmena Nelson, prin. Fax 566-3572
Adult S McClellan Center Adult
5703 Skvarla Ave 95652 916-566-2785
Jackie White, dir. Fax 566-3524
Other Schools – See North Highlands, Rio Linda, Sacramento

**Mc Cloud, Siskiyou, Pop. 1,075**
Siskiyou UNHSD
Supt. — See Mount Shasta
McCloud HS 50/9-12
PO Box 1530 96057 530-964-2181
Ed Stokes, prin. Fax 964-2011

**Mc Farland, Kern, Pop. 12,620**
McFarland USD 3,300/K-12
601 2nd St 93250 661-792-3081
Victor Hopper, supt. Fax 792-2447
www.mcfarlandusd.com
Mc Farland HS 800/9-12
259 W Sherwood Ave 93250 661-792-3126
Brian Bell, prin. Fax 792-2315
McFarland Independent S 50/Alt
599 5th St 93250 661-792-6312
Lori Schultz, admin. Fax 792-6758

Mc Farland MS 700/6-8
405 Mast Ave 93250 661-792-3340
Manuel Cantu, prin. Fax 792-5681
San Joaquin HS 100/Alt
599 5th St 93250 661-792-6312
Lori Schultz, prin. Fax 792-6758

**Mc Kinleyville, Humboldt, Pop. 14,503**
McKinleyville UNESD 1,100/K-8
2275 Central Ave 95519 707-839-1549
Al Rosell, supt. Fax 839-1540
www.nohum.k12.ca.us/msd
McKinleyville MS 400/6-8
2285 Central Ave 95519 707-839-1508
Wendy Pearcy, prin. Fax 839-2548

Northern Humboldt UNHSD 1,600/K-12
2755 McKinleyville Ave 95519 707-839-6470
Chris Hartley, supt. Fax 839-6457
www.nohum.k12.ca.us
Mc Kinleyville HS 600/9-12
1300 Murray Rd 95519 707-839-6400
Roger Macdonald, prin. Fax 839-6407
Tsurai HS 50/Alt
1300 Murray Rd 95519 707-839-6480
Tom Pender, prin. Fax 839-6494
Other Schools – See Arcata

**Madera, Madera, Pop. 60,700**
Golden Valley USD 1,900/K-12
37479 Avenue 12, 559-645-7500
Kevin Hatch, supt. Fax 645-7144
www.gvusd.k12.ca.us
Centennial Independent Study 50/Alt
12150 Road 36, 559-645-3580
Kuljeet Mann, admin.
Independence Continuation HS 50/Alt
12150 Road 36, 559-645-3580
Kuljeet Mann, prin. Fax 645-3581
Liberty HS 600/9-12
12220 Road 36, 559-645-3500
Kirk Dalmas, prin. Fax 645-4769
Lincoln Community Day S 50/Alt
12150 Road 36, 559-645-3580
Kuljeet Mann, admin.
Ranchos MS 300/7-8
12455 Road 35 1/2, 559-645-3550
Felipe Piedra, prin. Fax 645-3565
Valley Teen Ranch 50/Alt
12150 Road 36, 559-645-3580
Kuljeet Mann, admin.

Madera County Office of Education 800/
1105 S Madera Ave 93637 559-673-6051
Cecilia Massetti Ed.D., supt. Fax 673-5569
www.maderacoe.k12.ca.us
Enterprise Secondary S 100/Alt
1105 S Madera Ave 93637 559-661-3570
Alyson Crafton, prin. Fax 673-5569

Madera USD 19,800/K-12
1902 Howard Rd 93637 559-675-4500
Edward Gonzalez, supt. Fax 661-7764
www.maderausd.org
Desmond MS 900/7-8
26490 Martin St 93638 559-664-1775
Marvin Baker, prin. Fax 664-1308
Furman HS 200/Alt
955 W Pecan Ave 93637 559-675-4482
David Raygoza, prin. Fax 675-3811
Jefferson MS 1,000/7-8
1407 Sunset Ave 93637 559-673-9286
Jesse Carrasco, prin. Fax 673-6930
King MS 700/7-8
601 Lilly St 93638 559-674-4681
Sabrina Rodriquez, prin. Fax 674-4261
Madera HS North Campus 2,200/9-12
200 S L St 93637 559-675-4444
Alan Hollman, prin. Fax 675-4531
Madera HS South Campus 2,700/9-12
705 W Pecan Ave 93637 559-675-4450
Oracio Rodriguez, prin. Fax 675-9985
Mountain Vista HS Alt
29551 Avenue 8 93637 559-675-4580
Aimee Anderson, prin. Fax 674-2566
Ripperdan Community Day S Alt
26133 Avenue 7 93637 559-674-0059
Fermin Guzman, prin. Fax 674-7422
Madera Adult S Adult
955 W Pecan Ave 93637 559-675-4425
David Raygoza, prin. Fax 675-4562

---

Madera Beauty College Post-Sec.
325 N Gateway Dr 93637 559-673-9201

**Madison, Yolo, Pop. 493**
Esparto USD
Supt. — See Esparto
Madison Community HS 50/Alt
17923 Stephens St 95653 530-787-3165
Veronica Michael, prin. Fax 662-1521

**Mad River, Trinity, Pop. 402**
Southern Trinity JUSD 100/K-12
680 Van Duzen Rd, 707-574-6237
Peggy Canale, supt. Fax 574-6538
www.southerntrinityusd.org
Mt. Lassic HS 50/Alt
600 Van Duzen Rd, 707-574-6239
Peggy Canale, prin. Fax 574-6538
Southern Trinity HS 50/9-12
600 Van Duzen Rd, 707-574-6239
Peggy Canale, prin. Fax 574-1067

**Magalia, Butte, Pop. 10,902**
Paradise USD
Supt. — See Paradise
Ridgeview HS 100/Alt
13665 Skyway 95954 530-872-6478
Michael Lerch, prin. Fax 872-6481

Pines Christian Academy 50/PK-12
PO Box 1821 95954 530-873-1412
Douglas Crowder, head sch

**Malibu, Los Angeles, Pop. 12,292**
Santa Monica-Malibu USD
Supt. — See Santa Monica
Malibu MSHS 1,200/6-12
30215 Morning View Dr 90265 310-457-6801
Brandon Gallagher, prin. Fax 457-4984

Pepperdine University Post-Sec.
24255 Pacific Coast Hwy 90263 310-506-4000

**Mammoth Lakes, Mono, Pop. 8,104**
Mammoth USD 1,200/K-12
PO Box 3509 93546 760-934-6802
Lois Klein, supt. Fax 934-6803
www.mammothusd.org
Mammoth HS 300/9-12
PO Box 3149 93546 760-934-8541
Chris Powell, prin. Fax 934-3008
Mammoth MS 300/6-8
PO Box 2429 93546 760-934-7072
Annie Rinaldi, prin. Fax 934-7073
Sierra Continuation HS 50/Alt
PO Box 3509 93546 760-934-3702
Lois Klein, supt. Fax 924-0062

Mono County Office of Education
Supt. — See Bridgeport
Work Community S 200/Alt
451 Sierra Park Rd 93546 760-934-0031
Janet Hunt, prin. Fax 934-1443
Mono County Adult S Adult
451 Sierra Park Rd 93546 760-934-0031
Janet Hunt, prin. Fax 934-1443

**Manhattan Beach, Los Angeles, Pop. 33,631**
Manhattan Beach USD 7,200/PK-12
325 S Peck Ave 90266 310-318-7345
Dr. Michael Matthews, supt. Fax 303-3822
www.mbusd.org
Manhattan Beach MS 1,400/6-8
325 S Peck Ave 90266 310-545-4878
John Jackson, prin. Fax 303-3829
Mira Costa HS 2,400/9-12
325 S Peck Ave 90266 310-318-7337
Dr. Ben Dale, prin. Fax 303-3814

**Manteca, San Joaquin, Pop. 64,370**
Manteca USD 22,800/K-12
PO Box 32 95336 209-825-3200
Jason Messer, supt. Fax 858-7570
www.mantecausd.net
Calla Continuation HS 200/Alt
130 S Austin Rd 95336 209-858-7230
Kathy Crouse, prin. Fax 858-7505
East Union HS 1,500/9-12
1700 N Union Rd 95336 209-858-7270
Raul Mora, prin. Fax 825-3148
Manteca Community Day S 50/Alt
737 W Yosemite Ave 95337 209-858-7380
Gerald Braxton, prin. Fax 858-7526
Manteca HS 1,600/9-12
450 E Yosemite Ave 95336 209-858-7340
Frank Gonzales, prin. Fax 825-3158
Manteca Unified Vocational Academy Vo/Tech
2271 W Louise Ave 95337 209-858-7460
Diane Medeiros, prin. Fax 858-7524
McParland S 800/3-8
1601 Northgate Dr 95336 209-858-7290
Dale Borgeson, prin. Fax 858-7510
Sierra HS 1,400/9-12
1700 Thomas St 95337 209-858-7410
Steve Clark, prin. Fax 825-3198
Manteca Adult S Adult
2271 W Louise Ave 95337 209-858-7330
Diane Medeiros, prin. Fax 858-7524
Other Schools – See Lathrop, Stockton

**Maricopa, Kern, Pop. 1,126**
Maricopa USD 1,100/K-12
955 Stanislaus St 93252 661-769-8231
Scott Meier, supt. Fax 769-8168
maricopaschools.org
Maricopa HS 100/9-12
955 Stanislaus St 93252 661-769-8231
Scott Meier, prin. Fax 769-8168
Maricopa MS 6-8
955 Stanislaus St 93252 661-769-8231
Fax 769-8168

**Marina, Monterey, Pop. 17,783**
Monterey Peninsula USD
Supt. — See Monterey
Los Arboles MS 600/6-8
294 Hillcrest Ave 93933 831-384-3550
Rebecca Tyson, prin. Fax 384-6353
Marina HS 600/9-12
298 Patton Pkwy 93933 831-583-2060
Joseph Williams, prin. Fax 384-2288

**Mariposa, Mariposa, Pop. 2,123**
Mariposa County Office of Education 50/
PO Box 8 95338 209-742-0250
Robin Hopper, supt. Fax 966-4549
www.mariposa.k12.ca.us
Community S, 5171 Silva Rd 95338 50/Alt
Jeff Aranguena, admin. 209-742-0290
Fremont Community Day 50/Alt
4802 State Highway 140 95338 209-742-0290
Jeff Aranguena, prin. Fax 742-0292

Mariposa County USD 1,600/K-12
PO Box 8 95338 209-742-0250
Robin Hopper, supt. Fax 966-4549
www.mariposa.k12.ca.us/
Mariposa County HS 600/9-12
PO Box 127 95338 209-742-0260
Celeste Azevedo, prin. Fax 742-0264
Other Schools – See Coulterville, Yosemite National Park

Summit Christian S 50/K-12
PO Box 1445 95338 209-966-7636
Kristin Montgomery, dir.

**Markleeville, Alpine, Pop. 204**
Alpine County Office of Education 50/
43 Hawkside Dr 96120 530-694-2230
Patrick Traynor, supt. Fax 694-2379
www.alpinecoe.k12.ca.us
Alpine County Opportunity S 50/Alt
43 Hawkside Dr 96120 530-694-2230
Patrick Traynor, prin. Fax 694-2379

Alpine County USD 100/K-12
43 Hawkside Dr 96120 530-694-2230
Patrick Traynor, supt. Fax 694-2379
www.alpinecoe.k12.ca.us
Alpine County Community Day S Alt
43 Hawkside Dr 96120 530-694-9423
Patrick Traynor, prin.

**Martinez, Contra Costa, Pop. 34,098**
Contra Costa County Office of Education
Supt. — See Pleasant Hill
Golden Gate Community S 100/Alt
222 Glacier Dr 94553 925-313-2950
Edward Brown, prin. Fax 313-2955

Martinez USD 4,100/K-12
921 Susana St 94553 925-335-5800
Rami Muth, supt. Fax 335-5961
www.martinezusd.net
Alhambra HS 1,300/9-12
150 E St 94553 925-335-5810
Tom Doppe, prin. Fax 335-5870
Briones S 100/K-12
614 F St 94553 925-228-9232
Lori O'Connor, prin. Fax 335-5889
Martinez Continuation HS 100/Alt
614 F St 94553 925-228-9232
Lori O'Connor, prin. Fax 335-5889
Martinez JHS 900/6-8
1600 Court St 94553 925-335-5820
Michael DeFrancesco, prin. Fax 335-5829
Martinez Adult Center Adult
600 F St 94553 925-228-3276
Kathy Farwell, dir. Fax 228-6989

Martinez Adult Education Post-Sec.
600 F St 94553 925-228-3276

**Marysville, Yuba, Pop. 11,483**
Marysville JUSD 9,500/K-12
1919 B St 95901 530-741-6000
Gay Todd Ed.D., supt. Fax 741-7894
www.mjusd.com
Foothill IS 200/7-8
5351 Fruitland Rd 95901 530-741-6130
Kathleen Hansen, prin. Fax 741-6017
Marysville Community Day S Alt
1919 B St 95901 530-749-6919
Ginger Rogers, prin.
Marysville HS 900/9-12
12 E 18th St 95901 530-741-6180
Gary Cena, prin. Fax 741-7828
McKenney IS 500/6-8
1904 Huston St 95901 530-741-6187
Shevaun Mathews, prin. Fax 741-6004
Other Schools – See Olivehurst

Yuba County Office of Education 600/
935 14th St 95901 530-749-4900
Josh Harris, supt. Fax 741-6500
www.yuba.net/
Mathews Community S 100/Alt
1010 I St 95901 530-741-6349
Christopher Reyna, prin.

Yuba College Post-Sec.
2088 N Beale Rd 95901 530-741-6700

**Mather, Sacramento, Pop. 4,082**
Folsom-Cordova USD
Supt. — See Rancho Cordova
Mather Youth Academy 100/Alt
4420 Monhegan Way 95655 916-363-5019
Allen Sims, coord. Fax 364-1637

Regional Occupational Center & Program
Supt. — None
Sacramento County ROP Vo/Tech
10474 Mather Blvd 95655 916-228-2500
Tim Taylor, admin. Fax 228-2459

Sacramento County Office of Education 300/
10474 Mather Blvd 95655 916-228-2500
David Gordon, supt. Fax 228-2403
www.scoe.net
Other Schools – See Sacramento

**Maxwell, Colusa, Pop. 1,095**
Maxwell USD 300/K-12
PO Box 788 95955 530-438-2291
Rich Rhodes, supt. Fax 438-2693
www.maxwell.k12.ca.us
Maxwell HS 100/7-12
PO Box 788 95955 530-438-2291
Rich Rhodes, prin. Fax 438-2693

**Maywood, Los Angeles, Pop. 27,328**
Los Angeles USD
Supt. — See Los Angeles
Maywood Academy 1,300/9-12
6125 Pine Ave 90270 323-838-6000
Felipe Caceres, prin. Fax 560-9206

**Mendocino, Mendocino, Pop. 866**
Mendocino USD 500/K-12
PO Box 1154 95460 707-937-5868
Jason Morse, supt. Fax 937-0714
www.mendocinousd.org/
Mendocino Alternative S 50/Alt
PO Box 1154 95460 707-937-3703
Gail Dickenson, prin. Fax 937-6806
Mendocino HS 200/9-12
PO Box 226 95460 707-937-5871
Gail Dickenson, prin. Fax 937-1552
Mendocino Sunrise HS 50/Alt
PO Box 226 95460 707-937-9232
Gail Dickenson, prin. Fax 937-5629

**Mendota, Fresno, Pop. 10,983**
Mendota USD 2,900/K-12
115 McCabe Ave 93640 559-655-4942
Paul Lopez, supt. Fax 655-4944
www.musdaztecs.com
Mendota Continuation HS 50/Alt
211 Smoot Ave 93640 559-655-4471
Rebecca Gamez, prin. Fax 655-2440
Mendota HS 700/9-12
1200 Belmont Ave 93640 559-655-1993
Carlos Arredondo, prin. Fax 655-0223
Mendota JHS 400/7-8
1258 Belmont Ave 93640 559-655-4301
Travis Kirby, prin. Fax 655-1229

**Menifee, Riverside, Pop. 75,080**
Menifee UNESD 9,200/PK-12
30205 Menifee Rd 92584 951-672-1851
Steve Kennedy Ed.D., supt. Fax 672-1385
www.menifeeusd.org
Bell Mountain MS 1,100/6-8
28525 La Piedra Rd 92584 951-301-8496
Ernie Lizzarraga, prin. Fax 301-5286
Christensen MS 900/6-8
27625 Sherman Rd, 951-679-8356
Michelle Randall, prin. Fax 679-4090
Menifee Valley MS 900/6-8
26255 Garbani Rd 92584 951-672-6400
Ed Resnick, prin. Fax 672-6415

Perris UNHSD
Supt. — See Perris
Paloma Valley HS 2,700/9-12
31375 Bradley Rd 92584 951-672-6030
Brian Morris, prin. Fax 672-6037

Romoland ESD
Supt. — See Homeland
Chase MS 6-8
28100 Calm Horizon Dr, 951-566-4400
Chris Hernandez, prin. Fax 639-5943

Revival Christian Academy 100/K-12
29220 Scott Rd 92584 951-246-5657
Diana Miller, dir. Fax 672-9187

**Menlo Park, San Mateo, Pop. 30,400**
Las Lomitas ESD 1,400/K-8
1011 Altschul Ave 94025 650-854-2880
Lisa Cesario, supt. Fax 854-0882
www.llesd.k12.ca.us
La Entrada MS 700/4-8
2200 Sharon Rd 94025 650-854-3962
Shannon Potts, prin. Fax 854-5947

Menlo Park City ESD
Supt. — See Atherton
Hillview MS 800/6-8
1100 Elder Ave 94025 650-326-4341
Willy Haug, prin. Fax 325-3861

Sequoia UNHSD
Supt. — See Redwood City
Sequoia District Adult S Adult
3247 Middlefield Rd 94025 650-306-8866
Lionel de Maine, admin. Fax 365-2420

Mid-Peninsula HS 100/9-12
1340 Willow Rd 94025 650-321-1991
Dr. Douglas Thompson, head sch Fax 321-9921
St. Patrick's Seminary & University Post-Sec.
320 Middlefield Rd 94025 650-325-5621

**Merced, Merced, Pop. 76,840**
Merced City ESD 10,800/K-8
444 W 23rd St 95340 209-385-6600
Rosemary Parga Duran Ed.D., supt. Fax 385-6316
www.mcsd.k12.ca.us
Cruickshank MS 900/7-8
601 Mercy Ave 95340 209-385-6330
Jill Settera, prin. Fax 385-6338
Hoover MS 900/7-8
800 E 26th St 95340 209-385-6631
Julie Rivard, prin. Fax 385-6799
Rivera MS 800/7-8
945 Buena Vista Dr 95348 209-385-6680
Sergio Mendez, prin. Fax 385-6702
Tenaya MS 900/7-8
760 W 8th St 95341 209-385-6687
Anthony Arista, prin. Fax 385-6365

Merced County Office of Education 1,400/
632 W 13th St 95341 209-381-6600
Steven Gomes Ed.D., supt. Fax 381-6767
www.mcoe.org
Valley Community S 500/Alt
632 W 13th St 95341 209-381-4500
Derrek Dean, prin. Fax 385-8308

Other Schools – See Atwater, Livingston, Los Banos

Merced UNHSD
Supt. — See Atwater
El Capitan HS 9-12
100 Farmland Ave 95340 209-384-5500
Anthony Johnson, prin.
Golden Valley HS 2,100/9-12
PO Box 2188 95344 209-385-8000
Kevin Swartwood, prin. Fax 385-8002
Independence HS 200/Alt
1900 G St 95340 209-385-6515
Cristi Schumacher, prin. Fax 385-6435
Merced HS 2,800/9-12
PO Box 2167 95344 209-385-6465
John Olson, prin. Fax 385-6556
Sequoia HS 100/Alt
123 E 18th St 95340 209-385-8950
Jon Schaefer, prin. Fax 385-6535
Yosemite Continuation HS 300/Alt
1900 G St 95340 209-385-6425
Cristi Schumacher, prin. Fax 385-6435
Merced Adult S Adult
50 E 20th St 95340 209-385-6524
Debbie Glass, prin. Fax 385-6430

Regional Occupational Center & Program
Supt. — None
Merced County ROP Vo/Tech
632 W 13th St 95341 209-381-6677
Holly Newlon, supt. Fax 381-6766

Weaver UNSD 2,600/PK-8
3076 E Childs Ave 95341 209-723-7606
John Curry, supt. Fax 725-7128
www.weaverusd.k12.ca.us
Weaver MS 800/6-8
3076 E Childs Ave 95341 209-723-2174
Elias Villa M.A., prin. Fax 725-7116

---

Merced College Post-Sec.
3600 M St 95348 209-384-6000
Sierra College of Beauty Post-Sec.
1340 W 18th St 95340 209-723-2989
Stone Ridge Christian HS 100/9-12
500 Buena Vista Dr 95348 209-386-0322
Sandra Mobley, admin. Fax 386-0334
University of California Post-Sec.
5200 N Lake Rd 95343 209-228-4400
WestMed College-Merced Post-Sec.
330 E Yosemite Ave 95340 209-386-6300

**Middletown, Lake, Pop. 1,281**
Middletown USD 1,700/K-12
20932 Big Canyon Rd 95461 707-987-4100
Catherine Stone, supt. Fax 987-4105
www.middletownusd.org
Loconoma Vally HS 50/Alt
20932 Big Canyon Rd 95461 707-987-4170
Catherine Stone, prin. Fax 987-4171
Middletown HS 500/9-12
20932 Big Canyon Rd 95461 707-987-4140
Bill Roderick, prin. Fax 987-4146
Middletown MS 300/7-8
20932 Big Canyon Rd 95461 707-987-4160
Mitch Tucker, prin. Fax 987-4162

---

Middletown Christian S 100/K-12
PO Box 989 95461 707-987-2556
Anna Mayfield, admin. Fax 987-2126

**Midway City, Orange, Pop. 8,289**

---

Huntington College of Dental Technology Post-Sec.
14848 Monroe St 92655

**Millbrae, San Mateo, Pop. 20,615**
Millbrae ESD 2,300/K-8
555 Richmond Dr 94030 650-697-5693
Linda Luna, supt. Fax 697-6865
www.millbraeschooldistrict.org
Taylor MS 900/6-8
850 Taylor Blvd 94030 650-697-4096
Alicia Magallanes, prin. Fax 697-8435

San Mateo UNHSD
Supt. — See San Mateo
Mills HS 1,300/9-12
400 Murchison Dr 94030 650-558-2599
Paul Belzer, prin. Fax 558-2552

**Mill Valley, Marin, Pop. 13,420**
Mill Valley ESD 3,000/K-8
411 Sycamore Ave 94941 415-389-7700
Paul Johnson, supt. Fax 389-7773
www.mvschools.org
Mill Valley MS 900/6-8
425 Sycamore Ave 94941 415-389-7711
Anna Lazzarini, prin. Fax 389-7780

Tamalpais UNHSD
Supt. — See Larkspur
Tamalpais HS 1,200/9-12
700 Miller Ave 94941 415-388-3292
Julie Synyard, prin. Fax 380-3526

---

Golden Gate Baptist Theological Seminary Post-Sec.
201 Seminary Dr 94941 415-380-1300

**Milpitas, Santa Clara, Pop. 64,272**
Milpitas USD 10,100/PK-12
1331 E Calaveras Blvd 95035 408-635-2600
Cary Matsuoka, supt. Fax 635-2616
www.musd.org
Calaveras Hills HS 200/Alt
1331 E Calaveras Blvd 95035 408-635-2690
Carl Stice, prin. Fax 635-2615
Milpitas HS 3,000/9-12
1285 Escuela Pkwy 95035 408-635-2800
Cheryl Lawton, prin. Fax 635-2851
Rancho Milpitas MS 700/7-8
1915 Yellowstone Ave 95035 408-635-2656
Casey McMurray, prin. Fax 635-2661
Russell MS 700/7-8
1500 Escuela Pkwy 95035 408-635-2864
Damon James, prin. Fax 635-2869
Milpitas Adult S Adult
1331 E Calaveras Blvd 95035 408-635-2692
Usha Narayanan, prin. Fax 635-2611

---

Heald College Post-Sec.
341 Great Mall Pkwy 95035 408-934-4900

**Miranda, Humboldt, Pop. 496**
Southern Humbolt JUSD 700/PK-12
PO Box 650 95553 707-943-1789
Catherine Scott, supt. Fax 943-1921
www.humboldt.k12.ca.us/sohumb_usd/school/
Miranda JHS 100/7-8
PO Box 188 95553 707-943-3144
Jim Stewart, prin. Fax 943-3129
Osprey Learning Center 50/Alt
PO Box 188 95553 707-943-3144
Jim Stewart, prin. Fax 943-3627
South Fork HS 200/9-12
PO Box 188 95553 707-943-3144
Jim Stewart, prin. Fax 943-3129

**Mission Hills, Los Angeles, Pop. 3,460**
Los Angeles USD
Supt. — See Los Angeles
North Valley Occupational Center Vo/Tech
11450 Sharp Ave 91345 818-365-9645
Carlynn Huddleston, prin. Fax 365-2695

---

Bishop Alemany HS 1,700/9-12
11111 Alemany Dr 91345 818-363-3925
David Chambers, prin. Fax 365-2064

**Mission Viejo, Orange, Pop. 89,770**
Capistrano USD
Supt. — See San Juan Capistrano
Capistrano Valley HS 2,700/9-12
26301 Via Escolar 92692 949-364-6100
Josh Hill, prin. Fax 347-0514
Newhart MS 1,400/6-8
25001 Veterans Way 92692 949-855-0162
Jeff Jones, prin. Fax 770-1262

Saddleback Valley USD 30,900/PK-12
25631 Peter A Hartman Way 92691 949-586-1234
Clint Harwick Ed.D., supt. Fax 951-0994
svwp.svusd.org
La Paz IS 1,000/7-8
25151 Pradera Dr 92691 949-830-1720
Jean Carroll, prin. Fax 830-3320
Los Alisos IS 900/7-8
25171 Moor Ave 92691 949-830-9700
Rich Freda, prin. Fax 472-3968
Mira Monte Alternative HS 100/Alt
25632 Peter A Hartman Way 92691 949-830-8857
Darrell De Leon, prin. Fax 462-0352
Mission Viejo HS 2,600/9-12
25025 Chrisanta Dr 92691 949-837-7722
Ray Gatfield, prin. Fax 830-0782
Silverado Continuation HS 300/Alt
25632 Peter A Hartman Way 92691 949-586-8800
David Gordon, prin. Fax 583-9865
Trabuco Hills HS 3,200/9-12
27501 Mustang Run 92691 949-768-1934
Craig Collins, prin. Fax 588-0763
Adult Education Center Adult
25598 Peter A Hartman Way 92691 949-837-8830
David Gordon, dean Fax 837-1921
Other Schools – See Laguna Hills, Lake Forest, Rancho Santa Margarita

---

Master's Academy 50/K-12
23052 Alicia Pkwy Ste H107 92692 949-500-3059
Rebekah Milligan, admin. Fax 888-7420
Saddleback College Post-Sec.
28000 Marguerite Pkwy 92692 949-582-4500

**Modesto, Stanislaus, Pop. 192,307**
Empire UNESD 2,900/PK-8
116 N McClure Rd 95357 209-521-2800
David Garcia, supt. Fax 526-6421
www.empire.k12.ca.us
Glick MS 500/7-8
400 Frazine Rd 95357 209-577-3945
C.W. Smith, prin. Fax 577-3975

Modesto CSD 29,900/K-12
426 Locust St 95351 209-576-4011
Pamela Able, supt. Fax 576-4184
www.monet.k12.ca.us
Beyer HS 2,000/9-12
1717 Sylvan Ave 95355 209-576-4311
Dan park, prin. Fax 576-4352
Davis HS 1,800/9-12
1200 W Rumble Rd 95350 209-576-4500
Mike Rich, prin. Fax 576-4028
Downey HS 2,000/9-12
1000 Coffee Rd 95355 209-576-4211
Richard Baum, prin. Fax 576-4258
Elliott Alternative & Continuing Educ 700/Alt
1440 Sunrise Ave 95350 209-569-2890
David Houck, prin. Fax 576-4863
Enochs HS 2,500/9-12
3201 Sylvan Ave 95355 209-550-3400
Deborah Rowe, prin. Fax 550-3413
Gregori HS 1,400/9-12
3701 Pirrone Rd 95356 209-550-3420
Jeff Albritton, prin. Fax 550-3433
Hanshaw MS 700/7-8
1725 Las Vegas St 95358 209-576-4847
Sam DeLaRosa, prin. Fax 576-4723
Johansen HS 1,800/9-12
641 Norseman Dr 95357 209-576-4702
Nathan Schar, prin. Fax 576-4752
La Loma JHS 700/7-8
1800 Encina Ave 95354 209-576-4627
Marie McDonald, prin. Fax 576-4631
Modesto HS 2,500/9-12
18 H St 95351 209-576-4401
Jason Manning, prin. Fax 576-4434
Roosevelt JHS 800/7-8
1330 College Ave 95350 209-576-4871
David Sanchez, prin. Fax 569-2713
Twain JHS 800/7-8
707 S Emerald Ave 95351 209-576-4814
Mike Berhorst, prin. Fax 576-4843

Regional Occupational Center & Program
Supt. — None
Yosemite ROP, 1100 H St 95354 Vo/Tech
Cindy Young, admin. 209-238-1500

Stanislaus County Office of Education 1,300/
1100 H St 95354 209-238-1700
Tom Changnon, supt. Fax 238-4201
www.stancoe.org/
Petersen Alternative Center 300/Alt
715 13th St 95354 209-238-6717
John Luis, prin. Fax 238-6796
Other Schools – See Ceres, Turlock

Stanislaus UNESD 3,100/K-8
2410 Janna Ave 95350 209-529-9546
Britta Skavdahl, supt. Fax 529-0243
www.stanunion.k12.ca.us
Prescott JHS 600/7-8
2243 W Rumble Rd 95350 209-529-9892
Harjinder Singh, prin. Fax 529-4406

Sylvan Union ESD 8,100/K-8
605 Sylvan Ave 95350 209-574-5000
Debra Hendricks, supt. Fax 524-2672
www.sylvan.k12.ca.us
Savage MS 1,100/6-8
1900 Maid Mariane Ln 95355 209-552-3300
Mitch Wood, prin. Fax 552-3305
Somerset MS 900/6-8
1037 Floyd Ave 95350 209-574-5300
Mary Smyth, prin. Fax 529-1110
Ustach MS 1,000/6-8
2701 Kodiak Dr 95355 209-552-3000
Sean Greene, prin. Fax 552-3010

---

Adrian's Beauty College Post-Sec.
124 Floyd Ave 95350 209-526-2040
Big Valley Christian S 700/PK-12
4040 Tully Rd Ste D 95356 209-527-3481
Tim Cannon, pres. Fax 571-4810
Brethren Heritage S 100/K-12
3549 Dakota Ave 95358 209-543-7860
James Shuman, prin. Fax 543-7862
California Beauty College Post-Sec.
1115 15th St 95354 209-524-5184
Central Catholic HS 400/9-12
200 S Carpenter Rd 95351 209-524-9611
Russell Antracoli, prin. Fax 524-4913
Community Business College Post-Sec.
3800 McHenry Ave 95356 209-529-3648
Computer Tutor Business & Technical Inst Post-Sec.
4306 Sisk Rd 95356 209-545-5200
Institute of Technology - Modesto Campus Post-Sec.
5601 Stoddard Rd 95356 209-545-3100
Modesto Christian HS 300/9-12
5755 Sisk Rd 95356 209-343-2330
Charles Howell, prin. Fax 545-0584
Modesto Christian MS 100/6-8
5901 Sisk Rd 95356 209-529-5510
Rev. Matt Diehl, prin. Fax 545-1369
Modesto Junior College Post-Sec.
435 College Ave 95350 209-575-6550
Western Pacific Truck School Post-Sec.
2316 Nickerson Dr 95358 209-531-9226

**Mojave, Kern, Pop. 4,110**
Mojave USD 2,400/K-12
3500 Douglas Ave 93501 661-824-4001
Dr. Aaron Haughton, supt. Fax 824-2686
www.mojave.k12.ca.us/
Mojave JSHS 300/7-12
15732 O St 93501 661-824-4088
Scott Small, prin. Fax 824-3406
Other Schools – See California City

Regional Occupational Center & Program
Supt. — None
Kern County ROP Vo/Tech
15926 K St 93501 661-824-9313
Tom Anspach, admin. Fax 824-9316

---

National Test Pilot School Post-Sec.
PO Box 658 93502 661-824-2977

**Monrovia, Los Angeles, Pop. 35,498**
Monrovia USD 5,900/PK-12
325 E Huntington Dr 91016 626-471-2000
Dr. Katherine F. Thorossian, supt. Fax 471-2077
www.monroviaschools.net
Canyon Oaks HS 100/Alt
930 Royal Oaks Dr 91016 626-471-3000
Flint Fertig, dir. Fax 471-3033
Clifton MS 700/6-8
226 S Ivy Ave 91016 626-471-2600
Jennifer Jackson, prin. Fax 471-2610
Monrovia HS 1,700/9-12
845 W Colorado Blvd 91016 626-471-2800
Kirk McGinnis, prin. Fax 471-2810

Mountain Park S 100/Alt
950 S Mountain Ave 91016 626-471-3029
Flint Fertig, dir. Fax 471-3077
Santa Fe MS 600/6-8
148 W Duarte Rd 91016 626-471-2700
Dr. Caroline Sweeney, prin. Fax 471-2710
Monrovia Community Adult Education Adult
920 S Mountain Ave 91016 626-471-3035
Flint Fertig, dir. Fax 471-3036

---

Mt. Sierra College Post-Sec.
101 E Huntington Dr 91016 626-873-2144

**Montclair, San Bernardino, Pop. 36,107**

Chaffey JUNHSD
Supt. — See Ontario
Montclair HS 3,300/9-12
4725 Benito St 91763 909-621-6781
Martin Alvarado, prin. Fax 621-1882

Ontario-Montclair SD
Supt. — See Ontario
Serrano MS 700/7-8
4725 San Jose St 91763 909-624-0029
Mauricio Gormaz, prin. Fax 445-1687
Vernon MS 800/7-8
9775 Vernon Ave 91763 909-624-5036
Sarah Niemann, prin. Fax 445-1720

San Bernardino Co. Office of Education
Supt. — See San Bernardino
West End Community S 200/Alt
5033 Holt Blvd 91763 909-447-4501
Judi Benjamin, dir. Fax 447-4391

**Montebello, Los Angeles, Pop. 62,028**

Montebello USD 30,600/K-12
123 S Montebello Blvd 90640 323-887-7900
Susanna Contreras Smith, supt. Fax 887-5890
www.montebello.k12.ca.us
Applied Technology Center Vo/Tech
1200 W Mines Ave 90640 323-248-2500
Sterling Schubert, prin. Fax 727-0739
Eastmont IS 1,100/6-8
400 Bradshawe St 90640 323-721-5133
Cecilia Ramirez, prin. Fax 887-3058
La Merced IS 1,300/6-8
215 E Avenida De La Merced 90640 323-722-7262
Alice Jacquez, prin. Fax 887-5816
Montebello Community Day S 100/Alt
123 S Montebello Blvd 90640 323-887-7900
Benedetta Kennedy, dir. Fax 887-5895
Montebello HS 3,300/9-12
2100 W Cleveland Ave 90640 323-728-0121
Helen Meltzer, prin. Fax 887-7848
Montebello IS 1,300/6-8
1600 W Whittier Blvd 90640 323-721-5111
Leticia Alvidrez, prin. Fax 887-3192
Schurr HS 3,300/9-12
820 N Wilcox Ave 90640 323-887-3090
Francisco Arregui, prin. Fax 887-3097
Vail Continuation HS 400/Alt
1230 S Vail Ave 90640 323-728-1940
Horacio Perez, prin. Fax 887-3004
Montebello Adult Education Adult
149 N 21st St 90640 323-887-7844
Joe Torres, prin. Fax 724-8175
Schurr Adult Education Adult
820 N Wilcox Ave 90640 323-887-3088
Luz Hernandez, prin. Fax 887-3098
Other Schools – See Bell Gardens, Monterey Park

---

Cantwell-Sacred Heart of Mary HS 500/9-12
329 N Garfield Ave 90640 323-887-2066
Robert Fraley, prin. Fax 724-4332
Montebello Beauty College Post-Sec.
2201 W Whittier Blvd 90640 323-727-7851

**Monterey, Monterey, Pop. 26,593**

Monterey Peninsula USD 10,900/PK-12
PO Box 1031 93942 831-645-1200
Dr. Daniel Diffenbaugh, supt. Fax 649-4175
www.mpusd.k12.ca.us
Colton MS 700/6-8
100 Toda Vis 93940 831-649-1951
Janet Mikkelsen, prin. Fax 649-4692
Monterey HS 1,300/9-12
101 Herrmann Dr 93940 831-392-3801
Marcie Plummer, prin. Fax 649-1154
Other Schools – See Marina, Seaside

---

Monterey Institute of Intl. Studies Post-Sec.
460 Pierce St 93940 831-647-4100
Monterey Peninsula College Post-Sec.
980 Fremont St 93940 831-646-4000
Santa Catalina S 500/PK-12
1500 Mark Thomas Dr 93940 831-655-9300
Sr. Claire Barone, head sch Fax 649-3056
Trinity Christian HS 100/9-12
601 E Franklin St 93940 831-656-9434
Rick Fitzgerald, prin. Fax 656-9670
York S 200/8-12
9501 York Rd 93940 831-372-7338
Chuck Harmon, head sch Fax 372-8055

**Monterey Park, Los Angeles, Pop. 59,435**

Los Angeles County Office of Education
Supt. — See Downey
East Los Angeles Community Day S 300/Alt
1260 Monterey Pass Rd 91754 323-262-2263
Ray Donahue, prin.

Montebello USD
Supt. — See Montebello
Macy IS 900/6-8
2101 Lupine Ave 91755 323-722-0260
Jacinto Zavala, prin. Fax 887-3068

---

East Los Angeles College Post-Sec.
1301 Avenida Cesar Chavez 91754 323-265-8650

**Montrose, See La Crescenta**

---

St. Monica Academy 200/1-12
2361 Del Mar Rd 91020 818-369-7310
Marguerite Grimm, hdmstr. Fax 369-7305

**Moorpark, Ventura, Pop. 33,338**

Moorpark USD 7,000/K-12
5297 Maureen Ln 93021 805-378-6300
Dr. Kelli Hays, supt. Fax 529-8592
www.mrpk.org
Chaparral MS 700/6-8
280 Poindexter Ave 93021 805-378-6302
Joshua Stephenson, prin. Fax 378-6324
Community Continuation HS 100/Alt
4500 Tierra Rejada Rd 93021 805-378-6304
Carrie Pentis, prin. Fax 531-6448
Mesa Verde MS 800/6-8
14000 Peach Hill Rd 93021 805-378-6309
Adam Rauch, prin. Fax 531-6622
Moorpark HS 2,200/9-12
4500 Tierra Rejada Rd 93021 805-378-6305
Carrie Pentis, prin. Fax 531-6498
HS at Moorpark College 100/Alt
7075 Campus Rd 93021 805-378-1444
Ruby Delery, prin. Fax 378-1440

---

Moorpark College Post-Sec.
7075 Campus Rd 93021 805-378-1400

**Moraga, Contra Costa, Pop. 15,277**

Acalanes UNHSD
Supt. — See Lafayette
Campolindo HS 1,300/9-12
300 Moraga Rd 94556 925-280-3950
John Walker, prin. Fax 280-3951

Moraga ESD 1,800/K-8
1540 School St 94556 925-376-5943
Bruce K. Burns, supt. Fax 376-8132
www.moraga.k12.ca.us
Moraga IS 600/6-8
1010 Camino Pablo 94556 925-376-7206
Joan Danilson, prin. Fax 376-6836

---

St. Mary's College of California Post-Sec.
1928 Saint Marys Rd 94556 925-631-4000

**Moreno Valley, Riverside, Pop. 186,933**

Moreno Valley USD 35,400/K-12
25634 Alessandro Blvd 92553 951-571-7500
Dr. Judy D. White, supt. Fax 571-7550
www.mvusd.net
Alessandro S 100/Alt
23311 Dracaea Ave 92553 951-571-4510
Karen Tomei, admin. Fax 571-4515
Badger Springs MS 1,400/6-8
24750 Delphinium Ave 92553 951-571-4200
Jason Barney, prin. Fax 571-4205
Canyon Springs HS 2,600/9-12
23100 Cougar Canyon Dr 92557 951-571-4760
Tamara Kerr, prin. Fax 571-4765
Landmark MS 1,400/6-8
15261 Legendary Dr 92555 951-571-4220
Vicky Dudek, prin. Fax 571-4225
March Mountain HS 400/Alt
24551 Dracaea Ave 92553 951-571-4800
Sean McMurray, prin. Fax 571-4805
March Valley HS 200/Alt
24551 Dracaea Ave 92553 951-571-4800
Sean McMurray, prin. Fax 571-4805
Moreno Valley HS 2,400/9-12
23300 Cottonwood Ave 92553 951-571-4820
Robert Brough, prin. Fax 571-4825
Mountain View MS 1,300/6-8
13130 Morrison St 92555 951-571-4240
LaToysha Brown, prin. Fax 571-4245
Palm MS 1,300/6-8
11900 Slawson Ave 92557 951-571-4260
Erik Swanson, prin. Fax 571-4265
Sunnymead MS 1,500/6-8
23996 Eucalyptus Ave 92553 951-571-4280
Jennifer Castillo, prin. Fax 571-4285
Valley View HS 2,600/9-12
13135 Nason St 92555 951-571-4850
Kristen Hunter, prin. Fax 571-4855
Vista Del Lago HS 2,600/9-12
15150 Lasselle St 92551 951-571-4880
Dr. Janelle Woodward, prin. Fax 571-4885
Vista Heights MS 1,400/6-8
23049 Old Lake Dr 92557 951-571-4300
Mark Hasson, prin. Fax 571-4305
Moreno Valley Community Adult S Adult
13350 Indian St 92553 951-571-4790
Dr. Tammy Guzzetta, prin. Fax 571-4795

Val Verde USD
Supt. — See Perris
March MS 800/6-8
15800 Indian St 92551 951-490-0430
Jim Owen, prin. Fax 490-0435
Rancho Verde HS 3,200/9-12
17750 Lasselle St 92551 951-485-6200
Ross Godfrey, prin. Fax 485-6218
Val Verde/Student Success Academy 50/Alt
25100 Red Maple Ln 92551 951-443-2450
Vanessa Karwan, prin.
Vista Verde MS 900/6-8
25777 Krameria St 92551 951-485-6270
Esperanza Arce, prin. Fax 485-6278

---

Calvary Chapel Christian S 300/K-12
11960 Pettit St 92555 951-485-6088
Tim Hamilton, prin. Fax 485-6718
Elegante Beauty College Post-Sec.
24741 Alessandro Blvd 92553 951-247-2047
Moreno Valley College Post-Sec.
16130 Lasselle St 92551 951-571-6100
Sage College Post-Sec.
12125 Day St Ste L 92557 951-781-2727
Westech College Post-Sec.
22515 Alessandro Blvd 92553 951-653-8300

**Morgan Hill, Santa Clara, Pop. 36,440**

Morgan Hill USD 9,300/K-12
15600 Concord Cir 95037 408-201-6000
Steve Betando, supt. Fax 201-6007
www.mhusd.org
Britton MS 700/7-8
80 W Central Ave 95037 408-201-6160
Chris Moore, prin. Fax 201-6175
Central HS 200/Alt
85 Tilton Ave 95037 408-201-6300
Vera Gomes, prin. Fax 201-6310
Live Oak HS 1,200/9-12
1505 E Main Ave 95037 408-201-6100
Lloyd Webb, prin. Fax 201-6143
Sobrato HS 1,500/9-12
401 Burnett Ave 95037 408-201-6200
Courtney Macko, prin. Fax 201-6241
Community Adult Education Adult
17940 Monterey St 95037 408-201-6520
Dennis Browne, prin. Fax 201-6525
Other Schools – See San Jose

---

Oakwood S 400/PK-12
105 John Wilson Way 95037 408-782-7177
Fax 782-7138

**Morro Bay, San Luis Obispo, Pop. 10,002**

San Luis Coastal USD
Supt. — See San Luis Obispo
Morro Bay HS 800/9-12
235 Atascadero Rd 93442 805-771-1845
Dr. Kyle Pruitt, prin. Fax 772-5944

**Moss Landing, Monterey, Pop. 194**

North Monterey County USD 4,400/K-12
8142 Moss Landing Rd 95039 831-633-3343
Kari Yeater, supt. Fax 633-2937
www.nmcusd.org
Other Schools – See Castroville, Salinas

**Mountain House, San Joaquin, Pop. 9,039**

Lammersville USD
Supt. — See Tracy
Mountain House HS 500/9-10
1090 S Central Pkwy 95391 209-836-7460
Ben Fobert, admin. Fax 836-7462

**Mountain View, Santa Clara, Pop. 70,771**

Mountain View Whisman SD 4,900/K-8
750A San Pierre Way 94043 650-526-3500
Ayinde Rudolph, supt. Fax 964-8907
www.mvwsd.org
Crittenden MS 600/6-8
1701 Rock St 94043 650-903-6945
Geoffrey Chang, prin. Fax 967-1707
Graham MS 800/6-8
1175 Castro St 94040 650-526-3570
Kim Thompson, prin. Fax 965-9278

Mountain View-Los Altos UNHSD 3,600/9-12
1299 Bryant Ave 94040 650-940-4650
Dr. Jeff Harding, supt. Fax 961-1346
www.mvla.net/
Alta Vista HS 100/Alt
1325 Bryant Ave 94040 650-691-2433
Bill Pierce, prin. Fax 691-2469
Mountain View HS 1,800/9-12
3535 Truman Ave 94040 650-940-4600
David Grissom, prin. Fax 961-6349
Mountain View/Los Altos Adult Education Adult
333 Moffett Blvd 94043 650-940-1333
Keith Moody, dir. Fax 967-4699
Other Schools – See Los Altos

---

German International S of Silicon Valley 400/PK-12
310 Easy St 94043 650-254-0748
Mountain View Academy 100/9-12
360 S Shoreline Blvd 94041 650-967-2324
Gerald Corson, prin. Fax 967-6886
St. Francis HS 1,700/9-12
1885 Miramonte Ave 94040 650-968-1213
Patricia Tennant, prin. Fax 968-1706
Waldorf S of the Peninsula 100/6-12
180 N Rengstorff Ave 94043 650-417-7600
Sue Levine, admin. Fax 417-7676

**Mount Madonna, Santa Cruz**

---

Mount Madonna S 200/PK-12
491 Summit Rd, 408-847-2717
Mary McDonald, head sch Fax 847-5633

**Mount Shasta, Siskiyou, Pop. 3,264**

Siskiyou UNHSD 600/9-12
624 Everitt Memorial Hwy 96067 530-926-3006
Michael Matheson, supt. Fax 926-3113
www.sisuhsd.net/
Jefferson Continuation HS 50/Alt
720 Rockfellow Dr 96067 530-926-0425
Ed Stokes, prin. Fax 926-0586
Mount Shasta HS 300/9-12
710 Everitt Memorial Hwy 96067 530-926-2614
Dr. Jennifer McKinnon, prin. Fax 926-5162
South County Community Day S 50/Alt
720 Rockfellow Dr 96067 530-926-0425
Ed Stokes, prin. Fax 926-0586
Siskiyou Adult S Adult
720 Rockfellow Dr 96067 530-926-0425
Ed Stokes, prin. Fax 926-0586
Other Schools – See Happy Camp, Mc Cloud, Weed

**Murrieta, Riverside, Pop. 99,237**
Murrieta Valley USD 20,500/K-12
41870 McAlby Ct 92562 951-696-1600
Patrick Kelley, supt. Fax 304-1523
www.murrieta.k12.ca.us
Creekside HS 200/Alt
24150 Hayes Ave 92562 951-696-1409
Jared Rogers, prin. Fax 304-1665
McElhinney MS 1,100/6-8
35125 Briggs Rd 92563 951-304-1885
Thomas Patane, prin. Fax 304-1889
Murrieta Mesa HS 2,200/9-12
24801 Monroe Ave 92562 951-677-0568
Steve Ellis, prin. Fax 304-1895
Murrieta Valley HS 2,300/9-12
42200 Nighthawk Way 92562 951-696-1408
Eric Mooney, prin. Fax 304-1803
Shivela MS 1,400/6-8
24515 Lincoln Ave 92562 951-696-1406
Mark Pettengill, prin. Fax 304-1643
Tenaja Canyon Academy 100/Alt
24150 Hayes Ave 92562 951-304-1661
Jared Rogers, dir. Fax 304-1665
Thompson MS 1,800/6-8
24040 Hayes Ave 92562 951-696-1410
Dale Velk, prin. Fax 304-1691
Vista Murrieta HS 3,200/9-12
28251 Clinton Keith Rd 92563 951-894-5750
Mick Wager, prin. Fax 304-1832
Warm Springs MS 1,000/6-8
39245 Calle de Fortuna 92563 951-696-3503
Terry Picchiottino, prin. Fax 304-1611
Murrieta Valley Adult S Adult
24150 Hayes Ave 92562 951-696-3805
Tom Petrich, coord. Fax 304-1664

Temecula Valley USD
Supt. — See Temecula
Bella Vista MS 1,300/6-8
31650 Browning St 92563 951-294-6600
Shery Stewart, prin. Fax 294-6624

---

Calvary Murrieta Christian S 700/PK-12
24225 Monroe Ave 92562 951-834-9190
Desmond Starr, supt. Fax 698-4896
Veritas Evangelical Seminary Post-Sec.
39407 Murrieta Hot Springs 92563 951-698-6389

**Napa, Napa, Pop. 75,253**
Napa County Office of Education 200/
2121 Imola Ave 94559 707-253-6800
Barbara Nemko, supt. Fax 253-6841
www.napacoe.org
Napa County Community S 100/Alt
2121 Imola Ave 94559 707-253-6817
Caroline Wilson, dir. Fax 253-6983

Napa Valley USD 17,900/K-12
2425 Jefferson St 94558 707-253-3511
Patrick Sweeney, supt. Fax 253-3855
www.nvusd.k12.ca.us
Harvest Magnet MS 800/6-8
2449 Old Sonoma Rd 94558 707-259-8866
Carlos Flores, prin. Fax 253-4013
Napa HS 2,100/9-12
2475 Jefferson St 94558 707-253-3711
Annie Petrie, prin. Fax 253-3906
Napa Valley Independent Studies Alt
3310 Linda Vista Ave 94558 707-259-8577
Susan Hartman, prin. Fax 259-8494
New Technology HS Vo/Tech
920 Yount St 94559 707-259-8557
Riley Johnson, prin. Fax 253-8558
Redwood MS 1,000/6-8
3600 Oxford St 94558 707-253-3415
Maryanne Christoffersen, prin. Fax 259-0718
Silverado MS 800/6-8
1133 Coombsville Rd 94558 707-253-3688
Jen Kohl, prin. Fax 253-3830
Valley Oak HS 200/Alt
1600 Myrtle Ave 94558 707-253-3791
Maria Cisneros, prin. Fax 253-3437
Vintage HS 1,900/9-12
1375 Trower Ave 94558 707-253-3601
Mike Pearson, prin. Fax 253-3604
Napa Valley Adult Education Adult
1600 Lincoln Ave 94558 707-253-3594
Rhonda Slota, prin. Fax 253-3828
Other Schools – See American Canyon

Regional Occupational Center & Program
Supt. — None
Napa County ROP Vo/Tech
2121 Imola Ave 94559 707-253-6830
Tammie Holloway, dir. Fax 253-6917

---

Justin-Siena HS 600/9-12
4026 Maher St 94558 707-255-0950
John Bordelon, prin. Fax 255-1334
Kolbe Academy Trinity Prep 100/K-12
2055 Redwood Rd 94558 707-258-9030
Brian Muth, prin. Fax 258-9031
Napa Christian S 100/K-12
2201 Pine St 94559 707-255-5233
Justine Leonie, prin. Fax 255-8530
Napa State Hospital Post-Sec.
2100 Napa Vallejo Hwy 94558 707-253-5428
Napa Valley College Post-Sec.
2277 Napa Vallejo Hwy 94558 707-253-3000

**National City, San Diego, Pop. 57,012**
Sweetwater UNHSD
Supt. — See Chula Vista
Granger JHS 1,100/7-9
2101 Granger Ave 91950 619-472-6000
Richard Carreon, prin. Fax 267-4107
National City MS 700/7-8
1701 D Ave 91950 619-336-2600
Arturo Montano, prin. Fax 474-1756
Sweetwater HS 2,400/9-12
2900 Highland Ave 91950 619-474-9700
Maribel Gavin, prin. Fax 474-7635
National City Adult S Adult
517 Mile of Cars Way 91950 619-336-9400
Bernard Balanay, prin. Fax 336-0641

---

Bellus Academy Post-Sec.
1520 E Plaza Blvd 91950 619-474-6607
ITT Technical Institute Post-Sec.
401 Mile of Cars Way # 100 91950 619-327-1800
San Diego Academy 300/K-12
2800 E 4th St 91950 619-267-9550
Winston Morgan, prin. Fax 267-8662

**Needles, San Bernardino, Pop. 4,672**
Needles USD 700/K-12
1900 Erin Dr 92363 760-326-3891
Mary McNeil, supt. Fax 326-4218
www.needlesusd.org
Educational Training Center 50/Alt
1900 Erin Dr 92363 760-326-2092
Amy Avila, prin. Fax 326-2191
Needles Community Day S Alt
1900 Erin Dr 92363 760-326-3891
Marie Armijo, prin.
Needles HS 300/9-12
1900 Erin Dr 92363 760-326-2191
Amy Avila, prin. Fax 326-1212
Needles MS 200/6-8
1900 Erin Dr 92363 760-326-3894
Amy Avila, prin. Fax 326-4052

**Nevada City, Nevada, Pop. 2,983**
Nevada City ESD 1,000/K-8
800 Hoover Ln 95959 530-265-1820
Trisha Dellis, supt. Fax 265-1822
www.ncsd.k12.ca.us
Seven Hills IS 500/5-8
700 Hoover Ln 95959 530-265-1840
David Figuly, prin. Fax 265-1846

Nevada County Office of Education 3,000/
112 Nevada City Hwy 95959 530-478-6400
Holly Hermansen, supt. Fax 478-6410
www.nevco.org/
Other Schools – See Grass Valley

---

Ananda Living Wisdom S 100/PK-12
14618 Tyler Foote Rd 95959 530-478-7640
Diane Atwell, dir. Fax 478-7646
Woolman Semester S 50/11-12
13075 Woolman Ln 95959 530-273-3183
Gray Horwitz, head sch Fax 273-3183

**Newark, Alameda, Pop. 40,127**
Newark USD 6,600/K-12
5715 Musick Ave 94560 510-818-4103
Dr. Dave Marken, supt. Fax 794-2199
www.newarkunified.org
Bridgepoint Continuation HS 100/Alt
35753 Cedar Blvd 94560 510-818-3200
Marc Lopes, prin. Fax 818-3255
Crossroads HS 50/Alt
35753 Cedar Blvd 94560 510-818-3720
Marc Lopes, prin. Fax 818-3255
Newark JHS 1,000/7-8
6201 Lafayette Ave 94560 510-818-3050
Mark Neal, prin. Fax 794-2079
Newark Memorial HS 1,900/9-12
39375 Cedar Blvd 94560 510-818-4350
Phillip Morales, prin. Fax 794-2120
Newark Adult S Adult
35753 Cedar Blvd 94560 510-818-3700
Marc Lopes, prin. Fax 818-3738

**Newbury Park, See Thousand Oaks**
Conejo Valley USD
Supt. — See Thousand Oaks
Conejo Valley HS Alt/Continuation 200/Alt
1872 Newbury Rd 91320 805-498-6646
Martin Manzer, prin. Fax 498-1423
Newbury Park HS 2,600/9-12
456 N Reino Rd 91320 805-498-3676
Josh Eby, prin. Fax 499-3549
Sequoia MS 1,100/6-8
2855 Borchard Rd 91320 805-498-3617
Steve Lepire, prin. Fax 375-5605

---

Newbury Park Adventist Academy 200/9-12
180 Academy Dr 91320 805-498-2191
Steve Laing, prin. Fax 499-1165

**New Cuyama, Santa Barbara, Pop. 510**
Cuyama JUSD 200/K-12
2300 Highway 166 93254 661-766-2482
F. Paul Chounet, supt. Fax 766-2255
www.cuyamaunified.org
Cuyama Valley HS 100/9-12
2300 Highway 166 93254 661-766-2293
F. Paul Chounet, prin. Fax 766-2593
Sierra Madre Continuation HS 50/Alt
2300 Highway 166 93254 661-766-2293
F. Paul Chounet, prin. Fax 766-2593

**Newhall, See Santa Clarita**
William S. Hart UNHSD
Supt. — See Santa Clarita
Hart HS 2,100/9-12
24825 Newhall Ave 91321 661-259-7575
Dr. Collyn Nielsen, prin. Fax 254-6436
Placerita JHS 1,100/7-8
25015 Newhall Ave 91321 661-259-1551
Jan Hayes-Rennels, prin. Fax 287-9748

---

Master's College and Seminary Post-Sec.
21726 Placerita Canyon Rd 91321 661-259-3540

**Newman, Stanislaus, Pop. 10,029**
Newman-Crows Landing USD 2,300/PK-12
1162 Main St 95360 209-862-2933
Randy Fillpot, supt. Fax 862-0113
www.nclusd.k12.ca.us/
Foothill Community Day S 50/Alt
890 Main St 95360 209-862-2309
Rick Gonzalez, prin. Fax 862-2316
Newman Independent Study 50/Alt
890 Main St 95360 209-862-2309
Rick Gonzalez, prin. Fax 862-2316
Orestimba HS 800/9-12
707 Hardin Rd 95360 209-862-2916
Justin Pruett, prin. Fax 862-0259
Westside Valley Continuation HS 50/Alt
890 Main St 95360 209-862-2309
Rick Gonzalez, prin. Fax 862-2316
Yolo MS 600/6-8
901 Hoyer Rd 95360 209-862-2984
Eva Luna, prin. Fax 862-3734

**Newport Beach, Orange, Pop. 82,964**
Newport - Mesa USD
Supt. — See Costa Mesa
Corona Del Mar JSHS 2,400/7-12
2101 Eastbluff Dr 92660 949-515-6000
Kathy Scott, prin. Fax 515-6070
Ensign IS 1,200/7-8
2000 Cliff Dr 92663 949-515-6910
Michael Sciacca, prin. Fax 515-3370
Newport Harbor HS 2,500/9-12
600 Irvine Ave 92663 949-515-6300
Sean Boulton, prin. Fax 515-6370

---

Interior Designers Institute Post-Sec.
1061 Camelback St 92660 949-675-4451
Southern States University Post-Sec.
1601 Dove St Ste 105 92660 949-833-8868

**Newport Coast, Orange**

---

Sage Hill S 400/9-12
20402 Newport Coast Dr 92657 949-219-0100
Gordon McNeill, pres. Fax 219-1399

**Nicolaus, Sutter, Pop. 204**
East Nicolaus JUNHSD 300/9-12
2454 Nicolaus Ave 95659 530-656-2255
Karen Villalobos, supt. Fax 656-1065
www.eastnicolaus.k12.ca.us
East Nicolaus HS 300/9-12
2454 Nicolaus Ave 95659 530-656-2255
Karen Villalobos, prin. Fax 656-1065

**Nipomo, San Luis Obispo, Pop. 16,314**
Lucia Mar USD
Supt. — See Arroyo Grande
Central Coast New Tech HS 9-12
525 N Thompson Ave 93444
Daniel Neff, prin.
Nipomo HS 1,100/9-12
525 N Thompson Ave 93444 805-474-3300
John Denno, prin. Fax 929-2551

**Norco, Riverside, Pop. 26,516**
Corona-Norco USD 52,800/K-12
2820 Clark Ave 92860 951-736-5000
Michael H. Lin Ed.D., supt. Fax 736-5015
www.cnusd.k12.ca.us
Kennedy HS 600/10-12
1951 3rd St 92860 951-738-2200
Sarah Ragusa, prin. Fax 738-2212
Norco HS 2,200/9-12
2065 Temescal Ave 92860 951-736-3241
Rob Ibbetson, prin. Fax 736-3282
Norco IS 700/7-8
2711 Temescal Ave 92860 951-736-3206
Amy Shainman, prin. Fax 736-3208
Other Schools – See Corona, Eastvale

---

Norco College Post-Sec.
2001 3rd St 92860 951-372-7000

**Norden, Nevada**

---

Sugar Bowl Academy 50/6-12
PO Box 68 95724 530-426-1844
Tracy Keller, head sch Fax 426-1860

**North Edwards, Kern, Pop. 1,016**
Muroc JUSD 2,100/PK-12
17100 Foothill Ave 93523 760-769-4821
Dr. Michael McCoy Ph.D., supt. Fax 769-4241
www.muroc.k12.ca.us
Other Schools – See Boron, Edwards

**North Fork, Madera**
Chawanakee USD 700/K-12
PO Box 400 93643 559-877-6209
Darren Sylvia, supt. Fax 877-2065
www.chawanakee.k12.ca.us
Cougar Springs Community Day S 50/Alt
PO Box 339 93643 559-877-6209
Robert Nelson, prin. Fax 877-4430
Manzanita Community Day S 50/Alt
PO Box 339 93643 559-877-6209
Gary Talley, prin. Fax 877-4430
Mountain Oaks HS 50/9-12
PO Box 339 93643 559-877-4440
Gary Talley, prin. Fax 877-4430
Other Schools – See O Neals

**North Highlands, Sacramento, Pop. 40,275**
Twin Rivers USD
Supt. — See Mc Clellan

Highlands HS 900/9-12
6601 Guthrie St 95660 916-566-3465
Darryl Hawthrone, prin. Fax 566-7810
Pacific Career & Technology HS Vo/Tech
6560 Melrose Dr 95660 916-566-2715
Shane Yang, prin. Fax 566-3558

**North Hills, Los Angeles**
Los Angeles USD
Supt. — See Los Angeles
Einstein Continuation HS 100/Alt
15938 Tupper St 91343 818-892-4367
Flor Ayala, prin. Fax 893-3423
Monroe HS 2,500/9-12
9229 Haskell Ave 91343 818-830-4200
Christopher Rosas, prin. Fax 892-5622
Sepulveda MS 1,600/6-8
15330 Plummer St 91343 818-920-2130
L.G. Garrett, prin. Fax 891-5754

---

Centers of Learning 100/PK-12
PO Box 2037 91393 818-894-3213
Debra Grill, prin. Fax 893-8074
Heritage Christian S South Campus 700/6-12
9825 Woodley Ave 91343 818-894-5742
Lance Haliday, prin. Fax 892-5018

**North Hollywood, See Los Angeles**
Los Angeles USD
Supt. — See Los Angeles
Earhart Continuation S 100/Alt
5355 Colfax Ave 91601 818-769-4877
John Berns, prin. Fax 980-1794
East Valley HS 1,000/9-12
5525 Vineland Ave 91601 818-753-4400
Carrie Allen, prin. Fax 487-6922
Madison MS 1,600/6-8
13000 Hart St 91605 818-255-5200
Estelle Baptiste, prin. Fax 765-4692
North Hollywood HS 3,100/9-12
5231 Colfax Ave 91601 818-753-6200
Ricardo Rosales, prin. Fax 508-7124
Reed MS 1,700/6-8
4525 Irvine Ave 91602 818-487-7600
Jeanne Gamba, prin. Fax 766-9069
Romer MS 1,300/6-8
6501 Laurel Canyon Blvd 91606 818-505-2200
Manuel Diaz, prin. Fax 761-9343

---

Anderson Medical Career College Post-Sec.
10752 Burbank Blvd 91601 818-762-7095
Art Institute of California - Hollywood Post-Sec.
5250 Lankershim Blvd 91601 818-299-5100
Campbell Hall S 1,100/K-12
4533 Laurel Canyon Blvd 91607 818-980-7280
Rev. Julian Bull, hdmstr. Fax 505-5362
Concorde Career College Post-Sec.
12412 Victory Blvd 91606 818-766-8151
Harvard-Westlake HS 900/10-12
3700 Coldwater Canyon Ave 91604 818-980-6692
Jeanne Huybrechts, head sch Fax 487-6631
Kaplan College Post-Sec.
6180 Laurel Canyon Ste 101 91606 818-763-2563
Marinello School of Beauty Post-Sec.
6219 Laurel Canyon Blvd 91606 818-980-1300
Oakwood S 500/7-12
11600 Magnolia Blvd 91601 818-732-3000
Dr. James Astman, hdmstr.
Southern California Health Institute Post-Sec.
5200 Lankershim Blvd 91601 818-980-8990
Valley Torah Girls HS 200/9-12
12003 Riverside Dr 91607 818-755-1697
West Coast University Post-Sec.
12215 Victory Blvd 91606 818-299-5500

**Northridge, See Los Angeles**
Los Angeles USD
Supt. — See Los Angeles
Holmes MS 1,600/6-8
9351 Paso Robles Ave 91325 818-678-4100
Blanca Hernandez, prin. Fax 886-3358
Northridge Academy HS 1,100/9-12
9601 Zelzah Ave 91325 818-700-2222
Nidia Castro, prin. Fax 718-2239
Northridge MS 800/6-8
17960 Chase St 91325 818-678-5100
Adrienne Shaha, prin. Fax 885-1461

---

CA National University Advanced Studies Post-Sec.
8550 Balboa Blvd Ste 210 91325 800-782-2422
California State University-Northridge Post-Sec.
18111 Nordhoff St 91330 818-677-1200
Highland Hall Waldorf S 300/PK-12
17100 Superior St 91325 818-349-1394
San Fernando Valley Academy 100/PK-12
17601 Lassen St 91325 818-349-1373
Jerlene Johnson-Thorne, prin. Fax 773-6353

**Norwalk, Los Angeles, Pop. 103,851**
Little Lake City SD
Supt. — See Santa Fe Springs
Lakeside MS 700/6-8
11000 Kenney St 90650 562-868-9422
Ana Gutierrez, prin. Fax 863-9252

Norwalk-La Mirada USD 20,100/PK-12
12820 Pioneer Blvd 90650 562-868-0431
Dr. Hasmik Danielian Ed.D., supt. Fax 864-9857
www.nlmusd.k12.ca.us
Corvallis MS 900/6-8
11032 Leffingwell Rd 90650 562-868-2678
Bob Easton, prin. Fax 863-4755
Glenn HS 1,900/9-12
13520 Shoemaker Ave 90650 562-868-0431
Greg Puccia, prin. Fax 802-1596
Los Alisos MS 1,100/6-8
14800 Jersey Ave 90650 562-868-0865
Mike Garcia, prin. Fax 864-2967
Norwalk HS 2,200/9-12
11356 Leffingwell Rd 90650 562-868-0431
Dr. Ryan Smith, prin. Fax 864-0796
Waite MS 800/6-8
14320 Norwalk Blvd 90650 562-921-7981
Dr. Susan Newcomb, prin. Fax 921-8114
Norwalk Adult S Adult
15711 Pioneer Blvd 90650 562-868-9858
Sharon Todd, dir. Fax 863-2159
Other Schools – See La Mirada, Whittier

Regional Occupational Center & Program
Supt. — None
Southeast ROP Vo/Tech
12940 Foster Rd 90650 562-860-1927
Gilbert Montano, prin. Fax 929-2474

---

ATI College Post-Sec.
12440 Firestone Blvd # 2001 90650 562-864-0506
Cerritos College Post-Sec.
11110 Alondra Blvd 90650 562-860-2451
New Harvest Christian S 100/PK-12
PO Box 529 90651 562-929-6034
Nancy Salazar, admin. Fax 484-3260
NTMA Training Center of Southern CA Post-Sec.
14926 Bloomfield Ave 90650 562-921-3722

**Novato, Marin, Pop. 49,983**
Novato USD 7,700/K-12
1015 7th St 94945 415-897-4201
Jim Hogeboom, supt. Fax 898-5790
www.nusd.org
Marin Oaks HS 100/Alt
720 Diablo Ave 94947 415-892-8733
Kessa Early, prin. Fax 897-4229
Nexus Academy Alt
720 Diablo Ave 94949 415-506-3066
Kessa Early, prin.
Nova Education Center/Adult Education 100/Alt
720 Diablo Ave 94947 415-897-7653
Kessa Early, prin. Fax 897-5603
Novato HS 1,400/9-12
625 Arthur St 94947 415-898-2125
Matt Baldwin, prin. Fax 897-4242
San Jose MS 700/6-8
1000 Sunset Pkwy 94949 415-883-7831
Justin Mori, prin. Fax 883-0624
San Marin HS 900/9-12
15 San Marin Dr 94945 415-898-2121
Adam Littlefield, prin. Fax 892-8284
Sinaloa MS 800/6-8
2045 Vineyard Rd 94947 415-897-2111
Jim Larson, prin. Fax 892-1201

---

College of Marin Post-Sec.
1800 Ignacio Blvd 94949 415-457-8811
North Bay Christian Academy 100/K-12
6965 Redwood Blvd 94945 415-892-8921
Pamela Carraher, prin. Fax 899-1300

**Nuevo, Riverside, Pop. 6,326**
Nuview UNESD 1,900/K-12
29780 Lakeview Ave 92567 951-928-0066
David Pyle, supt. Fax 928-0324
www.nuview.k12.ca.us
Mountain Shadows MS 400/7-8
30401 Reservoir Ave 92567 951-928-3836
Debra Orona, prin. Fax 928-3015

**Oakdale, Stanislaus, Pop. 20,174**
Oakdale JUSD 5,300/K-12
168 S 3rd Ave 95361 209-848-4884
Marc Malone, supt. Fax 847-0155
www.ojusd.org
East Stanislaus HS 100/Alt
250 Hinkley Ave 95361 209-847-1735
Dennis Hitch, prin. Fax 847-9627
Oakdale HS 1,600/9-12
739 W G St 95361 209-847-3007
Michael Moore, prin. Fax 848-0314
Oakdale JHS 800/7-8
400 S Maag Ave 95361 209-847-2294
Jon Webb, prin. Fax 847-8521
Valley Oak JSHS 100/Alt
200 Hinkley Ave 95361 209-847-3097
Dennis Hitch, prin. Fax 848-4359

**Oak Hills, San Bernardino, Pop. 8,716**
Hesperia USD
Supt. — See Hesperia
Oak Hills HS 2,300/9-12
7625 Cataba Rd, 760-244-2283
Larry Porras, prin. Fax 244-0351

**Oakhurst, Madera, Pop. 2,743**
Bass Lake JUNESD 900/K-8
40096 Indian Springs Rd 93644 559-642-1555
Glenn Reid, supt. Fax 642-1556
www.basslakeschooldistrict.com/
Oak Creek IS 200/6-8
40094 Indian Springs Rd 93644 559-642-1570
Brad Barcus, prin. Fax 683-7279

Yosemite USD 2,200/K-12
50200 Road 427 93644 559-683-8801
James Sargent, supt. Fax 683-4160
www.yosemiteusd.com/
Ahwahnee Continuation HS 50/Alt
50200 Road 427 93644 559-683-8801
Dr. Randy Haggard, prin. Fax 658-2034
Campbell High Community Day S 50/Alt
50200 Road 427 93644 559-683-8801
Dr. Randy Haggard, prin. Fax 658-2359
Evergreen HS 50/Alt
50200 Road 427 93644 559-683-5544
Dr. Randy Haggard, prin. Fax 658-2359
Yosemite HS 800/9-12
50200 Road 427 93644 559-683-4667
Randy Seals, prin. Fax 683-8392
Yosemite Adult HS Adult
50200 Road 427 93644 559-683-8801
Dr. Randy Haggard, prin. Fax 642-4334
Other Schools – See Coarsegold, Raymond

**Oakland, Alameda, Pop. 373,354**
Oakland USD 39,600/PK-12
2111 International Blvd 94606 510-434-7790
Antwan Wilson, supt.
www.ousd.org
Alliance Academy 400/6-8
1800 98th Ave 94603 510-639-2893
Stacey Wyatt, prin. Fax 639-3387
Brewer MS 800/6-8
3748 13th Ave 94610 510-531-6600
Aubrey Lane, prin. Fax 531-6626
Bunche Continuation S 50/Alt
1240 18th St 94607 510-874-3300
Betsye Steele, prin. Fax 874-3305
Castlemont HS 100/9-12
8601 MacArthur Blvd 94605 510-639-1466
William Chavarin, prin. Fax 639-4271
Claremont MS 500/6-8
5750 College Ave 94618 510-654-7337
Jonathan Mayer, prin. Fax 654-7341
Coliseum College Prep Academy 400/6-12
1390 66th Ave 94621 510-639-3201
Amy Carozza, prin. Fax 639-3214
Community Day MSHS 50/Alt
4917 Mountain Blvd 94619 510-531-6800
Mekael Johnson, prin. Fax 482-7144
Dewey Academy 200/Alt
1111 2nd Ave 94606 510-874-3660
Robin Glover, prin. Fax 874-3661
Elmhurst Community Prep S 400/6-8
1800 98th Ave 94603 510-639-2888
Kilian Betlach, prin. Fax 639-2891
Fremont HS 9-12
4610 Foothill Blvd 94601 510-434-5257
Pamela Watson, prin. Fax 434-2018
Frick MS 400/6-8
2845 64th Ave 94605 510-729-7736
Jeffrey Taylor, prin. Fax 729-7739
Gateway to College S 100/Alt
900 Fallon St 94607 510-986-6941
Rogeair Purnell, prin. Fax 464-3231
Harte MS 600/6-8
3700 Coolidge Ave 94602 510-531-6400
Bianca D'Allesandro, prin. Fax 482-7272
LIFE Academy 300/6-12
2101 35th Ave 94601 510-534-0282
Aryn Bowman, prin. Fax 534-0283
Madison Park Academy 300/6-12
400 Capistrano Dr 94603 510-636-2701
Lucinda Taylor, prin. Fax 636-2704
McClymonds HS 200/9-12
2608 Myrtle St 94607 510-238-8607
Steve Henderson, prin. Fax 874-3796
MetWest HS 200/Alt
314 East Tenth St 94606 510-451-5902
Charlie Plant, prin. Fax 451-5903
Montera MS 900/6-8
5555 Ascot Dr 94611 510-531-6070
Darren Avent, prin. Fax 531-6354
Oakland HS 1,700/9-12
1023 MacArthur Blvd 94610 510-874-3676
Matin Abdel-Qawi, prin. Fax 874-3675
Oakland International HS 300/Alt
4521 Webster St 94609 510-597-4287
Carmelita Welsh-Reyes, prin. Fax 597-4292
Oakland Technical HS Vo/Tech
4351 Broadway 94611 510-450-5400
Staci Ross-Morrison, prin. Fax 450-5428
Roosevelt MS 700/6-8
1926 E 19th St 94606 510-535-2877
Clifford Hong, prin. Fax 535-2883
ROOTS International Academy 400/6-8
1390 66th Ave 94621 510-639-3226
Geoff Vu, prin. Fax 639-3214
Rudsdale Continuation S 100/Alt
8251 Fontaine St 94605 510-729-4303
Willie Thompson, prin. Fax 569-7402
Skyline HS 1,800/9-12
12250 Skyline Blvd 94619 510-482-7109
Kevin Taylor, prin. Fax 482-7296
Sojourner Truth S 200/Alt
8251 Fontaine St 94605 510-729-4308
Willie Thompson, prin. Fax 636-4701
Street Academy 100/Alt
417 29th St 94609 510-874-3630
Gina Hill, prin. Fax 874-3633
United for Success Academy 400/6-8
2101 35th Ave 94601 510-535-3880
Nicole Pierce, prin. Fax 535-7139
Urban Promise Academy 300/6-8
3031 E 18th St 94601 510-436-3636
Claire Fisher, prin. Fax 436-3638
Westlake MS 600/6-8
2629 Harrison St 94612 510-879-2130
Misha Karigica, prin. Fax 835-7170
West Oakland MS 200/6-8
991 14th St 94607 510-874-6788
Neha Ummat, prin. Fax 874-6790
Neighborhood Centers Adult S Adult
750 International Blvd 94606 510-451-7300
Chris Nelson, prin. Fax 451-7320

---

Academy of Chinese Culture & Health Sci. Post-Sec.
1601 Clay St 94612 510-763-7787
American University of Armenia Post-Sec.
300 Lakeside Dr Fl 12 94612 510-987-9452
Bishop O'Dowd HS 1,100/9-12
9500 Stearns Ave 94605 510-577-9100
Pamela Shay, prin. Fax 638-3259
College Preparatory S 400/9-12
6100 Broadway 94618 510-652-0111
Monique DeVane, head sch Fax 652-7467

DeVry University Post-Sec.
505 14th St Ste 100 94612 510-267-1340
Head-Royce S 800/K-12
4315 Lincoln Ave 94602 510-531-1300
Robert Lake, head sch Fax 531-2649
Holy Names HS 200/9-12
4660 Harbord Dr 94618 510-450-1110
Dr. Connie Hubbard, prin. Fax 547-3111
Holy Names University Post-Sec.
3500 Mountain Blvd 94619 510-436-1000
ITT Technical Institute Post-Sec.
7901 Oakport St Ste 3000 94621 510-553-2800
Laney College Post-Sec.
900 Fallon St 94607 510-834-5740
Lincoln University Post-Sec.
401 15th St 94612 510-628-8010
Merritt College Post-Sec.
12500 Campus Dr 94619 510-531-4911
Mills College Post-Sec.
5000 MacArthur Blvd 94613 510-430-2255
Moler Barber College Post-Sec.
3815 Telegraph Ave 94609 510-652-4177
Morgan S for Girls 200/6-8
PO Box 9966 94613 510-632-6000
Sandra Luna, head sch Fax 632-6301
Muhammad University of Islam 100/K-12
5277 Foothill Blvd 94601 510-436-0206
Keith Muhammad, dir.
Patten Academy of Christian Education 100/K-12
2430 Coolidge Ave 94601 510-533-3121
Dr. Sharon Anderson, prin. Fax 535-9381
Patten University Post-Sec.
2433 Coolidge Ave 94601 510-261-8500
St. Andrew Missionary Baptist S 50/K-12
2608 West St 94612 510-922-1924
Dr. Robert Lacy, dir. Fax 788-4017
St. Elizabeth HS 200/9-12
1530 34th Ave 94601 510-532-8947
Martin Procaccio, prin. Fax 532-9754
St. Martin de Porres S 100/6-8
1630 10th St 94607 510-832-1757
Dr. Hollis Pierce-Jenkins, pres. Fax 832-6481
Samuel Merritt University Post-Sec.
3100 Telegraph Ave Ste 1000 94609 510-869-6511
SUM Bible College & Theological Seminary Post-Sec.
735 105th Ave 94603 510-567-6174

**Oakley, Contra Costa, Pop. 33,914**
Liberty UNHSD
Supt. — See Brentwood
Freedom HS 2,500/9-12
1050 Neroly Rd 94561 925-625-5900
Kelly Manke, prin. Fax 625-0396

Oakley UNESD 4,700/K-8
91 Mercedes Ln 94561 925-625-0700
Pamela Conklin Ed.D., supt. Fax 625-1863
www.ouesd.k12.ca.us
Delta Vista MS 800/6-8
4901 Frank Hengel Way 94561 925-625-6840
Harvey Yurkovich, prin. Fax 625-6850
O'Hara Park MS 800/6-8
1100 OHara Ave 94561 925-625-5060
Colleen Creswell, prin. Fax 625-5096

**Oak Park, Ventura, Pop. 13,435**
Oak Park USD 4,100/PK-12
5801 Conifer St 91377 818-735-3200
Dr. Anthony Knight, supt. Fax 879-0372
www.oakparkusd.org/
Medea Creek MS 1,100/6-8
1002 Doubletree Rd 91377 818-707-7922
Brad Benioff, prin. Fax 865-8641
Oak Park HS 1,400/9-12
899 Kanan Rd 91377 818-735-3300
Kevin Buchanan, prin. Fax 707-7970
Oak Park Independent S Alt
5801 Conifer St 91377 818-735-3260
Stewart McGugan, prin. Fax 735-3290
Oak View HS 50/Alt
5701 Conifer St 91377 818-735-3217
Stewart McGugan, prin. Fax 735-3290

**Oceanside, San Diego, Pop. 159,148**
Oceanside USD 21,000/K-12
2111 Mission Ave 92058 760-966-4000
Dr. Duane Coleman, supt. Fax 433-8620
ousd.ca.schoolloop.com
Chavez MS 800/6-8
202 Oleander Dr 92057 760-966-4900
Jenny Morgan, prin. Fax 945-4665
El Camino HS 3,000/9-12
400 Rancho Del Oro Dr 92057 760-901-8000
Alexander Bennet, prin. Fax 757-5321
Jefferson MS 1,000/6-8
823 Acacia Ave 92058 760-966-4700
Marie Higareda de Ochoa, prin. Fax 757-5791
King MS 1,400/6-8
1290 Ivey Ranch Rd 92057 760-901-8800
Dr. Greg Smedley, prin. Fax 967-4154
Lincoln MS 900/6-8
2000 California St 92054 760-901-8900
Steve Bessant, prin. Fax 433-2035
Ocean Shores HS 200/Alt
3131 Oceanside Blvd 92056 760-901-8600
Tina Cornish, prin. Fax 439-5588
Oceanside HS 2,400/9-12
1 Pirates Cove Way 92054 760-722-8201
Ron Pirayoff, prin. Fax 757-2419

Vista USD
Supt. — See Vista
Madison MS 1,300/6-8
4930 Lake Blvd 92056 760-940-0176
Susan Ford, prin. Fax 940-2081
Mission Vista HS 900/9-12
1306 Melrose Dr 92057 760-758-6800
Craig Wiblemo, prin. Fax 758-6832

Roosevelt MS 1,100/6-8
850 Sagewood Dr 92057 760-726-8003
Fax 726-8596

MediaTech Institute Post-Sec.
302 Oceanside Blvd 92054 760-231-5368
MiraCosta College Post-Sec.
1 Barnard Dr 92056 760-757-2121
Oceanside College of Beauty Post-Sec.
1575 S Coast Hwy 92054 760-757-6161

**Ojai, Ventura, Pop. 7,310**
Ojai USD 2,900/PK-12
PO Box 878 93024 805-640-4300
Dr. Hank Bangser, supt. Fax 640-4419
www.ojai.k12.ca.us
Chaparral Continuation HS 50/Alt
PO Box 878 93024 805-640-4330
Becky Beckett, lead tchr. Fax 640-4341
Matilija JHS 500/7-8
703 El Paseo Rd 93023 805-640-4355
Bill Rosen, prin. Fax 640-4398
Nordhoff HS 900/9-12
1401 Maricopa Hwy 93023 805-640-4343
Greg Bayless, prin. Fax 640-4336

Besant Hill S 100/9-12
PO Box 850 93024 805-646-4343
Randy Bertin, head sch Fax 646-4371
Laurel Springs S 1,600/K-12
302 El Paseo Rd 93023 805-646-2473
Darby Carr, head sch Fax 646-0186
Oak Grove S 200/PK-12
220 W Lomita Ave 93023 805-646-8236
Meredy Benson Rice, head sch Fax 646-6509
Ojai Valley S 300/PK-12
723 El Paseo Rd 93023 805-646-1423
Michael Hall-Mounsey, pres. Fax 646-0362
Thacher S 300/9-12
5025 Thacher Rd 93023 805-646-4377
Michael Mulligan, head sch Fax 646-9490
Villanova Preparatory HS 300/9-12
12096 N Ventura Ave 93023 805-646-1464
Carol Hoffer, hdmstr. Fax 646-4430

**Olivehurst, Yuba, Pop. 13,017**
Marysville JUSD
Supt. — See Marysville
Lindhurst HS 1,200/9-12
4446 Olive Ave 95961 530-741-6150
Bob Eckardt, prin. Fax 741-6171
South Lindhurst Continuation HS 100/Alt
4446 Olive Ave 95961 530-741-6918
David Jones, prin. Fax 741-7875
Yuba Gardens IS 700/7-8
1964 11th Ave 95961 530-741-6194
Kari Ylst, prin. Fax 741-7847

New Life Christian S 100/PK-12
5736 Arboga Rd 95961 530-742-3033
John Lewallen, admin. Fax 741-8221

**Olympic Valley, Placer**

Squaw Valley Academy 100/9-12
PO Box 2667 96146 530-583-9393
Donald Rees, hdmstr. Fax 581-1111

**O Neals, Madera**
Chawanakee USD
Supt. — See North Fork
Minarets HS 300/9-12
PO Box 186 93645 559-868-8689
Daniel Ching, prin. Fax 868-3407
Chawanakee Adult Education Adult
PO Box 186 93645 559-868-4200
Gary Talley, prin. Fax 868-4222

**Ontario, San Bernardino, Pop. 161,020**
Chaffey JUNHSD 25,000/9-12
211 W 5th St 91762 909-988-8511
Mathew Holton, supt. Fax 984-1164
cjuhsd-ca.schoolloop.com
Chaffey Community Day S 50/Alt
1802 E 7th St 91764 909-460-5663
Bart Goldstein, prin.
Chaffey HS 3,600/9-12
1245 N Euclid Ave 91762 909-988-5560
Dr. George Matamala, prin. Fax 988-0146
Colony HS 2,200/9-12
3850 E Riverside Dr 91761 909-930-2929
Dr. Kern Oduro, prin. Fax 460-5856
Ontario HS 2,800/9-12
901 W Francis St 91762 909-988-7411
Eduardo Zaldivar, prin. Fax 986-2181
Valley View Continuation HS 700/Alt
1801 E 6th St 91764 909-985-0966
Bart Goldstein, prin. Fax 946-5586
Chaffey Adult S Adult
211 W 5th St 91762 909-988-8511
Todd Haag, prin. Fax 983-9916
Other Schools – See Alta Loma, Etiwanda, Montclair, Rancho Cucamonga

Chino Valley USD
Supt. — See Chino
Woodcrest JHS 500/7-8
2725 S Campus Ave 91761 909-923-3455
Sue Pederson, prin. Fax 548-6059

Mountain View ESD 2,800/K-8
2585 S Archibald Ave 91761 909-947-2205
Dr. Rick Carr, supt. Fax 947-2291
www.mtnview.k12.ca.us
Yokley MS, 2947 S Turner Ave 91761 1,000/6-8
Lisa Alcala, prin. 909-947-6774

Ontario-Montclair SD 22,200/PK-8
950 W D St 91762 909-459-2500
Dr. James Hammond, supt. Fax 459-2542
www.omsd.net
Danks MS 1,000/7-8
1020 N Vine Ave 91762 909-983-2691
Anthony Ortiz, prin. Fax 459-2959
De Anza MS 600/7-8
1450 S Sultana Ave 91761 909-986-8577
Marco Villegas, prin. Fax 459-2673
Oaks MS 900/7-8
1221 S Oaks Ave 91762 909-988-2050
Dave Foley, prin. Fax 988-2081
Wiltsey MS 700/6-8
1450 E G St 91764 909-986-5838
William Corrette, prin. Fax 459-2834
Other Schools – See Montclair

American Career College Post-Sec.
3130 Sedona Ct 91764 909-218-3253
Argosy University Inland Empire Post-Sec.
3401 Centre Lake Dr Ste 200 91761 909-472-0800
Everest College Post-Sec.
1460 S Milliken Ave 91761 909-984-5027
Everest College Post-Sec.
1819 Excise Ave 91761 909-484-4311
Franklin Career College Post-Sec.
1274 Slater Cir 91761 909-937-9007
Marinello School of Beauty Post-Sec.
940 N Mountain Ave 91762 909-984-5884
NTMA Training Center of Southern CA Post-Sec.
1717 S Grove Ave 91761 909-947-9363
Ontario Christian HS 500/9-12
931 W Philadelphia St 91762 909-984-1756
Tim Hoekstra, prin. Fax 460-0176
Platt College Post-Sec.
3700 Inland Empire Ste 400 91764 909-941-9410
Richard's Beauty College Post-Sec.
200 N Euclid Ave 91762 909-988-7584
San Antonio Christian S 100/K-10
1722 E 8th St 91764 909-982-2301
Janet Lopez, prin. Fax 982-0921
West Coast University Post-Sec.
2855 E Guasti Rd 91761 909-467-6100
Westech College Post-Sec.
3491 Concours 91764 909-980-4474

**Orange, Orange, Pop. 133,187**
Orange USD 29,500/PK-12
PO Box 11022 92856 714-628-4040
Michael Christenson Ed.D., supt. Fax 628-4041
www.orangeusd.org/
Career Education Center Vo/Tech
250 S Yorba St 92869 714-997-6066
Germaine Martell, coord. Fax 997-6035
El Modena HS 2,200/9-12
3920 E Spring St 92869 714-997-6331
Dustin Saxton, prin. Fax 997-0705
Orange HS 2,100/9-12
525 N Shaffer St 92867 714-997-6211
Dennis McCuistion, prin. Fax 633-6460
OUSD Community Day S Alt
250 S Yorba St 92869 714-628-5479
Germaine Martell, prin. Fax 538-8941
Portola MS 800/6-8
270 N Palm Dr 92868 714-997-6361
Jill Katevas, prin. Fax 978-0274
Richland Continuation HS 300/Alt
615 N Lemon St 92867 714-997-6167
Elsie Simonovski, prin. Fax 771-5967
Yorba MS 500/7-8
935 N Cambridge St 92867 714-997-6161
Tracy Knibb, prin. Fax 532-4759
Other Schools – See Anaheim, Villa Park

Argosy University Orange County Post-Sec.
601 S Lewis St 92868 714-620-3700
Chapman University Post-Sec.
1 University Dr 92866 714-997-6815
CNI College Post-Sec.
702 W Town and Country Rd 92868 714-437-9697
COBA Academy Post-Sec.
102 N Glassell St 92866 714-633-5950
Eldorado S for the Gifted Child 100/PK-12
4100 E Walnut Ave 92869 714-633-4774
Russell Ludwick, dir. Fax 744-3304
ITT Technical Institute Post-Sec.
4000 W Metropolitan Dr #100 92868 714-941-2400
Lutheran HS of Orange County 1,300/9-12
2222 N Santiago Blvd 92867 714-998-5151
Leslie Smith M.Ed., prin. Fax 998-1371
St. Joseph Hospital Post-Sec.
1100 W Stewart Dr 92868 714-771-8111
Santiago Canyon College Post-Sec.
8045 E Chapman Ave 92869 714-628-4900
South Coast College Post-Sec.
2011 W Chapman Ave 92868 866-266-8779

**Orange Cove, Fresno, Pop. 9,005**
Kings Canyon JUSD
Supt. — See Reedley
Citrus MS 600/6-8
1400 Anchor Ave 93646 559-305-7370
Patricia Ledesma, prin. Fax 626-7255
Orange Cove HS 600/9-12
1700 Anchor Ave 93646 559-626-5900
Angel Durazo, prin. Fax 626-7217

**Orangevale, Sacramento, Pop. 32,766**
San Juan USD
Supt. — See Carmichael
Carnegie MS 1,000/6-8
5820 Illinois Ave 95662 916-971-7853
Mark Siewert, prin. Fax 971-7849
Casa Roble Fundamental HS 1,500/9-12
9151 Oak Ave 95662 916-971-5452
Michele Lorenzo, prin. Fax 971-5495

Pasteur MS 700/6-8
8935 Elm Ave 95662 916-971-7891
Janet Deal, prin. Fax 971-7893

**Orcutt, Santa Barbara, Pop. 28,086**
Orcutt UNESD 5,000/K-12
500 Dyer St 93455 805-938-8900
Deborah Blow, supt. Fax 938-8919
www.orcutt-schools.net
Orcutt JHS 500/7-8
608 Pinal Ave 93455 805-938-8700
Kelly Osborne, prin. Fax 938-8749
Other Schools – See Santa Maria

**Orinda, Contra Costa, Pop. 16,885**
Acalanes UNHSD
Supt. — See Lafayette
Miramonte HS 1,200/9-12
750 Moraga Way 94563 925-280-3930
Julie Parks, prin. Fax 280-3931

Orinda UNESD 2,400/K-8
8 Altarinda Rd 94563 925-254-4901
Joe Jaconette Ed.D., supt. Fax 254-5261
www.orindaschools.org/
Orinda IS 900/6-8
80 Ivy Dr 94563 925-258-3090
Michael Randall, prin. Fax 631-7985

---

Orinda Academy 100/8-12
19 Altarinda Rd 94563 925-254-7553

**Orland, Glenn, Pop. 7,173**
Orland JUSD 2,200/K-12
1320 6th St 95963 530-865-1200
Dr. Ken Geisick, supt. Fax 865-1202
www.orlandusd.net
North Valley HS 50/Alt
1320 6th St 95963 530-865-1285
Jason Bramson, prin. Fax 865-1285
Orland Community Day S 50/Alt
1320 6th St 95963 530-865-1264
Jason Bramson, prin.
Orland HS 700/9-12
1320 6th St 95963 530-865-1210
Victor Perry, prin. Fax 865-1215
Price IS 500/6-8
1320 6th St 95963 530-865-1225
Kelly Haight, prin. Fax 865-1227

---

Providence Christian S 100/K-12
1148 E Walker St 95963 530-865-4924
Gordon Wiens, supt. Fax 865-4926

**Orosi, Tulare, Pop. 8,702**
Cutler-Orosi JUSD 4,100/K-12
12623 Avenue 416 93647 559-528-4763
Yolanda Valdez, supt. Fax 528-3132
www.cojusd.org
Cutler-Orosi Community Day S 50/Alt
12623 Avenue 416 93647 559-528-4703
Martha Calderon, prin. Fax 528-0102
El Monte MS 900/6-8
12623 Avenue 416 93647 559-528-3017
Michelle Kettle, prin. Fax 528-2822
Esperanza HS 100/Alt
12623 Avenue 416 93647 559-528-4703
Martha Calderon, prin. Fax 528-0102
Orosi HS 900/9-12
12623 Avenue 416 93647 559-528-4731
Roberto Vaca, prin. Fax 528-4930
Cutler-Orosi Adult S Adult
12623 Avenue 416 93647 559-528-4763
Melissa Calvero, dir.
Other Schools – See Cutler

**Oroville, Butte, Pop. 14,775**
Butte County Office of Education 1,400/
1859 Bird St 95965 530-532-5650
Tim Taylor, supt. Fax 532-5762
www.bcoe.org
Table Mountain S 50/Alt
41 County Center Dr 95965 530-532-5688
Karen Stiles, admin. Fax 532-5697
Other Schools – See Paradise

Oroville City ESD 2,600/PK-8
2795 Yard St 95966 530-532-3000
Penny Chennell-Carter, supt. Fax 532-3050
www.ocesd.org
Central MS 300/7-8
2565 Mesa Ave 95966 530-532-3002
Mikeial Williamson, prin. Fax 532-3042
Ishi Hills MS 400/6-8
1 Ishi Hills Way 95966 530-532-3078
Chris Renzullo, prin. Fax 532-3040

Oroville UNHSD 2,600/9-12
2211 Washington Ave 95966 530-538-2300
Dr. Corey Willenberg, supt. Fax 538-2308
www.ouhsd.org
Las Plumas HS 1,300/9-12
2380 Las Plumas Ave 95966 530-538-2310
Dana Ramos, prin. Fax 534-5974
Oroville Community Day S 50/Alt
2120 2nd St 95965 530-538-2330
Jeff Ochs, dir. Fax 533-2338
Oroville HS 1,200/9-12
1535 Bridge St 95966 530-538-2320
Jeff Peek, prin. Fax 534-6203
Prospect Continuation HS 200/Alt
2060 2nd St 95965 530-538-2330
Jeff Ochs, dir. Fax 533-2338
Oroville Adult Education Adult
2750 Mitchell Ave 95966 530-538-5350
Jeff Ochs, dir. Fax 538-5396

Thermalito UNESD 1,300/K-8
400 Grand Ave 95965 530-538-2900
Julian Diaz, supt. Fax 538-2908
www.thermalito.org/
Heritage Community Day S 50/Alt
2080 6th St 95965 530-532-4376
Jim Walters, prin. Fax 538-2949
Nelson Avenue MS 400/6-8
2255 6th St 95965 530-538-2940
Jim Walters, prin. Fax 538-2949

---

Butte College Post-Sec.
3536 Butte Campus Dr 95965 530-895-2511
Northwest Lineman College Post-Sec.
2009 Challenger Ave 95965 530-534-7260

**Oxnard, Ventura, Pop. 194,223**
Hueneme ESD
Supt. — See Port Hueneme
Blackstock JHS 1,200/6-8
701 E Bard Rd 93033 805-488-3644
Tom Beneke, prin. Fax 488-1250
Green JHS 1,100/6-8
3739 S C St 93033 805-986-8750
Heidi Haines, prin. Fax 986-8756

Ocean View ESD 2,600/PK-8
4200 Olds Rd 93033 805-488-4441
Craig Helmstedter Ed.D., supt. Fax 986-6797
www.oceanviewsd.org
Ocean View JHS 800/6-8
4300 Olds Rd 93033 805-488-6421
Heather Hendrix, prin. Fax 488-4132

Oxnard SD 16,100/K-8
1051 S A St 93030 805-385-1501
Dr. Cesar Morales, supt. Fax 483-7426
www.oxnardsd.org
Frank MS 1,200/6-8
701 N Juanita Ave 93030 805-385-1536
Dr. Liam Joyce, prin. Fax 981-1754
Fremont MS 1,100/6-8
1130 N M St 93030 805-385-1539
Greg Brisbine, prin. Fax 485-2486
Haydock MS 700/6-8
647 Hill St 93033 805-385-1545
Dr. Edd Bond, prin. Fax 487-7159

Oxnard UNHSD 16,800/K-12
309 S K St 93030 805-385-2500
Gabe Soumakian Ed.D., supt. Fax 483-3069
www.ouhsd.k12.ca.us
Channel Islands HS 2,700/9-12
1400 Raiders Way 93033 805-385-2787
Ray Senesac, prin. Fax 385-2748
Hueneme HS 2,000/9-12
500 W Bard Rd 93033 805-385-2667
Oscar Hernandez Ed.D., prin. Fax 385-2817
Oxnard HS 3,000/9-12
3400 W Gonzales Rd, 805-278-2907
Eric Riegert, prin. Fax 278-2912
Pacifica HS 3,300/9-12
600 E Gonzales Rd, 805-278-5000
Bijou Beltran, prin. Fax 278-7187
Rio Mesa HS 2,000/9-12
545 Central Ave, 805-278-5500
Ray Gonzales, prin. Fax 278-5525
Oxnard Adult S Adult
1101 W 2nd St 93030 805-385-2578
Diana Batista, prin. Fax 385-2581
Other Schools – See Camarillo

Rio SD 4,600/PK-8
2500 E Vineyard Ave, 805-485-3111
Dr. John Puglisi, supt. Fax 981-7736
rioschools.org
Rio Del Valle MS 700/6-8
3100 N Rose Ave, 805-485-3119
Joanne Davidson, prin. Fax 981-7737
Rio Vista MS 700/6-8
3050 Thames River Dr, 805-981-1507
Matt Klinefelter, prin. Fax 981-6791

---

Charter College - Oxnard Post-Sec.
2000 Outlet Center Dr # 150, 805-973-1240
ITT Technical Institute Post-Sec.
2051 Solar Dr Ste 150, 805-988-0143
Laurus College Post-Sec.
2351 Lockwood St, 805-267-1690
Modern Beauty Academy Post-Sec.
699 S C St 93030 805-483-4994
Oxnard College Post-Sec.
4000 S Rose Ave 93033 805-986-5800
Pacific Coast Trade School Post-Sec.
1690 Universe Cir 93033 805-487-9260
St. John's Regional Medical Center Post-Sec.
1600 N Rose Ave 93030 805-988-2500
Santa Clara HS 300/9-12
2121 Saviers Rd 93033 805-483-9502
Dr. Edward Robillard, prin. Fax 483-1588

**Pacifica, San Mateo, Pop. 35,016**
Jefferson UNHSD
Supt. — See Daly City
Oceana HS 600/9-12
401 Paloma Ave 94044 650-550-7300
Caro Pemberton, prin. Fax 550-7310
Terra Nova HS 1,200/9-12
1450 Terra Nova Blvd 94044 650-550-7600
Dorene Basuino, prin. Fax 550-7690

Pacifica SD 3,200/PK-8
375 Reina Del Mar Ave 94044 650-738-6600
Dr. Wendy Tukloff, supt. Fax 557-9672
www.pacificasd.org/
Lacy MS 600/6-8
1427 Palmetto Ave 94044 650-738-6665
Daniel Lyttle, prin. Fax 738-6669

---

Alma Heights Christian S 300/K-12
1295 Seville Dr 94044 650-359-0555
Dr. David Gross, dir. Fax 359-5020

**Pacific Grove, Monterey, Pop. 14,485**
Pacific Grove USD 2,000/K-12
435 Hillcrest Ave 93950 831-646-6520
Ralph Porras, supt. Fax 646-6500
pgusd.org
Community HS 50/Alt
435 Hillcrest Ave 93950 831-646-6535
Matt Bell, prin. Fax 648-8417
Pacific Grove HS 600/9-12
615 Sunset Dr 93950 831-646-6590
Matt Bell, prin. Fax 646-6660
Pacific Grove MS 400/6-8
835 Forest Ave 93950 831-646-6568
Sean Roach, prin. Fax 646-6652
Pacific Grove Adult Education Adult
1025 Lighthouse Ave 93950 831-646-6580
Craig Beller, prin. Fax 646-6578

---

Stanford University Hopkins Marine Post-Sec.
120 Ocean View Blvd 93950 831-655-6200

**Pacoima, See Los Angeles**
Los Angeles USD
Supt. — See Los Angeles
MacLay MS 900/6-8
12540 Pierce St 91331 818-686-3800
Carlos Tobar, prin. Fax 834-1012
Pacoima MS 1,600/6-8
9919 Laurel Canyon Blvd 91331 818-686-4200
Marsha Hamm, prin. Fax 834-2021
Pacoima Skills Center Adult
13545 Van Nuys Blvd 91331 818-896-9558
Juan Jimenez, admin. Fax 899-7087

**Palermo, Butte, Pop. 5,130**
Palermo UNESD 1,300/K-8
7390 Bulldog Way 95968 530-533-4842
Dr. Bryan Caples, supt. Fax 532-1047
www.palermoschools.org
Palermo MS 400/6-8
7350 Bulldog Way 95968 530-533-4708
Kathleen Andoe, prin. Fax 532-7801

**Palmdale, Los Angeles, Pop. 148,782**
Antelope Valley UNHSD
Supt. — See Lancaster
Highland HS 3,200/9-12
39055 25th St W 93551 661-538-0304
Steve Ford, prin. Fax 538-0405
Knight HS 3,400/9-12
37423 70th St E 93552 661-533-9000
Richie Romero, prin. Fax 533-0111
Palmdale HS 3,100/9-12
2137 E Avenue R 93550 661-273-3181
Kristina Ramos, prin. Fax 273-1093
Parris Continuation HS 500/Alt
38801 Clock Tower Plaza Dr 93550 661-274-1230
Will Laird, prin. Fax 274-1168
Phoenix HS Community Day 100/Alt
2270 E Avenue Q 93550 661-274-4619
Will Laird, prin.

Palmdale ESD 20,100/K-12
39139 10th St E 93550 661-947-7191
Raul Maldonado, supt. Fax 273-5137
www.palmdalesd.org
Cactus IS 300/7-8
3243 E Avenue R8 93550 661-273-0847
Ruth James, prin. Fax 273-5514
Desert Willow IS 800/7-8
36555 Sunny Ln 93550 661-285-5866
Melanie Culver, prin. Fax 456-1145
Millen IS 7-8
39221 22nd St W 93551 661-947-3075
Brian Williams, prin. Fax 538-9035
Shadow Hills IS 1,100/7-8
37315 60th St E 93552 661-533-7400
Barbara Gaines, prin. Fax 533-7445

Regional Occupational Center & Program
Supt. — None
Antelope Valley ROP Vo/Tech
1156 E Avenue S 93550 661-575-1026
Betsy McKinstry, dir. Fax 575-1037

Westside UNESD
Supt. — See Quartz Hill
Hillview MS 1,000/7-8
40525 Peonza Ln 93551 661-722-9993
Rodney Lots, prin. Fax 722-9483

Wilsona SD 1,400/K-8
18050 E Avenue O 93591 661-264-1111
Teresa Grey, supt. Fax 261-3259
www.wilsonasd.net
Other Schools – See Lancaster

---

DeVry University Post-Sec.
39115 Trade Center Dr # 100 93551 866-986-9388

**Palm Desert, Riverside, Pop. 47,665**
Desert Sands USD
Supt. — See La Quinta
Palm Desert HS 2,000/9-12
74910 Aztec Rd 92260 760-862-4300
Bob Hicks, prin. Fax 862-4390

---

College of the Desert Post-Sec.
43500 Monterey Ave 92260 760-346-8041
Xavier College Preparatory S 500/9-12
34200 Cook St 92211 760-601-3900
Jimmy Tricco, prin. Fax 601-3901

**Palm Springs, Riverside, Pop. 43,639**
Palm Springs USD 22,700/K-12
980 E Tahquitz Canyon Way 92262 760-416-6000
Dr. Christine Anderson, supt. Fax 416-6015
www.psusd.us
Cree MS 1,000/6-8
1011 E Vista Chino 92262 760-416-8283
Tracy Piper, prin. Fax 416-8287
Desert Learning Academy 50/Alt
2248 E Ramon Rd 92264 760-778-0487
Dr. Todd Reed, prin. Fax 778-0497
Palm Springs HS 2,200/9-12
2401 E Baristo Rd 92262 760-778-0400
Ryan Woll, prin. Fax 778-0481
Other Schools – See Cathedral City, Desert Hot Springs, Rancho Mirage

---

California Nurses Educational Institute Post-Sec.
5200 E Ramon Rd Ste I1 92264 760-416-5955
Desert Chapel Christian S 200/K-12
630 S Sunrise Way 92264 760-327-2772
Frank Marshall, admin. Fax 325-7048
Kaplan College Post-Sec.
2475 E Tahquitz Canyon Way 92262 760-778-3540

**Palo Alto, Santa Clara, Pop. 61,626**
Palo Alto USD 12,100/K-12
25 Churchill Ave 94306 650-329-3700
Glenn McGee Ph.D., supt. Fax 329-3803
www.pausd.org
Gunn HS 1,900/9-12
780 Arastradero Rd 94306 650-354-8200
Denise Herrmann, prin. Fax 493-7801
Jordan MS 1,000/6-8
750 N California Ave 94303 650-494-8120
Tom Jacoubowsky, prin. Fax 858-1310
Palo Alto HS 1,900/9-12
50 Embarcadero Rd 94301 650-329-3701
Kim Diorio, prin. Fax 329-3753
Stanford MS 1,000/6-8
480 E Meadow Dr 94306 650-856-5188
Sharon Ofek, prin. Fax 856-3248
Terman MS 700/6-8
655 Arastradero Rd 94306 650-856-9810
Pier Angeli La Place, prin. Fax 856-9878
Palo Alto Adult S Adult
50 Embarcadero Rd 94301 650-329-3752
Katya Villalobos, prin. Fax 329-8515

---

Bay Area College of Nursing Post-Sec.
824 San Antonio Rd 94303 650-858-6810
Castilleja S 400/6-12
1310 Bryant St 94301 650-328-3160
Nanci Kauffman, head sch Fax 326-8036
Girls' MS 200/6-8
3400 W Bayshore Rd 94303 650-968-8338
Jennifer Ayer, head sch Fax 968-4775
Kehillah Jewish HS 200/9-12
3900 Fabian Way 94303 650-213-9600
Rabbi Darren Kleinberg Ph.D., head sch Fax 213-9601
Meira Academy 9-12
3921 Fabian Way 94303 650-485-3589
Devorah Lewis, prin.
Palo Alto University Post-Sec.
1791 Arastradero Rd 94304 800-818-6136
Sofia University Post-Sec.
1069 E Meadow Cir 94303 650-493-4430

**Palo Cedro, Shasta, Pop. 1,232**
Shasta UNHSD
Supt. — See Redding
Foothill HS 1,300/9-12
9733 Deschutes Rd 96073 530-547-1700
Jim Bartow, prin. Fax 245-2700
Foothill Plus HS 50/Alt
9733 Deschutes Rd 96073 530-245-2715
Jim Bartow, prin. Fax 245-2700

---

Redding Christian S 500/PK-12
21945 Old 44 Dr 96073 530-547-5600
Erika Piper, prin. Fax 547-5655

**Palos Verdes Estates, Los Angeles, Pop. 12,975**
Palos Verdes Peninsula USD 11,800/PK-12
375 Via Almar 90274 310-378-9966
Donald Austin Ed.D., supt. Fax 378-0732
www.pvpusd.net
Palos Verdes HS 1,700/9-12
600 Cloyden Rd 90274 310-378-8471
Charles Park Ed.D., prin. Fax 378-0311
Palos Verdes IS 1,000/6-8
2161 Via Olivera 90274 310-544-4816
Frank Califano, prin. Fax 265-5944
Other Schools – See Rancho Palos Verdes, Rolling Hills

**Palos Verdes Peninsula, See Rolling Hills Estates**

---

Chadwick S 800/K-12
26800 Academy Dr 90274 310-377-1543
Ted Hill, hdmstr. Fax 377-0380

**Panorama City, See Los Angeles**
Los Angeles USD
Supt. — See Los Angeles
Burke HS 200/Alt
14630 Lanark St 91402 818-781-7665
Phillip Koch, prin. Fax 781-3226
Panorama HS 2,000/9-12
8015 Van Nuys Blvd 91402 818-909-4500
Elias De La Torre, prin. Fax 786-6991

---

St. Genevieve HS 600/9-12
13967 Roscoe Blvd 91402 818-894-6417
Dan Horn, prin. Fax 892-9853
Western Beauty Institute Post-Sec.
8700 Van Nuys Blvd 91402 818-894-9550

**Paradise, Butte, Pop. 25,494**
Butte County Office of Education
Supt. — See Oroville
Paradise IS - RISE Alt
5657 Recreation Dr 95969 530-532-5642
Cheri Gamette, prin. Fax 532-5794

Paradise USD 4,400/K-12
6696 Clark Rd 95969 530-872-6400
Donna Colosky, supt. Fax 872-6409
www.pusdk12.org
Honey Run Academy Alt
622 Pearson Rd 95969 530-872-6461
Dena Kapsalis, prin. Fax 872-9708
Paradise HS 1,200/9-12
5911 Maxwell Dr 95969 530-872-6425
John Christie, prin. Fax 872-6427
Paradise IS 500/6-8
5657 Recreation Dr 95969 530-872-6465
Frederick Light, prin. Fax 876-1852
Paradise Adult S Adult
622 Pearson Rd 95969 530-872-6424
Mary Ficcardi, dir. Fax 872-9708
Other Schools – See Magalia

---

Paradise Adventist Academy 200/K-12
PO Box 2169 95967 530-877-6540
Lance Taggart, prin. Fax 877-0870

**Paramount, Los Angeles, Pop. 53,159**
Paramount USD 15,900/K-12
15110 California Ave 90723 562-602-6000
David Verdugo, supt. Fax 602-8123
www.paramount.k12.ca.us
Alondra MS 900/6-8
16200 Downey Ave 90723 562-602-8004
Lynn Butler, prin. Fax 602-8005
Jackson MS 800/4-8
7220 Jackson St 90723 562-602-8020
Kelly Anderson, prin. Fax 602-8021
Paramount Alternative Education Center Alt
3701 Michelson St, 562-602-8160
Andrea Aguilar, prin. Fax 602-8161
Paramount Community Day S 50/Alt
14507 Paramount Blvd 90723 562-602-8084
Jerry King, prin. Fax 602-8085
Paramount HS 3,700/10-12
14429 Downey Ave 90723 562-602-6064
Greg Buckner Ed.D., prin. Fax 602-6099
Paramount HS - West Campus 1,300/9-9
14708 Paramount Blvd 90723 562-602-8073
Morrie Kosareff, prin. Fax 602-8075
Paramount Park MS 800/6-8
14608 Paramount Blvd 90723 562-602-8052
Kevin Longworth, prin. Fax 602-8053
Zamboni MS 900/6-8
15733 Orange Ave 90723 562-602-8048
Elizabeth Salcido, prin. Fax 602-8049
Paramount Adult Education Adult
14507 Paramount Blvd 90723 562-602-8080
Jerry King, prin. Fax 602-8081
Other Schools – See Lakewood

---

Infotech Career College Post-Sec.
8527 Alondra Blvd Ste 174 90723 562-804-1239
Marinello School of Beauty Post-Sec.
8527 Alondra Blvd Ste 129 90723 714-998-7461

**Parlier, Fresno, Pop. 14,454**
Parlier USD 3,300/K-12
900 S Newmark Ave 93648 559-646-2731
Gerardo Alvarez, supt. Fax 646-0626
www.parlierunified.org
Parlier HS 800/9-12
603 3rd St 93648 559-646-3573
Alan Macedo, prin. Fax 646-2856
Parlier JHS 500/7-8
1200 E Parlier Ave 93648 559-646-1660
Julissa Alvarado, prin. Fax 646-1633
San Joaquin Valley HS 100/Alt
900 S Newmark Ave 93648 559-646-2723
Israel Almendarez, prin. Fax 888-0210

**Pasadena, Los Angeles, Pop. 132,725**
Pasadena USD 19,300/K-12
351 S Hudson Ave 91101 626-396-3600
Dr. Brian McDonald, supt. Fax 795-5309
www.pusd.us/
Blair HS 1,000/7-12
1135 5th St Ste A 91106 626-396-5820
Trudell Skinner, prin. Fax 799-2189
Center for Independent Study 200/Alt
2925 E Sierra Madre Blvd 91107 626-396-5883
Jack Loos, dir. Fax 398-8793
Marshall Fundamental JSHS 1,900/6-12
990 N Allen Ave 91104 626-396-5810
Dr. Mark Anderson, prin. Fax 798-0643
Muir HS 1,100/9-12
1905 Lincoln Ave 91103 626-396-5600
Timothy Sippel, prin. Fax 791-3499
Pasadena HS 2,000/9-12
2925 E Sierra Madre Blvd 91107 626-798-8901
Dr. Gilbert Barraza, prin. Fax 798-1875
Rose City HS 300/Alt
351 S Hudson Ave 91101 626-396-5620
Jack Loos, prin. Fax 683-9309
Washington MS 600/6-8
1505 N Marengo Ave 91103 626-396-5830
Dr. Merian Stewart, prin. Fax 798-2844
Wilson MS 700/6-8
300 Madre St 91107 626-396-5800
Sarah Rudchenko, prin. Fax 584-9895
Other Schools – See Altadena, Sierra Madre

---

AGBU Vatche & Tamar Manoukian HS 200/9-12
2495 E Mountain St 91104 626-794-0363
Dr. Armine Movsisyan, prin. Fax 240-0818
Art Center College of Design Post-Sec.
1700 Lida St 91103 626-396-2200
California Institute of Technology Post-Sec.
1200 E California Blvd 91125 626-395-6811
Fuller Theological Seminary Post-Sec.
135 N Oakland Ave 91182 626-584-5200
Huntington Memorial Hospital Post-Sec.
100 W California Blvd 91105 626-397-5000
Judson International S 100/K-12
1610 E Elizabeth St 91104 626-398-2476
Diana Bjoraker, prin. Fax 398-2222
La Salle HS 700/9-12
3880 E Sierra Madre Blvd 91107 626-351-8951
Christopher Brady, prin. Fax 351-0275
Le Cordon Bleu College of Culinary Arts Post-Sec.
530 E Colorado Blvd 91101 626-229-1300
Los Angeles College of Music Post-Sec.
370 S Fair Oaks Ave 91105 626-568-8850
Maranatha HS 600/9-12
169 S Saint John Ave 91105 626-817-4000
Dr. Michelle Purghart, prin. Fax 817-4040
Mayfield Senior S 300/9-12
500 Bellefontaine St 91105 626-799-9121
Kate Morin, head sch Fax 799-8576
North-West College Post-Sec.
530 E Union St 91101 626-796-5815
Pacific Oaks College Post-Sec.
55 Eureka St 91103 626-529-8061
Pasadena City College Post-Sec.
1570 E Colorado Blvd 91106 626-585-7123
Polytechnic S 900/K-12
1030 E California Blvd 91106 626-396-6300
John Bracker, head sch Fax 796-2249
Providence Christian College Post-Sec.
1539 E Howard St 91104 866-323-0233
Waverly S 100/PK-12
67 W Bellevue Dr 91105 626-792-5940
Heidi Johnson, head sch Fax 683-5460
Westridge S 500/4-12
324 Madeline Dr 91105 626-799-1153
Elizabeth McGregor, head sch Fax 799-9236

**Paso Robles, San Luis Obispo, Pop. 20,187**
Paso Robles JUSD 6,700/K-12
PO Box 7010 93447 805-769-1000
Chris Williams, supt. Fax 237-3339
www.pasoschools.org
Culinary Arts Academy Vo/Tech
PO Box 7010 93447 805-769-1133
Gregg Wangard, dir. Fax 237-3449
Flamson MS 700/6-8
PO Box 7010 93447 805-769-1400
Gene Miller, prin. Fax 237-3427
Independence HS 200/Alt
PO Box 7010 93447 805-769-1620
Paul Press, dir. Fax 237-3374
Lewis MS 700/6-8
PO Box 7010 93447 805-769-1450
Stuart Hamill, prin. Fax 237-3458
Liberty Continuation HS 100/Alt
PO Box 7010 93447 805-769-1600
Paul Press, dir. Fax 237-3466
Paso Robles HS 2,000/9-12
PO Box 7010 93447 805-769-1500
Randall Nelson, prin. Fax 237-3424

---

ACTS Advanced Christian Training S 100/K-12
3025 Adelaida Rd 93446 805-239-0707
Dr. William Thompson, supt. Fax 238-1133

**Patterson, Stanislaus, Pop. 19,584**
Patterson JUSD 5,800/PK-12
510 Keystone Blvd 95363 209-895-7700
Philip M. Alfano, supt. Fax 892-5803
www.patterson.k12.ca.us/
Creekside MS 1,200/6-8
535 Peregrine Dr 95363 209-892-4710
Kerry McWilliams, prin. Fax 892-7101
Del Puerto HS 100/Alt
640 M St 95363 209-892-4720
Jose Sanchez, prin. Fax 892-3533
Patterson HS 1,600/9-12
200 N 7th St 95363 209-892-4750
Tonya Bibbins, prin. Fax 892-7093

**Patton, San Bernardino, Pop. 1,000**

---

Patton State Hospital Post-Sec.
3102 E Highland Ave 92369 909-425-7297

**Pearblossom, Los Angeles**
Keppel UNESD 2,700/K-8
PO Box 186 93553 661-944-2155
Steve Doyle, supt. Fax 944-2933
www.keppel.k12.ca.us
Other Schools – See Littlerock

**Pebble Beach, Monterey, Pop. 3,600**

---

Stevenson S 500/9-12
3152 Forest Lake Rd 93953 831-625-8300
Dr. Kevin Hicks, pres. Fax 625-5208

**Penn Valley, Nevada, Pop. 1,545**
Penn Valley Union ESD 500/K-12
14806 Pleasant Valley Rd 95946 530-432-7311
Torie England Ed.D., supt. Fax 432-7314
www.pennvalleyschools.k12.ca.us/pages/Penn_Valley_Union_Elem_SD
Pleasant Valley S 300/4-8
14685 Pleasant Valley Rd 95946 530-432-7333
Teena Corker, prin. Fax 432-7338

**Perris, Riverside, Pop. 66,780**
Perris UNHSD 10,300/6-12
155 E 4th St 92570 951-943-6369
Dr. Jonathan Greenberg, supt. Fax 940-5378
www.puhsd.org

Academy Community Day S 100/Alt
515 E 7th St 92570 951-657-2174
Pauline Garcia, prin. Fax 657-8102
Perris HS 2,500/9-12
175 E Nuevo Rd 92571 951-657-2171
Nick Hilton, prin. Fax 940-5717
Perris Lake HS 400/Alt
418 W Ellis Ave 92570 951-657-7357
Dean Hauser, prin. Fax 940-5305
Pinacate MS 1,200/7-8
1990 S A St 92570 951-943-6441
Loretta Houston, prin. Fax 940-5344
Other Schools – See Menifee, Sun City

Val Verde USD 18,900/PK-12
975 Morgan St 92571 951-940-6100
Michael McCormick, supt. Fax 940-6121
www.valverde.edu
Citrus Hill HS 2,200/9-12
18150 Wood Rd 92570 951-490-0400
Nereyda Gonzalez, prin. Fax 490-0405
Lakeside MS 1,200/7-8
27720 Walnut St 92571 951-443-2440
John Parker, prin. Fax 443-2445
Rivera MS 1,000/6-8
21675 Martin St 92570 951-940-8570
Esteban Lizarraga, prin. Fax 940-6133
Val Verde Continuation HS 500/Alt
972 Morgan St 92571 951-940-6155
Steve Coelho, prin. Fax 940-6158
Other Schools – See Moreno Valley

**Pescadero, San Mateo, Pop. 633**
La Honda-Pescadero USD 300/PK-12
PO Box 189 94060 650-879-0286
Amy Wooliever, supt. Fax 879-0816
www.lhpusd.com
Pescadero MSHS 100/6-12
PO Box 730 94060 650-879-0274
Patricia Talbot, prin. Fax 879-0589

**Petaluma, Sonoma, Pop. 56,146**
Petaluma SD 7,700/K-12
200 Douglas St 94952 707-778-4604
Gary Callahan, supt. Fax 778-4736
www.petalumacityschools.org
Carpe Diem HS 50/Alt
199 Fair St 94952 707-778-4796
Greg Stevenson, prin. Fax 762-7099
Casa Grande HS 1,700/9-12
333 Casa Grande Rd 94954 707-778-4677
Eric Backman, prin. Fax 778-4687
Crossroads S 50/Alt
700 Bantam Way 94952 707-778-4793
Kenilworth JHS 900/7-8
800 Riesling Rd 94954 707-778-4710
Bennett Holley, prin. Fax 766-8231
Petaluma HS 1,300/9-12
201 Fair St 94952 707-778-4651
David Stirrrat, prin. Fax 778-4767
Petaluma JHS 600/7-8
700 Bantam Way 94952 707-778-4724
Renee Semik, prin. Fax 778-4600
San Antonio HS 100/Alt
500 Vallejo St 94952 707-778-4758
Rebecca Lofton, prin. Fax 778-4899
Sonoma Mountain HS 50/Alt
299 Casa Grande Rd 94954 707-778-4738
Greg Stevenson, prin. Fax 778-1350
Valley Oaks Alternative S 100/Alt
540 Vallejo St 94952 707-778-4794
Rebecca Lofton, prin. Fax 778-4898
Petaluma Adult S Adult
200 Douglas St 94952 707-778-4633
Carol Waxman, prin. Fax 778-4785

---

St. Vincent de Paul HS 300/9-12
849 Keokuk St 94952 707-763-1032
Dr. John Walker, prin. Fax 763-9448
Santa Rosa Junior College Post-Sec.
680 Sonoma Mountain Pkwy 94954 707-778-2415

**Petrolia, Humboldt**
Mattole USD 700/PK-12
PO Box 211 95558 707-629-3311
Richard Graey, supt. Fax 629-3575
www.humboldt.k12.ca.us/mattole_usd
Mattole Triple Junction HS 50/9-12
PO Box 211 95558 707-629-3250
Karen Ashmore, prin. Fax 629-3551

**Phelan, San Bernardino, Pop. 13,933**
Snowline JUSD 8,300/K-12
PO Box 296000 92329 760-868-5817
Eric Johnston, supt. Fax 868-5309
www.snowlineschools.com/
Chaparral HS 200/Alt
PO Box 296000 92329 760-868-5400
Dave Smith, prin. Fax 868-4725
Eagle Summit Community S 100/Alt
PO Box 296000 92329 760-868-3442
Dave Smith, coord. Fax 868-6402
Pinon Mesa MS 800/6-8
PO Box 296000 92329 760-868-3126
Burt Umstead, prin. Fax 868-3033
Quail Valley MS 1,000/6-8
PO Box 296000 92329 760-949-4888
Dennis Zimmerman, prin. Fax 949-3663
Serrano HS 2,500/9-12
PO Box 296000 92329 760-868-3222
Sharon Schlegel, prin. Fax 868-3803
Snowline Virtual S 100/Alt
PO Box 296000 92329 760-868-6277
Dave Smith, prin. Fax 868-4024

**Pico Rivera, Los Angeles, Pop. 62,624**
El Rancho USD 9,900/PK-12
9333 Loch Lomond Dr 90660 562-942-1500
Martin Galindo, supt. Fax 949-2821
erusd.org
El Rancho HS 3,000/9-12
6501 Passons Blvd 90660 562-801-5295
Sam Genis, prin. Fax 801-5293
North Park Academy of the Arts 900/6-8
4450 Durfee Ave 90660 562-801-5137
Priscilla Rodriguez, prin. Fax 801-5143
Rivera MS 800/6-8
7200 Citronell Ave 90660 562-801-5088
Yvette Ventura-Rincon, prin. Fax 801-9158
Salazar Continuation HS 200/Alt
9115 Balfour St 90660 562-801-5021
Reynaldo Reyes, prin. Fax 942-9458
STEAM Academy @ Burke 600/6-8
8101 Orange Ave 90660 562-801-5059
Elias Vargas, prin. Fax 801-5067
El Rancho Adult Education Center Adult
9515 Haney St 90660 562-801-5009
Charles Collings, prin. Fax 948-2041

---

Armenian Mesrobian S 200/PK-12
8420 Beverly Rd 90660 562-699-2057
David Ghoogasian, prin. Fax 699-0757

**Piedmont, Alameda, Pop. 10,117**
Piedmont City USD 2,500/K-12
760 Magnolia Ave 94611 510-594-2600
Constance Hubbard, supt. Fax 654-7374
www.piedmont.k12.ca.us
Millennium HS 100/Alt
760 Magnolia Ave 94611 510-594-2703
Ting Hsu Engelman, prin. Fax 594-2791
Piedmont HS 800/9-12
800 Magnolia Ave 94611 510-594-2626
Brent Daniels, prin. Fax 450-0425
Piedmont MS 600/6-8
740 Magnolia Ave 94611 510-594-2660
Ryan Fletcher, prin. Fax 595-3523
Piedmont Adult S Adult
740 Magnolia Ave 94611 510-594-2655
Michael Brady, dir. Fax 595-8173

**Pinecrest, Tuolumne**
Summerville UNHSD
Supt. — See Tuolumne
Mountain HS 50/Alt
2 Pinecrest School Rd 95364 209-965-4046
David Johnstone, prin. Fax 928-1422

**Pine Valley, San Diego, Pop. 1,469**
Mountain Empire USD 1,800/PK-12
3291 Buckman Springs Rd 91962 619-473-9022
Dr. Kathy Granger, supt. Fax 473-9728
meusd.schoolwires.net
Mountain Empire HS 400/9-12
3305 Buckman Springs Rd 91962 619-473-8601
Patrick Keeley, prin. Fax 473-8038
Pine Valley MS 100/6-8
PO Box 571 91962 619-473-8693
Gary Brannon, prin. Fax 473-8026
Other Schools – See Jacumba

**Pinole, Contra Costa, Pop. 17,432**
West Contra Costa USD
Supt. — See Richmond
Pinole MS 700/7-8
1575 Mann Dr 94564 510-231-1436
Denise Van Hook, prin. Fax 724-9583
Pinole Valley HS 1,500/9-12
2900 Pinole Valley Rd 94564 510-231-1442
Sue Kahn, prin. Fax 758-6054

**Pismo Beach, San Luis Obispo, Pop. 7,494**
Lucia Mar USD
Supt. — See Arroyo Grande
Judkins MS 500/7-8
680 Wadsworth Ave 93449 805-474-3600
Ian Penton, prin. Fax 473-4376

---

Coastal Christian S 200/K-12
1005 N Oak Park Blvd 93449 805-489-1213
Dave Rehnberg M.A., prin. Fax 489-5394

**Pittsburg, Contra Costa, Pop. 60,137**
Pittsburg USD 11,200/PK-12
2000 Railroad Ave 94565 925-473-2300
Janet Schulze Ed.D., supt. Fax 473-4274
www.pittsburg.k12.ca.us
Black Diamond HS 300/Alt
1131 Stoneman Ave 94565 925-473-2510
Brian Wilson, prin.
Hillview JHS 1,200/6-8
333 Yosemite Dr 94565 925-473-2380
Maria Gonzalez, prin. Fax 473-4406
King JHS, 2012 Carion Ct 94565 800/6-8
Angela Stevenson, prin. 925-473-2500
Pittsburg HS 2,700/9-12
1750 Harbor St 94565 925-473-2390
Todd Whitmire, prin. Fax 473-4183
Rancho Medanos JHS 1,200/6-8
2301 Range Rd 94565 925-473-2490
Eric Peyko, prin. Fax 473-1060
Pittsburg Adult Education Center Adult
1151 Stoneman Ave 94565 925-473-4460
Lynne Nicodemus, prin. Fax 473-4470

---

Light the Bay Christian Academy 100/PK-12
1210 Stoneman Ave 94565 925-439-2552
Edward Marquardt, prin. Fax 439-2555
Los Medanos College Post-Sec.
2700 E Leland Rd 94565 925-439-2181

**Pixley, Tulare, Pop. 3,289**
Pixley UNESD 1,100/PK-8
300 N School St 93256 559-757-5207
Dr. Heather Elick, supt. Fax 757-0705
www.pixley.k12.ca.us/
Pixley MS 300/6-8
1520 E Court Ave 93256 559-757-3018
Monty Dunbar, prin. Fax 757-3507

**Placentia, Orange, Pop. 49,404**
Placentia-Yorba Linda USD 25,500/K-12
1301 E Orangethorpe Ave 92870 714-986-7000
Doug Domene, supt. Fax 524-3034
www.pylusd.org/
El Camino Real Continuation HS 200/Alt
1351 E Orangethorpe Ave 92870 714-986-7060
Gordon Chamberlin, prin. Fax 996-0294
El Dorado HS 2,000/9-12
1651 Valencia Ave 92870 714-986-7580
Carey Cecil, prin. Fax 524-2458
Kraemer MS 900/6-8
645 N Angelina Dr 92870 714-996-1551
Keith Carmona, prin. Fax 996-8407
Tuffree MS 700/7-8
2151 N Kraemer Blvd 92870 714-986-7480
Rosie Baldwin-Shirey, prin. Fax 993-6359
Valadez MS Academy 700/6-8
161 E La Jolla St 92870 714-986-7440
James Hardin, prin. Fax 238-9159
Valencia HS 2,600/9-12
500 N Bradford Ave 92870 714-996-4970
Rick Lopez, prin. Fax 996-3159
Other Schools – See Anaheim, Yorba Linda

**Placerville, El Dorado, Pop. 10,089**
El Dorado County Office of Education 700/
6767 Green Valley Rd 95667 530-622-7130
Jeremy Meyers, supt. Fax 621-2543
www.edcoe.org
El Dorado COE Adult Education Adult
6767 Green Valley Rd 95667 530-295-0007
David Publicover, dir. Fax 621-1395

El Dorado UNHSD 6,800/9-12
4675 Missouri Flat Rd 95667 530-622-5081
Stephen Wehr, supt. Fax 642-0806
www.eduhsd.k12.ca.us
El Dorado HS 1,400/9-12
561 Canal St 95667 530-622-3634
Chas Prior, prin. Fax 622-1802
Vista HS 100/Alt
561 Canal St 95667 530-622-3634
Leslie Redkey, prin. Fax 622-1802
Other Schools – See Diamond Springs, El Dorado, El Dorado Hills, Shingle Springs

Gold Oak UNESD 400/PK-8
3171 Pleasant Valley Rd 95667 530-626-3150
Wendy Neade, supt. Fax 626-3145
www.gousd.org
Pleasant Valley MS 100/6-8
4120 Pleasant Valley Rd 95667 530-644-9620
Wendy Neade, prin. Fax 644-9622

Gold Trail UNESD 500/K-8
1575 Old Ranch Rd 95667 530-626-3194
Joe Murchison, supt. Fax 626-3199
www.gtusd.org
Gold Trail MS 300/4-8
889 Cold Springs Rd 95667 530-626-2595
Scott Lyons, head sch Fax 626-3289

Mother Lode UNESD 1,200/K-8
3783 Forni Rd 95667 530-622-6464
Marcy Guthrie, supt. Fax 622-6163
www.mlusd.net
Green MS 500/5-8
3781 Forni Rd 95667 530-622-4668
Jason Harm, prin. Fax 622-4680

Placerville UNSD 1,300/K-8
1032 Thompson Way 95667 530-622-7216
Eric Bonniksen, supt. Fax 622-0336
www.pusdk8.us/
Markham MS 400/6-8
2800 Moulton Dr 95667 530-622-0403
Terry Edinger, prin. Fax 622-5584

Regional Occupational Center & Program
Supt. — None
Central Sierra ROP Vo/Tech
4675 Missouri Flat Rd 95667 530-621-0123
Carolyn Zachary, dir.

---

El Dorado Adventist S 200/K-12
1900 Broadway 95667 530-622-3560

**Planada, Merced, Pop. 4,571**
Planada ESD 800/PK-8
PO Box 236 95365 209-382-0756
Jose L. Gonzalez, supt. Fax 382-1750
www.planada.k12.ca.us/
Chavez MS 200/6-8
PO Box 236 95365 209-382-0768
Jose Duran, prin. Fax 382-0775

**Playa Del Rey, See Los Angeles**

---

St. Bernard HS 400/9-12
9100 Falmouth Ave 90293 310-823-4651
Dr. Cynthia Hoepner, prin. Fax 827-3365

**Pleasant Hill, Contra Costa, Pop. 31,678**
Contra Costa County Office of Education 1,000/
77 Santa Barbara Rd 94523 925-942-3388
Dr. Karen Sakata, supt. Fax 472-0875
www.cocoschools.org
Other Schools – See Martinez, Richmond

Mount Diablo USD
Supt. — See Concord
College Park HS 2,000/9-12
201 Viking Dr 94523 925-682-7670
Paul Gengler, prin. Fax 676-7892
Horizons 200/Alt
1 Santa Barbara Rd 94523 925-938-2564
Sharon Brockman, admin. Fax 937-6271
Pleasant Hill MS 800/6-8
1 Santa Barbara Rd 94523 925-256-0791
Terry McCormick, prin. Fax 937-6271
Prospect HS 50/Alt
1 Santa Barbara Rd 94523 925-945-7902
Sharon Brockman, admin. Fax 937-6271
Sequoia MS 900/6-8
265 Boyd Rd 94523 925-934-8174
Kevin Honey, prin. Fax 946-9063
Valley View MS 800/6-8
181 Viking Dr 94523 925-686-6136
Ean Ainsworth, prin. Fax 687-5381
Pleasant Hill Adult Center Adult
1 Santa Barbara Rd 94523 925-937-1530
Fax 937-6271

Regional Occupational Center & Program
Supt. — None
Contra Costa County ROP Vo/Tech
77 Santa Barbara Rd 94523 925-942-3368
Janet Haun, dir. Fax 934-1057

---

Carrington College California Post-Sec.
380 Civic Dr Ste 300 94523 925-298-6299
Diablo Valley College Post-Sec.
321 Golf Club Rd 94523 925-685-1230
John F. Kennedy University Post-Sec.
100 Ellinwood Way 94523 925-969-3300
Pleasant Hill Adventist Academy 200/K-12
796 Grayson Rd 94523 925-934-9261
Susan Walters, prin. Fax 934-5871

**Pleasanton, Alameda, Pop. 67,470**
Pleasanton USD 14,900/K-12
4665 Bernal Ave 94566 925-462-5500
James Hansen, supt. Fax 484-3591
pleasantonusd.net
Amador Valley HS 2,600/9-12
1155 Santa Rita Rd 94566 925-461-6100
Thomas Drescher, prin. Fax 461-6133
Foothill HS 2,200/9-12
4375 Foothill Rd 94588 925-461-6650
Jason Krolikowski, prin. Fax 461-6633
Hart MS 1,100/6-8
4433 Willow Rd 94588 925-426-3102
Terry Conde, prin. Fax 460-0799
Harvest Park MS 1,200/6-8
4900 Valley Ave 94566 925-426-4444
Jill Butler, prin. Fax 426-9613
Pleasanton MS 1,200/6-8
5001 Case Ave 94566 925-426-4390
Aileen Parsons, prin. Fax 426-1382
Village Continuation HS 200/Alt
4645 Bernal Ave 94566 925-426-4260
Dana Chavez, prin. Fax 426-8394

**Plumas Lake, Yuba, Pop. 5,494**
Plumas Lake ESD 1,100/K-8
2743 Plumas School Rd, 530-743-4428
Jeff Roberts, supt. Fax 743-1408
www.plusd.org
Riverside Meadows IS 300/6-8
1751 Cimarron Dr, 530-743-1271
Jason Hofhenke, prin. Fax 743-8970

**Point Arena, Mendocino, Pop. 438**
Point Arena SD 500/K-12
PO Box 87 95468 707-882-2803
Brent Cushenbery Ed.D., supt. Fax 882-2848
www.pointarenaschools.org
Point Arena HS 200/9-12
PO Box 7 95468 707-882-2134
Rebekah Barakos-Cartwrig, prin. Fax 882-3453
South Coast Continuation HS 50/Alt
PO Box 87 95468 707-882-2307
Leah Martini, prin. Fax 882-2309

**Pollock Pines, El Dorado, Pop. 6,676**
Pollock Pines ESD 700/K-8
2701 Amber Trl 95726 530-644-5416
Kevin Monsma, supt. Fax 644-5483
www.ppesd.org
Sierra Ridge MS 300/5-8
2700 Amber Trl 95726 530-644-2031
Kim Little, prin. Fax 644-0198

**Pomona, Los Angeles, Pop. 146,537**
Los Angeles County Office of Education
Supt. — See Downey
International Polytechnic HS 500/Alt
3801 W Temple Ave 91768 909-869-4567
Bruce Petersen, prin. Fax 869-2202

Pomona USD 26,000/PK-12
PO Box 2900 91769 909-397-4800
Richard Martinez, supt. Fax 397-4881
www.pusd.org
Diamond Ranch HS 1,900/9-12
100 Diamond Ranch Rd 91766 909-397-4715
S. Steinsefer-Ripley, prin. Fax 591-9374
Emerson MS 600/6-8
635 Lincoln Ave 91767 909-397-4516
Jesus Altamirano, prin. Fax 397-5280
Fremont Academy of Engineering & Design Vo/Tech
725 W Franklin Ave 91766 909-397-4521
Elizabeth Harper, prin. Fax 620-6229
Ganesha HS 1,300/9-12
1151 Fairplex Dr 91768 909-397-4400
Jennifer Francev, prin. Fax 629-4069
Garey HS 1,700/9-12
321 W Lexington Ave 91766 909-397-4451
Stacey Wilkins, prin. Fax 620-1575
Marshall MS 600/6-8
1921 Arroyo Ave 91768 909-397-4532
Juan Ortiz, prin. Fax 629-8275
Palomares Academy of Health Sciences Vo/Tech
2211 N Orange Grove Ave 91767 909-397-4539
Camille Ramos-Beal, prin. Fax 625-0337
Park West HS 200/Alt
1460 E Holt Ave Ste 100 91767 909-397-4900
Neville Brown, prin. Fax 865-2423
Pomona Alternative S 50/Alt
1460 E Holt Ave Ste 100 91767 909-397-4900
Neville Brown, prin. Fax 865-2423
Pomona Community Day S Alt
605 North Park Ave 91766 909-397-4491
Tom Sweeney, dir.
Pomona HS 1,400/9-12
475 Bangor St 91767 909-397-4498
Roger Fasting, prin. Fax 629-1410
Simons MS 700/6-8
900 E Franklin Ave 91766 909-397-4544
Cristine Goens, prin. Fax 623-4691
Village Academy HS Vo/Tech
1444 E Holt Ave 91767 909-397-4900
Marco Sanchez, prin. Fax 865-9250
Pomona Adult & Career Education Adult
1515 W Mission Blvd 91766 909-469-2333
Dr. Enrique Medina, dir. Fax 623-3841
Other Schools – See Diamond Bar

Regional Occupational Center & Program
Supt. — None
San Antonio ROP Vo/Tech
1425 E Holt Ave Ste 101 91767 909-469-2304
Enrique Medina, dir.

---

California State Polytechnic University Post-Sec.
3801 W Temple Ave 91768 909-869-7659
Carrington College California Post-Sec.
901 Corporate Center Dr 300 91768 909-366-4122
City of Knowledge S 200/PK-12
3285 N Garey Ave 91767 909-392-0251
Dr. Haleema Shaikley, prin. Fax 392-0295
DeVry University Post-Sec.
901 Corporate Center Dr 91768 909-622-8866
North-West College Post-Sec.
134 W Holt Ave 91768 909-623-1552
Pomona Catholic HS 300/6-12
533 W Holt Ave 91768 909-623-5297
Samuel Torres, prin. Fax 620-6057
Western University of Health Sciences Post-Sec.
309 E 2nd St 91766 909-623-6116

**Porterville, Tulare, Pop. 53,236**
Burton ESD 4,500/K-12
264 N Westwood St 93257 559-781-8020
Sharon Kamberg Ed.D., supt. Fax 781-1403
www.burtonschools.org
Burton Community Day S Alt
264 N Westwood St 93257 559-781-8020
Jean Miller, dir. Fax 781-1403
Burton MS 600/7-8
1155 N Elderwood St 93257 559-781-2671
Chastity Lollis Ed.D., prin. Fax 788-6424

Pleasant View ESD 800/PK-8
14004 Road 184 93257 559-784-6769
Mark Odsather, supt. Fax 784-6819
www.pleasant-view.org
Pleasant View West S 400/4-8
14004 Road 184 93257 559-784-6769
Mark Odsather, supt. Fax 784-6819

Porterville USD 13,500/K-12
600 W Grand Ave 93257 559-793-2400
John Snavely Ed.D., supt. Fax 793-1088
www.portervilleschools.org
Bartlett MS 500/7-8
600 W Grand Ave 93257 559-782-7100
Mike Tsuboi, prin. Fax 784-3432
Citrus Continuation HS 200/Alt
600 W Grand Ave 93257 559-782-7130
Scott Braden, prin. Fax 782-3643
Granite Hills HS 1,100/9-12
600 W Grand Ave 93257 559-782-7075
Apolinar Marroquin, prin. Fax 789-9357
Monache HS 1,900/9-12
600 W Grand Ave 93257 559-782-7150
Eric Barba Ed.D., prin. Fax 781-3377
Pioneer MS 500/6-8
600 W Grand Ave 93257 559-782-7200
Angel Valdez, prin. Fax 784-3507
Porterville HS 1,800/9-12
600 W Grand Ave 93257 559-782-7210
Jose Valdez, prin. Fax 782-7215
Prospect Education Center 100/Alt
600 W Grand Ave 93257 559-782-7095
Dawn Crater, dir. Fax 781-6846
Sequoia MS 500/7-8
600 W Grand Ave 93257 559-788-0925
Joe Santos Ed.D., prin. Fax 788-0927
Vine Street Community Day S 50/Alt
600 W Grand Ave 93257 559-782-6650
Monty Newkirk, prin. Fax 782-6652
Porterville Adult S Adult
600 W Grand Ave 93257 559-782-7030
Fernando Carrera, dir. Fax 781-4943
Other Schools – See Strathmore

Regional Occupational Center & Program
Supt. — None
Tulare Co. Organization/Vocational Educ Vo/Tech
600 W Grand Ave 93257 559-793-2406
Melinda Brown, dir.

---

Porterville College Post-Sec.
100 E College Ave 93257 559-791-2200

**Port Hueneme, Ventura, Pop. 20,969**
Hueneme ESD 8,200/K-8
205 N Ventura Rd 93041 805-488-3588
Dr. Jerry Dannenberg, supt. Fax 986-8755
www.huensd.k12.ca.us
Other Schools – See Oxnard

**Portola, Plumas, Pop. 2,059**
Plumas USD
Supt. — See Quincy
Beckwourth HS 50/Alt
155 6th Ave 96122 530-832-4284
Terry Oestreich, prin. Fax 832-5582
Portola JSHS 200/7-12
155 6th Ave 96122 530-832-4284
Sara Sheridan, prin. Fax 832-5582

**Portola Valley, San Mateo, Pop. 4,271**
Portola Valley ESD 700/K-8
4575 Alpine Rd 94028 650-851-1777
Dr. Lisa Gonzales, supt. Fax 851-3700
www.pvsd.net
Corte Madera MS 400/4-8
4575 Alpine Rd 94028 650-851-1777
Cyndi Maijala, prin. Fax 529-8553

---

Woodside Priory HS 300/9-12
302 Portola Rd 94028 650-851-8221
Brian Schlaak, prin. Fax 851-2839
Woodside Priory MS 100/6-8
302 Portola Rd 94028 650-851-8221
Caitha Ambler, prin. Fax 851-2839

**Potter Valley, Mendocino, Pop. 628**
Potter Valley Community USD 200/PK-12
PO Box 219 95469 707-743-2101
Damon Dickinson, supt. Fax 743-1930
www.pottervalleyschools.us
Centerville HS 50/Alt
PO Box 219 95469 707-743-1762
Mindi Juszczak, prin. Fax 743-2879
Potter Valley JSHS 100/7-12
PO Box 219 95469 707-743-1142
Mindi Juszczak, prin. Fax 743-2879

**Poway, San Diego, Pop. 46,170**
Poway USD
Supt. — See San Diego
Abraxas Continuation HS 200/Alt
12450 Glenoak Rd 92064 858-748-5900
David MacLeod, prin. Fax 679-1739
Meadowbrook MS 1,300/6-8
12320 Meadowbrook Ln 92064 858-748-0802
Miguel Carrillo, prin. Fax 679-0149
Poway HS 2,400/9-12
15500 Espola Rd 92064 858-748-0245
Ron Garrett, prin. Fax 679-6879
Twin Peaks MS 1,300/6-8
14640 Tierra Bonita Rd 92064 858-748-5131
Kelly Burke, prin. Fax 679-6823
Poway Adult S Adult
13626 Twin Peaks Rd 92064 858-668-4024
Kathleen Porter, dir. Fax 748-7423

---

Poway Academy of Hair Design Post-Sec.
13266 Poway Rd 92064 858-748-1490

**Prather, Fresno, Pop. 30**
Sierra USD 1,000/K-12
29143 Auberry Rd 93651 559-855-3662
Dr. Melissa Ireland, supt. Fax 855-3585
www.sierrausd.org
Other Schools – See Tollhouse

**Princeton, Colusa, Pop. 299**
Princeton JUSD 200/K-12
PO Box 8 95970 530-439-2261
Cody Walker, supt. Fax 439-2113
www.pjusd.org
Princeton JSHS 100/7-12
PO Box 8 95970 530-439-2261
Cody Walker, prin. Fax 439-2113

**Prunedale, Monterey, Pop. 16,965**

---

Prunedale Christian Academy 100/PK-12
8145 Prunedale North Rd 93907 831-663-2211
Dr. E.L. Moon, admin. Fax 663-1663

**Quartz Hill, Los Angeles, Pop. 10,599**
Antelope Valley UNHSD
Supt. — See Lancaster
Quartz Hill HS 3,100/9-12
6040 W Avenue L 93536 661-718-3100
Matt Anderson, prin. Fax 943-8203

Westside UNESD 8,500/K-8
41914 50th St W 93536 661-722-0716
Regina Rossall, supt. Fax 206-3645
www.westside.k12.ca.us
Walker MS 900/7-8
5632 W Avenue L8 93536 661-943-3258
Steve Wood, prin. Fax 943-2969
Other Schools – See Lancaster, Palmdale

**Quincy, Plumas, Pop. 1,652**
Plumas County Office of Education 50/
1446 E Main St 95971 530-283-6500
Terry Oestreich, admin. Fax 283-6530
www.pcoe.k12.ca.us
Plumas County Community S 50/Alt
1446 E Main St 95971 530-283-6500
Kristy Warren, prin. Fax 283-6509
Plumas County Opportunity S 50/Alt
1446 E Main St 95971 530-283-6500
Fax 283-6530

Plumas USD 2,000/K-12
1446 E Main St 95971 530-283-6500
Terry Oestreich, supt. Fax 283-6530
www.pcoe.k12.ca.us
Quincy JSHS 300/7-12
6 Quincy Junction Rd 95971 530-283-6510
Dr. Sue Segura, prin. Fax 283-6519
Other Schools – See Chester, Greenville, Portola

Regional Occupational Center & Program
Supt. — None
Plumas County ROP Vo/Tech
50 Church St Ste B 95971 530-283-6500
Terry Oestreich, dir. Fax 283-6509

---

Feather River College Post-Sec.
570 Golden Eagle Ave 95971 530-283-0202

**Ramona, San Diego, Pop. 19,844**
Ramona USD 6,000/K-12
720 9th St 92065 760-787-2000
Dr. Bob Graeff, supt. Fax 789-9168
www.ramonausd.net/
Future Bound Independent Study Alt
720 Ninth St 92065 760-787-2068
Dave Lohman, prin. Fax 788-3754
Montecito HS 100/Alt
720 9th St 92065 760-787-4300
Dave Lohman, prin. Fax 789-0928
Peirce MS 800/7-8
1521 Hanson Ln 92065 760-787-2400
Pauline Leavitt, prin. Fax 788-5014
Ramona Community S 600/Alt
1010 Ramona St 92065 760-788-5130
Kathryn Gunderson, prin. Fax 788-5918
Ramona HS 1,900/9-12
1401 Hanson Ln 92065 760-787-4000
Chris King, prin. Fax 789-4596

**Rancho Cordova, Sacramento, Pop. 60,932**
Folsom-Cordova USD 19,100/PK-12
1965 Birkmont Dr 95742 916-294-9000
Debbie Bettencourt, supt. Fax 294-9020
www.fcusd.org
Cordova HS 1,800/9-12
2239 Chase Dr 95670 916-294-2450
Dan Anklam, prin. Fax 294-9080
Kinney Continuation HS 200/Alt
2710 Kilgore Rd 95670 916-635-1292
Dana Carrigan, prin. Fax 635-0719
Mills MS 800/6-8
10439 Coloma Rd 95670 916-363-6544
Peter Maroon, prin. Fax 361-3744
Mitchell MS 800/6-8
2100 Zinfandel Dr 95670 916-635-8460
Jim Huber, prin. Fax 635-8979
Walnutwood Independent Study HS 200/Alt
10850 Gadsten Way 95670 916-638-2598
Charlie Linebarger, prin. Fax 635-6147
Folsom-Cordova Adult Education Adult
10850 Gadsten Way 95670 916-635-6810
Charlie Linebarger, prin. Fax 635-0905
Other Schools – See Folsom, Mather

---

California Northstate Coll of Pharmacy Post-Sec.
10811 International Dr 95670 916-631-8108
Heald College Post-Sec.
2910 Prospect Park Dr 95670 916-638-1616
ITT Technical Institute Post-Sec.
10863 Gold Center Dr 95670 916-851-3900
National Career Education Post-Sec.
11080 White Rock Rd Ste 100 95670 916-969-4900
San Joaquin Valley College Post-Sec.
11050 Olson Dr Ste 210 95670 916-638-7582

**Rancho Cucamonga, San Bernardino, Pop. 159,896**
Central ESD 4,800/K-8
10601 Church St Ste 112 91730 909-989-8541
Donna Libutti, supt. Fax 941-1732
www.csd-ca.schoolloop.com
Cucamonga MS 900/6-8
7611 Hellman Ave 91730 909-987-1788
Jeff Koenig, prin. Fax 483-3201
Musser MS 1,000/5-8
10789 Terra Vista Pkwy 91730 909-980-1230
Mary Kate Perez, prin. Fax 980-3042

Chaffey JUNHSD
Supt. — See Ontario
Los Osos HS 3,300/9-12
6001 Milliken Ave 91737 909-477-6900
Susan Petrocelli, prin. Fax 460-5872
Rancho Cucamonga HS 3,200/9-12
11801 Lark Dr 91701 909-989-1600
Cary Willborn, prin. Fax 945-5355

Cucamonga ESD 2,600/K-8
8776 Archibald Ave 91730 909-987-8942
Janet Temkin, supt. Fax 980-3628
www.cucamonga-ca.schoolloop.com
Rancho Cucamonga MS 900/6-8
8776 Archibald Ave 91730 909-980-0969
Bruce LaVallee, prin. Fax 481-5381

Regional Occupational Center & Program
Supt. — None
Baldy View ROP Vo/Tech
8265 Aspen St Ste 100 91730 909-980-6490
Shelley Adams, supt. Fax 980-8364

---

Chaffey College Post-Sec.
5885 Haven Ave 91737 909-652-6000
San Joaquin Valley College Post-Sec.
10641 Church St 91730 909-948-7582
Universal Technical Institute Post-Sec.
9494 Haven Ave 91730 909-484-1929
Upland Christian Academy 400/K-12
10900 Civic Center Dr 91730 909-758-8747
Tim Hoy, supt. Fax 204-4555

**Rancho Mirage, Riverside, Pop. 16,964**
Palm Springs USD
Supt. — See Palm Springs
Rancho Mirage HS 9-12
31001 Rattler Rd 92270 760-202-6455
Ken Wagner Ed.D., prin.

---

Eisenhower Memorial Hospital Post-Sec.
39000 Bob Hope Dr 92270 760-340-3911
Palm Valley S 400/PK-12
35525 Da Vall Dr 92270 760-328-0861
Robert E. Graves, head sch Fax 770-4541
Santa Barbara Business College Post-Sec.
34275 Monterey Ave 92270 866-749-7222

**Rancho Palos Verdes, Los Angeles, Pop. 39,919**
Los Angeles USD
Supt. — See Los Angeles
Dodson MS 1,800/6-8
28014 S Montereina Dr 90275 310-241-1900
John Vladovic, prin. Fax 832-4709

Palos Verdes Peninsula USD
Supt. — See Palos Verdes Estates
Miraleste IS 900/6-8
29323 Palos Verdes Dr E 90275 310-732-0900
Brent Kuykendall, prin. Fax 521-8915
Ridgecrest IS 900/6-8
28915 Northbay Rd 90275 310-544-2747
Kelli Keller, prin. Fax 265-1716

---

Marymount California University Post-Sec.
30800 Palos Verdes Dr E 90275 310-377-5501
Salvation Army College Officer Training Post-Sec.
30840 Hawthorne Blvd 90275 310-377-0481

**Rancho Santa Fe, San Diego, Pop. 3,061**
Rancho Sante Fe ESD 600/K-8
PO Box 809 92067 858-756-1141
Lindy Delaney, supt. Fax 756-0912
www.rsfschool.net/
Rowe MS 200/6-8
PO Box 809 92067 858-756-1141
Garrett Corduan, prin. Fax 759-0712

---

Horizon Prep 500/PK-12
PO Box 9070 92067 858-756-5599
Dr. Ken Kush, head sch Fax 759-5827

**Rancho Santa Margarita, Orange, Pop. 46,094**
Capistrano USD
Supt. — See San Juan Capistrano
Las Flores MS 1,100/6-8
25862 Antonio Pkwy 92688 949-589-6543
Robert Miller, prin. Fax 589-9286
Tesoro HS 2,400/9-12
1 Tesoro Creek Rd 92688 949-234-5310
Marc Patterson, prin. Fax 766-3370

Saddleback Valley USD
Supt. — See Mission Viejo
Rancho Santa Margarita IS 1,600/7-8
21931 Alma Aldea 92688 949-459-8253
Rick Jameson, prin. Fax 459-8258

---

Santa Margarita HS 1,600/9-12
22062 Antonio Pkwy 92688 949-766-6000
Ray Dunne, prin. Fax 766-6005

**Raymond, Madera**
Yosemite USD
Supt. — See Oakhurst
Raymond Granite HS 50/Alt
PO Box 228 93653 559-689-3490
Dr. Randy Haggard, prin.

**Red Bluff, Tehama, Pop. 13,607**
Antelope ESD 700/K-8
22630 Antelope Blvd 96080 530-527-1272
Richard Hassay, supt. Fax 527-2931
www.antelopeschools.org/
Berrendos MS 200/6-8
401 Chestnut Ave 96080 530-527-6700
Jim Weber, prin. Fax 527-2506

Red Bluff JUNHSD 1,600/9-12
PO Box 1507 96080 530-529-8700
Todd Brose, supt. Fax 529-8709
www.rbhsd.org
Red Bluff HS 1,400/9-12
1260 Union St 96080 530-529-8710
Ron Fisher, prin. Fax 529-8739
Salisbury HS 100/Alt
1050 Kimball Rd 96080 530-529-8766
Barbara Thomas, prin. Fax 529-8840

Red Bluff UNESD 1,900/K-8
1755 Airport Blvd 96080 530-527-7200
William McCoy, supt. Fax 527-9308
www.rbuesd.org
Vista Preparatory Academy 400/6-8
1770 S Jackson St 96080 530-527-7840
Isaac Scharaga, prin. Fax 527-9374

Regional Occupational Center & Program
Supt. — None
Tehama County ROP Vo/Tech
PO Box 689 96080 530-528-7341
Larry Champion, admin. Fax 529-4120

---

Mercy HS 100/9-12
233 Riverside Way 96080 530-527-8314
Paul Weber, prin. Fax 527-3058

**Redding, Shasta, Pop. 86,489**
Columbia ESD 1,000/PK-8
10140 Old Oregon Trl 96003 530-223-1915
Clay Ross, supt. Fax 223-4168
www.columbiasd.com
Mountain View MS 400/5-8
675 Shasta View Dr 96003 530-221-5224
Shannon Angstadt, prin. Fax 221-5620

Enterprise ESD 3,500/PK-8
1155 Mistletoe Ln 96002 530-224-4100
Brian Winstead Ed.D., supt. Fax 224-4101
www.eesd.net/
Parsons JHS 600/6-8
750 Hartnell Ave 96002 530-224-4190
Tony Moebes, prin. Fax 224-4191

Gateway USD 3,900/PK-12
4411 Mountain Lakes Blvd 96003 530-245-7900
James Harrell, supt. Fax 245-7920
www.gateway-schools.org
Gateway Educational Options 100/Alt
3500 Tamarack Dr 96003 530-245-7960
Ryan Johnson, prin. Fax 245-7963
Other Schools – See Shasta Lake

Pacheco UNESD 500/K-8
7424 Pacheco School Rd 96002 530-224-4599
Jason Provence, supt. Fax 224-4591
www.pacheco.k12.ca.us
Pacheco S 300/4-8
7430 Pacheco School Rd 96002 530-224-4585
Jason Provence, prin. Fax 224-4588

Redding ESD 3,300/K-12
5885 E Bonnyview Rd 96001 530-225-0011
Rick Fauss, supt. Fax 225-0015
www.reddingschools.net/
Sequoia MS 800/4-8
5885 E Bonnyview Rd 96001 530-225-0020
Cindy Bishop, prin. Fax 225-0029

Regional Occupational Center & Program
Supt. — None
Shasta-Trinity ROP Vo/Tech
4659 Eastside Rd 96001 530-246-3302
Charlie Hoffman, supt. Fax 246-3306

Shasta County Office of Education 200/
1644 Magnolia Ave 96001 530-225-0200
Tom Armelino, supt. Fax 225-0329
www.shastacoe.org
Career Pathways to Success Alt
3711 Oasis Rd 96003 530-225-0360
James Burger, prin. Fax 225-0366

Shasta UNHSD 5,700/6-12
2200 Eureka Way Ste B 96001 530-241-3261
Jim Cloney, supt. Fax 225-8499
www.suhsd.net
Enterprise HS 1,300/9-12
3411 Churn Creek Rd 96002 530-222-6601
Eric Peterson, prin. Fax 222-5138
Enterprise Plus HS 50/Alt
3411 Churn Creek Rd 96002 530-245-2714
Eric Peterson, prin. Fax 222-5138
Freedom HS 50/Alt
2650 8th St 96001 530-243-1880
Elsbeth Prigmore, prin. Fax 243-0753
North State Independence HS 200/Alt
2200 Eureka Way Ste B 96001 530-245-2760
Elsbeth Prigmore, prin. Fax 245-2761
Pioneer Continuation HS 200/Alt
2650 8th St 96001 530-243-1880
Elsbeth Prigmore, prin. Fax 243-0753
Shasta HS 1,500/9-12
2500 Eureka Way 96001 530-241-4161
Milan Woollard, prin. Fax 241-9571
Shasta Plus HS 50/Alt
2500 Eureka Way 96001 530-245-2716
Milan Woollard, prin. Fax 241-9571
Shasta Adult S Adult
590 Mary St 96001 530-245-2626
Kyle Turner, admin. Fax 245-2682
Other Schools – See Palo Cedro

---

Institute of Technology - Redding Campus Post-Sec.
1755 Hilltop Dr 96002 530-224-1000
Liberty Christian S 200/PK-12
3782 Churn Creek Rd 96002 530-222-2232
Mike Engstrom, supt. Fax 222-1784
Shasta Bible College & Graduate School Post-Sec.
2951 Goodwater Ave 96002 530-221-4275
Shasta College Post-Sec.
PO Box 496006 96049 530-242-7500
Simpson University Post-Sec.
2211 College View Dr 96003 530-224-5600

**Redlands, San Bernardino, Pop. 66,575**
Redlands USD 21,200/K-12
PO Box 3008 92373 909-307-5300
Lori Rhodes, supt. Fax 748-6711
www.redlands.k12.ca.us
Citrus Valley HS 2,200/9-12
PO Box 3008 92373 909-799-2300
Rhonda Bruce, prin. Fax 799-2349
Clement MS 1,000/6-8
501 E Pennsylvania Ave 92374 909-307-5400
Robert Clarey, prin. Fax 307-5414
Cope MS 1,300/6-8
1000 W Cypress Ave 92373 909-307-5420
Lisa Bruich, prin. Fax 307-5436
Moore MS 1,100/6-8
1550 E Highland Ave 92374 909-307-5440
Jamie Cortz, prin. Fax 307-5453
Orangewood HS 300/Alt
515 Texas St 92374 909-307-5380
Carol Ruhm, prin. Fax 307-5384
Redlands East Valley HS 2,400/9-12
31000 Colton Ave 92374 909-389-2500
John Maloney, prin. Fax 389-2517
Redlands HS 2,600/9-12
840 E Citrus Ave 92374 909-307-5500
Katherine Pearne, prin. Fax 307-5524

Redlands Adult S Adult
820 W Stuart Ave 92374 909-748-6930
David Finley, prin. Fax 307-5393
Other Schools – See Highland

Regional Occupational Center & Program
Supt. — None
Colton-Redlands-Yucaipa ROP Vo/Tech
PO Box 8640 92375 909-793-3115
Stephanie Houston, supt. Fax 793-6901

San Bernardino Co. Office of Education
Supt. — See San Bernardino
East Valley Community S 100/Alt
1812 W Park Ave 92373 909-748-0259
Bernadine Hollingsworth, dir. Fax 748-6451

---

Ashdown College of Health Sciences Post-Sec.
101 E Redlands Blvd Ste 285 92373 909-793-4263
Citrus Valley Christian Academy 100/1-12
PO Box 8037 92375 909-556-7201
Cheryl Van Gelder, admin.
Community Christian College Post-Sec.
1849 N Wabash Ave 92374 909-335-8863
Packinghouse Christian Academy 200/K-12
27165 San Bernardino Ave 92374 909-793-4984
Jeff Lindeman, prin. Fax 307-1852
Redlands Adventist Academy 500/K-12
130 Tennessee St 92373 909-793-1000
Linda Woolley, prin. Fax 793-9862
Redlands Christian S 400/7-12
105 Tennessee St 92373 909-793-0601
Daniel Cole, head sch Fax 792-5691
University of Redlands Post-Sec.
PO Box 3080 92373 909-793-2121

**Redondo Beach, Los Angeles, Pop. 63,466**
Redondo Beach Unified SD 8,600/K-12
1401 Inglewood Ave 90278 310-379-5449
Steven Keller Ed.D., supt. Fax 798-8610
www.rbusd.org
Adams MS 900/6-8
2600 Ripley Ave 90278 310-798-8636
Anthony Taranto, prin. Fax 318-3064
Parras MS 900/6-8
200 N Lucia Ave 90277 310-798-8616
Dr. Lars Nygren, prin. Fax 798-8620
Redondo Shores HS 100/Alt
1000 Del Amo St 90277 310-798-8690
Sue Hall, prin. Fax 798-5287
Redondo Union HS 2,500/9-12
1 Sea Hawk Way 90277 310-798-8665
Dr. Nicole Wesley, prin. Fax 798-4685
South Bay Adult S Adult
3401 Inglewood Ave 90278 310-937-3340
Vivian Ibarra, dir. Fax 937-3345

**Redwood City, San Mateo, Pop. 73,481**
Redwood City ESD 9,200/PK-8
750 Bradford St 94063 650-423-2200
Jan Christensen, supt. Fax 423-2204
www.rcsdk8.net
Kennedy MS 800/6-8
2521 Goodwin Ave 94061 650-365-4611
David Paliughi, prin. Fax 367-4362
McKinley Institute of Technology 400/6-8
400 Duane St 94062 650-366-3827
Thomas Ekno, prin. Fax 367-4363
North Star Academy 500/3-8
400 Duane St 94062 650-482-5973
Leslie Crane, prin. Fax 482-5980

Regional Occupational Center & Program
Supt. — None
San Mateo County ROP Vo/Tech
101 Twin Dolphin Dr 94065 650-598-2000
Ken San Filippo, dir. Fax 802-5414

San Mateo County Office of Education 200/
101 Twin Dolphin Dr 94065 650-802-5300
Anne Campbell, supt. Fax 802-5564
www.smcoe.org
Other Schools – See San Mateo

Sequoia UNHSD 8,700/9-12
480 James Ave 94062 650-369-1411
James Lianides, supt. Fax 306-8870
www.seq.org
Redwood HS 300/Alt
1968 Old County Rd 94063 650-369-1411
Frank Wells, prin. Fax 261-0213
Sequoia HS 2,000/9-12
1201 Brewster Ave 94062 650-367-9780
Sean Priest, prin. Fax 368-5180
Other Schools – See Atherton, Belmont, Menlo Park, Woodside

---

Canada College Post-Sec.
4200 Farm Hill Blvd 94061 650-306-3100

**Redwood Valley, Mendocino, Pop. 1,695**
Ukiah USD
Supt. — See Ukiah
Eagle Peak MS 400/5-8
8601 West Rd 95470 707-472-5250
Dan Stearns, prin. Fax 485-9542

**Reedley, Fresno, Pop. 23,944**
Kings Canyon JUSD 9,900/PK-12
675 W Manning Ave 93654 559-305-7010
Juan Garza, supt. Fax 637-1292
www.kcusd.com
Grant MS 500/6-8
360 N East Ave 93654 559-305-7330
Sharon Matsuzaki, prin. Fax 638-6772
Mountain View S 400/Alt
877 E North Ave 93654 559-305-7080
Judi Szpor, dir. Fax 637-7778

Navelencia MS 300/6-8
22620 Wahtoke Ave 93654 559-305-7350
Josh Darnell, prin. Fax 637-1316
Reedley HS 1,900/9-12
740 W North Ave 93654 559-305-7100
Roberto Gutierrez, prin. Fax 637-0458
Reedly Middle College HS 9-12
995 N Reed Ave 93654 559-305-7010
Lori Botkin, prin. Fax 637-1292
Kings Canyon Adult S Adult
675 W Manning Ave 93654 559-305-7085
Ron Pack, dir. Fax 637-9486
Other Schools – See Orange Cove

---

Immanuel S 400/K-12
1128 S Reed Ave 93654 559-638-2529
Ryan Wood, supt. Fax 638-7030
Reedley College Post-Sec.
995 N Reed Ave 93654 559-638-3641

**Rescue, El Dorado**
Rescue UNESD 4,000/K-8
2390 Bass Lake Rd 95672 530-677-4461
David Swart, supt. Fax 677-0719
www.rescueusd.org
Pleasant Grove MS 600/6-8
2540 Green Valley Rd 95672 530-672-4400
Hope Migliaccio, prin. Fax 677-5829
Other Schools – See El Dorado Hills

**Reseda, See Los Angeles**
Los Angeles USD
Supt. — See Los Angeles
Grey Continuation S 200/Alt
18230 Kittridge St 91335 818-758-3769
Harold Starr, prin. Fax 758-3714
Reseda HS 2,000/9-12
18230 Kittridge St 91335 818-758-3600
Jose Rodriguez, prin. Fax 776-0452
Sherman Oaks Ctr for Enriched Studies 2,100/4-12
18605 Erwin St 91335 818-758-5600
Judith Henderson, prin. Fax 344-5909
Wooden HS 100/Alt
18741 Elkwood St 91335 818-345-0203
Laura Novak, prin. Fax 996-9008
Reseda Adult Education Adult
18230 Kittridge St 91335 818-758-3700
Andrea Rodriguez, prin. Fax 758-3719

---

Everest College Post-Sec.
18040 Sherman Way Ste 400 91335 818-774-0550
Marinello School of Beauty Post-Sec.
18442 Sherman Way 91335 818-881-2521

**Rialto, San Bernardino, Pop. 97,244**
Rialto USD 26,700/K-12
182 E Walnut Ave 92376 909-820-7700
Dr. Cuauhtemoc Avila, supt. Fax 873-0448
www.rialto.k12.ca.us
Carter HS 2,400/9-12
2630 N Linden Ave 92377 909-854-4100
Christine Foote, prin. Fax 574-7313
Eisenhower HS 2,400/9-12
1321 N Lilac Ave 92376 909-820-7777
Scott Sparks, prin. Fax 421-7640
Frisbie MS 1,200/6-8
1442 N Eucalyptus Ave 92376 909-820-7887
Akinlana Osonduagwuike, prin. Fax 820-7885
Kolb MS 1,000/6-8
2351 N Spruce Ave 92377 909-820-7849
Carolyn Eide, prin. Fax 875-0374
Kucera MS 1,300/6-8
2140 W Buena Vista Dr 92377 909-421-7662
Monique Conway, prin. Fax 421-7681
Milor Continuation HS 300/Alt
266 W Randall Ave 92376 909-820-7785
Andres Luna, prin. Fax 421-7617
Rialto HS 3,000/9-12
595 S Eucalyptus Ave 92376 909-421-7500
Arnie Ayala, prin. Fax 421-7584
Rialto MS 1,200/6-8
1262 W Rialto Ave 92376 909-879-7308
Rhea McIver-Gibbs, prin. Fax 877-4893
Zupanic HS 100/Alt
266 W Randall Ave 92376 909-820-7955
Andres Luna, admin. Fax 421-7617
Rialto Adult S Adult
595 S Eucalyptus Ave 92376 909-879-6010
Veronica Smith-Iszard, dir. Fax 879-6011
Other Schools – See Colton

San Bernardino Co. Office of Education
Supt. — See San Bernardino
Murphy County Community S 100/Alt
149 N Arrowhead Ave 92376 909-421-7810
Bernadine Hollingsworth, dir.

**Richmond, Contra Costa, Pop. 99,595**
Contra Costa County Office of Education
Supt. — See Pleasant Hill
Contra Costa Adult S Adult
5555 Giant Hwy 94806 510-262-4340
Angela Hatter, prin. Fax 262-4343

West Contra Costa USD 29,200/PK-12
1108 Bissell Ave 94801 510-231-1100
Bruce Harter, supt. Fax 236-6784
www.wccusd.net
De Anza HS 800/9-12
5000 Valley View Rd 94803 510-231-1440
Summer Sigler, prin. Fax 223-7984
DeJean MS 600/7-8
3400 MacDonald Ave 94805 510-231-1430
William McGee, prin. Fax 236-6680
Kennedy HS 900/9-12
4300 Cutting Blvd 94804 510-231-1433
Roxanne Brown-Garcia, prin. Fax 235-1915

Richmond HS 1,500/9-12
1250 23rd St 94804 510-231-1450
Jose DeLeon, prin. Fax 235-0316
West CC Adult Ed - Serra Adult
6028 Ralston Ave 94805 510-215-4666
Valerie Garrett, prin. Fax 215-0430
Other Schools – See El Cerrito, El Sobrante, Hercules, Pinole, San Pablo

---

Kaiser Permanente Medical Center Post-Sec.
938 Marina Way S 94804 510-231-5000
Salesian HS 600/9-12
2851 Salesian Ave 94804 510-234-4433
Tim Chambers, prin. Fax 236-4636

**Ridgecrest, Kern, Pop. 26,434**
Sierra Sands USD 5,000/K-12
113 W Felspar Ave 93555 760-499-1600
Ernest Bell, supt. Fax 375-3338
www.ssusdschools.org
Burroughs HS 1,500/9-12
500 E French Ave 93555 760-499-1800
Bryan Auld, prin. Fax 375-1735
Mesquite Continuation HS 100/Alt
140 Drummond Ave 93555 760-499-1810
JoAnne McClelland, prin. Fax 446-3328
Monroe MS 500/6-8
340 W Church Ave 93555 760-499-1830
Bonny Porter, prin. Fax 375-8781
Murray MS 600/6-8
921 E Inyokern Rd 93555 760-446-5525
Kirsti Smith, prin. Fax 446-3838
Sierra Sands Adult S Adult
1327 N Norma St Ste 143 93555 760-499-1725
JoAnne McClelland, prin. Fax 446-1391

---

Cerro Coso Community College Post-Sec.
3000 College Heights Blvd 93555 760-384-6100
Immanuel Christian S 200/K-12
201 W Graaf Ave 93555 760-446-6114
Lisa Waddill, prin. Fax 284-8320

**Rio Dell, Humboldt, Pop. 3,219**
Rio Dell ESD 300/K-8
95 Center St 95562 707-764-5694
Leslie Yale, supt. Fax 764-2656
riodell.schoolwires.com
Monument MS 100/6-8
95 Center St 95562 707-764-3783
Leslie Yale, supt. Fax 764-2656

**Rio Linda, Sacramento, Pop. 14,536**
Twin Rivers USD
Supt. — See Mc Clellan
Rio Linda HS 1,800/9-12
6309 Dry Creek Rd 95673 916-566-2725
Ed Delgado, prin. Fax 566-1718
Rio Linda Preparatory Academy 500/5-8
1101 G St 95673 916-566-2720
Cindy Harrison, prin. Fax 566-3578

**Rio Vista, Solano, Pop. 7,140**
River Delta USD 2,300/K-12
445 Montezuma St 94571 707-374-1700
Don Beno, supt. Fax 374-2995
www.rdusd.org
Rio Vista HS 400/9-12
410 S 4th St 94571 707-374-6336
Vicky Turk, prin. Fax 374-6810
River Delta S 50/Alt
400 Elm Way 94571 707-374-1719
Pierre Laleau, prin. Fax 374-5623
Riverview MS 300/6-8
525 S 2nd St 94571 707-374-2345
Sonia Rambo, prin. Fax 374-5623
Wind River Adult S Adult
525 S 2nd St 94571 707-374-1731
Pierre Laleau, prin. Fax 374-1723
Other Schools – See Clarksburg, Courtland

**Ripon, San Joaquin, Pop. 13,864**
Ripon USD 3,100/PK-12
304 N Acacia Ave 95366 209-599-2131
Ziggy Robeson Ed.D., supt. Fax 599-6271
www.riponusd.net
Harvest HS, 729 W Main St 95366 Alt
Sergei Samborski, prin. 209-599-5009
Ripon HS 900/9-12
301 N Acacia Ave 95366 209-599-4287
Lance Morrow, prin. Fax 599-6410
Ripon Adult S Adult
304 N Acacia Ave 95366 209-599-2131

---

Ripon Christian HS 200/9-12
435 Maple Ave 95366 209-599-2155
Eric Segaar, prin. Fax 599-2170

**Riverbank, Stanislaus, Pop. 22,058**
Riverbank USD 2,400/K-12
6715 7th St 95367 209-869-2538
Dr. Daryl Camp, supt. Fax 869-1487
www.riverbank.k12.ca.us
Adelante Continuation HS 100/Alt
6801 7th St 95367 209-869-2383
Rebecca Evans, prin. Fax 869-7433
Cardozo MS 500/6-8
3525 Santa Fe St 95367 209-869-2591
Kevin Bizzini, prin. Fax 869-2714
Riverbank HS 700/9-12
6200 Claus Rd 95367 209-869-1891
Sean Richey, prin. Fax 869-2116

**Riverdale, Fresno, Pop. 3,092**
Riverdale JUSD 1,600/K-12
PO Box 1058 93656 559-867-8200
Jeff Percell, supt. Fax 867-6722
www.rjusd.org

Horizon HS 50/Alt
PO Box 726 93656 559-867-3614
Aaron Luoma, prin. Fax 867-4575
Riverdale ES 500/4-8
PO Box 338 93656 559-867-3589
Melissa Locke, prin. Fax 867-3393
Riverdale HS 500/9-12
PO Box 726 93656 559-867-3562
Aaron Luoma, prin. Fax 867-4750

**Riverside, Riverside, Pop. 295,499**
Alvord USD 20,200/K-12
10365 Keller Ave 92505 951-509-5070
Sid Salazar, supt. Fax 509-6070
www.alvord.k12.ca.us
Alvord Alternative Continuation HS Alt
10365 Keller Ave 92505 951-509-6120
Jason Marquez, admin. Fax 509-6119
Alvord Continuation HS 200/Alt
10365 Keller Ave 92505 951-358-1715
Sandy Fielding, prin. Fax 358-1716
Arizona MS 1,200/6-8
10365 Keller Ave 92505 951-358-1675
Jason Jones, prin. Fax 358-1676
Hillcrest HS 500/9-12
10365 Keller Ave 92505 951-358-1755
Jennifer Radeka, prin. Fax 358-1756
La Sierra HS 3,300/9-12
10365 Keller Ave 92505 951-358-1725
Errol Garnett, prin. Fax 358-1726
Loma Vista MS 1,100/6-8
10365 Keller Ave 92505 951-358-1685
Sherri Duckworth-Kemp, prin. Fax 358-1686
Norte Vista HS 2,300/9-12
10365 Keller Ave 92505 951-358-1740
Susan Boyd, prin. Fax 358-1741
Villegas MS 1,400/6-8
10365 Keller Ave 92505 951-358-1695
Joshua Moss, prin. Fax 358-1696
Wells MS 1,000/6-8
10365 Keller Ave 92505 951-358-1705
David Ferguson, prin. Fax 358-1706

Regional Occupational Center & Program
Supt. — None
Riverside County ROP Vo/Tech
PO Box 868 92502 951-826-6797
Nancy Pavelsky, dir. Fax 826-6440

Riverside USD 42,100/K-12
PO Box 2800 92516 951-788-7135
David Hansen Ed.D., supt. Fax 778-5668
www.rusdlink.org
Arlington HS 2,200/9-12
2951 Jackson St 92503 951-352-8316
Betsy Schmechel, prin. Fax 328-7311
Central MS 700/7-8
4795 Magnolia Ave 92506 951-788-7282
Lynn McCown, prin. Fax 328-2580
Chemawa MS 1,000/7-8
8830 Magnolia Ave 92503 951-352-8244
Raul Ayala, prin. Fax 328-2980
Earhart MS 1,000/7-8
20202 Aptos St 92508 951-697-5700
Sean Curtin, prin. Fax 328-7580
Gage MS 1,000/7-8
6400 Lincoln Ave 92506 951-788-7350
Dr. Keyisha Holmes, prin. Fax 328-5680
King HS 3,100/9-12
9301 Wood Rd 92508 951-789-5690
Michael West, prin. Fax 778-5680
Lincoln HS 300/Alt
4341 Victoria Ave 92507 951-788-7371
Pamela Mshana, prin. Fax 328-2931
Miller MS 900/7-8
17925 Krameria Ave 92504 951-789-8181
Chuck Hiroto, prin. Fax 328-2912
North HS 2,500/9-12
1550 3rd St 92507 951-788-7311
Dr. Lynne Sheffield, prin. Fax 328-2581
Polytechnic HS 2,900/9-12
5450 Victoria Ave 92506 951-788-7203
Dr. Michael Roe, prin. Fax 328-2901
Raincross HS 100/Alt
6401 Lincoln Ave 92506 951-276-7670
Dennis Deets, dir. Fax 778-5623
Ramona HS 2,200/9-12
7675 Magnolia Ave 92504 951-352-8429
Dr. Jamie Angulo, prin. Fax 328-2532
Riverside STEM Academy 300/5-9
4466 Mt Vernon Ave 92507 951-788-7308
Dale Moore, prin. Fax 328-2513
Sierra MS 900/7-8
4950 Central Ave 92504 951-788-7501
Steven Ybarra, prin. Fax 328-2552
Summit View S 700/Alt
6401 Lincoln Ave 92506 951-276-7670
Dennis Deets, dir. Fax 276-7685
University Heights MS 800/7-8
1155 Massachusetts Ave 92507 951-788-7388
Coleman Kells, prin. Fax 328-2566
Riverside Adult S Adult
6735 Magnolia Ave 92506 951-788-7185
James Dawson, prin. Fax 328-2523

Bethel Christian S 200/PK-12
2425 Van Buren Blvd 92503 951-359-1123
Dr. Michael Crites, supt. Fax 359-1719
California Baptist University Post-Sec.
8432 Magnolia Ave 92504 951-689-5771
Kaplan College Post-Sec.
4040 Vine St 92507 951-276-1704
La Sierra Academy 700/K-12
4900 Golden Ave 92505 951-351-1445
Walter Lancaster, prin. Fax 689-3708
La Sierra University Post-Sec.
4500 Riverwalk Pkwy 92505 951-785-2000
North-West College Post-Sec.
4550 La Sierra Ave 92505 951-351-7750
Notre Dame HS 500/9-12
7085 Brockton Ave 92506 951-275-5896
Matt Luttringer, prin. Fax 781-9020
Platt College Post-Sec.
6465 Sycamore Canyon # 100 92507 626-300-5444
Riverside Christian S 600/PK-12
8775 Magnolia Ave 92503 951-687-0077
Rev. John Moran, supt. Fax 687-3340
Riverside City College Post-Sec.
4800 Magnolia Ave 92506 951-222-8000
The Fab School Post-Sec.
2001 3rd St Ste E 92507 951-782-0567
United Education Institute Post-Sec.
1860 University Ave 92507 851-300-5500
University of California Post-Sec.
900 University Ave 92521 951-827-1012
Woodcrest Christian S 500/7-12
18401 Van Buren Blvd 92508 951-780-2010
Jim Sullivan, supt. Fax 780-2079

**Rocklin, Placer, Pop. 54,666**
Rocklin USD 11,200/PK-12
2615 Sierra Meadows Dr 95677 916-624-2428
Roger Stock, supt. Fax 630-2229
www.rocklinusd.org
Granite Oaks MS 900/7-8
2600 Wyckford Blvd 95765 916-315-9009
Jay Holmes, prin. Fax 315-9885
Rocklin HS 1,800/9-12
5301 Victory Ln 95765 916-632-1600
Davis Stewart, prin. Fax 632-0305
Spring View MS 800/7-8
5040 5th St 95677 916-624-3381
Elizabeth Davidson, prin. Fax 624-5737
Victory HS 100/Alt
3250 Victory Dr 95765 916-632-3195
Mark Williams, prin. Fax 632-8630
Whitney HS 1,800/9-12
701 Wildcat Blvd 95765 916-632-6500
Debra Hawkins, prin. Fax 435-2542

Sierra College Post-Sec.
5000 Rocklin Rd 95677 916-624-3333
William Jessup University Post-Sec.
333 Sunset Blvd 95765 916-577-2200

**Rodeo, Contra Costa, Pop. 8,152**
John Swett USD 1,600/K-12
400 Parker Ave 94572 510-245-4300
Rob Stockberger, supt. Fax 245-4312
www.jsusd.org
Other Schools – See Crockett

**Rohnert Park, Sonoma, Pop. 39,217**
Cotati-Rohnert Park USD 5,200/K-12
7165 Burton Ave 94928 707-792-4722
Robert Haley, supt. Fax 792-4537
www.crpusd.org
El Camino HS, 5450 Snyder Ln 94928 200/Alt
Amie Carter, prin. 707-792-4750
Jones MS 900/6-8
5154 Snyder Ln 94928 707-588-5600
Laurie Mason, prin. Fax 588-5607
Rancho Cotate HS 1,500/9-12
5450 Snyder Ln 94928 707-792-4750
Amie Carter, prin. Fax 792-4758
Technology HS Vo/Tech
1801 E Cotati Ave 94928 707-792-4825
Robert Steffen, prin. Fax 792-4727
Technology MS 100/6-8
7165 Burton Ave 94928 707-792-4800
Ashley Tatman, prin. Fax 792-4516

Bergin University of Canine Studies Post-Sec.
5860 Labath Ave 94928 707-545-3647
Sonoma State University Post-Sec.
1801 E Cotati Ave 94928 707-664-2880

**Rolling Hills, Los Angeles, Pop. 1,810**
Palos Verdes Peninsula USD
Supt. — See Palos Verdes Estates
Palos Verdes Peninsula HS 2,500/9-12
27118 Silver Spur Rd 90274 310-377-4888
Mitzi Cress, prin. Fax 544-4378
Rancho Del Mar HS 100/Alt
38 Crest Rd W 90274 310-377-6691
Rosemary Humphrey, prin. Fax 544-5526
PVPUSD Adult Education Adult
38 Crest Rd W 90274 310-541-7626
Rosemary Humphrey, prin. Fax 265-5967

**Rosamond, Kern, Pop. 17,416**
Southern Kern USD 3,000/K-12
PO Box CC 93560 661-256-5000
Jeffrey Weinstein, supt. Fax 256-1247
www.skusd.k12.ca.us
Lincoln Alternative Education 100/Alt
PO Box CC 93560 661-256-5090
Patrick Holmes, lead tchr. Fax 256-6868
Rare Earth Continuation HS 100/Alt
PO Box CC 93560 661-256-5090
Patrick Holmes, lead tchr. Fax 256-6868
Rosamond HS 800/9-12
PO Box CC 93560 661-256-5020
Harold Roney, prin. Fax 256-6880
Tropico MS 600/6-8
PO Box CC 93560 661-256-5040
Trinidad Gonzales, prin. Fax 256-0630

**Rosemead, Los Angeles, Pop. 53,367**
El Monte UNHSD
Supt. — See El Monte
Rosemead HS 1,900/9-12
9063 Mission Dr 91770 626-286-3141
Dr. Brian Bristol, prin. Fax 286-6396
Garvey ESD 5,300/K-8
2730 Del Mar Ave 91770 626-307-3400
Anita Chu, supt. Fax 307-1964
www.garvey.k12.ca.us
Garvey IS 700/7-8
2720 Jackson Ave 91770 626-307-3385
Gema Macias, prin. Fax 307-3443
Temple IS 500/7-8
8470 Fern Ave 91770 626-307-3360
Robert Boyd, prin. Fax 307-8162

Rosemead ESD 2,800/PK-8
3907 Rosemead Blvd 91770 626-312-2900
Amy Enomoto-Perez Ed.D., supt. Fax 312-2906
www.rosemead.k12.ca.us
Muscatel MS 600/7-8
4201 Ivar Ave 91770 626-287-1139
Jessica Ancona, prin. Fax 307-6185

Don Bosco Technical Institute Post-Sec.
1151 San Gabriel Blvd 91770 626-307-6500
Don Bosco Technical Institute 500/9-12
1151 San Gabriel Blvd 91770 626-940-2000
Xavier Jimenez, prin. Fax 940-2001
Rosemead Beauty School Post-Sec.
8531 Valley Blvd 91770 626-286-2147
University of the West Post-Sec.
1409 Walnut Grove Ave 91770 626-571-8811

**Roseville, Placer, Pop. 114,218**
Center JUSD
Supt. — See Antelope
Riles MS 700/7-8
4747 PFE Rd 95747 916-787-8100
Joyce Frisch, prin. Fax 773-4131

Dry Creek JESD 6,500/K-8
9707 Cook Riolo Rd 95747 916-770-8800
Brad Tooker, supt. Fax 771-0650
www.drycreek.k12.ca.us
Silverado MS 1,000/6-8
2525 Country Club Dr 95747 916-780-2620
Priscilla Rasanen, prin. Fax 780-2635
Other Schools – See Antelope

Eureka UNSD
Supt. — See Granite Bay
Olympus JHS 600/7-8
2625 La Croix Dr 95661 916-782-1667
Sean Healy, prin. Fax 782-1339

Roseville City ESD 9,300/K-8
1050 Main St 95678 916-771-1600
Derk Garcia, supt. Fax 771-1620
www.rcsdk8.org
Buljan MS 1,200/6-8
100 Hallissy Dr 95678 916-771-1720
Ryan Hartsoch, prin. Fax 773-2696
Chilton MS 6-8
4501 Bob Doyle Dr 95747 916-771-1870
Jeff Ancker, prin. Fax 771-1871
Cooley MS 1,100/6-8
9300 Prairie Woods Way 95747 916-771-1740
Karen Calkins, prin. Fax 786-3003
Eich MS 500/6-8
1509 Sierra Gardens Dr 95661 916-771-1770
Marc Buljan, prin. Fax 783-7292

Roseville JUNHSD 9,600/9-12
1750 Cirby Way 95661 916-786-2051
Ron Severson, supt. Fax 786-2681
www.rjuhsd.us
Adelante HS 100/Alt
350 Atlantic St 95678 916-782-3155
Amy Lloyd, prin. Fax 782-4064
Independence HS 200/Alt
125 Berry St 95678 916-786-0793
Debbie Latteri, prin. Fax 786-3389
Oakmont HS 1,600/9-12
1710 Cirby Way 95661 916-782-3781
Rob Hasty, prin. Fax 782-4943
Roseville HS 2,000/9-12
1 Tiger Way 95678 916-782-3753
David Byrd, prin. Fax 786-3846
Woodcreek HS 2,200/9-12
2551 Woodcreek Oaks Blvd 95747 916-771-6565
Jess Borjon, prin. Fax 771-6596
Roseville Adult S Adult
200 Branstetter St 95678 916-782-3952
Joyce Lude, dir. Fax 782-4361
Other Schools – See Antelope, Granite Bay

Christian Life Academy 100/K-12
1301 Coloma Way 95661 916-956-4662
Gary Gubitz, prin. Fax 786-7916
Heald College Post-Sec.
7 Sierra Gate Plz 95678 916-789-8600
Valley Christian Academy 300/PK-12
301 W Whyte Ave 95678 916-728-5500
Dr. Brad Gunter, admin. Fax 721-3305

**Ross, Marin, Pop. 2,341**

Branson S 300/9-12
PO Box 887 94957 415-454-3612
Ellen Moceri, head sch Fax 454-2327

**Rowland Heights, Los Angeles, Pop. 48,135**
Rowland USD 15,100/K-12
1830 Nogales St 91748 626-965-2541
Julie Mitchell, supt. Fax 854-8302
www.rowlandschools.org
Alvarado IS 900/7-8
1901 Desire Ave 91748 626-964-2358
Karen Magana, prin. Fax 810-5579
Community Day S 50/Alt
1928 Nogales St 91748 626-935-8210
Dr. Melissa Neal, prin. Fax 964-6450

Rowland HS 2,400/9-12
2000 Otterbein Ave 91748 626-965-3448
Mitch Brunyer, prin. Fax 810-4859
Rowland Adult & Continuing Education Adult
2100 Lerona Ave 91748 626-965-5975
Rocky Bettar, dir. Fax 854-1191
Other Schools – See La Puente, West Covina

---

Oxford S 100/7-12
18760 Colima Rd 91748 626-964-9588
Marylee Hull, prin. Fax 913-3919
Southlands Christian S 400/PK-12
18550 Farjardo St 91748 909-598-9733
Glenn Duncan, pres. Fax 468-9943

**Sacramento, Sacramento, Pop. 437,732**

Elk Grove USD
Supt. — See Elk Grove
Calvine HS 300/Alt
8333 Vintage Park Dr 95828 916-689-7502
Joe Airoso, prin. Fax 689-7546
Daylor HS 200/Alt
6131 Orange Ave 95823 916-427-5428
Katherine Whiteside, prin. Fax 391-2017
Florin HS 1,600/9-12
7956 Cottonwood Ln 95828 916-689-8600
Don Ross, prin. Fax 689-7430
Jackman MS 900/7-8
7925 Kentwall Dr 95823 916-393-2352
Michael Anderson, prin. Fax 393-4053
Las Flores Independent Study 300/Alt
5900 Bamford Dr 95823 916-422-5604
Ralph Robles, admin. Fax 428-8307
Rio Cazadero HS 300/Alt
7825 Grandstaff Dr 95823 916-422-3058
Douglas Wendle, prin. Fax 422-0604
Rutter MS 900/7-8
7350 Palmer House Dr 95828 916-422-7590
Kenneth Smith, prin. Fax 422-8354
Sheldon HS 2,300/9-12
8333 Kingsbridge Dr 95829 916-681-7500
Paula Duncan, prin. Fax 681-7505
Smedberg MS 1,100/7-8
8239 Kingsbridge Dr 95829 916-681-7525
Richard Wall, prin. Fax 681-7530
Valley HS 1,500/9-12
6300 Ehrhardt Ave 95823 916-689-6500
Chelsea Bowler-Shelton, prin. Fax 682-1528
Adult/Community Education Adult
8401 Gerber Rd 95828 916-686-7717
Kathy Hamilton, dir. Fax 689-5752

Natomas USD 12,300/PK-12
1901 Arena Blvd 95834 916-567-5400
Chris Evans, supt. Fax 567-5405
www.natomas.k12.ca.us
Discovery HS 100/Alt
3401 Fong Ranch Rd 95834 916-928-5200
Christopher Morris, prin. Fax 928-5222
Inderkum HS 1,600/9-12
2500 New Market Dr 95835 916-567-5640
Dan Motherspaw, prin. Fax 567-5649
Natomas HS 1,200/9-12
3301 Fong Ranch Rd 95834 916-641-4960
Yuri Penermon, prin. Fax 641-5455
Natomas MS 900/7-8
3200 N Park Dr 95835 916-567-5540
Shea Borges Ed.D., prin. Fax 567-5549

Sacramento City USD 43,900/PK-12
PO Box 246870 95824 916-643-9000
Jose Banda, supt. Fax 643-9480
www.scusd.edu
American Legion HS 300/Alt
3801 Broadway 95817 916-277-6600
Stan Echols, prin. Fax 277-6800
Bacon MS 700/7-8
4140 Cuny Ave 95823 916-433-5000
Mary Coronado, prin. Fax 433-5166
Benjamin Health Professions HS 400/9-12
451 McClatchy Way 95818 916-264-3262
Marla Johnson, prin. Fax 264-3245
Brannan MS 600/7-8
5301 Elmer Way 95822 916-264-4350
Enrique Flores, prin. Fax 264-4481
Burbank HS 1,800/9-12
3500 Florin Rd 95823 916-433-5100
Jim Peterson, prin. Fax 433-5199
California MS 700/7-8
1600 Vallejo Way 95818 916-264-4550
Andrea Egan, prin. Fax 264-4477
Capital City Independent Study 800/Alt
7222 24th St 95822 916-433-5187
Michael Salman, prin. Fax 433-5195
Carson MS 400/7-8
5301 N St 95819 916-277-6750
Santiago Chapa, prin. Fax 277-6550
Einstein MS 700/7-8
9325 Mirandy Dr 95826 916-228-5800
Garrett Kirkland, prin. Fax 228-5813
Johnson HS 1,600/9-12
6879 14th Ave 95820 916-277-6300
Kal Phan, prin. Fax 277-6740
Kennedy HS 2,100/9-12
6715 Gloria Dr 95831 916-433-5200
David Van Natten, prin. Fax 433-5511
McClatchy HS 2,300/9-12
3066 Freeport Blvd 95818 916-264-4400
Peter Lambert, prin. Fax 264-4499
Rosemont HS 1,400/9-12
9594 Kiefer Blvd 95827 916-228-5844
Elizabeth Vigil, prin. Fax 228-5733
School of Engineering and Sciences 400/7-12
7345 Gloria Dr 95831 916-433-2960
Jim Hays, prin. Fax 433-2959

Success Academy 50/Alt
5601 47th Ave 95824 916-643-2338
Cyndi Swindle, prin. Fax 433-5301
Sutter MS 1,400/7-8
3150 I St 95816 916-264-4150
Cristin Tahara-Martin, prin. Fax 264-3436
West Campus HS 900/9-12
5022 58th St 95820 916-277-6400
David Rodriguez, prin. Fax 277-6593
Wood MS 700/7-8
6201 Lemon Hill Ave 95824 916-382-5900
Tuan Duong, prin. Fax 382-5914
Jones Skills Center Adult
5451 Lemon Hill Ave 95824 916-433-2600
Susan Gilmore, dir. Fax 433-2640
McClaskey Adult Education Center Adult
5241 J St 95819 916-277-6625
Susan Gilmore, prin. Fax 277-6810

Sacramento County Office of Education
Supt. — See Mather
Gerber JSHS 100/Alt
PO Box 269003 95826 916-228-2329
Sharon Barnes, contact Fax 689-3730
Hickey JSHS 100/Alt
PO Box 269003 95826 916-566-2074
Lisa Alcala, prin. Fax 566-2018
North Area Community S 50/Alt
PO Box 269003 95826 916-566-1302
Lisa Alcala, prin. Fax 566-1304

San Juan USD
Supt. — See Carmichael
Arcade Fundamental MS 600/6-8
3500 Edison Ave 95821 916-971-7300
LeeAnn Hopton, prin. Fax 971-7821
Arden MS 900/6-8
1640 Watt Ave 95864 916-971-7306
Jeff Banks, prin. Fax 971-7830
El Camino Fundamental HS 1,700/9-12
4300 El Camino Ave 95821 916-971-7430
Shelley Friery, prin. Fax 971-7429
Encina Preparatory HS 1,100/6-12
1400 Bell St 95825 916-971-7538
Richard Judge, prin. Fax 971-7555
La Entrada Continuation HS 100/Alt
5320 Hemlock St 95841 916-971-7590
Fax 971-7302
Mira Loma HS 1,600/9-12
4000 Edison Ave 95821 916-971-7465
Rich Nichols, prin. Fax 971-7483
Rio Americano HS 1,600/9-12
4540 American River Dr 95864 916-971-7494
Brian Ginter, prin. Fax 971-7513

Twin Rivers USD
Supt. — See Mc Clellan
Foothill HS 1,200/9-12
5000 McCloud Dr 95842 916-566-3445
Brian Welborn, prin. Fax 566-3526
Foothill Ranch MS 700/5-8
5001 Diablo Dr 95842 916-566-3440
Howard Holcomb, prin. Fax 566-3574
Grant Union HS 2,000/9-12
1400 Grand Ave 95838 916-566-3450
Darris Hinson, prin. Fax 566-3501
King Technology Academy 400/7-8
3051 Fairfield St 95815 916-566-3490
Xay Phongmany, prin. Fax 566-7815
Norwood JHS 800/6-8
4601 Norwood Ave 95838 916-566-2710
Diedre Barlow, prin. Fax 566-3529
NOVA Opportunity S 50/Alt
2035 North Ave 95838 916-566-2750
Bob Wilkerson, prin. Fax 566-3541
Rio Tierra JHS 600/6-8
3201 Northstead Dr 95833 916-566-2730
Paul Orlando, prin. Fax 566-3533
Vista Nueva Career & Tech HS Vo/Tech
2035 North Ave 95838 916-566-2750
Bob Wilkerson, prin. Fax 566-3542

---

Al-Arqam Islamic S 300/PK-12
6990 65th St 95823 916-391-3333
Fax 391-3334
Alliant International University Post-Sec.
2030 W El Camino Ave # 200 95833 916-565-2955
American River College Post-Sec.
4700 College Oak Dr 95841 916-484-8011
Anthem College Post-Sec.
9738 Lincoln Village # 100 95827 916-929-9700
Art Institute of California - Sacramento Post-Sec.
2850 Gateway Oaks Dr # 100 95833 800-477-1957
Bradshaw Christian S 1,200/PK-12
8324 Bradshaw Rd 95829 916-688-0521
Michelle Reynolds, supt. Fax 688-0502
California State University-Sacramento Post-Sec.
6000 J St 95819 916-278-6011
Capital Christian S 1,100/PK-12
9470 Micron Ave 95827 916-856-5611
Todd W. Jacobs, supt. Fax 856-5951
Carrington College California Post-Sec.
8909 Folsom Blvd 95826 916-361-1660
Christian Brothers HS 1,000/9-12
4315 Mrtn Lthr King Jr Blvd 95820 916-733-3600
Mary Hesser, prin. Fax 733-3657
Cornerstone Christian S 200/K-12
5073 Andrea Blvd 95842 916-334-6236
Richard Batista, hdmstr. Fax 334-6200
Cosumnes River College Post-Sec.
8401 Center Pkwy 95823 916-691-7344
Cristo Rey HS 300/9-12
8475 Jackson Rd 95826 916-733-2660
Andreas Agos, prin. Fax 739-1310
Emergency Medical Sciences Training Inst Post-Sec.
3105 Fite Cir Ste 108 95827 800-500-0711
Epic Bible College Post-Sec.
4330 Auburn Blvd 95841 916-348-4689

Federico College of Hairstyling Post-Sec.
1515 Sports Dr 95834 916-929-4242
Kaplan College Post-Sec.
4330 Watt Ave Ste 400 95821 916-649-8168
Le Cordon Bleu Academy of Culinary Arts Post-Sec.
2450 Del Paso Rd 95834 888-807-8222
MTI College Post-Sec.
5221 Madison Ave 95841 916-339-1500
My-Le's Beauty College Post-Sec.
5972 Stockton Blvd 95824 916-422-0223
Sacramento City College Post-Sec.
3835 Freeport Blvd 95822 916-558-2111
Sacramento Country Day S 500/PK-12
2636 Latham Dr 95864 916-481-8811
Stephen Repsher, hdmstr. Fax 481-6016
St. Francis HS 1,100/9-12
5900 Elvas Ave 95819 916-452-3461
Theresa Rodgers, prin. Fax 452-1591
Truck Driving Academy Post-Sec.
3100 Fite Cir Ste 105 95827 916-381-2285
Union Institute & University Post-Sec.
160 Promenade Cir Ste 115 95834 916-564-3100
Unitek College Post-Sec.
1111 Howe Ave Ste 300 95825 818-518-6601
Universal Technical Institute Post-Sec.
4100 Duckhorn Dr 95834 916-263-9100
Western Pacific Truck School Post-Sec.
8720 Fruitridge Rd 95826 800-333-1233

**Saint Helena, Napa, Pop. 5,723**

St. Helena USD 1,400/K-12
465 Main St 94574 707-967-2708
Marylou Wilson Ed.D., supt. Fax 963-1335
www.sthelena.k12.ca.us
St. Helena HS 500/9-12
1401 Grayson Ave 94574 707-967-2740
Ben Scinto, prin. Fax 967-2735
Stevenson MS 300/6-8
1316 Hillview Pl 94574 707-967-2725
Elizabeth Chacon, prin. Fax 967-2734

---

Culinary Institute of America Greystone Post-Sec.
2555 Main St 94574 707-967-1100

**Salida, Stanislaus, Pop. 13,232**

Salida UNESD 2,700/K-8
4801 Sisk Rd 95368 209-545-0339
Twila Tosh, supt. Fax 545-2682
www.salida.k12.ca.us/
Salida MS - Vella Campus 1,000/6-8
5041 Toomes Rd 95368 209-545-1633
Dean Way, prin. Fax 545-0831

---

Heald College Modesto Post-Sec.
5260 Pirrone Ct 95368 209-416-3700
Kaplan College Post-Sec.
5172 Kiernan Ct 95368 209-543-7000
San Joaquin Valley College Post-Sec.
5380 Pirrone Rd 95368 209-543-8800

**Salinas, Monterey, Pop. 147,570**

Monterey County Office of Education 1,300/
PO Box 80851 93912 831-755-0300
Dr. Nancy Kotowski, supt. Fax 753-6473
www.monterey.k12.ca.us
Salinas Community S 300/Alt
1420 Natividad Rd 93906 831-755-3790
Faris Sabbah, prin. Fax 753-1042

North Monterey County USD
Supt. — See Moss Landing
Central Bay Continuation HS 100/Alt
17500 Pesante Rd 93907 831-663-2997
Aida Ramirez, prin. Fax 663-1151
N Monterey Co. Ctr for Independent Study 100/K-12
17500 Pesante Rd 93907 831-663-7050
Aida Ramirez, prin. Fax 663-6184

Regional Occupational Center & Program
Supt. — None
Mission Trails ROP Vo/Tech
867 E Laurel Dr 93905 831-753-4209
Randy Bangs, dir. Fax 422-5115

Salinas UNHSD 13,400/7-12
431 W Alisal St 93901 831-796-7000
Tim Vanoli, supt. Fax 796-7005
www.salinas.k12.ca.us
Alisal HS 2,400/9-12
777 Williams Rd 93905 831-796-7600
Ernesto Garcia, prin. Fax 796-7605
Carr Lake Community Day S 50/Alt
10 Sherwood Pl 93906 831-796-7770
Richard Moreno, prin.
El Puente S, 20 Sherwood Dr 93901 Alt
August Caresani, prin. 831-796-7770
El Sausal MS 900/7-8
1155 E Alisal St 93905 831-796-7200
Francisco Huerta, prin. Fax 796-7205
Everret Alvarez HS 2,300/9-12
1900 Independence Blvd 93906 831-796-7800
Jacqui Axtell, prin. Fax 796-7805
Harden MS 1,200/7-8
1561 McKinnon St 93906 831-796-7300
Alberto Verduzco, prin. Fax 796-7305
La Paz MS 900/7-8
1300 N Sanborn Rd 93905 831-796-7900
Irelia Dominguez, prin. Fax 796-7905
Mount Toro HS 400/Alt
10 Sherwood Pl 93906 831-796-7700
Richarad Moreno, prin. Fax 424-7325
North Salinas HS 1,900/9-12
55 Kip Dr 93906 831-796-7500
Barabara Emanuel, prin. Fax 796-7505
Salinas HS 2,500/9-12
726 S Main St 93901 831-796-7400
Judith Peterson, prin. Fax 796-7405

Washington MS 1,000/7-8
560 Iverson St 93901 831-796-7100
Anthony Hinton, prin. Fax 796-7105
Salinas Adult S Adult
20 Sherwood Pl 93906 831-796-6900
Todd Farr, prin. Fax 796-6905

Santa Rita UNSD 3,100/K-8
57 Russell Rd 93906 831-443-7200
Dr. Shelly Morr, supt. Fax 442-1729
www.santaritaschools.org
Bolsa Knolls MS 400/6-8
1031 Rogge Rd 93906 831-443-3300
John Gutierrez, prin. Fax 443-4766
Gavilan View MS 500/6-8
18250 Van Buren Ave 93906 831-443-7212
Abel Valdez, prin. Fax 443-0908

Spreckels UNESD
Supt. — See Spreckels
Buena Vista MS 400/6-8
18250 Tara Dr 93908 831-455-8936
Eric Tarallo, prin. Fax 455-8832

Washington UNESD 1,000/K-8
43 San Benancio Rd 93908 831-484-2166
Dr. Kevin Vaughn, supt. Fax 484-2828
www.washingtonusd.org
San Benancio MS 300/6-8
43 San Benancio Rd 93908 831-484-1172
Gina Uccelli, prin. Fax 484-6509

---

Hartnell College Post-Sec.
411 Central Ave 93901 831-755-6700
Heald College Post-Sec.
1450 N Main St 93906 831-443-1700
Notre Dame HS 300/9-12
455 Palma Dr 93901 831-751-1850
Colleen Eagleson, prin. Fax 757-5749
Palma HS 500/7-12
919 Iverson St 93901 831-422-6391
David Sullivan, prin. Fax 422-5065

**Salton City, Imperial, Pop. 3,695**
Coachella Valley USD
Supt. — See Thermal
West Shores HS 400/7-12
2381 Shore Hawk Ave, 760-848-1360
Richard Pimentel, prin. Fax 394-0971

**San Andreas, Calaveras, Pop. 2,665**
Calaveras County Office of Education
Supt. — See Angels Camp
Calaveras River Academy 100/Alt
PO Box 249 95249 209-754-1996
Mike Nagano, prin. Fax 754-4261
Oakendell S 50/Alt
PO Box 249 95249 209-754-1961
Mike Nagano, prin. Fax 754-1659
Calaveras County Adult Education Adult
PO Box 249 95249 209-754-1996
Mike Nagano, prin. Fax 754-4261

Calaveras USD 3,200/K-12
PO Box 788 95249 209-754-2300
Mark Campbell, supt. Fax 754-2215
www.calaveras.k12.ca.us
Calaveras HS 1,000/9-12
PO Box 607 95249 209-754-1811
Michael Merrill, prin. Fax 754-0276
Gold Strike Continuation HS 50/Alt
PO Box 788 95249 209-754-2123
Kathy Griggs, prin. Fax 754-1268
Other Schools – See Valley Springs

**San Anselmo, Marin, Pop. 11,931**
Ross Valley ESD 2,100/K-8
110 Shaw Dr 94960 415-454-2160
Dr. Rick E. Bagley Ed.D., supt. Fax 454-6840
rossvalleyschools.org
Other Schools – See Fairfax

Tamalpais UNHSD
Supt. — See Larkspur
Sir Francis Drake HS 1,000/9-12
1327 Sir Francis Drake Blvd 94960 415-453-8770
Liz Seabury, prin. Fax 458-3429

---

San Domenico HS 100/9-12
1500 Butterfield Rd 94960 415-258-1990
John Berry, prin. Fax 258-1901
San Domenico MS 200/6-8
1500 Butterfield Rd 94960 415-258-1908
Carrie Robley, prin. Fax 258-1901
San Francisco Theological Seminary Post-Sec.
105 Seminary Rd 94960 415-451-2800

**San Bernardino, San Bernardino, Pop. 204,762**
Regional Occupational Center & Program
Supt. — None
San Bernadino County ROP Vo/Tech
601 N E St 92415 909-386-2449
Kit Alvarez, admin. Fax 386-2479

San Bernardino City USD 51,300/PK-12
777 N F St 92410 909-381-1100
Dr. Dale Marsden, supt. Fax 885-6392
www.sbcusd.k12.ca.us/
Arrowview MS 800/7-8
2299 N G St 92405 909-881-8109
Berenice Rios, prin. Fax 881-8119
Arroyo Valley HS 2,900/9-12
1881 W Base Line St 92411 909-381-4295
Samaro Oramas, prin. Fax 386-2577
Cajon HS 2,700/9-12
1200 W Hill Dr 92407 909-881-8120
Toni Miller, prin. Fax 881-8141
Chavez MS 1,200/6-8
6650 Magnolia Ave 92407 909-386-2050
Ernestine Hopwood, prin. Fax 473-8443

Curtis MS 1,000/6-8
1050 Del Rosa Ave 92410 909-388-6332
Marlene Bicondova, prin. Fax 388-6339
Del Vallejo MS 900/6-8
1885 E Lynwood Dr 92404 909-881-8280
William Prudhomme, prin. Fax 881-8285
Golden Valley MS 1,100/6-8
3800 N Waterman Ave 92404 909-881-8168
Kristen Vicondova, prin. Fax 881-5196
Indian Springs HS 9-12
650 N Del Rosa Dr 92410 909-383-1360
Dr. Alan Kay, prin. Fax 383-1750
King MS 900/6-8
1250 Medical Center Dr 92411 909-388-6350
Maria Jauregui, prin. Fax 388-6361
Middle College HS 200/9-12
1260 Esperanza St 92410 909-888-4041
James Espinoza, prin.
Pacific HS 2,200/9-12
1020 Pacific St 92404 909-388-6419
Hector Vasquez, prin. Fax 388-6427
Richardson Prep MS 600/6-8
455 S K St 92410 909-388-6438
Natalie Raymundo, prin. Fax 383-0368
Rodriguez Prep MS 600/6-8
1985 Guthrie St 92404 909-884-6030
Teenya Bishop, prin. Fax 863-7869
San Bernardino HS 2,200/9-12
1850 N E St 92405 909-881-8217
Antoinette Fulcher Gutie, prin. Fax 881-8245
San Gorgonio HS 2,700/9-12
2299 Pacific St 92404 909-388-6524
Dion Clark, prin. Fax 388-6498
Shandin Hills MS 1,100/6-8
4301 Little Mountain Dr 92407 909-880-6666
Victoria Flores, prin. Fax 880-6672
Sierra HS 600/Alt
570 E 9th St 92410 909-388-6478
Rose Lalama, prin. Fax 889-4188
San Bernardino Adult S Adult
1200 N E St 92405 909-388-6000
Karen Bautista, prin. Fax 381-2887
Other Schools – See Highland

San Bernardino Co. Office of Education 2,000/
601 N E St 92415 909-386-2704
Ted Alejandre, supt. Fax 386-2478
www.sbcss.k12.ca.us
Other Schools – See Montclair, Redlands, Rialto, Victorville

---

Aquinas HS 400/9-12
2772 Sterling Ave 92404 909-886-4659
Christopher Barrows, prin. Fax 886-7717
California State Univ.-San Bernadino Post-Sec.
5500 University Pkwy 92407 909-537-5000
Concorde Career College Post-Sec.
201 E Airport Dr # A 92408 909-884-8891
Dikaios Christian Academy 200/K-12
PO Box 9067 92427 909-881-8310
Jerry Sommerville, dir. Fax 881-8315
Everest College Post-Sec.
217 E Club Center Dr Ste A 92408 909-777-3300
Hair Masters University of Beauty Post-Sec.
208 W Highland Ave 92405 909-882-2987
ITT Technical Institute Post-Sec.
670 Carnegie Dr 92408 909-806-4600
Marinello School of Beauty Post-Sec.
721 W 2nd St Ste E 92410 909-884-8747
Rock Christian S 100/K-10
2345 S Waterman Ave 92408 909-825-8887
San Bernardino Valley College Post-Sec.
701 S Mount Vernon Ave 92410 909-384-4400
The Art Institute of CA - Inland Empire Post-Sec.
674 E Brier Dr 92408 909-915-2100

**San Bruno, San Mateo, Pop. 37,955**
San Bruno Park ESD 2,100/K-8
500 Acacia Ave 94066 650-624-3100
Cheryl Olson, supt. Fax 266-9626
sbpsd.k12.ca.us
Parkside MS 500/6-8
1801 Niles Ave 94066 650-624-3180
Ethan Cheever, prin. Fax 877-8195

San Mateo UNHSD
Supt. — See San Mateo
Capuchino HS 1,100/9-12
1501 Magnolia Ave 94066 650-558-2799
Shamar Shanks, prin. Fax 558-2752
Peninsula Alternative HS 300/Alt
300 Piedmont Ave 94066 650-558-2499
Ron Campana, prin. Fax 866-4120

---

Skyline College Post-Sec.
3300 College Dr 94066 650-738-4100

**San Carlos, San Mateo, Pop. 27,121**
San Carlos ESD 3,300/K-8
1200 Industrial Rd Ste 9 94070 650-508-7333
Dr. Craig Baker, supt. Fax 508-7340
www.scsdk8.org
Central MS 600/5-8
757 Cedar St 94070 650-508-7321
Steven Kaufman, prin. Fax 508-7342

**San Clemente, Orange, Pop. 61,767**
Capistrano USD
Supt. — See San Juan Capistrano
Ayer MS 900/6-8
1271 Calle Sarmentoso 92673 949-366-9607
Nick Stever, prin. Fax 366-1519
San Clemente HS 3,000/9-12
700 Avenida Pico 92673 949-492-4165
Chris Carter, prin. Fax 361-5175
Shorecliffs MS 1,100/6-8
240 Via Socorro 92672 949-498-1660
Heidi Crowley, prin. Fax 498-0826

Vista del Mar MS 500/6-8
1130 Avenida Talega 92673 949-234-5955
Michelle Benham, prin. Fax 940-0262

**San Diego, San Diego, Pop. 1,256,111**
Poway USD 34,400/K-12
15250 Avenue of Science 92128 858-521-2800
Dr. John Collins, supt.
www.powayusd.com
Bernardo Heights MS 1,400/6-8
12990 Paseo Lucido 92128 858-485-4850
Tim Biland, prin. Fax 485-4865
Black Mountain MS 1,400/6-8
9353 Oviedo St 92129 858-484-1300
Charan Kirpalani, prin. Fax 538-9440
Del Norte HS 1,600/9-12
16601 Nighthawk Ln 92127 858-487-0877
Greg Mizel, prin. Fax 487-2443
Mesa Verde MS 1,300/6-8
8375 Entreken Way 92129 858-538-5478
Cliff Mitchell, prin. Fax 538-8636
Mt. Carmel HS 2,000/9-12
9550 Carmel Mountain Rd 92129 858-484-1180
Greg Magno, prin. Fax 538-9426
Oak Valley MS 1,400/6-8
16055 Winecreek Rd 92127 858-487-2939
Casey Currigan, prin. Fax 457-0991
Rancho Bernardo HS 2,300/9-12
13010 Paseo Lucido 92128 858-485-4800
David LeMaster, prin. Fax 485-4822
Westview HS 2,400/9-12
13500 Camino Del Sur 92129 858-780-2000
Todd Cassen, prin. Fax 780-2054
Other Schools – See Poway

Regional Occupational Center & Program
Supt. — None
San Diego County ROP Vo/Tech
6401 Linda Vista Rd Ste 408 92111 858-292-3500
Steve Pinning, dir. Fax 268-9726

San Diego County Office of Education 1,500/
6401 Linda Vista Rd 92111 858-292-3500
Randolph Ward, supt. Fax 292-3653
www.sdcoe.net
Monarch S 100/K-12
1625 Newton Ave 92113 858-652-4100
Fax 652-4107

Other Schools – See San Marcos

San Diego USD 127,800/PK-12
4100 Normal St 92103 619-725-8000
Cindy Marten, supt. Fax 291-7182
www.sandi.net
A. L. B. A. S 50/Alt
4041 Oregon St 92104 619-344-3900
Andy Trakas, prin. Fax 344-3940
Bell MS 1,000/6-8
620 Briarwood Rd 92139 619-430-1000
Precious Hubbard-Jackson, prin. Fax 470-6054
Challenger MS 1,100/6-8
10810 Parkdale Ave 92126 858-586-7001
Diane Ryan, prin. Fax 271-5203
Clairemont HS 1,200/9-12
4150 Ute Dr 92117 858-273-0201
Jennifer Roberson, prin. Fax 272-4219
Clark MS 1,100/6-8
4388 Thorn St 92105 619-344-4200
Thomas Liberto, prin. Fax 344-4274
Correia MS 800/7-8
4302 Valeta St 92107 619-222-0476
Jonathan McDade, prin. Fax 221-0147
Crawford HS 300/9-12
4191 Colts Way 92115 619-362-3700
Richard Lawrence, dir. Fax 593-9207
Creative Performing & Media Arts S 1,000/6-8
5050 Conrad Ave 92117 858-800-5550
Scott Thomason, prin.
De Portola MS 1,000/6-8
11010 Clairemont Mesa Blvd 92124 858-496-8080
Ryan Brock, prin. Fax 576-4419
Farb MS 600/6-8
4880 La Cuenta Dr 92124 858-697-6750
Courtney Rizzo, prin. Fax 697-6790
Foster Construction Tech Academy 400/9-12
7651 Wellington Way 92111 858-496-8370
Ana Diaz-Booz, dir. Fax 496-4907
Garfield HS 300/Alt
1255 16th St 92101 619-362-4500
Jolie Pickett, prin. Fax 362-4549
Henry HS 2,500/9-12
6702 Wandermere Dr 92120 619-286-7700
Elizabeth Gillingh, prin. Fax 229-0370
Hoover HS 2,000/9-12
4474 El Cajon Blvd 92115 619-344-4500
Joe Austin, prin. Fax 344-4649
Innovation MS 500/7-8
5095 Arvinels Ave 92117 858-278-5948
Nicola Labas, prin.
Kearny Digital Media and Design HS 500/9-12
7651 Wellington Way 92111 858-496-8370
Ana Diaz-Booz, prin. Fax 278-6349
Kearny HS of International Business 500/9-12
7651 Wellington Way 92111 858-496-8370
Ana Diaz-Booz, prin. Fax 496-8379
Kearny Science Connections & Tech HS 400/9-12
7651 Wellington Way 92111 858-496-8370
Ana Diaz-Booz, dir. Fax 715-9504
Lewis MS 1,100/6-8
5170 Greenbrier Ave 92120 619-583-3233
Brad Callahan, prin. Fax 229-1338
Lincoln HS, 4777 Imperial Ave 92113 1,900/9-12
John Ross, prin. 619-266-6500
Madison HS 1,200/9-12
4833 Doliva Dr 92117 858-496-8410
Richard Nash, prin. Fax 496-8421
Mann MS 1,000/6-8
4345 54th St 92115 619-582-8990
Allen Teng, prin. Fax 583-2637

Marshall MS 1,500/6-8
9700 Avenue of Nations 92131 858-549-5400
Michelle Irwin, prin. Fax 549-5490
Marston MS 800/6-8
3799 Clairemont Dr 92117 858-273-2030
Dr. John Gollias, prin. Fax 272-3460
Memorial Prep for Scholars & Athletes 500/6-8
2850 Logan Ave 92113 619-344-4350
Mirna Estrada, prin. Fax 344-4424
Millennial Tech MS 600/6-8
1110 Carolina Ln 92102 619-527-6933
William Neil, prin.
Mira Mesa HS 2,600/9-12
10510 Reagan Rd 92126 858-566-2262
Scott Giusti, prin. Fax 549-9541
Mission Bay HS 1,400/9-12
2475 Grand Ave 92109 858-273-1313
Ernest Remillard, prin. Fax 270-8294
Montgomery MS 400/6-8
2470 Ulric St 92111 858-397-6600
Stephanie Brown, prin. Fax 397-6642
Morse HS 2,000/9-12
6905 Skyline Dr 92114 619-262-0763
Harry Shelton, prin. Fax 262-6835
Mt. Everest Academy 200/Alt
4350 Mount Everest Blvd 92117 858-496-8778
Courtney Browne, prin. Fax 496-8797
Muir S 400/Alt
4431 Mount Herbert Ave 92117 858-268-1954
Laura Bellofato, prin. Fax 627-9289
New Dawn 100/Alt
5650 Mount Ackerly Dr 92111 858-496-1655
Georgina Barajas-Aguirre, prin.
Pacific Beach MS 700/6-8
4676 Ingraham St 92109 858-273-9070
Kimberly Meng, prin. Fax 270-8063
Pershing MS 800/6-8
8204 San Carlos Dr 92119 619-465-3234
Susan Levy, prin. Fax 461-5447
Point Loma HS 2,000/9-12
2335 Chatsworth Blvd 92106 619-223-3121
Barbara Samilson, prin. Fax 225-1298
Roosevelt International MS 900/6-8
3366 Park Blvd 92103 619-293-4450
Dr. Christina Casillas, prin. Fax 497-0918
San Diego Early College S 100/Alt
1425 Russ Blvd Ste T-112D 92101 619-525-2000
Elizabeth Larkin, prin.
San Diego HS of Business 500/9-12
1405 Park Blvd 92101 619-525-7461
Carmen Garcia, prin. Fax 525-7337
San Diego International Studies HS 600/9-12
1405 Park Blvd 92101 619-525-7464
Carmen Garcia, prin. Fax 744-7651
San Diego Metro Career & Tech HS Vo/Tech
7250 Mesa College Dr 92111 619-388-2299
Sara Leonard, prin.
San Diego Science & Technology HS 500/9-12
1405 Park Blvd 92101 619-525-7459
Dianne Cordero, prin. Fax 744-7677
School of Creative & Performing Arts 1,400/6-12
2425 Dusk Dr 92139 619-470-0555
Tim Farson, prin. Fax 470-9430
Scripps Ranch HS 2,400/9-12
10410 Treena St 92131 858-621-9020
Ann Menna, prin. Fax 621-0646
Serra HS 2,000/9-12
5156 Santo Rd 92124 858-496-8342
Vincent Mays, prin. Fax 571-3457
Standley MS 1,100/6-8
6298 Radcliffe Dr 92122 858-455-0550
William Pearson, prin. Fax 546-7627
Taft MS 500/6-8
9191 Gramercy Dr 92123 858-935-2650
Michael George, prin. Fax 496-8138
TRACE S 500/Alt
2555 Camino del Rio S 92108 619-574-1073
Amy Perez, prin.
Twain HS 300/Alt
6402 Linda Vista Rd 92111 858-800-5300
Emma Martinez, prin. Fax 800-5340
University City HS 1,800/9-12
6949 Genesee Ave 92122 858-457-3040
Jeff Olivero, prin. Fax 458-9432
Wangenheim MS 1,000/6-8
9230 Gold Coast Dr 92126 858-578-1400
Matthew Fallon, prin. Fax 578-9481
Whittier S, 3401 Clairemont Dr 92117 100/Alt
Cathie Whitley, prin. 858-490-2770
Wilson MS 600/6-8
3838 Orange Ave 92105 619-362-3400
David Downey, prin. Fax 362-3474
Other Schools – See La Jolla

San Dieguito UNHSD
Supt. — See Encinitas
Canyon Crest Academy 1,800/9-12
5951 E Village Center Loop 92130 858-350-0253
Brian Kohn, prin. Fax 350-0280
Carmel Valley MS 1,500/7-8
3800 Mykonos Ln 92130 858-481-8221
Cara Dolnik, prin. Fax 481-8256
Pacific Trails MS 7-8
5975 Village Center Loop Rd 92130 760-509-1000
Mary Anne Nuskin, prin. Fax 509-1005
Torrey Pines HS 2,700/9-12
3710 Del Mar Heights Rd 92130 858-755-0125
Brett Killeen, prin. Fax 481-0098

Sweetwater UNHSD
Supt. — See Chula Vista
Mar Vista Academy 1,100/Alt
1267 Thermal Ave 92154 619-628-5100
Thomas Winters, prin. Fax 423-8431
Montgomery HS 1,700/9-12
3250 Palm Ave 92154 619-628-3800
Tom Rodrigo, prin. Fax 424-6473

Montgomery MS 900/7-8
1051 Picador Blvd 92154 619-662-8200
Louie Zumstein, prin. Fax 428-6517
San Ysidro HS 2,400/9-12
5353 Airway Rd 92154 619-710-2300
Hector Espinoza, prin. Fax 710-2318
Southwest HS 1,700/9-12
1685 Hollister St 92154 619-628-3600
Lee Romero, prin. Fax 423-8253
Southwest MS 600/7-8
2710 Iris Ave 92154 619-628-4000
Oscar Medina, prin. Fax 423-1151
Montgomery Adult S Adult
3240 Palm Ave 92154 619-600-3800
Kevin McClelland, prin. Fax 423-7876

---

Academy of Our Lady of Peace 800/9-12
4860 Oregon St 92116 619-297-2266
Lauren Lek, prin. Fax 297-2473
Alliant International University Post-Sec.
10455 Pomerado Rd 92131 866-825-5426
Argosy University San Diego Post-Sec.
1615 Murray Canyon Ste 100 92108 619-321-3000
Art Institute of California - San Diego Post-Sec.
7650 Mission Valley Rd 92108 858-598-1200
Associated Technical College Post-Sec.
707 Broadway Ste 300 92101 619-234-2181
Avance Beauty College Post-Sec.
750 Beyer Way Ste B 92154 619-575-1511
Balboa City S 100/1-12
525 Hawthorn St 92101 619-298-2990
Dr. Stephen Parker, dir. Fax 295-8886
Bethel Seminary Post-Sec.
6116 Arosa St 92115 619-325-5200
Cal Coast Academy 50/6-12
11555 Clews Ranch Rd 92130 858-481-0882
Jan Dunning, head sch Fax 481-8583
California College San Diego Post-Sec.
2820 Camino Del Rio S # 300 92108 619-293-0190
CA International Business University Post-Sec.
520 W Ash St 92101 619-702-9400
California Miramar University Post-Sec.
9750 Miramar Rd Ste 180 92126 858-653-3000
California Univ of Management & Sciences Post-Sec.
8525 Gibbs Dr Ste 105 92123 858-277-6700
California Western School of Law Post-Sec.
225 Cedar St 92101 619-239-0391
Cambridge S 100/PK-10
PO Box 720508 92172 858-484-3488
Jean Kim, head sch Fax 484-3458
Career College of San Diego Post-Sec.
3350 Market St 92102 619-338-0813
Cathedral Catholic HS 1,700/9-12
5555 Del Mar Heights Rd 92130 858-523-4000
Kevin Calkins, prin. Fax 523-4097
Childrens Creative/Performing Arts Acad 200/PK-12
3051 El Cajon Blvd 92104 619-584-2454
Janet Cherif, dir. Fax 584-2422
Coleman University Post-Sec.
8888 Balboa Ave 92123 858-499-0202
Concorde Career Institute Post-Sec.
4393 Imperial Ave Ste 100 92113 619-688-0800
Design Institute of San Diego Post-Sec.
8555 Commerce Ave 92121 858-566-1200
DeVry University Post-Sec.
2655 Camino Del Rio N #350 92108 619-683-2446
FIDM Fashion Institute of Design Post-Sec.
350 10th Ave Fl 3 92101 619-235-2049
High Tech High Graduate School of Educ Post-Sec.
2855 Farragut Rd 92106 619-398-4902
Horizon JSHS 500/7-12
5331 Mount Alifan Dr 92111 858-244-0333
Chris Johnson, prin. Fax 654-3054
Horizon University Post-Sec.
5331 Mount Alifan Dr 92111 858-695-8587
International Prof School of Body Work Post-Sec.
9025 Balboa Ave Ste 130 92123 858-505-1000
John Paul the Great Catholic University Post-Sec.
10174 Old Grove Rd Ste 200 92131 858-653-6740
Kaplan College Post-Sec.
9055 Balboa Ave 92123 800-935-1857
Kuyper Preparatory S 50/K-12
7997 Paradise Valley Rd 92139 877-458-9737
Gabriela Lozoya, admin. Fax 458-9737
Maranatha Christian S 500/PK-12
9050 Maranatha Dr 92127 858-759-9737
Jess Hetherington, supt. Fax 759-4001
Marinello School of Beauty Post-Sec.
7550 Miramar Rd Ste 440 92126 858-547-9260
Maritime Institute Post-Sec.
1310 Rosecrans St Ste G 92106 619-225-1783
Mueller College Post-Sec.
123 Camino De La Reina 92108 619-291-9811
Newschool of Architecture & Design Post-Sec.
1249 F St 92101 619-684-8800
Ocean View Christian Academy 300/PK-12
2460 Palm Ave 92154 619-424-7875
Stephen Johnson, prin. Fax 621-5274
Pacific College of Oriental Medicine Post-Sec.
7445 Mission Valley Rd #105 92108 619-574-6909
Parker S 800/6-12
6501 Linda Vista Rd 92111 858-569-7900
Kevin Yaley, head sch Fax 569-0621
Platt College Post-Sec.
6250 El Cajon Blvd 92115 619-265-0107
Point Loma Nazarene University Post-Sec.
3900 Lomaland Dr 92106 619-849-2200
Rock Academy 400/PK-12
2277 Rosecrans St 92106 619-764-5205
Dr. Scott Marshall, head sch Fax 764-5204
Sage College Post-Sec.
2820 Camino Del Rio S # 100 92108 619-683-2727
St. Augustine HS 700/9-12
3266 Nutmeg St 92104 619-282-2184
Jim Horne, prin. Fax 282-1203
San Diego City College Post-Sec.
1313 Park Blvd 92101 619-388-3400

San Diego Jewish Academy 600/PK-12
11860 Carmel Creek Rd 92130 858-704-3700
Chaim Heller, head sch Fax 704-3850
San Diego Mesa College Post-Sec.
7250 Mesa College Dr 92111 619-388-2600
San Diego Miramar College Post-Sec.
10440 Black Mountain Rd 92126 619-388-7800
San Diego State University Post-Sec.
5500 Campanile Dr 92182 619-594-5200
Southern States University Post-Sec.
123 Camino De La Reina #100 92108 619-298-1829
Thomas Jefferson School of Law Post-Sec.
1155 Island Ave 92101 619-297-9700
Torah HS of San Diego 50/9-12
9001 Towne Centre Dr 92122 858-558-6880
Rabbi Michoel Peikes, head sch Fax 558-6835
Travel University International Post-Sec.
3625 Ruffin Rd Ste 308 92123 858-292-9755
University of San Diego Post-Sec.
5998 Alcala Park 92110 619-260-4600
Veterans Affairs Medical Center Post-Sec.
3350 La Jolla Village Dr 92161 858-552-8585
Waldorf S of San Diego 300/PK-12
3547 Altadena Ave 92105 619-280-8016
Johannes Lasthaus, admin. Fax 280-8071
Warren-Walker MS 100/6-8
2231 Camino Del Rio S 92108 619-260-3663
Suzanne Pettigrew, dean Fax 260-3573

**San Dimas, Los Angeles, Pop. 32,412**
Bonita USD 9,800/K-12
115 W Allen Ave 91773 909-971-8200
Kurt Madden, supt. Fax 971-8329
www.bonita.k12.ca.us
Chaparral HS 100/Alt
115 W Allen Ave 91773 909-971-8240
Christine Black, prin. Fax 971-8249
Lone Hill MS 900/6-8
115 W Allen Ave 91773 909-971-8270
Chris Regan, prin. Fax 971-8279
San Dimas HS 1,300/9-12
115 W Allen Ave 91773 909-971-8230
Michael Kelly, prin. Fax 971-8239
Vista Alternative S 50/Alt
115 W Allen Ave 91773 909-971-8242
Christine Black, prin. Fax 971-8249
Other Schools – See La Verne

---

ITT Technical Institute Post-Sec.
650 W Cienega Ave 91773 909-971-2300
Life Pacific College Post-Sec.
1100 W Covina Blvd 91773 800-356-0001

**San Fernando, Los Angeles, Pop. 23,530**
Los Angeles USD
Supt. — See Los Angeles
Academy of Scientific Exploration 9-12
1001 Arroyo St 91340 818-838-3926
Dana Neill, prin. Fax 838-3945
Arts, 1001 Arroyo St 91340 9-12
John Lawler, prin. 818-837-6428
Mission Continuation HS 100/Alt
11015 Omelveny Ave 91340 818-361-1777
Santiago Vides, prin. Fax 365-2592
San Fernando HS 2,700/9-12
11133 Omelveny Ave 91340 818-898-7600
Kenneth Lee, prin. Fax 365-7255
San Fernando Institute of Applied Media 100/6-8
130 N Brand Blvd 91340 818-837-5455
Pearl Arredondo, prin. Fax 365-8911
San Fernando MS 1,600/6-8
130 N Brand Blvd 91340 818-837-5400
Freddy Ortiz, prin. Fax 365-8911
Social Justice Humanities Academy 9-12
1001 Arroyo St 91340 818-838-3915
Jose Navarro, prin. Fax 838-6759
Teacher Preparation Academy 9-12
1001 Arroyo St 91340 818-838-3946
Elizabeth Beltran, prin.

**San Francisco, San Francisco, Pop. 773,534**
Regional Occupational Center & Program
Supt. — None
San Francisco County ROP Vo/Tech
750 25th Ave 94121 415-355-7711
Sharon Zimmern, coord. Fax 355-7744

San Francisco County Office of Education 100/
555 Franklin St 94102 415-241-6000
Richard Carranza, supt. Fax 241-6012
www.sfusd.edu
Civic Center Secondary S 100/Alt
727 Golden Gate Ave 94102 415-241-3000
Elisa Villafuerte, prin. Fax 241-6192

San Francisco USD 55,700/PK-12
555 Franklin St 94102 415-241-6000
Richard Carranza, supt. Fax 241-6012
www.sfusd.edu
Academy of Arts & Sciences 300/9-12
555 Portola Dr 94131 415-695-5700
Gregory Markwith, prin. Fax 695-5326
Aptos MS 1,000/6-8
105 Aptos Ave 94127 415-469-4520
Doug Dent, prin. Fax 333-9038
Asawa San Francisco S of the Arts 600/9-12
555 Portola Dr 94131 415-695-5700
Carmelo Sgarlato, prin. Fax 695-5326
Balboa HS 1,400/9-12
1000 Cayuga Ave 94112 415-469-4090
Susan Ritter, prin. Fax 469-0859
Brown MS 6-8
2055 Silver Ave 94124 415-642-8901
Bill Kappenhagen, prin. Fax 641-1120
Burton Academic HS 900/9-12
400 Mansell St 94134 415-469-4550
William Kappenhagen, prin. Fax 239-6806

Civic Center Secondary S 50/Alt
727 Golden Gate Ave 94102 415-241-3000
Elisa Villafuerte, prin. Fax 241-6192
Denman MS 600/6-8
241 Oneida Ave 94112 415-469-4535
Teresa Kohler, prin. Fax 585-8402
Downtown HS 300/9-12
693 Vermont St 94107 415-695-5860
Ellen Wong, prin. Fax 695-5863
Everett MS 300/6-8
450 Church St 94114 415-241-6344
Richard Curci, prin. Fax 241-6361
Francisco MS 600/6-8
2190 Powell St 94133 415-291-7900
Patricia Theel, prin. Fax 291-7910
Galileo Academy of Science & Technology 2,100/9-12
1150 Francisco St 94109 415-749-3430
Michael Reimer, prin. Fax 771-2322
Giannini MS 1,200/6-8
3151 Ortega St 94122 415-759-2770
Michael Reichle, prin. Fax 664-8541
Hoover MS 1,100/6-8
2290 14th Ave 94116 415-759-2783
Thomas Graven, prin. Fax 759-2881
Independence HS 300/Alt
1350 7th Ave 94122 415-242-2528
Robert Maass, prin. Fax 242-2533
International Studies Academy 400/Alt
655 De Haro St 94107 415-695-5866
Darlene Martin, prin. Fax 695-5864
Jordan S for Equity 300/Alt
325 La Grande Ave 94112 415-452-4922
Matt Alexander, admin. Fax 452-4927
King Academic MS 500/6-8
350 Girard St 94134 415-330-1500
Michael Essien, prin. Fax 468-7295
Lick MS 600/6-8
1220 Noe St 94114 415-695-5675
Bita Nazarian, prin. Fax 695-5360
Lilienthal S Winifred Scott Campus 400/Alt
3630 Divisadero St 94123 415-749-3516
Tyler Graff, prin. Fax 749-3431
Lincoln HS 2,000/9-12
2162 24th Ave 94116 415-759-2700
Barnaby Payne, prin. Fax 566-2224
Lowell HS 2,600/9-12
1101 Eucalyptus Dr 94132 415-759-2730
Andrew Ishibashi, prin. Fax 759-2742
Marina MS 800/6-8
3500 Fillmore St 94123 415-749-3495
Joanna Fong, prin. Fax 921-7539
Marshall HS 600/9-12
45 Conkling St 94124 415-695-5612
Martha Torres, prin. Fax 695-5438
Mission HS 900/9-12
3750 18th St 94114 415-241-6240
Eric Guthertz, prin. Fax 626-1641
O'Connell HS 500/9-12
2355 Folsom St 94110 415-695-5370
Mark Alvarado, prin. Fax 695-5379
Presidio MS 1,200/6-8
450 30th Ave 94121 415-750-8435
Tony Payne, prin. Fax 750-8445
Rooftop Alternative S - Mayeda Campus 300/Alt
500 Corbett Ave 94114 415-522-6757
Jeff Slater, prin. Fax 522-6763
Roosevelt MS 700/6-8
460 Arguello Blvd 94118 415-750-8446
Michael Stachon, prin. Fax 750-8455
San Francisco International HS 200/9-12
1050 York St 94110 415-695-5781
Julia Kessler, prin. Fax 695-5402
Visitacion Valley MS 400/6-8
450 Raymond Ave 94134 415-469-4590
Joe Truss, prin. Fax 469-4703
Wallenberg HS 600/9-12
40 Vega St 94115 415-749-3469
Cheryl Foster, prin. Fax 346-7303
Washington HS 2,100/9-12
600 32nd Ave 94121 415-750-8400
Ericka Lovrin, prin. Fax 750-8417
Wells HS 200/Alt
1099 Hayes St 94117 415-241-6315
Catherine Pringle, prin. Fax 241-6317

---

Academy of Art University Post-Sec.
79 New Montgomery St Fl 4 94105 415-274-2200
Alliant International University Post-Sec.
1 Beach St Ste 100 94133 415-955-2100
Alliant International University Post-Sec.
20 Haight St 94102 415-626-5550
American Coll of Traditional Chinese Med Post-Sec.
455 Arkansas St 94107 415-282-7600
American Conservatory Theater Post-Sec.
30 Grant Ave Fl 6 94108 415-439-2350
Archbishop Riordan HS 600/9-12
175 Phelan Ave 94112 415-586-8200
Vittorio Anastasio, prin. Fax 587-1310
Art Institute of California - San Fran Post-Sec.
1170 Market St 94102 888-493-3261
Bay Area Medical Academy Post-Sec.
1 Hallidie Plz Ste 406 94102 415-217-0077
Bay S of San Francisco 300/9-12
35 Keyes Ave 94129 415-561-5800
Luke Felker, hdmstr. Fax 561-5808
California College of the Arts Post-Sec.
1111 8th St 94107 415-703-9500
California Institute of Integral Studies Post-Sec.
1453 Mission St 94103 415-575-6100
City College of San Francisco Post-Sec.
50 Phelan Ave 94112 415-239-3000
Convent of the Sacred Heart HS 200/9-12
2222 Broadway St 94115 415-563-2900
Rachel Simpson, prin. Fax 931-0244
Cornerstone Academy Cambridge Campus 300/6-12
501 Cambridge St 94134 415-585-5183
Derrick Wong, head sch Fax 469-9600

De Marillac Academy 100/4-8
175 Golden Gate Ave 94102 415-552-5220
Christopher Giangregorio, prin. Fax 520-6969
Drew S 300/9-12
2901 California St 94115 415-409-3739
Sam Cuddeback, head sch Fax 346-0720
FIDM Fashion Institute of Design Post-Sec.
55 Stockton St 94108 415-675-5200
French-American International S 1,000/PK-12
150 Oak St 94102 415-558-2000
Melinda Bihn, head sch Fax 558-2024
Golden Gate University Post-Sec.
536 Mission St 94105 415-442-7000
Heald College Post-Sec.
875 Howard St Ste 100 94103 415-808-3000
Immaculate Conception Academy 200/9-12
3625 24th St 94110 415-824-2052
Lisa Graham, prin. Fax 821-4677
Jewish Community HS of the Bay 200/9-12
1835 Ellis St 94115 415-345-9777
Rabbi Howard Ruben, head sch Fax 345-1888
Kampner Hebrew Academy 100/1-12
645 14th Ave 94118 415-752-7333
Katheryn Schopp, prin. Fax 752-5851
Le Cordon Bleu College of Culinary Arts Post-Sec.
350 Rhode Island St 94103 415-771-3500
Lick-Wilmerding HS 400/9-12
755 Ocean Ave 94112 415-333-4021
Eric Temple, head sch Fax 586-0737
Lycee Francais de San Francisco 900/6-12
1201 Ortega St 94122 415-661-5232
Philippe Legendre, hdmstr. Fax 661-0246
Mercy HS 400/9-12
3250 19th Ave 94132 415-334-0525
Dr. Dorothy McCrea, prin. Fax 334-9726
New Charter University Post-Sec.
543 Howard St Fl 5 94105 415-813-5970
Olivet University Post-Sec.
250 4th St 94103 415-371-0002
Presidio Graduate School Post-Sec.
36 Lincoln Blvd 94129 415-561-6555
Proof S, 555 Post St 94102 50/6-10
Sam Vandervelde, head sch 415-747-5252
Sacred Heart Cathedral Prep S 1,300/9-12
1055 Ellis St 94109 415-775-6626
Gary Cannon, prin. Fax 931-6941
SAE Institute - San Francisco Post-Sec.
450 Bryant St 94107 415-344-0886
St. Ignatius College Prep S 1,400/9-12
2001 37th Ave 94116 415-731-7500
Patrick Ruff, prin. Fax 731-2227
St. John of San Fran Orthodox Academy 100/PK-12
6210 Geary Blvd 94121 415-221-3484
San Francisco Art Institute Post-Sec.
800 Chestnut St 94133 415-771-7020
San Francisco Christian S 200/K-12
25 Whittier St 94112 415-586-1117
Mark Asire, admin. Fax 841-0833
San Francisco Conservatory of Music Post-Sec.
50 Oak St 94102 800-899-7326
San Francisco State University Post-Sec.
1600 Holloway Ave 94132 415-338-1111
San Francisco University HS 400/9-12
3065 Jackson St 94115 415-447-3100
Julia Eells, head sch Fax 447-5801
San Francisco Waldorf HS 100/9-12
470 W Portal Ave 94127 415-431-2736
Caleb Buckley, admin. Fax 431-1712
Saybrook University Post-Sec.
747 Front St Fl 3 94111 800-825-4480
Sterne S, 245 Valencia St 94103 100/5-12
Ed McManis, head sch 415-701-1500
Stuart Hall HS 100/9-12
1715 Octavia St 94109 415-345-5811
Anthony Farrell, prin. Fax 563-3005
University of California Post-Sec.
513 Parnassus Ave # S-126 94143 415-476-9000
University of CA Hastings College of Law Post-Sec.
200 McAllister St 94102 415-565-4600
University of San Francisco Post-Sec.
2130 Fulton St 94117 415-422-5555
Urban S of San Francisco 400/9-12
1563 Page St 94117 415-626-2919
Mark Salkind, head sch Fax 626-1125
Woodside International S 100/9-12
1555 Irving St 94122 415-564-1063

**San Gabriel, Los Angeles, Pop. 39,114**
Alhambra USD
Supt. — See Alhambra
San Gabriel HS 2,400/9-12
801 S Ramona St 91776 626-943-6810
Debbie Stone, prin. Fax 308-2332

San Gabriel USD 5,400/K-12
408 Junipero Serra Dr 91776 626-451-5400
John Pappalardo Ed.D., supt. Fax 451-5494
www.sgusd.k12.ca.us
Del Mar HS 100/Alt
312 S Del Mar Ave 91776 626-291-5723
Lon Sellers, prin. Fax 291-2540
Gabrielino HS 1,800/9-12
1327 S San Gabriel Blvd 91776 626-573-2453
Sharron Heinrich, prin. Fax 573-5089
Jefferson MS 1,200/6-8
1372 E Las Tunas Dr 91776 626-287-5260
Dr. Matthew Arnold, prin. Fax 285-5387

---

San Gabriel Academy 500/PK-12
8827 E Broadway 91776 626-292-1156
Paul Negrete, prin. Fax 285-4949
San Gabriel Mission HS 200/9-12
254 S Santa Anita Ave 91776 626-282-3181
Marielle Sallo, prin. Fax 282-4209

**Sanger, Fresno, Pop. 24,008**
Regional Occupational Center & Program
Supt. — None

Valley ROP Vo/Tech
1305 Q St 93657 559-876-2122
Deborah Marvin-Deeter, dir. Fax 876-2102

Sanger USD 10,600/K-12
1905 7th St 93657 559-524-6521
Matt Navo, supt. Fax 875-0311
www.sanger.k12.ca.us/
Community Day S 50/Alt
818 L St 93657 559-524-6630
Johnny Gonzalez, prin. Fax 875-6379
Kings River Continuation HS 100/Alt
1801 7th St 93657 559-524-6490
Rick Church, prin. Fax 875-0676
Sanger HS 2,700/9-12
1045 Bethel Ave 93657 559-524-7121
Dan Chacon, prin. Fax 875-5721
Taft Independent Study 100/Alt
1801 7th St 93657 559-524-6490
Rick Church, prin. Fax 875-0676
Washington Academic MS 1,600/6-8
1705 10th St 93657 559-524-7015
Jamie Nino, prin. Fax 875-6365
Sanger Adult S Adult
1045 Bethel Ave 93657 559-524-7203
Nancy Penny, prin. Fax 875-1820

**San Jacinto, Riverside, Pop. 42,978**
San Jacinto USD 9,300/PK-12
2045 S San Jacinto Ave 92583 951-929-7700
Diane Perez, supt. Fax 658-3574
www.sanjacinto.k12.ca.us/
Monte Vista MS 900/6-8
181 N Ramona Blvd 92583 951-654-9361
Janet Covacevich, prin. Fax 654-0173
Mountain View HS Mountain Heights Acad 300/Alt
1000 N Ramona Blvd 92582 951-487-7710
Cliff Weaver, prin. Fax 487-7718
North Mountain MS 1,000/6-8
1202 E 7th St 92583 951-487-7797
Dr. Karen Kirschinger, prin. Fax 487-7799
San Jacinto HS 2,300/9-12
500 Idyllwild Dr 92583 951-654-7374
Jordan Reeves, prin. Fax 654-7702
San Jacinto Leadership Academy 100/6-8
1599 Malaga Dr 92583 951-929-1954
Col. Francis Sick, prin.

---

Mt. San Jacinto College Post-Sec.
1499 N State St 92583 951-487-6752

**San Joaquin, Fresno, Pop. 3,985**
Golden Plains USD 1,900/K-12
PO Box 937 93660 559-693-1115
Martin Macias, supt. Fax 693-2526
www.gpusd.org
Other Schools – See Helm, Tranquillity

**San Jose, Santa Clara, Pop. 914,803**
Alum Rock UNESD 12,000/PK-8
2930 Gay Ave 95127 408-928-6800
Dr. Hilaria Bauer Ph.D., supt. Fax 928-6400
www.arusd.org
Fischer MS 600/6-8
1720 Hopkins Dr 95122 408-928-7500
Dr. Imee Almazan Ed.D., prin. Fax 928-7501
George MS 600/6-8
277 Mahoney Dr 95127 408-928-7600
Barbara Campbell, prin. Fax 928-7601
Mathson MS 700/6-8
2050 Kammerer Ave 95116 408-928-7950
Oscar Leon, prin. Fax 928-7951
Ocala MS 600/6-8
2800 Ocala Ave 95148 408-928-8350
Tracy Leathers, prin. Fax 928-8351
Renaissance Academy at Fischer 300/6-8
1720 Hopkins Dr 95122 408-928-1950
Doug Kleinhenz, prin. Fax 928-1951
Renaissance Academy at Mathson 6-8
2050 Kammerer Ave 95116 408-928-8500
Doug Kleinhenz, prin. Fax 928-8501
Sheppard MS 800/6-8
480 Rough and Ready Rd 95133 408-928-8800
Jackie Montejano, prin. Fax 928-8801

Berryessa UNESD 8,100/K-8
1376 Piedmont Rd 95132 408-923-1800
Will Ector, supt. Fax 923-0623
www.berryessa.k12.ca.us
Morrill MS 900/6-8
1970 Morrill Ave 95132 408-923-1930
Anjanette Winckler, prin. Fax 946-0776
Piedmont MS 800/6-8
955 Piedmont Rd 95132 408-923-1945
Deanne Parrish, prin. Fax 251-2392
Sierramont MS 1,100/6-8
3155 Kimlee Dr 95132 408-923-1955
Chris Mosley, prin. Fax 729-5840

Campbell UNESD
Supt. — See Campbell
Monroe MS 1,000/5-8
1055 S Monroe St 95128 408-556-0360
Dawnel Sonntag, prin. Fax 341-7020

Campbell UNHSD 7,400/9-12
3235 Union Ave 95124 408-371-0960
Patrick Gaffney, supt. Fax 558-3006
www.cuhsd.org/
Boynton Alternative HS 300/Alt
901 Boynton Ave 95117 408-626-3404
Sarah Thomas, prin. Fax 984-8917
Branham HS 1,400/9-12
1570 Branham Ln 95118 408-626-3407
Fax 267-2676
Camden Community Day S 50/Alt
2223 Camden Ave 95124 408-626-3409
Sarah Thomas, prin. Fax 558-3000

Del Mar HS 1,200/9-12
1224 Del Mar Ave Ste A 95128 408-626-3403
Jennifer Baldwin, prin. Fax 295-9476
Leigh HS 1,600/9-12
5210 Leigh Ave 95124 408-626-3405
Pam Hoult, prin. Fax 265-7525
Campbell Adult & Community Education Adult
1224 Del Mar Ave 95128 408-371-0960
Dr. Bob Harper Ed.D., dir. Fax 947-2342
Other Schools – See Campbell, Saratoga

Cupertino UNSD
Supt. — See Cupertino
Miller MS 1,300/6-8
6151 Rainbow Dr 95129 408-252-3755
Steven Burrell, prin. Fax 255-5269

East Side UNHSD 25,400/K-12
830 N Capitol Ave 95133 408-347-5000
Chris Funk, supt. Fax 347-5045
www.esuhsd.org
Apollo Continuation HS 200/Alt
1835 Cunningham Ave 95122 408-928-5400
Vito Chiala, dir.
Calero HS 100/9-12
420 Calero Ave 95123 408-347-7600
Robert Ibarra, prin. Fax 347-5015
Evergreen Valley HS 2,600/9-12
3300 Quimby Rd 95148 408-347-7000
Lauren Kelly, prin. Fax 347-7175
Foothill HS 400/Alt
230 Pala Ave 95127 408-928-9100
Lynne Murray, prin. Fax 928-9115
Hill HS 2,200/9-12
3200 Senter Rd 95111 408-347-4100
Jose Hernandez, prin. Fax 347-4115
Independence HS 3,300/9-12
1776 Educational Park Dr 95133 408-928-9500
Grettel Castro-Sta, prin. Fax 928-9515
Lick HS 1,300/9-12
57 N White Rd 95127 408-347-4400
Kelly Daugherty, prin. Fax 347-4415
Mt. Pleasant HS 1,600/9-12
1750 S White Rd 95127 408-937-2800
Martha Guerrero, prin. Fax 937-2815
Oak Grove HS 2,100/9-12
285 Blossom Hill Rd 95123 408-347-6500
Martha Brazil, prin. Fax 347-6515
Overfelt HS 1,500/9-12
1835 Cunningham Ave 95122 408-347-5900
Vito Chiala, prin. Fax 347-5915
Pegasus HS 100/Alt
1776 Educational Park Dr 95133 408-928-9597
Grettel Castro-Stanley, coord. Fax 928-9535
Phoenix HS 100/Alt
6150 Snell Ave 95123 408-347-6291
Greg Louie, prin. Fax 347-6295
Piedmont Hills HS 2,200/9-12
1377 Piedmont Rd 95132 408-347-3800
Traci Williams, prin. Fax 347-3805
Santa Teresa HS 2,200/9-12
6150 Snell Ave 95123 408-347-6200
Greg Louie, prin. Fax 347-6215
Silver Creek HS 2,400/9-12
3434 Silver Creek Rd 95121 408-347-5600
Adolfo Laguna, prin. Fax 347-5615
Yerba Buena HS 1,700/9-12
1855 Lucretia Ave 95122 408-347-4700
Tom Huynh, prin. Fax 347-4715
East Side Adult Center Adult
1835 Cunningham Ave 95122 408-928-9300
Richard Uribe, dir. Fax 928-9309

Evergreen ESD 13,300/K-8
3188 Quimby Rd 95148 408-270-6800
Kathy Gomez, supt. Fax 274-3894
www.eesd.org/
Chaboya MS 1,100/7-8
3276 Fowler Rd 95135 408-270-6900
Derrick Watkins, prin. Fax 270-6916
LeyVa IS 900/7-8
1865 Monrovia Dr 95122 408-270-4993
James Sherman, prin. Fax 270-5462
Quimby Oak MS 1,000/7-8
3190 Quimby Rd 95148 408-270-6735
Phil Bond, prin. Fax 223-4533

Franklin-McKinley ESD 10,000/K-8
645 Wool Creek Dr 95112 408-283-6000
Dr. Juan Cruz, supt. Fax 283-6022
www.fmsd.org
Sylvandale MS 800/7-8
653 Sylvandale Ave 95111 408-363-5700
Dan Fowler, prin. Fax 363-5649

Fremont UNHSD
Supt. — See Sunnyvale
Lynbrook HS 1,800/9-12
1280 Johnson Ave 95129 408-366-7700
John Dwyer, prin. Fax 257-0551

Moreland SD 4,400/K-8
4711 Campbell Ave 95130 408-874-2900
Mary Kay Going, supt. Fax 374-8863
www.moreland.org
Moreland MS 1,000/6-8
4600 Student Ln 95130 408-875-3300
Ann Doumanian, prin. Fax 379-3622

Morgan Hill USD
Supt. — See Morgan Hill
Murphy MS 600/7-8
141 Avenida Espana 95139 408-201-6260
Heather Nursement, prin. Fax 201-6270

Mount Pleasant ESD 2,500/PK-8
3434 Marten Ave 95148 408-223-3700
Mariann Engle, supt. Fax 223-3715
www.mountpleasant.k12.ca.us
Boeger MS 700/6-8
1944 Flint Ave 95148 408-223-3770
Mia Cruz, prin. Fax 223-6959

Oak Grove ESD 11,500/K-8
6578 Santa Teresa Blvd 95119 408-227-8300
Jose Manzo, supt. Fax 629-7183
www.ogsd.net
Academy 50/Alt
6578 Santa Teresa Blvd 95119 408-226-2350
Oscar Ortiz, prin. Fax 227-2719
Bernal IS 800/7-8
6610 San Ignacio Ave 95119 408-578-5731
Jamal Splane, prin. Fax 578-7367
Davis IS 800/7-8
5035 Edenview Dr 95111 408-227-0616
Kim Kianidehkian, prin. Fax 224-8957
Herman IS 900/5-8
5955 Blossom Ave 95123 408-226-1886
Laura Meusel, prin. Fax 226-1897

Regional Occupational Center & Program
Supt. — None
Silicon Valley Career Technical Ed Vo/Tech
760 Hillsdale Ave 95136 408-723-6464
Susan Glass, supt. Fax 723-7266

San Jose USD 33,200/K-12
855 Lenzen Ave 95126 408-535-6000
Dr. Vincent Matthews, supt. Fax 535-2362
www.sjusd.org
Broadway HS 200/Alt
4825 Speak Ln 95118 408-535-6285
Giovanni Bui, prin. Fax 264-6392
Burnett Academy 900/6-8
850 N 2nd St 95112 408-535-6267
Fax 298-1675
Castillero MS 1,300/6-8
6384 Leyland Park Dr 95120 408-535-6385
Darbi O'Connell, prin. Fax 268-4489
Gunderson HS 1,100/9-12
622 Gaundabert Ln 95136 408-535-6340
Fax 224-2209
Gunderson Plus Continuation HS 50/Alt
622 Gaundabert Ln 95136 408-972-8629
Cecilia Molina, prin.
Harte MS 1,200/6-8
7050 Bret Harte Dr 95120 408-535-6270
Tina VanLaarhoven, prin. Fax 927-0698
Hoover MS 1,100/6-8
1635 Park Ave 95126 408-535-6274
Don McCloskey, prin. Fax 286-4864
Leland HS 1,800/9-12
6677 Camden Ave 95120 408-535-6290
Deepa Mukherjee, prin. Fax 927-6448
Leland Plus Continuation HS 50/Alt
6677 Camden Ave 95120 408-535-6100
Cecilia Molina, prin.
Liberty MSHS 400/Alt
5845 Allen Ave 95123 408-229-0722
Cecilia Molina, prin. Fax 225-5348
Lincoln HS 1,800/9-12
555 Dana Ave 95126 408-535-6300
Matt Hewitson, prin. Fax 535-2352
Lincoln Plus S, 1999 Olive Ave 95128 50/Alt
Cecilia Molina, prin. 408-292-3794
Middle College HS 50/Alt
2100 Moorpark Ave 95128 408-288-3100
Cecilia Molina, prin.
Muir MS 1,100/6-8
1260 Branham Ln 95118 408-535-6281
Jeannette Harding, prin. Fax 535-2319
O'Connor Career Academy Vo/Tech
2105 Forest Ave 95128 408-947-2852
Cecilia Molina, prin.
Pioneer HS 1,600/9-12
1290 Blossom Hill Rd 95118 408-535-6310
Stefani Garino, prin. Fax 535-2357
Pioneer Plus Continuation HS 50/Alt
1290 Blossom Hill Rd 95118 408-264-4428
Cecilia Molina, prin.
San Jose Community Day S 50/Alt
1155 E Julian St 95116 408-279-2550
Rosa Nieto, prin. Fax 280-7306
San Jose High Academy Plus 50/Alt
275 N 24th St 95116 408-287-1631
Cecilia Molina, prin.
San Jose HS Academy 1,100/9-12
275 N 24th St 95116 408-535-6320
Gloria Marchant, prin. Fax 535-2355
Willow Glen HS 1,500/9-12
2001 Cottle Ave 95125 408-535-6330
Phil Roark, prin. Fax 535-2353
Willow Glen MS 1,300/6-8
2105 Cottle Ave 95125 408-535-6277
Paul Slayton, prin. Fax 535-2353
Willow Glen Plus HS 50/Alt
2001 Cottle Ave 95125 408-264-4422
Cecilia Molina, prin.

Union ESD 5,000/K-8
5175 Union Ave 95124 408-377-8010
Denise Clay Ed.D., supt. Fax 377-7182
www.unionsd.org
Dartmouth MS 800/6-8
5575 Dartmouth Dr 95118 408-264-1122
Randy Martino, prin. Fax 264-9332
Union MS 800/6-8
2130 Los Gatos Almaden Rd 95124 408-371-0366
Todd Feinberg, prin. Fax 371-1217

---

Apostles Lutheran S 200/PK-12
5828 Santa Teresa Blvd 95123 408-578-4800
Joel Walker M.Ed., prin. Fax 225-0720
Archbishop Mitty HS 1,700/9-12
5000 Mitty Way 95129 408-252-6610
Timothy Brosnan, prin. Fax 252-6967
BASIS Independent Silicon Valley 600/5-12
1290 Parkmoor Ave 95126 408-291-0907
Toby Walker, head sch
Bellarmine College Prep S 1,600/9-12
960 W Hedding St 95126 408-294-9224
Kristina Luscher, prin. Fax 297-5585
Carrington College California Post-Sec.
6201 San Ignacio Ave 95119 408-360-0840
Center of Employment Training Post-Sec.
701 Vine St 95110 408-287-7924
Cristo Rey HS 100/9-12
1390 Five Wounds Ln 95116 408-293-0425
Joe Albers, prin.
DeVry University Post-Sec.
2160 Lundy Ave Ste 250 95131 408-571-3760
Evergreen Valley College Post-Sec.
3095 Yerba Buena Rd 95135 408-274-7900
Five Branches University Post-Sec.
3031 Tisch Way Ste 507 95128 408-260-0208
Harker MS 400/6-8
3800 Blackford Ave 95117 408-248-2510
Christopher Nikoloff, head sch Fax 248-2502
Harker Upper S 700/9-12
500 Saratoga Ave 95129 408-249-2510
Christopher Nikoloff, hdmstr. Fax 984-2325
International Technological University Post-Sec.
355 W San Fernando St 95110 888-488-4968
Liberty Baptist S 200/PK-12
2790 S King Rd 95122 408-274-5613
National Hispanic University Post-Sec.
14271 Story Rd 95127 408-254-6900
Notre Dame HS 600/9-12
596 S 2nd St 95112 408-294-1113
Mary Beth Riley, prin. Fax 293-9779
Palmer College of Chiropractic West Cmps Post-Sec.
90 E Tasman Dr 95134 866-303-7939
Presentation HS 800/9-12
2281 Plummer Ave 95125 408-264-1664
Mary Miller, prin. Fax 266-3028
Sacred Heart Nativity Schools 100/6-8
310 Edwards Ave 95110 408-993-1293
Lorraine Shepherd, prin. Fax 993-0675
San Jose City College Post-Sec.
2100 Moorpark Ave 95128 408-298-2181
San Jose State University Post-Sec.
1 Washington Sq 95192 408-924-1000
Silicon Valley University Post-Sec.
2160 Lundy Ave Ste 110 95131 408-435-8989
Stratford MS, 1718 Andover Ln 95124 200/6-8
Maggie Schwartz, prin. 408-626-0001
Valley Christian HS 1,300/9-12
100 Skyway Dr Ste 110 95111 408-513-2400
Mark Lodewyk, prin. Fax 513-2527
Valley Christian JHS 500/6-8
100 Skyway Dr Ste 140 95111 408-513-2460
Lisa Arnett, prin. Fax 513-2472
WestMed College-San Jose Post-Sec.
3031 Tisch Way 95128 408-236-1170

**San Juan Bautista, San Benito, Pop. 1,810**
Aromas/San Juan USD 1,200/PK-12
2300 San Juan Hwy 95045 831-623-4500
Ruben Zepeda, supt. Fax 623-4907
www.asjusd.k12.ca.us
Anzar HS 400/9-12
2000 San Juan Hwy 95045 831-623-7660
Charlene McKowen, prin. Fax 623-7676

**San Juan Capistrano, Orange, Pop. 33,954**
Capistrano USD 51,000/K-12
33122 Valle Rd 92675 949-234-9200
Kirsten Vital, supt. Fax 493-8729
capousd.ca.schoolloop.com
Forster MS 1,400/6-8
25601 Camino Del Avion 92675 949-234-5907
Carrie Bertini, prin. Fax 488-3567
Junipero Serra HS 200/Alt
31422 Camino Capistrano 92675 949-489-7216
Rich Bellante, prin. Fax 496-2007
San Juan Hills HS 1,900/9-12
29211 Vista Montana 92675 949-234-5900
Jennifer Smalley, prin. Fax 488-9727
Capistrano Unified Adult Education Adult
31431 El Camino Real 92675 949-493-0658
Jolene Dougherty, prin. Fax 489-1421
Other Schools – See Aliso Viejo, Dana Point, Ladera Ranch, Laguna Niguel, Mission Viejo, Rancho Santa Margarita, San Clemente

Regional Occupational Center & Program
Supt. — None
South Coast ROP Vo/Tech
33122 Valle Rd Ste 1000 92675 949-234-9464
Kimberly Thomason, dir.

---

Capistrano Valley Christian S 400/PK-12
32032 Del Obispo St 92675 949-493-5683
Dr. Ronald Sipus, head sch Fax 493-6057
JSerra HS 1,000/9-12
26351 Junipero Serra Rd 92675 949-493-9307
Eric Stroupe, admin. Fax 493-9308
Saddleback Valley Christian S 900/PK-12
26333 Oso Rd 92675 949-443-4050
Robert Metz, supt. Fax 443-3941
St. Margaret Episcopal S 1,100/PK-12
31641 La Novia Ave 92675 949-661-0108
William Moseley, head sch Fax 661-8637

**San Leandro, Alameda, Pop. 81,465**
San Leandro USD 8,800/K-12
14735 Juniper St 94579 510-667-3500
Dr. Mike McLaughlin, supt. Fax 667-3569
www.sanleandro.k12.ca.us

Bancroft MS 1,000/6-8
1150 Bancroft Ave 94577 510-618-4380
Valentin Del Rio, prin. Fax 895-4113
Lincoln HS 100/Alt
2600 Teagarden St 94577 510-618-4600
Benjamin Redmond, prin. Fax 614-2018
Muir MS 1,000/6-8
1444 Williams St 94577 510-618-4400
Vernon Walton, prin. Fax 667-3545
San Leandro HS 2,800/9-12
2200 Bancroft Ave 94577 510-618-4600
Reginald Richardson, prin. Fax 347-1064
San Leandro Adult S Adult
1448 Williams St 94577 510-667-6287
Bradley Frazier, prin. Fax 357-8794

San Lorenzo USD
Supt. — See San Lorenzo
Washington Manor MS 900/6-8
1170 Fargo Ave 94579 510-317-5500
Theresa Armada, prin. Fax 317-5597

---

Carrington College California Post-Sec.
15555 E 14th St Ste 500 94578 510-276-3888

**San Lorenzo, Alameda, Pop. 22,527**
San Lorenzo USD 12,100/K-12
15510 Usher St 94580 510-317-4600
Dr. Fred Brill, supt. Fax 278-4344
www.slzusd.org
Arroyo HS 1,800/9-12
15701 Lorenzo Ave 94580 510-317-4000
James Gray, prin. Fax 278-9067
Bohannon MS 900/6-8
800 Bockman Rd 94580 510-317-3800
Margaret Arman, prin. Fax 278-7794
Edendale MS 600/6-8
16160 Ashland Ave 94580 510-317-5100
Evelyn Baffico, prin. Fax 317-5190
San Lorenzo HS 1,400/9-12
50 E Lewelling Blvd 94580 510-317-3000
Tovi Scruggs, prin. Fax 278-0547
San Lorenzo Adult S Adult
820 Bockman Rd 94580 510-317-4200
John Kelly, prin. Fax 317-4291
Other Schools – See Hayward, San Leandro

---

Redwood Christian MSHS 400/6-12
1000 Paseo Grande 94580 510-317-8990
Al Hearne, prin. Fax 278-5064

**San Luis Obispo, San Luis Obispo, Pop. 43,697**
San Luis Coastal USD 7,200/PK-12
1500 Lizzie St 93401 805-549-1200
Dr. Eric Prater, supt. Fax 549-9074
www.slcusd.org
Laguna MS 700/7-8
11050 Los Osos Valley Rd 93405 805-596-4055
John Calandro, prin. Fax 544-2449
Pacific Beach HS 100/Alt
11950 Los Osos Valley Rd 93405 805-596-4023
Andrew Marinello, prin.
San Luis Obispo HS 1,400/9-12
1499 San Luis Dr 93401 805-596-4040
Leslie O'Connor, prin. Fax 542-9075
Adult S Adult
1500 Lizzie St Bldg G 93401 805-549-1222
Sally Ames, coord. Fax 544-0638
Other Schools – See Los Osos, Morro Bay

---

California Polytechnic State University Post-Sec.
1 Grand Ave 93407 805-756-1111
Central CA School of Continuing Educ. Post-Sec.
3195 McMillan Ave Ste F 93401 805-543-9123
Cuesta College Post-Sec.
PO Box 8106 93403 805-546-3100
Laurus College Post-Sec.
81 Higuera St Ste 110 93401 805-267-1690
Mission College Preparatory Catholic HS 300/9-12
682 Palm St 93401 805-543-2131
James Childs, prin. Fax 543-4359
San Luis Obispo Classical Academy 300/K-12
PO Box 3601 93403 805-548-8700
Susan Theule, dir.

**San Marcos, San Diego, Pop. 80,807**
San Diego County Office of Education
Supt. — See San Diego
North Coastal Consortium S PK-12
255 Pico Ave 92069 760-761-5110
John Kramer, prin.

San Marcos USD 19,100/K-12
255 Pico Ave Ste 250 92069 760-752-1299
Kevin Holt Ed.D., supt.
www.smusd.org/
Foothills HS 100/Alt
158 Cassou Rd 92069 760-290-2544
Mary Bunker, prin. Fax 736-2221
Mission Hills HS 2,500/9-12
1 E Mission Hills Ct 92069 760-290-2700
Courtney Goode, prin. Fax 290-2680
San Elijo MS 1,500/6-8
1600 Schoolhouse Way 92078 760-290-2800
Gary DeBora, prin. Fax 290-2828
San Marcos HS 2,200/9-12
1615 W San Marcos Blvd 92078 760-290-2200
Tiffany Campbell, prin. Fax 736-8275
San Marcos MS 1,400/6-8
650 W Mission Rd 92069 760-290-2500
Spencer Wavra, prin. Fax 744-0893
Twin Oaks HS 200/Alt
158 Cassou Rd 92069 760-290-2555
Mary Bunker, prin. Fax 736-2221
Woodland Park MS 1,300/6-8
1270 Rock Springs Rd 92069 760-290-2455
Josh Way, prin. Fax 741-6178

---

California State University-San Marcos Post-Sec.
333 S Twin Oaks Valley Rd 92096 760-750-4000
Coleman University Post-Sec.
1284 W San Marcos Blvd 92078 760-747-3990
Palomar College Post-Sec.
1140 W Mission Rd 92069 760-744-1150
Palomar Institute of Cosmetology Post-Sec.
355 Via Vera Cruz Ste 3 92078 760-744-7900
St. Joseph Academy K-12
500 Las Flores Dr 92078 760-305-8505
Anthony Biese, prin. Fax 305-8466
Univ of St. Augustine for Health Science Post-Sec.
700 Windy Point Dr 92069 800-241-1027

**San Marino, Los Angeles, Pop. 12,791**
San Marino USD 3,100/K-12
1665 West Dr 91108 626-299-7000
Alex Cherniss, supt. Fax 299-7010
www.smusd.us
Huntington MS 800/6-8
1700 Huntington Dr 91108 626-299-7060
Jason Kurtenbach, prin. Fax 299-7064
San Marino HS 1,100/9-12
2701 Huntington Dr 91108 626-299-7020
D.R. Moreland, prin. Fax 299-7037

---

Southwestern Academy 200/6-12
2800 Monterey Rd 91108 626-799-5010
Kenneth R. Veronda, hdmstr. Fax 799-0407

**San Mateo, San Mateo, Pop. 91,447**
San Mateo County Office of Education
Supt. — See Redwood City
Gateway Center 100/Alt
35 Tower Rd 94402 650-598-2150
Rebecca Vichiquis, prin. Fax 598-2191

San Mateo UNHSD 8,200/9-12
650 N Delaware St 94401 650-558-2299
Dr. Kevin Skelly, supt. Fax 762-0249
www.smuhsd.org
Aragon HS 1,500/9-12
900 Alameda De Las Pulgas 94402 650-558-2999
Patricia Kurtz, prin. Fax 558-2952
Hillsdale HS 1,300/9-12
3115 Del Monte St 94403 650-558-2699
Jeff Gilbert, prin. Fax 574-4173
San Mateo HS 1,400/9-12
506 N Delaware St 94401 650-558-2399
Yvonne Shiu, prin. Fax 558-2352
San Mateo Adult S Adult
789 E Poplar Ave 94401 650-558-2100
Lawrence Teshara, dir. Fax 762-0232
Other Schools – See Burlingame, Millbrae, San Bruno

San Mateo-Foster City ESD
Supt. — See Foster City
Abbott MS 800/6-8
600 36th Ave 94403 650-312-7600
Cathy Ennon, prin. Fax 312-7605
Bayside S.T.E.M. Academy 500/6-8
2025 Kehoe Ave 94403 650-312-7660
Joanne Day, prin. Fax 312-7634
Borel MS 900/6-8
425 Barneson Ave 94402 650-312-7670
Kenyetta Cook, prin. Fax 312-7644

---

College of San Mateo Post-Sec.
1700 W Hillsdale Blvd 94402 650-574-6161
Dawn Christian Academy 100/K-12
525 42nd Ave 94403 650-212-4222
Chris Chu, prin.
Gurnick Academy of Medical Arts Post-Sec.
2121 S El Camino Real 94403 650-685-6616
Junipero Serra HS 900/9-12
451 W 20th Ave 94403 650-345-8207
Dr. Barry Thornton, prin. Fax 573-6638
Pacific Rim International S 100/PK-12
454 Peninsula Ave 94401 650-685-1881
Rita Tang, dir. Fax 685-1820

**San Pablo, Contra Costa, Pop. 28,206**
West Contra Costa USD
Supt. — See Richmond
Helms MS 900/7-8
2500 Road 20 94806 510-233-3988
Jessica Petrilli, prin. Fax 234-5977
Middle College HS 300/9-12
2600 Mission Bell Dr 94806 510-215-3881
Hattie Smith, prin. Fax 215-7927
Vista S 200/Alt
2625 Barnard St 94806 510-231-1431
Sylvia Greenwood, prin. Fax 222-8357

---

Contra Costa College Post-Sec.
2600 Mission Bell Dr 94806 510-235-7800

**San Pedro, See Los Angeles**
Los Angeles USD
Supt. — See Los Angeles
Angels Gate Continuation S 100/Alt
3607 S Gaffey St 90731 310-221-4600
Joan D'Amore, prin. Fax 221-4629
Dana MS 1,500/6-8
1501 S Cabrillo Ave 90731 310-241-1100
Steven Gebhart, prin. Fax 514-9925
Johnston Community Day S 200/7-12
2210 N Taper Ave 90731 310-832-0376
Barbara Politz, prin. Fax 832-7914
San Pedro HS 3,000/9-12
1001 W 15th St 90731 310-241-5800
Jeanette Stevens, prin. Fax 547-3183
Harbor Community Adult S Adult
950 W Santa Cruz St 90731 310-547-4425
Lanny Nelms, prin. Fax 832-3489
Harbor Occupational Center Adult
740 N Pacific Ave 90731 310-547-5551
Gertrude Hawkins, prin. Fax 547-4979

---

Mary Star of the Sea HS 500/9-12
2500 N Taper Ave 90731 310-547-1138
Rita Dever, prin. Fax 547-1827
Rolling Hills Preparatory S 200/6-12
1 Rolling Hills Prep Way 90732 310-791-1101
Peter McCormack, head sch Fax 373-4931

**San Rafael, Marin, Pop. 55,927**
Dixie ESD 1,800/PK-8
380 Nova Albion Way 94903 415-492-3700
Dr. Thomas Lohwasser, supt. Fax 492-3707
dixieschooldistrict.org
Miller Creek MS 600/6-8
2255 Las Gallinas Ave 94903 415-492-3760
Kristy Treewater, prin. Fax 492-3765

Marin County Office of Education 300/
PO Box 4925 94913 415-472-4110
Mike Grant, supt. Fax 491-6625
www.marinschools.org/
Marin County Community S 100/Alt
PO Box 4925 94913 415-491-0581
Raquel Rose, dir. Fax 491-0981

Regional Occupational Center & Program
Supt. — None
Marin County ROP Vo/Tech
PO Box 4925 94913 415-499-5892
Gene Abbott, coord. Fax 491-6622

San Rafael CSD 6,000/PK-12
310 Nova Albion Way 94903 415-492-3233
Dr. Michael Watenpaugh, supt. Fax 492-3245
www.srcs.org
Davidson MS 900/6-8
280 Woodland Ave 94901 415-485-2400
Robert Marcucci, prin. Fax 485-2476
Madrone Continuation HS 50/Alt
185 Mission Ave 94901 415-485-2435
Jane Songer, prin. Fax 485-2438
San Rafael HS 900/9-12
185 Mission Ave 94901 415-485-2330
Glenn Dennis, prin. Fax 485-2345
Terra Linda HS 1,100/9-12
320 Nova Albion Way 94903 415-492-3100
Katy Dunlap, prin. Fax 492-3105

---

Dominican University of California Post-Sec.
50 Acacia Ave 94901 415-457-4440
Marin Academy 400/9-12
1600 Mission Ave 94901 415-453-4550
Travis Brownley, head sch Fax 453-8538
Marin S 100/9-12
150 N San Pedro Rd 94903 415-339-9336
Barbara J. Brown Ed.D., head sch Fax 339-9337

**San Ramon, Contra Costa, Pop. 68,811**
San Ramon Valley USD
Supt. — See Danville
California HS 2,600/9-12
9870 Broadmoor Dr 94583 925-803-3200
Sarah Cranford, prin. Fax 803-9341
Dougherty Valley HS 2,000/9-12
10550 Albion Rd, 925-479-6400
Daniel Hillman, prin. Fax 479-6597
Gale Ranch MS 800/6-8
6400 Main Branch Rd, 925-479-1500
Susan Goldman, prin. Fax 479-1595
Iron Horse MS 1,000/6-8
12601 Alcosta Blvd 94583 925-790-2500
Joe Nguyen, prin. Fax 824-2830
Pine Valley MS 900/6-8
3000 Pine Valley Rd 94583 925-479-7700
Jason Law, prin. Fax 828-1972
Venture Independent Study S 300/Alt
10540 Albion Rd, 925-479-1200
Matt Chamberlain, prin. Fax 479-1297
Windemere Ranch MS 1,000/6-8
11611 E Branch Pkwy, 925-479-7400
David Bolin, prin. Fax 479-7469

**Santa Ana, Orange, Pop. 321,180**
Garden Grove USD
Supt. — See Garden Grove
Fitz IS 700/7-8
4600 W McFadden Ave 92704 714-663-6351
Mischelle Repsher, prin. Fax 663-6527

Regional Occupational Center & Program
Supt. — None
Central Orange County CTE Partnership Vo/Tech
2323 N Broadway Ste 301 92706 714-996-3528
Al Mijares, dir.

Santa Ana USD 57,100/PK-12
1601 E Chestnut Ave 92701 714-558-5501
Rick Miller Ph.D., supt. Fax 558-5610
www.sausd.us
Carr IS 1,600/6-8
2120 W Edinger Ave 92704 714-480-4100
Jose Luis Pedroza, prin. Fax 957-8766
Century HS 2,000/9-12
1401 S Grand Ave 92705 714-568-7000
Michael Parra, prin. Fax 568-7038
Chavez HS 300/Alt
2128 Cypress Ave 92707 714-430-5700
Matthew Cruz, prin. Fax 430-5799
Community Day S 100/Alt
804 N Fairview St 92703 714-796-9000
Trucker Clark, prin. Fax 796-9099
Godinez Fundamental HS 2,600/9-12
3002 W Centennial Rd 92704 714-433-6600
Cindy Landsiedel, prin. Fax 433-6731
Lathrop IS 1,200/6-8
1111 S Broadway 92707 714-567-3300
Julie Infante, prin. Fax 567-3399
MacArthur Fundamental IS 1,300/6-8
600 W Alton Ave 92707 714-568-7700
David Casper, prin. Fax 568-7799

McFadden IS 1,400/6-8
2701 S Raitt St 92704 714-479-4000
Ignacio Muniz, prin. Fax 479-4099
Mendez Fundamental IS 1,400/6-8
2000 N Bristol St 92706 714-972-7800
Dennis Cole, prin. Fax 972-7899
Middle College HS 300/9-12
1530 W 17th St 92706 714-953-3900
Kathy Apps Ed.D., prin. Fax 953-3999
Saddleback HS 2,000/9-12
2802 S Flower St 92707 714-569-6300
Edward Bustamante Ed.D., prin. Fax 569-6399
Santa Ana HS 3,000/9-12
520 W Walnut St 92701 714-567-4900
Jeff Bishop, prin. Fax 567-4952
Segerstrom HS 2,400/9-12
2301 W MacArthur Blvd 92704 714-241-5000
Duncan McCulloch, prin. Fax 241-5099
Sierra Preparatory Academy 900/6-8
2021 N Grand Ave 92705 714-567-3500
Jesse Church, prin. Fax 567-3591
Spurgeon IS 1,200/6-8
2701 W 5th St 92703 714-480-2200
Todd Irving, prin. Fax 480-2215
Valley HS 2,300/9-12
1801 S Greenville St 92704 714-241-6410
David Richey, prin. Fax 241-6599
Villa Fundamental IS 1,400/6-8
1441 E Chestnut Ave 92701 714-558-5100
Jonathan Swanson, prin. Fax 558-5199
Willard IS 900/6-8
1342 N Ross St 92706 714-480-4800
Amy Scruton, prin. Fax 480-4899

Tustin USD
Supt. — See Tustin
Foothill HS 2,400/9-12
19251 Dodge Ave 92705 714-730-7464
Nick Stephany, prin. Fax 573-9376
Hewes MS 1,000/6-8
13232 Hewes Ave 92705 714-730-7348
Eric Kilian, prin. Fax 730-7315

---

Art Institute of California - Orange Co. Post-Sec.
3601 W Sunflower Ave 92704 714-830-0200
Bethel Baptist S 200/PK-12
901 S Euclid St 92704 714-839-3600
Dr. Terry Cantrell, admin. Fax 839-4953
California Coast University Post-Sec.
925 N Spurgeon St 92701 888-228-8648
Calvary Chapel S 1,500/K-12
3800 S Fairview St 92704 714-662-7485
Jay Henry, supt. Fax 979-3515
Colleen O'Hara's Beauty Academy Post-Sec.
109 W 4th St Fl 2 92701 714-568-5399
Everest College Post-Sec.
500 W Santa Ana Blvd 92701 714-656-1000
Mater Dei HS 2,000/9-12
1202 W Edinger Ave 92707 714-754-7711
Frances Clare, prin. Fax 754-1880
Newbridge College Post-Sec.
1840 E 17th St Ste 140 92705 714-550-8000
Santa Ana College Post-Sec.
1530 W 17th St 92706 714-564-6000
Taft Law School Post-Sec.
3700 S Susan St Ste 200 92704 714-850-4800

**Santa Barbara, Santa Barbara, Pop. 86,425**
Regional Occupational Center & Program
Supt. — None
Santa Barbara County ROP Vo/Tech
PO Box 6307 93160 805-937-8427
Tony Bauer, dir. Fax 569-2507

Santa Barbara County Office of Education 200/
PO Box 6307 93160 805-964-4711
William Cirone, supt. Fax 964-4712
www.sbceo.org
Other Schools – See Santa Maria

Santa Barbara SD 15,100/PK-12
720 Santa Barbara St 93101 805-963-4338
Dr. David Cash, supt. Fax 962-3146
www.sbunified.org
Alta Vista Alternative HS 100/Alt
215 E Ortega St 93101 805-965-1916
Elise Simmons, prin.
La Colina JHS 800/7-8
4025 Foothill Rd 93110 805-967-4506
David Ortiz, prin. Fax 967-3056
La Cuesta Continuation HS 100/Alt
710 Santa Barbara St 93101 805-966-0883
Elise Simmons, prin. Fax 963-8006
La Cumbre JHS 600/7-8
2255 Modoc Rd 93101 805-687-0761
Jo Ann Caines, prin. Fax 563-4636
San Marcos HS 1,800/9-12
4750 Hollister Ave 93110 805-967-4581
Ed Behrens, prin. Fax 967-8358
Santa Barbara HS 2,200/9-12
700 E Anapamu St 93103 805-966-9101
John Becchio, prin. Fax 965-6872
Santa Barbara JHS 800/7-8
721 E Cota St 93103 805-963-7751
Lito Garcia, prin. Fax 962-7196
Other Schools – See Goleta

---

Anacapa S 50/7-12
814 Santa Barbara St 93101 805-965-0228
Gordon Sichi, head sch Fax 899-2758
Antioch University Santa Barbara Post-Sec.
602 Anacapa St 93101 805-962-8179
Avalon Beauty College Post-Sec.
504 N Milpas St 93103 805-966-1931
Bishop Garcia Diego HS 300/9-12
4000 La Colina Rd 93110 805-967-1266
Dr. Paul Harrington, head sch Fax 964-3178

Fielding Graduate University Post-Sec.
2020 De La Vina St 93105 805-687-1099
Garden Street Academy 100/K-12
2300 Garden St 93105 805-687-3717
Angela Jevons, admin. Fax 456-1897
Laguna Blanca S 300/PK-12
4125 Paloma Dr 93110 805-687-1752
Rob Hereford, head sch Fax 682-2553
Providence Santa Barbara Christian S 100/7-12
630 E Canon Perdido St 93103 805-962-4400
Timothy Loomer, head sch Fax 962-0132
Santa Barbara Business College Post-Sec.
506 Chapala St 93101 866-749-7222
Santa Barbara City College Post-Sec.
721 Cliff Dr 93109 805-965-0581
Santa Barbara Cottage & Gen. Hosp. Post-Sec.
PO Box 689 93102 805-569-7290
Santa Barbara MS 100/6-9
1321 Alameda Padre Serra 93103 805-682-2989
Brian McWilliams, hdmstr. Fax 682-0893
University of California 93106 Post-Sec.
805-893-8000
Westmont College Post-Sec.
955 La Paz Rd 93108 805-565-6000

**Santa Clara, Santa Clara, Pop. 111,315**
Santa Clara USD 15,200/K-12
PO Box 397 95052 408-423-2000
Dr. Stanley Rose, supt. Fax 423-2285
www.santaclarausd.org
Buchser MS 1,000/6-8
1111 Bellomy St 95050 408-423-3000
Monica Stoffal, prin. Fax 423-3080
Cabrillo MS 800/6-8
2550 Cabrillo Ave 95051 408-423-3700
Stan Garber, prin. Fax 423-3780
New Valley Continuation HS 200/Alt
1875 Lawrence Rd 95051 408-423-2300
Gilbert Montiel, prin. Fax 423-2380
Santa Clara Community Day S Alt
3450 Brookdale Dr 95051 408-423-2090
Deborah Bauer, prin.
Santa Clara HS 1,900/9-12
3000 Benton St 95051 408-423-2600
Greg Shelby, prin. Fax 423-2681
Wilcox HS 1,900/9-12
3250 Monroe St 95051 408-423-2400
Bonnie Billings, prin. Fax 423-2480
Wilson Alternative S 300/Alt
1840 Benton St 95050 408-423-3600
Rochelle Kelly, dir. Fax 423-3580
Santa Clara Adult Education Adult
1840 Benton St 95050 408-423-3500
Kathy Martarano, dir. Fax 423-3580
Other Schools – See Sunnyvale

---

California Cosmetology College Post-Sec.
955 Monroe St 95050 408-247-2200
Henley-Putnam University Post-Sec.
2804 Mission Coll Blvd #240 95054 408-453-9900
Institute for Business and Technology Post-Sec.
2400 Walsh Ave 95051 800-915-3562
Mission College Post-Sec.
3000 Mission College Blvd 95054 408-988-2200
St. Lawrence Academy 200/9-12
2000 Lawrence Ct 95051 408-296-3013
Bridget McGarry, prin. Fax 296-3794
Santa Clara University Post-Sec.
500 El Camino Real 95053 408-554-4000

**Santa Clarita, Los Angeles, Pop. 171,060**
Regional Occupational Center & Program
Supt. — None
Hart District ROP Vo/Tech
21515 Centre Pointe Pkwy 91350 661-259-0033
Dave LeBarron, coord. Fax 260-1909

William S. Hart UNHSD 26,100/7-12
21380 Centre Pointe Pkwy 91350 661-259-0033
Victoria Engbrecht, supt. Fax 254-8653
www.hartdistrict.org
Academy of the Canyons 400/Alt
26455 Rockwell Canyon Rd 91355 661-362-3056
Pete Getz, prin. Fax 255-2954
Bowman Continuation HS 500/Alt
21508 Centre Pointe Pkwy 91350 661-253-4400
Robin Geissler, prin. Fax 253-4125
Golden Valley HS 2,200/9-12
27051 Robert C Lee Pkwy 91350 661-298-8140
Sal Frias, prin. Fax 250-8362
La Mesa JHS 1,200/7-8
26623 May Way 91351 661-250-0022
Michele Krantz, prin. Fax 252-3326
Learning Post HS 100/Alt
26455 Rockwell Canyon Rd 91355 661-255-8338
Pete Getz, prin. Fax 255-3801
Rio Norte JHS 1,200/7-8
28771 Rio Norte Dr 91354 661-295-3700
Vince Ferry, prin. Fax 257-1413
Other Schools – See Canyon Country, Newhall, Saugus, Stevenson Ranch, Valencia

---

Advantage Preparatory S 100/K-12
PO Box 802274 91380 661-296-5466
Cindee Grant, admin.
College of the Canyons Post-Sec.
26455 Rockwell Canyon Rd 91355 661-259-7800

**Santa Cruz, Santa Cruz, Pop. 57,302**
Live Oak SD 2,100/PK-12
984 Bostwick Ln Ste 1 95062 831-475-6333
Tamra Taylor, supt. Fax 475-2638
www.losd-ca.schoolloop.com/
Shoreline MS 500/6-8
855 17th Ave 95062 831-475-6565
Colleen Martin, prin. Fax 462-1653

Regional Occupational Center & Program
Supt. — None
Santa Cruz County ROP Vo/Tech
399 Encinal St 95060 831-466-5760
Mark Hodges, dir. Fax 466-5769

Santa Cruz CSD
Supt. — See Soquel
Alternative Family Education 200/Alt
840 N Branciforte Ave 95062 831-429-3898
Lysa Tabachnick, prin. Fax 429-3912
ARK Independent S 100/Alt
840 N Branciforte Ave 95062 831-429-3432
Lysa Tabachnick, prin. Fax 429-3912
Branciforte MS 500/6-8
315 Poplar Ave 95062 831-429-3883
Kristin Pfotenhauer, prin. Fax 429-3962
Costanoa Continuation HS 100/Alt
840 N Branciforte Ave 95062 831-429-3898
Lysa Tabachnick, prin. Fax 429-3912
Harbor HS 1,000/9-12
300 La Fonda Ave 95062 831-429-3810
Richard Davis, prin. Fax 429-3982
Mission Hill MS 600/6-8
425 King St 95060 831-429-3860
Julia Hodges, prin. Fax 427-4846
Santa Cruz HS 1,100/9-12
415 Walnut Ave 95060 831-429-3960
Karen Edmonds, prin. Fax 429-3944
Santa Cruz Adult Education Adult
319 La Fonda Ave 95062 831-429-3966
Lysa Tabachnick, prin. Fax 429-3061

Santa Cruz County Office of Education 1,100/
400 Encinal St 95060 831-466-5600
Michael Watkins, supt. Fax 466-5607
www.santacruz.k12.ca.us
Santa Cruz County Community S 400/Alt
400 Encinal St 95060 831-466-5728
Johnny Rice, dir. Fax 466-5730

---

Five Branches University Post-Sec.
200 7th Ave 95062 831-476-9424
Kirby Preparatory S 200/6-12
425 Encinal St 95060 831-423-0658
University of California Post-Sec.
1156 High St 95064 831-459-0111

**Santa Fe Springs, Los Angeles, Pop. 16,058**
Little Lake City SD 4,700/K-8
10515 S Pioneer Blvd 90670 562-868-8241
Phillip Perez Ed.D., supt. Fax 868-1192
www.llcsd.net
Lake Center MS 1,000/6-8
10503 Pioneer Blvd 90670 562-868-4977
William Crean Ed.D., prin. Fax 929-4527
Other Schools – See Norwalk

Whittier UNHSD
Supt. — See Whittier
Santa Fe HS 2,700/9-12
10400 Orr and Day Rd 90670 562-698-8121
Kevin Jamero, prin. Fax 868-8277

---

Presbyterian Theological Seminary Post-Sec.
15605 Carmenita Rd 90670 562-926-1023
St. Paul HS 700/9-12
9635 Greenleaf Ave 90670 562-698-6246
Kate Aceves, prin. Fax 696-8396

**Santa Maria, Santa Barbara, Pop. 97,930**
Orcutt UNESD
Supt. — See Orcutt
Lakeview JHS 600/7-8
3700 Orcutt Rd 93455 805-938-8600
Ted Lyon, prin. Fax 938-8649

Santa Barbara County Office of Education
Supt. — See Santa Barbara
Fitzgerald Community S 300/7-12
402 Farnel Rd 93458 805-928-0698
Fax 928-5414

Santa Maria JUNHSD 7,600/9-12
2560 Skyway Dr 93455 805-922-4573
Mark Richardson Ed.D., supt. Fax 928-9916
www.smjuhsd.k12.ca.us
Delta HS 500/Alt
4893 Bethany Ln 93455 805-937-6356
Esther Prieto-Chavez, prin. Fax 934-4743
Pioneer Valley HS 2,600/9-12
675 Panther Dr 93454 805-922-1305
Shanda Herrera, prin. Fax 928-9916
Righetti HS 2,200/9-12
941 E Foster Rd 93455 805-937-2051
Karen Rotondi, prin. Fax 934-0819
Santa Maria HS 2,300/9-12
901 S Broadway 93454 805-925-2567
Joseph Domingues, prin. Fax 922-0215

Santa Maria-Bonita ESD 14,600/K-8
708 S Miller St 93454 805-928-1783
Matt Beecher, supt. Fax 928-7874
www.smbsd.org
Arellanes JHS 600/7-8
1890 Sandalwood Dr 93455 805-361-6820
Stacie Rivera, prin. Fax 346-8535
El Camino JHS 700/7-8
219 W El Camino St 93458 805-361-7800
Betty Romero, prin. Fax 346-1851
Fesler JHS 800/7-8
1100 E Fesler St 93454 805-361-7880
Brian Zimmerman, prin. Fax 346-1849
Kunst JHS 800/7-8
930 Hidden Pines Way 93458 805-361-5800
Sharon Shell, prin. Fax 925-8239

---

Allan Hancock College Post-Sec.
800 S College Dr 93454 805-922-6966

Laurus College — Post-Sec.
325 E Betteravia Rd Ste B8 93454 — 805-267-1690
St. Joseph HS — 500/9-12
4120 S Bradley Rd 93455 — 805-937-2038
Joanne Poloni, prin. — Fax 937-4248
Santa Barbara Business College — Post-Sec.
303 Plaza Dr 93454 — 866-749-7222
Valley Christian Academy — 300/PK-12
2970 Santa Maria Way 93455 — 805-937-6317

### Santa Monica, Los Angeles, Pop. 86,130

Santa Monica-Malibu USD — 11,400/PK-12
1651 16th St 90404 — 310-450-8338
Sandra Lyon, supt. — Fax 450-1667
www.smmusd.org
Adams MS — 1,100/6-8
2425 16th St 90405 — 310-452-2326
Steven Richardson, prin. — Fax 452-5352
Lincoln MS — 1,100/6-8
1501 California Ave 90403 — 310-393-9227
Dr. Florence Culpepper, prin. — Fax 393-4297
Olympic Continuation HS — 100/Alt
721 Ocean Park Blvd 90405 — 310-392-2494
Dr. Anthony Fuller, prin. — Fax 392-9741
Santa Monica HS — 3,100/9-12
601 Pico Blvd 90405 — 310-395-3204
Eva Mayoral, prin. — Fax 395-5842
Santa Monica-Malibu Adult Education — Adult
2510 Lincoln Blvd 90405 — 310-664-6222
Dr. Anthony Fuller, prin. — Fax 664-6220
Other Schools – See Malibu

---

Art Institute of California-Los Angeles — Post-Sec.
2900 31st St 90405 — 310-752-4700
Crossroads S for Arts & Sciences — 1,100/K-12
1714 21st St 90404 — 310-829-7391
Bob Riddle, head sch — Fax 828-5636
Emperor's Coll. of Trad. Oriental Med. — Post-Sec.
1807 Wilshire Blvd Ste 200 90403 — 310-453-8300
Lighthouse Christian Academy — 100/9-12
1424 Yale St 90404 — 310-829-2522
Jack Mefford, prin. — Fax 829-5544
New Roads HS — 400/9-12
3131 Olympic Blvd 90404 — 310-828-5582
Luthern Williams, head sch — Fax 828-2582
New Roads MS — 200/6-8
3131 Olympic Blvd 90404 — 310-828-5582
Luthern Williams, head sch — Fax 828-2582
Pacifica Christian HS — 200/9-12
1730 Wilshire Blvd 90403 — 310-828-7015
Jim Knight, head sch — Fax 829-2063
Pardee RAND Grad Sch of Policy Studies — Post-Sec.
1776 Main St 90401 — 310-393-0411
St. Monica HS — 500/9-12
1030 Lincoln Blvd 90403 — 310-394-3701
Alex Chacon, prin. — Fax 458-1353
Santa Monica College — Post-Sec.
1900 Pico Blvd 90405 — 310-434-4000

### Santa Paula, Ventura, Pop. 29,121

Briggs ESD — 600/PK-8
12465 Foothill Rd 93060 — 805-525-7540
Deborah Cuevas, supt. — Fax 933-1111
www.briggsesd.org
Briggs MS — 300/5-8
14438 W Telegraph Rd 93060 — 805-525-7151
Samuel Pacheco, prin. — Fax 933-3565

Santa Paula USD — 5,300/K-12
201 S Steckel Dr 93060 — 805-933-8800
Alfonso Gamino, supt. — Fax 933-8026
www.santapaulaunified.org
Isbell MS — 1,100/6-8
221 S 4th St 93060 — 805-933-8880
George Alessi, prin. — Fax 933-5582
Renaissance Continuation HS — 100/Alt
333 N Palm Ave 93060 — 805-525-4407
Robin Gillette, prin. — Fax 525-2294
Santa Paula HS — 1,500/9-12
404 N 6th St 93060 — 805-525-4400
Elizabeth Garcia, prin. — Fax 525-1690

---

Thomas Aquinas College — Post-Sec.
10000 Ojai Rd 93060 — 800-634-9797

### Santa Rosa, Sonoma, Pop. 161,788

Regional Occupational Center & Program
Supt. — None
Sonoma County ROP — Vo/Tech
5340 Skylane Blvd 95403 — 707-524-2720
Stephen Jackson, dir. — Fax 524-2789

Santa Rosa CSD — 16,700/PK-12
211 Ridgway Ave 95401 — 707-528-5388
Socorro Shiels, supt. — Fax 528-5440
www.srcs.k12.ca.us
Allen HS — 1,000/9-12
599 Bellevue Ave 95407 — 707-528-5020
Mary Gail Stablein, prin. — Fax 528-5023
Carillo HS — 1,600/9-12
6975 Montecito Blvd 95409 — 707-528-5790
Vicki Zands, prin. — Fax 528-5789
Comstock MS — 300/7-8
2750 W Steele Ln 95403 — 707-528-5266
Laura Hendrickson, prin. — Fax 528-5480
Cook MS — 400/7-8
2480 Sebastopol Rd 95407 — 707-528-5156
Linsey Gannon, prin. — Fax 528-5163
Grace Necessary Small HS — 100/Alt
1702 Fulton Rd 95403 — 707-528-5756
Tony Negri, prin. — Fax 528-5246
Lewis Opportunity S — 50/Alt
2230 Lomitas Ave 95404 — 707-284-8225
Tracy Anderson, prin. — Fax 284-8232
Mesa Necessary Small HS — 100/Alt
1237 Mendocino Ave 95401 — 707-528-5227
Brad Coscarelli, prin. — Fax 528-5724
Midrose Necessary Small HS — 100/Alt
597 Bellevue Ave 95407 — 707-528-5041
Tony Negri, prin. — Fax 528-5027
Montgomery HS — 1,700/9-12
1250 Hahman Dr 95405 — 707-528-5191
Laurie Fong, prin. — Fax 528-5056
Nueva Vista Necessary Small HS — 50/Alt
2232 Lomitas Ave 95404 — 707-522-3291
Tracy Anderson, prin. — Fax 522-3293
Piner HS — 1,000/9-12
1700 Fulton Rd 95403 — 707-528-5245
Tim Zalunardo, prin. — Fax 528-5246
Ridgway Continuation HS — 300/Alt
325 Ridgway Ave 95401 — 707-528-5325
Gabriel Albavera, prin. — Fax 528-5717
Rincon Valley MS — 800/7-8
4650 Badger Rd 95409 — 707-528-5255
Matt Marshall, prin. — Fax 528-5644
Santa Rosa HS — 2,000/9-12
1235 Mendocino Ave 95401 — 707-528-5291
Brad Coscarelli, prin. — Fax 528-5724
Santa Rosa MS — 600/7-8
500 E St 95404 — 707-528-5281
Tom Fierro, prin. — Fax 528-5283
Slater MS — 800/7-8
3500 Sonoma Ave 95405 — 707-528-5241
Rachele Cunningham, prin. — Fax 528-5733

---

Cardinal Newman HS — 700/9-12
50 Ursuline Rd 95403 — 707-546-6470
Graham Rutherford, prin. — Fax 544-8502
Empire College — Post-Sec.
3035 Cleveland Ave 95403 — 707-546-4000
Lytle's Redwood Empire Beauty College — Post-Sec.
186 Wikiup Dr 95403 — 707-545-8490
Redwood Adventist Academy — 100/K-12
385 Mark West Springs Rd 95404 — 707-545-1697
Rob Fenderson, prin. — Fax 545-8020
Rincon Valley Christian S — 400/PK-12
4585 Badger Rd 95409 — 707-539-1486
Paul Eggenberger, admin. — Fax 539-1493
Santa Rosa Junior College — Post-Sec.
1501 Mendocino Ave 95401 — 707-527-4011
Sonoma Academy — 200/9-12
2500 Farmers Ln 95404 — 707-545-1770
Janet Durgin, head sch — Fax 636-2474
Summerfield Waldorf S — 400/PK-12
655 Willowside Rd 95401 — 707-575-7194
Jeffrey Westman, pres. — Fax 575-3217

### Santa Ynez, Santa Barbara, Pop. 4,319

Santa Ynez Valley UNHSD — 1,000/9-12
PO Box 398 93460 — 805-688-6487
Scott Cory, supt. — Fax 686-4454
www.syvuhsd.org
Refugio HS — 50/Alt
PO Box 398 93460 — 805-688-6487
Scott Cory, prin. — Fax 686-5627
Santa Ynez Valley Union HS — 1,000/9-12
PO Box 398 93460 — 805-688-6487
Mark Swanitz, prin. — Fax 688-1913

### Santee, San Diego, Pop. 51,246

Grossmont UNHSD
Supt. — See La Mesa
Santana HS — 1,400/9-12
9915 N Magnolia Ave 92071 — 619-956-0200
Tim Schwuchow, prin. — Fax 449-3119
West Hills HS — 2,000/9-12
8756 Mast Blvd 92071 — 619-956-0400
Robin Ballarin, prin. — Fax 258-3750

### San Ysidro, See San Diego

San Ysidro ESD — 4,400/PK-8
4350 Otay Mesa Rd 92173 — 619-428-4476
Julio Fonseca Ed.D., supt. — Fax 428-1505
www.sysd.k12.ca.us
San Ysidro MS — 800/7-8
4345 Otay Mesa Rd 92173 — 619-428-5551
Rouba Tay, prin. — Fax 690-2837

Sweetwater UNHSD
Supt. — See Chula Vista
San Ysidro Adult S — Adult
4220 Otay Mesa Rd 92173 — 619-428-7200
Sheryl Sanchez, prin. — Fax 428-0295

### Saratoga, Santa Clara, Pop. 28,911

Campbell UNHSD
Supt. — See San Jose
Prospect HS — 1,300/9-12
18900 Prospect Rd 95070 — 408-626-3408
Joell Hanson, prin. — Fax 973-1759

Los Gatos-Saratoga JUNHSD
Supt. — See Los Gatos
Saratoga HS — 1,400/9-12
20300 Herriman Ave 95070 — 408-867-3411
Paul Robinson, prin. — Fax 867-3577

Saratoga UNESD — 2,100/K-8
20460 Forrest Hills Dr 95070 — 408-867-3424
Nancy Johnson, supt. — Fax 867-2312
www.saratogausd.org
Redwood MS — 900/6-8
13925 Fruitvale Ave 95070 — 408-867-3042
Barbara Neal, prin. — Fax 867-3195

---

West Valley College — Post-Sec.
14000 Fruitvale Ave 95070 — 408-867-2200

### Saugus, See Santa Clarita

William S. Hart UNHSD
Supt. — See Santa Clarita
Saugus HS — 2,400/9-12
21900 Centurion Way 91350 — 661-297-3900
Bill Bolde, prin. — Fax 297-7491

### Scotts Valley, Santa Cruz, Pop. 11,122

Scotts Valley USD — 2,500/K-12
4444 Scotts Valley Dr # 5B 95066 — 831-438-1820
Penny Weaver, supt. — Fax 438-2314
www.scottsvalleyusd.org
Scotts Valley HS — 800/9-12
555 Glenwood Dr 95066 — 831-439-9555
Valerie Bariteau, prin. — Fax 439-9501
Scotts Valley MS — 600/6-8
8 Bean Creek Rd 95066 — 831-438-0610
Mary Lonhart, prin. — Fax 439-8935

### Seaside, Monterey, Pop. 30,879

Monterey Peninsula USD
Supt. — See Monterey
Central Coast HS — 100/Alt
200 Coe Ave 93955 — 831-392-3560
Alan Crawford, prin. — Fax 392-3561
Monterey Peninsula Community Day S — 50/Alt
200 Coe Ave 93955 — 831-392-3822
Alan Crawford, admin. — Fax 649-6621
Seaside HS — 1,000/9-12
2200 Noche Buena St 93955 — 831-392-3530
Carlos Moran, prin. — Fax 899-0212
Seaside MS — 800/6-8
999 Coe Ave 93955 — 831-899-7080
Manuel Nunez, prin. — Fax 899-0663
Adult Education — Adult
1713 Broadway Ave 93955 — 831-392-3565
Alan Crawford, admin.

---

California State University-Monterey Bay — Post-Sec.
100 Campus Ctr 93955 — 831-582-3000
Chartwell S — 100/2-12
2511 Numa Watson Rd 93955 — 831-394-3468
Nora Lee, head sch — Fax 394-6809

### Sebastopol, Sonoma, Pop. 7,156

Gravenstein UNESD — 700/K-8
3840 Twig Ave 95472 — 707-823-7008
Linda LaMarre, supt. — Fax 823-2108
www.grav.k12.ca.us/
Hillcrest MS — 300/6-8
725 Bloomfield Rd 95472 — 707-823-7653
David Fichera, prin. — Fax 823-4630

Sebastopol UNESD — 1,000/K-8
7611 Huntley St 95472 — 707-829-4570
Linda Irving, supt. — Fax 829-7427
www.sebastopolschools.org
Brook Haven MS — 400/5-8
7905 Valentine Ave 95472 — 707-829-4590
Deborah Hanks, prin. — Fax 829-6285

West Sonoma County UNHSD — 2,200/9-12
462 Johnson St 95472 — 707-824-6403
Dr. Steven Kellner, supt. — Fax 824-6499
wscuhsd.k12.ca.us
Analy HS — 1,300/9-12
6950 Analy Ave 95472 — 707-824-2300
Chris Heller, prin. — Fax 827-7936
Laguna Continuation HS — 100/Alt
445 Taft St 95472 — 707-824-6485
Kent Cromwell, prin. — Fax 829-7910
Other Schools – See Forestville

### Selma, Fresno, Pop. 22,943

Selma USD — 6,300/PK-12
3036 Thompson Ave 93662 — 559-898-6500
Dr. Tanya A. Fisher Ed.D., supt. — Fax 896-7147
www.selmausd.org
Heartland Alternative HS — 100/Alt
2269 Sylvia St 93662 — 559-898-6670
Drew Sylvia, prin. — Fax 896-4635
Lincoln MS — 1,000/7-8
1239 Nelson Blvd 93662 — 559-898-6600
Charles Coleman, prin. — Fax 896-0733
Selma HS — 1,700/9-12
3125 Wright St 93662 — 559-898-6550
Mark Babiarz, prin. — Fax 896-1110
Selma Adult S — Adult
3125 Wright St 93662 — 559-898-6590
Drew Sylvia, dir. — Fax 896-4333

### Shafter, Kern, Pop. 16,846

Kern UNHSD
Supt. — See Bakersfield
Central Valley Continuation HS — 100/Alt
526 Mannel Ave 93263 — 661-746-4281
John Brown, admin. — Fax 746-0521
Shafter HS — 1,500/9-12
526 Mannel Ave 93263 — 661-746-4961
Russell Shipley, prin. — Fax 746-6743

Richland UNESD — 3,300/PK-8
331 N Shafter Ave 93263 — 661-746-8600
Raquel Posadas-Gonzalez, supt. — Fax 746-8614
www.richland.k12.ca.us
Richland JHS — 600/7-8
331 N Shafter Ave 93263 — 661-746-8630
Kenneth Wright, prin. — Fax 746-8614

### Shandon, San Luis Obispo, Pop. 1,278

Shandon JUSD — 300/K-12
PO Box 79 93461 — 805-238-0286
Teresa Taylor, supt. — Fax 238-0777
www.shandonschools.org
Shandon HS — 100/9-12
PO Box 79 93461 — 805-238-0286
Teresa Taylor, supt. — Fax 238-0777

### Shasta Lake, Shasta, Pop. 9,765

Gateway USD
Supt. — See Redding
Central Valley HS — 800/9-12
4066 La Mesa Ave 96019 — 530-275-7075
Ryan Johnson, prin. — Fax 275-7065
Mountain Lakes HS — 100/Alt
17752 Shasta Dam Blvd 96019 — 530-275-7000
Mark Telles, prin. — Fax 275-7006

**Sherman Oaks, See Los Angeles**
Los Angeles USD
Supt. — See Los Angeles
Millikan MS 2,200/6-8
5041 Sunnyslope Ave 91423 818-528-1600
John Plevack, prin. Fax 990-7651

Buckley S 800/K-12
3900 Stansbury Ave 91423 818-783-1610
Dr. James Busby, head sch Fax 461-6714
DeVry University Post-Sec.
15301 Ventura Blvd Ste 100 91403 818-713-8111
Notre Dame HS 1,200/9-12
13645 Riverside Dr 91423 818-933-3600
Stephanie Connelly, prin. Fax 501-0507

**Shingle Springs, El Dorado, Pop. 4,277**
El Dorado UNHSD
Supt. — See Placerville
Ponderosa HS 1,900/9-12
3661 Ponderosa Rd 95682 530-677-2281
Lisa Garrett, prin. Fax 676-1401

Latrobe SD 200/K-8
7900 S Shingle Rd 95682 530-677-0260
Natalie Miller, supt. Fax 672-0463
www.latrobeschool.com
Miller's Hill S 100/4-8
7900 S Shingle Rd 95682 530-677-0260
Natalie Miller, admin. Fax 672-0463

**Shingletown, Shasta, Pop. 2,210**
Black Butte UNESD 200/K-8
7752 Ponderosa Way 96088 530-474-3125
Don Aust, supt. Fax 474-3118
www.blackbutteschool.org
Black Butte JHS 100/6-8
7946 Ponderosa Way 96088 530-474-3441
Don Aust, prin. Fax 474-1361

**Shoshone, Inyo, Pop. 30**
Death Valley USD 100/K-12
PO Box 217 92384 760-852-4303
James Copeland, supt. Fax 852-4395
www.inyo.k12.ca.us
Death Valley Academy 50/7-12
PO Box 217 92384 760-852-4303
Craig Hill, prin. Fax 852-4395
Shoshone Continuation HS 50/Alt
PO Box 217 92384 760-852-4303
Craig Hill, prin. Fax 852-4395

**Sierra Madre, Los Angeles, Pop. 10,555**
Pasadena USD
Supt. — See Pasadena
Sierra Madre MS 200/6-8
160 N Canon Ave 91024 626-836-2947
Garret Newson, prin. Fax 836-2964

Alverno HS 200/9-12
200 N Michillinda Ave 91024 626-355-3463
Julia Fanara, head sch Fax 355-3153

**Sierraville, Sierra, Pop. 200**
Regional Occupational Center & Program
Supt. — None
Rouse ROP Vo/Tech
PO Box 157 96126 530-994-1044
Stan Hardeman, supt. Fax 994-1045

**Signal Hill, Los Angeles, Pop. 10,477**
Long Beach USD
Supt. — See Long Beach
Nelson Academy 6-8
1951 Cherry Ave, 562-591-6041
Sparkle Peterson, prin. Fax 591-8690

American University of Health Science Post-Sec.
1600 E Hill St Bldg 1, 562-988-2278

**Silverado, Orange**

St. Michaels Preparatory S 100/9-12
19292 El Toro Rd 92676 949-858-0222
Fr. Victor Szczurek, hdmstr. Fax 858-7365

**Simi Valley, Ventura, Pop. 120,233**
Simi Valley USD 19,100/K-12
875 Cochran St 93065 805-520-6500
Dr. Jason Peplinski, supt. Fax 520-6504
www.simivalleyusd.org
Apollo HS 300/Alt
3150 School St 93065 805-520-6150
Shanna Sarris, prin. Fax 520-6655
Hillside MS 900/6-8
2222 Fitzgerald Rd 93065 805-520-6810
Jerry Block, prin. Fax 520-6156
Monte Vista S 100/Alt
1220 4th St 93065 805-579-6326
Stephen Pietrolungo Ed.D., prin. Fax 579-6329
Royal HS 2,300/9-12
1402 Royal Ave 93065 805-306-4875
Keith Derrick, prin. Fax 520-6644
Santa Susana HS 1,300/9-12
3570 Cochran St 93063 805-520-6800
Wendy Mayea, prin. Fax 579-6385
Simi Valley HS 2,600/9-12
5400 Cochran St 93063 805-577-1400
Dean May, prin. Fax 520-6633
Sinaloa MS 1,100/6-8
601 Royal Ave 93065 805-520-6830
Diana Janke, prin. Fax 520-6835
Valley View MS 1,300/6-8
3347 Tapo St 93063 805-520-6820
Michael Hall, prin. Fax 520-6157
Simi Valley Adult Education Adult
1880 Blackstock Ave 93065 805-579-6200
Michele Arso, dir. Fax 522-8902

Eternity Bible College Post-Sec.
2136 Winifred St 93063 805-581-1233
Grace Brethren JSHS 400/7-12
1350 Cherry Ave 93065 805-522-4667
John Hynes, prin. Fax 522-5617
Heritage Christian Academy 100/K-12
1559 Rosita Dr 93065 805-428-2511
Robert Neher, prin.
Simi Valley Adult Education Post-Sec.
1880 Blackstock Ave 93065 805-579-6200
Stoneridge Preparatory S 50/6-12
1625 Tierra Rejada Rd 93065 805-581-9110
Maria Arnold, dir. Fax 581-2864

**Solana Beach, San Diego, Pop. 12,580**
San Dieguito UNHSD
Supt. — See Encinitas
Warren MS 700/7-8
155 Stevens Ave 92075 858-755-1558
Adam Camacho, prin. Fax 755-0891

Santa Fe Christian S 1,000/PK-12
838 Academy Dr 92075 858-755-8900
Dr. Tom Bennett, head sch Fax 755-2480

**Soledad, Monterey, Pop. 25,398**
Soledad USD 4,600/PK-12
1261 Metz Rd 93960 831-678-3987
Dr. Rupi Boyd Ed.D., supt. Fax 678-2866
www.soledadusd.org
Main Street MS 700/PK-PK, 7-
441 Main St 93960 831-678-6460
Jessie Swift, prin. Fax 678-0797
Pinnacles HS 100/Alt
690 Main St 93960 831-678-6300
Jeffrey Lopez, prin. Fax 678-0162
Soledad HS 1,300/9-12
425 Gabilan Dr 93960 831-678-6400
Elizabeth Austin, prin. Fax 678-0449

**Somerset, El Dorado**
Pioneer UNESD 300/K-8
6862 Mount Aukum Rd 95684 530-620-3556
Lisa Fontana, supt. Fax 620-4932
www.pioneerusd.org
Mountain Creek MS 100/5-8
6862 Mount Aukum Rd 95684 530-620-4393
Lisa Fontana, prin. Fax 620-6509

**Sonoma, Sonoma, Pop. 10,444**
Sonoma Valley USD 4,700/K-12
17850 Railroad Ave 95476 707-935-6000
Louann Carlomagno Ph.D., supt. Fax 939-2235
svusdca.org/
Altimira MS 500/6-8
17805 Arnold Dr 95476 707-935-6020
William Deeths, prin. Fax 935-6027
Creekside HS 50/Alt
20000 Broadway 95476 707-933-4046
Sydney Smith, prin. Fax 933-4095
Harrison MS 400/6-8
1150 Broadway 95476 707-935-6080
Mary Ann Spitzer, prin. Fax 935-6083
Sonoma Valley HS 1,300/9-12
20000 Broadway 95476 707-933-4010
Kathleen Hawing, prin. Fax 935-4205

**Sonora, Tuolumne, Pop. 4,736**
Sonora UNHSD 1,300/9-12
100 School St 95370 209-533-8510
Patrick Chabot, supt. Fax 532-4513
www.sonorahs.k12.ca.us/
Bird HS 100/Alt
251 Barretta St 95370 209-532-2923
Roy Morlan, prin. Fax 533-0980
Cassina Continuation HS 100/Alt
251 Barretta St 95370 209-532-1587
Roy Morlan, prin. Fax 533-0980
Sonora HS 1,100/9-12
430 N Washington St 95370 209-532-5511
Ben Howell, prin. Fax 533-1158

Columbia College Post-Sec.
11600 Columbia College Dr 95370 209-588-5100
Mother Lode Adventist Junior Academy 100/K-10
80 N Forest Rd 95370 209-532-2855
Patrice Osborne, prin. Fax 532-7757

**Soquel, Santa Cruz, Pop. 9,255**
Santa Cruz CSD 7,000/K-12
405 Old San Jose Rd 95073 831-429-3410
Kris Munro, supt. Fax 429-3439
sccs.net
Soquel HS 1,000/9-12
401 Old San Jose Rd 95073 831-429-3909
Gail Atlansky, prin. Fax 429-3311
Other Schools – See Santa Cruz

**South Dos Palos, Merced, Pop. 1,600**
Dos Palos Oro Loma JUSD
Supt. — See Dos Palos
Westside HS 50/Alt
22369 6th St 93665 209-392-0280
Frank Lemos, prin. Fax 392-1043

**South El Monte, Los Angeles, Pop. 19,998**
El Monte UNHSD
Supt. — See El Monte
South El Monte HS 1,500/9-12
1001 Durfee Ave 91733 626-442-0218
Dr. Amy Avina, prin. Fax 442-4794

Valle Lindo ESD 1,100/K-8
1431 Central Ave 91733 626-580-0610
Dr. Mary Labrucherie, supt. Fax 575-1534
www.vallelindo.k12.ca.us
Shively MS 600/5-8
1431 Central Ave 91733 626-580-0610
Lynn Bulgin, prin. Fax 575-1534

**South Gate, Los Angeles, Pop. 94,017**
Los Angeles USD
Supt. — See Los Angeles
International Studies Learning Center 900/6-12
5225 Tweedy Blvd 90280 323-357-7521
Guillermina Jauregui, prin. Fax 569-7139
Odyssey Continuation HS 100/Alt
8693 Dearborn Ave 90280 323-567-5536
Julieta Badgley, prin. Fax 563-3468
Rodia Continuation HS 100/Alt
2701 Sequoia Dr 90280 323-569-7140
Regina Awtry, prin. Fax 569-7139
Science Tech Engineering Arts & Math HS 9-12
5225 Tweedy Blvd 90280 323-357-7500
Carla Barrera-Ortiz, prin. Fax 564-8371
South East HS 2,900/9-12
2720 Tweedy Blvd 90280 323-568-3400
Jesus Nunez, prin. Fax 566-7918
Southeast MS 1,300/6-8
2560 Tweedy Blvd 90280 323-568-3100
Wanda Sequeira, prin. Fax 564-9398
South Gate HS 3,300/9-12
3351 Firestone Blvd 90280 323-568-5600
German Cerda, prin. Fax 249-0237
South Gate MS 2,600/6-8
4100 Firestone Blvd 90280 323-568-4000
Janet Mack, prin. Fax 564-7434
Visual and Performing Arts HS 9-12
5225 Tweedy Blvd 90280 323-357-7500
Alison Miller, prin. Fax 564-8371
South Gate Adult Education Adult
2525 Firestone Blvd 90280 323-568-5700
Anna Madrid, prin. Fax 568-5716

Advanced College Post-Sec.
13180 Paramount Blvd 90280 562-408-6969
Career College of America Post-Sec.
5612 Imperial Hwy 90280 562-861-8702
GDS Institute Post-Sec.
7916 Long Beach Blvd 90280 323-585-5577

**South Lake Tahoe, El Dorado, Pop. 20,898**
Lake Tahoe USD 3,900/PK-12
1021 Al Tahoe Blvd 96150 530-541-2850
Dr. James Tarwater, supt. Fax 541-5930
www.ltusd.org/
Mt. Tallac Continuation HS 100/Alt
1735 Lake Tahoe Blvd 96150 530-543-2245
Thomas Houck, prin. Fax 542-1036
South Tahoe HS 1,100/9-12
1735 Lake Tahoe Blvd 96150 530-541-4111
Chad Houck, prin. Fax 541-4157
South Tahoe MS 800/6-8
2940 Lake Tahoe Blvd 96150 530-541-6404
John Simons, prin. Fax 541-4624
Transition Learning Center 100/Alt
1735 Lake Tahoe Blvd 96150 530-543-2264
Chad Houck, prin. Fax 542-1036

Lake Tahoe Community College Post-Sec.
1 College Dr 96150 530-541-4660

**South Pasadena, Los Angeles, Pop. 24,612**
South Pasadena USD 4,600/PK-12
1020 El Centro St 91030 626-441-5810
Geoff Yantz, supt. Fax 441-5815
www.spusd.net
South Pasadena HS 1,600/9-12
1401 Fremont Ave 91030 626-441-5820
Janet Anderson, prin. Fax 441-5825
South Pasadena MS 1,100/6-8
1500 Fair Oaks Ave 91030 626-441-5830
Dave Kubela, prin. Fax 441-5835

**South San Francisco, San Mateo, Pop. 60,202**
South San Francisco USD 9,300/K-12
398 B St 94080 650-877-8700
Shawnterra Moore, supt. Fax 583-4717
www.ssfusd.org
Alta Loma MS 800/6-8
116 Romney Ave 94080 650-877-8797
Lou Delorio, prin. Fax 877-8824
Baden HS 100/Alt
825 Southwood Dr 94080 650-877-8769
Michael Coyne, prin. Fax 737-9072
Community Day S Alt
201 W Orange Ave 94080 650-616-3882
Michael Coyne, prin.
El Camino HS 1,500/9-12
1320 Mission Rd 94080 650-877-8806
David Lunt, prin. Fax 589-2343
Parkway Heights MS 600/6-8
650 Sunset Ave 94080 650-877-8788
Marco Lopez, prin. Fax 225-9427
South San Francisco HS 1,500/9-12
400 B St 94080 650-877-8754
Anthony Limoges, prin. Fax 871-7943
Westborough MS 700/6-8
2570 Westborough Blvd 94080 650-877-8848
Ed Colucci, prin. Fax 871-5356
South San Francisco Adult Adult
825 Southwood Dr 94080 650-877-8844
Michael Coyne, prin. Fax 877-8786

NCP College of Nursing Post-Sec.
257 Longford Dr Ste 5 94080 650-871-0701

**Spreckels, Monterey, Pop. 663**
Spreckels UNESD 1,000/K-8
PO Box 7362 93962 831-455-2550
Eric Tarallo Ed.D., supt. Fax 455-1871
Other Schools – See Salinas

**Spring Valley, San Diego, Pop. 26,795**
Grossmont UNHSD
Supt. — See La Mesa

Monte Vista HS 1,800/9-12
3230 Sweetwater Springs Blv 91977 619-660-3000
Randy Montesanto, prin. Fax 670-9749
Mt. Miguel HS 1,600/9-12
8585 Blossom Ln 91977 619-667-6400
Kimberlee Hedrick Ed.D., prin. Fax 697-0794

La Mesa-Spring Valley SD
Supt. — See La Mesa
Spring Valley MS 600/7-8
3900 Conrad Dr 91977 619-668-5750
Margaret Jacobsen, prin. Fax 668-8302
STEAM Academy @ La Presa 500/4-8
1001 Leland St 91977 619-668-5720
Mike Allmann, prin. Fax 668-8305

**Stanford, Santa Clara, Pop. 12,819**

Stanford University Post-Sec.
450 Serra Mall 94305 650-723-2300

**Stevenson Ranch, Los Angeles, Pop. 16,902**
William S. Hart UNHSD
Supt. — See Santa Clarita
Rancho Pico JHS 1,000/7-8
26250 Valencia Blvd 91381 661-284-3260
Erum Jones, prin. Fax 255-7623
West Ranch HS 2,800/9-12
26255 Valencia Blvd 91381 661-222-1220
Mark Crawford, prin. Fax 290-2676

**Stockton, San Joaquin, Pop. 279,493**
Lincoln USD 9,000/PK-12
2010 W Swain Rd 95207 209-953-8700
Thomas Uslan, supt. Fax 474-7817
www.lusd.net
Lincoln HS 2,700/9-12
6844 Alexandria Pl 95207 209-953-8920
Terry Asplund, prin. Fax 952-4646
McCandless STEM Charter S Alt
2020 W Swain Rd 95207 209-953-8740
Phyllis Kahl, prin.
Sierra MS 600/7-8
6768 Alexandria Pl 95207 209-953-8749
Scott Tatum, prin. Fax 953-8747
Village Oaks HS 200/Alt
1900 W Swain Rd 95207 209-953-8687
Josef Schallberger, prin. Fax 953-8741

Linden USD
Supt. — See Linden
Pride Continuation HS 50/Alt
100 N Jack Tone Rd 95215 209-887-3894
Jane Steinkamp, prin.
Waterloo MS 400/5-8
7007 Pezzi Rd 95215 209-931-0818
Jesse Calvo, prin. Fax 931-2915

Lodi USD
Supt. — See Lodi
Bear Creek HS 1,900/9-12
10555 Thornton Rd 95209 209-953-8234
William Atterberry, prin. Fax 953-8247
Delta Sierra MS 400/7-8
2255 Wagner Heights Rd 95209 209-953-8510
Brad Watson, prin. Fax 953-8139
Elkhorn MS 300/4-8
10505 Davis Rd 95209 209-953-8312
Pat White, prin. Fax 953-8319
McAuliffe MS 900/7-8
3880 Iron Canyon Cir 95209 209-953-9431
Pierre Kirby, prin. Fax 953-9430
McNair HS 1,800/9-12
9550 Ronald E McNair Way 95210 209-953-9245
Jim Davis, prin. Fax 953-9261
Middle College HS 200/9-12
5151 Pacific Ave 95207 209-954-5790
Sherry Balian, prin. Fax 954-5875
Morada MS 700/7-8
5001 Eastview Dr 95212 209-953-8490
Janet Perez, prin. Fax 953-8502
Plaza Robles Continuation HS 200/Alt
9434 Thornton Rd 95209 209-953-8068
Mark Dawson, prin. Fax 953-8064

Manteca USD
Supt. — See Manteca
Great Valley Annex S 500/7-8
4550 Star Way 95206 209-938-6310
Patricia Boutte, prin. Fax 938-6383
New Vision HS 200/Alt
4726 McCuen Ave 95206 209-938-6225
Sonya Arellano, prin. Fax 938-6394
Weston Ranch HS 1,200/9-12
4606 McCuen Ave 95206 209-938-6245
Jose Fregoso, prin. Fax 938-6397

Regional Occupational Center & Program
Supt. — None
San Joaquin County ROC/P Vo/Tech
PO Box 213030 95213 209-468-5930
Christopher Kleinert, dir.

Stockton USD 35,100/PK-12
701 N Madison St 95202 209-933-7000
Dr. Julie Penn, supt. Fax 933-7071
www.stocktonusd.net
Chavez HS 2,100/9-12
2929 Windflower Ln 95212 209-933-7480
William Nelson, prin. Fax 475-9097
Edison HS 2,000/9-12
1425 S Center St 95206 209-933-7425
Brain Biedermann, prin. Fax 942-2106
Franklin HS 2,200/9-12
300 N Gertrude Ave 95215 209-933-7435
Juan Salas, prin. Fax 464-4708
Frederick Continuation S 300/Alt
1141 E Weber Ave 95205 209-933-7340
Chris Anderson, prin. Fax 933-7341

Merlo Institute of Environmental Tech 200/9-12
1670 E 6th St 95206 209-933-7190
Bukky Oyebade, prin. Fax 469-3740
Stagg HS 1,600/9-12
1621 Brookside Rd 95207 209-933-7445
Andre Phillips, prin. Fax 954-9037
Weber Institute Vo/Tech
302 W Weber Ave 95203 209-933-7330
Katrina Johnson Leon, dir. Fax 464-4917
School for Adults Adult
1525 Pacific Ave 95204 209-933-7455
Carol Hirota, prin. Fax 464-4917

Brookside Christian S 200/K-12
915 Rosemarie Ln 95207 209-954-7650
Jessica Carter, prin. Fax 954-7670
Carrington College California Post-Sec.
1313 W Robinhood Dr Ste B 95207 209-956-1240
Heald College Post-Sec.
1605 E March Ln 95210 209-473-5200
Humphreys College Post-Sec.
6650 Inglewood Ave 95207 209-478-0800
MTI Business College of Stockton Post-Sec.
6006 N El Dorado St 95207 209-957-3030
St. Mary HS 1,000/9-12
PO Box 7247 95267 209-957-3340
Kathy Smith, prin. Fax 957-0861
San Joaquin Delta College Post-Sec.
5151 Pacific Ave 95207 209-954-5151
San Joaquin General Hospital Post-Sec.
PO Box 1020 95201 209-468-6600
Stockton Christian S 200/K-12
9021 West Ln 95210 209-957-3043
Rachel Regnart, admin. Fax 957-4120
Teachers College of San Joaquin Post-Sec.
2857 Transworld Dr 95206 209-468-9155
University of the Pacific Post-Sec.
3601 Pacific Ave 95211 209-946-2285
Western Pacific Truck School Post-Sec.
1002 N Broadway Ave 95205 209-465-1191

**Strathmore, Tulare, Pop. 2,793**
Porterville USD
Supt. — See Porterville
Strathmore HS 300/9-12
22568 Avenue 196 93267 559-568-1731
John Buckley, prin. Fax 568-0091

Strathmore UNESD 800/K-8
PO Box 247 93267 559-568-1283
Shelly Long Ed.D., supt. Fax 568-1262
www.suesd.k12.ca.us
Strathmore MS 300/5-8
PO Box 247 93267 559-568-9293
Joanie Stone, prin. Fax 568-2944

**Studio City, See Los Angeles**

Bridges Academy 100/4-12
3921 Laurel Canyon Blvd 91604 818-506-1091
Carl Sabatino M.A., head sch Fax 506-8094

**Sugarloaf, San Bernardino**
Bear Valley USD
Supt. — See Big Bear Lake
Big Bear HS 800/9-12
351 Maple Ln 92386 909-585-6892
Mike Ghelber, prin. Fax 585-6809
Chautauqua HS 100/Alt
525 Maple Ln 92386 909-585-2521
Paulina Ugo, prin. Fax 585-3311

**Suisun City, Solano, Pop. 25,805**
Fairfield-Suisun USD
Supt. — See Fairfield
Crystal MS 900/6-8
400 Whispering Bay Ln 94585 707-435-5800
Monifa Williams, prin. Fax 435-5806

**Sun City, Riverside, Pop. 14,930**
Perris UNHSD
Supt. — See Perris
Heritage HS 2,700/9-12
26001 Briggs Rd 92585 951-940-5447
Frank Arce, prin. Fax 325-5449

**Sunland, See Los Angeles**
Los Angeles USD
Supt. — See Los Angeles
Mt. Gleason MS 1,200/6-8
10965 Mount Gleason Ave 91040 818-951-2580
Deborah Acosta, prin. Fax 352-6209

**Sunnyvale, Santa Clara, Pop. 134,677**
Cupertino UNSD
Supt. — See Cupertino
Cupertino MS 1,300/6-8
1650 S Bernardo Ave 94087 408-245-0303
Kara Butler, prin. Fax 732-4152

Fremont UNHSD 10,500/9-12
589 W Fremont Ave 94087 408-522-2200
Polly Bove, supt. Fax 245-5325
www.fuhsd.org
Fremont HS 2,000/9-12
1279 Sunnyvale Saratoga Rd 94087 408-522-2400
Bryan Emmert, prin. Fax 522-2401
Adult & Community Education Adult
591 W Fremont Ave 94087 408-522-2700
Peggy Raun-Linde, prin. Fax 522-2799
Other Schools – See Cupertino, San Jose

Santa Clara USD
Supt. — See Santa Clara
Peterson MS 900/6-8
1380 Rosalia Ave 94087 408-423-2800
Susan Harris, prin. Fax 423-2880

Sunnyvale ESD 6,600/K-8
PO Box 3217 94088 408-522-8200
Benjamin Picard Ed.D., supt. Fax 522-8221
www.sesd.org
Columbia MS 800/6-8
739 Morse Ave 94085 408-522-8247
Mary Beth Allmann, prin. Fax 522-8254
Sunnyvale MS 1,100/6-8
1080 Mango Ave 94087 408-522-8288
Nabil Shahin, prin. Fax 522-8296

Art Institute of California - Sunnyvale Post-Sec.
1120 Kifer Rd 94086 408-962-6400
Cogswell Polytechnical College Post-Sec.
1175 Bordeaux Dr 94089 408-541-0100
King's Academy 900/6-12
562 N Britton Ave 94085 408-481-9900
Scott Meadows, prin. Fax 481-9932
University of East West Medicine Post-Sec.
595 Lawrence Expy 94085 408-733-1878

**Sun Valley, See Los Angeles**
Los Angeles USD
Supt. — See Los Angeles
Byrd MS 1,700/6-8
8501 Arleta Ave 91352 818-394-4300
Deborah Wiltz, prin. Fax 768-1837
Francis Polytechnic HS 3,000/9-12
12431 Roscoe Blvd 91352 818-394-3600
Ari Bennett, prin. Fax 771-0452
Lewis Continuation S 100/Alt
12508 Wicks St 91352 818-394-3980
Robert Eiseman, prin. Fax 394-3981
Sun Valley HS 900/9-12
9171 Telfair Ave 91352 818-394-4600
Clara Herran, prin. Fax 767-8125
Sun Valley MS 1,200/6-8
7330 Bakman Ave 91352 818-255-5100
Roberto Lee, prin. Fax 503-9846
N Hollywood/Poly Cas Adult
12431 Roscoe Blvd 91352 818-394-3950
Carl Badeau, prin. Fax 394-3961

Village Christian HS 400/9-12
8930 Village Ave 91352 818-768-5540
Village Christian MS 200/6-8
8930 Village Ave 91352 818-768-1588

**Susanville, Lassen, Pop. 17,110**
Lassen UNHSD 900/7-12
1000 Main St 96130 530-257-5134
Willard McCabe, supt. Fax 251-0473
www.lassenhigh.org
Lassen Community Day S 50/Alt
1110 Main St 96130 530-257-2141
Christopher Mothorn, prin. Fax 257-5852
Lassen HS 900/9-12
1110 Main St 96130 530-257-2141
Robbin Pedrett, prin. Fax 251-1173
Diploma Gold Adult S Adult
1000 Main St 96130 530-257-5134
Robbin Pedrett, prin. Fax 251-0473

Regional Occupational Center & Program
Supt. — None
Lassen County ROP Vo/Tech
472-013 Johnstonville Rd 96130 530-252-1673
Rich Duvarney, dir.

Susanville ESD 1,000/K-8
109 S Gilman St 96130 530-257-8200
Jason Waddell, supt. Fax 257-8246
www.susanvillesd.org
Diamond View MS 300/6-8
850 Richmond Rd 96130 530-257-5144
Holly Theobald, prin. Fax 257-7232

Lassen Community College Post-Sec.
PO Box 3000 96130 530-257-6181

**Sutter, Sutter, Pop. 2,803**
Sutter UNHSD 700/9-12
PO Box 498 95982 530-822-5161
Ryan Robison, supt. Fax 822-5168
www.sutterhigh.k12.ca.us/
Butte View HS 50/Alt
PO Box 498 95982 530-822-5161
Ryan Robison, prin. Fax 822-5168
Sutter HS 700/9-12
PO Box 498 95982 530-822-5161
Ryan Robison, prin. Fax 822-5168

**Sutter Creek, Amador, Pop. 2,442**
Amador County Office of Education
Supt. — See Jackson
County Community S 100/Alt
525 Independence Dr 95685 209-257-5100
Frank Wagner, prin. Fax 245-3864

Amador County USD
Supt. — See Jackson
Amador HS 600/9-12
330 Spanish St 95685 209-257-7300
Jared Critchfield, prin. Fax 267-5942
Independence HS 100/Alt
525 Independence Dr 95685 209-257-5100
Butch Wagner, prin. Fax 267-5497
North Star S Alt
525 Independence Dr 95685 209-257-5150
Dr. Thomas Littlefair, prin. Fax 267-5847

**Sylmar, See Los Angeles**
Los Angeles USD
Supt. — See Los Angeles
Evergreen Continuation S 100/Alt
13101 Dronfield Ave 91342 818-367-5989
Robinson Acosta, prin. Fax 367-2796

Olive Vista MS 1,400/6-8
14600 Tyler St 91342 818-833-3900
Rodney Wright, prin. Fax 367-8273
Sylmar Biotech Health Academy 9-12
13050 Borden Ave 91342 818-833-3723
Maria Herrera, prin. Fax 833-5121
Sylmar HS 2,700/9-12
13050 Borden Ave 91342 818-833-3700
James Lee, prin. Fax 364-1037

---

Concordia JSHS 200/7-12
13570 Eldridge Ave 91342 818-362-5861
Ruth Peterson, prin. Fax 367-0043
Delphi Academy of Los Angeles 200/PK-12
11341 Brainard Ave 91342 818-583-1070
Karen Dale, head sch Fax 583-1082
ITT Technical Institute Post-Sec.
12669 Encinitas Ave 91342 818-364-5151
Los Angeles Mission College Post-Sec.
13356 Eldridge Ave 91342 818-364-7600
Olive View/UCLA Medical Centers Post-Sec.
14445 Olive View Dr 91342 818-364-4224

**Taft, Kern, Pop. 9,099**
Regional Occupational Center & Program
Supt. — None
West Side ROP Vo/Tech
PO Box 1337 93268 661-763-2390
Dale Countryman, dir. Fax 763-1445

Taft CSD 2,100/K-8
820 6th St 93268 661-763-1521
Julie Graves, supt. Fax 763-1495
www.taftcity.org
Lincoln JHS 700/6-8
810 6th St 93268 661-765-2127
Brandi Swearengin, prin. Fax 763-3970

Taft UNHSD 1,000/9-12
701 Wildcat Way 93268 661-763-2300
Blanca Cavazos, supt. Fax 763-1445
www.taft.k12.ca.us/
Buena Vista Continuation HS 100/Alt
701 Wildcat Way 93268 661-763-2383
Monica Toro, prin. Fax 763-2393
Taft Union HS 1,000/9-12
701 Wildcat Way 93268 661-763-2300
Bernardo Valenzuel, prin. Fax 763-4736

---

Taft College Post-Sec.
29 Emmons Park Dr 93268 661-763-7700

**Tahoe City, Placer, Pop. 1,643**
Tahoe-Truckee USD
Supt. — See Truckee
Cold Stream Alternative S 50/Alt
740 Timberland Ln 96145 530-582-2640
Greg Wohlman, prin. Fax 581-3457
North Tahoe HS 300/9-12
PO Box 5099 96145 530-581-7000
Joanna Mitchell, prin. Fax 581-3252
North Tahoe MS 400/5-8
PO Box 794 96145 530-581-7050
Fax 581-1237

**Tarzana, See Los Angeles**
Los Angeles USD
Supt. — See Los Angeles
Portola MS 1,900/6-8
18720 Linnet St 91356 818-654-3300
Stephanie McClay, prin. Fax 996-0292

---

Columbia College Hollywood Post-Sec.
18618 Oxnard St 91356 800-785-0585
Hypnosis Motivation Institute Post-Sec.
18607 Ventura Blvd Ste 310 91356 800-479-9464

**Tehachapi, Kern, Pop. 14,166**
Tehachapi USD 4,500/K-12
300 S Robinson St 93561 661-822-2100
Susan Andreas-Bervel, supt. Fax 822-2159
www.teh.k12.ca.us
Jacobsen MS 1,000/6-8
711 Anita Dr 93561 661-822-2150
Paul Kaminski, prin. Fax 822-2156
Monroe HS 200/Alt
126 S Snyder Ave 93561 661-822-2124
Laura Barba, prin. Fax 822-2188
Tehachapi HS 1,300/9-12
801 S Dennison Rd 93561 661-822-2130
Scott Heitman, prin. Fax 822-1854
Tehachapi Adult S Adult
126 S Snyder Ave 93561 661-822-2112
Laura Barba, prin. Fax 822-2188

---

Heritage Oak S 100/K-12
20915 Schout Rd 93561 661-823-0885
Amy Walker, head sch Fax 823-0863

**Temecula, Riverside, Pop. 95,946**
Temecula Valley USD 29,800/K-12
31350 Rancho Vista Rd 92592 951-676-2661
Timothy Ritter, supt. Fax 695-7121
www.tvusd.k12.ca.us
Chaparral HS 3,100/9-12
27215 Nicolas Rd 92591 951-695-4200
Gil Compton, prin. Fax 695-4219
Day MS 1,000/6-8
40775 Camino Campos Verde 92591 951-699-8138
Tina Miller, prin. Fax 699-4198
Gardner MS 1,100/6-8
45125 Via Del Coronado 92592 951-699-0080
Kristen Larson, prin. Fax 699-0081
Great Oak HS 3,400/9-12
32555 Deer Hollow Way 92592 951-294-6450
Marc Horton, prin. Fax 294-6477
Margarita MS 1,000/6-8
30600 Margarita Rd 92591 951-695-7370
Fax 695-7378
Nelson S 200/Alt
32225 Pio Pico Rd 92592 951-695-7360
Greg Cooke, prin. Fax 294-6303
Rancho Vista HS 200/Alt
32225 Pio Pico Rd 92592 951-695-7320
Greg Cooke, prin. Fax 294-6304
Temecula MS 1,200/6-8
42075 Meadows Pkwy 92592 951-302-5151
Rob Sousa, prin. Fax 302-5160
Temecula Valley HS 2,700/9-12
31555 Rancho Vista Rd 92592 951-695-7300
Allen Williams, prin. Fax 695-7311
Vail Ranch MS 1,200/6-8
33340 Camino Piedra Rojo 92592 951-302-5188
Kevin Groepper, prin. Fax 302-5195
Temecula Valley Adult S Adult
43000 Margarita Rd 92592 951-294-6512
Greg Cooke, prin. Fax 294-6521
Other Schools – See Murrieta

---

Health Staff Training Institute Post-Sec.
28671 Calle Cortez Ste F 92590 951-694-4784
Linfield Christian S 700/PK-12
31950 Pauba Rd 92592 951-676-8111
Drake Charles, head sch Fax 695-1291
Professional Golfers Career College Post-Sec.
26109 Ynez Rd 92591 800-877-4380
Rancho Christian S 500/PK-12
31300 Rancho Community Way 92592
951-303-1408
Jim Kunau, dir. Fax 302-1580
Royale College of Beauty Post-Sec.
27485 Commerce Center Dr 92590 951-676-0833

**Temple City, Los Angeles, Pop. 34,921**
Temple City USD 5,700/K-12
9700 Las Tunas Dr 91780 626-548-5000
Kathryn Perini, supt. Fax 548-5022
www.tcusd.net
Oak Avenue IS 900/7-8
6623 Oak Ave 91780 626-548-5060
Lawton Gray, prin. Fax 548-5170
Sears Learning Center 50/Alt
9229 Pentland St 91780 626-548-5113
Chris Sewell, prin. Fax 548-5118
Temple City HS 2,000/9-12
9501 Lemon Ave 91780 626-548-5040
Mary Jo Fosselman-King, prin. Fax 548-5045
Temple City Adult Education Adult
9229 Pentland St 91780 626-548-5050
Chris Sewell, prin. Fax 548-5118

---

United Beauty College Post-Sec.
10229 Lower Azusa Rd 91780 626-443-0900

**Templeton, San Luis Obispo, Pop. 7,486**
Templeton USD 2,200/PK-12
960 Old County Rd 93465 805-434-5800
Joe Koski, supt. Fax 434-5879
tusd.ca.schoolloop.com/
Eagle Canyon HS 50/9-12
950 Old County Rd 93465 805-434-5833
Joe Koski, prin. Fax 434-3879
Templeton HS 700/9-12
1200 S Main St 93465 805-434-5888
Kari Gibson, prin. Fax 434-0743
Templeton Independent Study HS 100/Alt
960 Old County Rd 93465 805-434-5846
Joe Koski, prin. Fax 434-5848
Templeton MS 500/6-8
925 Old County Rd 93465 805-434-5813
Kristina Benson, prin. Fax 434-5812

**Terra Bella, Tulare, Pop. 3,287**
Terra Bella UNESD 900/PK-8
9121 Road 240 93270 559-535-4451
Frank Betry, supt. Fax 535-0314
www.tbuesd.org
Smith MS 300/6-8
23825 Avenue 92 93270 559-535-4451
Guadalupe Roman, prin. Fax 535-0829

**Thermal, Riverside, Pop. 2,856**
Coachella Valley USD 18,300/K-12
PO Box 847 92274 760-399-5137
Darryl Adams, supt. Fax 399-1052
www.cvusd.us
Coachella Valley HS 2,700/9-12
83800 Airport Blvd 92274 760-399-5183
Victor Uribe, prin. Fax 399-0089
Desert Mirage HS 1,900/9-12
86150 Avenue 66 92274 760-397-2255
Maria McLeod, prin. Fax 397-8760
La Familia Continuation HS 100/Alt
56-615 Olive St 92274 760-399-5929
Arthur Kimball, prin. Fax 399-5169
Toro Canyon MS 1,000/7-8
86150 Avenue 66 92274 760-397-2244
Charles Housewright, prin. Fax 397-8760
Other Schools – See Coachella, Salton City

**Thousand Oaks, Ventura, Pop. 122,978**
Conejo Valley USD 20,700/PK-12
1400 E Janss Rd 91362 805-497-9511
Ann Bonitatibus Ed.D., supt. Fax 371-9170
www.conejousd.org
Century Academy 50/Alt
1025 Old Farm Rd 91360 805-496-0286
Martin Manzer, prin. Fax 496-5169
Colina MS 1,100/6-8
1500 E Hillcrest Dr 91362 805-495-7429
Shane Frank, prin. Fax 374-1163
Los Cerritos MS 1,000/6-8
2100 E Ave De Las Flores 91362 805-492-3538
Jason Klinger, prin. Fax 493-8854
Redwood MS 1,100/6-8
233 W Gainsborough Rd 91360 805-497-7264
Shauna Ashmore, prin. Fax 497-3734
Thousand Oaks HS 2,400/9-12
2323 N Moorpark Rd 91360 805-495-7491
Lou Lichtl, prin. Fax 374-1165
Conejo Valley Adult Education Adult
1025 Old Farm Rd 91360 805-497-2761
Michael Sanders, prin. Fax 374-1167
Other Schools – See Newbury Park, Westlake Village

---

California Lutheran University Post-Sec.
60 W Olsen Rd 91360 805-492-2411
Hillcrest Christian S 300/PK-12
384 Erbes Rd 91362 805-497-7501
Kathy Horan J.D., prin. Fax 494-9355
La Reina HS 600/7-12
106 W Janss Rd 91360 805-495-6494
Dr. Michael Bates, head sch Fax 494-4966
Trinity Pacific Christian S 400/K-12
3389 Camino Calandria 91360 805-492-0863
Barbara Richert, admin.

**Tiburon, Marin, Pop. 8,606**
Reed UNESD 1,400/K-8
277 Karen Way Ste A 94920 415-381-1112
Dr. Nancy Lynch, supt. Fax 384-0890
www.reedschools.org
Del Mar MS 400/6-8
105 Avenida Miraflores 94920 415-435-1468
Dr. Alan Vann Gardner, prin. Fax 435-6190

**Tollhouse, Fresno**
Sierra USD
Supt. — See Prather
Oak Meadow Community Day S 50/Alt
33411 Lodge Rd 93667 559-855-4347
Ara Keledjian, prin. Fax 855-4348
Sandy Bluffs Alternative Education Ctr. 50/Alt
33280 Lodge Rd 93667 559-855-3020
Ara Keledjian, prin. Fax 855-3081
Sierra HS 600/9-12
33326 Lodge Rd 93667 559-855-8311
Julia Reese, prin. Fax 855-2162
Sierra JHS 100/7-8
33326 Lodge Rd 93667 559-855-8311
Julia Reese, prin. Fax 855-2162

**Tomales, Marin, Pop. 200**
Shoreline USD 600/K-12
PO Box 198 94971 707-878-2266
Nancy Neu, supt. Fax 878-2554
www.shorelineunified.org
Tomales HS 200/9-12
PO Box 25 94971 707-878-2286
Adam Jennings, prin. Fax 878-2787

**Torrance, Los Angeles, Pop. 138,782**
Regional Occupational Center & Program
Supt. — None
Southern California ROC Vo/Tech
2300 Crenshaw Blvd 90501 310-224-4220
Laurie St. Gean, supt. Fax 320-1029

Torrance USD 24,000/PK-12
2335 Plaza Del Amo 90501 310-972-6500
George Mannon Ed.D., supt. Fax 972-6012
www.tusd.org
Calle Mayor MS 800/6-8
4800 Calle Mayor 90505 310-533-4548
David Mosley, prin. Fax 972-6389
Casimir MS 700/6-8
17220 Casimir Ave 90504 310-533-4498
Susan Holmes, prin. Fax 972-6391
Hull MS 700/6-8
2080 W 231st St 90501 310-533-4516
Patty Girgis, prin. Fax 972-6397
Jefferson MS 600/6-8
21717 Talisman St 90503 310-533-4794
Kara Heinrich-Daugherty, prin. Fax 972-6398
Lynn MS 800/6-8
5038 Halison St 90503 310-533-4495
Leroy Jackson, prin. Fax 972-6401
Madrona MS 700/6-8
21364 Madrona Ave 90503 310-533-4562
Chris Lipsey, prin. Fax 972-6402
Magruder MS 700/6-8
4100 W 185th St 90504 310-533-4527
Chris Sheck, prin. Fax 972-6403
North HS 2,200/9-12
3620 W 182nd St 90504 310-533-4412
Ronald Richardson, prin. Fax 972-6404
Richardson MS 700/6-8
23751 Nancylee Ln 90505 310-533-4790
Ian Drummond, prin. Fax 972-6405
Shery Continuation HS 100/Alt
2600 Vine Ave 90501 310-533-4440
Jamie Jimenez, prin. Fax 972-6408
South HS 2,100/9-12
4801 Pacific Coast Hwy 90505 310-533-4352
Scott McDowell, prin. Fax 972-6454
Torrance Community Day S 50/Alt
2291 Washington Ave 90501 310-972-6962
Jamie Jimenez, prin. Fax 972-6964
Torrance HS 2,100/9-12
2200 W Carson St 90501 310-533-4396
Karim Girgis, prin. Fax 972-6455
West HS 2,200/9-12
20401 Victor St 90503 310-533-4299
Pamela Metz, prin. Fax 972-6483
Griffith Adult Education Center Adult
2291 Washington Ave 90501 310-533-4454
James Jones, prin. Fax 972-6394
Hamilton Adult Education Center Adult
2606 W 182nd St 90504 310-533-4459
Wayne Diulio, dir. Fax 972-6395
Levy Adult Education Center Adult
3420 W 229th Pl 90505 310-533-4689
James Jones, prin. Fax 972-6399

Ambassador HS 100/9-12
540 Maple Ave 90503 310-356-0950
Dr. Michael Barker Ed.D., head sch Fax 618-8985
Bishop Montgomery HS 1,000/9-12
5430 Torrance Blvd 90503 310-540-2021
Rosemary Libbon, prin. Fax 792-1273
El Camino College Post-Sec.
16007 Crenshaw Blvd 90506 310-532-3670
Everest College Post-Sec.
1231 Cabrillo Ave Ste 201 90501 310-320-3200
ITT Technical Institute Post-Sec.
2555 W 190th St Ste 125 90504 310-965-5900
Los Angeles Co. Harbor UCLA Medical Ctr. Post-Sec.
1000 W Carson St 90502 310-533-2101
South Bay Junior Academy 200/PK-10
4400 Del Amo Blvd 90503 310-370-6215
Susan Vlach, prin. Fax 793-8665
Westwood College - South Bay Campus Post-Sec.
19700 S Vermont Ave Ste 100 90502 310-965-0888

**Tracy, San Joaquin, Pop. 78,298**
Jefferson ESD 2,500/K-8
1219 Whispering Wind Dr 95377 209-836-3388
James W. Bridges Ed.D., supt. Fax 836-2930
www.jeffersonschooldistrict.com
Jefferson S 400/5-8
7500 W Linne Rd 95304 209-835-3053
Alyssa Wooten, prin. Fax 835-4419

Lammersville USD 1,600/PK-10
111 S De Anza Blvd 95391 209-836-7400
Dr. Kirk Nicholas, supt. Fax 836-7402
www.lammersvilleschooldistrict.net
Other Schools – See Mountain House

Tracy JUSD 17,300/K-12
1875 W Lowell Ave 95376 209-830-3200
Brian Stephens, supt. Fax 830-3204
www.tracy.k12.ca.us
Duncan-Russell Continuation S 50/Alt
164 W Grant Line Rd 95376 209-830-3357
Dave Pickering, prin. Fax 830-3358
Kimball HS 2,000/9-12
3200 Jaguar Run 95377 209-832-6600
Cheryl Domenichelli, prin. Fax 832-6601
Monte Vista MS 900/6-8
751 W Lowell Ave 95376 209-830-3340
Susan O'Hara-Jones, prin. Fax 830-3341
Stein Continuation HS 200/Alt
650 W 10th St 95376 209-830-3395
Cynthia Johannes, prin. Fax 830-3396
Tracy HS 1,900/9-12
315 E 11th St 95376 209-830-3360
Jason Noll, prin. Fax 830-3361
West HS 2,200/9-12
1775 W Lowell Ave 95376 209-830-3370
Troy Brown, prin. Fax 830-3371
Williams MS 1,200/6-8
1600 Tennis Ln 95376 209-830-3345
Barbara Montgomery, prin. Fax 830-3346
Willow Community Day S 50/Alt
164 W Grant Line Rd 95376 209-830-3357
Dave Pickering, admin. Fax 830-3358
Tracy Adult S Adult
1895 W Lowell Ave 95376 209-830-3384
Dave Pickering, prin. Fax 830-3385

**Tranquillity, Fresno, Pop. 794**
Golden Plains USD
Supt. — See San Joaquin
Tranquillity HS 500/9-12
PO Box 457 93668 559-698-7205
James Reed, prin. Fax 698-7632

**Trona, San Bernardino, Pop. 18**
Trona JUSD 300/K-12
83600 Trona Rd 93562 760-372-2861
David Olney, supt. Fax 372-4534
www.trona.k12.ca.us/
Trona Community Day S 50/Alt
83600 Trona Rd 93562 760-372-2895
David Olney, prin. Fax 372-4534
Trona HS 100/7-12
83600 Trona Rd 93562 760-372-2824
David Olney, prin. Fax 372-4504

**Truckee, Nevada, Pop. 15,914**
Tahoe-Truckee USD 4,000/K-12
11603 Donner Pass Rd 96161 530-582-2500
Robert Leri Ed.D., supt. Fax 582-7606
www.ttusd.org
Alder Creek MS 500/6-8
10931 Alder Dr 96161 530-582-2750
Hein Larson, prin. Fax 582-7640
Sierra HS 50/Alt
11661 Donner Pass Rd 96161 530-582-2640
Greg Wohlman, prin. Fax 582-7687
Tahoe-Truckee HS 600/9-12
11725 Donner Pass Rd 96161 530-582-2600
John Carlson, prin. Fax 582-7636
Other Schools – See Tahoe City

**Tujunga, See Los Angeles**
Los Angeles USD
Supt. — See Los Angeles
Mt. Lukens Continuation HS 100/Alt
7705 Summitrose St 91042 818-352-4039
Jeeda Gabriel, prin. Fax 352-2499
Verdugo Hills HS 1,800/9-12
10625 Plainview Ave 91042 818-951-5400
Edward Trimis, prin. Fax 352-3577

**Tulare, Tulare, Pop. 58,086**
Tulare CSD 9,900/K-8
600 N Cherry St 93274 559-685-7200
Clare Gist Ed.D., supt. Fax 685-7287
www.tcsdk8.org/
Cherry Avenue MS 700/6-8
540 N Cherry St 93274 559-685-7320
Greg Anderson, prin. Fax 685-5621
Live Oak MS 600/7-8
980 N Laspina St 93274 559-685-7310
Michelle McPhetridge, prin. Fax 685-7313
Los Tules MS 600/6-8
801 W Gail Ave 93274 559-687-3156
Ira Porchia, prin. Fax 685-7374
Mulcahy MS 600/5-8
1001 W Sonora Ave 93274 559-685-7250
Tracey Jenkins, prin. Fax 687-6412

Tulare JUNHSD 4,800/9-12
426 N Blackstone St 93274 559-688-2021
Dr. Sarah Koligian, supt. Fax 687-7317
www.tjuhsd.org
Countryside HS Community Day School 50/Alt
1084 S Pratt St 93274 559-687-7400
Steve Ramirez, prin. Fax 687-7414
Mission Oak HS 1,400/9-12
3442 E Bardsley Ave 93274 559-687-7308
Michele Borges, prin. Fax 687-7383
Tulare Technical Preparatory S Vo/Tech
737 W Bardsley Ave 93274 559-687-7400
Steve Ramirez, prin. Fax 687-7414
Tulare Union HS 1,800/9-12
755 E Tulare Ave 93274 559-686-4761
Dr. Michelle Nunley, prin. Fax 687-7367
Tulare Western HS 1,700/9-12
824 W Maple Ave 93274 559-686-8751
Kevin Covert, prin. Fax 687-7341
Tulare Adult S Adult
575 W Maple Ave 93274 559-686-0225
Bill Edminster, dir. Fax 687-7447

Tulare Beauty College Post-Sec.
1400 W Inyo Ave 93274 559-688-2901

**Tulelake, Siskiyou, Pop. 985**
Tulelake Basin JUSD 500/K-12
PO Box 640 96134 530-667-2295
Vanessa Jones, supt. Fax 667-4298
www.tulelake.k12.ca.us
Tulelake Continuation HS 50/Alt
PO Box 640 96134 530-667-2280
Dean Teig, prin. Fax 667-4298
Tulelake HS 200/7-12
PO Box 640 96134 530-667-2292
Dean Teig, prin. Fax 667-4298

**Tuolumne, Tuolumne**
Summerville UNHSD 1,000/K-12
17555 Tuolumne Rd 95379 209-928-3498
Robert Griffith, supt. Fax 928-1321
www.summbears.k12.ca.us
Summerville HS 600/9-12
17555 Tuolumne Rd 95379 209-928-4228
David Johnstone, prin. Fax 928-1422
Other Schools – See Long Barn, Pinecrest, Twain Harte

**Turlock, Stanislaus, Pop. 66,239**
Chatom UNESD 600/PK-8
7201 Clayton Rd 95380 209-664-8505
Cherise Olvera, supt. Fax 664-8508
www.chatom.k12.ca.us
Other Schools – See Crows Landing

Stanislaus County Office of Education
Supt. — See Modesto
Allard Community S Alt
350 North Kilroy Rd 95380 209-238-6600
Daniel Vannest, prin. Fax 238-6699

Turlock USD 13,500/K-12
PO Box 819013 95381 209-667-0632
Dana Trevethan Ed.D., supt. Fax 667-6520
www.turlock.k12.ca.us
Dutcher MS 700/7-8
1441 Colorado Ave 95380 209-667-8817
Scott Lucas, prin. Fax 667-1332
Pitman HS 2,200/9-12
2525 W Christoffersen Pkwy 95382 209-656-1592
Amy Curd, prin. Fax 656-1639
Roselawn HS 200/Alt
312 S Roselawn Ave 95380 209-634-9311
Felipe Meraz, prin. Fax 634-8730
Turlock HS 2,100/9-12
1600 E Canal Dr 95380 209-667-2055
Dana Trevethan, prin. Fax 634-2698
Turlock JHS 1,300/7-8
3951 N Walnut Rd 95382 209-667-0881
Robert Ruiz, prin. Fax 668-3985
Turlock Adult Education Adult
1574 E Canal Dr 95380 209-667-0643
Alice Pollard, prin. Fax 667-0695

Adrian's Beauty College of Turlock Post-Sec.
1340 W Main St 95380 209-632-2233
California State University-Stanislaus Post-Sec.
1 University Cir 95382 209-667-3122
Turlock Christian JSHS 200/7-12
PO Box 1540 95381 209-632-2337
Steve Doerksen, prin. Fax 632-5859

**Tustin, Orange, Pop. 73,165**
Tustin USD 22,800/K-12
300 S C St 92780 714-730-7305
Dr. Gregory Franklin Ed.D., supt. Fax 730-7436
www.tustin.k12.ca.us
Columbus Tustin MS 900/6-8
17952 Beneta Way 92780 714-730-7352
Maggie Burdette, prin. Fax 730-7512
Currie MS 700/6-8
1402 Sycamore Ave 92780 714-730-7360
Erick Fineberg, prin. Fax 730-7593
Hillview HS 200/Alt
15400 Lansdowne Rd 92782 714-730-7356
Tim O'Donoghue, prin. Fax 730-7584
Pioneer MS 1,300/6-8
2700 Pioneer Rd 92782 714-730-7534
Tracey VanderHayden, prin. Fax 730-5405
Tustin Adult/Sycamore HS 50/Alt
15400 Landsdowne Rd 92782 714-730-7395
Tim O'Donoghue, prin. Fax 730-4895
Tustin HS 2,200/9-12
1171 El Camino Real 92780 714-730-7414
Christine Matos, prin. Fax 730-7568
Utt MS 900/6-8
13601 Browning Ave 92780 714-730-7573
Dean Jennings, prin. Fax 750-7576
Other Schools – See Irvine, Santa Ana

Spirit Christian Academy 200/K-12
1372 Irvine Blvd 92780 714-731-2630
Robin Gammie, admin. Fax 731-2639

**Twain Harte, Tuolumne, Pop. 2,173**
Summerville UNHSD
Supt. — See Tuolumne
South Fork HS 50/Alt
25611 Lyons Dam Rd 95383 209-586-5672
David Johnstone, prin. Fax 928-1422

**Twentynine Palms, San Bernardino, Pop. 23,540**
Morongo USD 8,700/K-12
PO Box 1209 92277 760-367-9191
Tom Baumgarten, supt. Fax 367-7189
www.morongousd.com
Twentynine Palms HS 800/9-12
72750 Wild Cat Way 92277 760-367-9591
Justin Monical, prin. Fax 367-2106
Twentynine Palms JHS 500/7-8
5798 Utah Trl 92277 760-367-9507
Stacy Smalling, prin. Fax 367-0742
Other Schools – See Yucca Valley

**Twin Peaks, San Bernardino**

Lake Arrowhead Christian S 100/K-12
PO Box 870 92391 909-337-3739
Linda Huffman M.Ed., prin. Fax 337-4550

**Ukiah, Mendocino, Pop. 15,561**
Mendocino County Office of Education 100/
2240 Old River Rd 95482 707-467-5000
Warren Galletti, supt. Fax 462-0379
www.mcoe.us
Mendocino County Community S 100/Alt
2240 Old River Rd 95482 707-467-5155
Antonio Lopez, dir. Fax 467-5164
Orr Creek S 50/Alt
2240 Old River Rd 95482 707-467-2517
Barbara Bloom, dir. Fax 467-2531

Regional Occupational Center & Program
Supt. — None
Mendocino County ROP Vo/Tech
2240 Old River Rd 95482 707-467-5123
Dennis Aseltyne, dir. Fax 468-8212

Ukiah USD 6,200/PK-12
511 S Orchard Ave 95482 707-472-5000
Debra Kubin, supt. Fax 463-2120
www.uusd.net
Pomolita MS 700/6-8
740 N Spring St 95482 707-472-5350
Bryan Barrett, prin. Fax 463-5203
South Valley Continuation HS 200/Alt
429 S Dora St 95482 707-472-5150
Fax 462-9654
Ukiah HS 1,600/9-12
1000 Low Gap Rd 95482 707-472-5750
Gordon Oslund, prin. Fax 463-4859
Ukiah Independent Study Academy Alt
1000 Low Gap Rd 95482 707-472-5062
Holly Rodgers, prin. Fax 463-2120
Ukiah Adult Education Adult
1056 N Bush St 95482 707-463-5217
Holly Rodgers, dir. Fax 463-0718
Other Schools – See Redwood Valley

Instilling Goodness Developing Virtue S 100/K-12
4951 Bodhi Way 95482 707-468-1138
Mendocino College Post-Sec.
1000 Hensley Creek Rd 95482 707-468-3000
Ukiah Junior Academy 100/K-10
180 Stipp Ln 95482 707-462-6350
Eric Stubbert, prin. Fax 462-4026

**Union City, Alameda, Pop. 65,266**
New Haven USD 12,600/K-12
34200 Alvarado Niles Rd 94587 510-471-1100
Dr. A. Smith, supt. Fax 471-7108
www.nhusd.k12.ca.us
Alvarado MS 1,400/6-8
31604 Alvarado Blvd 94587 510-489-0700
Heather Thorner, prin. Fax 475-3936
Chavez MS 1,500/6-8
2801 Hop Ranch Rd 94587 510-487-1700
Mireya Casarez, prin. Fax 475-3938
Decoto School for Independent Study Alt
600 G St 94587 510-476-2696
Grace Kim, coord.
Logan HS 4,100/9-12
1800 H St 94587 510-471-2520
Abhi Brar, prin. Fax 471-0514
New Haven Adult S Adult
600 G St 94587 510-489-2185
Jessica Wilder, prin. Fax 471-0554
Other Schools – See Hayward

**Upland, San Bernardino, Pop. 71,871**
Upland USD 11,900/K-12
390 N Euclid Ave 91786 909-985-1864
Nancy Kelly Ed.D., supt. Fax 949-7872
www.upland.k12.ca.us
Hillside HS 300/Alt
1558 W 9th St 91786 909-949-8400
Jerry Adams, prin. Fax 949-7840

Pioneer JHS 1,000/7-8
245 W 18th St 91784 909-949-7770
Aaron Dover, prin. Fax 949-7778
Upland HS 3,600/9-12
565 W 11th St 91786 909-949-7880
Garry Cameron, prin. Fax 949-7895
Upland JHS 1,000/7-8
444 E 11th St 91786 909-949-7810
Pam Chavira, prin. Fax 949-7817
Upland Adult S Adult
565 W 11th St 91786 909-949-7880

---

Western Christian HS 400/9-12
100 W 9th St 91786 909-920-5858
John Attwood, prin. Fax 985-3449
Westwood College - Inland Empire Post-Sec.
20 W 7th St 91786 909-931-7550

**Upper Lake, Lake, Pop. 1,026**
Upper Lake UNESD 500/K-8
PO Box 36 95485 707-275-2357
Valerie Gardner, supt. Fax 275-2205
www.uluesd.lake.k12.ca.us/
Upper Lake Union MS 200/6-8
PO Box 36 95485 707-275-0223
Tony Loumena, prin. Fax 275-2911

Upper Lake UNHSD 400/9-12
675 Clover Valley Rd 95485 707-275-2655
Patrick Iaccino, supt. Fax 275-0239
www.ulhs.k12.ca.us
Clover Valley HS 50/Alt
682 Clover Valley Rd 95485 707-275-0840
Don Boyd, lead tchr. Fax 275-0208
Upper Lake Community Day HS 50/Alt
675 Clover Valley Rd 95485 707-275-0840
Don Boyd, lead tchr. Fax 275-0208
Upper Lake HS 300/9-12
675 Clover Valley Rd 95485 707-275-2338
Patrick Iaccino, prin. Fax 275-0239

**Vacaville, Solano, Pop. 87,007**
Vacaville USD 12,500/K-12
401 Nut Tree Rd 95687 707-453-6100
Jane Shamieh, supt. Fax 453-7114
www.vacavilleusd.org
Country HS 200/Alt
100 McClellan St Ste B 95688 707-453-6215
Mike Sullivan, prin. Fax 451-3875
Jepson MS 1,000/7-8
580 Elder St 95688 707-453-6280
Kelley Birch, prin. Fax 447-7128
Vaca Pena MS 900/7-8
200 Keith Way 95687 707-453-6270
Jeff Crane, prin. Fax 451-9501
Vacaville HS 2,000/9-12
100 W Monte Vista Ave 95688 707-453-6011
Ed Santopadre, prin. Fax 447-5604
Wood HS 1,700/9-12
998 Marshall Rd 95687 707-453-6900
Cliff DeGraw, prin. Fax 451-3656
Adult Education Adult
100 McClellan St Ste A 95688 707-453-6018
Mark Frazier, prin. Fax 453-6959

---

Blake Austin College Post-Sec.
611 Orange Dr Ste K 95687 707-455-0557
Vacaville Christian S 1,000/PK-12
1117 Davis St 95687 707-446-1776
Paul Harrell, head sch Fax 446-1538

**Valencia, See Santa Clarita**
Castaic UNSD 2,900/K-8
28131 Livingston Ave 91355 661-257-4500
Janene Maxon, supt. Fax 257-3596
castaicusd.com
Other Schools – See Castaic

William S. Hart UNHSD
Supt. — See Santa Clarita
Arroyo Seco JHS 1,300/7-8
27171 Vista Delgado Dr 91354 661-296-0991
Rhondi Durand, prin. Fax 296-3436
Valencia HS 3,000/9-12
27801 Dickason Dr 91355 661-294-1188
John Costanzo, prin. Fax 294-3828
Golden Oak Adult S Adult
23201 Dalbey Dr 91355 661-253-0583
Ron Rudzinski, admin. Fax 260-1371

---

California Institute of the Arts Post-Sec.
24700 McBean Pkwy 91355 661-255-1050
Trinity Classical Academy 200/PK-12
28310 Kelly Johnson Pkwy 91355 661-296-2601
Liz Caddow, head sch Fax 607-0664

**Vallejo, Solano, Pop. 108,826**
Vallejo City USD 14,600/K-12
665 Walnut Ave 94592 707-556-8921
Ramona Bishop, supt. Fax 649-3907
www.vallejo.k12.ca.us
Bethel HS 2,000/9-12
1800 Ascot Pkwy 94591 707-556-5700
Lloyd Cartwright, prin. Fax 556-5703
Franklin MS 1,000/6-8
501 Starr Ave 94590 707-556-8470
Michelle Jordan-Faucett, prin. Fax 556-8475
Hogan MS 1,100/6-8
850 Rosewood Ave 94591 707-556-8510
Jocelyn Hendrix, prin. Fax 556-8529
Peoples Continuation HS 200/Alt
233 Hobbs Ave 94589 707-556-8670
Ernani Santos, prin. Fax 556-8674
Solano MS 800/6-8
1025 Corcoran Ave 94589 707-556-8600
Shayla Bowman, prin. Fax 556-8615
Vallejo Education Academy Alt
301 Farragut Ave 94590 707-649-3909
Linda Combs, prin.
Vallejo HS 1,900/9-12
840 Nebraska St 94590 707-556-1700
Roxanne Brown-Garcia, prin. Fax 556-8729
Vallejo Adult Education Adult
2833 Tennessee St 94591 707-556-8620
Paul Jacobs, prin. Fax 556-8624

---

California Maritime Academy Post-Sec.
200 Maritime Academy Dr 94590 707-654-1000
North Hills Christian S 300/PK-12
200 Admiral Callaghan Ln 94591 707-644-5284
Florence Wright, supt. Fax 644-5295
St. Patrick-St. Vincent HS 500/9-12
1500 Benicia Rd 94591 707-644-4425
Dave Perry, pres. Fax 644-3107
Touro University - California Post-Sec.
1310 Club Dr 94592 707-638-5200

**Valley Center, San Diego, Pop. 9,007**
Valley Center-Pauma USD 4,100/K-12
28751 Cole Grade Rd 92082 760-749-0464
Mary Gorsuch, supt. Fax 749-1208
www.vcpusd.net
Oak Glen HS 100/Alt
28751 Cole Grade Rd 92082 760-751-0455
Mike Schanze, prin. Fax 749-0767
Valley Center HS 1,300/9-12
28751 Cole Grade Rd 92082 760-751-5500
Ron McCowan, prin. Fax 751-5509
Valley Center MS 900/6-8
28751 Cole Grade Rd 92082 760-751-4295
Jon Peterson, prin. Fax 751-4259
Valley Center Prep S Alt
28751 Cole Grade Rd 92082 760-751-5590
Dennis Zabinsky, prin.

**Valley Glen, Los Angeles**

---

Los Angeles Valley College Post-Sec.
5800 Fulton Ave, 818-947-2600
Summit View S 100/1-12
6455 Coldwater Canyon Ave, 818-623-6300
Keri Borzello, head sch Fax 623-6390

**Valley Springs, Calaveras, Pop. 3,427**
Calaveras USD
Supt. — See San Andreas
Toyon MS 500/7-8
PO Box 1510 95252 209-754-2137
Amy Hasselwander, prin. Fax 754-5327

**Valley Village, See Los Angeles**

---

Valley Torah Boys HS 100/9-12
12517 Chandler Blvd 91607 818-505-7999
Rabbi Avrohom Stulberger, head sch Fax 505-7997

**Vandenberg AFB, Santa Barbara, Pop. 3,111**
Lompoc USD
Supt. — See Lompoc
Vandenberg MS 800/7-8
Mountain View Blvd 93437 805-742-2700
Joel Jory, prin. Fax 742-2759

**Van Nuys, See Los Angeles**
Los Angeles USD
Supt. — See Los Angeles
Fulton College Prep S 2,200/6-12
7477 Kester Ave 91405 818-947-2100
Raquel George, prin. Fax 994-2284
Grant HS 2,400/9-12
13000 Oxnard St 91401 818-756-2700
Pamela Damonte, prin. Fax 908-0774
Independence Continuation HS 100/Alt
6501 Balboa Blvd 91406 818-881-7737
Jason Camp, prin. Fax 609-0764
London HS 100/Alt
12924 Oxnard St 91401 818-756-2794
Walter Weronka, prin. Fax 902-9671
Mulholland MS 1,600/6-8
17120 Vanowen St 91406 818-609-2500
Gregory Vallone, prin. Fax 345-1933
Pearl Journalism & Communications HS 300/9-12
6649 Balboa Blvd 91406 818-654-3775
Deborah Smith, prin. Fax 654-3701
Rogers Continuation HS 200/Alt
14711 Gilmore St 91411 818-778-6895
Sunshine Sepulveda-Klus, prin. Fax 904-0675
Valley Alternative S 600/Alt
6701 Balboa Blvd 91406 818-342-6133
Yela Dirlam, prin. Fax 342-8645
Van Nuys HS 2,800/9-12
6535 Cedros Ave 91411 818-778-6800
Yolanda Gardea, prin. Fax 781-5181
Van Nuys MS 1,300/6-8
5435 Vesper Ave 91411 818-267-5900
Cristina Serrano, prin. Fax 909-7274
Vista MS 1,500/6-8
15040 Roscoe Blvd 91402 818-901-2727
Guiseppe Nardulli, prin. Fax 901-2740
Van Nuys Community Adult S Adult
6535 Cedros Ave 91411 818-778-6000
Bernadine Gonzalez, prin. Fax 778-6015

---

American Pacific College Post-Sec.
14435 Sherman Way Ste 210 91405 818-781-0001
California Institute of Locksmithing Post-Sec.
14719 1/2 Oxnard St 91411 818-994-7425
Casa Loma College Post-Sec.
6725 Kester Ave 91405 818-785-2726
Help Group's North Hills Prep S 100/1-12
15339 Saticoy St 91406 818-267-2600
Elin Bradley, dir. Fax 988-9143
ICDC College Post-Sec.
14434 Sherman Way 91405 818-787-0008
National Career College Post-Sec.
6850 Van Nuys Blvd Fl 3 91405 888-988-2301
Nick Harris Detective Academy Post-Sec.
14721 Oxnard St 91411 818-343-6611
The Kings University Post-Sec.
14800 Sherman Way 91405 818-779-8040

**Venice, See Los Angeles**
Los Angeles USD
Supt. — See Los Angeles
Venice Adult Skills Center Adult
611 5th Ave 90291 310-664-5820
Carl Badeau, prin. Fax 392-3461

**Ventura, Ventura, Pop. 103,287**
Ventura USD 17,300/K-12
255 W Stanley Ave Ste 100 93001 805-641-5000
Michael Babb, supt. Fax 653-7855
www.venturausd.org
Anacapa MS 900/6-8
100 S Mills Rd 93003 805-289-7900
Barbara Boggio, prin. Fax 289-7909
Balboa MS 1,300/6-8
247 S Hill Rd 93003 805-289-1800
Teresa Gern, prin. Fax 289-1806
Buena HS 2,100/9-12
5670 Telegraph Rd 93003 805-289-1826
Bobbi Powers, prin. Fax 289-1854
Cabrillo MS 1,000/6-8
1426 E Santa Clara St 93001 805-641-5155
Lorelle Dawes, prin. Fax 641-5377
De Anza Academy 700/6-8
2060 Cameron St 93001 805-641-5165
Hector Guerrero, prin. Fax 641-5282
El Camino HS 300/9-12
61 Day Rd 93003 805-289-7955
Cheryl Burns, prin. Fax 658-6315
Foothill Technology HS Vo/Tech
100 Day Rd 93003 805-289-0023
Joe Bova, prin. Fax 289-0029
Pacific HS 200/Alt
501 College Dr 93003 805-289-7950
Kenny Loo, prin. Fax 289-7962
Ventura HS 2,100/9-12
2 N Catalina St 93001 805-641-5116
Carlos Cohen, prin. Fax 641-5310
Ventura Adult and Continuing Education Adult
5200 Valentine Rd 93003 805-289-7925
Teresa Johnson, prin. Fax 289-7931

---

Brooks Institute Post-Sec.
5301 N Ventura Ave 93001 805-585-8000
St. Augustine Academy 100/K-12
PO Box 4506 93007 805-672-0411
Michael Van Hecke, hdmstr. Fax 672-0177
St. Bonaventure HS 600/9-12
3167 Telegraph Rd 93003 805-648-6836
Marc Groff, prin. Fax 648-4903
Santa Barbara Business College Post-Sec.
4839 Market St 93003 866-749-7222
Santa Barbara Business College - Online Post-Sec.
1834 Palma Dr 93003 866-749-7222
Ventura College Post-Sec.
4667 Telegraph Rd 93003 805-654-6400
Ventura County Christian S 50/K-12
96 MacMillan Ave 93001 805-641-0187
Tanja Geue, admin. Fax 641-0252

**Victorville, San Bernardino, Pop. 111,837**
Adelanto ESD
Supt. — See Adelanto
Mesa Linda MS 1,000/7-8
13001 Mesa Linda Ave 92392 760-246-6363
Debra French, prin. Fax 956-7456

San Bernardino Co. Office of Education
Supt. — See San Bernardino
Desert Mountain Community S 100/Alt
15733 First St 92392 760-843-5490
Bernadine Hollingsworth, dir.

Victor Valley UNHSD 13,000/7-12
16350 Mojave Dr, 760-955-3200
Ron Williams, supt. Fax 245-3128
www.vvuhsd.org
Adelanto HS 1,200/9-12
13853 Seneca Rd 92392 760-246-3909
Ebony Purcell, prin. Fax 261-7023
Cobalt Institute of Math & Science 600/7-12
14045 Topaz Rd 92392 760-955-2530
Dr. Melda Gaskins, prin. Fax 955-2437
Goodwill Education Center 400/Alt
16350 Mojave Dr, 760-955-3440
Kevan Loyd, prin. Fax 843-7384
Hook JHS 800/7-8
15000 Hook Blvd 92394 760-955-3360
Maura Balmaceda, prin. Fax 245-5839
Lakeview MS 900/7-8
12484 Tamarisk Rd, 760-955-3400
Lonnie Keeter, prin. Fax 955-1992
Silverado HS 3,900/9-12
14048 Cobalt Rd 92392 760-955-3353
Heather Conkle, prin. Fax 955-3439
University Preparatory S 1,100/Alt
13853 Seneca Rd 92392 760-243-5940
Valerie Hatcher, prin. Fax 951-2803
Victor Valley HS 2,700/9-12
16500 Mojave Dr, 760-955-3300
Chris Douglass, prin. Fax 955-3319
Victor Valley Adult Education Adult
13853 Seneca Rd 92392 760-955-3440
Kevan Loyd, coord. Fax 241-0115

---

Four-D College Post-Sec.
16534 Victor St, 760-962-1325
Victor Valley Beauty College Post-Sec.
16515 Mojave Dr, 760-245-2522

Victor Valley Christian S — 300/PK-12
15260 Nisqually Rd, — 760-241-8827
Deb Clarkson, admin. — Fax 243-0654
Victor Valley College — Post-Sec.
18422 Bear Valley Rd, — 760-245-4271
Westech College — Post-Sec.
14554 7th St, — 760-951-5050

**Villa Park, Orange, Pop. 5,691**
Orange USD
Supt. — See Orange
Cerro Villa MS — 1,000/7-8
17852 Serrano Ave 92861 — 714-997-6251
Lisa Ogan Ed.D., prin. — Fax 921-9331
Villa Park HS — 2,500/9-12
18042 Taft Ave 92861 — 714-532-8020
Ed Howard, prin. — Fax 628-4302

**Visalia, Tulare, Pop. 121,741**
Visalia USD — 27,300/K-12
5000 W Cypress Ave 93277 — 559-730-7300
Craig Wheaton Ed.D., supt. — Fax 730-7508
www.vusd.org/
Divisadero MS — 900/7-8
1200 S Divisadero St 93277 — 559-730-7661
Irene Del Cid, prin. — Fax 730-7908
El Diamante HS — 1,800/9-12
5100 W Whitendale Ave 93277 — 559-735-3501
Angela Sanchez, prin. — Fax 735-3579
Golden West HS — 1,700/9-12
1717 N McAuliff St 93292 — 559-730-7801
Jose Fregoso, prin. — Fax 730-7408
Green Acres MS — 1,200/7-8
1147 N Mooney Blvd 93291 — 559-730-7671
Andy Di Meo, prin. — Fax 730-7918
La Joya MS — 1,000/7-8
4711 W La Vida Ave 93277 — 559-730-7921
Travis Hambleton, prin. — Fax 730-7505
Mt. Whitney HS — 1,600/9-12
900 S Conyer St 93277 — 559-730-7602
Rick Hamilton, prin. — Fax 730-7679
Redwood HS — 2,000/9-12
1001 W Main St 93291 — 559-730-7367
Matt Shin, prin. — Fax 730-7741
Sequoia HS — 300/Alt
901 N Mooney Blvd 93291 — 559-730-7649
Adolfo Reyes, prin. — Fax 730-7487
Valley Oak MS — 900/7-8
2000 N Lovers Ln 93292 — 559-730-7681
Michael Hernandez, prin. — Fax 730-7822
Visalia Technical Early College HS — Vo/Tech
2049 S Linwood St 93277 — 559-622-3212
Victoria Porter, prin. — Fax 322-6214
Visalia Adult Education — Adult
3110 E Houston Ave 93292 — 559-730-7655
John Werner, prin. — Fax 635-0372

---

Advanced Career Institute — Post-Sec.
1728 N Kelsey St 93291 — 559-651-1978
Central Valley Christian S — 900/PK-12
5600 W Tulare Ave 93277 — 559-734-9481
Dr. John DeLeeuw, supt. — Fax 734-7963
College of the Sequoias — Post-Sec.
915 S Mooney Blvd 93277 — 559-730-3700
Estes Inst. Cosmetology Arts & Sciences — Post-Sec.
324 E Main St 93291 — 559-733-3617
Milan Institute of Cosmetology — Post-Sec.
6500 S Mooney Blvd Unit A 93277 — 559-735-3829
San Joaquin Valley College — Post-Sec.
8400 W Mineral King Ave 93291 — 559-651-2500

**Vista, San Diego, Pop. 90,562**
Vista USD — 24,200/K-12
1234 Arcadia Ave 92084 — 760-726-2170
Dr. Devin Vodicka, supt. — Fax 758-7838
www.vistausd.org
Alta Vista HS — 200/Alt
1575 Bonair Rd 92084 — 760-724-3775
Michael Sterner, prin. — Fax 724-0410
Murray Continuation S — 200/Alt
215 N Melrose Dr 92083 — 760-631-2502
Chuck Hoover, prin. — Fax 643-2685
Rancho Buena Vista HS — 2,800/9-12
1601 Longhorn Dr, — 760-727-7284
Chuck Schindler, prin. — Fax 598-7062
Rancho Minerva MS — 900/6-8
2245 Foothill Dr 92084 — 760-631-4500
Benjamin Gaines, prin. — Fax 643-2490
Vista HS — 2,700/9-12
1 Panther Way 92084 — 760-726-5611
Anthony Barela, prin. — Fax 630-9738
Vista Innovation & Design Academy — 700/6-8
740 Olive Ave 92083 — 760-724-7115
Dr. Eric Chagala, prin. — Fax 941-6912
Vista Magnet MS — 600/6-8
151 Civic Center Dr 92084 — 760-726-5766
Anne Green, prin. — Fax 945-4273
Vista Visions Academy — Alt
305 E Bobier Dr 92084 — 760-724-4785
Fax 630-4206
Vista Adult S — Adult
510 Sunset Dr, — 760-758-7122
Elizabeth O'Shea-West, prin. — Fax 726-3277
Other Schools – See Oceanside

---

Kaplan College — Post-Sec.
2022 University Dr 92083 — 760-630-1555
Tri City Christian S — 600/PK-12
302 N Emerald Dr 92083 — 760-630-8227
Clark Gilbert, supt. — Fax 724-6643

**Walnut, Los Angeles, Pop. 28,480**
Walnut Valley USD — 14,700/K-12
880 S Lemon Ave 91789 — 909-595-1261
Dr. Robert Taylor, supt. — Fax 444-3435
www.wvusd.k12.ca.us
Hockwalt Academies — 50/Alt
476 S Lemon Ave 91789 — 909-595-1261
Donna Hunter, prin. — Fax 594-1272
South Pointe MS — 1,000/6-8
20671 Larkstone Dr 91789 — 909-595-8171
Susan Arzola, prin. — Fax 468-5201
Suzanne MS — 1,400/6-8
525 Suzanne Rd 91789 — 909-594-1657
Lester Ojeda, prin. — Fax 598-6741
Walnut HS — 3,000/9-12
400 Pierre Rd 91789 — 909-594-1333
Brandon Dade, prin. — Fax 598-7282
Other Schools – See Diamond Bar

---

Mt. San Antonio College — Post-Sec.
1100 N Grand Ave 91789 — 909-594-5611

**Walnut Creek, Contra Costa, Pop. 61,759**
Acalanes UNHSD
Supt. — See Lafayette
Acalanes Center for Independent Study — 100/9-12
1963 Tice Valley Blvd 94595 — 925-280-3945
Mark Uhrenholt, dir. — Fax 280-3947
Las Lomas HS — 1,500/9-12
1460 S Main St 94596 — 925-280-3920
Matt Campbell, prin. — Fax 280-3921
Acalanes Adult S & Center — Adult
1963 Tice Valley Blvd 94595 — 925-280-3980
Mark Uhrenholt, dir. — Fax 395-3981

Mount Diablo USD
Supt. — See Concord
Foothill MS — 1,000/6-8
2775 Cedro Ln 94598 — 925-939-8600
April Bush, prin. — Fax 256-4281
Northgate HS — 1,600/9-12
425 Castle Rock Rd 94598 — 925-938-0900
Michael McAlister, prin. — Fax 945-6429

Walnut Creek ESD — 3,500/K-8
960 Ygnacio Valley Rd 94596 — 925-944-6850
Patricia Wool Ed.D., supt. — Fax 944-1768
www.walnutcreeksd.org
Walnut Creek IS — 1,200/6-8
2425 Walnut Blvd 94597 — 925-944-6840
Michael Cannon, prin. — Fax 933-1922

---

Berean Christian HS — 500/9-12
245 El Divisadero Ave 94598 — 925-945-6464
Dr. Nelson Noriega, prin. — Fax 945-7473
Contra Costa Christian S — 300/PK-12
2721 Larkey Ln 94597 — 925-934-4964
Brian Meek, head sch — Fax 934-4966

**Walnut Park, Los Angeles, Pop. 15,927**
Los Angeles USD
Supt. — See Los Angeles
Science Tech Engineering & Math Academy — 6-8
7500 Marbrisa Ave 90255 — 323-277-2600
Linda Park, prin. — Fax 589-1529
S of Social Justice and Service Learning — 6-8
7500 Marbrisa Ave 90255 — 323-277-2600
Aida Coronado-Delon, prin. — Fax 589-1529

**Warner Springs, San Diego**
Warner USD — 300/PK-12
PO Box 8 92086 — 760-782-3517
Melissa Brown M.Ed., supt. — Fax 782-9117
www.warnerusd.net
Warner JSHS — 100/7-12
PO Box 8 92086 — 760-782-3517
Melissa Brown M.Ed., supt. — Fax 782-0605

**Wasco, Kern, Pop. 25,343**
Regional Occupational Center & Program
Supt. — None
North Kern Vocational Training Center — Vo/Tech
2150 7th St 93280 — 661-758-3045
Amy Bean, dir. — Fax 758-5956

Wasco UNESD — 3,300/K-8
1102 5th St 93280 — 661-758-7100
Kelly Richers, supt. — Fax 758-7110
www.wuesd.org
Jefferson MS — 700/7-8
1102 5th St 93280 — 661-758-7140
Regina Green, prin. — Fax 758-9366

Wasco UNHSD — 1,800/9-12
2100 7th St 93280 — 661-758-8447
Lori Albrecht, supt. — Fax 758-4946
www.wascouhsd.org
Independence HS — 100/Alt
1445 Poso Dr 93280 — 661-758-7450
Martin Lonza, prin. — Fax 758-7451
Wasco HS — 1,600/9-12
1900 7th St 93280 — 661-758-7400
Kevin Tallon, prin. — Fax 758-9201

**Waterford, Stanislaus, Pop. 8,248**
Waterford USD — 3,600/K-12
219 N Reinway Ave 95386 — 209-874-1809
Don Davis, supt. — Fax 874-3109
www.waterford.k12.ca.us
Sentinel HS — 50/Alt
121 S Reinway Ave 95386 — 209-874-9017
Peggy Herndon, prin. — Fax 874-9065
Waterford HS — 600/9-12
121 S Reinway Ave 95386 — 209-874-9060
Don Davis, prin. — Fax 874-9065
Waterford MS — 200/7-8
12916 Bentley St 95386 — 209-874-2382
Paul Patterson, prin. — Fax 874-3652

**Watsonville, Santa Cruz, Pop. 50,582**
Pajaro Valley USD — 17,200/K-12
294 Green Valley Rd 95076 — 831-786-2100
Dorma Baker, supt. — Fax 728-4288
www.pvusd.net
Chavez MS — 200/6-8
440 Arthur Rd 95076 — 831-761-7699
Benjamin Benavidez, prin. — Fax 728-6477
Hall MS — 600/6-8
201 Brewington Ave 95076 — 831-728-6270
Adelina Cervero, prin. — Fax 761-6150
Lakeview MS — 700/6-8
2350 E Lake Ave 95076 — 831-728-6454
Dr. Rosa Hernandez, prin. — Fax 728-6480
New S — 100/Alt
165 Harkins Slough Rd 95076 — 831-761-6140
Artemisa Cortez, prin. — Fax 761-6188
Pajaro MS — 400/6-8
250 Salinas Rd 95076 — 831-728-6238
Dr. Victoria Sorensen, prin. — Fax 728-6219
Rolling Hills MS — 600/6-8
130 Herman Ave 95076 — 831-728-6341
Rick Ito, prin. — Fax 724-7323
Watsonville HS — 2,000/9-12
250 E Beach St 95076 — 831-728-6390
Elaine Legorreta, prin. — Fax 761-6013
Adult Education Green Valley Center — Adult
294 Green Valley Rd 95076 — 831-786-2160
Dr. Nancy Bilicich, dir. — Fax 786-2193
Other Schools – See Aptos, La Selva Beach

---

Green Valley Christian S — 200/K-12
376 S Green Valley Rd 95076 — 831-724-6505
Sharon Harris, admin. — Fax 288-0214
Monte Vista Christian S — 800/6-12
2 School Way 95076 — 831-722-8178
Stephen Sharp, head sch — Fax 722-6003
St. Francis Central Coast Catholic HS — 200/9-12
PO Box 2649 95077 — 831-724-5933
Patrick Lee, prin. — Fax 724-5995

**Weaverville, Trinity, Pop. 3,455**
Trinity Alps USD — 800/PK-12
PO Box 1227 96093 — 530-623-6104
Tom Barnett, supt. — Fax 623-3418
www.tausd.org
Alps View HS — 50/Alt
PO Box 1227 96093 — 530-623-6104
Tom Barnett, supt. — Fax 623-3418
Trinity HS — 400/9-12
PO Box 1060 96093 — 530-623-6127
Bob Anderson, prin. — Fax 623-6661
Trinity Adult S — Adult
PO Box 1227 96093 — 530-623-6104
Tom Barnett, supt. — Fax 623-3418

**Weed, Siskiyou, Pop. 2,802**
Siskiyou UNHSD
Supt. — See Mount Shasta
Weed HS — 200/9-12
909 Hillside Dr 96094 — 530-938-4774
Mike Matheson, prin. — Fax 938-1319

---

College of the Siskiyous — Post-Sec.
800 College Ave 96094 — 530-938-5555

**West Covina, Los Angeles, Pop. 103,993**
Covina-Valley USD
Supt. — See Covina
South Hills HS — 2,000/9-12
645 S Barranca St 91791 — 626-974-6220
Matt Dalton, prin. — Fax 974-6245
Traweek MS — 1,000/6-8
1941 E Rowland Ave 91791 — 626-974-7400
Mathew Kodama, prin. — Fax 974-7415
Tri Community Adult Ed.-Pioneer Center — Adult
1651 E Rowland Ave 91791 — 626-974-6821
Dan Gribbon, prin. — Fax 974-6830

Regional Occupational Center & Program
Supt. — None
East San Gabriel Valley ROP — Vo/Tech
1501 Del Norte St 91790 — 626-962-5080
Dr. Laurel Adler, supt. — Fax 472-5145

Rowland USD
Supt. — See Rowland Heights
Giano IS — 700/7-8
3223 S Giano Ave 91792 — 626-965-2461
Fax 854-2212

West Covina USD — 10,200/K-12
1717 W Merced Ave 91790 — 626-939-4600
Dr. Charles Hinman Ed.D., supt. — Fax 939-4701
www.wcusd.org
Coronado Alternative HS — 200/Alt
1500 E Francisquito Ave 91791 — 626-931-1810
Armando Marentes, prin. — Fax 931-1819
Edgewood HS — 400/9-12
1301 Trojan Way 91790 — 626-939-4900
Veronica Maddox, prin. — Fax 939-0800
Edgewood MS — 600/6-8
1625 W Durness St 91790 — 626-939-4900
Veronica Maddox, prin. — Fax 939-4999
Hollencrest MS — 700/6-8
2101 E Merced Ave 91791 — 626-931-1760
Hector Galicia, prin. — Fax 931-1762
Walnut Grove IS — 500/7-8
614 W Vine Ave 91790 — 626-919-7018
Rich Nambu, prin. — Fax 919-7207
West Covina HS — 2,700/9-12
1609 E Cameron Ave 91791 — 626-859-2900
Marc Trovatore, prin. — Fax 859-3950

---

American Beauty College — Post-Sec.
646 S Sunset Ave 91790
Marinello School of Beauty — Post-Sec.
118 Plaza Dr 91790 — 626-962-1021
North-West College — Post-Sec.
2121 W Garvey Ave N 91790 — 626-960-5046
South Hills Academy — 300/PK-10
1600 E Francisquito Ave 91791 — 626-919-2000
Nancy Jepsen, prin. — Fax 918-7730

**West Hills, Los Angeles**

Chaminade College Prep HS 1,300/9-12
7500 Chaminade Ave 91304 818-347-8300
Br. Stephen Lepire, prin. Fax 348-8374
de Toledo HS 400/9-12
22622 Vanowen St 91307 818-348-0048
Dr. Bruce Powell, head sch Fax 348-0092
West Valley Christian S 200/PK-12
22450 Sherman Way 91307 818-884-4710
Derek Swales, admin. Fax 884-4749

**West Hollywood, Los Angeles, Pop. 33,330**

Cedars-Sinai Graduate Program Post-Sec.
8700 Beverly Blvd Atrium 90048 310-423-8294
Pacific Hills S 200/6-12
8628 Holloway Dr 90069 310-276-3068
Ann Wagner, dir. Fax 657-3831
Touro College Los Angeles Post-Sec.
1317 N Crescent Hts Blvd 90046 323-822-9700

**Westlake Village, Los Angeles, Pop. 8,064**
Conejo Valley USD
Supt. — See Thousand Oaks
Westlake HS 2,400/9-12
100 N Lakeview Canyon Rd 91362 805-497-6711
Jason Branham, prin. Fax 497-2606

Malibu Cove Private S 100/K-12
860 Hampshire Rd 91361 805-267-4818
Joanne Alfonso, admin.
Oaks Christian S 1,400/5-12
31749 La Tienda Rd 91362 818-575-9900
Dr. Scott Lisea, head sch Fax 575-9951

**Westminster, Orange, Pop. 87,394**
Garden Grove USD
Supt. — See Garden Grove
La Quinta HS 2,200/9-12
10372 McFadden Ave 92683 714-663-6315
Denise Halstead, prin. Fax 775-7307
McGarvin IS 800/7-8
9802 Bishop Pl 92683 714-663-6218
Margaret Feliciani, prin. Fax 663-6163

Huntington Beach UNHSD
Supt. — See Huntington Beach
Westminster HS 2,700/9-12
14325 Goldenwest St 92683 714-893-1381
Joseph Fraser, prin. Fax 898-4721

Westminster SD 9,600/PK-8
14121 Cedarwood St 92683 714-894-7311
Dr. Marian Phelps, supt. Fax 899-2781
www.wsdk8.us
Johnson MS 800/6-8
13603 Edwards St 92683 714-894-7244
Daniel Owens, prin. Fax 379-0784
Warner MS 1,000/6-8
14171 Newland St 92683 714-894-7281
Amy Kwon, prin. Fax 895-2378
Other Schools – See Huntington Beach

Asian American Intl Beauty College Post-Sec.
7871 Westminster Blvd 92683 714-891-0508

**West Sacramento, Yolo, Pop. 45,910**
Washington USD 7,400/PK-12
930 Westacre Rd 95691 916-375-7600
Linda Luna Ed.D., supt. Fax 375-7619
www.wusd.k12.ca.us
River City HS 2,000/9-12
1 Raider Ln 95691 916-375-7800
Stan Mojsich, prin. Fax 375-7809
West Sacramento S for Independent Study 50/Alt
1200 Anna St 95605 916-375-7650
Alejandro Ramos, dir. Fax 375-7771
Yolo HS 100/Alt
919 Westacre Rd 95691 916-375-7740
Alejandro Ramos, prin. Fax 375-0928
Washington Adult S Adult
919 Westacre Rd 95691 916-375-7740
Alejandro Ramos, prin. Fax 375-7744

WyoTech Post-Sec.
980 Riverside Pkwy 95605 916-376-8888

**Westwood, Lassen, Pop. 1,610**
Westwood USD 400/K-12
PO Box 1225 96137 530-256-2311
Randy Bobby, supt. Fax 256-3539
www.westwoodusd.org/
Westwood HS 100/8-12
PO Box 1510 96137 530-256-3235
Marci Johnson, prin. Fax 256-3693

**Wheatland, Yuba, Pop. 3,292**
Wheatland SD 800/PK-8
111 Main St 95692 530-633-3130
Craig Guensler, supt. Fax 633-4807
www.wheatlandsd.com/
Bear River S 300/4-8
100 Wheatland Park Dr 95692 530-633-3135
Angela Gouker, prin. Fax 633-3142

Wheatland UNHSD 700/9-12
1010 Wheatland Rd 95692 530-633-3100
Vic Ramos Ed.D., supt. Fax 633-3109
www.wheatlandhigh.org
Wheatland Union HS 700/9-12
1010 Wheatland Rd 95692 530-633-3100
Vic Ramos Ed.D., prin. Fax 633-3109

**Whitethorn, Humboldt**
Leggett Valley USD
Supt. — See Leggett
Whale Gulch HS 50/9-12
76811 Usal Rd 95589 707-925-6285
Anthony Loumena, prin.

**Whittier, Los Angeles, Pop. 84,209**
East Whittier City ESD 9,000/PK-8
14535 Whittier Blvd 90605 562-907-5959
Mary Branca, supt. Fax 696-9256
www.ewcsd.org/
East Whittier MS 1,200/6-8
14421 Whittier Blvd 90605 562-789-7220
Gabriela Aldana, prin. Fax 945-3542
Granada MS 1,100/6-8
15337 Lemon Dr 90604 562-464-2330
Justin Mayernik, prin. Fax 943-5413
Hillview MS 900/6-8
10931 Stamy Rd 90604 562-789-2000
Wendy Davio, prin. Fax 946-3066

Lowell JSD 3,200/PK-8
11019 Valley Home Ave 90603 562-943-0211
Dr. Bonnie Bell, supt. Fax 947-7874
www.ljsd.org
Rancho-Starbuck IS 700/7-8
16430 Woodbrier Dr 90604 562-902-4261
Linda Takacs, prin. Fax 947-9911

Norwalk-La Mirada USD
Supt. — See Norwalk
El Camino HS 400/Alt
14625 Keese Dr 90604 562-868-0431
Bill Seals, prin. Fax 944-1843

Regional Occupational Center & Program
Supt. — None
Tri-Cities ROP Vo/Tech
10800 Ben Avon St 90606 562-698-9571
Maura Murabito, supt. Fax 696-5352

South Whittier ESD 3,500/K-8
11200 Telechron Ave 90605 562-944-6231
Gail Baxter, supt. Fax 946-4301
www.swhittier.k12.ca.us
Graves MS 700/7-8
13243 Los Nietos Rd 90605 562-944-0135
Dr. Matthew Fraijo, prin. Fax 944-9433

Whittier City ESD 6,400/K-8
7211 Whittier Ave 90602 562-789-3075
Dr. Ron Carruth, supt. Fax 698-6534
www.whittiercity.net
Dexter MS 1,200/6-8
11532 Floral Dr 90601 562-789-3090
Robert Allard Ed.D., prin. Fax 789-3095
Edwards MS 900/6-8
6812 Norwalk Blvd 90606 562-789-3120
Andrew Alvidrez, prin. Fax 789-3133

Whittier UNHSD 13,400/9-12
9401 Painter Ave 90605 562-698-8121
Sandra Thorstenson, supt. Fax 693-0221
www.wuhsd.org
California HS 3,100/9-12
9800 Mills Ave 90604 562-698-8121
Bill Schloss, prin. Fax 946-6094
Frontier HS 600/Alt
9401 Painter Ave 90605 562-698-8121
Margie Moriarty, prin. Fax 945-7451
La Serna HS 2,700/9-12
15301 Youngwood Dr 90605 562-698-8121
Ann Fitzgerald, prin. Fax 698-6918
Pioneer HS 1,400/9-12
10800 Ben Avon St 90606 562-698-8121
Monica Oviedo, prin. Fax 692-9194
Sierra Vista Alternative HS 400/Alt
9401 Painter Ave 90605 562-698-8121
Nicki Buchholz, dir. Fax 698-0004
Whittier HS 2,400/9-12
12417 Philadelphia St 90601 562-698-8121
Lori Eshilian, prin. Fax 698-8925
Adult Education Center Adult
9401 Painter Ave 90605 562-698-8121
Debbie Roberts, dir. Fax 693-5354
Other Schools – See Santa Fe Springs

Marinello School of Beauty Post-Sec.
6538 Greenleaf Ave 90601 562-698-0068
Remnant Christian S 50/9-12
7346 Painter Ave 90602 562-464-2554
James Turnbough, admin. Fax 464-2556
Rio Hondo College Post-Sec.
3600 Workman Mill Rd 90601 562-692-0921
Southern CA University of Health Science Post-Sec.
16200 Amber Valley Dr 90604 562-947-8755
Whittier Christian JHS 100/7-8
6548 Newlin Ave 90601 562-698-0527
Mike Ely, prin. Fax 698-2859
Whittier College Post-Sec.
PO Box 634 90608 562-907-4200

**Wildomar, Riverside, Pop. 31,160**
Lake Elsinore USD
Supt. — See Lake Elsinore
Brown MS 1,000/6-8
21861 Grand Ave 92595 951-253-7430
Karen Gaither, prin. Fax 253-7437
Elsinore HS 2,300/9-12
21800 Canyon Dr 92595 951-253-7200
Jon Hurst Ed.D., prin. Fax 253-7209

California Lutheran HS 100/9-12
PO Box 1570 92595 951-678-7000
Andrew Aguilar, supt. Fax 678-0172
Cornerstone Christian S 200/PK-12
34570 Monte Vista Dr 92595 951-674-9381
Sharon Privett, head sch Fax 674-8462
Faith Baptist Academy 200/K-12
PO Box 1030 92595 951-245-8748
Greg Beil, admin.

**Williams, Colusa, Pop. 5,073**
Williams USD 1,100/PK-12
PO Box 7 95987 530-473-2550
Jennifer Foglesong, supt. Fax 473-5894
www.williamsusd.net
Mid Valley HS 50/Alt
PO Box 7 95987 530-473-5369
Nicholas Richter, prin. Fax 473-5540
Williams JSHS 400/7-12
PO Box 7 95987 530-473-5369
Dr. Nicholas Richter, prin. Fax 473-5540

**Willits, Mendocino, Pop. 4,738**
Willits USD 1,800/K-12
1277 Blosser Ln 95490 707-459-5314
Patricia Johnson, supt. Fax 459-7862
www.willitsunified.com
Baechtel Grove MS 300/6-8
1150 Magnolia St 95490 707-459-2417
Maria Mungia, prin. Fax 459-7881
New Horizons S 50/Alt
120 N Main St 95490 707-459-4801
Robert Chavez, prin. Fax 459-6580
Sanhedrin Continuation HS 50/Alt
120 N Main St 95490 707-459-4801
Robert Chavez, prin. Fax 459-6580
Willits HS 500/9-12
299 N Main St 95490 707-459-7700
Robert Chavez, prin. Fax 459-7741

**Willows, Glenn, Pop. 6,043**
Glenn County Office of Education 200/
311 S Villa Ave 95988 530-934-6575
Tracey Quarne, supt. Fax 934-6576
www.glenncoe.org
Glenn Adult Program Adult
451 S Villa Ave 95988 530-934-6320
Jhan Dunn, dir. Fax 934-6325

Regional Occupational Center & Program
Supt. — None
Glenn County ROP Vo/Tech
311 S Villa Ave 95988 530-934-6575
John Dunn, dir. Fax 934-6576

Willows USD 1,400/K-12
823 W Laurel St 95988 530-934-6600
Dr. Mort Geivett, supt. Fax 934-6609
www.willowsunified.org
Willows Community HS 50/Alt
823 W Laurel St 95988 530-934-6605
Dr. Mort Geivett, prin. Fax 934-6609
Willows HS 500/9-12
203 N Murdock Ave 95988 530-934-6611
Shane Humphreys, prin. Fax 934-6619
Willows IS 300/6-8
1145 W Cedar St 95988 530-934-6633
Steve Sailsbery, prin. Fax 934-6697

**Wilmington, See Los Angeles**
Los Angeles USD
Supt. — See Los Angeles
Avalon Continuation HS 100/Alt
1425 N Avalon Blvd 90744 310-549-2112
David Bonneau, prin. Fax 549-3287
Banning Academies Creative Science 9-12
1527 Lakme Ave 90744 310-847-3789
Paul Valanis, prin. Fax 830-5515
Banning HS 3,100/9-12
1527 Lakme Ave 90744 310-847-3700
Rudy Mendoza, prin. Fax 830-5515
Harbor Teacher Preparation Academy 400/Alt
1111 Figueroa Pl 90744 310-834-3932
Jan Murata, admin. Fax 834-4194
Wilmington MS 1,900/6-8
1700 Gulf Ave 90744 310-847-1500
Myrna Brutti, prin. Fax 549-5307

Los Angeles Harbor College Post-Sec.
1111 Figueroa Pl 90744 310-233-4000
Pacific Harbor Christian S 200/PK-12
1530 N Wilmington Blvd 90744 310-835-5665
Amie Gray, prin. Fax 835-6316

**Wilton, Sacramento, Pop. 5,148**

Wilton Christian S 100/PK-12
9697 Dillard Rd 95693 916-687-7693
Rev. Clint Jeffcott, admin. Fax 687-6587

**Windsor, Sonoma, Pop. 26,016**
Windsor USD 5,300/PK-12
9291 Old Redwood Hwy 95492 707-837-7700
Steve Jorgensen, supt. Fax 838-4031
www.wusd.org
Windsor HS 1,700/9-12
8695 Windsor Rd 95492 707-837-7767
Marc Elin, prin. Fax 837-7773
Windsor MS 900/6-8
9500 Brooks Rd S 95492 707-837-7737
Shannyn Vehmeyer, prin. Fax 837-7743
Windsor Oaks Academy 100/Alt
8681 Windsor Rd 95492 707-837-7771
Marc Elin, prin. Fax 837-7770

**Winterhaven, Imperial, Pop. 381**
San Pasqual Valley USD 800/K-12
676 Base Line Rd 92283 760-572-0222
Dr. David Bealer, supt. Fax 572-0711
www.spvusd.org/
Manes HS 50/Alt
676 Base Line Rd 92283 760-572-0095
Paul Keegan, prin. Fax 572-0829
San Pasqual Valley HS 100/9-12
676 Base Line Rd 92283 760-572-0222
Paul Keegan, prin. Fax 572-0881
San Pasqual Valley MS 200/6-8
676 Base Line Rd 92283 760-572-0222
Vicki Gill, prin. Fax 572-0829

**Winters, Yolo, Pop. 6,490**
Winters JUSD 1,600/K-12
909 W Grant Ave 95694 530-795-6100
Dr. Todd Cutler, supt. Fax 795-6114
www.wintersjusd.org
Winters HS 500/9-12
101 Grant Ave 95694 530-795-6140
Dr. Paul Fawcett, prin. Fax 795-6147
Winters MS 300/6-8
425 Anderson Ave 95694 530-795-6130
John Barsotti, prin. Fax 795-6137
Wolfskill Continuation HS 100/Alt
200 Baker St 95694 530-795-6154
Matt Moran, lead tchr. Fax 795-6162

**Winton, Merced, Pop. 10,450**
Merced River UNESD 200/PK-8
4402 Oakdale Rd 95388 209-358-5679
Richard Lopez, supt. Fax 358-2855
www.mrusd.us
Washington MS 100/4-8
4402 Oakdale Rd 95388 209-358-5679
Richard Lopez, supt. Fax 358-2855

Winton SD 1,800/PK-8
PO Box 8 95388 209-357-6175
Randall Heller, supt. Fax 357-1994
www.winton.k12.ca.us
Winton MS 600/6-8
PO Box 1299 95388 209-357-6189
Kristie Warner, prin. Fax 358-5889

**Woodlake, Tulare, Pop. 7,217**
Woodlake USD 2,300/K-12
300 W Whitney Ave 93286 559-564-8081
Drew Sorensen, supt. Fax 564-3831
www.w-usd.org
Bravo Lake HS 50/Alt
450 W Sequoia Ave 93286 559-564-8716
Tony Casares, prin. Fax 564-2695
Woodlake Community Day S 50/Alt
36220 Millwood Dr 93286 559-564-8716
Tony Casares, dir. Fax 564-2695
Woodlake Union HS 800/9-12
400 W Whitney Ave 93286 559-564-3307
Ricardo Rodriguez, admin. Fax 564-3320
Woodlake Valley MS 500/6-8
497 N Palm St 93286 559-564-8061
Antonio Rivera, prin. Fax 564-0702

**Woodland, Yolo, Pop. 54,082**
Regional Occupational Center & Program
Supt. — None
Yolo County ROP Vo/Tech
1280 Santa Anita Ct Ste 100 95776 530-668-3770
Ronda Adams, coord. Fax 668-3850

Woodland JUSD 10,300/K-12
435 6th St 95695 530-662-0201
Dr. Maria Armstrong, supt. Fax 662-6956
www.wjusd.org
Douglass MS 900/7-8
525 Granada Dr 95695 530-666-2191
Derek Cooper, prin. Fax 668-9217
Lee MS 600/7-8
520 West St 95695 530-662-0251
Armando Olvera, prin. Fax 662-9423
Pioneer HS 1,600/9-12
1400 Pioneer Ave 95776 530-406-1148
Sandra Reese, prin. Fax 662-3661
Woodland HS 1,400/9-12
21 N West St 95695 530-662-4678
Karrie Sequeira, prin. Fax 662-7464
Woodland Adult Education Adult
575 Hays St 95695 530-662-0798
Susan Moylan, prin. Fax 662-8039
Other Schools – See Yolo

Yolo County Office of Education 300/
1280 Santa Anita Ct Ste 100 95776 530-668-6700
Jesse Ortiz, supt. Fax 668-3848
www.ycoe.org
Chavez Community S 50/Alt
255 W Beamer St 95695 530-668-3090
Angelina Arias, dir. Fax 662-6873

---

Cambridge Junior College Post-Sec.
501 Main St 95695 855-564-2293
Woodland Christian HS 200/6-12
1787 Matmor Rd 95776 530-406-8800
Justin Smith, admin. Fax 406-0900
Woodland Community College Post-Sec.
2300 E Gibson Rd 95776 530-661-5700

**Woodland Hills, See Los Angeles**
Los Angeles USD
Supt. — See Los Angeles
Thoreau Continuation HS 100/Alt
5429 Quakertown Ave 91364 818-340-4395
Douglas Franklin, prin. Fax 347-4235
Woodland Hills Academy 1,300/6-8
20800 Burbank Blvd 91367 818-226-2900
Ted Yamane, prin. Fax 716-0649
West Valley Occupational Center Adult
6200 Winnetka Ave 91367 818-346-3540
Candace Lee, prin. Fax 346-3858

---

Los Angeles Pierce College Post-Sec.
6201 Winnetka Ave 91371 818-347-0551
Louisville HS 400/9-12
22300 Mulholland Dr 91364 818-346-8812
Myra McPartland, pres. Fax 346-9483

**Woodside, San Mateo, Pop. 5,153**
Sequoia UNHSD
Supt. — See Redwood City
Woodside HS 1,800/9-12
199 Churchill Ave 94062 650-367-9750
Diane Burbank, prin. Fax 367-7263

**Yermo, San Bernardino**
Silver Valley USD 2,500/PK-12
PO Box 847 92398 760-254-2916
Jill Kemock, supt. Fax 254-2091
www.svusdk12.net
Silver Valley HS 500/9-12
PO Box 847 92398 760-254-2963
Marc Lacey, prin. Fax 254-3043
Other Schools – See Daggett, Fort Irwin

**Yolo, Yolo, Pop. 447**
Woodland JUSD
Supt. — See Woodland
Cache Creek HS 200/Alt
PO Box 298 95697 530-662-4331
William Jarrel, prin. Fax 666-9082

**Yorba Linda, Orange, Pop. 62,269**
Placentia-Yorba Linda USD
Supt. — See Placentia
La Entrada HS 100/Alt
4175 Fairmont Blvd 92886 714-779-4170
Carrie Bisgard, prin. Fax 779-6825
Yorba Linda HS 1,800/9-12
19900 Bastanchury Rd 92886 714-986-7500
Dave Flynn, prin. Fax 986-7501
Yorba Linda MS 900/6-8
4777 Casa Loma Ave 92886 714-986-7080
Cameron Malotte, prin. Fax 996-2752
Yorba MS 800/7-8
5350 Fairmont Blvd 92886 714-986-7400
Ken Valburg, prin. Fax 970-1647

---

Friends Christian MS 400/5-8
4231 Rose Dr 92886 714-524-5240
Jim Lugenbuehl, prin. Fax 524-5784

**Yosemite National Park, Mariposa**
Mariposa County USD
Supt. — See Mariposa
Yosemite Park HS 50/9-12
9670 Rancheria Flat Rd 95389 209-372-2382
Sean Jacobs, lead tchr. Fax 379-9138

**Yreka, Siskiyou, Pop. 7,387**
Regional Occupational Center & Program
Supt. — None
Siskiyou County ROP Vo/Tech
431 Knapp St 96097 530-842-6155
Kim Greene, dir. Fax 842-1759

Yreka UNHSD 700/9-12
400 Preece Way 96097 530-842-2521
Mark Greenfield, supt. Fax 842-1759
www.yuhsd.net
Discovery HS 50/9-12
400 Preece Way 96097 530-842-1659
Randy Baker, prin. Fax 841-1057
Yreka HS 700/9-12
400 Preece Way 96097 530-842-6151
Marie Caldwell, prin. Fax 841-0740
Yreka Union Community Day S Alt
400 Preece Way 96097 530-842-1659
Randy Baker, prin.
Yreka Union HS Adult Education Adult
400 Preece Way 96097 530-842-7829
Randy Baker, dir. Fax 842-1759

Yreka UNSD 800/K-8
309 Jackson St 96097 530-842-1168
Dave Parsons, supt. Fax 842-4576
www.yrekausd.net
Jackson Street ES 400/4-8
405 Jackson St 96097 530-842-3561
Chris Harris, prin. Fax 842-1716

**Yuba City, Sutter, Pop. 62,225**
Regional Occupational Center & Program
Supt. — None
Tri-County ROP Vo/Tech
970 Klamath Ln 95993 530-822-2952
Randy Page, dir. Fax 822-3003

Sutter County Office of Education 400/
970 Klamath Ln 95993 530-822-2900
Bill Cornelius, supt. Fax 671-3422
www.sutter.k12.ca.us
Feather River Academy 100/Alt
1895 Lassen Blvd 95993 530-822-2400
Gayelynn Gerhart, prin. Fax 822-3267

Yuba City USD 13,200/PK-12
750 N Palora Ave 95991 530-822-5200
Nancy Aaberg, supt. Fax 671-2454
www.ycusd.org
Gray Avenue MS 700/6-8
808 Gray Ave 95991 530-822-5240
Brian Gault, prin. Fax 822-5057
Powell Continuation HS 200/Alt
1875 Clark Ave 95991 530-822-5210
Jen Cates, prin. Fax 822-5053
River Valley HS 1,700/9-12
801 El Margarita Rd 95993 530-822-2500
Tom Reusser, prin. Fax 822-2589
Yuba City HS 1,800/9-12
850 B St 95991 530-674-4900
Martin Ramirez, prin. Fax 671-7814
Yuba City Unified Alternative S 100/Alt
984 B St 95991 530-822-5244
Bruce Morton, prin. Fax 822-5096

---

Cambridge Junior College Post-Sec.
990 Klamath Ln Ste A 95993 530-674-9199
Faith Christian JSHS 200/7-12
PO Box 1690 95992 530-674-5474
Steve Finlay, prin. Fax 674-0194

**Yucaipa, San Bernardino, Pop. 50,145**
Yucaipa-Calimesa JUSD 9,200/K-12
12797 3rd St 92399 909-797-0174
Cali Binks, supt. Fax 797-5751
www.yucaipaschools.com
Green Valley Continuation HS 100/Alt
35948 Susan St 92399 909-790-8580
Cara Prentiss, prin. Fax 790-8584
Green Valley Independent Study 100/Alt
35948 Susan St 92399 909-790-8580
Cara Prentiss, prin.
Oak View HS & Education Center 100/Alt
12358 6th St 92399 909-797-7931
Sam Spencer, prin. Fax 797-7962
Park View MS 700/7-8
34875 Tahoe Dr 92399 909-790-3285
Frank Tucci, prin. Fax 790-3295
Yucaipa HS 2,800/9-12
33000 Yucaipa Blvd 92399 909-797-0106
Shad Kirkland, prin. Fax 790-3200
Yucaipa Adult S Adult
35948 Susan St 92399 909-797-0121
Cara Prentiss, prin. Fax 790-6115
Other Schools – See Calimesa

---

Crafton Hills College Post-Sec.
11711 Sand Canyon Rd 92399 909-794-2161

**Yucca Valley, San Bernardino, Pop. 20,139**
Morongo USD
Supt. — See Twentynine Palms
Black Rock HS 100/Alt
59273 Sunnyslope Dr 92284 760-369-6310
Vonda Viland, prin. Fax 365-3366
La Contenta MS 700/7-8
7050 La Contenta Rd 92284 760-228-1802
Garrett Gruwell, prin. Fax 369-6324
Yucca Valley HS 1,500/9-12
7600 Sage Ave 92284 760-365-3391
Carl Phillips, prin. Fax 365-1845

---

Joshua Springs Christian S 200/PK-12
57373 Joshua Ln 92284 760-365-3599
Fern Ontiveros, admin. Fax 369-0315

# COLORADO

## COLORADO DEPARTMENT OF EDUCATION
**201 E Colfax Ave, Denver 80203-1704**
**Telephone 303-866-6646**
**Fax 303-830-0793**
**Website http://www.cde.state.co.us**

Commissioner of Education Robert Hammond

## COLORADO BOARD OF EDUCATION
**201 E Colfax Ave, Denver 80203-1704**

Chairperson Bob Schaffer

## BOARDS OF COOPERATIVE EDUCATIONAL SERVICES (BOCES)

Adams County BOCES
Eric Wiant, dir. 303-286-7294
1400 W 122nd Ave Ste 110 Fax 286-9079
Denver 80234
www.aboces.org

Centennial BOCES
Dr. Randy Zila, dir. 970-352-7404
2020 Clubhouse Dr, Greeley 80634 Fax 352-7350
www.cboces.org

Colorado Digital BOCES
Kindra Whitmyre, dir., 4035 Tutt Blvd 719-418-5276
Colorado Springs 80922
www.cdboces.org/

East Central BOCES
Don Anderson, dir. 719-775-2342
PO Box 910, Limon 80828 Fax 775-9714
www.ecboces.org

Expeditionary BOCES
Chad Burns, dir. 303-759-2076
1700 S Holly St, Denver 80222 Fax 757-7442
www.rmsel.org/

Front Range BOCES
Hi Howard, dir. 303-561-5096
6500 Arapahoe Rd, Boulder 80303 Fax 375-5813
www.frboces.org

Grand Valley BOCES
Bridgitte Sunderman, dir. 970-255-2700
2508 Blichman Ave Fax 255-2626
Grand Junction 81505

Mountain BOCES
Troy Lange, dir. 719-486-2603
1713 Mount Lincoln Dr W Fax 486-2109
Leadville 80461
www.mtnboces.org/

Mount Evans BOCES
Terri Jones, dir. 303-567-4467
PO Box 3399, Idaho Springs 80452 Fax 567-2208
mtevansboces.com

Northeast Colorado BOCES
Tim Sanger, dir. 970-774-6152
PO Box 98, Haxtun 80731 Fax 774-6157
www.neboces.org

Northwest Colorado BOCES
Paul McCarty, dir., PO Box 773390 970-879-0391
Steamboat Springs 80477 Fax 879-0442
www.nwboces.org/

Pikes Peak BOCES
Deborah Montgomery, dir. 719-570-7474
2883 S Circle Dr Fax 380-9685
Colorado Springs 80906
www.ppboces.org

Rio Blanco BOCES
Teresa Schott, dir. 970-675-2064
402 W Main St Ste 219 Fax 675-5738
Rangely 81648
www.rioblancoboces.org/

San Juan BOCES
Mary Rubadeau, dir. 970-247-3261
201 E 12th St, Durango 81301 Fax 247-8333
www.sjboces.org

San Luis Valley BOCES
Nita McAuliffe, dir. 719-589-5851
2261 Enterprise Dr, Alamosa 81101 Fax 589-5007
www.slvbocs.org

Santa Fe Trail BOCES
Sandy Malouff, dir. 719-383-2623
PO Box 980, La Junta 81050 Fax 383-2627

South Central BOCES
Kevin Schott, dir. 719-647-0023
323 S Purcell Blvd, Pueblo 81007 Fax 647-0136
www.sc-boces.org/

Southeastern BOCES
Loraine Saffer, dir. 719-336-9046
PO Box 1137, Lamar 81052 Fax 336-9679
www.seboces.org

Uncompahgre BOCS
Tammy Johnson, dir. 970-626-2977
PO Box 728, Ridgway 81432 Fax 626-2978
www.unbocs.org/

Ute Pass BOCES
Marcy Palmer, dir., 405 El Monte Pl 719-685-2640
Manitou Springs 80829 Fax 685-4536
www.upboces.org/

## PUBLIC, PRIVATE AND CATHOLIC SECONDARY SCHOOLS

**Aguilar, Las Animas, Pop. 527**
Aguilar RSD 6 100/PK-12
PO Box 567 81020 719-941-4188
Dr. Stacy Houser, supt. Fax 941-4279
www.aguilarschools.org
Aguilar JSHS 50/7-12
PO Box 567 81020 719-941-4188
Dr. Stacy Houser, supt. Fax 941-4279

**Akron, Washington, Pop. 1,685**
Akron SD R-1 300/PK-12
PO Box 429 80720 970-345-2053
Brian Christensen, supt. Fax 345-6508
akronrams.schoolwires.net
Akron JSHS 100/7-12
600 Elm Ave 80720 970-345-2268
Ed Lundquist, prin. Fax 345-6508

**Alamosa, Alamosa, Pop. 8,620**
Alamosa SD RE-11J 1,000/K-12
209 Victoria Ave 81101 719-587-1600
Rob Alejo, supt. Fax 587-1712
www.alamosa.k12.co.us/
Alamosa HS 500/9-12
805 Craft Dr 81101 719-587-6000
Andy Lavier, prin. Fax 587-6069
Alamosa Ombudsman S of Excellence 100/Alt
2431 Main St 81101 719-937-2112
Ortega MS 500/6-8
401 Victoria Ave 81101 719-587-1650
Greg Koers, prin. Fax 587-1721

---

Adams State University Post-Sec.
208 Edgemont Blvd 81101 719-587-7011

**Anton, Washington, Pop. 40**
Arickaree SD R-2 100/PK-12
12155 County Road NN 80801 970-383-2202
S. Shane Walkinshaw, supt. Fax 383-2205
www.arickaree.org
Arickaree JSHS 50/7-12
12155 County Road NN 80801 970-383-2202
S. Shane Walkinshaw, supt. Fax 383-2205

**Antonito, Conejos, Pop. 772**
South Conejos SD RE-10 200/K-12
PO Box 398 81120 719-376-5512
Carla Archuleta, supt. Fax 376-5425
sc-sd.org
Antonito HS 100/9-12
PO Box 398 81120 719-376-5468
Angela Montoya, prin. Fax 376-5425
Antonito MS 50/7-8
PO Box 398 81120 719-376-5407
Angela Montoya, prin. Fax 376-5425

**Arvada, Jefferson, Pop. 104,595**
Jefferson County SD R-1
Supt. — See Golden
Arvada HS 1,000/9-12
7951 W 65th Ave 80004 303-982-0162
Georgina Yacovetta-Rivas, prin. Fax 982-0163
Arvada West HS 1,700/9-12
11595 Allendale Dr 80004 303-982-1303
Robert Bishop, prin. Fax 982-1304
Drake MS 700/7-8
12550 W 52nd Ave 80002 303-982-1510
Rod Pugnetti, prin. Fax 982-1511
Moore MS 500/7-8
8455 W 88th Ave 80005 303-982-0400
Dr. Michelle McAteer, prin. Fax 982-0462
North Arvada MS 400/7-8
7285 Pierce St 80003 303-982-0528
Sohne Van Selus, prin. Fax 982-0529
Oberon MS 500/7-8
7300 Quail St 80005 303-982-2020
Tara Pena, prin. Fax 982-2021
Pomona HS 1,500/9-12
8101 W Pomona Dr 80005 303-982-0710
Andy Geise, prin. Fax 982-0709
Ralston Valley HS 1,700/9-12
13355 W 80th Ave 80005 303-982-5600
Gordon Goodrich, prin. Fax 982-5601
Warren Tech North Vo/Tech
11325 Allendale Dr 80004 303-982-9360
Fax 982-9361

---

Faith Christian Academy 300/6-8
6250 Wright St 80004 303-424-7310
Terrie Simmons, prin. Fax 403-2720
Faith Christian Academy 400/9-12
4890 Carr St 80002 303-424-7310
Andrew Hasz, prin. Fax 403-2730

**Aspen, Pitkin, Pop. 6,573**
Aspen SD RE-1 1,700/PK-12
235 High School Rd 81611 970-925-3760
Dr. John Maloy, supt. Fax 925-5721
www.aspenk12.net/
Aspen HS 600/9-12
235 High School Rd 81611 970-925-3760
Tharyn Mulberry, prin. Fax 925-1205
Aspen MS 500/5-8
235 High School Rd 81611 970-925-3760
Craig Rogers, prin. Fax 925-8374

**Ault, Weld, Pop. 1,488**
Ault-Highland SD RE-9 800/K-12
PO Box 68 80610 970-834-1345
Robert Ring, supt. Fax 834-1347
www.weldre9.k12.co.us
Highland HS 200/9-12
PO Box 68 80610 970-834-2816
Randy Yaussi, prin. Fax 834-2858
Highland MS 200/6-8
PO Box 68 80610 970-834-2829
Clay Naughton, prin. Fax 834-2663

**Aurora, Arapahoe, Pop. 313,203**
Aurora SD 38,100/PK-12
15701 E 1st Ave 80011 303-344-8060
Rico Munn, supt. Fax 326-1280
aurorak12.org
Aurora Central HS 2,200/9-12
11700 E 11th Ave 80010 303-340-1600
Geraldo De La Garza, prin. Fax 326-1270
Aurora Hills MS 900/6-8
1009 S Uvalda St 80012 303-341-7450
Darla Stumpp, prin. Fax 326-1250
Aurora West College Preparatory S 1,000/6-12
10100 E 13th Ave 80010 303-366-2671
Brian Duwe, prin. Fax 326-1260
Columbia MS 800/6-8
17600 E Columbia Ave 80013 303-690-6570
Steve Hamilton, prin. Fax 326-1251
East MS 1,000/6-8
1275 Fraser St 80011 303-340-0660
Biaze Houston, prin. Fax 326-1252
Futures Academy 100/Alt
14707 E 2nd Ave Ste 260 80011 720-949-0253
Joy Smith, prin.
Gateway HS 1,700/9-12
1300 S Sable Blvd 80012 303-755-7160
Dackri Davis, prin. Fax 326-1272

Hinkley HS 2,100/9-12
1250 Chambers Rd 80011 303-340-1500
Matthew Willis, prin. Fax 326-1274
Mrachek MS 900/6-8
1955 S Telluride St 80013 303-750-2836
Michelle Davis, prin. Fax 326-1254
North MS 700/6-8
12095 Montview Blvd 80010 303-364-7411
Courtney Goertz, prin. Fax 326-1256
Options S 1,900/Alt
11351 Montview Blvd 80010 303-340-0666
Joe Burton, prin. Fax 326-1281
Rangeview HS 2,200/9-12
17599 E Iliff Ave 80013 303-695-6848
Ron Fay, prin. Fax 326-1276
Smith HS 300/9-12
400 Airport Blvd 80011 303-364-8715
David Roll, prin. Fax 326-1278
South MS 700/6-8
12310 E Parkview Dr 80011 303-364-7623
Eryn Osterhaus, prin. Fax 326-1258
Vista PEAK Preparatory HS 9-12
24500 E 6th Ave 80018 303-340-0121
Garrett Rosa, prin. Fax 326-1262

Cherry Creek SD 5
Supt. — See Greenwood Village
Cherokee Trail HS 2,500/9-12
25901 E Arapahoe Rd 80016 720-886-1900
Kim Rauh, prin. Fax 886-1989
Falcon Creek MS 1,000/6-8
6100 S Genoa St 80016 720-886-7700
Lisa Ruiz, prin. Fax 886-7788
Fox Ridge MS 900/6-8
26301 E Arapahoe Rd 80016 720-886-4400
Marquetta Thomas, prin. Fax 886-4488
Grandview HS 2,600/9-12
20500 E Arapahoe Rd 80016 720-886-6500
Sarah Grobbel, prin. Fax 886-6698
Horizon Community MS 1,000/6-8
3981 S Reservoir Rd 80013 720-886-6100
Nickie Bell, prin. Fax 886-6253
I Team - Estate Alt
4360 S Pitkin St 80015 720-886-5850
Allison Witkin, prin. Fax 886-5865
I Team - Manor Alt
1820 S Joliet St 80012 720-747-2955
Allison Witkin, prin. Fax 747-2951
I Team - Ranch Alt
7250 S Gartrell Rd 80016 720-886-6880
Allison Witkin, prin. Fax 886-6888
Laredo MS 1,200/6-8
5000 S Laredo St 80015 720-886-5000
Edie Alvarez, prin. Fax 886-5298
Liberty MS 1,100/6-8
21500 E Dry Creek Rd 80016 720-886-2400
Carla Stearns, prin. Fax 886-2688
Overland HS 2,200/9-12
12400 E Jewell Ave 80012 720-747-3700
Leon Lundie, prin. Fax 747-3895
Prairie MS 1,700/6-8
12600 E Jewell Ave 80012 720-747-3000
David Gonzales, prin. Fax 747-3097
Sky Vista MS 800/6-8
4500 S Himalaya St 80015 720-886-4700
Greg Connellan, prin. Fax 886-4788
Smoky Hill HS 2,200/9-12
16100 E Smoky Hill Rd 80015 720-886-5300
Chuck Puga, prin. Fax 886-5408
Thunder Ridge MS 1,200/6-8
5250 S Picadilly St 80015 720-886-1500
Angie Zehner, prin. Fax 886-1582

---

American Sentinel University Post-Sec.
2260 S Xanadu Way Ste 310 80014 303-991-1575
Anthem College Post-Sec.
350 Blackhawk St 80011 720-859-7900
CedarWood Christian Academy 100/K-12
PO Box 111389 80042 303-361-6456
Gene Oborny, admin.
Colorado Technical University Post-Sec.
3151 S Vaughn Way 80014 303-632-2300
Community College of Aurora Post-Sec.
16000 E Centretech Pkwy 80011 303-360-4700
Concorde Career College Post-Sec.
111 Havana St 80010 303-861-1151
Ecotech Institute Post-Sec.
1400 S Abilene St 80012 877-326-5576
Everest College Post-Sec.
14280 E Jewell Ave Ste 100 80012 303-745-6244
ITT Technical Institute Post-Sec.
12500 E Iliff Ave Ste 100 80014 303-695-6317
Pickens Technical Center Post-Sec.
500 Airport Blvd 80011 303-344-4910
Pima Medical Institute Post-Sec.
13750 E Mississippi Ave 80012 303-368-7462
Platt College Post-Sec.
3100 S Parker Rd 80014 303-369-5151
Regis Jesuit HS for Boys 1,600/9-12
6400 S Lewiston Way 80016 303-269-8000
Alan Carruthers, prin. Fax 766-2240
Regis Jesuit HS for Girls 700/9-12
6300 S Lewiston Way 80016 303-269-8100
Gretchen Kessler, prin. Fax 221-4772
Xenon International Post-Sec.
2231 S Peoria St 80014 303-752-1560

**Bailey, Park, Pop. 150**
Platte Canyon SD 1 1,100/PK-12
PO Box 1069 80421 303-838-7666
Dr. Brenda Krage Ed.D., supt. Fax 679-7504
www.plattecanyonschools.org
Fitzsimmons MS 300/6-8
PO Box 1069 80421 303-838-7666
Rim Watson, prin. Fax 679-7506
Platte Canyon HS 300/9-12
PO Box 1069 80421 303-838-7666
Michael Schmidt, prin. Fax 679-7497

**Basalt, Pitkin, Pop. 3,792**
Roaring Fork SD RE-1
Supt. — See Glenwood Springs
Basalt HS 400/9-12
600 Southside Dr 81621 970-384-5959
David Schmid, prin. Fax 384-5955
Basalt MS 400/5-8
51 School St 81621 970-384-5900
Jeremy Voss, prin. Fax 384-5905

**Bayfield, LaPlata, Pop. 2,294**
Bayfield SD 10 JT-R 1,400/PK-12
24 S Clover Ln 81122 970-884-2496
Troy Zabel, supt. Fax 884-4284
www.bayfield.k12.co.us
Bayfield HS 400/9-12
24 S Clover Ln 81122 970-884-9521
Leon Hanhardt, prin. Fax 884-4226
Bayfield MS 300/6-8
24 S Clover Ln 81122 970-884-9592
Tod Lokey, prin. Fax 884-4110

**Bennett, Adams, Pop. 2,268**
Bennett SD 29J 1,000/PK-12
610 7th St 80102 303-644-3234
Dennis Veal, supt. Fax 644-4121
www.bennett29j.k12.co.us
Bennett HS 300/9-12
610 7th St 80102 303-644-3234
Rich Campbell, prin. Fax 644-3894
Bennett MS 200/6-8
455 8th St 80102 303-644-3234
Zachary Stall, admin. Fax 644-4398

**Berthoud, Larimer, Pop. 5,034**
Thompson SD R-2J
Supt. — See Loveland
Berthoud HS 600/9-12
850 Spartan Ave 80513 970-613-7700
Chris Garcia, prin. Fax 613-7728
Turner MS 500/6-8
950 Massachusetts Ave 80513 970-613-7400
Derrick Martin, prin. Fax 613-7420

**Bethune, Kit Carson, Pop. 236**
Bethune SD R-5 100/PK-12
PO Box 127 80805 719-346-7513
Shila Adolf, supt. Fax 346-5048
bethuneschool.com/
Bethune JSHS 100/7-12
PO Box 127 80805 719-343-7513
Shila Adolf, prin. Fax 346-5048

**Black Hawk, Gilpin, Pop. 118**
Gilpin County SD RE-1 400/PK-12
10595 Highway 119 80422 303-582-3444
Dr. David MacKenzie, supt. Fax 582-3346
www.gilpin.k12.co.us
Gilpin County JSHS 200/6-12
10595 Highway 119 80422 303-582-3444
Alexis Donaldson, prin. Fax 582-3346

**Blanca, Costilla, Pop. 380**
Sierra Grande SD R-30 300/K-12
17523 E Highway 160 81123 719-379-3259
Darren Edgar, supt. Fax 379-2572
www.sierragrandeschool.net
Sierra Grande HS 100/9-12
17523 E Highway 160 81123 719-379-3257
Brandon Mizokami, prin. Fax 379-2572
Sierra Grande MS 100/6-8
17523 E Highway 160 81123 719-379-3257
Lauren Sheldrake, prin. Fax 379-2572

**Boulder, Boulder, Pop. 95,063**
Boulder Valley SD RE-2 29,300/PK-12
PO Box 9011 80301 303-447-1010
Bruce Messinger Ph.D., supt. Fax 561-5134
www.bvsd.org
Arapahoe Campus 200/9-12
6600 Arapahoe Rd 80303 720-561-5220
Joan Bludorn, prin. Fax 561-5258
Boulder HS 1,800/9-12
1604 Arapahoe Ave 80302 720-561-2200
James Hill, prin. Fax 561-5317
Casey MS 500/6-8
1301 High St 80304 720-561-2700
Justin McMillan, prin. Fax 561-2701
Centennial MS 600/6-8
2205 Norwood Ave 80304 720-561-5441
Dana Ellis, prin. Fax 561-2090
Fairview HS 2,100/9-12
1515 Greenbriar Blvd 80305 720-561-3100
Don Stensrud, prin. Fax 561-5353
Manhattan S of Arts and Academics 500/6-8
290 Manhattan Dr 80303 720-561-6300
John Riggs, prin. Fax 561-6301
New Vista HS 300/9-12
700 20th St 80302 720-561-8700
Kirk Quitter, prin. Fax 561-8701
Platt MS 500/6-8
6096 Baseline Rd 80303 720-561-5536
Theo Robison, prin. Fax 561-6898
Southern Hills MS 500/6-8
1500 Knox Dr 80305 720-561-3400
Chavonne Gloster, prin. Fax 561-3401
Other Schools – See Broomfield, Lafayette, Louisville, Nederland

---

Naropa University Post-Sec.
2130 Arapahoe Ave 80302 303-444-0202
Rolf Institute of Structural Integration Post-Sec.
5055 Chaparral Ct Ste 103 80301 303-449-5903
September HS 50/9-12
1902 Walnut St 80302 303-443-9933
Shining Mountain Waldorf S 300/PK-12
999 Violet Ave 80304 303-444-7697
Jane Zeender, dir. Fax 444-7701
Southwest Acupuncture College Post-Sec.
6620 Gunpark Dr 80301 303-581-9955
Tara Performing Arts HS 50/9-12
4180 19th St 80304 303-440-4510
University of Colorado Boulder 80309 Post-Sec.
303-492-1411

Watershed S 100/6-12
1661 Alpine Ave 80304 303-440-7520
Greg Bamford, head sch Fax 440-7521

**Branson, Las Animas, Pop. 73**
Branson RSD 82 400/K-12
PO Box 128 81027 719-946-5531
Brad Caldwell, supt. Fax 946-5619
www.bransonschoolonline.com
Branson S 50/K-12
PO Box 128 81027 719-946-5531
Brad Caldwell, prin. Fax 946-5620
Branson S Online 400/Alt
PO Box 128 81027 719-946-5531
Leanna Christians, prin. Fax 946-5619

**Briggsdale, Weld, Pop. 225**
Briggsdale SD RE-10 200/PK-12
PO Box 129 80611 970-656-3417
Rick Mondt, supt. Fax 656-3479
www.briggsdaleschool.org/
Briggsdale JSHS 100/6-12
PO Box 129 80611 970-656-3417
Fax 656-3479

**Brighton, Adams, Pop. 32,801**
Brighton SD 27J 14,900/PK-12
18551 E 160th Ave 80601 303-655-2900
Chris Fiedler Ed.D., supt. Fax 655-2870
www.sd27j.org/
Brighton Heritage Academy 100/Alt
830 E Bridge St 80601 303-655-2850
Kenlyn Newman, prin. Fax 655-2886
Brighton HS 1,700/9-12
270 S 8th Ave 80601 303-655-4200
John Biner, prin. Fax 655-2883
Overland Trail MS 700/6-8
455 N 19th Ave 80601 303-655-4000
Eric Lambright, prin. Fax 655-2880
Vikan MS 600/6-8
879 Jessup St 80601 303-655-4050
Trina Norris-Buck, prin. Fax 655-2881
Other Schools – See Commerce City, Henderson

---

Brighton Adventist Academy 100/K-10
820 S 5th Ave 80601 303-659-1223
Heather Blaire, prin. Fax 558-8774
Elmwood Baptist Academy 100/PK-12
13100 E 144th Ave 80601 303-659-3818

**Broomfield, Boulder, Pop. 54,716**
Adams 12 Five Star SD
Supt. — See Thornton
Legacy HS 2,100/9-12
2701 W 136th Ave, 720-972-6700
James Ellis, prin. Fax 972-6897
Westlake MS 1,000/6-8
2800 W 135th Ave 80020 720-972-5200
Michael MacDonnell, prin. Fax 972-5239

Boulder Valley SD RE-2
Supt. — See Boulder
Broomfield Heights MS 600/6-8
1555 Daphne St 80020 720-561-8400
Chris Meyer, prin. Fax 561-8401
Broomfield HS 1,300/9-12
1 Eagle Way 80020 720-561-8100
Ginger Ramsey, prin. Fax 561-5390

---

Holy Family HS 600/9-12
5195 W 144th Ave, 303-410-1411
Tim Gallic, prin. Fax 466-1935
Redstone College Post-Sec.
10851 W 120th Ave 80021 303-466-1714
Westwood College - Online Post-Sec.
10249 Church Ranch Way 80021 720-887-8888

**Brush, Morgan, Pop. 5,401**
Brush SD RE-2(J) 1,500/PK-12
PO Box 585 80723 970-842-5176
Dr. Bill Wilson, supt. Fax 842-4481
www.brushschools.org
Brush HS 400/9-12
PO Box 585 80723 970-842-5171
Rocky Schneider, prin. Fax 842-2804
Brush MS 300/7-8
PO Box 585 80723 970-842-5035
Connie Dreitz, prin. Fax 842-3009

**Buena Vista, Chaffee, Pop. 2,579**
Buena Vista SD R-31 1,000/PK-12
PO Box 2027 81211 719-395-7000
Sue Holmes, supt. Fax 395-7007
www.bvschools.org
Buena Vista HS 300/9-12
PO Box 2027 81211 719-395-7100
Brian Yates, prin. Fax 395-7106
Chaffee County HS 50/Alt
PO Box 2027 81211 719-395-4064
Mike Post, prin. Fax 395-8267
McGinnis MS 200/6-8
PO Box 2027 81211 719-395-7060
John Emilsson, prin. Fax 395-7090

---

Link S 50/9-12
18885 County Road 367 81211 719-395-6797
Bobby Lewis, prin. Fax 395-6797
Patterson Christian Academy 100/PK-12
PO Box 1243 81211 719-395-6046
Erik Ritschard, admin. Fax 395-2055

**Burlington, Kit Carson, Pop. 4,206**
Burlington SD RE-6J 800/PK-12
PO Box 369 80807 719-346-8737
Tom Satterly, supt. Fax 346-8541
www.burlingtonk12.org/
Burlington HS 200/9-12
380 Mike Lounge Dr 80807 719-346-8455
Michael Clark, prin. Fax 346-5599
Burlington MS 200/5-8
2600 Rose Ave 80807 719-346-5440
Pam Pekarek, prin. Fax 346-7900

**Byers, Arapahoe, Pop. 1,139**
Byers SD 32J 500/PK-12
444 E Front St 80103 303-822-5292
Tom Turrell, supt. Fax 822-9592
www.byers32j.k12.co.us
Byers HS 200/7-12
444 E Front St 80103 303-822-5292
Don Frenzen, prin. Fax 822-8616

**Calhan, El Paso, Pop. 759**
Calhan SD RJ-1 500/PK-12
780 8th St 80808 719-347-2541
Linda Miller, supt. Fax 347-2144
calhanschool.org/
Calhan HS 200/9-12
780 8th St 80808 719-347-2766
David Slothower, prin. Fax 347-2108
Calhan MS 100/6-8
780 8th St 80808 719-347-2766
David Slothower, prin. Fax 347-2108

**Campo, Baca, Pop. 109**
Campo SD RE-6 100/PK-12
PO Box 70 81029 719-787-2226
Nikki Johnson, supt. Fax 787-0140
www.campok12.org
Campo JSHS 50/6-12
PO Box 70 81029 719-787-2226
Kim Jenkins, prin. Fax 787-0140

**Canon City, Fremont, Pop. 16,140**
Canon City SD RE-1 3,600/K-12
101 N 14th St 81212 719-276-5700
Dr. Robin Gooldy, supt. Fax 276-5739
www.canoncityschools.org/
Canon City HS 1,100/9-12
1313 College Ave 81212 719-276-5870
Bret Meuli, prin. Fax 276-5950
Canon City MS 400/6-8
1215 Main St 81212 719-276-5740
Ken Trujillo, prin. Fax 276-5795

**Carbondale, Garfield, Pop. 6,354**
Roaring Fork SD RE-1
Supt. — See Glenwood Springs
Bridges HS 100/Alt
455 S 3rd St 81623 970-384-6160
Lyn Blair, prin. Fax 384-6165
Carbondale MS 300/5-8
180 Snowmass Dr 81623 970-384-5700
Jennifer Lamont, prin. Fax 384-5705
Roaring Fork HS 300/9-12
2270 Highway 133 81623 970-384-5757
Drew Adams, prin. Fax 384-5755

---

Colorado Rocky Mountain S 200/9-12
1493 County Road 106 81623 970-963-2562
Jeff Leahy, head sch Fax 963-9865

**Castle Rock, Douglas, Pop. 47,126**
Douglas County SD RE-1 60,000/PK-12
620 Wilcox St 80104 303-387-0100
Dr. Elizabeth Celania-Fagen, supt. Fax 387-0107
www.dcsdk12.org
Castle Rock MS 800/7-8
2575 Meadows Pkwy, 303-387-1300
LeeAnn Hayen, prin. Fax 387-1301
Castle View HS 1,700/9-12
5254 Meadows Dr, 303-387-9000
James Calhoun, prin. Fax 387-9001
Douglas County HS 1,800/9-12
2842 Front St 80104 303-387-1000
Tony Kappas, prin. Fax 387-1001
Mesa MS 900/7-8
365 N Mitchell St 80104 303-387-4750
Anthony Jackowski, prin. Fax 387-4751
Oakes HS 200/Alt
961 Plum Creek Blvd 80104 303-387-0650
Derek Fleshman, prin. Fax 387-0651
Other Schools – See Highlands Ranch, Littleton, Lonetree, Parker

**Cedaredge, Delta, Pop. 2,222**
Delta County SD 50(J)
Supt. — See Delta
Cedaredge HS 300/9-12
575 SE Deer Creek Dr 81413 970-856-6882
Randy Brown, prin. Fax 856-6616
Cedaredge MS 200/6-8
845 SE Deer Creek Dr 81413 970-856-3118
Delaine Hudson, prin. Fax 856-3235

**Centennial, Arapahoe, Pop. 97,891**
Cherry Creek SD 5
Supt. — See Greenwood Village
Eaglecrest HS 2,300/9-12
5100 S Picadilly St 80015 720-886-1000
Gwen Hansen-Vigil, prin. Fax 886-1029
Endeavor Academy Alt
14076 E Briarwood Ave 80112 720-886-7200
Mark Morgan, prin. Fax 886-7288

Littleton SD
Supt. — See Littleton
Arapahoe HS 2,200/9-12
2201 E Dry Creek Rd 80122 303-347-6000
Natalie Pramenko, prin. Fax 347-6004
Newton MS 700/6-8
4001 E Arapahoe Rd 80122 303-347-7900
James O'Tremba, prin. Fax 347-3945

---

College for Financial Planning Post-Sec.
9000 E Nichols Ave Ste 200 80112 303-220-1200
Jones International University Post-Sec.
9697 E Mineral Ave 80112 303-784-8904

**Center, Saguache, Pop. 2,207**
Center Consolidated SD 26JT 600/PK-12
550 Sylvester Ave 81125 719-754-3442
George Welsh, supt. Fax 754-3952
www.center.k12.co.us
Academic Recovery Center 50/Alt
550 Sylvester Ave 81125 719-251-3334
Joy Werner, dir. Fax 754-3952
Center HS 100/9-12
550 Sylvester Ave 81125 719-754-2232
Kevin Jones, prin. Fax 754-2856
Skoglund MS 100/6-8
550 Sylvester Ave 81125 719-754-2232
Luis Murillo, prin. Fax 754-2856

**Cheraw, Otero, Pop. 245**
Cheraw SD 31 200/PK-12
PO Box 160 81030 719-853-6655
Tonya Rodwell, supt. Fax 853-6322
cheraw.k12.co.us
Cheraw HS 100/9-12
PO Box 160 81030 719-853-6655
Todd Werner, prin. Fax 853-6322
Cheraw MS 100/6-8
PO Box 160 81030 719-853-6655
Todd Werner, prin. Fax 853-6322

**Cheyenne Wells, Cheyenne, Pop. 839**
Cheyenne County SD RE-5 200/PK-12
PO Box 577 80810 719-767-5866
Glen Bradshaw, supt. Fax 767-8773
www.cheyennesd.net/
Cheyenne Wells HS 100/9-12
PO Box 577 80810 719-767-5612
Mike Miller, prin. Fax 767-5749
Cheyenne Wells MS 50/7-8
PO Box 577 80810 719-767-5656
Mike Miller, prin. Fax 767-5136

**Clifton, Mesa, Pop. 19,453**
Mesa County Valley SD 51
Supt. — See Grand Junction
Mt. Garfield MS 600/6-8
3475 Front St 81520 970-254-4720
Hal Templeton, prin. Fax 464-0536

---

Christian Community S 100/PK-12
3240 I70 Frontage Rd Ste B 81520 970-434-0205
Debbie Childs, admin. Fax 434-3847

**Collbran, Mesa, Pop. 699**
Plateau Valley SD 50 500/PK-12
56600 Highway 330 81624 970-487-3547
Gregory Randall, supt. Fax 487-3876
www.pvsd50.org
Grand Mesa HS 100/Alt
56600 Highway 330 81624 970-487-2017
Kristi Mease, prin.
Plateau Valley HS 100/9-12
56600 Highway 330 81624 970-487-3547
Leroy Gutierrez, prin. Fax 487-3876
Plateau Valley MS 100/6-8
56600 Highway 330 81624 970-487-3547
Leroy Gutierrez, prin. Fax 487-3876

**Colorado City, Pueblo, Pop. 2,165**
Pueblo County SD 70
Supt. — See Pueblo
Craver MS 200/6-8
PO Box 19369 81019 719-676-3030
Alexandra Strunk, prin. Fax 676-3511

**Colorado Springs, El Paso, Pop. 400,464**
Academy SD 20 25,600/PK-12
1110 Chapel Hills Dr 80920 719-234-1200
Dr. Mark Hatchell, supt. Fax 234-1299
www.asd20.org/
Aspen Valley HS 100/9-12
1450 Chapel Hills Dr 80920 719-234-6000
George Stone, prin. Fax 234-6099
Challenger MS 700/6-8
10215 Lexington Dr 80920 719-234-3000
Tony Scott, prin. Fax 234-3199
Discovery Canyon Campus 2,300/PK-12
1810 N Gate Blvd 80921 719-234-1800
Jim Bailey, prin. Fax 234-1899
Eagleview MS 900/6-8
1325 Vindicator Dr 80919 719-234-3400
John Jamison, prin. Fax 234-3599
Liberty HS 1,500/9-12
8720 Scarborough Dr 80920 719-234-2200
Alan Thimmig, prin. Fax 234-2399
Mountain Ridge MS 1,100/6-8
9150 Lexington Dr 80920 719-234-3200
Jeff Sterk, prin. Fax 234-3399
Pine Creek HS 1,500/9-12
10750 Thunder Mountain Ave 80908 719-234-2600
Kolette Back, prin. Fax 234-2799
Rampart HS 1,600/9-12
8250 Lexington Dr 80920 719-234-2000
Pete Alvarez, prin. Fax 234-2199
Timberview MS 1,100/6-8
8680 Scarborough Dr 80920 719-234-3600
Brett Smith, prin. Fax 234-3799
Other Schools – See USAF Academy

Cheyenne Mountain SD 12 4,800/PK-12
1775 LaClede St 80905 719-475-6100
Dr. Walter Cooper, supt. Fax 475-6106
www.cmsd.k12.co.us
Cheyenne Mountain HS 1,300/9-12
1200 Cresta Rd 80906 719-475-6110
Don Fortenberry, prin. Fax 475-6116
Cheyenne Mountain JHS 600/7-8
1200 W Cheyenne Rd 80906 719-475-6120
Greg Watkins, prin. Fax 475-6123

Colorado Springs SD 11 27,800/PK-12
1115 N El Paso St 80903 719-520-2000
Dr. Nicholas Gledich, supt. Fax 577-4546
www.d11.org
Bijou S 100/Alt
2115 Afton Way 80909 719-328-7900
Kathryn Presnal, dir. Fax 630-3379
Coronado HS 1,400/9-12
1590 W Fillmore St 80904 719-328-3600
Darin Smith, prin. Fax 328-3601
Digital HS Alt
2115 Afton Way 80909 719-328-3000
John Bailey, prin. Fax 328-3071
Doherty HS 2,200/9-12
4515 Barnes Rd 80917 719-328-6400
Kevin Gardner, prin. Fax 328-6401
Early College HS 9-12
2115 Afton Way 80909 719-328-2000
Aurora Umana-Arko, prin. Fax 328-2029
Galileo S of Math & Science 700/6-8
1600 N Union Blvd 80909 719-328-2200
Richard Law, prin. Fax 448-0498
Holmes MS 700/6-8
2455 Mesa Rd 80904 719-328-3800
Robert Utter, prin. Fax 448-0358
Jenkins MS 900/6-8
6410 Austin Bluffs Pkwy, 719-328-5300
Darren Joiner, prin. Fax 266-5276
Mann MS 500/6-8
1001 E Van Buren St 80907 719-328-2300
Peggy Layh, prin. Fax 488-0354
Mitchell HS 1,000/9-12
1205 Potter Dr 80909 719-328-6600
Scott Noller, prin. Fax 328-6601
North MS 700/6-8
612 E Yampa St 80903 719-328-2400
Bryan Relich, prin. Fax 448-0268
Palmer HS 2,000/9-12
301 N Nevada Ave 80903 719-328-5000
Lara Disney, prin. Fax 328-5001
Russell MS 700/6-8
3825 Montebello Dr W 80918 719-328-5200
Julie Johnson, prin. Fax 531-5520
Sabin MS 800/6-8
3605 N Carefree Cir 80917 719-328-7000
Jared Welch, prin. Fax 573-4960
Springs Community Night S Alt
2115 Afton Way 80909 719-328-6700
Tanya Nash, prin.
Swigert Aerospace Academy 500/6-8
4220 E Pikes Peak Ave 80909 719-328-6900
James Nason, prin. Fax 573-5094
Tesla Educational Opportunity Center 200/Alt
2115 Afton Way 80909 719-520-2701
Greg Wiley, prin. Fax 630-0243
West MS 300/6-8
1920 W Pikes Peak Ave 80904 719-328-3900
Shalah Sims, prin. Fax 448-0141
Adult Education Center Adult
2115 Afton Way 80909 719-328-3000
M. Burkhardt-Shields, prin. Fax 630-2286

Falcon SD 49
Supt. — See Falcon
Horizon MS 600/6-8
1750 Piros Dr 80915 719-495-5210
Dustin Horras, prin. Fax 495-5209
Sand Creek HS 1,200/9-12
7005 N Carefree Cir 80922 719-495-1160
Ron Hamilton, prin. Fax 495-1196
Skyview MS 1,000/6-8
6350 Windom Peak Blvd, 719-495-5566
Catherine Tinucci, prin. Fax 495-5569
Vista Ridge HS 1,100/9-12
6888 Black Forest Rd, 719-494-8800
Bruce Grose, prin. Fax 494-8838

Hanover SD 28 200/PK-12
17050 S Peyton Hwy 80928 719-683-2247
Paul McCarty, supt. Fax 683-2299
www.hanoverhornets.org
Hanover JSHS 100/5-12
17050 S Peyton Hwy 80928 719-683-2247
Danielle Van Esselstine, prin. Fax 683-3805

Harrison SD 2 10,800/PK-12
1060 Harrison Rd 80905 719-579-2000
Andre Spencer Ed.D., supt. Fax 579-2019
www.hsd2.org
Carmel MS 400/6-8
1740 Pepperwood Dr 80910 719-579-3210
Steve Thiessen, prin. Fax 579-2695
Fox Meadow MS 500/6-8
1450 Cheyenne Meadows Rd 80906 719-527-7100
John Rogerson, prin. Fax 576-0918
Harrison HS 900/9-12
2755 Janitell Rd 80906 719-579-2080
Cheri Martinez, prin. Fax 538-4832
High School Preparatory Academy Alt
2250 Jet Wing Dr 80916 719-579-2580
Damon DiFabio, prin. Fax 579-2582
Panorama MS 500/6-8
2145 S Chelton Rd 80916 719-579-3220
Elizabeth Domangue, prin. Fax 579-2756
Sierra HS 900/9-12
2250 Jet Wing Dr 80916 719-579-2090
Aaron Griffen, prin. Fax 579-2536

Widefield SD 3 9,100/PK-12
1820 Main St 80911 719-391-3000
Scott Campbell, supt. Fax 390-4372
www.wsd3.org
Discovery HS 100/Alt
701 Widefield Dr 80911 719-391-3121
Charles Poncelow, prin. Fax 391-3091
Mesa Ridge HS 1,300/9-12
6070 Mesa Ridge Pkwy 80911 719-391-3600
Kathi Mata, prin. Fax 390-9697
Sproul JHS 600/6-8
235 Sumac Dr 80911 719-391-3215
Maureen di Stasio, prin. Fax 391-3215
Watson JHS 600/6-8
136 Fontaine Blvd 80911 719-391-3255
Justin Lee, prin. Fax 392-3419
Widefield HS 1,300/9-12
615 Widefield Dr 80911 719-391-3200
Aaron Hoffman, prin. Fax 391-8072
Other Schools – See Fountain

---

CollegeAmerica - Colorado Springs Post-Sec.
2020 N Academy Blvd 80909 719-227-0170

Colorado Acad of Veterinary Technology Post-Sec.
2766 Janitell Rd 80906 719-219-9636
Colorado College Post-Sec.
14 E Cache La Poudre St 80903 719-389-6000
Colorado School for the Deaf and Blind Post-Sec.
33 N Institute St 80903 719-578-2100
Colorado Springs Christian S 800/K-12
4855 Mallow Rd 80907 719-599-3553
Dr. Roland DeRenzo, supt. Fax 268-2184
Colorado Springs S 300/PK-12
21 Broadmoor Ave 80906 719-475-9747
Aaron Schubach, head sch Fax 475-9864
Colorado Technical University Post-Sec.
4435 N Chestnut St 80907 719-598-0200
DeVry University Post-Sec.
1175 Kelly Johnson Blvd 80920 719-632-3000
Evangelical Christian Academy 200/7-12
4052 S Nonchalant Cir 80917 719-597-3675
Jim Johnson, supt. Fax 597-6983
Everest College Post-Sec.
1815 Jet Wing Dr 80916 719-638-6580
Fountain Valley S of Colorado 200/9-12
6155 Fountain Valley School 80911 719-390-7035
William Webb, head sch Fax 391-9039
IntelliTec College Post-Sec.
2315 E Pikes Peak Ave 80909 719-632-7626
IntelliTec Medical Institute Post-Sec.
6805 Corporate Dr Ste 100 80919 719-596-7400
International Salon and Spa Academy Post-Sec.
5705 N Academy Blvd 80918 719-597-1413
National American University Post-Sec.
1915 Jamboree Dr Ste 185 80920 719-590-8300
Nazarene Bible College Post-Sec.
1111 Academy Park Loop 80910 719-884-5000
Pikes Peak Christian S 400/PK-12
5905 Flintridge Dr 80918 719-598-8610
Pikes Peak Community College Post-Sec.
5675 S Academy Blvd 80906 719-502-2000
St. Mary HS 300/9-12
2501 E Yampa St 80909 719-635-7540
Jim Felice, prin. Fax 471-7623
Toni & Guy Hairdressing Academy Post-Sec.
332 Main St 80911 719-390-9898
UCH Memorial Hospital School of Rad Tech Post-Sec.
1400 E Boulder St 80909 719-365-8291
University of Colorado Colorado Springs Post-Sec.
1420 Austin Bluffs Pkwy 80918 719-255-8227
University of the Rockies Post-Sec.
555 E Pikes Peak Ave # 108 80903 719-442-0505
University S of Colorado Springs 100/K-12
2713 W Cucharras St 80904 719-302-3751

**Commerce City, Adams, Pop. 45,019**
Adams County SD 14 7,200/PK-12
5291 E 60th Ave 80022 303-853-3333
Pat Sanchez, supt. Fax 286-9753
www.adams14.org/
Adams City HS 1,700/9-12
7200 Quebec Pkwy 80022 303-289-3111
Gionni Thompson, prin. Fax 288-6113
Adams City MS 700/6-8
4451 E 72nd Ave 80022 303-289-5881
Matt Schwartz, prin. Fax 288-8574
Arnold HS 300/9-12
6500 E 72nd Ave 80022 303-289-2983
Paul Sandos, prin. Fax 289-7167
Kearney MS 700/6-8
6160 Kearney St 80022 303-287-0261
Veronica Jeffers, prin. Fax 287-0432

Brighton SD 27J
Supt. — See Brighton
Stuart MS 600/6-8
15955 E 101st Way 80022 720-685-5500
Richard Patterson, prin. Fax 685-5506

---

Rocky Mountain Lutheran HS 100/9-12
10391 Luther Ct 80022 303-346-1947
Rick Lohmiller, prin. Fax 451-0817

**Conifer, Jefferson, Pop. 600**
Jefferson County SD R-1
Supt. — See Golden
Conifer HS 900/9-12
10441 Highway 73 80433 303-982-5255
Wesley Paxton, prin. Fax 982-5256
West Jefferson MS 500/6-8
9449 Barnes Ave 80433 303-982-3056
Becky Brown, prin. Fax 982-3057

**Cortez, Montezuma, Pop. 8,328**
Montezuma-Cortez SD RE-1 2,800/PK-12
PO Box R 81321 970-565-7522
Alex Carter, supt. Fax 565-2161
www.cortez.k12.co.us
Cortez MS 600/6-8
450 W 2nd St 81321 970-565-7824
Glenn Smith, prin. Fax 565-5120
Montezuma-Cortez HS 700/9-12
418 S Sligo St 81321 970-565-3722
Dr. Jason Wayman, prin. Fax 565-5118

**Cotopaxi, Fremont, Pop. 45**
Cotopaxi SD RE-3 100/PK-12
PO Box 385 81223 719-942-4131
Randy Bohlander, supt. Fax 942-4134
www.cotopaxire3.org/
Cotopaxi S 100/PK-12
PO Box 385 81223 719-942-4131
Jackie Crabtree, prin. Fax 942-4134

**Craig, Moffat, Pop. 9,327**
Moffat County SD RE-1 2,300/PK-12
775 Yampa Ave 81625 970-824-3268
Brent Curtice, supt. Fax 824-6655
moffatsd.org/
Craig MS 500/6-8
915 Yampa Ave 81625 970-824-3289
Dave Grabowski, prin. Fax 824-3858
Moffat County HS 600/9-12
900 Finley Ln 81625 970-824-7036
Kelly McCormick, prin. Fax 824-3130

**Creede, Mineral, Pop. 412**
Creede Consolidated SD 1 100/PK-12
PO Box 429 81130 719-658-2220
Buck Stroh, supt. Fax 658-2942
www.creedek12.net
Creede MSHS 50/6-12
PO Box 429 81130 719-658-2220
John Goss, prin. Fax 658-2942

**Crested Butte, Gunnison, Pop. 1,477**
Gunnison Watershed SD RE 1J
Supt. — See Gunnison
Crested Butte Community S 600/K-12
PO Box 339 81224 970-641-7720
Stephanie Niemi, prin. Fax 641-7729

**Cripple Creek, Teller, Pop. 1,167**
Cripple Creek-Victor SD RE-1 400/PK-12
PO Box 897 80813 719-689-2685
Leslie Lindauer, supt. Fax 689-2256
www.ccvschools.org
Cripple Creek-Victor JSHS 200/7-12
PO Box 897 80813 719-689-2661
Dr. Tory Richey, prin. Fax 389-2256

**De Beque, Mesa, Pop. 499**
De Beque SD 49JT 100/PK-12
PO Box 70 81630 970-283-5418
Alan Dillon, supt. Fax 283-5213
www.dbschools.org
De Beque JSHS 50/7-12
PO Box 70 81630 970-283-5596
Jonathan Watts, prin. Fax 283-5598

**Deer Trail, Arapahoe, Pop. 538**
Deer Trail SD 26J 200/PK-12
PO Box 129 80105 303-769-4421
Kevin Schott, supt. Fax 769-4600
www.dt26j.org
Deer Trail JSHS 100/6-12
PO Box 129 80105 303-769-4421
Kevin Schott, prin. Fax 769-4600

**Del Norte, Rio Grande, Pop. 1,670**
Del Norte SD C-7 400/K-12
770 11th St 81132 719-657-4040
Nathan Smith, supt. Fax 657-2546
delnorte.schoolfusion.us
Del Norte HS 200/9-12
770 11th St 81132 719-657-4020
Brian Herman, prin. Fax 657-4024
Del Norte MS 100/5-8
770 11th St 81132 719-657-4030
Amy Duda, prin. Fax 657-9087

**Delta, Delta, Pop. 8,798**
Delta County SD 50(J) 4,500/PK-12
7655 2075 Rd 81416 970-874-4438
Caryn Gibson, supt. Fax 874-5744
www.deltaschools.com
Delta Academy of Applied Learning 50/Alt
PO Box 224 81416 970-874-0835
Kim Egging, dir. Fax 874-8684
Delta County Opportunity S 100/Alt
822 Grand Ave 81416 970-874-2753
Fax 874-6852
Delta HS 600/9-12
1400 Pioneer Rd 81416 970-874-8031
Derek Carlson, prin. Fax 874-8034
Delta MS 400/6-8
910 Grand Ave 81416 970-874-8046
Adam Truitt, prin. Fax 874-8049
Other Schools – See Cedaredge, Hotchkiss, Paonia

**Denver, Denver, Pop. 585,815**
Adams County SD 50
Supt. — See Westminster
Carpenter MS 600/6-8
7001 Lipan St 80221 303-428-8583
Chad Anderson, prin. Fax 657-3962
Ranum MS 800/6-8
2401 W 80th Ave 80221 303-428-9577
Shannon Willy, prin. Fax 657-3952

Denver County SD 1 75,400/PK-12
1860 Lincoln St 80203 720-423-3200
Tom Boasberg, supt. Fax 423-3413
www.dpsk12.org/
CEC Middle College of Denver Vo/Tech
2650 Eliot St 80211 720-423-6600
Scott Springer, prin. Fax 423-6604
Collegiate Prep Academy at Noel 400/9-12
5290 Kittredge St 80239 720-424-0850
Martha Gustafson, prin. Fax 424-0945
Compass Academy 6-8
911 S Hazel Ct 80219 720-424-0096
Marcia Fulton, dir.
Compassion Road Academy 9-12
1000 Cherokee St 80204 720-424-2200
Kimberly Ortiz, prin.
Contemporary Learning Academy 200/Alt
200 E 9th Ave 80203 720-423-6900
Shawne Anderson, prin. Fax 423-6999
Crittenton HS 200/Alt
96 S Zuni St 80223 303-733-7686
Shirley Algiene, admin. Fax 733-4119
DCIS at Montbello 200/6-12
5000 Crown Blvd 80239 720-423-5900
Julie Murgal, prin. Fax 423-5390
Denver Center for 21st Century Learning 200/Alt
1690 Williams St 80218 720-424-2980
Christian DeLaOliva, prin. Fax 424-3005
Denver Center for International Studies 700/6-12
574 W 6th Ave 80204 720-423-9000
Therese McCorquodale, prin. Fax 423-9075
Denver Discovery S 6-8
3480 Syracuse St 80238 720-424-4790
Kristen Atwood, prin. Fax 424-4791
Denver Montessori JSHS 7-12
4250 Shoshone St 80211 720-424-2600
Katy Myers, prin.
S of Innovation & Sustainable Design 9-12
150 S Pearl St 80209 720-424-2000
Danny Medved, prin.

Denver S of the Arts 1,100/6-12
7111 Montview Blvd 80220 720-424-1700
William Kohut, prin. Fax 424-1845
East HS 2,300/9-12
1600 City Park Esplanade 80206 720-423-8300
Andy Mendelsberg, prin. Fax 423-8306
Escuela Tlatelolco 100/Alt
2949 Federal Blvd 80211 303-964-8993
Nita Gonzales, prin. Fax 964-9795
Excel Academy 9-12
1825 S Federal Blvd 80219 720-424-2250
Cynthia Navarro, prin.
Gilliam S 50/Alt
2844 Downing St 80205 303-291-8929
Kim Ortiz, dir. Fax 292-9348
Grant Beacon MS 400/6-8
1751 S Washington St 80210 720-423-9360
Alex Magana, prin. Fax 423-9385
Griffith HS, 1860 Lincoln St 80203 600/Alt
David Daves, prin. 720-423-4900
Hamilton MS 900/6-8
8600 E Dartmouth Ave 80231 720-423-9500
Nickolas Dawkins, prin. Fax 423-9445
Henry World MS 900/6-8
3005 S Golden Way 80227 720-423-9560
Steve Goldstein, prin. Fax 423-9585
High Tech Early College 100/9-12
11200 E 45th Ave 80239 720-424-2450
Jarod Schott, prin.
Hill MS Campus of Arts & Sciences 900/6-8
451 Clermont St 80220 720-423-9680
Sean Kavanaugh, prin. Fax 423-9705
Jefferson HS 1,000/9-12
3950 S Holly St 80237 720-423-7000
Suzanne Morris-Sherer, prin. Fax 423-7047
Kennedy HS 1,200/9-12
2855 S Lamar St 80227 720-423-4300
Jeannie Peppel, prin. Fax 423-4309
Kepner MS 1,200/6-8
911 S Hazel Ct 80219 720-424-0000
Elza Guajardo, prin. Fax 424-0023
King Early College HS 1,200/6-12
19535 E 46th Ave 80249 720-424-0420
Kimberly Grayson, prin. Fax 424-0496
Kunsmiller Creative Arts Academy 600/K-12
2250 S Quitman Way 80219 720-424-0200
Peter Castillo, prin. Fax 424-0145
Lake International MS 300/6-8
1820 Lowell Blvd 80204 720-424-0260
Rebecca Marques-Guerrero, prin. Fax 424-0380
Legacy Options HS Alt
6850 N Argonne St 80249 720-424-3100
Anthony McWright, prin. Fax 424-3103
Lincoln HS 1,900/9-12
2285 S Federal Blvd 80219 720-423-5000
Larry Irvin, prin. Fax 423-5098
Manual HS 400/9-12
1700 E 28th Ave 80205 720-423-6300
Don Roy, prin. Fax 423-6301
McAuliffe International MS 6-8
2540 Holly St 80207 720-424-1540
Kurt Dennis, prin. Fax 424-1565
Merrill MS 500/6-8
1551 S Monroe St 80210 720-424-0600
Amy Bringedahl, prin. Fax 424-0625
Morey MS 700/6-8
840 E 14th Ave 80218 720-424-0700
Noah Tonk, prin. Fax 424-0727
Noel Community Arts S 200/6-12
5000 Crown Blvd 80239 720-423-5840
Stacy Miller, prin. Fax 423-5863
Northfield HS 9-12
5500 Central Park Blvd 80238 720-423-8000
Avi Tropper, prin.
North HS 900/9-12
2960 N Speer Blvd 80211 720-423-2700
Nicole Veltze, prin. Fax 423-2708
North HS Engagement Center Alt
2960 N Speer Blvd 80211 720-423-2700
Teresa Steele, prin. Fax 423-2708
P.R.E.P. Academy 100/Alt
2727 Columbine St 80205 720-424-8451
Jamie Lafaro, prin. Fax 424-8477
P.U.S.H. Academy Alt
4501 Airport Way 80239 720-423-7200
Angela Robertson, prin. Fax 423-7259
Randolph MSHS 900/6-12
3955 Steele St 80205 720-424-1080
Cesar Cedillo, prin. Fax 424-1241
Respect Academy at Lincoln Alt
2285 S Federal Blvd 80219 720-423-5203
Wendy Lanier, prin.
RiseUp Community HS Alt
1801 Federal Blvd 80204 303-587-4713
Lucas Ketzer, prin.
Skinner MS 400/6-8
3435 W 40th Ave 80211 720-424-1420
Michelle Koyama, prin. Fax 424-1446
South HS 1,300/9-12
1700 E Louisiana Ave 80210 720-423-6000
Kristin Waters, prin. Fax 423-6280
Summit Academy 200/Alt
3001 S Federal Blvd 80236 720-424-2400
Bobby Thomas, prin.
Vista Academy 200/6-12
4800 Telluride St 80249 720-423-7650
Rhonda Juett, prin. Fax 423-7667
Washington HS 1,500/9-12
655 S Monaco Pkwy 80224 720-423-8600
Jose Martinez, prin. Fax 423-8614
West Career Academy Alt
951 Elati St 80204 720-423-5390
Jessica Newman, prin.
West Generation Academy 6-12
951 Elati St 80204 720-423-5300
Domonic Martinez, prin.
West Leadership Academy 6-12
951 Elati St 80204 720-423-5300
Teresa Klava, prin.

Jefferson County SD R-1
Supt. — See Golden
D'Evelyn JSHS 1,000/7-12
10359 W Nassau Ave 80235 303-982-2600
Anthony Edwards, prin. Fax 982-2601

Mapleton SD 1 6,900/PK-12
591 E 80th Ave 80229 303-853-1000
Charlotte Ciancio, supt. Fax 853-1087
www.mapleton.us
Global Leadership Academy 400/K-12
7480 Broadway 80221 303-853-1930
Dave Sauer, dir. Fax 853-1956
Other Schools – See Thornton

Sheridan SD 2
Supt. — See Sheridan
Ft. Logan Northgate S 300/3-8
4000 S Lowell Blvd 80236 720-833-6853
Nelson Van Vranken, prin. Fax 833-6746
S.O.A.R. Academy Alt
3201 W Oxford Ave 80236 720-833-6796
Christian Ramaker, dir.
Sheridan HS 500/9-12
3201 W Oxford Ave 80236 720-833-6987
Michele Kelley, prin. Fax 833-6833

---

Accelerated Schools 50/K-12
2160 S Cook St 80210 303-758-2003
American Pathways University Post-Sec.
2227 Franklin St 80205 303-839-2551
American University of Paris Post-Sec.
700 Colorado Blvd # 502 80206 303-993-4326
Argosy University / Denver Post-Sec.
7600 E Eastman Ave 80231 303-923-4110
Arrupe Jesuit HS 300/9-12
4343 Utica St 80212 303-455-7449
Michael O'Hagan, prin. Fax 455-7453
Art Institute of Colorado Post-Sec.
1200 Lincoln St 80203 303-837-0825
Aspen University Post-Sec.
720 S Colorado Blvd #1150N 80246 800-441-4746
Bel-Rea Institute of Animal Technology Post-Sec.
1681 S Dayton St, 303-751-8700
Beth Jacob HS of Denver 100/9-12
5100 W 14th Ave 80204 303-893-1333
Bishop Machebeuf Catholic HS 400/9-12
458 Uinta Way 80230 303-344-0082
Marc Nestorick, prin. Fax 344-1582
Centura-St. Anthony Hospital Post-Sec.
4231 W 16th Ave 80204 303-629-4350
CollegeAmerica - Denver Post-Sec.
1385 S Colorado Blvd Fl 5 80222 303-534-0226
Colorado Academy 900/PK-12
3800 S Pierce St 80235 303-986-1501
Michael Davis Ph.D., hdmstr. Fax 914-2583
Colorado Ctr for Medical Laboratory Sci. Post-Sec.
1719 E 19th Ave 80218 303-839-6485
Colorado Heights University Post-Sec.
3001 S Federal Blvd 80236 303-937-4225
CO Sch of Traditional Chinese Medicine Post-Sec.
1441 York St Ste 202 80206 303-329-6355
Community College of Denver Post-Sec.
PO Box 173363 80217 303-556-2600
Denver Academy 400/1-12
4400 E Iliff Ave 80222 303-777-5870
Mark Twarogowski, hdmstr. Fax 777-5893
Denver Academy of Torah 100/PK-12
6825 E Alameda Ave 80224 720-859-6806
Denver Health Medical Center Post-Sec.
660 Bannock St 80204 303-436-6611
Denver Jewish Day School 400/K-12
2450 S Wabash St 80231 303-369-0663
Avi Halzel, head sch Fax 369-0664
Denver Waldorf S 300/PK-12
2100 S Pennsylvania St 80210 303-777-0531
Kelly Church, admin. Fax 744-1216
Emily Griffith Opportunity School Post-Sec.
1250 Welton St 80204 720-423-4700
Heritage College Post-Sec.
12 Lakeside Ln 80212 303-477-7240
Iliff School of Theology Post-Sec.
2201 S University Blvd 80210 303-744-1287
Johnson & Wales University-Denver Campus Post-Sec.
7150 Montview Blvd 80220 303-256-9300
Lincoln College of Technology Post-Sec.
11194 E 45th Ave 80239 303-722-5724
Metropolitan State University Post-Sec.
PO Box 173362 80217 303-556-2400
Mullen HS 800/9-12
3601 S Lowell Blvd 80236 303-761-1764
Janell Kloostermann, prin. Fax 761-0502
National American University Post-Sec.
1325 S Colorado Blvd #100 80222 303-876-7100
Phlebotomy Learning Center Post-Sec.
1780 S Bellaire St Ste 780 80222 303-584-0575
Pima Medical Institute Post-Sec.
7475 Dakin St 80221 303-426-1800
Regis University Post-Sec.
3333 Regis Blvd 80221 303-458-4100
Rocky Mountain College of Art & Design Post-Sec.
1600 Pierce St 80214 800-888-2787
St. John Vianney Theological Seminary Post-Sec.
1300 S Steele St 80210 303-282-3427
University of Colorado Denver Post-Sec.
1250 14th St 80202 303-556-2400
University of Denver Post-Sec.
2199 S University Blvd 80210 303-871-2000
Westwood College - Denver North Post-Sec.
7350 Broadway 80221 303-650-5050
Westwood College - Denver South Post-Sec.
3150 S Sheridan Blvd 80227 303-934-1122
William Howard Taft University Post-Sec.
600 S Cherry St Ste 525 80246 303-867-1155
Yeshiva Toras Chaim HS 100/9-12
PO Box 40067 80204 303-629-8200
Yeshiva Toras Chaim Talmudical Seminary Post-Sec.
1555 Stuart St 80204 303-629-8200

**Dolores, Montezuma, Pop. 903**
Dolores SD RE-4A 700/PK-12
PO Box 727 81323 970-882-7255
Dr. Scott Cooper, supt. Fax 882-7685
www.doloresschools.org
Dolores HS 200/9-12
PO Box 727 81323 970-882-7288
Jenifer Hufman, prin. Fax 882-7685
Dolores MS 200/7-8
PO Box 727 81323 970-882-7288
Jimmie Lankford, admin. Fax 882-7289

**Dove Creek, Dolores, Pop. 714**
Dolores County SD RE-2J 300/PK-12
PO Box 459 81324 970-677-2522
Bruce Hankins, supt. Fax 677-2712
www.dc2j.org
Dove Creek HS 100/6-12
PO Box 459 81324 970-677-2237
Ty Gray, prin. Fax 677-2927

**Durango, LaPlata, Pop. 16,541**
Durango SD 9-R 4,600/PK-12
201 E 12th St 81301 970-247-5411
Dan Snowberger, supt. Fax 247-9581
www.durangoschools.org
Durango Big Picture HS 100/9-12
2390 Main Ave 81301 970-259-0203
Alain Henry, prin. Fax 382-0588
Durango HS 1,300/9-12
2390 Main Ave 81301 970-259-1630
LeAnne Garcia, prin. Fax 385-1493
Escalante MS 500/6-8
141 Baker Ln 81303 970-247-9490
Tim Arnold, prin. Fax 385-1194
Miller MS 400/6-8
2608 Junction St 81301 970-247-1418
Cito Nuhn, prin. Fax 385-1191

---

Fort Lewis College Post-Sec.
1000 Rim Dr 81301 970-247-7010

**Eads, Kiowa, Pop. 605**
Eads SD RE-1 200/PK-12
210 W 10th St 81036 719-438-2218
Glenn Smith, supt. Fax 438-2272
www.eadseagles.org
Eads HS 100/9-12
210 W 10th St 81036 719-438-2214
Betsy Barnett, prin. Fax 438-2272
Eads MS 50/6-8
900 Maine St 81036 719-438-2216
Betsy Barnett, prin. Fax 438-2272

**Eagle, Eagle, Pop. 6,436**
Eagle County SD RE-50 5,800/PK-12
PO Box 740 81631 970-328-6321
Jason Glass, supt. Fax 328-1024
www.eagleschools.net
Eagle Valley MS 300/6-8
PO Box 1019 81631 970-328-6224
Katie Jarnot, prin. Fax 328-8915
Other Schools – See Edwards, Gypsum

**Eaton, Weld, Pop. 4,298**
Eaton SD RE-2 1,800/K-12
211 1st St 80615 970-454-3402
Randy Miller Ed.D., supt. Fax 454-5193
www.eaton.k12.co.us
Eaton HS 500/9-12
114 Park Ave 80615 970-454-3374
Mark Naill, prin. Fax 454-5190
Eaton MS 400/6-8
225 Juniper Ave 80615 970-454-3358
Jim Orth, prin. Fax 454-1337

**Edgewater, Jefferson, Pop. 5,086**
Jefferson County SD R-1
Supt. — See Golden
Jefferson HS 600/7-12
2305 Pierce St 80214 303-982-6056
Michael James, prin. Fax 982-6057

**Edwards, Eagle, Pop. 10,187**
Eagle County SD RE-50
Supt. — See Eagle
Battle Mountains HS 700/9-12
151 Miller Ranch Rd 81632 970-328-2930
Philip Qualman, prin. Fax 328-2935
Berry Creek MS 400/6-8
1000 Miller Ranch Rd 81632 970-328-2960
Amy Vanwel, prin. Fax 926-4137
Red Canyon HS 100/Alt
1002 Miller Ranch Rd 81632 970-328-2852
Wade Hill, prin. Fax 328-2855

---

Vail Christian HS 100/9-12
31621 Highway 6 81632 970-926-3015
Jeremy Lowe, prin. Fax 766-3016

**Elbert, Elbert, Pop. 225**
Elbert SD 200 200/PK-12
PO Box 38 80106 303-648-3030
Kelli Thompson, supt. Fax 648-3652
elbertschool.org
Elbert JSHS 100/7-12
PO Box 38 80106 303-648-3030
Shawn Graves, prin. Fax 648-3652

**Elizabeth, Elbert, Pop. 1,335**
Elizabeth SD C-1 2,500/PK-12
PO Box 610 80107 303-646-1836
Douglas Bissonette, supt. Fax 646-0337
elizabeth.k12.co.us/
Elizabeth HS 700/9-12
34500 County Road 13 80107 303-646-4616
Rod Blunck, prin. Fax 646-6030
Elizabeth MS 500/6-8
34427 County Road 13 80107 303-646-4520
Jodi Elkins, prin. Fax 646-0980
Frontier HS 100/Alt
589 S Banner St 80107 303-646-1798
Robert McMullen, dir. Fax 646-1329

**Ellicott, El Paso, Pop. 1,094**
Ellicott SD 22 1,000/PK-12
322 S Ellicott Hwy 80808 719-683-2700
Patrick Cullen Ed.D., supt. Fax 683-4442
www.ellicottschools.org
Ellicott HS 300/9-12
375 S Ellicott Hwy 80808 719-683-2700
Mark McPherson, prin. Fax 683-2705
Ellicott MS 200/6-8
350 S Ellicott Hwy 80808 719-683-2700
Chris Smith, prin. Fax 683-5430

**Englewood, Arapahoe, Pop. 29,512**
Cherry Creek SD 5
Supt. — See Greenwood Village
Campus MS 1,400/6-8
4785 S Dayton St 80111 720-554-2677
Dr. Enrique Rosales, prin. Fax 554-2795

Englewood SD 1 2,800/PK-12
4101 S Bannock St 80110 303-761-7050
Wendy Rubin Ed.D., supt. Fax 806-2064
www.englewoodschools.net
Colorado's Finest Alternative HS 300/Alt
300 W Chenango Ave 80110 303-934-5786
Bobbie Skaggs, prin. Fax 934-9183
Englewood HS 600/9-12
3800 S Logan St, 303-806-2266
Jon Fore, prin. Fax 806-2296
Englewood Leadership Academy 100/6-8
3800 S Logan St, 303-806-2266
Jon Fore, prin. Fax 806-2296
Englewood MS 300/7-8
3800 S Logan St, 303-781-7817
Mandy Braun, prin. Fax 806-2399

---

Columbia HealthOne Post-Sec.
501 E Hampden Ave, 303-788-6484
Elliot Christian S 100/6-12
8505 S Valley Hwy 80112 303-922-0011
Wayne Embry, admin. Fax 922-0159
Kent Denver S 700/6-12
4000 E Quincy Ave, 303-770-7660
Dr. Randal Harrington, head sch Fax 770-7137
St. Mary's Academy 700/PK-12
4545 S University Blvd, 303-762-8300
Deirdre Cryor, pres. Fax 783-6201

**Erie, Weld, Pop. 17,723**
St. Vrain Valley SD RE-1J
Supt. — See Longmont
Erie HS 800/9-12
3180 County Road 5 80516 303-828-4213
Matt Buchler, prin. Fax 494-3869
Erie MS 600/6-8
650 Main St 80516 303-828-3391
Todd Bissell, prin. Fax 652-8293

**Estes Park, Larimer, Pop. 5,792**
Estes Park SD R-3 1,100/PK-12
1605 Brodie Ave 80517 970-586-2361
Sheldon Rosenkrance, supt. Fax 586-1108
www.estesschools.org
Estes Park HS 400/9-12
1600 Manford Ave 80517 970-586-5321
Charles Scott, prin. Fax 586-1102
Estes Park MS 200/6-8
1500 Manford Ave 80517 970-586-4439
Ruby Bode, prin. Fax 586-1100

---

Eagle Rock S 100/9-12
2750 Notaiah Rd 80517 970-586-0600
Jeff Liddle, head sch Fax 586-4805

**Evans, Weld, Pop. 18,255**
Weld County SD 6
Supt. — See Greeley
Prairie Heights MS 6-8
3737 65th Ave 80620 970-348-3600
Dr. Dawn Hillman Ed.D., admin. Fax 348-3632

**Evergreen, Jefferson, Pop. 8,923**
Clear Creek SD RE-1
Supt. — See Idaho Springs
Clear Creek HS 300/9-12
185 Beaver Brook Canyon Rd 80439 303-679-4600
Elizabeth Gardner, prin. Fax 679-4603
Clear Creek MS 100/7-8
185 Beaver Brook Canyon Rd 80439 303-670-4600
Jeff Miller, prin. Fax 670-4690

Jefferson County SD R-1
Supt. — See Golden
Evergreen HS 1,000/9-12
29300 Buffalo Park Rd 80439 303-982-5140
Ryan Alsup, prin. Fax 982-5141
Evergreen MS 700/6-8
2059 Hiwan Dr 80439 303-982-5020
Joelle Broberg, prin. Fax 982-5021

**Fairplay, Park, Pop. 659**
Park County SD RE-2 600/PK-12
PO Box 189 80440 719-836-3111
Becky Minnis, supt. Fax 836-2275
www.parkcountyre2.org/
South Park HS 100/9-12
PO Box 189 80440 719-836-2006
Jane Newman, prin. Fax 836-4429
South Park MS 100/6-8
PO Box 189 80440 719-836-4406
Jane Newman, prin. Fax 836-2275

**Falcon, El Paso, Pop. 200**
Falcon SD 49 16,300/PK-12
10850 E Woodmen Rd 80831 719-495-1100
Peter Hilts, admin. Fax 494-8900
www.d49.org
Other Schools – See Colorado Springs, Peyton

**Firestone, Weld, Pop. 9,981**
St. Vrain Valley SD RE-1J
Supt. — See Longmont

Coal Ridge MS 900/6-8
6201 Booth Dr 80504 303-833-4176
Brian Young, prin. Fax 494-3813

**Flagler, Kit Carson, Pop. 558**
Arriba-Flagler SD C-20 100/PK-12
PO Box 218 80815 719-765-4684
Valorie McCleary, supt. Fax 765-4418
flaglerschools.co.afs.schoolinsites.com
Flagler S 100/PK-12
PO Box 218 80815 719-765-4684
Valorie McCleary, prin. Fax 765-4418

**Fleming, Logan, Pop. 408**
Frenchman SD RE-3 200/PK-12
506 N Fremont Ave 80728 970-265-2111
Steve McCracken, supt. Fax 265-2815
www.flemingschools.org
Fleming HS 100/7-12
506 N Fremont Ave 80728 970-265-2111
Stacy McDaniel, prin. Fax 265-2815

**Florence, Fremont, Pop. 3,816**
Florence SD RE-2 1,600/K-12
403 W 5th St 81226 719-784-6312
Rhonda Roberts, supt. Fax 784-4140
www.re-2.org/
Florence HS 500/9-12
2006 Highway 67 81226 719-784-6414
Brian Schipper, prin. Fax 784-2727
Fremont MS 400/6-8
215 Maple St 81226 719-784-4856
Andy Fieth, prin. Fax 784-3821

**Fort Carson, El Paso, Pop. 13,113**
Fountain-Fort Carson SD 8
Supt. — See Fountain
Carson MS 700/6-8
6200 Prussman Blvd, 719-382-1610
Josh Hobgood, prin. Fax 382-8526

**Fort Collins, Larimer, Pop. 140,582**
Poudre SD R-1 27,100/PK-12
2407 Laporte Ave 80521 970-482-7420
Dr. Sandra Smysor, supt. Fax 490-3514
www.psdschools.org
Blevins MS 500/6-8
2101 S Taft Hill Rd 80526 970-488-4000
David Linehan, prin. Fax 488-4011
Boltz MS 600/6-8
720 Boltz Dr 80525 970-472-3700
Brett Larsen, prin. Fax 472-3730
Centennial HS 100/Alt
330 E Laurel St 80524 970-488-4940
Mike Roberts, prin. Fax 488-4942
Fort Collins HS 1,700/9-12
3400 Lambkin Way 80525 970-488-8021
Mark Eversole, prin. Fax 488-8008
Fossil Ridge HS 2,000/9-12
5400 Ziegler Rd 80528 970-488-6260
Will Allen, prin. Fax 488-6263
Kinard Core Knowledge MS 800/6-8
3002 E Trilby Rd 80528 970-488-5400
Jesse Morrill, prin. Fax 488-5402
Lesher MS 700/6-8
1400 Stover St 80524 970-472-3800
Thomas Dodd, prin. Fax 472-3880
Lincoln MS 500/6-8
1600 Lancer Dr 80521 970-488-5700
Penny Stires, prin. Fax 488-5752
Polaris Expeditionary Learning S 300/K-12
1905 Orchard Pl 80521 970-488-8260
Joe Gawronski, prin. Fax 488-8262
Poudre Community Academy 100/Alt
2540 LaPorte Ave 80521 970-490-3295
Troy Krotz, prin. Fax 490-3402
Poudre HS 1,800/9-12
201 S Impala Dr 80521 970-488-6000
Kathy Mackay, prin. Fax 488-6060
Preston MS 900/6-8
4901 Corbett Dr 80528 970-488-7300
Scott Nielsen, prin. Fax 488-7307
Rocky Mountain HS 2,000/9-12
1300 W Swallow Rd 80526 970-488-7023
Craig Woodall, prin. Fax 488-7001
Webber MS 800/6-8
4201 Seneca St 80526 970-488-7800
Christopher Keiffer, prin. Fax 488-7811
Other Schools – See Laporte, Wellington

---

At-Home Professions Post-Sec.
2001 Lowe St 80525 970-225-6300
CollegeAmerica - Fort Collins Post-Sec.
4601 S Mason St 80525 970-221-2769
Colorado State University Post-Sec.
1062 Campus Delivery 80523 970-491-6909
Front Range Baptist Academy 100/PK-12
625 E Harmony Rd 80525 970-223-2173
Front Range Community College Post-Sec.
4616 S Shields St 80526 970-226-2500
Hair Dynamics Education Center Post-Sec.
PO Box 272389 80527 970-223-9943
Heritage Christian Academy 200/PK-12
2506 Zurich Dr 80524 970-494-1022
Mike Cuckler, admin. Fax 494-1025
Institute of Business & Medical Careers Post-Sec.
3842 S Mason St 80525 970-223-2669
McKinley College Post-Sec.
2001 Lowe St 80525 970-207-4550
US Career Institute Post-Sec.
2001 Lowe St 80525 800-347-7899

**Fort Lupton, Weld, Pop. 7,284**
Weld County SD RE-8 2,500/PK-12
301 Reynolds St 80621 303-857-3200
John Hoag, supt. Fax 857-3219
www.weld8.org
Fort Lupton HS 600/9-12
530 Reynolds St 80621 303-857-7100
Alan Kaylor, prin. Fax 857-7179
Fort Lupton MS 500/6-8
201 S McKinley Ave 80621 303-857-7200
Candace Kensinger, prin. Fax 857-7287

**Fort Morgan, Morgan, Pop. 11,188**
Ft. Morgan SD RE-3 3,200/PK-12
715 W Platte Ave 80701 970-867-5633
Ron Echols, supt. Fax 867-0262
www.morgan.k12.co.us
Fort Morgan HS 900/9-12
709 E Riverview Ave 80701 970-867-5648
Ben Bauman, prin. Fax 867-3347
Fort Morgan MS 500/7-8
300 Deuel St 80701 970-867-8253
Jason Frasco, prin. Fax 867-4876
Lincoln HS 50/Alt
230 Walnut St 80701 970-867-2924
Vicki Davis, prin. Fax 867-4958

---

Morgan Community College Post-Sec.
920 Barlow Rd 80701 970-542-3100

**Fountain, El Paso, Pop. 24,314**
Fountain-Fort Carson SD 8 7,600/PK-12
10665 Jimmy Camp Rd 80817 719-382-1300
Cheryl Serrano, supt. Fax 382-7338
www.ffc8.org
Fountain-Fort Carson HS 1,600/9-12
900 Jimmy Camp Rd 80817 719-382-1640
Burnie Hibbard, prin. Fax 382-4792
Fountain MS 1,000/6-8
515 N Santa Fe Ave 80817 719-382-1580
Deb Keiley, prin. Fax 382-9065
Welte Education Center 100/Alt
330 Lyckman Pl 80817 719-382-1550
Sally Conboy, prin. Fax 382-5782
Other Schools – See Fort Carson

Widefield SD 3
Supt. — See Colorado Springs
Janitell JHS 700/6-8
7635 Fountain Mesa Rd 80817 719-391-3295
David Gish, prin. Fax 390-7869

**Fowler, Otero, Pop. 1,170**
Fowler SD R-4J 400/K-12
PO Box 218 81039 719-263-4224
Steven Grasmick, supt. Fax 263-4625
www.fowler.k12.co.us/
Fowler HS 100/9-12
PO Box 218 81039 719-263-4279
Russell Bates, prin. Fax 263-4625
Fowler JHS 100/7-8
PO Box 218 81039 719-263-4224
Russell Bates, prin. Fax 263-4625

**Frederick, Weld, Pop. 8,509**
St. Vrain Valley SD RE-1J
Supt. — See Longmont
Frederick HS 800/9-12
5690 Tipple Pkwy 80530 303-833-3533
Peter Vargas, prin. Fax 494-3887

**Frisco, Summit, Pop. 2,654**
Summit SD RE-1 3,100/PK-12
PO Box 7 80443 970-368-1000
Dr. Heidi Pace, supt. Fax 368-1049
www.summit.k12.co.us
Snowy Peaks HS, PO Box 7 80443 50/Alt
James Smith, prin. 970-368-1145
Summit HS 800/9-12
PO Box 7 80443 970-368-1100
Drew Adkins, prin. Fax 368-1199
Summit MS 600/6-8
PO Box 7 80443 970-368-1200
Joel Rivera, prin. Fax 368-1299

---

Peak S, PO Box 550 80443 50/6-12
Steven Coleman, head sch 970-368-5601

**Fruita, Mesa, Pop. 12,442**
Mesa County Valley SD 51
Supt. — See Grand Junction
Fruita 8th & 9th Grade S 700/8-9
1835 J Rd 81521 970-254-6720
Jason Plantiko, prin. Fax 858-7751
Fruita Monument HS 1,300/10-12
1102 Wildcat Ave 81521 970-254-6600
Todd McClaskey, prin. Fax 858-9661

**Gateway, Mesa, Pop. 7,510**
Mesa County Valley SD 51
Supt. — See Grand Junction
Gateway S 50/K-12
PO Box 240 81522 970-254-7080
Fax 931-2883

**Gilcrest, Weld, Pop. 1,023**
Weld County SD RE-1 1,900/PK-12
PO Box 157 80623 970-737-2403
Don Rangel, supt. Fax 737-2516
www.weld-re1.k12.co.us
Valley HS 500/9-12
PO Box 156 80623 970-737-2494
Rich Dalgliesh, prin. Fax 737-2203
Other Schools – See La Salle, Platteville

**Glenwood Springs, Garfield, Pop. 9,485**
Roaring Fork SD RE-1 5,400/PK-12
1405 Grand Ave 81601 970-384-6000
Diana Sirko, supt. Fax 384-6005
www.rfschools.com
Glenwood Springs HS 800/9-12
1521 Grand Ave 81601 970-384-5555
Paul Freeman, prin. Fax 384-5556
Glenwood Springs MS 500/6-8
120 Soccer Field Rd 81601 970-384-5500
Sandy DeCrow, prin. Fax 384-5505
Other Schools – See Basalt, Carbondale

---

Colorado Mountain College Post-Sec.
802 Grand Ave 81601 970-945-8691
Glenwood Beauty Academy Post-Sec.
51241 Highway 6 Ste 1 81601 970-945-0485

**Golden, Jefferson, Pop. 18,494**
Jefferson County SD R-1 83,000/PK-12
PO Box 4001 80402 303-982-6500
Dan McMinimee, supt. Fax 982-6814
www.jeffcopublicschools.org/
Bell MS 500/6-8
1001 Ulysses St 80401 303-982-4280
Bridget Jones, prin. Fax 982-4281
Golden HS 1,200/9-12
701 24th St 80401 303-982-4200
Brian Conroy, prin. Fax 982-4201
Manning Options S 400/Alt
13200 W 32nd Ave 80401 303-982-6340
Barb Bares, prin. Fax 982-6341
Other Schools – See Arvada, Conifer, Denver, Edgewater, Evergreen, Lakewood, Littleton, Westminster, Wheat Ridge

---

Colorado School of Mines Post-Sec.
1500 Illinois St 80401 303-273-3000
Holmes Institute of Consciousness Stds Post-Sec.
573 Park Point Dr 80401 720-496-1370

**Granada, Prowers, Pop. 515**
Granada SD RE-1 200/PK-12
PO Box 259 81041 719-734-5492
Ty Kemp, supt. Fax 734-5495
www.granadaschools.org
Granada JSHS 100/7-12
PO Box 259 81041 719-734-5492
Ty Kemp, prin. Fax 734-5495

**Granby, Grand, Pop. 1,839**
East Grand SD 2 1,300/PK-12
PO Box 125 80446 970-887-2581
Jody Mimmack, supt. Fax 887-2635
www.egsd.org
East Grand MS 300/6-8
PO Box 2210 80446 970-887-3382
Jenny Rothboeck, prin. Fax 887-9234
Middle Park HS 300/9-12
PO Box 130 80446 970-887-2104
Thom Schnellinger, prin. Fax 887-9454

**Grand Junction, Mesa, Pop. 57,510**
Mesa County Valley SD 51 21,300/PK-12
2115 Grand Ave 81501 970-254-5100
Steven Schultz, supt. Fax 245-2714
www.d51schools.org
Bookcliff MS 600/6-8
540 29 1/4 Rd 81504 970-254-6220
Jim Butterfield, prin. Fax 245-7812
Career Center Vo/Tech
2935 North Ave 81504 970-254-6000
Lee Searcy, prin. Fax 255-8465
Central HS 1,600/9-12
550 Warrior Way 81504 970-254-6200
Lanc Sellden, prin. Fax 254-6169
East MS 500/6-8
830 Gunnison Ave 81501 970-254-5020
Leah Gonyeau, prin. Fax 242-0513
Grand Junction HS 1,800/9-12
1400 N 5th St 81501 970-254-6900
Ari Goldberg, prin. Fax 241-5154
Grand Mesa MS 600/6-8
585 31 1/2 Rd 81504 970-254-6270
Terrie ReQua, prin. Fax 523-5938
Orchard Mesa MS 500/6-8
2736 C Rd 81503 970-254-6320
Cheryl Vana, prin. Fax 245-7343
R-5 HS 200/Alt
310 N 7th St 81501 970-254-6880
Donald Trujillo, prin. Fax 242-4465
Redlands MS 600/6-8
2200 Broadway, 970-254-7000
Kelly Reed, prin. Fax 245-1985
Valley S West Alt
2508 Blichmann Ave 81505 970-255-2708
Brenda Witte, prin. Fax 255-2711
West MS 400/6-8
123 W Orchard Ave 81505 970-254-5090
Vernon Walker, prin. Fax 243-0574
Other Schools – See Clifton, Fruita, Gateway, Palisade

---

Colorado Mesa University Post-Sec.
1100 North Ave 81501 970-248-1020
Grand Valley Christian HS 50/9-12
PO Box 2013 81502 970-241-4126
Steve Kautzsch, prin.
IntelliTec College Post-Sec.
772 Horizon Dr 81506 970-245-8101

**Greeley, Weld, Pop. 91,409**
Weld County SD 6 19,100/PK-12
1025 9th Ave 80631 970-348-6000
Dr. Deirdre Pilch Ed.D., supt. Fax 348-6231
www.greeleyschools.org
Brentwood MS 700/6-8
2600 24th Avenue Ct 80634 970-348-3000
Nicole Petersen, prin. Fax 348-3030
Early College Academy 9-12
5590 W 11th St 80634 970-348-5800
Gordon Boschman, admin.
Franklin MS 700/6-8
818 35th Ave 80634 970-348-3200
Chris Ingram, prin. Fax 348-3230
Greeley Central HS 1,400/9-12
1515 14th Ave 80631 970-348-5000
Mark Cousins, prin. Fax 348-5030
Greeley-Evans Alternative Program Alt
1113 10th Ave 80631 970-348-4900
Dave Shaffer, admin. Fax 348-4930
Greeley West HS 1,500/9-12
2401 35th Ave 80634 970-348-5400
Shelli Robins, prin. Fax 348-5430
Heath MS 700/6-8
2223 16th St 80631 970-348-3400
Dr. Blakley Wallace, prin. Fax 348-3430
Jefferson HS 300/9-12
1315 4th Ave 80631 970-348-1600
Larry Green, prin. Fax 348-1630

Northridge HS 1,000/9-12
100 N 71st Ave 80634 970-348-5200
Insoon Olson, prin. Fax 348-5230
Other Schools – See Evans

---

Academy of Natural Therapy Post-Sec.
625 8th Ave 80631 970-352-1181
Aims Community College Post-Sec.
5401 W 20th St 80634 970-330-8008
Cheeks Intl Academy of Beauty Culture Post-Sec.
2547 11th Ave Ste B 80631 970-352-4500
Dayspring Christian Academy 300/PK-12
3734 W 20th St 80634 970-330-1151
Weston Kurz, dir. Fax 330-0565
Institute of Business & Medical Careers Post-Sec.
2863 35th Ave 80634 970-356-4733
University of Northern Colorado Post-Sec.
501 20th St 80639 970-351-1890

**Greenwood Village, Arapahoe, Pop. 13,663**
Cherry Creek SD 5 51,100/PK-12
4700 S Yosemite St 80111 303-773-1184
Dr. Harry Bull, supt. Fax 773-9370
www.cherrycreekschools.org
Cherry Creek HS 3,500/9-12
9300 E Union Ave 80111 720-554-2285
Ryan Silva, prin. Fax 554-2239
West MS 1,100/6-8
5151 S Holly St 80121 720-554-5180
Kate Bergles, prin. Fax 554-5181
Other Schools – See Aurora, Centennial, Englewood

---

Colorado State University Global Campus Post-Sec.
8000 E Maplewood Bdg 5 #250 80111
720-279-0159
DeVry University Post-Sec.
6312 S Fiddlers Green #150E 80111 303-329-3000
Tri-County Health Nutrition Services Post-Sec.
6162 S Willow Dr Ste 100 80111 303-220-9200

**Grover, Weld, Pop. 137**
Pawnee SD RE-12 100/PK-12
PO Box 220 80729 970-895-2222
Bret Robinson, supt. Fax 895-2221
www.pawneeschool.org
Pawnee S 50/PK-12
PO Box 220 80729 970-895-2222
Bret Robinson, prin. Fax 895-2221

**Gunnison, Gunnison, Pop. 5,730**
Gunnison Watershed SD RE 1J 1,800/PK-12
800 N Boulevard St 81230 970-641-7770
Doug Tredway, supt. Fax 641-7777
www.gunnisonschools.net/
Gunnison HS 300/9-12
800 W Ohio Ave 81230 970-641-7700
Andy Hanks, prin. Fax 641-7709
Gunnison MS 300/6-8
1099 N 11th St 81230 970-641-7710
Todd Witzel, prin. Fax 641-7739
Other Schools – See Crested Butte

---

Western State Colorado University Post-Sec.
600 N Adams St 81231 970-943-0120

**Gypsum, Eagle, Pop. 6,422**
Eagle County SD RE-50
Supt. — See Eagle
Eagle Valley HS 700/9-12
PO Box 188 81637 970-328-8960
Greg Doan, prin. Fax 328-8965
Gypsum Creek MS 400/6-8
PO Box 5129 81637 970-328-8980
David Russell, prin. Fax 328-8985

**Haxtun, Phillips, Pop. 937**
Haxtun SD RE-2J 300/PK-12
201 W Powell St 80731 970-774-6111
Darcy Garretson, supt. Fax 774-7568
www.haxtunschools.com
Haxtun HS 100/9-12
201 W Powell St 80731 970-774-6111
Alan Nall, prin. Fax 774-7568

**Hayden, Routt, Pop. 1,785**
Hayden SD RE-1 400/PK-12
PO Box 70 81639 970-276-3864
Trudy Vader, supt. Fax 276-4217
www.haydenschools.org/
Hayden HS 100/9-12
PO Box 70 81639 970-276-3761
Regina Zabel, prin. Fax 276-4374
Hayden MS 100/6-8
PO Box 70 81639 970-276-3762
Regina Zabel, prin. Fax 276-7235

**Henderson, Adams, Pop. 500**
Brighton SD 27J
Supt. — See Brighton
Prairie View HS 1,600/9-12
12909 E 120th Ave 80640 303-655-8800
Jaime White, prin. Fax 655-8920
Prairie View MS 800/6-8
12915 E 120th Ave 80640 720-685-5400
Tom Delgado, prin. Fax 685-5404

---

American Institute of Technology Post-Sec.
9239 Brighton Rd Unit 201 80640 303-558-3152

**Highlands Ranch, Douglas, Pop. 94,597**
Douglas County SD RE-1
Supt. — See Castle Rock
Cresthill MS 900/7-8
9195 Cresthill Ln 80130 303-387-2800
Sid Rundle, prin. Fax 387-2801
Highlands Ranch HS 1,700/9-12
9375 Cresthill Ln 80130 303-387-2500
Chris Page, prin. Fax 387-2501
Mountain Ridge MS 1,000/7-8
10590 Mountain Vista Rdg 80126 303-387-1800
Shannon Clarke, prin. Fax 387-1801
Mountain Vista HS 2,000/9-12
10585 Mountain Vista Rdg 80126 303-387-1500
Michael Weaver, prin. Fax 387-1501
Ranch View MS 1,000/7-8
1731 W Wildcat Reserve Pkwy 80129 303-387-2300
Tanner Fitch, prin. Fax 387-2301
STEM S and Academy 500/6-12
8773 Ridgeline Blvd 80129 303-683-7836
Dr. Penny Eucker, prin. Fax 683-2099
ThunderRidge HS 1,900/9-12
1991 W Wildcat Reserve Pkwy 80129 303-387-2000
Chris Tabeling, prin. Fax 387-2001
Eagle Academy Adult
9375 Cresthill Ln 80130 303-387-2700
Chris Eberhardt, prin. Fax 470-7376

---

Mile High Academy 100/PK-12
1733 Dad Clark Dr 80126 303-744-1069
Valor Christian HS 800/9-12
3775 Grace Blvd 80126 303-471-3000
Kurt Unruh, head sch Fax 471-3001

**Hoehne, Las Animas, Pop. 111**
Hoehne RSD 3 200/K-12
PO Box 91 81046 719-846-4457
Christine Barela, supt. Fax 846-2208
www.hoehnesd.org/
Hoehne S 200/K-12
PO Box 91 81046 719-846-4457
Joseph DeAngelis, prin. Fax 846-2208

**Holly, Prowers, Pop. 799**
Holly SD RE-3 300/PK-12
PO Box 608 81047 719-537-6616
Carlyn Yokum, supt. Fax 537-0315
www.hollyschool.org/
Holly JSHS 100/7-12
PO Box 608 81047 719-537-6512
Randy Holmen, prin. Fax 537-6519

**Holyoke, Phillips, Pop. 2,299**
Holyoke SD RE-1J 600/K-12
435 S Morlan Ave 80734 970-854-3634
Fax 854-4049
holyoke.schoolfusion.us
Holyoke Alternative HS Alt
545 E Hale St 80734 970-854-2284
Cindi Beavers, dir. Fax 854-4578
Holyoke JSHS 300/7-12
545 E Hale St 80734 970-854-2284
Susan Ortner, prin. Fax 854-4578

**Hotchkiss, Delta, Pop. 933**
Delta County SD 50(J)
Supt. — See Delta
Hotchkiss HS 200/9-12
438 Bulldog St 81419 970-872-3882
Mike Beard, prin. Fax 872-2390

**Hugo, Lincoln, Pop. 718**
Genoa-Hugo SD C113 200/PK-12
PO Box 247 80821 719-743-2428
Frank Reeves, supt. Fax 743-2194
www.genoahugo.org
Genoa-Hugo HS 50/9-12
PO Box 247 80821 719-743-2428
Shari Humphrey, prin. Fax 743-2194
Genoa-Hugo MS 50/6-8
PO Box 247 80821 719-743-2428
Shari Humphrey, prin. Fax 743-2194

**Idaho Springs, Clear Creek, Pop. 1,695**
Clear Creek SD RE-1 1,000/PK-12
PO Box 3399 80452 303-567-3850
Roslin Marshall, supt. Fax 567-3861
www.ccsdre1.org/
Other Schools – See Evergreen

**Idalia, Yuma, Pop. 88**
Idalia SD RJ-3 200/PK-12
PO Box 40 80735 970-354-7298
Tim Krause, supt. Fax 354-7416
www.idaliaco.us
Idalia JSHS 50/6-12
PO Box 40 80735 970-354-7298
Tim Krause, admin. Fax 354-7416

**Ignacio, LaPlata, Pop. 652**
Ignacio SD 11 JT 700/K-12
PO Box 460 81137 970-563-0500
Rocco Fuschetto Ed.D., supt. Fax 563-4524
www.ignacioschools.org
Ignacio HS 200/9-12
PO Box 460 81137 970-563-0515
Melanie Taylor, prin. Fax 563-9463
Ignacio MS 100/6-8
PO Box 460 81137 970-563-0600
Chris deKay, prin. Fax 563-0234

**Iliff, Logan, Pop. 261**
Valley SD RE-1
Supt. — See Sterling
Caliche JSHS 100/7-12
26308 County Road 65 80736 970-522-8200
Doug Stutzman, prin. Fax 522-9400

**Joes, Yuma, Pop. 78**
Liberty SD J-4 100/PK-12
PO Box 112 80822 970-358-4288
John McCleary, supt. Fax 358-4282
www.libertyschoolj4.com
Liberty JSHS 50/7-12
PO Box 112 80822 970-358-4288
John McCleary, prin. Fax 358-4282

**Johnstown, Weld, Pop. 9,738**
Weld County SD RE-5J
Supt. — See Milliken
Roosevelt HS 700/9-12
616 N 2nd St 80534 970-587-6000
Trevor Long, prin. Fax 587-2608

**Julesburg, Sedgwick, Pop. 1,216**
Julesburg SD RE-1 300/PK-12
102 W 6th St 80737 970-474-3365
Shawn Ehnes, supt. Fax 474-3742
www.julesburg.org
Julesburg JSHS 100/7-12
102 W 6th St 80737 970-474-3364
Shawn Ehnes, prin. Fax 474-3742

**Karval, Lincoln, Pop. 50**
Karval SD RE-23 200/PK-12
PO Box 5 80823 719-446-5311
Brenda Smith, supt. Fax 446-5332
www.karvalschool.org
Karval JSHS 50/6-12
PO Box 5 80823 719-446-5311
Brenda Smith, supt. Fax 446-5332

**Keenesburg, Weld, Pop. 1,112**
Weld County SD RE-3J 2,300/PK-12
PO Box 269 80643 303-536-2000
Dr. Greg Rabenhorst, supt. Fax 536-2010
www.re3j.com
Weld Central HS 600/9-12
4715 County Road 59 80643 303-536-2100
Dan Kennedy, prin. Fax 536-2110
Weld Central MS 500/6-8
4977 County Road 59 80643 303-536-2700
Jamie Jeffery, prin. Fax 536-2710

**Kersey, Weld, Pop. 1,432**
Weld County SD RE-7 1,100/PK-12
PO Box 485 80644 970-336-8500
Dr. E. Glenn McClain Ed.D., supt. Fax 336-8511
www.plattevalley.k12.co.us
Platte Valley HS 300/9-12
PO Box 487 80644 970-336-8700
Brad Joens, prin. Fax 336-8794
Platte Valley MS 300/6-8
PO Box 515 80644 970-336-8610
Jason Taylor, prin. Fax 336-8635

**Kim, Las Animas, Pop. 73**
Kim RSD 88 100/PK-12
PO Box 100 81049 719-643-5295
Monica Johnson, supt. Fax 643-5299
www.kimk12.org
Kim JSHS 50/7-12
PO Box 100 81049 719-643-5295
Monica Johnson, prin. Fax 643-5299

**Kiowa, Elbert, Pop. 708**
Kiowa SD C-2 400/PK-12
PO Box 128 80117 303-621-2220
Jason Westfall, supt. Fax 621-2239
www.kiowaschool.org
Kiowa HS 100/9-12
PO Box 128 80117 303-621-2115
Amy Smith, prin. Fax 621-2566
Kiowa MS 100/6-8
PO Box 128 80117 303-621-2785
Amy Smith, prin. Fax 621-2239

**Kit Carson, Cheyenne, Pop. 230**
Kit Carson SD R-1 100/K-12
PO Box 185 80825 719-962-3219
Gerald Keefe, supt. Fax 962-3317
www.kcsdr1.org
Carson JSHS 100/6-12
PO Box 185 80825 719-962-3219
Gerald Keefe, prin. Fax 962-3317

**Kremmling, Grand, Pop. 1,417**
West Grand SD 1-JT 400/K-12
PO Box 515 80459 970-724-3217
Mike Page, supt. Fax 724-9373
www.wgsd.us
West Grand HS 100/9-12
PO Box 515 80459 970-724-3425
Mike Page, prin. Fax 724-3450

**Lafayette, Boulder, Pop. 23,902**
Boulder Valley SD RE-2
Supt. — See Boulder
Angevine MS 600/6-8
1150 W South Boulder Rd 80026 720-561-7100
Mike Medina, prin. Fax 561-7101
Centaurus HS 1,000/9-12
10300 E South Boulder Rd 80026 720-561-7500
Rhonda Haniford, prin. Fax 561-5368

---

Dawson S 500/K-12
10455 Dawson Dr 80026 303-665-6679
George Moore, head sch Fax 665-0757

**La Jara, Conejos, Pop. 805**
North Conejos SD RE-1J 1,000/PK-12
PO Box 72 81140 719-274-5174
Curt Wilson, supt. Fax 274-5621
www.northconejos.com
Centauri HS 300/9-12
17889 US Highway 285 81140 719-274-5178
Brian Loch, prin. Fax 274-5637
Centauri MS 200/6-8
17891 US Highway 285 81140 719-274-4301
Tyler Huffaker, prin. Fax 274-4306
North Conejos Alternative Program 100/Alt
PO Box 72 81140 719-274-4220
Susan Hamilton, admin. Fax 274-3809

**La Junta, Otero, Pop. 6,961**
East Otero SD R-1 1,100/K-12
301 Raton Ave 81050 719-384-6900
Rick Lovato, supt. Fax 384-6910
www.lajuntaschools.org
La Junta JSHS 600/7-12
1817 Smithland Ave 81050 719-384-4467
John Haberman, prin. Fax 384-2581

---

Otero Junior College Post-Sec.
1802 Colorado Ave 81050 719-384-6831

**Lake City, Hinsdale, Pop. 393**
Hinsdale County SD RE 1 100/PK-12
PO Box 39 81235 970-944-2314
Dr. Leslie Nichols, supt. Fax 944-2662
www.lakecityschool.org/
Lake City Community S 100/PK-12
PO Box 39 81235 970-944-2314
Dr. Leslie Nichols, prin. Fax 944-2662

**Lakewood, Jefferson, Pop. 140,229**
Jefferson County SD R-1
Supt. — See Golden
Alameda International JSHS 800/7-12
1255 S Wadsworth Blvd 80232 303-982-8160
Susie VanScoyk, prin. Fax 982-8161
Bear Creek HS 1,900/9-12
9800 W Dartmouth Pl 80227 303-982-8855
Kevin Carroll, prin. Fax 982-8856
Brady Exploration S 300/Alt
5220 W Ohio Ave 80226 303-982-6722
Troy Braley, prin. Fax 982-6723
Carmody MS 700/7-8
2050 S Kipling St 80227 303-982-8930
Wendy Doran, prin. Fax 982-8931
Creighton MS 700/7-8
50 S Kipling St 80226 303-982-6282
Nick Kemmer, prin. Fax 982-6283
Dunstan MS 600/7-8
1855 S Wright St 80228 303-982-9270
Jennifer Kirksey, prin. Fax 982-9269
Green Mountain HS 1,200/9-12
13175 W Green Mountain Dr 80228 303-982-9500
Colleen Owens, prin. Fax 982-9501
Jefferson County Open S 300/PK-12
7655 W 10th Ave 80214 303-982-7045
Scott Bain, prin. Fax 982-7046
Lakewood HS 2,100/9-12
9700 W 8th Ave 80215 303-982-7096
Lisa Ritchey, prin. Fax 982-7097
Long View HS 100/Alt
13301 W 2nd Pl 80228 303-982-8523
Fax 982-8568
McClain Community HS 200/Alt
13600 W 2nd Pl 80228 303-982-7460
Steve Johnson, prin. Fax 982-7494
Warren Tech S Vo/Tech
13300 W 2nd Pl 80228 303-982-8600
Joe Shaw, prin. Fax 982-8622

---

Colorado Christian University Post-Sec.
8787 W Alameda Ave 80226 303-963-3000
Colorado School of Healing Arts Post-Sec.
7655 W Mississippi #100 80226 303-986-2320
Colorado School of Trades Post-Sec.
1575 Hoyt St 80215 303-233-4697
Denver Christian S 200/PK-12
3898 S Teller St 80235 303-733-2421
Dr. Steven Kortenhoeven, dir. Fax 733-7734
Ohio Center for Broadcasting - Colorado Post-Sec.
404 S Upham St 80226 303-937-7070
Red Rocks Community College Post-Sec.
13300 W 6th Ave 80228 303-914-6600

**Lamar, Prowers, Pop. 7,721**
Lamar SD RE-2 1,700/PK-12
210 W Pearl St 81052 719-336-3251
Dave Tecklenburg, supt. Fax 336-2817
www.lamarschools.org
Lamar HS 400/9-12
1900 S 11th St 81052 719-336-3488
Rocky Robbins, prin. Fax 336-3026
Lamar MS 300/6-8
104 W Park St 81052 719-336-7436
Matt Snyder, prin. Fax 336-5457

---

Lamar Community College Post-Sec.
2401 S Main St 81052 719-336-2248

**Laporte, Larimer, Pop. 2,391**
Poudre SD R-1
Supt. — See Fort Collins
Cache La Poudre MS 300/6-8
3515 W County Road 54G 80535 970-488-7400
Alicia Bono, prin. Fax 488-7433

**La Salle, Weld, Pop. 1,932**
Weld County SD RE-1
Supt. — See Gilcrest
North Valley MS 300/6-8
300 2nd Ave 80645 970-284-5508
Richard Dufault, prin. Fax 284-6595

**Las Animas, Bent, Pop. 2,388**
Las Animas SD RE-1 500/PK-12
1021 2nd St 81054 719-456-0161
Elsie Goines, supt. Fax 456-1117
la-schools.com
Las Animas HS 100/9-12
300 Grove Ave 81054 719-456-0211
Tom Meardon, prin. Fax 456-0932
Las Animas JHS 100/7-8
1021 2nd St 81054 719-456-0228
Elsie Goines, prin. Fax 456-0241

**La Veta, Huerfano, Pop. 774**
La Veta SD RE-2 200/PK-12
PO Box 85 81055 719-742-3562
Bree Lessar, supt. Fax 742-3959
www.laveta.k12.co.us
La Veta JSHS 100/6-12
PO Box 85 81055 719-742-3662
Bree Lessar, prin. Fax 742-5799

**Leadville, Lake, Pop. 2,564**
Lake County SD R-1 1,200/PK-12
107 Spruce St 80461 719-486-6800
Wendy Wyman, supt. Fax 486-2048
www.lakecountyschools.net/
Lake County HS 300/7-12
1000 W 4th St 80461 719-486-6950
Christina Gosselin, prin. Fax 486-8157

**Limon, Lincoln, Pop. 1,854**
Limon SD RE-4J 400/K-12
PO Box 249 80828 719-775-2350
Dave Marx, supt. Fax 775-9052
www.limonbadgers.com/
Limon JSHS 300/6-12
PO Box 249 80828 719-775-2350
Traci Weisensee, prin. Fax 775-9052

**Littleton, Arapahoe, Pop. 40,946**
Douglas County SD RE-1
Supt. — See Castle Rock
Rocky Heights MS 1,300/6-8
11033 Monarch Blvd 80124 303-387-3300
Jason Sears, prin. Fax 387-3301

Jefferson County SD R-1
Supt. — See Golden
Chatfield HS 1,900/9-12
7227 S Simms St 80127 303-982-3670
Chad Broer, prin. Fax 982-3671
Columbine HS 1,600/9-12
6201 S Pierce St 80123 303-982-4400
K.C. Somers, prin. Fax 982-4401
Dakota Ridge HS 1,500/9-12
13399 W Coal Mine Ave 80127 303-982-1970
Dr. James Jelinek, prin. Fax 982-1971
Deer Creek MS 500/6-8
9201 W Columbine Dr 80128 303-982-3820
Rob Hoover, prin. Fax 982-3821
Falcon Bluffs MS 600/6-8
8449 S Garrison St 80128 303-982-9900
Summer Guerrina, prin. Fax 982-9901
Ken Caryl MS 600/7-8
6509 W Ken Caryl Ave 80128 303-982-4710
Patrick Sandos, prin. Fax 982-4711
Summit Ridge MS 800/7-8
11809 W Coal Mine Ave 80127 303-982-9013
Daniel Brennan, prin. Fax 982-8998

Littleton SD 15,700/PK-12
5776 S Crocker St 80120 303-347-3300
Brian Ewert, supt. Fax 347-4350
www.littletonpublicschools.net
Euclid MS 700/6-8
777 W Euclid Ave 80120 303-347-7800
Gary Hein, prin. Fax 347-7830
Goddard MS 800/6-8
3800 W Berry Ave 80123 303-347-7850
Bryan Breuer, prin. Fax 347-7880
Heritage HS 1,700/9-12
1401 W Geddes Ave 80120 303-347-7600
Stacey Riendeau, prin. Fax 347-7604
Littleton HS 1,500/9-12
199 E Littleton Blvd 80121 303-347-7700
Amy Oaks Ed.D., prin. Fax 347-3772
Options Secondary HS Program 100/Alt
6558 S Acoma St 80120 303-347-3580
Greg Sumlin, prin. Fax 347-3590
Options Secondary MS Program Alt
6557 S Acoma St 80120 303-347-4725
Ashley Broer, prin. Fax 347-4747
Powell MS 900/6-8
8000 S Corona Way 80122 303-347-7950
Steve Wolf, prin. Fax 347-3975
Other Schools – See Centennial

---

Arapahoe Community College Post-Sec.
PO Box 9002 80160 303-797-4222
Denver Seminary Post-Sec.
6399 S Santa Fe Dr 80120 303-761-2482
Front Range Christian S 400/PK-12
6657 W Ottawa Ave Ste A17 80128 720-922-3269
David Cooper, head sch Fax 922-3296
Truth Christian Academy 50/PK-12
PO Box 621961 80162 303-670-3360
Stanley Silverman, admin. Fax 670-8069

**Lonetree, See Littleton**
Douglas County SD RE-1
Supt. — See Castle Rock
Rock Canyon HS 1,700/9-12
5810 McArthur Ranch Rd 80124 303-387-3000
Andrew Abner, prin. Fax 387-3021

---

University of Phoenix Post-Sec.
10004 Park Meadows Dr 80124 303-755-9090

**Longmont, Boulder, Pop. 84,733**
St. Vrain Valley SD RE-1J 25,500/PK-12
395 S Pratt Pkwy 80501 303-776-6200
Don Haddad Ed.D., supt. Fax 682-7396
www.svvsd.org
Altona MS 600/6-8
4600 Clover Basin Dr 80503 720-494-3980
Jeremy LaCrosse, prin. Fax 494-3989
Career Development Center Vo/Tech
1200 S Sunset St 80501 303-772-3333
Deniece Cook, prin. Fax 494-3977
Longmont HS 1,200/9-12
1040 Sunset St 80501 303-776-6014
Rick Olsen, prin. Fax 494-3916
Longs Peak MS 400/5-8
1500 14th Ave 80501 303-776-5611
Tim Bishop, prin. Fax 494-3663
Mead HS 700/9-12
12750 County Road 7 80504 720-494-3940
Linda Rawlings, prin. Fax 494-3959
Olde Columbine HS 100/Alt
1200 S Sunset St 80501 720-494-3961
Deniece Cook, prin. Fax 494-3968
Silver Creek HS 1,000/9-12
4901 Nelson Rd 80503 720-494-3721
Erick Finnestead, prin. Fax 494-3730
Skyline HS 1,200/9-12
600 E Mountain View Ave 80504 720-494-3741
Heidi Ringer, prin. Fax 682-7382
Sunset MS 600/6-8
1300 S Sunset St 80501 303-776-3963
Dr. Dawn Macy, prin. Fax 494-3703
Trail Ridge MS 600/6-8
1000 Button Rock Dr 80504 720-494-3820
Eddie Cloke, prin. Fax 494-3829
Westview MS 600/6-8
1651 Airport Rd 80503 303-772-3134
Mark Spencer, prin. Fax 494-3786
Other Schools – See Erie, Firestone, Frederick, Lyons, Mead, Niwot

---

Faith Baptist S 100/K-12
833 15th Ave 80501 303-776-5677
Institute of Business & Medical Careers Post-Sec.
2315 Main St 80501 303-651-6819
Longmont Christian S 300/PK-12
1440 Collyer St 80501 303-776-3254
Donnie Bennett, prin. Fax 485-6937

**Louisville, Boulder, Pop. 17,982**
Boulder Valley SD RE-2
Supt. — See Boulder
Louisville MS 600/6-8
1341 Main St 80027 720-561-7400
Ginny Vidulich, prin. Fax 561-7401
Monarch HS 1,500/9-12
329 Campus Dr 80027 720-561-4200
Jerry Anderson, prin. Fax 561-5650

---

Institute of Taoist Educ & Acupuncture Post-Sec.
325 W South Boulder Rd # 2 80027 720-890-8922

**Loveland, Larimer, Pop. 65,828**
Thompson SD R-2J 14,100/PK-12
800 S Taft Ave 80537 970-613-5000
Dr. Stan Scheer, supt. Fax 613-5095
www.thompsonschools.org
Ball MS 600/6-8
2660 Monroe Ave 80538 970-613-7300
Tiffany Miller, prin. Fax 613-7341
Clark MS 500/6-8
2605 Carlisle Dr 80537 970-613-5400
Christine Smith, prin. Fax 613-5420
Erwin MS 900/6-8
4700 Lucerne Ave 80538 970-613-7600
Diane Worner, prin. Fax 613-7619
Ferguson HS 100/Alt
1101 Hilltop Dr 80537 970-613-5300
Sheila Pottorff, prin. Fax 613-5395
Loveland HS 1,500/9-12
920 W 29th St 80538 970-613-5200
Todd Ball, prin. Fax 613-7191
Mountain View HS 1,100/9-12
3500 Mountain Lion Dr 80537 970-613-7800
Kim Young, prin. Fax 613-7820
Reed MS 700/6-8
370 W 4th St 80537 970-613-7200
Arnold Jahnke, prin. Fax 613-7287
Thompson Valley HS 1,300/9-12
1669 Eagle Dr 80537 970-613-7900
Lanny Hass, prin. Fax 613-7909
Other Schools – See Berthoud

---

Campion Academy 200/9-12
300 42nd St SW 80537 970-667-5592
Don Reeder B.S., prin. Fax 667-5104
Resurrection Christian S 800/PK-12
6508 E Crossroads Blvd 80538 970-612-0674
Rev. Allen Howlett M.A., supt. Fax 612-0975

**Lyons, Boulder, Pop. 2,004**
St. Vrain Valley SD RE-1J
Supt. — See Longmont
Lyons MSHS 400/6-12
100 McConnell Dr 80540 303-823-6631
Greg Winger, prin. Fax 494-3855

**Mc Clave, Bent, Pop. 150**
McClave SD RE-2 300/PK-12
PO Box 1 81057 719-829-4517
Terry Weber, supt. Fax 829-4430
www.mcclaveschool.org
Mc Clave JSHS 100/7-12
PO Box 1 81057 719-829-4517
Rachel Dunning, prin. Fax 829-4430

**Mancos, Montezuma, Pop. 1,302**
Mancos SD RE-6 400/PK-12
395 Grand Ave 81328 970-533-7748
Brian Hanson, supt. Fax 533-7954
www.mancosre6.edu
Mancos HS 100/9-12
355 Grand Ave 81328 970-533-7746
Adam Priestley, prin. Fax 533-7537
Mancos MS 100/6-8
100 S Beech St 81328 970-533-9143
Adam Priestley, prin. Fax 533-1463

---

San Juan Basin Technical College Post-Sec.
33057 Highway 160 81328 970-565-8457

**Manitou Springs, El Paso, Pop. 4,882**
Manitou Springs SD 14 1,500/PK-12
405 El Monte Pl 80829 719-685-2024
Ed Longfield, supt. Fax 685-4536
www.mssd14.org/
Manitou Springs HS 500/9-12
401 El Monte Pl 80829 719-685-2074
Glenn Hard, prin. Fax 685-4755
Manitou Springs MS 400/6-8
415 El Monte Pl 80829 719-685-2127
Chris Burr, prin. Fax 685-4552

**Manzanola, Otero, Pop. 429**
Manzanola SD 3J 200/K-12
PO Box 148 81058 719-462-5527
Tom Wilke, supt. Fax 462-5708
www.manzanola.k12.co.us/
Manzanola JSHS 100/7-12
PO Box 148 81058 719-462-5528
Tom Wilke, admin. Fax 462-5115

**Mead, Weld, Pop. 3,346**
St. Vrain Valley SD RE-1J
Supt. — See Longmont
Mead MS 400/6-8
620 Welker Ave 80542 970-535-4446
Joshua Barnett, prin. Fax 494-3686

**Meeker, Rio Blanco, Pop. 2,417**
Meeker SD RE-1 700/PK-12
PO Box 1089 81641 970-878-9040
Chris Selle, supt. Fax 878-3682
www.meeker.k12.co.us
Barone MS 200/6-8
PO Box 690 81641 970-878-9060
Jim Hanks, prin. Fax 878-4291
Meeker HS 200/9-12
PO Box 159 81641 970-878-9070
Amy Chinn, prin. Fax 878-3633

**Merino, Logan, Pop. 281**
Merino SD RE-4J 300/K-12
PO Box 198 80741 970-522-7424
Robert Sanders, supt. Fax 522-1541
www.merino-sd.schoolfusion.us/
Merino JSHS 200/7-12
PO Box 198 80741 970-522-7424
Lonnie Brungardt, prin. Fax 522-1541

**Milliken, Weld, Pop. 5,520**
Weld County SD RE-5J 3,300/PK-12
110 Centennial Dr Ste A 80543 970-587-6050
Dr. Martin Foster, supt. Fax 587-2607
www.weldre5j.k12.co.us
Milliken MS 600/6-8
PO Box 339 80543 970-587-6300
Ron Hruby, prin. Fax 587-5749
Other Schools – See Johnstown

**Moffat, Saguache, Pop. 116**
Moffat SD 2, PO Box 428 81143 200/PK-12
Kirk Banghart, supt. 719-256-4710
www.moffatschools.org
Moffat S, PO Box 127 81143 50/PK-12
Michelle Hashbarger, prin. 719-256-4710

**Monte Vista, Rio Grande, Pop. 4,392**
Monte Vista SD C-8 1,000/PK-12
349 E Prospect Ave 81144 719-852-5996
Robert Webb, supt. Fax 852-6184
www.monte.k12.co.us
Monte Vista HS 300/9-12
295 E Prospect Ave 81144 719-852-3586
Scott Wiedeman, prin. Fax 852-6121
Monte Vista MS 200/6-8
3720 Sherman Ave 81144 719-852-5984
Tom Tichy, prin. Fax 852-6199

Sargent SD RE-33J 400/K-12
7090 N County Road 2 E 81144 719-852-4023
Steven Marantino, supt. Fax 852-9890
www.sargent.k12.co.us
Sargent JSHS 100/7-12
7090 N County Road 2 E 81144 719-852-4025
Ronna Cochran, prin. Fax 852-9672

**Montrose, Montrose, Pop. 18,812**
Montrose County SD RE-1J 6,300/PK-12
PO Box 10000 81402 970-249-7726
Steve Schiell, supt. Fax 249-7173
www.mcsd.org
Centennial MS 500/6-8
PO Box 10000 81402 970-249-2576
Joe Simo, prin. Fax 240-6461
Columbine MS 500/6-8
PO Box 10000 81402 970-249-2581
Ben Stephenson, prin. Fax 240-6404
Montrose HS 1,400/9-12
PO Box 10000 81402 970-249-6636
James Barnhill, prin. Fax 240-6414
Other Schools – See Olathe

---

Colorado West Christian S 100/PK-12
2705 Sunnyside Rd 81401 970-249-1094

**Monument, El Paso, Pop. 5,337**
Lewis-Palmer SD 38 5,300/PK-12
PO Box 40 80132 719-488-4700
Karen Brofft, supt. Fax 488-4704
www.lewispalmer.org
Lewis-Palmer HS 900/9-12
1300 Higby Rd 80132 719-488-4720
Sandi Brandl, prin. Fax 488-4723
Lewis-Palmer MS 800/7-8
1776 Woodmoor Dr 80132 719-488-4776
Seann O'Connor, prin. Fax 488-4780
Palmer Ridge HS 1,100/9-12
19255 Monument Hill Rd 80132 719-867-8600
Gary Gabel, prin. Fax 867-8605

**Mosca, Alamosa, Pop. 180**
Sangre De Cristo SD RE-22J 300/PK-12
8751 Lane 7 N 81146 719-378-2321
Brady Stagner, supt. Fax 378-2327
www.sdc.schoolfusion.us
Sangre De Cristo JSHS 100/7-12
8751 Lane 7 N 81146 719-378-2321
John Stephens, prin. Fax 378-2327

**Nederland, Boulder, Pop. 1,417**
Boulder Valley SD RE-2
Supt. — See Boulder
Nederland MSHS 300/6-12
597 County Road 130 80466 720-561-4900
Adam Fels, prin. Fax 561-4901

**New Castle, Garfield, Pop. 4,478**
Garfield SD RE-2
Supt. — See Rifle
Coal Ridge HS 500/9-12
35947 Highway 6 81647 970-665-6700
Rick Elertson, prin. Fax 665-6701
Riverside MS 700/5-8
215 Alder Ave 81647 970-665-7800
Lacey Moser, prin. Fax 665-7846

**New Raymer, Weld, Pop. 95**
Prairie SD RE-11 200/PK-12
PO Box 68 80742 970-437-5351
Joe Kimmel, supt. Fax 437-5732
www.prairieschool.org/
Prairie JSHS 100/6-12
PO Box 68 80742 970-437-5351
Tabitha Piel, prin. Fax 437-5732

**Niwot, Boulder, Pop. 3,929**
St. Vrain Valley SD RE-1J
Supt. — See Longmont
Niwot HS 1,300/9-12
8989 Niwot Rd 80503 303-652-2550
Eric Rauschkolb, prin. Fax 494-3928

**Northglenn, Adams, Pop. 35,024**
Adams 12 Five Star SD
Supt. — See Thornton
Crossroads Alternative S 100/Alt
10900 Huron St 80234 720-972-5900
Alan Hollenbeck, prin. Fax 972-5919
Northglenn HS 1,700/9-12
601 W 100th Pl 80260 720-972-4600
Sharee Blunt, prin. Fax 972-4739
Northglenn MS 700/6-8
1123 Muriel Dr 80233 720-972-5080
Jami Miller, prin. Fax 972-5119
Vantage Point HS 500/Alt
10900 Huron St 80234 720-972-5800
Alan Hollenbeck, prin. Fax 972-5814

---

Community Christian S 200/PK-12
11980 Irma Dr 80233 303-452-7514
Wes Pavy, admin. Fax 452-4904

**Norwood, San Miguel, Pop. 505**
Norwood SD R-2J 300/PK-12
PO Box 448 81423 970-327-4336
David Crews, supt. Fax 327-4116
www.npsmavs.com
Norwood HS 100/6-12
PO Box 448 81423 970-327-4336
Fax 327-4116

**Nucla, Montrose, Pop. 704**
West End SD RE-2 300/PK-12
PO Box 570 81424 970-864-7350
Michael Epright, supt. Fax 864-7269
www.westendschools.org
Nucla HS 100/9-12
PO Box 570 81424 970-864-7350
Michael Epright, supt. Fax 864-7269

**Oak Creek, Routt, Pop. 865**
South Routt SD RE-3 400/PK-12
PO Box 158 80467 970-736-2313
Darci Mohr, supt. Fax 736-2458
www.southroutt.k12.co.us
Soroco HS 100/9-12
PO Box 158 80467 970-736-2531
Lynda McCarty, prin. Fax 736-0211
Soroco MS 100/6-8
PO Box 158 80467 970-736-8531
Lynda McCarty, prin. Fax 736-0182

**Olathe, Montrose, Pop. 1,821**
Montrose County SD RE-1J
Supt. — See Montrose
Olathe HS 400/9-12
410 Highway 50 81425 970-252-7950
Scot Brown, prin. Fax 323-5947
Olathe MS 300/6-8
410 Highway 50 81425 970-252-7950
Scot Brown, prin. Fax 323-5947

**Ordway, Crowley, Pop. 1,058**
Crowley County SD RE-1-J 500/K-12
117 W 3rd St 81063 719-267-3117
Scott Cuckow, supt. Fax 267-3130
www.cck12.net/
Crowley County HS 100/9-12
602 Main St 81063 719-267-3582
Lisa Bauer, prin. Fax 267-3585
Crowley County MS 100/6-8
602 Main St 81063 719-267-9880
Lisa Bauer, prin. Fax 267-9881

**Otis, Washington, Pop. 462**
Lone Star SD 101 100/K-12
44940 County Road 54 80743 970-848-2778
Susan Sonnenberg, supt. Fax 848-0340
www.lonestarschool.net
Lone Star JSHS 50/6-12
44940 County Road 54 80743 970-848-2778
Michael Bowers, prin. Fax 848-0340

Otis SD R-3 200/PK-12
518 Dungan St 80743 970-246-3413
Mike Warren, supt. Fax 246-0518
www.osdco.com
Otis JSHS 100/7-12
301 Work St 80743 970-246-3486
Michael Warren, supt. Fax 246-3487

**Ouray, Ouray, Pop. 990**
Ouray SD R-1 200/PK-12
PO Box N 81427 970-325-4505
Scott Pankow, supt. Fax 325-7343
www.ouray.k12.co.us/
Ouray HS 100/9-12
PO Box N 81427 970-325-4505
Scott Pankow, prin. Fax 325-7343
Ouray MS 50/7-8
PO Box N 81427 970-325-4505
Scott Pankow, prin. Fax 325-7343

**Ovid, Sedgwick, Pop. 314**
Platte Valley SD RE-3 100/PK-12
500 Main St 80744 970-463-5477
Sharon Green, supt. Fax 503-2318
www.plattevalley.schoolfusion.us

Revere JSHS 100/7-12
500 Main St 80744 970-463-5477
Chuck Bunner, prin. Fax 503-2318

**Pagosa Springs, Archuleta, Pop. 1,685**
Archuleta SD 50 JT 1,400/K-12
PO Box 1498 81147 970-264-2228
Linda Reed, supt. Fax 264-4631
www.mypagosaschools.com
Pagosa Springs HS 500/9-12
PO Box 1498 81147 970-264-2231
Sean O'Donnell, prin. Fax 264-2239
Pagosa Springs MS 400/5-8
PO Box 1498 81147 970-264-2794
Chris Hinger, prin. Fax 264-6112

**Palisade, Mesa, Pop. 2,644**
Mesa County Valley SD 51
Supt. — See Grand Junction
Palisade HS 1,000/9-12
3679 G Rd 81526 970-254-4800
Dan Bollinger, prin. Fax 464-5102

**Paonia, Delta, Pop. 1,427**
Delta County SD 50(J)
Supt. — See Delta
Paonia JSHS 300/7-12
846 Grand Ave 81428 970-527-4882
Randal Palmer, prin. Fax 527-4080

**Parachute, Garfield, Pop. 1,062**
Garfield County SD 16 900/PK-12
PO Box 68 81635 970-285-5701
Dr. Ken Haptonstall, supt. Fax 285-5711
www.garfield16.org
Grand Valley HS 300/9-12
PO Box 68 81635 970-285-5705
Ryan Frink, prin. Fax 285-5715
Grand Valley MS 200/6-8
PO Box 68 81635 970-285-5707
Jory Sorensen, prin. Fax 285-5717

**Parker, Douglas, Pop. 44,230**
Douglas County SD RE-1
Supt. — See Castle Rock
Chaparral HS 2,100/9-12
15655 Brookstone Dr 80134 303-387-3500
Greg Gotchey, prin. Fax 387-3501
Cimarron MS 900/7-8
12130 Canterberry Pkwy 80138 303-433-0120
Christopher Zimmerman, prin. Fax 433-0121
Legend HS 1,800/9-12
22219 Hilltop Rd 80138 303-387-4500
Jason Jacob, prin. Fax 387-4501
Ponderosa HS 1,200/9-12
7007 Bayou Gulch Rd 80134 303-387-4000
David Haggerty, prin. Fax 387-4101
Sagewood MS 1,000/6-8
4725 Fox Sparrow Rd 80134 303-387-4300
Daniel Winsor, prin. Fax 387-4301
Sierra MS 1,000/7-8
6651 E Pine Ln 80138 303-387-3800
Kathyrn Teel, prin. Fax 387-3801

---

Lutheran HS 200/9-12
11249 Newlin Gulch Blvd 80134 303-841-5551
David Ness, prin. Fax 842-1015
Rocky Vista University Post-Sec.
8401 S Chambers Rd 80134 303-373-2008

**Peetz, Logan, Pop. 237**
Peetz Plateau SD RE-5 200/PK-12
311 Coleman Ave 80747 970-334-2361
Mark Collard, supt. Fax 334-2360
www.peetzschool.org
Peetz JSHS 100/7-12
311 Coleman Ave 80747 970-334-2361
Mark Collard, prin. Fax 334-2360

**Peyton, El Paso, Pop. 247**
Falcon SD 49
Supt. — See Falcon
Falcon HS 1,200/9-12
10255 Lambert Rd 80831 719-495-5522
Cheryl DeGeorge, prin. Fax 495-5521
Falcon MS 900/6-8
9755 Towner Ave 80831 719-495-5232
Brian Smith, prin. Fax 495-5237
Patriot Learning Center 200/Alt
11990 Swingline Rd 80831 719-495-5505
Thomas Wilke, prin. Fax 495-5506

Peyton SD 23 JT 700/PK-12
13990 Bradshaw Rd 80831 719-749-2330
Tim Kistler, supt. Fax 749-2368
www.peyton.k12.co.us/
Peyton JSHS 300/7-12
13885 Bradshaw Rd 80831 719-749-0417
Brian Rea, prin. Fax 749-0150

**Platteville, Weld, Pop. 2,448**
Weld County SD RE-1
Supt. — See Gilcrest
South Valley MS 200/6-8
1004 Main St 80651 970-785-2205
Jeff Angus, prin. Fax 785-2182

**Pritchett, Baca, Pop. 140**
Pritchett SD RE-3 100/PK-12
PO Box 7 81064 719-523-4045
Jim Boydstun, supt. Fax 523-6991
www.pritchettschool.com/
Pritchett HS 50/9-12
PO Box 7 81064 719-523-4045
Kyle Boydstun, lead tchr. Fax 523-6991
Pritchett JHS 50/6-8
PO Box 7 81064 719-523-4045
Kyle Boydstun, lead tchr. Fax 523-6991

**Pueblo, Pueblo, Pop. 104,988**
Pueblo CSD 60 16,700/PK-12
315 W 11th St 81003 719-549-7100
Dr. Constance Jones, supt. Fax 549-7112
www.pueblocityschools.us

Centennial HS 1,200/9-12
2525 Mountview Dr 81008 719-549-7335
Javin Baker, prin. Fax 549-7634
Central HS 1,000/9-12
216 E Orman Ave 81004 719-549-7300
Dr. Lynn Seifert, prin. Fax 549-7306
Corwin International Magnet MS 600/4-8
1500 Lakeview Ave 81004 719-549-7400
Sulema James, prin. Fax 253-5264
East HS 1,000/9-12
9 MacNeil Rd 81001 719-549-7222
Dr. Patrick Krumholz, prin. Fax 253-5248
Health Academy 9-12
2525 Mountview Dr 81008 719-549-7632
William McAuliffe, coord.
Heaton MS 700/6-8
6 Adair Rd 81001 719-549-7420
Jayme Cardinal, prin. Fax 549-7838
Pueblo Academy of Arts 300/6-8
29 Lehigh Ave 81005 719-549-7430
Karen Ortiz, prin. Fax 549-7878
Risley International Academy 400/6-8
625 N Monument Ave 81001 719-549-7440
Charlotte Macaluso, prin. Fax 549-7926
Roncalli STEM Academy 600/6-8
4202 W State Highway 78 81005 719-549-7450
Marci Imes, prin. Fax 549-7469
South HS 1,400/9-12
1801 Hollywood Dr 81005 719-549-7255
Aaron Bravo, prin. Fax 549-7759

Pueblo County SD 70 8,700/PK-12
24951 E US Highway 50 81006 719-542-0220
C. Edward Smith, supt. Fax 542-0225
www.district70.org
Pleasant View MS 300/6-8
23600 Everett Rd 81006 719-542-7813
Ronda Rein, prin. Fax 545-6291
Pueblo County HS 900/9-12
1050 35th Ln 81006 719-948-3351
Terrie Tafoya, prin. Fax 948-0196
Vineland MS 300/6-8
1132 36th Ln 81006 719-948-3336
Sandy Gibbs, prin. Fax 948-2323
Other Schools – See Colorado City, Pueblo West, Rye

---

Colorado State University - Pueblo Post-Sec.
2200 Bonforte Blvd 81001 719-549-2100
IntelliTec College Post-Sec.
3673 Parker Blvd Ste 250 81008 719-542-3181
Parkview Medical Center Post-Sec.
400 W 16th St 81003 719-584-4573
Pueblo Community College Post-Sec.
900 W Orman Ave 81004 719-549-3200
St. Therese Catholic S 200/PK-12
320 Goodnight Ave 81004 719-561-1121
John Brainard, prin. Fax 561-2252

**Pueblo West, Pueblo, Pop. 29,092**
Pueblo County SD 70
Supt. — See Pueblo
Liberty Point International S 500/6-8
484 S Maher Dr 81007 719-547-3752
Brian Dilka, prin. Fax 547-0499
Pueblo West HS 1,300/9-12
661 W Capistrano Ave 81007 719-547-8050
Martha Nogare, prin. Fax 547-8041
Skyview MS 600/6-8
1047 S Camino De Bravo 81007 719-547-1175
Robert DiPietro, prin. Fax 647-9667

**Rangely, Rio Blanco, Pop. 2,325**
Rangely SD RE-4 500/PK-12
402 W Main St 81648 970-675-2207
Matt Scoggins, supt. Fax 675-5023
www.rangelyk12.org/
Rangely JSHS 200/6-12
234 S Jones Ave 81648 970-675-2253
Dr. Kevin Gates, prin. Fax 675-5403

---

Colorado Northwestern Community College Post-Sec.
500 Kennedy Dr 81648 800-562-1105

**Ridgway, Ouray, Pop. 910**
Ridgway SD R-2 400/PK-12
1115 Clinton St 81432 970-626-4320
Steve Smith, supt. Fax 626-4337
www.ridgway.k12.co.us/
Ridgway HS 100/9-12
1200 Green St 81432 970-626-5788
Chuck Siefken, prin. Fax 626-3249
Ridgway MS 100/6-8
1200 Green St 81432 970-626-5788
Chuck Siefken, prin. Fax 626-3249

**Rifle, Garfield, Pop. 9,029**
Garfield SD RE-2 4,600/PK-12
839 Whiteriver Ave 81650 970-665-7600
Susan Birdsey, supt. Fax 665-7623
www.garfieldre2.org/
Rifle HS 700/9-12
1350 Prefontaine Ave 81650 970-665-7725
Todd Ellis, prin. Fax 665-7785
Rifle MS 800/5-8
753 Railroad Ave 81650 970-665-7900
Kevin Marlatt, prin. Fax 665-7930
Other Schools – See New Castle

**Rocky Ford, Otero, Pop. 3,914**
Rocky Ford SD R-2 900/PK-12
601 S 8th St 81067 719-254-7423
Kermit Snyder, supt. Fax 254-7425
www.rockyfordk12.org
Rocky Ford JSHS 300/7-12
601 S 8th St 81067 719-254-7431
Cindy Cowan, prin. Fax 254-7436

**Rush, El Paso, Pop. 100**
Miami-Yoder SD 60 JT 200/PK-12
420 S Rush Rd 80833 719-478-2186
Rick Walter, supt. Fax 478-5380
www.miamiyoder.org
Miami-Yoder JSHS 100/6-12
420 S Rush Rd 80833 719-478-2186
Sharon Webb, prin. Fax 478-5380

**Rye, Pueblo, Pop. 153**
Pueblo County SD 70
Supt. — See Pueblo
Rye HS 200/9-12
PO Box 10 81069 719-489-2271
Michelle Mann, prin. Fax 489-2278

**Saguache, Saguache, Pop. 479**
Mountain Valley SD RE-1 100/PK-12
PO Box 127 81149 719-655-2578
Corey Doss, supt. Fax 655-2875
www.mountainvalleyschool.org
Mountain Valley HS 50/9-12
PO Box 127 81149 719-655-2578
Travis Garoutte, prin. Fax 655-2875
Mountain Valley MS 50/6-8
PO Box 127 81149 719-655-2578
Travis Garoutte, prin. Fax 655-2875

**Salida, Chaffee, Pop. 5,163**
Salida SD R-32 1,000/PK-12
349 E 9th St 81201 719-530-5200
Darryl Webb, supt. Fax 539-6220
salidaschools.com
Horizons Exploratory Academy 50/Alt
349 E 9th St 81201 719-530-5204
Albert Lionelle, prin. Fax 539-6220
Salida HS 300/9-12
26 Jones Ave 81201 719-530-5400
Tami Thompson, prin. Fax 539-2407
Salida MS 300/5-8
520 Milford St 81201 719-530-5300
Will Wooddell, prin. Fax 530-5364

**Sanford, Conejos, Pop. 874**
Sanford SD 6J 400/PK-12
PO Box 39 81151 719-274-5167
Kevin Edgar M.Ed., supt. Fax 274-5830
www.sanfordschools.org/
Sanford JSHS 100/7-12
PO Box 39 81151 719-274-5167
David Judd, prin. Fax 274-5830

**San Luis, Costilla, Pop. 618**
Centennial SD R-1 200/PK-12
PO Box 350 81152 719-672-3322
Brian Crowther, supt. Fax 672-3345
www.centennialschool.net
Centennial HS 100/9-12
PO Box 350 81152 719-672-3322
Arlen Arguello, prin. Fax 672-3345
Centennial JHS 50/6-8
PO Box 350 81152 719-672-3322
Arlen Arguello, prin. Fax 672-3345

**Seibert, Kit Carson, Pop. 178**
Hi-Plains SD R-23 100/PK-12
PO Box 238 80834 970-664-2636
Michael Warren, supt. Fax 664-2283
www.hp-patriots.com/
Hi-Plains JSHS 100/7-12
PO Box 238 80834 970-664-2616
Michael Warren, admin. Fax 664-2622

**Sheridan, Arapahoe, Pop. 5,532**
Sheridan SD 2 1,600/PK-12
4150 S Hazel Ct 80110 720-833-6616
Michael Clough, supt. Fax 833-6650
www.ssd2.org
Other Schools – See Denver

**Sheridan Lake, Kiowa, Pop. 88**
Plainview SD RE-2 100/K-12
13997 County Road 71 81071 719-729-3331
Jennifer Wilson, supt. Fax 729-3451
www.plainviewhawks.org
Plainview JHSH 50/6-12
13997 County Road 71 81071 719-729-3331
Jennifer Wilson, prin. Fax 729-3451

**Silverton, San Juan, Pop. 625**
Silverton SD 1 100/K-12
PO Box 128 81433 970-387-5543
Kim White, supt. Fax 387-5791
www.silvertonschool.org
Silverton HS 50/9-12
PO Box 128 81433 970-387-5543
Kim White, admin. Fax 387-5791
Silverton MS 50/6-8
PO Box 128 81433 970-387-5543
Kim White, prin. Fax 387-5791

**Simla, Elbert, Pop. 614**
Big Sandy SD 100J 200/PK-12
PO Box 68 80835 719-541-2292
Steve Wilson, supt. Fax 541-2186
bigsandy100j.com
Simla JSHS 100/6-12
PO Box 68 80835 719-541-2291
Sammi Swennes, prin. Fax 541-2443

**Springfield, Baca, Pop. 1,423**
Springfield SD RE-4 300/PK-12
389 Tipton St 81073 719-523-6654
Richard Hargrove, supt. Fax 523-4192
www.spre4.org
Springfield HS 100/9-12
389 Tipton St 81073 719-523-6522
Kirk Salmela, prin. Fax 523-4361
Springfield JHS 50/7-8
389 Tipton St 81073 719-523-6522
Kirk Salmela, prin. Fax 523-4361

**Steamboat Springs, Routt, Pop. 11,946**
Northwest Colorado BOCES 50/
PO Box 773390 80477 970-879-0391
Paul McCarty, dir. Fax 879-0442
www.nwboces.org/
Yampa Valley HS 50/Alt
PO Box 773390 80477 970-879-0391
Jane Toothaker, dir.

Steamboat Springs SD RE-2 2,300/K-12
325 7th St 80487 970-871-3199
Dr. Brad Meeks, supt. Fax 879-3943
www.sssd.k12.co.us
Steamboat Springs HS 600/9-12
45 Maple St 80487 970-879-1562
Kevin Taulman, prin. Fax 879-8039
Steamboat Springs MS 500/6-8
39510 Amethyst St 80487 970-879-1058
Jerry Buelter, prin. Fax 870-0368
Yampa Valley HS 50/Alt
325 7th St 80487 970-871-3299
Chuck Rosemond, lead tchr. Fax 871-3943

---

Heritage Christian S 100/K-12
27285 Brandon Cir 80487 970-879-1760
David Entwistle, admin. Fax 879-5511
Steamboat Mountain S 100/9-12
42605 County Road 36 80487 970-879-1350
Meg Morse, head sch Fax 879-0506

**Sterling, Logan, Pop. 14,616**
Valley SD RE-1 2,300/PK-12
301 Hagen St 80751 970-522-0792
Jan DeLay Ph.D., supt. Fax 522-0525
www.re1valleyschools.org/
Sterling HS 600/9-12
407 W Broadway St 80751 970-522-2944
Dianna Chrisman, prin. Fax 522-1540
Sterling MS 400/6-8
1177 Pawnee Ave 80751 970-522-1041
Robert Hall, prin. Fax 522-0209
Other Schools – See Iliff

---

Northeastern Junior College Post-Sec.
100 College Ave 80751 970-521-6600

**Strasburg, Adams, Pop. 2,413**
Strasburg SD 31J 1,000/PK-12
56729 Colorado Ave 80136 303-622-9211
Edward Vandertook, supt. Fax 622-9224
www.strasburg31j.com
Hemphill MS 200/6-8
2100 Wagner St 80136 303-622-9213
Sara Turrell, prin. Fax 622-2613
Strasburg HS 300/9-12
56729 Colorado Ave 80136 303-622-9211
Jeffrey Rasp, prin. Fax 622-6921

**Stratton, Kit Carson, Pop. 658**
Stratton SD R-4 200/PK-12
219 Illinois Ave 80836 719-348-5369
Jeff Durbin, supt. Fax 348-5555
www.strattonschools.org
Stratton HS 50/9-12
219 Illinois Ave 80836 719-348-5369
Dave Gottmann, prin. Fax 348-5555
Stratton MS 50/6-8
219 Illinois Ave 80836 719-348-5369
Dave Gottmann, prin. Fax 348-5555

**Swink, Otero, Pop. 607**
Swink SD 33 400/K-12
PO Box 487 81077 719-384-8103
Libby Hiza, supt. Fax 384-5471
www.swinkk12.net/
Swink JSHS 200/7-12
PO Box 487 81077 719-384-8103
Nancy Westfall, prin. Fax 384-5471

**Tabernash, Grand, Pop. 408**

---

Winter Park Christian S 50/K-12
PO Box 518 80478 970-887-9784
Ed Beckerle, hdmstr. Fax 887-9785

**Telluride, San Miguel, Pop. 2,291**
Telluride SD R-1 600/PK-12
725 W Colorado Ave 81435 970-728-6617
Mike Gass, supt. Fax 728-9490
www.tellurideschool.org
Telluride MSHS 200/7-12
725 W Colorado Ave 81435 970-728-4377
Mike Conran, prin. Fax 728-0257

---

Telluride Mountain S 100/PK-12
200 San Miguel River Dr 81435 970-728-1969
Karen Walker, head sch Fax 369-4412

**Thornton, Adams, Pop. 116,276**
Adams 12 Five Star SD 42,200/PK-12
1500 E 128th Ave 80241 720-972-4000
Chris Gdowski, supt. Fax 972-4008
www.adams12.org
Bollman Technical Education Center Vo/Tech
9451 Washington St 80229 720-972-5820
Janet Renden, prin. Fax 972-5869
Century MS 1,100/6-8
13000 Lafayette St 80241 720-972-5240
Howard Holbrook, prin. Fax 972-5279
Horizon HS 1,900/9-12
5321 E 136th Ave 80602 720-972-4400
David Shadwell, prin. Fax 972-4598
International S at Thornton MS 700/6-8
9451 Hoffman Way 80229 720-972-5160
Jessica Fiedler, prin. Fax 972-5199
Pathways S, 550 E 124th Ave 80241 Alt
Matthew Schmidt, prin. 720-972-4723
Rocky Top MS 1,100/6-8
14150 York St 80602 720-972-2200
Chelsea Behana, prin. Fax 972-2303
Shadow Ridge MS 1,000/6-8
12551 Holly St 80241 720-972-5040
Susie Wickham, prin. Fax 972-5079
Thornton HS 1,700/9-12
9351 Washington St 80229 720-972-4800
Jennifer Skrobela, prin. Fax 972-4999
Other Schools – See Broomfield, Northglenn, Westminster

Mapleton SD 1
Supt. — See Denver
Academy HS 300/9-12
8970 York St 80229 303-853-1730
Sheri Kangas, dir. Fax 853-1779
Mapleton Early College HS 200/9-12
8980 York St 80229 303-853-1960
James Long, dir. Fax 853-1996
Mapleton Expeditionary S of the Arts 600/7-12
8980 York St 80229 303-853-1270
Doug Seligman, dir. Fax 853-1296
York International S 700/K-12
9200 York St 80229 303-853-1600
Laura Nelson, dir. Fax 853-1656
North Valley S for Young Adults Adult
8990 York St 80229 303-853-1790
Chris Byrd, dir. Fax 853-1798

---

Empire Beauty School Post-Sec.
3811 E 120th Ave 80233 303-451-5808
Everest College Post-Sec.
9065 Grant St 80229 303-457-2757
HealthONE North Suburban Medical Center Post-Sec.
9191 Grant St 80229 303-451-7800

**Trinidad, Las Animas, Pop. 8,973**
Trinidad SD 1 1,100/PK-12
612 Park St 81082 719-846-3324
Scott Mader, supt. Fax 846-2957
www.tsd1.org
Trinidad HS 400/9-12
816 West St 81082 719-846-2971
George Dasko, prin. Fax 846-7488
Trinidad MS 300/6-8
607 Miner Dr 81082 719-846-4411
Deana Pachelli, prin. Fax 846-4740

---

Grace Christian Center S 50/K-12
1001 Obregon St 81082 719-846-6133
Jean Griffis, prin. Fax 846-6133
Trinidad State Junior College Post-Sec.
600 Prospect St 81082 719-846-5011

**USAF Academy, El Paso, Pop. 9,062**
Academy SD 20
Supt. — See Colorado Springs
Air Academy HS 1,400/9-12
6910 Carlton Dr, 719-234-2400
Dan Olson, prin. Fax 234-2599

---

United States Air Force Academy Post-Sec.
2304 Cadet Dr Ste 2300, 800-443-9266

**Vail, Eagle, Pop. 5,245**

---

Vail Mountain S 300/K-12
3000 Booth Falls Rd 81657 970-476-3850
Mike Imperi, head sch Fax 476-3860

**Vilas, Baca, Pop. 112**
Vilas SD RE-5 300/PK-12
PO Box 727 81087 719-523-6738
Mark Carara, supt. Fax 523-4818
www.vilasre5.us
Vilas Undivided HS 50/7-12
PO Box 727 81087 719-523-6738
Ryan Stredny, dean Fax 523-4818

**Walden, Jackson, Pop. 599**
North Park SD R-1 200/PK-12
PO Box 798 80480 970-723-3300
Jim Anderson, supt. Fax 723-8486
npsd.schoolfusion.us
North Park JSHS 100/6-12
PO Box 798 80480 970-723-3300
Kathleen Henschke, prin. Fax 723-4702

**Walsenburg, Huerfano, Pop. 3,036**
Huerfano SD RE-1 600/PK-12
201 E 5th St 81089 719-738-1520
Mike Moore, supt. Fax 738-3148
huerfano.k12.co.us
Mall HS 100/9-12
335 W Pine St 81089 719-738-1610
George Purnell, prin. Fax 738-2541

**Walsh, Baca, Pop. 543**
Walsh SD RE-1 200/PK-12
PO Box 68 81090 719-324-5632
Kyle Hebberd, supt. Fax 324-5426
www.walsheagles.com
Walsh JSHS 100/7-12
PO Box 68 81090 719-324-5221
Patrick McDonald, prin. Fax 324-5734

**Weldona, Morgan, Pop. 139**
Weldon Valley SD RE-20(J) 200/PK-12
911 North Ave 80653 970-645-2411
Doug Pfau M.S., supt. Fax 645-2377
www.weldonvalley.org/
Weldon Valley HS 100/9-12
911 North Ave 80653 970-645-2411
Doug Pfau, admin. Fax 645-2377
Weldon Valley JHS 50/7-8
911 North Ave 80653 970-645-2411
Doug Pfau, admin. Fax 645-2377

**Wellington, Larimer, Pop. 6,177**
Poudre SD R-1
Supt. — See Fort Collins
Wellington MS 400/6-8
4001 Wilson Ave 80549 970-488-6600
Alicia Durand, prin. Fax 488-6602

**Westcliffe, Custer, Pop. 555**
Custer County SD 1 400/PK-12
PO Box 730 81252 719-783-2357
Mark Payler, supt. Fax 783-2334
www.custercountyschools.org
Custer County HS 200/9-12
PO Box 730 81252 719-783-2291
Barb Jones, prin. Fax 783-4944
Custer County JHS 100/6-8
PO Box 730 81252 719-783-2291
Barb Jones, prin. Fax 783-4944

**Westminster, Adams, Pop. 103,933**
Adams 12 Five Star SD
Supt. — See Thornton
Mountain Range HS 2,000/9-12
12500 Huron St 80234 720-972-6300
Julie Enger, prin. Fax 972-6529
Silver Hills MS 1,100/6-8
12400 Huron St 80234 720-972-5000
Julie Evans, prin. Fax 972-5039

Adams County SD 50 10,100/PK-12
6933 Raleigh St 80030 303-428-3511
Dr. Pamela Swanson, supt. Fax 428-2810
www.adams50.org
Colorado STEM Academy 3-8
7281 Irving St 80030 303-429-7836
Anthony Matthews, prin.
Hidden Lake HS 300/Alt
7300 Lowell Blvd 80030 303-428-2600
James Steward, prin. Fax 428-2142
Shaw Heights MS 600/6-8
8780 Circle Dr 80031 303-428-9533
Mike Carlson, prin. Fax 657-3973
Westminster HS 2,400/9-12
6933 Raleigh St 80030 303-657-3980
Kiffany Kiewiet, prin. Fax 657-3989
Other Schools – See Denver

Jefferson County SD R-1
Supt. — See Golden
Carle MS 300/7-8
10200 W 100th Ave 80021 303-982-9070
John White, prin. Fax 982-9071
Mandalay MS 400/7-8
9651 Pierce St 80021 303-982-9802
John Schalk, prin. Fax 982-9813
Standley Lake HS 1,500/9-12
9300 W 104th Ave 80021 303-982-3311
Jeff Pierson, prin. Fax 982-3312

---

Belleview Christian S 300/PK-12
3455 W 83rd Ave 80031 303-427-5459
Dr. Peggy Polson, prin. Fax 426-6768
Cornerstone Christian Academy 200/PK-12
12000 Zuni St 80234 303-451-1421
Larry Zimbelman, prin.
DeVry University Post-Sec.
1870 W 122nd Ave 80234 303-280-7400
Front Range Community College Post-Sec.
3645 W 112th Ave 80031 303-404-5000
Hyland Christian S 100/K-12
5255 W 98th Ave 80020 303-466-1673
ITT Technical Institute Post-Sec.
8620 Wolff Ct Ste 100 80031 303-288-4488
LIFE Christian Academy 200/PK-12
11500 Sheridan Blvd 80020 303-438-1260
Cheri Strong, admin. Fax 438-1866
Prince Institute Post-Sec.
9051 Harlan St Ste 20 80031 303-427-5292

**Weston, Las Animas, Pop. 54**
Primero RSD RE-2 200/PK-12
20200 State Highway 12 81091 719-868-2715
Denille LePlatt, supt. Fax 868-2241
www.primeroschool.org
Primero JSHS 100/6-12
20200 State Highway 12 81091 719-868-2715
Heidi Dasko, prin. Fax 868-2241

**Wheat Ridge, Jefferson, Pop. 29,601**
Jefferson County SD R-1
Supt. — See Golden
Everitt MS 500/7-8
3900 Kipling St 80033 303-982-1580
Jeff Gomez, prin. Fax 982-1581
Wheat Ridge HS 1,300/9-12
9505 W 32nd Ave 80033 303-982-7695
Griff Wirth, prin. Fax 982-7696

---

Beth Eden Baptist S 200/K-12
2600 Wadsworth Blvd 80033 303-232-2313

**Wiggins, Morgan, Pop. 888**
Wiggins SD RE-50(J) 400/PK-12
320 Chapman St 80654 970-483-7762
Gary Bruntz, supt. Fax 483-6205
www.wiggins50.k12.co.us/
Wiggins MSHS 100/6-12
320 Chapman St 80654 970-483-7763
Trent Kerr, prin. Fax 483-7796

**Wiley, Prowers, Pop. 402**
Wiley SD RE-13 JT 100/PK-12
PO Box 247 81092 719-829-4806
Dave Eastin, supt. Fax 829-4808
www.wileyschool.org
Wiley S 100/PK-12
PO Box 247 81092 719-829-4806
Michelle Wallace, prin. Fax 829-4805

**Windsor, Weld, Pop. 18,391**
Weld County SD RE-4 4,100/PK-12
PO Box 609 80550 970-686-8000
Dan Seegmiller, supt. Fax 686-8001
www.weldre4.k12.co.us
Severance MS 400/6-8
1801 Avery Plaza St 80550 970-674-5200
Jay Tapia, prin. Fax 674-5201
Windsor HS 1,100/9-12
1100 Main St 80550 970-686-8100
Michelle Scallon, prin. Fax 686-0935
Windsor MS 600/6-8
900 Main St 80550 970-686-8200
Eric Johnson, prin. Fax 686-7122

**Woodland Park, Teller, Pop. 7,047**
Woodland Park SD RE-2 2,800/PK-12
PO Box 99 80866 719-686-2000
Jed Bowman Ph.D., supt. Fax 687-8408
www.wpsdk12.org/
Woodland Park HS 900/9-12
PO Box 6820 80866 719-686-2067
Del Garrick, prin. Fax 687-3880
Woodland Park MS 600/6-8
PO Box 6790 80866 719-686-2200
Jeff Wallingford, prin. Fax 687-8458

**Woodrow, Washington, Pop. 20**
Woodlin SD R-104 100/PK-12
15400 County Road L 80757 970-386-2223
Rose Cronk, supt. Fax 386-2241
www.woodlinschool.com
Woodlin Undivided HS 50/6-12
15400 County Road L 80757 970-386-2223
Rose Cronk, supt. Fax 386-2241

**Wray, Yuma, Pop. 2,328**
Wray SD RD-2 700/PK-12
30222 County Road 35 80758 970-332-5764
Levi Kramer, admin. Fax 332-5773
www.wrayschools.org
Buchanan MS 200/5-8
620 W 7th St 80758 970-332-3600
Laurie Unger, prin. Fax 332-3356
Wray HS 200/9-12
30074 County Road 35 80758 970-332-3767
Rick Ward, prin. Fax 332-4476

**Yoder, El Paso, Pop. 40**
Edison SD 54 JT 200/PK-12
14550 Edison Rd 80864 719-478-2125
Patrick Bershinsky, supt. Fax 478-3000
www.edison54jt.schoolfusion.us
Edison JSHS 100/6-12
14550 Edison Rd 80864 719-478-2125
Rachel Paul, prin. Fax 478-3000

**Yuma, Yuma, Pop. 3,498**
Yuma SD - 1 700/PK-12
PO Box 327 80759 970-848-5831
Dianna Chrisman, supt. Fax 848-2256
www.yumaschools.org
Yuma HS 200/9-12
1000 S Albany St 80759 970-848-5488
Matt Pounds, prin. Fax 848-0314
Yuma MS 100/5-8
500 S Elm St 80759 970-848-2000
Cynthia Rios, prin. Fax 848-4261

# CONNECTICUT

## CONNECTICUT DEPARTMENT OF EDUCATION
**165 Capitol Ave, Hartford 06106-1659**
**Telephone 860-713-6500**
**Fax 860-713-7001**
**Website http://www.sde.ct.gov**

Commissioner of Education   Stefan Pryor

## CONNECTICUT BOARD OF EDUCATION
**165 Capitol Ave, Hartford 06106-1659**

Chairperson   Allan Taylor

## REGIONAL EDUCATIONAL SERVICE CENTERS

Area Coop. Educational Services RESC
Dr. Craig Edmondson, dir. 203-498-6800
350 State St, North Haven 06473 Fax 498-6890
www.aces.org

Capitol Region Education Council RESC
Dr. Bruce Douglas, dir. 860-524-4063
111 Charter Oak Ave Fax 548-9924
Hartford 06106
www.crec.org

Cooperative Educational Services RESC
Dr. Evan Pitkoff, supt. 203-365-8803
40 Lindeman Dr, Trumbull 06611 Fax 365-8804
www.ces.k12.ct.us

Eastconn RESC
Paula Colen, dir. 860-455-0707
376 Hartford Tpke, Hampton 06247 Fax 455-8026
www.eastconn.org

Education Connection RESC
Dr. Danuta Thibodeau Ph.D., dir. 860-567-0863
PO Box 909, Litchfield 06759 Fax 567-3381
www.educationconnection.org

Learn RESC
Dr. Eileen Howley, dir. 860-434-4800
44 Hatchetts Hill Rd Fax 434-4820
Old Lyme 06371
www.learn.k12.ct.us

## PUBLIC, PRIVATE AND CATHOLIC SECONDARY SCHOOLS

**Ansonia, New Haven, Pop. 18,821**
Ansonia SD 2,400/K-12
42 Grove St 06401 203-736-5095
Carol Merlone Ed.D., supt. Fax 736-5098
www.ansonia.org
Ansonia HS 700/9-12
20 Pulaski Hwy 06401 203-736-5060
Joseph Dobbins, prin. Fax 736-5068
Ansonia MS 400/7-8
115 Howard Ave 06401 203-736-5070
Amy O'Brien, prin. Fax 736-1044

Connecticut Technical HS System
Supt. — See Middletown
O'Brien Technical HS Vo/Tech
141 Prindle Ave 06401 203-732-1800
Laurie Lebouthillier, prin. Fax 735-6236

**Avon, Hartford**
Avon SD 3,500/PK-12
34 Simsbury Rd 06001 860-404-4700
Gary Mala, supt. Fax 404-4702
www.avon.k12.ct.us
Avon HS 1,100/9-12
510 W Avon Rd 06001 860-404-4740
Chris Tranberg, prin. Fax 404-4743
Avon MS 600/7-8
375 W Avon Rd 06001 860-404-4770
Marco Famiglietti, prin. Fax 404-4773

---

Avon Old Farms S 400/9-12
500 Old Farms Rd 06001 860-404-4100
Kenneth LaRocque, hdmstr. Fax 404-4135

**Baltic, New London, Pop. 1,192**

---

Academy of the Holy Family 100/9-12
PO Box 691 06330 860-822-9272
Mary Riquier, prin. Fax 822-1318

**Beacon Falls, New Haven**
Regional SD 16
Supt. — See Prospect
Woodland Regional HS 700/9-12
135 Back Rimmon Rd 06403 203-881-5551
Kurt Ogren, prin. Fax 881-2015

**Berlin, Hartford**
Berlin SD 3,000/PK-12
238 Kensington Rd 06037 860-828-6581
David B. Erwin, supt. Fax 829-0832
www.berlinschools.org
Berlin HS 1,000/9-12
139 Patterson Way 06037 860-828-6577
Francis Kennedy, prin. Fax 829-2169
McGee MS 700/6-8
899 Norton Rd 06037 860-828-0323
Salvatore Urso, prin. Fax 828-0676

**Bethany, New Haven**
Regional SD 5
Supt. — See Woodbridge
Amity Regional MS 400/7-8
190 Luke Hill Rd 06524 203-393-3102
Richard Dellinger, prin. Fax 393-0583

**Bethel, Fairfield, Pop. 9,266**
Bethel SD 3,000/PK-12
PO Box 253 06801 203-794-8601
Dr. Christine Carver, supt. Fax 794-8723
www.bethel.k12.ct.us
Bethel HS 900/9-12
300 Whittlesey Dr 06801 203-794-8600
Christopher Troetti, prin. Fax 778-7448
Bethel MS 700/6-8
600 Whittlesey Dr 06801 203-794-8670
Derek Muharem, prin. Fax 830-7318

**Bethlehem, Litchfield**

---

Woodhall S 50/9-12
PO Box 550 06751 203-266-7788
Matthew C. Woodhall, head sch Fax 266-5896

**Bloomfield, Hartford, Pop. 7,200**
Bloomfield SD 2,000/PK-12
1133 Blue Hills Ave 06002 860-769-4200
Dr. James Thompson, supt. Fax 769-4215
www.bloomfieldschools.org
Arace MS 300/7-8
390 Park Ave 06002 860-286-2622
Trevor Ellis, prin. Fax 242-0347
Bloomfield HS 600/9-12
5 Huckleberry Ln 06002 860-286-2630
Daniel Moleti, prin. Fax 242-9491
Global Experience Magnet S 100/6-12
44 Griffin Rd S 06002 860-769-6600
Sabin Loveland, prin. Fax 769-6605

Capitol Region Education Council RESC
Supt. — See Hartford
Metropolitan Learning Center 700/6-12
1551 Blue Hills Ave 06002 860-242-7834
Sasha Douglas, prin. Fax 242-0732

**Bolton, Tolland**
Bolton SD 900/PK-12
72 Brandy St 06043 860-643-1569
Kristin Heckt, supt. Fax 647-8452
www.boltonpublicschools.com/
Bolton HS 300/9-12
72 Brandy St 06043 860-643-2768
Joseph Maselli, prin. Fax 645-8374

**Branford, New Haven, Pop. 27,603**
Branford SD 3,300/PK-12
1111 Main St 06405 203-315-7809
Hamlet Hernandez, supt. Fax 315-3505
www.branfordschools.org/
Branford HS 1,100/9-12
185 E Main St 06405 203-488-7291
Lee Panagoulias, prin. Fax 315-6740
Walsh IS 1,000/5-8
185 Damascus Rd 06405 203-488-8317
Robin Goeler, prin. Fax 481-2785

---

Branford Hall Career Institute Post-Sec.
1 Summit Pl 06405 203-488-2525
Porter and Chester Institute Post-Sec.
221 W Main St 06405 203-315-1060

**Bridgeport, Fairfield, Pop. 139,433**
Bridgeport SD 17,800/PK-12
45 Lyon Ter Rm 203 06604 203-275-1000
Frances Rabinowitz, supt. Fax 576-8488
www.bridgeportedu.com
Bassick HS 1,100/9-12
1181 Fairfield Ave 06605 203-275-3080
Peggy Moore, prin. Fax 337-0143
Bridgeport Learning Center 50/Alt
280 Tesiny Ave 06606 203-275-1136
Marilyn Earle, admin. Fax 337-0189
Bridgeport Military Academy 9-12
641 Mill Hill Ave 06610 203-337-2513
Diana Soares, prin.
Bridgeport Regional-Aquaculture S Vo/Tech
60 Saint Stephens Rd 06605 203-275-2926
Lea Catherman, dir. Fax 337-0168
Central HS 2,200/9-12
1 Lincoln Blvd 06606 203-275-1502
Eric Graf, prin. Fax 337-0173
FWC Information Technology HS 9-12
840 Old Town Rd 06606 203-275-3373
Victor Black, prin.
FWC Physical Science HS 9-12
840 Old Town Rd 06606 203-275-3343
Joseph Lipp, prin.
FWC Zoological Science HS 9-12
840 Old Town Rd 06606 203-275-3436
Michael Watson, prin.
Harding HS 1,300/9-12
1734 Central Ave 06610 203-275-2751
Carmen McPherson, prin. Fax 337-0177

Connecticut Technical HS System
Supt. — See Middletown
Bullard-Havens Technical HS Vo/Tech
500 Palisade Ave 06610 203-579-6333
Richard Cavallaro, prin. Fax 579-6904

---

Bridgeport Hospital Post-Sec.
267 Grant St 06610 203-384-3464
Bridgeport Hospital School of Nursing Post-Sec.
200 Mill Hill Ave 06610 203-384-3022
Cathedral Academy - St. Augustine Campus 100/4-8
63 Pequonnock St 06604 203-366-6500
Larry DiPalma, prin. Fax 362-2934
Housatonic Community College Post-Sec.
900 Lafayette Blvd 06604 203-332-5000
Kolbe Cathedral HS 300/9-12
33 Calhoun Pl 06604 203-335-2554
Henry Rondon, prin. Fax 335-2556
Leon Institute of Hair Design Post-Sec.
111 Wall St 06604 203-333-1465
New England Tractor Trailer Training Sch Post-Sec.
510 Barnum Ave Ste 4 06608 203-368-9069
St. Vincent's College Post-Sec.
2800 Main St 06606 203-576-5235
University of Bridgeport Post-Sec.
126 Park Ave 06604 800-392-3582

**Bristol, Hartford, Pop. 59,288**
Bristol SD 7,300/PK-12
PO Box 450 06011 860-584-7000
Ellen W. Solek Ed.D., supt. Fax 584-7611
www.bristol.k12.ct.us
Bristol Central HS 1,300/9-12
PO Box 700 06011 860-584-7735
Peter Wininger, prin. Fax 584-7713
Bristol Eastern HS 1,300/9-12
PO Box 580 06011 860-584-7876
Carly Fortin, prin. Fax 584-4886
Bristol Prep Academy Alt
632 King St 06010 860-584-7709
Ed Mongeon, coord. Fax 584-7763
Chippins Hill MS 800/6-8
551 Peacedale St 06010 860-584-3881
Matthew Harnett, prin. Fax 584-4833
Northeast MS 600/6-8
530 Stevens St 06010 860-584-7839
Daniel Sonstrom, prin. Fax 584-7837

Connecticut Technical HS System
Supt. — See Middletown
Bristol Technical Education Center Vo/Tech
431 Minor St 06010 860-584-8433
Luz Manson, admin. Fax 584-0795

---

St. Paul Catholic HS 300/9-12
1001 Stafford Ave 06010 860-584-0911
Cary Dupont, pres. Fax 585-8815

**Broad Brook, Hartford, Pop. 3,997**
East Windsor SD
Supt. — See East Windsor
East Windsor MS 400/5-8
38 Main St 06016 860-623-4488
Kimberly Hellerich, prin. Fax 654-1915

**Brookfield, Fairfield**
Brookfield SD 2,800/PK-12
PO Box 5194 06804 203-775-7620
John Barile, supt. Fax 740-3195
www.brookfieldps.org
Brookfield HS 1,000/9-12
45 Long Meadow Hill Rd 06804 203-775-7725
Marc Balanda, prin. Fax 775-7773
Whisconier MS 900/5-8
17 W Whisconier Rd 06804 203-775-7710
Deane Renda, prin. Fax 775-7615

**Brooklyn, Windham, Pop. 976**
Brooklyn SD 900/PK-8
119 Gorman Rd 06234 860-774-9153
Dr. Louise Berry J.D., supt. Fax 774-6938
www.brooklynschools.org/
Brooklyn MS 400/5-8
119 Gorman Rd 06234 860-774-9153
Alan Yanku, prin. Fax 774-6938

**Burlington, Hartford**
Regional SD 10 2,700/PK-12
24 Lyon Rd 06013 860-673-2538
Alan Beitman, supt. Fax 673-7534
www.region10ct.org
Har-Bur MS 900/5-8
26 Lyon Rd 06013 860-673-6163
Kenneth Smith, prin. Fax 673-3481
Mills HS 800/9-12
26 Lyon Rd 06013 860-673-0423
Pamela Lazaroski, prin. Fax 673-9128

**Canterbury, Windham**
Canterbury SD 500/PK-8
45 Westminster Rd 06331 860-546-6950
Dr. Lois Knapton, supt. Fax 546-6423
www.canterburypublicschools.org/
Baldwin MS 200/5-8
45 Westminster Rd 06331 860-546-9421
Brian Tedeschi, prin. Fax 546-6289

**Central Village, Windham**
Plainfield SD
Supt. — See Plainfield
Plainfield HS 800/9-12
PO Box 218 06332 860-564-6422
James Worth, prin. Fax 564-2116

**Chaplin, Windham**
Regional SD 11 300/7-12
304 Parish Hill Rd 06235 860-455-9306
Keneth Henrici, supt. Fax 455-1263
www.parishhill.org/
Parish Hill JSHS 300/7-12
304 Parish Hill Rd 06235 860-455-9584
Dori Smith, prin. Fax 455-9081

**Cheshire, New Haven, Pop. 25,684**
Cheshire SD 4,800/PK-12
29 Main St 06410 203-250-2420
Greg Florio Ed.D., supt. Fax 250-2453
www.cheshire.k12.ct.us
Cheshire HS 1,500/9-12
525 S Main St 06410 203-250-2511
Jeffrey Solan, prin. Fax 250-2563
Dodd MS 800/7-8
100 Park Pl 06410 203-272-3249
Michael Woods, prin. Fax 250-7614

---

Cheshire Academy 300/8-12
10 Main St 06410 203-272-5396
John Nozell, head sch Fax 250-7209

**Clinton, Middlesex, Pop. 3,326**
Clinton SD 2,000/PK-12
137B Glenwood Rd 06413 860-664-6500
Jack Cross, supt. Fax 664-6580
www.clintonpublic.org
Eliot MS 500/6-8
69 Fairy Dell Rd 06413 860-664-6503
Linda Tucker, prin. Fax 664-6583
Morgan S 600/9-12
27 Killingworth Tpke 06413 860-664-6504
Keri Hagness, prin. Fax 664-6548

**Colchester, New London, Pop. 4,696**
Colchester SD 3,000/PK-12
127 Norwich Ave Ste 202 06415 860-537-7260
Jeffry Mathieu, supt. Fax 537-1252
www.colchesterct.org/
Bacon Academy 1,000/9-12
611 Norwich Ave 06415 860-537-2378
Matthew Peel, prin. Fax 537-5410
Johnston MS 700/6-8
360 Norwich Ave 06415 860-537-2313
Christopher Bennett, prin. Fax 537-6258

**Collinsville, Hartford, Pop. 3,705**
Canton SD 1,700/PK-12
4 Market St Ste 100 06019 860-693-7704
Kevin Case, supt. Fax 693-7706
www.cantonschools.org
Canton HS 500/9-12
76 Simonds Ave 06019 860-693-7707
Andrew DiPippo, prin. Fax 693-7812
Canton MS 300/7-8
76 Simonds Ave 06019 860-693-7712
Pamela Hamad, prin. Fax 693-7812

**Coventry, Tolland, Pop. 10,063**
Coventry SD 1,800/PK-12
1700 Main St 06238 860-742-7317
David Petrone, supt. Fax 742-4567
www.coventrypublicschools.org/
Coventry HS 500/9-12
78 Ripley Hill Rd 06238 860-742-7346
Michele Mullaly, prin. Fax 742-4591
Hale MS 500/6-8
1776 Main St 06238 860-742-7334
Dena DeJulius, prin. Fax 742-4565

**Cromwell, Middlesex**
Cromwell SD 2,000/PK-12
9 Mann Memorial Dr 06416 860-632-4830
Dr. Paula Talty, supt. Fax 632-4865
www.cromwell.k12.ct.us/
Cromwell HS 500/9-12
1 Donald Harris Dr 06416 860-632-4841
Frances DiFiore, prin. Fax 613-3363
Cromwell MS 500/6-8
9 Mann Memorial Dr 06416 860-632-4853
Ann Cocchiola, prin. Fax 632-4855

---

Holy Apostles College and Seminary Post-Sec.
33 Prospect Hill Rd 06416 860-632-3010
Lincoln Technical Institute Post-Sec.
106 Sebethe Dr 06416 860-613-3350

**Danbury, Fairfield, Pop. 77,029**
Connecticut Technical HS System
Supt. — See Middletown
Abbott Technical HS Vo/Tech
21 Hayestown Ave 06811 203-797-4460
Stacy Butkus, prin. Fax 797-4382

Danbury SD 10,300/PK-12
63 Beaver Brook Rd 06810 203-797-4701
Sal Pascarella Ed.D., supt. Fax 830-6560
www.danbury.k12.ct.us
Alternative Center for Excellence 100/Alt
26 Locust Ave 06810 203-797-4786
Sandra Atanasoff, prin. Fax 830-6544
Broadview MS 1,100/6-8
72 Hospital Ave 06810 203-797-4861
Edward Robbs, prin. Fax 790-2856
Danbury HS 2,900/9-12
43 Clapboard Ridge Rd 06811 203-797-4800
Gary Bocaccio, prin. Fax 797-4730
Rogers Park MS 1,100/6-8
21 Memorial Dr 06810 203-797-4880
Patricia Joaquim, prin. Fax 790-2829
Westside MS Academy 6-8
1 School Ridge Rd 06810 203-329-6700
Dr. Frank LaBanca, prin.

---

Danbury Hospital Post-Sec.
24 Hospital Ave 06810 203-797-7210
Immaculate HS 400/9-12
73 Southern Blvd 06810 203-744-1510
Joe Carmen, prin. Fax 744-1275
Paul Mitchell the School Post-Sec.
109 South St 06810 203-744-0900
Ridley-Lowell Business & Technical Inst Post-Sec.
44 Shelter Rock Rd 06810 203-797-0551
Western Connecticut State University Post-Sec.
181 White St 06810 203-837-8200
Wooster S 300/PK-12
91 Miry Brook Rd 06810 203-830-3900
Matt Byrnes, head sch Fax 790-7147

**Danielson, Windham, Pop. 3,941**
Connecticut Technical HS System
Supt. — See Middletown
Ellis Technical HS Vo/Tech
613 Upper Maple St 06239 860-412-7500
Dr. Brian Mignault, prin. Fax 779-2565

---

Quinebaug Valley Community College Post-Sec.
742 Upper Maple St 06239 860-412-7200

**Darien, Fairfield, Pop. 20,500**
Darien SD 4,800/PK-12
PO Box 1167 06820 203-656-7412
Dr. Dan Brenner, supt. Fax 656-3052
www.darienps.org
Darien HS 1,300/9-12
80 High School Ln 06820 203-655-3981
Ellen Dunn, prin. Fax 656-3631
Middlesex MS 1,200/6-8
204 Hollow Tree Ridge Rd 06820 203-655-2518
Deborah Boccanfuso, prin. Fax 655-1627

**Dayville, Windham**
Killingly SD
Supt. — See Killingly
Killingly HS 800/9-12
226 Putnam Pike 06241 860-779-6620
Michael Vose Ph.D., prin. Fax 774-0846
Killingly IS 800/5-8
1599 Upper Maple St 06241 860-779-6700
Heather Taylor, prin. Fax 779-9639

**Deep River, Middlesex, Pop. 2,444**
Regional SD 4 1,000/7-12
PO Box 187 06417 860-526-2417
Dr. Ruth Levy, supt. Fax 526-5469
www.reg4.k12.ct.us
Valley Regional HS 600/9-12
256 Kelsey Hill Rd 06417 860-526-5328
Kristina Martineau, prin. Fax 526-8123
Winthrop MS 300/7-8
PO Box 187 06417 860-526-9546
William Duffy, prin. Fax 526-3721

**Derby, New Haven, Pop. 12,664**
Derby SD 1,300/PK-12
PO Box 373 06418 203-736-5027
Matthew Conway, supt. Fax 736-5031
www.derbyps.org/
Derby HS 400/9-12
8 Nutmeg Ave 06418 203-736-5032
Martin Pascale, prin. Fax 736-5031
Derby MS 300/6-8
10 Nutmeg Ave 06418 203-736-1426
Arnold Frank, prin. Fax 736-3234

**Durham, Middlesex, Pop. 2,900**
Regional SD 13 2,000/PK-12
135A Pickett Ln 06422 860-349-7200
Kathryn Veronesi Ed.D., supt. Fax 349-7203
www.rsd13ct.org/
Coginchaug Regional HS 600/9-12
PO Box 280 06422 860-349-7215
Brian Falcone, prin. Fax 349-7136
Strong MS 400/7-8
PO Box 435 06422 860-349-7222
Scott Sadinsky, prin. Fax 349-7225

---

Lake Grove School at Durham Post-Sec.
459R Wallingford Rd 06422 860-349-3467

**East Granby, Hartford**
East Granby SD 800/PK-12
PO Box 674 06026 860-653-6486
Dr. Christine Mahoney, supt. Fax 413-9075
www.eastgranby.k12.ct.us/
East Granby HS 300/9-12
95 S Main St 06026 860-653-2541
David Peling, prin. Fax 413-9092
East Granby MS 200/6-8
95 S Main St 06026 860-653-7113
Melissa Bavaro-Grande, prin. Fax 413-9126

**East Hampton, Middlesex, Pop. 2,637**
East Hampton SD 1,900/PK-12
94 Main St 06424 860-365-4000
Mark Winzler, supt. Fax 365-4004
www.easthamptonps.org
East Hampton HS 600/9-12
15 N Maple St 06424 860-365-4030
John Fidler, prin. Fax 365-4034
East Hampton MS 500/6-8
19 Childs Rd 06424 860-365-4060
Jason Lehmann, prin. Fax 365-4064

**East Hartford, Hartford, Pop. 50,077**
Capitol Region Education Council RESC
Supt. — See Hartford
Two Rivers Magnet MS 700/6-8
337 E River Dr 06108 860-290-5320
Jill Wnuk, prin. Fax 509-3609

East Hartford SD 7,100/PK-12
1110 Main St 06108 860-622-5107
Nathan Quesnel M.A., supt. Fax 622-5119
www.easthartford.org
CT International Baccalaureate Academy 200/9-12
857 Forbes St 06118 860-622-5560
Caryn Stedman, prin. Fax 622-5555
East Hartford HS 1,700/9-12
869 Forbes St 06118 860-622-5200
Matt Ryan, prin. Fax 622-5223
East Hartford MS 1,100/6-8
777 Burnside Ave 06108 860-622-5600
Anthony Menard, prin. Fax 622-5619
Stevens Alternative HS 200/Alt
40 Butternut Dr 06118 860-622-5999
Craig Outhouse, prin. Fax 622-5990

Hartford SD
Supt. — See Hartford
Pathways Academy of Technology & Design 300/9-12
2 Pent Rd 06118 860-695-9450
David Goldblum, prin. Fax 569-5569

Learn RESC
Supt. — See Old Lyme
Connecticut River Academy 400/9-12
9 Riverside Dr 06118 860-913-2200
Linda Dadona, prin.

---

Connecticut Training Center Post-Sec.
1137 Main St 06108 860-291-0250
Goodwin College Post-Sec.
1 Riverside Dr 06118 860-528-4111
New Testament Baptist Church S 100/PK-12
111 Ash St 06108 860-290-6696
Dr. Michael Stoddard, prin. Fax 290-6698
Stone Academy Post-Sec.
745 Burnside Ave 06108 860-569-0618

**East Haven, New Haven, Pop. 28,923**
East Haven SD 3,100/K-12
35 Wheelbarrow Ln 06513 203-468-3261
Dr. Portia S. Bonner, supt. Fax 468-3918
www.east-haven.k12.ct.us
East Haven Academy 300/3-8
67 Hudson St 06512 203-468-3219
Marianne Johnson, prin. Fax 468-3961
East Haven HS 900/9-12
35 Wheelbarrow Ln 06513 203-468-3267
Vincent DeNuzzo, prin. Fax 468-3818
Melillo MS 600/6-8
67 Hudson St 06512 203-468-3227
Laura Lynn, prin. Fax 468-3866

**East Lyme, New London**
East Lyme SD 2,900/PK-12
PO Box 176 06333 860-739-3966
James Lombardo Ed.D., supt. Fax 739-1215
www.eastlymeschools.org
East Lyme HS 1,200/9-12
PO Box 210 06333 860-739-6946
Michael Susi, prin. Fax 739-1241
Other Schools – See Niantic

**Easton, Fairfield**
Easton SD 1,100/PK-8
PO Box 500 06612 203-261-2513
Thomas McMorran Ed.D., supt. Fax 261-7936
www.er9.org
Keller MS 400/6-8
360 Sport Hill Rd 06612 203-268-8651
Susan Kaplan, prin. Fax 268-6105

Redding SD 1,100/K-8
PO Box 500 06612 203-261-2513
Thomas McMorran, supt. Fax 261-7936
www.er9.org
Other Schools – See Redding

Regional SD 9 1,000/9-12
PO Box 500 06612 203-261-2513
Thomas McMorran Ed.D., supt. Fax 261-4549
www.er9.org
Other Schools – See Redding

**East Windsor, Hartford**
East Windsor SD 1,300/PK-12
70 S Main St 06088 860-623-3346
Dr. Theresa Kane, supt. Fax 292-6817
www.eastwindsork12.org
East Windsor HS 400/9-12
76 S Main St 06088 860-623-3361
Edward Keleher, prin. Fax 623-7197
Other Schools – See Broad Brook

---

Lincoln Technical Institute Post-Sec.
97 Newberry Rd 06088 800-243-4242

**Ellington, Tolland**
Ellington SD 2,700/PK-12
PO Box 179 06029 860-896-2300
Dr. Scott Nicol, supt. Fax 896-2312
www.ellingtonpublicschools.org
Ellington HS 800/9-12
PO Box 149 06029 860-896-2352
Neil Rinaldi, prin. Fax 896-2366
Ellington MS 400/7-8
46 Middle Butcher Rd 06029 860-896-2339
David Pearson, prin. Fax 896-2351

**Enfield, Hartford, Pop. 45,500**
Capitol Region Education Council RESC
Supt. — See Hartford
Public Safety Academy 400/6-12
1617 King St 06082 860-253-0274
Jeff Larson, prin. Fax 741-0841

Enfield SD 5,500/PK-12
27 Shaker Rd 06082 860-253-6500
Dr. Jeffrey A. Schumann, supt. Fax 253-6510
www.enfieldschools.org
Enfield HS 700/9-12
1264 Enfield St 06082 860-253-5540
Andrew Longey, prin. Fax 253-5555
Fermi HS 1,100/9-12
124 N Maple St 06082 860-763-8800
Paul Newton, prin. Fax 763-8810
Kennedy MS 1,200/6-8
155 Raffia Rd 06082 860-763-8855
Steve Sargalski, prin. Fax 763-8888

---

Asnuntuck Community College Post-Sec.
170 Elm St 06082 860-253-3000
Porter and Chester Institute Post-Sec.
132 Weymouth Rd 06082 860-741-2561

**Fairfield, Fairfield, Pop. 54,400**
Fairfield SD 10,300/PK-12
PO Box 320189, 203-255-8371
Dr. David Title Ed.D., supt. Fax 255-8245
fairfieldschools.org
Fairfield Ludlowe HS 1,500/9-12
785 Unquowa Rd, 203-255-7201
Greg Hatzis, hdmstr. Fax 255-7213
Fairfield Warde HS 1,400/9-12
755 Melville Ave, 203-255-8449
David Ebling, hdmstr. Fax 255-8284
Fairfield Woods MS 800/6-8
1115 Fairfield Woods Rd, 203-255-8334
Dr. Gary Rosato, prin. Fax 255-8210
Ludlowe MS 1,000/6-8
689 Unquowa Rd, 203-255-8345
Meg Tiley, prin. Fax 255-8214
Tomlinson MS 800/6-8
200 Unquowa Rd, 203-255-8336
Sally Bonina, prin. Fax 255-8211

---

Fairfield College Prep S 900/9-12
1073 N Benson Rd, 203-254-4200
Dr. Robert Perrotta, prin. Fax 254-4108
Fairfield University Post-Sec.
1073 N Benson Rd, 203-254-4000
Notre Dame HS 400/9-12
220 Jefferson St, 203-372-6521
Christopher Cipriano, prin. Fax 374-4167
Sacred Heart University Post-Sec.
5151 Park Ave, 203-371-7999

**Falls Village, Litchfield, Pop. 534**
Regional SD 1 500/9-12
246 Warren Tpke 06031 860-824-0855
Patricia Chamberlain, supt. Fax 824-1271
www.region1schools.org
Housatonic Valley Regional HS 500/9-12
246 Warren Tpke 06031 860-824-5123
Dr. Jose Martinez, prin. Fax 824-5419

**Farmington, Hartford, Pop. 2,500**
Farmington SD 4,000/PK-12
1 Monteith Dr 06032 860-673-8268
Kathleen Greider, supt. Fax 673-8224
www.fpsct.org
Farmington HS 1,300/9-12
10 Monteith Dr 06032 860-673-2514
Dr. Bill Silva, prin. Fax 673-7284

Robbins MS 700/7-8
20 Wolf Pit Rd 06032 860-677-2683
Ted Donahue, prin. Fax 676-0697

---

Miss Porter's S 300/9-12
60 Main St 06032 860-409-3500
Katherine Windsor Ed.D., head sch Fax 409-3525
Tunxis Community College Post-Sec.
271 Scott Swamp Rd 06032 860-255-3500
University of Connecticut Health Center Post-Sec.
263 Farmington Ave 06030 860-679-2000

**Gales Ferry, New London, Pop. 1,137**
Ledyard SD
Supt. — See Ledyard
Ledyard MS 400/7-8
1860 Route 12 06335 860-464-3188
Christopher Pomroy, prin. Fax 464-2155

**Glastonbury, Hartford, Pop. 27,901**
Glastonbury SD 6,700/PK-12
PO Box 191 06033 860-652-7951
Dr. Alan Bookman, supt. Fax 652-7982
www.glastonburyus.org
Glastonbury HS 2,200/9-12
330 Hubbard St 06033 860-652-7200
Dr. Nancy Bean, prin. Fax 652-7267
Smith MS 1,100/7-8
216 Addison Rd 06033 860-652-7040
Donna Schilke, prin. Fax 652-4450

**Granby, Hartford**
Granby SD 2,200/PK-12
15B N Granby Rd 06035 860-844-5250
Dr. Alan Addley, supt. Fax 844-6081
www.granby.k12.ct.us
Granby Memorial HS 800/9-12
315 Salmon Brook St 06035 860-844-3014
Dr. Mary Jocelyn-Gadd, prin. Fax 844-3026
Granby Memorial MS 400/7-8
321 Salmon Brook St 06035 860-844-3029
Sue Henneberry, prin. Fax 844-3039

**Greens Farms, Fairfield**

---

Greens Farms Academy 700/PK-12
PO Box 998, 203-256-0717
Janet Hartwell, head sch Fax 256-7501

**Greenwich, Fairfield, Pop. 12,646**
Greenwich SD 8,800/K-12
290 Greenwich Ave 06830 203-625-7400
Dr. William McKersie, supt. Fax 618-9379
www.greenwich.k12.ct.us
Central MS 600/6-8
9 Indian Rock Ln 06830 203-661-8500
Shelley Somers, prin. Fax 661-2576
Greenwich HS 2,700/9-12
10 Hillside Rd 06830 203-625-8000
Chris Winters, hdmstr. Fax 863-8888
Western MS 500/6-8
1 Western Junior Hwy 06830 203-531-5700
Gordon Beinstein, prin. Fax 531-5220
Other Schools – See Riverside

---

Brunswick S 900/PK-12
100 Maher Ave 06830 203-625-5800
Daniel Griffin, dir. Fax 625-5889
Convent of Sacred Heart S 700/PK-12
1177 King St 06831 203-531-6500
Pamela Hayes, head sch Fax 531-5206
Greenwich Academy 900/PK-12
200 N Maple Ave 06830 203-625-8900
Molly King, head sch Fax 869-4921
Stanwich S 400/PK-12
257 Stanwich Rd 06830 203-542-0000
Charlie Sachs, head sch Fax 542-0025

**Griswold, See Jewett City**
Griswold SD 2,000/PK-12
211 Slater Ave 06351 860-376-7600
Paul Smith, supt. Fax 376-7607
www.griswold.k12.ct.us
Griswold Alternative S Alt
1553 Glasgo Rd 06351 860-376-9129
Erin Palonen, prin. Fax 376-9122
Griswold HS 700/9-12
267 Slater Ave 06351 860-376-7640
Dr. Mark Frizzell Ph.D., prin. Fax 376-7684
Griswold MS 600/5-8
211 Slater Ave 06351 860-376-7630
Michele Raynor, prin. Fax 376-7631

**Groton, New London, Pop. 9,886**
Connecticut Technical HS System
Supt. — See Middletown
Grasso Technical HS Vo/Tech
189 Fort Hill Rd 06340 860-448-0220
Patricia Feeney, prin. Fax 446-9895

Groton SD
Supt. — See Mystic
Fitch HS 1,200/9-12
101 Groton Long Point Rd 06340 860-449-7200
Joseph Arcarese, prin. Fax 449-7255
West Side MS 300/6-8
250 Brandegee Ave 06340 860-449-5630
John Jones, prin. Fax 449-5628

Learn RESC
Supt. — See Old Lyme
Marine Science Magnet HS 100/9-12
130 Shennecossett Rd 06340 860-446-9380
Dr. Nicholas Spera, prin. Fax 446-9381

---

Connecticut Center for Massage Therapy Post-Sec.
1154 Poquonnock Rd 06340 877-295-2268
University of Connecticut Post-Sec.
1084 Shennecossett Rd 06340 860-405-9000

**Guilford, New Haven, Pop. 19,848**
Guilford SD 3,700/PK-12
PO Box 367 06437 203-453-8200
Dr. Paul Freeman Ed.D., supt. Fax 453-8211
www.guilfordschools.org
Adams MS 600/7-8
233 Church St 06437 203-453-2755
Catherine Walker, prin. Fax 453-8446
Guilford HS 1,100/9-12
605 New England Rd 06437 203-453-2741
Rick Misenti, prin. Fax 453-6768

**Hamden, New Haven, Pop. 52,600**
Area Coop. Educational Services RESC
Supt. — See North Haven
Whitney HS East/West Alt
261 Skiff St 06517 203-281-3577
Gina Drury, prin. Fax 248-8312
Whitney HS North 100/Alt
205 Skiff St 06517 203-407-4500
Mark Dougherty, prin. Fax 407-4592

Connecticut Technical HS System
Supt. — See Middletown
Whitney Technical HS Vo/Tech
100 Fairview Ave 06514 203-397-4031
Dr. Mary Moran, prin. Fax 397-4129

Hamden SD 6,000/PK-12
60 Putnam Ave 06517 203-407-2000
Jody Goeler, supt. Fax 407-2001
www.hamden.org
Hamden HS 1,900/9-12
2040 Dixwell Ave 06514 203-407-2040
Gary Highsmith, prin. Fax 407-2041
Hamden MS 900/7-8
2623 Dixwell Ave 06518 203-407-3140
Dan Levy, prin. Fax 407-3141
Other Schools – See New Haven

---

Eli Whitney Tech. High School Post-Sec.
71 Jones Rd 06514 203-397-4031
Hamden Hall Country Day S 600/PK-12
1108 Whitney Ave 06517 203-752-2600
Robert Izzo, head sch Fax 752-2651
Paier College of Art Post-Sec.
20 Gorham Ave 06514 203-287-3031
Quinnipiac University Post-Sec.
275 Mount Carmel Ave 06518 203-582-8200
Sacred Heart Academy 500/9-12
265 Benham St 06514 203-288-2309
Sr. Maureen Flynn, prin. Fax 230-9680
Sawyer School Post-Sec.
1125 Dixwell Ave 06514 203-865-2900
West Woods Christian Academy 100/PK-12
2105 State St 06517 203-562-9922
William Kane, prin. Fax 786-4730

**Hartford, Hartford, Pop. 121,829**
Capitol Region Education Council RESC 3,800/
111 Charter Oak Ave 06106 860-524-4063
Dr. Bruce Douglas, dir. Fax 548-9924
www.crec.org
Greater Hartford Academy of Math/Science 200/9-12
15 Vernon St 06106 860-757-6300
Paul Brenton, prin. Fax 757-6399
Greater Hartford Academy of the Arts 400/9-12
15 Vernon St 06106 860-757-6300
Jeffrey Ostroff, prin. Fax 757-6382
Greater Hartford Academy of the Arts MS 6-8
140 Huyshope Ave 06106 860-724-0685
Bo Ryan, prin.
Two Rivers Magnet HS 9-12
15 Van Dyke Ave 06106 860-422-7095
Robert McCain, prin.
Other Schools – See Bloomfield, East Hartford, Enfield, New Britain, Windsor

Connecticut Technical HS System
Supt. — See Middletown
Connecticut Aero Tech HS Vo/Tech
500 Lindbergh Dr 06114 860-566-1234
Robert Sartoris, prin. Fax 566-1350
Prince Technical HS Vo/Tech
401 Flatbush Ave 06106 860-951-7112
Sheila Williams, prin. Fax 951-1529

Hartford SD 20,600/PK-12
960 Main St 06103 860-695-8000
Dr. Beth Schiavino-Narvaez, supt. Fax 722-6161
www.hartfordschools.org
Bulkeley Lower HS 600/9-10
300 Wethersfield Ave 06114 860-695-1000
Oscar Padua, prin. Fax 722-6601
Bulkeley Upper HS 400/11-12
300 Wethersfield Ave 06114 860-695-1000
Gayle Allen-Greene, prin. Fax 247-3491
Capital Community College Magnet Academy 11-12
950 Main St 06103 860-906-5122
Christian Arsenault, prin.
Capital Preparatory Magnet S 500/PK-12
1304 Main St 06103 860-695-9800
Kitsia Ferguson, prin. Fax 722-8520
Classical Magnet S 700/9-12
85 Woodland St 06105 860-695-9100
Zandralyn Gordon, prin. Fax 722-6449
Culinary Arts Academy 300/9-12
85 Sigourney St 06105 860-695-1733
Timothy Goodwin, prin.
Global Communications Academy 400/K-12
85 Edwards St 06120 860-695-6020
Kimberly Stone-Keaton, prin.
Hartford Magnet Trinity College Academy 700/6-12
53 Vernon St 06106 860-695-7201
Sally Biggs, prin. Fax 722-6954
High School Inc. 300/9-12
275 Asylum St 06103 860-695-7100
Audrey Boutaugh, prin. Fax 768-1487
HPHS Academy of Nursing & Health Science 400/9-12
55 Forest St 06105 860-695-1325
Melony Brady-Shanley, prin. Fax 722-8764

HPHS Engineering & Green Technology Acad 400/9-12
55 Forest St 06105 860-695-1315
Michael Maziarz, prin. Fax 722-8765
HPHS Law and Government Academy 400/9-12
55 Forest St 06105 860-695-1320
Jose Colon, prin. Fax 722-8768
Journalism and Media Academy 300/9-12
150 Tower Ave 06120 860-695-7564
Leonard Epps, prin.
Kinsella Sch of Performing Arts 700/PK-12
65 Van Block Ave 06106 860-695-4140
Kenneth O'Brien, prin. Fax 522-0004
McDonough Expeditionary Learning S 500/6-8
111 Hillside Ave 06106 860-695-4260
Bethany Sullivan, prin. Fax 722-8825
Middle Grades Academy 200/5-8
305 Greenfield St 06112 860-695-5557
Lynn Estey, prin.
Renzulli Gifted & Talented Academy 100/4-8
110 Washington St 06106 860-695-2140
Paula Erickson, prin. Fax 722-6984
Sports & Medical Sciences Academy 600/6-12
280 Huyshope Ave 06106 860-695-6900
John Laverty, prin. Fax 722-8017
University HS of Science & Engineering 400/9-12
351 Mark Twain Dr 06112 860-695-9020
Martin Folam, prin. Fax 722-6408
Other Schools – See East Hartford, Manchester

---

Capital Community College Post-Sec.
950 Main St 06103 860-906-5000
Connecticut Childrens Medical Center Post-Sec.
282 Washington St 06106 860-545-8514
Connecticut Institute for the Blind Post-Sec.
120 Holcomb St 06112 860-242-2274
Covenant Preparatory S 5-8
135 Broad St 06105 860-547-0289
Glenn Winfree, head sch Fax 547-0361
Hartford Area SDA S 100/PK-10
474 Woodland St 06112 860-724-5777
Grafton B. Jones, prin. Fax 548-9252
Hartford Hospital Post-Sec.
PO Box 5037 06102 860-545-2100
Hartford Seminary Post-Sec.
77 Sherman St 06105 860-509-9500
Institute of Living Schools Post-Sec.
400 Washington St 06106
Lincoln Technical Institute Post-Sec.
85 Sigourney St 06105 800-762-4337
Prince Regional Vocational Tech School Post-Sec.
500 Brookfield St 06106 860-246-8594
Rensselaer at Hartford Post-Sec.
275 Windsor St 06120 860-548-2400
Sawyer School Post-Sec.
141 Washington St 06106 860-247-4440
Trinity Academy 3-8
120 Sigourney St 06105 860-251-8337
Myron Congdon, head sch Fax 527-2863
Trinity College Post-Sec.
300 Summit St 06106 860-297-2000
Watkinson S 200/6-12
180 Bloomfield Ave 06105 860-236-5618
Teri Schrader, head sch Fax 233-8295

**Hebron, Tolland**
Regional SD 8 1,800/7-12
PO Box 1438 06248 860-228-2115
Dr. Robert Siminski Ed.D., supt. Fax 228-4346
www.reg8.k12.ct.us/
RHAM HS 1,200/9-12
85 Wall St 06248 860-228-9474
Scott Leslie, prin. Fax 228-5312
RHAM MS 600/7-8
25 RHAM Rd 06248 860-228-9423
Dr. Michael Seroussi, prin. Fax 228-5316

**Higganum, Middlesex, Pop. 1,666**
Regional SD 17 2,400/PK-12
57 Little City Rd 06441 860-345-4534
Howard Thiery, supt. Fax 345-2817
rsd17.org
Haddam-Killingworth HS 700/9-12
95 Little City Rd 06441 860-345-8541
Donna Hayward, prin. Fax 345-8252
Other Schools – See Killingworth

**Kent, Litchfield**

---

Kent S 600/9-12
PO Box 2006 06757 860-927-6111
Rev. Richardson Schell, hdmstr. Fax 927-6109
Marvelwood S 200/9-12
PO Box 3001 06757 860-927-0047
Arthur Goodearl, head sch Fax 927-5325

**Killingly, Windham**
Killingly SD 2,700/PK-12
PO Box 210 06239 860-779-6600
Kevin Farr, supt. Fax 779-3798
www.killinglyschools.org
Other Schools – See Dayville

**Killingworth, Middlesex**
Regional SD 17
Supt. — See Higganum
Haddam-Killingworth MS 800/5-8
451 Route 81 06419 860-663-1241
Dr. Jennifer Olsen, prin. Fax 663-2071

**Lakeville, Litchfield, Pop. 909**

---

Hotchkiss S 600/9-12
11 Interlaken Rd 06039 860-435-2591
G. Peter O'Neill, hdmstr. Fax 435-8056

**Lebanon, New London**
Lebanon SD 1,300/PK-12
891 Exeter Rd 06249 860-642-7795
Robert Angeli, supt. Fax 642-4589
www.lebanonct.org
Lebanon MS 400/5-8
891 Exeter Rd 06249 860-642-4702
Robert Laskarzewski, prin. Fax 642-3534
Lyman Memorial HS 400/9-12
917 Exeter Rd 06249 860-642-7567
James Apicelli, prin. Fax 642-3521

**Ledyard, New London**
Ledyard SD 2,600/PK-12
4 Blonder Blvd 06339 860-464-9255
Cathy Patterson, supt. Fax 464-8589
ledyard.net/
Ledyard HS 900/9-12
24 Gallup Hill Rd 06339 860-464-9600
Amanda Fagan, prin. Fax 464-1990
Other Schools – See Gales Ferry

**Litchfield, Litchfield, Pop. 1,239**
Litchfield SD 1,100/PK-12
PO Box 110 06759 860-567-7500
Lynn McMullin, supt. Fax 567-7508
www.litchfieldschools.org
Litchfield HS 500/9-12
PO Box 110 06759 860-567-7530
Kristen Della Volpe, prin. Fax 567-7538
Litchfield MS 200/7-8
PO Box 110 06759 860-567-7530
Stephanie Kubisek, admin. Fax 567-7538

Regional SD 6 1,100/PK-12
98 Wamogo Rd 06759 860-567-7400
Edward Drapp, supt. Fax 567-6652
www.rsd6.org
Wamogo Regional JSHS 600/7-12
98 Wamogo Rd 06759 860-567-7410
Jody Lambert, prin. Fax 567-6651

---

Connecticut Junior Republic Post-Sec.
PO Box 161 06759

**Madison, New Haven, Pop. 15,485**
Madison SD 3,500/K-12
PO Box 71 06443 203-245-6300
Thomas Scarice, supt. Fax 245-6336
www.madison.k12.ct.us
Hand HS 1,300/9-12
286 Green Hill Rd 06443 203-245-6350
Anthony Salutari, prin. Fax 245-6356
Polson MS 600/7-8
302 Green Hill Rd 06443 203-245-6480
Frank Henderson, prin. Fax 245-6494

**Manchester, Hartford, Pop. 29,743**
Connecticut Technical HS System
Supt. — See Middletown
Cheney Technical HS Vo/Tech
791 Middle Tpke W 06040 860-649-5396
Robert Sartoris, prin. Fax 649-5263

Hartford SD
Supt. — See Hartford
Great Path Academy 200/9-12
PO Box 1046 06045 860-512-3700
Tory Niles-Outler, prin. Fax 512-3701

Manchester SD 5,800/PK-12
45 N School St, 860-647-3441
Matt Geary, supt. Fax 647-5042
publicschools.manchesterct.gov
Bentley Alternative Education S Alt
134 Middle Tpke E 06040 860-647-3342
Fax 647-5038
Illing MS 800/7-8
227 Middle Tpke E 06040 860-647-3400
Beth Hayes, prin. Fax 647-5008
Manchester HS 1,800/9-12
134 Middle Tpke E 06040 860-647-3530
Jill Krieger, prin. Fax 646-3727

---

Cornerstone Christian S 200/PK-12
236 Main St, 860-643-0792
Tonya Snyder, prin. Fax 647-9291
East Catholic HS 700/9-12
115 New State Rd, 860-649-5336
Jason Hartling, prin. Fax 649-7191
Manchester Community College Post-Sec.
PO Box 1046 06045 860-512-3000

**Meriden, New Haven, Pop. 59,747**
Area Coop. Educational Services RESC
Supt. — See North Haven
Edison MS 700/6-8
1355 N Broad St 06450 203-639-8403
Karen Habegger, prin. Fax 639-8323

Connecticut Technical HS System
Supt. — See Middletown
Wilcox Technical HS Vo/Tech
298 Oregon Rd 06451 203-238-6260
Joyce Mowrey, prin. Fax 238-6602

Meriden SD 8,200/PK-12
22 Liberty St 06450 203-630-4171
Mark Benigni Ed.D., supt. Fax 630-0110
www.meridenk12.org
Lincoln MS 700/6-8
164 Centennial Ave 06451 203-238-2381
Dianne Vumback, prin. Fax 238-7258
Maloney HS 1,300/9-12
121 Gravel St 06450 203-238-2334
Jennifer Straub, prin. Fax 630-7011
Platt HS 1,100/9-12
220 Coe Ave 06451 203-235-7962
Robert Montemurro, prin. Fax 630-4011
Washington MS 800/6-8
1225 N Broad St 06450 203-235-6606
Raymond Southland, prin. Fax 235-6040

---

Marinello School of Beauty Post-Sec.
1231 E Main St 06450 203-237-6683

**Middlebury, New Haven, Pop. 4,100**
Regional SD 15 4,200/PK-12
PO Box 395 06762 203-758-8259
Regina Botsford, supt. Fax 758-1908
www.region15.org
Memorial MS 500/6-8
PO Box 903 06762 203-758-2496
John Sieller, prin. Fax 758-9594
Other Schools – See Southbury

---

Westover S 200/9-12
PO Box 847 06762 203-758-2423
Julie Faulstich, head sch Fax 577-4585

**Middletown, Middlesex, Pop. 46,173**
Connecticut Technical HS System
25 Industrial Park Rd 06457 860-807-2200
Dr. Nivea Torres, supt. Fax 807-2196
www.cttech.org
Vinal Technical HS Vo/Tech
60 Daniels St 06457 860-344-7100
Richard Shellman, prin. Fax 344-2622
Other Schools – See Ansonia, Bridgeport, Bristol, Danbury, Danielson, Groton, Hamden, Hartford, Manchester, Meriden, Milford, New Britain, Norwich, Stamford, Stratford, Torrington, Waterbury, Willimantic

Middletown SD 5,000/PK-12
311 Hunting Hill Ave 06457 860-638-1401
Patricia Charles Ed.D., supt. Fax 638-1495
www.middletownschools.org
Middletown HS 1,300/9-12
200 La Rosa Ln 06457 860-704-4500
Colleen Weiner, prin. Fax 347-2044
Wilson MS 700/7-8
370 Hunting Hill Ave 06457 860-347-8594
Robert Conroy, prin. Fax 347-2158

---

Mercy HS 700/9-12
1740 Randolph Rd 06457 860-346-6659
Sr. Mary McCarthy, pres. Fax 344-9887
Middlesex Community College Post-Sec.
100 Training Hill Rd 06457 860-343-5800
Wesleyan University 06459 Post-Sec.
860-685-2000
Xavier HS 900/9-12
181 Randolph Rd 06457 860-346-7735
Br. Brian Davis, hdmstr. Fax 346-6859

**Milford, New Haven, Pop. 50,507**
Connecticut Technical HS System
Supt. — See Middletown
Platt Technical HS Vo/Tech
600 Orange Ave, 203-783-5300
Scott Zito, prin. Fax 783-3970

Milford SD 6,700/K-12
70 W River St 06460 203-783-3402
Dr. Elizabeth E. Feser, supt. Fax 783-3475
www.milforded.org
Academy 100/Alt
140 Gulf St 06460 203-783-3652
Annaleise Spaziano, dir. Fax 783-3679
East Shore MS 500/6-8
240 Chapel St 06460 203-783-3559
Catherine Williams, prin. Fax 301-5060
Foran HS 1,000/9-12
80 Foran Rd 06460 203-783-3502
Max Berkowitz, prin. Fax 783-3635
Harborside MS 600/6-8
175 High St 06460 203-783-3523
Steve Gottlieb, prin. Fax 783-3687
Law HS 1,000/9-12
20 Lansdale Ave 06460 203-783-3574
Francis Thompson, prin. Fax 783-3586
West Shore MS 600/6-8
70 Kay Ave 06460 203-783-3553
Vince Scarpetti, prin. Fax 783-3696

---

Academy of Our Lady of Mercy 500/9-12
200 High St 06460 203-877-2786
Cynthia Gallant, prin. Fax 876-9760

**Monroe, Fairfield**
Monroe SD 3,600/PK-12
375 Monroe Tpke 06468 203-452-2860
James Agostine, supt. Fax 452-5818
www.monroeps.org
Jockey Hollow S 900/6-8
365 Fan Hill Rd 06468 203-452-2905
John Ceccolini, prin. Fax 452-2444
Masuk HS 1,300/9-12
1014 Monroe Tpke 06468 203-452-5823
Joe Kobza, prin. Fax 452-5835

**Montville, New London**
Montville SD
Supt. — See Oakdale
Palmer Building 50/Alt
PO Box 27 06353 860-848-7816
Heather Mileski, prin. Fax 848-9159

**Moodus, Middlesex, Pop. 1,397**
East Haddam SD 1,300/PK-12
PO Box 401 06469 860-873-5090
Brian Reas, supt. Fax 873-5092
www.easthaddamschools.org
Hale-Ray HS 400/9-12
PO Box 404 06469 860-873-5065
Eric Spencer, prin. Fax 873-5074
Hale-Ray MS 500/4-8
PO Box 363 06469 860-873-5081
Jason Peacock, prin. Fax 873-5086

**Mystic, New London, Pop. 4,136**
Groton SD 4,500/PK-12
1300 Flanders Rd 06355 860-572-2100
Michael Graner Ph.D., supt. Fax 572-2107
www.groton.k12.ct.us
Cutler MS 400/6-8
160 Fishtown Rd 06355 860-572-5830
Peter Bass, prin. Fax 572-5834

Other Schools – See Groton

Stonington SD
Supt. — See Old Mystic
Mystic MS 400/5-8
204 Mistuxet Ave 06355 860-536-9613
Gregory Keith, prin. Fax 536-4508

**Naugatuck, New Haven, Pop. 31,134**
Naugatuck SD 4,100/PK-12
380 Church St 06770 203-720-5265
Sharon Locke, supt. Fax 720-5272
www.naugy.net
City Hill MS 700/7-8
441 City Hill St 06770 203-720-5246
Brian Hendrickson, prin. Fax 720-5256
Naugatuck HS 1,300/9-12
543 Rubber Ave 06770 203-720-5400
Janice Saam, prin. Fax 720-5444

**New Britain, Hartford, Pop. 71,606**
Capitol Region Education Council RESC
Supt. — See Hartford
Medical Professions & Teacher Prep Acad 300/PK-PK, 6-
600 Slater Rd 06053 860-223-0726
Andrew Skarzynski, prin. Fax 223-0742

Connecticut Technical HS System
Supt. — See Middletown
Goodwin Regional Technical HS Vo/Tech
735 Slater Rd 06053 860-827-7736
Daniel Mello, prin. Fax 827-7862

New Britain SD 10,000/PK-12
PO Box 1960 06050 860-827-2203
Kelt Cooper, supt. Fax 612-1533
www.csdnb.org/
HALS Academy 200/6-8
40 Goodwin St 06051 860-826-1866
Leona Clerkin, prin. Fax 826-1867
New Britain HS 2,500/9-12
110 Mill St 06051 860-225-6300
David Chambers, prin. Fax 225-6350
Pulaski MS 500/6-8
757 Farmington Ave 06053 860-225-7665
Wanda Lickwar, prin. Fax 223-3840
Slade MS 700/6-8
183 Steele St 06052 860-225-6395
Richard Reyes, prin. Fax 826-7894

Central Connecticut State University Post-Sec.
1615 Stanley St 06053 860-832-3200
Charter Oak State College Post-Sec.
55 Paul Manafort Dr 06053 860-515-3800
Lincoln Technical Institute Post-Sec.
200 John Downey Dr 06051 860-225-8641

**New Canaan, Fairfield, Pop. 17,864**
New Canaan SD 4,200/PK-12
39 Locust Ave 06840 203-594-4000
Dr. Bryan D. Luizzi, supt. Fax 594-4035
www.newcanaan.k12.ct.us
New Canaan HS 1,300/9-12
11 Farm Rd 06840 203-594-4600
Dr. William Egan, prin. Fax 972-4700
Saxe MS 1,200/5-8
468 South Ave 06840 203-594-4500
Greg Macedo, prin. Fax 594-4565

St. Luke's S 500/5-12
377 N Wilton Rd 06840 203-966-5612
Mark Davis, head sch Fax 972-3409

**New Fairfield, Fairfield, Pop. 12,911**
New Fairfield SD 2,900/PK-12
3 Brush Hill Rd 06812 203-312-5770
Dr. Alicia Roy, supt. Fax 312-5609
www.newfairfieldschools.org
New Fairfield HS 1,000/9-12
54 Gillotti Rd 06812 203-312-5800
Mariana Coelho, prin. Fax 312-5803
New Fairfield MS 700/6-8
56 Gillotti Rd 06812 203-312-5885
Christine Baldelli, prin. Fax 312-5887

**New Haven, New Haven, Pop. 126,396**
Area Coop. Educational Services RESC
Supt. — See North Haven
Educational Center for the Arts 300/9-12
55 Audubon St 06510 203-777-5451
Alice Schilling, prin. Fax 782-3596

Hamden SD
Supt. — See Hamden
Hamden Collaborative Learning Center 50/Alt
306 Circular Ave 06514 203-407-2134
Jonathan Pearce, coord.

New Haven SD 19,500/PK-12
54 Meadow St 06519 203-936-5200
Garth Harries, supt. Fax 946-7300
www.nhps.net
Brennan/Rogers S of Arts and Sciences 200/3-8
200 Wilmot Rd 06515 203-946-8640
Dr. Gail DeBlasio, prin. Fax 946-7516
Cooperative Arts & Humanities HS 700/9-12
177 College St 06510 203-691-2400
Frank Costanzo, prin. Fax 691-2404
Cross HS 1,200/9-12
181 Mitchell Dr 06511 203-497-7400
Edith Johnson, prin. Fax 946-6932
Dixwell New Light HS 50/Alt
21 Wooster Pl 06511 203-946-5617
Larry Conaway, prin. Fax 946-5821
DOMUS Academy 50/Alt
560 Ella T Grasso Blvd 06519 203-492-0750
Marc Donald, prin. Fax 946-2343
Engineering & Science S 200/6-12
130B Leeder Hill Dr 06517 203-946-6610
Medria Blue-Ellis, prin. Fax 946-8440
High School in the Community 300/9-12
175 Water St 06511 203-946-7022
Matthew Brown, admin. Fax 946-7132
Hillhouse HS 1,000/9-12
480 Sherman Pkwy 06511 203-497-7500
David Diah, prin. Fax 946-8487
Hill Regional Career HS 700/9-12
140 Legion Ave 06519 203-946-5845
Dr. Madeline Negron, prin. Fax 946-5949
Hooker MS 300/3-8
691 Whitney Ave 06511 203-497-7200
Sheryl Hershonik, prin. Fax 497-7205
Hyde Leadership Academy 200/9-12
60 Sargent Dr 06511 203-497-7060
Dr. Zakia Parrish, prin. Fax 946-6161
McCabe Center 50/Alt
400 Canner St 06511 203-691-3484
Belinda Carberry, prin. Fax 946-5374
Metropolitan Business HS 300/9-12
115 Water St 06511 203-497-7700
Judy Puglisi, prin. Fax 497-7705
New Haven Academy 300/9-12
804 State St 06511 203-946-8995
Greg Baldwin, prin. Fax 946-8428
New Horizons HS Alt
103 Hallock Ave 06519 203-946-7342
Maureen Bransfield, prin. Fax 946-7317
Riverside Educational Academy 100/9-12
560 Ella T Grasso Blvd 06519 203-946-7180
Wanda Gibbs, prin. Fax 946-2380
Ross Arts MS 500/5-8
150 Kimberly Ave 06519 203-946-8974
Shawn True, prin. Fax 946-5824
Sound HS 300/9-12
60 S Water St 06519 203-946-6937
Rebecca Gratz, prin. Fax 946-6874
Adult & Continuing Education Center Adult
580 Ella T Grasso Blvd 06519 203-492-0213
Glen Worthy, prin. Fax 492-6384

Albertus Magnus College Post-Sec.
700 Prospect St 06511 203-773-8550
Berkeley Divinity School Post-Sec.
409 Prospect St 06511 203-432-9285
Gateway Community College Post-Sec.
20 Church St 06510 203-285-2000
Hopkins S 700/7-12
986 Forest Rd 06515 203-397-1001
Barbara Riley, head sch Fax 389-3506
St. Martin de Porres Academy 100/5-8
208 Columbus Ave 06519 203-772-2424
Kelly O'Leary, prin. Fax 772-2425
Southern Connecticut State University Post-Sec.
501 Crescent St 06515 203-392-5200
Yale-New Haven Hospital Post-Sec.
20 York St 06510 203-785-5074
Yale University Post-Sec.
38 Hillhouse Ave 06511 203-432-4771
Yeshiva of New Haven HS 50/9-12
765 Elm St 06511 203-777-7199

**Newington, Hartford, Pop. 30,076**
Newington SD 4,400/PK-12
131 Cedar St 06111 860-665-8610
Dr. William C. Collins, supt. Fax 665-8616
www.npsct.org
Kellogg MS 600/5-8
155 Harding Ave 06111 860-666-5418
Jason Lambert, prin. Fax 666-5925
Newington HS 1,500/9-12
605 Willard Ave 06111 860-666-5611
James Wenker, prin. Fax 666-8224
Wallace MS 700/5-8
71 Halleran Dr 06111 860-667-5888
David Milardo, prin. Fax 667-5893

Connecticut Center for Massage Therapy Post-Sec.
75 Kitts Ln 06111 860-667-1886
Hanger Orthopedic Group Post-Sec.
181 Patricia M Genova Dr 06111 860-667-5304

**New London, New London, Pop. 26,373**
New London SD 2,600/PK-12
134 Williams St 06320 860-447-6000
Dr. Manuel J. Rivera, supt. Fax 447-6016
www.newlondon.org
Jackson MS 600/6-8
36 Waller St 06320 860-437-6480
Dr. Alison Burdick, prin. Fax 437-6494
New London HS 900/9-12
490 Jefferson Ave 06320 860-437-6400
Tommy Thompson, prin. Fax 271-4321
Science & Technology Magnet HS of SE CT 9-12
490 Jefferson Ave 06320 860-437-6496
Laurelle Texidor, dir. Fax 439-7774
New London Adult Education Adult
3 Shaws Cv 06320 860-437-2385
Maria Pukas, dir. Fax 437-6460

Connecticut College Post-Sec.
270 Mohegan Ave 06320 860-447-1911
Mitchell College Post-Sec.
437 Pequot Ave 06320 860-701-5000
Ridley-Lowell Business & Technical Inst. Post-Sec.
470 Bank St 06320 860-443-7441
United States Coast Guard Academy Post-Sec.
31 Mohegan Ave 06320 800-883-8724

**New Milford, Litchfield, Pop. 6,408**
New Milford SD 4,700/PK-12
50 East St 06776 860-355-8406
JeanAnn Paddyfote Ph.D., supt. Fax 210-4132
www.newmilfordps.org
New Milford HS 1,500/9-12
388 Danbury Rd 06776 860-350-6647
Greg Shugrue, prin. Fax 210-2256
Schaghticoke MS 700/7-8
23 Hipp Rd 06776 860-354-2204
Dana Ford, prin. Fax 210-2217

Canterbury HS 300/9-12
101 Aspetuck Ave 06776 860-210-3800
Thomas Sheehy, hdmstr. Fax 350-4425
Faith Preparatory S 100/K-12
600 Danbury Rd Ste 2 06776 860-210-3677
Josephine DuBois, prin. Fax 210-3685

**Newtown, Fairfield, Pop. 1,929**
Newtown SD 4,800/PK-12
3 Primrose St 06470 203-426-7600
Dr. Joseph Erardi Ed.D., supt. Fax 270-6199
www.newtown.k12.ct.us
Newtown MS 900/7-8
11 Queen St 06470 203-426-7642
Thomas Einhorn, prin. Fax 270-6102
Other Schools – See Sandy Hook

**Niantic, New London, Pop. 3,074**
East Lyme SD
Supt. — See East Lyme
East Lyme MS 900/5-8
31 Society Rd 06357 860-739-4491
Dr. Judy DeLeeuw, prin. Fax 691-5400

**North Branford, New Haven, Pop. 12,996**
North Branford SD
Supt. — See Northford
North Branford HS 600/9-12
49 Caputo Rd 06471 203-484-1465
Todd Stoeffler, prin. Fax 484-1233
North Branford IS 600/6-8
654 Foxon Rd 06471 203-484-1500
Alan Davis, prin. Fax 484-1505

**Northford, New Haven, Pop. 3,200**
North Branford SD 2,200/K-12
PO Box 129 06472 203-484-1440
Scott Schoonmaker, supt. Fax 484-1445
www.northbranfordschools.org
Other Schools – See North Branford

**North Grosvenordale, Windham, Pop. 1,481**
Thompson SD 1,200/PK-12
785 Riverside Dr 06255 860-923-9581
Michael Jolin Ph.D., supt. Fax 923-9638
www.thompsonpublicschools.org/
Thompson MS 400/5-8
785 Riverside Dr 06255 860-923-9380
Tina Chahanovich, prin. Fax 923-9638
Tourtellotte Memorial HS 300/9-12
785 Riverside Dr 06255 860-923-9303
Megan Baker, prin. Fax 923-3752

**North Haven, New Haven, Pop. 23,822**
Area Coop. Educational Services RESC 1,900/
350 State St 06473 203-498-6800
Dr. Craig Edmondson, dir. Fax 498-6890
www.aces.org
Other Schools – See Hamden, Meriden, New Haven

North Haven SD 3,500/PK-12
5 Linsley St 06473 203-239-2581
Robert Cronin Ph.D., supt. Fax 234-9811
www.north-haven.k12.ct.us/
North Haven HS 1,200/9-12
221 Elm St 06473 203-239-1641
Russell Dallai Ph.D., prin. Fax 234-2602
North Haven MS 800/6-8
55 Bailey Rd 06473 203-239-1683
Philip Piazza, prin. Fax 234-2846

Gal Mar Academy of Hairdressing Post-Sec.
97 Washington Ave Ste 8 06473 203-281-4477

**North Stonington, New London**
North Stonington SD 800/PK-12
297 Norwich Westerly Rd 06359 860-535-2800
Peter Nero, supt. Fax 535-1470
www.northstonington.k12.ct.us
Wheeler HS 200/9-12
298 Norwich Westerly Rd 06359 860-535-0377
Kristen St. Germain, prin. Fax 535-2536
Wheeler MS 200/6-8
298 Norwich Westerly Rd 06359 860-535-0377
Kristen St. Germain, prin. Fax 535-2536

North Stonington Christian Academy 100/PK-12
12 Stillman Rd 06359 860-599-5071
Pamela Wilkinson, dir. Fax 599-2815

**Norwalk, Fairfield, Pop. 84,099**
Norwalk SD 11,200/PK-12
PO Box 6001 06852 203-854-4000
Dr. Steven Adamowski, supt. Fax 838-3299
www.norwalkps.org
Briggs HS 100/Alt
350 Main Ave 06851 203-899-2820
Marie Allan, prin. Fax 899-2824
Center for Global Studies 200/9-12
300 Highland Ave 06854 203-852-9488
Roslynne McCarthy, dir. Fax 854-0832
Hale MS 600/6-8
176 Strawberry Hill Ave 06851 203-899-2910
Dr. Albert Sackey, prin. Fax 899-2914
McMahon HS 1,700/9-12
300 Highland Ave 06854 203-852-9488
Suzanne Koroshetz, prin. Fax 899-2813
Norwalk HS 1,500/9-12
23 Calvin Murphy Dr 06851 203-838-4481
Reginald Roberts, prin. Fax 899-2815
Ponus Ridge MS 600/6-8
21 Hunters Ln 06850 203-847-3557
Dr. Damon Lewis, prin. Fax 899-2924
Roton MS 400/6-8
201 Highland Ave 06853 203-899-2930
Joseph Vellucci, prin. Fax 899-2934
West Rocks MS 700/6-8
81 W Rocks Rd 06851 203-899-2970
Dr. Lynne Moore, prin. Fax 899-2974

Norwalk Community College Post-Sec.
188 Richards Ave 06854 203-857-7000

Norwalk Hospital Post-Sec.
24 Stevens St 06850 203-852-2211

**Norwich, New London, Pop. 38,601**
Connecticut Technical HS System
Supt. — See Middletown
Norwich Technical HS Vo/Tech
7 Mahan Dr 06360 860-889-8453
Dr. Nikitoula Menounos, prin. Fax 886-4632

Endowed & Incorporated Academies 2,300/9-12
305 Broadway 06360 860-425-5500
David Klein, head sch Fax 887-2004
www.norwichfreeacademy.com
Norwich Free Academy 2,300/9-12
305 Broadway 06360 860-887-2505
David Klein, head sch Fax 887-2004

Learn RESC
Supt. — See Old Lyme
Three Rivers Middle College HS 100/11-12
574 New London Tpke 06360 860-215-9055
Brad Columbus, prin. Fax 215-9913

Norwich SD 3,900/PK-8
90 Town St 06360 860-823-4245
Abby I. Dolliver, supt. Fax 823-1880
www.norwichpublicschools.org
Kelly MS 600/7-8
25 Mahan Dr 06360 860-823-4211
William Peckrul, prin. Fax 892-4302

---

Three Rivers Community College Post-Sec.
574 New London Tpke 06360 860-886-0177

**Oakdale, New London**
Montville SD 2,600/PK-12
800 Old Colchester Rd 06370 860-848-1228
Brian Levesque, supt. Fax 848-0589
www.montvilleschools.org
Montville HS 800/9-12
800 Old Colchester Rd 06370 860-848-9208
Jeffrey Theodoss, prin. Fax 848-3872
Tyl MS 600/6-8
166 Chesterfield Rd 06370 860-848-2822
Mary Jane Dix, prin. Fax 848-8854
Other Schools – See Montville

---

St. Thomas More S 100/8-12
45 Cottage Rd 06370 860-859-1900
James Hanrahan M.Ed., hdmstr. Fax 859-2989

**Oakville, Litchfield, Pop. 8,924**
Watertown SD
Supt. — See Watertown
Swift MS 800/6-8
250 Colonial St 06779 860-945-4830
Marylu Lerz, prin. Fax 945-6449

**Old Lyme, New London**
Learn RESC 900/
44 Hatchetts Hill Rd 06371 860-434-4800
Dr. Eileen Howley, dir. Fax 434-4820
www.learn.k12.ct.us
Other Schools – See East Hartford, Groton, Norwich, Waterford

Regional SD 18 1,400/PK-12
49 Lyme St 06371 860-434-7238
Ian Neviaser, supt. Fax 434-9959
www.region18.org
Lyme-Old Lyme HS 400/9-12
69 Lyme St 06371 860-434-1651
James Wygonik, prin. Fax 434-8234
Lyme-Old Lyme MS 400/6-8
53 Lyme St 06371 860-434-2568
Michelle Dean, prin. Fax 434-0717

---

Lyme Academy College of Fine Arts Post-Sec.
84 Lyme St 06371 860-434-5232

**Old Mystic, New London, Pop. 3,422**
Stonington SD 2,400/K-12
PO Box 479 06372 860-572-0506
Dr. Van Riley, supt. Fax 572-1470
www.stoningtonschools.org
Other Schools – See Mystic, Pawcatuck

**Old Saybrook, Middlesex, Pop. 9,552**
Old Saybrook SD 1,600/PK-12
50 Sheffield St 06475 860-395-3157
Jan Perruccio, supt. Fax 395-3162
www.oldsaybrook.k12.ct.us
Old Saybrook HS 500/9-12
1111 Boston Post Rd 06475 860-395-3175
Sheila Riffle, prin. Fax 395-3179
Old Saybrook MS 600/4-8
60 Sheffield St 06475 860-395-3168
Mandy Ryan, prin. Fax 395-3350

**Orange, New Haven, Pop. 13,774**
Regional SD 5
Supt. — See Woodbridge
Amity Regional MS 400/7-8
100 Ohman Ave 06477 203-392-3200
Kathleen Fuller-Cutler, prin. Fax 387-7603

---

Southern Connecticut Hebrew Academy 100/K-11
261 Derby Ave 06477 203-795-5261

**Oxford, New Haven**
Oxford SD 2,100/PK-12
1 Great Hill Rd 06478 203-888-7754
Anna Ortiz, supt. Fax 888-5955
www.oxfordpublicschools.org
Great Oak MS 500/6-8
50 Great Oak Rd 06478 203-888-5418
Anthony Hibbert, prin. Fax 888-7798
Oxford HS 600/9-12
61 Quaker Farms Rd 06478 203-888-2468
Fax 881-5250

**Pawcatuck, New London, Pop. 5,474**
Stonington SD
Supt. — See Old Mystic
Pawcatuck MS 400/5-8
40 Field St 06379 860-599-5696
Tim Smith, prin. Fax 599-8948
Stonington HS 800/9-12
176 S Broad St 06379 860-599-5781
Mark Friese, prin. Fax 599-5784

**Plainfield, Windham, Pop. 14,363**
Plainfield SD 2,600/PK-12
651 Norwich Rd 06374 860-564-6403
Kenneth DiPietro, supt. Fax 564-6412
www.plainfieldschools.org
Plainfield Central S 600/6-8
75 Canterbury Rd 06374 860-564-6437
Scott Gagnon, prin. Fax 564-1147
Other Schools – See Central Village

**Plainville, Hartford, Pop. 17,932**
Plainville SD 2,400/PK-12
1 Central Sq 06062 860-793-3210
Dr. Jeffrey Kitching, supt. Fax 747-6790
www.plainvilleschools.org
Plainville HS 800/9-12
47 Robert Holcomb Way 06062 860-793-3220
Steven LePage, prin. Fax 793-3224
MS of Plainville 500/6-8
150 Northwest Dr 06062 860-793-3250
Matthew Guarino, prin. Fax 793-3265

**Plantsville, Hartford, Pop. 7,000**
Southington SD
Supt. — See Southington
Kennedy MS 800/6-8
1071 S Main St 06479 860-628-3275
Richard Terino, prin. Fax 628-3404

**Pomfret, Windham**

---

Pomfret S 400/9-12
398 Pomfret St 06258 860-963-6100
Timothy Richards, head sch Fax 963-2086

**Portland, Middlesex, Pop. 5,757**
Portland SD 1,400/PK-12
33 E Main St 06480 860-342-6790
Dr. Philip O'Reilly, supt. Fax 342-6791
www.portlandctschools.org
Portland HS 400/9-12
95 High St 06480 860-342-1720
Kathryn Lawson, prin. Fax 342-2906
Portland MS 200/7-8
93 High St 06480 860-342-1880
Scott Giegerich, prin. Fax 342-3934

**Preston, New London**
Preston SD 400/PK-8
325 Shetucket Tpke 06365 860-889-6098
Dr. John Welch, supt. Fax 889-8685
www.prestonschools.org/
Preston Plains MS 100/6-8
1 Route 164 06365 860-889-3831
Ivy Davis-Tomczuk, prin. Fax 204-0126

**Prospect, New Haven, Pop. 7,775**
Regional SD 16 2,500/PK-12
207 New Haven Rd 06712 203-758-6671
Michael Yamin, supt. Fax 758-5797
www.region16ct.org
Long River MS 600/6-8
38 Columbia Ave 06712 203-758-4421
Jayne Lanphear, prin. Fax 758-6948
Other Schools – See Beacon Falls

**Putnam, Windham, Pop. 7,034**
Putnam SD 1,300/PK-12
126 Church St 06260 860-963-6900
William Hull, supt. Fax 963-6903
www.putnam.k12.ct.us/
Putnam HS 300/9-12
152 Woodstock Ave 06260 860-963-6905
Joseph Ptaszynski, prin. Fax 963-6911
Putnam MS 300/6-8
35 Wicker St 06260 860-963-6920
Teri Bruce, prin. Fax 963-6921

**Redding, Fairfield**
Redding SD
Supt. — See Easton
Read MS 600/5-8
486 Redding Rd 06896 203-938-2533
Diane Martin, prin. Fax 938-8667

Regional SD 9
Supt. — See Easton
Barlow HS 1,000/9-12
100 Black Rock Tpke 06896 203-938-2508
Gina Pin, prin. Fax 938-0327

**Ridgefield, Fairfield, Pop. 7,542**
Ridgefield SD 5,300/PK-12
70 Prospect St 06877 203-894-5550
Dr. Karen Baldwin, supt. Fax 431-2811
www.ridgefield.org
East Ridge MS 800/6-8
10 E Ridge Rd 06877 203-894-5500
Martin Fiedler, prin. Fax 431-2843
Ridgefield HS 1,800/9-12
700 N Salem Rd 06877 203-894-5725
Dr. Stacey Gross, prin. Fax 431-2891
Scotts Ridge MS 500/6-8
750 N Salem Rd 06877 203-894-5725
Tim Salem, prin. Fax 894-3411

**Riverside, Fairfield, Pop. 8,283**
Greenwich SD
Supt. — See Greenwich
Eastern MS 800/6-8
51 Hendrie Ave 06878 203-637-1744
Ralph Mayo, prin. Fax 637-3567

**Rocky Hill, Hartford, Pop. 16,554**
Rocky Hill SD 2,500/PK-12
PO Box 627 06067 860-258-7701
Dr. Mark Zito, supt. Fax 258-7710
www.rockyhillps.com
Griswold MS 600/5-8
144 Bailey Rd 06067 860-258-7741
Richard Watson, prin. Fax 258-7746
Rocky Hill HS 800/9-12
50 Chapin Ave 06067 860-258-7721
Mario Almeida, prin. Fax 258-7735

---

Porter and Chester Institute Post-Sec.
30 Waterchase Dr 06067 860-529-2519

**Salisbury, Litchfield**

---

Salisbury S 300/9-12
251 Canaan Rd 06068 860-435-5700
Chisholm Chandler, hdmstr. Fax 435-5750

**Sandy Hook, Fairfield**
Newtown SD
Supt. — See Newtown
Newtown HS 1,700/9-12
12 Berkshire Rd 06482 203-426-7646
Lorrie Rodrigue, prin. Fax 426-6573

**Seymour, New Haven, Pop. 14,288**
Seymour SD 2,000/PK-12
98 Bank St 06483 203-888-4565
Christine Syriac, supt. Fax 888-1704
www.seymourschools.org
Seymour HS 600/9-12
2 Botsford Rd 06483 203-888-2561
James Freund, prin. Fax 888-7476
Seymour MS 600/6-8
211 Mountain Rd 06483 203-888-4513
Bernadette Hamad, prin. Fax 881-7535

**Shelton, Fairfield, Pop. 39,118**
Shelton SD 5,300/PK-12
382 Long Hill Ave 06484 203-924-1023
Freeman Burr, supt. Fax 924-5894
www.sheltonpublicschools.org
Shelton HS 1,600/9-12
120 Meadow St 06484 203-922-3004
Dr. Beth Smith, hdmstr. Fax 924-8236
Shelton IS 900/7-8
675 Constitution Blvd N 06484 203-926-2000
Kenneth Saranich, hdmstr. Fax 926-2017

---

Lincoln Technical Institute Post-Sec.
8 Progress Dr 06484 203-929-0592

**Simsbury, Hartford, Pop. 22,023**
Simsbury SD 4,600/PK-12
933 Hopmeadow St 06070 860-651-3361
Matthew Curtis, supt. Fax 651-4343
www.simsbury.k12.ct.us
James Memorial MS 800/7-8
155 Firetown Rd 06070 860-651-3341
Brian White, prin. Fax 658-3629
Simsbury HS 1,600/9-12
34 Farms Village Rd 06070 860-658-0451
Neil Sullivan, prin. Fax 658-2439

---

Walker S 200/6-12
230 Bushy Hill Rd 06070 860-408-4200
Stephen Dunn, admin. Fax 408-4201
Westminster S 400/9-12
995 Hopmeadow St 06070 860-408-3000
William Philip, hdmstr. Fax 408-3001

**Somers, Tolland, Pop. 1,774**
Somers SD 1,600/PK-12
1 Vision Blvd 06071 860-749-2270
Dr. Maynard Suffredini, supt. Fax 763-0748
www.somers.k12.ct.us
Avery MS 400/6-8
1 Vision Blvd 06071 860-749-2270
Clay Krevolin, prin. Fax 763-2073
Somers HS 600/9-12
5 Vision Blvd 06071 860-749-2270
Gary Cotzin, prin. Fax 749-9264

---

New England Tractor Trailer Training Post-Sec.
32 Field Rd 06071 860-749-0711

**Southbury, New Haven, Pop. 15,818**
Regional SD 15
Supt. — See Middlebury
Pomperaug Regional HS 1,300/9-12
234 Judd Rd 06488 203-262-3200
Glenn Lungarini, prin. Fax 262-6806
Rochambeau MS 500/6-8
100 Peter Rd 06488 203-264-2711
Michael Bernardi, prin. Fax 264-6638

**Southington, Hartford, Pop. 39,200**
Southington SD 6,700/PK-12
200 N Main St 06489 860-628-3200
Timothy J. Connellan, supt. Fax 821-8056
www.southingtonschools.org
ALTA at Pyne Center Alt
242 N Main St 06489 860-628-3379
Jess Levin, dir. Fax 628-3458
DePaolo MS 800/6-8
385 Pleasant St 06489 860-628-3260
Frank Pepe, prin. Fax 628-3403
Southington HS 2,000/9-12
720 Pleasant St 06489 860-628-3229
Brian Stranieri, prin. Fax 628-3397
Other Schools – See Plantsville

---

Branford Hall Career Institute Post-Sec.
35 N Main St 06489 860-276-0600
Lincoln College of New England Post-Sec.
2279 Mount Vernon Rd 06489 860-628-4751

**South Kent, Litchfield**

---

South Kent S 200/9-12
40 Bulls Bridge Rd 06785 860-927-3539
Andrew Vadnais, head sch Fax 803-0040

**South Windsor, Hartford, Pop. 22,090**
South Windsor SD 4,300/PK-12
1737 Main St 06074 860-291-1200
Kate Carter Ed.D., supt. Fax 291-1291
www.southwindsorschools.org
Edwards MS 1,100/6-8
100 Arnold Way 06074 860-648-5030
Nancy Larson, prin. Fax 648-5029
South Windsor HS 1,500/9-12
161 Nevers Rd 06074 860-648-5000
Daniel Sullivan, prin. Fax 648-5013

**Stafford Springs, Tolland, Pop. 4,869**
Stafford SD 1,800/PK-12
16 Levinthal Run 06076 860-684-2208
Dr. Patricia Collin, supt. Fax 684-5172
www.stafford.k12.ct.us
Stafford HS 500/9-12
145 Orcuttville Rd 06076 860-684-4233
Marco Pelliccia, prin. Fax 684-0424
Stafford MS 400/6-8
21 Levinthal Run 06076 860-684-2785
Fax 684-4671

**Stamford, Fairfield, Pop. 120,428**
Connecticut Technical HS System
Supt. — See Middletown
Wright Technical HS Vo/Tech
120 Bridge St 06905 203-356-0189
Eric Hilversum, dir. Fax 674-5801

Stamford SD 15,500/PK-12
888 Washington Blvd Fl 5 06901 203-977-4105
Dr. Winifred Hamilton, supt. Fax 977-5964
www.stamfordpublicschools.org/
Academy of Info Technology & Engineering 700/9-12
411 High Ridge Rd 06905 203-977-4336
Tina Rivera, prin. Fax 977-6638
Cloonan MS 600/6-8
11 W North St 06902 203-977-4544
David Tate, prin. Fax 977-4867
Dolan MS 500/6-8
51 Toms Rd 06906 203-977-4441
Charmaine Tourse, prin. Fax 977-4880
Rippowam MS 600/5-8
381 High Ridge Rd 06905 203-977-5255
Jason Martin, prin. Fax 977-5154
Scofield Magnet MS 600/5-8
641 Scofieldtown Rd 06903 203-977-2750
Scott Clayton, prin. Fax 977-2766
Stamford HS 1,900/9-12
55 Strawberry Hill Ave 06902 203-977-4223
Raymond Manka, prin. Fax 356-1720
Turn of River MS 600/6-8
117 Vine Rd 06905 203-977-4284
Brendan Fox, prin. Fax 977-5037
Westhill HS 2,300/9-12
125 Roxbury Rd 06902 203-977-4477
Camille Figluizzi, prin. Fax 977-4996

---

Beth Benjamin Academy of Connecticut Post-Sec.
132 Prospect St 06901 203-325-4351
Jewish HS of Connecticut 9-12
1937 W Main St 06902 203-357-0850
Dr. Paul Castle, prin.
King Low Heywood Thomas S 700/PK-12
1450 Newfield Ave 06905 203-322-3496
Thomas Main, hdmstr. Fax 461-9988
St. Basil College Seminary Post-Sec.
195 Glenbrook Rd 06902 203-324-4578
Stamford Hospital Post-Sec.
PO Box 9317 06904 203-276-7877
Trinity Catholic HS 400/9-12
926 Newfield Ave 06905 203-322-3401
Dr. Mark Karagus, prin. Fax 322-5330
Trinity Catholic MS 200/6-8
948 Newfield Ave 06905 203-322-7383
Dr. Patricia Lawler, prin. Fax 324-4435
Yeshiva Bais Binyomin 100/9-12
132 Prospect St 06901 203-325-4351

**Storrs, Tolland, Pop. 14,985**
Mansfield SD 1,300/PK-8
4 S Eagleville Rd 06268 860-429-3350
Fax 429-3379
www.mansfieldct.org/mboe/index.php
Mansfield MS 600/5-8
205 Spring Hill Rd 06268 860-429-9341
Candace Morell, prin. Fax 429-1020

Regional SD 19 1,200/9-12
1235 Storrs Rd 06268 860-487-1862
Bruce Silva, supt. Fax 429-0085
www.eosmith.org
Smith HS 1,200/9-12
1235 Storrs Rd 06268 860-487-0877
Dr. Louis DeLoreto, prin. Fax 429-7892

---

University of Connecticut 06269 Post-Sec.
860-486-2000

**Stratford, Fairfield, Pop. 50,391**
Connecticut Technical HS System
Supt. — See Middletown
Stratford S for Aviation Maintenance Vo/Tech
200 Great Meadow Rd 06615 203-381-9250
Scott Zito, prin. Fax 381-0764

Stratford SD 7,400/PK-12
1000 E Broadway 06615 203-385-4210
Dr. Janet Robinson, supt. Fax 381-2012
stratfordk12.org
Bunnell HS 1,200/9-12
1 Bulldog Blvd 06614 203-385-4250
Dr. Nancy Dowling, prin. Fax 381-2014
Flood MS 600/7-8
490 Chapel St 06614 203-385-4280
Lea Ann Bradford, prin. Fax 381-2033
Stratford HS 1,100/9-12
45 N Parade St 06615 203-385-4230
John Dellapiano, prin. Fax 381-2021
Wooster MS 500/7-8
150 Lincoln St 06614 203-385-4275
Bryan Darcy, prin. Fax 381-6918

---

Porter and Chester Institute Post-Sec.
670 Lordship Blvd 06615 203-375-4463

**Suffield, Hartford**
Suffield SD 2,500/PK-12
350 Mountain Rd 06078 860-668-3800
Karen Berasi, supt. Fax 668-3805
www.suffield.org
Suffield MS 600/6-8
350 Mountain Rd 06078 860-668-3820
Damon Pearce, prin. Fax 668-3088
Other Schools – See West Suffield

---

Suffield Academy 400/9-12
185 N Main St 06078 860-386-4400
Charles Cahn, hdmstr. Fax 386-4411

**Terryville, Litchfield, Pop. 5,299**
Plymouth SD 1,600/PK-12
77 Main St 06786 860-314-8005
Dr. Martin Semmel, supt. Fax 314-2766
www.plymouth.k12.ct.us
Terry MS 400/6-8
21 N Main St 06786 860-314-2790
Angela Suffridge, prin. Fax 314-2768
Terryville HS 500/9-12
33 N Harwinton Ave 06786 860-314-2777
Michael Hults, prin. Fax 314-2785

**Thomaston, Litchfield, Pop. 1,888**
Thomaston SD 1,100/PK-12
PO Box 166 06787 860-283-4796
Francine Coss, supt. Fax 283-6708
www.thomastonschools.net/
Thomaston HS 500/7-12
185 Branch Rd 06787 860-283-3030
John Perrucci, prin. Fax 283-3040

**Thompson, Windham**

---

Marianapolis Prep S 300/9-12
PO Box 304 06277 860-923-9565
Joseph Hanrahan, hdmstr. Fax 923-3730

**Tolland, Tolland**
Tolland SD 3,000/PK-12
51 Tolland Grn 06084 860-870-6850
Walter Willett Ph.D., supt. Fax 870-7737
www.tolland.k12.ct.us
Tolland HS 900/9-12
1 Eagle Hill Dr 06084 860-870-6818
Domonique Fox, prin. Fax 870-8168
Tolland MS 700/6-8
1 Falcon Way 06084 860-870-6860
Daniel Uriano, prin. Fax 870-5737

**Torrington, Litchfield, Pop. 35,694**
Connecticut Technical HS System
Supt. — See Middletown
Wolcott Technical HS Vo/Tech
75 Oliver St 06790 860-496-5300
Robert Axon, prin. Fax 496-9022

Torrington SD 4,400/PK-12
355 Migeon Ave 06790 860-489-2327
Lynda T. Reitman, supt. Fax 489-0726
www.torrington.org
Torrington HS 1,100/9-12
50 Major Besse Dr 06790 860-489-2294
Eric Baim, prin. Fax 489-2853
Torrington MS 1,100/6-8
200 Middle School Dr 06790 860-496-4050
Eric Baim, prin. Fax 496-1089

**Trumbull, Fairfield, Pop. 35,588**
Trumbull SD 6,900/PK-12
6254 Main St 06611 203-452-4300
Gary Cialfi, supt. Fax 452-4305
www.trumbullps.org
Hillcrest MS 700/6-8
530 Daniels Farm Rd 06611 203-452-4466
Stafford Thomas, prin. Fax 452-4479
Madison MS 900/6-8
4630 Madison Ave 06611 203-452-4499
Valerie Forshaw, prin. Fax 452-4490
Trumbull HS 2,200/9-12
72 Strobel Rd 06611 203-452-4555
Marc Guarino, prin. Fax 452-4593

---

Christian Heritage S 500/K-12
575 White Plains Rd 06611 203-261-6230
Dr. Brian Modarelli, head sch Fax 452-1531
St. Joseph HS 800/9-12
2320 Huntington Tpke 06611 203-378-9378
Kenneth Mayo, prin. Fax 378-7306

**Uncasville, New London, Pop. 2,975**

---

St. Bernard S 400/6-12
1593 Norwich New London Tpk 06382
860-848-3007
Thomas Doherty, hdmstr. Fax 848-0261

**Vernon Rockville, Tolland, Pop. 28,900**
Vernon SD 3,500/PK-12
PO Box 600 06066 860-870-6000
Dr. Mary Conway, supt. Fax 870-6005
vernonpublicschools.org
Rockville HS 1,100/9-12
70 Loveland Hill Rd 06066 860-870-6050
Andrew Rockett, prin. Fax 870-6314
Vernon Center MS 700/6-8
777 Hartford Tpke 06066 860-870-6070
James Harrison, prin. Fax 870-6318

**Wallingford, New Haven, Pop. 41,700**
Wallingford SD 6,300/PK-12
43 Hall Ave 06492 203-949-6500
Dr. Salvatore Menzo, supt. Fax 949-6550
www.wallingford.k12.ct.us
Hall HS 1,100/9-12
70 Pond Hill Rd 06492 203-294-5350
David Bryant, prin. Fax 294-5353
Hammarskjold MS 700/6-8
106 Pond Hill Rd 06492 203-294-3700
Sashi Govin, prin. Fax 294-3749
Moran MS 800/6-8
141 Hope Hill Rd 06492 203-741-2900
Joseph Piacentini, prin. Fax 741-2939
Sheehan HS 900/9-12
142 Hope Hill Rd 06492 203-294-5900
Rosemary Duthie, prin. Fax 294-5980

---

Choate Rosemary Hall 800/9-12
333 Christian St 06492 203-697-2000
Dr. Alex Curtis, hdmstr. Fax 697-2720

**Washington, Litchfield**
Regional SD 12
Supt. — See Washington Depot
Shepaug Valley JSHS 300/6-12
159 South St 06793 860-868-7326
Kimberly Gallo, prin. Fax 868-6260

---

Devereux Center in Connecticut Post-Sec.
81 Sabbaday Ln 06793 860-868-7377
Gunnery 300/9-12
99 Green Hill Rd 06793 860-868-7334
Peter Becker, head sch Fax 868-1614

**Washington Depot, Litchfield**
Regional SD 12 900/PK-12
PO Box 386 06794 860-868-6100
Patricia Cosentino Ed.D., supt. Fax 868-6103
www.region-12.org
Other Schools – See Washington

**Waterbury, New Haven, Pop. 106,427**
Connecticut Technical HS System
Supt. — See Middletown
Kaynor Technical HS Vo/Tech
43 Tompkins St 06708 203-596-4302
David Telesca, prin. Fax 596-4308

Waterbury SD 17,400/PK-12
236 Grand St 06702 203-574-8000
Dr. Kathleen Ouellette, supt. Fax 574-8010
www.waterbury.k12.ct.us
Crosby HS 1,400/9-12
300 Pierpont Rd 06705 203-574-8061
Jade Gopie, prin. Fax 574-8072
Enlightenment S 200/Alt
30 Church St 06702 203-574-8050
Gwendolyn Gonzalez, prin. Fax 573-6634
Kennedy HS 1,400/9-12
422 Highland Ave 06708 203-574-8153
Robert Johnston, prin. Fax 574-8154
North End MS 1,200/6-8
534 Bucks Hill Rd 06704 203-574-8097
Jacquelyn Gilmore, prin. Fax 574-8203
Wallace MS 1,200/6-8
3465 E Main St 06705 203-574-8140
Michael LoRusso, prin. Fax 574-8141
Waterbury Arts Magnet S 500/6-12
16 S Elm St 06706 203-573-6300
Lauren Elias, prin. Fax 573-6325
Waterbury Career Academy HS Vo/Tech
175 Birch St 06704 203-574-6000
Dr. Louis Padua, prin.
West Side MS 1,100/6-8
483 Chase Pkwy 06708 203-574-8120
Maria Burns, prin. Fax 574-8130
Wilby HS 1,300/9-12
460 Bucks Hill Rd 06704 203-574-8100
Michele Buerkle, prin. Fax 574-6896

---

Bais Yaakov of Waterbury HS 9-11
66 Buckingham St 06710 917-757-6410
Ita Selengut, prin.
Chase Collegiate S 500/PK-12
565 Chase Pkwy 06708 203-236-9500
Dr. Polly Peterson Ph.D., head sch Fax 236-9539
Holy Cross HS 700/9-12
587 Oronoke Rd 06708 203-757-9248
Margaret Leger, prin. Fax 757-3423
Industrial Management and Training Post-Sec.
233 Mill St 06706 203-753-7910
Mesivta of Waterbury 9-12
359 Cooke St 06710 203-756-1800
Naugatuck Valley Community College Post-Sec.
750 Chase Pkwy 06708 203-575-8040
Post University Post-Sec.
PO Box 2540 06723 203-596-4500
Sacred Heart HS 300/9-12
142 S Elm St 06706 203-753-1605
Anthony Azzara, prin. Fax 597-1686
St. Mary's Hospital Post-Sec.
56 Franklin St 06706 203-574-6300
Stone Academy Post-Sec.
101 Pierpont Rd 06705 203-756-5500
University of Connecticut Post-Sec.
99 E Main St 06702 203-236-9800

**Waterford, New London, Pop. 2,818**
Learn RESC
Supt. — See Old Lyme
Dual Language & Arts Magnet MS 100/6-8
51 Daniels Ave 06385 860-443-0461
Susan Goldstein, dir. Fax 443-0468

Waterford SD — 2,600/K-12
15 Rope Ferry Rd 06385 — 860-444-5801
Dr. H. Kaye Griffin, supt. — Fax 444-5870
www.waterfordschools.org
Clark Lane MS — 700/6-8
105 Clark Ln 06385 — 860-443-2837
James Sachs, prin. — Fax 437-6985
Waterford HS — 900/9-12
20 Rope Ferry Rd 06385 — 860-437-6956
Andre Hauser, prin. — Fax 447-7928

**Watertown, Litchfield, Pop. 6,000**
Watertown SD — 3,100/PK-12
10 Deforest St 06795 — 860-945-4801
Dr. B. Heston Carnemolla, supt. — Fax 945-2775
www.watertownps.org/
Watertown HS — 1,000/9-12
324 French St 06795 — 860-945-4810
Paul Jones Ed.D., prin. — Fax 945-3348
Other Schools – See Oakville

---

Porter and Chester Institute — Post-Sec.
320 Sylvan Lake Rd 06779 — 860-274-9294
Taft S — 600/9-12
110 Woodbury Rd 06795 — 860-945-7777
William MacMullen, hdmstr. — Fax 945-7720

**Westbrook, Middlesex, Pop. 2,342**
Westbrook SD — 900/PK-12
158 McVeagh Rd 06498 — 860-399-6432
Patricia Ciccone, supt. — Fax 399-8817
www.westbrookctschools.org/
Westbrook HS — 300/9-12
156 McVeagh Rd 06498 — 860-399-6214
Tara Winch, prin. — Fax 399-2007
Westbrook MS — 300/5-8
154 McVeagh Rd 06498 — 860-399-2010
Cori DiMaggio, prin. — Fax 399-2006

---

Oxford Academy — 50/9-12
1393 Boston Post Rd 06498 — 860-399-6247
Philip Cocchiola, head sch — Fax 399-5555

**West Hartford, Hartford, Pop. 61,804**
West Hartford SD — 10,000/PK-12
50 S Main St, — 860-561-6600
Thomas Moore, supt. — Fax 561-6910
www.whps.org
Bristow MS — 400/6-8
34 Highland St, — 860-231-2100
Steven Cook, prin. — Fax 231-2107
Conard HS — 1,500/9-12
110 Beechwood Rd, — 860-231-5000
Julio Duarte, prin. — Fax 521-6699
Hall HS — 1,500/9-12
975 N Main St, — 860-232-4561
Dan Zittoun, prin. — Fax 236-0366
King Philip MS — 900/6-8
100 King Philip Dr, — 860-233-8236
Joy Wright, prin. — Fax 233-0812
Sedgwick MS — 900/6-8
128 Sedgwick Rd, — 860-521-0610
Andrew Clapsaddle, prin. — Fax 521-7502

---

American Institute — Post-Sec.
99 South St, — 860-947-2299
American School for the Deaf — Post-Sec.
139 N Main St, — 860-570-2309
Kingswood Oxford S — 500/6-12
170 Kingswood Rd, — 860-233-9631
Dennis Bisgaard, head sch — Fax 236-3651
Northwest Catholic HS — 600/9-12
29 Wampanoag Dr, — 860-236-4221
Margaret Williamson, prin. — Fax 586-0911
St. Timothy MS — 100/6-8
225 King Philip Dr, — 860-236-0614
Tara Bellefleur M.Ed., prin. — Fax 920-0293
University of Hartford — Post-Sec.
200 Bloomfield Ave, — 860-768-4100
University of Saint Joseph — Post-Sec.
1678 Asylum Ave, — 860-232-4571

**West Haven, New Haven, Pop. 54,140**
West Haven SD — 6,000/PK-12
PO Box 26010 06516 — 203-937-4310
Neil Cavallaro, supt. — Fax 937-4315
www.whschools.org
Bailey MS — 900/7-8
106 Morgan Ln 06516 — 203-937-4380
Anthony Cordone Ed.D., prin. — Fax 937-4385
West Haven HS — 1,500/9-12
1 McDonough Plz 06516 — 203-937-4360
Pamela Gardner, prin. — Fax 934-4370

---

Notre Dame HS — 600/9-12
24 Ricardo St 06516 — 203-933-1673
Patrick Clifford, prin. — Fax 933-2474
Stone Academy — Post-Sec.
560 Saw Mill Rd 06516 — 203-288-7474
University of New Haven — Post-Sec.
300 Boston Post Rd 06516 — 203-932-7000

**Weston, Fairfield**
Weston SD — 2,500/PK-12
24 School Rd 06883 — 203-291-1400
Colleen Palmer Ph.D., supt. — Fax 291-1415
www.westonps.org
Weston HS — 800/9-12
115 School Rd 06883 — 203-291-1600
Lisa Deorio, prin. — Fax 291-1603
Weston MS — 600/6-8
135 School Rd 06883 — 203-291-1500
Dan Doak, prin. — Fax 291-1516

**Westport, Fairfield, Pop. 25,982**
Westport SD — 5,700/PK-12
110 Myrtle Ave 06880 — 203-341-1010
Dr. Elliott Landon, supt. — Fax 341-1029
www.westport.k12.ct.us/
Bedford MS — 900/6-8
88 North Ave 06880 — 203-341-1510
Adam Rosen, prin. — Fax 341-1508
Coleytown MS — 500/6-8
255 North Ave 06880 — 203-341-1600
Kris Szabo, prin. — Fax 341-1614
Staples HS — 1,800/9-12
70 North Ave 06880 — 203-341-1200
Mark Karagus, prin. — Fax 341-1202

---

Connecticut Center for Massage Therapy — Post-Sec.
25 Sylvan Rd S 06880 — 203-221-7325
Pierrepont S, 1 Sylvan Rd N 06880 — 100/K-12
Nancy Webber, head sch — 203-226-1891

**West Simsbury, Hartford, Pop. 2,411**

---

Master's S — 300/PK-12
36 Westledge Rd 06092 — 860-651-9361
Ray Lagan, admin. — Fax 651-9363

**West Suffield, Hartford**
Suffield SD
Supt. — See Suffield
Suffield HS — 900/9-12
1060 Sheldon St 06093 — 860-668-3810
Steve Moccio, prin. — Fax 668-3037

**Wethersfield, Hartford, Pop. 26,301**
Wethersfield SD — 3,600/PK-12
127 Hartford Ave 06109 — 860-571-8100
Michael Emmett, supt. — Fax 571-8130
www.wethersfield.k12.ct.us/
Deane MS — 600/7-8
551 Silas Deane Hwy 06109 — 860-571-8300
Susan Czapla, prin. — Fax 563-0563
Wethersfield HS — 1,100/9-12
411 Wolcott Hill Rd 06109 — 860-571-8200
Thomas Moore, prin. — Fax 571-8240

---

Connecticut Childrens Medical Center — Post-Sec.
170 Ridge Rd 06109 — 860-545-8551

**Willimantic, Windham, Pop. 17,404**
Connecticut Technical HS System
Supt. — See Middletown
Windham Technical HS — Vo/Tech
210 Birch St 06226 — 860-456-3879
Mark Ambruso, prin. — Fax 450-0630

Windham SD — 2,900/PK-12
322 Prospect St 06226 — 860-465-2300
Patricia Garcia Ph.D., supt. — Fax 456-2311
www.windham.k12.ct.us/
Windham HS — 700/9-12
355 High St 06226 — 860-465-2480
Dorothy Potter, prin. — Fax 465-2463
Windham MS — 700/6-8
123 Quarry St 06226 — 860-465-2351
Thanh Nguyen, prin. — Fax 465-2353

---

Eastern Connecticut State University — Post-Sec.
83 Windham St 06226 — 860-456-5000
Windham Community Memorial Hospital — Post-Sec.
112 Mansfield Ave 06226 — 860-456-6800

**Willington, Tolland**
Willington SD — 500/PK-8
40 Old Farms Rd Ste A 06279 — 860-487-3130
David Harding, supt. — Fax 487-3132
www.willingtonpublicschools.org
Hall Memorial MS — 300/4-8
111 River Rd 06279 — 860-429-9391
Deborah Sullivan, prin. — Fax 429-5682

**Wilton, Fairfield, Pop. 7,200**
Wilton SD — 4,300/PK-12
PO Box 277 06897 — 203-762-3381
Kevin Smith, supt. — Fax 762-2177
www.wilton.k12.ct.us
Middlebrook MS — 1,100/6-8
131 School Rd 06897 — 203-762-8388
Maria Coleman, prin. — Fax 762-1716
Wilton HS — 1,300/9-12
395 Danbury Rd 06897 — 203-762-0381
Robert O'Donnell, prin. — Fax 834-0164

**Windsor, Hartford, Pop. 27,817**
Capitol Region Education Council RESC
Supt. — See Hartford
Academy of Aerospace & Engineering — 6-12
1101 Kennedy Rd 06095 — 860-243-0857
Paul Brenton, prin. — Fax 286-2842

Windsor SD — 2,700/PK-12
601 Matianuck Ave 06095 — 860-687-2000
Dr. Craig Cooke, supt. — Fax 687-2009
www.windsorct.org
Sage Park MS — 800/6-8
25 Sage Park Rd 06095 — 860-687-2030
Paul Cavaliere, prin. — Fax 687-2039
Windsor HS — 1,200/9-12
50 Sage Park Rd 06095 — 860-687-2020
Russell Sills, prin. — Fax 687-2029

---

Branford Hall Career Institute — Post-Sec.
995 Day Hill Rd 06095 — 860-683-4900
Loomis Chaffee S — 700/9-12
4 Batchelder Rd 06095 — 860-687-6000
Sheila Culbert, head sch — Fax 687-6552
Praise Power & Prayer Christian S — 100/K-12
PO Box 474 06095 — 860-285-8898
Rev. Raymond McMahon, prin.
Trinity Christian S — 200/PK-12
180 Park Ave 06095 — 860-688-2008
Kasinda Bristol, hdmstr. — Fax 687-9737

**Windsor Locks, Hartford, Pop. 12,219**
Windsor Locks SD — 1,700/PK-12
58 S Elm St 06096 — 860-292-5000
Susan Bell, supt. — Fax 292-5003
www.wlps.org
Windsor Locks HS — 600/9-12
58 S Elm St 06096 — 860-292-5032
Steven Swensen, prin. — Fax 292-5039
Windsor Locks MS — 400/6-8
7 Center St 06096 — 860-292-5012
David Prinstein, prin. — Fax 292-5017

**Winsted, Litchfield, Pop. 7,586**
Endowed & Incorporated Academies — 500/7-12
200 Williams Ave 06098 — 860-379-8521
Dr. Anthony Serio Ed.D., supt. — Fax 379-6163
gilbertschool.org
Gilbert S — 500/7-12
200 Williams Ave 06098 — 860-379-8521
Alan J. Strauss, prin. — Fax 379-6163

Regional SD 7 — 1,100/7-12
PO Box 656 06098 — 860-379-1084
Dr. Judith Palmer, supt. — Fax 379-0618
www.nwr7.com
Northwestern Regional HS — 700/9-12
100 Battistoni Rd 06098 — 860-379-8525
Kenneth Chichester, prin. — Fax 738-6059
Northwestern Regional MS — 400/7-8
100 Battistoni Rd 06098 — 860-379-7243
Candy Perez, prin. — Fax 738-6205

---

Northwestern CT Comm. Technical College — Post-Sec.
2 Park Pl 06098 — 860-738-6300

**Wolcott, New Haven, Pop. 13,700**
Wolcott SD — 2,600/PK-12
154 Center St 06716 — 203-879-8183
Joseph Macary, supt. — Fax 879-8182
www.wolcottps.org
Tyrrell MS — 700/6-8
500 Todd Rd 06716 — 203-879-8151
Arline Tansley, prin. — Fax 879-8419
Wolcott HS — 900/9-12
457 Bound Line Rd 06716 — 203-879-8164
Joseph Monroe, prin. — Fax 879-8167

---

Connecticut Institute of Hair Design — Post-Sec.
1681 Meriden Rd 06716 — 203-879-4247

**Woodbridge, New Haven, Pop. 7,924**
Regional SD 5 — 2,400/7-12
25 Newton Rd 06525 — 203-392-2106
Charles Dumais, supt. — Fax 397-4864
www.amityregion5.org
Amity Regional HS — 1,700/9-12
25 Newton Rd 06525 — 203-397-4830
Charles Britton, prin. — Fax 397-4866
Other Schools – See Bethany, Orange

**Woodbury, Litchfield, Pop. 8,131**
Regional SD 14 — 2,000/PK-12
PO Box 469 06798 — 203-263-4330
Dr. Anna Leonard, supt. — Fax 263-0372
www.ctreg14.org
Nonnewaug HS — 800/9-12
5 Minortown Rd 06798 — 203-263-2186
Andrew O'Brien, prin. — Fax 263-3570
Woodbury MS — 400/6-8
67 Washington Ave 06798 — 203-263-4306
Alice Jones, prin. — Fax 263-0825

**Woodstock, Windham**
Endowed & Incorporated Academies — 1,100/9-12
57 Academy Rd 06281 — 860-928-6575
Christopher Sandford, hdmstr. — Fax 963-7222
www.woodstockacademy.org
Woodstock Academy — 1,100/9-12
57 Academy Rd 06281 — 860-928-6575
Christopher Sandford, hdmstr. — Fax 963-7222

Woodstock SD — 900/PK-8
147A Route 169 06281 — 860-928-7453
Viktor Toth, supt. — Fax 928-0206
www.woodstockschools.net
Woodstock MS — 400/5-8
147B Route 169 06281 — 860-963-6575
Paul Gamache, prin. — Fax 963-6577

---

Hyde S - Woodstock — 200/9-12
PO Box 237 06281 — 860-963-9096
Robert Felt, dir. — Fax 963-0164

# DELAWARE

## DELAWARE DEPARTMENT OF EDUCATION

**401 Federal St Ste 2, Dover 19901-3639**
**Telephone 302-735-4000**
**Fax 302-739-4654**
**Website http://www.doe.k12.de.us**

Secretary of Education  Mark Murphy

## DELAWARE BOARD OF EDUCATION

**1006 Tulip Tree Ln, Newark 19713-1128**

President  Teri Quinn Gray

## PUBLIC, PRIVATE AND CATHOLIC SECONDARY SCHOOLS

**Bear, New Castle, Pop. 18,842**

---

Academy of Massage & Bodywork  Post-Sec.
1218 Pulaski Hwy Ste 324  19701  302-392-6768
Aquinas Academy  100/PK-12
2370 Red Lion Rd  19701  302-838-9601
John Moore, prin.  Fax 838-9602
Caravel Academy  1,200/PK-12
2801 Del Laws Rd  19701  302-834-8938
Fairwinds Christian S  200/PK-12
801 Seymour Rd  19701  302-328-7404
Glasgow Christian Academy  200/PK-12
2880 Summit Bridge Rd  19701  302-392-1090
Red Lion Christian Academy  700/PK-12
1390 Red Lion Rd  19701  302-834-2526
Sam Osbourn, prin.  Fax 836-6346

**Bridgeville, Sussex, Pop. 1,988**
Woodbridge SD  2,300/PK-12
16359 Sussex Hwy  19933  302-337-7990
Heath Chasanov, supt.  Fax 337-7998
www.wsd.k12.de.us
Woodbridge MS  700/6-8
307 S Laws St  19933  302-337-8289
Delores Tunstall, prin.  Fax 337-0631
Other Schools – See Greenwood

**Camden, Kent, Pop. 3,311**
Caesar Rodney SD
Supt. — See Wyoming
Fifer MS  900/6-8
109 E Camden Wyoming Ave  19934  302-698-8400
Brian Smith, prin.  Fax 698-8409
Postlethwait MS  800/6-8
2841 S State St  19934  302-698-8410
Derek Prillaman, prin.  Fax 698-8419
Rodney HS  2,100/9-12
239 Old North Rd  19934  302-697-2161
Sherry Kijowski Ed.D., prin.  Fax 697-6888

**Claymont, New Castle, Pop. 8,108**
Brandywine SD
Supt. — See Wilmington
Brandywine Community S  Alt
500 Darley Rd  19703  302-792-3920
Dr. Kim Allen, dir.  Fax 792-3814

---

Archmere Academy  500/9-12
3600 Philadelphia Pike  19703  302-798-6632
John Jordan, prin.  Fax 798-7290

**Dagsboro, Sussex, Pop. 782**
Indian River SD
Supt. — See Selbyville
Indian River HS  900/9-12
29772 Armory Rd  19939  302-732-1500
Bennett Murray, prin.  Fax 732-1514

**Delmar, Sussex, Pop. 1,524**
Delmar SD  1,300/5-12
200 N 8th St  19940  302-846-9544
David Ring Ed.D., supt.  Fax 846-2793
www.delmar.k12.de.us
Delmar HS  600/9-12
200 N 8th St  19940  302-846-9544
Ashley Giska, prin.  Fax 846-5056
Delmar MS  700/5-8
200 N 8th St  19940  302-846-9544
Charity Phillips, prin.  Fax 846-5056

**Dover, Kent, Pop. 34,742**
Caesar Rodney SD
Supt. — See Wyoming
Dover AFB MS  200/6-8
3100 Hawthorne Dr  19901  302-674-3284
David Santore Ed.D., prin.  Fax 730-4283

Capital SD  6,100/PK-12
198 Commerce Way  19904  302-672-1500
Dr. Dan Shelton, supt.  Fax 672-1714
www.capital.k12.de.us
Central MS  900/7-8
211 Delaware Ave  19901  302-672-1772
Shan Green, prin.  Fax 672-1733
Dover HS, 1 Dover High Dr  19904  1,500/9-12
Dr. Courtney Voshell, prin.  302-241-2400
Kent County Alternative S  100/Alt
631 Ridgely St  19904  302-736-5355
William Buczynski, prin.  Fax 736-5263

---

Bayhealth Medical Center  Post-Sec.
640 S State St  19901  302-674-7001
Calvary Christian Academy  300/PK-12
1143 E Lebanon Rd  19901  302-697-7860
Aaron Coon, admin.  Fax 697-0284
Delaware State University  Post-Sec.
1200 N Dupont Hwy  19901  302-857-6060
Delaware Technical & Community College  Post-Sec.
100 Campus Dr  19904  302-857-1000
Harris School of Business  Post-Sec.
97 Commerce Way Ste 105  19904  302-674-8060
Wesley College  Post-Sec.
120 N State St  19901  302-736-2300

**Felton, Kent, Pop. 1,251**
Lake Forest SD  3,800/PK-12
5423 Killens Pond Rd  19943  302-284-3020
Dr. Brenda Wynder, supt.  Fax 284-4491
www.lf.k12.de.us
Lake Forest HS  900/9-12
5407 Killens Pond Rd  19943  302-284-9291
Theodora White, prin.  Fax 284-5833
Other Schools – See Harrington

**Frankford, Sussex, Pop. 835**
Indian River SD
Supt. — See Selbyville
Carver Educational Center  Alt
30207 Frankford School Rd  19945  302-732-3800
Judi Brittingham, prin.  Fax 732-3790

**Georgetown, Sussex, Pop. 6,322**
Indian River SD
Supt. — See Selbyville
Georgetown MS  500/6-8
301 W Market St  19947  302-856-1900
Mike Williams, prin.  Fax 856-1915
Sussex Central HS  1,200/9-12
26026 Patriots Way  19947  302-934-3166
Bradley Layfield Ed.D., prin.  Fax 934-3234

Sussex Technical SD
PO Box 351  19947  302-856-2541
Dr. A.J. Lathbury Ed.D., supt.  Fax 856-7078
www.sussexvt.k12.de.us
Sussex Technical HS  Vo/Tech
PO Box 351  19947  302-856-0961
John Demby Ed.D., prin.  Fax 856-1760
Sussex Extended Learning Division  Adult
PO Box 351  19947  302-856-9035
Dr. Michael Owens, admin.  Fax 856-7875

---

Delaware Technical & Community College  Post-Sec.
PO Box 610  19947  302-856-5400
Delmarva Christian HS  200/9-12
21777 Sussex Pines Rd  19947  302-856-4040
Mike Vonhof, prin.  Fax 856-6878

**Greenville, New Castle, Pop. 2,293**
Red Clay Consolidated SD
Supt. — See Wilmington
DuPont HS  1,300/9-12
50 Hillside Rd  19807  302-651-2626
Kevin Palladinetti, prin.  Fax 651-2757
DuPont MS  500/6-8
3130 Kennett Pike  19807  302-651-2690
Theodore Boyer, prin.  Fax 425-4585

**Greenwood, Sussex, Pop. 943**
Woodbridge SD
Supt. — See Bridgeville
Woodbridge HS  600/9-12
14712 Woodbridge Rd  19950  302-232-3333
Robert Adams, prin.  Fax 349-0237

---

Greenwood Mennonite S  200/PK-12
12802 Mennonite School Rd  19950  302-349-4131
Duane Miller, admin.  Fax 349-5076

**Harrington, Kent, Pop. 3,428**
Lake Forest SD
Supt. — See Felton
Chipman MS  1,000/6-8
101 W Center St  19952  302-398-8197
Douglas Brown, prin.  Fax 398-8375

**Hockessin, New Castle, Pop. 13,327**
Red Clay Consolidated SD
Supt. — See Wilmington
DuPont MS  900/6-8
735 Meeting House Rd  19707  302-239-3420
Aaron Selekman, prin.  Fax 239-3450

---

Sanford S  600/PK-12
6900 Lancaster Pike  19707  302-235-6500
Mark J. Anderson, head sch  Fax 239-5389
Wilmington Christian S  500/PK-12
825 Loveville Rd  19707  302-239-2121
William Stevens, head sch  Fax 239-2778

**Laurel, Sussex, Pop. 3,540**
Laurel SD  2,200/PK-12
1160 S Central Ave  19956  302-875-6100
Shawn Larrimore, supt.  Fax 875-6106
www.laurel.k12.de.us
Laurel HS  500/9-12
1133 S Central Ave  19956  302-875-6120
Dr. Richard Evans, prin.  Fax 875-6123
Laurel MS  300/5-8
1131 S Central Ave  19956  302-875-6110
Dr. Richard Evans, prin.  Fax 875-6109

**Lewes, Sussex, Pop. 2,714**
Cape Henlopen SD  4,800/K-12
1270 Kings Hwy  19958  302-645-6686
Robert S. Fulton M.Ed., supt.  Fax 645-6684
www.capehenlopenschools.com/
Beacon MS  500/6-8
19483 John J Williams Hwy  19958  302-645-6288
David Frederick, prin.  Fax 644-6118
Cape Henlopen HS  1,300/9-12
1250 Kings Hwy  19958  302-645-7711
Brian Donahue, prin.  Fax 645-1356
Other Schools – See Milton

---

American College Delaware  Post-Sec.
404 E Savannah Rd  19958  302-793-1101
Beebe Medical Center School of Nursing  Post-Sec.
424 Savannah Rd  19958  302-645-3251

**Magnolia, Kent, Pop. 218**

---

St. Thomas More Academy  200/9-12
133 Thomas More Dr  19962  302-697-8100
Rachael Casey, prin.  Fax 697-8122

**Middletown, New Castle, Pop. 18,390**
Appoquinimink SD
Supt. — See Odessa
Appoquinimink HS  1,500/9-12
1080 Bunker Hill Rd  19709  302-449-3840
Keisha Brinkley, prin.  Fax 378-5130
Meredith MS  700/6-8
504 S Broad St  19709  302-378-5001
T.J. Vari, prin.  Fax 378-5008
Middletown HS  1,200/9-12
120 Silver Lake Rd  19709  302-376-4141
Matt Donovan Ed.D., prin.  Fax 378-5268
Redding MS  700/6-8
201 New St  19709  302-378-5030
Chris Beck, prin.  Fax 378-5080
Waters MS  800/6-8
1235 Cedar Lane Rd  19709  302-449-3490
Thomas Poehlmann, prin.

New Castle County Voc-Tech SD
Supt. — See Wilmington
St. Georges Technical HS  Vo/Tech
555 Hyetts Corner Rd  19709  302-449-3360
Shanta Reynolds, prin.  Fax 376-6796

St. Andrew's S 300/9-12
350 Noxontown Rd 19709 302-378-9511
Daniel Roach, hdmstr. Fax 378-7120

**Milford, Sussex, Pop. 9,349**
Milford SD 2,600/PK-12
906 Lakeview Ave 19963 302-422-1600
Dr. Phyllis Kohel, supt. Fax 422-1608
www.milfordschooldistrict.org/
Milford Central Academy 300/6-8
1021 N Walnut St 19963 302-424-7900
Dr. Nancy Carnevale, prin. Fax 424-4163
Milford HS 800/9-12
1019 N Walnut St 19963 302-422-1610
Dr. Kelly Green, prin. Fax 424-5463

**Millsboro, Sussex, Pop. 3,755**
Indian River SD
Supt. — See Selbyville
Millsboro MS 600/6-8
302 E State St 19966 302-934-3200
Renee Jerns Ed.D., prin. Fax 934-3215

**Milton, Sussex, Pop. 2,504**
Cape Henlopen SD
Supt. — See Lewes
Mariner MS 500/6-8
16391 Harbeson Rd 19968 302-684-8516
Fred Best, prin. Fax 684-5606

**Newark, New Castle, Pop. 30,774**
Christina SD
Supt. — See Wilmington
Christiana HS 1,000/9-12
190 Salem Church Rd 19713 302-631-2400
Noreen LaSorsa, prin. Fax 454-3490
Gauger-Cobbs MS 1,200/6-8
50 Gender Rd 19713 302-454-2358
Carolyn Chambliss, prin. Fax 454-3482
Glasgow HS 1,100/9-12
1901 S College Ave 19702 302-631-5600
Dr. Dean Ivory, prin. Fax 454-5453
Kirk MS 800/6-8
140 Brennen Dr 19713 302-454-2164
Timothy Slade, prin. Fax 454-3491
Networks S for Entrepreneurial Sciences Vo/Tech
30 Blue Hen Dr 19713 302-454-2233
Norma Brister, prin. Fax 454-5446
Newark HS 1,400/9-12
750 E Delaware Ave 19711 302-631-4700
Curtis Bedford, prin. Fax 454-2155
Shue-Medill MS 1,000/6-8
1500 Capitol Trl 19711 302-454-2171
Michele Savage, prin. Fax 454-3492

New Castle County Voc-Tech SD
Supt. — See Wilmington
Hodgson Vocational-Technical HS Vo/Tech
2575 Glasgow Ave 19702 302-834-0990
Jerry Lamey Ed.D., prin. Fax 834-0598

---

Delaware Technical & Community College Post-Sec.
400 Stanton Christiana Rd 19713 302-454-3900
Schilling-Douglas School of Hair Design Post-Sec.
70 Amstel Ave 19711 302-737-5100
University of Delaware Post-Sec.
210 S College Ave 19716 302-831-2792

**New Castle, New Castle, Pop. 5,184**
Colonial SD 9,600/K-12
318 E Basin Rd 19720 302-323-2700
Dolon Blakey Ed.D., supt. Fax 323-2748
www.colonial.k12.de.us
Bedford MS 1,100/6-8
801 Cox Neck Rd 19720 302-832-6280
Andrew Moffett, prin. Fax 834-6729
McCullough MS 700/6-8
20 Chase Ave 19720 302-429-4000
Elizabeth Fleetwood, prin. Fax 429-4005
Penn HS 1,900/9-12
713 E Basin Rd 19720 302-323-2800
Brian Erskine, prin. Fax 323-2955
Read MS 800/6-8
314 E Basin Rd 19720 302-323-2760
Holly Sage, prin. Fax 323-2763
Wallin S Alt
701 E Basin Rd 19720 302-323-2952
Ige Purnell, prin. Fax 323-2787

---

Serviam Girls Academy 50/5-8
14 Halcyon Dr 19720 302-651-9700
Kate Lucyk, prin. Fax 651-9703
Tall Oaks Classical S 200/K-12
903 E Basin Rd 19720 302-738-3337
Dr. Timothy J. Dernlan, hdmstr. Fax 328-7886

Wilmington University Post-Sec.
320 N Dupont Hwy 19720 302-356-4636

**Odessa, New Castle, Pop. 353**
Appoquinimink SD 8,600/PK-12
PO Box 4010 19730 302-376-4128
Matthew Burrows, supt. Fax 378-5016
www.apposchooldistrict.com
Other Schools – See Middletown

**Seaford, Sussex, Pop. 6,739**
Seaford SD 3,200/K-12
390 N Market St 19973 302-629-4587
David Perrington, supt. Fax 629-2619
www.seafordbluejays.org/
Seaford HS 800/9-12
399 N Market St 19973 302-629-4587
Teresa Carson, prin. Fax 628-4417
Seaford Intensive Learning Center Alt
1 Delaware Pl 19973 302-629-4587
Dr. Sharon DiGoralamo, dir. Fax 629-2619
Seaford MS 700/6-8
500 E Stein Hwy 19973 302-629-4587
Dr. Stephanie Smith, prin. Fax 628-4485

---

Seaford Christian Academy 50/PK-12
110 Holly St 19973 302-629-7161

**Selbyville, Sussex, Pop. 2,147**
Indian River SD 8,700/PK-12
31 Hosier St 19975 302-436-1000
Susan Bunting Ed.D., supt. Fax 436-1034
www.irsd.net/
Selbyville MS 600/6-8
80 Bethany Rd 19975 302-436-1020
Jason Macrides, prin. Fax 436-1035
Other Schools – See Dagsboro, Frankford, Georgetown, Millsboro

**Smyrna, Kent, Pop. 9,689**
Smyrna SD 5,500/PK-12
82 Monrovia Ave 19977 302-653-8585
Deborah Wicks, supt. Fax 653-3149
www.smyrna.k12.de.us
Smyrna HS 1,400/9-12
500 Duck Creek Pkwy 19977 302-653-8581
Stacy Cook, prin. Fax 653-3139
Smyrna MS 800/7-8
700 Duck Creek Pkwy 19977 302-653-8584
Steven Gott, prin. Fax 653-3424

**Wilmington, New Castle, Pop. 69,534**
Brandywine SD 10,300/K-12
1311 Brandywine Blvd 19809 302-793-5000
Dr. Mark Holodick, supt. Fax 792-3823
www.brandywineschools.org
Brandywine HS 1,000/9-12
1400 Foulk Rd 19803 302-479-1600
James Simmons, prin. Fax 479-1604
Concord HS 1,300/9-12
2501 Ebright Rd 19810 302-475-3951
Yolanda McKinney, prin. Fax 529-3094
DuPont MS 900/6-8
701 W 34th St 19802 302-762-7146
Lewis Cheatwood, prin. Fax 762-7196
Mt. Pleasant HS 900/9-12
5201 Washington Blvd 19809 302-762-7125
Heather Austin, prin. Fax 762-7042
Springer MS 800/6-8
2220 Shipley Rd 19803 302-479-1621
Jacquelyn Biggs, prin. Fax 479-1628
Talley MS 800/6-8
1110 Cypress Rd 19810 302-475-3976
Dr. Richard Carter, prin. Fax 475-3998
Other Schools – See Claymont

Christina SD 16,100/PK-12
600 N Lombard St 19801 302-552-2600
Dr. Robert Andrzejewski, supt. Fax 429-3944
www.christina.k12.de.us/
Bayard MS 500/6-8
200 S Dupont St 19805 302-429-4118
Eric Stancell, prin. Fax 429-4153
Douglas S 50/Alt
1800 Prospect Rd 19805 302-429-4146
John Martin, admin. Fax 429-4920
Pyle Academy 100/Alt
501 N Lombard St 19801 302-429-4158
Kristina MacBury, prin. Fax 429-3959
Other Schools – See Newark

New Castle County Voc-Tech SD
1417 Newport Rd 19804 302-995-8050
Victoria Gehrt Ed.D., supt. Fax 995-1579
www.nccvotech.com
Delcastle Technical HS Vo/Tech
1417 Newport Rd 19804 302-995-8100
Dr. Clifton Hayes, prin. Fax 995-8197
Howard HS of Technology Vo/Tech
401 E 12th St 19801 302-571-5400
Stanley Spoor Ed.D., prin. Fax 571-5843
Delaware Skills Center Adult
13th & Clifford Brown Walk 19801 302-654-5392
Eric Wells, head sch Fax 654-9418
Other Schools – See Middletown, Newark

Red Clay Consolidated SD 18,400/PK-12
1502 Spruce Ave 19805 302-552-3700
Dr. Mervin Daugherty, supt. Fax 992-7820
www.redclayschools.com
Calloway S of Arts 900/6-12
100 N Dupont Rd 19807 302-651-2700
Julie Rumschlag, dean Fax 425-4594
Conrad S of Science 1,000/6-12
201 Jackson Ave 19804 302-992-5545
Mark Pruitt, prin. Fax 992-5585
Dickinson HS 600/9-12
1801 Milltown Rd 19808 302-992-5500
Byron Murphy, prin. Fax 992-5506
McKean HS 900/9-12
301 Mckennans Church Rd 19808 302-992-5520
Brian Mattix, prin. Fax 992-5525
Skyline MS 800/6-8
2900 Skyline Dr 19808 302-454-3410
Frank Rumford, prin. Fax 454-3541
Stanton MS 700/6-8
1800 Limestone Rd 19804 302-992-5540
Tawanda Bond, prin. Fax 992-5586
Groves Adult Education Adult
1621 Telegraph Rd 19804 302-651-2709
Kellie Tetrick, prin. Fax 658-7137
Other Schools – See Greenville, Hockessin

---

Christiana Care Health Services Post-Sec.
PO Box 1668 19899 302-428-2571
Concord Christian Academy 200/PK-12
2510 Marsh Rd 19810 302-475-3247
Dawn Career Institute Post-Sec.
3700 Lancaster Pike 19805 302-633-9075
Delaware College of Art and Design Post-Sec.
600 N Market St 19801 302-622-8000
Delaware Technical & Community College Post-Sec.
333 N Shipley St 19801 302-571-5300
Goldey-Beacom College Post-Sec.
4701 Limestone Rd 19808 302-998-8814
Harris School of Business Post-Sec.
1413 Foulk Rd 19803 302-478-8890
National Massage Therapy Institute Post-Sec.
1601 Concord Pike 19803 800-509-5058
Nativity Preparatory S 50/5-8
1515 Linden St 19805 302-777-1015
Paul Webster, prin. Fax 777-1225
Padua Academy 600/9-12
905 N Broom St 19806 302-421-3739
Cindy Hayes-Mann, head sch Fax 421-3748
St. Elizabeth HS 400/9-12
1500 Cedar St 19805 302-656-3369
Shirley Bounds, prin. Fax 656-7513
St. Marks HS 1,100/9-12
2501 Pike Creek Rd 19808 302-738-3300
Richard Bayhan, prin. Fax 738-5132
Salesianum S 1,000/9-12
1801 N Broom St 19802 302-654-2495
Rev. Christian Beretta, prin. Fax 654-7767
Tatnall S 700/PK-12
1501 Barley Mill Rd 19807 302-998-2292
Charles Tierney, head sch Fax 892-4389
Tower Hill S 800/PK-12
2813 W 17th St 19806 302-575-0550
Harry Baetjer, hdmstr. Fax 657-8366
Ursuline Academy 500/PK-12
1106 Pennsylvania Ave 19806 302-658-7158
Cathie Field-Lloyd, pres. Fax 658-4297
Widener University School of Law Post-Sec.
PO Box 7474 19803 302-477-2162
Wilmington Friends S 800/PK-12
101 School Rd 19803 302-576-2900
Ken Aldridge, head sch Fax 576-2939

**Woodside, Kent, Pop. 178**
POLYTECH SD
PO Box 22 19980 302-697-2170
Dr. Deborah Zych, supt. Fax 697-6749
www.polytechpanthers.com
POLYTECH HS, PO Box 97 19980 Vo/Tech
Dr. Jason Peel, prin. 302-697-3255

**Wyoming, Kent, Pop. 1,263**
Caesar Rodney SD 7,500/K-12
7 Front St 19934 302-698-4800
Kevin Fitzgerald Ed.D., supt. Fax 697-3406
www.cr.k12.de.us
Other Schools – See Camden, Dover

# DISTRICT OF COLUMBIA

## DISTRICT OF COLUMBIA PUBLIC SCHOOLS

**1200 1st St NE, Washington 20002-3361**
**Telephone 202-442-5885**
**Fax 202-442-5026**
**Website dcps.dc.gov/**

Chancellor Kaya Henderson

## DISTRICT OF COLUMBIA BOARD OF EDUCATION

**441 4th St NW Ste 723N, Washington 20002**

President Laura Slover

## PUBLIC, PRIVATE AND CATHOLIC SECONDARY SCHOOLS

**Washington, District of Columbia, Pop. 587,406**

District of Columbia SD 42,600/PK-12
1200 1st St NE 20002 202-442-5885
Kaya Henderson, chncllr. Fax 442-5026
dcps.dc.gov

Anacostia HS 800/9-12
1601 16th St SE 20020 202-698-2155
Lloyd Bryant, prin. Fax 698-2188

Ballou HS 1,000/9-12
3401 4th St SE 20032 202-645-3400
Yetunde Reeves, prin. Fax 645-3397

Banneker HS 400/9-12
800 Euclid St NW 20001 202-671-6320
Anita Berger, prin. Fax 673-2231

Brookland MS 6-8
1150 Michigan Ave NE 20017 202-759-1999
Norah Lycknell, prin. Fax 671-6251

Cardozo HS 500/6-12
1200 Clifton St NW 20009 202-673-7385
Tanya Roane, prin. Fax 673-2232

CHOICE Academy 50/Alt
1720 1st St NE 20002 202-939-4350
Gary Washington, dir. Fax 673-8123

Columbia Heights Education Campus 1,200/6-12
3101 16th St NW 20010 202-939-7700
Maria Tukeva, prin. Fax 576-9147

Coolidge HS 500/9-12
6315 5th St NW 20011 202-671-6080
Richard Jackson, prin. Fax 576-3147

Deal MS 1,000/6-8
3815 Fort Dr NW 20016 202-939-2010
James Albright, prin. Fax 282-1116

Dunbar HS 600/9-12
101 N St NW 20001 202-698-3762
Abdullah Zaki, prin. Fax 673-2233

Eastern HS 800/9-12
1700 E Capitol St NE 20003 202-698-4500
Rachel Skerritt, prin. Fax 698-4800

Eliot-Hine MS 400/6-8
1830 Constitution Ave NE 20002 202-939-5380
Tynika Young, prin. Fax 673-8063

Ellington HS of the Arts 500/9-12
2501 11th St NW 20001 202-282-0123
Desepe De Vargas, prin. Fax 337-7847

Ellington HS of the Arts 9-12
2001 10th St NW 20001 202-282-0123
Desepe de Vargas, prin. Fax 337-7847

Hardy MS 400/6-8
1819 35th St NW 20007 202-729-4350
Patricia Pride, prin. Fax 576-9443

Hart MS 500/6-8
601 Mississippi Ave SE 20032 202-671-6426
Charlette Butler, prin. Fax 645-3426

Jefferson MS Academy 200/6-8
801 7th St SW 20024 202-729-3270
Natalie Gordon, prin. Fax 724-2459

Johnson MS 300/6-8
1400 Bruce Pl SE 20020 202-939-3140
Courtney Aldridge, prin. Fax 645-5882

Kramer MS 300/6-8
1700 Q St SE 20020 202-939-3150
Roman Smith, prin. Fax 698-1169

McKinley MS 6-8
151 T St NE 20002 202-281-3950
Mary Louise Jones, prin. Fax 832-1293

McKinley Technology HS Vo/Tech
151 T St NE 20002 202-281-3950
Mary Jones, prin. Fax 576-6279

Miller MS 300/6-8
301 49th St NE 20019 202-388-6870
Kortni Stafford, prin. Fax 727-8330

Moore HS 300/Alt
1001 Monroe St NE 20017 202-281-3600
Jada Langston, prin. Fax 526-5022

Oyster-Adams Bilingual MS 300/4-8
2020 19th St NW 20009 202-673-7311
Mayra Canizales, prin. Fax 673-6500

Phelps Architecture Construction & Eng S 300/9-12
704 26th St NE 20002 202-729-4360
Willie Jackson, prin. Fax 442-8438

Roosevelt HS 500/9-12
4400 Iowa Ave NW 20011 202-576-6130
Sha Brown, prin. Fax 541-6449

School Without Walls HS 500/9-12
2130 G St NW 20037 202-645-9690
Richard Trogisch, prin. Fax 724-8536

Sousa MS 400/6-8
3650 Ely Pl SE 20019 202-729-3260
Clarence Humes, prin. Fax 645-0456

Stuart-Hobson MS 400/6-8
410 E St NE 20002 202-671-6010
Dawn Clemens, prin. Fax 698-4720

Washington Metropolitan HS 300/Alt
300 Bryant St NW 20001 202-939-3610
Rinaldo Murray, prin. Fax 671-2101

Wilson HS 1,600/9-12
3950 Chesapeake St NW 20016 202-282-0120
Kimberly Martin, prin. Fax 282-0077

Woodson HS 800/9-12
540 55th St NE 20019 202-939-2030
Darrin Slade, prin. Fax 645-4193

Youth Services Center 100/Alt
1000 Mount Olivet Rd NE 20002 202-576-8388
Soncyree Lee, prin. Fax 576-9073

Ballou STAY HS Adult
3401 4th St SE 20032 202-645-3390
Cara Fuller, prin. Fax 645-3935

Roosevelt STAY HS Adult
4400 Iowa Ave NW 20011 202-576-8399
Eugenia Young, prin. Fax 576-8478

---

Academia de la Recta Porta Christian S 100/K-12
7614 Georgia Ave NW 20012 202-726-8737
Annette Miles M.A., admin. Fax 726-8759

American University Post-Sec.
4400 Massachusetts Ave NW 20016 202-885-1000

Archbishop Carroll HS 500/9-12
4300 Harewood Rd NE 20017 202-529-0900
Mary Blaufuss, pres. Fax 526-8879

Bennett Career Institute Post-Sec.
700 Monroe St NE 20017 202-526-1400

British S of Washington 400/PK-12
2001 Wisconsin Ave NW 20007 202-829-3700
David Rowsell, head sch Fax 829-6522

Burke S 300/6-12
4101 Connecticut Ave NW 20008 202-362-8882
Damian Jones, head sch Fax 362-1914

Catholic University of America Post-Sec.
620 Michigan Ave NE 20064 202-319-5000

Chicago Sch of Professional Psychology Post-Sec.
901 15th St NW 20005 202-706-5052

Corcoran College of Art & Design Post-Sec.
500 17th St NW 20006 202-639-1800

Cornerstone S of Washington DC 100/PK-12
3742 Ely Pl SE 20019 202-575-0027
Derrick Max, head sch Fax 575-0669

Dudley Beauty College Post-Sec.
2031 Rhode Island Ave NE 20018 202-269-3666

Field S 300/6-12
2301 Foxhall Rd NW 20007 202-295-5800
Dale Johnson, hdmstr. Fax 295-5858

Gallaudet University Post-Sec.
800 Florida Ave NE 20002 202-651-5000

Georgetown Day HS 500/9-12
4200 Davenport St NW 20016 202-274-3200
Russell Shaw, head sch Fax 364-9603

Georgetown University Post-Sec.
37th and O St NW 20057 202-687-0100

Georgetown Visitation Prep HS 500/9-12
1524 35th St NW 20007 202-337-3350
Daniel Kerns, hdmstr. Fax 342-5733

George Washington University Post-Sec.
2121 I St NW 20052 202-994-1000

Gonzaga College HS 1,000/9-12
19 I St NW 20001 202-336-7100
Thomas Every, hdmstr. Fax 336-7164

Graduate School USA Post-Sec.
600 Maryland Ave SW 20024 202-314-3300

Howard University Post-Sec.
2400 6th St NW 20059 202-806-6100

Howard University School of Divinity Post-Sec.
1400 Shepherd St NE 20017 202-806-0500

Johns Hopkins University Post-Sec.
1740 Massachusetts Ave NW 20036 202-663-5600

Lab S of Washington 200/1-12
4759 Reservoir Rd NW 20007 202-965-6600
Katherine Schantz, head sch Fax 965-5015

Levine School of Music Post-Sec.
2801 Upton St NW 20008 202-686-8000

Maret S 600/K-12
3000 Cathedral Ave NW 20008 202-939-8800
Marjo Talbott, hdmstr. Fax 939-8884

Medtech College Post-Sec.
529 14th St NW 20045 202-872-4700

Model Secondary School for the Deaf Post-Sec.
800 Florida Ave NE 20002 202-651-5031

National Cathedral S 600/4-12
3612 Woodley Rd NW 20016 202-537-6300
Kathleen Jamieson, head sch Fax 537-5743

National Conservatory of Dramatic Arts Post-Sec.
1556 Wisconsin Ave NW 20007 202-333-2202

Pontifical Faculty Immaculate Conception Post-Sec.
487 Michigan Ave NE 20017 202-495-3820

Pontifical John Paul II Institute Post-Sec.
620 Michigan Ave NE 20064 202-526-3799

Radians College Post-Sec.
1025 Vermont Ave NW Ste 200 20005 202-291-9020

St. Albans S 600/4-12
Mount Saint Alban 20016 202-537-6435
Vance Wilson, hdmstr. Fax 537-6434

St. Anselms Abbey S 200/6-12
4501 S Dakota Ave NE 20017 202-269-2350
Bill Crittenberger, hdmstr. Fax 269-2373

St. Johns College HS 1,000/9-12
2607 Military Rd NW 20015 202-363-2316
Br. Michael Andrejko, prin. Fax 380-1754

San Miguel MS 100/6-8
7705 Georgia Ave NW 20012 202-232-8345
Dave Palank, prin. Fax 232-3987

Sidwell Friends S 1,100/PK-12
3825 Wisconsin Ave NW 20016 202-537-8100
Bryan Garman, head sch Fax 537-8138

Strayer University Post-Sec.
1133 15th St NW Ste 200 20005 202-408-2400

Technical Learning Center Post-Sec.
1720 I St NW Ste 200 20006 202-223-3500

The Institute of World Politics Post-Sec.
1521 16th St NW 20036 202-462-2101

Trinity University Post-Sec.
125 Michigan Ave NE 20017 202-884-9000

University of the District of Columbia Post-Sec.
4200 Connecticut Ave NW 20008 202-274-5000

University of the Potomac Post-Sec.
1401 H St NW Ste 100 20005 202-686-0876

Walter Reed Medical Center Post-Sec.
6825 16th St NW 20306 202-782-6104

Washington International S 500/6-12
3100 Macomb St NW 20008 202-243-1800
Clayton Lewis, head sch Fax 243-1802

Washington Jesuit Academy 100/5-8
900 Varnum St NE 20017 202-832-7679
Marcus Washington, hdmstr. Fax 832-8098

Washington MS for Girls 100/4-8
1901 Mississippi Ave SE 20020 202-678-1113
Sr. Mary Bourdon, prin. Fax 678-1114

Washington Theological Union Post-Sec.
1600 Webster St NE 20017 202-526-1221

Wesley Theological Seminary Post-Sec.
4500 Massachusetts Ave NW 20016 202-885-8600

# FLORIDA

**FLORIDA DEPARTMENT OF EDUCATION**
**325 W Gaines St, Tallahassee 32399-0400**
**Telephone 850-245-0505**
**Fax 850-245-9667**
**Website http://www.fldoe.org/**

Commissioner of Education Pam Stewart

**FLORIDA BOARD OF EDUCATION**
**325 W Gaines St, Tallahassee 32399-0400**

Chairperson Kathleen Shanahan

## PUBLIC, PRIVATE AND CATHOLIC SECONDARY SCHOOLS

**Alachua, Alachua, Pop. 8,873**
Alachua County SD
Supt. — See Gainesville
Mebane MS 400/6-8
16401 NW 140th St 32615 386-462-1648
Manda Bessner, prin. Fax 462-9094
Santa Fe HS 1,100/9-12
16213 NW US Highway 441 32615 386-462-1125
Dr. Beth LeClear, prin. Fax 462-1711

Forest Grove Christian Academy 100/PK-12
22575 NW 94th Ave 32615 386-462-3921

**Altamonte Springs, Seminole, Pop. 40,483**
Seminole County SD
Supt. — See Sanford
Lake Brantley HS 2,800/9-12
991 Sand Lake Rd 32714 407-746-3450
Mike Gaudreau, prin. Fax 746-3600
Teague MS 1,400/6-8
1350 Mcneil Rd 32714 407-320-1550
Leon McCants, prin. Fax 320-1545

Altamonte Christian S 300/K-12
601 Palm Springs Dr 32701 407-831-0950
City College Post-Sec.
177 Montgomery Rd 32714 407-831-9816
Everglades University Post-Sec.
887 E Altamonte Dr 32701 407-277-0311

**Altha, Calhoun, Pop. 529**
Calhoun County SD
Supt. — See Blountstown
Altha S 600/PK-12
25793 N Main St 32421 850-762-3121
Sue Price, prin. Fax 762-9502

**Apopka, Orange, Pop. 40,626**
Orange County SD
Supt. — See Orlando
Amikids Orlando 50/Alt
1461 S Lake Pleasant Rd 32703 407-886-5405
William Tovine, prin.
Apopka HS 2,900/9-12
555 Martin St 32712 407-905-5500
Douglas Guthrie, prin. Fax 814-6130
Apopka MS 1,100/6-8
425 N Park Ave 32712 407-884-2208
Kelly Pelletier, prin. Fax 884-2217
Piedmont Lakes MS 1,100/6-8
2601 Lakeville Rd 32703 407-884-2265
Edward Thompson, prin. Fax 884-2287
Wekiva HS 2,200/9-12
2501 N Hiawassee Rd 32703 407-297-4900
Michele Erickson, prin. Fax 297-4970
Wolf Lake MS 1,100/6-8
1725 W Ponkan Rd 32712 407-464-3317
Laura Beusse, prin. Fax 464-3336

Champion Preparatory Academy 300/PK-12
1935 S Orange Blossom Trl 32703 407-788-0018
Community Christian Learning Center 100/K-12
750 Roger Williams Rd 32703 407-410-0049
Forest Lake Academy 400/9-12
500 Education Loop 32703 407-862-8411
Golf Academy of America Post-Sec.
510 S Hunt Club Blvd 32703 800-342-7342

**Arcadia, DeSoto, Pop. 7,533**
De Soto County SD 4,500/PK-12
PO Box 2000 34265 863-494-4222
Dr. Karyn Gary, supt. Fax 494-0389
www.desotoschools.com
DeSoto HS 1,100/9-12
1710 E Gibson St 34266 863-494-3434
Darrell Milstead, prin. Fax 494-7867
DeSoto MS 1,000/6-8
420 E Gibson St 34266 863-494-4133
Denise Schultz, prin. Fax 494-6263
DeSoto County Adult Education Center Adult
310 W Whidden St 34266 863-993-1333
Kathy Severson, prin. Fax 993-9181

**Atlantic Beach, Duval, Pop. 12,332**
Duval County SD
Supt. — See Jacksonville
Marine Science Education Center Vo/Tech
1347 Palmer St 32233 904-247-5973
Donald Nelson, prin. Fax 247-5976
Mayport MS 800/6-8
2600 Mayport Rd 32233 904-247-5977
Katrina McCray, prin. Fax 247-5987

**Auburndale, Polk, Pop. 13,305**
Polk County SD
Supt. — See Bartow
Auburndale HS 1,500/9-12
1 Bloodhound Trl 33823 863-965-6200
John Hill, prin. Fax 965-6245
Stambaugh MS 900/6-8
226 N Main St 33823 863-965-5494
Trish Butler, prin. Fax 965-5496
East Area Adult S Adult
300 E Bridgers Ave 33823 863-965-5475
Loretta Cameron, prin. Fax 965-5477

Southern Technical College Post-Sec.
298 Havendale Blvd 33823 407-438-6000

**Ave Maria, Collier**

Ave Maria University Post-Sec.
5050 Ave Maria Blvd 34142 877-283-8648

**Avon Park, Highlands, Pop. 8,676**
Highlands County SD
Supt. — See Sebring
Avon Park HS 900/9-12
700 E Main St 33825 863-452-4311
Tealy Williams, prin. Fax 452-4324
Avon Park MS 700/6-8
401 S Lake Ave 33825 863-452-4333
Seth Lambert, prin. Fax 452-4341
Career Academy Vo/Tech
600 W College Dr 33825 863-784-7209
Karen Pella, lead tchr. Fax 784-7211

South Florida State College Post-Sec.
600 W College Dr 33825 863-453-6661
Walker Memorial Academy 200/PK-12
1525 W Avon Blvd 33825 863-453-3131

**Babson Park, Polk, Pop. 1,321**

Webber International University Post-Sec.
PO Box 96 33827 863-638-1431

**Baker, Okaloosa**
Okaloosa County SD
Supt. — See Fort Walton Beach
Baker S 1,300/K-12
1369 14th St 32531 850-689-7279
Michael Martello, prin. Fax 689-7416

**Baldwin, Duval, Pop. 1,376**
Duval County SD
Supt. — See Jacksonville
Baldwin MSHS 1,100/6-12
291 Mill St W 32234 904-266-1200
Denise Hall, prin. Fax 266-1220

**Bartow, Polk, Pop. 17,008**
Polk County SD 95,500/PK-12
PO Box 391 33831 863-534-0500
Kathryn LeRoy, supt. Fax 519-8231
www.polk-fl.net
Bartow HS 2,000/9-12
1270 S Broadway Ave 33830 863-534-7400
Emilean Clemons, prin. Fax 534-0077
Bartow MS 800/6-8
550 E Clower St 33830 863-534-7415
Dr. Leigh Anne Cooley, prin. Fax 534-7418
Bartow Youth Academy Alt
2415 Bob Phillips Rd 33830 863-519-3770
Brett Butler, prin. Fax 519-3771
Gause Academy of Leadership 200/6-12
1395 Polk St 33830 863-534-7425
Daraford Jones, prin. Fax 519-3716
International Baccalaureate HS at Bartow 200/9-12
1270 S Broadway Ave 33830 863-534-0194
Brenda Hardman, prin. Fax 534-0077
Summerlin Academy 9-12
1500 S Jackson Ave 33830 863-519-7504
Steve Cochran, prin. Fax 519-8774
Union Academy 400/6-8
1795 E Wabash St 33830 863-534-7435
Joel McGuire, prin. Fax 534-7487
Other Schools – See Auburndale, Davenport, Dundee, Eagle Lake, Fort Meade, Frostproof, Haines City, Lake Alfred, Lakeland, Lake Wales, Mulberry, Poinciana, Winter Haven

**Bell, Gilchrist, Pop. 455**
Gilchrist County SD
Supt. — See Trenton
Bell HS 700/6-12
930 S Main St 32619 352-463-3232
Sherry Lindsey, prin. Fax 463-3294

**Belle Glade, Palm Beach, Pop. 17,323**
Palm Beach County SD
Supt. — See West Palm Beach
Crossroads Academy 200/Alt
225 SW 12th St 33430 561-993-8400
Diane Howard, prin. Fax 993-8450
Glades Central Community HS 1,100/9-12
1001 SW Avenue M 33430 561-993-4400
Angela Avery-Moore, prin. Fax 993-9462
Lake Shore MS 700/6-8
425 W Canal St N 33430 561-829-1100
Anthony Lockhart, prin. Fax 829-1130

Glades Day S 300/PK-12
400 Gator Blvd 33430 561-996-6769

**Belleview, Marion, Pop. 4,408**
Marion County SD
Supt. — See Ocala
Belleview HS 1,600/9-12
10400 SE 36th Ave 34420 352-671-6210
Mike Kelly, prin. Fax 671-6212
Belleview MS 1,100/6-8
10500 SE 36th Ave 34420 352-671-6235
David Ellers, prin. Fax 671-6239

Souls Harbor Christian Academy 200/PK-12
12650 SE County Highway 484 34420 352-245-6252
Taylor College Post-Sec.
5190 SE 125th St 34420 352-245-4119

**Blountstown, Calhoun, Pop. 2,466**
Calhoun County SD 2,200/PK-12
20859 Central Ave E Ste G20 32424 850-674-5927
Ralph Yoder, supt. Fax 674-5814
www.calhounflschools.org
Blountstown HS 400/9-12
18597 NE State Road 69 32424 850-674-5724
Debbie Williams, prin. Fax 674-8865
Blountstown MS 300/6-8
17586 Main St N 32424 850-674-8234
Neva Miller, prin. Fax 674-6480
Calhoun County Adult Education Center Adult
17283 NW Charlie Johns St 32424 850-674-6490
Other Schools – See Altha

**Boca Raton, Palm Beach, Pop. 83,145**
Palm Beach County SD
Supt. — See West Palm Beach
Boca Raton Community HS 3,000/9-12
1501 NW 15th Ct 33486 561-338-1400
Geoffrey McKee, prin. Fax 338-1440
Boca Raton Community MS 1,300/6-8
1251 NW 8th St 33486 561-416-8700
Peter Slack, prin. Fax 416-8777
Eagles Landing MS 1,300/6-8
19500 Coral Ridge Dr 33498 561-470-7000
Cynthia Chiapetta, prin. Fax 470-7030
Estridge High Tech MS 1,200/6-8
1798 NW Spanish River Blvd 33431 561-989-7800
Laura Riopelle, prin. Fax 989-7810
Loggers Run Community MS 1,100/6-8
11584 W Palmetto Park Rd 33428 561-883-8000
Francis Giblin, prin. Fax 883-8027
Olympic Heights Community HS 2,100/9-12
20101 Lyons Rd 33434 561-852-6900
Dave Clark, prin. Fax 852-6974

Omni MS 1,600/6-8
5775 Jog Rd 33496 561-989-2800
Gerald Riopelle, prin. Fax 981-9651
Spanish River Community HS 2,400/9-12
5100 Jog Rd 33496 561-241-2200
William Latson, prin. Fax 241-2236
West Boca Raton Community HS 2,200/9-12
12811 Glades Rd 33498 561-672-2001
Craig Sommer, prin. Fax 672-2014

---

Boca Raton Christian S 500/PK-12
315 NW 4th St 33432 561-391-2727
Robert Tennies Ed.D., hdmstr. Fax 226-0617
Boca Raton Prep International S 200/PK-12
10333 Diego Dr S 33428 561-852-1410
Stan Daniel, head sch Fax 479-1731
Digital Media Arts College Post-Sec.
5400 Broken Sound Blvd NW 33487 561-391-1148
Everglades University Post-Sec.
5002 T Rex Ave Ste 100 33431 561-912-1211
Florida Atlantic University Post-Sec.
PO Box 3091 33431 561-297-3000
Garden of the Sahaba Academy 300/PK-11
3100 NW 5th Ave 33431 561-395-3011
Grandview Preparatory S 200/PK-12
336 NW Spanish River Blvd 33431 561-416-9737
Klein Jewish Academy 700/K-12
9701 Donna Klein Blvd 33428 561-852-3300
Lynn University Post-Sec.
3601 N Military Trl 33431 561-237-7000
PC Professor Post-Sec.
7056 Beracasa Way 33433 561-750-7879
St. Andrew's S 1,300/PK-12
3900 Jog Rd 33434 561-210-2000
Peter Benedict, head sch Fax 210-2007
Saint John Paul II Academy 500/9-12
4001 N Military Trl 33431 561-314-2100
Br. Dan Aubin, pres. Fax 989-8582
Weinbaum Yeshiva HS 300/9-12
7902 Montoya Cir N 33433 561-417-7422
West Boca Medical Center Post-Sec.
21644 State Road 7 33428 561-488-8000

**Bonifay, Holmes, Pop. 2,723**
Holmes County SD 3,300/PK-12
701 E Pennsylvania Ave 32425 850-547-9341
Eddie Dixon, supt. Fax 547-0381
www.hdsb.org
Bethlehem S 500/PK-12
2767 Highway 160 32425 850-547-3621
Brent Jones, prin. Fax 547-4856
Bonifay MS 500/5-8
401 Mclaughlin Ave 32425 850-547-2754
Donald Etheridge, prin. Fax 547-3685
Graduate Alternative S Alt
401 McLaughlin Ave 32425 850-547-0470
Ron Dixon, prin. Fax 547-0474
Holmes County HS 500/9-12
825 W Highway 90 32425 850-547-9000
Mickey Hudson, prin. Fax 547-6694
Other Schools – See Graceville, Ponce de Leon

**Bonita Springs, Lee, Pop. 43,637**
Lee County SD
Supt. — See Fort Myers
Bonita Springs MS for the Arts 700/6-8
10141 W Terry St 34135 239-992-4422
Linda Mitchell, prin. Fax 992-9157

**Boynton Beach, Palm Beach, Pop. 66,992**
Palm Beach County SD
Supt. — See West Palm Beach
Boynton Beach Community HS 1,500/9-12
4975 Park Ridge Blvd 33426 561-752-1200
Alfred Barch, prin. Fax 752-1205
Congress MS 1,000/6-8
101 S Congress Ave 33426 561-374-5600
Denise O'Conner, prin. Fax 374-5642
McAuliffe MS 1,300/6-8
6500 Le Chalet Blvd, 561-374-6600
Jeff Silverman, prin. Fax 374-6636
Odyssey MS 1,000/6-8
6161 W Woolbright Rd 33437 561-752-1300
Bonnie Fox, prin. Fax 752-1305

---

Bethesda Memorial Hospital Post-Sec.
2815 S Seacrest Blvd 33435 561-737-7733
Florida Career College Post-Sec.
1743 N Congress Ave 33426 561-634-7400
Lake Worth Christian S 500/PK-12
7592 High Ridge Rd 33426 561-493-3100
Jim Harwood, supt. Fax 493-3848
St. Vincent DePaul Regional Seminary Post-Sec.
10701 S Military Trl 33436 561-732-4424

**Bradenton, Manatee, Pop. 48,642**
Manatee County SD 43,700/PK-12
PO Box 9069 34206 941-708-8770
Dr. Diana Green, supt. Fax 708-8686
www.manateeschools.net
Bayshore HS 1,500/9-12
5401 34th St W 34210 941-751-7004
David Underhill, prin. Fax 753-0953
Braden River HS 2,000/9-12
6545 State Road 70 E 34203 941-751-8230
Jennifer Gilray, prin. Fax 751-8250
Braden River MS 900/6-8
6215 River Club Blvd 34202 941-751-7080
Randy Petrilla, prin. Fax 751-7085
Haile MS 1,000/6-8
9501 E State Road 64 34212 941-714-7240
Sharon Scarbrough, prin. Fax 714-7245
Harllee MS 500/6-8
6423 9th St E 34203 941-751-7027
Verdya Bradley, prin. Fax 751-7030
Horizons Academy 400/Alt
1910 27th St E 34208 941-714-7470
Omar Edwards, dir. Fax 708-6417
Johnson MS 500/6-8
2121 26th Ave E 34208 941-741-3344
Carl Auckerman, prin. Fax 741-3345
King MS 1,100/6-8
600 75th St NW 34209 941-798-6820
Michele Romeo, prin. Fax 798-6835
Lakewood Ranch HS 1,900/9-12
5500 Lakewood Ranch Blvd 34211 941-727-6100
Craig Little, prin. Fax 727-6099
Lee MS 900/6-8
4000 53rd Ave W 34210 941-727-6500
Scott Cooper, prin. Fax 727-6513
Manatee HS 2,300/9-12
902 33rd Street Ct W 34205 941-714-7300
Don Sauer, prin. Fax 741-3443
Manatee Technical Institute East Vo/Tech
5520 Lakewood Ranch Blvd 34211 941-752-8100
Doug Wagner, dir. Fax 727-6257
Manatee Technical Institute - Main Vo/Tech
6305 State Road 70 E 34203 941-751-7900
Doug Wagner, dir. Fax 405-1367
Manatee Technical Institute - West Vo/Tech
5505 34th St W 34210 941-209-6800
Doug Wagner, dir. Fax 751-7927
Nolan MS 900/6-8
6615 Greenbrook Blvd 34202 941-751-8200
Scot Boice, prin. Fax 751-8210
Southeast HS 1,300/9-12
1200 37th Ave E 34208 941-741-3366
Jim Pauley, prin. Fax 741-3372
Sugg MS 800/6-8
3801 59th St W 34209 941-741-3157
Darlene Proue, prin. Fax 741-3514
Other Schools – See Palmetto

---

Bradenton Christian S 500/PK-12
3304 43rd St W 34209 941-792-5454
Dan Vande Pol, supt. Fax 795-7190
Community Christian S 200/PK-12
5500 18th St E 34203 941-756-8748
Edison Academics 100/6-12
7700 Cortez Rd W 34209 941-792-7500
Paula Cavitt-Jackson, admin. Fax 792-7559
Florida College of Natural Health Post-Sec.
616 67th Street Cir E 34208 941-744-1244
Gulfcoast Christian Academy 50/K-12
1700 51st Ave E 34203 941-755-0332
Carol Pope, admin. Fax 981-1564
GUTI - Bradenton Post-Sec.
4212 Cortez Rd W 34210 941-761-4400
IMG Academy 600/PK-12
5693 Bollettieri Blvd 34210 941-739-3964
Richard Odell, hdmstr. Fax 752-2433
Inspiration Academy 50/6-12
7900 40th Ave W 34209 941-795-5466
ITT Technical Institute Post-Sec.
8039 Cooper Creek Blvd 34201 941-309-9200
Lake Erie College\Osteopathic Medicine Post-Sec.
5000 Lakewood Ranch Blvd 34211 941-756-0690
Manatee Learning Academy 200/PK-10
6210 17th Ave W 34209 941-794-0088
Manatee Technical Institute Post-Sec.
5603 34th St W 34210 941-751-7900
St. Stephen's Episcopal S 600/PK-12
315 41st St W 34209 941-746-2121
Dr. Janet Pullen, head sch Fax 746-5699
State College of FL Manatee-Sarasota Post-Sec.
PO Box 1849 34206 941-752-5000

**Brandon, Hillsborough, Pop. 100,869**
Hillsborough County SD
Supt. — See Tampa
Brandon HS 2,000/9-12
1101 Victoria St 33510 813-744-8120
Carl Green, prin. Fax 744-8129
Burns MS 1,300/6-8
615 Brooker Rd 33511 813-744-8383
Matthew DiPrima, prin. Fax 740-3623
Mann MS 1,100/6-8
409 E Jersey Ave 33510 813-744-8400
Barbara Fillhart, prin. Fax 744-6707
McLane MS 1,000/6-8
306 N Knights Ave 33510 813-744-8100
Dina Langston, prin. Fax 744-8135
Brandon Adult Education Adult
1101 Victoria St 33510 813-744-8131
Susan Balke, admin. Fax 664-8393

---

Central Baptist Christian S 300/PK-12
402 E Windhorst Rd 33510 813-689-6133
Dan Martin, prin. Fax 689-0011
Faith Baptist Christian S 100/K-12
1118 N Parsons Ave 33510 813-654-4936
Southern Technical College Post-Sec.
608 E Bloomingdale Ave 33511 813-654-8800

**Branford, Suwannee, Pop. 686**
Suwannee County SD
Supt. — See Live Oak
Branford HS 700/6-12
405 Reynolds St NE 32008 386-935-5600
Jimmy Wilkerson, prin. Fax 935-3867

**Bristol, Liberty, Pop. 982**
Liberty County SD 1,500/PK-12
PO Box 429 32321 850-643-2275
David Summers, supt. Fax 643-2533
www.lcsbonline.org
Liberty County HS 300/9-12
PO Box 519 32321 850-643-2241
Aaron Day, prin. Fax 643-4153
Liberty County Adult S Adult
PO Box 429 32321 850-643-1016
Terrell Sykes, prin.

**Bronson, Levy, Pop. 1,084**
Levy County SD 5,700/PK-12
PO Box 129 32621 352-486-5231
Robert Hastings, supt. Fax 486-5237
www.levy.k12.fl.us
Bronson MSHS 600/6-12
8691 NE 90th St 32621 352-486-5260
John Lott, prin. Fax 486-5263
Levy Learning Academy 6-12
320 Mongo St 32621 352-486-5388
Dennis Webber, prin.
Other Schools – See Cedar Key, Chiefland, Williston

**Brooksville, Hernando, Pop. 7,591**
Hernando County SD 20,800/PK-12
919 N Broad St 34601 352-797-7000
Dr. Lori Romano Ph.D., supt. Fax 797-7101
www.hernandoschools.org
Central HS 1,400/9-12
14075 Ken Austin Pkwy 34613 352-797-7020
John Stratton, prin. Fax 797-7120
Discovery Academy Alt
14063 Ken Austin Pkwy 34613 352-797-7013
Latressa Jones, prin. Fax 797-7113
Endeavor Academy 50/Alt
14063 Ken Austin Pkwy 34613 352-797-7013
Latressa Jones, prin. Fax 797-7113
Hernando HS 1,400/9-12
700 Bell Ave 34601 352-797-7015
Leechele Booker, prin. Fax 797-7115
Nature Coast Technical HS Vo/Tech
4057 California St 34604 352-797-7088
Tony-Ann Noyes, prin. Fax 797-7188
Parrott MS 800/6-8
19220 Youth Dr 34601 352-797-7075
Brent Gaustad, prin. Fax 797-7175
Powell MS 1,000/6-8
4100 Barclay Ave 34609 352-797-7095
Thomas Dye, prin. Fax 797-7195
West Hernando MS 1,000/6-8
14325 Ken Austin Pkwy 34613 352-797-7035
Lori Lessley, prin. Fax 797-7135
Other Schools – See Spring Hill, Weeki Wachee

---

Hernando Christian Academy 200/PK-12
7200 Emerson Rd 34601 352-796-0616
Ken Alvarez, supt. Fax 799-3400
Pasco-Hernando Community College Post-Sec.
11415 Ponce De Leon Blvd 34601 352-796-6726

**Bunnell, Flagler, Pop. 2,615**
Flagler County SD 12,800/PK-12
PO Box 755 32110 386-437-7526
Jacob Oliva, supt. Fax 586-2351
www.flaglerschools.com
Other Schools – See Palm Coast

**Bushnell, Sumter, Pop. 2,367**
Sumter County SD 7,200/PK-12
2680 W C 476 33513 352-793-2315
Richard Shirley, supt. Fax 793-4180
www.sumter.k12.fl.us
South Sumter HS 1,100/9-12
706 N Main St 33513 352-793-3131
Dr. Preston Morgan, prin. Fax 793-2992
Other Schools – See Sumterville, Webster, Wildwood

**Callahan, Nassau, Pop. 1,111**
Nassau County SD
Supt. — See Fernandina Beach
Callahan MS 800/6-8
450121 Old Dixie Hwy 32011 904-491-7935
Kimberly Harrison, prin. Fax 879-2860
West Nassau County HS 1,000/9-12
1 Warrior Dr 32011 904-491-7942
Curtis Gaus, prin. Fax 879-5843

---

Sonshine Christian Academy 300/PK-12
PO Box 5026 32011 904-879-1260

**Cantonment, Escambia, Pop. 4,500**
Escambia County SD
Supt. — See Pensacola
Ransom MS 1,400/6-8
1000 W Kingsfield Rd 32533 850-937-2220
Brent Brummet, prin. Fax 937-2232
Tate HS 1,900/9-12
1771 Tate Rd 32533 850-937-2300
Rick Shackle, prin. Fax 937-2328

**Cape Coral, Lee, Pop. 151,800**
Lee County SD
Supt. — See Fort Myers
Alternative Learning Center West 100/Alt
380 Santa Barbara Blvd N 33993 239-574-1678
Ken Burns, prin. Fax 574-4751
Baker HS 1,700/9-12
3500 Agualinda Blvd 33914 239-458-6690
Jami Covert, prin. Fax 458-6691
Caloosa MS 900/6-8
610 Del Prado Blvd S 33990 239-574-3232
Dr. Ann Cole, prin. Fax 574-2660
Cape Coral HS 1,500/9-12
2300 Santa Barbara Blvd 33991 239-574-6766
Scott Cook, prin. Fax 574-7799
Cape Coral Technical College Vo/Tech
360 Santa Barbara Blvd N 33993 239-574-4440
Brian Mangan, prin. Fax 458-3721
Challenger MS 1,100/6-8
624 SW Trafalgar Pkwy 33991 239-242-4341
Teri Cannady, prin. Fax 242-7217
Diplomat MS 800/6-8
1039 NE 16th Ter 33909 239-574-5257
Maura Bennington, prin. Fax 574-4008
Gulf MS 800/6-8
1809 SW 36th Ter 33914 239-549-0606
Donnie Hopper, prin. Fax 549-2806
Island Coast HS 1,700/9-12
2125 De Navarra Pkwy 33909 239-458-0362
Kristin Bueno, prin. Fax 772-8405
Mariner HS 1,500/9-12
701 Chiquita Blvd N 33993 239-772-3324
Robert Butz, prin. Fax 772-4880
Mariner MS 900/6-8
425 Chiquita Blvd N 33993 239-772-1848
Rachel Gould, prin. Fax 242-1256
Trafalgar MS 800/6-8
2120 SW Trafalgar Pkwy 33991 239-283-2001
Dr. Michael Galbreath, prin. Fax 283-5620

---

Cape Coral Christian S 100/PK-12
811 Santa Barbara Blvd 33991 239-574-3707
Lee County High Tech Center North Post-Sec.
360 Santa Barbara Blvd N 33993 239-574-4440

**Casselberry, Seminole, Pop. 25,625**
Seminole County SD
Supt. — See Sanford
South Seminole MS 1,200/6-8
101 S Winter Park Dr 32707 407-746-1350
Dr. Mia Coleman-Baker, prin. Fax 746-1420

---

Aviation Institute of Maintenance Post-Sec.
2725 S US Highway 17/92 32707 888-349-5387
Florida Institute of Animal Arts Post-Sec.
493 Semoran Blvd 32707 407-869-7387

**Cedar Key, Levy, Pop. 698**
Levy County SD
Supt. — See Bronson
Cedar Key S 200/PK-12
951 Whiddon Ave 32625 352-543-5223
Darby Allen, prin. Fax 543-5988

**Celebration, Osceola, Pop. 7,281**
Osceola County SD
Supt. — See Kissimmee
Celebration HS 1,900/9-12
1809 Celebration Blvd 34747 321-939-6600
Mytron Lisby, prin. Fax 939-6658

**Century, Escambia, Pop. 1,651**
Escambia County SD
Supt. — See Pensacola
Northview HS 500/9-12
4100 W Highway 4 32535 850-327-6681
Gayle Weaver, prin. Fax 327-6106

**Chiefland, Levy, Pop. 2,173**
Levy County SD
Supt. — See Bronson
Chiefland HS 500/9-12
808 N Main St 32626 352-493-6000
Matt McLelland, prin. Fax 493-6018
Chiefland MS 300/6-8
811 NW 4th Dr 32626 352-493-6025
Matt McLelland, prin. Fax 493-6048
Adult HS Adult
114 Rodgers Blvd 32626 352-493-9533
Fax 493-9994

**Chipley, Washington, Pop. 3,525**
Washington County SD 3,400/PK-12
652 3rd St 32428 850-638-6222
Joseph Taylor, supt. Fax 638-6226
www.wcsdschools.com
Chipley HS 600/9-12
1545 Brickyard Rd 32428 850-638-6100
Kyle Newsom, prin. Fax 638-6017
Roulhac MS 600/5-8
1535 Brickyard Rd 32428 850-638-6170
Nancy Holley, prin. Fax 638-6319
Washington-Holmes Tech Center Vo/Tech
757 Hoyt St 32428 850-638-1180
Martha Compton, dir. Fax 638-6177
Washington Inst for Specialized Educ 50/Alt
680 2nd St 32428 850-638-6020
Sam Cox, lead tchr. Fax 415-5024
Other Schools – See Vernon

---

Washington County Christian S 100/PK-12
1405 Brickyard Rd 32428 850-638-9227
Jason Haddock, admin. Fax 638-9234

**Citra, Marion**
Marion County SD
Supt. — See Ocala
North Marion HS 1,400/9-12
151 W Highway 329 32113 352-671-6010
Ben Whitehouse, prin. Fax 671-6011
North Marion MS 800/6-8
2085 W Highway 329 32113 352-671-6035
John Kerley, prin. Fax 671-6044

**Citrus Springs, Citrus, Pop. 8,462**
Citrus County SD
Supt. — See Inverness
Citrus Springs MS 800/6-8
150 W Citrus Springs Blvd 34434 352-344-2244
David Roland, prin. Fax 249-2111

**Clearwater, Pinellas, Pop. 105,537**
Pinellas County SD
Supt. — See Largo
Bayside HS 400/Alt
14405 49th St N 33762 727-507-4730
Patricia Fuller, prin. Fax 507-4735
Clearwater Fundamental MS 900/6-8
1660 Palmetto St 33755 727-298-1609
Linda Burris, prin. Fax 298-1614
Clearwater HS 2,000/9-12
540 S Hercules Ave 33764 727-298-1620
Keith Mastorides, prin. Fax 469-5981
Clearwater IS 400/Alt
1220 Palmetto St 33755 727-298-1616
Philip Wirth, prin. Fax 469-4189
Countryside HS 2,200/9-12
3000 State Road 580 33761 727-725-7956
Gerald Schlereth, prin. Fax 725-7990
Oak Grove MS 1,200/6-8
1370 S Belcher Rd 33764 727-524-4430
Dr. Dawn Coffin, prin. Fax 524-4416
PTEC Clearwater Vo/Tech
6100 154th Ave N 33760 727-538-7167
Arlene Corbin, dir. Fax 507-4423
Clearwater Adult Education Center Adult
540 S Hercules Ave 33764 727-469-4190
Christy Richards, admin. Fax 469-4193

---

Allendale Academy 800/K-12
2655 Ulmerton Rd Ste 402 33762 727-531-2481
Calvary Christian HS 200/9-12
110 N McMullen Booth Rd 33759 727-449-2247
David Kilgore, head sch Fax 461-5421
Church of Scientology Cadet S 100/6-12
1875 Drew St 33765 727-639-1080
Clearwater Academy International 200/PK-12
801 Drew St 33755 727-446-1722
Clearwater Central Catholic HS 500/9-12
2750 Haines Bayshore Rd 33760 727-531-1449
James Deputy, prin. Fax 535-7034
Clearwater Christian College Post-Sec.
3400 Gulf To Bay Blvd 33759 727-726-1153
Florida Career College Post-Sec.
410 Park Place Blvd 33759 727-724-1037
Iva Christian S 100/K-12
1430 Bellair Rd 33756 727-442-2424
Lakeside Christian S 300/K-12
1897 Sunset Point Rd 33765 727-461-3311
Jim Jensen, head sch Fax 445-1835
National Aviation Academy Post-Sec.
6225 Ulmerton Rd 33760 727-531-2080
Pinellas Technical Education Center Post-Sec.
6100 154th Ave N 33760 727-538-7167
St. Petersburg Theological Seminary Post-Sec.
3190 Gulf to Bay Blvd 33759 727-399-0276
Sunstate Academy Post-Sec.
2525 Drew St 33765 727-538-3827
Ultimate Medical Academy Post-Sec.
1255 Cleveland St 33755 727-298-8685
Washburn Academy 100/PK-12
222 S Lincoln Ave 33756 727-647-1668

**Clermont, Lake, Pop. 27,603**
Lake County SD
Supt. — See Tavares
Clermont MS 700/6-8
301 East Ave 34711 352-243-2460
Steven Benson, prin. Fax 243-1407
East Ridge HS 2,300/9-12
13322 Excalibur Rd 34711 352-242-2080
Julie Robinson-Leuallen, prin. Fax 242-2090
East Ridge MS 1,100/6-8
13201 Excalibur Rd 34711 352-536-8020
Charlie McDaniel, prin. Fax 536-8039
Windy Hill MS 1,200/6-8
3575 Hancock Rd 34711 352-394-2123
William Roberts, prin. Fax 394-7901

---

Family Christian S of Clermont 200/K-12
2500 S Hwy 27 34711 352-241-0323
Real Life Christian Academy 300/PK-12
1501 Steves Rd 34711 352-394-5575
Dr. Steven Long, admin. Fax 394-7860

**Clewiston, Hendry, Pop. 7,087**
Hendry County SD
Supt. — See LaBelle
Clewiston HS 900/9-12
1501 S Francisco St 33440 863-983-1520
George Duckstein, prin. Fax 983-2168
Clewiston MS 700/6-8
601 W Pasadena Ave 33440 863-983-1530
R. Scott Cooper, prin. Fax 983-1541

**Cocoa, Brevard, Pop. 16,719**
Brevard County SD
Supt. — See Melbourne
Cocoa HS 900/7-12
2000 Tiger Trl 32926 321-632-5300
Dr. Stephanie Soliven, prin. Fax 636-1218
Space Coast JSHS 1,700/7-12
6150 Banyan St 32927 321-638-0750
Robert Spinner, prin. Fax 638-0766
Clearlake Education Center Adult
1225 Clearlake Rd 32922 321-633-3660
Jeff Arnott, prin. Fax 633-3488

---

Eastern Florida State College Post-Sec.
1519 Clearlake Rd 32922 321-632-1111
Space Coast Christian Academy 100/PK-12
1950 Michigan Ave 32922 321-636-0883
Chad Perdue, prin. Fax 634-5318

**Cocoa Beach, Brevard, Pop. 11,096**
Brevard County SD
Supt. — See Melbourne
Cocoa Beach JSHS 1,400/7-12
1500 Minutemen Cswy 32931 321-783-1776
Tim Cool, prin. Fax 868-6602

**Coconut Creek, Broward, Pop. 51,291**
Broward County SD
Supt. — See Fort Lauderdale
Atlantic Technical Center HS Vo/Tech
4700 Coconut Creek Pkwy 33063 754-321-5100
Robert Crawford, prin. Fax 321-5380
Coconut Creek HS 1,600/9-12
1400 NW 44th Ave 33066 754-322-0350
Scott Fiske, prin. Fax 322-0480
Lyons Creek MS 1,900/6-8
4333 Sol Press Blvd 33073 754-322-3700
Horace Hamm, prin. Fax 322-3785
Monarch HS 2,100/9-12
5050 Wiles Rd 33073 754-322-1400
James Neer, prin. Fax 322-1530
Thomas Education Center West Alt
4690 Coconut Creek Pkwy 33063 754-321-6800
Tracy Lockhart-Talley, prin. Fax 321-6840

---

Atlantic Technical Center Post-Sec.
4700 Coconut Creek Pkwy 33063 754-321-5100
Broward College Post-Sec.
1000 Coconut Creek Blvd 33066 954-201-2240
North Broward Preparatory S 1,400/PK-12
7600 Lyons Rd 33073 954-247-0179
Elise Ecoff, head sch Fax 247-0012

**Coconut Grove, See Miami**

---

Carrollton S of the Sacred Heart 800/PK-12
3747 Main Hwy 33133 305-446-5673
Olen Kalkus, hdmstr. Fax 592-6533
Ransom Everglades S 1,100/6-12
3575 Main Hwy 33133 305-460-8800
Penny Townsend, head sch Fax 854-1846

**Cooper City, Broward, Pop. 28,003**
Broward County SD
Supt. — See Fort Lauderdale
Cooper City HS 2,300/9-12
9401 Stirling Rd 33328 754-323-0200
Wendy Doll, prin. Fax 323-0330
Pioneer MS 1,400/6-8
5350 SW 90th Ave 33328 754-323-4100
Michael Consaul, prin. Fax 323-4185

---

Cooper City Christian Academy 100/K-12
5201 S Flamingo Rd 33330 954-779-6221
Nur Ul-Islam Academy 300/PK-12
10600 SW 59th St 33328 954-434-3288
Westlake Preparatory S & Academy 100/K-12
8950 Stirling Rd 33024 954-236-2300

**Coral Gables, Miami-Dade, Pop. 46,270**
Miami-Dade County SD
Supt. — See Miami
Carver MS 1,000/6-8
4901 Lincoln Dr 33133 305-444-7388
Shelley Stroleny, prin. Fax 529-5148
Coral Gables HS 3,300/9-12
450 Bird Rd 33146 305-443-4871
Adolfo Costa, prin. Fax 441-8094
De Leon MS 1,200/6-8
5801 Augusto St 33146 305-661-1611
Martha Chang, prin. Fax 666-3140
International Studies Preparatory Acad 100/9-12
1570 Madruga Ave 33146 305-663-7200
Alejandro Perez, prin. Fax 661-0196
Coral Gables Adult Education Center Adult
450 Bird Rd 33146 305-443-4871
Alan Bashaw, prin. Fax 446-2507

---

New Professions Technical Institute Post-Sec.
4000 W Flagler St 33134 305-461-2223
Riviera Day S and Riviera Preparatory S 600/PK-12
6800 Nervia St 33146 305-666-1856
Lawrence Cohen, dir. Fax 661-5437
SABER Post-Sec.
3990 W Flagler St Ste 103 33134 305-443-9170
University of Miami Post-Sec.
PO Box 248006 33124 305-284-2211
University of Southernmost Florida Post-Sec.
2222 Ponce De Leon Ste 500 33134 305-443-9654

**Coral Springs, Broward, Pop. 117,909**
Broward County SD
Supt. — See Fort Lauderdale
Coral Glades HS 2,300/9-12
2700 Sportsplex Dr 33065 754-322-1250
Steven Carruth, prin. Fax 322-1380
Coral Springs HS 2,500/9-12
7201 W Sample Rd 33065 754-322-0500
Susan Leon, prin. Fax 322-0630
Coral Springs MS 1,600/6-8
10300 Wiles Rd 33076 754-322-3000
Ian Murray, prin. Fax 322-3085
Forest Glen MS 1,500/6-8
6501 Turtle Run Blvd 33067 754-322-3400
Ronald Foresman, prin. Fax 322-3485
Ramblewood MS 1,500/6-8
8505 W Atlantic Blvd 33071 754-322-4300
Cory Smith, prin. Fax 322-4385
Sawgrass Springs MS 1,300/6-8
12500 W Sample Rd 33065 754-322-4500
James Cecil, prin. Fax 322-4585
Taravella HS 3,000/9-12
10600 Riverside Dr 33071 754-322-2300
Shawn Cerra, prin. Fax 322-2430

---

Coral Springs Christian Academy 900/PK-12
2251 Riverside Dr 33065 954-755-3217
Joseph E. Sanelli, head sch Fax 346-1112
Florida Medical Training Institute Post-Sec.
7451 Wiles Rd Ste 105 33067 954-752-1414
Mesivta of Coral Springs 9-12
1730 N University Dr 33071 954-464-0416
Rabbi Yosef Eizicovics, prin. Fax 208-0788
Phyl's Academy Preparatory S 50/7-12
11411 NW 56th Dr 33076 954-731-7524

**Cottondale, Jackson, Pop. 899**
Jackson County SD
Supt. — See Marianna
Cottondale JSHS 500/6-12
2680 Levy St 32431 850-482-9821
Ken Granger, prin. Fax 482-9827

**Crawfordville, Wakulla, Pop. 3,618**
Wakulla County SD 4,800/PK-12
PO Box 100 32326 850-926-0065
Robert Pearce, supt. Fax 926-0123
wakulla.schooldesk.net
Riversprings MS 500/6-8
800 Spring Creek Hwy 32327 850-926-2300
Michele Yeomans, prin. Fax 926-2111
Wakulla County HS 1,200/9-12
3237 Coastal Hwy 32327 850-926-7125
Michael Barwick, prin. Fax 926-8571
Wakulla MS 600/6-8
22 Jean Dr 32327 850-926-7143
Richard Myhre, prin. Fax 926-3752

**Crescent City, Putnam, Pop. 1,539**
Putnam County SD
Supt. — See Palatka
Crescent City JSHS 900/7-12
2201 S US Highway 17 32112 386-698-1629
Mechele Higginbotham, prin. Fax 698-3073

**Crestview, Okaloosa, Pop. 20,112**
Okaloosa County SD
Supt. — See Fort Walton Beach
Crestview HS 1,900/9-12
1250 N Ferdon Blvd 32536 850-689-7177
Dexter Day, prin. Fax 689-7332
Davidson MS 900/6-8
6261 Old Bethel Rd 32536 850-683-7500
Jay Sanders, prin. Fax 683-7523
Shoal River MS 900/6-8
3200 E Redstone Ave 32539 850-689-7229
Cheree Davis, prin. Fax 689-7245

**Cross City, Dixie, Pop. 1,699**
Dixie County SD 2,000/PK-12
16077 NE Highway 19 32628 352-498-6131
Mark Rains, supt. Fax 498-1308
www.dixie.k12.fl.us/
Dixie County HS 500/9-12
16077 SE Highway 19 32628 352-498-6410
Jerry Evans, prin. Fax 498-1287
Rains MS 400/6-8
981 SE Highway 351 32628 352-498-1346
Alexa Mills, prin. Fax 498-1283
Other Schools – See Old Town

**Crystal River, Citrus, Pop. 3,056**
Citrus County SD
Supt. — See Inverness
Crystal River HS 1,200/9-12
3195 Crystal River High Dr 34428 352-795-4641
Dr. Linda Connors, prin. Fax 249-2106
Crystal River MS 800/6-8
344 NE Crystal St 34428 352-795-2116
Gloria Bishop, prin. Fax 249-2108

**Cutler Bay, Miami-Dade, Pop. 39,453**
Miami-Dade County SD
Supt. — See Miami
Cutler Bay HS 900/9-12
8601 SW 212th St, 305-235-1581
Lucas DelaTorre, prin. Fax 234-8071
Cutler Bay MS 700/6-8
19400 Gulfstream Rd, 305-235-4761
Paul Pfeiffer, prin. Fax 254-3746

College of Business & Technology Post-Sec.
19151 S Dixie Hwy, 305-764-3165
Fortis College Post-Sec.
19600 S Dixie Hwy Ste B, 786-345-5300

**Dade City, Pasco, Pop. 6,339**
Pasco County SD
Supt. — See Land O Lakes
Centennial MS 700/6-8
38505 Centennial Rd 33525 352-524-9700
Rick Saylor, prin. Fax 524-9791
Irvin Education Center 100/Alt
35830 State Road 52 33525 352-524-5700
Nancy Guss, prin. Fax 524-5791
Pasco HS 1,400/9-12
36850 State Road 52 33525 352-524-5500
Kari Kadluv, prin. Fax 524-5591
Pasco MS 900/6-8
13925 14th St 33525 352-524-8400
Jeffrey Wolff, prin. Fax 524-8491
Moore-Mickens Education Center Adult
38301 Martin Luther King Bl 33525 352-524-9000
Nancy Guss, prin. Fax 524-9091

East Pasco Adventist Academy 100/PK-10
38434 Centennial Rd 33525 352-567-3646
Pasco-Hernando Community College Post-Sec.
36727 Blanton Rd 33523 352-567-6701

**Dania Beach, Broward, Pop. 29,112**
Broward County SD
Supt. — See Fort Lauderdale
Olsen MS 1,100/6-8
330 SE 11th Ter 33004 754-323-3800
Valerie Harris, prin. Fax 323-3885

Key College Post-Sec.
225 E Dania Beach Blvd 33004 800-581-8292

**Davenport, Polk, Pop. 2,854**
Polk County SD
Supt. — See Bartow
Davenport Community Campus Alt
8 W Palmetto St 33837 863-419-3486
Fax 419-3491
Ridge Community HS 2,200/9-12
500 Orchid Dr 33837 863-419-3315
Russell Donnelly, prin. Fax 419-3321

Ridge Christian Academy 200/PK-12
41219 Highway 27 33837 863-420-2885

**Davie, Broward, Pop. 90,050**
Broward County SD
Supt. — See Fort Lauderdale
College Academy 300/11-12
3501 Davie Rd 33314 754-321-6900
Deborah Davey, prin. Fax 321-6940
Indian Ridge MS 2,000/6-8
1355 S Nob Hill Rd 33324 754-323-3300
Frank Zagari, prin. Fax 323-3385
McFatter Technical HS Vo/Tech
6500 Nova Dr 33317 754-321-5700
Jeanette Johnson, prin. Fax 321-5980
Nova HS 2,200/9-12
3600 College Ave 33314 754-323-1650
John LaCasse, prin. Fax 323-1780
Nova MS 1,200/6-8
3602 College Ave 33314 754-323-3700
Jermaine Fleming, prin. Fax 323-3785
Western HS 3,000/9-12
1200 SW 136th Ave 33325 754-323-2400
Jimmy Arrojo, prin. Fax 323-2530

American Preparatory Academy 100/K-12
4850 S Pine Island Rd 33328 954-434-8936
ASM Beauty World Academy Post-Sec.
6423 Stirling Rd 33314 954-321-8411
Broward College Post-Sec.
3501 Davie Rd 33314 954-201-6800
Nova Southeastern University Post-Sec.
3301 College Ave 33314 954-262-7300
Posnack Jewish Day S 500/K-12
5810 S Pine Island Rd 33328 954-583-6100
Trinity International University Post-Sec.
8190 W State Road 84 33324 954-382-6400

**Daytona Beach, Volusia, Pop. 59,727**
Volusia County SD
Supt. — See De Land
Campbell MS, 625 S Keech St 32114 1,000/6-8
Kelly Lewis, prin. 386-258-4661
Hinson MS 1,000/6-8
1860 N Clyde Morris Blvd 32117 386-258-4682
Robert Ouellette, prin. Fax 506-5064
Mainland HS 1,700/9-12
1255 W Intl Speedway Blvd 32114 386-258-4665
Dr. Cheryl Salerno, prin. Fax 506-5069
Riverview Learning Center 50/Alt
801 N Wild Olive Ave 32118 386-258-4673
Kevin Tucker, prin. Fax 239-6218
Seabreeze HS 1,700/9-12
2700 N Oleander Ave 32118 386-258-4674
Joseph Rawlings, prin. Fax 506-5071

Bethune-Cookman University Post-Sec.
640 Dr Mary Mcleod Bthn Blvd 32114 386-481-2000
Daytona State College Post-Sec.
PO Box 2811 32120 386-506-3000
Embry-Riddle Aeronautical University Post-Sec.
600 S Clyde Morris Blvd 32114 800-222-3728
Embry-Riddle Aeronautical Univ-Worldwide Post-Sec.
600 S Clyde Morris Blvd 32114 800-522-6787
Father Lopez HS 300/9-12
3918 LPGA Blvd 32124 386-253-5213
Lee Sayago, prin. Fax 252-6101
Halifax Academy 100/4-12
275 N Williamson Blvd 32114 386-252-9557
Halifax Medical Center Post-Sec.
PO Box 2830 32120 386-254-4065
Keiser University Post-Sec.
1800 Business Park Blvd 32114 386-274-5060
Phoenix East Aviation Post-Sec.
561 Pearl Harbor Dr 32114 386-258-0703

**De Bary, Volusia, Pop. 19,046**
Volusia County SD
Supt. — See De Land
Highbanks Learning Center 50/Alt
336 E Highbanks Rd 32713 386-968-0039
Kevin Tucker, prin.

**Deerfield Beach, Broward, Pop. 72,542**
Broward County SD
Supt. — See Fort Lauderdale
Deerfield Beach HS 2,500/9-12
910 SW 15th St 33441 754-322-0650
Jon Marlow, prin. Fax 322-0780
Deerfield Beach MS 1,200/6-8
701 SE 6th Ave 33441 754-322-3300
Francine Baugh, prin. Fax 322-3385

ITT Technical Institute Post-Sec.
700 W Hillsboro Blvd 33441 954-360-4701
South Florida Bible College Post-Sec.
1100 S Federal Hwy 33441 954-545-4500
Zion Lutheran Christian S 500/PK-12
959 SE 6th Ave 33441 954-421-3146
Joann Halem, prin. Fax 421-4250

**De Funiak Springs, Walton, Pop. 5,054**
Walton County SD 7,500/PK-12
145 S Park St Ste 2 32435 850-892-1100
Carlene Anderson, supt. Fax 892-1191
www.walton.k12.fl.us
Emerald Coast Technical College Vo/Tech
761 N 20th St 32433 850-892-1240
Mike Davis, dir. Fax 892-1249
Walton HS 800/9-12
449 Walton Rd 32433 850-892-1270
Russell Hughes, prin. Fax 892-1279
Walton Learning Center Alt
286 Gene Hurley Rd 32435 850-892-1100
Alexis Tibbetts, prin. Fax 892-8584
Walton MS 600/6-8
555 Walton Rd 32433 850-892-1281
Jason Campbell, prin. Fax 892-1289
Other Schools – See Freeport, Paxton, Santa Rosa Beach

**De Land, Volusia, Pop. 26,549**
Volusia County SD 56,300/PK-12
PO Box 2118 32721 386-734-7190
James Russell, supt. Fax 822-6790
myvolusiaschools.org
DeLand HS 2,500/9-12
800 N Hill Ave 32724 386-822-6909
Mitch Moyer, prin. Fax 626-0556
DeLand MS 1,100/6-8
1400 Aquarius Ave 32724 386-822-5678
William Dunnigan, prin. Fax 822-6583
Southwestern MS 700/6-8
605 W New Hampshire Ave 32720 386-822-6815
Mamie Oatis, prin. Fax 822-6708
Other Schools – See Daytona Beach, De Bary, Deltona, New Smyrna Beach, Orange City, Ormond Beach, Pierson, Port Orange

Florida Technical College Post-Sec.
1199 S Woodland Blvd 32720 386-734-3303
Lighthouse Christian Academy 200/PK-12
126 S Ridgewood Ave 32720 386-734-5380
Stetson University Post-Sec.
421 N Woodland Blvd 32723 386-822-7000

**Delray Beach, Palm Beach, Pop. 59,547**
Palm Beach County SD
Supt. — See West Palm Beach
Atlantic Community HS 2,200/9-12
2455 W Atlantic Ave 33445 561-243-1500
Tara Ocampo, prin. Fax 243-1532
Carver Community MS 900/6-8
101 Barwick Rd 33445 561-638-2100
Kiwana Prophete, prin. Fax 638-2181
Village Academy 800/K-12
400 SW 12th Ave 33444 561-243-6100
Latoya Dixon, prin. Fax 243-6150

American Heritage S Boca Delray 1,200/PK-12
6200 Linton Blvd 33484 561-495-7272
Cambridge Institute Allied Health/Tech Post-Sec.
5150 Linton Blvd Ste 340 33484 561-381-4990

**Deltona, Volusia, Pop. 83,518**
Volusia County SD
Supt. — See De Land
Deltona HS 1,700/9-12
100 Wolf Pack Run 32725 386-575-4153
Carolyn Carbonell, prin. Fax 968-0014
Deltona MS 1,200/6-8
250 Enterprise Rd 32725 386-575-4150
Dr. Rick Inge, prin. Fax 968-0015
Galaxy MS 1,100/6-8
2400 Eustace Ave 32725 386-575-4144
Patricia Corr, prin. Fax 968-0016
Heritage MS 1,200/6-8
1001 Parnell Ct 32738 386-575-4113
Thomas Vaughan, prin. Fax 708-0020
Pine Ridge HS 1,800/9-12
926 Howland Blvd 32738 386-575-4195
John Atkinson, prin. Fax 688-9502

Deltona Christian S 200/PK-12
1200 Providence Blvd 32725 386-574-1971
Trinity Christian Academy 600/PK-12
875 Elkcam Blvd 32725 386-789-4515
Dr. Dennis Robinson, hdmstr. Fax 789-0210

**Destin, Okaloosa, Pop. 11,900**
Okaloosa County SD
Supt. — See Fort Walton Beach
Destin MS 600/5-8
4608 Legendary Marina Dr 32541 850-833-7655
Charlie Marello, prin. Fax 833-7677

**Doral, Miami-Dade, Pop. 45,331**
Miami-Dade County SD
Supt. — See Miami
Reagan/Doral HS 2,300/9-12
8600 NW 107th Ave, 305-805-1900
Juan Silva, prin. Fax 805-1901

Divine Savior Lutheran Academy 400/PK-12
10311 NW 58th St, 305-597-4545
Benjamin Troge, head sch Fax 597-4077
Miami-Dade College Post-Sec.
3800 NW 115th Ave, 305-237-8000
Millenia Atlantic University Post-Sec.
3801 NW 97th Ave, 786-331-1000
Polytechnic University of Puerto Rico Post-Sec.
8180 NW 36th St Ste 401, 305-418-4220
San Ignacio College Post-Sec.
10395 NW 41st St Ste 125, 305-629-2929

**Dover, Hillsborough, Pop. 3,664**
Hillsborough County SD
Supt. — See Tampa
Strawberry Crest HS 2,000/9-12
4691 Gallagher Rd 33527 813-707-7522
David Brown, prin. Fax 707-7526

**Dundee, Polk, Pop. 3,628**
Polk County SD
Supt. — See Bartow
Dundee Ridge Middle Academy 900/6-8
5555 Lake Trask Rd 33838 863-419-3088
Stacy Gideons, prin. Fax 419-3157
Woods Opportunity Center 100/Alt
213 Lake Ave 33838 863-421-3325
Rodney Bellamy, prin. Fax 421-3390

**Dunedin, Pinellas, Pop. 34,705**
Pinellas County SD
Supt. — See Largo
Dunedin Highland MS 1,200/6-8
70 Patricia Ave 34698 727-469-4112
Chris Bates, prin. Fax 469-4115
Dunedin HS 1,400/9-12
1651 Pinehurst Rd 34698 727-469-4100
Kyle Johnson, prin. Fax 469-4143

Cornerstone Christian S 100/PK-12
317 Milwaukee Ave 34698 727-733-1438

**Dunnellon, Marion, Pop. 1,711**
Marion County SD
Supt. — See Ocala
Dunnellon HS 1,200/9-12
10055 SW 180th Avenue Rd 34432 352-465-6745
Ken McAteer, prin. Fax 465-6746
Dunnellon MS 700/6-8
21005 Chestnut St 34431 352-465-6720
Delbert Smallridge, prin. Fax 465-6721

Dunnellon Christian Academy 200/PK-12
20831 Powell Rd 34431 352-489-7716
Kristy Nelson, admin. Fax 489-5760

**Eagle Lake, Polk, Pop. 2,207**
Polk County SD
Supt. — See Bartow
Lake Region HS 1,900/9-12
1995 Thunder Rd 33839 863-297-3099
Deborah Kindel, prin. Fax 297-3097

Bethel's Christian Academy 50/PK-10
75 Don Polston Dr 33839 863-875-5572
Dr. Frank O'Harroll, prin. Fax 875-5574

**Eastpoint, Franklin, Pop. 2,298**
Franklin County SD 1,300/K-12
85 School Rd Ste 1 32328 850-670-2810
Nina Marks, supt. Fax 670-2859
www.franklincountyschools.org/
Franklin County S 900/K-12
1250 US Highway 98 32328 850-670-2800
Kris Bray, prin. Fax 670-2801
Franklin County Adult S Adult
85 School Rd Ste 1 32328 850-670-2810
Nick O'Grady, dir. Fax 670-2859

**El Portal, Miami-Dade, Pop. 2,243**
Miami-Dade County SD
Supt. — See Miami
Academy for Community Education 100/Alt
8950 NW 2nd Ave 33150 305-460-2946
Dr. Deborah Carter, prin. Fax 460-2944

**Englewood, Sarasota, Pop. 14,723**
Charlotte County SD
Supt. — See Port Charlotte
Lemon Bay HS 1,300/9-12
2201 Placida Rd 34224 941-474-7702
Bob Bedford, prin. Fax 475-5260

**Estero, Lee, Pop. 22,447**
Lee County SD
Supt. — See Fort Myers
Estero HS 1,500/9-12
21900 River Ranch Rd 33928 239-947-9400
Clayton Simmons, prin. Fax 947-5017

**Eustis, Lake, Pop. 18,227**
Lake County SD
Supt. — See Tavares
Eustis HS - Curtright Campus 400/9-9
1801 Bates Ave 32726 352-589-1510
Nancy Velez, prin. Fax 589-1605
Eustis MS 1,000/6-8
18725 Bates Ave 32736 352-357-3366
Johnathan Owens, prin. Fax 357-5963
Eustis SHS 900/10-12
1300 E Washington Ave 32726 352-357-4147
Nancy Velez, prin. Fax 357-7449

---

Lake Technical Center Post-Sec.
2001 Kurt St 32726 352-589-2250

**Everglades City, Collier**
Collier County SD
Supt. — See Naples
Everglades City S 200/PK-12
PO Box 170 34139 239-377-9800
James Ragusa, prin. Fax 377-9801

**Fernandina Beach, Nassau, Pop. 11,315**
Nassau County SD 11,100/PK-12
1201 Atlantic Ave 32034 904-491-9900
Dr. John Ruis, supt. Fax 277-9042
www.nassau.k12.fl.us
Fernandina Beach HS 900/9-12
435 Citrona Dr 32034 904-491-7937
Dr. Spencer Lodree, prin. Fax 277-3754
Fernandina Beach MS 700/6-8
315 Citrona Dr 32034 904-491-7938
Dr. John Mazzella, prin. Fax 261-8919
Nassau County Adult S Adult
1201 Atlantic Ave 32034 904-491-9899
Brent Lemond, prin. Fax 548-4499
Other Schools – See Callahan, Hilliard, Yulee

**Fern Park, Seminole, Pop. 7,563**

---

Lincoln Tech Fern Park Campus Post-Sec.
7275 Estapona Cir 32730 407-673-7406

**Florahome, Putnam**
Putnam County SD
Supt. — See Palatka
Roberts JSHS 200/7-12
901 State Road 100 32140 386-659-1737
Dr. Melissa Coleman, prin. Fax 659-1986

**Fort Lauderdale, Broward, Pop. 162,648**
Broward County SD 245,200/PK-12
600 SE 3rd Ave 33301 754-321-0000
Robert Runcie, supt. Fax 321-2701
www.browardschools.com
Atlantic Technical Center - A Ashe Camps Vo/Tech
1701 NW 23rd Ave 33311 754-322-2800
Robert Crawford, prin. Fax 322-2880
Dandy MS 900/6-8
2400 NW 26th St 33311 754-322-3200
Shernette Grant, prin. Fax 322-3285
Dillard MSHS 1,700/6-12
2501 NW 11th St 33311 754-322-0800
Cassandra Robinson, prin. Fax 322-0930
Fort Lauderdale HS 1,800/9-12
1600 NE 4th Ave 33305 754-322-1100
Priscilla Ribeiro, prin. Fax 322-1230
New River MS 1,300/6-8
3100 Riverland Rd 33312 754-323-3600
Melinda Wessinger, prin. Fax 323-3685
Pine Ridge Education Center 100/Alt
1251 SW 42nd Ave 33317 754-321-7250
Belinda Hope, prin. Fax 321-7290
Stranahan HS 1,800/9-12
1800 SW 5th Pl 33312 754-323-2100
Deborah Owens, prin. Fax 323-2230
Sunrise MS 1,100/6-8
1750 NE 14th St 33304 754-322-4700
Michael Walker, prin. Fax 322-4785
Whiddon-Rodgers Education Center 600/Alt
700 SW 26th St 33315 754-321-7550
Wylie Howard, prin. Fax 321-7590
Other Schools – See Coconut Creek, Cooper City, Coral Springs, Dania Beach, Davie, Deerfield Beach, Hallandale Beach, Hollywood, Lauderdale Lakes, Lauderhill, Margate, Miramar, North Lauderdale, Oakland Park, Parkland, Pembroke Pines, Plantation, Pompano Beach, Sunrise, Tamarac, Weston

---

Alternative Education Foundation Prep S 200/PK-12
4650 SW 61st Ave 33314 954-581-8222
Archbishop Edward McCarthy HS 1,500/9-12
5451 S Flamingo Rd 33330 954-434-8820
Richard Jean, prin. Fax 680-4835
Art Institute of Fort Lauderdale Post-Sec.
1799 SE 17th St 33316 954-463-3000
Atlantic Institute of Oriental Medicine Post-Sec.
100 E Broward Blvd Ste 100 33301 954-763-9840
Calvary Christian Academy 1,700/PK-12
2401 W Cypress Creek Rd 33309 954-905-5100
Chapin Marsh, supt. Fax 653-2991
Cardinal Gibbons HS 1,100/9-12
2900 NE 47th St 33308 954-491-2900
Paul Ott, prin. Fax 772-1025
City College Post-Sec.
2000 W Commercial Blvd #200 33309 954-492-5353
Coral Ridge Training School Post-Sec.
2121 W Oakland Park Blvd 33311 954-714-0061
DeVry University Post-Sec.
600 Corporate Dr Ste 200 33334 954-938-3083
Fortis College Post-Sec.
4850 W Oakland Park Ste 200 33313 954-587-7100
Fort Lauderdale Preparatory S 200/PK-12
3275 W Oakland Park Blvd 33311 954-485-7500
ITT Technical Institute Post-Sec.
3401 S University Dr 33328 954-476-9300
Keiser University Post-Sec.
1500 NW 49th St 33309 954-776-4456
Knox Theological Seminary Post-Sec.
5554 N Federal Hwy 33308 954-771-0376
NSU University S 1,900/PK-12
3375 SW 75th Ave 33314 954-262-4506
Dr. William Kopas, head sch
Pine Crest S 2,700/PK-12
1501 NE 62nd St 33334 954-492-4100
Dr. Dana Markham, pres. Fax 492-4177
St. Thomas Aquinas HS 2,200/9-12
2801 SW 12th St 33312 954-581-0700
Denise Aloma, prin. Fax 581-8263
Sanford-Brown College Post-Sec.
1201 W Cypress Creek Rd 33309 954-308-7400
Strayer University Post-Sec.
2307 W Broward Blvd Ste 100 33312 954-745-6960
Westminster Academy 900/PK-12
5601 N Federal Hwy 33308 954-771-4600

**Fort Meade, Polk, Pop. 5,552**
Polk County SD
Supt. — See Bartow
Fort Meade MSHS 700/6-12
700 Edgewood Dr N 33841 863-285-1180
Amy Hardee, prin. Fax 285-1186

**Fort Myers, Lee, Pop. 60,807**
Lee County SD 79,900/PK-12
2855 Colonial Blvd 33966 239-337-8300
Gregory Adkins Ed.D., supt. Fax 337-8301
www.leeschools.net
Alternative Learning Center Central 100/Alt
3650 Michigan Ave 33916 239-334-3416
Ken Burns, prin. Fax 332-7772
Cypress Lake HS 1,500/9-12
6750 Panther Ln 33919 239-481-2233
Angela Roles, prin. Fax 481-9838
Cypress Lake MS 700/6-8
8901 Cypress Lake Dr 33919 239-481-1533
Kelly Maniscalco, prin. Fax 481-3121
Dunbar HS 1,000/9-12
3800 Edison Ave 33916 239-461-5322
Carl Burnside, prin. Fax 461-5110
Dunbar MS 900/6-8
4750 Winkler Avenue Ext, 239-334-1357
Dr. Nathan Shaker, prin. Fax 334-7633
Fort Myers HS 1,800/9-12
2635 Cortez Blvd 33901 239-334-2167
David LaRosa, prin. Fax 334-3095
Fort Myers Middle Academy 600/6-8
3050 Central Ave 33901 239-936-1759
Ron Schuyler, prin. Fax 936-4350
Fort Myers Technical College Vo/Tech
3800 Michigan Ave 33916 239-334-4544
William McCormick, prin. Fax 332-4839
Lexington MS 900/6-8
16351 Summerlin Rd 33908 239-454-6130
Linda Caprarotta, prin. Fax 489-3419
Oak Hammock MS 1,300/6-8
5321 Tice St 33905 239-693-0469
Jennifer Sneddon, prin. Fax 694-4089
Riverdale HS 1,800/6-12
2600 Buckingham Rd 33905 239-694-4141
Gerald Demming, prin. Fax 694-3527
South Fort Myers HS 1,800/9-12
14020 Plantation Rd 33912 239-561-0060
Melissa Layner, prin. Fax 561-3612
Southwest Florida Public Service Academy Vo/Tech
4312 Michigan Ave 33905 239-334-3897
Todd Everly, prin. Fax 334-8794
Three Oaks MS 900/6-8
18500 3 Oaks Pkwy, 239-267-5757
Mike Carson, prin. Fax 267-4007
Adult & Community Education Adult
2855 Colonial Blvd, 239-939-6310
Rita Effing, dir. Fax 334-4568
Dunbar Community S Adult
1857 High St 33916 239-334-2941
Herman Williams, admin. Fax 334-3519
Other Schools – See Bonita Springs, Cape Coral, Estero, Lehigh Acres, North Fort Myers

---

Bishop Verot Catholic HS 600/9-12
5598 Sunrise Dr 33919 239-274-6700
Dr. Denny Denison, prin. Fax 274-6798
Canterbury S 600/PK-12
8141 College Pkwy 33919 239-481-4323
John Anthony Paulus, head sch Fax 481-8339
Crestwell S 200/PK-10
1901 Park Meadows Dr 33907 239-481-4478
Edison State College Post-Sec.
8099 College Pkwy 33919 239-489-9300
Evangelical Christian S 800/PK-12
8237 Beacon Blvd 33907 239-936-3319
Florida Gulf Coast University Post-Sec.
10501 FGCU Blvd 33965 239-590-1000
Fort Myers Institute of Technology Post-Sec.
3800 Michigan Ave 33916 239-334-4544
Heritage Institute Post-Sec.
6630 Orion Dr Ste 200 33912 239-936-5822
ITT Technical Institute Post-Sec.
13500 Powers Ct Ste 100 33912 239-603-8700
Keiser University Post-Sec.
9100 Forum Corporate Pkwy 33905 239-277-1336
Rasmussen College Post-Sec.
9160 Forum Corporate # 100 33905 239-477-2100
Sonshine Christian Academy 200/PK-12
12925 Palm Beach Blvd 33905 239-694-8882
Southwest Florida Christian Academy 500/K-12
3750 Colonial Blvd, 239-936-8865
Lisa Kleinmann, hdmstr. Fax 936-7095
Southwest Florida College Post-Sec.
1685 Medical Ln 33907 239-939-4766
Sunstate Academy Post-Sec.
2040 Colonial Blvd 33907 239-278-1311

**Fort Pierce, Saint Lucie, Pop. 40,874**
St. Lucie County SD 39,500/PK-12
4204 Okeechobee Rd 34947 772-429-3600
E. Wayne Gent, supt. Fax 429-3916
www.stlucieschools.org
Forest Grove MS 700/6-8
3201 S 25th St 34981 772-468-5885
Terrance Davis, prin. Fax 595-1187
Fort Pierce Central HS 2,300/9-12
4101 S 25th St 34981 772-468-5888
Todd Smith, prin. Fax 468-5761
Fort Pierce Westwood HS 1,200/9-12
1801 Panther Ln 34947 772-468-5400
John Lynch, prin. Fax 468-5465
Lincoln Park Academy 1,800/6-12
1806 Avenue I 34950 772-468-5474
Henry Sanabria, prin. Fax 468-5485
McCarty MS 600/6-8
1201 Mississippi Ave 34950 772-468-5700
Felicia Nixon, prin. Fax 468-5737
Performance Based Preparatory Academy Alt
2909 Delaware Ave 34950 772-468-5880
Letty Richardson, admin. Fax 468-5795
Other Schools – See Port Saint Lucie

---

Aviator College of Aeronautical Sci/Tech Post-Sec.
3800 Saint Lucie Blvd 34946 800-635-9032
Fort Pierce Beauty Academy Post-Sec.
3028 S US 1 34982 772-464-4885
Indian River State College Post-Sec.
3209 Virginia Ave 34981 772-462-4772
John Carroll HS 400/9-12
3402 Delaware Ave 34947 772-464-5200
Ben Hopper, prin. Fax 464-5233
Liberty Baptist Academy 500/PK-12
3660 W Midway Rd 34981 772-461-2731
St. Andrew's Episcopal Academy 200/PK-12
210 S Indian River Dr 34950 772-461-7689
Trina Angelone, head sch Fax 461-4683

**Fort Walton Beach, Okaloosa, Pop. 18,836**
Okaloosa County SD 28,900/PK-12
120 Lowery Pl SE 32548 850-833-3100
Mary Beth Jackson, supt. Fax 833-3436
www.okaloosaschools.com
Bruner MS 800/6-8
322 Holmes Blvd NW 32548 850-833-3266
Dr. Cynthia Hudson, prin. Fax 833-3434
Choctawhatchee HS 1,700/9-12
110 Racetrack Rd NW 32547 850-833-3614
Cindy Gates, prin. Fax 833-3410
CHOICE HS & Technical Center Vo/Tech
1976 Lewis Turner Blvd 32547 850-833-3500
Jerry Sansom, prin. Fax 833-3466
Fort Walton Beach HS 1,800/9-12
400 Hollywood Blvd SW 32548 850-833-3300
John Spolski, prin. Fax 833-3311
Pryor MS 600/6-8
201 Racetrack Rd NW 32547 850-833-3613
Grant Meyer, prin. Fax 833-4276
Other Schools – See Baker, Crestview, Destin, Laurel Hill, Niceville, Shalimar, Valparaiso

---

Calvary Christian Academy 200/PK-12
535 Clifford St 32547 850-862-1414
John Policastro, admin. Fax 862-9826

**Fort White, Columbia, Pop. 554**
Columbia County SD
Supt. — See Lake City
Fort White HS 1,200/6-12
17828 SW State Road 47 32038 386-497-5952
Keith Couey, prin. Fax 497-5951

**Freeport, Walton, Pop. 1,743**
Walton County SD
Supt. — See De Funiak Springs
Freeport HS 300/9-12
12615 331 Business 32439 850-892-1200
Tripp Hope, prin. Fax 892-1209
Freeport MS 400/5-8
360 Kylea Laird Dr 32439 850-892-1221
Charlie Morse, prin. Fax 892-1229

**Frostproof, Polk, Pop. 2,965**
Polk County SD
Supt. — See Bartow
Frostproof MSHS 1,100/6-12
1000 N Palm Ave 33843 863-635-7809
Kyle Windham, prin. Fax 635-7812

**Fruitland Park, Lake, Pop. 3,984**

Holy Trinity Episcopal S 50/6-12
2201 Spring Lake Rd 34731 352-787-8855
Dr. Nancy Bryson Ed.D., head sch Fax 787-8063

**Gainesville, Alachua, Pop. 121,031**
Alachua County SD 26,200/PK-12
620 E University Ave 32601 352-955-7300
Dr. Owen Roberts, supt. Fax 955-6700
www.sbac.edu
Bishop MS 700/6-8
1901 NE 9th St 32609 352-955-6701
Mike Gamble, prin. Fax 955-6966
Buchholz HS 2,100/9-12
5510 NW 27th Ave 32606 352-955-6702
Vincente Perez, prin. Fax 955-7285
Eastside HS 1,300/9-12
1201 SE 43rd St 32641 352-955-6704
Jeff Charbonnet, prin. Fax 955-7291
Ft. Clarke MS 900/6-8
9301 NW 23rd Ave 32606 352-333-2800
Donna Kidwell, prin. Fax 333-2806
Gainesville HS 1,800/9-12
1900 NW 13th St 32609 352-955-6707
David Shelnutt, prin. Fax 955-7283
Kanapaha MS 900/6-8
5005 SW 75th St 32608 352-955-6960
Sherry Estes, prin. Fax 955-6858
Lincoln MS 700/6-8
1001 SE 12th St 32641 352-955-6711
Don Lewis, prin. Fax 955-7133
Professional Academies Magnet at Loften Vo/Tech
3000 E University Ave 32641 352-955-6839
Bill McElroy, prin. Fax 955-6999
Westwood MS 1,000/6-8
3215 NW 15th Ave 32605 352-955-6718
James Tenbieg, prin. Fax 955-6897
Other Schools – See Alachua, Hawthorne, Newberry

Academy for Five Element Acupuncture Post-Sec.
305 SE 2nd Ave 32601 352-335-2332
City College Post-Sec.
7001 NW 4th Blvd 32607 352-335-4000
Cornerstone Academy 200/PK-12
PO Box 357430 32635 352-378-9337
Doug Lawson, hdmstr. Fax 378-7708
Countryside Christian S 100/PK-12
10926 NW 39th Ave 32606 352-332-1493
Dragon Rises College Oriental Medicine Post-Sec.
1000 NE 16th Ave Bldg F 32601 352-371-2833
Florida School of Massage Post-Sec.
6421 SW 13th St 32608 352-378-7891
Oak Hall Upper S 400/6-12
8009 SW 14th Ave 32607 352-332-3609
Richard Gehman, hdmstr. Fax 332-4975
Rock S 300/PK-12
9818 SW 24th Ave 32607 352-331-7625
St. Francis HS 200/9-12
4100 NW 115th Ter 32606 352-376-6545
Ernest Herrington, prin. Fax 248-0418
Santa Fe College Post-Sec.
3000 NW 83rd St 32606 352-395-5000
Sung SDA S 50/K-12
2115 NW 39th Ave 32605 352-376-6040
University of Florida Post-Sec.
PO Box 114000 32611 352-392-3261

**Gibsonton, Hillsborough, Pop. 13,940**
Hillsborough County SD
Supt. — See Tampa
East Bay HS 2,000/9-12
7710 Old Big Bend Rd 33534 813-671-5134
Maria Gsell, prin. Fax 671-5139
Eisenhower MS 1,400/6-8
7620 Old Big Bend Rd 33534 813-671-5121
Darrell Faver, prin. Fax 671-5039

**Glen Saint Mary, Baker, Pop. 430**
Baker County SD
Supt. — See Macclenny
Baker County HS 1,300/9-12
1 Wildcat Dr 32040 904-259-6286
Allen Murphy, prin. Fax 259-5617

**Gotha, Orange, Pop. 1,873**

Central Florida Preparatory S 200/PK-12
1450 Citrus Oaks Ave 34734 407-290-8073
Crenshaw S 50/PK-12
2342 Hempel Ave 34734 407-877-7412
Brenda Crenshaw, head sch Fax 877-0541

**Graceville, Jackson, Pop. 2,229**
Holmes County SD
Supt. — See Bonifay
Poplar Springs S 400/PK-12
3726 Atomic Dr 32440 850-263-6260
Gordon Wells, prin. Fax 263-1252

Jackson County SD
Supt. — See Marianna
Graceville JSHS 400/6-12
5539 Brown St 32440 850-263-4451
Larry Moore, prin. Fax 263-3605

The Baptist College of Florida Post-Sec.
5400 College Dr 32440 800-328-2660

**Greenacres, Palm Beach, Pop. 36,906**
Palm Beach County SD
Supt. — See West Palm Beach
Leonard HS 2,500/9-12
4701 10th Ave N 33463 561-641-1200
Edward Tierney, prin. Fax 491-8350
Swain MS 1,100/6-8
5332 Lake Worth Rd 33463 561-649-6900
James Thomas, prin. Fax 649-6906
Tradewinds MS 1,200/6-8
5090 S Haverhill Rd 33463 561-493-6400
Rebecca Subin, prin. Fax 493-6410

Greenacres Christian Academy 100/PK-12
4982 Cambridge St 33463 561-965-0363
Southeastern College Post-Sec.
6812 Forest Hill Blvd # D1 33413 561-433-2330

**Green Cove Springs, Clay, Pop. 6,779**
Clay County SD 34,100/PK-12
900 Walnut St 32043 904-284-6500
Charlie Van Zant, supt. Fax 284-6525
www.oneclay.net
Bannerman Learning Center 100/Alt
608 Mill St 32043 904-529-2100
Mike Elia, prin. Fax 529-1025
Clay HS 1,400/9-12
2025 State Road 16 W 32043 904-529-3000
Cary Dicks, prin. Fax 529-3214
Green Cove Springs JHS 900/7-8
1220 Bonaventure Ave 32043 904-529-2140
Jen Halter, prin. Fax 529-2144
Lake Asbury JHS 1,100/7-8
2851 Sandridge Rd 32043 904-291-5582
Becky Murphy, prin. Fax 291-5593
Other Schools – See Keystone Heights, Middleburg, Orange Park, Starke

**Groveland, Lake, Pop. 8,373**
Lake County SD
Supt. — See Tavares
Gray MS 1,000/6-8
205 E Magnolia St 34736 352-429-3322
Pam Chateauneuf, prin. Fax 429-0133
South Lake HS 1,700/9-12
15600 Silver Eagle Rd 34736 352-394-2100
Rob McCue, prin. Fax 394-1972

**Gulf Breeze, Santa Rosa, Pop. 5,682**
Santa Rosa County SD
Supt. — See Milton
Gulf Breeze HS 1,500/9-12
675 Gulf Breeze Pkwy 32561 850-916-4100
Dan Brothers, prin. Fax 916-4109
Gulf Breeze MS 900/6-8
649 Gulf Breeze Pkwy 32561 850-934-4080
Michael Brandon, prin. Fax 934-4085
Woodlawn Beach MS 1,100/6-8
1500 Woodlawn Way 32563 850-934-4010
Victor Lowrimore, prin. Fax 934-4015

**Gulfport, Pinellas, Pop. 11,800**
Pinellas County SD
Supt. — See Largo
Boca Ciega HS 1,500/9-12
924 58th St S 33707 727-893-2780
Michael Vigue, prin. Fax 893-1382

**Haines City, Polk, Pop. 20,261**
Polk County SD
Supt. — See Bartow
Boone MS 900/6-8
225 S 22nd St 33844 863-421-3302
Kathryn Raub, prin. Fax 421-3305
Haines City HS 2,100/9-12
2800 Hornet Dr 33844 863-421-3281
Adam Lane, prin. Fax 421-3283
Haines City HS - IB 200/9-12
2800 Hornet Dr 33844 863-419-3371
Adam Lane, prin. Fax 419-3373
Jenkins Academy of Technology 500/6-8
701 Ledwith Ave 33844 863-421-3267
Brad Tarver, prin. Fax 421-3269

Landmark Christian S 200/PK-12
2020 E Hinson Ave 33844 863-422-2037
NorthRidge Christian Academy 100/K-10
2250 State Road 17 S 33844 863-422-3473
Dr. David Myers, admin. Fax 421-5584

**Hallandale Beach, Broward, Pop. 36,609**
Broward County SD
Supt. — See Fort Lauderdale
Gulfstream MS 400/6-8
120 SW 4th Ave, 754-323-4700
Robert Pappas, prin. Fax 323-4785
Hallandale HS 1,300/9-12
720 NW 9th Ave, 754-323-0900
Estella Eckhardt, prin. Fax 323-1030
Lanier-James Education Center 100/Alt
1050 NW 7th Ct, 754-321-7350
Kelvin Lee, prin. Fax 321-7390
Hallandale Adult Center Adult
1000 SW 3rd St, 754-321-7050
Bardetta Haygood, prin. Fax 321-7135

**Havana, Gadsden, Pop. 1,746**
Gadsden County SD
Supt. — See Quincy
East Gadsden HS 900/9-12
27001 Blue Star Hwy 32333 850-662-2300
Dr. Melvin Roberts, prin. Fax 539-2863

Tallavana Christian S 200/PK-12
5840 Havana Hwy 32333 850-539-5300
Diane Townsend, prin. Fax 539-8785

**Hawthorne, Alachua, Pop. 1,398**
Alachua County SD
Supt. — See Gainesville
Hawthorne MSHS 300/6-12
21403 SE 69th Ave 32640 352-481-1900
Libby Hartwell, prin. Fax 481-4859

**Hialeah, Miami-Dade, Pop. 224,295**
Miami-Dade County SD
Supt. — See Miami
American HS 2,000/9-12
18350 NW 67th Ave 33015 305-557-3770
Francisco Garnica, prin. Fax 828-7380
Filer MS 1,200/6-8
531 W 29th St 33012 305-822-6601
Emirce Ladaga, prin. Fax 822-2063
Hialeah HS 2,900/9-12
251 E 47th St 33013 305-822-1500
Herberto Sanchez, prin. Fax 828-5513
Hialeah-Miami Lakes HS 1,700/9-12
7977 W 12th Ave 33014 305-823-1330
Eric Acosta, prin. Fax 362-4188
Hialeah MS 900/6-8
6027 E 7th Ave 33013 305-681-3527
Lourdes Diaz, prin. Fax 681-6225
Marti MAST 6-12 Academy 500/6-12
5701 W 24th Ave 33016 305-557-5931
Jose Enriquez, prin. Fax 556-6917
Palm Springs MS 1,200/6-9
1025 W 56th St 33012 305-821-2460
Leonard Torres, prin. Fax 828-3987
Westland Hialeah HS 1,900/9-12
4000 W 18th Ave 33012 305-818-3000
Giovanna Blanco, prin. Fax 818-3002
American Adult Education Adult
18350 NW 67th Ave 33015 305-557-3770
Alexis Cazanas, prin. Fax 827-7935
Hialeah HS Adult Education Center Adult
251 E 47th St 33013 305-822-1500
Manuel Gonzalez, prin. Fax 821-6018
Hialeah-Miami Lakes Adult Ed Center Adult
7977 W 12th Ave 33014 305-823-1330
Alexis Cazanas, prin. Fax 828-8929

Advance Science Institute Post-Sec.
3750 W 12th Ave 33012 305-827-5452
American Christian S 100/PK-12
5888 W 20th Ave 33016 305-827-6544
Dr. Marcela Chavarri, prin. Fax 827-6620
Beauty Academy of South Florida Post-Sec.
1305 W 49th St 33012 305-817-3577
Beauty Schools of America Post-Sec.
1060 W 49th St 33012 305-362-9003
Champagnat Catholic S 300/PK-12
1851 Palm Ave 33010 305-888-3760
College of Business & Technology Post-Sec.
935 W 49th St 33012 305-764-3165
Compu-Med Vocational Careers Post-Sec.
2900 W 12th Ave 3rd Flr 33012 305-888-9200
Dade Medical College Post-Sec.
5875 NW 163rd St Ste 101 33014 786-363-3340
Edison Private S 400/PK-12
3720 E 4th Ave 33013 305-824-0303
Florida Career College Post-Sec.
3750 W 18th Ave 33012 305-825-3231
Florida National University Post-Sec.
4425 W 20th Ave 33012 305-821-3333
Florida National University Post-Sec.
4206 W 12th Ave 33012 305-231-3326
Florida National University Online Post-Sec.
4425 W 20th Ave 33012 305-821-3333
Futura Career Institute Post-Sec.
4512 W 12th Ave 33012 305-825-7660
Horeb Christian S 200/PK-12
795 W 68th St 33014 305-557-6811
La Belle Beauty School Post-Sec.
1495 W 49th St 33012 305-558-0562
Lincoln-Marti S 300/1-12
1750 E 4th Ave 33010 305-884-1570
Miami-Dade College Post-Sec.
1780 W 49th St 33012 305-237-8700
Nouvelle Institute Post-Sec.
500 W 49th St Fl 2 33012 305-557-3017
Total International Career Institute Post-Sec.
3060 W 12th Ave 33012 305-681-6622
Trinity Christian Academy 100/PK-12
1498 W 84th St 33014 305-819-8999

**Hialeah Gardens, Miami-Dade, Pop. 21,719**
Miami-Dade County SD
Supt. — See Miami
Hialeah Gardens HS 2,600/9-12
11700 Hialeah Gardens Blvd 33018 305-698-5000
Dr. Louis Algaze, prin. Fax 698-5001
Hialeah Gardens MS 1,900/6-8
11690 NW 92nd Ave 33018 305-817-0017
Maritza Jimenez, prin. Fax 817-0018

**Hilliard, Nassau, Pop. 3,050**
Nassau County SD
Supt. — See Fernandina Beach
Hilliard MSHS 800/6-12
1 Flashes Ave 32046 904-491-7940
Dr. Brent Tilley, prin. Fax 845-7662

**Hobe Sound, Martin, Pop. 11,387**

Hobe Sound Bible College Post-Sec.
11298 SE Gomez Ave 33455 772-546-5534
Hobe Sound Christian Academy 200/PK-12
PO Box 1065 33475 772-545-1455
Pine S 200/K-12
12350 SE Federal Hwy 33455 772-675-7005
Phyllis Parker, hdmstr. Fax 675-7006

**Holiday, Pasco, Pop. 21,981**
Pasco County SD
Supt. — See Land O Lakes
Anclote HS 1,200/9-12
1540 Sweetbriar Dr 34691 727-246-3000
Elaine Williams, prin. Fax 246-3091
Smith MS 1,100/6-8
1410 Sweetbriar Dr 34691 727-246-3200
Susan Seibert, prin. Fax 246-3291

**Hollywood, Broward, Pop. 137,985**
Broward County SD
Supt. — See Fort Lauderdale
Apollo MS 1,100/6-8
6800 Arthur St 33024 754-323-2900
Shawn Aycock, prin. Fax 323-2985
Attucks MS 800/6-8
3500 N 22nd Ave 33020 754-323-3000
Errol Evans, prin. Fax 323-3085
Driftwood MS 1,600/6-8
2751 NW 70th Ter 33024 754-323-3100
Steven Williams, prin. Fax 323-3185
Hollywood Hills HS 1,700/9-12
5400 Stirling Rd 33021 754-323-1050
Lourdes Gonzalez, prin. Fax 323-1180

McArthur HS 2,200/9-12
6501 Hollywood Blvd 33024 754-323-1200
Todd LaPace, prin. Fax 323-1330
McNicol MS 800/6-8
1602 S 27th Ave 33020 754-323-3400
Melissa Gurreonero, prin. Fax 323-3485
Sheridan Technical Center Vo/Tech
5400 Sheridan St 33021 754-321-5400
Daniel Boegli, prin. Fax 321-5680
South Broward HS 2,200/9-12
1901 N Federal Hwy 33020 754-323-1800
Olayemi Awofadeju, prin. Fax 323-1930

---

Chaminade-Madonna College Prep HS 600/9-12
500 E Chaminade Dr 33021 954-989-5150
Raiza Echemendia, prin. Fax 983-4663
City College Post-Sec.
6565 Taft St Ste 200 33024 954-744-1777
Dade Medical College Post-Sec.
6837 Taft St 33024 954-843-7930
Hollywood Christian S 300/PK-12
1708 N State Road 7 33021 954-322-4375
Dr. Mike Hill Ed.D., head sch Fax 322-4383
Sheridan Hills Christian S 500/PK-12
3751 Sheridan St 33021 954-966-7995
William Hewlett, head sch Fax 961-1359
Sheridan Technical Center Post-Sec.
5400 Sheridan St 33021 754-321-5400

**Homestead, Miami-Dade, Pop. 59,655**
Miami-Dade County SD
Supt. — See Miami
Center for International Education 9-12
900 NE 23 Ave 33033 305-248-7911
Lisa Pizzimenti-Bradshaw, prin. Fax 248-3518
Homestead HS 2,000/9-12
2351 SE 12th Ave 33034 305-245-7000
Guillermo Munoz, prin. Fax 247-5757
Homestead MS 600/6-8
650 NW 2nd Ave 33030 305-247-4221
Keith Anderson, prin. Fax 247-1098
Medical Academy for Science & Technology 300/9-12
1220 NW 1st Ave 33030 305-257-4500
Lisa Noffo, prin. Fax 257-4501
Redland MS 600/6-8
16001 SW 248th St 33031 305-247-6112
Charles Hankerson, prin. Fax 248-0628
School for Advanced Studies - Homestead 100/11-12
500 College Ter 33030 305-237-5062
Dr. Omar Monteagudo, prin. Fax 237-5232
South Dade HS 3,400/9-12
28401 SW 167th Ave 33030 305-247-4244
Javier Perez, prin. Fax 248-3867
South Dade MS 1,300/4-8
29100 SW 194th Ave 33030 305-224-5200
Maria Medina, prin. Fax 224-5201
South Dade Skill Center Vo/Tech
28300 SW 152nd Ave 33033 305-247-7839
Dr. Susana Mauri, prin. Fax 247-2375
South Dade Technical S Adult
109 NE 8th St 33030 305-248-5723
Dr. Susana Mauri, prin. Fax 248-9164

---

Colonial Christian S 200/PK-12
17105 SW 296th St 33030 305-246-8608
Terri Morrissey, admin. Fax 246-1542
Dade Medical College Post-Sec.
381 N Krome Ave 33030 786-454-9070
Faith Fellowship S 50/PK-12
28945 SW 187th Ave 33030 305-246-5534
Monica Upegui B.A., prin. Fax 246-5586
Miami-Dade College Post-Sec.
500 College Ter 33030 305-237-5000
Redland Christian Academy 300/PK-12
17700 SW 280th St 33031 305-247-7399

**Hudson, Pasco, Pop. 12,006**
Pasco County SD
Supt. — See Land O Lakes
Fivay HS 1,600/9-12
12115 Chicago Ave 34669 727-246-4000
Marsha VanHook, prin. Fax 246-4091
Hudson HS 1,100/9-12
14410 Cobra Way 34669 727-774-4200
David LaRoche, prin. Fax 774-4291
Hudson MS 900/6-8
14540 Cobra Way 34669 727-774-8200
Joseph Musselman, prin. Fax 774-8291

---

Grace Christian S 100/K-12
9403 Scot St 34669 727-863-1825
Glenwood Pratt, prin. Fax 862-4484

**Immokalee, Collier, Pop. 23,830**
Collier County SD
Supt. — See Naples
Immokalee HS 1,400/9-12
701 Immokalee Dr 34142 239-377-1800
Ken Fairbanks, prin. Fax 377-1801
Immokalee MS 800/6-8
401 N 9th St 34142 239-377-4200
Abel Jaimes, prin. Fax 377-4201
Immokalee Technical Center Vo/Tech
508 N 9th St 34142 239-377-9900
Dorin Oxender, prin. Fax 377-7101

**Indialantic, Brevard, Pop. 2,676**
Brevard County SD
Supt. — See Melbourne
Hoover MS 500/7-8
2000 Hawk Haven Dr 32903 321-727-1611
Lena Wiebelt, prin. Fax 725-0076

**Indiantown, Martin, Pop. 6,057**
Martin County SD
Supt. — See Stuart
Indiantown MS 400/5-8
16303 SW Farm Rd 34956 772-597-2146
Jeff Raimann, prin. Fax 597-5854

**Interlachen, Putnam, Pop. 1,381**
Putnam County SD
Supt. — See Palatka
Interlachen HS 800/9-12
126 N County Road 315 32148 386-684-2116
Thomas Bolling, prin. Fax 684-3915
Price MS 500/6-8
140 N County Road 315 32148 386-684-2113
Leah Lundy, prin. Fax 684-3908

**Inverness, Citrus, Pop. 7,057**
Citrus County SD 15,400/PK-12
1007 W Main St 34450 352-726-1931
Sandra Himmel, supt. Fax 726-4418
www.citrus.k12.fl.us
Citrus HS 1,600/9-12
600 W Highland Blvd 34452 352-726-2241
Rich Hilgert, prin. Fax 249-2102
Inverness MS 1,100/6-8
1950 Highway 41 N 34450 352-726-1471
Patricia Douglas, prin. Fax 249-2133
Withlacoochee Technical Institute Vo/Tech
1201 W Main St 34450 352-726-2430
Denise Willis, dir. Fax 249-2157
Other Schools – See Citrus Springs, Crystal River, Lecanto

---

Inverness Christian Academy 200/PK-12
4222 S Florida Ave 34450 352-726-3759

**Islamorada, Monroe, Pop. 1,220**

---

Island Christian S 200/PK-12
83400 Overseas Hwy 33036 305-664-4933

**Jacksonville, Duval, Pop. 800,944**
Duval County SD 118,400/PK-12
1701 Prudential Dr 32207 904-390-2000
Dr. Nikolai Vitti Ed.D., supt. Fax 390-2586
www.duvalschools.org
Anderson HS of the Arts 1,100/9-12
2445 San Diego Rd 32207 904-346-5620
Jackie Cornelius, prin. Fax 346-5636
Arlington MS 800/6-8
8141 Lone Star Rd 32211 904-720-1680
Yolonda Sanders, prin. Fax 720-1702
Atlantic Coast HS Vo/Tech
9735 R G Skinner Pkwy 32256 904-538-5120
Debra Lynch, prin. Fax 538-5159
Bridge to Success MS Alt
1840 W 9th St 32209 904-630-6640
Aleya Prier, prin. Fax 630-6653
Butler MS 700/6-8
900 Acorn St 32209 904-630-6900
Truitte Moreland, prin. Fax 630-6913
Darnell-Cookman MSHS 1,100/6-12
1701 N Davis St 32209 904-630-6805
Carol Daniels, prin. Fax 630-6811
Davis MS 1,200/6-8
7050 Melvin Rd 32210 904-573-1060
Nidia Ashby, prin. Fax 573-1066
DuPont MS 800/6-8
2710 Dupont Ave 32217 904-739-5200
Marilyn Barnwell, prin. Fax 739-5321
Englewood HS 1,800/9-12
4412 Barnes Rd 32207 904-739-5212
Sara Bravo, prin. Fax 739-5324
First Coast HS 2,100/9-12
590 Duval Station Rd 32218 904-757-0080
Alvin Brennan, prin. Fax 696-8721
Ft. Caroline MS 800/6-8
3787 University Club Blvd 32277 904-745-4927
Maysha Shelton, prin. Fax 745-4937
Gilbert MS 500/6-8
1424 Franklin St 32206 904-630-6700
Jamelle Goodwin, prin. Fax 630-6713
Grand Park Education Center 100/Alt
2335 W 18th St 32209 904-630-6894
Tyrone Blue, prin. Fax 630-6898
Highlands MS 900/6-8
10913 Pine Estates Rd E 32218 904-696-8771
Jackie Simmons, prin. Fax 696-8782
Jackson HS 800/9-12
3816 N Main St 32206 904-630-6950
Evan Daniels, prin. Fax 630-6955
Johnson College Prep MS 1,100/6-8
3276 Norman E Thagard Blvd 32254 904-693-7600
Sharwonda Peek, prin. Fax 693-7661
Kernan MS 1,300/6-8
2271 Kernan Blvd S 32246 904-220-1350
Julie Hemphill, prin. Fax 220-1355
Kirby-Smith MS 900/6-8
2034 Hubbard St 32206 904-630-6600
June Marshall, prin. Fax 630-6605
Lake Shore MS 1,300/6-8
2519 Bayview Rd 32210 904-381-7440
Christopher Begley, prin. Fax 381-7437
Landmark MS 1,400/6-8
101 Kernan Blvd N 32225 904-221-7125
David Gilmore, prin. Fax 221-8847
Landon MS 700/6-8
1819 Thacker Ave 32207 904-346-5650
Timothy Feagins, prin. Fax 346-5657
LaVilla S of the Arts 1,100/6-8
501 N Davis St 32202 904-633-6069
Lianna Knight, prin. Fax 633-8089
Lee HS 1,700/9-12
1200 McDuff Ave S 32205 904-381-3930
Scott Schneider, prin. Fax 381-3945
Mandarin HS 2,800/9-12
4831 Greenland Rd 32258 904-260-3911
Donna Richardson, prin. Fax 260-5439
Mandarin MS 1,500/6-8
5100 Hood Rd 32257 904-292-0555
James Ledford, prin. Fax 260-5415
Northwestern MS 500/6-8
2100 W 45th St 32209 904-924-3100
Tyrus Lyles, prin. Fax 924-3284
Oceanway MS 1,300/6-8
143 Oceanway Ave 32218 904-714-4680
Tonya Marx, prin. Fax 714-4685

Parker HS 1,700/9-12
7301 Parker School Rd 32211 904-720-1650
Megan Pardue, prin. Fax 720-1700
Paxon HS for Advanced Studies 1,500/9-12
3239 Norman E Thagard Blvd 32254 904-693-7583
Royce Turner, prin. Fax 693-7597
Peterson Academy of Technology Vo/Tech
7450 Wilson Blvd 32210 904-573-1150
Cathy Barnes, prin. Fax 573-3206
Raines HS 1,000/9-12
3663 Raines Ave 32209 904-924-3049
Vincent Hall, prin. Fax 924-3058
Randolph Academies of Technology Vo/Tech
1157 Golfair Blvd 32209 904-924-3011
Robert Lewis, prin. Fax 924-3125
Ribault HS 1,000/9-12
3701 Winton Dr 32208 904-924-3092
Christopher Jackson, prin. Fax 924-3154
Ribault MS 600/6-8
3610 Ribault Scenic Dr 32208 904-924-3062
Angela Maxey, prin. Fax 924-3167
Rutherford Alternative Education Center 100/Alt
1514 Hubbard St 32206 904-630-6782
Maurice Nesmith, prin. Fax 630-6789
Sandalwood HS 3,100/9-12
2750 John Prom Blvd 32246 904-646-5100
Vickie Schultz, prin. Fax 646-5126
Schools for the Future Academy Alt
1824 N Pearl St 32206 904-354-7799
Vincent Foster, prin. Fax 359-2637
Southside MS 900/6-8
2948 Knights Ln E 32216 904-739-5238
Zeina Spaulding, prin. Fax 739-5244
Stanton College Preparatory HS 1,600/9-12
1149 W 13th St 32209 904-630-6760
Nongongoma Majova-Seane, prin. Fax 630-6758
Stilwell MS 1,200/6-8
7840 Burma Rd 32221 904-693-7523
Jennifer Campese, prin. Fax 693-7539
Stuart MS 900/6-8
4815 Wesconnett Blvd 32210 904-573-1000
Sadie Milliner-Smith, prin. Fax 573-3213
Twin Lakes Academy MS 1,500/6-8
8050 Point Meadows Dr 32256 904-538-0825
Tamara Tuschhoff, prin. Fax 538-0840
Westside HS 1,200/9-12
5530 Firestone Rd 32244 904-573-1170
Gregory Bostic, prin. Fax 573-1177
White HS 1,800/9-12
1700 Old Middleburg Rd N 32210 904-693-7620
Jason Bloom, prin. Fax 693-7639
Wolfson HS 1,500/9-12
7000 Powers Ave 32217 904-739-5265
Terry Connor, prin. Fax 739-5272
Other Schools – See Atlantic Beach, Baldwin, Jacksonville Beach, Neptune Beach

---

Arlington Country Day S 400/PK-12
5725 Fort Caroline Rd 32277 904-762-0123
Deborah Condit, head sch Fax 762-0125
Art Institute of Jacksonville Post-Sec.
8775 Baypine Rd 32256 904-486-3000
Austin Christian Academy 100/PK-12
6901 N Main St 32208 904-647-5065
Audrey White, prin. Fax 643-2245
Baptist Medical Centers Post-Sec.
800 Prudential Dr 32207 904-393-2001
Baptist/St. Vincent's Health System Post-Sec.
1 Shircliff Way 32204 904-387-7300
Bishop John J. Snyder HS 500/9-12
5001 Samaritan Way 32210 904-771-1029
David Yazdiya, prin. Fax 908-8988
Bishop Kenny HS 1,200/9-12
1055 Kingman Ave 32207 904-398-7545
Todd Orlando, prin. Fax 398-5728
Bolles S - Bartrum Campus 400/6-8
2264 Bartram Rd 32207 904-724-8850
Dave Farace, head sch Fax 724-8862
Bolles S - San Jose Campus 1,600/9-12
7400 San Jose Blvd 32217 904-733-9292
Dave Farace, head sch Fax 739-9363
Cedar Creek Christian S 300/PK-12
1372 Lane Ave S 32205 904-781-9151
Chamberlain College of Nursing Post-Sec.
5200 Belfort Rd 32256 904-251-8100
Chatman's Early Learning Christian Acdmy 200/PK-12
1614 Leonid Rd 32218 904-751-9803
Christ's Church Academy 400/K-12
10850 Old Saint Augustine 32257 904-268-8667
Dr. Madison Nichols, head sch Fax 880-3251
Concorde Career Institute Post-Sec.
7259 Salisbury Rd 32256 904-725-0525
Cornerstone Christian S 300/PK-12
9039 Beach Blvd 32216 904-730-5500
Donna Stables, prin. Fax 730-5502
Dade Medical College Post-Sec.
9550 Regency Sq Blvd # 1200 32225 904-345-5678
DeVry University Post-Sec.
5200 Belfort Rd Ste 175 32256 904-367-4942
Eagle's View Academy 400/K-12
7788 Ramona Blvd W 32221 904-786-1411
Edward Waters College Post-Sec.
1658 Kings Rd 32209 904-470-8000
Episcopal S of Jacksonville 900/6-12
4455 Atlantic Blvd 32207 904-396-5751
Charles F. Zimmer, head sch Fax 396-7209
Esprit De Corps Center for Learning 200/K-12
9840 Wagner Rd 32219 904-924-2000
Dr. Jeannette Holmes-Vann, admin. Fax 766-8870
Everest University - Jacksonville Campus Post-Sec.
8226 Philips Hwy 32256 904-731-4949
First Coast Christian S 600/PK-12
7587 Blanding Blvd 32244 904-777-3040
Richard Spain, admin. Fax 777-3045
Florida Career College Post-Sec.
6600 Youngerman Cir 32244 904-573-1900
Florida Coastal School of Law Post-Sec.
8787 Baypine Rd 32256 904-680-7700
Florida State College Post-Sec.
3939 Roosevelt Blvd 32205 904-381-3400

Florida State College Post-Sec.
4501 Capper Rd 32218 904-766-6500
Florida State College Post-Sec.
11901 Beach Blvd 32246 904-646-2111
Florida State College - Jacksonville Post-Sec.
101 State St W 32202 904-646-2300
Fortis Institute Post-Sec.
5995 University Blvd W #2 32216 904-443-6300
Foundation Academy 200/PK-12
3675 San Pablo Rd S 32224 904-493-7300
Nadia Hionides, prin. Fax 821-1247
Greenwood S 200/6-12
9920 Regency Square Blvd 32225 904-726-5000
Harvest Community S 200/PK-12
2360 Saint Johns Bluff Rd S 32246 904-997-1882
Patty Wilcox, admin. Fax 997-1862
Heart to Heart Christian Academy 100/K-12
8247 W Ramona Blvd 32221 904-783-8638
Heritage Institute Post-Sec.
4130 Salisbury Rd Ste 1100 32216 904-332-0910
ITT Technical Institute Post-Sec.
7011 A C Skinner Pkwy #140 32256 904-573-9100
Jacksonville University Post-Sec.
2800 University Blvd N 32211 904-256-8000
Jones College Post-Sec.
5353 Arlington Expy 32211 904-743-1122
Jones College Post-Sec.
1195 Edgewood Ave S 32205 904-743-1122
Kaplan College Post-Sec.
7450 Beach Blvd 32216 904-855-2400
Keiser University Post-Sec.
6430 Southpoint Pkwy 32216 904-296-3440
Normandy Beauty School of Jacksonville Post-Sec.
5373 Lenox Ave 32205 904-786-6250
North Florida Educational Institute 300/PK-12
580 Lawton Ave 32208 904-764-0084
Old Plank Christian Academy 200/PK-12
8964 Old Plank Rd 32220 904-783-4888
Parsons Christian Academy 200/PK-12
5705 Fort Caroline Rd 32277 904-745-4588
Providence S 1,400/PK-12
2701 Hodges Blvd 32224 904-223-5270
Dr. Julie Giardino, head sch Fax 223-3028
St. Luke's Hospital/Mayo Clinic Post-Sec.
4201 Belfort Rd 32216 904-296-3733
Sanford-Brown Institute Post-Sec.
10255 Fortune Pkwy Ste 501 32256 904-363-6221
Seacoast Christian Academy 200/6-12
8057 Arlington Expy 32211 904-722-1738
Dr. Elton Brooke, prin. Fax 725-5085
Shands Jacksonville Medical Center Post-Sec.
655 W 8th St 32209 904-244-0411
Southeastern College Post-Sec.
6700 Southpoint Pkwy # 400 32216 904-448-9499
Stenotype Institute Post-Sec.
3563 Phillips Hwy Ste 501 32207 904-398-4141
Temple Christian Academy 200/K-12
4200 Georgetown Rd 32210 904-778-8655
Trinity Baptist College Post-Sec.
800 Hammond Blvd 32221 800-786-2206
Trinity Christian Academy 1,500/PK-12
800 Hammond Blvd 32221 904-596-2400
Dr. Clay Lindstam, admin. Fax 596-2531
Tulsa Welding School Post-Sec.
3500 Southside Blvd 32216 904-646-9353
University Christian S 500/PK-12
5520 University Blvd W 32216 904-737-6330
Beverly Bandy, prin. Fax 483-3572
University of North Florida Post-Sec.
1 U N F Dr 32224 904-620-1000
University of Southernmost Florida Post-Sec.
9550 Regency Square Blvd 32225 877-722-3381
Victory Christian Academy 200/PK-12
10613 Lem Turner Rd 32218 904-764-7781
Virginia College Post-Sec.
5940 Beach Blvd 32207 904-520-7400

**Jacksonville Beach, Duval, Pop. 20,925**
Duval County SD
Supt. — See Jacksonville
Fletcher MS 1,100/6-8
2000 3rd St N 32250 904-247-5929
Teresa Mowbray, prin. Fax 247-5940

**Jasper, Hamilton, Pop. 4,513**
Hamilton County SD 1,600/PK-12
5683 US Highway 129 S # 1 32052 386-792-1228
Thomas Moffses, supt. Fax 792-3681
www.hamiltonfl.com
Hamilton County HS 600/7-12
5683 US Highway 129 S 32052 386-792-6540
Kip McLeod, prin. Fax 792-6594

---

Corinth Christian Academy 100/K-12
7042 SW 41st Ave 32052 386-938-2270

**Jay, Santa Rosa, Pop. 529**
Santa Rosa County SD
Supt. — See Milton
Jay JSHS 500/7-12
3741 School St 32565 850-675-4507
Brad Marcilliat, prin. Fax 675-8573

**Jensen Beach, Martin, Pop. 11,571**
Martin County SD
Supt. — See Stuart
Jensen Beach HS 1,600/9-12
2875 NW Goldenrod Rd 34957 772-232-3500
Lori Vogel, prin. Fax 232-3699

**Jupiter, Palm Beach, Pop. 54,490**
Palm Beach County SD
Supt. — See West Palm Beach
Independence MS 1,300/6-8
4001 Greenway Dr 33458 561-799-7500
Kathy Koerner, prin. Fax 799-7505
Jupiter Community HS 2,800/9-12
500 Military Trl 33458 561-744-7900
Daniel Frank, prin. Fax 744-7978
Jupiter MS 1,300/6-8
15245 Military Trl 33458 561-745-7200
Colleen Iannitti, prin. Fax 745-7246

---

Jupiter Christian S 600/PK-12
700 S Delaware Blvd 33458 561-746-7800
Dr. James P. Colman, pres. Fax 746-1955

**Key Biscayne, Miami-Dade, Pop. 12,269**
Miami-Dade County SD
Supt. — See Miami
Maritime & Science Technology Academy 600/9-12
3979 Rickenbacker Cswy 33149 305-365-6278
Josephine Otero, prin. Fax 361-0996

**Keystone Heights, Clay, Pop. 1,326**
Clay County SD
Supt. — See Green Cove Springs
Keystone Heights JSHS 1,200/7-12
900 Orchid Ave, 352-473-2761
Angela Gentry, prin. Fax 473-5920

**Key West, Monroe, Pop. 24,199**
Monroe County SD 7,700/PK-12
241 Trumbo Rd 33040 305-293-1400
Mark Porter, supt. Fax 293-1407
keysschools.schoolfusion.us/
Key West HS 1,200/9-12
2100 Flagler Ave 33040 305-293-1549
Amber Bosco, prin. Fax 293-1547
Other Schools – See Marathon, Tavernier

---

Florida Keys Community College Post-Sec.
5901 College Rd 33040 305-296-9081

**Kissimmee, Osceola, Pop. 58,578**
Osceola County SD 54,400/PK-12
817 Bill Beck Blvd 34744 407-870-4600
Melba Luciano, supt. Fax 870-4010
www.osceola.k12.fl.us
Challenger Learning Center 200/Alt
2320 New Beginnings Rd 34744 407-518-8140
Beth Rattie, dir. Fax 518-8141
Denn John MS 1,200/6-8
2001 Denn John Ln 34744 407-935-3560
Hank Hoyle, prin. Fax 935-3572
Discovery IS 1,300/6-8
5350 San Miguel Rd 34758 407-343-7300
Alan Ramos, prin. Fax 343-7310
Endeavor HS 50/Alt
2320 New Beginnings Rd 34744 407-518-8140
Beth Rattie, dir. Fax 518-8141
Gateway HS 2,300/9-12
93 Panther Paws Trl 34744 407-935-3600
Larry Meadows, prin. Fax 935-3609
Horizon MS 1,200/6-8
2020 Ham Brown Rd 34746 407-943-7240
Michelle Henninger, prin. Fax 943-7250
Kissimmee MS 1,200/6-8
2410 Dyer Blvd 34741 407-870-0857
Gary Weeden, prin. Fax 870-5669
Liberty HS 2,100/9-12
4250 Pleasant Hill Rd 34746 407-933-3910
Evelith Olmeda-Garcia, prin. Fax 933-9990
Neptune MS 1,400/6-8
2727 Neptune Rd 34744 407-935-3500
Cindy Mohen, prin. Fax 935-3519
New Beginnings Educational Center 300/Alt
2599 W Vine St 34741 407-348-4466
Nina Wehmeyer, prin. Fax 348-4069
Osceola County S for the Arts 800/6-12
3151 N Orange Blossom Trl 34744 407-931-4803
Jonathan Rasmussen, prin. Fax 931-3019
Osceola HS 2,100/9-12
420 S Thacker Ave 34741 407-518-5400
Edward Jones, prin. Fax 943-7909
Parkway MS 900/6-8
857 Florida Pkwy 34743 407-344-7000
Megan Gould, prin. Fax 348-2797
PATHS @ TECO Vo/Tech
501 Simpson Rd 34744 407-518-5407
Paula Evans, prin. Fax 344-2467
Poinciana HS 1,400/9-12
2300 S Poinciana Blvd 34758 407-870-4860
Michael Meechin, prin. Fax 870-0382
Technical Education Center Vo/Tech
501 Simpson Rd 34744 407-344-5080
Jeanette Eddy, dir. Fax 344-5089
Zenith MS 100/Alt
2218 E Irlo Bronson Mem Hwy 34744 407-846-3976
Robert Studly, prin. Fax 933-9920
Adult Learning Center Adult
2320 New Beginnings Rd 34744 407-518-8140
Beth Rattie, dir. Fax 518-8141
Other Schools – See Celebration, Saint Cloud

---

American Inst Coll of Health Professions Post-Sec.
1420 Celebration Blvd 34747 407-738-4488
City of Life Christian Academy 400/PK-12
2874 E Irlo Bronson Mem Hwy 34744 407-847-5184
Dr. Kathy Harkema, prin. Fax 870-2679
Florida Technical College Post-Sec.
3831 W Vine St 34741 407-483-5700
Freedomland Christian Academy PK-12
1210 N Main St 34744 407-935-9088
Heritage Christian S 500/K-12
1500 E Vine St 34744 407-847-4087
Johnson University Florida Post-Sec.
1011 Bill Beck Blvd 34744 407-847-8966
Life Christian Academy 300/PK-12
2269 Partin Settlement Rd 34744 407-847-8222
North Kissimmee Christian S 100/PK-12
425 W Donegan Ave 34741 407-847-2877
PHA Preparatory S 200/PK-12
1820 Armstrong Blvd 34741 407-343-1905
Pleasant Hill Academy 300/PK-12
PO Box 582409 34758 407-350-5974
Carmen Ruiz, admin. Fax 350-5984
Southland Christian S 400/PK-12
2440 Fortune Rd 34744 407-201-7999

**LaBelle, Hendry, Pop. 4,611**
Hendry County SD 6,700/PK-12
PO Box 1980 33975 863-674-4642
Paul K. Puletti, supt. Fax 674-4090
www.hendry-schools.org
La Belle HS 1,000/9-12
4050 E Cowboy Way 33935 863-674-4120
Robert Egley, prin. Fax 674-4571
La Belle MS 700/6-8
8000 E Cowboy Way 33935 863-674-4646
Kenneth Pickles, prin. Fax 674-4645
Other Schools – See Clewiston

**Lake Alfred, Polk, Pop. 4,919**
Polk County SD
Supt. — See Bartow
Lake Alfred-Addair MS 700/6-8
925 N Buena Vista Dr 33850 863-295-5988
Charles Thacker, prin. Fax 295-5989

**Lake Butler, Union, Pop. 1,869**
Union County SD 2,200/PK-12
55 SW 6th St 32054 386-496-2045
Carlton Faulk, supt. Fax 496-2580
www.union.k12.fl.us
Lake Butler MS 700/5-8
150 SW 6th St 32054 386-496-3046
Carolyn Parrish, prin. Fax 496-4352
Union County HS 600/9-12
1000 S Lake Ave 32054 386-496-3040
Mike Ripplinger, prin. Fax 496-4187
Union County Adult HS Adult
208 SE 6th St 32054 386-496-1300
Barry Sams, dir. Fax 496-4919

**Lake City, Columbia, Pop. 11,774**
Columbia County SD 9,700/PK-12
372 W Duval St 32055 386-755-8000
Terry Huddleston, supt. Fax 755-8008
www.columbia.k12.fl.us
Challenge Learning Center 100/Alt
1301 NW LaBonte Ln 32055 386-755-8296
Lex Carswell, prin. Fax 755-8291
Columbia HS 1,700/9-12
469 SE Fighting Tiger Dr 32025 386-755-8080
Donnie Harrison, prin. Fax 755-8082
Lake City MS 1,100/6-8
843 SW Arlington Blvd 32025 386-758-4800
Sonja Judkins, prin. Fax 758-4839
Richardson MS 600/6-8
646 SE Pennsylvania St 32025 386-755-8130
Angela Coppock, prin. Fax 755-8154
Career and Adult Education Adult
409 SW Saint Johns St 32025 386-758-4872
Keith Hatcher, dir. Fax 758-4967
Other Schools – See Fort White

---

Florida Gateway College Post-Sec.
149 SE College Pl 32025 386-752-1822
Lake City Christian Academy 100/PK-12
3035 SW Pinemount Rd 32024 386-758-0055
Tana Norris, dir. Fax 758-3018
New Generation Christian S 200/K-12
608 SW Marvin Burnett Rd 32025 386-758-4710

**Lakeland, Polk, Pop. 95,497**
Polk County SD
Supt. — See Bartow
Chiles Middle Academy 700/6-8
400 N Florida Ave 33801 863-499-2742
Brian Andrews, prin. Fax 499-2774
Crystal Acad of Science and Engineering 6-8
2410 N Crystal Lake Dr 33801 863-668-3055
Ronda Cotter, prin.
Crystal Lake MS 900/6-8
2410 N Crystal Lake Dr 33801 863-499-2970
Ronda Cotter, prin. Fax 603-6267
Duncan Opportunity Center 100/Alt
3333 Winter Lake Rd 33803 863-499-2860
Wanda Brokenburr, prin. Fax 499-2863
Harrison S for the Arts 400/9-12
750 Hollingsworth Rd 33801 863-499-2855
Daryl Ward, prin. Fax 499-2938
Jenkins HS 2,300/9-12
6000 Lakeland Highlands Rd 33813 863-648-3566
Buddy Thomas, prin. Fax 648-3573
Kathleen HS 1,900/9-12
1100 Red Devil Way 33815 863-499-2655
Donna Drisdom, prin. Fax 499-2726
Kathleen MS 800/6-8
3627 Kathleen Pnes 33810 863-853-6040
Sheila Gregory, prin. Fax 853-6037
Lake Gibson HS 1,800/9-12
7007 N Socrum Loop Rd 33809 863-853-6100
Tami Dawson, prin. Fax 853-6108
Lake Gibson MS 1,200/6-8
6901 N Socrum Loop Rd 33809 863-853-6151
Kathy Conely, prin. Fax 853-6171
Lakeland Highlands MS 1,300/6-8
740 Lake Miriam Dr 33813 863-648-3500
Telay Kendrick, prin. Fax 648-3580
Lakeland HS 2,000/9-12
726 Hollingsworth Rd 33801 863-499-2900
Arthur Martinez, prin. Fax 499-2917
PACE Center for Girls 50/Alt
101 W Main St 33815 863-688-5596
Xuchitl Coso, prin. Fax 688-9566
Sleepy Hill MS 900/6-8
2215 Sleepy Hill Rd 33810 863-815-6577
Kathryn Blackburn, prin. Fax 815-6586
Southwest MS 900/6-8
2815 Eden Pkwy 33803 863-499-2840
Tye Bruno, prin. Fax 499-2762
Tenoroc HS 1,300/9-12
4905 Saddle Creek Rd 33801 863-614-9183
Jason Looney, prin. Fax 614-9192
Traviss Career Center Vo/Tech
3225 Winter Lake Rd 33803 863-499-2700
Wayne Dickens, prin. Fax 499-2706
West Area Adult & Community S Adult
604 S Central Ave 33815 863-499-2835
Loretta Cameron, prin. Fax 499-2727

---

Everest University - Lakeland Campus Post-Sec.
995 E Memorial Blvd Ste 110 33801 863-686-1444
Excel Christian Academy 200/PK-12
6505 Odom Rd 33809 863-853-9235
Florida Southern College Post-Sec.
111 Lake Hollingsworth Dr 33801 863-680-4111
Florida Technical College Post-Sec.
4715 S Florida Ave Ste 4 33813 863-619-6200
Geneva Classical Academy 100/PK-12
4204 Lakeland Highlands Rd 33813 863-644-1408
Rich Cali, hdmstr. Fax 619-5841
Keiser University Post-Sec.
2400 Interstate Dr 33805 863-682-6020
Lakeland Christian S 1,000/PK-12
1111 Forest Park St 33803 863-688-2771
Dr. Michael Sligh, hdmstr. Fax 682-5637
Lakeland Regional Medical Center Post-Sec.
1324 Lakeland Hills Blvd 33805 863-687-1100
Santa Fe Catholic HS 300/9-12
3110 US Highway 92 E 33801 863-665-4188
Matthew Franzino, prin. Fax 665-4151
Sonrise Christian S 100/PK-12
3151 Hardin Combee Rd 33801 863-665-4187
Southeastern University Post-Sec.
1000 Longfellow Blvd 33801 863-667-5000
Traviss Career Center Post-Sec.
3225 Winter Lake Rd 33803 863-499-2700
Victory Christian Academy 300/PK-12
1401 Griffin Rd 33810 863-858-5614

**Lake Mary, Seminole, Pop. 13,545**
Seminole County SD
Supt. — See Sanford
Greenwood Lakes MS 900/6-8
601 Lake Park Dr 32746 407-320-7650
Debra Abbott, prin. Fax 320-7699
Lake Mary HS 2,600/9-12
655 Longwood Lake Mary Rd 32746 407-320-9550
Michael Kotkin, prin. Fax 320-9512
Markham Woods MS 1,000/6-8
6003 Markham Woods Rd 32746 407-871-1750
Byron Durias, prin. Fax 871-1799

---

ITT Technical Institute Post-Sec.
1400 S International Pkwy 32746 407-660-2900
Lake Mary Preparatory S 700/PK-12
650 Rantoul Ln 32746 407-805-0095
Remington College of Nursing Post-Sec.
660 Century Pt Ste 1050 32746 800-294-4434
Remington College - Online Post-Sec.
500 International Pkwy #200 32746 800-560-6192

**Lake Park, Palm Beach, Pop. 7,949**

---

Palm Beach Academy of Health & Beauty Post-Sec.
1220 10th St Ste A 33403 561-845-1400

**Lake Placid, Highlands, Pop. 2,195**
Highlands County SD
Supt. — See Sebring
Lake Placid HS 800/9-12
202 Green Dragon Dr 33852 863-699-5010
Toni Stivender, prin. Fax 699-5094
Lake Placid MS 700/6-8
201 S Tangerine Ave 33852 863-699-5030
Chris Doty, prin. Fax 699-5029

**Lake Wales, Polk, Pop. 13,989**
Polk County SD
Supt. — See Bartow
McLaughlin MS of Fine Arts Academy 800/6-8
800 4th St S 33853 863-678-4233
Eileen Killebrew, prin. Fax 678-4033
Roosevelt Academy 200/6-12
115 E St 33853 863-678-4252
Debra Edwards, prin. Fax 678-4250

---

Candlelight Christian Academy 200/K-12
209 E Sessoms Ave 33853 863-676-0049
Endtime Christian S of Excellence 50/PK-12
200 S 3rd St 33853 863-676-8299
Betty Hill, prin. Fax 678-1193
Warner University Post-Sec.
13895 Hwy 27 33859 863-638-1426

**Lakewood Ranch, Manatee**

---

Out of Door Academy 400/6-12
5950 Deer Dr, 941-349-3223
David Mahler, hdmstr. Fax 907-1251

**Lake Worth, Palm Beach, Pop. 34,358**
Palm Beach County SD
Supt. — See West Palm Beach
Intensive Transition South S 100/Alt
1509 Barton Rd 33460 561-202-0600
Reginald Jeudy, prin. Fax 202-0650
Lake Worth Community HS 2,100/9-12
1701 Lake Worth Rd 33460 561-533-6300
George Lockhart, prin. Fax 493-0888
Lake Worth MS 900/6-8
1300 Barnett Dr 33461 561-540-5500
Mike Williams, prin. Fax 540-5559
Park Vista Community HS 2,900/9-12
7900 S Jog Rd 33467 561-491-8400
Reginald Myers, prin. Fax 493-6854
Woodlands MS 1,200/6-8
5200 Lyons Rd 33467 561-357-0300
Jeffrey Eassa, prin. Fax 357-0307

---

Academy of Palm Beach Post-Sec.
3141 S Military Trl 33463 561-965-5550
Palm Beach State College Post-Sec.
4200 S Congress Ave 33461 561-967-7222
Trinity Christian Academy 600/PK-12
7259 S Military Trl 33463 561-967-1900
Tobi Manke, prin. Fax 965-4347

**Land O Lakes, Pasco, Pop. 31,370**
Pasco County SD 61,900/PK-12
7227 Land O Lakes Blvd 34638 813-794-2000
Kurt Browning, supt. Fax 794-2716
www.pasco.k12.fl.us
Land O'Lakes HS 1,600/9-12
20325 Gator Ln, 813-794-9400
Ric Mellin, prin. Fax 794-9491
Pine View MS 800/6-8
5334 Parkway Blvd 34639 813-794-4800
Jennifer Crosby, prin. Fax 794-4891
Rushe MS 1,300/6-8
18654 Mentmore Blvd, 813-346-1200
David Salerno, prin. Fax 346-1291
Sunlake HS 1,600/9-12
3023 Sunlake Blvd, 813-346-1000
Michael Cloyd, prin. Fax 346-1091
Other Schools – See Dade City, Holiday, Hudson, New Port Richey, Port Richey, Wesley Chapel, Zephyrhills

---

Academy at the Lakes - McCormick 200/5-12
2331 Collier Pkwy 34639 813-948-7600
Mark Heller, head sch Fax 949-0563
Land O' Lakes Christian S 200/PK-12
5105 School Rd, 813-995-9040

**Lantana, Palm Beach, Pop. 10,206**
Palm Beach County SD
Supt. — See West Palm Beach
Lantana Community MS 800/6-8
1225 W Drew St 33462 561-540-3400
Edward Burke, prin. Fax 540-3435
Santaluces Community HS 2,300/9-12
6880 Lawrence Rd 33462 561-642-6200
Tameka Robinson, prin. Fax 642-6255

---

Kentwood Preparatory S 200/1-12
6210 S Congress Ave 33462 561-649-6141

**Largo, Pinellas, Pop. 76,001**
Pinellas County SD 101,000/PK-12
301 4th St SW 33770 727-588-6000
Dr. Michael Grego, supt. Fax 588-6200
www.pcsb.org
Fitzgerald MS 1,400/6-8
6410 118th Ave 33773 727-547-4526
Michael Hernandez, prin. Fax 549-6631
Largo HS 1,700/9-12
410 Missouri Ave N 33770 727-588-3758
Bradley Finkbiner, prin. Fax 588-4037
Largo MS 900/6-8
155 8th Ave SE 33771 727-588-4600
Stephanie Joyner, prin. Fax 588-3720
Pinellas Gulf Coast Academy 300/Alt
1197 E Bay Dr 33770 727-474-8836
Bonnie Solinsky, prin. Fax 581-9557
Pinellas Park HS 2,100/9-12
6305 118th Ave 33773 727-538-7410
Brett Patterson, prin. Fax 507-4563
Other Schools – See Clearwater, Dunedin, Gulfport, Palm Harbor, Pinellas Park, Safety Harbor, Saint Petersburg, Seminole, Tarpon Springs

---

ATA Career Education Post-Sec.
12360 66th St 33773 727-576-9597
Everest University - Largo Campus Post-Sec.
1199 E Bay Dr 33770 727-725-2688
Fortis College Post-Sec.
6565 Ulmerton Rd 33771 727-531-5900
Indian Rocks Christian S 800/PK-12
12685 Ulmerton Rd 33774 727-596-4342
Walter Weller, supt. Fax 593-8778
Schiller International University Post-Sec.
8560 Ulmerton Rd 33771 800-261-9751
Westside Christian S 100/K-12
11633 137th St N 33774 727-517-2153
Rev. Huey Davis, prin. Fax 593-7700

**Lauderdale Lakes, Broward, Pop. 31,785**
Broward County SD
Supt. — See Fort Lauderdale
Anderson HS 2,000/9-12
3050 NW 41st St 33309 754-322-0200
Angel Almanzar, prin. Fax 322-0330
Lauderdale Lakes MS 1,000/6-8
3911 NW 30th Ave 33309 754-322-3500
James Griffin, prin. Fax 322-3585

---

Florida Career College Post-Sec.
3383 N State Road 7 33319 954-535-8700

**Lauderhill, Broward, Pop. 65,234**
Broward County SD
Supt. — See Fort Lauderdale
Lauderhill MSHS 600/6-12
1901 NW 49th Ave 33313 754-322-3600
Dr. Ryan Reardon, prin. Fax 322-3685
Parkway MS 1,200/6-8
3600 NW 5th Ct 33311 754-322-4000
Bradford Mattair, prin. Fax 322-4085

---

Intl School of Health Beauty and Tech Post-Sec.
5950 W Oakland Park Blvd 33313 954-741-0088
University of Fort Lauderdale Post-Sec.
4093 NW 16th St 33313 954-486-7728

**Laurel Hill, Okaloosa, Pop. 532**
Okaloosa County SD
Supt. — See Fort Walton Beach
Laurel Hill S 500/PK-12
8078 4th St 32567 850-652-4111
Lee Martello, prin. Fax 652-4659

**Lecanto, Citrus, Pop. 5,799**
Citrus County SD
Supt. — See Inverness
Citrus County Renaissance Center 100/Alt
3630 W Educational Path 34461 352-527-4567
Heather Nieb, prin. Fax 249-2144
Lecanto HS 1,800/9-12
3810 W Educational Path 34461 352-746-2334
Jeff Davis, prin. Fax 249-2136
Lecanto MS 700/6-8
3800 W Educational Path 34461 352-746-2050
Danita Eatman, prin. Fax 249-2138

---

Seven Rivers Christian S 300/PK-12
4221 W Gulf to Lake Hwy 34461 352-746-5696

**Leesburg, Lake, Pop. 19,677**
Lake County SD
Supt. — See Tavares
Carver MS 800/6-8
1200 Beecher St 34748 352-787-7868
Mollie Cunningham, prin. Fax 787-1339
Leesburg HS 1,700/9-12
1401 Yellow Jacket Way 34748 352-787-5047
Dennis Neal, prin. Fax 787-9040
Oak Park MS 600/6-8
2101 South St 34748 352-787-3232
Barbara Longo, prin. Fax 326-2177

---

Beacon College Post-Sec.
105 E Main St 34748 352-787-7660
First Academy-Leesburg 300/PK-12
219 N 13th St 34748 352-787-7762
Gregory Frescoln, admin. Fax 323-1773
Lake-Sumter State College Post-Sec.
9501 US Highway 441 34788 352-787-3747

**Lehigh Acres, Lee, Pop. 85,066**
Lee County SD
Supt. — See Fort Myers
East Lee County HS 1,700/9-12
715 Thomas Sherwin Ave S, 239-369-2932
Susan Zellers, prin. Fax 369-3213
Harns Marsh MS 6-8
1820 Unice Ave N 33971 239-690-2025
Dr. Charles Luckey, prin. Fax 690-2028
Lehigh Acres MS 1,100/6-8
104 Arthur Ave 33936 239-369-6108
Neketa Watson, prin. Fax 369-8808
Lehigh HS 1,600/9-12
901 Gunnery Rd N 33971 239-693-5353
Jackie Corey, prin. Fax 693-6702
Varsity Lakes MS 1,100/6-8
801 Gunnery Rd N 33971 239-694-3464
Daman Essert, prin. Fax 694-7093

**Lithia, Hillsborough**
Hillsborough County SD
Supt. — See Tampa
Barrington MS 1,100/6-8
5925 Village Center Dr 33547 813-657-7266
Amy Rappleyea, prin. Fax 657-7369
Newsome HS 2,300/9-12
16550 Fishhawk Blvd 33547 813-740-4600
Carla Bruning, prin. Fax 740-4604
Randall MS 1,300/6-8
16510 Fishhawk Blvd 33547 813-740-3900
Claire Mawhinney, prin. Fax 740-3910

**Live Oak, Suwannee, Pop. 6,744**
Suwannee County SD 6,000/PK-12
702 2nd St NW 32064 386-647-4600
Jerry Scarborough, supt. Fax 364-2635
suwannee.schooldesk.net
Riveroak Technical College Vo/Tech
415 Pinewood Dr SW 32064 386-647-4200
Walter Boatright, prin. Fax 364-4698
Suwannee HS 1,300/9-12
1314 Pine Ave SW 32064 386-647-4000
Malcolm Hines, prin. Fax 364-2794
Suwannee MS 1,100/6-8
1730 Walker Ave SW 32064 386-647-4500
Jay Jolicoeur, prin. Fax 208-1474
Other Schools – See Branford

---

Melody Christian Academy 200/PK-12
PO Box 100 32064 386-364-4800
Westwood Christian S 100/PK-12
920 11th St SW 32064 386-362-3735
Darlene Galloway, prin. Fax 364-6486

**Longwood, Seminole, Pop. 13,382**
Seminole County SD
Supt. — See Sanford
Lyman HS 2,300/9-12
865 S Ronald Reagan Blvd 32750 407-746-2050
Brian Urichko, prin. Fax 746-2024
Milwee MS 1,300/6-8
1341 S Ronald Reagan Blvd 32750 407-746-3850
James Kubis, prin. Fax 746-3899
Rock Lake MS 900/6-8
250 Slade Dr 32750 407-746-9350
Pamela Shellman, prin. Fax 746-9399

---

One S of the Arts 100/PK-12
1675 Dixon Rd 32779 407-774-0168
Kristen Campbell, hdmstr. Fax 774-1750

**Loxahatchee, Palm Beach**
Palm Beach County SD
Supt. — See West Palm Beach
Osceola Creek MS 800/6-8
6775 180th Ave N 33470 561-422-2500
Nicole Daly, prin. Fax 422-2510
Seminole Ridge Community HS 2,500/9-12
4601 Seminole Pratt Whitney 33470 561-422-2600
James Campbell, prin. Fax 422-2623

**Lutz, Hillsborough, Pop. 19,035**
Hillsborough County SD
Supt. — See Tampa
Martinez MS 1,100/6-8
5601 W Lutz Lake Fern Rd 33558 813-558-1190
Scott Weaver, prin. Fax 558-1226
Steinbrenner HS 2,200/9-12
5575 W Lutz Lake Fern Rd 33558 813-792-5131
Kelly King, prin. Fax 792-5135

Tampa Christian Community S 100/PK-12
960 W Lutz Lake Fern Rd 33548 813-949-2144
Melissa Walker, prin. Fax 877-3111

**Lynn Haven, Bay, Pop. 18,004**
Bay County SD
Supt. — See Panama City
Mosley HS 1,800/9-12
501 Mosley Dr 32444 850-767-4400
Sandy Harrison, prin. Fax 872-4453
Mowat MS 900/6-8
1903 W Highway 390 32444 850-767-4040
Ed Sheffield, prin. Fax 265-2179

**Macclenny, Baker, Pop. 6,242**
Baker County SD 5,000/PK-12
392 South Blvd E 32063 904-259-6251
Sherrie Raulerson, supt. Fax 259-1387
www.baker.k12.fl.us
Baker County MS 1,100/6-8
211 E Jonathan St 32063 904-259-2226
Debbie Fraser, prin. Fax 259-7955
Baker County Adult Center Adult
270 South Blvd E 32063 904-259-6251
Ann Watts, prin. Fax 259-0378
Other Schools – See Glen Saint Mary

**Madison, Madison, Pop. 2,801**
Madison County SD 2,500/PK-12
210 NE Duval Ave 32340 850-973-5022
Doug Brown, supt. Fax 973-5027
www.madison.k12.fl.us
Madison Co. Excel Alternative Ed. Center 50/Alt
2523 W US 90 32340 850-973-5054
Jada Williams, prin. Fax 973-5047
Madison County HS 700/9-12
2649 W US 90 32340 850-973-5061
Ben Killingsworth, prin. Fax 973-5066

North Florida Community College Post-Sec.
325 NW Turner Davis Dr 32340 850-973-2288

**Maitland, Orange, Pop. 15,449**
Orange County SD
Supt. — See Orlando
Maitland MS 1,000/6-8
701 N Thistle Ln 32751 407-623-1462
Dr. Stefanie Shames, prin. Fax 623-1474

Florida College of Natural Health Post-Sec.
2600 Lake Lucien Dr Ste 140 32751 407-261-0319
Orangewood Christian S 700/PK-12
1300 W Maitland Blvd 32751 407-339-0223
Dr. Donald Larson, head sch Fax 339-4148

**Malone, Jackson, Pop. 2,054**
Jackson County SD
Supt. — See Marianna
Malone S 500/PK-12
PO Box 68 32445 850-482-9950
Doug Powell, prin. Fax 482-9981

**Marathon, Monroe, Pop. 8,204**
Monroe County SD
Supt. — See Key West
Marathon MSHS 600/6-12
350 Sombrero Beach Rd 33050 305-289-2480
Wendy McPherson, prin. Fax 289-2486

**Margate, Broward, Pop. 51,792**
Broward County SD
Supt. — See Fort Lauderdale
Margate MS 1,200/6-8
500 NW 65th Ave 33063 754-322-3800
Ernest Toliver, prin. Fax 322-3885

American Institute Post-Sec.
5000 Coconut Creek Pkwy # C 33063 888-283-1671
Florida Career College Post-Sec.
3271 N State Road 7 33063 954-862-7260
Margate School of Beauty Post-Sec.
5281 Coconut Creek Pkwy 33063 954-972-9630

**Marianna, Jackson, Pop. 5,957**
Jackson County SD 6,800/PK-12
PO Box 5958 32447 850-482-1200
Steve Benton, supt. Fax 482-1299
www.jcsb.org
Jackson Alternative S 100/Alt
2701 Technology Cir 32448 850-482-9666
Rex Suggs, prin. Fax 482-9800
Marianna HS 800/9-12
3546 Caverns Rd 32446 850-482-9605
Connie Brisolara, prin. Fax 482-1247
Marianna MS 700/6-8
4144 South St 32448 850-482-9609
Eddie Ellis, prin. Fax 482-9795
Adult Education Adult
2971 Guyton St 32446 850-482-9617
John Ellerbee, prin. Fax 482-1201
Other Schools – See Cottondale, Graceville, Malone, Sneads

Chipola College Post-Sec.
3094 Indian Cir 32446 850-526-2761
Dayspring Christian Academy 200/PK-12
4685 Meadowview Rd 32446 850-526-4919

**Mayo, Lafayette, Pop. 1,208**
LaFayette County SD 1,200/PK-12
363 NE Crawford St 32066 386-294-1351
Robert Edwards, supt. Fax 294-3072
lafayette.schooldesk.net
LaFayette JSHS 600/6-12
160 NE Hornet Ln 32066 386-294-1701
Ray Hancock, prin. Fax 294-4197
Adult Education Adult
363 NE Crawford St 32066 386-294-1649
Stephen Clark, admin. Fax 294-4197

Lighthouse Christian Academy 100/PK-12
772 N State Road 51 32066 386-294-2994
Bobby Ur, hdmstr. Fax 294-3449

**Melbourne, Brevard, Pop. 74,011**
Brevard County SD 68,600/PK-12
2700 Judge Fran Jamieson 32940 321-633-1000
Dr. Desmond Blackburn, supt. Fax 633-3432
www.edline.net/pages/Brevard_County_Schools
Eau Gallie HS 1,600/9-12
1400 Commodore Blvd 32935 321-242-6400
Jeremy Salmon, prin. Fax 242-6427
Johnson MS 800/7-8
2155 Croton Rd 32935 321-242-6430
Robert Fish, prin. Fax 242-6436
Melbourne HS 2,000/9-12
74 Bulldog Blvd 32901 321-952-5880
James Kirk, prin. Fax 952-5898
Palm Bay HS 1,700/9-12
101 Pirate Ln 32901 321-952-5900
John Thomas, prin. Fax 676-2891
Stone MS 800/7-8
1101 E University Blvd 32901 321-723-0741
Mary Bland, prin. Fax 951-1497
West Shore JSHS 1,000/7-12
250 Wildcat Aly 32935 321-242-4730
Eric Fleming, prin. Fax 242-4740
Palm Bay Adult Center Adult
101 Pirate Ln 32901 321-952-5914
John Thomas, prin. Fax 676-2891
South Area Adult Center Adult
1362 S Babcock St 32901 321-952-5977
Jeff Arnott, prin. Fax 952-5831
Other Schools – See Cocoa, Cocoa Beach, Indialantic, Merritt Island, Palm Bay, Rockledge, Satellite Beach, Titusville, Viera, West Melbourne

Central Catholic HS 400/9-12
100 E Florida Ave 32901 321-727-0793
Thomas Armstrong, prin. Fax 727-1134
Community Christian S 100/K-12
1616 Ferndale Ave 32935 321-259-1590
Laurel Earls, prin. Fax 259-5301
Everest University - Melbourne Campus Post-Sec.
2401 N Harbor City Blvd 32935 321-253-2929
Florida Institute of Technology Post-Sec.
150 W University Blvd 32901 321-674-8000
Florida Prep 300/6-12
1950 Academy Dr 32901 321-723-3211
James Dwight, pres. Fax 676-9548
Holy Trinity Episcopal Academy 500/7-12
5625 Holy Trinity Dr 32940 321-723-8323
Nancy Giangrisostomi, head sch Fax 308-9077
Keiser University Post-Sec.
900 S Babcock St 32901 321-409-4800
New Covenant S 100/K-12
1990 W New Haven Ave # 306 32904 321-724-9603
Sandra Hancock, prin. Fax 724-6932
Shiloh Christian Academy 100/PK-12
155 E University Blvd 32934 321-956-1404
West Melbourne Christian Academy 100/K-12
3150 Milwaukee Ave 32904 321-725-3743

**Merritt Island, Brevard, Pop. 33,904**
Brevard County SD
Supt. — See Melbourne
Edgewood JSHS 900/7-12
180 E Merritt Ave 32953 321-454-1030
Dr. Kenneth Winn, prin. Fax 452-1176
Jefferson MS 600/7-8
1275 S Courtenay Pkwy 32952 321-453-5154
Dr. Lori Spinner, prin. Fax 459-2854
Merritt Island HS 1,500/9-12
100 Mustang Way 32953 321-454-1000
Mollie Vega, prin. Fax 454-1013

Avalon School of Cosmetology Post-Sec.
2088 N Courtenay Pkwy 32953 321-452-8490
Brevard Private Academy 100/7-12
508 S Plumosa St 32952 321-459-3466
Merritt Island Christian S 500/PK-12
140 Magnolia Ave 32952 321-453-2710
Dr. Nanci Dettra, supt. Fax 452-6580

**Miami, Miami-Dade, Pop. 396,081**
Miami-Dade County SD 333,100/PK-12
1450 NE 2nd Ave 33132 305-995-1000
Alberto Carvalho, supt. Fax 995-1488
www.dadeschools.net/
Ammons MS 1,200/6-8
17990 SW 142nd Ave 33177 305-971-0158
Maria Costa, prin. Fax 971-0179
Andover MS 1,200/6-8
121 NE 207th St 33179 305-654-2727
Rennina Turner, prin. Fax 654-2728
Arvida MS 1,300/6-8
10900 SW 127th Ave 33186 305-385-7144
Nancy Aragon, prin. Fax 383-9472
Baker Aviation S Vo/Tech
3275 NW 42nd Ave 33142 305-871-3143
Rene Mantilla, prin. Fax 871-5840
Bell MS 700/6-8
11800 NW 2nd St 33182 305-220-2075
Ingrid Soto, prin. Fax 229-0798
BioTECH @ Richmond Heights HS 9-12
15015 SW 103rd Ave 33176 786-573-5353
Barbara Mendizabel, prin. Fax 573-5350
Braddock HS 3,200/9-12
3601 SW 147th Ave 33185 305-225-9729
Manuel Garcia, prin. Fax 221-3312
Brownsville MS 500/7-9
4899 NW 24th Ave 33142 305-633-1481
Ebony Dunn, prin. Fax 635-8702
Canosa MS 2,000/6-8
15735 SW 144th St 33196 305-252-5900
Elio Falcon, prin. Fax 252-5901
Chiles MS 1,000/6-8
8190 NW 197th St 33015 305-816-9101
Nelson Izquierdo, prin. Fax 816-9248
Citrus Grove MS 1,000/6-8
2153 NW 3rd St 33125 305-642-5055
Cory Rodriguez, prin. Fax 642-9349
C.O.P.E. Center North 100/Alt
9950 NW 19th Ave 33147 305-836-3300
Dr. Colleen Del Terzo, prin. Fax 835-8818
Coral Reef HS 3,200/9-12
10101 SW 152nd St 33157 305-232-2044
Thomas Ennis, prin. Fax 252-3454
Country Club MS 1,400/6-8
18305 NW 75th Pl 33015 305-820-8800
Jose Fernandez, prin. Fax 820-8801
Curry MS 1,100/6-8
15750 SW 47th St 33185 305-222-2775
Jean Baril, prin. Fax 229-1521
Dario MS 700/6-8
350 NW 97th Ave 33172 305-226-0179
Dr. Verona McCarthy, prin. Fax 559-0919
De Diego MS 500/6-8
3100 NW 5th Ave 33127 305-573-7229
Dr. April Williams, prin. Fax 573-6415
Design & Architectural Magnet HS 500/9-12
4001 NE 2nd Ave 33137 305-573-7135
Dr. Stacy Mancuso, prin. Fax 573-8253
Ferguson HS 4,200/9-12
15900 SW 56th St 33185 305-408-2700
Rafael Villalobos, prin. Fax 408-6487
Glades MS 1,100/6-8
9451 SW 64th Ter 33173 305-271-3342
Cynthia Valdes-Garcia, prin. Fax 271-0402
Hammocks MS 1,200/6-8
9889 Hammocks Blvd 33196 305-385-0896
Deborah Leal, prin. Fax 382-0861
Highland Oaks MS 1,200/6-8
2375 NE 203rd St 33180 305-932-3810
Cheryl Kushi, prin. Fax 932-0676
Hopkins Technical Center Vo/Tech
750 NW 20th St 33127 305-324-6070
Nyce Daniel, prin. Fax 545-6397
IPreparatory Academy 50/9-12
1500 Biscayne Blvd 33132 305-995-1928
Alberto Carvalho, prin. Fax 523-0736
iTech @ Thomas A. Edison Educational Ctr 9-12
6101 NW 2nd Ave 33127 305-762-5000
Layda Nasr, prin. Fax 757-2219
Jefferson MS 300/7-9
525 NW 147th St 33168 305-681-7481
Robin Atkins, prin. Fax 688-5912
Jones-Ayers MS 600/6-8
1331 NW 46th St 33142 305-634-9787
Bernard Edwards, prin. Fax 638-8254
Kinloch Park MS 1,200/6-8
4340 NW 3rd St 33126 305-445-5467
Scott Weiner, prin. Fax 445-3110
Krop HS 2,800/9-12
1410 NE 215th St 33179 305-652-6808
Dr. Allison Harley, prin. Fax 651-8043
Law Enforcement Officers Memorial HS 300/9-12
300 NW 2nd Ave 33128 305-371-0400
Christopher Shinn, prin. Fax 371-0401
Madison MS 600/6-8
3400 NW 87th St 33147 305-836-2610
Uwezo Frazier, prin. Fax 696-5249
Mann MS 800/6-8
8950 NW 2nd Ave 33150 305-757-9537
Leon Maycock, prin. Fax 754-0724
MAST @ FIU Biscayne Bay 9-12
3000 NE 151st St 33181 305-919-4450
Dr. Matthew Welker, prin. Fax 919-4456
Mays Conservatory of the Arts 400/6-12
11700 SW 216th St 33170 305-233-2300
Martin Reid, prin. Fax 251-5462
McMillan MS 800/6-8
13100 SW 59th St 33183 305-385-6877
Hilca Thomas, prin. Fax 387-9641
Miami Arts Studio 6-12 6-12
15015 SW 24th St 33185 305-485-2323
Dr. Miguel Balsera, prin. Fax 485-2324
Miami Central HS 1,800/9-12
1781 NW 95th St 33147 305-696-4161
Gregory Bethune, prin. Fax 836-2872
Miami Coral Park HS 2,900/9-12
8865 SW 16th St 33165 305-226-6565
Alicia Hidalgo, prin. Fax 553-4658
Miami Edison HS 900/9-12
6161 NW 5th Ct 33127 305-751-7337
Trynegwa Diggs, prin. Fax 759-4561
Miami HS 2,700/9-12
2450 SW 1st St 33135 305-649-9800
Benny Valdes, prin. Fax 649-9475
Miami Jackson HS 1,200/9-12
1751 NW 36th St 33142 305-634-2621
Carlos Rios, prin. Fax 634-7477
Miami Killian HS 2,800/9-12
10655 SW 97th Ave 33176 305-271-3311
Magda Pereira, prin. Fax 275-5494
Miami Norland HS 1,400/9-12
1050 NW 195th St 33169 305-653-1416
Reginald Lee, prin. Fax 651-6175
Miami Northwestern HS 1,600/9-12
1100 NW 71st St 33150 305-836-0991
Wallace Aristide, prin. Fax 691-4955
Miami Southridge HS 2,200/9-12
19355 SW 114th Ave 33157 305-238-6110
Humberto Miret, prin. Fax 253-4456
Miami Sunset HS 2,400/9-12
13125 SW 72nd St 33183 305-385-4255
John Lux, prin. Fax 385-6458
New World S of the Arts 500/9-12
25 NE 2nd St 33132 305-237-3135
Evonne Alvarez, prin. Fax 237-3794
Norland MS 700/6-8
1235 NW 192nd Ter 33169 305-653-1210
Ronald Redmon, prin. Fax 654-1237
Richmond Heights MS 700/6-8
15015 SW 103rd Ave 33176 305-238-2316
Kristal Hickmon, prin. Fax 251-3712
Riviera MS 800/6-8
10301 SW 48th St 33165 305-226-4286
Dr. Winston Whyte, prin. Fax 226-1025

Rockway MS 1,300/6-8
9393 SW 29th Ter 33165 305-221-8212
Melanie Megias, prin. Fax 221-5940
School for Advanced Studies - North 100/11-12
11380 NW 27th Ave Ste 1111 33167 305-237-1089
Dr. Omar Monteagudo, prin. Fax 237-1610
School for Advanced Studies-South 200/11-12
11011 SW 104th St Ste 706 33176 305-237-0510
Dr. Omar Monteagudo, prin. Fax 237-0511
School for Advanced Studies-Wolfson 100/11-12
25 NE 2nd St 33132 305-237-7270
Dr. Omar Monteagudo, prin. Fax 237-7271
Shenandoah MS 1,200/6-8
1950 SW 19th St 33145 305-856-8282
Bianca Calzadilla, prin. Fax 856-7049
South Miami HS 2,200/9-12
6856 SW 53rd St 33155 305-666-5871
Gilberto Bonce, prin. Fax 666-6359
Southwest Miami HS 3,000/9-12
8855 SW 50th Ter 33165 305-274-0181
Carlos Diaz, prin. Fax 596-7370
TERRA Environmental Research Institute 1,300/9-12
11005 SW 84th St 33173 305-412-5800
Caridad Montano, prin. Fax 412-5801
Thomas MS 700/6-8
13001 SW 26th St 33175 305-995-3800
Allen Breeding, prin. Fax 995-3537
Turner Technical Arts HS Vo/Tech
10151 NW 19th Ave 33147 305-691-8324
Lavette Hunter, prin. Fax 693-9463
Varela HS 3,000/9-12
15255 SW 96th St 33196 305-752-7900
Nery Fins, prin. Fax 386-8987
Wallace C.O.P.E. Center 100/Alt
10225 SW 147th Ter 33176 305-233-1044
Annette Burks, prin. Fax 256-8694
Washington HS 1,000/9-12
1200 NW 6th Ave 33136 305-324-8900
William Aristide, prin. Fax 324-4676
West Miami MS 1,100/6-8
7525 SW 24th St 33155 305-261-8383
Katyna Lopez-Martin, prin. Fax 267-8204
Westview MS 400/6-8
1901 NW 127th St 33167 305-681-6647
Dr. David Moore, prin. Fax 685-3192
Young Mens Preparatory Academy 100/6-12
3001 NW 2nd Ave 33127 305-571-1111
Pierre Edouard, prin. Fax 571-1112
Young Women's Preparatory Academy 400/6-12
1150 SW 1st St 33130 305-575-1200
Concepcion Martinez, prin. Fax 325-8071
Dorsey Education Center Adult
7100 NW 17th Ave 33147 305-693-2490
Dr. Angela Thomas-Dupree, prin. Fax 691-7492
English Center Adult
3501 SW 28th St 33133 305-445-7731
Yamila Carballo, prin. Fax 441-2150
Miami Coral Park Adult Education Ctr Adult
8865 SW 16th St 33165 305-226-6565
Robert Novak, prin. Fax 559-7415
Miami Jackson Adult Education Center Adult
1751 NW 36th St 33142 305-634-2621
Joey Bautista, prin. Fax 633-8191
Miami Palmetto Adult Education Center Adult
7460 SW 118th St 33156 305-235-1360
Dr. Barbara Hawkins, prin. Fax 253-3898
Miami Senior Adult Education Center Adult
2450 SW 1st St 33135 305-649-9800
Alan Bashaw, prin. Fax 643-2395
Miami Sunset Adult Education Center Adult
13125 SW 72nd St 33183 305-385-4255
Julian Cazanas, prin. Fax 386-9218
Southwest Adult Education Ctr. Adult
8855 SW 50th Ter 33165 305-274-0181
Robert Novak, prin. Fax 274-3351
Turner Tech Adult Ed Center Adult
10151 NW 19th Ave 33147 305-691-8324
Lavette Hunter, prin. Fax 693-9463
Other Schools – See Coral Gables, Cutler Bay, Doral, El Portal, Hialeah, Hialeah Gardens, Homestead, Key Biscayne, Miami Beach, Miami Gardens, Miami Lakes, Miami Springs, Naranja, North Miami, North Miami Beach, Opa Locka, Palmetto Bay, Perrine, Pinecrest, South Miami

---

Acupuncture & Massage College Post-Sec.
10506 N Kendall Dr 33176 305-595-9500
American HS Academy 600/6-12
10300 SW 72nd St Ste 427 33173 305-270-1440
American Medical Acadmey Post-Sec.
12215 SW 112th St 33186 305-271-6555
Archbishop Coleman Carroll HS 500/9-12
10300 SW 167th Ave 33196 305-388-6700
Sr. Margaret Ann, prin. Fax 388-4371
Archbishop Curley-Notre Dame HS 300/9-12
4949 NE 2nd Ave 33137 305-751-8367
Douglas Romanik, prin. Fax 751-3517
Beis Chana S for Girls 500/9-12
17330 NW 7th Ave 33169 305-653-8770
Rabbi Benzion Korf, prin. Fax 653-6790
Belen Jesuit Preparatory HS 1,500/6-12
500 SW 127th Ave 33184 305-223-8600
Dr. Maria Reyes-Garcia, prin. Fax 227-2565
Brito Miami Private S 300/PK-12
2732 SW 32nd Ave 33133 305-448-1463
Brother Rice Academy 6-8
4949 NE 2nd Ave 33137 305-751-8367
Douglas Romanik, prin. Fax 751-3517
Calusa Preparatory S 200/K-12
12515 SW 72nd St 33183 305-596-3787
Carlos Albizu University Post-Sec.
2173 NW 99th Ave 33172 305-593-1223
Center of Cinematography Art & TV Post-Sec.
1637 NW 27th Ave 33125 305-634-0550
Champagnat Catholic S 200/PK-12
2609 NW 7th St 33125 305-642-4132
City College Post-Sec.
9300 S Dadeland Blvd # 200 33156 305-666-9242
College of Business & Technology Post-Sec.
8230 W Flagler St 33144 305-764-3165
College of Business & Technology Post-Sec.
8765 SW 165th Ave Ste 114 33193 305-764-3165
Columbus HS 1,400/9-12
3000 SW 87th Ave 33165 305-223-5650
David Pugh, prin. Fax 559-4306
Compu-Med Vocational Careers Post-Sec.
9738 SW 24th St 33165 305-553-2898
Dade Christian S 900/PK-12
6601 NW 167th St 33015 305-822-7690
Dade Medical College Post-Sec.
3721 NW 7th St Ste 1 33126 786-363-4910
DeVry University Post-Sec.
8700 W Flagler St Ste 100 33174 305-229-4833
Educating Hands School of Massage Post-Sec.
3883 Biscayne Blvd 33137 305-285-6991
Eureka Institute of Health and Beauty Post-Sec.
11373 W Flagler St Ste 209 33174 305-480-1005
Everest Institute Post-Sec.
9020 SW 137th Ave 33186 305-386-9900
Everest Institute Post-Sec.
111 NW 183rd St Ste 200 33169 305-949-9500
Florida Career College Post-Sec.
1321 SW 107th Ave Ste 201B 33174 305-553-6065
Florida Career College Post-Sec.
11731 Mills Dr Bldg 2 33183 888-852-7272
Florida Christian S 1,400/PK-12
4200 SW 89th Ave 33165 305-226-8152
Dr. Robert Andrews, hdmstr. Fax 226-8166
Florida College of Natural Health Post-Sec.
7925 NW 12th St Ste 201 33126 305-597-9599
Florida International University Post-Sec.
11200 SW 8th St 33199 305-348-2000
Florida National University Post-Sec.
11865 SW 26th St Ste H3 33175 305-266-9999
Fortis College Post-Sec.
7757 W Flagler St 33144 305-717-7000
Future Tech Institute Post-Sec.
3446 SW 8th St Ste 213 33135 305-774-0227
George T. Baker Aviation School Post-Sec.
3275 NW 42nd Ave 33142 305-871-3143
Grace Christian Preparatory S 100/K-12
11000 SW 216th St 33170 305-259-1929
Greater Miami Adventist Academy 300/PK-12
500 NW 122nd Ave 33182 305-220-5955
Hope Center Post-Sec.
1411 NW 14th Ave 33125 305-545-7572
Immaculata - La Salle HS 800/9-12
3601 S Miami Ave 33133 305-854-2334
Sr. Kim Keraitis, prin. Fax 858-5971
International Training Careers Post-Sec.
7360 Coral Way 33155 800-649-8139
ITT Technical Institute Post-Sec.
7955 NW 12th St Ste 119 33126 305-477-3080
Jackson Memorial Medical Center Post-Sec.
1611 NW 12th Ave 33136 305-585-6754
Keiser University Post-Sec.
2101 NW 117th Ave 33172 305-596-2226
Keystone National HS 800/9-12
12840 NW 1st Ct 33168 866-257-6011
Killian Oaks Academy 100/PK-12
10545 SW 97th Ave 33176 305-274-2221
La Belle Beauty Academy Post-Sec.
2960 SW 8th St 33135 305-649-2800
La Progressiva Presbyterian S 400/PK-12
2480 NW 7th St 33125 305-642-8600
Lincoln-Marti S 1,100/PK-12
931 SW 1st St 33130 305-324-4060
Lindsey Hopkins Technical Education Ctr Post-Sec.
750 NW 20th St 33127 305-324-6070
Management Resources Institute Post-Sec.
10 NW 42nd Ave Ste 400 33126 305-442-9223
Marti S 100/4-8
1685 SW 32nd Ave 33145 305-441-0565
Edith Ysada, prin. Fax 443-9359
Miami Christian S 300/PK-12
200 NW 109th Ave 33172 305-221-7754
Lorena Morrison Ed.D., head sch Fax 221-7783
Miami Country Day S 1,000/PK-12
601 NE 107th St 33161 305-759-2843
Dr. John Davies, head sch Fax 397-0370
Miami Dade College Post-Sec.
300 NE 2nd Ave 33132 305-237-8888
Miami-Dade College Post-Sec.
950 NW 20th St 33127 305-237-4160
Miami-Dade College Post-Sec.
11380 NW 27th Ave 33167 305-237-1000
Miami-Dade College Post-Sec.
11011 SW 104th St 33176 305-237-2000
Miami-Dade College Post-Sec.
627 SW 27th Ave 33135 305-237-6000
Miami International Univ of Art & Design Post-Sec.
1501 Biscayne Blvd Ste 100 33132 305-428-5700
New Concept Massage & Beauty School Post-Sec.
2022 SW 1st St 33135 305-642-3020
New World School of the Arts Post-Sec.
300 NE 2nd Ave 33132 305-237-7007
Northwest Christian Academy 300/PK-12
951 NW 136th St 33168 305-685-8734
Jerry Nelson, admin. Fax 685-5341
Nouvelle Institute Post-Sec.
3271 NW 7th St Ste 106 33125 305-643-3360
Our Lady of Lourdes Academy 800/9-12
5525 SW 84th St 33143 305-667-1623
Sr. Kathryn Donze, prin. Fax 663-3121
Professional Training Center Post-Sec.
13926 SW 47th St 33175 305-220-4120
Revelation S of Florida 500/PK-12
10680 SW 186th St 33157 305-969-9448
Riviera Preparatory S 200/6-12
9775 SW 87 Ave 33176 786-300-0300
St. Brendan HS 1,200/9-12
2950 SW 87th Ave 33165 305-223-5181
Dr. Jose Rodelgo-Bueno, prin. Fax 220-7434
St. John Vianney College Seminary Post-Sec.
2900 SW 87th Ave 33165 305-223-4561
South Florida Institute of Technology Post-Sec.
720 NW 27th Ave Fl 2 33125 305-649-2050
The Praxis Institute Post-Sec.
1850 SW 8th St 33135 305-642-4104
Universal Beauty School Post-Sec.
10720 W Flagler St Ste 21 33174 305-485-7700
Westwood Christian S 500/PK-12
5801 SW 120th Ave 33183 305-274-3380
Worshipers House of Prayer Academy 100/K-12
8350 NW 7th Ave 33150 305-200-3245
Marie Zizi, prin. Fax 460-8045

**Miami Beach, Miami-Dade, Pop. 86,463**
Miami-Dade County SD
Supt. — See Miami
Miami Beach HS 2,400/9-12
2231 Prairie Ave 33139 305-532-4515
John Donohue, prin. Fax 531-9209
Nautilus MS 800/7-8
4301 N Michigan Ave 33140 305-532-3481
Rene Bellmas, prin. Fax 532-8906
Miami Beach Adult Center Adult
1424 Drexel Ave 33139 305-531-0451
Judith DelGado, prin. Fax 531-2352

---

Hebrew Academy (RASG) 500/PK-12
2400 Pine Tree Dr 33140 305-532-6421
Rabbi Zvi Kahn, head sch Fax 672-6191
Klurman Mesivta HS 100/7-12
1140 Alton Rd 33139 305-653-8770
Mechina HS of South Florida 100/7-12
4000 Alton Rd 33140 305-534-7050
Miami Ad School Post-Sec.
955 Alton Rd 33139 305-538-3193
Mt. Sinai Medical Center Post-Sec.
4300 Alton Rd 33140 305-674-2222
Talmudic University Post-Sec.
4000 Alton Rd 33140 305-534-7050
Yeshiva Gedolah Rabbinical College Post-Sec.
1140 Alton Rd 33139 305-653-8770

**Miami Gardens, Miami-Dade, Pop. 105,806**
Miami-Dade County SD
Supt. — See Miami
Carol City MS 700/6-8
3737 NW 188th St, 305-624-2652
Sonia Romero, prin. Fax 623-2955
Lake Stevens MS 600/6-8
18484 NW 48th Pl, 305-620-1294
Dr. Mark Soffian, prin. Fax 620-1345
Miami Carol City HS 1,800/9-12
3301 Miami Gardens Dr, 305-621-5681
Jamarv Dunn, prin. Fax 620-8862
North Dade MS 700/6-8
1840 NW 157th St, 305-624-8415
Fabrice Laguerre, prin. Fax 628-2954

---

Azure College Post-Sec.
1525 NW 167th St, 305-751-0001
College of Business and Technology Post-Sec.
5190 NW 167th St 33014 305-764-3165
Florida Memorial University Post-Sec.
15800 NW 42nd Ave, 305-626-3600
Monsignor Edward Pace HS 900/9-12
15600 NW 32nd Ave, 305-624-8534
Ana Garcia, prin. Fax 521-0185
St. Thomas University Post-Sec.
16401 NW 37th Ave, 305-628-6546

**Miami Lakes, Miami-Dade, Pop. 29,182**
Miami-Dade County SD
Supt. — See Miami
Goleman HS 2,100/9-12
14100 NW 89th Ave 33018 305-362-0676
Joaquin Hernandez, prin. Fax 827-0249
Miami Lakes Educational Center Vo/Tech
5780 NW 158th St 33014 305-557-1100
James Parker, prin. Fax 827-9317
Miami Lakes MS 800/6-8
6425 Miami Lakeway N 33014 305-557-3900
Dr. Manuel Sanchez, prin. Fax 828-6753

---

Southeastern College Post-Sec.
17395 NW 59th Ave 33015 305-820-5003

**Miami Shores, Miami-Dade, Pop. 10,271**

---

Barry University Post-Sec.
11300 NE 2nd Ave 33161 305-899-3000

**Miami Springs, Miami-Dade, Pop. 13,739**
Miami-Dade County SD
Supt. — See Miami
Miami Springs HS 1,900/9-12
751 Dove Ave 33166 305-885-3585
Edward Smith, prin. Fax 884-2632
Miami Springs MS 1,600/6-8
150 S Royal Poinciana Blvd 33166 305-888-6457
Kimberly Emmanuel, prin. Fax 887-5281
Miami Springs Adult Education Center Adult
751 Dove Ave 33166 305-885-3585
Miguel Veloso, prin. Fax 884-2632

**Middleburg, Clay, Pop. 12,797**
Clay County SD
Supt. — See Green Cove Springs
Middleburg HS 1,700/9-12
3750 County Road 220 32068 904-213-2100
Robert Feltner, prin. Fax 291-5462
Wilkinson JHS 700/7-8
5025 County Road 218 32068 904-291-5500
Christina Cornwell, prin. Fax 291-5510

**Milton, Santa Rosa, Pop. 8,470**
Santa Rosa County SD 25,400/PK-12
5086 Canal St 32570 850-983-5000
Tim Wyrosdick, supt. Fax 983-5013
www.santarosa.k12.fl.us/
Avalon MS 800/6-8
5445 King Arthurs Way 32583 850-983-5540
David Sigurnjak, prin. Fax 983-5545
Central S 500/K-12
6180 Central School Rd 32570 850-983-5640
Sean Twitty, prin. Fax 983-5645
Hobbs MS 800/6-8
5317 Glover Ln 32570 850-983-5630
Floyd Smith, prin. Fax 983-5635

King MS 500/6-8
5928 Stewart St 32570 850-983-5660
Darren Brock, prin. Fax 983-5665
Learning Academy 100/Alt
5880 Stewart St 32570 850-983-3495
Kara Whitney, admin. Fax 983-8098
Locklin Technical Center Vo/Tech
5330 Berryhill Rd 32570 850-983-5700
Maria LaDouceur, prin. Fax 983-5715
Milton HS 1,800/9-12
5445 Stewart St 32570 850-983-5600
Tim Short, prin. Fax 983-5610
Santa Rosa HS Adult
5330 Berryhill Rd 32570 850-983-5710
Donna Christopher, prin. Fax 983-5345
Other Schools – See Gulf Breeze, Jay, Navarre, Pace

Radford M. Locklin Technical Center Post-Sec.
5330 Berryhill Rd 32570 850-983-5700
Santa Rosa Christian S 300/PK-12
6331 Chestnut St 32570 850-623-4671
West Florida Baptist Academy 200/K-12
5621 Highway 90 32583 850-623-9307

**Minneola, Lake, Pop. 9,082**
Lake County SD
Supt. — See Tavares
Lake Minneola HS 1,300/9-12
101 N Hancock Rd, 352-394-9600
Linda Shepherd-Miller, prin. Fax 394-9601

**Miramar, Broward, Pop. 118,644**
Broward County SD
Supt. — See Fort Lauderdale
Everglades HS 2,700/9-12
17100 SW 48th Ct 33027 754-323-0500
Haleh Darbar, prin. Fax 323-0640
Glades MS 1,600/6-8
16700 SW 48th Ct 33027 754-323-4600
Krista Herrera, prin. Fax 323-4685
Miramar HS 2,600/9-12
3601 SW 89th Ave 33025 754-323-1350
Maria Formoso, prin. Fax 323-1480
New Renaissance MS 1,200/6-8
10701 Miramar Blvd 33025 754-323-3500
Janet Morales, prin. Fax 323-3585
Perry MS 700/6-8
3400 Wildcat Way 33023 754-323-3900
Davida Johnson, prin. Fax 323-3985

Brown Mackie College - Miami Post-Sec.
3700 Lakeside Dr 33027 305-341-6600
Chamberlain College of Nursing Post-Sec.
2300 SW 145th Ave 33027 954-885-3510
Concorde Career Institute Post-Sec.
10933 Marks Way 33025 954-731-8880
DeVry University Post-Sec.
2300 SW 145th Ave 33027 954-499-9700
Le Cordon Bleu College of Culinary Arts Post-Sec.
3221 Enterprise Way 33025 954-438-8882
Unilatina International College Post-Sec.
3130 Commerce Pkwy 33025 954-607-4344

**Monticello, Jefferson, Pop. 2,477**
Jefferson County SD 1,000/PK-12
1490 W Washington St 32344 850-342-0100
Al Cooksey, supt. Fax 342-0108
www.jeffersonschooldistrict.org
Jefferson County MSHS 400/6-12
50 David Rd 32344 850-997-3555
Dr. Baron McCombs, prin. Fax 997-4773
Turning Point Alternative S Alt
575 S Water St 32344 850-342-0100
Nancy Whitty, prin.
Jefferson County Adult Center Adult
575 S Water St 32344 850-342-0100
Sherman Stroman, prin. Fax 342-0108

Aucilla Christian Academy 300/PK-12
7803 Aucilla Rd 32344 850-997-3597

**Montverde, Lake, Pop. 1,436**

Montverde Academy 900/PK-12
17235 7th St 34756 407-469-2561
Dr. Kasey Kesselring, hdmstr. Fax 469-3711

**Moore Haven, Glades, Pop. 1,667**
Glades County SD 1,400/PK-12
PO Box 459 33471 863-946-0202
Scott Bass, supt. Fax 946-1529
www.gladesedu.org
Moore Haven MSHS 300/6-12
PO Box 99 33471 863-946-0811
Tim Wilder, prin. Fax 946-1532

**Mount Dora, Lake, Pop. 12,205**
Lake County SD
Supt. — See Tavares
Mount Dora HS 1,100/9-12
700 N Highland St 32757 352-383-2177
Dr. Rhonda Boone, prin. Fax 383-6466
Mount Dora MS 800/6-8
1405 Lincoln Ave 32757 352-383-6101
Jacob Stein, prin. Fax 383-4949

Mount Dora Christian Academy 600/PK-12
301 W 13th Ave 32757 352-383-2155
Dr. Brad Moser, hdmstr. Fax 383-3112
Solid Rock Christian S 100/PK-12
21951 US Highway 441 32757 352-735-5777
Southern Technical College Post-Sec.
2799 W Old US Highway 441 32757 352-383-4242

**Mulberry, Polk, Pop. 3,765**
Polk County SD
Supt. — See Bartow
Mulberry HS 1,000/9-12
1 NE 4th Cir 33860 863-701-1104
Michael Young, prin. Fax 701-1109
Mulberry MS 1,000/6-8
500 Dr MLK Jr Ave 33860 863-701-1066
Cynthia Cangelose, prin. Fax 701-1068
New Horizons S 50/Alt
6980 State Road 37 S 33860 863-428-1520
Brett Butler, prin. Fax 428-2204

Fortis Institute Post-Sec.
5925 Imperial Pkwy Ste 200 33860 863-646-1400

**Naples, Collier, Pop. 19,366**
Collier County SD 42,000/PK-12
5775 Osceola Trl 34109 239-377-0001
Dr. Kamela Patton, supt. Fax 377-0206
www.collierschools.com
Beacon HS 300/Alt
3710 Estey Ave 34104 239-377-1060
Dr. Cynthia Janssen, prin. Fax 377-1051
Collier HS 1,800/9-12
5600 Cougar Dr 34109 239-377-1200
Jose Hernandez, prin. Fax 377-1201
Corkscrew MS 700/6-8
1165 County Road 858 34120 239-377-3400
Dennis Snider, prin. Fax 377-3401
Cypress Palm MS 800/6-8
4255 18th Ave NE 34120 239-377-5200
John Kasten, prin. Fax 377-5201
East Naples MS 1,000/6-8
4100 Estey Ave 34104 239-377-3600
Darren Burkett, prin. Fax 377-3601
Golden Gate HS 1,400/9-12
2925 Titan Way 34116 239-377-1600
Dr. Tobin Walcott, prin. Fax 377-1601
Golden Gate MS 900/6-8
2701 48th Ter SW 34116 239-377-3800
Dr. Mason Clark, prin. Fax 377-3801
Gulf Coast HS 1,900/9-12
7878 Shark Way 34119 239-377-1400
Joseph Mikulski, prin. Fax 377-1401
Gulfview MS 700/6-8
255 6th St S 34102 239-377-4000
Kevin Huelsman, prin. Fax 377-4001
Lely HS 1,500/9-12
1 Lely High School Blvd 34113 239-377-2000
Ryan Nemeth, prin. Fax 377-2001
Manatee MS 800/6-8
1920 Manatee Rd 34114 239-377-4400
Pamela Vickaryous, prin. Fax 377-4401
Naples HS 1,600/9-12
1100 Golden Eagle Cir 34102 239-377-2200
Kevin Saba, prin. Fax 377-2201
New Beginnings S - Naples 50/Alt
3710 Estey Ave 34104 239-377-1050
Eric Peltz, lead tchr. Fax 377-1051
North Naples MS 900/6-8
16165 Learning Ln 34110 239-377-4600
Margaret Jackson, prin. Fax 377-4601
Oakridge MS 1,100/6-8
14975 Collier Blvd 34119 239-377-4800
Kimberly Lonergan, prin. Fax 377-4801
Palmetto Ridge HS 1,900/9-12
1655 Victory Ln 34120 239-377-2400
Jon Bremseth, prin. Fax 377-2401
Pine Ridge MS 1,000/6-8
1515 Pine Ridge Rd 34109 239-377-5000
Sean Kinsley, prin. Fax 377-5001
Walker Technical HS Vo/Tech
3702 Estey Ave 34104 239-377-3300
Yolanda Flores, prin. Fax 377-3301
Other Schools – See Everglades City, Immokalee

Ave Maria School of Law Post-Sec.
1025 Commons Cir 34119 239-687-5300
Community S of Naples 700/PK-12
13275 Livingston Rd 34109 239-597-7575
Dr. David Watson, head sch Fax 598-2973
First Baptist Academy 500/PK-12
3000 Orange Blossom Dr 34109 239-597-2233
Thomas Rider, admin. Fax 597-4187
Hodges University Post-Sec.
2655 Northbrooke Dr 34119 239-513-1122
Lorenzo Walker Institute of Technology Post-Sec.
3702 Estey Ave 34104 239-377-0900
Nicaea Academy 200/PK-12
14785 Collier Blvd 34119 239-353-9099
St. John Neumann Catholic HS 200/9-12
3000 53rd St SW 34116 239-455-3044
Sr. Patricia Roche, prin. Fax 455-2966
Seacrest Country Day S 500/PK-12
7100 Davis Blvd 34104 239-793-1986
D. John Watson Ph.D., head sch Fax 793-1460
Wolford College Post-Sec.
1336 Creekside Blvd Ste 2 34108 239-513-1135

**Naranja, Miami-Dade, Pop. 8,180**
Miami-Dade County SD
Supt. — See Miami
Miami MacArthur South HS 100/Alt
13990 SW 264th St 33032 305-258-7200
Gregory Beckford, prin. Fax 258-7201

**Navarre, Santa Rosa, Pop. 30,113**
Santa Rosa County SD
Supt. — See Milton
Holley-Navarre MS 700/6-8
1976 Williams Creek Dr 32566 850-936-6040
Joie DeStefano, prin. Fax 936-6049
Navarre HS 1,900/9-12
8600 High School Blvd 32566 850-936-6080
Brian Noack, prin. Fax 936-6088

**Neptune Beach, Duval, Pop. 6,907**
Duval County SD
Supt. — See Jacksonville
Fletcher HS 2,300/9-12
700 Seagate Ave 32266 904-247-5905
Donald Nelson, prin. Fax 247-5920

Beaches Chapel Christian S 300/PK-12
610 Florida Blvd 32266 904-241-4211

**Newberry, Alachua, Pop. 4,851**
Alachua County SD
Supt. — See Gainesville
Newberry HS 600/9-12
400 SW 258th St 32669 352-472-1101
Kevin Purvis, prin. Fax 472-1116
Oak View MS 600/6-8
1203 SW 250th St 32669 352-472-1102
Katherine Munn, prin. Fax 472-1131

**New Port Richey, Pasco, Pop. 14,612**
Pasco County SD
Supt. — See Land O Lakes
Bayonet Point MS 800/6-8
11125 Little Rd 34654 727-774-7400
Shelley Carrino, prin. Fax 774-7491
Gulf HS 1,300/9-12
5355 School Rd 34652 727-774-3300
Kim Davis, prin. Fax 774-3391
Gulf MS 800/6-8
6419 Louisiana Ave 34653 727-774-8000
Jason Joens, prin. Fax 774-8091
Marchman Technical Education Center Vo/Tech
7825 Campus Dr 34653 727-774-1700
Robert Aguis, prin. Fax 774-1791
Mitchell HS 1,800/9-12
2323 Little Rd 34655 727-774-9200
James Michaels, prin. Fax 774-9291
Ridgewood HS 1,100/9-12
7650 Orchid Lake Rd 34653 727-774-3900
Angie Murphy, prin. Fax 774-3991
River Ridge HS 1,600/9-12
11646 Town Center Rd 34654 727-774-7200
Toni Zetzsche, prin. Fax 774-7291
River Ridge MS 1,100/6-8
11646 Town Center Rd 34654 727-774-7000
Marcy Nettles, prin. Fax 774-7291
Seven Springs MS 1,300/6-8
2441 Little Rd 34655 727-774-6700
Christopher Dunning, prin. Fax 774-6791
Schwettman Education Center Adult
5520 Grand Blvd 34652 727-774-0000
Randy Koenigsfeld, prin. Fax 774-0091

Benes International School of Beauty Post-Sec.
7027 US Highway 19 34652 727-848-8415
Elfers Christian S 200/PK-12
5630 Olympia St 34652 727-845-0235
Genesis Preparatory S 100/6-12
7710 Osteen Rd 34653 727-846-8407
Millennium Academy 100/K-12
1005 Ridge Rd 34654 727-845-8150
New Port Richey SDA S 100/PK-12
4416 Thys Rd 34653 727-842-8919
Keith Nelson, prin. Fax 842-8919
Pasco-Hernando Community College Post-Sec.
10230 Ridge Rd 34654 727-847-2727
Rasmussen College Post-Sec.
8661 Citizens Dr 34654 727-942-0069
Southeastern College Post-Sec.
6014 US Highway 19 Ste 250 34652 727-487-6855

**New Smyrna Beach, Volusia, Pop. 22,191**
Volusia County SD
Supt. — See De Land
New Smyrna Beach HS 1,900/9-12
1015 10th St 32168 386-424-2555
Karen Chenoweth, prin. Fax 424-2505
New Smyrna Beach MS 1,300/6-8
1200 S Myrtle Ave 32168 386-424-2550
Elizabeth Johnson, prin. Fax 424-2504

Knight's Christian Academy 50/PK-12
310 Douglas St 2nd Floor 32168 386-426-0800
Wanda Conley, admin. Fax 426-0805

**Niceville, Okaloosa, Pop. 12,288**
Okaloosa County SD
Supt. — See Fort Walton Beach
Niceville HS 1,900/9-12
800 John Sims Pkwy E 32578 850-833-4114
Jeff Palmer, prin. Fax 833-4267
Ruckel MS 900/6-8
201 Partin Dr N 32578 850-833-4142
Paul Whiddon, prin. Fax 833-3291

Northwest Florida State College Post-Sec.
100 College Blvd E 32578 850-678-5111
Rocky Bayou Christian S 600/PK-12
2101 Partin Dr N 32578 850-729-7227
Michael Mosley Ph.D., supt. Fax 729-2513

**North Fort Myers, Lee, Pop. 39,050**
Lee County SD
Supt. — See Fort Myers
North Fort Myers HS 1,600/9-12
5000 Orange Grove Blvd 33903 239-995-2117
Matthew Mederios, prin. Fax 995-1243

Temple Christian S 100/PK-12
18841 State Road 31 33917 239-543-3222

**North Lauderdale, Broward, Pop. 39,771**
Broward County SD
Supt. — See Fort Lauderdale
Silver Lakes MS 500/6-8
7600 Tam Oshanter Blvd 33068 754-322-4600
Alison Trautmann, prin. Fax 322-4685

**North Miami, Miami-Dade, Pop. 57,562**
Miami-Dade County SD
Supt. — See Miami
North Miami HS 2,600/9-12
13110 NE 8th Ave 33161 305-891-6590
Daryl Branton, prin. Fax 895-1788
North Miami MS 700/7-9
700 NE 137th St 33161 305-891-5611
Patrick Lacouty, prin. Fax 891-4057
North Miami Adult Education Center Adult
13110 NE 8th Ave 33161 305-981-6774
Jean Ridore, prin. Fax 895-6248

Johnson & Wales University Post-Sec.
1701 NE 127th St 33181 305-892-7000
Miami Union Academy 300/PK-12
12600 NW 4th Ave 33168 305-953-9907

**North Miami Beach, Miami-Dade, Pop. 40,525**
Miami-Dade County SD
Supt. — See Miami
Kennedy MS 1,400/6-8
1075 NE 167th St 33162 305-947-1451
Mary Parton, prin. Fax 949-9046
Mourning HS 1,600/9-12
2601 NE 151st St 33160 305-919-2000
Lisa Garcia, prin. Fax 919-2001
North Miami Beach HS 2,200/9-12
1247 NE 167th St 33162 305-949-8381
Randy Milliken, prin. Fax 949-0491

Allison Academy 100/6-12
1881 NE 164th St 33162 305-940-3922
Dr. Sarah Allison, dir. Fax 940-1820
Bais Yaakov S for Girls 300/6-12
1110 NE 163rd St 33162 305-957-1670
Chames HS 100/9-12
1025 NE Miami Gardens Dr 33179 305-944-5344
Rohr MS 6-8
1051 N Miami Beach Blvd 33162 305-947-7779
Rabbi Ephraim Palgon, prin. Fax 947-7221
SAE Institute of Technology Post-Sec.
16051 W Dixie Hwy Ste 200 33160 305-944-7494
Scheck Hillel Community S 900/PK-12
19000 NE 25th Ave, Miami FL 33180 305-931-2831
Dr. Ezra Levy, hdmstr. Fax 932-7463
Sha'arei Bina Torah Academy for Girls 50/6-12
1557 NE 164th St Ste 206 33162 305-956-3755
Rabbi Elchonon Abramchik, prin. Fax 956-3758
Union Institute & University Post-Sec.
16853 NE 2nd Ave Ste 102 33162 305-653-7141

**North Palm Beach, Palm Beach, Pop. 11,885**

Baldwin Prep S 100/K-12
200 Castlewood Dr 33408 561-844-7700
Benjamin S 1,300/PK-12
11000 Ellison Wilson Rd 33408 561-626-3747
Robert Goldberg, head sch Fax 626-8752

**North Port, Sarasota, Pop. 56,337**
Sarasota County SD
Supt. — See Sarasota
Heron Creek MS 1,100/6-8
6501 W Price Blvd, 941-480-3371
Matthew Gruhl, prin. Fax 480-3398
North Port HS 2,300/9-12
6400 W Price Blvd, 941-423-8558
David Jones, prin. Fax 480-3199
Woodland MS 700/6-8
2700 Panacea Blvd 34289 941-240-8590
Cindy Hall, prin. Fax 240-8589

**Oakland Park, Broward, Pop. 40,410**
Broward County SD
Supt. — See Fort Lauderdale
Northeast HS 2,100/9-12
700 NE 56th St 33334 754-322-1550
Anthony Valachovic, prin. Fax 322-1680
Rickards MS 800/6-8
6000 NE 9th Ave 33334 754-322-4400
Washington Collado, prin. Fax 322-4485

**Ocala, Marion, Pop. 55,278**
Marion County SD 40,600/PK-12
PO Box 670 34478 352-671-7700
George Tomyn, supt. Fax 671-7581
www.marion.k12.fl.us
Forest HS 2,200/9-12
5000 SE Maricamp Rd 34480 352-671-4700
Brent Carson, prin. Fax 671-4702
Fort King MS 1,200/6-8
545 NE 17th Ave 34470 352-671-4725
Gary Smallridge, prin. Fax 671-4726
Horizon Academy - Marion Oak 800/5-8
365 Marion Oaks Dr 34473 352-671-6290
Troy Sanford, prin. Fax 671-6291
Howard MS 1,100/6-8
1655 NW 10th St 34475 352-671-7225
Robert Hensel, prin. Fax 671-7226
Lake Weir HS 1,700/9-12
10351 SE Maricamp Rd 34472 352-671-4820
Wayne Livingston, prin. Fax 671-4829
Liberty MS 1,100/6-8
4773 SW 95th St 34476 352-291-7930
Jennifer Sibbald, prin. Fax 291-7931
Marion Technical Institute 50/9-12
1614 E Fort King St 34471 352-671-4765
Jim Wohrley, prin. Fax 671-4766
Osceola MS 1,000/6-8
526 SE Tuscawilla Ave 34471 352-671-7100
Suzette Parker, prin. Fax 671-7101
Vanguard HS 1,800/9-12
7 NW 28th St 34475 352-671-4900
Cindy Repp, prin. Fax 671-4903
West Port HS 2,300/9-12
3733 SW 80th Ave 34481 352-291-4000
Jayne Ellspermann, prin. Fax 291-4001
Comm Adult Education Center Adult
1014 SW 7th Rd 34471 352-671-7200
Debbie Jenkins, dir. Fax 629-1117
Other Schools – See Belleview, Citra, Dunnellon, Summerfield

College of Central Florida Post-Sec.
3001 SW College Rd 34474 352-873-5800
First Assembly Christian S 300/PK-12
1827 NE 14th St 34470 352-351-1913
Marion Co. School Radiologic Technology Post-Sec.
1014 SW 7th Rd 34471 352-671-7200
Meadowbrook Academy 300/K-12
4741 SW 20th St Bldg 1 34474 352-861-0700
Tina Stelogeannis, prin. Fax 861-0533
Ocala Christian Academy 400/PK-12
1714 SE 36th Ave 34471 352-694-4178
Rev. Tim Rowe, admin. Fax 694-7192
Rasmussen College Post-Sec.
4755 SW 46th Ct 34474 352-629-1941
Redeemer Christian S 200/PK-10
155 SW 87th Pl 34476 352-854-2999
St. John Lutheran S 400/PK-12
1915 SE Lake Weir Ave 34471 352-622-7275
Tim Schmidt, prin. Fax 433-2540
Trinity Catholic HS 500/9-12
2600 SW 42nd St 34471 352-622-9025
Louis Pereira, pres. Fax 861-8164

**Ocoee, Orange, Pop. 34,484**
Orange County SD
Supt. — See Orlando
Ocoee HS 2,400/9-12
1925 Ocoee Crown Point Pkwy 34761 407-905-3000
William Floyd, prin. Fax 905-3099
Ocoee MS 1,600/6-8
300 S Bluford Ave 34761 407-877-5035
Dr. Mark Shanoff, prin. Fax 877-5045

Victory Christian Academy 200/K-12
1601 A D Mims Rd 34761 407-656-1295

**Odessa, Hillsborough, Pop. 7,133**
Hillsborough County SD
Supt. — See Tampa
Walker MS 700/6-8
8282 N Mobley Rd 33556 813-631-4726
Anthony Jones, prin. Fax 631-4738

Odessa Christian S 200/K-12
19521 Michigan Ave 33556 813-792-1825
Erin Ciulla, head sch Fax 749-6690

**Okeechobee, Okeechobee, Pop. 5,542**
Okeechobee County SD 6,400/PK-12
700 SW 2nd Ave 34974 863-462-5000
Ken Kenworthy, supt. Fax 462-5151
www.okee.k12.fl.us/
Okeechobee Achievement Academy 200/Alt
1000 NW 34th St 34972 863-462-5125
Randal Weigum, prin. Fax 462-5295
Okeechobee HS 1,200/10-12
2800 US Highway 441 N 34972 863-462-5025
Dylan Tedders, prin. Fax 462-5037
Okeechobee HS Freshman Campus 500/9-9
610 SW 2nd Ave 34974 863-462-5288
Carol Revels, head sch Fax 462-5258
Osceola MS 900/6-8
825 SW 28th St 34974 863-462-5070
Sean Downing, prin. Fax 462-5076
Yearling MS 700/6-8
925 NW 23rd Ln 34972 863-462-5056
Andy Brewer, prin. Fax 462-5062

Okeechobee Christian Academy 100/PK-12
701 S Parrott Ave 34974 863-763-3072
Sabina Guthrie, prin. Fax 213-1339

**Oldsmar, Pinellas, Pop. 13,296**

Oldsmar Christian S 200/PK-12
650 Burbank Rd 34677 813-855-5746

**Old Town, Dixie**
Dixie County SD
Supt. — See Cross City
Dixie County Adult Center Adult
328 SE 349 Ave 32680 352-498-6141
Fax 498-1279

Dixie County Learning Academy 100/K-12
1357 NE 82nd Ave 32680 352-542-3306
Dr. Sylvia Lamenta, prin. Fax 542-7291

**Opa Locka, Miami-Dade, Pop. 15,115**
Miami-Dade County SD
Supt. — See Miami
Mann Opportunity S 200/Alt
16101 NW 44th Ct 33054 305-625-0855
Samuel Johnson, prin. Fax 625-1605

Betesda Christian S 100/K-12
PO Box 540392 33054 305-685-8255
Rev. Justo P. Armas, admin. Fax 685-5338

**Orange City, Volusia, Pop. 10,438**
Volusia County SD
Supt. — See De Land
eLearning West 50/Alt
1000 W Rhode Island Ave 32763 386-968-0037
Melissa Carr, dir. Fax 968-0033
River Springs MS 1,400/6-8
900 W Ohio Ave 32763 386-968-0011
Stacy Gotlib, prin. Fax 456-5355
University HS 2,600/9-12
1000 W Rhode Island Ave 32763 386-968-0013
Dr. Julian Jones, prin. Fax 968-0019

**Orange Park, Clay, Pop. 8,196**
Clay County SD
Supt. — See Green Cove Springs
Fleming Island HS 2,000/9-12
2233 Village Square Pkwy 32003 904-541-2100
Tom Pittman, prin. Fax 541-2085
Lakeside JHS 900/7-8
2750 Moody Ave 32073 904-213-2980
David McDonald, prin. Fax 213-2987
Oakleaf HS 1,800/9-12
4035 Plantation Oaks Blvd 32065 904-218-1900
Treasure Pickett, prin. Fax 272-8599
Oakleaf JHS 900/7-8
4085 Plantation Oaks Blvd 32065 904-213-5500
Anthony Williams, prin. Fax 291-2549
Orange Park HS 1,700/9-12
2300 Kingsley Ave 32073 904-272-8110
Clayton Anderson, prin. Fax 272-8181
Orange Park JHS 700/7-8
1500 Gano Ave 32073 904-278-2000
Al DeJesus, prin. Fax 278-2009
Ridgeview HS 1,600/9-12
466 Madison Ave 32065 904-213-5203
Debbie Segreto, prin. Fax 213-3033

Everest University Post-Sec.
805 Wells Rd 32073 904-264-9122
Fortis College Post-Sec.
560 Wells Rd 32073 904-269-7086
National Heavy Equipment Operator School Post-Sec.
PO Box 65789 32065 904-272-4000
R. Webber Institute for Worship Studies Post-Sec.
151 Kingsley Ave 32073 904-264-2172
St. Johns Country Day S 600/PK-12
3100 Doctors Lake Dr 32073 904-264-9572
Edward Ellison, hdmstr. Fax 264-0375

**Orlando, Orange, Pop. 231,839**
Orange County SD 175,100/PK-12
445 W Amelia St 32801 407-317-3200
Dr. Barbara Jenkins, supt. Fax 317-3401
www.ocps.net
Acceleration Academy 400/Alt
2274 S Semoran Blvd 32822 407-992-0917
Douglas Loftus, prin. Fax 207-4961
Acceleration Academy West Alt
2751 Lake Stanley Rd 32818 407-521-2358
George Morse, prin. Fax 521-2369
Avalon MS 1,600/6-8
13914 Mailer Blvd 32828 407-207-7839
Karen Furno, prin. Fax 207-7872
Boone HS 2,900/9-12
1000 E Kaley St 32806 407-893-7200
Dusty Johns, prin. Fax 897-2466
Carver MS 700/6-8
4500 Columbia St 32811 407-296-5110
Hector Maestre, prin. Fax 296-6407
Chain of Lakes MS 1,400/6-8
8700 Conroy Windermere Rd 32835 407-909-5400
Cheron Anderson, prin. Fax 909-5410
Colonial 9th Grade Center 900/9-9
7775 Valencia College Ln 32807 407-249-6369
Jose Martinez, prin. Fax 249-6297
Colonial HS 2,400/10-12
6100 Oleander Dr 32807 407-482-6300
Jose Martinez, prin. Fax 737-1450
Conway MS 1,100/6-8
4600 Anderson Rd 32812 407-249-6420
Michael Hanson, prin. Fax 249-6429
Corner Lake MS 1,300/6-8
1700 Chuluota Rd 32820 407-568-0510
Luis Tousent, prin. Fax 568-0920
Cypress Creek HS 3,200/9-12
1101 Bear Crossing Dr 32824 407-852-3400
Walton McHale, prin. Fax 850-5160
Discovery MS 900/6-8
601 Woodbury Rd 32828 407-384-1555
Gloria Fernandez, prin. Fax 384-1580
Drop Back In 700/Alt
228 N Semoran Blvd 32807 407-658-9555
Shannon Folsom, prin. Fax 658-9559
East Orlando Education Center 50/Alt
2510 Gulfstream Rd 32805 407-245-1555
William Tovine, prin. Fax 245-1561
East River HS 1,900/9-12
650 E River Falcons Way 32833 407-956-8550
Heather Hilton, prin. Fax 956-8565
Edgewater HS 1,700/9-12
3100 Edgewater Dr 32804 407-835-4900
Howard Hepburn, prin. Fax 245-2758
Evans HS 2,100/9-12
4949 Silver Star Rd 32808 407-522-3400
Jenny Gibson-Linkh, prin. Fax 522-3458
Freedom HS 3,100/9-12
2500 W Taft Vineland Rd 32837 407-816-5600
Rolando Bailey, prin. Fax 816-5616
Freedom MS 1,100/6-8
2850 W Taft Vineland Rd 32837 407-858-6130
Cheri Godek, prin. Fax 858-6132
Glenridge MS 1,400/6-8
2900 Upper Park Rd 32814 407-623-1415
Trevor Honahan, prin. Fax 623-1427
Howard MS 600/6-8
800 E Robinson St 32801 407-245-1780
Michael Martucci, prin. Fax 245-1785
Hunters Creek MS 1,100/6-8
13400 Town Loop Blvd 32837 407-858-4620
Amy McHale, prin. Fax 858-4621
Jackson MS 1,300/6-8
6000 Stonewall Jackson Rd 32807 407-249-6430
Dr. Jhunu Mohapatra, prin. Fax 249-6438
Jones HS 900/9-12
801 S Rio Grande Ave 32805 407-835-2300
Roderick Walton, prin. Fax 245-2765
Lake Nona HS 1,800/9-12
12500 Narcoossee Rd 32832 407-956-8300
Margaret Nampon, prin. Fax 956-8315
Lake Nona MS 1,200/6-8
13700 Narcoossee Rd 32832 407-858-5522
Stephanie Minter, prin. Fax 858-5530
Lee MS 900/6-8
1201 Maury Rd 32804 407-245-1800
Cynthia Haupt, prin. Fax 245-1809
Legacy MS 900/6-8
11398 Lake Underhill Rd 32825 407-658-5330
Shannon Battoe, prin. Fax 658-5334
Liberty MS 1,100/6-8
3405 S Chickasaw Trl 32829 407-249-6440
James Russo, prin. Fax 249-6449
Lockhart MS 800/6-8
3411 Dr Love Rd 32810 407-296-5120
Alison Kirby, prin. Fax 296-6549
Meadowbrook MS 1,100/6-8
6000 North Ln 32808 407-296-5130
Robin Brown, prin. Fax 296-5139
Meadow Woods MS 1,100/6-8
1800 Rhode Island Woods Cir 32824 407-850-5180
Marisol Mendez, prin. Fax 850-5190

Memorial MS 700/6-8
2220 29th St 32805 407-245-1810
Jennifer Bellinger, prin. Fax 245-1820
Mid Florida Tech Vo/Tech
2900 W Oak Ridge Rd 32809 407-251-6000
Alex Heidelberg, prin. Fax 251-6197
Oak Ridge HS 1,700/9-12
700 W Oak Ridge Rd 32809 407-852-3200
Dr. Leigh Ann Bradshaw, prin. Fax 850-5152
Odyssey MS 900/6-8
9290 Lee Vista Blvd 32829 407-207-3850
Ann Hembrook, prin. Fax 207-3871
Olympia HS 3,000/9-12
4301 S Apopka Vineland Rd 32835 407-905-6400
Guy Swenson, prin. Fax 905-6465
Orlando Tech Ctr Vo/Tech
301 W Amelia St 32801 407-246-7060
Andrew Jenkins, dir. Fax 317-3372
Pace Center for Girls 100/Alt
728 Gear Lake Ave 32803 407-992-0456
William Tovine, admin. Fax 992-0455
Phillips HS 3,600/9-12
6500 Turkey Lake Rd 32819 407-355-3200
Suzanne Knight, prin. Fax 370-7232
Positive Pathways Transition Center Alt
6125 N Orange Blossom Tr 32810 407-992-0599
Francis Pons, prin. Fax 992-0914
Robinswood MS 1,300/6-8
6305 Balboa Dr 32818 407-296-5140
Marcia Newsome, prin. Fax 296-5148
Simon Youth Academy Alt
5253 International Dr 32819 407-858-6114
William Tovine, prin. Fax 858-6119
South Creek MS 1,000/6-8
3801 Wetherbee Rd 32824 407-251-2413
Sean Brown, prin. Fax 251-2464
Southwest MS 1,200/6-8
6450 Dr Phillips Blvd 32819 407-370-7200
Matthew Arnold, prin. Fax 370-7210
Timber Creek HS 3,000/9-12
1001 Avalon Park South Blvd 32828 321-235-7800
Gabriel Berrio, prin. Fax 253-7821
Union Park MS 1,000/6-8
1844 Westfall Dr 32817 407-249-6309
Melanie May, prin. Fax 249-4404
Universal Education Center Alt
1000 Universal Studios Plz 32819 407-224-6634
William Tovine, prin. Fax 224-6636
University HS 2,800/9-12
2450 Cougar Way 32817 407-482-8700
Dr. Anne Carcara, prin. Fax 737-1455
Walker MS 900/6-8
150 Amidon Ln 32809 407-858-3210
Julio Valle, prin. Fax 858-3218
Westridge MS 1,100/6-8
3800 W Oak Ridge Rd 32809 407-354-2640
Christopher Camacho, prin. Fax 354-2637
Avalon Center for Tech Excellence Adult
2201 Crown Hill Blvd 32828 407-281-5100
Jayne Lychako, prin. Fax 281-5127
Other Schools – See Apopka, Maitland, Ocoee, Windermere, Winter Garden, Winter Park

---

Adventist University of Health Sciences Post-Sec.
671 Winyah Dr 32803 407-303-9798
Agape Christian Academy 400/PK-12
2425 N Hiawassee Rd 32818 407-298-1111
Anthem College Post-Sec.
3710 Maguire Blvd 32803 407-893-7400
Asbury Theological Seminary Post-Sec.
8401 Valencia College Ln 32825 407-482-7500
Avalon S 100/K-12
5002 Andrus Ave 32804 407-297-4353
Bishop Moore HS 1,100/9-12
3901 Edgewater Dr 32804 407-293-7561
Scott Brogan, prin. Fax 296-8135
Central Florida Blood Bank Post-Sec.
8669 Commodity Cir 32819 407-849-6100
Central Florida Christian Academy 200/PK-12
700 Good Homes Rd 32818 407-850-2322
Dr. Clayton Cloer, pres. Fax 293-6914
Centura Institute Post-Sec.
6359 Edgewater Dr 32810 407-275-9696
Concorde Career Institute Post-Sec.
3444 McCrory Pl 32803 407-812-3060
Conrad Academy 200/K-12
PO Box 678207 32867 407-243-2211
DAVE School Post-Sec.
2500 Universal Studios # 25 32819 855-328-3839
Devereux-Florida Treatment Network Post-Sec.
5850 T G Lee Blvd Ste 400 32822 407-812-4555
DeVry University Post-Sec.
4000 Millenia Blvd 32839 407-345-2800
DeVry University Post-Sec.
1800 Pembrook Dr Ste 160 32810 407-659-0900
Downey Christian S 300/PK-12
10201 E Colonial Dr 32817 407-275-0340
Dr. C.C. Dees, admin. Fax 275-1481
Eastland Christian S 300/PK-12
9000 Lake Underhill Rd 32825 407-277-5858
Everest University - North Orlando Cmps Post-Sec.
5421 Diplomat Cir 32810 407-628-5870
Everest University-South Orlando Campus Post-Sec.
9200 Southpark Center Loop 32819 407-851-2525
Faith Christian Academy 400/PK-12
9307 Curry Ford Rd 32825 407-275-8031
Family Christian Academy 100/K-10
9580 Curry Ford Rd 32825 407-568-9837
Dana Paynter, admin.
FCC Anthem College Post-Sec.
989 N Semoran Blvd 32807 407-628-5870
First Academy 1,000/PK-12
2667 Bruton Blvd 32805 407-206-8600
Dr. Steve Whitaker, head sch
Florida College of Integrative Medicine Post-Sec.
7100 Lake Ellenor Dr 32809 407-888-8689
Florida Technical College Post-Sec.
12900 Challenger Pkwy 32826 407-447-7300
Heritage Prep S 200/PK-12
6000 W Colonial Dr 32808 407-293-6000
ITT Technical Institute Post-Sec.
8301 Southpark Cir Ste 100 32819 407-371-6000
Keiser University Post-Sec.
5600 Lake Underhill Rd 32807 407-273-5800
Lake Highland Preparatory S 2,000/PK-12
901 Highland Ave 32803 407-206-1900
Warren Hudson, pres. Fax 206-1933
Leaders Preparatory S 200/PK-12
1021 N Goldenrod Rd 32807 407-382-9900
Le Cordon Bleu College of Culinary Arts Post-Sec.
8511 Commodity Cir # 100 32819 407-888-4000
Medtech Institute Post-Sec.
2000 N Alafaya Trl Ste 300 32826 407-691-3391
Mt. Sinai Jr Academy 100/K-10
2610 Orange Center Blvd 32805 407-298-7871
Orlando Christian Prep S 400/PK-12
500 S Semoran Blvd 32807 407-823-9744
Orlando Medical Institute Post-Sec.
6220 S Orange Blossom #410 32809 407-251-0007
Pine Castle Christian Academy 200/PK-12
7101 Lake Ellenor Dr 32809 407-313-7222
Tom Wittkamper, admin. Fax 313-7226
Saints Academy 100/K-12
821 S Kirkman Rd 32811 407-683-5537
Sanford-Brown College Post-Sec.
6039 S Rio Grande Ave 32809 407-857-2300
Southern Technical College Post-Sec.
1485 Florida Mall Ave 32809 407-438-6000
South Orlando Christian Academy 200/PK-12
5815 Makoma Dr 32839 407-859-9511
Stenotype Institute Post-Sec.
1636 W Oak Ridge Rd 32809 407-816-5573
Strayer University Post-Sec.
2200 N Alafaya Trl Ste 500 32826 407-926-2000
Treasure of Knowledge Christian Academy 200/PK-11
13001 Landstar Blvd 32824 407-859-8755
Universal Technical Institute Post-Sec.
2202 W Taft Vineland Rd 32837 321-281-9810
University of Central Florida Post-Sec.
PO Box 160000 32816 407-823-2000
Valencia College Post-Sec.
PO Box 3028 32802 407-299-5000
Victory Christian Academy 100/K-12
240 N Ivey Ln 32811 407-295-3332
West Oaks Academy 200/PK-12
8624 A D Mims Rd 32818 407-292-8481

**Ormond Beach, Volusia, Pop. 37,607**
Volusia County SD
Supt. — See De Land
Ormond Beach MS 1,100/6-8
151 Domicilio Ave 32174 386-258-4667
Matt Krajewski, prin. Fax 676-1258

---

Calvary Christian Academy 400/PK-12
1687 W Granada Blvd 32174 386-672-2081
Daytona College Post-Sec.
425 S Nova Rd 32174 386-267-0565
Harry Wendelstedt Umpire School Post-Sec.
88 S Saint Andrews Dr 32174 800-818-1690
Riverbend Academy 300/PK-12
2080 W Granada Blvd 32174 386-615-0986
Jason Karr, hdmstr. Fax 672-7945
WyoTech Post-Sec.
470 Destination Daytona Ln 32174 386-255-0295

**Oviedo, Seminole, Pop. 32,607**
Seminole County SD
Supt. — See Sanford
Chiles MS 1,300/6-8
1240 Sanctuary Dr 32766 407-871-7050
Linda Mumey, prin. Fax 871-7099
Hagerty HS 2,400/9-12
3225 Lockwood Blvd 32765 407-871-0750
Dr. Mary Williams, prin. Fax 871-0749
Jackson Heights MS 1,200/6-8
41 Academy Ave 32765 407-320-4550
Sarah Mansur, prin. Fax 320-4599
Oviedo HS 2,200/9-12
601 King St 32765 407-320-4050
Joe Trybus, prin. Fax 320-4000
Tuskawilla MS 1,100/6-8
1801 Tuskawilla Rd 32765 407-746-8550
Kate Eglof, prin. Fax 746-8599

---

Master's Academy 900/PK-12
1500 Lukas Ln 32765 407-971-2221
Dr. Mitchell Salerno, supt. Fax 706-0254
Reformed Theological Seminary Post-Sec.
1231 Reformation Dr 32765 407-366-9493

**Pace, Santa Rosa, Pop. 19,523**
Santa Rosa County SD
Supt. — See Milton
Pace HS 1,900/9-12
4065 Norris Rd 32571 850-995-3600
Stephen Shell, prin. Fax 995-3620
Sims MS 900/6-8
5500 Education Dr 32571 850-995-3676
Emily Donalson, prin. Fax 995-3696

**Pahokee, Palm Beach, Pop. 5,609**
Palm Beach County SD
Supt. — See West Palm Beach
Pahokee HS 500/9-12
900 Larrimore Rd 33476 561-924-6400
Adrian Ocampo, prin. Fax 924-6457
Pahokee MS 300/6-8
850 Larrimore Rd 33476 561-924-6500
Adrian Ocampo, prin. Fax 924-6550

**Palatka, Putnam, Pop. 10,395**
Putnam County SD 10,700/PK-12
200 Reid St 32177 386-329-0510
Phyllis Criswell, supt. Fax 329-0520
www.putnamschools.org
Jenkins MS 500/7-8
1100 N 19th St 32177 386-329-0588
Dr. Richard Surrency, prin. Fax 329-0636
Palatka HS 1,400/9-12
302 Mellon Rd 32177 386-329-0577
Mary Beth Hedstrom, prin. Fax 329-0624
Other Schools – See Crescent City, Florahome, Interlachen

---

Hillcrest Academy 50/K-12
2009 President St 32177 386-328-6514
Lisa Yaunk, admin.
Peniel Baptist Academy 300/PK-12
110 Peniel Church Rd 32177 386-328-1707
St. John's River State College Post-Sec.
5001 Saint Johns Ave 32177 386-312-4200

**Palm Bay, Brevard, Pop. 100,267**
Brevard County SD
Supt. — See Melbourne
Bayside HS 1,700/9-12
1901 Degroodt Rd SW 32908 321-956-5000
Christine Moore, prin. Fax 956-5021
Heritage HS 1,800/9-12
2351 Malabar Rd NW 32907 321-722-4178
Dr. John Harris, prin. Fax 722-4198
Southwest MS 1,000/7-8
451 Eldron Blvd SE 32909 321-952-5800
Todd Scheuerer, prin. Fax 952-5819

---

Covenant Christian S 300/PK-12
720 Emerson Dr NE 32907 321-727-2661
Ken Ingraham, hdmstr. Fax 728-9574
Darlyne McGee's Academy of Cosmetology Post-Sec.
1975 Palm Bay Rd NE Ste 106 32905 321-951-0595

**Palm Beach, Palm Beach, Pop. 8,309**

---

Palm Beach Day Academy 200/4-9
241 Seaview Ave 33480 561-655-1188
Dr. Rebecca van der Bogert, hdmstr. Fax 655-5794

**Palm Beach Gardens, Palm Beach, Pop. 47,764**
Palm Beach County SD
Supt. — See West Palm Beach
Duncan MS 1,400/6-8
5150 117th Ct N 33418 561-776-3500
Phillip Damico, prin. Fax 776-3550
Dwyer HS 2,300/9-12
13601 N Military Trl 33410 561-625-7800
Glenda Sheffield, prin. Fax 625-7870
Palm Beach Gardens Community HS 2,500/9-12
4245 Holly Dr 33410 561-694-7300
Larry Clawson, prin. Fax 691-0515
Watkins MS 600/6-8
9480 MacArthur Blvd 33403 561-776-3600
Don Hoffman, prin. Fax 776-3603

---

Strayer University Post-Sec.
11025 RCA Center Dr Ste 200 33410 561-904-3000

**Palm City, Martin, Pop. 22,880**
Martin County SD
Supt. — See Stuart
Hidden Oaks MS 1,100/6-8
2801 SW Martin Hwy 34990 772-219-1655
Jeri Eckler, prin. Fax 219-1663

**Palm Coast, Flagler, Pop. 73,538**
Flagler County SD
Supt. — See Bunnell
Flagler Palm Coast HS 2,400/9-12
5500 E Highway 100 32164 386-437-7540
Dustin Sims, prin. Fax 437-7546
Flagler Technical Institute Vo/Tech
5400 E Highway 100 32164 386-446-7612
Kevin McCarthy, dir. Fax 446-7620
Indian Trails MS 900/7-8
5505 Belle Terre Pkwy 32137 386-446-6732
Paul Peacock, prin. Fax 446-7662
Matanzas HS 1,600/9-12
3535 Old Kings Rd N 32137 386-447-1575
Earl Johnson, prin. Fax 447-1597
Taylor MS 1,000/7-8
4500 Belle Terre Pkwy 32164 386-446-6700
Nathan Lovelette M.Ed., prin. Fax 446-6711

**Palmetto, Manatee, Pop. 12,420**
Manatee County SD
Supt. — See Bradenton
Buffalo Creek MS 900/6-8
7320 69th St E 34221 941-721-2260
Anthony Losada, prin. Fax 721-2275
Lincoln MS 600/6-8
305 17th St E 34221 941-721-6840
Ed Hundley, prin. Fax 721-6853
Manatee Technical Institute - North Vo/Tech
801 9th St W 34221 941-845-2092
Doug Wagner, dir. Fax 845-2102
Palmetto HS 1,700/9-12
1200 17th St W 34221 941-723-4848
Willie Clark, prin. Fax 723-4952

**Palmetto Bay, Miami-Dade**
Miami-Dade County SD
Supt. — See Miami
Southwood MS 1,500/6-8
16301 SW 80th Ave, 305-251-5361
Raul Garcia, prin. Fax 251-7464

---

Palmer Trinity S 700/6-12
7900 SW 176th St, 305-251-2230
Patrick Roberts, head sch Fax 251-2917
Westminster Christian S 1,000/PK-12
6855 SW 152nd St, 305-233-2030
Peter Cabrera, supt. Fax 238-2259

**Palm Harbor, Pinellas, Pop. 56,551**
Pinellas County SD
Supt. — See Largo
Carwise MS 1,200/6-8
3301 Bentley Dr 34684 727-724-1442
Robert Vicari, prin. Fax 724-1446
Palm Harbor MS 1,400/6-8
1800 Tampa Rd 34683 727-669-1146
Victoria Hawkins, prin. Fax 669-1244

Palm Harbor University HS 2,500/9-12
1900 Omaha St 34683 727-669-1131
Christen Gonzalez, prin. Fax 725-7936
Palm Harbor Community S Adult
1900 Omaha St 34683 727-669-1140
Anne Sarver, prin. Fax 725-7936

**Panama City, Bay, Pop. 35,536**
Bay County SD 25,400/PK-12
1311 Balboa Ave 32401 850-767-4100
William Husfelt, supt.
www.bay.k12.fl.us
Arnold HS 1,400/9-12
550 N Alf Coleman Rd 32407 850-767-3700
Keith Bland, prin. Fax 236-3068
Bay HS 1,300/9-12
1200 Harrison Ave 32401 850-767-4600
Billy May, prin. Fax 767-4651
Bozeman S 1,300/K-12
13410 Highway 77 32409 850-767-1300
Josh Balkom, prin. Fax 265-5377
Brown MS 800/6-8
5044 Merritt Brown Way 32404 850-767-3976
Charlotte Marshall, prin. Fax 872-7625
Everitt MS 800/6-8
608 School Ave 32401 850-767-3776
Phillip Mullins, prin. Fax 872-7721
Haney Technical Center Vo/Tech
3016 Highway 77 32405 850-767-5500
Ann Leonard, dir. Fax 747-5555
Jinks MS 700/6-8
600 W 11th St 32401 850-767-4695
Britt Smith, prin. Fax 872-7612
Rosenwald HS 300/9-12
924 Bay Ave 32401 850-767-4580
Chandra Tyson, prin. Fax 872-7615
Rutherford HS 1,300/9-12
1000 School Ave 32401 850-767-4500
L. Coy Pilson, prin. Fax 872-4827
Surfside MS 900/6-8
300 Nautilus St 32413 850-767-5180
Dr. Sue Harrell, prin. Fax 233-5193
Washington Academy 100/Alt
924 Bay Ave 32401 850-767-5576
Todd Harless, prin. Fax 914-6429
Other Schools – See Lynn Haven

---

Covenant Christian S 300/PK-12
2350 Frankford Ave 32405 850-769-7448
Glenda Delmar, prin. Fax 763-2104
Gooding Institute of Nurse Anesthesia Post-Sec.
615 N Bonita Ave 32401 850-747-6918
Gulf Coast State College Post-Sec.
5230 W Highway 98 32401 850-769-1551
Panama City Advanced S 100/PK-12
3332 Token Rd 32405 850-784-2520

**Parkland, Broward, Pop. 23,535**
Broward County SD
Supt. — See Fort Lauderdale
Stoneman Douglas HS 3,000/9-12
5901 Pine Island Rd 33076 754-322-2150
Ty Thompson, prin. Fax 322-2280
Westglades MS 1,500/6-8
11000 Holmberg Rd 33076 754-322-4800
Jack Vesey, prin. Fax 322-4885

**Paxton, Walton, Pop. 626**
Walton County SD
Supt. — See De Funiak Springs
Paxton S 600/PK-12
21893 US Highway 331 N 32538 850-892-1230
Beth Tucker, prin. Fax 892-1239

**Pembroke Pines, Broward, Pop. 151,189**
Broward County SD
Supt. — See Fort Lauderdale
Flanagan HS 3,100/9-12
12800 Taft St 33028 754-323-0650
Michelle Kefford, prin. Fax 323-0780
Pines MS 1,500/6-8
200 NW Douglas Rd 33024 754-323-4000
Carlton Campbell, prin. Fax 323-4085
Silver Trail MS 1,500/6-8
18300 Sheridan St 33331 754-323-4300
Stephen Frazier, prin. Fax 323-4385
West Broward HS 2,800/9-12
500 NW 209th Ave 33029 754-323-2600
Teresa Hall, prin. Fax 323-2730
Young MS 1,400/6-8
901 NW 129th Ave 33028 754-323-4500
Harold Osborn, prin. Fax 323-4585

---

Broward College Post-Sec.
7200 Pines Blvd 33024 954-201-8100
Florida Career College Post-Sec.
7891 Pines Blvd 33024 954-965-7272
Florida Technical College Post-Sec.
12520 Pines Blvd 33027 954-556-1900
Jose Maria Vargas University Post-Sec.
8300 S Palm Dr 33025 954-322-4460
Keiser University Post-Sec.
1640 SW 145th Ave 33027 954-431-4300
Pelican Flight Training Center Post-Sec.
1601 SW 75th Ave 33023 954-966-9750

**Pensacola, Escambia, Pop. 50,807**
Escambia County SD 38,400/PK-12
75 N Pace Blvd 32505 850-432-6121
Malcolm Thomas, supt. Fax 469-6379
www.escambia.k12.fl.us
Bailey MS 1,400/6-8
4110 Bauer Rd 32506 850-492-6136
Janet Penrose, prin. Fax 492-9860
Bellview MS 1,100/6-8
6201 Mobile Hwy 32526 850-941-6080
Melia Adams, prin. Fax 941-6089
Brown-Barge MS 500/6-8
201 Hancock Ln 32503 850-494-5640
Dr. Joy McMichael, prin. Fax 494-5699
Escambia HS 1,800/9-12
1310 N 65th Ave 32506 850-453-3221
Frank Murphy, prin. Fax 453-9381
Ferry Pass MS 900/6-8
8355 Yancey Ave 32514 850-494-5650
Sherri Mims, prin. Fax 494-5653
PACE Center for Girls 100/Alt
1028 Underwood Ave 32504 850-478-7060
Laurie Rodgers, prin. Fax 494-0840
Pensacola HS 1,600/9-12
500 W Maxwell St 32501 850-595-1500
David Williams, prin. Fax 595-1519
Pine Forest HS 1,700/9-12
2500 Longleaf Dr 32526 850-941-6150
Laura Touchstone, prin. Fax 941-6163
Stone Career Center Vo/Tech
2400 Longleaf Dr 32526 850-941-6200
Thomas Rollins, prin. Fax 941-6215
Washington HS 1,600/9-12
6000 College Pkwy 32504 850-475-5257
Dr. Michael Roberts, prin. Fax 494-7297
West Florida HS of Advanced Technology 1,300/9-12
2400 Longleaf Dr 32526 850-941-6221
Sheena Payne, prin. Fax 941-6210
Woodham MS 900/6-8
150 E Burgess Rd 32503 850-494-7140
Wilson Taylor, prin. Fax 494-7484
Workman MS 900/6-8
6299 Lanier Dr 32504 850-494-5665
Traci Ursery, prin. Fax 494-5697
Andrews Center Adult
129 N Merritt St 32507 850-453-7462
LaDon Boyd, prin.
Other Schools – See Cantonment, Century, Walnut Hill, Warrington

---

Aletheia Christian Academy 200/PK-12
PO Box 10568 32524 850-969-0088
Jeff Caulfield-James, admin. Fax 969-0906
East Hill Christian S 200/PK-12
1301 E Gonzalez St 32501 850-438-7746
Glenn Dickson, hdmstr. Fax 434-7384
Florida Institute of Ultrasound Post-Sec.
8800 University Pkwy Ste A4 32514 850-478-7300
Fortis Institute Post-Sec.
4081 E Olive Rd Ste B 32514 850-476-7607
George Stone Vocational Technical Ctr. Post-Sec.
2400 Longleaf Dr 32526 850-941-6200
ITT Technical Institute Post-Sec.
6913 N 9th Ave 32504 850-483-5700
Jones Christian Academy 200/PK-12
100 Boeing St 32507 850-456-2249
Pensacola Catholic HS 600/9-12
3043 W Scott St 32505 850-436-6400
Sr. Kierstin Martin, prin. Fax 436-6405
Pensacola Christian Academy 2,300/PK-12
10 Brent Ln 32503 850-478-8483
Pensacola Christian College Post-Sec.
PO Box 18000 32523 850-478-8496
Pensacola School of Massage Therapy Post-Sec.
2409 Creighton Rd 32504 850-474-1330
Pensacola State College Post-Sec.
1000 College Blvd 32504 850-484-1000
Trinitas Christian S 200/K-12
3301 E Johnson Ave 32514 850-484-3515
University of West Florida Post-Sec.
11000 University Pkwy 32514 850-474-2000
Virginia College Post-Sec.
19 W Garden St 32502 850-436-8444

**Perrine, Miami-Dade, Pop. 15,576**
Miami-Dade County SD
Supt. — See Miami
Morgan Educational Center HS Vo/Tech
18180 SW 122nd Ave 33177 305-253-9920
Kimberly Davis, prin. Fax 259-1495

**Perry, Taylor, Pop. 6,889**
Taylor County SD 3,000/PK-12
318 N Clark St 32347 850-838-2500
Paul Dyal, supt. Fax 838-2501
www.taylor.k12.fl.us
Taylor County HS 700/9-12
900 N Johnson Stripling Rd 32347 850-838-2525
Audie Ash, prin. Fax 838-2521
Taylor County MS 600/6-8
610 E Lafayette St 32347 850-838-2516
Kiki Puhl, prin. Fax 838-2559
Taylor Technical Institute Vo/Tech
3233 S Byron Butler Pkwy 32348 850-838-2535
Judy Johnson, coord. Fax 838-2546

---

Taylor Technical Institute Post-Sec.
3233 S Byron Butler Pkwy 32348 850-838-2545

**Pierson, Volusia, Pop. 1,725**
Volusia County SD
Supt. — See De Land
Taylor MSHS 1,000/6-12
100 E Washington Ave 32180 386-749-9800
Ron Pagano, prin. Fax 626-0051

**Pinecrest, Miami-Dade**
Miami-Dade County SD
Supt. — See Miami
Miami Palmetto HS 2,900/9-12
7460 SW 118th St 33156 305-235-1360
Victoria Dobbs, prin. Fax 235-7169
Palmetto MS 800/7-9
7351 SW 128th St 33156 305-238-3911
Jesus Gonzalez, prin. Fax 233-4849

---

Gulliver Academy - Montgomery Dr Campus 100/5-8
7500 SW 120th St 33156 305-238-3424
Frank Steel, head sch Fax 675-7744
Gulliver Preparatory S 800/9-12
6575 N Kendall Dr 33156 305-666-7937
Frank Steel, head sch Fax 665-3791

**Pinellas Park, Pinellas, Pop. 47,904**
Pinellas County SD
Supt. — See Largo
Pinellas Park MS 900/6-8
6940 70th Ave N 33781 727-545-6400
David Rosenberger, prin. Fax 547-7894
Pinellas Secondary S 100/Alt
8570 66th St N 33781 727-549-6550
Darren Hammond, prin. Fax 549-6555

---

Classical Christian S for the Arts 100/K-12
PO Box 1455 33780 727-547-6820
Cortiva Institute-Florida Post-Sec.
4045 Park Blvd N 33781 727-865-4940
National University of Health Sciences Post-Sec.
9200 113th St 33781 800-826-6285

**Plantation, Broward, Pop. 82,808**
Broward County SD
Supt. — See Fort Lauderdale
Plantation HS 2,300/9-12
6901 NW 16th St 33313 754-322-1850
Alona Dipaolo, prin. Fax 322-1980
Plantation MS 1,000/6-8
6600 W Sunrise Blvd 33313 754-322-4100
Sherri Wilson, prin. Fax 322-4185
Seminole MS 1,300/6-8
6200 SW 16th St 33317 754-323-4200
Kathryn Marlow, prin. Fax 323-4285
South Plantation HS 2,300/9-12
1300 Paladin Way 33317 754-323-1950
Christine Henschel, prin. Fax 323-2080

---

Allied Health Institute Post-Sec.
51 N State Road 7 33317 877-959-3570
American Heritage S 2,300/PK-12
12200 W Broward Blvd 33325 954-472-0022
William Laurie, pres. Fax 472-0616

**Plant City, Hillsborough, Pop. 34,205**
Hillsborough County SD
Supt. — See Tampa
Durant HS 2,200/9-12
4748 Cougar Path 33567 813-757-9075
Pamela Bowden, prin. Fax 707-7079
Marshall MS 900/6-8
18 S Maryland Ave, 813-757-9360
Daphne Blanton, prin. Fax 707-7385
Plant City HS 2,000/9-12
1 Raider Pl, 813-757-9370
Susan Sullivan, prin. Fax 757-9135
Simmons Career Center Vo/Tech
1202 W Grant St, 813-707-7430
Cleto Chazares, prin. Fax 707-7435
Tomlin MS 1,600/6-8
501 N Woodrow Wilson St, 813-757-9400
Traci Durrance, prin. Fax 707-7024
Turkey Creek MS 1,000/6-8
5005 Turkey Creek Rd 33567 813-757-9442
Fredda Johnson, prin. Fax 757-9451
Plant City Adult Education Adult
1 Raider Pl, 813-707-7147
Valerie Henry, prin. Fax 707-7149

---

Hillsborough Community College Post-Sec.
1206 N Park Rd, 813-757-2100

**Poinciana, Osceola, Pop. 51,604**
Polk County SD
Supt. — See Bartow
Lake Marion Creek MS 800/5-8
3055 Lake Marion Creek Dr 34759 863-427-1471
Maryjo Costine, prin. Fax 427-1502

**Pompano Beach, Broward, Pop. 97,655**
Broward County SD
Supt. — See Fort Lauderdale
Blanche Ely HS 1,900/9-12
1201 NW 6th Ave 33060 754-322-0950
Karlton Johnson, prin. Fax 322-1080
Crystal Lake MS 1,500/6-8
3551 NE 3rd Ave 33064 754-322-3100
Sabine Phillips, prin. Fax 322-3185
Cypress Run Education Center 100/Alt
2800 NW 30th Ave 33069 754-321-6500
Gastride Harrigan, prin. Fax 321-6540
Pompano Beach HS 1,300/9-12
600 NE 13th Ave 33060 754-322-2000
Hudson Thomas, prin. Fax 322-2130
Pompano Beach MS 1,100/6-8
310 NE 6th St 33060 754-322-4200
Sonja Braziel, prin. Fax 322-4285
Thomas Education Center East Adult
180 SW 2nd St 33060 754-321-6750
Wade Edmond, prin. Fax 321-6790

---

Everest University-Pompano Beach Campus Post-Sec.
225 N Federal Hwy 33062 954-783-7339
Florida Barber Academy Post-Sec.
3269 N Federal Hwy 33064 954-781-6066
Florida College of Natural Health Post-Sec.
2001 W Sample Rd Ste 100 33064 954-975-6400
Highlands Christian Academy 500/PK-12
501 NE 48th St 33064 954-421-1747
New Life Preparatory Academy 100/9-12
2111 NW 2nd Ave 33069 954-440-8333
Progressive Training Center Post-Sec.
98 E McNab Rd Ste 98 33060 954-946-2022

**Ponce de Leon, Holmes, Pop. 585**
Holmes County SD
Supt. — See Bonifay
Ponce De Leon JSHS 400/6-12
1477 Ammons Rd 32455 850-836-4242
Brian Morgan, prin. Fax 836-5388

**Ponte Vedra Beach, Saint Johns**
St. Johns County SD
Supt. — See Saint Augustine
Landrum MS 1,200/6-8
230 Landrum Ln 32082 904-547-8410
Jewel Johnson, prin. Fax 547-8415
Nease HS 1,600/9-12
10550 Ray Rd, 904-547-8300
Kyle Dresback, prin. Fax 547-8305

Ponte Vedra HS 1,500/9-12
460 Davis Park Rd, 904-547-7350
Steve McCormick, prin. Fax 547-7355

**Port Charlotte, Charlotte, Pop. 53,337**
Charlotte County SD 16,500/PK-12
1445 Education Way 33948 941-255-0808
Steve Dionisio, supt. Fax 255-7571
yourcharlotteschools.net
Academy Alt
18300 Cochran Blvd 33948 941-255-7545
Jack Ham, prin. Fax 255-7548
Charlotte Technical Center Vo/Tech
18150 Murdock Cir 33948 941-255-7500
DeeLynn Bennett, dir. Fax 255-7509
Murdock MS 800/6-8
17325 Mariner Way 33948 941-255-7525
Demetrius Revelas, prin. Fax 255-7533
Port Charlotte HS 1,800/9-12
18200 Cochran Blvd 33948 941-255-7485
Lou Long, prin. Fax 255-7493
Port Charlotte MS 800/6-8
23000 Midway Blvd 33952 941-255-7460
Maria Gifford, prin. Fax 255-7469
Adult & Community Education Adult
1441 Tamiami Trl Unit 365 33948 941-255-7430
Jack Ham, dir. Fax 255-7433
Other Schools – See Englewood, Punta Gorda, Rotonda West

Community Christian S 300/PK-12
20035 Quesada Ave 33952 941-625-8977
Dr. Sarah Mielke, head sch Fax 625-1735
Port Charlotte Adventist S 100/K-12
2100 Loveland Blvd 33980 941-625-5237
Port Charlotte Christian S 50/K-12
3279 Sherwood Rd 33980 941-625-4450
Elizabeth Kolenda, prin. Fax 243-0586
Southwest Florida College Post-Sec.
950 Tamiami Trl Unit 109 33953 877-270-9786

**Port Orange, Volusia, Pop. 55,114**
Volusia County SD
Supt. — See De Land
Atlantic HS 1,100/9-12
1250 Reed Canal Rd 32129 386-322-6100
JamesTager, prin. Fax 506-0001
Creekside MS 1,100/6-8
6801 Airport Rd 32128 386-322-6155
John Cash, prin. Fax 506-0002
eLearning East 50/Alt
1250 Reed Canal Rd 32129 386-506-0014
Melissa Carr, dir. Fax 506-5048
Silver Sands MS 1,200/6-8
1300 Herbert St 32129 386-322-6175
Rose Roland, prin. Fax 322-7574
Spruce Creek HS 2,800/9-12
801 Taylor Rd 32127 386-322-6272
Todd Sparger, prin. Fax 506-5045

Palmer College of Chiropractic FL Campus Post-Sec.
4777 City Center Pkwy 32129 866-585-9677

**Port Richey, Pasco, Pop. 2,626**
Pasco County SD
Supt. — See Land O Lakes
Chasco MS 700/6-8
7702 Ridge Rd 34668 727-774-1300
David Huyck, prin. Fax 774-1391

**Port Saint Joe, Gulf, Pop. 3,399**
Gulf County SD 2,000/PK-12
150 Middle School Dr 32456 850-229-8256
Jim Norton, supt. Fax 229-6089
www.gulf.k12.fl.us
Port Saint Joe JSHS 500/7-12
100 Shark Dr 32456 850-229-8251
Duane McFarland, prin. Fax 227-1803
Gulf County Adult S Adult
150 Middle School Dr 32456 850-229-8256
Billy Hoover, coord. Fax 229-6089
Other Schools – See Wewahitchka

**Port Saint Lucie, Saint Lucie, Pop. 160,756**
St. Lucie County SD
Supt. — See Fort Pierce
College Preparatory Academy 9-12
501 NW California Blvd 34986 772-323-3747
Erika Rains, admin.
Port Saint Lucie HS 1,900/9-12
1201 SE Jaguar Ln 34952 772-337-6770
Bridgette Hargadine, prin. Fax 337-6780
St. Lucie West Centennial HS 2,500/9-12
1485 SW Cashmere Blvd 34986 772-344-4400
Andrea Popwell, prin. Fax 785-6679
Southern Oaks MS 1,000/6-8
5500 NE Saint James Dr 34983 772-785-5640
Lisa Sullivan, prin. Fax 785-5660
Southport MS 900/6-8
2420 SE Morningside Blvd 34952 772-337-5900
Nicole Telese, prin. Fax 337-5903
Treasure Coast HS 2,500/9-12
1000 SW Darwin Blvd 34953 772-807-4300
Susan Seal, prin. Fax 807-4320

Barnabas Christian Academy 100/K-12
1860 SW Fountainview Blvd 34986 772-344-1643
Bill Reed, admin. Fax 344-1443
Keiser University Post-Sec.
10330 S US Highway 1 34952 772-398-9990
Morningside Academy 200/6-12
1631 SE Greendon Ave 34952 772-335-2096
Port St. Lucie Beauty Academy Post-Sec.
7644 S US 1 34983 772-340-3540

**Princeton, Miami-Dade, Pop. 21,761**

Princeton Christian S 300/PK-12
PO Box 924916 33092 305-257-3644

**Punta Gorda, Charlotte, Pop. 16,453**
Charlotte County SD
Supt. — See Port Charlotte
Charlotte HS 1,900/9-12
1250 Cooper St 33950 941-575-5450
Cathy Corsaletti, prin. Fax 575-5464
Punta Gorda MS 1,100/6-8
1001 Education Ave 33950 941-575-5485
Justina Dionisio, prin. Fax 575-5491

**Quincy, Gadsden, Pop. 7,889**
Gadsden County SD 5,900/PK-12
35 Martin Luther King Jr Bl 32351 850-627-9651
Reginald James, supt. Fax 627-2760
www.gcps.k12.fl.us
Carter-Paramore Academy 200/Alt
631 S Stewart St 32351 850-627-6030
Keith Dowdell, prin. Fax 875-3197
Gadsden Central Academy 50/Alt
655 S Stewart St 32351 850-875-7249
Rebecca Gaines, admin. Fax 627-1802
Gadsden Technical Institute Vo/Tech
201 Martin Luther King Jr 32351 850-875-8324
Dr. Sylvia Jackson, dir. Fax 875-7297
Shanks MS 600/6-8
1400 W King St 32351 850-875-8737
Juanita Ellis, prin. Fax 875-8775
West Gadsden HS 400/7-12
200 Providence Rd 32351 850-442-9500
Pauline West, prin. Fax 442-6126
Other Schools – See Havana

Munroe Day S 200/PK-12
91 Old Mt Pleasant Rd 32352 850-856-5500
Suzanne Johnson, head sch Fax 856-5856

**Riverview, Hillsborough, Pop. 68,857**
Hillsborough County SD
Supt. — See Tampa
Giunta MS 1,000/6-8
4202 S Falkenburg Rd, 813-740-4888
Michael Bobo, prin. Fax 740-4892
Riverview HS 2,300/9-12
11311 Boyette Rd 33569 813-671-5011
Danielle Shotwell, prin. Fax 671-5012
Rodgers MS 1,000/6-8
11910 Tucker Rd 33569 813-671-5288
Michael Miranda, prin. Fax 671-5245
Spoto HS 1,200/9-12
8538 Eagle Palm Dr, 813-672-5405
David New, prin. Fax 672-5423

Florida Career College Post-Sec.
2662 S Falkenburg Rd, 813-621-5775
Providence Christian S 200/PK-12
5416 Providence Rd, 813-661-0588
David Hubbart, admin. Fax 681-3852

**Riviera Beach, Palm Beach, Pop. 31,825**
Palm Beach County SD
Supt. — See West Palm Beach
Kennedy MS 600/6-8
1901 Avenue S 33404 561-845-4500
Corey Brooks, prin. Fax 845-4537
Riviera Beach Prep & Achievement Academy 100/Alt
7071 Garden Rd 33404 561-881-4740
Elaine Hubbard-Williams, prin. Fax 881-4731
Suncoast HS 1,500/9-12
1717 Avenue S 33404 561-882-3400
Linda Cartlidge, prin. Fax 882-3443

North Technical Education Center Post-Sec.
7071 Garden Rd 33404 561-881-4600

**Rockledge, Brevard, Pop. 24,317**
Brevard County SD
Supt. — See Melbourne
Kennedy MS 700/7-8
2100 S Fiske Blvd 32955 321-633-3500
Richard Myers, prin. Fax 633-3509
McNair Magnet MS 600/7-8
1 Challenger Dr 32955 321-633-3630
Rosette Brown, prin. Fax 633-3639
Rockledge HS 1,300/9-12
220 Raider Rd 32955 321-636-3711
Anthony Hines, prin. Fax 632-6064

**Rosemary Beach, Walton**

Ohana Institute 100/3-12
82 S Barret Sq 32461 850-231-1140

**Rotonda West, Charlotte**
Charlotte County SD
Supt. — See Port Charlotte
Ainger MS 900/6-8
245 Cougar Way 33947 941-697-5800
Marcia Louden, prin. Fax 697-5470

**Royal Palm Beach, Palm Beach, Pop. 33,307**
Palm Beach County SD
Supt. — See West Palm Beach
Crestwood MS 1,200/6-8
64 Sparrow Dr 33411 561-753-5000
Stephanie Nance, prin. Fax 753-5035
Royal Palm Beach Community HS 2,100/9-12
10600 Okeechobee Blvd 33411 561-753-4000
Jesus Armas, prin. Fax 753-4015

South University Post-Sec.
9801 Belvedere Rd 33411 561-273-6500

**Ruskin, Hillsborough, Pop. 16,985**
Hillsborough County SD
Supt. — See Tampa
Lennard HS 1,600/9-12
2342 E Shell Point Rd 33570 813-641-5611
Mary Freitas, prin. Fax 641-5610
Shields MS 1,400/6-8
15732 Beth Shields Way 33573 813-672-5338
Tia Brown, prin. Fax 672-5342
South County Career Center Vo/Tech
2810 John Sherman Way 33570 813-233-3335
Tibor Kovacs, prin. Fax 233-3339
Lennard Adult Education Adult
2342 E Shell Point Rd 33570 813-658-2075
Sandra Tune, prin. Fax 658-2078

Hillsborough Community College Post-Sec.
551 24th St NE 33570 813-253-7000
Ruskin Christian S 200/PK-12
820 W College Ave 33570 813-645-6441

**Safety Harbor, Pinellas, Pop. 16,579**
Pinellas County SD
Supt. — See Largo
Safety Harbor MS 1,400/6-8
901 1st Ave N 34695 727-724-1400
Alison Kennedy, prin. Fax 724-1407

**Saint Augustine, Saint Johns, Pop. 12,760**
St. Johns County SD 30,800/PK-12
40 Orange St 32084 904-547-7500
Joseph Joyner Ed.D., supt. Fax 547-7515
www.stjohns.k12.fl.us
Gaines and Transition S 50/Alt
1 Christopher St 32084 904-547-8560
Tish McMahon, prin. Fax 547-8555
Menendez HS 1,400/9-12
600 State Road 206 W 32086 904-547-8660
Dr. Clay Carmichael, prin. Fax 547-8675
Murray MS 700/6-8
150 N Holmes Blvd 32084 904-547-8470
Tom Schwarm, prin. Fax 547-8475
Pacetti Bay MS 1,000/6-8
245 Meadowlark Ln 32092 904-547-8760
Jay Willets, prin. Fax 547-8765
Rogers MS 900/6-8
6250 US Highway 1 S 32086 904-547-8700
Greg Bergamasco, prin. Fax 547-8705
Saint Augustine HS 1,700/9-12
3205 Varella Ave 32084 904-547-8530
Dr. DeArmas Graham, prin. Fax 547-8535
St. Johns Technical HS Vo/Tech
2980 Collins Ave 32084 904-547-8500
Cynthia Williams, prin. Fax 547-8505
Sebastian MS 700/6-8
2955 Lewis Speedway 32084 904-547-3840
Kelly Battel, prin. Fax 547-3845
Other Schools – See Ponte Vedra Beach, Saint Johns

Beacon of Hope Christian S 100/K-12
1230 Kings Estate Rd 32086 904-797-6996
First Coast Technical College Post-Sec.
2980 Collins Ave 32084 904-547-3282
Flagler College Post-Sec.
74 King St 32084 904-829-6481
Florida School for the Deaf and Blind Post-Sec.
207 San Marco Ave 32084 904-827-2200
St. Joseph Academy 300/9-12
155 State Road 207 32084 904-824-0431
Todd DeClemente, prin. Fax 826-4477
Univ. of St. Augustine for Health Sci. Post-Sec.
1 University Blvd 32086 904-826-0084

**Saint Cloud, Osceola, Pop. 34,423**
Osceola County SD
Supt. — See Kissimmee
Harmony HS 1,900/9-12
3601 Arthur Gallagher Blvd 34771 407-933-9900
Grover Butler, prin. Fax 933-9901
Narcoossee MS 1,000/6-8
2700 N Narcoossee Rd 34771 407-891-6600
Frank Telemko, prin. Fax 891-6610
Saint Cloud HS 1,900/9-12
2000 Bulldog Ln 34769 407-891-3100
Nathaniel Fancher, prin. Fax 891-3114
Saint Cloud MS 1,200/6-8
1975 Michigan Ave 34769 407-891-3200
Cynthia Chiavini, prin. Fax 891-3206

**Saint Johns, Saint Johns**
St. Johns County SD
Supt. — See Saint Augustine
Bartram Trail HS 1,700/9-12
7399 Longleaf Pine Pkwy, 904-547-8340
Chris Phelps, prin. Fax 547-8359
Creekside HS 1,700/9-12
100 Knights Ln, 904-547-7300
Randy Johnson, prin. Fax 547-7305
Fruit Cove MS 1,500/6-8
3180 Race Track Rd, 904-547-7880
Lynn O'Connor, prin. Fax 547-7885
Switzerland Point MS 1,000/6-8
777 Greenbriar Rd, 904-547-8650
Lisa Kunze, prin. Fax 547-8645

**Saint Leo, Pasco, Pop. 1,297**

St. Leo University Post-Sec.
33701 State Road 52 33574 352-588-8200

**Saint Petersburg, Pinellas, Pop. 239,351**
Pinellas County SD
Supt. — See Largo
Azalea MS 1,100/6-8
7855 22nd Ave N 33710 727-893-2606
Connie Kolosey, prin. Fax 893-2624
Bay Point MS 1,100/6-8
2151 62nd Ave S 33712 727-893-1153
Jason Shedrick, prin. Fax 893-1181
Gibbs HS 1,400/9-12
850 34th St S 33711 727-893-5452
Reuben Hepburn, prin. Fax 893-5461
Hollins HS 1,700/9-12
4940 62nd St N 33709 727-547-7876
Robert Florio, prin. Fax 547-7727
Hopkins MS 1,000/6-8
701 16th St S 33705 727-893-2400
Barry Brown, prin. Fax 893-1600
Lakewood HS 1,300/9-12
1400 54th Ave S 33705 727-893-2916
Erin Savage, prin. Fax 893-1387

Lealman Innovation Academy 400/6-12
4900 28th St N 33714 727-528-5802
Busara Pitts, prin. Fax 528-5807
Marshall Fundamental MS 900/6-8
3901 22nd Ave S 33711 727-552-1737
Dr. Solomon Lowery, prin. Fax 552-1741
Meadowlawn MS 1,200/6-8
6050 16th St N 33703 727-570-3097
Claudius Effiom, prin. Fax 570-3396
Northeast HS 1,900/9-12
5500 16th St N 33703 727-570-3138
Kevin Hendrick, prin. Fax 217-7318
PTEC St. Petersburg Vo/Tech
901 34th St S 33711 727-893-2500
Boe Norwood, dir. Fax 893-2776
St. Petersburg HS 2,200/9-12
2501 5th Ave N 33713 727-893-1842
Albert Bennett, prin. Fax 893-1399
Tyrone MS 900/6-8
6421 22nd Ave N 33710 727-893-1819
Robin Mobley, prin. Fax 893-1946
Hollins Evening Adult Education Ctr Adult
4940 62nd St N 33709 727-547-7872
Brenda Vlach, admin. Fax 547-7873
Lakewood Community S Adult
1400 54th Ave S 33705 727-893-2955
Sharon Snow, admin. Fax 893-1375
Northeast Community S Adult
1717 54th Ave N 33714 727-570-3193
Dr. Kathy Gregg, admin. Fax 217-7449
Tomlinson Adult Learning Center Adult
296 Mirror Lake Dr N 33701 727-893-2723
Godfrey Watson, dir. Fax 893-2782

---

Admiral Farragut Academy 400/PK-12
501 Park St N 33710 727-384-5500
Robert Fine, hdmstr. Fax 347-5160
Bayfront Medical Center Post-Sec.
701 6th St S 33701 727-893-6604
Canterbury S of Florida -Knowlton Campus 300/5-12
990 62nd Ave NE 33702 727-525-1419
Mac Hall, head sch Fax 525-2545
Eckerd College Post-Sec.
4200 54th Ave S 33711 727-867-1166
ITT Technical Institute Post-Sec.
877 Executive Ctr Dr W #100 33702 727-209-4700
Keswick Christian S 500/PK-12
10101 54th Ave N 33708 727-393-9100
Nick Stratis, supt. Fax 397-5378
Loraine's Academy Post-Sec.
1012 58th St N 33710 727-347-4247
Northside Christian S 600/PK-12
7777 62nd Ave N 33709 727-541-7593
Dr. Don James, hdmstr. Fax 546-5836
Pinellas Technical Education Center Post-Sec.
901 34th St S 33711 727-893-2500
Poynter Institute for Media Studies Post-Sec.
801 3rd St S 33701 888-769-6837
St. Petersburg Catholic HS 500/9-12
6333 9th Ave N 33710 727-344-4065
Rev. Richard Rosin, prin. Fax 343-9311
St. Petersburg College Post-Sec.
PO Box 13489 33733 727-341-4772
Shorecrest Preparatory S 1,000/PK-12
5101 1st St NE 33703 727-522-2111
Michael Murphy, hdmstr. Fax 527-4191
Southeastern College Post-Sec.
11208 Blue Heron Blvd Ste A 33716 727-576-6500
University of South Florida Post-Sec.
140 7th Ave S 33701 727-873-4873

**Sanford, Seminole, Pop. 52,277**
Seminole County SD 63,700/PK-12
400 E Lake Mary Blvd 32773 407-320-0000
Dr. Walt Griffin, supt. Fax 320-0281
www.scps.k12.fl.us
Crooms Academy of Information Technology 600/9-12
2200 W 13th St 32771 407-320-5750
Demetria Faison, prin. Fax 320-5798
Journeys Academy 200/Alt
1722 W Airport Blvd 32771 407-320-7850
Kenneth Bevan, prin. Fax 320-7849
Millennium MS 1,700/6-8
21 Lakeview Ave 32773 407-320-6550
Dr. Maggie Gunderson, prin. Fax 320-6599
Polk Alternative S Alt
211 Bush Blvd 32773 407-665-1405
Dr. Erica Pooler, prin.
Sanford MS 1,500/6-8
1700 S French Ave 32771 407-320-6150
Randy Shuler, prin. Fax 320-6265
Seminole HS 3,400/9-12
2701 Ridgewood Ave 32773 407-320-5050
Dr. Connie Collins, prin. Fax 320-5024
Other Schools – See Altamonte Springs, Casselberry, Lake Mary, Longwood, Oviedo, Winter Park, Winter Springs

---

Aerosim Flight Academy Post-Sec.
2700 Flightline Ave 32773 407-330-7020
Holy Cross Academy 5-9
100 Aero Ln 32771 407-936-3636
Rob Sinninger, prin. Fax 936-0041
Liberty Christian S 100/PK-12
2626 S Palmetto Ave 32773 407-323-1583
Fax 323-1588
Seminole State College of Florida Post-Sec.
100 Weldon Blvd 32773 407-708-4722
Southern Technical College Post-Sec.
2910 S Orlando Dr 32773 407-323-4141

**Santa Rosa Beach, Walton**
Walton County SD
Supt. — See De Funiak Springs
Emerald Coast MS 500/5-8
6694 W County Highway 30A 32459 850-622-5025
Jeff Infinger, prin. Fax 622-5027
South Walton HS 600/9-12
645 Greenway Trl 32459 850-622-5020
Alexis Tibbetts, prin. Fax 622-5039

**Sarasota, Sarasota, Pop. 51,038**
Sarasota County SD 39,600/PK-12
1960 Landings Blvd 34231 941-927-9000
Lori White, supt.
sarasotacountyschools.net
Booker HS 1,000/9-12
3201 N Orange Ave 34234 941-355-2967
Dr. Rachel Shelley, prin. Fax 359-5757
Booker MS 800/6-8
2250 Myrtle St 34234 941-359-5824
LaShawn Houston-Frost, prin. Fax 359-5898
Brookside MS 900/6-8
3636 S Shade Ave 34239 941-361-6472
Kristine Lawrence, prin. Fax 361-6508
McIntosh MS 900/6-8
701 McIntosh Rd 34232 941-361-6520
Dr. Harriet Moore, prin. Fax 361-6340
Riverview HS 2,600/9-12
1 Ram Way 34231 941-923-1484
Eric Jackson, prin. Fax 361-6175
Sarasota HS 2,000/9-12
1000 S School Ave 34237 941-955-0181
Jeff Hradek, prin. Fax 361-6380
Sarasota MS 1,100/6-8
4826 Ashton Rd 34233 941-361-6464
Karen Rose, prin. Fax 361-6798
Suncoast Polytechnical HS Vo/Tech
4650 Beneva Rd 34233 941-921-3981
Trent Terry, dir. Fax 921-9900
Suncoast Technical College Vo/Tech
4748 Beneva Rd 34233 941-924-1365
Dr. Todd Bowden, dir. Fax 921-7902
YMCA Triad North/South 100/Alt
4430 Beneva Rd 34233 941-925-6693
Margaret King, dir. Fax 925-6696
Other Schools – See North Port, Venice

---

Argosy University/Sarasota Post-Sec.
5250 17th St 34235 941-379-0404
Cardinal Mooney Catholic HS 500/9-12
4171 Fruitville Rd 34232 941-371-4917
Stephen Christie, prin. Fax 371-6924
East West College of Natural Medicine Post-Sec.
3808 N Tamiami Trl 34234 941-355-9080
Everglades University Post-Sec.
6001 Lake Osprey Dr Ste 110 34240 941-907-2262
Fashion Focus Hair Academy Post-Sec.
2184 Gulf Gate Dr 34231 941-921-4877
Keiser University Post-Sec.
6151 Lake Osprey Dr 34240 941-907-3900
Meridian College Post-Sec.
7020 Professional Pkwy E 34240 941-377-4880
New College of Florida Post-Sec.
5800 Bay Shore Rd 34243 941-487-5000
NewGate S 100/PK-12
5237 Ashton Rd 34233 941-922-4949
Potter's Wheel Academy 100/K-12
PO Box 50203 34232 941-284-4076
Reed Palmer, dir. Fax 605-7024
Providence Community S 200/PK-12
5600 Deer Dr 34240 941-727-6860
Ringling College of Art & Design Post-Sec.
2700 N Tamiami Trl 34234 941-351-5100
Sarasota Christian S 400/PK-12
5415 Bahia Vista St 34232 941-371-6481
Larry Litwiller, head sch Fax 371-0898
Sarasota County Technical Institute Post-Sec.
4748 Beneva Rd 34233 941-924-1365
Sarasota Memorial Hospital Post-Sec.
1700 S Tamiami Trl 34239 941-917-1080
Sarasota School of Massage Therapy Post-Sec.
5899 Whitfield Ave Ste 301 34243 941-957-0577
University of S Florida Sarasota-Manatee Post-Sec.
8350 N Tamiami Trl 34243 941-359-4200

**Satellite Beach, Brevard, Pop. 9,911**
Brevard County SD
Supt. — See Melbourne
DeLaura MS 700/7-8
300 Jackson Ave 32937 321-773-7581
Robert Pruett, prin. Fax 773-0702
Satellite HS 1,200/9-12
300 Scorpion Ct 32937 321-779-2000
Mark Elliott, prin. Fax 773-0703

**Sebastian, Indian River, Pop. 21,634**
Indian River County SD
Supt. — See Vero Beach
Sebastian River HS 1,900/9-12
9001 90th Ave 32958 772-564-4170
Todd Racine, prin. Fax 564-4182
Sebastian River MS 1,000/6-8
9400 County Road 512 32958 772-564-5111
Jody Idlette, prin. Fax 564-5225

**Sebring, Highlands, Pop. 10,311**
Highlands County SD 11,600/PK-12
426 School St 33870 863-471-5555
Wally Cox, supt. Fax 471-5600
www.highlands.k12.fl.us
Hill-Gustat MS 700/6-8
4700 Schumacher Rd 33872 863-471-5437
Jackie Allen, prin. Fax 314-5245
Sebring HS 1,600/9-12
3514 Kenilworth Blvd 33870 863-471-5500
Anne Lindsay, prin. Fax 471-5507
Sebring MS 700/6-8
500 E Center Ave 33870 863-471-5700
Sandi Whidden, prin. Fax 471-5710
Other Schools – See Avon Park, Lake Placid

---

Highlands University Preparatory S 100/PK-12
1160 Persimmon Ave 33870 863-385-3850
Laura Young, prin. Fax 385-5752

**Seffner, Hillsborough, Pop. 7,410**
Hillsborough County SD
Supt. — See Tampa
Armwood HS 1,700/9-12
12000 E US Highway 92 33584 813-744-8040
Joseph Castelli, prin. Fax 744-8048
Brandon Alternative S 200/Alt
1019 N Parsons Ave 33584 813-651-2165
Nancy Lind, admin. Fax 651-2173
Burnett MS 1,000/6-8
1010 N Kingsway Rd 33584 813-744-6745
Dante Jones, prin. Fax 744-8973
Jennings MS 900/6-8
9325 Governors Run Dr 33584 813-740-4575
Richard Scionti, prin. Fax 740-4579

---

Seffner Christian Academy 700/PK-12
11605 E US Highway 92 33584 813-626-0001
Roger Duncan, admin. Fax 627-0330

**Seminole, Pinellas, Pop. 17,030**
Pinellas County SD
Supt. — See Largo
Career Academies of Seminole Vo/Tech
12611 86th Ave 33776 727-545-6405
Barbara Clare, prin. Fax 545-6408
Osceola Fundamental HS 1,700/9-12
9751 98th St 33777 727-547-7717
Michael Bohnet, prin. Fax 545-6412
Osceola MS 1,200/6-8
9301 98th St 33777 727-547-7689
Susan Arsenault, prin. Fax 547-7667
Seminole HS 2,200/9-12
8401 131st St 33776 727-547-7536
Thomas Brittain, prin. Fax 547-7503
Seminole MS 1,300/6-8
8701 131st St 33776 727-547-4520
Wendy Bryan, prin. Fax 547-7741

**Shalimar, Okaloosa, Pop. 699**
Okaloosa County SD
Supt. — See Fort Walton Beach
Meigs MS 500/6-8
150 Richbourg Ave 32579 850-833-4301
Dr. Lee Hale, prin. Fax 833-9392

**Sneads, Jackson, Pop. 1,817**
Jackson County SD
Supt. — See Marianna
Sneads HS 400/9-12
8066 Old Spanish Trl 32460 850-482-9007
John Shouse, prin. Fax 482-9058

**South Daytona, Volusia, Pop. 12,013**

---

International Academy Post-Sec.
2550 S Ridgewood Ave 32119 386-767-4600
Warner Christian Academy 700/PK-12
1730 S Ridgewood Ave 32119 386-767-5451
Mark Tress, supt. Fax 760-6834

**South Miami, Miami-Dade, Pop. 11,508**
Miami-Dade County SD
Supt. — See Miami
South Miami MS 700/6-8
6750 SW 60th St 33143 305-661-3481
Juan Boue, prin. Fax 665-6728

**Spring Hill, Hernando, Pop. 96,871**
Hernando County SD
Supt. — See Brooksville
Fox Chapel MS 700/6-8
9412 Fox Chapel Ln 34606 352-797-7025
Ray Pinder, prin. Fax 797-7125
Springstead HS 1,800/9-12
3300 Mariner Blvd 34609 352-797-7010
Carmine Ruffa, prin. Fax 797-7110

---

ATA Career Education Post-Sec.
7355 Spring Hill Dr 34606 352-684-3007
Bene's International School of Beauty Post-Sec.
1486 Pinehurst Dr 34606 352-263-2744
Bishop McLaughlin HS 200/9-12
13651 Hays Rd 34610 727-857-2600
Camille Jowanna, prin. Fax 857-2610
Pasco-Hernando Community College Post-Sec.
450 Beverly Ct 34606 352-688-8798
Spring Hill Christian Academy 300/PK-12
3140 Mariner Blvd 34609 352-683-8485
Michael Willis, prin. Fax 683-5087
West Hernando Christian S 300/PK-12
2250 Osowaw Blvd 34607 352-688-9918
Wider Horizons S 100/PK-12
4060 Castle Ave 34609 352-686-1934

**Starke, Bradford, Pop. 5,317**
Bradford County SD 3,300/PK-12
501 W Washington St 32091 904-966-6018
Chad Farnsworth, supt. Fax 966-6030
www.bradfordschools.org
Bradford HS 800/9-12
581 N Temple Ave 32091 904-966-6075
Bryan Boyer, prin. Fax 966-6020
Bradford MS 700/6-8
527 N Orange St 32091 904-966-6705
Mallory McConnell, prin. Fax 966-6714
Bradford Union Career Technical Center Vo/Tech
609 N Orange St 32091 904-966-6766
David Harris, coord. Fax 966-6786

Clay County SD
Supt. — See Green Cove Springs
Florida Youth Challenge Academy 200/Alt
5629 State Road 16 W 32091 904-682-4000
Fax 682-3990

---

Bradford-Union Area Vo-Tech Center Post-Sec.
609 N Orange St 32091 904-966-6764
Hope Christian Academy 200/PK-12
3900 SE State Road 100 32091 352-473-4040
Angie Davis, prin. Fax 473-2024
Northside Christian Academy 200/PK-12
7415 NW County Road 225 32091 904-964-7124
Alicia Etheridge, head sch Fax 966-2350

**Stuart, Martin, Pop. 15,329**
Martin County SD 17,700/PK-12
500 SE Ocean Blvd 34994 772-219-1200
Laurie Gaylord, supt. Fax 219-1231
www.martinschools.org
Anderson MS 1,000/6-8
7000 SE Atlantic Ridge Dr 34997 772-221-7100
Timothy Aitken, prin. Fax 221-7149
Martin County HS 2,000/9-12
2801 S Kanner Hwy 34994 772-219-1800
Al Fabrizio, prin. Fax 219-1821
Murray MS 700/6-8
4400 SE Murray St 34997 772-219-1670
Amy Laws, prin. Fax 219-1677
South Fork HS 1,800/9-12
10000 SW Bulldog Way 34997 772-219-1840
Dave Hall, prin. Fax 219-1860
Spectrum JSHS 100/Alt
800 SE Bahama Ave 34994 772-219-1870
Janice Mills, prin. Fax 219-1873
Stuart MS 900/6-8
575 SE Georgia Ave 34994 772-219-1685
David Krakoff, prin. Fax 219-1690
Stuart Community Adult HS Adult
1150 SE Saint Josephs Ave 34996 772-219-1296
Melissa Eversdyke, coord. Fax 219-1299
Other Schools – See Indiantown, Jensen Beach, Palm City

---

Chapman School of Seamanship Post-Sec.
4343 SE Saint Lucie Blvd 34997 772-283-8130
Community Christian Academy 300/PK-12
777 SE Salerno Rd 34997 772-288-7227
Star Academy for Pet Stylists Post-Sec.
2201 SE Indian St Unit C6 34997 772-221-9330

**Summerfield, Marion**
Marion County SD
Supt. — See Ocala
Lake Weir MS 1,300/6-8
10220 SE Sunset Harbor Rd 34491 352-671-6120
Stephanie Calloway, prin. Fax 671-6121

**Sumterville, Sumter**
Sumter County SD
Supt. — See Bushnell
Sumter Alternative S Alt
709 N West St 33585 352-568-1113
James Presley, prin. Fax 793-6508
Sumter County Adult Center Adult
1425 CR 526A 33585 352-793-5719
Chris Burk, prin. Fax 793-6508

**Sunrise, Broward, Pop. 82,120**
Broward County SD
Supt. — See Fort Lauderdale
Bair MS 900/6-8
9100 NW 21st Mnr 33322 754-322-2900
James McDermott, prin. Fax 322-2985
Piper HS 2,500/9-12
8000 NW 44th St 33351 754-322-1700
Angel Gomez, prin. Fax 322-1830
Westpine MS 1,400/6-8
9393 NW 50th St 33351 754-322-4900
Paula Meadows, prin. Fax 322-4985

**Tallahassee, Leon, Pop. 177,584**
Leon County SD 32,200/PK-12
2757 W Pensacola St 32304 850-487-7100
Jackie Pons, supt. Fax 487-7141
www.leonschools.net
Chiles HS 2,000/9-12
7200 Lawton Chiles Ln 32312 850-488-1756
Joe Burgess, prin. Fax 488-1218
Cobb MS 800/6-8
915 Hillcrest Ave 32308 850-488-3364
Tonja Fitzgerald, prin. Fax 922-2452
Deerlake MS 900/6-8
9902 Deer Lk W 32312 850-922-6545
Laura Brooks, prin. Fax 488-3275
Fairview MS 900/6-8
3415 Zillah St 32305 850-488-6880
Scott Hansen, prin. Fax 922-6326
Godby HS 1,100/9-12
1717 W Tharpe St 32303 850-617-4700
Shelly Bell, prin. Fax 922-4162
Griffin MS 500/6-8
800 Alabama St 32304 850-617-5353
Gwendolyn Lynn-Thomas, prin. Fax 617-5354
Leon HS 1,900/9-12
550 E Tennessee St 32308 850-617-5700
Billy Epting, prin. Fax 922-5311
Lincoln HS 1,900/9-12
3838 Trojan Trl 32311 850-487-2110
Allen Burch, prin. Fax 922-4173
Lively-Technical Center Vo/Tech
500 Appleyard Dr 32304 850-487-7555
Vernea Randolph, prin. Fax 922-3880
Montford MS 1,100/6-8
5789 Pimlico Dr 32309 850-922-6011
Lewis Blessing, prin. Fax 922-7974
Nims MS 500/6-8
723 W Orange Ave 32310 850-488-5960
Desmond Cole, prin. Fax 922-0203
Raa MS 900/6-8
401 W Tharpe St 32303 850-488-6287
Giselle Marsh, prin. Fax 922-5835
Rickards HS 1,300/9-12
3013 Jim Lee Rd 32301 850-414-5500
Doug Cook, prin. Fax 922-7104
SAIL HS 400/9-12
2006 Jackson Bluff Rd 32304 850-488-2468
Tiffany Thomas, prin. Fax 922-8483
Second Chance S Alt
860 Blountstown St 32304 850-488-2087
Richard Richardson, prin. Fax 410-1531
Success Academy at Ghazvini Learning Ctr 100/Alt
854 Blountstown St 32304 850-488-2087
Joe Pons, prin. Fax 410-3353
Swift Creek MS 700/6-8
2100 Pedrick Rd 32317 850-414-2670
Sue Rishell, prin. Fax 414-2650
Adult & Community Education Adult
283 Trojan Trl 32311 850-922-5343
Regina Browning, prin. Fax 922-5352

---

Betton Hills S 100/1-12
2205 Thomasville Rd 32308 850-656-9211
Caroline Accorsini, dir. Fax 656-9602
Community Christian S 300/PK-12
4859 Kerry Forest Pkwy 32309 850-893-6628
David Pinson, hdmstr. Fax 668-3966
Core Institute Post-Sec.
223 W Carolina St 32301 866-830-0108
Florida A&M University Post-Sec.
1601 Martin Luther King Jr 32307 850-599-3000
Florida State University Post-Sec.
600 W College Ave 32306 850-644-2525
ITT Technical Institute Post-Sec.
2639 N Monroe St Ste 100 32303 850-422-6300
John Paul II Catholic HS 100/9-12
5100 Terrebonne Dr 32311 850-201-5744
Sr. Maureen Martin, prin. Fax 205-3299
Keiser University Post-Sec.
1700 Halstead Blvd Ste 2 32309 850-906-9494
Lively Area Vocational Technical School Post-Sec.
500 Appleyard Dr 32304 850-487-7555
Maclay S 900/PK-12
3737 N Meridian Rd 32312 850-893-2138
James Milford, head sch Fax 893-7434
North Florida Christian S 800/PK-12
3000 N Meridian Rd 32312 850-386-6327
Dr. Tom Phillips, admin. Fax 386-8409
North Florida Cosmetology Institute Post-Sec.
2424 Allen Rd 32312 850-878-5269
Tallahassee Community College Post-Sec.
444 Appleyard Dr 32304 850-201-6200
Tallahassee Memorial Hospital Post-Sec.
1300 Miccosukee Rd 32308 850-681-5385

**Tamarac, Broward, Pop. 59,173**
Broward County SD
Supt. — See Fort Lauderdale
Millennium MS 1,500/6-8
5803 NW 94th Ave 33321 754-322-3900
Dr. Cheryl Cendan, prin. Fax 322-3985

**Tampa, Hillsborough, Pop. 328,173**
Hillsborough County SD 192,200/PK-12
PO Box 3408 33601 813-272-4000
Jeff Eakins, supt. Fax 272-4510
www.sdhc.k12.fl.us
Adams MS 1,200/6-8
10201 N Boulevard 33612 813-975-7665
Heath Beauregard, prin. Fax 632-6889
Alonso HS 2,400/9-12
8302 Montague St 33635 813-356-1525
Kenneth Hart, prin. Fax 356-1529
Benito MS 1,100/6-8
10101 Cross Creek Blvd 33647 813-631-4694
John Sanders, prin. Fax 631-4706
Blake HS 1,600/9-12
1701 N Boulevard 33607 813-272-3422
Jesse Salters, prin. Fax 272-3715
Bowers/Whitley Career Center Vo/Tech
13609 N 22nd St 33613 813-558-1750
Dr. Anthony Colucci, prin. Fax 558-1761
Buchanan MS 700/6-8
1001 W Bearss Ave 33613 813-975-7600
Scott Hilgenberg, prin. Fax 975-7610
Chamberlain HS 1,900/9-12
9401 N Boulevard 33612 813-975-7677
Celeste Liccio, prin. Fax 975-7687
Coleman MS 900/6-8
1724 S Manhattan Ave 33629 813-872-5335
Michael Hoskinson, prin. Fax 872-5338
Davidsen MS 1,100/6-8
10501 Montague St 33626 813-558-5300
Brent McBrien, prin. Fax 558-5299
Dowdell MS 700/6-8
1208 Wishing Well Way 33619 813-744-8322
Roger Stanley, prin. Fax 740-3616
Farnell MS 1,300/6-8
13912 Nine Eagles Dr 33626 813-356-1640
John Cobb, prin. Fax 356-1644
Ferrell Girls Prep Academy 300/6-8
4302 N 24th St 33610 813-276-5608
Karen French, prin. Fax 276-5615
Franklin Boys Prep Academy 300/6-8
3915 E 21st Ave 33605 813-744-8108
John Haley, prin. Fax 744-8579
Freedom HS 2,100/9-12
17410 Commerce Park Blvd 33647 813-558-1185
Kevin Stephenson, prin. Fax 558-1189
Gaither HS 2,000/9-12
16200 N Dale Mabry Hwy 33618 813-975-7340
Thomas Morrill, prin. Fax 975-7349
Hill MS 1,000/6-8
5200 Ehrlich Rd 33624 813-975-7325
Ronald Mason, prin. Fax 975-4819
Hillsborough HS 1,900/9-12
5000 N Central Ave 33603 813-276-5620
Gary Brady, prin. Fax 276-5629
Jefferson HS 1,700/9-12
4401 W Cypress St 33607 813-872-5241
Robert Quinn, prin. Fax 872-5250
King HS 1,800/9-12
6815 N 56th St 33610 813-744-8333
Michael Rowan, prin. Fax 744-8343
Leto HS 1,700/9-12
4409 W Sligh Ave 33614 813-872-5300
Hilda Genco, prin. Fax 872-5314
Liberty MS 1,200/6-8
17400 Commerce Park Blvd 33647 813-558-1180
James Ammirati, prin. Fax 558-1184
Madison MS 800/6-8
4444 W Bay Vista Ave 33611 813-272-3050
Joseph Brown, prin. Fax 233-2796
Memorial MS 700/6-8
4702 N Central Ave 33603 813-872-5230
Henry Lefler, prin. Fax 872-5238
Middleton HS 1,200/9-12
4801 N 22nd St 33610 813-233-3360
Kim Moore, prin. Fax 233-3364
Monroe MS 600/6-8
4716 W Montgomery Ave 33616 813-272-3020
Peter Megara, prin. Fax 272-3027
North Tampa Alternative S 200/Alt
8602 N Armenia Ave 33604 813-631-4426
Angela Vickers, prin. Fax 631-4429
Orange Grove Magnet MS 500/6-8
3415 N 16th St 33605 813-276-5717
Shannon Butler, prin. Fax 276-5857
Pierce MS 1,100/6-8
5511 N Hesperides St 33614 813-872-5344
Raymond Padgett, prin. Fax 871-7978
Plant HS 2,400/9-12
2415 S Himes Ave 33629 813-272-3033
Robert Nelson, prin. Fax 272-0624
Progress Village MS 800/6-8
8113 Zinnia Dr 33619 813-671-5110
Andrew Olson, prin. Fax 671-5240
Robinson HS 1,500/9-12
6311 S Lois Ave 33616 813-272-3006
Johnny Bush, prin. Fax 272-3014
Sickles HS 2,000/9-12
7950 Gunn Hwy 33626 813-631-4742
Jake Russell, prin. Fax 631-4754
Sligh MS 700/6-8
2011 E Sligh Ave 33610 813-276-5596
Shellie Blackwood-Green, prin. Fax 276-5606
Smith MS 1,100/6-8
14303 Citrus Pointe Dr 33625 813-792-5125
JoAnn Johnson, prin. Fax 792-5129
Stewart MS 900/6-8
1125 W Spruce St 33607 813-276-5691
Baretta Wilson, prin. Fax 276-5698
Tampa Bay Technical HS 2,000/9-12
6410 Orient Rd 33610 813-744-8360
Michael Ippolito, prin. Fax 744-8368
Van Buren MS 600/6-8
8715 N 22nd St 33604 813-975-7652
Derrick Gaines, prin. Fax 631-4312
Waters Career Center Vo/Tech
2704 N Highland Ave 33602 813-233-2655
Veronica Knight, admin. Fax 233-2659
Webb MS 900/6-8
6035 Hanley Rd 33634 813-872-5351
Frank Diaz, prin. Fax 872-5359
Wharton HS 2,400/9-12
20150 Bruce B Downs Blvd 33647 813-631-4710
Bradley Woods, prin. Fax 631-4722
Williams MS 800/6-8
5020 N 47th St 33610 813-744-8600
Arlene Castelli, prin. Fax 744-8665
Wilson MS 600/6-8
1005 W Swann Ave 33606 813-276-5682
Colleen Faucett, prin. Fax 233-2540
Young Magnet MS 600/6-8
1807 E Dr Martn Lthr King 33610 813-276-5739
Nadine Johnson, prin. Fax 276-5893
Aparicio/Levy Tech Center Adult
10119 E Ellicott St 33610 813-740-4884
AnnMarie Courtney, prin. Fax 740-4885
Bowers/Whitley Adult Education Adult
13609 N 22nd St 33613 813-463-9528
Dr. Sheila Washington, prin. Fax 558-1761
Brewster Tech Center Adult
2222 N Tampa St 33602 813-276-5448
Paul Gansemer, prin. Fax 276-5756
Chamberlain Adult Education Adult
9401 N Boulevard 33612 813-631-4500
Marcia Monk, prin. Fax 631-4513
Erwin Tech Center Adult
2010 E Hillsborough Ave 33610 813-769-5180
James Rich, prin. Fax 769-5185
Gary Adult S Adult
5101 N 40th St 33610 813-740-7660
Edward Cristiano, prin. Fax 740-7674
Jefferson Adult S Adult
4401 W Cypress St 33607 813-356-1288
Pam Elles, prin. Fax 356-1291
Learey Technical Center Adult
7010 N Manhattan Ave 33614 813-769-2123
AnnMarie Courtney, prin. Fax 769-4615
Leto Adult Education Adult
4409 W Sligh Ave 33614 813-872-5300
Dr. Olaniyio Popoola, prin. Fax 356-1010
Other Schools – See Brandon, Dover, Gibsonton, Lithia, Lutz, Odessa, Plant City, Riverview, Ruskin, Seffner, Temple Terrace, Valrico

---

Academy of the Holy Names HS 400/9-12
3319 Bayshore Blvd 33629 813-839-5371
Sr. Ann Regan, prin. Fax 839-3924
Academy Prep Center of Tampa 100/5-8
1407 E Columbus Dr 33605 813-248-5600
American Youth Academy 400/PK-12
5905 E 130th Ave 33617 813-987-9282
Dr. Abdulmajid Biuk, prin. Fax 987-9262
Argosy University/Tampa Post-Sec.
1403 N Howard Ave 33607 813-393-5290
Art Institute of Tampa Post-Sec.
4401 N Himes Ave Ste 150 33614 813-873-2112
Bayshore Christian S 200/PK-12
3909 S MacDill Ave 33611 813-839-4297
Melanie Humenansky, head sch Fax 835-1404
Berkeley Preparatory S 1,300/PK-12
4811 Kelly Rd 33615 813-885-1673
Joseph Seivold, hdmstr. Fax 886-6933
Cambridge Christian S 600/PK-12
6101 N Habana Ave 33614 813-872-6744
Tim Euler, head sch Fax 872-6013
Carrollwood Day S 800/PK-12
1515 W Bearss Ave 33613 813-920-2288
Ryan Kelly, head sch Fax 960-9269
Citrus Park Christian S 400/PK-12
7705 Gunn Hwy 33625 813-920-3960
Concorde Career Institute Post-Sec.
4202 W Spruce St 33607 813-874-0094
DeVry University Post-Sec.
5540 W Executive Dr Ste 100 33609 813-287-6700
DeVry University Post-Sec.
6700 Lakeview Center # 150 33619 813-664-4260

Everest University - Brandon Campus Post-Sec.
3924 Coconut Palm Dr 33619 813-621-0041
Everest University - Tampa Campus Post-Sec.
3319 W Hillsborough Ave 33614 813-879-6000
Faith Outreach Academy 200/PK-12
7607 Sheldon Rd 33615 813-887-5546
Gateway Christian Academy 100/PK-12
14205 N Florida Ave 33613 813-964-9800
Maritza Maldonado, prin. Fax 964-9808
Henry W. Brewster Technical Center Post-Sec.
2222 N Tampa St 33602 813-276-5448
Hillsborough Community College Post-Sec.
10414 E Columbus Dr 33619 813-253-7802
Hillsborough Community College Post-Sec.
PO Box 30030 33630 813-253-7000
Hillsborough Community College Ybor Camp Post-Sec.
2112 N 15th St 33605 813-253-7601
ITT Technical Institute Post-Sec.
4809 Memorial Hwy 33634 813-885-2244
James Haley Veteran's Hospital Post-Sec.
13000 Bruce B Downs Blvd 33612 813-972-2000
Jesuit HS 700/9-12
4701 N Himes Ave 33614 813-877-5344
Barry Neuburger, prin. Fax 872-1853
Keiser University Post-Sec.
5002 W Waters Ave 33634 813-885-4900
LaSalle Computer Learning Center Post-Sec.
1111 N West Shore Blvd #110 33607 888-482-6877
Manhattan Beauty School Post-Sec.
2317 E Fletcher Ave 33612 813-264-3535
Manhattan Hairstyling Academy Post-Sec.
1906 W Platt St 33606 813-837-2525
Rasmussen College Post-Sec.
4042 Park Oaks Blvd Ste 100 33610 813-246-7600
Remington College Post-Sec.
6302 E ML King Blvd Ste 400 33619 813-935-5700
Sanford-Brown College Post-Sec.
7702 Woodland Center # 100 33614 847-781-3600
Sanford-Brown Institute Post-Sec.
3725 W Grace St 33607 813-881-0007
Southeastern College Post-Sec.
5225 Memorial Hwy 33634 813-961-2837
Southwest Florida College Post-Sec.
3910 Riga Blvd 33619 813-630-4401
Strayer University Post-Sec.
6302 E M L King Blvd # 450 33619 813-663-0100
Strayer University Post-Sec.
4902 Eisenhower Blvd # 100 33634 813-882-0100
Tampa Adventist Academy 100/PK-10
3205 N Boulevard 33603 813-228-7950
Tampa Bay Christian Academy 300/PK-12
6815 N Rome Ave 33604 813-343-0600
Natasha Sherwood, hdmstr. Fax 343-0601
Tampa Catholic HS 700/9-12
4630 N Rome Ave 33603 813-870-0860
Thomas Reidy, prin. Fax 877-9136
Tampa General Hospital Post-Sec.
PO Box 1289 33601 813-844-7985
Tampa Preparatory S 600/6-12
727 W Cass St 33606 813-251-8481
Kevin Plummer, hdmstr. Fax 254-2106
The Salon Professional Academy Post-Sec.
4802 Gunn Hwy Ste 144 33624 813-908-8020
Ultimate Medical Academy Post-Sec.
9309 N Florida Ave Ste 100 33612 813-386-6350
Universal Academy of Florida 400/PK-12
6801 Orient Rd 33610 813-664-0695
University of South Florida Post-Sec.
4202 E Fowler Ave 33620 813-974-2011
University of Tampa Post-Sec.
401 W Kennedy Blvd 33606 813-253-3333
West Gate Christian S 100/PK-12
5121 Kelly Rd 33615 813-884-5147

**Tarpon Springs, Pinellas, Pop. 23,056**
Pinellas County SD
Supt. — See Largo
East Lake HS 2,300/9-12
1300 Silver Eagle Dr 34688 727-942-5419
Carmela Haley, prin. Fax 942-5441
East Lake MS Academy of Engineering 6-8
1200 Silver Eagle Dr 34688 727-940-7624
Karen Huzar, prin. Fax 942-5441
Tarpon Springs HS 1,700/9-12
1411 Gulf Rd 34689 727-943-4900
James Joyer, prin. Fax 943-4907
Tarpon Springs MS 1,100/6-8
501 N Florida Ave 34689 727-943-5511
Raquel Giles, prin. Fax 943-5519

---

St. Petersburg College Post-Sec.
600 E Klosterman Rd 34689 727-791-2400

**Tavares, Lake, Pop. 13,762**
Lake County SD 38,700/PK-12
201 W Burleigh Blvd 32778 352-253-6500
Susan Moxley Ed.D., supt. Fax 253-6503
www.lake.k12.fl.us/
Tavares HS 1,300/9-12
603 N New Hampshire Ave 32778 352-343-3007
Dr. Janice Boyd, prin. Fax 343-0892
Tavares MS 1,000/6-8
1335 Lane Park Cutoff 32778 352-343-4545
Trella Mott, prin. Fax 343-7212
Other Schools – See Clermont, Eustis, Groveland, Leesburg, Minneola, Mount Dora, Umatilla

---

Adventure Christian Academy 100/K-12
3800 State Road 19 32778 352-742-4543
Gary Johnson, admin. Fax 343-3820
Liberty Christian Prep 200/PK-12
2451 Dora Ave 32778 352-343-0061

**Tavernier, Monroe, Pop. 2,111**
Monroe County SD
Supt. — See Key West
Coral Shores HS 800/9-12
89901 Overseas Hwy 33070 305-853-3222
Blake Fry, prin. Fax 853-3228

**Temple Terrace, Hillsborough, Pop. 23,889**
Hillsborough County SD
Supt. — See Tampa
Greco MS 900/6-8
6925 E Fowler Ave 33617 813-987-6926
Yinka Alege, prin. Fax 987-6863

---

Florida College Post-Sec.
119 N Glen Arven Ave 33617 813-988-5131

**Titusville, Brevard, Pop. 42,761**
Brevard County SD
Supt. — See Melbourne
Astronaut HS 1,200/9-12
800 War Eagle Blvd 32796 321-264-3000
Krista Miller, prin. Fax 264-3013
Jackson MS 600/7-8
1515 Knox Mcrae Dr 32780 321-269-1812
Annetha Jones, prin. Fax 269-7811
Madison MS 500/7-8
3375 Dairy Rd 32796 321-264-3120
Sherry Tomlinson, prin. Fax 264-3124
Titusville HS 1,400/9-12
150 Terrier Trl S 32780 321-264-3100
Gary Preisser, prin. Fax 264-3103
South Lake Education Center Adult
3755 Garden St 32796 321-264-3088
Jeff Arnott, prin. Fax 264-3042

---

Bristow Academy Post-Sec.
365 Golden Knights Blvd 32780 321-567-0382
Melbourne Beauty School Post-Sec.
106 Julia St 32796 - -
Temple Christian S 100/PK-12
1400 N Washington Ave 32780 321-269-2837

**Trenton, Gilchrist, Pop. 1,949**
Gilchrist County SD 2,500/PK-12
310 NW 11th Ave 32693 352-463-3200
Robert G. Rankin, supt. Fax 463-3276
www.gilchristschools.org
Trenton HS 600/6-12
1013 N Main St 32693 352-463-3210
Cheri Langford, prin. Fax 463-3264
Other Schools – See Bell

**Trinity, Pasco, Pop. 10,776**

---

Trinity College of Florida Post-Sec.
2430 Welbilt Blvd 34655 727-376-6911

**Umatilla, Lake, Pop. 3,433**
Lake County SD
Supt. — See Tavares
Umatilla HS 900/9-12
320 N Trowell Ave 32784 352-669-3131
Randy Campbell, prin. Fax 669-6606
Umatilla MS 600/6-8
305 E Lake St 32784 352-669-3171
Thomas Sanders, prin. Fax 669-5424

**Valparaiso, Okaloosa, Pop. 4,829**
Okaloosa County SD
Supt. — See Fort Walton Beach
Okaloosa STEMM Academy 6-8
379 Edge Ave 32580 850-833-4120
Wanda Avery, admin. Fax 833-4177

**Valrico, Hillsborough, Pop. 34,795**
Hillsborough County SD
Supt. — See Tampa
Bloomingdale HS 2,400/9-12
1700 Bloomingdale Ave, 813-744-8018
Susan Burkett, prin. Fax 744-8026
Mulrennan MS 1,200/6-8
4215 Durant Rd, 813-651-2100
Tim Ducker, prin. Fax 651-2104

---

Foundation Christian Academy 200/PK-12
3955 Lithia Pinecrest Rd, 813-654-2969
Grace Christian S 200/PK-12
1425 N Valrico Rd 33594 813-689-8815
Manhattan Hairstyling Academy Post-Sec.
3244 Lithia Pinecrest #103 33594 813-655-4545

**Venice, Sarasota, Pop. 20,602**
Sarasota County SD
Supt. — See Sarasota
Venice HS 1,900/9-12
1 Indian Ave 34285 941-488-6726
Jack Turgeon, prin. Fax 486-2034
Venice MS 600/6-8
1900 Center Rd 34292 941-486-2100
Dr. Karin Schmidt, prin. Fax 486-2108

---

Venice Christian S 200/PK-12
1200 Center Rd 34292 941-496-4411
Jerry Frimmel, admin. Fax 408-8362

**Vernon, Washington, Pop. 673**
Washington County SD
Supt. — See Chipley
Vernon HS 400/9-12
3232 Moss Hill Rd 32462 850-535-2046
Brian Riviere, prin. Fax 535-6244
Vernon MS 400/6-8
3206 Moss Hill Rd 32462 850-535-2807
Kimberly Register, prin. Fax 535-1683

**Vero Beach, Indian River, Pop. 15,009**
Indian River County SD 16,800/PK-12
1990 25th St 32960 772-564-3000
Dr. Mark Rendell, supt. Fax 569-0424
www.indianriverschools.org
Alternative Center for Education 100/Alt
4680 28th Ct 32967 772-564-6240
Denny Hart, prin. Fax 564-6265
Gifford MS 1,000/6-8
4530 28th Ct 32967 772-564-3550
Roxanne Decker, prin. Fax 564-3561
Oslo MS 900/6-8
480 20th Ave SW 32962 772-564-3980
Beth Hofer, prin. Fax 564-4029
Storm Grove MS 800/6-8
6400 57th St 32967 772-564-6400
Tosha Jones, prin. Fax 564-6321
Vero Beach Freshman Learning Center 9-9
1507 19th St 32960 772-564-5800
Shawn O'Keefe, prin. Fax 564-4928
Vero Beach HS 1,900/10-12
1707 16th St 32960 772-564-5400
Shawn O'Keefe, prin. Fax 564-5553
Technical Center for Career & Adult Ed Adult
1426 19th St 32960 772-564-4970
Christi Shields, prin. Fax 564-4977
Other Schools – See Sebastian

---

FlightSafety Academy Post-Sec.
2805 Airport Dr 32960 772-564-7600
Glendale Christian S 100/PK-12
790 27th Ave 32968 772-569-1095
Dr. Mark Richardson, hdmstr. Fax 562-4919
Master's Academy 200/PK-12
1105 58th Ave 32966 772-794-4655
Wayne Smith, hdmstr. Fax 562-9808
St. Edward's S 500/PK-12
1895 Saint Edwards Dr 32963 772-231-4136
Michael Mersky, head sch Fax 231-2427

**Viera, Brevard**
Brevard County SD
Supt. — See Melbourne
Viera HS 2,200/9-12
6103 Stadium Pkwy 32940 321-632-1770
Miguel Alba, prin. Fax 433-4338

**Walnut Hill, Escambia**
Escambia County SD
Supt. — See Pensacola
Ward MS 500/6-8
7650 Highway 97 32568 850-327-4283
Nancy Perry, prin. Fax 327-4991

**Warrington, Escambia, Pop. 14,034**
Escambia County SD
Supt. — See Pensacola
Warrington MS 700/6-8
450 S Old Corry Field Rd, Pensacola FL 32507
850-453-7440
Dr. Reggie Lipnick, prin. Fax 453-7572

**Wauchula, Hardee, Pop. 4,954**
Hardee County SD 5,000/PK-12
PO Box 1678 33873 863-773-9058
David Durastanti, supt. Fax 773-0069
www.hardee.k12.fl.us
Hardee HS 1,300/9-12
830 Altman Rd 33873 863-773-3181
Dr. Michele Polk Ed.D., prin. Fax 773-4390
Hardee JHS 1,100/6-8
2401 US Highway 17 N 33873 863-773-3147
Doug Herron, prin. Fax 773-3167
Other Schools – See Zolfo Springs

**Webster, Sumter, Pop. 770**
Sumter County SD
Supt. — See Bushnell
South Sumter MS 800/6-8
773 NW 10th Ave 33597 352-793-2232
Allen Shirley, prin. Fax 793-3976

**Weeki Wachee, Hernando, Pop. 12**
Hernando County SD
Supt. — See Brooksville
Weeki Wachee HS 900/9-12
12150 Vespa Way 34614 352-797-7029
Troy LaBarbara, prin. Fax 797-7129

**Wellington, Palm Beach, Pop. 55,375**
Palm Beach County SD
Supt. — See West Palm Beach
Emerald Cove MS 1,200/6-8
9950 Stribling Way 33414 561-803-8000
Eugina Feaman, prin. Fax 803-8050
Palm Beach Central HS 2,900/9-12
8499 Forest Hill Blvd, 561-304-1000
Darren Edgecomb, prin. Fax 304-1017
Polo Park MS 1,100/6-8
11901 Lake Worth Rd, 561-333-5500
Ann Clark, prin. Fax 333-5505
Wellington Community HS 2,400/9-12
2101 Greenview Shores Blvd 33414 561-795-4900
Mario Crocetti, prin. Fax 795-4948
Wellington Landings MS 1,300/6-8
1100 Aero Club Dr 33414 561-792-8100
Blake Bennett, prin. Fax 792-8106

**Wesley Chapel, Pasco, Pop. 42,858**
Pasco County SD
Supt. — See Land O Lakes
Long MS 1,500/6-8
2025 Mansfield Blvd 33543 813-346-6200
Christine Wolff, prin. Fax 346-6291
Weightman MS 1,200/6-8
30649 Wells Rd, 813-794-0200
Brandon Bracciale, prin. Fax 794-0291
Wesley Chapel HS 1,400/9-12
30651 Wells Rd, 813-794-8700
Carin Nettles, prin. Fax 794-8791
Wiregrass Ranch HS 2,000/9-12
2909 Mansfield Blvd 33543 813-346-6000
Robyn White, prin. Fax 346-6091

---

Saddlebrook Preparatory S 100/3-12
5700 Saddlebrook Way 33543 813-907-4500
Larry Robison, hdmstr. Fax 991-4713

**West Melbourne, Brevard, Pop. 17,945**
Brevard County SD
Supt. — See Melbourne
Central MS 1,300/7-8
2600 Wingate Blvd 32904 321-722-4150
Gregory Potter, prin. Fax 722-4165

Bethany Christian S 300/PK-12
1100 Dorchester Ave 32904 321-727-2038

**West Miami, Miami-Dade, Pop. 5,942**

Florida Education Institute Post-Sec.
5818 SW 8th St 33144 305-263-9990

**Weston, Broward, Pop. 64,228**
Broward County SD
Supt. — See Fort Lauderdale
Cypress Bay HS 4,200/9-12
18600 Vista Park Blvd 33332 754-323-0350
Charles Neely, prin. Fax 323-0363
Falcon Cove MS 2,500/6-8
4251 Bonaventure Blvd 33332 754-323-3200
Dr. Mark Kaplan, prin. Fax 323-3285
Tequesta Trace MS 1,500/6-8
1800 Indian Trce 33326 754-323-4400
Paul Micensky, prin. Fax 323-4485

American InterContinental University Post-Sec.
2250 N Commerce Pkwy 33326 954-446-6100
Sagemont S - Upper School Campus 500/6-12
2585 Glades Cir 33327 954-389-2454

**West Palm Beach, Palm Beach, Pop. 98,081**
Palm Beach County SD 171,900/PK-12
3300 Forest Hill Blvd 33406 561-434-8000
Robert Avossa Ed.D., supt. Fax 434-8571
www.palmbeachschools.org/
Bak MS of the Arts 1,400/6-8
1725 Echo Lake Dr 33407 561-882-3870
Sally Rozanski, prin. Fax 882-3879
Bear Lakes MS 700/6-8
3505 Shenandoah Rd 33409 561-615-7700
Kirk Howell, prin. Fax 615-7756
Conniston Community MS 1,100/6-8
3630 Parker Ave 33405 561-802-5400
Oscar Otero, prin. Fax 802-5409
Dreyfoos S of the Arts 1,300/9-12
501 S Sapodilla Ave 33401 561-802-6000
Susan Atherley, prin. Fax 802-6059
Forest Hill Community HS 1,800/9-12
6901 Parker Ave 33405 561-540-2400
Mary Stratos, prin. Fax 540-2440
Gold Coast Community S 100/Alt
4260 Westgate Ave 33409 561-687-6300
Timothy Abrams, prin. Fax 687-6350
Jeaga MS 1,200/6-8
3777 N Jog Rd 33411 561-242-8000
Kevin Gatlin, prin. Fax 242-8005
Okeeheelee MS 1,400/6-8
2200 Pinehurst Dr 33413 561-434-3200
David Samore, prin. Fax 434-3244
PACE Center for Girls 50/Alt
1225 S Military Trl Ste D 33415 561-472-1990
Fax 472-1991
Palm Beach Lakes Community HS 1,700/9-12
3505 Shiloh Dr 33407 561-640-5000
Dr. Cheryl McKeever, prin. Fax 688-5340
Palm Springs Community MS 1,500/6-8
1560 Kirk Rd 33406 561-434-3300
Sandra Jinks, prin. Fax 434-3303
Roosevelt Community MS 1,200/6-8
1900 N Australian Ave 33407 561-822-0200
Moneek McTier, prin. Fax 882-0222
Turning Points Academy 100/Alt
1950 Benoist Farms Rd 33411 561-681-3700
Anthony Allen Ph.D., prin. Fax 681-3750
Western Pines MS 1,200/6-8
5949 140th Ave N 33411 561-792-2500
Robert Hatcher, prin. Fax 792-2530
Adult Education Center of Palm Beach Adult
2161 N Military Trl 33409 561-616-7800
Rickey Swearingen, prin. Fax 616-7850
Other Schools – See Belle Glade, Boca Raton, Boynton Beach, Delray Beach, Greenacres, Jupiter, Lake Worth, Lantana, Loxahatchee, Pahokee, Palm Beach Gardens, Riviera Beach, Royal Palm Beach, Wellington

Academy for Nursing & Health Occupations Post-Sec.
5154 Okechobee Blvd #201 33417 561-683-1400
Atlantic Christian Academy 300/PK-12
4900 Summit Blvd 33415 561-686-8081
Jim Rozendal, hdmstr. Fax 640-7613
Berean Christian S 600/PK-12
8350 Okeechobee Blvd 33411 561-798-9300
William Dupere, hdmstr. Fax 792-3073
Cardinal Newman HS 700/9-12
512 Spencer Dr 33409 561-683-6266
Dr. Christine Higgins, prin. Fax 683-7307
Dade Medical College Post-Sec.
2601 S Military Trl 33415 561-345-7240
Florida Career College Post-Sec.
6058 Okeechobee Blvd 33417 561-689-0550
Health Career Institute Post-Sec.
1764 N Congress Ave 33409 561-586-0121
ITT Technical Institute Post-Sec.
1756 N Congress Ave 33409 561-233-4900
Keiser University Post-Sec.
2085 Vista Pkwy 33411 561-471-6000
King's Academy 1,000/PK-12
8401 Belvedere Rd 33411 561-686-4244
Jeffrey Loveland, pres. Fax 686-8017
Lincoln College of Technology Post-Sec.
2410 Metrocentre Blvd 33407 561-842-8324
MCI Institute of Technology Post-Sec.
3650 Shawnee Ave Ste 12 33409 888-318-9310
Northwood University Post-Sec.
2600 N Military Trl 33409 800-458-8325
Oxbridge Academy 300/9-12
3151 N Military Trl 33409 561-972-9600
Bob Parsons, pres.
Palm Beach Atlantic University Post-Sec.
901 S Flagler Dr 33401 888-468-6722
PC Professor Post-Sec.
6080 Okeechobee Blvd #200 33417 561-684-3333

**Wewahitchka, Gulf, Pop. 1,928**
Gulf County SD
Supt. — See Port Saint Joe
Wewahitchka JSHS 400/7-12
1 Gator Cir 32465 850-639-2228
Jay Bidwell, prin. Fax 639-5394

**Wildwood, Sumter, Pop. 6,607**
Sumter County SD
Supt. — See Bushnell
Wildwood MSHS 700/6-12
700 Huey St 34785 352-748-1314
Larry Woodward, prin. Fax 748-7668

**Williston, Levy, Pop. 2,726**
Levy County SD
Supt. — See Bronson
Williston HS 600/9-12
427 W Noble Ave 32696 352-528-3542
Eulin Gibbs, prin. Fax 528-2723
Williston MS 400/6-8
20550 NE 42nd Pl 32696 352-528-2941
Kelly Gore, prin. Fax 528-2941

**Windermere, Orange, Pop. 2,437**
Orange County SD
Supt. — See Orlando
Gotha MS 1,200/6-8
9155 Gotha Rd 34786 407-521-2360
Patrice Knowles, prin. Fax 521-2361

Windermere Preparatory S 1,100/PK-12
6189 Winter Garden Vineland 34786 407-905-7737
Dr. Thomas Marcy, hdmstr. Fax 905-7710

**Winter Garden, Orange, Pop. 33,427**
Orange County SD
Supt. — See Orlando
Bridgewater MS 1,500/6-8
5600 Tiny Rd 34787 407-905-3710
Lisa James, prin. Fax 905-3858
Lakeview MS 1,400/6-8
1200 W Bay St 34787 407-877-5010
Athena Adams, prin. Fax 877-5019
Sunridge MS 6-8
14955 Sunridge Blvd 34787 407-656-0794
Patricia Bowen-Painter, prin. Fax 656-0806
West Orange HS 3,300/9-12
1625 Beulah Rd 34787 407-905-2400
Douglas Szcinski, prin. Fax 656-4970
Westside Tech Ctr Vo/Tech
955 E Story Rd 34787 407-905-2000
Crystal Davidson, dir. Fax 656-3970

Foundation Academy - South Campus 400/6-12
15304 Tilden Rd 34787 407-877-2744
Dr. Lorne Wenzel, hdmstr. Fax 877-1985
Professional Golfers Career College Post-Sec.
16349 Phil Ritson Way 34787 407-905-2200

**Winter Haven, Polk, Pop. 33,292**
Polk County SD
Supt. — See Bartow
Denison MS 900/6-8
400 Avenue A SE 33880 863-291-5353
Terri Christian, prin. Fax 291-5347
Jewett Middle Academy 600/6-8
601 Avenue T NE 33881 863-291-5320
Jacquelyn Moore, prin. Fax 297-3049
Ridge Career Center Vo/Tech
7700 State Road 544 33881 863-419-3060
Lisa Harden, prin. Fax 419-3062
Westwood MS 1,000/6-8
3520 Avenue J NW 33881 863-965-5484
Todd Bennett, prin. Fax 965-5585
Winter Haven HS 1,600/9-12
600 6th St SE 33880 863-291-5330
Gina Williams, prin. Fax 297-3024

All Saints' Academy 600/PK-12
5001 State Road 540 W 33880 863-293-5980
Carolyn Baldwin, hdmstr. Fax 294-2819
Heritage Christian Academy 100/PK-10
244 Avenue D SW 33880 863-293-0012
John Scott, admin. Fax 299-4146
Oasis Christian Academy 200/PK-12
151 King Rd 33880 863-293-0930
Matt Wiggins, admin. Fax 293-0429
Polk Community College Post-Sec.
999 Avenue H NE 33881 863-297-1000
Ridge Career Center Post-Sec.
7700 State Road 544 33881 863-419-3060
Winter Haven Christian S 200/PK-10
1700 Buckeye Loop Rd 33881 863-294-4135

**Winter Park, Orange, Pop. 27,399**
Orange County SD
Supt. — See Orlando
Winter Park 9th Grade Center 900/9-9
528 Huntington Ave 32789 407-623-1476
Timothy Smith, prin. Fax 623-1485
Winter Park Education Center Alt
1045 Azalea Ln 32789 407-245-1555
William Tovine, prin. Fax 245-1561
Winter Park HS 2,500/10-12
2100 Summerfield Rd 32792 407-622-3200
Timothy Smith, prin. Fax 975-2434
Winter Park Tech Center Vo/Tech
901 W Webster Ave 32789 407-622-2900
Jayne Lychako, prin. Fax 975-2435

Seminole County SD
Supt. — See Sanford
Lake Howell HS 2,300/9-12
4200 Dike Rd 32792 407-746-9050
Frank Casillo, prin. Fax 746-9025

Fortis College Post-Sec.
1573 W Fairbanks Ave #100 32789 407-843-3984
Full Sail University Post-Sec.
3300 University Blvd 32792 407-679-0100
Geneva S 500/PK-12
2025 State Road 436 32792 407-332-6363
Rev. Robert Ingram, hdmstr. Fax 332-1664
Herzing University Post-Sec.
1865 State Road 436 32792 407-478-0500
International Community S 400/PK-12
4800 Howell Branch Rd 32792 407-645-2343
Robyn Terwilleger, prin.
Rollins College Post-Sec.
1000 Holt Ave 32789 407-646-2000
Trinity Preparatory S 800/6-12
5700 Trinity Prep Ln 32792 407-671-4140
Craig Maughan, hdmstr. Fax 671-6935
Walden Community S 50/5-12
4595 Howell Branch Rd 32792 407-677-8225

**Winter Springs, Seminole, Pop. 32,650**
Seminole County SD
Supt. — See Sanford
Indian Trails MS 1,100/6-8
415 Tuskawilla Rd 32708 407-320-4350
Dr. Lesley Sileo Robinson, prin. Fax 320-4399
Winter Springs HS 2,100/9-12
130 Tuskawilla Rd 32708 407-320-8750
Dr. Mickey Reynolds, prin. Fax 320-8700

**Yulee, Nassau, Pop. 11,311**
Nassau County SD
Supt. — See Fernandina Beach
Yulee HS 1,000/9-12
85375 Miner Rd 32097 904-491-7949
Natasha Drake, prin. Fax 225-8658
Yulee MS 900/6-8
85439 Miner Rd 32097 904-491-7944
Jeremy Boatright, prin. Fax 225-0104

**Zellwood, Orange, Pop. 2,799**

Hampden DuBose Academy 100/K-12
PO Box 639 32798 407-880-4321
Rev. Michael Jackson, admin. Fax 886-2297

**Zephyrhills, Pasco, Pop. 13,107**
Pasco County SD
Supt. — See Land O Lakes
Stewart MS 1,000/6-8
38505 10th Ave, 813-794-6500
Shae Davis, prin. Fax 794-6591
Zephyrhills HS 1,600/9-12
6335 12th St, 813-794-6100
Angela Stone, prin. Fax 794-6191

Zephyrhills Christian Academy 100/K-12
34927 Eiland Blvd 33541 813-779-1648

**Zolfo Springs, Hardee, Pop. 1,811**
Hardee County SD
Supt. — See Wauchula
Pioneer Career Academy 50/Alt
2630 Academy Dr 33890 863-735-2300
Gilbert Vasquez, dir. Fax 735-2155

# GEORGIA

## GEORGIA DEPARTMENT OF EDUCATION
**2066 Twin Towers E, Atlanta 30334**
**Telephone 404-656-2800**
**Fax 404-651-8737**
**Website http://www.doe.k12.ga.us**

State Superintendent of Schools John Barge

## GEORGIA BOARD OF EDUCATION
**2053 Twin Towers East, Atlanta 30334**

Chief Executive Officer John Barge

## REGIONAL EDUCATIONAL SERVICE AGENCIES (RESA)

Central Savannah River Area RESA
Gene Sullivan, dir. 706-556-6225
4683 Augusta Hwy, Dearing 30808 Fax 556-8891
www.csraresa.net

Chattahoochee-Flint RESA
Norman Carter, dir. 229-937-5341
PO Box 1150, Ellaville 31806 Fax 937-5754
www.ciclt.net

Coastal Plains RESA
Harold Chambers, dir. 229-546-4094
245 N Robinson St, Lenox 31637 Fax 546-4167
www.cpresa.org

First District RESA
Dr. Whit Myers, dir. 912-842-5000
PO Box 780, Brooklet 30415 Fax 842-5161
www.fdresa.org/

Griffin RESA
Dr. Stephanie Gordy, dir. 770-229-3247
440 Tilney Ave, Griffin 30224 Fax 228-7316
www.griffinresa.net/

Heart of Georgia RESA
Dr. Steven Miletto, dir. 478-374-2240
1141 Cochran Hwy Fax 374-1524
Eastman 31023
www.hgresa.org/

Metro RESA
Leigh Ann Putman, dir. 770-432-2404
1870 Teasley Dr SE, Smyrna 30080 Fax 432-6105
www.ciclt.net/mresa

Middle Georgia RESA
Carolyn Williams, dir. 478-988-7170
80 Cohen Walker Dr Fax 988-7176
Warner Robins 31088
www.mgresa.org/

Northeast Georgia RESA
Dr. Keith Everson, dir. 706-742-8292
375 Winter St, Winterville 30683 Fax 742-8928
www.negaresa.org

North Georgia RESA
Larry Harmon, dir. 706-276-1111
4731 Old Highway 5 S Fax 276-1114
Ellijay 30540
www.ngresa.org/

Northwest Georgia RESA
Dexter Mills, dir. 706-295-6189
3167 Cedartown Hwy SE Fax 295-6098
Rome 30161
www.nwgaresa.com/

Oconee RESA
Dr. Hayward Cordy, dir. 478-552-5178
206 S Main St, Tennille 31089 Fax 552-6499
www.oconeeresa.org

Okefenokee RESA
Dr. Peggy Stovall, dir. 912-285-6151
1450 N Augusta Ave Fax 287-6650
Waycross 31503
www.okresa.org

Pioneer RESA
Justin Old, dir. 706-865-2141
PO Box 1789, Cleveland 30528 Fax 865-6748
www.pioneerresa.org/

Southwest Georgia RESA
Tim Helms, dir. 229-207-0600
570 Martin Luther King Jr Fax 336-2888
Camilla 31730
www.ciclt.net/sn/clt/swresa/default.aspx?ClientCode=swresa

West Georgia RESA
Rachel Spates, dir. 770-583-2528
99 Brown School Dr Fax 583-3223
Grantville 30220
www.garesa.org/

## PUBLIC, PRIVATE AND CATHOLIC SECONDARY SCHOOLS

**Abbeville, Wilcox, Pop. 2,863**
Wilcox County SD 1,300/PK-12
395 College St W 31001 229-467-2141
Steve Smith, supt. Fax 467-2302
www.wilcox.k12.ga.us/
Other Schools – See Rochelle

**Acworth, Cobb, Pop. 19,875**
Cobb County SD
Supt. — See Marietta
Allatoona HS 1,900/9-12
3300 Dallas Acworth Hwy NW 30101 770-975-6503
John Kelly, prin. Fax 529-7744
Barber MS 1,000/6-8
4222 Cantrell Rd NW 30101 770-975-6764
Dr. Lisa Williams, prin. Fax 529-0325
Durham MS 1,100/6-8
2891 Mars Hill Rd NW 30101 770-975-6641
Dr. Patricia Alford, prin. Fax 975-6643

---

Chattahoochee Technical College Post-Sec.
5198 Ross Rd SE 30102 770-975-4000
Cornerstone Preparatory Academy 400/K-12
3588 Hickory Grove Rd 30101 770-529-7077
Jeanne Borders, head sch Fax 529-7477

**Adairsville, Bartow, Pop. 4,584**
Bartow County SD
Supt. — See Cartersville
Adairsville HS 1,000/9-12
519 Old Highway 41 NW 30103 770-606-5841
Bruce Mulkey, prin. Fax 773-2722
Adairsville MS 700/6-8
485 Old Highway 41 NW 30103 770-606-5842
Dr. Brian Knuchel, prin. Fax 606-5179

**Adel, Cook, Pop. 5,286**
Cook County SD 3,300/PK-12
1109 N Parrish Ave 31620 229-896-2294
Lance Heard, supt. Fax 896-3443
www.cook.k12.ga.us/
Cook HS 900/9-12
9900 Highway 37 31620 229-896-2213
Keith Croft, prin. Fax 896-3423
Other Schools – See Sparks

**Ailey, Montgomery, Pop. 429**
Montgomery County SD
Supt. — See Mount Vernon
Montgomery County MS 200/6-8
800 Martin Luther King Dr 30410 912-583-2351
Juanita Boatwright, prin. Fax 583-4469

**Alamo, Wheeler, Pop. 2,788**
Wheeler County SD 1,000/PK-12
18 McRae St 30411 912-568-7198
Dr. Mark Davidson, supt. Fax 568-1985
www.wheelercountyschools.org
Wheeler County MSHS 500/6-12
50 Snowhill Rd 30411 912-568-7166
Hal Ford, prin. Fax 568-7141

**Albany, Dougherty, Pop. 76,579**
Dougherty County SD 13,900/PK-12
200 Pine Ave 31701 229-431-1285
Dr. David Mosely, supt. Fax 431-1276
www.docoschools.org
Albany HS 900/9-12
801 W Residence Ave 31701 229-431-3300
Rodney Bullard, prin. Fax 431-3481
Albany MS 500/6-8
1700 Cordell Ave 31705 229-431-3325
Eddie Johnson, prin. Fax 431-3474
Cross MS 600/6-8
324 Lockett Station Rd, 229-431-3362
Thelma Chunn, prin. Fax 431-3476
Dougherty HS 900/9-12
1800 Pearce Ave 31705 229-431-3310
Dr. Jeffrey Ross, prin. Fax 431-1302
Merry Acres MS 800/6-8
1601 Florence Dr 31707 229-431-3338
Dr. Gail Griffin, prin. Fax 431-1204
Monroe HS 1,200/9-12
900 Lippitt Dr 31701 229-431-3316
Vinson Davis, prin. Fax 431-3380
Radium Springs MS 700/6-8
2600 Radium Springs Rd 31705 229-431-3346
Dr. Valerie Williams, prin. Fax 431-3552
South GA Regional Achievement Center Alt
1001 W Highland Ave 31701 229-431-1218
Dr. David Hamilton, prin. Fax 431-3478
Southside MS 400/6-8
1615 Newton Rd 31701 229-431-3351
Dr. Frederick Polite, prin. Fax 431-1209
Westover HS 1,200/9-12
2600 Partridge Dr 31707 229-431-3320
William Chunn, prin. Fax 431-3349

---

Albany State University Post-Sec.
504 College Dr 31705 229-430-4600
Albany Technical College Post-Sec.
1704 S Slappey Blvd 31701 229-430-3500
Byne Christian S 100/PK-12
2832 Ledo Rd 31707 229-436-0173
Darton State College Post-Sec.
2400 Gillionville Rd 31707 229-317-6000
Deerfield-Windsor S 800/PK-12
PO Box 71149 31708 229-435-1301
David Davies, hdmstr. Fax 435-4118
Sherwood Christian Academy 400/PK-12
1418 Old Pretoria Rd, 229-883-5677
Dr. Brian Dougherty, hdmstr. Fax 883-5794

**Alma, Bacon, Pop. 3,400**
Bacon County SD 2,000/PK-12
102 W 4th St 31510 912-632-7363
Dr. Laine Reichert, supt. Fax 632-2454
www.bcraiders.com/
Bacon County HS 500/9-12
1190 US Highway 1 S 31510 912-632-4414
Ross New, prin. Fax 632-6603
Bacon County MS 400/6-8
1188 US Highway 1 S 31510 912-632-4662
Stephanie Deen Cooks, prin. Fax 632-6603

**Alpharetta, Fulton, Pop. 56,130**
Fulton County SD
Supt. — See Atlanta
Alpharetta HS 2,300/9-12
3595 Webb Bridge Rd 30005 770-521-7640
Shannon Kersey, prin. Fax 521-7653
Haynes Bridge MS 700/6-8
10665 Haynes Bridge Rd 30022 470-254-7030
Lauren Seidman, prin. Fax 254-2842
Holcomb Bridge MS 700/6-8
2700 Holcomb Bridge Rd 30022 470-254-5280
Christopher Shearer, prin. Fax 254-3333
Independence HS Alt
86 School Dr 30009 470-254-7611
Tabatha Taylor, prin. Fax 254-7621
Webb Bridge MS 1,400/6-8
4455 Webb Bridge Rd 30005 470-254-2940
Susan Opferman, prin. Fax 254-2948

---

DeVry University Post-Sec.
2555 Northwinds Pkwy 30009 770-619-3600
King's Ridge Christian S 700/PK-12
2765 Bethany Bnd 30004 770-754-5738
David Rhodes, hdmstr. Fax 754-5544
Mill Springs Academy 300/1-12
13660 New Providence Rd 30004 770-360-1336
Robert Moore, hdmstr. Fax 360-1341

**Americus, Sumter, Pop. 16,892**
Sumter County SD 4,400/PK-12
100 Learning Ln, 229-931-8500
Donnie Smith, supt. Fax 931-8555
www.sumterschools.org
Americus Sumpter HS South Campus 900/10-12
805 Harrold Ave 31709 229-924-3653
Kimothy Hadley, prin. Fax 924-1556
Americus Sumter HS North Campus 400/9-9
200 Industrial Blvd, 229-924-5914
Coleman Price, prin. Fax 924-0532
Ombudsman Learning Center Alt
1540 E Forsyth St 31709 229-931-9771
Arthur Young, prin. Fax 931-9772
Staley MS 500/6-8
915 N Lee St, 229-924-3168
Sharron Marcus, prin. Fax 928-2135
Sumter County MS 700/6-8
439 Bumphead Rd, 229-924-1010
Stacy Favors, prin. Fax 928-5571

---

Georgia Southwestern State University Post-Sec.
800 GSW State University Dr 31709 229-928-1273
South Georgia Technical College Post-Sec.
900 S Georgia Tech Pkwy 31709 229-931-2394
Southland Academy 600/PK-12
PO Box 1127 31709 229-924-4406

**Armuchee, Floyd**
Floyd County SD
Supt. — See Rome
Armuchee MS 500/6-8
471 Floyd Springs Rd NE 30105 706-378-7924
Steve Turrentine, prin. Fax 378-7983

**Ashburn, Turner, Pop. 4,108**
Turner County SD 1,600/PK-12
423 N Cleveland St 31714 229-567-3338
Tommy Day, supt. Fax 567-3285
www.turner.k12.ga.us/
Turner County HS 400/9-12
316 Lamar St 31714 229-567-4377
Mike Simmons, prin. Fax 567-9243
Turner County MS 400/6-8
316 Lamar St 31714 229-567-4343
Mike Simmons, prin. Fax 567-9243
Turner County Specialty S 200/Alt
330 Gilmore St 31714 229-567-3412
Patricia Hargress, prin. Fax 567-2877

**Athens, Clarke, Pop. 113,262**
Clarke County SD 11,900/PK-12
PO Box 1708 30603 706-546-7721
Dr. Philip Lanoue, supt. Fax 208-9124
www.clarke.k12.ga.us
Burney-Harris-Lyons MS 600/6-8
1600 Tallassee Rd 30606 706-548-7208
Melanie Sigler, prin. Fax 357-5263
Cedar Shoals HS 1,500/9-12
1300 Cedar Shoals Dr 30605 706-546-5375
Dr. Tony Price, prin. Fax 357-5291
Clarke Central HS 1,500/9-12
350 S Milledge Ave 30605 706-357-5200
Dr. Robbie Hooker, prin. Fax 357-5269
Clarke MS 500/6-8
1235 Baxter St 30606 706-543-6547
Theodore MacMillan, prin. Fax 548-0257
Classic City Performance Learning Center 100/Alt
440 Dearing Ext Bldg 3 30606 706-353-2323
Dr. David Cole, dir. Fax 353-3877
Coile MS 600/6-8
110 Old Elberton Rd 30601 706-357-5318
Dwight Manzy, prin. Fax 357-5321
Hilsman MS 700/6-8
870 Gaines School Rd 30605 706-548-7281
Dr. Selena Blankenship, prin. Fax 357-5295

---

Athens Academy 1,000/PK-12
PO Box 6548 30604 706-549-9225
John Thorsen, head sch Fax 354-3775
Athens Christian S 800/PK-12
1270 Highway 29 N 30601 706-549-7586
Steve Cummings, head sch Fax 549-2899
Athens Technical College Post-Sec.
800 Highway 29 N 30601 706-355-5000
Georgia Institute of Cosmetology Post-Sec.
3529 Atlanta Hwy 30606 706-549-6400
Msgr. Walter J. Donovan HS 100/9-12
590 Lavender Rd 30606 706-433-0223
Patrick Yuran, prin. Fax 433-0229
University of Georgia Post-Sec.
0 UGA 30602 706-542-3000

**Atlanta, Fulton, Pop. 412,360**
Atlanta CSD 45,200/PK-12
130 Trinity Ave SW 30303 404-802-3500
Meria Carstarphen Ed.D., supt. Fax 802-1803
www.atlantapublicschools.us
B.E.S.T. Academy 200/6-12
1890 D L Hollowell Pkwy NW 30318 404-802-4950
Dr. Timothy Jones, prin.
Brown MS, 765 Peeples St SW 30310 600/6-8
Tiauna Crooms, prin. 404-802-6800
Bunche MS 800/6-8
1925 Niskey Lake Rd SW 30331 404-802-6700
Mario Watkins, prin.
Carver Early College HS 300/9-12
55 McDonough Blvd SE 30315 404-802-4405
Marcene Thornton, prin.
Carver HS 400/9-12
55 McDonough Blvd SE 30315 404-802-5500
Marvin Pryor, prin.
Crim Open Campus HS 400/Alt
256 Clifton St SE 30317 404-802-5800
Dawn Parker, prin. Fax 371-4889
Douglass HS 1,000/9-12
225 Hamilton E Holmes Dr NW 30318 404-802-3100
DeMarcos Holland, prin. Fax 799-8022
Forrest Hill Academy 300/Alt
2930 Forrest Hills Dr SW 30315 404-802-6950
Zawadaski Robinson, prin. Fax 559-0947
Grady HS 1,500/9-12
929 Charles Allen Dr NE 30309 404-802-3001
Timothy Guiney, prin. Fax 802-3090
Harper-Archer MS 500/6-8
3399 Collier Dr NW 30331 404-802-6500
Marques Stewart, prin. Fax 699-4569
Inman MS 900/6-8
774 Virginia Ave NE 30306 404-802-3200
Paula Herrema, prin. Fax 802-3299
Jackson HS 800/9-12
801 Glenwood Ave SE 30316 404-802-5200
Stephanie Johnson, prin. Fax 802-5299
King MS 600/6-8
1550 Hosea L Williams Dr NE 30317 404-802-5400
Paul Brown, prin.
King Young Womens Leadership Academy 200/6-12
1190 Northwest Dr NW 30318 404-802-4900
Erin Barksdale, prin.
Long MS 600/6-8
3200 Latona Dr SW 30354 404-802-4800
Lisa Hill, prin. Fax 802-4899
Mays HS 1,400/9-12
3450 Benjamin E Mays Dr SW 30331
Richard Fowler, prin. 404-802-5100
North Atlanta HS 300/9-12
4111 Northside Pkwy NW 30327 404-802-4700
Dr. Curtiss Douglass, prin.
Price MS 600/6-8
1670 B W Bickers Dr SE 30315 404-802-6300
Duane Hale, prin. Fax 624-5137
South Atlanta HS 300/9-12
800 Hutchens Rd SE 30354 404-802-5000
Dr. Patricia Ford, prin.
Sutton MS 1,300/6-8
2875 Northside Dr NW 30305 404-802-5600
Woodbridge Greene, prin.
Sylvan Hills MS 400/6-8
1461 Sylvan Rd SW 30310 404-802-6200
Artesa Portee, prin. Fax 802-6299
Therrell HS 400/9-12
3099 Panther Trl SW 30311 404-802-5300
Shelly Powell, prin.
Washington HS 300/9-12
45 Whitehouse Dr SW 30314 404-802-4600
Tasharah Wilson, prin. Fax 752-6063
West End Academy Alt
1445 Maynard Rd NW 30331 404-802-2900
Dr. Evelyn Mobley, prin. Fax 802-2949
Young MS 800/6-8
3116 Benjamin E Mays Dr SW 30311 404-802-5900
DeMarco Mitchell, prin. Fax 802-5999

DeKalb County SD
Supt. — See Stone Mountain
Cross Keys HS 1,000/9-12
1626 N Druid Hills Rd NE 30319 678-874-6102
Jason Heard, prin. Fax 874-6110
Druid Hills HS 1,800/9-12
1798 Haygood Dr NE 30307 678-874-6302
Brittany Cunningham, prin. Fax 874-6310
Henderson MS 1,500/6-8
2830 Henderson Mill Rd 30341 678-874-2902
Rochelle Patillo, prin. Fax 874-2910
Lakeside HS 1,900/9-12
3801 Briarcliff Rd NE 30345 678-874-6702
Jason Clyne, prin. Fax 874-6710
McNair HS 800/9-12
1804 Bouldercrest Rd SE 30316 678-874-4902
Loukisha Walker, prin. Fax 874-4910

Fulton County SD 87,800/PK-12
6201 Powers Ferry Road NW 30339 470-254-3600
Kenneth Zeff, supt. Fax 254-1246
www.fultonschools.org
Sandtown MS 1,100/6-8
5400 Campbellton Rd SW 30331 404-346-6500
Valerie Andrews, prin. Fax 346-6510
Westlake HS 1,900/9-12
2400 Union Rd SW 30331 470-254-6400
Alexandra Bates, prin. Fax 254-6410
Other Schools – See Alpharetta, College Park, East Point, Fairburn, Johns Creek, Milton, Roswell, Sandy Springs

---

American InterContinental University Post-Sec.
6600 Peachtree Dunwoody Rd 30328 404-965-6500
Anthem College Post-Sec.
2450 Piedmont Rd NE 30324 678-279-7000
Argosy University/Atlanta Post-Sec.
980 Hammond Dr Ste 100 30328 770-671-1200
Art Institute of Atlanta Post-Sec.
6600 Peachtree Dunwoody Rd 30328 770-394-8300
Atlanta Country Day S 50/7-12
8725 Dunwoody Pl 30350 770-998-0311
Mark Cox, hdmstr. Fax 998-0313
Atlanta Girls' S 200/6-12
3254 Northside Pkwy NW 30327 404-845-0900
Ayanna Hill-Gill, hdmstr. Fax 869-9718
Atlanta International S 1,000/PK-12
2890 N Fulton Dr NE 30305 404-841-3840
Kevin Glass, hdmstr. Fax 841-3896
Atlanta Jewish Academy Upper S 100/9-12
5200 Northland Dr 30342 770-451-5299
Dr. Paul Oberman, prin. Fax 451-5571
Atlanta Medical Center Post-Sec.
303 Parkway Dr NE 30312 404-265-4203
Atlanta Metro State College Post-Sec.
1630 Metropolitan Pkwy SW 30310 404-756-4000
Atlanta School of Massage Post-Sec.
2 Dunwoody Park 30338 877-291-4485
Atlanta's John Marshall Law School Post-Sec.
1422 W Peachtree St NW 30309 404-872-3593
Atlanta Technical College Post-Sec.
1560 Metropolitan Pkwy SW 30310 404-225-4400
Bauder College Post-Sec.
384 Northyards Blvd NW #190 30313 404-237-7573
Beulah Heights University Post-Sec.
PO Box 18145 30316 404-627-2681
Brandon Hall S 100/6-12
1701 Brandon Hall Dr 30350 770-394-8177
Johnny Graham, head sch Fax 868-1444
Bright Futures Academy 100/6-12
1300 Joseph E Boone Blvd NW 30314
Eddie Echols, prin. 404-564-7751
Brown College of Court Reporting Post-Sec.
1900 Emery St NW Ste 200 30318 404-876-1227
Brown Mackie College Post-Sec.
4370 Peachtree Rd NE 30319 404-799-4500
Carver College Post-Sec.
3870 Cascade Rd SW 30331 404-527-4520
Chamberlain College of Nursing Post-Sec.
5775 Peachtree Dunwdy A100 30342 404-250-8500
Clark Academy 100/5-8
228 Margaret St SE 30315 678-651-2100
Clark Atlanta University Post-Sec.
223 James P Brawley Dr 30314 404-880-8000
Cristo Rey Atlanta Jesuit HS 9-10
680 W Peachtree St NW 30308 404-637-2800
Rev. James Van Dyke, prin. Fax 637-2888
DeVry University Post-Sec.
5775 Peachtree Dunwoody NE 30342 404-236-1310
DeVry University Post-Sec.
100 Galleria Pkwy SE #100 30339 770-916-3704
Emory University Post-Sec.
201 Dowman Dr 30322 404-727-6123
Everest College Post-Sec.
2841 Greenbriar Pkwy SW 30331 678-500-3400
Franklin Academy 100/9-12
1585 Clifton Rd NE 30329 404-633-7404
Dr. Martha Burdette, head sch Fax 321-0610
Galloway S 700/PK-12
215 W Wieuca Rd NW 30342 404-252-8389
Suzanna Jemsby, head sch Fax 252-7770
Georgia Christian University Post-Sec.
6789 Peachtree Industrial 30360 770-279-0507
Georgia Institute of Technology Post-Sec.
225 North Ave NW 30332 404-894-2000
Georgia Perimeter College Post-Sec.
2101 Womack Rd 30338 770-274-5000
Georgia State University Post-Sec.
PO Box 3965 30302 404-413-2000
Grady Health System Post-Sec.
PO Box 26189 30303 404-616-4252
Greater Atlanta Adventist Academy 200/9-12
401 Hamilton E Holmes Dr NW 30318 404-799-0337
Johnny Holliday, prin. Fax 225-7250
Herzing University Post-Sec.
3393 Peachtree Rd NE # 1003 30326 404-816-4533
Holy Innocents' Episcopal S 1,300/PK-12
805 Mount Vernon Hwy 30327 404-255-4026
Paul Barton, head sch Fax 250-0815
Holy Spirit College Post-Sec.
4465 Northside Dr NW 30327 678-904-4959
Holy Spirit Preparatory S 600/PK-12
4449 Northside Dr NW 30327 678-904-2811
Kyle Pietrantonio, head sch Fax 904-4983
Interdenominational Theological Center Post-Sec.
700 Mrtn Lthr King Jr Dr SW 30314 404-527-7700
International School Skin Nail Massage Post-Sec.
5600 Roswell Rd 30342 404-843-1005
ITT Technical Institute Post-Sec.
485 Oak Pl Ste 800 30349 770-765-4600
Keller Graduate School of Management Post-Sec.
3575 Piedmont Rd NE Lvl 100 30305 404-760-1400
Lovett S 1,600/K-12
4075 Paces Ferry Rd NW 30327 404-262-3032
William Peebles, hdmstr. Fax 261-1967
Marist S 1,100/7-12
3790 Ashford Dunwoody Rd NE 30319 770-457-7201
Fr. Joel Konzen, prin. Fax 457-8402
Medtech Institute Post-Sec.
4501 Circle 75 Pkwy SE 30339 770-859-9779
Medtech Institute Post-Sec.
2800 Century Pkwy NE # 100 30345 770-938-4711
Mercer University - Day Grad/Prof Campus Post-Sec.
3001 Mercer University Dr 30341 678-547-6000
Mohammed Schools of Atlanta 200/PK-12
735 Fayetteville Rd SE 30316 404-378-4219
Qur'an Shakir, prin. Fax 378-4600
Morehouse College Post-Sec.
830 Westview Dr SW 30314 404-681-2800
Morehouse School of Medicine Post-Sec.
720 Westview Dr SW 30310 404-752-1500
Mt. Vernon Presbyterian S 700/PK-12
471 Mount Vernon Hwy NE 30328 404-252-3448
Dr. Brett Jacobsen, head sch Fax 252-6777
Oglethorpe University Post-Sec.
4484 Peachtree Rd NE 30319 404-261-1441
Omnitech Institute Post-Sec.
1800 Phoenix Blvd 30349 404-888-1800
Pace Academy 1,000/K-12
966 W Paces Ferry Rd NW 30327 404-262-1345
Frederick Assaf, hdmstr. Fax 264-9376
Paideia S 1,000/PK-12
1509 Ponce De Leon Ave NE 30307 404-377-3491
Paul Bianchi, hdmstr. Fax 377-0032
Portfolio Center Post-Sec.
125 Bennett St NW 30309 404-351-5055
Richmont Graduate University Post-Sec.
2055 Mount Paran Rd NW 30327 404-233-3949
SAE Institute Post-Sec.
215 Peachtree St NE Ste 300 30303 404-526-9366
St. Joseph's Hospital Post-Sec.
5665 Pchtree Dunwoody Rd 30342 404-851-7120
St. Pius X HS 1,100/9-12
2674 Johnson Rd NE 30345 404-636-3023
Steven Spellman, prin. Fax 633-8387
Sanford-Brown College Post-Sec.
1140 Hammond Dr Ste A1150 30328 770-576-4498
Savannah College of Art & Design Post-Sec.
PO Box 77300 30357 404-253-2700
Sophia Academy 100/PK-12
2880 Dresden Dr 30341 404-303-8722
Jenni Ellis, head sch Fax 303-8883
Southwest Atlanta Christian Academy 200/PK-12
PO Box 310750 31131 404-346-2080
Spelman College Post-Sec.
350 Spelman Ln SW 30314 404-681-3643
Strayer University Post-Sec.
3355 Northeast Expy NE #100 30341 770-454-9270
Strayer University Post-Sec.
3101 TowerCreek Pkwy SE 700 30339 770-612-2170

Temima HS 100/9-12
1985B Lavista Rd NE Ste B 30329 404-315-0507
University of Atlanta Post-Sec.
6685 Peachtree Industrial 30360 770-744-0370
Weber Jewish Community HS 200/9-12
6751 Roswell Rd 30328 404-917-2500
Rabbi Ed Harwitz, head sch Fax 917-2501
Westminster S 1,900/K-12
1424 W Paces Ferry Rd NW 30327 404-355-8673
Keith Evans, pres. Fax 355-6606
Westwood College Post-Sec.
1100 Spring St NW Ste 102 30309 404-745-9862
Westwood College Post-Sec.
2309 Parklake Dr NE 30345 770-743-3000
Yeshiva Ohr Yisrael of Atlanta 50/9-12
1458 Holly Ln NE 30329 404-320-1444

**Augusta, Richmond, Pop. 193,101**
Richmond County SD 31,600/PK-12
864 Broad St 30901 706-826-1000
Dr. Angela Pringle, supt. Fax 826-4612
www.rcboe.org
Academy of Richmond County 1,300/9-12
910 Russell St 30904 706-737-7152
Criston Jensen, prin. Fax 737-7155
Alternative Education Center at Lamar Alt
970 Baker Ave 30904 706-796-4965
Charles Givens, prin. Fax 796-4643
Butler HS 900/9-12
2011 Lumpkin Rd 30906 706-796-4959
Dr. Stacey Mabray, prin. Fax 796-4780
Cross Creek HS 1,300/9-12
3855 Old Waynesboro Rd 30906 706-772-8140
Dr. Jason Moore, prin. Fax 772-8153
Davidson Fine Arts Magnet JSHS 800/6-12
615 12th St 30901 706-823-6924
Dr. Renee Kelly, prin. Fax 823-4373
Glenn Hills HS 1,000/9-12
2840 Glenn Hills Dr 30906 706-796-4924
Dr. Bobby Williams, prin. Fax 796-4932
Glenn Hills MS 800/6-8
2941 Glenn Hills Dr 30906 706-796-4705
Dr. Bernard Chatman, prin. Fax 796-4716
Johnson Health Science HS 600/6-12
1324 Laney Walker Blvd 30901 706-823-6933
Charlie Tudor, prin. Fax 823-6931
Josey HS 800/9-12
1701 15th St 30901 706-737-7360
Isaac Lee, prin. Fax 737-7363
Laney HS 700/9-12
1740 Walton Way 30904 706-823-6900
Jonathan Woods, prin. Fax 823-6918
Langford MS 600/6-8
3019 Walton Way Ext 30909 706-737-7301
Victoria Reese, prin. Fax 737-7302
Richmond Co. Technical Career Magnet S Vo/Tech
32000B Augusta Tech Dr 30906 706-823-5580
Mylinthia Renee-Kelly, prin. Fax 796-4889
Sego MS 700/6-8
3420 Julia Ave 30906 706-796-4944
Pauline Andrews, prin. Fax 796-4670
Tutt MS 600/6-8
495 Boy Scout Rd 30909 706-737-7288
Angela Sheahan, prin. Fax 481-1620
Westside HS 800/9-12
1002 Patriots Way 30907 706-868-4030
Scott McClintock, prin. Fax 868-4005
Performance Learning Center Adult
1740 Walton Way 30904 706-796-4965
Gregory Thompson, admin. Fax 796-4643
Other Schools – See Hephzibah

Alleluia Community S 200/K-12
2819 Peach Orchard Rd 30906 706-793-9663
Aquinas HS 300/9-12
1920 Highland Ave 30904 706-736-5516
Maureen Lewis, admin. Fax 736-2678
Augusta Technical College Post-Sec.
3200 Augusta Tech Dr 30906 706-771-4000
Curtis Baptist S 400/PK-12
1326 Broad St 30901 706-828-6624
Glenn Smith, head sch Fax 828-6627
Georgia Regents University Post-Sec.
1120 15th St 30912 706-721-0211
Miller-Motte Technical College Post-Sec.
621 NW Frontage Rd 30907 706-396-8000
Paine College Post-Sec.
1235 15th St 30901 706-821-8200
University Hospital Health System Post-Sec.
1350 Walton Way 30901 706-722-9011
Virginia College Post-Sec.
2807 Wylds Road Ext 30909 706-288-2500
Westminster S of Augusta 500/PK-12
3067 Wheeler Rd 30909 706-731-5260
Stephen O'Neil, hdmstr. Fax 731-5274

**Austell, Cobb, Pop. 6,416**
Cobb County SD
Supt. — See Marietta
Cooper MS 800/6-8
4605 Ewing Rd 30106 770-819-2438
Dr. Vanessa Watkins, prin. Fax 819-2440
Garrett MS 900/6-8
5235 Austell Pwdr Sprgs Rd 30106 770-819-2466
Kimberly Jackson, prin. Fax 819-2468
South Cobb HS 2,000/9-12
1920 Clay Rd 30106 770-819-2611
Ashley Hosey, prin. Fax 819-2613

**Avondale Estates, DeKalb, Pop. 2,893**
DeKalb County SD
Supt. — See Stone Mountain
DeKalb S of the Arts 300/8-12
1192 Clarendon Ave 30002 678-676-2502
Susan McCauley, prin. Fax 676-2510

**Bainbridge, Decatur, Pop. 12,559**
Decatur County SD 5,500/PK-12
100 S West St, 229-248-2200
Dr. Fred Rayfield, supt. Fax 248-2252
www.dcboe.com
Bainbridge HS 1,500/9-12
1 Bearcat Blvd, 229-248-2230
Tommie Howell, prin. Fax 248-2260
Bainbridge MS 800/7-8
1301 E College St, 229-248-2206
John Wooden, prin. Fax 248-2817

Bainbridge College Post-Sec.
PO Box 990, 229-248-2500
Grace Christian Academy 300/PK-12
1302 Lake Douglas Rd, 229-243-8851
Joan Shiver, admin. Fax 243-0515

**Barnesville, Lamar, Pop. 6,625**
Lamar County SD 2,600/PK-12
100 Victory Ln 30204 770-358-5891
Dr. Jute Wilson, supt. Fax 358-5858
www.lamar.k12.ga.us
Lamar County HS 700/9-12
1 Trojan Way 30204 770-358-8641
Matt Adams, prin. Fax 358-8649
Lamar County MS 600/6-8
100 Burnette Rd 30204 770-358-8652
Dr. Julie Steele, prin. Fax 358-8657

Gordon State College Post-Sec.
419 College Dr 30204 678-359-5555

**Baxley, Appling, Pop. 4,360**
Appling County SD 3,500/PK-12
249 Blackshear Hwy 31513 912-367-8600
Dr. Scarlett Copeland, supt. Fax 367-1011
www.appling.k12.ga.us
Appling County HS 1,000/9-12
482 Blackshear Hwy 31513 912-367-8610
Dr. Gene Starr, prin. Fax 367-9877
Appling County MS 800/6-8
2997 Blackshear Hwy 31513 912-367-8630
Chris Roppe, prin. Fax 367-8803

**Bellville, Evans, Pop. 123**

Pinewood Christian Academy 600/PK-12
PO Box 7 30414 912-739-1272
Harold Roach, hdmstr. Fax 739-2321

**Bethlehem, Barrow, Pop. 594**
Barrow County SD
Supt. — See Winder
Snodon Prep HS Alt
54 Star St W 30620 770-868-1072
Chuck Torbett, prin. Fax 867-1341

Bethlehem Christian Academy 400/PK-12
PO Box 187 30620 770-307-1574
Rhonda Whiting, head sch Fax 425-6553

**Black Creek, Bryan**
Bryan County SD 7,800/PK-12
8810 US Highway 280 E 31308 912-851-4000
Dr. Paul Brooksher, supt. Fax 851-4093
www.bryan.k12.ga.us/
Other Schools – See Pembroke, Richmond Hill

**Blackshear, Pierce, Pop. 3,390**
Pierce County SD 3,600/PK-12
PO Box 349 31516 912-449-2044
Terri DeLoach, supt. Fax 449-2046
www.pierce.k12.ga.us/
Pierce County HS 1,000/9-12
4850 County Farm Rd 31516 912-449-2055
Dara Bennett, prin. Fax 449-2061
Pierce County MS 900/6-8
5216 County Farm Rd 31516 912-449-2077
Perry Tison, prin. Fax 449-2075

**Blairsville, Union, Pop. 642**
Union County SD 2,600/PK-12
124 Hughes St 30512 706-745-2322
Gary Steppe, supt. Fax 745-5025
www.ucschools.org
Union County HS 700/9-12
153 Panther Cir 30512 706-745-2216
John Hill, prin. Fax 745-4122
Union County MS 600/6-8
367 Wellborn St 30512 706-745-2483
Gwen Stafford, prin. Fax 781-6200
Other Schools – See Suches

Lighthouse Christian Academy 50/K-12
772 John Smith Rd E 30512 706-745-1606
Donna Mizell, admin. Fax 745-1606
North Georgia Technical College Post-Sec.
121 Meeks Ave 30512 706-439-6300

**Blakely, Early, Pop. 5,032**
Early County SD 2,200/PK-12
11927 Columbia St, 229-723-4337
Bronwyn Ragan-Martin Ed.D., supt. Fax 723-8183
www.early.k12.ga.us
Early County HS 600/9-12
12020 Columbia St, 229-723-3006
David Ferry, prin. Fax 723-8690
Early County MS 500/6-8
12053 Columbia St, 229-723-3746
Anthony Yarbrough, prin. Fax 723-3942
Learning and Opportunity Academy Alt
544 Howell St, 229-723-3943
James McCoy, prin. Fax 723-6385

**Bloomingdale, Chatham, Pop. 2,668**
Savannah-Chatham County SD
Supt. — See Savannah
New Hampstead HS 9-12
2451 Little Neck Rd 31302 912-395-6789
Tawn Foltz, prin. Fax 201-7699

**Blue Ridge, Fannin, Pop. 1,269**
Fannin County SD 3,000/K-12
2290 E First St 30513 706-632-3771
Mark Henson, supt. Fax 632-7583
www.fannin.k12.ga.us
Fannin County HS 900/9-12
360 Rebels Cir 30513 706-632-2081
Erik Cioffi, prin. Fax 632-6908
Fannin County MS 700/6-8
4560 Old Highway 76 30513 706-632-6100
Lori Chastain, prin. Fax 632-0461

**Bogart, Clarke, Pop. 1,021**
Oconee County SD
Supt. — See Watkinsville
Malcom Bridge MS 700/6-8
2500 Malcom Bridge Rd 30622 706-310-1992
Billy Heaton, prin. Fax 310-1993
North Oconee HS 1,000/9-12
1081 Rocky Branch Rd 30622 706-769-7760
Dr. Philip Brown, prin. Fax 769-4766

Prince Avenue Christian S 700/PK-12
2201 Ruth Jackson Rd 30622 678-726-2300
Seth Hathaway, head sch Fax 726-2301

**Bonaire, Houston**
Houston County SD
Supt. — See Perry
Bonaire MS 900/6-8
125 GA Highway 96 E 31005 478-929-6235
Cindy Randall, prin. Fax 929-6245

**Bowdon, Carroll, Pop. 1,987**
Carroll County SD
Supt. — See Carrollton
Bowdon HS 500/9-12
504 W College St 30108 770-258-5408
Travis Thomas, prin. Fax 258-7278
Bowdon MS 300/6-8
129 N Jonesville Rd 30108 770-258-1778
Scott Estes, prin. Fax 258-4374

**Braselton, Jackson, Pop. 7,379**

Braselton Christian Academy 50/K-12
401 Zion Church Rd 30517 706-824-9943
Penney Smith, dir. Fax 824-9975
Heritage Academy 200/K-12
2001 Cherry Dr 30517 770-658-3020
David Douglas, hdmstr. Fax 658-3039

**Bremen, Haralson, Pop. 6,130**
Bremen CSD 2,000/PK-12
501 Pacific Ave 30110 770-537-5508
Dr. David Hicks, supt. Fax 537-0610
www.bremencs.com
Bremen Crossroad Academy Alt
504 Georgia Ave S 30110 770-537-2592
Beth Garrett, dir.
Bremen HS 600/9-12
504 Georgia Ave S 30110 770-537-2592
Tim Huff, prin. Fax 537-0714
Bremen MS 500/6-8
2440 Crosstown Pkwy 30110 770-537-4874
Silas Brown, prin. Fax 537-5043

**Brooklet, Bulloch, Pop. 1,369**
Bulloch County SD
Supt. — See Statesboro
Southeast Bulloch HS 900/9-12
9184 Brooklet Denmark Rd 30415 912-842-8440
Donna Clifton, prin. Fax 842-9411
Southeast Bulloch MS 700/6-8
9124 Brooklet Denmark Rd 30415 912-842-8400
Torian White, prin. Fax 842-9559

**Brunswick, Glynn, Pop. 15,115**
Glynn County SD, PO Box 1677 31521 13,000/PK-12
Howard Mann, supt. 912-267-4100
www.glynn.k12.ga.us
Brunswick HS 1,800/9-12
3885 Altama Ave 31520 912-267-4200
Toriano Gilbert, prin. Fax 261-4433
Coastal Education HS 50/Alt
3700 Altama Ave 31520 912-279-5777
Jill Smith, prin.
Glynn Academy 1,700/9-12
1001 Mansfield St 31520 912-267-4210
Dr. Scott Spence, prin. Fax 267-4246
Glynn MS 1,000/6-8
635 Lanier Blvd 31520 912-267-4150
Matthew Blackstone, prin. Fax 267-4158
Jackson Learning Center Alt
1405 H St 31520 912-280-4030
Robert Pope, lead tchr. Fax 261-7917
Macon MS 900/6-8
201 McKenzie Dr 31523 912-265-3337
Michele Seals, prin. Fax 267-4118
Needwood MS 600/6-8
669 Harry Driggers Blvd 31525 912-261-4488
Jim Pulos, prin. Fax 261-4491
Risley MS 200/6-8
707 S Port Pkwy 31523 912-280-4020
Lori Joiner, prin. Fax 261-3252

Brunswick Christian Academy 200/PK-12
4231 US Highway 17 N 31525 912-264-4546
College of Coastal Georgia Post-Sec.
1 College Dr 31520 912-279-5700
Heritage Christian Academy 200/PK-12
4265 Norwich Street Ext 31520 912-264-5491
Cindy Zangla, admin. Fax 264-0799

**Buena Vista, Marion, Pop. 2,149**
Marion County SD 1,400/PK-12
PO Box 391 31803 229-649-2234
Richard McCorkle, supt. Fax 649-7423
www.marion.k12.ga.us/
Marion County MSHS 700/6-12
1 Eagle Dr 31803 229-649-7520
Glenn Tidwell, prin. Fax 649-5945

**Buford, Gwinnett, Pop. 12,025**
Buford CSD 3,500/K-12
2625 Sawnee Ave 30518 770-945-5035
Dr. Geye Hamby, supt. Fax 945-4629
www.bufordcityschools.org

Buford HS 1,000/9-12
2750 Sawnee Ave 30518 770-945-6768
Dr. Banks Bitterman, prin. Fax 932-7570
Buford MS 800/6-8
2700 Robert Bell Pkwy 30518 770-904-3690
Melanie Reed, prin. Fax 904-3689

Gwinnett County SD
Supt. — See Suwanee
Jones MS 1,300/6-8
3575 Ridge Rd 30519 770-904-5450
Dr. Richard Holland, prin. Fax 904-5452
Twin Rivers MS 1,500/6-8
2300 Braselton Hwy 30519 678-407-7550
Linda Boyd, prin. Fax 407-7560

**Butler, Taylor, Pop. 1,959**
Taylor County SD 1,500/PK-12
PO Box 1930 31006 478-862-5224
Dr. Gary Gibson, supt. Fax 862-5818
www.taylor.k12.ga.us
Taylor County HS 500/9-12
PO Box 1930 31006 478-862-3314
Ken Camp, prin. Fax 862-3099
Taylor County MS 200/7-8
PO Box 580 31006 478-862-5285
Shonda Green, prin. Fax 862-5368

**Byron, Peach, Pop. 4,436**
Peach County SD
Supt. — See Fort Valley
Byron MS 400/6-8
201 Linda Dr 31008 478-825-9660
Dr. Jeff Bell, prin. Fax 956-3916

**Cairo, Grady, Pop. 9,480**
Grady County SD 4,600/PK-12
122 N Broad St, 229-377-3701
Dr. Kermit Gilliard, supt. Fax 377-3437
www.grady.k12.ga.us
Cairo HS 1,100/9-12
455 5th St SE, 229-377-2222
Christopher Lokey, prin. Fax 377-2812
Washington MS 600/6-8
1277 Martin Luther King Jr, 229-377-2106
Tilda Brimm, prin. Fax 377-7779

**Calhoun, Gordon, Pop. 15,378**
Calhoun CSD 3,600/PK-12
380 Barrett Rd 30701 706-629-2900
Dr. Michele Taylor, supt. Fax 629-3235
www.calhounschools.org
Calhoun HS 900/9-12
355 S River St 30701 706-602-6770
Greg Green, prin. Fax 602-6652
Calhoun MS 800/6-8
399 S River St 30701 706-629-3340
Michelle Knight, prin. Fax 629-0236

Gordon County SD 7,000/PK-12
PO Box 12001 30703 706-629-7366
Dr. Susan Remillard, supt. Fax 625-5671
www.gcbe.org
Ashworth MS 700/6-8
PO Box 12001 30703 706-625-9545
Scott McClanahan, prin. Fax 879-5073
College and Career Academy Vo/Tech
PO Box 12001 30703 706-879-5370
Dr. Amy Parker, prin. Fax 879-5371
Gordon Central HS 800/9-12
PO Box 12001 30703 706-629-7391
Doug Clark, prin. Fax 879-5399
Sonoraville HS 1,000/8-12
PO Box 12001 30703 706-602-0320
Bruce Potts, prin. Fax 879-5165

---

Georgia Cumberland Academy 200/9-12
397 Academy Dr SW 30701 706-629-4591
Dr. Greg Gerard, prin. Fax 629-1272
Georgia Northwestern Technical College Post-Sec.
1151 Highway 53 Spur SW 30701 706-624-1100

**Camilla, Mitchell, Pop. 5,311**
Mitchell County SD 1,700/PK-12
108 S Harney St 31730 229-336-2100
Victor Hill, supt. Fax 336-3870
www.mitchell.k12.ga.us
Mitchell County HS 400/9-12
1000 Newton Rd 31730 229-336-0970
Robert Adams, prin. Fax 336-2171
Mitchell County MS 400/6-8
55 Griffin Rd 31730 229-336-0980
Patricia English, prin. Fax 336-2139

---

Westwood S 400/PK-12
255 Fuller St 31730 229-336-7992
Ross Worsham, hdmstr. Fax 336-0982

**Canton, Cherokee, Pop. 22,432**
Cherokee County SD 35,400/PK-12
111 Academy St 30114 770-479-1871
Dr. Frank Petruzielo, supt. Fax 479-7758
www.cherokee.k12.ga.us
ACE Academy Alt
8871 Knox Bridge Hwy 30114 770-345-2005
Richard Landolt, prin. Fax 345-2214
Cherokee HS 2,100/9-12
930 Marietta Hwy 30114 770-721-5300
Todd Miller, prin. Fax 479-8421
Creekland MS 1,400/6-8
1555 Owens Store Rd 30115 770-479-3200
Dr. Deborah Wiseman, prin. Fax 479-3210
Creekview HS 1,700/9-12
1550 Owens Store Rd 30115 770-720-7600
Dr. Adrian Thomason, prin. Fax 720-7644
Freedom MS 1,100/6-8
10550 Bells Ferry Rd 30114 770-345-4100
Sheila Grimes, prin. Fax 345-4140
Rusk MS 800/7-8
4695 Hickory Rd 30115 770-345-2832
Cindy Cooper, prin. Fax 345-5073

Sequoyah HS 1,600/9-12
4485 Hickory Rd 30115 770-721-3200
Elliott Berman, prin. Fax 345-5498
Teasley MS 800/6-8
151 Hickory Log Dr 30114 770-721-5420
Dr. Susan Zinkil, prin. Fax 479-3275
Other Schools – See Woodstock

**Carnesville, Franklin, Pop. 574**
Franklin County SD 3,200/PK-12
280 Busha Rd 30521 706-384-4554
Dr. Ruth O'Dell, supt. Fax 384-7472
www.franklin.k12.ga.us
Franklin County HS 1,100/9-12
6570 Highway 145 30521 706-384-4525
Brad Roberts, prin. Fax 384-3534
Franklin County MS 900/6-8
485 Turkey Creek Rd 30521 706-384-4581
Lucy Floyd, prin. Fax 384-2285

**Carrollton, Carroll, Pop. 23,838**
Carroll County SD 14,400/PK-12
164 Independence Dr 30116 770-832-3568
Scott Cowart, supt. Fax 834-6399
www.carrollcountyschools.com/
Central HS 1,100/9-12
113 Central High Rd 30116 770-834-3386
Jared Griffis, prin. Fax 832-0103
Central MS 900/6-8
155 Whooping Creek Rd 30116 770-832-8114
Jimmy LeBlanc, prin. Fax 836-2782
GOAL Program Alt
1095 Newnan Rd 30116 770-830-5012
Deaidra Wilson, prin. Fax 830-8634
Mount Zion HS 400/9-12
280 Eureka Church Rd 30117 770-834-6654
Tracey Barrow, prin. Fax 832-9497
Other Schools – See Bowdon, Mount Zion, Temple, Villa Rica

Carrollton CSD 4,300/PK-12
106 Trojan Dr 30117 770-832-9633
Dr. Kent Edwards, supt. Fax 836-9950
www.carrolltoncityschools.net/
Carrollton HS 1,300/9-12
202 Trojan Dr 30117 770-834-7726
Dr. Mark Albertus, prin. Fax 834-8714
Carrollton JHS 700/7-8
510 Ben Scott Blvd 30117 770-832-6535
Dr. Todd Simpson, prin. Fax 832-7003
Performance Learning Center Alt
510 Ben Scott Blvd 30117 770-836-2842
Aprill Jones-Byrd, prin.

---

Oak Mountain Academy 200/PK-12
222 Cross Plains Rd 30116 770-834-6651
Paula Gillispie, head sch Fax 834-6785
University of West Georgia Post-Sec.
1601 Maple St 30118 678-839-5000
West Georgia Technical College Post-Sec.
997 Newnan Rd 30116 770-836-6800

**Cartersville, Bartow, Pop. 19,341**
Bartow County SD 14,200/PK-12
PO Box 200007 30120 770-606-5800
John Harper Ed.D., supt. Fax 606-5855
www.bartow.k12.ga.us
Bartow County College & Career Academy Vo/Tech
738 Grassdale Rd NW 30121 770-606-5175
Dr. Paul Sabin, admin. Fax 606-5180
Cass MS 1,100/6-8
195 Fire Tower Rd NW 30120 770-606-5846
Dr. Kristy Arnold, prin. Fax 606-3835
Woodland HS 1,700/9-12
800 Old Alabama Rd SE 30120 770-606-5870
Dr. Melissa Williams, prin. Fax 606-2080
Other Schools – See Adairsville, Emerson, Euharlee, White

Cartersville CSD 4,000/PK-12
PO Box 3310 30120 770-382-5880
Dr. J. Howard Hinesley, supt. Fax 387-7476
www.cartersville.k12.ga.us
Cartersville HS 1,100/9-12
320 E Church St 30120 770-382-3200
Marc Feuerbach, prin. Fax 382-0701
Cartersville MS 900/6-8
825 Douthit Ferry Rd 30120 770-382-3666
Jeff Hogan, prin. Fax 387-7495

---

Excel Christian Academy 300/K-12
325 Old Mill Rd 30120 770-382-9488
Trinity S 100/PK-12
814 West Ave 30120 770-386-7479

**Cave Spring, Floyd, Pop. 1,186**

---

Georgia School for the Deaf Post-Sec.
232 Perry Farm Rd SW 30124 706-777-2200

**Cedartown, Polk, Pop. 9,595**
Polk County SD 7,000/PK-12
612 S College St 30125 770-748-3821
Dr. William A. Hunter, supt. Fax 748-5131
www.polk.k12.ga.us/
Cedartown HS 1,100/9-12
167 Frank Lott Dr 30125 770-748-0490
Dr. Darrell Wetherington, prin. Fax 749-1872
Cedartown MS 900/6-8
1664 Syble W Brannon Pkwy 30125 770-749-8850
Tamra Walker, prin. Fax 749-2795
Other Schools – See Rockmart

**Centerville, Houston, Pop. 6,978**
Houston County SD
Supt. — See Perry
Thomson MS 800/6-8
301 Thomson St 31028 478-953-0489
Dr. Walter Stephens, prin. Fax 953-0484

**Chamblee, DeKalb, Pop. 9,782**
DeKalb County SD
Supt. — See Stone Mountain
Chamblee MS 1,000/6-8
3601 Sexton Woods Dr 30341 678-874-8202
Jose DeJesus, prin. Fax 874-8210

---

Interactive College of Technology Post-Sec.
5303 New Peachtree Rd 30341 770-216-2960
Iverson Institute Post-Sec.
5522 New Peachtree Rd # 114 30341 770-446-1333

**Chatsworth, Murray, Pop. 4,251**
Murray County SD 7,600/PK-12
PO Box 40 30705 706-695-4531
Dr. Vickie Reed, supt. Fax 695-8425
www.murray.k12.ga.us
Bagley MS 600/7-8
4600 Highway 225 N 30705 706-695-1115
Shalina Cochran, prin. Fax 695-7289
Gladden MS 600/7-8
700 Old Dalton Ellijay Rd 30705 706-695-7448
Dr. Ardith Bates, prin. Fax 517-2479
Murray County HS 900/9-12
1001 Green Rd 30705 706-695-1414
Gina Linder, prin. Fax 517-2625
North Murray HS 1,000/9-12
2568 Mount Carmel Church Rd 30705 706-695-7760
Dr. Maria Bradley, prin. Fax 517-5526
Other Schools – See Eton

**Chickamauga, Walker, Pop. 3,044**
Chickamauga CSD 1,400/K-12
402 Cove Rd 30707 706-382-3100
Melody Day, supt. Fax 375-5364
chickamaugacityschools.org
Lee HS 500/9-12
105 Lee Cir 30707 706-382-3100
C.R. Simmons, prin. Fax 375-5881
Lee MS 400/6-8
300 Crescent Ave 30707 706-382-3100
Benny Ashley, prin. Fax 375-1020

**Chula, Tift**

---

Tiftarea Academy 500/PK-12
PO Box 10 31733 229-382-0436

**Clarkesville, Habersham, Pop. 1,712**
Habersham County SD 6,300/PK-12
PO Box 70 30523 706-754-2118
Matthew Cooper, supt. Fax 754-1549
www.habershamschools.com/
North Habersham MS 500/6-8
1500 Wall Bridge Rd 30523 706-754-2915
Elizabeth Tuck, prin. Fax 754-8218
Other Schools – See Cornelia, Demorest, Mount Airy

---

North Georgia Technical College Post-Sec.
PO Box 65 30523 706-754-7700

**Clarkston, DeKalb, Pop. 7,202**
DeKalb County SD
Supt. — See Stone Mountain
Clarkston HS 1,300/9-12
618 N Indian Creek Dr 30021 678-676-5302
Michelle Jones, prin. Fax 676-5310

---

Atlanta Area School for the Deaf Post-Sec.
890 N Indian Creek Dr 30021 404-296-7101
Georgia Perimeter College Post-Sec.
555 N Indian Creek Dr 30021 678-891-3200
Georgia Piedmont Technical College Post-Sec.
495 N Indian Creek Dr 30021 404-297-9522

**Claxton, Evans, Pop. 2,710**
Evans County SD 1,200/PK-12
613 W Main St 30417 912-739-3544
Dr. Joy Collins, supt. Fax 739-2492
www.evans.k12.ga.us
Claxton HS 400/9-12
102 N Clark St 30417 912-739-3993
Dr. Justin Russell, prin. Fax 739-2029
Claxton MS 400/6-8
600 Hendrix St 30417 912-739-3646
Dr. Diane Holland, prin. Fax 739-7217

**Cleveland, White, Pop. 3,334**
White County SD 3,600/PK-12
136 Warriors Path 30528 706-865-2315
Jeffrey Wilson Ed.D., supt. Fax 865-7784
www.white.k12.ga.us
White County HS 800/10-12
2600 Highway 129 N 30528 706-865-2312
John Osborne, prin. Fax 865-5981
White County MS 600/6-8
283 Old Blairsville Rd 30528 706-865-4060
Kristi Gerrells, prin. Fax 865-1947
White County Ninth Grade Academy 300/9-9
328 Old Blairsville Rd 30528 706-865-0727
John Osborne, prin. Fax 865-0737

---

Truett McConnell College Post-Sec.
100 Alumni Dr 30528 706-865-2134

**Cochran, Bleckley, Pop. 5,096**
Bleckley County SD 2,300/PK-12
PO Box 516 31014 478-934-2821
Steve Smith, supt. Fax 934-9595
www.bleckley.k12.ga.us
Bleckley County HS 700/9-12
155 Highway 87 Byp S 31014 478-934-6258
Dr. Trey Belflower, prin. Fax 934-9707
Bleckley County MS 600/6-8
590 GA Highway 26 E 31014 478-934-7270
Michele Dyal, prin. Fax 934-6502
Bleckley County Success Academy Alt
140 Country Club Rd 31014 478-934-1685
Denise Warren, prin.

**College Park, Fulton, Pop. 13,682**
Clayton County SD
Supt. — See Jonesboro

North Clayton HS 900/9-12
1525 Norman Dr, 770-994-4035
Lonnie Farmer, prin. Fax 994-4038
North Clayton MS 800/6-8
5517 W Fayetteville Rd, 770-994-4025
Shakira Rice, prin. Fax 994-4028

Fulton County SD
Supt. — See Atlanta
Banneker HS 1,200/9-12
6015 Feldwood Rd, 770-969-3410
Duke Bradley, prin. Fax 969-3418
Camp Creek MS 800/6-8
4345 Welcome All Rd SW, 470-254-8030
Keynun Campbell, prin. Fax 254-8228
McClarin Alternative HS 300/Alt
3605 Main St 30337 470-254-8080
Dr. Leteshia Woodley, prin. Fax 254-8089
McNair MS 700/6-8
2800 Burdett Rd, 470-254-4160
Luqman Abdur-Rahman, prin. Fax 254-4165

---

Woodward Academy 2,800/PK-12
1662 Rugby Ave 30337 404-765-4000
F. Stuart Gulley Ph.D., pres. Fax 765-4009

**Colquitt, Miller, Pop. 1,979**
Miller County SD 1,100/PK-12
96 Perry St, 229-758-5592
Dr. Allen Kicklighter, supt. Fax 758-6040
www.millercountyschools.schoolinsites.com
Miller County HS 300/9-12
996 Phillipsburg Rd, 229-758-4130
David Kirkland, prin. Fax 758-3244
Miller County MS 200/6-8
996 Phillipsburg Rd, 229-758-4130
Robert Melton, prin. Fax 758-3244

**Columbus, Muscogee, Pop. 184,779**
Muscogee County SD 31,200/PK-12
PO Box 2427 31902 706-748-2000
Dr. David Lewis, supt. Fax 748-2001
www.muscogee.k12.ga.us
Arnold Magnet Academy 800/6-8
2011 51st St 31904 706-748-2436
Dr. Brenda Badura, prin. Fax 748-2435
Baker MS 300/6-8
1215 Benning Dr 31903 706-683-8721
Ramona Horn, prin. Fax 683-8731
Blackmon Road MS 900/6-8
7251 Blackmon Rd 31909 706-565-2998
Penny Bowen, prin. Fax 565-3006
Carver STEM HS 1,000/9-12
3100 8th St 31906 706-748-2499
Chris Lindsey, prin. Fax 748-2512
Columbus HS 1,300/9-12
1700 Cherokee Ave 31906 706-748-2534
Dr. Marvin Crumbs, prin. Fax 748-2546
Double Churches MS 400/6-8
7611 Whitesville Rd 31904 706-748-2678
Craig Fitts, prin. Fax 748-2682
Early College Academy 200/9-12
2701 11th Ave 31904 706-748-2948
Susan Willard, dean Fax 748-2951
East Columbus Magnet Academy 700/6-8
6100 Georgetown Dr 31907 706-565-3026
Tamura Magwood, prin. Fax 565-3031
Eddy MS 400/6-8
2100 S Lumpkin Rd 31903 706-683-8782
Shermaine Derrick, prin. Fax 683-8789
Fort MS 600/6-8
2900 Woodruff Farm Rd 31907 706-569-3740
Sonja Coaxum, prin. Fax 569-3616
Hardaway HS 1,800/9-12
2901 College Dr 31906 706-748-2766
Matt Bell, prin. Fax 748-2776
Jordan Vocational HS 800/9-12
3200 Howard Ave 31904 706-748-2819
Alton White, prin. Fax 748-2829
Kendrick HS 800/9-12
6015 Georgetown Dr 31907 706-565-2960
Dr. Alonzo James, prin. Fax 565-2971
Northside HS 1,600/9-12
2002 American Way 31909 706-748-2920
Martin Richburg, prin. Fax 748-2931
Richards MS 800/6-8
2892 Edgewood Rd 31906 706-569-3697
Lance Henderson, prin. Fax 569-3704
Rothschild Leadership Academy 500/6-8
1136 Hunt Ave 31907 706-569-3709
Dr. Michael Forte, prin. Fax 569-3717
St. Elmo Center for Gifted Education K-12
2101 18th Ave 31901 706-748-3115
Paula Cash, dir. Fax 748-3118
Shaw HS 1,200/9-12
7579 Raider Way 31909 706-569-3638
Michael Barden, prin. Fax 569-3648
Spencer HS 800/9-12
4340 Victory Dr 31903 706-683-8701
Dr. Johnny Freeman, prin. Fax 683-8716
Veterans Memorial MS 700/6-8
2008 Old Guard Rd 31909 706-748-3203
Melanie Knight, prin. Fax 748-3211
Other Schools – See Midland

---

Brookstone S 800/PK-12
440 Bradley Park Dr 31904 706-324-1392
Dr. Frank Brown, hdmstr. Fax 571-0178
Calvary Christian S 600/PK-12
7556 Old Moon Rd 31909 706-323-0467
Dr. Ricky Smith, hdmstr. Fax 323-1941
Columbus State University Post-Sec.
4225 University Ave 31907 706-507-8800
Columbus Technical College Post-Sec.
928 Manchester Expy 31904 706-649-1800
Grace Christian S 100/PK-12
2915 14th Ave 31904 706-323-9161
Medical Center Post-Sec.
PO Box 951 31902 706-571-1200
Miller-Motte Technical College Post-Sec.
1800 Box Rd 31907 706-225-5002

Rivertown School of Beauty Post-Sec.
4747 Hamilton Rd Ste B 31904 706-653-8032
St. Anne Pacelli S 500/PK-12
2020 Kay Cir 31907 706-561-8232
Gayla Arrington, prin. Fax 563-0211
Southeastern Beauty School Post-Sec.
PO Box 12483 31917 706-687-1054
Virginia College Post-Sec.
5601 Veterans Pkwy 31904 762-207-1600

**Comer, Madison, Pop. 1,110**
Madison County SD
Supt. — See Danielsville
Madison County MS 1,000/6-8
3215 Highway 172 30629 706-783-2400
Chuck Colquitt, prin. Fax 783-4390

**Commerce, Jackson, Pop. 6,437**
Commerce CSD 1,500/PK-12
PO Box 29 30529 706-335-5500
Dr. Joy Tolbert, supt. Fax 335-5214
www.commerce-city.k12.ga.us
Commerce HS 400/9-12
272 Lakeview Dr 30529 706-335-5942
Donald Drew, prin. Fax 336-6955
Commerce MS 400/5-8
7690 Jefferson Rd 30529 706-335-5594
Bill Ruma, prin. Fax 335-6222

Jackson County SD
Supt. — See Jefferson
East Jackson Comprehensive HS 1,000/9-12
1435 Hoods Mill Rd 30529 706-336-8900
Jamie Dixon, prin. Fax 335-2928
East Jackson MS 400/6-8
1880 Hoods Mill Rd 30529 706-335-2083
Tiffany Barnett, prin. Fax 335-0935

**Conyers, Rockdale, Pop. 14,890**
Rockdale County SD 15,600/PK-12
PO Box 1199 30012 770-860-4211
Richard Autry, supt. Fax 860-4285
www.rockdale.k12.ga.us
Alpha Alternative S Alt
1045 North St NW 30012 770-922-8636
Alex Guilford, prin. Fax 918-0248
Conyers MS 1,000/6-8
400 Sigman Rd NW 30012 770-483-3371
Allison Barbour, prin. Fax 483-9448
Edwards MS 1,000/6-8
2633 Stanton Rd SE 30094 770-483-3255
Fred Middleton, prin. Fax 483-3676
Heritage HS 1,600/9-12
2400 Granade Rd SW 30094 770-483-5428
Greg Fowler, prin. Fax 483-9435
Magnet S for Science/Technology 9-12
1174 Bulldog Cir NE 30012 770-483-8737
Dr. Debra Arnold, dir. Fax 483-7379
Memorial MS 800/6-8
3205 Underwood Rd SE 30013 770-922-0139
Michell Glover, prin. Fax 922-6192
Open Campus S Alt
1115 West Ave SW 30012 770-388-5727
Frank Daniels, prin. Fax 388-5728
Rockdale County HS 1,800/9-12
1174 Bulldog Cir NE 30012 770-483-8754
Mary Ann Suddeth, prin. Fax 483-8708
Salem HS 1,500/9-12
3551 Underwood Rd SE 30013 770-929-0176
Tonya Bloodworth, prin. Fax 922-1292
Other Schools – See Stockbridge

---

GDA Inc Post-Sec.
1448 V F W Dr SW 30012 770-918-8501
Georgia Career Institute Post-Sec.
1820 Highway 20 SE Ste 208 30013 770-922-7653
Victory Christian S 100/PK-12
1151 Flat Shoals Rd SE 30013 770-929-3758
Young Americans Christian S 600/PK-12
1701 Honey Creek Rd SE 30013 770-760-7902
Dr. David Taylor Ed.D., admin. Fax 760-7981

**Cordele, Crisp, Pop. 11,020**
Crisp County SD 2,600/K-12
PO Box 729 31010 229-276-3400
Dr. David Mims, supt. Fax 276-3406
www.crispschools.org
Crisp County HS 1,100/9-12
2402 Cougar Aly 31015 229-276-3430
Dr. Rusty Sowell, prin. Fax 276-3436
Crisp County MS 900/6-8
1116 E 24th Ave 31015 229-276-3460
Brandon Williams, prin. Fax 276-3466

---

Crisp Academy 200/PK-12
150 Crisp Academy Dr 31015 229-273-6330
Dr. Kip Stevens, hdmstr. Fax 273-4141
South Georgia Technical College Post-Sec.
402 N Midway Rd 31015 229-271-4040

**Cornelia, Habersham, Pop. 4,030**
Habersham County SD
Supt. — See Clarkesville
South Habersham MS 500/6-8
237 Old Athens Hwy 30531 706-778-7121
Daphne Penick, prin. Fax 778-2110

**Covington, Newton, Pop. 12,895**
Newton County SD 17,800/PK-12
PO Box 1469 30015 770-787-1330
Samantha Fuhrey, supt. Fax 784-2950
www.newtoncountyschools.org
Alcovy HS 2,000/9-12
14567 Highway 36 30014 770-784-4995
Dr. Sandra Owens, prin. Fax 625-6117
Clements MS 700/6-8
66 Jack Neely Rd 30016 770-784-2934
Joy Scavella, prin. Fax 784-2992
Cousins MS 900/6-8
8187 Carlton Trl NW 30014 770-786-7311
Dr. Makeba Clark, prin. Fax 784-2991

Eastside HS 1,400/9-12
10245 Eagle Dr 30014 770-784-2920
Jeff Cher, prin. Fax 784-2918
Indian Creek MS 1,000/6-8
11051 Covington by Pass Rd 30014 770-385-6453
Dr. Renee Mallard, prin. Fax 385-6456
Liberty MS 1,000/6-8
5225 Salem Rd 30016 678-625-6617
Keisa Taylor, prin. Fax 625-6200
Newton HS 1,900/9-12
1 Ram Way 30014 770-787-2250
John Ellenberg, prin. Fax 784-2957
Veterans Memorial MS 700/6-8
13357 Brown Bridge Rd 30016 770-385-6893
James Peek, prin. Fax 385-6899

---

Georgia Perimter College Post-Sec.
239 Cedar Ln 30014 770-278-1200
Peachtree Academy 200/PK-12
14101 Highway 278 E 30014 678-729-9111
Dr. ShaRonda McRae, prin. Fax 729-9118

**Crawford, Oglethorpe, Pop. 804**
Oglethorpe County SD
Supt. — See Lexington
Oglethorpe County MS 500/6-8
270 Buddy Faust Rd 30630 706-743-8146
Beverley Levine, prin. Fax 743-0849

**Cumming, Forsyth, Pop. 5,371**
Forsyth County SD 36,900/PK-12
1120 Dahlonega Hwy 30040 770-887-2461
Dr. Jeff Bearden, supt. Fax 781-6632
www.forsyth.k12.ga.us
Forsyth Central HS 1,400/9-12
520 Tribble Gap Rd 30040 770-887-8151
Mitch Young, prin. Fax 781-2289
Gateway Academy Alt
136 Elm St 30040 770-781-2299
Betty Pope, dir. Fax 888-1193
Lakeside MS 900/6-8
2565 Echols Rd 30041 678-965-5080
Debbie Sarver, prin. Fax 965-5081
Liberty MS 900/6-8
7465 Wallace Tatum Rd 30028 770-781-4889
Cheryl Riddle, prin. Fax 513-3877
Little Mill MS 900/6-8
6800 Little Mill Rd 30041 678-965-5000
Connie McCrary, prin. Fax 965-5001
North Forsyth HS 2,300/9-12
3635 Coal Mountain Dr 30028 770-781-6637
Jeff Cheney, prin. Fax 888-0934
North Forsyth MS 900/6-8
3645 Coal Mountain Dr 30028 770-889-0743
Jeff Hunt, prin. Fax 888-1210
Otwell MS 900/6-8
605 Tribble Gap Rd 30040 770-887-5248
Steve Miller, prin. Fax 888-1214
Piney Grove MS 1,000/6-8
8135 Majors Rd 30041 678-965-5010
Terri North, prin. Fax 965-5011
South Forsyth HS 1,900/9-12
585 Peachtree Pkwy 30041 770-781-2264
Laura Wilson, prin. Fax 888-1224
South Forsyth MS 900/6-8
4670 Windermere Pkwy 30041 770-888-3170
Sandy Tinsley, prin. Fax 888-3175
Vickery Creek MS 1,200/6-8
6240 Post Rd 30040 770-667-2580
Drew Hayes, prin. Fax 667-2593
West Forsyth HS 2,100/9-12
4155 Drew Rd 30040 770-888-3470
Heather Gordy, prin. Fax 888-3471
Other Schools – See Suwanee

---

Covenant Christian Academy 200/PK-12
6905 Post Rd 30040 770-674-2990
Johnathan Arnold, hdmstr. Fax 674-2989
Fideles Christian S 100/PK-12
1390 Weber Industrial Dr 30041 770-888-6705
Jonny Whisenant, dir. Fax 888-9720
Horizon Christian Academy 300/K-12
PO Box 2715 30028 678-947-0711
Gary Bennett, admin. Fax 947-0721
Pinecrest Academy 800/PK-12
955 Peachtree Pkwy 30041 770-888-4477
Paul Parker, head sch Fax 888-0404

**Cusseta, Chattahoochee, Pop. 1,258**
Chattahoochee County SD 900/PK-12
326 Broad St 31805 706-989-3774
David McCurry, supt. Fax 989-3776
www.chattco.org
ACE Academy Alternative S Alt
326 Broad St 31805 706-989-3243
Jim Sims, dir. Fax 989-3776
Chattahoochee County HS 500/9-12
360 GA Highway 26 31805 706-989-3678
James Sims, prin. Fax 989-0649
Chattahoochee County MS 100/6-8
360 GA Highway 26 31805 706-989-3678
Jim Sims, prin. Fax 989-0649

**Cuthbert, Randolph, Pop. 3,851**
Randolph County SD 1,100/PK-12
98 School Dr, 229-732-3601
Dr. Marvin Howard, supt. Fax 732-3840
www.sowegak12.org/
Randolph-Clay HS 300/9-12
3451 GA Highway 266, 229-732-2101
Willie Williams, prin. Fax 732-5633
Randolph-Clay MS 200/6-8
3451 GA Highway 266, 229-732-2790
Ronald Gadson, prin. Fax 732-5633

---

Andrew College Post-Sec.
501 College St, 229-732-2171

**Dacula, Gwinnett, Pop. 4,365**
Gwinnett County SD
Supt. — See Suwanee

Dacula HS 1,800/9-12
123 Broad St 30019 770-963-6664
Dr. Bryan Long, prin. Fax 338-4665
Dacula MS 1,600/6-8
137 Dacula Rd 30019 770-963-1110
Dr. Kellye Riggins, prin. Fax 338-4632

---

Dacula Classical Academy 100/PK-12
PO Box 986 30019 678-377-0080
Hebron Christian Academy 600/6-12
775 Dacula Rd 30019 770-963-9250
Timothy Hillen, hdmstr. Fax 277-3581

**Dahlonega, Lumpkin, Pop. 5,151**
Lumpkin County SD 3,800/PK-12
56 Indian Dr 30533 706-864-3611
Dewey Moye, supt. Fax 864-3755
lumpkincounty.schoolinsites.com
Lumpkin County HS 1,100/9-12
2001 Indian Dr 30533 706-864-6186
Rick Conner, prin. Fax 864-4929
Lumpkin County MS 900/6-8
44 School Dr 30533 706-864-6189
Chris Froggatt, prin. Fax 864-0199

---

North Georgia College & State University Post-Sec.
82 College Cir 30597 706-864-1400

**Dallas, Paulding, Pop. 11,233**
Paulding County SD 27,900/PK-12
3236 Atlanta Hwy 30132 770-443-8000
Cliff Cole, supt. Fax 443-8089
www.paulding.k12.ga.us
East Paulding HS 1,600/9-12
3320 E Paulding Dr 30157 770-445-5100
Jason Freeman, prin. Fax 443-6357
East Paulding MS 900/6-8
2945 Hiram Acworth Hwy 30157 770-443-7000
Brett Taylor, prin. Fax 443-0116
Jones MS 800/6-8
100 Stadium Dr 30132 770-443-8024
Craig Wilcox, prin. Fax 443-8026
McClure MS 1,100/6-8
315 Bob Grogan Dr 30132 770-505-3700
Jaynath Hayes, prin. Fax 505-7253
Moses MS 900/6-8
1066 Old County Farm Rd 30132 770-443-8727
Scott Viness, prin. Fax 443-8078
New Hope Education Center Alt
4555 Dallas Acworth Hwy 30132 770-445-2656
Vladimir Labossiere, prin. Fax 443-7006
North Paulding HS 1,800/9-12
300 N Paulding Dr 30132 770-443-9400
Dr. Mark Crowe, prin. Fax 363-8544
Paulding County HS 1,500/9-12
1297 Villa Rica Hwy 30157 770-443-8008
Dr. Paul McMahon, prin. Fax 443-7030
Ritch MS 6-8
60 Old Country Trl 30157 770-443-1449
Christine Carson, prin. Fax 443-4339
Scoggins MS 800/6-8
1663 Mulberry Rock Rd 30157 770-456-4188
Tammy Allen, prin. Fax 456-4189
South Paulding MS 500/6-8
592 Nebo Rd 30157 770-445-8500
Sandra Webb, prin. Fax 445-9989
Other Schools – See Douglasville, Hiram, Powder Springs

**Dalton, Whitfield, Pop. 32,710**
Dalton CSD 7,200/PK-12
PO Box 1408 30722 706-876-4000
Jim Hawkins Ph.D., supt. Fax 226-4583
www.daltonpublicschools.com/
Dalton HS 1,400/9-12
1500 Manly St 30720 706-876-4800
Steve Bartoo, prin. Fax 226-2430
Dalton MS 1,600/6-8
1250 Cross Plains Trl 30721 706-278-3903
Brian Suits, prin. Fax 428-7852
Morris Innovative HS 300/Alt
104 Fort Hill Ter 30721 706-876-4150
Pat Hunt, prin. Fax 278-4998

Whitfield County SD 12,500/PK-12
PO Box 2167 30722 706-217-6780
Dr. Judy Gilreath, supt. Fax 217-6755
www.whitfield.k12.ga.us
Coahulla Creek HS 700/9-12
3361 Crow Rd NE 30721 706-694-4900
Tracy Mardis, prin. Fax 694-5033
Crossroads Academy Alt
2818 Airport Rd 30721 706-271-2495
Donna Harris, prin. Fax 271-2496
Eastbrook MS 600/6-8
1382 Eastbrook Rd SE 30721 706-278-6135
Dr. Gregory Bailey, prin. Fax 226-9859
New Hope MS 600/6-8
1111 New Hope Rd NW 30720 706-673-2295
Joe Barnett, prin. Fax 673-2086
North Whitfield MS 900/6-8
3264 Cleveland Rd 30721 706-259-3381
Andrea Bradley, prin. Fax 259-8168
Southeast Whitfield County HS 1,200/9-12
1954 Riverbend Rd 30721 706-876-7000
Denise Pendley, prin. Fax 278-3433
Valley Point MS 500/6-8
3796 S Dixie Rd 30721 706-277-9662
Stephanie Hungerpiller, prin. Fax 277-7035
Phoenix HS Adult
2300 Maddox Chapel Rd NE 30721 706-260-2206
Fred Toney, prin. Fax 260-2200
Other Schools – See Rocky Face, Tunnel Hill

---

Christian Heritage S 400/K-12
PO Box 2066 30722 706-277-1198
Gerald Porter, head sch Fax 277-2300
Dalton State College Post-Sec.
650 College Dr 30720 706-272-4436
Georgia Beauty Academy Post-Sec.
PO Box 3516 30719 866-418-4522
Georgia Northwestern Technical College Post-Sec.
2310 Maddox Chapel Rd NE 30721 706-272-2966

**Damascus, Early, Pop. 251**

---

Southwest Georgia Academy 400/PK-12
14105 GA Highway 200, 229-725-4792

**Danielsville, Madison, Pop. 548**
Madison County SD 4,700/PK-12
800 Madison St 30633 706-795-2191
Dr. Allen McCannon, supt. Fax 795-5029
www.madison.k12.ga.us
Madison County HS 1,400/9-12
600 Madison St 30633 706-795-2197
George Bullock, prin. Fax 795-3116
Other Schools – See Comer

**Darien, McIntosh, Pop. 1,951**
McIntosh County SD 1,700/PK-12
200 Pine St SE 31305 912-437-6645
Dr. Tina Kirby, supt. Fax 437-2140
www.mcintosh.k12.ga.us/
McIntosh County Academy 500/9-12
8945 US Highway 17 31305 912-437-6691
Terrance Haywood, prin. Fax 437-3077
McIntosh County MS 400/6-8
500 Greene St 31305 912-437-6685
Carolyn Smith, prin. Fax 437-5676

**Dawson, Terrell, Pop. 4,502**
Terrell County SD 1,500/PK-12
PO Box 151, 229-995-4425
Robert Aaron, supt. Fax 995-4632
www.terrell.k12.ga.us
Terrell County HS 400/9-12
201 Greenwave Blvd, 229-995-2544
Douglas Bell, prin. Fax 995-4523
Terrell County MS 400/6-8
201 Greenwave Blvd, 229-995-2828
Valencia Gardner, prin. Fax 995-5418

---

Terrell Academy 300/K-12
602 Academy Dr SE, 229-995-4242

**Dawsonville, Dawson, Pop. 2,501**
Dawson County SD 3,400/PK-12
28 Main St 30534 706-265-3246
Dr. Damon Gibbs, supt. Fax 265-1226
www.dawsoncountyschools.org/
Dawson County HS 1,000/9-12
PO Box 129 30534 706-265-6555
Richard Crumley, prin. Fax 265-3936
Dawson County MS 400/6-8
332 Highway 9 N 30534 706-216-5801
Jeffrey Clapper, prin. Fax 265-7252
Hightower Academy Alt
175 Tiger Cir 30534 706-265-1244
Richard Crumley, prin. Fax 265-2867
Riverview MS 400/6-8
5126 Highway 9 S 30534 706-216-4849
Dr. Randi Sagona, prin. Fax 265-1426

**Decatur, DeKalb, Pop. 18,866**
City Schools of Decatur 3,500/PK-12
125 Electric Ave 30030 404-371-3601
Dr. Phyllis Edwards, supt. Fax 371-5579
www.csdecatur.net
Decatur HS 800/9-12
310 N McDonough St 30030 404-370-4420
Arlethea Williams, prin. Fax 370-4434
Renfroe MS 700/6-8
220 W College Ave 30030 404-370-4440
Johnathan Clark, prin. Fax 370-4449

DeKalb County SD
Supt. — See Stone Mountain
Bethune MS 1,000/6-8
5200 Covington Hwy 30035 678-875-0302
Myron Broome, prin. Fax 875-0310
Cedar Grove MS 1,000/6-8
2300 Wildcat Rd 30034 678-874-4202
Candace Alexander, prin. Fax 874-4210
Chapel Hill MS 1,000/6-8
3535 Dogwood Farm Rd 30034 678-676-8502
Lisa McGhee, prin. Fax 676-8510
Columbia HS 1,300/9-12
2106 Columbia Dr 30032 678-874-0802
Stephanie Amey, prin. Fax 874-0810
Columbia MS 1,200/6-8
3001 Columbia Dr 30034 678-875-0502
Keith Jones, prin. Fax 875-0510
DeKalb HS of Technology South Vo/Tech
3303 Panthersville Rd 30034 678-874-4502
Dr. Vikki Williams, prin. Fax 874-4510
Druid Hills MS 1,000/6-8
3100 Mount Olive Dr 30033 678-874-7602
Jacqueline Taylor, prin. Fax 874-7610
International Student Center 100/Alt
3318 Midway Rd 30032 678-676-0902
Terry Segovis, prin. Fax 676-6608
McNair MS 800/6-8
2190 Wallingford Dr 30032 678-874-5102
Ronald Mitchell, prin. Fax 874-5110
Miller Grove MS 1,000/6-8
2215 Miller Rd 30035 678-676-8902
Thaddeus Dixon, prin. Fax 676-8910
Southwest DeKalb HS 1,500/9-12
2863 Kelley Chapel Rd 30034 678-874-1902
Thomas Glanton, prin. Fax 874-1910
Towers HS 1,100/9-12
3919 Brookcrest Cir 30032 678-874-2202
Vincent Denson, prin. Fax 874-2210

---

Academe of the Oaks 100/9-12
146 New St 30030 404-405-2173
Eva Handschin, dir. Fax 377-7178
Agnes Scott College Post-Sec.
141 E College Ave 30030 404-471-6000
American Professional Institute Post-Sec.
141 Sams St 30030 404-371-3338
Columbia Theological Seminary Post-Sec.
PO Box 520 30031 404-378-8821
DeKalb Medical Center Post-Sec.
2701 N Decatur Rd 30033 404-501-5206
DeVry University Post-Sec.
1 W Court Sq Ste 100 30030 404-270-2706
Georgia Perimeter College Post-Sec.
3251 Panthersville Rd 30034 678-891-2300
Greenforest-McCalep Christian Academy 500/PK-12
3250 Rainbow Dr 30034 404-486-6737
Millicent Black Ph.D., prin. Fax 486-1127
Gupton-Jones College of Funeral Service Post-Sec.
5141 Snapfinger Woods Dr 30035 770-593-2257
Laurus Technical Institute Post-Sec.
523 Church St 30030 404-303-2929

**Demorest, Habersham, Pop. 1,780**
Habersham County SD
Supt. — See Clarkesville
Wilbanks MS 600/6-8
3115 Demorest Mt Airy Hwy 30535 706-894-1341
Marybeth Thomas, prin. Fax 894-1342

---

Piedmont College Post-Sec.
PO Box 10 30535 706-778-3000

**Dexter, Laurens, Pop. 568**
Laurens County SD
Supt. — See Dublin
West Laurens HS 1,200/9-12
3692 GA Highway 257 31019 478-875-1000
Clifford Garnto, prin. Fax 875-2860

**Donalsonville, Seminole, Pop. 2,610**
Seminole County SD 1,600/PK-12
800 S Woolfork Ave, 229-524-2433
Monroe Bonner, supt. Fax 524-2212
www.seminole.k12.ga.us
Seminole County MSHS 800/6-12
5582 GA Highway 39, 229-524-5135
Dr. H. Brinson Register, prin. Fax 524-5178

**Doraville, DeKalb, Pop. 8,200**
DeKalb County SD
Supt. — See Stone Mountain
Sequoyah MS 900/6-8
3456 Aztec Rd 30340 678-676-7902
Sedrick Anthony, prin. Fax 676-7910

**Douglas, Coffee, Pop. 11,434**
Coffee County SD 7,800/PK-12
1311 Peterson Ave S 31533 912-384-2086
Dr. Morris Leis, supt. Fax 383-5333
coffee.k12.ga.us
Carver HS Freshman Campus 600/9-9
1020 Gaskin Ave S 31533 912-384-1342
Abe Morris, prin. Fax 383-4160
Coffee Alternative Education Center Alt
1303 Peterson Ave S 31533 912-383-4100
Tonya LeSure, dir. Fax 383-4124
Coffee County Career Academy Vo/Tech
1303 Peterson Ave S 31533 912-389-6851
Scott Gillis, prin. Fax 720-9849
Coffee HS 1,400/10-12
159 Trojan Way 31533 912-384-2094
Dr. Rowland Cummings, prin. Fax 383-4142
Coffee MS 1,800/6-8
901 Connector 206 N 31533 912-720-1011
Sherri Berry, dir. Fax 720-1032

---

Citizens Christian Academy 200/PK-12
PO Box 1064 31534 912-384-8862
South Georgia State College Post-Sec.
100 College Park Dr W 31533 912-260-4200

**Douglasville, Douglas, Pop. 30,224**
Douglas County SD 23,200/K-12
PO Box 1077 30133 770-651-2000
Dr. Gordon Pritz, supt. Fax 920-4159
www.douglas.k12.ga.us
Alexander HS 1,700/9-12
6500 Alexander Pkwy 30135 770-651-6000
Nathan Hand, prin. Fax 920-4514
Chapel Hill HS 1,200/9-12
4899 Chapel Hill Rd 30135 770-651-6200
Dr. Sean Kelly, prin. Fax 947-7512
Chapel Hill MS 1,100/6-8
3989 Chapel Hill Rd 30135 770-651-5000
Dr. Jolene Morris, prin. Fax 920-4242
Chestnut Log MS 700/6-8
2544 Pope Rd 30135 770-651-5100
Dr. Nicole Hayes, prin. Fax 651-5103
Douglas County HS 1,800/9-12
8705 Campbellton St 30134 770-651-6500
Andre Weaver, prin. Fax 920-4456
Factory Shoals MS 800/6-8
3301 Shoals School Rd 30135 770-651-5800
Angela Carter, prin. Fax 920-4356
Fairplay MS 600/6-8
8311 Highway 166 30135 770-651-5300
Yvonne Kidney, prin. Fax 920-4599
New Manchester HS 1,700/9-12
4925 Highway 92/166 30135 770-651-2700
Connie Craft, prin.
Stewart MS 500/6-8
8138 Malone St 30134 770-651-5400
Robyn Scott, prin. Fax 920-4229
Yeager MS 600/6-8
4000 Kings Hwy 30135 770-651-5600
Dr. Fred Ervin, prin. Fax 947-7374
Other Schools – See Lithia Springs, Winston

Paulding County SD
Supt. — See Dallas
Austin MS 900/6-8
3490 Ridge Rd 30134 770-942-0316
Gary Plunkett, prin. Fax 942-0548
South Paulding HS 1,800/9-12
1364 Winn Rd 30134 770-949-9221
Dr. Keith Rowland, prin. Fax 949-9239

Harvester Christian Academy 300/PK-12
4241 Central Church Rd 30135 770-942-1583
Joel Slater, hdmstr. Fax 942-9332
Heirway Christian Academy 200/PK-12
6758 Spring St 30134 770-489-4392
ITT Technical Institute Post-Sec.
5905 Stewart Pkwy 30135 678-715-2100
Kings Way Christian S 300/PK-12
6456 The Kings Way 30135 770-949-0812
Dr. Ray Conway, admin. Fax 949-1045
Strayer University Post-Sec.
4655 Timber Ridge Dr 30135 678-715-2200
West Georgia Technical College Post-Sec.
4600 Timber Ridge Dr 30135 770-947-7200

**Dublin, Laurens, Pop. 16,025**
Dublin CSD 2,400/PK-12
207 Shamrock Dr 31021 478-272-3440
Dr. Chuck Ledbetter, supt. Fax 272-1249
www.dublincityschools.us/
Dublin HS 700/9-12
1127 Hillcrest Pkwy 31021 478-272-4727
Robert Hunter, prin. Fax 277-9829
Dublin MS 500/6-8
1501 N Jefferson St 31021 478-272-8122
Mike Mallette, prin. Fax 277-9828
Moore Street S 50/Alt
1405 W Moore St 31021 478-277-4189
Emory Bostic, prin.

Laurens County SD 6,700/PK-12
467 Firetower Rd 31021 478-272-4767
Rob Johnson, supt. Fax 277-2619
www.lcboe.net
East Laurens HS 600/9-12
920 US Highway 80 E 31027 478-272-3144
Eddie Morris, prin. Fax 274-1032
East Laurens MS 500/6-8
920 US Highway 80 E 31027 478-272-1201
Ernest Holmes, prin. Fax 609-2176
West Laurens MS 1,000/6-8
332 W Laurens School Rd 31021 478-272-8452
Tim Franks, prin. Fax 609-2202
Other Schools – See Dexter, Rentz

Oconee Fall Line Technical College Post-Sec.
560 Pinehill Rd 31021 478-275-6589
Trinity Christian S 400/K-12
200 Trinity Rd 31021 478-272-7699

**Duluth, Gwinnett, Pop. 25,917**
Gwinnett County SD
Supt. — See Suwanee
Duluth HS 2,500/9-12
3737 Brock Rd 30096 770-476-5206
Anthony Smith, prin. Fax 232-3332
Duluth MS 1,900/6-8
3200 Pleasant Hill Rd 30096 770-476-3372
Deborah Fusi, prin. Fax 232-3295
Hull MS 2,300/6-8
1950 Old Peachtree Rd 30097 770-232-3200
Denise Showell, prin. Fax 232-3203
Radloff MS 1,700/6-8
3939 Shackleford Rd 30096 678-245-3400
Dr. Sarah Skinner, prin. Fax 245-3403

Atlanta Adventist Academy 200/9-12
PO Box 4088 30096 404-699-1400
Atlanta Institute of Music Post-Sec.
2875 Breckinridge Blvd #700 30096 770-242-7717
Aviation Institute of Maintenance Post-Sec.
2025 Satellite Pointe 30096 678-377-5600
Childcare Education Institute Post-Sec.
3059 Peachtree Indstrl #100 30097 800-499-9907
DeVry University Post-Sec.
3505 Koger Blvd Ste 170 30096 770-381-4400
ITT Technical Institute Post-Sec.
10700 Abbotts Bridge # 190 30097 678-957-8510

**Dunwoody, DeKalb, Pop. 45,357**
DeKalb County SD
Supt. — See Stone Mountain
Dunwoody HS 1,500/9-12
5035 Vermack Rd 30338 678-874-8502
Tom McFerrin, prin. Fax 874-8510

Empire Beauty School Post-Sec.
4719 Ashford-Dunwoody #205 30338 770-672-2448

**Eastman, Dodge, Pop. 4,921**
Dodge County SD 3,300/K-12
720 College St 31023 478-374-3783
Dr. Melinda Dennis, supt. Fax 374-6697
www.dodge.k12.ga.us
Dodge County HS 900/9-12
350 Pearl Bates Ave 31023 478-374-7711
Dr. Susan Long, prin. Fax 374-6987
Dodge County MS 700/6-8
5911 Oak St 31023 478-374-6492
Mike Hilliard, prin. Fax 374-6484

**East Point, Fulton, Pop. 33,152**
Fulton County SD
Supt. — See Atlanta
Tri-Cities HS 1,800/9-12
2575 Harris St 30344 470-254-8200
Dan Sims, prin. Fax 254-8158
West MS 800/6-8
2376 Headland Dr 30344 470-254-8130
Pammy Darden, prin. Fax 254-8121
Woodland MS 1,200/6-8
2745 Stone Rd 30344 404-305-2182
Jason Stamper, prin. Fax 305-2190

**Eatonton, Putnam, Pop. 6,410**

Gatewood S 400/PK-12
139 Phillips Dr 31024 706-485-8231

**Edison, Calhoun, Pop. 1,517**
Calhoun County SD
Supt. — See Morgan
Calhoun County HS 300/9-12
700 Manry St, 229-213-0148
Henry Acres, prin. Fax 213-5000
Calhoun County MS 200/6-8
PO Box 364, 229-213-0146
Craveous Butler, prin. Fax 213-0146

**Elberton, Elbert, Pop. 4,600**
Elbert County SD 1,900/PK-12
50 Laurel Dr 30635 706-213-4000
Charles Bell, supt. Fax 283-6674
www.elbert.k12.ga.us
Elbert County Comprehensive HS 900/9-12
600 Abernathy Cir 30635 706-213-4100
Jason Kouns, prin. Fax 283-1183
Elbert County MS 700/5-8
1108 Athens Tech Rd 30635 706-213-4200
Jon Jarvis, prin. Fax 283-1117
Elberton Education Center 50/Alt
600 Abernathy Cir 30635 706-213-4165
Tammy Mason, admin.

**Ellaville, Schley, Pop. 1,796**
Schley County SD 1,400/PK-12
PO Box 66 31806 229-937-2405
Adam Hathaway, supt. Fax 937-5180
www.schleyk12.org/
Schley County MSHS 700/6-12
2131 US Highway 19 S 31806 229-937-0560
Jim Langley, prin. Fax 937-0565

**Ellenwood, Clayton**
DeKalb County SD
Supt. — See Stone Mountain
Cedar Grove HS 900/9-12
2360 River Rd 30294 678-874-4002
Pamela Benford, prin. Fax 874-4010

Anointed Word Christian S International 50/PK-12
3800 Linecrest Rd 30294 404-241-8200
Markell Davis-Haynes, admin. Fax 328-9801

**Ellijay, Gilmer, Pop. 1,600**

North Georgia Christian Academy 100/PK-12
191 Harold Pritchett Rd 30540 706-635-6422
Mary Pierce, admin. Fax 635-6425

**Emerson, Bartow, Pop. 1,449**
Bartow County SD
Supt. — See Cartersville
South Central MS 700/6-8
224 Old Alabama Rd SE 30137 770-606-5865
Neil Howell, prin. Fax 606-5168

**Eton, Murray, Pop. 907**
Murray County SD
Supt. — See Chatsworth
Mountain Creek Academy 200/Alt
273 Harris St 30724 706-517-5355
Marcus Richardson, prin. Fax 517-5339

**Euharlee, Bartow, Pop. 4,058**
Bartow County SD
Supt. — See Cartersville
Woodland MS 900/6-8
1061 Euharlee Rd, 770-606-5871
Lamar Barnes, prin. Fax 606-2092

**Evans, Columbia, Pop. 28,398**
Columbia County SD 22,500/PK-12
4781 Hereford Farm Rd 30809 706-541-0650
Dr. Sandra Carraway, supt. Fax 541-2723
www.ccboe.net
CCBOE Alternative S Alt
628 Gibbs Rd 30809 706-868-5715
Dr. Ja'net Bishop, prin. Fax 854-5819
Evans HS 1,700/9-12
4550 Cox Rd 30809 706-863-1198
Michael Johnson, prin. Fax 854-5807
Evans MS 800/6-8
4785 Hereford Farm Rd 30809 706-863-2275
Sandra Thompson, prin. Fax 854-5810
Greenbrier HS 1,700/9-12
5114 Riverwood Pkwy 30809 706-650-6040
Chris Segraves, prin. Fax 855-3886
Greenbrier MS 600/6-8
5120 Riverwood Pkwy 30809 706-650-6080
Chip Fulmer, prin. Fax 854-5800
Lakeside HS 1,700/9-12
533 Blue Ridge Dr 30809 706-863-0027
Steven Cummings, prin. Fax 854-5802
Lakeside MS 700/6-8
527 Blue Ridge Dr 30809 706-855-6900
Felicia Turner, prin. Fax 854-5805
Riverside MS 700/6-8
1095 Furys Ferry Rd 30809 706-868-3712
Yvette Foster, prin. Fax 854-5824
Other Schools – See Grovetown, Harlem, Martinez

Augusta School of Massage Post-Sec.
608 Ponder Place Dr 30809 706-863-4799

**Fairburn, Fulton, Pop. 12,742**
Fulton County SD
Supt. — See Atlanta
Bear Creek MS 1,100/6-8
7415 Herndon Rd 30213 470-254-6080
Anthony Newbold, prin. Fax 254-3584
Creekside HS 1,400/9-12
7405 Herndon Rd 30213 470-254-4300
Ronald Maxwell, prin. Fax 254-4313
Hughes HS 1,900/9-12
7510 Hall Rd 30213 770-774-3620
Brady Reeves, prin. Fax 774-3633
Renaissance MS 1,100/6-8
7155 Hall Rd 30213 770-306-4330
Tricia Rock, prin. Fax 306-4338

Arlington Christian S 300/K-12
4500 Ridge Rd 30213 770-964-9871
Landmark Christian S 800/PK-12
50 SE Broad St 30213 770-306-0647
Mike Titus, hdmstr. Fax 969-6551

**Fayetteville, Fayette, Pop. 15,530**
Fayette County SD 18,800/PK-12
PO Box 879 30214 770-460-3535
Dr. Joseph Barrow, supt. Fax 460-8191
www.fcboe.org
Bennetts Mill MS 600/6-8
210 Lester Rd 30215 770-716-3982
Marcus Broadhead, prin. Fax 716-3983
Fayette County Alternative S Alt
450 Grady Ave 30214 770-460-3551
Tim Carder, prin. Fax 460-3905
Fayette County HS 1,400/9-12
1 Tiger Trl 30214 770-460-3540
Dr. Dan Lane, prin. Fax 460-3410
Rising Starr MS 1,000/6-8
183 Panther Path 30215 770-486-2721
Nancy Blair, prin. Fax 486-2727
Starr's Mill HS 1,500/9-12
193 Panther Path 30215 770-486-2710
Allen Leonard, prin. Fax 486-2716
Whitewater HS 1,500/9-12
100 Wildcat Way 30215 770-460-3935
Roy Rabold, prin. Fax 716-3973
Whitewater MS 800/6-8
1533 Highway 85 S 30215 770-460-3450
Connie Baldwin, prin. Fax 460-0362
Other Schools – See Peachtree City, Tyrone

Fayette Beauty Academy Post-Sec.
386 Glynn St N 30214 770-461-4669
GRACE Christian Academy 200/PK-12
355 McDonough Rd 30214 770-461-0137
Our Lady of Mercy Catholic HS 400/9-12
861 Highway 279 30214 770-461-2202
Brian Newhall, prin. Fax 461-9353
Solid Rock Academy 200/PK-12
106 Commerce St 30214 770-997-9744

**Fitzgerald, Ben Hill, Pop. 8,940**
Ben Hill County SD 3,200/PK-12
509 W Palm St 31750 229-409-5500
Nancy Whidden, supt. Fax 409-5513
www.ben-hill.k12.ga.us
Ben Hill County MS 800/6-8
134 JC Hunter Rd 31750 229-409-5578
Dawn Clements, prin. Fax 409-5580
Fitzgerald HS 800/9-12
601 W Cypress St 31750 229-409-5530
Stacey Bell, prin. Fax 409-5534

**Flintstone, Walker**
Walker County SD
Supt. — See La Fayette
Chattanooga Valley MS 500/6-8
847 Allgood Rd 30725 706-820-0735
Wade Breeden, prin. Fax 820-0736

**Flowery Branch, Hall, Pop. 5,590**
Hall County SD
Supt. — See Gainesville
Davis MS 1,200/6-8
4450 Hog Mountain Rd 30542 770-965-3020
Eddie Millwood, prin. Fax 965-3025
South Hall MS 1,200/6-8
4335 Falcon Pkwy 30542 770-532-4416
Paula Stubbs, prin. Fax 967-5852

North Georgia Christian S 200/PK-12
5285 Strickland Rd 30542 678-828-8350
Carol Cox, head sch Fax 828-8357

**Folkston, Charlton, Pop. 2,443**
Charlton County SD 1,500/PK-12
1259 Third St 31537 912-496-2596
Dr. John Lairsey, supt. Fax 496-2595
www.charlton.k12.ga.us
Bethune MS 600/4-8
285 Little Phoebe Church Rd 31537 912-496-2360
Nora Nettles, prin. Fax 496-3766
Charlton County HS 400/9-12
994 Indian Trl 31537 912-496-2501
Dr. Joshua Howard, prin. Fax 496-3732

**Forest Park, Clayton, Pop. 18,177**
Clayton County SD
Supt. — See Jonesboro
Babb MS 800/6-8
5500 Reynolds Rd 30297 404-473-3248
Brenda Ross, prin. Fax 473-3252
Forest Park HS 1,700/9-12
5452 Phillips Dr 30297 770-473-2775
Dr. Derrick Manning, prin. Fax 473-3228
Forest Park MS 700/6-8
930 Finley Dr 30297 770-472-2817
Monique Drewry, prin. Fax 472-2833

Arnold/Padrick's Univ of Cosmetology Post-Sec.
4971 Courtney Dr 30297 404-361-5641
Beauty College of America Post-Sec.
1171 Main St 30297 404-361-4098

**Forsyth, Monroe, Pop. 3,748**
Monroe County SD 3,600/PK-12
PO Box 1308 31029 478-994-2031
Anthony Pack, supt. Fax 994-3364
www.monroe.k12.ga.us
Monroe County Achievement Ctr Alt
25 Brooklyn Ave 31029 478-994-7072
Grady Caldwell, coord. Fax 994-7074
Monroe County MS - Banks Stephens Campus 300/7-8
66 Thornton Rd 31029 478-994-6186
Efrem Yarber, prin. Fax 994-7061
Persons HS 1,200/9-12
300 Montpelier Ave 31029 478-994-2812
Jim Finch, prin. Fax 994-7065

**Fort Gaines, Clay, Pop. 1,094**
Clay County SD 300/PK-10
111 Commerce St E, 229-768-2232
Johnnie Grimsley, supt. Fax 768-3654
www.clay.k12.ga.us
Clay County MSHS 100/6-10
200 Hobbs Ln, 229-768-2234
Michelle Oliver, prin. Fax 768-2363

**Fort Oglethorpe, Catoosa, Pop. 9,051**
Catoosa County SD
Supt. — See Ringgold
Lakeview-Fort Oglethorpe HS 1,000/9-12
1850 Battlefield Pkwy 30742 706-866-0342
Terri Vandiver, prin. Fax 861-6645
Performance Learning Center Alt
2 Barnhardt Cir 30742 706-861-2772
Sharon Vaughn, prin. Fax 861-6643

**Fort Valley, Peach, Pop. 9,695**
Peach County SD 3,900/K-12
523 Vineville St 31030 478-825-5933
Daryl Fineran, supt. Fax 825-9970
www.peachschools.org
Fort Valley MS 500/6-8
712 Peggy Dr 31030 478-825-2413
Damika Glover, prin. Fax 825-1332
Peach County HS 1,100/9-12
900 Campus Dr 31030 478-825-8258
Bruce Mackey, prin. Fax 825-2290
Other Schools – See Byron

---

Fort Valley State University Post-Sec.
1005 State University Dr 31030 478-825-6211

**Franklin, Heard, Pop. 969**
Heard County SD 2,100/PK-12
PO Box 1330 30217 706-675-3320
Jerry Prince, supt. Fax 675-3357
www.heard.k12.ga.us
Heard County Comprehensive HS 600/9-12
545 Main St 30217 706-675-3656
Rodney Kay, prin. Fax 675-8729
Heard County MS 500/6-8
269 Old Field Rd 30217 706-675-9247
Mike Roberts, prin. Fax 675-9255

**Franklin Springs, Franklin, Pop. 938**

---

Emmanuel College Post-Sec.
PO Box 129 30639 800-860-8800

**Gainesville, Hall, Pop. 33,306**
Gainesville CSD 7,200/PK-12
508 Oak St 30501 770-536-5275
Dr. Wanda Creel, supt. Fax 287-2019
www.gcssk12.net/
Gainesville HS 1,500/9-12
830 Century Pl 30501 770-536-4441
Tom Smith, prin. Fax 287-2031
Gainesville MS 1,400/6-8
1581 Community Way 30501 770-534-4237
Dr. Rose Prejean-Harris, prin. Fax 287-2022

Hall County SD 25,900/PK-12
711 Green St NW 30501 770-534-1080
Will Schofield, supt. Fax 535-7404
www.hallco.org
Chestatee HS 1,100/9-12
3005 Sardis Rd 30506 770-532-1162
Suzanne Jarrard, prin. Fax 532-2202
Da Vinci Academies of Discovery 6-8
3215 Poplar Springs Rd 30507 770-533-4004
Paula Stubbs, prin. Fax 533-4018
East Hall HS 1,000/9-12
3534 E Hall Rd 30507 770-536-9921
Jeff Cooper, prin. Fax 535-1184
East Hall MS 900/6-8
4120 E Hall Rd 30507 770-531-9457
Kristin Finley, prin. Fax 531-2327
Johnson HS 1,200/9-12
3305 Poplar Springs Rd 30507 770-536-2394
Stan Lewis, prin. Fax 531-3046
Lanier Career Academy Alt
2723 Tumbling Creek Rd 30504 770-531-2330
Dr. Cindy Blakley, prin. Fax 450-5978
North Hall HS 1,100/9-12
4885 Mount Vernon Rd 30506 770-983-7331
Jamey Moore, prin. Fax 983-7941
North Hall MS 900/6-8
4856 Rilla Rd 30506 770-983-9749
Dr. Shane Rayburn, prin. Fax 983-9993
Other Schools – See Flowery Branch, Oakwood

---

Brenau University Post-Sec.
500 Washington St SE 30501 800-252-5119
Interactive College of Technology Post-Sec.
2323 Browns Bridge Rd 30504 678-450-0550
Lakeview Academy 500/PK-12
796 Lakeview Dr 30501 770-532-4383
Dr. John Kennedy, head sch Fax 536-6142
Riverside Military Academy 400/7-12
2001 Riverside Dr 30501 800-462-2338
Dr. James Benson, pres. Fax 291-3364

**Georgetown, Quitman, Pop. 912**
Quitman County SD 400/PK-12
PO Box 248, 229-334-4189
Allen Fort, supt. Fax 334-2109
www.quitman.k12.ga.us/
Quitman HS 100/9-12
173 Kaigler Rd, 229-334-4298
Jon-Erik Jones, prin. Fax 334-4700

**Glennville, Tattnall, Pop. 3,528**
Tattnall County SD
Supt. — See Reidsville
Glennville MS 300/6-8
721 E Barnard St 30427 912-654-1467
Cindy Boyett, prin. Fax 654-1300

**Gray, Jones, Pop. 3,239**
Jones County SD 4,900/PK-12
125 Stewart Ave 31032 478-986-3032
William Mathews, supt. Fax 986-4412
jones.schooldesk.net/
Gray Station MS 800/6-8
324 GA Highway 18 E 31032 478-986-2090
Wes Cavender, prin. Fax 986-2099
Jones County HS 1,100/9-12
339 Railroad St 31032 478-986-5444
Chuck Gibson, prin. Fax 986-1589
Other Schools – See Macon

**Grayson, Gwinnett, Pop. 2,619**
Gwinnett County SD
Supt. — See Suwanee
Bay Creek MS 1,000/6-8
821 Cooper Rd 30017 678-344-7570
Dr. Maggie Fehrman, prin. Fax 736-6908
Couch MS 1,000/6-8
1777 Grayson Hwy 30017 678-407-7272
Devon Williams, prin. Fax 407-7326

**Greensboro, Greene, Pop. 3,310**
Greene County SD 1,800/PK-12
101 E Third St 30642 706-453-7688
Philip Mellor, supt. Fax 453-9019
www.greene.k12.ga.us
Carson MS 400/6-8
1010 S Main St 30642 706-453-3308
Brock Miller, prin. Fax 453-4674
Greene County HS 500/9-12
1002 S Main St 30642 706-453-2271
Corey Stephens, prin. Fax 453-3311

**Greenville, Meriwether, Pop. 862**
Meriwether County SD 3,200/PK-12
PO Box 70 30222 706-672-4297
Dr. Tim Dixon, supt. Fax 672-1618
www.mcssga.org
Greenville MSHS 300/7-12
17656 Roosevelt Hwy 30222 706-672-4930
Thaddeus Jackson, prin. Fax 672-1424
Other Schools – See Manchester

**Griffin, Spalding, Pop. 23,259**
Griffin Spalding County School System 10,600/PK-12
PO Box N 30224 770-229-3700
Jim Smith, supt. Fax 229-3708
www.spalding.k12.ga.us
Carver Road MS 500/6-8
2185 Carver Rd 30224 770-229-3739
Tiffany Taylor, prin. Fax 229-3712
Cowan Road MS 600/6-8
1185 Cowan Rd 30223 770-229-3722
Laura Jordan, prin. Fax 227-8583
Griffin HS 1,300/9-12
1617 W Poplar St 30224 770-229-3752
Darrell Evans, prin. Fax 467-4644
Kennedy Road MS 500/6-8
280 Kennedy Rd 30223 770-229-3760
Dexter Sands, prin. Fax 467-4626
Rehoboth Road MS 700/6-8
1500 Rehoboth Rd 30224 770-229-3727
Larry Jones, prin. Fax 229-3770
Spalding HS 1,200/9-12
433 Wilson Rd 30224 770-229-3775
Lindy Pruitt, prin. Fax 227-6899

---

Southern Crescent Technical College Post-Sec.
501 Varsity Rd 30223 770-228-7348

**Grovetown, Columbia, Pop. 10,773**
Columbia County SD
Supt. — See Evans
Columbia MS 800/6-8
2013 Raider Way 30813 706-541-1252
Eli Putnam, prin. Fax 854-5820
Grovetown HS 1,400/9-12
2010 Warrior Way 30813 706-541-2723
Craig Baker, prin. Fax 447-2109
Grovetown MS 900/6-8
5463 Harlem Grovetown Rd 30813 706-855-2514
Tom Smallwood, prin. Fax 854-5822

**Guyton, Effingham, Pop. 1,661**
Effingham County SD
Supt. — See Springfield
Effingham County MS 900/6-8
1659 GA Highway 119 S 31312 912-772-7001
Billy Hughes, prin. Fax 772-7005
South Effingham HS 1,500/9-12
1220 Noel C Conaway Rd 31312 912-728-7511
Dr. Mark Winters, prin. Fax 728-7529
South Effingham MS 900/6-8
1200 Noel C Conaway Rd 31312 912-728-7500
April Hodges, prin. Fax 728-7508

**Hahira, Lowndes, Pop. 2,695**
Lowndes County SD
Supt. — See Valdosta
Hahira MS 800/6-8
101 S Nelson St 31632 229-794-2838
Janet Hendley, prin. Fax 794-3564

---

Valwood S 400/PK-12
4380 Old US 41 N 31632 229-242-8491
Dr. Darren Pascavage, hdmstr. Fax 245-7894

**Hamilton, Harris, Pop. 1,001**
Harris County SD 5,100/PK-12
132 Barnes Mill Rd 31811 706-628-4206
Fax 628-5609
www.harris.k12.ga.us
Educational Opportunity Center Alt
PO Box 388 31811 706-628-7452
Sanders Denham, prin. Fax 628-7480
Harris County - Carver MS 800/7-8
11696 US Highway 27 E 31811 706-628-4951
Stacey Carlisle, prin. Fax 628-5737
Harris County HS 1,500/9-12
8281 GA Highway 116 31811 706-628-4278
Roger Couch, prin. Fax 628-4335

**Hampton, Henry, Pop. 6,827**
Clayton County SD
Supt. — See Jonesboro
Lovejoy HS 2,000/9-12
1587 Mcdonough Rd 30228 770-473-2920
Dr. Keith Colbert, prin. Fax 473-2928
Lovejoy MS 600/6-8
1588 Lovejoy Rd 30228 770-473-2933
Debra Bostick-Smtih, prin. Fax 603-5777

Henry County SD
Supt. — See Mc Donough
Dutchtown HS 1,300/9-12
149 Mitchell Rd 30228 770-515-7510
Nicole Shaw, prin. Fax 515-7518
Dutchtown MS 1,100/6-8
155 Mitchell Rd 30228 770-515-7500
April Madden, prin. Fax 515-7505
Hampton HS 9-12
795 Hampton Locust Grove Rd 30228 770-946-7461
Todd Finn, prin. Fax 946-7468
Hampton MS 800/6-8
799 Hampton Locust Grove Rd 30228 770-707-2130
Dr. Carolyn Flemister-Bell, prin. Fax 946-3545

---

Bible Baptist Christian S 200/PK-12
2780 Mount Carmel Rd 30228 770-946-4700

**Harlem, Columbia, Pop. 2,608**
Columbia County SD
Supt. — See Evans
Harlem HS 700/9-12
1070 Appling Harlem Rd 30814 706-556-5980
Dietmar Perez, prin. Fax 854-5813
Harlem MS 600/6-8
375 W Forrest St 30814 706-556-5990
Carla Shelton, prin. Fax 854-5816

**Hartwell, Hart, Pop. 4,400**
Hart County SD 3,300/K-12
PO Box 696 30643 706-376-5141
Jerry Bell, supt. Fax 376-7046
www.hart.k12.ga.us
Hart County HS 900/9-12
59 Fifth St 30643 706-376-5461
Kevin Gaines, prin. Fax 856-7237
Hart County MS 800/6-8
176 Powell Rd 30643 706-376-5431
Dr. David Buddenbaum, prin. Fax 376-2207

**Hawkinsville, Pulaski, Pop. 4,540**
Pulaski County SD 1,300/PK-12
72 Warren St 31036 478-783-7200
Jane Williams, supt. Fax 783-7204
www.pulaski.k12.ga.us
Alternative Learning Center Alt
Warren St 31036 478-783-7265
Marvin Hill, dir. Fax 783-7204
Hawkinsville HS 400/9-12
24 Red Devil Dr 31036 478-783-7210
Russell Lawley, prin. Fax 783-7251
Pulaski County MS 300/6-8
8 Red Devil Dr 31036 478-892-7215
Natasha Kilgore, prin. Fax 783-7297

**Hazlehurst, Jeff Davis, Pop. 4,181**
Jeff Davis County SD 3,100/PK-12
PO Box 1780 31539 912-375-6700
Dr. Rob Brown, supt. Fax 375-6703
www.jeff-davis.k12.ga.us
Davis HS 700/9-12
156 Collins St 31539 912-375-6760
Cecelia McLoon, prin. Fax 375-0945
Davis MS 700/6-8
93 Collins St 31539 912-375-6750
Barry Waller, prin. Fax 375-6756

**Hephzibah, Richmond, Pop. 3,910**
Richmond County SD
Supt. — See Augusta
Hephzibah HS 1,100/9-12
4558 Brothersville Rd 30815 706-592-2089
Dr. Larina Thomas, prin. Fax 592-3975
Hephzibah MS 500/6-8
2427 Mims Rd 30815 706-592-4534
Doug Frierson, prin. Fax 592-3979
Morgan Road MS 600/6-8
3635 Hiers Blvd 30815 706-796-4992
Dr. Shontier Barnes, prin. Fax 560-3947
Pine Hill MS 600/6-8
2147 McElmurray Rd 30815 706-592-3730
Glenda Collingsworth, prin. Fax 592-3741
Spirit Creek MS 500/6-8
115 Dolphin Way 30815 706-592-3987
Dr. Melissa Shepard, prin. Fax 592-3999

**Hiawassee, Towns, Pop. 877**
Towns County SD 1,100/PK-12
67 Lakeview Cir Ste C 30546 706-896-2279
Dr. Darren Berrong, supt. Fax 896-2632
www.towns.k12.ga.us
Towns County HS 300/9-12
1400 Highway 76 E 30546 706-896-4131
Dr. Connie Hobbs, prin. Fax 896-6628
Towns County MS 300/6-8
1400 Highway 76 E 30546 706-896-4131
Erica Chastain, prin. Fax 896-6628

**Hinesville, Liberty, Pop. 31,826**
Liberty County SD 9,500/PK-12
200 Bradwell St 31313 912-876-2161
Dr. Valya Lee, supt. Fax 368-6201
www.liberty.k12.ga.us/
Bradwell Institute HS 1,800/9-12
100 Pafford St 31313 912-876-6121
Scott Carrier, prin. Fax 876-6914
Frasier MS 800/6-8
910 Long Frasier Dr 31313 912-877-5367
Jermaine Williams, prin. Fax 877-3291
Liberty County HS 1,200/9-12
3216 E Oglethorpe Hwy 31313 912-876-4316
Paula Scott, prin. Fax 876-4303

Snelson-Golden MS 800/6-8
465 Coates Rd 31313 912-877-3112
Dr. Sonia Bacon, prin. Fax 368-5342
Other Schools – See Midway

---

First Presbyterian Christian Academy 300/PK-12
308 E Court St 31313 912-876-0441

**Hiram, Paulding, Pop. 3,455**
Paulding County SD
Supt. — See Dallas
Hiram HS 1,700/9-12
702 Virgie Ballentine Dr 30141 770-443-1182
Misty Cooksey, prin. Fax 439-5053

---

Grace Christian Academy 300/PK-12
5790 Powder Springs/Dallas 30141 770-222-8955
Eddie Fincher, hdmstr. Fax 222-3321
Vogue Beauty School Post-Sec.
3655 Macland Rd 30141 770-943-6811

**Hogansville, Troup, Pop. 3,003**
Troup County SD
Supt. — See LaGrange
Callaway HS 800/9-12
221 Whitfield Rd 30230 706-845-2070
Jonathan Laney, prin. Fax 845-2071

**Homer, Banks, Pop. 1,123**
Banks County SD 2,900/K-12
102 Highway 51 S 30547 706-677-2224
Stan Davis, supt. Fax 677-2223
www.banks.k12.ga.us
Banks County HS 800/9-12
1486 Historic Homer Hwy # A 30547 706-677-2221
Dr. Joseph Goodroe, prin. Fax 677-2688
Banks County MS 700/6-8
712 Thompson St 30547 706-677-2277
Hank Ramey, prin. Fax 677-5227

**Homerville, Clinch, Pop. 2,408**
Clinch County SD 1,400/PK-12
46 S College St 31634 912-487-5321
Dr. Donna Ryan, supt. Fax 487-5068
www.clinchcounty.com/
Clinch County HS 400/8-12
863 Carswell St 31634 912-487-5366
Denise Brown, prin. Fax 487-3272

**Hoschton, Jackson, Pop. 1,352**
Gwinnett County SD
Supt. — See Suwanee
Mill Creek HS 3,500/9-12
4400 Braselton Hwy 30548 678-714-5850
Jason Lane, prin. Fax 714-5863
Osborne MS 1,600/6-8
4404 Braselton Hwy 30548 770-904-5400
Kenney Wells, prin. Fax 765-5981

**Irwinton, Wilkinson, Pop. 587**
Wilkinson County SD 1,600/PK-12
PO Box 206 31042 478-946-5521
Dr. Aaron Geter, supt. Fax 946-5565
www.wilkinson.k12.ga.us/
Wilkinson County HS 400/9-12
PO Box 547 31042 478-946-2441
Jerome Miles, prin. Fax 946-7134
Wilkinson County MS 400/6-8
PO Box 527 31042 478-946-2541
Dr. Angela Smith, prin. Fax 946-8981

**Jackson, Butts, Pop. 4,955**
Butts County SD 3,500/PK-12
181 N Mulberry St 30233 770-504-2300
Robert Costley, supt. Fax 504-2305
www.butts.k12.ga.us
Henderson MS 800/6-8
494 George Tate Dr 30233 770-504-2310
Renee Burgdorf, prin. Fax 504-2315
Jackson HS 1,000/9-12
717 S Harkness St 30233 770-504-2340
Jay Homan, prin. Fax 504-2341

**Jasper, Pickens, Pop. 3,647**
Pickens County SD 4,400/K-12
100 D B Carrol 30143 706-253-1700
Dr. Lula Mae Perry, supt. Fax 253-1705
www.pickenscountyschools.org
Jasper MS 500/6-8
339 W Church St 30143 706-253-1760
Shane Purdy, prin. Fax 253-1765
Pickens County HS 1,200/9-12
500 Dragon Dr 30143 706-253-1800
Chris LeMieux, prin. Fax 253-1805
Pickens County MS 500/6-8
1802 Refuge Rd 30143 706-253-1830
Pennie Fowler, prin. Fax 253-1835

---

Chattahoochee Technical College Post-Sec.
100 Campus Dr 30143 706-253-4500

**Jefferson, Jackson, Pop. 9,285**
Jackson County SD 6,800/PK-12
1660 Winder Hwy 30549 706-367-5151
April Howard Ed.D., supt. Fax 367-9457
www.jackson.k12.ga.us
Jackson County Comprehensive HS 1,000/9-12
1668 Winder Hwy 30549 706-367-5003
Pete Jones, prin. Fax 367-5007
West Jackson MS 800/6-8
400 Gum Springs Church Rd 30549 706-654-2775
Joe Cobb, prin. Fax 824-1969
Other Schools – See Commerce

Jefferson CSD 2,800/PK-12
345 Storey Ln 30549 706-367-2880
Dr. John Jackson, supt. Fax 367-2291
www.jeffcityschools.org/
Jefferson HS 800/9-12
575 Washington St 30549 706-367-2881
Dr. Kevin Smith, prin. Fax 367-1884
Jefferson MS 600/6-8
100 Dragon Dr 30549 706-367-2882
Kenneth Martin, prin. Fax 367-5207

**Jeffersonville, Twiggs, Pop. 1,016**
Twiggs County SD 900/PK-12
PO Box 232 31044 478-945-3127
Elgin Dixon, supt. Fax 945-3078
www.twiggs.k12.ga.us
Twiggs County HS 300/9-12
375 Watson Dr 31044 478-945-3112
Jamie Paulk, prin. Fax 945-3140
Twiggs County MS 300/5-8
375 Watson Dr 31044 478-945-3113
Trendie Spires, prin. Fax 945-3140

---

Twiggs Academy 100/PK-12
961 Hamlin Floyd Rd 31044 478-945-3175

**Jesup, Wayne, Pop. 10,029**
Wayne County SD 5,400/PK-12
555 Sunset Blvd 31545 912-427-1000
Dr. Jay Brinson, supt. Fax 427-1004
www.wayne.k12.ga.us
Puckett MS 600/6-8
475 Durrence Rd 31545 912-427-1061
Dr. Pam Shuman, prin. Fax 427-1069
Wayne County HS 1,400/9-12
1 Jacket Dr 31545 912-427-1088
Hubert Adams, prin. Fax 427-1081
Williams MS 500/6-8
1175 S US Highway 301 31546 912-427-1025
Dr. Reggie Burgess, prin. Fax 427-1032

---

Altamaha Technical College Post-Sec.
1777 W Cherry St 31545 912-427-5800

**Johns Creek, Fulton, Pop. 74,864**
Fulton County SD
Supt. — See Atlanta
Autrey Mill MS 1,400/6-8
4110 Old Alabama Rd, 770-521-7622
Trey Martin, prin. Fax 521-7630
Chattahoochee HS 1,900/9-12
5230 Taylor Rd, 770-521-7600
Tim Corrigan, prin. Fax 521-7659
Johns Creek HS 1,800/9-12
5575 State Bridge Rd, 770-623-2138
Jimmy Zoll, prin. Fax 623-2139
Northview HS 1,800/9-12
10625 Parsons Rd, 770-497-3828
Brian Downey, prin. Fax 497-3844
River Trail MS 1,500/6-8
10795 Rogers Cir, 470-254-3860
Dawn Melin, prin. Fax 254-3866
Taylor Road MS 1,000/6-8
5150 Taylor Rd, 470-254-7090
Ed Williamson, prin. Fax 254-5609

---

Mt. Pisgah Christian S 800/PK-12
9820 Nesbit Ferry Rd, 678-336-3443
John Marshall, head sch Fax 336-3399

**Jonesboro, Clayton, Pop. 4,639**
Clayton County SD 50,800/PK-12
1058 5th Ave 30236 770-473-2700
Luvenia Jackson, supt. Fax 473-2706
www.clayton.k12.ga.us
Jonesboro HS 1,300/9-12
7728 Mount Zion Blvd 30236 770-473-2855
Felicia Brown, prin. Fax 603-5177
Jonesboro MS 800/6-8
1308 Arnold St 30236 678-610-4331
Lisa Hightower, prin. Fax 610-4347
Kendrick MS 800/6-8
7971 Kendrick Rd 30238 770-472-8400
Kimberly Dugger, prin. Fax 472-8413
Mt. Zion HS 1,600/9-12
2535 Mount Zion Pkwy 30236 770-473-2940
Melvin Blocker, prin. Fax 473-2784
Mundy's Mill HS 1,700/9-12
9652 Fayetteville Rd 30238 678-817-3000
Dr. William Greene, prin. Fax 817-3007
Mundy's Mill MS 800/6-8
1251 Mundys Mill Rd 30238 770-473-2880
Sharra Cunningham, prin. Fax 603-5779
Perry Learning Center Alt
137 Spring St 30236 770-515-7601
Dr. Terry Young, dir. Fax 515-7689
Pointe South MS 800/6-8
8495 Thomas Rd 30238 770-473-2890
Sandra Nicholson, prin. Fax 477-4603
Roberts MS 700/6-8
1905 Walt Stephens Rd 30236 678-479-0100
Charmine Johnson, prin. Fax 479-0114
Stillwell Fine Arts Magnet HS 9-12
2530 Mount Zion Pkwy 30236 770-472-2838
Michael Robinson, prin.
Other Schools – See College Park, Forest Park, Hampton, Morrow, Rex, Riverdale

---

Everest Institute Post-Sec.
6431 Tara Blvd 30236 770-603-0000
Laurus Technical Institute Post-Sec.
9540 Tara Blvd 30236 770-477-2799

**Kathleen, Houston**
Houston County SD
Supt. — See Perry
Mossy Creek MS 700/6-8
200 Danny Carpenter Dr 31047 478-988-6171
Dr. Andy Gentry, prin. Fax 218-7538
Veterans HS 1,300/9-12
340 Piney Grove Rd 31047 478-218-7537
Christopher Brown, prin. Fax 217-7570

**Kennesaw, Cobb, Pop. 28,907**
Cobb County SD
Supt. — See Marietta
Awtrey MS 900/6-8
3601 Nowlin Rd NW 30144 770-975-6615
Jeffrey Crawford, prin. Fax 975-6617
Harrison HS 2,000/9-12
4500 Due West Rd NW 30152 678-594-8104
Ashlynn Campbell, prin. Fax 594-8106
Kennesaw Mountain HS 2,000/9-12
1898 Kennesaw Due West NW 30152 678-594-8190
Dr. Mark Trachtenbroit, prin. Fax 594-8192
Lost Mountain MS 1,000/6-8
700 Old Mountain Rd NW 30152 678-594-8224
Candace Wilkes, prin. Fax 594-8226
McClure MS 1,100/6-8
3660 Old Stilesboro Rd NW 30152 678-331-8131
Kelly Metcalfe, prin. Fax 331-8132
North Cobb HS 2,700/9-12
3400 Highway 293 N 30144 770-975-6685
Joseph Horton, prin. Fax 975-6687
Palmer MS 1,000/6-8
690 N Booth Rd NW 30144 770-591-5020
Lisa Jackson, prin. Fax 591-5032
Pine Mountain MS 700/6-8
2720 Pine Mountain Cir NW 30152 678-594-8252
Dr. Jasmine Kullar, prin. Fax 594-8254

---

Cobb Beauty College Post-Sec.
3096 Cherokee St NW 30144 770-424-6915
Devereux-Georgia Treatment Network Post-Sec.
PO Box 1688 30156 800-342-3357
Empire Beauty School Post-Sec.
425 Ernest Barrett Pkwy #H2 30144 770-419-2303
ITT Technical Institute Post-Sec.
2065 ITT Tech Way NW 30144 770-426-2300
Kennesaw State University Post-Sec.
1000 Chastain Rd NW 30144 770-423-6000
Mount Paran Christian S 1,200/PK-12
1275 Stanley Rd NW 30152 770-578-0182
North Cobb Christian S 800/PK-12
4500 Eagle Dr 30144 770-975-0252
Todd Clingman, head sch Fax 975-8446
Shiloh Hills Christian S 300/PK-12
260 Hawkins Store Rd NE 30144 770-926-7729
Terry Farrant, admin. Fax 926-3762
TLE Christian Academy 50/1-12
2765 S Main St 30144 770-218-1790

**Kingsland, Camden, Pop. 15,425**
Camden County SD 9,400/PK-12
311 S East St 31548 912-729-5687
Dr. William Hardin, supt. Fax 729-1489
www.camden.k12.ga.us
Camden County HS 2,800/9-12
6300 Laurel Island Pkwy 31548 912-729-7318
Dr. John Tucker, prin. Fax 729-7627
Camden MS 1,100/6-8
1300 Middle School Rd 31548 912-729-3113
Thoms McClendon, prin. Fax 729-7489
Other Schools – See Saint Marys

**La Fayette, Walker, Pop. 6,986**
Walker County SD 9,200/PK-12
201 S Duke St 30728 706-638-1240
Damon Raines, supt. Fax 638-7827
www.walkerschools.org
La Fayette HS 1,200/9-12
100 Rambler Dr 30728 706-638-2342
Mike Culberson, prin. Fax 638-4767
La Fayette MS 900/6-8
419 Roadrunner Blvd 30728 706-638-6440
Karen Hughes, prin. Fax 638-7616
Other Schools – See Flintstone, Rossville

**LaGrange, Troup, Pop. 29,111**
Troup County SD 11,900/PK-12
PO Box 1228 30241 706-812-7900
Dr. Cole Pugh, supt. Fax 812-7904
www.troup.org/
Callaway MS 700/6-8
2244 Hammett Rd 30241 706-845-2080
Melissa Trimeloni, prin. Fax 845-2081
Gardner Newman MS 1,000/6-8
101 Shannon Dr 30241 706-883-1535
Derek Pitts, prin. Fax 883-1562
Hope Academy Alt
200 Mooty Bridge Rd 30240 706-812-7988
Karla Fagg, prin. Fax 812-7927
La Grange HS 1,400/9-12
516 N Greenwood St 30240 706-883-1590
Dr. Penny Johnson, prin. Fax 812-7976
Long Cane MS 1,000/6-8
326 Long Cane Rd 30240 706-845-2085
Chip Giles, prin. Fax 845-2086
Troup County Comprehensive HS 1,300/9-12
1920 Hamilton Rd 30241 706-812-7957
Chip Medders, prin. Fax 812-7960
Other Schools – See Hogansville

---

Lafayette Christian S 300/PK-12
1904 Hamilton Rd 30241 706-884-6684
John Cipolla, hdmstr. Fax 882-2515
LaGrange Academy 200/PK-12
1501 Vernon Rd 30240 706-882-8097
Carl Parke, head sch Fax 882-8640
LaGrange College Post-Sec.
601 Broad St 30240 706-880-8000
West Georgia Technical College Post-Sec.
1 College Cir 30240 706-845-4323

**Lakeland, Lanier, Pop. 3,308**
Lanier County SD 1,800/PK-12
247 S Highway 221 31635 229-482-3966
Dr. Keith Humphrey, supt. Fax 482-3020
www.lanier.k12.ga.us/
Lanier County HS 400/9-12
52 W Patten Ave 31635 229-482-3868
Gene Culpepper, prin. Fax 482-3368
Lanier County MS 400/6-8
52 W Patten Ave 31635 229-482-8247
Reada Hamm, prin. Fax 482-3643

**Lawrenceville, Gwinnett, Pop. 27,847**
Gwinnett County SD
Supt. — See Suwanee

Archer HS 1,900/9-12
2255 New Hope Rd 30045 678-407-7700
Ken Johnson, prin. Fax 407-7725
Central Gwinnett HS 2,600/9-12
564 W Crogan St 30046 770-963-8041
Maryanne Grimes, prin. Fax 442-5152
Creekland MS 2,300/6-8
170 Russell Rd 30043 770-338-4700
Dr. Eddie Maresh, prin. Fax 338-4703
Crews MS 1,200/6-8
1000 Old Snellville Hwy 30044 770-982-6940
Dr. Stacey Schepens, prin. Fax 982-6942
Discovery HS 9-12
1335 Old Norcross Rd 30046 678-226-4250
John Campbell, prin. Fax 377-3983
Five Forks MS 1,100/6-8
3250 River Dr 30044 770-972-1506
Christine Douthart, prin. Fax 736-4547
Gwinnett InterVention Education Ctr East 200/Alt
723 Hi Hope Rd 30043 770-338-4855
Durrant Williams, prin. Fax 338-4899
Jordan MS 6-8
8 Village Way 30046 770-822-6500
Melissa Walker, prin. Fax 407-8889
Maxwell HS of Technology Vo/Tech
990 McElvaney Ln 30044 770-963-6838
Dr. Jeff Hall, prin. Fax 338-4612
Moore MS 900/6-8
1221 Lawrenceville Hwy 30046 678-226-7100
Lamont Mays, prin. Fax 226-7103
Mountain View HS 1,900/9-12
2351 Sunny Hill Rd 30043 678-407-7600
Keith Chaney, prin. Fax 407-7605
Phoenix HS 600/9-12
501 W Pike St 30046 770-513-6862
Donna Scott, prin. Fax 513-6864
Richards MS 1,400/6-8
3555 Sugarloaf Pkwy 30044 770-995-7133
Mark McCain, prin. Fax 338-4791
Sweetwater MS 1,700/6-8
3500 Cruse Rd 30044 770-923-4131
Dr. Gene Taylor, prin. Fax 806-8930

---

Empire Beauty School Post-Sec.
1455 Pleasant Hill Rd #105 30044 770-564-0725
Georgia Gwinnett College Post-Sec.
1000 University Center Ln 30043 678-407-5000
Gerard Preparatory S 200/PK-12
263 Jackson St 30043 770-277-4722
J.G. Sinclair, admin. Fax 277-4365
Gwinnett Technical College Post-Sec.
5150 Sugarloaf Pkwy 30043 770-962-7580
Strong Wall Academy 100/PK-12
PO Box 1647 30046 678-679-3070
Anthony Knight, hdmstr. Fax 679-3075

**Leesburg, Lee, Pop. 2,853**
Lee County SD 6,000/PK-12
PO Box 399 31763 229-903-2100
Dr. Lawrence Walters, supt. Fax 903-2130
www.lee.k12.ga.us
Lee County 9th Grade Campus 500/9-9
370 Leslie Hwy 31763 229-903-3590
Tim Mears, prin. Fax 903-3595
Lee County HS 1,200/10-12
1 Trojan Way 31763 229-903-2260
Kevin Dowling, prin. Fax 903-2291
Lee County MS East 6-8
185 Firetower Rd 31763 229-903-3500
Kelli Duke, prin. Fax 903-3521
Lee County MS West 1,500/6-8
190 Smithville Rd N 31763 229-903-2140
John Savelle, prin. Fax 903-2160
Transitional Learning Center Alt
190 Smithville Rd N 31763 229-903-3920
Vince Grace, dir. Fax 903-3925

**Lexington, Oglethorpe, Pop. 225**
Oglethorpe County SD 2,300/PK-12
735 Athens Rd 30648 706-743-8128
Beverly Levine, supt. Fax 743-3211
www.oglethorpe.k12.ga.us
Oglethorpe County HS 700/9-12
749 Athens Rd 30648 706-743-8124
Susie Johnson, prin. Fax 743-3536
Other Schools – See Crawford

**Lilburn, Gwinnett, Pop. 11,365**
Gwinnett County SD
Supt. — See Suwanee
Berkmar HS 3,000/9-12
405 Pleasant Hill Rd NW 30047 770-806-3700
Alfred Taylor, prin. Fax 806-3715
Berkmar MS 1,000/6-8
4355 Lawrenceville Hwy NW 30047 770-638-2300
Nicole Tubbs, prin. Fax 638-2309
Lilburn MS 1,400/6-8
4994 Lawrenceville Hwy NW 30047 770-921-1776
Dr. Yvette Arthur, prin. Fax 806-3866
Parkview HS 2,700/9-12
998 Cole Dr SW 30047 770-921-2874
David Smith, prin. Fax 806-3797
Trickum MS 1,900/6-8
130 Killian Hill Rd SW 30047 770-921-2705
Kay Sands, prin. Fax 806-3742

---

Al-Falah Academy 200/PK-10
4805 Lawrenceville Hwy #220 30047 678-502-7211
Sr. Jelena Naim, prin. Fax 430-3513
Gwinnett College Post-Sec.
4230 Lawrencevll Hwy NW #11 30047 770-381-7200
Killian Hill Christian S 400/K-12
151 Arcado Rd SW 30047 770-921-3224
Providence Christian Academy 600/K-12
4575 Lawrenceville Hwy NW 30047 770-279-7200
Dr. James Vaught, hdmstr. Fax 279-8258

**Lincolnton, Lincoln, Pop. 1,557**
Lincoln County SD 1,200/PK-12
PO Box 39 30817 706-359-3742
Brian Campbell, supt. Fax 359-7938
www.lincolncountyschools.org
Lincoln County HS 400/9-12
200 Charles Ward Elam Dr 30817 706-359-3121
Howie Gunby, prin. Fax 359-3552
Lincoln County MS 300/6-8
200B Charles Ward Elam Dr 30817 706-359-3069
Pam Carmichael, prin. Fax 359-2200

**Lindale, Floyd, Pop. 4,135**
Floyd County SD
Supt. — See Rome
Pepperell HS 800/9-12
3 Dragon Dr SE 30147 706-236-1844
Phil Ray, prin. Fax 236-1846
Pepperell MS 800/6-8
200 Hughes Dairy Rd SE 30147 706-236-1849
Becky McCoy, prin. Fax 802-6776

**Lithia Springs, Douglas, Pop. 15,167**
Douglas County SD
Supt. — See Douglasville
Lithia Springs HS 1,500/9-12
2520 E County Line Rd 30122 770-651-6700
Dr. Garrick Askew, prin. Fax 732-2644
Turner MS 600/6-8
7101 Turner Dr 30122 770-651-5500
Darron Franklin, prin. Fax 651-5503

---

Colonial Hills Christian S 300/PK-12
7131 Mount Vernon Rd 30122 770-941-6342
David Hicks, admin. Fax 941-2090
Lithia Christian Academy 200/PK-12
2548 Vulcan Dr 30122 770-941-5406
Lanier Motes, admin. Fax 941-9599

**Lithonia, DeKalb, Pop. 1,901**
DeKalb County SD
Supt. — See Stone Mountain
Arabia Mountain HS 1,600/9-12
6610 Browns Mill Rd 30038 678-875-3602
Rodney Swanson, prin. Fax 875-3610
King HS 1,500/9-12
3991 Snapfinger Rd 30038 678-874-5402
Kerby Bullard, prin. Fax 874-5410
Lithonia HS 1,300/9-12
2440 Phillips Rd 30058 678-676-2902
Yolanda Peek, prin. Fax 676-2910
Lithonia MS 1,200/6-8
2451 Randall Ave 30058 678-875-0702
Debra Phillips, prin. Fax 875-0710
Miller Grove HS 1,600/9-12
2645 DeKalb Medical Pkwy 30058 678-875-1102
Matthew Priester, prin. Fax 875-1110
Redan MS 900/6-8
1775 Young Rd 30058 678-874-7902
Dr. Donald Mason, prin. Fax 874-7910
Salem MS 1,100/6-8
5333 Salem Rd 30038 678-676-9402
Terrence Harvey, prin. Fax 676-9410

---

Luther Rice University and Seminary Post-Sec.
3038 Evans Mill Rd 30038 770-484-1204

**Locust Grove, Henry, Pop. 5,279**
Henry County SD
Supt. — See Mc Donough
Locust Grove HS 1,100/9-12
3275 S Ola Rd 30248 770-898-1452
Lisa Gugino, prin. Fax 898-7076
Locust Grove MS 1,000/6-8
3315 S Ola Rd 30248 770-957-6055
Tony Townsend, prin. Fax 957-7160
Luella HS 2,000/9-12
603 Walker Dr 30248 770-898-9822
Jerry Smith, prin. Fax 898-9625
Luella MS 800/6-8
2075 Hmpton Locust Grove Rd 30248 678-583-8919
Mary Carol Stanley, prin. Fax 583-8920

---

Strong Rock Christian S 700/PK-12
4200 Strong Rock Pkwy 30248 678-833-1200
Patrick Stuart M.A., head sch Fax 833-1395

**Loganville, Walton, Pop. 10,219**
Gwinnett County SD
Supt. — See Suwanee
Grayson HS 2,600/9-12
50 Hope Hollow Rd 30052 770-554-1071
Dana Pugh, prin. Fax 554-1074
McConnell MS 1,500/6-8
550 Ozora Rd 30052 770-554-1000
Clent Chatham, prin. Fax 554-1003
Snell MS 1,200/6-8
3800 Brushy Fork Rd 30052 770-554-7750
Allen Craine, prin. Fax 554-7749

Walton County SD
Supt. — See Monroe
Loganville HS 1,500/9-12
100 Trident Trl 30052 678-684-2880
Mike Robison, prin. Fax 684-2955
Loganville MS 1,100/6-8
4869 Bay Creek Church Rd 30052 678-684-2960
Christy Bowman, prin. Fax 684-2983
Walnut Grove HS 1,200/9-12
4863 Guthrie Cemetery Rd 30052 678-507-3900
Dr. Sean Callahan, prin. Fax 507-3901
Walton County Alternative Education Alt
4869 Bay Creek Church Rd 30052 678-684-2980
Meredith Cannon, dir. Fax 684-2983
Youth MS 1,100/6-8
1804 Highway 81 30052 678-684-2710
David Todd, prin. Fax 466-8596

---

Covenant Christian Academy 300/PK-12
3425 Loganville Hwy 30052 770-466-7890
Emmaline McKinnon, admin. Fax 466-2833
Gwinnett Christian Academy 100/PK-12
3156 Langley Rd 30052 770-982-3773
Rev. Rick McClain, head sch Fax 982-3773
Loganville Christian Academy 600/PK-12
2575 Highway 81 30052 770-554-9888
Christy Monda, admin. Fax 554-9881

**Lookout Mountain, Walker, Pop. 1,588**

---

Covenant College Post-Sec.
14049 Scenic Hwy 30750 706-820-1560

**Louisville, Jefferson, Pop. 2,485**
Jefferson County SD 2,900/PK-12
1001 Peachtree St 30434 478-625-7626
Dr. Molly Howard, supt. Fax 625-7459
www.jefferson.k12.ga.us
Hi Tech S Alt
1200 School St 30434 478-625-7764
Ken Hildebrant, prin. Fax 625-3120
Jefferson County HS 800/9-12
1157 Warrior Trl 30434 478-625-9991
Dr. Alan Long, prin. Fax 625-8988
Louisville MS 300/6-8
1200 School St 30434 478-625-7764
Ken Hildebrant, prin. Fax 625-3120
Other Schools – See Wrens

---

Jefferson Academy 200/K-12
2264 US Highway 1 N 30434 478-625-8861

**Ludowici, Long, Pop. 1,650**
Long County SD 2,100/PK-12
PO Box 428 31316 912-545-2367
Dr. Robert Waters, supt. Fax 545-2380
www.longcountyps.com
Long County HS 600/9-12
PO Box 579 31316 912-545-2135
Scotty Hattaway, prin. Fax 545-2136
Long County MS 6-8
PO Box 729 31316 912-545-2069
Heath Crane, prin. Fax 545-2775

**Lumpkin, Stewart, Pop. 2,722**
Stewart County SD 500/PK-12
PO Box 547 31815 229-838-4329
Valerie Roberts, supt. Fax 838-6984
www.stewart.k12.ga.us/
Stewart County HS 100/9-12
PO Box 547 31815 229-838-4301
SaJuanna Williams, admin. Fax 838-4352
Stewart County MS 100/6-8
PO Box 547 31815 229-838-4301
SaJuana Williams, prin. Fax 838-4352

**Lyons, Toombs, Pop. 4,285**
Toombs County SD 3,000/PK-12
117 E Wesley Ave 30436 912-526-3141
Sonya Ross, supt. Fax 526-3291
www.toombscountyschools.org
Toombs County HS 700/9-12
500 Bulldog Rd 30436 912-526-6068
Chris Bell, prin. Fax 526-4612
Toombs County MS 700/6-8
701 Bulldog Rd 30436 912-526-8363
Pam Sears, prin. Fax 526-0240

---

Toombs Christian Academy 300/PK-12
PO Box 227 30436 912-526-8938

**Mableton, Cobb, Pop. 36,289**
Cobb County SD
Supt. — See Marietta
Floyd MS 900/6-8
4803 Floyd Rd SW 30126 770-819-2453
Dr. Teresa Hargrett, prin. Fax 819-2455
Lindley MS 1,300/7-8
50 Veterans Memorial Hwy SE 30126 770-819-2496
Lisa Williams, prin. Fax 819-2498
Pebblebrook HS 2,000/9-12
991 Old Alabama Rd SW 30126 770-819-2521
Travis Joshua, prin. Fax 819-2523

---

Cumberland Christian Academy 100/6-8
4900 Floyd Rd SW 30126 678-426-1600
Dr. Lee Campbell, hdmstr. Fax 819-9091
Whitefield Academy 700/PK-12
1 Whitefield Dr SE 30126 678-305-3000
Kevin Bracher Ph.D., hdmstr. Fax 305-3010

**Mc Donough, Henry, Pop. 21,578**
Henry County SD 39,700/PK-12
33 N Zack Hinton Pkwy 30253 770-957-6601
Rodney Bowler, supt. Fax 914-6178
www.henry.k12.ga.us
Eagle's Landing HS 1,100/9-12
301 Tunis Rd 30253 770-954-9515
Gabriel Crerie, prin. Fax 914-9789
Eagle's Landing MS 900/6-8
295 Tunis Rd 30253 770-914-8189
Derrick Thomas, prin. Fax 914-2989
Henry County HS 1,000/9-12
401 Tomlinson St 30253 770-957-3943
Scott John, prin. Fax 957-5052
Henry County MS 800/6-8
166 Holly Smith Dr 30253 770-957-3945
Dr. Kimberly Anderson, prin. Fax 898-4986
Mainstay Academy Alt
354 N Ola Rd 30252 678-432-2310
Debbie Rush, dir. Fax 507-6259
Ola HS 1,500/9-12
357 N Ola Rd 30252 770-288-3222
David Shedd, prin. Fax 288-3230
Ola MS 1,100/6-8
353 N Ola Rd 30252 770-288-2108
Kathleen Truitt, prin. Fax 288-2114
Union Grove HS 1,600/9-12
120 E Lake Rd 30252 678-583-8502
Ryan Meeks, prin. Fax 583-8850
Union Grove MS 1,200/6-8
210 E Lake Rd 30252 678-583-8978
Dr. Matt Isenberg, prin. Fax 583-8580
Other Schools – See Hampton, Locust Grove, Stockbridge

---

Creekside Christian Academy 500/PK-12
175 Foster Dr 30253 770-961-9300
Rodney Knox, hdmstr. Fax 960-1875

Eagle's Landing Christian Academy 1,100/PK-12
2400 Highway 42 N 30253 770-957-2927
Chuck Gilliam, admin. Fax 957-2290

**Macon, Bibb, Pop. 90,157**
Bibb County SD 24,700/PK-12
484 Mulberry St 31201 478-765-8711
Dr. Curtis Jones, supt. Fax 765-8549
www.bcsdk12.net
Appling MS 600/6-8
1210 Shurling Dr 31211 478-779-2200
Dr. Christopher Ridley, prin. Fax 779-2202
Ballard-Hudson MS 500/6-8
1070 Anthony Rd 31204 478-779-3400
Eclan David, prin. Fax 779-3396
Burghard Opportunity Center Alt
6020 Bloomfield Rd 31206 478-779-2900
Chanelle Sweet, prin.
Central HS 1,000/9-12
2155 Napier Ave 31204 478-779-2300
Emanuel Frazier, prin. Fax 779-2307
Howard HS 1,200/9-12
6400 Forsyth Rd 31210 478-779-4850
Dr. Shannon Norfleet, prin. Fax 779-4860
Howard MS 1,000/6-8
6600 Forsyth Rd 31210 478-779-3500
Lindsey Allen, prin. Fax 779-3458
Hutchings College & Career Academy Vo/Tech
2011 Riverside Dr 31204 478-779-2550
Darrick McCray, coord. Fax 779-2540
Miller Magnet MS 800/6-8
751 Hendley St 31204 478-779-4050
Dr. Sherri Flagg, prin. Fax 779-4032
Northeast HS 700/9-12
1646 Upper River Rd 31211 478-779-4100
Steven Jones, prin. Fax 779-4136
Rutland HS 1,100/9-12
6250 Skipper Rd 31216 478-779-3100
Kent Sparks, prin. Fax 779-3045
Rutland MS 1,000/6-8
6260 Skipper Rd 31216 478-779-4400
Richard Key, prin. Fax 779-4373
Southwest HS 1,000/9-12
1775 Williamson Rd 31206 478-779-4500
Dexter Martin, prin. Fax 779-4484
Weaver MS 1,000/6-8
2570 Heath Rd 31206 478-779-4650
Jim Montgomery, prin. Fax 779-4627
Westside HS 1,200/9-12
2851 Heath Rd 31206 478-779-3800
Dr. Julia Daniely, prin. Fax 779-3832

Jones County SD
Supt. — See Gray
Clifton Ridge MS 500/6-8
169 Dusty Ln 31211 478-743-5182
Charles Lundy, prin. Fax 743-8282

---

American Professional Institute Post-Sec.
1667 Eisenhower Pkwy 31206 478-314-4444
Central Fellowship Christian Academy 300/PK-12
8460 Hawkinsville Rd 31216 478-788-6909
Central Georgia Technical College Post-Sec.
3300 Macon Tech Dr 31206 478-757-3400
Covenant Academy 400/PK-12
4652 Ayers Rd 31210 478-471-0285
First Presbyterian Day S 1,000/PK-12
5671 Calvin Dr 31210 478-477-6505
Georgia Academy for the Blind Post-Sec.
2895 Vineville Ave 31204 478-751-6083
Medical Center of Central Georgia Post-Sec.
777 Hemlock St 31201 478-633-1234
Mercer University in Macon Post-Sec.
1400 Coleman Ave 31207 478-301-2700
Middle Georgia Christian S 100/PK-12
5859 Thomaston Rd 31220 478-757-9585
Middle Georgia State College Post-Sec.
100 College Station Dr 31206 478-471-2700
Miller-Motte Technical College Post-Sec.
175 Tom Hill Sr Blvd 31210 478-803-4800
Montessori of Macon 100/PK-12
855 Tolliver Pl 31210 478-757-8927
Mount de Sales Academy 700/6-12
851 Orange St 31201 478-751-3240
David Held, pres. Fax 751-3241
Stratford Academy 900/PK-12
6010 Peake Rd 31220 478-477-8073
Dr. Robert Veto, head sch Fax 477-0299
Tattnall Square Academy 600/PK-12
111 Trojan Trl 31210 478-477-6760
Dr. Brenda Shuman-Riley, head sch Fax 474-7887
Virginia College Post-Sec.
1901 Paul Walsh Dr 31206 478-803-4600
Wesleyan College Post-Sec.
4760 Forsyth Rd 31210 800-447-6610
Windsor Academy 200/PK-12
4150 Jones Rd 31216 478-781-1621

**Mc Rae, Telfair, Pop. 5,685**
Telfair County SD 1,800/PK-12
PO Box 240 31055 229-868-5661
Lenard Harrelson, supt. Fax 868-5549
www.telfairschools.org
Telfair County HS 400/9-12
PO Box 240 31055 229-868-6096
Daymond Ray, prin. Fax 868-7221
Telfair County MS 400/6-8
PO Box 240 31055 229-868-7465
Christopher Ellis, prin. Fax 868-2616

**Manchester, Meriwether, Pop. 4,197**
Meriwether County SD
Supt. — See Greenville
Manchester HS 500/9-12
405 N 5th Ave 31816 706-846-8445
Nicole Kendrick, prin. Fax 846-2082
Manchester MS 400/6-8
231 W Perry St 31816 706-846-2846
Lashanda Acres, prin. Fax 846-8242

**Marietta, Cobb, Pop. 54,999**
Cobb County SD 105,700/PK-12
514 Glover St SE 30060 770-426-3300
Chris Ragsdale, supt. Fax 426-3329
www.cobb.k12.ga.us
Daniell MS 1,000/6-8
2900 Scott Rd 30066 678-594-8048
David Nelson, prin. Fax 594-8050
Dickerson MS 1,200/6-8
855 Woodlawn Dr NE 30068 770-578-2710
Dr. Carole Brink, prin. Fax 578-2712
Dodgen MS 1,200/6-8
1725 Bill Murdock Rd 30062 770-578-2726
Dr. Loralee Hill, prin. Fax 578-2728
East Cobb MS 1,300/6-8
380 Holt Rd NE 30068 770-578-2740
Leetonia Young, prin. Fax 578-2742
Hightower Trail MS 1,000/6-8
3905 Post Oak Tritt Rd 30062 770-578-7225
Laura Montgomery, prin. Fax 578-7227
Kell HS 1,700/9-12
4770 Lee Waters Rd 30066 678-494-7844
Ed Wagner, prin. Fax 494-7846
Lassiter HS 2,000/9-12
2601 Shallowford Rd 30066 678-494-7863
Dr. Chris Richie, prin. Fax 494-7865
Mabry MS 800/6-8
2700 Jims Rd NE 30066 770-928-5546
Merrilee Heflin, prin. Fax 928-5548
McCleskey MS 700/6-8
4080 Maybreeze Rd 30066 770-928-5560
Claire Lyons, prin. Fax 928-5562
Oakwood Digital Academy 100/Alt
1560 Joyner Ave SE 30060 678-594-8240
David Pearce, prin. Fax 594-8241
Osborne HS 1,700/9-12
2451 Favor Rd SW 30060 770-437-5900
Josh Morreale, prin. Fax 437-5902
Performance Learning Center Alt
1560 Joyner Ave SE 30060 678-331-1098
Lugenia Purnell, prin. Fax 331-1058
Pope HS 1,700/9-12
3001 Hembree Rd NE 30062 770-578-7900
Dr. Robert Downs, prin. Fax 578-7902
Simpson MS 900/6-8
3340 Trickum Rd NE 30066 770-971-4711
Dr. Andrew Bristow, prin. Fax 971-4507
Smitha MS 900/6-8
2025 Powder Springs Rd SW 30064 678-594-8267
Clint Terza, prin. Fax 594-8269
Sprayberry HS 1,800/9-12
2525 Sandy Plains Rd 30066 770-578-3200
Joseph Sharp, prin. Fax 578-3202
Wheeler HS 2,100/9-12
375 Holt Rd NE 30068 770-578-3266
Dr. Peter Giles, prin. Fax 578-3268
Adult Education Center Adult
240 Barber Rd SE 30060 678-594-8011
Francia Browne, admin. Fax 594-8015
Other Schools – See Acworth, Austell, Kennesaw, Mableton, Powder Springs, Smyrna

Marietta CSD 8,200/K-12
250 Howard St NE 30060 770-422-3500
Dr. Emily Lembeck, supt. Fax 425-4095
www.marietta-city.org
Marietta HS 2,000/9-12
1171 Whitlock Ave SW 30064 770-428-2631
Forrestella Taylor, prin. Fax 429-3151
Marietta MS 1,200/7-8
121 Winn St NW 30064 770-422-0311
Gabe Carmona, prin. Fax 429-3162
Marietta Performance Learning Center Alt
353 Lemon St NE Ste B 30060 770-429-3188
Tammie Roach, admin. Fax 429-3189

---

Chattahoochee Technical College Post-Sec.
980 S Cobb Dr SE 30060 770-528-4545
Covenant Christian Ministries Academy 100/PK-12
PO Box 4065 30061 770-919-0022
Vanessa Anderson, supt. Fax 919-2098
Cumberland Christian Academy 100/9-12
2115 Pair Rd SW 30008 678-426-1600
Dr. Lee Campbell, hdmstr. Fax 423-0366
Dominion Christian HS 200/6-12
4607 Burnt Hickory Rd NW 30064 770-420-2153
Michael Lightner, prin. Fax 420-2510
Everest Institute Post-Sec.
1600 Terrell Rd Ste G 30067 770-303-7997
Life University Post-Sec.
1269 Barclay Cir SE 30060 770-426-2600
Lincoln College of Technology Post-Sec.
2359 Windy Hill Rd Ste 100 30067 770-226-0056
Mt. Bethel Christian Academy 500/PK-12
4385 Lower Roswell Rd 30068 770-971-0245
Jim Callis, head sch Fax 971-3770
Southern Polytech State University Post-Sec.
1100 S Marietta Pkwy SE 30060 678-915-7778
Toni & Guy Hairdressing Academy Post-Sec.
1355 Roswell Rd Ste 150 30062 770-565-3285
Walker S 1,100/PK-12
700 Cobb Pkwy N 30062 770-427-2689
Jack Hall, head sch Fax 514-8122

**Martinez, Columbia, Pop. 34,798**
Columbia County SD
Supt. — See Evans
Stallings Island MS 500/6-8
3830 Blackstone Camp Rd 30907 706-447-2106
Don Putnam, prin. Fax 447-2103

---

Augusta Christian S 500/PK-12
313 Baston Rd 30907 706-863-2905
Dr. David Piccolo, head sch Fax 860-6618
Augusta Preparatory Day S 500/PK-12
285 Flowing Wells Rd 30907 706-863-1906
Ferrell Singleton, head sch Fax 863-6198

**Metter, Candler, Pop. 4,108**
Candler County SD 2,100/PK-12
210 S College St 30439 912-685-5713
Dr. Thomas Bigwood, supt. Fax 685-3068
www.metter.org
Metter HS 500/9-12
34905 GA Highway 129 S 30439 912-685-2134
John Jordan, prin. Fax 685-2897
Metter MS 400/6-8
33661 GA Highway 129 S 30439 912-685-5580
Ralph Carlyle, prin. Fax 685-4970

**Midland, Muscogee**
Muscogee County SD
Supt. — See Columbus
Cohn MS 6-8
7352 Garrett Rd 31820 706-569-3801
Richard Green, prin. Fax 569-3825
Midland MS 700/6-8
6990 Warm Springs Rd 31820 706-569-3673
Barrie Clarke, prin. Fax 569-3678

**Midway, Liberty, Pop. 2,059**
Liberty County SD
Supt. — See Hinesville
Midway MS 800/6-8
425 Edgewater Dr 31320 912-884-6677
Debra Frazier, prin. Fax 884-5944

**Milledgeville, Baldwin, Pop. 17,451**
Baldwin County SD 5,700/PK-12
PO Box 1188 31059 478-453-4176
Dr. Noris Price, supt. Fax 457-3327
www.baldwin-county-schools.com
Baldwin HS 1,300/9-12
155 GA Highway 49 W 31061 478-453-6429
Dr. Cloise Williams, prin. Fax 451-3032
Oak Hill MS 1,100/6-8
356 Blandy Rd NW 31061 478-457-3370
Dr. Linda Ramsey, prin. Fax 457-2422

---

American Professional Institute Post-Sec.
2485 N Columbia St Ste 114 31061 478-452-3900
Central Georgia Technical College Post-Sec.
54 GA Highway 22 W 31061
Georgia College & State University Post-Sec.
231 W Hancock St 31061 478-445-5004
Georgia Military College Post-Sec.
201 E Greene St 31061 478-387-4900
Georgia Military College Prep S 500/6-12
201 E Greene St 31061 478-387-4900
Milledge Academy 500/PK-12
197 Log Cabin Rd NE 31061 478-452-5570
Mark Hopkins, hdmstr. Fax 452-5000

**Millen, Jenkins, Pop. 3,092**
Jenkins County SD 1,500/PK-12
1152 E Winthrope Ave 30442 478-982-6000
Tara Cooper, supt. Fax 982-6002
www.jchs.com/
Jenkins County Alternative S Alt
Barney Ave 30442 478-982-6023
Rob Gray, prin. Fax 982-6002
Jenkins County HS 400/9-12
433 Barney Ave 30442 478-982-4791
Rob Gray, prin. Fax 982-6015
Jenkins County MS 300/6-8
409 Barney Ave 30442 478-982-1063
Rob Gray, prin. Fax 982-6015

**Milner, Lamar, Pop. 597**

---

Rock Springs Christian Academy 200/PK-12
219 Rock Springs Rd 30257 678-692-0192

**Milton, Fulton, Pop. 31,916**
Fulton County SD
Supt. — See Atlanta
Cambridge HS 9-12
2845 Bethany Bnd, 770-667-2883
Dr. Edward Spurka, prin. Fax 667-2927
Hopewell MS 1,300/6-8
13060 Cogburn Rd, 678-297-3240
Michael LeMoyne, prin. Fax 297-3250
Milton HS 2,700/9-12
13025 Birmingham Hwy, 770-740-7000
Brian Jones, prin. Fax 667-2844
Northwestern MS 1,300/6-8
12805 Birmingham Hwy, 470-254-2870
Leonard Forti, prin. Fax 254-2878

**Monroe, Walton, Pop. 12,993**
Walton County SD 13,300/PK-12
200 Double Spring Church SW 30656 770-266-4417
Gary Hobbs, supt. Fax 266-4420
www.walton.k12.ga.us
Carver MS 900/6-8
1095 Good Hope Rd 30655 770-207-3333
Dr. Dawn Spruill, prin. Fax 207-3332
Monroe Area HS 1,100/9-12
300 Double Springs Church 30656 770-266-4599
Bryan Hicks, prin. Fax 266-4598
Other Schools – See Loganville

---

Walton Academy 900/PK-12
1 Bulldog Dr 30655 770-267-7578

**Montezuma, Macon, Pop. 3,439**
Macon County SD
Supt. — See Oglethorpe
Macon County HS 500/9-12
611 Vienna Rd 31063 478-472-8579
Rickey Edmond, prin. Fax 472-6206
Macon County MS 400/6-8
615 Vienna Rd 31063 478-472-7045
Issiah Ross, prin. Fax 472-2549

**Monticello, Jasper, Pop. 2,623**
Jasper County SD 2,300/PK-12
1411 College St 31064 706-468-6350
Dr. Mike Newton, supt. Fax 468-0045
www.jasper.k12.ga.us

Jasper County HS 600/9-12
14477 GA Highway 11 N 31064 706-468-5016
Robyn Mullis, prin. Fax 468-5021
Jasper County MS 500/6-8
1289 College St 31064 706-468-2227
Dianna Blizzard, prin. Fax 468-1847

Piedmont Academy 300/PK-12
PO Box 231 31064 706-468-8818

**Morgan, Calhoun, Pop. 236**
Calhoun County SD 700/PK-12
PO Box 39 39866 229-213-0189
Dr. Yolanda Turner, supt. Fax 213-3837
www.calhoun.k12.ga.us
Other Schools – See Edison

**Morganton, Union, Pop. 300**

Mountain Area Christian Academy 200/PK-12
14090 Old Highway 76 30560 706-374-6222

**Morrow, Clayton, Pop. 6,303**
Clayton County SD
Supt. — See Jonesboro
Morrow HS 1,800/9-12
2299 Old Rex Morrow Rd 30260 770-473-3241
Dr. Pamela Pitts, prin. Fax 473-3244
Morrow MS 800/6-8
5934 Trammell Rd 30260 770-210-4001
Matthew Smith, prin. Fax 210-4002

Clayton State University Post-Sec.
2000 Clayton State Blvd 30260 678-466-4000
Interactive College of Technology Post-Sec.
1580 Southlake Pkwy Ste C 30260 770-960-1298

**Moultrie, Colquitt, Pop. 14,082**
Colquitt County SD 9,500/PK-12
PO Box 2708 31776 229-890-6200
Dr. Samuel A. DePaul, supt. Fax 890-6246
www.colquitt.k12.ga.us/
Achievement Center 100/Alt
1800 Park Ave SE 31768 229-890-6197
Darius Dawson, prin. Fax 890-6181
Gray JHS 1,300/8-9
812 11th Ave NW 31768 229-890-6189
Frederick Smith, prin. Fax 890-6123
Other Schools – See Norman Park

Moultrie Technical College Post-Sec.
800 Veterans Pkwy N, 229-891-7000

**Mount Airy, Habersham, Pop. 1,271**
Habersham County SD
Supt. — See Clarkesville
Habersham Central SHS 1,300/10-12
2059 Highway 197 30563 706-778-7161
Wes McGee, prin. Fax 778-1258
Habersham Ninth Grade Academy 500/9-9
171 Raider Cir 30563 706-778-0830
Connie Franklin, prin. Fax 778-0848
Habersham Success Academy 50/6-12
171 Raider Cir 30563 706-894-3056
Doug Westmoreland, prin. Fax 778-0848

**Mount Berry, Floyd**

Berry College Post-Sec.
2277 Martha Berry Hwy NW 30149 706-232-5374

**Mount Vernon, Montgomery, Pop. 2,411**
Montgomery County SD 1,000/PK-12
703 Dobbins St 30445 912-583-2301
Dr. Randy Rodgers, supt. Fax 583-4822
www.montgomery.k12.ga.us
Montgomery County HS 300/9-12
701 Dobbins St 30445 912-583-2296
Pamela Richards, prin. Fax 583-2302
Other Schools – See Ailey

Brewton-Parker College Post-Sec.
PO Box 197 30445 912-583-2241

**Mount Zion, Carroll, Pop. 1,655**
Carroll County SD
Supt. — See Carrollton
Mount Zion MS 300/6-8
132 Eagle Dr 30150 770-834-3389
Connie Robison, prin. Fax 214-7794

**Nahunta, Brantley, Pop. 1,033**
Brantley County SD 3,600/PK-12
272 School Cir 31553 912-462-6176
Dr. Greg Jacobs, supt. Fax 462-6731
www.brantley.k12.ga.us
Brantley County HS 900/9-12
10804 Highway 82 31553 912-462-5121
Nehemiah Cummings, prin. Fax 462-5123
Brantley County MS 600/7-8
10990 Highway 82 31553 912-462-7092
Dr. Angela Haney, prin. Fax 462-6785

**Nashville, Berrien, Pop. 4,886**
Berrien County SD 3,200/PK-12
810 S Dogwood Dr 31639 229-686-2081
Danny Hayes, supt. Fax 686-9002
www.berrien.k12.ga.us
Berrien HS 800/9-12
500 E Smith Ave 31639 229-686-7428
Angie Lovein, prin. Fax 686-6251
Berrien MS 700/6-8
800 Tifton Hwy 31639 229-686-2021
Margo Mathis, prin. Fax 686-6546

**Newborn, Newton, Pop. 690**

Shiloh Christian Academy 50/K-12
9595 Highway 142 30056 706-468-2606

**Newnan, Coweta, Pop. 32,285**
Coweta County SD 22,500/PK-12
PO Box 280 30264 770-254-2800
Dr. Steve Barker, supt. Fax 254-2807
www.cowetaschools.org
Arnall MS 900/6-8
700 Lora Smith Rd 30265 770-254-2765
Dr. Jan Franks, prin. Fax 254-2770
Brown MS Alt
32 Clark St 30263 770-304-5930
Skip Seagraves, prin. Fax 254-2806
Dowdell Academy Alt
1 Dowdell St 30263 770-254-2870
Kevin Jones, prin. Fax 304-5919
Evans MS 800/6-8
41 Evans Dr 30263 770-254-2780
Vera Perry-Harris, prin. Fax 254-2783
Madras MS 1,000/6-8
240 Edgeworth Rd 30263 770-254-2744
Lorraine Johnson, prin. Fax 304-5928
Newnan HS 2,300/9-12
190 Lagrange St 30263 770-254-2880
Chase Puckett, prin. Fax 254-2797
Northgate HS 1,800/9-12
3220 Fischer Rd 30265 770-463-5585
Bill Harrison, prin. Fax 463-4982
Smokey Road MS 800/6-8
965 Smokey Rd 30263 770-254-2840
Keafer Triplett, prin. Fax 304-5933
Other Schools – See Senoia, Sharpsburg

Heritage S 400/PK-12
2093 Highway 29 N 30263 770-253-9898
J.P. Watson, head sch Fax 253-4850
West Georgia Technical College Post-Sec.
160 Martin Luther King Dr 30263 770-755-7440

**Newton, Baker, Pop. 647**
Baker County SD 300/PK-12
PO Box 40, 229-734-5346
Dr. Torrance Choates, supt. Fax 734-3064
bck12.baker.k12.ga.us/
Baker County S 300/PK-12
260 GA Highway 37 SW, 229-734-5274
Dr. Torrance Choates, prin. Fax 734-3071

**Norcross, Gwinnett, Pop. 8,915**
Gwinnett County SD
Supt. — See Suwanee
Gwinnett InterVention Education Ctr West 300/Alt
5550 Peachtree Industrial 30071 770-246-5300
Todd Marschke, prin. Fax 246-5348
Meadowcreek HS 2,700/9-12
4455 Steve Reynolds Blvd 30093 770-381-9680
Tommy Welch, prin. Fax 806-2230
Norcross HS 3,300/9-12
5300 Spalding Dr 30092 770-448-3674
William Bishop, prin. Fax 447-2664
Summerour MS 1,200/6-8
321 Price Pl 30071 770-448-3045
Dorothy Parker-Jarrett, prin. Fax 417-2476

Ashworth College Post-Sec.
6625 the Corners Pkwy # 500 30092 770-729-8400
Everest Institute Post-Sec.
1750 Beaver Ruin Rd Ste 500 30093 770-921-1085
Greater Atlanta Christian S 1,900/PK-12
1575 Indian Trail Lilburn 30093 770-243-2000
Dr. David Fincher, pres. Fax 243-2268
Professional Career Development Inst Post-Sec.
6625 the Corners Pkey # 500 30092 800-957-5412
Wesleyan S 1,100/K-12
5405 Spalding Dr 30092 770-448-7640
Chris Cleveland, hdmstr. Fax 448-3699

**Norman Park, Colquitt, Pop. 956**
Colquitt County SD
Supt. — See Moultrie
Colquitt County HS 1,600/10-12
105 Darbyshire Rd 31771 229-890-6141
Stephanie Terrell, prin. Fax 890-6166

**Oakwood, Hall, Pop. 3,904**
Hall County SD
Supt. — See Gainesville
West Hall HS 1,100/9-12
5500 McEver Rd 30566 770-967-9826
Scott Justus, prin. Fax 967-4864
West Hall MS 900/6-8
5470 McEver Rd 30566 770-967-4871
Rodney Stephens, prin. Fax 967-4874

Lanier Technical College Post-Sec.
2990 Landrum Education Dr 30566 770-531-6300

**Ocilla, Irwin, Pop. 3,380**
Irwin County SD 1,700/PK-12
PO Box 225 31774 229-468-7485
Dr. Thad Clayton, supt. Fax 468-7220
www.irwin.k12.ga.us/
Irwin County HS 400/9-12
149 Chieftain Cir 31774 229-468-9421
Kerry Billingsley, prin. Fax 468-9423
Irwin County MS 400/6-8
149 Chieftain Cir 31774 229-468-5517
Edd Cunningham, prin. Fax 468-3134

**Oglethorpe, Macon, Pop. 1,323**
Macon County SD 1,800/PK-12
PO Box 488 31068 478-472-8188
Dr. D. Ray Hill, supt. Fax 472-2042
www.macon.k12.ga.us/
Other Schools – See Montezuma

**Peachtree City, Fayette, Pop. 33,616**
Fayette County SD
Supt. — See Fayetteville
Booth MS 1,000/6-8
250 S Peachtree Pkwy 30269 770-631-3240
Steve Greene, prin. Fax 631-3245

McIntosh HS 1,600/9-12
201 Walt Banks Rd 30269 770-631-3232
Lisa Fine, prin. Fax 631-3278

**Peachtree Crnrs, Gwinnett**
Gwinnett County SD
Supt. — See Suwanee
Pinckneyville MS 1,300/6-8
5440 W Jones Bridge Rd, 770-263-0860
Marci Sledge, prin. Fax 447-2617

**Pearson, Atkinson, Pop. 2,082**
Atkinson County SD 1,500/PK-12
98 Roberts Ave E 31642 912-422-7373
Tim Cochran, supt. Fax 422-7369
www.atkinson.k12.ga.us/
Atkinson County HS 400/9-12
145 Rebel Ln 31642 912-422-3267
Shane Miller, prin. Fax 422-7889
Atkinson County MS 400/6-8
145 Rebel Ln 31642 912-422-3267
Anthony Davis, prin. Fax 422-3348

**Pelham, Mitchell, Pop. 3,877**
Pelham CSD 1,500/PK-12
203 Mathewson Ave SW 31779 229-294-8715
Floyd Fort, supt. Fax 294-2760
www.pelham-city.k12.ga.us
Pelham City HS 400/9-12
720 Barrow Ave SW 31779 229-294-8623
Dr. Russ Chesser, prin. Fax 294-6069
Pelham City MS 400/6-8
209 Mathewson Ave SW 31779 229-294-6063
John Hamilton, prin. Fax 294-6046

**Pembroke, Bryan, Pop. 2,165**
Bryan County SD
Supt. — See Black Creek
Bryan County MS 500/6-8
600 Payne Dr 31321 912-626-5050
Dr. Michael Tinney, prin. Fax 653-2705
Byran County HS 500/9-12
1234 Camellia Dr 31321 912-626-5060
Cari DeLaTorre, prin. Fax 653-2858

**Perry, Houston, Pop. 13,635**
Houston County SD 26,000/PK-12
PO Box 1850 31069 478-988-6200
Dr. Mark Scott, supt. Fax 988-6259
www.hcbe.net
Perry HS 1,200/9-12
1307 North Ave 31069 478-988-6298
Dr. Darryl Albritton, prin. Fax 988-6381
Perry MS 800/6-8
495 Perry Pkwy 31069 478-988-6285
Thomas Moore, prin. Fax 988-6345
Other Schools – See Bonaire, Centerville, Kathleen, Warner Robins

Westfield S 600/PK-12
2005 US Highway 41 S 31069 478-987-0547
William Carroll, hdmstr. Fax 987-7379

**Pinehurst, Dooly, Pop. 452**
Dooly County SD
Supt. — See Vienna
Dooly County MS 300/6-8
11949 US Highway 41 31070 229-645-3421
Dr. Kelvin Butts, prin. Fax 645-3840

Fullington Academy 300/PK-12
PO Box B 31070 229-645-3383
Ken Shealy, hdmstr. Fax 645-3386

**Pooler, Chatham, Pop. 18,668**
Savannah-Chatham County SD
Supt. — See Savannah
West Chatham MS 1,000/6-8
800 Pine Barren Rd 31322 912-395-3650
Julian Childers, prin. Fax 201-7688

**Portal, Bulloch, Pop. 637**
Bulloch County SD
Supt. — See Statesboro
Portal MSHS 400/6-12
27245 US Highway 80 W 30450 912-842-8360
Dr. Karen Doty, prin. Fax 865-5659

**Port Wentworth, Chatham, Pop. 5,224**
Savannah-Chatham County SD
Supt. — See Savannah
Rice Creek S 3-8
100 Mulberry Ave 31407 912-395-4100
Dr. Troy Brown, prin. Fax 201-5068

**Powder Springs, Cobb, Pop. 13,580**
Cobb County SD
Supt. — See Marietta
Hillgrove HS 2,100/9-12
4165 Luther Ward Rd 30127 678-331-3961
Christian Suttle, prin. Fax 331-8128
Lovinggood MS 1,200/6-8
3825 Luther Ward Rd 30127 678-331-3015
Angela Stewart, prin. Fax 331-3016
McEachern HS 2,200/9-12
2400 New Macland Rd 30127 770-222-3710
Regina Montgomery, prin. Fax 222-3712
Tapp MS 700/6-8
3900 Macedonia Rd 30127 770-222-3758
Tiffany Honore, prin. Fax 222-3760

Paulding County SD
Supt. — See Dallas
Dobbins MS 900/6-8
637 Williams Lake Rd 30127 770-443-4835
Cartess Ross, prin. Fax 439-1672

Powder Springs Beauty College Post-Sec.
4114 Austell Powder Springs 30127 770-439-9432
Praise Academy 300/PK-12
4052 Hiram Lithia Springs 30127 770-943-2484
Joe White M.Ed., admin. Fax 943-9458

**Quitman, Brooks, Pop. 3,809**
Brooks County SD 2,200/PK-12
1081 Barwick Rd 31643 229-263-7531
Owen Clemons, supt. Fax 263-5206
www.brookscountyschools.com/
Brooks County HS 600/9-12
1801 Moultrie Hwy 31643 229-263-8923
Dr. Elena Ponder, prin. Fax 263-7049
Brooks County MS 500/6-8
2171 Moultrie Hwy 31643 229-263-7521
Djana Goss, prin. Fax 263-9038

**Rabun Gap, Rabun**

Rabun Gap-Nacoochee S 300/5-12
339 Nacoochee Dr 30568 706-746-7467
Dr. Anthony Sgro, head sch Fax 746-2594

**Reidsville, Tattnall, Pop. 4,920**
Tattnall County SD 3,400/PK-12
PO Box 157 30453 912-557-4726
Dr. Gina Williams, supt. Fax 557-3036
www.tattnallschools.org
Reidsville MS 300/6-8
148 W Brazell St 30453 912-557-3993
Gwenda Johnson, prin. Fax 557-4124
Tattnall County HS 900/9-12
1 Battle Creek Warrior Blvd 30453 912-557-4374
Glenn Stewart, prin. Fax 557-4542
Other Schools – See Glennville

**Rentz, Laurens, Pop. 289**
Laurens County SD
Supt. — See Dublin
Crossroads Alternative S Alt
1046 Emily Currie Rd 31075 478-984-4253
Brian Howell, prin. Fax 984-4831

**Rex, Clayton**
Clayton County SD
Supt. — See Jonesboro
Adamson MS 600/6-8
3187 Rex Rd 30273 770-968-2925
Chuck Wilkerson, prin. Fax 968-2949
Rex Mill MS 1,100/6-8
6380 Evans Dr 30273 770-474-0702
Caryn Turner, prin. Fax 474-5812

**Richmond Hill, Bryan, Pop. 8,989**
Bryan County SD
Supt. — See Black Creek
Richmond Hill HS 1,700/9-12
1 Wildcat Dr 31324 912-459-5151
Debi McNeal, prin. Fax 756-4958
Richmond Hill MS 1,400/6-8
503 Warren Hill Rd 31324 912-459-5130
Dr. William McGrath, prin. Fax 756-5369

**Rincon, Effingham, Pop. 8,590**
Effingham County SD
Supt. — See Springfield
Ebenezer MS 900/6-8
1100 Ebenezer Rd 31326 912-754-7757
Amie Dickerson, prin. Fax 754-4012

**Ringgold, Catoosa, Pop. 3,500**
Catoosa County SD 10,900/PK-12
PO Box 130 30736 706-965-2297
Denia Reese, supt. Fax 965-8913
www.catoosa.k12.ga.us
Heritage HS 1,300/9-12
3960 Poplar Springs Rd 30736 706-937-6464
Ronnie Bradford, prin. Fax 937-6477
Heritage MS 1,000/6-8
4005 Poplar Springs Rd 30736 706-937-3568
Chris Lusk, prin. Fax 937-2483
Ringgold HS 1,000/9-12
29 Tiger Trl 30736 706-935-2254
J.R. Jones, prin. Fax 965-8910
Ringgold MS 800/6-8
217 Tiger Trl 30736 706-935-3381
Mike Sholl, prin. Fax 965-8908
Other Schools – See Fort Oglethorpe, Rossville

**Riverdale, Clayton, Pop. 14,852**
Clayton County SD
Supt. — See Jonesboro
Drew HS 1,600/9-12
6237 Garden Walk Blvd 30274 770-472-2820
Gary Townsend, prin. Fax 472-2825
Riverdale HS 1,200/9-12
160 Roberts Dr 30274 770-473-2905
Jamille Miller-Brown, prin. Fax 473-2913
Riverdale MS 800/6-8
400 Roberts Dr 30274 770-994-4045
Adrian Courtland, prin. Fax 994-4467
Sequoyah MS 900/6-8
95 Valley Hill Rd SW 30274 770-515-7524
Lonnie White, prin. Fax 515-7540

Southern Regional Medical Center Post-Sec.
11 Upper Riverdale Rd SW 30274 770-991-8053

**Roberta, Crawford, Pop. 993**
Crawford County SD 1,900/PK-12
PO Box 8 31078 478-836-3131
John Douglas, supt. Fax 836-3114
crawfordcounty.schoolinsites.com
Crawford County Comprehensive HS 500/9-12
400 E Agency St 31078 478-836-3126
Mike Campbell, prin. Fax 836-4853
Crawford County MS 400/6-8
401 Lowe Rd 31078 478-836-3181
Dr. Anthony English, prin. Fax 836-3795

**Rochelle, Wilcox, Pop. 1,171**
Wilcox County SD
Supt. — See Abbeville
Wilcox County HS 400/9-12
186 7th Ave 31079 229-365-7231
Chad Davis, prin. Fax 365-7461
Wilcox County MS 300/6-8
114 7th Ave 31079 229-365-2331
Chad Davis, prin. Fax 365-2641

**Rockmart, Polk, Pop. 4,119**
Polk County SD
Supt. — See Cedartown
Rockmart HS 800/9-12
990 Cartersville Hwy 30153 770-684-5432
DeAnna Williams, prin. Fax 684-4768
Rockmart MS 800/6-8
60 Knox Mountain Rd 30153 678-757-1479
Robyn Teems, prin. Fax 757-9868

Georgia Northwestern Technical College Post-Sec.
466 Brock Rd 30153 770-684-5696

**Rock Spring, Walker**

Georgia Northwestern Technical College Post-Sec.
265 Bicentennial Trl 30739 706-764-3510

**Rocky Face, Whitfield**
Whitfield County SD
Supt. — See Dalton
Westside MS 500/6-8
580 Lafayette Rd 30740 706-673-2611
Angela Hargis, prin. Fax 673-5349

**Rome, Floyd, Pop. 35,635**
Floyd County SD 10,500/PK-12
600 Riverside Pkwy NE 30161 706-234-1031
Dr. Jeff McDaniel, supt. Fax 236-1824
www.floydboe.net
Armuchee HS 600/9-12
4203 Martha Berry Hwy NW 30165 706-236-1886
Dr. James Burris, prin. Fax 802-6757
Coosa HS 700/9-12
4454 Alabama Hwy NW 30165 706-236-1870
Trevor Hubbard, prin. Fax 290-8142
Coosa MS 600/6-8
212 Eagle Dr NW 30165 706-236-1856
Dr. Lisa Landrum, prin. Fax 802-6766
Model HS 700/9-12
3252 Calhoun Rd NE 30161 706-236-1895
Dr. Glenn White, prin. Fax 802-6750
Model MS 600/6-8
164 Barron Rd NE 30161 706-290-8150
David Tucker, prin. Fax 802-6775
Other Schools – See Armuchee, Lindale

Rome CSD 5,800/PK-12
508 E 2nd St 30161 706-236-5050
Dr. Michael Buck, supt. Fax 802-4311
www.rcs.rome.ga.us
Rome HS 1,500/9-12
1000 Veterans Memorial NE 30161 706-235-9653
Dr. J. Tygar Evans, prin. Fax 236-5078
Rome MS 800/7-8
1020 Veterans Memorial NE 30161 706-235-4695
Greg Christian, prin. Fax 234-5903
Rome Transitional Academy Alt
1162 Spider Webb Dr SE 30161 706-802-4326
Jennifer Perkins, prin. Fax 802-4327

Darlington S 800/PK-12
1014 Cave Spring Rd SW 30161 706-235-6051
Brent Bell, hdmstr. Fax 232-3600
Georgia Highlands College Post-Sec.
3175 Cedartown Hwy SE 30161 706-802-5000
Georgia Northwestern Technical College Post-Sec.
1 Maurice Culberson Dr SW 30161 706-295-6963
Shorter University Post-Sec.
315 Shorter Ave SW 30165 800-868-6980
Unity Christian S 400/PK-12
2960 New Calhoun Hwy NE 30161 706-292-0700
Eric Munn, head sch Fax 292-0772

**Rossville, Walker, Pop. 4,039**
Catoosa County SD
Supt. — See Ringgold
Lakeview MS 800/6-8
416 Cross St 30741 706-866-1040
Steve McClure, prin. Fax 861-6644

Walker County SD
Supt. — See La Fayette
Ridgeland HS 1,300/9-12
2478 Happy Valley Rd 30741 706-820-9361
Glen Brown, prin. Fax 820-1342
Rossville MS 700/6-8
316 Bull Dog Trl 30741 706-820-0638
Jason Pelham, prin. Fax 820-0696

**Roswell, Fulton, Pop. 86,448**
Fulton County SD
Supt. — See Atlanta
Centennial HS 1,900/9-12
9310 Scott Rd 30076 770-650-4230
Kibbey Crumbley, prin. Fax 650-4250
Crabapple MS 800/6-8
10700 Crabapple Rd 30075 470-254-4520
Rako Morrissey, prin. Fax 254-4524
Elkins Pointe MS 900/6-8
11290 Elkins Rd 30076 470-254-2892
Kindra Smith, prin. Fax 254-2898
Roswell HS 2,500/9-12
11595 King Rd 30075 470-254-4500
Jerome Huff, prin. Fax 254-4509

Blessed Trinity Catholic HS 1,000/9-12
11320 Woodstock Rd 30075 678-277-9083
Frank Moore, prin. Fax 277-9756
Chrysalis Experiential Academy 100/5-12
10 Mansell Ct E Ste 500 30076 404-513-9914
Fellowship Christian S 700/PK-12
10965 Woodstock Rd 30075 770-993-1650
Kathy Teston, admin. Fax 993-9262
St. Francis Day S 900/PK-12
9375 Willeo Rd 30075 770-641-8257
Strayer University Post-Sec.
100 Mansell Ct E 30076 770-650-3000

**Saint Marys, Camden, Pop. 16,595**
Camden County SD
Supt. — See Kingsland
Saint Marys MS 900/6-8
205 Martha Dr 31558 912-882-8626
Michael Wooden, prin. Fax 882-5473

**Saint Simons Island, Glynn, Pop. 12,646**

Frederica Academy 400/PK-12
200 Murray Way 31522 912-638-9981
John Thomas, head sch Fax 638-1442

**Sandersville, Washington, Pop. 5,844**
Washington County SD 3,200/PK-12
PO Box 716 31082 478-552-3981
Dr. Donna Hinton, supt. Fax 552-3128
www.washington.k12.ga.us/
Elder MS 700/6-8
902 Linton Rd 31082 478-552-2007
Rev. Manzie Broxton, prin. Fax 552-7388
Washington County Alternative S Alt
446 Riddleville Rd 31082 478-553-1243
Dr. Vincent Jackson, prin. Fax 553-1245
Washington County HS 900/9-12
420 Riddleville Rd 31082 478-552-2324
Dr. Al Gray, prin. Fax 552-3140

Brentwood S 400/PK-12
PO Box 955 31082 478-552-5136
Oconee Fall Line Technical College Post-Sec.
1189 Deepstep Rd 31082 478-553-2050

**Sandy Springs, Fulton, Pop. 91,346**
Fulton County SD
Supt. — See Atlanta
North Springs Charter HS 1,600/9-12
7447 Roswell Rd 30328 770-551-2490
Dr. Eddie Ruiz, prin. Fax 551-2498
Ridgeview Charter MS 900/6-8
5340 Trimble Rd, 404-843-7710
Lisa Hastey, prin. Fax 847-3292
Riverwood International Charter HS 1,600/9-12
5900 Raider Dr 30328 470-254-1980
Robert Shaw, prin. Fax 254-8709
Sandy Springs MS 900/6-8
8750 Pride Pl 30350 470-254-4970
Charles Gardner, prin. Fax 254-3334

Gwinnett College - Sandy Springs Post-Sec.
6690 Roswell Rd Ste 2200 30328 770-457-2021

**Savannah, Chatham, Pop. 133,567**
Savannah-Chatham County SD 33,400/PK-12
208 Bull St 31401 912-395-5600
Dr. Thomas Lockamy, supt. Fax 201-9073
www.savannah.chatham.k12.ga.us/
Beach HS 1,100/9-12
3001 Hopkins St 31405 912-395-5330
Derrick Muhammad, prin. Fax 201-5322
Building Bridges Academy HS Alt
402 Market St 31408 912-395-2540
Marcus Scott, admin. Fax 201-5065
Building Bridges Academy MS Alt
100 Priscilla D Pkwy 31408 912-395-6780
Dr. Janice Williams, admin.
Coastal MS 700/6-8
4595 US Highway 80 E 31410 912-395-3950
Allison Schuster-Jones, prin. Fax 898-3951
DeRenne MS 700/6-8
1009 Clinch St 31405 912-395-5900
Carol Mobley, prin. Fax 201-5903
Groves HS 1,500/9-12
100 Priscilla D Thomas Way 31408 912-395-2520
Dr. Ellis Duncan, prin. Fax 201-5840
Hubert MS 600/6-8
768 Grant St 31401 912-395-5235
Wilhelmenia Manning, prin. Fax 201-5238
Islands HS 700/9-12
170 Whitemarsh Island Rd 31410 912-395-2000
Kerry Coursey, prin.
Jenkins HS 1,300/9-12
1800 E De Renne Ave 31406 912-395-6300
Heather Handy, prin. Fax 303-6331
Johnson HS 1,000/9-12
3012 Sunset Blvd 31404 912-395-6400
Bernadette Ball-Oliver, prin. Fax 395-6418
Mercer MS 700/6-8
201 Rommel Ave 31408 912-395-6700
Horace Magwood, prin. Fax 201-5979
Myers MS 600/6-8
2025 E 52nd St 31404 912-395-6600
Ericka Washington, prin. Fax 303-6604
Savannah Arts Academy 800/9-12
500 Washington Ave 31405 912-395-5000
Gif Lockley, prin. Fax 201-4160
Savannah Early College HS 100/9-12
400 Pennsylvania Ave 31404 912-395-2535
Caroline Gordon-Jelks, admin. Fax 201-7585
School of Liberal Studies 800/9-12
400 Pennsylvania Ave 31404 912-395-5050
Tammy Broadnax, prin. Fax 201-5054
Southwest MS 700/6-8
6030 Ogeechee Rd 31419 912-395-3540
Craig Daughtry, prin. Fax 201-5831
STEM Academy 800/6-8
207 E Montgomery Xrd 31406 912-395-3500
Peter Ulrich, prin. Fax 201-4161
Windsor Forest HS 1,200/9-12
12419 Largo Dr 31419 912-395-3400
Derrick Butler, prin. Fax 961-3422
Woodville-Tompkins Tech & Career HS Vo/Tech
151 Coach Joe Turner St 31408 912-395-6750
Alfred McGuire, prin. Fax 965-6768
Other Schools – See Bloomingdale, Pooler, Port Wentworth

Armstrong Atlantic State University Post-Sec.
11935 Abercorn St 31419 912-344-2576
Benedictine Military S 300/9-12
6502 Seawright Dr 31406 912-644-7000
Rev. Frank Ziemkiewicz, hdmstr. Fax 356-3527

Bethesda Academy 100/6-12
PO Box 13039 31416 912-351-2055
Megan Kicklighter, prin. Fax 351-2062
Bible Baptist S 300/PK-12
4700 Skidaway Rd 31404 912-352-3067
Calvary Day S 700/PK-12
4625 Waters Ave 31404 912-644-5080
Dr. James Taylor, hdmstr. Fax 351-2280
Habersham S 100/PK-12
505 E 54th St 31405 912-509-0540
Memorial Day S 300/PK-12
6500 Habersham St 31405 912-352-4535
Mercer University Post-Sec.
4700 Waters Ave 31404
Providence Christian S 200/PK-12
401 Tibet Ave 31406 912-335-7976
Ramah SDA Junior Academy 200/PK-10
3400 Florance St 31405 912-233-3101
St. Andrew's S 400/PK-12
601 Penn Waller Rd 31410 912-897-4941
Mark Toth, hdmstr. Fax 897-4943
St. Vincent's Academy 300/9-12
207 E Liberty St 31401 912-236-5508
Mary Anne Hogan, prin. Fax 236-7877
Savannah Christian Preparatory S 1,300/PK-12
PO Box 2848 31402 912-234-1653
Dr. David Pitre, hdmstr. Fax 234-0491
Savannah College of Art & Design Post-Sec.
PO Box 3146 31402 912-525-5100
Savannah Country Day S 900/PK-12
824 Stillwood Dr 31419 912-925-8800
Kef Wilson, head sch Fax 920-7800
Savannah State University Post-Sec.
3219 College St 31404 912-358-4778
Savannah Technical College Post-Sec.
5717 White Bluff Rd 31405 912-443-5700
South University Post-Sec.
709 Mall Blvd 31406 912-201-8000
Virginia College Post-Sec.
14045 Abercorn St Ste 1503 31419 912-721-5600

**Scottdale, DeKalb, Pop. 10,220**

Fugees Academy, PO Box 388 30079 100/6-12
Luma Mufleh, dir. 678-358-0547

**Senoia, Coweta, Pop. 3,245**
Coweta County SD
Supt. — See Newnan
East Coweta MS 700/6-8
6291 Highway 16 30276 770-599-6607
Dr. Schwanda Jackson, prin. Fax 599-1051

**Sharpsburg, Coweta, Pop. 336**
Coweta County SD
Supt. — See Newnan
East Coweta HS 2,700/9-12
400 McCollum-Sharpsburg Rd 30277 770-254-2850
Steve Allen, prin. Fax 254-2857
Lee MS 900/6-8
370 Willis Rd 30277 770-251-1547
Dr. Cindy Bennett, prin. Fax 253-8381

Central Christian S 100/K-12
3613 Highway 34 E 30277 770-252-1234
Bill Parsons, head sch Fax 304-9576
Trinity Christian S of Sharpsburg 1,000/PK-12
8817 Highway 54 W 30277 770-251-6770
Dean Demos, hdmstr. Fax 251-6714

**Siloam, Greene, Pop. 278**

Greene Academy 200/PK-12
PO Box 109 30665 706-467-2147
Robert Bradley, head sch Fax 467-2147

**Smyrna, Cobb, Pop. 49,900**
Cobb County SD
Supt. — See Marietta
Campbell HS 2,300/9-12
5265 Ward St SE 30080 678-842-6850
Dr. Jeanne Walker, prin. Fax 842-6852
Campbell MS 1,200/6-8
3295 Atlanta Rd SE 30080 678-842-6873
Jonathan Tanner, prin. Fax 842-6875
Griffin MS 1,100/6-8
4010 King Springs Rd SE 30082 678-842-6917
Paul Gillihan, prin. Fax 842-6919

Medix School Post-Sec.
2108 Cobb Pkwy SE 30080 770-980-0002

**Snellville, Gwinnett, Pop. 17,762**
Gwinnett County SD
Supt. — See Suwanee
Brookwood HS 3,300/9-12
1255 Dogwood Rd 30078 770-972-7642
William Ford, prin. Fax 978-5075
Shiloh HS 2,000/9-12
4210 Shiloh Rd 30039 770-972-8471
Dr. Danyel Dollard, prin. Fax 736-4345
Shiloh MS 1,700/6-8
4285 Shiloh Rd 30039 770-972-3224
Dr. Eli Welch, prin. Fax 736-4563
Snellville MS 900/6-8
3155 Pate Rd 30078 770-972-1530
Katise Menchan, prin. Fax 736-4444
South Gwinnett HS 2,400/9-12
2288 Main St E 30078 770-972-4840
Eric Thigpen, prin. Fax 736-4329

**Social Circle, Walton, Pop. 4,199**
Social Circle CSD 1,700/PK-12
147 Alcova Dr 30025 770-464-2731
Dr. Todd McGhee, supt. Fax 464-4920
www.socialcircleschools.com/
Social Circle HS 500/9-12
154 Alcova Dr 30025 770-464-2611
Dr. Carrie Ann Booher, prin. Fax 464-2612
Social Circle MS 400/6-8
154 Alcova Dr 30025 770-464-1932
Dr. Charcia Nichols, prin. Fax 464-2612

**Soperton, Treutlen, Pop. 3,093**
Treutlen County SD 1,200/PK-12
5040 S Third St 30457 912-529-7101
Cheryl Conley, supt. Fax 529-4226
www.treutlen.k12.ga.us
Treutlen MSHS 600/6-12
7892 GA Highway 29 30457 912-529-7132
Christopher Watkins, prin. Fax 529-6121

**Sparks, Cook, Pop. 2,024**
Cook County SD
Supt. — See Adel
Cook MS 800/6-8
1601 N Elm St 31647 229-549-5999
Dr. David Boland, prin. Fax 549-5986

**Sparta, Hancock, Pop. 1,390**
Hancock County SD 1,100/PK-12
PO Box 488 31087 706-444-5775
Dr. Charles Culver, supt. Fax 444-7026
www.hancockcountyschools.net/
CrossRoads Alternative S Alt
PO Box 488 31087 706-444-7009
Dr. Shirley Harper, dir. Fax 444-7026
Hancock Central HS 400/9-12
11311 GA Highway 15 31087 706-444-7009
Dr. Tanger Ward, prin. Fax 444-9918
Hancock Central MS 200/6-8
11311 GA Highway 15 31087 706-444-6652
Dr. Tanger Ward, prin. Fax 444-4344

**Springfield, Effingham, Pop. 2,815**
Effingham County SD 11,500/PK-12
405 N Ash St 31329 912-754-6491
Dr. Randy Shearouse, supt. Fax 754-7033
www.effingham.k12.ga.us
Effingham County HS 1,800/9-12
1589 GA Highway 119 S 31329 912-754-6404
Yancy Ford, prin. Fax 754-6893
Other Schools – See Guyton, Rincon

**Statenville, Echols, Pop. 1,016**
Echols County SD 400/PK-12
216 US Highway 129 N 31648 229-559-5734
Dr. Virginia Jewell, admin. Fax 559-0484
www.echols.k12.ga.us
Echols County HS 200/9-12
PO Box 40 31648 229-559-5437
Dave Rosser, prin. Fax 559-3491

**Statesboro, Bulloch, Pop. 27,883**
Bulloch County SD 9,700/PK-12
150 Williams Rd Ste A 30458 912-212-8500
Charles Wilson, supt. Fax 212-8529
www.bulloch.k12.ga.us
James MS 600/6-8
18809 US Highway 80 W 30458 912-212-8820
Mike Yawn, prin. Fax 489-5916
Langston Chapel MS 600/6-8
156 Langston Chapel Rd 30458 912-212-8720
Dr. Evelyn Gamble-Hilton, prin. Fax 681-6416
Statesboro HS 1,400/9-12
10 Lester Rd 30458 912-212-8860
Dr. Ken LeCain, prin. Fax 489-5965
Transitions Learning Center Alt
150 Williams Rd Ste B 30458 912-212-8610
Tim Rountree, admin. Fax 489-9978
Other Schools – See Brooklet, Portal

Bulloch Academy 500/PK-12
873 Westside Rd 30458 912-764-6297
Georgia Southern University Post-Sec.
PO Box 8024 30460 912-478-5391
Ogeechee Technical College Post-Sec.
1 Joseph E Kennedy Blvd 30458 912-681-5500
Trinity Christian S 200/PK-12
571 E Main St 30461 912-489-1375

**Statham, Barrow, Pop. 2,353**
Barrow County SD
Supt. — See Winder
Bear Creek MS 6-8
228 Jefferson St 30666 770-725-5575
Dr. Jennifer Wood, prin. Fax 725-7656

**Stillmore, Emanuel, Pop. 530**

Emanuel Academy 200/K-12
PO Box 400 30464 912-562-4405

**Stockbridge, Henry, Pop. 24,827**
Henry County SD
Supt. — See Mc Donough
Austin Road MS 800/6-8
100 Austin Rd 30281 770-507-5407
Gabriel Wiley, prin. Fax 507-5413
Henry Academy North 200/Alt
109 S Lee St 30281 770-507-6414
George Eckerle, prin. Fax 507-6259
Stockbridge HS 1,300/9-12
1151 Old Conyers Rd 30281 770-474-8747
Eric Watson, prin. Fax 474-4727
Stockbridge MS 700/6-8
533 Old Conyers Rd 30281 770-474-5710
Purvis Jackson, prin. Fax 507-8406
Woodland HS 1,500/9-12
800 Moseley Dr 30281 770-389-2784
Bret Cook, prin. Fax 389-2790
Woodland MS 700/6-8
820 Moseley Dr 30281 770-389-2774
Legena Williams, prin. Fax 389-2780

Rockdale County SD
Supt. — See Conyers
Davis MS 900/6-8
3375 E Fairview Rd SW 30281 770-388-5675
Michael Mauriello, prin. Fax 388-5676

Community Christian S 900/PK-12
2001 Jodeco Rd 30281 678-432-0191
DeVry University Post-Sec.
675 Southcrest Pkwy Ste 100 30281 678-284-4700

**Stone Mountain, DeKalb, Pop. 5,717**
DeKalb County SD 98,400/PK-12
1701 Mountain Industrial Bl 30083 678-676-1200
Dr. R. Stephen Green, supt. Fax 676-0785
www.dekalb.k12.ga.us
Andrews HS 700/Alt
1701 Mountain Industrial 30083 678-676-2602
Merlon Jones, prin. Fax 676-2610
Champion MS 600/6-8
5265 Mimosa Dr 30083 678-875-1502
Antoine Rhodes, prin. Fax 875-1510
DeKalb Alternative S 200/Alt
5855 Memorial Dr 30083 678-676-2302
Margie Smith, prin. Fax 676-2310
DeKalb Early College Academy 300/9-12
1701 Mountain Industrial Bl 30083 678-875-2402
Edward Conner, dir.
Freedom MS 1,000/6-8
505 S Hairston Rd 30088 678-874-8702
Marchell Boston, prin. Fax 874-8710
Redan HS 1,200/9-12
5247 Redan Rd 30088 678-676-3602
Janice Boger, prin. Fax 676-3610
Stephenson HS 1,500/9-12
701 Stephenson Rd 30087 678-676-4202
Michael Jones, prin. Fax 676-4210
Stephenson MS 1,100/6-8
922 Stephenson Rd 30087 678-676-4402
Carolyn Williams, prin. Fax 676-4410
Stone Mountain HS 1,100/9-12
4555 Central Dr 30083 678-676-6302
Dr. James Jones, prin. Fax 676-6310
Stone Mountain MS 1,100/6-8
4301 Sarr Pkwy 30083 678-676-4802
Dr. Vincent Hinton, prin. Fax 676-4810
Other Schools – See Atlanta, Avondale Estates, Chamblee, Clarkston, Decatur, Doraville, Dunwoody, Ellenwood, Lithonia, Tucker

Pro Way Hair School Post-Sec.
5684 Memorial Dr 30083 404-299-5156

**Suches, Union**
Union County SD
Supt. — See Blairsville
Woody Gap S 100/K-12
2331 State Highway 60 30572 706-747-2401
Sheila Collins, prin. Fax 747-1419

**Sugar Hill, Gwinnett, Pop. 18,185**
Gwinnett County SD
Supt. — See Suwanee
Lanier HS 1,200/9-12
918 Buford Hwy 30518 678-765-4040
Dr. Reuben Gresham, prin. Fax 765-4049
Lanier MS 1,200/6-8
6482 Suwanee Dam Rd 30518 770-945-8419
Todd Hamilton, prin. Fax 271-5108
North Gwinnett MS 2,000/6-8
170 Peachtree Industrial Bl 30518 678-745-2300
Wanda Law, prin. Fax 745-2348

**Summerville, Chattooga, Pop. 4,440**
Chattooga County SD 2,300/PK-12
33 Middle School Rd 30747 706-857-3447
Jimmy Lenderman, supt. Fax 857-3440
chattooga.schoolfusion.us
Chattooga CrossRoads Academy 100/Alt
989 Highway 114 30747 706-857-1112
Barry Peppers, prin. Fax 857-6644
Chattooga HS 700/9-12
989 Highway 114 30747 706-857-2402
Jeff Martin, prin. Fax 857-2565
Summerville MS 400/6-8
200 Middle School Rd 30747 706-857-2444
Kevin Muskett, prin. Fax 857-7769

**Suwanee, Gwinnett, Pop. 15,041**
Forsyth County SD
Supt. — See Cumming
Lambert HS 2,100/9-12
805 Nichols Rd 30024 678-965-5050
Dr. Gary Davison, prin. Fax 965-5051
Riverwatch MS 1,300/6-8
610 James Burgess Rd 30024 678-455-7311
Kathy Carpenter, prin. Fax 455-7316

Gwinnett County SD 165,500/PK-12
437 Old Peachtree Rd NW 30024 678-301-6000
J. Alvin Wilbanks, supt. Fax 301-6030
www.gwinnett.k12.ga.us/
Collins Hill HS 3,200/9-12
50 Taylor Rd 30024 770-682-4100
Kerensa Wing, prin. Fax 682-4105
Northbrook MS 6-8
1221 Northbrook Pkwy 30024 678-407-7140
Dr. Keith Thompson, prin. Fax 407-7157
North Gwinnett HS 2,500/9-12
20 Level Creek Rd 30024 770-945-9558
Nathan Vallantine, prin. Fax 271-5185
Peachtree Ridge HS 3,200/9-12
1555 Old Peachtree Rd NW 30024 678-957-3100
Dr. Jeff Matthews, prin. Fax 957-3108
Other Schools – See Buford, Dacula, Duluth, Grayson, Hoschton, Lawrenceville, Lilburn, Loganville, Norcross, Peachtree Crnrs, Snellville, Sugar Hill

Friendship Christian S 200/PK-12
3160 Old Atlanta Rd 30024 678-845-0418
Dr. Rick Johnson Ph.D., head sch Fax 845-0417

**Swainsboro, Emanuel, Pop. 7,222**
Emanuel County SD 4,000/PK-12
PO Box 130 30401 478-237-6674
Dr. Kevin A. Judy, supt. Fax 419-1102
www.emanuel.k12.ga.us
Swainsboro HS 800/9-12
689 S Main St 30401 478-237-2267
Dr. Denise Warnock, prin. Fax 419-1134
Swainsboro MS 600/6-8
200 Tiger Trl 30401 478-237-8047
Dr. Willie Gibson, prin. Fax 419-1148

Other Schools – See Twin City

---

East Georgia State College — Post-Sec.
131 College Cir 30401 — 478-289-2000
Swainsboro Technical College — Post-Sec.
346 Kite Rd 30401 — 478-289-2200

**Sylvania, Screven, Pop. 2,925**
Screven County SD — 2,500/PK-12
PO Box 1668 30467 — 912-451-2000
William Bland, supt. — Fax 451-2001
www.screven.k12.ga.us
Screven County HS — 700/9-12
110 Halcyondale Rd 30467 — 912-451-2300
Brett Warren, prin. — Fax 451-2301
Screven County MS — 600/6-8
126 Friendship Rd 30467 — 912-451-2200
Dr. Bobby Costlow, prin. — Fax 451-2201

**Sylvester, Worth, Pop. 6,122**
Worth County SD — 3,200/PK-12
103 Eldridge St 31791 — 229-776-8600
Kay Mathews, supt. — Fax 776-8603
www.worthschools.net
Worth County Comprehensive HS — 900/9-12
406 W King St 31791 — 229-776-8625
Scott Chafin, prin. — Fax 776-8614
Worth County MS — 900/6-8
1305 N Isabella St 31791 — 229-776-8620
Tiffany Sevier, prin. — Fax 776-8624

**Talbotton, Talbot, Pop. 965**
Talbot County SD — 500/K-12
PO Box 308 31827 — 706-665-8528
Dr. Jack Catrett, supt. — Fax 665-3620
www.talbot.k12.ga.us/
Central S — 500/K-12
PO Box 308 31827 — 706-665-8577
Jake Golden, prin. — Fax 665-3946

**Tallapoosa, Haralson, Pop. 3,111**
Haralson County SD — 3,600/PK-12
299 Robertson Ave 30176 — 770-574-2500
Dr. Janet Goodman, supt. — Fax 574-2225
www.haralson.k12.ga.us
Haralson County HS — 1,000/9-12
1655 Georgia Highway 120 30176 — 770-574-7647
Topher Byrnes, prin. — Fax 574-7648
Haralson County MS — 800/6-8
2633 Georgia Highway 120 30176 — 770-646-8600
Dr. Brian Ridley, prin. — Fax 646-0108

**Tallulah Falls, Rabun, Pop. 164**

---

Tallulah Falls S — 300/6-12
PO Box 10 30573 — 706-754-0400
Larry Peevy, head sch — Fax 754-3595

**Temple, Paulding, Pop. 4,145**
Carroll County SD
Supt. — See Carrollton
Temple HS — 600/9-12
589 Sage St 30179 — 770-562-3218
Tim Gribben, prin. — Fax 562-1510
Temple MS — 500/6-8
275 Rainey Rd 30179 — 770-562-6001
Gail Parmer, prin. — Fax 562-6002
Villa Rica MS — 500/6-8
614 Tumlin Lake Rd 30179 — 770-459-0407
Greta Jackson, prin. — Fax 459-5496

**Thomaston, Upson, Pop. 9,037**
Thomaston-Upson County SD — 4,400/PK-12
205 Civic Center Dr 30286 — 706-647-9621
Dr. Maggie Shook, supt. — Fax 647-7154
www.upson.k12.ga.us
Upson-Lee Alternative S — Alt
300 Adams St 30286 — 706-647-5738
Cristina Cunningham, prin. — Fax 646-3160
Upson-Lee HS — 1,300/9-12
268 Knight Trl 30286 — 706-647-8171
Tracy Caldwell, prin. — Fax 647-3708
Upson-Lee MS — 1,100/6-8
101 Holston Dr 30286 — 706-647-6256
Rhonda Gulley, prin. — Fax 647-3631

**Thomasville, Thomas, Pop. 18,212**
Thomas County SD — 5,300/PK-12
200 N Pinetree Blvd 31792 — 229-225-4380
Dr. George Kornegay, supt. — Fax 225-5012
www.thomas.k12.ga.us
Thomas County Central HS — 1,500/9-12
4686 US Highway 84 Byp W 31792 — 229-225-5050
Trista Jones, prin. — Fax 227-2422
Thomas County MS — 1,700/5-8
4681 US Highway 84 Byp W 31792 — 229-225-4394
Kathy Keown, prin. — Fax 225-4378

Thomasville CSD — 3,100/PK-12
404 N Broad St Ste 3 31792 — 229-225-2600
Sabrina Boykins-Everett, supt. — Fax 225-2696
www.tcitys.org
MacIntyre Park MS — 600/6-8
117 Glenwood Dr 31792 — 229-225-2628
Tina McBride, prin. — Fax 225-3502
Scholars Academy — 6-12
820 E Washington St 31792 — 229-228-3397
Dr. Dale Graham, dir. — Fax 225-3525
Thomasville HS — 700/9-12
315 S Hansell St 31792 — 229-225-2634
Todd Mobley, prin. — Fax 225-2663

---

Brookwood S — 500/PK-12
301 Cardinal Ridge Rd 31792 — 229-226-8070
Dr. Randolph Watts, hdmstr. — Fax 227-0326
Southwest Georgia Technical College — Post-Sec.
15689 US Highway 19 N 31792 — 229-225-4096
Thomas University — Post-Sec.
1501 Millpond Rd 31792 — 229-226-1621

**Thomson, McDuffie, Pop. 6,688**
McDuffie County SD — 4,200/PK-12
716 Lee St 30824 — 706-986-4000
Dr. Mychele Rhodes, supt. — Fax 986-4001
www.mcduffie.k12.ga.us
McDuffie Achievement Center — Alt
614 Martin Luther King St 30824 — 706-986-4070
Dr. Roderick Hilton, prin. — Fax 595-4733
Thomson HS — 1,100/9-12
PO Box 1077 30824 — 706-986-4200
Claude Powell, prin. — Fax 986-4201
Thomson-McDuffie MS — 1,000/6-8
1191 White Oak Rd 30824 — 706-986-4300
Anita Cummings, prin. — Fax 986-4301

**Tifton, Tift, Pop. 16,154**
Tift County SD — 7,500/PK-12
PO Box 389 31793 — 229-387-2400
Patrick Atwater, supt. — Fax 386-1020
www.tiftschools.com
Eighth Street MS — 1,200/7-8
700 8th St W 31794 — 229-387-2445
Dr. Chad Stone, prin. — Fax 386-1036
Sixth Street Academy — Alt
805 6th St W 31794 — 229-387-2485
Tom Mark, dir. — Fax 386-1066
Tift County HS — 1,400/10-12
1 Blue Devil Way 31794 — 229-387-2475
Kim Seigler, prin. — Fax 386-1022
Tift County HS Northeast Campus — 600/9-9
3021 Fulwood Rd 31794 — 229-387-2450
Scott Haskins, prin. — Fax 386-1038

---

Abraham Baldwin Agriculture College — Post-Sec.
2802 Moore Hwy 31793 — 229-391-5001
Moultrie Technical College — Post-Sec.
52 Tech Dr 31794 — 229-391-2600

**Tiger, Rabun, Pop. 402**
Rabun County SD — 1,700/PK-12
963 Tiger Connector 30576 — 706-212-4350
Melissa Williams, supt. — Fax 782-6224
www.rabun.k12.ga.us
Rabun County HS — 700/9-12
230 Wildcat Hill Dr 30576 — 706-782-4526
Jonathan Gibson, prin. — Fax 782-7550
Rabun County MS — 400/7-8
95 Wildcat Pride Way 30576 — 706-782-5470
Vicki Tyler, prin. — Fax 782-4520

**Toccoa, Stephens, Pop. 8,279**
Stephens County SD — 4,000/PK-12
2332 Mize Rd 30577 — 706-886-9415
Bryan Dorsey, supt. — Fax 886-3882
www.stephens.k12.ga.us/
Crossroads Success Academy — Alt
191 Big A School Rd 30577 — 706-886-3114
Jerry Brown, dir. — Fax 886-3127
Stephens County HS — 1,100/9-12
323 Indian Trl 30577 — 706-886-6825
Sandy Steele, prin. — Fax 886-8765
Stephens County MS — 1,000/6-8
1315 Rose Ln 30577 — 706-886-2880
Donna Collins, prin. — Fax 886-2882

---

North Georgia Technical College — Post-Sec.
8989 Highway 17 30577 — 706-779-8100

**Toccoa Falls, Stephens**

---

Toccoa Falls College — Post-Sec.
107 Kincaid Dr, Toccoa GA 30577 — 706-886-6831

**Trenton, Dade, Pop. 2,264**
Dade County SD — 2,400/PK-12
PO Box 188 30752 — 706-657-4361
Cherie Swader, supt. — Fax 657-4572
www.dadecountyschools.org/
Dade County HS — 700/9-12
300 Tradition Ln 30752 — 706-657-7517
Josh Ingle, prin. — Fax 657-4854
Dade MS — 500/6-8
250 Pace Dr 30752 — 706-657-6491
Jamison Griffin, prin. — Fax 657-3055

**Trion, Chattooga, Pop. 1,797**
Trion CSD — 1,400/PK-12
239 Simmons St 30753 — 706-734-2363
Dr. Phil Williams, supt. — Fax 734-3397
www.trionschools.org/
Trion HS — 400/9-12
919 Allgood St Ste 3 30753 — 706-734-7316
Bryan Edge, prin. — Fax 734-7692
Trion MS — 300/6-8
919 Allgood St Ste 2 30753 — 706-734-7433
Cindy Anderson, prin. — Fax 734-7517

**Tucker, DeKalb, Pop. 26,961**
DeKalb County SD
Supt. — See Stone Mountain
Tucker HS — 1,600/9-12
5036 Lavista Rd 30084 — 678-874-3702
James Jackson, prin. — Fax 874-3746
Tucker MS — 1,300/6-8
2160 Idlewood Rd 30084 — 678-875-0902
Dr. Kathy Cunningham, prin. — Fax 875-0910

---

Le Cordon Bleu College of Culinary Arts — Post-Sec.
1927 Lakeside Pkwy 30084 — 770-938-4711

**Tunnel Hill, Whitfield, Pop. 854**
Whitfield County SD
Supt. — See Dalton
Northwest Whitfield County HS — 1,300/9-12
1651 Tunnel Hill Varnell Rd 30755 — 706-516-2200
Britt Adams, prin. — Fax 673-7098

**Twin City, Emanuel, Pop. 1,730**
Emanuel County SD
Supt. — See Swainsboro

Emanuel County Institute — 600/6-12
PO Box 218 30471 — 478-763-2673
Barry Joiner, prin. — Fax 763-3834

**Tyrone, Fayette, Pop. 6,701**
Fayette County SD
Supt. — See Fayetteville
Flat Rock MS — 800/6-8
325 Jenkins Rd 30290 — 770-969-2830
Jade Bolton, prin. — Fax 969-2835
Sandy Creek HS — 1,200/9-12
360 Jenkins Rd 30290 — 770-969-2840
Robert Hunter, prin. — Fax 969-2838

**Valdosta, Lowndes, Pop. 53,506**
Lowndes County SD — 10,800/PK-12
1592 Norman Dr 31601 — 229-245-2250
Wes Taylor, supt. — Fax 245-2255
www.lowndes.k12.ga.us
Lowndes HS — 3,000/9-12
1606 Norman Dr 31601 — 229-245-2260
Jay Floyd, prin. — Fax 245-2468
Lowndes MS — 900/6-8
2379 Copeland Rd 31601 — 229-245-2280
Dr. Derald Jones, prin. — Fax 245-2470
Mathis Learning Center — 400/Alt
1606 Norman Dr 31601 — 229-245-2271
Sol Summerlin, dir. — Fax 259-2273
Pine Grove MS — 700/6-8
4159 River Rd 31605 — 229-219-3234
Ken Overman, prin. — Fax 219-3233
Other Schools – See Hahira

Valdosta CSD — 7,600/PK-12
PO Box 5407 31603 — 229-333-8500
Dr. William Todd Cason, supt. — Fax 247-7757
www.gocats.org
Horne Learning Center — 200/Alt
PO Box 5407 31603 — 229-333-8597
Michael Roberts, prin. — Fax 333-0313
Newbern MS — 700/6-8
PO Box 5407 31603 — 229-333-8566
Fax 245-5655
Valdosta Early College Academy — 6-12
PO Box 5407 31603 — 229-671-8455
Dr. Mae McKinney, prin. — Fax 247-7689
Valdosta HS — 1,800/9-12
PO Box 5407 31603 — 229-333-8540
Dr. Janice Richardson, prin. — Fax 333-8584
Valdosta MS — 900/6-8
PO Box 5407 31603 — 229-333-8555
Beth DeLoach, prin. — Fax 245-5656

---

Georgia Christian S — 200/PK-12
4359 Dasher Rd 31601 — 229-559-5131
Burt Copeland, prin. — Fax 559-7401
Highland Christian Academy — 200/K-12
2206 E Hill Ave 31601 — 229-245-8111
Ron Kooy, prin. — Fax 245-8110
Open Bible Christian S — 300/PK-12
3992 N Oak Street Ext 31605 — 229-244-6694
Valdosta State University — Post-Sec.
1500 N Patterson St 31698 — 229-333-5800
Wiregrass Georgia Technical College — Post-Sec.
4089 Val Tech Rd 31602 — 229-333-2100

**Vidalia, Toombs, Pop. 10,364**
Vidalia CSD — 2,600/PK-12
301 Adams St 30474 — 912-537-3088
Dr. J. Garrett Wilcox, supt. — Fax 538-0938
www.vidaliacity.schoolinsites.com
Trippe MS — 600/6-8
2200 McIntosh St 30474 — 912-537-3813
Gwen Warren, prin. — Fax 537-3223
Vidalia Comprehensive HS — 700/9-12
1001 North St W 30474 — 912-537-7931
John Sharpe, prin. — Fax 537-3006

---

Southeastern Technical College — Post-Sec.
3001 E 1st St 30474 — 912-538-3100
Vidalia Heritage Academy — 100/PK-12
PO Box 2005 30475 — 912-537-6679
Jeff McCormick, admin.

**Vienna, Dooly, Pop. 3,989**
Dooly County SD — 1,500/PK-12
202 E Cotton St 31092 — 229-268-4761
Julie Harrelson, supt. — Fax 268-6148
www.doolyschools.org
Dooly County HS — 300/9-12
715 N 3rd St 31092 — 229-268-8181
Dr. Ed Mashburn, prin. — Fax 268-1916
Other Schools – See Pinehurst

**Villa Rica, Carroll, Pop. 13,578**
Carroll County SD
Supt. — See Carrollton
Bay Springs MS — 800/6-8
122 Bay Springs Rd 30180 — 770-459-2098
Marti Stephens, prin. — Fax 459-2097
Villa Rica HS — 1,500/9-12
600 Rocky Branch Rd 30180 — 770-459-5185
Glen Harding, prin. — Fax 459-2119

**Waco, Haralson, Pop. 513**

---

West Georgia Technical College — Post-Sec.
176 Murphy Campus Blvd 30182 — 770-537-6000

**Waleska, Cherokee, Pop. 623**

---

Reinhardt University — Post-Sec.
7300 Reinhardt Cir 30183 — 770-720-5600

**Warner Robins, Houston, Pop. 64,686**
Houston County SD
Supt. — See Perry
Edge Academy, 400 Elberta Rd 31093 — Alt
Shirley Randall, admin. — 478-929-7801
Feagin Mill MS — 700/6-8
1200 Feagin Mill Rd 31088 — 478-953-0430
Dr. Jesse Davis, prin. — Fax 953-0438

Houston County Crossroads Center — Alt
215 Scott Blvd 31088 — 478-929-7828
Dr. Ronnie Walker, prin. — Fax 929-7118
Houston County HS — 1,800/9-12
920 GA Highway 96 31088 — 478-988-6340
Dr. Douglas Rizer, prin. — Fax 988-6341
Huntington MS — 800/6-8
206 Wellborn Rd 31088 — 478-542-2240
Dr. Gwen Taylor, prin. — Fax 542-2247
Northside HS — 1,700/9-12
926 Green St 31093 — 478-929-7858
Dr. Greg Peavy, prin. — Fax 929-7813
Northside MS — 600/6-8
500 Johnson Rd 31093 — 478-929-7845
Jan Melnick, prin. — Fax 929-7124
Warner Robins HS — 1,800/9-12
401 S Davis Dr 31088 — 478-929-7877
Steve Monday, prin. — Fax 929-7769
Warner Robins MS — 800/6-8
425 Mary Ln 31088 — 478-929-7832
Brett Wallace, prin. — Fax 929-7834

---

Central Geogia Technical College — Post-Sec.
80 Cohen Walker Dr 31088 — 478-988-6800
Westside Christian Academy — 200/PK-12
1101 Dunbar Rd 31093 — 478-784-9153
Chuck Lewis, head sch — Fax 785-1099

**Warrenton, Warren, Pop. 1,925**
Warren County SD — 700/PK-12
PO Box 228 30828 — 706-465-3383
Carole Carey, supt. — Fax 465-9141
www.warren.k12.ga.us/
Warren County HS — 200/9-12
1253 Atlanta Hwy 30828 — 706-465-3742
Trevor Roberson, prin. — Fax 465-0901
Warren County MS — 100/6-8
1253 Atlanta Hwy 30828 — 706-465-3742
Truett Abbott, prin. — Fax 465-0901

---

Briarwood Academy — 300/PK-12
4859 Thomson Hwy 30828 — 706-595-5641

**Washington, Wilkes, Pop. 4,057**
Wilkes County SD — 1,700/PK-12
313 N Alexander Ave Ste A 30673 — 706-678-2718
Dr. Rosemary Caddell, supt. — Fax 678-3799
www.wilkes.k12.ga.us
Washington-Wilkes Comprehensive HS — 500/9-12
1182 Tignall Rd 30673 — 706-678-2426
Robert Wheeler, prin. — Fax 678-2628
Washington-Wilkes MS — 400/6-8
1180 Tignall Rd 30673 — 706-678-7131
Deleki Lee, prin. — Fax 678-3546

**Watkinsville, Oconee, Pop. 2,786**
Oconee County SD — 6,500/K-12
PO Box 146 30677 — 706-769-5130
Dr. Jason Branch, supt. — Fax 769-3500
www.oconeeschools.org/
Oconee County HS — 1,000/9-12
2721 Hog Mountain Rd 30677 — 706-769-6655
Ben Wiggins, prin. — Fax 310-2003
Oconee County MS — 800/6-8
1101 Mars Hill Rd 30677 — 706-769-3575
Dr. Suzanne Miller, prin. — Fax 310-2001
Other Schools – See Bogart

---

Westminster Christian Academy — 300/PK-12
PO Box 388 30677 — 706-769-9372
Jared Clark, head sch — Fax 769-2050

**Waycross, Ware, Pop. 14,397**
Ware County SD — 5,800/PK-12
1301 Bailey St 31501 — 912-283-8656
Jim LeBrun, supt. — Fax 283-8698
www.ware.k12.ga.us
Ware County HS — 1,500/9-12
700 Victory Dr 31503 — 912-287-2351
Bert Smith, prin. — Fax 287-2358
Ware County MS — 800/6-8
2301 Cherokee St 31503 — 912-287-2341
Dr. Darlene Tanner, prin. — Fax 287-2353
Waycross MS — 600/6-8
700 Central Ave 31501 — 912-287-2333
David Hitt, prin. — Fax 287-2352

---

Okefenokee Technical College — Post-Sec.
1701 Carswell Ave 31503 — 912-287-6584
South Georgia State College — Post-Sec.
2001 S Georgia Pkwy W 31503 — 912-449-7600
Southside Christian S — 100/PK-12
3439 Knight Ave 31503 — 912-285-5438

**Waynesboro, Burke, Pop. 5,700**
Burke County SD — 4,500/PK-12
789 Burke Veterans Pkwy 30830 — 706-554-5101
Rudy Falana, supt. — Fax 554-8051
www.burke.k12.ga.us
Burke County Academy of Success — Alt
PO Box 1005 30830 — 706-554-8046
Dr. Chiquita Brady, prin. — Fax 554-8081
Burke County HS — 1,200/9-12
1057 Burke Veterans Pkwy 30830 — 706-554-6691
Sam Adkins, prin. — Fax 554-8070
Burke County MS — 900/6-8
356 Southside Dr 30830 — 706-554-3532
Dr. Mona Reynolds, prin. — Fax 554-8063

---

Burke Academy — 400/PK-12
PO Box 787 30830 — 706-554-4479
Faith Christian Academy — 100/PK-12
726 GA Highway 24 S 30830 — 706-554-1577
Amy Grubb, prin. — Fax 554-2566

**West Point, Troup, Pop. 3,435**

---

Point University — Post-Sec.
507 W 10th St 31833 — 706-385-1000

**White, Bartow, Pop. 658**
Bartow County SD
Supt. — See Cartersville
Cass HS — 1,400/9-12
1000 Colonel Way NE 30184 — 770-606-5845
Mike Nelson, prin. — Fax 606-5467

**Winder, Barrow, Pop. 13,757**
Barrow County SD — 11,900/PK-12
179 W Athens St 30680 — 770-867-4527
Dr. Chris McMichael, supt. — Fax 867-4540
www.barrow.k12.ga.us
Apalachee HS — 1,600/9-12
940 Haymon Morris Rd 30680 — 770-586-5111
Dr. Sheila Kahrs, prin. — Fax 307-3726
Barrow Co. Alternative Education Program — Alt
106 Church St 30680 — 770-867-2900
Chuck Torbett, coord. — Fax 867-1264
Haymon-Morris MS — 700/6-8
1008 Haymon Morris Rd 30680 — 678-963-0602
Dr. James Bowen, prin. — Fax 867-1854
Russell MS — 700/6-8
84 W Midland Ave 30680 — 770-867-8181
Paul DeFoor, prin. — Fax 868-1215
Sims Academy of Innovation & Technology — Vo/Tech
985 Austin Rd 30680 — 770-867-7467
Marc Dastous, prin.
Westside MS — 700/6-8
240 Matthews School Rd 30680 — 770-307-2972
Valorie Rolader, prin. — Fax 307-2976
Winder-Barrow HS — 1,800/9-12
272 N 5th Ave 30680 — 770-867-4519
Dr. Al Darby, prin. — Fax 867-6412
Other Schools – See Bethlehem, Statham

**Winston, Douglas**
Douglas County SD
Supt. — See Douglasville
Mason Creek MS — 800/6-8
7777 Mason Creek Rd 30187 — 770-651-2500
Eric Collins, prin. — Fax 920-4278

**Woodbury, Meriwether, Pop. 960**

---

Flint River Academy — 300/PK-12
11556 Highway 85 E 30293 — 706-553-2541

**Woodstock, Cherokee, Pop. 23,245**
Cherokee County SD
Supt. — See Canton
Booth MS — 1,200/6-8
6550 Putnam Ford Dr 30189 — 770-926-5707
Dawn Weinbaum, prin. — Fax 928-2908
Etowah HS — 2,200/9-12
6565 Putnam Ford Dr 30189 — 770-721-3120
Keith Ball, prin. — Fax 926-4157
Mill Creek MS — 1,100/6-8
442 Arnold Mill Rd 30188 — 770-721-6400
Dr. Kerry Martin, prin. — Fax 926-5439
Polaris Evening Program — 200/Alt
2010 Towne Lake Hls S Dr 30189 — 770-721-3100
Dr. Curt Ashley, admin. — Fax 592-3509
River Ridge HS — 1,100/9-12
400 Arnold Mill Rd 30188 — 770-721-6500
Darrell Herring, prin. — Fax 721-6590
Woodstock HS — 2,000/9-12
2010 Towne Lake Hills S Dr 30189 — 770-721-3000
Mark Smith, prin. — Fax 592-3509
Woodstock MS — 1,100/6-8
2000 Towne Lake Hills S Dr 30189 — 770-721-3060
David Childress, prin. — Fax 591-8054

---

Cherokee Christian S — 400/K-12
3075 Trickum Rd 30188 — 678-494-5464
Michael Lee, supt. — Fax 592-4881

**Wrens, Jefferson, Pop. 2,160**
Jefferson County SD
Supt. — See Louisville
Wrens MS — 300/6-8
PO Box 585 30833 — 706-547-6580
Julia Wells, prin. — Fax 547-6224

**Wrightsville, Johnson, Pop. 2,174**
Johnson County SD — 1,200/PK-12
PO Box 110 31096 — 478-864-3302
Rebecca Thomas, supt. — Fax 864-4053
www.johnson.k12.ga.us/
Johnson County HS — 300/9-12
150 Trojan Way 31096 — 478-864-2222
Gary Price, prin. — Fax 864-4054
Johnson County MS — 300/6-8
150 Trojan Way 31096 — 478-864-2222
Gary Price, prin. — Fax 864-4054

**Young Harris, Towns, Pop. 891**

---

Young Harris College — Post-Sec.
PO Box 68 30582 — 706-379-3111

**Zebulon, Pike, Pop. 1,154**
Pike County SD — 3,500/PK-12
PO Box 386 30295 — 770-567-8489
Dr. Michael Duncan, supt. — Fax 567-8349
www.pike.k12.ga.us/
Pike County Alternative Program — Alt
PO Box 405 30295 — 770-567-2915
John Welch, admin.
Pike County HS — 1,100/9-12
331 Pirate Dr 30295 — 770-567-8770
Michael Maddox, prin. — Fax 567-3303
Pike County MS — 900/6-8
609 Hughley Rd 30295 — 770-567-3353
Dr. Vickie Smith, prin. — Fax 567-5054

# HAWAII

## HAWAII DEPARTMENT OF EDUCATION
**PO Box 2360, Honolulu 96804-2360**
**Telephone 808-586-3230**
**Fax 808-586-3234**
**Website doe.k12.hi.us**

Superintendent of Education Kathryn Matayoshi

## HAWAII BOARD OF EDUCATION
**PO Box 2360, Honolulu 96804-2360**

Chairperson Donald Horner

### PUBLIC, PRIVATE AND CATHOLIC SECONDARY SCHOOLS

**Aiea, Honolulu, Pop. 7,258**
Hawaii SD
Supt. — See Honolulu
Aiea HS 1,100/9-12
98-1276 Ulune St 96701 808-483-7300
Kim Sanders, prin. Fax 483-7303
Aiea IS 600/7-8
99-600 Kulawea St 96701 808-483-7230
Tom Kurashige, prin. Fax 483-7235

---

Calvary Chapel Christian S 100/PK-12
98-1016 Komo Mai Dr 96701 808-524-0846
Rev. Edwin Arcalas, dir. Fax 275-5193

**Ewa Beach, Honolulu, Pop. 10,071**
Hawaii SD
Supt. — See Honolulu
Campbell HS 2,800/9-12
91-980 North Rd 96706 808-689-1200
Naomi Takamari, prin. Fax 689-1242
Ewa Makai MS 800/7-8
91-6291 Kapolei Pkwy 96706 808-687-9500
Edward Oshiro, prin. Fax 685-2052
Ilima IS 700/7-8
91-884 Fort Weaver Rd 96706 808-687-9300
Christopher Bonilla, prin. Fax 689-1258

---

Friendship Christian S 300/PK-12
91-1207 Renton Rd 96706 808-681-8838
Lanakila Baptist HS 100/7-12
91-1219 Renton Rd 96706 808-681-3146
Rick Denham, dir. Fax 681-0704

**Hana, Maui, Pop. 446**
Hawaii SD
Supt. — See Honolulu
Hana S 300/K-12
PO Box 128 96713 808-248-4815
Richard Paul, prin. Fax 248-4819

**Hilo, Hawaii, Pop. 26,125**
Hawaii SD
Supt. — See Honolulu
Hilo HS 1,200/9-12
556 Waianuenue Ave 96720 808-974-4021
Robert Dircks, prin. Fax 974-4036
Hilo IS 500/7-8
587 Waianuenue Ave 96720 808-974-4955
Heather Dansdill, prin. Fax 974-6184
Waiakea HS 1,200/9-12
155 W Kawili St 96720 808-974-4888
Kelcy Koga, prin. Fax 974-4880
Waiakea IS 900/6-8
200 W Puainako St 96720 808-981-7231
Lisa Souza, prin. Fax 981-7237
Hilo Community S Adult
155 W Kawili St # P27 96720 808-974-4100
Chad Okinaka, prin. Fax 974-6170

---

Hawaii College or Oriental Medicine Post-Sec.
93 Banyan Dr Rm 504 96720 808-981-2790
Hawaii Community College Post-Sec.
200 W Kawili St 96720 808-934-2500
St. Joseph JSHS 100/7-12
1000 Ululani St 96720 808-935-4936
Llewellyn Young, prin. Fax 969-9019
University of Hawaii at Hilo Post-Sec.
200 W Kawili St 96720 808-974-7414

**Honokaa, Hawaii, Pop. 1,529**
Hawaii SD
Supt. — See Honolulu
Honoka'a HS 700/7-12
45-527 Pakalana St 96727 808-775-8800
Rachelle Matsumura, prin. Fax 775-8803

**Honolulu, Honolulu, Pop. 378,155**
Hawaii SD 179,900/PK-12
PO Box 2360 96804 808-586-3230
Kathryn Matayoshi, supt. Fax 586-3234
www.hawaiipublicschools.org
Aliamanu MS 700/7-8
3271 Salt Lake Blvd 96818 808-421-4100
Robert Eggleston, prin. Fax 421-4103
Central MS 400/6-8
1302 Queen Emma St 96813 808-587-4400
Cindy Yun-Kim, prin. Fax 587-4409
Dole MS 800/6-8
1803 Kamehameha IV Rd 96819 808-832-3340
Mavis Tasaka, prin. Fax 832-3349
Farrington HS 2,500/9-12
1564 N King St 96817 808-832-3600
Alfredo Carganilla, prin. Fax 832-3587
Jarrett MS 200/6-8
1903 Palolo Ave 96816 808-733-4888
Reid Kuba, prin. Fax 733-4894
Kaimuki HS 1,000/9-12
2705 Kaimuki Ave 96816 808-733-4900
Wade Araki, prin. Fax 733-4929
Kaimuki MS 1,000/6-8
631 18th Ave 96816 808-733-4800
Frank Fernandes, prin. Fax 733-4810
Kaiser HS 1,200/9-12
511 Lunalilo Home Rd 96825 808-394-1200
Justin Mew, prin. Fax 394-1201
Kalakaua MS 1,000/6-8
821 Kalihi St 96819 808-832-3130
Lorelei Aiwohi, prin. Fax 832-3140
Kalani HS 1,200/9-12
4680 Kalanianaole Hwy 96821 808-377-7744
Mitchell Otani, prin. Fax 377-2483
Kawananakoa MS 900/6-8
49 Funchal St 96813 808-587-4430
Ann Sugibayashi, prin. Fax 587-4443
Kula Kaiapuni O Anuenue S 400/K-12
2528 10th Ave 96816 808-733-8465
Glen Miyasato, prin. Fax 733-8467
McKinley HS 1,800/9-12
1039 S King St 96814 808-594-0400
Ron Okamura, prin. Fax 594-0407
Moanalua HS 2,000/9-12
2825 Ala Ilima St 96818 808-837-8455
Robin Martin, prin. Fax 831-7919
Moanalua MS 800/7-8
1289 Mahiole St 96819 808-831-7850
Lisa Nagamine, prin. Fax 831-7859
Niu Valley MS 800/6-8
310 Halemaumau St 96821 808-377-2440
Sean Tajima, prin. Fax 377-2444
Radford HS 1,300/9-12
4361 Salt Lake Blvd 96818 808-421-4200
James Sunday, prin. Fax 421-4210
Roosevelt HS 1,400/9-12
1120 Nehoa St 96822 808-531-9500
Sean Wong, prin. Fax 587-4637
Stevenson MS 600/6-8
1202 Prospect St 96822 808-587-4520
Linell Dilwith, prin. Fax 587-4523
Washington MS 800/6-8
1633 S King St 96826 808-973-0177
Michael Harano, prin. Fax 973-0181
Farrington Community S Adult
1101 Kalihi St 96819 808-832-3595
Kenneth Furukawa, prin. Fax 832-3598
McKinley Community S Adult
634 Pensacola St Ste 216 96814 808-594-0540
Helen Sanpei, prin. Fax 594-0544
Moanalua Community S Adult
2825 Ala Ilima St Ste A 96818 808-837-8466
Lance Jyo, prin. Fax 831-7926
Other Schools – See Aiea, Ewa Beach, Hana, Hilo, Honokaa, Hoolehua, Kahuku, Kahului, Kailua, Kailua Kona, Kaneohe, Kapaa, Kapaau, Kapolei, Keaau, Kealakekua, Kihei, Lahaina, Lanai City, Laupahoehoe, Lihue, Makawao, Mililani, Pahala, Pahoa, Pearl City, Wahiawa, Waialua, Waianae, Wailuku, Waimea, Waipahu

---

Argosy University/Hawaii Post-Sec.
1001 Bishop St Ste 400 96813 808-536-5555
Assets S 400/K-12
1 Ohana Nui Way 96818 808-423-1356
Dr. Paul Singer, hdmstr. Fax 422-1920
Babel University Professional School Post-Sec.
1833 Kalakaua Ave 96815 808-946-3773
Chaminade University of Honolulu Post-Sec.
3140 Waialae Ave 96816 808-735-4711
Christian Academy 400/PK-12
3400 Moanalua Rd 96819 808-836-0233
Linda Kim, prin. Fax 836-4415
Damien Memorial S 400/6-12
1401 Houghtailing St 96817 808-841-0195
Bernard Ho, pres. Fax 847-1401
Hawaiian Mission Academy 100/9-12
1438 Pensacola St 96822 808-536-2207
Hawaii Baptist Academy 200/7-8
420 Wyllie St 96817 808-595-6302
Richard Bento, pres.
Hawaii Baptist Academy 500/9-12
420 Wyllie St 96817 808-595-6301
Richard Bento, pres. Fax 595-6354
Hawaii Institute of Hair Design Post-Sec.
1128 Nuuanu Ave Ste 102 96817 808-533-6596
Hawaii Pacific University Post-Sec.
1164 Bishop St 96813 808-544-0200
Hawaii School for the Deaf and the Blind Post-Sec.
3440 Leahi Ave 96815 808-733-4999
Hawaii Tokai International College Post-Sec.
2241 Kapiolani Blvd 96826 808-983-4100
Heald College Post-Sec.
1500 Kapiolani Blvd 96814 808-955-1500
Honolulu Community College Post-Sec.
874 Dillingham Blvd 96817 808-845-9211
Honolulu Waldorf HS 100/9-12
5257 Kalanianaole Hwy 96821 808-735-9311
Helen Platell, dir. Fax 373-4982
Institute of Clinical Acupuncture Post-Sec.
100 N Beretania St Ste 203B 96817 808-521-2288
Iolani S 1,900/K-12
563 Kamoku St 96826 808-949-5355
Dr. Timothy Cottrell Ph.D., head sch Fax 943-2297
Kaimuki Christian S 300/PK-12
1117 Koko Head Ave 96816 808-732-1781
Dr. Mark Gallagher, prin. Fax 735-1354
Kamehameha S - Kapalama Campus 3,200/K-12
1887 Makuakane St 96817 808-842-8211
Earl Kim, head sch Fax 842-8411
Kapiolani Community College Post-Sec.
4303 Diamond Head Rd 96816 808-734-9000
La Pietra - Hawaii S for Girls 200/6-12
2933 Poni Moi Rd 96815 808-922-2744
Mahina Eleneki Hugo, head sch Fax 923-4514
Lutheran HS of Hawaii 100/6-12
1404 University Ave 96822 808-949-5302
Fax 947-3701
Maryknoll HS 600/9-12
1526 Alexander St 96822 808-952-7200
Darcie Kawamura, prin. Fax 952-7201
Medical Assisting School of Hawaii Post-Sec.
33 S King St Ste 223 96813 808-524-3363
Mid-Pacific Institute 1,500/PK-12
2445 Kaala St 96822 808-973-5000
Paul Turnbull Ph.D., pres. Fax 973-5099
New Hope Christian College - Hawaii Post-Sec.
290 Sand Island Access Rd 96819 808-853-1040
Pacific Buddhist Academy 100/9-12
1710 Pali Hwy 96813 808-532-2649
Josh Hernandez Morse, head sch Fax 522-7395
Punahou S 3,700/K-12
1601 Punahou St 96822 808-944-5711
Dr. James Scott, pres. Fax 944-5762
Remington College Post-Sec.
1111 Bishop St Ste 400 96813 808-942-1000
Sacred Hearts Academy 1,100/PK-12
3253 Waialae Ave 96816 808-734-5058
Betty White, prin. Fax 737-7867
St. Andrew's S 400/PK-12
224 Queen Emma Sq 96813 808-536-6102
Sandra Theunick, head sch Fax 538-1035
St. Francis S 300/PK-12
2707 Pamoa Rd 96822 808-988-4111
Sr. Joan of Arc Souza, prin. Fax 988-5497
St. Louis S 600/6-12
3142 Waialae Ave 96816 808-739-7777
Judge Walter Kirimitsu, pres. Fax 739-4853
Travel Institute of the Pacific Post-Sec.
1314 S King St Ste 1164 96814 808-591-2708
University of Hawaii at Manoa Post-Sec.
2500 Campus Rd 96822 808-956-8111
World Medicine Institute Post-Sec.
1073 Hind Iuka Dr 96821 808-373-2849

**Hoolehua, Maui**
Hawaii SD
Supt. — See Honolulu
Moloka'i HS 300/9-12
PO Box 158 96729 808-567-6950
Stan Hao, prin. Fax 567-6960
Moloka'i MS 200/7-8
PO Box 443 96729 808-567-6940
Dawn Mains, prin. Fax 567-6939

**Kahuku, Honolulu, Pop. 995**
Hawaii SD
Supt. — See Honolulu
Kahuku JSHS 1,500/7-12
56-490 Kamehameha Hwy 96731 808-293-8950
Pauline Masaniai, prin. Fax 293-8960

**Kahului, Maui, Pop. 18,567**
Hawaii SD
Supt. — See Honolulu
Maui HS 1,800/9-12
660 Lono Ave 96732 808-873-3000
Bruce Anderson, prin. Fax 873-3010
Maui Waena IS 1,100/6-8
795 Onehee Ave 96732 808-873-3070
Jamie Yap, prin. Fax 873-3066
Maui Community S for Adults Adult
179 W Kaahumanu Ave 96732 808-873-3082
Kurt Ginoza, prin. Fax 873-3046

---

Ka'ahumanu Hou Christian Schools of Maui 50/PK-12
777 Mokulele Hwy 96732 808-871-2477
Joni Uemura, prin. Fax 871-5668
Maui College Post-Sec.
310 W Kaahumanu Ave 96732 808-984-3500

**Kailua, Honolulu, Pop. 26,779**
Hawaii SD
Supt. — See Honolulu
Kailua HS 900/9-12
451 Ulumanu Dr 96734 808-266-7900
Francine Honda, prin. Fax 266-7915
Kailua IS 700/7-8
145 S Kainalu Dr 96734 808-263-1500
Lisa DeLong, prin. Fax 266-7984
Kalaheo HS 800/9-12
730 Iliaina St 96734 808-254-7900
Susan Hummel, prin. Fax 254-7907
Olomana JSHS 100/7-12
42-522 Kalanianaole Hwy 96734 808-266-7866
Stacey Oshio, prin. Fax 266-7873
Windward School for Adults Adult
730 Iliaina St 96734 808-254-7955
John Vannatta, prin. Fax 254-7958

---

Le Jardin Academy 800/PK-12
917 Kalanianaole Hwy 96734 808-261-0707
Louis Young, hdmstr. Fax 262-9339
Trinity Christian S 300/PK-12
875 Auloa Rd 96734 808-262-8501
Stephen Sprague, hdmstr. Fax 261-3916

**Kailua Kona, Hawaii, Pop. 7,780**
Hawaii SD
Supt. — See Honolulu
Kealakehe HS 1,500/9-12
74-5000 Puohulihuli St 96740 808-327-4300
Wilfred Murakami, prin. Fax 327-4307
Kealakehe IS 800/6-8
74-5062 Onipaa St 96740 808-327-4314
Joyce Crisafi, prin. Fax 327-4315
Kona Community S Adult
74-5000 Puohulihuli St 96740 808-327-4692
John Vannatta, prin. Fax 327-4693

---

Makua Lani Christian Academy 100/8-12
74-4966 Kealaka'a St 96740 808-329-4898
Thaddea Pitts, prin. Fax 329-5898
Mauna Loa Helicopter Post-Sec.
73-310 UU St 96740 808-334-0234

**Kamuela, Hawaii, Pop. 5,972**

---

Hawaii Preparatory Academy 600/K-12
65-1692 Kohala Mountain Rd 96743 808-885-7321
Robert McKendry, head sch Fax 881-4003
Parker S 300/K-12
65-1224 Lindsey Rd 96743 808-885-7933
Carl Sturges Ph.D., hdmstr. Fax 885-6233

**Kaneohe, Honolulu, Pop. 22,238**
Hawaii SD
Supt. — See Honolulu
Castle HS 1,200/9-12
45-386 Kaneohe Bay Dr 96744 808-233-5600
Bernadette Tyrell, prin. Fax 233-5623
King IS 600/7-8
46-155 Kamehameha Hwy 96744 808-233-5727
Wendy Matsuzaki, prin. Fax 233-5747

---

Koolau Baptist Academy 200/K-12
PO Box 1642 96744 808-233-2900
Windward Community College Post-Sec.
45-720 Keaahala Rd 96744 808-235-7400

**Kapaa, Kauai, Pop. 7,352**
Hawaii SD
Supt. — See Honolulu
Kapa'a HS 1,000/9-12
4695 Mailihuna Rd 96746 808-821-4400
Daniel Hamada, prin. Fax 821-4420
Kapa'a MS 600/6-8
4867 Olohena Rd 96746 808-821-4460
Nathan Aiwohi, prin. Fax 821-6967

**Kapaau, Hawaii, Pop. 1,135**
Hawaii SD
Supt. — See Honolulu
Kohala HS 300/9-12
54-3611 Akoni Pule Hwy 96755 808-889-7117
Janette Snelling, prin. Fax 889-7120
Kohala MS 200/6-8
PO Box 777 96755 808-889-7119
Alan Brown, prin. Fax 889-7121

**Kapolei, Honolulu, Pop. 8,781**
Hawaii SD
Supt. — See Honolulu
Kapolei HS 2,000/9-12
91-5007 Kapolei Pkwy 96707 808-692-8200
Elden Esmeralda, prin. Fax 692-8255
Kapolei MS 1,400/6-8
91-5335 Kapolei Pkwy 96707 808-693-7025
Bruce Naguwa, prin. Fax 693-7030

---

American Renaissance Academy 100/K-12
PO Box 75357 96707 808-682-7337
Wendi Bayudan, prin. Fax 682-7336

Island Pacific Academy 700/K-12
909 Haumea St 96707 808-674-3563
Gerald Teramae, head sch Fax 674-3575
University of Hawaii - West Oahu Post-Sec.
91-1001 Farrington Hwy 96707 808-689-2800

**Keaau, Hawaii, Pop. 1,591**
Hawaii SD
Supt. — See Honolulu
Kea'au HS 900/9-12
16-725 Keaau Pahoa Rd 96749 808-982-4220
Dean Cevallos, prin. Fax 982-4224
Kea'au MS 600/6-8
16-565 Keaau Pahoa Rd 96749 808-982-4200
Elna Gomes, prin. Fax 982-4219

---

Christian Liberty S 300/PK-12
16-675 Milo St 96749 808-966-8445
Troy Rimel, dir. Fax 966-8866
Kamehameha S - Hawaii Campus 1,100/K-12
16-716 Volcano Rd 96749 808-982-0000
Monica Naeole-Wong Ed.D., hdmstr. Fax 982-0010

**Kealakekua, Hawaii, Pop. 1,317**
Hawaii SD
Supt. — See Honolulu
Konawaena HS 700/9-12
81-1043 Konawaena School Rd 96750
808-323-4500
Shawn Suzuki, prin. Fax 323-4515
Konawaena MS 500/6-8
81-1045 Konawaena School Rd 96750
808-323-4566
Teddy Burgess, prin. Fax 323-4574

**Kihei, Maui, Pop. 16,763**
Hawaii SD
Supt. — See Honolulu
Lokelani IS 600/6-8
1401 Liloa Dr 96753 808-875-6800
Donna Whitford, prin. Fax 875-6835

**Koloa, Kauai, Pop. 1,524**

---

Kahili Adventist S K-12
2-4035 Kaumualii Hwy 96756 808-742-9294

**Kula, Maui, Pop. 5,082**

---

Haleakala Waldorf S 200/PK-12
4160 Lower Kula Rd 96790 808-878-2511
Antje Bojarsky, chrpsn. Fax 878-3341

**Lahaina, Maui, Pop. 8,745**
Hawaii SD
Supt. — See Honolulu
Lahaina IS 700/6-8
871 Lahainaluna Rd 96761 808-662-3965
Stacy Bookland, prin. Fax 662-3968
Lahainaluna HS 1,100/9-12
980 Lahainaluna Rd 96761 808-662-4000
Emily DeCosta, prin. Fax 662-3997

---

Maui Preparatory Academy 200/PK-12
PO Box 186 96761 808-665-9966

**Laie, Honolulu, Pop. 2,912**

---

Brigham Young University Post-Sec.
55-220 Kulanui St 96762 808-675-3211

**Lanai City, Maui, Pop. 2,317**
Hawaii SD
Supt. — See Honolulu
Lanai S 500/K-12
PO Box 630630 96763 808-565-7900
Elton Kinoshita, prin. Fax 565-7904

**Laupahoehoe, Hawaii, Pop. 416**
Hawaii SD
Supt. — See Honolulu
Laupahoehoe Community Public Charter S 9-12
PO Box 189 96764 808-962-2200
Nely Caberto, prin. Fax 962-2202

**Lihue, Kauai, Pop. 4,702**
Hawaii SD
Supt. — See Honolulu
Kamakahelei MS 900/6-8
4431 Nuhou St 96766 808-241-3200
Debra Badua, prin. Fax 241-3210
Kaua'i HS 1,200/9-12
3577 Lala Rd 96766 808-274-3160
Anne Kane, prin. Fax 274-3170
Kauai Community S for Adults Adult
3607A Lala Rd Ste P-12 96766 808-274-3390
Helen Sanpei, prin. Fax 274-3393

---

Island S 400/PK-12
3-1875 Kaumualii Hwy 96766 808-246-0233
L. Shannon Graves M.Ed., head sch Fax 245-6053
Kauai Community College Post-Sec.
3-1901 Kaumualii Hwy 96766 808-245-8311

**Makawao, Maui, Pop. 4,664**
Hawaii SD
Supt. — See Honolulu
Kalama IS 800/6-8
120 Makani Rd 96768 808-573-8735
John Costales, prin. Fax 573-8748
Kekaulike HS 1,100/9-12
121 Kula Hwy 96768 808-573-8710
Mark Elliott, prin. Fax 573-2231

---

Seabury Hall 400/6-12
480 Olinda Rd 96768 808-572-7235
Sarah Bakhiet, head sch Fax 572-7196

**Mililani, Honolulu, Pop. 19,872**
Hawaii SD
Supt. — See Honolulu

Mililani HS 2,400/9-12
95-1200 Meheula Pkwy 96789 808-627-7747
Fred Murphy, prin. Fax 627-7375
Mililani MS 1,700/6-8
95-1140 Lehiwa Dr 96789 808-626-7355
Elynne Chung, prin. Fax 626-7358

---

Hanalani S 700/PK-12
94-294 Anania Dr 96789 808-625-0737
Mark Sugimoto, head sch Fax 625-0691

**Pahala, Hawaii, Pop. 832**
Hawaii SD
Supt. — See Honolulu
Ka'u HS & Pahala ES 600/K-12
963150 Pikake St 96777 808-313-4100
Sharon Beck, prin. Fax 928-2092

**Pahoa, Hawaii, Pop. 606**
Hawaii SD
Supt. — See Honolulu
Pahoa JSHS 700/7-12
15-3038 Puna Rd 96778 808-313-4300
Darlene Bee, prin. Fax 965-2153

**Paia, Maui, Pop. 1,965**

---

Todd Memorial Christian S 200/PK-12
519 Baldwin Ave 96779 808-579-9237
Carolyn Moore, prin. Fax 579-9449

**Pearl City, Honolulu, Pop. 36,969**
Hawaii SD
Supt. — See Honolulu
Highlands IS 1,000/7-8
1460 Hoolaulea St 96782 808-453-6480
Amy Martinson, prin. Fax 453-6484
Pearl City HS 1,800/9-12
2100 Hookiekie St 96782 808-454-5500
Aaron Tominaga, prin. Fax 453-6521

---

Leeward Community College Post-Sec.
96-045 Ala Ike St 96782 808-455-0011

**Pukalani, Maui, Pop. 4,987**

---

Kamehemaha Schools Maui 1,000/K-12
270 Aapueo Pkwy, 808-572-3100
Lee Ann DeLima, hdmstr. Fax 573-7062

**Wahiawa, Honolulu, Pop. 11,315**
Hawaii SD
Supt. — See Honolulu
Leilehua HS 1,900/9-12
1515 California Ave 96786 808-305-3000
Jason Nakamoto, prin. Fax 622-6554
Wahiawa MS 800/6-8
275 Rose St 96786 808-622-6500
Ursula Kawaguchi, prin. Fax 622-6506
Wheeler MS 900/6-8
2 Wheeler Army Airfield 96786 808-622-6525
Brenda Vierra-Chun, prin. Fax 622-6529
Wahiawa Community S Adult
1515 California Ave 96786 808-305-3200
Wanelle Kaneshiro-Erdman, prin. Fax 621-7765

**Waialua, Honolulu, Pop. 2,839**
Hawaii SD
Supt. — See Honolulu
Waialua JSHS 600/7-12
67-160 Farrington Hwy 96791 808-637-8200
Avis Nanbu, prin. Fax 637-8209

**Waianae, Honolulu, Pop. 4,907**
Hawaii SD
Supt. — See Honolulu
Nanakuli JSHS 1,000/7-12
89-980 Nanakuli Ave 96792 808-668-5823
Darin Pilialoha, prin. Fax 668-5828
Wai'anae HS 1,700/9-12
85-251 Farrington Hwy 96792 808-697-9400
Disa Hauge, prin. Fax 697-7018
Wai'anae IS 900/7-8
85-626 Farrington Hwy 96792 808-697-7121
Raechelle Fabrao, prin. Fax 697-7124

**Wailuku, Maui, Pop. 10,085**
Hawaii SD
Supt. — See Honolulu
Baldwin HS 1,600/9-12
1650 Kaahumanu Ave 96793 808-984-5656
Catherine Kilborn, prin. Fax 984-5674
Iao IS 900/6-8
260 S Market St 96793 808-984-5610
Norma Barroga, prin. Fax 984-5617

---

St. Anthony JSHS 100/7-12
1618 Lower Main St 96793 808-244-4190
Betsey Gunderson, head sch Fax 242-8081

**Waimea, Kauai, Pop. 1,080**
Hawaii SD
Supt. — See Honolulu
Niihau S 50/K-12
PO Box 339 96796 808-338-6800
Nely Caberto, prin. Fax 338-6807
Waimea Canyon MS 400/6-8
PO Box 518 96796 808-338-6830
Melissa Speetjens, prin. Fax 338-6832
Waimea HS 600/9-12
PO Box 339 96796 808-338-6800
Mahina Anguay, prin. Fax 338-6807

**Waipahu, Honolulu, Pop. 28,747**
Hawaii SD
Supt. — See Honolulu
Waipahu HS 2,400/9-12
94-1211 Farrington Hwy 96797 808-528-9555
Keith Hayashi, prin. Fax 675-0257
Waipahu IS 1,200/7-8
94-455 Farrington Hwy 96797 808-675-0177
Randell Dunn, prin. Fax 675-0181
Waipahu Community S Adult
94-1211 Farrington Hwy 96797 808-528-9577
John Vannatta, prin. Fax 675-0259

# IDAHO

## IDAHO DEPARTMENT OF EDUCATION
**PO Box 83720, Boise 83720-0003**
**Telephone 208-332-6800**
**Fax 208-334-2228**
**Website http://www.sde.idaho.gov**

Superintendent of Public Instruction Tom Luna

## IDAHO BOARD OF EDUCATION
**PO Box 83720, Boise 83720-0003**

President Kenneth Edmunds

## PUBLIC, PRIVATE AND CATHOLIC SECONDARY SCHOOLS

**Aberdeen, Bingham, Pop. 1,945**
Aberdeen SD 58 800/PK-12
PO Box 610 83210 208-397-4113
Jane Ward, supt. Fax 397-4114
aberdeen58.org/
Aberdeen HS 200/9-12
PO Box 610 83210 208-397-4152
Travis Pincock, prin. Fax 397-4439
Aberdeen MS 200/6-8
PO Box 610 83210 208-397-3280
Ann Mennear, prin. Fax 397-3281

**American Falls, Power, Pop. 4,393**
American Falls JSD 381 1,500/PK-12
827 Fort Hall Ave 83211 208-226-5173
Dr. Ron Bolinger, supt. Fax 226-5754
www.sd381.k12.id.us
American Falls Academy 50/Alt
598 Lincoln St 83211 208-226-5008
Cliff Hart, prin. Fax 226-3194
American Falls HS 400/9-12
2966 S Frontage Rd 83211 208-226-2531
Travis Hansen, prin. Fax 226-5853
Thomas MS 300/6-8
355 Bannock Ave 83211 208-226-5203
Randy Jensen, prin. Fax 226-5274

**Ammon, Bonneville, Pop. 13,621**
Bonneville JSD 93
Supt. — See Idaho Falls
Hillcrest HS 1,300/9-12
2800 Owen St 83406 208-525-4429
Doug McLaren, prin. Fax 525-4437
Sandcreek MS 800/7-8
2955 Owen St 83406 208-525-4416
Lyndon Oswald, prin. Fax 525-4438

**Arco, Butte, Pop. 974**
Butte County JSD 111 400/PK-12
PO Box 89 83213 208-527-8235
Spencer Larsen, supt. Fax 527-8950
www.butteschooldistrict.org/
Butte County HS 100/9-12
PO Box 655 83213 208-527-8237
Robert Chambers, prin. Fax 527-8246
Butte County JHS 100/6-8
PO Box 695 83213 208-527-8237
Robert Chambers, prin. Fax 527-8246

---

Wisdom Ranch S 50/9-12
PO Box 166 83213 208-527-4750

**Arimo, Bannock, Pop. 334**
Marsh Valley JSD 21 1,300/PK-12
PO Box 180 83214 208-254-3306
Marvin Hansen, supt. Fax 254-9243
www.mvsd21.org
Marsh Valley Alternative S 50/Alt
12655 S Old Highway 91 83214 208-254-3711
Mike Welch, admin. Fax 254-9230
Marsh Valley HS 400/9-12
12655 S Old Highway 91 83214 208-254-3711
Mike Welch, prin. Fax 254-9230
Marsh Valley MS 200/7-8
12805 S Old Highway 91 83214 208-254-3260
Jason Brower, prin. Fax 254-3631

**Ashton, Fremont, Pop. 1,114**
Fremont County JSD 215
Supt. — See Saint Anthony
North Fremont JSHS 300/6-12
3581 E 1300 N 83420 208-652-7468
Drex Hathaway, prin. Fax 652-7784

**Bancroft, Caribou, Pop. 366**
North Gem SD 149 200/PK-12
PO Box 70 83217 208-648-7848
Curry Donaldson, supt. Fax 648-7895
www.sd149.com
North Gem JSHS 100/7-12
PO Box 70 83217 208-648-7848
Jamie Holyoak, admin. Fax 648-7895

**Blackfoot, Bingham, Pop. 11,732**
Blackfoot SD 55 4,300/PK-12
270 E Bridge St 83221 208-785-8800
Brian Kress, supt. Fax 785-8809
www.d55.k12.id.us
Blackfoot HS 1,100/9-12
870 S Fisher Ave 83221 208-785-8810
Roger Thomas, prin. Fax 785-2329
Independence Alternative HS 200/Alt
155 E Francis St 83221 208-785-8825
Mark Kartchner, prin. Fax 785-8893
Mountain View MS 600/7-8
645 Mitchell Ln 83221 208-785-8820
Wes Jensen, prin. Fax 785-8823

Snake River SD 52 1,700/PK-12
103 S 900 W 83221 208-684-3001
Mark Gabrylczyk, supt. Fax 684-3003
www.snakeriver.org
Snake River HS 500/9-12
922 W Highway 39 83221 208-684-3061
Ed Jackson, prin. Fax 684-3074
Snake River JHS 300/7-8
918 W Highway 39 83221 208-684-3018
Odila Conica, prin. Fax 684-3047

**Bliss, Gooding, Pop. 316**
Bliss JSD 234 100/K-12
PO Box 115 83314 208-352-4447
Kevin Lancaster, supt. Fax 352-4649
www.bliss234.org
Bliss S 100/K-12
601 Highway 30 83314 208-352-4445
Kevin Lancaster, prin. Fax 352-4649

**Boise, Ada, Pop. 200,322**
ISD of Boise City 25,500/PK-12
8169 W Victory Rd 83709 208-854-4000
Dr. Don Coberly, supt. Fax 854-4003
www.boiseschools.org
Boise SHS 1,500/10-12
1010 W Washington St 83702 208-854-4270
Robb Thompson, prin. Fax 854-4271
Borah SHS 1,400/10-12
6001 W Cassia St 83709 208-854-4370
Tim Standlee, prin. Fax 854-4371
Capital SHS 1,300/10-12
8055 W Goddard Rd 83704 208-854-4490
Sandy Winters, prin. Fax 854-4491
Church HS 500/Alt
8051 W Salt Creek Dr 83709 208-854-5650
Derek Gardner, prin. Fax 854-5651
East JHS 500/7-9
5600 E Warm Springs Ave 83716 208-854-4730
David Greene, prin. Fax 854-4731
Fairmont JHS 800/7-9
2121 N Cole Rd 83704 208-854-4790
Brian Walker, prin. Fax 854-4791
Hillside JHS 500/7-9
3536 W Hill Rd 83703 208-854-5120
Nate Dennis, prin. Fax 854-5121
Les Bois JHS 600/7-9
4150 E Grand Forest Dr 83716 208-854-5340
Rich Clements, prin. Fax 854-5341
North JHS 900/7-9
1105 N 13th St 83702 208-854-5740
Jeff Roberts, prin. Fax 854-5741
Professional-Technical Education Center Vo/Tech
8201 W Victory Rd 83709 208-854-5810
Dr. Irene Westrick, prin. Fax 854-5811
Riverglen JHS 600/7-9
6801 Gary Ln 83714 208-854-5910
Deb Watts, prin. Fax 854-5911
South JHS 700/7-9
3101 W Cassia St 83705 208-854-6110
Jeff Hultberg, prin. Fax 854-6111
Timberline SHS 1,100/10-12
701 E Boise Ave 83706 208-854-6230
Ted Hettinga, prin. Fax 854-6232
Treasure Valley Math & Science Center 100/7-12
6801 Gary Ln 83714 208-854-6800
Dr. Holly MacLean, prin. Fax 854-6801
West JHS 900/7-9
8371 W Salt Creek Dr 83709 208-854-6450
Janet Cherry, prin. Fax 854-6451
Boise Evening S Adult
8051 W Salt Creek Dr 83709 208-854-6700
Jeff Lamping, admin. Fax 854-5676

West Ada SD
Supt. — See Meridian
Centennial HS 1,700/9-12
12400 W Mcmillan Rd 83713 208-855-4250
David Moser, prin. Fax 855-4273
Lake Hazel MS 1,200/6-8
11625 W La Grange St 83709 208-855-4375
Bret Heller, prin. Fax 855-4399
Scott MS 1,100/6-8
13600 W Mcmillan Rd 83713 208-350-4060
Linda Ventura, prin. Fax 350-4074

---

Bishop Kelly HS 700/9-12
7009 W Franklin Rd 83709 208-375-6010
Mike Caldwell M.Ed., prin. Fax 375-3626
Boise Bible College Post-Sec.
8695 W Marigold St 83714 800-893-7755
Boise State University Post-Sec.
1910 University Dr 83725 208-426-1000
Brown Mackie College - Boise Post-Sec.
9050 W Overland Rd Ste 100 83709 208-321-8800
Carrington College Post-Sec.
1122 N Liberty St 83704 877-206-2106
ITT Technical Institute Post-Sec.
12302 W Explorer Dr 83713 208-322-8844
Milan Institute Post-Sec.
8590 W Fairview Ave 83704 208-672-9500
Riverstone International School 300/PK-12
5521 E Warm Springs Ave 83716 208-424-5000
Bob Carignan, head sch Fax 424-0033
St. Alphonsus Regional Medical Center Post-Sec.
1055 N Curtis Rd 83706 208-378-2000
Stevens-Henager College Post-Sec.
1444 S Entertainment Ave 83709 208-336-7671

**Bonners Ferry, Boundary, Pop. 2,493**
Boundary County SD 101 1,500/PK-12
7188 Oak St 83805 208-267-3146
Dr. Richard Conley, supt. Fax 267-7217
www.bcsd101.com
Bonners Ferry HS 500/9-12
6485 Tamarack Ln 83805 208-267-3149
Tim Gering, prin. Fax 267-5171
Boundary County MS 300/6-8
6577 Main St Ste 100 83805 208-267-5852
David Miles, prin. Fax 267-8099

**Bruneau, Owyhee**
Bruneau-Grand View JSD 365 300/PK-12
39678 State Highway 78 83604 208-834-2260
Dennis Wilson, supt. Fax 834-2516
www.sd365.us
Rimrock JSHS 200/6-12
39678 State Highway 78 83604 208-834-2260
Dennis Wilson, prin. Fax 834-2516

**Buhl, Twin Falls, Pop. 4,067**
Buhl JSD 412 1,300/PK-12
920 Main St 83316 208-543-6436
Ronald Anthony, supt. Fax 543-6360
www.buhlschools.org
Buhl HS 400/9-12
1 Indian Territory 83316 208-543-8262
Ryan Bowman, prin. Fax 543-8705
Buhl MS 300/6-8
525 Sawtooth Ave 83316 208-543-8292
Suzanne Wilkin, prin. Fax 543-5137

**Burley, Cassia, Pop. 10,210**
Cassia County JSD 151 5,200/PK-12
3650 Overland Ave 83318 208-878-6600
Dr. Gaylen Smyer Ph.D., supt. Fax 878-4231
www.cassiaschools.org
Burley HS 800/9-12
1 Bobcat Blvd 83318 208-878-6606
Levi Power, prin. Fax 878-6647
Burley JHS 500/7-8
700 W 16th St 83318 208-878-6613
Steve Copmann, prin. Fax 878-6624
Cassia JSHS 100/Alt
1010 W 17th St 83318 208-878-6630
Lauri Heward, prin. Fax 878-0822
Cassia Regional Technical Center Vo/Tech
1143 W 16th St 83318 208-878-6610
Curtis Richins, prin. Fax 878-6641
Other Schools – See Declo, Malta, Oakley

**Caldwell, Canyon, Pop. 45,339**
Caldwell SD 132 5,900/K-12
1502 Fillmore St 83605 208-455-3300
Tim Rosandick, supt. Fax 455-3302
www.caldwellschools.org/
Caldwell HS 1,200/9-12
3401 S Indiana Ave 83605 208-455-3304
Anita Wilson, prin. Fax 455-3256
Canyon Springs HS 400/Alt
516 N 11th Ave 83605 208-455-3325
Monica White, prin. Fax 455-3341
Jefferson MS 600/6-8
3311 S 10th Ave 83605 208-455-3309
Moss Strong, prin. Fax 459-6773

Syringa MS 700/6-8
1100 Willow St 83605 208-455-3305
Shay Swan, prin. Fax 455-3353

Vallivue SD 139 7,400/PK-12
5207 S Montana Ave 83607 208-454-0445
Dr. Pat Charlton, supt. Fax 454-0293
www.vallivue.org
Rivervue Academy 100/Alt
21985 Dixie River Rd 83607 208-454-8899
Mary Ann VandeBrake, prin. Fax 454-8261
Vallivue Academy 100/Alt
6123 Timbre Pl 83607 208-455-1917
Mark Layne, prin. Fax 455-3567
Vallivue HS 1,800/9-12
1407 E Homedale Rd 83607 208-454-9253
Dick Brulotte, prin. Fax 459-7114
Vallivue MS 700/6-8
16412 S 10th Ave 83607 208-454-1426
Brian Lee, prin. Fax 454-7846
Other Schools – See Nampa

---

Gem State Academy 100/9-12
16115 S Montana Ave 83607 208-459-1627
The College of Idaho Post-Sec.
2112 Cleveland Blvd 83605 208-459-5011

**Cambridge, Washington, Pop. 325**
Cambridge JSD 432 100/PK-12
PO Box 39 83610 208-257-3321
Ed Schumacher, supt. Fax 257-3323
www.cambridge432.org/
Cambridge MSHS 100/7-12
PO Box 39 83610 208-257-3311
Ed Schumacher, supt. Fax 257-3323

**Carey, Blaine, Pop. 598**
Blaine County SD 61
Supt. — See Hailey
Carey S 200/K-12
20 Panther Ln 83320 208-823-4391
John Peck, prin. Fax 823-4310

**Cascade, Valley, Pop. 926**
Cascade SD 422 300/PK-12
PO Box 291 83611 208-630-6057
Pal Sartori, supt. Fax 382-3797
www.cascadeschools.org
Cascade JSHS 200/7-12
PO Box 291 83611 208-630-6057
Diana Wold, prin. Fax 382-3797

**Castleford, Twin Falls, Pop. 224**
Castleford JSD 417 300/PK-12
500 Main St 83321 208-537-6511
Lyle Bayley, supt. Fax 537-6855
www.castlefordschools.com
Castleford S 300/PK-12
500 Main St 83321 208-537-6511
Lyle Bayley, supt. Fax 537-6855

**Challis, Custer, Pop. 1,066**
Challis JSD 181 400/K-12
PO Box 304 83226 208-879-4231
Peter McPherson, supt. Fax 879-5473
www.d181.k12.id.us
Challis JSHS 200/7-12
PO Box 304 83226 208-879-2255
Russ Bradshaw, prin. Fax 879-5801

**Chubbuck, Bannock, Pop. 13,624**

---

The School of Hairstyling Post-Sec.
141 E Chubbuck Rd 83202 208-232-9170

**Clark Fork, Bonner, Pop. 519**
Lake Pend Oreille SD 84
Supt. — See Ponderay
Clark Fork JSHS 100/7-12
121 E 4th St 83811 208-255-7177
Phil Kemink, prin. Fax 266-1692

**Coeur d Alene, Kootenai, Pop. 43,078**
Coeur D'Alene SD 271 9,800/PK-12
1400 N Northwood Center Ct 83814 208-664-8241
Matthew Handelman, supt. Fax 664-1748
www.cdaschools.org
Canfield MS 800/6-8
1800 E Dalton Ave 83815 208-664-9188
Nick Lilyquist, prin. Fax 769-2951
Coeur D'Alene HS 1,400/9-12
5530 N 4th St 83815 208-667-4507
Warren Olson, prin. Fax 664-5785
Lake City HS 1,500/9-12
6101 N Ramsey Rd 83815 208-769-0769
Deanne Clifford, prin. Fax 769-2944
Lakes Magnet MS 600/6-8
930 N 15th St 83814 208-667-4544
Jeff Bengtson, prin. Fax 769-2982
Project CDA/Bridge Academy 50/Alt
1619 N 9th St 83814 208-667-7460
Fax 765-2299
Woodland MS 800/6-8
2101 W Saint Michelle 83815 208-667-5996
David Serwat, prin. Fax 667-5997

---

Lake City Junior Academy 200/PK-10
111 E Locust Ave 83814 208-667-0877
North Idaho College Post-Sec.
1000 W Garden Ave 83814 208-769-3300
The Headmasters School of Hair Design Post-Sec.
317 Coeur DAlene Lake Dr 83814 208-664-0541

**Cottonwood, Idaho, Pop. 891**
Cottonwood JSD 242 400/PK-12
PO Box 158 83522 208-962-3971
Rene' Forsmann, supt. Fax 962-7780
www.sd242.org
Prairie JSHS 200/7-12
PO Box 540 83522 208-962-3901
Carrie Nygaard, prin. Fax 962-7702

---

Summit Academy 100/PK-12
PO Box 427 83522 208-962-5650
James Hickel, prin. Fax 962-7129

**Council, Adams, Pop. 826**
Council SD 13 200/PK-12
PO Box 468 83612 208-253-4217
Murray Dalgleish, supt. Fax 253-4297
www.csd13.org/
Council JSHS 100/7-12
PO Box 468 83612 208-253-4217
Murray Dalgleish, supt. Fax 253-4297

**Craigmont, Lewis, Pop. 493**
Highland JSD 305 200/PK-12
PO Box 130 83523 208-924-5211
Brad Baumberger M.Ed., supt. Fax 924-5614
www.sd305.org
Highland S 200/PK-12
PO Box 130 83523 208-924-5211
Dr. Sarah Hatfield, prin. Fax 924-5614

**Culdesac, Nez Perce, Pop. 380**
Culdesac JSD 342 100/PK-12
600 Culdesac Ave 83524 208-843-5413
Alan Felgenhauer, supt. Fax 843-2719
pass.culsch.org
Culdesac S 100/PK-12
600 Culdesac Ave 83524 208-843-5413
Shannon Morris M.A., prin. Fax 843-2719

**Dayton, Franklin, Pop. 454**
West Side JSD 202 600/PK-12
PO Box 39 83232 208-747-3502
Spencer Barzee, supt. Fax 747-3705
www.wssd.k12.id.us
Lee MS 100/6-8
PO Box 140 83232 208-747-3303
Spencer Barzee, prin. Fax 747-3637
West Side HS 200/9-12
PO Box 39 83232 208-747-3411
Tyler Telford, prin. Fax 747-3990

**Deary, Latah, Pop. 490**
Whitepine JSD 288 200/K-12
PO Box 249 83823 208-877-1408
Tera Reeves, supt. Fax 877-1570
www.sd288.k12.id.us/
Deary S 200/4-12
PO Box 9 83823 208-877-1151
Darrah Eggers, prin. Fax 877-1366

**Declo, Cassia, Pop. 341**
Cassia County JSD 151
Supt. — See Burley
Declo HS 300/9-12
505 E Main St 83323 208-654-2030
Roland Bott, prin. Fax 654-2404
Declo JHS 300/6-8
205 E Main St 83323 208-654-9960
Scott Muir, prin. Fax 654-2070

**Dietrich, Lincoln, Pop. 330**
Dietrich SD 314 200/PK-12
406 N Park St 83324 208-544-2158
Neal Hollingshead, supt. Fax 544-2832
www.sd314.k12.id.us/
Dietrich S 200/PK-12
406 N Park St 83324 208-544-2158
Neal Hollingshead, prin. Fax 544-2832

**Driggs, Teton, Pop. 1,636**
Teton County SD 401 1,500/K-12
PO Box 775 83422 208-354-2207
Monte Woolstenhulme, supt. Fax 354-2250
tsd401.org
Basin JSHS Alt
510 N 1st E 83422 208-354-4800
LeaAnn Gomez, prin. Fax 354-2250
Teton HS 400/9-12
555 E Ross Ave 83422 208-354-2952
Frank Mello, prin. Fax 354-2907
Teton MS 400/6-8
935 N 5th E 83422 208-354-2971
Steven Burch, prin. Fax 354-8685

**Dubois, Clark, Pop. 673**
Clark County SD 161 200/PK-12
PO Box 237 83423 208-374-5215
Daniel Lantis, supt. Fax 374-5234
www.clarkcountyschools161.org/
Clark County JSHS 100/6-12
PO Box 237 83423 208-374-5215
Daniel Lantis, supt. Fax 374-5234

**Eagle, Ada, Pop. 19,545**
West Ada SD
Supt. — See Meridian
Eagle Academy 100/Alt
100 S Academy Ave 83616 208-350-4220
James Buschine, prin. Fax 350-4234
Eagle HS 1,600/9-12
574 Park Ln 83616 208-350-4235
Terry Beck, prin. Fax 350-4254
Eagle MS 1,200/6-8
1000 W Floating Feather Rd 83616 208-350-4255
Tony Nelson, prin. Fax 350-4269
Idaho Fine Arts Academy 6-12
3467 W Flint Dr 83616
Tina Perry, prin.

**Emmett, Gem, Pop. 6,420**
Emmett ISD 221 2,400/K-12
400 S Pine St Ste 1 83617 208-365-6301
Wayne Rush, supt. Fax 365-2961
emmettschools.org
Black Canyon Alternative HS 100/Alt
400 S Pine St Ste 2 83617 208-365-5552
Stephen Joyner, prin. Fax 365-5085
Emmett HS 700/9-12
721 W 12th St 83617 208-365-6323
Wade Carter, prin. Fax 365-6100
Emmett MS 600/5-8
301 E 4th St 83617 208-365-2921
Bob Hyde, prin. Fax 365-2427

**Fairfield, Camas, Pop. 404**
Camas County SD 121 100/K-12
610 Soldier Rd 83327 208-764-2625
Jim Cobble, supt. Fax 764-9218
www.camascountyschools.org/
Camas County HS 50/9-12
610 Soldier Rd 83327 208-764-2472
Jeff Rast, prin. Fax 764-2018

**Filer, Twin Falls, Pop. 2,469**
Filer SD 413 1,400/PK-12
700B Stevens Ave 83328 208-326-5981
Dr. John Graham, supt. Fax 326-3350
www.filer.k12.id.us
Filer HS 400/9-12
3915 Wildcat Way 83328 208-326-5945
Leon Madsen, prin. Fax 326-3419
Filer MS 200/7-8
299 Highway 30 83328 208-326-5906
Shane Hild, prin. Fax 326-3385

**Firth, Bingham, Pop. 462**
Firth SD 59 700/PK-12
319 Lincoln St 83236 208-346-6815
Sid Tubbs, supt. Fax 346-6814
www.firthschools.org
Firth HS 200/9-12
329 Lincoln St 83236 208-346-6812
Jeff Gee, prin. Fax 346-6987
Firth MS 200/5-8
410 Roosevelt St 83236 208-346-6240
David Mecham, prin. Fax 346-4306

**Fruitland, Payette, Pop. 4,599**
Fruitland SD 373 1,500/PK-12
PO Box A 83619 208-452-3595
Teresa Fabricius, supt. Fax 452-6430
www.fruitlandschools.org
Fruitland Alternative S 50/Alt
PO Box A 83619 208-452-3360
Gayle VanWeerdhuizen, admin.
Fruitland HS 500/9-12
PO Box A 83619 208-452-4411
Mike Fitch, prin. Fax 452-4485
Fruitland MS 400/6-8
PO Box A 83619 208-452-3350
Kimi Fitch, prin. Fax 452-4063

**Garden Valley, Boise, Pop. 390**
Garden Valley SD 71 200/PK-12
PO Box 710 83622 208-462-3756
Marc Gee, supt. Fax 462-3570
www.gvsd.net
Garden Valley S 200/PK-12
PO Box 710 83622 208-462-3756
Marc Gee, supt. Fax 462-3570

**Genesee, Latah, Pop. 930**
Genesee JSD 282 300/K-12
PO Box 98 83832 208-285-1161
Wendy Moore, supt. Fax 285-1495
www.sd282.org/
Genesee S 300/K-12
PO Box 98 83832 208-285-1162
Kelly Caldwell, prin. Fax 285-1495

**Glenns Ferry, Elmore, Pop. 1,301**
Glenns Ferry JSD 192 500/PK-12
800 Old Highway 30 83623 208-366-7436
Cody Fisher, supt. Fax 366-7455
www.glennsferryschools.org/
Glenns Ferry HS 100/9-12
639 N Bannock St 83623 208-366-7434
Cody Fisher, prin. Fax 366-2056
Glenns Ferry MS 100/6-8
639 N Bannock St 83623 208-366-7438
Rob Spriggs, prin. Fax 366-2056

**Gooding, Gooding, Pop. 3,514**
Gooding JSD 231 1,100/PK-12
507 Idaho St 83330 208-934-4321
Mary Larson, supt. Fax 934-4403
www.goodingschools.org
Gooding HS 300/9-12
1050 7th Ave W 83330 208-934-4831
Benjamin Hardcastle, prin. Fax 934-4347
Gooding MS 300/6-8
1045 7th Ave W 83330 208-934-8443
Collin Robertson, prin. Fax 934-4898

---

Idaho State School for the Deaf/Blind Post-Sec.
1450 Main St 83330 208-934-4457

**Grace, Caribou, Pop. 908**
Grace JSD 148 400/PK-12
PO Box 347 83241 208-425-3984
Jamie Holyoak, supt. Fax 425-3809
www.sd148.org/
Grace JSHS 200/7-12
PO Box 348 83241 208-425-3731
Stephen Brady, prin. Fax 425-3063

**Grangeville, Idaho, Pop. 3,096**
Mountain View SD 244 1,200/PK-12
714 Jefferson St 83530 208-983-0990
Kent Stokes, supt. Fax 983-1245
www.sd244.org
Grangeville HS 300/9-12
910 S D St 83530 208-983-0580
Steve Higgins, prin. Fax 983-3786
Other Schools – See Kooskia

**Greenleaf, Canyon, Pop. 835**

---

Greenleaf Friends Academy 200/PK-12
PO Box 368 83626 208-459-6346
Jeff Metcalf M.Ed., prin. Fax 459-7700

**Hagerman, Gooding, Pop. 864**
Hagerman JSD 233 400/K-12
324 N 2nd Ave 83332 208-837-6344
Eric Anderson, supt. Fax 837-6380
www.hagerman.k12.id.us
Hagerman JSHS 200/7-12
150 Lake St W 83332 208-837-4572
Mark Kress, prin. Fax 837-6502

**Hailey, Blaine, Pop. 7,880**
Blaine County SD 61 3,200/K-12
118 W Bullion St 83333 208-578-5000
Dr. GwenCarol Holmes, supt. Fax 578-5110
www.blaineschools.org/
Silver Creek HS 50/Alt
1060 Fox Acres Rd Ste 1000 83333 208-578-5060
Mike Glenn, admin. Fax 578-5160
Wood River HS 800/9-12
1250 Fox Acres Rd 83333 208-578-5020
John Pearce, prin. Fax 578-5120

Wood River MS 700/6-8
900 N 2nd Ave 83333 208-578-5030
Fritz Peters, prin. Fax 578-5130
Other Schools – See Carey

**Hansen, Twin Falls, Pop. 1,129**
Hansen SD 415 400/PK-12
550 Main St S 83334 208-423-6387
Kristin Beck, supt. Fax 423-6808
www.hansen.k12.id.us
Hansen JSHS 200/7-12
550 Main St S 83334 208-423-5593
Kayla Kelly, prin. Fax 423-6808

**Harrison, Kootenai, Pop. 203**
Kootenai SD 274 200/K-12
13030 E Ogara Rd 83833 208-689-3631
Lynette Ferguson, supt. Fax 689-3641
www.sd274.com
Kootenai JSHS 100/6-12
13030 E Ogara Rd 83833 208-689-3311
Tim Schultz, prin. Fax 689-9072

**Hayden, Kootenai, Pop. 13,034**

---

North Idaho Christian S 200/1-12
251 W Miles Ave 83835 208-772-7546
Cal Booth, admin. Fax 719-3000

**Hazelton, Jerome, Pop. 738**
Valley SD 262 600/PK-12
882 Valley Rd 83335 208-829-5333
Arlyn Bodily, supt. Fax 829-5548
www.valleyvikings.org
Valley S 600/PK-12
882 Valley Rd 83335 208-829-5353
Arlyn Bodily, admin. Fax 829-5548

**Heyburn, Minidoka, Pop. 3,058**
Minidoka County JSD 331
Supt. — See Rupert
Mt. Harrison JSHS 200/Alt
1431 17th St 83336 208-436-6252
Shanna Lindsay, prin. Fax 436-4746

**Homedale, Owyhee, Pop. 2,586**
Homedale JSD 370 1,200/K-12
116 E Owyhee Ave 83628 208-337-4611
Rob Sauer, supt. Fax 337-4911
www.homedaleschools.org
Homedale HS 400/9-12
203 E Idaho Ave 83628 208-337-4613
Matt Holtry, prin. Fax 337-4933
Homedale MS 400/5-8
3437 Johnstone Rd 83628 208-337-5780
Amy Winters, prin. Fax 337-5782

**Horseshoe Bend, Boise, Pop. 696**
Horseshoe Bend SD 73 200/PK-12
398 School Dr 83629 208-793-2225
Fax 793-2449
www.hsbschools.org
Horseshoe Bend HS 100/9-12
398 School Dr 83629 208-793-2225
Dennis Chesnut, prin. Fax 793-2449

**Idaho City, Boise, Pop. 473**
Basin SD 72 400/PK-12
PO Box 227 83631 208-392-4183
John McFarlane, supt. Fax 392-9954
www.idahocityschools.net/
Idaho City MSHS 200/7-12
PO Box 227 83631 208-392-4183
John McFarlane, prin. Fax 392-9954

**Idaho Falls, Bonneville, Pop. 55,872**
Bonneville JSD 93 9,800/PK-12
3497 N Ammon Rd 83401 208-525-4400
Dr. Chuck Shackett, supt. Fax 529-0104
www.d93schools.org
Bonneville HS 1,300/9-12
3165 E Iona Rd 83401 208-525-4406
Heath Jackson, prin. Fax 523-7014
Lincoln Alternative HS 200/Alt
3175 E Lincoln Rd 83401 208-525-4447
Gordon Howard, prin. Fax 525-4446
Rocky Mountain MS 700/7-8
3443 N Ammon Rd 83401 208-525-4403
Jason Lords, prin. Fax 525-4469
Technical Careers HS Vo/Tech
3497 N Ammon Rd 83401 208-525-4433
Craig Miller, prin. Fax 525-4434
Telford Academy 50/Alt
2017 E 49th N 83401 208-542-0283
John Pymm, prin. Fax 524-2429
Other Schools – See Ammon

Idaho Falls SD 91 9,400/PK-12
690 John Adams Pkwy 83401 208-525-7500
George Boland, supt. Fax 525-7596
www.d91.k12.id.us
Compass Academy 300/9-12
955 Garfield St 83401 208-525-7720
Matthew Bertasso, dir.
Eagle Rock MS 600/7-8
2020 Pancheri Dr 83402 208-525-7700
Matt Hancock, prin. Fax 525-7703
Eastern Idaho Professional Technical HS Vo/Tech
390 John Adams Pkwy 83401 208-525-7549
Bobbi Crosser Finlayson, coord. Fax 525-7596
Emerson Alternative HS 100/Alt
335 5th St 83401 208-524-7800
Robin Busch, prin. Fax 525-7795
Idaho Falls HS 1,100/9-12
601 S Holmes Ave 83401 208-525-7740
Bob Devine, prin. Fax 525-7768
Skyline HS 1,000/9-12
1767 Blue Sky Dr 83402 208-525-7770
W. Jeff Sanders, prin. Fax 525-7778
Taylorview MS 600/7-8
350 Castlerock Ln 83404 208-524-7850
Kathy Smith, prin. Fax 524-7851

---

Eastern Idaho Technical College Post-Sec.
1600 S 25th E 83404 208-524-3000
Stevens-Henager College Post-Sec.
901 Pier View Dr Ste 105 83402 208-522-0887

Watersprings S 500/PK-12
4250 S 25th E 83404 208-542-6250
Rick Brown, supt. Fax 441-6806

**Jerome, Jerome, Pop. 10,745**
Jerome JSD 261 3,400/PK-12
125 4th Ave W 83338 208-324-2392
Dale Layne, supt. Fax 324-7609
www.jeromeschools.org
Jerome HS 900/9-12
104 Tiger Dr 83338 208-324-8137
Keelie Campbell, prin. Fax 324-1266
Jerome MS 800/6-8
520 10th Ave W 83338 208-324-8134
Ryan Ellsworth, prin. Fax 324-7458
Northside Alternative JSHS 50/Alt
125 4th Ave W 83338 208-324-8137
Dale Layne, prin. Fax 324-1266

**Juliaetta, Latah, Pop. 565**
Kendrick JSD 283 200/PK-12
305 4th St 83535 208-289-4211
Dr. Lindsay Park, supt. Fax 289-4201
www.dist283.org/
Other Schools – See Kendrick

**Kamiah, Lewis, Pop. 1,246**
Kamiah JSD 304 600/PK-12
1102 Hill St 83536 208-935-2991
Fred Mercer, supt. Fax 935-4005
www.kamiah.org/
Kamiah HS 100/9-12
1102 Hill St 83536 208-935-4067
Michael Roberts, prin. Fax 935-4068
Kamiah MS 200/5-8
1102 Hill St 83536 208-935-4040
Michael Roberts, prin. Fax 935-4041

**Kellogg, Shoshone, Pop. 2,083**
Kellogg JSD 391 1,300/K-12
800 Bunker Ave 83837 208-784-1348
Woody Woodford, supt. Fax 786-3331
www.kelloggschools.org
Kellogg HS 400/9-12
2 Jacobs Gulch Rd 83837 208-784-1371
Curt Bayer, prin. Fax 783-0741
Kellogg MS 300/6-8
810 Bunker Ave 83837 208-784-1311
Scott Ross, prin. Fax 784-0134

---

Silver Valley Christian Academy 50/PK-12
15 E Mullan Ave 83837 208-783-3791
Brenda Erikson, sec. ed. Fax 783-3791

**Kendrick, Latah, Pop. 297**
Kendrick JSD 283
Supt. — See Juliaetta
Kendrick JSHS 100/7-12
2001 Highway 3 83537 208-289-4202
Steven Kirkland, prin. Fax 289-4213

**Kimberly, Twin Falls, Pop. 3,233**
Kimberly SD 414 1,500/K-12
141 Center St W 83341 208-423-4170
Luke Schroeder, supt. Fax 423-6155
www.kimberly.edu/
Kimberly HS 400/9-12
141 Center St W 83341 208-423-4170
Lisa Senecal, prin. Fax 423-5181
Kimberly MS 300/6-8
141 Center St W 83341 208-423-4170
Mathew Schvaneveldt, prin. Fax 423-6155

**Kooskia, Idaho, Pop. 590**
Mountain View SD 244
Supt. — See Grangeville
Clearwater Valley JSHS 200/6-12
PO Box 130 83539 208-926-4511
Randall Miskin, prin. Fax 926-4807

**Kuna, Ada, Pop. 14,851**
Kuna JSD 3 4,400/PK-12
711 E Porter St 83634 208-922-1000
Wendy Johnson, supt. Fax 922-5646
www.kunaschools.org
Initial Point HS 100/Alt
1080 N Ten Mile Rd 83634 208-472-9721
Lora Seabaugh, prin. Fax 472-9730
Kuna HS 1,300/9-12
637 E Deer Flat Rd 83634 208-955-0200
Brian Graves, prin. Fax 922-2178
Kuna MS 700/7-8
1360 Boise St 83634 208-922-1002
Deb McGrath, prin. Fax 922-1030

**Lapwai, Nez Perce, Pop. 1,098**
Lapwai SD 341 500/PK-12
404 S Main St 83540 208-843-2622
Dr. David Aiken, supt. Fax 843-7746
www.lapwaidistrict.org/
Lapwai JSHS 200/6-12
404 S Main St 83540 208-843-2241
D'Lisa Pinkham, prin. Fax 843-5289

**Leadore, Lemhi, Pop. 105**
South Lemhi SD 292 100/PK-12
PO Box 119 83464 208-768-2441
Erica J. Kemery, supt. Fax 768-2797
www.leadoreschool.org
Leadore S 100/PK-12
PO Box 119 83464 208-768-2441
Erica J. Kemery, prin. Fax 768-2797

**Lewiston, Nez Perce, Pop. 31,213**
Lewiston ISD 1 4,800/PK-12
3317 12th St 83501 208-748-3000
Dr. Robert Donaldson, supt. Fax 748-3059
www.lewistonschools.net
Jenifer JHS 600/7-9
1213 16th St 83501 208-748-3300
JoAnne Greear, prin. Fax 748-3349
Lewiston SHS 1,000/10-12
1114 9th Ave 83501 208-748-3100
Kevin Driskill, prin. Fax 748-3149
Sacajawea JHS 600/7-9
3610 12th St 83501 208-748-3400
Phil Uhlorn, prin. Fax 748-3449
Tammany Alternative Learning Center 100/Alt
1982 Tammany Creek Rd 83501 208-748-3270
Greg Kramasz, admin. Fax 748-3299

---

Confluence Christian HS 50/9-12
PO Box 1852 83501 208-731-6320
Ross Carlton, prin.
Lewis-Clark State College Post-Sec.
500 8th Ave 83501 208-792-5272
Mr. Leon's School of Hair Design Post-Sec.
205 10th St 83501 208-743-6822
The Headmasters School of Hair Design Post-Sec.
602 Main St 83501 208-743-1512

**Mc Call, Valley, Pop. 2,959**
McCall-Donnelly JSD 421 900/PK-12
120 Idaho St 83638 208-634-2161
Jim Foudy, supt. Fax 634-4075
www.mdsd.org
Heartland Alternative S 50/Alt
124 Idaho St 83638 208-634-3686
David Pickard, prin. Fax 634-1512
McCall-Donnelly HS 300/9-12
401 N Mission St 83638 208-634-2218
Tim Thomas, prin. Fax 634-7505
Payette Lakes MS 200/6-8
111 S Samson Trl 83638 208-634-5994
Susan Buescher, prin. Fax 634-5231

**Mackay, Custer, Pop. 515**
Mackay JSD 182 200/PK-12
PO Box 390 83251 208-588-2896
Leigh Patterson, supt. Fax 588-2269
Mackay JSHS 100/7-12
PO Box 390 83251 208-588-2262
Leigh Patterson, prin. Fax 588-2549

**Malad City, Oneida, Pop. 2,070**
Oneida County SD 351 900/PK-12
25 E 50 S Ste A 83252 208-534-6080
Dr. David Risenmay, supt. Fax 534-6080
www.oneidaschooldistrict.org
Malad HS 200/9-12
181 Jenkins Ave 83252 208-497-2588
Dr. David Risenmay, prin. Fax 497-2588
Malad MS 200/6-8
175 Jenkins Ave 83252 208-497-5877
Sheldon Vaughan, prin. Fax 497-5877
Oneida Alternative HS 50/Alt
300 W 450 N 83252 208-497-5877
Terri Sorensen, prin. Fax 497-5877

**Malta, Cassia, Pop. 193**
Cassia County JSD 151
Supt. — See Burley
Raft River JSHS 100/7-12
PO Box 68 83342 208-645-2220
Eric Boden, prin. Fax 645-2640

**Marsing, Owyhee, Pop. 1,018**
Marsing JSD 363 900/K-12
PO Box 340 83639 208-896-4111
Norm Stewart, supt. Fax 896-4790
www.marsingschools.org/
Marsing HS 200/9-12
PO Box 340 83639 208-896-4111
Tim Little, prin. Fax 896-4457
Marsing MS 200/6-8
PO Box 340 83639 208-896-4111
Jacob Skousen, prin. Fax 896-5128

**Melba, Canyon, Pop. 503**
Melba JSD 136 700/PK-12
PO Box 185 83641 208-495-1141
Andy Grover, supt. Fax 495-1142
www.melbaschools.org
Melba JSHS 300/7-12
PO Box 185 83641 208-495-2221
Todd Shumway, prin. Fax 495-2188

**Menan, Jefferson, Pop. 728**
Jefferson County JSD 251
Supt. — See Rigby
Jefferson Alternative HS 100/Alt
529 N 3470 E 83434 208-754-4550
Richard Young, prin. Fax 754-4581

**Meridian, Ada, Pop. 73,335**
West Ada SD 34,700/PK-12
1303 E Central Dr 83642 208-855-4500
Dr. Linda Clark, supt. Fax 350-5962
www.westada.org
Central Academy 100/Alt
6075 N Locust Grove Rd, 208-855-4325
Donell McNeal, prin. Fax 855-4324
Crossroads MS 100/Alt
650 N Nola Rd 83642 208-855-4275
Karen Harr, prin. Fax 855-4284
Heritage MS 1,000/6-8
4990 N Meridian Rd, 208-350-4130
Susan McInerney, prin. Fax 350-4139
Lewis & Clark MS 1,100/6-8
4141 E Pine Ave 83642 208-350-4270
Kelly Davies, prin. Fax 350-4284
Meridian Academy 100/Alt
2311 E Lanark St 83642 208-855-4315
Dustin Barrett, prin. Fax 855-4326
Meridian HS 1,400/9-12
1900 W Pine Ave 83642 208-350-4160
Geoff Stands, prin. Fax 350-4179
Meridian MS 1,100/6-8
1507 W 8th St 83642 208-855-4225
Lisa Austin, prin. Fax 888-3038
Mountain View HS 2,100/9-12
2000 S Millenium Way 83642 208-855-4050
Aaron Maybon, prin. Fax 855-4074
Pathways MS 200/Alt
1855 E Heritage Park Ln, 208-350-4040
Eric Eschen, prin. Fax 350-4059
Rebound School of Opportunity 50/Alt
1450 E Watertower St 83642 208-350-5232
Fax 350-5179
Renaissance HS 500/9-12
1307 E Central Dr 83642 208-350-4380
Shana Hawkins, prin. Fax 350-4399
Rocky Mountain HS 2,100/9-12
5450 N Linder Rd, 208-350-4340
Mike Hirano, prin. Fax 350-4369
Sawtooth MS 1,000/6-8
3730 N Linder Rd, 208-855-4200
Kevin Leishman, prin. Fax 855-4224
Other Schools – See Boise, Eagle

---

Ambrose S 400/K-12
6100 N Locust Grove Rd, 208-323-3888
Kirk VanderLeest, hdmstr. Fax 672-0522
Broadview College Post-Sec.
2750 E Gala St 83642 208-577-2900
Cole Valley Christian S 300/7-12
200 E Carlton Ave 83642 208-947-1212
Brad Carr, supt. Fax 898-9016
Covenant Academy 50/K-12
2400 E Fairview Ave 83642 208-890-0881
David Barrett, admin. Fax 362-8061
Guardian College Post-Sec.
2150 E Fairview Ave Ste 100 83642 208-321-4744
Northwest Lineman College Post-Sec.
7600 S Meridian Rd 83642 208-888-4817
Sheridan Academy 50/6-12
2273 E Gala St Ste 120 83642 208-331-2044
Leigh Wilson, dir. Fax 331-7724

**Middleton, Canyon, Pop. 5,406**
Middleton SD 134 3,100/PK-12
5 S 3rd Ave W 83644 208-585-3027
Dr. Rich Bauscher, supt. Fax 585-3028
www.msd134.org
ATLAS S 50/Alt
200 S 4th Ave W 83644 208-585-3027
Christine McMillan, hdmstr. Fax 585-3028
Middleton HS 1,000/9-12
1538 Emmett Rd 83644 208-585-6657
Mike Williams, prin. Fax 585-3362
Middleton MS 700/6-8
511 W Main St 83644 208-585-3251
Andrew Horning, prin. Fax 585-2098

**Midvale, Washington, Pop. 169**
Midvale SD 433 100/K-12
PO Box 130 83645 208-355-2234
James Warren, supt. Fax 355-2347
www.midvalerangers.org
Midvale Alternative S 50/Alt
PO Box 130 83645 208-355-2234
James Warren, prin. Fax 355-2347
Midvale S 100/K-12
PO Box 130 83645 208-355-2234
James Warren, prin. Fax 355-2347

**Montpelier, Bear Lake, Pop. 2,578**
Bear Lake County SD 33
Supt. — See Paris
Bear Lake HS 300/9-12
330 Boise St 83254 208-847-0294
David Chamberlain, prin. Fax 847-0144
Bear Lake MS 200/6-8
633 Washington St 83254 208-847-2255
Steve Heeder, prin. Fax 847-3626

**Moscow, Latah, Pop. 23,195**
Moscow SD 281 1,900/PK-12
650 N Cleveland St 83843 208-882-1120
Greg Bailey, supt. Fax 883-4440
www.msd281.org
Moscow HS 600/9-12
402 E 5th St 83843 208-882-2591
Robert Celebrezze, prin. Fax 892-1136
Moscow MS 400/6-8
1410 E D St 83843 208-882-3577
Kevin Hill, prin. Fax 892-1182
Paradise Creek Regional HS 50/Alt
1314 S Main St 83843 208-882-3687
Edward Norman, prin. Fax 882-6815

---

Mr. Leon's School of Hair Design Post-Sec.
618 S Main St 83843 208-882-2923
New Saint Andrews College Post-Sec.
PO Box 9025 83843 208-882-1566
University of Idaho Post-Sec.
PO Box 444264 83844 208-885-6111

**Mountain Home, Elmore, Pop. 13,628**
Mountain Home SD 193 3,100/PK-12
PO Box 1390 83647 208-587-2580
Tim McMurtrey, supt. Fax 587-9896
www.mtnhomesd.org
Mountain Home JHS 300/8-9
1600 E 6th S 83647 208-587-2590
Sam Gunderson, prin. Fax 587-2597
Mountain Home SHS 700/10-12
300 S 11th E 83647 208-587-2570
Jeff Johnson, prin. Fax 587-2579

**Mullan, Shoshone, Pop. 674**
Mullan SD 392 100/K-12
PO Box 71 83846 208-744-1118
Robin Stanley, supt. Fax 744-1119
www.mullanschools.com
Mullan JSHS 50/7-12
PO Box 71 83846 208-744-1126
Tom Durbin, prin. Fax 744-1128

**Murtaugh, Twin Falls, Pop. 114**
Murtaugh JSD 418 200/PK-12
PO Box 117 83344 208-432-5451
Michele Capps, supt. Fax 432-5477
www.murtaugh.k12.id.us/
Murtaugh HS 100/9-12
PO Box 117 83344 208-432-5451
Adam Johnson, prin. Fax 432-5477
Murtaugh MS 100/6-8
PO Box 117 83344 208-432-5451
Adam Johnson, prin. Fax 432-5477

**Nampa, Canyon, Pop. 79,667**
Nampa SD 131 14,500/PK-12
619 S Canyon St 83686 208-468-4600
David Peterson, supt. Fax 468-4638
www.nsd131.org/
Alpha One Alternative HS 50/Alt
141 Smith Ave 83651 208-468-4775
Pat Berg, prin. Fax 468-4776
Columbia HS 1,300/9-12
301 S Happy Valley Rd 83687 208-498-0571
Cory Woolstenhulme, prin. Fax 498-0573
East Valley MS 900/6-8
4085 E Greenhurst Rd 83686 208-468-4760
Matt Crist, admin. Fax 461-4069
Gateways Alternative S Alt
141 Smith Ave 83651 208-498-0557
Cyndi Cook, prin. Fax 498-0568
Lone Star MS 800/6-8
11055 Lone Star Rd 83651 208-468-4745
Greg Heideman, prin. Fax 442-4763
Nampa HS 1,400/9-12
203 Lake Lowell Ave 83686 208-498-0551
Byron Holtry, prin. Fax 466-1240
Skyview HS 1,300/9-12
1303 E Greenhurst Rd 83686 208-498-0561
Kim Bekkedahl, prin. Fax 468-7822
South MS 900/6-8
229 W Greenhurst Rd 83686 208-468-4740
Stuart Vickers, prin. Fax 465-2779
Union HS 100/Alt
506 Fletcher Dr 83686 208-498-0559
Carleen Schnitker, prin. Fax 468-2832
West MS 700/6-8
28 S Midland Blvd 83651 208-468-4750
Stefanie Duby, prin. Fax 465-2776

Vallivue SD 139
Supt. — See Caldwell
Sage Valley MS 900/6-8
18070 Santa Ana Ave 83687 208-468-4919
Sean Smith, prin. Fax 468-4904

---

Calvary Chapel Christian S 100/PK-12
1210 N Middleton Rd 83651 208-467-7116
College of Western Idaho Post-Sec.
5500 Opportunity Dr 83687 208-562-3000
Milan Institute Post-Sec.
1021 W Hemingway Blvd 83651 208-461-0616
Nampa Christian HS 200/7-12
11920 W Flamingo Ave 83651 208-466-8451
Greg Wiles, supt. Fax 475-1741
Northwest Nazarene University Post-Sec.
623 S University Blvd 83686 208-467-8011
Razzle Dazzle College of Hair Design Post-Sec.
721 E Roosevelt Ave 83686 208-465-7660

**New Meadows, Adams, Pop. 492**
Meadows Valley SD 11 200/PK-12
PO Box F 83654 208-347-2411
Mike Howard, supt. Fax 347-2624
www.mvsd11.org
Meadows Valley S 200/PK-12
PO Box F 83654 208-347-2118
Mike Howard, supt. Fax 347-2624

**New Plymouth, Payette, Pop. 1,508**
New Plymouth SD 372 900/PK-12
103 SE Avenue 83655 208-278-5740
Ryan Kerby, supt. Fax 278-3069
www.npschools.us
New Plymouth HS 300/9-12
207 S Plymouth Ave 83655 208-278-5311
Kevin Barker, prin. Fax 278-5313
New Plymouth MS 200/6-8
4400 SW 2nd Ave 83655 208-278-5788
Christine Collins, prin. Fax 278-3773

**Nezperce, Lewis, Pop. 463**
Nezperce JSD 302 100/PK-12
PO Box 279 83543 208-937-2551
Dennis Kachelmier, supt. Fax 937-2136
www.nezpercesd.us/
Nezperce S 100/PK-12
PO Box 279 83543 208-937-2551
Les Wells, prin. Fax 937-2136

**Notus, Canyon, Pop. 520**
Notus SD 135 400/K-12
PO Box 256 83656 208-459-7442
Craig Woods, supt. Fax 453-1027
www.notusschools.org
Notus JSHS 200/7-12
PO Box 256 83656 208-459-4633
Craig Woods, prin. Fax 459-6304

**Oakley, Cassia, Pop. 762**
Cassia County JSD 151
Supt. — See Burley
Oakley JSHS 200/7-12
455 W Main St 83346 208-862-3328
Michael Corbett, prin. Fax 862-3330

**Oldtown, Bonner, Pop. 183**

---

House of the Lord Christian Academy 100/PK-12
754 Silver Birch Ln 83822 208-437-2184
Candace Craddick, prin. Fax 437-0441

**Orofino, Clearwater, Pop. 3,071**
Orofino JSD 171 1,000/PK-12
PO Box 2259 83544 208-476-5593
Robert Vian, supt. Fax 476-7293
www.sd171.k12.id.us
Orofino HS 300/7-12
300 Dunlap Rd 83544 208-476-5557
Dan Hull, prin. Fax 476-0147
Other Schools – See Weippe

**Paris, Bear Lake, Pop. 510**
Bear Lake County SD 33 1,100/PK-12
PO Box 300 83261 208-945-2891
Dr. Gary Brogan, supt. Fax 945-2893
blsd.net
Other Schools – See Montpelier

**Parma, Canyon, Pop. 1,955**
Parma SD 137 1,000/K-12
805 E McConnell Ave 83660 208-722-5115
Jim Norton, supt. Fax 722-7937
www.parmaschools.org
Parma HS 300/9-12
137 Panther Way 83660 208-722-5115
David Carson, prin. Fax 722-7153
Parma MS 300/5-8
905 E McConnell Ave 83660 208-722-5115
Peggy Sharkey, prin. Fax 722-6913

**Paul, Minidoka, Pop. 1,146**
Minidoka County JSD 331
Supt. — See Rupert
West Minico MS 400/6-8
155 S 600 W 83347 208-438-5018
Tim Perrigot, prin. Fax 438-8513

**Payette, Payette, Pop. 7,244**
Payette JSD 371 1,500/PK-12
20 N 12th St 83661 208-642-9366
Pauline King, supt. Fax 642-9006
www.payetteschools.org/
McCain MS 400/6-8
400 N Iowa Ave 83661 208-642-4122
Rick Hale, prin. Fax 642-2171
Payette HS 400/9-12
1500 6th Ave S 83661 208-642-3327
Mark Heleker, prin. Fax 642-3368

**Plummer, Benewah, Pop. 956**
Plummer/Worley JSD 44 400/PK-12
PO Box 130 83851 208-686-1621
Judi Sharrett, supt. Fax 686-2108
www.pwsd44.com
Lakeside JSHS 100/7-12
PO Box 130 83851 208-686-1937
Jennifer Hall, prin. Fax 686-2207

**Pocatello, Bannock, Pop. 53,083**
Pocatello/Chubbuck SD 25 12,400/PK-12
3115 Pole Line Rd 83201 208-232-3563
Dr. Douglas Howell, supt. Fax 235-3280
www.sd25.us
Alameda MS 6-8
3115 Pole Line Rd 83201 208-235-6800
Brandon Vaughan, prin. Fax 235-6801
Century HS 1,200/9-12
7801 W Diamond Back Dr 83204 208-478-6863
Sheryl Brockett, prin. Fax 478-6870
Franklin MS 800/6-8
2271 E Terry St 83201 208-233-5590
Patrick Vereecken, prin. Fax 233-1024
Hawthorne MS 800/6-8
1025 W Eldredge Rd 83201 208-237-1680
Dr. Heidi Kessler, prin. Fax 237-1682
Highland HS 1,300/9-12
1800 Bench Rd 83201 208-237-1300
Dian Swanson, prin. Fax 237-1350
Irving MS 700/6-8
911 N Grant Ave 83204 208-232-3039
Tonya Wilkes, prin. Fax 232-0379
New Horizon HS 100/Alt
955 W Alameda Rd 83201 208-237-2233
Bradley Wallace, prin. Fax 238-3635
Pocatello HS 1,100/9-12
325 N Arthur Ave 83204 208-233-2056
Lisa Delonas, prin. Fax 232-0365

---

Idaho State University Post-Sec.
921 S 8th Ave 83209 208-282-0211

**Ponderay, Bonner, Pop. 1,102**
Lake Pend Oreille SD 84 3,800/PK-12
901 N Triangle Dr 83852 208-263-2184
Shawn Woodward, supt. Fax 263-5053
www.lposd.org/
Other Schools – See Clark Fork, Sandpoint

**Post Falls, Kootenai, Pop. 26,948**
Post Falls SD 273 5,600/PK-12
PO Box 40 83877 208-773-1658
Jerry Keane, supt. Fax 773-3218
www.pfsd.com
New Vision Alternative S 100/Alt
PO Box 40 83877 208-773-3541
Dawn Mackesy, prin. Fax 773-3542
Post Falls HS 1,500/9-12
PO Box 40 83877 208-773-0581
Chris Sensel, prin. Fax 773-0587
Post Falls MS 700/6-8
PO Box 40 83877 208-773-7554
Deborah Davis, prin. Fax 773-0884
River City MS 500/6-8
PO Box 40 83877 208-457-0933
Michael Yovetich, prin. Fax 457-1673

---

American Institute of Clinical Massage Post-Sec.
4365 E Inverness Dr 83854 208-773-5890
Genesis Preparatory Academy 100/K-12
PO Box 1237 83877 208-691-0712
Chris Finch, prin. Fax 777-8853

**Potlatch, Latah, Pop. 786**
Potlatch SD 285 400/K-12
130 6th St 83855 208-875-0327
Jeffrey A. Cirka, supt. Fax 875-1028
www.potlatchschools.org
Potlatch JSHS 200/7-12
130 6th St 83855 208-875-1231
Cheryl Riedinger, prin. Fax 875-1028

**Preston, Franklin, Pop. 5,154**
Preston JSD 201 2,500/PK-12
120 E 2nd S 83263 208-852-0283
Joel Wilson, supt. Fax 852-3976
www.prestonidahoschools.org
Franklin County HS 100/Alt
594 N State St 83263 208-852-2272
Ken Gifford, prin. Fax 852-3976
Preston HS 700/9-12
151 E 2nd S 83263 208-852-0280
Jeff Lords, prin. Fax 852-0080
Preston JHS 600/6-8
450 E Valley View Dr 83263 208-852-0751
Curtis Jenson, prin. Fax 852-3510

**Priest River, Bonner, Pop. 1,684**
West Bonner County SD 83 1,200/PK-12
134 Main St 83856 208-448-4439
Paul Anselmo, supt. Fax 448-4629
www.sd83.org
PREP Alternative HS 50/Alt
134 Main St 83856 208-448-1405
Leoni Johnson, prin. Fax 448-0630
Priest River JHS 200/7-8
5709 Highway 2 83856 208-448-1118
Leoni Johnson, prin. Fax 448-1119
Priest River Lamanna HS 400/9-12
596 Highway 57 83856 208-448-1211
Roy Reynolds, prin. Fax 448-1212

**Rathdrum, Kootenai, Pop. 6,685**
Lakeland SD 272 4,300/PK-12
PO Box 39 83858 208-687-0431
Brad Murray, supt. Fax 687-1884
web.lakeland272.org

Kootenai Technical Education Center Vo/Tech
6838 W Lancaster Rd 83858 208-712-4733
Fax 712-6004

Lakeland HS 700/9-12
PO Box 69 83858 208-687-0181
Conrad Underdahl, prin. Fax 687-1313
Lakeland JHS 400/7-8
PO Box 98 83858 208-687-0661
Todd Spear, prin. Fax 687-1510
Mountain View Alternative HS 100/Alt
PO Box 39 83858 208-687-0025
Paul Uzzi, admin. Fax 687-2843
Other Schools – See Spirit Lake

**Rexburg, Madison, Pop. 25,087**
Madison SD 321 4,900/PK-12
PO Box 830 83440 208-359-3300
Geoffrey Thomas, supt. Fax 359-3345
www.d321.k12.id.us
Central HS 100/Alt
379 S 2nd E 83440 208-359-2337
Rodger Hampton M.Ed., prin. Fax 359-2521
Madison Academy 50/Alt
379 S 2nd E 83440 208-359-2337
Rodger Hampton M.Ed., admin. Fax 359-2521
Madison JHS 1,100/7-9
134 Madison Ave 83440 208-359-3310
Rex Fullmer M.Ed., prin. Fax 372-0105
Madison SHS 1,000/10-12
2300 University Blvd 83440 208-359-3305
Mike Bennett M.Ed., prin. Fax 359-3346

---

Brigham Young University - Idaho Post-Sec.
525 S Center St 83460 208-496-1411

**Richfield, Lincoln, Pop. 478**
Richfield SD 316 200/PK-12
555 N Tiger Dr 83349 208-487-2241
Mike Smith, supt. Fax 487-2240
sites.google.com/site/richfieldtigers
Richfield S 200/PK-12
555 N Tiger Dr 83349 208-487-2790
Mike Smith, admin. Fax 487-2055

**Rigby, Jefferson, Pop. 3,876**
Jefferson County JSD 251 4,200/PK-12
3850 E 300 N 83442 208-745-6693
Dr. Lisa Sherick, supt. Fax 745-0848
www.sd251.org/
Rigby HS 900/9-12
3833 Rigby High Ln 83442 208-745-7704
Dr. Yvonne Thurber, prin. Fax 745-7707
Rigby MS 300/6-8
290 N 3800 E 83442 208-745-6674
Sherry Simmons, prin. Fax 745-6675
Other Schools – See Menan

**Riggins, Idaho, Pop. 415**
Salmon River JSD 243 100/PK-12
PO Box 872 83549 208-630-6027
Jim Doramus, supt. Fax 630-6026
www.jsd243.org
Salmon River JSHS 100/6-12
PO Box 872 83549 208-630-6025
Jim Doramus, supt. Fax 630-6028

**Ririe, Jefferson, Pop. 653**
Ririe JSD 252 400/PK-12
PO Box 508 83443 208-538-7482
Chad Williams, supt. Fax 538-7363
www.ririeschools.org
Ririe JSHS 200/7-12
PO Box 568 83443 208-538-7311
Chad Williams, prin. Fax 538-7860

**Rockland, Power, Pop. 294**
Rockland SD 382 200/K-12
PO Box 119 83271 208-548-2221
Chester Bradshaw, supt. Fax 548-2224
www.rbulldogs.org
Rockland S 200/K-12
PO Box 119 83271 208-548-2221
Chester Bradshaw, prin. Fax 548-2224

**Rupert, Minidoka, Pop. 5,482**
Minidoka County JSD 331 3,900/K-12
310 10th St 83350 208-436-4727
Dr. Kenneth Cox, supt. Fax 436-6593
www.minidokaschools.org
East Minico MS 400/6-8
310 10th St 83350 208-436-3178
Bryan McKinney, prin. Fax 436-3235
Minico HS 1,000/9-12
310 10th St 83350 208-436-4721
Suzette Miller, prin. Fax 436-3266
Other Schools – See Heyburn, Paul

**Saint Anthony, Fremont, Pop. 3,512**
Fremont County JSD 215 2,100/PK-12
945 W 1st N 83445 208-624-7542
Dr. Garry Parker, supt. Fax 624-3385
www.sd215.net

South Fremont HS 500/9-12
855 N Bridge St 83445 208-624-3416
Larry Bennett, prin. Fax 624-4898
South Fremont JHS 400/6-8
550 N 1st W 83445 208-624-7880
David Marotz, prin. Fax 624-4386
Other Schools – See Ashton

**Saint Maries, Benewah, Pop. 2,361**
Saint Maries JSD 41 1,000/PK-12
PO Box 384 83861 208-245-2579
Joseph Kren, supt. Fax 245-3970
www.sd41.org
Saint Maries Community Education Center 50/Alt
422 Hells Gulch Rd 83861 208-245-2152
John Cordell, prin. Fax 245-0212
Saint Maries HS 300/9-12
424 Hells Gulch Rd 83861 208-245-2142
John Cordell, prin. Fax 245-5650
Saint Maries MS 200/6-8
1315 W Jefferson Ave 83861 208-245-3495
Jeffrey Andersen, prin. Fax 245-0506

**Salmon, Lemhi, Pop. 3,067**
Salmon SD 291 600/PK-12
907 Sharkey St 83467 208-756-4271
Jim Smith, supt. Fax 756-6695
www.salmonschools.com
Salmon Alternative HS 50/Alt
1401 S Bean Ln 83467 208-756-6277
Fax 756-6695
Salmon JSHS 300/5-12
401 S Warpath 83467 208-756-2415
Shawn Hendrickson, prin. Fax 756-3484

**Sandpoint, Bonner, Pop. 7,221**
Lake Pend Oreille SD 84
Supt. — See Ponderay
Lake Pend Oreille Alternative HS 100/Alt
1005 N Boyer Ave 83864 208-263-6121
Geoffrey Penrose, prin. Fax 265-5734
Sandpoint HS 1,000/9-12
410 S Division Ave 83864 208-263-3034
Tom Albertson, prin. Fax 263-5321
Sandpoint MS 500/7-8
310 S Division Ave 83864 208-265-4169
Kim Keaton, prin. Fax 263-5525

**Shelley, Bingham, Pop. 4,332**
Shelley JSD 60 1,800/PK-12
545 Seminary Ave 83274 208-357-3411
Dr. Bryan Jolley, supt. Fax 357-5741
www.shelleyschools.org
Hobbs MS 300/7-8
350 E Pine St 83274 208-357-7667
Mike Messick, prin. Fax 357-3003
Shelley HS 600/9-12
570 W Fir St 83274 208-357-7400
Dale Clark, prin. Fax 357-5585

**Shoshone, Lincoln, Pop. 1,444**
Shoshone JSD 312 400/PK-12
61 E Highway 24 83352 208-886-2381
Rob Waite, supt. Fax 886-2038
www.shoshonesd.org
Shoshone JSHS 100/6-12
61 E Highway 24 83352 208-886-2381
Kelly Chapman, prin. Fax 886-2742

**Soda Springs, Caribou, Pop. 3,009**
Soda Springs JSD 150 800/K-12
250 E 2nd S 83276 208-547-3371
Dr. Molly Stein, supt. Fax 547-4878
www.sodaschools.org
Soda Springs HS 200/9-12
300 E 1st N 83276 208-547-4308
Robert Daniel, prin. Fax 547-3327
Tigert MS 200/5-8
250 E 2nd S Ste B 83276 208-547-4922
Debra Daniels, prin. Fax 547-2619

**Spirit Lake, Kootenai, Pop. 1,910**
Lakeland SD 272
Supt. — See Rathdrum
Timberlake HS 500/9-12
PO Box 909 83869 208-623-6303
Kurt Hoffman, prin. Fax 623-6203
Timberlake JHS 300/7-8
PO Box 1080 83869 208-623-2582
Chris McDougall, prin. Fax 623-2750

**Sugar City, Madison, Pop. 1,499**
Sugar-Salem JSD 322 1,500/PK-12
PO Box 150 83448 208-356-8802
Alan Dunn, supt. Fax 356-7237
www.sugarsalem.org
Sugar-Salem HS 400/9-12
1 S Digger Dr 83448 208-356-0274
Jared Jenks, prin. Fax 359-3167
Sugar-Salem JHS 200/7-8
PO Box 180 83448 208-356-4437
Kevin Schultz, prin. Fax 358-9717
Valley View Alt HS 50/Alt
1 S Digger Dr 83448 208-356-6845
Jay Miller, prin. Fax 356-3167

**Sun Valley, Blaine, Pop. 1,392**

---

Community S 300/PK-12
PO Box 2118 83353 208-622-3955
David Holmes, head sch Fax 622-3962

**Terreton, Jefferson**
West Jefferson SD 253 600/PK-12
1256 E 1500 N 83450 208-663-4542
Dwight Richins, supt. Fax 663-4543
www.wjsd.org
West Jefferson HS 200/9-12
1260 E 1500 N 83450 208-663-4391
Wes Woodward, prin. Fax 663-4390

**Troy, Latah, Pop. 841**
Troy SD 287 300/K-12
PO Box 280 83871 208-835-3791
Dr. Christy Castro, supt. Fax 835-3790
www.sd287.k12.id.us
Troy JSHS 200/7-12
101 Trojan Dr 83871 208-835-2361
Brad Malm, prin. Fax 835-2441

**Twin Falls, Twin Falls, Pop. 43,303**
Twin Falls SD 411 7,700/PK-12
201 Main Ave W 83301 208-733-6900
Wiley Dobbs, supt. Fax 733-6987
www.tfsd.k12.id.us
Canyon Ridge HS 1,100/9-12
300 N College Rd W 83301 208-732-7555
Kasey Teske, prin. Fax 732-7556
Magic Valley HS 100/Alt
512 Main Ave N 83301 208-733-8823
Roger Keller, prin. Fax 733-8505
O'Leary JHS 900/6-8
2350 Elizabeth Blvd 83301 208-733-2155
Jess Johnson, prin. Fax 733-8666
Stuart JHS 800/6-8
644 Caswell Ave W 83301 208-733-4875
Amy McBride, prin. Fax 733-4949
Twin Falls HS 1,000/9-12
1615 Filer Ave E 83301 208-733-6551
Dan Vogt, prin. Fax 733-8192

---

College of Southern Idaho Post-Sec.
PO Box 1238 83303 208-733-9554
Lighthouse Christian S 300/PK-12
960 Eastland Dr 83301 208-737-1425
Kevin Newbry, supt. Fax 737-4671
Mr. Juan's College of Hair Design Post-Sec.
586 Blue Lakes Blvd N 83301 208-733-7777
Twin Falls Christian Academy 100/K-12
798 Eastland Dr N 83301 208-733-1452
Brent Walker, prin. Fax 734-1417

**Wallace, Shoshone, Pop. 769**
Wallace SD 393 500/PK-12
405 7th St 83873 208-753-4515
Dr. Robert Ranells, supt. Fax 753-4151
www.wsd393.org/
Wallace JSHS 200/7-12
1 Miners Aly 83873 208-753-5315
Don Almquist, prin. Fax 753-7105

**Weippe, Clearwater, Pop. 439**
Orofino JSD 171
Supt. — See Orofino
Timberline S 300/PK-12
22869 Highway 11 83553 208-435-4411
Shaun Ball, prin. Fax 435-4846

**Weiser, Washington, Pop. 5,415**
Weiser SD 431 1,600/PK-12
925 Pioneer Rd 83672 208-414-0616
Wil Overgaard, supt. Fax 414-1265
www.weiserschools.org
Weiser HS 500/9-12
690 W Indianhead Rd 83672 208-414-2595
David Davies, prin. Fax 414-1795
Weiser MS 400/6-8
320 E Galloway Ave 83672 208-414-2620
Jason Hunter, prin. Fax 414-2094

**Wendell, Gooding, Pop. 2,752**
Wendell SD 232 1,100/PK-12
PO Box 300 83355 208-536-2418
Greg Lowe, supt. Fax 536-2629
www.wendellschools.org
Wendell HS 300/9-12
850 E Main St 83355 208-536-2100
Jon Goss, prin. Fax 536-2124
Wendell MS 400/5-8
920 E Main St 83355 208-536-5531
Luke Kelsey, prin. Fax 536-5957

**Wilder, Canyon, Pop. 1,528**
Wilder SD 133 400/K-12
210 A Ave 83676 208-482-6228
Jeff Dillon, supt. Fax 482-6980
www.wilderschools.org
Wilder MSHS 200/6-12
419 Huff Rd 83676 208-482-6229
Tim Jensen, prin. Fax 482-7421

# ILLINOIS

## ILLINOIS DEPARTMENT OF EDUCATION
**100 N 1st St, Springfield 62777-0002**
**Telephone 866-262-6663**
**Fax 217-524-8585**
**Website http://www.isbe.state.il.us**

Superintendent of Education Dr. Christopher Koch

## ILLINOIS BOARD OF EDUCATION
**100 N 1st St, Springfield 62777-0002**

Chairperson Gery Chico

## REGIONAL OFFICES OF EDUCATION (ROE)

Adam/Brwn/Cass/Morgn/Pik/Sctt ROE
Deborah Niederhauser, supt. 217-277-2080
507 Vermont St, Quincy 62301 Fax 277-2092
www.wc4.org

Alxndr/Jcksn/Pulsk/Prry/Union ROE
Donna Boros, supt., 1001 Walnut St 618-687-7290
Murphysboro 62966 Fax 687-7296
www.roe30.org

Bond/Christn/Effingham/Fayette/Mtgmy ROE
Julie Wollerman, supt. 618-283-5011
300 S 7th St, Vandalia 62471 Fax 283-5013
www.roe3.org

Boone/Winnebago ROE
Dr. Lori Fanello, supt. 815-636-3060
300 Heart Blvd, Loves Park 61111 Fax 636-3069
www.bwroe.org

Bureau/Henry/Stark ROE
Angie Zarvell, supt. 309-936-7890
107 S State St, Atkinson 61235 Fax 936-1111
www.bhsroe.org

Calhoun/Greene/Jersey/Macoupin ROE
Larry Pfeiffer, supt. 217-854-4016
225 E Nicholas St, Carlinville 62626 Fax 854-2032
www.roe40.com

Carroll/Jo Daviess/Stephenson ROE
Aaron Mercier, supt. 815-599-1408
27 S State Ave Ste 101 Fax 297-9032
Freeport 61032
www.roe8.com

Champaign/Ford ROE
Jane Quinlan, supt. 217-893-3219
200 S Fredrick St, Rantoul 61866 Fax 893-0024
www.roe9.k12.il.us/

Clay/Crawford/Jspr/Lwrnce/Rchlnd ROE
Monte Newlin, supt. 618-392-4631
103 W Main St Ste 23, Olney 62450 Fax 392-3993
www.roe12.net

Clintn/Jeffrsn/Marin/Washngtn ROE
Keri Jo Garrett, supt. 618-594-2432
930 Fairfax St Ste B, Carlyle 62231 Fax 594-7192
www.roe13.k12.il.us

Clk/Cls/Cumb/Dglas/Edg/Mlt/Shlb ROE
Dr. Bobbi Mattingly, supt. 217-348-0151
730 7th St, Charleston 61920 Fax 348-0171
www.roe11.k12.il.us/

DeKalb ROE
Amanda Christensen, supt. 815-217-0460
2500 N Annie Glidden Rd Fax 217-0467
DeKalb 60115
www.dekalbcounty.org/roe

DeWitt/Livingston/Logan/McLean ROE
Mark Jontry, supt. 309-888-5120
200 W Front St Ste 500 Fax 862-0420
Bloomington 61701
www.roe17.org

Dupage ROE
Darlene Ruscitti, supt. 630-407-5800
421 N County Farm Rd Fax 407-5801
Wheaton 60187
www.dupage.k12.il.us/

Edwds/Gtn/Hdn/Pope/Sln/Wbsh/Wyn/Wt ROE
Lawrence Fillingim, supt. 618-253-5581
512 N Main St, Harrisburg 62946 Fax 252-8472
www.roe20.k12.il.us/

Franklin-Johnson-Massac-Williamson ROE
Matt Donkin, supt. 618-438-9711
202 W Main St, Benton 62812 Fax 435-2861
www.roe21.org

Grundy/Kendall ROE
Christopher Mehochko, supt. 815-941-3247
1320 Union St, Morris 60450 Fax 942-5384
www.roe24.org

Hancck/Fultn/Schuylr/McDonogh ROE
John Meixner, supt. 309-837-4821
130 S Lafayette St Ste 200 Fax 837-2887
Macomb 61455
www.roe26.net

Henderson/Knox/Mercer/Warren ROE
Jodi Scott, supt. 309-734-6822
105 N E St Ste 1, Monmouth 61462 Fax 734-2452
www.roe33.net

Iroquois/Kankakee ROE
Greg Murphy, supt. 815-937-2950
189 E Court St Ste 600 Fax 937-2921
Kankakee 60901
www.i-kan.org

Kane ROE
Patricia Dal Santo, supt. 630-232-5955
210 S 6th St, Geneva 60134 Fax 208-5100
www.kaneroe.org/

Lake ROE
Dr. Roycealee Wood, supt. 847-543-7833
800 Lancer Ln Ste E128 Fax 543-7832
Grayslake 60030
www.lake.k12.il.us

LaSalle/Marshall/Putnam ROE
Christopher Dvorak, supt. 815-434-0780
119 W Madison St, Ottawa 61350 Fax 434-2453
www.roe35.org

Lee/Ogle/Whiteside ROE
Robert Sondgeroth, supt. 815-625-2054
1001 W 23rd St, Sterling 61081 Fax 625-1625
www.roe47.org

Macon/Piatt ROE 39
Matthew Snyder, supt. 217-872-3721
1690 Huston Dr, Decatur 62526 Fax 872-0239
www.maconpiattroe.com/

Madison County ROE
Dr. Robert Daiber, supt. 618-296-4530
157 N Main St, Edwardsville 62025 Fax 692-7018
www.roe41.org

Mason-Tazewell-Woodford ROE
Gail Owen, supt. 309-477-2290
414 Court St Ste 100, Pekin 61554 Fax 347-3735
www.roe53.net

McHenry ROE
Leslie Schermerhorn, supt. 815-334-4475
2200 N Seminary Ave Fax 338-0475
Woodstock 60098
www.mchenryroe.org/

Menard/Sangamon ROE
Jeff Vose, supt. 217-753-6620
200 S 9th St Ste 303 Fax 535-3166
Springfield 62701
www.roe51.org

Monroe-Randolph ROE
Kelton Davis, supt. 618-939-5650
107 E Mill St, Waterloo 62298 Fax 939-5332
www.roe45.org

North Cook Intermediate Service Center
Dr. Bruce Brown, dir. 847-824-8300
2340 S River Rd Fax 824-1033
Des Plaines 60018
www.ncisc.org

Peoria ROE
Gerald Brookhart, supt. 309-672-6906
324 Main St Ste 401, Peoria 61602 Fax 672-6053
www.co.peoria.il.us/roe

Rock Island ROE
Tammy Muerhoff, supt. 309-736-1111
3430 Avenue of the Cities Fax 736-1127
Moline 61265
www.riroe.com/

Saint Clair ROE
Susan Sarfaty, supt. 618-825-3900
1000 S Illinois St, Belleville 62220 Fax 825-3999
www.stclair.k12.il.us/

South Cook Intermediate Service Center
Dr. Vanessa Kinder, supt. 708-754-6600
253 W Joe Orr Rd Fax 754-8687
Chicago Heights 60411
www.s-cook.org

Vermilion ROE
Cheryl Reifsteck, supt. 217-431-2668
200 S College St Ste B Fax 431-2671
Danville 61832
www.roe54.k12.il.us/

West Suburb Intermediate Service Center
Kay Poyner Brown, dir. 708-449-4284
4413 Roosevelt Rd Ste 104 Fax 449-4288
Hillside 60162
www.west40.org

Will ROE
Shawn Walsh, supt. 815-740-8360
702 W Maple St, New Lenox 60451 Fax 740-4788
www.willroe.org

## PUBLIC, PRIVATE AND CATHOLIC SECONDARY SCHOOLS

**Abingdon, Knox, Pop. 3,272**
Abingdon-Avon CUSD 276 800/PK-12
401 W Latimer St 61410 309-462-2301
Chad Willlis, supt. Fax 462-3870
www.d217.net
Abingdon-Avon HS 200/9-12
600 W Martin St 61410 309-462-2338
Shane Gordon, prin. Fax 462-2492
Other Schools – See Avon

**Addison, DuPage, Pop. 36,491**
Addison SD 4 4,200/PK-8
222 N JF Kennedy Dr 60101 630-458-2500
John Langton, supt. Fax 628-8829
www.asd4.org
Indian Trail JHS 1,400/6-8
222 N JF Kennedy Dr Frnt 1 60101 630-458-2600
Craig Bennett, prin. Fax 628-2841

DAOES
301 S Swift Rd 60101 630-691-7590
Jim Thorne, dir. Fax 691-7592
www.tcdupage.org
Technology Center of Dupage Vo/Tech
301 S Swift Rd Ste B 60101 630-620-8770
Steven Carr, prin. Fax 691-7592

DuPage HSD 88 4,000/9-12
2 Friendship Plz 60101 630-530-3980
Dr. Scott Helton, supt. Fax 832-0198
www.dupage88.net/
Addison Trail HS 1,900/9-12
213 N Lombard Rd 60101 630-628-3302
Adam Cibulka, prin. Fax 628-0177
Other Schools – See Villa Park

---

Chamberlain College of Nursing Post-Sec.
1221 N Swift Rd 60101 630-953-3680
DeVry University Post-Sec.
1221 N Swift Rd 60101 630-953-1300

**Albion, Edwards, Pop. 1,965**
Edwards County CUSD 1 1,000/PK-12
361 W Main St Ste 100 62806 618-445-2814
David Cowger, supt. Fax 445-2272
www.edwardscountyschools.org
Edwards County HS 300/9-12
361 W Main St 62806 618-445-2325
Preston Nelson, prin. Fax 445-3154

**Aledo, Mercer, Pop. 3,626**
Mercer County SD 404 1,300/PK-12
1002 SW 6th St 61231 309-582-2238
Alan Boucher, supt. Fax 582-7428
www.mercerschools.org
Mercer County HS 400/9-12
1500 S College Ave 61231 309-582-2223
Stacey Day, prin. Fax 582-5920
Other Schools – See Joy

**Alexander, Morgan**
Franklin CUSD 1 — 300/PK-12
PO Box 140 62601 — 217-478-3011
Andy Stremlau, supt. — Fax 478-4921
www.franklinhigh.com
Other Schools – See Franklin

**Algonquin, McHenry, Pop. 29,616**
CUSD 300 — 19,500/PK-12
2550 Harnish Dr 60102 — 847-551-8300
Fred Heid, supt. — Fax 551-8413
www.d300.org
Algonquin MS — 500/6-8
520 Longwood Dr 60102 — 847-658-2545
Andrew Reincke, prin. — Fax 658-2547
Jacobs HS — 2,200/9-12
2601 Bunker Hill Dr 60102 — 847-658-2500
Barb Valle, prin. — Fax 658-3203
Other Schools – See Carpentersville, Hampshire, West Dundee

Consolidated SD 158 — 9,000/PK-12
650 Academic Dr 60102 — 847-659-6158
Dr. John Burkey, supt. — Fax 659-6121
www.district158.org/
Heineman MS — 800/6-8
725 Academic Dr 60102 — 847-659-4300
Jake Litchfield, prin. — Fax 659-4320
Other Schools – See Huntley, Lake in the Hills

**Alsip, Cook, Pop. 19,017**
Alsip-Hazelgreen-Oaklawn SD 126 — 1,500/K-8
11900 S Kostner Ave 60803 — 708-389-1900
Craig Gwaltney, supt. — Fax 396-3793
www.dist126.org
Prairie JHS — 400/7-8
11910 S Kostner Ave 60803 — 708-371-3080
Maureen Paulmeyer, prin. — Fax 396-3798

Atwood Heights SD 125 — 700/PK-8
12150 S Hamlin Ave 60803 — 708-371-0080
Dr. Thomas Livingston, supt. — Fax 371-7847
www.ahsd125.org
Hamlin Upper Grade Center — 200/6-8
12150 S Hamlin Ave 60803 — 708-597-1550
Dr. Lisa West, prin. — Fax 396-0515

**Altamont, Effingham, Pop. 2,313**
Altamont CUSD 10 — 800/PK-12
7 S Ewing St 62411 — 618-483-6195
Jeff Fritchtnitch, supt. — Fax 483-6303
www.altamontschools.org
Altamont HS — 300/9-12
7 S Ewing St 62411 — 618-483-6194
Jerry Tkachuk, prin. — Fax 483-5399

**Alton, Madison, Pop. 26,887**
Alton CUSD 11 — 6,400/PK-12
PO Box 9028 62002 — 618-474-2600
Dr. Kenneth Spells, supt. — Fax 463-2126
www.altonschools.org
Alton HS — 2,000/9-12
4200 Humbert Rd 62002 — 618-474-2700
Dr. Russell Tepen, prin. — Fax 463-2000
Alton MS — 1,400/6-8
2200 College Ave 62002 — 618-474-2200
Dr. Steven Sandbothe, prin. — Fax 463-2127

---

CALC Institute of Technology — Post-Sec.
200 N Center Dr Ste A 62002 — 618-474-0616
Marquette HS — 400/9-12
219 E 4th St 62002 — 618-463-0580
Michael Slaughter, prin. — Fax 465-4029
Mississippi Valley Christian S — 100/PK-12
2009 Seminary St 62002 — 618-462-1071
Jerry Fair, prin. — Fax 462-9877
St. Mary MS — 100/6-8
1015 Milton Rd 62002 — 618-465-9719
Judy Kulp, prin. — Fax 465-9726

**Amboy, Lee, Pop. 2,480**
Amboy CUSD 272 — 800/PK-12
11 E Hawley St 61310 — 815-857-2164
Jeff Thake, supt. — Fax 857-4434
www.amboy.net/
Amboy HS — 300/9-12
11 E Hawley St 61310 — 815-857-3632
Ron Gruber, prin. — Fax 857-3631
Amboy JHS — 200/5-8
140 S Appleton Ave 61310 — 815-857-3528
Joyce Schamberger, prin. — Fax 857-4603

**Anna, Union, Pop. 4,407**
Anna CCSD 37 — 700/K-8
301 S Green St 62906 — 618-833-6812
Charles Goforth, supt. — Fax 833-3205
anna37.com/
Anna JHS — 300/5-8
301 S Green St 62906 — 618-833-6812
Mark Laster, prin. — Fax 833-6535

Anna-Jonesboro Community HSD 81 — 500/9-12
608 S Main St 62906 — 618-833-8421
Rob Wright, supt. — Fax 833-4239
aj81.net
Anna-Jonesboro HS — 500/9-12
608 S Main St 62906 — 618-833-8502
Brett Detering, prin. — Fax 833-5931

**Annawan, Henry, Pop. 875**
Annawan CUSD 226 — 400/PK-12
501 W South St 61234 — 309-935-6781
Joseph Buresh, supt. — Fax 935-6065
www.annawan226.org
Annawan HS — 100/9-12
501 W South St 61234 — 309-935-6781
Wayne Brau, prin. — Fax 935-6065

**Antioch, Lake, Pop. 14,166**
Antioch CCSD 34 — 3,000/PK-8
964 Spafford St 60002 — 847-838-8400
Dr. Jay Marino, supt. — Fax 838-8404
www.antioch34.com
Antioch Upper Grade S — 1,000/6-8
800 Highview Dr 60002 — 847-838-8310
Mike Zarco, prin. — Fax 838-8304

Community HSD 117
Supt. — See Lake Villa
Antioch Community HS — 1,400/9-12
1133 Main St 60002 — 847-395-1421
Bradford Hubbard, prin. — Fax 395-2435

**Arcola, Douglas, Pop. 2,899**
Arcola CUSD 306 — 800/PK-12
351 W Washington St 61910 — 217-268-4963
Thomas Mulligan, supt. — Fax 268-3809
www.arcola.k12.il.us
Arcola JSHS — 300/7-12
351 W Washington St 61910 — 217-268-4962
Lisa Sigrist, prin. — Fax 268-4483

---

Pleasant View S — 50/K-12
184 N County Road 300E 61910 — 217-268-3886
Allen Miller, admin.

**Argenta, Macon, Pop. 935**
Argenta-Oreana CUSD 1 — 1,000/PK-12
PO Box 440 62501 — 217-795-2313
Damian Jones, supt. — Fax 795-2174
www.argenta-oreana.org/
Argenta-Oreana HS — 300/9-12
PO Box 469 62501 — 217-795-4821
Sean German, prin. — Fax 795-4550
Argenta-Oreana MS — 200/6-8
PO Box 439 62501 — 217-795-2163
Amanda Ryder, prin. — Fax 795-4502

**Arlington Heights, Cook, Pop. 74,142**
Arlington Heights SD 25 — 5,100/PK-8
1200 S Dunton Ave 60005 — 847-758-4900
Dr. Lori Bein, supt. — Fax 758-4907
www.sd25.org
South MS — 900/6-8
400 S Highland Ave 60005 — 847-398-4250
Piper Boston, prin. — Fax 394-6260
Thomas MS — 900/6-8
1430 N Belmont Ave 60004 — 847-398-4260
Brian Kaye, prin. — Fax 394-6843

CCSD 59 — 6,500/PK-8
2123 S Arlington Heights Rd 60005 — 847-593-4300
Art Fessler, supt. — Fax 593-4409
www.ccsd59.org
Other Schools – See Des Plaines, Elk Grove Village, Mount Prospect

Township HSD 214 — 12,100/9-12
2121 S Goebbert Rd 60005 — 847-718-7600
David Schuler Ph.D., supt. — Fax 718-7609
www.d214.org
Academy at Forest View — 100/Alt
2121 S Goebbert Rd 60005 — 847-718-7771
Kara Kendrick, dir. — Fax 718-7773
Hersey HS — 2,000/9-12
1900 E Thomas St 60004 — 847-718-4800
Gordon Sisson, prin. — Fax 718-4817
Vanguard S — 100/Alt
2121 S Goebbert Rd 60005 — 847-718-7888
Kate Kraft, dir. — Fax 718-7869
Other Schools – See Buffalo Grove, Elk Grove Village, Mount Prospect, Rolling Meadows, Wheeling

---

Christian Liberty Academy — 400/PK-12
502 W Euclid Ave 60004 — 847-259-4444
Thad Bennett, hdmstr. — Fax 259-9972
ITT Technical Institute — Post-Sec.
3800 N Wilke Rd Ste 100 60004 — 847-454-1800
Northwest Community Hospital — Post-Sec.
800 W Central Rd 60005 — 847-618-1000
Robert Morris University — Post-Sec.
2123 S Goebbert Rd 60005 — 800-762-5960
St. Viator HS — 1,000/9-12
1213 E Oakton St 60004 — 847-392-4050
Eileen Manno, prin. — Fax 392-4329

**Armstrong, Vermilion**
Armstrong Twp. HSD 225 — 100/9-12
PO Box 37 61812 — 217-569-2122
Bill Mulvaney, supt. — Fax 569-2171
www.armstrong.k12.il.us
Armstrong HS — 100/9-12
PO Box 37 61812 — 217-569-2122
Darren Loschen, prin. — Fax 569-2171

**Arthur, Douglas, Pop. 2,280**
Arthur CUSD 305 — 700/PK-12
301 E Columbia St 61911 — 217-543-2511
Kenneth Schwengel, supt. — Fax 543-2210
www.cusd305.org
Arthur-Lovington-Atwood-Hammond HS — 100/9-12
301 E Columbia St 61911 — 217-543-2146
Buck Condill, prin. — Fax 543-2174

---

Arthur Christian S — 100/PK-12
1710 State Highway 133 61911 — 217-543-2397
Greg Mast, prin. — Fax 543-3781

**Ashkum, Iroquois, Pop. 755**
Central CUSD 4 — 1,100/PK-12
PO Box 158 60911 — 815-698-2212
Tonya Evans, supt. — Fax 694-2844
www.clifton-u4.k12.il.us
Other Schools – See Clifton

**Ashland, Cass, Pop. 1,324**
A-C Central CUSD 262 — 500/PK-12
PO Box 260 62612 — 217-476-8112
Timothy Page, supt. — Fax 476-8100
a-ccentral.com
A-C Central HS — 100/9-12
PO Box 260 62612 — 217-476-3312
Fax 476-3730

Other Schools – See Chandlerville

**Ashton, Lee, Pop. 967**
Ashton-Franklin Center CUSD 275 — 600/PK-12
611 Western Ave 61006 — 815-453-7461
John Zick, supt. — Fax 453-7462
www.afcschools.net
Ashton-Franklin Center JSHS — 200/7-12
611 Western Ave 61006 — 815-453-7461
Tammy Harvey, prin. — Fax 453-7462

**Assumption, Christian, Pop. 1,158**
Central A & M CUSD 21 — 900/K-12
105 N College St 62510 — 217-226-4042
Dr. DeAnn Heck, supt. — Fax 226-4133
camraiders.com
Central A & M MS — 200/6-8
404 Colegrove St 62510 — 217-226-4241
Ryan Scott, prin. — Fax 226-4442
Other Schools – See Moweaqua

**Astoria, Fulton, Pop. 1,131**
Astoria CUSD 1 — 400/PK-12
402 N Jefferson St 61501 — 309-329-2156
Don Willett, supt. — Fax 329-2214
www.astoria.fulton.k12.il.us
Astoria HS — 100/9-12
402 N Jefferson St 61501 — 309-329-2156
Don Willett, prin. — Fax 329-2246
Astoria JHS — 100/6-8
402 N Jefferson St 61501 — 309-329-2158
Dave Crouse, prin. — Fax 329-2963

**Athens, Menard, Pop. 1,956**
Athens CUSD 213 — 1,100/PK-12
1 Warrior Way 62613 — 217-636-8761
Dr. Scott Laird, supt. — Fax 636-8851
www.athens-213.org
Athens HS — 300/9-12
1 Warrior Way 62613 — 217-636-8314
Bill Reed, prin. — Fax 636-8851
Athens JHS — 200/7-8
1 Warrior Way 62613 — 217-636-8380
Matt Rhoades, prin. — Fax 636-8851

**Auburn, Sangamon, Pop. 4,722**
Auburn CUSD 10 — 1,500/PK-12
606 W North St 62615 — 217-438-6164
Darren Root, supt. — Fax 438-6483
www.auburn.k12.il.us
Auburn HS — 400/9-12
511 N 7th St 62615 — 217-438-6817
Nathan Essex, prin. — Fax 438-6153
Other Schools – See Divernon

**Augusta, Hancock, Pop. 586**
Southeastern CUSD 337 — 500/PK-12
PO Box 215 62311 — 217-392-2172
Todd Fox, supt. — Fax 392-2174
www.southeastern337.com/
Southeastern JSHS — 200/7-12
PO Box 155 62311 — 217-392-2125
Cyle Rigg, prin. — Fax 392-2229

**Aurora, Kane, Pop. 194,432**
Aurora East Unit SD 131 — 14,200/PK-12
417 5th St 60505 — 630-299-5550
Dr. Michael Popp, supt. — Fax 299-5500
www.d131.org
Cowherd MS — 1,100/6-8
441 N Farnsworth Ave 60505 — 630-299-5900
Crystal England, prin. — Fax 299-5901
East HS — 3,300/9-12
500 Tomcat Ln 60505 — 630-299-8000
Spencer Byrd, prin. — Fax 299-8199
Rodgers Magnet Academy — 3-8
157 N Root St 60505 — 630-299-7175
Angela Rowley, prin.
Simmons MS — 1,100/6-8
1130 Sheffer Rd 60505 — 630-299-4150
Mechelle Patterson, prin. — Fax 299-4151
Waldo MS — 1,000/6-8
56 Jackson St 60505 — 630-299-8400
Sandra Katula, prin. — Fax 299-8401

Aurora West Unit SD 129 — 12,400/PK-12
80 S River St 60506 — 630-301-5000
Dr. Jeff Craig, supt. — Fax 844-5710
www.sd129.org/
Herget MS — 800/6-8
1550 Deerpath Rd 60506 — 630-301-5006
Cindy Larry, prin. — Fax 301-5222
Jefferson MS — 700/6-8
1151 Plum St 60506 — 630-301-5009
Shawn Munos, prin. — Fax 844-5711
Success Academy Blackhawk Campus — Alt
1720 N Randall Rd 60506 — 630-301-5355
Melinda Lasky, prin. — Fax 264-3376
Washington MS — 600/6-8
231 S Constitution Dr 60506 — 630-301-5017
Brett Burton, prin. — Fax 844-5712
West Aurora HS — 3,500/9-12
1201 W New York St 60506 — 630-301-5600
Dr. Chuck Hiscock, prin. — Fax 844-4505
Other Schools – See North Aurora

CUSD 308
Supt. — See Oswego
Bednarcik JHS — 1,000/6-8
3025 Heggs Rd, — 630-636-2500
Sharon Alexander, prin. — Fax 636-2591

Indian Prairie CUSD 204 — 28,600/PK-12
780 Shoreline Dr 60504 — 630-375-3000
Dr. Karen Sullivan, supt. — Fax 375-3009
ipsdweb.ipsd.org
Fischer MS — 1,000/6-8
1305 Long Grove Dr 60504 — 630-375-3100
Jennifer Nonnemacher, prin. — Fax 375-3101
Granger MS — 1,000/6-8
2721 Stonebridge Blvd, — 630-375-1010
Laurie Fiorenza, prin. — Fax 375-1110
Indian Plains HS — 50/Alt
1322 N Eola Rd, — 630-375-3375
Cecilia Tobin, prin. — Fax 375-3361
Metea Valley HS — 2,500/9-12
1801 N Eola Rd, — 630-375-5900
Dr. Darrell Echols, prin. — Fax 375-5901
Still MS — 800/6-8
787 Meadowridge Dr 60504 — 630-375-3900
Kimberly Cornish, prin. — Fax 375-3901
Waubonsie Valley HS — 1,900/10-12
2590 Ogden Ave 60504 — 630-375-3300
Jason Stipp, prin. — Fax 375-3301
Other Schools – See Naperville

John C. Dunham STEM Partnership SD — 3-8
405 S Gladstone Ave 60506 — 630-947-1240
Dr. Ed Howerton, admin.
www.stem.aurora.edu
Dunham STEM Partnership S — 3-8
405 S Gladstone Ave 60506 — 630-947-1240
Dr. Ed Howerton, admin.

---

Aurora Central Catholic HS — 600/9-12
1255 N Edgelawn Dr 60506 — 630-907-0095
Rev. F. William Etheredge, admin. — Fax 907-1076
Aurora Christian S — 600/PK-12
2255 Sullivan Rd 60506 — 630-892-1551
Collette House, supt. — Fax 892-1692
Aurora University — Post-Sec.
347 S Gladstone Ave 60506 — 630-892-6431
Marmion Academy — 500/9-12
1000 Butterfield Rd, — 630-897-6936
Anthony Tinerella, head sch — Fax 897-7086
Rasmussen College — Post-Sec.
2363 Sequoia Dr Ste 131 60506 — 630-888-3500
Robert Morris University — Post-Sec.
905 Meridian Lake Dr 60504 — 800-762-5960
Rosary HS — 400/9-12
901 N Edgelawn Dr 60506 — 630-896-0831
Sr. Ann Brummel, prin. — Fax 896-8372

**Avon, Fulton, Pop. 778**
Abingdon-Avon CUSD 276
Supt. — See Abingdon
Abingdon-Avon MS — 100/6-8
320 E Woods St 61415 — 309-465-3621
Chad Cox, prin. — Fax 465-7194

**Barrington, Cook, Pop. 10,188**
Barrington CUSD 220 — 9,000/PK-12
310 James St 60010 — 847-381-6300
Dr. Brian Harris, supt. — Fax 381-6337
www.barrington220.org
Barrington HS — 3,000/9-12
616 W Main St 60010 — 847-381-1400
Steve McWilliams, prin. — Fax 304-3937
Barrington MS Prairie Campus — 1,200/6-8
40 E Dundee Rd 60010 — 847-304-3990
Travis Lobbins, prin. — Fax 304-3986
Barrington MS Station Campus — 1,000/6-8
215 Eastern Ave 60010 — 847-756-6400
Dr. Craig Winkelman, prin. — Fax 842-1343

**Barry, Pike, Pop. 1,297**
Western CUSD 12 — 600/PK-12
401 McDonough St 62312 — 217-335-2323
Terry Robertson, supt. — Fax 335-2212
www.westerncusd12.org
Western HS — 200/9-12
401 McDonough St 62312 — 217-335-2323
Constance Thomas, prin. — Fax 335-2211
Other Schools – See Kinderhook

**Bartlett, Cook, Pop. 40,574**
SD U-46
Supt. — See Elgin
Bartlett HS — 2,700/9-12
701 W Schick Rd 60103 — 630-372-4700
Dr. Richard Lebron, prin. — Fax 372-4682
Eastview MS — 1,000/7-8
321 N Oak Ave 60103 — 630-213-5550
Donald Donner, prin. — Fax 213-5563

**Bartonville, Peoria, Pop. 6,361**
Limestone Community HSD 310 — 1,100/9-12
4201 Airport Rd 61607 — 309-697-6271
Allan Gresham, supt. — Fax 697-9635
www.limestone.k12.il.us
Limestone Community HS — 1,100/9-12
4201 Airport Rd 61607 — 309-697-6271
Jill Warren, admin. — Fax 697-9635

Oak Grove SD 68 — 400/PK-8
4812 Pfeiffer Rd 61607 — 309-697-3367
Loren Baele, supt. — Fax 633-2381
www.og68.org
Oak Grove West JHS — 100/5-8
6018 W Lancaster Rd 61607 — 309-697-0621
Kyra Fancher, prin. — Fax 697-0721

**Batavia, Kane, Pop. 25,733**
Batavia Unit SD 101 — 6,300/PK-12
335 W Wilson St 60510 — 630-937-8800
Dr. Lisa Hichens, supt. — Fax 937-8801
www.bps101.net
Batavia HS — 1,900/9-12
1200 Main St 60510 — 630-937-8600
Dr. JoAnne Smith, prin. — Fax 937-8601
Rotolo MS — 1,500/6-8
1501 S Raddant Rd 60510 — 630-937-8700
Bryan Zwemke, prin. — Fax 937-8701

**Beach Park, Lake, Pop. 13,341**
Beach Park CCSD 3 — 2,400/PK-8
11315 W Wadsworth Rd 60099 — 847-599-5070
Dr. Nancy Wagner, supt. — Fax 263-2133
www.bpd3.org
Beach Park MS — 900/6-8
40667 N Green Bay Rd 60099 — 847-596-5860
John Fredrickson, prin. — Fax 731-2402

**Beardstown, Cass, Pop. 6,084**
Beardstown CUSD 15 — 1,600/PK-12
500 E 15th St 62618 — 217-323-3099
Reggie Clinton, supt. — Fax 323-5190
www.beardstown.com/
Beardstown JSHS — 700/5-12
500 E 15th St 62618 — 217-323-3665
Scott Riddle, prin. — Fax 323-3667

**Bedford Park, Cook, Pop. 575**

---

Fox College — Post-Sec.
6640 S Cicero Ave 60638 — 708-444-4500

**Beecher, Will, Pop. 4,314**
Beecher CUSD 200U — 1,100/K-12
PO Box 338 60401 — 708-946-2266
Jeffrey McCartney, supt. — Fax 946-3404
www.beecher200u.org/
Beecher HS — 400/9-12
PO Box 338 60401 — 708-946-2266
Nathan Schilling, prin. — Fax 946-3403
Beecher JHS — 200/6-8
101 E Church Rd 60401 — 708-946-3412
Michael Meyer, prin. — Fax 946-2763

**Beecher City, Effingham, Pop. 461**
Beecher City CUSD 20 — 300/PK-12
438 E State Highway 33 62414 — 618-487-5100
Scott Cameron, supt. — Fax 487-5242
www.bcity.effingham.k12.il.us/
Beecher City JSHS — 200/6-12
438 E State Highway 33 62414 — 618-487-5117
Phil Lark, prin.

**Belleville, Saint Clair, Pop. 43,276**
Belleville SD 118 — 3,700/PK-8
105 W A St 62220 — 618-233-2830
Matt Klosterman, supt. — Fax 233-8355
www.belleville118.org
Central JHS — 400/7-8
1801 Central School Rd 62220 — 618-233-5377
Rocky Horrighs, prin. — Fax 233-5440
West JHS — 300/7-8
840 Royal Heights Rd 62226 — 618-234-8200
Gustavo Cotto, prin. — Fax 234-8220

Belleville Township HSD 201 — 4,900/9-12
920 N Illinois St 62220 — 618-222-8200
Dr. Jeff Dosier, supt. — Fax 233-7586
bths201.org/
Belleville HS East — 2,500/9-12
2555 West Blvd 62221 — 618-222-3700
Jason Karstens, prin. — Fax 222-3799
Belleville HS West — 2,200/9-12
4063 Frank Scott Pkwy W 62223 — 618-222-7500
Rich Mertens, prin. — Fax 235-2484
Belleville Night/Alternative S — 100/Alt
4063 Frank Scott Pkwy W 62223 — 618-222-7660
Andrea Gannon, admin. — Fax 235-2484

Harmony Emge SD 175 — 800/PK-8
7401 Westchester Dr 62223 — 618-397-8444
Pam Leonard, supt. — Fax 397-8446
www.harmony175.org/
Emge JHS — 400/7-8
7401 Westchester Dr 62223 — 618-397-6557
Matt Graham, prin. — Fax 397-3011

Whiteside SD 115 — 1,400/PK-8
111 Warrior Way 62221 — 618-239-0000
Peggy Burke, supt. — Fax 239-9240
www.whiteside.stclair.k12.il.us
Whiteside MS — 600/5-8
111 Warrior Way 62221 — 618-239-0000
Ron Trelow, prin. — Fax 239-9240

---

Althoff Catholic HS — 400/9-12
5401 W Main St 62226 — 618-235-1100
David Harris, prin. — Fax 235-9535
Alvareita's College of Cosmetology — Post-Sec.
5400 W Main St 62226 — 618-257-9193
French Academy — 200/PK-12
219 W Main St 62220 — 618-233-7542
Phillip Paeltz, hdmstr. — Fax 233-0541
St. Elizabeth Hospital — Post-Sec.
211 S 3rd St 62220 — 618-234-2120
Southwestern Illinois College — Post-Sec.
2500 Carlyle Ave 62221 — 618-235-2700

**Bellwood, Cook, Pop. 18,875**
Bellwood SD 88 — 2,800/PK-8
640 Eastern Ave 60104 — 708-344-9344
Rosemary Hendricks, supt. — Fax 344-9416
sd88.org
Roosevelt MS — 500/6-8
2500 Oak St 60104 — 708-544-3318
Mark Holder, prin. — Fax 544-0192

**Belvidere, Boone, Pop. 25,242**
Belvidere CUSD 100 — 8,200/PK-12
1201 5th Ave 61008 — 815-544-0301
Dr. Michael Houselog, supt. — Fax 544-4260
www.district100.com
Belvidere Central MS — 1,100/6-8
8787 Beloit Rd 61008 — 815-544-0190
Nicole Difford, prin. — Fax 544-1128
Belvidere HS — 1,200/9-12
1500 East Ave 61008 — 815-547-6345
Matt Zickert, prin. — Fax 547-7304
Belvidere North HS — 1,500/9-12
9393 Beloit Rd 61008 — 815-544-2636
Marc Eckmann, prin. — Fax 547-2916
Belvidere South MS — 900/6-8
919 E 6th St 61008 — 815-544-3175
Ben Commore, prin. — Fax 544-2780

**Bement, Piatt, Pop. 1,710**
Bement CUSD 5 — 400/PK-12
201 S Champaign St 61813 — 217-678-4200
Sheila Greenwood, supt. — Fax 678-4251
www.bement.k12.il.us
Bement HS — 100/9-12
201 S Champaign St 61813 — 217-678-4200
Douglas Kepley, prin. — Fax 678-4251
Bement MS — 100/6-8
201 S Champaign St 61813 — 217-678-4200
Douglas Kepley, prin. — Fax 678-4251

**Bensenville, DuPage, Pop. 18,131**
Bensenville SD 2 — 1,500/PK-8
210 S Church Rd 60106 — 630-766-5940
Dr. James Stelter Ed.D., supt. — Fax 766-6099
www.bsd2.org
Blackhawk MS — 700/6-8
250 S Church Rd 60106 — 630-766-2601
Perry Finch, prin. — Fax 766-7612

Fenton Community HSD 100 — 1,500/9-12
1000 W Green St 60106 — 630-860-6257
Dr. Kathie Pierce, supt. — Fax 766-3178
www.fenton100.org
Fenton HS — 1,500/9-12
1000 W Green St 60106 — 630-766-2500
James Ongtengco, prin. — Fax 766-3178

---

Robert Morris University — Post-Sec.
1000 Tower Ln # 200 60106 — 630-787-7800

**Benson, Woodford, Pop. 423**
Roanoke-Benson CUSD 60
Supt. — See Roanoke
Roanoke-Benson JHS — 200/5-8
PO Box 137 61516 — 309-394-2233
John Streit, prin. — Fax 394-2612

**Benton, Franklin, Pop. 7,012**
Benton CCSD 47 — 1,200/PK-8
1403 S Main St 62812 — 618-439-3136
Dr. Jay Goble, supt. — Fax 435-4840
www.benton47.org/
Benton MS — 400/5-8
1000 Forrest St 62812 — 618-438-4011
Tammy McCollum, prin. — Fax 435-2152

Benton Consolidated HSD 103 — 600/9-12
511 E Main St 62812 — 618-439-6415
Dr. Aaron Mattox, supt. — Fax 438-8091
www.bentonhighschool.org
Benton Consolidated HS — 600/9-12
511 E Main St 62812 — 618-439-3103
Mark Miller, prin. — Fax 438-2915

**Berkeley, Cook, Pop. 5,108**
Berkeley SD 87 — 2,800/PK-8
1200 N Wolf Rd 60163 — 708-449-3350
Dr. Terri Bresnahan, supt. — Fax 547-3341
www.berkeley87.org
MacArthur MS — 500/6-8
1310 N Wolf Rd 60163 — 708-449-3185
Dr. Kermit Blakley, prin. — Fax 649-3780
Other Schools – See Northlake

**Berwyn, Cook, Pop. 56,069**
Berwyn North SD 98 — 3,400/PK-8
6633 16th St 60402 — 708-484-6200
Dr. Carmen Ayala, supt. — Fax 795-2482
www.bn98.org
Lincoln MS — 1,100/6-8
6432 16th St 60402 — 708-795-2475
Michelle Smith, prin. — Fax 795-2880

Berwyn South SD 100 — 3,900/PK-8
3401 Gunderson Ave 60402 — 708-795-2300
Dr. Stanley Fields, supt. — Fax 795-2317
www.bsd100.org
Freedom MS — 600/6-8
3016 Ridgeland Ave 60402 — 708-795-5800
James Calabrese, prin. — Fax 795-5806
Heritage MS — 600/6-8
6850 31st St 60402 — 708-749-6110
Susan Butler, prin. — Fax 749-6124

J. S. Morton HSD 201
Supt. — See Cicero
Morton West HS — 3,400/9-12
2400 Home Ave 60402 — 708-780-4100
Josh McMahon, prin. — Fax 222-5903

**Bethalto, Madison, Pop. 9,426**
Bethalto CUSD 8 — 2,500/PK-12
610 Texas Blvd 62010 — 618-377-7200
Charles Stegall, supt. — Fax 377-2845
www.bethalto.org
Civic Memorial HS — 800/9-12
200 School St 62010 — 618-377-7220
Debra Pitts, prin. — Fax 377-7001
Trimpe MS — 600/6-8
910 2nd St 62010 — 618-377-7240
Kimberly Wilks, prin. — Fax 377-7218

**Bethany, Moultrie, Pop. 1,345**
Okaw Valley CUSD 302 — 500/PK-12
PO Box 97 61914 — 217-665-3232
Kent Stauder, supt. — Fax 665-3601
www.okawvalley.org
Okaw Valley HS — 200/9-12
PO Box 249 61914 — 217-665-3631
Matthew Shoaff, prin. — Fax 665-3863
Other Schools – See Findlay

**Biggsville, Henderson, Pop. 300**
West Central CUSD 235 — 1,000/PK-12
RR 1 Box 72 61418 — 309-627-2371
Paula Markey, supt. — Fax 627-2453
www.wc235.k12.il.us

West Central HS 300/9-12
RR 1 Box 72 61418 309-627-2377
Scott Schneider, prin. Fax 627-2120
Other Schools – See Stronghurst

**Big Rock, Kane, Pop. 710**
Hinckley-Big Rock CUSD 429
Supt. — See Hinckley
Hinckley-Big Rock MS 200/6-8
PO Box 247 60511 630-556-4180
Jeff Strouss, prin. Fax 556-4181

**Bismarck, Vermilion, Pop. 578**
Bismarck-Henning CUSD 1 900/K-12
PO Box 350 61814 217-759-7261
Scott Watson, supt. Fax 759-7942
www.bismarck.k12.il.us
Bismarck-Henning HS 400/9-12
PO Box 350 61814 217-759-7291
Brent Rademacher, prin. Fax 759-7815
Bismarck-Henning JHS 300/5-8
PO Box 350 61814 217-759-7301
Rusty Campbell, prin. Fax 759-7313

**Bloomingdale, DuPage, Pop. 21,714**
Bloomingdale SD 13 1,200/PK-8
164 Euclid Ave 60108 630-893-9590
Dr. Jon Bartelt, supt. Fax 893-1818
www.sd13.org
Westfield MS 400/6-8
149 Fairfield Way 60108 630-529-6211
Stefan Larsson, prin. Fax 893-9336

CCSD 93 3,900/PK-8
230 Covington Dr 60108 630-893-9393
William Shields Ed.D., supt. Fax 539-3450
www.ccsd93.com
Stratford MS 700/6-8
251 Butterfield Dr 60108 630-980-9898
James Doyle, prin. Fax 980-9914
Other Schools – See Carol Stream

---

Pivot Point International Academy Post-Sec.
144 E Lake St Ste C 60108 847-985-5900

**Bloomington, McLean, Pop. 74,597**
Bloomington SD 87 5,500/PK-12
300 E Monroe St 61701 309-827-6031
Dr. Barry Reilly, supt. Fax 827-5717
www.district87.org
Bloomington HS 1,400/9-12
1202 E Locust St 61701 309-828-5201
Tim Moore, prin. Fax 829-1078
Bloomington JHS 1,100/6-8
901 Colton Ave 61701 309-827-0086
Sherri Thomas, prin. Fax 829-0084

McLean County Unit SD 5
Supt. — See Normal
Evans JHS 700/6-8
2901 Morrissey Dr 61704 309-557-4406
Trevor Chapman, prin. Fax 557-4507

McLean/Dewitt Regional Vocational System
PO Box 5187 61701 309-829-8671
Tom Frazier, supt.
Bloomington Area Career Center Vo/Tech
PO Box 5187 61702 309-829-8671
Tom Frazier, dir. Fax 828-3546

---

Central Catholic HS 400/9-12
1201 Airport Rd 61704 309-661-7000
Sean Foster, prin. Fax 661-7010
Cornerstone Christian Academy 400/PK-12
PO Box 1608 61702 309-662-9900
Becky Shamess, hdmstr. Fax 662-9904
Hairmasters Institute of Cosmetology Post-Sec.
506 S McClun St 61701 309-827-6971
Illinois Wesleyan University Post-Sec.
1312 Park St 61701 309-556-1000

**Blue Island, Cook, Pop. 23,417**
Community HSD 218
Supt. — See Oak Lawn
Eisenhower HS 1,800/9-12
12700 Sacramento Ave 60406 708-597-6300
Dr. Gary Rauch, prin. Fax 597-9958

Cook County SD 130 3,700/PK-8
12300 Greenwood Ave 60406 708-385-6800
Dr. Tina Halliman, supt. Fax 385-8467
www.district130.org/
Kerr MS 400/6-8
12915 Maple Ave 60406 708-385-5959
Bridgette McNeal, prin. Fax 371-6812
Veterans Memorial MS 400/6-8
12320 Greenwood Ave 60406 708-489-6630
Leonora Gora, prin. Fax 489-3522
Other Schools – See Crestwood

---

Cannella School of Hair Design Post-Sec.
12840 Western Ave 60406 708-388-4949

**Blue Mound, Macon, Pop. 1,145**
Meridian CUSD 15
Supt. — See Macon
Meridian MS 300/6-8
PO Box 320 62513 217-692-2148
Andrew Pygott, prin. Fax 692-2039

**Bluffs, Scott, Pop. 708**
Scott-Morgan CUSD 2 300/PK-12
PO Box 230 62621 217-754-3351
Kevin Blankenship, supt. Fax 754-3908
www.bluffs-school.com/
Bluffs HS 100/9-12
PO Box 230 62621 217-754-3815
Joseph Kuhlmann, prin. Fax 754-3908
Bluffs JHS 100/6-8
PO Box 230 62621 217-754-3815
Joseph Kuhlmann, prin. Fax 754-3908

**Bluford, Jefferson, Pop. 685**
Bluford Unit SD 318 300/K-12
901 6th St 62814 618-732-8242
John Ashby, supt. Fax 732-6114
www.busd318.org
Webber HS 100/9-12
PO Box 110 62814 618-732-6121
Brock Harris, prin. Fax 732-8784

**Bolingbrook, Will, Pop. 71,637**
Valley View CUSD 365U
Supt. — See Romeoville
Addams MS 700/6-8
905 Lily Cache Ln 60440 630-759-7200
Dr. Jason Pascavage, prin. Fax 759-6362
Bolingbrook HS 3,600/9-12
365 Raider Way 60440 630-759-6400
Yolanda Jordan, prin. Fax 759-2650
Brooks MS 1,200/6-8
350 Blair Ln 60440 630-759-6340
Dr. Keith Wood, prin. Fax 759-6360
Humphrey MS 700/6-8
777 Falconridge Way 60440 630-972-9240
Dan Laverty, prin. Fax 739-8521

**Bourbonnais, Kankakee, Pop. 18,268**
Bourbonnais ESD 53 2,500/PK-8
281 W John Casey Rd 60914 815-929-5100
Daniel R. Hollowell, supt. Fax 939-0481
www.besd53.org
Bourbonnais Upper Grade Center 600/7-8
200 W John Casey Rd 60914 815-929-5200
Jeffrey Gindy, prin. Fax 935-7849

Kankakee Area Career Center
PO Box 570 60914 815-939-4971
Donald Fay, supt. Fax 939-7598
www.kacc-il.org
Kankakee Area Career Center Vo/Tech
PO Box 570 60914 815-939-4971
Bosa Goodale, prin. Fax 939-7598

---

Olivet Nazarene University Post-Sec.
1 University Ave 60914 815-939-5011

**Bradford, Stark, Pop. 767**
Bradford CUSD 1 200/PK-8
115 High St 61421 309-897-2801
Dr. Ellin Lotspeich Ed.D., supt. Fax 897-4451
www.edline.net/pages/bradford_schools_1
Bradford JHS 100/6-8
115 High St 61421 309-897-2801
Dr. Ellin Lotspeich Ed.D., admin. Fax 897-4451

**Bradley, Kankakee, Pop. 15,644**
Bradley SD 61 1,700/PK-8
111 N Crosswell Ave 60915 815-933-3371
Scott Goselin, supt. Fax 939-6601
www.bradleyschools.com/
Bradley Central MS 500/6-8
260 N Wabash Ave 60915 815-939-3564
Mark Kohl, prin. Fax 939-6603

Bradley-Bourbonnais Comm. HSD 307 2,100/9-12
700 W North St 60915 815-937-3707
Dr. Scott Wakeley, supt. Fax 937-0156
www.bbchs.org
Bradley-Bourbonnais Community HS 2,100/9-12
700 W North St 60915 815-937-3707
Dr. Brian Wright, prin. Fax 937-0156

---

Paul Mitchell The School Post-Sec.
605 E North St 60915 815-932-5049

**Braidwood, Will, Pop. 6,143**
Reed-Custer CUSD 255U 1,700/PK-12
255 Comet Dr 60408 815-458-2307
Mark Mitchell, supt. Fax 458-4106
www.rc255.net
Reed-Custer HS 500/9-12
249 Comet Dr 60408 815-458-2166
Tim Ricketts, prin. Fax 458-4138
Reed-Custer MS 400/6-8
407 Comet Dr 60408 815-458-2868
Shane Trager, prin. Fax 458-4118

**Breese, Clinton, Pop. 4,414**
Central Community HSD 71 600/9-12
7740 Old US Highway 50 62230 618-526-4510
Kevin Meyer, supt. Fax 526-2521
www.centralcougars.org/
Central Community HS 600/9-12
7740 Old US Highway 50 62230 618-526-4578
B. Kent Jones, prin. Fax 526-7647

---

Mater Dei HS 500/9-12
900 Mater Dei Dr 62230 618-526-7216
Dennis Litteken, prin. Fax 526-8310

**Bridgeport, Lawrence, Pop. 1,874**
Red Hill CUSD 10 1,100/PK-12
1250 Judy Ave 62417 618-945-2061
Jakie Walker, supt. Fax 945-7607
redhill.cusd10.org
Red Hill JSHS 400/7-12
908 Church St 62417 618-945-2521
Clarence Gross, prin. Fax 945-7151

**Bridgeview, Cook, Pop. 16,102**

---

AQSA S 200/PK-12
7361 W 92nd St 60455 708-598-2700
Tammie Ismail, prin. Fax 598-2731
Northwestern Business College Post-Sec.
7725 S Harlem Ave 60455 888-205-2283
Universal S 600/PK-12
7350 W 93rd St 60455 708-599-4100
Hanan Abdallah M.Ed., admin. Fax 599-1588

**Brighton, Macoupin, Pop. 2,236**
Southwestern CUSD 9 1,500/PK-12
PO Box 728 62012 618-372-3813
Mark Skertich, supt. Fax 372-4681
www.piasabirds.net
Other Schools – See Piasa

**Brimfield, Peoria, Pop. 851**
Brimfield CUSD 309 800/PK-12
PO Box 380 61517 309-446-3378
Joseph Blessman, supt. Fax 446-3716
www.brimfield309.com/
Brimfield HS 200/9-12
PO Box 380 61517 309-446-3349
Joseph Blessman, prin. Fax 446-3716

**Broadlands, Champaign, Pop. 347**
Heritage CUSD 8
Supt. — See Homer
Heritage HS 200/9-12
PO Box 260 61816 217-834-3392
Ryan Peyton, prin. Fax 834-3016

**Brookfield, Cook, Pop. 18,709**
Brookfield Lagrange Park SD 95 1,100/K-8
3524 Maple Ave 60513 708-485-0606
Dr. Mark Kuzniewski, supt. Fax 485-8066
www.district95.org
Gross MS 400/6-8
3524 Maple Ave 60513 708-485-0600
Kevin Nicholson, prin. Fax 485-0638

**Brownstown, Fayette, Pop. 753**
Brownstown CUSD 201 300/PK-12
421 S College Ave 62418 618-427-3355
Adam Bussard, supt. Fax 427-3704
www.bcusd201.com
Brownstown JSHS 100/7-12
421 S College Ave 62418 618-427-3839
Michael Shackelford, prin. Fax 427-3704

**Brussels, Calhoun, Pop. 140**
Brussels CUSD 42 100/K-12
PO Box 128 62013 618-883-2131
Dr. Mark Martin, supt. Fax 883-2514
Brussels HS 100/7-12
PO Box 128 62013 618-883-2131
Andy Stumpf, prin. Fax 883-2514

**Buckley, Iroquois, Pop. 593**

---

Christ Lutheran HS 50/9-12
PO Box 8 60918 217-394-2547
Sandy Spitz, prin. Fax 394-2097

**Buda, Bureau, Pop. 531**
Bureau Valley CUSD 340
Supt. — See Manlius
Bureau Valley South S 200/3-8
PO Box 277 61314 309-895-2037
Kristal LeRette, prin. Fax 895-2200

**Buffalo, Sangamon, Pop. 499**
Tri-City CUSD 1 600/PK-12
324 W Charles St 62515 217-364-4811
Jill Larson, supt. Fax 364-4896
www.tricityschools.org
Tri-City HS 200/9-12
324 W Charles St 62515 217-364-4530
Christy Kindel, prin. Fax 364-4812
Tri-City JHS 100/6-8
324 W Charles St 62515 217-364-4530
Christy Kindel, prin. Fax 364-4812

**Buffalo Grove, Cook, Pop. 40,915**
Aptakisic-Tripp CCSD 102 2,000/PK-8
1231 Weiland Rd 60089 847-353-5660
Dr. Theresa Dunkin, supt. Fax 634-5334
www.d102.org
Aptakisic JHS 500/7-8
1231 Weiland Rd 60089 847-353-5500
Jessica McIntyre, prin. Fax 634-5347

Kildeer Countryside CCSD 96 3,100/PK-8
1050 Ivy Hall Ln 60089 847-459-4260
Julie Schmidt, supt. Fax 459-2344
www.kcsd96.org
Twin Groves MS 600/6-8
2600 N Buffalo Grove Rd 60089 847-821-8946
Jessica Barnes, prin. Fax 821-8949
Other Schools – See Long Grove

Township HSD 214
Supt. — See Arlington Heights
Buffalo Grove HS 2,100/9-12
1100 W Dundee Rd 60089 847-718-4000
Jeff Wardle, prin. Fax 718-4122

Wheeling CCSD 21
Supt. — See Wheeling
Cooper MS 700/6-8
1050 Plum Grove Cir 60089 847-520-2750
Robert Gurney, prin. Fax 419-3071

**Bunker Hill, Macoupin, Pop. 1,760**
Bunker Hill CUSD 8 500/PK-12
504 E Warren St 62014 618-585-3116
Dr. Victor Buehler, supt. Fax 585-3212
bhschools.org
Bunker Hill HS 200/9-12
314 S Meissner St 62014 618-585-3232
Matthew Smith, prin. Fax 585-3241

**Burbank, Cook, Pop. 28,566**
Burbank SD 111 3,300/PK-8
7600 S Central Ave 60459 708-496-0500
Dr. Franzy Fleck, supt. Fax 496-0510
www.bsd111.org
Liberty JHS 800/7-8
5900 W 81st St 60459 708-952-3255
Mark Antkiewicz, prin. Fax 229-0659

Reavis Township HSD 220 — 1,800/9-12
6034 W 77th St 60459 — 708-599-7200
Dr. Daniel Riordan, supt. — Fax 599-8751
www.reavisd220.org
Reavis HS — 1,800/9-12
6034 W 77th St 60459 — 708-599-7200
Dr. Daniel Riordan, prin. — Fax 599-8751

---

Queen of Peace HS — 400/9-12
7659 Linder Ave 60459 — 708-458-7600
Mary Nickels, prin. — Fax 458-5734
St. Laurence HS — 600/9-12
5556 W 77th St 60459 — 708-458-6900
Jim Muting, prin. — Fax 458-7898

**Burlington, Kane, Pop. 618**
Central CUSD 301 — 3,100/PK-12
PO Box 396 60109 — 847-464-6005
Dr. Todd Stirn, supt. — Fax 464-6021
www.burlington.k12.il.us/
Central HS — 1,100/9-12
PO Box 68 60109 — 847-464-6030
Chris Testone, prin. — Fax 464-6039
Central MS — 100/8-8
PO Box 397 60109 — 847-464-6000
Carie Walter, prin. — Fax 464-0233

**Burr Ridge, DuPage, Pop. 10,371**
CCSD 180 — 600/PK-8
15W451 91st St 60527 — 630-734-6600
Dr. Thomas Schneider, supt. — Fax 325-6450
www.ccsd180.org
Burr Ridge MS — 300/5-8
15W451 91st St 60527 — 630-325-5454
Julie Bartell, prin. — Fax 325-6450

Gower SD 62
Supt. — See Willowbrook
Gower MS — 400/5-8
7941 S Madison St 60527 — 630-323-8275
Tracy Murphy, prin. — Fax 323-2055

Pleasantdale SD 107 — 800/PK-8
7450 Wolf Rd 60527 — 708-784-2013
Dr. David Palzet, supt. — Fax 246-0161
www.d107.org
Pleasantdale MS — 300/5-8
7450 Wolf Rd 60527 — 708-246-3210
John Glimco, prin. — Fax 352-0092

---

Everest College — Post-Sec.
6880 N Frontage Rd 60527 — 630-920-1102

**Bushnell, McDonough, Pop. 3,074**
Bushnell-Prairie City CUSD 170 — 800/PK-12
845 Walnut St 61422 — 309-772-9461
Kathy Dinger, supt. — Fax 772-9462
bpcschools.org
Bushnell-Prairie City HS — 200/9-12
845 Walnut St 61422 — 309-772-2113
Jon Lamb, prin. — Fax 772-2104
Bushnell-Prairie City JHS — 200/6-8
847 Walnut St 61422 — 309-772-3123
Mike Snowden, prin. — Fax 772-2666

**Byron, Ogle, Pop. 3,700**
Byron CUSD 226 — 1,600/PK-12
696 N Colfax St 61010 — 815-234-5491
Dr. James Hammack, supt. — Fax 234-4106
www.byron226.org
Byron HS — 500/9-12
696 N Colfax St 61010 — 815-234-5491
Jay Mullens, prin. — Fax 234-4106
Byron MS — 400/6-8
850 N Colfax St 61010 — 815-234-5491
Zack Ettelbrick, prin. — Fax 234-4225

**Cahokia, Saint Clair, Pop. 14,938**
Cahokia CUSD 187 — 2,800/K-12
1700 Jerome Ln 62206 — 618-332-3700
Arthur Ryan, supt. — Fax 332-3706
www.cusd187.org
Cahokia HS — 900/9-12
800 Range Ln 62206 — 618-332-3730
Kevin Bement, prin. — Fax 332-3747
8th Grade Academy — 8-8
1900 Mousette Ln 62206 — 618-332-5900
Melissa Rebmann, prin. — Fax 332-3725

**Cairo, Alexander, Pop. 2,772**
Cairo Unit SD 1 — 500/PK-12
4201 Sycamore St 62914 — 618-734-4102
Andrea Evers, supt. — Fax 734-4047
www.cairoschooldistrict1.com
Cairo JSHS — 200/6-12
4201 Sycamore St 62914 — 618-734-2187
Zena Madison, prin. — Fax 734-2189

**Calumet City, Cook, Pop. 36,556**
Calumet City SD 155 — 1,200/K-8
540 Superior Ave 60409 — 708-862-7665
Dr. Troy Paraday, supt. — Fax 868-7555
www.calumetcity155.org/
Wentworth JHS — 400/6-8
560 Superior Ave 60409 — 708-862-0750
Ermetra Olawumi, prin. — Fax 862-1194

Dolton SD 149 — 2,100/PK-8
292 Torrence Ave 60409 — 708-868-7861
Dr. Shelly Davis-Jones, supt. — Fax 868-7850
www.schooldistrict149.org/
Creative Communications Academy — 7-8
1650 Pulaski Rd 60409 — 708-868-7585
Gerald Scott, prin. — Fax 868-7589
School of Fine Arts — 7-8
1650 Pulaski Rd 60409 — 708-868-7565
Dellnora Winters, prin. — Fax 868-7589
STEM Academy — 7-8
1650 Pulaski Rd 60409 — 708-868-7595
Michael Steele, prin. — Fax 868-7589

Hoover-Schrum Memorial SD 157 — 900/PK-8
1255 Superior Ave 60409 — 708-868-7500
Dr. Michele Morris, supt. — Fax 868-7511
www.hsdist157.org
Schrum Memorial MS — 300/6-8
485 165th St 60409 — 708-862-4236
Dr. Bennie Knott, prin. — Fax 862-4580

Thornton Fractional Township HSD 215 — 3,600/9-12
1601 Wentworth Ave 60409 — 708-585-2321
Dr. Creg Williams, supt. — Fax 585-2317
www.tfd215.org/
Center for Academics & Technology — Vo/Tech
1605 Wentworth Ave 60409 — 708-585-2353
Kent Farlow, prin. — Fax 585-2356
Thornton Fractional North HS — 1,600/9-12
755 Pulaski Rd 60409 — 708-585-1000
Dr. Dwayne Evans, prin. — Fax 585-1010
Other Schools – See Lansing

---

Westwood College — Post-Sec.
80 River Oaks Ctr Ste 111 60409 — 708-832-1988

**Calumet Park, Cook, Pop. 7,781**
Calumet Public SD 132 — 1,100/PK-8
1440 W Vermont Ave 60827 — 708-388-8920
Dr. Elizabeth Reynolds, supt. — Fax 388-2138
www.sd132.org
Calumet MS — 400/6-8
1440 W Vermont Ave 60827 — 708-388-8820
Andrea Delaney, prin. — Fax 388-8557

**Cambridge, Henry, Pop. 2,137**
Cambridge CUSD 227 — 500/PK-12
300 S West St 61238 — 309-937-2144
Thomas Akers, supt. — Fax 937-5128
cambridge.il.schoolwebpages.com/
Cambridge Community JSHS — 200/7-12
300 S West St 61238 — 309-937-2051
Robert Reagan, prin. — Fax 937-5128

**Campbell Hill, Jackson, Pop. 333**
Trico CUSD 176 — 1,000/PK-12
PO Box 220 62916 — 618-426-1111
Jackie L. Smith, supt. — Fax 426-3625
www.trico176.org
Trico HS — 300/9-12
PO Box 336 62916 — 618-426-1111
Mike Denault, prin. — Fax 426-3701
Trico JHS — 200/6-8
PO Box 335 62916 — 618-426-1111
Ronald Coleman, prin. — Fax 426-3712

**Camp Point, Adams, Pop. 1,120**
Central CUSD 3 — 900/K-12
2110 Highway 94 N 62320 — 217-593-7116
Martin Cook, supt. — Fax 593-7026
www.cusd3.com/
Central HS — 300/9-12
2110 Highway 94 N 62320 — 217-593-7731
Jeff Waggener, prin. — Fax 593-7025
Central JHS — 300/5-8
2110 Highway 94 N 62320 — 217-593-7741
Erica Smith, prin. — Fax 593-7028

**Canton, Fulton, Pop. 14,563**
Canton Union SD 66 — 2,600/PK-12
20 W Walnut St 61520 — 309-647-9411
Roy Webb, supt. — Fax 649-5036
www.cantonusd.org
Canton HS — 700/9-12
1001 N Main St 61520 — 309-647-1820
Jennifer Watts, prin. — Fax 649-5039
Ingersoll MS — 800/5-8
1605 E Ash St 61520 — 309-647-6951
Wayne Krus, prin. — Fax 647-6959

---

Graham Hospital — Post-Sec.
210 W Walnut St 61520 — 309-647-4086
Spoon River College — Post-Sec.
23235 N County Highway 22 61520 — 309-647-4645

**Carbondale, Jackson, Pop. 25,058**
Carbondale Community HSD 165 — 1,100/9-12
330 S Giant City Rd 62902 — 618-457-4722
Stephen Murphy, supt. — Fax 457-3353
www.cchs165.jacksn.k12.il.us/
Carbondale Community HS — 1,100/9-12
1301 E Walnut St 62901 — 618-457-3371
Daniel Booth, prin. — Fax 549-1686

Carbondale ESD 95 — 1,400/PK-8
925 S Giant City Rd 62902 — 618-457-3591
Michael Shimshak, supt. — Fax 457-2043
www.ces95.org
Carbondale MS — 400/6-8
1150 E Grand Ave 62901 — 618-457-2174
Marilynn Ross, prin. — Fax 457-2176

---

Southern Illinois University — Post-Sec.
1263 Lincoln Dr 62901 — 618-453-2121
Trinity Christian S — 100/PK-12
1218 W Freeman St 62901 — 618-529-3733
Dr. Betsy George, prin. — Fax 549-8252

**Carlinville, Macoupin, Pop. 5,852**
Carlinville CUSD 1 — 1,400/PK-12
829 W Main St 62626 — 217-854-9823
Mike Kelly, supt. — Fax 854-2777
www.carlinvilleschools.net/
Carlinville HS — 400/9-12
829 W Main St 62626 — 217-854-3104
Patrick Drew, prin. — Fax 854-5260
Carlinville MS — 300/7-8
110 Illinois Ave 62626 — 217-854-3106
Roy Kulenkamp, prin. — Fax 854-4503

---

Blackburn College — Post-Sec.
700 College Ave 62626 — 217-854-3231

**Carlyle, Clinton, Pop. 3,259**
Carlyle CUSD 1 — 1,200/PK-12
1400 13th St 62231 — 618-594-8283
Joe Novsek, supt. — Fax 594-8285
www.carlyle.k12.il.us
Carlyle HS — 400/9-12
1461 12th St 62231 — 618-594-2453
Joe Wilkerson, prin. — Fax 594-8286
Carlyle JHS — 400/5-8
1631 12th St 62231 — 618-594-8292
Dustin Bilbruck, prin. — Fax 594-8294

Clintn/Jeffrsn/Marin/Washngtn ROE
930 Fairfax St Ste B 62231 — 618-594-2432
Keri Jo Garrett, supt. — Fax 594-7192
www.roe13.k12.il.us
Other Schools – See Centralia

**Carmi, White, Pop. 5,196**
Carmi-White County CUSD 5 — 1,300/PK-12
211 W Robinson St 62821 — 618-382-2341
Brad Lee, supt. — Fax 384-3207
www.carmischools.org
Carmi-White County HS — 400/9-12
800 W Main St 62821 — 618-382-4661
Jarrod Newell, prin. — Fax 382-2453
Carmi-White County JHS — 200/7-8
800 W Main St 62821 — 618-382-4661
Bart King, prin. — Fax 382-2453

**Carol Stream, DuPage, Pop. 38,894**
CCSD 93
Supt. — See Bloomingdale
Stream MS — 600/6-8
283 El Paso Ln 60188 — 630-462-8940
Peter LaChance, prin. — Fax 462-9224

Glenbard Township HSD 87
Supt. — See Glen Ellyn
Glenbard North HS — 2,600/9-12
990 Kuhn Rd 60188 — 630-653-7000
Dr. John Mensik, prin. — Fax 653-7259

**Carpentersville, Kane, Pop. 37,150**
CUSD 300
Supt. — See Algonquin
Carpentersville MS — 700/7-8
100 Cleveland Ave 60110 — 847-426-1380
Asia Gurney, prin. — Fax 426-1404
Dundee-Crown HS — 2,500/9-12
1500 Kings Rd 60110 — 847-426-1415
Devon Larosa, prin. — Fax 426-1245
Oak Ridge S — 50/Alt
300 Cleveland Ave 60110 — 847-426-4052
Stacy Wilkinson, prin. — Fax 426-4474

**Carrier Mills, Saline, Pop. 1,618**
Carrier Mills-Stonefort CUSD 2 — 500/PK-12
7071 US 45 S 62917 — 618-994-2392
Richard Morgan, supt. — Fax 994-2929
Carrier Mills-Stonefort HS — 100/9-12
7071 US 45 S 62917 — 618-994-2392
Richard Morgan, prin. — Fax 994-2929

**Carrollton, Greene, Pop. 2,475**
Carrollton CUSD 1 — 600/PK-12
950A 3rd St 62016 — 217-942-5314
Dr. Kerry Cox, supt. — Fax 942-9259
www.c-hawks.net
Carrollton HS — 200/9-12
950 3rd St 62016 — 217-942-6913
Leslee Frazier, prin. — Fax 942-6835

**Carterville, Williamson, Pop. 5,368**
Carterville CUSD 5 — 1,400/PK-12
306 Virginia Ave 62918 — 618-985-4826
Keith Liddell, supt. — Fax 985-2041
www.c-ville.wilmsn.k12.il.us
Carterville HS — 500/9-12
1415 W Grand Ave 62918 — 618-985-2940
Todd Rogers, prin. — Fax 985-2741
Carterville JHS — 300/7-8
816 S Division St 62918 — 618-985-2940
Jeff Hartford, prin. — Fax 985-2492

---

John A. Logan College — Post-Sec.
700 Logan College Dr 62918 — 618-985-3741

**Carthage, Hancock, Pop. 2,577**
Carthage ESD 317 — 400/PK-8
210 S Adams St 62321 — 217-357-3922
Vicki Hardy, supt. — Fax 357-6793
www.cesd317.org
Carthage MS — 200/5-8
210 S Adams St 62321 — 217-357-3914
Jerry Butcher, prin. — Fax 357-3755

Hancck/Fultn/Schuylr/McDonogh ROE
Supt. — See Macomb
Hancock County Academy — 50/Alt
553 Main St 62321 — 217-575-3226

Illini West HSD 307 — 400/9-12
600 Miller St 62321 — 217-357-9607
Kim Schilson, supt. — Fax 357-9609
www.illiniwest.org
Illini West HS — 400/9-12
600 Miller St 62321 — 217-357-2136
Brad Gooding, prin. — Fax 357-3569

**Cary, McHenry, Pop. 17,990**
Cary CCSD 26 — 2,800/PK-8
2115 Crystal Lake Rd 60013 — 224-357-5100
Brian Coleman, supt. — Fax 639-3898
www.cary26.org
Cary JHS — 1,100/6-8
2109 Crystal Lake Rd 60013 — 224-357-5150
Linda Goeglein, prin. — Fax 516-5507

Community HSD 155
Supt. — See Crystal Lake
Cary-Grove HS 1,800/9-12
2208 3 Oaks Rd 60013 847-639-3825
Jay Sargeant, prin. Fax 639-3873

---

Trinity Oaks Christian Academy 200/PK-12
233 Trinity Oaks Way 60013 847-462-5971
Dr. Paul Wrobbel, head sch Fax 462-5972

**Casey, Clark, Pop. 2,756**
Casey-Westfield CUSD C4 800/PK-12
502 E Delaware Ave 62420 217-932-2184
Dee Scott, supt. Fax 932-5553
www.caseywestfield.org
Casey-Westfield JSHS 300/7-12
306 E Edgar Ave 62420 217-932-2175
James Sullivan, prin. Fax 932-2004

**Catlin, Vermilion, Pop. 2,025**
Salt Fork CUSD 512
Supt. — See Sidell
Salt Fork HS 100/9-12
701 W Vermilion St 61817 217-427-5331
Darin Chambliss, prin. Fax 427-2468

**Centralia, Marion, Pop. 12,732**
Centralia HSD 200 1,000/9-12
2100 E Calumet St 62801 618-532-7391
Chuck Lane, supt. Fax 532-8952
www.centraliahs.org
Centralia HS 1,000/9-12
2100 E Calumet St 62801 618-532-7391
Reid Shipley, prin. Fax 532-8952

Centralia SD 135 1,400/PK-8
400 S Elm St 62801 618-532-1907
Craig Clark, supt. Fax 532-4986
www.ccs135.com
Centralia JHS 600/5-8
900 S Pine St 62801 618-533-7130
Tron Young, prin. Fax 533-7123

Clintn/Jeffrsn/Marin/Washngtn ROE
Supt. — See Carlyle
Alternative Learning Academy Alt
1000 E Third St 62801 618-533-3935
Brad Weathers, dir. Fax 533-3936

---

Christ Our Rock Lutheran HS 100/9-12
9545 Shatuc Rd 62801 618-226-3315
Don Duensing, prin. Fax 226-3312
Kaskaskia College Post-Sec.
27210 College Rd 62801 618-545-3000

**Cerro Gordo, Piatt, Pop. 1,398**
Cerro Gordo CUSD 100 600/PK-12
PO Box 79 61818 217-763-5221
Brett Robinson, supt. Fax 763-6562
www.cgbroncos.org
Cerro Gordo JSHS 200/7-12
PO Box 79 61818 217-763-2711
Steve Cline, prin. Fax 763-6287

**Chadwick, Carroll, Pop. 548**
Chadwick-Milledgeville CUSD 399 500/PK-12
15 School St 61014 815-684-5191
Timothy Schurman, supt. Fax 684-5241
www.dist399.net
Chadwick JHS 100/6-8
19 School St 61014 815-684-5191
Timothy Schurman, prin. Fax 684-5241
Other Schools – See Milledgeville

**Champaign, Champaign, Pop. 78,771**
Champaign CUSD 4 9,400/PK-12
703 S New St 61820 217-351-3800
Dr. Judy Wiegand, supt. Fax 352-3590
www.champaignschools.org
Centennial HS 1,400/9-12
913 Crescent Dr 61821 217-351-3951
Gregory Johnson, prin. Fax 351-3730
Central HS 1,200/9-12
610 W University Ave 61820 217-351-3911
Joe Williams, prin. Fax 351-3919
Edison MS 600/6-8
306 W Green St 61820 217-351-3771
Angela Schoonover, prin. Fax 355-2564
Franklin MS 600/6-8
817 N Harris Ave 61820 217-351-3819
Sara Sanders, prin. Fax 351-3729
Jefferson MS 700/6-8
1115 Crescent Dr 61821 217-351-3790
Angelica Franklin, prin. Fax 351-3754
Novak Academy 100/Alt
815 N Randolph St 61820 217-352-4328
Tony Maltbia, prin. Fax 352-7292

---

High School of St. Thomas More 300/9-12
3901 N Mattis Ave 61822 217-352-7210
Ryan Bustle, prin. Fax 352-7213
Judah Christian S 500/PK-12
908 N Prospect Ave 61820 217-359-1701
Mike Chitty, admin. Fax 359-0214
Parkland College Post-Sec.
2400 W Bradley Ave 61821 217-351-2200

**Chandlerville, Cass, Pop. 551**
A-C Central CUSD 262
Supt. — See Ashland
A-C Central MS 100/5-8
191 S Bluff St 62627 217-476-3312
Fax 476-3730

**Channahon, Will, Pop. 12,437**
Channahon SD 17 1,500/PK-8
24920 S Sage St 60410 815-467-4315
Nicholas Henkle, supt. Fax 467-4343
csd17.org
Channahon JHS 400/7-8
24917 W Sioux Dr 60410 815-467-4314
Dr. Chad Uphoff, prin. Fax 467-2188

Minooka Community HSD 111 2,500/9-12
26655 W Eames St 60410 815-467-2557
Dr. Jim Blanche, supt. Fax 467-9733
www.mchs.net/
Minooka Community HS South Campus 1,300/9-10
26655 W Eames St 60410 815-521-4001
Ron Kiesewetter, prin. Fax 467-6120
Other Schools – See Minooka

---

Families of Faith Christian Academy 100/PK-12
24466 W Eames St 60410 815-521-1381
Rev. Clark Llewellyn, prin. Fax 467-4476

**Charleston, Coles, Pop. 21,496**
Charleston CUSD 1 2,800/PK-12
410 W Polk Ave 61920 217-639-1000
Jim Littleford, supt. Fax 639-1005
www.charleston.k12.il.us
Charleston HS 800/9-12
1615 Lincoln Ave 61920 217-639-5000
Trevor Doughty, prin. Fax 639-5005
Charleston MS 400/7-8
920 Smith Dr 61920 217-639-6000
Chad Burgett, prin. Fax 639-6005

---

Eastern Illinois University Post-Sec.
600 Lincoln Ave 61920 217-581-5000

**Chatham, Sangamon, Pop. 11,317**
Ball Chatham CUSD 5 4,500/PK-12
201 W Mulberry St 62629 217-483-2416
Dr. Douglas A Wood, supt. Fax 483-2940
www.chathamschools.org
Glenwood HS 1,300/9-12
1501 E Plummer Blvd 62629 217-483-2424
Jim Lee, prin. Fax 483-5402
Glenwood MS 700/7-8
595 Chatham Rd 62629 217-483-2481
Christina Root, prin. Fax 483-4940

**Chester, Randolph, Pop. 8,526**
Chester CUSD 139 1,000/PK-12
1940 Swanwick St 62233 618-826-4509
William Riley, supt. Fax 826-4500
www.chester139.com
Chester HS 300/9-12
1901 Swanwick St 62233 618-826-2302
Dr. Sarah Gass, prin. Fax 826-3723

**Chicago, Cook, Pop. 2,654,865**
City of Chicago SD 299 407,100/PK-12
42 W Madison St 60602 773-553-1000
Forrest Claypool, supt. Fax 535-1502
www.cps.edu
Air Force Academy HS 300/9-12
3630 S Wells St 60609 773-535-1590
Yashika Eggleston, prin. Fax 535-1847
Albany Park Multicultural MS 300/7-8
4929 N Sawyer Ave 60625 773-534-5108
Hiliana Araceli Leon, prin. Fax 534-5178
Alcott College Prep 200/9-12
2957 N Hoyne Ave 60618 773-534-5979
Elias Estrada, prin. Fax 534-5789
Amundsen HS 1,500/9-12
5110 N Damen Ave 60625 773-534-2320
Anna Pavichevich, prin. Fax 534-2330
Austin Polytechnical Academy 200/9-12
231 N Pine Ave 60644 773-534-6300
Ali Muhammad, prin. Fax 534-6046
Back of the Yards IB HS 300/9-12
2111 W 47th St 60609 773-535-7320
Patricia Barrera Brekke, prin. Fax 535-6880
Banner West Academy HS 100/Alt
819 N Leamington Ave 60651 773-854-1188
Eric Carlton, prin. Fax 854-1196
Bogan Computer Tech HS 1,600/9-12
3939 W 79th St 60652 773-535-2180
Alahrie Aziz-Sims, prin. Fax 535-2165
Bowen HS 300/9-12
2710 E 89th St 60617 773-535-7650
Nia Abdullah, prin. Fax 535-6489
Bronzeville Scholastic Institute 600/9-12
4934 S Wabash Ave 60615 773-535-1150
Leeandra Khan, prin. Fax 535-1228
Brooks College Prep Academy 800/9-12
250 E 111th St 60628 773-535-9930
Andre Weaver, prin. Fax 535-9939
Camelot Safe Academy 50/4-8
7877 S Coles Ave 60649 773-902-2487
Joseph Haley, prin. Fax 902-7961
Camelot Safe Academy Garfield Park Alt
125 S Clark St 60603
Lisa Sykes, prin.
Camelot Safe Academy HS 50/Alt
7877 S Coles Ave 60649 773-902-2487
Joseph Haley, prin. Fax 902-7961
Carver Military Academy 500/9-12
13100 S Doty Ave 60827 773-535-5250
Steven Rouse, prin. Fax 535-5037
Castellanos MS 500/4-8
2524 S Central Park Ave 60623 773-534-1620
Virginia Jimenez, prin. Fax 534-1611
Chicago Academy HS 500/9-12
3400 N Austin Ave 60634 773-534-0146
Joshua VanderJagt, prin. Fax 534-0192
Chicago Excel Academy HS 300/Alt
1257 W 111th St 60643 773-629-8379
Tyree Booker, prin. Fax 629-8736
Chicago HS for Agricultural Sciences 600/9-12
3857 W 111th St 60655 773-535-2500
William Hook, prin. Fax 535-2507
Chicago HS for the Arts 400/9-12
2714 W Augusta Blvd 60622 773-534-9710
Nicole Fishman, prin. Fax 534-9720
Chicago Military Academy 500/9-12
3519 S Giles Ave 60653 773-534-9750
Richard Miller, prin. Fax 534-9760
Chicago Technology Academy 300/9-12
1301 W 14th St 60608 773-534-7755
Linnea Garrett, prin. Fax 534-7757
Chicago Vocational Career Academy Vo/Tech
2100 E 87th St 60617 773-535-6100
Douglas Maclin, prin. Fax 535-6975
Clark Academic Prep HS 700/7-12
5101 W Harrison St 60644 773-534-6250
Beulah McLoyd, prin. Fax 534-6292
Clemente Community Academy 1,000/9-12
1147 N Western Ave 60622 773-534-4000
Marcey Sorensen, prin. Fax 534-4012
Collins Academy HS 400/9-12
1313 S Sacramento Dr 60623 773-534-1840
Erin Galfer, prin. Fax 542-6471
Community Services West Academy Vo/Tech
1239 S Pulaski Rd 60623 773-522-5133
Bertha Buchanan, prin. Fax 522-5250
Corliss HS 600/9-12
821 E 103rd St 60628 773-535-5115
Leonard Harris, prin. Fax 535-5511
Crane Medical Preparatory HS 300/9-12
2245 W Jackson Blvd 60612 773-534-7600
Fareeda Jahaan Shabazz, prin. Fax 534-7612
Curie Metropolitan HS 3,300/9-12
4959 S Archer Ave 60632 773-535-2100
Phillip Perry, prin. Fax 535-2049
DeVry Advantage Academy 200/11-12
3300 N Campbell Ave 60618 773-697-2216
Carolyn Eggert, prin. Fax 327-4262
Disney II Magnet HS 200/7-10
3900 N Lawndale Ave 60618 773-553-1000
Bogdana Gueorgieva, prin.
Douglass Academy 300/9-12
543 N Waller Ave 60644 773-534-6176
Vanessa Perry, prin. Fax 534-6172
Dunbar Vocational Career Academy Vo/Tech
3000 S King Dr 60616 773-534-9000
Gerald Morrow, prin. Fax 534-9250
Dyett Academic Center 50/Alt
555 E 51st St 60615 773-535-1825
Charles Campbell, prin. Fax 535-1037
Evergreen Academy MS 400/6-8
3537 S Paulina St 60609 773-535-4836
Marian Strok, prin. Fax 535-4853
Excel Acadamy-Englewood HS 300/9-12
7141 S Morgan St 60621 773-535-4773
Kevin Sweetland, prin.
Excel Academy - Southwest 100/9-9
7014 S Washtenaw Ave 60629 773-424-0721
Glenda Forbes, prin. Fax 424-0746
Farragut Career Academy Vo/Tech
2345 S Christiana Ave 60623 773-534-1300
Tonya Hammaker, prin. Fax 534-1336
Fenger Academy HS 700/9-12
11220 S Wallace St 60628 773-535-5430
Elizabeth Dozier, prin. Fax 535-5444
Field ES 400/4-8
7019 N Ashland Blvd 60626 773-534-2030
Adrian Dobbins, prin. Fax 534-2189
Foreman HS 1,700/9-12
3235 N Leclaire Ave 60641 773-534-3400
Daniel Zimmerman, prin. Fax 534-3684
Gage Park HS 1,000/9-12
5630 S Rockwell St 60629 773-535-9230
Brian Metcalf, prin. Fax 535-9411
Gary ES 1,200/PK-PK, 3-
3740 W 31st St 60623 773-534-1455
Alberto Juarez, prin. Fax 534-1435
Goode STEM Academy 200/9-11
7651 S Homan Ave 60652 773-535-7875
Matsuo Marti, prin. Fax 535-7877
Hancock College Prep HS 1,000/9-12
4034 W 56th St 60629 773-535-2410
Dr. Karen Boran, prin. Fax 535-2434
Harlan Community Academy HS 1,200/7-12
9652 S Michigan Ave 60628 773-535-5400
Reginald Evans, prin. Fax 535-5061
Harper HS 600/9-12
6520 S Wood St 60636 773-535-9150
Leonetta Sanders, prin. Fax 535-9090
Hernandez MS for Advancement of Sciences 1,000/6-8
3510 W 55th St 60632 773-535-8850
Raul Bermejo, prin. Fax 535-8851
Hirsch Metro HS 400/9-12
7740 S Ingleside Ave 60619 773-535-3100
Afina Lockhart, prin. Fax 535-3240
Hope College Prep HS 600/9-12
5515 S Lowe Ave 60621 773-535-3160
Michael Durr, prin. Fax 535-3444
Hubbard HS 1,600/9-12
6200 S Hamlin Ave 60629 773-535-2200
Nancy Wiley, prin. Fax 535-2218
Hyde Park Academy HS 1,400/9-12
6220 S Stony Island Ave 60637 773-535-0880
Antonio Ross, prin. Fax 535-0633
Infinity Math/Science Tech HS 400/9-12
3120 S Kostner Ave 60623 773-535-4225
Charles Smith, prin. Fax 535-4270
Jefferson Alternative S 200/Alt
1100 S Hamilton Ave 60612 312-433-7110
Beryl Shingles, prin. Fax 433-4442
Johnson - Brainerd HS 100/Alt
8908 S Ashland Ave 60620
Sandra Smith, dir.
Johnson - Englewood HS 100/Alt
845 W 69th St 60621 773-962-9256
Veriner James, dir. Fax 969-9995
Johnson - Humboldt Park HS 100/Alt
2421 W Division St 60622 773-276-0620
Ursula Ricketts, dir. Fax 276-0692
Johnson - North Lawndale HS 200/9-12
3222 W Roosevelt Rd 60624 773-826-1136
John Shenberger, prin. Fax 826-1180

Johnson - Roseland HS 100/Alt
10928 S Halstead Ave 60628 773-468-1480
Raashida Washington, dir. Fax 468-1507
Jones College Prep HS 900/9-12
700 S State St 60605 773-534-8600
Dr. Joseph Powers, prin. Fax 534-8625
Juarez Community Academy 1,700/9-12
2150 S Laflin St 60608 773-534-7030
Juan Ocon, prin. Fax 534-7058
Julian HS 1,200/9-12
10330 S Elizabeth St 60643 773-535-5170
Careda Taylor, prin. Fax 535-5230
Kelly HS 2,800/9-12
4136 S California Ave 60632 773-535-4900
James Coughlin, prin. Fax 535-4841
Kelvyn Park HS 1,200/7-12
4343 W Wrightwood Ave 60639 773-534-4200
Allyson Fox-Crump, prin. Fax 534-4507
Kennedy HS 1,600/9-12
6325 W 56th St 60638 773-535-2325
George Szkapiak, prin. Fax 535-2485
Kenwood Academy HS 1,800/7-12
5015 S Blackstone Ave 60615 773-535-1350
Gregory Jones, prin. Fax 535-1360
King College Prep HS 900/9-12
4445 S Drexel Blvd 60653 773-535-1180
David Narain, prin. Fax 535-1658
Lake View HS 1,500/9-12
4015 N Ashland Ave 60613 773-534-5440
Scott Grens, prin. Fax 534-5585
Lane Tech HS 4,300/7-12
2501 W Addison St 60618 773-534-5400
Christopher Dignam, prin. Fax 534-5544
Lincoln Park HS 2,300/9-12
2001 N Orchard St 60614 773-534-8130
Michael Boraz, prin. Fax 534-8218
Lindblom Math/Science Academy 900/7-12
6130 S Wolcott Ave 60636 773-535-9300
Alan Mather, prin. Fax 535-9314
Madero MS 300/6-8
3202 W 28th St 60623 773-535-4466
Jose Illanes, prin. Fax 535-4469
Mandela Alternative HS 100/Alt
7847 S Jeffery Blvd 60649 773-375-0529
Nancy Jackson, prin. Fax 375-0610
Manley Career Academy Vo/Tech
2935 W Polk St 60612 773-534-6900
Trista Harper, prin. Fax 534-6924
Marine Academy 400/10-12
145 S Campbell Ave 60612 773-534-7818
Fred Aguirre, prin. Fax 534-0877
Marine Leadership Academy - Ames 600/7-12
1920 N Hamlin Ave 60647 773-534-4970
Col. Robert Sprague, admin. Fax 534-4975
Marshall Metro HS 700/9-12
3250 W Adams St 60624 773-534-6455
Dr. Lori Campbell, prin. Fax 534-6409
Marshall MS 400/7-8
3900 N Lawndale Ave 60618 773-534-5200
Januario Gutierrez, prin. Fax 534-5292
Mather HS 1,600/9-12
5835 N Lincoln Ave 60659 773-534-2350
Christie Jones, prin. Fax 534-2424
Morgan Park JSHS 1,600/7-12
1744 W Pryor Ave 60643 773-535-2550
Carolyn Epps, prin. Fax 535-2706
Multicultural Academy of Scholarship HS 300/9-12
3120 S Kostner Ave 60623 773-535-4242
James Clarke, prin. Fax 535-4273
North-Grand HS 900/9-12
4338 W Wabansia Ave 60639 773-534-8520
Jason Nault, prin. Fax 534-8535
Northside College Prep HS 1,100/9-12
5501 N Kedzie Ave 60625 773-534-3954
Kelly Mest, prin. Fax 534-3964
Northwest MS 600/6-8
5252 W Palmer St 60639 773-534-3250
Marilyn Strojny, prin. Fax 534-3251
Ogden International HS 600/6-12
1250 W Erie St, 773-534-0866
Shane Smith, prin. Fax 534-0869
Ombudsman - Northwest HS 200/Alt
7500 N Harlem Ave 60631 312-806-9022
Sue Fila, prin. Fax 940-2197
Ombudsman - South HS 500/Alt
6057 S Western Ave 60636 773-498-5085
Sue Fila, prin. Fax 424-7291
Ombudsman - West HS 400/Alt
2401 W Congress Pkwy 60612 312-243-1550
Sue Fila, prin. Fax 243-1562
Orr Academy HS 800/9-12
730 N Pulaski Rd 60624 773-534-6500
Tyese Sims, prin. Fax 534-6504
Pathways in Education Brighton Park 300/Alt
3124 W 47th St 60632
Andrew Morgan, prin.
Pathways in Education HS 200/Alt
3284 W 87th St 60652 773-434-6300
Andrew Morgan, prin. Fax 434-6301
Pathways in Education HS - Avondale 300/Alt
3100 W Belmont Ave 60618 773-588-5007
Andrew Morgan, prin. Fax 588-5009
Pathways in Education Lincoln Square Alt
4820 N Western Ave 60625
Joe Zotto, prin.
Payton College Prep HS 900/9-12
1034 N Wells St 60610 773-534-0034
Timothy Devine, prin. Fax 534-0035
Peace and Education Coalition HS 200/Alt
4946 S Paulina St 60609 773-535-9023
Brigitte Lee Swenson, prin. Fax 535-9477
Phillips Academy HS 500/9-12
244 E Pershing Rd 60653 773-535-1603
Matthew Sullivan, prin. Fax 535-1605
Phoenix Military Academy 500/9-12
145 S Campbell Ave 60612 773-534-7275
Ferdinand Wipachit, prin. Fax 534-7273

Prosser Career Academy Vo/Tech
2148 N Long Ave 60639 773-534-3200
Linda Pierzchalski, prin. Fax 534-3382
Raby HS 500/9-12
3545 W Fulton Blvd 60624 773-534-6755
Femi Skanes, prin. Fax 534-6938
Richards Career Academy Vo/Tech
5009 S Laflin St 60609 773-535-4945
Durrell Anderson, prin. Fax 535-4883
Rickover Naval Academy HS 400/9-12
5900 N Glenwood Ave 60660 773-534-2890
Michael Biela, prin. Fax 534-2895
Robeson HS 700/9-12
6835 S Normal Blvd 60621 773-535-3800
Melanie Beatty-Sevier, prin. Fax 535-3620
Roosevelt HS 1,400/9-12
3436 W Wilson Ave 60625 773-534-5000
Pilar Vazquez-Vialva, prin. Fax 534-5044
Schurz HS 2,300/9-12
3601 N Milwaukee Ave 60641 773-534-3420
Daniel Kramer, prin. Fax 534-3573
Senn HS 1,000/9-12
5900 N Glenwood Ave 60660 773-534-2365
Susan Lofton, prin. Fax 534-2369
Shields MS 700/5-8
2611 W 48th St 60632 773-535-7115
Peter Auffant, prin. Fax 535-7296
Simeon Career Academy Vo/Tech
8147 S Vincennes Ave 60620 773-535-3200
Dr. Sheldon House, prin. Fax 535-3465
Simpson Academy for Young Women 200/Alt
1321 S Paulina St 60608 773-534-7812
Marisa Velasquez, prin. Fax 534-7819
Social Justice HS 400/9-12
3120 S Kostner Ave 60623 773-535-4300
Kathy Farr, prin. Fax 535-4271
Solorio Academy HS 600/9-12
5400 S Saint Louis Ave 60632 773-535-9070
Victor Iturralde, prin. Fax 535-9073
South Shore International S 300/9-12
1955 E 75th St 60649 773-535-8350
Janice Elaine Wells, prin.
Spry Community Links HS 200/9-12
2400 S Marshall Blvd 60623 773-534-1997
Francisco Borras, prin. Fax 534-0354
Steinmetz College Prep HS 1,800/9-12
3030 N Mobile Ave 60634 773-534-3030
Stephen Ngo, prin. Fax 534-3151
Sullivan HS 800/9-12
6631 N Bosworth Ave 60626 773-534-2000
Chad Adams, prin. Fax 534-2141
Taft HS 2,900/7-12
6530 W Bryn Mawr Ave 60631 773-534-1000
Mark Grishaber, prin. Fax 534-1027
TEAM Englewood Academy 400/9-12
6201 S Stewart Ave 60621 773-535-3530
Rodney Bly, prin. Fax 535-3586
Tilden Career Community HS 400/9-12
4747 S Union Ave 60609 773-535-1625
Maurice Swinney, prin. Fax 535-1866
Uplift Community HS 400/9-12
900 W Wilson Ave 60640 773-534-2875
Stephanie Moore, prin. Fax 534-2876
VOISE Academy HS 400/9-12
231 N Pine Ave 60644 773-534-0660
Ali Muhammad, prin. Fax 534-0667
Von Steuben Metro HS 1,600/9-12
5039 N Kimball Ave 60625 773-534-5100
Laura Lemone, prin. Fax 534-5210
Washington HS 1,500/9-12
3535 E 114th St 60617 773-535-5725
Kevin Gallick, prin. Fax 535-5038
Wells Community Academy HS 600/9-12
936 N Ashland Ave 60622 773-534-7010
Rituparna Raichoudhuri, prin. Fax 534-7078
Westinghouse College Prep HS 800/9-12
3223 W Franklin Blvd 60624 773-534-6400
Patrick McGill, prin. Fax 534-6422
Williams Prep S of Medicine 300/9-12
4934 S Wabash Ave 60615 773-535-1120
Jullanar Naselli, prin. Fax 535-1023
World Language HS 400/9-12
3120 S Kostner Ave 60623 773-535-4334
Brian Rogers, prin. Fax 254-8470
Young Magnet JSHS 2,200/7-12
211 S Laflin St 60607 773-534-7500
Dr. Joyce Kenner, prin. Fax 534-7261

---

Adler School of Professional Psychology Post-Sec.
17 N Dearborn St 60602 312-662-4000
Advocate Illinois Masonic Post-Sec.
836 W Wellington Ave 60657 773-296-8950
Advocate Trinity Hospital Post-Sec.
2320 E 93rd St 60617 773-978-2000
American Academy of Art Post-Sec.
332 S Michigan Ave Ste 3 60604 312-461-0600
American Floral Art School Post-Sec.
2519 W Altgeld St Ste 100 60647 312-922-9328
American Health Information Management Post-Sec.
233 N Michigan Ave Ste 2150 60601 312-233-1100
Argosy University/Chicago Post-Sec.
225 N Michigan Ave Ste 1300 60601 312-777-7600
ATS Institute of Technology Post-Sec.
25 E Washington St Ste 200 60602 312-214-2000
Bais Yaakov HS for Girls 200/9-12
5800 N Kimball Ave 60659 773-267-1494
Shulamis Keller, prin. Fax 267-4798
Bexley Seabury Post-Sec.
8765 W Higgins Rd 60631 773-380-6780
Bnos Rabbeinu HS 50/9-12
6237 N Whipple St 60659 773-338-3214
Tsyrl Turen, prin. Fax 772-1688
British S of Chicago 800/PK-12
814 W Eastman St, 773-506-2097
Michael Horton, prin.
Brother Rice HS 800/9-12
10001 S Pulaski Rd 60655 773-429-4300
James Antos, prin. Fax 779-5239

Cain's Barber College Post-Sec.
365 E 51st St 60615 773-536-4441
Cannella School of Hair Design Post-Sec.
9012 S Commercial Ave 60617 773-221-4700
Cannella School of Hair Design Post-Sec.
4269 S Archer Ave 60632 773-890-0412
Cannella School of Hair Design Post-Sec.
4217 W North Ave 60639 773-278-4477
Capri Beauty College Post-Sec.
2653 W 63rd St 60629 773-778-1077
Catholic Theological Union Post-Sec.
5401 S Cornell Ave 60615 773-371-5400
Chamberlain College of Nursing Post-Sec.
3300 N Campbell Ave 60618 773-961-3000
Chicago Academy for the Arts 100/9-12
1010 W Chicago Ave, 312-421-0202
Jason Patera, prin. Fax 421-3816
Chicago Hope Academy 100/9-12
2189 W Bowler St 60612 312-491-1600
Robert Muzikowski, pres. Fax 491-1616
Chicago Jesuit Academy 100/5-8
5058 W Jackson Blvd 60644 773-638-6103
Thomas Beckley, prin. Fax 638-6107
Chicago Sch. of Professional Psychology Post-Sec.
325 N Wells St 60654 312-329-6600
Chicago State University Post-Sec.
9501 S King Dr 60628 773-995-2000
Chicago Theological Seminary Post-Sec.
1407 E 60th St 60637 773-896-2400
Chicago Waldorf S 400/PK-12
1300 W Loyola Ave 60626 773-465-2662
Luke Goodwin, admin. Fax 465-6648
Christ the King Jesuit College Prep S 300/9-12
5088 W Jackson Blvd 60644 773-261-7505
Temple Payne, prin. Fax 261-7507
Columbia College Post-Sec.
600 S Michigan Ave 60605 312-369-1000
Computer Systems Institute Post-Sec.
318 W Adams St Fl 10 60606 312-346-6774
Cook County Hospital Post-Sec.
1825 W Harrison St 60612 312-633-8533
Cortiva Institute-School of Massage Thpy Post-Sec.
17 N State St Fl 5 60602 312-753-7900
Coyne College Post-Sec.
330 N Green St 60607 800-999-5220
Cristo Rey Jesuit HS 500/9-12
1852 W 22nd Pl 60608 773-890-6800
Patricia Garrity, prin. Fax 890-6801
CS Academy College Prep S 100/K-12
1443 W 63rd St 60636 312-675-8691
Domonique Ziegler, admin. Fax 737-4865
De La Salle Institute - Institute Campus 1,100/9-12
3434 S Michigan Ave 60616 312-842-7355
Diane Brown, prin. Fax 842-5640
De La Salle Institute - Lourdes Campus 500/9-12
1040 W 32nd Pl 60608 773-650-6800
Diane Brown, prin. Fax 650-9722
DePaul College Prep S 400/9-12
3633 N California Ave 60618 773-539-3600
Dr. James Quaid, prin. Fax 539-9158
De Paul University Post-Sec.
1 E Jackson Blvd 60604 312-362-8000
DeVry University Post-Sec.
3300 N Campbell Ave 60618 773-929-8500
DeVry University Post-Sec.
225 W Washington St Ste 100 60606 312-372-4900
DeVry University Post-Sec.
8550 W Bryn Mawr Ave # 450 60631 773-695-1000
East-West University Post-Sec.
816 S Michigan Ave 60605 312-939-0111
Erikson Institute Post-Sec.
451 N La Salle Dr 60654 312-755-2250
Everest College Post-Sec.
7414 S Cicero Ave 60629 708-793-4600
GCE - Lab S 50/6-12
1535 N Dayton St, 312-643-0991
Eric Davis, dir. Fax 643-0975
Greater West Comm Development Project Post-Sec.
500 N Sacramento Blvd 60612 312-432-9595
Hales Franciscan HS 100/9-12
4930 S Cottage Grove Ave 60615 773-285-8400
Nichole Jackson, prin. Fax 285-7025
Hanna Sacks Girls HS 100/9-12
3021 W Devon Ave 60659 773-338-9222
Tobie Teller, prin. Fax 338-2405
Harold S. Washington College Post-Sec.
30 E Lake St 60601 312-553-5600
Harrington College of Design Post-Sec.
200 W Madison St Lbby 2 60606 312-939-4975
Harry S. Truman College Post-Sec.
1145 W Wilson Ave 60640 773-907-4000
Holy Trinity HS 300/9-12
1443 W Division St, 773-278-4212
Marianne Lynch, prin. Fax 278-0144
Ida Crown Jewish Academy 300/9-12
2828 W Pratt Blvd 60645 773-973-1450
Rabbi Leonard Matanky, dean Fax 973-6131
Illinois Center for Broadcasting Post-Sec.
530 S State St 60605 312-884-8000
Illinois College of Optometry Post-Sec.
3241 S Michigan Ave 60616 312-225-1700
Illinois Institute of Technology Post-Sec.
3300 S Federal St 60616 312-567-3000
Illinois School of Health Careers Post-Sec.
11 E Adams St Ste 200 60603 312-913-1230
Institute for Clinical Social Work Post-Sec.
401 S State St Ste 822 60605 312-935-4232
John Marshall Law School Post-Sec.
315 S Plymouth Ct 60604 312-427-2737
Josephinum Academy 200/6-12
1501 N Oakley Blvd 60622 773-276-1261
Julie Raino, prin. Fax 292-3963
Kendall College Post-Sec.
900 N North Branch St, 888-905-3632
Kennedy-King College Post-Sec.
6301 S Halsted St 60621 773-602-5000
Latin S of Chicago 1,100/PK-12
59 W North Blvd 60610 312-582-6000
Randall Dunn, head sch Fax 582-6011

Le Cordon Bleu College of Culinary Arts Post-Sec.
361 W Chestnut St 60610 312-944-0882
Leo HS 100/9-12
7901 S Sangamon St 60620 773-224-9600
Philip Mesina, prin. Fax 224-3856
Lexington College Post-Sec.
310 S Peoria St 60607 312-226-6294
Loyola University Chicago Post-Sec.
1032 W Sheridan Rd 60660 773-274-3000
Lubavitch Girls HS 100/9-12
6350 N Whipple St 60659 773-743-7716
Kreindel Pinkhus, prin. Fax 743-7735
Lubavitch Mesivta of Chicago 100/9-12
2756 W Morse Ave 60645 773-262-0430
Rabbi Moshe Perlstein, dean Fax 338-2209
Lutheran School of Theology at Chicago Post-Sec.
1100 E 55th St 60615 773-256-0700
Luther North College Preparatory HS 200/9-12
5700 W Berteau Ave 60634 773-286-3600
Wayne Wenzel, prin. Fax 286-0304
Lycee Francais de Chicago 600/PK-12
1929 W Wilson Ave 60640 773-665-0066
Eric Veteau, pres. Fax 665-1725
MacCormac College Post-Sec.
29 E Madison St 60602 312-922-1884
Malcolm X College Post-Sec.
1900 W Van Buren St 60612 312-850-7000
Marist HS 1,800/9-12
4200 W 115th St 60655 773-881-5300
Larry Tucker, prin. Fax 881-0595
McCormick Theological Seminary Post-Sec.
5460 S University Ave 60615 800-228-4687
Meadville Lombard Theological School Post-Sec.
610 S Michigan Ave 60605 773-256-3000
Midwest College of Oriental Medicine Post-Sec.
4334 N Hazel St Ste 206 60613 262-554-2010
Moody Bible Institute Post-Sec.
820 N La Salle Dr 60610 312-329-4000
Morgan Park Academy 400/PK-12
2153 W 111th St 60643 773-881-6700
Mercedes Z. Sheppard, head sch Fax 881-8409
Mother McAuley Liberal Arts HS 1,400/9-12
3737 W 99th St 60655 773-881-6500
Eileen Boyce, prin. Fax 881-6562
Mt. Carmel HS 800/9-12
6410 S Dante Ave 60637 773-324-1020
John Stimler, prin. Fax 324-9235
National Latino Education Institute Post-Sec.
2011 W Pershing Rd 60609 773-247-0707
National-Louis University Post-Sec.
122 S Michigan Ave 60603 888-658-8632
Northeastern Illinois University Post-Sec.
5500 N Saint Louis Ave 60625 773-583-4050
North Park University Post-Sec.
3225 W Foster Ave 60625 773-244-6200
North Shore SDA Jr. Academy 100/PK-12
5220 N California Ave 60625 773-769-0733
Harley Peterson, prin. Fax 769-0928
Northside Catholic Academy 100/5-8
5525 N Magnolia Ave 60640 773-271-2008
Fax 271-3101
Northwestern College Post-Sec.
4829 N Lipps Ave 60630 888-205-2283
Northwestern Memorial Hospital Post-Sec.
514 N Fairbanks 9th Floor 60611 312-926-2215
Northwestern University Post-Sec.
303 E Chicago Ave 60611 312-503-8649
Notre Dame HS 100/9-12
3115 N Mason Ave 60634 773-622-9494
Irene Heidelbauer, dir. Fax 622-2807
Olive-Harvey College Post-Sec.
10001 S Woodlawn Ave 60628 773-291-6100
Our Lady of Tepeyac HS 200/9-12
2228 S Whipple St 60623 773-522-0023
Becca Noonan, prin. Fax 522-0508
Pacific College of Oriental Medicine Post-Sec.
65 E Wacker Pl Fl 21 60601 773-477-4822
Parker S 900/PK-12
330 W Webster Ave 60614 773-353-3000
Daniel Frank Ph.D., prin. Fax 549-4669
Providence - St. Mel S 500/PK-12
119 S Central Park Blvd 60624 773-722-4600
Jeanette DiBella, prin. Fax 722-9004
Pyramid Career Institute Post-Sec.
3051 N Lincoln Ave 60657 773-975-9898
Ravenswood Baptist Christian S 100/K-12
4437 N Seeley Ave 60625 773-561-6576
Karl Engle, prin. Fax 561-3080
Resurrection College Prep HS 600/9-12
7500 W Talcott Ave 60631 773-775-6616
Maria Hawk, prin. Fax 775-0611
Resurrection University Post-Sec.
1431 N Claremont Ave 60622 773-252-6464
Richard J. Daley College Post-Sec.
7500 S Pulaski Rd 60652 773-838-7500
Robert Morris University Post-Sec.
401 S State St 60605 312-935-6800
Roosevelt University Post-Sec.
430 S Michigan Ave 60605 312-341-3500
Rosel School of Cosmetology Post-Sec.
2446 W Devon Ave 60659 773-508-5600
Rush University Post-Sec.
600 S Paulina St # 440 60612 312-942-7100
St. Augustine College Post-Sec.
1333 W Argyle St 60640 773-878-8756
St. Benedict Prep S 200/9-12
3900 N Leavitt St 60618 773-539-0066
Ericka Mickelburgh, hdmstr. Fax 539-3397
St. Francis De Sales HS 200/9-12
10155 S Ewing Ave 60617 773-731-7272
John Kimec, prin. Fax 731-7888
St. Ignatius College Prep HS 1,400/9-12
1076 W Roosevelt Rd 60608 312-421-5900
Brianna Latko, prin. Fax 421-7124
St. Mary of Providence School Post-Sec.
4200 N Austin Ave 60634 773-545-8300
St. Patrick HS 800/9-12
5900 W Belmont Ave 60634 773-282-8844
Jon Baffico, prin. Fax 282-2361

St. Rita of Cascia HS 700/9-12
7740 S Western Ave 60620 773-925-6600
Brendan Conroy, prin. Fax 925-2451
St. Xavier University Post-Sec.
3700 W 103rd St 60655 773-298-3000
Sanford-Brown College Post-Sec.
1 N State St Ste 500 60602 312-980-9200
San Miguel MS 100/6-8
1954 W 48th St 60609 773-890-1481
Thaddeus Smith, prin. Fax 254-3382
School of the Art Institute of Chicago Post-Sec.
37 S Wabash Ave 60603 312-899-5100
Shimer College Post-Sec.
3424 S State St 60616 312-235-3500
Spertus Institute for Jewish Learning Post-Sec.
610 S Michigan Ave 60605 312-322-1700
Steven Papageorge Hair Academy Post-Sec.
1113 W Belmont Ave # 15 60657 773-883-5100
Taylor Business Institute Post-Sec.
318 W Adams St Fl 5 60606 312-658-5100
Telshe HS 100/9-12
3535 W Foster Ave 60625 773-463-7738
Rabbi Shmuel Adler, dir. Fax 463-2849
Telshe Yeshiva-Chicago Post-Sec.
3535 W Foster Ave 60625 773-463-7738
The Illinois Institute of Art Post-Sec.
350 N Orleans St Lbby 136 60654 312-280-3500
Toyota Technological Inst at Chicago Post-Sec.
6045 S Kenwood Ave 60637 773-834-2500
Tribeca Flashpoint Media Arts Academy Post-Sec.
28 N Clark St Ste 500 60602 312-332-0707
University of Chicago Post-Sec.
5801 S Ellis Ave 60637 773-702-1234
University of Chicago Lab S 1,800/PK-12
1362 E 59th St 60637 773-702-9450
Robin Appleby, dir. Fax 702-7455
University of Illinois at Chicago Post-Sec.
1200 W Harrison St 60607 312-996-7000
Univ. of Chicago Hospital/Roosevelt U. Post-Sec.
5841 S Maryland Ave 60637 773-702-6240
VanderCook College of Music Post-Sec.
3140 S Federal St 60616 800-448-2655
Warde S - Holy Name Cathedral 400/4-8
751 N State St 60654 312-466-0700
Michael Kennedy, head sch Fax 337-7180
Westwood College Post-Sec.
8501 W Higgins Rd Ste 100 60631 773-380-6800
Westwood College Post-Sec.
1 N State St Ste 1000 60602 312-739-0890
Wilbur Wright College North Post-Sec.
4300 N Narragansett Ave 60634 773-777-7900
Yeshivas Meor HaTorah of Chicago 50/9-12
3635 W Devon Ave 60659 773-465-0419

**Chicago Heights, Cook, Pop. 29,817**

Bloom Township HSD 206 3,300/9-12
100 W 10th St 60411 708-755-7010
Dr. Lenell Navarre, supt. Fax 755-1149
www.sd206.org
Bloom HS 1,700/9-12
101 W 10th St 60411 708-755-1122
Krystal Thomas, prin. Fax 755-1149
Bloom Trail HS 1,600/9-12
22331 Cottage Grove Ave 60411 708-758-7000
Dr. Debra Graham, prin. Fax 758-8372
District 206 Alternative HS 100/Alt
100 W 10th St 60411 708-754-4095
Michael Campbell, prin. Fax 754-4099

Flossmoor SD 161 2,400/PK-8
41 E Elmwood Dr 60411 708-647-7000
Craig Doster, supt. Fax 754-2153
www.sd161.org
Other Schools – See Flossmoor

Park Forest SD 163
Supt. — See Park Forest
Obama S of Leadership and STEM 400/4-8
401 Concord Dr 60411 708-668-9100
Ericka Patterson, prin. Fax 283-2358

---

Marian Catholic HS 1,400/9-12
700 Ashland Ave 60411 708-755-7565
Steve Tortorello, prin. Fax 755-0042
Prairie State College Post-Sec.
202 S Halsted St 60411 708-709-3500

**Chicago Ridge, Cook, Pop. 13,978**

Chicago Ridge SD 127-5 1,400/PK-8
6135 108th St 60415 708-636-2000
Dr. Kevin B. Russell, supt. Fax 636-0916
www.crsd1275.org
Finley JHS 400/6-8
10835 Lombard Ave 60415 708-636-2005
Laura Grachan, prin. Fax 636-0045

**Chillicothe, Peoria, Pop. 6,048**

Illinois Valley Central Unit SD 321 1,700/PK-12
1300 W Sycamore St 61523 309-274-5418
Chad Allison, supt. Fax 274-5046
www.ivcschools.com/
Chillicothe Elementary & JHS 200/4-8
914 W Truitt Ave 61523 309-274-6266
Patrick Auge, prin. Fax 274-2010
Illinois Valley Central HS 700/9-12
1300 W Sycamore St 61523 309-274-5481
Kenton Bergman, prin. Fax 274-8613

**Chrisman, Edgar, Pop. 1,339**

Edgar County CUSD 6 300/K-12
23231 IL Highway 1 61924 217-269-2513
Dr. Steven Poznic, supt. Fax 269-3231
www.chrisman.k12.il.us
Chrisman HS 100/9-12
23231 IL Highway 1 61924 217-269-2823
Nancy Dalenberg, prin. Fax 269-2329
Chrisman-Scottland JHS 100/6-8
23231 IL Highway 1 61924 217-269-3980
Nancy Dalenberg, prin. Fax 269-3231

**Christopher, Franklin, Pop. 2,363**

Christopher Unit SD 99 700/PK-12
1 Bearcat Dr 62822 618-724-9461
Richard Towers, supt. Fax 724-9400
www.cpher.frnkln.k12.il.us
Christopher HS 300/9-12
1 Bearcat Dr 62822 618-724-9461
Jeff Johnston, prin. Fax 724-9400

**Cicero, Cook, Pop. 83,518**

Cicero SD 99 13,300/PK-8
5110 W 24th St 60804 708-863-4856
Rodolfo Hernandez, supt. Fax 652-8105
www.cicd99.edu
Unity JHS 2,700/7-8
2115 S 54th Ave 60804 708-863-8268
Donata Heppner, prin. Fax 656-5652

J. S. Morton HSD 201 8,200/9-12
5041 W 31st St 60804 708-780-2110
Dr. Michael Kuzniewski, supt. Fax 780-2111
morton201.org
Morton Alternative S 50/Alt
1874 S 54th Ave 60804 708-222-3080
Erin Kelly, prin. Fax 222-3070
Morton East HS 3,500/10-12
2423 S Austin Blvd 60804 708-780-4000
Jose Gamboa, prin. Fax 222-3090
Morton Freshman Center 1,300/9-9
1801 S 55th Ave 60804 708-863-7900
Mayra Barahona-Arroyo, prin. Fax 863-2244
Other Schools – See Berwyn

---

Morton College Post-Sec.
3801 S Central Ave 60804 708-656-8000

**Cisne, Wayne, Pop. 671**

North Wayne CUSD 200 400/PK-12
PO Box 235 62823 618-673-2151
Julie Healy, supt. Fax 673-2152
Cisne HS 100/9-12
1456 US Highway 45 62823 618-673-2154
Kevin Bowen, prin. Fax 673-2155
Cisne MS 100/5-8
PO Box 69 62823 618-673-2156
Julie Healy, prin. Fax 673-2152

**Cissna Park, Iroquois, Pop. 841**

Cissna Park CUSD 6 300/K-12
511 N 2nd St 60924 815-457-2171
Dr. Daniel Hylbert, supt. Fax 457-3033
www.cissnapark.k12.il.us
Cissna Park HS 100/9-12
511 N 2nd St 60924 815-457-2171
Mark Portwood, prin. Fax 457-3033
Cissna Park JHS 100/6-8
511 N 2nd St 60924 815-457-2171
Mark Portwood, prin. Fax 457-3033

**Clarendon Hills, DuPage, Pop. 8,292**

CCSD 181 4,000/PK-8
115 55th St 60514 630-861-4900
Dr. Don White, supt. Fax 887-1079
www.d181.org
Clarendon Hills MS 700/6-8
301 Chicago Ave 60514 630-861-4800
Griffin Sonntag, prin. Fax 887-4267
Other Schools – See Hinsdale

**Clay City, Clay, Pop. 956**

Clay City CUSD 10 300/PK-12
PO Box 542 62824 618-676-1431
Cathy Croy, supt. Fax 676-1430
www.claycityschools.org
Clay City HS 100/9-12
PO Box 542 62824 618-676-1522
Ben Borries, prin. Fax 676-1481
Clay City JHS 100/6-8
PO Box 542 62824 618-676-1431
Ben Borries, prin. Fax 676-1537

**Clifton, Iroquois, Pop. 1,441**

Central CUSD 4
Supt. — See Ashkum
Central HS 400/9-12
1134 E 3100 North Rd 60927 815-694-2321
Marc Shaner, prin. Fax 694-2709
Nash MS 300/5-8
1134 E 3100 North Rd 60927 815-694-2323
Victoria Marquis, prin. Fax 694-2830

**Clinton, DeWitt, Pop. 7,123**

Clinton CUSD 15 1,900/PK-12
680 Illini Dr 61727 217-935-8321
Curt Nettles, supt. Fax 935-2300
www.cusd15.org
Clinton HS 500/9-12
1200 State Route 54 W 61727 217-935-8337
Jerry Wayne, prin. Fax 935-4029
Clinton JHS 500/6-8
701 Illini Dr 61727 217-935-2103
Drew Goebel, prin. Fax 937-1918

**Coal City, Grundy, Pop. 5,546**

Coal City CUSD 1 2,100/PK-12
100 S Baima St 60416 815-634-2287
Dr. Kent Bugg, supt. Fax 634-8775
www.coalcity.k12.il.us
Coal City HS 600/9-12
655 W Division St 60416 815-634-2396
Mitch Hamann, prin. Fax 634-2313
Coal City MS 500/6-8
500 S Carbon Hill Rd 60416 815-634-5039
Travis Johnson, prin. Fax 634-5049

**Cobden, Union, Pop. 1,130**

Cobden Unit SD 17 500/K-12
413 N Appleknocker St 62920 618-893-2313
Edwin Shoemate, supt. Fax 893-4772
www.cobdenappleknockers.com

Cobden HS 100/9-12
413 N Appleknocker St 62920 618-893-4031
Crystal Housman, prin. Fax 893-2138
Cobden JHS 100/6-8
413 N Appleknocker St 62920 618-893-4031
Crystal Housman, prin. Fax 893-2138

**Colchester, McDonough, Pop. 1,398**
West Prairie CUSD 103 700/PK-12
204 S Hun St 62326 309-776-3180
Dr. Jonathan Heerboth, supt. Fax 776-3194
www.westprairie.org/
West Prairie MS 200/5-8
600 S Hun St 62326 309-776-3220
Caitlin Watson, prin. Fax 776-3115
Other Schools – See Sciota

**Colfax, McLean, Pop. 1,054**
Ridgeview CUSD 19 500/PK-12
300 S Harrison St 61728 309-723-5111
Guy Gradert, supt. Fax 723-6395
www.ridgeview19.org
Ridgeview JSHS 200/6-12
202 E Wood St 61728 309-723-2951
Jim Campbell, prin. Fax 723-4851

**Collinsville, Madison, Pop. 25,082**
Collinsville CUSD 10 6,600/PK-12
201 W Clay St 62234 618-346-6350
Robert Green, supt. Fax 343-3657
www.kahoks.org
Collinsville Area Vocational Center Vo/Tech
2201 S Morrison Ave 62234 618-346-6140
Dr. Tricia Blackard, prin. Fax 346-6241
Collinsville HS 2,000/9-12
2201 S Morrison Ave 62234 618-346-6320
David Snider, prin. Fax 346-6341
Collinsville MS 1,000/7-8
9649 Collinsville Rd 62234 618-343-2100
Kimberly Jackson, prin. Fax 343-2102

---

Collinsville Christian Academy 100/1-12
1203 Vandalia St 62234 618-345-4224
Deedra Mager, admin. Fax 345-4470

**Columbia, Monroe, Pop. 9,637**
Columbia CUSD 4 2,000/PK-12
5 Veterans Pkwy 62236 618-281-4772
Dr. Gina Segobiano, supt. Fax 281-4570
www.columbia4.org
Columbia HS 600/9-12
77 Veterans Pkwy 62236 618-281-5001
Jason Dandurand, prin. Fax 281-8081
Columbia MS 600/5-8
100 Eagle Dr 62236 618-281-4993
Brian Reeves, prin. Fax 281-4964

**Concord, Morgan, Pop. 167**
Triopia CUSD 27 400/PK-12
2204 Concord Arenzville Rd 62631 217-457-2283
Steve Eisenhauer, supt. Fax 457-2277
www.triopiacusd27.org/
Triopia JSHS 200/7-12
2204 Concord Arenzville Rd 62631 217-457-2281
Adam Dean, prin. Fax 457-2277

**Coulterville, Randolph, Pop. 930**
Coulterville Unit SD 1 200/PK-12
PO Box 396 62237 618-758-2881
Karyn Albers, supt. Fax 758-2330
Coulterville HS 100/9-12
PO Box 396 62237 618-758-2881
Brandon Taylor, prin. Fax 758-2330
Coulterville JHS 100/6-8
PO Box 396 62237 618-758-2881
Brandon Taylor, prin. Fax 758-2330

**Country Club Hills, Cook, Pop. 16,299**
Bremen Community HSD 228
Supt. — See Midlothian
Hillcrest HS 1,300/9-12
17401 Crawford Ave 60478 708-799-7000
Renee Simms, prin. Fax 799-0402

Country Club Hills SD 160 1,300/PK-8
4411 185th St 60478 708-957-6200
Dr. Sandra Thomas, supt. Fax 957-8686
www.cch160.org
Southwood MS 300/7-8
18635 Lee St 60478 708-957-6230
Kim Edwards, prin. Fax 799-4033

**Cowden, Shelby, Pop. 628**
Cowden-Herrick Community USD 3A 200/PK-12
PO Box 188 62422 217-783-2126
Darrell Gordon, supt. Fax 783-2126
www.cowden-herrick.k12.il.us
Cowden-Herrick JSHS 100/PK-PK, 6-
PO Box 188 62422 217-783-2125
Seth Schuler, prin. Fax 783-2124

**Crest Hill, Will, Pop. 20,552**
Richland SD 88A 1,000/PK-8
1919 Caton Farm Rd, 815-744-7288
Dr. Michael Early, supt. Fax 744-6196
www.d88a.org
Richland JHS 400/5-8
1919 Caton Farm Rd, 815-744-6166
Kelly Whyte, prin. Fax 725-8491

**Crestwood, Cook, Pop. 10,823**
Cook County SD 130
Supt. — See Blue Island
Hale MS 300/6-8
5220 135th St 60445 708-385-6690
John Dudzik, prin. Fax 385-2417

**Crete, Will, Pop. 8,098**
Crete-Monee CUSD 201U 5,000/PK-12
1500 S Sangamon St 60417 708-367-8300
Nathaniel Cunningham, supt. Fax 672-2698
www.cm201u.org
Crete-Monee HS 1,700/9-12
1515 W Exchange St 60417 708-367-8200
Dr. James Harden, prin. Fax 672-2888
Other Schools – See Monee, University Park

---

Illinois Lutheran HS 100/7-12
1610 Main St 60417 708-672-3262
Joe Archer, prin. Fax 672-0512

**Creve Coeur, Tazewell, Pop. 5,361**
Creve Coeur SD 76 700/PK-8
400 N Highland St 61610 309-698-3600
Shayne Aldridge, supt. Fax 698-9827
www.cc76.k12.il.us
Parkview JHS 300/5-8
800 Groveland St 61610 309-698-3610
Don Bockler, prin. Fax 698-3902

Mason-Tazewell-Woodford ROE
Supt. — See Pekin
Tazewell Academy Alt
107 Riverview Dr 61610 309-698-8034
Lorna Sherwood, coord. Fax 698-8062

**Crystal Lake, McHenry, Pop. 40,164**
Community HSD 155 7,100/9-12
1 Virginia Rd 60014 815-455-8500
Johnnie Thomas, supt. Fax 459-5022
www.d155.org
Crystal Lake Central HS 1,600/9-12
45 W Franklin Ave 60014 815-459-2505
Steve Olson, prin. Fax 459-2536
Crystal Lake South HS 1,900/9-12
1200 S McHenry Ave 60014 815-455-3860
Scott Shepard, prin. Fax 455-5706
Prairie Ridge HS 1,600/9-12
6000 Dvorak Dr 60012 815-479-0404
Steven Koch, prin. Fax 459-8993
Other Schools – See Cary

Crystal Lake CCSD 47 8,200/PK-8
300 Commerce Dr 60014 815-459-6070
Kathy Hinz, supt. Fax 459-0263
www.d47.org
Beardsley MS 1,000/6-8
515 E Crystal Lake Ave 60014 815-477-5897
Cathy Alberth, prin. Fax 479-5119
Bernotas MS 1,000/6-8
170 N Oak St 60014 815-459-9210
Jeff Prickett, prin. Fax 479-5116
Lundahl MS 1,000/6-8
560 Nash Rd 60014 815-459-5971
Angela Compere, prin. Fax 479-5113

Prairie Grove Consolidated SD 46 900/K-8
3223 IL Route 176 60014 815-459-3023
Dr. Phil Bender, supt. Fax 356-0519
www.dist46.org/
Prairie Grove JHS 400/6-8
3225 IL Route 176 60014 815-459-3557
Victor Wight, prin. Fax 459-3785

---

Cosmetology & Spa Institute Post-Sec.
700 E Terra Cotta Ave 60014 815-455-5900
Faith Lutheran HS 100/9-12
174 S McHenry Ave 60014 815-479-9305
Chris Schoenleb, prin. Fax 479-9300
McHenry County College Post-Sec.
8900 US Highway 14 60012 815-455-3700

**Cuba, Fulton, Pop. 1,288**
CUSD 3 Fulton County 500/PK-12
PO Box 79 61427 309-785-5021
Brad Kenser, supt. Fax 785-5432
www.cusd3.net
Cuba HS 100/9-12
20325 N State Route 97 61427 309-785-5023
Jeff Braun, prin. Fax 785-5102
Cuba MS 100/6-8
20325 N State Route 97 61427 309-785-5023
Jeff Braun, prin. Fax 785-5102

**Cullom, Livingston, Pop. 554**
Tri-Point CUSD 6-J
Supt. — See Kempton
Tri-Point HS 200/9-12
PO Box 316 60929 815-689-2110
Kellee Hill, prin. Fax 689-2377

**Dakota, Stephenson, Pop. 499**
Dakota CUSD 201 800/PK-12
400 Campus Dr 61018 815-449-2832
Robert Prusator, supt. Fax 449-2459
www.dakota201.com
Dakota JSHS 400/7-12
300 Campus Dr 61018 815-449-2812
Eric Rankin, prin. Fax 449-2322

**Danville, Vermilion, Pop. 32,053**
Danville CCSD 118 6,200/PK-12
516 N Jackson St 61832 217-444-1000
Dr. Alicia Geddis, supt. Fax 444-1006
www.danville118.org
Bailey Academy Alt
502 E Main St 61832 217-477-0300
Tracy Cherry, prin. Fax 477-0399
Danville HS 1,600/9-12
202 E Fairchild St 61832 217-444-1500
Kim Norton, prin. Fax 444-1529
North Ridge MS 700/6-8
1619 N Jackson St 61832 217-444-3400
Chris Rice, prin. Fax 444-3488
South View MS 600/6-8
133 E 9th St 61832 217-444-1800
Sharon Phillips, prin. Fax 444-1882

Oakwood CUSD 76
Supt. — See Oakwood
Oakwood JHS 100/7-8
21600 N 900 East Rd 61834 217-443-2883
John Tosh, prin. Fax 776-2228

Vermilion Vocational Education Delivery
2000 E Main St 61832 217-443-8742
Nick Chatterton, dir.
www.dacc.edu/dual/college-express
College Express Vo/Tech
2000 E Main St 61832 217-443-8742
Nick Chatterton, prin.

---

Concept College of Cosmetology Post-Sec.
2500 Georgetown Rd 61832 217-442-9329
Danville Area Community College Post-Sec.
2000 E Main St 61832 217-443-3222
First Baptist Christian S 200/PK-12
1211 N Vermilion St 61832 217-442-2434
Robert Lazzell, prin. Fax 442-8731
Lakeview College of Nursing Post-Sec.
903 N Logan Ave 61832 217-709-0920
Schlarman Academy 500/PK-12
2112 N Vermilion St 61832 217-442-2725
Gail Lewis, prin. Fax 442-0293

**Darien, DuPage, Pop. 21,762**
Cass SD 63 800/PK-8
8502 Bailey Rd 60561 630-985-2000
Dr. Kerry Foderaro, supt. Fax 985-0225
www.cassd63.org
Cass JHS 400/5-8
8502 Bailey Rd 60561 630-985-1900
Christine Marcinkewicz, prin. Fax 985-2881

Darien SD 61 1,600/PK-8
7414 S Cass Ave 60561 630-968-7505
Dr. Robert Carlo, supt. Fax 968-0872
www.darien61.org
Eisenhower JHS 600/6-8
1410 75th St 60561 630-964-5200
Mike Fitzgerald, prin. Fax 968-8002

Hinsdale Township HSD 86
Supt. — See Hinsdale
Hinsdale South HS 1,800/9-12
7401 Clarendon Hills Rd 60561 630-468-4000
Stephanie Palmer, prin. Fax 920-8649

**Decatur, Macon, Pop. 73,849**
Decatur SD 61 8,500/PK-12
101 W Cerro Gordo St 62523 217-362-3000
Lisa Taylor, supt. Fax 424-3009
www.dps61.org/
Decatur MS 400/7-8
1 Educational Park 62526 217-876-8021
Deloris Brown, prin. Fax 424-3169
Eisenhower HS, 1200 S 16th St 62521 1,000/9-12
Dr. Amy Zahm, prin. 217-362-3100
Jefferson MS 500/7-8
4735 E Cantrell St 62521 217-424-3190
Nathan Sheppard, prin. Fax 424-3037
MacArthur HS 1,200/9-12
1499 W Grand Ave 62522 217-362-3151
Paul Ranstead, prin. Fax 423-4336
Phoenix Academy 100/Alt
1900 E Cleveland Ave 62521 217-424-3090
Janice Ranzy-Allen, prin. Fax 424-3092
Adult Education & Training Center Adult
300 E Eldorado St 62523 217-424-3085
Fax 424-3004

Heartland Region
1 College Park 62521 217-872-4050
www.tech-academy.org
Heartland Technical Academy Vo/Tech
1 College Park 62521 217-872-4050
Bret Hitchings, prin.

---

Lutheran School Association 500/K-12
2001 E Mound Rd 62526 217-233-2001
Kyle Karsten, supt. Fax 233-2002
Millikin University Post-Sec.
1184 W Main St 62522 800-373-7733
Mr. John's School of Cosmetology Post-Sec.
1745 E Eldorado St 62521 217-423-8173
Richland Community College Post-Sec.
1 College Park 62521 217-875-7200
St. Teresa HS 300/9-12
2710 N Water St 62526 217-875-2431
Dr. Ken Hendriksen, prin. Fax 875-2436

**Deerfield, Lake, Pop. 18,034**
Deerfield SD 109 3,100/PK-8
517 Deerfield Rd 60015 847-945-1844
Dr. Michael Lubelfeld, supt. Fax 945-1853
www.dps109.org
Caruso MS 500/6-8
1801 Montgomery Rd 60015 847-945-8430
Dr. Brian Bullis, prin. Fax 945-1963
Shepard MS 500/6-8
440 Grove Ave 60015 847-948-0620
Dr. John Filippi, prin. Fax 948-8589

Township HSD 113
Supt. — See Highland Park
Deerfield HS 1,600/9-12
1959 Waukegan Rd 60015 224-632-3000
Dr. Christopher Dignam, prin. Fax 632-3700

---

Chicagoland Jewish HS 200/9-12
1095 Lake Cook Rd 60015 847-470-6700
Tony Frank, hdmstr. Fax 324-3701
Trinity International University Post-Sec.
2065 Half Day Rd 60015 847-945-8800

**DeKalb, DeKalb, Pop. 43,053**
DeKalb CUSD 428 6,000/PK-12
901 S 4th St 60115 815-754-2350
Dr. Douglas Moeller, supt. Fax 758-6933
dist428.org
DeKalb HS 1,700/9-12
501 W Dresser Rd 60115 815-754-2100
Tamra Ropeter, prin. Fax 758-0931

Huntley MS 600/6-8
1515 S 4th St 60115 815-754-2241
Dr. Thomas Kim, prin. Fax 758-6062
Rosette MS 600/6-8
650 N 1st St 60115 815-754-2226
Tim Vincent, prin. Fax 758-1097

Northern Illinois University 60115 Post-Sec.
815-753-1000

**De Land, Piatt, Pop. 442**
Deland-Weldon CUSD 57 200/PK-12
304 E IL Route 10 61839 217-736-2311
Dr. Jeffrey Holmes, supt. Fax 736-2654
www.dwschools.org
Deland-Weldon HS 50/9-12
304 E IL Route 10 61839 217-664-3314
Amanda Geary, prin. Fax 736-2654
Other Schools – See Weldon

**Delavan, Tazewell, Pop. 1,679**
Delavan CUSD 703 500/PK-12
907 Locust St 61734 309-244-8283
Dr. Andrew Brooks, supt. Fax 244-7696
www.delavanschools.com
Delavan HS 200/9-12
907 Locust St 61734 309-244-8285
Matt Gordon, prin. Fax 244-8694
Delavan JHS 100/7-8
907 Locust St 61734 309-244-8285
Matt Gordon, prin. Fax 244-8694

**De Pue, Bureau, Pop. 1,815**
DePue Unit SD 103 500/PK-12
PO Box 800 61322 815-447-2121
Randall Otto, supt. Fax 447-2067
depueschools.org
DePue HS 100/9-12
PO Box 800 61322 815-447-2121
Randall Otto, supt. Fax 447-2067

**Des Plaines, Cook, Pop. 57,381**
CCSD 59
Supt. — See Arlington Heights
Friendship JHS 700/6-8
550 Elizabeth Ln 60018 847-593-4350
Jodi Megerle, prin. Fax 593-7182

CCSD 62 4,700/PK-8
777 E Algonquin Rd 60016 847-824-1136
Dr. Jane Westerhold, supt. Fax 824-0612
www.d62.org
Algonquin MS 700/6-8
767 E Algonquin Rd 60016 847-824-1205
John Swanson, prin. Fax 824-1270
Chippewa MS 600/6-8
123 N 8th Ave 60016 847-824-1503
Dr. Leah Kimmelman, prin. Fax 824-1514

East Maine SD 63 3,600/PK-8
10150 Dee Rd 60016 847-299-1900
Dr. Scott Clay, supt. Fax 299-9963
www.emsd63.org
Other Schools – See Niles

Maine Township HSD 207
Supt. — See Park Ridge
Maine West HS 1,700/9-12
1755 S Wolf Rd 60018 847-827-6176
Dr. Audrey Haugan, prin. Fax 296-4916

Oakton Community College Post-Sec.
1600 E Golf Rd 60016 847-635-1600
Willows Academy 200/6-12
1015 Rose Ave 60016 847-824-6900
Jeanne Petros, dir. Fax 824-7089

**Dieterich, Effingham, Pop. 615**
Dieterich CUSD 30 400/K-12
PO Box 187 62424 217-925-5249
Cary Jackson, supt. Fax 925-5447
www.dieterich.k12.il.us/
Dieterich JSHS 200/7-12
PO Box 187 62424 217-925-5247
Kevin Haarman, prin. Fax 925-5447

**Divernon, Sangamon, Pop. 1,159**
Auburn CUSD 10
Supt. — See Auburn
Auburn JHS 300/6-8
303 E Kenney St 62530 217-628-3414
Mark Dudley, prin. Fax 628-3814

**Dixmoor, Cook, Pop. 3,616**
West Harvey-Dixmoor SD 147
Supt. — See Harvey
Parks MS 400/6-8
14700 Robey Ave 60426 708-371-9575
Taiyuan Banks-Tillmon, prin. Fax 371-1412

**Dixon, Lee, Pop. 15,509**
Dixon Unit SD 170 2,700/PK-12
1335 Franklin Grove Rd 61021 815-284-7722
Margo Empen, supt. Fax 284-8576
www.dixonschools.org
Dixon HS 800/9-12
300 Lincoln Statue Dr 61021 815-284-7723
Dr. Michael Grady, prin. Fax 284-4297
Reagan MS 700/6-8
620 Division St 61021 815-284-7725
Andrew Bullock, prin. Fax 284-1711

Faith Christian S 100/K-12
7571 S Ridge Rd 61021 815-652-4806
Linda Foster, prin. Fax 652-4871
Jack Mabley Development Center Post-Sec.
1120 Washington Ave 61021 815-288-8300
Sauk Valley Community College Post-Sec.
173 IL Route 2 61021 815-288-5511

**Dolton, Cook, Pop. 22,862**
Dolton SD 148
Supt. — See Riverdale
Lincoln JHS 200/7-8
14151 Lincoln Ave 60419 708-201-2075
Van King, prin. Fax 849-3758
Roosevelt JHS 200/7-8
111 W 146th St 60419 708-201-2071
Fax 849-1285

Thornton Township HSD 205
Supt. — See South Holland
Thornridge HS 1,300/9-12
15000 Cottage Grove Ave 60419 708-271-4401
James Walton, prin. Fax 271-5028

**Dongola, Union, Pop. 707**
Dongola Unit SD 66 300/PK-12
PO Box 190 62926 618-827-3841
Dr. Paige Maginel, supt. Fax 827-4641
dongolaschool.com
Dongola HS 100/9-12
PO Box 190 62926 618-827-3524
John Goddard, prin. Fax 827-4422
Dongola JHS 50/7-8
PO Box 190 62926 618-827-3524
John Goddard, prin. Fax 827-4422

**Donovan, Iroquois, Pop. 304**
Donovan CUSD 3 400/PK-12
PO Box 186 60931 815-486-7397
Lucas Schroeder, supt. Fax 486-7060
www.donovan.k12.il.us
Donovan HS 100/9-12
PO Box 186 60931 815-486-7395
Jason Bauer, admin. Fax 486-7060
Donovan JHS 100/7-8
PO Box 186 60931 815-486-7395
Jason Bauer, admin. Fax 486-7060

**Downers Grove, DuPage, Pop. 47,147**
Center Cass SD 66 1,100/PK-8
699 Plainfield Rd 60516 630-783-5000
Tim Arnold, supt. Fax 910-0980
www.ccsd66.org/
Lakeview JHS 400/6-8
701 Plainfield Rd 60516 630-985-2700
Paul Windsor, prin. Fax 985-1545

Community HSD 99 5,100/9-12
6301 Springside Ave 60516 630-795-7100
Dr. Mark McDonald, supt. Fax 795-7199
www.csd99.org
Downers Grove North HS 2,100/9-12
4436 Main St 60515 630-795-8400
Scott Kasik, prin. Fax 795-8499
Downers Grove South HS 3,000/9-12
1436 Norfolk St 60516 630-795-8500
Edward Schwartz, prin. Fax 795-8599

Downers Grove SD 58 5,000/PK-8
1860 63rd St 60516 630-719-5800
Dr. Kari Cremascoli, supt. Fax 719-9857
www.dg58.org
Herrick MS 600/7-8
4435 Middaugh Ave 60515 630-719-5810
Matt Neustadt, prin. Fax 719-1628
O'Neill MS 500/7-8
635 59th St 60516 630-719-5815
Matthew Durbala, prin. Fax 719-1436

DeVry University Post-Sec.
3005 Highland Pkwy Ste 100 60515 630-515-3000
DeVry University Online Education Center Post-Sec.
3005 Highland Pkwy Ste 100 60515 630-515-3000
Marquette Manor Baptist Academy 200/PK-12
333 75th St 60516 630-964-5363
Donald Sherwin, admin. Fax 964-5385
Midwestern University Post-Sec.
555 31st St 60515 630-969-4400

**Downs, McLean, Pop. 986**
Tri-Valley CUSD 3 1,000/PK-12
410 E Washington St 61736 309-378-2351
Dr. David Mouser, supt. Fax 378-2223
tri-valley3.org
Tri-Valley HS 300/9-12
503 E Washington St 61736 309-378-2911
Benjamin Derges, prin. Fax 378-3202
Tri-Valley MS 400/4-8
505 E Washington St 61736 309-378-3414
Doug Roberts, prin. Fax 378-3214

**Dunlap, Peoria, Pop. 1,372**
Dunlap CUSD 323
Supt. — See Peoria
Dunlap HS 1,200/9-12
PO Box 365 61525 309-243-7751
Thomas Welsh, prin. Fax 243-9565
Dunlap MS 400/6-8
13120 Route 91 61525 309-243-7778
Zac Chatterton, prin. Fax 243-1136
Dunlap Valley MS 400/6-8
PO Box 366 61525 309-243-1034
Jason Holmes, prin. Fax 243-9829

**Dupo, Saint Clair, Pop. 4,069**
Dupo CUSD 196 1,200/PK-12
600 Louisa Ave 62239 618-286-3812
Dr. Stephen Smith, supt. Fax 286-5554
www.dupo196.org
Dupo HS, 600 Louisa Ave 62239 300/9-12
Matt Hickam, prin. 618-286-3214
Dupo JHS, 600 Louisa Ave 62239 200/7-8
William Harris, prin. 618-286-3214

**Du Quoin, Perry, Pop. 5,956**
Du Quoin CUSD 300 1,500/PK-12
845 E Jackson St 62832 618-542-3856
Dr. Gary Kelly, supt. Fax 542-6614
www.duquoinschools.org

Du Quoin HS 400/9-12
500 E South St 62832 618-542-4744
Matt Hickam, prin. Fax 542-8822
Du Quoin MS 400/5-8
845 E Jackson St 62832 618-542-2646
Aaron Hill, prin. Fax 542-4373

Christian Fellowship S 100/PK-12
PO Box 227 62832 618-542-6800

**Durand, Winnebago, Pop. 1,423**
Durand CUSD 322 700/PK-12
200 W South St 61024 815-248-2171
Kurt Alberstett, supt. Fax 248-2599
www.durandbulldogs.com
Durand HS 200/9-12
200 W South St 61024 815-248-2171
Michael Leskowich, prin. Fax 248-2599
Durand JHS 100/7-8
200 W South St 61024 815-248-2171
Michael Leskowich, prin. Fax 248-2599

**Dwight, Livingston, Pop. 4,231**
Dwight Township HSD 230 300/9-12
801 S Franklin St 60420 815-584-6200
Dr. Richard Jancek, supt. Fax 584-2950
www.dwight.k12.il.us
Dwight Township HS 300/9-12
801 S Franklin St 60420 815-584-6200
Dr. Richard Jancek, supt. Fax 584-2950

**Earlville, LaSalle, Pop. 1,691**
Earlville CUSD 9 400/PK-12
PO Box 539 60518 815-246-8361
Wade Winekauf, supt. Fax 246-8672
Earlville HS 100/9-12
PO Box 539 60518 815-246-8361
Rich Faivre, prin. Fax 246-8672

**East Alton, Madison, Pop. 6,171**
East Alton SD 13 800/PK-8
210 E Saint Louis Ave 62024 618-433-2051
Virgil Moore, supt. Fax 433-2054
www.easd13.org/
East Alton MS 200/6-8
1000 3rd St 62024 618-433-2201
Alyssa Smith, prin. Fax 433-2203

**East Dubuque, Jo Daviess, Pop. 1,681**
East Dubuque Unit SD 119 600/PK-12
100 N School Rd 61025 815-747-2111
Greg Herbst, supt. Fax 747-3516
www.edbqhs.org
East Dubuque HS 200/7-12
200 Parklane Dr 61025 815-747-3188
Darren Sirianni, prin. Fax 747-3516

**East Moline, Rock Island, Pop. 20,814**
East Moline SD 37 2,500/PK-8
3451 Morton Dr 61244 309-792-2887
Kristin Humphries, supt. Fax 792-6010
www.emsd37.org
Glenview MS 1,100/5-8
3100 7th St 61244 309-755-1919
Ron Harris, prin. Fax 752-2551

Silvis SD 34
Supt. — See Silvis
Northeast JHS 200/6-8
4280 4th Ave 61244 309-203-1300
Jim Widdop, prin. Fax 203-1322

United Township Area Career Center
1275 Avenue of the Cities 61244 309-752-1691
Larry Shimmin, admin. Fax 752-1692
uths.net/
United Township Area Career Center Vo/Tech
1275 Avenue of the Cities 61244 309-752-1691
Larry Shimmin, dir. Fax 752-1692

United Township HSD 30 1,600/9-12
1275 Avenue of the Cities 61244 309-752-1611
Jay Morrow Ed.D., supt. Fax 752-1615
uths.net/hs
United Township HS 1,600/9-12
1275 Avenue of the Cities 61244 309-752-1633
Carl Johnson, prin. Fax 752-1608

East Moline Christian S 400/PK-12
900 46th Ave 61244 309-796-1485
La' James College of Hairstyling Post-Sec.
485 Avenue of the Cities 61244 888-880-2106

**East Peoria, Tazewell, Pop. 23,021**
East Peoria Community HSD 309 1,200/9-12
1401 E Washington St 61611 309-694-8300
Dr. Chuck Nagel, supt. Fax 694-8322
www.ep309.org
East Peoria Community HS 1,200/9-12
1401 E Washington St 61611 309-694-8300
Dr. Chuck Nagel, supt. Fax 694-8322

East Peoria SD 86 1,700/PK-8
601 Taylor St 61611 309-427-5100
Tony Ingold, supt. Fax 698-1364
www.epd86.org
Central JHS 600/6-8
601 Taylor St 61611 309-427-5200
Jason Warner, prin. Fax 699-2595

Illinois Central College Post-Sec.
1 College Dr, Peoria IL 61635 309-694-5422
Midwest Technical Institute Post-Sec.
280 High Point Ln 61611 800-814-5124
Oehrlein School of Cosmetology Post-Sec.
100 Meadow Ave 61611 309-699-1561

**East Saint Louis, Saint Clair, Pop. 26,776**
East St. Louis SD 189 4,900/PK-12
1005 State St 62201 618-646-3000
Arthur Culver, supt. Fax 583-7186
www.estl189.com

East Saint Louis 9th Grade Center 400/9-9
3939 Caseyville Ave 62204 618-646-3760
Tira Brockman, prin. Fax 646-3768
East Saint Louis HS 1,000/10-12
4901 State St 62205 618-646-3700
Lelon Seaberry, prin. Fax 646-3958
Lincoln MS 700/6-8
12 S 10th St 62201 618-646-3770
Eric Harris, prin. Fax 646-3778
Mason-Clark MS 700/6-8
5510 State St 62203 618-646-3750
Darnell Spencer, prin. Fax 646-3758

---

Vee's School of Beauty Culture Post-Sec.
2701 State St 62205 618-274-1751

**Edinburg, Christian, Pop. 1,060**
Edinburg CUSD 4 300/PK-12
100 E Martin St 62531 217-623-5603
Fred Lamkey, supt. Fax 623-5604
www.ecusd4.com
Edinburg HS 100/9-12
100 E Martin St 62531 217-623-5603
Michelle Reiss, prin. Fax 623-5604
Edinburg JHS 50/7-8
100 E Martin St 62531 217-623-5603
Michelle Reiss, prin. Fax 623-5604

**Edwardsville, Madison, Pop. 23,810**
Edwardsville CUSD 7 7,400/PK-12
PO Box 250 62025 618-656-1182
Dr. Lynda Andre, supt. Fax 692-7423
www.ecusd7.org
Edwardsville HS 2,400/9-12
6161 Center Grove Rd 62025 618-656-7100
Dennis Cramsey, prin. Fax 655-1037
EHS South 100/Alt
6148 Center Grove Rd 62025 618-692-7466
Paul Stuart, admin. Fax 656-4859
Liberty MS 900/6-8
1 District Dr 62025 618-655-6800
Hillary Stanifer, prin. Fax 655-6801
Lincoln MS 800/6-8
145 West St 62025 618-656-0485
Steve Stuart, prin. Fax 659-1268

---

Alvareita's College of Cosmetology Post-Sec.
333 S Kansas St 62025 618-656-2593
Metro East Lutheran HS 200/9-12
6305 Center Grove Rd 62025 618-656-0043
Dr. Jay Krause, prin. Fax 656-3315
Southern Illinois Univ. Edwardsville Post-Sec.
State Route 157 62026 800-447-7483

**Effingham, Effingham, Pop. 12,212**
Bond/Christn/Effingham/Fayette/Mtgmy ROE
Supt. — See Vandalia
Aspire Alternative S Alt
900 Edgar St 62401 217-342-2865
Amber Kidd, prin. Fax 342-9840

Effingham CUSD 40 2,600/K-12
PO Box 130 62401 217-540-1500
Mark Doan, supt. Fax 540-1510
www.effingham.k12.il.us
Effingham HS 800/9-12
1301 W Grove Ave 62401 217-540-1100
Jason Fox, prin. Fax 540-1102
Effingham JHS 600/6-8
600 S Henrietta St 62401 217-540-1300
Bill Myers, prin. Fax 540-1362

---

St. Anthony of Padua HS 200/9-12
304 E Roadway Ave 62401 217-342-6969
Greg Fearday, prin. Fax 342-6997

**Eldorado, Saline, Pop. 4,079**
Eldorado CUSD 4 1,300/PK-12
2200A Illinois Ave 62930 618-273-6394
Ryan Hobbs, supt. Fax 273-9311
www.eldorado.k12.il.us/
Eldorado HS 400/9-12
2200 Illinois Ave 62930 618-273-2881
Ryan Hobbs, prin. Fax 273-8153
Eldorado MS 200/6-8
1907 1st St 62930 618-273-8056
Billy Tippett, dean Fax 273-2943

**Elgin, Kane, Pop. 106,496**
SD U-46 40,300/PK-12
355 E Chicago St 60120 847-888-5000
Tony Sanders, admin. Fax 608-4173
www.u-46.org
Abbott MS 500/7-8
949 Van St 60123 847-888-5160
Kathy Davis, prin. Fax 608-2740
Elgin HS 2,400/9-12
1200 Maroon Dr 60120 847-888-5100
Jerry Cook, prin. Fax 888-6997
Ellis MS 600/7-8
225 S Liberty St 60120 847-888-5151
Perry Hayes, prin. Fax 608-2744
Gifford Street HS 200/Alt
46 S Gifford St 60120 847-888-5000
Lourdes Baker, prin. Fax 888-5087
Kimball MS 700/7-8
451 N Mclean Blvd 60123 847-888-5290
Alan Tamburrino, prin. Fax 608-2749
Larkin HS 2,000/9-12
1475 Larkin Ave 60123 847-888-5200
Dr. Jon Tuin, prin. Fax 888-6996
Larsen MS 700/7-8
665 Dundee Ave 60120 847-888-5250
Gina Crespo, prin. Fax 888-7172
Other Schools – See Bartlett, South Elgin, Streamwood

---

Cannella School of Hair Design Post-Sec.
117 W Chicago St 60123 847-742-6611
DeVry University Post-Sec.
2250 Point Blvd Ste 250 60123 847-649-3980

Einstein Academy 100/PK-12
747 Davis Rd 60123 847-697-3836
Cathy Ilani, prin. Fax 697-6085
Elgin Academy 500/PK-12
350 Park St 60120 847-695-0300
Seth Hanford, hdmstr. Fax 695-5017
Elgin Community College Post-Sec.
1700 Spartan Dr 60123 847-697-1000
Harvest Christian Academy 600/PK-12
1000 N Randall Rd 60123 847-214-3500
Marc Abbatacola, dir. Fax 214-3501
Judson University Post-Sec.
1151 N State St 60123 847-628-2500
Robert Morris University Post-Sec.
1707 N Randall Rd Ste 180 60123 800-762-5960
St. Edward Central Catholic HS 400/9-12
335 Locust St 60123 847-741-7535
Matthew DeBlock, prin. Fax 695-4682
Westminster Christian S 500/PK-12
2700 W Highland Ave, 847-695-0310
Steve Bell, head sch Fax 695-0135

**Elizabeth, Jo Daviess, Pop. 746**
Carroll/Jo Daviess/Stephenson ROE
Supt. — See Freeport
Regional Alternative Program Elizabeth Alt
950 Hwy 20 W 61028 815-599-1408
Brandy Howard, coord. Fax 297-9032

Jo Daviess-Carroll AVC
950 US Highway 20 W 61028 815-858-2203
Nancy Jogerst, dir. Fax 858-2316
www.jdcavc.org
Jo Daviess-Carroll AVC Vo/Tech
950 US Highway 20 W 61028 815-858-2203
Nancy Jogerst, dir. Fax 858-2316

**Elizabethtown, Hardin, Pop. 296**
Hardin County CUSD 1 600/PK-12
PO Box 218 62931 618-287-2411
David Reavis, supt. Fax 287-2421
Hardin County HS 200/9-12
PO Box 218 62931 618-287-2141
Richard Ozment, prin. Fax 287-8381
Hardin County JHS 100/6-8
PO Box 218 62931 618-287-2411
Richard Ozment, prin. Fax 287-8381

**Elk Grove Village, Cook, Pop. 32,640**
CCSD 59
Supt. — See Arlington Heights
Grove JHS 800/6-8
777 W Elk Grove Blvd 60007 847-593-4367
John Harrington, prin. Fax 472-3001

Schaumburg CCSD 54
Supt. — See Schaumburg
Mead JHS 600/7-8
1765 Biesterfield Rd 60007 847-357-6000
Jillian Sagan, prin. Fax 357-6001

Township HSD 214
Supt. — See Arlington Heights
Elk Grove HS 2,000/9-12
500 W Elk Grove Blvd 60007 847-718-4400
Paul Kelly, prin. Fax 718-4417

**Elkville, Jackson, Pop. 899**
Elverado CUSD 196 500/PK-12
PO Box 130 62932 618-568-1321
Kevin Spain, supt. Fax 568-1152
www.elv196.com
Elverado HS 200/9-12
PO Box 217 62932 618-568-1104
Jeremy Pierce, prin. Fax 568-1551
Other Schools – See Vergennes

**Elmhurst, DuPage, Pop. 43,533**
Elmhurst SD 205 8,300/PK-12
162 S York St 60126 630-834-4530
Dr. David Moyer, supt. Fax 617-2345
www.elmhurst205.org/
Bryan MS 700/6-8
111 W Butterfield Rd 60126 630-617-2350
Jason Crockett, admin. Fax 617-2232
Churchville MS 500/6-8
155 E Victory Pkwy 60126 630-832-8682
Gina Pogue Reeder, prin. Fax 617-2387
Sandburg MS 700/6-8
345 E Saint Charles Rd 60126 630-834-4534
Linda Fehrenbacher, prin. Fax 617-2380
York Community HS 2,600/9-12
355 W Saint Charles Rd 60126 630-617-2400
Diana Smith, prin. Fax 617-2399

---

Elmhurst College Post-Sec.
190 S Prospect Ave 60126 630-279-4100
I C Catholic Prep 300/9-12
217 S Cottage Hill Ave 60126 630-530-3460
Pamela Levar, prin. Fax 530-2290
Timothy Christian HS 400/9-12
1061 S Prospect Ave 60126 630-833-7575
Brad Mitchell, prin. Fax 833-9821

**Elmwood, Peoria, Pop. 2,079**
Elmwood CUSD 322 700/PK-12
301 W Butternut St 61529 309-742-8464
Chad Wagner, supt. Fax 742-8812
elmwood322.com
Elmwood HS 200/9-12
301 W Butternut St 61529 309-742-2851
Stan Matheny, prin. Fax 742-8350
Elmwood JHS 100/7-8
301 W Butternut St 61529 309-742-2851
Stan Matheny, prin. Fax 742-8350

**Elmwood Park, Cook, Pop. 24,650**
Elmwood Park CUSD 401 2,700/PK-12
8201 W Fullerton Ave 60707 708-452-7292
Dr. Kevin M. Anderson, supt. Fax 452-9504
www.epcusd401.org/

Elm MS 500/7-8
7607 W Cortland St 60707 708-452-3550
Dr. Kathleen Porreca, prin. Fax 452-0662
Elmwood Park HS 800/9-12
8201 W Fullerton Ave 60707 708-452-7272
James Jennings, prin. Fax 452-0732

**El Paso, Woodford, Pop. 2,782**
El Paso-Gridley CUSD 11 1,200/PK-12
97 W 5th St 61738 309-527-4410
Michael Lindy, supt. Fax 527-4040
www.unit11.org/
El Paso-Gridley HS 400/9-12
600 N Elm St 61738 309-527-4415
Brian Quam, prin. Fax 527-4411
Other Schools – See Gridley

**Elsah, Jersey, Pop. 651**

---

Principia College Post-Sec.
1 Maybeck Pl 62028 618-374-2131

**Erie, Whiteside, Pop. 1,588**
Erie CUSD 1 700/PK-12
520 5th Ave 61250 309-659-2239
Bradley Cox, supt. Fax 659-2230
www.ecusd.info
Erie HS 200/9-12
435 6th Ave 61250 309-659-2239
Tim McConnell, prin. Fax 659-2514
Erie MS 200/5-8
500 5th Ave 61250 309-659-2239
Keith Morgan, prin. Fax 659-7254

**Eureka, Woodford, Pop. 5,225**
Eureka CUSD 140 1,600/PK-12
109 W Cruger Ave 61530 309-467-3737
Robert Bardwell, supt. Fax 467-2377
www.district140.org
Eureka HS 500/9-12
200 W Cruger Ave 61530 309-467-2361
Richard Wherley, prin. Fax 467-2648
Eureka MS 500/5-8
2005 S Main St 61530 309-467-3771
Kelly Nichols, prin. Fax 467-2052

---

Eureka College Post-Sec.
300 E College Ave 61530 309-467-3721

**Evanston, Cook, Pop. 71,880**
Evanston Township HSD 202 3,000/9-12
1600 Dodge Ave 60201 847-424-7000
Dr. Eric Witherspoon, supt. Fax 424-7220
www.eths.k12.il.us
Evanston Township HS 3,000/9-12
1600 Dodge Ave 60201 847-424-7000
Marcus Campbell, prin. Fax 424-7200

Evanston/Skokie SD 65 7,300/PK-8
1500 McDaniel Ave 60201 847-859-8000
Dr. Paul Goren, supt. Fax 866-7241
www.district65.net
Chute MS 600/6-8
1400 Oakton St 60202 847-859-8600
James McHolland, prin. Fax 492-7956
Haven MS 700/6-8
2417 Prairie Ave 60201 847-859-8200
Kathleen Roberson, prin. Fax 492-9983
Nichols MS 500/6-8
800 Greenleaf St 60202 847-859-8660
Adrian Harries, prin. Fax 492-7880

---

Beacon Academy 50/9-12
622 Davis St 60201 224-999-1177
Jeff Bell, head sch Fax 241-3052
Garrett Evangelical Theological Seminary Post-Sec.
2121 Sheridan Rd 60201 847-866-3900
Northwestern University Post-Sec.
633 Clark St 60208 847-491-3741
Pivot Point International Post-Sec.
1560 Sherman Ave Ste 700 60201 847-866-0500
Roycemore S 300/PK-12
1200 Davis St 60201 847-866-6055
Kevin Smith, hdmstr. Fax 866-6545
St. Francis Hospital Post-Sec.
355 Ridge Ave 60202 847-492-4000

**Evansville, Randolph, Pop. 690**

---

Christ our Savior Lutheran HS 50/9-12
810 Soldiers Way 62242 618-853-7300
John Christman, admin. Fax 853-7361

**Evergreen Park, Cook, Pop. 19,576**
Evergreen Park Community HSD 231 800/9-12
9901 S Kedzie Ave 60805 708-424-7400
Dr. James Dunlap, supt. Fax 424-7497
www.evergreenpark.org
Evergreen Park HS 800/9-12
9901 S Kedzie Ave 60805 708-424-7400
Bill Sanderson, prin. Fax 424-7497

Evergreen Park ESD 124 1,800/PK-8
2929 W 87th St 60805 708-423-0950
Robert Machak Ed.D., supt. Fax 423-4292
www.d124.org
Central MS 400/7-8
9400 S Sawyer Ave 60805 708-424-0148
Rita Sparks, prin. Fax 229-8406

**Fairbury, Livingston, Pop. 3,720**
Prairie Central CUSD 8 2,100/PK-12
605 N 7th St 61739 815-692-2504
Dr. John Capasso, supt. Fax 692-3195
www.prairiecentral.org
Prairie Central HS 600/9-12
411 N 7th St 61739 815-692-2355
Dan Casillas, prin. Fax 692-2438
Other Schools – See Forrest

**Fairfield, Wayne, Pop. 5,118**
Fairfield Community HSD 225 400/9-12
300 W King St 62837 618-842-2649
Jill Fulkerson, supt. Fax 842-4465
www.fchsmules.com
Fairfield Community HS 400/9-12
300 W King St 62837 618-842-2649
Jill Fulkerson, prin. Fax 842-5187

Fairfield SD 112 600/PK-8
806 N 1st St 62837 618-842-6501
Diana Zurliene, supt. Fax 842-2932
fairfieldcolts.com
Center Street S 300/4-8
200 W Center St 62837 618-842-2679
Bill Wrenn, prin. Fax 842-4719

---

Frontier Community College Post-Sec.
2 Frontier Dr 62837 618-842-3711

**Fairview Heights, Saint Clair, Pop. 16,671**
Grant CCSD 110 700/PK-8
10110 Old Lincoln Trl 62208 618-398-5577
Matt Stines, supt. Fax 398-5578
dist110.com
Grant MS 300/5-8
10110 Old Lincoln Trl 62208 618-397-2764
Carla Lasley, prin. Fax 397-7809

Pontiac-William Holliday SD 105 700/PK-8
400 Ashland Ave 62208 618-233-2320
Dr. Julie Brown, supt. Fax 233-0918
www.pwh105.org
Pontiac JHS 200/6-8
400 Ashland Ave 62208 618-233-6004
Joanna Luehmann, prin. Fax 233-0918

**Farina, Fayette, Pop. 518**
South Central CUSD 401
Supt. — See Kinmundy
South Central HS 200/9-12
800 W Washington St 62838 618-245-3363
Steve Phillips, prin. Fax 245-6165

**Farmer City, DeWitt, Pop. 2,018**
Blue Ridge CUSD 18 600/PK-12
411 N John St 61842 309-928-9141
Susan Wilson, supt. Fax 928-5478
www.blueridge18.org
Blue Ridge HS 200/9-12
411 N John St 61842 309-928-2622
John Lawrence, prin. Fax 928-5301
Other Schools – See Mansfield

**Farmington, Fulton, Pop. 2,424**
Farmington Central CUSD 265 1,500/PK-12
212 N Lightfoot Rd 61531 309-245-1000
Dr. John Asplund, supt. Fax 245-9161
www.dist265.com/
Farmington Central JHS 300/6-8
300 N Lightfoot Rd 61531 309-245-1000
Perry Miller, prin. Fax 245-9162
Farmington HS 400/9-12
310 N Lightfoot Rd 61531 309-245-1000
Perry Miller, prin. Fax 245-9163

**Findlay, Shelby, Pop. 676**
Okaw Valley CUSD 302
Supt. — See Bethany
Okaw Valley MS 200/5-8
501 W Division St 62534 217-756-8521
Ross Forlines, prin. Fax 756-8599

**Fisher, Champaign, Pop. 1,871**
Fisher CUSD 1 600/K-12
PO Box 700 61843 217-897-6125
Barbara Thompson, supt. Fax 897-6676
www.fisher.k12.il.us
Fisher JSHS 300/7-12
211 W Division St 61843 217-897-1225
Tom Shallenberger, prin. Fax 897-1708

**Fithian, Vermilion, Pop. 480**
Oakwood CUSD 76
Supt. — See Oakwood
Oakwood HS 300/9-12
5870 US Route 150 61844 217-354-2358
Tim Lee, prin. Fax 354-2603

**Flanagan, Livingston, Pop. 1,105**
Flanagan-Cornell Unit SD 74 400/PK-12
202 E Falcon Hwy 61740 815-796-2233
Jerry Farris, supt. Fax 796-2856
www.fc74.org
Flanagan-Cornell HS 100/9-12
202 E Falcon Hwy 61740 815-796-2291
Brian Yoder, prin. Fax 796-2856

**Flora, Clay, Pop. 5,018**
Flora CUSD 35 1,400/PK-12
444 S Locust St 62839 618-662-2412
Joel Hackney, supt. Fax 662-4587
www.floraschools.com
Flora HS 400/9-12
600 S Locust St 62839 618-662-8316
Toby Pearce, prin. Fax 662-2725
Henson JHS 300/6-8
609 N Stanford Rd 62839 618-662-8394
Janette Schade, prin. Fax 662-8395

**Flossmoor, Cook, Pop. 9,246**
Flossmoor SD 161
Supt. — See Chicago Heights
Parker JHS 900/6-8
2810 School St 60422 708-647-5400
David Kennedy, prin. Fax 799-9207

Homewood-Flossmoor Community HSD 233 2,800/9-12
999 Kedzie Ave 60422 708-799-3000
Dr. Von Mansfield, supt. Fax 799-8552
www.hfhighschool.org
Homewood-Flossmoor HS 2,800/9-12
999 Kedzie Ave 60422 708-799-3000
Dr. Ryan Pitcock, prin. Fax 335-6995

**Ford Heights, Cook, Pop. 2,726**
Ford Heights SD 169 400/PK-8
910 Woodlawn Ave 60411 708-758-1370
Dr. Gregory Jackson, supt. Fax 758-1372
www.fordheights169.org
Cottage Grove Upper Grade Center 200/5-8
800 E 14th St 60411 708-758-1400
Sharon Rivers, prin. Fax 758-0711

**Forest Park, Cook, Pop. 13,818**
Forest Park SD 91 900/PK-8
424 Des Plaines Ave 60130 708-366-5700
Dr. Louis Cavallo, supt. Fax 366-5761
www.forestparkschools.org
Forest Park MS 300/6-8
925 Beloit Ave 60130 708-366-5703
Joseph Pisano, prin. Fax 366-2091

Proviso Township HSD 209 4,900/9-12
8601 Roosevelt Rd 60130 708-338-5912
Dr. Nettie Collins-Hart, supt. Fax 338-5999
www.pths209.org
Proviso Math & Science Academy 800/9-12
8601 Roosevelt Rd 60130 708-338-4100
Dr. Bessie Karvelas, prin. Fax 338-4199
Other Schools – See Hillside, Maywood

**Forrest, Livingston, Pop. 1,217**
Prairie Central CUSD 8
Supt. — See Fairbury
Prairie Central JHS 300/7-8
800 N Wood St 61741 815-657-8660
Tonya Dieken, prin. Fax 657-8677

**Forreston, Ogle, Pop. 1,426**
Forrestville Valley CUSD 221 800/PK-12
PO Box 665 61030 815-938-2036
Sheri Smith, supt. Fax 938-9028
www.fvvsd221.org
Forreston JSHS 500/6-12
PO Box 665 61030 815-938-2175
Michael Mandzen, prin. Fax 938-2546

**Forsyth, Macon, Pop. 3,456**

---

Decatur Christian S 200/PK-12
137 S Grant St 62535 217-877-5636
Randy Grigg, supt. Fax 877-7627

**Fox Lake, Lake, Pop. 10,448**
Fox Lake Grade SD 114
Supt. — See Spring Grove
Stanton MS 300/5-8
101 Hawthorne Ln 60020 847-973-4200
Jeff Sefcik, prin. Fax 973-4210

Grant Community HSD 124 1,800/9-12
285 E Grand Ave 60020 847-587-2561
Dr. Christine Sefcik, supt. Fax 587-2991
www.grant.lake.k12.il.us/
Grant Community HS 1,800/9-12
285 E Grand Ave 60020 847-587-2561
Jeremy Schmidt, prin. Fax 587-2991

**Fox River Grove, McHenry, Pop. 4,788**
Fox River Grove SD 3 500/PK-8
403 Orchard St 60021 847-516-5100
Dr. Tim Mahaffy, supt. Fax 516-9169
www.dist3.org
Fox River Grove MS 200/5-8
401 Orchard St 60021 847-516-5105
Eric Runck, prin. Fax 516-5104

**Frankfort, Will, Pop. 17,612**
Frankfort CCSD 157C 2,400/PK-8
10482 Nebraska St 60423 815-469-5922
Dr. Maura Zinni, supt. Fax 469-8988
www.fsd157c.org
Hickory Creek MS 800/6-8
22150 116th Ave 60423 815-469-4474
Dr. Kevin Suchinski, prin. Fax 469-7930

Lincoln-Way Community HSD 210
Supt. — See New Lenox
Lincoln-Way East HS 2,200/9-12
201 Colorado Ave 60423 815-464-4000
Dr. Sharon Michalak, prin. Fax 464-4132
Lincoln-Way North HS 1,800/9-12
19900 S Harlem Ave 60423 815-534-3000
Dr. Mark Cohen, prin. Fax 534-3009

Summit Hill SD 161 3,100/PK-8
20100 S Spruce Dr 60423 815-464-2230
Barb Rains, supt. Fax 469-0566
www.summithill.org/
Summit Hill JHS 900/7-8
7260 W North Ave 60423 815-469-4330
Daniel Pierson, prin. Fax 464-1596

**Franklin, Morgan, Pop. 598**
Franklin CUSD 1
Supt. — See Alexander
Franklin JSHS 200/6-12
110 State 62638 217-675-2395
Jason Courier, prin. Fax 675-2396

**Franklin Park, Cook, Pop. 18,209**
Franklin Park SD 84 1,300/PK-8
2915 Maple St 60131 847-455-4230
Dr. David H. Katzin, supt. Fax 455-9094
www.d84.org
Hester JHS 400/6-8
2836 Gustav St 60131 847-455-2150
Giffen Trotter, prin. Fax 455-0945

Leyden Community HSD 212 3,400/9-12
3400 Rose St 60131 847-451-3020
Dr. Nick Polyak, supt. Fax 671-9079
www.leyden212.org
East Leyden HS 1,700/9-12
3400 Rose St 60131 847-451-3023
Jason Markey, prin. Fax 233-9928
Other Schools – See Northlake

Mannheim SD 83 2,600/PK-8
10401 Grand Ave 60131 847-455-4413
Kim Petrasek, supt. Fax 451-8290
www.d83.org/
Other Schools – See Melrose Park

**Freeburg, Saint Clair, Pop. 4,312**
Freeburg CCSD 70 800/PK-8
408 S Belleville St 62243 618-539-3188
Tomi Diefenbach, supt. Fax 539-5795
www.frg70.org
Freeburg ES 500/3-8
408 S Belleville St 62243 618-539-3188
Theresa Goscinski, prin. Fax 539-5795

Freeburg Community HSD 77 600/9-12
401 S Monroe St 62243 618-539-5533
Andrew Lehman, supt. Fax 539-4887
www.fchs77.org/district.cfm
Freeburg HS 600/9-12
401 S Monroe St 62243 618-539-5533
Greg Frerking, prin. Fax 539-4887

**Freeport, Stephenson, Pop. 24,738**
Carroll/Jo Daviess/Stephenson ROE
27 S State Ave Ste 101 61032 815-599-1408
Aaron Mercier, supt. Fax 297-9032
www.roe8.com
Regional Alternative Program Freeport Alt
27 S State St 61032 815-599-1408
Brandy Howard, prin. Fax 297-9032
Other Schools – See Elizabeth

Freeport SD 145 3,800/K-12
501 E South St 61032 815-232-0300
Michael Schiffman, supt. Fax 235-4177
www.fsd145.org
Freeport Alternative HS 50/Alt
1330 S Locust Ave 61032 815-233-0796
Dana Dinderman, admin. Fax 232-2311
Freeport HS 1,200/9-12
701 W Moseley St 61032 815-232-0400
Dr. Beth Summers, prin. Fax 232-0629
Freeport MS 700/5-8
701 W Empire St 61032 815-232-0500
Nick Swords, prin. Fax 232-0536
Sandburg MS 500/5-8
1717 W Eby St 61032 815-232-0340
Dr. Kathy Jenkins, prin. Fax 232-1241

---

Aquin Central Catholic HS 200/7-12
1419 S Galena Ave 61032 815-235-3154
Rosemarie Brubaker, admin. Fax 235-3185
Highland Community College Post-Sec.
2998 W Pearl City Rd 61032 815-235-6121

**Fulton, Whiteside, Pop. 3,442**
River Bend CUSD 2 900/PK-12
1110 3rd St 61252 815-589-2711
Darryl Hogue Ed.D., supt. Fax 589-4630
www.riverbendschools.org
Fulton HS 300/9-12
1207 12th St 61252 815-589-3511
Chris Tennyson, prin. Fax 589-3412
River Bend MS 200/6-8
415 12th St 61252 815-589-2611
Kathleen Schipper, prin. Fax 589-3130

---

Unity Christian HS 100/7-12
711 10th St 61252 815-589-3912
Christopher Pluister, prin. Fax 589-4430

**Galatia, Saline, Pop. 925**
Galatia CUSD 1 400/PK-12
200 N Hickory St 62935 618-268-6371
Dr. Beth Rister, supt. Fax 268-4196
www.galatiak12.org
Galatia HS 100/9-12
200 N McKinley St 62935 618-268-4194
John Cummins, prin. Fax 268-4196
Galatia JHS 100/7-8
200 N McKinley St 62935 618-268-4194
John Cummins, prin. Fax 268-4196

**Galena, Jo Daviess, Pop. 3,404**
Galena Unit SD 120 800/PK-12
1206 Franklin St 61036 815-777-3086
Dr. Sharon Olds, supt. Fax 777-0303
www.gusd120.k12.il.us
Galena HS 200/9-12
1206 Franklin St 61036 815-777-0917
Elizabeth Murphy, prin. Fax 777-2089
Galena MS 200/5-8
1230 Franklin St 61036 815-777-2413
Ben Soat, prin. Fax 777-4259

---

Tri-State Christian S 200/PK-12
11084 W US Highway 20 61036 815-777-3800
Tad Nuce, prin. Fax 777-2991

**Galesburg, Knox, Pop. 31,321**
Galesburg AVC
1135 W Fremont St 61401 309-343-3733
Jeff Houston, dir. Fax 343-1305
www.gavc.weebly.com
Galesburg AVC Vo/Tech
1135 W Fremont St 61401 309-343-3733
Jeff Houston, dir. Fax 343-1305

Galesburg CUSD 205 — 4,500/PK-12
PO Box 1206 61402 — 309-343-1151
Ralph Grimm, supt. — Fax 343-1319
www.galesburg205.org
Churchill JHS — 500/6-8
905 Maple Ave 61401 — 309-973-2002
Tom Hawkins, prin. — Fax 342-6384
Galesburg HS — 1,300/9-12
1135 W Fremont St 61401 — 309-973-2001
Roy VanMeter, prin. — Fax 343-7122
Galesburg HS North — Alt
1017 W Dayton St 61401 — 309-973-2003
Jason Spring, prin. — Fax 343-1237
Lombard MS — 500/6-8
1220 E Knox St 61401 — 309-973-2004
Nick Sutton, prin. — Fax 342-7135

---

Carl Sandburg College — Post-Sec.
2400 Tom L Wilson Blvd 61401 — 309-344-2518
Galesburg Christian S — 100/PK-12
746 Hawkinson Ave 61401 — 309-343-8008
Robert Nutzhorn, admin. — Fax 342-0235
Knox College — Post-Sec.
2 E South St 61401 — 309-341-7000

**Galva, Henry, Pop. 2,565**
Galva CUSD 224 — 600/PK-12
224 Morgan Rd 61434 — 309-932-2108
Doug O'Riley, supt. — Fax 932-8326
www.galva224.org
Galva JSHS — 300/7-12
224 Morgan Rd 61434 — 309-932-2151
Jerry Becker, prin. — Fax 932-2152

**Gardner, Grundy, Pop. 1,442**
Gardner-South Wilmington Twp. HSD 73 — 200/9-12
500 E Main St 60424 — 815-237-2176
Michael Perrott, supt. — Fax 237-2842
www.gswhs.grundy.k12.il.us
Gardner-South Wilmington Twp. HS — 200/9-12
500 E Main St 60424 — 815-237-2176
John Engelman, prin. — Fax 237-2842

**Geneseo, Henry, Pop. 6,533**
Geneseo CUSD 228 — 2,700/PK-12
648 N Chicago St 61254 — 309-945-0450
Scott Kuffel, supt. — Fax 945-0445
www.dist228.org
Geneseo HS — 900/9-12
700 N State St 61254 — 309-945-0399
Michael Haugse, prin. — Fax 945-0374
Geneseo MS — 600/6-8
333 E Ogden Ave 61254 — 309-945-0599
Nathan O'Dell, prin. — Fax 945-0580

**Geneva, Kane, Pop. 21,261**
Geneva CUSD 304 — 5,900/PK-12
227 N 4th St 60134 — 630-463-3000
Dr. Kent Mutchler, supt. — Fax 463-3009
www.geneva304.org
Geneva Community HS — 1,900/9-12
416 McKinley Ave 60134 — 630-463-3800
Thomas Rogers, prin. — Fax 463-3809
Geneva MS North — 700/6-8
1357 Viking Dr 60134 — 630-463-3700
Lawrence Bidlack, prin. — Fax 463-3709
Geneva MS South — 700/6-8
1415 Viking Dr 60134 — 630-463-3600
Terry Bleau, prin. — Fax 463-3609

**Genoa, DeKalb, Pop. 5,138**
Genoa-Kingston CUSD 424 — 1,900/PK-12
980 Park Ave 60135 — 815-784-6222
Joe Burgess, supt. — Fax 784-6059
www.gkschools.org
Genoa-Kingston HS — 600/9-12
980 Park Ave 60135 — 815-784-5111
Brett McPherson, prin. — Fax 784-3124
Genoa-Kingston MS — 500/6-8
941 W Main St 60135 — 815-784-5222
Angelo Lekkas, prin. — Fax 784-4323

**Georgetown, Vermilion, Pop. 3,408**
Georgetown-Ridge Farm CUSD 4 — 900/PK-12
502 W Mulberry St 61846 — 217-662-8488
Jean Neal, supt. — Fax 662-3402
www.grf.k12.il.us
Georgetown-Ridge Farm HS — 300/9-12
500 W Mulberry St 61846 — 217-662-6716
Brad Russell, prin. — Fax 662-3404
Miller JHS — 300/6-8
414 W West St 61846 — 217-662-6606
Lisa Gocken, prin. — Fax 662-6345

**Germantown Hills, Woodford, Pop. 3,399**
Germantown Hills SD 69 — 900/K-8
103 Warrior Way, — 309-383-2121
Dan Mair, supt. — Fax 383-2123
ghills.metamora.k12.il.us
Germantown Hills JHS — 300/6-8
103 Warrior Way, — 309-383-2121
Dave Raffel, prin. — Fax 383-4739

**Gibson City, Ford, Pop. 3,366**
Gibson City-Melvin-Sibley CUSD 5 — 1,100/PK-12
307 N Sangamon Ave 60936 — 217-784-8296
Anthony Galindo, supt. — Fax 784-8558
www.gcmsk12.org
GCMS HS — 300/9-12
815 N Church St 60936 — 217-784-4292
Christopher Garard, prin. — Fax 784-8293
GCMS MS — 300/6-8
316 E 19th St 60936 — 217-784-8731
Jeremy Darnell, prin. — Fax 784-8726

**Gillespie, Macoupin, Pop. 3,280**
Gillespie CUSD 7 — 1,300/PK-12
510 W Elm St 62033 — 217-839-2464
Joseph Tieman, supt. — Fax 839-3353
www.joomla.gcusd7.org
Gillespie HS — 400/9-12
612 Broadway St 62033 — 217-839-2114
Lori Emmons, prin. — Fax 839-4302
Gillespie MS, 412 Oregon St 62033 — 300/6-8
Lori Emmons, prin. — 217-839-2116

**Gilman, Iroquois, Pop. 1,793**
Iroquois West CUSD 10 — 1,000/PK-12
PO Box 67 60938 — 815-265-4642
Dr. Linda Dvorak, supt. — Fax 265-7008
www.iwest.k12.il.us/
Iroquois West HS — 300/9-12
PO Box 67 60938 — 815-265-4229
Joshua Houberg, prin. — Fax 265-8108
Other Schools – See Onarga

**Girard, Macoupin, Pop. 2,085**
North Mac CUSD 34 — 1,600/PK-12
525 N 3rd St 62640 — 217-627-2915
Marica Cullen, supt. — Fax 627-3519
www.northmacschools.org
North Mac IS — 300/3-8
525 N 3rd St 62640 — 217-627-2419
Dennis McMillin, prin. — Fax 627-3409
Other Schools – See Virden

**Glasford, Peoria, Pop. 1,015**
Illini Bluffs CUSD 327 — 900/PK-12
9611 S Hanna City Glsfrd Rd 61533 — 309-389-2231
Dr. Roger Alvey, supt. — Fax 389-2251
www.illinibluffs.com
Illini Bluffs HS — 300/9-12
9611 S Hanna City Glsfrd Rd 61533 — 309-389-5681
Keith Brown, prin. — Fax 389-4681
Illini Bluffs MS — 200/6-8
9611 S Hanna City Glsfrd Rd 61533 — 309-389-3451
Karen Peterson, prin. — Fax 389-3454

**Glen Carbon, Madison, Pop. 12,692**

---

Gateway Legacy Christian Academy — 100/PK-12
97 Oaklawn Dr 62034 — 618-288-0452
Melissa Morrison, prin. — Fax 288-0453
McGivney Catholic HS — 9-10
7190 Bouse Rd 62034 — 618-855-9010
Mike Scholz, prin. — Fax 855-9011

**Glencoe, Cook, Pop. 8,600**
Glencoe SD 35 — 1,300/K-8
620 Greenwood Ave 60022 — 847-835-7800
Dr. Catherine Wang, supt. — Fax 835-7805
www.glencoeschools.org
Central S — 600/5-8
620 Greenwood Ave 60022 — 847-835-7600
Dr. Ryan Mollet, prin. — Fax 835-7605

**Glendale Heights, DuPage, Pop. 33,478**
Marquardt SD 15 — 2,700/PK-8
1860 Glen Ellyn Rd 60139 — 630-469-7615
Dr. Jerry O'Shea Ed.D., supt. — Fax 790-1650
www.d15.us/
Marquardt MS — 800/6-8
1912 Glen Ellyn Rd 60139 — 630-858-3850
Meredith Haugens, prin. — Fax 790-5042

Queen Bee SD 16 — 2,000/PK-8
1560 Bloomingdale Rd 60139 — 630-260-6100
Victoria Tabbert, supt. — Fax 260-6103
www.queenbee16.org
Glenside MS — 600/6-8
1560 Bloomingdale Rd 60139 — 630-260-6112
Christopher Collins, prin. — Fax 510-8568

**Glen Ellyn, DuPage, Pop. 27,048**
CCSD 89 — 2,000/PK-8
22W600 Butterfield Rd 60137 — 630-469-8900
Dr. John Perdue, supt. — Fax 469-8936
www.ccsd89.org
Glen Crest MS — 700/6-8
725 Sheehan Ave 60137 — 630-469-5220
Kim Price, prin. — Fax 469-5250

Glen Ellyn SD 41 — 3,600/PK-8
793 N Main St 60137 — 630-790-6400
Dr. Paul Gordon, supt. — Fax 790-1867
www.d41.org
Hadley JHS — 1,200/6-8
240 Hawthorne Blvd 60137 — 630-790-6450
Steve Diveley, prin. — Fax 790-6469

Glenbard Township HSD 87 — 8,700/9-12
596 Crescent Blvd 60137 — 630-469-9100
Dr. David Larson, supt. — Fax 469-9107
glenbard87.org/
Glenbard South HS — 1,400/9-12
23w200 Butterfield Rd 60137 — 630-469-6500
Sandra Coughlin, prin. — Fax 469-6572
Glenbard West HS — 2,300/9-12
670 Crescent Blvd 60137 — 630-469-8600
Peter Monoghan, prin. — Fax 469-8615
Other Schools – See Carol Stream, Lombard

---

College of DuPage — Post-Sec.
425 Fawell Blvd 60137 — 630-942-2800

**Glenview, Cook, Pop. 44,009**
Glenview CCSD 34 — 4,800/PK-8
1401 Greenwood Rd 60026 — 847-998-5000
Dr. Mike Nicholson, supt. — Fax 998-1629
www.glenview34.org
Attea MS — 800/6-8
2500 Chestnut Ave 60026 — 847-486-7700
Mark Richter, prin. — Fax 729-6251
Springman MS — 800/6-8
2701 Central Rd 60025 — 847-998-5020
Allyson Thorne, prin. — Fax 998-4032

Northfield Township HSD 225 — 4,700/9-12
3801 W Lake Ave 60026 — 847-486-4700
Dr. Michael Riggle, supt. — Fax 486-4733
www.glenbrook225.org
Glenbrook South HS — 2,600/9-12
4000 W Lake Ave 60026 — 847-486-4559
Dr. Brian Wegley, prin. — Fax 486-4462
Glenbrook Evening HS — Adult
4000 W Lake Ave 60026 — 847-486-4709
Frank Santa, prin. — Fax 486-4733
Other Schools – See Northbrook

**Glenwood, Cook, Pop. 8,797**
Brookwood SD 167 — 1,200/PK-8
201 E Glenwood Dyer Rd 60425 — 708-758-5190
Dr. Valorie Moore, supt. — Fax 757-2104
www.brookwood167.org
Brookwood JHS — 300/7-8
201 E Glenwood Lansing Rd 60425 — 708-758-5252
Bethany Lindsay, prin. — Fax 758-3954

**Godfrey, Madison, Pop. 17,742**

---

Alvareita's College of Cosmetology — Post-Sec.
3048 Godfrey Rd 62035 — 618-466-8952
Lewis & Clark Community College — Post-Sec.
5800 Godfrey Rd 62035 — 618-468-7000

**Golconda, Pope, Pop. 665**
Pope County CUSD 1 — 500/PK-12
125 State Highway 146 W 62938 — 618-683-2301
Charles Bleyer, supt. — Fax 683-5181
www.popek12.org
Pope County HS — 100/9-12
125 State Highway 146 W 62938 — 618-683-3071
Ryan Fritch, prin. — Fax 683-9956

**Goreville, Johnson, Pop. 1,046**
Goreville CUSD 1 — 600/PK-12
201 S Ferne Clyffe Rd 62939 — 618-995-9831
Dr. Steve Webb, supt. — Fax 995-9832
www.gorevilleschools.com
Goreville HS — 200/9-12
201 S Ferne Clyffe Rd 62939 — 618-995-2142
Jeri Miller, prin. — Fax 995-1188

**Granite City, Madison, Pop. 29,332**
Granite City CUSD 9 — 5,200/PK-12
1947 Adams St 62040 — 618-451-5800
Jim Greenwald, supt. — Fax 451-6135
www.gcsd9.net
Coolidge JHS — 600/7-8
3231 Nameoki Rd 62040 — 618-451-5826
Patrick Curry, prin. — Fax 876-5154
Granite City HS — 1,900/9-12
3101 Madison Ave 62040 — 618-451-5808
Daren DePew, prin. — Fax 451-6296

**Grant Park, Kankakee, Pop. 1,318**
Grant Park CUSD 6 — 600/PK-12
PO Box 549 60940 — 815-465-6013
John Palan, supt. — Fax 465-2505
www.grantpark.k12.il.us
Grant Park HS — 200/9-12
PO Box 549 60940 — 815-465-2181
Tom Sanidas, prin. — Fax 465-2505

**Granville, Putnam, Pop. 1,410**
Putnam County CUSD 535 — 900/PK-12
400 E Silverspoon Ave 61326 — 815-882-2800
Jay McCracken, supt. — Fax 882-2802
www.pcschools535.org/
Putnam County HS — 300/9-12
402 E Silverspoon Ave 61326 — 815-882-2800
Bob Peterson, prin. — Fax 339-2628
Other Schools – See Mc Nabb

**Grayslake, Lake, Pop. 20,539**
CCSD 46 — 3,800/K-8
565 Frederick Rd 60030 — 847-223-3650
Ellen Correll, supt. — Fax 223-3695
www.d46.k12.il.us
Grayslake MS — 800/7-8
440 Barron Blvd 60030 — 847-223-3680
Marcus Smith, prin. — Fax 223-3526

Grayslake Community HSD 127 — 2,900/9-12
400 N Lake St 60030 — 847-986-3400
Dr. Catherine Finger, supt. — Fax 231-6838
www.d127.org/
Grayslake Community HS - Central Campus — 1,400/9-12
400 N Lake St 60030 — 847-986-3300
Daniel Landry, prin. — Fax 223-8690
Grayslake Community HS - North Campus — 1,600/9-12
1925 N Route 83 60030 — 847-986-3100
Dr. James Roscoe, prin. — Fax 986-3023

Lake County HS Technology Campus
19525 W Washington St 60030 — 847-223-6681
Steve Clark, dir. — Fax 223-7363
www.techcampus.org
Lake County HS Technology Campus — Vo/Tech
19525 W Washington St 60030 — 847-223-6681
Steve Clark, dir. — Fax 223-7363

---

College of Lake County — Post-Sec.
19351 W Washington St 60030 — 847-543-2000
Westlake Christian Academy — 200/PK-12
275 S Lake St 60030 — 847-548-6209
Dr. Michael Healan, prin. — Fax 548-6481

**Grayville, White, Pop. 1,656**
Grayville CUSD 1 — 300/PK-12
728 W North St 62844 — 618-375-7214
Sarah Emery, supt. — Fax 375-5202
www.grayville.white.k12.il.us
Grayville JSHS — 100/6-12
728 W North St 62844 — 618-375-7114
Sarah Emery, prin. — Fax 375-6521

**Greenfield, Greene, Pop. 1,063**
Greenfield CUSD 10 — 500/PK-12
311 Mulberry St 62044 — 217-368-2447
Kevin Bowman, supt. — Fax 368-2724
www.greenfieldschools.org/
Greenfield HS — 200/9-12
502 East St 62044 — 217-368-2219
Beth Bettis, prin. — Fax 368-2230

**Green Valley, Tazewell, Pop. 698**
Midwest Central CUSD 191
Supt. — See Manito
Midwest Central MS — 200/6-8
121 N Church St 61534 — 309-352-2300
Erin Stone, prin. — Fax 352-2903

**Greenview, Menard, Pop. 765**
Greenview CUSD 200 — 300/PK-12
147 E Palmer St 62642 — 217-968-2295
Dr. Janice Kunz, supt. — Fax 968-2297
www.greenviewschools.org
Greenview JSHS — 100/6-12
147 E Palmer St 62642 — 217-968-2295
Ryan Heavner, prin. — Fax 968-2297

**Greenville, Bond, Pop. 6,851**
Bond County CUSD 2 — 2,000/PK-12
1008 N Hena St 62246 — 618-664-0170
Wes Olson, supt. — Fax 664-5000
www.bccu2.org
Bond City Comm Unit 2 HS — 600/9-12
1000 E State Route 140 62246 — 618-664-1370
Wendy Porter, prin. — Fax 664-4786
Greenville JHS — 300/6-8
1200 Junior High Dr 62246 — 618-664-1226
Gary Brauns, prin. — Fax 664-5071

---

Greenville College — Post-Sec.
315 E College Ave 62246 — 618-664-2800

**Gridley, McLean, Pop. 1,415**
El Paso-Gridley CUSD 11
Supt. — See El Paso
El Paso-Gridley JHS — 300/6-8
403 McLean St 61744 — 309-747-2156
Robby Tomlinson, prin. — Fax 747-2938

**Griggsville, Pike, Pop. 1,219**
Griggsville-Perry CUSD 4 — 400/PK-12
PO Box 439 62340 — 217-833-2352
Dr. Janet Gladu, supt. — Fax 833-2354
www.griggsvilleperry.org
Griggsville-Perry HS — 100/9-12
PO Box 439 62340 — 217-833-2352
Jeff Bourne, prin. — Fax 833-2354
Other Schools – See Perry

**Gurnee, Lake, Pop. 30,557**
Gurnee SD 56 — 2,100/PK-8
3706 Florida Ave 60031 — 847-336-0800
Dr. John Hutton, supt. — Fax 336-1110
www.d56.org
Viking MS — 600/6-8
4460 Old Grand Ave 60031 — 847-336-2108
Patrick Jones, prin. — Fax 249-0719

Warren Township HSD 121 — 4,400/9-12
34090 N Almond Rd 60031 — 847-662-1400
John Ahlgrim, supt. — Fax 548-0564
www.d121.org
Warren Township HS — 2,200/9-10
500 N OPlaine Rd 60031 — 847-662-1400
Greg Meyer, prin. — Fax 599-4848
Warren Township HS — 2,200/11-12
34090 N Almond Rd 60031 — 847-662-1400
Patrick Keeley, prin. — Fax 548-6444

Woodland CCSD 50 — 8,800/PK-8
1105 N Hunt Club Rd 60031 — 847-596-5600
Joy Swoboda, supt. — Fax 856-0311
www.dist50.net
Woodland MS — 2,300/6-8
7000 Washington St 60031 — 847-856-3400
Scott Snyder, prin. — Fax 856-1306

---

DeVry University — Post-Sec.
1075 Tri State Pkwy Ste 800 60031 — 847-855-2649

**Hamilton, Hancock, Pop. 2,918**
Hamilton CCSD 328 — 600/PK-12
270 N 10th St 62341 — 866-332-3880
Joe Yurko, supt. — Fax 847-3915
www.hhs328.com
Hamilton HS — 200/9-12
1100 Keokuk St 62341 — 866-332-3880
Shelli Jennings, prin. — Fax 847-3474
Hamilton JHS — 100/7-8
1100 Keokuk St 62341 — 866-332-3880
Shelli Jennings, prin. — Fax 847-3915

**Hampshire, Kane, Pop. 5,507**
CUSD 300
Supt. — See Algonquin
Hampshire HS — 1,100/9-12
1600 Big Timber Rd 60140 — 847-792-3500
Brett Bending, prin. — Fax 792-3515
Hampshire MS — 700/6-8
560 S State St 60140 — 847-683-2522
Kurt Rohlwing, prin. — Fax 683-1030

**Hanover, Jo Daviess, Pop. 828**
River Ridge CUSD 210 — 500/PK-12
4141 IL Route 84 S 61041 — 815-858-9005
Bradley Albrecht, supt. — Fax 858-9006
www.riverridge210.org
River Ridge HS — 200/9-12
4141 IL Route 84 S 61041 — 815-858-9005
Michael Foltz, prin. — Fax 858-9006
River Ridge MS — 100/6-8
4141 IL Route 84 S 61041 — 815-858-9005
Michael Foltz, prin. — Fax 858-9006

**Hanover Park, Cook, Pop. 37,237**
Keeneyville SD 20 — 1,600/PK-8
5540 Arlington Dr E 60133 — 630-894-2250
Dr. Michael Connolly, supt. — Fax 894-5187
www.esd20.org
Spring Wood MS — 600/6-8
5540 Arlington Dr E 60133 — 630-893-8900
Craig Barringer, prin. — Fax 894-9658

---

Hanover Park College of Beauty Culture — Post-Sec.
1166 E Lake St 60133 — 630-830-6560

**Hardin, Calhoun, Pop. 960**
Calhoun CUSD 40 — 500/K-12
PO Box 387 62047 — 618-576-2722
Dr. Kate Sievers, supt. — Fax 576-2641
www.calhoun.k12.il.us
Calhoun HS — 200/9-12
PO Box 387 62047 — 618-576-2229
Cheri Burris, prin. — Fax 576-8031

**Harrisburg, Saline, Pop. 8,789**
Edwds/Gtn/Hdn/Pope/Sln/Wbsh/Wyn/Wt ROE
512 N Main St 62946 — 618-253-5581
Lawrence Fillingim, supt. — Fax 252-8472
www.roe20.k12.il.us/
Harrisburg Learning Alternative S — Alt
512 N Main St 62946 — 618-253-7622
Dave Norris, prin. — Fax 253-7516

Harrisburg CUSD 3 — 2,100/PK-12
40 S Main St 62946 — 618-253-7637
Mike Gauch, supt. — Fax 253-2095
www.hbg.saline.k12.il.us
Harrisburg HS — 600/9-12
333 W College St 62946 — 618-253-7637
Scott Dewar, prin. — Fax 252-0994
Harrisburg MS — 500/6-8
312 Bulldog Blvd 62946 — 618-253-7637
John Crabb, prin. — Fax 253-2093

---

Southeastern Illinois College — Post-Sec.
3575 College Rd 62946 — 618-252-5400

**Hartsburg, Montgomery, Pop. 309**
Hartsburg-Emden CUSD 21 — 200/PK-12
400 W Front St 62643 — 217-642-5244
Donald Beard, supt. — Fax 642-5333
www.logan.k12.il.us/hartsem.html
Hartsburg-Emden JSHS — 100/6-12
400 W Front St 62643 — 217-642-5244
Terry Wisniewski, prin. — Fax 642-5333

**Harvard, McHenry, Pop. 9,314**
Harvard CUSD 50 — 2,500/PK-12
401 N Division St 60033 — 815-943-4022
Dr. Lauri Tobias, supt. — Fax 943-4282
www.cusd50.org
Harvard HS — 700/9-12
1103 N Jefferson St 60033 — 815-943-6461
Rob Zielinski, prin. — Fax 943-8506
Harvard JHS — 500/6-8
1301 Garfield St 60033 — 815-943-6466
Margaret Segersten, prin. — Fax 943-8521

**Harvey, Cook, Pop. 24,990**
Harvey SD 152 — 2,400/PK-8
16001 Lincoln Ave 60426 — 708-333-0300
Dr. Denean Adams, supt. — Fax 333-0349
www.harvey152.org
Brooks MS — 500/7-8
14741 Wallace St 60426 — 708-333-6390
Frank Kuzniewski, prin. — Fax 333-3177

Thornton Township HSD 205
Supt. — See South Holland
Thornton Township HS — 2,000/9-12
15001 Broadway Ave 60426 — 708-225-4109
Tony Ratliff, prin. — Fax 225-5014

West Harvey-Dixmoor SD 147 — 1,400/PK-8
191 W 155th Pl 60426 — 708-339-9500
J. Kay Giles, supt. — Fax 596-7020
www.whd147.org
Other Schools – See Dixmoor

---

Ingalls Memorial Hospital — Post-Sec.
1 Ingalls Dr 60426 — 708-333-2300

**Havana, Mason, Pop. 3,277**
Havana CUSD 126 — 1,100/PK-12
501 S McKinley St 62644 — 309-543-3384
Mathew Plater, supt. — Fax 543-3385
mason.k12.il.us/havana126
Havana HS — 300/9-12
501 S McKinley St 62644 — 309-543-3337
David McKinney, prin. — Fax 543-6721
Havana JHS — 300/5-8
801 E Laurel Ave 62644 — 309-543-6677
Chris Snider, prin. — Fax 543-6678

**Hawthorn Woods, Lake, Pop. 7,541**
Lake Zurich CUSD 95
Supt. — See Lake Zurich
Lake Zurich MS North Campus — 700/6-8
95 Hubbard Ln 60047 — 847-719-3600
Todd Jakowitsch, prin. — Fax 719-3620

**Hebron, McHenry, Pop. 1,203**
Alden Hebron SD 19 — 400/PK-12
11915 Price Rd 60034 — 815-648-2442
Dr. Debbie Ehlenburg, supt. — Fax 648-2339
www.alden-hebron.org
Alden-Hebron HS — 100/9-12
9604 Illinois St 60034 — 815-648-2442
Tim Hayunga, prin. — Fax 648-2339
Alden-Hebron MS — 100/6-8
9604 Illinois St 60034 — 815-648-2442
Tim Hayunga, prin. — Fax 648-2339

**Henry, Marshall, Pop. 2,442**
Henry-Senachwine CUSD 5 — 600/PK-12
1023 College St 61537 — 309-364-3614
Dr. Michael Miller, supt. — Fax 364-2990
www.hscud5.org
Henry-Senachwine Consolidated HS — 200/9-12
1023 College St 61537 — 309-364-2829
Weston Wolven, prin. — Fax 364-2990

**Herrin, Williamson, Pop. 12,262**
Herrin CUSD 4 — 2,500/PK-12
500 N 10th St 62948 — 618-988-8024
Dr. Mark Collins, supt. — Fax 942-6998
www.herrinunit.org
Herrin HS — 800/9-12
700 N 10th St 62948 — 618-942-6606
Dr. Terry Ryker, prin. — Fax 942-7562
Herrin MS — 500/6-8
700 S 14th St 62948 — 618-942-7461
Steve Robinson, prin. — Fax 988-8821

**Herscher, Kankakee, Pop. 1,577**
Herscher CUSD 2 — 1,100/PK-12
PO Box 504 60941 — 815-426-2162
Dr. Richard Decman, supt. — Fax 426-2872
www.hcusd2.org
Herscher HS — 700/9-12
PO Box 504 60941 — 815-426-2103
George McKenna, prin. — Fax 426-2957
Other Schools – See Kankakee

**Heyworth, McLean, Pop. 2,807**
Heyworth CUSD 4 — 1,000/PK-12
522 E Main St 61745 — 309-473-3727
Dr. Ty Wolf, supt. — Fax 473-2220
www.husd4.org
Heyworth JSHS — 400/7-12
308 W Cleveland St 61745 — 309-473-2322
Jeff Asmus, prin. — Fax 473-2323

**Hickory Hills, Cook, Pop. 13,836**
North Palos SD 117
Supt. — See Palos Hills
Conrady JHS — 1,000/6-8
7950 W 97th St 60457 — 708-233-4500
Andy Anderson, prin. — Fax 430-8964

**Highland, Madison, Pop. 9,807**
Highland CUSD 5 — 3,100/PK-12
400 Broadway 62249 — 618-654-2106
Michael Sutton, supt. — Fax 654-5424
www.highlandcusd5.org
Highland HS — 1,000/9-12
400 Broadway 62249 — 618-654-7131
Dr. Karen Gauen, prin. — Fax 654-6548
Highland MS — 500/6-8
400 Broadway 62249 — 618-651-8800
Erick Baer, prin. — Fax 654-1551

**Highland Park, Lake, Pop. 29,398**
North Shore SD 112 — 4,500/PK-8
1936 Green Bay Rd 60035 — 224-765-3000
Michael Bregy, supt. — Fax 765-3083
www.nssd112.org
Edgewood MS — 600/6-8
929 Edgewood Rd 60035 — 224-765-3200
Matt Eriksen, prin. — Fax 765-3208
Elm Place MS — 400/6-8
2031 Sheridan Rd 60035 — 224-765-3300
Richard Schroeder, prin. — Fax 765-3308
Northwood JHS — 400/6-8
945 North Ave 60035 — 224-765-3600
Sandra Arreguin, prin. — Fax 765-3608

Township HSD 113 — 3,700/9-12
1040 Park Ave W 60035 — 224-765-1000
Dr. Christopher Dignam, supt. — Fax 765-1060
www.dist113.org
Highland Park HS — 2,000/9-12
433 Vine Ave 60035 — 224-765-2000
Dr. Thomas Koulentes, prin. — Fax 765-2700
Other Schools – See Deerfield

**Hillsboro, Montgomery, Pop. 6,176**
Hillsboro CUSD 3 — 1,900/PK-12
1311 Vandalia Rd 62049 — 217-532-2942
David Powell, supt. — Fax 532-3137
www.hillsboroschools.net
Hillsboro HS — 500/9-12
522 E Tremont St 62049 — 217-532-2841
Janet Ward, prin. — Fax 532-5142
Hillsboro JHS — 400/6-8
909 Rountree St 62049 — 217-532-3742
Mark Fenske, prin. — Fax 532-6211

**Hillside, Cook, Pop. 8,034**
Proviso Township HSD 209
Supt. — See Forest Park
Proviso West HS — 2,200/9-12
4701 Harrison St 60162 — 708-449-6400
Oscar Hawthorne, prin. — Fax 449-3636

**Hinckley, DeKalb, Pop. 2,046**
Hinckley-Big Rock CUSD 429 — 700/PK-12
700 E Lincoln Ave 60520 — 815-286-7578
Travis McGuire, supt. — Fax 286-7577
www.hbr429.org
Hinckley-Big Rock HS — 200/9-12
700 E Lincoln Ave 60520 — 815-286-7500
Jay Brickman, prin. — Fax 286-7505
Other Schools – See Big Rock

**Hines, Cook**

---

Edward Hines Veterans Admin. Hospital — Post-Sec.
PO Box 5000 60141 — 708-216-2153

**Hinsdale, DuPage, Pop. 16,548**
CCSD 181
Supt. — See Clarendon Hills
Hinsdale MS — 800/6-8
100 S Garfield Ave 60521 — 630-861-4700
Ruben Pena, prin. — Fax 655-9754

Hinsdale Township HSD 86 4,500/9-12
5500 S Grant St 60521 630-655-6100
Dr. Bruce Law, supt. Fax 325-9153
www.hinsdale86.org
Hinsdale Central HS 2,800/9-12
5500 S Grant St 60521 630-570-8000
Dr. Mark Kolkman, prin. Fax 887-1362
Other Schools – See Darien, Willowbrook

---

Hinsdale Adventist Academy 300/PK-12
631 E Hickory St 60521 630-323-9211

**Hoffman Estates, Cook, Pop. 50,808**
Schaumburg CCSD 54
Supt. — See Schaumburg
Eisenhower JHS 600/7-8
800 Hassell Rd, 847-357-5500
Steve Kern, prin. Fax 357-5501

Township HSD 211
Supt. — See Palatine
Conant HS 2,400/9-12
700 E Cougar Trl, 847-755-3600
Julie Nowak, prin. Fax 755-3623
Higgins Education Center 50/Alt
1030 W Higgins Rd, 847-755-6840
Amy Friel, admin. Fax 755-6842
Hoffman Estates HS 2,000/9-12
1100 W Higgins Rd, 847-755-5600
James Britton, prin. Fax 755-5623

---

Ambria College of Nursing Post-Sec.
5210 Trillium Blvd 60192 847-397-0300
Montessori Academy of North Hoffman 100/PK-12
1250 Freeman Rd 60192 847-705-1234
Valeo Academy 100/K-12
2500 Beverly Rd 60192 847-645-9300
Rachelle Crawford, prin. Fax 645-3986

**Homer, Champaign, Pop. 1,182**
Heritage CUSD 8 400/K-12
512 W 1st St 61849 217-896-2041
Thomas Davis, supt. Fax 896-2338
www.heritage.k12.il.us
Other Schools – See Broadlands

**Homer Glen, Will**
Homer CCSD 33C 3,700/PK-8
15733 S Bell Rd, 708-226-7600
Dr. Kara Coglianese, supt. Fax 226-7616
www.homerschools.org
Homer JHS 800/7-8
15711 S Bell Rd, 708-226-7800
Troy Mitchell, prin. Fax 226-7859

**Homewood, Cook, Pop. 18,862**
Homewood SD 153 1,900/PK-8
18205 Aberdeen St 60430 708-799-5661
Dr. Dale Mitchell, supt. Fax 799-1377
www.hsd153.org
Hart JHS 500/7-8
18220 Morgan St 60430 708-799-5544
Dr. Scott McAllister, prin. Fax 799-8360

**Hoopeston, Vermilion, Pop. 5,322**
Hoopeston Area CUSD 11 1,400/PK-12
615 E Orange St 60942 217-283-6668
Hank Hornbeck, supt. Fax 283-5431
www.hoopeston.k12.il.us
Hoopeston Area HS 400/9-12
615 E Orange St 60942 217-283-6662
Larry Maynard, prin. Fax 283-5431
Hoopeston Area MS 200/7-8
615 E Orange St 60942 217-283-6664
Anne Burton, prin. Fax 283-5431

**Hume, Edgar, Pop. 377**
Shiloh CUSD 1 400/PK-12
21751 N 575th St 61932 217-887-2364
Dr. Allen Hall, supt. Fax 887-2448
www.shiloh1.us
Shiloh JSHS 200/6-12
21751 N 575th St 61932 217-887-2364
Elizabeth Harbaugh, prin. Fax 887-2448

**Huntley, McHenry, Pop. 23,973**
Consolidated SD 158
Supt. — See Algonquin
Huntley HS 2,400/9-12
13719 Harmony Rd 60142 847-659-6600
Scott Rowe, prin. Fax 659-6620

**Hutsonville, Crawford, Pop. 551**
Hutsonville CUSD 1 400/PK-12
500 W Clover St 62433 618-563-4912
Julie Kraemer, supt. Fax 563-9122
hutsonvilletigers.net
Hutsonville HS 100/9-12
500 W Clover St 62433 618-563-4913
Guy Rumler, prin. Fax 563-9122

**Illiopolis, Sangamon, Pop. 880**
Sangamon Valley CUSD 9
Supt. — See Niantic
Sangamon Valley MS 200/6-8
341 Matilda St 62539 217-486-2241
Jonathan Field, prin. Fax 486-6038

**Ina, Jefferson, Pop. 2,329**
Spring Garden Community Cons SD 178
Supt. — See Mount Vernon
Spring Garden MS 100/4-8
PO Box 129 62846 618-437-5361
Monte Jo Clark, prin. Fax 437-5333

---

Rend Lake College Post-Sec.
468 N Ken Gray Pkwy 62846 618-437-5321

**Ingleside, See Fox Lake**
Big Hollow SD 38 1,300/PK-8
26051 W Nippersink Rd 60041 847-740-1490
Robert Gold, supt. Fax 587-2663
www.bighollow.us
Big Hollow MS 600/5-8
26051 W Nippersink Rd 60041 847-740-5322
Christine Arndt, prin. Fax 740-9021

Gavin SD 37 900/PK-8
25775 W IL Route 134 60041 847-546-2916
Dr. John Ahlemeyer, supt. Fax 546-9584
www.gavin37.org
Gavin South MS 500/5-8
25775 W IL Route 134 60041 847-546-9336
Jason Jurgaitis, prin. Fax 546-9338

**Island Lake, McHenry, Pop. 7,988**
Wauconda CUSD 118
Supt. — See Wauconda
Matthews MS 500/6-8
PO Box 920 60042 847-526-6210
Robert Taterka, prin. Fax 526-8918

**Itasca, DuPage, Pop. 8,539**
Itasca SD 10 900/PK-8
200 N Maple St 60143 630-773-1232
Craig Benes, supt. Fax 773-1342
www.itasca.k12.il.us
Peacock MS 300/6-8
301 E North St 60143 630-773-0335
Heidi Weeks, prin. Fax 285-7460

---

Environmental Technical Institute Post-Sec.
1101 W Thorndale Ave 60143 630-285-9100

**Jacksonville, Morgan, Pop. 19,003**
Jacksonville SD 117 3,300/PK-12
516 Jordan St 62650 217-243-9411
Steve Ptacek, supt. Fax 243-6844
www.jsd117.org
Jacksonville HS 1,000/9-12
1211 N Diamond St 62650 217-243-4384
Mike McGiles, prin. Fax 245-0445
Turner JHS 500/7-8
664 Lincoln Ave 62650 217-243-3383
Beth Brockschmidt, prin. Fax 243-3459

---

Illinois College Post-Sec.
1101 W College Ave 62650 217-245-3000
Illinois School for the Deaf Post-Sec.
125 S Webster Ave 62650 217-479-4200
Illinois School for Visually Impaired Post-Sec.
658 E State St 62650 217-479-4400
MacMurray College Post-Sec.
447 E College Ave 62650 217-479-7000
Mr. John's School of Cosmetology & Nails Post-Sec.
1429 S Main St 62650 217-243-1744
Routt Catholic HS 100/9-12
500 E College Ave 62650 217-243-8563
Nicholas Roscetti, prin. Fax 243-3138

**Jerseyville, Jersey, Pop. 8,349**
Jersey CUSD 100 2,300/PK-12
100 Lincoln Ave 62052 618-498-5561
Dr. Lori Franke-Hopkins, supt. Fax 498-5265
www.jersey100.k12.il.us/
Jersey Community HS 1,100/8-12
801 N State St 62052 618-498-5521
Lisa Schuenke, prin. Fax 498-5332

**Johnsburg, McHenry, Pop. 6,290**
Johnsburg CUSD 12 2,300/PK-12
2222 Church St, 815-385-6916
Dr. Dan Johnson, supt. Fax 385-4715
www.johnsburg12.org
Johnsburg HS 800/9-12
2002 W Ringwood Rd, 815-385-9233
Kevin Shelton, prin. Fax 344-0451
Johnsburg JHS 700/6-8
2220 Church St, 815-385-6210
Nancy Hurckes, prin. Fax 344-7106

**Johnston City, Williamson, Pop. 3,492**
Johnston City CUSD 1 1,200/PK-12
PO Box 147 62951 618-983-8021
Kathy Clark, supt. Fax 983-6034
www.jcindians.org
Johnston City HS 300/9-12
1500 Jefferson Ave 62951 618-983-4700
Joey Ohnesorge, prin. Fax 983-6812
Washington MS 400/5-8
100 E 12th St 62951 618-983-7581
Patty Hilliard, prin. Fax 983-6409

**Joliet, Will, Pop. 145,165**
Joliet SD 86 11,200/PK-8
420 N Raynor Ave 60435 815-740-3196
Charles Coleman Ed.D., supt. Fax 740-6520
www.joliet86.org
Dirksen JHS 600/6-8
203 S Midland Ave 60436 815-729-1566
Rolland Jasper, prin. Fax 744-2346
Gompers JHS 800/6-8
1501 Copperfield Ave 60432 815-727-5276
Constance Russell, prin. Fax 726-5341
Hufford JHS 1,000/6-8
1125 N Larkin Ave 60435 815-725-3540
Pam Surprenant, prin. Fax 744-5974
Washington JHS & Academy 700/6-8
402 Richards St 60433 815-727-5271
Michael Latting, prin. Fax 740-5451

Joliet Township HSD 204 5,800/9-12
300 Caterpillar Dr 60436 815-727-6970
Dr. Cheryl McCarthy, supt. Fax 727-1277
www.jths.org
Joliet Central HS 2,900/9-12
201 E Jefferson St 60432 815-727-6740
Shad Hallihan, prin. Fax 727-6824
Joliet Township Alternative HS 100/Alt
110 Collins St 60432 815-727-6810
LaTanya Harris, prin.
Joliet West HS 2,800/9-12
401 N Larkin Ave 60435 815-727-6940
Teresa Gibson, prin. Fax 744-3070

Plainfield CCSD 202
Supt. — See Plainfield
Aux Sable MS 1,100/6-8
2001 Wildspring Pkwy 60431 815-439-7092
Dr. Edward Boswell, prin. Fax 577-9476

---

Joliet Catholic Academy 700/9-12
1200 N Larkin Ave 60435 815-741-0500
Jeffrey Budz, prin. Fax 741-9530
Joliet Junior College Post-Sec.
1215 Houbolt Rd 60431 815-729-9020
Professional Choice Hair Design Academy Post-Sec.
2719 W Jefferson St 60435 815-741-8224
University of St. Francis Post-Sec.
500 Wilcox St 60435 800-735-7500

**Joppa, Massac, Pop. 354**
Joppa-Maple Grove CUSD 38 300/PK-12
PO Box 10 62953 618-543-9023
Bill Biggerstaff, supt. Fax 543-9264
joppa38.com
Joppa JSHS 100/7-12
PO Box 10 62953 618-543-7589
Landon Sommer, prin. Fax 543-9264

**Joy, Mercer, Pop. 416**
Mercer County SD 404
Supt. — See Aledo
Mercer County JHS 200/7-8
203 N Washington St 61260 309-584-4174
Robert Reed, prin. Fax 584-4257

**Junction, Gallatin, Pop. 129**
Gallatin CUSD 7 800/PK-12
5175 Highway 13 62954 618-272-3821
Lucinda Schmitt, supt. Fax 272-4101
Gallatin HS 200/9-12
5175 Highway 13 62954 618-272-5141
Judy Kaegi, prin. Fax 272-4101
Gallatin JHS 200/5-8
5175 Highway 13 62954 618-272-7341
Chris Fromm, prin. Fax 272-4101

**Justice, Cook, Pop. 12,733**
Indian Springs SD 109 2,800/PK-8
7540 S 86th Ave 60458 708-496-8700
Dr. Jon Nebor, supt. Fax 496-8641
www.isd109.org
Wilkins JHS 600/7-8
8001 S 82nd Ave 60458 708-496-8708
Joseph Porrey, prin. Fax 728-3114

**Kankakee, Kankakee, Pop. 26,896**
Herscher CUSD 2
Supt. — See Herscher
Limestone MS 300/5-8
963 N 5000W Rd 60901 815-933-2243
Michelle Chavers, prin. Fax 936-4123

Kankakee SD 111 5,200/PK-12
240 Warren Ave 60901 815-802-7700
Dr. Genevra A. Walters, supt. Fax 936-8944
www.k111.k12.il.us
Kankakee HS 1,100/9-12
1200 W Jeffery St 60901 815-802-5500
Greg Merrill, contact Fax 933-9149
Kankakee JHS 700/7-8
2250 E Crestwood St 60901 815-802-5700
Charles Hensley, prin. Fax 935-7272

---

Bishop McNamara HS 400/9-12
550 W Brookmont Blvd 60901 815-932-7413
Terry Granger, prin. Fax 932-0926
Grace Christian Academy 200/PK-12
2499 Waldron Rd 60901 815-939-4579
Stephen Bull, prin. Fax 939-1334
Kankakee Community College Post-Sec.
100 College Dr 60901 815-802-8100
Kankakee Trinity Academy 200/PK-12
1580 Butterfield Trl 60901 815-935-8080
Brad Prairie, prin. Fax 935-0280

**Kansas, Edgar, Pop. 784**
Kansas CUSD 3 200/PK-12
PO Box 350 61933 217-948-5174
John Hasten, supt. Fax 948-5577
www.kansas.k12.il.us
Kansas JSHS 100/7-12
PO Box 350 61933 217-948-5175
Michael Lowery, prin. Fax 948-5577

**Kempton, Ford, Pop. 229**
Tri-Point CUSD 6-J 500/PK-12
PO Box 128 60946 815-253-6299
Jeff Bryan, supt. Fax 253-6298
www.tripointschools.org
Other Schools – See Cullom, Piper City

**Kewanee, Henry, Pop. 12,667**
Kewanee CUSD 229 1,700/PK-12
1001 N Main St 61443 309-853-3341
Christopher Sullens Ed.D., supt. Fax 852-5504
www.kcud229.org/
Central JHS 400/4-8
215 E Central Blvd 61443 309-853-4290
Jason Anderson, prin. Fax 853-3195
Kewanee HS 500/9-12
1211 E 3rd St 61443 309-853-3328
James Bryan, prin. Fax 854-0210

Wethersfield CUSD 230 — 700/PK-12
439 Willard St 61443 — 309-853-4860
Shane Kazubowski, supt. — Fax 856-7976
www.geese230.com
Wethersfield JSHS — 300/7-12
439 Willard St 61443 — 309-853-4205
Jeremiah Johnston, prin. — Fax 856-7800

**Kincaid, Christian, Pop. 1,483**
South Fork SD 14 — 400/PK-12
PO Box 20 62540 — 217-237-4333
Ron Graham, supt. — Fax 237-2245
www.southforkschools.com/
South Fork JSHS — 200/6-12
PO Box 20 62540 — 217-237-4333
Chris Clark, prin. — Fax 237-4370

**Kinderhook, Pike, Pop. 216**
Western CUSD 12
Supt. — See Barry
Western JHS — 100/6-8
PO Box 189 62345 — 217-432-8324
Jerud VanDyke, prin. — Fax 432-8003

**Kinmundy, Marion, Pop. 794**
South Central CUSD 401 — 700/PK-12
PO Box 189 62854 — 618-547-3414
Kerry Herdes, supt. — Fax 547-7790
southcentralschools.org/
South Central MS — 200/5-8
PO Box 40 62854 — 618-547-7734
Greg Grinestaff, prin. — Fax 547-7441
Other Schools – See Farina

**Kirkland, DeKalb, Pop. 1,732**
Hiawatha CUSD 426 — 600/PK-12
PO Box 428 60146 — 815-522-6676
Dr. William Mattingly, supt. — Fax 522-6619
www.hiawatha426.k12.il.us
Hiawatha HS — 200/9-12
PO Box 428 60146 — 815-522-3335
Mark Zych, prin. — Fax 522-9918

**Knoxville, Knox, Pop. 2,888**
Knoxville CUSD 202 — 1,100/PK-12
809 E Main St 61448 — 309-289-2328
Steve Wilder, supt. — Fax 289-9614
www.bluebullets.org
Knoxville HS — 300/9-12
600 E Main St 61448 — 309-289-2324
Chad Bahnks, prin. — Fax 289-9466
Knoxville JHS — 300/5-8
701 E Mill St 61448 — 309-289-4126
Daniel Powell, prin. — Fax 289-4128

**La Grange, Cook, Pop. 15,333**
La Grange SD 105 — 1,300/PK-8
701 7th Ave 60525 — 708-482-2700
Glenn Schlichting Ph.D., supt. — Fax 482-2727
www.d105.net
Gurrie MS — 300/7-8
1001 S Spring Ave 60525 — 708-482-2720
Edmond Hood, prin. — Fax 482-2724

Lyons Township HSD 204 — 3,900/9-12
100 S Brainard Ave 60525 — 708-579-6451
Dr. Timothy Kilrea, supt. — Fax 579-6768
www.lths.net
Lyons Township HS North Campus — 1,900/11-12
100 S Brainard Ave 60525 — 708-579-6300
Dr. Brian Waterman, prin. — Fax 579-3187
Other Schools – See Western Springs

**Lagrange Hlds, Cook**
La Grange Highlands SD 106 — 900/PK-8
1750 W Plainfield Rd 60525 — 708-246-3085
Patricia Viniard, supt. — Fax 246-0220
www.district106.net
Highlands MS — 300/6-8
1850 W Plainfield Rd 60525 — 708-579-6890
Michael Papierski, prin. — Fax 485-3593

**La Grange Park, Cook, Pop. 13,395**
La Grange SD 102 — 3,100/PK-8
333 N Park Rd 60526 — 708-482-2400
Dr. Kyle A. Schumacher, supt. — Fax 482-2402
www.dist102.k12.il.us
Park JHS — 700/7-8
325 N Park Rd 60526 — 708-482-2500
Philip Abraham, prin. — Fax 352-1170

---

Nazareth Academy — 800/9-12
1209 W Ogden Ave 60526 — 708-354-0061
Deborah Tracy, prin. — Fax 354-0109

**La Harpe, Hancock, Pop. 1,230**
La Harpe Community SD 347 — 200/PK-8
404 W Main St 61450 — 217-659-7739
Dr. Ryan Olson, supt. — Fax 659-7730
www.laharpeeagles.org
La Harpe JHS — 100/6-8
404 W Main St 61450 — 217-659-3713
Lila McKeown, prin. — Fax 659-7730

**Lake Bluff, Lake, Pop. 5,647**
Lake Bluff ESD 65 — 900/PK-8
900 W North Shore Dr # 220 60044 — 847-234-9400
Dr. Jean Sophie, supt. — Fax 234-6237
www.lb65.org
Lake Bluff MS — 300/6-8
31 E Sheridan Pl 60044 — 847-234-9407
Nathan Blackmer, prin. — Fax 615-9144

**Lake Forest, Lake, Pop. 19,130**
Lake Forest Community HSD 115 — 1,700/9-12
300 S Waukegan Rd 60045 — 847-235-9657
Michael Simeck, supt. — Fax 234-2372
www.lfhs.org/
Lake Forest HS — 1,700/9-12
1285 N McKinley Rd 60045 — 847-582-7315
Dr. Chala Holland, prin. — Fax 582-7797

Lake Forest SD 67 — 2,000/K-8
300 S Waukegan Rd 60045 — 847-235-9657
Michael Simeck, supt. — Fax 234-5132
www.lf67.org
Deer Path MS - West — 600/7-8
155 W Deerpath 60045 — 847-604-7400
Renee DeVore, prin. — Fax 234-2389

---

Lake Forest Academy — 400/9-12
1500 W Kennedy Rd 60045 — 847-234-3210
Dr. John Strudwick, head sch — Fax 615-3202
Lake Forest College — Post-Sec.
555 N Sheridan Rd 60045 — 847-234-3100
Lake Forest Graduate Sch. of Management — Post-Sec.
1905 W Field Ct 60045 — 847-234-5005
School of St. Mary MS — 300/4-8
185 E Illinois Rd 60045 — 847-234-0371
Dr. Venette Biancalana, admin. — Fax 234-9593
Woodlands Academy Sacred Heart — 200/9-12
760 E Westleigh Rd 60045 — 847-234-4300
Gerald Grossman, head sch — Fax 234-4348

**Lake in the Hills, McHenry, Pop. 28,527**
Consolidated SD 158
Supt. — See Algonquin
Marlowe MS — 1,300/6-8
9625 Haligus Rd 60156 — 847-659-4700
Adam Zehr, prin. — Fax 659-4720

**Lake Villa, Lake, Pop. 8,603**
Community HSD 117 — 2,800/9-12
1625 Deep Lake Rd Ste A 60046 — 847-838-7100
Jim McKay, supt. — Fax 395-7553
www.chsd117.org
Lakes Community HS — 1,400/9-12
1600 Eagle Way 60046 — 847-838-7100
David Newberry, prin. — Fax 395-7553
Other Schools – See Antioch

Lake Villa CCSD 41 — 3,100/PK-8
131 McKinley Ave 60046 — 847-356-2385
Dr. Lynette Zimmer, supt. — Fax 356-2670
www.district41.org
Palombi MS — 800/PK-PK, 7-
133 McKinley Ave 60046 — 847-356-2118
Victor Wight, prin. — Fax 356-0833

**Lake Zurich, Lake, Pop. 19,359**
Lake Zurich CUSD 95 — 5,900/PK-12
400 S Old Rand Rd 60047 — 847-438-2831
Dr. Mike Egan, supt. — Fax 438-6702
www.lz95.org
Lake Zurich HS — 2,100/9-12
300 Church St 60047 — 847-438-5155
Kent Nightlinger, prin. — Fax 438-5989
Lake Zurich MS South Campus — 700/6-8
435 W Cuba Rd 60047 — 847-540-7070
Dave Gardner, prin. — Fax 540-9438
Other Schools – See Hawthorn Woods

---

Quentin Road Christian S — 200/PK-12
60 Quentin Rd 60047 — 847-438-4494
Karen Scudder, admin.

**La Moille, Bureau, Pop. 722**
La Moille CUSD 303 — 300/K-12
801 S Main St 61330 — 815-638-2144
Dr. Ricardo Espinoza, supt. — Fax 638-2392
www.lamoilleschools.org
Allen JHS — 100/4-8
801 S Main St 61330 — 815-638-2233
Chawn Huffaker, prin. — Fax 638-2886
La Moille HS — 100/9-12
801 S Main St 61330 — 815-638-2144
Brent Ziegler, prin. — Fax 638-2392

**Lanark, Carroll, Pop. 1,444**
Eastland CUSD 308 — 400/PK-12
500 S School Dr 61046 — 815-493-6301
Dr. Mark Hansen, supt. — Fax 493-6303
www.eastland308.com
Eastland JSHS — 200/7-12
500 S School Dr 61046 — 815-493-6341
Monica Burkholder, prin. — Fax 493-6343

**Lansing, Cook, Pop. 27,924**
Lansing ESD 158 — 2,400/PK-8
18300 Greenbay Ave 60438 — 708-474-6700
Cecilia Heiberger Ed.D., supt. — Fax 474-9976
www.d158.net
Memorial JHS — 800/6-8
2721 Ridge Rd 60438 — 708-474-2383
Dr. Keli Ross, prin. — Fax 474-8463

Sunnybrook SD 171 — 1,000/PK-8
19266 Burnham Ave 60438 — 708-895-0750
Dr. Hughes George, supt. — Fax 895-8580
www.sd171.org
Heritage MS — 500/5-8
19250 Burnham Ave 60438 — 708-895-0790
Juan Gardner, prin. — Fax 895-8580

Thornton Fractional Township HSD 215
Supt. — See Calumet City
Thornton Fractional South HS — 1,900/9-12
18500 Burnham Ave 60438 — 708-585-2000
Judy Whalen, prin. — Fax 585-2009

---

American School — Post-Sec.
2200 E 170th St 60438 — 708-418-2800
Illiana Christian HS — 600/9-12
2261 Indiana Ave 60438 — 708-474-0515
Peter Boonstra, prin. — Fax 474-0581

**La Salle, LaSalle, Pop. 9,462**
La Salle ESD 122 — 1,000/PK-8
1165 Saint Vincents Ave 61301 — 815-223-0786
Daniel Marenda, supt. — Fax 223-8740
www.lasalleschools.net
Lincoln JHS — 300/6-8
1165 Saint Vincents Ave 61301 — 815-223-0786
Brian DeBernardi, prin. — Fax 223-8740

La Salle-Peru Township HSD 120 — 1,200/9-12
541 Chartres St 61301 — 815-223-1721
Steven Wrobleski, supt. — Fax 223-3444
www.lphs.net
Lasalle-Peru Area Career Center — Vo/Tech
541 Chartres St 61301 — 815-223-2454
Mary Stouffer, prin. — Fax 224-5066
La Salle-Peru Township HS — 1,200/9-12
541 Chartres St 61301 — 815-223-1721
Deb Nelson, prin. — Fax 223-3444

---

Educators of Beauty — Post-Sec.
122 Wright St 61301 — 815-223-7326
LaSalle-Peru Christian S — 100/PK-12
PO Box 1043 61301 — 815-223-1037
Wesley Waddle, prin.

**Lawrenceville, Lawrence, Pop. 4,300**
Lawrence County CUSD 20 — 1,200/PK-12
1802 Cedar St 62439 — 618-943-2326
Doug Daugherty, supt. — Fax 943-4092
www.cusd20.com
Lawrenceville HS — 400/9-12
2200 James St 62439 — 618-943-3389
Paul Higginbotham, prin. — Fax 943-4925
Parkview JHS — 300/6-8
1802 Cedar St 62439 — 618-943-2327
Jeremy Brush, prin. — Fax 943-4092

**Lebanon, Saint Clair, Pop. 4,302**
Lebanon CUSD 9 — 600/PK-12
200 W Schuetz St 62254 — 618-537-4611
Patrick Keeney, supt. — Fax 537-9588
lcusd9.org/
Lebanon HS — 300/6-12
200 W Schuetz St 62254 — 618-537-4423
Leigh Jackson, prin. — Fax 537-9588

---

McKendree University — Post-Sec.
701 College Rd 62254 — 618-537-4481

**Leland, LaSalle, Pop. 971**
Leland CUSD 1 — 300/PK-12
370 N Main St 60531 — 815-495-3821
Jodi Moore, admin. — Fax 495-4611
www.leland1.org
Leland HS — 100/9-12
370 N Main St 60531 — 815-495-3231
Jodi Moore, admin. — Fax 495-4611

**Lemont, DuPage, Pop. 15,866**
Lemont Township HSD 210 — 1,500/9-12
800 Porter St 60439 — 630-257-5838
Dr. Mary Ticknor, supt. — Fax 257-7603
www.lhs210.net
Lemont HS — 1,500/9-12
800 Porter St 60439 — 630-257-5838
Eric Michaelsen, prin. — Fax 243-0310

Lemont-Bromberek Combined SD 113A — 2,400/K-8
16100 W 127th St 60439 — 630-257-2286
Dr. Courtney Orzel, supt. — Fax 243-3005
www.sd113a.org
Old Quarry MS — 1,100/6-8
16100 W 127th St 60439 — 630-257-2286
Johnny Billingsley, prin. — Fax 243-3004

**Lena, Stephenson, Pop. 2,887**
Lena Winslow CUSD 202 — 900/PK-12
401 Fremont St 61048 — 815-369-3100
Dr. Tom Chiles, supt. — Fax 369-3102
www.le-win.net
Lena-Winslow HS — 300/9-12
516 Fremont St 61048 — 815-369-3115
Mark Kuehl, prin. — Fax 369-3165
Lena-Winslow JHS — 200/6-8
517 Fremont St 61048 — 815-369-3114
Andrew Lobdell, prin. — Fax 369-3162

**Le Roy, McLean, Pop. 3,530**
Le Roy CUSD 2 — 800/PK-12
600 E Pine St 61752 — 309-962-4211
Gary Tipsord, supt. — Fax 962-9312
www.leroyk12.org
Le Roy HS — 200/9-12
505 E Center St 61752 — 309-962-2911
Steve Reschke, prin. — Fax 962-8421
Le Roy JHS — 100/7-8
505 E Center St 61752 — 309-962-2911
Jeff Baughman, prin. — Fax 962-8421

**Lewistown, Fulton, Pop. 2,366**
Lewistown SD 97 — 700/PK-12
15501 E Avenue L 61542 — 309-547-5826
Jeanne Davis, supt. — Fax 547-5235
www.cusd97.fulton.k12.il.us
Central MS, 15501 E Avenue L 61542 — 300/5-8
Jan Braun, prin. — 309-547-2231
Lewistown Community HS — 200/9-12
15205 N State 100 Hwy 61542 — 309-547-2288
Clay Ginglen, prin. — Fax 547-9870

**Lexington, McLean, Pop. 2,036**
Lexington CUSD 7 — 500/PK-12
202 E Greenwich St 61753 — 309-365-4141
Dwight Stricklin, supt. — Fax 365-7381
www.lexington.k12.il.us
Lexington HS — 200/9-12
100 E Wall St 61753 — 309-365-2711
Dwight Stricklin, prin. — Fax 365-5032
Lexington JHS — 100/6-8
100 E Wall St 61753 — 309-365-2711
Paul Deters, prin. — Fax 365-5032

**Liberty, Adams, Pop. 512**
Liberty CUSD 2 700/PK-12
505 N Park St 62347 217-645-3433
Kelle Bunch, supt. Fax 645-3241
www.libertyschool.net
Liberty HS 300/7-12
505 N Park St 62347 217-645-3433
Karen Jirjis, prin. Fax 645-3389

**Libertyville, Lake, Pop. 20,013**
Community HSD 128
Supt. — See Vernon Hills
Libertyville HS 2,000/9-12
708 W Park Ave 60048 847-327-7000
Dr. Marina Scott, prin. Fax 367-2573

Libertyville SD 70 2,500/PK-8
1381 Lake St 60048 847-362-9695
Dr. Guy Schumacher, supt. Fax 362-3003
www.d70schools.org
Highland MS 1,000/6-8
310 W Rockland Rd 60048 847-362-9020
Jon Hallmark, prin. Fax 362-0870

**Lincoln, Logan, Pop. 14,271**
Lincoln Community HSD 404 800/9-12
1000 Railer Way 62656 217-732-4131
Robert Bagby, supt. Fax 735-3963
www.lchs.k12.il.us
Lincoln Community HS 800/9-12
1000 Railer Way 62656 217-732-4131
Todd Poelker, prin. Fax 735-3963

Lincoln ESD 27 1,300/PK-8
304 8th St 62656 217-732-2522
Dr. Kent Froebe, supt. Fax 732-2198
lincoln27.homestead.com/
Lincoln JHS 400/6-8
208 Broadway St 62656 217-732-3535
Michael Workman, prin. Fax 732-2685

Lincolnland Technical Education Center
1000 Primm Rd 62656 217-732-4131
Robert Bagby, dir. Fax 735-3963
Lincolnland Technical Education Center Vo/Tech
1000 Primm Rd 62656 217-732-4131
Robert Bagby, dir. Fax 735-3963

---

Lincoln Christian University Post-Sec.
100 Campus View Dr 62656 217-732-3168
Lincoln College Post-Sec.
300 Keokuk St 62656 217-732-3155

**Lincolnshire, Lake, Pop. 7,186**
Adlai E. Stevenson HSD 125 4,000/9-12
2 Stevenson Dr 60069 847-415-4000
Dr. Eric Twadell, supt. Fax 634-0239
www.d125.org/
Stevenson HS 4,000/9-12
1 Stevenson Dr 60069 847-415-4106
Troy Gobble, prin. Fax 634-7309

Lincolnshire-Prairieview SD 103 1,600/PK-8
1370 N Riverwoods Rd 60069 847-295-4030
Dr. Scott Warren, supt. Fax 295-9196
www.d103.org
Wright JHS 800/5-8
1370 N Riverwoods Rd 60069 847-295-1560
Michelle Blackley, prin. Fax 295-7136

**Lincolnwood, Cook, Pop. 12,270**
Lincolnwood SD 74 1,200/PK-8
6950 N East Prairie Rd 60712 847-675-8234
Dr. Joseph F. Bailey, supt. Fax 675-4207
www.sd74.org
Lincoln Hall MS 400/6-8
6855 N Crawford Ave 60712 847-675-8240
Dr. Jean Weiss, prin. Fax 675-8124

**Lindenhurst, Lake, Pop. 14,182**
Millburn CCSD 24
Supt. — See Wadsworth
Millburn MS 200/6-8
640 Freedom Way 60046 847-245-1600
Jake Jorgenson, prin. Fax 265-8198

**Lisle, DuPage, Pop. 21,980**
Lisle CUSD 202 1,600/PK-12
5211 Center Ave 60532 630-493-8000
Keith Filipiak, supt. Fax 971-4054
www.lisle.dupage.k12.il.us/
Lisle HS 500/9-12
1800 Short St 60532 630-493-8300
Jeffery Howard, prin. Fax 968-0182
Lisle JHS 400/6-8
5207 Center Ave 60532 630-493-8200
David Kearney, prin. Fax 493-8209

Naperville CUSD 203
Supt. — See Naperville
Kennedy JHS 1,000/6-8
2929 Green Trails Dr 60532 630-420-3220
Brian Valek, prin. Fax 420-6960

---

Benedictine University Post-Sec.
5700 College Rd 60532 630-829-6000
Benet Academy 1,400/9-12
2200 Maple Ave 60532 630-719-2782
Stephen Marth, prin. Fax 719-2849
Universal Technical Institute Post-Sec.
2611 Corporate West Dr 60532 630-529-2662

**Litchfield, Montgomery, Pop. 6,861**
Litchfield CUSD 12 1,500/PK-12
1702 N State St 62056 217-324-2157
Jeffrey Strieker, supt. Fax 324-2158
litchfieldpanthers.org
Litchfield HS 500/9-12
1705 N State St 62056 217-324-3955
Dr. Deann Heck, prin. Fax 324-5851
Litchfield MS 300/6-8
1701 N State St 62056 217-324-4668
Jennifer Thompson, prin. Fax 324-5693

---

Tri-County Beauty Academy Post-Sec.
219 N State St 62056 217-324-9062

**Lockport, Will, Pop. 24,568**
Lockport SD 91 600/PK-8
808 Adams St 60441 815-838-0737
Donna Gray, supt. Fax 834-4339
www.d91.net/
Kelvin Grove MS 400/4-8
808 Adams St 60441 815-838-0737
John Jennings, prin. Fax 834-4339

Lockport Township HSD 205 3,700/9-12
1323 E 7th St 60441 815-588-8100
Dr. Todd Wernet, supt. Fax 588-8109
www.lths.org
Lockport Township HS Central Campus 900/9-9
1222 S Jefferson St 60441 815-588-8200
Kerri Green, prin. Fax 588-8209
Lockport Township HS East Campus 2,800/10-12
1333 E 7th St 60441 815-588-8300
Dennis Hicks, prin. Fax 588-8309

Will County SD 92 1,800/PK-8
708 N State St 60441 815-838-8031
Dr. Peter Sullivan, supt. Fax 838-8034
www.d92.org
Oak Prairie JHS 600/6-8
15161 S Gougar Rd, 815-836-2724
Mark Murray, prin. Fax 834-2178

**Lombard, DuPage, Pop. 42,433**
Glenbard Township HSD 87
Supt. — See Glen Ellyn
Glenbard East HS 2,500/9-12
1014 S Main St 60148 630-627-9250
Shahe Bagdasarian, prin. Fax 627-9264

Lombard SD 44 3,100/PK-8
150 W Madison St 60148 630-827-4400
Dr. Michael Robey, supt. Fax 620-3798
www.sd44.org
Glenn Westlake MS 1,000/6-8
1514 S Main St 60148 630-827-4500
Philip Wieczorek, prin. Fax 620-3791

---

College Preparatory S of America 400/PK-12
331 W Madison St 60148 630-889-8000
Dr. Riaz Ahmad, prin. Fax 889-8012
Illinois Center for Broadcasting Post-Sec.
455 Eisenhower Ln S Ste 200 60148 630-916-1700
Montini Catholic HS 700/9-12
19W070 16th St 60148 630-627-6930
Maryann O'Neill, prin. Fax 627-0537
National University of Health Sciences Post-Sec.
200 E Roosevelt Rd 60148 630-629-2000
Northern Seminary Post-Sec.
660 E Butterfield Rd 60148 630-620-2180

**London Mills, Fulton, Pop. 391**
Spoon River Valley CUSD 4 400/PK-12
35265 N IL Route 97 61544 309-778-2204
K. Scot Reynolds, supt. Fax 778-2655
www.spoon-river.k12.il.us
Spoon River Valley HS 100/9-12
35265 N IL Route 97 61544 309-778-2201
Chris Janssen, prin. Fax 778-2655
Spoon River Valley JHS 100/7-8
35265 N IL Route 97 61544 309-778-2201
Chris Janssen, prin. Fax 778-2655

**Long Grove, Lake, Pop. 7,912**
Kildeer Countryside CCSD 96
Supt. — See Buffalo Grove
Woodlawn MS 600/6-8
6362 Gilmer Rd 60047 847-353-8500
Greg Grana, prin. Fax 949-8237

**Louisville, Clay, Pop. 1,135**
North Clay CUSD 25 700/PK-12
PO Box C 62858 618-665-3358
Monty Aldrich, supt. Fax 665-3893
members.wabash.net/~northclay/
North Clay Community HS 200/9-12
PO Box 220 62858 618-665-3102
Keith Price, prin. Fax 665-4270

**Lovejoy, Saint Clair, Pop. 732**
Brooklyn Unit SD 188 200/PK-12
PO Box 250 62059 618-271-1014
Dr. Henrietta Young, supt. Fax 271-9108
www.lovejoy.stclair.k12.il.us
Lovejoy MS 50/6-8
PO Box 250 62059 618-271-1014
Dr. Henrietta Young, prin. Fax 271-9108
Lovejoy Technology Academy 50/9-12
PO Box 250 62059 618-271-1014
Dr. Henrietta Young, prin. Fax 271-9108

**Loves Park, Winnebago, Pop. 23,555**
Harlem Unit SD 122
Supt. — See Machesney Park
Harlem MS 1,100/7-8
735 Windsor Rd 61111 815-654-4510
Matthew Cascio, prin. Fax 654-4540

**Lyons, Cook, Pop. 10,580**
Lyons SD 103 2,300/K-8
4100 Joliet Ave 60534 708-783-4100
Kyle Hastings, supt. Fax 780-9725
www.sd103.com/
Washington MS 700/6-8
8101 Ogden Ave 60534 708-783-4200
Johnny Billingsley, prin. Fax 780-9757

**Mc Henry, McHenry, Pop. 26,740**
McHenry CCSD 15 4,800/PK-8
1011 N Green St 60050 815-385-7210
R. Alan Hoffman Ed.D., supt. Fax 344-7121
www.d15.org
McHenry MS 800/6-8
2120 W Lincoln Rd 60051 815-385-2522
Mike Glover, prin. Fax 578-2101
Parkland S 800/6-8
1802 N Ringwood Rd 60050 815-385-8810
Mike Adams, prin. Fax 363-5023

McHenry Community HSD 156 2,500/9-12
4716 W Crystal Lake Rd 60050 815-385-7900
Dr. Michael Roberts, supt. Fax 344-7153
www.dist156.org
McHenry HS - East 900/9-12
1012 N Green St 60050 815-385-1145
Eric Blake, prin. Fax 363-8435
McHenry HS - West 1,600/9-12
4724 W Crystal Lake Rd 60050 815-385-7077
Marsha Potthoff, prin. Fax 363-8651

---

Montini MS 200/4-8
1405 N Richmond Rd 60050 815-385-1022
Michael Shukis, prin. Fax 363-7536

**Machesney Park, Winnebago, Pop. 23,071**
Harlem Unit SD 122 7,200/PK-12
8605 N 2nd St 61115 815-654-4500
Dr. Julie Morris, supt. • Fax 654-4600
www.harlem122.org
Harlem HS 2,300/9-12
1 Huskie Cir 61115 815-654-4511
Terrell Yarbrough, prin. Fax 654-4525
Other Schools – See Loves Park

**Mackinaw, Tazewell, Pop. 1,936**
Deer Creek-Mackinaw CUSD 701 1,100/PK-12
401 E 5th St 61755 309-359-8965
Scott Dearman, supt. Fax 359-5291
www.deemack.org/
Deer Creek-Mackinaw HS 300/9-12
401 E 5th St 61755 309-359-4421
Mary Lanier, prin. Fax 359-3125

**Mc Leansboro, Hamilton, Pop. 2,863**
Hamilton County CUSD 10 1,300/PK-12
PO Box 369 62859 618-643-2328
Jeff Fetcho, supt. • Fax 643-2015
www.unit10.com
Hamilton County JSHS 500/7-12
1 Fox Ln 62859 618-643-2328
Travis McCollum, prin. Fax 643-2307

**Mc Nabb, Putnam, Pop. 278**
Putnam County CUSD 535
Supt. — See Granville
Putnam County JHS 200/6-8
13183 N 350th Ave 61335 815-882-2800
Michael Olson, prin. Fax 882-2299

**Macomb, McDonough, Pop. 18,862**
Hanck/Fultn/Schuylr/McDonogh ROE
130 S Lafayette St Ste 200 61455 309-837-4821
John Meixner, supt. Fax 837-2887
www.roe26.net
Academy for Secondary Education 50/Alt
341 S Johnson St 61455 309-575-3226
Other Schools – See Carthage

Macomb CUSD 185 2,000/PK-12
323 W Washington St 61455 309-833-4161
Dr. Patrick Twomey, supt. Fax 836-2133
macomb185.org/
Macomb HS 600/9-12
1525 S Johnson St 61455 309-837-2331
John Rumley, prin. Fax 836-1034
Macomb JHS 300/7-8
1525 S Johnson St 61455 309-833-2074
Dana Isackson, prin. Fax 836-1034

---

McDonough District Hospital Post-Sec.
525 E Grant St 61455 309-833-4101
Western Illinois University Post-Sec.
1 University Cir 61455 309-298-1414

**Macon, Macon, Pop. 1,126**
Meridian CUSD 15 1,100/PK-12
PO Box 347 62544 217-764-5269
Daniel Brue, supt. Fax 764-5291
www.meridianhawks.net
Meridian HS 300/9-12
PO Box 380 62544 217-764-5233
Eric Hurelbrink, prin. Fax 764-5282
Other Schools – See Blue Mound

**Madison, Madison, Pop. 3,816**
Madison CUSD 12 400/PK-12
602 Farrish St 62060 618-877-1712
Evelyn Kelly, supt. Fax 877-2690
www.madisoncusd12.org
Madison HS 200/9-12
600 Farrish St 62060 618-876-7010
Rob Miller, prin. Fax 877-2694
Madison JHS 100/6-8
600 Farrish St 62060 618-876-6409
Rob Miller, prin. Fax 877-2693
Madison Student Support Center 50/Alt
1003 Farrish St 62060 618-876-6409
David Jackson, coord. Fax 877-2693

**Mahomet, Champaign, Pop. 7,188**
Mahomet-Seymour CUSD 3 2,900/PK-12
PO Box 229 61853 217-586-2161
Rick Johnston, supt. Fax 586-7591
www.mscusd.org
Mahomet-Seymour HS 900/9-12
PO Box 1098 61853 217-586-4962
Shannon Cheek, prin. Fax 586-6844

Mahomet-Seymour JHS 700/6-8
PO Box 560 61853 217-586-4415
Heather Landrus, prin. Fax 586-5869

**Malta, DeKalb, Pop. 1,142**

---

Kishwaukee College Post-Sec.
21193 Malta Rd 60150 815-825-2086

**Manhattan, Will, Pop. 6,984**
Manhattan SD 114 1,200/PK-8
25440 S Gougar Rd 60442 815-478-6093
Russell Ragon, supt. Fax 478-7660
www.manhattan114.org
Manhattan JHS 400/6-8
15606 W Smith Rd 60442 815-478-6090
Ron Pacheco, prin. Fax 478-6094

---

Community Christian S 100/PK-12
22811 S Cedar Rd 60442 815-485-2379
Pat Quinn, dean

**Manito, Mason, Pop. 1,628**
Midwest Central CUSD 191 1,100/PK-12
1010 S Washington St 61546 309-968-6868
Todd Hellrigel, supt. Fax 968-7916
www.midwestcentral.org/
Midwest Central HS 300/9-12
910 S Washington St 61546 309-968-6766
Jay Blair, prin. Fax 968-6340
Other Schools – See Green Valley

**Manlius, Bureau, Pop. 356**
Bureau Valley CUSD 340 1,100/PK-12
PO Box 289 61338 815-445-3101
Dr. Stephen Endress, supt. Fax 445-2802
www.bv340.org
Bureau Valley HS 400/9-12
PO Box 329 61338 815-445-4004
Eric Lawson, prin. Fax 445-3017
Other Schools – See Buda

**Mansfield, Piatt, Pop. 902**
Blue Ridge CUSD 18
Supt. — See Farmer City
Blue Ridge IS & JHS 100/4-8
PO Box 69 61854 217-489-5201
Fax 489-9051

**Manteno, Kankakee, Pop. 9,119**
Manteno CUSD 5 2,000/PK-12
84 N Oak St 60950 815-928-7000
Lisa Harrod, supt. Fax 468-6439
www.manteno5.org/
Manteno HS 600/9-12
443 N Maple St 60950 815-928-7101
Roger Schnitzler, prin. Fax 468-2344
Manteno MS 700/5-8
250 N Poplar St 60950 815-928-7154
David Conrad, prin. Fax 468-8082

**Maple Park, Kane, Pop. 1,296**
Fox Valley Career Center
47W326 Keslinger Rd 60151 630-365-5113
Dr. Rick Burchell Ed.D., dir. Fax 365-9088
www.kaneland.org/shared/fvcc
Fox Valley Career Center Vo/Tech
47W326 Keslinger Rd 60151 630-365-5113
Dr. Rick Burchell, dir. Fax 365-9088

Kaneland CUSD 302 4,800/PK-12
47W326 Keslinger Rd 60151 630-365-5111
Dr. Todd Leden, supt. Fax 365-9428
www.kaneland.org
Kaneland HS 1,300/9-12
47W326 Keslinger Rd 60151 630-365-5100
Jill Maras, prin. Fax 365-8421
Other Schools – See Sugar Grove

**Marengo, McHenry, Pop. 7,571**
Marengo Community HSD 154 800/9-12
110 Franks Rd 60152 815-568-6511
Dr. Dan Bertrand, supt. Fax 568-6510
www.mchs154.org
Marengo HS 800/9-12
110 Franks Rd 60152 815-568-6511
Angela Fink, prin. Fax 568-6510

Marengo-Union Consolidated ESD 165 800/PK-8
816 E Grant Hwy 60152 815-568-8323
Lea Damisch, supt. Fax 568-8367
www.marengo165.org
Marengo Community MS 400/6-8
816 E Grant Hwy 60152 815-568-5720
Tracy Beam, prin. Fax 568-7572

**Marion, Williamson, Pop. 16,859**
Crab Orchard CUSD 3 500/PK-12
19189 Bailey St 62959 618-982-2181
Derek Hutchins, supt. Fax 982-2080
www.cocusd3.org/
Crab Orchard HS 100/9-12
19189 Bailey St 62959 618-982-2181
Sy Stone, prin. Fax 982-2080

Marion CUSD 2 3,900/PK-12
1700 W Cherry St 62959 618-993-2321
Dr. Keith Oates, supt. Fax 997-0943
www.marionunit2.org
Marion HS 1,100/9-12
1501 S Carbon St 62959 618-993-8196
Jason Varner, prin. Fax 997-8749
Marion JHS 800/6-8
1609 W Main St 62959 618-997-1317
Rebecca Moss, prin. Fax 997-0477

---

Agape Christian HS 100/9-12
5208 Meadowland Pkwy Ste A 62959 618-997-9302
Seth Knox, prin. Fax 997-9304

**Marissa, Saint Clair, Pop. 1,970**
Marissa CUSD 40 600/PK-12
1 E Marissa St 62257 618-295-2313
Dr. Kevin Cogdill, supt. Fax 295-2609
www.marissa40.org
Marissa JSHS 200/7-12
300 School View Dr 62257 618-295-2393
Mark Heuring, prin. Fax 295-2276

**Markham, Cook, Pop. 12,287**
Prairie-Hills ESD 144 2,200/PK-8
3015 W 163rd St, 708-210-2888
Dr. Kimako Patterson, supt. Fax 210-9925
phsd144.net/
Prairie-Hills JHS 600/6-8
3035 W 163rd St, 708-210-2860
Kenndell Smith, prin. Fax 210-9208

**Maroa, Macon, Pop. 1,775**
Maroa-Forsyth CUSD 2 1,200/PK-12
PO Box 738 61756 217-794-3488
Mike Williams, supt. Fax 794-3878
www.mfschools.org
Maroa-Forsyth HS 300/9-12
PO Box 738 61756 217-794-3463
Scott Adreon, prin. Fax 794-5459
Maroa-Forsyth MS 300/6-8
PO Box 738 61756 217-794-5115
Brice Stewart, prin. Fax 794-3351

**Marquette Heights, Tazewell, Pop. 2,798**
North Pekin & Marquette Hts SD 102 700/PK-8
51 Yates Rd 61554 309-382-2172
Byron Sondgeroth, supt. Fax 382-2122
www.dist102.org/
Georgetowne MS 200/6-8
51 Yates Rd 61554 309-382-3456
Bob Ketcham, prin. Fax 382-2122

**Marshall, Clark, Pop. 3,915**
Marshall CUSD 2C 1,400/PK-12
503 Pine St 62441 217-826-5912
Kevin Ross, supt. Fax 826-5170
www.marshall.k12.il.us/
Marshall HS 400/9-12
806 N 6th St 62441 217-826-2395
Tim Pearison, prin. Fax 826-5511
Marshall JHS 200/7-8
806 N 6th St 62441 217-826-2812
John Ritchey, prin. Fax 826-6065

**Martinsville, Clark, Pop. 1,153**
Martinsville CUSD 3C 400/PK-12
PO Box K 62442 217-382-4321
Jill Rogers, supt. Fax 382-4183
www.martinsville.k12.il.us/
Martinsville JSHS 200/7-12
PO Box K 62442 217-382-4132
Jeff Thompson, prin. Fax 382-4761

**Mascoutah, Saint Clair, Pop. 7,258**
Mascoutah CUSD 19 3,600/PK-12
421 W Harnett St 62258 618-566-7414
Dr. Craig Fiegel, supt. Fax 566-4507
www.mascoutah19.k12.il.us
Mascoutah HS 1,000/9-12
1313 W Main St 62258 618-566-8523
Sandra Jouglard, prin. Fax 566-8693
Mascoutah MS 800/6-8
846 N 6th St 62258 618-566-2305
Bob Stone, prin. Fax 566-2307

**Mason City, Mason, Pop. 2,332**
Illini Central CUSD 189 800/PK-12
208 N West Ave 62664 217-482-5180
Beau Fretueg, supt. Fax 482-3121
www.illinicentral.org
Illini Central HS 300/9-12
208 N West Ave 62664 217-482-3252
Jennifer Durbin, prin. Fax 482-3323
Illini Central MS 200/6-8
208 N West Ave 62664 217-482-3252
Jennifer Durbin, prin. Fax 482-3323

**Matteson, Cook, Pop. 18,630**
ESD 159 1,900/PK-8
6202 Vollmer Rd 60443 708-720-1300
Barbara Suggs-Mason, supt. Fax 720-3218
www.dist159.com
Powell MS 700/6-8
20600 Matteson Ave 60443 708-283-9600
Kimberly Johnson, prin. Fax 283-1885

Matteson ESD 162
Supt. — See Richton Park
Huth MS 600/7-8
3718 213th Pl 60443 708-748-0470
Corey Levy, prin. Fax 503-1119

**Mattoon, Coles, Pop. 18,262**
Mattoon CUSD 2 3,400/K-12
1701 Charleston Ave 61938 217-238-8850
Larry Lilly, supt. Fax 238-8855
www.mattoon.k12.il.us
Mattoon HS 1,000/9-12
2521 Walnut Ave 61938 217-238-7800
Michele Sinclair, prin. Fax 238-7805
Mattoon MS 800/6-8
1200 S 9th St 61938 217-238-5800
Jeremie Smith, prin. Fax 238-5805

---

Lake Land College Post-Sec.
5001 Lake Land Blvd 61938 217-234-5253

**Maywood, Cook, Pop. 23,814**
Maywood-Melrose Park-Broadview SD 89
Supt. — See Melrose Park
Irving MS 400/6-8
805 S 17th Ave 60153 708-450-2015
Adrian Harries, prin. Fax 343-0762

Proviso Township HSD 209
Supt. — See Forest Park
Proviso East HS 1,800/9-12
807 S 1st Ave 60153 708-344-7000
Tony Valente, prin. Fax 344-5942

**Mazon, Grundy, Pop. 1,011**
Mazon-Verona-Kinsman ESD 2C 300/PK-8
1013 North St 60444 815-448-2200
Nancy Dillow, supt. Fax 448-3005
www.mvkmavericks.org
Mazon-Verona-Kinsman MS 200/5-8
1013 North St 60444 815-448-2127
Debra Paulsen, prin. Fax 448-3005

**Melrose Park, Cook, Pop. 25,229**
Mannheim SD 83
Supt. — See Franklin Park
Mannheim JHS 800/6-8
2600 Hyde Park Ave 60164 847-455-5020
Timothy Daley, prin. Fax 455-2038

Maywood-Melrose Park-Broadview SD 89 5,300/PK-8
906 Walton St 60160 708-450-2460
Dr. David Negron, supt. Fax 450-2461
www.maywood89.org
Stevenson MS 1,000/6-8
1630 N 20th Ave 60160 708-450-2053
James Parker, prin. Fax 344-1356
Other Schools – See Maywood

---

Everest College Post-Sec.
1101 W North Ave Ste 1 60160 708-731-4400
Lincoln College of Technology Post-Sec.
8317 W North Ave 60160 708-344-4700
Walther Christian Academy - Upper S 300/9-12
900 Chicago Ave 60160 708-344-0404
Jim Craven, hdmstr. Fax 344-0525

**Mendon, Adams, Pop. 949**
CUSD 4 700/PK-12
PO Box 200 62351 217-936-2111
Brian Kurz, supt. Fax 936-2643
www.cusd4.com
Unity HS 200/9-12
PO Box 200 62351 217-936-2116
William Dorethy, prin. Fax 936-2117
Unity MS 300/4-8
PO Box 200 62351 217-936-2727
Seth Klusmeyer, prin. Fax 936-2730

**Mendota, LaSalle, Pop. 7,312**
Mendota CCSD 289 1,300/PK-8
1806 Guiles Ave 61342 815-539-7631
Kristen School, supt. Fax 538-2927
www.mendota289.org/
Northbrook S 600/PK-PK, 5-
1804 Guiles Ave 61342 815-539-6237
Beth Wackerlin, prin. Fax 538-3090

Mendota Township HSD 280 600/9-12
2300 W Main St 61342 815-539-7446
Jeff Prusator, supt. Fax 539-3103
mendotahs.org/
Mendota Township HS 600/9-12
2300 W Main St 61342 815-539-7446
Denise Aughenbaugh, prin. Fax 539-3103

**Meredosia, Morgan, Pop. 1,040**
Meredosia-Chambersburg CUSD 11 300/PK-12
PO Box 440 62665 217-584-1744
Ron Gilbert, supt. Fax 584-1129
www.mcsd11.net
Meredosia-Chambersburg HS 100/9-12
PO Box 440 62665 217-584-1291
Daniel Carie, prin. Fax 584-1741
Meredosia-Chambersburg JHS 50/6-8
PO Box 440 62665 217-584-1291
Daniel Carie, prin. Fax 584-1741

**Merrionette Park, Cook, Pop. 1,874**

---

Everest College Post-Sec.
11560 S Kedzie Ave 60803 708-239-0055

**Metamora, Woodford, Pop. 3,585**
Metamora Township HSD 122 1,000/9-12
PO Box 109 61548 309-367-4151
Randall G. Toepke, supt. Fax 367-4351
mths.metamora.k12.il.us/
Metamora Twp HS 1,000/9-12
PO Box 109 61548 309-367-4151
Randall Toepke, supt. Fax 367-4154

**Metropolis, Massac, Pop. 6,368**
Massac Unit SD 1 2,100/PK-12
PO Box 530 62960 618-524-9376
Dennis Smith, supt. Fax 524-4432
www.massac.org
Massac County HS 600/9-12
2841 Old Marion Rd 62960 618-524-3440
Jason Hayes, prin. Fax 524-3131
Massac JHS 300/7-8
3028 Old Marion Rd 62960 618-524-2645
Kelli Ward, prin. Fax 524-2765

**Midlothian, Cook, Pop. 14,581**
Bremen Community HSD 228 5,300/9-12
15233 Pulaski Rd 60445 708-389-1175
Bill Kendall, supt. Fax 389-2552
www.bhsd228.com
Bremen HS 1,400/9-12
15203 Pulaski Rd 60445 708-371-3600
David Kibelkis, prin. Fax 371-7194
Other Schools – See Country Club Hills, Oak Forest, Tinley Park

**Milford, Iroquois, Pop. 1,300**
Milford Area SD 124 200/PK-12
PO Box 304 60953 815-889-5176
Dr. Dale Hastings, supt. Fax 889-5221
www.mpsk12.org

Milford HS 200/9-12
124 E Jones St 60953 815-889-4184
Stephen Totheroh, prin. Fax 889-4871

**Millbrook, Kendall, Pop. 329**
Newark CCSD 66
Supt. — See Newark
Millbrook JHS 100/5-8
8411 Fox River Dr 60536 630-553-5435
Demetra Turman, prin. Fax 553-1027

**Milledgeville, Carroll, Pop. 1,027**
Chadwick-Milledgeville CUSD 399
Supt. — See Chadwick
Milledgeville HS 100/9-12
100 E 8th St 61051 815-225-7141
Paula Rademacher, prin. Fax 225-7847

**Mill Shoals, Wayne, Pop. 214**
Wabash CUSD 348
Supt. — See Mount Carmel
Mill Shoals Learning Alternative S Alt
590 East St 62862 618-896-5525
Cindy Baumgart, prin. Fax 896-7312

**Millstadt, Saint Clair, Pop. 3,983**
Millstadt CCSD 160 900/PK-8
211 W Mill St 62260 618-476-1803
Jonathan Green, supt. Fax 476-1893
www.mccsd160.com
Millstadt Consolidated S 600/3-8
211 W Mill St 62260 618-476-1681
Josh Lane, prin. Fax 476-3401

**Minonk, Woodford, Pop. 2,068**
Fieldcrest CUSD 6 1,200/PK-12
1 Dornbush Dr 61760 309-432-2177
Dan Oakley, supt. Fax 432-3377
www.fieldcrest.k12.il.us
Fieldcrest HS 400/9-12
1 Dornbush Dr 61760 309-432-2529
William Lapp, prin. Fax 432-2064

**Minooka, Grundy, Pop. 10,784**
Minooka CCSD 201 4,000/PK-8
PO Box 467 60447 815-467-6121
Dr. Kris Monn, supt. Fax 467-9544
www.min201.org
Minooka JHS 800/7-8
333 W McEvilly Rd 60447 815-467-2136
Sarah Massey, prin. Fax 467-5087

Minooka Community HSD 111
Supt. — See Channahon
Minooka Community HS 1,200/11-12
301 S Wabena Ave 60447 815-467-2140
Ron Kiesewetter, prin. Fax 467-2431

**Mokena, Will, Pop. 18,589**
Mokena SD 159 1,800/PK-8
11244 Willow Crest Ln 60448 708-342-4900
Dr. Omar Castillo, supt. Fax 479-3143
www.mokena159.org
Mokena JHS 700/6-8
19815 Kirkstone Way 60448 708-342-4870
Dr. Michael Rolinitis, prin. Fax 479-3122

Rasmussen College Post-Sec.
8650 Spring Lake Dr 60448 815-534-3300

**Moline, Rock Island, Pop. 42,701**
Moline-Coal Valley CUSD 40 7,400/PK-12
1619 11th Ave 61265 309-743-1600
Lanty McGuire, supt. Fax 757-3476
www.molineschools.org
Deere MS 800/6-8
2035 11th St 61265 309-743-1622
Dr. Dusti Adrian, prin. Fax 757-3668
Moline HS 2,100/9-12
3600 Avenue of the Cities 61265 309-743-1624
Dan McGuire, prin. Fax 757-3667
Moline HS - Coolidge Campus 100/Alt
3432 Avenue of the Cities 61265 309-743-8587
Lyle Goldensoph, prin. Fax 757-3536
Wilson MS 900/6-8
1301 48th St 61265 309-743-1623
Robert Beem, prin. Fax 757-3586

Black Hawk College Post-Sec.
6600 34th Ave 61265 309-796-5000
Midwest Technical Institute Post-Sec.
3620 Avenue of the Cities 61265 800-814-5124
Quad Cities Christian S 100/6-12
4000 11th St 61265 309-762-3800
Mark Sullivan, admin. Fax 762-8150

**Momence, Kankakee, Pop. 3,244**
Momence CUSD 1 1,300/PK-12
400 N Pine St 60954 815-472-3501
Gary Miller, supt. Fax 472-3516
www.momence.k12.il.us
Momence HS 400/9-12
101 N Franklin St 60954 815-472-6477
Shannon Anderson, prin. Fax 472-2055
Momence JHS 400/PK-PK, 5-
801 W 2nd St 60954 815-472-4184
Jeremy Heck, prin. Fax 472-3517

**Monee, Will, Pop. 5,063**
Crete-Monee CUSD 201U
Supt. — See Crete
Monee Education Center Alt
5154 Main St 60449 708-367-2660
Brian Wortel, coord. Fax 672-2764

**Monmouth, Warren, Pop. 9,279**
Monmouth-Roseville CUSD 238 1,700/PK-12
105 N E St 61462 309-734-4712
Edward Fletcher, supt. Fax 734-4755
www.mr238.org

Monmouth-Roseville HS 500/9-12
325 W 1st Ave 61462 309-734-5118
Jay Melton, prin. Fax 734-2918
Other Schools – See Roseville

United CUSD 304 1,000/PK-12
1905 100th St 61462 309-734-9413
Jeffrey Whitsitt, supt. Fax 734-0223
united.k12.il.us/
United HS 300/9-12
1905 100th St 61462 309-734-9411
Amy Schmitz, prin. Fax 734-6090
United JHS 300/6-8
2140 State Highway 135 61462 309-734-8511
Joseph Nichols, prin. Fax 734-6094

Monmouth College Post-Sec.
700 E Broadway 61462 800-747-2687

**Monticello, Piatt, Pop. 5,493**
Monticello CUSD 25 1,700/PK-12
2 Sage Dr 61856 217-762-8511
Dr. Victor Zimmerman, supt. Fax 762-8534
www.sages.us
Monticello HS 600/9-12
1 Sage Dr 61856 217-762-8511
Tip Reedy, prin. Fax 762-7421
Monticello MS 400/6-8
2015 E Washington St 61856 217-762-8511
Jeanne Handley, prin. Fax 762-7765

**Mooseheart, Kane**

Mooseheart S 200/PK-12
255 W James J Davis Dr 60539 630-906-3646

**Morris, Grundy, Pop. 13,509**
Grundy Area Vocational Center
1002 Union St 60450 815-942-4390
Lance Copes, dir. Fax 942-6650
www.gavc-il.org
Grundy AVC Vo/Tech
1002 Union St 60450 815-942-4390
Lance Copes, dir. Fax 942-6650

Grundy/Kendall ROE
1320 Union St 60450 815-941-3247
Christopher Mehochko, supt. Fax 942-5384
www.roe24.org
Premier Academy 100/6-12
7700 Ashley Rd 60450 815-416-0377
Sherri Frost, prin.

Morris Community HSD 101 900/9-12
1000 Union St 60450 815-942-1294
Dr. Patrick Halloran, supt. Fax 941-5407
www.morrishs.org
Morris HS 900/9-12
1000 Union St 60450 815-942-1294
Kelly Hussey, prin. Fax 941-5405

Morris SD 54 1,200/PK-8
54 White Oak Dr 60450 815-942-0056
Dr. Teri Shaw, supt. Fax 942-0240
www.morris54.org
Shabbona MS 400/6-8
725 School St 60450 815-942-0056
Christopher Maier, prin. Fax 416-0581

**Morrison, Whiteside, Pop. 4,151**
Morrison CUSD 6 1,100/PK-12
643 Genesee Ave 61270 815-772-2064
Scott Vance, supt. Fax 772-4644
www.morrisonschools.org
Morrison HS 300/9-12
643 Genesee Ave 61270 815-772-4071
Kay Harwood, prin. Fax 772-4644
Morrison JHS 300/6-8
300 Academic Dr 61270 815-772-7264
Joe Robbins, prin. Fax 772-2531

Morrison Institute of Technology Post-Sec.
701 Portland Ave 61270 815-772-7218

**Morrisonville, Christian, Pop. 1,053**
Morrisonville CUSD 1 300/PK-12
PO Box 13 62546 217-526-4431
Gary DePatis, supt. Fax 526-4433
www.mohawks.net
Morrisonville HS 100/9-12
PO Box 13 62546 217-526-4432
Ann Little, prin. Fax 526-4452
Morrisonville JHS 50/7-8
PO Box 13 62546 217-526-4432
Ann Little, prin. Fax 526-4452

**Morton, Tazewell, Pop. 16,106**
Morton CUSD 709 2,800/PK-12
1050 S 4th Ave Ste 200 61550 309-263-2581
Dr. Lindsey Hall, supt. Fax 266-6320
www.morton709.org
Morton HS 1,000/9-12
350 N Illinois Ave 61550 309-266-7182
Marjorie Johnson, prin. Fax 263-2168
Morton JHS 400/7-8
225 E Jackson St 61550 309-266-6522
Lee Hoffman, prin. Fax 284-5031

**Morton Grove, Cook, Pop. 22,739**
Golf ESD 67 600/PK-8
9401 Waukegan Rd 60053 847-966-8200
Dr. Beth Flores, supt. Fax 966-8290
www.golf67.net
Golf MS 200/5-8
9401 Waukegan Rd 60053 847-965-3740
Karen Chvojka, prin. Fax 966-9493

**Mounds, Pulaski, Pop. 797**
Meridian CUSD 101 500/PK-12
1401 Mounds Rd 62964 618-342-6776
Spencer Byrd, supt. Fax 342-6856
www.meridian101.com

Meridian HS 200/9-12
1401 Mounds Rd 62964 618-342-6778
Tim Turner, prin. Fax 342-6856

**Mount Carmel, Wabash, Pop. 7,195**
Wabash CUSD 348 1,600/K-12
218 W 13th St 62863 618-262-4181
Tim Buss, supt. Fax 262-7912
www.wabash348.com
Mount Carmel HS 600/9-12
201 N Pear St 62863 618-262-5104
Pat Cheesman, prin. Fax 262-8781
Mount Carmel MS 400/6-8
1520 Poplar St 62863 618-262-5699
Steven Holt, prin. Fax 263-9096
Other Schools – See Mill Shoals

Wabash Valley College Post-Sec.
2200 College Dr 62863 618-262-8641

**Mount Carroll, Carroll, Pop. 1,702**
West Carroll CUSD 314 1,300/PK-12
642 S East St 61053 815-734-3374
Craig Mathers, supt. Fax 244-0211
www.wc314.org/
West Carroll MS 300/5-8
633 S East St 61053 815-244-2002
Julie Katzenberger, prin. Fax 244-1051
Other Schools – See Savanna

**Mount Morris, Ogle, Pop. 2,953**
Oregon CUSD 220
Supt. — See Oregon
Rahn JHS 200/7-8
105 W Brayton Rd 61054 815-734-5300
Kip Crandall, prin. Fax 734-7129

**Mount Olive, Macoupin, Pop. 2,093**
Mount Olive CUSD 5 500/PK-12
804 W Main St 62069 217-999-7831
Patrick Murphy, supt. Fax 999-2150
www.mtoliveschools.org
Mount Olive HS 200/9-12
804 W Main St 62069 217-999-4231
Shane Schuricht, prin. Fax 999-4302

**Mount Prospect, Cook, Pop. 53,352**
CCSD 59
Supt. — See Arlington Heights
Holmes JHS 500/6-8
1900 W Lonnquist Blvd 60056 847-593-4390
Dr. Robert Bohanek, prin. Fax 593-7386

Mount Prospect SD 57 2,100/PK-8
701 W Gregory St 60056 847-394-7300
Dr. Elaine Aumiller, supt. Fax 394-7311
www.d57.org
Lincoln MS 700/6-8
700 W Lincoln St 60056 847-394-7350
Jason Kaiz, prin. Fax 394-7358

River Trails SD 26 1,200/PK-8
1900 E Kensington Rd 60056 847-297-4120
Dane Delli Ph.D., supt. Fax 297-4124
www.rtsd26.org
River Trails MS 400/6-8
1000 N Wolf Rd 60056 847-298-1750
Keir Rogers, prin. Fax 298-2639

Township HSD 214
Supt. — See Arlington Heights
Prospect HS 2,100/9-12
801 W Kensington Rd 60056 847-718-5200
Michelle Dowling, prin. Fax 718-5216

Christian Life College Post-Sec.
400 E Gregory St 60056 847-259-1840

**Mount Pulaski, Logan, Pop. 1,560**
Mount Pulaski CUSD 23 500/PK-12
119 N Garden St Ste 2 62548 217-792-7222
Todd Hamm, supt. Fax 792-5551
www.mtpulaski.k12.il.us
Mount Pulaski HS 200/9-12
206 S Spring St 62548 217-792-3209
Terry Morgan, prin. Fax 792-3248

**Mount Sterling, Brown, Pop. 2,006**
Brown County CUSD 1 700/PK-12
503 NW Cross St 62353 217-773-3359
Vicki Phillips, supt. Fax 773-2121
www.bchornets.com/
Brown County HS 200/9-12
500 E Main St 62353 217-773-3345
Ann Logan, prin. Fax 773-2128
Brown County MS 200/5-8
504 E Main St 62353 217-773-9152
Ann Logan, prin. Fax 773-9121

**Mount Vernon, Jefferson, Pop. 14,904**
Mount Vernon Area Vocational Center
320 S 7th St 62864 618-246-5602
Robert Knutson, dir. Fax 244-8049
Mount Vernon Area Vocational Center Vo/Tech
320 S 7th St 62864 618-246-5602
Robert Knutson, dir. Fax 244-8049

Mount Vernon CSD 80 1,700/PK-8
2710 North St 62864 618-244-8080
Fax 244-8082
www.mtv80.org
Casey MS 500/6-8
1829 Broadway St 62864 618-244-8060
Mary McGreer, prin. Fax 244-8014

Mount Vernon Township HSD 201 1,300/9-12
320 S 7th St 62864 618-244-3700
Dr. Michael Smith, supt. Fax 244-3047
www.mvths.org
Mount Vernon HS 1,300/9-12
320 S 7th St 62864 618-244-3700
Rowdy Fatheree, prin. Fax 244-8047

Spring Garden Community Cons SD 178 100/K-8
14975 E Bakersville Rd 62864 618-244-8070
Monte Jo Clark, supt. Fax 244-8071
springgarden178.weebly.com
Other Schools – See Ina

---

DuQuoin Beauty College Post-Sec.
212 S 20th St 62864 618-542-9777

**Mount Zion, Macon, Pop. 5,766**
Mount Zion CUSD 3 2,500/PK-12
455 Elm St 62549 217-864-2366
Dr. Travis Roundcount, supt. Fax 864-2200
www.mtzion.k12.il.us
Mount Zion HS 800/9-12
305 S Henderson St 62549 217-864-2363
Kraig Garber, prin. Fax 864-5815
Mount Zion JHS 400/7-8
315 S Henderson St 62549 217-864-2369
Jerry Birkey, prin. Fax 864-6829

**Moweaqua, Shelby, Pop. 1,822**
Central A & M CUSD 21
Supt. — See Assumption
Central A & M HS 300/9-12
229 E Pine St 62550 217-768-3866
Charles Brown, prin. Fax 768-3797

**Mulberry Grove, Bond, Pop. 626**
Mulberry Grove CUSD 1 400/PK-12
801 W Wall St 62262 618-326-8812
Brad Turner, supt. Fax 326-8482
www.mgschools.com
Mulberry Grove JSHS 100/6-12
801 W Wall St 62262 618-326-8221
Brad Turner, prin. Fax 326-8482

**Mundelein, Lake, Pop. 30,630**
Diamond Lake SD 76 1,100/PK-8
500 Acorn Ln 60060 847-566-9221
Dr. Bhavna Sharma-Lewis, supt. Fax 566-5689
www.d76.lake.k12.il.us/
West Oak MS 400/5-8
500 Acorn Ln 60060 847-566-9220
Christopher Willeford, prin. Fax 970-3534

Fremont SD 79 2,200/PK-8
28855 N Fremont Center Rd 60060 847-566-0169
Dr. Jill Gildea, supt. Fax 566-7280
www.fsd79.org
Fremont MS 800/6-8
28871 N Fremont Center Rd 60060 847-566-9384
Pam Motsenbocker, prin. Fax 566-7805

Mundelein Consolidated HSD 120 2,200/9-12
1350 W Hawley St 60060 847-949-2200
Dr. Kevin Myers Ph.D., supt. Fax 949-4756
www.d120.org/
Mundelein Consolidated HS 2,200/9-12
1350 W Hawley St 60060 847-949-2200
Dr. Kevin Myers, supt. Fax 949-0599

Mundelein ESD 75 1,700/PK-8
470 N Lake St 60060 847-949-2700
Dr. Andy Henrikson, supt. Fax 949-2727
www.district75.org
Sandburg MS 600/PK-PK, 6-
855 W Hawley St 60060 847-949-2707
Mark Pilut, prin. Fax 949-2716

---

Carmel HS 1,400/9-12
1 Carmel Pkwy 60060 847-566-3000
Mark Ostap, prin. Fax 566-8465
University of St. Mary of the Lake Post-Sec.
1000 E Maple Ave 60060 847-566-6401

**Murphysboro, Jackson, Pop. 7,754**
Alxndr/Jcksn/Pulsk/Prry/Union ROE
1001 Walnut St 62966 618-687-7290
Donna Boros, supt. Fax 687-7296
www.roe30.org
Cope Alternative S Alt
1725-B Shomaker Dr 62966 618-684-2913
Stephen Schumacher, prin.

Murphysboro CUSD 186 2,100/K-12
593 Ava Rd 62966 618-684-3781
Christopher Grode, supt. Fax 684-2465
www.cusd186.org
Murphysboro HS 600/9-12
50 Blackwood Dr 62966 618-687-2336
Tony Wilson, prin. Fax 687-3532
Murphysboro MS 500/6-8
2125 Spruce St 62966 618-684-3041
Jeff Keener, prin. Fax 687-1042

**Naperville, DuPage, Pop. 138,897**
Indian Prairie CUSD 204
Supt. — See Aurora
Crone MS 1,200/6-8
4020 111th St 60564 630-428-5600
Melissa Couch, prin. Fax 428-5601
Gregory MS 1,000/6-8
2621 Springdale Cir 60564 630-428-6300
Stephen Severson, prin. Fax 428-6301
Hill MS 900/6-8
1836 Brookdale Rd 60563 630-428-6200
Michael Dutdut, prin. Fax 428-6201
Neuqua Valley HS 4,100/9-12
2360 95th St 60564 630-428-6000
Dr. Robert McBride, prin. Fax 428-6001
Scullen MS 1,100/6-8
2815 Mistflower Ln 60564 630-428-7000
James Seput, prin. Fax 428-7001

Naperville CUSD 203 17,700/PK-12
203 W Hillside Rd 60540 630-420-6300
Dan Bridges, supt. Fax 420-1066
www.naperville203.org
Jefferson JHS 1,000/6-8
1525 N Loomis St 60563 630-420-6307
Nancy Voise, prin. Fax 420-6930
Lincoln JHS 800/6-8
1320 Olympus Dr 60565 630-420-6370
Patrick Gaskin, prin. Fax 637-4582
Madison JHS 700/6-8
1000 River Oak Dr 60565 630-420-4257
Erin Anderson, prin. Fax 420-6402
Naperville Central HS 2,900/9-12
440 Aurora Ave 60540 630-420-6420
William Wiesbrook, prin. Fax 369-6247
Naperville North HS 3,100/9-12
899 N Mill St 60563 630-420-6484
Stefanie Posey, prin. Fax 420-4255
Washington JHS 600/6-8
201 N Washington St 60540 630-420-6390
Jon Vogel, prin. Fax 420-6474
Other Schools – See Lisle

---

DeVry University Post-Sec.
2056 Westings Ave Ste 40 60563 630-428-9086
Naperville Christian Academy 50/PK-12
1451 Raymond Dr Ste 200 60563 630-637-9622
Rebecca Ruff, dir. Fax 355-1828
North Central College Post-Sec.
30 N Brainard St 60540 630-637-5100

**Nashville, Washington, Pop. 3,221**
Nashville Community HSD 99 400/9-12
1300 S Mill St 62263 618-327-8286
Ernie Fowler, supt. Fax 327-4512
www.county.washington.k12.il.us
Nashville Community HS 400/9-12
1300 S Mill St 62263 618-327-8286
Brian Pasero, prin. Fax 327-4512

**Neoga, Cumberland, Pop. 1,622**
Neoga CUSD 3 600/PK-12
PO Box 280 62447 217-895-2201
Dr. Elizabeth Pressler, supt. Fax 895-3476
www.neoga.k12.il.us
Neoga JSHS 200/6-12
PO Box 280 62447 217-895-2205
Benjamin Johnson, prin. Fax 895-3957

**Newark, Kendall, Pop. 984**
Newark CCSD 66 200/K-8
503 Chicago Rd 60541 815-695-5143
Dr. Diane Cepela, supt. Fax 695-5776
www.newarkdistrict66.org
Other Schools – See Millbrook

Newark Community HSD 18 200/9-12
413 Chicago Rd 60541 815-695-5164
Amy Smith, supt. Fax 695-5752
www.newarkhs.k12.il.us
Newark Community HS 200/9-12
413 Chicago Rd 60541 815-695-5164
Jim Still, prin. Fax 695-5752

**New Athens, Saint Clair, Pop. 2,032**
New Athens CUSD 60 500/PK-12
501 Hanft St 62264 618-475-2174
Brian Karraker, supt. Fax 475-2176
www.na60.org
New Athens HS 200/9-12
501 Hanft St 62264 618-475-2173
Dan Lehman, prin. Fax 475-2176
New Athens JHS 100/6-8
501 Hanft St 62264 618-475-2172
Jim Marlow, prin. Fax 475-2176

**New Berlin, Sangamon, Pop. 1,336**
New Berlin CUSD 16 900/PK-12
600 N Cedar St 62670 217-488-2040
Adam Ehrman, supt. Fax 488-2043
www.pretzelpride.com
New Berlin HS 200/9-12
PO Box 230 62670 217-488-6012
Hattie Doyle, prin. Fax 488-3207
New Berlin JHS 200/6-8
PO Box 230 62670 217-488-6011
Megan Doerfler, prin. Fax 488-3207

**New Lenox, Will, Pop. 24,189**
Lincoln-Way Community HSD 210 7,300/9-12
1801 E Lincoln Hwy 60451 815-462-2100
Dr. R. Scott Tingley, supt. Fax 462-2519
www.lw210.org
Lincoln-Way Central HS 2,000/9-12
1801 E Lincoln Hwy 60451 815-462-2100
Dr. Steven Provis, prin. Fax 485-7648
Lincoln Way West HS 1,300/9-12
21701 Gougar Rd 60451 815-717-3500
Dr. Monica Schmitt, prin. Fax 717-3509
Other Schools – See Frankfort

New Lenox SD 122 5,200/K-8
102 S Cedar Rd 60451 815-485-2169
Dr. Margaret Manville, supt. Fax 485-2236
www.nlsd122.org
Liberty JHS 700/7-8
151 Lenox St 60451 815-462-7951
Shane Street, prin. Fax 462-0672
Martino JHS 600/7-8
731 E Joliet Hwy 60451 815-485-7593
Dr. Bonnie Groen, prin. Fax 485-9578

---

Providence Catholic HS 1,200/9-12
1800 W Lincoln Hwy 60451 815-717-3179
Dr. John Harper, prin. Fax 485-2709

**Newton, Jasper, Pop. 2,823**
Jasper County CUSD 1 1,300/PK-12
609 S Lafayette St 62448 618-783-8459
Marilyn Holt, supt. Fax 783-3679
www.cusd1.jasper.k12.il.us
Jasper County JHS 200/7-8
1104 W Jourdan St 62448 618-783-4202
Travis Wyatt, prin. Fax 783-4257
Newton Community HS 500/9-12
201 Westend Ave 62448 618-783-2303
Beth Probst, prin. Fax 783-3783

**Niantic, Macon, Pop. 703**
Sangamon Valley CUSD 9 800/PK-12
PO Box 200 62551 217-668-2338
Ernie Fowler, supt. Fax 668-2406
www.sv.k12.il.us
Sangamon Valley HS 200/9-12
PO Box 200 62551 217-668-2392
Bob Meadows, prin. Fax 668-2406
Other Schools – See Illiopolis

**Niles, Cook, Pop. 29,272**
East Maine SD 63
Supt. — See Des Plaines
Gemini JHS 800/7-8
8955 N Greenwood Ave 60714 847-827-1181
Richard Groeling, prin. Fax 827-3499

Park Ridge-Niles CCSD 64
Supt. — See Park Ridge
Emerson MS 800/6-8
8101 N Cumberland Ave 60714 847-318-8110
Dr. Jim Morrison, prin. Fax 318-8701

---

Logos Christian Academy 200/PK-12
7280 N Caldwell Ave 60714 847-647-9456
Larry Murg, prin. Fax 647-7916
Niles School of Cosmetology Post-Sec.
8057 N Milwaukee Ave 60714 847-965-8061
Northridge Preparatory S 300/6-12
8320 W Ballard Rd 60714 847-375-0600
John Kestler, prin. Fax 375-0606
Notre Dame College Prep S 800/9-12
7655 W Dempster St 60714 847-965-2900
Daniel Tully, pres. Fax 965-2975

**Nokomis, Montgomery, Pop. 2,240**
Nokomis CUSD 22 600/PK-12
511 Oberle St 62075 217-563-7311
Dr. Scott Doerr, supt. Fax 563-2549
www.nokomis.k12.il.us
Nokomis JSHS 200/6-12
511 Oberle St 62075 217-563-2014
Eric Bruder, prin. Fax 563-2671

**Normal, McLean, Pop. 51,379**
ISU Lab SD 1,000/PK-12
ISU Campus Box 5300 61790 309-438-8542
Dr. Jeffrey Hill, supt. Fax 438-3813
www.uhigh.ilstu.edu/labschool/unitwide.html
University HS 600/9-12
ISU Campus Box 7100 61790 309-438-8542
Dr. Jeffrey Hill, prin. Fax 438-5198

McLean County Unit SD 5 13,100/PK-12
1809 Hovey Ave 61761 309-557-4000
Dr. Mark Daniel, supt. Fax 557-4501
www.unit5.org
Chiddix JHS 600/6-8
300 S Walnut St 61761 309-557-4405
Timothy Green, prin. Fax 557-4506
Field Vocational Training Center Vo/Tech
412 E Cypress St 61761 309-557-4440
Jane Collins, coord. Fax 557-4534
Kingsley JHS 900/6-8
303 Kingsley St 61761 309-557-4407
Shelly Erickson, prin. Fax 557-4508
Normal Community HS 1,900/9-12
3900 E Raab Rd 61761 309-557-4401
David Bollmann, prin. Fax 557-4502
Normal Community West HS 1,600/9-12
501 N Parkside Rd 61761 309-557-4402
David Johnson, prin. Fax 557-4503
Parkside JHS 700/6-8
101 N Parkside Rd 61761 309-557-4408
Dan Lamboley, prin. Fax 557-4509
Other Schools – See Bloomington

---

Calvary Christian Academy 300/PK-12
1017 N School St 61761 309-452-7912
Mike Sturgill, head sch Fax 451-0033
Heartland Community College Post-Sec.
1500 W Raab Rd 61761 309-268-8000
Illinois State University Post-Sec.
Campus Box 4000 61790 309-438-2111

**Norridge, Cook, Pop. 14,463**
Ridgewood Community HSD 234 800/9-12
7500 W Montrose Ave 60706 708-456-4242
Dr. Jennifer Kelsall, supt. Fax 456-8238
www.ridgenet.org
Ridgewood Community HS 800/9-12
7500 W Montrose Ave 60706 708-456-4242
John Bolger, prin. Fax 456-8238

**Norris City, White, Pop. 1,272**
Norris City-Omaha-Enfield CUSD 3 700/PK-12
PO Box 399 62869 618-378-3222
Matthew Vollman, supt. Fax 378-3286
www.ncoecusd.white.k12.il.us
Norris City-Omaha-Enfield HS 200/9-12
PO Box 399 62869 618-378-3312
Todd Haley, prin. Fax 378-3364

**North Aurora, Kane, Pop. 16,455**
Aurora West Unit SD 129
Supt. — See Aurora
Jewel MS 700/6-8
1501 Waterford Rd 60542 630-301-5010
Dr. Greg Scalia, prin. Fax 907-3161

---

Everest College Post-Sec.
150 S Lincolnway Ste 100 60542 630-896-2140

**Northbrook, Cook, Pop. 32,798**
Northbrook ESD 27 1,200/PK-8
1250 Sanders Rd 60062 847-498-2610
Dr. David Kroeze, supt. Fax 498-5916
www.nb27.org
Wood Oaks JHS 400/6-8
1250 Sanders Rd 60062 847-272-1900
Robert McElligott, prin. Fax 480-4834

Northbrook SD 28 1,700/PK-8
1475 Maple Ave 60062 847-498-7900
Dr. Larry Hewitt, supt. Fax 498-7970
www.northbrook28.net
Northbrook JHS 600/6-8
1475 Maple Ave 60062 847-498-7920
Scott Meek, prin. Fax 656-1712

Northbrook/Glenview SD 30 1,100/K-8
2374 Shermer Rd 60062 847-498-4190
Dr. Brian Wegley, supt. Fax 498-8981
www.district30.org
Maple S 400/6-8
2370 Shermer Rd 60062 847-400-8900
Dr. Nathan Carter, prin. Fax 272-0979

Northfield Township HSD 225
Supt. — See Glenview
Glenbrook North HS 2,100/9-12
2300 Shermer Rd 60062 847-509-2400
Paul Pryma, prin. Fax 509-2411

West Northfield SD 31 900/K-8
3131 Techny Rd 60062 847-272-6880
Dr. Alexandra Nicholson, supt. Fax 272-4818
www.district31.net/
Field MS 300/6-8
2055 Landwehr Rd 60062 847-272-6884
Erin Murphy, prin. Fax 272-1050

**North Chicago, Lake, Pop. 31,474**
North Chicago SD 187 3,400/PK-12
2000 Lewis Ave 60064 847-689-8150
Dr. Ben Martindale, supt. Fax 689-6328
d187.org
Neal Math Science Academy 500/6-8
1905 Argonne Dr 60064 847-689-6313
Victorene King, prin. Fax 689-6332
North Chicago Community HS 800/9-12
1717 17th St 60064 847-578-7400
Venessa Simmons-Woods, prin. Fax 689-7473

---

R. Franklin University of Medicine Post-Sec.
3333 Green Bay Rd 60064 847-578-3000

**Northfield, Cook, Pop. 5,375**
New Trier Township HSD 203 4,200/9-12
7 Happ Rd 60093 847-446-7000
Dr. Linda Yonke, supt. Fax 446-0874
www.newtrier.k12.il.us
New Trier Township HS -Northfield Campus 1,100/9-9
7 Happ Rd 60093 847-446-7000
Paul Waechtler, prin. Fax 784-7500
Other Schools – See Winnetka

Sunset Ridge SD 29 400/K-8
525 Sunset Ridge Rd 60093 847-881-9456
Dr. Edward Stange, supt.
www.sunsetridge29.net
Sunset Ridge MS 300/4-8
525 Sunset Ridge Rd 60093 847-881-9400
Dr. Shelley Carey, prin.

---

Christian Heritage Academy 500/PK-12
315 Waukegan Rd 60093 847-446-5252
Dr. David Roth Ed.D., admin. Fax 446-5267

**Northlake, Cook, Pop. 12,227**
Berkeley SD 87
Supt. — See Berkeley
Northlake MS 400/6-8
202 S Lakewood Ave 60164 708-449-3195
Dr. Sunil Mody, prin. Fax 547-2548

Leyden Community HSD 212
Supt. — See Franklin Park
West Leyden HS 1,700/9-12
1000 N Wolf Rd 60164 847-451-3154
Dr. Tatiana Bonuma, prin. Fax 451-3180

**Oak Brook, DuPage, Pop. 7,720**
Butler SD 53 400/PK-8
2801 York Rd 60523 630-573-2887
Dr. Heidi Wennstrom, supt. Fax 573-5374
www.butler53.com
Butler JHS 200/6-8
2801 York Rd 60523 630-573-2760
Amy Read, prin. Fax 573-1725

---

Hair Professionals Acad of Cosmetology Post-Sec.
1200 Harger Rd Ste 100 60523 630-653-6630
ITT Technical Institute Post-Sec.
800 Jorie Blvd Ste 100 60523 630-472-7000

**Oakbrook Terrace, DuPage, Pop. 2,106**

---

John Hancock University Post-Sec.
1 Mid America Plz Ste 130 60181 877-355-4762

**Oak Forest, Cook, Pop. 27,551**
Arbor Park SD 145 1,500/PK-8
17301 Central Ave 60452 708-687-8040
Allen Jebens, supt. Fax 687-9498
www.arbor145.org
Arbor Park MS 700/5-8
17303 Central Ave 60452 708-687-5330
Mary Beth Sexton, prin. Fax 535-4527

Bremen Community HSD 228
Supt. — See Midlothian
Oak Forest HS 1,400/9-12
15201 Central Ave 60452 708-687-0500
Brad Sikora, prin. Fax 687-0594

Forest Ridge SD 142 1,700/PK-8
15000 Laramie Ave 60452 708-687-3334
Dr. Paul McDermott, supt. Fax 687-2970
www.d142.org
Hille MS 600/6-8
5800 151st St 60452 708-687-5550
John Orth, prin. Fax 687-8569

---

Capri Beauty College Post-Sec.
15815 Rob Roy Dr 60452 708-687-3020
John Amico's School of Hair Design Post-Sec.
15301 Cicero Ave 60452 708-687-7800

**Oakland, Coles, Pop. 873**
Oakland CUSD 5 300/PK-12
310 Teeter St 61943 217-346-2555
Lance Landeck, supt. Fax 346-2267
www.oak.k12.il.us
Oakland HS 100/9-12
310 Teeter St 61943 217-346-2118
Adam Clapp, prin. Fax 346-2267

**Oak Lawn, Cook, Pop. 55,942**
Community HSD 218 5,600/9-12
10701 Kilpatrick Ave 60453 708-424-2000
Dr. Ty Harting, supt. Fax 424-6389
www.chsd218.org
Richards HS 1,700/9-12
10601 Central Ave 60453 708-499-2550
John Hallberg, prin. Fax 499-6941
Other Schools – See Blue Island, Palos Heights, Robbins

Oak Lawn Community HSD 229 1,900/9-12
9400 Southwest Hwy 60453 708-424-5200
Dr. Michael Riordan, supt. Fax 424-5297
www.olchs.org
Oak Lawn Community HS 1,900/9-12
9400 Southwest Hwy 60453 708-424-5200
Dr. Michael Riordan, prin. Fax 424-5263

Oak Lawn-Hometown SD 123 3,000/PK-8
4201 W 93rd St 60453 708-423-0150
Dr. Paul Enderle, supt. Fax 423-0160
www.d123.org/
Oak Lawn-Hometown MS 1,100/6-8
5345 W 99th St 60453 708-499-6400
Kristin Simpkins, prin. Fax 499-7684

Ridgeland SD 122 2,300/PK-8
6500 W 95th St 60453 708-599-5550
Julie Shellberg, supt. Fax 599-5626
www.ridgeland122.com
Simmons MS 700/6-8
6450 W 95th St 60453 708-599-8540
Tracy Flood, prin. Fax 599-8015

---

Cameo Beauty Academy Post-Sec.
9714 S Cicero Ave 60453 708-636-4660
Southside Baptist S 100/PK-12
5220 W 105th St 60453 708-425-3435
Robert Burckart, prin. Fax 425-9016

**Oak Park, Cook, Pop. 50,159**
Oak Park ESD 97 5,500/PK-8
970 Madison St 60302 708-524-3000
Dr. Carol Kelley, supt. Fax 524-3019
www.op97.org
Brooks MS 900/6-8
325 S Kenilworth Ave 60302 708-524-3050
LeeAndra Khan, prin. Fax 524-3036
Julian MS 900/6-8
416 S Ridgeland Ave 60302 708-524-3040
Dr. Todd Fitzgerald, prin. Fax 524-3035

Oak Park-River Forest SD 200 3,200/9-12
201 N Scoville Ave 60302 708-383-0700
Dr. Steven Isoye, supt. Fax 434-3917
www.oprfhs.org
Oak Park-River Forest HS 3,200/9-12
201 N Scoville Ave 60302 708-383-0700
Nathaniel Rouse, prin. Fax 434-3917

---

Fenwick HS 1,200/9-12
505 Washington Blvd 60302 708-386-0127
Peter Groom, prin. Fax 386-3052

**Oakwood, Vermilion, Pop. 1,576**
Oakwood CUSD 76 1,100/PK-12
12190 US Route 150 61858 217-446-6081
Gary Lewis, supt. Fax 446-6218
www.oakwood.k12.il.us
Other Schools – See Danville, Fithian

**Oblong, Crawford, Pop. 1,457**
Oblong CUSD 4 600/PK-12
PO Box 40 62449 618-592-3933
Jeffery Patchett, supt. Fax 592-3427
www.oblongschools.net
Oblong HS 200/9-12
700 S Range St 62449 618-592-4235
Jeffery Patchett, prin. Fax 592-3540

**Odin, Marion, Pop. 1,064**
Odin SD 722 300/PK-12
102 S Merritt St 62870 618-775-8266
Jeffrey Humes, supt. Fax 775-8268
www.odinpublicschools.org
Odin HS 100/9-12
102 S Merritt St 62870 618-775-8266
Sam Alli, prin. Fax 775-8268

**O Fallon, Saint Clair, Pop. 27,465**
Central SD 104 600/PK-8
309 Hartman Ln 62269 618-632-6336
John Bute, supt. Fax 632-0263
www.central104.org
Arthur MS 200/5-8
160 Saint Ellen Mine Rd 62269 618-632-6336
Jered Weh, prin. Fax 622-8691

O'Fallon CCSD 90 3,500/PK-8
118 E Washington St 62269 618-632-3666
Carrie Hruby, supt. Fax 632-7864
www.of90.net/pages/O_Fallon_C_C_School_District_9
Carriel JHS 700/6-8
450 N 7 Hills Rd 62269 618-632-3666
Ellen Hays, prin. Fax 622-2940

Fulton JHS 500/6-8
307 Kyle Rd 62269 618-628-0090
Joi Wills, prin. Fax 624-9390

O'Fallon Township HSD 203 2,500/9-12
600 S Smiley St 62269 618-632-3507
Dr. Darcy Benway, supt. Fax 632-9730
www.oths.k12.il.us/
O'Fallon HS - Milburn 600/9-9
650 Milburn School Rd 62269 618-622-9647
Richard Bickel, prin. Fax 622-9630
O'Fallon HS - Smiley 1,800/10-12
600 S Smiley St 62269 618-632-3507
Richard Bickel, prin. Fax 206-2468

---

First Baptist Academy 200/K-12
1111 E Highway 50 62269 618-726-6040
Jackye Biehl, admin. Fax 632-8029

**Oglesby, LaSalle, Pop. 3,742**
Oglesby ESD 125 600/PK-8
755 Bennett Ave 61348 815-883-9297
Michael Pillion, supt. Fax 883-3568
www.ops125.net
Washington MS 200/6-8
212 W Walnut St 61348 815-883-3517
Cindy Pozzi, prin. Fax 883-9282

---

Illinois Valley Community College Post-Sec.
815 N Orlando Smith St 61348 815-224-2720

**Ohio, Bureau, Pop. 504**
Ohio Community HSD 505 50/9-12
PO Box 478 61349 815-376-4414
Sharon Sweger, supt. Fax 376-2102
www.bhsroe.org
Ohio Community HS 50/9-12
PO Box 478 61349 815-376-4414
Jason Wilt, prin. Fax 376-2102

**Okawville, Washington, Pop. 1,424**
West Washington County CUSD 10 500/K-12
PO Box 27 62271 618-243-6454
Scott Fuhrhop, supt. Fax 243-6454
www.okawville-k12.org
Okawville JSHS 300/7-12
400 S Hanover St 62271 618-243-5201
Mike Rumsey, prin. Fax 243-6110

**Olney, Richland, Pop. 9,020**
Richland County CUSD 1 2,100/PK-12
1100 E Laurel St 62450 618-395-2324
Larry Bussard, supt. Fax 392-4147
www.ercu1.net
Richland County HS 600/9-12
1200 E Laurel St 62450 618-393-2191
Chad LeCrone, prin. Fax 395-1256
Richland County MS 400/6-8
1099 N Van St 62450 618-395-4372
Cris Edwards, prin. Fax 392-3399

---

Olney Central College Post-Sec.
305 N West St 62450 618-395-7777

**Olympia Fields, Cook, Pop. 4,901**
Rich Township HSD 227 3,900/9-12
20550 S Cicero Ave 60461 708-679-5800
Ronald Patton, supt. Fax 679-5740
www.rich227.org
Rich Central HS 1,500/9-12
3600 W 203rd St 60461 708-679-5600
Venesa Woods, prin. Fax 679-5632
Other Schools – See Park Forest, Richton Park

**Onarga, Iroquois, Pop. 1,354**
Iroquois West CUSD 10
Supt. — See Gilman
Iroquois West MS 200/6-8
303 N Evergreen St 60955 815-268-4355
Duane Ehmen, prin. Fax 268-7608

**Oneida, Knox, Pop. 697**
ROWVA CUSD 208 700/PK-12
PO Box 69 61467 309-483-3711
Joe Sornberger, supt. Fax 483-6123
www.rowva.k12.il.us
ROWVA HS 200/9-12
PO Box 69 61467 309-483-6371
Joe Peters, prin. Fax 483-8223
ROWVA JHS 100/7-8
PO Box 69 61467 309-483-6376
N. Hroziencik, prin. Fax 483-6378

**Orangeville, Stephenson, Pop. 784**
Orangeville CUSD 203 400/PK-12
201 S Orange St 61060 815-789-4289
Dr. Doug DeSchepper, supt. Fax 789-4709
www.orangevillecusd.com/
Orangeville HS 100/9-12
201 S Orange St 61060 815-789-4289
Andrew Janecke, prin. Fax 789-4709
Orangeville JHS 100/6-8
201 S Orange St 61060 815-789-4289
Andrew Janecke, prin. Fax 789-4709

**Oregon, Ogle, Pop. 3,686**
Oregon CUSD 220 1,500/PK-12
206 S 10th St 61061 815-732-5300
Thomas Mahoney, supt. Fax 732-2187
www.ocusd.net
Oregon HS 500/9-12
210 S 10th St 61061 815-732-5300
Andrew Nelson, prin. Fax 732-3361
Other Schools – See Mount Morris

**Orion, Henry, Pop. 1,846**
Orion CUSD 223 1,100/PK-12
PO Box 189 61273 309-526-3388
David Deets, supt. Fax 526-3711
orionschools.us/

Orion HS 300/9-12
PO Box 39 61273 309-526-3361
Nathan DeBaillie, prin. Fax 526-3854
Orion MS 200/6-8
PO Box 129 61273 309-526-3392
Scott Briney, prin. Fax 526-3872

**Orland Hills, Cook, Pop. 7,042**
Consolidated HSD 230
Supt. — See Orland Park
Andrew HS 2,200/9-12
9001 171st St, 708-342-5800
Robert Nolting, prin. Fax 532-7383

**Orland Park, Cook, Pop. 56,112**
Consolidated HSD 230 8,200/9-12
15100 S 94th Ave 60462 708-745-5203
Dr. James Gay, supt. Fax 349-2105
www.d230.org
Sandburg HS 3,500/9-12
13300 S La Grange Rd 60462 708-671-3100
Deborah Baker, prin. Fax 361-9714
Other Schools – See Orland Hills, Palos Hills

Orland SD 135 5,100/K-8
15100 S 94th Ave 60462 708-364-3306
Dr. Janet Stutz, supt. Fax 873-6479
www.orland135.org
Century JHS 800/6-8
10801 W 159th St 60467 708-364-3500
Brian Horn, prin. Fax 349-5840
Jerling JHS 600/6-8
8851 W 151st St 60462 708-364-3700
Kevin Brown, prin. Fax 873-6457
Orland JHS 500/6-8
14855 West Ave 60462 708-364-4200
Linda Kane, prin. Fax 349-5843

---

ITT Technical Institute Post-Sec.
11551 184th Pl 60467 708-326-3200
Robert Morris University Post-Sec.
43 Orland Square Dr 60462 800-762-5960

**Oswego, Kendall, Pop. 29,822**
CUSD 308 17,000/PK-12
4175 State Route 71 60543 630-636-3080
Dr. Matthew Wendt, supt. Fax 636-3688
www.sd308.org
Oswego East HS 2,000/9-12
1525 Harvey Rd 60543 630-636-2200
Scott Savage, prin. Fax 636-2454
Oswego HS 2,400/9-12
4250 State Route 71 60543 630-636-2000
Mike Wayne, prin. Fax 636-2199
Plank JHS 900/6-8
510 Secretariat Ln 60543 630-551-9400
James Martin, prin. Fax 551-9691
Thompson JHS 900/6-8
440 Boulder Hill Pass 60543 630-636-2600
Shannon Leuders, prin. Fax 636-2691
Traughber JHS 1,000/6-8
570 Colchester Dr 60543 630-636-2700
Tarah Fowler, prin. Fax 636-2791
Other Schools – See Aurora, Plainfield

---

Hair Professionals School of Cosmetology Post-Sec.
PO Box 40 60543 630-554-2266

**Ottawa, LaSalle, Pop. 18,544**
Ottawa ESD 141 2,100/PK-8
320 W Main St 61350 815-433-1133
Cleve Threadgill, supt. Fax 433-1888
www.oes141.org
Shepherd MS 400/7-8
701 E McKinley Rd 61350 815-434-7925
Lori Kimes, prin. Fax 433-9447

Ottawa Township HSD 140 1,400/9-12
211 E Main St 61350 815-433-1323
Michael Cushing, supt. Fax 433-1338
www.ottawahigh.com
Ottawa Township HS 1,400/9-12
211 E Main St 61350 815-433-1323
Mike Cushing, prin. Fax 433-1338

---

Marquette Academy 400/K-12
1000 Paul St 61350 815-433-0125
Brooke Rick, prin. Fax 433-2632

**Palatine, Cook, Pop. 67,495**
Palatine CCSD 15 12,400/PK-8
580 N 1st Bank Dr 60067 847-963-3000
Scott Thompson Ed.D., supt. Fax 963-3200
www.ccsd15.net
Sundling JHS 700/7-8
1100 N Smith St 60067 847-963-3700
Jason Dietz, prin. Fax 963-3706
Winston Campus JHS 700/7-8
120 N Babcock Dr 60074 847-963-7400
Matt Warren, prin. Fax 963-7508
Other Schools – See Rolling Meadows

Township HSD 211 12,500/9-12
1750 S Roselle Rd 60067 847-755-6600
Dr. Daniel Cates, supt. Fax 755-6810
adc.d211.org
District 211 Academy - North 50/Alt
335 E Illinois Ave 60067 847-755-6700
Francesca Anderson, admin. Fax 755-6858
Fremd HS 2,800/9-12
1000 S Quentin Rd 60067 847-755-2600
Dr. Kurt Tenopir, prin. Fax 755-2623
Palatine HS 2,800/9-12
1111 N Rohlwing Rd 60074 847-755-1600
Gary Steiger, prin. Fax 755-1623
Other Schools – See Hoffman Estates, Schaumburg

---

William Rainey Harper College Post-Sec.
1200 W Algonquin Rd 60067 847-925-6000

**Palestine, Crawford, Pop. 1,359**
Palestine CUSD 3 400/PK-12
100 S Main St 62451 618-586-2713
Chris Long, supt. Fax 586-2905
www.palestine-pioneers.net
Palestine HS 100/9-12
102 N Main St 62451 618-586-2712
Tangi Waldrop, dean Fax 586-5328

**Palmyra, Macoupin, Pop. 692**
Northwestern CUSD 2 300/PK-12
30953 Route 111 62674 217-436-2210
Patrick Bowman, supt. Fax 436-2701
www.northwestern.k12.il.us
Northwestern HS 100/9-12
30889 Route 111 62674 217-436-2011
Brandi Maxedon, prin. Fax 436-9112
Northwestern JHS 100/7-8
30889 Route 111 62674 217-436-2011
Brandi Maxedon, prin. Fax 436-9112

**Palos Heights, Cook, Pop. 12,393**
Community HSD 218
Supt. — See Oak Lawn
Shepard HS 1,900/9-12
13049 S Ridgeland Ave 60463 708-371-1111
Dr. Josh Barron, prin. Fax 371-7688

Palos Heights SD 128 800/PK-8
12809 S McVickers Ave 60463 708-597-9040
Dr. Dawn Green, supt. Fax 597-9089
www.palos128.org
Independence JHS 300/6-8
6610 W Highland Dr 60463 708-448-0737
Kevin Kirk, prin. Fax 448-0179

---

Chicago Christian HS 400/9-12
12001 S Oak Park Ave 60463 708-388-7650
Sue Tameling, prin. Fax 388-0154
Trinity Christian College Post-Sec.
6601 W College Dr 60463 708-597-3000

**Palos Hills, Cook, Pop. 17,273**
Consolidated HSD 230
Supt. — See Orland Park
Stagg HS 2,500/9-12
8015 W 111th St 60465 708-974-7400
Eric Olsen, prin. Fax 974-0803

North Palos SD 117 3,000/PK-8
7825 W 103rd St 60465 708-598-5500
Dr. Jeannie Stachowiak, supt. Fax 598-5539
www.npd117.net/
Other Schools – See Hickory Hills

---

Hair Professionals Career College Post-Sec.
10321 S Roberts Rd 60465 708-430-1755
Moraine Valley Community College Post-Sec.
9000 W College Pkwy 60465 708-974-4300

**Palos Park, Cook, Pop. 4,788**
Palos CCSD 118 1,900/PK-8
8800 W 119th St 60464 708-448-4800
Dr. Anthony Scarsella, supt. Fax 448-4880
www.palos118.org
Palos South MS 700/6-8
13100 S 82nd Ave 60464 708-448-5971
Stuart Wrzesinski, prin. Fax 448-0754

**Pana, Christian, Pop. 5,807**
Pana CUSD 8 1,400/PK-12
PO Box 377 62557 217-562-1500
Dr. David Lett, supt. Fax 562-1501
www.panaschools.com
Pana HS 500/9-12
PO Box 377 62557 217-562-6600
Gayle McRoberts, prin. Fax 562-6714
Pana JHS 200/6-8
PO Box 377 62557 217-562-6500
Paul Lauff, prin. Fax 562-6712

**Paris, Edgar, Pop. 8,761**
Paris CUSD 4 500/PK-8
15601 US Highway 150 61944 217-465-5391
Lorraine Bailey, supt. Fax 466-1225
www.crestwood.k12.il.us
Crestwood JHS 200/6-8
15601 US Highway 150 61944 217-465-5391
Danette Young, prin. Fax 466-1225

Paris-Union SD 95 1,600/PK-12
300 S Eads Ave 61944 217-465-8448
Connie Sutton, supt. Fax 463-2243
www.paris95.k12.il.us
Mayo MS 300/6-8
310 E Wood St 61944 217-466-3050
Jeremy Larson, prin. Fax 466-3905
Paris Cooperative HS 600/9-12
14040 E 1200th Rd 61944 217-466-1175
Dave Meister, dir. Fax 466-1903

**Park Forest, Cook, Pop. 21,337**
Park Forest SD 163 1,700/PK-8
242 S Orchard Dr 60466 708-668-9400
Dr. Joyce Carmine, supt. Fax 748-9359
www.sd163.com
Obama S of Technology and the Arts 400/4-8
215 Wilson St 60466 708-668-9600
Cheryl Muench, prin. Fax 503-2297
Other Schools – See Chicago Heights

Rich Township HSD 227
Supt. — See Olympia Fields
Rich East Campus HS 1,200/9-12
300 Sauk Trl 60466 708-679-6100
Mark Kramer, prin. Fax 679-7330

**Park Ridge, Cook, Pop. 37,078**
Maine Township HSD 207 5,000/9-12
1177 S Dee Rd 60068 847-696-3600
Dr. Kenneth Wallace, supt. Fax 696-3254
www.maine207.org

Frost Academy 50/Alt
1177 S Dee Rd 60068 847-292-6521
Edward Pieczynski, dir. Fax 692-8132
Maine East HS 1,400/9-12
2601 Dempster St 60068 847-825-4484
Dr. Michael Pressler, prin. Fax 825-1636
Maine South HS 1,900/9-12
1111 S Dee Rd 60068 847-825-7711
Shawn Messmer, prin. Fax 825-0677
Other Schools – See Des Plaines

Park Ridge-Niles CCSD 64 4,300/PK-8
164 S Prospect Ave 60068 847-318-4300
Dr. Laurie Heinz, supt. Fax 318-4351
www.d64.org
Lincoln MS 700/6-8
200 S Lincoln Ave 60068 847-318-4215
Dr. Anthony Murray, prin. Fax 318-4210
Other Schools – See Niles

**Patoka, Marion, Pop. 584**
Patoka CUSD 100 300/PK-12
1220 Kinoka Rd 62875 618-432-5440
David Rademacher, supt. Fax 432-5306
pcusd100.sharpschool.net
Patoka HS 100/9-12
1220 Kinoka Rd 62875 618-432-5440
Bryan Rainey, prin. Fax 432-5306
Patoka JHS 50/7-8
1220 Kinoka Rd 62875 618-432-5200
Bryan Rainey, prin. Fax 432-5306

**Pawnee, Sangamon, Pop. 2,672**
Pawnee CUSD 11 500/PK-12
810 4th St 62558 217-625-2471
Gary Alexander, supt. Fax 625-2251
www.pawneeschools.com/
Pawnee JSHS 200/7-12
810 4th St 62558 217-625-2471
Tim Kratochvil, prin. Fax 625-2251

**Paw Paw, Lee, Pop. 862**
Paw Paw CUSD 271 300/K-12
PO Box 508 61353 815-627-2841
Stan Adcock, supt. Fax 627-2971
www.2paws.net
Paw Paw JSHS 100/7-12
PO Box 37 61353 815-627-2671
Chuck Schneider, prin. Fax 627-8481

**Paxton, Ford, Pop. 4,437**
Paxton-Buckley-Loda CUSD 10 1,500/PK-12
PO Box 50 60957 217-379-3314
Clifford McClure, supt. Fax 379-2862
pblunit10.com
Paxton-Buckley-Loda HS 400/9-12
PO Box 50 60957 217-379-4331
Travis Duley, prin. Fax 379-2491
Paxton-Buckley-Loda JHS 300/6-8
PO Box 50 60957 217-379-9202
Josh Didier, prin. Fax 379-9169

**Payson, Adams, Pop. 1,023**
Payson CUSD 1 500/PK-12
406 W State St 62360 217-656-3323
Donna Veile, supt. Fax 656-4042
www.cusd1.org
Seymour JSHS 200/7-12
420 W Brainard St 62360 217-656-3355
Dawn VanCamp, prin. Fax 656-3584

**Pearl City, Stephenson, Pop. 832**
Pearl City CUSD 200 500/PK-12
PO Box 9 61062 815-443-2715
Timothy Thill, supt. Fax 443-2237
www.pcwolves.net/
Pearl City HS 200/9-12
PO Box 9 61062 815-443-2715
Kelly Mandrell, prin. Fax 443-2237
Pearl City JHS 100/7-8
PO Box 9 61062 815-443-2715
Kelly Mandrell, prin. Fax 443-2237

**Pecatonica, Winnebago, Pop. 2,172**
Pecatonica CUSD 321 1,000/PK-12
PO Box 419 61063 815-239-1639
William Faller, supt. Fax 239-2125
www.pecschools.com/
Pecatonica Community MS 300/5-8
PO Box 419 61063 815-239-2612
Timothy King, prin. Fax 239-1274
Pecatonica HS 300/9-12
PO Box 419 61063 815-239-2611
Todd France, prin. Fax 239-9128

**Pekin, Tazewell, Pop. 33,678**
Mason-Tazewell-Woodford ROE
414 Court St Ste 100 61554 309-477-2290
Gail Owen, supt. Fax 347-3735
www.roe53.net
Other Schools – See Creve Coeur

Pekin Community HSD 303 2,000/9-12
320 Stadium Dr 61554 309-477-4222
Dr. Danielle Owens, supt. Fax 477-4376
www.pekinhigh.net
Pekin Community HS 2,000/9-12
1903 Court St 61554 309-347-4101
Amy Hubner, prin. Fax 477-4377

Pekin SD 108 3,800/PK-8
501 Washington St 61554 309-477-4700
Dr. Bill Link, supt. Fax 477-4701
www.pekin.net
Broadmoor JHS 400/7-8
501 Maywood Ave 61554 309-477-4731
Ty Goss, prin. Fax 477-4739
Edison JHS 400/7-8
1400 Earl St 61554 309-477-4732
Bill Heisel, prin. Fax 477-4738

---

Faith Baptist Christian S — 100/PK-12
1501 Howard Ct 61554 — 309-347-6178
Ken Seest, prin. — Fax 347-8716

**Peoria, Peoria, Pop. 111,234**
Dunlap CUSD 323 — 3,700/PK-12
3020 W Willow Knolls Dr 61614 — 309-691-3955
Dr. Lisa Parker, supt. — Fax 691-6764
www.dunlapcusd.net
Other Schools – See Dunlap

Norwood ESD 63 — 500/PK-8
6521 W Farmington Rd 61604 — 309-676-3523
David Black, supt. — Fax 676-6099
www.norwood63.org
Norwood MS — 200/5-8
6521 W Farmington Rd 61604 — 309-676-3683
Joel Kilgus, prin. — Fax 676-6099

Peoria SD 150 — 12,900/PK-12
3202 N Wisconsin Ave 61603 — 309-672-6768
Sharon Desmoulin-Kherat, supt. — Fax 672-6708
www.psd150.org
Bills MS — 200/5-8
6001 N Frostwood Pkwy 61615 — 309-693-4437
Laura Rodgers, prin. — Fax 693-4438
Knoxville Center for Student Success — 100/Alt
2628 N Knoxville Ave 61604 — 309-439-0000
Eric Thomas, prin. — Fax 282-0007
Lindbergh MS — 300/5-8
6327 N Sheridan Rd 61614 — 309-693-4427
Susan Malahy, prin. — Fax 693-0499
Manual Academy — 1,100/8-12
811 S Griswold St 61605 — 309-672-6600
Heather Young, prin. — Fax 672-6605
Peoria HS — 1,300/9-12
1615 N North St 61604 — 309-672-6630
Brett Elliott, prin. — Fax 685-5803
Richwoods HS — 1,500/9-12
6301 N University St 61614 — 309-693-4400
Cindy Clark, prin. — Fax 693-4414
Rolling Acres MS — 300/5-8
5617 N Merrimac Ave 61614 — 309-689-1100
Michael Barber, prin. — Fax 693-4423
Sterling MS — 300/5-8
2315 N Sterling Ave 61604 — 309-672-6557
Joe Gallo, prin. — Fax 681-8286
Von Steuben MS — 300/5-8
801 E Forrest Hill Ave 61603 — 309-672-6561
Denise Smith, prin. — Fax 685-7631
Washington Gifted MS — 300/5-8
3706 N Grand Blvd 61614 — 309-672-6563
David Poehls, prin. — Fax 672-6564
Woodruff Career & Technical Center — Vo/Tech
1800 NE Perry Ave 61603 — 309-672-6665
Thomas Blumer, prin. — Fax 282-5260
Other Schools – See West Peoria

Pleasant Valley SD 62 — 500/PK-8
3314 W Richwoods Blvd 61604 — 309-679-0634
Dr. Allen Johnson, supt. — Fax 674-0165
www.pv62.com
Pleasant Valley MS — 300/PK-K, 5-8
3314 W Richwoods Blvd 61604 — 309-679-0634
Dr. Allen Johnson, admin. — Fax 679-0652

---

Bradley University — Post-Sec.
1501 W Bradley Ave 61625 — 309-676-7611
Daarul Uloom Islamic S — 200/PK-10
4125 W Charter Oak Rd 61615 — 309-691-9089
Mona Rustom, prin.
Methodist College — Post-Sec.
415 NE Saint Mark Ct 61603 — 309-672-5513
Midstate College — Post-Sec.
411 W Northmoor Rd 61614 — 309-692-4092
Peoria Christian S — 900/PK-12
3506 N California Ave 61603 — 309-686-4500
Becky Gardner, admin. — Fax 686-2569
Peoria Notre Dame HS — 800/9-12
5105 N Sheridan Rd 61614 — 309-691-8741
Randy Simmons, prin. — Fax 691-0875
Robert Morris University — Post-Sec.
211 Fulton St 61602 — 800-762-5960
St. Francis Medical Center — Post-Sec.
530 NE Glen Oak Ave 61637 — 309-655-2000
St. Francis Medical Ctr. Coll./Nursing — Post-Sec.
511 NE Greenleaf St 61603 — 309-655-2201

**Peoria Heights, Peoria, Pop. 5,986**
Peoria Heights CUSD 325 — 800/PK-12
500 E Glen Ave 61616 — 309-686-8800
Eric Heath, supt. — Fax 686-8801
www.phcusd325.net
Peoria Heights HS — 200/9-12
508 E Glen Ave 61616 — 309-686-8803
Joseph Stoner, prin. — Fax 686-8808

---

Peoria Christian S - Monroe — 300/5-8
3725 N Monroe Ave 61616 — 309-681-0500
Thomas Schlich, prin. — Fax 807-3353

**Peotone, Will, Pop. 4,103**
Peotone CUSD 207U — 1,600/PK-12
212 W Wilson St 60468 — 708-258-0991
Steve Stein, supt. — Fax 258-0994
www.peotoneschools.org
Peotone HS — 700/9-12
605 W North St 60468 — 708-258-3236
Tyler Hesh, prin. — Fax 258-6991
Peotone JHS — 500/6-8
1 Blue Devil Dr 60468 — 708-258-3246
Scott Wenzel, prin. — Fax 258-6669

**Perry, Pike, Pop. 397**
Griggsville-Perry CUSD 4
Supt. — See Griggsville
Griggsville-Perry MS — 100/5-8
PO Box 98 62362 — 217-236-9161
Pollee Craven, prin. — Fax 236-7221

**Peru, LaSalle, Pop. 10,189**
Peru ESD 124 — 1,000/PK-8
1800 Church St 61354 — 815-223-0486
Mark Cross, supt. — Fax 223-0490
www.perued.net
Parkside MS — 500/5-8
1800 Church St 61354 — 815-223-7723
Lori Madden, prin. — Fax 223-0285

---

St. Bede Academy — 300/9-12
24 W US Highway 6 61354 — 815-223-3140
Michelle Mershon, prin. — Fax 223-8580

**Petersburg, Menard, Pop. 2,232**
PORTA CUSD 202 — 1,200/PK-12
PO Box 202 62675 — 217-632-3803
Matthew Brue, supt. — Fax 632-3221
www.porta202.org
PORTA HS — 400/9-12
PO Box 202 62675 — 217-632-3216
Darren Hartry, prin. — Fax 632-5446
PORTA JHS — 200/7-8
PO Box 202 62675 — 217-632-3219
Amy McMahan, prin. — Fax 632-5448

**Phoenix, Cook, Pop. 1,934**
South Holland SD 151
Supt. — See South Holland
Coolidge MS — 500/6-8
15500 7th Ave 60426 — 708-339-5300
Patricia Payne, prin. — Fax 339-5327

**Piasa, Macoupin**
Southwestern CUSD 9
Supt. — See Brighton
Southwestern HS — 500/9-12
PO Box 100 62079 — 618-729-3211
Mark Bearley, prin. — Fax 729-4276
Southwestern MS — 300/7-8
PO Box 70 62079 — 618-729-3217
Scott Hopkins, prin. — Fax 729-9231

**Pinckneyville, Perry, Pop. 5,604**
Pinckneyville Community HSD 101 — 400/9-12
600 E Water St 62274 — 618-357-5013
Keith Hagene, supt. — Fax 357-6045
www.pchspanthers.com
Pinckneyville Community HS — 400/9-12
600 E Water St 62274 — 618-357-5013
Dustin Foutch, prin. — Fax 357-6045

Pinckneyville SD 50 — 600/PK-8
301 W Mulberry St 62274 — 618-357-9096
Tim O'Leary, supt. — Fax 357-8731
www.p50.perry.k12.il.us
Pinckneyville MS — 300/5-8
700 E Water St 62274 — 618-357-2724
Mark Rohlfing, prin.

**Piper City, Ford, Pop. 823**
Tri-Point CUSD 6-J
Supt. — See Kempton
Tri-Point MS — 200/K-K, 4-8
PO Box 158 60959 — 815-686-2247
Jay Bennett, prin. — Fax 686-2663

**Pittsfield, Pike, Pop. 4,559**
Pikeland CUSD 10 — 1,300/PK-12
512 S Madison St 62363 — 217-285-2147
Paula Hawley, supt. — Fax 285-5059
www.pikeland.net
Pikeland Community S — 600/3-8
601 Piper Ln 62363 — 217-285-9462
Lisa Jockisch, prin. — Fax 285-9551
Pittsfield HS — 400/9-12
201 E Higbee St 62363 — 217-285-6888
Angie Greger, prin. — Fax 285-9583

**Plainfield, Will, Pop. 38,856**
CUSD 308
Supt. — See Oswego
Murphy JHS — 6-8
26923 W Grande Park Blvd, — 630-608-5100
Brent Anderson, prin. — Fax 608-5191

Plainfield CCSD 202 — 28,800/PK-12
15732 S Howard St 60544 — 815-577-4000
Dr. Ronald Abrell, supt. — Fax 436-7824
www.psd202.org
Drauden Point MS — 1,000/6-8
1911 Drauden Rd, — 815-577-4900
Patrick Flynn, prin. — Fax 439-9385
Heritage Grove MS — 900/6-8
12425 S Van Dyke Rd, — 815-439-4810
Shannon Miller, prin. — Fax 436-4661
Indian Trail MS — 800/6-8
14723 S Eastern Ave 60544 — 815-436-6128
Christian Rivara, prin. — Fax 436-7536
Jones MS — 900/6-8
15320 W Wallin Dr 60544 — 815-267-3600
Thomas Novinski, prin. — Fax 439-7201
Kennedy MS — 1,200/6-8
12350 Essington Rd, — 815-439-8024
Amandeep Hundal, prin. — Fax 254-7375
Plainfield Academy — 200/Alt
23930 W Lockport St 60544 — 815-439-5521
Tod Schnowske, prin. — Fax 439-7014
Plainfield Central HS — 2,200/9-12
24120 W Fort Beggs Dr 60544 — 815-436-3200
Robert Smith, prin. — Fax 439-2882
Plainfield East HS — 1,900/9-12
12001 Naperville Rd, — 815-577-0324
Anthony Manville, prin. — Fax 577-0979
Plainfield North HS — 2,000/9-12
12005 S 248th Ave, — 815-609-8506
Raymond Epperson, prin. — Fax 254-6138
Plainfield South HS — 2,400/9-12
7800 Caton Farm Rd, — 815-439-5555
Robert Yanello, prin. — Fax 436-5108
Timber Ridge MS — 1,000/6-8
2101 S Bronk Rd, — 815-439-3410
Dean Kariotakis, prin. — Fax 439-3412

Other Schools – See Joliet

Troy CCSD 30C — 4,500/PK-8
5800 Theodore Dr, — 815-577-6760
Todd Koehl Ph.D., supt. — Fax 577-3795
troywebs.troy30c.org
Troy MS — 900/7-8
5800 Theodore Dr, — 815-230-9920
Renee Marski, prin. — Fax 577-2867

**Plano, Kendall, Pop. 10,709**
Plano CUSD 88 — 2,300/PK-12
800 S Hale St 60545 — 630-552-8978
Dr. Hector Garcia, supt. — Fax 552-8548
www.plano88.org/
Plano HS — 600/9-12
704 W Abe St 60545 — 630-552-3178
Eric Benson, prin. — Fax 552-8824
Plano MS — 300/7-8
804 S Hale St 60545 — 630-552-3608
Mark Heller, prin. — Fax 552-3802

**Pleasant Hill, Pike, Pop. 964**
Pleasant Hill CUSD 3 — 300/PK-12
PO Box 277 62366 — 217-734-2311
Ron Edwards, supt. — Fax 734-2629
www.phwolves.com
Pleasant Hill HS — 100/9-12
PO Box 277 62366 — 217-734-2311
Ron Edwards, prin. — Fax 734-2725

**Pleasant Plains, Sangamon, Pop. 790**
Pleasant Plains CUSD 8 — 1,300/PK-12
PO Box 20 62677 — 217-626-1041
Matt Runge, supt. — Fax 626-1082
www.ppcusd8.org
Pleasant Plains HS — 500/9-12
PO Box 320 62677 — 217-626-1044
Luke Brooks, prin. — Fax 626-1667
Pleasant Plains MS — 400/5-8
2455 N Farmingdale Rd 62677 — 217-626-1061
Ben Theilen, prin. — Fax 626-2272

**Polo, Ogle, Pop. 2,326**
Polo CUSD 222 — 700/PK-12
100 S Union Ave 61064 — 815-946-3815
Christopher Rademacher, supt. — Fax 946-2493
www.polo222.org/
Aplington MS — 100/6-8
610 E Mason St 61064 — 815-946-2519
Mark Downey, prin. — Fax 946-2537
Polo Community HS — 200/9-12
100 S Union Ave 61064 — 815-946-3314
Andy Faivre, prin. — Fax 946-2493

**Pontiac, Livingston, Pop. 11,777**
Livingston Area Career Center
1100 E Indiana Ave 61764 — 815-842-2557
Tera Graves, dir. — Fax 842-1005
www.lacc.k12.il.us
Livingston Area Career Center — Vo/Tech
1100 E Indiana Ave 61764 — 815-842-2557
Tera Graves, dir. — Fax 842-1005

Pontiac CCSD 429 — 1,300/PK-8
117 W Livingston St 61764 — 815-842-1533
Brian Dukes, supt. — Fax 844-5773
www.pontiac429.org
Pontiac JHS — 400/6-8
600 N Morrow St 61764 — 815-842-4343
Brian Hensley, prin. — Fax 844-6230

Pontiac Township HSD 90 — 800/9-12
1100 E Indiana Ave 61764 — 815-844-6113
Jon Kilgore, supt. — Fax 844-6116
www.pontiac90.org
Pontiac HS — 800/9-12
1100 E Indiana Ave 61764 — 815-844-6113
Eric Bohm, prin. — Fax 844-6116

**Poplar Grove, Boone, Pop. 4,959**
North Boone CUSD 200 — 1,700/K-12
6248 N Boone School Rd 61065 — 815-765-3322
Dr. Ted Rehl, supt. — Fax 765-2053
www.nbcusd.org
North Boone HS — 500/9-12
17823 Poplar Grove Rd 61065 — 815-765-3311
Jacob Hubert, prin. — Fax 765-3316
North Boone MS — 300/7-8
17641 Poplar Grove Rd 61065 — 815-765-9274
Jamison Pearce, prin. — Fax 765-9275

**Port Byron, Rock Island, Pop. 1,628**
Riverdale CUSD 100 — 1,200/PK-12
9624 256th St N 61275 — 309-523-3184
Ronald Jacobs, supt. — Fax 523-3550
riverdaleschools.org
Riverdale HS — 300/9-12
9622 256th St N 61275 — 309-523-3181
Rick Dwyer, prin. — Fax 523-2885
Riverdale MS — 200/6-8
9822 256th St N 61275 — 309-523-3131
James Jennings, prin. — Fax 523-3934

**Posen, Cook, Pop. 5,912**
Posen-Robbins ESD 143-5 — 1,700/PK-8
14025 S Harrison Ave 60469 — 708-388-7200
Dr. Anthony Edison Ed.D., supt. — Fax 388-3868
www.prsd1435.org
Other Schools – See Robbins

**Princeton, Bureau, Pop. 7,583**
Princeton ESD 115 — 800/PK-8
506 E Dover Rd 61356 — 815-875-3162
Tim Smith, supt. — Fax 875-3101
www.princeton115schools.org
Logan JHS — 400/5-8
302 W Central Ave 61356 — 815-875-6415
Amanda Carr, prin. — Fax 872-0034

Princeton HSD 500 600/9-12
103 S Euclid Ave 61356 815-875-3308
Kirk Haring, supt. Fax 875-8525
www.phs-il.org
Princeton HS 600/9-12
103 S Euclid Ave 61356 815-875-3308
Andy Berlinski, prin. Fax 875-8525

**Princeville, Peoria, Pop. 1,723**
Princeville CUSD 326 800/PK-12
909 N Town Ave 61559 309-385-2213
Shannon Duling, supt. Fax 385-1823
www.princeville326.org/
Princeville HS 200/9-12
302 Cordis Ave 61559 309-385-4660
Richard Thole, prin. Fax 385-1110

**Prophetstown, Whiteside, Pop. 2,069**
Prophetstown-Lyndon-Tampico CUSD 3 800/PK-12
79 Grove St 61277 815-537-5101
Dave Rogers, supt. Fax 537-5102
plt3.org
PLT MS 200/6-8
38 Ferry St 61277 815-537-5084
Chad Colmone, prin. Fax 537-5085
Prophetstown HS 300/9-12
310 W Riverside Dr 61277 815-537-5161
Josh Johnson, prin. Fax 537-5102

**Prospect Heights, Cook, Pop. 16,131**
Prospect Heights SD 23 1,500/PK-8
700 N Schoenbeck Rd 60070 847-870-3850
Dr. Deb Wilson, supt. Fax 870-3896
www.d23.org/
MacArthur MS 500/6-8
700 N Schoenbeck Rd 60070 847-870-3879
Steven Lee, prin. Fax 870-3881

**Quincy, Adams, Pop. 39,738**
Quincy Area Vocational Technical Center
219 Baldwin Dr 62301 217-224-3775
Mark Pfleiger, dir. Fax 221-4800
www.qps.org/qavtc/
Quincy Area Vocational Technical Center Vo/Tech
219 Baldwin Dr 62301 217-224-3775
Mark Pfleiger, dir. Fax 221-4800

Quincy SD 172 7,100/PK-12
1416 Maine St 62301 217-223-8700
Dr. Calvin Lee, supt. Fax 228-7162
www.qps.org
Quincy JHS 1,400/7-9
100 S 14th St 62301 217-222-3073
Dan Sparrow, prin. Fax 228-7185
Quincy SHS 1,400/10-12
3322 Maine St 62301 217-224-3770
Danielle Edgar, prin. Fax 228-7149

---

Blessing Hospital Post-Sec.
PO Box 7005 62305 217-223-8400
Blessing-Rieman College of Nursing Post-Sec.
PO Box 7005 62305 217-228-5520
Gem City College Post-Sec.
700 State St 62301 217-222-0391
John Wood Community College Post-Sec.
1301 S 48th St 62305 217-224-6500
Quincy Christian S 100/PK-12
PO Box 3643 62305 217-223-5698
Ryan Norsworthy, pres. Fax 223-5724
Quincy Notre Dame HS 400/9-12
1400 S 11th St 62301 217-223-2479
Mark McDowell, prin. Fax 223-0023
Quincy University Post-Sec.
1800 College Ave 62301 217-222-8020
Vatterott College Post-Sec.
3609 N Marx Dr 62305 217-224-0600

**Ramsey, Fayette, Pop. 1,024**
Ramsey CUSD 204 500/PK-12
702 W 6th St 62080 618-423-2335
Melissa Ritter, supt. Fax 423-2314
www.ramsey.fayette.k12.il.us
Ramsey HS 100/9-12
702 W 6th St 62080 618-423-2333
Ginger Edwards, prin. Fax 423-2314

**Rantoul, Champaign, Pop. 12,421**
Rantoul CSD 137 1,500/PK-12
400 E Wabash Ave 61866 217-893-4171
Michelle Ramage, supt. Fax 892-4313
www.rcs.k12.il.us
Eater JHS, 400 E Wabash Ave 61866 500/6-8
Ryan Green, prin. 217-892-2115
Thompson Learning Academy Alt
201 S Frederick St 61866 217-892-1112
Mike Penicook, prin.

Rantoul Township HSD 193 700/9-12
200 S Sheldon St 61866 217-892-2151
Scott Amerio, supt. Fax 892-4442
www.rths.k12.il.us
Rantoul Township HS 700/9-12
200 S Sheldon St 61866 217-892-2151
Todd Wilson, prin. Fax 892-4442

**Raymond, Montgomery, Pop. 996**
Panhandle CUSD 2 500/PK-12
509 N Prairie St 62560 217-229-4215
Aaron Hopper, supt. Fax 229-4216
www.panhandleschools.com
Lincolnwood HS 100/9-12
507 N Prairie St 62560 217-229-4237
Kendal Elvidge, prin. Fax 229-3005
Lincolnwood JHS 100/6-8
507 N Prairie St 62560 217-229-4237
Kendal Elvidge, prin. Fax 229-3005

**Red Bud, Randolph, Pop. 3,675**
Red Bud CUSD 132 1,000/PK-12
815 Locust St 62278 618-282-3507
Jonathan Tallman, supt. Fax 282-6151
www.redbud132.org
Red Bud HS 400/9-12
815 Locust St 62278 618-282-3826
Dustin Nail, prin. Fax 282-6828

**Richmond, McHenry, Pop. 1,854**
Nippersink SD 2 1,400/PK-8
4213 US Highway 12 60071 815-678-4242
Dr. Dan Oest, supt. Fax 675-0413
www.nippersinkdistrict2.org
Nippersink MS 500/6-8
10006 N Main St 60071 815-678-7129
Tim Molitor, prin. Fax 678-7210

Richmond-Burton Community HSD 157 800/9-12
4213 US Highway 12 60071 815-678-4525
Dr. Dan Oest, supt. Fax 678-4324
www.rbchs.com
Richmond-Burton HS 800/9-12
8311 IL Route 31 60071 815-678-4525
Tom Lind, prin. Fax 678-4324

**Richton Park, Cook, Pop. 13,324**
Matteson ESD 162 3,100/PK-8
14601 Sauk Trl Ste 2 60471 708-748-0100
Dr. Blondean Davis, supt. Fax 748-7302
www.sd162.org
Other Schools – See Matteson

Rich Township HSD 227
Supt. — See Olympia Fields
Rich South Campus HS 1,300/9-12
5000 Sauk Trl 60471 708-679-3000
Jennifer Bednarczyk, prin. Fax 679-3168

**Riverdale, Cook, Pop. 13,395**
Dolton SD 148 2,400/PK-8
114 W 144th St 60827 708-841-2290
Dr. Saundra R. Mickles, supt. Fax 841-5048
www.district148.net
Washington JHS 200/7-8
13900 S School St 60827 708-201-2078
Dorothy Jeter, prin. Fax 201-2148
Other Schools – See Dolton

**River Forest, Cook, Pop. 10,962**
River Forest SD 90 1,300/PK-8
7776 Lake St 60305 708-771-8282
Edward Condon Ph.D., supt. Fax 771-8291
www.district90.org/
Roosevelt JHS 600/5-8
7560 Oak Ave 60305 708-366-9230
Larry Garstki, prin. Fax 771-3962

---

Concordia University Chicago Post-Sec.
7400 Augusta St 60305 708-771-8300
Dominican University Post-Sec.
7900 Division St 60305 708-366-2490
Trinity HS 500/9-12
7574 Division St 60305 708-771-8383
Dr. Antonia Bouillette, prin. Fax 488-2014

**River Grove, Cook, Pop. 10,116**

---

Guerin College Preparatory HS 500/9-12
8001 Belmont Ave 60171 708-453-6233
Karen Booth, prin. Fax 453-6296
Triton College Post-Sec.
2000 5th Ave 60171 708-456-0300

**Riverside, Cook, Pop. 8,771**
Riverside Brookfield Township HSD 208 1,400/9-12
160 Ridgewood Rd 60546 708-442-7500
Dr. Kevin Skinkis, supt. Fax 447-5570
www.rbhs208.net
Riverside Brookfield Township HS 1,400/9-12
160 Ridgewood Rd 60546 708-442-7500
Kristin Smetana, prin. Fax 442-7840

Riverside SD 96 1,500/PK-8
63 Woodside Rd 60546 708-447-5007
Dr. Griff Powell, supt. Fax 447-3252
www.district96.org
Hauser JHS 500/6-8
65 Woodside Rd 60546 708-447-3896
April Mahy, prin. Fax 447-5180

**Riverton, Sangamon, Pop. 3,413**
Riverton CUSD 14 1,500/PK-12
PO Box 1010 62561 217-629-6009
Dr. Lance Thurman, supt. Fax 629-6008
www.rivertonschools.org
Riverton HS 400/9-12
PO Box 560 62561 217-629-6003
Matt Moore, prin. Fax 629-6020
Riverton MS 500/5-8
PO Box 530 62561 217-629-6002
Chris Koerwitz, prin. Fax 629-6017

**Roanoke, Woodford, Pop. 2,057**
Roanoke-Benson CUSD 60 600/PK-12
PO Box 320 61561 309-923-8921
Rohn Peterson, supt. Fax 923-7508
www.rb60.com/
Roanoke-Benson HS 200/9-12
PO Box 320 61561 309-923-8401
Michael Tresnak, prin. Fax 923-7508
Other Schools – See Benson

---

Linn Mennonite Christian S 50/K-12
1594 County Road 1700 N 61561 309-923-5641
Matthew Kennell, pres.

**Robbins, Cook, Pop. 5,299**
Community HSD 218
Supt. — See Oak Lawn
Delta Learning Center 200/Alt
3940 W Midlothian 60472 708-371-1880
Joe Fowler, prin. Fax 371-4782

Posen-Robbins ESD 143-5
Supt. — See Posen
Kellar JHS 500/6-8
14123 S Lydia Ave 60472 708-388-7201
Rochelle James M.A., prin. Fax 388-6177

**Robinson, Crawford, Pop. 7,621**
Robinson CUSD 2 1,600/PK-12
PO Box 190 62454 618-544-7511
Josh Quick, supt. Fax 544-7511
www.robinsonschools.com/
Nuttall MS 400/6-8
PO Box 190 62454 618-544-8618
Craig Beals, prin. Fax 544-8618
Robinson HS 500/9-12
PO Box 190 62454 618-544-9510
Troy Hickey, prin. Fax 544-9510

---

Lincoln Trail College Post-Sec.
11220 State Highway 1 62454 618-544-8657

**Rochelle, Ogle, Pop. 9,466**
Rochelle CCSD 231 1,700/PK-8
444 N 8th St 61068 815-562-6363
Todd Prusator, supt. Fax 562-5500
www.d231.rochelle.net
Rochelle MS 500/6-8
111 School Ave 61068 815-562-7997
Mike Valentine, prin. Fax 562-8527

Rochelle Township HSD 212 900/9-12
1401 Flagg Rd 61068 815-562-4161
Richard Craven, supt. Fax 562-6693
www.rths.rochelle.net/
Rochelle Township HS 900/9-12
1401 Flagg Rd 61068 815-562-4161
Jason Harper, prin. Fax 562-6693

**Rochester, Sangamon, Pop. 3,622**
Rochester CUSD 3A 2,300/PK-12
4 Rocket Dr 62563 217-498-6210
Dr. Thomas Bertrand, supt. Fax 498-8045
www.rochester3a.net
Rochester HS 700/9-12
1 Rocket Dr 62563 217-498-9761
Brent Ashbaugh, prin. Fax 498-9825
Rochester JHS 400/7-8
3 Rocket Dr 62563 217-498-9761
Kim Poole, prin. Fax 498-6204

**Rock Falls, Whiteside, Pop. 9,103**
Rock Falls ESD 13 1,000/PK-8
602 4th Ave 61071 815-626-2604
Dan Arickx, supt. Fax 626-2627
www.rfsd13.org
Rock Falls MS 300/6-8
1701 12th Ave 61071 815-626-2626
Kyle Ackman, prin. Fax 626-3198

Rock Falls Township HSD 301 600/9-12
101 12th Ave 61071 815-625-3886
Ron McCord, supt. Fax 625-3889
www.wside.k12.il.us/rfhs
Rock Falls Township HS 600/9-12
101 12th Ave 61071 815-625-3886
Mike Berentes, prin. Fax 625-3889

**Rockford, Winnebago, Pop. 148,827**
Rockford SD 205 27,200/PK-12
501 7th St 61104 815-966-3000
Dr. Ehren Jarrett, supt. Fax 966-3193
www.rps205.com
Auburn HS 1,800/9-12
5110 Auburn St 61101 815-966-3300
Janice Hawkins, prin. Fax 966-3911
Eisenhower MS 1,000/6-8
3525 Spring Creek Rd 61107 815-229-2450
Jeff Carlson, prin. Fax 229-2456
Flinn MS 1,000/6-8
2525 Ohio Pkwy 61108 815-229-2800
Randy Bay, prin. Fax 229-2894
Guilford HS 1,900/9-12
5620 Spring Creek Rd 61114 815-654-4870
Jennifer Lawrence, prin. Fax 654-4901
Jefferson HS 1,700/9-12
4145 Samuelson Rd 61109 815-874-9536
Don Rundall, prin. Fax 921-0306
Kennedy MS 700/6-8
520 Pierpont Ave 61103 815-654-4880
Renneth Richardson, prin. Fax 654-4874
Lincoln MS 700/6-8
1500 Charles St 61104 815-229-2400
Jason Grey, prin. Fax 229-2420
Marshall S 400/4-8
4664 N Rockton Ave 61103 815-490-5400
Jill Faber, prin. Fax 490-5405
Rockford East HS 1,500/9-12
2929 Charles St 61108 815-229-2100
Peter Verona, prin. Fax 229-2113
Rockford Environmental Science Academy 1,100/6-8
1800 Ogilby Rd 61102 815-489-5509
William Ady, prin. Fax 966-5360
Roosevelt Community Education Center 300/Alt
978 Haskell Ave 61103 815-966-3265
Dr. Heidi Houy, prin. Fax 966-3105
West MS 700/6-8
1900 N Rockton Ave 61103 815-966-3200
Maurice Davis, prin. Fax 966-3216

---

Berean Baptist Christian S 200/PK-12
5626 Safford Rd 61101 815-962-4841
Douglas Swanson, admin. Fax 962-4851
Boylan Central Catholic HS 1,200/9-12
4000 Saint Francis Dr 61103 815-877-0531
Jerry Kerrigan, prin. Fax 877-2544
Christian Life Schools 700/PK-12
5950 Spring Creek Rd 61114 815-877-5749
Mark Perry, supt. Fax 877-4358
Educators of Beauty Post-Sec.
2601B N Mulford Rd 61114 815-639-9200

Keith Country Day S 300/PK-12
1 Jacoby Pl 61107 815-399-8823
Dr. Debra Dimke, hdmstr. Fax 399-2470
North Love Christian S 200/PK-12
5301 E Riverside Blvd 61114 815-877-6021
Tony Cotelleso, admin. Fax 877-6076
Our Lady of the Sacred Heart Academy 50/PK-12
3218 11th St 61109 815-399-3021
Lou Bageanis, prin.
Rasmussen College Post-Sec.
6000 E State St Fl 4 61108 815-316-4800
Rockford Career College Post-Sec.
1130 S Alpine Rd Ste 100 61108 815-965-8616
Rockford Christian S 1,200/PK-12
1401 N Bell School Rd 61107 815-391-8000
Randy Taylor, supt. Fax 391-8004
Rockford IQRA S 200/PK-12
5925 Darlene Dr 61109 815-397-6899
Huda Ghazal, prin. Fax 397-1681
Rockford Lutheran JSHS 600/6-12
3411 N Alpine Rd 61114 815-877-9551
Don Kortze, prin. Fax 636-4429
Rockford Memorial Hospital Post-Sec.
2400 N Rockton Ave 61103 815-971-5000
Rockford University Post-Sec.
5050 E State St 61108 815-226-4000
Rock Valley College Post-Sec.
3301 N Mulford Rd 61114 815-921-7821
St. Anthony College of Nursing Post-Sec.
5658 E State St 61108 815-395-5091
St. Anthony Medical Center Post-Sec.
5666 E State St 61108 815-226-2000
Spectrum S 200/PK-12
2909 N Main St 61103 815-877-1600
Christine Klekamp, dir. Fax 877-1685
Swedish-American Hospital Post-Sec.
1401 E State St 61104 815-968-4400

**Rock Island, Rock Island, Pop. 37,879**
Rock Island-Milan SD 41 6,400/PK-12
2101 6th Ave 61201 309-793-5900
Dr. Michael Oberhaus, supt. Fax 793-5905
rockislandschools.org
Edison JHS 400/7-8
4141 9th St 61201 309-793-5920
Gary Flecker, prin. Fax 793-5919
Marshall Center 100/Alt
600 11th Ave 61201 309-793-5924
Phillip Ambrose, prin. Fax 793-5979
Rock Island HS 1,600/9-12
1400 25th Ave 61201 309-793-5950
Tim Wernentin, prin. Fax 793-9866
Washington JHS 500/7-8
3300 18th Ave 61201 309-793-5915
Kristin Allen, prin. Fax 793-5917

---

Alleman HS 500/9-12
1103 40th St 61201 309-786-7793
David Hobin, prin. Fax 786-7834
Augustana College Post-Sec.
639 38th St 61201 309-794-7000
Trinity College of Nursing Post-Sec.
2122 25th Ave 61201 309-779-7700

**Rockton, Winnebago, Pop. 7,573**
Hononegah Community HSD 207 2,100/9-12
307 Salem St 61072 815-624-5010
Lynn Gibson, supt. Fax 624-5029
www.hononegah.org
Hononegah Community HS 2,100/9-12
307 Salem St 61072 815-624-5005
Eric Flohr, prin. Fax 624-5025

Rockton SD 140 1,500/PK-8
1050 E Union St 61072 815-624-7143
Dr. Robert Willis, supt. Fax 624-4640
rockton140.org
Mack MS 500/6-8
11810 Old River Rd 61072 815-624-2611
Kindyl Etnyre, prin. Fax 624-5900

**Rolling Meadows, Cook, Pop. 23,765**
Palatine CCSD 15
Supt. — See Palatine
Plum Grove JHS 800/7-8
2600 Plum Grove Rd 60008 847-963-7600
Kerry Wilson Ed.D., prin. Fax 963-7606
Sandburg JHS 500/7-8
2600 Martin Ln 60008 847-963-7800
Erika Johansen, prin. Fax 963-7806

Township HSD 214
Supt. — See Arlington Heights
Rolling Meadows HS 1,800/9-12
2901 Central Rd 60008 847-718-5600
Eileen Hart, prin. Fax 718-5617
Young Adult Program 100/Alt
2901 Central Rd 60008 847-718-5787
Dan Williams, dir. Fax 718-5617

**Romeoville, Will, Pop. 38,967**
Valley View CUSD 365U 17,500/PK-12
755 Dalhart Ave 60446 815-886-2700
Dr. James Mitchem, supt. Fax 886-7294
www.vvsd.org/
Lukancic MS 600/6-8
725 W Normantown Rd 60446 815-886-2216
Tricia Rollerson, prin. Fax 886-2264
Martinez MS 800/6-8
590 Belmont Dr 60446 815-886-6100
Sarah DeDonato, prin. Fax 886-7264
Romeoville HS 1,800/9-12
100 N Independence Blvd 60446 815-886-1800
Derek Kinder, prin. Fax 886-7272
Other Schools – See Bolingbrook

Wilco Area Career Center
500 Wilco Blvd 60446 815-838-6941
Katrina Plese, dir. Fax 838-1163
www.wilco.k12.il.us
Wilco Area Career Center Vo/Tech
500 Wilco Blvd 60446 815-838-6941
Katrina Plese, dir. Fax 838-1163

---

Illinois Welding School Post-Sec.
1315 Enterprise Dr Ste E 60446 630-679-0566
Lewis University Post-Sec.
1 University Pkwy 60446 815-838-0500
Rasmussen College Post-Sec.
1400 W Normantown Rd 60446 815-306-2600
Romeoville Christian Academy 100/PK-12
301 W Normantown Rd 60446 815-886-4850
Mark Widmer, prin.

**Roscoe, Winnebago, Pop. 10,602**
Kinnikinnick CCSD 131 1,600/PK-8
5410 Pine Ln 61073 815-623-2837
Keli Freedlund, supt. Fax 623-9285
www.kinn131.org
Roscoe MS 800/6-8
6121 Elevator Rd 61073 815-623-2837
Julie Cropp, prin. Fax 623-7604

**Roselle, DuPage, Pop. 22,408**
Lake Park Community HSD 108 2,800/9-12
590 Medinah Rd 60172 630-529-4500
Lynne Panega, supt. Fax 295-5414
www.lphs.org
Lake Park HS East 1,400/9-10
600 Medinah Rd 60172 630-529-4500
Jim Roberts, prin. Fax 295-5212
Lake Park HS West 1,400/11-12
500 W Bryn Mawr Ave 60172 630-595-5322
Janet Constien, prin. Fax 351-2932

Medinah SD 11 600/K-8
700 E Granville Ave 60172 630-893-3737
Dr. John Butts, supt. Fax 893-4947
www.medinah11.org
Medinah MS 200/6-8
700 E Granville Ave 60172 630-893-3838
George Gouriotis, prin. Fax 893-5198

Roselle SD 12 700/K-8
100 E Walnut St 60172 630-529-2091
Dr. M. Kaczkowski, supt. Fax 529-2467
www.sd12.k12.il.us/
Roselle MS 200/6-8
500 S Park St 60172 630-529-1600
Kathleen Schneiter, prin. Fax 529-1882

**Roseville, Warren, Pop. 986**
Monmouth-Roseville CUSD 238
Supt. — See Monmouth
Monmouth-Roseville JHS 200/7-8
200 E Gossett St 61473 309-426-2682
Donald Farr, prin. Fax 426-2303

**Round Lake, Lake, Pop. 17,862**
Round Lake Area SD 116 7,100/PK-12
884 W Nippersink Rd 60073 847-270-9000
Dr. Constance Collins, supt. Fax 546-3538
www.rlas-116.org
Magee MS 700/6-8
500 N Cedar Lake Rd 60073 847-546-8800
Dr. Lisa Steffen, prin. Fax 740-3836
Round Lake HS 1,900/9-12
800 High School Dr 60073 847-270-9300
Dr. Donn Mendoza, prin. Fax 546-5872
Other Schools – See Round Lake Heights

**Round Lake Heights, Lake, Pop. 2,629**
Round Lake Area SD 116
Supt. — See Round Lake
Round Lake MS 1,000/6-8
2000 Lotus Dr 60073 847-270-9400
David Higgs, prin. Fax 270-9419

**Roxana, Madison, Pop. 1,531**
Roxana CUSD 1 1,900/PK-12
401 Chaffer Ave 62084 618-254-7544
Debra Kreutztrager, supt. Fax 254-7547
www.roxanaschools.org
Roxana HS 600/9-12
401 Chaffer Ave 62084 618-254-7553
Tom Roth, prin. Fax 254-7580
Roxana JHS 400/6-8
401 Chaffer Ave 62084 618-254-7560
Steve Mayerhofer, prin. Fax 254-8107

**Royal, Champaign, Pop. 293**
Prairieview-Ogden CCSD 197 200/K-8
PO Box 27 61871 217-583-3300
Victor White, supt. Fax 583-3391
www.pvo.k12.il.us/
Other Schools – See Thomasboro

**Rushville, Schuyler, Pop. 3,179**
Schuyler-Industry CUSD 5 1,200/PK-12
740 Maple Ave 62681 217-322-4311
Dr. Tami Roskamp, supt. Fax 322-4398
www.sid5.com/
Rushville-Industry HS 300/9-12
730 N Congress St 62681 217-322-4311
Carl Spath, prin. Fax 322-2844
Schuyler-Industry MS 400/5-8
750 N Congress St 62681 217-322-4311
Jim Shepherd, prin. Fax 322-3938

**Saint Anne, Kankakee, Pop. 1,243**
Saint Anne Community HSD 302 200/9-12
PO Box 630 60964 815-422-5022
Richard Levek, supt. Fax 422-5023
www.sachs.k12.il.us/
Saint Anne Community HS 200/9-12
PO Box 630 60964 815-427-8141
Ramie Kolitwenzew, prin. Fax 427-8609

**Saint Charles, Kane, Pop. 32,580**
Saint Charles CUSD 303 13,500/PK-12
201 S 7th St 60174 331-228-2000
Dr. Donald Schlomann, supt. Fax 228-2001
www.d303.org
Haines MS 1,200/6-8
305 S 9th St 60174 331-228-3100
Pamela Jensen, prin. Fax 228-3101
Saint Charles East HS 2,300/9-12
1020 Dunham Rd 60174 331-228-4000
Charlie Kyle, prin. Fax 228-4001
Saint Charles North HS 2,000/9-12
255 Red Gate Rd 60175 331-228-4400
Audra Christenson, prin. Fax 228-4401
Thompson MS 900/6-8
705 W Main St 60174 331-228-3400
Timothy Loversky, prin. Fax 228-3401
Wredling MS 1,300/6-8
1200 Dunham Rd 60174 331-228-3400
Steve Morrill, prin. Fax 228-3401

**Saint Elmo, Fayette, Pop. 1,414**
Saint Elmo CUSD 202 500/PK-12
1200 N Walnut St 62458 618-829-3264
Deborah Philpot, supt. Fax 829-5161
www.stelmo.org
Saint Elmo HS 100/9-12
300 W 12th St 62458 618-829-3227
Brian Garrard, prin. Fax 829-5161
Saint Elmo JHS 100/7-8
300 W 12th St 62458 618-829-3227
Brian Garrard, prin. Fax 829-5161

**Saint Jacob, Madison, Pop. 1,092**
Triad CUSD 2
Supt. — See Troy
Triad MS 800/6-8
9539 US Highway 40 62281 618-644-5511
Matt Noyes, prin. Fax 644-9435

**Saint Joseph, Champaign, Pop. 3,931**
Saint Joseph CCSD 169 900/PK-8
PO Box 409 61873 217-469-2291
Todd Pence, supt. Fax 469-8906
www.stjoe.k12.il.us
Saint Joseph MS 400/5-8
PO Box 409 61873 217-469-2334
Chris Graham, prin. Fax 469-2537

Saint Joseph-Ogden Community HSD 305 500/9-12
PO Box 890 61873 217-469-2586
Brian Brooks, supt.
www.sjo.k12.il.us
Saint Joseph-Ogden HS 500/9-12
PO Box 890 61873 217-469-2332
Gary Page, prin. Fax 469-8290

**Salem, Marion, Pop. 7,393**
Salem Community HSD 600 800/9-12
1200 N Broadway Ave 62881 618-548-0727
Brad Detering, supt. Fax 548-8021
www.salemhigh.com
Salem Community HS 800/9-12
1200 N Broadway Ave 62881 618-548-0727
John Boles, prin. Fax 548-8021

Salem SD 111 1,000/PK-8
1300 Hawthorn Rd 62881 618-548-7702
Leslie Foppe, supt. Fax 548-7714
www.salem111.com
Franklin Park MS 600/PK-PK, 4-
1325 N Franklin St 62881 618-548-7704
Matt Sturgeon, prin. Fax 548-7712

**Sandoval, Marion, Pop. 1,257**
Sandoval CUSD 501 500/PK-12
859 W Missouri Ave 62882 618-247-3233
Jennifer Garrison, supt. Fax 247-3243
www.sandoval501.org
Sandoval HS 200/9-12
859 W Missouri Ave 62882 618-247-3361
Annie Gray, prin. Fax 247-3235
Sandoval JHS 100/7-8
859 W Missouri Ave 62882 618-247-3361
Annie Gray, prin. Fax 247-3235

**Sandwich, DeKalb, Pop. 7,330**
Indian Valley Vocational Center
600 Lions Rd 60548 815-786-9873
Ron Pieper, dir. Fax 786-6928
www.ivvc.net
Indian Valley Vocational Center Vo/Tech
600 Lions Rd 60548 815-786-9873
Ron Pieper, dir. Fax 786-6928

Sandwich CUSD 430 2,300/PK-12
720 S Wells St 60548 815-786-2187
Rick Schmitt, supt. Fax 786-6229
www.sandwich430.org
Sandwich Community HS 800/9-12
515 E Lions Rd 60548 815-786-2157
Tom Sodaro, prin. Fax 786-2632
Sandwich MS 600/6-8
600 S Wells St 60548 815-786-2138
B.J. Richardson, prin. Fax 786-6606

**Sauk Village, Cook, Pop. 10,221**
CCSD 168 1,700/PK-8
21899 Torrence Ave 60411 708-758-1610
Dr. Donna Leak, supt. Fax 758-5929
www.d168.org
Rickover JHS 600/6-8
22151 Torrence Ave 60411 708-758-1900
Myra Patterson, prin. Fax 758-1601

**Savanna, Carroll, Pop. 3,017**
West Carroll CUSD 314
Supt. — See Mount Carroll
West Carroll HS 400/9-12
500 Cragmoor St 61074 815-273-7715
Adam Brumbaugh, prin. Fax 273-7819

**Scales Mound, Jo Daviess, Pop. 373**
Scales Mound CUSD 211 — 300/PK-12
210 Main St 61075 — 815-845-2215
William Caron, supt. — Fax 845-2238
www.scalesmound.net
Scales Mound HS — 100/9-12
210 Main St 61075 — 815-845-2215
Dr. Matthew Wiederholt, prin. — Fax 845-2238
Scales Mound JHS — 50/6-8
210 Main St 61075 — 815-845-2215
Dr. Matthew Wiederholt, prin. — Fax 845-2238

**Schaumburg, Cook, Pop. 72,713**
Schaumburg CCSD 54 — 14,000/PK-8
524 E Schaumburg Rd 60194 — 847-357-5000
Andrew DuRoss, supt. — Fax 357-5152
www.sd54.org
Addams JHS — 700/7-8
700 S Springinsguth Rd 60193 — 847-357-5900
Chris Bingen, prin. — Fax 357-5901
Frost JHS — 600/7-8
320 W Wise Rd 60193 — 847-357-6800
Scott Ross, prin. — Fax 357-6801
Keller JHS — 500/7-8
820 Bode Rd 60194 — 847-357-6500
Heather Wilson, prin. — Fax 357-6501
Other Schools – See Elk Grove Village, Hoffman Estates

Township HSD 211
Supt. — See Palatine
Schaumburg HS — 2,400/9-12
1100 W Schaumburg Rd 60194 — 847-755-4600
Timothy Little, prin. — Fax 755-4623

---

American Intercontinental Univ Online — Post-Sec.
231 N Martingale Rd Fl 6 60173 — 877-701-3800
Argosy University/Schaumburg — Post-Sec.
999 N Plaza Dr Ste 111 60173 — 847-969-4900
DeVry University — Post-Sec.
1051 Perimeter Dr Fl 9 60173 — 847-330-0040
Lake Forest Graduate Sch. of Management — Post-Sec.
1300 E Woodfield Rd Ste 600 60173 — 847-234-5005
Prince Institute — Post-Sec.
1300 E Woodfield Rd Ste 110 60173 — 847-592-6600
Robert Morris University — Post-Sec.
1000 E Woodfield Rd 60173 — 800-225-1520
Roosevelt University — Post-Sec.
1400 N Roosevelt Blvd 60173 — 847-619-7300
Schaumburg Christian S — 1,200/PK-12
200 N Roselle Rd 60194 — 847-885-3230
The Illinois Institute of Art — Post-Sec.
1000 N Plaza Dr Ste 100 60173 — 847-619-3450

**Schiller Park, Cook, Pop. 11,679**
Schiller Park SD 81 — 1,300/PK-8
9760 Soreng Ave 60176 — 847-671-1816
Dr. Kimberly Boryszewski, supt. — Fax 671-1872
www.sd81.org
Lincoln MS — 300/6-8
9750 Soreng Ave 60176 — 847-678-2916
Constance Stavrou, prin. — Fax 678-4059

**Sciota, McDonough, Pop. 61**
West Prairie CUSD 103
Supt. — See Colchester
West Prairie HS — 200/9-12
18575 E 800th St 61475 — 309-456-3750
Scott Sullivan, prin. — Fax 456-3997

**Seneca, LaSalle, Pop. 2,330**
Seneca CCSD 170 — 500/PK-8
174 Oak St 61360 — 815-357-8744
Eric Misener, supt. — Fax 357-1516
www.sgs170.org
Seneca MS South Campus — 200/5-8
174 Oak St 61360 — 815-357-8744
Shane Severson, prin. — Fax 357-1078

Seneca Township HSD 160 — 400/9-12
PO Box 20 61360 — 815-357-5000
Dr. Jim Carlson, supt. — Fax 357-5050
www.senecahs.org
Seneca HS — 400/9-12
PO Box 20 61360 — 815-357-5000
Marty Voiles, prin. — Fax 357-5050

**Serena, LaSalle**
Serena CUSD 2 — 800/K-12
PO Box 107 60549 — 815-496-2850
Marty Felesena, supt. — Fax 496-2987
www.unit2.net
Serena Community HS — 300/9-12
PO Box 107 60549 — 815-496-2361
Steve Hanson, prin. — Fax 496-2987

**Sesser, Franklin, Pop. 1,900**
Sesser-Valier CUSD 196 — 800/PK-12
4626 State Highway 154 62884 — 618-625-5105
Dr. Jason D. Henry, supt. — Fax 625-6696
sv196.org
Sesser-Valier HS — 200/9-12
4626 State Highway 154 62884 — 618-625-5105
Natalie Page, prin. — Fax 625-6696
Sesser-Valier JHS — 200/6-8
4626 State Highway 154 62884 — 618-625-5105
Judy L. Logsdon, prin. — Fax 625-3040

**Shabbona, DeKalb, Pop. 921**
Indian Creek CUSD 425 — 800/PK-12
506 S Shabbona Rd 60550 — 815-824-2197
Pamela Rockwood, supt. — Fax 824-2199
www.indiancreekschools.org
Indian Creek HS — 200/9-12
506 S Shabbona Rd 60550 — 815-824-2197
Sarah Montgomery, prin. — Fax 824-2199
Other Schools – See Waterman

**Shelbyville, Shelby, Pop. 4,676**
Shelbyville CUSD 4 — 1,200/PK-12
720 W Main St 62565 — 217-774-4626
Denise Bence, supt. — Fax 774-2521
www.shelbyville.k12.il.us/
Moulton MS — 400/4-8
1101 W North 6th St 62565 — 217-774-2169
Russell Tomblin, prin. — Fax 774-3042
Shelbyville HS — 300/9-12
1001 W North 6th St 62565 — 217-774-3926
Richard Stuart, prin. — Fax 774-5836

**Sherrard, Mercer, Pop. 637**
Sherrard CUSD 200 — 1,500/PK-12
PO Box 369 61281 — 309-593-4075
Dr. Samuel Light, supt. — Fax 593-4078
www.sherrard.us
Sherrard HS — 500/9-12
4701 176th Ave 61281 — 309-593-2175
Kevin Parker, prin. — Fax 593-2775
Sherrard JHS — 200/7-8
4701 176th Ave 61281 — 309-593-2135
Brad Hulick, prin. — Fax 593-2143

**Shiloh, Saint Clair, Pop. 12,229**
Shiloh Village SD 85 — 600/PK-8
125 Diamond Ct 62269 — 618-632-7434
Dale Sauer, supt. — Fax 632-8343
www.shiloh.stclair.k12.il.us
Shiloh MS — 300/5-8
1 Wildcat Xing 62269 — 618-632-7434
Jeff Alt, prin. — Fax 622-9350

**Sidell, Vermilion, Pop. 607**
Salt Fork CUSD 512 — 400/PK-12
7087 N 600 East Rd 61876 — 217-288-9306
Dr. Phil Harrison, supt. — Fax 288-9393
www.saltfork.k12.il.us
Salt Fork JHS — 100/6-8
7087 N 600 East Rd 61876 — 217-288-9394
Brian Allensworth, prin.
Other Schools – See Catlin

**Silvis, Rock Island, Pop. 7,322**
Silvis SD 34 — 600/PK-8
1305 5th Ave 61282 — 309-792-9325
Dr. Terri VandeWiele Ed.D., supt. — Fax 792-8092
silvis34.net
Other Schools – See East Moline

**Skokie, Cook, Pop. 62,756**
Niles Township HSD 219 — 4,700/9-12
7700 Gross Point Rd 60077 — 847-626-3000
Dr. Anne Roloff, supt. — Fax 626-3090
www.niles219.org
Niles Central S — 50/Alt
7700 Gross Point Rd 60077 — 847-626-3120
Dr. Anne Hellmer, dir. — Fax 626-3080
Niles North HS — 2,100/9-12
9800 Lawler Ave 60077 — 847-626-2000
Dr. Ryan McTague, prin. — Fax 626-3424
Niles West HS — 2,600/9-12
5701 Oakton St 60077 — 847-626-2500
Dr. Jason Ness, prin. — Fax 626-3700

Skokie SD 68 — 1,700/PK-8
9440 Kenton Ave 60076 — 847-676-9000
Dr. James Garwood, supt. — Fax 676-9232
www.skokie68.org
Old Orchard JHS — 700/PK-PK, 6-
9310 Kenton Ave 60076 — 847-676-9010
Robyn Huemmer, prin. — Fax 676-3827

Skokie SD 69 — 1,700/PK-8
5050 Madison St 60077 — 847-675-7666
Margaret Clauson, supt. — Fax 675-7675
www.skokie69.net
Lincoln JHS — 500/6-8
7839 Lincoln Ave 60077 — 847-676-3545
Mark Rasar, prin. — Fax 676-3595

Skokie SD 73-5 — 1,100/PK-8
8000 E Prairie Rd 60076 — 847-324-0509
Kate Donegan, supt. — Fax 673-1282
www.sd735.org
McCracken MS — 400/6-8
8000 E Prairie Rd 60076 — 847-673-1220
Allison Stein, prin. — Fax 673-1282

---

Computer Systems Institute — Post-Sec.
8930 Gross Point Rd 60077 — 847-967-5030
Everest College — Post-Sec.
9811 Woods Dr Ste 200 60077 — 847-470-0277
Fasman Yeshiva HS — 100/9-12
7135 Carpenter Rd 60077 — 847-982-2500
Hebrew Theological College — Post-Sec.
7135 Carpenter Rd 60077 — 847-982-2500
Knowledge Systems Institute — Post-Sec.
3420 Main St 60076 — 847-679-3135
Zarem/Golde ORT Technical Institute — Post-Sec.
5440 Fargo Ave 60077 — 847-324-5588

**Somonauk, DeKalb, Pop. 1,867**
Somonauk CUSD 432 — 900/PK-12
501 W Market St 60552 — 815-498-2314
Jay Streicher, supt. — Fax 498-9523
www.somonauk.net
Somonauk HS — 300/9-12
501 W Market St 60552 — 815-498-2314
Laura Hatch, prin. — Fax 498-9841
Somonauk MS — 300/5-8
501 W Market St 60552 — 815-498-1866
Justin Snider, prin. — Fax 498-1647

**South Beloit, Winnebago, Pop. 7,705**
Prairie Hill CCSD 133 — 800/K-8
6605 Prairie Hill Rd 61080 — 815-389-3957
Wes Heiar, supt. — Fax 389-6107
www.prairiehill.org
Willowbrook MS — 400/5-8
6605 Prairie Hill Rd 61080 — 815-389-3957
Steve Heidel, prin. — Fax 389-6107

South Beloit CUSD 320 — 1,000/PK-12
850 Hayes Ave 61080 — 815-389-3478
Scott Fisher, supt. — Fax 389-3477
www.sbsobos.org/
South Beloit HS — 300/9-12
245 Prairie Hill Rd 61080 — 815-389-9004
Clint Czizek, prin. — Fax 389-9268
South Beloit JHS — 200/7-8
840 Blackhawk Blvd 61080 — 815-389-1421
Michael McCoy, prin. — Fax 389-8811

**South Elgin, Kane, Pop. 21,549**
SD U-46
Supt. — See Elgin
Kenyon Woods MS — 1,000/7-8
1515 Raymond St 60177 — 847-289-6685
Mike Demovsky, prin. — Fax 628-6166
South Elgin HS — 2,700/9-12
760 E Main St 60177 — 847-289-3760
James Edwards, prin. — Fax 888-7014

**South Holland, Cook, Pop. 21,729**
South Holland SD 150 — 1,000/PK-8
848 E 170th St 60473 — 708-339-4240
Dr. Jerry Jordan, supt. — Fax 339-4244
www.sd150.org
McKinley JHS — 400/4-8
16949 Cottage Grove Ave 60473 — 708-339-8500
William Kolloway, prin. — Fax 331-5805

South Holland SD 151 — 1,400/PK-8
525 E 162nd St 60473 — 708-339-1516
Dr. Teresa D. Hill, supt. — Fax 331-7600
www.shsd151.org
Other Schools – See Phoenix

Thornton Township HSD 205 — 5,200/9-12
465 E 170th St 60473 — 708-225-4000
Leotis Swopes Ed.D., supt. — Fax 225-4004
www.district205.net
Thornwood HS — 1,900/9-12
17101 S Park Ave 60473 — 708-225-4701
Dennis Willis, prin. — Fax 225-5033
Other Schools – See Dolton, Harvey

---

Seton Academy — 200/9-12
16100 Seton Dr 60473 — 708-333-6300
Earl McKay, prin. — Fax 333-1534
South Suburban College of Cook County — Post-Sec.
15800 State St 60473 — 708-596-2000

**South Roxana, Madison, Pop. 2,033**

---

Bethel Christian Academy — 100/PK-12
PO Box 87207 62087 — 618-254-0188
RaNell Consiglio, prin. — Fax 254-2067

**Sparland, Marshall, Pop. 403**
Midland CUSD 7 — 800/PK-12
901 Hilltop Dr 61565 — 309-469-2061
Rolf Sivertsen, supt. — Fax 469-2063
midland-7.info
Midland MS — 200/5-8
901 Hilltop Dr 61565 — 309-469-3131
Rolf Silvertsen, prin. — Fax 469-5701
Other Schools – See Varna

**Sparta, Randolph, Pop. 4,242**
Sparta CUSD 140 — 1,300/PK-12
203B Dean Ave 62286 — 618-443-5331
Dr. Larry Beattie, supt. — Fax 443-2023
www.sparta.k12.il.us
Sparta HS — 400/9-12
205 W Hood St 62286 — 618-443-4341
R. Scott Beckley, prin. — Fax 443-5059

**Springfield, Sangamon, Pop. 113,193**
Capital Area Career Center
2201 Toronto Rd Ste B, — 217-529-5431
Jodi Ferriell, dir. — Fax 529-7861
capital.tec.il.us
Capital Area Career Center — Vo/Tech
2201 Toronto Rd Ste B, — 217-529-5431
Molly Kosbab, prin. — Fax 529-7861

Menard/Sangamon ROE
200 S 9th St Ste 303 62701 — 217-753-6620
Jeff Vose, supt. — Fax 535-3166
www.roe51.org
Sangamon County Learning Academy — Alt
2201 Toronto Rd, — 217-529-3390
Julie Sullivan, prin.

Springfield SD 186 — 13,800/PK-12
1900 W Monroe St 62704 — 217-525-3000
Jennifer Gill, supt. — Fax 525-3005
www.sps186.org/
Douglas S — 50/Alt
444 W Reynolds St 62702 — 217-525-4400
Kari Borders, prin. — Fax 525-4401
Franklin MS — 700/6-8
1200 Outer Park Dr 62704 — 217-787-3006
Tod Davis, prin. — Fax 525-7937
Grant MS — 600/6-8
1800 W Monroe St 62704 — 217-525-3170
Cindy Baugher, prin. — Fax 525-3390
Jefferson MS — 500/6-8
3001 S Allis St 62703 — 217-585-5810
Karen Stapleton-Crump, prin. — Fax 525-3293
Lanphier HS — 1,100/9-12
1300 N 11th St 62702 — 217-525-3080
Artie Doss, prin. — Fax 525-3084
Lee S — 200/PK-12
1201 Bunn Ave 62703 — 217-585-5828
Nathan Kochanowski, prin. — Fax 535-2755
Lincoln Magnet MS — 300/6-8
300 S 11th St 62703 — 217-525-3236
Nichole Heyen, prin. — Fax 525-3294
Springfield HS — 1,400/9-12
101 S Lewis St 62704 — 217-525-3100
Michael Grossen, prin. — Fax 525-3122

Springfield Learning Academy 100/Alt
101 E Laurel St 62704 217-525-3358
Reiko Hurd, prin. Fax 525-3090
Springfield Southeast HS 1,300/9-12
2350 E Ash St 62703 217-525-3130
Jason Wind, prin. Fax 525-3139
Washington MS 600/6-8
2300 E Jackson St 62703 217-525-3182
Chris Barham, prin. Fax 525-3319
Lawrence Education Center Adult
101 E Laurel St 62704 217-525-3144
Kathi Lee, prin. Fax 525-3090

---

Calvary Academy 300/PK-12
1730 W Jefferson St 62702 217-546-5987
Dr. Jay Hinckley, prin. Fax 321-1063
ITT Technical Institute Post-Sec.
2501 Wabash Ave 62704 217-547-5700
Lincoln Land Community College Post-Sec.
PO Box 19256 62794 217-786-2200
Lutheran HS 200/9-12
3500 W Washington St, 217-546-6363
Glenn Rollins, prin. Fax 546-6489
Midwest Technical Institute Post-Sec.
2731 N Farmers Market Rd 62707 800-814-5124
Robert Morris University Post-Sec.
3101 Montvale Dr 62704 800-762-5960
Sacred Heart-Griffin HS 800/9-12
1200 W Washington St 62702 217-787-1595
Sr. Margaret Joanne Grueter, prin. Fax 787-9856
St. John's College Post-Sec.
729 E Carpenter St 62702 217-525-5628
St. John's Hospital Post-Sec.
800 E Carpenter St 62769 217-544-6464
University of Illinois at Springfield Post-Sec.
1 University Plz 62703 217-206-6600

**Spring Grove, McHenry, Pop. 5,732**
Fox Lake Grade SD 114 700/PK-8
29067 W Grass Lake Rd 60081 847-973-4114
John Donnellan, supt. Fax 973-4010
www.foxlake114.org
Other Schools – See Fox Lake

**Spring Valley, Bureau, Pop. 5,488**
Hall HSD 502 400/9-12
800 W Erie St 61362 815-664-4500
Michael Struna, supt. Fax 664-2300
www.hallhighschool.org
Hall HS 400/9-12
800 W Erie St 61362 815-664-2100
Michael Struna, prin. Fax 664-2300

**Stanford, McLean, Pop. 590**
Olympia CUSD 16 1,900/PK-12
903 E 800 North Rd 61774 309-379-6011
Dr. Andrew S. Wise, supt. Fax 379-2328
www.olympia.org
Olympia HS 600/9-12
7832 N 100 East Rd 61774 309-379-5911
Ed Jodlowski, prin. Fax 379-2583
Olympia MS 400/6-8
911 E 800 North Rd 61774 309-379-5941
Andrew Walsh, prin. Fax 379-5411

**Staunton, Macoupin, Pop. 5,081**
Staunton CUSD 6 1,300/PK-12
801 N Deneen St 62088 618-635-2962
Dan Cox, supt. Fax 635-2994
www.stauntonschools.org
Staunton HS 400/9-12
801 N Deneen St 62088 618-635-3838
Brett Allen, prin. Fax 635-2834
Staunton JHS 300/6-8
801 N Deneen St 62088 618-635-3831
Brooke Wiemers, prin. Fax 635-4637

**Steeleville, Randolph, Pop. 2,076**
Steeleville CUSD 138 400/PK-12
609 S Sparta St 62288 618-965-3469
Dr. Stephanie Mulholland, supt. Fax 965-3433
www.steeleville138.org
Steeleville HS 100/9-12
701 S Sparta St 62288 618-965-3432
Jennifer Hagel, prin. Fax 965-3433

**Steger, Will, Pop. 9,382**
Steger SD 194 1,600/PK-8
3753 Park Ave 60475 708-755-0022
Dave Thieman, supt. Fax 755-9512
www.sd194.org/
Columbia Central MS 600/5-8
94 Richton Rd 60475 708-755-0021
Mike Smith, prin. Fax 755-1877

**Sterling, Whiteside, Pop. 15,098**
Sterling CUSD 5 3,300/PK-12
410 E Le Fevre Rd 61081 815-626-5050
Tad Everett, supt. Fax 622-4113
www.sterlingpublicschools.org
Challand MS 800/6-8
1700 6th Ave 61081 815-626-3300
Matt Birdsley, prin. Fax 622-4173
Sterling HS 1,000/9-12
1608 4th Ave 61081 815-625-6800
Jason Austin, prin. Fax 622-4157

Whiteside Area Career Center
1608 5th Ave 61081 815-626-5810
Kim Purvis, supt.
Whiteside Area Career Center Vo/Tech
1608 5th Ave 61081 815-626-5810
Kim Purvis, prin.

---

Educators of Beauty Post-Sec.
211 E 3rd St 61081 815-625-0247
Newman Central Catholic HS 300/9-12
1101 W 23rd St 61081 815-625-0500
Kathleen Howard, prin. Fax 625-8444

**Stillman Valley, Ogle, Pop. 1,114**
Meridian CUSD 223 2,000/PK-12
207 W Main St 61084 815-645-2230
Phillip Caposey, supt. Fax 645-4325
www.meridian223.org
Meridian JHS 500/6-8
207 W Main St 61084 815-645-2230
Jill Davis, prin. Fax 645-8181
Stillman Valley HS 600/9-12
425 S Pine St 61084 815-645-2230
Leslie Showers, prin. Fax 645-8145

**Stockton, Jo Daviess, Pop. 1,848**
Stockton CUSD 206 600/PK-12
540 N Rush St 61085 815-947-3391
Dr. David Gilliland, supt. Fax 947-2673
www.stocktonschools.com
Stockton HS 200/9-12
540 N Rush St 61085 815-947-3323
Dr. David Gilliland, prin. Fax 947-2673
Stockton MS 200/5-8
500 N Rush St 61085 815-947-3702
Brad Fox, prin. Fax 947-2114

**Strasburg, Shelby, Pop. 465**
Stewardson-Strasburg CUSD 5A 300/PK-12
2806 E 600 North Rd 62465 217-682-3355
Michele Lindenmeyer, supt. Fax 682-3305
www.stew-stras.org
Stewardson-Strasburg JSHS 100/7-12
2806 E 600 North Rd 62465 217-682-3355
Justin Deters, prin. Fax 682-3305

**Streamwood, Cook, Pop. 39,124**
SD U-46
Supt. — See Elgin
Canton MS 700/7-8
1100 Sunset Cir 60107 630-213-5525
Jeff Smith, prin. Fax 213-5709
Streamwood HS 2,100/9-12
701 W Schaumburg Rd 60107 630-213-5500
Ariel Correa, prin. Fax 483-5909
Tefft MS 800/7-8
1100 Shirley Ave 60107 630-213-5535
Lavonne Smiley, prin. Fax 213-5646

**Streator, LaSalle, Pop. 13,509**
Streator ESD 44 1,500/PK-8
1520 N Bloomington St 61364 815-672-2926
Matthew Wilkinson, supt. Fax 673-2032
www.ses44.net/
Northlawn JHS 600/5-8
202 E 1st St 61364 815-672-4558
Keri Jancek, prin. Fax 672-8109

Streator Twp. HSD 40 900/9-12
202 W Lincoln Ave 61364 815-672-0545
Matt Seaton, supt. Fax 673-3637
www.streatorhs.org
Streator Twp. HS 900/9-12
202 W Lincoln Ave 61364 815-672-0545
Amy Mascal, prin. Fax 673-3637

Woodland CUSD 5 500/PK-12
5800 E 3000 North Rd 61364 815-672-5974
Ryan McGuckin, supt. Fax 673-1630
www.woodland5.org
Woodland HS 100/9-12
5800 E 3000 North Rd 61364 815-672-2900
Debra Derby, prin.

**Stronghurst, Henderson, Pop. 875**
West Central CUSD 235
Supt. — See Biggsville
West Central MS 200/6-8
PO Box 179 61480 309-924-1681
Julia Burns, prin. Fax 924-1122

**Sugar Grove, Kane, Pop. 8,881**
Kaneland CUSD 302
Supt. — See Maple Park
Harter MS 1,100/6-8
1601 N Esker Dr 60554 630-466-8400
Brian Faulkner, prin. Fax 466-1999

---

Waubonsee Community College Post-Sec.
Route 47 at Waubonsee Dr 60554 630-466-7900

**Sullivan, Moultrie, Pop. 4,417**
Sullivan CUSD 300 1,100/PK-12
725 N Main St 61951 217-728-8341
Brad Tuttle, supt. Fax 728-4139
home.sullivan.k12.il.us
Sullivan HS 400/9-12
725 N Main St 61951 217-728-8311
Erik Young, prin. Fax 728-4139
Sullivan MS 300/6-8
713 N Main St 61951 217-728-8381
Ted Walk, prin. Fax 728-4139

**Summit, Cook**
Summit SD 104 1,800/PK-8
6021 S 74th Ave 60501 708-458-0505
Dr. Troy J. Whalen, supt. Fax 458-0532
www.sd104.us
Heritage MS 500/6-8
6021 S 74th Ave 60501 708-458-7590
Robert Bassett, prin. Fax 728-3111

**Summit Argo, Cook, Pop. 10,942**
Argo Community HSD 217 1,800/9-12
7329 W 63rd St 60501 708-728-3200
Dr. Kevin O'Mara, supt. Fax 728-3155
www.argohs.net
Argo Community HS 1,800/9-12
7329 W 63rd St 60501 708-728-3200
Tim Clark, prin. Fax 728-3155

**Swansea, Saint Clair, Pop. 13,123**
Wolf Branch SD 113 800/K-8
410 Huntwood Rd 62226 618-277-2100
Scott Harres, supt. Fax 235-2376
www.wbsd113.org
Wolf Branch MS 300/5-8
410 Huntwood Rd 62226 618-277-2100
Jeff Burkett, prin. Fax 277-5461

**Sycamore, DeKalb, Pop. 17,257**
Sycamore CUSD 427 3,800/K-12
245 W Exchange St Ste 1 60178 815-899-8100
Kathy Countryman, supt. Fax 899-8110
www.syc427.org
Sycamore HS 1,200/9-12
427 Spartan Trl 60178 815-899-8131
Tim Carlson, prin. Fax 899-8166
Sycamore MS 900/6-8
150 Maplewood Dr 60178 815-899-8170
Jim Cleven, prin. Fax 899-8177

---

Cornerstone Christian Academy 300/PK-12
355 N Cross St 60178 815-895-8522
Tom Olmstead, admin. Fax 895-8717
Hair Professionals Career College Post-Sec.
2245 Gateway Dr 60178 815-756-3596

**Table Grove, Fulton, Pop. 410**
V I T CUSD 2 400/PK-12
1502 E US Highway 136 61482 309-758-5138
Michael Curry, supt. Fax 758-5298
www.vit2.org
V I T HS 100/9-12
1500 E US Highway 136 61482 309-758-5136
Tracey Korsmeyer, prin. Fax 758-5126
V I T JHS 100/7-8
1500 E US Highway 136 61482 309-758-5136
Tracey Korsmeyer, prin. Fax 758-5126

**Tamms, Alexander, Pop. 620**
Egyptian CUSD 5 500/PK-12
20023 Diswood Rd 62988 618-776-5306
Brad Misner, supt. Fax 776-5122
www.egyptianschool.com
Egyptian HS 100/9-12
20023 Diswood Rd 62988 618-776-5251
Bret Gowin, prin. Fax 776-5122
Egyptian JHS 100/6-8
20023 Diswood Rd 62988 618-776-5251
Bret Gowin, prin. Fax 776-5122

Five County Regional Vocational System
130 Washington St 62988 618-747-2703
Jerry Ohlau, dir. Fax 747-2872
Five County Regional Vocational Center Vo/Tech
130 Washington St 62988 618-747-2703
Jerry Ohlau, dir. Fax 747-2872

**Taylor Ridge, Rock Island**
Rockridge CUSD 300 800/PK-12
14110 134th Ave W 61284 309-793-8001
Jack Bambrick, supt. Fax 795-1719
rockridgeschools.org
Rockridge HS 400/9-12
14110 134th Ave W 61284 309-793-8020
Katy Hasson, prin. Fax 795-1763
Rockridge JHS 200/6-8
14110 134th Ave W 61284 309-793-8040
Mike Ruff, prin. Fax 795-9823

**Taylorville, Christian, Pop. 11,116**
Taylorville CUSD 3 1,900/PK-12
512 W Spresser St 62568 217-824-4951
Dr. Greggory Fuerstenau, supt. Fax 824-5157
www.taylorvilleschools.com
Taylorville HS 800/9-12
815 W Springfield Rd 62568 217-824-2268
Robert Richardson, prin. Fax 824-3352
Taylorville JHS 600/5-8
120 E Bidwell St 62568 217-824-4924
Kirk Kettelkamp, prin. Fax 824-7180

---

VisionWay Christian S 200/PK-12
1124 N Webster St 62568 217-824-6722
Glenna Tolliver, prin. Fax 824-6622

**Teutopolis, Effingham, Pop. 1,530**
Teutopolis CUSD 50 1,100/PK-12
PO Box 607 62467 217-857-3535
William Fritcher, supt. Fax 857-6265
www.teutopolisschools.org/
Teutopolis HS 400/9-12
801 W Main St 62467 217-857-3139
Greg Beck, prin. Fax 857-3473
Teutopolis JHS 200/7-8
904 W Water St 62467 217-857-6678
Patrick Drees, prin. Fax 857-6051

**Thomasboro, Champaign, Pop. 1,098**
Prairieview-Ogden CCSD 197
Supt. — See Royal
Prairieview-Ogden JHS 100/7-8
2499 County Road 2100 E 61878 217-694-4122
Steve Fiscus, prin. Fax 694-4123

**Thompsonville, Franklin, Pop. 542**
Thompsonville CUSD 174 300/K-12
21191 Shawneetown Rd 62890 618-627-2446
Chris Grant, supt. Fax 627-2302
thompsonville.il.schoolwebpages.com/
Thompsonville HS 100/9-12
21191 Shawneetown Rd 62890 618-627-2301
Chris Grant, prin. Fax 627-2302

---

Thompsonville Christian S 50/K-10
PO Box 53 62890 618-627-2065
Evelyn Hainey, prin. Fax 627-2726

**Tinley Park, Cook, Pop. 56,069**
Bremen Community HSD 228
Supt. — See Midlothian
Tinley Park HS 1,300/9-12
6111 175th St 60477 708-532-1900
Theresa Nolan, prin. Fax 532-4332

CCSD 146 2,400/PK-8
6611 171st St 60477 708-614-4500
Dr. Jeff Stawick, supt. Fax 614-8992
www.district146.org
Central MS 800/6-8
18146 Oak Park Ave 60477 708-614-4510
Randy Fortin, prin. Fax 614-7271

Kirby SD 140 3,700/PK-8
16931 Grissom Dr 60477 708-532-6462
Dr. Michael Byrne, supt. Fax 532-1512
www.ksd140.org
Grissom MS 600/6-8
17000 80th Ave 60477 708-429-3030
Deborah Broadwell, prin. Fax 532-8529
Prairie View MS 700/6-8
8500 175th St, 708-532-8540
Kristine Roth, prin. Fax 532-8544

---

DeVry University Post-Sec.
18624 W Creek Dr 60477 708-342-3300
Fox College Post-Sec.
18020 Oak Park Ave 60477 708-444-4500
Paul Mitchell The School Post-Sec.
18454 W Creek Dr 60477 708-478-6907

**Toledo, Cumberland, Pop. 1,235**
Cumberland CUSD 77 900/PK-12
1496 Illinois Route 121 62468 217-923-3132
Todd Butler, supt. Fax 923-3132
www.cumberland.k12.il.us
Cumberland HS 300/9-12
1496 Illinois Route 121 62468 217-923-3133
Kevin Maynard, prin. Fax 923-5514
Cumberland MS 200/5-8
1496 Illinois Route 121 62468 217-923-3135
Stacy Keyser, prin. Fax 923-5449

**Tolono, Champaign, Pop. 3,389**
Tolono CUSD 7 1,700/PK-12
PO Box 720 61880 217-485-6510
Andrew Larson, supt. Fax 485-3091
www.unitsevenschools.com
Unity HS 500/9-12
1127 County Road 800 N 61880 217-485-6230
Phil Morrison, prin. Fax 485-6220
Unity JHS 400/6-8
1121 County Road 800 N 61880 217-485-6735
Laura Fitzgerald, prin. Fax 485-3218

**Toulon, Stark, Pop. 1,289**
Stark County CUSD 100
Supt. — See Wyoming
Stark County HS 300/9-12
PO Box 419 61483 309-286-4451
William Lamb, prin. Fax 286-3321
Stark County JHS, PO Box 659 61483 200/6-8
William Lamb, prin. 309-286-3451

**Tremont, Tazewell, Pop. 2,212**
Tremont CUSD 702 1,000/PK-12
400 W Pearl St 61568 309-925-3461
Jeff Hinman, supt. Fax 925-5817
www.tremont702.net
Tremont HS 300/9-12
400 W Pearl St 61568 309-925-3823
Sean Berry, prin. Fax 925-5817
Tremont MS 300/5-8
400 W Pearl St 61568 309-925-3823
Jeremy Garrett, prin. Fax 925-5817

**Trenton, Clinton, Pop. 2,693**
Wesclin CUSD 3 1,200/PK-12
699 Wesclin Rd 62293 618-224-7583
Jennifer Filyaw, supt. Fax 588-9106
www.wesclin.k12.il.us
Wesclin HS 400/9-12
699 Wesclin Rd 62293 618-224-7341
John Isenhower, prin. Fax 588-9106
Wesclin MS 200/4-8
10003 State Route 160 62293 618-224-7355
Roger Freeze, prin. Fax 224-7085

**Troy, Madison, Pop. 9,707**
Triad CUSD 2 3,600/PK-12
203 E Throp St 62294 618-667-5400
Leigh Lewis, supt. Fax 667-8854
www.triadunit2.org
Triad HS 1,200/9-12
703 E US Highway 40 62294 618-667-5409
Rodney Winslow, prin. Fax 667-8853
Other Schools – See Saint Jacob

**Tuscola, Douglas, Pop. 4,425**
Tuscola CUSD 301 1,000/PK-12
409 S Prairie St 61953 217-253-4241
Michael Smith, supt. Fax 253-4522
www.tuscola.k12.il.us/
East Prairie JHS 300/5-8
409 S Prairie St 61953 217-253-2828
Carol Munson, prin. Fax 253-3236
Tuscola HS 300/9-12
500 S Prairie St 61953 217-253-2377
Brad Allen, prin. Fax 253-4861

**Ullin, Pulaski, Pop. 448**
Century CUSD 100 400/K-12
4721 Shawnee College Rd 62992 618-845-3447
Leslie Varble, supt. Fax 845-3476
www.centuryschooldistrict100.com/
Century JSHS 200/6-12
4721 Shawnee College Rd 62992 618-845-3518
Leslie Varble, prin. Fax 845-3476

---

Shawnee Community College Post-Sec.
8364 Shawnee College Rd 62992 618-634-3200

**Union, McHenry, Pop. 576**
McHenry ROE
Supt. — See Woodstock

Evergreen Academy Alt
6506 National St 60180 815-923-2789
Cheryl Horn, prin. Fax 923-4450

**University Park, Will, Pop. 6,997**
Crete-Monee CUSD 201U
Supt. — See Crete
Crete-Monee MS 700/7-8
635 Olmstead Ln, 708-367-2400
Kokona Chrisos, prin. Fax 672-2777

---

Governors State University Post-Sec.
1 University Pkwy, 708-534-5000

**Urbana, Champaign, Pop. 39,989**
University of IL Lab S 300/8-12
1212 W Springfield Ave 61801 217-333-2870
Dr. Jeffrey Wakington, supt.
University of Illinois HS 300/8-12
1212 W Springfield Ave 61801 217-333-2870
Susan Kovacs, dir.

Urbana SD 116 4,200/PK-12
PO Box 3039 61803 217-384-3636
Donald Owen Ed.D., supt. Fax 337-4973
www.usd116.org
Urbana HS 1,000/9-12
1002 S Race St 61801 217-384-3505
Matthew Stark, prin. Fax 384-3532
Urbana MS 800/6-8
1201 S Vine St 61801 217-384-3685
Scott Woods, prin. Fax 367-3156

---

Concept College of Cosmetology Post-Sec.
129 N Race St 61801 217-344-7550
Kingswood S 50/K-12
PO Box 834 61803 217-344-5540
Marsh Jones, hdmstr. Fax 344-5535
University of Illinois Post-Sec.
901 W Illinois St 61801 217-333-1000

**Utica, LaSalle, Pop. 1,346**
Waltham Community CESD 185 100/K-8
946 N 33rd Rd 61373 815-667-4790
Dr. Larry Carlton, supt. Fax 667-4462
www.wesd185.org
Waltham North S 100/3-8
946 N 33rd Rd 61373 815-667-4417
Kristine Eager, prin. Fax 667-4462

**Valmeyer, Monroe, Pop. 1,250**
Valmeyer CUSD 3 500/PK-12
300 S Cedar Bluff Dr 62295 618-935-2100
Eric Frankford, supt. Fax 935-2108
www.valmeyerk12.org
Valmeyer HS 100/9-12
300 S Cedar Bluff Dr 62295 618-935-2100
Eric Frankford, prin. Fax 935-2108
Valmeyer JHS 100/6-8
300 S Cedar Bluff Dr 62295 618-939-2100
Teena Riechmann, prin. Fax 939-2108

**Vandalia, Fayette, Pop. 6,969**
Bond/Christn/Effingham/Fayette/Mtgmy ROE
300 S 7th St 62471 618-283-5011
Julie Wollerman, supt. Fax 283-5013
www.roe3.org
New Approach Alternative HS Alt
1500 Jefferson St 62471 618-283-9311
Laura Benhoff, prin. Fax 283-9339
Other Schools – See Effingham

Okaw Area Vocational Center
1109 N 8th St 62471 618-283-5150
Nick Casey, supt. Fax 283-2014
www.vcs.fayette.k12.il.us/OKAW
Okaw Area Vocational Center Vo/Tech
1109 N 8th St 62471 618-283-5150
Nick Casey, prin. Fax 283-2014

Vandalia CUSD 203 1,500/PK-12
1109 N 8th St 62471 618-283-4525
Rich Well, supt. Fax 283-4107
www.vcs.fayette.k12.il.us/
Vandalia Community HS 500/9-12
1109 N 8th St 62471 618-283-5155
Randy Protz, prin. Fax 283-9855
Vandalia JHS 500/4-8
1011 W Fletcher St 62471 618-283-5151
Brian Kern, prin. Fax 283-8165

**Varna, Marshall, Pop. 382**
Midland CUSD 7
Supt. — See Sparland
Midland HS 200/9-12
1830 State Route 17 61375 309-463-2095
Jeremy Gauwitz, prin. Fax 463-2630

**Vergennes, Jackson, Pop. 291**
Elverado CUSD 196
Supt. — See Elkville
Elverado JHS 100/6-8
PO Box 35 62994 618-684-3527
Belinda Conner, prin. Fax 687-3363

**Vernon Hills, Lake, Pop. 24,688**
Community HSD 128 3,300/9-12
50 Lakeview Pkwy Ste 101 60061 847-247-4500
Dr. Prentiss Lea, supt. Fax 247-4543
www.d128.org/
Vernon Hills HS 1,400/9-12
145 Lakeview Pkwy 60061 847-932-2000
Dr. Jon Guillaume, prin. Fax 932-2049
Other Schools – See Libertyville

Hawthorn CCSD 73 3,900/K-8
841 W End Ct 60061 847-990-4200
Nicholas Brown, supt. Fax 367-3290
www.hawthorn73.org
Hawthorn MS North 600/6-8
201 W Hawthorn Pkwy 60061 847-990-4400
Robert Collins, prin. Fax 367-8124

Hawthorn MS South 600/6-8
600 N Aspen Dr 60061 847-990-4100
Robert Natale, prin. Fax 816-9259

**Vienna, Johnson, Pop. 1,414**
Vienna HSD 133 300/9-12
601 N 1st St 62995 618-658-4461
Joshua Stafford, supt. Fax 658-9727
www.viennahighschool.com
Vienna HS 300/9-12
601 N 1st St 62995 618-658-4461
Joshua Stafford, admin. Fax 658-9727

**Villa Grove, Douglas, Pop. 2,492**
Villa Grove CUSD 302 600/PK-12
400 N Sycamore St 61956 217-832-2261
Norm Tracy, supt. Fax 832-8615
www.vg302.org
Villa Grove HS 200/9-12
400 N Sycamore St 61956 217-832-2321
Stephen Killion, prin. Fax 832-8689
Villa Grove JHS 100/7-8
400 N Sycamore St 61956 217-832-2261
Stephen Killion, prin. Fax 832-8615

**Villa Park, DuPage, Pop. 21,596**
DuPage County SD 45 3,300/PK-8
255 W Vermont St 60181 630-516-7700
Anthony Palmisao, supt. Fax 530-1624
www.d45.org/
Jackson MS 700/6-8
301 W Jackson St 60181 630-516-7600
Renee Reynolds, prin. Fax 530-6271
Jefferson MS 400/6-8
255 W Vermont St 60181 630-516-7800
Raul Gaston, prin. Fax 993-6348

DuPage HSD 88
Supt. — See Addison
Willowbrook HS 2,100/9-12
1250 S Ardmore Ave 60181 630-530-3439
Daniel Krause, prin. Fax 530-3401

Salt Creek SD 48 500/PK-8
1110 S Villa Ave 60181 630-279-8400
Dr. John Correll, supt. Fax 279-6167
www.saltcreek48.org
Albright MS 200/5-8
1110 S Villa Ave 60181 630-279-6160
Scott Jackson, prin. Fax 279-1614

---

Cannella School of Hair Design Post-Sec.
617 W North Ave 60181 630-833-6118
Islamic Foundation S 700/PK-12
300 W Highridge Rd 60181 630-941-8800
Omar Qureshi, dir. Fax 941-8804
Ms. Robert's Academy of Beauty Culture Post-Sec.
17 E Park Blvd 60181 630-941-3880

**Virden, Macoupin, Pop. 3,404**
North Mac CUSD 34
Supt. — See Girard
North Mac HS 400/9-12
231 W Fortune St 62690 217-965-4127
Rob Horn, prin. Fax 965-4006

**Virginia, Cass, Pop. 1,600**
Virginia CUSD 64 400/PK-12
651 S Morgan St 62691 217-452-3085
Brent ODaniell, supt. Fax 452-3088
virginia64.com
Virginia JSHS 100/6-12
651 S Morgan St 62691 217-452-3087
Aaron Llewellyn, prin. Fax 452-3088

**Wadsworth, Lake, Pop. 3,763**
Millburn CCSD 24 900/PK-8
18550 W Millburn Rd 60083 847-356-8331
Jason Lind, supt. Fax 356-9722
www.millburn24.net/
Other Schools – See Lindenhurst

**Waltonville, Jefferson, Pop. 432**
Waltonville CUSD 1 400/PK-12
804 W Knob St 62894 618-279-7211
Alan Estes, supt. Fax 279-3291
www.wcusd1.org
Waltonville HS 100/9-12
804 W Knob St 62894 618-279-7211
Alan Estes, admin. Fax 279-3291

**Warren, Jo Daviess, Pop. 1,421**
Warren CUSD 205 400/PK-12
311 S Water St 61087 815-745-2653
Shawn Teske, supt. Fax 745-2037
www.205warren.net
Warren JSHS 200/6-12
311 S Water St 61087 815-745-2641
Steve Rickert, prin. Fax 745-2654

**Warrensburg, Macon, Pop. 1,195**
Warrensburg-Latham CUSD 11 1,000/PK-12
430 W North St 62573 217-672-3514
Dr. Kristen Kendrick-Weikle, supt. Fax 672-8468
www.wl.k12.il.us
Warrensburg-Latham HS 300/9-12
427 W North St 62573 217-672-3531
Ken Hatcher, prin. Fax 672-3261
Warrensburg-Latham MS 200/6-8
425 W North St 62573 217-672-3321
Paul Hoffman, prin. Fax 672-3770

**Warrenville, DuPage, Pop. 12,933**
CUSD 200
Supt. — See Wheaton
Hubble MS 800/6-8
3S600 Herrick Rd 60555 630-821-7900
Dr. Jon Pilkington, prin. Fax 821-7901

---

Carmel Montessori Academy 50/PK-12
3S238 State Route 59 60555 630-393-2995
Jacob LaFranzo, admin.

**Warsaw, Hancock, Pop. 1,585**
Warsaw CUSD 316 500/PK-12
340 S 11th St 62379 217-256-4282
Bob Gound, supt. Fax 256-4282
warsawschool.com
Warsaw HS, 340 S 11th St 62379 200/9-12
Brad Froman, prin. 217-256-4281

**Washburn, Marshall, Pop. 1,146**
Lowpoint-Washburn CUSD 21 400/PK-12
PO Box 580 61570 309-248-7522
Parker Deitrich, supt. Fax 248-7518
www.washburn.k12.il.us
Lowpoint-Washburn JSHS 200/7-12
PO Box 580 61570 309-248-7521
Mark Zulz, prin. Fax 248-7410

**Washington, Tazewell, Pop. 14,931**
Central SD 51 1,100/PK-8
1301 Eagle Ave 61571 309-444-3943
Dale Heidbreder, supt. Fax 444-9898
www.central51.net
Central IS 600/4-8
1301 Eagle Ave 61571 309-444-3943
Brian Hoelscher, prin. Fax 444-3414

District 50 Schools 800/PK-8
304 E Almond Dr 61571 309-745-8914
Dr. Chad Allaman, supt. Fax 745-5417
www.d50schools.com
Manor MS, 1014 School St 61571 400/4-8
Angela Ludlum, prin. 309-745-3921

Washington Community HSD 308 1,200/9-12
115 Bondurant St 61571 309-444-7704
Dr. Kyle Freeman, supt. Fax 444-5767
www.wacohi.net
Washington Comm HS 1,200/9-12
115 Bondurant St 61571 309-444-3167
Dr. Kyle Freeman, admin. Fax 444-5767

Washington SD 52 900/PK-8
303 Jackson St 61571 309-444-4182
Dr. John Tignor, supt. Fax 444-8538
www.d52schools.com
Washington MS 400/5-8
1100 N Main St 61571 309-444-3361
Jon Smith, prin. Fax 444-3941

**Waterloo, Monroe, Pop. 9,722**
Waterloo CUSD 5 2,700/PK-12
302 Bellefontaine Dr 62298 618-939-3453
Brian Charron, supt. Fax 939-4578
www.wcusd5.net
Waterloo HS 900/9-12
505 E Bulldog 62298 618-939-3455
Lori Costello, prin. Fax 939-5180
Waterloo JHS 600/6-8
200 Bellefontaine Dr 62298 618-939-3457
Nick Schwartz, prin. Fax 939-1383

---

Gibault Catholic HS 200/9-12
501 Columbia Ave 62298 618-939-3883
Russell Hart, prin. Fax 939-7215

**Waterman, DeKalb, Pop. 1,482**
Indian Creek CUSD 425
Supt. — See Shabbona
Indian Creek MS 200/5-8
425 S Elm St 60556 815-264-7712
Steven Simpson, prin. Fax 264-7826

**Watseka, Iroquois, Pop. 5,192**
Iroquois County CUSD 9 1,100/K-12
1411 W Lafayette St 60970 815-432-4931
Kenneth Lee, supt. Fax 432-6889
www.watseka-u9.k12.il.us
Raymond MS 300/6-8
101 W Mulberry St 60970 815-432-2115
Ryan McGuckin, prin. Fax 432-6896
Watseka Community HS 400/9-12
138 S Belmont Ave 60970 815-432-2486
James Bunting, prin. Fax 432-5578

**Wauconda, Lake, Pop. 13,421**
Wauconda CUSD 118 4,400/PK-12
555 N Main St 60084 847-526-7690
Dr. Daniel J. Coles, supt. Fax 526-1019
www.d118.org
Wauconda HS 1,300/9-12
555 N Main St 60084 847-526-6611
Daniel Klett, prin. Fax 487-3595
Wauconda MS 500/6-8
215 Slocum Lake Rd 60084 847-526-2122
Daniel Stoller, prin. Fax 487-3597
Other Schools – See Island Lake

---

Frassati Academy 6-8
316 W Mill St 60084 847-487-5600
Dr. Diane Vida, prin. Fax 487-5611

**Waukegan, Lake, Pop. 87,117**
Waukegan CUSD 60 16,600/PK-12
1201 N Sheridan Rd 60085 224-303-1000
Dr. Donaldo Batiste, supt.
www.wps60.org
Abbott MS 800/6-8
1319 Washington St 60085 224-303-2360
Timothy Bryner, prin. Fax 399-8512
Benny MS 600/6-8
1401 Montesano Ave 60087 224-303-2460
Minerva Cruz-Familar, prin. Fax 399-8524
Jefferson MS 900/6-8
600 S Lewis Ave 60085 224-303-2560
Lee Gaiser, prin. Fax 399-8516
Juarez MS 700/6-8
201 N Butrick St 60085 224-303-2660
Kwing Lee, prin. Fax 399-8506
Waukegan Alternative S 100/Alt
1020 Glen Rock Ave 60085 224-303-2860
Grant Flink, dir. Fax 399-8520
Waukegan HS 3,200/9-12
2325 Brookside Ave 60085 224-303-3000
Brian Riegler, prin. Fax 399-8542
Webster MS 600/6-8
930 New York St 60085 224-303-2760
Yvonne Brown, prin. Fax 399-8540

---

Cristo Rey St. Martin College Prep HS 200/9-12
515 S Martin Luther King Jr 60085 847-623-5500
Michael Odiotti, prin. Fax 623-5604
Lake County Baptist S 200/PK-12
1550 W Yorkhouse Rd 60087 847-623-7600
Timothy Kowach, prin. Fax 623-2085
Robert Morris University Post-Sec.
1507 S Waukegan Rd 60085 800-762-5960

**Waverly, Morgan, Pop. 1,296**
Waverly CUSD 6 400/PK-12
201 N Miller St 62692 217-435-8121
Dustin Day, supt. Fax 435-3431
www.waverlyscotties.com
Waverly HS 100/7-12
201 N Miller St 62692 217-435-2211
Tamara Hermes, prin. Fax 435-3431

**Wayne City, Wayne, Pop. 1,023**
Wayne City CUSD 100 400/PK-12
PO Box 457 62895 618-895-3103
Jeff Mitchell, supt. Fax 895-2331
www.waynecity100.org
Wayne City JSHS 200/7-12
PO Box 457 62895 618-895-3103
Tony Richardson, prin. Fax 895-2331

**Weldon, DeWitt, Pop. 425**
Deland-Weldon CUSD 57
Supt. — See De Land
Deland-Weldon MS 50/7-8
2311 N 300 East Rd 61882 217-736-2401
Amanda Geary, prin. Fax 736-2654

**Westchester, Cook, Pop. 16,532**
Westchester SD 92-5 1,200/K-8
9981 Canterbury St 60154 708-450-2700
Rachel Dziallo, supt. Fax 450-2718
www.sd925.org
Westchester MS 400/6-8
1620 Norfolk Ave 60154 708-450-2735
Gregory Leban, prin. Fax 450-2752

---

St. Joseph HS 800/9-12
10900 W Cermak Rd 60154 708-562-4433
Ronald Hoover, prin. Fax 562-4459

**West Chicago, DuPage, Pop. 26,802**
Benjamin SD 25 700/PK-8
28W250 Saint Charles Rd 60185 630-876-7800
Dr. Philip Ehrhardt, supt. Fax 876-3325
www.bendist25.org
Benjamin MS 400/5-8
28W300 Saint Charles Rd 60185 630-876-7820
Michael Fitzgerald, prin. Fax 231-3886

Community HSD 94 2,200/9-12
326 Joliet St 60185 630-876-6200
Dr. Douglas Domeracki, supt. Fax 876-6241
www.d94.org
Community HS 2,200/9-12
326 Joliet St 60185 630-876-6200
Dr. Moses Cheng, prin. Fax 876-6241

West Chicago ESD 33 4,000/PK-8
312 E Forest Ave 60185 630-293-6000
Dr. Charles Johns, supt. Fax 293-6088
www.wego33.org
Leman MS 800/6-8
238 E Hazel St 60185 630-293-6060
Marc Campbell, prin. Fax 562-2586

---

Central Medical Education Post-Sec.
550 E Washington St 60185 630-682-1600
Wheaton Academy 600/9-12
900 Prince Crossing Rd 60185 630-562-7500
Dr. Gene Frost, head sch Fax 231-0842

**West Dundee, Kane**
CUSD 300
Supt. — See Algonquin
Dundee MS 900/6-8
4200 W Main St 60118 847-426-1485
Jeff Herb, prin. Fax 426-4008

---

Hair Professionals Academy Post-Sec.
825 Village Quarter Rd # B 60118 847-836-5900

**Western Springs, Cook, Pop. 12,882**
Lyons Township HSD 204
Supt. — See La Grange
Lyons Township HS South Campus 2,000/9-10
4900 Willow Springs Rd 60558 708-579-6500
Dr. Brian Waterman, prin. Fax 588-7473

Western Springs SD 101 1,500/PK-8
4335 Howard Ave 60558 708-246-3700
Dr. Brian Barnhart, supt. Fax 482-2581
www.d101.org
McClure JHS 500/6-8
4225 Wolf Rd 60558 708-246-7590
F. Daniel Chick, prin. Fax 246-4370

**West Frankfort, Franklin, Pop. 8,100**
Frankfort CUSD 168 1,900/PK-12
900 N Cherry St 62896 618-937-2421
Gregory Goins, supt. Fax 932-2025
www.wfschools.org
Central JHS 300/7-8
1600 E 9th St 62896 618-937-2444
Charley Cass, prin. Fax 937-2445
Frankfort Community HS 500/9-12
601 E Main St 62896 618-932-3126
Bethany Shaw, prin. Fax 932-6515

**Westmont, DuPage, Pop. 24,243**
CUSD 201 1,500/PK-12
133 S Grant St 60559 630-468-8000
Kevin Carey, supt. Fax 969-9022
www.cusd201.org
Westmont HS 500/9-12
909 Oakwood Dr 60559 630-468-8100
Jack Baldermann, prin. Fax 654-2758
Westmont JHS 400/6-8
944 Oakwood Dr 60559 630-468-8200
John Jonak, prin. Fax 654-2203

Maercker SD 60 1,300/PK-8
1 S Cass Ave Ste 202 60559 630-515-4840
Dr. Jamie Reilly, supt. Fax 515-4845
www.maercker.org
Other Schools – See Willowbrook

**West Peoria, Peoria, Pop. 4,328**
Peoria SD 150
Supt. — See Peoria
Coolidge MS 300/5-8
2708 W Rohmann Ave 61604 309-672-6506
Mervyn Swanson, prin. Fax 673-7605

**Westville, Vermilion, Pop. 3,171**
Westville CUSD 2 1,300/PK-12
125 W Ellsworth St 61883 217-267-3141
Dr. Seth Miller, supt. Fax 267-3144
www.westville.k12.il.us
Westville HS 400/9-12
918 N State St 61883 217-267-2183
Guy Goodlove, prin. Fax 267-7593
Westville JHS 200/7-8
412 Moses Ave 61883 217-267-2185
Jared Ellison, prin. Fax 267-3621

**Wheaton, DuPage, Pop. 51,936**
CUSD 200 13,400/PK-12
130 W Park Ave 60189 630-682-2002
Dr. Jeff Schuler, supt. Fax 682-2068
www.cusd200.org
Edison MS 700/6-8
1125 S Wheaton Ave 60189 630-682-2050
Rachel Bednar, prin. Fax 682-2337
Franklin MS 800/6-8
211 E Franklin St 60187 630-682-2060
David Bendis, prin. Fax 682-2340
Monroe MS 700/6-8
1855 Manchester Rd 60187 630-682-2285
Bryan Buck, prin. Fax 682-2331
Wheaton North HS 2,200/9-12
701 W Thomas Rd 60187 630-784-7300
Matt Biscan, prin. Fax 682-2158
Wheaton/Warrenville South HS 2,300/9-12
1920 S Wiesbrook Rd 60189 630-784-7200
Dave Claypool, prin. Fax 682-2042
Other Schools – See Warrenville

---

St. Francis HS 800/9-12
2130 W Roosevelt Rd 60187 630-668-5800
Raeann Huhn, prin. Fax 668-5893
Wheaton College Post-Sec.
501 College Ave 60187 630-752-5000

**Wheeling, Cook, Pop. 37,130**
Township HSD 214
Supt. — See Arlington Heights
Wheeling HS 1,800/9-12
900 S Elmhurst Rd 60090 847-718-7000
Angela Sisi, prin. Fax 718-7007

Wheeling CCSD 21 6,700/PK-8
999 W Dundee Rd 60090 847-537-8270
Dr. Kate Hyland, supt. Fax 520-2848
www.ccsd21.org
Holmes MS 700/6-8
221 S Wolf Rd 60090 847-520-2790
Martin Hopkins, prin. Fax 419-3073
London MS 700/6-8
1001 W Dundee Rd 60090 847-520-2745
Luis Correa, prin. Fax 520-2842
Other Schools – See Buffalo Grove

---

SOLEX College Post-Sec.
350 E Dundee Rd 60090 847-229-9595
Worsham College of Mortuary Science Post-Sec.
495 Northgate Pkwy 60090 847-808-8444

**White Hall, Greene, Pop. 2,509**
North Greene Unit SD 3 600/PK-12
407 N Main St 62092 217-374-2842
Lawrence Coultas, supt. Fax 374-2849
www.northgreene.com
North Greene JSHS 300/7-12
546 N Main St 62092 217-374-2131
Keppen Clanton, prin. Fax 374-2132

**Williamsfield, Knox, Pop. 574**
Williamsfield CUSD 210 300/PK-12
PO Box 179 61489 309-639-2219
Tim Farquer, supt. Fax 639-2618
www.billtown.org
Williamsfield HS, PO Box 179 61489 100/9-12
Zack Binder, prin. 309-639-2216
Williamsfield MS, PO Box 179 61489 100/6-8
Zack Binder, prin. 309-639-2216

**Williamsville, Sangamon, Pop. 1,465**
Williamsville CUSD 15 1,400/PK-12
800 S Walnut St 62693 217-566-2014
David Root, supt. Fax 566-2183
www.wcusd15.org
Williamsville HS 400/9-12
900 S Walnut St 62693 217-566-3361
Doug Furlow, prin. Fax 566-3792
Williamsville JHS 400/6-8
500 S Walnut St 62693 217-566-3600
Clay Shoufler, prin. Fax 566-2475

**Willowbrook, DuPage, Pop. 8,420**
Gower SD 62 900/PK-8
7700 Clarendon Hills Rd 60527 630-986-5383
Dr. Victor Simon, supt. Fax 323-3074
www.gower62.com
Other Schools – See Burr Ridge

Hinsdale Township HSD 86
Supt. — See Hinsdale
Transition Center Adult
42 63rd St 60527 630-323-9673
Tammy Prentiss, admin. Fax 323-9676

Maercker SD 60
Supt. — See Westmont
Westview Hills MS 500/6-8
630 65th St 60527 630-515-4830
Sean Nugent, prin. Fax 515-4835

**Wilmette, Cook, Pop. 26,500**
Avoca SD 37 600/PK-8
2921 Illinois Rd 60091 847-251-3587
Kevin Jauch, supt. Fax 251-7742
avoca37.org
Murphy MS 200/PK-PK, 6-
2921 Illinois Rd 60091 847-251-3617
Matthew Palcer, prin. Fax 251-4179

Wilmette SD 39 3,700/PK-8
615 Locust Rd 60091 847-256-2450
Ray Lechner, supt. Fax 256-1920
www.wilmette39.org
Wilmette JHS 800/7-8
620 Locust Rd 60091 847-256-7280
Kelly Jackson, prin. Fax 256-0204

---

Loyola Academy 2,100/9-12
1100 Laramie Ave 60091 847-256-1100
Kathryn Baal Ph.D., prin. Fax 853-4512
Regina Dominican HS 300/9-12
701 Locust Rd 60091 847-256-7660
Meg Bigane, prin. Fax 256-3726

**Wilmington, Will, Pop. 5,660**
Wilmington CUSD 209U 1,400/PK-12
209U Wildcat Ct 60481 815-926-1751
Jay Plese, supt. Fax 926-1692
www.wilmington.will.k12.il.us
Wilmington HS 500/9-12
209 Wildcat Ct 60481 815-926-1752
Kevin Feeney, prin. Fax 926-1691
Wilmington MS 300/6-8
715 S Joliet St 60481 815-476-2189
Adam Spicer, prin. Fax 476-1941

**Winchester, Scott, Pop. 1,579**
Winchester CUSD 1 700/PK-12
149 S Elm St 62694 217-742-3175
David Roberts, supt. Fax 742-3312
www.winchesterschools.net
Winchester HS, 200 W Cross St 62694 200/9-12
Dennis Vortman, prin. 217-742-3151

**Windsor, Shelby, Pop. 1,177**
Windsor CUSD 1 400/PK-12
1424 Minnesota Ave 61957 217-459-2636
Gavin Sronce, supt. Fax 459-2661
www.windsor.k12.il.us
Windsor JSHS 200/7-12
1424 Minnesota Ave 61957 217-459-2636
Erik Van Hoveln, prin. Fax 459-2794

**Winfield, DuPage, Pop. 8,924**
Winfield SD 34 400/PK-8
0S150 Winfield Rd 60190 630-909-4900
Dr. Gwynne Kell, supt. Fax 260-2382
www.winfield34.org/
Winfield Central S 200/3-8
0S150 Park St 60190 630-909-4960
Dawn Reinke, prin. Fax 933-9236

**Winnebago, Winnebago, Pop. 3,067**
Winnebago CUSD 323 1,600/PK-12
304 E McNair Rd 61088 815-335-2456
Scott Bloomquist, supt. Fax 335-7574
www.winnebagoschools.org
Winnebago HS 600/9-12
200 E McNair Rd 61088 815-335-2336
Ronald Gruber, prin. Fax 335-7548
Winnebago MS 300/6-8
407 N Elida St 61088 815-335-2364
Catherine Finley, prin. Fax 335-1437

**Winnetka, Cook, Pop. 12,045**
New Trier Township HSD 203
Supt. — See Northfield
New Trier Township HS - Winnetka Campus 3,100/10-12
385 Winnetka Ave 60093 847-446-7000
Denise Dubravec, prin. Fax 835-9851

Winnetka SD 36 1,800/K-8
1235 Oak St 60093 847-446-9400
Trisha Kocanda, supt. Fax 446-9408
www.winnetka36.org
Washburne MS 500/7-8
515 Hibbard Rd 60093 847-446-5892
Dave Kanne, prin. Fax 446-1380

---

Hadley School for the Blind Post-Sec.
700 Elm St 60093 847-446-8111
Music Center of the North Shore Post-Sec.
300 Green Bay Rd 60093 847-446-3822
North Shore Country Day S 500/PK-12
310 Green Bay Rd 60093 847-446-0674
Thomas Doar, hdmstr. Fax 446-0675

**Winthrop Harbor, Lake, Pop. 6,595**
Winthrop Harbor SD 1 600/K-8
500 North Ave 60096 847-731-3085
Patricia Goodwin, supt. Fax 731-3156
www.whsd1.org
North Prairie JHS 300/5-8
500 North Ave 60096 847-731-3089
Carrie Nottingham, prin. Fax 731-3152

**Wolf Lake, Union**
Shawnee CUSD 84 400/PK-12
3365 N State Route 3 62998 618-833-5709
Shelly Clover-Hill, supt. Fax 833-4171
www.shawneedistrict84.com/
Shawnee JSHS 100/6-12
3365 N State Route 3 62998 618-833-5307
Mike Hanson, prin. Fax 833-5468

**Wood Dale, DuPage, Pop. 13,602**
Wood Dale SD 7 1,200/PK-8
543 N Wood Dale Rd 60191 630-595-9510
Dr. John Corbett, supt. Fax 595-5625
www.wd7.org
Wood Dale JHS 300/6-8
655 N Wood Dale Rd 60191 630-766-6210
Shelly Skarzynski, prin. Fax 766-1839

**Woodhull, Henry, Pop. 803**
Alwood CUSD 225 400/PK-12
301 E 5th Ave 61490 309-334-2719
Shannon Bumann, supt. Fax 334-2925
www.alwood.net
Alwood MSHS 200/6-12
301 E 5th Ave 61490 309-334-2102
David Mills, prin. Fax 334-2632

**Woodlawn, Jefferson, Pop. 691**
Woodlawn Unit SD 209 200/PK-12
300 N Central St 62898 618-735-2631
David Larkin, supt. Fax 735-2032
www.woodlawngs.org
Woodlawn HS 200/9-12
300 N Central St 62898 618-735-2631
Thomas Rude, prin. Fax 735-2032

**Woodridge, DuPage, Pop. 34,058**
Woodridge SD 68 2,900/PK-8
7925 Janes Ave 60517 630-985-7925
Dr. Cathy Skinner, supt. Fax 910-2060
www.woodridge68.org
Jefferson JHS 600/7-8
7200 Janes Ave 60517 630-852-8010
Dr. William Schmidt, prin. Fax 969-7168

---

Westwood College Post-Sec.
7155 Janes Ave 60517 630-434-7655

**Wood River, Madison, Pop. 10,543**
East Alton-Wood River Community HSD 14 600/9-12
777 N Wood River Ave 62095 618-254-3151
Dr. John Pearson, supt. Fax 254-9113
www.eawr.net
East Alton-Wood River HS 600/9-12
777 N Wood River Ave 62095 618-254-3151
Leigh Robinson, prin. Fax 254-9113

Wood River-Hartford ESD 15 800/PK-8
501 E Lorena Ave 62095 618-254-0607
Patrick Anderson Ph.D., supt. Fax 254-9048
www.wrh15.org/
Lewis-Clark JHS 200/6-8
501 E Lorena Ave 62095 618-254-4355
Heather Johnson, prin. Fax 254-7600

**Woodstock, McHenry, Pop. 24,445**
McHenry ROE
2200 N Seminary Ave 60098 815-334-4475
Leslie Schermerhorn, supt. Fax 338-0475
www.mchenryroe.org/
Other Schools – See Union

Woodstock CUSD 200 6,300/PK-12
227 W Judd St 60098 815-338-8200
Michael Moan Ed.D., supt. Fax 338-2005
www.woodstockschools.org/
Creekside MS 800/6-8
3201 Hercules Rd 60098 815-337-5200
Robert Hackbart, prin. Fax 206-0476
Northwood MS 600/6-8
2121 N Seminary Ave 60098 815-338-4900
Jake Wakitsch, prin. Fax 337-2150
Woodstock HS 1,000/9-12
501 W South St 60098 815-338-4370
Justin Smith Ed.D., prin. Fax 334-0811
Woodstock North HS 900/9-12
3000 Raffel Rd 60098 815-334-2100
Brian McAdow, prin. Fax 334-2101

---

Marian Central Catholic HS 700/9-12
1001 McHenry Ave 60098 815-338-4220
Andreas Edmondson, admin. Fax 338-4253

**Worth, Cook, Pop. 10,649**
Worth SD 127 1,000/PK-8
11218 S Ridgeland Ave 60482 708-448-2800
Dr. Rita Wojtylewski, supt. Fax 448-6215
www.worthschools.org
Worth JHS 300/6-8
11151 S New England Ave 60482 708-448-2803
Joseph Zampillo, prin. Fax 448-6155

**Wyoming, Stark, Pop. 1,418**
Stark County CUSD 100 800/PK-12
300 W Van Buren St 61491 309-695-6123
Jerry Klooster, supt.
www.stark100.com
Other Schools – See Toulon

**Yorkville, Kendall, Pop. 16,715**
Yorkville CUSD 115 5,000/PK-12
PO Box 579 60560 630-553-4382
Dr. Tim Shimp, supt. Fax 553-4398
www.y115.org
Yorkville HS 1,200/10-12
797 Game Farm Rd 60560 630-553-4380
David Travis, prin. Fax 553-4397
Yorkville HS Academy 9-9
702 Game Farm Rd 60560 630-553-4385
David Travis, prin. Fax 553-4592
Yorkville MS 800/7-8
920 Prairie Crossing Dr 60560 630-553-4544
Lisa Adler, prin. Fax 553-5181

---

Parkview Christian Academy 200/PK-12
201 W Center St 60560 630-553-5158
Deborah Benson, supt. Fax 553-3370

**Zeigler, Franklin, Pop. 1,781**
Zeigler-Royalton CUSD 188 600/PK-12
PO Box 38 62999 618-596-5841
George Wilkerson, supt. Fax 596-6789
www.zr188.org
Zeigler-Royalton HS 200/9-12
PO Box 38 62999 618-596-5841
Quent Hamilton, prin. Fax 596-6789
Zeigler-Royalton JHS 100/7-8
PO Box 87 62999 618-596-2121
Leigh Bailey, prin. Fax 596-2075

**Zion, Lake, Pop. 23,535**
Zion ESD 6 2,700/PK-8
2200 Bethesda Blvd 60099 847-872-5455
Dr. Keely Roberts, supt. Fax 746-1280
www.zion6.com
Zion Central JHS 600/7-8
1716 27th St 60099 847-746-1431
Joseph Kent, prin. Fax 746-9750

Zion-Benton Township HSD 126 2,700/9-12
3901 21st St 60099 847-731-9300
Dr. Chris Clark, supt. Fax 731-4441
www.zbths.org
New Tech High @ Zion-Benton East 300/9-12
1634 23rd St 60099 847-731-9800
David Frusher, prin. Fax 746-5428
Zion-Benton Township HS 2,400/9-12
3901 21st St 60099 847-731-9300
Chris Pawelczyk, prin. Fax 731-4408

# INDIANA

## INDIANA DEPARTMENT OF EDUCATION
**151 W Ohio St Ste X, Indianapolis 46204-2564**
**Telephone 317-232-6610**
**Fax 317-232-8004**
**Website http://www.doe.in.gov**

Superintendent of Public Instruction Glenda Ritz

## INDIANA BOARD OF EDUCATION
**200 W Washington St Ste 229, Indianapolis 46204-2798**

Chairperson Tony Bennett

## EDUCATIONAL SERVICE CENTERS (ESC)

Central Indiana ESC
Dr. Kevin M. Caress, dir. 317-759-5555
6036 Lakeside Blvd Bldg A
Indianapolis 46278
www.ciesc.k12.in.us

East Central ESC
Larry John, dir., 1601 Indiana Ave 765-825-1247
Connersville 47331 Fax 825-2532
www.ecesc.k12.in.us/

Northern Indiana ESC
Ted Chittum, dir. 574-254-0111
56535 Magnetic Dr Fax 254-0148
Mishawaka 46545
www.niesc.k12.in.us/

Northwest Indiana ESC
Edward Schoenfelt, dir. 219-926-5555
48 W 900 N, Chesterton 46304 Fax 926-5553
www.nwiesc.k12.in.us/

Region 8 ESC
Joshua Wenning, dir. 260-724-6200
251 W 850 N, Decatur 46733 Fax 244-6201
www.r8esc.k12.in.us/

Southern Indiana ESC
Judy Bueckert, dir. 812-482-6641
1102 Tree Lane Dr, Jasper 47546 Fax 482-6652
www.siec.k12.in.us/

Wabash Valley ESC
Dr. Dennis Cahill, dir. 765-463-1589
3061 Benton St Fax 463-1580
West Lafayette 47906
www.esc5.k12.in.us/

West Central ESC
Valerie Buchanan, dir. 765-653-2727
PO Box 21, Greencastle 46135 Fax 653-7897
www.wciesc.k12.in.us/

William E. Wilson ESC
Dr. Phil Partenheimer, dir. 812-256-8000
PO Box 217, Charlestown 47111 Fax 256-8012
www.wesc.k12.in.us/

## PUBLIC, PRIVATE AND CATHOLIC SECONDARY SCHOOLS

**Akron, Kosciusko, Pop. 1,159**
Tippecanoe Valley SC 2,100/K-12
8343 S State Road 19 46910 574-353-7741
Brett Boggs, supt. Fax 353-7743
www.tvsc.k12.in.us
Tippecanoe Valley HS 600/9-12
8345 S State Road 19 46910 574-353-7031
Kirk Doehrmann, prin. Fax 353-1016
Tippecanoe Valley MS 500/6-8
11303 W 800 S 46910 574-353-7353
Blaine Conley, prin. Fax 353-7189

**Albion, Noble, Pop. 2,325**
Central Noble Community SC 1,300/K-12
200 E Main St 46701 260-636-2175
Alan Middleton, supt. Fax 636-7918
centralnoble.k12.in.us
Central Noble JSHS 400/6-12
401 E Highland St 46701 260-636-2117
Geoff Brose, prin. Fax 636-2791

**Alexandria, Madison, Pop. 5,088**
Alexandria Community SC 1,600/PK-12
202 E Washington St 46001 765-724-4496
Dr. Alice Johnson, supt. Fax 724-5049
www.alex.k12.in.us
Alexandria-Monroe JSHS 800/7-12
1 Burden Ct 46001 765-724-4413
Thomas Johns, prin. Fax 724-5041

**Anderson, Madison, Pop. 54,768**
Anderson Community SC 4,800/PK-12
1600 Hillcrest Ave 46011 765-641-2000
Terry Thompson, supt. Fax 641-2080
www.acsc.net
Anderson HS 1,500/9-12
4610 Madison Ave 46013 765-641-2037
Alex Brandon, prin. Fax 641-2041
D26 Career Center Vo/Tech
325 W 38th St 46013 765-641-2046
Julie Morse, dir. Fax 641-2041
Highland MS 1,100/6-8
2108 E 200 N 46012 765-641-2059
David Tijerina, prin. Fax 641-2064

Frankton-Lapel Community SD 2,900/PK-12
7916 W 300 N 46011 765-734-1261
Bobby Fields, supt. Fax 734-1129
www.flcs.k12.in.us/
Other Schools – See Frankton, Lapel

---

Anderson Christian S 200/PK-12
5401 S Madison Ave 46013 765-649-0123
Thomas Snell, admin. Fax 649-3844
Anderson University Post-Sec.
1100 E 5th St 46012 765-649-9071
Apex School of Beauty Culture Post-Sec.
333 Jackson St 46016 765-642-7560
Harrison College Post-Sec.
140 E 53rd St 46013 765-644-7514
Indiana Christian Academy 100/PK-12
432 W 300 N 46012 765-643-7884
Kevin Plew, prin. Fax 683-4200
Liberty Christian HS 300/7-12
2323 Columbus Ave 46016 765-644-7774
Stacy Scott, prin. Fax 644-7779

**Angola, Steuben, Pop. 8,487**
Metropolitan SD of Steuben County 3,100/K-12
400 S Martha St 46703 260-665-2854
Dr. Brent Wilson, supt. Fax 665-9155
www.msdsteuben.k12.in.us
Angola HS 900/9-12
350 S John McBride Ave 46703 260-665-2186
Travis Heavin, prin. Fax 665-7012
Angola MS 700/6-8
1350 E Maumee St 46703 260-665-9581
Ann Rice, prin. Fax 665-9583

---

Trine University Post-Sec.
1 University Ave 46703 260-665-4100

**Arcadia, Hamilton, Pop. 1,652**
Hamilton Heights SC 2,300/PK-12
PO Box 469 46030 317-984-3538
Dr. Derek Arrowood, supt. Fax 984-3042
www.hhschuskies.org
Hamilton Heights HS 700/9-12
PO Box 379 46030 317-984-3551
Jarrod Mason, prin. Fax 984-3554
Hamilton Heights MS 500/6-8
PO Box 609 46030 317-984-3588
Bret Bailey, prin. Fax 984-3231

**Argos, Marshall, Pop. 1,665**
Argos Community SD 700/PK-12
410 N First St 46501 574-892-5139
Michele Riise, supt. Fax 892-6527
www.argos.k12.in.us/
Argos Community JSHS 300/7-12
500 Yearick St 46501 574-892-5137
Nick Medich, prin. Fax 892-6527

**Attica, Fountain, Pop. 3,214**
Attica Consolidated SC 900/PK-12
205 E Sycamore St 47918 765-762-7000
Derek Marshall, supt. Fax 762-7007
www.attica.k12.in.us
Attica JSHS 400/7-12
211 E Sycamore St 47918 765-762-7000
Johnathan Hoke, prin. Fax 762-7017

**Auburn, DeKalb, Pop. 12,632**

---

Lakewood Park Christian S 500/PK-12
5555 County Road 29 46706 260-925-1393
Dr. Ed Yoder, supt. Fax 925-5010

**Aurora, Dearborn, Pop. 3,721**
South Dearborn Community SC 2,800/PK-12
6109 Squire Pl 47001 812-926-2090
Dr. John Mehrle, supt. Fax 926-4216
www.sdcsc.k12.in.us
South Dearborn HS 900/9-12
5770 Highlander Pl 47001 812-926-2090
Brad Stoneking, prin. Fax 926-4162
South Dearborn MS 500/7-8
5850 Squire Pl 47001 812-926-2090
Jason Cheek, prin. Fax 926-2149

**Austin, Scott, Pop. 4,251**
Scott County SD 1 1,300/K-12
PO Box 9 47102 812-794-8750
Robert Anderson, supt. Fax 794-8765
www.scsd1.com/
Austin HS 400/9-12
401 S Highway 31 47102 812-794-8730
Sherman Smith, prin. Fax 794-8739
Austin MS 300/6-8
401 S Highway 31 47102 812-794-8740
David Deaton, prin. Fax 794-8739

**Avon, Hendricks, Pop. 12,177**
Avon Community SC 7,900/K-12
7203 E US Highway 36 46123 317-544-6000
Dr. Margaret Hoernemann, supt. Fax 544-6001
www.avon-schools.org
Avon HS 2,600/9-12
7575 E County Road 150 S 46123 317-544-5000
Matt Shockley, prin. Fax 544-5001
Avon MS North 700/7-8
1251 N Dan Jones Rd 46123 317-544-5500
Susan Green, prin. Fax 544-5501
Avon MS South 700/7-8
7199 E US Highway 36 46123 317-544-5700
Dan Chapin, prin. Fax 544-5701

**Bainbridge, Putnam, Pop. 737**
North Putnam Community SD 1,700/PK-12
PO Box 169 46105 765-522-6218
Daniel Noel Ed.D., supt. Fax 522-3562
www.nputnam.k12.in.us
Other Schools – See Greencastle, Roachdale

**Batesville, Franklin, Pop. 6,459**
Batesville Community SC 1,900/PK-12
PO Box 121 47006 812-934-2194
Dr. James Roberts, supt. Fax 933-0833
www.batesvilleinschools.com
Batesville HS 700/9-12
1 Bulldog Blvd 47006 812-934-4384
Andy Allen, prin. Fax 934-5964
Batesville MS 500/6-8
201 N Mulberry St 47006 812-934-5175
Dave Strouse, prin. Fax 933-0834

**Bedford, Lawrence, Pop. 13,252**
North Lawrence Community SD 5,300/PK-12
PO Box 729 47421 812-279-3521
Gary Conner, supt. Fax 275-1577
www.nlcs.k12.in.us
Bedford MS 600/6-8
1501 N St 47421 812-279-9781
David Schlegel, prin. Fax 277-3218
Bedford-North Lawrence HS 1,600/9-12
595 Stars Blvd 47421 812-279-9756
Daniel Dyke, prin. Fax 279-9304
North Lawrence Career Ctr Vo/Tech
258 BNL Dr 47421 812-279-3561
Tim Day, prin. Fax 275-1578
Shawswick MS 200/6-8
71 Shawswick School Rd 47421 812-275-6121
James Pentzer, prin. Fax 275-3458
Other Schools – See Oolitic

**Beech Grove, Marion, Pop. 13,930**
Beech Grove CSD 2,700/PK-12
5334 Hornet Ave 46107 317-788-4481
Dr. Paul Kaiser, supt. Fax 782-4065
www.bgcs.k12.in.us
Beech Grove HS 800/9-12
5330 Hornet Ave 46107 317-786-1447
Elizabeth Walters, prin. Fax 781-2920
Beech Grove MS 400/7-8
1248 Buffalo St 46107 317-784-6649
Thomas Gearhart, prin. Fax 781-2926

St. Francis Hospital Center Post-Sec.
1600 Albany St 46107 317-783-8220

**Berne, Adams, Pop. 3,972**
South Adams SD 1,400/PK-12
1075 Starfire Way 46711 260-589-3133
Scott Litwiller, supt. Fax 589-2065
www.southadams.k12.in.us
South Adams HS 400/9-12
1000 Parkway St 46711 260-589-3131
Trent Lehman, prin. Fax 589-3042
South Adams MS 400/6-8
1212 Starfire Way 46711 260-589-1102
Jeff Rich, prin. Fax 589-2112

**Bicknell, Knox, Pop. 2,893**
North Knox SC 1,300/K-12
11110 N State Road 159 47512 812-735-4434
Darrel Bobe, supt. Fax 328-6262
www.nknox.k12.in.us
North Knox JSHS 600/7-12
10890 N State Road 159 47512 812-735-2990
Matt Sandefer, prin. Fax 328-2155

**Bloomfield, Greene, Pop. 2,386**
Bloomfield SD 1,000/K-12
PO Box 266 47424 812-384-4507
Daniel Sichting, supt. Fax 384-0172
www.bsd.k12.in.us
Bloomfield JSHS 500/7-12
PO Box 266 47424 812-384-4550
David Dean, prin. Fax 384-1422

Eastern Greene SD 1,300/PK-12
1471 N State Road 43 47424 812-825-5722
Ted Baechtold, supt. Fax 825-9413
www.egreene.k12.in.us/
Eastern Greene HS 400/9-12
11064 E State Road 54 47424 812-825-5621
Kevin Frank, prin. Fax 825-6661
Eastern Greene MS 400/5-8
10503 E State Road 54 47424 812-825-5010
Doug Lewis, prin. Fax 825-7386

**Bloomington, Monroe, Pop. 78,128**
Monroe County Community SC 10,500/PK-12
315 E North Dr 47401 812-330-7700
Judith DeMuth Ed.D., supt. Fax 330-7813
www.mccsc.edu
Academy of Science & Entrepreneurship 200/9-12
444 S Patterson Dr 47403 812-330-2480
Jessica Willis, prin. Fax 330-2481
Batchelor MS 500/7-8
900 W Gordon Pike 47403 812-330-7763
Eric Gilpin, prin. Fax 330-7766
Bloomington Graduation S 100/Alt
705 W Coolidge Dr 47403 812-330-7708
Eric Jackson, dir. Fax 330-2433
Bloomington HS North 1,500/9-12
3901 N Kinser Pike 47404 812-330-7724
Jeffry Henderson, prin. Fax 330-7805
Bloomington HS South 1,700/9-12
1965 S Walnut St 47401 812-330-7714
Mark Fletcher, prin. Fax 330-7810
Hoosier Hills Career Center Vo/Tech
3070 N Prow Rd 47404 812-330-7730
Alan Dafoe, dir. Fax 330-7807
Jackson Creek MS 500/7-8
3980 S Sare Rd 47401 812-330-2451
David Pillar, prin. Fax 330-2457
Tri-North MS 500/7-8
1000 W 15th St 47404 812-330-7745
Dr. Gale Hill, prin. Fax 330-7799
Broadview Learning Center Adult
705 W Coolidge Dr 47403 812-330-7731
Robert Moore, dir. Fax 330-7789

Bloomington Hospital Post-Sec.
PO Box 1149 47402 812-336-6821
Hair Arts Academy Post-Sec.
1681 N College Ave 47404 812-339-1117
Harmony S 200/PK-12
PO Box 1787 47402 812-334-8349
Steve Bonchek, dir. Fax 333-3435
Indiana University Post-Sec.
107 S Indiana Ave 47405 812-855-4848
Ivy Tech Community College - Bloomington Post-Sec.
200 N Daniels Way 47404 812-332-1559
Lighthouse Christian Academy 200/K-12
1201 W That Rd 47403 812-824-2000
Joyce Huck B.A., prin. Fax 824-2017

**Bluffton, Wells, Pop. 9,806**
Metro SD of Bluffton-Harrison 1,400/PK-12
805 E Harrison Rd 46714 260-824-2620
Wayne Barker, supt. Fax 824-6011
www.bhmsd.org
Bluffton-Harrison MS 400/5-8
1500 Stogdill Rd 46714 260-824-3536
Claire Paul, prin. Fax 824-6014
Bluffton HS 500/9-12
1 Tiger Trl 46714 260-824-3724
Steve Baker, prin. Fax 824-6001

**Boone Grove, Porter**
Porter Township SC
Supt. — See Valparaiso
Boone Grove MS 400/6-8
325 W 550 S 46302 219-464-4828
Robert Lichtenberger, prin. Fax 465-0999

**Boonville, Warrick, Pop. 6,171**
Warrick County SC 9,900/K-12
PO Box 809 47601 812-897-0400
Brad Schneider, supt. Fax 897-6033
www.warrick.k12.in.us/
Boonville HS 900/9-12
300 N 1st St 47601 812-897-4701
Mike Whitten, prin. Fax 897-6061
Boonville MS 700/6-8
555 N Yankeetown Rd 47601 812-897-1420
Abbie Redmon, prin. Fax 897-6584
Other Schools – See Lynnville, Newburgh

**Borden, Clark, Pop. 799**
West Clark Community SC
Supt. — See Sellersburg
Borden JSHS 400/7-12
PO Box 260 47106 812-967-2087
Lisa Nale, prin. Fax 967-2086

**Bourbon, Marshall, Pop. 1,801**
Triton SC 1,000/K-12
100 Triton Dr 46504 574-342-2255
Donna Burroughs, supt. Fax 342-8165
www.triton.k12.in.us/
Triton JSHS 500/7-12
300 Triton Dr 46504 574-342-6505
Robert Ross, prin. Fax 342-8175

**Brazil, Clay, Pop. 7,835**
Clay Community SD 4,400/PK-12
1013 S Forest Ave 47834 812-443-4461
Jeffery Fritz, supt. Fax 442-0849
www.clay.k12.in.us
North Clay MS 800/6-8
3450 W State Road 340 47834 812-448-1530
Robert Boltinghouse, prin. Fax 442-0608
Northview HS 1,100/9-12
3150 W State Road 340 47834 812-448-2661
Christopher Mauk, prin. Fax 446-2647
Other Schools – See Clay City

**Bremen, Marshall, Pop. 4,550**
Bremen Public SD 1,500/K-12
512 W Grant St 46506 574-546-3929
Dr. James White, supt. Fax 546-6303
www.bps.k12.in.us
Bremen HS 500/9-12
511 W Grant St 46506 574-546-3511
Bruce Jennings, prin. Fax 546-5477

**Bristol, Elkhart, Pop. 1,559**

Kessington Christian S 50/PK-12
19153 County Road 104 46507 574-848-4987
Nancy Stump, admin.

**Brookville, Franklin, Pop. 2,579**
Franklin County Community SC 2,900/PK-12
225 E 10th St 47012 765-647-4128
Dr. Debbie Howell, supt. Fax 647-2417
www.fccsc.k12.in.us
Brookville MS 500/5-8
9092 Wildcat Ln 47012 765-647-6040
Christopher Bundy, prin. Fax 647-4960
Franklin County HS 900/9-12
1 Wildcat Ln 47012 765-647-4101
Keith Isaacs, prin. Fax 647-2732

**Brownsburg, Hendricks, Pop. 20,984**
Brownsburg Community SC 7,600/PK-12
310 S Stadium Dr 46112 317-852-5726
Jim Snapp, supt. Fax 852-1015
www.brownsburg.k12.in.us
Brownsburg East MS 1,100/6-8
1250 Airport Rd 46112 317-852-2386
Shane Hacker, prin. Fax 852-1023
Brownsburg HS 2,300/9-12
1000 S Odell St 46112 317-852-2258
Bret Daghe, prin. Fax 852-1490
Brownsburg West MS 700/6-8
1555 S Odell St 46112 317-852-3143
Laurie Johnson, prin. Fax 858-4100
Harris Academy Alt
725 S Green St Ste A 46112 317-852-1010
Lynn Lodwick, dir. Fax 852-1012

Bethesda Christian S 400/PK-12
7950 N County Road 650 E 46112 317-858-2820
Don Criss, supt. Fax 858-2819

**Brownstown, Jackson, Pop. 2,921**
Brownstown Central Community SC 1,700/PK-12
608 W Commerce St 47220 812-358-4271
Greg Walker, supt. Fax 358-5303
www.btownccs.k12.in.us
Brownstown Central HS 600/9-12
500 N Elm St 47220 812-358-3453
Joseph Sheffer, prin. Fax 358-5318
Brownstown Central MS 400/6-8
520 W Walnut St 47220 812-358-4947
Doug McClure, prin. Fax 358-3940

**Bunker Hill, Miami, Pop. 866**
Maconaquah SC 2,300/PK-12
7932 S Strawtown Pike 46914 765-689-9131
Dr. Douglas Arnold, supt. Fax 689-0995
www.maconaquah.k12.in.us
Maconaquah HS 700/9-12
256 E 800 S 46914 765-689-9131
Chad Carlson, prin. Fax 689-9528
Maconaquah MS 500/6-8
594 E 800 S 46914 765-689-9131
Craig Jernagan, prin. Fax 689-9360

**Butler, DeKalb, Pop. 2,658**
DeKalb County Eastern Community SD 1,500/K-12
300 E Washington St 46721 260-868-2125
Dr. Jeffrey Stephens, supt. Fax 868-2562
www.dekalbeastern.com
Eastside JSHS 700/7-12
603 E Green St 46721 260-868-2186
Larry Yoder, prin. Fax 868-5773

**Cambridge City, Wayne, Pop. 1,861**
Western Wayne SD
Supt. — See Pershing
Lincoln HS 400/9-12
205 E Parkway Dr 47327 765-478-5916
Jason Bodnar, prin. Fax 478-3262
Lincoln MS 200/6-8
205 E Parkway Dr 47327 765-478-5840
Jasoin Bodnar, prin. Fax 478-3265

**Campbellsburg, Washington, Pop. 579**
West Washington SC 800/K-12
9699 W Mount Tabor Rd 47108 812-755-4996
Keith Nance, supt. Fax 755-4843
www.wwcs.k12.in.us
West Washington JSHS 400/7-12
8028 W Batts Rd 47108 812-755-4996
Mary Knapp, prin. Fax 755-4460

**Cannelton, Perry, Pop. 1,540**
Cannelton CSD 200/PK-12
109 S 3rd St Ste A 47520 812-547-2637
Alva Sibbitt, supt. Fax 547-4142
www.cannelton.k12.in.us
Cannelton JSHS 100/6-12
109 S 3rd St 47520 812-547-3296
Brian Garrett, prin. Fax 548-2288

**Carmel, Hamilton, Pop. 77,695**
Carmel Clay SD 15,600/PK-12
5201 E Main St 46033 317-844-9961
Dr. Nicholas D. Wahl, supt. Fax 844-9965
www.ccs.k12.in.us
Carmel HS 4,600/9-12
520 E Main St 46032 317-846-7721
John Williams, prin. Fax 571-4066
Carmel MS 1,200/6-8
300 S Guilford Rd 46032 317-846-7331
Lila Jay, prin. Fax 571-4067
Clay MS 1,200/6-8
5150 E 126th St 46033 317-844-7251
Todd Crosby, prin. Fax 571-4020
Creekside MS 1,400/6-8
3525 W 126th St 46032 317-733-6420
Tom Harmas, prin. Fax 733-6422

University HS of Indiana 300/9-12
2825 W 116th St 46032 317-733-4475
Charles Webster, head sch Fax 733-4484

**Castleton, Marion, Pop. 36**

Kaye Beauty College Post-Sec.
6346 E 82nd St 46250 317-576-0224

**Cayuga, Vermillion, Pop. 1,146**
North Vermillion Community SC 700/K-12
5551 N Falcon Dr 47928 765-492-4033
Michael Turner, supt. Fax 492-7001
www.nvc.k12.in.us
North Vermillion JSHS 400/7-12
5555 N Falcon Dr 47928 765-492-3364
Jayne Ann Virostko, prin. Fax 492-7006

**Cedar Lake, Lake, Pop. 11,431**
Hanover Community SC 2,100/K-12
PO Box 645 46303 219-374-3500
Thomas Taylor, supt. Fax 374-4411
www.hanover.k12.in.us
Hanover Central HS 600/9-12
10120 W 133rd Ave 46303 219-374-3800
Mary Ann West, prin. Fax 374-4408
Hanover Central MS 500/6-8
10631 W 141st Ave 46303 219-374-3900
Tony Hiatt, prin. Fax 374-8926

**Centerville, Wayne, Pop. 2,522**
Centerville-Abington Community SD 1,700/PK-12
115 W South St 47330 765-855-3475
Philip Stevenson, supt. Fax 855-2524
www.centerville.k12.in.us
Centerville-Abington JHS 300/7-8
509 Willow Grove Rd 47330 765-855-5113
Rick Schauss, prin. Fax 855-5207
Centerville HS 500/9-12
507 Willow Grove Rd 47330 765-855-3481
Mikel McCoy, prin. Fax 855-3484

**Chalmers, White, Pop. 504**
Frontier SC 800/K-12
PO Box 809 47929 219-984-5009
Cathy Rowe, supt. Fax 984-5022
www.frontier.k12.in.us
Frontier JSHS 400/7-12
1 Falcon Dr 47929 219-984-5437
Jeff Hettinger, prin. Fax 984-5360

**Charlestown, Clark, Pop. 7,449**
Greater Clark County SD
Supt. — See Jeffersonville
Charlestown HS 700/9-12
1 Pirate Pl 47111 812-256-3328
Mark Laughner, prin. Fax 256-7274
Charlestown MS 600/6-8
8804 High Jackson Rd 47111 812-256-6363
Karen Wesely, prin. Fax 256-7282

**Charlottesville, Hancock**
Eastern Hancock County Community SC 1,100/K-12
10370 E County Road 250 N 46117 317-467-0064
Steve Welsh, supt. Fax 936-5516
www.easternhancock.org

Eastern Hancock HS — 400/9-12
10320 E County Road 250 N 46117 — 317-936-5595
David Pfaff, prin. — Fax 936-5050
Eastern Hancock MS — 300/6-8
10380 E County Road 250 N 46117 — 317-936-5324
David Pfaff, prin. — Fax 936-5050

**Chesterton, Porter, Pop. 12,902**
Duneland SC — 5,900/K-12
601 W Morgan Ave 46304 — 219-983-3600
Dr. David Pruis, supt. — Fax 983-3614
www.duneland.k12.in.us
Chesterton HS — 2,000/9-12
2125 S 11th St 46304 — 219-983-3730
James Goetz, prin. — Fax 983-3775
Chesterton MS — 1,000/7-8
651 W Morgan Ave 46304 — 219-983-3776
Craig Stafford, prin. — Fax 983-3798

**Churubusco, Whitley, Pop. 1,774**
Smith-Green Community SD — 1,200/PK-12
222 W Tulley St 46723 — 260-693-2007
Galen Mast, supt. — Fax 693-6434
www.sgcs.k12.in.us/
Churubusco JSHS — 700/6-12
1 Eagle Dr 46723 — 260-693-2131
Jim Folland, prin. — Fax 693-3673

**Cicero, Hamilton, Pop. 4,762**

---

Indiana Academy — 100/9-12
24815 State Road 19 46034 — 317-984-3575
Steve Baughman, prin. — Fax 984-5081

**Clarksville, Clark, Pop. 21,221**
Clarksville Community SC — 1,400/PK-12
200 Ettel Ln 47129 — 812-282-7753
Dr. Kim Knott, supt. — Fax 282-7754
www.ccsc.k12.in.us/
Clarksville HS — 400/9-12
800 Dr Dot Lewis Dr 47129 — 812-282-8231
Dan Butler, prin. — Fax 282-8234
Clarksville MS — 400/5-8
101 Ettel Ln 47129 — 812-282-8235
Nikki Bullington, prin. — Fax 280-5004

---

Our Lady of Providence JSHS — 500/7-12
707 Providence Way 47129 — 812-945-2538
Melinda Ernstberger, prin. — Fax 981-2538
PJ's College of Cosmetology — Post-Sec.
1414 Blackiston Mill Rd 47129 — 812-282-0459

**Clay City, Clay, Pop. 856**
Clay Community SD
Supt. — See Brazil
Clay City JSHS — 400/7-12
601 Lankford St 47841 — 812-939-2154
Jeff Bell, prin. — Fax 939-3170

**Clayton, Hendricks, Pop. 965**
Mill Creek Community SC — 1,600/PK-12
6631 S County Road 200 W 46118 — 317-539-9200
Jim Diagostino, supt. — Fax 539-9215
www.mccsc.k12.in.us/
Cascade HS — 500/9-12
6565 S County Road 200 W 46118 — 317-539-9315
Jon Acton, prin. — Fax 539-9350
Cascade MS — 400/6-8
6423 S County Road 200 W 46118 — 317-539-9285
Eric Sieferman, prin. — Fax 539-9310

**Clinton, Vermillion, Pop. 4,826**
South Vermillion Community SC — 1,900/PK-12
PO Box 387 47842 — 765-832-2426
David Chapman, supt. — Fax 832-7391
www.svcs.k12.in.us
South Vermillion HS — 600/9-12
770 Wildcat Dr 47842 — 765-832-3551
Don Harman, prin. — Fax 832-5310
South Vermillion MS — 400/6-8
900 Wildcat Dr 47842 — 765-832-7727
Angela Harris, prin. — Fax 832-5316

**Cloverdale, Putnam, Pop. 2,143**
Cloverdale Community SD — 1,300/PK-12
310 E Logan St 46120 — 765-795-4664
Greg Linton, supt. — Fax 795-5166
www.cloverdale.k12.in.us
Cloverdale HS — 400/9-12
205 E Market St 46120 — 765-795-4203
Sonny Stoltz, prin. — Fax 795-4381
Cloverdale MS — 400/5-8
312 E Logan St 46120 — 765-795-2900
Stacey Baugh, prin. — Fax 795-2901

**Columbia City, Whitley, Pop. 8,635**
Whitley County Consolidated SD — 3,600/PK-12
107 N Walnut St 46725 — 260-244-5772
Dr. Patricia O'Connor, supt. — Fax 244-4099
www.wccs.k12.in.us
Columbia City HS — 1,100/9-12
600 N Whitley St 46725 — 260-244-6136
Jennifer Reiff, prin. — Fax 244-7326
Eagle Tech Academy — 400/9-12
107 N Walnut St 46725 — 260-244-5707
Braden Mullett, admin. — Fax 248-4403
Indian Springs MS — 800/6-8
1692 S State Road 9 46725 — 260-244-5148
Jan Boylen, prin. — Fax 244-4710

**Columbus, Bartholomew, Pop. 43,281**
Bartholomew Consolidated SC — 11,300/PK-12
1200 Central Ave 47201 — 812-376-4220
Dr. John Quick, supt. — Fax 376-4486
www.bcsc.k12.in.us
Central MS — 800/7-8
725 7th St 47201 — 812-376-4287
Randall Gratz, prin. — Fax 376-4511
Columbus Area Career Connection — Vo/Tech
1400 25th St 47201 — 812-376-4240
Gene Hack, dir. — Fax 376-4699
Columbus East HS — 1,500/9-12
230 S Marr Rd 47201 — 812-376-4369
Mark Newell, prin. — Fax 376-4358
Columbus North HS — 2,000/9-12
1400 25th St 47201 — 812-376-4432
David Clark, prin. — Fax 376-4291
Columbus Signature Acad - NewTech — 9-12
2205 25th St 47201 — 812-376-4595
Mike Reed, prin. — Fax 376-4599
McDowell Educational Center — Alt
2700 McKinley Ave 47201 — 812-376-4451
Andrea Quick, dir. — Fax 376-4512
Northside MS — 800/7-8
1400 27th St 47201 — 812-376-4405
Amy Dixon, prin. — Fax 376-4479

---

Columbus Christian S — 200/PK-12
3170 Indiana Ave 47201 — 812-372-3780
Rev. Kendall Wildey, admin. — Fax 372-3878
Columbus Regional Hospital — Post-Sec.
2400 17th St 47201 — 812-376-5439
Harrison College — Post-Sec.
2222 Poshard Dr 47203 — 812-379-9000
Ivy Tech Community College - Columbus — Post-Sec.
4475 Central Ave 47203 — 812-372-9925

**Connersville, Fayette, Pop. 13,304**
Fayette County SC — 4,000/PK-12
1401 Spartan Dr 47331 — 765-825-2178
Dr. Russell Hodges, supt. — Fax 825-8060
www.fayette.k12.in.us
Connersville HS — 1,200/9-12
1100 Spartan Dr 47331 — 765-825-1151
Randal Judd, prin. — Fax 825-0777
Connersville MS — 600/7-8
1900 N Grand Ave 47331 — 765-825-1139
Beth Denham, prin. — Fax 827-4346
Whitewater Technical Career Center — Vo/Tech
1300 Spartan Dr 47331 — 765-825-0521
Steven Dungan, dir. — Fax 827-0836

**Converse, Miami, Pop. 1,252**
Oak Hill United SC — 1,600/K-12
PO Box 550 46919 — 765-395-3341
Joel Martin, supt. — Fax 395-3343
www.ohusc.k12.in.us
Oak Hill HS — 500/9-12
7756 W Delphi Pike Ste 27 46919 — 765-384-4381
Michael McDivitt, prin. — Fax 384-5414
Oak Hill JHS — 200/7-8
7760 W Delphi Pike Ste 27 46919 — 765-384-4385
Greg Perkins, prin. — Fax 384-4386

**Corydon, Harrison, Pop. 3,080**
South Harrison Community SD — 3,000/K-12
315 S Harrison Dr 47112 — 812-738-2168
Dr. Mark Eastridge, supt. — Fax 738-2158
www.shcsc.k12.in.us/
Corydon Central HS — 700/9-12
375 Country Club Rd 47112 — 812-738-4181
Keith Marshall, prin. — Fax 738-1145
Corydon Central JHS — 400/7-8
377 Country Club Rd 47112 — 812-738-4184
Mark Black, prin. — Fax 738-5752
Other Schools – See Elizabeth

**Covington, Fountain, Pop. 2,619**
Covington Community SC — 1,000/PK-12
601 Market St 47932 — 765-793-4877
Kirk Booe M.S., supt. — Fax 793-5209
www.covington.k12.in.us/
Covington Community HS — 300/9-12
1017 6th St 47932 — 765-793-2286
Adam Welchans, prin. — Fax 793-5200
Covington MS — 200/6-8
514 Railroad St 47932 — 765-793-4451
Steve Reynolds, prin. — Fax 793-5217

**Crawfordsville, Montgomery, Pop. 15,708**
Crawfordsville Community SD — 2,500/PK-12
1000 Fairview Ave 47933 — 765-362-2342
Scott Bowling, supt. — Fax 364-3237
www.cville.k12.in.us
Crawfordsville HS — 700/9-12
1 W Athenian Dr 47933 — 765-362-2340
Gregory Hunt, prin. — Fax 364-3200
Crawfordsville MS — 6-8
705 Wallace Ave 47933 — 765-362-2992
Jay Strickland, prin. — Fax 364-3212

North Montgomery Community SC — 2,100/PK-12
480 W 580 N 47933 — 765-359-2112
Dr. Colleen Moran, supt. — Fax 359-2111
www.nm.k12.in.us/
North Montgomery HS — 600/9-12
5945 N US Highway 231 47933 — 765-362-5140
Michael Cox, prin. — Fax 362-6710
Northridge MS — 500/6-8
482 W 580 N 47933 — 765-364-1071
Benjamin Moore, prin. — Fax 362-7985

South Montgomery Community SC — 1,800/K-12
6425 US 231 S 47933 — 765-866-0203
Dr. Shawn Greiner, supt. — Fax 866-0736
www.southmont.k12.in.us
Southmont HS — 600/9-12
6425 S US Highway 231 47933 — 765-866-0350
Kevin Stewart, prin. — Fax 866-2044
Southmont JHS — 300/7-8
6460 S US Highway 231 47933 — 765-866-2023
Mike Tricker, prin. — Fax 866-2045

---

Wabash College — Post-Sec.
301 W Wabash Ave 47933 — 765-361-6100

**Crothersville, Jackson, Pop. 1,577**
Crothersville Community SD — 500/K-12
201 S Preston St 47229 — 812-793-2601
Dr. Terry Goodin, supt. — Fax 793-3004
www.crothersville.k12.in.us
Crothersville JSHS — 300/6-12
109 N Preston St 47229 — 812-793-2051
David Schill, prin. — Fax 793-3004

**Crown Point, Lake, Pop. 27,010**
Crown Point Community SC — 7,700/PK-12
200 E North St 46307 — 219-663-3371
Dr. Teresa Eineman, supt. — Fax 662-3414
www.cps.k12.in.us
Colonel John Wheeler MS — 900/6-8
401 W Joliet St 46307 — 219-663-2173
Timothy Vassar, prin. — Fax 662-4378
Crown Point HS — 2,600/9-12
1500 S Main St 46307 — 219-663-4885
Chip Pettit, prin. — Fax 662-5661
Taft MS — 900/6-8
1000 S Main St 46307 — 219-663-1507
Michael Hazen, prin. — Fax 662-4349

---

St. Anthony School of Echocardiography — Post-Sec.
1201 S Main St 46307 — 219-757-6132

**Culver, Marshall, Pop. 1,330**
Culver Community SC — 1,000/K-12
PO Box 231 46511 — 574-842-3364
Dr. Vicki McGuire, supt. — Fax 842-4615
www.culver.k12.in.us
Culver Community HS — 300/9-12
701 School St 46511 — 574-842-3391
Brett Berndt, prin. — Fax 842-3392
Culver Community MS — 200/7-8
1 Cavalier Dr 46511 — 574-842-5690
Brett Berndt, prin. — Fax 842-5691

---

Culver Academies — 800/9-12
1300 Academy Rd 46511 — 574-842-7000
John Buxton, head sch — Fax 842-8161

**Daleville, Delaware, Pop. 1,631**
Daleville Community SD — 800/K-12
14300 W 2nd St 47334 — 765-378-3329
Paul Garrison M.S., supt. — Fax 378-3649
www.daleville.k12.in.us
Daleville JSHS — 400/7-12
8400 S Bronco Dr 47334 — 765-378-3371
Eric Douglas M.A., prin. — Fax 378-4076

**Danville, Hendricks, Pop. 8,895**
Danville Community SC — 2,600/PK-12
200 Warrior Way 46122 — 317-745-2212
Dr. Tracey Shafer, supt. — Fax 745-3924
www.danville.k12.in.us
Central Normal Campus — Alt
49 N Wayne St 46122 — 317-745-7942
James Bryant, dir. — Fax 745-3886
Danville Community HS — 800/9-12
100 Warrior Way 46122 — 317-745-6431
Paul Hamann, prin. — Fax 745-3908
Danville Community MS — 800/5-8
1425 W Lincoln St 46122 — 317-745-5491
Marsha Webster, prin. — Fax 745-3949

**Decatur, Adams, Pop. 9,334**
North Adams Community SD — 1,900/PK-12
625 Stadium Dr 46733 — 260-724-7146
Brent Lehman, supt. — Fax 724-4777
www.nadams.k12.in.us
Bellmont HS — 800/9-12
1000 E North Adams Dr 46733 — 260-724-7121
Kimberly Harsh, prin. — Fax 724-7826
Bellmont MS — 500/5-8
1200 E North Adams Dr 46733 — 260-724-3137
Scott Miller, prin. — Fax 724-4495

**Delphi, Carroll, Pop. 2,860**
Delphi Community SC — 1,600/PK-12
501 Armory Rd 46923 — 765-564-2100
Ralph Walker, supt. — Fax 564-6919
www.delphi.k12.in.us/
Delphi Community HS — 500/9-12
301 Armory Rd 46923 — 765-564-3481
Ann-Marie Circle, prin. — Fax 564-3260
Delphi Community MS — 400/6-8
401 Armory Rd 46923 — 765-564-3411
Ann Circle, prin. — Fax 564-2135

**Demotte, Jasper, Pop. 3,774**

---

Covenant Christian HS — 100/9-12
PO Box 430 46310 — 219-987-7651
Clarence Oudman, admin. — Fax 987-7652

**Denver, Miami, Pop. 480**
North Miami Community SD — 1,000/K-12
PO Box 218 46926 — 765-985-3891
Nicholas Eccles, supt. — Fax 985-3904
www.nmcs.k12.in.us/
North Miami MSHS — 500/7-12
570 E 900 N 46926 — 765-985-2931
Nathan Stauffer, prin. — Fax 985-2056

**Donaldson, Marshall**

---

Ancilla College — Post-Sec.
PO Box 1 46513 — 574-936-8898

**Dubois, Dubois, Pop. 488**
Northeast Dubois County SC — 1,000/PK-12
5379 E Main St 47527 — 812-678-2781
William Hochgesang, supt. — Fax 678-4418
www.nedubois.k12.in.us
Dubois MS — 300/5-8
4550 N 4th St 47527 — 812-678-2181
Ryan Case, prin. — Fax 678-2282

Northeast Dubois HS 300/9-12
4711 N Dubois Rd NE 47527 812-678-2251
Rick Gladish, prin. Fax 678-3991

**Dugger, Sullivan, Pop. 917**
Dugger Union Community School Corp K-12
7356 E County Road 50 S 47848 812-648-7109
Ross Martin, supt. Fax 648-7112
www.duggerunionschools.org
Dugger Union Community S K-12
7356 E County Road 50 S 47848 812-789-2096
Ross Martin, prin. Fax 648-7109

**Dunkirk, Jay, Pop. 2,346**
Jay SC
Supt. — See Portland
West Jay MS 300/6-8
140 E Highland Ave 47336 765-768-7648
Mike Crull, prin. Fax 768-6152

**Dyer, Lake, Pop. 16,198**
Lake Central SC
Supt. — See Saint John
Kahler MS 1,200/5-8
600 Joliet St 46311 219-865-3535
Ken Newton, prin. Fax 865-4428

---

Heritage Christian HS 50/9-12
10790 Calumet Ave 46311 219-558-2660
Ralph Medema, admin. Fax 558-2664
Mid-America Reformed Seminary Post-Sec.
229 Seminary Dr 46311 219-864-2400

**East Chicago, Lake, Pop. 29,444**
School City of East Chicago 5,700/PK-12
1401 E 144th St 46312 219-391-4100
Dr. Youssef Yomtoob, supt. Fax 391-4126
www.scec.k12.in.us
Block MS 700/7-8
2700 Cardinal Dr 46312 219-391-4084
Dee Etta Wright, prin. Fax 391-4282
East Chicago Central HS 1,400/9-12
1100 W Columbus Dr 46312 219-391-4000
Shaunna Finley, prin. Fax 391-4049
West Side MS 300/7-8
4001 Indianapolis Blvd 46312 219-391-4068
Veronica Williams, prin. Fax 391-4284

**Edinburgh, Johnson, Pop. 4,440**
Edinburgh Community SC 900/PK-12
202 Keeley St 46124 812-526-2681
Dr. William A. Glentzer, supt. Fax 526-0271
www.ecsc.k12.in.us
Edinburgh Community HS 300/9-12
300 Keeley St 46124 812-526-5501
Kevin Rockey, prin. Fax 526-3439
Edinburgh Community MS 200/6-8
300 Keeley St 46124 812-526-3418
Jon Price, prin. Fax 526-3439

**Elizabeth, Harrison, Pop. 161**
South Harrison Community SD
Supt. — See Corydon
South Central JSHS 300/6-12
6675 E Highway 11 SE 47117 812-969-2941
David Beaver, prin. Fax 969-3019

**Elkhart, Elkhart, Pop. 49,305**
Baugo Community SD 2,000/K-12
29125 County Road 22 46517 574-293-8583
James DuBois, supt. Fax 294-2171
www.baugo.org/
Jimtown HS 600/9-12
59021 County Road 3 46517 574-295-2343
Jeffrey Ziegler, prin. Fax 294-2171
Jimtown JHS 300/7-8
58903 County Road 3 46517 574-294-6586
Michael Stout, prin. Fax 294-8557

Concord Community SD 4,900/K-12
59040 Minuteman Way 46517 574-875-5161
John Trout, supt. Fax 875-8762
www.concord.k12.in.us
Concord Community HS 1,500/9-12
59117 Minuteman Way 46517 574-875-6524
Dan Cunningham, prin. Fax 875-8580
Concord JHS 800/7-8
59397 County Road 11 46517 574-875-5122
Rob Zook, prin. Fax 875-1089

Elkhart Community SD 12,500/PK-12
2720 California Rd 46514 574-262-5500
Dr. Robert Haworth, supt. Fax 262-5733
www.elkhart.k12.in.us
Elkhart Area Career Ctr Vo/Tech
2424 California Rd 46514 574-262-5650
Dr. David Benak, dir. Fax 262-5801
Elkhart Central HS 1,800/9-12
1 Blazer Blvd 46516 574-295-4700
Frank Serge, prin. Fax 295-4712
Elkhart Memorial HS 1,800/9-12
2608 California Rd 46514 574-262-5600
Cary Anderson, prin. Fax 262-5625
Moran MS 600/7-8
200 W Lusher Ave 46517 574-295-4805
Cynthia Bonner, prin. Fax 295-4807
North Side MS 700/7-8
300 Lawrence St 46514 574-262-5570
Sara Jackowiak, prin. Fax 262-5573
West Side MS 700/7-8
101 S Nappanee St 46514 574-295-4815
Kristie Stutsman, prin. Fax 295-4812

---

Anabaptist Mennonite Biblical Seminary Post-Sec.
3003 Benham Ave 46517 800-964-2627
Elkhart Christian Academy 400/PK-12
25943 County Road 22 46517 574-293-1609
Sue Alberts, supt. Fax 293-3238
Harrison College Post-Sec.
56075 Parkway Ave 46516 574-522-0397

**Ellettsville, Monroe, Pop. 6,255**
Richland-Bean Blossom Community SC 2,800/PK-12
600 Edgewood Dr 47429 812-876-7100
Dr. Mike Wilcox, supt. Fax 876-7020
www.rbbcsc.k12.in.us/
Edgewood HS 800/9-12
601 S Edgewood Dr 47429 812-876-2277
Dirk Ackerman, prin. Fax 876-9163
Edgewood JHS 600/6-8
851 W Edgewood Dr 47429 812-876-2005
Rod Hite, prin. Fax 876-8985

**Elnora, Daviess, Pop. 631**
North Daviess Community SD 1,100/K-12
5494 E State Road 58 47529 812-636-8000
Robert Bell, supt. Fax 636-7546
www.ndaviess.k12.in.us
North Daviess JSHS 500/7-12
5494 E State Road 58 47529 812-636-8000
Jed Jerrels, prin. Fax 636-7255

**Elwood, Madison, Pop. 8,510**
Elwood Community SC 1,600/PK-12
1306 N Anderson St 46036 765-552-9861
Dr. Christopher Daughtry, supt. Fax 552-8088
www.elwood.k12.in.us
Elwood JSHS 500/7-12
1137 N 19th St 46036 765-552-9854
David Retherford, prin. Fax 552-1044
Hinds Career Center Vo/Tech
1105 N 19th St 46036 765-552-9881
James Pearson, dir. Fax 552-2021

**Eminence, Morgan**
Eminence Community SC 500/K-12
PO Box 135 46125 765-528-2101
Jeff Gibboney, supt. Fax 528-2262
www.eminence.k12.in.us
Eminence JSHS 300/6-12
PO Box 105 46125 765-528-2221
Corey Scott, prin. Fax 528-2276

**Evansville, Vanderburgh, Pop. 114,065**
Evansville-Vanderburgh SC 21,600/PK-12
951 Walnut St 47713 812-435-8453
Dr. David Smith, supt. Fax 435-8421
www.evscschools.com/
Academy for Innovative Studies 300/Alt
3013 N 1st Ave 47710 812-435-8316
Karen Scheessele, prin. Fax 435-8517
Bosse HS 800/9-12
1300 Washington Ave 47714 812-477-1661
Sheila Huff, prin. Fax 474-6976
Central HS 1,300/9-12
5400 N 1st Ave 47710 812-435-8292
Andrea Campbell, prin. Fax 435-8515
Harrison HS 1,500/9-12
211 Fielding Rd 47715 812-477-1046
Elizabeth Wells, prin. Fax 474-4125
Helfrich Park MS 600/6-8
2603 W Maryland St 47712 812-435-8246
Timothy McIntosh, prin. Fax 435-8249
McGary MS 300/6-8
1535 Joyce Ave 47714 812-476-3035
Dale Naylor, prin. Fax 474-6919
New Tech Institute 200/9-12
1901 Lynch Rd 47711 812-435-0967
Christpher Gibson, prin. Fax 435-8568
North HS 1,600/9-12
15331 Highway 41 N 47725 812-435-8283
John Skinner, prin. Fax 435-8349
North JHS 800/7-8
15325 Highway 41 N 47725 812-435-0975
Aaron Huff, prin. Fax 435-8887
Perry Heights MS 500/6-8
5800 Hogue Rd 47712 812-435-8326
Charles Goodman, prin. Fax 435-8363
Plaza Park MS 700/6-8
7301 Lincoln Ave 47715 812-476-4971
Shane Browder, prin. Fax 474-6922
Reitz HS 1,400/9-12
350 Dreier Blvd 47712 812-435-8206
Beth Carnahan, prin. Fax 435-8217
Southern IN Career and Technical Center Vo/Tech
1901 Lynch Rd 47711 812-435-8438
Dr. Cory Herrin, prin. Fax 435-8366
Thompkins MS 800/6-8
1300 W Mill Rd 47710 812-435-8323
Nichole Alcorn, prin. Fax 435-8588
Washington MS 400/6-8
1801 Washington Ave 47714 812-477-8983
Michele Branson, prin. Fax 474-6930

---

Evansville Day S 50/PK-12
3400 N Green River Rd 47715 812-476-3039
Jarin Jaffee, head sch Fax 476-4061
Harrison College Post-Sec.
4601 Theatre Dr 47715 812-476-6000
Ivy Tech Community College - Southwest Post-Sec.
3501 N 1st Ave 47710 812-426-2865
Mater Dei HS 500/9-12
1300 Harmony Way 47720 812-426-2258
Darin Knight, prin. Fax 421-5717
Reitz Memorial HS 800/9-12
1500 Lincoln Ave 47714 812-476-4973
Cyndi Schneider, prin. Fax 474-2942
Roger's Academy of Hair Design Post-Sec.
2903 Mount Vernon Ave 47712 812-429-0110
University of Evansville Post-Sec.
1800 Lincoln Ave 47714 812-488-2000
University of Southern Indiana Post-Sec.
8600 University Blvd 47712 812-464-8600
Westside Catholic S St. Boniface Campus 100/4-8
2031 W Michigan St 47712 812-422-1014
Tracey Unfried, prin. Fax 422-1057

**Fairland, Shelby, Pop. 314**
Northwestern Cons SC of Shelby County 1,400/PK-12
4920 W 600 N 46126 317-835-7461
Chris Hoke, supt. Fax 835-4441
www.nwshelbyschools.org
Triton Central HS 500/9-12
4774 W 600 N 46126 317-835-3000
Cary Chandler, prin. Fax 480-1887
Triton Central MS 500/5-8
4740 W 600 N 46126 317-835-3006
Bobby Thompson, prin. Fax 835-3008

**Fairmount, Grant, Pop. 2,932**
Madison-Grant United SC 1,300/PK-12
11580 S E 00 W 46928 765-948-4143
Dr. Scott Deetz Ph.D., supt. Fax 948-4150
www.mgusc.k12.in.us
Madison-Grant HS 500/9-12
11700 S E 00 W 46928 765-948-4141
Anna Roth, prin. Fax 948-4874
Madison-Grant JHS 200/7-8
11640 S E 00 W 46928 765-948-5132
Chris Smedley, prin. Fax 948-3671

**Farmersburg, Sullivan, Pop. 1,110**
Northeast SC
Supt. — See Hymera
North Central HS 500/9-12
910 E County Road 975 N 47850 812-397-2132
Monty Kirk, prin. Fax 397-2133

**Ferdinand, Dubois, Pop. 2,150**
Southeast Dubois County SC 1,400/PK-12
432 E 15th St 47532 812-817-0900
Richard Allen, supt. Fax 367-1075
www.sedubois.k12.in.us
Forest Park JSHS 700/7-12
1440 Michigan St 47532 812-817-0900
James Mehling, prin. Fax 367-1172

**Fishers, Hamilton, Pop. 75,207**
Hamilton Southeastern SD 18,200/K-12
13485 Cumberland Rd 46038 317-594-4100
Fax 594-4109
www.hse.k12.in.us
Fall Creek JHS 7-8
12001 Olio Rd, 317-594-4390
Kim Lippe, prin. Fax 594-4399
Fishers HS 2,300/9-12
13000 Promise Rd 46038 317-915-4290
Jason Urban, prin. Fax 915-4299
Fishers JHS 1,000/7-8
13257 Cumberland Rd 46038 317-594-4150
Crystal Thorpe, prin. Fax 594-4159
Hamilton Southeastern Freshman Center 9-9
12001 Olio Rd, 317-594-4390
Kim Lippe, prin. Fax 594-4399
Hamilton Southeastern HS 2,100/10-12
13910 E 126th St, 317-594-4190
Matt Kegley, prin. Fax 594-4199
Hamilton Southeastern Intermediate JHS 1,000/7-8
12278 Cyntheanne Rd, 317-594-4120
Tim Mankin, prin. Fax 594-4129
Riverside JHS 1,000/7-8
10910 Eller Rd 46038 317-915-4280
Rob Huesing, prin. Fax 915-4289

**Flora, Carroll, Pop. 2,010**
Carroll Consolidated SC 1,100/K-12
2 S 3rd St 46929 574-967-4113
Christopher Lagoni, supt. Fax 967-3831
www.carroll.k12.in.us/
Carroll JSHS 500/7-12
2362 E State Road 18 46929 574-967-4157
Tiffany Myers, prin. Fax 967-4027

**Floyds Knobs, Floyd**
New Albany Floyd County Consolidated SD
Supt. — See New Albany
Floyd Central HS 1,700/9-12
6575 Old Vincennes Rd 47119 812-542-8504
Janie Whaley, prin. Fax 542-4795

**Fort Branch, Gibson, Pop. 2,743**
South Gibson SC 2,000/K-12
1029 W 650 S 47648 812-753-4230
Dr. Stacey Humbaugh, supt. Fax 753-4081
www.sgibson.k12.in.us
Gibson Southern HS 700/9-12
3499 W 800 S 47648 812-753-3011
Scott Reid, prin. Fax 753-4862

**Fortville, Hancock, Pop. 3,887**
Mt. Vernon Community SC 3,500/PK-12
1776 W State Road 234 46040 317-485-3100
Dr. Shane Robbins, admin. Fax 485-3113
www.mvcsc.k12.in.us
8th Grade Academy 300/8-8
8112 N 200 W 46040 317-485-3131
Scott Shipley, prin. Fax 482-0027
Mt. Vernon HS 1,100/9-12
8112 N 200 W 46040 317-485-3131
Bernie Campbell, prin. Fax 485-3154

**Fort Wayne, Allen, Pop. 246,159**
East Allen County SD
Supt. — See New Haven
East Allen University 9-12
6501 Wayne Trce 46816 260-446-0240
Doug Hicks, prin. Fax 446-0249
Harding JHS 300/7-8
6501 Wayne Trce 46816 260-446-0240
Fax 446-0249

Fort Wayne Community SD 30,700/PK-12
1200 S Clinton St 46802 260-467-1000
Dr. Wendy Robinson, supt. Fax 467-1980
www.fwcs.k12.in.us
Anthis Career Center Vo/Tech
1200 Barr St 46802 260-467-1010
Larry Gerardot, prin. Fax 425-7609

Blackhawk MS 800/6-8
7200 E State Blvd 46815 260-467-4885
Kara Froning, prin. Fax 467-4943
Jefferson MS 700/6-8
5303 Wheelock Rd 46835 260-467-4825
Jeff King, prin. Fax 467-4883
Kekionga MS 500/6-8
2929 Engle Rd 46809 260-467-6600
Robin Peterman, prin. Fax 467-6658
Lakeside MS 500/6-8
2100 Lake Ave 46805 260-467-8625
Alan Jones, prin. Fax 467-8672
Lane MS 600/6-8
4901 Vance Ave 46815 260-467-4400
Mark Bailey, prin. Fax 467-4437
Memorial Park MS 600/6-8
2200 Maumee Ave 46803 260-467-5300
Tim Rayl, prin. Fax 467-5298
Miami MS 800/6-8
8100 Amherst Dr 46819 260-467-8560
Adam Swinford, prin. Fax 467-8606
Northrop HS 2,200/9-12
7001 Coldwater Rd 46825 260-467-2300
Kevin Simmons, prin. Fax 467-2301
North Side HS 1,700/9-12
475 E State Blvd 46805 260-467-2800
Chad Hissong, prin. Fax 467-2690
Northwood MS 700/6-8
1201 E Washington Center Rd 46825 260-467-2930
Austin Couch, prin. Fax 467-2987
Portage MS 500/6-8
3521 Taylor St 46802 260-467-4500
Michael Christner, prin. Fax 467-4497
Shawnee MS 800/6-8
1000 E Cook Rd 46825 260-467-6525
Matt Schiebel, prin. Fax 467-6527
Snider HS 1,900/9-12
4600 Fairlawn Pass 46815 260-467-4600
Nicole Chisley, prin. Fax 467-4729
South Side HS 1,500/9-12
3601 S Calhoun St 46807 260-467-2600
Carlton Mable, prin. Fax 467-2663
Ward Education Center Alt
3501 Warsaw St 46806 260-467-4570
Gradlin Pruitt, prin. Fax 467-5497
Wayne HS 1,500/9-12
9100 Winchester Rd 46819 260-467-6400
John Houser, prin. Fax 467-6490

Metro SD of Southwest Allen County 6,900/K-12
4824 Homestead Rd 46814 260-431-2051
Dr. Philip Downs, supt. Fax 431-2063
www.sacs.k12.in.us
Homestead HS 2,200/9-12
4310 Homestead Rd 46814 260-431-2200
Park Ginder, prin. Fax 431-2299
Summit MS 700/6-8
4509 Homestead Rd 46814 260-431-2502
Josh St. John, prin. Fax 431-2599
Woodside MS 1,000/6-8
2310 W Hamilton Rd S 46814 260-431-2701
Jerry Schillinger, prin. Fax 431-2799

Northwest Allen County SD 6,500/PK-12
13119 Coldwater Rd 46845 260-637-3155
Christopher Himsel, supt. Fax 637-8355
www.nacs.k12.in.us/
Allen County Youth Services Center 50/Alt
11805 Lima Rd 46818 260-449-3561
Deb Neumeyer, admin. Fax 449-7943
Carroll Freshman Center 500/9-9
3905 Carroll Rd 46818 260-637-0064
Sam DiPrimio, prin. Fax 637-5868
Carroll HS 1,400/10-12
3701 Carroll Rd 46818 260-637-3161
Samuel DiPrimio, prin. Fax 637-8356
Carroll MS 900/6-8
4027 Hathaway Rd 46818 260-637-5159
John Miller, prin. Fax 637-5478
Maple Creek MS 700/6-8
425 Union Chapel Rd 46845 260-338-0802
Bill Toler, prin. Fax 338-0369

---

Bishop Dwenger HS 1,000/9-12
1300 E Washington Center Rd 46825 260-496-4700
Jason Schiffli, prin. Fax 496-4702
Bishop Luers HS 600/9-12
333 E Paulding Rd 46816 260-456-1261
Tiffany Albertson, prin. Fax 456-1262
Blackhawk Christian S 700/PK-12
7400 E State Blvd 46815 260-493-7400
Linda Pearson, admin. Fax 749-8527
Brown Mackie College Post-Sec.
3000 E Coliseum Blvd 46805 260-484-4400
Canterbury S 900/PK-12
3210 Smith Rd 46804 260-436-0746
Jonathan Hancock, hdmstr. Fax 436-5137
Concordia Lutheran HS 700/9-12
1601 Saint Joe River Dr 46805 260-483-1102
Terry Breininger, dir. Fax 471-0180
Concordia Theological Seminary Post-Sec.
6600 N Clinton St 46825 260-452-2100
Fort Wayne School of Radiography Post-Sec.
700 Broadway 46802 260-425-3990
Harrison College Post-Sec.
6413 N Clinton St 46825 260-471-7667
Indiana Tech Post-Sec.
1600 E Washington Blvd 46803 260-422-5561
Indiana Univ-Purdue Univ at Fort Wayne Post-Sec.
2101 E Coliseum Blvd 46805 260-481-6100
International Business College Post-Sec.
5699 Coventry Ln 46804 260-459-4500
ITT Technical Institute Post-Sec.
2810 Dupont Commerce Ct 46825 260-497-6200
Ivy Tech Community College - Northeast Post-Sec.
3800 N Anthony Blvd 46805 260-482-9171
MedTech College Post-Sec.
7230 Engle Rd Ste 200 46804 260-436-3272
National College Post-Sec.
6131 N Clinton St 46825 260-483-1605
Ravenscroft Beauty College Post-Sec.
6110 Stellhorn Rd 46815 260-486-8868
Rudae's School of Beauty Culture Post-Sec.
5317 Coldwater Rd 46825 260-483-2466
The Masters of Cosmetology College Post-Sec.
1732 Bluffton Rd 46809 260-747-6667
University of St. Francis Post-Sec.
2701 Spring St 46808 260-399-7999

**Fountain City, Wayne, Pop. 783**
Northeastern Wayne SD 1,100/PK-12
PO Box 406 47341 765-847-2821
Laura Blessing, supt. Fax 847-5355
www.nws.k12.in.us
Northeastern HS 600/9-12
7295 N US Highway 27 47341 765-847-2591
Steve Angel, prin. Fax 847-2875
Northeastern MS 6-8
7295 N US Highway 27 47341 765-847-2591
Dawn Sonsini, admin. Fax 847-2875

**Fowler, Benton, Pop. 2,292**
Benton Community SC 1,900/PK-12
PO Box 512 47944 765-884-0850
Gregg Hoover, supt. Fax 884-1614
www.benton.k12.in.us
Other Schools – See Oxford

**Francesville, Pulaski, Pop. 873**
West Central SC 900/K-12
PO Box 578 47946 219-567-9161
Don Street, supt. Fax 567-9761
www.wcsc.k12.in.us
West Central HS 300/9-12
1852 S US Highway 421 47946 219-567-9119
Pat Culp, prin. Fax 567-2597
West Central MS 200/6-8
1850 S US Highway 421 47946 219-567-2534
Pat Culp, prin. Fax 567-9535

**Frankfort, Clinton, Pop. 16,300**
Clinton Prairie SC 1,000/K-12
4431 W Old State Road 28 46041 765-659-1339
John Sampson, supt. Fax 659-5305
www.clintonprairie.com
Clinton Prairie JSHS 400/7-12
2400 S County Road 450 W 46041 765-659-3305
Brent Miler, prin. Fax 659-3205

Frankfort Community SC 3,200/PK-12
2400 E Wabash St 46041 765-654-5585
Donald DeWeese, supt. Fax 659-6220
www.frankfortschools.org
Frankfort HS 900/9-12
1 S Maish Rd 46041 765-654-8545
Steve Edwards, prin. Fax 654-9224
Frankfort MS 700/6-8
329 N Maish Rd 46041 765-659-3321
Kelly Berenda, prin. Fax 659-6260

**Franklin, Johnson, Pop. 23,366**
Franklin Community SC 4,800/PK-12
998 Grizzly Cub Dr 46131 317-738-5800
David Clendening, supt. Fax 738-5812
www.franklinschools.org
Franklin Community HS 1,700/9-12
2600 Cumberland Dr 46131 317-738-5700
Doug Harter, prin. Fax 738-5703
Franklin Community MS 800/7-8
625 Grizzly Cub Dr 46131 317-346-8400
Steve Ahaus, prin. Fax 346-8411

---

Franklin College Post-Sec.
101 Branigin Blvd 46131 317-738-8000

**Frankton, Madison, Pop. 1,842**
Frankton-Lapel Community SD
Supt. — See Anderson
Frankton JSHS 700/7-12
610 E Clyde St 46044 765-754-7879
Greg Granger, prin. Fax 754-8594

**Fremont, Steuben, Pop. 2,131**
Fremont Community SD 1,000/K-12
PO Box 665 46737 260-495-5005
Loraine K. Vaughn, supt. Fax 495-9798
fremontcommunityschoolsindiana.org
Fremont HS 400/9-12
PO Box 655 46737 260-495-9876
Mark Sherbondy, prin. Fax 495-1838
Fremont MS 300/5-8
PO Box 770 46737 260-495-6100
Mark Fowerbaugh, prin. Fax 495-7301

**French Lick, Orange, Pop. 1,754**
Springs Valley Community SC 1,000/K-12
498 S Larry Bird Blvd 47432 812-936-4474
Anthony Whitaker, supt. Fax 936-9392
www.svalley.k12.in.us
Springs Valley Community JSHS 500/6-12
326 S Larry Bird Blvd 47432 812-936-9984
James Bush, prin. Fax 936-9266

**Fulton, Fulton, Pop. 332**
Caston SC 800/K-12
PO Box 8 46931 574-857-2035
Lucinda Douglass, supt. Fax 857-6035
www.caston.k12.in.us/
Caston JSHS 400/7-12
PO Box 128 46931 574-857-3505
Chuck Evans, prin. Fax 857-6795

**Garrett, DeKalb, Pop. 6,210**
Garrett-Keyser-Butler Community SD 1,700/K-12
801 E Houston St 46738 260-357-3185
Dennis Stockdale, supt. Fax 357-4565
www.gkb.k12.in.us
Garrett HS 600/9-12
801 E Houston St 46738 260-357-4114
Matthew Smith, prin. Fax 357-5000
Garrett MS 500/6-8
801 E Houston St 46738 260-357-5745
Lucas Fielden, prin. Fax 357-3575
Other Schools – See Kendallville

**Gary, Lake, Pop. 78,995**
Gary Community SC 9,200/PK-12
1988 Polk St 46407 219-881-5401
Dr. Cheryl Pruitt, supt. Fax 881-4102
www.garycsc.k12.in.us
Gary Career Center Vo/Tech
1800 E 35th Ave 46409 219-962-7571
Robert Doctor, prin. Fax 962-6269
New Tech S Vo/Tech
1800 E 35th Ave 46409 219-963-2901
Lydia Colaire, prin. Fax 963-2937
West Side Leadership Academy 1,500/7-12
900 Gerry St 46406 219-977-2100
Terrance Little, prin. Fax 977-2168
Wirt/Emerson Visual Performing Arts JSHS 700/6-12
210 N Grand Blvd 46403 219-938-1161
Dr. Adrian Richie, prin. Fax 938-7544

Lake Ridge New Tech SC 1,900/K-12
6111 W Ridge Rd 46408 219-838-1819
Dr. Sharon Johnson-Shirley, supt. Fax 989-7802
www.lakeridge.k12.in.us
Calumet New Tech HS 600/9-12
3900 Calhoun St 46408 219-838-6990
Cynthia Mose-Trevino, prin. Fax 989-7849
Lake Ridge New Tech MS 400/6-8
3601 W 41st Ave 46408 219-980-0730
Torry Ivey, prin. Fax 980-0731

---

Ambassador Christian Academy 300/PK-12
900 W Ridge Rd 46408 219-887-4473
Dr. Vercena Stewart, admin. Fax 887-1749
Indiana University Northwest Post-Sec.
3400 Broadway 46408 219-980-6500
Ivy Tech Community College - Northwest Post-Sec.
1440 E 35th Ave 46409 219-981-1111

**Gas City, Grant, Pop. 5,872**
Mississinewa Community SC 2,500/PK-12
424 E South A St 46933 765-674-8528
Michael Powell, supt. Fax 674-8529
www.olemiss.k12.in.us
Baskett MS 600/6-8
125 N Broadway St 46933 765-674-8536
Jamie Eckstein, prin. Fax 677-4452
Mississinewa HS 700/9-12
1 Indian Trail Dr 46933 765-674-2248
Steve Quaderer, prin. Fax 677-4424

**Gaston, Delaware, Pop. 858**
Wes-Del Community SD 800/K-12
10290 N County Road 600 W 47342 765-358-4006
Michael Bush, supt. Fax 358-4065
www.wes-del.k12.in.us/
Wes-Del MSHS 500/6-12
10000 N County Road 600 W 47342 765-358-4091
Kyle Mealy, prin. Fax 358-3514

**Georgetown, Floyd, Pop. 2,851**
New Albany Floyd County Consolidated SD
Supt. — See New Albany
Highland Hills MS 1,500/5-8
3492 Edwardsville Galena Rd 47122 812-542-8501
Steve Griffin, prin. Fax 542-4792

**Goshen, Elkhart, Pop. 31,231**
Fairfield Community SD 2,100/K-12
67240 County Road 31 46528 574-831-2188
Steve Thalheimer, supt. Fax 831-5698
www.fairfield.k12.in.us
Fairfield JSHS 900/7-12
67530 US Highway 33 46526 574-831-2184
Amy Bertram, prin. Fax 831-2187

Goshen Community SD 6,400/PK-12
613 E Purl St 46526 574-533-8631
Dr. Diane Woodworth, supt. Fax 533-2505
www.goshenschools.org/
Goshen HS 1,800/9-12
401 Lincolnway E 46526 574-533-8651
Dr. Barry Younghans, prin. Fax 534-1567
Goshen MS 1,400/6-8
1216 S Indiana Ave 46526 574-533-0391
Lori Shreiner, prin. Fax 534-3042

---

Bethany Christian S 300/4-12
2904 S Main St 46526 574-534-2567
Hank Willems, prin. Fax 533-0150
Clinton Christian S 100/PK-12
61763 County Road 35 46528 574-642-3940
Gail Schrock, admin. Fax 642-3674
Goshen College Post-Sec.
1700 S Main St 46526 574-535-7000

**Granger, Saint Joseph, Pop. 29,968**
Penn-Harris-Madison SC
Supt. — See Mishawaka
Discovery MS 900/6-8
10050 Brummitt Rd 46530 574-674-6010
Sheryll Harper, prin. Fax 679-4214

---

Granger Christian S 200/K-12
52025 Gumwood Rd 46530 574-272-5815
Mary Kane, lead tchr. Fax 968-2664

**Greencastle, Putnam, Pop. 10,164**
Greencastle Community SC 2,100/PK-12
PO Box 480 46135 765-653-9771
Dawn Puckett, supt. Fax 653-1282
www.greencastle.k12.in.us

Greencastle HS — 600/9-12
910 E Washington St 46135 — 765-653-9711
Russell Hesler, prin. — Fax 653-4773
Greencastle MS — 500/6-8
400 Percy L Julian Dr 46135 — 765-653-9774
S. Wooden, prin. — Fax 653-5381

North Putnam Community SD
Supt. — See Bainbridge
Area 30 Career Center — Vo/Tech
1 N Calbert Way 46135 — 765-653-3515
Lora Busch, dir. — Fax 653-6110

South Putnam Community SD — 900/K-12
3999 S US Highway 231 46135 — 765-653-3119
Bruce Bernhardt, supt. — Fax 653-7476
www.sputnam.k12.in.us
South Putnam MSHS — 600/6-12
1780 E US Highway 40 46135 — 765-653-3148
Michael Schimpf, prin. — Fax 653-3149

---

DePauw University — Post-Sec.
PO Box 37 46135 — 765-658-4800

**Greenfield, Hancock, Pop. 20,372**
Greenfield-Central Community SD — 4,000/PK-12
110 W North St 46140 — 317-462-4434
Dr. Harold Olin, supt. — Fax 467-4227
www.gcsc.k12.in.us
Greenfield-Central HS — 1,400/9-12
810 N Broadway St 46140 — 317-462-9211
Steven Bryant, prin. — Fax 467-6723
Greenfield Central JHS — 700/7-8
1440 N Franklin St 46140 — 317-477-4616
Dan Jack, prin. — Fax 477-4617

---

Hancock Memorial Hospital — Post-Sec.
801 N State St 46140 — 317-462-0457
PJ's College of Cosmetology — Post-Sec.
1400 W Main St 46140 — 317-462-9239

**Greensburg, Decatur, Pop. 11,380**
Decatur County Community SD — 2,100/PK-12
2020 N Montgomery Rd 47240 — 812-663-4595
Johnny Budd, supt. — Fax 663-4168
www.decaturco.k12.in.us
North Decatur JSHS — 600/7-12
3172 N State Road 3 47240 — 812-663-4204
Charlie McCoy, prin. — Fax 663-9606
South Decatur JSHS — 500/7-12
8885 S State Road 3 47240 — 812-591-3330
Jim Jameson, prin. — Fax 591-3331

Greensburg Community SC — 2,300/K-12
1312 W Westridge Pkwy 47240 — 812-663-4774
Tom Hunter, supt. — Fax 663-5713
www.greensburg.k12.in.us
Greensburg Community HS — 700/9-12
1000 E Central Ave 47240 — 812-663-7176
Grant Peters, prin. — Fax 663-8911
Greensburg Community JHS — 600/6-8
505 E Central Ave 47240 — 812-663-7523
Matt Clifford, prin. — Fax 663-9425

**Greentown, Howard, Pop. 2,402**
Eastern Howard SC — 1,400/K-12
221 W Main St Ste 1 46936 — 765-628-3391
Tracy Caddell Ed.D., supt. — Fax 628-5017
www.eastern.k12.in.us
Eastern HS — 700/9-12
421 S Harrison St 46936 — 765-628-3333
Keith Richie Ed.D., prin. — Fax 628-5021
Eastern MS — 6-8
421 S Harrison St 46936 — 765-628-5030
Lindsey Brown, prin. — Fax 628-5031

**Greenwood, Johnson, Pop. 48,867**
Center Grove Community SC — 7,600/K-12
4800 W Stones Crossing Rd 46143 — 317-881-9326
Dr. Richard Arkanoff, supt. — Fax 881-0241
www.centergrove.k12.in.us
Center Grove HS — 2,400/9-12
2717 S Morgantown Rd 46143 — 317-881-0581
Doug Bird, prin. — Fax 885-4509
Center Grove MS Central — 900/6-8
4900 W Stones Crossing Rd 46143 — 317-882-9391
Craig Smith, prin. — Fax 885-4534
Center Grove MS North — 900/6-8
202 N Morgantown Rd 46142 — 317-885-8800
Scott Johnson, prin. — Fax 885-3388

Central Nine Career Center SD
1999 US Highway 31 S 46143 — 317-888-4401
Dr. David Edds, dir. — Fax 865-8670
www.central9.k12.in.us
Central Nine Career Center — Vo/Tech
1999 US Highway 31 S 46143 — 317-888-4401
Lawrence Courtney, prin. — Fax 885-8670

Clark-Pleasant Community SC
Supt. — See Whiteland
Clark Pleasant MS — 900/7-8
1354 E Worthsville Rd 46143 — 317-535-7121
Tim Rinehold, prin. — Fax 535-2064

Greenwood Community SC — 3,800/PK-12
605 W Smith Valley Rd 46142 — 317-889-4060
Dr. Kent DeKoninck, supt. — Fax 889-4068
gws.k12.in.us
Greenwood Community HS — 1,100/9-12
615 W Smith Valley Rd 46142 — 317-889-4000
Todd Garrison, prin. — Fax 889-4039
Greenwood MS — 900/6-8
523 S Madison Ave 46142 — 317-889-4040
Chris Sutton, prin. — Fax 889-4044

---

Greenwood Christian Academy — 400/PK-12
835 W Worthsville Rd 46143 — 317-215-5300
Bruce Peters, hdmstr. — Fax 535-1070

MedTech College — Post-Sec.
1500 American Way 46143 — 317-534-0322

**Griffith, Lake, Pop. 16,641**
Griffith Public SD — 2,600/PK-12
PO Box 749 46319 — 219-924-4250
Dr. Peter Morikis, supt. — Fax 922-5933
www.griffith.k12.in.us
Griffith HS — 900/9-12
600 N Wiggs St 46319 — 219-924-4281
Brian Orkis, prin. — Fax 922-5920
Griffith MS — 400/7-8
600 N Raymond St 46319 — 219-924-4280
Dustin Nelson, prin. — Fax 922-5927

---

Calumet Christian S — PK-12
826 N Harvey St 46319 — 219-922-8428
Dan Obinger, dir.

**Hagerstown, Wayne, Pop. 1,765**
Nettle Creek SC — 1,200/PK-12
297 E Northmarket St 47346 — 765-489-4543
Dr. William Doering, supt. — Fax 489-4914
www.nettlecreek.k12.in.us
Hagerstown JSHS — 500/7-12
701 Baker Rd 47346 — 765-489-4511
Mark Childs, prin. — Fax 489-4333

**Hamilton, DeKalb, Pop. 1,521**
Hamilton Community SD — 400/K-12
903 S Wayne St 46742 — 260-488-2513
Jon Willman, supt. — Fax 488-2348
www.hcs.k12.in.us
Hamilton Community HS — 200/7-12
903 S Wayne St 46742 — 260-488-2161
Tim Holcomb, prin. — Fax 488-3149

**Hamlet, Starke, Pop. 787**
Oregon-Davis SC — 600/PK-12
5998 N 750 E 46532 — 574-867-2111
Gregory Briles, supt. — Fax 867-8191
www.od.k12.in.us
Oregon-Davis JSHS — 300/7-12
5990 N 750 E 46532 — 574-867-4561
Timothy Pletcher, prin. — Fax 867-2481

**Hammond, Lake, Pop. 79,563**
Hammond CSD — 13,700/PK-12
41 Williams St 46320 — 219-933-2400
Dr. Walter Watkins, supt. — Fax 933-2495
www.hammond.k12.in.us
Area Career Center — Vo/Tech
5727 Sohl Ave 46320 — 219-933-2428
Michael Zimmerman, prin. — Fax 554-4570
Eggers MS — 600/6-8
5825 Blaine Ave 46320 — 219-933-2449
Rhoderick Poats, prin. — Fax 554-4575
Gavit MSHS — 1,600/6-12
1670 175th St 46324 — 219-989-7328
Michelle Ondas, prin. — Fax 554-4573
Hammond HS — 800/9-12
5926 Calumet Ave 46320 — 219-933-2442
Mescha Lammy, prin. — Fax 933-1688
Morton HS — 1,200/9-12
6915 Grand Ave 46323 — 219-989-7316
Kenneth Easton, prin. — Fax 554-4574
Scott MS — 800/6-8
3635 173rd St 46323 — 219-989-7340
Colleen Bergren, prin. — Fax 554-4576
Other Schools – See Whiting

---

Bishop Noll Institute — 500/9-12
1519 Hoffman St 46327 — 219-932-9058
Craig Stafford, prin. — Fax 853-1736
Kaplan College — Post-Sec.
7833 Indianapolis Blvd 46324 — 219-844-0100
Purdue University Calumet — Post-Sec.
2200 169th St 46323 — 219-989-2400
St. Margaret Hospital — Post-Sec.
5454 Hohman Ave 46320 — 219-932-2300

**Hanover, Jefferson, Pop. 3,496**
Southwestern-Jefferson County Cons SC — 1,300/K-12
239 S Main Cross St 47243 — 812-866-6250
Trevor Jones, supt. — Fax 866-6256
www.swjcs.us
Southwestern HS — 400/9-12
167 S Main Cross St 47243 — 812-866-6230
Jeff Bates, prin. — Fax 866-6233
Southwestern MS — 300/6-8
167 S Main Cross St 47243 — 812-866-6220
Trevor Jones, prin. — Fax 866-4680

---

Hanover College — Post-Sec.
PO Box 108 47243 — 812-866-7000

**Hartford City, Blackford, Pop. 6,115**
Blackford County SD — 1,900/PK-12
668 W 200 S 47348 — 765-348-7550
Dr. Scot Croner, supt. — Fax 348-7552
www.bcs.k12.in.us
Blackford HS — 600/9-12
2392 N State Road 3 47348 — 765-348-7560
Scott Shimer, prin. — Fax 348-7568
Blackford JHS — 300/7-8
800 W Van Cleve St 47348 — 765-348-7590
Melissa Blossom, prin. — Fax 348-7593

**Hebron, Porter, Pop. 3,695**
Metro SD of Boone Township — 1,100/K-12
307 S Main St 46341 — 219-996-4771
Dr. Nathan H. Kleefisch, supt. — Fax 996-5777
www.hebronschools.k12.in.us/
Hebron HS — 300/9-12
509 S Main St 46341 — 219-996-4771
Mark Lutze, prin. — Fax 996-5777
Hebron MS — 300/6-8
307 S Main St 46341 — 219-996-4771
Jeff Brooks, prin. — Fax 996-5777

**Henryville, Clark, Pop. 1,892**
West Clark Community SC
Supt. — See Sellersburg
Henryville JSHS — 500/7-12
213 N Ferguson St 47126 — 812-294-1455
Troy Albert, prin. — Fax 294-4276

**Highland, Lake, Pop. 23,446**
Town of Highland SD — 3,100/K-12
9145 Kennedy Ave 46322 — 219-924-7400
Brian J. Smith, supt. — Fax 922-5637
www.highland.k12.in.us
Highland HS — 1,200/9-12
9135 Erie St 46322 — 219-922-5610
Patrick Weil, prin. — Fax 922-5636
Highland MS — 500/6-8
2941 41st St 46322 — 219-922-5620
Terry Mucha, prin. — Fax 922-2270

---

Creative Hair Styling Academy — Post-Sec.
2549 Highway Ave 46322 — 219-838-2004

**Hobart, Lake, Pop. 28,672**
Hobart CSD — 3,700/PK-12
32 E 7th St 46342 — 219-942-8885
Dr. Peggy Buffington, supt. — Fax 942-0081
www.hobart.k12.in.us
Hobart HS — 1,200/9-12
2211 E 10th St 46342 — 219-942-8521
Brent Martinson, prin. — Fax 942-3326
Hobart MS — 1,000/6-8
36 E 8th St 46342 — 219-942-8541
Carolie Warren, prin. — Fax 947-7194

River Forest Community SC — 1,600/K-12
3250 Michigan St 46342 — 219-962-2909
Dr. Steven Disney, supt. — Fax 962-4951
www.rfcsc.k12.in.us
River Forest HS — 700/9-12
3300 Indiana St 46342 — 219-962-7551
Randall Horka, prin. — Fax 962-8338
River Forest MS — 400/6-8
3300 Indiana St 46342 — 219-962-7751
Randall Horka, prin. — Fax 962-8338

---

College of Court Reporting — Post-Sec.
111 W 10th St Ste 111 46342 — 866-294-3974

**Hope, Bartholomew, Pop. 2,080**
Flat Rock-Hawcreek SC — 900/PK-12
9423 N State Road 9 47246 — 812-546-4922
Shawn Price, supt. — Fax 546-5617
www.flatrock.k12.in.us
Hauser JSHS — 400/7-12
9273 N State Road 9 47246 — 812-546-4421
James Mayer, prin. — Fax 546-2005

**Howe, Lagrange, Pop. 791**

---

Howe Military Academy — 100/7-12
PO Box 240 46746 — 260-562-2131
Leon Baker, hdmstr. — Fax 562-3678

**Huntingburg, Dubois, Pop. 6,020**
Southwest Dubois County SC — 1,700/PK-12
113 N Jackson St 47542 — 812-683-3971
Mike Eineman, supt. — Fax 683-2752
www.swdubois.k12.in.us
Southridge HS — 500/9-12
1110 S Main St 47542 — 812-683-2272
Kelly Murphy, prin. — Fax 683-2010
Southridge MS — 400/6-8
1112 S Main St 47542 — 812-683-3372
Annette Altmeyer, prin. — Fax 683-2817

**Huntington, Huntington, Pop. 17,196**
Huntington County Community SC — 6,200/K-12
2485 Waterworks Rd 46750 — 260-356-8312
Randy Harris, supt. — Fax 358-2222
www.hccsc.k12.in.us
Crestview MS — 700/6-8
1151 W 500 N 46750 — 260-356-6210
Chuck Werth, prin. — Fax 358-2232
Huntington North HS — 1,900/9-12
450 MacGahan St 46750 — 260-356-6104
Chad Daugherty, prin. — Fax 358-2210
Riverview MS — 700/6-8
2465 Waterworks Rd 46750 — 260-356-0910
Curt Crago, prin. — Fax 358-2243

---

Huntington University — Post-Sec.
2303 College Ave 46750 — 260-356-6000

**Hymera, Sullivan, Pop. 795**
Northeast SC — 1,400/PK-12
PO Box 493 47855 — 812-383-5761
Dr. Mark Baker, supt. — Fax 383-4591
www.nesc.k12.in.us/
Other Schools – See Farmersburg, Shelburn

**Indianapolis, Marion, Pop. 800,178**
Franklin Township Community SC — 7,900/PK-12
6141 S Franklin Rd 46259 — 317-862-2411
Dr. Flora Reichanadter, supt. — Fax 862-7238
www.ftcsc.k12.in.us
Franklin Central HS — 2,500/9-12
6215 S Franklin Rd 46259 — 317-862-6646
Kevin Koers, prin. — Fax 862-7262
Franklin Township MS East — 1,100/6-8
10440 Indian Creek Rd S 46259 — 317-803-8100
Chase Huotari, prin. — Fax 803-8199
Franklin Township MS West — 900/6-8
7620 E Edgewood Ave 46239 — 317-862-2446
Matthew Vandermark, prin. — Fax 862-7271

Indianapolis SD 26,200/PK-12
120 E Walnut St 46204 317-226-4000
Dr. Lewis Ferebee, supt. Fax 226-4936
www.ips.k12.in.us
Arlington Community HS 7-12
4825 N Arlington Ave 46226 317-226-2345
Stanley Law, prin.
Arsenal Technical HS 2,100/9-12
1500 E Michigan St 46201 317-693-5300
Julie Blakehorn, admin. Fax 226-3932
Attucks Medical Magnet HS 400/6-12
1140 Dr Mrtn Lthr Kng Jr St 46202 317-226-2800
Lauren Franklin, prin. Fax 226-3495
Broad Ripple HS for Arts & Humanities 500/6-12
1115 Broad Ripple Ave 46220 317-693-5700
Briant Williams, prin. Fax 226-3783
Harshman Magnet MS 400/7-8
1501 E 10th St 46201 317-226-4101
James Larkin, prin. Fax 226-3444
IPS Career Technology Center Vo/Tech
725 N Oriental St 46202 317-693-5430
Ben Carter, dir. Fax 226-3709
Key Learning Community S 100/K-12
777 S White River Pky West 46203 317-226-4992
Michael Akers, prin. Fax 226-3049
Marshall Community HS 500/7-12
10101 E 38th St 46235 317-693-5460
Ashauna Short, prin. Fax 226-3718
Northwest HS 800/7-12
5525 W 34th St 46224 317-693-5600
Michelle Britian - Watts, prin. Fax 226-3409
Shortridge HS 300/6-12
3401 N Meridian St 46208 317-226-2810
Shane O'Day, prin. Fax 226-3725
Washington Community HS 300/7-12
2215 W Washington St 46222 317-693-5555
Linda Gagyi, prin. Fax 226-3273

Metro SD of Decatur Township 6,300/PK-12
5275 Kentucky Ave 46221 317-856-5265
Nathan Davis Ed.D., admin. Fax 856-2156
www.msddecatur.k12.in.us
Decatur Central HS 1,800/9-12
5251 Kentucky Ave 46221 317-856-5288
Scott DeFreese, prin. Fax 856-2157
Decatur MS 900/7-8
5108 S High School Rd 46221 317-856-5274
Kyle Barrentine, prin. Fax 856-2163

Metro SD of Pike Township 10,900/PK-12
6901 Zionsville Rd 46268 317-293-0393
Nathaniel Jones, supt. Fax 297-7896
www.pike.k12.in.us
Guion Creek MS 900/6-8
4401 W 52nd St 46254 317-293-4549
Maggie Bishop, prin. Fax 298-2794
Lincoln MS 900/6-8
5353 W 71st St 46268 317-291-9499
Dan Kuznik, prin. Fax 297-1673
New Augusta Public Academy North 800/6-8
6450 Rodebaugh Rd 46268 317-388-7700
Kim Mills, prin. Fax 388-7786
Pike Freshman Center 800/9-9
6801 Zionsville Rd 46268 317-347-8600
Troy Inman, prin. Fax 347-8555
Pike HS 2,200/10-12
5401 W 71st St 46268 317-291-5250
Troy Inman, prin. Fax 328-7239
Pike Prep Academy Alt
7140 Waldemar Dr 46268 317-347-8352
Roy Dobbs, prin. Fax 298-0681

Metro SD of Warren Township 10,900/PK-12
975 N Post Rd 46219 317-869-4300
Dr. Dena Cushenberry, supt. Fax 869-4348
www.warren.k12.in.us
Creston MS 600/7-8
10925 Prospect St 46239 317-532-6800
Chad Reedy, prin. Fax 532-6899
Raymond Park MS 500/7-8
8575 E Raymond St 46239 317-532-8900
Dr. John Kleine, prin. Fax 532-8999
Renaissance S 300/Alt
8931 E 30th St 46219 317-532-2975
Masimba Taylor, dir. Fax 532-2951
Stonybrook MS 600/7-8
11300 Stony Brook Dr 46229 317-532-8800
Pam Griffin, prin. Fax 532-8899
Walker Career Center Vo/Tech
9651 E 21st St 46229 317-532-6150
Cindy Frey, dir. Fax 532-6199
Warren Central HS 3,700/9-12
9500 E 16th St 46229 317-532-6200
Rich Shepler, prin. Fax 532-6459

Metropolitan SD of Lawrence Township 14,900/PK-12
6501 Sunnyside Rd 46236 317-423-8200
Dr. Shawn Smith, supt. Fax 543-3534
www.ltschools.org/
Belzer MS 1,100/7-8
7555 E 56th St 46226 317-964-6200
Andrew Harsha, prin. Fax 543-3355
Fall Creek Valley MS 1,100/7-8
9701 E 63rd St 46236 317-964-6600
Kathryn Luessow, prin. Fax 823-5497
Lawrence Central HS 2,500/9-12
7300 E 56th St 46226 317-964-7400
Rocco Valadez, prin. Fax 543-3348
Lawrence North HS 2,300/9-12
7802 Hague Rd 46256 317-964-7700
Brett Crousore, prin. Fax 576-6406
McKenzie Career Center Vo/Tech
7250 E 75th St 46256 317-964-8000
Frank Svarczkopf, prin. Fax 849-2546

Metropolitan SD of Washington Township 11,000/PK-12
8550 Woodfield Crossing 46240 317-845-9400
Dr. Nikki Woodson, supt. Fax 205-3384
www.msdwt.k12.in.us
Eastwood MS 700/6-8
4401 E 62nd St 46220 317-259-5401
Matt Kaiser, prin. Fax 259-5407
Light Career Center Vo/Tech
1901 E 86th St 46240 317-259-5265
Shawn Wright-Browner, dir. Fax 259-5298
North Central HS 3,600/9-12
1801 E 86th St 46240 317-259-5301
Bryant Branigan, prin. Fax 259-5369
Northview MS 800/6-8
8401 Westfield Blvd 46240 317-259-5421
Tina Merriweather, prin. Fax 259-5431
Westlane MS 900/6-8
1301 W 73rd St 46260 317-259-5412
Linda Lawrence, prin. Fax 259-5409

Metropolitan SD of Wayne Township 16,100/PK-12
1220 S High School Rd 46241 317-988-8600
Jeffrey Butts Ph.D., supt. Fax 243-5744
www.wayne.k12.in.us
Area 31 Career Center Vo/Tech
1200 N Girls School Rd 46214 317-988-7230
Patrick Biggerstaff, prin. Fax 988-7298
Chapel Hill 7th & 8th Grade Center 1,200/7-8
7320 W 10th St 46214 317-988-8800
Sheri Patterson, prin. Fax 988-8949
Davis 9th Grade Center 1,200/9-9
1150 N Girls School Rd 46214 317-988-7500
Steve Samuel, prin. Fax 484-3124
Davis HS 3,300/10-12
1200 N Girls School Rd 46214 317-988-7000
Sandra Squire, prin. Fax 988-7311
Davis University HS 300/10-12
1155 S High School Rd 46241 317-988-7800
Rebecca Daugherty, prin. Fax 243-5683
Lynhurst 7th & 8th Grade Center 1,100/7-8
2805 S Lynhurst Dr 46241 317-988-8100
Dan Wilson, prin. Fax 243-5532

Perry Township SD 14,400/PK-12
6548 Orinoco Ave 46227 317-789-3700
Dr. Thomas Little, supt. Fax 789-3709
www.msdpt.k12.in.us
Perry Meridian HS 2,300/9-12
401 W Meridian School Rd 46217 317-789-4400
Rolland Abraham, prin. Fax 789-4479
Perry Meridian MS 1,100/7-8
202 W Meridian School Rd 46217 317-789-4100
David Rohl, prin. Fax 865-2710
Southport HS 2,200/9-12
971 E Banta Rd 46227 317-789-4800
Barbara Brouwer, prin. Fax 780-4325
Southport MS 1,100/7-8
5715 S Keystone Ave 46227 317-789-4600
Brian Knight, prin. Fax 780-4302

---

American College of Education Post-Sec.
101 W Ohio St Ste 1200 46204 800-280-0307
Art Institute of Indianapolis Post-Sec.
3500 Depauw Blvd 46268 317-613-4800
Aviation Institute of Maintenance Post-Sec.
7251 W McCarty St 46241 317-243-4519
Bishop Chatard HS 700/9-12
5885 Crittenden Ave 46220 317-251-1451
Rick Wagner, prin. Fax 251-3648
Brebeuf Jesuit Prep S 800/9-12
2801 W 86th St 46268 317-524-7128
Greg VanSlambrook, prin. Fax 524-7148
Brown Mackie College Post-Sec.
1200 N Meridian St Ste 100 46204 317-554-8300
Butler University Post-Sec.
4600 Sunset Ave 46208 317-940-8000
Calvary Christian S 200/PK-12
3639 S Keystone Ave 46227 317-789-8710
Charles Barcus, admin. Fax 789-8718
Cardinal Ritter JSHS 600/7-12
3360 W 30th St 46222 317-924-4333
Jo Hoy, prin. Fax 927-7929
Cathedral HS 1,300/9-12
5225 E 56th St 46226 317-968-7337
David Worland, prin. Fax 543-5050
Central Christian Academy 200/PK-12
2565 Villa Ave 46203 317-788-1587
Daniel Pride, hdmstr. Fax 781-4758
Chamberlain College of Nursing Post-Sec.
9100 Keystone Xing 46240 317-816-7335
Christian Theological Seminary Post-Sec.
1000 W 42nd St 46208 317-924-1331
Colonial Christian S 200/PK-12
8140 Union Chapel Rd 46240 317-253-0649
Dr. Kevin Suiter, admin. Fax 254-2840
Community Hospital of Indianapolis Post-Sec.
1500 N Ritter Ave 46219 317-355-5529
Covenant Christian HS 300/9-12
7525 W 21st St 46214 317-390-0202
Andy Goodwin, prin. Fax 390-6823
Crosspointe Christian Academy 200/PK-12
220 Country Club Rd 46234 317-271-1600
Crossroads Bible College Post-Sec.
601 N Shortridge Rd 46219 317-789-8255
DeVry University Post-Sec.
9100 Keystone Xing Ste 100 46240 317-581-8854
Empire Beauty School Post-Sec.
3810 E Southport Rd 46237 317-781-0959
Fortis College Post-Sec.
9001 Wesleyan Rd Ste 101 46268 317-808-4800
Franklin University Post-Sec.
8415 Allison Pointe Ste 400 46250 319-429-3100
Harrison College Post-Sec.
550 E Washington St 46204 317-447-6200
Harrison College Post-Sec.
6300 Technology Center Dr 46278 317-873-6500
Harrison College Post-Sec.
8150 Brookville Rd 46239 317-375-8000
Harrison College - Online Post-Sec.
500 N Meridian St Ste 500 46204 317-217-6815
Heritage Christian S 1,400/PK-12
6401 E 75th St 46250 317-849-3441
Jeff Freeman, admin. Fax 594-5863
Horizon Christian S 300/PK-12
7702 Indian Lake Rd 46236 317-823-4538
Michael Slack, head sch Fax 823-2396
Indiana School for the Deaf Post-Sec.
1200 E 42nd St 46205 317-924-4374
Indiana State School for the Blind Post-Sec.
7725 N College Ave 46240 317-253-1481
Indiana University School of Allied Hlth Post-Sec.
1140 W Michigan St 46202 317-274-4702
Indiana Univ-Purdue Univ at Indianapolis Post-Sec.
355 Lansing St 46202 317-274-5555
International Business College Post-Sec.
7205 Shadeland Sta 46256 317-813-2300
International S of Indiana 600/PK-12
4330 Michigan Rd 46208 317-923-1951
David Garner, hdmstr. Fax 923-1910
ITT Technical Institute Post-Sec.
9511 Angola Ct 46268 317-875-8640
ITT Technical Institute Post-Sec.
2525 N Shadeland Ave Ste 10 46219 317-351-3800
Ivy Tech Community College - Central IN Post-Sec.
50 W Fall Creek Pkwy N Dr 46208 317-921-4800
Kaplan College Post-Sec.
4200 S East St 46227 317-782-0315
Lincoln College of Technology Post-Sec.
7225 Winton Dr # 128 46268 317-632-5553
Lutheran HS 200/9-12
5555 S Arlington Ave 46237 317-787-5474
Michael Brandt, head sch Fax 787-2794
Marian University Post-Sec.
3200 Cold Spring Rd 46222 317-955-6000
Martin University Post-Sec.
PO Box 18567 46218 317-543-3235
MedTech College Post-Sec.
6612 E 75th St Ste 300 46250 317-845-0100
Methodist Hosp/Clarian Health Partners Post-Sec.
PO Box 1367 46206 317-929-5900
National College Post-Sec.
6060 Castleway West Dr 46250 317-578-7353
Park Tudor S 1,000/PK-12
7200 N College Ave 46240 317-415-2700
Dr. Matthew Miller, head sch Fax 254-2714
Providence Cristo Rey HS 100/9-12
75 N Belleview Pl 46222 317-860-1000
Michael Brooks, prin.
Reppert School of Auctioneering Post-Sec.
6851 Madison Ave 46227 317-300-1075
Roncalli HS 1,100/9-12
3300 Prague Rd 46227 317-787-8277
Chuck Weisenbach, prin. Fax 788-4095
Scecina Memorial HS 300/9-12
5000 Nowland Ave 46201 317-356-6377
John Hegarty, prin. Fax 322-4287
Southside Christian S K-12
329 W Banta Rd 46217 317-258-6363
Mark Petty, prin.
Suburban Christian S 100/PK-12
722 E County Line Rd 46227 317-888-3366
TCM International Institute Post-Sec.
PO Box 24560 46224 317-299-0333
The Chef's Academy Post-Sec.
644 E Washington St 46204 800-919-2500
Trinity Christian S 100/K-12
440 Saint Peter St 46201 317-631-3194
Sharon Ragan, prin. Fax 631-7230
University of Indianapolis Post-Sec.
1400 E Hanna Ave 46227 317-788-3368

**Jasonville, Greene, Pop. 2,204**

Metro SD Shakamak 900/K-12
9233 Shakamak School Rd 47438 812-665-3550
Mike Mogan, supt. Fax 665-5001
www.shakamak.k12.in.us/
Shakamak JSHS 400/7-12
9233 Shakamak School Rd 47438 812-665-3550
Dennis Moody, prin. Fax 665-5001

**Jasper, Dubois, Pop. 14,939**

Greater Jasper Consolidated SD 3,300/PK-12
1520 Saint Charles St 47546 812-482-1801
Dr. Tracy Lorey, supt. Fax 482-3388
www.gjcs.k12.in.us
Jasper HS 1,000/9-12
1600 Saint Charles St 47546 812-482-6050
Brian Wilson, prin. Fax 634-3971
Jasper MS 800/6-8
3600 N Portersville Rd 47546 812-482-6454
David Hubster, prin. Fax 482-6457

**Jeffersonville, Clark, Pop. 43,626**

Greater Clark County SD 10,500/PK-12
2112 Utica Sellersburg Rd 47130 812-283-0701
Dr. Andrew Melin, supt. Fax 288-4804
www.gcs.k12.in.us
Clark County MSHS 100/6-12
2710 E 10th St 47130 812-288-4837
Jeff Griffith, prin. Fax 288-4829
Corden Porter S 100/Alt
630 Meigs Ave 47130 812-288-4891
Laura Morris, prin. Fax 288-4843
Jeffersonville HS 2,100/9-12
2315 Allison Ln 47130 812-282-6601
Julie Straight, prin. Fax 288-4812
Parkview MS 800/6-8
1600 Brigman Ave 47130 812-288-4844
Amy Hasselbring, prin. Fax 288-2849
River Valley MS 900/6-8
2220 Veterans Pkwy 47130 812-288-4848
Michelle Dyer, prin. Fax 288-4851
Other Schools – See Charlestown, New Washington

---

Mid-America College of Funeral Service Post-Sec.
3111 Hamburg Pike 47130 812-288-8878

Ottawa University — Post-Sec.
287 Quartermaster Ct 47130 — 812-280-7271

**Jonesboro, Grant, Pop. 1,733**

King's Academy — 100/K-12
1201 S Water St 46938 — 765-674-1722
Tony Miner, hdmstr. — Fax 674-7322

**Kendallville, Noble, Pop. 9,716**
East Noble SC — 3,800/PK-12
126 W Rush St 46755 — 260-347-2502
Ann Linson, supt. — Fax 347-0111
www.eastnoble.net
Alternative Learning Center — Alt
702 Dowling St 46755 — 260-349-0814
Belinda Justus, dir. — Fax 347-1242
East Noble HS — 1,200/9-12
901 Garden St 46755 — 260-347-2032
Steve Peterson, prin. — Fax 347-2362
East Noble MS — 600/7-8
401 E Diamond St 46755 — 260-347-0100
Andrew Deming, prin. — Fax 347-7168

Garrett-Keyser-Butler Community SD
Supt. — See Garrett
Four County Area Voc Coop — Vo/Tech
1607 Dowling St 46755 — 260-349-0250
Jim Walmsley, prin. — Fax 349-0240

**Kentland, Newton, Pop. 1,729**
South Newton SC — 900/PK-12
13232 S 50 E 47951 — 219-474-5184
Kenneth Rudnick, supt. — Fax 474-6966
www.newton.k12.in.us/
South Newton HS — 300/9-12
13102 S 50 E 47951 — 219-474-5167
Charles Huckstep, prin. — Fax 474-6592
South Newton MS — 200/6-8
13100 S 50 E 47951 — 219-474-5167
Tansey Mulligan, prin. — Fax 474-3624

**Knightstown, Henry, Pop. 2,153**
C.A. Beard Memorial SC — 1,200/K-12
8139 W US Highway 40 46148 — 765-345-5101
Jediah Behny, supt. — Fax 345-5103
www.cabeard.k12.in.us
Knightstown HS — 400/9-12
8149 W US Highway 40 46148 — 765-345-5153
Scott Ritchie, prin. — Fax 345-7977
Knightstown IS — 400/4-8
1 Panther Trl 46148 — 765-345-5455
K. Gardner, prin. — Fax 345-5523

**Knox, Starke, Pop. 3,653**
Knox Community SC — 2,000/PK-12
2 Redskin Trl 46534 — 574-772-1600
A.J. Gappa, supt. — Fax 772-1608
www.knox.k12.in.us
Knox Community HS — 600/9-12
1 Redskin Trl 46534 — 574-772-1670
Dr. Elizabeth Ratliff, prin. — Fax 772-1681
Knox Community MS — 500/6-8
901 S Main St 46534 — 574-772-1654
David Miller, prin. — Fax 772-1664

**Kokomo, Howard, Pop. 44,079**
Kokomo SC — 7,100/PK-12
PO Box 2188 46904 — 765-455-8000
Dr. Jeff Hauswald, supt. — Fax 455-8018
www.kokomo.k12.in.us
Bon Air 1-1 Middle Technology Academy — 300/6-8
2796 N Apperson Way 46901 — 765-454-7025
Angela Blessing, prin. — Fax 454-7034
Central International (KEY) MS — 700/6-8
303 E Superior St 46901 — 765-454-7000
Holly Herrera, prin. — Fax 454-7007
International Program — 10-12
303 E Superior St 46901 — 765-454-7000
Kokomo Area Career Center — Vo/Tech
2415 S Berkley Rd 46902 — 765-455-8021
Jonathan Schuck, dir. — Fax 454-7014
Kokomo HS — 1,900/9-12
2501 S Berkley Rd 46902 — 765-455-8040
Anthony Harl, prin. — Fax 455-8060
Maple Crest Middle STEM S — 700/6-8
2727 S Washington St 46902 — 765-455-8085
Kathryn Reckard, prin. — Fax 455-8062
McKinley Alternative HS — Alt
1217 W Carter St 46901 — 765-454-7080
Idowu Ikudabo, coord. — Fax 454-7081
Twilight Alternative HS — Alt
2501 S Berkley Rd 46902 — 765-454-8040
Rick Hagenow, dir.

Northwestern SC — 1,700/K-12
3075 N Washington St 46901 — 765-452-3060
Ryan Snoddy, supt. — Fax 452-3065
nwsc.k12.in.us
Northwestern HS — 600/9-12
3431 N 400 W 46901 — 765-454-2332
Kristen Bilkey, prin. — Fax 454-2333
Northwestern MS — 300/7-8
3431 N 400 W 46901 — 765-454-2323
Brett Davis, prin. — Fax 457-2324

Taylor Community SC — 1,400/PK-12
3750 E 300 S 46902 — 765-453-3035
Chris Smith, supt. — Fax 455-8531
www.taylor.k12.in.us
Taylor HS — 400/9-12
3794 E 300 S 46902 — 765-453-1101
Eric Hartman, prin. — Fax 455-5163
Taylor MS — 300/6-8
3794 E 300 S 46902 — 765-455-5186
Heather Hord, prin. — Fax 455-5157

Indiana University at Kokomo — Post-Sec.
2300 S Washington St 46902 — 765-453-2000
Ivy Tech Community College - Kokomo — Post-Sec.
PO Box 1373 46903 — 765-459-0561
Rudae's School of Beauty Culture — Post-Sec.
208 W Jefferson St 46901 — 765-459-4197
St. Joseph Hospital & Health Center — Post-Sec.
1907 W Sycamore St 46901 — 765-452-5611

**Kouts, Porter, Pop. 1,870**
East Porter County SC — 2,400/K-12
PO Box 370 46347 — 219-766-2214
Dr. Rod Gardin, supt. — Fax 766-2885
epcsc.schoolwires.net/
Kouts MSHS — 500/6-12
PO Box 699 46347 — 219-766-2231
Thomas Stoner, prin. — Fax 766-3763
Other Schools – See Valparaiso

**La Crosse, LaPorte, Pop. 550**
Tri Township School Corp
Supt. — See Wanatah
La Crosse HS — 100/9-12
PO Box 360 46348 — 219-754-2461
Timothy Somers, prin. — Fax 754-2511

**Lafayette, Tippecanoe, Pop. 65,793**
Lafayette SC — 7,000/K-12
2300 Cason St 47904 — 765-771-6000
Les Huddle, supt. — Fax 771-6049
www.lsc.k12.in.us
Jefferson HS — 2,000/9-12
1801 S 18th St 47905 — 765-772-4700
Mark Preston, prin. — Fax 772-4713
Oakland HS — 100/9-12
1100 Elizabeth St 47904 — 765-807-8550
Clare Lutgen, prin. — Fax 807-8551
Tecumseh JHS — 1,000/7-8
2101 S 18th St 47905 — 765-772-4750
Brandon Hawkins, prin. — Fax 772-4763

Tippecanoe SC — 11,500/K-12
21 Elston Rd 47909 — 765-474-2481
Dr. Scott Hanback, supt. — Fax 474-0533
www.tsc.k12.in.us
East Tipp MS — 500/6-8
7501 E 300 N 47905 — 765-589-3566
Shaad Buss, prin. — Fax 589-3129
McCutcheon HS — 1,800/9-12
4951 Old US Highway 231 S 47909 — 765-474-1488
John Beeker, prin. — Fax 477-9710
Southwestern MS — 400/6-8
2100 W 800 S 47909 — 765-538-3025
Karen Smith, prin. — Fax 538-2877
Wainwright MS — 300/6-8
7501 E 700 S 47905 — 765-269-8350
Dr. Neal McCutcheon, prin. — Fax 269-8359
Wea Ridge MS — 600/6-8
4410 S 150 E 47909 — 765-471-2164
Cory Marshall, prin. — Fax 474-5347
Other Schools – See West Lafayette

Central Catholic JSHS — 400/7-12
2410 S 9th St 47909 — 765-474-2496
Neil Wagner, prin. — Fax 474-8752
Faith Christian S — 700/PK-12
5526 State Road 26 E 47905 — 765-447-2727
Scott Grass, supt. — Fax 449-3737
Harrison College — Post-Sec.
4705 Meijer Ct 47905 — 765-447-9550
Ivy Tech Community College - Lafayette — Post-Sec.
PO Box 6299 47903 — 765-269-5000
Lafayette Beauty Academy — Post-Sec.
833 Ferry St 47901 — 765-742-0068
St. Elizabeth School of Nursing — Post-Sec.
1508 Tippecanoe St 47904 — 765-423-6400

**Lagrange, Lagrange, Pop. 2,609**
Lakeland SC — 2,200/K-12
825 E 075 N 46761 — 260-499-2400
Risa Herber, supt. — Fax 463-4800
www.lakeland.k12.in.us
Lakeland HS — 700/9-12
805 E 075 N 46761 — 260-499-2470
Eva Merkel, prin. — Fax 463-4058
Lakeland MS — 500/6-8
1055 E 075 N 46761 — 260-499-2480
Karen Lake, prin. — Fax 463-2648

Prairie Heights Community SC — 1,400/K-12
305 S 1150 E 46761 — 260-351-3214
Jeff Reed, supt. — Fax 351-3614
www.ph.k12.in.us/
Prairie Heights HS — 500/9-12
245 S 1150 E 46761 — 260-351-3214
Jeremy Swander, prin. — Fax 351-3848
Prairie Heights MS — 400/5-8
395 S 1150 E 46761 — 260-351-3214
Damon Witherspoon, prin. — Fax 351-2182

**Lake Station, Lake, Pop. 12,350**
Lake Station Community SD — 1,500/K-12
2500 Pike St 46405 — 219-962-1159
Dr. Tom Cripliver, supt. — Fax 962-4011
www.lakes.k12.in.us
Edison JSHS — 700/7-12
3304 Parkside Ave 46405 — 219-962-8531
Bruce Bush, prin. — Fax 962-2064

**Lakeville, Saint Joseph, Pop. 778**
Union-North United SC — 1,200/K-12
22601 Tyler Rd 46536 — 574-784-8141
Mitchell Mawhorter, supt. — Fax 784-2181
www.unorth.k12.in.us
Laville JSHS — 600/7-12
69969 US Highway 31 46536 — 574-784-3151
Nathan McKeand, prin. — Fax 784-8695

**Lanesville, Harrison, Pop. 557**
Lanesville Community SC — 700/K-12
2725 Crestview Ave NE 47136 — 812-952-2555
Steve Morris, supt. — Fax 952-3762
www.lanesville.k12.in.us/
Lanesville JSHS — 300/7-12
2725 Crestview Ave NE 47136 — 812-952-2555
Steve Morris, prin. — Fax 952-3762

**Lapel, Madison, Pop. 2,035**
Frankton-Lapel Community SD
Supt. — See Anderson
Lapel HS — 400/9-12
1850 S 900 W 46051 — 765-534-3036
Chad Kemerly, prin. — Fax 203-9943
Lapel MS — 300/6-8
2883 S State Road 13 46051 — 765-534-3137
Bill Chase, prin. — Fax 203-9937

**La Porte, LaPorte, Pop. 21,655**
La Porte Community SC — 6,300/K-12
1921 A St 46350 — 219-362-7056
Mark Francesconi, supt. — Fax 324-9347
www.lpcsc.k12.in.us
Boston MS — 800/6-8
1000 Harrison St 46350 — 219-326-6930
Deborah Carter, prin. — Fax 324-7108
Kesling MS — 800/6-8
306 E 18th St 46350 — 219-362-7507
Bill Wilmsen, prin. — Fax 324-5712
La Porte HS — 1,900/9-12
602 F St 46350 — 219-362-3102
Benjamin Tonagel, prin. — Fax 324-2142

La Lumiere S — 200/9-12
6801 N Wilhelm Rd 46352 — 219-326-7450
Dr. Charles Clark, hdmstr. — Fax 325-3185

**Larwill, Whitley, Pop. 280**
Whitko Community SC — 1,800/K-12
710 N State Road 5 Ste B 46764 — 574-594-2658
Steven Clason, supt. — Fax 594-2326
www.whitko.org
Whitko MS — 400/6-8
710 N State Road 5 46764 — 260-327-3603
Parrish Kruger, prin. — Fax 327-3805
Other Schools – See South Whitley

**Lawrenceburg, Dearborn, Pop. 4,938**
Lawrenceburg Community SC — 1,900/K-12
300 Tiger Blvd 47025 — 812-537-7200
Karl Galey, supt. — Fax 537-0759
www.lburg.k12.in.us
Greendale MS — 400/6-8
200 Tiger Blvd 47025 — 812-537-7259
Jayme Herbert, prin. — Fax 537-6385
Lawrenceburg HS — 600/9-12
100 Tiger Blvd 47025 — 812-537-7219
Bill Snyder, prin. — Fax 537-7221

**Lebanon, Boone, Pop. 15,595**
Lebanon Community SC — 3,500/K-12
1810 N Grant St 46052 — 765-482-0380
Dr. Robert Taylor, supt. — Fax 483-3053
www.leb.k12.in.us/
Lebanon HS — 1,000/9-12
510 Essex Dr 46052 — 765-482-0400
Kevin O'Rourke, prin. — Fax 483-3040
Lebanon MS — 800/6-8
1800 N Grant St 46052 — 765-482-3400
Doyle Dunshee, prin. — Fax 483-3049

**Leo, Allen**
East Allen County SD
Supt. — See New Haven
Leo JSHS — 1,300/7-12
14600 Amstutz Rd 46765 — 260-446-0180
Dr. Neal Brown, prin. — Fax 446-0189

**Leopold, Perry**
Perry Central Community SC — 1,200/PK-12
18677 Old State Road 37 47551 — 812-843-5576
Mary Roberson, supt. — Fax 843-4746
www.pccs.k12.in.us/
Perry Central JSHS — 500/7-12
18677 Old State Road 37 47551 — 812-843-5121
Seth Clark, prin. — Fax 843-4198

**Liberty, Union, Pop. 2,110**
Union County/College Corner JSD — 1,300/K-12
107 S Layman St 47353 — 765-458-7471
Dr. Zach Rozelle, supt. — Fax 458-5647
www.uc.k12.in.us/
Union County HS — 400/9-12
410 Patriot Blvd 47353 — 765-458-5136
Connie Rosenberger, prin. — Fax 458-6315
Union County MS — 400/6-8
488 E State Road 44 47353 — 765-458-7438
Ronald Ross, prin. — Fax 458-6041

**Ligonier, Noble, Pop. 4,376**
West Noble SC — 2,300/K-12
5050 N US Highway 33 46767 — 260-894-3191
Dr. Dennis VanDuyne, supt. — Fax 894-3260
westnoble.k12.in.us/
West Noble HS — 700/9-12
5094 N US Highway 33 46767 — 260-894-3191
Dr. Greg Baker, prin. — Fax 894-4708
West Noble MS — 800/5-8
5194 N US Highway 33 46767 — 260-894-3191
Melanie Tijerina, prin. — Fax 894-4703

**Lincoln City, Spencer**
North Spencer County SC — 2,000/PK-12
PO Box 316 47552 — 812-937-2400
Daniel Scherry, supt. — Fax 937-7187
www.nspencer.k12.in.us
Heritage Hills HS — 700/9-12
3644 E County Road 1600 N 47552 — 812-937-4472
Nick Alcorn, prin. — Fax 937-4878

Heritage Hills MS 300/7-8
PO Box 1777 47552 812-937-4472
Chad Schnieders, prin. Fax 937-4327

**Linton, Greene, Pop. 5,354**
Linton-Stockton SC 1,400/K-12
801 1st St NE 47441 812-847-6020
Nick Karazsia, supt. Fax 847-8659
www.lssc.k12.in.us/
Linton-Stockton HS 400/9-12
10 H St NE 47441 812-847-6024
Nathan Moore, prin. Fax 847-6037
Linton-Stockton MS 300/6-8
109 I St NE 47441 812-847-6022
Jeff Sparks, prin. Fax 847-6032

**Lizton, Hendricks, Pop. 481**
North West Hendricks SD 1,900/PK-12
PO Box 70 46149 317-994-4100
Richard King, supt. Fax 994-5963
www.hendricks.k12.in.us/
Tri-West HS 600/9-12
7883 N State Road 39 46149 317-994-4000
Adam Benner, prin. Fax 994-5106
Tri-West MS 400/6-8
555 W US Highway 136 46149 317-994-4200
Ryan Nickoli, prin. Fax 994-4230

**Logansport, Cass, Pop. 18,151**
Logansport Community SC 4,200/PK-12
2829 George St 46947 574-722-2911
Michele Starkey, supt. Fax 753-0143
www.lcsc.k12.in.us
Century Career Center Vo/Tech
2500 Hopper St 46947 574-722-3811
Clark Miller, dir. Fax 753-7649
Columbia MS 400/6-8
1300 N 3rd St 46947 574-753-3797
Greg Grostefon, prin. Fax 753-6159
Lincoln MS 500/6-8
2901 Usher St 46947 574-753-7115
Jeff Canady, prin. Fax 753-5826
Logansport Community HS 1,300/9-12
1 Berry Ln 46947 574-753-0441
Matt Jones, prin. Fax 753-3688

**Loogootee, Martin, Pop. 2,735**
Loogootee Community SC 1,000/K-12
PO Box 282 47553 812-295-2595
Dr. Joan Keller, supt. Fax 295-5595
www.loogootee.k12.in.us/
Loogootee HS 500/9-12
201 Brooks Ave 47553 812-295-3254
Chip Mehaffey, prin. Fax 295-3694
Loogootee MS 100/5-8
201 Brooks Ave 47553 812-295-3254
Lacey Wade, prin. Fax 295-3694

**Lowell, Lake, Pop. 9,196**
Tri-Creek SC 3,600/K-12
195 W Oakley Ave 46356 219-696-6661
Dr. Debra K. Howe, supt. Fax 696-2150
www.tricreek.k12.in.us/
Lowell HS 1,300/9-12
2051 E Commercial Ave 46356 219-696-7733
Lori Pavell, prin. Fax 696-0042
Lowell MS 900/6-8
19250 Cline St 46356 219-696-7701
Rebecca Pavich, prin. Fax 690-2620

**Lynn, Randolph, Pop. 1,088**
Randolph Southern SC 500/K-12
1 Rebel Dr 47355 765-874-1181
Donnie Bowsman, supt. Fax 874-1298
www.rssc.k12.in.us
Randolph Southern JSHS 300/7-12
2 Rebel Dr 47355 765-874-2541
Donald Knotts, prin. Fax 874-1298

**Lynnville, Warrick, Pop. 881**
Warrick County SC
Supt. — See Boonville
Tecumseh JSHS 400/7-12
5244 W State Route 68 47619 812-922-3237
Josh Susott, prin. Fax 922-3608

**Madison, Jefferson, Pop. 11,775**
Madison Consolidated SD 2,900/K-12
2421 Wilson Ave 47250 812-274-8001
Dr. Ginger Bolinger, supt. Fax 274-8507
www.madison.k12.in.us
Madison Consolidated HS 1,000/9-12
743 Clifty Dr 47250 812-274-8002
Kevin Yancey, prin. Fax 274-8788
Madison Consolidated JHS 800/6-8
701 8th St 47250 812-274-8003
Jill Mires, prin. Fax 274-8503

---

Christian Academy of Madison 100/PK-12
477 W Hutchinson Ln 47250 812-273-5000
Anna Gosman, admin. Fax 265-0700
Ivy Tech Community College - Southeast Post-Sec.
590 Ivy Tech Dr 47250 812-265-2580
King's Daughter's Hospital Post-Sec.
PO Box 447 47250 812-265-5211
Shawe Memorial JSHS 200/7-12
201 W State St 47250 812-273-2150
Steve Hesse, prin. Fax 273-8975

**Marengo, Crawford, Pop. 809**
Crawford County Community SC 1,600/PK-12
5805 E Administration Rd 47140 812-365-2135
Woodrow DeRossett, supt. Fax 365-2783
www.cccs.k12.in.us/
Crawford County JSHS 700/7-12
1130 S State Road 66 47140 812-365-2125
Brandon Johnson, prin. Fax 365-2127

**Marion, Grant, Pop. 29,023**
Eastbrook Community SC 1,700/K-12
560 S 900 E 46953 765-664-0624
Brett Garrett, supt. Fax 664-0626
www.eastbrookschools.net
Eastbrook HS 600/9-12
560 S 900 E 46953 765-664-1214
Patrick McLaughlin, prin. Fax 664-1216
Eastbrook JHS 300/7-8
560 S 900 E 46953 765-668-7136
Elizabeth Duckwall, prin. Fax 668-7137

Marion Community SD 3,900/PK-12
750 W 26th St 46953 765-662-2546
Brad Lindsay, supt. Fax 651-2043
www.marion.k12.in.us
Marion HS 1,200/9-12
750 W 26th St 46953 765-664-9051
Keith Burke, prin. Fax 662-0383
McCulloch JHS 600/7-8
3528 S Washington St 46953 765-674-6917
Dawn Morgan, prin. Fax 674-8943
Tucker Career & Technology Center Vo/Tech
107 S Pennsylvania St 46952 765-664-9091
Michael Ripperger, dir. Fax 651-2048

---

Indiana Wesleyan University Post-Sec.
4201 S Washington St 46953 765-674-6901
Lakeview Christian S 300/PK-12
5318 S Western Ave 46953 765-677-4266
Dr. Douglas Ballinger, admin. Fax 677-4269

**Marshall, Parke, Pop. 323**
North Central Parke Community SC 1,300/K-12
1497 E State Road 47 47859 765-597-2750
Dr. Thomas Rohr, supt. Fax 597-2755
www.ncp.k12.in.us
Turkey Run JSHS 300/7-12
1551 E State Road 47 47859 765-597-2700
Fax 597-4202
Other Schools – See Rockville

**Martinsville, Morgan, Pop. 11,701**
Metro SD of Martinsville 5,400/PK-12
460 S Main St 46151 765-342-6641
Dr. Michele Moore, supt. Fax 342-6877
www.msdmartinsville.org
Bell - East MS 700/6-8
1459 E Columbus St 46151 765-342-6675
Eric Bowlen, prin. Fax 349-5236
Hammons S 50/Alt
389 E Jackson St 46151 765-342-0120
Melody Bentley, lead tchr. Fax 349-5256
Martinsville HS 1,600/9-12
1360 E Gray St 46151 765-342-5571
Nicholas Sears, prin. Fax 349-5256
Martinsville West MS 600/6-8
109 E Garfield Ave 46151 765-342-6628
Suzie Lipps, prin. Fax 349-5232

---

Tabernacle Christian S 100/PK-12
2189 Burton Ln 46151 765-342-0501
Kenny Roll, prin. Fax 342-0502

**Medora, Jackson, Pop. 677**
Medora Community SC 200/PK-12
PO Box 369 47260 812-966-2210
Roger Bane, supt. Fax 966-2217
www.medorahornets.org/
Medora JSHS 100/6-12
PO Box 248 47260 812-966-2201
Chrystal Street, prin. Fax 966-2209

**Merrillville, Lake, Pop. 34,497**
Merrillville Community SC 6,900/K-12
6701 Delaware St 46410 219-650-5300
Dr. Mark B. Sperling, supt. Fax 650-5320
www.mvsc.k12.in.us
Merrillville HS 2,400/9-12
276 E 68th Pl 46410 219-650-5307
Michael Krutz, prin. Fax 650-5391
Pierce MS 1,100/7-8
199 E 70th Ave 46410 219-650-5308
Christine Kibler-Wheeler, prin. Fax 650-5483

---

Andrean HS 600/9-12
5959 Broadway 46410 219-887-5281
Richard Piwowarski, prin. Fax 981-5072
Brown Mackie College Post-Sec.
1000 E 80th Pl Ste 205M 46410 219-769-3321
DeVry University Post-Sec.
1000 E 80th Pl Ste 222N 46410 219-736-7440
ITT Technical Institute Post-Sec.
8488 Georgia St 46410 219-738-6100
Merrillville Beauty College Post-Sec.
48 W 67th Pl 46410 219-769-2232
Success School Post-Sec.
8101 Polo Club Dr 46410 219-736-9999

**Michigan City, LaPorte, Pop. 30,502**
Michigan City Area SD 4,800/PK-12
408 S Carroll Ave 46360 219-873-2000
Dr. Barbara Eason-Watkins, supt. Fax 873-2072
www.mcas.k12.in.us
Barker MS 300/7-8
319 Barker Rd 46360 219-873-2057
Karen Puchalski, prin. Fax 873-3099
Krueger MS 200/7-8
2001 Springland Ave 46360 219-873-2061
Vera Jones, prin. Fax 873-2063
Michigan City HS 1,900/9-12
8466 W Pahs Rd 46360 219-873-2044
Wendell McCollum, prin. Fax 873-2055
Smith Area Career Center Vo/Tech
817 Lafayette St 46360 219-873-2120
Audra Peterson, dir. Fax 873-2068

---

Brown Mackie College Post-Sec.
1001 E US Highway 20 46360 219-877-3100
Lakeshore Medical Lab Training Programs Post-Sec.
402 Franklin St 46360 219-872-7032
Marquette Catholic HS 200/9-12
306 W 10th St 46360 219-873-1325
James White, prin. Fax 873-1327

**Michigantown, Clinton, Pop. 463**
Clinton Central SC 1,000/K-12
PO Box 118 46057 765-249-2515
Dr. Jeffery Studebaker, supt. Fax 249-2504
www.clinton.k12.in.us/
Clinton Central JSHS 500/7-12
PO Box 178 46057 765-249-2255
Wendy Haag, prin. Fax 249-0214

**Middlebury, Elkhart, Pop. 3,377**
Middlebury Community SD 4,400/K-12
56853 Northridge Dr 46540 574-825-9425
Jane Allen, supt. Fax 825-9426
www.mcsin-k12.org/
Northridge HS 1,300/9-12
56779 Northridge Dr 46540 574-825-2142
Andrew Wood, prin. Fax 825-1473
Northridge MS 1,100/6-8
56691 Northridge Dr 46540 574-825-9531
Robby Goodman, prin. Fax 825-9154

**Middletown, Henry, Pop. 2,295**
Shenandoah SC 1,400/PK-12
5100 N Raider Rd 47356 765-354-2266
Ron Green, supt. Fax 354-2274
www.shenandoah.k12.in.us/
Shenandoah HS 400/9-12
7354 W US Highway 36 47356 765-354-6640
Jacob Wiese, prin. Fax 354-3110
Shenandoah MS 300/6-8
5156 N Raider Rd 47356 765-354-6638
Greg Allen, prin. Fax 354-3120

**Milan, Ripley, Pop. 1,874**
Milan Community SC 1,200/K-12
412 E Carr St 47031 812-654-2365
Paul Ketcham M.S., supt. Fax 654-2441
www.milan.k12.in.us
Milan HS 400/9-12
609 N Warpath Dr 47031 812-654-3096
Ryan Langferman, prin. Fax 654-2368
Milan MS 300/6-8
609 N Warpath Dr 47031 812-654-1616
Patrick Murphy, prin. Fax 654-2368

**Mishawaka, Saint Joseph, Pop. 46,961**
Penn-Harris-Madison SC 10,500/K-12
55900 Bittersweet Rd 46545 574-259-7941
Dr. Jerry Thacker, supt. Fax 258-9547
www.phmschools.org
Grissom MS 700/6-8
13881 Kern Rd 46544 574-633-4061
Nathan Boyd, prin. Fax 633-2134
Penn HS 3,400/9-12
56100 Bittersweet Rd 46545 574-259-7961
Steve Hope, prin. Fax 258-9543
Schmucker MS 1,000/6-8
56045 Bittersweet Rd 46545 574-259-5661
Sean Galiher, prin. Fax 259-0807
Other Schools – See Granger

School City of Mishawaka 5,100/K-12
1402 S Main St 46544 574-254-4500
Dr. A. Dean Speicher, supt. Fax 254-4585
www.mishawaka.k12.in.us
Mishawaka HS 1,500/9-12
1202 Lincolnway E 46544 574-254-7300
Jerome Calderone, prin. Fax 254-7481
Young MS 700/7-8
1801 N Main St 46545 574-254-3600
C. Mike Fisher, prin. Fax 258-3021

---

Bais Yaakov of Indiana 50/9-12
206 W 8th St 46544 574-257-0689
Dena Gewirtz, admin.
Bethel College Post-Sec.
1001 Bethel Cir 46545 574-807-7000
Marian HS 700/9-12
1311 S Logan St 46544 574-259-5257
Mark Kirzeder, prin. Fax 258-7668

**Mitchell, Lawrence, Pop. 4,315**
Mitchell Community SD 1,900/PK-12
441 N 8th St 47446 812-849-4481
Dr. Steve Phillips, supt. Fax 849-2133
www.mitchell.k12.in.us
Mitchell HS 600/9-12
1000 W Bishop Blvd 47446 812-849-3663
Sean Vandeventer, prin. Fax 849-5368
Mitchell JHS 400/6-8
1010 W Bishop Blvd 47446 812-849-3747
Jennifer Caruso, prin. Fax 849-5841

**Modoc, Randolph, Pop. 190**
Union SC 400/K-12
8707 W US Highway 36 47358 765-853-5464
Allen Hayne, supt. Fax 853-5070
www.usc.k12.in.us
Union JSHS 200/7-12
8707 W US Highway 36 47358 765-853-5421
Allen Hayne, prin. Fax 853-6057

**Monon, White, Pop. 1,750**
North White SC 700/PK-12
402 E Broadway St 47959 219-253-6618
Dr. Teresa L. Gremaux, supt. Fax 253-6488
www.nwhite.k12.in.us/
North White JSHS 400/7-12
305 E Broadway St 47959 219-253-6638
Anthony Cassel, prin. Fax 253-7004
Other Schools – See Monticello

**Monroe, Adams, Pop. 839**
Adams Central Community SD 1,200/K-12
222 W Washington St 46772 260-692-6193
Dr. Lori M. Stiglitz, supt. Fax 692-6198
www.accs.k12.in.us/
Adams Central HS 400/9-12
222 W Washington St 46772 260-692-6151
Jason Witzigreuter, prin. Fax 692-6192
Adams Central MS 200/6-8
222 W Washington St 46772 260-692-6151
Jason Witzigreuter, prin. Fax 692-6192

**Monroeville, Allen, Pop. 1,229**
East Allen County SD
Supt. — See New Haven
Heritage JSHS 900/7-12
13608 Monroeville Rd 46773 260-446-0140
Matt Widenhoefer, prin. Fax 446-0146

**Monrovia, Morgan, Pop. 1,058**
Monroe-Gregg SD 1,500/PK-12
135 S Chestnut St 46157 317-996-3720
Dr. William Roberson, supt. Fax 996-2977
www.m-gsd.org/
Monrovia HS 500/9-12
135 S Chestnut St 46157 317-996-2259
Mike Springer, prin. Fax 996-3519
Monrovia MS 400/6-8
135 S Chestnut St 46157 317-996-2352
Yolanda Goodpaster, prin. Fax 996-3429

**Montezuma, Parke, Pop. 1,013**
Southwest Parke Community SC 900/K-12
4851 S Coxville Rd 47862 765-569-2073
Leonard Orr, supt. Fax 569-0309
www.swparke.k12.in.us
Riverton Parke JSHS 500/7-12
4907 S Coxville Rd 47862 765-569-2045
Kyle Kersey, prin. Fax 569-2047

**Montgomery, Daviess, Pop. 341**
Barr-Reeve Community SD 700/K-12
PO Box 97 47558 812-486-3220
Travis Madison, supt. Fax 486-3509
www.barr.k12.in.us
Barr-Reeve MSHS 300/6-12
PO Box 129 47558 812-486-3265
Jeff Doyle, prin. Fax 486-2829

**Monticello, White, Pop. 5,324**
North White SC
Supt. — See Monon
White County Academic Skills Center Adult
315 N Illinois St 47960 574-583-5158
Suzy Karberg, dir. Fax 583-4231

Twin Lakes SC 2,200/PK-12
565 S Main St 47960 574-583-7211
Dr. Thomas Fletcher, supt. Fax 583-2679
www.twinlakes.k12.in.us/
Roosevelt MS 600/6-8
721 W Broadway St 47960 574-583-5552
Rod Coffing, prin. Fax 583-3675
Twin Lakes HS 800/9-12
300 S 3rd St 47960 574-583-7108
Jennifer Miller, prin. Fax 583-2679

**Mooresville, Morgan, Pop. 9,219**
Mooresville Consolidated SC 4,500/PK-12
11 W Carlisle St 46158 317-831-0950
David Marcotte, supt. Fax 831-9202
www.mooresvilleschools.org
Hadley MS 700/7-8
200 W Carlisle St 46158 317-831-9208
Jacob Allen, prin. Fax 831-9249
Mooresville HS 1,300/9-12
550 N Indiana St 46158 317-831-9203
Brian Disney, prin. Fax 831-9206

**Morocco, Newton, Pop. 1,125**
North Newton SC 1,500/K-12
PO Box 8 47963 219-285-2228
Destin Haas, supt. Fax 285-2708
www.nn.k12.in.us/
North Newton JSHS 700/7-12
1641 W 250 N 47963 219-285-2252
Chris Enyeart, prin. Fax 285-2881

**Morristown, Shelby, Pop. 1,211**
Shelby Eastern SD
Supt. — See Shelbyville
Morristown JSHS 400/6-12
PO Box 960 46161 765-763-1221
Ken Howell, prin. Fax 763-7170

**Mount Summit, Henry, Pop. 346**
Blue River Valley SD 700/PK-12
PO Box 217 47361 765-836-4816
Stephen Welsh, supt. Fax 836-4817
www.brv.k12.in.us
Other Schools – See New Castle

**Mount Vernon, Posey, Pop. 6,543**
Metro SD of Mt. Vernon 2,200/PK-12
1000 W 4th St 47620 812-838-4471
Dr. Tom Kopatich, supt. Fax 833-5179
www.msdmv.k12.in.us
Mount Vernon HS 800/9-12
700 Harriett St 47620 812-838-4356
Tom Russell, prin. Fax 833-2099
Mount Vernon JHS 500/6-8
701 Tile Factory Rd 47620 812-833-2077
Chad Rodgers, prin. Fax 833-2083

**Muncie, Delaware, Pop. 68,179**
Cowan Community SC 800/K-12
9401 S Nottingham St 47302 765-289-4866
Dennis Chambers, supt. Fax 284-0315
www.cowan.k12.in.us
Cowan JSHS 300/7-12
9401 S Nottingham St 47302 765-289-7128
Patrick Bloom, prin. Fax 741-5954

Delaware Community SC 2,600/K-12
7821 N State Road 3 47303 765-284-5074
Reece Mann, supt. Fax 284-5259
www.delcomschools.org
Delta HS 800/9-12
3400 E State Road 28 47303 765-288-5597
Christopher Conley, prin. Fax 288-8498
Delta MS 600/6-8
9800 N County Road 200 E 47303 765-747-0869
Kelly Brown, prin. Fax 213-2131

Muncie Community SD 6,700/K-12
2501 N Oakwood Ave 47304 765-747-5211
Tim Heller, supt. Fax 747-5341
www.muncie.k12.in.us
Muncie Area Career Center Vo/Tech
2500 N Elgin St 47303 765-747-5250
JoAnn McCowan, dir. Fax 747-5455
Muncie Central HS 900/9-12
801 N Walnut St 47305 765-747-5260
Tom Jarvis, prin. Fax 747-5314
Muncie Southside MS 1,000/6-8
1601 E 26th St 47302 765-747-5320
Kelli Turner, prin. Fax 747-5325
Northside MS 800/6-8
2400 W Bethel Ave 47304 765-747-5290
Jackie Samuels, prin. Fax 751-0616

University Schools, Supt. — None
Dr. William Sharp, supt.
Burris Laboratory S 600/K-12
2201 W University Ave 47306 765-285-1131
Dawn Miller, prin. Fax 285-8620
IN Academy for Science Math & Humanities 300/11-12
301 N Talley Ave 47303 765-285-7457
Dr. Jeffrey Smith, prin. Fax 285-2777

---

Ball Memorial Hospital Post-Sec.
2401 W University Ave 47303 765-747-3393
Ball State University Post-Sec.
2000 W University Ave 47306 765-289-1241
Heritage Hall Christian S 200/PK-12
6401 W River Rd 47304 765-289-6371
David Stein, admin. Fax 213-2245
Ivy Tech Community College - East Centrl Post-Sec.
4301 S Cowan Rd 47302 765-289-2291
PJ's College of Cosmetology Post-Sec.
3100 W Kilgore Ave 47304 765-289-6144

**Munster, Lake, Pop. 23,303**
Town of Munster SD 4,100/K-12
8616 Columbia Ave 46321 219-836-9111
Dr. Jeffrey Hendrix, supt. Fax 836-3215
www.munster.k12.in.us
Munster HS 1,600/9-12
8808 Columbia Ave 46321 219-836-3200
Michael Wells, prin. Fax 836-3203
Wright MS 900/6-8
8650 Columbia Ave 46321 219-836-6260
Timothy Sopko, prin. Fax 836-0501

**Nappanee, Elkhart, Pop. 6,570**
Wa-Nee Community SD 3,100/K-12
1300 N Main St 46550 574-773-3131
Joe Sabo, supt. Fax 773-5593
www.wanee.org
Northwood HS 900/9-12
2101 N Main St 46550 574-773-4127
David Maugel, prin. Fax 773-4099
Other Schools – See Wakarusa

---

United Christian S 100/K-12
29522 County Road 52 46550 574-773-7505
Terrill Yoder, admin. Fax 773-7513

**Nashville, Brown, Pop. 795**
Brown County SC 1,900/PK-12
PO Box 38 47448 812-988-6601
David Shaffer, supt. Fax 988-5403
www.brownco.k12.in.us
Brown County HS 700/9-12
PO Box 68 47448 812-988-6606
Shane Killinger, prin. Fax 988-5422
Brown County JHS 300/7-8
PO Box 578 47448 812-988-6605
Brian Garman, prin. Fax 988-5415

**New Albany, Floyd, Pop. 35,385**
New Albany Floyd County Consolidated SD
11,500/PK-12
PO Box 1087 47151 812-949-4200
Dr. Bruce Hibbard, supt. Fax 949-6900
www.nafcs.k12.in.us
Hazelwood MS 1,000/5-8
1021 Hazelwood Ave 47150 812-542-8502
Jessica Waters, prin. Fax 542-4793
New Albany HS 2,000/9-12
1020 Vincennes St 47150 812-542-8506
Janet Page, prin. Fax 542-4797
Prosser Career Education Center Vo/Tech
4202 Charlestown Rd 47150 812-542-8508
Alan Taylor, prin. Fax 542-4799
Scribner MS 1,000/5-8
910 Old Vincennes Rd 47150 812-542-8503
Keith Bush, prin. Fax 542-4794
Other Schools – See Floyds Knobs, Georgetown

---

Christian Academy of Indiana 700/PK-12
1000 Academy Dr 47150 812-944-6200
Darin Long, prin. Fax 944-6903
Indiana University Southeast Post-Sec.
4201 Grant Line Rd 47150 812-941-2333

**Newburgh, Warrick, Pop. 3,276**
Warrick County SC
Supt. — See Boonville
Castle HS 1,900/9-12
3344 State Route 261 47630 812-853-3331
Doug Gresham, prin. Fax 853-9886
Castle North MS 700/6-8
2800 State Route 261 47630 812-853-7347
John Bertram, prin. Fax 858-1089
Castle South MS 700/6-8
3711 Casey Rd 47630 812-490-7930
Jim Hood, prin. Fax 490-7925
Warrick Education Center Alt
3199 State Route 261 47630 812-858-4309
Drew Gerth, prin. Fax 858-3420

---

ITT Technical Institute Post-Sec.
10999 Stahl Rd 47630 812-858-1600

**New Carlisle, Saint Joseph, Pop. 1,830**
New Prairie United SC 2,800/K-12
5327 N Cougar Rd 46552 574-654-7273
Dr. Paul White, supt. Fax 654-7274
www.npusc.k12.in.us
New Prairie HS 900/9-12
5333 N Cougar Rd 46552 574-654-7271
Greg Dettinger, prin. Fax 654-3390
New Prairie MS 700/6-8
5325 N Cougar Rd 46552 574-654-3070
Janet Scott, prin. Fax 654-7009

**New Castle, Henry, Pop. 17,809**
Blue River Valley SD
Supt. — See Mount Summit
Blue River Valley JSHS 300/7-12
4741 N Hillsboro Rd 47362 765-836-4811
Ken Howell, prin. Fax 836-3255

New Castle Community SC 3,600/K-12
322 Elliott Ave 47362 765-521-7201
Stephen Fisher, supt. Fax 521-7268
www.nccsc.k12.in.us
New Castle Chrysler HS 1,100/9-12
801 Parkview Dr 47362 765-593-6670
Christopher Walker, prin. Fax 593-6585
New Castle MS 600/7-8
601 Parkview Dr 47362 765-521-7230
Jaci Hadsell, prin. Fax 521-7269

**New Haven, Allen, Pop. 14,574**
East Allen County SD 9,200/PK-12
1240 State Road 930 E 46774 260-446-0100
Kenneth Folks, supt. Fax 446-0107
www.eacs.k12.in.us
East Allen Alternative S Alt
800 Homestead Dr 46774 260-446-0260
Jeff Kline, prin. Fax 446-0263
New Haven HS 1,100/9-12
1300 Green Rd 46774 260-446-0220
Greg Mohler, prin. Fax 446-0228
New Haven MS 600/6-8
900 Prospect Ave 46774 260-446-0230
Doug Pickett, prin. Fax 446-0236
Other Schools – See Fort Wayne, Leo, Monroeville, Woodburn

**New Palestine, Hancock, Pop. 2,034**
Southern Hancock County Community SC 3,200/PK-12
PO Box 508 46163 317-861-4463
Dr. Lisa Lantrip, supt. Fax 861-2142
corp.newpal.k12.in.us/
Doe Creek MS 600/7-8
PO Box 478 46163 317-861-4487
James Voelz, prin. Fax 861-2136
New Palestine HS 1,100/9-12
PO Box 448 46163 317-861-4417
Keith Fessler, prin. Fax 861-2125

**New Washington, Clark, Pop. 563**
Greater Clark County SD
Supt. — See Jeffersonville
New Washington MSHS 500/6-12
226 N Highway 62 47162 812-293-3368
Ben Ledbetter, prin. Fax 293-5803

**Noblesville, Hamilton, Pop. 51,089**
Noblesville SD 8,600/PK-12
18025 River Rd, 317-773-3171
Dr. Beth Niedermeyer, supt. Fax 773-7845
www.noblesvilleschools.org
Noblesville East MS 1,400/6-8
1625 Field Dr 46060 317-773-0782
Ryan Rich, prin. Fax 776-6261
Noblesville HS 2,600/9-12
18111 Cumberland Rd 46060 317-773-4680
Jeff Bryant, prin. Fax 776-6289
Noblesville West MS 700/6-8
19900 Hague Rd, 317-776-7792
Stacey Swan, prin. Fax 776-7797

---

Kaye Beauty College Post-Sec.
1111 S 10th St 46060 317-773-6189
St. Theodore Guerin HS 700/9-12
15300 N Gray Rd, 317-582-0120
James McNeany, prin. Fax 582-0140

**North Judson, Starke, Pop. 1,752**
North Judson-San Pierre SC 1,300/K-12
801 Campbell Dr 46366 574-896-2155
Lynn Johnson, supt. Fax 896-2156
www.njsp.k12.in.us
North Judson MS 300/6-8
950 Campbell Dr 46366 574-896-2167
Kelly Shepherd, prin. Fax 896-3036
North Judson-San Pierre HS 400/9-12
1 Bluejay Dr 46366 574-896-2158
Annette Zupin, prin. Fax 896-3945

**North Manchester, Wabash, Pop. 6,040**
Manchester Community SD 1,500/K-12
404 W 9th St 46962 260-982-7518
Dr. Bill Reichhart, supt. Fax 982-4583
www.mcs.k12.in.us
Manchester JSHS 600/7-12
1 Squire Dr 46962 260-982-2196
Nancy Alspaugh, prin. Fax 982-1034

---

Manchester University — Post-Sec.
604 E College Ave 46962 — 260-982-5000

**North Vernon, Jennings, Pop. 6,629**
Jennings County SC — 4,900/K-12
34 W Main St 47265 — 812-346-4483
Dr. Terry Sargent, supt. — Fax 346-4490
www.jcsc.org
Jennings County HS — 1,500/9-12
800 W Walnut St 47265 — 812-346-5588
Tom Black, prin. — Fax 346-4232
Jennings County MS — 800/7-8
820 W Walnut St 47265 — 812-346-4940
George Grubbs, prin. — Fax 346-4497

**Notre Dame, Saint Joseph, Pop. 5,766**

---

Holy Cross College — Post-Sec.
PO Box 308 46556 — 574-239-8377
St. Mary's College 46556 — Post-Sec.
574-284-4000
University of Notre Dame — Post-Sec.
220 Main Building 46556 — 574-631-5000

**Oakland City, Gibson, Pop. 2,406**
East Gibson SC — 1,000/PK-12
941 S Franklin St 47660 — 812-749-4755
Dr. Henry Brewster, supt. — Fax 749-3343
www.egsc.k12.in.us
Wood Memorial HS — 300/9-12
943 S Franklin St 47660 — 812-749-4757
Roger Benson, prin. — Fax 749-3512
Wood Memorial JHS — 200/7-8
945A S Franklin St 47660 — 812-749-4715
Roger Benson, prin. — Fax 749-4988

---

Oakland City University — Post-Sec.
138 N Lucretia St 47660 — 812-749-4781

**Oldenburg, Franklin, Pop. 669**

---

Oldenburg Academy — 200/9-12
1 Twister Cir 47036 — 812-934-4440
Bettina Rose, prin. — Fax 934-4838

**Oolitic, Lawrence, Pop. 1,177**
North Lawrence Community SD
Supt. — See Bedford
Oolitic MS — 400/6-8
903 Hoosier Ave 47451 — 812-275-7551
Steve Underwood, prin. — Fax 277-3219

**Orleans, Orange, Pop. 2,135**
Orleans Community SD — 800/K-12
173 Marley St 47452 — 812-865-2688
Gary McClintic, supt. — Fax 865-3428
www.orleans.k12.in.us/
Orleans JSHS — 400/7-12
200 W Wilson St 47452 — 812-865-2688
Roy Kline, prin. — Fax 865-3532

**Osgood, Ripley, Pop. 1,609**
Jac-Cen-Del Community SC — 900/PK-12
723 N Buckeye St 47037 — 812-689-4114
Timothy W. Taylor, supt. — Fax 689-7423
www.jaccendel.k12.in.us
Jac-Cen-Del MSHS — 400/7-12
4586 N US Highway 421 47037 — 812-689-4643
Daryl Werner, prin. — Fax 689-0152

**Ossian, Wells, Pop. 3,255**
Northern Wells Community SD — 2,500/PK-12
312 N Jefferson St 46777 — 260-622-4125
Dr. Scott Mills, supt. — Fax 622-7893
www.nwcs.k12.in.us
Norwell HS — 800/9-12
1100 E US Highway 224 46777 — 260-543-2213
Mark Misch, prin. — Fax 543-2591
Norwell MS — 600/6-8
1100 E US Highway 224 46777 — 260-543-2218
Tim Wilson, prin. — Fax 543-2510

**Oxford, Benton, Pop. 1,155**
Benton Community SC
Supt. — See Fowler
Benton Central JSHS — 900/7-12
4241 E 300 S 47971 — 765-884-1600
Corey Robb, prin. — Fax 884-8445

**Paoli, Orange, Pop. 3,640**
Lost River Career Cooperative SD
600 Elm St Ste 1 47454 — 812-723-4818
David Embree, supt. — Fax 723-4822
Lost River Career Cooperative S — Vo/Tech
600 Elm St Ste 1 47454 — 812-723-4818
David Embree, prin. — Fax 723-4822

Paoli Community SC — 1,600/PK-12
501 Elm St 47454 — 812-723-4717
Casey Brewster, supt. — Fax 723-5100
www.paoli.k12.in.us
Paoli JSHS — 700/7-12
501 Elm St 47454 — 812-723-3905
Todd Hitchcock, prin. — Fax 723-4459

**Parker City, Randolph, Pop. 1,400**
Monroe Central SC — 1,000/K-12
1918 N 1000 W 47368 — 765-468-6868
Adrian Moulton, supt. — Fax 468-6578
www.monroecentral.org
Monroe Central JSHS — 500/7-12
1878 N 1000 W 47368 — 765-468-7545
Scott Ritchie, prin. — Fax 468-8878

**Pekin, Washington, Pop. 1,385**
East Washington SC — 1,600/K-12
1050 N Eastern School Rd 47165 — 812-967-3926
Steve Darnell, supt. — Fax 967-5797
www.ewsc.k12.in.us
Eastern HS — 500/9-12
1100 N Eastern School Rd 47165 — 812-967-3931
Darin Farris, prin. — Fax 967-5767
East Washington MS — 500/5-8
1100 N Eastern School Rd 47165 — 812-967-5000
Amber Sater, prin. — Fax 967-5737

**Pendleton, Madison, Pop. 4,212**
South Madison Community SC — 4,400/PK-12
203 S Heritage Way 46064 — 765-778-2152
Joseph Buck, supt. — Fax 778-8207
www.smadison.k12.in.us
Pendleton Heights HS — 1,300/9-12
1 Arabian Dr 46064 — 765-778-2161
Mark Hall, prin. — Fax 778-0605
Pendleton Heights MS — 700/7-8
7450 S 300 W 46064 — 765-778-2139
Daniel Joyce, prin. — Fax 778-0557

**Pershing, Wayne, Pop. 406**
Western Wayne SD — 1,100/K-12
PO Box 217 47370 — 765-478-5375
Dr. Robert Mahon, supt. — Fax 478-4577
www.wwayne.k12.in.us
Other Schools – See Cambridge City

**Peru, Miami, Pop. 11,168**
Peru Community SC — 2,000/PK-12
35 W 3rd St 46970 — 765-473-3081
Sam Watkins, supt. — Fax 472-5129
www.peru.k12.in.us
KEYS Academy — Alt
19 Park Dr 46970 — 765-472-5150
Kristy Eddy, dir. — Fax 472-5157
Peru HS — 700/9-12
401 N Broadway 46970 — 765-472-3301
Jason Cary, prin. — Fax 472-5148
Peru JHS — 300/7-8
30 Daniel St 46970 — 765-473-3084
Sheri Spiker, prin. — Fax 473-4007

**Petersburg, Pike, Pop. 2,365**
Pike County SC — 2,000/PK-12
907 E Walnut St 47567 — 812-354-8731
Suzanne Blake, supt. — Fax 354-8733
www.pcsc.k12.in.us
Pike Central HS — 600/9-12
1810 E State Road 56 47567 — 812-354-8478
Chad Whitehead, prin. — Fax 789-2992
Pike Central MS — 500/6-8
1814 E State Road 56 47567 — 812-354-8478
Chad Whitehead, prin. — Fax 354-9559

**Plainfield, Hendricks, Pop. 27,200**
Plainfield Community SC — 4,800/PK-12
985 Longfellow Ln 46168 — 317-839-2578
Scott Olinger, supt. — Fax 838-3664
www.plainfield.k12.in.us
Plainfield Community MS — 1,100/6-8
709 Stafford Rd 46168 — 317-838-3966
Jerry Goldsberry, prin. — Fax 838-3965
Plainfield HS — 1,500/9-12
1 Red Pride Dr 46168 — 317-839-7711
Melvin Siefert, prin. — Fax 838-3671

---

PJ's College of Cosmetology — Post-Sec.
2026 Stafford Rd 46168 — 317-839-2761

**Plymouth, Marshall, Pop. 9,894**
Plymouth Community SC — 3,600/PK-12
611 Berkley St 46563 — 574-936-3115
Daniel Tyree, supt. — Fax 936-3160
www.plymouth.k12.in.us/
Lincoln JHS — 600/7-8
220 N Liberty St 46563 — 574-936-3113
Reid Gault, prin. — Fax 936-3574
Plymouth HS — 1,100/9-12
1 Big Red Dr 46563 — 574-936-2178
Jim Condon, prin. — Fax 936-4842

**Poneto, Wells, Pop. 166**
Southern Wells Community SD — 800/K-12
9120 S 300 W 46781 — 765-728-5537
James Craig, supt. — Fax 728-8124
www.swraiders.com
Southern Wells JSHS — 400/7-12
9120 S 300 W 46781 — 765-728-5534
Chad Yencer, prin. — Fax 728-8124

**Portage, Porter, Pop. 36,264**
Portage Township SD — 8,100/K-12
6240 US Highway 6 46368 — 219-762-6511
Dr. Richard Weigel, supt. — Fax 762-3263
www.portage.k12.in.us
Fegely MS — 700/6-8
5384 Stone Ave 46368 — 219-763-8150
Tom Martin, prin. — Fax 763-8157
Portage HS — 2,600/9-12
6450 US Highway 6 46368 — 219-763-8100
Jennifer Sass, prin. — Fax 764-6062
Willowcreek MS — 1,200/6-8
5962 Central Ave 46368 — 219-763-8090
Michelle Stewart, prin. — Fax 762-3455

---

Portage Christian S — 200/PK-12
PO Box 28 46368 — 219-762-8962
Larry Pender, supt. — Fax 763-9931

**Portland, Jay, Pop. 6,162**
Jay SC — 3,600/PK-12
1976 W Tyson Rd 47371 — 260-726-9341
Dr. Timothy Long, supt. — Fax 726-4959
www.jayschools.k12.in.us
East Jay MS — 600/6-8
225 E Water St 47371 — 260-726-9371
Lee Newman, prin. — Fax 726-2383
Jay County HS — 1,100/9-12
2072 W State Road 67 47371 — 260-726-9306
Phil Ford, prin. — Fax 726-9760
Other Schools – See Dunkirk

**Poseyville, Posey, Pop. 1,039**
Metro SD of North Posey County — 1,300/PK-12
101 N Church St 47633 — 812-874-2243
Dr. Todd Camp, supt. — Fax 874-8806
www.northposey.k12.in.us/
North Posey HS — 500/9-12
5900 High School Rd 47633 — 812-673-4242
Dr. Scott Strieter, prin. — Fax 673-6616
North Posey JHS — 200/7-8
5800 High School Rd 47633 — 812-673-4244
Steve Kavanaugh, prin. — Fax 673-6622

**Princeton, Gibson, Pop. 8,390**
North Gibson SC — 2,100/PK-12
1108 N Embree St 47670 — 812-385-4851
Dr. Brian Harmon, supt. — Fax 386-1531
www.ngsc.k12.in.us
Princeton Community HS — 700/9-12
1101 N Main St 47670 — 812-385-2591
Steve Hauger, prin. — Fax 386-1535
Princeton Community MS — 500/6-8
1106 N Embree St 47670 — 812-385-2020
Noah Velthouse, prin. — Fax 386-6746

**Ramsey, Harrison**
North Harrison Community SC — 2,300/PK-12
1260 Highway 64 NW 47166 — 812-347-2407
D. John Thomas, supt. — Fax 347-2870
www.nhcs.k12.in.us
North Harrison HS — 700/9-12
1070 Highway 64 NW 47166 — 812-347-2741
Stephen Hatton, prin. — Fax 347-2875
North Harrison MS — 500/6-8
1180 Highway 64 NW 47166 — 812-347-2421
Nathan Freed, prin. — Fax 347-2835

**Rensselaer, Jasper, Pop. 5,800**
Rensselaer Central SC — 1,700/PK-12
900 E Washington St 47978 — 219-866-7822
Ned Speicher, supt. — Fax 866-8360
www.rensselaerschools.org
Rensselaer Central HS — 500/9-12
1106 E Grace St 47978 — 219-866-5175
Andrew Jones, prin. — Fax 866-5135
Rensselaer Central MS — 400/6-8
1106 E Bomber Dr 47978 — 219-866-4661
Eric Huffman, prin. — Fax 866-2103

---

St. Joseph's College — Post-Sec.
PO Box 870 47978 — 219-866-6000

**Richmond, Wayne, Pop. 35,381**
Richmond Community SC — 3,800/PK-12
300 Hub Etchison Pkwy 47374 — 765-973-3300
Todd Terrill, supt. — Fax 973-3417
www.rcs.k12.in.us
Community Youth Services — 100/Alt
315 NW 3rd St 47374 — 765-973-3496
Carrie Wolfe, prin. — Fax 935-6303
Hibberd Building — Alt
900 S L St 47374 — 765-973-3412
Gwinn Gibbs, prin. — Fax 973-3712
Richmond HS — 1,500/9-12
380 Hub Etchison Pkwy 47374 — 765-973-3424
Rae Woolpy, prin. — Fax 973-3716
Test IS — 400/5-8
33 S 22nd St 47374 — 765-973-3412
Stacy Mopps, prin. — Fax 973-3712
Worth IS — 400/5-8
222 NW 7th St 47374 — 765-973-3495
Richard Bryant, prin. — Fax 973-3703
Richmond Adult Education Center — Adult
302 N 7th St 47374 — 765-973-3486
Rusty Hensley, prin. — Fax 935-1825

---

Bethany Theological Seminary — Post-Sec.
615 National Rd W 47374 — 800-287-8822
David Demuth Institute of Cosmetology — Post-Sec.
1301 S 8th Pl 47374 — 765-935-7964
Earlham Coll. & Earlham Sch. of Religion — Post-Sec.
801 National Rd W 47374 — 765-983-1200
Indiana University East — Post-Sec.
2325 Chester Blvd 47374 — 765-973-8200
Ivy Tech Community College - Richmond — Post-Sec.
2357 Chester Blvd 47374 — 765-966-2656
New Creations Christian S — 100/K-12
6400 National Rd E 47374 — 765-935-2790
Rev. Bev Hodgin, prin. — Fax 935-3961
PJ's College of Cosmetology — Post-Sec.
115 N 9th St 47374 — 765-962-3005
Reid Hospital & Health Care Services — Post-Sec.
1401 Chester Blvd 47374 — 765-983-3167
Seton Catholic JSHS — 100/7-12
233 S 5th St 47374 — 765-965-6956
Rick Ruhl, prin. — Fax 935-9930

**Rising Sun, Ohio, Pop. 2,292**
Rising Sun-Ohio County Community SD — 900/K-12
110 S Henrietta St 47040 — 812-438-2655
Branden Roeder, supt. — Fax 438-4636
www.risingsunschools.com/
Rising Sun HS — 300/9-12
210 S Henrietta St 47040 — 812-438-2652
Noel Bostic, prin. — Fax 438-2431

**Roachdale, Putnam, Pop. 922**
North Putnam Community SD
Supt. — See Bainbridge
North Putnam HS — 600/9-12
8869 N County Road 250 E 46172 — 765-522-6282
Jason Chew, prin. — Fax 522-2862
North Putnam MS — 400/6-8
8905 N County Road 250 E 46172 — 765-522-2900
Scott Miller, prin. — Fax 522-2863

**Rochester, Fulton, Pop. 6,144**

Rochester Community SC 1,900/PK-12
PO Box 108 46975 574-223-2159
Jana Vance, supt. Fax 223-4909
www.zebras.net

Rochester Community HS 600/9-12
PO Box 108 46975 574-223-2176
Adam Strasser, prin. Fax 223-3401

Rochester Community MS 400/6-8
PO Box 108 46975 574-223-2280
Oscar Haughs, prin. Fax 223-1531

**Rockport, Spencer, Pop. 2,241**

South Spencer County SC 1,500/PK-12
PO Box 26 47635 812-649-2591
Candis Haskell, supt. Fax 649-4249
www.sspencer.k12.in.us

South Spencer HS 500/9-12
1142 N Orchard Rd 47635 812-649-9157
Angela Gladish, prin. Fax 649-2214

South Spencer MS 300/6-8
1298 N Orchard Rd 47635 812-649-2203
Scot French, prin. Fax 649-9630

**Rockville, Parke, Pop. 2,594**

North Central Parke Community SC
Supt. — See Marshall

Rockville JSHS 400/7-12
506 N Beadle St 47872 765-569-5686
Dwight Ashley, prin. Fax 569-1047

**Rolling Prairie, LaPorte, Pop. 580**

---

Sacred Heart Apostolic S 50/7-12
PO Box 7 46371 219-778-4596

**Rossville, Clinton, Pop. 1,638**

Rossville Consolidated SD 1,000/K-12
PO Box 11 46065 765-379-2990
Dr. James Hanna, supt. Fax 379-3014
www.rcsd.k12.in.us

Rossville MSHS 300/6-12
PO Box 530 46065 765-379-2551
Michael Gick, prin. Fax 379-2556

**Royal Center, Cass, Pop. 854**

Pioneer Regional SC 1,000/K-12
PO Box 577 46978 574-643-2605
Dr. David Bess, supt. Fax 643-9977
www.pioneer.k12.in.us/

Pioneer JSHS 400/7-12
PO Box 547 46978 574-643-3145
Jeremy Tucker, prin. Fax 643-2020

**Rushville, Rush, Pop. 6,250**

Rush County SD 2,800/PK-12
330 W 8th St 46173 765-932-4186
Matthew Vance, supt. Fax 938-1608
rcs.rushville.k12.in.us/

Rush MS 400/7-8
1601 N Sexton St 46173 765-932-2968
Marla Stevens, prin. Fax 938-2011

Rushville Consolidated HS 800/9-12
1201 Lions Path 46173 765-932-3901
Robert Hadley, prin. Fax 932-4051

**Russiaville, Howard, Pop. 1,087**

Western SC 2,600/K-12
2600 S 600 W 46979 765-883-5576
Randy McCracken, supt. Fax 883-7946
www.western.k12.in.us

Western HS 800/9-12
2600 S 600 W 46979 765-883-5541
Rick Davis, prin. Fax 883-4522

Western MS 600/6-8
2600 S 600 W 46979 765-883-5566
Tracy Horrell, prin. Fax 883-4531

**Saint John, Lake, Pop. 14,717**

Lake Central SC 10,000/PK-12
8260 Wicker Ave 46373 219-365-8507
Dr. Lawrence Veracco, supt. Fax 365-6406
www.lcsc.us

Clark MS 1,100/5-8
8915 W 93rd Ave 46373 219-365-9203
Scott Graber, prin. Fax 365-9348

Lake Central HS 3,200/9-12
8400 Wicker Ave 46373 219-365-8551
Robin Tobias, prin. Fax 365-7156

Other Schools – See Dyer, Schererville

**Saint Leon, Franklin, Pop. 670**

Sunman-Dearborn Community SC 4,100/K-12
1 Trojan Pl Ste B, Brookville IN 47012 812-623-2291
Dr. Andrew Jackson, supt. Fax 623-3341
www.sunmandearborn.k12.in.us

East Central HS 1,400/9-12
1 Trojan Pl Ste A, Brookville IN 47012 812-576-4811
Robert Shipley, prin. Fax 576-2047

Sunman-Dearborn MS 700/6-8
8356 Schuman Rd, Brookville IN 47012
812-576-3500
Matt Maple, prin. Fax 576-3506

**Saint Mary of the Woods, Vigo, Pop. 793**

---

St. Mary-of-the-Woods College Post-Sec.
1 St Mary of Woods Coll 47876 812-535-5151

**Saint Meinrad, Spencer, Pop. 700**

---

St. Meinrad School of Theology Post-Sec.
200 Hill Dr 47577 812-357-6611

**Salem, Washington, Pop. 6,263**

Salem Community SD 2,000/K-12
500 N Harrison St 47167 812-883-4437
Dr. D. Lynn Reed, supt. Fax 883-1031
www.salemschools.com/

Salem HS 600/9-12
700 N Harrison St 47167 812-883-3904
Derek Smith, prin. Fax 883-3905

Salem MS 500/6-8
1001 N Harrison St 47167 812-883-3808
Ray Oppel, prin. Fax 883-8049

**Schererville, Lake, Pop. 28,917**

Lake Central SC
Supt. — See Saint John

Grimmer MS 900/5-8
225 W 77th Ave 46375 219-865-6985
John Alessia, prin. Fax 865-4423

---

Don Roberts Beauty Academy Post-Sec.
152 E US Highway 30 46375 219-864-1600

**Scottsburg, Scott, Pop. 6,707**

Scott County SD 2 2,800/PK-12
375 E Mcclain Ave 47170 812-752-8946
Dr. Marc Slaton, supt. Fax 752-8951
www.scsd2.k12.in.us/

Scottsburg HS 900/9-12
500 S Gardner St 47170 812-752-8927
Ric Manns, prin. Fax 752-6207

Scottsburg MS 700/6-8
425 S 3rd St 47170 812-752-8926
Kristin Nass, prin. Fax 752-8864

**Sellersburg, Clark, Pop. 6,055**

West Clark Community SC 4,800/PK-12
601 Renz Ave 47172 812-246-3375
Dr. Chad Schenck, supt. Fax 246-9731
www.wclark.k12.in.us

Silver Creek HS 700/9-12
557 Renz Ave 47172 812-246-3391
Michael Crabtree, prin. Fax 246-8184

Silver Creek MS 600/6-8
495 N Indiana Ave 47172 812-246-4421
Al Eckert, prin. Fax 246-7430

West Clark Education Center Alt
206 N New Albany St 47172 812-248-7130
Tate Enlow, dir.

Other Schools – See Borden, Henryville

---

Ivy Tech Community College - Southern Post-Sec.
8204 Highway 311 47172 812-246-3301

**Selma, Delaware, Pop. 856**

Liberty-Perry Community SC 1,100/K-12
PO Box 337 47383 765-282-5615
Bryan Rausch, supt. Fax 281-3733
www.libertyperry.org

Selma MS 300/6-8
10501 E County Road 167 S 47383 765-288-7242
Dennis Thompson, prin. Fax 281-3727

Wapahani HS 400/9-12
10401 E County Road 167 S 47383 765-289-7323
Dr. Mark Fahey, prin. Fax 281-3724

**Seymour, Jackson, Pop. 17,275**

Seymour Community SD 4,300/PK-12
1638 S Walnut St 47274 812-522-3340
Robert Hooker, supt. Fax 522-8031
www.scsc.k12.in.us

Seymour HS 1,200/9-12
1350 W 2nd St 47274 812-522-4384
Greg Prange, prin. Fax 523-2347

Seymour MS 900/6-8
920 N Obrien St 47274 812-522-5453
Doug McClure, prin. Fax 523-8134

---

Trinity Lutheran HS 100/9-12
7120 N County Road 875 E 47274 812-524-8547
Daniel Sievert, prin. Fax 524-8523

**Sharpsville, Tipton, Pop. 600**

Tri-Central Community School Corporation 900/PK-12
4774 N 200 W 46068 765-963-2585
Dr. Tim Garland Ph.D., supt. Fax 963-3042
www.tccs.k12.in.us/

Tri Central MSHS 500/6-12
2115 W 500 N 46068 765-963-2560
Dave Driggs, prin. Fax 963-6844

**Shelburn, Sullivan, Pop. 1,220**

Northeast SC
Supt. — See Hymera

Northeast MS 200/6-8
620 N Washington St 47879 812-397-5390
J.T. Roberts, prin. Fax 397-2886

**Shelbyville, Shelby, Pop. 18,951**

Shelby Eastern SD 1,300/PK-12
2451 N 600 E 46176 765-544-2246
Dr. Robert Evans, supt. Fax 544-2247
www.ses.k12.in.us

Other Schools – See Morristown, Waldron

Shelbyville Central SD 3,900/PK-12
803 Saint Joseph St 46176 317-392-2505
Dr. David Adams, supt. Fax 392-5737
www.shelbycs.k12.in.us

Shelbyville HS 1,100/9-12
2003 S Miller St 46176 317-398-9731
Kathleen Miltz, prin. Fax 392-5709

Shelbyville MS 900/6-8
1200 W McKay Rd 46176 317-392-2551
Ryan Mikus, prin. Fax 392-5713

Southwestern Cons SD of Shelby County 700/K-12
3406 W 600 S 46176 317-729-5746
Dr. Paula Maurer, supt. Fax 729-5330
www.swshelby.k12.in.us

Southwestern JSHS 300/7-12
3406 W 600 S 46176 317-729-5122
Curtis Chase, prin. Fax 729-2424

**Sheridan, Hamilton, Pop. 2,630**

Sheridan Community SD 1,100/PK-12
24795 Hinesley Rd 46069 317-758-4172
Dr. David Mundy, supt. Fax 758-6248
www.scs.k12.in.us/

Sheridan HS 400/9-12
24185 Hinesley Rd 46069 317-758-4431
Jane Newblom, prin. Fax 758-2406

Sheridan MS 300/6-8
3030 W 246th St 46069 317-758-6780
Jane Newblom, prin. Fax 758-2435

**Shoals, Martin, Pop. 746**

Shoals Community SC 600/PK-12
11741 Ironton Rd 47581 812-247-2060
Candace Roush, supt. Fax 247-2278
shoals.k12.in.us/

Shoals Community JSHS 300/7-12
7900 US Highway 50 47581 812-247-2090
Lucas Calhoun, prin. Fax 247-2056

**South Bend, Saint Joseph, Pop. 97,691**

South Bend Community SC 19,300/PK-12
215 S Saint Joseph St 46601 574-283-8000
Dr. Carole Schmidt, supt. Fax 283-8143
www.sbcsc.k12.in.us

Adams HS 1,600/9-12
808 S Twyckenham Dr 46615 574-283-7700
James Seitz, prin. Fax 283-7704

Brown Intermediate Center 500/4-8
737 Beale St 46616 574-287-9680
Joseph Somers, prin. Fax 283-5581

Clay HS 1,400/9-12
19131 Darden Rd 46637 574-243-7000
Mansour Eid, prin. Fax 243-7005

Clay Intermediate Center 600/5-8
52900 Lily Rd 46637 574-243-7145
Frances Beard, prin. Fax 243-7151

CTE Vo/Tech
3206 Sugar Maple Ct 46628 574-283-7505
Laura Marzotto, dir. Fax 283-7549

Dickinson Intermediate Fine Arts Academy 600/5-8
4404 Elwood Ave 46628 574-283-7625
Thomas Sims, prin. Fax 283-7633

Edison Intermediate Center 600/5-8
2701 Eisenhower Ave 46615 574-283-8900
Elizabeth Lake, prin. Fax 283-8903

Greene Intermediate Center 400/5-8
24702 Roosevelt Rd 46614 574-283-7900
Amanda Davis, prin. Fax 283-7903

Jackson Intermediate Center 600/5-8
5001 Miami St 46614 574-231-5600
Gretchen McEndarfer, prin. Fax 231-5605

Jefferson Traditional S 500/5-8
528 S Eddy St 46617 574-283-8700
Carmen Williams, prin. Fax 283-8703

LaSalle Intermediate Academy 800/5-8
2701 Elwood Ave 46628 574-283-7500
George Azar, prin. Fax 283-7513

Marshall Intermediate Center 500/5-8
1433 Byron Dr 46614 574-231-5801
Tiana Batiste-Waddell, prin. Fax 231-5804

Navarre Intermediate Center 600/5-8
4702 Ford St 46619 574-283-7345
Matthew Emery, prin. Fax 283-7351

Riley HS 1,400/9-12
1902 Fellows St 46613 574-283-8400
Francois Bayingana, prin. Fax 283-8405

Rise Up Academy 200/Alt
19010 Adams Rd 46637 574-243-7300
Terry Moore, prin. Fax 243-7303

Washington HS 1,200/9-12
4747 W Washington St 46619 574-283-7200
Byron Sanders, prin. Fax 283-7205

---

Brown Mackie College Post-Sec.
3454 Douglas Rd 46635 574-237-0774

Community Baptist Christian S 200/PK-12
5715 Miami St 46614 574-291-3620
Matt Fenton, admin. Fax 291-3648

Indiana University South Bend Post-Sec.
PO Box 7111 46634 574-520-4872

ITT Technical Institute Post-Sec.
17390 Dugdale Dr 46635 574-247-8300

Ivy Tech Community College North Central Post-Sec.
220 Dean Johnson Blvd 46601 574-289-7001

National College Post-Sec.
1030 E Jefferson Blvd 46617 574-307-7100

Purdue University-College of Technology Post-Sec.
PO Box 7111 46634 574-520-4180

Radiological Technologies University-VT Post-Sec.
100 E Wayne St Ste 140 46601 574-232-2408

St. Joseph HS 800/9-12
435 N Notre Dame Ave 46617 574-233-6137
Susan Richter, prin. Fax 232-3482

Trinity S at Greenlawn 200/7-12
107 S Greenlawn Ave 46617 574-287-5590

**South Whitley, Whitley, Pop. 1,743**

Whitko Community SC
Supt. — See Larwill

Whitko HS 600/9-12
1 Big Blue Ave 46787 260-723-5146
David Parker, prin. Fax 723-4724

**Speedway, Marion, Pop. 11,556**

Town of Speedway SD 1,600/PK-12
5335 W 25th St 46224 317-244-0236
Kenneth Hull, supt. Fax 486-4843
www.speedwayschools.org

Speedway HS 500/9-12
5357 W 25th St 46224 317-244-7238
Kyle Trebley, prin. Fax 486-4838

Speedway JHS 200/7-8
5151 W 14th St 46224 317-244-3359
John Dizney, prin. Fax 486-4845

**Spencer, Owen, Pop. 2,205**
Spencer-Owen Community SD 2,800/PK-12
205 E Hillside Ave 47460 812-829-2233
Dr. Chad Briggs, supt. Fax 829-6614
www.socs.k12.in.us
Owen Valley HS 800/9-12
622 W State Highway 46 47460 812-829-2266
Rhonda Schafer, prin. Fax 829-6605
Owen Valley MS 500/7-8
626 W State Highway 46 47460 812-829-2249
Aaron LaGrange, prin. Fax 829-6635

**Straughn, Henry, Pop. 222**
South Henry SC 800/K-12
6972 S State Road 103 47387 765-987-7882
Wesley Hammond, supt. Fax 987-7589
www.shenry.k12.in.us/
Tri JSHS 400/7-12
6972 S State Road 103 47387 765-987-7988
Tony Benson, prin. Fax 987-8446

**Sullivan, Sullivan, Pop. 4,203**
Southwest SC 1,700/PK-12
110 N Main St 47882 812-268-6311
Chris Stitzle, supt. Fax 268-6312
www.swest.k12.in.us/
Sullivan HS 500/9-12
902 N Section St 47882 812-268-6301
Dr. Tara Jenkins, prin. Fax 268-6303
Sullivan MS 300/6-8
415 W Frakes St 47882 812-268-4000
Dustin Hitt, prin. Fax 268-5368

**Switz City, Greene, Pop. 291**
White River Valley SD 800/K-12
PO Box 1470 47465 812-659-1424
Robert Hacker, supt. Fax 659-2278
www.wrv.k12.in.us
White River Valley JSHS 400/7-12
PO Box 1470 47465 812-659-2274
Kevin Smith, prin. Fax 659-2283

**Syracuse, Kosciusko, Pop. 2,781**
Wawasee Community SC 3,200/PK-12
1 Warrior Path Bldg 2 46567 574-457-3188
Dr. Thomas Edington, supt. Fax 457-4962
www.wawasee.k12.in.us/
Wawasee HS 900/9-12
1 Warrior Path Bldg 1 46567 574-457-3147
Michael Schmidt, prin. Fax 457-4364
Wawasee MS 500/6-8
9850 N State Road 13 46567 574-457-8839
Susan Mishler, prin. Fax 457-3575

**Tell City, Perry, Pop. 7,212**
Tell City-Troy Township SC 1,500/PK-12
837 17th St 47586 812-547-3300
John Scioldo, supt. Fax 547-9704
www.tellcity.k12.in.us
Tell City JSHS 700/7-12
900 12th St 47586 812-547-3131
Brad Ramsey, prin. Fax 547-9705

**Terre Haute, Vigo, Pop. 59,043**
Vigo County SC 15,400/PK-12
PO Box 3703 47803 812-462-4011
Daniel Tanoos, supt. Fax 462-4115
www.vigoschools.org/
Honey Creek MS 800/6-8
6601 S Carlisle St 47802 812-462-4372
Nolan Cox, prin. Fax 462-4367
McLean Alternative HS 200/Alt
961 Lafayette Ave 47804 812-462-4330
Jeanne Conley, prin. Fax 462-4017
Otter Creek MS 800/6-8
4801 N Lafayette St 47805 812-462-4391
Sarah Gore, prin. Fax 462-4388
Scott MS 400/6-8
1000 Grant St 47802 812-462-4381
Scotia Brown, prin. Fax 462-4370
Terre Haute North Vigo HS 2,000/9-12
3434 Maple Ave 47804 812-462-4312
Robin Smith, prin. Fax 462-4204
Terre Haute South Vigo HS 1,800/9-12
3737 S 7th St 47802 812-462-4252
Dr. Tammy Rowshandel, prin. Fax 462-4408
Washington Alternative HS 50/Alt
3707 S 7th St 47802 812-462-4427
Dr. Karen Andrews, prin. Fax 462-4066
Wilson MS 800/6-8
301 S 25th St 47803 812-462-4396
Susan Mardis, prin. Fax 232-2217
Other Schools – See West Terre Haute

---

Harrison College Post-Sec.
1378 S State Road 46 47803 812-877-2100
Indiana State University Post-Sec.
200 N 7th St 47809 812-237-6311
Ivy Tech Community College Wabash Valley Post-Sec.
8000 S Education Dr 47802 812-299-1121
Rose-Hulman Institute of Technology Post-Sec.
5500 Wabash Ave 47803 812-877-1511
Terre Haute Adventist S 50/K-10
900 S 29th St 47803 812-232-1339
Karen Shinn, prin.

**Thorntown, Boone, Pop. 1,514**
Western Boone County Community SD 1,800/PK-12
1201 N State Road 75 46071 765-482-6333
Dr. Judi Hendrix, supt. Fax 482-0890
www.weboschools.org/
Western Boone JSHS 900/7-12
1205 N State Road 75 46071 765-482-6143
Rob Ramey, prin. Fax 482-6146

**Tipton, Tipton, Pop. 5,058**
Tipton Community SC 1,700/K-12
1051 S Main St 46072 765-675-2147
Kevin Emsweller, supt. Fax 675-3857
www.tcsc.k12.in.us
Tipton HS 500/9-12
619 S Main St 46072 765-675-7431
Joe Rushton, prin. Fax 675-9519
Tipton MS 400/6-8
817 S Main St 46072 765-675-7521
Shayne Clark, prin. Fax 675-9027

**Topeka, Lagrange, Pop. 1,128**
Westview SC 2,400/K-12
1545 S 600 W 46571 260-768-4404
Dr. Randall Zimmerly, supt. Fax 768-7368
www.westview.k12.in.us
Westview JSHS 800/7-12
1635 S 600 W 46571 260-768-4146
Rich Cory, prin. Fax 768-7611

**Trafalgar, Johnson, Pop. 1,089**
Nineveh-Hensley-Jackson United SC 1,900/K-12
802 S Indian Creek Dr 46181 317-878-2100
Dr. Tim Edsell, supt. Fax 878-5765
www.nhj.k12.in.us
Indian Creek HS 600/9-12
803 W Indian Creek Dr 46181 317-878-2110
Fax 878-2112
Indian Creek MS 500/6-8
801 W Indian Creek Dr 46181 317-878-2130
Sean Zachery, prin. Fax 878-2149

**Union City, Randolph, Pop. 3,547**
Randolph Eastern SC 700/K-12
731 N Plum St 47390 765-964-4994
Lisa Smith, supt. Fax 964-6590
www.resc.k12.in.us/
Union City Community JSHS 300/7-12
603 N Walnut St 47390 765-964-4840
Aaron Black, prin. Fax 964-3775

**Union Mills, LaPorte**
South Central Community SC 900/K-12
9808 S 600 W 46382 219-767-2263
Linda Wiltfong, supt. Fax 767-2260
www.scentral.k12.in.us/
South Central JSHS 500/7-12
9808 S 600 W 46382 219-767-2266
Sandra Wood, prin. Fax 767-2260

**Upland, Grant, Pop. 3,790**

---

Taylor University Post-Sec.
236 W Reade Ave 46989 800-882-3456

**Valparaiso, Porter, Pop. 31,160**
East Porter County SC
Supt. — See Kouts
Morgan Township MSHS 400/6-12
299 S State Road 49 46383 219-462-5883
Chris George, prin. Fax 462-4014
Washington Township MSHS 400/6-12
381 E State Road 2 46383 219-464-3598
Jerry Hale, prin. Fax 462-3372

Porter Township SC 1,200/K-12
248 S 500 W 46385 219-477-4933
Dr. Stacey Schmidt, supt. Fax 477-4834
www.ptsc.k12.in.us
Boone Grove HS 500/9-12
260 S 500 W 46385 219-306-8600
Clay Corman, prin. Fax 306-8659
Other Schools – See Boone Grove

Union Township SC 1,600/K-12
599 W 300 N Ste A 46385 219-759-2531
John Hunter, supt. Fax 759-3250
www.union.k12.in.us
Union Township MS 400/6-8
599 W 300 N 46385 219-759-2562
Jerry Lasky, prin. Fax 759-4359
Wheeler HS 600/9-12
587 W 300 N 46385 219-759-2561
Donald Gandy, prin. Fax 759-5602

Valparaiso Community SC 6,400/K-12
3801 Campbell St 46385 219-531-3000
Dr. E. Ric Frataccia Ed.D., supt. Fax 531-3009
www.valpo.k12.in.us
Franklin MS 800/6-8
605 Campbell St 46385 219-531-3020
Christopher Fields, prin. Fax 531-3026
Jefferson MS 700/6-8
1600 Roosevelt Rd 46383 219-531-3140
Elizabeth Krutz, prin. Fax 531-3146
Porter County Career Ctr Vo/Tech
1005 Franklin St 46383 219-531-3170
Jon Groth, prin. Fax 531-3173
Valparaiso HS 2,200/9-12
2727 Campbell St 46385 219-531-3070
Dr. Reid Amones, prin. Fax 531-3076

---

Don Roberts Beauty School Post-Sec.
1354 Lincolnway 46385 219-462-5189
Porter Memorial Hospital Post-Sec.
814 Laporte Ave 46383 219-465-4883
South Haven Christian S 100/PK-12
786 Juniper Rd 46385 219-759-5313
Michael Owney, prin. Fax 759-1577
Valparaiso University 46383 Post-Sec.
219-464-5000
Victory Christian Academy 300/PK-12
3805 LaPorte Ave 46383 219-548-8803
Joyce Folk, admin. Fax 548-7413

**Veedersburg, Fountain, Pop. 2,156**
Southeast Fountain SC 1,200/K-12
744 E US Highway 136 47987 765-294-2254
Doug Allison, supt. Fax 294-3200
www.sefschools.org/
Fountain Central JSHS 600/7-12
750 E US Highway 136 47987 765-294-2206
Bill Chestnut, prin. Fax 294-3204

**Versailles, Ripley, Pop. 2,089**
South Ripley Community SC 1,200/K-12
PO Box 690 47042 812-689-6282
Robert D. Moorhead, supt. Fax 689-6760
www.sripley.k12.in.us
South Ripley HS 400/9-12
1589 S Benham Rd 47042 812-689-5303
Dr. David Wintin, prin. Fax 689-6715
South Ripley JHS 200/7-8
1589 S Benham Rd 47042 812-689-0909
Destiny Rutzel, prin. Fax 689-6970

Southeastern Career SC 812-689-5253
901 W US Highway 50 47042 Fax 689-6977
Bradley Street, supt.
www.sccusa.org
Southeastern Career Center Vo/Tech
901 W US Highway 50 47042 812-689-5253
Brad Street, prin. Fax 689-6977

**Vevay, Switzerland, Pop. 1,662**
Switzerland County SC 1,400/PK-12
1040 W Main St 47043 812-427-2611
Michael Jones, supt. Fax 427-2044
www.switzerland.k12.in.us
Switzerland County HS 400/9-12
1020 W Main St 47043 812-427-2626
Gregg Goewert, prin. Fax 427-3445
Switzerland County MS 200/7-8
1004 W Main St 47043 812-427-3809
Sean McGarvey, prin. Fax 427-3807

**Vincennes, Knox, Pop. 18,142**
South Knox SC 1,200/K-12
6116 E State Road 61 47591 812-726-4440
Tim Grove, supt. Fax 743-2110
www.sknox.k12.in.us
South Knox MSHS 500/7-12
6136 E State Road 61 47591 812-726-4450
Jeff Dhonau, prin. Fax 726-4545

Twin Rivers Career & Technical Education
PO Box 1266 47591 812-882-0801
Brandon R. Small, dir. Fax 882-0802
www.twinriversarea.org
Twin Rivers Career & Technical Education Vo/Tech
PO Box 1266 47591 812-882-0801
Brandon R. Small, dir. Fax 882-0802

Vincennes Community SC 2,700/K-12
1712 S Quail Run Rd 47591 812-882-4844
Gregory T. Parsley, supt. Fax 885-1427
www.vcsc.k12.in.us
Clark MS 600/6-8
1926 S Richard Bauer Dr 47591 812-882-5172
Ryan Clark, prin. Fax 885-1419
Lincoln HS 800/9-12
1545 S Hart Street Rd 47591 812-882-8480
Stephen Combs, prin. Fax 885-1431

---

Good Samaritan Hospital Post-Sec.
520 S 7th St 47591 812-885-3195
Rivet MSHS 200/6-12
210 Barnett St 47591 812-882-6215
Janice Jones, prin. Fax 886-1939
Vincennes Beauty College Post-Sec.
12 S 2nd St 47591 812-882-1086
Vincennes University Post-Sec.
1002 N 1st St 47591 812-888-8888

**Wabash, Wabash, Pop. 10,549**
Heartland Career Center SD
79 S 200 W 46992 260-563-7481
Mark Hobbs, supt. Fax 563-5544
www.hcc.k12.in.us
Heartland Career Ctr Vo/Tech
79 S 200 W 46992 260-563-7481
Jon Higgins, prin. Fax 563-5544

Metro SD of Wabash County 2,100/K-12
204 N 300 W 46992 260-563-8050
Dr. Sandra Weaver, supt. Fax 569-6836
www.msdwc.k12.in.us
Northfield JSHS 500/7-12
154 W 200 N 46992 260-563-8050
Paul Voigt, prin. Fax 569-6839
Southwood JSHS 600/7-12
564 E State Road 124 46992 260-563-8050
Tim Drake, prin. Fax 569-6843
Whites JSHS 100/Alt
5233 S 50 E 46992 260-563-1158
Troy Friedersdorf, prin. Fax 563-5272

Wabash CSD 1,500/PK-12
PO Box 744 46992 260-563-2151
Jason Callahan, supt. Fax 563-2066
www.apaches.k12.in.us
Wabash HS 500/9-12
580 N Miami St 46992 260-563-4131
Josh Blossom, prin. Fax 563-6806
Wabash MS 300/5-8
150 Colerain St 46992 260-563-4137
Scott Bumgardener, prin. Fax 569-9805

**Wakarusa, Elkhart, Pop. 1,739**
Wa-Nee Community SD
Supt. — See Nappanee
Northwood MS 700/6-8
PO Box 367 46573 574-862-2710
Bart Rice, prin. Fax 862-2327

**Waldron, Shelby, Pop. 796**
Shelby Eastern SD
Supt. — See Shelbyville
Waldron JSHS 400/6-12
PO Box 369 46182 765-525-6822
Gary Brown, prin. Fax 525-9727

**Walkerton, Saint Joseph, Pop. 2,125**
John Glenn SC 1,900/PK-12
101 John Glenn Dr 46574 574-586-3129
Richard Reese, supt. Fax 586-2660
www.jgsc.k12.in.us
Glenn HS 600/9-12
201 John Glenn Dr 46574 574-586-3195
William Morton, prin. Fax 586-3905
Urey MS 300/7-8
407 Washington St 46574 574-586-3184
Mark Maudlin, prin. Fax 586-3714

**Walton, Cass, Pop. 1,033**
Southeastern SC 1,500/K-12
100 S Main St 46994 574-626-2525
Trudie Hedrick, supt. Fax 626-2751
www.sesc.k12.in.us
Cass JSHS 700/7-12
6422 E State Road 218 46994 574-626-2511
Shay Bonnell, prin. Fax 626-2172

**Wanatah, LaPorte, Pop. 1,033**
Tri Township School Corp 300/K-12
PO Box 249 46390 219-754-2461
Tim Somers, supt. Fax 754-2511
www.tritownship.k12.in.us
Other Schools – See La Crosse

**Warsaw, Kosciusko, Pop. 13,362**
Warsaw Community SC 6,900/PK-12
1 Administration Dr 46580 574-371-5098
David Hoffert Ed.D., supt. Fax 371-5046
www.warsaw.k12.in.us
Edgewood MS 500/7-8
900 S Union St 46580 574-371-5096
JoElla Smyth, prin. Fax 371-5010
Gateway Educational Center Alt
201 N Union St 46580 574-371-5019
Steve Ferber, prin. Fax 371-5033
Lakeview MS 500/7-8
848 E Smith St 46580 574-269-7211
Jon Lippe, prin. Fax 371-5013
Warsaw Community HS 2,100/9-12
1 Tiger Ln 46580 574-371-5099
Troy Akers, prin. Fax 371-5012

**Washington, Daviess, Pop. 11,354**
Washington Community SD 2,500/K-12
301 E South St 47501 812-254-5536
Dr. Dan Roach, supt. Fax 254-8346
www.wcs.k12.in.us
Washington HS 800/9-12
608 E Walnut St 47501 812-254-3860
LeAnne Kelley, prin. Fax 254-8374
Washington JHS 400/7-8
210 NE 6th St 47501 812-254-2682
Mark Arnold, prin. Fax 254-8381

---

Washington Catholic MSHS 100/5-12
201 NE 2nd St 47501 812-254-2050
Karie Craney, prin. Fax 254-8746

**Waterloo, DeKalb, Pop. 2,205**
DeKalb County Central United SC 3,900/PK-12
3326 County Road 427 46793 260-920-1011
Dr. Sherry Grate Ed.D., supt. Fax 837-7767
www.dekalbcentral.net
DeKalb HS 1,300/9-12
3424 County Road 427 46793 260-920-1012
Matthew Toth, prin. Fax 837-7841
DeKalb MS 900/6-8
3338 County Road 427 46793 260-920-1013
Kimberly Fifer, prin. Fax 837-7812

**Westfield, Hamilton, Pop. 29,609**
Westfield Washington SD 6,400/PK-12
322 W Main St 46074 317-867-8000
Dr. Mark Keen, supt. Fax 867-0929
www.wws.k12.in.us
Westfield HS 1,800/9-12
18250 N Union St 46074 317-867-6800
Dr. Stacy McGuire, prin. Fax 867-2909
Westfield MS 900/7-8
345 W Hoover St 46074 317-867-6600
Ryan Haughey, prin. Fax 867-1407

**West Lafayette, Tippecanoe, Pop. 29,004**
Tippecanoe SC
Supt. — See Lafayette
Battle Ground MS 500/6-8
6100 N 50 W 47906 765-269-8140
Dr. BeAnn Younker, prin. Fax 269-8215
Harrison HS 1,700/9-12
5701 N 50 W 47906 765-463-3511
Allen Remaly, prin. Fax 463-1477
Klondike MS 400/6-8
3307 Klondike Rd 47906 765-463-2544
Christine Cannon, prin. Fax 497-9413

West Lafayette Community SC 2,100/K-12
1130 N Salisbury St 47906 765-746-1602
Dr. Rocky Killion, supt. Fax 746-1644
www.wl.k12.in.us/
West Lafayette JSHS 700/7-12
1105 N Grant St 47906 765-746-0400
Ronald Shriner, prin. Fax 746-0420

---

Purdue University Post-Sec.
610 Purdue Mall 47907 765-494-4600

**West Lebanon, Warren, Pop. 721**
Metro SD of Warren County
Supt. — See Williamsport
Seeger Memorial JSHS 600/7-12
1222 S State Road 263 47991 765-893-4445
Dan Nelson, prin. Fax 893-8354

**West Terre Haute, Vigo, Pop. 2,213**
Vigo County SC
Supt. — See Terre Haute
West Vigo HS 600/9-12
4590 W Sarah Myers Dr 47885 812-462-4282
Tom Balitewicz, prin. Fax 462-4090
West Vigo MS 400/6-8
4750 W Sarah Myers Dr 47885 812-462-4361
Julie Lautenschlager, prin. Fax 462-4358

**Westville, LaPorte, Pop. 5,829**
Metro SD of New Durham Township 900/K-12
207 E Valparaiso St 46391 219-785-2239
Dr. Curtiss Strietelmeier, supt. Fax 785-4584
www.westville.k12.in.us/
Westville JSHS 400/7-12
207 E Valparaiso St 46391 219-785-2531
Alissa Schnick, prin. Fax 785-2990

---

Purdue University North Central Post-Sec.
1401 S US Highway 421 46391 219-785-5200

**Wheatfield, Jasper, Pop. 846**
Kankakee Valley SC 3,500/K-12
PO Box 278 46392 219-987-4711
Aaron Case, supt. Fax 987-4710
www.kv.k12.in.us
Kankakee Valley HS 1,100/9-12
3923 W State Road 10 46392 219-956-3143
Michael Spagna, prin. Fax 956-4639
Kankakee Valley MS 900/6-8
5258 W State Road 10 46392 219-987-8810
Michael Cornwell, prin. Fax 987-2540

**Whiteland, Johnson, Pop. 4,117**
Clark-Pleasant Community SC 5,900/K-12
50 Center St 46184 317-535-7579
Dr. Patrick Spray, supt. Fax 535-4931
www.cpcsc.k12.in.us
Clark Pleasant Academy Alt
129 N US Highway 31 46184 317-535-3240
Lisa Morris, dir. Fax 535-0189
Whiteland Community HS 1,700/9-12
300 Main St 46184 317-535-7562
Tom Zobel, prin. Fax 535-7509
Other Schools – See Greenwood

**Whitestown, Boone, Pop. 2,806**
Zionsville Community SC
Supt. — See Zionsville
Zionsville West MS 900/5-8
5565 S 700 E 46075 317-873-1240
Kris Devereaux, prin. Fax 769-6909

---

Traders Point Christian Academy 600/PK-12
6600 S Indianapolis Rd 46075 317-769-2450
Ron Evans, head sch Fax 769-2456

**Whiting, Lake, Pop. 4,948**
Hammond CSD
Supt. — See Hammond
Clark MSHS 1,500/6-12
1921 Davis Ave 46394 219-659-3522
Robert Wilson, prin. Fax 554-4571
Whiting CSD 1,100/PK-12
1500 Center St 46394 219-659-0656
Dr. Sandra Martinez Ph.D., supt. Fax 473-4008
www.whiting.k12.in.us
Whiting HS 400/9-12
1751 Oliver St 46394 219-659-0255
Julie Fregien, prin. Fax 473-1341
Whiting MS 200/6-8
1800 New York Ave 46394 219-473-1344
Kevin Spitler, prin. Fax 473-4017

---

Calumet College of St. Joseph Post-Sec.
2400 New York Ave 46394 219-473-7770

**Williamsport, Warren, Pop. 1,888**
Metro SD of Warren County 1,200/K-12
101 N Monroe St 47993 765-762-3364
Ralph Shrader, supt. Fax 762-6623
www.msdwarco.k12.in.us/
Other Schools – See West Lebanon

**Winamac, Pulaski, Pop. 2,467**
Eastern Pulaski Community SC 1,300/K-12
711 School Dr 46996 574-946-4010
Dan L. Foster, supt. Fax 946-4510
www.epulaski.k12.in.us/
Winamac Community HS 400/9-12
715 School Dr 46996 574-946-6151
Rick Defries, prin. Fax 946-4219
Winamac Community MS 300/6-8
715 School Dr 46996 574-946-6525
Ryan Dickinson, prin. Fax 946-4219

**Winchester, Randolph, Pop. 4,890**
Randolph Central SC 1,600/K-12
103 N East St 47394 765-584-1401
Dr. Gregory Hinshaw, supt. Fax 584-1403
www.rc.k12.in.us
Driver MS 400/6-8
700 N Union St 47394 765-584-4671
Thomas Osborn, prin. Fax 584-8204
Winchester Community HS 500/9-12
700 N Union St 47394 765-584-8201
Tom Osborn, prin. Fax 584-8204

**Winona Lake, Kosciusko, Pop. 4,854**

---

Grace College & Seminary Post-Sec.
200 Seminary Dr 46590 574-372-5100
Lakeland Christian Academy 100/7-12
1093 S 250 E 46590 574-267-7265
Joy Lavender, admin. Fax 267-5687

**Wolcott, White, Pop. 982**
Tri-County SC 800/K-12
105 N 2nd St 47995 219-279-2418
Dr. Kathy Goad, supt. Fax 279-2242
www.trico.k12.in.us
Tri-County JSHS 300/7-12
11298 W 100 S 47995 219-279-2105
Shawn McCracken, prin. Fax 279-2108

**Woodburn, Allen, Pop. 1,511**
East Allen County SD
Supt. — See New Haven
Woodlan JSHS 800/7-12
17215 Woodburn Rd 46797 260-446-0290
Ron Kammeyer, prin. Fax 446-0298

**Yorktown, Delaware, Pop. 9,307**
Yorktown Community SC 2,300/K-12
2311 S Broadway St 47396 765-759-2720
Jennifer McCormick, supt. Fax 759-7894
www.yorktown.k12.in.us
Yorktown HS 800/9-12
1100 S Tiger Dr 47396 765-759-2550
Stacey Brewer, prin. Fax 759-4040
Yorktown MS 500/6-8
8820 W Smith St 47396 765-759-2660
Heath Dudley, prin. Fax 759-3243

**Zionsville, Boone, Pop. 13,972**
Zionsville Community SC 5,800/PK-12
900 Mulberry St 46077 317-873-2858
Scott Robison, supt. Fax 873-8003
www.zcs.k12.in.us
Zionsville Community HS 1,800/9-12
1000 Mulberry St 46077 317-873-3355
Tim East, prin. Fax 873-8002
Zionsville MS 1,000/5-8
900 N Ford Rd 46077 317-873-2426
Sean Conner, prin. Fax 733-4001
Other Schools – See Whitestown

# IOWA

## IOWA DEPARTMENT OF EDUCATION
**400 E 14th St, Des Moines 50319-0146**
**Telephone 515-281-5294**
**Fax 515-242-5988**
**Website educateiowa.gov/**

Director of Education Dr. Brad Buck

## IOWA BOARD OF EDUCATION
**400 E 14th St, Des Moines 50319-9000**

President Rosie Hussey

## AREA EDUCATION AGENCIES (AEA)

AEA 267
Dr. Dean Meier, admin. 319-273-8200
3712 Cedar Heights Dr Fax 273-8229
Cedar Falls 50613
www.aea267.k12.ia.us
Grant Wood AEA 10
Joe Crozier, admin., 4401 6th St SW 319-399-6700
Cedar Rapids 52404 Fax 399-6457
www.aea10.k12.ia.us/
Great Prairie AEA
Dr. Jon Sheldahl, admin. 641-682-8591
2814 N Court St, Ottumwa 52501 Fax 682-9083
www.gpaea.k12.ia.us
Green Hills AEA
Dr. Lane Plugge, admin. 800-432-5804
PO Box 1109, Council Bluffs 51502 Fax 366-7772
www.ghaea.org
Heartland AEA 11
Dr. Paula Vincent, admin. 515-270-9030
6500 Corporate Dr Fax 270-5383
Johnston 50131
www.heartlandaea.org
Keystone AEA 1
Patrick Heiderscheit, admin. 563-245-1480
1400 2nd St NW, Elkader 52043 Fax 245-1484
www.aea1.k12.ia.us
Mississippi Bend AEA 9
William Decker, admin. 563-359-1371
729 21st St, Bettendorf 52722 Fax 359-5967
www.aea9.k12.ia.us
Northwest AEA
Dr. Tim Grieves, admin. 712-222-6000
1520 Morningside Ave Fax 222-6123
Sioux City 51106
www.nwaea.k12.ia.us/
Prairie Lakes AEA 8
Jeff Herzberg, admin. 712-335-3588
PO Box 802, Pocahontas 50574 Fax 335-4600
www.aea8.k12.ia.us/

## PUBLIC, PRIVATE AND CATHOLIC SECONDARY SCHOOLS

**Ackley, Hardin, Pop. 1,584**
AGWSR Community SD 600/PK-12
918 4th Ave 50601 641-847-2611
Marty Jimmerson, supt. Fax 847-2612
www.agwsr.org
AGWSR HS 200/9-12
918 4th Ave 50601 641-847-2633
Sheryl Arends, prin. Fax 847-3345

**Adair, Guthrie, Pop. 778**
Adair-Casey Community SD 300/PK-12
3384 Indigo Ave 50002 641-746-2241
Steve Smith, supt. Fax 746-2243
accs.k12.ia.us
Adair-Casey JSHS 100/7-12
3384 Indigo Ave 50002 641-746-2241
Cynthia Jensen, prin. Fax 746-2243

**Adel, Dallas, Pop. 3,654**
Adel DeSoto Minburn Community SD 1,300/PK-12
801 Nile Kinnick Dr S 50003 515-993-4283
Greg Dufoe, supt. Fax 993-4866
www.adm.k12.ia.us
ADM HS 500/9-12
801 Nile Kinnick Dr S 50003 515-993-4584
Lee Greibel, prin. Fax 993-3025
ADM MS 300/6-8
801 Nile Kinnick Dr S 50003 515-993-3490
Kim Timmerman, prin. Fax 993-1956

**Afton, Union, Pop. 842**
East Union Community SD 400/PK-12
1916 High School Dr 50830 641-347-5215
Lance Ridgely, supt. Fax 347-5514
www.east-union.k12.ia.us
East Union MSHS 200/6-12
1916 High School Dr 50830 641-347-8421
Mark Weis, prin. Fax 347-5514

**Akron, Plymouth, Pop. 1,468**
Akron Westfield Community SD 600/PK-12
PO Box 950 51001 712-568-2616
Randy Collins, supt. Fax 568-2997
akron-westfield.com
Akron Westfield HS 200/9-12
PO Box 950 51001 712-568-2020
Derek Briggs, prin. Fax 568-2997
Akron Westfield MS 100/6-8
PO Box 950 51001 712-568-2020
Derek Briggs, prin. Fax 568-2997

**Albia, Monroe, Pop. 3,726**
Albia Community SD 1,200/PK-12
701 Washington Ave E 52531 641-932-2161
Kevin Crall, supt. Fax 932-5192
www.albia.k12.ia.us
Albia HS 400/9-12
503 B Ave E 52531 641-932-2161
Richard Montgomery, prin. Fax 932-7069
Albia JHS 200/7-8
505 C Ave E 52531 641-932-2161
Richard Montgomery, prin. Fax 932-7069

**Alburnett, Linn, Pop. 663**
Alburnett Community SD 600/PK-12
PO Box 400 52202 319-842-2266
Dani Trimble, supt. Fax 842-2398
www.alburnettcsd.org
Alburnett JSHS 300/6-12
PO Box 400 52202 319-842-2263
Joshua Henriksen, prin. Fax 842-2398

**Algona, Kossuth, Pop. 5,513**
Algona Community SD 1,500/PK-12
600 S Hale St 50511 515-295-3528
Marty Fonley, supt. Fax 295-5166
www.algona.k12.ia.us
Algona HS 500/9-12
601 S Hale St 50511 515-295-7207
Jared Cecil, prin. Fax 295-9273
Algona MS 400/5-8
601 S Hale St 50511 515-295-7207
James Rotert, prin. Fax 295-9273

Bishop Garrigan HS 200/4-12
1224 N McCoy St 50511 515-295-3521
Christina Peterson, prin. Fax 295-7739

**Alleman, Polk, Pop. 426**
North Polk Community SD 1,200/PK-12
13960 NE 6th Ave 50007 515-984-3400
Dr. Dan Mart, supt. Fax 685-2002
www.northpolk.org
North Polk HS 400/9-12
13960 NE 6th Ave 50007 515-984-3400
Derrick Joel, prin. Fax 685-2004
North Polk MS 200/6-8
315 NE 141st Ave 50007 515-984-3400
Jon Richards, prin. Fax 685-3520

**Allison, Butler, Pop. 1,024**
North Butler Community SD 700/PK-12
PO Box 428 50602 319-267-2205
Joel Foster, supt. Fax 267-2926
www.northbutler.k12.ia.us/
Other Schools – See Greene

**Alta, Buena Vista, Pop. 1,871**
Alta Community SD 500/PK-12
101 W 5th St 51002 712-200-1010
Lynn Evans, supt. Fax 200-1602
www.alta.k12.ia.us
Alta-Aurelia HS 200/9-12
1009 S Main St 51002 712-200-1331
Tom Ryherd, prin. Fax 200-1602

**Alton, Sioux, Pop. 1,209**
MOC-Floyd Valley Community SD
Supt. — See Orange City
MOC-Floyd Valley MS 300/6-8
1104 5th Ave 51003 712-756-4128
Cam Smith, prin. Fax 756-4100

**Ames, Story, Pop. 57,846**
Ames Community SD 4,400/PK-12
415 Stanton Ave 50014 515-268-6600
Dr. Tim Taylor, supt. Fax 268-6633
www.ames.k12.ia.us
Ames HS 1,400/9-12
1921 Ames High Dr 50010 515-817-0600
Spence Evans, prin. Fax 817-0627
Ames MS 900/6-8
3915 Mortensen Rd 50014 515-268-2400
Pam Stangeland, prin. Fax 268-2419

Antioch School of Church Planting Post-Sec.
2400 Oakwood Rd 50014 515-292-9694
Iowa State University 50011 Post-Sec.
515-294-4111
Professional Cosmetology Institute Post-Sec.
309 Kitty Hawk Dr 50010 515-232-7250

**Anamosa, Jones, Pop. 5,484**
Anamosa Community SD 1,200/PK-12
200 S Garnavillo St 52205 319-462-4321
Lisa Beames, supt. Fax 462-4322
www.anamosa.k12.ia.us
Anamosa HS 400/9-12
209 Sadie St 52205 319-462-3594
Jacqueline Lahey, prin. Fax 462-2332
Anamosa MS 300/5-8
200 S Garnavillo St 52205 319-462-3553
Linda Vaughn, prin. Fax 462-3309

**Andrew, Jackson, Pop. 431**
Andrew Community SD 200/PK-8
PO Box 230 52030 563-672-3221
Andy Crozier, supt. Fax 672-9750
www.andrew.k12.ia.us
Andrew MS 50/6-8
PO Box 230 52030 563-672-3221
Tara Notz, prin. Fax 672-9750

**Anita, Cass, Pop. 970**
CAM Community SD 400/PK-12
1000 Victory Park Rd 50020 712-762-3231
Dr. Casey Berlau, supt. Fax 762-3713
www.camcougars.org
CAM HS 100/9-12
1000 Victory Park Rd 50020 712-762-3231
Dominic Giegerich, prin. Fax 762-3713
Other Schools – See Massena

**Ankeny, Polk, Pop. 45,034**
Ankeny Community SD 10,400/PK-12
PO Box 189 50021 515-965-9600
Dr. Bruce Kimpston, supt. Fax 965-4234
www.ankenyschools.org/
Ankeny Centennial HS 1,000/10-12
2220 NW State St, 515-965-9610
Dr. Jen Lindaman, prin. Fax 964-5070
Ankeny HS 1,700/10-12
1155 SW Cherry St, 515-965-9630
Dr. Jeff Hawkins, prin. Fax 965-2975
Northview MS 1,300/8-9
1302 N Ankeny Blvd, 515-965-9700
Bev Kuehn, prin. Fax 965-9639
Southview MS 600/8-9
1020 SW Cherry St, 515-965-9635
Dan Meyer, admin. Fax 965-9223

---

Ankeny Christian Academy 300/PK-12
1604 W 1st St, 515-965-8114
Joyce Hansen, admin. Fax 965-8210
Des Moines Area Community College Post-Sec.
2006 S Ankeny Blvd, 515-964-6200
Faith Baptist Bible College Post-Sec.
1900 NW 4th St, 515-964-0601
INSTE Bible College Post-Sec.
2302 SW 3rd St, 515-289-9200

**Anthon, Woodbury, Pop. 561**
Maple Valley-Anthon Oto Community SD
Supt. — See Mapleton
Maple Valley-Anthon Oto MS 100/6-8
110 W Division St 51004 712-373-5244
Jane Ellis, prin. Fax 373-5326

**Aplington, Butler, Pop. 1,123**
Aplington-Parkersburg Community SD
Supt. — See Parkersburg
Aplington-Parkersburg MS 200/6-8
215 10th St 50604 319-347-6621
Brian Buseman, prin. Fax 347-2395

**Arlington, Fayette, Pop. 428**
Starmont Community SD 600/PK-12
3202 40th St 50606 563-933-4598
Allan Nelson, supt. Fax 933-2134
www.starmont.k12.ia.us
Starmont HS 200/9-12
3202 40th St 50606 563-933-2218
Marc Snavely, prin. Fax 933-2134
Starmont MS 100/6-8
3202 40th St 50606 563-933-2218
Marc Snavely, prin. Fax 933-2134

**Armstrong, Emmet, Pop. 919**
North Union SD
Supt. — See Fenton
North Union HS 100/9-12
PO Box 75 50514 712-868-3542
Robert Zotz, prin. Fax 868-3550

**Arnolds Park, Dickinson, Pop. 1,120**
Okoboji Community SD
Supt. — See Milford
Okoboji MS 300/5-8
10 W Broadway St 51331 712-332-5641
Ryan Cunningham, prin. Fax 332-7180

**Atlantic, Cass, Pop. 7,038**
Atlantic Community SD 1,500/PK-12
1100 Linn St 50022 712-243-4252
Mike Amstein Ed.D., supt. Fax 243-8023
www.atlanticiaschools.org/
Atlantic HS 500/9-12
1201 E 14th St 50022 712-243-5358
Heather McKay, prin. Fax 243-8007
Atlantic MS 300/6-8
1100 Linn St 50022 712-243-1330
Josh Rasmussen, prin. Fax 243-7732
Cass County Educational Opportunity Ctr 50/Alt
1209 Sunnyside Ln 50022 712-243-3535
Fax 243-8069

**Audubon, Audubon, Pop. 2,169**
Audubon Community SD 600/PK-12
800 3rd Ave 50025 712-563-2607
Brett Gibbs, supt. Fax 563-3607
www.audubon.k12.ia.us/
Audubon MSHS 400/5-12
800 3rd Ave 50025 712-563-2607
Eric Trager, prin. Fax 563-3607

**Aurelia, Cherokee, Pop. 1,026**
Aurelia Community SD 300/PK-8
PO Box 367 51005 712-434-2284
Lynn Evans, supt. Fax 434-2053
www.aurelia.k12.ia.us
Aurelia MS 200/6-8
PO Box 367 51005 712-434-5595
Ann Sandine, prin. Fax 434-2053

**Avoca, Pottawattamie, Pop. 1,501**
A-H-S-T Community SD 600/PK-12
PO Box 158 51521 712-343-6364
Jesse Ulrich, supt. Fax 343-2170
www.ahst.k12.ia.us
A-H-S-T HS 300/7-12
PO Box 158 51521 712-343-6364
Cynthia Phillips, prin. Fax 343-6915

**Baxter, Jasper, Pop. 1,091**
Baxter Community SD 400/K-12
PO Box 189 50028 641-227-3102
Todd Martin, supt. Fax 227-3217
www.baxter.k12.ia.us
Baxter JSHS 200/6-12
PO Box 189 50028 641-227-3103
Robert Luther, prin. Fax 227-3217

**Bedford, Taylor, Pop. 1,430**
Bedford Community SD 500/PK-12
PO Box 234 50833 712-523-2656
Joe Drake, supt. Fax 523-3166
www.bedford.k12.ia.us
Bedford MSHS 300/6-12
PO Box 234 50833 712-523-2656
Michael Irvin, prin. Fax 523-2308

**Belle Plaine, Benton, Pop. 2,512**
Belle Plaine Community SD 600/PK-12
707 7th St 52208 319-444-3611
Chad Straight, supt. Fax 444-3617
www.belle-plaine.k12.ia.us
Belle Plaine JSHS 200/7-12
610 13th Ave 52208 319-444-3720
Todd Werner, prin. Fax 444-4507

**Bellevue, Jackson, Pop. 2,180**
Bellevue Community SD 700/PK-12
1601 State St 52031 563-872-4913
Dr. Tom Meyer, supt. Fax 872-3216
www.bellevue.k12.ia.us
Bellevue MSHS 400/7-12
1601 State St 52031 563-872-4001
Jeff Recker, prin. Fax 872-3298

---

Marquette HS 100/9-12
502 Franklin St 52031 563-872-3356
Geoff Kaiser, prin. Fax 872-3285

**Belmond, Wright, Pop. 2,355**
Belmond-Klemme Community SD 800/PK-12
411 10th Ave NE 50421 641-444-4300
Kirk Nelson, supt. Fax 444-4524
www.bkcsd.org
Belmond-Klemme Alternative S 50/Alt
411 10th Ave NE 50421 641-444-4300
Eric Dockstader, prin. Fax 444-4097
Belmond-Klemme Community JSHS 300/7-12
411 10th Ave NE 50421 641-444-4300
Eric Dockstader, prin. Fax 444-4097

**Bettendorf, Scott, Pop. 32,699**
Bettendorf Community SD 4,500/PK-12
PO Box 1150 52722 563-359-3681
Dr. Theron Schutte, supt. Fax 359-3685
www.bettendorf.k12.ia.us
Bettendorf HS 1,400/9-12
3333 18th St 52722 563-332-7001
Jimmy Casas, prin. Fax 332-2326
Bettendorf MS 1,100/6-8
2030 Middle Rd 52722 563-359-3686
Lisa Reid, prin. Fax 359-3855
Edison Academy Alt
438 16th St 52722 563-359-9375
Tammy Chelf, coord. Fax 359-5565

Pleasant Valley Community SD 3,700/PK-12
525 Belmont Rd 52722 563-332-5550
Jim Spelhaug, supt. Fax 332-4372
www.pleasval.k12.ia.us
Other Schools – See Le Claire, Riverdale

---

Brown Mackie College Post-Sec.
2119 Kimberly Rd 52722 563-344-1500
Morning Star Academy 200/PK-12
1426 Tanglefoot Ln 52722 563-359-5700
Fax 359-5737
Rivermont Collegiate 200/PK-12
1821 Sunset Dr 52722 563-359-1366
Curtis Fee, hdmstr. Fax 359-7576
Scott Community College Post-Sec.
500 Belmont Rd 52722 563-441-4001

**Bloomfield, Davis, Pop. 2,620**
Davis County Community SD 1,200/PK-12
608 S Washington St 52537 641-664-2200
Dan Maeder, supt. Fax 664-2221
www.dcmustangs.com/
Davis County HS 400/9-12
503 E Locust St 52537 641-664-2200
Jeff Graves, prin. Fax 664-1763
Davis County MS 400/5-8
500 E North St 52537 641-664-2200
Brad Nelson, prin. Fax 664-1767

**Bonaparte, Van Buren, Pop. 432**
Harmony Community SD 300/PK-12
602 8th St 52620 319-592-3600
Kerry Phillips, supt. Fax 592-3690
www.harmonycsd.org
Other Schools – See Farmington

**Bondurant, Polk, Pop. 3,802**
Bondurant-Farrar Community SD 1,400/PK-12
300 Garfield St SW 50035 515-967-7819
Dr. Richard Powers, supt. Fax 967-7847
www.bondurant.k12.ia.us/
Bondurant-Farrar HS 400/9-12
1000 Grant St N 50035 515-957-8191
Michael Kramer, prin. Fax 957-8224
Bondurant-Farrar MS 300/6-8
300 Garfield St SW 50035 515-967-3711
Chad Carlson, prin. Fax 957-9924

**Boone, Boone, Pop. 12,525**
Boone Community SD 2,200/PK-12
500 7th St 50036 515-433-0750
Dr. Bradley Manard, supt. Fax 433-0753
boone.k12.ia.us/
Boone HS 700/9-12
400 7th St 50036 515-433-0890
Kristopher Byam, prin. Fax 433-0989
Boone MS 700/5-8
1640 1st St 50036 515-433-0020
Scott Kelley, prin. Fax 433-0026
Futures HS 50/Alt
727 W Mamie Eisenhower Ave 50036 515-433-0885
Kristopher Byam, prin. Fax 433-0753

---

Des Moines Area Community College Post-Sec.
1125 Hancock Dr 50036 515-432-7203

**Britt, Hancock, Pop. 2,051**
West Hancock Community SD 700/PK-12
PO Box 278 50423 641-843-3833
Wayne Kronemann, supt. Fax 843-4717
www.whancock.org/
West Hancock HS 200/9-12
PO Box 278 50423 641-843-3863
Dan Peterson, prin. Fax 843-4633
Other Schools – See Kanawha

**Brooklyn, Poweshiek, Pop. 1,455**
Brooklyn-Guernsey-Malcom Community SD 600/PK-12
1090 Jackson St 52211 641-522-7058
Brad Hohensee, supt. Fax 522-7211
www.brooklyn.k12.ia.us
Brooklyn-Guernsey-Malcom JSHS 300/7-12
1090 Jackson St 52211 641-522-7058
Rick Radcliffe, prin. Fax 522-7211

**Buffalo Center, Winnebago, Pop. 902**
North Iowa Community SD 500/PK-12
111 3rd Ave NW 50424 641-562-2525
Cory Myer, supt. Fax 562-2921
www.northiowa.org
North Iowa HS 200/9-12
111 3rd Ave NW 50424 641-562-2525
Keri Bergeson, prin. Fax 562-2921
North Iowa MS 100/5-8
111 3rd Ave NW 50424 641-562-2525
Jill Schutjer, prin. Fax 562-2921

**Burlington, Des Moines, Pop. 24,989**
Burlington Community SD 3,800/PK-12
1429 West Ave 52601 319-753-6791
Patrick Coen, supt. Fax 753-6796
www.bcsds.org
Burlington Alternative HS 100/Alt
2132 Madison Ave 52601 319-753-5092
David Keane, prin. Fax 753-6962
Burlington Community HS 1,100/9-12
421 Terrace Dr 52601 319-753-2211
David Keane, prin. Fax 753-6634
Leopold MS 500/6-8
3075 Sunnyside Ave 52601 319-752-8390
Mark Yeoman, prin. Fax 752-8447
Stone MS 6-8
3000 Mason Rd 52601 319-752-4393
Brian Johnson, prin. Fax 752-7437

---

Great River Christian S 100/PK-12
426 Harrison Ave 52601 319-753-2255
Jon Frischkorn, admin. Fax 753-2030
Notre Dame HS 200/6-12
702 S Roosevelt Ave 52601 319-754-8431
Bill Maupin, prin. Fax 752-8690

**Burnside, Webster**
Southeast Webster-Grand Community SD 600/PK-8
PO Box 49 50521 515-359-2235
Rich Stoffers, supt. Fax 359-2236
www.se-webster.k12.ia.us
Other Schools – See Dayton

**Bussey, Marion, Pop. 420**
Twin Cedars Community SD 400/PK-12
2204 Highway G71 50044 641-944-5241
Brian VanderSluis, supt. Fax 944-5824
www.twincedarscsd.org
Twin Cedars JSHS 200/7-12
2204 Highway G71 50044 641-944-5243
David Roby, prin. Fax 944-5225

**Calmar, Winneshiek, Pop. 970**
South Winneshiek Community SD 600/PK-12
PO Box 430 52132 563-562-3269
Clark Goltz, supt. Fax 562-3260
www.southwinn.com
South Winneshiek HS 300/9-12
PO Box 430 52132 563-562-3226
Mary Recker, prin. Fax 562-3228
Other Schools – See Ossian

---

Northeast Iowa Community College Post-Sec.
PO Box 400 52132 563-562-3263

**Camanche, Clinton, Pop. 4,417**
Camanche Community SD 1,100/PK-12
702 13th Ave 52730 563-259-3000
Thomas Parker, supt. Fax 259-3005
www.camanche.k12.ia.us
Camanche HS 300/9-12
937 9th Ave 52730 563-259-3008
Chuck Wiebenga, prin. Fax 259-3048
Camanche MS 300/5-8
1400 9th St 52730 563-259-3014
Justin Shaffer, prin. Fax 259-3031

**Carlisle, Warren, Pop. 3,818**
Carlisle Community SD 2,000/PK-12
430 School St 50047 515-989-3589
Bryce Amos, supt. Fax 989-3075
www.carlisle.k12.ia.us
Carlisle HS 600/9-12
430 School St 50047 515-989-0831
Matthew Blackmore, prin. Fax 989-3075
Carlisle MS 500/6-8
325 Scotch Ridge Rd 50047 515-989-0833
John Elkin, prin. Fax 989-4521

**Carroll, Carroll, Pop. 9,988**
Carroll Community SD 1,800/PK-12
1026 N Adams St 51401 712-792-8001
Rob Cordes, supt. Fax 792-8008
www.carroll.k12.ia.us
Carroll HS 600/9-12
2809 N Grant Rd 51401 712-792-8010
Tammie McKenzie, prin. Fax 792-8118
Carroll MS 400/5-8
3203 N Grant Rd 51401 712-792-8020
Jerry Raymond, prin. Fax 792-8024

---

Des Moines Area Community College Post-Sec.
906 N Grant Rd 51401 712-792-1755
Kuemper Catholic HS 300/9-12
109 S Clark St 51401 712-792-3596
Penny Miller, prin. Fax 792-8070
Kuemper Catholic MS 200/6-8
1519 N West St 51401 712-792-2123
Ted Garringer, prin. Fax 792-3365

**Carson, Pottawattamie, Pop. 809**
Riverside Community SD 500/PK-12
PO Box 218 51525 712-484-2212
Dr. James Sutton Ed.D., supt. Fax 484-3957
www.riversideschools.org
Other Schools – See Oakland

**Cascade, Dubuque, Pop. 2,146**
Western Dubuque Community SD
Supt. — See Farley
Cascade JSHS 400/7-12
505 Johnson St NW 52033 563-852-3201
Greg VanderLugt, prin. Fax 852-7186

**Cedar Falls, Black Hawk, Pop. 38,680**
Cedar Falls Community SD 4,800/PK-12
1002 W 1st St 50613 319-553-3000
Dr. Andy Pattee, supt. Fax 277-0614
www.cfschools.org/
Cedar Falls SHS 1,100/10-12
1015 Division St 50613 319-553-2500
Jason Wedgbury, prin. Fax 277-4604
Holmes JHS 500/7-9
505 Holmes Dr 50613 319-553-2650
David Welter, prin. Fax 277-0571
Peet JHS 600/7-9
525 E Seerley Blvd 50613 319-553-2710
Bill Boevers, prin. Fax 266-8839

---

Kaplan University Post-Sec.
7009 Nordic Dr 50613 319-277-0220
La' James International College Post-Sec.
6322 University Ave 50613 319-277-2150
University of Northern Iowa Post-Sec.
1227 W 27th St 50614 319-273-2311
Valley Lutheran HS 100/6-12
4520 Rownd St 50613 319-266-4565
Glenn Rollins, dir. Fax 266-4054

**Cedar Rapids, Linn, Pop. 122,869**
Cedar Rapids Community SD 15,800/PK-12
2500 Edgewood Rd NW 52405 319-558-2000
Dr. Brad Buck, supt. Fax 558-2224
www.cr.k12.ia.us
Franklin MS 600/6-8
300 20th St NE 52402 319-558-2452
Lucas Ptacek, prin. Fax 398-2454
Harding MS 900/6-8
4801 Golf St NE 52402 319-558-2254
Linda Reysack, prin. Fax 378-0671
Jefferson HS 1,500/9-12
1243 20th St SW 52404 319-558-2435
Charles McDonnell, prin. Fax 398-2442
Kennedy HS 1,800/9-12
4545 Wenig Rd NE 52402 319-558-2251
Jason Kline, prin. Fax 294-1118
McKinley MS 600/6-8
620 10th St SE 52403 319-558-2348
Steve Goodall, prin. Fax 398-2347
Metro HS 500/Alt
1212 7th St SE 52401 319-558-2193
Dr. Carlos Grant, prin. Fax 398-2117
Polk Alternative Education Center Alt
1500 B Ave NE 52402 319-558-2475
Deb Scott, dir.
Roosevelt MS 500/6-8
300 13th St NW 52405 319-558-2153
Autumn Pino, prin. Fax 398-2424
Taft MS 700/6-8
5200 E Ave NW 52405 319-558-2243
Gary Hatfield, prin. Fax 654-8619
Washington HS 1,400/9-12
2205 Forest Dr SE 52403 319-558-2161
Dr. Ralph Plagman, prin. Fax 398-2016
Wilson MS 300/6-8
2301 J St SW 52404 319-558-2156
Andrew Eley, prin. Fax 398-2368

College Community SD 5,000/PK-12
401 76th Ave SW 52404 319-848-5200
John Speer, supt. Fax 848-4019
www.prairiepride.org
Prairie HS 1,000/10-12
401 76th Ave SW 52404 319-848-5340
Erik Anderson, prin. Fax 848-5201
Prairie Point MS/9th Grade Academy 1,100/7-9
401 76th Ave SW 52404 319-848-5500
Greg Leytem, prin. Fax 848-5520

---

Capri College Post-Sec.
2945 Williams Pkwy SW 52404 319-364-1541
Cedar Valley Christian S 200/PK-12
3636 Cottage Grove Ave SE 52403 319-366-7462
Jeffrey Pospisil, prin. Fax 247-0037
Coe College Post-Sec.
1220 1st Ave NE 52402 319-399-8000
Holy Family - LaSalle MS 100/6-8
3700 1st Ave NW 52405 319-396-7792
Nick Duffy, prin. Fax 390-6527
ITT Technical Institute Post-Sec.
3735 Queen Ct SW 52404 319-297-3400
Kaplan University Post-Sec.
3165 Edgewood Pkwy SW 52404 319-363-0481
Kirkwood Community College Post-Sec.
PO Box 2068 52406 319-398-5411
Mercy-St. Luke's Hospital Post-Sec.
1026 A Ave NE 52402 319-369-7204
Mt. Mercy University Post-Sec.
1330 Elmhurst Dr NE 52402 319-363-8213
Regis MS 500/6-8
735 Prairie Dr NE 52402 319-363-1968
Beth Globokar, prin. Fax 247-6099
Xavier HS 800/9-12
6300 42nd St NE 52411 319-294-6635
Tom Keating, prin. Fax 294-6712

**Center Point, Linn, Pop. 2,394**
Center Point-Urbana Community SD 1,500/PK-12
PO Box 296 52213 319-849-1102
Alan Marshall, supt. Fax 849-2312
www.cpuschools.org/
Center Point-Urbana HS 400/9-12
PO Box 296 52213 319-849-1102
Rob Libolt, prin. Fax 849-2068
Center Point-Urbana MS 300/6-8
PO Box 296 52213 319-849-1102
Brent Winterhof, prin. Fax 443-2764

**Centerville, Appanoose, Pop. 5,460**
Centerville Community SD 1,200/PK-12
PO Box 370 52544 641-856-0601
Anthony Ryan, supt. Fax 856-0656
www.centervilleschools.org
Appanoose County Campus 50/Alt
PO Box 370 52544 641-856-0890
Roger Raum, prin.
Centerville HS 400/9-12
600 CHS Dr 52544 641-856-0813
Roger Raum, prin. Fax 856-0809
Howar JHS 200/7-8
850 S Park Ave 52544 641-856-0760
Bruce Karpen, prin. Fax 856-0761

---

Indian Hills Community College Post-Sec.
721 N 1st St 52544 641-856-2143

**Central City, Linn, Pop. 1,249**
Central City Community SD 400/PK-12
400 Barber St 52214 319-438-6181
Dr. Tim Cronin, supt. Fax 438-6110
www.central-city.k12.ia.us
Central City HS 100/9-12
400 Barber St 52214 319-438-6181
Jason McLaughlin, prin. Fax 438-6110
Central City MS 100/7-8
400 Barber St 52214 319-438-6181
Jason McLaughlin, prin. Fax 438-6110

**Chariton, Lucas, Pop. 4,293**
Chariton Community SD 1,400/PK-12
PO Box 738 50049 641-774-5967
Paula Wright, supt. Fax 774-8511
www.chariton.k12.ia.us/
Chariton HS 500/9-12
501 N Grand St 50049 641-774-5066
Tracy Hall, prin. Fax 774-3404
Chariton MS 300/6-8
1300 N 16th St 50049 641-774-5114
Andy Fuhs, prin. Fax 774-4109

**Charles City, Floyd, Pop. 7,583**
Charles City Community SD 1,500/PK-12
500 N Grand Ave 50616 641-257-6500
Dr. Dan Cox, supt. Fax 257-6509
www.charlescityschools.org
Charles City HS 500/9-12
1 Comet Dr 50616 641-257-6510
Josh Johnson, prin. Fax 257-1175
Charles City MS 300/6-8
500 N Grand Ave 50616 641-257-6530
Rick Gabel, prin. Fax 228-9842

**Charter Oak, Crawford, Pop. 501**
Charter Oak-Ute Community SD 300/PK-12
321 Main St 51439 712-678-3325
Rollie Wiebers, supt. Fax 678-3626
www.charter-oak-ute.k12.ia.us/
Charter Oak-Ute HS 100/9-12
321 Main St 51439 712-678-3325
Adam Eggeling, prin. Fax 678-3626
Charter Oak-Ute JHS 100/6-8
321 Main St 51439 712-678-3325
Adam Eggeling, prin. Fax 678-3626

**Cherokee, Cherokee, Pop. 5,205**
Cherokee Community SD 1,000/PK-12
600 W Bluff St 51012 712-225-6767
Kimberly Lingenfelter, supt. Fax 225-6769
www.ccsd.k12.ia.us/
Cherokee MS 300/5-8
206 Indian St 51012 712-225-6750
Neil Phipps, prin. Fax 225-4841
Washington HS 300/9-12
600 W Bluff St 51012 712-225-6755
Scot Aden, prin. Fax 225-6765

**Churdan, Greene, Pop. 379**
Paton-Churdan Community SD 200/PK-12
PO Box 157 50050 515-389-3111
Kreg Lensch, supt. Fax 389-3113
www.paton-churdan.k12.ia.us
Paton-Churdan JSHS 100/6-12
PO Box 157 50050 515-389-3111
Annie Smith, prin. Fax 389-3113

**Clarence, Cedar, Pop. 966**
North Cedar Community SD
Supt. — See Stanwood
North Cedar JSHS 300/7-12
PO Box 310 52216 563-452-3179
Mark Dohmen, prin. Fax 452-3972

**Clarinda, Page, Pop. 5,483**
Clarinda Community SD 1,200/PK-12
PO Box 59 51632 712-542-5165
Paul Honnold, supt. Fax 542-3802
www.clarinda.k12.ia.us
Clarinda Alternative HS 50/Alt
PO Box 59 51632 712-542-5165
Teresa Nook, prin. Fax 542-3802
Clarinda HS 300/9-12
PO Box 59 51632 712-542-5167
Teresa Nook, prin. Fax 542-4305
Clarinda MS 300/5-8
PO Box 59 51632 712-542-2132
Josh Porter, prin. Fax 542-5949

---

Iowa Western Community College Post-Sec.
923 E Washington St 51632 712-542-5117

**Clarion, Wright, Pop. 2,837**
Clarion-Goldfield-Dows Community SD 900/PK-12
319 3rd Ave NE 50525 515-532-3423
Dr. Robert Olson, supt. Fax 532-2628
www.clargold.org
Clarion-Goldfield-Dows HS 300/9-12
1111 Willow Dr 50525 515-532-2895
Dennis March, prin. Fax 532-2897
Clarion-Goldfield-Dows MS 200/6-8
300 3rd Ave NE 50525 515-532-2412
Steve Haberman, prin. Fax 532-2741

**Clarksville, Butler, Pop. 1,422**
Clarksville Community SD 300/PK-12
318 N Mather St 50619 319-278-4008
Randy Strabala, supt. Fax 278-4618
www.clarksville.k12.ia.us/
Clarksville JSHS 200/6-12
318 N Mather St 50619 319-278-4273
Robert Saathoff, prin. Fax 278-4981

**Clear Lake, Cerro Gordo, Pop. 7,667**
Clear Lake Community SD 1,400/PK-12
1529 3rd Ave N 50428 641-357-2181
Anita Micich, supt. Fax 357-2182
www.clearlakeschools.org
Clear Lake HS 500/9-12
125 N 20th St 50428 641-357-5235
Chris Murphy, prin. Fax 357-6218
Clear Lake MS 300/6-8
1601 3rd Ave N 50428 641-357-6114
Steve Kwikkel, prin. Fax 357-8353

**Clinton, Clinton, Pop. 26,311**
Clinton Community SD 3,800/PK-12
1401 12th Ave N 52732 563-243-9600
Deborah Olson, supt. Fax 243-2415
www.clinton.k12.ia.us
Clinton HS 1,100/9-12
817 8th Ave S 52732 563-243-7540
John Ryan Kuch, prin. Fax 243-9612
Clinton MS, 1350 14th St NW 52732 6-8
Dan Boyd, prin. 563-243-0466

---

Ashford University Post-Sec.
400 N Bluff Blvd 52732 866-711-1700
Clinton Community College Post-Sec.
1000 Lincoln Blvd 52732 563-244-7000
Prince of Peace Catholic S 300/PK-12
312 S 4th St 52732 563-242-1663
Nancy Peart, prin. Fax 243-8272

**Clive, Polk, Pop. 15,239**
West Des Moines Community SD
Supt. — See West Des Moines
Indian Hills JHS 700/7-8
9401 Indian Hills Dr 50325 515-633-4700
Shane Christensen, prin. Fax 633-4799

---

ITT Technical Institute Post-Sec.
1860 NW 118th St Ste 110 50325 515-327-5500

**Colfax, Jasper, Pop. 2,079**
Colfax-Mingo Community SD 600/PK-12
204 N League Rd 50054 515-674-3646
Tracy Hook, supt. Fax 674-3921
www.colfax-mingo.k12.ia.us
Colfax-Mingo JSHS 200/7-12
204 N League Rd 50054 515-674-4111
Todd Jones, prin. Fax 674-4940

**College Springs, Page, Pop. 207**
South Page Community SD 200/PK-12
PO Box 98 51637 712-582-3212
Gregg Cruickshank, supt. Fax 582-3217
www.southpageschools.com
South Page JSHS 100/6-12
PO Box 98 51637 712-582-3211
Denise Green, prin. Fax 582-3217

**Colo, Story, Pop. 872**
Colo-Nesco Comm SD 400/PK-12
PO Box 136 50056 641-377-2284
Jim Verlengia, supt. Fax 377-2283
www.colo-nesco.k12.ia.us
Colo-Nesco JSHS 200/7-12
919 West St 50056 641-377-2282
Brandon Kelley, prin. Fax 377-2283

**Columbus Junction, Louisa, Pop. 1,878**
Columbus Community SD 900/PK-12
1208 Colton St 52738 319-728-2911
Gary Benda, supt. Fax 728-8750
www.columbuscsd.org
Columbus Community HS 300/9-12
1004 Colton St 52738 319-728-2231
Gary Benda, prin. Fax 728-2205
Columbus Community JHS 100/7-8
1004 Colton St 52738 319-728-2233
Gary Benda, prin. Fax 728-2205

**Conrad, Grundy, Pop. 1,100**
BCLUW Community SD 600/K-12
PO Box 670 50621 641-366-2819
Ben Petty, supt. Fax 366-2175
www.bcluw.k12.ia.us
BCLUW HS 200/9-12
PO Box 670 50621 641-366-2810
Kristyn Kell, prin. Fax 366-2951
Other Schools – See Union

**Coon Rapids, Carroll, Pop. 1,296**
Coon Rapids-Bayard Community SD 400/PK-12
PO Box 297 50058 712-999-2207
Dr. Tom Ward, supt. Fax 999-7740
www.crbcrusaders.org

Coon Rapids-Bayard Intermediate JSHS 300/5-12
PO Box 297 50058 712-999-2208
Larry Frakes, prin. Fax 999-7740

**Coralville, Johnson, Pop. 18,406**
Iowa City Community SD
Supt. — See Iowa City
Northwest JHS 600/7-8
1507 8th St 52241 319-688-1060
Laura Cottrell, prin. Fax 688-1069

**Corning, Adams, Pop. 1,626**
Southwest Valley SD
Supt. — See Villisca
Southwest Valley HS 200/9-12
904 8th St 50841 641-322-4245
James Craig, prin. Fax 322-5149

**Correctionville, Woodbury, Pop. 815**
River Valley Community SD 500/PK-12
PO Box 8 51016 712-372-4420
Ken Slater, supt. Fax 372-4677
www.rvwolverines.org
River Valley JSHS 200/7-12
PO Box 8 51016 712-372-4656
Steve Sauvain, prin. Fax 372-4784

**Corydon, Wayne, Pop. 1,578**
Wayne Community SD 600/PK-12
102 N Dekalb St 50060 641-872-2184
Dave Daughton, supt. Fax 872-2091
www.wayne.k12.ia.us
Wayne Community JSHS 200/7-12
102 N Dekalb St 50060 641-872-2184
Stacy Snyder, prin. Fax 872-2091

**Council Bluffs, Pottawattamie, Pop. 61,150**
Council Bluffs Community SD 8,800/PK-12
300 W Broadway Ste 1600 51503 712-328-6446
Dr. Martha Bruckner, supt. Fax 328-6548
www.cbcsd.org/
Jefferson HS 1,300/9-12
2501 W Broadway 51501 712-328-6493
Todd Barnett, prin. Fax 328-6497
Kanesville Alternative Learning Ctr 300/Alt
807 Avenue G 51503 712-328-6510
Jesse Tvrdy, prin. Fax 328-6511
Kirn MS 900/6-8
100 North Ave 51503 712-328-6454
Kerry Newman, prin. Fax 328-6554
Lincoln HS 1,300/9-12
1205 Bonham St 51503 712-328-6481
Bridgette Bellows, prin. Fax 328-6485
Tucker Career & College Center Vo/Tech
815 N 18th St 51501 712-328-6408
Cyle Forney, prin. Fax 328-6425
Wilson MS 900/6-8
715 N 21st St 51501 712-328-6476
Kim Kazmierczak, prin. Fax 328-6479

Lewis Central Community SD 3,200/PK-12
4121 Harry Langdon Blvd 51503 712-366-8202
Dr. Mark Schweer, supt. Fax 366-8315
www.lewiscentral.org/
Lewis Central HS 900/9-12
3504 Harry Langdon Blvd 51503 712-366-8322
Joel Beyenhof, prin. Fax 366-8340
Lewis Central MS 700/6-8
3820 Harry Langdon Blvd 51503 712-366-8251
Jim Dermody, prin. Fax 366-8324

---

EQ School of Hair Design Post-Sec.
536 W Broadway 51503 712-328-2613
Heartland Christian S 100/PK-12
400 Wright Rd 51501 712-322-5817
Gary Wilson, dir. Fax 322-4287
Iowa School for the Deaf Post-Sec.
3501 Harry Langdon Blvd 51503 712-366-0571
Iowa Western Community College Post-Sec.
2700 College Rd 51503 712-325-3200
Jennie Edmundson Memorial Hospital Post-Sec.
933 E Pierce St 51503 712-328-6239
St. Albert HS 300/7-12
400 Gleason Ave 51503 712-328-2316
David Schweitzer, prin. Fax 328-8316

**Cresco, Howard, Pop. 3,829**
Howard-Winneshiek Community SD 1,000/PK-12
1000 Schroder Dr 52136 563-547-2762
John Carver, supt. Fax 547-5973
www.howard-winn.k12.ia.us
Crestwood Alternative S 50/Alt
1000 Schroder Dr 52136 563-547-2764
Julie Montgomery, lead tchr.
Crestwood HS 500/9-12
1000 Schroder Dr 52136 563-547-2764
Christopher Rogne, prin. Fax 547-4650

---

Total Look Sch of Cosmetology & Massage Post-Sec.
806 3rd St W 52136 563-547-3624

**Creston, Union, Pop. 7,756**
Creston Community SD 1,400/PK-12
801 N Elm St 50801 641-782-7028
Steve McDermott, supt. Fax 782-7020
www.crestonschools.org
Creston HS 500/9-12
601 W Townline St 50801 641-782-2116
Bill Messerole, prin. Fax 782-9502
Creston MS 300/6-8
805 Academic Ave 50801 641-782-2129
Brad Baker, prin. Fax 782-6983

---

Southwestern Community College Post-Sec.
1501 W Townline St 50801 641-782-7081

**Dakota City, Humboldt, Pop. 834**
Humboldt Community SD 1,200/PK-12
PO Box 130 50529 515-332-1330
Greg Darling, supt. Fax 332-4478
www.humboldt.k12.ia.us
Other Schools – See Humboldt

**Dallas Center, Dallas, Pop. 1,610**
Dallas Center-Grimes Community SD 2,000/K-12
PO Box 512 50063 515-992-3866
Scott Grimes, supt. Fax 992-3079
dcgschools.com
Other Schools – See Grimes

**Danville, Des Moines, Pop. 929**
Danville Community SD 600/PK-12
419 S Main St 52623 319-392-4221
Gary DeLacy, supt. Fax 392-8390
www.danvillecsd.org
Danville JSHS 300/7-12
419 S Main St 52623 319-392-4221
Theresa Ritters, prin. Fax 392-8704

**Davenport, Scott, Pop. 96,534**
Davenport Community SD 15,300/PK-12
1606 Brady St 52803 563-336-5000
Arthur Tate, supt. Fax 336-5080
www.davenportschools.org
Central HS 1,400/9-12
1120 N Main St 52803 563-323-9900
Scott McKissick, prin. Fax 323-3110
Keystone Academy Davenport Learning Ctr 200/Alt
1002 W Kimberly Rd 52806 563-386-5840
Sheri Womack, prin. Fax 386-9764
Mid City HS 9-12
3801 Marquette St 52806 563-336-7000
Dr. Jake Klipsch, prin. Fax 391-0357
North HS 1,000/9-12
626 W 53rd St 52806 563-388-9880
Jay Chelf, prin. Fax 388-9456
Smart IS 500/6-8
1934 W 5th St 52802 563-323-1837
Todd Hawley, prin. Fax 323-3093
Sudlow IS 800/6-8
1414 E Locust St 52803 563-326-3502
Bruce Potts, prin. Fax 326-2248
West HS 1,900/9-12
3505 W Locust St 52804 563-386-5500
Virginia Weipert, prin. Fax 386-5508
Williams IS 800/6-8
3040 N Division St 52804 563-391-6550
Garet Egel, prin. Fax 391-0149
Wood IS 700/6-8
5701 N Division St 52806 563-391-6350
Sheri Simpson-Schultz, prin. Fax 391-4416
Other Schools – See Walcott

---

Assumption HS 400/9-12
1020 W Central Park Ave 52804 563-326-5313
Bridget Murphy, prin. Fax 326-3510
Capri College Post-Sec.
2540 E 53rd St 52807 563-388-6642
Hamilton Technical College Post-Sec.
1011 E 53rd St 52807 563-386-3570
Kaplan University Post-Sec.
1801 E Kimberly Rd Ste 1 52807 563-355-3500
La' James College of Hairstyling Post-Sec.
5205 N Brady St 52806 563-441-7900
Palmer College of Chiropractic Post-Sec.
1000 Brady St 52803 563-884-5000
St. Ambrose University Post-Sec.
518 W Locust St 52803 563-333-6000

**Dayton, Webster, Pop. 832**
Southeast Webster-Grand Community SD
Supt. — See Burnside
Southeast Valley MS 100/5-8
30850 Paragon Ave 50530 515-359-2235
Dan Fox, prin. Fax 359-2236

**Decorah, Winneshiek, Pop. 8,056**
Decorah Community SD 1,600/PK-12
510 Winnebago St 52101 563-382-4208
Michael Haluska, supt. Fax 387-0753
decorah.k12.ia.us/
Decorah HS 600/9-12
100 E Claiborne Dr 52101 563-382-3643
Kim Sheppard, prin. Fax 382-3107
Decorah MS 400/5-8
405 Winnebago St 52101 563-382-8427
Leona Hoth, prin. Fax 387-4052

North Winneshiek Community SD 200/PK-8
3495 N Winn Rd 52101 563-735-5411
Tim Dugger, supt. Fax 735-5430
www.n-winn.k12.ia.us/
North Winneshiek MS 50/6-8
3495 N Winn Rd 52101 563-735-5411
Tim Dugger, prin. Fax 735-5430

---

Luther College Post-Sec.
700 College Dr 52101 563-387-2000

**Delhi, Delaware, Pop. 456**
Maquoketa Valley Community SD 700/PK-12
PO Box 186 52223 563-922-9422
Doug Tuetken, supt. Fax 922-9502
www.maquoketa-v.k12.ia.us
Maquoketa Valley HS 200/9-12
PO Box 186 52223 563-922-2091
Doug Tuetken, prin. Fax 922-3026
Maquoketa Valley MS 200/6-8
PO Box 186 52223 563-922-9411
Tracy Morrison, prin. Fax 922-9502

**Denison, Crawford, Pop. 8,238**
Denison Community SD 2,100/K-12
819 N 16th St 51442 712-263-2176
Michael Pardun, supt. Fax 263-5233
www.denison.k12.ia.us
Denison Alternative HS 50/Alt
10 Opportunity Dr 51442 712-265-2349
Lynn Torr, prin. Fax 265-2397
Denison HS 700/9-12
819 N 16th St 51442 712-263-3101
Lynn Torr, prin. Fax 263-6009
Denison MS 400/6-8
1201 N 16th St 51442 712-263-9393
Dave Wiebers, prin. Fax 263-5418

**Denver, Bremer, Pop. 1,773**
Denver Community SD 800/PK-12
PO Box 384 50622 319-984-6323
Brad Laures, supt. Fax 984-5345
www.denver.k12.ia.us
Denver HS 200/9-12
PO Box 384 50622 319-984-5639
Paul Gebel, prin. Fax 984-5630
Denver MS 200/6-8
PO Box 384 50622 319-984-6041
Paul Gebel, prin. Fax 984-5630

**Des Moines, Polk, Pop. 197,701**
Des Moines Independent Community SD 30,300/PK-12
2323 Grand Ave 50312 515-242-7911
Thomas Ahart, supt. Fax 242-7679
www.dmschools.org
Brody MS 700/6-8
2501 Park Ave 50321 515-242-8443
Thomas Hoffman, prin. Fax 244-0927
Callanan MS 600/6-8
3010 Center St 50312 515-242-8101
Dawn Stahly, prin. Fax 242-8103
Des Moines Alternative Center Alt
1801 Grand Ave 50309 515-242-7781
Randi Oleson, prin. Fax 323-8617
Des Moines Central Campus 50/Alt
1800 Grand Ave 50309 515-242-7846
Gary G. McClanahan, prin. Fax 242-7598
East HS 2,200/9-12
815 E 13th St 50316 515-242-7788
Morris Leslie, prin. Fax 242-7958
Goodrell MS 600/6-8
3300 E 29th St 50317 515-242-8444
Craig Leager, prin. Fax 264-9057
Harding MS 500/6-8
203 E Euclid Ave 50313 515-242-8445
Joy Linquist, prin. Fax 244-3566
Hiatt MS 600/6-8
1430 University Ave 50314 515-242-8450
Debra Chapman, prin. Fax 266-6390
Hoover HS 1,100/9-12
4800 Aurora Ave 50310 515-242-7300
Cynthia Flesch, prin. Fax 242-7308
Hoyt MS 500/6-8
2700 E 42nd St 50317 515-242-8446
Deborah Markert, prin. Fax 265-5059
Lincoln HS 2,200/9-12
2600 SW 9th St 50315 515-242-7500
Paul Williamson, prin. Fax 242-7517
McCombs MS 600/6-8
201 County Line Rd 50320 515-242-8447
Nancy Croy, prin. Fax 287-2644
Meredith MS 700/6-8
4827 Madison Ave 50310 515-242-7250
David Johns, prin. Fax 242-8291
Merrill MS 700/6-8
5301 Grand Ave 50312 515-242-8448
Alex Hanna, prin. Fax 274-9691
North HS 1,100/9-12
501 Holcomb Ave 50313 515-242-7200
Michael Vukovich, prin. Fax 242-7319
Roosevelt HS 1,700/9-12
4419 Center St 50312 515-242-7272
Kevin Biggs, prin. Fax 242-7350
Scavo HS 300/Alt
1800 Grand Ave 50309 515-242-7589
Richard Blonigan, prin. Fax 242-7591
Weeks MS 700/6-8
901 E Park Ave 50315 515-242-8449
Audrey Rieken, prin. Fax 288-6755

Saydel Community SD 1,200/PK-12
5740 NE 14th St 50313 515-264-0866
Doug Wheeler, supt. Fax 264-0869
www.saydel.k12.ia.us
Saydel HS 500/9-12
5601 NE 7th St 50313 515-262-9325
Kevin Schulte, prin. Fax 266-8497
Woodside MS 300/5-8
5810 NE 14th St 50313 515-265-3451
Joshua Heyer, prin. Fax 265-0950

---

AIB College of Business Post-Sec.
2500 Fleur Dr 50321 515-244-4221
Des Moines University Post-Sec.
3200 Grand Ave 50312 515-271-1400
Drake University Post-Sec.
2507 University Ave 50311 515-271-2011
Grand View Christian S 200/K-12
2905 NE 46th Ave 50317 319-777-3977
Dotty Van Hooser, prin.
Grand View University Post-Sec.
1200 Grandview Ave 50316 515-263-2800
Iowa Methodist Medical Center Post-Sec.
1200 Pleasant St 50309 515-241-6201
Iowa School of Beauty Post-Sec.
3305 70th St 50322 515-278-9939
Mercy College of Health Sciences Post-Sec.
928 6th Ave 50309 515-643-3180
Vatterott College - Des Moines Post-Sec.
7000 Fleur Dr 50321 515-309-9000

**De Witt, Clinton, Pop. 5,259**
Central Community SD 1,500/PK-12
PO Box 110 52742 563-659-0700
Dr. Dan Peterson, supt. Fax 659-0707
www.central-csd.org
Central Alternative Program 50/Alt
PO Box 110 52742 563-659-4713
George Pickup, prin. Fax 659-0714
Central HS 500/9-12
PO Box 110 52742 563-659-0715
George Pickup, prin. Fax 659-0714
Central MS 200/7-8
PO Box 110 52742 563-659-0735
Tim Bradley, prin. Fax 659-0766

**Diagonal, Ringgold, Pop. 330**
Diagonal Community SD 100/PK-12
403 W 2nd St 50845 641-734-5331
Karleen Stephens, supt. Fax 734-5729
www.diagonal.k12.ia.us
Diagonal JSHS 100/6-12
403 W 2nd St 50845 641-734-5331
Lorna Paxson, prin. Fax 734-5729

**Dike, Grundy, Pop. 1,205**
Dike-New Hartford Community SD 900/PK-12
PO Box D 50624 319-989-2552
Larry Hunt, supt. Fax 989-2735
www.dnhcsd.org
Dike-New Hartford HS 200/9-12
PO Box D 50624 319-989-2485
Irvin Laube, prin. Fax 989-2735
Other Schools – See New Hartford

**Donnellson, Lee, Pop. 907**
Central Lee Community SD 1,000/PK-12
2642 Highway 218 52625 319-835-9510
John Henriksen, supt. Fax 835-3910
www.centrallee.org
Central Lee HS 300/9-12
2642 Highway 218 52625 319-835-9510
Nicole Herdrich, prin. Fax 835-5709
Central Lee MS 200/6-8
2642 Highway 218 52625 319-835-9510
Kim Ensminger, prin. Fax 835-5020

**Dubuque, Dubuque, Pop. 56,421**
Dubuque Community SD 10,500/PK-12
2300 Chaney Rd 52001 563-552-3000
Stan Rheingans, supt. Fax 552-3026
www.dbqschools.org
Dubuque SHS 1,600/9-12
1800 Clarke Dr 52001 563-552-5500
Dr. Daniel Johnson, prin. Fax 552-5502
Hempstead HS 1,700/9-12
3715 Pennsylvania Ave 52002 563-552-5200
Lee Kolker, prin. Fax 552-5231
Jefferson MS 600/6-8
1105 Althauser Ave 52001 563-552-4700
Kelly Molony, prin. Fax 552-4701
Roosevelt MS 1,100/6-8
2001 Radford Rd 52002 563-552-5000
Dale Lass, prin. Fax 552-5001
Washington MS 700/6-8
51 N Grandview Ave 52001 563-552-4800
Mark Burns, prin. Fax 552-4801

---

Capri College Post-Sec.
395 Main St 52001 563-588-2379
Clarke University Post-Sec.
1550 Clarke Dr 52001 563-588-6300
Emmaus Bible College Post-Sec.
2570 Asbury Rd 52001 563-588-8000
Loras College Post-Sec.
1450 Alta Vista St 52001 563-588-7100
Mazzuchelli Catholic MS 400/6-8
2005 Kane St 52001 563-582-1198
Phil Bormann, prin. Fax 582-5428
University of Dubuque Post-Sec.
2000 University Ave 52001 563-589-3000
Wahlert Catholic HS 600/9-12
2005 Kane St 52001 563-583-9771
Ronald Meyers, prin. Fax 583-9775
Wartburg Theological Seminary Post-Sec.
PO Box 5004 52004 563-589-0200

**Dunkerton, Black Hawk, Pop. 848**
Dunkerton Community SD 500/PK-12
509 S Canfield St 50626 319-822-4295
Jim Stanton, supt. Fax 822-9456
www.dunkerton.k12.ia.us
Dunkerton JSHS 200/7-12
509 S Canfield St 50626 319-822-4295
Justin Urbanek, prin. Fax 822-9456

**Dunlap, Harrison, Pop. 1,032**
Boyer Valley Community SD 400/PK-12
1102 Iowa Ave 51529 712-643-5702
Doug Gee, supt. Fax 643-2279
www.boyer-valley.k12.ia.us
Boyer Valley MSHS 200/PK-PK, 6-
1102 Iowa Ave 51529 712-643-2258
Mike Weber, prin. Fax 643-2279

**Durant, Cedar, Pop. 1,820**
Durant Community SD 700/K-12
408 7th St 52747 563-785-4432
Duane Bennett, supt. Fax 785-4611
www.durant.k12.ia.us
Durant HS 200/9-12
408 7th St 52747 563-785-4431
Anthony Neumann, prin. Fax 785-6558
Durant MS 200/5-8
408 7th St 52747 563-785-4433
Rebecca Stineman, prin. Fax 785-6558

**Dyersville, Dubuque, Pop. 4,031**

---

Beckman HS 500/7-12
1325 9th St SE 52040 563-875-7188
Patrick Meade, prin. Fax 875-7242

**Dysart, Tama, Pop. 1,367**
Union Community SD
Supt. — See La Porte City
Union MS 300/6-8
PO Box 159 52224 319-476-5100
Mark Albertsen, prin. Fax 476-2385

**Eagle Grove, Wright, Pop. 3,540**
Eagle Grove Community SD 800/PK-12
325 N Commercial Ave 50533 515-448-4749
Jess Toliver, supt. Fax 448-3156
www.eagle-grove.k12.ia.us
Blue MS 200/5-8
1015 NW 2nd St 50533 515-448-4767
Scott Jeske, prin. Fax 448-5527
Eagle Grove HS 200/9-12
415 NW 2nd St 50533 515-448-5143
Jeff Siebersma, prin. Fax 448-3583

**Earlham, Madison, Pop. 1,435**
Earlham Community SD 600/PK-12
PO Box 430 50072 515-758-2235
Mike Wright, supt. Fax 758-2215
home.ecsdcards.com/
Earlham HS 200/9-12
PO Box 430 50072 515-758-2235
Jennifer Knight, prin. Fax 758-2215
Earlham MS 100/7-8
PO Box 430 50072 515-758-2214
Jennifer Knight, prin. Fax 758-2215

**Early, Sac, Pop. 548**
Schaller-Crestland Community SD
Supt. — See Schaller
Ridge View MS 200/6-8
PO Box 377 50535 712-273-5192
Ellen Pickhinke, prin. Fax 273-5120

**Eddyville, Wapello, Pop. 1,011**
Eddyville-Blakesburg-Fremont Comm SD 900/PK-12
PO Box 429 52553 641-969-4226
Dean Cook, supt. Fax 969-4547
www.rocketsk12.org
Eddyville-Blakesburg-Fremont HS 300/9-12
1301 Berdan Ext 52553 641-969-4288
Donna Keesling, prin. Fax 969-4574
Eddyville-Blakesburg-Fremont JHS 100/7-8
1301 Berdan Ext 52553 641-938-2202
Donna Keesling, prin. Fax 938-2613

**Edgewood, Clayton, Pop. 857**
Edgewood-Colesburg Community SD 600/PK-12
PO Box 315 52042 563-928-6411
Rob Busch, supt. Fax 928-6414
www.edge-cole.k12.ia.us
Edgewood-Colesburg JSHS 300/7-12
PO Box 316 52042 563-928-6412
Dawn Voss, prin. Fax 928-6414

**Eldon, Wapello, Pop. 923**
Cardinal Community SD 600/PK-12
4045 Ashland Rd 52554 641-652-7531
Joel Pedersen, supt. Fax 652-3143
www.cardinalcomet.com
Cardinal MSHS 300/6-12
4045 Ashland Rd 52554 641-652-7531
Jeremy Hissem, prin. Fax 652-3143

**Eldora, Hardin, Pop. 2,695**
Eldora-New Providence Community SD 600/PK-12
1010 Edgington Ave 50627 641-939-5631
Jay Mathis, supt. Fax 939-3667
Eldora-New Providence HS 300/9-12
1800 24th St 50627 641-939-3421
Michael Rundall, prin. Fax 939-3423

**Eldridge, Scott, Pop. 5,557**
North Scott Community SD 3,000/PK-12
251 E Iowa St 52748 563-285-4819
Joe Stutting, supt. Fax 285-6075
www.north-scott.k12.ia.us
North Scott HS 1,000/9-12
200 S 1st St 52748 563-285-9631
Shane Knoche, prin. Fax 285-9308
North Scott JHS 500/7-8
502 S 5th St 52748 563-285-8272
John Hawley, prin. Fax 285-6045

**Elgin, Fayette, Pop. 680**
Valley Community SD 200/K-8
23493 Canoe Rd 52141 563-426-5501
Duane Willhite, supt. Fax 426-5502
www.valley.k12.ia.us
North Fayette Valley MS 100/7-8
23493 Canoe Rd 52141 563-426-5551
Micah Gearhart, prin. Fax 426-5502

**Elkader, Clayton, Pop. 1,265**
Central Community SD 500/PK-12
400 1st St NW 52043 563-245-1751
Nick Trenkamp, supt. Fax 245-1763
www.central.k12.ia.us/
Central Community JSHS 300/6-12
400 1st St NW 52043 563-245-1750
Dan Yanda, prin. Fax 245-1763

**Elk Horn, Shelby, Pop. 661**
Exira-Elk Horn-Kimballton Community SD 200/PK-12
PO Box 388a 51531 712-764-4616
Dean Schnoes, supt. Fax 764-4626
www.exira-ehk.k12.ia.us/
Exira-Elk Horn-Kimballton HS 100/9-12
PO Box 388a 51531 712-764-4606
Dean Schnoes, supt. Fax 764-4626
Other Schools – See Exira

**Emmetsburg, Palo Alto, Pop. 3,872**
Emmetsburg Community SD 700/PK-12
205 King St 50536 712-852-3201
Amanda Schmidt, supt. Fax 852-3338
www.e-hawks.org
Emmetsburg HS 200/9-12
205 King St 50536 712-852-2966
Mike Embrock, prin. Fax 852-3317
Emmetsburg MS 200/5-8
205 King St 50536 712-852-2892
Tracie Christensen, prin. Fax 852-3811

---

Iowa Lakes Community College Post-Sec.
3200 College Dr 50536 712-852-3554

**Epworth, Dubuque, Pop. 1,855**
Western Dubuque Community SD
Supt. — See Farley
Western Dubuque HS 800/9-12
PO Box 379 52045 563-876-3442
Dave Hoeger, prin. Fax 876-5512

---

Divine Word College Post-Sec.
PO Box 380 52045 563-876-3353

**Essex, Page, Pop. 789**
Essex Community SD 200/PK-12
111 Forbes St 51638 712-379-3117
Paul Croghan, supt. Fax 379-3200
www.ehs-ees.com/
Essex JSHS 100/6-12
111 Forbes St 51638 712-379-3115
Rob Brecht, prin. Fax 379-3200

**Estherville, Emmet, Pop. 6,305**
Estherville Lincoln Central Comm SD 1,400/PK-12
1814 7th Ave S 51334 712-362-2692
Tara Paul, supt. Fax 362-2410
www.estherville.k12.ia.us
Estherville Lincoln Central HS 400/9-12
1520 Central Ave 51334 712-362-2659
Brad Leonard, prin. Fax 362-2406
Estherville Lincoln Central MS 400/5-8
1430 1st Ave S 51334 712-362-2335
David McCaulley, prin. Fax 362-7822

---

Iowa Lakes Community College Post-Sec.
300 S 18th St 51334 712-362-7945

**Evansdale, Black Hawk, Pop. 4,640**
Waterloo Community SD
Supt. — See Waterloo
Bunger MS 400/6-8
157 S Roosevelt Rd 50707 319-433-2550
Rachel Savage, prin. Fax 433-2564

**Everly, Clay, Pop. 602**
Clay Central/Everly Community SD
Supt. — See Royal
Clay Central/Everly JSHS 100/7-12
PO Box 110 51338 712-834-2227
Curt Busch, prin. Fax 834-2193

**Exira, Audubon, Pop. 839**
Exira-Elk Horn-Kimballton Community SD
Supt. — See Elk Horn
Exira-Elk Horn-Kimballton MS 200/PK-K, 4-8
PO Box 335 50076 712-268-5318
Stephen Humphrey, prin. Fax 268-5319

**Fairbank, Buchanan, Pop. 1,107**
Wapsie Valley Community SD 800/PK-12
2535 Viking Ave 50629 319-638-6711
Chad Garber, supt. Fax 638-7061
www.wapsievalleyschools.com/
Wapsie Valley JSHS 300/7-12
2535 Viking Ave 50629 319-638-6711
Ross Bauer, prin. Fax 638-7061

**Fairfield, Jefferson, Pop. 9,274**
Fairfield Community SD 1,700/PK-12
403 S 20th St 52556 641-472-2655
Dr. Laurie Noll, supt. Fax 472-0269
www.fairfieldsfuture.org/
Fairfield HS 500/9-12
605 E Broadway Ave 52556 641-472-2059
Aaron Becker, prin. Fax 472-4703
Fairfield MS 500/5-8
404 W Fillmore Ave 52556 641-472-5019
Laura Atwood, prin. Fax 472-5301

---

Maharishi S of the Age of Enlightenment 200/PK-12
804 Dr Robert Keith Wallace 52556 641-472-9400
Richard Beall Ph.D., head sch Fax 472-1211
Maharishi University of Management Post-Sec.
1000 N 4th St 52557 641-472-7000

**Farley, Dubuque, Pop. 1,531**
Western Dubuque Community SD 2,900/PK-12
PO Box 68 52046 563-744-3885
Rick Colpitts, supt. Fax 744-3093
www.wdbqschools.org
Drexler Middle IS 700/5-8
PO Box 279 52046 563-744-3371
Mary Jane Maher, prin. Fax 744-3711
Other Schools – See Cascade, Epworth

---

Seton Catholic - St. Joseph S 100/6-8
PO Box 249 52046 563-744-3290
Mary Smock, prin. Fax 744-3450

**Farmington, Van Buren, Pop. 661**
Harmony Community SD
Supt. — See Bonaparte
Harmony JSHS 100/6-12
33727 Route J40 52626 319-592-3192
Stephanie Vititoe, prin. Fax 592-3135

**Farragut, Fremont, Pop. 484**
Nishnabotna SD
Supt. — See Hamburg
Nishnabotna JSHS 100/6-12
PO Box 36 51639 712-385-8131
Dr. Lisa Spencer, prin. Fax 385-8135

**Fayette, Fayette, Pop. 1,319**

---

Upper Iowa University Post-Sec.
PO Box 1857 52142 563-425-5200

**Fenton, Kossuth, Pop. 279**
North Union SD 300/PK-12
PO Box 109 50539 515-868-3590
Matthew Berninghaus, supt. Fax 889-2264
www.northunion.k12.ia.us
Other Schools – See Armstrong, Swea City

**Fontanelle, Adair, Pop. 671**
Nodaway Valley Community SD
Supt. — See Greenfield
Nodaway Valley MS 200/5-8
112 S 1st St 50846 641-745-2291
Lanny Kliefoth, prin. Fax 745-3501

**Forest City, Winnebago, Pop. 4,101**
Forest City Community SD 1,200/PK-12
PO Box 270 50436 641-585-2323
Darwin Lehmann, supt. Fax 585-5218
www.forestcity.k12.ia.us
Forest City HS 400/9-12
206 W School St 50436 641-585-2324
Ken Baker, prin. Fax 585-3034
Forest City MS 300/6-8
216 W School St 50436 641-585-4772
Zach Dillavou, prin. Fax 585-3432

---

Forest City Christian S 50/PK-12
305 Walnut St 50436 641-585-3233
Ivon Tokheim, admin. Fax 585-3233
Waldorf College Post-Sec.
106 S 6th St 50436 800-292-1903

**Fort Dodge, Webster, Pop. 24,736**
Fort Dodge Community SD 3,000/PK-12
104 S 17th St 50501 515-576-1161
Dr. Douglas Van Zyl, supt. Fax 576-1988
www.fort-dodge.k12.ia.us
Fort Dodge HS 1,100/9-12
819 N 25th St 50501 515-955-1770
David Keane, prin. Fax 955-3374
Willard Alternative Education HS 50/Alt
819 N 25th St 50501 515-576-7305
David Keane, prin. Fax 576-7305

---

Iowa Central Community College Post-Sec.
1 Triton Cir 50501 515-576-7201
La' James International College Post-Sec.
2419 5th Ave S 50501 515-576-3119
St. Edmond HS 400/6-12
501 N 22nd St 50501 515-955-5850
Linda Mitchell, prin. Fax 955-3569

**Fort Madison, Lee, Pop. 10,836**
Fort Madison Community SD 1,700/PK-12
PO Box 1423 52627 319-372-7252
Kenneth Marang, supt. Fax 372-7255
www.fmcsd.org
Fort Madison HS 600/9-12
2001 Avenue B 52627 319-372-1862
Greg Smith, prin. Fax 372-1325
Fort Madison MS 500/4-8
502 48th St 52627 319-372-4687
Todd Dirth, prin. Fax 372-0378

---

Holy Trinity HS 200/7-12
2600 Avenue A 52627 319-372-2486
Michael Sheerin, prin. Fax 372-6310

**Fredericksburg, Chickasaw, Pop. 923**
Sumner-Fredericksburg Community SD
Supt. — See Sumner
Sumner-Fredericksburg MS 200/6-8
401 E High St 50630 563-237-5334
Jill Glenn, prin. Fax 237-6329

**Garden Grove, Decatur, Pop. 208**
Mormon Trail Community SD
Supt. — See Humeston
Mormon Trail JSHS 100/7-12
PO Box 177 50103 641-443-3425
Steve Hunt, prin. Fax 443-2644

**Garnavillo, Clayton, Pop. 742**
Clayton Ridge Community SD
Supt. — See Guttenberg
Clayton Ridge MS 200/5-8
PO Box 9 52049 563-964-2321
Shane Wahls, prin. Fax 964-2756

**Garner, Hancock, Pop. 3,097**
Garner-Hayfield-Ventura Community SD 800/PK-12
PO Box 449 50438 641-923-2718
Tyler Williams, supt. Fax 923-3825
www.garner.k12.ia.us
Garner-Hayfield-Ventura HS 300/9-12
PO Box 449 50438 641-923-2632
Jim Haag, prin. Fax 923-4005
Other Schools – See Ventura

**Garwin, Tama, Pop. 518**
GMG Community SD 500/PK-12
306 Park St 50632 641-499-2239
Ben Petty, supt. Fax 499-2159
www.garwin.k12.ia.us
GMG JSHS 200/7-12
306 Park St 50632 641-499-2005
Mark Polich, prin. Fax 499-2552

**George, Lyon, Pop. 1,076**
George-Little Rock Community SD 500/PK-12
PO Box 6 51237 712-475-3311
Steve Barber, supt. Fax 475-3574
george-littlerock.org/
George-Little Rock HS 100/9-12
PO Box 6 51237 712-475-3311
Kevin Range, prin. Fax 475-6573
Other Schools – See Little Rock

**Gilbert, Story, Pop. 1,068**
Gilbert Community SD 1,300/PK-12
103 Mathews Dr 50105 515-232-3740
Lindsey Beecher, supt. Fax 827-5400
www.gilbert.k12.ia.us
Gilbert HS 400/9-12
312 Gretten St 50105 515-232-3738
Layne Billings, prin. Fax 827-1298
Gilbert MS 400/6-8
201 E Mathews Dr 50105 515-232-0540
Chris Billings, prin. Fax 827-7420

**Gilbertville, Black Hawk, Pop. 708**

---

Don Bosco HS 200/9-12
405 16th Ave 50634 319-296-1692
Rick Blackwell, prin. Fax 296-1693
Immaculate Conception S 200/3-8
311 16th Ave 50634 319-296-1089
Sharon Mayer, prin. Fax 296-3847

**Gilman, Marshall, Pop. 508**
East Marshall Community SD 800/PK-12
PO Box 159 50106 641-498-7481
Dianne Anderson, supt. Fax 498-2035
www.e-marshall.k12.ia.us
East Marshall MS 300/4-8
PO Box 159 50106 641-498-7483
Robert Schelp, prin. Fax 498-2180
Other Schools – See Le Grand

**Glenwood, Mills, Pop. 5,209**
Glenwood Community SD 2,100/PK-12
103 Central St Ste 300 51534 712-527-9034
Devin Embray, supt. Fax 527-4287
www.glenwoodschools.org
Glenwood HS 700/9-12
504 Sharp St 51534 712-527-4897
Richard Hutchinson, prin. Fax 527-9554
Glenwood MS 400/6-8
400 Sivers Rd 51534 712-527-4887
Heidi Stanley, prin. Fax 527-3411

**Glidden, Carroll, Pop. 1,142**
Glidden-Ralston Community SD 400/PK-12
PO Box 488 51443 712-659-3411
Kreg Lensch, supt. Fax 659-2248
www.glidden-ralston.k12.ia.us
Glidden-Ralston JSHS 200/7-12
PO Box 488 51443 712-659-2205
Dirk Troutman, prin. Fax 659-2248

**Goose Lake, Clinton, Pop. 238**
Northeast Community SD 800/PK-12
PO Box 66 52750 563-577-2249
James Cox, supt. Fax 577-2450
www.northeast.k12.ia.us
Northeast MSHS 500/6-12
PO Box 70 52750 563-577-2249
Alicia Christiansen, prin. Fax 577-2248

**Gowrie, Webster, Pop. 1,027**
Prairie Valley Community SD 700/PK-12
PO Box 49 50543 515-352-5575
Lois Irwin, supt. Fax 352-5573
www.prairievalley.k12.ia.us
Southeast Valley HS 300/7-12
PO Box 49 50543 515-352-3142
Jim Henrich, prin. Fax 352-3143

**Graettinger, Palo Alto, Pop. 839**
Graettinger-Terril Community SD 200/PK-12
PO Box 58 51342 712-859-3286
Andrew Woiwood, supt. Fax 859-3509
www.gtschools.k12.ia.us/
Graettinger-Terril MSHS 100/6-12
PO Box 58 51342 712-859-3286
Jeremy Simington, prin. Fax 859-3509

**Granger, Dallas, Pop. 1,237**
Woodward-Granger Community SD 1,100/PK-12
1904 State St 50109 515-999-8022
Brad Anderson, supt. Fax 999-8025
www.woodward-granger.k12.ia.us
Other Schools – See Woodward

**Greene, Butler, Pop. 1,121**
North Butler Community SD
Supt. — See Allison
North Butler JSHS 200/7-12
PO Box 190 50636 641-816-5631
Dan Huff, prin. Fax 816-5921

**Greenfield, Adair, Pop. 1,975**
Nodaway Valley Community SD 700/PK-12
410 NW 2nd St 50849 641-743-6127
Casey Berlau, supt. Fax 343-7173
www.nodawayvalley.org/
Nodaway Valley HS 200/9-12
410 NW 2nd St 50849 641-743-6141
Lanny Kliefoth, prin. Fax 343-7040
Other Schools – See Fontanelle

**Grimes, Polk, Pop. 8,166**
Dallas Center-Grimes Community SD
Supt. — See Dallas Center
Dallas Center-Grimes Community HS 400/10-12
2555 W 1st St 50111 515-986-9747
Cary Justmann, prin. Fax 986-9734
Dallas Center-Grimes Meadows 8-9
2555 W 1st St Ste 200 50111 515-986-0105
Lori Phillips, prin. Fax 986-3155

**Grinnell, Poweshiek, Pop. 9,024**
Grinnell-Newburg Community SD 1,800/PK-12
1333 Sunset St 50112 641-236-2700
Todd Abrahamson, supt. Fax 236-2699
www.grinnell-k12.org
Grinnell Community HS 600/9-12
1333 Sunset St 50112 641-236-2720
Kevin Seney, prin. Fax 236-2692
Grinnell Community MS 500/5-8
132 East St S 50112 641-236-2750
Sara Hegg-Dunne, prin. Fax 236-2732

---

Grinnell College Post-Sec.
PO Box 805 50112 641-269-4000

**Griswold, Cass, Pop. 1,029**
Griswold Community SD 600/PK-12
PO Box 280 51535 712-778-2152
Dana Kunze, supt. Fax 778-4145
www.griswoldschools.org/
Griswold MSHS 300/6-12
PO Box 280 51535 712-778-2154
T. J. Dunphy, prin. Fax 778-2161

**Grundy Center, Grundy, Pop. 2,679**
Grundy Center Community SD 500/PK-12
1301 12th St 50638 319-825-5418
Jerry Schutz, supt. Fax 825-5419
www.spartanpride.net
Grundy Center MSHS 200/5-12
1006 M Ave 50638 319-825-5449
Dr. Ann Lebo, prin. Fax 825-6415

**Guthrie Center, Guthrie, Pop. 1,559**
Guthrie Center Community SD 600/PK-12
906 School St 50115 641-332-2972
Steve Smith, supt. Fax 332-2973
www.guthrie.k12.ia.us
Guthrie Center HS 200/9-12
906 School St 50115 641-332-2236
Garold Thomas, prin. Fax 332-2973
Guthrie Center JHS 100/7-8
906 School St 50115 641-332-2236
Shane Arp, prin. Fax 332-2973

**Guttenberg, Clayton, Pop. 1,910**
Clayton Ridge Community SD 600/PK-12
PO Box 520 52052 563-252-2341
Shane Wahls, supt. Fax 252-2656
www.claytonridge.k12.ia.us
Clayton Ridge HS 200/9-12
PO Box 520 52052 563-252-2342
Andy Peterson, prin. Fax 252-2656
Other Schools – See Garnavillo

**Hamburg, Fremont, Pop. 1,176**
Nishnabotna SD 400/PK-12
309 S St 51640 712-382-2703
Dr. Mike Wells, supt. Fax 382-1922
www.nishbd.org/
Other Schools – See Farragut

**Hampton, Franklin, Pop. 4,420**
Hampton-Dumont Community SD 1,200/PK-12
601 12th Ave NE 50441 641-456-2175
Todd Lettow, supt. Fax 456-5750
www.hampton-dumont.k12.ia.us/
Hampton-Dumont HS 400/9-12
101 12th Ave NW 50441 641-456-4893
Steve Madson, prin. Fax 456-4569
Hampton-Dumont MS 400/4-8
601 12th Ave NE 50441 641-456-4735
Anthony Spradlin, prin. Fax 456-2023

**Harlan, Shelby, Pop. 5,057**
Harlan Community SD 1,600/PK-12
2102 Durant St 51537 712-755-2152
Justin Wagner, supt. Fax 755-7312
www.harlan.k12.ia.us
Harlan Community HS 500/9-12
2102 Durant St 51537 712-755-3101
John Connell, prin. Fax 755-7705
Harlan Community MS 400/6-8
2108 Durant St 51537 712-755-3196
Bill Mueller, prin. Fax 755-3699

**Hartley, O'Brien, Pop. 1,644**
Hartley-Melvin-Sanborn Community SD 600/PK-12
300 N 8th Ave W 51346 712-928-3406
Bill Thompson, supt. Fax 928-3536
www.hartley-ms.k12.ia.us
Hartley-Melvin-Sanborn HS 200/9-12
PO Box 206 51346 712-928-3406
Rusty Shockley, prin. Fax 928-2152
Other Schools – See Sanborn

**Hastings, Mills, Pop. 151**
East Mills Community SD 300/PK-12
58962 380th St 51540 712-624-8700
Paul Croghan, supt. Fax 624-8279
www.emschools.org
East Mills Learning Center 50/Alt
58962 380th St 51540 712-624-8696
Paul Croghan, supt. Fax 624-8279
Other Schools – See Malvern

**Hawarden, Sioux, Pop. 2,534**
West Sioux Community SD 600/PK-12
1300 Falcon Dr 51023 712-551-1461
Randy Collins, supt. Fax 551-1367
www.westsiouxschools.org/
West Sioux HS 200/9-12
1300 Falcon Dr 51023 712-551-1181
Ryan Kramer, prin. Fax 551-1514
West Sioux MS 100/6-8
1300 Falcon Dr 51023 712-551-1022
Ryan Kramer, prin. Fax 551-1367

**Hinton, Plymouth, Pop. 925**
Hinton Community SD 700/PK-12
PO Box 128 51024 712-947-4329
Pete Stuerman, supt. Fax 947-4427
www.hintonschool.com/
Hinton HS 200/9-12
PO Box 128 51024 712-947-4328
Betty Wendt, prin. Fax 947-4427
Hinton MS 300/4-8
PO Box 128 51024 712-947-4328
Brian DeJong, prin. Fax 947-4947

**Holstein, Ida, Pop. 1,384**
Galva-Holstein Community SD 500/PK-12
PO Box 320 51025 712-368-4353
Jon Wiebers, supt. Fax 368-4843
www.rvraptors.org/
Ridge View HS 200/9-12
PO Box 320 51025 712-368-4353
Bret Warnke, prin. Fax 368-4843

**Holy Cross, Dubuque, Pop. 372**

LaSalle Catholic S - Holy Cross Center 100/4-8
PO Box 368 52053 563-870-2405
Susan Hucker, prin. Fax 870-4101

**Hubbard, Hardin, Pop. 843**
Hubbard-Radcliffe Community SD 400/PK-8
PO Box 129 50122 641-864-2211
Patricia Heinz, supt. Fax 864-2422
www.hubbard.k12.ia.us
South Hardin MS 200/6-8
PO Box 129 50122 641-864-2211
Duane Harding, prin. Fax 864-2422

**Hudson, Black Hawk, Pop. 2,275**
Hudson Community SD 600/K-12
PO Box 240 50643 319-988-3233
Dr. Anthony Voss, supt. Fax 988-3235
hudsonpiratepride.com
Hudson JSHS 200/7-12
PO Box 240 50643 319-988-4226
Jeff Dieken, prin. Fax 988-4174

**Hull, Sioux, Pop. 2,161**
Boyden-Hull Community SD 600/K-12
PO Box 678 51239 712-439-2711
Steve Grond, supt. Fax 439-1419
www.boyden-hull.k12.ia.us
Boyden-Hull JSHS 300/7-12
PO Box 678 51239 712-439-2440
Dan Pottebaum, prin. Fax 439-1419

Western Christian HS 300/9-12
PO Box 658 51239 712-439-1013
Dan Barkel, prin. Fax 439-1407

**Humboldt, Humboldt, Pop. 4,652**
Humboldt Community SD
Supt. — See Dakota City
Humboldt HS 500/9-12
1500 Wildcat Rd 50548 515-332-1430
Lori Westhoff, prin. Fax 332-7150
Humboldt MS 300/5-8
1400 Wildcat Rd 50548 515-332-2812
Brenda Geitzenauer, prin. Fax 332-2023

**Humeston, Wayne, Pop. 485**
Mormon Trail Community SD 200/PK-12
PO Box 156 50123 641-877-2521
Lorna Paxson, supt. Fax 877-3400
www.mormontrailcsd.org/
Other Schools – See Garden Grove

**Huxley, Story, Pop. 3,264**
Ballard Community SD 1,600/PK-12
PO Box 307 50124 515-597-2811
Herman Maxey, supt. Fax 597-2965
www.ballard.k12.ia.us/
Ballard Community HS 500/9-12
PO Box 307 50124 515-597-2971
John Ronca, prin. Fax 597-2964
Ballard Community MS 400/6-8
PO Box 307 50124 515-597-2815
Thomas Maher, prin. Fax 597-2818

**Ida Grove, Ida, Pop. 2,129**
Odebolt-Arthur/Battle Creek-Ida Grove SD 900/PK-12
900 John Montgomery Dr 51445 712-364-3687
Terry Kenealy, supt. Fax 364-3609
www.oabcig.org
Odebolt-Arthur/Battle Creek-Ida Grove HS 300/9-12
900 John Montgomery Dr 51445 712-364-3371
Patrick Miller, prin. Fax 364-4463
Other Schools – See Odebolt

**Independence, Buchanan, Pop. 5,911**
Independence Community SD 1,300/PK-12
1207 1st St W 50644 319-334-7400
Jean Peterson, supt. Fax 334-7404
www.independence.k12.ia.us/
Independence JSHS 600/7-12
700 20th Ave SW 50644 319-334-7405
John Howard, prin. Fax 332-1296

**Indianola, Warren, Pop. 14,597**
Indianola Community SD 3,500/PK-12
1304 E 2nd Ave 50125 515-961-9500
Art Sathoff, supt. Fax 961-9505
www.indianola.k12.ia.us
Indianola HS 1,000/9-12
1304 E 1st Ave 50125 515-961-9510
Craig Calhoun, prin. Fax 961-9519
Indianola MS 800/6-8
403 S 15th St 50125 515-961-9530
Annette Jauron, prin. Fax 961-9535

Simpson College Post-Sec.
701 N C St 50125 515-961-6251

**Inwood, Lyon, Pop. 809**
West Lyon Community SD 900/PK-12
1787 Iowa 182 Ave 51240 712-753-4917
Jim Hargens, supt. Fax 753-4928
www.wlwildcats.org
West Lyon HS 200/9-12
1787 Iowa 182 Ave 51240 712-753-4917
Doug Jiskoot, prin. Fax 753-4928
West Lyon JHS 100/7-8
1787 Iowa 182 Ave 51240 712-753-4917
Doug Jiskoot, prin. Fax 753-4928

**Iowa City, Johnson, Pop. 66,297**
Iowa City Community SD 12,000/PK-12
1725 N Dodge St 52245 319-688-1000
Stephen Murley, supt. Fax 688-1009
www.iowacityschools.org
Iowa City HS 1,400/9-12
1900 Morningside Dr 52245 319-688-1040
John Bacon, prin. Fax 688-1049
Southeast JHS 700/7-8
2501 Bradford Dr 52240 319-688-1070
Amber Boyd, prin. Fax 688-1079
Tate HS 200/Alt
1528 Mall Dr 52240 319-688-1080
Ann Browning, prin. Fax 688-1089
West HS 1,900/9-12
2901 Melrose Ave 52246 319-688-1050
Gregg Shoultz Ph.D., prin. Fax 688-1059
Other Schools – See Coralville, North Liberty

La' James International College Post-Sec.
227 E Market St 52245 319-337-2109
Regina HS 400/7-12
2150 Rochester Ave 52245 319-338-5436
Glenn Plummer, prin. Fax 887-3817
University of Iowa Post-Sec.
107 Calvin Hall 52242 319-335-3500

**Iowa Falls, Hardin, Pop. 5,192**
Iowa Falls Community SD 1,100/PK-12
710 North St 50126 641-648-6400
Dr. John Robbins, supt. Fax 648-6401
www.ifacadets.net
Iowa Falls - Alden HS 400/9-12
1903 Taylor Ave 50126 641-648-6440
Clyde Tarrence, prin. Fax 648-3222
Riverbend MS 200/7-8
1124 Union St 50126 641-648-6430
Jeff Burchfield, prin. Fax 648-6432

Ellsworth Community College Post-Sec.
1100 College Ave 50126 800-322-9235

**Janesville, Bremer, Pop. 923**
Janesville Consolidated SD 300/PK-12
PO Box 478 50647 319-987-2581
B.J. Meaney, supt. Fax 987-2824
www.janesville.k12.ia.us
Janesville JSHS 100/6-12
PO Box 478 50647 319-987-2581
Jen Poock, prin. Fax 987-2824

**Jefferson, Greene, Pop. 4,314**
Greene County Community SD 1,000/PK-12
204 W Madison St 50129 515-386-4168
Tim Christensen, supt. Fax 386-3591
www.jefferson-scranton.k12.ia.us
Greene County HS 300/9-12
101 Ram Dr 50129 515-386-2188
Brian Phillips, prin. Fax 386-2159
Greene County MS 200/7-8
203 W Harrison St 50129 515-386-8126
Shawn Zanders, prin. Fax 386-4412

**Jesup, Buchanan, Pop. 2,492**
Jesup Community SD 900/PK-12
PO Box 287 50648 319-827-1700
Nathan Marting, supt. Fax 827-3905
www.jesup.k12.ia.us
Jesup HS 200/9-12
PO Box 287 50648 319-827-1700
Rodney Chamberlin, prin. Fax 827-3905
Jesup MS 200/5-8
PO Box 287 50648 319-827-1700
Lisa Loecher, prin. Fax 827-3905

**Jewell, Hamilton, Pop. 1,204**
South Hamilton Community SD 700/PK-12
315 Division St 50130 515-827-5479
Kenneth Howard, supt. Fax 827-5368
www.s-hamilton.k12.ia.us
South Hamilton MSHS 300/7-12
315 Division St 50130 515-827-5418
W. Scott Dryer, prin. Fax 827-5368

**Johnston, Polk, Pop. 17,014**
Johnston Community SD 6,300/PK-12
PO Box 10 50131 515-278-0470
Dr. Corey Lunn, supt. Fax 278-5884
www.johnston.k12.ia.us
Johnston HS 1,300/10-12
PO Box 10 50131 515-278-0449
Ryan Woods, prin. Fax 276-5795
Johnston MS 1,000/8-9
PO Box 10 50131 515-278-0476
Brent Riessen, prin. Fax 278-0130

La' James International College Post-Sec.
8805 Chambery Blvd 50131 515-278-2208

**Kalona, Washington, Pop. 2,347**
Mid-Prairie Community SD
Supt. — See Wellman
Mid-Prairie MS 300/6-8
713 F Ave 52247 319-656-2241
Marc Pennington, prin. Fax 656-2207

Iowa Mennonite HS 100/9-12
1421 540th St SW 52247 319-656-2586
Tim Lehman, prin. Fax 656-2073
Shiloh University Post-Sec.
100 Shiloh Dr 52247 319-656-2447

**Kanawha, Hancock, Pop. 646**
West Hancock Community SD
Supt. — See Britt
West Hancock MS 200/5-8
PO Box 130 50447 641-762-3261
Ruth Verbrugge, prin. Fax 843-4717

**Keokuk, Lee, Pop. 10,499**
Keokuk Community SD 1,500/PK-12
1721 Franklin St 52632 319-524-1402
Tim Hood, supt. Fax 524-1114
www.keokukschools.org
Keokuk HS 700/9-12
2285 Middle Rd 52632 319-524-2542
Zach Wigle, prin. Fax 524-1784
Keokuk MS 400/6-8
2002 Orleans Ave 52632 319-524-3737
Brad McCloskey, prin. Fax 524-1511

Southeastern Community College Post-Sec.
PO Box 6007 52632 319-524-3221

**Keosauqua, Van Buren, Pop. 1,003**
Van Buren Community SD 600/PK-12
503 Henry St 52565 319-293-3334
Dr. Pam Ewell, supt. Fax 293-3301
www.van-buren.k12.ia.us
Van Buren Community JSHS 200/7-12
405 4th St 52565 319-293-3183
Chuck Banks, prin. Fax 293-3345

**Keota, Keokuk, Pop. 998**
Keota Community SD 300/PK-12
PO Box 88 52248 641-636-2189
Mark Schneider, supt. Fax 636-3009
www.keota.k12.ia.us/
Keota JSHS 100/7-12
PO Box 88 52248 641-636-3491
Nathan Carlson, prin. Fax 636-2210

**Kingsley, Plymouth, Pop. 1,392**
Kingsley-Pierson Community SD 500/K-12
PO Box 520 51028 712-378-2861
Scott Bailey, supt. Fax 378-3729
www.k-pcsd.org
Kingsley-Pierson HS 100/9-12
PO Box 520 51028 712-378-2861
Scott Bailey, prin. Fax 378-3729
Other Schools – See Pierson

**Knoxville, Marion, Pop. 7,242**
Knoxville Community SD 1,300/PK-12
309 W Main St 50138 641-842-6551
Cassi Murra, supt. Fax 842-2109
www.knoxville.k12.ia.us
Knoxville HS 600/9-12
1811 W Madison St 50138 641-842-2173
Tracy Wilkins, prin. Fax 842-2066
Knoxville MS 400/6-8
102 N Lincoln St 50138 641-842-3315
Brian McNeill, prin. Fax 842-5754

**Lake City, Calhoun, Pop. 1,715**
South Central Calhoun Community SD
Supt. — See Rockwell City
South Central Calhoun HS 300/9-12
PO Box 45 51449 712-464-7211
Randy Martin, prin. Fax 464-1012

**Lake Mills, Winnebago, Pop. 2,090**
Lake Mills Community SD 700/PK-12
102 S 4th Ave E 50450 641-592-0881
Chad Kohagen, supt. Fax 592-0883
www.lake-mills.org
Lake Mills HS 200/9-12
102 S 4th Ave E 50450 641-592-0893
James Scholbrock, prin. Fax 592-0883
Lake Mills MS 200/6-8
102 S 4th Ave E 50450 641-592-0894
James Scholbrock, prin. Fax 592-0883

**Lake Park, Dickinson, Pop. 1,094**
Harris-Lake Park Community SD 400/PK-12
PO Box 8 51347 712-832-3809
Dennis Peters, supt. Fax 832-3812
www.harris-lp.k12.ia.us
Harris-Lake Park MSHS 200/6-12
PO Box 8 51347 712-832-3809
Travis Popken, prin. Fax 832-3812

**Lake View, Sac, Pop. 1,137**
East Sac County SD 1,000/PK-12
PO Box 110 51450 712-665-5000
Barb Kruthoff, supt. Fax 665-5021
www.eastsac.k12.ia.us/
East Sac County HS 300/9-12
PO Box 110 51450 712-665-5001
Kevin Litterer, prin. Fax 665-5022
Other Schools – See Sac City

**Lamoni, Decatur, Pop. 2,266**
Lamoni Community SD 400/PK-12
202 N Walnut St 50140 641-784-3342
Chris Coffelt, supt. Fax 784-6548
lamoni.k12.ia.us
Lamoni HS 100/9-12
202 N Walnut St 50140 641-784-3351
Andy Peterson, prin. Fax 784-6548
Lamoni MS 100/6-8
202 N Walnut St 50140 641-784-7299
Andy Peterson, prin. Fax 784-6548

Graceland University Post-Sec.
1 University Pl 50140 641-784-5000

**Lansing, Allamakee, Pop. 998**
Eastern Allamakee Community SD 400/PK-12
569 Center St 52151 563-538-4201
Dale Crozier, supt. Fax 538-4969
www.e-allamakee.k12.ia.us/
Kee HS 100/9-12
569 Center St 52151 563-538-4201
Mary Hogan, prin. Fax 538-4969
Lansing MS 100/6-8
569 Center St 52151 563-538-4201
Mary Hogan, prin. Fax 538-4969

**La Porte City, Black Hawk, Pop. 2,264**
Union Community SD 1,200/PK-12
200 Adams St 50651 319-342-2674
Neil Mullen, supt. Fax 342-2393
www.union.k12.ia.us/
Union HS 400/9-12
200 Adams St 50651 319-342-2697
Travis Fleshner, prin. Fax 342-2393
Other Schools – See Dysart

**Latimer, Franklin, Pop. 507**
CAL Community SD 300/PK-12
1441 Gull Ave 50452 641-579-6087
Steve Lane, supt. Fax 579-6408
www.cal.k12.ia.us
CAL HS 100/6-12
1441 Gull Ave 50452 641-579-6086
Scott Striegel, prin. Fax 579-6408

**Laurens, Pocahontas, Pop. 1,251**
Laurens-Marathon Community SD 300/PK-12
300 W Garfield St 50554 712-841-5000
Jeff Kruse, supt. Fax 841-5010
www.laurens-marathon.k12.ia.us
Laurens-Marathon HS 100/9-12
300 W Garfield St 50554 712-841-5000
Troy Oehlertz, prin. Fax 841-5010
Laurens-Marathon MS 100/6-8
300 W Garfield St 50554 712-841-5000
Troy Oehlertz, prin. Fax 841-5010

**Lawton, Woodbury, Pop. 902**
Lawton-Bronson Community SD 600/PK-12
100 Tara Way 51030 712-944-5183
Jeff Thelander, supt. Fax 944-5568
www.lb-eagles.org
Lawton JSHS 300/7-12
100 Tara Way 51030 712-944-5181
Rachel Leavitt, prin. Fax 944-5568

**Le Claire, Scott, Pop. 3,701**
Pleasant Valley Community SD
Supt. — See Bettendorf
Pleasant Valley JHS 600/7-8
3501 Wisconsin St 52753 563-332-0200
Trampus Budde, prin. Fax 332-0205

**Le Grand, Marshall, Pop. 933**
East Marshall Community SD
Supt. — See Gilman
East Marshall HS 300/9-12
PO Box A 50142 641-479-2785
Matthew Rasmusson, prin. Fax 479-2601

**Le Mars, Plymouth, Pop. 9,729**
Le Mars Community SD 2,100/PK-12
940 Lincoln St SW 51031 712-546-4155
Dr. Todd Wendt, supt. Fax 546-5934
www.lemars.k12.ia.us
Individualized Learning Center 50/Alt
940 Lincoln St SW 51031 712-546-5858
Dr. Mark Iverson, prin. Fax 546-5934
Le Mars HS 700/9-12
940 Lincoln St SW 51031 712-546-4153
Dr. Mark Iverson, prin. Fax 546-9581
Le Mars MS 500/6-8
940 Lincoln St SW 51031 712-546-7022
Steve Shanks, prin. Fax 546-7024

---

Gehlen Catholic HS 200/7-12
709 Plymouth St NE 51031 712-546-5126
Jeff Alesch, prin. Fax 546-9384

**Lenox, Taylor, Pop. 1,401**
Lenox Community SD 500/PK-12
600 S Locust St 50851 641-333-2244
David Henrichs, supt. Fax 333-2247
www.lenox.k12.ia.us
Lenox JSHS 200/7-12
600 S Locust St 50851 641-333-2244
Mike Still, prin. Fax 333-2247

**Leon, Decatur, Pop. 1,972**
Central Decatur Community SD 700/PK-12
1201 NE Poplar St 50144 641-446-4819
Chris Coffelt, supt. Fax 446-7990
www.centraldecatur.org
Central Decatur JSHS 300/7-12
1201 NE Poplar St 50144 641-446-4816
Rudy Evertsen, prin. Fax 446-7990

**Letts, Louisa, Pop. 371**
Louisa-Muscatine Community SD 900/PK-12
14478 170th St 52754 319-726-3541
Mike Van Sickle, supt. Fax 726-3334
www.lmcsd.org
Louisa-Muscatine JSHS 300/7-12
14354 170th St 52754 319-726-3421
Chris Parkhurst, prin. Fax 726-3649

**Liberty Center, Warren**
Southeast Warren Community SD 500/PK-12
PO Box 19 50145 641-466-3510
Delane Galvin, supt. Fax 466-3525
www.se-warren.k12.ia.us
Southeast Warren JSHS 200/7-12
PO Box 19 50145 641-466-3331
Delane Galvin, prin. Fax 466-3525

**Lisbon, Linn, Pop. 2,132**
Lisbon Community SD 600/PK-12
PO Box 839 52253 319-455-2075
Patrick Hocking, supt. Fax 455-2733
www.lisbon.k12.ia.us
Lisbon HS 200/9-12
PO Box 839 52253 319-455-2106
Ian Dye, prin. Fax 455-3208
Lisbon MS 100/7-8
PO Box 839 52253 319-455-2659
Ian Dye, prin. Fax 455-2733

**Little Rock, Lyon, Pop. 458**
George-Little Rock Community SD
Supt. — See George
George-Little Rock MS 100/6-8
PO Box 247 51243 712-479-2771
Molly Schilling, prin. Fax 479-2770

**Logan, Harrison, Pop. 1,523**
Logan-Magnolia Community SD 700/PK-12
1200 N 2nd Ave 51546 712-644-2250
Tom Ridder, supt. Fax 644-2934
www.lomaschools.org
Logan-Magnolia JSHS 300/7-12
1200 N 2nd Ave 51546 712-644-2250
Christi Gochenour, prin. Fax 644-2934

**Lone Tree, Johnson, Pop. 1,281**
Lone Tree Community SD 500/PK-12
PO Box 520 52755 319-629-4212
Michael Reeves, supt. Fax 629-4324
www.lone-tree.k12.ia.us
Lone Tree JSHS 300/6-12
PO Box 520 52755 319-629-4610
Amber Jacque, prin. Fax 629-4324

**Mc Gregor, Clayton, Pop. 856**
MFL MarMac Community SD
Supt. — See Monona
MFL MarMac MS 200/4-8
PO Box 504 52157 563-873-3463
Denise Mueller, prin. Fax 873-2371

**Madrid, Boone, Pop. 2,521**
Madrid Community SD 700/K-12
201 N Main St 50156 515-795-1400
Brian Horn, supt. Fax 795-2121
madrid.k12.ia.us
Madrid HS 200/9-12
599 N Kennedy Ave 50156 515-795-3240
Kevin Williams, prin. Fax 795-4408
Madrid JHS 100/7-8
599 N Kennedy Ave 50156 515-795-3240
Kevin Williams, prin. Fax 795-4408

**Malvern, Mills, Pop. 1,127**
East Mills Community SD
Supt. — See Hastings
East Mills JSHS 200/7-12
1505 E 15th St 51551 712-624-8645
Linda Rempe, prin. Fax 624-8124

**Manchester, Delaware, Pop. 5,134**
West Delaware County Community SD 1,500/PK-12
701 New St 52057 563-927-3515
Dr. Kristen Rickey, supt. Fax 927-2785
www.w-delaware.k12.ia.us
West Delaware HS 500/9-12
605 New St 52057 563-927-3515
Tim Felderman, prin. Fax 927-6222
West Delaware MS 500/5-8
1101 Doctor St 52057 563-927-3515
Lisa Wunn, prin. Fax 927-9115

**Manly, Worth, Pop. 1,311**
Central Springs Community SD 800/PK-12
PO Box 190 50456 641-454-2211
Steve Ward, supt. Fax 454-2212
www.centralsprings.net/
Central Springs HS 300/9-12
PO Box 190 50456 641-454-2208
Ken Estes, prin. Fax 454-2212
Other Schools – See Nora Springs

**Manning, Carroll, Pop. 1,493**
IKM-Manning Community SD 800/PK-12
209 10th St 51455 712-655-3781
Thomas Ward, supt. Fax 655-3311
www.ikm-manning.k12.ia.us/
IKM-Manning HS 200/9-12
209 10th St 51455 712-655-3781
Brian Wall, prin. Fax 655-3311
IKM-Manning MS 200/4-8
209 10th St 51455 712-655-3761
Sharon Whitson, prin. Fax 654-9282

**Manson, Calhoun, Pop. 1,685**
Manson Northwest Webster Community SD 800/PK-12
PO Box 387 50563 712-469-2202
Mark Egli, supt. Fax 469-2298
www.mnwcougars.com
Manson Northwest Webster MSHS 400/7-12
1601 15th St 50563 712-469-2245
Kevin Wood, prin. Fax 469-3131

**Mapleton, Monona, Pop. 1,204**
Maple Valley-Anthon Oto Community SD 700/PK-12
501 S 7th St 51034 712-881-1315
Steve Oberg, supt. Fax 881-1316
www.mvaoschool.com
Maple Valley-Anthon Oto HS 300/9-12
501 S 7th St 51034 712-881-1317
Dan Dougherty, prin. Fax 881-1321
Other Schools – See Anthon

**Maquoketa, Jackson, Pop. 5,978**
Maquoketa Community SD 1,500/PK-12
612 S Vermont St 52060 563-652-4984
Chris Hoover, supt. Fax 652-6958
www.maquoketa.k12.ia.us
Maquoketa HS 600/9-12
600 Washington St 52060 563-652-2451
Mark Vervaecke, prin. Fax 652-5324
Maquoketa MS 300/6-8
200 E Locust St 52060 563-652-4956
Christine Snell, prin. Fax 652-6885

**Marcus, Cherokee, Pop. 1,110**
Marcus-Meriden-Cleghorn Community SD 400/PK-12
PO Box 667 51035 712-376-4171
Jan Brandhorst, supt. Fax 376-4302
www.mmccsd.org
Marcus-Meriden-Cleghorn Community HS 200/7-12
PO Box 667 51035 712-376-4172
Jason Toenges, prin. Fax 376-4302

**Marengo, Iowa, Pop. 2,516**
Iowa Valley Community SD 600/PK-12
359 E Hilton St 52301 319-642-7714
Donita Joens, supt. Fax 642-3023
www.iowa-valley.k12.ia.us
Iowa Valley JSHS 300/7-12
359 E Hilton St 52301 319-642-3332
Shawn Kreman, prin. Fax 642-3023

**Marion, Linn, Pop. 34,170**
Linn-Mar Community SD 6,700/PK-12
2999 N 10th St 52302 319-447-3000
Quintin Shepherd Ph.D., supt. Fax 377-9252
www.linnmar.k12.ia.us/
Excelsior MS 800/6-8
3555 10th St 52302 319-447-3130
John Christian, prin. Fax 373-4930
Linn-Mar HS 1,800/9-12
3111 10th St 52302 319-447-3040
Jeffrey Gustason Ph.D., prin. Fax 377-0486
Oak Ridge MS 700/6-8
4901 Alburnett Rd 52302 319-447-3410
Erica Rausch, prin. Fax 373-3222

Marion ISD 1,700/PK-12
PO Box 606 52302 319-377-4691
Joseph Chris Dyer, supt. Fax 377-4692
www.marion-isd.org
Marion HS 600/9-12
675 S 15th St 52302 319-377-9891
Greg Semler, prin. Fax 377-7621
Vernon MS 500/5-8
1350 4th Ave 52302 319-377-9401
Phillip Cochran, prin. Fax 377-7670

**Marshalltown, Marshall, Pop. 27,096**
Marshalltown Community SD 5,100/PK-12
1002 S 3rd Ave 50158 641-754-1000
Dr. Marvin Wade, supt. Fax 754-1003
www.marshalltown.k12.ia.us
Marshalltown HS 1,600/9-12
1602 S 2nd Ave 50158 641-754-1130
Jacquline Wyant, prin. Fax 754-1136
Miller MS 700/7-8
125 S 11th St 50158 641-754-1110
Jacy Large, prin. Fax 754-1115

---

Iowa School of Beauty Post-Sec.
112 Nicholas Dr 50158 641-752-4223
Marshalltown Community College Post-Sec.
3700 S Center St 50158 641-752-7106

**Martensdale, Warren, Pop. 462**
Martensdale-St. Marys Community SD 500/PK-12
PO Box 350 50160 641-764-2466
Tom Wood, supt. Fax 764-2100
www.mstm.us/
Martensdale-St. Marys JSHS 200/7-12
PO Box 350 50160 641-764-2486
Josh Moser, prin. Fax 764-2100

**Mason City, Cerro Gordo, Pop. 27,653**
Mason City Community SD 3,600/PK-12
1515 S Pennsylvania Ave 50401 641-421-4400
Anita Micich, supt. Fax 421-4448
www.masoncityschools.org
Adams MS 600/7-8
29 S Illinois Ave 50401 641-421-4420
Jerry Siglin, prin. Fax 421-4476
Alternative HS 100/Alt
19 N Illinois Ave 50401 641-421-4426
David Ciccetti, prin. Fax 421-3362
Mason City HS 1,100/9-12
1700 4th St SE 50401 641-421-4431
Dan Long, prin. Fax 421-4523

---

Kaplan University Post-Sec.
2570 4th St SW 50401 641-423-2530
La' James College Post-Sec.
24 2nd St NE 50401 641-424-2161
Newman HS 200/9-12
2445 19th St SW 50401 641-423-6939
Tony Adams, prin. Fax 423-6653
North Iowa Area Community College Post-Sec.
500 College Dr 50401 641-423-1264
North Iowa Christian S 50/K-12
811 N Kentucky Ave 50401 641-423-6440
Janna Voss, admin. Fax 423-6440
North Iowa Mercy Health Center Post-Sec.
1000 4th St SW 50401 641-422-7722
World Wide College of Auctioneering Post-Sec.
PO Box 949 50402 800-423-5242

**Massena, Cass, Pop. 355**
CAM Community SD
Supt. — See Anita
CAM MS 100/6-8
207 E 6th St 50853 712-779-2212
Larry Hunt, prin. Fax 779-3365

**Maxwell, Story, Pop. 916**
Collins-Maxwell Community SD — 500/PK-12
400 Metcalf St 50161 — 515-387-1115
Jason Ellingson, supt. — Fax 387-8842
www.collins-maxwell.k12.ia.us
Collins-Maxwell MSHS — 300/6-12
400 Metcalf St 50161 — 515-387-1115
Jordan Nelson, prin. — Fax 387-8842

**Maynard, Fayette, Pop. 516**
West Central Community SD — 300/PK-12
PO Box 54 50655 — 563-637-2283
Rick Pederson, supt. — Fax 637-2294
www.w-central.k12.ia.us/
West Central HS — 100/9-12
PO Box 54 50655 — 563-637-2283
Stuart Fuhs, prin. — Fax 637-2294

**Mediapolis, Des Moines, Pop. 1,547**
Mediapolis Community SD — 900/PK-12
PO Box 358 52637 — 319-394-3101
Greg Ray, supt. — Fax 394-3021
www.meposchools.org/
Mediapolis HS — 300/9-12
725 N Northfield St 52637 — 319-394-3101
Roger Thornburg, prin. — Fax 394-9198
Mediapolis MS — 200/6-8
725 N Northfield St 52637 — 319-394-3101
Roger Thornburg, prin. — Fax 394-9198

**Melcher, Marion, Pop. 1,280**
Melcher-Dallas Community SD — 400/PK-12
PO Box 489 50163 — 641-947-3731
Randy Alger, supt. — Fax 947-5002
mdcsd-ia.schoolloop.com
Melcher-Dallas HS — 100/9-12
PO Box 158 50163 — 641-947-3731
Randy Alger, prin. — Fax 947-2203
Melcher-Dallas JHS — 50/6-8
PO Box 158 50163 — 641-947-3731
Randy Alger, prin. — Fax 947-2203

**Milford, Dickinson, Pop. 2,878**
Okoboji Community SD — 1,000/PK-12
PO Box 147 51351 — 712-338-4757
Gary Janssen, supt. — Fax 338-4758
www.okoboji.k12.ia.us
Okoboji HS — 300/9-12
PO Box 147 51351 — 712-338-2446
Brian Downing, prin. — Fax 338-2550
Other Schools – See Arnolds Park

**Missouri Valley, Harrison, Pop. 2,810**
Missouri Valley Community SD — 800/PK-12
109 E Michigan St 51555 — 712-642-2706
Deidre Drees, supt. — Fax 642-2456
www.movalleyschools.org
Missouri Valley HS — 300/9-12
605 Lincoln Hwy 51555 — 712-642-4149
Kristie Kruckman, prin. — Fax 642-4624
Missouri Valley MS — 200/6-8
607 Lincoln Hwy 51555 — 712-642-2707
Brent Hoesing, prin. — Fax 642-3738

**Mondamin, Harrison, Pop. 398**
West Harrison Community SD — 300/PK-12
410 Pine St 51557 — 712-646-2231
Lyle Schwartz, supt. — Fax 646-2891
www.w-harrison.k12.ia.us/
West Harrison MSHS — 200/4-12
410 Pine St 51557 — 712-646-2231
Fred Matlage, prin. — Fax 646-2891

**Monona, Clayton, Pop. 1,540**
MFL MarMac Community SD — 700/PK-12
PO Box 1040 52159 — 563-539-4795
Dr. Dale Crozier, supt. — Fax 539-4913
www.mflmarmac.k12.ia.us
MFL MarMac HS — 200/9-12
PO Box 1040 52159 — 563-539-2031
David Ross, prin. — Fax 539-4694
Other Schools – See Mc Gregor

**Monroe, Jasper, Pop. 1,825**
PCM Community SD — 1,100/PK-12
PO Box 610 50170 — 641-259-2751
Brad Jermeland, supt. — Fax 259-2753
www.pcmonroe.k12.ia.us
PCM HS — 300/9-12
PO Box 610 50170 — 641-259-2315
Scott Bridges, prin. — Fax 259-2317
Other Schools – See Prairie City

**Montezuma, Poweshiek, Pop. 1,455**
Montezuma Community SD — 500/PK-12
PO Box 580 50171 — 641-623-5185
Dave Versteeg, supt. — Fax 623-5733
montezuma-schools.org
Montezuma HS — 200/9-12
PO Box 580 50171 — 641-623-5121
Brian Moretz, prin. — Fax 623-5733
Montezuma JHS — 100/7-8
PO Box 580 50171 — 641-623-5121
Brian Moretz, prin. — Fax 623-5733

**Monticello, Jones, Pop. 3,779**
Monticello Community SD — 1,100/PK-12
711 S Maple St 52310 — 319-465-5963
Chris Anderson, supt. — Fax 465-4092
www.monticello.k12.ia.us/
Monticello HS — 300/9-12
850 E Oak St 52310 — 319-465-6597
Joan Young, prin. — Fax 465-4253
Monticello MS — 300/5-8
217 S Maple St 52310 — 319-465-3575
Brent Meier, prin. — Fax 465-6959

**Moravia, Appanoose, Pop. 658**
Moravia Community SD — 400/PK-12
505 N Trussell Ave 52571 — 641-724-3241
Brad Breon, supt. — Fax 724-0629
www.moravia.k12.ia.us
Moravia JSHS — 200/7-12
505 N Trussell Ave 52571 — 641-724-3241
Kathleen Carr, prin. — Fax 724-0629

**Moulton, Appanoose, Pop. 600**
Moulton-Udell Community SD — 200/PK-12
305 E 8th St 52572 — 641-642-3665
Brian VanderSluis, supt. — Fax 642-3461
www.moulton-udell.k12.ia.us
Moulton-Udell JSHS — 100/7-12
305 E 8th St 52572 — 641-642-8131
Randy Alger, prin. — Fax 642-3461

**Mount Ayr, Ringgold, Pop. 1,687**
Mount Ayr Community SD — 600/PK-12
1001 E Columbus St 50854 — 641-464-0500
Joe Drake, supt. — Fax 464-2325
www.mtayrschools.org
Mount Ayr JSHS — 300/7-12
1001 E Columbus St 50854 — 641-464-0510
Lynne Wallace, prin. — Fax 464-2325

**Mount Pleasant, Henry, Pop. 8,462**
Mount Pleasant Community SD — 2,100/PK-12
400 E Madison St 52641 — 319-385-7750
Fax 385-7788
www.mt-pleasant.k12.ia.us
Mount Pleasant HS — 600/9-12
2104 S Grand Ave 52641 — 319-385-7700
Todd Liechty, prin. — Fax 385-7789
Mount Pleasant MS — 500/6-8
400 E Madison St 52641 — 319-385-7730
Jason Martinez, prin. — Fax 385-7735
WisdomQuest Education Center — 50/Alt
400 E Madison St 52641 — 319-385-7709
Melissa Shull, lead tchr. — Fax 385-7715

---

Iowa Wesleyan College — Post-Sec.
601 N Main St 52641 — 319-385-8021
Mount Pleasant Christian S — 100/PK-12
1505 E Washington St 52641 — 319-385-8613
Tina Hill, admin. — Fax 385-8415

**Mount Vernon, Linn, Pop. 4,439**
Mount Vernon Community SD — 1,300/PK-12
525 Palisades Rd SW 52314 — 319-895-8845
Dr. Gary O'Malley, supt. — Fax 895-8875
www.mountvernon.k12.ia.us
Mount Vernon HS — 400/9-12
731 Palisades Rd SW 52314 — 319-895-8843
Steve Brand, prin. — Fax 895-6185
Mount Vernon MS — 400/5-8
525 Palisades Rd SW 52314 — 319-895-6254
Bob Haugse, prin. — Fax 895-8134

---

Cornell College — Post-Sec.
600 1st St SW 52314 — 319-895-4000

**Moville, Woodbury, Pop. 1,596**
Woodbury Central Community SD — 600/PK-12
408 S 4th St 51039 — 712-873-3128
Doug Glackin, supt. — Fax 873-3162
www.woodbury-central.k12.ia.us
Woodbury Central HS — 200/9-12
408 S 4th St 51039 — 712-873-3128
Dan Bormann, prin. — Fax 873-3162
Woodbury Central MS — 100/6-8
408 S 4th St 51039 — 712-873-3128
Don Bormann, prin. — Fax 873-3162

**Murray, Clarke, Pop. 756**
Murray Community SD — 300/PK-12
PO Box 187 50174 — 641-447-2517
Alan Miller, supt. — Fax 447-2313
www.murraycsd.org
Murray JSHS — 100/7-12
PO Box 187 50174 — 641-447-2517
Tara Page, dean — Fax 447-2313

**Muscatine, Muscatine, Pop. 22,599**
Muscatine Community SD — 5,300/PK-12
2900 Mulberry Ave 52761 — 563-263-7223
Dr. Jerry Riibe, supt. — Fax 263-7729
www.muscatineschools.org
Central MS — 600/6-8
901 Cedar St 52761 — 563-263-7784
Terry Hogenson, prin. — Fax 263-0145
Muscatine HS — 1,600/9-12
2705 Cedar St 52761 — 563-263-6141
Mike McGrory, prin. — Fax 264-1794
West MS — 600/6-8
600 Kindler Ave 52761 — 563-263-0411
Perry Rodocker, prin. — Fax 263-6645

---

Muscatine Community College — Post-Sec.
152 Colorado St 52761 — 563-288-6001

**Nashua, Chickasaw, Pop. 1,656**
Nashua-Plainfield Community SD — 600/PK-12
PO Box 569 50658 — 641-435-4835
Randy Strabala, supt. — Fax 435-4835
www.nashua-plainfield.k12.ia.us
Nashua-Plainfield JSHS — 200/7-12
PO Box 569 50658 — 641-435-4166
Erik Smith, prin. — Fax 435-4167

**Neola, Pottawattamie, Pop. 840**
Tri-Center Community SD — 800/PK-12
33980 310th St 51559 — 712-485-2257
Dr. Tony Weers, supt. — Fax 485-2411
www.tctrojans.org
Tri-Center HS — 200/9-12
33980 310th St 51559 — 712-485-2257
Angela Huseman, prin. — Fax 485-2411
Tri-Center MS — 200/6-8
33980 310th St 51559 — 712-485-2211
Angie Huseman, prin. — Fax 485-2402

**Nevada, Story, Pop. 6,711**
Nevada Community SD — 1,600/PK-12
1035 15th St 50201 — 515-382-2783
Dr. Steven Gray, supt. — Fax 382-2836
www.nevadacubs.org
Nevada HS — 400/9-12
1035 15th St 50201 — 515-382-3521
Justin Gross, prin. — Fax 382-2935
Nevada MS — 400/5-8
1035 15th St 50201 — 515-382-2751
Chris Schmidt, prin. — Fax 382-2836

**Newell, Buena Vista, Pop. 875**
Newell-Fonda Community SD — 300/PK-12
PO Box 297 50568 — 712-272-3324
Rob Olsen, supt. — Fax 272-4276
www.newell-fonda.k12.ia.us
Newell-Fonda HS — 100/9-12
PO Box 297 50568 — 712-272-3325
Alynn Coppock, prin. — Fax 272-4276

**New Hampton, Chickasaw, Pop. 3,557**
New Hampton Community SD — 1,100/PK-12
710 W Main St 50659 — 641-394-2134
Jay Jurrens, supt. — Fax 394-2921
www.new-hampton.k12.ia.us
Education Options — 50/Alt
710 W Main St 50659 — 641-394-2144
Sarah Updegraff, prin.
New Hampton HS — 400/9-12
710 W Main St 50659 — 641-394-2144
Sarah Updegraff, prin. — Fax 394-6046
New Hampton MS — 300/5-8
206 W Main St 50659 — 641-394-2259
Susan Anderson, prin. — Fax 394-2662

**New Hartford, Butler, Pop. 512**
Dike-New Hartford Community SD
Supt. — See Dike
Dike-New Hartford JHS — 300/6-8
PO Box 214 50660 — 319-983-2206
Jerold Martinek, prin. — Fax 983-2207

**New London, Henry, Pop. 1,877**
New London Community SD — 500/PK-12
PO Box 97 52645 — 319-367-0512
Steve McAllister, supt. — Fax 367-0513
www.new-london.k12.ia.us
New London JSHS — 300/6-12
PO Box 97 52645 — 319-367-0500
Scott Kracht, prin. — Fax 367-0501

**New Sharon, Mahaska, Pop. 1,287**
North Mahaska Community SD — 600/PK-12
PO Box 89 50207 — 641-637-4187
Angela Livezey, supt. — Fax 637-4559
www.n-mahaska.k12.ia.us
North Mahaska JSHS — 300/7-12
PO Box 89 50207 — 641-637-4187
Douglas Ray, prin. — Fax 637-4559

**Newton, Jasper, Pop. 15,101**
Newton Community SD — 2,900/PK-12
700 N 4th Ave E 50208 — 641-792-5809
Bob Callaghan, supt. — Fax 792-9159
www.newton.k12.ia.us
Basics & Beyond Alternative S — 100/Alt
700 N 4th Ave E 50208 — 641-792-0335
Laura Selover, prin. — Fax 792-0332
Berg MS — 400/7-8
1900 N 5th Ave E 50208 — 641-792-7741
Lisa Sharp, prin. — Fax 792-7779
Newton HS — 800/9-12
800 E 4th St S 50208 — 641-792-5797
Bill Peters, prin. — Fax 792-0005

---

Des Moines Area Community College — Post-Sec.
600 N 2nd Ave W 50208 — 641-791-3622

**Nora Springs, Floyd, Pop. 1,424**
Central Springs Community SD
Supt. — See Manly
Central Springs MS — 200/6-8
PO Box 367 50458 — 641-749-5301
Robert Hoffman, prin. — Fax 749-5898

**North English, Iowa, Pop. 1,037**
English Valleys Community SD — 500/PK-12
PO Box 490 52316 — 319-664-3634
Donita Joens, supt. — Fax 664-3636
www.english-valleys.k12.ia.us
English Valleys JSHS — 200/7-12
PO Box 490 52316 — 319-664-3631
Heather Lightfoot, prin. — Fax 664-3670

**North Liberty, Johnson, Pop. 13,098**
Iowa City Community SD
Supt. — See Iowa City
North Central JHS — 400/7-8
180 Forevergreen Rd E 52317 — 319-688-1210
Jane Fry, prin. — Fax 688-1219

**Northwood, Worth, Pop. 1,968**
Northwood-Kensett Community SD — 500/PK-12
PO Box 289 50459 — 641-324-2021
Michael Crozier, supt. — Fax 324-2092
www.nwood-kensett.k12.ia.us
Northwood-Kensett JSHS — 200/7-12
PO Box 289 50459 — 641-324-2142
Keith Fritz, prin. — Fax 324-2174

**Norwalk, Warren, Pop. 8,841**
Norwalk Community SD — 2,100/PK-12
380 Wright Rd 50211 — 515-981-0676
Dennis Wulf, supt. — Fax 981-0559
www.norwalk.k12.ia.us/

Eastview 8/9 S 8-9
1600 North Ave 50211 515-981-9655
Dr. Jody Ratigan, prin. Fax 981-9706
Norwalk HS 600/10-12
1201 North Ave 50211 515-981-4201
Chris Basinger, prin. Fax 981-9875

**Oakland, Pottawattamie, Pop. 1,517**
Riverside Community SD
Supt. — See Carson
Riverside Community HS 200/7-12
PO Box 428 51560 712-482-6464
David Gute, prin. Fax 482-3074

**Odebolt, Sac, Pop. 1,011**
Odebolt-Arthur/Battle Creek-Ida Grove SD
Supt. — See Ida Grove
Odebolt-Arthur/Battle Creek-Ida Grove MS 100/6-8
600 S Maple St 51458 712-668-2827
Doug Mogensen, prin. Fax 668-2631

**Oelwein, Fayette, Pop. 6,310**
Oelwein Community SD 1,300/PK-12
307 8th Ave SE 50662 319-283-3536
Dan Diercks, supt. Fax 283-4497
www.oelwein.k12.ia.us
Oelwein HS 400/9-12
315 8th Ave SE 50662 319-283-2731
Josh Ehn, prin. Fax 283-1689
Oelwein MS 300/6-8
300 12th Ave SE 50662 319-283-3015
Mary Beth Steggall, prin. Fax 283-9813

**Ogden, Boone, Pop. 2,032**
Ogden Community SD 700/PK-12
PO Box 250 50212 515-275-2894
Tim Hoffman, supt. Fax 275-4537
www.ogdenschools.org
Ogden HS 200/9-12
PO Box 250 50212 515-275-4034
Jenn Peter, prin. Fax 275-4972
Ogden MS 200/5-8
PO Box 250 50212 515-275-2912
Dave Neubauer, prin. Fax 275-2908

**Onawa, Monona, Pop. 2,968**
West Monona Community SD 500/PK-12
1314 15th St 51040 712-433-2043
Lyle Schwartz, supt. Fax 433-3803
www.westmonona.org
West Monona HS 200/9-12
1314 15th St 51040 712-433-2453
Tim Chesnut, prin. Fax 433-3803
West Monona MS 100/6-8
1314 15th St 51040 712-433-9098
Tim Chesnut, prin. Fax 433-1142

**Orange City, Sioux, Pop. 5,966**
MOC-Floyd Valley Community SD 1,300/PK-12
PO Box 257 51041 712-737-4873
Russ Adams, supt. Fax 737-8789
www.moc-fv.k12.ia.us/
MOC-Floyd Valley HS 400/9-12
615 8th St SE 51041 712-737-4871
Mike Mulder, prin. Fax 737-3933
Other Schools – See Alton

---

Northwestern College Post-Sec.
101 7th St SW 51041 712-707-7000
Unity Christian HS 300/9-12
216 Michigan Ave SW 51041 712-737-4114
Wayne Dykstra, prin. Fax 737-2686

**Orient, Adair, Pop. 408**
Orient-Macksburg Community SD 100/PK-12
PO Box 129 50858 641-337-5061
Clark Wicks, supt. Fax 337-5013
www.o-mschools.org
Orient-Macksburg Community S 100/PK-12
PO Box 129 50858 641-337-5061
Teresa Thompson, prin. Fax 337-5606

**Osage, Mitchell, Pop. 3,601**
Osage Community SD 900/PK-12
820 Sawyer Dr 50461 641-732-5381
Barbara Schwamman, supt. Fax 732-5381
www.osage.k12.ia.us
Osage HS 300/9-12
820 Sawyer Dr 50461 641-732-3102
Tim Hejhal, prin. Fax 732-3456
Osage MS 300/5-8
820 Sawyer Dr 50461 641-732-3127
Jay Marley, prin. Fax 732-5450

**Osceola, Clarke, Pop. 4,887**
Clarke Community SD 1,500/PK-12
802 N Jackson St 50213 641-342-4969
Steve Seid, supt. Fax 342-6101
www.clarke.k12.ia.us
Clarke Community HS 400/9-12
800 N Jackson St 50213 641-342-6505
Shane Stephens, prin. Fax 342-2213
Clarke Learning Center 50/Alt
802 N Jackson St 50213 641-342-2804
Shane Stephens, prin.
Clarke MS 200/7-8
800 N Jackson St 50213 641-342-4221
Jeff Sogard, prin. Fax 342-1528

**Oskaloosa, Mahaska, Pop. 11,273**
Oskaloosa Community SD 2,300/PK-12
PO Box 710 52577 641-673-8345
Russell Reiter, supt. Fax 673-8370
www.oskaloosa.k12.ia.us
Oskaloosa HS 700/9-12
1816 N 3rd St 52577 641-673-3407
Stacy Bandy, prin. Fax 672-2440
Oskaloosa MS 500/6-8
1704 N 3rd St 52577 641-673-8308
Andy Hotek, prin. Fax 673-3779

---

William Penn University Post-Sec.
201 Trueblood Ave 52577 800-677-9076

**Ossian, Winneshiek, Pop. 842**
South Winneshiek Community SD
Supt. — See Calmar
South Winneshiek MS 100/6-8
PO Box 298 52161 563-532-9365
Barb Schwamman, prin. Fax 532-9855

**Ottumwa, Wapello, Pop. 24,651**
Ottumwa Community SD 4,400/PK-12
1112 N Van Buren 52501 641-684-6596
Tom Rubel, supt. Fax 684-6522
www.ottumwaschools.com
Accelerated College Career Academy Alt
15260 Truman St 52501 641-683-1342
John Ohlinger, admin. Fax 684-6854
Evans MS 1,000/6-8
812 Chester Ave 52501 641-684-6511
Melissa Carson-Roark, prin. Fax 684-7386
Ottumwa HS 1,300/9-12
501 E 2nd St 52501 641-683-4444
Mark Hanson, prin. Fax 682-7528

---

Indian Hills Community College Post-Sec.
525 Grandview Ave 52501 641-683-5111
Iowa School of Beauty Post-Sec.
609 W 2nd St 52501 641-684-6504

**Oxford, Johnson, Pop. 790**
Clear Creek Amana Community SD 1,800/PK-12
PO Box 487 52322 319-828-4510
Tim Kuehl, supt. Fax 828-4743
www.ccaschools.org
Other Schools – See Tiffin

**Packwood, Jefferson, Pop. 200**
Pekin Community SD 600/PK-12
1062 Birch Ave 52580 319-695-3707
Dennis Phelps, supt. Fax 695-5130
www.pekincsd.org
Pekin HS 200/6-12
1062 Birch Ave 52580 319-695-3705
Tim Hadley, prin. Fax 661-2353

**Panora, Guthrie, Pop. 1,114**
Panorama Community SD 500/PK-12
PO Box 39 50216 641-755-4144
Shawn Holloway, supt. Fax 755-3008
www.panorama.k12.ia.us
Panorama MSHS 200/6-12
PO Box 39 50216 641-755-2317
Mark Johnston, prin. Fax 755-3008

**Parkersburg, Butler, Pop. 1,860**
Aplington-Parkersburg Community SD 900/PK-12
610 N Johnson St 50665 319-346-1571
Jon Thompson, supt. Fax 346-1012
www.a-pcsd.net
Aplington-Parkersburg HS 300/9-12
610 N Johnson St 50665 319-346-1571
Aaron Thomas, prin. Fax 346-1012
Other Schools – See Aplington

**Paullina, O'Brien, Pop. 1,052**
South O'Brien Community SD 600/PK-12
PO Box 638 51046 712-949-2115
Dan Moore, supt. Fax 949-2149
www.s-obrien.k12.ia.us
South O'Brien Secondary S 300/7-12
PO Box 638 51046 712-949-3454
Steven Bruder, prin. Fax 949-3453

**Pella, Marion, Pop. 10,224**
Pella Community SD 2,300/PK-12
PO Box 468 50219 641-628-1111
Greg Ebeling, supt. Fax 628-1116
www.pellaschools.org
Pella Community HS 700/9-12
212 E University St 50219 641-628-3870
Eric Nelson, prin. Fax 628-7402
Pella Community MS 400/7-8
613 E 13th St 50219 641-628-4784
Josh Manning, prin. Fax 628-6804

---

Central College Post-Sec.
812 University St 50219 641-628-9000
Pella Christian HS 300/9-12
300 Eagle Ln 50219 641-628-4440
Darryl De Ruiter, prin. Fax 628-3530

**Peosta, Dubuque, Pop. 1,367**

---

Northeast Iowa Community College Post-Sec.
8342 NICC Dr 52068 563-556-5110

**Perry, Dallas, Pop. 7,599**
Perry Community SD 1,800/PK-12
1102 Willis Ave Ste 200 50220 515-465-4656
Lynn Ubben, supt. Fax 465-4025
www.perry.k12.ia.us/
Perry HS 600/9-12
1200 18th St 50220 515-465-3503
Dan Marburger, prin. Fax 465-5977
Perry MS 400/6-8
1200 18th St 50220 515-465-3531
Shaun Kruger, prin. Fax 465-8555

**Pierson, Woodbury, Pop. 361**
Kingsley-Pierson Community SD
Supt. — See Kingsley
Pierson MS 100/6-8
321 4th St 51048 712-375-5939
Robert Wiese, prin. Fax 375-5771

**Pleasant Hill, Polk, Pop. 8,612**
Southeast Polk Community SD 5,900/PK-12
8379 NE University Ave 50327 515-967-4294
Dirk Halupnik, supt. Fax 967-4257
www.southeastpolk.org/
Southeast Polk HS 1,800/9-12
7945 NE University Ave 50327 515-967-6631
Stephen Pettit, prin. Fax 967-5117
Southeast Polk JHS 1,000/7-8
8325 NE University Ave 50327 515-967-5509
Mike Dailey, prin. Fax 967-1676

**Pleasantville, Marion, Pop. 1,681**
Pleasantville Community SD 700/PK-12
415 Jones St 50225 515-848-0555
Dr. Tony Aylsworth, supt. Fax 848-0561
www.pleasantville.k12.ia.us
Pleasantville HS 200/9-12
415 Jones St 50225 515-848-0541
Gary Friday, prin. Fax 848-0562
Pleasantville MS 200/6-8
415 Jones St 50225 515-848-0528
Gary Friday, prin. Fax 848-0561

**Pocahontas, Pocahontas, Pop. 1,776**
Pocahontas Area Community SD 400/PK-12
202 1st Ave SW 50574 712-335-4311
Joseph Kramer, supt. Fax 335-4206
www.pocahontas.k12.ia.us/
Pocahontas Area JSHS 200/7-12
205 2nd Ave NW 50574 712-335-4848
Roger Francis, prin. Fax 335-3420
Pocahontas Area Reg Learning Center 50/Alt
202 1st Ave SW 50574 712-335-5971
Roger Francis, prin.

**Postville, Allamakee, Pop. 2,192**
Postville Community SD 500/PK-12
PO Box 717 52162 563-864-7651
Abe Maske, supt. Fax 864-7659
www.postville.k12.ia.us
Mott HS 100/7-12
PO Box 717 52162 563-864-7651
Brendan Knudtson, prin. Fax 864-7659

**Prairie City, Jasper, Pop. 1,659**
PCM Community SD
Supt. — See Monroe
PCM MS 200/6-8
PO Box 490 50228 515-994-2686
Stephanie Langstraat, prin. Fax 994-2686

**Preston, Jackson, Pop. 1,004**
Easton Valley SD 400/PK-12
321 W School St 52069 563-689-4221
Andy Crozier, supt. Fax 689-5823
www.eastonvalleycsd.com
Easton Valley HS 100/7-12
321 W School St 52069 563-689-4221
Tony Johnson, prin. Fax 689-4222

**Redfield, Dallas, Pop. 817**
West Central Valley Community SD
Supt. — See Stuart
West Central Valley MS 200/6-8
PO Box B 50233 515-833-2331
Anthony Lohse, prin. Fax 833-2629

**Red Oak, Montgomery, Pop. 5,681**
Red Oak Community SD 1,200/PK-12
2011 N 8th St 51566 712-623-6600
Tom Messinger, supt. Fax 623-6603
www.redoakschooldistrict.com
Red Oak HS 400/9-12
2011 N 8th St 51566 712-623-6610
Jeff Spotts, prin. Fax 623-6613
Red Oak MS 300/6-8
308 E Corning St 51566 712-623-6620
Nathan Perrien, prin. Fax 623-6626

**Reinbeck, Grundy, Pop. 1,657**
Gladbrook-Reinbeck Community SD 600/PK-12
300 Cedar St 50669 319-345-2712
Jay Mathis, supt. Fax 345-2242
www.gr-rebels.net
Gladbrook-Reinbeck JSHS 200/7-12
600 Blackhawk St 50669 319-345-2921
Scot Aden, prin. Fax 345-6432

**Remsen, Plymouth, Pop. 1,653**
Remsen-Union Community SD 400/PK-12
511 Roosevelt Ave 51050 712-786-1101
Jan Brandhorst, supt. Fax 786-1104
www.rurockets.org
Remsen-Union HS 100/9-12
511 Roosevelt Ave 51050 712-786-1101
Tobias Young, prin. Fax 786-1104
Remsen-Union MS 100/6-8
511 Roosevelt Ave 51050 712-786-1101
Tobias Young, prin. Fax 786-1104

---

St. Marys HS 100/9-12
523 Madison St 51050 712-786-1433
Pete Haefs, prin. Fax 786-2499

**Riceville, Howard, Pop. 779**
Riceville Community SD 100/K-12
912 Woodland Ave 50466 641-985-2288
Dr. Steve Nicholson, supt. Fax 985-4171
www.riceville.k12.ia.us
Riceville Community S 100/K-12
912 Woodland Ave 50466 641-985-2288
Cory Schumann, prin. Fax 985-4171

**Riverdale, Scott, Pop. 403**
Pleasant Valley Community SD
Supt. — See Bettendorf
Pleasant Valley HS 1,200/9-12
604 Belmont Rd 52722 563-332-5151
David Zimmer, prin. Fax 332-8525

**Riverside, Washington, Pop. 985**
Highland Community SD 700/PK-12
1715 Vine Ave 52327 319-648-3822
Chris Armstrong, supt. Fax 648-4055
www.highland.k12.ia.us
Highland HS 200/9-12
1715 Vine Ave 52327 319-648-2891
Angela Hazelett, prin. Fax 648-3310
Highland MS 200/6-8
1715 Vine Ave 52327 319-648-5018
Joel Diederichs, prin. Fax 648-4055

**Rockford, Floyd, Pop. 856**
Rudd-Rockford-Marble Rock Community SD 500/PK-12
PO Box 218 50468 641-756-3610
Keith Turner, supt. Fax 756-2369
www.rockford.k12.ia.us
Rockford JSHS 200/7-12
PO Box 218 50468 641-756-3813
Keith Turner, prin. Fax 756-2369

**Rock Rapids, Lyon, Pop. 2,533**
Central Lyon Community SD 700/PK-12
PO Box 471 51246 712-472-2664
David Ackerman, supt. Fax 472-2115
www.centrallyon.org
Central Lyon HS 200/9-12
PO Box 471 51246 712-472-4051
David Ackerman, admin. Fax 472-2115
Central Lyon MS 100/6-8
PO Box 471 51246 712-472-4041
Jason Engleman, prin. Fax 472-2346

**Rock Valley, Sioux, Pop. 3,334**
Rock Valley Community SD 800/PK-12
1712 20th Ave 51247 712-476-2701
Chad Janzen, supt. Fax 476-2125
www.rvcsd.org
Rock Valley JSHS 400/6-12
1712 20th Ave 51247 712-476-2701
Nicole Roder, prin. Fax 476-2125

---

Netherlands Reformed Christian S 400/K-12
712 20th Ave SE 51247 712-476-2821
Daniel Breuer, prin. Fax 476-5438

**Rockwell, Cerro Gordo, Pop. 1,034**
West Fork SD 700/PK-12
PO Box 60 50469 641-882-3236
Darrin Strike, supt. Fax 822-4882
www.westforkschool.org/
West Fork MS 200/5-8
PO Box 60 50469 641-822-3264
Tracy Peterson, prin. Fax 822-3273
Other Schools – See Sheffield

**Rockwell City, Calhoun, Pop. 1,695**
South Central Calhoun Community SD 900/PK-12
1000 Tonawanda St 50579 712-297-7341
Jeff Kruse, supt. Fax 297-7320
www.scc.k12.ia.us
South Central Calhoun MS 300/4-8
1000 Tonawanda St 50579 712-297-8111
Marc DeMoss, prin. Fax 297-7320
Other Schools – See Lake City

**Roland, Story, Pop. 1,275**
Roland-Story Community SD
Supt. — See Story City
Roland-Story MS 300/5-8
206 S Main St 50236 515-388-4348
John Sheahan, prin. Fax 388-4435

**Royal, Clay, Pop. 436**
Clay Central/Everly Community SD 400/PK-12
PO Box 110 51357 712-933-2241
Dennis McClain, supt. Fax 933-2243
www.claycentraleverly.new.rschooltoday.com
Other Schools – See Everly

**Ruthven, Palo Alto, Pop. 734**
Ruthven-Ayrshire Community SD 300/PK-12
PO Box 159 51358 712-837-5211
Andrew Woiwood, supt. Fax 837-5210
www.ruthven.k12.ia.us
Ruthven-Ayrshire JSHS 100/7-12
PO Box 159 51358 712-837-5212
Jon Josephson, prin. Fax 837-5210

**Sac City, Sac, Pop. 2,191**
East Sac County SD
Supt. — See Lake View
East Sac County MS 300/5-8
300 S 11th St 50583 712-662-3259
Denny Olhausen, prin. Fax 662-4323
Sac County Flex Ed Center Alt
400 S 16th St 50583 712-662-4907
Gene Coon, lead tchr. Fax 662-7602

**Saint Ansgar, Mitchell, Pop. 1,101**
St. Ansgar Community SD 700/PK-12
PO Box 398 50472 641-713-4681
Jody Gray, supt. Fax 713-4042
www.st-ansgar.k12.ia.us
Saint Ansgar HS 200/9-12
PO Box 398 50472 641-713-4720
Lynn Baldus, prin. Fax 713-2449
Saint Ansgar MS 200/6-8
PO Box 398 50472 641-713-4720
Lynn Baldus, prin. Fax 713-4042

**Sanborn, O'Brien, Pop. 1,402**
Hartley-Melvin-Sanborn Community SD
Supt. — See Hartley
Hartley-Melvin-Sanborn MS 200/5-8
PO Box 557 51248 712-930-3281
Mark Dorhout, prin. Fax 930-5414

**Schaller, Sac, Pop. 764**
Schaller-Crestland Community SD 400/PK-8
PO Box 249 51053 712-275-4267
Jon Wiebers, supt. Fax 275-4269
www.rvraptors.org
Other Schools – See Early

**Schleswig, Crawford, Pop. 871**
Schleswig Community SD 200/PK-8
PO Box 250 51461 712-676-3313
Brian Johnson, supt. Fax 676-3539
www.schleswig.k12.ia.us
Schleswig MS 100/5-8
PO Box 250 51461 712-676-3313
David Galvin, prin. Fax 676-3539

**Sergeant Bluff, Woodbury, Pop. 4,152**
Sergeant Bluff-Luton Community SD 1,500/PK-12
201 Port Neal Rd 51054 712-943-4338
Rod Earleywine, supt. Fax 943-1131
www.sblschools.com
Sergeant Bluff-Luton HS 500/9-12
708 Warrior Rd 51054 712-943-5561
Jason Klingingsmith, prin. Fax 943-5887
Sergeant Bluff-Luton MS 300/6-8
208 Port Neal Rd 51054 712-943-4235
Bill McKelvey, prin. Fax 943-8780

**Seymour, Wayne, Pop. 696**
Seymour Community SD 200/PK-12
100 S Park Ave 52590 641-898-2291
Brad Breon, supt. Fax 898-7500
www.seymour.k12.ia.us/
Seymour JSHS 100/7-12
100 S Park Ave 52590 641-898-2291
Jamie Houser, prin. Fax 898-7500

**Sheffield, Franklin, Pop. 1,165**
West Fork SD
Supt. — See Rockwell
West Fork HS 200/9-12
PO Box 617 50475 641-892-4461
Randy Bushbaum, prin. Fax 892-4335

**Sheldon, O'Brien, Pop. 5,156**
Sheldon Community SD 1,000/PK-12
1700 E 4th St 51201 712-324-2504
Robin Spears, supt. Fax 324-5607
www.sheldon.k12.ia.us
Sheldon HS 300/9-12
1700 E 4th St 51201 712-324-2501
Sherrie Zeutenhorst, prin. Fax 324-5607
Sheldon MS 300/5-8
310 23rd Ave 51201 712-324-4346
Cindy Barwick, prin. Fax 324-4347

---

Northwest Iowa Community College Post-Sec.
603 W Park St 51201 712-324-5061

**Shenandoah, Page, Pop. 5,088**
Shenandoah Community SD 1,000/PK-12
304 W Nishna Rd 51601 712-246-1581
Dr. Kerri Nelson Ed.D., supt. Fax 246-3722
www.shenandoah.k12.ia.us
Shenandoah HS 300/9-12
1000 Mustang Dr 51601 712-246-4727
Sandy Hilding, prin. Fax 246-2842
Shenandoah MS 300/5-8
601 Dr Creighton Cir 51601 712-246-2520
Jason Shaffer, prin. Fax 246-6390

**Sibley, Osceola, Pop. 2,785**
Sibley-Ocheyedan Community SD 800/PK-12
120 11th Ave NE 51249 712-754-2533
Bill Boer, supt. Fax 754-2534
www.thegenerals.org
Sibley-Ocheyedan HS 200/9-12
120 11th Ave NE 51249 712-754-3601
Brent Town, prin. Fax 754-2534
Sibley-Ocheyedan MS 200/5-8
120 11th Ave NE 51249 712-754-2542
Fax 754-3651

**Sidney, Fremont, Pop. 1,125**
Sidney Community SD 400/PK-12
PO Box 609 51652 712-374-2141
Gregg Cruickshank, supt. Fax 374-2013
sidneyschools.org
Sidney JSHS 200/7-12
PO Box 609 51652 712-374-2731
Bill Huntington, prin. Fax 374-2013

**Sigourney, Keokuk, Pop. 2,051**
Sigourney Community SD 500/PK-12
909 E Pleasant Valley St 52591 641-622-2025
Dave Harper, supt. Fax 622-2319
www.sigourneyschools.com
Sigourney JSHS 300/7-12
907 E Pleasant Valley St 52591 641-622-2010
Shannon Webb, prin. Fax 622-2047

**Sioux Center, Sioux, Pop. 7,004**
Sioux Center Community SD 1,100/PK-12
550 9th St NE 51250 712-722-2985
Patrick O'Donnell, supt. Fax 722-2986
www.sioux-center.k12.ia.us
Sioux Center HS 300/9-12
550 9th St NE 51250 712-722-2981
Gary McEldowney, prin. Fax 722-2930
Sioux Center MS 300/5-8
550 9th St NE 51250 712-722-3783
Julie Schley, prin. Fax 722-3782

---

Dordt College Post-Sec.
498 4th Ave NE 51250 712-722-6000

**Sioux City, Woodbury, Pop. 80,564**
Sioux City Community SD 12,100/PK-12
627 4th St 51101 712-279-6667
Dr. Paul Gausman, supt. Fax 279-6690
www.siouxcityschools.org/
East HS 1,300/9-12
5011 Mayhew Ave 51106 712-274-4000
Richard Todd, prin. Fax 274-4670
East MS 1,100/6-8
5401 Lorraine Ave 51106 712-274-4030
Dr. Michael Rogers, prin. Fax 274-4668
North HS 1,300/9-12
4200 Cheyenne Blvd 51104 712-239-7000
Ryan Dumkreiger, prin. Fax 239-8270
North MS 1,000/6-8
2101 Outer Dr N 51108 712-279-6804
Shawn Chesteen, prin. Fax 277-5941
West HS 1,200/9-12
2001 Casselman St 51103 712-279-6772
Scott Cole, prin. Fax 279-6790
West MS 900/6-8
3301 W 19th St 51103 712-279-6813
Cynthia Washinowski, prin. Fax 277-6138

---

Bio-Chi Institute Post-Sec.
1925 Geneva St 51103 712-252-1157
Bishop Heelan HS 500/9-12
1021 Douglas St 51105 712-252-0573
Chris Bork, prin. Fax 252-4897
Briar Cliff University Post-Sec.
3303 Rebecca St 51104 712-279-5321
Holy Cross S / Blessed Sacrament Ctr 300/3-8
3030 Jackson St 51104 712-277-4739
Michael Sweeney, prin. Fax 258-3698
Iowa School of Beauty Post-Sec.
3320 Line Dr 51106 712-274-9733
Mater Dei S - Nativity Center 100/5-8
4243 Natalia Way 51106 712-274-0268
Mary Fischer, prin. Fax 274-0377
Mercy Medical Center - Sioux City Post-Sec.
801 5th St 51101 712-279-2018
Morningside College Post-Sec.
1501 Morningside Ave 51106 712-274-5000
St. Luke's College Post-Sec.
2720 Stone Park Blvd 51104 712-279-3149
Siouxland Community Christian S 200/PK-12
6100 Morningside Ave 51106 712-276-4732
Steven Peters, supt. Fax 276-4752
Western Iowa Tech Community College Post-Sec.
4647 Stone Ave 51106 712-274-6400

**Sioux Rapids, Buena Vista, Pop. 775**
Sioux Central Community SD 600/PK-12
4440 US Highway 71 50585 712-283-2571
Scott Williamson, supt. Fax 283-2989
www.siouxcentral.org
Sioux Central HS 200/9-12
4440 US Highway 71 50585 712-283-2571
Jeff Scharn, prin. Fax 283-2285
Sioux Central MS 100/7-8
4440 US Highway 71 50585 712-283-2571
Jeff Scharn, prin. Fax 283-2285

**Sloan, Woodbury, Pop. 970**
Westwood Community SD 600/PK-12
1000 Rebel Way 51055 712-428-3355
Jay Lutt, supt. Fax 428-3246
www.wwrebels.org
Westwood JSHS 300/7-12
1000 Rebel Way 51055 712-428-3303
Matt Drees, prin. Fax 428-3246

**Solon, Johnson, Pop. 2,019**
Solon Community SD 1,400/PK-12
301 S Iowa St 52333 319-624-3401
Davis Eidahl, supt. Fax 624-2518
www.solon.k12.ia.us
Solon HS 400/9-12
600 W 5th St 52333 319-624-3401
Nathan Wear, prin. Fax 624-4091
Solon MS 400/5-8
313 S Iowa St 52333 319-624-3401
Mike Herdliska, prin. Fax 624-2518

**Spencer, Clay, Pop. 11,130**
Spencer Community SD 1,300/PK-12
PO Box 200 51301 712-262-8950
Terry Hemann, supt. Fax 262-1116
www.spenceriowaschools.com/
Spencer HS 600/9-12
PO Box 200 51301 712-262-1700
Elli Wiemers, prin. Fax 262-5704
Spencer MS 300/6-8
PO Box 200 51301 712-262-3345
Pat Hamilton, prin. Fax 264-3444

---

Iowa Lakes Community College Post-Sec.
1900 Grand Ave Ste B1 51301 712-262-7141

**Spillville, Winneshiek, Pop. 366**

---

C F S Consolidated S 100/4-8
PO Box 68 52168 563-562-3617
Kathryn Schmitt, prin. Fax 562-3292

**Spirit Lake, Dickinson, Pop. 4,786**
Spirit Lake Community SD 1,300/PK-12
2701 Hill Ave 51360 712-336-2820
Dr. David Smith Ed.D., supt. Fax 336-4641
www.spirit-lake.k12.ia.us/
Spirit Lake HS 400/9-12
2701 Hill Ave 51360 712-336-3707
Angela Olsen, prin. Fax 336-3714
Spirit Lake MS 400/5-8
2701 Hill Ave 51360 712-336-1370
Terry Bruinsma, prin. Fax 336-4758

The Faust Institute of Cosmetology — Post-Sec.
1543 18th St Ste 15 51360 — 712-336-0512

**Springville, Linn, Pop. 1,066**
Springville Community SD — 400/K-12
400 Academy St 52336 — 319-854-6197
Pat Hocking, supt. — Fax 854-6199
www.springville.k12.ia.us
Springville JSHS — 200/6-12
400 Academy St 52336 — 319-854-6196
Nick Merritt, prin. — Fax 854-7891

**Stanton, Montgomery, Pop. 688**
Stanton Community SD — 200/K-12
PO Box 400 51573 — 712-829-2162
Dr. Chris Herrick, supt. — Fax 829-2164
www.stantonschools.com
Stanton MSHS — 100/6-12
PO Box 400 51573 — 712-829-2162
Kevin Blunt, prin. — Fax 829-2164

**Stanwood, Cedar, Pop. 676**
North Cedar Community SD — 800/PK-12
PO Box 247 52337 — 563-942-3358
Mike Cooper, supt. — Fax 942-0014
www.north-cedarstu.org
Other Schools – See Clarence

**State Center, Marshall, Pop. 1,450**
West Marshall Community SD — 900/PK-12
PO Box 670 50247 — 641-483-2660
Nicloe Kooiker, supt. — Fax 483-2665
www.w-marshall.k12.ia.us
West Marshall HS — 300/9-12
PO Box 670 50247 — 641-483-2136
Kristian Einsweiler, prin. — Fax 483-2172
West Marshall MS — 200/6-8
PO Box 340 50247 — 641-483-2165
Jeff Barry, prin. — Fax 483-3095

**Storm Lake, Buena Vista, Pop. 10,411**
Storm Lake Community SD — 2,300/PK-12
PO Box 638 50588 — 712-732-8060
Dr. Carl Turner Ed.D., supt. — Fax 732-8063
www.slcsd.org
Storm Lake HS — 700/9-12
PO Box 638 50588 — 712-732-8065
Beau Ruleaux, prin. — Fax 732-8068
Storm Lake MS — 600/5-8
PO Box 638 50588 — 712-732-8080
Jay Slight, prin. — Fax 732-8084

Buena Vista University — Post-Sec.
610 W 4th St 50588 — 712-749-2351
St. Mary MSHS — 200/5-12
304 Seneca St 50588 — 712-732-4166
Steven Lueck, prin. — Fax 732-4590
The Faust Institute of Cosmetology — Post-Sec.
1290 Lake Ave 50588 — 712-732-6571

**Story City, Story, Pop. 3,411**
Roland-Story Community SD — 1,000/PK-12
1009 Story St 50248 — 515-733-4301
Matt Patton, supt. — Fax 733-2131
www.roland-story.k12.ia.us
Roland-Story HS — 300/9-12
1009 Story St 50248 — 515-733-4329
Steve Schlatter, prin. — Fax 733-2131
Other Schools – See Roland

**Stuart, Guthrie, Pop. 1,630**
West Central Valley Community SD — 900/PK-12
3299 White Pole Rd 50250 — 515-523-2187
Dr. David Arnold, supt. — Fax 523-1166
www.wcv.k12.ia.us
West Central Valley HS — 300/9-12
3299 White Pole Rd 50250 — 515-523-1313
Debbie Wilson, prin. — Fax 523-2765
Other Schools – See Redfield

**Sully, Jasper, Pop. 821**
Lynnville-Sully Community SD — 500/K-12
PO Box 210 50251 — 641-594-4445
Shane Ehresman, supt. — Fax 594-2770
www.lshawks.org
Lynnville-Sully HS — 200/9-12
PO Box 210 50251 — 641-594-4445
Shane Ehresman, prin. — Fax 594-2770
Lynnville-Sully MS — 100/6-8
PO Box 210 50251 — 641-594-4445
Teri Bowlin, prin. — Fax 594-2770

**Sumner, Bremer, Pop. 2,021**
Sumner-Fredericksburg Community SD — 800/PK-12
802 W 6th St 50674 — 563-578-3341
Rick Pederson, supt. — Fax 578-3424
www.sfcougars.k12.ia.us
Sumner-Fredericksburg HS — 300/9-12
802 W 6th St 50674 — 563-578-3341
Allan Eckelman, prin. — Fax 578-3424
Other Schools – See Fredericksburg

**Swea City, Kossuth, Pop. 535**
North Union SD
Supt. — See Fenton
North Union MS — 100/6-8
PO Box 567 50590 — 515-272-4361
Mike Landstrum, prin. — Fax 272-4391

**Tabor, Fremont, Pop. 1,036**
Fremont-Mills Community SD — 500/PK-12
PO Box 310 51653 — 712-629-2325
Dr. Christopher Herrick, supt. — Fax 629-5155
www.fmtabor.org
Fremont-Mills MSHS — 200/7-12
PO Box 310 51653 — 712-629-2325
Jeremy Christiansen, prin. — Fax 629-5155

**Tama, Tama, Pop. 2,803**
South Tama County Community SD — 1,500/PK-12
1702 Harding St 52339 — 641-484-4811
Mary Jones, supt. — Fax 484-4861
www.s-tama.k12.ia.us/
Partnership HS — 50/Alt
215 W 9th St 52339 — 641-484-3085
Fax 484-3924
South Tama County HS — 400/9-12
1715 Harding St 52339 — 641-484-4345
Roy Frakes, prin. — Fax 484-5152
Other Schools – See Toledo

**Thornburg, Keokuk, Pop. 67**
Tri-County Community SD — 200/PK-12
PO Box 17 50255 — 641-634-2408
Dennis Phelps, supt. — Fax 634-2145
www.tri-countyschools.com
Tri-County HS — 100/9-12
PO Box 17 50255 — 641-634-2636
Alessandra Steinke, prin. — Fax 634-2145
Tri-County JHS — 100/7-8
PO Box 17 50255 — 641-634-2636
Alessandra Steinke, prin. — Fax 634-2145

**Tiffin, Johnson, Pop. 1,895**
Clear Creek Amana Community SD
Supt. — See Oxford
Clear Creek Amana HS — 500/9-12
PO Box 199 52340 — 319-545-2361
Mark Moody, prin. — Fax 545-2863
Clear Creek Amana MS — 400/6-8
PO Box 530 52340 — 319-545-4490
Brad Fox, prin. — Fax 545-4094

**Tipton, Cedar, Pop. 3,193**
Tipton Community SD — 900/PK-12
400 E 6th St 52772 — 563-886-6121
Marlene Johnson, supt. — Fax 886-2341
www.tipton.k12.ia.us
Tipton HS — 300/9-12
400 E 6th St 52772 — 563-886-6027
Chris Habben, prin. — Fax 886-2341
Tipton MS — 200/5-8
400 E 6th St 52772 — 563-886-6025
Sue O'Donnell, prin. — Fax 886-2555

**Toledo, Tama, Pop. 2,265**
South Tama County Community SD
Supt. — See Tama
South Tama County MS — 300/5-8
201 S Green St 52342 — 641-484-4121
Benjamin Adams, prin. — Fax 484-2699

**Traer, Tama, Pop. 1,686**
North Tama County Community SD — 500/K-12
605 Walnut St 50675 — 319-478-2265
David Hill, supt. — Fax 478-2917
www.n-tama.k12.ia.us
North Tama JSHS — 300/7-12
605 Walnut St 50675 — 319-478-2265
Paul Rea, prin. — Fax 478-2917

**Treynor, Pottawattamie, Pop. 919**
Treynor Community SD — 800/K-12
PO Box 369 51575 — 712-487-3414
Kevin Elwood, supt. — Fax 487-3332
www.treynorschools.org
Treynor HS — 200/9-12
PO Box 369 51575 — 712-487-3804
Gary McNeal, prin. — Fax 487-3332
Treynor MS — 200/6-8
PO Box 369 51575 — 712-487-3181
Jenny Berens, prin. — Fax 487-3567

**Tripoli, Bremer, Pop. 1,304**
Tripoli Community SD — 500/PK-12
209 8th Ave SW 50676 — 319-882-4201
Troy Heller, supt. — Fax 882-3103
www.tripoli.k12.ia.us
Tripoli JSHS — 300/6-12
209 8th Ave SW 50676 — 319-882-4202
Troy Heller, supt. — Fax 882-3103

**Troy Mills, Linn**
North Linn Community SD — 500/PK-12
PO Box 200 52344 — 319-224-3291
Karl Kurt, supt. — Fax 224-3727
www.northlinn.k12.ia.us
North Linn HS — 200/9-12
PO Box 200 52344 — 319-224-3291
Scott Beaty, prin. — Fax 224-3232
North Linn MS — 100/6-8
PO Box 200 52344 — 319-224-3291
Scott Beaty, prin. — Fax 224-3232

**Truro, Madison, Pop. 481**
Interstate 35 Community SD — 900/PK-12
PO Box 79 50257 — 641-765-4291
Kevin Fiene, supt. — Fax 765-4593
www.i-35.k12.ia.us
Interstate 35 HS — 300/9-12
PO Box 79 50257 — 641-765-4818
Steve Kaster, prin. — Fax 765-4820
Interstate 35 MS — 200/6-8
PO Box 200 50257 — 641-765-4908
Steve Kaster, prin. — Fax 765-4905

**Underwood, Pottawattamie, Pop. 909**
Underwood Community SD — 800/PK-12
PO Box 130 51576 — 712-566-2332
Edward Hawks, supt. — Fax 566-2070
www.underwoodeagles.org/
Underwood HS — 200/9-12
PO Box 130 51576 — 712-566-2703
Matt McDonough, prin. — Fax 566-2712
Underwood MS — 200/6-8
PO Box 130 51576 — 712-566-2332
J. Lewis Curtis, prin. — Fax 566-2070

**Union, Hardin, Pop. 394**
BCLUW Community SD
Supt. — See Conrad
BCLUW MS — 200/5-8
704 Commercial St 50258 — 641-486-5371
Dirk Borgman, prin. — Fax 486-5372

**Urbandale, Polk, Pop. 38,851**
Urbandale Community SD — 3,900/PK-12
11152 Aurora Ave 50322 — 515-457-5000
Steve Bass, supt. — Fax 457-5018
www.urbandaleschools.com
Urbandale HS — 1,200/9-12
7111 Aurora Ave 50322 — 515-457-6800
Dr. Brian Coppess, prin. — Fax 457-6810
Urbandale MS — 900/6-8
7701 Aurora Ave 50322 — 515-457-6600
Loren DeKruyf, prin. — Fax 457-6610

Des Moines Christian S — 1,000/PK-12
13007 Douglas Pkwy Ste 100 50323 — 515-252-2480
Glenn Vos, supt. — Fax 251-6911
Kaplan University — Post-Sec.
4655 121st St 50323 — 515-727-2100

**Van Horne, Benton, Pop. 678**
Benton Community SD — 1,600/PK-12
PO Box 70 52346 — 319-228-8701
Gary Zittergruen, supt. — Fax 228-8254
www.benton.k12.ia.us
Benton Community HS — 500/9-12
PO Box 70 52346 — 319-228-8701
James Bieschke, prin. — Fax 228-8747
Benton Community MS — 200/7-8
PO Box 70 52346 — 319-228-8701
Kal Goodchild, prin. — Fax 228-8747

**Van Meter, Dallas, Pop. 1,006**
Van Meter Community SD — 600/K-12
PO Box 257 50261 — 515-996-9960
Deron Durflinger, supt. — Fax 996-9954
www.vmbulldogs.com/
Van Meter HS — 400/9-12
PO Box 257 50261 — 515-996-2221
Deron Durflinger, prin. — Fax 996-2488
Van Meter MS — 700/6-8
PO Box 257 50261 — 515-996-2221
Adam Lamoureux, prin. — Fax 996-2488

**Ventura, Cerro Gordo, Pop. 712**
Garner-Hayfield-Ventura Community SD
Supt. — See Garner
Garner-Hayfield-Ventura JHS — 7-8
110 S Main St 50482 — 641-829-4484
Debra Steenhard, prin. — Fax 829-3995

**Victor, Iowa, Pop. 887**
H-L-V Community SD — 400/PK-12
PO Box B 52347 — 319-647-2161
Brad Hohensee, supt. — Fax 647-2164
www.hlv.k12.ia.us
H-L-V JSHS — 100/7-12
PO Box B 52347 — 319-647-2161
Cory Lahndorf, prin. — Fax 647-2164

**Villisca, Montgomery, Pop. 1,244**
Southwest Valley SD — 700/PK-12
406 E 3rd St 50864 — 712-826-2552
William Stone, supt. — Fax 826-4072
www.southwestvalley.org
Southwest Valley MS — 200/6-8
406 E 3rd St 50864 — 712-826-2552
Lora Top, prin. — Fax 826-4072
Other Schools – See Corning

**Vinton, Benton, Pop. 5,202**
Vinton-Shellsburg Community SD — 1,700/PK-12
1502 C Ave 52349 — 319-436-4728
Mary Jo Hainstock, supt. — Fax 472-3889
www.vscsd.org
Vinton-Shellsburg HS — 500/9-12
210 W 21st St 52349 — 319-436-4728
Matt Kingsbury, prin. — Fax 472-5704
Vinton-Shellsburg MS — 400/6-8
212 W 15th St 52349 — 319-436-4728
Shelly Petersen, prin. — Fax 472-4014

Iowa Braille and Sight Saving School — Post-Sec.
1002 G Ave 52349 — 319-472-5221

**Walcott, Scott, Pop. 1,613**
Davenport Community SD
Supt. — See Davenport
Walcott IS — 400/6-8
545 E James St 52773 — 563-284-6253
Mike Lawler, prin. — Fax 284-5081

**Wapello, Louisa, Pop. 2,049**
Wapello Community SD — 700/PK-12
406 Mechanic St 52653 — 319-523-3641
Mike Peterson, supt. — Fax 523-8151
www.wapello.k12.ia.us
Wapello HS — 200/9-12
501 Buchanan Ave 52653 — 319-523-3241
Steve Bohlen, prin. — Fax 523-4408
Wapello JHS — 100/7-8
501 Buchanan Ave 52653 — 319-523-8131
Steve Bohlen, prin. — Fax 523-4408

**Washington, Washington, Pop. 7,169**
Washington Community SD — 1,300/PK-12
PO Box 926 52353 — 319-653-6543
Jeff Dicks, supt. — Fax 653-5685
www.washington.k12.ia.us
Washington HS — 400/9-12
PO Box 271 52353 — 319-653-2143
Erik Buchholz, prin. — Fax 653-6751
Washington MS — 300/6-8
PO Box 490 52353 — 319-653-5414
Curt Mayer, prin. — Fax 653-7350

**Waterloo, Black Hawk, Pop. 66,424**
Waterloo Community SD 10,100/PK-12
1516 Washington St 50702 319-433-1800
Dr. Jane Lindaman, supt. Fax 433-1886
www.waterloo.k12.ia.us
Carver Academy 500/6-8
1505 Logan Ave 50703 319-433-2500
Mike Landers, prin. Fax 433-2548
Central MS 500/6-8
1350 Katoski Dr 50701 319-433-2100
Alissa Richards, prin. Fax 433-2149
East HS 1,000/9-12
214 High St 50703 319-433-2400
Marla Padget, prin. Fax 433-2498
Expo Alternative Learning Center 400/Alt
1410 Independence Ave 50703 319-433-1930
Cary Wieland, prin. Fax 433-1933
Hoover MS 800/6-8
630 Hillcrest Rd 50701 319-433-2830
Michael Fisher, prin. Fax 433-2843
West HS 1,600/9-12
425 E Ridgeway Ave 50702 319-433-2700
Andrew Miehe, prin. Fax 433-2749
Other Schools – See Evansdale

---

Allen College Post-Sec.
1825 Logan Ave 50703 319-226-2000
Blessed Maria Assunta Pallotta MS 6-8
3225 W 9th St 50702 319-232-6592
Kim Graven, prin. Fax 232-6963
College of Hair Design Post-Sec.
722 Water St Ste 201 50703 319-232-9995
Columbus HS 300/9-12
3231 W 9th St 50702 319-233-3358
Tom Ulses, prin. Fax 235-0733
Covenant Medical Center Post-Sec.
3421 W 9th St 50702 319-272-7296
Hawkeye Community College Post-Sec.
PO Box 8015 50704 319-296-2320
Waterloo Christian S 100/PK-12
1307 W Ridgeway Ave 50701 319-235-9309
Fax 833-4780

**Waucoma, Fayette, Pop. 253**
Turkey Valley Community SD 400/PK-12
3219 Highway 24 52171 563-776-6011
Clark Goltz, supt. Fax 776-4271
www.turkey-v.k12.ia.us
Turkey Valley JSHS 200/7-12
3219 Highway 24 52171 563-776-6011
Carol Knoll, prin. Fax 776-4271

**Waukee, Dallas, Pop. 13,637**
Waukee Community SD 6,300/PK-12
560 SE University Ave 50263 515-987-5161
Dr. David Wilkerson, supt. Fax 987-2701
www.waukeeschools.org
Prairieview S 400/8-9
655 SE University Ave 50263 515-987-2770
Juley Murphy-Tiernan, prin. Fax 987-2789
Timberline S 700/8-9
2605 SE LA Grant Pkwy 50263 515-987-5161
Brady Fleming, prin.
Waukee SHS 1,100/10-12
555 SE University Ave 50263 515-987-5163
Kirk Johnson, prin. Fax 987-2784

**Waukon, Allamakee, Pop. 3,873**
Allamakee Community SD 1,200/PK-12
1059 3rd Ave NW 52172 563-568-3409
Dave Herold, supt. Fax 568-2677
www.allamakee.k12.ia.us/
Waukon HS 400/9-12
1061 3rd Ave NW 52172 563-568-3466
Mike Hardy, prin. Fax 568-3165
Waukon MS 200/6-8
1059 3rd Ave NW 52172 563-568-6321
Jennifer Garin, prin. Fax 568-2677

**Waverly, Bremer, Pop. 9,752**
Waverly-Shell Rock Community SD 1,700/PK-12
1415 4th Ave SW 50677 319-352-3630
Dr. Ed Klamfoth, supt. Fax 352-5676
www.wsr.k12.ia.us
Greenview Alternative S 50/Alt
1405 4th Ave SW 50677 319-352-9273
Jeremy Langner, prin.
Waverly-Shell Rock HS 600/9-12
1405 4th Ave SW 50677 319-352-2087
David Fox, prin. Fax 352-2098
Waverly-Shell Rock MS 300/5-8
501 Heritage Way 50677 319-352-3632
Roger Wilcox, prin. Fax 352-5199

---

Wartburg College Post-Sec.
PO Box 1003 50677 319-352-8200

**Wayland, Henry, Pop. 957**
Waco Community SD 500/PK-12
PO Box 158 52654 319-256-6200
Frederick Whipple, supt. Fax 256-6213
www.wacocsd.org
Waco JSHS 200/7-12
PO Box 158 52654 319-256-6200
Jeff Nance, prin. Fax 256-6211

**Webster City, Hamilton, Pop. 7,961**
Webster City Community SD 1,600/PK-12
PO Box 10 50595 515-832-9200
Mike Sherwood, supt. Fax 832-9204
www.webster-city.k12.ia.us
Webster City HS 500/9-12
PO Box 10 50595 515-832-9210
Becky Hacker-Kluver, prin. Fax 832-9215
Webster City MS 500/5-8
PO Box 10 50595 515-832-9220
Becky Hacker-Kluver, prin. Fax 832-9225

**Wellman, Washington, Pop. 1,387**
Mid-Prairie Community SD 1,200/PK-12
PO Box 150 52356 319-646-6093
Mark Schneider, supt. Fax 646-2093
www.mid-prairie.k12.ia.us
Alternative Learning Center 50/Alt
PO Box 150 52356 319-646-6096
Amy Shalla, prin. Fax 646-2093
Mid-Prairie HS 300/9-12
PO Box 150 52356 319-646-6091
James Cayton, prin. Fax 646-6097
Other Schools – See Kalona

**West Bend, Palo Alto, Pop. 779**
West Bend - Mallard Community SD 300/K-12
PO Box 247 50597 515-887-7821
Amanda Schmidt, supt. Fax 887-7853
www.west-bend.k12.ia.us
West Bend - Mallard HS 100/9-12
PO Box 247 50597 515-887-7831
Paul Peppmeier, prin. Fax 887-7853
West Bend - Mallard MS 100/5-8
PO Box 247 50597 515-887-7831
Paul Peppmeier, prin. Fax 887-7853

**West Branch, Cedar, Pop. 2,295**
West Branch Community SD 800/PK-12
148 N Oliphant St 52358 319-643-7213
Kevin Hatfield, supt. Fax 643-7122
www.west-branch.k12.ia.us
West Branch HS 300/9-12
900 W Main St 52358 319-643-7216
Shannon Bucknell, prin. Fax 643-2415
West Branch MS 200/5-8
225 N Maple St 52358 319-643-5324
Sara Oswald, prin. Fax 643-5447

---

Scattergood Friends S 100/9-12
1951 Delta Ave 52358 319-643-7600
Thomas Weber, head sch Fax 643-7485

**West Burlington, Des Moines, Pop. 2,909**
West Burlington ISD 800/PK-12
607 Ramsey St 52655 319-752-8747
David Schmitt, supt. Fax 754-9382
www.wbschools.us
West Burlington HS 200/9-12
408 W Van Weiss Blvd 52655 319-752-7138
Bruce Snodgrass, prin. Fax 754-0075
West Burlington JHS 200/6-8
408 W Van Weiss Blvd 52655 319-752-7138
Bruce Snodgrass, prin. Fax 754-0075

---

Southeastern Community College Post-Sec.
PO Box 180 52655 319-752-2731

**West Des Moines, Polk, Pop. 55,623**
West Des Moines Community SD 8,800/PK-12
3550 Mills Civic Pkwy 50265 515-633-5000
Dr. Lisa Remy, supt. Fax 633-5099
www.wdmcs.org
Stilwell JHS 700/7-8
1601 Vine St 50265 515-633-6000
Eric Boyle, prin. Fax 633-6099
Valley HS 2,000/10-12
3650 Woodland Ave 50266 515-633-4000
Tim Miller, prin. Fax 633-4099
Valley Southwoods Freshman HS 700/9-9
625 S 35th St 50265 515-633-4500
Mitch Kuhnert, prin. Fax 633-4599
Walnut Creek Alternative HS 200/Alt
1020 8th St 50265 515-633-6480
Dr. Kim Davis, prin. Fax 633-6499
Other Schools – See Clive

---

Dowling Catholic HS 1,400/9-12
1400 Buffalo Rd 50265 515-225-3000
Matt Meendering, prin. Fax 222-1056
Iowa Christian Academy 300/PK-12
2501 Vine St 50265 515-221-3999
Dr. Brenda Hillman, admin. Fax 225-2387

**West Liberty, Muscatine, Pop. 3,704**
West Liberty Community SD 1,200/PK-12
111 W 7th St 52776 319-627-2116
Steve Hanson, supt. Fax 627-2963
www.wl.k12.ia.us
West Liberty HS 300/9-12
310 W Maxson Ave 52776 319-627-2115
James Hamilton, prin. Fax 627-2046
West Liberty MS 300/6-8
203 E 7th St 52776 319-627-2118
Vicki Vernon, prin. Fax 627-2092

**Westside, Crawford, Pop. 299**
Ar-We-Va Community SD 100/PK-12
108 Clinton St 51467 712-663-4311
Kurt Brosamle, supt. Fax 663-4312
www.ar-we-va.k12.ia.us
Westside JSHS 100/6-12
108 Clinton St 51467 712-663-4312
Kurt Brosamle, prin. Fax 663-4312

**West Union, Fayette, Pop. 2,464**
North Fayette Community SD 700/PK-12
PO Box 73 52175 563-422-3851
Duane Willhite, supt. Fax 422-3854
www.nfvschools.com
North Fayette Valley HS 300/9-12
PO Box 73 52175 563-422-3852
Todd Wolverton, prin. Fax 422-5798

**Wheatland, Clinton, Pop. 762**
Calamus-Wheatland Community SD 500/PK-12
PO Box 279 52777 563-374-1292
Lonnie Luepker, supt. Fax 374-1080
www.cal-wheat.k12.ia.us
Calamus-Wheatland JSHS 200/7-12
PO Box 279 52777 563-374-1292
Christine Meyer, prin. Fax 374-1080

**Whiting, Monona, Pop. 758**
Whiting Community SD 200/PK-12
PO Box 295 51063 712-455-2468
Jeff Thelander, supt. Fax 455-2601
www.whitingcsd.org
Whiting JSHS 100/6-12
PO Box 295 51063 712-455-2468
Al Laboranti, prin. Fax 455-2601

**Williamsburg, Iowa, Pop. 3,044**
Williamsburg Community SD 1,000/PK-12
PO Box 120 52361 319-668-1059
Dr. Carol Montz, supt. Fax 668-9311
www.williamsburg.k12.ia.us
Williamsburg JSHS 600/7-12
PO Box 120 52361 319-668-1050
Lynell O'Connor, prin. Fax 668-9311

**Wilton, Muscatine, Pop. 2,767**
Wilton Community SD 900/PK-12
1002 Cypress St 52778 563-732-2035
Joe Burnett, supt. Fax 732-4121
www.wiltoncsd.org/
Wilton JSHS 400/7-12
1002 Cypress St 52778 563-732-2629
Ken Crawford, prin. Fax 732-4121

**Winfield, Henry, Pop. 1,123**
Winfield-Mt. Union Community SD 400/PK-12
PO Box E 52659 319-257-7700
Jeff Maeder, supt. Fax 257-7714
wmucsd.org
Winfield-Mt. Union JSHS 300/6-12
PO Box E 52659 319-257-7701
David Edwards, prin. Fax 257-7703

**Winterset, Madison, Pop. 5,159**
Winterset Community SD 1,800/PK-12
PO Box 30 50273 515-462-2718
Dr. Susan Meade, supt. Fax 462-2732
www.winterset.k12.ia.us
Winterset HS 500/9-12
624 Husky Dr 50273 515-462-3320
Lee Schipull, prin. Fax 462-2178
Winterset JHS 300/7-8
720 Husky Dr 50273 515-462-3336
Doug Hinrichs, prin. Fax 462-2178

**Winthrop, Buchanan, Pop. 845**
East Buchanan Community SD 600/PK-12
414 5th St N 50682 319-935-3767
Dan Fox, supt. Fax 935-3749
www.east-buc.k12.ia.us
East Buchanan HS 200/9-12
414 5th St N 50682 319-935-3367
Travis Schueller, prin. Fax 935-3615
East Buchanan MS 100/6-8
414 5th St N 50682 319-935-3367
Travis Schueller, prin. Fax 935-3615

**Woodbine, Harrison, Pop. 1,455**
Woodbine Community SD 500/PK-12
501 Weare St 51579 712-647-2411
Doug Gee, supt. Fax 647-2526
sites.google.com/a/woodbine.k12.ia.us/flashy-tiger
Woodbine HS 200/7-12
501 Weare St 51579 712-647-2227
Sam Swenson, prin. Fax 647-2279

**Woodward, Dallas, Pop. 1,006**
Woodward-Granger Community SD
Supt. — See Granger
Woodward Academy 300/Alt
1251 334th St 50276 515-438-3481
Jeremy Hilbert, prin. Fax 438-3489
Woodward-Granger HS 200/9-12
306 W 3rd St 50276 515-438-2115
Robert Boley, prin. Fax 438-2497
Woodward-Granger MS 200/6-8
306 W 3rd St 50276 515-438-4653
Bret Miller, prin. Fax 438-4329

**Wyoming, Jones, Pop. 513**
Midland Community SD 300/PK-12
PO Box 109 52362 563-488-2292
Brian Rodenberg, supt. Fax 488-2253
www.midland.k12.ia.us
Midland MSHS 200/6-12
PO Box 109 52362 563-488-2292
Carol Reilly, prin. Fax 488-2253

# KANSAS

## KANSAS DEPARTMENT OF EDUCATION
**900 SW Jackson St, Topeka 66612**
**Telephone 785-296-3202**
**Fax 785-296-7933**
**Website http://www.ksde.org**

Commissioner of Education Dr. Diane DeBacker

## KANSAS BOARD OF EDUCATION
**120 SE 10th Ave, Topeka 66612-1103**

Chairperson David Dennis

## PUBLIC, PRIVATE AND CATHOLIC SECONDARY SCHOOLS

**Abilene, Dickinson, Pop. 6,690**
Abilene USD 435 1,600/PK-12
PO Box 639 67410 785-263-2630
Dr. Denise Guy, supt. Fax 263-7610
www.abileneschools.org/
Abilene HS 500/9-12
1300 N Cedar St 67410 785-263-1260
Ben Smith, prin. Fax 263-3327
Abilene MS 400/6-8
500 NW 14th St 67410 785-263-1471
Ron Wilson, prin. Fax 263-4443

**Agra, Phillips, Pop. 263**
Thunder Ridge SD
Supt. — See Kensington
Thunder Ridge MS 100/PK-PK, 4-
941 Kansas Ave 67621 785-638-2244
Beth Norris, prin. Fax 638-2254

**Allen, Lyon, Pop. 176**
North Lyon County USD 251
Supt. — See Americus
Northern Heights HS 100/9-12
1208 Highway 56 66833 620-528-3521
Russell Swisher, prin. Fax 528-3392

**Alma, Wabaunsee, Pop. 821**
Mill Creek Valley USD 329 500/PK-12
PO Box 157 66401 785-765-3394
Brad Starnes, supt. Fax 765-3624
www.usd329.com
Wabaunsee HS 100/9-12
912 Missouri Ave 66401 785-765-3315
Jeff Stuewe, prin. Fax 765-3523
Other Schools – See Paxico

**Almena, Norton, Pop. 407**
Northern Valley USD 212 200/PK-12
PO Box 217 67622 785-669-2445
Steve Taylor, supt. Fax 669-2263
www.nvhuskies.org
Northern Valley HS 50/9-12
PO Box 217 67622 785-669-2445
Steve Taylor, prin. Fax 669-2263
Other Schools – See Long Island

**Altamont, Labette, Pop. 1,042**
Labette County USD 506 1,700/PK-12
PO Box 189 67330 620-784-5326
Dr. John Wyrick, supt. Fax 784-5879
www.usd506.org
Labette County HS 500/9-12
PO Box 407 67330 620-784-5321
Shane Holtzman, prin. Fax 784-2682

**Americus, Lyon, Pop. 875**
North Lyon County USD 251 400/PK-12
PO Box 527 66835 620-443-5116
Aron Dody, supt. Fax 443-5659
www.usd251.org
Other Schools – See Allen

**Andale, Sedgwick, Pop. 920**
Renwick USD 267 1,900/PK-12
PO Box 68 67001 316-444-2165
Tracy Bourne, supt. Fax 445-2241
www.usd267.com
Andale HS 400/9-12
PO Box 28 67001 316-444-2607
Stan May, prin. Fax 445-2501
Other Schools – See Garden Plain

**Andover, Butler, Pop. 11,537**
Andover USD 385 5,300/PK-12
1432 N Andover Rd 67002 316-218-4660
Greg Rasmussen, supt. Fax 733-3604
www.usd385.org
Andover Central HS 700/9-12
603 E Central Ave 67002 316-218-4700
Cheryl Hochhalter, prin. Fax 733-7798
Andover Central MS 600/6-8
903 E Central Ave 67002 316-218-4710
Tim Hayden, prin. Fax 733-8563
Andover HS 800/9-12
1744 N Andover Rd 67002 316-218-4600
Bob Baier, prin. Fax 733-3681
Andover MS 600/6-8
1628 N Andover Rd 67002 316-218-4610
Deb Regier, prin. Fax 733-4165

**Anthony, Harper, Pop. 2,226**
Anthony-Harper USD 361 800/PK-12
PO Box 486 67003 620-842-5183
Josh Swartz, supt. Fax 842-5307
www.usd361.org/
Chaparral HS 200/9-12
467 N State Road 14 67003 620-842-5155
Ron Levan, prin. Fax 896-2927

**Argonia, Sumner, Pop. 493**
Argonia USD 359 200/PK-12
202 E Allen St 67004 620-435-6311
Dr. Julie McPherrron, supt. Fax 435-6623
www.argonia359.org
Argonia JSHS 100/6-12
202 E Allen St 67004 620-435-6611
Aaron Dewlen, prin. Fax 435-6358

**Arkansas City, Cowley, Pop. 11,966**
Arkansas City USD 470 2,700/PK-12
PO Box 1028 67005 620-441-2000
Ron Ballard, supt. Fax 441-2009
www.usd470.com
Arkansas City HS 800/9-12
1200 W Radio Ln 67005 620-441-2010
Dr. David Zumwalt, prin. Fax 441-2021
Arkansas City MS 600/6-8
400 E Kansas Ave 67005 620-441-2030
William Pfannenstiel, prin. Fax 441-2036

---

Ark City Christian Academy 100/PK-12
PO Box 1181 67005 620-442-0022
Tamen Eis, prin. Fax 442-0034
Cowley County Community College Post-Sec.
PO Box 1147 67005 620-442-0430

**Arma, Crawford, Pop. 1,474**
Northeast USD 246 500/K-12
PO Box 669 66712 620-347-4116
Greg Gorman, supt. Fax 347-4087
www.usd246.org
Northeast HS 200/9-12
PO Box 669 66712 620-347-4115
Jason Clemensen, prin. Fax 347-4149

**Ashland, Clark, Pop. 841**
Ashland USD 220 200/PK-12
PO Box 187 67831 620-635-2220
Dr. Calvin Jones, supt. Fax 635-2637
www.ashland.k12.ks.us
Ashland HS 100/9-12
PO Box 187 67831 620-635-2814
Dr. Calvin Jones, prin. Fax 635-2637
Ashland JHS 50/7-8
PO Box 187 67831 620-635-2814
Fax 635-2637

**Atchison, Atchison, Pop. 10,700**
Atchison USD 409 1,700/PK-12
626 Commercial St 66002 913-367-4384
Dr. Susan Myers, supt. Fax 367-2246
www.usd409.net
Atchison Alternative S 50/Alt
215 N 8th St 66002 913-360-6540
Gerre Martin, prin. Fax 367-2860
Atchison HS 400/9-12
1500 Riley St 66002 913-367-4162
Bryon Hanson, prin. Fax 367-0415
Atchison MS 300/6-8
301 N 5th St 66002 913-367-5363
Chad Bilderback, prin. Fax 367-1302

---

Benedictine College Post-Sec.
1020 N 2nd St 66002 913-367-5340
Highland Community College-Technical Ctr Post-Sec.
1501 Riley St 66002 913-367-6204
Maur Hill - Mount Academy 200/9-12
1000 Green St 66002 913-367-5482
Monika King, prin. Fax 367-5096

**Attica, Harper, Pop. 621**
Attica USD 511 100/PK-12
PO Box 415 67009 620-254-7661
Dale Adams, supt. Fax 254-7872
www.usd511.net
Attica JSHS 50/7-12
PO Box 415 67009 620-254-7915
Joshua Lanning, prin. Fax 254-7872

**Atwood, Rawlins, Pop. 1,181**
Rawlins County USD 105 300/PK-12
205 N 4th St Ste 1 67730 785-626-3236
Jerry Hodson, supt. Fax 626-3083
www.usd105.org
Rawlins County JSHS 200/7-12
100 N 8th St 67730 785-626-3289
Matthew Dunning, prin. Fax 626-1022

**Augusta, Butler, Pop. 9,098**
Augusta USD 402 2,200/PK-12
2345 Greyhound Dr 67010 316-775-5484
Dr. John Black, supt. Fax 775-5035
www.usd402.com
Augusta HS 600/9-12
2020 Ohio St 67010 316-775-5461
Donna Zerr, prin. Fax 775-3484
Augusta MS 600/6-8
1001 State St 67010 316-775-6383
Matthew Ward, prin. Fax 775-3853

**Axtell, Marshall, Pop. 393**
Prairie Hills USD 113
Supt. — See Sabetha
Axtell HS 100/9-12
504 Pine St 66403 785-736-2237
Duane Ford, prin. Fax 736-2295

**Baldwin City, Douglas, Pop. 4,416**
Baldwin City USD 348 1,400/PK-12
PO Box 67 66006 785-594-2721
Paul Dorathy, supt. Fax 594-3408
www.usd348.com/
Baldwin HS 400/9-12
PO Box 67 66006 785-594-2725
Rob McKim, prin. Fax 594-2858
Baldwin JHS 300/6-8
PO Box 67 66006 785-594-2448
Joe Sample, prin. Fax 594-2449

---

Baker University Post-Sec.
PO Box 65 66006 785-594-6451

**Barnes, Washington, Pop. 159**
Barnes USD 223 400/PK-12
PO Box 188 66933 785-763-4231
Brian Cordel, supt. Fax 763-4461
www.usd223.org
Other Schools – See Hanover, Linn

**Basehor, Leavenworth, Pop. 4,548**
Basehor-Linwood USD 458 2,100/K-12
PO Box 282 66007 913-724-1396
David Howard, supt. Fax 724-2709
www.usd458.org
Basehor-Linwood HS 700/9-12
2108 N 155th St 66007 913-724-2266
Sherry Reeves, prin. Fax 724-2040
Basehor-Linwood MS 500/6-8
15900 Conley Rd 66007 913-724-2976
Amy Garver, prin. Fax 955-7074

**Baxter Springs, Cherokee, Pop. 3,956**
Baxter Springs USD 508 800/PK-12
1108 Military Ave 66713 620-856-2375
David Pendergraft, supt. Fax 856-3943
www.usd508.org
Baxter Springs HS 300/7-12
100 N Military Ave 66713 620-856-3366
Cory White, prin. Fax 856-2918

**Bel Aire, Sedgwick, Pop. 6,561**
Wichita USD 259
Supt. — See Wichita
Northeast Magnet HS 600/9-12
5550 N Lycee St 67226 316-973-2300
Matt Creasman, prin. Fax 973-2307

Sunrise Christian Academy 500/PK-12
5500 E 45th St N 67220 316-744-9262
Dr. Robert Lindsted, supt. Fax 744-7449

**Belle Plaine, Sumner, Pop. 1,652**
Belle Plaine USD 357 600/PK-12
PO Box 760 67013 620-488-2288
Dr. Rose Kane, supt. Fax 488-3517
www.usd357.org
Belle Plaine HS 200/9-12
PO Box 8 67013 620-488-2421
Monte Stewart, prin. Fax 488-3536
Belle Plaine MS 200/5-8
PO Box 457 67013 620-488-2222
Morey Balzer, prin. Fax 488-3391

**Belleville, Republic, Pop. 1,978**
Republic County USD 109 400/K-12
PO Box 469 66935 785-527-5621
Michael Couch, supt. Fax 527-5375
www.usd109.org/
Republic County JSHS 200/6-12
PO Box 469 66935 785-527-2281
Alan Sheets, prin. Fax 527-5505

**Beloit, Mitchell, Pop. 3,807**
Beloit USD 273 800/PK-12
PO Box 547 67420 785-738-3261
Jeff Travis, supt. Fax 738-4103
www.usd273.org
Alternative Learning Center Alt
PO Box 506 67420 785-738-5275
Karen Niemczyk, prin. Fax 738-9967
Beloit JSHS 400/7-12
PO Box 606 67420 785-738-3593
Casey Seyfert, prin. Fax 738-5566

North Central Kansas Technical College Post-Sec.
PO Box 507 67420 785-738-2276
St. John Catholic HS 100/7-12
209 S Cherry St 67420 785-738-2942
Marcy Kee, prin. Fax 738-4462

**Bennington, Ottawa, Pop. 670**
Twin Valley USD 240 600/PK-12
PO Box 38 67422 785-488-3325
Janet Neufeld, supt. Fax 488-3326
www.usd240.org
Bennington HS 100/7-12
PO Box 8 67422 785-488-3321
Steve Rivers, prin. Fax 488-2939
Other Schools – See Tescott

**Benton, Butler, Pop. 874**
Circle USD 375
Supt. — See Towanda
Circle MS 300/7-8
14697 SW 20th St 67017 316-778-1470
Brenda Young, prin. Fax 536-2249

**Bird City, Cheyenne, Pop. 441**
Cheylin USD 103 100/K-12
PO Box 28 67731 785-734-2341
Shelly Angelos, supt. Fax 734-2489
www.cheylin.com/
Cheylin West JSHS 100/7-12
PO Box 28 67731 785-734-2341
Shelly Angelos, prin. Fax 734-2489

**Blue Rapids, Marshall, Pop. 1,010**
Valley Heights USD 498
Supt. — See Waterville
Valley Heights JSHS 100/7-12
2274 6th Rd 66411 785-363-2508
Trenton Horn, prin. Fax 363-2072

**Bonner Springs, Wyandotte, Pop. 7,122**
Bonner Springs USD 204 2,500/PK-12
PO Box 435 66012 913-422-5600
Daniel Brungardt, supt. Fax 422-4193
www.usd204.net
Bonner Springs HS 700/9-12
PO Box 216 66012 913-422-5121
Joe Hornback, prin. Fax 422-7284
Clark MS 600/6-8
PO Box 336 66012 913-422-5115
Rick Moulin, prin. Fax 422-1644

**Brewster, Thomas, Pop. 303**
Brewster USD 314 100/PK-12
PO Box 220 67732 785-694-2236
Shea Rothchild, supt. Fax 694-2746
www.usd314.k12.ks.us
Brewster HS 50/7-12
PO Box 220 67732 785-694-2236
Shea Rothchild, prin. Fax 694-2746

**Brookville, Saline, Pop. 257**
Ell-Saline USD 307 500/K-12
PO Box 157 67425 785-225-6813
Jerry Minneman, supt. Fax 225-6815
www.ellsaline.org
Ell-Saline MSHS 200/7-12
414 E Anderson St 67425 785-225-6633
Susan Wildeman, prin. Fax 225-6694

**Bucklin, Ford, Pop. 775**
Bucklin USD 459 300/PK-12
PO Box 8 67834 620-826-3828
Dr. Kelly Arnberger, supt. Fax 826-3377
www.bucklinschools.com
Bucklin HS 100/5-12
PO Box 8 67834 620-826-3241
Carol Whisman, prin. Fax 826-9966

**Buffalo, Wilson, Pop. 229**
Altoona-Midway USD 387 200/PK-12
20584 US 75 Hwy 66717 620-537-7721
Terence Wilson, supt. Fax 537-7721
www.usd387.org
Altoona-Midway MSHS 100/5-12
20704 US 75 Hwy 66717 620-537-7711
Darrin Ashmore, prin. Fax 537-2641

**Buhler, Reno, Pop. 1,319**
Buhler USD 313 2,300/PK-12
PO Box 320 67522 620-543-2258
Mike Berblinger, supt. Fax 543-2510
www.buhlerschools.org
Buhler HS 600/9-12
611 N Main St 67522 620-543-2255
Mike Ellegood, prin. Fax 543-2853
Other Schools – See Hutchinson

**Burden, Cowley, Pop. 531**
Central USD 462 300/PK-12
PO Box 128 67019 620-438-2218
Marian Hedges, supt. Fax 438-2217
www.usd462.org
Central JSHS 100/7-12
PO Box 128 67019 620-438-2215
Shane Walter, prin. Fax 438-2217

**Burlingame, Osage, Pop. 917**
Burlingame USD 454 300/PK-12
100 Bloomquist Dr Ste A 66413 785-654-3328
Allen Konicek, supt. Fax 654-3570
www.usd454.net
Burlingame JSHS 200/7-12
100 Bloomquist Dr Ste A 66413 785-654-3315
Tammy Baird, prin. Fax 654-3191

**Burlington, Coffey, Pop. 2,635**
Burlington USD 244 900/PK-12
200 S 6th St 66839 620-364-8478
Cliff Williams, supt. Fax 364-8548
www.usd244ks.org
Burlington HS 300/9-12
830 Cross St 66839 620-364-8672
Don Hilliard, prin. Fax 364-8680
Burlington MS 300/5-8
720 Cross St 66839 620-364-2156
Matt Thomsen, prin. Fax 364-8560

**Burrton, Harvey, Pop. 886**
Burrton USD 369 300/PK-12
PO Box 369 67020 620-463-3840
Jeff Shearon, supt. Fax 463-2636
www.burrton.usd369.org
Burrton MSHS 100/6-12
PO Box 369 67020 620-463-3820
Joan Simoneau, prin. Fax 463-2096

**Bushton, Rice, Pop. 274**
Central Plains USD 112
Supt. — See Holyrood
Central Plains MS 100/5-8
500 S Main St 67427 620-562-3596
Jane Oeser, prin. Fax 562-3248

**Caldwell, Sumner, Pop. 1,059**
Caldwell USD 360 200/PK-12
22 N Webb St 67022 620-845-2585
Alan Jamison, supt. Fax 845-2610
www.usd360.com
Caldwell Secondary S 100/6-12
31 N Osage St 67022 620-845-2585
Kevin Schmidt, prin. Fax 845-2534

**Caney, Montgomery, Pop. 2,080**
Caney Valley USD 436 900/PK-12
700 E Bullpup Blvd 67333 620-879-9200
Blake Vargas, supt. Fax 879-9209
www.caney.com
Caney Valley JSHS 400/7-12
601 E Bullpup Blvd 67333 620-879-9220
William Ellis, prin. Fax 879-9227

**Canton, McPherson, Pop. 732**
Canton-Galva USD 419 400/K-12
PO Box 317 67428 620-628-4901
Bill Seidl, supt. Fax 628-4380
usd419.org
Canton-Galva JSHS 100/7-12
PO Box 275 67428 620-628-4401
Shawn Koehn, prin. Fax 628-4951

**Carbondale, Osage, Pop. 1,411**
Santa Fe Trail USD 434 1,100/PK-12
1663 E US Highway 56 66414 785-665-7168
Steve Pegram, supt. Fax 665-7164
www.usd434.org
Carbondale Attendance Center 300/5-8
315 N 4th St 66414 785-836-7188
Michael Flax, prin. Fax 836-7696
Santa Fe Trail HS 400/9-12
15701 S California Rd 66414 785-665-7161
Patrick Graham, prin. Fax 665-7193

**Cawker City, Mitchell, Pop. 462**
Waconda USD 272 300/PK-12
PO Box 326 67430 785-781-4328
Troy Damman, supt. Fax 781-4318
www.usd272.org
Other Schools – See Downs

**Cedar Vale, Chautauqua, Pop. 554**
Cedar Vale USD 285 100/PK-12
PO Box 458 67024 620-758-2265
Lance Rhodd, supt. Fax 758-2647
www.cvs285.net
Cedar Vale JSHS 100/6-12
PO Box 458 67024 620-758-2791
Jackie Burdette, prin. Fax 758-2704

**Centralia, Nemaha, Pop. 501**
Vermillion USD 380
Supt. — See Vermillion
Centralia JSHS 100/7-12
507 John Riggins Ave 66415 785-857-3324
Larry Glatczak, prin. Fax 857-3847

**Chanute, Neosho, Pop. 8,951**
Chanute USD 413 1,900/PK-12
315 Chanute 35 Pkwy 66720 620-432-2500
Richard Proffitt, supt. Fax 431-6810
www.usd413.org
Chanute HS 600/9-12
1501 W 36th St 66720 620-432-2510
John Lawrence, prin. Fax 431-3020
Royster MS 400/6-8
400 W Main St 66720 620-432-2520
Lori Kiblinger, prin. Fax 431-7841

Neosho County Community College Post-Sec.
800 W 14th St 66720 620-431-2820

**Chapman, Dickinson, Pop. 1,368**
Chapman USD 473 1,100/K-12
PO Box 249 67431 785-922-6521
Lacee Sell, supt. Fax 922-6446
usd473.net
Chapman HS 300/9-12
PO Box 249 67431 785-922-6561
Kevin Suther, prin. Fax 922-7162
Chapman MS 300/6-8
PO Box 249 67431 785-922-6555
Bruce Hurford, prin. Fax 922-6601

**Chase, Rice, Pop. 461**
Chase-Raymond USD 401 200/PK-12
313 E Avenue C 67524 620-938-2913
Carl Helm, supt. Fax 938-2622
www.usd401.com/
Chase HS 50/9-12
313 E Avenue C 67524 620-938-2923
Glenna Grinstead, prin. Fax 938-2456
Raymond JHS 50/7-8
313 E Avenue C 67524 620-938-2923
Glenna Grinstead, prin. Fax 938-2456

**Cheney, Sedgwick, Pop. 2,072**
Cheney USD 268 800/PK-12
100 W 6th Ave 67025 316-542-3512
David Grover, supt. Fax 542-0326
www.cheney268.com
Cheney HS 300/9-12
100 W 6th Ave 67025 316-542-3113
Greg Rosenhagen, prin. Fax 542-3789
Cheney MS 200/6-8
100 W 6th Ave 67025 316-542-0060
Amy Wallace, prin. Fax 542-0608

**Cherokee, Crawford, Pop. 696**
Cherokee USD 247 600/PK-12
506 S Smelter St 66724 620-457-8350
Brad Miner, supt. Fax 457-8428
www.usd247.com
Southeast HS 200/9-12
126 W 400 Hwy 66724 620-457-8365
Larry Malle, prin. Fax 457-8389
Southeast JHS 300/5-8
206 W Magnolia St 66724 620-457-8315
Joseph Martin, prin. Fax 457-8380

**Cherryvale, Montgomery, Pop. 2,326**
Cherryvale USD 447 900/PK-12
618 E 4th St 67335 620-336-8130
George Owens, supt. Fax 336-8133
www.usd447.org
Cherryvale MSHS 400/7-12
700 S Carson St 67335 620-336-8100
Scott Lambdin, prin. Fax 336-8110

**Chetopa, Labette, Pop. 1,068**
Chetopa - St. Paul USD 505 400/PK-12
430 Elm St 67336 620-236-7244
Dr. Bobbi Williams, supt. Fax 236-4271
www.usd505.org
Chetopa HS 100/6-12
430 Elm St 67336 620-236-7244
Lonnie Moser, prin. Fax 236-4271
Other Schools – See Saint Paul

**Cimarron, Gray, Pop. 2,164**
Cimarron-Ensign USD 102 700/K-12
PO Box 489 67835 620-855-7743
Mike Waters, supt. Fax 855-7745
www.cimarronschools.net
Cimarron JSHS 300/7-12
PO Box 489 67835 620-855-3323
John Luhrs, prin. Fax 855-3219

**Claflin, Barton, Pop. 637**
Central Plains USD 112
Supt. — See Holyrood
Central Plains HS 100/9-12
PO Box 348 67525 620-587-3801
Toby Holmes, prin. Fax 587-3677

**Clay Center, Clay, Pop. 4,283**
Clay Center USD 379 1,300/K-12
PO Box 97 67432 785-632-3176
Michael Folks, supt. Fax 632-5020
www.usd379.org/
Clay Center Community HS 300/9-12
1630 9th St 67432 785-632-2131
Bud Young, prin. Fax 632-2076
Clay Center Community MS 300/6-8
935 Prospect St 67432 785-632-3232
Keith Hoffman, prin. Fax 632-6013
Other Schools – See Wakefield

**Clearwater, Sedgwick, Pop. 2,443**
Clearwater USD 264 1,200/PK-12
PO Box 248 67026 620-584-2091
Paul Becker, supt. Fax 584-6705
www.usd264.org
Clearwater HS 400/9-12
PO Box 248 67026 620-584-2361
Bob Mellen, prin. Fax 584-2083

Clearwater MS — 200/7-8
PO Box 248 67026 — 620-584-2036
Danielle Hollas, prin. — Fax 584-2199

**Clyde, Cloud, Pop. 706**
Clifton-Clyde USD 224 — 300/PK-12
616 N High St Ste 2 66938 — 785-446-2098
Corey Reese, supt. — Fax 446-3000
www.usd224.com/
Clifton-Clyde HS — 100/8-12
616 N High St Ste 1 66938 — 785-446-3444
Corey Reese, prin. — Fax 446-3458

**Coffeyville, Montgomery, Pop. 9,654**
Coffeyville USD 445 — 1,800/PK-12
615 Ellis St 67337 — 620-252-6400
Craig A. Correll Ed.D., supt. — Fax 252-6807
cvilleschools.com
Field Kindley Memorial HS — 500/9-12
1110 W 8th St 67337 — 620-252-6410
Travis Stalford, prin. — Fax 252-6818
Horn Field Kindley Tech Academy — Alt
615 Ellis St 67337 — 620-252-6440
Travis Stalford, prin.
Roosevelt MS — 200/7-8
1000 W 8th St 67337 — 620-252-6420
Jeffrey Pegues, prin. — Fax 252-6844
LINC, 510 W 8th St 67337 — Adult
John Bally, lead tchr. — 620-251-9070

---

Coffeyville Community College — Post-Sec.
400 W 11th St 67337 — 620-251-7700

**Colby, Thomas, Pop. 5,323**
Colby USD 315 — 900/K-12
600 W 3rd St 67701 — 785-460-5000
Katina Brenn, supt. — Fax 460-5050
www.colbyeagles.org
Colby HS — 300/9-12
1890 S Franklin Ave 67701 — 785-460-5300
Troy Keiswetter, prin. — Fax 460-5350
Colby MS — 200/6-8
750 W 3rd St 67701 — 785-460-5200
Robb Ross, prin. — Fax 460-5250

---

Colby Community College — Post-Sec.
1255 S Range Ave 67701 — 785-462-3984
Heartland Christian S — 100/PK-12
1995 W 4th St 67701 — 785-460-6419
Dr. Mark Gundlach, admin. — Fax 460-8337

**Coldwater, Comanche, Pop. 813**
South Central USD 300 — 300/K-12
PO Box 721 67029 — 620-582-2181
Michael Baldwin, supt. — Fax 582-2540
www.usd300ks.com
South Central HS — 100/9-12
PO Box 578 67029 — 620-582-2158
Ty Theurer, prin. — Fax 582-2535
Other Schools – See Protection

**Colony, Anderson, Pop. 394**
Crest USD 479 — 200/K-12
PO Box 305 66015 — 620-852-3540
Chuck Mahon, supt. — Fax 852-3542
www.usd479.org
Crest HS — 100/9-12
PO Box 325 66015 — 620-852-3521
Chuck Mahon, prin. — Fax 852-3357

**Columbus, Cherokee, Pop. 3,208**
Columbus USD 493 — 1,100/PK-12
802 S Highschool Ave 66725 — 620-429-3661
David Carriger, supt. — Fax 429-2673
www.usd493.com
Central S — 400/4-8
810 S Highschool Ave 66725 — 620-429-3943
James Bolden, prin. — Fax 429-2882
Columbus HS — 300/9-12
124 S Highschool Ave 66725 — 620-429-3821
Tony Shearburn, prin. — Fax 429-3657

**Concordia, Cloud, Pop. 5,314**
Concordia USD 333 — 1,100/PK-12
217 W 7th St 66901 — 785-243-3518
Beverly Mortimer, supt. — Fax 243-8883
www.usd333.com
Concordia JSHS — 500/7-12
436 W 10th St 66901 — 785-243-2452
Bryce Wachs, prin. — Fax 243-8805

---

Cloud County Community College — Post-Sec.
2221 Campus Dr 66901 — 785-243-1435

**Conway Springs, Sumner, Pop. 1,251**
Conway Springs USD 356 — 600/K-12
110 N Monnett St 67031 — 620-456-2961
Clay Murphy, supt. — Fax 456-3173
www.usd356.org
Conway Springs HS — 200/9-12
607 W Saint Louis St 67031 — 620-456-2963
Brent Harrell, prin. — Fax 456-3314
Conway Springs MS — 100/6-8
112 N Cranmer St 67031 — 620-456-2965
Ryan Rusco, prin. — Fax 456-3313

**Copeland, Gray, Pop. 310**
Copeland USD 476 — 100/PK-8
PO Box 156 67837 — 620-668-5565
Jay Zehr, supt. — Fax 668-5568
www.usd476.org
South Gray JHS — 50/6-8
PO Box 156 67837 — 620-668-5565
Jay Zehr, prin. — Fax 668-5568

**Cottonwood Falls, Chase, Pop. 897**
Chase County USD 284 — 300/PK-12
PO Box 569 66845 — 620-273-6303
Jeffrey Kohlman, supt. — Fax 273-6717
www.usd284.org/
Chase County JSHS — 100/7-12
PO Box 400 66845 — 620-273-6354
Travis Githens, prin. — Fax 273-8337

**Council Grove, Morris, Pop. 2,159**
Morris County USD 417 — 800/PK-12
17 Wood St 66846 — 620-767-5192
Doug Conwell, supt. — Fax 767-5444
www.usd417.net
Council Grove JSHS — 200/7-12
129 Hockaday St 66846 — 620-767-5149
Kelly McDiffett, prin. — Fax 767-7280

**Courtland, Republic, Pop. 285**
Pike Valley USD 426
Supt. — See Scandia
Pike Valley JHS — 100/6-8
PO Box 320 66939 — 785-374-4221
Mike Gritten, prin. — Fax 374-4268

**Cunningham, Kingman, Pop. 450**
Cunningham USD 332 — 200/K-12
PO Box 67 67035 — 620-298-3271
Robert Reed, supt. — Fax 298-2562
www.usd332.org/
Cunningham HS — 100/9-12
PO Box 98 67035 — 620-298-2473
Robert Reed, prin. — Fax 298-5005

**Damar, Rooks, Pop. 131**
Palco USD 269 — 200/PK-12
PO Box 38 67632 — 785-737-4635
Larry Lysell M.S., supt. — Fax 737-4636
www.usd269.net
Other Schools – See Palco

**Deerfield, Kearny, Pop. 694**
Deerfield USD 216 — 300/PK-12
803 Beech 67838 — 620-426-8516
Dr. Daniel Slack, supt. — Fax 426-7890
www.usd216.org
Deerfield HS — 100/9-12
803 Beech 67838 — 620-426-8401
Tammie Sabata, prin. — Fax 426-6903
Deerfield MS — 100/6-8
803 Beech 67838 — 620-426-7901
Tammie Sabata, prin. — Fax 426-6903

**Derby, Sedgwick, Pop. 21,570**
Derby USD 260 — 6,700/PK-12
120 E Washington St 67037 — 316-788-8400
Craig Wilford, supt. — Fax 788-8526
www.derbyschools.com
Derby HS — 1,900/9-12
920 N Rock Rd 67037 — 316-788-8500
Tim Hamblin, prin. — Fax 788-8593
Derby MS — 1,000/7-8
801 E Madison Ave 67037 — 316-788-8580
Clinton Shipley, prin. — Fax 788-8553
Derby North MS — 6-8
3100 N Rock Rd 67037 — 316-788-8400
Jeff Smith, prin. — Fax 788-8527

**De Soto, Johnson, Pop. 5,615**
De Soto USD 232 — 6,800/PK-12
35200 W 91st St 66018 — 913-667-6200
Dr. Ron Wimmer, supt. — Fax 667-6201
www.usd232.org
De Soto HS — 700/9-12
35000 W 91st St 66018 — 913-667-6250
Dustin Mortenson, prin. — Fax 667-6251
Lexington Trails MS — 300/6-8
8800 Penner Ave 66018 — 913-667-6260
Steve Ludwig, prin. — Fax 667-6261
Other Schools – See Lenexa, Shawnee

**Dexter, Cowley, Pop. 275**
Dexter USD 471 — 100/PK-12
PO Box 97 67038 — 620-876-5415
K.B. Criss, supt. — Fax 876-5548
www.usd471.org
Dexter JSHS — 100/6-12
PO Box 97 67038 — 620-876-5415
K.B. Criss, prin. — Fax 876-5548

**Dighton, Lane, Pop. 1,017**
Dighton USD 482 — 300/PK-12
PO Box 878 67839 — 620-397-2835
Dr. Randy Freeman, supt. — Fax 397-5932
www.usd482.org
Dighton JSHS — 100/7-12
PO Box 939 67839 — 620-397-5333
Mark Penka, prin. — Fax 397-5338

**Dodge City, Ford, Pop. 26,977**
Dodge City USD 443 — 5,700/K-12
PO Box 460 67801 — 620-371-1070
Alan Cunningham, supt. — Fax 227-1687
www.usd443.org
Comanche MS — 300/6-8
1601 1st Ave 67801 — 620-371-1100
Marc Woofter, prin. — Fax 339-4802
Dodge City HS — 1,700/9-12
2201 W Ross Blvd 67801 — 620-227-1611
Jacque Feist, prin. — Fax 227-1680
Dodge City MS — 900/6-8
2000 6th Ave 67801 — 620-227-1610
Mike King, prin. — Fax 227-1731

---

Dodge City Community College — Post-Sec.
2501 N 14th Ave 67801 — 620-225-1321

**Douglass, Butler, Pop. 1,675**
Douglass USD 396 — 700/PK-12
921 E 1st St 67039 — 316-747-3300
Robert Reynolds, supt. — Fax 747-3305
www.usd396.net/
Douglass HS — 200/9-12
910 E 1st St 67039 — 316-747-3310
Scott Dunham, prin. — Fax 747-3315
Sisk MS — 200/6-8
950 E 1st St 67039 — 316-747-3340
Scott Dunham, prin. — Fax 747-3346

**Downs, Osborne, Pop. 896**
Waconda USD 272
Supt. — See Cawker City
Lakeside JSHS — 100/6-12
PO Box 247 67437 — 785-454-3332
Troy Damman, prin. — Fax 454-3747

**Easton, Leavenworth, Pop. 251**
Easton USD 449 — 600/PK-12
32502 Easton Rd 66020 — 913-651-9740
Charles Coblentz, supt. — Fax 324-5237
www.easton449.org
Pleasant Ridge HS — 300/9-12
32500 Easton Rd 66020 — 913-651-5556
Andy Metsker, prin. — Fax 254-3089
Pleasant Ridge MS — 200/6-8
32504 Easton Rd 66020 — 913-651-5522
Amanda Brimer, prin. — Fax 324-5237

**Effingham, Atchison, Pop. 540**
Atchison County Community USD 377 — 700/PK-12
PO Box 289 66023 — 913-833-5050
Stephen Wiseman, supt. — Fax 833-5210
www.usd377.org
Atchison County Community JSHS — 300/7-12
PO Box 289 66023 — 913-833-2240
Deanna Scherer, prin. — Fax 833-5210

**Elbing, Butler, Pop. 228**

---

Berean Academy — 300/PK-12
PO Box 70 67041 — 316-799-2211
Terry Tilson M.Ed., supt. — Fax 799-2601

**El Dorado, Butler, Pop. 12,711**
El Dorado USD 490 — 1,800/PK-12
124 W Central Ave 67042 — 316-322-4800
Sue Givens, supt. — Fax 322-4801
www.eldoradoschools.org
El Dorado HS — 600/9-12
401 McCollum Rd 67042 — 316-322-4810
Kevin House, prin. — Fax 322-4811
El Dorado MS — 400/6-8
440 E Wildcat Way 67042 — 316-322-4820
Karla King, prin. — Fax 322-4821

---

Butler Community College — Post-Sec.
901 S Haverhill Rd 67042 — 316-321-2222

**Elkhart, Morton, Pop. 2,178**
Elkhart USD 218 — 500/PK-12
PO Box 999 67950 — 620-697-2195
Rex Richardson, supt. — Fax 697-2607
www.usd218.org
Elkhart HS — 100/9-12
PO Box 999 67950 — 620-697-2193
Chris Hattabaugh, prin. — Fax 697-4415
Elkhart MS — 100/5-8
PO Box 999 67950 — 620-697-2197
Diane Finn, prin. — Fax 697-4828
Point Rock Alternative S — 50/Alt
PO Box 999 67950 — 620-697-1253
Antonia Villa, prin. — Fax 697-4642

**Ellinwood, Barton, Pop. 2,100**
Ellinwood USD 355 — 400/K-12
300 N Schiller Ave 67526 — 620-564-3226
Ben Jacobs, supt. — Fax 564-2206
www.usd355.org/
Ellinwood HS — 100/9-12
210 E 2nd St 67526 — 620-564-3136
Mark Cook, prin. — Fax 564-2816
Ellinwood MS — 100/7-8
210 E 2nd St 67526 — 620-564-3136
Mark Cook, prin. — Fax 564-2816

**Ellis, Ellis, Pop. 2,048**
Ellis USD 388 — 400/PK-12
PO Box 256 67637 — 785-726-4281
Robert Young, supt. — Fax 726-4677
www.usd388.k12.ks.us
Ellis HS — 100/7-12
PO Box 300 67637 — 785-726-3151
Corey Burton, prin. — Fax 726-3169

**Ellsworth, Ellsworth, Pop. 3,090**
Ellsworth USD 327 — 600/K-12
PO Box 306 67439 — 785-472-5561
Dale Brungardt, supt. — Fax 472-5563
www.usd327.org
Ellsworth JSHS — 200/7-12
211 W 11th St 67439 — 785-472-4471
Ken Windholz, prin. — Fax 472-8109

**Elwood, Doniphan, Pop. 1,173**
Riverside USD 114 — 700/PK-12
PO Box 49 66024 — 913-365-5632
Michael Newman, supt. — Fax 365-5967
www.usd114.org
Riverside MS — 100/6-8
PO Box 368 66024 — 913-365-6735
Robert Hampton, prin. — Fax 365-3503
Other Schools – See Wathena

**Emporia, Lyon, Pop. 24,437**
Emporia USD 253 — 4,200/PK-12
PO Box 1008 66801 — 620-341-2200
Theresa Davidson, supt. — Fax 341-2205
www.usd253.org
Emporia HS — 1,200/9-12
3302 W 18th Ave 66801 — 620-341-2365
Dr. Britton Hart, prin. — Fax 341-2376
Emporia MS — 900/6-8
2300 Graphic Arts Rd 66801 — 620-341-2335
Wendy Baumgardner, prin. — Fax 341-2341

Flint Hills Learning Center Alt
1624 Industrial Rd 66801 620-341-2251
Dr. Britton Hart, prin. Fax 343-6789

---

Emporia State University Post-Sec.
1200 Commercial St 66801 620-341-1200
Flint Hills Technical College Post-Sec.
3301 W 18th Ave 66801 620-343-4600

**Erie, Neosho, Pop. 1,145**
Erie-Galesburg USD 101 600/PK-12
PO Box 137 66733 620-244-3264
Steve Woolf, supt. Fax 244-3664
www.usd101.com
Other Schools – See Galesburg

**Eskridge, Wabaunsee, Pop. 526**
Mission Valley USD 330 400/PK-12
PO Box 158 66423 785-449-2282
William Clark, supt. Fax 409-6216
www.mv330.org
Mission Valley HS 200/7-12
12913 Mission Valley Rd 66423 866-557-6686
Charles Chesmore, prin. Fax 409-6218

**Eudora, Douglas, Pop. 5,992**
Eudora USD 491 1,500/PK-12
PO Box 500 66025 785-542-4910
Steve Splichal, supt. Fax 542-4909
www.eudoraschools.org/
Eudora - De Soto Technical Education Ctr Vo/Tech
PO Box 712 66025 785-542-4986
Ron Abel, prin. Fax 542-4970
Eudora HS 400/9-12
PO Box 712 66025 785-542-4980
Ron Abel, prin. Fax 542-4990
Eudora MS 400/6-8
PO Box 701 66025 785-542-4960
Denise Kendall, prin. Fax 542-4970

**Eureka, Greenwood, Pop. 2,592**
Eureka USD 389 700/PK-12
216 N Main St 67045 620-583-5588
Randy Corns, supt. Fax 583-8200
www.usd389.net
Eureka JSHS 300/7-12
815 N Jefferson St 67045 620-583-7428
Stacy Coulter, prin. Fax 583-8222

**Everest, Brown, Pop. 283**
South Brown County USD 430
Supt. — See Horton
Everest MS 200/5-8
221 S 7th St 66424 785-548-7536
Jackie Wenger, prin. Fax 548-7538

**Fort Leavenworth, Leavenworth, Pop. 1,300**
Ft. Leavenworth USD 207 1,900/PK-9
207 Education Way 66027 913-651-7373
Keith Mispagel, supt. Fax 758-6010
www.usd207.org
Patton JHS 400/7-9
1 Patton Cir 66027 913-651-7371
Ryan Wiebe, prin. Fax 758-6097

**Fort Riley, Geary, Pop. 7,475**
Geary County USD 475
Supt. — See Junction City
Fort Riley MS 700/6-8
4020 1st Division Rd 66442 785-717-4500
Heather Oentrich, prin. Fax 717-4501

**Fort Scott, Bourbon, Pop. 7,870**
Ft. Scott USD 234 1,900/PK-12
424 S Main St 66701 620-223-0800
Bob Beckham, supt. Fax 223-2760
www.usd234.org
Fort Scott HS 600/9-12
1005 S Main St 66701 620-223-0600
Shawn Thomas, prin. Fax 223-5368
Fort Scott MS 400/6-8
1105 E 12th St 66701 620-223-3262
Jim Howard, prin. Fax 223-8946

---

Fort Scott Community College Post-Sec.
2108 Horton St 66701 620-223-2700

**Fowler, Meade, Pop. 579**
Fowler USD 225 200/PK-12
PO Box 170 67844 620-646-5661
Tom Dolenz, supt. Fax 646-5713
www.usd225.org/
Fowler HS 100/7-12
PO Box 140 67844 620-646-5221
Tom Dolenz, prin. Fax 646-5295

**Frankfort, Marshall, Pop. 726**
Vermillion USD 380
Supt. — See Vermillion
Frankfort JSHS 100/7-12
PO Box 203 66427 785-292-4486
Dean Dalinghaus, prin. Fax 292-4636

**Fredonia, Wilson, Pop. 2,433**
Fredonia USD 484 700/PK-12
PO Box 539 66736 620-378-4177
Brian Smith, supt. Fax 378-4345
www.fredoniaks.com
Fredonia HS 200/9-12
916 Robinson St 66736 620-378-4172
Jamie Camacho, prin. Fax 378-4398
Fredonia MS 200/6-8
203 N 8th St 66736 620-378-4167
Laura Fitzmorris, prin. Fax 378-3635

**Frontenac, Crawford, Pop. 3,381**
Frontenac USD 249 900/PK-12
208 S Cayuga St 66763 620-231-7551
Rick Simoncic, supt. Fax 231-1312
www.frontenac249.org
Frontenac HS 300/9-12
201 S Crawford St 66763 620-231-7550
Ted Hessong, prin. Fax 231-2043
Frontenac JHS 200/6-8
208 S Cayuga St 66763 620-232-6370
Mike Martin, prin. Fax 231-1312

**Galena, Cherokee, Pop. 2,973**
Galena USD 499 800/PK-12
702 E 7th St 66739 620-783-4499
Brian Smith, supt. Fax 783-5547
www.usd499.org
Galena HS 200/9-12
702 E 7th St 66739 620-783-4499
Toby VanCleave, prin. Fax 783-1780
Galena MS 200/6-8
702 E 7th St 66739 620-783-4499
Toby VanCleave, prin. Fax 783-5214

**Galesburg, Neosho, Pop. 125**
Erie-Galesburg USD 101
Supt. — See Erie
Galesburg MS 100/6-8
PO Box 147 66740 620-763-2470
James Fox, prin. Fax 763-2224

**Garden City, Finney, Pop. 26,301**
Garden City USD 457 7,300/PK-12
1205 Fleming St 67846 620-805-7000
Dr. Steve Karlin Ed.D., supt. Fax 805-7190
www.gckschools.com
Garden City Alternate Education Center 100/Alt
1312 N 7th St 67846 620-805-8600
Mark Ronn, prin. Fax 805-8648
Garden City HS 2,000/9-12
2720 Buffalo Way Blvd 67846 620-805-5400
Steve Nordby, prin. Fax 805-5615
Good MS 600/7-8
1412 N Main St 67846 620-805-8100
Brad Springston, prin. Fax 805-8150
Henderson MS 600/Alt
2406 Fleming St 67846 620-805-8500
Glenda LaBarbera, prin. Fax 805-8598

---

Garden City Community College Post-Sec.
801 N Campus Dr 67846 620-276-7611

**Garden Plain, Sedgwick, Pop. 838**
Renwick USD 267
Supt. — See Andale
Garden Plain HS 200/9-12
PO Box 128 67050 316-531-2272
Matt Hoffman, prin. Fax 535-2727

**Gardner, Johnson, Pop. 18,628**
Gardner Edgerton USD 231 5,100/PK-12
PO Box 97 66030 913-856-2000
Pam Stranathan, supt. Fax 856-2069
www.usd231.com
Gardner Edgerton HS 1,300/9-12
425 N Waverly Rd 66030 913-856-2600
Mark Meyer, prin. Fax 856-2690
Pioneer Ridge MS 700/5-8
16200 S Kill Creek Rd 66030 913-856-3850
Tim Drake, prin. Fax 856-2097
Trail Ridge MS 5-8
495 E Grand St 66030 913-856-3550
John Martin, prin. Fax 856-3552
Wheatridge MS 800/5-8
318 E Washington St 66030 913-856-2900
Jim Brockway, prin. Fax 856-2980

**Garnett, Anderson, Pop. 3,385**
Garnett USD 365 1,100/PK-12
PO Box 328 66032 785-448-6155
Donald Blome, supt. Fax 448-6157
www.usd365.org
Anderson County JSHS 500/7-12
1100 W Highway 31 66032 785-448-3115
Kenny Kellstadt, prin. Fax 448-6670

**Girard, Crawford, Pop. 2,739**
Girard USD 248 1,100/PK-12
415 N Summit St 66743 620-724-4325
Blaise Bauer, supt. Fax 724-8446
www.girard248.org/
Girard HS 300/9-12
415 N Summit St 66743 620-724-4326
Todd Ferguson, prin. Fax 724-6136
Girard MS 200/6-8
415 N Summit St 66743 620-724-4114
Randy Heatherly, prin. Fax 724-4610

**Glasco, Cloud, Pop. 493**
Southern Cloud USD 334
Supt. — See Miltonvale
Glasco HS 100/9-12
PO Box 158 67445 785-568-2291
Regina Wallace, prin. Fax 568-2239

**Goddard, Sedgwick, Pop. 4,232**
Goddard USD 265 4,800/K-12
PO Box 249 67052 316-794-4000
Dr. Justin Henry, supt. Fax 794-2222
www.goddardusd.com
Eisenhower HS 700/9-12
PO Box 789 67052 316-794-4190
Bill Kelley, prin. Fax 794-4191
Eisenhower MS 400/7-8
PO Box 349 67052 316-794-4150
Jerold Longabaugh, prin. Fax 794-4063
Goddard Academy 9-12
PO Box 318 67052 316-794-4142
Sean Hollas, prin. Fax 794-4143
Goddard HS 900/9-12
PO Box 189 67052 316-794-4100
Doug Bridwell, prin. Fax 794-4130
Goddard MS 400/7-8
PO Box 279 67052 316-794-4230
Lisa Hogarth, prin. Fax 794-4254

**Goessel, Marion, Pop. 530**
Goessel USD 411 300/K-12
PO Box 68 67053 620-367-4601
John Fast, supt. Fax 367-4603
www.usd411.org
Goessel JSHS 100/6-12
PO Box 6 67053 620-367-2242
Scott Boden, prin. Fax 367-2571

**Goodland, Sherman, Pop. 4,416**
Goodland USD 352 900/PK-12
PO Box 509 67735 785-890-2397
Bill Biermann, supt. Fax 890-8504
www.usd352.org
Goodland JSHS 300/6-12
PO Box 509 67735 785-890-5656
Greg Ferguson, prin. Fax 890-8517

---

Northwest Kansas Technical College Post-Sec.
1209 Harrison St 67735 785-890-3641

**Grainfield, Gove, Pop. 277**
Wheatland USD 292 100/PK-12
PO Box 165 67737 785-673-4213
Gary Kraus, supt. Fax 673-4234
www.usd292.org
Wheatland HS 50/9-12
PO Box 149 67737 785-673-4223
Gary Kraus, prin. Fax 673-4234

**Great Bend, Barton, Pop. 15,763**
Great Bend USD 428 3,000/PK-12
201 S Patton Rd 67530 620-793-1500
Brad Reed, supt. Fax 793-1585
www.usd428.net
Great Bend HS 900/9-12
2027 Morton St 67530 620-793-1521
Tim Friess, prin. Fax 793-1537
Great Bend MS 500/7-8
1919 Harrison St 67530 620-793-1510
David Reiser, prin. Fax 793-1549

---

Barton County Community College Post-Sec.
245 NE 30 Rd 67530 620-792-2701

**Greensburg, Kiowa, Pop. 767**
Kiowa County USD 422 300/PK-12
710 S Main St 67054 620-723-2145
Darin Headrick, supt. Fax 723-2705
www.usd422.org
Kiowa County HS 100/9-12
720 S Main St 67054 620-723-2164
Randy Fulton, prin. Fax 723-2019

**Gridley, Coffey, Pop. 338**
Le Roy-Gridley USD 245
Supt. — See Le Roy
Southern Coffey County JHS 50/6-8
PO Box 426 66852 620-836-2151
Julie Rosenquist, prin. Fax 836-4041

**Grinnell, Gove, Pop. 259**
Grinnell USD 291 100/K-8
PO Box 68 67738 785-824-3277
Mike McDermeit, supt. Fax 824-3215
usd291.com
Grinnell MS 50/5-8
PO Box 68 67738 785-824-3277
Mike McDermeit, prin. Fax 824-3215

**Gypsum, Saline, Pop. 398**
Southeast of Saline USD 306 700/K-12
5056 E Highway K4 67448 785-536-4291
Greg Mann, supt. Fax 536-4247
www.usd306.k12.ks.us
Southeast Saline JSHS 400/7-12
5056 E Highway K4 67448 785-536-4286
Roger Stumpf, prin. Fax 536-4292

**Halstead, Harvey, Pop. 2,058**
Halstead-Bentley USD 440 800/K-12
521 W 6th St 67056 316-835-2641
Thomas Alstrom, supt. Fax 835-2305
www.usd440.com
Halstead HS 200/9-12
521 W 6th St 67056 316-835-2682
Joe Gerber, prin. Fax 835-3673
Halstead MS 300/4-8
221 W 6th St 67056 316-835-2694
Amy Wagoner, prin. Fax 835-2469

**Hamilton, Greenwood, Pop. 262**
Hamilton USD 390 100/K-12
2596 W Rd N 66853 620-678-3244
Greg Markowitz, supt. Fax 678-3321
www.hamilton390.net
Hamilton HS 50/7-12
2596 W Rd N 66853 620-678-3651
Diana Riley, prin. Fax 678-3651

**Hanover, Washington, Pop. 680**
Barnes USD 223
Supt. — See Barnes
Hanover HS 100/9-12
209 E North St 66945 785-337-2281
Doug Wilson, prin. Fax 337-2307

**Hartford, Lyon, Pop. 364**
Southern Lyon County USD 252 500/PK-12
PO Box 278 66854 620-392-5519
Dr. Michael Argabright, supt. Fax 392-5841
www.usd252.org/
Hartford JSHS 100/6-12
PO Box 218 66854 620-392-5515
Aaric Davis, prin. Fax 392-5960
Other Schools – See Olpe

**Haven, Reno, Pop. 1,205**
Haven USD 312 — 900/K-12
PO Box 130 67543 — 620-465-3445
Clark Wedel, supt. — Fax 465-3595
www.havenschools.com
Haven HS — 300/9-12
PO Box C 67543 — 620-465-2585
Marty Nienstedt, prin. — Fax 465-7729
Haven MS — 100/7-8
PO Box B 67543 — 620-465-2587
Marty Nienstedt, prin. — Fax 465-2588

**Haviland, Kiowa, Pop. 699**

---

Barclay College — Post-Sec.
607 N Kingman St 67059 — 620-862-5252

**Hays, Ellis, Pop. 20,202**
Hays USD 489 — 2,700/PK-12
323 W 12th St 67601 — 785-623-2400
Dean Katt, supt. — Fax 623-2409
www.usd489.com/
Hays HS — 800/9-12
2300 E 13th St 67601 — 785-623-2600
Martin Straub, prin. — Fax 623-2609
Hays MS — 500/6-8
201 E 29th St 67601 — 785-623-2450
Craig Pallister, prin. — Fax 623-2456

---

Fort Hays State University — Post-Sec.
600 Park St 67601 — 785-628-4000
Hays Academy of Hair Design — Post-Sec.
1214 E 27th St 67601 — 785-628-6624
Thomas More Prep-Marian JSHS — 200/7-12
1701 Hall St 67601 — 785-625-6577
Chad Meitner, prin. — Fax 625-3912

**Haysville, Sedgwick, Pop. 10,516**
Haysville USD 261 — 5,100/PK-12
1745 W Grand Ave 67060 — 316-554-2200
Dr. John Burke, supt. — Fax 554-2230
www.usd261.com
Haysville HS — Alt
106 Stewart Ave 67060 — 316-554-2231
Myron Regier, admin. — Fax 554-2328
Haysville MS — 500/6-8
900 W Grand Ave 67060 — 316-554-2251
Dr. Mike Maurer, prin. — Fax 554-2258
Haysville West MS — 700/6-8
1956 W Grand Ave 67060 — 316-554-2370
Ildo Martins, prin. — Fax 554-2377
Other Schools – See Wichita

**Healy, Lane, Pop. 233**
Healy USD 468 — 100/PK-12
5006 N Dodge Rd 67850 — 620-398-2248
Larry Lysell, supt. — Fax 398-2435
www.usd468.org
Healy JSHS — 50/7-12
5006 N Dodge Rd 67850 — 620-398-2248
Beverly Roemer, prin. — Fax 398-2435

**Herington, Dickinson, Pop. 2,456**
Herington USD 487 — 500/PK-12
19 N Broadway 67449 — 785-258-2263
John Thissen, supt. — Fax 258-2982
www.heringtonschools.org
Herington HS — 100/9-12
1401 N D St 67449 — 785-258-2261
Brandi Hendrix, prin. — Fax 258-3013
Herington MS — 100/6-8
1317 N D St 67449 — 785-258-2448
Brandi Hendrix, prin. — Fax 258-3976

**Hesston, Harvey, Pop. 3,645**
Hesston USD 460 — 800/K-12
PO Box 2000 67062 — 620-327-4931
Ben Proctor, supt. — Fax 327-7157
www.hesstonschools.org
Hesston HS — 300/9-12
PO Box 2000 67062 — 620-327-7122
Ty Rhodes, prin. — Fax 327-7138
Hesston MS — 300/5-8
PO Box 2000 67062 — 620-327-7111
Brandon Simmelink, prin. — Fax 327-7115

---

Hesston College — Post-Sec.
PO Box 3000 67062 — 620-327-4221

**Hiawatha, Brown, Pop. 3,067**
Hiawatha USD 415 — 900/PK-12
PO Box 398 66434 — 785-742-2224
Dr. Penny Hargrove, supt. — Fax 742-2301
www.hiawathaschools.org
Hiawatha HS — 300/9-12
600 Red Hawk Dr 66434 — 785-742-3312
Andrew Gaddis, prin. — Fax 742-7156
Hiawatha MS — 300/5-8
307 S Morrill Ave 66434 — 785-742-4172
David Coufal, prin. — Fax 742-1744

**Highland, Doniphan, Pop. 980**
Doniphan West USD 111 — 400/PK-12
PO Box 308 66035 — 785-442-3671
Rex Bollinger, supt. — Fax 442-3289
www.usd111.org
Doniphan West JSHS — 200/7-12
PO Box 308 66035 — 785-442-3286
Chris Lackey, prin. — Fax 442-3289

---

Highland Community College — Post-Sec.
606 W Main St 66035 — 785-442-6000

**Hill City, Graham, Pop. 1,438**
Graham County USD 281 — 400/PK-12
PO Box 309 67642 — 785-421-2135
Jim Hickel, supt. — Fax 421-5657
www.usd281.com
Hill City JSHS — 200/7-12
PO Box 160 67642 — 785-421-2117
Alan Stein, prin. — Fax 421-3029

**Hillsboro, Marion, Pop. 2,935**
Durham-Hillsboro-Lehigh USD 410 — 600/PK-12
416 S Date St 67063 — 620-947-3184
Dr. Steve Noble, supt. — Fax 947-3475
www.usd410.net
Hillsboro MSHS — 200/6-12
400 E Grand Ave 67063 — 620-947-3991
Clint Corby, prin. — Fax 947-3251

---

Tabor College — Post-Sec.
400 S Jefferson St 67063 — 620-947-3121

**Hoisington, Barton, Pop. 2,656**
Hoisington USD 431 — 800/PK-12
165 W 3rd St 67544 — 620-653-4134
Bill Lowry, supt. — Fax 653-4073
www.usd431.net/
Hoisington HS — 200/9-12
218 E 7th St 67544 — 620-653-2141
Joel Mason, prin. — Fax 653-4164
Hoisington MS — 200/5-8
360 W 11th St 67544 — 620-653-4951
Patricia Reinhardt, prin. — Fax 653-4483

**Holcomb, Finney, Pop. 2,058**
Holcomb USD 363 — 1,000/PK-12
PO Box 8 67851 — 620-277-2629
Jean Rush, supt. — Fax 277-2010
www.usd363.com/
Holcomb HS — 200/9-12
PO Box 38 67851 — 620-277-2063
Rob Schneeberger, prin. — Fax 277-0240
Holcomb MS — 200/6-8
PO Box 89 67851 — 620-277-2699
Chad Krug, prin. — Fax 277-2746

**Holton, Jackson, Pop. 3,248**
Holton USD 336 — 1,000/PK-12
PO Box 352 66436 — 785-364-3650
Dennis Stones, supt. — Fax 364-3975
www.holtonks.net
Holton HS — 300/9-12
901 New York Ave 66436 — 785-364-2181
Rod Wittmer, prin. — Fax 364-5360
Holton MS — 200/6-8
900 Iowa Ave 66436 — 785-364-2441
Michael Kimberlin, prin. — Fax 364-5460

North Jackson USD 335 — 400/PK-12
12692 266th Rd 66436 — 785-364-2194
Adrianne Walsh, supt. — Fax 364-4346
www.jhcobras.net
Jackson Heights MSHS — 200/7-12
12719 266th Rd 66436 — 785-364-2195
Darren Shupe, prin. — Fax 364-2487

**Holyrood, Ellsworth, Pop. 439**
Central Plains USD 112 — 400/PK-12
PO Box 168 67450 — 785-252-3695
Greg Clark, supt. — Fax 252-3697
www.usd112.org
Other Schools – See Bushton, Claflin, Wilson

**Hope, Dickinson, Pop. 357**
Rural Vista USD 481
Supt. — See White City
Hope HS — 100/9-12
PO Box 218 67451 — 785-366-7221
Mike Teeter, prin. — Fax 366-7115

**Horton, Brown, Pop. 1,718**
South Brown County USD 430 — 600/PK-12
522 Central Ave 66439 — 785-486-2611
Dr. Steven Davies, supt. — Fax 486-2496
usd430.k12.ks.us
Horton HS — 200/9-12
1120 1st Ave E 66439 — 785-486-2151
David Norman, prin. — Fax 486-2909
Other Schools – See Everest

**Howard, Elk, Pop. 671**
West Elk USD 282 — 300/PK-12
PO Box 607 67349 — 620-374-2113
Bert Moore, supt. — Fax 374-2414
Howard West Elk S — 300/PK-12
PO Box 278 67349 — 620-374-2147
Martin Burke, prin. — Fax 374-2116

**Hoxie, Sheridan, Pop. 1,186**
Hoxie USD 412 — 400/PK-12
PO Box 348 67740 — 785-675-3258
Scott Hoyt, supt. — Fax 675-2126
www.hoxie.org/
Hoxie JSHS — 100/7-12
PO Box 989 67740 — 785-675-3286
Gary Johnson, prin. — Fax 675-2270

**Hoyt, Jackson, Pop. 649**
Royal Valley USD 337
Supt. — See Mayetta
Royal Valley HS — 300/9-12
PO Box 128 66440 — 785-986-6251
James Holloman, prin. — Fax 986-6479

**Hugoton, Stevens, Pop. 3,876**
Hugoton USD 210 — 1,100/PK-12
205 E 6th St 67951 — 620-544-4397
Adrian Howie, supt. — Fax 544-7138
www.usd210.org
Hugoton HS — 300/9-12
215 W 11th St 67951 — 620-544-4311
John Girodat, prin. — Fax 544-7392
Hugoton MS — 200/7-8
115 W 11th St 67951 — 620-544-4341
Lance Custer, prin. — Fax 544-4856

**Humboldt, Allen, Pop. 1,917**
Humboldt USD 258 — 600/PK-12
801 New York St 66748 — 620-473-3121
Kay Lewis, supt. — Fax 473-2023
www.usd258.net
Humboldt HS — 200/9-12
1020 New York St 66748 — 620-473-2251
John Johnson, prin. — Fax 473-2086
Humboldt MS — 100/6-8
1105 Bridge St 66748 — 620-473-3348
Stephanie Splechter, prin. — Fax 473-3141
Humboldt Tech Building — Vo/Tech
1116 New York St 66748 — 620-473-2251
John Johnson, prin. — Fax 473-2086

**Hutchinson, Reno, Pop. 41,132**
Buhler USD 313
Supt. — See Buhler
Prairie Hills MS — 300/6-8
3200 Lucille Dr 67502 — 620-662-6027
Todd Fredrickson, prin. — Fax 694-1002

Hutchinson USD 308 — 4,500/PK-12
PO Box 1908 67504 — 620-615-4000
Dr. Shelly Kiblinger, supt. — Fax 615-4010
www.usd308.com
Hutchinson HS — 1,400/9-12
810 E 13th Ave 67501 — 620-615-4100
Ronn Roehm, prin. — Fax 615-4200
Hutchinson MS 8 — 400/8-8
200 W 14th Ave 67501 — 620-615-4800
David Patterson, prin. — Fax 615-4802

Nickerson USD 309 — 1,100/K-12
4501 W 4th Ave 67501 — 620-663-7141
Dr. William Hagerman, supt. — Fax 663-7148
www.usd309ks.org
Reno Valley MS — 200/7-8
1616 Wilshire Dr 67501 — 620-662-4573
Vince Naccarato, prin. — Fax 662-6708
Other Schools – See Nickerson

---

Central Christian S — 200/PK-12
1910 E 30th Ave 67502 — 620-663-2174
Tim Kuhns, supt. — Fax 663-2176
Hutchinson Community College — Post-Sec.
1300 N Plum St 67501 — 620-665-3500
Sidney's Hairdressing College — Post-Sec.
200 E 3rd Ave 67501 — 620-662-5481
Trinity Catholic HS — 300/7-12
1400 E 17th Ave 67501 — 620-662-5800
Joe Hammersmith, prin. — Fax 662-1233

**Independence, Montgomery, Pop. 9,137**
Independence USD 446 — 1,600/K-12
517 N 10th St 67301 — 620-332-1800
Rusty Arnold, supt. — Fax 332-1811
www.indyschools.com
Independence HS — 600/9-12
1301 N 10th St 67301 — 620-332-1815
Mario Sherrell, prin. — Fax 332-1831
Independence MS — 400/6-8
300 W Locust St 67301 — 620-332-1836
Mark Hayward, prin. — Fax 332-1841

---

Independence Community College — Post-Sec.
1057 W College Ave 67301 — 620-331-4100

**Ingalls, Gray, Pop. 304**
Ingalls USD 477 — 200/PK-12
PO Box 99 67853 — 620-335-5136
Dave Novack, supt. — Fax 335-5678
www.ingallsusd477.com/
Ingalls JSHS — 100/6-12
PO Box 99 67853 — 620-335-5135
Joe Meador, prin. — Fax 335-5801

**Inman, McPherson, Pop. 1,343**
Inman USD 448 — 500/PK-12
PO Box 129 67546 — 620-585-6424
Kevin Case, supt. — Fax 585-2689
www.usd448.com
Inman JSHS — 200/7-12
PO Box 279 67546 — 620-585-6441
Scott Friesen, prin. — Fax 585-2797

**Iola, Allen, Pop. 5,562**
Iola USD 257 — 1,300/PK-12
305 N Washington Ave 66749 — 620-365-4700
Jack Koehn, supt. — Fax 365-4708
www.usd257.org
Iola HS — 400/9-12
300 E Jackson Ave 66749 — 620-365-4715
Stacey Fager, prin. — Fax 365-4730
Iola Upper MS — 300/7-8
600 East St 66749 — 620-365-4785
Jack Stanley, prin. — Fax 365-4770

---

Allen Community College — Post-Sec.
1801 N Cottonwood St 66749 — 620-365-5116

**Jetmore, Hodgeman, Pop. 861**
Hodgeman County USD 227 — 300/PK-12
PO Box 398 67854 — 620-357-8301
Doug Chaney, supt. — Fax 357-8437
www.usd227.org/
Hodgeman County HS — 200/7-12
PO Box 100 67854 — 620-357-8378
Dexter Leach, prin. — Fax 357-6563

**Johnson, Stanton, Pop. 1,483**
Stanton County USD 452 — 500/PK-12
PO Box C 67855 — 620-492-6226
Kim Novack, supt. — Fax 492-1326
www.usd452.org
Stanton County JSHS — 200/7-12
PO Box C 67855 — 620-492-6284
Randall Jansonius, prin. — Fax 492-1326

**Junction City, Geary, Pop. 21,775**
Geary County USD 475 — 8,400/PK-12
PO Box 370 66441 — 785-717-4000
Dr. Corbin Witt, supt. — Fax 717-4003
web.usd475.org/
Dixon Center for Innovative Studies — Alt
920 W 6th St 66441 — 785-717-4710
Thomas Wesoloski, prin. — Fax 717-4711
Freshman Success Academy — 500/9-9
300 W 9th St 66441 — 785-717-4312
Jeff Tanner, pres.
Junction City HS — 1,700/9-12
900 N Eisenhower Dr 66441 — 785-717-4200
Melissa Sharp, prin. — Fax 717-4201
Junction City MS — 1,000/6-8
700 Wildcat Ln 66441 — 785-717-4400
Mary Wright, prin. — Fax 717-4401
Other Schools – See Fort Riley

St. Xaviers S — 200/K-12
200 N Washington St 66441 — 785-238-2841
Shawn Augustine, prin. — Fax 238-5021

**Kansas City, Wyandotte, Pop. 142,097**
Kansas City USD 500 — 19,200/PK-12
2010 N 59th St 66104 — 913-551-3200
Dr. Cynthia Lane, supt. — Fax 551-3217
www.kckps.org
Argentine MS — 600/6-8
2123 Ruby Ave 66106 — 913-627-6750
Jereme Brueggeman, prin. — Fax 627-6783
Arrowhead MS — 500/6-8
1715 N 82nd St 66112 — 913-627-6600
Laurie Boyd, prin. — Fax 627-6654
Central MS — 600/6-8
925 Ivandale St 66101 — 913-627-6150
Walt Thompson, prin. — Fax 627-6152
Coronado MS — 400/6-8
1735 N 64th Ter 66102 — 913-627-6300
Jewell Ragsdale, prin. — Fax 627-6358
Eisenhower MS — 500/6-8
2901 N 72nd St 66109 — 913-627-6450
Samia Guess, prin. — Fax 627-6455
Harmon HS — 1,200/9-12
2400 Steele Rd 66106 — 913-627-7050
Geoff Markos, prin. — Fax 627-7185
Northwest MS — 500/6-8
2400 N 18th St 66104 — 913-627-4000
Dr. Carnest Mitchell, prin. — Fax 627-4052
Rosedale MS — 600/6-8
3600 Springfield St 66103 — 913-627-6900
Travis Helm, prin. — Fax 627-6957
Schlagle HS — 800/9-12
2214 N 59th St 66104 — 913-627-7500
Yolanda Thompson, prin. — Fax 627-7555
Sumner Academy/Arts & Sciences — 900/8-12
1610 N 8th St 66101 — 913-627-7200
Jonathan Richard, prin. — Fax 627-7205
Washington HS — 1,000/9-12
7340 Leavenworth Rd 66109 — 913-627-7800
Dr. Maritza Paul, prin. — Fax 627-7850
West MS — 400/6-8
2600 N 44th St 66104 — 913-627-6000
Elvira Randle, prin. — Fax 627-6053
Wyandotte HS — 1,200/9-12
2501 Minnesota Ave 66102 — 913-627-7650
Mary Stewart, prin. — Fax 627-7700

Piper-Kansas City USD 203 — 1,600/PK-12
3130 N 122nd Ave 66109 — 913-721-2088
Tim Conrad, supt. — Fax 721-3573
www.piperschools.com
Piper HS — 500/9-12
4400 N 107th St 66109 — 913-721-2100
Jason Malaschak, prin. — Fax 721-3867
Piper MS — 400/6-8
4420 N 107th St 66109 — 913-721-1144
Stephen Mercer, prin. — Fax 721-1526

Turner USD 202 — 3,500/PK-12
800 S 55th St 66106 — 913-288-4100
Dr. Jason Dandoy, supt. — Fax 288-3401
www.turnerusd202.org/
Journey S of Choice — Alt
2540 Junction Rd 66106 — 913-288-3690
Rena Duewel, prin. — Fax 288-3691
Turner HS — 1,200/9-12
2211 S 55th St 66106 — 913-288-3300
Alan Penrose, prin. — Fax 288-3301
Turner MS — 600/7-8
1312 S 55th St 66106 — 913-288-4000
Shannon Adams, prin. — Fax 288-4001

Bishop Ward HS — 300/9-12
708 N 18th St 66102 — 913-371-1201
Karen Hopson, prin. — Fax 371-2145
Donnelly College — Post-Sec.
608 N 18th St 66102 — 913-621-8700
Kansas City Kansas Community College — Post-Sec.
7250 State Ave 66112 — 913-334-1100
Kansas State School for the Blind — Post-Sec.
1100 State Ave 66102 — 913-281-3308
University of Kansas Medical Center — Post-Sec.
3901 Rainbow Blvd 66160 — 913-588-5000

**Kensington, Smith, Pop. 463**
Thunder Ridge SD — 300/PK-12
128 S Kansas St 66951 — 785-476-2218
Jeff Yoxall, supt. — Fax 476-2258
usd110.net
Thunder Ridge HS — 100/9-12
209 E Ash St 66951 — 785-476-2217
Jeff Yoxall, prin. — Fax 476-2210
Other Schools – See Agra

**Kingman, Kingman, Pop. 3,142**
Kingman-Norwich USD 331 — 1,000/PK-12
115 N Main St 67068 — 620-532-3134
Dr. Robert Diepenbrock, supt. — Fax 532-3251
www.knusd331.com/
Kingman HS — 300/9-12
260 W Kansas Ave 67068 — 620-532-3136
Andy Albright, prin. — Fax 532-3027
Kingman MS — 200/6-8
607 N Spruce St 67068 — 620-532-3186
Brent Garrison, prin. — Fax 532-5137
Other Schools – See Norwich

**Kiowa, Barber, Pop. 1,012**
South Barber County USD 255 — 200/PK-12
512 Main St 67070 — 620-825-4115
Dr. Andi Williams, supt. — Fax 825-4145
www.southbarber.com
South Barber JSHS — 100/7-12
1220 N 8th St 67070 — 620-825-4214
Brent Shaffer, prin. — Fax 825-4250

**Kismet, Seward, Pop. 456**
Kismet-Plains USD 483 — 700/PK-12
17222 Mustang Rd 67859 — 620-563-7103
Elton Argo, supt. — Fax 563-7348
www.usd483.net
Southwestern Heights HS — 200/9-12
17222 Mustang Rd 67859 — 620-563-7292
Dan Frisby, prin. — Fax 563-7383
Southwestern Heights JHS — 200/6-8
17222 Mustang Rd 67859 — 620-563-7100
Kurt Stanfield, prin. — Fax 563-7342

**La Crosse, Rush, Pop. 1,335**
La Crosse USD 395 — 300/K-12
PO Box 778 67548 — 785-222-2505
Bill Keeley, supt. — Fax 222-3240
www.usd395.org
La Crosse HS — 100/9-12
PO Box 810 67548 — 785-222-2528
Kathy Keeley, prin. — Fax 222-3480
La Crosse MS — 50/7-8
PO Box 810 67548 — 785-222-3030
Kathy Keeley, prin. — Fax 222-3480

**LaCygne, Linn, Pop. 1,138**
Prairie View USD 362 — 900/PK-12
13799 KS Highway 152, — 913-757-2677
Chris Kleidosty, supt. — Fax 757-4442
www.pv362.org
Prairie View HS — 300/9-12
13731 KS Highway 152, — 913-757-4447
Timothy Weis, prin. — Fax 757-4443
Prairie View MS — 200/6-8
13667 KS Highway 152, — 913-757-4497
Ken Bolt, prin. — Fax 757-2728

**Lakin, Kearny, Pop. 2,182**
Lakin USD 215 — 600/PK-12
1003 W Kingman Ave 67860 — 620-355-6761
Mike Ward, supt. — Fax 355-7317
www.usd215.org
Lakin HS — 200/9-12
407 N Campbell St 67860 — 620-355-6411
Tim Robertson, prin. — Fax 355-6460
Lakin MS — 200/5-8
1201 W Kingman Ave 67860 — 620-355-6973
Mike Ward, prin. — Fax 355-8313

**Langdon, Reno, Pop. 42**
Fairfield USD 310 — 300/PK-12
16115 S Langdon Rd 67583 — 620-596-2152
Nathan Reed, supt. — Fax 596-2835
www.usd310.org
Fairfield HS — 100/9-12
16115 S Langdon Rd 67583 — 620-596-2152
Jason Briar, prin. — Fax 596-2835
Fairfield MS — 100/6-8
16115 S Langdon Rd 67583 — 620-596-2615
Jason Briar, prin. — Fax 596-2835

**Lansing, Leavenworth, Pop. 10,978**
Lansing USD 469 — 2,600/PK-12
200 E Mary St 66043 — 913-727-1100
Dr. Randal Bagby, supt. — Fax 727-1619
www.usd469.net
Lansing HS — 800/9-12
1412 147th St 66043 — 913-727-3357
Steve Dike, prin. — Fax 727-2001
Lansing MS — 600/6-8
509 Ida St 66043 — 913-727-1197
Kerry Brungardt, prin. — Fax 727-1349

**Larned, Pawnee, Pop. 3,979**
Ft. Larned USD 495 — 1,000/PK-12
120 E 6th St 67550 — 620-285-3185
Jon Flint, supt. — Fax 285-2973
www.usd495.net
Larned HS — 300/9-12
815 Corse Ave 67550 — 620-285-2151
Troy Langdon, prin. — Fax 285-7148
Larned MS — 300/5-8
904 Corse Ave 67550 — 620-285-8430
Shane Sundahl, prin. — Fax 285-8433

**Lawrence, Douglas, Pop. 84,434**
Lawrence USD 497 — 11,200/PK-12
110 McDonald Dr 66044 — 785-832-5000
Dr. Rick Doll, supt. — Fax 832-5016
www.usd497.org
Lawrence Free State HS — 1,500/9-12
4700 Overland Dr 66049 — 785-832-6050
Myron Graber, prin. — Fax 832-6099
Lawrence HS — 1,500/9-12
1901 Louisiana St 66046 — 785-832-5050
Matt Brungardt, prin. — Fax 832-5066
Lawrence Liberty Memorial Central MS — 400/6-8
1400 Massachusetts St 66044 — 785-832-5400
Jeff Harkin, prin. — Fax 832-5403
Lawrence South MS — 600/6-8
2734 Louisiana St 66046 — 785-832-5450
Jennifer Bessolo, prin. — Fax 832-5453
Lawrence Southwest MS — 600/6-8
2511 Inverness Dr 66047 — 785-832-5550
Kristen Ryan, prin. — Fax 832-5554
Lawrence West MS — 600/6-8
2700 Harvard Rd 66049 — 785-832-5500
Myron Melton, prin. — Fax 832-5504

Bishop Seabury Academy — 200/6-12
4120 Clinton Pkwy 66047 — 785-832-1717
Dr. Don Schawang, hdmstr. — Fax 832-1919
Haskell Indian Nations University — Post-Sec.
155 Indian Ave 66046 — 785-749-8404
Pinnacle Career Institute — Post-Sec.
1601 W 23rd St Ste 200 66046 — 785-841-9640
University of Kansas — Post-Sec.
1450 Jayhawk Blvd 66045 — 785-864-2700
Veritas Christian S — 100/K-12
256 N Michigan St 66044 — 785-749-0083
Kelli Huslig M.Ed., admin. — Fax 749-0580

**Leavenworth, Leavenworth, Pop. 33,833**
Leavenworth USD 453 — 3,700/PK-12
PO Box 969 66048 — 913-684-1400
Mike Roth, supt. — Fax 684-1407
www.usd453.org
Leavenworth HS — 1,300/9-12
2012 10th Ave 66048 — 913-684-1550
Dr. Thomas Barry, prin. — Fax 684-1555
Warren MS — 500/6-8
PO Box 7 66048 — 913-684-1530
Dr. Leeann Fitzgerald, prin. — Fax 684-1539

Immaculata HS — 100/9-12
600 Shawnee St 66048 — 913-682-3900
Richard Geraci, prin. — Fax 682-9036
University of Saint Mary — Post-Sec.
4100 S 4th St 66048 — 913-682-5151

**Leawood, Johnson, Pop. 31,391**
Blue Valley USD 229
Supt. — See Overland Park
Leawood MS — 500/6-8
2410 W 123rd St 66209 — 913-239-5300
Lana Gerber, prin. — Fax 239-5348
Prairie Star MS — 700/6-8
14201 Mission Rd 66224 — 913-239-5600
Heath Sigg, prin. — Fax 239-5648

**Lebo, Coffey, Pop. 937**
Lebo-Waverly USD 243
Supt. — See Waverly
Lebo HS — 100/7-12
PO Box 45 66856 — 620-256-6341
Richard Burkdoll, prin. — Fax 256-6342

**Lenexa, Johnson, Pop. 47,046**
De Soto USD 232
Supt. — See De Soto
Mill Creek MS — 600/6-8
8001 Mize Blvd 66227 — 913-667-3512
Larry Breedlove, prin. — Fax 422-9229

Brown Mackie College — Post-Sec.
9705 Lenexa Dr 66215 — 913-768-1900
Christ Preparatory Academy — 100/K-12
15700 W 87th Street Pkwy 66219 — 913-831-1345
Ron Lawlor, admin. — Fax 438-1402
St. James Academy — 700/9-12
24505 Prairie Star Pkwy 66227 — 913-254-4200
Karla Leibham, prin. — Fax 254-4221
The Art Institutes International — Post-Sec.
8208 Melrose Dr 66214 — 913-217-4600

**Leon, Butler, Pop. 678**
Bluestem USD 205 — 500/PK-12
625 S Mill Rd 67074 — 316-742-3261
Joel Lovesee, supt. — Fax 742-9265
www.usd205.com
Bluestem JSHS — 300/7-12
500 S Bluestem Dr 67074 — 316-742-3281
Brian Minks, prin. — Fax 742-3813

**Leoti, Wichita, Pop. 1,520**
Leoti USD 467 — 400/PK-12
PO Box 967 67861 — 620-375-4677
Keith Higgins, supt. — Fax 375-2304
www.leoti.org/
Wichita County JSHS — 200/7-12
PO Box K 67861 — 620-375-2213
Delbert Schmidt, prin. — Fax 375-4958

**Le Roy, Coffey, Pop. 552**
Le Roy-Gridley USD 245 — 200/PK-12
PO Box 278 66857 — 620-964-2212
Russ Mildward, supt. — Fax 964-2413
usd245ks.org/
Southern Coffey County HS — 100/9-12
PO Box 188 66857 — 620-964-2217
Russ Mildward, prin. — Fax 964-2410
Other Schools – See Gridley

**Liberal, Seward, Pop. 20,195**
Liberal USD 480 — 4,800/PK-12
PO Box 949 67905 — 620-604-1010
Renae Hickert, supt. — Fax 604-1011
www.usd480.net
Liberal HS — 1,200/9-12
1611 W 2nd St 67901 — 620-604-1200
Shiloh Vincent, prin. — Fax 604-1201
Liberal South MS — 300/7-8
950 S Grant Ave 67901 — 620-604-1300
Jason Diseker, prin. — Fax 604-1301
Liberal West MS — 400/7-8
500 N Western Ave 67901 — 620-604-1400
Troy McCarter, prin. — Fax 604-1401

Seward County Community College — Post-Sec.
PO Box 1137 67905 — 620-624-1951

**Lincoln, Lincoln, Pop. 1,283**
Lincoln USD 298 — 400/PK-12
PO Box 289 67455 — 785-524-4436
Kathy Robertson, supt. — Fax 524-3080
www.usd298.com
Lincoln JSHS — 200/7-12
PO Box 269 67455 — 785-524-4193
David Kirkendall, prin. — Fax 524-5114

**Lindsborg, McPherson, Pop. 3,384**
Smoky Valley USD 400 — 1,000/PK-12
126 S Main St 67456 — 785-227-2981
Glen Suppes, supt. — Fax 227-2982
www.smokyvalley.org/
Smoky Valley HS — 300/9-12
1 Viking Blvd 67456 — 785-227-2909
Bill Nelson, prin. — Fax 227-2900
Smoky Valley MS — 300/5-8
401 N Cedar St 67456 — 785-227-4249
John Denk, prin. — Fax 227-3650

Bethany College — Post-Sec.
335 E Swensson Ave 67456 — 785-227-3311

**Linn, Washington, Pop. 406**
Barnes USD 223
Supt. — See Barnes
Linn HS — 100/9-12
300 Parkview St 66953 — 785-348-5531
Mike Savage, prin. — Fax 348-5534

**Little River, Rice, Pop. 556**
Little River USD 444 — 300/PK-12
PO Box 218 67457 — 620-897-6325
Dr. Betty Summers, supt. — Fax 897-6788
usd444.ss5.sharpschool.com
Little River HS — 100/9-12
PO Box 8 67457 — 620-897-6201
Audrey Johnson, prin. — Fax 897-6203
Little River JHS — 100/6-8
PO Box 8 67457 — 620-897-6201
Audrey Johnson, prin. — Fax 897-6203

**Logan, Phillips, Pop. 588**
Logan USD 326 — 200/K-12
PO Box 98 67646 — 785-689-7595
Michael Gower, supt. — Fax 689-7517
www.logan326.net
Logan HS — 100/7-12
PO Box 98 67646 — 785-689-7574
Kellen Adams, prin. — Fax 689-7543

**Long Island, Phillips, Pop. 134**
Northern Valley USD 212
Supt. — See Almena
Long Island MS — 100/5-8
PO Box 98 67647 — 785-854-7681
Marvin Gebhard, prin. — Fax 854-7684

**Longton, Elk, Pop. 339**
Elk Valley USD 283 — 200/PK-12
PO Box 87 67352 — 620-642-2811
Jason Crawford, supt. — Fax 642-6551
www.usd283.org
Elk Valley HS — 100/6-12
PO Box 87 67352 — 620-642-2215
Jason Crawford, prin. — Fax 642-3361

**Lost Springs, Marion, Pop. 64**
Centre USD 397 — 300/K-12
PO Box 38 66859 — 785-983-4304
Susan Beeson, supt. — Fax 983-4352
www.usd397.com
Centre K-12 S — 300/K-12
2374 310th St 66859 — 785-983-4321
Susan Beeson, prin. — Fax 983-4377

**Louisburg, Miami, Pop. 4,257**
Louisburg USD 416 — 1,800/PK-12
PO Box 550 66053 — 913-837-1700
Dr. Brian Biermann, supt. — Fax 837-1701
www.usd416.org
Louisburg HS — 500/9-12
PO Box 399 66053 — 913-837-1720
Dr. Tammy Thomasson, prin. — Fax 837-1799
Louisburg MS — 400/6-8
PO Box 308 66053 — 913-837-1800
Michael Isaacsen, prin. — Fax 837-1801
Peoria Street Learning Center — 50/Alt
PO Box 550 66053 — 913-837-1700
Leonard Scotto, prin. — Fax 837-1701

**Lyndon, Osage, Pop. 1,040**
Lyndon USD 421 — 400/PK-12
PO Box 488 66451 — 785-828-4413
Cheryl Cook, supt. — Fax 828-3686
www.usd421.org
Lyndon HS — 100/9-12
PO Box 488 66451 — 785-828-4911
Brad Marcotte, prin. — Fax 828-4221

**Lyons, Rice, Pop. 3,662**
Lyons USD 405 — 800/PK-12
800 S Workman St 67554 — 620-257-5196
Bill Day, supt. — Fax 257-5197
www.usd405.com
Lyons HS — 200/9-12
601 E American Rd 67554 — 620-257-5114
Kelly Nusser, prin. — Fax 257-3194
Lyons MS — 200/6-8
501 E American Rd 67554 — 620-257-3961
Kevin Logan, prin. — Fax 257-3518
Rice County Learning Ctr — Alt
110 E 1st St 67554 — 620-257-7060
Larry Walker, dir. — Fax 257-7060

**Macksville, Stafford, Pop. 542**
Macksville USD 351 — 300/PK-12
PO Box 487 67557 — 620-348-3415
Greg Rinehart M.Ed., supt. — Fax 348-3217
www.usd351.com
Macksville MSHS — 100/7-12
PO Box 307 67557 — 620-348-2475
Stephanie Brandyberry, prin. — Fax 348-2631

**Mc Louth, Jefferson, Pop. 860**
Mc Louth USD 342 — 500/PK-12
PO Box 40 66054 — 913-796-2201
Steve Lilly, supt. — Fax 796-6440
www.mclouth.org
Mc Louth HS — 200/9-12
PO Box 40 66054 — 913-796-6122
Janna Davis, prin. — Fax 796-6124
Mc Louth MS — 100/6-8
PO Box 40 66054 — 913-796-6122
Janna Davis, prin. — Fax 796-6124

**Mc Pherson, McPherson, Pop. 12,895**
Mc Pherson USD 418 — 2,300/PK-12
514 N Main St 67460 — 620-241-9400
Mark Crawford, supt. — Fax 241-9410
www.mcpherson.com/418
Mc Pherson HS — 700/9-12
801 E 1st St 67460 — 620-241-9500
Brad Plackemeier, prin. — Fax 241-9506
Mc Pherson MS — 600/6-8
700 E Elizabeth St 67460 — 620-241-9450
Kelley Brake, prin. — Fax 241-9456

Central Christian College of Kansas — Post-Sec.
PO Box 1403 67460 — 620-241-0723
Elyria Christian S — 200/K-12
1644 Comanche Rd 67460 — 620-241-2994
Rhonda Stucky, admin. — Fax 241-1238
McPherson College — Post-Sec.
1600 E Euclid St 67460 — 620-242-0400

**Madison, Greenwood, Pop. 687**
Madison-Virgil USD 386 — 300/PK-12
PO Box 398 66860 — 620-437-2910
Ryan Bradbury, supt. — Fax 437-2916
www.usd386.net
Madison HS — 100/7-12
PO Box 398 66860 — 620-437-2912
Ryan Bradbury, prin. — Fax 437-2911

**Maize, Sedgwick, Pop. 3,313**
Maize USD 266 — 6,800/K-12
905 W Academy Ave 67101 — 316-722-0614
Chad Higgins, supt. — Fax 722-8538
www.usd266.com
Complete HS Maize — Alt
745 W Central St 67101 — 316-722-4790
Kristy Custer, prin. — Fax 729-0621
Maize HS — 1,500/9-12
11600 W 45th St N 67101 — 316-722-0441
Chris Botts, prin. — Fax 729-7743
Maize MS — 800/6-8
4600 N Maize Rd 67101 — 316-729-2464
Brian Thompson, prin. — Fax 729-2479
Other Schools – See Wichita

**Manhattan, Riley, Pop. 50,618**
Manhattan-Ogden USD 383 — 6,400/PK-12
2031 Poyntz Ave 66502 — 785-587-2000
Dr. Robert Shannon, supt. — Fax 587-2006
www.usd383.org
Anthony MS — 500/7-8
2501 Browning Ave 66502 — 785-587-2890
Vickie Kline, prin. — Fax 587-2899
Eisenhower MS — 400/7-8
800 Walters Dr 66502 — 785-587-2880
Tracy Newell, prin. — Fax 587-2888
Manhattan HS West/East Campus — 1,900/9-12
2100 Poyntz Ave 66502 — 785-587-2100
Greg Hoyt, prin. — Fax 587-2132

American Institute of Baking — Post-Sec.
PO Box 3999 66505 — 785-537-4750
Crum's Beauty College — Post-Sec.
512 Poyntz Ave 66502 — 785-776-4794
Flint Hills Christian S — 100/PK-12
3905 Green Valley Rd 66502 — 785-776-2223
Tim McDonald, admin. — Fax 776-3016
Kansas State University 66506 — Post-Sec.
785-532-6250
Manhattan Area Technical College — Post-Sec.
3136 Dickens Ave 66503 — 785-587-2800
Manhattan Christian College — Post-Sec.
1415 Anderson Ave 66502 — 785-539-3571

**Mankato, Jewell, Pop. 856**
Rock Hills USD 107 — 200/PK-12
109 E Main St 66956 — 785-378-3102
Nadine Smith, supt. — Fax 378-3438
www.usd107.org/
Rock Hills JSHS — 100/7-12
109 E Main St 66956 — 785-378-3126
Sam Meyers, prin. — Fax 378-3530

**Marion, Marion, Pop. 1,911**
Marion-Florence USD 408 — 500/K-12
101 N Thorp St 66861 — 620-382-2117
Lee Leiker, supt. — Fax 382-2118
www.usd408.com
Marion HS — 200/9-12
701 E Main St 66861 — 620-382-2168
Tod Gordon, prin. — Fax 382-6021
Marion MS — 100/7-8
125 S Lincoln St 66861 — 620-382-6070
Missy Stubenhofer, prin. — Fax 382-6073

**Marysville, Marshall, Pop. 3,251**
Marysville USD 364 — 700/PK-12
211 S 10th St 66508 — 785-562-5308
Bill Mullins, supt. — Fax 562-5309
www.usd364.org
Marysville JSHS — 200/7-12
1111 Walnut St 66508 — 785-562-5386
Darren Schroeder, prin. — Fax 562-5387

**Mayetta, Jackson, Pop. 325**
Royal Valley USD 337 — 900/PK-12
PO Box 219 66509 — 785-966-2246
John Rundle, supt. — Fax 966-2490
www.rv337.com/
Royal Valley MS — 300/5-8
PO Box 189 66509 — 785-966-2251
John Linn, prin. — Fax 966-2833
Other Schools – See Hoyt

**Meade, Meade, Pop. 1,700**
Meade USD 226 — 500/PK-12
PO Box 400 67864 — 620-873-2081
Kenneth Harshberger, supt. — Fax 873-2201
www.usd226.org/
Meade HS — 200/9-12
PO Box 400 67864 — 620-873-2981
Scott Moshier, prin. — Fax 873-2201

**Medicine Lodge, Barber, Pop. 1,980**
Barber County North USD 254 — 500/PK-12
PO Box 288 67104 — 620-886-3370
Mark Buck, supt. — Fax 886-3640
www.usd254.org/
Medicine Lodge JSHS — 200/7-12
400 W Eldorado Ave 67104 — 620-886-5667
Darryl Honas, prin. — Fax 886-3053

**Melvern, Osage, Pop. 380**
Marais Des Cygnes Valley USD 456 — 200/K-12
PO Box 158 66510 — 785-549-3521
Darrel Finch, supt. — Fax 549-3659
www.usd456.org
Marais Des Cygnes Valley MSHS — 100/6-12
PO Box 158 66510 — 785-549-3313
Thad Thurston, prin. — Fax 549-3576

**Meriden, Jefferson, Pop. 803**
Jefferson West USD 340 — 800/PK-12
PO Box 267 66512 — 785-484-3444
A. Patton Happer, supt. — Fax 484-3148
www.usd340.org
Jefferson West HS — 300/9-12
PO Box 268 66512 — 785-484-3331
Rhonda Frakes, prin. — Fax 484-2021
Jefferson West MS — 300/5-8
PO Box 410 66512 — 785-484-2900
John Hamon, prin. — Fax 484-2904

**Miltonvale, Cloud, Pop. 532**
Southern Cloud USD 334 — 200/K-12
PO Box 334 67466 — 785-427-3334
Roger Perkins, supt. — Fax 427-2422
www.sc334.org
Miltonvale HS — 50/7-12
PO Box 394 67466 — 785-427-3250
Roger Perkins, prin. — Fax 427-3181
Other Schools – See Glasco

**Minneapolis, Ottawa, Pop. 2,009**
North Ottawa County USD 239 — 600/K-12
PO Box 257 67467 — 785-392-2167
Chris Vignery, supt. — Fax 392-3038
www.usd239.org
Minneapolis JSHS — 300/7-12
PO Box 317 67467 — 785-392-2113
Jay Macy, prin. — Fax 392-2275

**Minneola, Clark, Pop. 728**
Minneola USD 219 — 300/K-12
PO Box 157 67865 — 620-885-4372
Mark Walker, supt. — Fax 885-4509
www.usd219.org/
Minneola HS — 100/9-12
PO Box 157 67865 — 620-885-4611
Brandon Haynes, prin. — Fax 885-4509

**Montezuma, Gray, Pop. 959**
Montezuma USD 371 — 200/PK-12
PO Box 355 67867 — 620-846-2283
Jay Zehr, supt. — Fax 846-2294
sghs.musd371.k12.ks.us
South Gray HS — 100/9-12
PO Box 355 67867 — 620-846-2281
Tim Skinner, prin. — Fax 846-2181

**Moran, Allen, Pop. 543**
Marmaton Valley USD 256 — 300/K-12
128 W Oak St 66755 — 620-237-4250
Kenneth McWhirter, supt. — Fax 237-8872
www.usd256.org
Marmaton Valley HS — 200/7-12
128 W Oak St 66755 — 620-237-4251
Kim Ensminger, prin. — Fax 237-4576

**Moscow, Stevens, Pop. 304**
Moscow USD 209 — 200/K-12
PO Box 158 67952 — 620-598-2205
Stuart Moore, supt. — Fax 598-2233
usd209.weebly.com
Moscow HS — 100/6-12
PO Box 160 67952 — 620-598-2250
Tina Salmans, prin. — Fax 598-2233

**Mound City, Linn, Pop. 679**
Jayhawk USD 346 — 500/PK-12
PO Box 278 66056 — 913-795-2247
Royce Powelson, supt. — Fax 795-2185
www.usd346.org/
Jayhawk-Linn JSHS — 200/7-12
PO Box D 66056 — 913-795-2224
Jim Dillon, prin. — Fax 795-9906

**Moundridge, McPherson, Pop. 1,722**
Moundridge USD 423 400/K-12
PO Box K 67107 620-345-5500
George Leary, supt. Fax 345-8617
www.usd423.org
Moundridge HS 200/9-12
PO Box 610 67107 620-345-5500
Hilarie Hecox, prin. Fax 345-5218
Moundridge MS 100/5-8
PO Box 607 67107 620-345-5500
JoAnn Browne, prin. Fax 345-5307

**Mulvane, Sedgwick, Pop. 5,964**
Mulvane USD 263 1,800/PK-12
PO Box 130 67110 316-777-1102
Brad Rahe, supt. Fax 777-1103
www.usd263.com
Mulvane HS 600/9-12
1900 N Rock Rd 67110 316-777-1183
Jay Ensley, prin. Fax 777-2228
Mulvane MS 400/6-8
915 Westview Dr 67110 316-777-2022
Traci Becker, prin. Fax 777-4967

**Natoma, Osborne, Pop. 333**
Paradise USD 399 100/PK-12
PO Box 100 67651 785-885-4843
Aaron Homburg, supt. Fax 885-4523
www.usd399.com
Natoma HS 100/7-12
PO Box 100 67651 785-885-4849
Aaron Homburg, prin. Fax 885-4523

**Neodesha, Wilson, Pop. 2,454**
Neodesha USD 461 800/PK-12
PO Box 88 66757 620-325-2610
Don Potter, supt. Fax 325-2368
www.neodesha.k12.ks.us
Neodesha JSHS 300/7-12
1000 N 8th St 66757 620-325-3015
Daryl Pruter, prin. Fax 325-2382

**Ness City, Ness, Pop. 1,441**
Ness City USD 303 300/PK-12
414 E Chestnut St 67560 785-798-2210
Derek Reinhardt, supt. Fax 798-3581
www.nesscityschools.org
Ness City JSHS 200/7-12
200 N 5th St 67560 785-798-3991
Tom Flax, prin. Fax 798-3064

**Newton, Harvey, Pop. 18,716**
Newton USD 373 2,800/K-12
308 E 1st St 67114 316-284-6200
Dr. Deborah Hamm, supt. Fax 284-6207
usd373-ks.schoolloop.com
Chisholm MS 500/7-8
900 E 1st St 67114 316-284-6260
Bobbi Jo Grieb, prin. Fax 284-6267
Newton HS 1,000/9-12
900 W 12th St 67114 316-284-6280
Roger Erickson, prin. Fax 284-6288

**Nickerson, Reno, Pop. 1,065**
Nickerson USD 309
Supt. — See Hutchinson
Nickerson HS 300/9-12
305 S Nickerson St 67561 620-422-3226
Rick Blosser, prin. Fax 422-3229

**North Newton, McPherson, Pop. 1,738**

---

Bethel College Post-Sec.
300 E 27th St 67117 316-283-2500

**Norton, Norton, Pop. 2,877**
Norton USD 211 700/PK-12
105 E Waverly St 67654 785-877-3386
Phillip Wilson, supt. Fax 877-2030
www.usd211.org/
Norton Community HS 200/9-12
513 W Wilberforce St 67654 785-877-3338
Rudy Perez, prin. Fax 877-6940
Norton JHS 100/7-8
706 Jones Ave 67654 785-877-5851
Dustin McEwen, prin. Fax 877-3771

**Norwich, Kingman, Pop. 478**
Kingman-Norwich USD 331
Supt. — See Kingman
Norwich HS 100/9-12
PO Box 10 67118 620-478-2235
Wayne Morrow, prin. Fax 478-2879
Norwich MS 100/6-8
PO Box 10 67118 620-478-2235
Wayne Morrow, prin. Fax 478-2879

**Oakley, Logan, Pop. 2,023**
Oakley USD 274 400/PK-12
621 Center Ave Ste 103 67748 785-671-4588
Bill Steiner, supt. Fax 671-3044
www.oakleyschoolsks.com/
Oakley HS 100/9-12
118 W 7th St 67748 785-671-3241
Marlo Klassen, prin. Fax 671-3743
Oakley MS 100/6-8
611 Center Ave 67748 785-671-3820
Craig Wamsley, prin. Fax 671-3010

**Oberlin, Decatur, Pop. 1,774**
Oberlin USD 294 400/PK-12
131 E Commercial St 67749 785-475-3805
Duane Dorshorst, supt. Fax 475-3076
www.usd294.org
Decatur Community JSHS 200/7-12
605 E Commercial St 67749 785-475-2231
Benjamin Jimenez, prin. Fax 475-2802

**Olathe, Johnson, Pop. 122,644**
Olathe USD 233 26,700/PK-12
PO Box 2000 66063 913-780-7000
Dr. Marlin Berry, supt. Fax 780-8011
www.olatheschools.com
California Trail MS 900/6-8
13775 W 133rd St 66062 913-780-7220
Mike Wiley, prin. Fax 780-7229
Chisholm Trail MS 700/6-8
16700 W 159th St 66062 913-780-7240
Mike Wolgast, prin. Fax 780-7249
Frontier Trail MS 800/6-8
15300 W 143rd St 66062 913-780-7210
Dr. Rod Smith, prin. Fax 780-7216
Indian Trail MS 700/6-8
1440 E 151st St 66062 913-780-7230
Dr. Sarah Guerrero, prin. Fax 780-7234
Mission Trail MS 6-8
1001 N Persimmon Dr 66061 913-780-7260
Rachelle Waters, prin. Fax 780-7269
Olathe Advance Technical Center Vo/Tech
611 N Nelson Rd 66061 913-780-7026
Amy McLain, admin. Fax 780-8239
Olathe East HS 2,000/9-12
14545 W 127th St 66062 913-780-7120
Dr. Bill Weber, prin. Fax 780-7137
Olathe North HS 1,900/9-12
600 E Prairie St 66061 913-780-7140
David Morford, prin. Fax 780-7837
Olathe Northwest HS 1,700/9-12
21300 College Blvd 66061 913-780-7150
Dr. Gwen Poss, prin. Fax 780-7159
Olathe South HS 2,000/9-12
1640 E 151st St 66062 913-780-7160
Phil Clark, prin. Fax 780-7170
Oregon Trail MS 400/6-8
1800 W Dennis Ave 66061 913-780-7250
Anne Hawks, prin. Fax 780-7256
Pioneer Trail MS 700/6-8
15100 W 127th St 66062 913-780-7270
Elaine Carpenter, prin. Fax 780-7278
Prairie Trail MS 700/6-8
21600 W 107th St 66061 913-780-7280
J.J. Libal, prin. Fax 780-7289
Santa Fe Trail MS 600/6-8
1100 N Ridgeview Rd 66061 913-780-7290
Kerry Lane, prin. Fax 780-7296

---

Kansas School for the Deaf Post-Sec.
450 E Park St 66061 913-791-0573
Mid-America Nazarene University Post-Sec.
2030 E College Way 66062 913-782-3750
Superior School of Hairdressing Post-Sec.
1215 E Santa Fe St 66061 913-782-4004

**Olpe, Lyon, Pop. 541**
Southern Lyon County USD 252
Supt. — See Hartford
Olpe JSHS 200/7-12
PO Box 206 66865 620-475-3223
Shane Clark, prin. Fax 475-3951

**Onaga, Pottawatomie, Pop. 694**
Onaga-Havensville-Wheaton USD 322 300/PK-12
PO Box 60 66521 785-889-4614
Adam McDaniel, supt. Fax 889-4662
www.usd322.org
Onaga HS 100/9-12
PO Box 458 66521 785-889-4251
Adam McDaniel, prin. Fax 889-4944

**Osage City, Osage, Pop. 2,899**
Osage City USD 420 700/K-12
520 Main St 66523 785-528-3176
Troy Hutton, supt. Fax 528-3932
www.usd420.org
Osage City HS 200/9-12
515 Ellinwood St 66523 785-528-3172
Tony Heward, prin. Fax 528-2980
Osage City MS 100/6-8
420 S 5th St 66523 785-528-3175
Tim Riemann, prin. Fax 528-2980

**Osawatomie, Miami, Pop. 4,349**
Osawatomie USD 367 1,200/PK-12
1200 Trojan Dr 66064 913-755-4172
Gary French, supt. Fax 755-2031
www.usd367.org/
Osawatomie HS 400/9-12
1200 Trojan Dr 66064 913-755-2191
Doug Chisam, prin. Fax 755-2645
Osawatomie MS 300/6-8
428 Pacific Ave 66064 913-755-4155
Dan Welch, prin. Fax 755-2197

**Osborne, Osborne, Pop. 1,422**
Osborne County USD 392 300/PK-12
213 W Adams 67473 785-346-2145
Keith Hall, supt. Fax 346-2448
www.usd392.com
Osborne JSHS 100/7-12
219 N 2nd St 67473 785-346-2143
Tom Conway, prin. Fax 346-2331

**Oskaloosa, Jefferson, Pop. 1,096**
Oskaloosa USD 341 500/PK-12
404 Park St 66066 785-863-2539
Jon Pfau, supt. Fax 863-3080
www.usd341.org
Oskaloosa JSHS 200/7-12
404 Park St 66066 785-863-2281
Brent Mumford, prin. Fax 863-3106

**Oswego, Labette, Pop. 1,768**
Oswego USD 504 500/PK-12
PO Box 129 67356 620-795-2126
Douglas Beisel, supt. Fax 795-4871
www.usd504.org
Oswego JSHS 100/6-12
PO Box 129 67356 620-795-2125
Mike Barbo, prin. Fax 795-2130

**Otis, Rush, Pop. 278**
Otis-Bison USD 403 200/PK-12
PO Box 227 67565 785-387-2201
Troy Piper, supt. Fax 387-2203
www.usd403.org/
Otis-Bison JSHS 100/7-12
PO Box 257 67565 785-387-2337
Mark Goodheart, prin. Fax 387-2557

**Ottawa, Franklin, Pop. 12,279**
Ottawa USD 290 2,400/PK-12
1404 S Ash St 66067 785-229-8010
Dr. Jeanne Stroh, supt. Fax 229-8019
www.usd290.org
Career Technology Educational Coop Vo/Tech
908 W 11th St 66067 785-229-8090
Dr. Ryan Cobbs, prin. Fax 229-8099
Ottawa HS 700/9-12
1120 S Ash St 66067 785-229-8020
Ryan Cobbs, prin. Fax 229-8029
Ottawa Learning Center Alt
1404 S Ash St 66067 785-229-8070
Dr. Ryan Cobbs, prin. Fax 229-8079
Ottawa MS 600/6-8
1230 S Ash St 66067 785-229-8030
Derek Bland, prin. Fax 229-8039

---

Bethel Christian Academy 50/K-12
3755 Nevada Rd 66067 785-242-1226
Donita Callahan, admin. Fax 242-1226
Ottawa University Post-Sec.
1001 S Cedar St 66067 785-242-5200

**Overland Park, Johnson, Pop. 169,666**
Blue Valley USD 229 19,900/PK-12
PO Box 23901 66283 913-239-4000
Dr. Al Hanna, supt. Fax 239-4150
www.bluevalleyk12.org
Aubry Bend MS 6-8
12501 W 175th St, 913-624-2300
Diana Tate, prin. Fax 624-2348
Blue Valley Academy Alt
7500 W 149th Ter 66223 913-239-4529
Valerie Jennings, prin. Fax 239-4534
Blue Valley MS 400/6-8
5001 W 163rd Ter, 913-239-5100
Roxana Rogers, prin. Fax 239-5148
Blue Valley North HS 1,500/9-12
12200 Lamar Ave 66209 913-239-3000
David Stubblefield, prin. Fax 239-3038
Blue Valley Northwest HS 1,700/9-12
13260 Switzer Rd 66213 913-239-3400
Amy Murphy Ed.D., prin. Fax 239-3555
Blue Valley Southwest HS 9-12
17600 S Quivira Rd, 913-624-2000
Scott Roberts, prin. Fax 624-2048
Blue Valley West HS 1,300/9-12
16200 Antioch Rd, 913-239-3700
Brett Potts, prin. Fax 239-3880
Center for Advanced Professional Studies 11-12
7511 W 149th Ter 66223 913-239-5900
Chad Ralston, dir. Fax 239-5948
Harmony MS 600/6-8
10101 W 141st St 66221 913-239-5200
Sheila Albers, prin. Fax 239-5248
Lakewood MS 700/6-8
6601 Edgewater Dr 66223 913-239-5800
Scott Currier, prin. Fax 239-5848
Overland Trail MS 600/6-8
6201 W 133rd St 66209 913-239-5400
Shelly Nielsen, prin. Fax 239-5448
Oxford MS 600/6-8
12500 Switzer Rd 66213 913-239-5500
Linda Crosthwait, prin. Fax 239-5548
Other Schools – See Leawood, Stilwell

---

American Academy of Hair Design Post-Sec.
11401 W 112th Ter 66210 - -
B-Street Design School of Intl Hair Stlg Post-Sec.
10324 Mastin St 66212 913-492-4114
Cleveland Chiropractic College Post-Sec.
10850 Lowell Ave 66210 913-234-0600
Heritage Christian Academy 400/PK-12
9333 W 159th St 66221 913-681-7622
ITT Technical Institute Post-Sec.
7600 W 119th St Ste 100 66213 913-253-1300
Johnson County Community College Post-Sec.
12345 College Blvd 66210 913-469-8500
Kansas City College and Bible School Post-Sec.
7401 Metcalf Ave 66204 913-722-0272
LaBaron Hairdressing Academy Post-Sec.
8119 Robinson St 66204 913-642-0077
Ottawa University Post-Sec.
4370 W 109th St Ste 200 66211 913-266-8600
Overland Christian S 100/PK-12
7401 Metcalf Ave 66204 913-722-0272
Chad Pollard, admin. Fax 403-0595
St. Thomas Aquinas HS 1,000/9-12
11411 Pflumm Rd 66215 913-345-1411
Craig Moss, pres. Fax 345-2319
Wright Career College Post-Sec.
10700 Metcalf Ave 66210 913-385-7700

**Oxford, Sumner, Pop. 1,034**
Oxford USD 358 300/PK-12
PO Box 937 67119 620-455-2227
Mark Whitener, supt. Fax 455-3680
www.usd358.com
Oxford JSHS 200/6-12
PO Box 970 67119 620-455-2410
Mark Whitener, prin. Fax 455-3741

**Palco, Rooks, Pop. 275**
Palco USD 269
Supt. — See Damar
Palco JSHS 50/6-12
PO Box 38 67657 785-737-4645
Roger Morris, prin. Fax 737-4646

**Paola, Miami, Pop. 5,476**
Paola USD 368 2,000/K-12
1115 E 303rd St 66071 913-294-8000
Judy Welter, supt. Fax 294-8001
www.usd368.org/
Paola HS 600/9-12
401 Angela St 66071 913-294-8010
Phil Bressler, prin. Fax 294-8011
Paola MS 400/6-8
405 N Hospital Dr 66071 913-294-8030
Mark Bloustine, prin. Fax 294-8031

**Parsons, Labette, Pop. 10,094**
Parsons USD 503 800/PK-12
PO Box 1056 67357 620-421-5950
Dr. Shelly Martin, supt. Fax 421-5954
www.vikingnet.net
Parsons HS 400/9-12
3030 Morton Ave 67357 620-421-3660
Matt Rogers, prin. Fax 423-8816
Parsons MS 300/6-8
2719 Main St 67357 620-421-4190
Larry Geist, prin. Fax 423-8822

---

Labette Community College Post-Sec.
200 S 14th St 67357 620-421-6700

**Paxico, Wabaunsee, Pop. 208**
Mill Creek Valley USD 329
Supt. — See Alma
Mill Creek Valley JHS 100/7-8
PO Box 128 66526 785-636-5353
Steve Oliver, prin. Fax 636-5116

**Peabody, Marion, Pop. 1,179**
Peabody-Burns USD 398 300/PK-12
506 N Elm St 66866 620-983-2198
Ron Traxson, supt. Fax 983-2247
www.usd398.net
Peabody-Burns JSHS 200/6-12
810 N Sycamore St 66866 620-983-2196
Ken Parry, prin. Fax 983-2773

**Perry, Jefferson, Pop. 910**
Perry USD 343 800/PK-12
PO Box 729 66073 785-597-5138
Dr. Denis Yoder, supt. Fax 597-2254
www.usd343.net
Perry-Lecompton HS 300/9-12
PO Box 18 66073 785-597-5124
Mike Copple, prin. Fax 597-5177
Perry-Lecompton MS 300/5-8
PO Box 31 66073 785-597-5159
Josh Woodward, prin. Fax 597-5014

**Phillipsburg, Phillips, Pop. 2,555**
Phillipsburg USD 325 600/PK-12
240 S 7th St 67661 785-543-5281
Mike Gower, supt. Fax 543-2271
www.usd325.com
Phillipsburg HS 200/9-12
410 S 7th St 67661 785-543-5251
Todd Bowman, prin. Fax 543-6305
Phillipsburg MS 200/5-8
647 7th St 67661 785-543-5114
Chris Look, prin. Fax 543-2934

**Pittsburg, Crawford, Pop. 19,561**
Pittsburg USD 250 2,700/K-12
PO Box 75 66762 620-235-3100
Destry Brown, supt. Fax 235-3106
www.usd250.org
Pittsburg HS 700/9-12
1978 E 4th St 66762 620-235-3200
Jon Bishop, prin. Fax 235-3210
Pittsburg MS 600/6-8
1310 N Broadway St 66762 620-235-3240
Terry Smith, prin. Fax 235-3248

---

Pittsburg State University Post-Sec.
1701 S Broadway St 66762 620-231-7000
St. Mary's Colgan HS 300/7-12
PO Box 266 66762 620-231-4690
Tom Compton, prin. Fax 231-0690

**Plainville, Rooks, Pop. 1,886**
Plainville USD 270 400/PK-12
203 SE Cardinal Ave 67663 785-434-4678
Gail Dunbar, supt. Fax 434-7404
www.usd270.net
Plainville HS 100/9-12
202 SE Cardinal Ave 67663 785-434-4547
Lisa Gehring, prin. Fax 434-4689

**Pleasanton, Linn, Pop. 1,187**
Pleasanton USD 344 300/K-12
PO Box 480 66075 913-352-8534
Travis Laver, supt. Fax 352-6588
www.usd344.org/
Pleasanton HS 100/7-12
PO Box 480 66075 913-352-8701
Mitch Shaw, prin. Fax 352-6588

**Pomona, Franklin, Pop. 819**
West Franklin USD 287 600/PK-12
510 E Franklin St 66076 785-566-3396
Jerry Turner, supt. Fax 566-8325
www.usd287.org
West Franklin HS 200/9-12
511 E Franklin St 66076 785-566-3392
Rick Smith, prin. Fax 566-8454
West Franklin MS 100/6-8
331 Tyler St 66076 785-566-3541
Rick Smith, prin. Fax 566-3634

**Prairie Village, Johnson, Pop. 21,158**

---

Kansas City Christian S 400/PK-12
4801 W 79th St 66208 913-648-5227
Bill Glotzbach, head sch Fax 648-5269

**Pratt, Pratt, Pop. 6,720**
Pratt USD 382 900/PK-12
401 S Hamilton St 67124 620-672-4500
Suzan Patton, supt. Fax 672-4509
www.usd382.com
Liberty MS 200/5-8
300 S Iuka St 67124 620-672-4530
Tony Helfrich, prin. Fax 672-4539
Pratt HS 300/9-12
400 S Hamilton St 67124 620-672-4540
Steve Blankenship, prin. Fax 672-4549

Skyline USD 438 400/PK-12
20269 W US Highway 54 67124 620-672-5651
Becca Flowers, supt. Fax 672-9377
skylineschools.org
Skyline JSHS 100/7-12
20269 W US Highway 54 67124 620-672-5651
Herb McPherson, prin. Fax 672-9377

---

Pratt Community College Post-Sec.
348 NE State Road 61 67124 620-672-5641

**Pretty Prairie, Reno, Pop. 669**
Pretty Prairie USD 311 300/PK-12
PO Box 218 67570 620-459-6241
Brad Wade, supt. Fax 459-6810
www.usd311.com
Pretty Prairie HS 100/9-12
PO Box 326 67570 620-459-6313
Randy Hendrickson, prin. Fax 459-6935
Pretty Prairie MS 100/5-8
PO Box 307 67570 620-459-6911
Randy Hendrickson, prin. Fax 459-6729

**Protection, Comanche, Pop. 508**
South Central USD 300
Supt. — See Coldwater
South Central MS 100/6-8
PO Box 38 67127 620-622-4545
Matt Jellison, prin. Fax 622-4844

**Quinter, Gove, Pop. 912**
Quinter USD 293 300/PK-12
PO Box 540 67752 785-754-2470
Linda Zeigler, supt. Fax 754-3365
www.quinterschools.org
Quinter JSHS 100/7-12
PO Box 459 67752 785-754-3660
Toby Countryman M.A., prin. Fax 754-3905

**Randolph, Riley, Pop. 158**
Blue Valley USD 384 200/K-12
PO Box 98 66554 785-293-5256
Brady Burton, supt. Fax 293-5607
www.usd384.org/
Blue Valley HS 100/9-12
PO Box 68 66554 785-293-5255
Marion Mazouch, prin. Fax 293-5372
Randolph MS 50/5-8
PO Box 38 66554 785-293-5253
Marion Mazouch, prin. Fax 293-5607

**Ransom, Ness, Pop. 292**
Western Plains USD 106 200/PK-12
100 School St 67572 785-731-2352
Jeff Jones, supt. Fax 731-2235
www.usd106.org
Western Plains HS 50/9-12
100 School St 67572 785-731-2352
Jeff Jones, prin. Fax 731-2235

**Rexford, Thomas, Pop. 229**
Golden Plains USD 316
Supt. — See Selden
Golden Plains HS 100/9-12
PO Box 100 67753 785-687-3265
Darrin Herl, prin. Fax 687-2285
Golden Plains MS 50/6-8
PO Box 100 67753 785-687-3265
Darrin Herl, prin. Fax 687-2285

**Richmond, Franklin, Pop. 461**
Central Heights USD 288 600/PK-12
3521 Ellis Rd 66080 785-869-3455
Brian Spencer, supt. Fax 869-2675
www.usd288.org
Central Heights HS 200/9-12
3521 Ellis Rd 66080 785-869-3455
Tom Horstick, prin. Fax 869-2675
Central Heights MS 200/6-8
3521 Ellis Rd 66080 785-869-3455
Buddy Welch, prin. Fax 869-2675

**Riley, Riley, Pop. 930**
Riley County USD 378 700/PK-12
PO Box 326 66531 785-485-4000
Nancy Meyer, supt. Fax 485-2860
www.usd378.org
Riley County HS 200/9-12
PO Box 38 66531 785-485-4020
Harold Oliver, prin. Fax 485-2426

**Riverton, Cherokee, Pop. 874**
Riverton USD 404 800/PK-12
PO Box 290 66770 620-848-3386
Todd Berry, supt. Fax 848-9853
www.usd404.org/
Riverton HS 200/9-12
PO Box 290 66770 620-848-3388
Chad Harper, prin. Fax 848-3609
Riverton MS 200/6-8
PO Box 260 66770 620-848-3355
Dr. Becky Murray, prin. Fax 848-3288

**Roeland Park, Johnson, Pop. 6,575**

---

Bishop Miege HS 700/9-12
5041 Reinhardt Dr 66205 913-262-2700
Randy Salisbury, prin. Fax 262-2752

**Rolla, Morton, Pop. 432**
Rolla USD 217 200/PK-12
PO Box 167 67954 620-593-4344
Kim Mauk, supt. Fax 593-4250
www.usd217.org
Rolla JSHS 100/6-12
PO Box 167 67954 620-593-4345
Gardell Schnable, prin. Fax 593-4204

**Rosalia, Butler, Pop. 169**
Flinthills USD 492 200/K-12
PO Box 188 67132 620-476-2237
Jeremy Boldra, supt. Fax 476-2253
www.usd492.org
Flinthills HS 100/9-12
PO Box 188 67132 620-476-2215
Bret Howard, prin. Fax 476-2244
Flinthills MS 50/7-8
PO Box 188 67132 620-476-2218
Larry Gawith, prin. Fax 476-2391

**Rose Hill, Butler, Pop. 3,842**
Rose Hill USD 394 1,700/PK-12
104 N Rose Hill Rd 67133 316-776-3300
Randal Chickadonz, supt. Fax 776-3309
www.usd394.com
Rose Hill HS 600/9-12
104 N Rose Hill Rd 67133 316-776-3360
Shannon Haydock, prin. Fax 776-3378
Rose Hill MS 400/6-8
104 N Rose Hill Rd 67133 316-776-3320
Kay Walker, prin. Fax 776-3319

**Rossville, Shawnee, Pop. 1,132**
Kaw Valley USD 321
Supt. — See Saint Marys
Rossville JSHS 300/7-12
PO Box 68 66533 785-584-6193
Toby McCullough, prin. Fax 584-6379

**Rozel, Pawnee, Pop. 156**
Pawnee Heights USD 496 100/K-12
PO Box 98 67574 620-527-4212
Daniel Binder, supt. Fax 527-4215
www.phtigers.net
Pawnee Heights S 100/K-12
PO Box 97 67574 620-527-4211
Daniel Binder, prin. Fax 527-4215

**Russell, Russell, Pop. 4,436**
Russell County USD 407 700/K-12
802 N Main St 67665 785-483-2173
Angela Lawrence, supt. Fax 483-2175
www.usd407.org
Ruppenthal MS 200/6-8
400 N Elm St 67665 785-483-3174
Gaylon Walter, prin. Fax 483-5386
Russell HS 200/9-12
565 E State St 67665 785-483-5631
Larry Bernard, prin. Fax 483-5636

**Sabetha, Nemaha, Pop. 2,538**
Prairie Hills USD 113 1,100/PK-12
1619 S Old Hwy 75 66534 785-284-2175
Todd Evans, supt. Fax 284-3739
www.usd113.org
Sabetha HS 200/9-12
1011 Blue Jay Blvd 66534 785-284-2155
Sheri Harmer, prin. Fax 284-2600
Sabetha MS 200/6-8
751 Blue Jay Blvd 66534 785-284-2151
Matthew Garber, prin. Fax 284-0061
Other Schools – See Axtell, Wetmore

**Saint Francis, Cheyenne, Pop. 1,327**
St. Francis Community USD 297 300/K-12
PO Box 1110 67756 785-332-8182
Robert Schiltz, supt. Fax 332-8181
www.usd297.org/
Saint Francis JSHS 100/7-12
PO Box 1110 67756 785-332-8153
David Morrow, prin. Fax 332-8177

**Saint George, Pottawatomie, Pop. 611**
Rock Creek USD 323
Supt. — See Westmoreland
Rock Creek JSHS 400/7-12
9355 Flush Rd 66535 785-494-8591
Eric Koppes, prin. Fax 494-8595

**Saint John, Stafford, Pop. 1,281**
St. John-Hudson USD 350 300/K-12
505 N Broadway St 67576 620-549-3564
Joshua P. Meyer, supt. Fax 549-3964
www.usd350.com
Saint John JSHS 100/7-12
505 N Broadway St 67576 620-549-3277
Mike Burgan, prin. Fax 549-6289

**Saint Marys, Pottawatomie, Pop. 2,562**
Kaw Valley USD 321 1,300/PK-12
411 W Lasley St 66536 785-437-2254
Kerry Lacock, supt. Fax 437-3155
www.kawvalley.k12.ks.us
Saint Marys JSHS 300/7-12
601 E Lasley St 66536 785-437-6257
David Cromer, prin. Fax 437-3460
Other Schools – See Rossville

**Saint Paul, Neosho, Pop. 622**
Chetopa - St. Paul USD 505
Supt. — See Chetopa

Saint Paul HS 100/7-12
318 1st St 66771 620-449-2245
Kim Bartelli, prin. Fax 449-8960

**Salina, Saline, Pop. 46,386**
Salina USD 305 6,900/PK-12
PO Box 797 67402 785-309-4700
William Hall, supt. Fax 309-4737
www.usd305.com
Lakewood MS 800/6-8
1135 E Lakewood Cir 67401 785-309-4000
Sherri Louthan, prin. Fax 309-4001
Opportunity Now Alt
219 S 3rd St 67401 785-309-5200
Jeff Hayes, coord. Fax 826-4746
Salina Central HS 1,000/9-12
650 E Crawford St 67401 785-309-3500
Shanna Rector, prin. Fax 309-3501
Salina South HS 1,100/9-12
730 E Magnolia Rd 67401 785-309-3700
Curtis Stevens, prin. Fax 309-3701
Salina South MS 800/6-8
2015 Simmons St 67401 785-309-3900
Beth Morrison, prin. Fax 309-3901
Salina West Education Center Alt
501 W Cloud St 67401 785-309-4900
Rex Boley, prin.
Salina Adult Education Center Adult
2620 Centennial Rd 67401 785-309-4660
Kelly Mobray, dir. Fax 309-4669

---

Academy of Hair Design Post-Sec.
115 S 5th St 67401 785-825-8155
Brown Mackie College Post-Sec.
2106 S 9th St 67401 800-365-0433
Kansas State University Post-Sec.
2310 Centennial Rd 67401 785-826-2640
Kansas Wesleyan University Post-Sec.
100 E Claflin Ave 67401 785-827-5541
Sacred Heart HS 300/7-12
234 E Cloud St 67401 785-827-4422
John Krajicek, prin. Fax 827-8648
St. Johns Military S 200/6-12
PO Box 5020 67402 785-823-7231
Andrew England, pres. Fax 309-5489
Salina Area Technical College Post-Sec.
2562 Centennial Rd 67401 785-309-3100
Salina Christian Academy 200/PK-12
1009 Highland Ave 67401 785-452-9929
Duane Custer, prin. Fax 825-2506

**Satanta, Haskell, Pop. 1,111**
Satanta USD 507 300/PK-12
PO Box 279 67870 620-649-2234
Jeff Bollinger, supt. Fax 649-2668
www.usd507.org
Satanta JSHS 100/6-12
PO Box 69 67870 620-649-2611
J.D. Johnson, prin. Fax 649-2658

**Scandia, Republic, Pop. 370**
Pike Valley USD 426 200/K-12
PO Box 291 66966 785-335-2206
Mary Treaster, supt. Fax 335-2219
www.pikevalley.com
Pike Valley HS 100/9-12
PO Box 139 66966 785-335-2294
Jeremy Luedke, prin. Fax 335-2386
Other Schools – See Courtland

**Scott City, Scott, Pop. 3,797**
Scott County USD 466 900/PK-12
PO Box 288 67871 620-872-7600
Jamie Rumford, supt. Fax 872-7609
www.usd466.com
Scott City HS 200/9-12
712 S Main St 67871 620-872-7620
Brad McCormick, prin. Fax 872-7629
Scott City MS 300/5-8
809 W 9th St 67871 620-872-7640
Jana Irvin, prin. Fax 872-7649

**Sedan, Chautauqua, Pop. 1,096**
Chautauqua County Community USD 286 400/PK-12
302 Sherman St 67361 620-725-3187
Nathan Hinrichs, supt. Fax 725-5642
www.usd286.org
Sedan HS 200/7-12
416 E Elm St 67361 620-725-3186
Kay Hill, prin. Fax 725-3188

**Sedgwick, Harvey, Pop. 1,672**
Sedgwick USD 439 500/K-12
PO Box K 67135 316-772-5783
Larry Roth, supt. Fax 772-0274
www.usd439.com
Sedgwick HS 200/9-12
PO Box K 67135 316-772-5155
Mike Hilliard, prin. Fax 772-0334

**Selden, Sheridan, Pop. 219**
Golden Plains USD 316 200/PK-12
PO Box 199 67757 785-386-4559
Darrn Herl, supt. Fax 386-4562
usd316.k12.ks.us/
Other Schools – See Rexford

**Seneca, Nemaha, Pop. 1,982**
Nemaha Central USD 115 500/PK-12
318 Main St 66538 785-336-6101
Darrel Kohlman, supt. Fax 336-2268
www.usd115.org
Nemaha Central HS 200/9-12
214 N 11th St 66538 785-336-3557
Patrick McKernan, prin. Fax 336-3672

**Sharon Springs, Wallace, Pop. 741**
Wallace County USD 241 200/PK-12
521 N Main St 67758 785-852-4252
Brian McVay, supt. Fax 852-4603
www.usd241.org/
Wallace County HS 100/9-12
521 N Main St 67758 785-852-4240
Brian McVay, prin. Fax 852-4603

**Shawnee, Johnson, Pop. 60,803**
De Soto USD 232
Supt. — See De Soto
Mill Valley HS 1,100/9-12
5900 Monticello Rd 66226 913-422-4351
Tobie Waldeck, prin. Fax 422-4039
Monticello Trails MS 700/6-8
6100 Monticello Rd 66226 913-422-1100
Brian Schwanz, prin. Fax 422-4990

---

Academy of Aesthetics Arts Post-Sec.
10316 Shawnee Mission Pkwy 66203 913-962-9772
Central Baptist Theological Seminary Post-Sec.
6601 Monticello Rd 66226 800-677-2287
Maranatha Christian Academy 200/7-12
6826 Lackman Rd 66217 913-631-0637
Mark Schultze, supt. Fax 631-0899
Midland Adventist Academy 100/K-12
6915 Maurer Rd 66217 913-268-7400

**Shawnee Mission, See Merriam**
Shawnee Mission USD 512 27,100/PK-12
7235 Antioch Rd 66204 913-993-6200
Dr. Jim Hinson, supt. Fax 993-6247
www.smsd.org
Hocker Grove MS 800/7-8
10400 Johnson Dr 66203 913-993-0200
Ben Pretz, prin. Fax 993-0399
Horizons HS Alt
5900 Lamar Ave 66202 913-993-9500
Paul Colwell, prin. Fax 993-9599
Indian Hills MS 800/7-8
6400 Mission Rd 66208 913-993-0400
Dr. Scott Sherman, prin. Fax 993-0599
Indian Woods MS 700/7-8
9700 Woodson Dr 66207 913-993-0600
David Conrady, prin. Fax 993-0799
Shawnee Mission East HS 1,800/9-12
7500 Mission Rd 66208 913-993-6600
John McKinney, prin. Fax 993-6899
Shawnee Mission North HS 1,600/9-12
7401 Johnson Dr 66202 913-993-6900
Richard Kramer, prin. Fax 993-7099
Shawnee Mission Northwest HS 1,800/9-12
12701 W 67th St 66216 913-993-7200
Lisa Gruman, prin. Fax 993-7499
Shawnee Mission South HS 1,400/9-12
5800 W 107th St 66207 913-993-7500
Todd Dain, prin. Fax 993-7799
Shawnee Mission West HS 1,900/9-12
8800 W 85th St 66212 913-993-7800
Steve Loe, prin. Fax 993-8099
Trailridge MS 800/7-8
7500 Quivira Rd 66216 913-993-1000
Bonnie Welty, prin. Fax 993-1199
Westridge MS 1,000/7-8
9300 Nieman Rd 66214 913-993-1200
Eric Rembold, prin. Fax 993-1399

**Silver Lake, Shawnee, Pop. 1,409**
Silver Lake USD 372 700/PK-12
PO Box 39 66539 785-582-4026
Tim Hallacy, supt. Fax 582-5259
www.silverlakeschools.org/
Silver Lake JSHS 300/7-12
PO Box 39 66539 785-582-4639
Brad Womack, prin. Fax 582-4265

**Smith Center, Smith, Pop. 1,647**
Smith Center USD 237 400/PK-12
216 S Jefferson St 66967 785-282-6665
Ron Meitler, supt. Fax 282-6518
www.usd237.com
Smith Center JSHS 200/7-12
300 Roger Barta Way 66967 785-282-6609
Greg Koelsch, prin. Fax 282-5206

**Solomon, Dickinson, Pop. 1,069**
Solomon USD 393 300/K-12
113 E 7th St 67480 785-655-2541
Justin Coup, supt. Fax 655-2505
www.usd393.net
Solomon HS 200/7-12
409 N Pine St 67480 785-655-2551
Dustin Dooley, prin. Fax 655-3011

**South Haven, Sumner, Pop. 360**
South Haven USD 509 200/PK-12
PO Box 229 67140 620-892-5216
Lynn Archer, supt. Fax 892-5814
www.usd509.org/
South Haven JSHS 100/6-12
PO Box 229 67140 620-892-5215
Lynn Archer, prin. Fax 892-5814

**Spearville, Ford, Pop. 771**
Spearville USD 381 400/K-12
PO Box 338 67876 620-385-2676
Daryl Stegman, supt. Fax 385-2614
www.usd381.org/
Spearville JSHS 200/6-12
PO Box 158 67876 620-385-2631
Patrick Crowdis, prin. Fax 385-2641

**Spring Hill, Johnson, Pop. 5,340**
Spring Hill USD 230 3,300/PK-12
101 E South St 66083 913-592-7200
Dr. Wayne Burke, supt. Fax 592-7270
www.usd230.org
Spring Hill HS 600/9-12
19701 S Ridgeview Rd 66083 913-592-7299
Marc Williams, prin. Fax 592-2847
Spring Hill MS 300/6-8
301 E South St 66083 913-592-7288
Rodney Sprague, prin. Fax 592-5424

**Stafford, Stafford, Pop. 1,029**
Stafford USD 349 200/PK-12
PO Box 400 67578 620-234-5243
Dr. Mary Jo Taylor, supt. Fax 234-6986
www.stafford349.com
Stafford MSHS 100/6-12
PO Box 370 67578 620-234-5248
Dallas Woolf, prin. Fax 234-6041

**Sterling, Rice, Pop. 2,287**
Sterling USD 376 500/PK-12
PO Box 188 67579 620-278-3621
Dr. Fred Dierksen, supt. Fax 278-3882
www.usd376.com
Sterling JSHS 200/7-12
308 E Washington Ave 67579 620-278-2171
Bill Anderson, prin. Fax 278-3237

---

Sterling College Post-Sec.
125 W Cooper St 67579 620-278-2173

**Stilwell, Johnson**
Blue Valley USD 229
Supt. — See Overland Park
Blue Valley HS 1,300/9-12
6001 W 159th St 66085 913-239-4800
Scott Bacon, prin. Fax 239-4835
Pleasant Ridge MS 500/6-8
9000 W 165th St 66085 913-239-5700
Phoebe Lewis, prin. Fax 239-5748

**Stockton, Rooks, Pop. 1,312**
Stockton USD 271 300/PK-12
201 N Cypress St 67669 785-425-6367
Allaire Homburg, supt. Fax 425-6923
www.usd271.com
Stockton HS 100/9-12
105 N Cypress St 67669 785-425-6784
S. Wayne, prin. Fax 425-6200

**Sublette, Haskell, Pop. 1,442**
Sublette USD 374 400/PK-12
PO Box 670 67877 620-675-2277
Rex Bruce, supt. Fax 675-2652
www.usd374.org/
Sublette MSHS 100/7-12
PO Box 460 67877 620-675-2232
Monty Marlin, prin. Fax 675-8347

**Sylvan Grove, Lincoln, Pop. 277**
Sylvan Grove USD 299 200/PK-12
504 W 4th St 67481 785-526-7175
Jude Stecklein, supt. Fax 526-7182
www.usd299.org/
Sylvan-Lucas Unified JSHS 100/7-12
504 W 4th St 67481 785-526-7175
Jeff Starkey, prin. Fax 526-7182

**Syracuse, Hamilton, Pop. 1,789**
Syracuse USD 494 500/PK-12
PO Box 1187 67878 620-384-7872
Kenneth Bridges, supt. Fax 384-7692
www.usd494.org
Syracuse JSHS 200/7-12
PO Box 1187 67878 620-384-7446
Paul Zuzelski, prin. Fax 384-6686

**Tecumseh, Shawnee**
Shawnee Heights USD 450 3,600/PK-12
4401 SE Shawnee Heights Rd 66542 785-379-5800
Dr. Martin Stessman, supt. Fax 379-5810
www.usd450.net
Shawnee Heights HS 1,100/9-12
4201 SE Shawnee Heights Rd 66542 785-379-5880
Ed West, prin. Fax 379-5967
Shawnee Heights MS 600/7-8
4335 SE Shawnee Heights Rd 66542 785-379-5830
Tim Urich, prin. Fax 379-5848

**Tescott, Ottawa, Pop. 315**
Twin Valley USD 240
Supt. — See Bennington
Tescott HS 100/9-12
PO Box 196 67484 785-283-4774
Dr. Becky Cheney, prin. Fax 283-4347

**Tipton, Mitchell, Pop. 210**

---

Tipton Catholic HS 50/9-12
PO Box 146 67485 785-373-5835
Gery Hake, prin. Fax 373-5637

**Tonganoxie, Leavenworth, Pop. 4,915**
Tonganoxie USD 464 1,900/K-12
330 E 24/40 Highway 66086 913-416-1400
Dr. Lyn Rantz, supt. Fax 416-1408
www.tong464.org
Tonganoxie HS 600/9-12
404 E 24/40 Highway 66086 913-416-1460
Mark Farrar, prin. Fax 416-1468
Tonganoxie MS 600/5-8
824 E Washington St 66086 913-416-1470
Mark Altman, prin. Fax 416-1478

---

Genesis Christian S 200/PK-12
PO Box 994 66086 913-845-9498
Sharon Beeman, prin. Fax 845-9498

**Topeka, Shawnee, Pop. 122,701**
Auburn Washburn USD 437 7,100/PK-12
5928 SW 53rd St 66610 785-339-4000
Dr. Scott McWilliams, supt. Fax 339-4025
www.usd437.net

Pathways Learning Center — Alt
4101 SW Martin Dr 66609 — 785-339-4270
Galen Craghead, prin. — Fax 339-4275
Washburn Rural Alternative HS — 1,200/Alt
5900 SW 61st St 66619 — 785-339-4900
Kelly Younger, prin. — Fax 339-4925
Washburn Rural HS — 1,800/9-12
5900 SW 61st St 66619 — 785-339-4100
Ed Raines, prin. — Fax 339-4125
Washburn Rural MS — 900/7-8
5620 SW 61st St 66619 — 785-339-4300
Gerald Meier, prin. — Fax 339-4325

Seaman USD 345 — 3,900/PK-12
901 NW Lyman Rd 66608 — 785-575-8600
Mike Mathes, supt. — Fax 575-8620
www.usd345.com
Seaman HS — 1,200/9-12
4850 NW Rochester Rd 66617 — 785-286-8300
Ron Vinduska, prin. — Fax 286-8320
Seaman MS — 600/7-8
5620 NW Topeka Blvd 66617 — 785-286-8400
Traci Hammes, prin. — Fax 286-8403

Topeka USD 501 — 13,300/PK-12
624 SW 24th St 66611 — 785-295-3000
Dr. Julie Ford, supt. — Fax 575-6161
www.topekapublicschools.net
Chase MS — 400/6-8
2250 NE State St 66616 — 785-295-3840
Keith Jones, prin. — Fax 575-6632
Eisenhower MS — 400/6-8
3305 SE Minnesota Ave 66605 — 785-274-6160
Rebecca Morrisey, prin. — Fax 274-4603
French MS — 600/6-8
5257 SW 33rd St 66614 — 785-438-4150
Kelli Hoffman, prin. — Fax 271-3609
Highland Park HS — 700/9-12
2424 SE California Ave 66605 — 785-274-6000
Dr. Beryl New, prin. — Fax 274-4896
Jardine MS — 500/6-8
2600 SW 33rd St 66611 — 785-274-6330
Mike Haire, prin. — Fax 274-4768
Landon MS — 500/6-8
731 SW Fairlawn Rd 66606 — 785-438-4220
David Boggs, prin. — Fax 271-3737
Robinson MS — 400/6-8
1125 SW 14th St 66604 — 785-295-3770
Tammy Hazelton, prin. — Fax 575-6720
Topeka HS — 1,700/9-12
800 SW 10th Ave 66612 — 785-295-3150
Dr. Linda Wiley, prin. — Fax 575-6255
Topeka West HS — 1,000/9-12
2001 SW Fairlawn Rd 66604 — 785-438-4000
Dustin Dick, prin. — Fax 271-3497
Washburn Institute of Technology — Vo/Tech
5724 SW Huntoon St 66604 — 785-273-7140
Dr. Clark Coco, dean — Fax 273-7080
Adult Education Center — Adult
5724 SW Huntoon St 66604 — 785-235-7690
Patricia Williamson, coord. — Fax 273-7080

---

Baker University School of Nursing — Post-Sec.
1500 SW 10th Ave 66604 — 888-866-4242
Bryan University — Post-Sec.
1527 SW Fairlawn Rd 66604 — 785-272-0889
Cair Paravel Latin S — 300/PK-12
635 SW Clay St 66606 — 785-232-3878
Melody Congdon, head sch — Fax 232-0047
Community College of Cosmetology — Post-Sec.
3602 SW Topeka Blvd 66611 — 785-267-7701
Hayden HS — 500/9-12
401 SW Gage Blvd 66606 — 785-272-5210
Mark Madsen, prin. — Fax 272-2975
Heritage Christian S — 200/PK-12
2000 NW Clay St 66608 — 785-286-0427
Janeal Lischke, prin. — Fax 286-9898
Washburn Institute of Technology — Post-Sec.
5724 SW Huntoon St 66604 — 785-273-7140
Washburn University — Post-Sec.
1700 SW College Ave 66621 — 785-670-1010
Wichita Technical Institute - Topeka — Post-Sec.
3712 SW Burlingame Rd 66609 — 785-354-4568

**Towanda, Butler, Pop. 1,426**
Circle USD 375 — 1,600/K-12
PO Box 9 67144 — 316-541-2577
James Johnson, supt. — Fax 536-2249
www.usd375.org
Circle HS — 500/9-12
PO Box 158 67144 — 316-541-2277
Todd Dreifort, prin. — Fax 536-2249
Other Schools – See Benton

**Troy, Doniphan, Pop. 1,001**
Troy USD 429 — 400/PK-12
PO Box 190 66087 — 785-985-3950
Brian Harris, supt. — Fax 985-3688
www.troyusd.org/
Troy MSHS — 200/7-12
PO Box 160 66087 — 785-985-3533
Jared Wigger, prin. — Fax 985-3885

**Tyro, Montgomery, Pop. 209**

---

Tyro Community Christian S — 100/K-12
PO Box 308 67364 — 620-289-4450
Terry Byrd, admin. — Fax 289-4283

**Udall, Cowley, Pop. 727**
Udall USD 463 — 400/PK-12
303 S Seymour St 67146 — 620-782-3355
Kim Stephens, supt. — Fax 782-9690
www.usd463.org/
Udall HS — 100/9-12
301 W 4th St 67146 — 620-782-3623
Brian Rowley, prin. — Fax 782-9689
Udall MS — 100/6-8
301 W 4th St 67146 — 620-782-3623
Brian Rowley, prin. — Fax 782-9689

**Ulysses, Grant, Pop. 6,107**
Ulysses USD 214 — 1,600/PK-12
111 S Baughman St 67880 — 620-356-3655
David Younger, supt. — Fax 356-5181
www.ulysses.org
Kepley MS — 400/6-8
113 N Colorado St 67880 — 620-356-3025
Juan Perez, prin. — Fax 356-3024
Ulysses HS — 400/9-12
501 N Mccall St 67880 — 620-356-1380
Mark Paul, prin. — Fax 356-5566

**Uniontown, Bourbon, Pop. 268**
Uniontown USD 235 — 500/PK-12
601 5th St 66779 — 620-756-4302
Janice Hedges, supt. — Fax 756-4492
www.uniontown235.org
Uniontown HS — 200/7-12
601 5th St 66779 — 620-756-4301
Janice Hedges, prin. — Fax 756-4340

**Valley Center, Sedgwick, Pop. 6,673**
Valley Center USD 262 — 2,600/PK-12
143 S Meridian Ave 67147 — 316-755-7000
Cory Gibson, supt. — Fax 755-7001
www.usd262.net
Valley Center HS — 800/9-12
9600 N Meridian Ave 67147 — 316-755-7070
Jamie Lewis, prin. — Fax 755-7071
Valley Center MS — 400/7-8
800 N Meridian Ave 67147 — 316-755-7060
Kent Hipp, prin. — Fax 755-7061

**Valley Falls, Jefferson, Pop. 1,187**
Valley Falls USD 338 — 400/PK-12
700 Oak St 66088 — 785-945-3214
Loren Feldkamp, supt. — Fax 945-6780
www.usd338.com
Valley Falls HS — 100/9-12
601 Elm St 66088 — 785-945-3229
Susan Grey, prin. — Fax 945-3220

**Vermillion, Marshall, Pop. 108**
Vermillion USD 380 — 600/PK-12
209 School St 66544 — 785-382-6216
Mischel Miller, supt. — Fax 382-6213
www.usd380.org
Other Schools – See Centralia, Frankfort

**Victoria, Ellis, Pop. 1,204**
Victoria USD 432 — 200/K-12
PO Box 139 67671 — 785-735-9212
David Ottley, supt. — Fax 735-9229
www.usd432.org/
Victoria JSHS — 100/7-12
PO Box 20 67671 — 785-735-9211
Stuart Moeckel, prin. — Fax 735-9208

**Wakeeney, Trego, Pop. 1,842**
WaKeeney USD 208 — 400/PK-12
527 Russell Ave 67672 — 785-743-2145
Dr. George Griffith, supt. — Fax 743-2071
www.tregoeagles.com/
Trego Community HS — 100/9-12
1200 Russell Ave 67672 — 785-743-2061
Craig Malsam, prin. — Fax 743-2449

**Wakefield, Clay, Pop. 948**
Clay Center USD 379
Supt. — See Clay Center
Wakefield HS — 100/9-12
PO Box 40 67487 — 785-461-5437
Brian Sturges, prin. — Fax 461-5892

**Wamego, Pottawatomie, Pop. 4,265**
Wamego USD 320 — 1,400/PK-12
510 E US Highway 24 66547 — 785-456-7643
Denise O'Dea, supt. — Fax 456-8125
www.usd320.com
Wamego HS — 400/9-12
801 Lincoln St 66547 — 785-456-2214
Tim Winter, prin. — Fax 456-7382
Wamego MS — 300/6-8
1701 Kaw Valley Rd 66547 — 785-456-7682
Vici Jennings, prin. — Fax 456-2944

**Washington, Washington, Pop. 1,122**
Washington County USD 108 — 400/PK-12
101 W College St 66968 — 785-325-2261
Michael Stegman, supt. — Fax 325-2771
www.usd108.org/
Washington County HS — 200/7-12
101 W College St 66968 — 785-325-2261
Carol Whisman, prin. — Fax 325-2138

**Waterville, Marshall, Pop. 672**
Valley Heights USD 498 — 300/K-12
PO Box 89 66548 — 785-363-2398
John Bergkamp, supt. — Fax 363-2269
www.valleyheights.org/
Other Schools – See Blue Rapids

**Wathena, Doniphan, Pop. 1,344**
Riverside USD 114
Supt. — See Elwood
Riverside HS — 200/9-12
PO Box 38 66090 — 785-989-4426
Robert Blair, prin. — Fax 989-3317

**Waverly, Coffey, Pop. 580**
Lebo-Waverly USD 243 — 500/PK-12
PO Box 457 66871 — 785-733-2651
Ted Vannocker, supt. — Fax 733-2707
www.usd243ks.org
Waverly HS — 100/7-12
PO Box 8 66871 — 785-733-2561
Susan Brenner, prin. — Fax 733-2756
Other Schools – See Lebo

**Wellington, Sumner, Pop. 7,956**
Wellington USD 353 — 1,600/K-12
PO Box 648 67152 — 620-326-4300
Rick Weiss, supt. — Fax 326-4304
www.usd353.com/
Roosevelt Education Center — Alt
201 N B St 67152 — 620-326-4330
Zachary Lawrence, dir. — Fax 326-4332
Wellington HS — 500/9-12
1700 E 16th St 67152 — 620-326-4310
Adam Hatfield, prin. — Fax 326-4383
Wellington MS — 400/6-8
605 N A St 67152 — 620-326-4320
Jamie Ybarra, prin. — Fax 326-4390

**Wellsville, Franklin, Pop. 1,818**
Wellsville USD 289 — 800/PK-12
602 Walnut St 66092 — 785-883-2388
Jerald Henn, supt. — Fax 883-4453
www.wellsville-usd289.org
Wellsville HS — 200/9-12
602 Walnut St 66092 — 785-883-2057
Josh Adams, prin. — Fax 883-2294
Wellsville MS — 200/6-8
602 Walnut St 66092 — 785-883-4350
Aaron Dardis, prin. — Fax 883-2260

**Weskan, Wallace, Pop. 159**
Weskan USD 242 — 100/PK-12
219 Coyote Blvd 67762 — 785-943-5222
Dave Hale, supt. — Fax 943-5303
www.weskanschools.org/
Weskan JSHS — 100/7-12
219 Coyote Blvd 67762 — 785-943-5222
Dave Hale, supt. — Fax 943-5303

**Westmoreland, Pottawatomie, Pop. 771**
Rock Creek USD 323 — 900/PK-12
PO Box 70 66549 — 785-457-3732
Dr. Darrel Stufflebeam, supt. — Fax 457-3701
www.rockcreekschools.org
Other Schools – See Saint George

**Wetmore, Nemaha, Pop. 364**
Prairie Hills USD 113
Supt. — See Sabetha
Wetmore HS — 100/9-12
PO Box AB 66550 — 785-866-2860
Janelle Boden, prin. — Fax 866-5450

**White City, Morris, Pop. 611**
Rural Vista USD 481 — 400/PK-12
PO Box 98 66872 — 785-349-2964
Ralph Blevins, supt. — Fax 349-2965
www.usd481.org
White City HS — 100/9-12
PO Box 98 66872 — 785-349-2211
Mike Teeter, prin. — Fax 349-2965
Other Schools – See Hope

**Whitewater, Butler, Pop. 694**
Remington-Whitewater USD 206 — 500/K-12
PO Box 243 67154 — 316-799-2115
James Regier, supt. — Fax 799-2307
www.usd206.org
Remington HS — 200/9-12
8850 NW Meadowlark Rd 67154 — 316-799-2123
Tim Bumgarner, prin. — Fax 799-2943
Remington MS — 100/5-8
PO Box 99 67154 — 316-799-2131
Bob Friesen, prin. — Fax 799-2581

**Wichita, Sedgwick, Pop. 369,464**
Haysville USD 261
Supt. — See Haysville
Haysville Campus HS — 1,500/9-12
2100 W 55th St S 67217 — 316-554-2236
Myron Regier, prin. — Fax 554-2241

Maize USD 266
Supt. — See Maize
Maize South HS — 700/9-12
3701 N Tyler Rd 67205 — 316-462-8000
Dave Hickerson, prin. — Fax 462-8001
Maize South MS — 900/6-8
3403 N Tyler Rd 67205 — 316-722-0421
Gillian Macias, prin. — Fax 722-4077

Wichita USD 259 — 46,400/PK-12
201 N Water St 67202 — 316-973-4000
John Allison, supt. — Fax 973-4595
www.usd259.org
Allison Traditional Magnet MS — 500/6-8
221 S Seneca St 67213 — 316-973-4800
Mitch Linn, prin. — Fax 973-4810
Brooks Technology & Arts Magnet MS — 600/6-8
3802 E 27th St N 67220 — 316-973-6450
Renee Erickson, prin. — Fax 973-6581
Coleman MS — 700/6-8
1544 N Governeour Rd 67206 — 316-973-6600
Jeff Freund, prin. — Fax 973-6699
Curtis MS — 700/6-8
1031 S Edgemoor St 67218 — 316-973-7350
Stephanie Wasko, prin. — Fax 973-7410
Hadley MS — 900/6-8
1101 N Dougherty Ave 67212 — 316-973-7800
Amy Johnson, prin. — Fax 973-7816
Hamilton MS — 500/6-8
1407 S Broadway St 67211 — 316-973-5350
Justin Kasel, prin. — Fax 973-5360
Jardine Technology Magnet MS — 400/6-8
3550 E Ross Pkwy 67210 — 316-973-4300
Lura Atherly, prin. — Fax 973-4310
Marshall MS — 500/6-8
1510 N Payne Ave 67203 — 316-973-9000
Ron Stubbs, prin. — Fax 973-9010
Mayberry Cultural & Fine Arts Magnet MS — 600/6-8
207 S Sheridan St 67213 — 316-973-5800
Eric Hofer-Holdeman, prin. — Fax 973-5808

| | |
|---|---|
| Mead MS | 500/6-8 |
| 2601 E Skinner St 67211 | 316-973-8500 |
| Toby Martin, prin. | Fax 973-8503 |
| Metro-Boulevard Alternative HS | 100/Alt |
| 1847 N Chautauqua Ave 67214 | 316-973-0500 |
| Leroy Parks, prin. | Fax 973-0510 |
| Metro-Meridian Alternative S | 100/Alt |
| 301 S Meridian Ave 67213 | 316-973-0550 |
| Ron Riley, prin. | Fax 973-0560 |
| Pleasant Valley MS | 600/6-8 |
| 2220 W 29th St N 67204 | 316-973-8000 |
| Victoria Manning, prin. | Fax 973-8008 |
| Robinson MS | 800/6-8 |
| 328 N Oliver Ave 67208 | 316-973-8600 |
| Amy Champlin, prin. | Fax 973-8625 |
| Sowers Alternative HS | 100/Alt |
| 2400 Wassall St 67216 | 316-973-1600 |
| Jackie Hultman, prin. | Fax 973-1610 |
| Stucky MS | 700/6-8 |
| 4545 N Broadview Cir 67220 | 316-973-8400 |
| Jennifer Sinclair, prin. | Fax 973-8410 |
| Truesdell MS | 900/6-8 |
| 2464 S Glenn Ave 67217 | 316-973-3900 |
| Terrell Davis, prin. | Fax 973-3904 |
| Wells Alternative MS | 50/Alt |
| 1221 E Galena St Ste 373 67216 | 316-973-7650 |
| Nancy Mueller, prin. | Fax 973-7673 |
| Wichita East HS | 2,300/9-12 |
| 2301 E Douglas Ave 67211 | 316-973-7200 |
| Ken Thiessen, prin. | Fax 973-7224 |
| Wichita Heights HS | 1,500/9-12 |
| 5301 N Hillside St 67219 | 316-973-1400 |
| Bruce Deterding, prin. | Fax 973-1410 |
| Wichita North HS | 2,000/9-12 |
| 1437 N Rochester St 67203 | 316-973-6300 |
| Sherman Padgett, prin. | Fax 973-6190 |
| Wichita Northwest HS | 1,400/9-12 |
| 1220 N Tyler Rd 67212 | 316-973-6000 |
| Gil Alvarez, prin. | Fax 973-6070 |
| Wichita Southeast HS | 1,600/9-12 |
| 903 S Edgemoor St 67218 | 316-973-2700 |
| Lori Doyle, prin. | Fax 973-2755 |
| Wichita South HS | 1,400/9-12 |
| 701 W 33rd St S 67217 | 316-973-5450 |
| Cara Ledy, prin. | Fax 973-5519 |
| Wichita West HS | 1,300/9-12 |
| 820 S Osage St 67213 | 316-973-3600 |
| Joel Hudson, prin. | Fax 973-3657 |
| Wilbur MS | 1,000/6-8 |
| 340 N Tyler Rd 67212 | 316-973-1100 |
| Mark Jolliffe, prin. | Fax 973-1090 |

Other Schools – See Bel Aire

---

| | |
|---|---|
| Bishop Carroll Catholic HS | 1,100/9-12 |
| 8101 W Central Ave 67212 | 316-722-2390 |
| Vanessa Harshberger, prin. | Fax 722-6670 |
| Classical S of Wichita | 100/K-12 |
| 6355 Willowbrook St 67218 | 316-773-9279 |
| Classic College of Hair Design | Post-Sec. |
| 1675 S Rock Rd Ste 101 67207 | 316-681-2288 |
| Friends University | Post-Sec. |
| 2100 W University Ave 67213 | 316-295-5000 |
| Heritage College | Post-Sec. |
| 2800 S Rock Rd 67210 | 316-681-1615 |
| Independent S | 500/PK-12 |
| 8317 E Douglas Ave 67207 | 316-686-0152 |
| ITT Technical Institute | Post-Sec. |
| 8111 E 32nd St N Ste 103 67226 | 316-609-4100 |
| Kansas College of Chinese Medicine | Post-Sec. |
| 9235 E Harry St Bldg 200 67207 | 316-691-8822 |
| Kapaun Mt. Carmel Catholic HS | 900/9-12 |
| 8506 E Central Ave 67206 | 316-634-0315 |
| Chris Bloomer, prin. | Fax 636-2437 |
| Newman University | Post-Sec. |
| 3100 W McCormick St 67213 | 316-942-4291 |
| Old Town Barber College | Post-Sec. |
| 1211 E Douglas Ave 67211 | 316-264-4891 |
| Paul Mitchell the School | Post-Sec. |
| 3242 N Rock Rd Ste 106 67226 | 316-630-0600 |
| Trinity Academy | 300/9-12 |
| 12345 E 21st St N 67206 | 316-634-0909 |
| Matt Brewer, hdmstr. | Fax 634-0928 |
| Vatterott College | Post-Sec. |
| 8853 E 37th St N 67226 | 316-634-0066 |
| Wichita Adventist Christian Academy | 50/K-10 |
| 2725 S Osage Ave 67217 | 316-267-9472 |
| Wichita Area Technical College | Post-Sec. |
| 4501 E 47th St S 67210 | 316-677-1500 |
| Wichita Area Technical College | Post-Sec. |
| 4004 N Webb Rd 67226 | 316-677-9400 |
| Wichita Area Technical College - Grove | Post-Sec. |
| 301 S Grove St 67211 | 316-677-9400 |
| Wichita Collegiate S | 1,000/PK-12 |
| 9115 E 13th St N 67206 | 316-634-0433 |
| Tom Davis, hdmstr. | Fax 634-0598 |
| Wichita State University | Post-Sec. |
| 1845 Fairmount St 67260 | 316-978-3456 |
| Wichita Technical Institute | Post-Sec. |
| 2051 S Meridian Ave 67213 | 316-943-2241 |
| Wichita Technical Institute - East | Post-Sec. |
| 6130 E Central Ave 67208 | 316-260-1030 |
| Wright Career College | Post-Sec. |
| 7700 E Kellogg Dr 67207 | 316-927-7700 |
| Xenon International Academy | Post-Sec. |
| 3804 W Douglas Ave 67203 | 316-943-5516 |

**Wilson, Ellsworth, Pop. 759**

| | |
|---|---|
| Central Plains USD 112 | |
| Supt. — See Holyrood | |
| Wilson JSHS | 100/7-12 |
| PO Box 220 67490 | 785-658-2202 |
| Kenroy Wilson, prin. | Fax 658-2205 |

**Winchester, Jefferson, Pop. 551**

| | |
|---|---|
| Jefferson County North USD 339 | 500/PK-12 |
| 310 5th St 66097 | 913-774-2000 |
| Denise Jennings, supt. | Fax 774-2027 |
| www.usd339.net | |
| Jefferson County North HS | 100/9-12 |
| 302 5th St 66097 | 913-774-8515 |
| Joe Worthington, prin. | Fax 774-8535 |

**Winfield, Cowley, Pop. 11,966**

| | |
|---|---|
| Winfield USD 465 | 2,500/PK-12 |
| 1407 Wheat Rd 67156 | 620-221-5100 |
| Dr. J.K. Campbell, supt. | Fax 221-0508 |
| www.usd465.com | |
| Winfield HS | 700/9-12 |
| 300 Viking Blvd 67156 | 620-221-5160 |
| Trenton Creeden, prin. | Fax 221-5165 |
| Winfield MS | 400/6-8 |
| 130 Viking Blvd 67156 | 620-221-5130 |
| David Hammer, prin. | Fax 221-5147 |

---

| | |
|---|---|
| Southwestern College | Post-Sec. |
| 100 College St 67156 | 620-229-6000 |

**Winona, Logan, Pop. 161**

| | |
|---|---|
| Triplains USD 275 | 100/PK-12 |
| PO Box 97 67764 | 785-846-7869 |
| Lamar Bergsten, supt. | Fax 846-7767 |
| triplains.weebly.com | |
| Winona HS | 50/9-12 |
| PO Box 97 67764 | 785-846-7496 |
| Lamar Bergsten, prin. | Fax 846-7767 |

**Yates Center, Woodson, Pop. 1,379**

| | |
|---|---|
| Woodson USD 366 | 500/PK-12 |
| PO Box 160 66783 | 620-625-8804 |
| Greg Brown, supt. | Fax 625-8806 |
| www.usd366.net | |
| Yates Center HS | 100/9-12 |
| PO Box 160 66783 | 620-625-8820 |
| Karl Hamm, prin. | Fax 625-8850 |

# KENTUCKY

## KENTUCKY DEPARTMENT OF EDUCATION
**500 Mero St, Frankfort 40601-1987**
**Telephone 502-564-4770**
**Fax 502-564-5680**
**Website http://www.education.ky.gov**

Commissioner of Education Terry Holliday Ph.D

## KENTUCKY BOARD OF EDUCATION
**500 Mero St Ste 1, Frankfort 40601-1957**

Chairperson David Karem

## PUBLIC, PRIVATE AND CATHOLIC SECONDARY SCHOOLS

**Albany, Clinton, Pop. 1,999**
Clinton County SD 1,800/PK-12
2353 N Highway 127 42602 606-387-6480
Charlotte Bernard, supt. Fax 387-5437
www.clinton.kyschools.us
Clinton County HS 500/9-12
65 High School Dr 42602 606-387-5569
Sheldon Harlan, prin. Fax 387-8659
Clinton County MS 500/5-8
169 Middle School Rd 42602 606-387-6466
Teresa Scott, prin. Fax 387-6469

Kentucky Tech System
Supt. — See Frankfort
Clinton County Area Technology Center Vo/Tech
151 Armstrong Honeycutt Dr 42602 606-387-6448
Stesha Flowers, prin. Fax 387-4035

**Alexandria, Campbell, Pop. 8,396**
Campbell County SD 4,800/PK-12
101 Orchard Ln 41001 859-635-2173
Glen Miller, supt. Fax 448-2439
www.campbell.kyschools.us/
Campbell County Day Treatment 50/Alt
51 Orchard Ln 41001 859-635-9113
Alvin Elsbernd, prin. Fax 448-2781
Campbell County HS 1,400/9-12
909 Camel Xing 41001 859-635-4161
Adam Ritter, prin. Fax 448-4886
Campbell County MS 1,200/6-8
8000 Alexandria Pike 41001 859-635-6077
Jason Smith, prin. Fax 448-4863

Kentucky Tech System
Supt. — See Frankfort
Campbell County Area Technology Center Vo/Tech
50 Orchard Ln 41001 859-635-4101
Joseph Amann, prin. Fax 635-2766

---

Bishop Brossart HS 400/9-12
4 Grove St 41001 859-635-2108
Dan Ridder, prin. Fax 635-2135

**Ashland, Boyd, Pop. 21,270**
Ashland ISD 3,100/PK-12
PO Box 3000 41105 606-327-2706
Stephen E. Gilmore, supt. Fax 327-2705
www.ashland.kyschools.us
Ashland MS 500/6-8
2800 Kansas St 41102 606-327-2727
David Greene, prin. Fax 327-2765
Blazer HS 900/9-12
1500 Blazer Blvd 41102 606-327-6040
Derek Runyon, prin. Fax 324-0517

Boyd County SD 3,400/PK-12
1104 Bob McCullough Dr 41102 606-928-4141
R. Brock Walter, supt. Fax 928-4771
www.boyd.kyschools.us
Boyd County Career & Technical Center Vo/Tech
12300 Midland Trail Rd 41102 606-928-7120
Doug Deborde, dir. Fax 928-6432
Boyd County Central Alternative S Alt
12307 Midland Trail Rd 41102 606-928-7110
Dara'Su Knipp, dir. Fax 928-1526
Boyd County HS 900/9-12
14375 Lions Ln 41102 606-928-7100
Thomas Holbrook, prin. Fax 928-1312
Boyd County MS 700/6-8
1226 Summitt Rd 41102 606-928-9547
Bill Boblett, prin. Fax 928-2067
Other Schools – See Rush

Fairview ISD 800/PK-12
2201 Main St W 41102 606-324-3877
Michael Taylor, supt. Fax 324-2288
www.fairview.kyschools.us
Fairview JSHS 400/7-12
2123 Main St W 41102 606-324-9226
Eric Hale, prin. Fax 325-1486

Raceland-Worthington ISD
Supt. — See Raceland
Ashland Day Treatment Center 50/Alt
1539 Greenup Ave 41101 606-920-2073
Marty Mills, prin. Fax 920-2075

---

Ashland Community and Technical College Post-Sec.
1400 College Dr 41101 606-326-2000
Holy Family S 100/PK-12
932 Winchester Ave 41101 606-324-7040
Matt Anderson, prin. Fax 324-6888
Rose Hill Christian S 200/PK-12
1001 Winslow Rd 41102 606-324-6105
Dr. Jerry Foster, prin. Fax 324-6420

**Augusta, Bracken, Pop. 1,171**
Augusta ISD 300/PK-12
307 Bracken St 41002 606-756-2545
Lisa McCane, supt. Fax 756-2149
www.augusta.kyschools.us
Augusta JSHS 100/7-12
207 Bracken St 41002 606-756-2105
Robin Kelsch, prin. Fax 756-3000

**Barbourville, Knox, Pop. 3,119**
Barbourville ISD 700/PK-12
PO Box 520 40906 606-546-3120
Larry Warren, supt. Fax 546-3452
www.barbourvilleind.com
Barbourville City S 700/PK-12
PO Box 520 40906 606-546-3129
Paul Middleton, prin. Fax 546-3337

Kentucky Tech System
Supt. — See Frankfort
Knox County Area Technology Center Vo/Tech
210 Wall St 40906 606-546-5320
Ralph Halcomb, prin. Fax 546-3818

Knox County SD 4,500/PK-12
200 Daniel Boone Dr 40906 606-546-3157
Kelly Sprinkles, supt. Fax 546-2819
www.knox.kyschools.us
Knox Central HS 900/9-12
100 Panther Way 40906 606-546-9253
Tim Melton, prin. Fax 546-5684
Knox County MS 500/7-8
311 N Main St 40906 606-545-5267
Jeremy Ledford, prin. Fax 546-2161
Other Schools – See Corbin

---

Union College Post-Sec.
310 College St 40906 606-546-4151

**Bardstown, Nelson, Pop. 11,437**
Bardstown ISD 2,800/PK-12
308 N 5th St 40004 502-331-8800
Brent Holsclaw, supt. Fax 331-8830
www.bardstown.kyschools.us
Bardstown HS 600/9-12
400 N 5th St 40004 502-331-8802
Chris Pickett, prin. Fax 331-8832
Bardstown MS 500/6-8
410 N 5th St 40004 502-331-8803
Bob Blackmon, prin. Fax 331-8833

Kentucky Tech System
Supt. — See Frankfort
Nelson County Area Technology Center Vo/Tech
1060 Bloomfield Rd 40004 502-348-9096
Jeremey Booher, prin. Fax 348-9097

Nelson County SD 4,800/PK-12
288 Wildcat Ln 40004 502-349-7000
Anthony Orr, supt. Fax 349-7004
nelson.kyschools.us
Horizons Academy 100/Alt
304 Wildcat Ln 40004 502-349-7045
Penny Bradley, prin. Fax 349-7044
Nelson County HS 1,400/9-12
1070 Bloomfield Rd 40004 502-349-7010
Shelly Hendricks, prin. Fax 349-7017
Nelson HS 9-12
2885 New Shepherdsville Rd 40004 502-349-4650
Wes Bradley, prin. Fax 349-4651
Old Kentucky Home MS 400/6-8
301 Wildcat Ln 40004 502-349-7040
Jesse Simpson, prin. Fax 349-7042
Other Schools – See Bloomfield

---

Bethlehem HS 300/9-12
309 W Stephen Foster Ave 40004 502-348-8594
Tom Hamilton, prin. Fax 349-1247

**Bardwell, Carlisle, Pop. 716**
Carlisle County SD 900/PK-12
4557 State Route 1377 42023 270-628-3800
Jay Simmons, supt. Fax 628-5477
www.carlisle.kyschools.us
Carlisle County HS 200/9-12
4557 State Route 1377 42023 270-628-3800
Kelli Edging, prin. Fax 628-3837
Carlisle County MS 200/6-8
4557 State Route 1377 42023 270-628-3800
DeeAnne Arant, prin. Fax 628-3974

**Barlow, Ballard, Pop. 654**
Ballard County SD 1,500/PK-12
3465 Paducah Rd 42024 270-665-8400
Casey Allen, supt. Fax 665-9844
www.ballard.kyschools.us
Ballard County MS 300/6-8
3565 Paducah Rd 42024 270-665-8400
Amber Parker, prin. Fax 665-5153
Ballard Memorial HS 400/9-12
3561 Paducah Rd 42024 270-665-8400
Leslee Davis, prin. Fax 665-5312

**Baxter, Harlan**
Harlan County SD
Supt. — See Harlan
Harlan County HS 1,100/9-12
4000 N US Highway 119 40806 606-574-2020
Edna Burkhart, prin. Fax 574-0493

**Beattyville, Lee, Pop. 1,296**
Kentucky Tech System
Supt. — See Frankfort
Lee County Area Technology Center Vo/Tech
PO Box B 41311 606-464-5018
Craig Herald, prin. Fax 464-0663

Lee County SD 1,100/K-12
PO Box 668 41311 606-464-5000
Dr. Jim Evans Ed.D., supt. Fax 464-5009
www.lee.kyschools.us
Lee County HS 400/9-12
PO Box J 41311 606-464-5005
Mark Murray, prin. Fax 464-5014
Lee County MS 200/6-8
PO Box N 41311 606-464-5010
Karen Angel, prin. Fax 464-5011

**Bedford, Trimble, Pop. 584**
Trimble County SD 1,400/K-12
PO Box 275 40006 502-255-3201
Fax 255-5105
www.trimble.kyschools.us
Trimble County HS 400/9-12
1029 Highway 421 N 40006 502-255-7781
Fax 255-5126
Trimble County MS 300/6-8
116 Wentworth Ave 40006 502-255-7361
Mike Genton, prin. Fax 255-5102

**Belfry, Pike**
Kentucky Tech System
Supt. — See Frankfort
Belfry Area Technology Center Vo/Tech
PO Box 280 41514 606-353-4951
Tom Ford, prin. Fax 353-0868

Pike County SD
Supt. — See Pikeville
Belfry HS 800/9-12
PO Box 160 41514 606-237-3900
Mark Gannon, prin. Fax 237-5119
Belfry MS 500/6-8
PO Box 850 41514 606-353-7230
Jeremy Howard, prin. Fax 353-0530

**Bellevue, Campbell, Pop. 5,875**
Bellevue ISD 800/PK-12
219 Center St 41073 859-261-2108
Robb Smith, supt. Fax 261-1708
www.bellevue.kyschools.us
Bellevue HS 400/6-12
201 Center St 41073 859-261-2980
Dave Eckstein, prin. Fax 261-1825

Daymar College Post-Sec.
119 Fairfield Ave 41073 859-291-0800

**Benton, Marshall, Pop. 4,312**
Marshall County SD 4,800/PK-12
86 High School Rd 42025 270-527-8628
Trent Lovett, supt. Fax 527-0804
www.marshall.kyschools.us
Benton MS 200/6-8
906 Joe Creason Dr 42025 270-527-9091
Jill Darnall, prin. Fax 527-9992
Marshall County HS 1,300/9-12
416 High School Rd 42025 270-527-1453
Amy Waggoner, prin. Fax 527-0578
Marshall County Technical Center Vo/Tech
341 High School Rd 42025 270-527-8648
Stacey Bradley, dir. Fax 527-1920
South Marshall MS 300/6-8
85 Sid Darnall Rd 42025 270-527-3828
Ryan Marchetti, prin. Fax 527-7616
STAR Academy 50/Alt
1308 US Highway 641 N 42025 270-252-1394
David Morris, dir. Fax 252-1394
Other Schools – See Calvert City

Christian Fellowship S 100/PK-12
1343 US Highway 68 E 42025 270-527-8377
Bill Rowley, admin. Fax 527-2872

**Berea, Madison, Pop. 13,252**
Berea ISD 900/PK-12
3 Pirate Pkwy 40403 859-986-8446
Mike Hogg, supt. Fax 986-1839
www.berea.kyschools.us/
Berea Community MSHS 300/6-12
1 Pirate Pkwy 40403 859-986-4911
Donna Lovell, prin. Fax 986-4640

Madison County SD
Supt. — See Richmond
Farristown MS 400/6-8
751 Farristown Industrial 40403 859-387-8600
Alicia Hunter, prin. Fax 986-3092
Foley MS 500/6-8
275 Glades Rd 40403 859-625-6140
Mark Wall, prin. Fax 986-3362
Madison Southern HS 1,100/9-12
279 Glades Rd 40403 859-625-6148
Brandon Watkins, prin. Fax 986-3092

Berea College Post-Sec.
101 Chestnut St 40403 859-985-3000

**Beverly, Bell**

Red Bird Christian S 200/PK-12
15420 S Highway 66 40913 606-598-2416
Michael R. Hensley, head sch Fax 598-7314

**Blackey, Letcher, Pop. 120**
Letcher County SD
Supt. — See Whitesburg
Letcher MS 100/6-8
160 Letcher High School Dr 41804 606-633-7812
Ricky Warf, prin. Fax 633-5731

**Bloomfield, Nelson, Pop. 831**
Nelson County SD
Supt. — See Bardstown
Bloomfield MS 400/6-8
96 Arnold Ln 40008 502-349-7201
Jim Beavers, prin. Fax 349-7203

**Booneville, Owsley, Pop. 81**
Owsley County SD 900/PK-12
14 Old KY 11 41314 606-593-6363
Dr. Timothy Bobrowski, supt. Fax 593-6368
www.owsley.kyschools.us
Owsley County JSHS 400/7-12
177 Shepherd Rd 41314 606-593-5185
Gary Cornett, prin. Fax 593-6312

**Bowling Green, Warren, Pop. 56,664**
Bowling Green ISD 4,000/PK-12
1211 Center St 42101 270-746-2200
Gary Fields, supt. Fax 746-2205
www.bgreen.kyschools.us/
Academy at 11th Street 50/Alt
877 E 11th Ave 42101 270-746-2321
Marisa Duarte, dir. Fax 746-2325
Bowling Green HS 1,200/9-12
1801 Rockingham Ave 42104 270-746-2300
William King, prin. Fax 746-2305
Bowling Green JHS 900/6-8
900 Campbell Ln 42104 270-746-2290
Cynthia West, prin. Fax 746-2295
Children's Stabilization Unit 50/Alt
501 Chestnut St 42101 270-781-3997
Josh Long, lead tchr. Fax 781-8987

Kentucky Tech System
Supt. — See Frankfort
Warren County Area Technology Center Vo/Tech
365 Technology Way 42101 270-746-7205
Eric Keeling, prin. Fax 746-7207

Warren County SD 13,800/PK-12
PO Box 51810 42102 270-781-5150
Rob Clayton, supt. Fax 781-2392
www.warrencountyschools.org/
Drakes Creek MS 600/7-8
704 Cypress Wood Ln 42104 270-843-0165
Daryl Woods, prin. Fax 782-6138
Greenwood HS 1,100/9-12
5065 Scottsville Rd 42104 270-842-3627
Greg Dunn, prin. Fax 842-2037
Jackson Academy Alt
877 Jackson St 42101 270-782-5410
Lighthouse Academy 100/Alt
877 Jackson St 42101 270-782-5410
Eric Wilson, prin. Fax 782-3240
Moss MS 500/7-8
2565 Russellville Rd 42101 270-843-0166
Jerry Nole, prin. Fax 843-8512
South Warren HS 900/9-12
8140 Nashville Rd 42101 270-467-7500
Jenny Hester, prin. Fax 467-7506
South Warren MS 600/7-8
295 Richpond Rd 42104 270-467-7510
Eddy Bushelman, prin. Fax 467-7516
Warren Central HS 1,000/9-12
559 Morgantown Rd 42101 270-781-2401
Brad Tolbert, prin. Fax 781-5115
Warren East HS 900/9-12
6867 Louisville Rd 42101 270-781-1277
Nicole Clark, prin. Fax 843-2610
Warren East MS 500/7-8
7031 Louisville Rd 42101 270-843-0181
David Cloyd, prin. Fax 781-8565

Anchored Christian S 100/PK-12
1807 Cave Mill Rd 42104 270-781-9077
Bowling Green Christian Academy 100/PK-12
1730 Destiny Ln 42104 270-782-9552
Cindy Moses, admin. Fax 782-9585
Daymar College Post-Sec.
2421 Industrial Dr 42101 270-843-6750
PJs College of Cosmetology Post-Sec.
1901 Russellville Rd 42101 270-842-8149
Southcentral Kentucky Comm & Tech Coll Post-Sec.
1845 Loop St 42101 270-901-1000
Southcentral Kentucky Comm Tech College Post-Sec.
1127 Morgantown Rd 42101 270-746-7807
Western Kentucky University Post-Sec.
1906 College Heights Blvd 42101 270-745-0111

**Brandenburg, Meade, Pop. 2,585**
Kentucky Tech System
Supt. — See Frankfort
Meade County Area Technology Center Vo/Tech
110 Greer St 40108 270-422-3955
Faye Campbell, prin. Fax 422-3307

Meade County SD 4,900/PK-12
1155 Old Ekron Rd 40108 270-422-7500
Dr. John Millay, supt. Fax 422-5494
www.meade.kyschools.us
Meade County HS 1,600/9-12
938 Old State Rd 40108 270-422-7515
William Adams, prin. Fax 422-3928
Pepper MS 800/7-8
1085 Old Ekron Rd 40108 270-422-7530
Chad Butler, prin. Fax 422-5515

**Brooksville, Bracken, Pop. 638**
Bracken County SD 1,200/PK-12
348 W Miami St 41004 606-735-2523
Jeff Aulick, supt. Fax 735-3640
www.bracken.k12.ky.us
Bracken County HS 300/9-12
PO Box 128 41004 606-735-3153
Dennis Maines, prin. Fax 735-2549
Bracken County MS 300/6-8
167 Parsley Dr 41004 606-735-3425
Leah Jefferson, prin. Fax 735-2057

**Brownsville, Edmonson, Pop. 829**
Edmonson County SD 2,000/PK-12
PO Box 129 42210 270-597-2101
Patrick Waddell, supt. Fax 597-2103
www.edmonson.k12.ky.us
Edmonson County HS 600/9-12
220 Wild Cat Way 42210 270-597-2151
Tommy Hodges, prin. Fax 597-2962
Edmonson County MS 300/7-8
210 Wild Cat Way 42210 270-597-2932
Brandon Prunty, prin. Fax 597-2182

**Buckhorn, Perry, Pop. 162**
Perry County SD
Supt. — See Hazard
Buckhorn S 400/K-12
18392 KY Highway 28 41721 606-398-7176
Tim Wooton, prin. Fax 398-7930

**Burgin, Mercer, Pop. 946**
Burgin ISD 500/PK-12
PO Box B 40310 859-748-4000
Martha Collier, supt. Fax 748-4010
www.burgin.kyschools.us
Burgin S 200/PK-12
PO Box B 40310 859-748-5282
Chris LeMonds, prin. Fax 748-4002

**Burkesville, Cumberland, Pop. 1,484**
Cumberland County SD 1,000/K-12
PO Box 420 42717 270-864-3377
Dr. Kirk Biggerstaff, supt. Fax 864-5803
www.cland.k12.ky.us
Cumberland County HS 300/9-12
PO Box 380 42717 270-864-3451
Angela Morrison, prin. Fax 864-1284
Cumberland County MS 200/6-8
PO Box 70 42717 270-864-5818
Tim Parson, prin. Fax 864-2590

**Burlington, Boone, Pop. 15,646**
Boone County SD
Supt. — See Florence
Camp Ernst MS 1,000/6-8
6515 Camp Ernst Rd 41005 859-534-4000
Stephanie Hagerty, prin. Fax 534-4001

**Burna, Livingston, Pop. 254**
Livingston County SD
Supt. — See Smithland
Livingston County MS 200/7-8
1370 US Highway 60 E 42028 270-988-3263
Lisa Huddleston, prin. Fax 988-2518

**Butler, Pendleton, Pop. 586**
Pendleton County SD
Supt. — See Falmouth
Sharp MS 600/6-8
35 Wright Rd 41006 859-472-7000
Rhonda Moore, prin. Fax 472-7011

**Cadiz, Trigg, Pop. 2,498**
Trigg County SD 2,100/PK-12
202 Main St 42211 270-522-6075
Travis Hamby, supt. Fax 522-7782
www.trigg.kyschools.us
Trigg County HS 600/9-12
203 Main St 42211 270-522-2200
Shannon Burcham, prin. Fax 522-2224
Trigg County MS 500/6-8
206 Lafayette St 42211 270-522-2210
Kristi Miller, prin. Fax 522-2203

**Calhoun, McLean, Pop. 758**
McLean County SD 1,600/K-12
PO Box 245 42327 270-273-5257
Stephen Riggs, supt. Fax 273-5259
www.mclean.kyschools.us/
McLean County HS 500/9-12
1859 State Route 136 E 42327 270-273-5278
Ashley Troutman, prin. Fax 273-5208
McLean County MS 400/6-8
1901 State Route 136 E 42327 270-273-5191
Shannon Lindsey, prin. Fax 273-9876

**Calvert City, Marshall, Pop. 2,542**
Marshall County SD
Supt. — See Benton
North Marshall MS 500/6-8
3110 US Highway 95 42029 270-395-7108
Aimee Lepisto, prin. Fax 395-5449

**Campbellsville, Taylor, Pop. 8,884**
Campbellsville ISD 1,100/PK-12
136 S Columbia Ave 42718 270-465-4162
Mike Deaton, supt. Fax 465-3918
www.cville.kyschools.us/
Campbellsville HS 300/9-12
230 W Main St 42718 270-465-8774
Kirby Smith, prin. Fax 789-4007
Campbellsville MS 300/4-8
230 W Main St 42718 270-465-5121
Elisha Rhodes, prin. Fax 789-3718
Eagle Academy 100/Alt
230 W Main St 42718 270-465-6337
Kirby Smith, admin. Fax 465-9777

Taylor County SD 2,700/PK-12
1209 E Broadway St 42718 270-465-5371
Roger D. Cook, supt. Fax 789-3954
www.taylor.kyschools.us
Taylor County HS 800/9-12
300 Ingram Ave 42718 270-465-4431
Laura Benningfield, prin. Fax 465-5731
Taylor County MS 600/6-8
1207 E Broadway St 42718 270-465-2877
Tony Jewell, prin. Fax 789-1753

Campbellsville University Post-Sec.
1 University Dr 42718 270-789-5000

**Campton, Wolfe, Pop. 434**
Wolfe County SD 1,300/K-12
PO Box 160 41301 606-668-8002
Kenny Bell, supt. Fax 668-8050
www.wolfe.kyschools.us
Wolfe County HS 400/9-12
PO Box 790 41301 606-668-8202
Greg Creech, prin. Fax 668-8250
Wolfe County MS 200/7-8
PO Box 460 41301 606-668-8152
Nick Brooks, prin. Fax 668-8100

**Carlisle, Nicholas, Pop. 1,984**
Nicholas County SD 1,200/PK-12
395 W Main St 40311 859-289-3770
Marty Feltner, supt. Fax 289-3777
www.nicholas.kyschools.us
Nicholas County JSHS 500/7-12
103 School Dr 40311 859-289-3780
Barbara Allison, prin. Fax 289-6429

Motif Beauty Academy Post-Sec.
225 Elderberry Dr 40311 859-745-5886

**Carrollton, Carroll, Pop. 3,854**
Carroll County SD 1,700/K-12
813 Hawkins St 41008 502-732-7070
Bill Hogan, supt. Fax 732-7073
www.carroll.kyschools.us
Carroll County Alternative S 50/Alt
519 Park Ave 41008 502-732-7112
Amy Sutter, lead tchr. Fax 732-7113
Carroll County HS 500/9-12
1706 Highland Ave 41008 502-732-7075
Tom Stephens, prin. Fax 732-7012
Carroll County MS 400/6-8
408 5th St 41008 502-732-7080
Dana Oak, prin. Fax 732-7107

Kentucky Tech System
Supt. — See Frankfort
Carroll County Area Technology Center Vo/Tech
1704 Highland Ave 41008 502-732-4479
Tony Jury, prin. Fax 732-4837

---

Christian Academy of Carrollton 100/PK-12
1703 Easter Day Rd 41008 502-732-4734
Katie Matson, admin. Fax 732-4732

**Cave City, Barren, Pop. 2,196**
Caverna ISD 800/PK-12
1102 N Dixie Hwy 42127 270-773-2530
Cornelius Faulkner, supt. Fax 773-2524
www.caverna.k12.ky.us
Other Schools – See Horse Cave

**Cecilia, Hardin, Pop. 563**
Hardin County SD
Supt. — See Elizabethtown
Central Hardin HS 1,800/9-12
3040 Leitchfield Rd 42724 270-737-6800
Tim Isaacs, prin. Fax 765-3889
West Hardin MS 600/6-8
10471 Leitchfield Rd 42724 270-862-3924
Mike Lawson, prin. Fax 862-3647

**Clinton, Hickman, Pop. 1,362**
Hickman County SD 800/PK-12
416 N Waterfield Dr 42031 270-653-2341
Casey Henderson, supt. Fax 653-6007
www.hickman.kyschools.us
Hickman County HS 300/7-12
301 James H Phillips Dr 42031 270-653-4044
Kevin Estes, prin. Fax 653-3200

---

Daymar College Post-Sec.
1171 US Highway 51 S 42031 270-653-9800

**Cloverport, Breckinridge, Pop. 1,138**
Cloverport ISD 400/PK-12
PO Box 37 40111 270-788-3910
Charles Proffitt, supt. Fax 788-6290
www.cloverport.kyschools.us
Fraize HS 100/9-12
301 Poplar St 40111 270-788-3388
Keith Haynes, prin. Fax 788-6640
Fraize MS 100/6-8
301 Poplar St 40111 270-788-3388
Keith Haynes, prin. Fax 788-6640

**Columbia, Adair, Pop. 4,378**
Adair County SD 2,600/PK-12
1204 Greensburg St 42728 270-384-2476
Alan Reed, supt. Fax 384-5841
www.adair.kyschools.us
Adair County HS 700/9-12
526 Indian Dr 42728 270-384-2751
Troy Young, prin. Fax 384-6900
Adair County MS 400/6-8
322 General John Adair Dr 42728 270-384-5308
Alma Rich, prin. Fax 384-2168
Adair County Youth Development Center 50/Alt
PO Box 39 42728 270-384-0811
Tamara Smith, prin. Fax 384-2122

---

Lindsey Wilson College Post-Sec.
210 Lindsey Wilson St 42728 270-384-2126

**Corbin, Whitley, Pop. 7,232**
Corbin ISD 2,800/PK-12
108 Roy Kidd Ave 40701 606-528-1303
Ed McNeel, supt. Fax 523-1747
www.corbinschools.org
Corbin Educational Center 50/Alt
709 Roy Kidd Ave 40701 606-523-4080
Tom Greer, admin. Fax 523-3614
Corbin HS 800/9-12
1901 Snyder St 40701 606-528-3902
John Crawford, prin. Fax 523-3627
Corbin MS 400/7-8
706 S Kentucky Ave 40701 606-523-3619
Cindy Davis, prin. Fax 523-3621

Kentucky Tech System
Supt. — See Frankfort
Corbin Area Technology Center Vo/Tech
1909 Snyder St 40701 606-528-5338
Patty Crawford, prin. Fax 528-0532

Knox County SD
Supt. — See Barbourville
Lynn Camp JSHS 400/7-12
100 N KY 830 40701 606-528-5429
Anthony Pennington, prin. Fax 528-4750

**Covington, Kenton, Pop. 39,321**
Covington ISD 3,900/PK-12
25 E 7th St 41011 859-392-1000
Alvin Garrison, supt. Fax 292-5970
covingtoncsd.ky.schoolwebpages.com
Holmes HS 800/9-12
2500 Madison Ave 41014 859-655-9545
Scott Hornblower, prin. Fax 581-7259
Holmes MS 700/6-8
2500 Madison Ave 41014 859-392-1100
Sean Bohannon, prin. Fax 292-5810

---

Calvary Christian S 400/PK-12
5955 Taylor Mill Rd 41015 859-356-9201
Dr. Bill Dickens, admin. Fax 356-8962
Covington Catholic HS 500/9-12
1600 Dixie Hwy 41011 859-491-2247
Bob Rowe, prin. Fax 448-2242
Covington Latin HS 200/8-12
21 E 11th St 41011 859-291-7044
Mo Woltering, hdmstr. Fax 291-1939

Holy Cross HS 400/9-12
3617 Church St 41015 859-431-1335
Michael Holtz, prin. Fax 655-2184

**Crestview Hills, Kenton, Pop. 3,111**

---

Thomas More College Post-Sec.
333 Thomas More Pkwy 41017 844-698-6248

**Crestwood, Oldham, Pop. 4,447**
Oldham County SD 11,700/PK-12
6165 W Highway 146 40014 502-241-3500
Rick McHargue, supt. Fax 241-3209
www.oldham.kyschools.us/
East Oldham MS 600/6-8
1201 E Highway 22 40014 502-222-8480
Mark Robson, prin. Fax 222-8489
South Oldham HS 1,200/9-12
5901 Veterens Memorial Pkwy 40014 502-241-6681
Jeff Griffin, prin. Fax 241-0955
South Oldham MS 700/6-8
6403 W Highway 146 40014 502-241-0320
Steve Emerson, prin. Fax 241-1438
Other Schools – See Goshen, La Grange

---

Trend Setter's Academy of Beauty Culture Post-Sec.
6539 W Highway 22 40014 502-241-0565

**Cumberland, Harlan, Pop. 2,210**

---

Southeast Kentucky Community/Tech Coll Post-Sec.
700 College Rd 40823 606-589-2145

**Cynthiana, Harrison, Pop. 6,302**
Harrison County SD 3,200/PK-12
308 Webster Ave 41031 859-234-7110
Andy Dotson, supt. Fax 234-8164
www.harrison.kyschools.us
Harrison County HS 900/9-12
320 Webster Ave 41031 859-234-7117
Amy Coleman, prin. Fax 234-0115
Harrison County MS 700/6-8
269 Education Dr 41031 859-234-7123
Michael McIntire, prin. Fax 234-8385

Kentucky Tech System
Supt. — See Frankfort
Harrison County Area Technology Center Vo/Tech
327 Webster Ave 41031 859-234-5286
Nicki Jones, prin. Fax 234-0658

**Danville, Boyle, Pop. 15,790**
Boyle County SD 2,800/PK-12
352 N Danville Byp 40422 859-236-6634
Mike LaFavers, supt. Fax 236-8624
www.boyle.kyschools.us
Boyle County Day Treatment Center 50/Alt
1637 Perryville Rd 40422 859-236-5047
LuAnn Littlefield, dir.
Boyle County HS 900/9-12
1637 Perryville Rd 40422 859-236-5047
Mark Wade, prin. Fax 236-7820
Boyle County MS 700/6-8
1651 Perryville Rd 40422 859-236-4212
Steve Karsner, prin. Fax 236-9596

Danville ISD 1,800/PK-12
152 E Martin L King Blvd 40422 859-238-1300
Dr. Keith Look, supt. Fax 238-1330
www.danvilleschools.net
Bate MS 400/6-8
460 Stanford Ave 40422 859-238-1305
Beth Lee, prin. Fax 238-1343
Danville HS 500/9-12
203 E Lexington Ave 40422 859-238-1308
Fax 936-8401

---

Centre College Post-Sec.
600 W Walnut St 40422 859-238-5200
Danville Christian Academy 200/PK-12
2170 Shakertown Rd 40422 859-236-2177
Debra Lucas, hdmstr. Fax 236-6759
Kentucky School for the Deaf Post-Sec.
S 2nd St 40422 859-239-7017
National College Post-Sec.
115 E Lexington Ave 40422 859-236-6991

**Dawson Springs, Hopkins, Pop. 2,724**
Dawson Springs ISD 700/PK-12
118 E Arcadia Ave 42408 270-797-3811
Leonard Whalen, supt. Fax 797-5201
www.dsprings.k12.ky.us
Dawson Springs HS 300/7-12
317 Eli St 42408 270-797-2957
Kevin Stockman, prin. Fax 797-5204

**Dayton, Campbell, Pop. 5,244**
Dayton ISD 900/PK-12
200 Clay St 41074 859-491-6565
Jay Brewer, supt. Fax 292-3995
www.dayton.kyschools.us
Dayton HS 300/7-12
200 Greendevil Ln 41074 859-292-7486
Jeremy Dodd, prin. Fax 261-1606

**Dixon, Webster, Pop. 785**
Kentucky Tech System
Supt. — See Frankfort
Webster County Area Technology Center Vo/Tech
PO Box 230 42409 270-639-5035
Lawrence Garrity, prin. Fax 639-5545

Webster County SD 2,100/PK-12
28 State Route 1340 42409 270-639-5083
Dr. Rachel Yarbrough, supt. Fax 639-0117
www.webster.kyschools.us
Webster County HS 600/9-12
1922 US Highway 41A S 42409 270-639-5092
Tara Howard, prin. Fax 639-0128

Webster County MS 300/7-8
1928 US Highway 41A S 42409 270-639-9496
Cyndi Boggs, prin. Fax 639-9497

**Dry Ridge, Grant, Pop. 2,166**
Grant County SD
Supt. — See Williamstown
Grant County HS 1,100/9-12
715 Warsaw Rd 41035 859-824-9739
Claudette Herald, prin. Fax 824-9756
Grant County MS 900/6-8
305 School Rd 41035 859-824-7161
John Preston, prin. Fax 824-7163

**Eastern, Floyd**
Floyd County SD
Supt. — See Prestonsburg
Allen Central HS 400/9-12
PO Box 139 41622 606-358-9543
Larry Begley, prin. Fax 358-9247
Allen Central MS 300/6-8
PO Box 193 41622 606-358-0110
Wes Halbert, prin. Fax 358-0112

**Eddyville, Lyon, Pop. 2,514**
Lyon County SD 800/K-12
217 Jenkins Rd 42038 270-388-9715
Russ Tilford, supt. Fax 388-4962
www.lyon.kyschools.us
Lyon County HS 300/9-12
209 W Fairview Ave 42038 270-388-9715
Ryan Amerson, prin. Fax 388-2296
Lyon County MS 200/6-8
111 W Fairview Ave 42038 270-388-9715
Robert Richey, prin. Fax 388-0517

**Edgewood, Kenton, Pop. 8,503**
Kenton County SD
Supt. — See Fort Wright
Dixie Heights HS 1,400/9-12
3010 Dixie Hwy 41017 859-341-7650
Karen Hendrix, prin. Fax 341-2531
Turkey Foot MS 1,000/6-8
3230 Turkeyfoot Rd 41017 859-341-0216
Debbie Obermeyer, prin. Fax 341-7217

---

St. Elizabeth Medical Center Post-Sec.
1 Medical Village Dr 41017 859-301-2170

**Edmonton, Metcalfe, Pop. 1,584**
Metcalfe County SD 700/PK-12
109 Sartin Dr 42129 270-432-3171
Dr. Benny Lile, supt. Fax 432-3170
www.metcalfe.kyschools.us
Metcalfe County HS 500/9-12
208 Randolph St 42129 270-432-2481
Kelly Bell, prin. Fax 432-2714
Metcalfe County MS 200/6-8
208 Randolph St Lot 1 42129 270-432-3359
Allen Trotter, prin. Fax 432-5828

**Elizabethtown, Hardin, Pop. 27,593**
Elizabethtown ISD 2,500/PK-12
219 Helm St 42701 270-765-6146
Jon Ballard, supt. Fax 765-2158
www.etown.k12.ky.us
Elizabethtown HS 800/9-12
620 N Mulberry St 42701 270-769-3381
Steve Smallwood, prin. Fax 769-2539
Stone MS 600/6-8
323 Morningside Dr 42701 270-769-6343
Jennifer Burnham, prin. Fax 769-6749
Valley View Education Center Alt
701 Hawkins Dr 42701 270-769-2359
Kristin Froedge, admin. Fax 769-3860

Hardin County SD 13,700/PK-12
65 W A Jenkins Rd 42701 270-769-8800
Nannette Johnston, supt. Fax 769-8888
www.hardin.kyschools.us/
Bluegrass MS 600/6-8
170 W A Jenkins Rd 42701 270-765-2658
Michael Elmore, prin. Fax 737-0450
Hardin Co. Early College & Career Center 300/10-12
200 University Dr 42701 270-769-7930
Dan Robbins, prin.
Hardin HS 1,000/9-12
384 W A Jenkins Rd 42701 270-769-8906
Mark Wells, prin. Fax 769-8996
Mulberry Helm Education Center 100/Alt
114 S Mulberry St 42701 270-769-8866
Eric Vowels, dir. Fax 769-8869
Other Schools – See Cecilia, Glendale, Radcliff, Vine Grove

---

Elizabethtown Beauty School Post-Sec.
308 N Miles St 42701 270-765-2118
Elizabethtown Community & Technical Coll Post-Sec.
600 College Street Rd 42701 270-769-2371
Trend Setter's Academy of Beauty Culture Post-Sec.
622B Westport Rd 42701 270-765-5243

**Elkton, Todd, Pop. 2,020**
Todd County SD 2,200/PK-12
205 Airport Rd 42220 270-265-2436
Wayne Benningfield, supt. Fax 265-5414
www.todd.kyschools.us
Todd County Central HS 600/9-12
806 S Main St 42220 270-265-2506
Jennifer Pope, prin. Fax 265-9408
Todd County MS 500/6-8
515 W Main St 42220 270-265-2511
Connie Wofford, prin. Fax 265-9414

**Eminence, Henry, Pop. 2,433**
Eminence ISD 600/PK-12
291 W Broadway St 40019 502-845-4788
Buddy Berry, supt. Fax 845-2339
www.eminence.kyschools.us/

Eminence JSHS 300/6-12
254 W Broadway St 40019 502-845-5427
Angie Deckard, prin. Fax 845-1310

**Erlanger, Kenton, Pop. 17,704**
Erlanger-Elsmere ISD 2,300/PK-12
500 Graves Ave 41018 859-727-2009
Dr. Kathlyn Burkhardt, supt. Fax 727-5653
www.erlanger.kyschools.us
Bartlett Educational Center 50/Alt
305 Bartlett Ave 41018 859-342-2460
Chris Klosinski, prin. Fax 342-2423
Lloyd HS 600/9-12
450 Bartlett Ave 41018 859-727-1555
John Riehemann, prin. Fax 727-5912
Tichenor MS 500/6-8
305 Bartlett Ave 41018 859-727-2255
Mac Cooley, prin. Fax 342-2425

St. Henry HS 500/9-12
3755 Scheben Dr 41018 859-525-0255
David Otte, prin. Fax 525-5855

**Fairdale, Jefferson, Pop. 6,563**
Jefferson County SD
Supt. — See Louisville
Fairdale HS Magnet Career Academy 1,000/9-12
1001 Fairdale Rd 40118 502-485-8248
Brad Weston, prin. Fax 485-8761

**Falmouth, Pendleton, Pop. 2,146**
Pendleton County SD 2,600/PK-12
2525 US Highway 27 N 41040 859-654-6911
R. Anthony Strong, supt. Fax 654-6143
pendleton.kyschools.us
Pendleton County HS 800/9-12
2359 US Highway 27 N 41040 859-654-3355
Chad Simms, prin. Fax 654-4235
Other Schools – See Butler

**Fern Creek, Jefferson, Pop. 16,406**
Jefferson County SD
Supt. — See Louisville
Fern Creek Traditional HS 1,400/9-12
9115 Fern Creek Rd 40291 502-485-8251
Dr. Nathan Meyer, prin. Fax 485-8032

**Flemingsburg, Fleming, Pop. 2,619**
Fleming County SD 2,300/K-12
211 W Water St 41041 606-845-5851
Brian Creasman, supt. Fax 849-3158
www.fleming.kyschools.us
Fleming County HS 700/9-12
1658 Elizaville Rd 41041 606-845-6601
Mark Leet, prin. Fax 845-3102
Simons MS 300/7-8
242 W Water St 41041 606-845-9331
Jessee Bacon, prin. Fax 849-2309

**Florence, Boone, Pop. 29,280**
Boone County SD 19,300/PK-12
8330 US Highway 42 41042 859-283-1003
Randy Poe Ed.D., supt. Fax 282-2376
www.boone.kyschools.us
Alternative Center for Education Alt
99 Center St 41042 859-282-2163
Jerome Gels, prin. Fax 282-2165
Boone County HS 1,400/9-12
7056 Burlington Pike 41042 859-282-5655
Mark Raleigh, prin. Fax 282-5653
Jones MS 700/6-8
8000 Spruce Dr 41042 859-282-4610
Tony Pastura, prin. Fax 282-2364
Ockerman MS 900/6-8
8300 US Highway 42 41042 859-282-3240
Michael Poiry, prin. Fax 282-3242
Other Schools – See Burlington, Hebron, Union

Beckfield College Post-Sec.
16 Spiral Dr 41042 859-371-9393
Gateway Community & Technical College Post-Sec.
500 Technology Way 41042 859-441-4500
Hair Design School Post-Sec.
7285 Turfway Rd 41042 859-283-2690
Heritage Academy 200/PK-12
7216 US Highway 42 41042 859-525-0213
Lincoln College of Technology Post-Sec.
8095 Connector Dr 41042 859-282-9999
National College Post-Sec.
7627 Ewing Blvd 41042 859-525-6510

**Fort Knox, Hardin, Pop. 9,669**

Sullivan University Post-Sec.
63 Quartermaster St 40121 502-942-8500

**Fort Mitchell, Kenton, Pop. 8,095**
Beechwood ISD 1,200/PK-12
50 Beechwood Rd 41017 859-331-3250
Dr. Mike Stacy, supt. Fax 331-7528
www.beechwood.kyschools.us/
Beechwood JSHS 600/7-12
54 Beechwood Rd 41017 859-331-1220
Alissa Ayres, prin. Fax 426-3744

Kenton County SD
Supt. — See Fort Wright
Kenton County Academies Vo/Tech
3234 Turkeyfoot Rd 41017 859-341-2266
Dr. Francis O'Hara, dir.

Brown Mackie College Post-Sec.
309 Buttermilk Pike 41017 859-341-5627

**Fort Thomas, Campbell, Pop. 16,124**
Fort Thomas ISD 2,800/PK-12
28 N Fort Thomas Ave 41075 859-781-3333
Gene Kirchner, supt. Fax 442-4016
www.fortthomas.kyschools.us/

Highlands HS 800/9-12
2400 Memorial Pkwy 41075 859-781-5900
Brian Robinson, prin. Fax 441-9271
Highlands MS 600/6-8
2350 Memorial Pkwy 41075 859-441-5222
Mark Goetz, prin. Fax 441-9371

**Fort Wright, Kenton, Pop. 5,642**
Kenton County SD 14,500/PK-12
1055 Eaton Dr 41017 859-344-8888
Dr. Terri Cox-Cruey, supt. Fax 344-1531
www.kenton.kyschools.us/
Other Schools – See Edgewood, Fort Mitchell, Independence, Taylor Mill

**Frankfort, Franklin, Pop. 24,820**
Frankfort ISD 700/PK-12
959 Leestown Ln 40601 502-875-8661
Fax 875-8663
www.frankfort.k12.ky.us
Capital City Preparatory 50/Alt
328 Shelby St 40601 502-875-8650
Alan Spade, dir. Fax 875-8652
Frankfort HS 200/9-12
328 Shelby St 40601 502-875-8655
Michael Godbey, prin. Fax 875-8657

Franklin County SD 6,000/PK-12
916 E Main St 40601 502-695-6700
Chrissy Jones, supt. Fax 695-6708
www.franklin.kyschools.us
Academy 50/Alt
400 Democrat Dr 40601 502-695-6720
Sarah Vivian, prin. Fax 695-9618
Bondurant MS 600/6-8
300 Bondurant Dr 40601 502-875-8440
Casey Sparrow, prin. Fax 875-8442
Elkhorn MS 700/6-8
1060 E Main St 40601 502-695-6740
Willie Bartley, prin. Fax 695-6745
Franklin Co. Career & Technical Center Vo/Tech
1106 E Main St 40601 502-695-6790
James Hardin, dir. Fax 695-6791
Franklin County HS 900/9-12
1100 E Main St 40601 502-695-6750
Stirling Sampson, prin. Fax 695-6755
Western Hills HS 800/9-12
100 Doctors Dr 40601 502-875-8400
Rita Rector, prin. Fax 227-4568

Kentucky Tech System
500 Mero St 40601 502-564-4286
Dr. Dale Winkler, cmmssnr. Fax 564-4800
www.kytech.ky.gov
Other Schools – See Albany, Alexandria, Barbourville, Bardstown, Beattyville, Belfry, Bowling Green, Brandenburg, Carrollton, Corbin, Cynthiana, Dixon, Glasgow, Greensburg, Greenup, Harned, Harrodsburg, Hartford, Hebron, Hickman, Hindman, Hyden, Inez, Jackson, Lancaster, Lebanon, Liberty, Mc Kee, Manchester, Martin, Mayfield, Maysville, Monticello, Morgantown, Mount Sterling, Mount Vernon, Murray, Paducah, Pikeville, Pineville, Princeton, Richmond, Russell, Russell Springs, Russellville, Shelbyville, Shepherdsville, Somerset, Stanford, Tompkinsville, West Liberty, Whitesburg, Winchester

Frankfort Christian Academy 300/PK-12
1349 US Highway 421 S 40601 502-695-0744
Carrie Beth Tigges, admin. Fax 695-8725
Kentucky State University Post-Sec.
400 E Main St 40601 502-597-6000

**Franklin, Simpson, Pop. 8,221**
Simpson County SD 3,000/PK-12
430 S College St 42134 270-586-8877
James Flynn, supt. Fax 586-2011
www.simpson.kyschools.us
Franklin Simpson HS 900/9-12
400 S College St 42134 270-586-3273
Tim Schlosser, prin. Fax 586-2021
Franklin Simpson HS West Campus 50/Alt
229 Joker Phillips St 42134 270-586-2039
Crystal Bayles, prin. Fax 586-2047
Franklin Simpson MS 700/6-8
322 S College St 42134 270-586-4401
Craig Delk, prin. Fax 586-2048

**Frenchburg, Menifee, Pop. 482**
Menifee County SD 1,000/PK-12
PO Box 110 40322 606-768-8002
Benny Patrick, supt. Fax 768-8050
www.menifee.kyschools.us/
Menifee County Academy Alt
6969 Tarr Ridge Rd 40322
Menifee County HS 300/9-12
119 Indian Creek Rd 40322 606-768-8102
Brenda Warren, prin. Fax 768-8200

**Fulton, Fulton, Pop. 2,370**
Fulton ISD 400/PK-12
304 W State Line St 42041 270-472-1553
Dr. Tamara Smith, supt. Fax 472-6921
www.fultonind.kyschools.us
Fulton Independent HS 200/6-12
700 Stephen Beale Dr 42041 270-472-1741
Donna Garland, prin. Fax 472-6135

**Georgetown, Scott, Pop. 28,525**
Scott County SD 8,300/PK-12
PO Box 578 40324 502-863-3663
Patricia Putty, supt. Fax 863-5367
www.scott.kyschools.us
Elkhorn Crossing HS 9-12
2001 Frankfort Rd 40324 502-570-4920
Michelle Nichols, prin. Fax 873-2610
Georgetown MS 500/6-8
730 S Hamilton St 40324 502-863-3805
Rhonda Schornick, prin. Fax 867-1372

Ninth Grade Center 600/9-9
1072 Cardinal Dr 40324 502-863-4635
Dwayne Ellison, prin. Fax 868-0515
Royal Spring MS 700/6-8
332 Champion Way 40324 502-570-2390
Shannon Gullett, prin. Fax 863-3621
Scott County Cardinal Academy Alt
1076 Cardinal Dr 40324 502-863-4057
Joretta Crowe, dir. Fax 863-4432
Scott County MS 700/6-8
1036 Cardinal Dr 40324 502-863-7202
Jennifer Sutton, prin. Fax 863-7452
Scott County SHS 1,700/10-12
1080 Cardinal Dr 40324 502-863-4131
Frank Howatt, prin. Fax 867-0544

Georgetown College Post-Sec.
400 E College St 40324 502-863-8000
Providence Christian Academy 300/PK-10
172 Southgate Dr 40324 502-868-9393
Rick White M.Ed., admin. Fax 370-4766

**Glasgow, Barren, Pop. 13,692**
Barren County SD 4,700/PK-12
202 W Washington St 42141 270-651-3787
Bo Matthews, supt. Fax 651-8836
www.barren.kyschools.us
Barren County HS 1,000/10-12
507 Trojan Trl 42141 270-651-6315
Brad Johnson, prin. Fax 651-9211
Barren County MS 600/7-8
555 Trojan Trl 42141 270-651-4909
Lori Downs, prin. Fax 651-5137
College Street Campus Alt
304 E College St 42141 270-629-6554
Dan Belding, dir. Fax 629-2267
Trojan Academy 9-9
505 Trojan Trl 42141 270-629-5505
Warren Cunningham, prin. Fax 629-5504

Glasgow ISD 2,000/PK-12
PO Box 1239 42142 270-651-6757
Sean Howard, supt. Fax 651-9791
www.glasgow.kyschools.us/
Glasgow HS 600/9-12
1601 Columbia Ave 42141 270-651-8801
Keith Hale, prin. Fax 651-5189
Glasgow MS 500/6-8
105 Scottie Dr 42141 270-651-2256
Scott Jones, prin. Fax 651-3090

Kentucky Tech System
Supt. — See Frankfort
Barren County Area Technology Center Vo/Tech
491 Trojan Trl 42141 270-651-2196
Ashley Bell, prin. Fax 651-2197

Glasgow Christian Academy 200/PK-12
600 Old Cavalry Dr 42141 270-651-7729
Tracy Shaw, admin. Fax 651-6811
PJs College of Cosmetology Post-Sec.
920 Happy Valley Rd 42141 270-651-6553
Southcentral Kentucky Comm Tech College Post-Sec.
129 State Ave 42141 270-651-5373

**Glendale, Hardin**
Hardin County SD
Supt. — See Elizabethtown
East Hardin MS 700/6-8
129 College St 42740 270-369-7370
Daniel Lockwood, prin. Fax 369-6380

**Goshen, Oldham, Pop. 900**
Oldham County SD
Supt. — See Crestwood
North Oldham HS 1,000/9-12
1815 S Highway 1793 40026 502-228-0158
Craig Wallace, prin. Fax 228-7735
North Oldham MS 800/6-8
1801 S Highway 1793 40026 502-228-9998
Carrie Pitsenberger, prin. Fax 228-0985

**Grayson, Carter, Pop. 4,170**
Carter County SD 4,900/PK-12
228 S Carol Malone Blvd 41143 606-474-6696
Ronnie Dotson, supt. Fax 474-6125
www.cartercountyschools.org
East Carter County HS 800/9-12
405 Hitchins Rd 41143 606-474-5714
Larry Kiser, prin. Fax 475-9200
East Carter MS 600/6-8
1 Spirit Ln 41143 606-474-5156
Jenny Stark, prin. Fax 474-4027
Other Schools – See Olive Hill

Kentucky Christian University Post-Sec.
100 Academic Pkwy 41143 606-474-3000

**Greensburg, Green, Pop. 2,133**
Green County SD 1,700/K-12
PO Box 369 42743 270-932-6601
Jim Frank, supt. Fax 932-3624
www.green.kyschools.us
Green County HS 500/9-12
PO Box 227 42743 270-932-6610
Karen Marcum, prin. Fax 932-3214
Green County MS 400/6-8
PO Box 176 42743 270-932-6615
Philip West, prin. Fax 932-7617

Kentucky Tech System
Supt. — See Frankfort
Green County Area Technology Center Vo/Tech
102 Carlisle Ave 42743 270-932-4263
LeeAnn Wall, prin. Fax 932-3072

**Greenup, Greenup, Pop. 1,174**
Greenup County SD 2,900/K-12
45 Musketeer Dr 41144 606-473-9819
Sherry Horsley, supt. Fax 473-5710
www.greenup.kyschools.us/
Greenup County HS 900/9-12
196 Musketeer Dr 41144 606-473-9812
Jason Smith, prin. Fax 473-7854
Other Schools – See South Shore, Wurtland

Kentucky Tech System
Supt. — See Frankfort
Greenup County Area Technology Center Vo/Tech
146 Musketeer Dr 41144 606-473-9344
Sarah Johnson, prin. Fax 473-9177

**Greenville, Muhlenberg, Pop. 4,256**
Muhlenberg County SD
Supt. — See Powderly
Muhlenberg County Career Alternative HS 100/Alt
3875 State Route 181 N 42345 270-338-5460
Paul Moore, prin. Fax 338-4918
Muhlenberg County Career & Tech Center Vo/Tech
501 Robert Draper Way 42345 270-338-0040
Donna Bumps, prin. Fax 338-2442
Muhlenberg County HS East Campus 700/9-10
2900 State Route 176 42345 270-338-9409
Donna Bumps, prin. Fax 338-9710
Muhlenberg County HS West Campus 700/11-12
501 Robert L Draper Way 42345 270-338-0040
Donna Bumps, prin. Fax 338-2442
Muhlenberg North MS 600/6-8
1000 N Main St 42345 270-338-3550
Jerry Rager, prin. Fax 338-2911
Muhlenberg South MS 600/6-8
200 Pritchett Dr 42345 270-338-4650
Brian Lile, prin. Fax 338-0151
Renaissance Center 50/Alt
203 Airport Rd 42345 270-338-0662
Alex Watkins, prin. Fax 338-2194

**Hagerhill, Johnson**

---

Piarist S 100/6-12
PO Box 369 41222 606-789-1967
Rev. Thomas Carroll, prin. Fax 789-1968

**Hardinsburg, Breckinridge, Pop. 2,302**
Breckinridge County SD 2,800/PK-12
86 Airport Rd 40143 270-756-3000
Janet L. Meeks, supt. Fax 756-6888
www.breck.kyschools.us
Other Schools – See Harned

**Harlan, Harlan, Pop. 1,720**
Harlan County SD 4,200/PK-12
251 Ball Park Rd 40831 606-573-4330
T. Michael Howard, supt. Fax 573-5767
www.harlan.kyschools.us
Other Schools – See Baxter

Harlan ISD 800/PK-12
420 E Central St 40831 606-573-8700
Charles Morton, supt. Fax 573-8711
www.harlan-ind.k12.ky.us
Harlan MSHS 500/5-12
420 E Central St 40831 606-573-8750
Stacy Noah, prin. Fax 573-8753

---

Jenny Lea Academy of Cosmetology Post-Sec.
114 N Cumberland Ave 40831 606-573-9817

**Harned, Breckinridge**
Breckinridge County SD
Supt. — See Hardinsburg
Breckinridge County HS 900/9-12
PO Box 10 40144 270-756-3080
Nick Carter, prin. Fax 756-3090
Breckinridge County MS 600/6-8
PO Box 39 40144 270-756-3060
Jayme Knochel, prin. Fax 756-3061

Kentucky Tech System
Supt. — See Frankfort
Breckinridge County Area Technology Ctr. Vo/Tech
PO Box 68 40144 270-756-2138
Thomas Thompson, prin. Fax 756-2878

**Harrodsburg, Mercer, Pop. 8,110**
Kentucky Tech System
Supt. — See Frankfort
Harrodsburg Area Technology Center Vo/Tech
PO Box 628 40330 859-734-9329
Tony Webb, prin. Fax 734-3613

Mercer County SD 2,800/PK-12
371 E Lexington St 40330 859-733-7000
Dennis Davis, supt. Fax 733-7004
www.mercer.kyschools.us/
Hughes Jones Harrodsburg Area Tech Ctr Vo/Tech
661 Tapp Rd 40330 859-734-9329
Tony Webb, prin. Fax 734-3613
King MS 700/6-8
937 Moberly Rd 40330 859-733-7060
Terry Gordon, prin. Fax 733-7064
Mercer Central Alternative S 50/Alt
371 E Lexington St 40330 859-733-7120
Christopher Souder, dir. Fax 733-7104
Mercer County HS 700/9-12
1124 Moberly Rd 40330 859-733-7160
Malissa Hutchins, prin. Fax 733-7164

**Hartford, Ohio, Pop. 2,636**
Kentucky Tech System
Supt. — See Frankfort
Ohio County Area Technology Center Vo/Tech
1406 S Main St 42347 270-274-9612
Brad Sisk, prin. Fax 274-9633

Ohio County SD 4,200/PK-12
PO Box 70 42347 270-298-3249
Scott Lewis, supt. Fax 298-3886
www.ohio.kyschools.us/
Ohio County HS 1,100/9-12
1400 S Main St 42347 270-274-3366
Greg Decker, prin. Fax 274-9482
Ohio County MS 600/7-8
1404 S Main St 42347 270-274-7893
Cheston Hoover, prin. Fax 274-7320

**Hawesville, Hancock, Pop. 930**
Hancock County SD 1,700/PK-12
83 State Route 3543 42348 270-927-6914
Kyle Estes, supt. Fax 927-6916
www.hancock.kyschools.us
Other Schools – See Lewisport

**Hazard, Perry, Pop. 4,362**
Hazard ISD 900/K-12
705 Main St 41701 606-436-3911
Sandra Johnson, supt. Fax 436-2742
www.hazard.kyschools.us
Hazard HS 300/9-12
157 Bulldog Ln 41701 606-439-1318
Donald Mobelini, prin. Fax 439-2285
Hazard MS 300/5-8
325 School St 41701 606-436-4421
Kevin Combs, prin. Fax 435-0407

Knott County SD
Supt. — See Hindman
Cordia HS 100/7-12
6050 Lotts Creek Rd 41701 606-785-4457
Jonathan Mullins, prin. Fax 785-4669

Perry County SD 3,500/PK-12
315 Park Ave 41701 606-439-5814
Jonathan Jett, supt. Fax 439-2512
www.perry.kyschools.us/
Perry County Central HS 1,000/9-12
305 Park Ave 41701 606-439-5888
Michelle Ritchie, prin. Fax 439-2825
Other Schools – See Buckhorn

---

Hazard Community & Technical College Post-Sec.
1 Community College Dr 41701 606-436-4282

**Hebron, Boone, Pop. 5,808**
Boone County SD
Supt. — See Florence
Conner HS 1,200/9-12
3310 Cougar Path 41048 859-334-4400
Tim Hitzfield, prin. Fax 334-4406
Conner MS 1,100/6-8
3300 Cougar Path 41048 859-334-4410
James Brewer, prin. Fax 334-4435

Kentucky Tech System
Supt. — See Frankfort
Boone County Area Technology Center Vo/Tech
3320 Cougar Path 41048 859-689-7855
Garry Harper, prin. Fax 689-7828

**Henderson, Henderson, Pop. 28,141**
Henderson County SD 7,000/PK-12
1805 2nd St 42420 270-831-5000
Marganna Stanley, supt. Fax 831-5009
www.henderson.kyschools.us/
Central Academy 100/Alt
851 Center St 42420 270-831-5100
Bob Lawson, prin. Fax 831-5103
Henderson County Area Technology Center Vo/Tech
2424 Zion Rd 42420 270-831-8850
Victor Doty, dir. Fax 831-8853
Henderson County HS 2,000/9-12
2424 Zion Rd 42420 270-831-8800
Sally Sugg, prin. Fax 831-8870
Henderson County North MS 800/6-8
1707 2nd St 42420 270-831-5060
Zack Windell, prin. Fax 831-5064
Henderson County South MS 700/6-8
800 S Alves St 42420 270-831-5050
Ryan Reusch, prin. Fax 831-5058

---

Henderson Community College Post-Sec.
2660 S Green St 42420 270-827-1867
Pat Wilson Beauty College Post-Sec.
326 N Main St 42420 270-826-5195

**Hickman, Fulton, Pop. 2,360**
Fulton County SD 600/PK-12
2780 Moscow Ave 42050 270-236-3923
Aaron Collins, supt. Fax 236-2184
www.fulton.kyschools.us
Fulton County HS 200/9-12
2740 Moscow Ave 42050 270-236-3904
Ellen Murphy, prin. Fax 236-9004

Kentucky Tech System
Supt. — See Frankfort
Fulton County Area Technology Center Vo/Tech
2720 Moscow Ave 42050 270-236-2517
Terry Sullivan, prin. Fax 236-9395

**Highland Heights, Campbell, Pop. 6,806**

---

Northern Kentucky University Post-Sec.
400 Nunn Dr 41099 859-572-5100

**Hi Hat, Floyd**
Floyd County SD
Supt. — See Prestonsburg
South Floyd MSHS 300/6-12
299 Mt Raider Dr 41636 606-452-9600
Stacy Shannon, prin. Fax 452-2155

**Hindman, Knott, Pop. 768**
Kentucky Tech System
Supt. — See Frankfort
Knott County Area Technology Center Vo/Tech
1996 Highway 160 S 41822 606-785-5350
Danny Vance, prin. Fax 785-5445

Knott County SD 2,500/PK-12
PO Box 869 41822 606-785-3153
Kimberly King, supt. Fax 785-0800
www.knott.kyschools.us/
Knott County Central HS 600/9-12
76 Patriot Ln 41822 606-785-3166
Bobby Pollard, prin. Fax 785-3169
Other Schools – See Hazard

**Hitchins, Carter**

---

Carter Christian Academy 50/PK-12
3547 State Highway 773 41146 606-475-1919
Nikki Lewis, prin. Fax 475-0551

**Hodgenville, Larue, Pop. 3,149**
LaRue County SD 2,300/PK-12
208 College St 42748 270-358-4111
Sam Sanders, supt. Fax 358-3053
www.larue.kyschools.us/
LaRue County HS 700/9-12
925 S Lincoln Blvd 42748 270-358-2210
Kyle Goodlett, prin. Fax 358-9469
LaRue County MS 600/6-8
911 S Lincoln Blvd 42748 270-358-3196
Jason Detre, prin. Fax 358-3946

**Hopkinsville, Christian, Pop. 30,860**
Christian County SD 8,900/K-12
PO Box 609 42241 270-887-7000
Mary Ann Gemmill, supt. Fax 887-1316
www.christian.kyschools.us/
Christian County Day Treatment Center 50/Alt
731 E 2nd St 42240 270-887-1147
Darrell Johnson, lead tchr. Fax 889-6561
Christian County HS 1,200/9-12
220 Glass Ave 42240 270-887-7050
Chris Bentzel, prin. Fax 887-1294
Christian County MS 800/7-8
215 Glass Ave 42240 270-887-7070
Kevin Crider, prin. Fax 887-1189
Gateway Academy to Innovation Vo/Tech
705 N Elm St 42240 270-887-7030
Penny Knight, prin. Fax 887-1242
Hopkinsville HS 1,200/9-12
430 Koffman Dr 42240 270-887-7110
Curtis Higgins, prin. Fax 887-1118
Hopkinsville MS 800/7-8
434 Koffman Dr 42240 270-887-7130
Wendy Duvall, prin. Fax 887-1234
21st Century Academy Alt
210 Glass Ave 42240 270-887-7401
Debbie Upton, prin.

---

Brown Mackie College Post-Sec.
4001 Fort Campbell Blvd 42240 270-886-1302
Heritage Christian Academy 500/PK-12
8349 Eagle Way 42240 270-885-2417
Linda Garris, hdmstr. Fax 885-0094
Hopkinsville Community College Post-Sec.
PO Box 2100 42241 270-707-3700
University Heights Academy 400/PK-12
1300 Academy Dr 42240 270-886-0254

**Horse Cave, Hart, Pop. 2,268**
Caverna ISD
Supt. — See Cave City
Caverna HS 200/9-12
2276 S Dixie St 42749 270-773-2828
Brad Phipps, prin. Fax 773-2825
Caverna MS 200/6-8
2278 S Dixie St 42749 270-773-4665
Barry Nesbitt, prin. Fax 773-4668

**Hyden, Leslie, Pop. 362**
Kentucky Tech System
Supt. — See Frankfort
Leslie County Area Technology Center Vo/Tech
PO Box 902 41749 606-672-2859
Dwight Lewis, prin. Fax 672-4943

Leslie County SD 1,600/PK-12
PO Box 949 41749 606-672-2397
Anthony Little, supt. Fax 672-4224
www.leslie.kyschools.us
Leslie County HS 500/9-12
PO Box 970 41749 606-672-2337
Robert Roark, prin. Fax 672-2858

---

Frontier Nursing University Post-Sec.
PO Box 528 41749 606-672-2312

**Independence, Kenton, Pop. 24,387**
Kenton County SD
Supt. — See Fort Wright
Kenton HS 1,600/9-12
11132 Madison Pike 41051 859-960-0100
John Popham, prin. Fax 960-0360
Twenhofel MS 700/6-8
11846 Taylor Mill Rd 41051 859-356-5559
Shannon Gross, prin. Fax 356-1137

---

Community Christian Academy 300/PK-12
11875 Taylor Mill Rd 41051 859-356-7990
Tara Bates, prin. Fax 356-7991

**Inez, Martin, Pop. 715**
Kentucky Tech System
Supt. — See Frankfort
Martin County Area Technology Center Vo/Tech
7900 Highway 645 41224 606-298-3879
Martha Williams, prin. Fax 298-7240

Martin County SD 1,900/PK-12
PO Box 366 41224 606-298-3572
Steve Meadows, supt. Fax 298-4427
www.martin.kyschools.us
Clark HS 600/9-12
388 Cardinal Ln 41224 606-298-3591
Lon Laney, prin. Fax 298-5148
Other Schools – See Warfield

**Irvine, Estill, Pop. 2,691**
Estill County SD 2,600/PK-12
PO Box 930 40336 606-723-2181
Jeff Saylor, supt. Fax 723-6029
www.estill.kyschools.us/
Estill County HS 700/9-12
397 Engineer Rd 40336 606-723-3537
Arthur Ballard, prin. Fax 723-4894
Estill County MS 500/6-8
51 Patriot Dr 40336 606-723-5136
Tim Burkhart, prin. Fax 723-2041

**Jackson, Breathitt, Pop. 2,211**
Breathitt County SD 1,900/PK-12
PO Box 750 41339 606-666-2491
Steve Meadows, supt. Fax 666-2493
www.breathitt.kyschools.us
Breathitt County Day Treatment Center 50/Alt
3826 Highway 15 S 41339 606-666-8820
Ronnie Combs, lead tchr. Fax 666-8597
Breathitt County HS 500/9-12
2307 Bobcat Ln 41339 606-666-7511
Derek McKnight, prin. Fax 666-7765
Cadet Leadership and Educ Alternative 50/Alt
2665 Highway 30 W 41339 606-295-2267
Dean Smith, lead tchr. Fax 295-2274
Sebastian MS 200/7-8
244 L B J Rd 41339 606-666-8894
Reggie Hamilton, prin. Fax 666-5336

Jackson ISD 400/PK-12
940 Highland Ave 41339 606-666-4979
Kyle Lively, supt. Fax 666-4350
www.jacksonind.kyschools.us/
Jackson City S 400/PK-12
940 Highland Ave 41339 606-666-5164
James Yount, prin. Fax 666-2555

Kentucky Tech System
Supt. — See Frankfort
Breathitt County Area Technology Center Vo/Tech
2303 Bobcat Ln 41339 606-666-5153
Joe Mayabb, prin. Fax 666-5394

---

Oakdale Christian Academy 50/7-12
5801 Beattyville Rd 41339 606-666-5422
Laura Mead, prin. Fax 666-5422

**Jamestown, Russell, Pop. 1,780**
Russell County SD 2,600/PK-12
404 S Main St 42629 270-343-3191
Michael Ford, supt. Fax 343-3072
www.russell.kyschools.us
Other Schools – See Russell Springs

**Jeffersontown, Jefferson, Pop. 25,990**
Jefferson County SD
Supt. — See Louisville
Jeffersontown HS Magnet Career Academy 1,300/9-12
9600 Old Six Mile Ln 40299 502-485-8275
Matt Kingsley, prin. Fax 485-8832

**Jenkins, Letcher, Pop. 2,198**
Jenkins ISD 600/PK-12
PO Box 74 41537 606-832-2183
Freddie Bowling, supt. Fax 832-2181
www.jenkins.kyschools.us
Jenkins MSHS 300/6-12
269 Old Highway 3086 41537 606-832-2184
David Lee, prin. Fax 832-4283

**La Grange, Oldham, Pop. 7,910**
Oldham County SD
Supt. — See Crestwood
Buckner Alternative HS 100/Alt
1350 N Highway 393 40031 502-222-3767
Beth Carter, prin. Fax 222-3769
Oldham County HS 1,400/9-12
1150 N Highway 393 40031 502-222-9461
Rich Graviss, prin. Fax 222-0558
Oldham County MS 800/6-8
4305 Brown Blvd 40031 502-222-1451
Chris Kraft, prin. Fax 222-5178

**Lancaster, Garrard, Pop. 3,397**
Garrard County SD 2,700/PK-12
322 W Maple Ave 40444 859-792-3018
Paul Mullins, supt. Fax 792-4733
www.garrard.kyschools.us
Garrard County HS 700/9-12
599 Industry Rd 40444 859-792-2146
Kalem Gresham, prin. Fax 792-4352
Garrard MS 600/6-8
304 W Maple Ave 40444 859-792-2108
Andrew Pickerill, prin. Fax 792-9618

Kentucky Tech System
Supt. — See Frankfort
Garrard County Area Technology Center Vo/Tech
306 W Maple Ave 40444 859-792-2144
Troy Watts, prin. Fax 792-4058

**Lawrenceburg, Anderson, Pop. 10,349**
Anderson County SD 4,000/PK-12
1160 Bypass N 40342 502-839-3406
Sheila Mitchell, supt. Fax 839-2501
www.anderson.kyschools.us
Anderson County HS 1,200/9-12
1 Bearcat Dr 40342 502-839-5118
Chris Glass, prin. Fax 839-3486
Anderson County MS 900/6-8
1 Mustang Trl 40342 502-839-9261
Jeanna Kidd, prin. Fax 839-2534

---

Christian Academy of Lawrenceburg 100/PK-12
126 N Main St 40342 502-839-9992
Jason Gribbins, admin. Fax 839-3728

**Lebanon, Marion, Pop. 5,374**
Kentucky Tech System
Supt. — See Frankfort
Marion County Area Technology Center Vo/Tech
721 E Main St 40033 270-692-3155
Brandon Bardin, prin. Fax 692-1357

Marion County SD 3,200/PK-12
755 E Main St 40033 270-692-3721
Taylora Schlosser, supt. Fax 692-1899
www.marion.kyschools.us/
Lebanon MS 400/6-8
200 Corporate Dr 40033 270-692-3441
Christina McRay, prin. Fax 692-0266
Marion County HS 1,000/9-12
735 E Main St 40033 270-692-6066
Mike Abell, prin. Fax 692-6248
St. Charles MS 300/6-8
1155 Highway 327 40033 270-692-4578
Buffy Mann, prin. Fax 692-1176
Spalding Academy 50/Alt
721 E Main St 40033 270-692-0690
Eric King, prin.

**Leitchfield, Grayson, Pop. 6,624**
Grayson County SD 4,300/PK-12
PO Box 4009 42755 270-259-4011
Doug Robinson, supt. Fax 259-4756
www.graysoncountyschools.com
Grayson County Alternative S 50/Alt
340 School House Rd 42754 270-259-2800
Kelly Shawn Majors, dir. Fax 259-2802
Grayson County HS 1,200/9-12
340 School House Rd 42754 270-259-4078
Todd Johnston, prin. Fax 259-6131
Grayson County MS 1,000/6-8
726 John Hill Taylor Dr 42754 270-259-4175
Jim Blain, prin. Fax 259-5875
Grayson County Technology Center Vo/Tech
252 School House Rd 42754 270-259-3195
Cynthia Smith, dir. Fax 259-8082

---

Leitchfield Christian Academy 100/PK-12
106 E Walnut St 42754 270-259-4076
Linda Gentry, prin. Fax 259-3240

**Lewisport, Hancock, Pop. 1,650**
Hancock County SD
Supt. — See Hawesville
Hancock County HS 500/9-12
80 State Route 271 S 42351 270-927-6953
Rick Lasley, prin. Fax 927-8677
Hancock County MS 400/6-8
100 State Route 271 S 42351 270-927-6255
Traci Sanders, prin. Fax 927-9895

**Lexington, Fayette, Pop. 288,987**
Fayette County SD 38,000/PK-12
1126 Russell Cave Rd 40505 859-381-4100
Emmanuel Caulk, supt. Fax 381-4303
www.fcps.net
Beaumont MS 1,100/6-8
2080 Georgian Way 40504 859-381-3094
Kate McAnelly, prin. Fax 381-3109
Bryan Station HS 1,900/9-12
201 Eastin Rd 40505 859-381-3308
James McMillin, prin. Fax 381-4939
Bryan Station MS 600/6-8
1865 Wickland Dr 40505 859-381-3288
Lester Diaz, prin. Fax 381-3292
Clark MS 900/6-8
3341 Clays Mill Rd 40503 859-381-3036
Cecil Combs, prin. Fax 381-3037
Clay HS 2,200/9-12
2100 Fontaine Rd 40502 859-381-3423
Greg Quenon, prin. Fax 381-3430
Crawford MS 400/6-8
1813 Charleston Dr 40505 859-381-3370
Mike Jones, prin. Fax 381-3378
Dunbar HS 2,100/9-12
1600 Man O War Blvd 40513 859-381-3546
Betsy Rains, prin. Fax 381-3560
Eastside Technical Center Vo/Tech
2208 Liberty Rd 40509 859-381-3740
Wade Stanfield, prin. Fax 381-3747
Hayes MS 900/6-8
260 Richardson Pl 40509 859-381-4920
Dave Hoskins, prin. Fax 381-4937
King Academy for Excellence 100/Alt
2200 Liberty Rd 40509 859-381-4040
Mark Sellers, dir. Fax 381-4031
Lafayette HS 1,900/9-12
401 Reed Ln 40503 859-381-3474
Bryne Jacobs, prin. Fax 381-3487
Learning Center at Linlee 100/Alt
2420 Spurr Rd 40511 859-381-0597
Chris Salyers, prin. Fax 246-1135
Leestown MS 600/6-8
2010 Leestown Rd 40511 859-381-3181
Cynthia Lawson, prin. Fax 381-3180
Lexington Traditional Magnet S 700/6-8
350 N Limestone 40508 859-381-3192
Jane Dreidame, prin. Fax 381-3199
Locust Trace AgriScience Center Vo/Tech
3591 Leestown Rd 40511 859-381-3990
Anne DeMott, prin. Fax 381-3989
Morton MS 800/6-8
1225 Tates Creek Rd 40502 859-381-3533
Ronda Runyon, prin. Fax 381-3536
Opportunity Middle College 100/11-12
1126 Russell Cave Rd 40505 859-246-6379
Frank LaBoone, prin. Fax 246-6889
School for Creative and Performing Arts 300/4-8
400 Lafayette Pkwy 40503 859-381-3332
Beth Randolph, prin. Fax 381-3334
Southern MS 700/6-8
400 Wilson Downing Rd 40517 859-381-3582
Frank Coffey, prin. Fax 381-3588
Southside Technical Center Vo/Tech
1800 Harrodsburg Rd 40504 859-381-3603
Daryn Morris, prin. Fax 381-3807
Stables Alt
1126 Russell Cave Rd 40505 859-333-5827
Racher Baker, dir. Fax 381-4312
STEAM Academy 200/9-12
123 E Sixth St 40508 859-381-3033
Tina Stevenson, dir. Fax 381-3059
Tates Creek HS 1,700/9-12
1111 Centre Pkwy 40517 859-381-3620
Sam Meaux, prin. Fax 381-3635
Tates Creek MS 800/6-8
1105 Centre Pkwy 40517 859-381-3052
Eric Thornsbury, prin. Fax 381-3053
Winburn MS 600/6-8
1060 Winburn Dr 40511 859-381-3967
Whitney Allison, prin. Fax 381-3971
Woodson Academy 200/Alt
1813 Charleston Dr 40505 859-381-3933
Jaynae Boateng, dir. Fax 381-4792

---

Blue Grass Baptist S 200/PK-12
3743 Red River Dr 40517 859-272-1217
Bluegrass Community & Technical College Post-Sec.
470 Cooper Dr 40506 859-246-6200
Employment Solutions Coll for Tech Educ Post-Sec.
1165 Centre Pkwy Ste 120 40517 859-272-5225
ITT Technical Institute Post-Sec.
2473 Fortune Dr Ste 180 40509 859-246-3300
Kaufman Beauty School Post-Sec.
701 E High St 40502 859-266-0693
Lexington Catholic HS 800/9-12
2250 Clays Mill Rd 40503 859-277-7183
Dr. Steve Angelucci, pres. Fax 276-5086
Lexington Christian Academy 1,600/PK-12
450 W Reynolds Rd 40503 859-422-5700
Lexington Junior Academy 50/K-10
968 Lane Allen Rd 40504 859-278-0295
Lexington Theological Seminary Post-Sec.
230 Lexington Green Cir 300 40503 859-252-0361
MedTech College Post-Sec.
1648 McGrathiana Pkwy # 200 40511 859-410-2110
National College Post-Sec.
2376 Sir Barton Way 40509 859-253-0621
St. Joseph's Hospital Post-Sec.
1 Saint Joseph Dr 40504 859-278-3436
Sayre S 500/PK-12
194 N Limestone 40507 859-254-1361
Stephen Manella, head sch Fax 231-0508
Spencerian College Post-Sec.
1575 Winchester Rd 40505 859-223-9608
Strayer University Post-Sec.
220 Lexington Green Cir 550 40503 859-971-4400
Sullivan University Post-Sec.
2355 Harrodsburg Rd 40504 859-276-4357
Transylvania University Post-Sec.
300 N Broadway 40508 859-233-8300
University of Kentucky 40506 Post-Sec.
859-257-9000
Univ. of Kentucky Chandler Medical Ctr. Post-Sec.
103 Administration Plz A311 40536 859-323-5126

**Liberty, Casey, Pop. 2,153**
Casey County SD 2,400/PK-12
1922 N US 127 42539 606-787-6941
Marion Sowders, supt. Fax 787-5231
www.casey.kyschools.us/
Casey County HS 700/9-12
1841 E KY 70 42539 606-787-6151
Joshua Blevins, prin. Fax 787-8654
Casey County MS 400/7-8
1673 E KY 70 42539 606-787-6769
Jeff Emerson, prin. Fax 787-5337

Kentucky Tech System
Supt. — See Frankfort
Casey County Area Technology Center Vo/Tech
1723 E KY 70 42539 606-787-6241
Carmela Clark, prin. Fax 787-6243

**Lick Creek, Pike, Pop. 221**
Pike County SD
Supt. — See Pikeville
East Ridge HS 600/9-12
19471 Lick Mountain Rd 41540 606-835-2811
Kevin Justice, prin. Fax 835-2899

**London, Laurel, Pop. 7,883**
Laurel County SD 9,300/PK-12
718 N Main St 40741 606-862-4600
Doug Bennett Ed.D., supt. Fax 862-4601
www.laurel.k12.ky.us
McDaniel Learning Center 50/Alt
275 S Laurel Rd 40744 606-862-4781
Jeremy Kidd, prin. Fax 862-4782
North Laurel HS 1,400/9-12
1300 E Hal Rogers Pkwy 40741 606-862-4699
Michael Black, prin. Fax 862-4701
North Laurel MS 1,100/6-8
101 Johnson Rd 40741 606-862-4715
Steve Morris, prin. Fax 862-4717
South Laurel HS 1,300/9-12
201 S Laurel Rd 40744 606-862-4727
Harmon Hodge, prin. Fax 862-4728
South Laurel MS 1,100/6-8
223 S Laurel Rd 40744 606-862-4745
Jeffrey Reed, prin. Fax 862-4746

**Lost Creek, Breathitt**

Riverside Christian S 50/K-12
114 Riverside School Rd 41348 606-666-2359
Meg Plummer, prin. Fax 666-5211

**Louisa, Lawrence, Pop. 2,448**
Lawrence County SD 2,400/PK-12
50 Bulldog Ln 41230 606-638-9671
Robbie Fletcher, supt. Fax 638-0128
www.lawrence.kyschools.us
Lawrence County HS 600/9-12
100 Bulldog Ln 41230 606-638-9676
Christy Moore, prin. Fax 638-3227
Louisa MS 400/6-8
9 Bulldog Ln 41230 606-638-4090
Thomas Castle, prin. Fax 638-4865

**Louisville, Jefferson, Pop. 248,762**
Jefferson County SD 96,500/PK-12
PO Box 34020 40232 502-485-3011
Dr. Donna Hargens, supt. Fax 485-3991
www.jcpsky.net
Academy @ Shawnee 500/6-12
4001 Herman St 40212 502-485-8326
Venita Benboe, prin. Fax 485-8738
Atherton HS 1,300/9-12
3000 Dundee Rd 40205 502-485-8202
Tom Aberli, prin. Fax 485-8985
Ballard HS 2,000/9-12
6000 Brownsboro Rd 40222 502-485-8206
Staci Eddleman, prin. Fax 485-8856
Barret Traditional MS 600/6-8
2561 Grinstead Dr 40206 502-485-8207
Tom Wortham, prin. Fax 485-8579
Breckinridge Metropolitan HS 100/Alt
1128 E Broadway 40204 502-485-6678
Stuart Cripe, prin. Fax 485-6680
Brown S 700/K-12
546 S 1st St 40202 502-485-8216
Angela Parsons, prin. Fax 485-8741
Butler Traditional HS 1,700/9-12
2222 Crums Ln 40216 502-485-8220
William Allen, prin. Fax 485-8517
Carrithers MS 500/6-8
4320 Billtown Rd 40299 502-485-8224
Marcela Williams, prin. Fax 485-8394
Central HS Magnet Career Academy 1,100/9-12
1130 W Chestnut St 40203 502-485-8226
Raymond Green, prin. Fax 485-7034
Conway MS 900/6-8
6300 Terry Rd 40258 502-485-8233
Gregory Fehr, prin. Fax 485-8076
Daniels Academy 200/Alt
1960 Bashford Manor Ln 40218 502-485-8316
Don Dillard, prin. Fax 485-8791
Doss HS Magnet Career Academy 900/9-12
7601 Saint Andrews Church 40214 502-485-8239
Marty Pollio, prin. Fax 485-8080
DuPont Manual HS 1,900/9-12
120 W Lee St 40208 502-485-8241
Jerry Mayes, prin. Fax 485-8035
DuValle Education Center 100/Alt
3610 Bohne Ave 40211 502-485-3558
Brian Clark, admin. Fax 485-6790
Farnsley MS 1,100/6-8
3400 Lees Ln 40216 502-485-8242
Linda Hudson, prin. Fax 485-8663
Highland MS 1,200/6-8
1700 Norris Pl 40205 502-485-8266
Steven Heckman, prin. Fax 485-8831
Iroquois HS Magnet Career Academy 1,100/9-12
4615 Taylor Blvd 40215 502-485-8269
Christopher Perkins, prin. Fax 485-8033
Jefferson County HS 600/Alt
900 S Floyd St 40203 502-485-3173
Jerry Keepers, prin. Fax 485-3671
Jefferson County Traditional MS 900/6-8
1418 Morton Ave 40204 502-485-8272
Teri Reed, prin. Fax 485-8635
Jefferson MS 1,000/6-8
1501 Rangeland Rd 40219 502-485-8273
Kimberly Gregory, prin. Fax 485-8045
Johnson Traditional MS 900/6-8
2509 Wilson Ave 40210 502-485-8277
Beverly Johnson, prin. Fax 485-8679
Kammerer MS 1,000/6-8
7315 Wesboro Rd 40222 502-485-8279
David Armour, prin. Fax 485-8618
Kennedy Metro MS 100/Alt
4515 Taylorsville Rd 40220 502-485-6950
Kevin Nix, prin. Fax 491-7290
Knight MS 400/6-8
9803 Blue Lick Rd 40229 502-485-8287
Catherine Gibbs, prin. Fax 485-8073
Lassiter MS 700/6-8
8200 Candleworth Dr 40214 502-485-8288
Jonathan Cesler, prin. Fax 485-8373
Liberty HS 300/Alt
3307 E Indian Trl 40213 502-485-7100
Iman Talaat, prin. Fax 485-7102
Louisville Male HS 1,700/9-12
4409 Preston Hwy 40213 502-485-8292
Jim Jury, prin. Fax 485-8770
Meyzeek MS 1,100/6-8
828 S Jackson St 40203 502-485-8299
Chris Burba, prin. Fax 485-8641
Moore Traditional MSHS 1,600/6-12
6415 Outer Loop 40228 502-485-8304
Vicki Lete, prin. Fax 485-8168
Myers MS 800/6-8
330 S Hubbards Ln 40207 502-485-8305
Katy Zeitz, prin. Fax 485-8157
Newburg MS 1,000/6-8
4901 Exeter Ave 40218 502-485-8306
Nicole Adell, prin. Fax 485-8883
Noe MS 1,300/6-8
121 W Lee St 40208 502-485-8307
Jennifer Cave, prin. Fax 485-8056
Olmsted Academy North 800/6-8
4530 Bellevue Ave 40215 502-485-8331
Ryan Rodosky, prin. Fax 485-8381
Olmsted Academy South 800/6-8
5650 Southern Pkwy 40214 502-485-8270
Angela Allen, prin. Fax 485-8380
Phoenix S of Discovery 300/Alt
3741 Pulliam Dr 40218 502-485-7700
Ken Moeller, prin. Fax 485-7701
Pleasure Ridge Park HS Magnet Academy 1,800/9-12
5901 Greenwood Rd 40258 502-485-8311
Kimberly Salyer, prin. Fax 485-8093
Ramsey MS 800/6-8
6409 Gellhaus Ln 40299 502-485-8391
Jennifer Colley, prin. Fax 485-8973
Seneca HS Magnet Career Academy 1,400/9-12
3510 Goldsmith Ln 40220 502-485-8323
Kim Harbolt, prin. Fax 485-8174
Southern HS Magnet Career Academy 1,200/9-12
8620 Preston Hwy 40219 502-485-8330
Bryce Hibbard, prin. Fax 485-8029
Waggener Traditional HS 800/9-12
330 S Hubbards Ln 40207 502-485-8340
Katy Zeitz, prin. Fax 485-8140
Western HS Early College 700/9-12
2501 Rockford Ln 40216 502-485-8344
Michael Newman, prin. Fax 485-8969
Western MS 300/6-8
2201 W Main St 40212 502-485-8345
Kymberly Rice, prin. Fax 485-8047
Westport MS 800/6-8
8100 Westport Rd 40222 502-485-8346
Jodie Zeller, prin. Fax 485-8590
Youth Performing Arts JSHS 7-12
1517 S 2nd St 40208 502-485-8355
Jerry Mayes, prin. Fax 485-8808
Other Schools – See Fairdale, Fern Creek, Jeffersontown, Middletown, Valley Station

Assumption HS 900/9-12
2170 Tyler Ln 40205 502-458-9551
Martha Tedesco, prin. Fax 454-8411
ATA College Post-Sec.
10180 Linn Station Rd #A200 40223 502-371-8383
Bellarmine University Post-Sec.
2001 Newburg Rd 40205 502-272-8131
Beth Haven Christian S 200/PK-12
5515 Johnsontown Rd 40272 502-937-3516
Diana Cahill, head sch Fax 937-3364
Brown Mackie College Post-Sec.
3605 Fern Valley Rd 40219 502-968-7191
Christian Academy of Louisville 1,700/PK-12
700 S English Station Rd 40245 502-244-3225
Linda Rafla, prin. Fax 244-1824
Covenant Classical Academy 50/K-12
13902 Factory Ln 40245 502-243-0404
R. Lance Harris, hdmstr.
Daymar College Post-Sec.
4112 Fern Valley Rd 40219 502-495-1040
Daymar College - Online Post-Sec.
3309 Collins Ln 40245 270-926-1188
DeVry University Post-Sec.
10172 Linn Station Rd # 300 40223 502-326-2860
Evangel Christian S 200/K-12
5400 Minor Ln 40219 502-968-7744
Dr. Roger Hoagland, supt. Fax 400-1906
Galen College of Nursing Post-Sec.
1031 Zorn Ave Ste 400 40207 502-410-6200
Hair Design School Post-Sec.
1049 Bardstown Rd 40204 502-459-8150
Hair Design School Post-Sec.
5120 Dixie Hwy 40216 502-447-0111
Hair Design School Post-Sec.
5314 Bardstown Rd 40291 502-499-0070
Holy Cross HS 200/9-12
5144 Dixie Hwy 40216 502-447-4363
Danielle Wiegandt, prin. Fax 448-1062
ITT Technical Institute Post-Sec.
9500 Ormsby Station Rd #100 40223 502-327-7424
Jefferson Community & Technical College Post-Sec.
109 E Broadway 40202 502-213-5333
Kentucky Country Day S 1,000/PK-12
4100 Springdale Rd 40241 502-423-0440
Brad Lyman, hdmstr. Fax 423-0445
Kentucky School for the Blind Post-Sec.
1867 Frankfort Ave 40206 502-897-1583
Louisville Bible College Post-Sec.
PO Box 91046 40291 502-231-5221
Louisville Collegiate S 700/PK-12
2427 Glenmary Ave 40204 502-479-0340
Dr. James Calleroz White, head sch Fax 454-8549
Louisville Jr. Academy 50/K-12
2988 Newburg Rd 40205 502-452-2965
David Matthews, prin. Fax 742-0829
Louisville Presbyterian Seminary Post-Sec.
1044 Alta Vista Rd 40205 502-895-3411
Mercy Academy 600/9-12
5801 Fegenbush Ln 40228 502-671-2010
Amy Elstone, prin. Fax 491-0661
National College Post-Sec.
4205 Dixie Hwy 40216 502-447-7634
Nativity Academy at St. Boniface 100/6-8
529 E Liberty St 40202 502-855-3300
Thomas Kallay, prin. Fax 562-2192
Paul Mitchell The School Post-Sec.
156 N Hurstbourne Pkwy 40222 502-583-1018
Portland Christian S East 200/K-12
8509 Westport Rd 40242 502-429-3727
Jodell Seay, dir. Fax 326-2682
Presentation Academy 300/9-12
861 S 4th St 40203 502-583-5935
Barbara Wine, prin. Fax 583-1342
Sacred Heart Academy 800/9-12
3175 Lexington Rd 40206 502-897-6097
Mary McCoy, prin. Fax 893-0120
Sacred Heart S for the Arts 200/K-12
3105 Lexington Rd 40206 502-897-1816
Dr. Anna Jo Paul, dir. Fax 896-3927
St. Francis DeSales HS 300/9-12
425 W Kenwood Dr 40214 502-368-6519
Suzanne Barnett, prin. Fax 366-6172
St. Francis S 100/PK-12
233 W Broadway 40202 502-736-1000
Alexandra Thurstone, head sch Fax 736-1049
St. Xavier HS 1,400/9-12
1609 Poplar Level Rd 40217 502-637-4712
Francisco Espinosa, prin. Fax 634-2171
Simmons College of Kentucky Post-Sec.
1018 S 7th St 40203 502-776-1443
Southern Baptist Theological Seminary Post-Sec.
2825 Lexington Rd 40280 502-897-4011
Spalding University Post-Sec.
845 S 3rd St 40203 502-585-9911
Spencerian College Post-Sec.
4627 Dixie Hwy 40216 502-447-1000
Sullivan College of Technology & Design Post-Sec.
3901 Atkinson Square Dr 40218 800-844-6528
Sullivan University Post-Sec.
3101 Bardstown Rd 40205 502-456-6505
Trend Setter's Academy of Beauty Culture Post-Sec.
7283 Dixie Hwy 40258 502-937-6816
Trend Setter's Academy of Beauty Culture Post-Sec.
8111 Preston Hwy 40219 502-962-7710
Trinity HS 1,300/9-12
4011 Shelbyville Rd 40207 502-895-9427
Daniel Zoeller, prin. Fax 895-6837
University of Louisville Post-Sec.
2301 S 3rd St 40208 502-852-5555
Valiant Christian Academy 100/PK-12
5627 New Cut Rd 40214 502-368-0080
Kristine Salvo, admin. Fax 361-5179
Valor Traditional Academy 100/K-12
11501 Schlatter Rd 40291 502-239-3345
Walden S 200/K-12
4238 Westport Rd 40207 502-893-0433
Ned Southworth, head sch Fax 895-8668
Whitefield Academy 700/PK-12
7711 Fegenbush Ln 40228 502-239-2509
Gary Mounce, head sch Fax 239-3144

**Ludlow, Kenton, Pop. 4,360**
Ludlow ISD 900/PK-12
525 Elm St 41016 859-261-8210
Mike Borchers, supt. Fax 291-6811
www.ludlow.kyschools.us/
Ludlow HS 400/7-12
515 Elm St 41016 859-261-8211
Travis Caudill, prin. Fax 655-7536

**Mc Kee, Jackson, Pop. 793**
Jackson County SD 2,300/PK-12
PO Box 217 40447 606-287-7181
Mike Smith, supt. Fax 287-8469
www.jackson.kyschools.us
Jackson County HS 600/9-12
PO Box 427 40447 606-287-7155
Keith Hays, prin. Fax 287-2123
Jackson County MS 500/6-8
PO Box 1329 40447 606-287-8351
Stephen Gabbard, prin. Fax 287-8360

Kentucky Tech System
Supt. — See Frankfort
Jackson County Area Technology Center Vo/Tech
PO Box 1509 40447 606-287-2163
Alonzo Moore, prin. Fax 287-7538

**Madisonville, Hopkins, Pop. 19,131**
Hopkins County SD 7,000/PK-12
320 S Seminary St 42431 270-825-6000
Linda Q. Zellich, supt. Fax 825-6072
www.hopkins.kyschools.us
Adolescent Day Treatment Center 50/Alt
110 Sugg St 42431 270-825-6059
Andy Belcher, prin. Fax 825-6053
Browning Springs MS 400/6-8
357 W Arch St 42431 270-825-6006
Jason Clark, prin. Fax 825-6009
Hopkins County Academy 50/Alt
150 School St 42431 270-825-6122
Andy Belcher, prin. Fax 825-6140
Hopkins County Central HS 900/9-12
6625 Hopkinsville Rd 42431 270-825-6133
Rick Snodgrass, prin. Fax 825-6135
Madison MS 500/6-8
510 Brown Rd 42431 270-825-6160
Timothy Roy, prin. Fax 825-6016
Madisonville North Hopkins HS 1,100/9-12
4515 Hanson Rd 42431 270-825-6017
Tommy Ransom, prin. Fax 825-6045
Other Schools – See Nortonville

Daymar College Post-Sec.
1105 National Mine Rd 42431 270-643-0312
Madisonville Community College Post-Sec.
2000 College Dr 42431 270-821-2250

**Manchester, Clay, Pop. 1,245**
Clay County SD 3,500/PK-12
128 Richmond Rd 40962 606-598-2168
William Sexton, supt. Fax 598-7829
www.clay.kyschools.us
Clay County HS 900/9-12
415 Clay County High Rd 40962 606-598-3737
Mike Gregory, prin. Fax 598-8976
Clay County MS 500/7-8
239 Richmond Rd 40962 606-598-1810
Steven Burchfield, prin. Fax 598-1230
Horse Creek Learning Center Alt S 50/Alt
1342 S Hwy 421 40962 606-598-1601
James Hollin, dir. Fax 599-0991

Kentucky Tech System
Supt. — See Frankfort
Clay County Area Technology Center Vo/Tech
1097 N Highway 11 40962 606-598-2194
Anthony Young, prin. Fax 598-4201

Southeast School of Cosmetology Post-Sec.
PO Box 493 40962 606-598-7901

**Marion, Crittenden, Pop. 3,006**
Crittenden County SD 1,300/K-12
601 W Elm St 42064 270-965-3525
Vince Clark, supt. Fax 965-9064
www.crittenden.kyschools.us/
Crittenden County HS 400/9-12
519 1/2 W Gum St 42064 270-965-2248
Curtis Brown, prin. Fax 965-2797
Crittenden County MS 300/6-8
519 W Gum St 42064 270-965-5221
Teresa Marshall, prin. Fax 965-5082

**Martin, Floyd, Pop. 630**
Floyd County SD
Supt. — See Prestonsburg
Renaissance Learning Center 50/Alt
PO Box 1390 41649 606-285-3634
Fax 285-3031

Kentucky Tech System
Supt. — See Frankfort
Floyd County Area Technology Center Vo/Tech
1024 KY Route 122 41649 606-285-3088
Lenville Martin, prin. Fax 285-0274

**Mayfield, Graves, Pop. 9,719**
Graves County SD 4,700/PK-12
2290 State Route 121 N 42066 270-328-2656
Kim Harrison, supt. Fax 328-1561
www.graves.kyschools.us
Gateway Academy HS 50/Alt
100 E Lockridge St 42066 270-328-4979
Donna Crouch, prin. Fax 247-0051
Graves County HS 1,400/9-12
1220 Eagles Way 42066 270-674-6242
Matt Madding, prin. Fax 247-8540
Graves County MS 700/7-8
625 Jimtown Rd 42066 270-674-4890
Jonathan Miller, prin. Fax 251-3693

Kentucky Tech System
Supt. — See Frankfort
Mayfield/Graves County Area Tech Center Vo/Tech
710 Douthitt St 42066 270-247-4710
Michael Miller, prin. Fax 247-4721

Mayfield ISD 1,500/PK-12
914 E College St 42066 270-247-3868
Lonnie Burgett, supt. Fax 247-3854
www.mayfield.kyschools.us/
Mayfield HS 400/9-12
700 Douthitt St 42066 270-247-4461
Don Hubbard, prin. Fax 247-9624
Mayfield MS 300/6-8
112 W College St 42066 270-247-7521
Kim Reed, prin. Fax 247-8297

Mid-Continent University Post-Sec.
99 E Powell Rd 42066 270-247-8521
Northside Baptist Christian S 100/PK-12
711 N 12th St 42066 270-247-0516
Shawn Marrs, prin. Fax 247-7125

**Maysville, Mason, Pop. 8,803**
Kentucky Tech System
Supt. — See Frankfort
Mason County Area Technology Center Vo/Tech
646 Kenton Station Rd 41056 606-759-7101
Jeremy McCloud, prin. Fax 759-7568

Mason County SD 2,900/PK-12
PO Box 130 41056 606-564-5563
Rick Ross, supt. Fax 564-5392
www.masoncoschools.com
Mason County HS 800/9-12
1320 US Highway 68 41056 606-564-3393
Chris O'Hearn, prin. Fax 564-5360
Mason County MS 700/6-8
420 Chenault Dr 41056 606-564-6748
Justin Moore, prin. Fax 564-5958

Maysville Community & Technical College Post-Sec.
1755 US Highway 68 41056 606-759-7141
St. Patrick S 300/PK-12
318 Limestone St 41056 606-564-5949
Anne Poe, prin. Fax 564-8795

**Middlesboro, Bell, Pop. 10,068**
Middlesboro ISD 1,300/PK-12
PO Box 959 40965 606-242-8800
Steve Martin, supt. Fax 242-8805
www.mboro.kyschools.us/
Middlesboro HS 400/9-12
4404 W Cumberland Ave 40965 606-242-8820
Bob Bennett, prin. Fax 242-8825
Middlesboro MS 300/5-8
4400 W Cumberland Ave 40965 606-242-8880
William Jones, prin. Fax 242-8885

Collins School of Cosmetology Post-Sec.
111 W Chester Ave 40965 606-248-3602

**Middletown, Jefferson, Pop. 7,092**
Jefferson County SD
Supt. — See Louisville
Crosby MS 1,400/6-8
303 Gatehouse Ln 40243 502-485-8235
Michael Kelly, prin. Fax 485-8424

Eastern HS 2,100/9-12
12400 Old Shelbyville Rd 40243 502-485-8243
Lana Kaelin, prin. Fax 485-3883

**Midway, Woodford, Pop. 1,609**

Midway College Post-Sec.
512 E Stephens St 40347 800-755-0031

**Monticello, Wayne, Pop. 6,123**
Kentucky Tech System
Supt. — See Frankfort
Wayne County Area Technology Center Vo/Tech
150 Cardinal Way 42633 606-348-8424
John Kinnett, prin. Fax 348-5090

Wayne County SD 1,800/PK-12
1025 S Main St 42633 606-348-8484
Wayne Roberts, supt. Fax 348-0734
www.wayne.kyschools.us
Lake Cumberland Youth Development Center 50/Alt
9000 Highway 1546 42633 606-348-4201
Tillie Slagle, lead tchr. Fax 348-7501
Otter Creek Academy 50/Alt
1441 Old Bethel Church Rd 42633 606-343-0203
Peggy Shearer, prin. Fax 343-0301
Wayne County HS 700/9-12
2 Kenny Davis Blvd 42633 606-348-5575
Brian Dishman, prin. Fax 348-3458
Wayne County MS 400/6-8
95 Champion Dr 42633 606-348-6691
Melissa Gossage, prin. Fax 348-5495

**Morehead, Rowan, Pop. 6,756**
Rowan County SD 3,300/PK-12
121 E 2nd St 40351 606-784-8928
Marvin Moore, supt. Fax 783-1011
www.rowan.kyschools.us/
Bluegrass Discovery Academy 50/Alt
415 W Sun St 40351 606-780-9992
Dr. Ray Ginter, prin. Fax 784-6167
Morehead Youth Development Center 50/Alt
495 Forest Hills Dr 40351 606-783-8575
Paula Stafford, prin. Fax 783-8572
Rowan County MS 700/6-8
555 Viking Dr 40351 606-784-8911
Jay Padula, prin. Fax 784-5579
Rowan County SHS 900/9-12
499 Viking Dr 40351 606-784-8956
Dr. Ray Ginter, prin. Fax 784-1067

Lakeside Christian Academy 200/PK-12
2535 US Highway 60 W 40351 606-784-2751
Adam Eldridge, admin. Fax 784-0056
Morehead State University Post-Sec.
150 University Blvd 40351 800-585-6781

**Morganfield, Union, Pop. 3,234**
Union County SD 2,300/PK-12
510 S Mart St 42437 270-389-1694
Patricia Sheffer, supt. Fax 389-9806
www.union.kyschools.us
Clements Victory Technical HS Vo/Tech
2302 US Highway 60 E 42437 270-389-2419
Holly Keeney, prin. Fax 389-9383
Union County HS 700/9-12
4464 US Highway 60 W 42437 270-389-1454
Evan Jackson, prin. Fax 389-2715
Union County Learning Academy 50/Alt
4464 US Highway 60 W 42437 270-389-3553
Brian Lovell, prin. Fax 389-3554
Union County MS 500/6-8
4465 US Highway 60 W 42437 270-389-0224
Jeremy Roach, prin. Fax 389-0245

**Morgantown, Butler, Pop. 2,380**
Butler County SD 2,100/PK-12
203 N Tyler St 42261 270-526-5624
Scott Howard, supt. Fax 526-5625
www.butlerschools.net
Butler County HS 600/9-12
1852 S Main St 42261 270-526-2204
Patrick O'Driscoll, prin. Fax 526-2268
Butler County Learning Center 50/Alt
178 Academic Way Ste 200 42261 270-526-2264
Ryan Emmick, lead tchr. Fax 526-2305
Butler County MS 500/6-8
PO Box 10 42261 270-526-5647
Tim Freeman, prin. Fax 526-3238

Kentucky Tech System
Supt. — See Frankfort
Butler County Area Technology Center Vo/Tech
179 Academic Way Ste 400 42261 270-526-2223
Ray Hammer, prin. Fax 526-2273

**Mount Olivet, Robertson, Pop. 297**
Robertson County SD 200/PK-12
1762 Sardis Rd 41064 606-724-5431
Sanford Holbrook, supt. Fax 724-5921
school.robertson.k12.ky.us
Robertson County S 200/PK-12
1760 Sardis Rd 41064 606-724-5421
Jamey Johnson, prin. Fax 724-5225

**Mount Sterling, Montgomery, Pop. 6,810**
Kentucky Tech System
Supt. — See Frankfort
Montgomery County Area Technology Ctr Vo/Tech
682 Woodford Dr 40353 859-498-1103
Melanie Jamison, prin. Fax 498-5960

Montgomery County SD 4,100/PK-12
640 Woodford Dr 40353 859-497-8760
Joshua Powell Ph.D., supt. Fax 497-8780
www.montgomery.kyschools.us
McNabb MS 800/7-8
3570 Indian Mound Dr 40353 859-497-8770
Larry Bailey, prin. Fax 497-9683
Montgomery County HS 1,300/9-12
724 Woodford Dr 40353 859-497-8765
Shannon White, prin. Fax 497-8705
Sterling S Alt
212 N Maysville St 40353 859-497-8761
Marty Dixon, admin. Fax 497-8780

Nu-Tek Academy of Beauty Post-Sec.
153 Evans Ave 40353 859-498-4460

**Mount Vernon, Rockcastle, Pop. 2,459**
Kentucky Tech System
Supt. — See Frankfort
Rockcastle County Area Technology Center Vo/Tech
1555 Lake Cumberland Rd 40456 606-256-4346
Ralph Baker, prin. Fax 256-4337

Rockcastle County SD 3,000/PK-12
245 Richmond St 40456 606-256-2125
David Pensol, supt. Fax 256-2126
www.rockcastle.kyschools.us/
Rockcastle Acad for Academic Achievement 50/Alt
PO Box 1730 40456 606-256-3846
Fax 256-1027
Rockcastle County HS 800/9-12
PO Box 1410 40456 606-256-4816
Jennifer Mattingly, prin. Fax 256-3755
Rockcastle County MS 600/6-8
PO Box 1730 40456 606-256-5118
Chris Hendrickson, prin. Fax 256-2622

**Mount Washington, Bullitt, Pop. 9,010**
Bullitt County SD
Supt. — See Shepherdsville
Bullitt East HS 1,300/9-12
11450 Highway 44 E 40047 502-869-6400
Willie Foster, prin. Fax 538-8368
Eastside MS 600/6-8
6925 Highway 44 E 40047 502-869-5000
Troy Wood, prin. Fax 538-0659
Mt. Washington MS 500/6-8
269 Water St 40047 502-869-5200
Dr. Denise Allen, prin. Fax 538-0703

**Munfordville, Hart, Pop. 1,588**
Hart County SD 2,400/PK-12
25 Quality St 42765 270-524-2631
Ricky Line, supt. Fax 524-2634
www.hart.kyschools.us
Hart County HS 700/9-12
1014 S Dixie Hwy 42765 270-524-9341
Greg Cecil, prin. Fax 524-3251

**Murray, Calloway, Pop. 17,409**
Calloway County SD 3,400/PK-12
PO Box 800 42071 270-762-7300
Tres Settle, supt. Fax 762-7310
www.calloway.kyschools.us
Alternative S Alt
2003 College Farm Rd 42071 270-762-7318
Travis Anderson, prin. Fax 762-7429
Calloway County HS 1,000/9-12
2108 College Farm Rd 42071 270-762-7374
Randy McCallon, prin. Fax 762-7380
Calloway County MS 700/6-8
2112 College Farm Rd 42071 270-762-7355
Amy Turner, prin. Fax 762-7360

Kentucky Tech System
Supt. — See Frankfort
Murray/Calloway County Area Tech Center Vo/Tech
1800 Sycamore St 42071 270-753-1870
James Hicks, prin. Fax 759-9656

Murray ISD 1,400/PK-12
208 S 13th St 42071 270-753-4363
Bob Rogers, supt. Fax 759-4906
www.murray.kyschools.us
Murray HS 400/9-12
501 Doran Rd 42071 270-753-5202
Teresa Speed, prin. Fax 753-8391
Murray MS 500/4-8
801 Main St 42071 270-753-5125
Lou Carter, prin. Fax 753-9039

Ezell's Cosmetology School Post-Sec.
PO Box 1431 42071 270-753-4723
Murray State University Post-Sec.
102 Curris Ctr 42071 800-272-4678

**Neon, Letcher, Pop. 749**
Letcher County SD
Supt. — See Whitesburg
Fleming Neon MS 100/6-8
PO Box 425 41840 606-855-7864
Terry Sturgill, prin. Fax 855-4485

**New Castle, Henry, Pop. 887**
Henry County SD 2,200/PK-12
326 S Main St 40050 502-845-8600
Tim Abrams, supt. Fax 845-8601
www.henry.kyschools.us
Henry County HS 700/9-12
1120 Eminence Rd 40050 502-845-8670
Shannon Sageser, prin. Fax 845-8671
Henry County MS 500/6-8
1124 Eminence Rd 40050 502-845-8660
Zach Woods, prin. Fax 845-8661

**Newport, Campbell, Pop. 14,797**
Newport ISD 1,800/PK-12
301 W 8th St 41071 859-292-3004
Kelly Middleton, supt. Fax 292-3073
www.newportwildcats.org/
Newport HS 400/9-12
900 E 6th St 41071 859-292-3023
Kyle Niederman, prin. Fax 292-8340
Newport MS 400/6-8
95 W 9th St 41071 859-292-3017
Tim Grayson, prin. Fax 292-3049

Newport Adult Learning Center — Adult
30 W 8th St 41071 — 859-292-3056
Nichole Braun, coord. — Fax 292-3099

---

Brighton Center for Employment Training — Post-Sec.
601 Washington Ave Ste 140 41071 — 859-491-8303
Holy Trinity JHS — 50/6-8
840 Washington Ave 41071 — 859-292-0487
James Hubbard, prin. — Fax 431-8745
Newport Central Catholic HS — 400/9-12
13 Carothers Rd 41071 — 859-292-0001
Jason Huther, prin. — Fax 292-0656

**Nicholasville, Jessamine, Pop. 27,423**
Jessamine County SD — 7,900/PK-12
871 Wilmore Rd 40356 — 859-885-4179
Kathy Fields, supt. — Fax 887-4811
www.jessamine.k12.ky.us
East Jessamine HS — 1,000/9-12
815 Sulphur Well Pike 40356 — 859-885-7240
Aaron Etherington, prin. — Fax 881-0161
East Jessamine MS — 900/6-8
901 Union Mill Rd 40356 — 859-885-5561
James Botts, prin. — Fax 887-1797
West Jessamine HS — 1,100/9-12
2101 Wilmore Rd 40356 — 859-887-2421
Dr. Scott Wells, prin. — Fax 887-8854
West Jessamine MS — 900/6-8
1400 Wilmore Rd 40356 — 859-885-2244
James Freeman, prin. — Fax 885-8078
Jessamine County Adult Education — Adult
200 Computrex Dr 40356 — 859-887-9052
Mary Davis, prin. — Fax 881-0521
Other Schools – See Wilmore

---

Barrett & Company School of Hair Design — Post-Sec.
973 Kimberly Sq 40356 — 859-885-9136

**Nortonville, Hopkins, Pop. 1,195**
Hopkins County SD
Supt. — See Madisonville
South Hopkins MS — 500/6-8
9140 Hopkinsville Rd 42442 — 270-825-6125
Stuart Fitch, prin. — Fax 825-6085

**Olive Hill, Carter, Pop. 1,580**
Carter County SD
Supt. — See Grayson
Carter County Career & Technical Center — Vo/Tech
15 Grahn Rd 41164 — 606-286-4022
Steve Stubbs, prin. — Fax 286-6333
West Carter County HS — 600/9-12
PO Box 1479 41164 — 606-286-2481
John Baumgardner, prin. — Fax 286-8026
West Carter County MS — 500/6-8
150 Warrior Dr 41164 — 606-286-5354
Ryan Tomolonis, prin. — Fax 286-8556

**Oneida, Clay, Pop. 406**

---

Oneida Baptist Institute — 300/K-12
PO Box 67 40972 — 606-847-4111
Rev. David Robinson M.Ed., prin. — Fax 847-4496

**Owensboro, Daviess, Pop. 55,842**
Daviess County SD — 11,400/PK-12
PO Box 21510 42304 — 270-852-7000
Owens Saylor, supt. — Fax 852-7010
www.daviess.kyschools.us/
Apollo HS — 1,300/9-12
2280 Tamarack Rd 42301 — 270-852-7100
Charles Broughton, prin. — Fax 852-7110
Beacon Central Alternative S — 100/Alt
3361 Buckland Sq 42301 — 270-852-7200
Michelle Ruckdeschel, dir. — Fax 852-7210
Burns MS — 800/6-8
4610 Goetz Dr 42301 — 270-852-7400
Dane Ferguson, prin. — Fax 852-7410
College View MS — 800/6-8
5061 New Hartford Rd 42303 — 270-852-7500
Jennifer Crume, prin. — Fax 852-7510
Daviess County HS — 1,600/9-12
4255 New Hartford Rd 42303 — 270-852-7300
Matt Mason, prin. — Fax 852-7310
Daviess County MS — 800/6-8
1415 E 4th St 42303 — 270-852-7600
Kelly Skeens, prin. — Fax 852-7610

Owensboro ISD — 4,500/PK-12
450 Griffith Ave 42301 — 270-686-1000
Dr. Nicholas Brake, supt. — Fax 684-5756
www.owensboro.kyschools.us
Gateway Academy — 50/Alt
2401 McConnell Ave 42303 — 270-686-1120
Melissa Brown, prin. — Fax 686-1036
Owensboro HS — 1,000/9-12
1800 Frederica St 42301 — 270-686-1110
John DeLacey, prin. — Fax 686-1019
Owensboro MS - North Campus — 600/7-8
1300 Booth Ave 42301 — 270-686-1130
George Powell, prin. — Fax 686-1173

---

Brescia University — Post-Sec.
717 Frederica St 42301 — 270-685-3131
Daymar College — Post-Sec.
3361 Buckland Sq 42301 — 270-926-4040
Kentucky Wesleyan College — Post-Sec.
3000 Frederica St 42301 — 270-926-3111
Mr. Jim's College of Cosmetology — Post-Sec.
1240 Carter Rd 42301 — 270-684-3505
Owensboro Catholic HS — 500/9-12
1524 W Parrish Ave 42301 — 270-684-3215
Gates Settle, prin. — Fax 684-7050
Owensboro Catholic MS — 200/7-8
2540 Christie Pl 42301 — 270-683-0480
David Kessler, prin. — Fax 683-0495
Owensboro Community & Technical College — Post-Sec.
4800 New Hartford Rd 42303 — 270-686-4400
Owensboro Mercy Health System — Post-Sec.
811 E Parrish Ave 42303 — 270-688-2100

**Owenton, Owen, Pop. 1,301**
Owen County SD — 1,900/PK-12
1600 Highway 22 E 40359 — 502-484-3934
Dr. Rob Stafford, supt. — Fax 484-9095
www.owen.kyschools.us
Bowling MS — 600/5-8
2380 Highway 22 E 40359 — 502-484-5701
Donette Gaines, prin. — Fax 484-3044
Owen County HS — 500/9-12
2340 Highway 22 E 40359 — 502-484-5509
Duane Kline, prin. — Fax 484-0444

**Owingsville, Bath, Pop. 1,507**
Bath County SD — 2,100/PK-12
405 W Main St 40360 — 606-674-6314
Harvey Tackett, supt. — Fax 674-2647
www.bath.kyschools.us
Bath County HS — 600/9-12
645 Chenault Dr 40360 — 606-674-6325
Paul Prater, prin. — Fax 674-9188
Bath County MS — 500/6-8
335 W Main St 40360 — 606-674-8165
John Slone, prin. — Fax 674-2676

**Paducah, McCracken, Pop. 24,294**
Kentucky Tech System
Supt. — See Frankfort
Paducah Area Technology Center — Vo/Tech
2400 Adams St 42003 — 270-443-6592
Donald Wann, prin. — Fax 442-6233

McCracken County SD — 5,200/PK-12
5347 Benton Rd 42003 — 270-538-4000
Quin Sutton, supt. — Fax 538-4001
www.mccracken.kyschools.us/
Commonwealth Middle College HS — 11-12
4810 Alben Barkley Dr 42001 — 270-534-3350
Mindy Wilham, prin.
Lone Oak MS — 800/6-8
225 John E Robinson Dr 42001 — 270-538-4130
Brent Buchanan, prin. — Fax 538-4131
McCracken County HS — 9-12
6530 US Highway 60 W 42001 — 270-538-4300
Michael Ceglinski, prin. — Fax 538-4301
Reidland MS — 400/6-8
5347 Benton Rd 42003 — 270-538-4190
Susan Nelson, prin. — Fax 538-4191
Other Schools – See West Paducah

Paducah ISD — 3,000/PK-12
PO Box 2550 42002 — 270-444-5600
Donald Shively, supt. — Fax 444-5607
www.paducah.kyschools.us/
Paducah MS — 600/6-8
342 Lone Oak Rd 42001 — 270-444-5710
Stacey Overlin, prin. — Fax 444-5709
Paducah Tilghman HS — 800/9-12
2400 Washington St 42003 — 270-444-5650
Arthur Davis, prin. — Fax 444-5659

---

Community Christian Academy — 200/K-12
110 Lebanon Church Rd 42003 — 270-554-1651
Anna Thomas, prin. — Fax 554-6968
Daymar College — Post-Sec.
509 S 30th St 42001 — 270-444-9950
St. Mary HS — 200/9-12
1243 Elmdale Rd 42003 — 270-442-1681
Lisa Aly, prin. — Fax 442-7920
St. Mary MS — 100/6-8
1243 Elmdale Rd 42003 — 270-442-1681
Lisa Aly, prin. — Fax 442-7920
West Kentucky Comm. & Technical College — Post-Sec.
4810 Alben Barkley Dr 42001 — 270-554-9200

**Paintsville, Johnson, Pop. 3,422**
Johnson County SD — 3,800/PK-12
253 N Mayo Trl 41240 — 606-789-2530
Thomas Salyer, supt. — Fax 789-2506
www.johnson.kyschools.us/
Johnson Central HS — 1,000/9-12
257 N Mayo Trl 41240 — 606-789-2500
Russell Halsey, prin. — Fax 789-2547
Johnson County Alternative S — 50/Alt
257 N Mayo Trl 41240 — 606-789-2077
Ben Hamilton, prin. — Fax 789-2525
Johnson County MS — 600/7-8
251 N Mayo Trl 41240 — 606-789-4133
Joey Estep, prin. — Fax 789-4135

Paintsville ISD — 800/PK-12
305 2nd St 41240 — 606-789-2654
Coy Samons, supt. — Fax 789-7412
www.paintsville.kyschools.us/
Paintsville MSHS — 300/7-12
225 2nd St 41240 — 606-789-2656
Chuck McClure, prin. — Fax 789-2582
Other Schools – See Prestonsburg

**Paris, Bourbon, Pop. 8,356**
Bourbon County SD — 3,000/PK-12
3343 Lexington Rd 40361 — 859-987-2180
Amy Baker, supt. — Fax 987-2182
www.bourbon.kyschools.us/
Bourbon County HS — 900/9-12
3341 Lexington Rd 40361 — 859-987-2185
David Horseman, prin. — Fax 987-5850
Bourbon County MS — 600/6-8
3339 Lexington Rd 40361 — 859-987-2189
Travis Earlywine, prin. — Fax 987-5854

Paris ISD — 700/PK-12
310 W 7th St 40361 — 859-987-2160
Gary Wiseman, supt. — Fax 987-6749
www.paris.kyschools.us
Paris HS — 200/9-12
308 W 7th St 40361 — 859-987-2168
Jami Dailey, prin. — Fax 987-2132
Paris MS — 200/6-8
304 W 7th St 40361 — 859-987-2163
Jami Dailey, prin. — Fax 987-2164

**Park Hills, Kenton, Pop. 2,906**

---

Notre Dame Academy — 600/9-12
1699 Hilton Dr 41011 — 859-261-4300
Dr. Laura Koehl, prin. — Fax 292-7722

**Phelps, Pike, Pop. 888**
Pike County SD
Supt. — See Pikeville
Phelps HS — 400/7-12
PO Box 925 41553 — 606-456-3482
Mike Hamilton, prin. — Fax 456-8988

**Pikeville, Pike, Pop. 6,797**
Kentucky Tech System
Supt. — See Frankfort
Millard Area Technology Center — Vo/Tech
7925 Millard Hwy 41501 — 606-437-6059
Jim Hamilton, prin. — Fax 437-0502

Pike County SD — 8,800/K-12
316 S Mayo Trl 41501 — 606-433-9200
David Lester, supt. — Fax 432-3321
www.pike.kyschools.us
Northpoint Academy — Alt
5279 N Mayo Trl 41501 — 606-433-0181
Harold Wallace, prin. — Fax 433-0626
Pike County Central HS — 700/9-12
100 Winners Circle Dr 41501 — 606-432-4352
David Rowe, prin. — Fax 432-7733
Shelby Valley HS — 600/9-12
125 Douglas Park 41501 — 606-639-0033
Greg Napier, prin. — Fax 639-2074
Other Schools – See Belfry, Lick Creek, Phelps

Pikeville ISD — 1,200/PK-12
148 2nd St 41501 — 606-432-8161
Jerry Green, supt. — Fax 432-2119
www.pikeville.kyschools.us
Pikeville JSHS — 500/7-12
120 Championship Dr 41501 — 606-432-0185
David Thomas, prin. — Fax 432-2022

---

East Kentucky Beauty College — Post-Sec.
5333 N Mayo Trl 41501 — 606-432-3627
National College — Post-Sec.
50 National College Blvd 41501 — 606-478-7200
Pikeville Medical Center — Post-Sec.
911 Bypass Rd 41501 — 606-437-3500
University of Pikeville — Post-Sec.
147 Sycamore St 41501 — 606-218-5250

**Pineville, Bell, Pop. 1,711**
Bell County SD — 3,000/PK-12
PO Box 340 40977 — 606-337-7051
Yvonne Gilliam, supt. — Fax 337-1412
www.bell.kyschools.us
Bell County Alternative S — 50/Alt
9828 US Highway 25 E 40977 — 606-337-0957
John Lefevers, prin. — Fax 337-7103
Bell County HS — 800/9-12
9824 US Highway 25 E 40977 — 606-337-7061
Richard Gambrel, prin. — Fax 337-0867

Kentucky Tech System
Supt. — See Frankfort
Bell County Area Technology Center — Vo/Tech
9828 US Highway 25 E 40977 — 606-337-3094
David Sowders, prin. — Fax 337-9053

Pineville ISD — 600/PK-12
401 W Virginia Ave 40977 — 606-337-5701
Terry Hayes, supt. — Fax 337-9983
www.pineville.kyschools.us
Pineville JSHS — 300/7-12
401 W Virginia Ave 40977 — 606-337-5701
William Keyes, prin. — Fax 337-3720

---

Clear Creek Baptist Bible College — Post-Sec.
300 Clear Creek Rd 40977 — 606-337-3196

**Pippa Passes, Knott, Pop. 530**

---

Alice Lloyd College — Post-Sec.
100 Purpose Rd 41844 — 606-368-6000
Buchanan S — 100/K-12
100 Purpose Rd 41844 — 606-368-6108

**Pleasureville, Henry, Pop. 817**
Shelby County SD
Supt. — See Shelbyville
Shelby County Education Center — 100/Alt
8472 Cropper Rd 40057 — 502-461-7540
Steve Coleman, prin. — Fax 461-9021

**Powderly, Muhlenberg, Pop. 738**
Muhlenberg County SD — 5,500/PK-12
510 W Main St 42367 — 270-338-2871
Randy McCarty, supt. — Fax 338-0529
www.mberg.k12.ky.us/
Other Schools – See Greenville

**Prestonsburg, Floyd, Pop. 3,226**
Floyd County SD — 5,900/K-12
106 N Front Ave 41653 — 606-886-2354
Henry Webb, supt. — Fax 886-8862
www.floyd.kyschools.us
Adams MS — 300/6-8
2520 S Lake Dr 41653 — 606-886-2671
Thomas Poe, prin. — Fax 886-7026
Prestonsburg HS — 600/9-12
825 Blackcat Blvd 41653 — 606-886-2252
Jerry Butcher, prin. — Fax 886-1745
Other Schools – See Eastern, Hi Hat, Martin, Stanville

Paintsville ISD
Supt. — See Paintsville
Perkins Job Corp Academy 100/Alt
478 Meadows Br 41653 606-886-1037
John Brown, prin. Fax 886-6048

---

Big Sandy Community & Technical College Post-Sec.
1 Bert Combs Dr 41653 606-886-3863

**Princeton, Caldwell, Pop. 6,185**
Caldwell County SD 2,100/PK-12
PO Box 229 42445 270-365-8000
Carrell Boyd, supt. Fax 365-5742
www.caldwell.kyschools.us/
Caldwell County HS 600/9-12
350 Beckner Ln 42445 270-365-8010
Christy Phelps, prin. Fax 365-9742
Caldwell County MS 400/6-8
440 Beckner Ln 42445 270-365-8020
Steve Smiley, prin. Fax 365-9573

Kentucky Tech System
Supt. — See Frankfort
Caldwell County Area Technology Center Vo/Tech
130 Vocational School Rd 42445 270-365-5563
Donna Wolfe, prin. Fax 365-5609

**Raceland, Greenup, Pop. 2,412**
Raceland-Worthington ISD 1,100/PK-12
600 Rams Blvd 41169 606-836-2144
Larry Coldiron, supt. Fax 833-5807
www.raceland.kyschools.us
Raceland-Worthington HS 500/7-12
500 Rams Blvd 41169 606-836-8221
Mickey Dixon, prin. Fax 494-2341
Other Schools – See Ashland

**Radcliff, Hardin, Pop. 20,329**
Hardin County SD
Supt. — See Elizabethtown
North Hardin HS 1,400/9-12
801 S Logsdon Pkwy 40160 270-351-3167
Lonnie Dennis, prin. Fax 352-4512
North MS 500/6-8
100 Trojan Way 40160 270-352-3340
Chris Bauer, prin. Fax 352-3341

---

North Hardin Christian S 500/PK-12
1298 Rogersville Rd 40160 270-351-7700

**Richmond, Madison, Pop. 30,594**
Kentucky Tech System
Supt. — See Frankfort
Madison County Area Technology Center Vo/Tech
PO Box 809 40476 859-624-4520
Diana Gordon, prin. Fax 624-9659

Madison County SD 10,100/PK-12
PO Box 768 40476 859-624-4500
Elmer Thomas, supt. Fax 624-4508
www.madison.kyschools.us
Caudill MS 600/6-8
1428 Robert R Martin Bypass 40475 859-625-6172
Che Haselwood, prin. Fax 623-2652
Clark-Moores MS 500/6-8
1143 Berea Rd 40475 859-624-4545
Vickie Fritz, prin. Fax 624-4534
Madison Central HS 1,700/9-12
705 N 2nd St 40475 859-625-6109
Drew Muntz, prin. Fax 623-3925
Madison MS 400/6-8
101 Summit St 40475 859-624-4550
Amie Gallion, prin. Fax 624-4543
Other Schools – See Berea

---

Eastern Kentucky University Post-Sec.
521 Lancaster Ave 40475 859-622-1000
National College Post-Sec.
125 S Killarney Ln 40475 859-623-8956

**Rush, Boyd**
Boyd County SD
Supt. — See Ashland
Ramey-Estep HS 100/7-12
2901 Pigeon Roost Rd 41168 606-928-5801
Elizabeth Brewster, prin. Fax 928-2145

**Russell, Greenup, Pop. 3,354**
Kentucky Tech System
Supt. — See Frankfort
Russell Area Technology Center Vo/Tech
705 Red Devil Ln 41169 606-836-1256
David Trimble, prin. Fax 836-3784

Russell ISD 2,200/PK-12
409 Belfonte St 41169 606-836-9679
M. Sean Horne, supt. Fax 836-2865
www.russellind.kyschools.us
Russell HS 600/9-12
709 Red Devil Ln 41169 606-836-9658
Anna Chaffin, prin. Fax 836-9650
Russell MS 500/6-8
707 Red Devil Ln 41169 606-836-8135
Shawn Moore, prin. Fax 836-0614

**Russell Springs, Russell, Pop. 2,403**
Kentucky Tech System
Supt. — See Frankfort
Lake Cumberland Area Technology Center Vo/Tech
2330 S Highway 127 42642 270-866-6175
Jeff Adams, prin. Fax 866-2424

Russell County SD
Supt. — See Jamestown
Russell County HS 900/9-12
2166 S Highway 127 42642 270-866-3341
Shannon Williams, prin. Fax 866-8830
Russell County MS 400/6-8
2258 S Highway 127 42642 270-866-2224
Wayne Ackerman, prin. Fax 866-8679

**Russellville, Logan, Pop. 6,795**
Kentucky Tech System
Supt. — See Frankfort
Russellville Area Technology Center Vo/Tech
1103 W 9th St 42276 270-726-8432
Elizabeth Frogue, prin. Fax 726-6303

Logan County SD 3,600/PK-12
PO Box 417 42276 270-726-2436
Dr. Kevin Hub, supt. Fax 726-8892
www.logan.kyschools.us
Logan County HS 1,100/9-12
2200 Bowling Green Rd 42276 270-726-8454
Wilson C. Jaynes, prin. Fax 726-1108

Russellville ISD 1,000/PK-12
355 S Summer St 42276 270-726-8405
Leon Smith, supt. Fax 726-4036
www.russellville.kyschools.us/
Russellville JSHS 400/6-12
1101 W 9th St 42276 270-726-8421
Kim McDaniel, prin. Fax 726-3685

---

Daymar College Post-Sec.
206 Sam Walton Dr 42276 270-726-8311

**Saint Catharine, Washington**

---

Saint Catharine College Post-Sec.
2735 Bardstown Rd 40061 859-336-5082

**Salyersville, Magoffin, Pop. 1,875**
Magoffin County SD 2,400/PK-12
PO Box 109 41465 606-349-6117
Stanley Holbrook, supt. Fax 349-3417
www.magoffin.kyschools.us
Magoffin County Career & Technical Ctr Vo/Tech
209 Hornet Dr 41465 606-349-5188
Vince Minix, dir. Fax 349-5345
Magoffin County HS 600/9-12
201 Hornet Dr 41465 606-349-2011
Tony Skaggs, prin. Fax 349-5345
Whitaker MS 300/7-8
221 Hornet Dr 41465 606-349-5190
Johnnie Johnson, prin. Fax 349-5139

**Sandy Hook, Elliott, Pop. 666**
Elliott County SD 1,100/K-12
PO Box 767 41171 606-738-8002
Dr. C. Thomas Potter Ed.D., supt. Fax 738-8050
www.elliott.kyschools.us
Elliott County JSHS 500/7-12
PO Box 687 41171 606-738-8052
Zachary Mayse, prin. Fax 738-8000

**Scottsville, Allen, Pop. 4,154**
Allen County SD 3,400/PK-12
570 Oliver St 42164 270-618-3181
Randall Jackson, supt. Fax 618-3185
www.allen.kyschools.us
Allen County Scottsville HS 900/9-12
1545 Bowling Green Rd 42164 270-622-4119
Shane Davis, prin. Fax 622-5882
Allen County Technical Center Vo/Tech
1585 Bowling Green Rd 42164 270-622-4711
Josephy Cosby, dir. Fax 622-7006
Bazzell MS 500/7-8
201 New Gallatin Rd 42164 270-622-7140
Melissa Towery, prin. Fax 622-4649

---

Daymar College Post-Sec.
1138 Old Gallatin Rd 42164 270-237-3577

**Shelbyville, Shelby, Pop. 13,656**
Kentucky Tech System
Supt. — See Frankfort
Shelby County Area Technology Center Vo/Tech
230 Rocket Ln 40065 502-633-6554
Steve Coleman, prin. Fax 633-4212

Shelby County SD 6,800/PK-12
PO Box 159 40066 502-633-2375
James Neihof, supt. Fax 633-1988
www.shelby.kyschools.us
Collins HS 1,200/8-12
801 Discovery Blvd 40065 502-647-1160
John Leeper, prin. Fax 647-1161
Shelby County HS 1,200/8-12
1701 Frankfort Rd 40065 502-633-2344
Eddie Oakley, prin. Fax 647-0238
Other Schools – See Pleasureville

---

Cornerstone Christian Academy 200/PK-12
3850 Frankfort Rd 40065 502-633-4070
David Ladner, hdmstr. Fax 633-4605

**Shepherdsville, Bullitt, Pop. 11,048**
Bullitt County SD 13,000/PK-12
1040 Highway 44 E 40165 502-869-8000
Keith Davis, supt. Fax 543-3608
www.bullittschools.org
Bernheim MS 500/6-8
700 Audubon Dr 40165 502-869-4000
Troy Kolb, prin. Fax 543-5299
Bullitt Central HS 1,200/9-12
1330 Highway 44 E 40165 502-869-6000
Jim Beavers, prin. Fax 543-1797
Bullitt Lick MS 400/6-8
555 W Blue Lick Rd 40165 502-869-5400
Lee Barger, prin. Fax 543-1685
Hebron MS 400/6-8
3300 E Hebron Ln 40165 502-869-4200
Steve Miracle, prin. Fax 957-6014
North Bullitt HS 1,300/9-12
3200 E Hebron Ln 40165 502-869-6200
Rob Fulk, prin. Fax 957-6762
Riverview Opportunity Center 100/Alt
383 High School Dr 40165 502-869-6600
Angela Bibelhauser, prin. Fax 543-1792

Zoneton MS 500/6-8
797 Old Preston Hwy N 40165 502-869-4400
Kathy House, prin. Fax 955-7027
Other Schools – See Mount Washington

Kentucky Tech System
Supt. — See Frankfort
Bullitt County Area Technology Center Vo/Tech
395 High School Dr 40165 502-543-7018
Brady Southwood, prin. Fax 543-1691

---

Little Flock Christian Academy 200/K-12
5500 N Preston Hwy 40165 502-957-7686
Rick Grice, prin. Fax 957-4122

**Silver Grove, Campbell, Pop. 1,083**
Silver Grove ISD 300/PK-12
PO Box 400 41085 859-441-3894
Ken Ellis, supt. Fax 441-4299
www.silvergrove.kyschools.us
Silver Grove S 300/PK-12
PO Box 400 41085 859-441-3873
Wes Murray, prin. Fax 441-4299

**Smithland, Livingston, Pop. 299**
Livingston County SD 1,300/PK-12
127 E Adair St 42081 270-928-2111
Darryl Chittenden, supt. Fax 928-2112
www.livingston.kyschools.us/
Livingston Central HS 400/9-12
750 US Highway 60 W 42081 270-928-2065
Scott Gray, prin. Fax 928-2066
Other Schools – See Burna

**Somerset, Pulaski, Pop. 11,017**
Kentucky Tech System
Supt. — See Frankfort
Pulaski County Area Technology Center Vo/Tech
3865 S Highway 27 Ste 101 42501 606-678-2998
Beth Hargis, prin. Fax 678-3032

Pulaski County SD 7,800/PK-12
PO Box 1055 42502 606-679-1123
Steve Butcher, supt. Fax 679-1438
www.pulaski.net
Northern MS 900/6-8
650 Oak Leaf Ln 42503 606-678-5230
Shelly Hargis, prin. Fax 678-2729
Pulaski County Day Treatment 100/Alt
500 Chandler St 42501 606-677-9986
Tammy Roberts, admin. Fax 677-9885
Pulaski County HS 1,100/9-12
511 E University Dr 42503 606-679-1574
Rodney McAninch, prin. Fax 677-2771
Southern MS 1,000/6-8
200 Enterprise Dr 42501 606-679-6855
Brett McQueary, prin. Fax 679-2270
Southwestern HS 1,200/9-12
1765 WTLO Rd 42503 606-678-9000
Danita Ellis, prin. Fax 678-9277

Somerset ISD 1,600/PK-12
305 College St 42501 606-679-4451
Boyd Randolph, supt. Fax 678-0864
www.somerset.kyschools.us
Meece MS 400/5-8
210 Barnett St 42501 606-678-5821
Calvin Rollyson, prin. Fax 678-2934
Somerset HS 500/9-12
301 College St 42501 606-678-4721
Wesley Cornett, prin. Fax 677-0087

---

Somerset Christian S 300/PK-12
815 Grand Central Blvd 42503 606-451-1600
John Hale, prin. Fax 677-9850
Somerset Community College Post-Sec.
808 Monticello St 42501 877-629-9722

**S Portsmouth, Greenup**

---

Harvest Christian Academy 100/K-12
PO Box 398 41174 606-932-3007
Ashley Pelfrey, admin. Fax 453-1635

**South Shore, Greenup, Pop. 1,096**
Greenup County SD
Supt. — See Greenup
McKell MS 300/6-8
129 Bulldog Ln 41175 606-932-3221
Nathan Sutton, prin. Fax 932-9844

**Springfield, Washington, Pop. 2,454**
Washington County SD 1,700/PK-12
PO Box 72 40069 859-336-5470
Dr. Robin Cochran Ed.D., supt. Fax 336-5480
www.washington.kyschools.us
Washington County HS 600/9-12
300 W US 150 Bypass 40069 859-336-5475
William Elmore, prin. Fax 336-5983
Washington County MS 200/6-8
603 Lincoln Park Rd 40069 859-336-5475
Tyler Howard, prin. Fax 336-5477

**Stanford, Lincoln, Pop. 3,439**
Kentucky Tech System
Supt. — See Frankfort
Lincoln County Area Technology Center Vo/Tech
422 Education Way 40484 606-365-8500
Amy Tracy, prin. Fax 365-8504

Lincoln County SD 4,100/PK-12
PO Box 265 40484 606-365-2124
Karen Hatter, supt. Fax 365-1660
www.lincoln.kyschools.us
Fort Logan Alternative JSHS 50/Alt
PO Box 265 40484 606-365-1333
Scott Montgomery, prin. Fax 365-4020
Lincoln County HS 1,100/9-12
60 Education Way 40484 606-365-9111
Fax 365-1750

Lincoln County MS 600/7-8
285 Education Way 40484 606-365-8400
Debbie Sims, prin. Fax 365-8600

**Stanton, Powell, Pop. 2,713**
Powell County SD 2,400/PK-12
PO Box 430 40380 606-663-3300
Michael Tate, supt. Fax 663-3303
www.powell.kyschools.us
Powell County Alternative S 50/Alt
PO Box 430 40380 606-663-3505
Kenny Rice, dir. Fax 663-3303
Powell County HS 700/9-12
700 W College Ave 40380 606-663-3320
Kendall Kearns, prin. Fax 663-3406
Powell County MS 500/6-8
770 W College Ave 40380 606-663-3308
Tiffany Anderson, prin. Fax 663-3307

**Stanville, Floyd**
Floyd County SD
Supt. — See Prestonsburg
Betsy Layne HS 400/9-12
554 Bobcat Blvd 41659 606-478-9138
Cassandra Akers, prin. Fax 478-3805

**Stearns, McCreary, Pop. 1,397**
McCreary County SD 3,100/PK-12
120 Raider Way 42647 606-376-2591
Michael Cash, supt. Fax 376-5584
www.mccreary.kyschools.us
McCreary Central Academy 100/Alt
400 Raider Way 42647 606-376-1477
Fax 376-1478
McCreary Central HS 800/9-12
400 Raider Way 42647 606-376-5051
Sharon Privett, prin. Fax 376-3005
McCreary County MS 400/7-8
180 Raider Way 42647 606-376-5081
Clint Taylor, prin. Fax 376-9580

**Taylor Mill, Kenton, Pop. 6,506**
Kenton County SD
Supt. — See Fort Wright
Scott HS 1,000/9-12
5400 Old Taylor Mill Rd 41015 859-356-3146
Dr. Brennon Sapp, prin. Fax 356-5516
Woodland MS 800/6-8
5399 Old Taylor Mill Rd 41015 859-356-7300
Fax 356-7595

**Taylorsville, Spencer, Pop. 749**
Spencer County SD 2,800/PK-12
207 W Main St 40071 502-477-3250
Charles Adams, supt. Fax 477-3259
publicschools.spencercounty.ky.gov
Hillview Academy 50/Alt
PO Box 249 40071 502-477-1530
Bob Hafendorfer, prin. Fax 477-1760
Spencer County HS 800/9-12
520 Taylorsville Rd 40071 502-477-3255
Curt Haun, prin. Fax 477-3212
Spencer County MS 600/6-8
1263 Mount Washington Rd 40071 502-477-3260
Matt Mercer, prin. Fax 477-6796

**Tompkinsville, Monroe, Pop. 2,360**
Kentucky Tech System
Supt. — See Frankfort
Monroe County Area Technology Center Vo/Tech
757 Old Mulkey Rd 42167 270-487-8261
Jerri Rowland, prin. Fax 487-0094

Monroe County SD 1,900/PK-12
309 Emberton St 42167 270-487-5456
Amy Thompson, supt. Fax 487-5571
www.monroe.kyschools.us
Falcon Academy Alt
401 W 4th St 42167 270-487-6181
Jordan Hale, prin. Fax 487-6181
Monroe County HS 600/9-12
755 Old Mulkey Rd 42167 270-487-6217
Max Petett, prin. Fax 487-8274
Monroe County MS 500/6-8
600 S Main St 42167 270-487-9624
Tony Harlan, prin. Fax 487-9534

**Union, Boone, Pop. 5,294**
Boone County SD
Supt. — See Florence
Cooper HS 1,000/9-12
2855 Longbranch Rd 41091 859-384-5040
Michael Wilson, prin. Fax 384-5049
Gray MS 1,000/6-8
10400 US Highway 42 41091 859-384-5333
Todd Novak, prin. Fax 384-5318
Ryle HS 1,600/9-12
10379 US Highway 42 41091 859-384-5300
Matthew Turner, prin. Fax 384-5312

**Valley Station, Jefferson, Pop. 22,840**
Jefferson County SD
Supt. — See Louisville
Stuart MS 1,000/6-8
4601 Valley Station Rd 40272 502-485-8334
Renee Bledsoe, prin. Fax 485-8713
Valley Traditional HS 900/9-12
10200 Dixie Hwy 40272 502-485-8339
Rob Stephenson, prin. Fax 485-8666

**Vanceburg, Lewis, Pop. 1,503**
Lewis County SD 2,400/PK-12
PO Box 159 41179 606-796-2811
J. Belinda Forman, supt. Fax 796-3081
www.lewis.kyschools.us/
Lewis County HS 700/9-12
PO Box 99 41179 606-796-2823
Jack Lykins, prin. Fax 796-3066

Lewis County MS 500/6-8
PO Box 69 41179 606-796-6228
Brenda Box, prin. Fax 796-6255
Meade Vocational Education Center Vo/Tech
PO Box 130 41179 606-796-6106
Brad Brammell, prin. Fax 796-9739

**Vancleve, Breathitt**

---

Kentucky Mountain Bible College Post-Sec.
PO Box 10 41385 606-693-5000
Mt. Carmel S 100/K-12
PO Box 2 41385 606-666-5008
John Mills, prin. Fax 666-4612

**Versailles, Woodford, Pop. 8,423**
Woodford County SD 3,900/PK-12
330 Pisgah Rd 40383 859-879-4600
D. Scott Hawkins, supt. Fax 873-1614
ilearn.woodfordschools.org/
Safe Harbor Academy 50/Alt
299 S Main St 40383 859-879-4694
Logan Culbertson, prin. Fax 873-1328
Woodford County HS 1,200/9-12
180 Frankfort St 40383 859-879-4630
Rob Akers, prin. Fax 873-7731
Woodford County MS 900/6-8
100 School House Rd 40383 859-879-4650
Tracy Bruno, prin. Fax 873-4436

**Villa Hills, Kenton, Pop. 7,410**

---

Villa Madonna Academy 9-12
2500 Amsterdam Rd 41017 859-331-6333
Pamela McQueen, prin. Fax 331-8615

**Vine Grove, Hardin, Pop. 4,350**
Hardin County SD
Supt. — See Elizabethtown
Alton MS 700/6-8
100 Country Club Rd 40175 270-877-2135
Jama Bennett, prin. Fax 877-6297
Brown Street Center 100/Alt
400 Brown St 40175 270-877-2100
Robert King, prin. Fax 877-2820

**Walton, Boone, Pop. 3,572**
Walton-Verona ISD 1,600/PK-12
16 School Rd 41094 859-485-4181
Dr. Robert Storer, supt. Fax 485-1810
wv.kyschools.us
Walton-Verona HS 500/9-12
30 School Rd 41094 859-485-7721
Joanne Estenfelder, prin. Fax 485-7739
Walton-Verona MS 500/5-8
32 School Rd 41094 859-485-7721
Eric Morwessel, prin. Fax 485-7739

**Warfield, Martin, Pop. 269**
Martin County SD
Supt. — See Inez
Martin County MS 200/6-8
130 Middle School Dr 41267 606-395-5900
Brent Haney, prin. Fax 395-5902

**Warsaw, Gallatin, Pop. 1,574**
Gallatin County SD 1,700/PK-12
75 Boardwalk 41095 859-567-2828
Travis Huber, supt. Fax 567-4528
www.gallatin.kyschools.us
Gallatin County HS 500/9-12
70 Wildcat Cir 41095 859-567-7640
Jon Jones, prin. Fax 567-8222
Gallatin County MS 400/6-8
88 Pawprint Path 41095 859-567-5860
Curt Bieger, prin. Fax 567-6107
Gallatin County Wildcat Academy 50/Alt
75 Boardwalk 41095 859-567-1820
Greg Ulasiewicz, dir.

**West Liberty, Morgan, Pop. 3,396**
Kentucky Tech System
Supt. — See Frankfort
Morgan County Area Technology Center Vo/Tech
PO Box 249 41472 606-743-8452
Garry Harper, prin. Fax 743-8500

Morgan County SD 2,100/K-12
212 University Dr 41472 606-743-8002
Deatrah Barnett, supt. Fax 743-8050
www.morgan.kyschools.us/
Morgan County HS 600/9-12
150 Road To Success 41472 606-743-8052
Joseph Gamble, prin. Fax 743-8100
Morgan County MS 500/6-8
380 Road To Success 41472 606-743-8102
Terry Whitt, prin. Fax 743-8150

**West Paducah, McCracken**
McCracken County SD
Supt. — See Paducah
Heath MS 400/6-8
4330 Metropolis Lake Rd 42086 270-538-4070
Matthew Blackwell, prin. Fax 538-4071

**Whitesburg, Letcher, Pop. 2,131**
Kentucky Tech System
Supt. — See Frankfort
Letcher County Area Technology Center Vo/Tech
515 Cougar Dr 41858 606-633-5053
Dejah Burton, prin. Fax 633-8084

Letcher County SD 2,900/PK-12
224 Parks St 41858 606-633-4455
Tony Sergent, supt. Fax 633-4724
www.letcher.kyschools.us
Letcher County Alternative S 50/Alt
185 Circle Dr Ste A 41858 606-633-5559
William Adams, lead tchr. Fax 633-2459
Letcher County Central HS 900/9-12
435 Cougar Dr 41858 606-633-2339
Gracie Maggard, prin. Fax 633-2447
Whitesburg MS 200/6-8
366 Parks St 41858 606-633-2761
Henry Frazier, prin. Fax 633-4137
Other Schools – See Blackey, Neon

---

Jenny Lea Academy of Cosmetology Post-Sec.
74 Parkway Plaza Loop 41858 606-633-8784

**Whitesville, Daviess, Pop. 544**

---

Trinity HS 100/9-12
10510 Main Cross St 42378 270-233-5184
Ron Williams, prin. Fax 233-9293

**Williamsburg, Whitley, Pop. 5,159**
Whitley County SD 4,600/PK-12
300 Main St 40769 606-549-7000
Scott Paul, supt. Fax 549-7006
www.whitley.kyschools.us
Whitley County Alternative S 50/Alt
351 Boulevard of Champions 40769 606-549-7050
Terry Huddleston, prin. Fax 549-7068
Whitley County HS 1,200/9-12
350 Boulevard Of Champions 40769 606-549-7025
Bob Lawson, prin. Fax 549-7035
Whitley County MS 600/7-8
351 Boulevard Of Champions 40769 606-549-7050
Stuart Conlin, prin. Fax 549-7055

Williamsburg ISD 800/PK-12
1000 Main St 40769 606-549-6044
Dennis Byrd, supt. Fax 549-6076
www.wburg.kyschools.us
Williamsburg Alternative Center 50/Alt
1000 Main St 40769 606-539-0414
Mike Maxey, lead tchr. Fax 539-9230
Williamsburg S 800/PK-12
1000 Main St 40769 606-549-6044
Gary Peters, prin. Fax 549-6076

---

University of the Cumberlands Post-Sec.
6178 College Station Dr 40769 606-549-2200

**Williamstown, Grant, Pop. 3,887**
Grant County SD 3,800/K-12
820 Arnie Risen Blvd 41097 859-824-3323
Ron Livingood, supt. Fax 824-3508
www.grant.kyschools.us
Eagle Creek Academy 50/Alt
1505 N Main St 41097 859-824-7706
Paul Bodenhamer, prin. Fax 824-7067
Other Schools – See Dry Ridge

Williamstown ISD 600/PK-12
300 Helton St 41097 859-824-7144
Sally Skinner, supt. Fax 824-3237
www.williamstown.kyschools.us/
Williamstown HS 200/9-12
300 Helton St 41097 859-824-4421
Brandy Feagan, admin. Fax 824-4736
Williamstown JHS 200/6-8
300 Helton St 41097 859-824-4421
Brandy Feagan, prin. Fax 824-3745

**Wilmore, Jessamine, Pop. 3,637**
Jessamine County SD
Supt. — See Nicholasville
Jessamine Career & Technology Center Vo/Tech
881 Wilmore Rd, 859-881-8324
C. Dexter Knight, prin. Fax 887-9051
Providence S 100/Alt
210 S Lexington Ave 40390 859-887-4600
Charlanne Pook, prin. Fax 858-9586

---

Asbury Theological Seminary Post-Sec.
204 N Lexington Ave 40390 800-227-2879
Asbury University Post-Sec.
1 Macklem Dr 40390 859-858-3511

**Winchester, Clark, Pop. 18,061**
Clark County SD 3,800/PK-12
1600 W Lexington Ave 40391 859-744-4545
Paul Christy, supt. Fax 745-3935
www2.clarkschools.net
Campbell JHS 400/7-8
620 Boone Ave 40391 859-745-5200
Dustin Howard, prin. Fax 745-2027
Clark County Area Technology Center Vo/Tech
2745 Boonesboro Rd 40391 859-744-1250
Michael Kindred, prin. Fax 744-9979
Clark HS 1,700/9-12
2745 Boonesboro Rd 40391 859-744-6111
David Bolen, prin. Fax 745-2418
Phoenix Academy 50/Alt
100 Vaught Rd 40391 859-744-4618
Jennifer Kincaid, prin. Fax 745-0150

Kentucky Tech System
Supt. — See Frankfort
Clark County Area Technology Center Vo/Tech
650 Boone Ave 40391 859-744-1250
Michael Kindred, prin. Fax 744-9979

**Wurtland, Greenup, Pop. 983**
Greenup County SD
Supt. — See Greenup
Wurtland MS 300/6-8
700 Center St 41144 606-836-1023
Amanda Powell, prin. Fax 836-3939

# LOUISIANA

## LOUISIANA DEPARTMENT OF EDUCATION
**PO Box 94064, Baton Rouge 70804-9064**
**Telephone 225-342-3602**
**Fax 225-342-7316**
**Website http://www.louisianaschools.net/default.html**

Superintendent of Education John White

## LOUISIANA BOARD OF EDUCATION
**PO Box 94064, Baton Rouge 70804-9064**

President Penny Dastugue

## PUBLIC, PRIVATE AND CATHOLIC SECONDARY SCHOOLS

**Abbeville, Vermilion, Pop. 12,038**
Vermilion Parish SD 9,200/PK-12
PO Box 520 70511 337-898-5770
Jerome Puyau, supt. Fax 898-0939
www.vrml.k12.la.us
Abbeville HS 600/9-12
1305 Wildcat Dr 70510 337-893-1874
Ivy Landry, prin. Fax 893-0935
Williams MS 700/6-8
1105 Prairie Ave 70510 337-893-3943
Dana Primeaux, prin. Fax 893-5190
Other Schools – See Erath, Gueydan, Kaplan, Maurice

South Louisiana Community College Post-Sec.
1301 Clover St 70510 337-893-4984
Vermilion Catholic HS 200/9-12
425 Park Ave 70510 337-893-6636
Michael Guilbeaux, prin. Fax 898-0394

**Albany, Livingston, Pop. 1,080**
Livingston Parish SD
Supt. — See Livingston
Albany HS 600/9-12
PO Box 1090 70711 225-567-9319
Jill Prokop, prin. Fax 567-9162
Albany MS 500/5-8
PO Box 1210 70711 225-567-5231
Rachel Jenkins, prin. Fax 567-9177

**Alexandria, Rapides, Pop. 46,974**
Rapides Parish SD 23,700/PK-12
PO Box 1230 71309 318-487-0888
Nason Authement, supt. Fax 449-3167
www.rpsb.us
Alexandria HS 1,100/9-12
800 Ola St 71303 318-448-8234
Duane Urbina, prin. Fax 487-9994
Alexandria Magnet MS 600/6-8
122 Maryland Ave 71301 318-445-5343
Monte Demars, prin. Fax 442-8650
Bolton HS 700/9-12
2101 Vance Ave 71301 318-448-3628
Clovis Christman, prin. Fax 448-4329
Brame MS 900/6-8
4800 Dawn St 71301 318-443-3688
Walter Fall, prin. Fax 442-3966
Peabody Magnet HS 700/9-12
2727 Jones Ave 71302 318-448-3457
Jamie Henagan, prin. Fax 487-0771
RAPPS S 50/Alt
4645 Lincoln Rd 71302 318-448-9899
Deidra Anderson, prin. Fax 449-4774
Smith Magnet MS 500/6-8
3100 Jones Ave 71302 318-445-6241
Dr. Norvella Williams, prin. Fax 445-9255
Other Schools – See Ball, Deville, Elmer, Glenmora, Lecompte, Lena, Pineville, Tioga

Blue Cliff College-Alexandria Post-Sec.
1505 Metro Dr Ste 1 71301 318-445-2778
Central Louisiana Technical College Post-Sec.
4311 S MacArthur Dr 71302 318-487-5439
Grace Christian S 400/PK-12
4900 Jackson St 71303 318-445-8735
Kay Blackburn, prin. Fax 443-1034
Holy Savior Menard HS 500/7-12
4603 Coliseum Blvd 71303 318-445-8233
Joel Desselle, prin. Fax 448-8170
Louisiana State University at Alexandria Post-Sec.
8100 Highway 71 S 71302 318-445-3672
Rapides Regional Medical Center Post-Sec.
PO Box 30101 71301 318-473-3150
University Academy of Central Louisiana 200/9-12
8100 Highway 71 S 71302 318-427-0123

**Amite, Tangipahoa, Pop. 4,112**
Tangipahoa Parish SD 18,300/PK-12
59656 Puleston Rd 70422 985-748-7153
Mark Kolwe, supt. Fax 748-8587
www.tangischools.org
Amite HS 500/9-12
403 S Laurel St 70422 985-748-9301
Terran Perry, prin. Fax 748-2814
West Side MS 400/5-8
401 W Oak St 70422 985-748-9073
Ashley Walker, prin. Fax 748-9225
Other Schools – See Hammond, Independence, Kentwood, Loranger, Ponchatoula, Tickfaw

Oak Forest Academy 700/PK-12
600 Walnut St 70422 985-748-4321

**Anacoco, Vernon, Pop. 864**
Vernon Parish SD
Supt. — See Leesville
Anacoco JSHS 400/7-12
4740 Port Arthur Ave 71403 337-239-3039
Lisa Lohman, prin. Fax 238-4228

**Arcadia, Bienville, Pop. 2,890**
Bienville Parish SD 2,300/PK-12
PO Box 418 71001 318-263-9416
William Britt, supt. Fax 263-3100
www.bpsb.us/
Arcadia JSHS 300/6-12
967 Daniel St 71001 318-263-2264
Jeffery Sampson, prin. Fax 263-9703
Other Schools – See Castor, Gibsland, Ringgold, Saline

**Archibald, Richland**
Richland Parish SD
Supt. — See Rayville
Richland Career Center Vo/Tech
3768 Highway 15 71218 318-248-2465
Lee McDonald, prin. Fax 248-3525

**Arnaudville, Saint Landry, Pop. 1,048**
St. Landry Parish SD
Supt. — See Opelousas
Arnaudville ES 300/5-8
PO Box 770 70512 337-754-5320
Elsie Semien, prin. Fax 754-5326
Beau Chene HS 800/9-12
7076 Highway 93 70512 337-662-5815
Keith James, prin. Fax 662-3688

**Athens, Claiborne, Pop. 242**

Mount Olive Christian S 100/PK-12
15349 Highway 9 71003 318-258-5661
Linda Lee Gantt, prin. Fax 258-5662

**Atlanta, Winn, Pop. 159**
Winn Parish SD
Supt. — See Winnfield
Atlanta S 300/PK-12
118 School Rd 71404 318-628-4613
Bridgette Bartlett, prin. Fax 628-4247

**Avondale, Jefferson, Pop. 4,884**
Jefferson Parish SD
Supt. — See Harvey
Ford MS 500/6-8
435 S Jamie Blvd 70094 504-436-2474
Faith Joseph, prin. Fax 436-0604
Taylor Science & Tech Academy 300/6-12
701 Church Hill Pkwy 70094 504-838-2249
Jaime Zapico, prin. Fax 436-0247

**Baker, East Baton Rouge, Pop. 13,732**
City of Baker SD 1,800/PK-12
14750 Plank Rd 70714 225-774-5795
Dr. Herman Brister, supt. Fax 774-5797
www.bakerschools.org
Baker HS 400/9-12
3200 Groom Rd 70714 225-775-1259
Traci Morgan, prin. Fax 775-4011
Baker MS 400/6-8
5903 Groom Rd 70714 225-775-9750
John Arrasmith, prin. Fax 775-9753

Bethany Christian S 200/PK-12
13855 Plank Rd 70714 225-774-0133
Carolyn DeSalvo, prin. Fax 774-0163

**Baldwin, Saint Mary, Pop. 2,394**
St. Mary Parish SD
Supt. — See Centerville
Boudreaux MS 300/6-8
18333 Highway 182 70514 337-924-7990
Magdalene Drexler, prin. Fax 924-7999
West St. Mary HS 400/9-12
PO Box 120 70514 337-924-7990
Dr. Derrick White, prin. Fax 924-7999

**Ball, Rapides, Pop. 3,932**
Rapides Parish SD
Supt. — See Alexandria
Tioga JHS 500/7-8
1150 Tioga Rd 71405 318-640-9412
Rebecca Pippen, prin. Fax 640-0126

**Basile, Evangeline, Pop. 1,791**
Evangeline Parish SD
Supt. — See Ville Platte
Basile JSHS 400/5-12
2835 2nd St 70515 337-432-5012
Tony Bertrand, prin. Fax 432-6414

**Bastrop, Morehouse, Pop. 11,255**
Morehouse Parish SD 4,400/PK-12
PO Box 872 71221 318-281-5784
George Noflin Ph.D., supt. Fax 283-3456
www.mpsb.us
Bastrop HS 1,100/8-12
402 Highland Ave 71220 318-281-0194
Dr. David Nordman, prin. Fax 281-0457
Morehouse Alternative S 50/Alt
1607 Martin L King S 71220 318-281-1407
Howard Loche, prin. Fax 283-3460
Morehouse JHS 500/6-8
1001 W Madison Ave 71220 318-281-0776
Shelia Minor, prin. Fax 283-1846

Bastrop Beauty School #1 Post-Sec.
117 S Vine St 71220 318-281-8652
Prairie View Academy 300/K-12
9942 Edwin St 71220 318-281-7044

**Baton Rouge, East Baton Rouge, Pop. 226,740**
Central Community SD 3,500/PK-12
PO Box 78094 70837 225-262-1919
Michael Faulk, supt. Fax 262-1989
www.centralcss.org
Central HS 1,200/9-12
10200 E Brookside Dr 70818 225-261-3438
Dave Prescott, prin. Fax 261-3501
Central MS 900/6-8
12656 Sullivan Rd 70818 225-261-2237
Jason Fountain, prin. Fax 261-9973

East Baton Rouge Parish SD 41,500/PK-12
PO Box 2950 70821 225-922-5400
Warren Drake, supt. Fax 922-5499
www.ebrschools.org
Arlington Prepatory Academy 100/Alt
931 Dean Lee Dr 70820 225-766-8188
Margot Morgan-Forbes, prin. Fax 757-1276
Baton Rouge Magnet HS 1,300/9-12
2825 Government St 70806 225-383-0520
Nanette McCann, prin. Fax 344-7413
Belaire HS 800/9-12
12121 Tams Dr 70815 225-272-1860
Roy Walker, prin. Fax 272-3782
Broadmoor HS 1,200/9-12
10100 Goodwood Blvd 70815 225-926-1420
Shalonda Simoneaux, prin. Fax 928-5472
Broadmoor MS 600/6-8
1225 Sharp Rd 70815 225-272-0540
Daniel Edwards, prin. Fax 272-0195
Brookstown Middle Magnet Academy 6-8
4375 East Brookstown Dr 70805 225-355-6556
James Smith, prin. Fax 355-6503
Capitol MS 600/6-8
5100 Greenwell Springs Rd 70806 225-231-9292
Viola Jackson, prin. Fax 231-9291
EBR Readiness Superintendent's Academy Alt
1919 Staring Ln 70810 225-757-9679
Delores Watts, prin. Fax 757-9682
Glasgow MS 600/6-8
1676 Glasgow Ave 70808 225-925-2942
Erin Howard, prin. Fax 928-3565
Glen Oaks HS 600/9-12
6650 Cedar Grove Dr 70812 225-356-4306
Ed Hunter, prin. Fax 359-6782
Greenville Alternative S at Beechwood Alt
2555 DeSoto Dr 70807 225-775-4285
Ronnie Knox, prin. Fax 356-4427
Greenville Superintendent's Academy Alt
1645 N Foster Dr 70806 225-357-0139
Sherwanda Johnson, prin. Fax 356-6358
Lee HS 600/9-12
4510 Bawell St 70808 225-924-9406
Nanette McCann, prin. Fax 924-9409

McKinley HS 1,400/9-12
800 E Mckinley St 70802 225-344-7696
Herman Brister, prin. Fax 387-5435
McKinley Magnet MS 700/6-8
1550 Eddie Robinson Sr Dr 70802 225-388-0089
Sean Joffrion, prin. Fax 387-1434
North Banks MS of Excellence 6-8
5959 Cadillac St 70811 225-357-3371
Fax 356-2665
Northdale Superintendents Academy 400/Alt
10755 Cletus Dr 70815 225-272-2036
Claudia Battley, prin. Fax 273-2125
Park Forest MS 900/6-8
3760 Aletha Dr 70814 225-275-6650
Curtis Walker, prin. Fax 275-3058
Scotlandville Magnet HS 1,200/9-12
9870 Scotland Ave 70807 225-775-3715
Tiffany Quiett, prin. Fax 774-3767
Scotlandville Pre-Engineering Academy 300/6-8
9147 Elm Grove Garden Dr 70807 225-775-0776
Shalika Scott, prin. Fax 775-2104
Sherwood MS Academic Magnet 800/6-8
1020 Marlbrook Dr 70815 225-272-3090
J. Noel, prin. Fax 273-9459
Southeast MS 900/6-8
15000 S Harrells Ferry Rd 70816 225-753-5930
Amber Boyd, prin. Fax 756-8601
Tara HS 900/9-12
9002 Whitehall Ave 70806 225-927-6100
Karen Triche, prin. Fax 928-0122
Westdale MS 900/6-8
5650 Claycut Rd 70806 225-924-1308
Jeremy Couvillon, prin. Fax 926-9929
Woodlawn HS 1,300/9-12
15755 Jefferson Hwy 70817 225-753-1200
Scott Stevens, prin. Fax 751-9269
Woodlawn MS 1,000/6-8
14939 Tiger Bend Rd 70817 225-751-0436
Shelly Colvin, prin. Fax 753-0159
Other Schools – See Pride

---

Baton Rouge Community College Post-Sec.
201 Community College Dr 70806 225-216-8000
Baton Rouge Community College Acadian Post-Sec.
3250 N Acadian Thruway E 70805 225-359-9201
Baton Rouge General Medical Center Post-Sec.
PO Box 2511 70821 225-387-7767
Baton Rouge International S 300/PK-12
5015 Auto Plex Dr 70809 225-293-4338
Baton Rouge School of Computers Post-Sec.
9352 Interline Ave 70809 225-923-2525
Brighton S 200/K-12
12108 Parkmeadow Ave 70816 225-291-2524
Camelot College Post-Sec.
2618 Wooddale Blvd # A 70805 225-928-3005
Catholic HS 1,000/8-12
855 Hearthstone Dr 70806 225-383-0397
Lisa Harvey, prin. Fax 383-0381
Christian Life Academy 600/PK-12
2037 Quail Dr 70808 225-769-6760
Delta College of Arts & Technology Post-Sec.
7380 Exchange Pl 70806 225-928-7770
Diesel Driving Academy Post-Sec.
8067 Airline Hwy 70815 225-929-9990
Domestic Health Care Institute Post-Sec.
4826 Jamestown Ave 70808 225-925-5312
Dunham S 800/PK-12
11111 Roy Emerson Dr 70810 225-767-7097
Steven Eagleton, hdmstr. Fax 767-7056
Episcopal S of Baton Rouge 900/PK-12
3200 Woodland Ridge Blvd 70816 225-753-3180
Hugh McIntosh, head sch Fax 756-0507
Family Christian Academy 200/K-12
PO Box 262550 70826 225-768-3026
ITI Technical College Post-Sec.
13944 Airline Hwy 70817 225-752-4230
ITT Technical Institute Post-Sec.
14111 Airline Hwy Ste 101 70817 225-754-5800
Lockworks Academie of Hairdressing Post-Sec.
2834 S Sherwood Forest Blvd 70816 225-295-1435
Louisiana Culinary Institute Post-Sec.
10550 Airline Hwy 70816 225-769-8820
Louisiana School for the Deaf Post-Sec.
PO Box 3074 70821 225-769-8160
Louisiana School/Visually Impaired Post-Sec.
PO Box 4328 70821 225-757-3482
Louisiana State University & A & M Coll. Post-Sec.
Louisiana State Univ 70803 225-578-3202
Louisiana State University Law Center Post-Sec.
1 E Campus Dr 70803 225-578-5292
Medical Training College Post-Sec.
10525 Plaza Americana Dr 70816 225-926-5820
MedVance Institute Post-Sec.
9255 Interline Ave 70809 225-248-1015
Our Lady of the Lake College Post-Sec.
5414 Brittany Dr 70808 225-768-1700
Our Lady of the Lake Medical Center Post-Sec.
5000 Hennessy Blvd 70808 225-769-7799
Parkview Baptist S 1,400/K-12
5750 Parkview Church Rd 70816 225-291-2500
Dr. Don Mayes, hdmstr. Fax 293-4135
Redemptorist HS 300/7-12
PO Box 2028 70821 225-357-0936
Dary Glueck, prin. Fax 357-4555
Remington College Post-Sec.
10551 Coursey Blvd 70816 225-236-3200
Riverdale Christian Academy 200/PK-12
2791 Oneal Ln 70816 225-753-6722
Runnels S 800/PK-12
17255 S Harrells Ferry Rd 70816 225-215-5706
St. Joseph's Academy 1,000/9-12
3015 Broussard St 70808 225-383-7207
Linda Harvison, prin. Fax 344-5714
St. Michael the Archangel HS 700/9-12
PO Box 86110 70879 225-753-9782
Ellen Lee, prin. Fax 753-0605
Southern University and A&M College Post-Sec.
Southern University 70813 225-771-4500
Virginia College Post-Sec.
9501 Cortana Pl 70815 225-236-3900

**Bell City, Calcasieu**
Calcasieu Parish SD
Supt. — See Lake Charles
Bell City S 600/K-12
PO Box 100 70630 337-217-4500
Reinette Guillory, prin. Fax 217-4501

**Belle Chasse, Plaquemines, Pop. 12,371**
Plaquemines Parish SD 3,900/PK-12
1484 Woodland Hwy 70037 504-595-6400
Denis Rousselle, supt. Fax 398-9990
www.ppsb.org
Belle Chasse HS 800/9-12
8346 Highway 23 70037 504-595-6600
Jemi Carlone, prin. Fax 393-1182
Belle Chasse MS 700/5-8
13476 Highway 23 70037 504-595-6640
Joe Williamson, prin. Fax 656-2399
Other Schools – See Braithwaite, Buras, Port Sulphur

**Belle Rose, Assumption, Pop. 1,892**
Assumption Parish SD
Supt. — See Napoleonville
Belle Rose MS 200/5-8
PO Box 229 70341 225-473-8917
Iris Breaux, prin. Fax 473-8429

**Benton, Bossier, Pop. 1,921**
Bossier Parish SD 20,700/PK-12
PO Box 2000 71006 318-549-5000
D.C. Machen, supt. Fax 549-5004
www.bossierschools.org
Benton HS 800/9-12
6136 Highway 3 71006 318-549-5240
Mitch Downey, prin. Fax 549-5252
Benton MS 700/6-8
6140 Highway 3 71006 318-549-5310
Dr. Kyle Machen, prin. Fax 549-5323
Other Schools – See Bossier City, Haughton, Plain Dealing

**Berwick, Saint Mary, Pop. 4,860**
St. Mary Parish SD
Supt. — See Centerville
Berwick HS 500/9-12
700 Pattie Dr 70342 985-384-8450
Buffy Fegenbush, prin. Fax 384-8505
Berwick JHS 500/6-8
3955 Bourgeois Dr 70342 985-384-5664
Tim Hymel, prin. Fax 384-5663

**Bogalusa, Washington, Pop. 12,052**
Bogalusa City SD 600/PK-12
1705 Sullivan Dr 70427 985-281-2100
Willie Breaux, supt. Fax 735-8828
www.bogschools.org
Bogalusa HS 400/6-12
PO Box 580 70429 985-281-2180
Lesley McKinley, prin. Fax 735-9768

---

Ben's Ford Christian School 500/PK-12
59253 Mount Pleasant Rd 70427 985-735-0387
Northshore Technical Community College Post-Sec.
1710 Sullivan Dr 70427 985-732-6640

**Bossier City, Bossier, Pop. 59,796**
Bossier Parish SD
Supt. — See Benton
Airline HS 1,600/9-12
2801 Airline Dr 71111 318-549-5080
Jason Rowland, prin. Fax 549-5093
Bossier HS 600/9-12
777 Bearkat Dr 71111 318-549-6680
David Thrash, prin. Fax 549-6693
Bossier Parish S for Technology Vo/Tech
1020 Innovation Dr 71111 318-759-2900
Jayda Spillers, prin. Fax 759-2956
Butler Educational Complex 100/Alt
649 Wyche St 71111 318-549-7050
Chuck Horton, admin. Fax 549-7063
Cope MS 700/6-8
4814 Shed Rd 71111 318-549-5380
Judy Grooms, prin. Fax 549-5393
Elm Grove MS 900/6-8
4301 Panther Dr 71112 318-759-2400
Ross Boyett, prin. Fax 759-2409
Greenacres MS 800/6-8
2220 Airline Dr 71111 318-549-6210
Arthur James, prin. Fax 549-6223
Parkway HS 1,100/9-12
2010 Colleen St 71112 318-759-2200
Dr. Nichole Bourgeois, prin. Fax 759-2213
Rusheon MS 500/6-8
2401 Old Minden Rd 71112 318-549-6610
Judy Madden, prin. Fax 549-6623

---

Bossier Parish Community College Post-Sec.
6220 E Texas St 71111 318-678-6000
Pat Goins Benton Road Beauty School Post-Sec.
1701 Old Minden Rd Ste 36 71111 318-746-7674
Virginia College Post-Sec.
2950 E Texas St Ste C 71111 318-741-8020

**Bourg, Terrebonne, Pop. 2,533**
Terrebonne Parish SD
Supt. — See Houma
South Terrebonne HS 1,100/9-12
3879 Highway 24 70343 985-868-7850
Mark Torbert, prin. Fax 868-1691

**Boutte, Saint Charles, Pop. 3,028**
St. Charles Parish SD
Supt. — See Luling
Hahnville HS 1,500/9-12
200 Tiger Dr 70039 985-758-7537
Ken Oertling, prin. Fax 758-9876

**Braithwaite, Plaquemines**
Plaquemines Parish SD
Supt. — See Belle Chasse
Phoenix S 200/PK-12
12700 Highway 39 70040 504-595-6480
Kristie Williams, prin. Fax 333-7073

**Breaux Bridge, Saint Martin, Pop. 8,038**
St. Martin Parish SD 7,900/PK-12
625 Corporate Blvd 70517 337-332-2105
Dr. Lottie Beebe, supt.
www.saintmartinschools.org
Breaux Bridge HS 800/9-12
1015 Breaux Bridge Sr High 70517 337-332-3131
Louis Blanchard, prin. Fax 332-4058
Breaux Bridge JHS 200/7-8
100 Martin St 70517 337-332-2844
Denise Frederick, prin. Fax 332-4831
Other Schools – See Cecilia, Parks, Saint Martinville

**Broussard, Lafayette, Pop. 8,078**
Lafayette Parish SD
Supt. — See Lafayette
Broussard MS 500/5-8
1325 S Morgan Ave 70518 337-521-7870
John Mouton, prin. Fax 521-7871

---

Episcopal S of Acadiana 500/PK-12
1557 Smede Hwy 70518 337-365-1416
Dr. Paul Baker Ph.D., hdmstr. Fax 367-9841

**Brusly, West Baton Rouge, Pop. 2,561**
West Baton Rouge Parish SD
Supt. — See Port Allen
Brusly HS 500/9-12
630 Frontage Rd 70719 225-749-2815
Walt Lemoine, prin. Fax 749-8563
Brusly MS 500/6-8
601 N Kirkland St 70719 225-749-3123
Callie Kershaw, prin. Fax 749-8570

**Bunkie, Avoyelles, Pop. 4,132**
Avoyelles Parish SD
Supt. — See Marksville
Bunkie HS 500/7-12
435 Evergreen St 71322 318-346-6216
David Moreau, prin. Fax 346-9611

**Buras, Plaquemines, Pop. 887**
Plaquemines Parish SD
Supt. — See Belle Chasse
South Plaquemines HS 400/7-12
34121 Highway 23 70041 504-595-6435
John Barthelemy, prin.

**Calhoun, Ouachita, Pop. 674**
Ouachita Parish SD
Supt. — See Monroe
Calhoun MS 500/6-8
191 Highway 80 E 71225 318-644-5840
Buddy Canal, prin. Fax 644-5418

**Calvin, Winn, Pop. 236**
Winn Parish SD
Supt. — See Winnfield
Calvin S 300/PK-12
PO Box 80 71410 318-727-8784
Paula Jones, prin. Fax 727-9224

**Cameron, Cameron, Pop. 399**
Cameron Parish SD 1,300/PK-12
PO Box 1548 70631 337-775-5784
Charles Adkins, supt. Fax 775-5097
www.camsch.org
Johnson Bayou S 100/PK-12
6304 Gulf Beach Hwy 70631 337-569-2138
Brenda Sanders, prin. Fax 569-2673
Other Schools – See Grand Chenier, Hackberry, Lake Charles

**Campti, Natchitoches, Pop. 1,035**
Natchitoches Parish SD
Supt. — See Natchitoches
Lakeview HS 300/9-12
PO Box 200 71411 318-476-3360
William Hymes, prin. Fax 476-2851

**Carencro, Lafayette, Pop. 7,438**
Lafayette Parish SD
Supt. — See Lafayette
Carencro MS 700/6-8
4301 N University Ave 70520 337-521-7880
Jeffrey Janette, prin. Fax 521-7881

**Castor, Bienville, Pop. 258**
Bienville Parish SD
Supt. — See Arcadia
Castor S 500/PK-12
PO Box 69 71016 318-544-7271
Dr. James Guin, prin. Fax 544-9077

**Cecilia, Saint Martin, Pop. 1,957**
St. Martin Parish SD
Supt. — See Breaux Bridge
Cecilia HS 700/9-12
PO Box 360 70521 337-667-6221
Daniel LeBoeuf, prin. Fax 667-6795
Cecilia JHS 400/7-8
PO Box 129 70521 337-667-6226
Charee Theriot, prin. Fax 667-7352

**Centerville, Saint Mary**
St. Mary Parish SD 9,300/PK-12
PO Box 170 70522 337-836-9661
Leonard Armato, supt. Fax 836-5461
www.stmaryk12.net
Centerville S 600/PK-12
PO Box 59 70522 337-836-5103
Mike Galler, prin. Fax 836-9594
Other Schools – See Baldwin, Berwick, Franklin, Morgan City, Patterson

**Central, East Baton Rouge, Pop. 26,615**

---

Central Private S 300/PK-12
12801 Centerra Ct, 225-261-3341

**Chalmette, Saint Bernard, Pop. 16,314**
St. Bernard Parish SD 6,900/PK-12
200 E Saint Bernard Hwy 70043 504-301-2000
Doris Voitier, supt. Fax 301-2010
www.stbernard.k12.la.us

Chalmette HS 1,500/9-12
1100 E Judge Perez Dr 70043 504-301-2600
Wayne Warner, prin. Fax 301-2610
Jackson MS 400/6-8
201 8th St 70043 504-301-1500
Montrelle Sinegar, prin. Fax 301-1510
Rowley Alternative S 200/Alt
49 Madison Ave 70043 504-301-4001
Andre Bonnafons, prin. Fax 301-4010
Other Schools – See Meraux, Saint Bernard

---

Nunez Community College Post-Sec.
3710 Paris Rd 70043 504-278-6200

**Chauvin, Terrebonne, Pop. 2,885**
Terrebonne Parish SD
Supt. — See Houma
Lacache MS 400/5-8
5266 Highway 56 70344 985-594-3945
Mark Thibodeaux, prin. Fax 594-4128

**Choudrant, Lincoln, Pop. 836**
Lincoln Parish SD
Supt. — See Ruston
Choudrant HS 300/7-12
PO Box 220 71227 318-768-2542
Lisa Bastion, prin. Fax 768-4182

**Church Point, Acadia, Pop. 4,487**
Acadia Parish SD
Supt. — See Crowley
Church Point HS 500/9-12
305 E Lougarre St 70525 337-684-5472
Lee Ward Bellard, prin. Fax 684-5137
Church Point MS 300/6-8
340 W Martin Luther King Dr 70525 337-684-6381
Cheri Baggett, prin. Fax 684-0123

**Clarks, Caldwell, Pop. 1,011**

---

Old Bethel Christian Academy 100/PK-12
PO Box 95 71415 318-649-0281
Sandra Richmond, prin. Fax 649-0281

**Clinton, East Feliciana, Pop. 1,628**
East Feliciana Parish SD 2,000/PK-12
PO Box 397 70722 225-683-8277
Henderson Lewis Ph.D., supt. Fax 683-3320
www.efpsb.k12.la.us
East Feliciana MS 300/6-8
PO Box 166 70722 225-683-3321
Karen Gipson, prin. Fax 683-5115
East Feliciana Parish Enrichment Academy 50/Alt
PO Box 166 70722 225-683-8198
Ella Philson, prin. Fax 683-4900
Other Schools – See Jackson

---

Silliman Institute 400/PK-12
PO Box 946 70722 225-683-5383

**Colfax, Grant, Pop. 1,531**
Grant Parish SD 3,300/PK-12
PO Box 208 71417 318-627-3274
Sheila Jackson, supt. Fax 627-5931
www.gpsb.org
Other Schools – See Dry Prong, Georgetown, Montgomery

**Columbia, Caldwell, Pop. 387**
Caldwell Parish SD 1,400/PK-12
PO Box 1019 71418 318-649-2689
Karla Tollett, supt. Fax 649-0636
www.caldwelledu.org/
Caldwell Parish HS 500/9-12
163 Spartan Dr 71418 318-649-2750
Russell Farrar, prin. Fax 649-0021
Caldwell Parish JHS 200/6-8
114 Trojan Dr 71418 318-649-2340
Fax 649-2341

**Converse, Sabine, Pop. 416**
Sabine Parish SD
Supt. — See Many
Converse S 500/K-12
PO Box 10 71419 318-567-2673
Winston Hodge, prin. Fax 567-3400

**Cottonport, Avoyelles, Pop. 1,987**

---

Central Louisiana Technical College Post-Sec.
508 Choupique Ln 71327 318-876-2401

**Coushatta, Red River, Pop. 1,958**
Red River Parish SD 1,500/PK-12
PO Box 1369 71019 318-932-4081
Kay Easley, supt. Fax 932-4367
www.rrbulldogs.com/
Red River HS 300/9-12
PO Box 409 71019 318-932-4913
Carroll Daniels, prin. Fax 932-5344
Red River JHS 300/6-8
915 E Carrol St 71019 318-932-5265
Danny Rester, prin. Fax 932-9959

---

Riverdale Academy 300/PK-12
100 Riverdale Rd 71019 318-932-5876

**Covington, Saint Tammany, Pop. 8,662**
St. Tammany Parish SD 36,300/PK-12
PO Box 940 70434 985-892-2276
Trey Folse, supt. Fax 898-3267
www.stpsb.org
Covington HS 1,500/9-12
73030 Lions Dr 70433 985-892-3422
Roslyn Hanson, prin. Fax 875-9699
Pitcher JHS 300/7-8
415 S Jefferson Ave 70433 985-892-3021
Raphael Tillman, prin. Fax 892-1188
Other Schools – See Folsom, Madisonville, Mandeville, Pearl River, Slidell

---

Archbishop Hannan HS 300/8-12
71324 Highway 1077 70433 985-249-6363
Fr. Charles Latour, prin. Fax 249-6370

Aveda Institute Post-Sec.
1355 Polders Ln 70433 985-892-9953
Christ Episcopal S 400/1-12
80 Christwood Blvd 70433 985-871-9902
Northlake Christian S 800/PK-12
70104 Wolverine Dr 70433 985-635-0400
Monty Fontenot M.Ed., head sch Fax 893-4363
St. Paul's HS 900/8-12
917 S Jahncke Ave 70433 985-892-3200
Trevor Watkins, prin. Fax 892-4048
St. Scholastica Academy 700/8-12
PO Box 1210 70434 985-892-2540
Mary Kathryn Villere, prin. Fax 893-5256

**Crowley, Acadia, Pop. 13,095**
Acadia Parish SD 9,600/PK-12
PO Box 309 70527 337-783-3664
John Bourque, supt. Fax 783-3761
www.acadia.k12.la.us/
Acadia Parish Alternative S 50/Alt
404 W 12th St 70526 337-783-7188
Carolla Jolivette, prin. Fax 785-0794
Crowley HS 700/9-12
263 Hensgens Rd 70526 337-783-5313
Perry Myles, prin. Fax 783-7796
Crowley MS 500/6-8
401 W Northern Ave 70526 337-783-5305
Chad Lemelle, prin. Fax 783-5338
Other Schools – See Church Point, Iota, Midland, Rayne

---

Acadiana Technical College Post-Sec.
1933 W Hutchinson Ave 70526 337-788-7521
Northside Christian S 300/K-12
809 E Northern Ave 70526 337-783-3620
Rev. Randy Trahan, prin. Fax 788-3461
Notre Dame HS 400/9-12
910 N Eastern Ave 70526 337-783-3519
Cindy Istre, prin. Fax 788-2115

**Cut Off, Lafourche, Pop. 5,828**
Lafourche Parish SD
Supt. — See Thibodaux
South Lafourche HS 1,200/9-12
16911 E Main St 70345 985-632-5721
Gaye Cheramie, prin. Fax 632-6723

**Delcambre, Vermilion, Pop. 1,846**
Iberia Parish SD
Supt. — See New Iberia
Delcambre JSHS 500/6-12
601 W Main St 70528 337-685-2595
Kimberly Messman, prin. Fax 685-6099

**Delhi, Richland, Pop. 2,885**
Richland Parish SD
Supt. — See Rayville
Delhi HS 200/9-12
413 Main St 71232 318-878-2235
Barbara Turner, prin. Fax 878-8967
Delhi MS 200/5-8
106 Toombs St 71232 318-878-3748
Shirley McDade, prin. Fax 878-3749

**Denham Springs, Livingston, Pop. 10,120**
Livingston Parish SD
Supt. — See Livingston
Denham Springs Freshman HS 700/9-9
940 N Range Ave 70726 225-665-7890
Ken Magee, prin. Fax 665-1865
Denham Springs JHS 900/6-8
401 Hatchell Ln 70726 225-665-8898
Bryan Wax, prin. Fax 665-8601
Denham Springs SHS 1,400/10-12
1000 N Range Ave 70726 225-665-8851
Kelly Jones, prin. Fax 665-4082
Juban Parc JHS 600/6-8
12470 Brown Rd 70726 225-664-1001
Jeff Frizell, prin. Fax 664-5000
Live Oak HS 1,200/9-12
36079 Hwy 16 70706 225-665-8858
Beth Jones, prin. Fax 665-8850
Southside JHS 500/6-8
26535 LA Highway 16 70726 225-664-4221
Carlos Williams, prin. Fax 664-3307

---

Community Christian Academy 100/PK-12
400 N River Rd 70726 225-665-5696
Denham Springs Beauty College Post-Sec.
923 Florida Ave SE 70726 225-665-6188

**Dequincy, Calcasieu, Pop. 3,178**
Calcasieu Parish SD
Supt. — See Lake Charles
DeQuincy HS 400/9-12
207 N Overton St 70633 337-217-4530
Craig Neal, prin. Fax 217-4531
DeQuincy MS 300/6-8
1603 W 4th St 70633 337-217-4770
Denise Doyle, prin. Fax 217-4771

**Deridder, Beauregard, Pop. 10,238**
Beauregard Parish SD 6,000/PK-12
PO Box 938 70634 337-463-5551
Timothy Cooley M.Ed., supt. Fax 463-6735
www.beau.k12.la.us/
Beauregard Alternative Program 50/Alt
506 Martin Luther King Dr 70634 337-462-2709
Cord Ensminger, prin. Fax 462-2710
DeRidder HS 800/9-12
723 ONeal St 70634 337-463-3266
Debbie Dixon, prin. Fax 463-9358
DeRidder JHS 600/6-8
415 N Frusha Dr 70634 337-463-9083
Eddie Joslin, prin. Fax 463-7696
East Beauregard HS 500/6-12
5364 Highway 113 70634 337-328-7511
Larry Hollie, prin. Fax 328-8132
Other Schools – See Longville, Merryville, Singer

---

Beckwith Christian S 100/PK-12
5525 Highway 27 70634 337-463-3437

**Destrehan, Saint Charles, Pop. 11,371**
St. Charles Parish SD
Supt. — See Luling
Destrehan HS 1,500/9-12
1 Wildcat Ln 70047 985-764-9946
Stephen Weber, prin. Fax 764-9948
Hurst MS 500/6-8
170 Road Runner Ln 70047 985-764-6367
Steven Guitterrez, prin. Fax 764-2678

**Deville, Rapides, Pop. 1,751**
Rapides Parish SD
Supt. — See Alexandria
Buckeye JSHS 1,100/6-12
PO Box 439 71328 318-466-5678
Doyle DeWayne Vines, prin. Fax 466-9269

**Dodson, Winn, Pop. 331**
Winn Parish SD
Supt. — See Winnfield
Dodson S 300/PK-12
PO Box 97 71422 318-628-2172
Mike Hearne, prin. Fax 628-7515

**Donaldsonville, Ascension, Pop. 7,399**
Ascension Parish SD 19,600/PK-12
PO Box 189 70346 225-391-7000
Patrice Pujol, supt. Fax 473-7820
www.apsb.org
Donaldsonville HS 500/9-12
100 Tiger Dr 70346 225-391-7900
Marvin Evans, prin. Fax 473-4496
Lowery MS 100/6-8
2389 Highway 1 S Ste A 70346 225-391-7550
Nicole Grimes, prin. Fax 473-2514
Other Schools – See Geismar, Gonzales, Prairieville, Saint Amant

---

Ascension Catholic HS 200/9-12
311 Saint Vincent St 70346 225-473-9227
Sandy Pizzolato, prin. Fax 473-9235

**Doyline, Webster, Pop. 803**
Webster Parish SD
Supt. — See Minden
Doyline S 500/PK-12
376 College St 71023 318-745-3673
Fax 745-3695

**Dry Prong, Grant, Pop. 434**
Grant Parish SD
Supt. — See Colfax
Grant HS 700/9-12
17779 Highway 167 71423 318-899-3331
Amanda Morrison, prin. Fax 899-5724
Grant JHS 400/7-8
17773 Highway 167 71423 318-899-5697
Robert Smith, prin. Fax 899-7346

**Dulac, Terrebonne, Pop. 1,389**
Terrebonne Parish SD
Supt. — See Houma
Grand Caillou MS 200/6-8
2161 Grand Caillou Rd, 985-876-7172
Judy Gaspard, prin. Fax 876-7279

**Duson, Lafayette, Pop. 1,682**
Lafayette Parish SD
Supt. — See Lafayette
Judice MS 600/6-8
2645 S Fieldspan Rd 70529 337-521-7890
Samuel Clay, prin. Fax 521-7891

**Edgard, Saint John the Baptist, Pop. 2,428**
St. John The Baptist Parish SD
Supt. — See Reserve
West St. John HS 200/8-12
PO Box 160 70049 985-497-3271
Claude Hill, prin. Fax 497-5009

**Elizabeth, Allen, Pop. 531**
Allen Parish SD
Supt. — See Oberlin
Elizabeth S 400/PK-12
PO Box 580 70638 318-634-5341
Keith Morgan, prin. Fax 634-5218

**Elmer, Rapides**
Rapides Parish SD
Supt. — See Alexandria
Oak Hill HS 400/K-12
7362 Highway 112 71424 318-793-2014
Kerry Rogers, prin. Fax 793-8589

**Elton, Jefferson Davis, Pop. 1,103**
Jefferson Davis Parish SD
Supt. — See Jennings
Elton JSHS 300/6-12
903 2nd St 70532 337-584-2991
Danielle Simien, prin. Fax 584-2244

**Epps, West Carroll, Pop. 844**
West Carroll Parish SD
Supt. — See Oak Grove
Epps S 300/PK-12
PO Box 277 71237 318-926-3624
Penny Hale, prin. Fax 926-5655

**Erath, Vermilion, Pop. 2,099**
Vermilion Parish SD
Supt. — See Abbeville
Erath HS 500/9-12
808 S Broadway St 70533 337-937-8451
Marc Turner, prin. Fax 937-5109
Erath MS 500/6-8
800 S Broadway St 70533 337-937-4441
Sandy Huval, prin. Fax 937-5125

**Eunice, Saint Landry, Pop. 10,256**
St. Landry Parish SD
Supt. — See Opelousas
Eunice Career & Technical Education Ctr. Vo/Tech
421 S 10th St 70535 337-457-8686
Kristina Joubert, prin. Fax 457-0307
Eunice HS 600/9-12
301 S Bobcat Dr 70535 337-457-3011
Mitchell Fontenot, prin. Fax 457-3720

Eunice JHS 400/7-8
751 W Oak Ave 70535 337-457-7386
Lakesha Miller, prin. Fax 457-1764

---

Louisiana Academy of Beauty Post-Sec.
550 E Laurel Ave 70535 337-457-7627
Louisiana State University Eunice Post-Sec.
2048 Johnson Hwy 70535 337-457-7311
St. Edmund HS 200/7-12
351 W Magnolia Ave 70535 337-457-2592
Laurie Doucet, prin. Fax 457-2510

**Evans, Vernon**
Vernon Parish SD
Supt. — See Leesville
Evans S 400/PK-12
18829 Highway 111 70639 337-286-5289
Ulita Watson, prin. Fax 286-9298

**Farmerville, Union, Pop. 3,818**
Union Parish SD 2,000/PK-12
PO Box 308 71241 318-368-9715
Dr. George Cannon, supt. Fax 368-1012
www.unionpsd.org
Union Parish HS 600/9-12
300 Anthony St 71241 318-368-2661
David Gray, prin. Fax 368-2229
Union Parish JHS 200/7-8
606 Bernice St 71241 318-368-9235
Kristi Auger, prin. Fax 368-1989

---

Union Christian Academy 200/PK-12
110 W Hill St 71241 318-368-8890

**Ferriday, Concordia, Pop. 3,491**
Concordia Parish SD
Supt. — See Vidalia
Concordia Education Center 50/Alt
160 Kindergarten Rd 71334 318-757-3941
Lillian Franklin, prin. Fax 757-3330
Ferriday HS 300/9-12
801 EE Wallace Blvd N 71334 318-757-8626
James Davis, prin. Fax 757-0763
Ferriday JHS 300/6-8
201 Martin Luther King Blvd 71334 318-757-8695
Arlana Davis, prin. Fax 757-8696

---

Central Louisiana Technical College Post-Sec.
PO Box 1465 71334 318-757-6501

**Florien, Sabine, Pop. 616**
Sabine Parish SD
Supt. — See Many
Florien S 600/PK-12
500 High School Rd 71429 318-586-3681
Eddie Jones, prin. Fax 586-3822

**Folsom, Saint Tammany, Pop. 708**
St. Tammany Parish SD
Supt. — See Covington
Folsom JHS 200/6-8
83055 Hay Hollow Rd 70437 985-796-3724
Sharon Garrett, prin. Fax 796-3701

**Forest, West Carroll, Pop. 348**
West Carroll Parish SD
Supt. — See Oak Grove
Forest S 500/PK-12
PO Box 368 71242 318-428-3672
James Harris, prin. Fax 428-8875

**Franklin, Saint Mary, Pop. 7,561**
St. Mary Parish SD
Supt. — See Centerville
Franklin HS 400/9-12
1401 Cynthia St 70538 337-828-0143
Tybus Burdett, prin. Fax 828-0184
Franklin JHS 300/6-8
525 Morris St 70538 337-828-0855
Molly Stadalis, prin. Fax 828-5095
St. Mary Parish Alternative S 100/Alt
131 Clausen Rd S 70538 337-836-9388
Harry Williams, admin. Fax 836-9397

---

Hanson Memorial HS 300/6-12
903 Anderson St 70538 337-828-3487
Kim Adams, prin. Fax 828-0787

**Franklinton, Washington, Pop. 3,833**
Washington Parish SD 5,400/PK-12
PO Box 587 70438 985-839-3436
Darrell Fairburn, supt. Fax 839-5464
www.wpsb.org
Franklinton HS 800/9-12
1 Demon Cir 70438 985-839-6781
Lisa Tanner, prin. Fax 839-9830
Franklinton JHS 700/6-8
617 Main St 70438 985-839-3501
Tiffany Hughes-Smith, prin. Fax 839-6912
Pine JSHS 600/6-12
1 Raider Dr 70438 985-848-5243
Jennifer Thomas, prin. Fax 848-9433
Other Schools – See Mount Hermon, Varnado

---

Bowling Green S 400/PK-12
700 Varnado St 70438 985-839-5317

**French Settlement, Livingston, Pop. 1,104**
Livingston Parish SD
Supt. — See Livingston
French Settlement JSHS 400/7-12
15875 LA Highway 16 70733 225-698-3561
Lance Hutson, prin. Fax 698-6458

**Geismar, Ascension**
Ascension Parish SD
Supt. — See Donaldsonville
Dutchtown HS 1,900/9-12
13165 Highway 73 70734 225-391-6200
Carli Francois, prin. Fax 677-8191
Dutchtown MS 700/6-8
13078 Highway 73 70734 225-391-7800
Doug Walker, prin. Fax 621-2351

**Georgetown, Grant, Pop. 323**
Grant Parish SD
Supt. — See Colfax
Georgetown S 300/PK-12
PO Box 99 71432 318-827-5306
Carla Lasyone Ph.D., prin. Fax 827-9481

**Gibsland, Bienville, Pop. 966**
Bienville Parish SD
Supt. — See Arcadia
Gibsland-Coleman S 200/K-12
PO Box 70 71028 318-843-6247
Samuel Andrews, prin. Fax 843-9804

**Glenmora, Rapides, Pop. 1,328**
Rapides Parish SD
Supt. — See Alexandria
Glenmora HS 300/K-12
PO Box 697 71433 318-748-8145
Carrol Babb, prin. Fax 748-8146
Plainview S 300/PK-12
10935 Highway 112 71433 318-634-5944
Sonia Rasmussen, prin. Fax 634-5389

**Golden Meadow, Lafourche, Pop. 2,060**
Lafourche Parish SD
Supt. — See Thibodaux
Golden Meadow MS 400/6-8
630 S Bayou Dr 70357 985-475-7314
Hennessy Melancon, prin. Fax 475-6623

**Gonzales, Ascension, Pop. 9,648**
Ascension Parish SD
Supt. — See Donaldsonville
Central MS 700/6-8
14101 Roddy Rd 70737 225-391-6400
Monica Hills, prin. Fax 621-2682
East Ascension HS 1,700/9-12
612 E Worthy St 70737 225-391-6100
Traci McCorkle, prin. Fax 621-2397
Gonzales MS 600/6-8
1502 W Orice Roth Rd 70737 225-391-6450
Lori Charlet, prin. Fax 621-2509

---

Ascension Christian HS 200/8-12
14408 E A Academy Rd 70737 225-622-2800
Mark Pellegrin M.S., supt. Fax 622-2875
St. Theresa S 300/4-8
212 E New River St 70737 225-647-2803
Christine Musso, prin. Fax 647-7814

**Grambling, Lincoln, Pop. 4,930**
Grambling State Lab Schools 300/K-12
407 Central Ave 71245 318-274-6153
Dr. Pamela Payne, admin. Fax 274-3215
Grambling State University Lab. HS 100/9-12
407 Central Ave 71245 318-274-6153
Dr. Pamela Payne, prin. Fax 274-3215
Grambling State University Lab. MS 100/6-8
407 Central Ave 71245 318-274-6531
Dr. Pamela Payne, prin. Fax 274-3360

---

Grambling State University Post-Sec.
403 Main St 71245 318-274-3811

**Grand Cane, DeSoto, Pop. 242**

---

Central S 100/K-12
PO Box 187 71032 318-858-3319

**Grand Chenier, Cameron**
Cameron Parish SD
Supt. — See Cameron
South Cameron S 300/PK-12
753 Oak Grove Hwy 70643 337-542-4628
Bobbye Delaney, prin. Fax 542-4419

**Grand Coteau, Saint Landry, Pop. 940**

---

School of the Sacred Heart 500/PK-12
PO Box 310 70541 337-662-5275
Michael Baber, head sch Fax 662-3011

**Grand Isle, Jefferson, Pop. 1,269**
Jefferson Parish SD
Supt. — See Harvey
Grand Isle S 200/PK-12
PO Box 995 70358 985-787-2577
Richard Augustin, prin. Fax 787-3878

**Grant, Allen**
Allen Parish SD
Supt. — See Oberlin
Fairview S 400/PK-12
PO Box 216 70644 318-634-5354
Pylla Turner, prin. Fax 634-5357

**Gray, Terrebonne, Pop. 5,450**
Terrebonne Parish SD
Supt. — See Houma
Bourgeois HS 1,100/9-12
1 Reservation Ct 70359 985-872-3277
Matthew Hodson, prin. Fax 872-3270

**Greensburg, Saint Helena, Pop. 714**
St. Helena Parish SD 800/PK-12
PO Box 540 70441 225-222-4349
Dr. Kelli Joseph, supt. Fax 222-4937
www.sthpk-12.net
St. Helena College and Career Academy 300/7-12
14340 Highway 37 70441 225-222-4402
Reginald Douglas, prin. Fax 222-6986

---

Northshore Technical Community College Post-Sec.
PO Box 1300 70441 225-222-4251

**Gretna, Jefferson, Pop. 17,467**
Jefferson Parish SD
Supt. — See Harvey
Gretna MS 600/6-8
910 Gretna Blvd 70053 504-366-0120
Scott Deemer, prin. Fax 366-8807
Jefferson HS 400/9-12
17 Gretna Blvd 70053 504-363-4300
Andrew Vincent, prin. Fax 361-1114

Ruppel Academy for Advanced Studies 300/6-8
815 Huey P Long Ave 70053 504-361-8905
Emily Miller, prin. Fax 361-0792

**Gueydan, Vermilion, Pop. 1,385**
Vermilion Parish SD
Supt. — See Abbeville
Gueydan HS 200/6-12
901 Main St 70542 337-536-6938
Luddy Herpin, prin. Fax 536-7000

**Hackberry, Cameron, Pop. 1,258**
Cameron Parish SD
Supt. — See Cameron
Hackberry S 200/PK-12
1390 School St 70645 337-762-3305
Charles Wilson, prin. Fax 762-3304

**Hammond, Tangipahoa, Pop. 19,799**
Tangipahoa Parish SD
Supt. — See Amite
Hammond High Magnet S 1,200/9-12
45168 River Rd 70401 985-345-7235
Dr. Beth Moulds, prin. Fax 345-5252
Hammond Jr High Magnet S 500/7-8
111 J W Davis Dr 70403 985-345-2654
Mildred Johnson, prin. Fax 542-4215
Tangipahoa Alternative Solutions Program 100/Alt
411 E Crystal St 70401 985-542-5634
Marilyn Dunn, prin. Fax 542-9987

---

Compass Career College Post-Sec.
42353 Deluxe Plz Ste 20 70403 985-419-2050
North Oaks Medical Center Post-Sec.
15790 Medical Arts Dr 70403 985-543-6600
Northshore Technical Community College Post-Sec.
PO Box 489 70404 985-543-4120
St. Thomas Aquinas HS 400/9-12
14520 Voss Dr 70401 985-542-7662
Jose Becerra, prin. Fax 542-4010
Southeastern Louisiana University Post-Sec.
PO Box 784 70404 985-549-2000

**Harrisonburg, Catahoula, Pop. 340**
Catahoula Parish SD 1,100/PK-12
PO Box 690 71340 318-744-5727
Dr. Gwile Freeman, supt. Fax 744-9221
cpsbla.org/
Harrisonburg HS 100/K-12
PO Box 710 71340 318-744-5273
S. Floyd, prin. Fax 744-5273
Other Schools – See Jonesville, Sicily Island

**Harvey, Jefferson, Pop. 20,018**
Jefferson Parish SD 43,900/PK-12
501 Manhattan Blvd 70058 504-349-7600
Isaac Joseph, supt. Fax 349-7960
www.jppss.k12.la.us
Cox HS 1,000/9-12
2200 Lapalco Blvd 70058 504-367-6388
Mark Perry, prin. Fax 367-3176
West Jefferson HS 1,200/9-12
2200 8th St 70058 504-368-6055
Vanessa Brown-Lewis, prin. Fax 368-0535
Other Schools – See Avondale, Grand Isle, Gretna, Jefferson, Kenner, Lafitte, Marrero, Metairie, Terrytown, Westwego

**Haughton, Bossier, Pop. 3,398**
Bossier Parish SD
Supt. — See Benton
Haughton HS 1,100/9-12
210 E McKinley Ave 71037 318-549-5450
Gene Couvillion, prin. Fax 549-5470
Haughton MS 1,000/6-8
395 S Elm St 71037 318-549-5560
Waylon Bates, prin. Fax 549-5573

**Haynesville, Claiborne, Pop. 2,308**
Claiborne Parish SD
Supt. — See Homer
Haynesville JSHS 400/4-12
9930 Highway 79 71038 318-624-0905
Tony Guirlando, prin. Fax 624-2488

---

Claiborne Academy 300/PK-12
6741 Highway 79 71038 318-927-2747

**Holden, Livingston**
Livingston Parish SD
Supt. — See Livingston
Holden S 700/K-12
30120 LA 441 Hwy 70744 225-567-9367
Paula Green, prin. Fax 567-5248

**Homer, Claiborne, Pop. 3,200**
Claiborne Parish SD 1,800/PK-12
PO Box 600 71040 318-927-3502
William Kennedy, supt. Fax 927-9184
www.claibornepsb.org
Homer HS 200/9-12
1008 N Main St 71040 318-927-2985
Lee Simms, prin. Fax 927-4733
Homer JHS 200/5-8
612 Pelican Dr 71040 318-927-2826
Sue Barfield, prin. Fax 927-4376
Other Schools – See Haynesville, Summerfield

**Hornbeck, Vernon, Pop. 464**
Vernon Parish SD
Supt. — See Leesville
Hornbeck S 500/PK-12
PO Box 9 71439 318-565-4440
Raymond Jones, prin. Fax 565-4136

**Houma, Terrebonne, Pop. 33,132**
Lafourche Parish SD
Supt. — See Thibodaux
Bayou Blue MS 500/5-8
196 Mazerac St 70364 985-851-1952
Andre Adams, prin. Fax 851-1849

Terrebonne Parish SD 17,300/PK-12
PO Box 5097 70361 985-876-7400
Philip Martin, supt. Fax 872-0054
www.tpsd.org
East Street Alternative S 50/Alt
609 East St 70363 985-876-1093
Tommy Salter, prin. Fax 851-7931
Ellender Memorial HS 900/9-12
3012 Patriot Dr 70363 985-868-7903
Blaise Pellegrin, prin. Fax 868-3503
Evergreen JHS 700/7-8
5000 W Main St 70360 985-876-2606
Kelly Burlette, prin. Fax 868-4395
Houma JHS 1,100/7-9
315 Saint Charles St 70360 985-872-1511
Darrell Dillard, prin. Fax 872-5121
Oaklawn JHS 400/7-8
2215 Acadian Dr 70363 985-872-2904
Charles Bergeron, prin. Fax 917-1917
Terrebonne Career & Tech HS Vo/Tech
3051 Patriot Dr 70363 985-851-1163
William Simmons, prin. Fax 851-4480
Terrebonne HS 1,000/10-12
7318 Main St 70360 985-879-3377
Julio Contreras, prin. Fax 223-2270
Bayou Cane Adult Education Adult
6484 W Main St 70360 985-876-3180
Marilyn Schwartz, coord. Fax 876-0411
Other Schools – See Bourg, Chauvin, Dulac, Gray, Montegut

---

Blue Cliff College-Houma Post-Sec.
803 Barrow St 70360 985-601-4000
Covenant Christian Academy 200/K-12
144 Rue Des Affaires 70364 985-851-7567
Jason Hutchinson M.Ed., prin. Fax 851-1087
Houma Christian S 400/PK-12
109 Valhi Blvd 70360 985-851-7423
James Champagne, prin. Fax 872-4958
Messiah Montessori International S 100/PK-12
PO Box 20027 70360 985-857-8808
Dr. Jules Boquet, head sch Fax 851-3116
Omega Institute of Cosmetology Post-Sec.
229 S Hollywood Rd 70360 985-876-9334
South Louisiana Beauty College Post-Sec.
300 Howard Ave 70363 985-873-8978
Vandebilt Catholic HS 900/8-12
209 S Hollywood Rd 70360 985-876-2551
Yvonne Weimer, prin. Fax 868-9774

**Independence, Saint Helena, Pop. 1,638**
Tangipahoa Parish SD
Supt. — See Amite
Independence HS 500/9-12
270 Tiger Ave 70443 985-878-9436
Mike Stant, prin. Fax 878-4831
Independence Middle Magnet S 300/5-8
300 W 2nd St 70443 985-878-4376
Alexa Hookfin, prin. Fax 878-4848

**Iota, Acadia, Pop. 1,481**
Acadia Parish SD
Supt. — See Crowley
Iota HS 400/9-12
456 S 5th St 70543 337-779-2534
Dr. Cindy Abshire, prin. Fax 779-2872
Iota MS 300/6-8
426 S 5th St 70543 337-779-2536
Lee Ann Wall, prin. Fax 779-2594

**Iowa, Calcasieu, Pop. 2,909**
Calcasieu Parish SD
Supt. — See Lake Charles
Iowa MSHS 500/6-12
401 W Miller Ave 70647 337-217-4380
Michael Oakley, prin. Fax 217-4381

**Jackson, East Feliciana, Pop. 3,776**
East Feliciana Parish SD
Supt. — See Clinton
East Feliciana HS 300/9-12
3501 Highway 10 70748 225-634-5931
Curt Green, prin. Fax 634-3207

---

Baton Rouge Community College Jackson Post-Sec.
3337 Highway 10 70748 225-634-2636

**Jeanerette, Iberia, Pop. 5,487**
Iberia Parish SD
Supt. — See New Iberia
Jeanerette HS 300/9-12
8217 E Old Spanish Trl 70544 337-276-6038
Linda Freeman, prin. Fax 276-5016

**Jefferson, Jefferson, Pop. 11,058**
Jefferson Parish SD
Supt. — See Harvey
Martyn Alternative S 50/Alt
1108 Shrewsbury Rd 70121 504-838-6933
Theresa Henderson, prin. Fax 831-0247
Riverdale HS 900/9-12
240 Riverdale Dr 70121 504-833-7288
Danielle Yunusah, prin. Fax 340-4531
Riverdale MS 800/6-8
3900 Jefferson Hwy 70121 504-828-2706
Randy Bennett, prin. Fax 833-5125

**Jena, LaSalle, Pop. 3,373**
LaSalle Parish SD 2,600/PK-12
PO Box 90 71342 318-992-2161
Roy Breithaupt, supt. Fax 992-8457
www.lasallepsb.com
Jena HS 400/9-12
PO Box 89 71342 318-992-5195
Glen Joiner, prin. Fax 992-4797
Jena JHS 300/6-8
PO Box 920 71342 318-992-5815
Rhonda Russell, prin. Fax 992-6392
Other Schools – See Olla, Urania

**Jennings, Jefferson Davis, Pop. 10,205**
Jefferson Davis Parish SD 5,800/PK-12
PO Box 640 70546 337-824-1834
Brian M. LeJeune, supt. Fax 824-9737
www.jeffersondavis.org
Hathaway S 500/PK-12
4040 Pine Island Hwy 70546 337-824-4452
Jeremy Fuselier, prin. Fax 824-2769
Jennings HS 900/7-12
2310 N Sherman St 70546 337-824-0642
Benjamin Oustalet, prin. Fax 824-5585
West End Instructional Center Alt
802 W Jefferson St 70546 337-824-9521
Kent Ray, prin. Fax 824-9978
Other Schools – See Elton, Lacassine, Lake Arthur, Roanoke, Welsh

---

Bethel Christian S 200/PK-12
15147 Highway 102 70546 337-824-0020
Dr. Blaine St. Germain, prin. Fax 824-0579

**Jonesboro, Jackson, Pop. 4,648**
Jackson Parish SD 2,300/PK-12
PO Box 705 71251 318-259-4456
Wayne Alford, supt. Fax 259-2527
www.jpsb.us/
Jonesboro-Hodge HS 300/9-12
225 Pershing Hwy 71251 318-259-4138
Michael Beck, prin. Fax 259-2701
Jonesboro-Hodge MS 300/5-8
440 Old Winnfield Rd 71251 318-259-6611
Norman Amos, prin. Fax 259-9699
Weston S 600/PK-12
213 Highway 505 71251 318-259-7313
Dr. Robin Potts, prin. Fax 259-1056
Other Schools – See Quitman

**Jonesville, Catahoula, Pop. 2,258**
Catahoula Parish SD
Supt. — See Harrisonburg
Block HS 300/8-12
300 Division St 71343 318-339-7996
Jeffrey Odom, prin. Fax 339-7901
Catahoula Parish Alternative S Alt
300 Division St 71343 318-339-7996
Andrea Cruse, prin. Fax 339-7901
Central S 100/K-12
244 Larto Bayou Rd 71343 318-339-7574
Johnnie Adams, prin. Fax 339-7925

**Kaplan, Vermilion, Pop. 4,526**
Vermilion Parish SD
Supt. — See Abbeville
Kaplan HS 500/9-12
200 E Pirates Ln 70548 337-643-6385
Janet Guerrini, prin. Fax 643-3543
Rost MS 400/5-8
112 W 6th St 70548 337-643-8545
David Dupuis, prin. Fax 643-7013

**Kenner, Jefferson, Pop. 65,713**
Jefferson Parish SD
Supt. — See Harvey
Bonnabel Magnet Academy HS 1,600/9-12
2801 Bruin Dr 70065 504-443-4564
Dawn Kalb, prin. Fax 443-3401
Roosevelt MS 600/6-8
3315 Maine Ave 70065 504-443-1361
John Olson, prin. Fax 443-3425

---

Herzing University Post-Sec.
2500 Williams Blvd 70062 504-733-0074
John Jay Kenner Academy Post-Sec.
2844 Tennessee Ave 70062 504-467-2951
Southwest University Post-Sec.
2200 Veterans Memorial Blvd 70062 504-468-2900

**Kentwood, Tangipahoa, Pop. 2,191**
Tangipahoa Parish SD
Supt. — See Amite
Kentwood High Magnet S 300/7-12
603 9th St 70444 985-229-2881
Rochell Bates, prin. Fax 229-6031
Sumner HS 500/9-12
15841 Highway 440 70444 985-229-8805
Walter Stuckey, prin. Fax 229-2043
Sumner MS 400/6-8
15649 Highway 440 70444 985-310-2152
Brenda Johnson, prin. Fax 229-4257

**Kilbourne, West Carroll, Pop. 412**
West Carroll Parish SD
Supt. — See Oak Grove
Kilbourne S 300/PK-12
PO Box 339 71253 318-428-3721
Brandon Smith, prin. Fax 428-3860

**Kinder, Allen, Pop. 2,412**
Allen Parish SD
Supt. — See Oberlin
Kinder HS 300/9-12
145 Highway 383 70648 337-738-2886
Loma Bertrand, prin. Fax 738-5665
Kinder MS 300/5-8
414 N 12th St 70648 337-738-3223
Tracey Odom, prin. Fax 738-3425

**Labadieville, Assumption, Pop. 1,837**
Assumption Parish SD
Supt. — See Napoleonville
Labadieville MS 300/5-8
2747 Highway 1 70372 985-526-4227
Corey Crochet, prin. Fax 526-4163

**Lacassine, Jefferson Davis, Pop. 475**
Jefferson Davis Parish SD
Supt. — See Jennings
Lacassine S 600/PK-12
PO Box 50 70650 337-588-4205
Christina Fontenot, prin. Fax 588-4283

**Lafayette, Lafayette, Pop. 118,722**
Lafayette Parish SD 30,300/PK-12
PO Box 2158 70502 337-521-7000
Dr. Donald Aguillard, supt. Fax 233-0977
www.lpssonline.com
Acadiana HS 1,700/9-12
315 Rue Du Belier 70506 337-521-7950
David LeJeune, prin. Fax 521-7951
Acadian MS 500/5-8
4201 Moss St 70507 337-521-7840
Linda Nance, prin. Fax 521-7841
Alleman MS 1,000/5-8
600 Roselawn Blvd 70503 337-521-7850
Jennifer Gardner, prin. Fax 521-7851
Breaux MS 800/6-8
1400 S Orange St 70501 337-521-7860
Stephen Judice, prin. Fax 521-7861
Carencro HS 1,200/9-12
721 W Butcher Switch Rd 70507 337-521-7960
Ken Roebuck, prin. Fax 521-7961
Comeaux HS 1,900/9-12
100 W Bluebird St 70508 337-521-7970
Mary Sonnier, prin. Fax 521-7971
Early College Academy 200/9-12
320 Devalcourt St 70506 337-521-8956
Anne Castille, prin. Fax 262-1940
Lafayette HS 2,400/9-12
3000 W Congress St 70506 337-521-7980
Dr. Donald Thornton, prin. Fax 521-7981
Lafayette MS 500/6-8
1301 W University Ave 70506 337-521-7900
Allison El Koubi, prin. Fax 521-7901
Martin MS 700/5-8
401 Broadmoor Blvd 70503 337-521-7910
Jeanne Hebert, prin. Fax 521-7911
Moss Preparatory Program Alt
801 Mudd Ave 70501 337-521-7580
Jody Duhon, admin. Fax 521-7581
Northside HS 800/9-12
301 Dunand St 70501 337-521-7990
Julia Williams, prin. Fax 521-7991
Smith Career Center Vo/Tech
200 18th St 70501 337-521-7570
Alicia Caesar, prin. Fax 521-7571
Thibodaux STEM Magnet Academy 400/6-12
805 Teurlings Dr 70501 337-521-7920
Jeff Debetaz, prin. Fax 521-7921
Other Schools – See Broussard, Carencro, Duson, Scott, Youngsville

---

Ascension Episcopal S 700/PK-12
1030 Johnston St 70501 337-233-9748
Paul Quick, hdmstr. Fax 269-9768
Blue Cliff College Post-Sec.
120 James Comeaux Rd 70508 337-269-0620
Cosmetology Training Center Post-Sec.
2516 Johnston St 70503 337-237-6868
Delta College of Arts & Technology Post-Sec.
200 Republic Ave Ste F 70508 337-988-5455
Lafayette Christian Academy 800/PK-12
220 Portland Ave 70507 337-234-9860
Lafayette General Medical Center Post-Sec.
PO Box 52009 70505 337-261-7381
Lockworks Academie of Hairdressing Post-Sec.
2922 Johnston St 70503 337-233-0511
Remington College Post-Sec.
303 Rue Louis XIV 70508 337-981-4010
Ronnie & Dorman's School of Hair Design Post-Sec.
201 Saint Joseph St 70506 337-232-1806
St. Genevieve MS 200/6-8
91 Teurlings Dr 70501 337-266-5553
Julie Zaunbrecher, prin. Fax 266-5775
St. Thomas More HS 1,000/9-12
450 E Farrel Rd 70508 337-988-3700
Richard Lavergne, prin. Fax 988-2911
South Louisiana Community College Post-Sec.
1101 Bertrand Dr 70506 337-521-9000
South Louisiana Community College Post-Sec.
320 Devalcourt St 70506 337-521-9000
Teurlings Catholic HS 700/9-12
139 Teurlings Dr 70501 337-235-5711
Michael Boyer, prin. Fax 234-8057
Unitech Training Academy Post-Sec.
3605 Ambassador Caffery Pky 70503 337-988-6764
University Medical Center Post-Sec.
2390 W Congress St 70506 337-261-6004
University of Louisiana at Lafayette Post-Sec.
104 E University Ave 70503 337-482-1000

**Lafitte, Jefferson, Pop. 956**
Jefferson Parish SD
Supt. — See Harvey
Fisher MSHS 400/6-12
2529 Jean Lafitte Blvd 70067 504-689-3665
Debbie Dantin, prin. Fax 689-7556

**Lake Arthur, Jefferson Davis, Pop. 2,693**
Jefferson Davis Parish SD
Supt. — See Jennings
Lake Arthur JSHS 400/7-12
4374 Tiger Ln 70549 337-774-5152
Amanda Fontenot, prin. Fax 774-2522

**Lake Charles, Calcasieu, Pop. 70,438**
Calcasieu Parish SD 32,500/PK-12
PO Box 800 70602 337-217-4000
Karl Bruchhaus, supt. Fax 217-4051
www.cpsb.org
Barbe HS 1,900/9-12
2200 W McNeese St 70605 337-217-4460
Shannon LaFargue, prin. Fax 217-4461
Calcasieu Parish Alternative HS 100/Alt
745 S Shattuck St 70601 337-217-4290
Kenny Brown, prin. Fax 217-4291
College Street T & I Vocational Ctr Vo/Tech
739 E College St 70607 337-217-4370
Justin Mahoney, prin. Fax 217-4371
Houston HS 1,200/9-12
880 Sam Houston Jones Pkwy 70611 337-217-4480
Shannon Foolkes, prin. Fax 217-4481
LaGrange HS 1,000/9-12
3420 Louisiana Ave 70607 337-217-4960
Rico Guillory, prin. Fax 217-4961
Lake Charles/Boston Academy 400/9-12
1509 Enterprise Blvd 70601 337-217-4390
Beth Fraser, prin. Fax 217-4391
Molo Magnet MS 400/6-8
2300 Medora St 70601 337-217-4710
Shonna Anderson, prin. Fax 217-4711
Moss Bluff MS 900/6-8
297 Park Rd 70611 337-217-4570
Kendall Fontenot, prin. Fax 217-4571

Oak Park MS 500/6-8
2200 Oak Park Blvd 70601 337-217-4830
Martin Guillory, prin. Fax 217-4831
STEPS HS 9-12
3820 Bennett Johnston Ave 70615 337-491-2607
Matthew Rion, prin. Fax 491-2649
Washington-Marion Magnet HS 700/9-12
2802 Pineview St 70615 337-217-4540
Jackie Shelton, prin. Fax 217-4541
Welsh MS 1,300/6-8
1500 W Mcneese St 70605 337-217-4410
Bobby Jack Thompson, prin. Fax 217-4412
White MS 600/6-8
1000 E McNeese St 70607 337-217-4810
Owen Clanton, prin. Fax 217-4811
Other Schools – See Bell City, Dequincy, Iowa, Starks, Sulphur, Vinton, Westlake

Cameron Parish SD
Supt. — See Cameron
Grand Lake S 800/PK-12
1039 Highway 384 70607 337-905-2231
Jackie Holmes, prin. Fax 905-2961

---

Covenant Grace Academy 50/K-12
2110 E McNeese St 70607 337-474-2424
Marla Pennick, admin. Fax 474-2424
Delta School of Business and Technology Post-Sec.
517 Broad St 70601 337-439-5765
Hamilton Christian Academy 300/PK-12
1415 8th St 70601 337-439-1178
Lake Charles Memorial Hospital Post-Sec.
1701 Oak Park Blvd 70601 337-494-3200
McNeese State University Post-Sec.
4205 Ryan St 70605 337-475-5000
St. Louis HS 600/9-12
1620 Bank St 70601 337-436-7275
Christopher Fontenot, pres. Fax 436-6792
St. Patrick's Hospital Post-Sec.
524 S Ryan St 70601 337-491-7730
Sowela Technical Community College Post-Sec.
3820 Senator Johnston Ave 70615 337-421-6565
Stage One - The Hair School Post-Sec.
209 W College St 70605 337-474-0533

**Lake Providence, East Carroll, Pop. 3,969**
East Carroll Parish SD 1,200/PK-12
PO Box 792 71254 318-559-2222
Dr. Voleria Millikin, supt. Fax 559-3864
www.e-carrollschools.org
Griffin Middle Academy 200/6-8
1205 Charles D Jones Blvd 71254 318-559-1395
Janice Harris, prin. Fax 559-0679
Trass HS 300/9-12
700 Martin Luther King Jr 71254 318-559-1984
Rickey Taylor, prin. Fax 559-5380

---

Briarfield Academy 200/PK-12
301 Riddle Ln 71254 318-559-2360

**Laplace, Saint John the Baptist, Pop. 29,464**

---

St. Charles Catholic HS 400/8-12
100 Dominican Rd 70068 985-652-3809
Andrew Cupit, prin. Fax 652-2609

**Larose, Lafourche, Pop. 7,283**
Lafourche Parish SD
Supt. — See Thibodaux
Larose-Cut Off MS 500/6-8
13356 W Main St 70373 985-693-3273
Samantha Lagarde, prin. Fax 693-3270

**Lecompte, Rapides, Pop. 1,209**
Rapides Parish SD
Supt. — See Alexandria
Rapides HS 300/9-12
PO Box 770 71346 318-776-9371
Jeff Hickman, prin. Fax 776-5844

---

Red River Academy 100/7-12
PO Box 1255 71346 318-776-5655

**Leesville, Vernon, Pop. 6,343**
Vernon Parish SD 10,100/PK-12
201 Belview Rd 71446 337-239-3401
James Williams, supt. Fax 238-5777
www.vpsb.k12.la.us
Hicks S 400/PK-12
1296 Hicks School Rd 71446 337-239-9645
Rhonda Roberts, prin. Fax 239-6149
Leesville HS 900/9-12
502 Berry Ave 71446 337-239-3464
Mark Freshley, prin. Fax 239-2485
Leesville JHS 500/7-8
480 Berry Ave 71446 337-239-3874
Robert Causey, prin. Fax 238-4113
Pickering JSHS 600/7-12
180 Lebleu Rd 71446 337-537-1555
Hubert Jordan, prin. Fax 537-3019
Vernon Parish Optional S 50/Alt
1100 Abe Allen Memorial Dr 71446 337-392-0008
Roger Rolon, prin. Fax 392-0009
Other Schools – See Anacoco, Evans, Hornbeck, Pitkin, Rosepine, Simpson

---

Central Louisiana Technical College Post-Sec.
15014 Lake Charles Hwy 71446 337-537-3135
Faith Training Christian Academy 400/PK-12
603 E Mechanic St 71446 337-329-1569

**Lena, Rapides**
Rapides Parish SD
Supt. — See Alexandria
Northwood HS 800/PK-12
8830 Highway 1 N 71447 318-793-8021
Jill Summers, prin. Fax 793-8503

**Livingston, Livingston, Pop. 1,758**
Livingston Parish SD 23,300/PK-12
PO Box 1130 70754 225-686-7044
John Watson, supt. Fax 686-3052
www.lpsb.org
Doyle JSHS 500/7-12
PO Box 160 70754 225-686-2318
Thomas Hodges, prin. Fax 686-2701
Other Schools – See Albany, Denham Springs, French Settlement, Holden, Maurepas, Springfield, Walker, Watson

**Livonia, Pointe Coupee, Pop. 1,418**
Pointe Coupee Parish SD
Supt. — See New Roads
Livonia HS 800/7-12
PO Box 549 70755 225-637-2532
Stacey Gueho, prin. Fax 637-3024

**Lockport, Lafourche, Pop. 2,549**
Lafourche Parish SD
Supt. — See Thibodaux
Lockport MS 300/6-8
720 Main St 70374 985-532-2597
Jarod Martin, prin. Fax 532-5811

**Logansport, DeSoto, Pop. 1,527**
DeSoto Parish SD
Supt. — See Mansfield
Logansport S 300/PK-12
PO Box 549 71049 318-697-4338
Matt LaFollette, prin. Fax 697-1120
Stanley S 400/PK-12
14323 Highway 84 71049 318-697-2664
Carolyn Phillips, prin. Fax 697-5984

**Longville, Beauregard, Pop. 621**
Beauregard Parish SD
Supt. — See Deridder
South Beauregard JSHS 700/7-12
151 Longville Church Rd 70652 337-725-3536
Tammy Crain, prin. Fax 725-6222

**Loranger, Tangipahoa**
Tangipahoa Parish SD
Supt. — See Amite
Loranger HS 600/9-12
19404 Hiatt St 70446 985-878-6271
Rhea Marrs, prin. Fax 878-4875
Loranger MS 600/5-8
54123 Allman St 70446 985-878-9455
Catherine Perry, prin. Fax 878-4907

**Loreauville, Iberia, Pop. 881**
Iberia Parish SD
Supt. — See New Iberia
Loreauville JSHS 400/7-12
PO Box 446 70552 337-229-4701
Karen Bashay, prin. Fax 229-4275

**Luling, Saint Charles, Pop. 11,952**
St. Charles Parish SD 8,200/PK-12
13855 River Rd 70070 985-785-6289
Felecia Gomez-Walker, supt. Fax 785-1025
www.stcharles.k12.la.us
Smith MS 300/6-8
281 Judge Edward Dufresne 70070 985-331-1018
Harold Blood, prin. Fax 331-9385
Other Schools – See Boutte, Destrehan, Paradis, Saint Rose

**Lutcher, Saint James, Pop. 3,521**
St. James Parish SD 3,700/PK-12
PO Box 338 70071 225-258-4500
Alonzo Luce Ph.D., supt. Fax 869-8845
www.stjames.k12.la.us
Career & Technology Center Vo/Tech
1410 Buddy Whitney St 70071 225-258-4571
Tracy Zeringue, dir. Fax 869-7935
Lutcher HS 1,000/7-12
1910 W Main St 70071 225-258-5300
Dr. Daryl Scoggin, prin. Fax 869-8872
Other Schools – See Saint James, Vacherie

**Madisonville, Saint Tammany, Pop. 704**
St. Tammany Parish SD
Supt. — See Covington
Madisonville JHS 500/6-8
PO Box 850 70447 985-845-3355
Dwayne Kern, prin. Fax 845-9018

**Mamou, Evangeline, Pop. 3,194**
Evangeline Parish SD
Supt. — See Ville Platte
Mamou JSHS 700/5-12
1008 7th St 70554 337-468-5793
Liz Chatelain, prin. Fax 468-2220

**Mandeville, Saint Tammany, Pop. 11,401**
St. Tammany Parish SD
Supt. — See Covington
Fontainebleau HS 1,600/9-12
100 Bulldog Dr 70471 985-892-7112
Johnny Vitrano, prin. Fax 892-9894
Fountainebleau JHS 900/7-8
100 Hurricane Aly 70471 985-875-7501
Dr. Timothy Schneider, prin. Fax 875-7650
Lakeshore HS 900/9-12
26301 Highway 1088 70448 985-624-5046
Christian Monson, prin. Fax 624-5202
Mandeville HS 1,700/9-12
1 Skipper Dr 70471 985-626-5225
Bruce Bundy, prin. Fax 626-5298
Mandeville JHS 700/7-8
639 Carondelet St 70448 985-626-4428
Mary Ann Cucchiara, prin. Fax 674-0401
Monteleone JHS 600/7-8
63000 Blue Marlin Dr 70448 985-951-8088
Sheri Jones, prin. Fax 951-8083

**Mangham, Richland, Pop. 672**
Richland Parish SD
Supt. — See Rayville
Mangham HS 200/9-12
PO Box 348 71259 318-248-2485
Connie Williams, prin. Fax 248-2406
Mangham JHS 200/6-8
810 McConnel St 71259 318-248-2729
Connie Williams, prin. Fax 248-2931

**Mansfield, DeSoto, Pop. 4,973**
DeSoto Parish SD 4,500/PK-12
201 Crosby St 71052 318-872-2836
Dr. Cade Brumley, supt. Fax 872-1324
www.desotopsb.com
DeSoto Alternative S 50/Alt
2269 Whaley St 71052 318-871-0493
Toras Hill, prin. Fax 871-0496
Mansfield HS 400/9-12
401 Kings Hwy 71052 318-872-0793
Sedric Clark, prin. Fax 872-2223
Mansfield MS 400/5-8
1915 McArthur Dr 71052 318-872-1309
Grayson Collins, prin. Fax 872-1319
Other Schools – See Logansport, Stonewall

---

Northwest Louisiana Technical College Post-Sec.
943 Oxford Rd 71052 318-872-2243

**Many, Sabine, Pop. 2,778**
Sabine Parish SD 4,100/PK-12
PO Box 1079 71449 318-256-9228
Dr. Sara Ebarb, supt. Fax 256-0105
www.sabine.k12.la.us
Many HS 300/9-12
100 Tiger Dr 71449 318-256-2114
Norman Booker, prin. Fax 256-0492
Many JHS 400/4-8
1801 Natchitoches Hwy 71449 318-256-3573
Madeline Owens, prin. Fax 256-2846
Sabine Career Academy Alt
910 W Mississippi Ave 71449 318-256-0582
Charlie Mason, prin. Fax 256-5470
Other Schools – See Converse, Florien, Negreet, Noble, Pleasant Hill, Zwolle

---

Northwest Louisiana Technical College Post-Sec.
PO Box 790 71449 318-256-4101

**Marksville, Avoyelles, Pop. 5,505**
Avoyelles Parish SD 5,900/PK-12
221 Tunica Dr W 71351 318-253-5982
Dwayne Lemoine, supt. Fax 253-5178
www.avoyellespsb.com
Marksville HS 900/7-12
407 W Bontemps St 71351 318-253-9356
Marvin Hall, prin. Fax 253-4256
Other Schools – See Bunkie, Moreauville

**Marrero, Jefferson, Pop. 32,762**
Jefferson Parish SD
Supt. — See Harvey
Cullier Career Center Vo/Tech
1429 Ames Blvd Ste B 70072 504-340-6963
Preston Gassery, prin. Fax 341-1022
Ehret HS 1,700/9-12
4300 Patriot St 70072 504-340-7651
Maria Landry, prin. Fax 340-7295
Higgins HS 1,500/9-12
7201 Lapalco Blvd 70072 504-341-2273
Randi Hindman, prin. Fax 341-8110
Marrero MS 900/6-8
4100 7th St 70072 504-341-5842
Christina Conforto, prin. Fax 341-0004
St. Ville-Douglass Connections 100/Alt
4300 Patriot St 70072 504-368-5962
Fax 362-1904
Truman MS 600/6-8
5417 Ehret Rd 70072 504-341-0961
Terry Johnson, prin. Fax 347-4497

---

Academy of Our Lady HS 500/8-12
5501 Westbank Expy 70072 504-341-6217
Sr. Michelle Geiger, prin. Fax 341-6229
Archbishop Shaw HS 500/8-12
1000 Barataria Blvd 70072 504-340-6727
George Hebert, prin. Fax 347-9883

**Maurepas, Livingston**
Livingston Parish SD
Supt. — See Livingston
Maurepas S 400/K-12
PO Box 39 70449 225-695-6111
Kenny Kraft, prin. Fax 695-3265

**Maurice, Vermilion, Pop. 953**
Vermilion Parish SD
Supt. — See Abbeville
North Vermilion HS 800/9-12
11609 LA Highway 699 70555 337-898-1491
Tommy Byler, prin. Fax 893-8684
North Vermilion MS 6-8
11609 LA Highway 699 70555 337-893-1583
Joan Romero, prin. Fax 893-1585

**Meraux, Saint Bernard, Pop. 5,703**
St. Bernard Parish SD
Supt. — See Chalmette
Trist MS 500/6-8
1 Pirates Cv 70075 504-872-9402
Denise Pritchard, prin. Fax 872-9426

**Merryville, Beauregard, Pop. 1,088**
Beauregard Parish SD
Supt. — See Deridder
Merryville HS 500/K-12
7061 Highway 110 W 70653 337-825-8046
Donnie Love, prin. Fax 825-6443

**Metairie, Jefferson, Pop. 136,499**
Jefferson Parish SD
Supt. — See Harvey
Adams MS 800/6-8
5525 Henican Pl 70003 504-887-5240
Fax 887-0173
East Jefferson HS 1,100/9-12
400 Phlox Ave 70001 504-888-7171
James Kytle, prin. Fax 888-2072
Harris MS 700/6-8
911 Elise Ave 70003 504-733-0867
Otis Guichet, prin. Fax 733-0953
Haynes Academy for Advanced Studies 700/6-12
1416 Metairie Rd 70005 504-837-8300
Karla Russo, prin. Fax 837-2110

King HS — 1,200/9-12
4301 Grace King Pl 70002 — 504-888-7334
Sharon Meggs-Hamilton, prin. — Fax 888-2082
Meisler MS — 800/6-8
3700 Cleary Ave 70002 — 504-888-5832
Semaj Allen-Raymond M.Ed., prin. — Fax 888-5855

---

Archbishop Chapelle HS — 900/8-12
8800 Veterans Memorial Blvd 70003 — 504-467-3105
John Serio, prin. — Fax 466-3191
Archbishop Rummel HS — 800/8-12
1901 Severn Ave 70001 — 504-834-5592
Michael Scalco, prin. — Fax 832-4016
Blue Cliff College — Post-Sec.
3200 Cleary Ave 70002 — 504-456-3141
Crescent City Christian S — 300/PK-12
4828 Utica St 70006 — 504-885-4700
Robert Brian, admin. — Fax 885-4703
Ecole Classique S — 300/PK-12
5236 Glendale St 70006 — 504-887-3507
Greater New Orleans Christian Academy — K-10
5220 Irving St 70006 — 504-302-7940
Rodil Capobres, prin.
Lutheran HS — 100/9-12
3864 17th St 70002 — 504-455-4062
Carol Christen, prin. — Fax 455-4453
Metairie Park Country Day S — 800/PK-12
300 Park Rd 70005 — 504-837-5204
Carolyn Chandler, hdmstr. — Fax 837-0015
Ridgewood Preparatory S — 300/PK-12
201 Pasadena Ave 70001 — 504-835-2545
St. Martin's Episcopal S — 500/PK-12
225 Green Acres Rd 70003 — 504-733-0353
Merry Sorrells, head sch — Fax 736-8800

**Midland, Acadia**
Acadia Parish SD
Supt. — See Crowley
Midland JSHS — 300/8-12
735 S Crocker St 70559 — 337-783-3310
Todd Briley, prin. — Fax 783-3332

**Minden, Webster, Pop. 12,925**
Webster Parish SD — 6,700/PK-12
PO Box 520 71058 — 318-377-7052
Dr. Daniel Rawls, supt. — Fax 377-4114
www.websterpsb.org
Minden HS — 900/9-12
PO Box 838 71058 — 318-377-2766
Robin Tucker, prin. — Fax 377-3236
Webster JHS — 500/7-8
700 E Union St 71055 — 318-377-3847
Elena Black, prin. — Fax 377-1943
Other Schools – See Doyline, Sarepta, Sibley, Springhill

---

Glenbrook S — 400/K-12
1674 Country Club Cir 71055 — 318-377-2135
Northwest Louisiana Technical College — Post-Sec.
PO Box 835 71058 — 318-371-3035

**Monroe, Ouachita, Pop. 48,278**
Monroe City SD — 8,100/PK-12
PO Box 4180 71211 — 318-325-0601
Brent Vidrine, supt. — Fax 812-3604
www.mcschools.net
Carroll Magnet HS — 600/9-12
2939 Renwick St 71201 — 318-387-8441
Patrick Taylor, prin. — Fax 325-6305
Carroll Magnet JHS — 300/7-8
2913 Renwick St 71201 — 318-322-1683
Tammye Turpin Ed.D., prin. — Fax 322-0833
King MS — 400/7-8
3716 Nutland Rd 71202 — 318-387-1825
Alvin Williams, prin. — Fax 325-4285
Lee JHS — 500/7-8
1600 N 19th St 71201 — 318-323-1143
Dana Mullins, prin. — Fax 325-5236
Monroe City Alternative S — 50/Alt
300 Sherrouse Ave 71203 — 318-343-3258
Robert Rash, prin. — Fax 343-6141
Neville HS — 1,000/9-12
600 Forsythe Ave 71201 — 318-323-2237
Whitney Martin, prin. — Fax 387-8774
Wossman HS — 700/9-12
1600 Arizona Ave 71202 — 318-387-2932
Sam Moore, prin. — Fax 322-1378

Ouachita Parish SD — 18,800/PK-12
PO Box 1642 71210 — 318-432-5000
Dr. Don Coker, supt. — Fax 432-5221
www.opsb.net
Ouachita JHS — 1,100/6-8
5500 Blanks St 71203 — 318-345-5100
Charles Wright, prin. — Fax 345-3308
Ouachita Parish HS — 1,200/9-12
681 Highway 594 71203 — 318-343-2769
Eddie Mahoney, prin. — Fax 343-9594
Richwood HS — 500/9-12
5901 Highway 165 Byp 71202 — 318-361-0467
Dr. Sharilynn Loche, prin. — Fax 361-9810
Richwood MS — 500/6-8
5855 Highway 165 Byp 71202 — 318-432-2000
Orlando Freemont, prin. — Fax 432-2049
Sterlington HS — 300/9-12
233 Keystone Rd 71203 — 318-665-2725
Dell Ashley, prin. — Fax 665-2727
Other Schools – See Calhoun, Sterlington, West Monroe

---

Career Technical College — Post-Sec.
2319 Louisville Ave 71201 — 318-323-2889
Cloyd's Beauty School #2 Inc. — Post-Sec.
1311 Winnsboro Rd 71202 — 318-322-5314
Cloyd's Beauty School #3 Inc. — Post-Sec.
2514 Ferrand St 71201 — 318-322-5314
Louisiana Delta Community College — Post-Sec.
7500 Millhaven Rd 71203 — 318-345-9000
Ouachita Christian S — 800/PK-12
7065 Highway 165 N 71203 — 318-325-6000
Bobby Stokes, hdmstr. — Fax 387-7000
River Oaks S — 300/PK-12
600 Finks Hideaway Rd 71203 — 318-343-4185
St. Francis Medical Center — Post-Sec.
PO Box 1901 71210 — 318-327-4141
St. Frederick HS — 300/7-12
3300 Westminister Ave 71201 — 318-323-9636
Dr. Robert Webber, prin. — Fax 323-7456
University of Louisiana at Monroe — Post-Sec.
700 University Ave 71209 — 318-342-1000

**Montegut, Terrebonne, Pop. 1,507**
Terrebonne Parish SD
Supt. — See Houma
Montegut MS — 600/5-8
138 Dolphin St 70377 — 985-594-5886
Jennifer Pitre, prin. — Fax 594-9666

**Monterey, Concordia, Pop. 437**
Concordia Parish SD
Supt. — See Vidalia
Monterey S — 500/PK-12
PO Box 127 71354 — 318-386-2214
Ralph Simmons, prin. — Fax 386-7356

**Montgomery, Grant, Pop. 714**
Grant Parish SD
Supt. — See Colfax
Montgomery HS — 300/7-12
PO Box 428 71454 — 318-646-2879
Patti Williams, prin. — Fax 646-3926

**Moreauville, Avoyelles, Pop. 900**
Avoyelles Parish SD
Supt. — See Marksville
Avoyelles HS — 800/7-12
287 Main St 71355 — 318-985-2361
Brent Whiddon, prin. — Fax 985-2786

**Morgan City, Saint Mary, Pop. 12,212**
St. Mary Parish SD
Supt. — See Centerville
Morgan City HS — 700/9-12
2400 Tiger Dr 70380 — 985-384-1754
Milton Fabre, prin. — Fax 384-7054
Morgan City JHS — 600/6-8
911 Marguerite St 70380 — 985-384-5922
Kenneth Holmes, prin. — Fax 385-4170

---

Central Catholic HS — 200/7-12
2100 Cedar St Unit 1 70380 — 985-385-5372
Vic Bonnaffee, prin. — Fax 385-3444
South Central Louisiana Technical Coll — Post-Sec.
900 Youngs Rd 70380 — 985-380-2957

**Mount Hermon, Washington**
Washington Parish SD
Supt. — See Franklinton
Mount Hermon S — 500/PK-12
36119 Highway 38 70450 — 985-877-4642
Debra Byrd, prin. — Fax 877-4710

**Napoleonville, Assumption, Pop. 653**
Assumption Parish SD — 3,900/PK-12
4901 Highway 308 70390 — 985-369-7251
Earl Martinez, supt. — Fax 369-2530
www.assumptionschools.com
Assumption HS — 1,100/10-12
4880 Highway 308 70390 — 985-369-2956
Niles Riche, prin. — Fax 369-6252
Napoleonville MS — 300/5-8
4847 Highway 1 70390 — 985-369-6587
Shawn Preston, prin. — Fax 369-6595
9th Grade Academy — 300/9-9
4880 Highway 308 70390 — 985-369-2956
Jessica Thibodeaux, prin.
Other Schools – See Belle Rose, Labadieville, Pierre Part

**Natchitoches, Natchitoches, Pop. 17,968**
Natchitoches Parish SD — 6,800/PK-12
PO Box 16 71458 — 318-352-2358
Dr. Jesse Skinner, supt. — Fax 352-8138
www.nat.k12.la.us/
East Natchitoches S — 500/4-8
1001 E 5th St 71457 — 318-352-4516
Alvin Brossette, prin. — Fax 352-4515
Jackson Technical Center — 100/Alt
1621 Welch St 71457 — 318-357-9410
Bobby Benjamin, prin. — Fax 357-8677
Natchitoches Central HS — 1,300/9-12
6513 Highway 1 Byp 71457 — 318-352-2211
William Gordy, prin. — Fax 357-8837
NSU Middle Lab S — 200/6-8
Tec Pod Bldg NSU 71497 — 318-357-4509
Ben LaGrone, prin. — Fax 357-4260
Other Schools – See Campti

---

Northwestern State University — Post-Sec.
175 Sam Sibley Dr 71497 — 318-357-6011
Northwest Louisiana Technical College — Post-Sec.
PO Box 657 71458 — 318-357-3162
St. Mary's S — 400/PK-12
1101 E 5th St 71457 — 318-352-8394
Jacque Horton, prin. — Fax 352-5798

**Negreet, Sabine**
Sabine Parish SD
Supt. — See Many
Negreet S — 500/PK-12
PO Box 14 71460 — 318-256-2349
Chad Crow, prin. — Fax 256-5868

**New Iberia, Iberia, Pop. 30,160**
Iberia Parish SD — 13,600/PK-12
1500 Jane St 70563 — 337-365-2341
Dale Henderson, supt. — Fax 365-6996
www.iberia.k12.la.us
Alternative Center for Education — 100/Alt
500 Bank Ave 70560 — 337-369-3696
Maxine Jones, prin. — Fax 365-5111
Anderson MS — 500/7-8
1059 Anderson St 70560 — 337-365-3932
Dwalyn Jackson, prin. — Fax 367-8285
Belle Place MS — 500/7-8
4110 Loreauville Rd 70563 — 337-364-2141
Curtis Coquat, prin. — Fax 365-9463
Iberia MS — 600/7-8
613 Weeks Island Rd 70560 — 337-364-3927
Gleacia Morales, prin. — Fax 365-9681
Iberia Parish Career Center — Vo/Tech
618 Recreation Dr 70560 — 337-365-7231
Chris Broussard, prin. — Fax 367-0875
New Iberia HS — 1,700/9-12
1301 E Admiral Doyle Dr 70560 — 337-369-6714
Curt Landry, prin. — Fax 364-6920
Westgate HS — 1,100/9-12
2305 Jefferson Island Rd 70560 — 337-365-2431
Neely Moore, prin. — Fax 364-3487
Other Schools – See Delcambre, Jeanerette, Loreauville

---

Assembly Christian S — 300/PK-12
4219 E Admiral Doyle Dr 70560 — 337-364-4340
Bristow Academy — Post-Sec.
1113 Vortex Dr 70560 — 337-364-8909
Catholic HS — 800/4-12
1301 Delasalle Dr 70560 — 337-364-5116
Ray Simon, prin. — Fax 364-5041
Highland Baptist Christian S — 500/PK-12
708 Angers St 70563 — 337-364-2273
Janie C. Lamothe, admin. — Fax 369-6303
Neill Institute — Post-Sec.
1301A W Saint Peter St 70560 — 337-365-6570
South Louisiana Community College — Post-Sec.
609 Ember Dr 70560 — 337-373-0172

**New Orleans, Orleans, Pop. 338,397**
Orleans Parish SD — 10,500/PK-12
3520 General Degaulle Dr 70114 — 504-304-3520
Henderson Lewis Ph.D., supt. — Fax 309-2865
www.opsb.us
McDonogh 35 HS — 900/7-12
4000 Cadillac St 70122 — 504-324-7600
Gerald DeBose, prin. — Fax 942-0276
McMain Magnet JSHS — 700/7-12
5712 S Claiborne Ave 70125 — 504-324-7500
Bridgette Frick, prin. — Fax 862-5123

---

Academy of the Sacred Heart HS — 300/9-12
4521 Saint Charles Ave 70115 — 504-891-1943
Dr. Yvonne Adler, prin. — Fax 891-9744
Academy of the Sacred Heart MS — 200/5-8
4521 Saint Charles Ave 70115 — 504-891-1943
Kim Duckworth, prin. — Fax 891-2755
Bishop McManus Academy — 200/PK-12
13123 I 10 Service Rd 70128 — 504-246-5121
Dr. Tonilynn Tyson, prin. — Fax 246-5564
Brother Martin HS — 1,200/7-12
4401 Elysian Fields Ave 70122 — 504-283-1561
Gregory Rando, prin. — Fax 286-8462
Cabrini HS — 500/8-12
1400 Moss St 70119 — 504-482-1193
Yvonne Hrapmann, prin. — Fax 483-8671
Cameron College — Post-Sec.
2740 Canal St 70119 — 504-821-5881
De La Salle HS — 400/8-12
5300 Saint Charles Ave 70115 — 504-895-5717
Dr. Myles Seghers, prin. — Fax 895-1300
Delgado Community College — Post-Sec.
615 City Park Ave 70119 — 504-671-5000
Dillard University — Post-Sec.
2601 Gentilly Blvd 70122 — 504-283-8822
Eastern College of Health Vocations — Post-Sec.
201 Evans Rd 70123 — 504-885-3353
Holy Cross S — 1,000/5-12
5500 Paris Ave 70122 — 504-942-3100
Charles DiGange, hdmstr. — Fax 286-5665
Holy Rosary HS — 100/8-12
2437 Jena St 70115 — 504-482-7173
Sr. Paulette Tiefenbrunn, prin. — Fax 482-7229
Jesuit HS — 1,400/8-12
4133 Banks St 70119 — 504-486-6631
Peter Kernion, prin. — Fax 483-3942
Louisiana State Univ. Health Sci. Center — Post-Sec.
433 Bolivar St 70112 — 504-568-4808
Loyola University New Orleans — Post-Sec.
6363 Saint Charles Ave 70118 — 504-865-2011
McGehee S — 500/PK-12
2343 Prytania St 70130 — 504-561-1224
Eileen Powers, head sch — Fax 525-7910
Medical Center of Louisiana/Charity Cmps — Post-Sec.
1541 Tulane Ave 70112 — 504-568-2311
Moler Beauty College — Post-Sec.
3968 Old Gentilly Rd 70126 — 504-282-2539
Mt. Carmel Academy — 1,200/8-12
7027 Milne Blvd 70124 — 504-288-7626
Beth Simno, prin. — Fax 288-7629
Newman S — 900/PK-12
1903 Jefferson Ave 70115 — 504-899-5641
Dale Smith, head sch — Fax 896-8597
New Orleans Baptist Theological Seminary — Post-Sec.
3939 Gentilly Blvd 70126 — 504-282-4455
Notre Dame Seminary — Post-Sec.
2901 S Carrollton Ave 70118 — 504-866-7426
Ochsner School of Allied Health Sciences — Post-Sec.
1514 Jefferson Hwy 70121 — 504-842-3267
Our Lady of Holy Cross College — Post-Sec.
4123 Woodland Dr 70131 — 504-394-7744
St. Augustine HS — 900/6-12
2600 A P Tureaud Ave 70119 — 504-944-2424
Sean Goodwin, prin. — Fax 947-7712
St. Katharine Drexel HS — 300/7-12
5116 Magazine St 70115 — 504-899-6061
Cherllyn Branche, prin. — Fax 891-8766
St. Marys Academy — 500/PK-12
6905 Chef Menteur Hwy 70126 — 504-245-0200
Sr. Jennie Jones, prin. — Fax 245-0422
St. Marys Dominican HS — 900/8-12
7701 Walmsley Ave 70125 — 504-865-9401
Carolyn Favre M.Ed., prin. — Fax 866-5958
Southern University at New Orleans — Post-Sec.
6400 Press Dr 70126 — 504-286-5000
Touro Infirmary — Post-Sec.
1401 Foucher St 70115 — 504-897-8244
Tulane University — Post-Sec.
6823 Saint Charles Ave 70118 — 504-865-5000
University of New Orleans — Post-Sec.
2000 Lakeshore Dr 70148 — 504-280-6000
Ursuline Academy HS — 400/8-12
2635 State St 70118 — 504-861-9150
Alice Bairnsfather, prin. — Fax 861-7392
Xavier University — Post-Sec.
1 Drexel Dr 70125 — 504-486-7411

**New Roads, Pointe Coupee, Pop. 4,804**
Pointe Coupee Parish SD 2,900/PK-12
PO Box 579 70760 225-638-8674
Linda D'Amico, supt. Fax 638-3237
www.pcpsb.net
Other Schools – See Livonia

Baton Rouge Community College New Roads Post-Sec.
605 Hospital Rd 70760 225-638-8613
Catholic HS of Pointe Coupee 300/7-12
504 4th St W 70760 225-638-9313
Colleen Caillet, prin. Fax 638-6471
False River Academy 500/PK-12
201 Major Pkwy 70760 225-638-3783

**Noble, Sabine, Pop. 244**
Sabine Parish SD
Supt. — See Many
Ebarb S 300/PK-12
5340 Highway 482 71462 318-645-9402
Darrin Dyess, prin. Fax 645-4689

**Oakdale, Allen, Pop. 7,688**
Allen Parish SD
Supt. — See Oberlin
Oakdale HS 300/9-12
101 N 13th St 71463 318-335-2338
Nancy Willis, prin. Fax 335-3257
Oakdale MS 400/5-8
124 S 13th St 71463 318-335-1558
Robbyn Tarver, prin. Fax 335-4690

Central Louisiana Technical College Post-Sec.
117 Highway 1152 71463 318-335-3944

**Oak Grove, West Carroll, Pop. 1,714**
West Carroll Parish SD 2,100/PK-12
314 E Main St 71263 318-428-2378
Richard Strong, supt. Fax 428-3775
www.wcpsb.com
Oak Grove JSHS 400/6-12
501 W Main St 71263 318-428-2308
Mike Gammill, prin. Fax 428-2311
Other Schools – See Epps, Forest, Kilbourne

**Oberlin, Allen, Pop. 1,727**
Allen Parish SD 4,300/PK-12
PO Box C 70655 337-639-4311
Michael Doucet, supt. Fax 639-2346
www.allen.k12.la.us
Oberlin HS 300/7-12
PO Box D 70655 337-639-4341
Tonya Rider, prin. Fax 639-2508
Other Schools – See Elizabeth, Grant, Kinder, Oakdale, Reeves

**Olla, LaSalle, Pop. 1,375**
LaSalle Parish SD
Supt. — See Jena
LaSalle HS 200/9-12
PO Box 458 71465 318-495-5165
Sheila King, prin. Fax 495-5503

**Opelousas, Saint Landry, Pop. 16,425**
St. Landry Parish SD 14,000/PK-12
PO Box 310 70571 337-948-3657
Edward Brown, supt. Fax 942-0204
www.slp.k12.la.us
Magnet Academy for Cultural Arts 300/7-12
1100 Leo St 70570 337-942-6195
Karen Olivier, prin. Fax 948-6310
Magnet Academy of Biomedical Sciences 9-12
PO Box 310 70571 337-948-3657
Fax 942-0204
Northwest HS 500/9-12
3746 Highway 104 70570 337-543-2001
Gregory Campbell, prin. Fax 543-8796
Opelousas HS 700/9-12
PO Box 1269 70571 337-942-5634
Dr. Rodney Johnson, prin. Fax 942-6219
Opelousas JHS 500/7-8
730 S Market St 70570 337-942-4957
Chastity Wilson, prin. Fax 942-2659
Plaisance ES 300/5-8
3264 Highway 167 70570 337-826-3335
Larry Watson, prin. Fax 826-7062
St. Landry Accelerated Transition S 100/Alt
152 Violet Dr 70570 337-942-4761
Charles Vidrine, prin. Fax 948-9792
Other Schools – See Arnaudville, Eunice, Port Barre, Sunset, Washington

Family Worship Christian Acadmey 100/PK-12
PO Box 1463 70571 337-942-1563
Opelousas Catholic S 700/PK-12
428 E Prudhomme St 70570 337-942-5404
John Cavell, prin. Fax 942-5922
Opelousas School of Cosmetology Post-Sec.
529 E Vine St 70570 337-942-6147
South Louisiana Community College Post-Sec.
332 E South St 70570 337-943-1518
Westminster Christian Academy 700/PK-12
186 Westminster Dr 70570 337-948-8607
Merida Brooks, supt. Fax 948-8983

**Paradis, Saint Charles, Pop. 1,269**
St. Charles Parish SD
Supt. — See Luling
Martin MS 600/6-8
434 South St 70080 985-758-7579
Erin Granier, prin. Fax 758-7570

**Parks, Saint Martin, Pop. 645**
St. Martin Parish SD
Supt. — See Breaux Bridge
Parks MS 400/5-8
1010 Saint Louis Dr Ste A 70582 337-845-4753
Dr. Wanda Phillips, prin. Fax 845-5532

**Patterson, Saint Mary, Pop. 6,020**
St. Mary Parish SD
Supt. — See Centerville
Patterson HS 500/9-12
2525 Main St 70392 985-395-2675
Rachael Wilson, prin. Fax 395-5453
Patterson JHS 500/4-8
1101 1st St 70392 985-395-6772
Suzanne Bergeron, prin. Fax 395-6773

**Pearl River, Saint Tammany, Pop. 2,460**
St. Tammany Parish SD
Supt. — See Covington
Creekside JHS 500/6-8
65434 Highway 41 70452 985-863-5882
Lisa Virga, prin. Fax 863-7658
Pearl River HS 800/9-12
39110 Rebel Ln 70452 985-863-2591
Michael Winkler, prin. Fax 863-5934

**Pierre Part, Assumption, Pop. 3,145**
Assumption Parish SD
Supt. — See Napoleonville
Pierre Part MS 300/5-8
3321 Highway 70 S 70339 985-252-6359
Wanda Templet, prin. Fax 252-3918

**Pine Prairie, Evangeline, Pop. 1,598**
Evangeline Parish SD
Supt. — See Ville Platte
Pine Prairie S 800/PK-12
PO Box 200 70576 337-599-2300
Anita West, prin. Fax 599-2003

**Pineville, Rapides, Pop. 14,277**
Rapides Parish SD
Supt. — See Alexandria
Pineville HS 1,300/9-12
1511 Line St 71360 318-442-8990
Dr. Karl Carpenter, prin. Fax 487-1984
Pineville JHS 600/7-8
501 Edgewood Dr 71360 318-640-0512
Dana Nolan, prin. Fax 640-9692
Rapides Training Academy 100/Alt
901 Crepe Myrtle St 71360 318-445-7017
Matt Byrnes, prin. Fax 445-5690

Louisiana College Post-Sec.
1140 College Dr 71360 318-487-7011
Pineville Beauty School Post-Sec.
1008 Main St 71360 318-445-1040

**Pitkin, Vernon, Pop. 566**
Vernon Parish SD
Supt. — See Leesville
Pitkin S 500/PK-12
7239 Highway 463 70656 318-358-3121
Kevin Lambright, prin. Fax 358-3580

**Plain Dealing, Bossier, Pop. 996**
Bossier Parish SD
Supt. — See Benton
Plain Dealing HS 300/6-12
300 E Vance St 71064 318-759-2700
Sandrina Isebaert, prin. Fax 759-2713

**Plaquemine, Iberville, Pop. 7,074**
Iberville Parish SD 4,600/PK-12
PO Box 151 70765 225-687-4341
Dr. P. Edward Cancienne, supt. Fax 687-5408
www.ipsb.net
Math Science & Arts Academy West Alt
57955 Saint Louis Rd 70764 225-687-6845
Elvis Cavalier, admin. Fax 687-6826
Plaquemine HS 1,200/7-12
59595 Belleview Dr 70764 225-687-6367
Chandler Smith, prin. Fax 687-4422
Other Schools – See Saint Gabriel, White Castle

Capital Area Technical College Post-Sec.
25250 Tenant Rd 70764 225-687-5500
St. John HS 200/7-12
24250 Regina St 70764 225-687-3056
Cherie Schlatre, prin. Fax 687-3530

**Plaucheville, Avoyelles, Pop. 243**

St. Joseph S 200/PK-12
PO Box 59 71362 318-922-3401
Bryan Runyan, prin. Fax 922-3776

**Pleasant Hill, Sabine, Pop. 710**
Sabine Parish SD
Supt. — See Many
Pleasant Hill S 300/PK-12
PO Box 8 71065 318-796-3670
Joseph Self, prin. Fax 796-2034

**Ponchatoula, Tangipahoa, Pop. 6,436**
Tangipahoa Parish SD
Supt. — See Amite
Ponchatoula HS 1,700/9-12
19452 Highway 22 70454 985-386-3514
Daniel Strickland, prin. Fax 386-0011
Ponchatoula JHS 700/7-8
315 E Oak St 70454 985-370-5322
Bobby Matthews, prin. Fax 370-5327

**Port Allen, West Baton Rouge, Pop. 5,131**
West Baton Rouge Parish SD 3,700/PK-12
3761 Rosedale Rd 70767 225-343-8309
Wes Watts, supt. Fax 387-2101
www.wbrschools.net
Devall MS 200/5-8
11851 N River Rd 70767 225-627-4268
Laree Taylor, prin. Fax 627-4278
Port Allen HS 400/9-12
3553 Rosedale Rd 70767 225-383-1107
James Jackson, prin. Fax 344-6312
Port Allen MS 200/6-8
610 Rosedale Rd 70767 225-383-5777
John Arrasmith, prin. Fax 346-5030
Other Schools – See Brusly

**Port Barre, Saint Landry, Pop. 2,017**
St. Landry Parish SD
Supt. — See Opelousas
Port Barre HS 500/5-12
PO Box 69 70577 337-585-7256
Timothy Villemarette, prin. Fax 585-2290

**Port Sulphur, Plaquemines, Pop. 1,706**
Plaquemines Parish SD
Supt. — See Belle Chasse
Plaquemines Parish Learning Center Alt
26892 Highway 23 70083 504-595-6410
John Vanison, prin. Fax 398-4366

**Prairieville, Ascension, Pop. 26,585**
Ascension Parish SD
Supt. — See Donaldsonville
Galvez MS 600/6-8
42018 Highway 933 70769 225-391-6350
Sandy Waguespack, prin. Fax 621-2434
Prairieville MS 800/6-8
16200 Highway 930 70769 225-391-6300
Dina Davis, prin. Fax 673-4883

**Pride, East Baton Rouge**
East Baton Rouge Parish SD
Supt. — See Baton Rouge
Northeast JSHS 600/7-12
13700 Pride Port Hudson Rd 70770 225-654-5808
Brandon Levatino, prin. Fax 654-5591

**Quitman, Jackson, Pop. 180**
Jackson Parish SD
Supt. — See Jonesboro
Quitman S 700/PK-12
PO Box 38 71268 318-259-2698
Steve Shovan, prin. Fax 259-1139

**Raceland, Lafourche, Pop. 10,053**
Lafourche Parish SD
Supt. — See Thibodaux
Central Lafourche HS 1,300/9-12
4820 Highway 1 70394 985-532-3319
Chris Kimball, prin. Fax 532-3822
Raceland MS 400/6-8
PO Box C 70394 985-537-5140
Hiram Bailey, prin. Fax 537-5182

**Rayne, Acadia, Pop. 7,834**
Acadia Parish SD
Supt. — See Crowley
Armstrong MS 400/6-8
700 Martin Luther King Blvd 70578 337-334-3377
Marshall Thibodeaux, prin. Fax 334-2681
Rayne HS 600/9-12
1016 N Polk St 70578 337-334-3691
John Prudhomme, prin. Fax 334-5568

**Rayville, Richland, Pop. 3,658**
Richland Parish SD 4,100/PK-12
PO Box 599 71269 318-728-5964
Sheldon Jones, supt. Fax 728-6366
www.richland.k12.la.us
Rayville HS 500/9-12
193 Highway 3048 71269 318-728-3296
Tommy Watson, prin. Fax 728-5652
Rayville JHS 300/6-8
225 Highway 3048 71269 318-728-3618
Nettie Ranel, prin. Fax 728-9374
Other Schools – See Archibald, Delhi, Mangham

Riverfield Academy 300/PK-12
115 Riverfield Dr 71269 318-728-3281

**Reeves, Allen, Pop. 230**
Allen Parish SD
Supt. — See Oberlin
Reeves S 300/PK-12
13770 Highway 113 70658 337-666-2414
Brenda Green, prin. Fax 666-2812

**Reserve, Saint John the Baptist, Pop. 9,667**
St. John The Baptist Parish SD 6,400/PK-12
PO Box AL 70084 985-536-1106
Kevin George, supt. Fax 536-1109
www.stjohn.k12.la.us
East St. John HS 1,400/9-12
1 Wildcat Dr 70084 985-536-4226
Cory Butler, prin. Fax 536-4286
St. John Alternative Program 100/Alt
1880 Highway 44 70084 985-536-4283
Phyllis Clark, prin. Fax 536-4527
Other Schools – See Edgard

Riverside Academy 800/PK-12
332 Railroad Ave 70084 985-536-4246
South Central Louisiana Technical Coll Post-Sec.
181 Regala Park Rd 70084 985-536-4418

**Ringgold, Bienville, Pop. 1,471**
Bienville Parish SD
Supt. — See Arcadia
Ringgold JSHS 200/6-12
4044 Bienville Rd Ste B 71068 318-894-2271
Eric Carter, prin. Fax 894-4444

**River Ridge, Jefferson, Pop. 13,340**

Curtis Christian S 800/PK-12
10125 Jefferson Hwy 70123 504-737-4621

**Roanoke, Jefferson Davis, Pop. 537**
Jefferson Davis Parish SD
Supt. — See Jennings
Welsh-Roanoke JHS 300/6-8
8150 Highway 90 70581 337-753-2317
Rae Daigle, prin. Fax 753-2245

**Rosepine, Vernon, Pop. 1,651**
Vernon Parish SD
Supt. — See Leesville
Rosepine JSHS 500/7-12
502 Louisiana Ave 70659 337-463-6079
Steve Thomas, prin. Fax 462-6132

**Ruston, Lincoln, Pop. 21,600**
Lincoln Parish SD 4,800/PK-12
410 S Farmerville St 71270 318-255-1430
Danny Bell, supt. Fax 255-3203
www.lincolnschools.org/
Ruston HS 1,100/9-12
900 Bearcat Dr 71270 318-255-0807
Ricky Durrett, prin. Fax 251-2202

Ruston JHS 600/7-8
481 Tarbutton Rd 71270 318-251-1601
Tim Nutt, prin. Fax 254-5235
Other Schools – See Choudrant, Simsboro

---

Bethel Christian S 100/PK-12
2901 Winona Dr 71270 318-255-1112
Nancy Stevenson, admin. Fax 513-1113
Cedar Creek S 600/PK-12
2400 Cedar Creek Dr 71270 318-255-7707
Andrew Yepson, head sch Fax 251-2846
Louisiana Tech University Post-Sec.
PO Box 3168 71272 318-257-0211
Pat Goins Ruston Beauty School Post-Sec.
213 W Alabama Ave 71270 318-255-2717

**Saint Amant, Ascension**
Ascension Parish SD
Supt. — See Donaldsonville
Saint Amant HS 1,700/9-12
12035 Highway 431 70774 225-391-6000
Mia Edwards, prin. Fax 621-2573
Saint Amant MS 500/6-8
44317 Highway 429 70774 225-391-6500
Christy Bourgeois, prin. Fax 621-2593

**Saint Benedict, Saint Tammany**

---

St. Joseph Seminary College Post-Sec.
75376 River Rd 70457 985-892-1800

**Saint Bernard, Saint Bernard**
St. Bernard Parish SD
Supt. — See Chalmette
Saint Bernard MS 300/6-8
2601 Torres Dr 70085 504-267-7878
Susan Deffes, prin. Fax 267-7886

**Saint Francisville, West Feliciana, Pop. 1,749**
West Feliciana Parish SD 2,100/PK-12
PO Box 1910 70775 225-635-3891
Hollis Milton, supt. Fax 635-0108
www.wfpsb.org
West Feliciana HS 600/9-12
PO Box 580 70775 225-635-4561
James Carroll, prin. Fax 635-5588
West Feliciana MS 500/6-8
PO Box 690 70775 225-635-3898
Jovanka Ganes, prin. Fax 635-6925

**Saint Gabriel, Iberville, Pop. 6,621**
Iberville Parish SD
Supt. — See Plaquemine
East Iberville S 500/PK-12
3285 Highway 75 70776 225-642-5410
Meshell Hill, prin. Fax 642-9607
Math Science & Arts Academy East 300/K-12
1400 Gordon Simon LeBlanc 70776 225-642-8457
Charles Johnson, dir.

**Saint James, Saint James, Pop. 827**
St. James Parish SD
Supt. — See Lutcher
Saint James HS 600/7-12
PO Box 101 70086 225-258-4900
Michael Kennedy, prin. Fax 265-2455

**Saint Joseph, Tensas, Pop. 1,163**
Tensas Parish SD 700/PK-12
PO Box 318 71366 318-766-3269
Carol S. Johnson, supt. Fax 766-3634
www.tensaspsb.org/
Tensas HS 200/7-12
PO Box 318 71366 318-766-3585
Dena Hale, prin. Fax 766-7988

---

Tensas Academy 200/PK-12
PO Box 555 71366 318-766-4384

**Saint Martinville, Saint Martin, Pop. 6,047**
St. Martin Parish SD
Supt. — See Breaux Bridge
St. Martinville HS 700/9-12
762 N Main St 70582 337-394-3135
Michael Kreamer, prin. Fax 394-8045
St. Martinville JHS 400/6-8
7190 Main Hwy 70582 337-394-4764
Elizabeth Thibeaux-Clay, prin. Fax 394-9619

**Saint Rose, Saint Charles, Pop. 8,003**
St. Charles Parish SD
Supt. — See Luling
Cammon MS 300/6-8
234 Pirate Dr 70087 504-467-4536
Tamika Green, prin. Fax 468-3873

---

ITT Technical Institute Post-Sec.
140 James Dr E 70087 504-463-0338

**Saline, Bienville, Pop. 271**
Bienville Parish SD
Supt. — See Arcadia
Saline S 300/PK-12
PO Box 129 71070 318-576-3215
Scott Canady, prin. Fax 576-9068

**Sarepta, Webster, Pop. 889**
Webster Parish SD
Supt. — See Minden
North Webster JHS 500/6-8
6041 Highway 2 71071 318-847-4301
Cyndi Hair, prin. Fax 847-4891

**Schriever, Terrebonne, Pop. 6,745**

---

Fletcher Technical Community College Post-Sec.
1407 Highway 311 70395 985-448-7900

**Scott, Lafayette, Pop. 8,472**
Lafayette Parish SD
Supt. — See Lafayette
Scott MS 700/5-8
116 Marie St 70583 337-521-7930
Candy Kelly, prin. Fax 521-7931

**Shreveport, Caddo, Pop. 196,498**
Caddo Parish SD 40,700/PK-12
PO Box 32000 71130 318-603-6300
Dr. T. Lamar Goree, supt. Fax 631-5241
www.caddoschools.org
Bickham MS 700/6-8
7240 Old Mooringsport Rd 71107 318-929-4106
Shannon Wall, prin. Fax 929-2416
Broadmoor MS Laboratory 600/6-8
441 Atlantic Ave 71105 318-861-2403
Billy Williams, prin. Fax 865-4142
Byrd HS 2,300/9-12
3201 Line Ave 71104 318-869-2567
Gerald Badgley, prin. Fax 869-2253
Caddo Career/Tech Center Vo/Tech
5950 Union Ave 71108 318-636-5150
Kenneth Berg, prin. Fax 621-9138
Caddo Middle Career & Technology S 800/7-8
6310 Clift Ave 71106 318-868-2753
Tellauance Graham, prin. Fax 868-2755
Caddo Ombudsman East Alt
1020 Shreveport Barksdale 71105 318-670-7461
John Sampson, dir.
Caddo Ombudsman North Alt
3000 N Market St 71107 318-220-8035
John Sampson, dir.
Caddo Ombudsman South Alt
8805 Jewella Ave 71108 318-220-4749
John Sampson, dir.
Caddo Ombudsman West Alt
3714 Greenwood Rd 71109 318-220-8354
John Sampson, dir.
Caddo Parish Magnet HS 1,200/9-12
1601 Viking Dr 71101 318-221-2501
Michael Ilgenfritz, prin. Fax 227-1393
Caddo Parish Magnet MS 1,200/6-8
7635 Cornelious Ln 71106 318-868-6588
Robin Debusk, prin. Fax 865-6125
Fair Park HS 1,100/9-12
3222 Greenwood Rd 71109 318-635-8181
Bruce Daigle, prin. Fax 631-1982
Green Oaks Performing Arts Academy 600/7-12
2550 Thomas E Howard Dr 71107 318-425-3411
Marvin Alexander, prin. Fax 425-3414
Huntington JSHS 1,200/7-12
6801 Rasberry Ln 71129 318-687-6655
Travis Smith, prin. Fax 687-0943
Lakeshore MS 600/7-8
1807 San Jacinto St 71109 318-635-1325
Dr. Matthew Mitchell, prin. Fax 635-1961
Northwood HS 1,000/9-12
5939 Old Mooringsport Rd 71107 318-929-3513
Darlene Simons, prin. Fax 929-7498
Oak Park MS 400/5-8
4331 Henry St 71109 318-635-2141
Julia Smith O'Neal, prin. Fax 636-6336
Ridgewood MS 600/6-8
2001 Ridgewood Dr 71118 318-686-0383
Scott Aymond, prin. Fax 686-0390
Shreve HS 1,400/9-12
6115 E Kings Hwy 71105 318-865-7137
Ginger Gustavson, prin. Fax 865-5041
Shreveport Job Corps Opportunity Center 300/Alt
2815 Lillian St 71109 318-227-9331
Lionel Fraser, dir. Fax 222-0768
Southwood HS 1,300/9-12
9000 Walker Rd 71118 318-686-9512
Jeff Roberts, prin. Fax 687-7588
Washington New Tech JSHS 600/7-12
2104 Milam St 71103 318-222-2186
Carter Bedford, prin. Fax 226-0628
Woodlawn Leadership Academy 1,000/9-12
7340 Wyngate Blvd 71106 318-686-3161
Betty Jordan, prin. Fax 687-6787
Youree Drive MS 1,100/6-8
6008 Youree Dr 71105 318-868-5324
Rick Carson, prin. Fax 861-5086
Other Schools – See Vivian

---

American Commercial College Post-Sec.
3014 Knight St 71105 866-648-2112
American School of Business Post-Sec.
702 Professional Dr N 71105 318-798-3333
Ayers Institute Post-Sec.
8820 Jewella Ave 71108 318-635-0280
Blue Cliff College Post-Sec.
8731 Park Plaza Dr 71105 318-798-6868
Calvary Baptist Academy 1,100/K-12
9333 Linwood Ave 71106 318-687-4923
Career Technical College Post-Sec.
1227 Shreveport Barksdale 71105 318-629-2889
Centenary College of Louisiana Post-Sec.
2911 Centenary Blvd 71104 318-869-5011
Diesel Driving Academy Post-Sec.
3523 Greenwood Rd 71109 318-636-6300
Evangel Christian Academy 800/PK-12
7425 Broadacres Rd 71129 318-688-7061
Guy's Academy Hair Skin and Nails Post-Sec.
1141 Shreveport Barksdale 71105 318-865-5591
Louisiana State University Post-Sec.
1 University Pl 71115 318-797-5000
Louisiana State Univ Health Sciences Ctr Post-Sec.
1501 Kings Hwy 71103 318-675-5000
Loyola College Prep S 500/9-12
921 Jordan St 71101 318-221-2675
John LeBlanc, prin. Fax 226-6334
Northwest Louisiana Technical College Post-Sec.
2010 N Market St 71107 318-676-7811
Overton Brooks VA Medical Center Post-Sec.
510 E Stoner Ave 71101 318-424-6037
Remington College Post-Sec.
2106 Bert Kouns Industrial 71118 318-671-4001
Southern University at Shreveport Post-Sec.
3050 M L King Dr 71107 318-670-6000

**Sibley, Webster, Pop. 1,205**
Webster Parish SD
Supt. — See Minden
Lakeside JSHS 400/7-12
9090 Highway 371 71073 318-377-2133
Johnny Rowland, prin. Fax 382-0733

**Sicily Island, Catahoula, Pop. 519**
Catahoula Parish SD
Supt. — See Harrisonburg
Sicily Island HS 100/PK-12
PO Box 128 71368 318-389-5337
Marguerita Krause, prin. Fax 389-5309

**Simpson, Vernon, Pop. 631**
Vernon Parish SD
Supt. — See Leesville
Simpson S 300/PK-12
PO Box 8 71474 337-383-7810
Lee Coriell, prin. Fax 383-7655

**Simsboro, Lincoln, Pop. 828**
Lincoln Parish SD
Supt. — See Ruston
Simsboro S 600/K-12
1 Tiger Dr 71275 318-247-6265
Dr. Lillie Williams-Hearn, prin. Fax 247-6276

**Singer, Beauregard, Pop. 282**
Beauregard Parish SD
Supt. — See Deridder
Singer HS 300/K-12
153 Highway 110 E 70660 337-463-5908
Theresa Harlow, prin. Fax 463-0199

**Slidell, Saint Tammany, Pop. 26,521**
St. Tammany Parish SD
Supt. — See Covington
Boyet JHS 700/7-8
59295 Rebel Dr 70461 985-643-3775
John Priola, prin. Fax 643-9470
Clearwood JHS 600/4-8
130 Clearwood Dr 70458 985-641-8200
Alan Bennett, prin. Fax 641-7122
Northshore HS 1,500/9-12
100 Panther Dr 70461 985-649-6400
Frank Jabbia, prin. Fax 649-3613
St. Tammany JHS 600/6-8
701 Cleveland Ave 70458 985-643-1592
Vincent DiCarlo, prin. Fax 643-5873
Salmen HS 900/9-12
300 Spartan Dr 70458 985-643-7359
Brennan McCurley, prin. Fax 645-8776
Slidell HS 1,700/9-12
1 Tiger Dr 70458 985-643-2992
William Percy, prin. Fax 649-6853
Slidell JHS 700/7-8
333 Pennsylvania Ave 70458 985-641-5914
Patrick Mackin, prin. Fax 641-6397

---

Academy of Creative Hair Design Post-Sec.
740 Oak Harbor Blvd 70458 985-643-2614
First Baptist Christian S 200/1-12
4141 Pontchartrain Dr 70458 985-643-3725
Mona Nelson, admin. Fax 641-9205
Pope John Paul II HS 300/9-12
1901 Jaguar Dr 70461 985-649-0914
Martha Mundine, prin. Fax 649-5494

**Sorrento, Ascension, Pop. 1,385**

---

River Parishes Community College Post-Sec.
PO Box 310 70778 225-675-8270

**Springfield, Livingston, Pop. 483**
Livingston Parish SD
Supt. — See Livingston
Springfield HS 300/9-12
PO Box 39 70462 225-294-3256
Spencer Harris, prin. Fax 294-4800
Springfield MS 400/5-8
PO Box 40 70462 225-294-3306
Dwayne Dykes, prin. Fax 294-3307

**Springhill, Webster, Pop. 5,214**
Webster Parish SD
Supt. — See Minden
North Webster HS 500/9-12
101 S Arkansas St 71075 318-539-2563
Jeff Franklin, prin. Fax 539-2569

**Starks, Calcasieu, Pop. 662**
Calcasieu Parish SD
Supt. — See Lake Charles
Starks S 400/PK-12
PO Box 69 70661 337-217-4820
Cary Smith, prin. Fax 217-4821

**Sterlington, Ouachita, Pop. 1,568**
Ouachita Parish SD
Supt. — See Monroe
Sterlington MS 300/6-8
206 High Ave 71280 318-432-2100
Chris Cox, prin. Fax 432-2149

**Stonewall, DeSoto, Pop. 1,797**
DeSoto Parish SD
Supt. — See Mansfield
North DeSoto HS 600/9-12
PO Box 430 71078 318-925-6917
Bart Weaver, prin. Fax 925-1940
North DeSoto MS 500/6-8
PO Box 310 71078 318-925-4520
Keith Simmons, prin. Fax 925-4719

**Sulphur, Calcasieu, Pop. 20,056**
Calcasieu Parish SD
Supt. — See Lake Charles
LeBlanc MS/Drost Special 400/6-8
1100 N Crocker St 70663 337-217-4510
Joe David, prin. Fax 217-4511
Lewis MS 900/6-8
1752 Cypress St 70663 337-217-4700
Dan Sylvest, prin. Fax 217-4701
Sulphur 9th Grade Campus 600/9-9
600 Willow Ave 70663 337-217-4440
Lee Crick, prin. Fax 217-4441
Sulphur SHS 1,400/10-12
100 Sycamore St 70663 337-217-4430
Robert Barrentine, prin. Fax 217-4434

**Summerfield, Claiborne**
Claiborne Parish SD
Supt. — See Homer
Summerfield S 300/PK-12
PO Box 158 71079 318-927-3621
Shane Lee, prin. Fax 927-9160

**Sunset, Saint Landry, Pop. 2,868**
St. Landry Parish SD
Supt. — See Opelousas
Sunset ES 400/5-8
236 Church Hill St 70584 337-662-3194
Marquet Rideau, prin. Fax 662-3478

**Tallulah, Madison, Pop. 7,266**
Madison Parish SD 1,900/PK-12
301 S Chestnut St 71282 318-574-3616
Clara Durr, supt. Fax 574-3667
www.madisonpsb.org
Christian Acres Alternative S 100/Alt
200 Bailey St 71282 318-574-1563
Natasha Mosley, prin. Fax 574-1563
Madison Alternative S Alt
507 Bayou Dr 71282
Natasha Mosley, prin.
Madison HS 500/9-12
1234 Madison High Dr S 71282 318-574-3529
Glenda Douglas, prin. Fax 574-2399
Madison MS 400/7-8
1233 Madison High Dr S 71282 318-574-0933
Benita Young, prin. Fax 574-9199

---

Tallulah Academy-Delta Christian S 300/PK-12
700 Wood St 71282 318-574-2606

**Terrytown, Jefferson, Pop. 22,887**
Jefferson Parish SD
Supt. — See Harvey
Livaudais MS 600/6-8
925 Lamar Ave 70056 504-393-7544
Davon Hayes, prin. Fax 393-9610

**Thibodaux, Lafourche, Pop. 14,384**
Lafourche Parish SD 14,100/PK-12
PO Box 879 70302 985-446-5631
Dr. Jo Ann Matthews, supt. Fax 446-0801
www.lpsd.k12.la.us
East Thibodaux MS 400/6-8
802 E 7th St 70301 985-446-5616
Tanya Richard, prin. Fax 446-5610
Sixth Ward MS 300/6-8
1865 Choctaw Rd 70301 985-633-2449
Kenneth Delcambre, prin. Fax 633-7373
Thibodaux HS 1,400/8-12
1355 Tiger Dr 70301 985-447-4071
Glenn Haydel, prin. Fax 447-4077
West Thiboudaux MS 500/6-8
1111 E 12th St 70301 985-446-6889
Gregory Cook, prin. Fax 447-1777
Other Schools – See Cut Off, Golden Meadow, Houma, Larose, Lockport, Raceland

---

Nicholls State University Post-Sec.
906 E 1st St 70310 985-446-8111
South Central Louisiana Technical Coll Post-Sec.
1425 Tiger Dr 70301 985-447-0924
White HS 700/8-12
555 Cardinal Dr 70301 985-446-8486
Michelle Chiasson, prin. Fax 448-1275

**Tickfaw, Tangipahoa, Pop. 685**
Tangipahoa Parish SD
Supt. — See Amite
Nesom MS 400/6-8
14417 Highway 442 W 70466 985-345-2166
Charlotte Tillman, prin. Fax 345-3731

**Tioga, Rapides**
Rapides Parish SD
Supt. — See Alexandria
Tioga HS 900/9-12
PO Box 1030 71477 318-640-9661
Allen Lacombe, prin. Fax 640-9757

**Urania, LaSalle, Pop. 1,308**
LaSalle Parish SD
Supt. — See Jena
LaSalle JHS 200/6-8
PO Box 520 71480 318-495-3474
Stephanie Clark, prin. Fax 495-3478

**Vacherie, Saint James, Pop. 2,354**
St. James Parish SD
Supt. — See Lutcher
Science & Math Academy 7-12
3125 Valcour Aime St 70090 225-258-4600
Pam Bourgeois, dir. Fax 265-7093

**Varnado, Washington, Pop. 1,459**
Washington Parish SD
Supt. — See Franklinton
Varnado HS 400/6-12
25543 Washington St, Angie LA 70426
985-732-2025
Randy Branch, prin. Fax 732-5198

**Vidalia, Concordia, Pop. 4,268**
Concordia Parish SD 3,800/PK-12
PO Box 950 71373 318-336-4226
Paul Nelson Ph.D., supt. Fax 336-5875
www.cpsbla.us/
Vidalia HS 500/9-12
2201 Murray Dr 71373 318-336-6231
Rick Brown, prin. Fax 336-6233
Vidalia JHS 400/6-8
210 Gillespie St 71373 318-336-6227
Whest Shirley, prin. Fax 336-6229
Other Schools – See Ferriday, Monterey

---

Vidalia Beauty School Post-Sec.
208 Westside Dr 71373 318-336-2377

**Ville Platte, Evangeline, Pop. 7,370**
Evangeline Parish SD 6,000/PK-12
1123 Te Mamou Rd 70586 337-363-6651
Toni Hamlin, supt. Fax 363-8086
www.epsb.com
Evangeline Central Alternative S 100/Alt
4587 Vidrine Rd 70586 337-363-6308
Dexter Brown, prin. Fax 363-6309
Ville Platte HS 900/5-12
210 W Cotton St 70586 337-363-3387
Kelli Lafleur, prin. Fax 363-7274
Other Schools – See Basile, Mamou, Pine Prairie

---

Christian Heritage Academy 100/PK-12
607 Prosper St 70586 337-363-7690
Sue Pomier, prin. Fax 363-7690
Sacred Heart HS 200/9-12
114 Trojan Ln 70586 337-363-1475
Dawn Shipp, prin. Fax 363-0348
South Louisiana Community College Post-Sec.
1124 Vocational Dr Ward 1 70586 337-363-2197

**Vinton, Calcasieu, Pop. 3,128**
Calcasieu Parish SD
Supt. — See Lake Charles
Vinton HS 300/9-12
1603 Grace Ave 70668 337-217-4400
Mitch Manuel, prin. Fax 217-4401
Vinton MS 200/6-8
900 Horridge St 70668 337-217-4720
Gena Granger, prin. Fax 217-4721

**Vivian, Caddo, Pop. 3,629**
Caddo Parish SD
Supt. — See Shreveport
North Caddo HS 300/9-12
201 Airport Dr 71082 318-375-3258
Annie Cherry, prin. Fax 222-8430

**Walker, Livingston, Pop. 6,061**
Livingston Parish SD
Supt. — See Livingston
Literacy and Technology Center 9-12
9261 Florida Blvd 70785 225-667-5268
Kim Albin, prin.
North Corbin JHS 700/6-8
32725 N Corbin Rd 70785 225-686-2038
Dennis DeLee, prin. Fax 686-2690
Pathways, 13330 Burgess Ave 70785 Alt
Lisa Kluka, prin. 225-665-6062
Pine Ridge S 50/Alt
PO Box 72 70785 225-664-4823
Tony Terry, prin. Fax 664-2984
Walker Freshman HS 400/9-9
PO Box 659 70785 225-664-0243
David Clark, prin. Fax 665-0512
Walker SHS 1,000/10-12
12646 Burgess Ave 70785 225-664-4825
Jason St. Pierre, prin. Fax 664-4321
Westside JHS 600/6-8
12615 Burgess Ave 70785 225-665-8259
Steve Link, prin. Fax 665-8283

**Washington, Saint Landry, Pop. 948**
St. Landry Parish SD
Supt. — See Opelousas
North Central HS 300/5-12
6579 Highway 10 70589 337-623-4239
Reginald Bush, prin. Fax 623-5360
Washington Career & Technical Center Vo/Tech
PO Box 430 70589 337-826-7360
Dr. Tracy Beard, prin. Fax 826-5264

**Watson, Livingston, Pop. 1,038**
Livingston Parish SD
Supt. — See Livingston
Live Oak MS 1,000/6-8
PO Box 470 70786 225-664-3211
Ryan Hodges, prin. Fax 664-1551

**Welsh, Jefferson Davis, Pop. 3,178**
Jefferson Davis Parish SD
Supt. — See Jennings
Welsh HS 300/9-12
306 Bourgeois St 70591 337-734-2361
Robin Primeaux, prin. Fax 734-4149

**Westlake, Calcasieu, Pop. 4,510**
Calcasieu Parish SD
Supt. — See Lake Charles
Arnett MS 500/6-8
400 Sulphur Ave 70669 337-217-4630
Max Caldarera, prin. Fax 217-4631
Westlake HS 500/9-12
1000 Garden Dr 70669 337-217-4950
Jason Van Metre, prin. Fax 217-4951
Westlake HS T & I Vo/Tech
2307 Jones St 70669 337-217-4375
Gary Singer, prin. Fax 217-4376

**West Monroe, Ouachita, Pop. 12,872**
Ouachita Parish SD
Supt. — See Monroe
Good Hope MS 700/6-8
400 Good Hope Rd 71291 318-396-9693
Twainna Calhoun, prin. Fax 397-5110
Ouachita Parish Alternative Center 100/Alt
1600 N 7th St 71291 318-323-5991
Scott Stone, prin. Fax 323-5946
Riser MS 500/6-8
100 Price Dr 71292 318-387-0567
Rodney Lloyd, prin. Fax 387-9072
West Monroe HS 2,000/9-12
201 Riggs St 71291 318-323-3771
Shelby Ainsworth, prin. Fax 388-4594
West Ouachita HS 1,000/9-12
4061 Caples Rd 71292 318-249-2117
Becky Oaks, prin. Fax 249-4774
West Ridge MS 700/6-8
6977 Cypress St 71291 318-397-8444
Jim McKay, prin. Fax 397-9376
Woodlawn JHS 300/6-8
175 Woodlawn School Rd 71292 318-325-1574
Charles Dykes, prin. Fax 325-9858

---

Claiborne Christian S 400/PK-12
334 Laird St 71291 318-396-7968
Cloyd's Beauty School #1 Inc. Post-Sec.
603 Natchitoches St 71291 318-322-5314
Northeast Baptist S 200/PK-12
5225 I 20 Service Rd 71292 318-325-2077
Anita Watson, prin. Fax 998-0193

**Westwego, Jefferson, Pop. 8,397**
Jefferson Parish SD
Supt. — See Harvey
Worley MS 600/6-8
801 Spartan Ln 70094 504-348-4964
Ira Wilson, prin. Fax 348-7057

**White Castle, Iberville, Pop. 1,872**
Iberville Parish SD
Supt. — See Plaquemine
White Castle HS 300/7-12
32695 Graham St 70788 225-545-3621
Charley Handy, prin. Fax 545-2964

**Winnfield, Winn, Pop. 4,766**
Winn Parish SD 2,300/PK-12
PO Box 430 71483 318-628-6936
Steve Bartlett, supt. Fax 628-2582
www.winnpsb.org
Winnfield HS 400/9-12
631 Thomas Mill Rd 71483 318-628-3506
Dr. Jane Griffin, prin. Fax 628-3417
Winnfield MS 400/6-8
685 Thomas Mill Rd 71483 318-628-2765
Brent Carpenter, prin. Fax 628-1838
Winn Parish Adult Learning Center Adult
403 W South Ave 71483 318-628-3492
Mike Austin, dir. Fax 628-7280
Other Schools – See Atlanta, Calvin, Dodson

---

Central Louisiana Technical College Post-Sec.
5960 Highway 167 N 71483 318-628-4342

**Winnsboro, Franklin, Pop. 4,862**
Franklin Parish SD 3,000/PK-12
7293 Prairie Rd 71295 318-435-9046
Dr. Lanny Johnson, supt. Fax 435-3392
www.fpsb.us
Franklin Parish HS 700/9-12
1600 Glover Dr 71295 318-435-5676
Patricia Sartin, prin. Fax 435-6493

---

Family Community Christian S 500/PK-12
2023 Highway 15 71295 318-435-4791
Franklin Academy 200/PK-12
2110 Loop Rd 71295 318-435-9520

**Youngsville, Lafayette, Pop. 8,025**
Lafayette Parish SD
Supt. — See Lafayette
Youngsville MS 800/5-8
600 Church St 70592 337-521-7940
Renee Nunez, prin. Fax 521-7941

---

Youngsville Christian S 100/PK-10
214 Church St 70592 337-856-8693
Daina Jackson, admin. Fax 856-8675

**Zachary, East Baton Rouge, Pop. 14,763**
Zachary Community SD 5,200/PK-12
3755 Church St 70791 225-658-4969
Scott Devillier, supt. Fax 658-5261
www.zacharyschools.org
Northwestern MS 1,200/7-8
5200 E Central Ave 70791 225-654-9201
Debby Brian, prin. Fax 658-2025
Zachary Career and Technical Center Vo/Tech
205 W Flonacher Rd 70791 225-658-7381
Johnathon Coats, admin. Fax 658-7385
Zachary HS 1,400/9-12
4100 Bronco Ln 70791 225-654-2776
Joe LeBlanc, prin. Fax 658-0010

**Zwolle, Sabine, Pop. 1,697**
Sabine Parish SD
Supt. — See Many
Zwolle JSHS 300/7-12
PO Box 188 71486 318-645-6104
Bradley McLaren, prin. Fax 645-4830

# MAINE

## MAINE DEPARTMENT OF EDUCATION
**23 State House Sta, Augusta 04333**
**Telephone 207-624-6600**
**Fax 207-624-6700**
**Website http://www.maine.gov/doe/**

Commissioner of Education Stephen Bowen

## MAINE BOARD OF EDUCATION
**23 State House Station, Augusta 04333-0023**

Chairperson Steven Pound

## PUBLIC, PRIVATE AND CATHOLIC SECONDARY SCHOOLS

**Ashland, Aroostook, Pop. 707**
RSU 32 / MSAD 32 200/PK-12
PO Box 289 04732 207-435-3661
Gehrig Johnson Ph.D., supt. Fax 435-8421
www.sad32.org/
Ashland District S 200/PK-12
PO Box 369 04732 207-435-3481
Joel Hall, prin. Fax 435-6417

**Auburn, Androscoggin, Pop. 22,603**
Auburn SD 3,700/PK-12
PO Box 800 04212 207-784-6431
Katherine Grondin, supt. Fax 333-6628
www.auburnschl.edu
Auburn MS 600/7-8
38 Falcon Dr 04210 207-333-6654
Celena Ranger, prin. Fax 784-1359
Franklin Alternative S 100/Alt
23 High St 04210 207-782-3242
Russell Barlow, prin. Fax 783-4189
Little HS 1,000/9-12
77 Harris St 04210 207-333-6652
James Miller, prin. Fax 784-9243
Merrill Hill Alternative S 50/Alt
23 High St 04210 207-783-3242
Russell Barlow, prin.

---

Central Maine Community College Post-Sec.
1250 Turner St 04210 207-755-5100
St. Dominic Academy 300/7-12
121 Gracelawn Rd 04210 207-782-6911
Joline Girouard, prin. Fax 795-6439

**Augusta, Kennebec, Pop. 18,710**
Augusta SD 2,300/PK-12
40 Pierce Dr 04330 207-626-2468
James Anastasio, supt. Fax 626-2444
www.augustaschools.org/
Capitol Area Technical Center Vo/Tech
40 Pierce Dr 04330 207-626-2475
Fax 626-2498
Cony JSHS 1,100/7-12
60 Pierce Dr 04330 207-626-2460
Kim Silsby, prin. Fax 626-2541

---

University of Maine at Augusta Post-Sec.
46 University Dr 04330 207-621-3000

**Baileyville, Washington**
AOS 90 - EMASS 800/PK-12
PO Box 580 04694 207-427-6913
William Braun, supt. Fax 427-3166
sites.google.com/site/aos90aos90
Woodland JSHS 200/7-12
14 First Ave 04694 207-427-3325
Patricia Metta, prin. Fax 427-3950
Other Schools – See Lee

**Bangor, Penobscot, Pop. 32,402**
Bangor SD 3,800/PK-12
73 Harlow St 04401 207-992-4152
Dr. Betsy Webb, supt. Fax 992-4163
www.bangorschools.net
Bangor HS 1,200/9-12
885 Broadway 04401 207-992-5500
Paul Butler, prin. Fax 941-6212
Cohen MS 400/6-8
304 Garland St 04401 207-941-6230
Gary Gonyar, prin. Fax 941-6235
Doughty MS 400/6-8
143 5th St 04401 207-941-6220
Ed Hackett, prin. Fax 947-7606
Career Technical Education
Supt. — None
United Technologies Center-Region 4 Vo/Tech
200 Hogan Rd 04401 207-942-5296
Fred Woodman, dir. Fax 942-0776

---

All Saints S - St. John Campus 100/4-8
PO Box 1749 04402 207-942-0955
Joseph Gallant, prin. Fax 942-2398
Bangor Christian S 300/PK-12
1476 Broadway 04401 207-947-7356
Jim Frost, hdmstr. Fax 262-9528
Bapst Memorial HS 500/9-12
100 Broadway 04401 207-947-0313
Melville MacKay, head sch Fax 941-2474
Beal College Post-Sec.
99 Farm Rd 04401 207-947-4591
Eastern Maine Community College Post-Sec.
354 Hogan Rd 04401 207-974-4600
Eastern Maine Medical Center Post-Sec.
489 State St 04401 207-973-7051
Empire Beauty School Post-Sec.
639 Broadway 04401 207-942-0039
Husson University Post-Sec.
1 College Cir 04401 207-941-7000
New England School of Communications Post-Sec.
1 College Cir 04401 207-941-7176

**Bar Harbor, Hancock, Pop. 2,528**

---

College of the Atlantic Post-Sec.
105 Eden St 04609 207-288-5015

**Bath, Sagadahoc, Pop. 8,327**
RSU 1 2,100/PK-12
34 Wing Farm Pkwy 04530 207-443-6601
Dr. Patrick Manuel, supt. Fax 443-8295
www.rsu1.org/
Bath MS 400/6-8
6 Old Brunswick Rd 04530 207-443-8270
Brandon Ward, prin. Fax 443-8273
Bath Regional Vocational Center Vo/Tech
800 High St 04530 207-443-8257
Joel Austin, prin. Fax 443-8256
Morse HS 700/9-12
826 High St 04530 207-443-8250
Jay Pinkerton, prin. Fax 443-8268

---

Hyde S - Bath 100/9-12
616 High St 04530 207-443-5584
Laura Gauld, head sch Fax 443-1450

**Belfast, Waldo, Pop. 6,555**
RSU 20
Supt. — See Searsport
Belfast Area HS 600/9-12
98 Waldo Ave 04915 207-338-1790
Stephen Fitzpatrick, prin. Fax 338-6713
Howard MS 400/6-8
173 Lincolnville Ave 04915 207-338-3320
Kimberly Buckheit, prin. Fax 338-5588
Adult Education Adult
6B Lions Way 04915 207-338-3197
Darrell Gilman Ed.D., prin. Fax 338-2960

**Bethel, Oxford**
RSU 44 / MSAD 44 800/K-12
1 Parkway Ste 204 04217 207-824-2185
David Murphy Ed.D., supt. Fax 824-2725
www.sad44.org
Telstar HS 300/9-12
284 Walkers Mills Rd 04217 207-824-2136
Ann Bell, prin. Fax 824-7130
Telstar MS 200/6-8
284 Walkers Mills Rd 04217 207-824-2136
Clark Rafford, prin. Fax 824-0496

---

Gould Academy 200/9-12
PO Box 860 04217 207-824-7700
Matt Ruby, head sch Fax 824-7711

**Biddeford, York, Pop. 20,950**
Biddeford SD 2,600/PK-12
18 Maplewood Ave 04005 207-282-8280
Jeremy Ray, supt. Fax 284-7956
www.biddefordschooldepartment.org
Biddeford HS 800/9-12
20 Maplewood Ave 04005 207-282-1596
Jerome Sirois, prin. Fax 282-8275
Biddeford MS 600/6-8
25 Tiger Way 04005 207-282-6400
Kyle Keenan, prin. Fax 282-6040
Biddeford Regional Center of Tech Vo/Tech
10 Maplewood Ave 04005 207-282-1501
Peg Levasseur, prin. Fax 282-7986

---

Heartwood College of Art Post-Sec.
2 Main St Bldg 17 Ste 223 04005 207-284-8800
University of New England Post-Sec.
11 Hills Beach Rd 04005 207-283-0171

**Bingham, Somerset, Pop. 749**
RSU 83 / MSAD 13 200/PK-12
PO Box 649 04920 207-672-5502
Virginia Rebar, supt. Fax 672-5502
www.sad13.org
Quimby MS 100/5-8
PO Box 649 04920 207-672-5500
Juliana Richard, prin. Fax 672-5502
Upper Kennebec Valley HS 100/9-12
PO Box 669 04920 207-672-3300
Juliana Richard, prin. Fax 672-4485

**Blue Hill, Hancock, Pop. 936**

---

Stevens Academy 300/9-12
23 Union St 04614 207-374-2808
Tim Seeley, head sch Fax 374-2982

**Boothbay Harbor, Lincoln, Pop. 1,073**
AOS 98 - RCSS 800/PK-12
51 Emery Ln 04538 207-633-2874
Eileen King, supt. Fax 633-5458
sites.google.com/site/boothbayschools/schools-of-union-49
Boothbay Region HS 200/9-12
236 Townsend Ave 04538 207-633-2421
Daniel Welch, prin. Fax 633-7129

**Brewer, Penobscot, Pop. 9,320**
Brewer SD 1,700/PK-12
261 Center St 04412 207-989-3160
Jay McIntire, supt. Fax 989-8622
www.breweredu.org/
Brewer HS 700/9-12
79 Parkway S 04412 207-989-4140
David Wall, prin. Fax 989-2657

**Bridgton, Cumberland, Pop. 2,035**
RSU 61 / MSAD 61 1,800/K-12
900 Portland Rd 04009 207-647-3048
Alan Smith, supt. Fax 647-5682
www.lakeregionschools.org
Other Schools – See Naples

**Brunswick, Cumberland, Pop. 14,835**
Brunswick SD 1,900/K-12
46 Federal St 04011 207-319-1900
Paul Perzanoski, supt. Fax 725-1700
www.brunswick.k12.me.us/
Brunswick HS 900/9-12
116 Maquoit Rd 04011 207-319-1910
Shanna Crofton, prin. Fax 798-5515
Brunswick JHS 500/6-8
65 Columbia Ave 04011 207-319-1930
Walter Wallace, prin. Fax 721-0602
Career Technical Education
Supt. — None
Maine Vocational Region 10 Vo/Tech
68 Church Rd 04011 207-729-6622
Barry Lohnes, dir. Fax 721-0907

---

Bowdoin College Post-Sec.
5000 College Sta 04011 207-725-3000

**Buckfield, Oxford**
RSU 10
Supt. — See Dixfield
Buckfield JSHS 300/7-12
160 Morrill St 04220 207-336-2151
George Reuter, prin. Fax 336-2460

**Bucksport, Hancock, Pop. 2,843**
RSU 25 1,100/PK-12
62 Mechanic St 04416 207-469-7311
James Boothby, supt. Fax 469-6640
www.rsu25.org/

Bucksport HS 400/9-12
102 Broadway 04416 207-469-6650
Bill Tracy, prin. Fax 469-2081
Bucksport MS 300/5-8
100 Miles Ln 04416 207-469-6647
Josh Tripp, prin. Fax 469-2068

**Buxton, York**
RSU 6 / MSAD 6 3,300/PK-12
94 Main St 04093 207-929-3831
Frank Sherburne, supt. Fax 929-5955
www.bonnyeagle.org
Bonny Eagle MS 900/6-8
92 Sokokis Trl 04093 207-929-3833
Michael Roy, prin. Fax 929-9181
Other Schools – See Standish

**Calais, Washington, Pop. 3,074**
Calais SD 600/PK-12
32 Blue Devil Hl 04619 207-454-7561
Raymond Freve, supt. Fax 454-2296
www.calaisschool.org
Calais MSHS 300/7-12
34 Blue Devil Hl Ste 2 04619 207-454-2591
Matt Clark, prin. Fax 454-0306
Saint Croix Regional Tech Center Vo/Tech
34 Blue Devil Hl Ste 1 04619 207-454-2581
Robert F. Moholland, admin. Fax 454-2597

---

Washington County Community College Post-Sec.
1 College Dr 04619 207-454-1000

**Camden, Knox, Pop. 3,526**
MSAD 28 / Five Town CSD 1,400/K-12
7 Lions Ln 04843 207-236-3358
Elaine Nutter, supt. Fax 236-7810
www.fivetowns.net
Camden-Rockport MS 400/5-8
34 Knowlton St 04843 207-236-7805
Jaime Stone, prin. Fax 236-7815
Other Schools – See Rockport

**Cape Elizabeth, Cumberland, Pop. 8,854**
Cape Elizabeth SD 1,700/K-12
320 Ocean House Rd 04107 207-799-2217
Meredith Nadeau, supt. Fax 799-2914
www.cape.k12.me.us
Cape Elizabeth HS 500/9-12
345 Ocean House Rd 04107 207-799-3309
Jeffrey Shedd, prin. Fax 767-8050
Cape Elizabeth MS 600/5-8
14 Scott Dyer Rd 04107 207-799-8176
Michael Tracy, prin. Fax 767-0832

**Carabaset Vly, Franklin**

---

Carrabassett Valley Academy 100/7-12
3197 Carrabassett Dr, 207-237-2250
Kate Punderson, head sch Fax 237-2213

**Caribou, Aroostook, Pop. 8,094**
Eastern Aroostook Regional Sch Unit 39 1,700/PK-12
75 Bennett Dr Ste 3 04736 207-496-6311
Timothy Doad, supt. Fax 498-3261
www.rsu39.org
Caribou HS 500/9-12
308 Sweden St 04736 207-493-4260
Travis Barnes, prin. Fax 493-4244
Caribou MS 300/6-8
21 Glenn St 04736 207-493-4240
Leland Caron, prin. Fax 493-4243
Caribou Regional Technology Center Vo/Tech
308 Sweden St Ste 1 04736 207-493-4270
Ralph Conroy, prin. Fax 493-4242
Adult Education Adult
75 Bennett Dr Ste 2 04736 207-493-4272
Dan MacDonald, dir.
Other Schools – See Limestone

---

Empire Beauty School Post-Sec.
30 Skyway Dr 04736 207-498-6067

**Carmel, Penobscot**
RSU 87 / MSAD 23 700/PK-8
44 Plymouth Rd 04419 207-848-5173
John Backus, supt. Fax 848-5196
www.rsu87.org
Caravel MS 200/5-8
520 Irish Rd 04419 207-848-3615
Mark Turner, prin. Fax 848-0884

**Castine, Hancock, Pop. 1,015**

---

Maine Maritime Academy Post-Sec.
66 Pleasant St 04420 207-326-4311

**Corinth, Penobscot**
RSU 64 / MSAD 64 1,200/K-12
PO Box 279 04427 207-285-3334
Rhonda Sperrey, supt. Fax 285-3307
www.rsu64schools.org
Central HS 300/9-12
PO Box 370 04427 207-285-3326
Brent Slowikowski, prin. Fax 285-4342
Central MS 300/6-8
PO Box 19 04427 207-285-3177
Jonathan Perry, prin. Fax 285-4350

**Cumberland Center, Cumberland, Pop. 2,477**
RSU 51 / MSAD 51 1,900/K-12
PO Box 6A 04021 207-829-4800
Jeff Porter, supt. Fax 829-4802
www.msad51.org
Greely HS 700/9-12
303 Main St 04021 207-829-4805
Dan McKeone, prin. Fax 829-2256
Greely MS 6-8 500/6-8
351 Tuttle Rd 04021 207-829-4815
Mar-E Trebilcock, prin. Fax 829-4819

**Danforth, Washington**
RSU 84 / MSAD 14 200/PK-12
31A Houlton Rd 04424 207-448-2882
Terry A. Comeau, supt. Fax 448-7235
www.eastgrandschool.org
East Grand S 200/PK-12
31 Houlton Rd 04424 207-448-2260
Dawn Matthews, prin. Fax 448-7880

**Deer Isle, Hancock**
Deer Isle - Stonington Community SD 400/K-12
251 N Deer Isle Rd 04627 207-348-9100
Mark Jenkins, supt. Fax 348-9103
Deer Isle - Stonington HS 100/9-12
251 N Deer Isle Rd 04627 207-348-2303
Todd West, prin. Fax 348-2304

**Dexter, Penobscot, Pop. 2,129**
AOS 94 - S46HRSD 700/PK-12
175 Fern Rd Ste 1 04930 207-924-6000
Kevin Jordan, supt. Fax 924-7660
www.aos94.org
Dexter HS 300/9-12
12 Abbott Hill Rd 04930 207-924-5536
Stephen Bell, prin. Fax 924-7673
Tri-County Regional Technology Center Vo/Tech
14 Abbott Hill Rd 04930 207-924-7670
Dr. Patrick O'Neill, dir. Fax 924-5539

**Dixfield, Oxford, Pop. 1,056**
RSU 10 2,800/PK-12
33 Nash St 04224 207-562-7254
Craig King Ed.D., supt. Fax 562-7059
district.rsu10.org
Dirigo HS 300/9-12
145 Weld St 04224 207-562-4251
Mike Poulin, prin. Fax 562-6074
Dirigo MS 200/6-8
45 Middle School Dr 04224 207-562-7552
Michael Poulin, prin. Fax 562-8329
Other Schools – See Buckfield, Mexico, Rumford

**Dover Foxcroft, Piscataquis, Pop. 3,077**
RSU 68 / MSAD 68 700/PK-8
63 Harrison Ave Ste C 04426 207-564-6535
Robert Lucy, supt. Fax 564-3487
www.sedomocha.org
Se Do Mo Cha MS 300/5-8
63 Harrison Ave 04426 207-564-6535
Julie Kimball, prin. Fax 564-6531

---

Foxcroft Academy 500/9-12
975 W Main St 04426 207-564-8351
Arnold Shorey, head sch Fax 564-8394

**Dyer Brook, Aroostook**
RSU 50 800/PK-12
922 Dyer Brook Rd, 207-757-8223
Larry Malone, supt. Fax 757-8257
www.rsu50.org
Southern Aroostook Community S 400/K-12
922 Dyer Brook Rd, 207-757-8206
Jon Porter, prin. Fax 757-8257
Other Schools – See Stacyville

**East Machias, Washington**

---

Washington Academy 400/9-12
PO Box 190 04630 207-255-8301
Judson McBrine, head sch Fax 255-8303

**East Millinocket, Penobscot, Pop. 1,552**
E Millinocket & Medway SD 400/K-12
45 North St 04430 207-746-3500
Dawn Pray M.Ed., supt. Fax 746-3516
eastmillinocketschools.org
Schenck HS 200/9-12
45 North St 04430 207-746-3511
Catherine Steeves M.Ed., prin. Fax 746-3516
Other Schools – See Medway

Millinocket SD 500/K-12
45 North St Ste 2 04430 207-723-6400
Frank Boynton, supt. Fax 447-6599
www.millinocketschools.org/
Other Schools – See Millinocket

**Easton, Aroostook**
Easton SD 200/PK-12
PO Box 126 04740 207-488-7700
Roger Shaw, supt. Fax 488-2840
eastonschools.org
Easton JSHS 100/7-12
PO Box 66 04740 207-488-7702
Cameron Adams, prin. Fax 488-7707

**Eastport, Washington, Pop. 1,291**
AOS 77 - SCSS 600/PK-12
PO Box 190 04631 207-853-2567
Kenneth Johnson, supt. Fax 853-6260
Shead HS 100/9-12
89 High St 04631 207-853-6254
Paul Theriault, prin. Fax 853-2919

---

Westlawn Institute of Marine Technology Post-Sec.
16 Deep Cove Rd 04631 207-853-6600

**East Waterboro, York**
RSU 57 / MSAD 57
Supt. — See Waterboro
Massabesic MS 800/6-8
134 Old Alfred Rd 04030 207-247-6121
Mark Fisher, prin. Fax 247-8621

**Eliot, York**
RSU 35 / MSAD 35 2,400/PK-12
180 Depot Rd 03903 207-439-2438
Dr. Mary Nash, supt. Fax 439-2531
www.rsu35.org

Marshwood MS 600/6-8
626 Harold L Dow Hwy 03903 207-439-1399
John Caverly, prin. Fax 439-3504
Other Schools – See South Berwick

**Ellsworth, Hancock, Pop. 7,675**
Ellsworth SD PK-12
66 Main St Ste 201 04605 207-664-7100
Daniel Higgins, supt.
www.ellsworthschools.org
Ellsworth HS 600/9-12
299 State St 04605 207-667-4722
Bruce Lindberg, prin. Fax 667-5027
Hancock County Technical Center Vo/Tech
112 Boggy Brook Rd 04605 207-667-9729
Amy Boles, dir. Fax 667-7138

**Fairfield, Kennebec, Pop. 2,598**
RSU 49 / MSAD 49 2,300/PK-12
8 School St 04937 207-453-4200
Dr. Dean Baker, supt. Fax 453-0110
www.msad49.org
Lawrence HS 700/9-12
9 School St 04937 207-453-4200
Mark Campbell, prin. Fax 453-4219
Lawrence JHS 400/7-8
7 School St 04937 207-453-4200
Roberta Hersom, prin. Fax 453-4214

---

Kennebec Valley Community College Post-Sec.
92 Western Ave 04937 207-453-5000

**Falmouth, Cumberland, Pop. 1,834**
Falmouth SD 2,000/K-12
51 Woodville Rd 04105 207-781-3200
Geoff Bruno, supt. Fax 781-5711
www.falmouthschools.org
Falmouth HS 700/9-12
74 Woodville Rd 04105 207-781-7429
Gregg Palmer, prin. Fax 781-3985
Falmouth MS 500/6-8
52 Woodville Rd 04105 207-781-3740
Janet Adams, prin. Fax 321-0108

RSU 14 - Windham Raymond
Supt. — See Windham
REAL S Alt
1 Mackworth Is 04105 207-781-6207
Pender Makin, dir. Fax 781-6206

---

Maine Educational Center for the Deaf Post-Sec.
Mackworth Island 04105 207-781-3165

**Farmingdale, Kennebec, Pop. 1,939**
RSU 2
Supt. — See Hallowell
Hall-Dale MSHS 200/6-12
111 Maple St 04344 207-622-4162
Mark Tinkham, prin. Fax 622-7515

**Farmington, Franklin, Pop. 4,199**
RSU 9 - Mt. Blue Regional SD 2,200/PK-12
115 Learning Ln 04938 207-778-6571
Dr. Thomas Ward, supt. Fax 778-4160
www.mtbluersd.org/
Foster Reg Applied Tech Center Vo/Tech
129 Seamon Rd 04938 207-778-3562
Glenn Kapiloff, prin. Fax 778-3562
Mt. Blue HS 700/9-12
129 Seamon Rd 04938 207-778-3561
Bruce Mochamer, prin. Fax 778-3564
Mt. Blue MS 400/6-8
269 Middle St 04938 207-778-3511
Gary Oswald, prin. Fax 778-5810

---

University of Maine Farmington Post-Sec.
111 South St 04938 207-778-7050

**Fort Fairfield, Aroostook, Pop. 1,799**
MSAD 20 1,000/PK-12
28 High School Dr Ste B 04742 207-473-4455
Marc Gendron, supt. Fax 473-4095
www.msad20.org/
Fort Fairfield MSHS 300/6-12
28 High School Dr Ste A 04742 207-472-3271
John Kaleta, prin. Fax 472-3281

**Fort Kent, Aroostook, Pop. 2,423**
MSAD 27 1,000/PK-12
84 Pleasant St Ste 1 04743 207-834-3189
Timothy Doak, supt. Fax 834-3395
www.sad27.org/
Fort Kent Community HS 300/9-12
84 Pleasant St 04743 207-834-5540
James Charette, prin. Fax 834-2723
Valley Rivers MS 6-8
84 Pleasant ST 04743 207-834-5540
Ralph Caron, prin.

---

University of Maine Fort Kent Post-Sec.
23 University Dr 04743 207-834-7500

**Freeport, Cumberland, Pop. 1,447**
RSU 5 1,900/PK-12
17 West St 04032 207-865-0928
Edward R. McDonough, supt. Fax 865-2855
rsu5.org/
Freeport HS 500/9-12
30 Holbrook St 04032 207-865-4706
Brian Campbell, prin. Fax 865-2900
Freeport MS 300/6-8
19 Kendall Ln 04032 207-865-6051
Raymond Grogan, prin. Fax 865-2902

---

Merriconeag Waldorf S 200/K-12
57 Desert Rd 04032 207-865-3900
Pine Tree Academy 200/PK-12
67 Pownal Rd 04032 207-865-4747

**Frenchville, Aroostook**
RSU 33 / MSAD 33 — 300/PK-12
PO Box 9 04745 — 207-543-7334
Dr. Fern Desjardins, supt. — Fax 543-6242
www.msad33.org
St. John Valley Tech Center — Vo/Tech
PO Box 509 04745 — 207-543-6606
David Morse, dir. — Fax 543-6115
Other Schools – See Saint Agatha

**Fryeburg, Oxford, Pop. 1,595**
RSU 72 / MSAD 72 — 800/PK-8
124 Portland St 04037 — 207-935-2600
Jay Robinson, supt. — Fax 935-3787
www.msad72.org
Ockett MS — 300/6-8
25 Molly Ockett Dr 04037 — 207-935-2401
Emily Kirkpatrick, prin. — Fax 935-4470

---

Fryeburg Academy — 600/9-12
745 Main St 04037 — 207-935-2001
Erin Mayo, head sch — Fax 935-4292

**Gardiner, Kennebec, Pop. 5,663**
MSAD 11 — 2,200/PK-12
150 Highland Ave 04345 — 207-582-5346
Patricia Hopkins, supt. — Fax 582-8305
www.msad11.org
Gardiner Area HS — 700/9-12
40 W Hill Rd 04345 — 207-582-3150
Chad Kempton, prin. — Fax 582-0434
Gardiner Regional MS — 500/6-8
161 Cobbossee Ave 04345 — 207-582-1326
Todd Sanders, prin. — Fax 582-6823

**Gorham, Cumberland, Pop. 6,775**
Gorham SD — 2,700/K-12
75 South St Ste 2 04038 — 207-222-1000
Theodore Sharpe, supt. — Fax 839-5003
www.gorhamschools.org/
Gorham HS — 900/9-12
41 Morrill Ave 04038 — 207-222-1100
Christopher Record, prin. — Fax 839-7742
Gorham MS — 600/6-8
106 Weeks Rd 04038 — 207-222-1220
Robert Riley, prin. — Fax 839-4092

**Gray, Cumberland, Pop. 877**
RSU 15 / MSAD 15 — 2,000/K-12
14 Shaker Rd 04039 — 207-657-3335
Bruce Beasley, supt. — Fax 657-2040
www.msad15.org/
Gray-New Gloucester HS — 600/9-12
10 Libby Hill Rd 04039 — 207-657-3323
Ted Finn, prin. — Fax 657-3329
Gray-New Gloucester MS — 600/5-8
31 Libby Hill Rd 04039 — 207-657-4994
Sherry Levesque, prin. — Fax 657-5219

**Greenville, Piscataquis, Pop. 1,245**
Greenville SD — 100/PK-12
PO Box 100 04441 — 207-695-3708
David Morrill, supt. — Fax 695-3709
www.ghslakers.org
Greenville Consolidated S — 100/PK-12
PO Box 100 04441 — 207-695-2666
Kelly MacFadyen, prin. — Fax 695-4614

**Guilford, Piscataquis, Pop. 885**
RSU 80 / MSAD 4 — 400/PK-12
31 High St Ste C 04443 — 207-876-3444
Ann Kirkpatrick, supt. — Fax 876-3446
www.sad4.org
Piscataquis Community Secondary S — 300/7-12
9 Campus Dr 04443 — 207-876-4625
John Keane, prin. — Fax 876-4628

**Hallowell, Kennebec, Pop. 2,343**
RSU 2 — 2,200/PK-12
7 Reed St 04347 — 207-622-6351
Virgel Hammonds, supt. — Fax 622-7866
www.kidsrsu.org
Other Schools – See Farmingdale, Monmouth, Richmond

**Hampden, Penobscot, Pop. 4,292**
RSU 22 / MSAD 22 — 2,100/PK-12
24 Main Rd N 04444 — 207-862-3255
Richard Lyons, supt. — Fax 862-2789
www.rsu22.us
Hampden Academy — 700/9-12
89 Western Ave 04444 — 207-862-3791
Ruey Yehle, prin. — Fax 862-4577
Reeds Brook MS — 300/6-8
28A Main Rd S 04444 — 207-862-3540
Regan Nickels, prin. — Fax 862-3551
Other Schools – See Winterport

**Harrington, Washington**
RSU 37 / MSAD 37 — 700/PK-12
1020 Sacarap Rd 04643 — 207-483-2734
Ronald Ramsay, supt. — Fax 483-6051
www.msad37.org/
Narraguagus HS — 200/7-12
1611 Main St 04643 — 207-483-2746
Lucille Willey, prin. — Fax 483-2771

**Hartland, Somerset, Pop. 799**
RSU 19
Supt. — See Newport
Somerset Valley MS — 300/5-8
45 Blake St 04943 — 207-938-4770
Don Roux, prin. — Fax 938-2114

**Hebron, Oxford**

---

Hebron Academy — 300/6-12
PO Box 309 04238 — 207-966-2100
John King, hdmstr. — Fax 966-1111

**Hermon, See Bangor**
Hermon SD — 1,200/PK-12
31 Billings Rd 04401 — 207-848-4000
Patricia Duran, supt. — Fax 848-5226
www.hermon.net
Hermon HS — 600/9-12
2415 Route 2 04401 — 207-848-4000
Brian Walsh, prin. — Fax 848-5591
Hermon MS — 300/5-8
29 Billings Rd 04401 — 207-848-4000
Gerald Kiesman, prin. — Fax 848-2163

**Hiram, Oxford**
RSU 55 / MSAD 55 — 1,100/K-12
137 S Hiram Rd 04041 — 207-625-2490
Carl Landry, supt. — Fax 625-7065
www.sad55.org
Sacopee Valley HS — 400/9-12
115 S Hiram Rd 04041 — 207-625-3208
Britt Wolfe, prin. — Fax 625-7869
Sacopee Valley MS — 400/4-8
137 S Hiram Rd 04041 — 207-625-2450
Michael Lynch, prin. — Fax 625-2465

**Hodgdon, Aroostook**
RSU 70 / MSAD 70 — 500/PK-12
175 Hodgdon Mills Rd 04730 — 207-532-3015
Scott Richardson, supt. — Fax 532-2679
www.msad70.org
Hodgdon HS — 100/9-12
174 Hodgdon Mills Rd 04730 — 207-532-2413
Mary Harbison, prin. — Fax 532-4043

**Holden, Penobscot**
RSU 63 / MSAD 63 — 600/PK-8
202 Kidder Hill Rd 04429 — 207-843-7851
Kenneth Smith, supt. — Fax 843-7295
www.edline.net/pages/rsu63
Holbrook MS — 300/5-8
202 Kidder Hill Rd 04429 — 207-843-7769
Richard Modery, prin. — Fax 843-4328

**Houlton, Aroostook, Pop. 4,790**
Career Technical Education
Supt. — None
Region 2 School of Applied Tech — Vo/Tech
PO Box 307 04730 — 207-532-9541
Dave Keaton, dir. — Fax 532-6975

RSU 29 / MSAD 29 — 1,300/PK-12
PO Box 190 04730 — 207-532-6555
Ellen Schneider, supt. — Fax 532-6481
www.sad29.k12.me.us/
Houlton MSHS — 400/6-12
7 Bird St 04730 — 207-532-6551
Martin Bouchard, prin. — Fax 532-6282

---

Greater Houlton Christian Academy — 100/PK-12
27 School St 04730 — 207-532-0736
R. Thomas Zimmerman, head sch — Fax 532-9553

**Howland, Penobscot, Pop. 1,083**
AOS 43
Supt. — See Lagrange
Hichborn MS — 100/6-8
23 Cross St 04448 — 207-732-3113
Carol Marcinkus, prin. — Fax 732-8331
Penobscot Valley HS — 200/9-12
23 Cross St 04448 — 207-732-3111
Carol Marcinkus, prin. — Fax 732-8328

**Islesboro, Waldo**
Islesboro SD — 100/K-12
PO Box 118 04848 — 207-734-6723
Dr. Joseph Mattos, supt. — Fax 734-8159
ics.islesboro.k12.me.us
Islesboro Central S — 100/K-12
PO Box 118 04848 — 207-734-2251
Heather Knight, prin. — Fax 734-8159

**Jackman, Somerset**
RSU 82 / MSAD 12 — 200/K-12
606 Main St 04945 — 207-668-5291
Dr. William Crumley, supt. — Fax 668-4482
www.sad12.com
Forest Hills Consolidated S — 200/K-12
606 Main St 04945 — 207-668-5291
Denise Plante, prin. — Fax 668-4482

**Jay, Franklin**
RSU 73
Supt. — See Livermore Falls
Spruce Mountain HS — 200/9-12
33 Community Dr 04239 — 207-897-4336
Thomas Plourde, prin. — Fax 897-9313
Spruce Mountain MS — 200/6-8
23 Community Dr 04239 — 207-897-4319
Scott Albert, prin. — Fax 897-3513

**Jonesport, Washington**
Moosabec Community SD Union 103 — 200/PK-12
127 Snare Creek Ln 04649 — 207-497-2154
William Shuttleworth, supt. — Fax 497-2703
www.union103.org
Jonesport-Beals HS — 100/9-12
180 Snare Creek Ln 04649 — 207-497-5454
Michael Kelley, prin. — Fax 497-3004

**Kennebunk, York, Pop. 5,151**
RSU 21 — 2,400/K-12
177 Alewive Rd 04043 — 207-985-1100
Katie Hawes, supt. — Fax 985-1104
www.rsu21.net
Kennebunk HS — 700/9-12
89 Fletcher St 04043 — 207-985-1110
Susan Cressey, prin. — Fax 985-1350
Kennebunk MS — 500/6-8
60 Thompson Rd 04043 — 207-467-8004
Jeff Rodman, prin. — Fax 467-9059

**Kennebunkport, York, Pop. 1,232**

---

The Landing School — Post-Sec.
PO Box 1490 04046 — 207-985-7976

**Kents Hill, Kennebec**

---

Kents Hill S — 200/9-12
PO Box 257 04349 — 207-685-4914
Patrick McInerney, head sch — Fax 685-9529

**Kittery, York, Pop. 4,483**
Kittery SD — 1,000/K-12
200 Rogers Rd 03904 — 207-475-1334
Allyn Hutton, supt. — Fax 439-5407
www.kitteryschools.com
Shapleigh MS — 400/4-8
43 Stevenson Rd 03904 — 207-439-2572
Anne Ellis, prin. — Fax 439-9958
Traip Academy — 300/9-12
12 Williams Ave 03904 — 207-439-1121
Eric Waddell, prin. — Fax 439-3789

**Lagrange, Penobscot**
AOS 43 — 1,300/PK-12
20 Howland Rd 04453 — 207-943-7317
Michael Wright, supt. — Fax 943-5314
www.aos43.com
Other Schools – See Howland, Milo

**Lee, Penobscot**
AOS 90 - EMASS
Supt. — See Baileyville
Mt. Jefferson JHS — 100/5-8
61 Winn Rd 04455 — 207-738-2866
Pamela Hamilton, prin. — Fax 738-3817

---

Lee Academy — 300/9-12
26 Winn Rd 04455 — 207-738-2252

**Lewiston, Androscoggin, Pop. 35,657**
Lewiston SD — 5,100/PK-12
36 Oak St 04240 — 207-795-4100
William T. Webster, supt. — Fax 795-4177
www.lewistonpublicschools.org/
Lewiston HS — 1,400/9-12
156 East Ave 04240 — 207-795-4190
Shawn Chabot, prin. — Fax 795-4119
Lewiston MS — 700/7-8
75 Central Ave 04240 — 207-795-4180
Jake Langlais, prin. — Fax 753-1789
Lewiston Regional Technical Center — Vo/Tech
156 East Ave 04240 — 207-795-4144
Robert Callahan, dir. — Fax 795-4147

---

Bates College — Post-Sec.
2 Andrews Rd 04240 — 207-786-6255
Central Maine Christian Academy — 100/PK-12
390 Main St 04240 — 207-777-0007
Patricia St. Hilaire, admin. — Fax 777-0007
College of Nursing & Health Professions — Post-Sec.
70 Middle St 04240 — 207-795-2840
Mr. Bernard's School of Hair Fashion — Post-Sec.
711 Lisbon St 04240 — 207-783-7765

**Limestone, Aroostook, Pop. 1,068**
Eastern Aroostook Regional Sch Unit 39
Supt. — See Caribou
Limestone Community S — 300/PK-12
93 High St 04750 — 207-325-4742
Susan White, prin. — Fax 325-4969

Maine School of Science & Mathematics — 100/10-12
95 High St 04750 — 207-325-3303
Luke Shorty, dir. — Fax 325-3340
www.mssm.org/
Maine S of Science & Mathematics — 100/10-12
95 High St 04750 — 207-325-3303
Luke C. Shorty, dir. — Fax 325-3340

**Lincoln, Penobscot, Pop. 2,837**
Career Technical Education
Supt. — None
North Penobscot Tech-Region 3 — Vo/Tech
35 W Broadway 04457 — 207-794-3004
Mary Hawkes, dir. — Fax 794-8049

RSU 67 — 1,100/PK-12
25 Reed Dr 04457 — 207-794-6500
Dr. Keith Laser, supt. — Fax 794-2600
www.rsu67.org
Mattanawcook Academy — 400/9-12
33 Reed Dr 04457 — 207-794-6711
Henry Pietras, prin. — Fax 794-3205
Mattanawcook JHS — 400/4-8
41 School St 04457 — 207-794-8935
Christopher Cowing, prin. — Fax 794-2601

**Lisbon, See Lisbon Falls**
Lisbon SD — 1,300/PK-12
19 Gartley St 04250 — 207-353-6711
Richard Green, supt. — Fax 353-3032
www.lisbonschoolsme.org/
Other Schools – See Lisbon Falls

**Lisbon Falls, Androscoggin, Pop. 4,031**
Lisbon SD
Supt. — See Lisbon
Lisbon HS — 400/9-12
2 Sugg Dr 04252 — 207-353-3030
Kenneth Healey, prin. — Fax 353-3032
Sugg MS — 300/6-8
4 Sugg Dr 04252 — 207-353-3055
Darren Akerman, prin. — Fax 353-3053

**Livermore Falls, Androscoggin, Pop. 1,558**
RSU 73 — 1,000/PK-12
9 Cedar St 04254 — 207-897-6722
Kenneth Healey, supt. — Fax 897-2362
rsu73.org

Other Schools – See Jay

**Machias, Washington, Pop. 1,257**
AOS 96 - MBASS 900/PK-12
291 Court St 04654 207-255-6585
Scott Porter, supt. Fax 255-8054
www.aos96.org
Machias Memorial HS 100/9-12
1 Bulldog Ln 04654 207-255-3812
Brian Leavitt, prin. Fax 255-3093

---

University of Maine at Machias Post-Sec.
116 OBrien Ave 04654 207-255-1200

**Madawaska, Aroostook, Pop. 2,953**
Madawaska SD 600/PK-12
328 Saint Thomas St Ste 201 04756 207-728-3346
Ginette Albert, supt. Fax 728-7823
www.madawaskaschools.org/
Madawaska MSHS 300/7-12
135 7th Ave 04756 207-728-3371
Wayne Anderson, prin. Fax 728-3636

**Madison, Somerset, Pop. 2,594**
RSU 59 / MSAD 59 800/PK-12
205 Main St 04950 207-696-3323
Todd LeRoy, supt. Fax 696-5631
sites.google.com/a/msad59.org/rsu59/
Madison Area Memorial HS 300/9-12
486 Main St 04950 207-696-3395
Bonnie Levesque, prin. Fax 696-5644
Madison JHS 200/5-8
205 Main St 04950 207-696-3381
Bonnie Levesque, prin. Fax 696-5640

**Mars Hill, Aroostook, Pop. 965**
MSAD 42, PO Box 1006 04758 PK-12
Elaine Boulier, supt. 207-425-3771
Central Aroostook JSHS 200/7-12
PO Box 310 04758 207-425-2811
Kay York, prin. Fax 429-8460

**Medway, Penobscot**
E Millinocket & Medway SD
Supt. — See East Millinocket
Medway MS 100/5-8
25 Middle School Dr 04460 207-746-3470
Dawn Pray M.Ed., prin. Fax 746-9435

**Mexico, Oxford, Pop. 1,718**
Career Technical Education
Supt. — None
Region 9 School of Applied Tech Vo/Tech
377 River Rd 04257 207-364-3764
Brenda Gammon, dir. Fax 364-2074

RSU 10
Supt. — See Dixfield
Mountain Valley MS 300/6-8
58 Highland Ter 04257 207-364-7926
Ryan Casey, prin. Fax 364-5608

**Millinocket, Penobscot, Pop. 4,427**
Millinocket SD
Supt. — See East Millinocket
Stearns JSHS 200/7-12
199 State St 04462 207-723-6430
Deborah Levesque, prin. Fax 723-6437

**Milo, Piscataquis, Pop. 1,832**
AOS 43
Supt. — See Lagrange
Penquis Valley HS 300/6-12
48 Penquis Dr 04463 207-943-7346
Jeremy Bousquet, prin. Fax 943-5333

**Monmouth, Kennebec**
RSU 2
Supt. — See Hallowell
Monmouth Academy 200/9-12
96 Academy Rd 04259 207-933-4416
Richard Amero, prin. Fax 933-7222
Monmouth MS 300/4-8
117 Academy Rd 04259 207-933-9002
Richard Amero, prin. Fax 933-7252

**Mount Desert, Hancock**
AOS 91 - MDIRSS 1,500/K-12
PO Box 60 04660 207-288-5049
Howard Colter, supt. Fax 288-5071
www.mdirss.org
Mt. Desert Island HS 500/9-12
PO Box 180 04660 207-288-5011
Matthew Haney, prin. Fax 288-0692

**Naples, Cumberland, Pop. 423**
RSU 61 / MSAD 61
Supt. — See Bridgton
Lake Region HS 600/9-12
1877 Roosevelt Trl 04055 207-693-6221
A. Erik Good, prin. Fax 693-4591
Lake Region MS 400/6-8
204 Kansas Rd 04055 207-647-8403
Matthew Lokken, prin. Fax 647-0991
Lake Region Vocational Center Vo/Tech
1879 Roosevelt Trl 04055 207-693-3864
Rosie Schacht, dir. Fax 693-3864

**Newcastle, Lincoln, Pop. 659**

---

Lincoln Academy 500/9-12
81 Academy Hl 04553 207-563-3596
David Sturdevant, hdmstr. Fax 563-1067

**Newport, Penobscot, Pop. 1,726**
RSU 19 2,300/PK-12
PO Box 40 04953 207-368-5091
Gregory Potter, supt. Fax 368-2192
www.rsu19.org

Nokomis Regional HS 700/9-12
266 Williams Rd 04953 207-368-4354
Mary Nadeau, prin. Fax 368-3276
Sebasticook Valley MS 300/5-8
337 Williams Rd 04953 207-368-4592
Jason Tardy, prin. Fax 368-4598
Other Schools – See Hartland

**Norridgewock, Somerset, Pop. 1,411**

---

Riverview Memorial S 50/K-10
201 Mercer Rd 04957 207-634-2641

**North Anson, Somerset**
RSU 74 / MSAD 74 700/PK-12
PO Box 219 04958 207-635-2727
Kenneth Coville, supt. Fax 635-3599
www.sad74.k12.me.us
Carrabec HS 200/9-12
PO Box 220 04958 207-635-2296
Dr. Regina Campbell, prin. Fax 635-2276

**North Berwick, York, Pop. 1,596**
RSU 60 / MSAD 60 2,500/K-12
PO Box 819 03906 207-676-2234
Steven Connolly, supt. Fax 676-3229
www.msad60.org
Noble HS 1,000/8-12
388 Somersworth Rd 03906 207-676-2843
Joseph Findlay, prin. Fax 676-2842

**North Bridgton, Cumberland**

---

Bridgton Academy 200/12-12
PO Box 292 04057 207-647-3322
Graydon Vigneau, hdmstr. Fax 514-0757

**North Haven, Knox**
RSU 7 / MSAD 7 100/PK-12
93 Pulpit Harbor Rd 04853 207-867-4707
Jay Bartner, supt. Fax 867-4438
www.northhavencommunityschool.org
North Haven Community S 100/PK-12
93 Pulpit Harbor Rd 04853 207-867-4707
Amy Marx, prin. Fax 867-4438

**Norway, Oxford, Pop. 2,676**
Career Technical Education
Supt. — None
Oxford Hills Tech-Region 11 Vo/Tech
PO Box 313 04268 207-743-7756
Shawn Lambert, dir. Fax 743-0667

**Oakland, Kennebec, Pop. 2,571**
RSU 18 3,000/PK-12
41 Heath St 04963 207-465-7384
Gary N. Smith, supt. Fax 465-9130
www.rsu18.org/
Messalonskee HS 800/9-12
131 Messalonskee High Dr 04963 207-465-7381
Jonathan Moody, prin. Fax 465-9151
Messalonskee MS 600/6-8
33 School Bus Dr 04963 207-465-2167
Mark Hatch, prin. Fax 465-9683
Other Schools – See South China

**Old Orchard Beach, York, Pop. 8,527**
RSU 23 2,900/PK-12
28 Jameson Hill Rd 04064 207-934-5751
Lloyd Crocker, supt. Fax 934-1917
www.rsu23.org
Loranger MS 300/3-8
148 Saco Ave 04064 207-934-4848
Michael Flaherty, prin. Fax 934-3712
Old Orchard Beach HS 300/9-12
40 E Emerson Cummings Blvd 04064 207-934-4461
John Suttie, prin. Fax 934-3705

**Old Town, Penobscot, Pop. 7,682**
RSU 34 1,500/PK-12
156 Oak St Ste 2 04468 207-827-7171
David Walker, supt. Fax 827-3922
www.rsu34.org/
Leonard MS 300/6-8
156 Oak St 04468 207-827-3900
Jennifer Cyr, prin. Fax 827-3922
Old Town HS 500/9-12
203 Stillwater Ave 04468 207-827-3910
Scott Gordon, prin. Fax 827-3918

**Orono, Penobscot, Pop. 9,316**
RSU 26 1,300/K-12
10 Goodridge Dr 04473 207-866-7110
Joanne Harriman, supt. Fax 866-4217
www.rsu26.org/
Orono HS 400/9-12
14 Goodridge Dr 04473 207-866-4916
Jim Chasse, prin. Fax 866-7116
Orono MS 100/6-8
14 Goodridge Dr 04473 207-866-2350
Jeffrey Paul, prin. Fax 866-7111

---

University of Maine 04469 Post-Sec.
207-581-1110

**Phillips, Franklin**
RSU 58 / MSAD 58 700/K-12
1401 Rangeley Rd 04966 207-639-2086
Dr. Erica Brouillet, supt. Fax 639-5120
www.msad58.org
Other Schools – See Salem

**Pittsfield, Somerset, Pop. 3,092**
RSU 53 / MSAD 53 800/PK-8
167 School St Ste A 04967 207-487-5107
Jason I. Tardy, supt. Fax 487-6310
www.msad53.org/
Warsaw MS 300/5-8
167 School St 04967 207-487-5145
Sharon Littlefield, prin. Fax 487-4511

---

Maine Central Institute 400/9-12
295 Main St 04967 207-487-3355
Christopher Hopkins, head sch Fax 487-3512

**Poland, Androscoggin**
RSU 16 1,700/PK-12
3 Aggregate Rd 04274 207-998-2727
Tina Meserve, supt. Fax 998-2753
www.rsu16.org
Poland Regional HS 500/9-12
1457 Maine St 04274 207-998-5400
Catherine Medd, prin. Fax 998-5060
Whittier MS 300/7-8
1457 Maine St 04274 207-998-5400
Shawn Vincent, prin. Fax 998-5060

**Portland, Cumberland, Pop. 64,466**
Portland SD 6,800/PK-12
353 Cumberland Ave 04101 207-874-8100
Jeanne Crocker, supt. Fax 874-8199
www2.portlandschools.org
Casco Bay HS 300/9-12
196 Allen Ave 04103 207-874-8160
Derek Pierce, prin. Fax 797-5437
Deering HS 900/9-12
370 Stevens Ave 04103 207-874-8260
Ira Waltz, prin. Fax 874-8153
King MS 500/6-8
92 Deering Ave 04102 207-874-8140
Michael McCarthy, prin. Fax 874-8290
Lincoln MS 500/6-8
522 Stevens Ave 04103 207-874-8145
Suellyn Santiago, prin. Fax 874-8288
Moore MS 500/6-8
171 Auburn St 04103 207-874-8150
Stephen Rogers, prin. Fax 874-8272
Portland Arts & Technology HS Vo/Tech
196 Allen Ave 04103 207-874-8165
Michael Johnson, dir. Fax 874-8170
Portland HS 900/9-12
284 Cumberland Ave 04101 207-874-8250
Deborah Migneault, prin. Fax 874-8248

---

Cheverus HS 500/9-12
267 Ocean Ave 04103 207-774-6238
John Mullen, prin. Fax 828-0207
Empire Beauty School Post-Sec.
319 Marginal Way 04101 207-774-9413
Inst for Doctoral Studies in Visual Arts Post-Sec.
130 Neal St 04102 207-879-8757
Maine College of Art Post-Sec.
522 Congress St Ste 4 04101 207-775-3052
McAuley HS 200/9-12
631 Stevens Ave 04103 207-797-3802
Kathryn Woodson Barr, prin. Fax 797-3804
Mercy Hospital Post-Sec.
144 State St 04101 207-879-3000
University of New England Post-Sec.
716 Stevens Ave 04103 207-797-7261
University of Southern Maine Post-Sec.
PO Box 9300 04104 207-780-4141
Waynflete S 600/PK-12
360 Spring St 04102 207-774-5721
Geoffrey Wagg, head sch Fax 772-4782

**Presque Isle, Aroostook, Pop. 9,565**
RSU 79 / MSAD 1 1,800/PK-12
PO Box 1118 04769 207-764-4101
Dr. Gehrig Johnson, supt. Fax 764-4103
www.sad1.org/
Presque Isle HS 600/9-12
16 Griffin St 04769 207-764-0121
Ben Greenlaw, prin. Fax 764-7720
Presque Isle MS 400/6-8
569 Skyway St 04769 207-764-4474
Anne Blanchard, prin. Fax 768-3447
Presque Isle Regional Tech Center Vo/Tech
79 Blake St 04769 207-764-1356
Tim Prescott, prin. Fax 764-8107

---

Cornerstone Christian Academy 50/PK-12
PO Box 743 04769 207-768-6222
Brigitte Morse, head sch Fax 768-6224
Northern Maine Community College Post-Sec.
33 Edgemont Dr 04769 207-768-2700
University of Maine at Presque Isle Post-Sec.
181 Main St 04769 207-768-9400

**Rangeley, Franklin**
RSU 78 200/K-12
43 Mendolia Rd 04970 207-864-3311
Jay McIntire, supt. Fax 864-2451
www.rangeleyschool.org
Rangeley Lakes Regional S 200/K-12
43 Mendolia Rd 04970 207-864-3311
Charles Brown, prin. Fax 864-2451

**Raymond, Cumberland**
RSU 14 - Windham Raymond
Supt. — See Windham
Jordan-Small MS 200/5-8
423 Webbs Mills Rd 04071 207-655-4743
Randolph Crockett, prin. Fax 655-6952

**Readfield, Kennebec**
RSU 38 1,200/PK-12
45 Millard Harrison Dr 04355 207-685-3336
Dr. Donna H. Wolfrom, supt. Fax 685-4703
www.maranacook.org/
Maranacook Community HS 400/9-12
2250 Millard Harrison Dr 04355 207-685-4923
Dwayne Conway, prin. Fax 685-9597
Maranacook Community MS 300/6-8
2100 Millard Harrison Dr 04355 207-685-3128
Cathy Jacobs, prin. Fax 685-9876

**Richmond, Sagadahoc, Pop. 1,737**
RSU 2
Supt. — See Hallowell
Richmond MSHS — 200/6-12
132 Main St 04357 — 207-737-4348
Steve Lavoie, prin. — Fax 737-8707

**Rockland, Knox, Pop. 7,144**
Career Technical Education
Supt. — None
Mid-Coast School of Tech-Region 8 — Vo/Tech
1 Main St 04841 — 207-594-2161
Elizabeth Fisher, dir. — Fax 594-7506

RSU 13 — 1,500/K-12
28 Lincoln St 04841 — 207-596-6620
John McDonald, supt. — Fax 596-2004
www.rsu13.org
Oceanside HS East — 300/10-12
400 Broadway 04841 — 207-596-2010
Renee Thompson, prin. — Fax 596-2028
Other Schools – See Thomaston

**Rockport, Knox**
MSAD 28 / Five Town CSD
Supt. — See Camden
Camden Hills Regional HS — 600/9-12
25 Keelson Dr 04856 — 207-236-7800
Nick Ithomitis, prin. — Fax 236-7813

**Rumford, Oxford, Pop. 4,160**
RSU 10
Supt. — See Dixfield
Mountain Valley HS — 400/9-12
799 Hancock St 04276 — 207-364-4547
Matthew Gilbert, prin. — Fax 364-3436

**Sabattus, Androscoggin**
RSU 4
Supt. — See Wales
Oak Hill MS — 400/6-8
40 Ball Park Rd 04280 — 207-375-6961
Jeff Ireland, prin. — Fax 375-8871

**Saco, York, Pop. 18,250**
Saco SD — K-12
90 Beach St 04072 — 207-284-4505
Mike Pulsifer, prin. — Fax 284-5951
sacoschools.org
Saco MS — 800/6-8
40 Buxton Rd 04072 — 207-282-4181
Laurie Wood, prin. — Fax 286-1807
Saco Transition Program — 50/Alt
80 Common St 04072 — 207-286-2091
Stephanie Jackson, lead tchr. — Fax 284-5951

---

Thornton Academy — 1,500/6-12
438 Main St 04072 — 207-282-3361
Rene Menard, hdmstr. — Fax 282-3508

**Saint Agatha, Aroostook**
RSU 33 / MSAD 33
Supt. — See Frenchville
Wisdom MSHS — 100/7-12
PO Box 69 04772 — 207-543-7717
Tammy LeBlanc, prin. — Fax 543-6316

**Salem, Franklin**
RSU 58 / MSAD 58
Supt. — See Phillips
Mt. Abram Regional HS — 200/9-12
1513 Salem Rd, — 207-678-2701
Marco Aliberti, prin. — Fax 678-2668

**Sanford, York, Pop. 9,565**
Sanford SD — 3,000/K-12
917 Main St Ste 200 04073 — 207-324-2810
David Theoharides, supt. — Fax 324-5742
www.sanford.org
Sanford HS — 1,100/9-12
52 Sanford High Blvd 04073 — 207-324-4050
Marianne Sylvain, prin. — Fax 324-3022
Sanford JHS — 500/6-8
708 Main St 04073 — 207-324-3114
Pam Lydon, prin. — Fax 490-5139
Sanford Regional Technical Center — Vo/Tech
52 Sanford High Blvd 04073 — 207-324-2942
Kathy Sargent, dir. — Fax 324-2957

**Scarborough, Cumberland, Pop. 4,340**
Scarborough SD — 3,300/K-12
PO Box 370 04070 — 207-730-4100
Dr. George Entwistle, supt. — Fax 730-4104
www.scarboroughschools.org
Scarborough HS — 1,100/9-12
11 Municipal Dr 04074 — 207-730-5000
David Creech, prin. — Fax 730-5007
Scarborough MS — 800/6-8
21 Quentin Dr 04074 — 207-730-4800
Barbara Hathorn, prin. — Fax 730-4804

**Searsport, Waldo, Pop. 985**
RSU 20 — 2,300/PK-12
6 Mortland Rd 04974 — 207-548-6643
Brian Carpenter, supt. — Fax 548-2310
www.rsu20.org/
Searsport District HS — 200/9-12
24 Mortland Rd 04974 — 207-548-2313
Kent Hoffman, prin. — Fax 548-2354
Searsport District MS — 200/6-8
26 Mortland Rd 04974 — 207-548-2313
Kent Hoffman, prin. — Fax 548-2354
Other Schools – See Belfast

**Skowhegan, Somerset, Pop. 6,196**
RSU 54 / MSAD 54 — 2,600/PK-12
196 W Front St 04976 — 207-474-9508
Brent Colbry, supt. — Fax 474-7422
www.msad54.org/
Skowhegan Area HS — 800/9-12
61 Academy Cir 04976 — 207-474-5511
Monique Poulin, prin. — Fax 474-0111
Skowhegan Area MS — 400/6-8
155 Academy Cir 04976 — 207-474-3339
Zachary Longyear, prin. — Fax 474-9588
Somerset Career & Technical Center — Vo/Tech
61 Academy Cir 04976 — 207-474-2151
David Dorr, prin. — Fax 858-4879

**South Berwick, York**
RSU 35 / MSAD 35
Supt. — See Eliot
Marshwood HS — 700/9-12
260 Dow Hwy 03908 — 207-384-4500
Paul Mehlhorn, prin. — Fax 384-4508

---

Berwick Academy — 600/PK-12
31 Academy St 03908 — 207-384-2164
Gregory Schneider, head sch — Fax 384-3332
Seacoast Christian S — 200/PK-12
224 Main St 03908 — 207-384-5759
Joseph Davis, admin. — Fax 384-2303

**South China, Kennebec**
RSU 18
Supt. — See Oakland
China MS — 200/5-8
773 Lakeview Dr 04358 — 207-445-1500
Lois Bowden, prin. — Fax 445-3278

---

Erskine Academy — 600/9-12
309 Windsor Rd 04358 — 207-445-2962

**South Paris, Oxford, Pop. 2,214**
RSU 17 / MSAD 17 — 3,400/PK-12
232 Main St # 2 04281 — 207-743-8972
Rick Colpitts, supt. — Fax 743-2878
www.sad17.k12.me.us/
Oxford Hills Comprehensive HS — 1,100/9-12
256 Main St 04281 — 207-743-8914
Theodore Moccia, prin. — Fax 743-5326
Oxford Hills MS — 500/7-8
100 Pine St 04281 — 207-743-5946
Troy Eastman, prin. — Fax 743-8048

**South Portland, Cumberland, Pop. 24,549**
South Portland SD — 3,100/PK-12
130 Wescott Rd 04106 — 207-871-0555
Ken Kunin, supt. — Fax 871-0559
www.spsd.org
Mahoney MS — 300/6-8
240 Ocean St 04106 — 207-799-7386
Carrie Stilphen, prin. — Fax 767-7731
Memorial MS — 400/6-8
120 Wescott Rd 04106 — 207-773-5629
Megan Welter, prin. — Fax 772-4597
South Portland HS — 900/9-12
637 Highland Ave 04106 — 207-767-3266
Ryan Caron, prin. — Fax 767-7713

---

Greater Portland Christian S — 100/PK-12
1338 Broadway 04106 — 207-767-5123
Fax 767-5124
Kaplan University — Post-Sec.
265 Western Ave 04106 — 207-774-6126
Maine Medical Center — Post-Sec.
SMTC Fort Rd 04106 — 207-767-9589
New England Bible College — Post-Sec.
879 Sawyer St 04106 — 207-799-5979
Southern Maine Community College — Post-Sec.
2 Fort Rd 04106 — 207-741-5500

**Stacyville, Penobscot**
RSU 50
Supt. — See Dyer Brook
Katahdin MSHS — 200/7-12
PO Box 50, — 207-365-4218
Jon Porter, prin. — Fax 365-6011

**Standish, Cumberland, Pop. 464**
RSU 6 / MSAD 6
Supt. — See Buxton
Bonny Eagle HS — 1,200/9-12
700 Saco Rd 04084 — 207-929-3840
Paul Penna, prin. — Fax 929-9147

---

St. Joseph's College of Maine — Post-Sec.
278 Whites Bridge Rd 04084 — 207-892-6766

**Sullivan, Hancock**
RSU 24 — 2,600/PK-12
2165 US Hwy 1 04664 — 207-667-8136
Michael Eastman, supt. — Fax 667-6493
www.rsu24.org
Sumner Memorial HS — 200/9-12
2456 US Hwy 1 04664 — 207-422-3510
Marianne Deraps, prin. — Fax 422-6463

**Thomaston, Knox, Pop. 1,856**
RSU 13
Supt. — See Rockland
Oceanside HS West — 100/8-9
47 Valley St 04861 — 207-354-2502
William Gifford, prin. — Fax 354-2369

**Thorndike, Waldo**
RSU 3 / MSAD 3
Supt. — See Unity
Mt. View HS — 400/9-12
577 Mount View Rd 04986 — 207-568-3255
Bill Tracy, prin. — Fax 568-4315
Mt. View MS — 400/6-8
575 Mount View Rd 04986 — 207-568-7561
Quinton Donahue, prin. — Fax 568-7590

**Topsham, Sagadahoc, Pop. 5,854**
RSU 75 / MSAD 75 — 2,600/K-12
50 Republic Ave 04086 — 207-729-9961
Bradley Smith, supt. — Fax 725-9354
www.link75.org/
Mt. Ararat HS — 900/9-12
73 Eagles Way 04086 — 207-729-2951
Donna Brunette Ph.D., prin. — Fax 729-2953
Mt. Ararat MS — 600/6-8
66 Republic Ave 04086 — 207-729-2950
Bill Zima, prin. — Fax 729-2964

**Turner, Androscoggin**
RSU 52 / MSAD 52 — 2,000/PK-12
486 Turner Ctr Rd 04282 — 207-225-1000
Dr. Henry Aliberti, supt. — Fax 225-5608
www.msad52.org
Leavitt Area HS — 600/9-12
21 Matthews Way 04282 — 207-225-1100
Eben Shaw, prin. — Fax 225-3978
Tripp MS — 300/7-8
65 Matthews Way 04282 — 207-225-1070
Gail Marine, prin. — Fax 225-2102

**Union, Knox**
RSU 40 / MSAD 40 — 1,900/PK-12
PO Box 701 04862 — 207-785-2277
Steve Nolan, supt. — Fax 785-3119
www.msad40.org
Other Schools – See Waldoboro

**Unity, Waldo, Pop. 459**
RSU 3 / MSAD 3 — 1,400/PK-12
84 School St 04988 — 207-948-6136
Heather Perry, supt. — Fax 948-6173
www.rsu3.org/
Other Schools – See Thorndike

---

Unity College — Post-Sec.
90 Quaker Hill Rd 04988 — 207-948-9100

**Van Buren, Aroostook, Pop. 1,897**
RSU 88 / MSAD 24 — 300/PK-12
169 Main St Ste 101 04785 — 207-868-2746
Lawrence Worcester, supt. — Fax 868-5420
www.msad24.org/
Van Buren District HS — 100/9-12
169 Main St Ste 102 04785 — 207-868-5274
Ben Lothrop, prin. — Fax 868-3537
Van Buren Regional Technology Center — Vo/Tech
169 Main St Ste 102 04785 — 207-868-2746
Ben Lothrop, dir. — Fax 868-5420

**Vinalhaven, Knox**
RSU 8 / MSAD 8 — 200/PK-12
22 Arcola Ln 04863 — 207-863-4800
Bruce Mailloux, supt. — Fax 863-4572
www.vinalhavenschool.org/
Vinalhaven S — 200/PK-12
22 Arcola Ln 04863 — 207-863-4800
Timothy Kane, prin. — Fax 863-4572

**Waldo, See Belfast**
Career Technical Education
Supt. — None
Waldo County Tech Center — Vo/Tech
1022 Waterville Rd 04915 — 207-342-5231
Chris Downing, dir. — Fax 342-4070

**Waldoboro, Lincoln, Pop. 1,207**
RSU 40 / MSAD 40
Supt. — See Union
Medomak MS — 300/7-8
318 Manktown Rd 04572 — 207-832-5028
Kate Race, prin. — Fax 832-5710
Medomak Valley HS — 600/9-12
320 Manktown Rd 04572 — 207-832-5389
Andrew Cavanaugh, prin. — Fax 832-2280

**Wales, Androscoggin**
RSU 4 — 1,300/PK-12
971 Gardiner Rd 04280 — 207-375-4273
James Hodgkin, supt. — Fax 375-2522
www.rsu4.org
Oak Hill HS — 500/9-12
PO Box 400 04280 — 207-375-4950
Patricia Doyle, prin. — Fax 375-4048
Other Schools – See Sabattus

**Washburn, Aroostook, Pop. 987**
RSU 45 / MSAD 45 — 400/PK-12
33 School St 04786 — 207-455-8301
Ed Buckley, supt. — Fax 455-8217
www.msad45.net/
Washburn District HS — 100/9-12
1359 Main St 04786 — 207-455-4501
Ron Erickson, prin. — Fax 455-4509

**Waterboro, York**
RSU 57 / MSAD 57 — 3,300/K-12
86 West Rd 04087 — 207-247-3221
Dr. John Davis, supt. — Fax 247-3477
www.rsu57.org
Massabesic HS — 1,000/9-12
88 West Rd 04087 — 207-247-3141
Christian Elkington, prin. — Fax 247-3146
Other Schools – See East Waterboro

**Waterville, Kennebec, Pop. 15,358**
AOS 92 - KVCS — 6,500/PK-12
25 Messalonskee Ave 04901 — 207-873-4281
Eric Haley, supt. — Fax 872-5531
www.aos92.org/
Mid Maine Technical Center — Vo/Tech
3 Brooklyn Ave 04901 — 207-873-0102
Peter Hallen, dir. — Fax 873-7057
Waterville HS — 1,200/9-12
1 Brooklyn Ave 04901 — 207-873-2751
Don Reiter, prin. — Fax 873-7058

Waterville JHS 800/6-8
100 W River Rd 04901 207-873-2144
Carol Gilley, prin. Fax 873-5752
Other Schools – See Winslow

---

Colby College Post-Sec.
4000 Mayflower Hill Dr 04901 207-859-4000
Empire Beauty School Post-Sec.
251 Kennedy Memorial Dr 04901 207-873-0682
Temple Academy 200/PK-12
60 W River Rd 04901 207-873-5325
Thomas College Post-Sec.
180 W River Rd 04901 207-859-1111

**Wells, York**
Wells-Ogunquit Community SD 1,400/K-12
1460 Post Rd 04090 207-646-8331
Ellen Schneider, supt. Fax 646-0314
www.k12wocsd.net/
Wells HS 400/9-12
200 Sanford Rd 04090 207-646-7011
James Daly, prin. Fax 646-4842
Wells JHS 400/5-8
1470 Post Rd 04090 207-646-5142
Christopher Chessie, prin. Fax 646-2899

---

York County Community College Post-Sec.
112 College Dr 04090 207-646-9282

**Westbrook, Cumberland, Pop. 17,059**
Westbrook SD 1,900/PK-12
117 Stroudwater St 04092 207-854-0800
Dr. Marc Gousse, supt. Fax 854-0809
www.westbrookschools.org
Westbrook HS 700/9-12
125 Stroudwater St 04092 207-854-0810
Jonathan Ross, prin. Fax 854-0812
Westbrook MS 600/5-8
471 Stroudwater St 04092 207-854-0830
Matthew Nelson, dean Fax 854-0858
Westbrook Regional Technology Center Vo/Tech
125 Stroudwater St 04092 207-854-0820
Todd Fields, dir. Fax 854-0822

**Windham, Cumberland, Pop. 13,020**
RSU 14 - Windham Raymond 3,300/K-12
228 Windham Center Rd 04062 207-892-1800
Sanford Prince, supt. Fax 892-1805
www.windham.k12.me.us
Windham HS 1,100/9-12
406 Gray Rd 04062 207-892-1810
Chris Howell, prin. Fax 892-1813
Windham MS 700/6-8
408 Gray Rd 04062 207-892-1820
Charles Haddock, prin. Fax 892-1826
Other Schools – See Falmouth, Raymond

---

Windham Christian Academy 100/PK-12
1051 Roosevelt Trl 04062 207-892-2244
Roy Mickelson, prin. Fax 893-1289

**Winslow, Kennebec, Pop. 7,626**
AOS 92 - KVCS
Supt. — See Waterville
Winslow HS 1,000/9-12
20 Danielson St 04901 207-872-1990
Chad Bell, prin. Fax 872-1993
Winslow JHS 600/6-8
6 Danielson St 04901 207-872-1973
Kevin Michaud, prin. Fax 872-1977

**Winterport, Waldo, Pop. 1,327**
RSU 22 / MSAD 22
Supt. — See Hampden
Wagner MS 100/5-8
19 Williams Way 04496 207-223-4309
Richard Glencross, prin. Fax 223-4325

**Winthrop, Kennebec, Pop. 2,622**
Winthrop SD 900/PK-12
17A Highland Ave 04364 207-377-2296
Gary Rosenthal, supt. Fax 377-2708
www.winthropschools.org
Winthrop HS 200/9-12
211 Rambler Rd 04364 207-377-2228
Keith Morin, prin. Fax 377-7486
Winthrop MS 200/6-8
400 Rambler Rd 04364 207-377-2249
Karen Criss, prin. Fax 377-3667

**Wiscasset, Lincoln, Pop. 1,086**
Wiscasset SD K-12
83 Federal St 04578 207-882-4104
Lyford Beverage, prin. Fax 882-4123
www.wiscassetschools.org
Wiscasset MSHS 200/7-12
272 Gardiner Rd 04578 207-882-7722
Cheri Towle, prin. Fax 882-8251

**Yarmouth, Cumberland, Pop. 5,801**
Yarmouth SD 1,400/K-12
101 McCartney St 04096 207-846-5586
Andrew Dolloff, supt. Fax 846-2339
www.yarmouthschools.org
Harrison MS 500/5-8
220 McCartney St 04096 207-846-2499
Bruce Brann, prin. Fax 846-2489
Yarmouth HS 500/9-12
286 W Elm St 04096 207-846-5535
Ted Hall, prin. Fax 846-2326

---

North Yarmouth Academy 300/PK-12
148 Main St 04096 207-846-9051
Ben Jackson, head sch Fax 846-8829

**York, York, Pop. 9,818**
York SD 1,900/K-12
469 US Route 1 03909 207-363-3403
Debra Dunn, supt. Fax 363-5602
www.yorkschools.org/
York HS 600/9-12
1 Robert Stevens Dr 03909 207-363-3621
Robert Stevens, prin. Fax 363-1809
York MS 600/5-8
30 Organug Rd 03909 207-363-4214
David Williams, prin. Fax 363-1815

# MARYLAND

## MARYLAND DEPARTMENT OF EDUCATION
**200 W Baltimore St, Baltimore 21201-2549**
**Telephone 410-767-0600**
**Fax 410-333-6033**
**Website http://www.marylandpublicschools.org**

Superintendent of Schools Lillian Lowery Ed.D

## MARYLAND BOARD OF EDUCATION
**200 W Baltimore St, Baltimore 21201-2549**

President Dr. Charlene Dukes

## PUBLIC, PRIVATE AND CATHOLIC SECONDARY SCHOOLS

**Aberdeen, Harford, Pop. 14,190**
Harford County SD
Supt. — See Bel Air
Aberdeen HS 1,400/9-12
251 Paradise Rd 21001 410-273-5500
Michael O'Brien, prin. Fax 273-5587
Aberdeen MS 1,000/6-8
111 Mount Royal Ave 21001 410-273-5510
Dr. Anthony Bess, prin. Fax 273-5542
Alternative Education Program 100/Alt
253 Paradise Rd 21001 410-273-5594
Kilo Mack, prin. Fax 273-5592

**Abingdon, Harford**

New Covenant Christian S 200/PK-12
128 Saint Marys Church Rd 21009 443-512-0771
Jean Armstrong, prin. Fax 569-3846

**Accident, Garrett, Pop. 323**
Garrett County SD
Supt. — See Oakland
Northern Garrett HS 500/9-12
86 Pride Pkwy 21520 301-746-8668
Gary Reichenbecher, prin. Fax 746-8942
Northern MS 400/6-8
371 Pride Pkwy 21520 301-746-8165
Karen DeVore, prin. Fax 746-8865

**Accokeek, Prince George's, Pop. 10,314**
Prince George's County SD
Supt. — See Upper Marlboro
Accokeek Academy 800/5-8
14500 Berry Rd 20607 301-203-3200
Judy Adams, prin. Fax 203-3207

**Adelphi, Prince George's, Pop. 14,821**
Prince George's County SD
Supt. — See Upper Marlboro
Buck Lodge MS 800/7-8
2611 Buck Lodge Rd 20783 301-431-6290
Kenneth Nance, prin. Fax 431-6294

University of Maryland University Coll Post-Sec.
3501 University Blvd E 20783 301-985-7000

**Annapolis, Anne Arundel, Pop. 37,674**
Anne Arundel County SD 76,500/PK-12
2644 Riva Rd 21401 410-222-5000
Dr. George Arlotto, supt. Fax 222-5602
www.aacps.org
Annapolis HS 1,500/9-12
2700 Riva Rd 21401 410-266-5240
Susan Chittim, prin. Fax 266-0687
Annapolis MS 600/6-8
1399 Forest Dr 21403 410-267-8658
Dennis Kelly, prin. Fax 267-8924
Bates MS 700/6-8
701 Chase St 21401 410-263-0270
Paul DeRoo, prin. Fax 263-0295
Broadneck HS 2,200/9-12
1265 Green Holly Dr, 410-757-1300
David Smith, prin. Fax 757-5621
Moss at Adams Academy 50/Alt
245 Clay St 21401 410-222-1639
Wendy Slaughter, prin.
Annapolis Evening HS Adult
2700 Riva Rd 21401 410-224-2924
Patricia Suriano, admin.
Other Schools – See Arnold, Baltimore, Edgewater, Fort Meade, Gambrills, Glen Burnie, Harwood, Linthicum Heights, Lothian, Millersville, Odenton, Pasadena, Severn, Severna Park

Key S 700/PK-12
534 Hillsmere Dr 21403 410-263-9231
Matthew Nespole, hdmstr. Fax 280-5516
St. John's College Post-Sec.
PO Box 2800 21404 410-263-2371
St. Mary's HS 500/9-12
113 Duke of Gloucester St 21401 410-263-3294
Mindi Imes, prin. Fax 269-7843
United States Naval Academy Post-Sec.
121 Blake Rd 21402 410-293-4361

**Arnold, Anne Arundel, Pop. 22,629**
Anne Arundel County SD
Supt. — See Annapolis
Magothy River MS 800/6-8
241 Peninsula Farm Rd 21012 410-544-0926
Christopher Mirenzi, prin. Fax 544-1867
Severn River MS 800/6-8
241 Peninsula Farm Rd 21012 410-544-0922
Richard Tubman, prin. Fax 315-8006

Anne Arundel Community College Post-Sec.
101 College Pkwy 21012 410-777-2222

**Baltimore, Baltimore, Pop. 609,299**
Anne Arundel County SD
Supt. — See Annapolis
Brooklyn Park MS 500/6-8
200 Hammonds Ln 21225 410-636-2967
Beth Shakan, prin. Fax 636-1774

Baltimore CSD 79,600/PK-12
200 E North Ave 21202 443-984-2000
Dr. Gregory Thornton, admin. Fax 396-8898
www.bcps.k12.md.us
Achievement Academy at Harbor City 400/9-12
2201 Pinewood Ave 21214 410-396-6241
Tajah Gross, prin.
Baltimore City College HS 1,300/9-12
3220 The Alameda 21218 410-396-6557
Cindy Harcum, prin. Fax 243-0669
Baltimore Community HS 300/Alt
6820 Fait Ave 21224 443-642-2035
Leslie Lewis, prin.
Baltimore Design S 6-12
1500 Barclay St 21202 443-642-2311
Melissa Patrylo, prin.
Baltimore Polytechnic Institute Vo/Tech
1400 W Cold Spring Ln 21209 410-396-7026
Jacqueline Williams, prin. Fax 235-5027
Baltimore S for the Arts 400/9-12
712 Cathedral St 21201 443-642-5165
Christopher Ford, prin.
Bard HS Early College 9-12
1101 N Wolfe St 21213 443-642-2062
Roscoe Bickford, prin.
Career Academy Vo/Tech
101 W 24th St 21218 410-396-7454
Gus Herrington, prin.
Carver Voc-Tech HS Vo/Tech
2201 Presstman St 21216 410-396-0553
Shionta Somerville, prin. Fax 396-0059
Digital Harbor HS 1,200/9-12
1100 Covington St 21230 443-984-1256
Shannon Mobley, prin. Fax 539-7270
Douglass HS 800/9-12
2301 Gwynns Falls Pkwy 21217 410-396-7821
Kelvin Bridgers, prin. Fax 523-7557
Dunbar HS 800/9-12
1400 Orleans St 21231 443-642-4478
Tammy Mays, prin. Fax 545-7526
Eager Street Academy 100/Alt
401 E Eager St 21202 410-209-4091
Laura D'Anna, prin. Fax 209-4268
Edmondson-Westside HS 1,000/9-12
501 N Athol Ave 21229 410-396-0685
Muriel Cole-Webber, prin. Fax 545-7715
Excel Academy 300/6-12
1001 W Saratoga St 21223 410-396-1290
Tammatha Woodhouse, prin. Fax 947-7941
Forest Park HS 600/9-12
3701 Eldorado Ave 21207 410-396-0753
Monica Dailey, prin. Fax 396-0143
Franklin HS, 1201 Cambria St 21225 300/9-12
Christopher Battaglia, prin. 410-396-1373
Friendship Academy of Engring & Tech 700/6-12
2500 E Northern Pkwy 21214 443-642-5616
Katrice Wiley, prin.
Green Street Academy 300/6-11
125 N Hilton St 21229 443-642-2068
Crystal Harden-Lindsey, prin.
Knowledge and Success Academy 400/6-12
2000 Edgewood St 21216 443-642-2670
Tony Edwards, prin.

Lewis HS, 6401 Pioneer Dr 21214 400/9-12
Janine Patterson, prin. 410-545-1746
Maritime Industries Academy HS 400/9-12
2700 Seamon Ave 21225 410-396-0242
Tawney Manning, prin.
Mergenthaler Vo-Tech HS Vo/Tech
3500 Hillen Rd 21218 410-396-6496
Craig Rivers, prin. Fax 243-5354
NACA Freedom and Democracy II 200/6-12
2500 E Northern Pkwy 21214 443-642-2031
Linda Johnson-Brown, prin.
Northwestern HS 700/9-12
6900 Park Heights Ave 21215 410-396-0646
Saeed Hill, prin. Fax 396-0866
Patterson HS 1,100/9-12
100 Kane St 21224 410-396-9276
Vance Benton, prin. Fax 633-0179
Savage Institute of Visual Arts 500/9-12
1500 Harlem Ave 21217 443-396-7701
Tracey Hicks, prin.
Stadium S, 1300 Gorsuch Ave 21218 300/6-8
Shana Hall, dir. 443-984-2682
Success Academy Alt
2201 Pinewood Ave 21214 443-642-2101
Rhonda Tapper, prin.
Thomas Medical Arts Academy 500/9-12
100 N Calhoun St 21223 410-984-2831
Stephanie Farmer, prin.
Vanguard Collegiate MS 200/6-8
5000 Truesdale Rd 21206 443-642-2069
Esther Wallace, prin.
Washington MS 300/6-8
1301 McCulloh St 21217 410-396-7734
Jessica Blackmon-Stewart, prin. Fax 396-0552
Western HS 1,000/9-12
4600 Falls Rd 21209 410-396-7040
Michelle White, prin. Fax 396-7492
Youth Opportunity S Alt
1510 W Lafayette Ave 21217 410-962-1905
Sandy Mason, prin.

Baltimore County SD
Supt. — See Towson
Arbutus MS 700/6-8
5525 Shelbourne Rd 21227 410-887-1402
Michelle Feeney, prin. Fax 536-1164
Carver Center for Arts & Technology 800/9-12
938 York Rd 21204 410-887-2775
Karen Steele, prin. Fax 769-9114
Catonsville Center/Alternative Studies 100/Alt
901 S Rolling Rd 21228 410-887-0934
David Lloyd, prin. Fax 747-1789
Catonsville HS 1,800/9-12
421 Bloomsbury Ave 21228 410-887-0808
Matthew Ames, prin. Fax 747-9473
Chesapeake HS 1,100/9-12
1801 Turkey Point Rd 21221 410-887-0100
Jess Grim, prin. Fax 682-3426
Crossroads Center 200/Alt
11640 Crossroads Cir 21220 410-887-2275
John Ward, prin. Fax 887-2449
Deep Creek MS 800/6-8
1000 S Marlyn Ave 21221 410-887-0112
Dwan Pinamonti, prin. Fax 391-6534
Dumbarton MS 900/6-8
300 Dumbarton Rd Ste 1 21212 410-887-3176
Susan Harris, prin. Fax 583-7020
Dundalk HS 1,200/9-12
1901 Delvale Ave 21222 410-887-7023
Kristin Anelli, prin. Fax 887-7025
Dundalk MS 500/6-8
7400 Dunmanway 21222 410-887-7018
Seth Barish, prin. Fax 887-7284
Eastern Technical HS 1,300/9-12
1100 Mace Ave 21221 410-887-0190
Christene Anderson, prin. Fax 887-0424
Golden Ring MS 600/6-8
6700 Kenwood Ave 21237 410-887-0130
Lawrence Rudolph, prin. Fax 682-6750
Holabird MS 700/6-8
1701 Delvale Ave 21222 410-887-7049
Julie Dellone, prin. Fax 887-7275

Kenwood HS 1,700/9-12
501 Stemmers Run Rd 21221 410-887-0153
Kandice Taylor, prin. Fax 887-6382
Lansdowne HS 1,200/9-12
3800 Hollins Ferry Rd 21227 410-887-1415
Kenneth Miller, prin. Fax 887-1461
Lansdowne MS 600/6-8
2400 Lansdowne Rd 21227 410-887-1411
Susan Evans, prin. Fax 887-1412
Loch Raven HS 900/9-12
1212 Cowpens Ave 21286 410-887-3525
Bonnie Lambert, prin. Fax 887-5898
Loch Raven Technical Academy 700/6-8
8101 La Salle Rd 21286 410-887-3518
Stacey Johnson, prin. Fax 821-6398
Meadowood Education Center 50/Alt
1849 Gwynn Oak Ave 21207 410-887-6888
Damien Ingram, prin. Fax 887-6889
Middle River MS 900/6-8
800 Middle River Rd 21220 410-887-0165
Shannon Parker, prin. Fax 887-0167
Milford Mill Academy 1,400/9-12
3800 Washington Ave 21244 410-887-0660
Roderick Harden, prin. Fax 887-0681
Old Court MS 600/6-8
4627 Old Court Rd 21208 410-887-0742
Kyria Joseph, prin. Fax 887-0670
Overlea HS 900/9-12
5401 Kenwood Ave 21206 410-887-5241
Marquis Dwarte, prin. Fax 661-0174
Parkville MS 1,100/6-8
8711 Avondale Rd 21234 410-887-5250
Erin O'Toole-Trivas, prin. Fax 887-5315
Patapsco HS & Center for the Arts 1,400/9-12
8100 Wise Ave 21222 410-887-7060
Craig Reed, prin. Fax 887-7062
Perry Hall HS 2,200/9-12
4601 Ebenezer Rd 21236 410-887-5108
Andrew Last, prin. Fax 887-5116
Perry Hall MS 1,600/6-8
4300 Ebenezer Rd 21236 410-887-5100
Allen Zink, prin. Fax 887-5152
Pikesville HS 900/9-12
7621 Labyrinth Rd 21208 410-887-1217
Sandra Reid, prin. Fax 486-8436
Pikesville MS 1,000/6-8
7701 7 Mile Ln 21208 410-887-1207
Diane Richmond, prin. Fax 887-1259
Pine Grove MS 900/6-8
9200 Old Harford Rd 21234 410-887-5270
Tina Nelson, prin. Fax 668-5237
Rosedale Center 100/Alt
8200 Old Philadelphia Rd 21237 410-887-0133
Paul Martin, prin. Fax 887-0473
Southwest Academy 700/6-8
6200 Johnnycake Rd 21207 410-887-0825
Karen Barnes, prin. Fax 887-0829
Sparrows Point HS 800/9-12
7400 N Point Rd 21219 410-887-7517
Emily Caster, prin. Fax 477-4311
Sparrows Point MS 500/6-8
7400 N Point Rd 21219 410-887-7524
Lisa Perry, prin. Fax 477-6953
Stemmers Run MS 700/6-8
201 Stemmers Run Rd 21221 410-887-0177
Bryan Thanner, prin. Fax 918-1787
Stricker MS 800/6-8
7855 Trappe Rd 21222 410-887-7038
Brian Wagner, prin. Fax 285-1864
Sudbrook Magnet MS 1,000/6-8
4300 Bedford Rd 21208 410-887-6720
Gordon Webb, prin. Fax 887-6737
Towson HS 1,400/9-12
69 Cedar Ave 21286 410-887-3608
Charlene Dimino, prin. Fax 583-1375
Western S of Technology 900/9-12
100 Kenwood Ave 21228 410-887-0840
Murray Parker, prin. Fax 887-1024
Windsor Mill MS 500/6-8
8300 Windsor Mill Rd 21244 410-887-0618
Harvey Chambers, prin. Fax 496-1308
Woodlawn HS 1,500/9-12
1801 Woodlawn Dr 21207 410-887-1309
Kirk Sykes, prin. Fax 887-1324
Woodlawn MS 600/6-8
3033 Saint Lukes Ln 21207 410-887-1304
Rochelle Archelus, prin. Fax 298-4352

---

All-State Career School Post-Sec.
2200 Broening Hwy Ste 160 21224 410-631-1818
Archbishop Curley HS 600/9-12
3701 Sinclair Ln 21213 410-485-5000
Brian Kohler, prin. Fax 483-2545
Arlington Baptist S 200/PK-12
3030 N Rolling Rd 21244 410-655-9300
Aimee Stiles, admin. Fax 496-3901
Bais HaMedrash & Mesivta of Baltimore Post-Sec.
6823 Old Pimlico Rd 21209 410-486-0006
Bais Hamedrash & Mesivta S of Baltimore 100/9-12
6823 Old Pimlico Rd 21209 410-486-0006
Yaakov Grossman, prin. Fax 602-9738
Bais Yaakov Eva Winer HS 400/9-12
6302 Smith Ave 21209 443-548-7700
Baltimore Actors Theatre Conservatory 50/K-12
300 Dumbarton Rd Ste 2 21212 410-337-8519
Dr. Walter Anderson, hdmstr. Fax 337-8582
Baltimore City Community College Post-Sec.
2901 Liberty Heights Ave 21215 410-462-8300
Baltimore Lab S 100/1-12
2220 Saint Paul St 21218 410-261-5500
Steve Buettner, head sch Fax 366-7680
Baltimore School of Massage Post-Sec.
517 Progress Dr Ste A-L 21207 410-944-8855
Baltimore Studio of Hair Design Post-Sec.
318 N Howard St 21201 410-539-1935
Baltimore-White Marsh Adventist S 50/PK-12
7427 Rossville Blvd 21237 410-663-1819
Dr. Rose Gamblin, prin. Fax 663-9009
Beren HS 200/9-12
400 Mount Wilson Ln 21208 410-484-7200
Jacob Schuchman, prin. Fax 484-3215
Beth Tfiloh Dahan Community S 900/PK-12
3300 Old Court Rd 21208 410-486-1905
Bnos Yisroel S of Baltimore 400/PK-12
6300 Park Heights Ave 21215 443-524-3200
Boys Latin S of Maryland 600/K-12
822 W Lake Ave 21210 410-377-5192
Christopher Post, hdmstr. Fax 377-4312
Broadcasting Institute of Maryland Post-Sec.
7200 Harford Rd 21234 410-254-2770
Bryn Mawr S 800/PK-12
109 W Melrose Ave 21210 410-323-8800
Maureen Walsh, hdmstr. Fax 377-8963
Calvert Hall College HS 1,200/9-12
8102 La Salle Rd 21286 410-825-4266
Charles Stembler, prin. Fax 825-6826
Catholic HS of Baltimore 300/9-12
2800 Edison Hwy 21213 410-732-6200
Marty Meyd, prin. Fax 732-7639
Coppin State University Post-Sec.
2500 W North Ave 21216 410-951-3000
Cristo Rey Jesuit HS 9-12
420 S Chester St 21231 410-727-3255
Thomas Malone, prin. Fax 573-9898
Faith Theological Seminary Post-Sec.
529 Walker Ave 21212 410-323-6211
Fortis Institute Post-Sec.
6901 Security Blvd Ste 21 21244 410-907-8110
Friends S of Baltimore 1,000/PK-12
5114 N Charles St 21210 410-649-3200
Matthew Micciche, head sch Fax 649-3213
Gilman S 1,000/K-12
5407 Roland Ave 21210 410-323-3800
Henry Smyth, hdmstr. Fax 864-2812
Goucher College Post-Sec.
1021 Dulaney Valley Rd 21204 410-337-6000
Greater Baltimore Medical Center Post-Sec.
6701 N Charles St 21204 410-828-2121
Institute of Notre Dame 300/9-12
901 N Aisquith St 21202 410-522-7800
Kathleen Casey, prin. Fax 522-7810
Johns Hopkins University Post-Sec.
3400 N Charles St 21218 410-516-8000
Loyola University Maryland Post-Sec.
4501 N Charles St 21210 800-221-9107
Maryland Beauty Academy of Essex Post-Sec.
505 Eastern Blvd 21221 410-686-4477
Maryland General Hospital Post-Sec.
827 Linden Ave 21201 410-995-8600
Maryland Institute College of Art Post-Sec.
1300 W Mount Royal Ave 21217 410-669-9200
Maryland School for the Blind Post-Sec.
3501 Taylor Ave 21236
Mercy HS 400/9-12
1300 E Northern Pkwy 21239 410-433-8880
Pegeen D'Agostino, pres. Fax 323-8816
Mercy Hospital Post-Sec.
301 Saint Paul St 21202 410-332-9202
Morgan State University Post-Sec.
1700 E Cold Spring Ln 21251 443-885-3333
Mother Seton Academy 100/6-8
2215 Greenmount Ave 21218 410-563-2833
Richard Gudel, prin. Fax 563-7354
Mt. St. Joseph HS 1,000/9-12
4403 Frederick Ave 21229 410-644-3300
David Norton, prin. Fax 646-6221
Mt. Zion Baptist Christian S 100/PK-12
2000 E Belvedere Ave 21239 410-426-2309
Ner Israel Rabbinical College Post-Sec.
400 Mount Wilson Ln 21208 410-484-7200
North American Trade Schools Post-Sec.
6901 Security Blvd Ste 16 21244 410-298-4844
Notre Dame of Maryland University Post-Sec.
4701 N Charles St 21210 410-435-0100
Our Lady of Mt. Carmel HS 200/9-12
1706 Old Eastern Ave 21221 410-686-1023
Kathleen Sipes, pres. Fax 686-2361
Park S of Baltimore 900/PK-12
2425 Old Court Rd 21208 410-339-7070
Daniel Paradis, hdmstr. Fax 339-4125
Peabody Institute Johns Hopkins Univ. Post-Sec.
1 E Mount Vernon Pl 21202 410-234-4500
Rabbi Benjamin Steinberg MS 300/6-8
6300 Smith Ave 21209 443-548-7700
Rabbi Naftoli Hexter, prin. Fax 548-0347
Roland Park Country S 700/PK-12
5204 Roland Ave 21210 410-323-5500
Jean Waller Brune, head sch Fax 323-2164
St. Frances Academy 200/9-12
501 E Chase St 21202 410-539-5794
Dr. Curtis Turner, prin. Fax 685-2650
St. Ignatius Loyola Academy 100/6-8
300 E Gittings St 21230 410-539-8268
Teresa Scott, prin. Fax 539-4821
St. Mary's Seminary & University Post-Sec.
5400 Roland Ave 21210 410-864-4000
Seton Keough HS 400/9-12
1201 S Caton Ave 21227 410-646-4444
Angela Calamari, prin. Fax 368-1591
Sisters Academy of Baltimore 100/5-8
139 1st Ave 21227 410-242-1212
Sr. Debra Liesen, prin. Fax 242-5104
Sojourner-Douglass College Post-Sec.
200 N Central Ave 21202 410-276-0306
Stratford University Post-Sec.
210 S Central Ave 21202 410-752-4710
Talmudical Academy 800/K-12
4445 Old Court Rd 21208 410-484-6600
TESST College of Technology Post-Sec.
1520 S Caton Ave 21227 410-644-6400
Union Memorial Hospital Post-Sec.
201 E University Pkwy 21218 410-554-2739
University of Baltimore Post-Sec.
1420 N Charles St 21201 410-837-4200
University of Maryland Baltimore Post-Sec.
620 W Lexington St 21201 410-706-3100
University of Maryland Baltimore County Post-Sec.
1000 Hilltop Cir 21250 410-455-1000

**Bel Air, Harford, Pop. 9,934**

Harford County SD 37,500/PK-12
102 S Hickory Ave 21014 410-838-7300
Barbara Canavan, supt. Fax 893-2478
www.hcps.org
Bel Air HS 1,600/9-12
100 Heighe St 21014 410-638-4600
Gregory Komondor, prin. Fax 638-4604
Bel Air MS 1,300/6-8
99 Idlewild St 21014 410-638-4140
Natalie Holloway, prin. Fax 638-4144
Harford Technical HS Vo/Tech
200 Thomas Run Rd 21015 410-638-3804
Charles Hagan, prin. Fax 638-3820
Patterson Mill HS 1,000/9-12
85 Patterson Mill Rd 21015 410-638-4640
Sean Abel, prin. Fax 638-4646
Patterson Mill MS 700/6-8
85 Patterson Mill Rd 21015 410-638-4640
Sean Abel, prin. Fax 638-4646
Southampton MS 1,300/6-8
1200 Moores Mill Rd 21014 410-638-4150
Glenn Jensen, prin. Fax 638-4305
Wright HS 1,500/9-12
1301 N Fountain Green Rd 21015 410-638-4110
Michael Thatcher, prin. Fax 638-4114
Other Schools – See Aberdeen, Edgewood, Fallston, Havre de Grace, Joppa, Pylesville

---

Harford Community College Post-Sec.
401 Thomas Run Rd 21015 443-412-2000
International Beauty School Post-Sec.
227 Archer St 21014 410-838-0845
John Carroll HS 700/9-12
703 E Churchville Rd 21014 410-879-2480
Richard O'Hara, pres. Fax 836-8514
St. Margaret MS 300/6-8
1716 E Churchville Rd Ste A 21015 410-877-9660
Madeleine Hobik, prin. Fax 420-9322

**Beltsville, Prince George's, Pop. 16,294**

Prince George's County SD
Supt. — See Upper Marlboro
High Point HS 2,200/9-12
3601 Powder Mill Rd 20705 301-572-6400
Sandra Jimenez, prin. Fax 572-6481
King MS 600/6-8
4545 Ammendale Rd 20705 301-572-0650
Robin Wiltison, prin. Fax 572-0668

---

TESST Technology Institute Post-Sec.
4600 Powder Mill Rd Ste 500 20705 301-937-8448

**Berlin, Worcester, Pop. 4,357**

Worcester County SD
Supt. — See Newark
Decatur HS 1,400/9-12
9913 Seahawk Rd 21811 410-641-2171
Tom Zimmer, prin. Fax 641-1135
Decatur MS 600/7-8
9815 Seahawk Rd 21811 410-641-2846
Lynne Barton, prin. Fax 641-3274

---

Worcester Preparatory S 500/PK-12
PO Box 1006 21811 410-641-3575
Dr. Barry Tull, hdmstr. Fax 641-3586

**Bethesda, Montgomery, Pop. 59,121**

Montgomery County SD
Supt. — See Rockville
Bethesda-Chevy Chase HS 1,800/9-12
4301 E West Hwy 20814 240-497-6300
Dr. Donna Jones, prin. Fax 497-6306
Johnson HS 2,200/9-12
6400 Rock Spring Dr 20814 301-803-7100
Jennifer Baker, prin. Fax 571-6916
North Bethesda MS 800/6-8
8935 Bradmoor Dr 20817 301-571-3883
Alton Sumner, prin. Fax 571-3881
Pyle MS 1,300/6-8
6311 Wilson Ln 20817 301-320-6540
Christopher Nardi, prin. Fax 320-6647
Westland MS 1,200/6-8
5511 Massachusetts Ave 20816 301-320-6515
Alison Serino, prin. Fax 320-7054
Whitman HS 1,900/9-12
7100 Whittier Blvd 20817 301-320-6600
Dr. Alan Goodwin, prin. Fax 320-6594

---

DeVry University Post-Sec.
4550 Montgomery Ave Ste 100 20814 301-652-8477
Holton-Arms S 600/3-12
7303 River Rd 20817 301-365-5300
Susanna Jones, hdmstr. Fax 365-6085
Landon S 700/3-12
6101 Wilson Ln 20817 301-320-3200
Jim Neill, hdmstr. Fax 320-2787
Lycee Rochambeau 1,100/PK-12
9600 Forest Rd 20814 301-530-8260
Catherine Levy, prin. Fax 564-5779
Stone Ridge S of the Sacred Heart 700/PK-12
9101 Rockville Pike 20814 301-657-4322
Catherine Karrels, hdmstr. Fax 657-4393
The SANS Technology Institute Post-Sec.
8120 Woodmont Ave Ste 205 20814 301-654-7267
Washington Conservatory of Music Post-Sec.
1 Westmoreland Cir 20816 301-320-2770
Washington Waldorf S 200/PK-12
4800 Sangamore Rd 20816 301-229-6107

**Bladensburg, Prince George's, Pop. 9,010**
Prince George's County SD
Supt. — See Upper Marlboro
Annapolis Road Academy 100/Alt
5150 Annapolis Rd 20710 301-209-3580
Agnes Brown-Jones, prin. Fax 209-3579
Bladensburg HS 1,800/9-12
4200 57th Ave 20710 301-887-6700
BernNadette Mahoney, prin. Fax 887-6710
Community Based Classroom 100/Alt
5150 Annapolis Rd 20710 301-985-5149
Dr. Tammy Williams, prin. Fax 985-1794

---

Elizabeth Seton HS 600/9-12
5715 Emerson St 20710 301-864-4532
Sr. Ellen Hagar, pres. Fax 864-8946

**Boonsboro, Washington, Pop. 3,310**
Washington County SD
Supt. — See Hagerstown
Boonsboro HS 900/9-12
10 Campus Ave 21713 301-766-8022
Dr. Sherry Hamilton, prin. Fax 432-2269
Boonsboro MS 800/6-8
1 J H Wade Dr 21713 301-766-8038
Gary Willow, prin. Fax 432-2644

**Bowie, Prince George's, Pop. 52,916**
Prince George's County SD
Supt. — See Upper Marlboro
Bowie HS 2,800/9-12
15200 Annapolis Rd 20715 301-805-2600
Derwanna Bey, prin. Fax 805-2619
Ogle MS 900/6-8
4111 Chelmont Ln 20715 301-805-2641
Glenise Marshall, prin. Fax 805-6674
Tall Oaks HS 100/Alt
2112 Church Rd 20721 301-390-0230
Dr. Larry McCray, prin. Fax 390-0228
Tasker MS 900/6-8
4901 Collington Rd 20715 301-805-2660
Ingrid Johnson, prin. Fax 805-2663

---

Belair Baptist Christian Academy 50/PK-12
2801 Belair Dr 20715 301-262-0578
Dr. Gary Kohl, admin. Fax 262-0579
Bowie State University Post-Sec.
14000 Jericho Park Rd 20715 301-860-4000

**Brandywine, Prince George's, Pop. 6,567**
Prince George's County SD
Supt. — See Upper Marlboro
Gwynn Park HS 1,100/9-12
13800 Brandywine Rd 20613 301-372-0140
Dr. Tracie Miller, prin. Fax 372-0149
Gwynn Park MS 600/6-8
8000 Dyson Rd 20613 301-372-0120
Danielle Moore, prin. Fax 372-0119

**Brooklandville, Baltimore**

---

Maryvale Prep HS 400/6-12
11300 Falls Rd 21022 410-252-3366
Donna Bridickas, prin. Fax 561-1826
St. Paul's S 800/PK-12
PO Box 8100 21022 410-825-4400
David Faus, hdmstr. Fax 427-0390
St. Paul's S for Girls 400/5-12
PO Box 8000 21022 410-823-6323
Penny Evins, head sch Fax 828-7238

**Brunswick, Frederick, Pop. 5,703**
Frederick County SD
Supt. — See Frederick
Brunswick HS 800/9-12
101 Cummings Dr 21716 240-236-8600
Nancy Doll, prin. Fax 236-8601
Brunswick MS 500/6-8
301 Cummings Dr 21716 240-236-5400
Barbara Keiling, prin. Fax 236-5401

**Buckeystown, Frederick, Pop. 1,012**

---

St. John's Catholic Prep S 300/9-12
PO Box 909 21717 301-662-4210
Marc Minsker, prin. Fax 892-6877

**Burtonsville, Montgomery, Pop. 8,050**
Montgomery County SD
Supt. — See Rockville
Banneker MS 800/6-8
14800 Perrywood Dr 20866 301-989-5747
Dr. Otis Lee, prin. Fax 879-1032
Paint Branch HS 1,800/9-12
14121 Old Columbia Pike 20866 301-388-9900
Dr. Myriam Rogers, prin. Fax 989-5609

**California, Saint Mary's, Pop. 11,416**

---

Blades School of Hair Design Post-Sec.
PO Box 226 20619 301-862-9797

**Callaway, Saint Mary's**

---

King's Christian Academy 300/PK-12
20738 Point Lookout Rd 20620 301-994-3080
Kevin Fry, admin. Fax 994-3087

**Cambridge, Dorchester, Pop. 12,038**
Dorchester County SD 4,600/PK-12
700 Glasgow St 21613 410-228-4747
Dr. Henry Wagner, supt. Fax 228-1847
www.dcps.k12.md.us
Cambridge-South Dorchester HS 800/9-12
2475 Cambridge Beltway 21613 410-228-9224
Dave Bromwell, prin. Fax 228-0724
Dorchester Career and Technology Center Vo/Tech
2465 Cambridge Beltway 21613 410-901-6950
Kermit Hines, prin. Fax 221-8589

Maces Lane MS 500/6-8
1101 Maces Ln 21613 410-228-2111
Susie Price, prin. Fax 221-5278
Other Schools – See Hurlock

**Capitol Heights, Prince George's, Pop. 4,271**
Prince George's County SD
Supt. — See Upper Marlboro
Central HS 900/9-12
200 Cabin Branch Rd 20743 301-499-7080
Daryl Kennedy, prin. Fax 499-7087
Fairmont Heights HS 800/9-12
1401 Nye St 20743 301-925-1360
Torrie Walker, prin. Fax 925-1371
Walker Mill MS 700/6-8
800 Karen Blvd 20743 301-808-4055
Nicole Clifton, prin. Fax 808-4039

---

Maple Springs Baptist Bible Coll. & Sem. Post-Sec.
4130 Belt Rd 20743 301-736-3631

**Catonsville, Baltimore, Pop. 40,573**
Baltimore County SD
Supt. — See Towson
Catonsville MS 700/6-8
2301 Edmondson Ave 21228 410-887-0803
Michael Thorne, prin. Fax 887-1036

---

Community College of Baltimore County Post-Sec.
800 S Rolling Rd 21228 443-840-2222
Mt. de Sales Academy 500/9-12
700 Academy Rd 21228 410-744-8498
Sr. Mary Huffman, prin. Fax 747-5105

**Centreville, Queen Anne's, Pop. 4,193**
Queen Anne's County SD 7,800/PK-12
202 Chesterfield Ave 21617 410-758-2403
Dr. Carol Williamson, supt. Fax 758-8200
qacps.schoolwires.net
Centreville MS 500/6-8
231 Ruthsburg Rd 21617 410-758-0883
Amy Hudock, prin. Fax 758-4447
Queen Anne's County HS 1,200/9-12
125 Ruthsburg Rd 21617 410-758-0500
Jacquelyn Wilhelm, prin. Fax 758-4454
Other Schools – See Stevensville, Sudlersville

---

Gunston S 100/9-12
PO Box 200 21617 410-758-0620
John Lewis, hdmstr. Fax 758-0628

**Cheltenham, Prince George's**
Prince George's County SD
Supt. — See Upper Marlboro
Croom Vocational HS Vo/Tech
9400 Surratts Rd 20623 301-372-8846
William Henderson, prin. Fax 372-3422

**Chesapeake City, Cecil, Pop. 671**
Cecil County SD
Supt. — See Elkton
Bohemia Manor HS 600/9-12
2755 Augustine Herman Hwy 21915 410-885-2075
Wanita Fleury, prin. Fax 885-2485
Bohemia Manor MS 500/6-8
2757 Augustine Herman Hwy 21915 410-885-2095
Dr. Ann Little, prin. Fax 885-2485

**Chestertown, Kent, Pop. 5,140**
Kent County SD
Supt. — See Rock Hall
Kent County MS 400/6-8
402 E Campus Ave 21620 410-778-1771
Janice Steffy, prin. Fax 778-6541

---

Washington College Post-Sec.
300 Washington Ave 21620 410-778-2800

**Clarksburg, Montgomery, Pop. 13,276**
Montgomery County SD
Supt. — See Rockville
Clarksburg HS 1,900/9-12
22500 Wims Rd 20871 301-444-3000
Stephen Whiting, prin. Fax 444-3595
Rocky Hill MS 1,000/6-8
22401 Brick Haven Way 20871 301-353-8282
Dr. Cynthia Eldridge, prin. Fax 601-3197

**Clarksville, Howard**
Howard County SD
Supt. — See Ellicott City
Clarksville MS 700/6-8
6535 S Trotter Rd 21029 410-313-7057
Joelle Miller, prin. Fax 531-5105
River Hill HS 1,400/9-12
12101 Clarksville Pike 21029 410-313-7120
Kathryn McKinley, prin. Fax 313-7406

**Clear Spring, Washington, Pop. 356**
Washington County SD
Supt. — See Hagerstown
Clear Spring HS 500/9-12
12630 Broadfording Rd 21722 301-766-8082
Darrell Marriott, prin. Fax 842-0082
Clear Spring MS 400/6-8
12628 Broadfording Rd 21722 301-766-8094
Matthew Noll, prin. Fax 842-3826

**Clinton, Prince George's, Pop. 35,163**
Prince George's County SD
Supt. — See Upper Marlboro
Decatur MS 600/6-8
8200 Pinewood Dr 20735 301-449-4950
William Blake, prin. Fax 449-2105
Surrattsville HS 800/9-12
6101 Garden Dr 20735 301-599-2453
Kristi Holden, prin. Fax 599-2565

---

Grace Brethren Christian S 600/PK-12
6501 Surratts Rd 20735 301-868-1600
George Hornickel, dir. Fax 868-9475

**Cockeysville, Baltimore, Pop. 20,195**
Baltimore County SD
Supt. — See Towson
Cockeysville MS 700/6-8
10401 Greenside Dr 21030 410-887-7626
Deborah Magness, prin. Fax 887-7628

**College Park, Prince George's, Pop. 29,403**

---

University of Maryland College Park Post-Sec.
20742 301-405-1000

**Colora, Cecil**

---

West Nottingham Academy 100/9-12
1079 Firetower Rd 21917 410-658-5556
Stephen Brotschul, head sch Fax 658-6790

**Columbia, Howard, Pop. 95,623**
Howard County SD
Supt. — See Ellicott City
Atholton HS 1,500/9-12
6520 Freetown Rd 21044 410-313-7065
JoAnn Hutchens, prin. Fax 313-7078
Hammond HS 1,300/9-12
8800 Guilford Rd 21046 410-313-7615
Marcy Leonard, prin. Fax 313-7632
Harper's Choice MS 500/6-8
5450 Beaverkill Rd 21044 410-313-6929
Adam Eldridge, prin. Fax 313-5612
Lake Elkhorn MS 6-8
6680 Cradlerock Way 21045 410-313-7600
Martin Vandenberge, prin. Fax 313-7633
Long Reach HS 1,300/9-12
6101 Old Dobbin Ln 21045 410-313-7117
David Burton, prin. Fax 313-7422
Oakland Mills HS 1,100/9-12
9410 Kilimanjaro Rd 21045 410-313-6945
Karim Shortridge, prin. Fax 313-6948
Oakland Mills MS 400/6-8
9540 Kilimanjaro Rd 21045 410-313-6937
Katherine Orlando, prin. Fax 313-7447
Wilde Lake HS 1,300/9-12
5460 Trumpeter Rd 21044 410-313-6965
James LeMon, prin. Fax 313-6972
Wilde Lake MS 500/6-8
10481 Cross Fox Ln 21044 410-313-6957
Anne Swartz, prin. Fax 313-6963

---

Atholton Adventist Academy 200/PK-10
6520 Martin Rd 21044 410-740-2425
Marilynn Peeke, prin. Fax 740-2545
Howard Community College Post-Sec.
10901 Little Patuxent Pkwy 21044 443-518-1200
Lincoln College of Technology Post-Sec.
9325 Snowden River Pkwy 21046 410-290-7100

**Cresaptown, Allegany, Pop. 4,546**
Allegany County SD
Supt. — See Cumberland
Center for Career & Technical Education Vo/Tech
14211 McMullen Hwy SW 21502 301-729-6486
Candy Canan, prin. Fax 729-0661

---

Calvary Christian Academy 300/PK-12
PO Box 5154 21505 301-729-0791
Daniel Thompson, admin. Fax 729-1648

**Crisfield, Somerset, Pop. 2,671**
Somerset County SD
Supt. — See Westover
Crisfield HS & Academy 400/8-12
210 N Somerset Ave 21817 410-968-0150
James Conrow, prin. Fax 968-1178

**Crownsville, Anne Arundel, Pop. 1,733**

---

Indian Creek S 200/9-12
1130 Anne Chambers Way 21032 410-849-5151
Richard Branson Ed.D., head sch Fax 841-2623

**Cumberland, Allegany, Pop. 20,280**
Allegany County SD 8,100/PK-12
PO Box 1724 21501 301-759-2000
Dr. David Cox Ed.D., supt. Fax 759-2029
www.acpsmd.org
Allegany HS 700/9-12
616 Sedgwick St 21502 301-777-8110
Michael Calhoun, prin. Fax 759-2534
Braddock MS 600/6-8
909 Holland St 21502 301-777-7990
Danny Carter, prin. Fax 777-9741
Ft. Hill HS 700/9-12
500 Greenway Ave 21502 301-777-2570
Joseph Carter, prin. Fax 777-2572
Washington MS 600/6-8
200 N Massachusetts Ave 21502 301-777-5360
Kendra Kenney, prin. Fax 777-8452
Other Schools – See Cresaptown, Frostburg, Lonaconing

---

Allegany College of Maryland Post-Sec.
12401 Willowbrook Rd 21502 301-784-5000
Bishop Walsh S 400/PK-12
700 Bishop Walsh Rd 21502 301-724-5360
Ann Workmeister, prin. Fax 722-0555
International Beauty School Post-Sec.
119 N Centre St 21502 301-777-3020
Lighthouse Christian Academy 100/PK-12
2020 Bedford St 21502 301-777-7375

**Damascus, Montgomery, Pop. 14,848**
Montgomery County SD
Supt. — See Rockville

Baker MS 500/7-8
25400 Oak Dr 20872 301-253-7010
Dr. Louise Worthington, prin. Fax 253-7020
Damascus HS 1,300/9-12
25921 Ridge Rd 20872 301-253-7030
Jennifer Webster, prin. Fax 253-7046

**Denton, Caroline, Pop. 4,304**
Caroline County SD 5,500/PK-12
204 Franklin St 21629 410-479-1460
John D. Ewald, supt. Fax 479-0108
cl.k12.md.us
Lockerman MS 800/6-8
410 Lockerman St 21629 410-479-2760
Lee Sutton, prin. Fax 479-3594
Other Schools – See Federalsburg, Ridgely

**Dundalk, Baltimore, Pop. 61,917**
Baltimore County SD
Supt. — See Towson
Sollers Point Technical HS Vo/Tech
1901 Delvale Ave 21222 410-887-7075
Michael Weglein, prin. Fax 887-7238

**Easton, Talbot, Pop. 15,604**
Talbot County SD 4,500/PK-12
PO Box 1029 21601 410-822-0330
Kelly Griffith, supt. Fax 820-4260
www.tcps.k12.md.us/
Easton HS 1,100/9-12
723 Mecklenburg Ave 21601 410-822-4180
David Stofa, prin. Fax 819-5814
Easton MS 700/6-8
201 Peach Blossom Ln 21601 410-822-2910
Norby Lee, prin. Fax 822-7210
Other Schools – See Saint Michaels

---

Chesapeake Christian S 100/PK-12
1009 N Washington St 21601 410-822-7600
SS. Peter & Paul HS 200/9-12
900 High St 21601 410-822-2275
James Nemeth, prin. Fax 822-1767

**Edgewater, Anne Arundel, Pop. 8,834**
Anne Arundel County SD
Supt. — See Annapolis
Center of Applied Technology-South Vo/Tech
211 Central Ave E 21037 410-956-5900
Thomas Milans, prin. Fax 956-5905
Central MS 1,100/6-8
221 Central Ave E 21037 410-956-5800
Mildred Beall, prin. Fax 956-1266
South River HS 2,200/9-12
201 Central Ave E 21037 410-956-5600
William Myers, prin. Fax 956-5137
South River Evening HS Adult
201 Central Ave E 21037 410-956-0462
Rosaria Jablonski, admin. Fax 956-5919

**Edgewood, Harford, Pop. 24,585**
Harford County SD
Supt. — See Bel Air
Edgewood HS 1,200/9-12
2415 Willoughby Beach Rd 21040 410-612-1500
Larissa Santos, prin. Fax 612-1585
Edgewood MS 1,100/6-8
2311 Willoughby Beach Rd 21040 410-612-1518
Patrice Brown, prin. Fax 612-1523

**Eldersburg, Carroll, Pop. 30,093**
Carroll County SD
Supt. — See Westminster
Liberty HS 1,200/9-12
5855 Bartholow Rd 21784 410-751-3560
Kenneth Goncz, prin. Fax 751-3564

**Elkridge, Howard, Pop. 15,025**
Howard County SD
Supt. — See Ellicott City
Elkridge Landing MS 700/6-8
7085 Montgomery Rd 21075 410-313-5040
Gina Cash, prin. Fax 313-5045
Mayfield Woods MS 700/6-8
7950 Red Barn Way 21075 410-313-5022
Melissa Shindel, prin. Fax 313-5029

**Elkton, Cecil, Pop. 14,914**
Cecil County SD 15,500/PK-12
201 Booth St 21921 410-996-5400
D'Ette Devine Ed.D., supt. Fax 996-5454
www.ccps.org
Cecil County S of Technology Vo/Tech
912 Appleton Rd 21921 410-392-8879
David Dollenger, prin. Fax 392-8880
Cherry Hill MS 500/6-8
2535 Singerly Rd 21921 410-996-5020
Albert Volpe, prin. Fax 996-5435
Elkton HS 1,100/9-12
110 James St 21921 410-996-5000
John Roush, prin. Fax 996-5646
Elkton MS 600/6-8
615 North St 21921 410-996-5010
Dr. Stuart Hutchinson, prin. Fax 996-5639
Other Schools – See Chesapeake City, North East, Perryville, Rising Sun

---

Tri-State Christian Academy 300/PK-12
146 Appleton Rd 21921 410-398-6444
Keith Wilson, head sch Fax 688-4847

**Ellicott City, Howard, Pop. 64,049**
Howard County SD 50,600/PK-12
10910 Clarksville Pike 21042 410-313-6600
Dr. Renee Foose, supt. Fax 313-6674
www.hcpss.org
Applications and Research Lab Vo/Tech
10920 Clarksville Pike 21042 410-313-6998
Rick Robb, admin. Fax 313-7000
Bonnie Branch MS 700/6-8
4979 Ilchester Rd 21043 410-313-2580
Cherolyn Jones, prin. Fax 313-2586
Burleigh Manor MS 600/6-8
4200 Centennial Ln 21042 410-313-2507
John DiPaula, prin. Fax 313-2513
Centennial HS 1,400/9-12
4300 Centennial Ln 21042 410-313-2856
Claire Hafets, prin. Fax 313-2861
Dunloggin MS 600/6-8
9129 Northfield Rd 21042 410-313-2831
Jeffrey Fink, prin. Fax 313-2530
Ellicott Mills MS 700/6-8
4445 Montgomery Rd 21043 410-313-2839
Christopher Rattay, prin. Fax 313-2845
Folly Quarter MS 600/6-8
13500 Triadelphia Rd 21042 410-313-1506
Richard Wilson, prin. Fax 313-1509
Homewood Center 100/Alt
10914 State Route 108 21042 410-313-7081
Tina Maddox, prin. Fax 313-7130
Howard HS 1,700/9-12
8700 Old Annapolis Rd 21043 410-313-2867
Nick Novak, prin. Fax 313-2870
Mt. Hebron HS 1,400/9-12
9440 Old Frederick Rd 21042 410-313-2880
Andrew Cockley, prin. Fax 313-2543
Patapsco MS 600/6-8
8885 Old Frederick Rd 21043 410-313-2848
Cynthia Dillon, prin. Fax 313-2852
Other Schools – See Clarksville, Columbia, Elkridge, Fulton, Glenelg, Glenwood, Hanover, Jessup, Laurel, Marriottsville

---

Glenelg Country S 800/PK-12
12793 Folly Quarter Rd 21042 410-531-8600
Gregory Ventre, hdmstr. Fax 531-7363

**Emmitsburg, Frederick, Pop. 2,774**

---

Mt. St. Mary's University Post-Sec.
16300 Old Emmitsburg Rd 21727 301-447-6122

**Fallston, Harford, Pop. 8,862**
Harford County SD
Supt. — See Bel Air
Fallston HS 1,100/9-12
2301 Carrs Mill Rd 21047 410-638-4120
Richard Jester, prin. Fax 638-4125
Fallston MS 900/6-8
2303 Carrs Mill Rd 21047 410-638-4129
Joseph Mascari, prin. Fax 638-4237

**Federalsburg, Caroline, Pop. 2,672**
Caroline County SD
Supt. — See Denton
Richardson HS 500/9-12
25320 Richardson Rd 21632 410-754-5575
Christal Harkowa, prin. Fax 754-3497
Richardson MS 400/6-8
25390 Richardson Rd 21632 410-754-5263
Lynn Willey, prin. Fax 754-5695

**Finksburg, Carroll**

---

Gerstell Academy 300/PK-12
2500 Old Westminster Pike 21048 410-861-3000
Dr. Lorraine Fulton, pres. Fax 861-3006

**Forestville, Prince George's, Pop. 12,138**
Prince George's County SD
Supt. — See Upper Marlboro
Forestville HS 700/9-12
7001 Beltz Dr 20747 301-817-0400
Nathaniel Laney, prin. Fax 817-0416
Suitland HS 2,100/9-12
5200 Silver Hill Rd 20747 301-817-0500
Nate Newman, prin. Fax 817-0515

---

Bishop McNamara HS 900/9-12
6800 Marlboro Pike 20747 301-735-8401
Dr. Robert Van der Waag, prin. Fax 735-0934

**Fort Meade, Anne Arundel, Pop. 8,776**
Anne Arundel County SD
Supt. — See Annapolis
MacArthur MS 1,200/6-8
3500 Rockenbach Rd 20755 410-674-0032
Eugene Whiting, prin. Fax 674-8021
Meade HS 2,300/9-12
1100 Clark Rd 20755 410-674-7710
John Yore, prin. Fax 551-8210
Meade MS 700/6-8
1103 26th St 20755 410-674-2355
Christine DeGuzman, prin. Fax 674-6590
Meade Evening HS Adult
1100 Clark Rd 20755 410-674-7415
Anthony Andrione, admin.

**Fort Washington, Prince George's, Pop. 23,036**
Prince George's County SD
Supt. — See Upper Marlboro
Friendly HS 1,300/9-12
10000 Allentown Rd 20744 301-449-4900
Raynah Adams, prin. Fax 449-4911
Gourdine MS 600/6-8
8700 Allentown Rd 20744 301-449-4940
Leatriz Covington, prin. Fax 449-4948
Oxon Hill MS 600/7-8
9570 Fort Foote Rd 20744 301-749-4270
Wendell Coleman, prin. Fax 749-4286

---

National Christian Academy 300/PK-12
6700 Bock Rd 20744 301-567-9507
Andrew Stewart M.Ed., prin. Fax 567-7332

**Frederick, Frederick, Pop. 63,120**
Frederick County SD 39,500/PK-12
191 S East St 21701 301-696-6820
Dr. Theresa Alban, supt. Fax 696-6823
www.fcps.org
Ballenger Creek MS 700/6-8
5525 Ballenger Creek Pike 21703 240-236-5700
Mita Badshah, prin. Fax 236-5701
Career and Technology Center Vo/Tech
7922 Opossumtown Pike 21702 240-236-8500
Michael Concepcion, prin. Fax 236-8501
Crestwood MS 500/6-8
7100 Foxcroft Dr 21703 240-566-9000
Donna Clabaugh, prin. Fax 566-9001
Frederick HS 1,400/9-12
650 Carroll Pkwy 21701 240-236-7000
Kathy Campagnoli, prin. Fax 236-7015
Heather Ridge S Alt
1445 Taney Ave 21702 240-236-8000
Denise Flora, prin. Fax 236-8001
Johnson HS 1,600/9-12
1501 N Market St 21701 240-236-8200
Jethro Reid, prin. Fax 236-8201
Johnson MS 500/6-8
1799 Schifferstadt Blvd 21701 240-236-4900
Neal Case, prin. Fax 236-4901
Linganore HS 1,600/9-12
12013 Old Annapolis Rd 21701 240-566-9700
Dave Kehne, prin. Fax 566-9701
Monocacy MS 800/6-8
8009 Opossumtown Pike 21702 240-236-4700
Brian Vasquenza, prin. Fax 236-4701
Tuscarora HS 1,500/9-12
5312 Ballenger Creek Pike 21703 240-236-6400
Andrew Kibler, prin. Fax 236-6401
West Frederick MS 800/6-8
515 W Patrick St 21701 240-236-4000
Frank Vetter, prin. Fax 236-4050
Other Schools – See Brunswick, Ijamsville, Middletown, New Market, Thurmont, Walkersville

---

Frederick Community College Post-Sec.
7932 Opossumtown Pike 21702 301-846-2400
Hood College Post-Sec.
401 Rosemont Ave 21701 301-663-3131
Maryland School for the Deaf Post-Sec.
PO Box 250 21705
New Life Christian S 200/K-12
5909 Jefferson Pike 21703 301-663-8418
Jason Burrell, hdmstr. Fax 698-1583

**Frostburg, Allegany, Pop. 8,847**
Allegany County SD
Supt. — See Cumberland
Eckhart Alternative S 100/Alt
17000 National Hwy SW 21532 301-689-3483
Tonya Detrick-Grove, coord. Fax 689-2567
Mountain Ridge HS 800/9-12
100 Dr Nancy S Grasmick Ln 21532 301-689-3377
Gene Morgan, prin. Fax 689-8709

---

Frostburg State University Post-Sec.
101 Braddock Rd 21532 301-687-4000

**Fruitland, Wicomico, Pop. 4,731**
Wicomico County SD
Supt. — See Salisbury
Bennett MS 900/6-8
532 S Division St 21826 410-677-5140
Liza Hastings, prin. Fax 677-5133

**Fulton, Howard, Pop. 1,957**
Howard County SD
Supt. — See Ellicott City
Lime Kiln MS 600/6-8
11650 Scaggsville Rd 20759 410-880-5988
Scott Conroy, prin. Fax 880-5996
Reservoir HS 1,500/9-12
11550 Scaggsville Rd 20759 410-888-8850
Patrick Saunderson, prin. Fax 888-8849

**Gaithersburg, Montgomery, Pop. 57,995**
Montgomery County SD
Supt. — See Rockville
Forest Oak MS 800/6-8
651 Saybrooke Oaks Blvd 20877 301-670-8242
Dr. Art Williams, prin. Fax 840-5322
Gaithersburg HS 2,000/9-12
101 Education Blvd 20877 301-284-4500
Dr. Christine Handy-Collins, prin. Fax 284-4701
Gaithersburg MS 400/7-8
2 Teachers Way 20877 301-840-4554
Ann Dolan Rindner, prin. Fax 840-4570
Lakelands Park MS 900/6-8
1200 Main St 20878 301-670-1400
Deborah Higdon, prin. Fax 670-1418
Montgomery Village MS 600/6-8
19300 Watkins Mill Rd 20886 301-840-4660
Dr. Edgar Malker, prin. Fax 840-6388
Quince Orchard HS 1,800/9-12
15800 Quince Orchard Rd 20878 301-840-4686
Carole Working, prin. Fax 840-4699
Ridgeview MS 500/7-8
16600 Raven Rock Dr 20878 301-406-1300
Monifa McKnight, prin. Fax 840-4679
Shady Grove MS 600/6-8
8100 Midcounty Hwy 20877 301-548-7540
Edward Owusu, prin. Fax 548-7535
Watkins Mill HS 1,500/9-12
10301 Apple Ridge Rd 20886 301-840-3959
Carol Goddard, prin. Fax 840-3980

---

Aesthetics Institutes of Cosmetology Post-Sec.
15958 Shady Grove Rd Unit C 20877 301-330-9252
Avalon S 200/K-12
200 W Diamond Ave 20877 301-963-8022
Kevin Davern, hdmstr. Fax 963-8027

Covenant Life S 300/PK-12
7503 Muncaster Mill Rd 20877 301-869-4500
Jamie Leach, hdmstr. Fax 948-4920
Sodexho Marriott Healthcare Mid-Atlantic Post-Sec.
9801 Washingtonian Blvd 20878 301-987-4127

**Gambrills, Anne Arundel, Pop. 2,747**
Anne Arundel County SD
Supt. — See Annapolis
Arundel HS 2,000/9-12
1001 Annapolis Rd 21054 410-674-6500
Gina Davenport, prin. Fax 672-3711
Crofton MS 1,100/6-8
2301 Davidsonville Rd 21054 410-793-0280
Nuria Williams, prin. Fax 793-0295

**Germantown, Montgomery, Pop. 83,263**
Montgomery County SD
Supt. — See Rockville
Clemente MS 1,200/6-8
18808 Waring Station Rd 20874 301-601-0344
Jeffrey Brown, prin. Fax 601-0370
King MS 600/6-8
13737 Wisteria Dr 20874 301-353-8080
Christopher Wynne, prin. Fax 601-0399
Kingsview MS 900/6-8
18909 Kingsview Rd 20874 301-601-4611
James D'Andrea, prin. Fax 601-4610
Neelsville MS 900/6-8
11700 Neelsville Church Rd 20876 301-353-8064
Vicky Lake-Parcan, prin. Fax 353-8094
Northwest HS 2,100/9-12
13501 Richter Farm Rd 20874 301-601-4660
Lance Dempsey, prin. Fax 601-4662
Seneca Valley HS 1,300/9-12
19401 Crystal Rock Dr 20874 301-353-8000
Marc Cohen, prin. Fax 353-8004

---

Montgomery College Post-Sec.
20200 Observation Dr 20876 240-567-7700

**Glen Burnie, Anne Arundel, Pop. 65,521**
Anne Arundel County SD
Supt. — See Annapolis
Corkran MS 600/6-8
7600 Quarterfield Rd 21061 410-222-6493
Adam Zetwick, prin. Fax 761-3853
Glen Burnie HS 2,000/9-12
7550 Baltimore Annapolis Bl 21060 410-761-8950
Vickie Plitt, prin. Fax 761-3711
Marley MS 800/6-8
10 Davis Ct 21060 410-761-0934
Kimberly Winterbottom, prin. Fax 761-0736
North County HS 1,900/9-12
10 1st Ave E 21061 410-222-6970
Julie Cares, prin. Fax 222-6976
Glen Burnie Evening HS Adult
7550 Baltimore Annapolis Bl 21060 410-761-3664
Holly Holman, admin. Fax 863-4531
North County Evening HS Adult
10 1st Ave E 21061 410-424-2102
Rebecca Bittman, admin.

**Glencoe, Baltimore**

---

Oldfields S 100/8-12
1500 Glencoe Rd 21152 410-472-4800
Dr. Parnell Hagerman, head sch Fax 472-3141

**Glenelg, Howard**
Howard County SD
Supt. — See Ellicott City
Glenelg HS 1,200/9-12
14025 Burntwoods Rd 21737 410-313-5528
Karl Schindler, prin. Fax 313-5540

**Glenwood, Howard**
Howard County SD
Supt. — See Ellicott City
Glenwood MS 600/6-8
2680 Route 97 21738 410-313-5520
Robert Motley, prin. Fax 313-5534

**Great Mills, Saint Mary's**
St. Mary's County SD
Supt. — See Leonardtown
Great Mills HS 1,700/9-12
21130 Great Mills Rd 20634 301-863-4001
Jake Heibel, prin. Fax 863-4006

**Greenbelt, Prince George's, Pop. 22,408**
Prince George's County SD
Supt. — See Upper Marlboro
Greenbelt MS 700/6-8
6301 Breezewood Dr 20770 301-513-5040
George Covington, prin. Fax 513-5097
Roosevelt HS 2,600/9-12
7601 Hanover Pkwy 20770 301-513-5400
Reginald McNeill, prin. Fax 486-3720

---

Lancaster Bible College Post-Sec.
7852 Walker Dr Ste 100 20770 301-552-1400

**Hagerstown, Washington, Pop. 37,853**
Washington County SD 22,200/PK-12
10435 Downsville Pike 21740 301-766-2800
Dr. Clayton Wilcox, supt. Fax 766-2829
www.wcps.k12.md.us/
Antietam Academy Alt
40 W Oak Ridge Dr 21740 301-766-8447
Tim Morrow, coord. Fax 766-8479
Hicks MS 800/6-8
1321 S Potomac St 21740 301-766-8110
Deron Crawford, prin. Fax 766-8116
Ingram S for the Arts 200/9-12
7 S Potomac St 21740 301-766-8840
Rob Hovermale, prin. Fax 766-8849
Northern MS 700/6-8
701 Northern Ave 21742 301-766-8258
Dr. Theresa Williamson, prin. Fax 797-5887
North Hagerstown HS 1,300/9-12
1200 Pennsylvania Ave 21742 301-766-8238
James Aleshire, prin. Fax 733-3158
South Hagerstown HS 1,300/9-12
1101 S Potomac St 21740 301-766-8369
Jeremy Jakoby, prin. Fax 766-8474
Washington County Technical HS Vo/Tech
50 W Oak Ridge Dr 21740 301-766-8050
Jeff Stouffer, prin. Fax 797-9743
Western Heights MS 700/6-8
1300 Marshall St 21740 301-766-8403
Matthew Mauriello, prin. Fax 791-4136
Evening HS Adult
40 W Oak Ridge Dr 21740 301-766-8059
Tim Morrow, admin.
Other Schools – See Boonsboro, Clear Spring, Hancock, Smithsburg, Williamsport

---

Award Beauty School Post-Sec.
26 E Antietam St 21740 301-733-4520
Broadfording Christian Academy 300/PK-12
13535 Broadfording Church 21740 301-797-8886
William Wyand, supt. Fax 797-3155
Grace Academy 400/PK-12
13321 Cearfoss Pike 21740 301-733-2033
Jack Appleby, hdmstr. Fax 733-4706
Hagerstown Community College Post-Sec.
11400 Robinwood Dr 21742 240-500-2530
Heritage Academy 200/PK-12
12215 Walnut Pt W 21740 301-582-2600
Greg Stegall, prin. Fax 582-2603
Highland View Academy 100/9-12
10100 Academy Dr 21740 301-739-8480
Kaplan University Post-Sec.
18618 Crestwood Dr 21742 301-766-3600
Paradise Mennonite S 200/1-10
19308 Air View Rd 21742 301-733-1368
Pittsburgh Institute of Aeronautics Post-Sec.
14516 Pennsylvania Ave 21742 800-444-1440
St. James S 200/8-12
17641 College Rd 21740 301-733-9330
Rev. D. Stuart Dunnan, hdmstr. Fax 739-1310
St. Maria Goretti HS 200/9-12
1535 Oak Hill Ave 21742 301-739-4266
Richard Fairley, pres. Fax 739-4261

**Hampstead, Carroll, Pop. 6,228**
Carroll County SD
Supt. — See Westminster
North Carroll HS 800/9-12
1400 Panther Dr 21074 410-751-3450
Thomas Clowes, prin. Fax 751-3457
North Carroll MS 600/6-8
2401 Hanover Pike 21074 410-751-3440
James Carver, prin. Fax 751-3464
Shiloh MS 700/6-8
3675 Willow St 21074 410-386-4570
Scott Lavender, prin. Fax 386-4579

**Hancock, Washington, Pop. 1,530**
Washington County SD
Supt. — See Hagerstown
Hancock MSHS 300/6-12
289 W Main St 21750 301-766-8186
Rodney Gayman, prin. Fax 678-7218

**Hanover, Anne Arundel**
Howard County SD
Supt. — See Ellicott City
Viaduct MS 6-8
7000 Banbury Dr 21076 410-313-8711
Shiney Ann John, prin. Fax 313-8091

---

ITT Technical Institute Post-Sec.
7030 Dorsey Rd Ste 100 21076 410-694-4700

**Harwood, Anne Arundel**
Anne Arundel County SD
Supt. — See Annapolis
Southern HS 1,100/9-12
4400 Solomons Island Rd 20776 410-867-7100
Kevin Hamlin, prin. Fax 867-7100

**Havre de Grace, Harford, Pop. 12,505**
Harford County SD
Supt. — See Bel Air
Havre De Grace HS 700/9-12
700 Congress Ave 21078 410-939-6600
James Reynolds, prin. Fax 939-6667
Havre De Grace MS 500/6-8
401 Lewis Ln 21078 410-939-6608
Chandra Krantz, prin. Fax 939-6613

**Huntingtown, Calvert**
Calvert County SD
Supt. — See Prince Frederick
Huntingtown HS 1,600/9-12
4125 Solomons Island Rd 20639 410-414-7036
Rick Weber, prin. Fax 535-2865
Plum Point MS 700/6-8
1475 Plum Point Rd 20639 410-535-7400
Kelley Adams, prin. Fax 535-7413
Adult Education Adult
4105 Old Town Rd 20639 410-535-7382
Edie McGreevy, coord. Fax 535-7383

---

Calverton S 400/PK-12
300 Calverton School Rd 20639 410-535-0216
Daniel Rocha, hdmstr. Fax 535-6934

**Hurlock, Dorchester, Pop. 2,049**
Dorchester County SD
Supt. — See Cambridge
North Dorchester HS 500/9-12
5875 Cloverdale Rd 21643 410-943-4511
Lynn Sorrells, prin. Fax 943-3499
North Dorchester MS 400/6-8
5745 Cloverdale Rd 21643 410-943-3322
Vaughn Evans, prin. Fax 943-3214

**Hyattsville, Prince George's, Pop. 17,068**
Prince George's County SD
Supt. — See Upper Marlboro
Hyattsville MS 700/6-8
6001 42nd Ave 20781 301-209-5830
Thornton Boone, prin. Fax 209-5849
Northwestern HS 2,300/9-12
7000 Adelphi Rd 20782 301-985-1820
Elaine Murray, prin. Fax 985-1833
Orem MS 700/6-8
6100 Editors Park Dr 20782 301-853-0840
Theresa Merrifield, prin. Fax 853-0839
Northwestern Evening HS Adult
7000 Adelphi Rd 20782 301-985-1460
William Kitchings, prin. Fax 985-5749

---

DeMatha Catholic HS 900/9-12
4313 Madison St 20781 240-764-2200
Dr. Daniel McMahon, prin. Fax 764-2275

**Ijamsville, Frederick, Pop. 350**
Frederick County SD
Supt. — See Frederick
Oakdale HS 900/9-12
5850 Eaglehead Dr 21754 240-566-9400
Jeff Marker, prin. Fax 566-9401
Oakdale MS 600/6-8
9840 Old National Pike 21754 240-236-5500
Stephanie Ware, prin. Fax 236-5501
Urbana HS 1,600/9-12
3471 Campus Dr 21754 240-236-7600
Jay Berno, prin. Fax 236-7601
Urbana MS 700/6-8
3511 Pontius Ct 21754 240-566-9200
Michelle Concepcion, prin. Fax 566-9201
Windsor Knolls MS 900/6-8
11150 Windsor Rd 21754 240-236-5000
T.C. Suter, prin. Fax 236-5001

---

Friends Meeting S 100/PK-12
3232 Green Valley Rd 21754 301-798-0288
Mara Y. Nicastro, hdmstr. Fax 798-0299

**Indian Head, Charles, Pop. 3,706**
Charles County SD
Supt. — See La Plata
Henson MS 500/6-8
3535 Livingston Rd 20640 301-375-8550
Christina Caballero, prin. Fax 375-9216
Lackey HS 1,200/9-12
3000 Chicamuxen Rd 20640 301-743-5431
Kathy Perriello, prin. Fax 743-9076
Smallwood MS 500/6-8
4990 Indian Head Hwy 20640 301-743-5422
Kathy Kiessling, prin. Fax 753-8421

**Jessup, Howard, Pop. 7,088**
Howard County SD
Supt. — See Ellicott City
Patuxent Valley MS 700/6-8
9151 Vollmerhausen Rd 20794 410-880-5840
Micah Humbert, prin. Fax 880-5846

**Joppa, Harford, Pop. 12,356**
Harford County SD
Supt. — See Bel Air
Joppatowne HS 900/9-12
555 Joppa Farm Rd 21085 410-612-1510
Pamela Zeigler, prin. Fax 612-1528
Magnolia MS 700/6-8
299 Fort Hoyle Rd 21085 410-612-1525
Melissa Mickey, prin. Fax 612-1598

**Kensington, Montgomery, Pop. 2,142**
Montgomery County SD
Supt. — See Rockville
Einstein HS 1,600/9-12
11135 Newport Mill Rd 20895 301-929-2200
James Fernandez, prin. Fax 962-1016
Newport Mill MS 600/6-8
11311 Newport Mill Rd 20895 301-929-2244
Panagiota Tsonis, prin. Fax 929-2274

---

Academy of the Holy Cross 600/9-12
4920 Strathmore Ave 20895 301-942-2100
Melissa Huey-Burns, prin. Fax 929-6440
Brookewood S 100/1-12
10401 Armory Ave 20895 301-949-7997
Joseph McPherson, hdmstr. Fax 949-0069

**Kingsville, Baltimore, Pop. 4,276**

---

Open Bible Christian Academy 200/PK-12
13 Open Bible Way 21087 410-593-9940
Jill Greenlee, admin. Fax 593-9942
Redeemer Classical Christian S 300/PK-12
6415 Mount Vista Rd 21087 410-592-9625
Terry Cellini, admin. Fax 817-6904

**Landover, Prince George's, Pop. 22,690**
Prince George's County SD
Supt. — See Upper Marlboro
Gholson MS 700/7-8
900 Nalley Rd 20785 301-883-8390
Jacqueline Marshall-Hall, prin. Fax 883-8394
Kenmoor MS 700/6-8
2500 Kenmoor Dr 20785 301-925-2300
Maha Fadli, prin. Fax 925-2317

---

Fortis College Post-Sec.
4351 Garden City Dr 20785 301-459-3650

**Lanham Seabrook, Prince George's, Pop. 16,792**
Prince George's County SD
Supt. — See Upper Marlboro

DuVal HS 1,600/9-12
9880 Good Luck Rd 20706 301-918-8600
Mark Covington, prin. Fax 918-8606
Johnson MS 900/6-8
5401 Barker Pl 20706 301-918-8680
Rodney McBride, prin. Fax 918-8688

---

Lanham Christian S 200/PK-12
8400 Good Luck Rd 20706 301-552-9102
Rev. Randy Burr, dir. Fax 552-2021

**La Plata, Charles, Pop. 8,508**
Charles County SD 26,700/PK-12
PO Box 2770 20646 301-932-6610
Kimberly Hill Ed.D., supt. Fax 932-6651
www.ccboe.com
La Plata HS 1,400/9-12
6035 Radio Station Rd 20646 301-934-1100
Douglass Dolan, prin. Fax 934-5657
Somers MS 900/6-8
300 Willow Ln 20646 301-934-4663
Carrie Akins, prin. Fax 934-2982
Other Schools – See Indian Head, Newburg, Pomfret, Waldorf

---

College of Southern Maryland Post-Sec.
PO Box 910 20646 301-934-2251

**Largo, Prince George's, Pop. 10,502**
Prince George's County SD
Supt. — See Upper Marlboro
Academy of Health Sciences at PGCC 100/9-12
301 Largo Rd Rm 119 20774 301-583-1593
Dr. Kathy Richard-Andrews, prin. Fax 583-5241

---

Prince George's Community College Post-Sec.
301 Largo Rd 20774 301-336-6000

**Laurel, Prince George's, Pop. 24,374**
Howard County SD
Supt. — See Ellicott City
Hammond MS 500/6-8
8100 Aladdin Dr 20723 410-880-5830
Kerry Dufresne, prin. Fax 880-5837
Murray Hill MS 700/6-8
9989 Winter Sun Rd 20723 410-880-5897
Josh Wasilewski, prin. Fax 317-5048

Prince George's County SD
Supt. — See Upper Marlboro
Eisenhower MS 700/6-8
13725 Briarwood Dr 20708 301-497-3620
John Mangrum, prin. Fax 497-3637
Laurel HS 1,800/9-12
8000 Cherry Ln 20707 301-497-2050
Dwayne Jones, prin. Fax 497-2068

---

Capitol College Post-Sec.
11301 Springfield Rd 20708 800-950-1992
Maryland Univ of Integrative Health Post-Sec.
7750 Montpelier Rd 20723 410-888-9048
St. Vincent Pallotti HS 500/9-12
113 Saint Marys Pl 20707 301-725-3228
Jeffrey Palumbo, prin. Fax 776-4343

**Leonardtown, Saint Mary's, Pop. 2,832**
St. Mary's County SD 17,400/PK-12
23160 Moakley St 20650 301-475-5511
James Smith, supt. Fax 475-4262
www.smcps.org
Fairlead Academy II Alt
24009 Point Lookout Rd 20650 301-475-0240
Wendy Zimmerman, dean Fax 475-0245
Forrest Technology Center Vo/Tech
24005 Point Lookout Rd 20650 301-475-0242
Michael Egan, dir. Fax 475-0245
Leonardtown HS 1,900/9-12
23995 Point Lookout Rd 20650 301-475-0200
Mike Watson, prin. Fax 475-0204
Leonardtown MS 900/6-8
24015 Point Lookout Rd 20650 301-475-0230
Lisa Bachner, prin. Fax 475-0237
Other Schools – See Great Mills, Lexington Park, Mechanicsville, Morganza

---

St. Mary's Ryken HS 700/9-12
22600 Camp Calvert Rd 20650 301-475-2814
Rick Wood, prin. Fax 373-4186

**Lexington Park, Saint Mary's, Pop. 11,085**
St. Mary's County SD
Supt. — See Leonardtown
Esperanza MS 800/6-8
22790 Maple Rd 20653 301-863-4016
Jill Snyder-Mills, prin. Fax 863-4020
Fairlead Academy I Alt
20833 Great Mills Rd 20653 301-863-4090
Rebecca Cline, dean Fax 863-4013
Spring Ridge MS 900/6-8
19856 Three Notch Rd 20653 301-863-4031
Angela Fulp, prin. Fax 863-4035

**Linthicum Heights, Anne Arundel, Pop. 2,980**
Anne Arundel County SD
Supt. — See Annapolis
Lindale MS 800/6-8
415 Andover Rd 21090 410-691-4344
Johnny Nash, prin. Fax 691-4359

**Lonaconing, Allegany, Pop. 1,197**
Allegany County SD
Supt. — See Cumberland
Westmar MS 300/6-8
16915 Lower Georges Creek 21539 301-463-5751
Toby Eirich, prin. Fax 463-2231

**Lothian, Anne Arundel**
Anne Arundel County SD
Supt. — See Annapolis

Southern MS 800/6-8
5235 Solomons Island Rd 20711 410-222-1659
Kevin Buckley, prin. Fax 867-0231

**Lusby, Calvert, Pop. 1,786**
Calvert County SD
Supt. — See Prince Frederick
Mill Creek MS 500/6-8
12200 Southern Connector 20657 410-535-7824
Abbe Gray, prin. Fax 535-7829
Patuxent HS 1,100/9-12
12485 Southern Connector 20657 410-535-7865
Sabrina Bergen, prin. Fax 535-7875
Southern MS 600/6-8
9615 H G Trueman Rd 20657 410-535-7877
Mandy Blackmon, prin. Fax 535-7879

**Lutherville, Baltimore, Pop. 6,362**
Baltimore County SD
Supt. — See Towson
Ridgely MS 1,100/6-8
121 E Ridgely Rd 21093 410-887-7650
Susan Truesdell, prin. Fax 887-7834

**Mc Henry, Garrett**

---

Garrett College Post-Sec.
687 Mosser Rd 21541 301-387-3000

**Manchester, Carroll, Pop. 4,742**
Carroll County SD
Supt. — See Westminster
Manchester Valley HS 800/9-12
3300 Maple Grove Rd 21102 410-386-1673
Kenneth Fischer, prin. Fax 386-1561

**Mardela Springs, Wicomico, Pop. 336**
Wicomico County SD
Supt. — See Salisbury
Mardela MSHS 700/6-12
24940 Delmar Rd 21837 410-677-5142
Rick Briggs, prin. Fax 677-5166

**Marion Station, Somerset**
Somerset County SD
Supt. — See Westover
Peyton Adult & Alt Learning Ctr 200/Alt
28573 Hudson Corner Rd 21838 410-623-2385
William Johnson, prin. Fax 623-2114

**Marriottsville, Howard**
Howard County SD
Supt. — See Ellicott City
Marriotts Ridge HS 1,300/9-12
12100 Woodford Dr 21104 410-313-5568
Adrianne Kaufman, prin. Fax 313-5574
Mount View MS 700/6-8
12101 Woodford Dr 21104 410-313-5545
Tammy Goldeisen, prin. Fax 313-5551

---

Chapelgate Christian Academy 400/PK-PK, 6-
2600 Marriottsville Rd 21104 410-442-5888
Robin Van Ness, hdmstr. Fax 442-5820

**Mechanicsville, Saint Mary's, Pop. 1,477**
St. Mary's County SD
Supt. — See Leonardtown
Brent MS 1,000/6-8
29675 Point Lookout Rd 20659 301-884-4635
Janet Fowler, prin. Fax 884-8937

**Middletown, Frederick, Pop. 4,076**
Frederick County SD
Supt. — See Frederick
Middletown HS 1,200/9-12
200 Schoolhouse Dr 21769 240-236-7400
Lee Jeffrey, prin. Fax 236-7450
Middletown MS 800/6-8
100 Martha Mason St 21769 240-236-4200
Everett Warren, prin. Fax 236-4250

**Millersville, Anne Arundel**
Anne Arundel County SD
Supt. — See Annapolis
Old Mill HS 2,200/9-12
600 Patriot Ln 21108 410-969-9010
James Todd, prin. Fax 969-1620
Old Mill MS North 900/6-8
610 Patriot Ln 21108 410-969-5950
Sean McElhaney, prin. Fax 969-2612
Old Mill MS South 700/6-8
620 Patriot Ln 21108 410-969-7000
Carolyn Burton-Page, prin. Fax 969-5157

---

Rockbridge Academy 300/K-12
911 Generals Hwy 21108 410-923-1171
Roy Griffith, hdmstr. Fax 923-6588
Strayer University Post-Sec.
1520 Jabez Run 21108 410-923-4500

**Mitchellville, Prince George's, Pop. 10,692**
Prince George's County SD
Supt. — See Upper Marlboro
Just MS 700/7-8
1300 Campus Way N 20721 301-808-4040
Dr. Keary Schoen, prin. Fax 808-4050

---

Woodstream Christian Academy 400/PK-12
9800 Lottsford Rd 20721 301-955-1160
Rachel Ballard Ph.D., head sch Fax 955-1169

**Monkton, Baltimore**
Baltimore County SD
Supt. — See Towson
Hereford MS 900/6-8
712 Corbett Rd 21111 410-887-7902
Cathryn Walrod, prin. Fax 887-7904

**Montgomery Village, Montgomery, Pop. 30,917**

---

Living Grace Christian S 100/K-12
20300 Pleasant Ridge Dr 20886 301-840-9830
Dr. Daniel Switzer, prin. Fax 840-8005

**Morganza, Saint Mary's**
St. Mary's County SD
Supt. — See Leonardtown
Chopticon HS 1,600/9-12
25390 Colton Point Rd 20660 301-475-0215
Garth Bowling, prin. Fax 475-0222

**Mount Airy, Carroll, Pop. 9,125**
Carroll County SD
Supt. — See Westminster
Mount Airy MS 600/6-8
102 Watersville Rd 21771 410-751-3554
Karl Streaker, prin. Fax 751-3556

---

Mount Airy Christian Academy 400/K-12
16700 Old Frederick Rd 21771 410-489-4321
Rory Rice, head sch Fax 489-4492

**Newark, Worcester, Pop. 331**
Worcester County SD 6,600/PK-12
6270 Worcester Hwy 21841 410-632-5000
Jerry Wilson Ph.D., supt. Fax 632-0364
www.worcesterk12.com
Worcester Technical HS Vo/Tech
6290 Worcester Hwy 21841 410-632-5050
Caroline Bloxom, prin. Fax 632-5059
Other Schools – See Berlin, Pocomoke City, Snow Hill

**Newburg, Charles**
Charles County SD
Supt. — See La Plata
Piccowaxen MS 500/6-8
12834 Rock Point Rd 20664 301-934-1977
Wendell Martin, prin. Fax 934-1628

**New Carrollton, Prince George's, Pop. 11,918**
Prince George's County SD
Supt. — See Upper Marlboro
Carroll MS 900/6-8
6130 Lamont Dr 20784 301-918-8640
David Curry, prin. Fax 918-8646

---

Hair Academy Post-Sec.
8435 Annapolis Rd 20784 301-459-2509

**New Market, Frederick, Pop. 644**
Frederick County SD
Supt. — See Frederick
New Market MS 500/6-8
125 W Main St 21774 240-236-4600
Jennifer Bingman, prin. Fax 236-4650

**New Windsor, Carroll, Pop. 1,365**
Carroll County SD
Supt. — See Westminster
New Windsor MS 400/6-8
1000 Green Valley Rd 21776 410-751-3355
David Bortz, prin. Fax 751-3358

**North Bethesda, Montgomery, Pop. 42,508**

---

Georgetown Preparatory S 500/9-12
10900 Rockville Pike 20852 301-493-5000
Jeffrey Jones, hdmstr. Fax 493-5905

**North East, Cecil, Pop. 3,496**
Cecil County SD
Supt. — See Elkton
North East HS 1,100/9-12
300 Irishtown Rd 21901 410-996-6200
David Foye, prin. Fax 996-6264
North East MS 700/6-8
200 E Cecil Ave 21901 410-996-6210
Denise Sopa, prin. Fax 996-6236
Rising Sun HS 1,200/9-12
100 Tiger Dr 21901 410-658-9115
Anne Gellrich, prin. Fax 658-9121

---

Cecil College Post-Sec.
1 Seahawk Dr 21901 410-287-1000
Tome S 500/K-12
581 S Maryland Ave 21901 410-287-2050

**Oakland, Garrett, Pop. 1,908**
Garrett County SD 3,700/PK-12
40 S 2nd St 21550 301-334-8900
Dr. Janet Wilson, supt. Fax 334-7621
garrettcountyschools.org
Southern Garrett HS 800/9-12
345 Oakland Dr 21550 301-334-9447
Jim Maddy, prin. Fax 334-5085
Southern MS 500/6-8
605 Harvey Winters Dr 21550 301-334-8881
Brooks Elliott, prin. Fax 334-2315
Other Schools – See Accident

**Odenton, Anne Arundel, Pop. 35,750**
Anne Arundel County SD
Supt. — See Annapolis
Arundel MS 900/6-8
1179 Hammond Ln 21113 410-674-6900
George Lindley, prin. Fax 674-6593

**Olney, Montgomery, Pop. 33,044**
Montgomery County SD
Supt. — See Rockville
Farquhar MS 600/6-8
16915 Batchellors Forest Rd 20832 301-924-3100
Joel Beidleman, prin. Fax 924-3152
Parks MS 900/6-8
19200 Olney Mill Rd 20832 301-924-3180
Jewel Sanders, prin. Fax 924-3288

Our Lady of Good Counsel HS 1,300/9-12
17301 Old Vic Blvd 20832 240-283-3200
Dr. Paul Barker, pres. Fax 283-3250
Washington Christian Academy 300/K-12
16227 Batchellors Forest Rd 20832 240-390-0429
Dave Hawes, head sch Fax 559-0115

**Owings, Calvert, Pop. 2,102**
Calvert County SD
Supt. — See Prince Frederick
Northern HS 1,500/9-12
2950 Chaneyville Rd 20736 410-257-1519
Kevin Howard, prin. Fax 257-1530
Northern MS 700/6-8
2954 Chaneyville Rd 20736 410-257-1622
Jaime Webster, prin. Fax 257-1623
Windy Hill MS 700/6-8
9560 Boyds Turn Rd 20736 410-257-1560
James Kurtz, prin. Fax 257-4586

**Owings Mills, Baltimore, Pop. 29,714**
Baltimore County SD
Supt. — See Towson
New Town HS 900/9-12
4931 New Town Blvd 21117 410-887-1614
Kevin Whatley, prin. Fax 654-8897
Owings Mills HS 1,000/9-12
124 Tollgate Rd 21117 410-887-1700
Abbey Campbell, prin. Fax 581-1713

Empire Beauty School Post-Sec.
9616 Reistertown Rd Ste 105 21117 866-232-2771
Garrison Forest S 600/PK-12
300 Garrison Forest Rd 21117 410-363-1500
Kim Roberts Ph.D., hdmstr. Fax 363-8441
ITT Technical Institute Post-Sec.
11301 Red Run Blvd 21117 443-394-7115
Jemicy S 100/9-12
11202 Garrison Forest Rd 21117 410-653-2700
Ben Shifrin, hdmstr. Fax 753-8085
McDonogh S 1,300/PK-12
8600 McDonogh Rd 21117 443-544-7000
Charles Britton, hdmstr. Fax 581-0155

**Oxon Hill, Prince George's, Pop. 17,298**
Prince George's County SD
Supt. — See Upper Marlboro
Oxon Hill HS 1,600/9-12
6701 Leyte Dr 20745 301-749-4300
Dr. Jean-Paul Cadet, prin. Fax 749-4320
Potomac HS 1,100/9-12
5211 Boydell Ave 20745 301-702-3900
Robynne Prince, prin. Fax 702-3886

**Parkton, Baltimore**
Baltimore County SD
Supt. — See Towson
Hereford HS 1,400/9-12
17301 York Rd 21120 410-887-1905
Louis Jira, prin. Fax 887-1944

**Parkville, Baltimore, Pop. 30,034**
Baltimore County SD
Supt. — See Towson
Parkville HS 1,500/9-12
2600 Putty Hill Ave 21234 410-887-5257
Maureen Astarita, prin. Fax 668-7503

**Pasadena, Anne Arundel, Pop. 23,755**
Anne Arundel County SD
Supt. — See Annapolis
Chesapeake Bay MS 1,100/6-8
4804 Mountain Rd 21122 410-437-2400
Michael Dunn, prin. Fax 437-9920
Chesapeake HS 1,600/9-12
4798 Mountain Rd 21122 410-255-9600
Stephen Gorski, prin. Fax 360-4364
Fox MS 900/6-8
7922 Outing Ave 21122 410-437-5512
Russell Austin, prin. Fax 360-1511
Northeast HS 1,300/9-12
1121 Duvall Hwy 21122 410-437-6400
Jason Williams, prin. Fax 437-7012

**Perry Hall, Baltimore, Pop. 27,923**

Perry Hall Christian S 300/PK-12
3919 Schroeder Ave 21128 410-256-4886
Steve Taylor, head sch Fax 256-5451

**Perryville, Cecil, Pop. 4,257**
Cecil County SD
Supt. — See Elkton
Perryville HS 800/9-12
1696 Perryville Rd 21903 410-996-6000
Charles Helm, prin. Fax 996-6027
Perryville MS 600/6-8
850 Aiken Ave 21903 410-996-6010
Justin Zimmerman, prin. Fax 996-6048

**Pocomoke City, Worcester, Pop. 4,103**
Worcester County SD
Supt. — See Newark
Pocomoke HS 300/9-12
1817 Old Virginia Rd 21851 410-632-5180
Annette Wallace, prin. Fax 632-5189
Pocomoke MS 400/4-8
800 8th St 21851 410-632-5150
Todd Hall, prin. Fax 632-5159

**Pomfret, Charles, Pop. 498**
Charles County SD
Supt. — See La Plata
McDonough HS 1,200/9-12
7165 Marshall Corner Rd 20675 301-934-2944
Bradley Snow, prin. Fax 753-8408
Stethem Educational Center 100/Alt
7775 Marshall Corner Rd 20675 301-753-1757
Evelyn Arnold, prin. Fax 934-0165

**Poolesville, Montgomery, Pop. 4,780**
Montgomery County SD
Supt. — See Rockville
Poole MS 400/6-8
17014 Tom Fox Ave 20837 301-972-7979
Robert Sinclair, prin. Fax 972-7982
Poolesville JSHS 1,200/7-12
17501 W Willard Rd 20837 301-972-7900
Deena Levine, prin. Fax 972-7943

**Potomac, Montgomery, Pop. 43,827**
Montgomery County SD
Supt. — See Rockville
Cabin John MS 900/6-8
10701 Gainsborough Rd 20854 301-469-1150
Dr. Paulette Smith, prin. Fax 469-1003
Churchill HS 2,100/9-12
11300 Gainsborough Rd 20854 301-469-1200
Dr. Joan Benz, prin. Fax 469-1208
Hoover MS 1,000/6-8
8810 Postoak Rd 20854 301-469-1010
Yong-Mi Kim, prin. Fax 469-1013

Bullis S 600/2-12
10601 Falls Rd 20854 301-299-8500
Dr. Gerald Boarman, hdmstr. Fax 299-9050
Connelly S of the Holy Child 300/6-12
9029 Bradley Blvd 20854 301-365-0955
Dr. Shannon Gomez, hdmstr. Fax 365-0981
German S Washington DC 600/PK-12
8617 Chateau Dr 20854 301-365-4400
Petra Palenzatis, head sch Fax 365-3905
Heights S 500/3-12
10400 Seven Locks Rd 20854 301-365-4300
Alvaro de Vicente, hdmstr. Fax 365-4303
McLean S 400/K-12
8224 Lochinver Ln 20854 301-299-8277
Michael Saxenian, head sch Fax 299-1639
Muslim Community S / Alim Academy 100/PK-12
7917 Montrose Rd 20854 301-340-6713
Somayyah Nahidian M.Ed., prin. Fax 340-7339
St. Andrew's Episcopal S 500/3-12
8804 Postoak Rd 20854 301-983-5200
Robert Kosasky, head sch Fax 983-4710

**Prince Frederick, Calvert, Pop. 2,434**
Calvert County SD 16,500/PK-12
1305 Dares Beach Rd 20678 410-535-1700
Dr. Daniel Curry, supt. Fax 535-7476
www.calvertnet.k12.md.us
Calvert HS 1,200/9-12
520 Fox Run Blvd 20678 410-535-7330
Susan Johnson, prin. Fax 535-7200
Calvert MS 600/6-8
655 Chesapeake Blvd 20678 410-535-7355
Zach Seawell, prin. Fax 535-7430
Career & Technology Academy Vo/Tech
330 Dorsey Rd 20678 410-535-7450
Mark Wilding, prin. Fax 535-7418
Other Schools – See Huntingtown, Lusby, Owings

**Princess Anne, Somerset, Pop. 3,212**
Somerset County SD
Supt. — See Westover
Washington HS & Academy 600/8-12
10902 Old Princess Anne Rd 21853 410-651-0480
Sidney Hankerson, prin. Fax 651-0235

University of Maryland Eastern Shore Post-Sec.
11868 Academic Oval 21853 410-651-2200

**Pylesville, Harford, Pop. 684**
Harford County SD
Supt. — See Bel Air
North Harford HS 1,400/9-12
211 Pylesville Rd 21132 410-638-3650
Colin Carr, prin. Fax 638-3666
North Harford MS 1,000/6-8
112 Pylesville Rd 21132 410-638-3658
Karl Wickman, prin. Fax 638-3669

**Randallstown, Baltimore, Pop. 31,696**
Baltimore County SD
Supt. — See Towson
Deer Park Magnet MS 1,200/6-8
9830 Winands Rd 21133 410-887-0726
Quinhon Goodlowe, prin. Fax 887-0704
Randallstown HS 1,100/9-12
4000 Offutt Rd 21133 410-887-0748
Aubrey Brown, prin. Fax 887-0759

**Reisterstown, Baltimore, Pop. 25,217**
Baltimore County SD
Supt. — See Towson
Franklin HS 1,500/9-12
12000 Reisterstown Rd 21136 410-887-1119
Patrick McCusker, prin. Fax 833-4434
Franklin MS 1,300/6-8
10 Cockeys Mill Rd 21136 410-887-1114
Charlyn Maul, prin. Fax 517-2548

Maryland Beauty Academy Post-Sec.
152 Chartley Dr 21136 410-517-0442

**Ridgely, Caroline, Pop. 1,595**
Caroline County SD
Supt. — See Denton
Caroline Career and Technology Center Vo/Tech
10855 Central Ave 21660 410-479-0100
Eugene Smith, prin. Fax 479-1308
North Caroline HS 1,000/9-12
10990 River Rd 21660 410-479-2332
Dr. Michael Smith, prin. Fax 479-2743

**Rising Sun, Cecil, Pop. 2,742**
Cecil County SD
Supt. — See Elkton
Rising Sun MS 700/6-8
289 Pearl St 21911 410-658-5535
Richard Edwards, prin. Fax 658-9173

**Riverdale, Prince George's, Pop. 5,120**
Prince George's County SD
Supt. — See Upper Marlboro
Parkdale HS 2,200/9-12
6001 Good Luck Rd 20737 301-513-5700
Tanya Washington, prin. Fax 513-5209
Wirt MS 800/6-8
62nd Pl and Tuckerman St 20737 301-985-1720
Roger Prince, prin. Fax 985-2135

**Rock Hall, Kent, Pop. 1,286**
Kent County SD 2,000/PK-12
5608 Boundary Ave 21661 410-778-7113
Dr. Karen Couch, supt. Fax 778-2350
www.kent.k12.md.us
Other Schools – See Chestertown, Worton

**Rockville, Montgomery, Pop. 59,311**
Montgomery County SD 144,500/PK-12
850 Hungerford Dr 20850 301-309-6277
Larry Bowers, supt. Fax 279-3205
www.montgomeryschoolsmd.org
Blair Ewing Center Alt
14501 Avery Rd 20853 301-279-4920
Dr. Ira Thomas, prin. Fax 279-4962
Frost MS 1,100/6-8
9201 Scott Dr 20850 301-279-3949
Dr. Joey Jones, prin. Fax 279-3956
Magruder HS 1,700/9-12
5939 Muncaster Mill Rd 20855 301-840-4600
Leroy Evans, prin. Fax 840-4617
Montgomery HS 2,100/9-12
250 Richard Montgomery Dr 20852 301-610-8000
Damon Monteleone, prin. Fax 279-8428
Parkland MS 800/6-8
4610 W Frankfort Dr 20853 301-438-5700
Khanny Yang, prin. Fax 460-2699
Redland MS 500/6-8
6505 Muncaster Mill Rd 20855 301-840-4680
Everett Davis, prin. Fax 670-2231
Rockville HS 1,300/9-12
2100 Baltimore Rd 20851 301-517-8105
Billie-Jean Bensen, prin. Fax 517-8288
Tilden MS 500/7-8
11211 Old Georgetown Rd 20852 301-230-5930
Irina LaGrange, prin. Fax 230-5991
West MS 1,100/6-8
651 Great Falls Rd 20850 301-279-3979
Craig Staton, prin. Fax 517-8216
Wood MS 900/6-8
14615 Bauer Dr 20853 301-460-2150
Dr. Traci Townsend, prin. Fax 460-2104
Wootton HS 2,300/9-12
2100 Wootton Pkwy 20850 301-279-8550
Dr. Michael Doran, prin. Fax 279-8569
Other Schools – See Bethesda, Burtonsville, Clarksburg, Damascus, Gaithersburg, Germantown, Kensington, Olney, Poolesville, Potomac, Sandy Spring, Silver Spring

Berman Hebrew Academy 700/PK-12
13300 Arctic Ave 20853 301-962-9400
Montgomery College Post-Sec.
51 Mannakee St 20850 240-567-5000
Montrose Christian S 200/PK-12
5100 Randolph Rd 20852 301-770-5335
Dr. Ken Fentress, chncllr. Fax 881-7345
Omega Studios School of Applied Arts Post-Sec.
5609 Fishers Ln 20852 301-230-9100
School for Tomorrow 50/4-12
4511 Bestor Dr 20853 301-460-4747
Alan Shusterman, head sch
Smith Jewish Day S 700/7-12
11710 Hunters Ln 20852 301-881-1400
Rabbi Mitchel Malkus, head sch Fax 230-1986
Strayer University Post-Sec.
4 Research Pl Ste 100 20850 301-548-5500

**Rosedale, Baltimore, Pop. 18,880**

Community College of Baltimore County Post-Sec.
7201 Rossville Blvd 21237 443-840-2222

**Saint Marys City, Saint Mary's, Pop. 3,200**

St. Mary's College of Maryland Post-Sec.
18952 E Fisher Rd 20686 240-895-2000

**Saint Michaels, Talbot, Pop. 1,017**
Talbot County SD
Supt. — See Easton
Saint Michaels MSHS 400/7-12
200 Seymour Ave 21663 410-745-2852
Helga Einhorn, prin. Fax 745-9939

**Salisbury, Wicomico, Pop. 29,461**
Wicomico County SD 14,500/PK-12
PO Box 1538 21802 410-677-4400
Dr. John Fredericksen, supt. Fax 677-4444
www.wcboe.org
Bennett HS 1,400/9-12
300 E College Ave 21804 410-677-5141
Steve Grudis, prin. Fax 677-5126
Career Technology Education Vo/Tech
1015 Beaglin Park Dr 21804 410-677-5144
Choices Academy Alt
28929 Adventist Dr 21801 410-677-5220
Christel Savage, prin. Fax 677-5225
Parkside HS 1,100/9-12
1015 Beaglin Park Dr 21804 410-677-5143
Kim Pinhey, prin. Fax 677-5104
Salisbury MS 900/6-8
607 Morris St 21801 410-677-5149
Amy Eskridge, prin. Fax 677-5122

Wicomico HS 1,100/9-12
201 Long Ave 21804 410-677-5146
Don Brady, prin. Fax 677-5151
Wicomico MS 600/6-8
635 E Main St 21804 410-677-5145
Kelley Springston, prin. Fax 677-5197
Evening HS Adult
201 Long Ave 21804 410-677-4537
David Harner, admin. Fax 677-4418
Other Schools – See Fruitland, Mardela Springs

---

Del-Mar-Va Beauty Academy Post-Sec.
111 Milford St 21804 410-742-7929
Salisbury Christian S 600/PK-12
807 Parker Rd 21804 410-546-0661
Dr. Robert Burris, hdmstr. Fax 546-4674
Salisbury School 300/PK-12
6279 Hobbs Rd 21804 410-742-4464
Ed Cowell, hdmstr. Fax 742-9875
Salisbury University Post-Sec.
1101 Camden Ave 21801 410-543-6000
Wor-Wic Community College Post-Sec.
32000 Campus Dr 21804 410-334-2800

**Sandy Spring, Montgomery, Pop. 3,092**
Montgomery County SD
Supt. — See Rockville
Sherwood HS 2,100/9-12
300 Olney Sandy Spring Rd 20860 301-924-3200
William Gregory, prin. Fax 924-3220

---

Sandy Spring Friends S 600/PK-12
16923 Norwood Rd 20860 301-774-7455
Thomas Gibian, hdmstr. Fax 924-1115

**Severn, Anne Arundel, Pop. 42,378**
Anne Arundel County SD
Supt. — See Annapolis
Center of Applied Technology-North Vo/Tech
800 Stevenson Rd 21144 410-969-3100
Dan Schaffhauser, prin. Fax 696-3684

---

Annapolis Area Christian S 800/PK-12
109 Burns Crossing Rd 21144 410-519-5300
Rick Kempton, supt. Fax 573-6866
Archbishop Spalding HS 1,200/9-12
8080 New Cut Rd 21144 410-969-9105
Lewis VanWambeke, prin. Fax 969-1026

**Severna Park, Anne Arundel, Pop. 37,032**
Anne Arundel County SD
Supt. — See Annapolis
Severna Park HS 1,900/9-12
60 Robinson Rd 21146 410-544-0900
Patrick Bathras, prin. Fax 647-2978
Severna Park MS 1,400/6-8
450 Jumpers Hole Rd 21146 410-647-7900
Sharon Hansen, prin. Fax 431-5376
Severna Park Evening HS Adult
60 Robinson Rd 21146 410-544-0182
Sonja Davenport, admin.

---

Severn S 600/6-12
201 Water St 21146 410-647-7700
Douglas Lagarde, hdmstr. Fax 544-9455

**Silver Spring, Montgomery, Pop. 69,258**
Montgomery County SD
Supt. — See Rockville
Argyle MS 800/6-8
2400 Bel Pre Rd 20906 301-460-2400
James Allrich, prin. Fax 460-2423
Blair HS 2,800/9-12
51 University Blvd E 20901 301-649-2800
Renay Johnson, prin. Fax 649-2830
Blake HS 1,800/9-12
300 Norwood Rd 20905 301-879-1300
Christopher Berry, prin. Fax 879-1306
Briggs-Chaney MS 900/6-8
1901 Rainbow Dr 20905 301-989-6000
Dr. Tamitha Campbell, prin. Fax 989-6020
Eastern MS 900/6-8
300 University Blvd E 20901 301-650-6650
Casey Crouse, prin. Fax 650-6657
Edison HS of Technology Vo/Tech
12501 Dalewood Dr 20906 301-929-2175
Peter Cahall, prin. Fax 929-2177
Kennedy HS 1,700/9-12
1901 Randolph Rd 20902 301-929-2100
Joe Rubens, prin. Fax 929-2240
Key MS 900/6-8
910 Schindler Dr 20903 301-422-5600
Yolanda Stanislaus, prin. Fax 434-1375
Lee MS 600/6-8
11800 Monticello Ave 20902 301-649-8100
Kimberly Hayden Williams, prin. Fax 649-8110
Loiederman MS 800/6-8
12701 Goodhill Rd 20906 301-929-2282
Nicole Sosik, prin. Fax 962-5993
Northwood HS 1,500/9-12
919 University Blvd W 20901 301-649-8088
Mildred Charley-Greene, prin. Fax 649-8285
Silver Spring International MS 800/6-8
313 Wayne Ave 20910 301-650-6544
Karen Bryant, prin. Fax 562-5244
Sligo MS 400/6-8
1401 Dennis Ave 20902 301-649-8121
Cary Dimmick, prin. Fax 649-8145
Springbrook HS 1,700/9-12
201 Valley Brook Dr 20904 301-989-5700
Samuel Rivera, prin. Fax 622-1875
Takoma Park MS 800/6-8
7611 Piney Branch Rd 20910 301-650-6444
Alicia Deeny, prin. Fax 650-6430
Wheaton HS 1,200/9-12
12601 Dalewood Dr 20906 301-929-2050
Dr. Debra Mugge, prin. Fax 929-2081

White Oak MS 700/6-8
12201 New Hampshire Ave 20904 301-989-5780
Virginia de los Santos, prin. Fax 989-5696

---

Barrie S 300/PK-12
13500 Layhill Rd 20906 301-576-2800
Dr. Charles Abelmann, hdmstr. Fax 576-2803
Columbia College Post-Sec.
12125 Veirs Mill Rd 20906 301-929-0565
Everest Institute Post-Sec.
8757 Georgia Ave Ste 650 20910 301-495-4400
Griggs International Academy Post-Sec.
PO Box 4437 20914 301-680-6570
Griggs University Post-Sec.
PO Box 4437 20914 301-680-6570
Holy Cross Hospital Post-Sec.
1500 Forest Glen Rd 20910 301-905-1216
Medtech College Post-Sec.
1100 Wayne Ave Ste 100 20910 301-608-2300
Montgomery Beauty School Post-Sec.
8736 Arliss St 20901 301-459-2509
National Labor College Post-Sec.
10000 New Hampshire Ave 20903 301-431-6400
Nora S 100/9-12
955 Sligo Ave 20910 301-495-6672
Dave Mullen, head sch Fax 495-7829
Siena S 100/4-12
1300 Forest Glen Rd 20901 301-244-3600
Jilly Darefsky, head sch Fax 244-3601
Yeshiva College of the Nations Capital Post-Sec.
1216 Arcola Ave 20902 301-593-2534
Yeshiva of Greater Washington - Boys Div 100/7-12
1216 Arcola Ave 20902 301-649-7077
Rabbi Yitzchok Merkin, hdmstr. Fax 649-7053
Yeshiva of Greater Washington-Girls Div 200/7-12
2010 Linden Ln 20910 301-962-5111
Rabbi Yitzchok Merkin, hdmstr. Fax 962-8372

**Smithsburg, Washington, Pop. 2,924**
Washington County SD
Supt. — See Hagerstown
Smithsburg HS 800/9-12
66 N Main St 21783 301-766-8337
Michael Chilcutt, prin. Fax 824-2617
Smithsburg MS 700/6-8
68 N Main St 21783 301-766-8353
Dr. Stephen Tarason, prin. Fax 824-5147

**Snow Hill, Worcester, Pop. 2,063**
Worcester County SD
Supt. — See Newark
Snow Hill HS 300/9-12
305 S Church St 21863 410-632-5270
Kimberly Purvis, prin. Fax 632-5279
Snow Hill MS 400/4-8
522 Coulbourne Ln 21863 410-632-5240
Christina Welch, prin. Fax 632-5249

**Spencerville, Montgomery, Pop. 1,516**

---

Spencerville Adventist Academy 300/PK-12
2502 Spencerville Rd 20868 301-421-9101
Brian Kittleson, prin. Fax 421-0007

**Springdale, Prince George's, Pop. 2,957**
Prince George's County SD
Supt. — See Upper Marlboro
Flowers HS 2,400/9-12
10001 Ardwick Ardmore Rd 20774 301-636-8000
Gorman Brown, prin. Fax 636-8008

**Stevenson, Baltimore**

---

St. Timothy's S 200/9-12
8400 Greenspring Ave 21153 410-486-7400
Randy Stevens, hdmstr. Fax 486-1167
Stevenson University Post-Sec.
1525 Greenspring Valley Rd 21153 410-486-7000

**Stevensville, Queen Anne's, Pop. 6,708**
Queen Anne's County SD
Supt. — See Centreville
Kent Island HS 1,200/9-12
900 Love Point Rd 21666 410-604-2070
John Schrecongost, prin. Fax 604-2089
Matapeake MS 400/6-8
671 Romancoke Rd 21666 410-643-7330
Dr. Angela Holocker, prin. Fax 643-7445
Stevensville MS 500/6-8
610 Main St 21666 410-643-3194
Kevin Kintop, prin. Fax 643-3046

**Sudlersville, Queen Anne's, Pop. 476**
Queen Anne's County SD
Supt. — See Centreville
Sudlersville MS 300/6-8
600 Charles St 21668 410-438-3151
John Lischner, prin. Fax 438-3489

**Suitland, Prince George's, Pop. 25,409**
Prince George's County SD
Supt. — See Upper Marlboro
Drew-Freeman MS 700/7-8
2600 Brooks Dr 20746 301-817-0900
LeTrecia Gloster, prin. Fax 817-0915
Green Valley Academy 100/Alt
2001 Shadyside Ave 20746 301-817-3100
Gordon Libby, prin. Fax 817-3176

**Sykesville, Carroll, Pop. 4,375**
Carroll County SD
Supt. — See Westminster
Century HS 1,200/9-12
355 Ronsdale Rd 21784 410-386-4400
Troy Barnes, prin. Fax 386-4413
Oklahoma Road MS 800/6-8
6300 Oklahoma Rd 21784 410-751-3600
Erin Brilhart, prin. Fax 751-3604

South Carroll HS 1,100/9-12
1300 W Old Liberty Rd 21784 410-751-3575
Diane Cooper, prin. Fax 751-3587
Sykesville MS 800/6-8
7301 Springfield Ave 21784 410-751-3545
Ralph Billings, prin. Fax 751-3573

**Takoma Park, Montgomery, Pop. 16,094**

---

Don Bosco Cristo Rey HS 300/9-12
1010 Larch Ave 20912 301-891-4750
Larry Savoy, prin. Fax 270-1459
Montgomery College Post-Sec.
7600 Takoma Ave 20912 240-567-5000
Takoma Academy 200/9-12
8120 Carroll Ave 20912 301-434-4700
Carla Thrower, prin. Fax 434-4814
Washington Adventist Hospital Post-Sec.
7600 Carroll Ave 20912 301-891-7600
Washington Adventist University Post-Sec.
7600 Flower Ave 20912 301-891-4000

**Taneytown, Carroll, Pop. 6,558**
Carroll County SD
Supt. — See Westminster
Northwest MS 500/6-8
99 Kings Dr 21787 410-751-3270
David Watkins, prin. Fax 751-3275

**Temple Hills, Prince George's, Pop. 7,677**
Prince George's County SD
Supt. — See Upper Marlboro
Crossland HS 1,300/9-12
6901 Temple Hill Rd 20748 301-449-4800
Theresa Moseley-Fax, prin. Fax 449-4801
Marshall MS 800/6-8
4909 Brinkley Rd 20748 301-702-7540
DeMarco Clark, prin. Fax 702-7555
Stoddert MS 600/6-8
2501 Olson St 20748 301-702-7500
Michael Gilchrist, prin. Fax 702-7515
Crossland Evening HS Adult
6901 Temple Hill Rd 20748 301-449-4994
William Kitchings, prin. Fax 449-2126

**Thurmont, Frederick, Pop. 6,091**
Frederick County SD
Supt. — See Frederick
Catoctin HS 1,000/9-12
14745 Sabillasville Rd 21788 240-236-8100
Bernard Quesada, prin. Fax 236-8101
Thurmont MS 700/6-8
408 E Main St 21788 240-236-5100
Jennifer Powell, prin. Fax 236-5101

**Timonium, Baltimore, Pop. 9,759**
Baltimore County SD
Supt. — See Towson
Dulaney HS 1,900/9-12
255 E Padonia Rd 21093 410-887-7633
Samuel Wynkoop, prin. Fax 666-8915

---

R. Paul Academy of Cosmetology Arts/Sci Post-Sec.
1811 York Rd Ste B 21093 410-252-4481

**Towson, Baltimore, Pop. 54,024**
Baltimore County SD 104,400/PK-12
6901 N Charles St 21204 410-887-4554
S. Dallas Dance Ph.D., supt. Fax 887-4309
www.bcps.org
Other Schools – See Baltimore, Catonsville, Cockeysville, Dundalk, Lutherville, Monkton, Owings Mills, Parkton, Parkville, Randallstown, Reisterstown, Timonium

---

Concordia Prep S 300/6-12
1145 Concordia Dr 21286 410-825-2323
Alan Freeman, admin. Fax 825-2506
Loyola Blakefield HS 1,000/6-12
500 Chestnut Ave 21204 410-823-0601
Anthony Day, pres. Fax 823-5277
Medix School Post-Sec.
700 York Rd 21204 410-337-5155
Notre Dame Preparatory S 800/6-12
815 Hampton Ln 21286 410-825-0590
Laurie Jones, prin. Fax 321-4809
TESST College of Technology Post-Sec.
803 Glen Eagles Ct 21286 410-296-5350
Towson State University Post-Sec.
8000 York Rd 21252 410-704-2000

**Union Bridge, Carroll, Pop. 956**
Carroll County SD
Supt. — See Westminster
Key HS 1,000/9-12
3825 Bark Hill Rd 21791 410-751-3320
John Baugher, prin. Fax 751-3325

**Upper Marlboro, Prince George's, Pop. 606**
Prince George's County SD 120,700/PK-12
14201 School Ln 20772 301-952-6000
Dr. Kevin Maxwell, admin. Fax 627-6576
www.pgcps.org
Douglass HS 1,100/9-12
8000 Croom Rd 20772 301-952-2400
Eddie Scott, prin. Fax 627-3377
Kettering MS 500/6-8
65 Herrington Dr 20774 301-808-4060
Amin Salaam, prin. Fax 499-3128
Largo HS 1,200/9-12
505 Largo Rd 20774 301-808-8880
Afie Mirshah-Nayar, prin. Fax 808-4066
Madison MS 900/6-8
7300 Woodyard Rd 20772 301-599-2422
Courtney King, prin. Fax 599-2562
Wise HS 2,500/9-12
12650 Brooke Ln 20772 301-780-2100
Charoscar Coleman, prin. Fax 780-2112

Other Schools – See Accokeek, Adelphi, Beltsville, Bladensburg, Bowie, Brandywine, Capitol Heights, Cheltenham, Clinton, Forestville, Fort Washington, Greenbelt, Hyattsville, Landover, Lanham Seabrook, Largo, Laurel, Mitchellville, New Carrollton, Oxon Hill, Riverdale, Springdale, Suitland, Temple Hills

---

Clinton Christian S 500/PK-12
6707 Woodyard Rd 20772 301-599-9600
Carlos Williams, prin. Fax 599-9603
Riverdale Baptist S 700/PK-12
1133 Largo Rd 20774 301-249-7000
Eric Harrison, head sch Fax 249-3425

**Waldorf, Charles, Pop. 64,982**
Charles County SD
Supt. — See La Plata
Davis MS 1,200/6-8
2495 Davis Rd 20603 301-638-0858
Kimberly McClarin, prin. Fax 638-3562
Hanson MS 800/6-8
12350 Vivian Adams Dr 20601 301-645-4520
Kathy-Lynn Kiessling, prin. Fax 870-1182
Mattawoman MS 1,000/6-8
10145 Berry Rd 20603 301-645-7708
Sonia Jones, prin. Fax 638-0043
North Point HS 2,200/9-12
2500 Davis Rd 20603 301-753-1759
Michael Simms, prin. Fax 885-2347
St. Charles HS 900/9-12
5305 Piney Church Rd 20602 301-753-2090
Richard Conley, prin. Fax 396-4135
Stoddert MS 700/6-8
2040 Saint Thomas Dr 20602 301-645-1334
Kenneth Schroeck, prin. Fax 870-1183
Stone HS 1,400/9-12
3785 Leonardtown Rd 20601 301-645-2601
Michael Meiser, prin. Fax 932-4278
Westlake HS 1,600/9-12
3300 Middletown Rd 20603 301-645-8857
Chrystal Benson, prin. Fax 932-8583

---

Aaron's Academy of Beauty Post-Sec.
11690 Doolittle Dr 20602 301-645-3681
Grace Christian Academy of Maryland 400/PK-12
13000 Zekiah Dr 20601 301-645-0406
Matt Duranske, dir. Fax 645-7463

**Walkersville, Frederick, Pop. 5,663**
Frederick County SD
Supt. — See Frederick
Walkersville HS 1,200/9-12
81 W Frederick St 21793 240-236-7200
Tracey Franklin, prin. Fax 236-7250
Walkersville MS 800/6-8
55 W Frederick St 21793 240-236-4400
Stacey Hiltner, prin. Fax 236-4401

**Westminster, Carroll, Pop. 18,162**
Carroll County SD 26,900/PK-12
125 N Court St 21157 410-751-3000
Stephen Guthrie, supt. Fax 751-3030
www.carrollk12.org/
Carroll County Career & Technology Ctr Vo/Tech
1229 Washington Rd 21157 410-751-3669
William Eckles, prin. Fax 751-3677
Crossroads MS Alt
45 Kate Wagner Rd 21157 410-751-3691
Bryan Wetzel, prin.
Gateway S 100/Alt
45 Kate Wagner Rd 21157 410-751-3691
Bryan Wetzel, admin. Fax 751-3687
Westminster East MS 700/6-8
121 Longwell Ave 21157 410-751-3656
Christian Roemer, prin. Fax 751-3660
Westminster HS 1,700/9-12
1225 Washington Rd 21157 410-751-3630
Jeffrey Hopkins, prin. Fax 751-3640
Westminster West MS 1,000/6-8
60 Monroe St 21157 410-751-3661
Amy Gromada, prin. Fax 751-3667
Winters Mill HS 1,200/9-12
560 Gorsuch Rd 21157 410-386-1500
Eric King, prin. Fax 386-1513
Other Schools – See Eldersburg, Hampstead, Manchester, Mount Airy, New Windsor, Sykesville, Taneytown, Union Bridge

---

Carroll Christian S 200/PK-12
550 Baltimore Blvd 21157 410-876-3838
Carroll Community College Post-Sec.
1601 Washington Rd 21157 410-386-8000
McDaniel College Post-Sec.
2 College Hl 21157 410-848-7000

**Westover, Somerset**
Somerset County SD 3,100/PK-12
7982A Tawes Campus Dr 21871 410-651-1616
Dr. John Gaddis, supt. Fax 651-2931
www.somerset.k12.md.us
Tawes Technology & Career Center Vo/Tech
7982 Tawes Campus Dr 21871 410-651-2285
David Elebash, prin. Fax 651-3154
Other Schools – See Crisfield, Marion Station, Princess Anne

---

Holly Grove Christian S 500/PK-12
7317 Mennonite Church Rd 21871 410-957-0222
Michael Rohrer, prin. Fax 957-4250

**White Plains, Charles, Pop. 3,560**

---

Southern Maryland Christian Academy 300/PK-12
PO Box 1668 20695 301-870-2550
Matthew Gaines, dir. Fax 934-2855

**Williamsport, Washington, Pop. 2,115**
Washington County SD
Supt. — See Hagerstown
Springfield MS 800/6-8
334 Sunset Ave 21795 301-766-8389
Jennifer Ruppenthal, prin. Fax 766-8401
Williamsport HS 1,000/9-12
5 S Clifton Dr 21795 301-766-8423
Heath Wilcox, prin. Fax 223-9610

---

Gateway Christian Academy 100/PK-12
PO Box 590 21795 301-582-4595
Renee Wyand, prin. Fax 223-5972

**Worton, Kent, Pop. 248**
Kent County SD
Supt. — See Rock Hall
Kent County HS 600/9-12
25301 Lambs Meadow Rd 21678 410-778-4540
Tracey Williams, prin. Fax 778-4266

**Wye Mills, Talbot**

---

Chesapeake College Post-Sec.
PO Box 8 21679 410-822-5400

# MASSACHUSETTS

## MASSACHUSETTS DEPARTMENT OF EDUCATION
**75 Pleasant St, Malden 02148-4906**
**Telephone 781-388-3000**
**Fax 781-388-3770**
**Website http://www.doe.mass.edu**

Commissioner of Education Mitchell Chester

## MASSACHUSETTS BOARD OF EDUCATION
**75 Pleasant St, Malden 02148-4906**

Chairperson Maura Banta

## PUBLIC, PRIVATE AND CATHOLIC SECONDARY SCHOOLS

**Abington, Plymouth, Pop. 15,563**
Abington SD 1,400/PK-12
171 Adams St 02351 781-982-2150
Peter Schafer, supt. Fax 982-2157
www.abingtonps.org
Abington HS 500/9-12
201 Gliniewicz Way 02351 781-982-2160
Teresa Sullivan-Cruz, prin. Fax 982-0061
Frolio MS 300/7-8
1071 Washington St 02351 781-982-2170
Roseanne Kurposka, prin. Fax 982-2173

**Acton, Middlesex**
Acton-Boxborough Regional SD 5,800/PK-12
16 Charter Rd 01720 978-264-4700
Glenn Brand, supt. Fax 264-3340
www.abschools.org
Acton-Boxborough Regional HS 2,000/9-12
36 Charter Rd 01720 978-264-4700
JoAnn Campbell, prin. Fax 264-3345
Grey JHS 1,000/7-8
16 Charter Rd 01720 978-264-4700
Andrew Shen, prin. Fax 264-3343

**Acushnet, Bristol, Pop. 3,170**
Acushnet SD 1,000/PK-8
708 Middle Rd Ste 1 02743 508-998-0260
Stephen Donovan Ed.D., supt. Fax 998-0262
www.acushnetschools.us
Ford MS 500/5-8
708 Middle Rd 02743 508-998-0265
Helder Angelo, prin. Fax 998-7316

**Agawam, Hampden, Pop. 28,599**
Agawam SD
Supt. — See Feeding Hills
Agawam HS 1,400/9-12
760 Cooper St 01001 413-821-0521
Steven Lemanski, prin. Fax 821-0536
Doering S 600/5-8
68 Main St 01001 413-789-1400
Susan Federico, prin. Fax 789-7337

**Amesbury, Essex, Pop. 12,109**
Amesbury SD 2,300/PK-12
5 Highland St 01913 978-388-0507
Gary S. Reese Ed.D., supt. Fax 388-8315
schools.amesburyma.gov
Amesbury HS 600/9-12
5 Highland St 01913 978-388-4800
Norman Hamond, prin. Fax 388-3393
Amesbury MS 700/5-8
220 Main St 01913 978-388-0515
Michael Curry, prin. Fax 388-1626

**Amherst, Hampshire, Pop. 17,824**
Amherst-Pelham SD 1,500/7-12
170 Chestnut St 01002 413-362-1810
Maria Geryk, supt. Fax 549-6108
www.arps.org/
Amherst Regional HS 1,100/9-12
21 Mattoon St 01002 413-362-1700
Mark Jackson, prin. Fax 549-9704
Amherst Regional MS 500/7-8
170 Chestnut St 01002 413-362-1850
Marisa Mendonsa, prin. Fax 549-9812

---

Amherst College Post-Sec.
PO Box 5000 01002 413-542-2000
Hampshire College Post-Sec.
893 West St 01002 413-549-4600
University of Massachusetts 01003 Post-Sec.
413-545-0111

**Andover, Essex, Pop. 8,592**
Andover SD 6,200/PK-12
36 Bartlet St 01810 978-623-8501
Sheldon Berman Ed.D., supt. Fax 623-8505
www.aps1.net
Andover HS 1,800/9-12
80 Shawsheen Rd 01810 978-623-8632
Philip Conrad, prin. Fax 623-8636
Andover West MS 500/6-8
70 Shawsheen Rd 01810 978-623-8700
Becky Franks, prin. Fax 623-8720
Doherty MS 600/6-8
50 Bartlet St 01810 978-623-8750
Robin Wilson, prin. Fax 623-8770
Wood Hill MS 400/6-8
11 Cross St 01810 978-623-8925
Patrick Bucco, prin. Fax 623-8929

Greater Lawrence Technical SD
57 River Rd 01810 978-686-0194
John Lavoie, supt. Fax 687-6209
www.glts.net
Greater Lawrence Technical S Vo/Tech
57 River Rd 01810 978-686-0194
Elizabeth Freedman, prin. Fax 687-6209

---

Massachusetts School of Law at Andover Post-Sec.
500 Federal St 01810 978-681-0800
Phillips Academy 1,100/9-12
180 Main St 01810 978-749-4000
John Palfrey, head sch Fax 749-4068

**Arlington, Middlesex, Pop. 41,750**
Arlington SD 4,800/PK-12
869 Massachusetts Ave 02476 781-316-3523
Kathleen Bodie, supt. Fax 316-3509
www.arlington.k12.ma.us
Arlington HS 1,200/9-12
869 Massachusetts Ave 02476 781-316-3591
Matthew Janger, prin. Fax 316-3504
Ottoson MS 1,000/6-8
63 Acton St 02476 781-316-3745
Timothy Ruggere, prin. Fax 641-5436

---

Arlington Catholic HS 700/9-12
16 Medford St 02474 781-646-7770
Stephen Biagioni, prin. Fax 648-8345

**Ashburnham, Worcester**
Ashburnham-Westminster Regional SD 2,300/PK-12
11 Oakmont Dr 01430 978-827-1434
Dr. Gary Mazzola, supt. Fax 827-5969
www.awrsd.org
Oakmont Regional HS 700/9-12
9 Oakmont Dr 01430 978-827-5907
David Uminski, prin. Fax 827-1413
Overlook MS 600/6-8
10 Oakmont Dr 01430 978-827-1425
Philip Saisa, prin. Fax 827-1423

---

Cushing Academy 400/9-12
PO Box 8000 01430 978-827-7000
Christopher Torino, hdmstr. Fax 827-7500

**Ashland, Middlesex, Pop. 12,066**
Ashland SD 2,700/PK-12
87 W Union St 01721 508-881-0150
James Adams, supt. Fax 881-0161
www.ashland.k12.ma.us
Ashland HS 700/9-12
65 E Union St 01721 508-881-0177
Kelley St. Coeur, prin. Fax 881-0186
Ashland MS 600/6-8
87 W Union St 01721 508-881-0167
David DiGirolamo, prin. Fax 881-0169

**Athol, Worcester, Pop. 8,127**
Athol-Royalston SD 1,400/PK-12
1062 Pleasant St 01331 978-249-2400
Anthony Polito, supt. Fax 249-2402
www.arrsd.org/
Athol HS 400/9-12
2363 Main St 01331 978-249-2435
Mitchel Aho, prin. Fax 249-7217
Athol-Royalston MS 400/5-8
1062 Pleasant St 01331 978-249-2430
Thomas Telicki, prin. Fax 249-0055

**Attleboro, Bristol, Pop. 42,657**
Attleboro SD 5,900/PK-12
100 Rathbun Willard Dr 02703 508-222-0012
Kenneth Sheehan, supt. Fax 223-1577
www.attleboroschools.com
Attleboro HS 1,800/9-12
100 Rathbun Willard Dr 02703 508-222-5150
William Runey, prin. Fax 223-1579
Brennan MS 600/5-8
320 Rathbun Willard Dr 02703 508-222-6260
Karen Saltzman, prin. Fax 223-1555
Coelho MS 700/5-8
99 Brown St 02703 508-761-7551
Andrew Boles, prin. Fax 399-6506
Wamsutta MS 500/5-8
300 Locust St 02703 508-223-1540
Joseph Connor, prin. Fax 226-2087

---

Bishop Feehan HS 1,000/9-12
70 Holcott Dr 02703 508-226-6223
Sean Kane, pres. Fax 226-7696

**Auburn, Worcester, Pop. 15,005**
Auburn SD 2,300/K-12
5 West St 01501 508-832-7755
Dr. Maryellen Brunelle, supt. Fax 832-7757
www.auburn.k12.ma.us
Auburn HS 700/9-12
99 Auburn St 01501 508-832-7711
Casey Handfield, prin. Fax 832-7710
Auburn MS 500/6-8
9 West St 01501 508-832-7722
Joseph Gagnon, prin. Fax 832-8655

**Avon, Norfolk, Pop. 4,558**
Avon SD 800/PK-12
1 Patrick Clark Dr 02322 508-588-0230
Paul Zinni, supt. Fax 559-1081
www.avon.k12.ma.us/
Avon MSHS 400/7-12
285 W Main St 02322 508-583-4822
Elizabeth York, prin. Fax 588-5501

**Ayer, Middlesex, Pop. 2,780**
Ayer Shirley SD 1,700/PK-12
115 Washington St 01432 978-772-8600
Dr. Mary Malone, supt. Fax 772-7444
www.asrsd.org
Ayer Shirley HS 300/9-12
141 Washington St 01432 978-772-8600
Albert Varga, prin. Fax 772-8615
Other Schools – See Shirley

**Babson Park, Norfolk**

---

Babson College Post-Sec.
231 Forest St 02457 781-235-1200

**Baldwinville, Worcester, Pop. 2,008**
Narragansett Regional SD 1,400/PK-12
462 Baldwinville Rd 01436 978-939-5661
Dr. Stephen Hemman, supt. Fax 939-5179
www.nrsd.org
Narragansett MS 500/5-8
460 Baldwinville Rd 01436 978-393-5928
Peter Cushing, prin. Fax 939-8422
Narragansett Regional HS 400/9-12
464 Baldwinville Rd 01436 978-939-5388
John Jasinski, prin. Fax 939-5723

**Barnstable, Barnstable, Pop. 48,854**

---

Trinity Christian Academy 100/PK-12
979 Mary Dunn Rd 02630 508-790-0114
Ben Haskell, hdmstr. Fax 790-1293

**Barre, Worcester, Pop. 998**
Quabbin SD 2,700/PK-12
872 South St 01005 978-355-4668
Dr. Maureen Marshall, supt. Fax 355-6756
www.qrsd.org
Quabbin Regional HS 800/9-12
800 South St 01005 978-355-4651
Gregory Devine, prin. Fax 355-0163
Quabbin Regional MS 500/7-8
800 South St 01005 978-355-5042
Susanne Musnicki, prin. Fax 355-6104

**Bedford, Middlesex, Pop. 12,996**
Bedford SD 2,400/K-12
97 McMahon Rd 01730 781-275-7588
Jonathan Sills, supt. Fax 275-0885
www.bedford.k12.ma.us

Bedford HS 800/9-12
9 Mudge Way 01730 781-275-1700
Henry Turner, prin. Fax 275-6664
Glenn MS 600/6-8
99 McMahon Rd 01730 781-275-3201
Kevin Tracey, prin. Fax 275-7632

Middlesex Community College Post-Sec.
591 Springs Rd 01730 781-280-3200
National Aviation Academy of New England Post-Sec.
150 Hanscom Dr 01730 781-274-8448

**Belchertown, Hampshire, Pop. 2,339**
Belchertown SD 2,500/PK-12
PO Box 841 01007 413-323-0423
Karol Coffin, supt. Fax 323-0448
www.belchertownps.org
Belchertown HS 800/9-12
142 Springfield Rd 01007 413-323-9419
Christine Vigneux, prin. Fax 323-9406
Jabish Brook MS 400/7-8
62 N Washington St 01007 413-323-0433
Thomas Ruscio, prin. Fax 323-0450

**Bellingham, Norfolk, Pop. 4,778**
Bellingham SD 2,500/PK-12
60 Harpin St 02019 508-883-1706
Peter Marano, supt. Fax 883-0180
www.bellinghamk12.org
Bellingham HS 700/9-12
60 Blackstone St 02019 508-966-3761
Lucas Giguere, prin. Fax 966-4182
Memorial MS 700/5-8
130 Blackstone St 02019 508-883-2330
William Tranter, prin. Fax 883-2037
Primavera Alternative HS 50/Alt
80 Harpin St 02019 508-883-5403
Jeffrey Croteau, dir. Fax 883-5408

**Belmont, Middlesex, Pop. 24,057**
Belmont SD 4,000/PK-12
644 Pleasant St 02478 617-993-5401
John Phelan, supt. Fax 993-5409
www.belmont.k12.ma.us
Belmont HS 1,100/9-12
221 Concord Ave 02478 617-993-5301
Dan Richards, prin. Fax 993-5909
Chenery MS 1,200/5-8
95 Washington St 02478 617-993-5800
Kristen St. George, prin. Fax 993-5809

Belmont Hill S 400/7-12
350 Prospect St 02478 617-484-4410
Dr. Richard Melvoin, hdmstr. Fax 484-4688
Waldorf HS of Massachusetts Bay 100/9-12
160 Lexington St 02478 617-489-6600

**Berkley, Bristol**
Berkley SD 900/PK-8
21 N Main St 02779 508-822-5220
Thomas Lynch, supt. Fax 823-1772
www.berkleypublicschools.org
Berkley MS 400/5-8
21 N Main St 02779 508-884-9434
Kimberly Hebert, prin. Fax 386-1044

**Beverly, Essex, Pop. 38,805**
Beverly SD 4,200/PK-12
502 Cabot St 01915 978-921-6100
Steven Hiersche, supt. Fax 922-6597
www.beverlyschools.org/index2.shtm
Beverly HS 1,300/9-12
100 Sohier Rd 01915 978-921-6132
Sean Gallagher, prin. Fax 927-9460
Briscoe MS 1,000/6-8
7 Sohier Rd 01915 978-921-6103
Matthew Poska, prin. Fax 927-7781

Endicott College Post-Sec.
376 Hale St 01915 978-927-0585
Montserrat College of Art Post-Sec.
23 Essex St 01915 978-921-4242
Waring S 200/6-12
35 Standley St 01915 978-927-8793
Tim Bakland, hdmstr. Fax 921-2107

**Billerica, Middlesex, Pop. 37,609**
Billerica SD 5,600/K-12
365 Boston Rd 01821 978-528-7900
Tim Piwowar, supt. Fax 528-7909
www.billerica.k12.ma.us
Billerica Memorial HS 1,500/9-12
35 River St 01821 978-528-8710
Thomas Murphy, prin. Fax 528-8719
Locke MS 700/6-8
110 Allen Rd 01821 978-528-8650
Anthony Garas, prin. Fax 528-8659
Marshall MS 800/6-8
15 Floyd St 01821 978-528-8671
Michael Rossi, prin. Fax 528-8679

Shawsheen Valley Vocational Technical SD
100 Cook St 01821 978-667-2111
Timothy Broadrick, supt. Fax 663-6272
www.shawsheentech.org
Shawsheen Valley Technical HS Vo/Tech
100 Cook St 01821 978-667-2111
Dr. Robert Kanellas, prin. Fax 663-6272

**Blackstone, Worcester, Pop. 8,023**
Blackstone-Millville Regional SD 1,900/PK-12
175 Lincoln St 01504 508-883-4400
Allen Himmelberger, supt. Fax 883-9892
www.bmrsd.info
Blackstone-Millville Regional HS 500/9-12
175 Lincoln St 01504 508-876-0117
Michael Dudek, prin. Fax 876-1035
Hartnett MS 500/6-8
35 Federal St 01504 508-876-0190
Justin Cameron, prin. Fax 876-0198

**Bolton, Worcester**
Nashoba Regional SD 3,100/PK-12
50 Mechanic St 01740 978-779-0539
Michael Wood Ed.D., supt. Fax 779-5537
www.nrsd.net
Nashoba Regional HS 1,000/9-12
12 Green Rd 01740 978-779-2257
Parry Graham, prin. Fax 779-2720
Other Schools – See Lancaster, Stow

**Boston, Suffolk, Pop. 592,375**
Boston SD 53,300/PK-12
26 Court St Ste 10 02108 617-635-9000
Tommy Chang, supt. Fax 635-9059
www.bostonpublicschools.org
Boston Arts Academy 400/9-12
174 Ipswich St 02215 617-635-6470
Anne Clark, hdmstr. Fax 635-8854
Boston Latin S 2,400/7-12
78 Avenue Louis Pasteur 02115 617-635-8895
Lynne Teta, hdmstr. Fax 635-7883
Boston Middle School Academy 50/Alt
215 Dorchester St 02127 617-635-1534
Yvonne Vest, dir. Fax 635-1539
Fenway HS 300/9-12
174 Ipswich St 02215 617-635-9911
Dr. Peggy Kemp, hdmstr. Fax 635-9204
Quincy Upper S 500/6-12
152 Arlington St 02116 617-635-8940
Richard Chang, prin. Fax 635-8945
Snowden International HS 400/9-12
150 Newbury St 02116 617-635-9989
Eugene Roundtree, hdmstr. Fax 635-9996
Boston Adult Technical Academy Adult
20 Church St 02116 617-635-1542
Benjamin Helfat, hdmstr. Fax 635-6362
Other Schools – See Brighton, Charlestown, Dorchester, East Boston, Hyde Park, Jamaica Plain, Mattapan, Roslindale, Roxbury, South Boston, West Roxbury

Bay State College Post-Sec.
122 Commonwealth Ave 02116 617-217-9000
Benjamin Franklin Inst. of Technology Post-Sec.
41 Berkeley St 02116 617-423-4630
Berklee College of Music Post-Sec.
1140 Boylston St 02215 617-266-1400
Beth Israel Healthcare Post-Sec.
330 Brookline Ave 02215 617-667-2539
Blaine The Beauty Career School Post-Sec.
30 West St 02111 617-266-2661
Boston Architectural College Post-Sec.
320 Newbury St 02115 617-262-5000
Boston Baptist College Post-Sec.
950 Metropolitan Ave 02136 617-364-3510
Boston College HS 1,600/7-12
150 William T Morrissey 02125 617-436-3900
Stephen Hughes, prin. Fax 474-5105
Boston Conservatory Post-Sec.
8 Fenway 02215 617-536-6340
Boston Trinity Academy 200/6-12
17 Hale St 02136 617-364-3700
Frank Guerra, hdmstr. Fax 364-3800
Boston University Post-Sec.
233 Bay State Rd 02215 617-353-2000
Boston University Academy 200/9-12
1 University Rd 02215 617-353-9000
Dr. Ari Betof, head sch Fax 353-8999
Brigham and Women's Hospital Post-Sec.
75 Francis St 02115 617-732-7493
British S of Boston 300/PK-12
416 Pond St 02130 617-522-2261
Paul Wiseman, hdmstr. Fax 522-0385
Bunker Hill Community College Post-Sec.
250 Rutherford Ave 02129 617-228-2000
Cathedral HS 300/7-12
74 Union Park St 02118 617-542-2325
Dr. Oscar Santos, prin. Fax 542-1745
Children's Hospital Post-Sec.
300 Longwood Ave 02115 617-355-6433
Commonwealth S 200/9-12
151 Commonwealth Ave 02116 617-266-7525
William Wharton, head sch Fax 266-5769
Cristo Rey HS 300/9-12
100 Savin Hill Ave 02125 617-825-2580
Jeff Thielman, pres. Fax 825-2613
Emerson College Post-Sec.
120 Boylston St 02116 617-824-8500
Emmanuel College Post-Sec.
400 Fenway 02115 617-735-9715
Fisher College Post-Sec.
118 Beacon St 02116 617-236-8800
Massachusetts College of Art and Design Post-Sec.
621 Huntington Ave 02115 617-879-7000
MCPHS University Post-Sec.
179 Longwood Ave 02115 617-732-2800
MGH Institute of Health Professions Post-Sec.
36 1st Ave 02129 617-726-2947
New England College of Business/Finance Post-Sec.
10 High St Ste 204 02110 617-951-2350
New England College of Optometry Post-Sec.
424 Beacon St 02115 800-824-5526
New England Conservatory of Music Post-Sec.
290 Huntington Ave 02115 617-585-1100
New England Law \ Boston Post-Sec.
154 Stuart St 02116 617-451-0010
New England School of Art & Design Post-Sec.
75 Arlington St 02116 617-573-8785
New England School of Photography Post-Sec.
537 Commonwealth Ave 02215 617-437-1868
Newman Preparatory S 300/9-12
247 Marlborough St 02116 617-267-4530
North Bennet Street School Post-Sec.
150 North St 02109 617-227-0155
Northeastern University Post-Sec.
360 Huntington Ave 02115 617-373-2000
St. Joseph Preparatory HS 200/9-12
617 Cambridge St 02134 617-254-8383
Thomas Nunan, head sch Fax 254-0240
School of the Museum of Fine Arts Post-Sec.
230 Fenway 02115 617-267-6100
Simmons College Post-Sec.
300 Fenway 02115 617-521-2000
Suffolk University Post-Sec.
8 Ashburton Pl 02108 617-573-8000
University of Massachusetts Boston Post-Sec.
100 William T Mrrissey Blvd 02125 617-287-5000
Urban College of Boston Post-Sec.
178 Tremont St 02111 617-348-6359
Veterans Administration Medical Center Post-Sec.
150 S Huntington Ave 02130 617-232-9500
Wentworth Institute of Technology Post-Sec.
550 Huntington Ave 02115 617-989-4590
Wheelock College Post-Sec.
200 Riverway 02215 617-879-2000
Winsor S 400/5-12
103 Pilgrim Rd 02215 617-735-9500
Rachel Friis Stettler, head sch Fax 912-1381

**Bourne, Barnstable, Pop. 1,380**
Bourne SD 2,200/PK-12
36 Sandwich Rd 02532 508-759-0660
Steven Lamarche, supt. Fax 759-1107
www.bourneps.org
Bourne HS 600/9-12
75 Waterhouse Rd 02532 508-759-0670
Amy Cetner, prin. Fax 759-0677
Bourne MS 700/5-8
77 Waterhouse Rd 02532 508-759-0690
Melissa Stafford, prin. Fax 759-0695

Upper Cape Cod Regional Vo-Tech SD
220 Sandwich Rd 02532 508-759-7711
Robert Dutch, supt. Fax 759-7208
www.uppercapetech.com
Upper Cape Cod Regional Technical S Vo/Tech
220 Sandwich Rd 02532 508-759-7711
Roger Forget, prin. Fax 759-7208

**Boxford, Essex, Pop. 2,307**
Masconomet SD 2,100/7-12
20 Endicott Rd 01921 978-887-2323
Kevin Lyons, supt. Fax 887-3573
www.masconomet.org
Masconomet Regional HS 1,300/9-12
20 Endicott Rd 01921 978-887-2323
Laurie Hodgdon, prin. Fax 887-7243
Masconomet Regional MS 800/7-8
20 Endicott Rd 01921 978-887-2323
Dorothy Flaherty, prin. Fax 887-1991

**Boylston, Worcester**
Berlin-Boylston SD 400/PK-12
215 Main St 01505 508-869-2837
Nadine Ekstrom, supt. Fax 869-0023
www.bbrsd.org
Tahanto Regional MSHS 400/6-12
1001 Main St 01505 508-869-2333
Diane Tucceri, prin. Fax 869-0175

**Bradford, See Haverhill**

Bradford Christian Academy 100/1-12
97 Oxford Ave 01835 978-373-7900
Victoria Kennedy, head sch Fax 373-7977

**Braintree, Norfolk, Pop. 33,800**
Braintree SD 5,500/K-12
348 Pond St 02184 781-380-0130
Frank Hackett Ed.D., supt. Fax 380-0146
www.braintreeschools.org
Braintree HS 1,500/9-12
128 Town St 02184 781-848-4000
James Lee, hdmstr. Fax 380-0116
East MS 700/6-8
305 River St 02184 781-380-0170
John Sheehan, prin. Fax 848-4522
South MS 600/6-8
232 Peach St 02184 781-380-0160
Damon Rainie, prin. Fax 380-0164

Archbishop Williams HS 500/9-12
80 Independence Ave 02184 781-843-3636
Dr. Carmen Mariano, prin. Fax 843-3782
Thayer Academy 700/6-12
745 Washington St 02184 781-843-3580
Ted Koskores, hdmstr. Fax 843-2916

**Bridgewater, Plymouth, Pop. 7,639**
Bridgewater-Raynham Regional SD 5,500/PK-12
166 Mount Prospect St 02324 508-279-2140
Derek Swenson, supt. Fax 697-7012
www.bridge-rayn.org
Bridgewater MS 600/7-8
166 Mount Prospect St 02324 508-279-2100
Lynn Bastoni, prin. Fax 279-2104
Bridgewater-Raynham Regional HS 1,600/9-12
415 Center St 02324 508-697-6902
Angela Watson, prin. Fax 279-2110
Other Schools – See Raynham

Bridgewater State University Post-Sec.
131 Summer St 02325 508-531-1000

**Brighton, See Boston**
Boston SD
Supt. — See Boston
Another Course to College S 200/9-12
20 Warren St 02135 617-635-8865
Michele Pellam, hdmstr. Fax 635-8866
Brighton HS 1,100/9-12
25 Warren St 02135 617-635-9873
Emily Bozeman, hdmstr. Fax 635-9892

Lyon HS 100/9-12
95 Beechcroft St 02135 617-635-8351
Jean-Dominique Anoh, prin. Fax 635-8353

---

Bais Yaakov of Boston HS 50/9-12
198 Strathmore Rd 02135 617-254-7547
Everest Institute Post-Sec.
1505 Commonwealth Ave 02135 888-741-4270
Margolis Mesivta of Greater Boston 100/9-12
34 Sparhawk St 02135 617-779-0166
Saint John's Seminary Post-Sec.
127 Lake St 02135 617-254-2610

**Brockton, Plymouth, Pop. 79,948**
Brockton SD 16,200/PK-12
43 Crescent St 02301 508-580-7000
Kathleen Smith, supt. Fax 580-7513
www.bpsma.org/
Ashfield MS 500/6-8
225 Coe Rd 02302 508-580-7268
Barbara Lovell, prin. Fax 580-7072
Brockton Champion HS 200/Alt
175 Warren Ave 02301 508-894-4377
Cynthia Burns, admin. Fax 894-4380
Brockton HS 4,100/9-12
470 Forest Ave 02301 508-580-7633
Michael Thomas, prin. Fax 580-7600
East MS 400/6-8
464 Centre St 02302 508-580-7351
Kelly Silva, prin. Fax 580-7090
Edison Academy 9-12
700 Belmont St 02301 508-580-7638
James Cobbs, prin. Fax 580-7987
Goddard Alternative S 100/Alt
20 Union St 02301 508-580-7203
John Lander, prin. Fax 580-7083
North MS 500/6-8
108 Oak St 02301 508-580-7371
Sean Ahern, prin. Fax 580-7088
Plouffe Academy 600/6-8
250 Crescent St 02302 508-894-4301
Michelle Nessralla, prin. Fax 894-4300
Russell Alternative S 100/Alt
175 Warren Ave 02301 508-580-7033
Cynthia Burns, prin. Fax 580-7943
South MS 500/6-8
105 Keith Avenue Ext 02301 508-580-7311
Kevin Karo, prin. Fax 580-7089
West MS 600/6-8
271 West St 02301 508-580-7381
Clifford Murray, prin. Fax 580-7307
Adult Learning Center Adult
211 Crescent St 02302 508-580-7475
Suzanne Martin, admin.

---

Ailano School of Cosmetology Post-Sec.
541 West St 02301 508-583-5433
Brockton Hospital Post-Sec.
680 Centre St 02302 508-941-7044
Cardinal Spellman HS 700/9-12
738 Court St 02302 508-583-6875
Paul Kelly, prin. Fax 580-1977
LaBaron Hairdressing Academy Post-Sec.
240 Liberty St 02301 508-583-1700
Lincoln Technical Institute Post-Sec.
365 Westgate Dr 02301 508-941-0730
Massasoit Community College Post-Sec.
1 Massasoit Blvd 02302 508-588-9100
Sullivan and Cogliano Training Center Post-Sec.
460 Belmont St 02301 508-584-9909
Trinity Catholic Academy - Upper Campus 200/4-8
37 Erie Ave 02302 508-583-6225
Annette Bailey, prin. Fax 583-6229

**Brookline, Norfolk, Pop. 57,031**
Brookline SD 6,800/PK-12
333 Washington St 02445 617-730-2401
Dr. William Lupini, supt. Fax 730-2601
www.brookline.k12.ma.us/
Brookline HS 1,800/9-12
115 Greenough St 02445 617-713-5000
Deborah Holman, prin. Fax 713-5005
Devotion Upper S 7-8
194 Boylston St 02445
Monica Crowley, prin.

---

Boston Graduate Sch for Psychoanalysis Post-Sec.
1581 Beacon St 02446 617-277-3915
Dexter Southfield S 400/PK-12
20 Newton St 02445 617-522-5544
Todd Vincent, hdmstr. Fax 522-8166
Hellenic College/Holy Cross Sch Theology Post-Sec.
50 Goddard Ave 02445 617-731-3500
Maimonides S 500/K-12
34 Philbrick Rd 02445 617-232-4452
Newbury College Post-Sec.
129 Fisher Ave 02445 617-730-7000
New England Institute of Art Post-Sec.
10 Brookline Pl 02445 617-739-1700

**Burlington, Middlesex, Pop. 24,055**
Burlington SD 3,500/K-12
123 Cambridge St 01803 781-270-1800
Dr. Eric Conti, supt. Fax 270-1773
www.bpsk12.org
Burlington HS 1,000/9-12
123 Cambridge St 01803 781-270-1836
Mark Sullivan, prin. Fax 229-4893
Simonds MS 800/6-8
114 Winn St 01803 781-270-1781
Richard Connors, prin. Fax 229-4980

**Buzzards Bay, Barnstable, Pop. 3,756**

---

Massachusetts Maritime Academy Post-Sec.
101 Academy Dr 02532 508-830-5000

**Byfield, Essex**
Triton Regional SD 3,000/PK-12
112 Elm St 01922 978-465-2397
Christopher Farmer, supt. Fax 465-8599
www.trsd.net
Triton Regional HS 800/9-12
112 Elm St 01922 978-462-8171
Kathryn Dawe, prin. Fax 465-6868
Triton Regional MS 400/7-8
112 Elm St 01922 978-463-5845
Alan Macrae, prin. Fax 465-6868

---

Governor's Academy 400/9-12
1 Elm St 01922 978-465-1763
Dr. Peter Quimby, hdmstr. Fax 463-9896

**Cambridge, Middlesex, Pop. 100,799**
Cambridge SD 5,000/PK-12
159 Thorndike St 02141 617-349-6400
Dr. Jeffrey Young, supt. Fax 349-6496
www.cpsd.us
Cambridge Rindge & Latin HS 1,600/9-12
459 Broadway 02138 617-349-6630
Damon Smith, prin. Fax 349-6749
Cambridge Street Upper S 6-8
850 Cambridge St 02141 617-349-3050
Manuel Fernandez, prin.
Putnam Avenue Upper S 6-8
158 Spring St 02141 617-349-7780
Mirko Chardin, prin.
Rindge Avenue Upper S 6-8
70 Rindge Ave 02140 617-349-4060
Ralph Watson, prin.
Vassal Lane Upper S 6-8
197 Vassal Ln 02138 617-349-6550
Barbara Boyle, prin.

---

Buckingham Browne & Nichols S 1,000/PK-12
80 Gerrys Landing Rd 02138 617-800-2135
Geordie Mitchell M.Ed., admin.
Cambridge College Post-Sec.
1000 Massachusetts Ave 02138 617-868-1000
Cambridge School of Culinary Arts Post-Sec.
2020 Massachusetts Ave 02140 617-354-2020
Episcopal Divinity School Post-Sec.
99 Brattle St 02138 617-868-3450
Harvard University Post-Sec.
Massachusetts Hall 02138 617-495-1000
Hult International Business School Post-Sec.
1 Education St 02141 617-746-1990
International School of Boston 600/PK-12
45 Matignon Rd 02140 617-499-1451
Dr. Richard Blumenthal Ph.D., head sch Fax 499-1454
Le Cordon Bleu College of Culinary Arts Post-Sec.
215 1st St 02142 888-394-6222
Lesley University Post-Sec.
29 Everett St 02138 617-868-9600
Massachusetts Institute of Technology Post-Sec.
77 Massachusetts Ave 02139 617-253-1000
Matignon HS 400/9-12
1 Matignon Rd 02140 617-876-1212
Joseph DiSarcina, prin. Fax 661-3905
St. Paul's Choir S 50/4-8
29 Mount Auburn St 02138 617-868-8658
William McIvor, hdmstr. Fax 354-7092

**Canton, Norfolk, Pop. 18,530**
Blue Hills Regional Vocational SD
800 Randolph St 02021 781-828-5800
James Quaglia, supt. Fax 828-3872
www.bluehills.org
Blue Hills Regional Technical S Vo/Tech
800 Randolph St 02021 781-828-5800
Jill Rossetti, prin. Fax 828-3872

Canton SD 3,300/PK-12
960 Washington St 02021 781-821-5060
Jennifer Henderson, supt. Fax 575-6500
www.cantonma.org
Canton HS 900/9-12
900 Washington St 02021 781-821-5050
Derek Folan, prin. Fax 821-5052
Galvin MS 800/6-8
55 Pecunit St 02021 781-821-5070
William Conard, prin. Fax 575-6509

---

Bay State School of Technology Post-Sec.
225 Turnpike St 02021 781-828-3434
Porter and Chester Institute Post-Sec.
5 Campanelli Cir 02021 781-830-0350

**Carver, Plymouth**
Carver SD 1,800/PK-12
3 Carver Square Blvd 02330 508-866-6160
Elizabeth Sorrell, supt. Fax 866-2920
www.carver.org
Carver MSHS 900/6-12
60 S Meadow Rd 02330 508-866-6140
Scott Knief, prin. Fax 866-5639

**Charlemont, Franklin**

---

Academy at Charlemont 100/7-12
1359 Route 2 E 01339 413-339-4912
Dr. Brian Bloomfield, hdmstr. Fax 339-4324

**Charlestown, See Boston**
Boston SD
Supt. — See Boston
Charlestown HS 900/9-12
240 Medford St 02129 617-635-9914
William Thomas, hdmstr. Fax 635-9928
Edwards MS 500/6-8
28 Walker St 02129 617-635-8516
Robert Rametti, prin. Fax 635-8522

**Charlton, Worcester**
Dudley-Charlton Regional SD
Supt. — See Dudley
Charlton MS 800/5-8
2 Oxford Rd 01507 508-248-1423
Dean Packard, prin. Fax 248-1418

Southern Worcester Co. Reg Vocational SD
57 Old Muggett Hill Rd 01507 508-248-5971
John Lafleche, supt. Fax 248-4747
www.baypath.tec.ma.us
Bay Path Regional Vocational Tech HS Vo/Tech
57 Old Muggett Hill Rd 01507 508-248-5971
Clifford Cloutier, prin. Fax 248-4747

**Chatham, Barnstable, Pop. 1,395**
Monomoy SD 1,900/PK-12
425 Crowell Rd 02633 508-945-5130
Scott Carpenter, supt. Fax 945-5133
www.monomoy.edu/
Other Schools – See Harwich

**Chelmsford, Middlesex, Pop. 33,858**
Chelmsford SD 5,100/PK-12
230 North Rd 01824 978-251-5100
Dr. Jay Lang, supt. Fax 251-5110
www.chelmsford.k12.ma.us
McCarthy MS 900/5-8
250 North Rd 01824 978-251-5122
Kurt McPhee, prin. Fax 251-5130
Parker MS 700/5-8
75 Graniteville Rd 01824 978-251-5133
Dr. Jeffrey Parks, prin. Fax 251-5140
Other Schools – See North Chelmsford

**Chelsea, Suffolk, Pop. 34,185**
Chelsea SD 5,700/PK-12
500 Broadway 02150 617-466-4477
Mary Bourque, supt. Fax 889-8361
chelseaschools.com
Browne S 600/5-8
180 Walnut St 02150 617-466-5235
David Liebowitz, prin. Fax 889-8459
Chelsea HS 1,300/9-12
299 Everett Ave 02150 617-466-5000
Priti Johari, prin. Fax 889-8468
Clark Avenue S 500/5-8
8 Clark Ave 02150 617-466-5100
Mary Leverone, prin. Fax 889-7539
Wright Science & Technology Acad 500/5-8
180 Walnut St 02150 617-466-5240
Andrew O'Brien, prin. Fax 889-8463

---

Everest Institute Post-Sec.
70 Everett Ave 02150 617-889-5999

**Cheshire, Berkshire, Pop. 507**
Adams-Cheshire Regional SD 1,300/PK-12
191 Church St 01225 413-743-2939
Kristen Gordon, supt. Fax 743-4135
www.acrsd.net
Hoosac Valley HS 600/6-12
125 Savoy Rd 01225 413-743-5200
Vinnie Regan, prin. Fax 743-8420

**Chestnut Hill, See Newton**

---

Beaver Country Day S 500/6-12
791 Hammond St 02467 617-738-2700
Peter Hutton, head sch Fax 738-2701
Boston College Post-Sec.
140 Commonwealth Ave 02467 617-552-8000
Brimmer and May S 400/PK-12
69 Middlesex Rd 02467 617-566-7462
Judy Guild, head sch Fax 734-5147
Pine Manor College Post-Sec.
400 Heath St 02467 617-731-7000

**Chicopee, Hampden, Pop. 54,468**
Chicopee SD 7,800/PK-12
180 Broadway St 01020 413-594-3410
Richard Rege, supt. Fax 594-3552
www.chicopeeps.org
Bellamy MS 1,000/6-8
314 Pendleton Ave 01020 413-594-3527
Matthew Francis, prin. Fax 594-1837
Chicopee Academy 100/Alt
12 DARE Way 01022 413-594-3449
John Leonard, prin. Fax 594-1863
Chicopee Comprehensive HS 1,400/9-12
617 Montgomery St 01020 413-594-3534
Derek Morrison, prin. Fax 594-3492
Chicopee HS 1,100/9-12
820 Front St 01020 413-594-3437
Roland Joyal, prin. Fax 594-3500
Dupont Memorial MS 6-8
650 Front St 01013 413-594-1881
Kristopher Theriault, prin. Fax 594-1897

---

College of Our Lady of Elms Post-Sec.
291 Springfield St 01013 413-594-2761
Holyoke Catholic HS 300/9-12
134 Springfield St 01013 413-331-2480
Maryann Linnehan, prin. Fax 331-2708
Porter and Chester Institute Post-Sec.
134 Dulong Cir 01022 413-593-3339
Salter College Post-Sec.
645 Shawinigan Dr 01020 413-206-0300

**Clinton, Worcester, Pop. 7,209**
Clinton SD 1,900/PK-12
150 School St 01510 978-365-4200
Terrance Ingano, supt. Fax 365-5037
clinton.k12.ma.us
Clinton HS 500/9-12
200 W Boylston St 01510 978-365-4208
James Hastings, prin. Fax 365-4237

Clinton MS 700/4-8
100 W Boylston St 01510 978-365-4220
Annmarie Sargent, prin. Fax 368-7256

**Cohasset, Norfolk, Pop. 7,075**
Cohasset SD 1,500/PK-12
143 Pond St 02025 781-383-6111
Barbara Cataldo, supt. Fax 383-6507
www.cohassetk12.org
Cohasset MSHS 700/6-12
143 Pond St 02025 781-383-6100
Carolyn Connolly, prin. Fax 383-4168

**Concord, Middlesex, Pop. 4,700**
Concord SD 2,000/PK-8
120 Meriam Rd 01742 978-318-1500
Diana Rigby, supt. Fax 318-1537
www.concordpublicschools.net
Concord MS 600/6-8
835 Old Marlboro Rd 01742 978-318-1380
Lynne Beattie, prin. Fax 318-1392

Concord-Carlisle SD 1,200/9-12
120 Meriam Rd 01742 978-318-1500
Diana Rigby, supt. Fax 318-1537
www.concordpublicschools.net
Concord-Carlisle HS 1,200/9-12
500 Walden St 01742 978-318-1400
Peter Badalament, prin. Fax 318-1435

---

Concord Academy 400/9-12
166 Main St 01742 978-402-2200
Richard G. Hardy, head sch Fax 402-2210
Fenn S 300/4-9
516 Monument St 01742 978-369-5800
Gerard J.G. Ward, admin. Fax 371-7520
Middlesex S 400/9-12
PO Box 9122 01742 978-369-2550
Kathleen Carroll Giles, head sch Fax 287-4759

**Conway, Franklin**

---

Conway School of Landscape Design Post-Sec.
PO Box 179 01341 413-369-4044

**Dalton, Berkshire, Pop. 7,155**
Central Berkshire Regional SD 1,800/PK-12
PO Box 299 01227 413-684-0320
Laurie Casna, supt. Fax 684-4088
www.cbrsd.org
Nessacus Regional MS 400/6-8
35 Fox Rd 01226 413-684-0780
John Martin, prin. Fax 684-4214
Wahconah Regional HS 600/9-12
150 Old Windsor Rd 01226 413-684-1330
James Conro, prin. Fax 684-5032

**Danvers, Essex, Pop. 26,232**
Danvers SD 3,600/PK-12
64 Cabot Rd 01923 978-777-4539
Lisa Dana, supt. Fax 777-8931
www.danvers.mec.edu
Danvers HS 1,000/9-12
60 Cabot Rd 01923 978-777-8925
Susan Ambrozavitch, prin. Fax 777-8931
Holten-Richmond MS 900/6-8
55 Conant St 01923 978-774-8590
Adam Federico, prin. Fax 762-8686

---

North Shore Community College Post-Sec.
1 Ferncroft Rd 01923 978-762-4000
St. Johns Preparatory S 1,200/9-12
72 Spring St 01923 978-774-1050
Keith Crowley Ph.D., prin. Fax 624-1315

**Dedham, Norfolk, Pop. 24,346**
Dedham SD 2,900/PK-12
100 Whiting Ave 02026 781-310-1100
Mike Welch, supt. Fax 320-0193
www.dedham.k12.ma.us
Dedham HS 800/9-12
140 Whiting Ave 02026 781-310-1100
Ron McCarthy, prin. Fax 320-8126
Dedham MS 600/6-8
70 Whiting Ave 02026 781-310-7000
Debra Gately, prin. Fax 461-0354

---

Noble And Greenough S 600/7-12
10 Campus Dr 02026 781-326-3700
Robert Henderson, hdmstr. Fax 320-1329
Ursuline Academy 400/7-12
85 Lowder St 02026 781-326-6161
Mary Jo Keaney, prin. Fax 326-4898

**Deerfield, Franklin, Pop. 620**

---

Deerfield Academy 600/9-12
PO Box 87 01342 413-772-0241
Dr. Margarita Curtis, hdmstr. Fax 772-1129
Eaglebrook S 300/6-9
PO Box 7 01342 413-774-7411
Andrew Chase, hdmstr. Fax 774-9136

**Dighton, Bristol**
Bristol County Agricultural SD
135 Center St 02715 508-669-6744
Stephen Dempsey, supt. Fax 669-6747
www.edline.net/pages/Bristol_County_Agr_High
Bristol County Agricultural HS Vo/Tech
135 Center St 02715 508-669-6744
Aaron Polansky, prin. Fax 669-6747

Dighton-Rehoboth Regional SD
Supt. — See North Dighton
Dighton MS 400/5-8
1250R Somerset Ave 02715 508-669-4200
Richard Wheeler, prin. Fax 669-4210

**Dorchester, See Boston**
Boston SD
Supt. — See Boston
Boston International HS 300/9-12
100 Maxwell St 02124 617-635-9373
Tony King, hdmstr. Fax 635-8224
Boston Latin Academy 1,700/7-12
205 Townsend St 02121 617-635-9957
Troy Henninger, hdmstr. Fax 635-6696
Burke HS 600/9-12
60 Washington St 02121 617-635-9837
Lindsa McIntyre, hdmstr. Fax 635-9852
Community Academy of Science & Health 400/9-12
11 Charles St 02122 617-635-8950
Tonya Freeman-Wisdom, prin. Fax 635-8948
Dearborn STEM Academy 200/6-12
60 Washington St 02121 617-635-8412
Lisa Gilbert-Smith, prin. Fax 635-8419
Dorchester Academy 400/9-12
11 Charles St 02122 617-635-9730
Melissa Malone Sanjeh, hdmstr. Fax 635-8847
Frederick MS 600/6-8
270 Columbia Rd 02121 617-635-1650
Pauline Lugira, prin. Fax 635-1637
Henderson Inclusion S 200/PK-12
18 Croftland Ave 02124 617-635-8725
Patricia Lampron, prin. Fax 635-8728
McCormack MS 700/6-8
315 Mount Vernon St 02125 617-635-8657
Jose Duarte, prin. Fax 635-9788
Newcomers Academy 200/9-12
100 Maxwell St 02124 617-635-7993
Nicole Bahnam, dir. Fax 635-7990
TechBoston Academy 900/6-12
9 Peacevale Rd 02124 617-635-1615
Keith Love, hdmstr. Fax 635-1622

---

Cross Factor Academy 200/PK-12
670 Washington St 02124 617-522-1841
Michael Dixon Ph.D., head sch Fax 524-9583
Epiphany S 100/5-8
154 Centre St 02124 617-326-0425
Rev. John Finley, head sch Fax 326-0424
Laboure College Post-Sec.
2120 Dorchester Ave 02124 617-296-8300
Mother Caroline Academy 100/4-8
515 Blue Hill Ave 02121 617-427-1177
Ed Hudner, dir. Fax 427-7788
Seton Academy 100/9-12
2220 Dorchester Ave 02124 617-296-1087
Maureen White Ph.D., prin. Fax 296-1089

**Douglas, Worcester**
Douglas SD 1,600/PK-12
21 Davis St 01516 508-476-7901
Norman Yvon, supt. Fax 476-3719
www.douglas.k12.ma.us/
Douglas HS 600/9-12
33 Davis St 01516 508-476-4100
Kevin Maines, prin. Fax 476-7310
Douglas MS 6-8
21 Davis St 01516 508-476-3332
Beverly Bachelder, prin. Fax 476-1604

**Dover, Norfolk, Pop. 2,253**
Dover-Sherborn SD 1,200/PK-12
157 Farm St 02030 508-785-0036
William McAlduff, supt. Fax 785-2239
www.doversherborn.org
Dover-Sherborn Regional HS 600/9-12
9 Junction St 02030 508-785-1730
John Smith, prin. Fax 785-8141
Dover-Sherborn Regional MS 600/6-8
155 Farm St 02030 508-785-0635
Scott Kellett, prin. Fax 785-0796

**Dracut, Middlesex, Pop. 25,594**
Dracut SD 3,800/PK-12
2063 Lakeview Ave 01826 978-957-2660
Steven Stone, supt. Fax 957-2682
www.dracutps.org
Dracut HS 1,100/9-12
1540 Lakeview Ave 01826 978-957-1500
Richard Manley, prin. Fax 957-9717
Richardson MS 700/6-8
1570 Lakeview Ave 01826 978-957-3330
Maria McGuinness, prin. Fax 957-4075

**Dudley, Worcester, Pop. 3,700**
Dudley-Charlton Regional SD 4,100/PK-12
68 Dudley Oxford Rd 01571 508-943-6888
Gregg Desto, supt. Fax 943-1077
www.dcrsd.org
Dudley MS 600/5-8
70 Dudley Oxford Rd 01571 508-943-2224
John Paire, prin. Fax 949-0720
Shepherd Hill Regional HS 1,100/9-12
68 Dudley Oxford Rd 01571 508-943-6700
Mary Pierangeli, prin. Fax 943-5956
Other Schools – See Charlton

---

Nichols College Post-Sec.
124 Center Rd 01571 508-213-1560

**Duxbury, Plymouth, Pop. 1,793**
Duxbury SD 3,200/PK-12
130 Saint George St 02332 781-934-7600
Dr. Benedict Tantillo, supt. Fax 934-7644
www.duxbury.k12.ma.us
Duxbury HS 1,000/9-12
130 Saint George St 02332 781-934-7650
Andrew Stephens, prin. Fax 934-7617
Duxbury MS 800/6-8
71 Alden St 02332 781-934-7640
Blake Dalton, prin. Fax 934-7608

**East Boston, See Boston**
Boston SD
Supt. — See Boston
East Boston HS 1,400/9-12
86 White St 02128 617-635-9896
Phil Brangiforte, hdmstr. Fax 635-9726

**East Bridgewater, Plymouth, Pop. 11,104**
East Bridgewater SD 1,700/PK-12
143 Plymouth St 02333 508-378-8200
Elizabeth Legault, supt. Fax 378-8225
www.ebps.net
East Bridgewater HS 600/7-12
143 Plymouth St 02333 508-378-8214
Paul Vieira, prin. Fax 378-8226

**East Falmouth, Barnstable, Pop. 5,768**
Falmouth SD 3,500/PK-12
340 Teaticket Hwy 02536 508-548-0151
Dr. Nancy Taylor, supt. Fax 457-9032
www.falmouth.k12.ma.us
Other Schools – See Falmouth

**Easthampton, Hampshire, Pop. 16,004**
Easthampton SD 1,600/PK-12
50 Payson Ave Ste 200 01027 413-529-1500
Nancy Follansbee, supt. Fax 529-1567
www.epsd.us
Easthampton HS 400/9-12
70 Williston Ave 01027 413-529-1585
Kevin Burke, prin. Fax 529-1591
White Brook MS 500/5-8
200 Park St 01027 413-529-1530
Meredith Balise, prin. Fax 529-1534

---

Williston Northampton S 500/7-12
19 Payson Ave 01027 413-529-3000
Robert W. Hill, head sch Fax 527-9494

**East Longmeadow, Hampden, Pop. 13,367**
East Longmeadow SD 2,800/PK-12
180 Maple St 01028 413-525-5450
Gordon Smith, supt. Fax 525-5456
www.eastlongmeadowma.gov/schools.htm
Birchland Park MS 700/6-8
50 Hanward Hl 01028 413-525-5480
Timothy Allen Ed.D., prin. Fax 525-5320
East Longmeadow HS 900/9-12
180 Maple St 01028 413-525-5460
Gina Flanagan Ed.D., prin. Fax 525-5496

**East Sandwich, Barnstable, Pop. 3,915**
Sandwich SD
Supt. — See Sandwich
Sandwich HS 1,000/9-12
365 Quaker Meeting House Rd 02537 508-888-4900
Ellin Booras, prin. Fax 833-8392
Sandwich STEM Academy 500/7-8
365 Quaker Meeting House Rd 02537
Gilbert Newton, dir. 508-888-5300

---

Riverview S 100/6-12
551 Route 6A 02537 508-888-0489
Nancy Hopkins, admin. Fax 833-7001

**East Walpole, Norfolk, Pop. 3,800**
Walpole SD
Supt. — See Walpole
Bird MS 500/6-8
625 Washington St 02032 508-660-7226
Bridget Gough, prin. Fax 660-7229

**East Wareham, Plymouth**
Wareham SD
Supt. — See Wareham
Wareham Cooperative S 100/Alt
27 Depot St 02538 508-291-3526
Allen McMurrey, prin.

**East Weymouth, Norfolk**
Weymouth SD
Supt. — See Weymouth
Chapman MS 1,100/7-8
1051 Commercial St 02189 781-337-4500
Paul Duprey, prin. Fax 340-2594

**Everett, Middlesex, Pop. 38,826**
Everett SD 6,500/PK-12
121 Vine St 02149 617-389-7950
Frederick Foresteire, supt. Fax 394-2408
www.everett.k12.ma.us/
Everett HS 1,800/9-12
100 Elm St 02149 617-394-2490
Erick Naumann, prin. Fax 389-5841

---

Pope John XXIII Central HS 300/9-12
888 Broadway 02149 617-389-0240
Dr. Thomas Ryan, prin. Fax 389-2201

**Fairhaven, Bristol, Pop. 16,132**
Fairhaven SD 1,700/PK-12
128 Washington St 02719 508-979-4000
Dr. Robert Baldwin, supt. Fax 979-4149
www.fairhavenps.org/
Fairhaven HS 600/9-12
12 Huttleston Ave 02719 508-979-4052
Tara Quirk, prin. Fax 979-4140
Hastings MS 500/6-8
30 School St 02719 508-979-4063
Wayne Miller, prin. Fax 979-4068

**Fall River, Bristol, Pop. 86,097**
Fall River SD 9,100/PK-12
417 Rock St 02720 508-675-8420
Meg Mayo-Brown, supt. Fax 675-8462
www.fallriverschools.org/
Durfee HS 2,200/9-12
360 Elsbree St 02720 508-675-8100
Maria Pontes, prin. Fax 675-8186
Kuss MS 600/6-8
52 Globe Mills Ave 02724 508-675-8335
Margaret Christ, prin. Fax 675-1984

Morton MS 500/6-8
1135 N Main St 02720 508-675-8340
Sheryl Rabbitt, prin. Fax 675-8414
Resiliancy MS Alt
290 Rock St 02720 508-675-8420
Joyce Paulo, prin. Fax 675-8462
Resiliency Preparatory S 200/Alt
276 Maple St 02720 508-675-8230
Magdalana Reis, prin. Fax 235-2661
Talbot Innovation MS 600/6-8
124 Melrose St 02723 508-675-8350
Renee Lewis, prin. Fax 675-8356

Greater Fall River Vocational SD
251 Stonehaven Rd 02723 508-678-2891
Marta Montleon, supt. Fax 679-6423
www.dimanregional.org/
Diman Regional Vocational Technical HS Vo/Tech
251 Stonehaven Rd 02723 508-678-2891
Kyle Alves, prin. Fax 679-6423

---

Bishop Connolly HS 300/9-12
373 Elsbree St 02720 508-676-1071
Christopher Myron, prin. Fax 676-8594
Bristol Community College Post-Sec.
777 Elsbree St 02720 508-678-2811
Rob Roy Academy Post-Sec.
260 S Main St 02721 508-672-4751
Salter School Post-Sec.
82 Hartwell St 02721 508-730-2740

**Falmouth, Barnstable, Pop. 3,663**
Falmouth SD
Supt. — See East Falmouth
Falmouth HS 900/9-12
874 Gifford Street Ext 02540 508-540-2200
Mary Gans, prin. Fax 548-7515
Lawrence MS 500/7-8
113 Lakeview Ave 02540 508-548-0606
Tom Bushy, prin. Fax 457-9778

---

Falmouth Academy 200/7-12
7 Highfield Dr 02540 508-457-9696
Steve Duffy, head sch Fax 457-4112
National Grad. Sch. Quality Systems Mgmt Post-Sec.
186 Jones Rd 02540 508-457-1313

**Feeding Hills, Hampden, Pop. 5,450**
Agawam SD 4,100/PK-12
1305 Springfield St Ste 1 01030 413-821-0548
William Sapelli, supt. Fax 789-1835
www.agawampublicschools.org
Agawam JHS 700/7-8
1305 Springfield St Ste 2 01030 413-821-0561
Norman Robbins, prin. Fax 786-4240
Other Schools – See Agawam

**Fiskdale, Worcester, Pop. 2,545**
Tantasqua SD 1,800/7-12
320 Brookfield Rd 01518 508-347-3077
Erin Nosek, supt. Fax 347-2697
www.tantasqua.org
Tantasqua Regional HS 800/9-12
319 Brookfield Rd 01518 508-347-9301
Michael Lucas, prin. Fax 347-1061
Tantasqua Regional JHS 600/7-8
320 Brookfield Rd 01518 508-347-7381
Christopher Starczewski, prin. Fax 347-3994
Tantasqua Regional Vocational HS Vo/Tech
319 Brookfield Rd 01518 508-347-3045
Mark Wood, prin. Fax 347-1061

**Fitchburg, Worcester, Pop. 39,363**
Fitchburg SD 4,600/PK-12
376 South St 01420 978-345-3200
Andre Ravenelle, supt. Fax 348-2305
www.fitchburgschools.org
Fitchburg HS 1,100/9-12
140 Arnhow Farm Rd 01420 978-345-3240
Jeremy Roche, prin. Fax 348-2303
Goodrich Academy Alt
111 Goodrich St 01420 978-345-3244
Raymond Dewar, prin. Fax 343-6127
Longsjo MS 600/5-8
98 Academy St 01420 978-343-2146
Craig Chalifoux, prin. Fax 348-2323
Memorial MS 700/5-8
615 Rollstone St 01420 978-345-3295
Francis Thomas, prin. Fax 343-2121

Montachusett Regional Vo/Tech HSD
1050 Westminster St 01420 978-345-9200
Tammy Lajoie, supt. Fax 345-9165
www.montytech.net
Montachusett Reg Vocational Technical HS Vo/Tech
1050 Westminster St 01420 978-345-9200
Tammy Lajoie, supt. Fax 348-1176

---

Fitchburg State University Post-Sec.
160 Pearl St 01420 978-345-2151
Henri's School of Hair Design Post-Sec.
PO Box 2244 01420 978-342-6061
Notre Dame HS 50/7-12
151 South St 01420 978-343-7635
Jeffrey Hammond, prin. Fax 343-4379
St. Bernards HS 300/9-12
45 Harvard St 01420 978-342-3212
Robert Blanchard, admin. Fax 345-8067

**Florence, See Northampton**
Northampton SD
Supt. — See Northampton
Kennedy MS 600/6-8
100 Bridge Rd 01062 413-587-1489
Lesley Wilson, prin. Fax 587-1495

**Foxboro, Norfolk, Pop. 5,706**
Foxborough SD 2,800/PK-12
60 South St 02035 508-543-1660
Debra Spinelli, supt. Fax 543-4793
www.foxborough.k12.ma.us
Ahern MS 900/5-8
111 Mechanic St 02035 508-543-1610
Susan Abrams, prin. Fax 543-1613
Foxborough HS 800/9-12
120 South St 02035 508-543-1616
Diana Myers-Pachla, prin. Fax 698-6517

**Framingham, Middlesex, Pop. 61,638**
Framingham SD 8,200/PK-12
73 Mount Wayte Ave Ste 5 01702 508-626-9117
Dr. Stacy Scott Ed.D., supt. Fax 877-4240
www.framingham.k12.ma.us
Cameron MS 500/6-8
215 Elm St 01701 508-879-2290
Michelle Melick, prin. Fax 788-3560
Framingham HS 2,100/9-12
115 A St 01701 508-620-4963
Elyse Torbert, prin. Fax 877-6603
Fuller MS 500/6-8
31 Flagg Dr 01702 508-620-4956
Sharon Seyller, prin. Fax 628-1308
Walsh MS 700/6-8
301 Brook St 01701 508-626-9180
Patrick Johnson, prin. Fax 877-1825

South Middlesex Regional Technical SD
750 Winter St 01702 508-416-2350
Jonathan Evans, supt. Fax 416-2342
www.keefetech.org
Keefe Technical HS Vo/Tech
750 Winter St 01702 508-416-2100
Shannon Snow, prin. Fax 416-2342

---

Blaine The Beauty Career School Post-Sec.
624 Worcester Rd 01702 508-370-3700
Blaine The Beauty Career School Post-Sec.
624 Worcester Rd 01702 508-370-7447
Framingham State College Post-Sec.
PO Box 9101 01701 508-620-1220
Marian HS 300/9-12
273 Union Ave 01702 508-875-7646
Sr. Catherine Clifford, prin. Fax 875-0838

**Franklin, Norfolk, Pop. 30,893**
Franklin SD 6,000/PK-12
355 E Central St 02038 508-541-5243
Maureen Sabolinski, supt. Fax 533-0321
franklindistrict.vt-s.net
Franklin HS 1,600/9-12
218 Oak St 02038 508-613-1400
Peter Light, prin. Fax 613-1510
Mann MS 500/6-8
224 Oak St 02038 508-553-0322
Rebecca Motte, prin. Fax 541-7071
Remington MS 500/6-8
628 Washington St 02038 508-541-2130
Brian Wildeman, prin. Fax 541-2124
Sullivan MS 500/6-8
500 Lincoln St 02038 508-553-0322
Beth Wittcoff, prin. Fax 542-2109

Tri-County Regional Vocational Tech SD
147 Pond St 02038 508-528-5400
Stephen Dockray, supt. Fax 528-6074
www.tri-county.tc
Tri-County Regional Vo-Tech HS Vo/Tech
147 Pond St 02038 508-528-5400
Michael Procaccini, prin. Fax 528-6074

---

Dean College Post-Sec.
99 Main St 02038 508-541-1508

**Gardner, Worcester, Pop. 19,860**
Gardner SD 2,400/PK-12
70 Waterford St 01440 978-632-1000
Denise Clemons M.Ed., supt. Fax 632-1164
www.gardnerk12.org
Gardner Academy for Learning/Technology 100/Alt
75 E Broadway 01440 978-632-1606
Timothy McCormick, prin. Fax 632-1164
Gardner HS 600/8-12
200 Catherine St 01440 978-632-1600
Mark Pellegrino, prin. Fax 630-4040

---

Mt. Wachusett Community College Post-Sec.
444 Green St 01440 978-632-6600

**Georgetown, Essex**
Georgetown SD 1,600/PK-12
51 North St 01833 978-352-5777
Carol Jacobs, supt. Fax 352-5778
www.georgetown-schools.org/
Georgetown MSHS 800/6-12
11 Winter St 01833 978-352-5790
Peter Lucia, prin. Fax 352-5798

**Gloucester, Essex, Pop. 28,371**
Gloucester SD 3,100/PK-12
2 Blackburn Dr 01930 978-281-9800
Richard Safier, supt. Fax 281-9899
www.gloucesterschools.com
Gloucester HS 1,000/9-12
32 Leslie O Johnson Rd 01930 978-281-9870
Erik Anderson, prin. Fax 281-9733
O'Maley MS 600/6-8
32 Cherry St 01930 978-281-9850
Debra Lucey, prin. Fax 281-9890

**Grafton, Worcester**
Grafton SD 2,400/PK-12
30 Providence Rd 01519 508-839-5421
James Cummings Ed.D., supt. Fax 839-7618
www.grafton.k12.ma.us

Grafton Memorial HS 700/9-12
24 Providence Rd 01519 508-839-5425
James Pignataro, prin. Fax 839-8544
Grafton MS 500/7-8
22 Providence Rd 01519 508-839-5420
Timothy Fauth, prin. Fax 839-8528

**Granby, Hampshire, Pop. 1,346**
Granby SD 1,100/PK-12
387 E State St 01033 413-467-7193
Dr. Judith Houle, supt. Fax 467-3909
www.granbyschoolsma.org
Granby JSHS 600/7-12
385 E State St 01033 413-467-7105
Jonathan Cavallo, prin. Fax 467-3909

---

MacDuffie S 200/6-12
66 School St, 413-255-0000
Steve Griffin, head sch Fax 467-1607

**Great Barrington, Berkshire, Pop. 2,177**
Berkshire Hills SD
Supt. — See Stockbridge
Monument Mountain Regional HS 500/9-12
600 Stockbridge Rd 01230 413-528-3346
Marianne Young, prin. Fax 528-9267
Monument Valley Regional MS 400/5-8
313 Monument Valley Rd 01230 413-644-2300
Ben Doren, prin. Fax 644-2394

---

Bard College at Simon's Rock Post-Sec.
84 Alford Rd 01230 413-644-4400

**Greenfield, Franklin, Pop. 14,016**
Greenfield SD 1,600/PK-12
141 Davis St 01301 413-772-1311
Jordana Harper, supt. Fax 774-7940
www.gpsk12.org
Greenfield HS 500/8-12
21 Barr Ave 01301 413-772-1350
Donna Woodcock, prin. Fax 774-6204

---

Greenfield Community College Post-Sec.
1 College Dr 01301 413-775-1000
Stoneleigh-Burnham S 100/7-12
574 Bernardston Rd 01301 413-774-2711
Sally Mixsell, head sch Fax 772-2602

**Groton, Middlesex, Pop. 1,106**
Groton-Dunstable Regional SD 2,700/PK-12
PO Box 729 01450 978-448-5505
Dr. Kristan Rodriguez, supt. Fax 448-9402
www.gdrsd.org
Groton-Dunstable Regional HS 900/9-12
PO Box 730 01450 978-448-6362
Michael Mastrullo, prin. Fax 448-0390
Groton-Dunstable Regional MS 900/5-8
PO Box 727 01450 978-448-6155
James Lin, prin. Fax 448-1201

---

Groton S 400/8-12
PO Box 991 01450 978-448-3363
Temba Maqubela, hdmstr. Fax 448-3100
Lawrence Academy 400/9-12
PO Box 992 01450 978-448-6535
Dan Scheibe, head sch Fax 448-9208

**Hadley, Hampshire**
Hadley SD 700/PK-12
125 Russell St 01035 413-586-0822
Anne McKenzie Ed.D., supt. Fax 582-6453
www.hadleyschools.org
Hopkins Academy 300/7-12
131 Russell St 01035 413-584-1106
Brian Beck, prin. Fax 582-6455

---

Hartsbrook S 300/PK-12
193 Bay Rd 01035 413-584-3198
Fax 586-9438

**Hamilton, Essex**
Hamilton-Wenham SD
Supt. — See Wenham
Hamilton-Wenham Regional HS 700/9-12
775 Bay Rd 01982 978-468-0400
Eric Tracy, prin. Fax 468-0241
Miles River MS 400/6-8
787 Bay Rd 01982 978-468-0362
Craig Hovey, prin. Fax 468-8454

**Hampden, Hampden**
Hampden-Wilbraham SD
Supt. — See Wilbraham
Burgess MS 300/5-8
85 Wilbraham Rd 01036 413-566-8950
Peter Dufresne, prin. Fax 566-2163

**Hanover, Plymouth, Pop. 11,912**
Hanover SD 2,700/PK-12
188 Broadway 02339 781-878-0786
Matthew Ferron Ed.D., supt. Fax 871-3374
www.hanoverschools.org
Hanover HS 700/9-12
287 Cedar St 02339 781-878-5450
Matthew Paquette, prin. Fax 871-0590
Hanover MS 900/5-8
45 Whiting St 02339 781-871-1122
Daniel Birolini, prin. Fax 871-8792

South Shore Regional Vo Tech SD
476 Webster St 02339 781-878-8822
Thomas Hickey Ed.D., supt. Fax 982-0281
www.ssvotech.org
South Shore Vocational Technical HS Vo/Tech
476 Webster St 02339 781-878-8822
Margaret Dutch, prin. Fax 982-0281

**Hanscom AFB, See Bedford**
Lincoln SD
Supt. — See Lincoln
Hanscom MS 200/4-8
2 Eglin St 01731 781-274-0050
Erich Ledebuhr, prin. Fax 274-7329

**Hanson, Plymouth, Pop. 2,089**
Whitman-Hanson SD
Supt. — See Whitman
Hanson MS 500/6-8
111 Liberty St 02341 781-618-7575
William Tranter, prin. Fax 618-8815

**Harvard, Worcester**
Harvard SD 1,300/PK-12
39 Mass Ave 01451 978-456-4140
Linda Dwight, supt. Fax 456-8592
www.psharvard.org
Bromfield S 800/6-12
14 Mass Ave 01451 978-456-4152
James O'Shea, prin. Fax 456-3013

**Harwich, Barnstable**
Cape Cod Regional Technical HSD
351 Pleasant Lake Ave 02645 508-432-4500
Robert Sanborn, supt. Fax 432-7916
capetech.us
Cape Cod Regional Technical HS Vo/Tech
351 Pleasant Lake Ave 02645 508-432-4500
Billy Terranova, prin. Fax 430-2430

Monomoy SD
Supt. — See Chatham
Monomoy Regional HS 300/8-12
75 Oak St 02645 508-430-7200
Bill Burkhead, prin.

**Hatfield, Hampshire, Pop. 1,311**
Hatfield SD 500/PK-12
34 School St 01038 413-247-5641
John Robert, supt. Fax 247-0201
hatfieldps.net
Smith Academy 200/7-12
34 School St 01038 413-247-5641
Andrew Berrios, prin. Fax 247-0201

**Hathorne, Essex**
Essex N Shore Agricultural & Tech HS
PO Box 346 01937 978-304-4700
Daniel O'Connell, supt. Fax 774-6530
www.essextech.net
Essex Technical HS Vo/Tech
PO Box 346 01937 978-304-4700
Brad Morgan, prin. Fax 774-6530

**Haverhill, Essex, Pop. 59,811**
Haverhill SD 7,700/PK-12
4 Summer St Ste 104 01830 978-374-3400
James Scully, supt. Fax 374-3422
www.haverhill-ps.org/
Haverhill Alternative S 50/Alt
415 Primrose St 01830 978-374-3482
John DePolo, prin. Fax 372-6070
Haverhill HS 1,700/9-12
137 Monument St 01832 978-374-5700
Elizabeth Kitsos, prin. Fax 374-5705
Hunking MS 400/6-8
100 Winchester St 01835 978-374-5787
Shannon Nolan, prin. Fax 372-5890
Nettle MS 500/5-8
150 Boardman St 01830 978-374-5792
Tim Corkery, prin. Fax 374-3441
Whittier MS 500/5-8
256 Concord St 01830 978-374-5782
Brian Gill, prin. Fax 372-5999

Whittier Regional Vocational SD
115 Amesbury Line Rd 01830 978-373-4101
Maureen Lynch, supt. Fax 521-0260
www.whittiertech.org
Whittier Regional Vocational HS Vo/Tech
115 Amesbury Line Rd 01830 978-373-4101
Chris Laganas, prin. Fax 521-0260

---

Northern Essex Community College Post-Sec.
100 Elliott St 01830 978-556-3000
Northpoint Bible College Post-Sec.
320 S Main St 01835 978-478-3400

**Hingham, Plymouth, Pop. 5,570**
Hingham SD 4,100/PK-12
220 Central St 02043 781-741-1500
Dorothy Galo, supt. Fax 749-7457
www.hinghamschools.org
Hingham HS 1,100/9-12
17 Union St 02043 781-741-1560
Paula Girouard McCann, prin. Fax 741-1515
Hingham MS 900/6-8
1103 Main St 02043 781-741-1550
Derek Smith, prin. Fax 749-6297

---

Notre Dame Academy 600/9-12
1073 Main St 02043 781-749-5930
Kathleen Colin, prin. Fax 749-8366

**Holbrook, Norfolk, Pop. 10,445**
Holbrook SD 1,200/PK-12
245 S Franklin St 02343 781-767-1226
Dr. Patricia Lally, supt. Fax 767-1312
www.holbrook.k12.ma.us/
Holbrook JSHS 400/7-12
245 S Franklin St 02343 781-767-4616
Mary Ann DeMello, prin. Fax 767-2697

**Holden, Worcester, Pop. 14,628**
Wachusett Regional SD
Supt. — See Jefferson
Mountview MS 800/6-8
270 Shrewsbury St 01520 508-829-5577
Erik Githmark, prin. Fax 829-3711
Wachusett Regional HS 2,100/9-12
1401 Main St 01520 508-829-6771
William Beando, prin. Fax 829-4895

**Holliston, Middlesex, Pop. 12,926**
Holliston SD 2,800/PK-12
370 Hollis St 01746 508-429-0654
Bradford Jackson, supt. Fax 429-0653
www.holliston.k12.ma.us/
Adams MS 700/6-8
323 Woodland St 01746 508-429-0657
Peter Botelho, prin. Fax 429-0690
Holliston HS 800/9-12
370 Hollis St 01746 508-429-0677
Nicole Bottomley, prin. Fax 429-8225

**Holyoke, Hampden, Pop. 39,370**
Holyoke SD 5,800/PK-12
57 Suffolk St Ste 101 01040 413-534-2005
Dr. Stephen Zrike, supt. Fax 534-2297
www.hps.holyoke.ma.us
Dean Vocational Technical HS Vo/Tech
1045 Main St 01040 413-534-2071
Bradley Bacom, prin. Fax 536-9694
Holyoke HS 1,300/9-12
500 Beech St 01040 413-534-2020
Stephen Sullivan, prin. Fax 534-2098
Peck ES 400/4-8
1916 Northampton St 01040 413-534-2040
Nancy Athas, prin. Fax 532-8563

Springfield SD
Supt. — See Springfield
Gateway to College @ HCC 100/9-12
303 Homestead Ave 01040 413-552-2176
Rhonda Jacobs, dir.

---

Holyoke Community College Post-Sec.
303 Homestead Ave 01040 413-538-7000

**Hopedale, Worcester, Pop. 3,687**
Hopedale SD 1,300/PK-12
25 Adin St 01747 508-634-2220
Pamela Smith, supt. Fax 478-1471
www.hopedaleschools.org
Hopedale JSHS 500/7-12
25 Adin St 01747 508-634-2217
Derek Atherton, prin. Fax 634-4319

**Hopkinton, Middlesex, Pop. 2,531**
Hopkinton SD 3,400/PK-12
89 Hayden Rowe St 01748 508-417-9360
Cathy Macleod, supt. Fax 497-9833
www.hopkinton.k12.ma.us
Hopkinton HS 1,100/9-12
90 Hayden Rowe St 01748 508-497-9820
Evan Bishop, prin. Fax 497-9829
Hopkinton MS 800/6-8
88 Hayden Rowe St 01748 508-497-9830
Alan Keller Ed.D., prin. Fax 497-9803

**Hudson, Middlesex, Pop. 14,374**
Hudson SD 2,500/PK-12
155 Apsley St 01749 978-567-6100
Dr. Judi Fortuna, supt. Fax 567-6123
www.hudson.k12.ma.us
Hudson JSHS 1,100/8-12
69 Brigham St 01749 978-567-6250
Brian Reagan, prin. Fax 567-6285

**Hull, Plymouth, Pop. 10,097**
Hull SD 1,100/PK-12
180 Harborview Rd 02045 781-925-4400
Kathleen Tyrell, supt. Fax 925-8042
www.town.hull.ma.us
Hull HS 300/9-12
180 Main St 02045 781-925-3000
Michael Devine, prin. Fax 925-3071
Memorial MS 200/6-8
81 Central Ave 02045 781-925-2040
Anthony Hrivnak, prin. Fax 925-8002

**Huntington, Hampshire, Pop. 920**
Gateway SD 900/PK-12
12 Littleville Rd 01050 413-685-1000
Dr. David Hopson, supt. Fax 667-8739
www.grsd.org
Gateway Regional JSHS 300/7-12
12 Littleville Rd 01050 413-685-1100
Jason Finnie, prin. Fax 667-5593

**Hyannis, Barnstable, Pop. 14,120**
Barnstable SD 4,000/PK-12
PO Box 955 02601 508-862-4953
Bill Butler, supt. Fax 790-6454
www.barnstable.k12.ma.us
Barnstable HS 2,000/8-12
744 W Main St 02601 508-790-6445
Patrick Clark, prin. Fax 790-6430

---

Blaine The Beauty Career School Post-Sec.
259 North St Ste 3 02601 508-771-1680
St. John Paul II HS & St. Xavier Prep 200/K-12
120 High School Rd 02601 508-862-6336
Christopher Keavy, prin. Fax 862-6339

**Hyde Park, See Boston**
Boston SD
Supt. — See Boston
Boston Community Leadership Academy 500/9-12
655 Metropolitan Ave 02136 617-635-8937
Brett Dickens, hdmstr. Fax 635-8942
New Mission HS 300/9-12
655 Metropolitan Ave 02136 617-635-6437
Naia Wilson, hdmstr. Fax 635-6332
Rogers MS 600/6-8
15 Everett St 02136 617-635-8700
Geoffrey Walker, prin. Fax 635-8708

**Indian Orchard, See Springfield**
Springfield SD
Supt. — See Springfield
Springfield Public Day HS 100/Alt
90 Berkshire St 01151 413-787-7036
Rhonda Jacobs, prin. Fax 787-6828

**Ipswich, Essex, Pop. 4,128**
Ipswich SD 2,100/PK-12
1 Lord Sq 01938 978-356-2935
Dr. William Hart, supt. Fax 356-0445
www.ipsk12.net
Ipswich HS 700/9-12
134 High St 01938 978-356-3137
David Dalton, prin. Fax 356-3720
Ipswich MS 500/6-8
130 High St 01938 978-356-3535
David Fabrizio, prin. Fax 412-8169

**Jamaica Plain, See Boston**
Boston SD
Supt. — See Boston
Community Academy 50/Alt
25 Glen Rd 02130 617-635-7734
Jennifer Levine, prin. Fax 635-7731
English HS 700/9-12
144 McBride St 02130 617-635-8979
Ligia Noriega-Murphy, prin. Fax 635-8988
Muniz Academy 9-12
20 Child St 02130 617-635-8198
Dr. Dania Vazquez, prin. Fax 635-7835

**Jefferson, Worcester**
Wachusett Regional SD 7,100/PK-12
1745 Main St 01522 508-829-1670
Dr. Darryll McCall Ed.D., supt. Fax 829-1680
www.wrsd.net
Other Schools – See Holden, Rutland, Sterling

**Kingston, Plymouth, Pop. 5,491**
Silver Lake Regional SD 1,800/7-12
250 Pembroke St 02364 781-585-4313
Joy Blackwood, supt. Fax 585-2994
www.slrsd.org
Silver Lake Regional HS 1,200/9-12
260 Pembroke St 02364 781-585-3844
James Mulcahy, prin. Fax 585-6544
Silver Lake Regional MS 600/7-8
256 Pembroke St 02364 781-582-3555
James Dupille, prin. Fax 582-3599

---

Sacred Heart HS 400/7-12
399 Bishops Hwy 02364 781-585-7511
Dr. Michael Gill, prin. Fax 396-3230

**Lakeville, Plymouth**
Freetown-Lakeville SD 2,900/PK-12
98 Howland Rd 02347 508-923-2000
Richard Medeiros, supt. Fax 923-0934
www.freelake.org/
Apponequet Regional HS 800/9-12
100 Howland Rd 02347 508-947-2660
Barbara Starkie, prin. Fax 946-2350
Freetown-Lakeville MS 800/6-8
96 Howland Rd 02347 508-923-3518
David Patota, prin. Fax 946-2050

**Lancaster, Worcester**
Nashoba Regional SD
Supt. — See Bolton
Burbank MS 200/6-8
1 Hollywood Dr 01523 978-365-4558
Laura Friend, prin. Fax 365-6882

**Lawrence, Essex, Pop. 75,608**
Lawrence SD 11,100/PK-12
233 Haverhill St 01841 978-975-5905
Jeffrey Riley, supt. Fax 722-8550
www.lawrence.k12.ma.us
Arlington MS 500/5-8
150 Arlington St 01841 978-975-5930
Robin Finn, prin. Fax 722-8519
Bruce S 600/3-8
135 Butler St 01841 978-975-5935
Cheryl Merz, prin. Fax 722-8521
Business Management & Finance HS 500/9-12
70-71 N Parish Rd 01843 978-946-0713
Sean McCarthy, prin. Fax 722-8501
Frost MS 500/5-8
33 Hamlet St 01843 978-722-8810
Ellen Baranowski, prin. Fax 722-8513
Guilmette MS 600/5-8
80 Bodwell St 01841 978-722-8270
Melissa Spash, prin. Fax 722-8524
Health & Human Services HS 500/9-12
70-71 N Parish Rd 01843 978-946-0735
Paul Neal, prin. Fax 722-8502
Humanities & Leadership Development HS 500/9-12
70-71 N Parish Rd 01843 978-946-0724
Edward Lombardi, prin. Fax 722-8503
International HS 500/9-12
70-71 N Parish Rd 01843 978-946-0712
Geraldo Acosta, prin. Fax 722-8504
HS Learning Center 200/9-12
233 E Haverhill St 01841 978-975-5917
Robert Cayer, prin. Fax 722-8531
Mathematics Science & Technology HS 500/9-12
70-71 N Parish Rd 01843 978-946-0719
Alyce Merlino, prin. Fax 722-8505
Parthum MS 500/5-8
255 E Haverhill St 01841 978-691-7224
Peter Lefebre, prin. Fax 722-8536
Performing & Fine Arts HS 500/9-12
70-71 N Parish Rd 01843 978-946-0766
Anne Callagy, prin. Fax 722-8506
Adult Learning Center Adult
147 Haverhill St 01840 978-722-8110

Bellesini Academy 100/5-8
94 Bradford St 01840 978-989-0004
Julie DeFillippo, dir. Fax 989-9404
Central Catholic HS 1,400/9-12
300 Hampshire St 01841 978-682-0260
Doreen Keller, prin. Fax 685-2707
Esperanza Academy 100/5-8
198 Garden St 01840 978-686-4673
Christopher Wilson, head sch Fax 681-1591
Notre Dame Cristo Rey HS 300/9-12
303 Haverhill St 01840 978-689-8222
Delia Duran-Clark, prin. Fax 689-8728

**Lee, Berkshire, Pop. 2,028**
Lee SD 800/PK-12
14 Park St 01238 413-243-0276
Alfred Skrocki, supt. Fax 243-4995
www.leepublicschools.net
Lee MSHS 400/7-12
300 Greylock St 01238 413-243-2781
Gregg Brighenti, prin. Fax 243-4105

**Leicester, Worcester, Pop. 10,191**
Leicester SD 1,800/PK-12
1078 Main St 01524 508-892-7040
Dr. Judith J. Paolucci, supt. Fax 892-7043
www.leicester.k12.ma.us/
Leicester HS 500/9-12
174 Paxton St 01524 508-892-7030
Tracey Hippert, prin. Fax 892-7034
Leicester MS 400/6-8
70 Winslow Ave 01524 508-892-7055
Fax 892-7047

**Lenox, Berkshire, Pop. 1,652**
Lenox SD 800/PK-12
6 Walker St Ste 3 01240 413-637-5550
Timothy Lee, supt. Fax 637-5559
www.lenoxps.org
Lenox Memorial HS 500/6-12
197 East St 01240 413-637-5560
Michael Knybel, prin. Fax 637-5564

Berkshire County Christian S 100/PK-12
PO Box 1980 01240 413-637-2474
Heidi Dickerson, prin.

**Leominster, Worcester, Pop. 39,624**
Leominster SD 6,200/PK-12
24 Church St 01453 978-534-7700
Jim Jolicoeur, supt. Fax 534-7775
www.leominster.mec.edu/
Leominster Center Technical Education Vo/Tech
122 Granite St 01453 978-534-7735
David Fiandaca, dir. Fax 537-7934
Leominster HS 1,200/9-12
122 Granite St 01453 978-534-7715
Christopher Lord, prin. Fax 537-1765
Samoset MS 500/6-8
100 DeCicco Dr 01453 978-534-7725
Colleen LeClair, prin. Fax 466-7421
Sky View MS 900/6-8
500 Kennedy Way 01453 978-534-7780
Timothy Blake, prin. Fax 840-8600

**Lexington, Middlesex, Pop. 30,568**
Lexington SD 6,400/PK-12
146 Maple St 02420 781-861-2580
Dr. Mary Czajkowski, supt. Fax 863-5829
lps.lexingtonma.org
Clarke MS 800/6-8
17 Stedman Rd 02421 781-861-2450
Anna Monaco, prin. Fax 674-2043
Diamond MS 800/6-8
99 Hancock St 02420 781-861-2460
Anne Carothers, prin. Fax 274-0174
Lexington HS 2,000/9-12
251 Waltham St 02421 781-861-2320
Laura Lasa, prin. Fax 861-2440

Minuteman Regional Vocational Tech SD
758 Marrett Rd 02421 781-861-6500
Dr. Edward Bouquillon, supt. Fax 863-1747
www.minuteman.org
Minuteman Regional Technical HS Vo/Tech
758 Marrett Rd 02421 781-861-6500
John Dillon, prin. Fax 863-1747

Lexington Christian Academy 300/6-12
48 Bartlett Ave 02420 781-862-7850
Timothy Russell, head sch Fax 863-8503

**Lincoln, Middlesex, Pop. 2,850**
Lincoln SD 1,100/PK-8
6 Ballfield Rd 01773 781-259-9400
Rebecca McFall, supt. Fax 259-9246
www.lincnet.org/
Other Schools – See Hanscom AFB

**Littleton, Middlesex, Pop. 2,867**
Littleton SD 1,600/PK-12
PO Box 1486 01460 978-540-2500
Kelly Clenchy, supt. Fax 486-9581
www.littletonps.org/
Littleton HS 400/9-12
56 King St 01460 978-952-2555
Dr. John Harrington, prin. Fax 486-0758
Littleton MS 400/6-8
55 Russell St 01460 978-486-8938
Dr. Mark Branco, prin. Fax 952-4547

**Longmeadow, Hampden, Pop. 15,594**
Longmeadow SD 3,000/PK-12
535 Bliss Rd 01106 413-565-4200
Marie Doyle, supt. Fax 565-4215
sites.longmeadow.k12.ma.us/www/
Glenbrook MS 400/6-8
110 Cambridge Cir 01106 413-565-4250
Nikcole Allen, prin. Fax 565-4277
Longmeadow HS 1,000/9-12
95 Grassy Gutter Rd 01106 413-565-4220
Thomas Landers, prin. Fax 565-4233
Williams MS 400/6-8
410 Williams St 01106 413-565-4260
Taylor Wrye, prin. Fax 565-4254

Bay Path College Post-Sec.
588 Longmeadow St 01106 413-565-1000

**Lowell, Middlesex, Pop. 102,517**
Lowell SD 13,200/PK-12
155 Merrimack St 01852 978-674-4320
Salah Khelfaoui Ph.D., supt. Fax 937-7609
www.lowell.k12.ma.us
Butler MS 600/5-8
1140 Gorham St 01852 978-937-8973
Teresa Soares-Pena, prin. Fax 937-2819
Daley MS 700/5-8
150 Fleming St 01851 978-937-8981
Liam Skinner, prin. Fax 937-7610
Lowell HS 2,300/9-12
50 Father Morissette Blvd 01852 978-937-8900
Brian Martin, hdmstr. Fax 937-8902
Lowell HS Career Academy Vo/Tech
125 Smith St 01851 978-970-3318
Margo Ferrick, coord. Fax 275-6399
O'Connell Alternative S Alt
21 Carter St 01852 978-446-7000
Liam Skinner, prin. Fax 937-7656
Robinson MS 600/5-8
110 June St 01850 978-937-8974
Thad King, prin. Fax 937-8988
Stoklosa MS 700/5-8
560 Broadway St 01854 978-275-6330
Nancy O'Loughlin, prin. Fax 275-6343
Sullivan MS 700/5-8
150 Draper St 01852 978-937-8993
Jacqueline Paton, prin. Fax 937-3278
Wang MS 700/5-8
365 W Meadow Rd 01854 978-937-7683
Matthew Stahl, prin. Fax 937-7680

Blaine The Beauty Career School Post-Sec.
231 Central St 01852 978-459-9959
Community Christian Academy 200/PK-12
105 Princeton Blvd 01851 978-453-4738
Jennifer Najem, prin. Fax 453-1506
Lincoln Technical Institute Post-Sec.
211 Plain St 01852 978-458-4800
Lowell Academy Hairstyling Institute Post-Sec.
136 Central St 01852 978-453-3235
Lowell Catholic HS 400/9-12
530 Stevens St 01851 978-452-1794
Maryellen DeMarco, prin. Fax 452-5646
University of Massachusetts Lowell Post-Sec.
1 University Ave 01854 978-934-4000

**Ludlow, Hampden, Pop. 18,820**
Ludlow SD 2,900/PK-12
63 Chestnut St 01056 413-583-8372
Todd Gazda, supt. Fax 583-5666
www.ludlowps.org
Baird MS 700/6-8
1 Rooney Rd 01056 413-583-5685
Joseph Langone, prin. Fax 583-5636
Ludlow HS 1,000/9-12
500 Chapin St 01056 413-589-9001
Lisa Nemeth, prin. Fax 583-5637

Jolie Hair and Beauty Academy Post-Sec.
44 Sewall St 01056 413-589-0747

**Lunenburg, Worcester, Pop. 1,728**
Lunenburg SD 1,200/PK-12
1025 Massachusetts Ave 01462 978-582-4100
Loxi Jo Calmes, supt. Fax 582-4103
www.lunenburgschools.net/
Lunenburg HS 500/8-12
1079 Massachusetts Ave 01462 978-582-4115
Brian Spadafino, prin. Fax 582-4153

Twin City Christian S 100/PK-12
194 Electric Ave 01462 978-582-4901
Jack Murray, admin. Fax 582-4978

**Lynn, Essex, Pop. 87,864**
Lynn SD 13,600/PK-12
100 Bennett St 01905 781-593-1680
Catherine Latham, supt. Fax 477-7487
www.lynnschools.org/
Breed MS 1,300/6-8
90 OCallaghan Way 01905 781-477-7330
Julie Louf, prin. Fax 581-6985
Classical HS 1,400/9-12
235 OCallaghan Way 01905 781-477-7404
Gene Constantino, prin. Fax 477-7212
English HS 1,700/9-12
50 Goodridge St 01902 781-477-7366
Thomas Strangie, prin. Fax 477-7365
Fecteau-Leary JSHS 200/7-12
33 N Common St 01902 781-268-3007
Maura Durgin-Scully, prin. Fax 268-3006
Lynn Vocational Technical Institute Vo/Tech
80 Neptune Blvd 01902 781-477-7431
Robert Buontempo, prin. Fax 477-7415
Marshall MS 900/6-8
19 Porter St 01902 781-477-7360
Molly Cohen, prin. Fax 477-7355
Pickering MS 600/6-8
70 Conomo Ave 01904 781-477-7440
Kevin Rittershaus, prin. Fax 477-7202

St. Mary JSHS 600/6-12
35 Tremont St 01902 781-595-7885
Grace Regan, head sch Fax 595-4471

**Lynnfield, Essex, Pop. 11,472**
Lynnfield SD 2,300/PK-12
525 Salem St 01940 781-334-9200
Jane Tremblay, supt. Fax 334-9209
www.lynnfield.k12.ma.us
Lynnfield HS 600/9-12
275 Essex St 01940 781-334-5820
Robert Cleary, prin. Fax 334-7207
Lynnfield MS 800/5-8
505 Main St 01940 781-334-5810
Stephen Ralston, prin. Fax 334-7203

**Malden, Middlesex, Pop. 56,660**
Malden SD 6,500/PK-12
200 Pleasant St 02148 781-397-7204
Dr. David DeRuosi, supt. Fax 397-7276
www.maldenps.org
Malden HS 1,800/9-12
77 Salem St 02148 781-397-7223
Dana Brown, prin. Fax 397-7224

Blaine The Beauty Career School Post-Sec.
347 Pleasant St 02148 781-397-7400
Malden Catholic HS 600/9-12
99 Crystal St 02148 781-322-3098
Br. Thomas Puccio, prin. Fax 397-0573
New England Hair Academy Post-Sec.
492 Main St # 500 02148 781-324-6799
Salter School Post-Sec.
2 Florence St 02148 781-324-5454

**Manchester, Essex, Pop. 5,286**
Manchester Essex Regional SD 1,400/PK-12
PO Box 1407 01944 978-526-4919
Pamela Beaudoin, supt. Fax 526-7585
www.mersd.org
Manchester Essex Regional HS 500/9-12
36 Lincoln St 01944 978-526-4412
Patricia Puglisi, prin. Fax 526-2046
Manchester Essex Regional MS 400/6-8
36 Lincoln St 01944 978-526-2022
Steven Guditus, prin. Fax 526-2046

**Mansfield, Bristol, Pop. 7,170**
Mansfield SD 4,700/K-12
2 Park Row 02048 508-261-7500
Zeffro Gianetti, supt. Fax 261-7509
www.mansfieldschools.com
Mansfield HS 1,400/9-12
250 East St 02048 508-261-7540
Michael Connolly, prin. Fax 339-0259
Qualters MS 1,100/6-8
240 East St 02048 508-261-7530
Suzanne Ryan, prin. Fax 261-7535

**Marblehead, Essex, Pop. 19,576**
Marblehead SD 3,200/PK-12
9 Widger Rd 01945 781-639-3141
Maryann Perry, supt. Fax 639-3149
www.marbleheadschools.org
Marblehead HS 900/9-12
2 Humphrey St 01945 781-639-3100
Layne Millington, prin. Fax 639-3105
Marblehead Veterans MS 500/7-8
217 Pleasant St 01945 781-639-3120
Matthew Fox, prin. Fax 639-3130

**Marion, Plymouth, Pop. 1,426**

Tabor Academy 500/9-12
66 Spring St 02738 508-748-2000
John Quirk, head sch Fax 291-6666

**Marlborough, Middlesex, Pop. 36,087**
Assabet Valley Regional Vocational SD
215 Fitchburg St 01752 508-485-9430
Ernest Houle, supt. Fax 460-3472
www.assabettech.com
Assabet Valley Regional Technical HS Vo/Tech
215 Fitchburg St 01752 508-485-9430
Mark Hollick, prin. Fax 460-3472

Marlborough SD 4,600/PK-12
17 Washington St 01752 508-460-3509
Richard Langlois, supt. Fax 485-1142
www.mps-edu.org
Hildreth S 100/Alt
85 Sawin St 01752 508-460-3505
Toby Peterson, dir. Fax 460-3746
Marlborough HS 1,100/9-12
431 Bolton St 01752 508-460-3500
Charles Caliri, prin. Fax 460-3501
Whitcomb MS 1,400/5-8
25 Union St 01752 508-460-3502
Brian Daniels, prin. Fax 460-3597

Hillside S 100/5-9
404 Robin Hill St 01752 508-485-2824
David Beecher, hdmstr. Fax 485-4420

**Marshfield, Plymouth, Pop. 4,261**
Marshfield SD 4,600/PK-12
76 S River St 02050 781-834-5000
Jeffrey Granatino, supt. Fax 834-5070
www.mpsd.org
Furnace Brook MS 1,100/6-8
500 Furnace St 02050 781-834-5020
Patrick Sullivan, prin. Fax 834-5899
Marshfield HS 1,400/9-12
167 Forest St 02050 781-834-5050
Robert Keuther, prin. Fax 834-5040

**Mashpee, Barnstable**
Mashpee SD 1,800/PK-12
150A Old Barnstable Rd 02649 508-539-1500
Brian Hyde, supt. Fax 477-5805
www.mashpee.k12.ma.us

Mashpee HS 500/9-12
500 Old Barnstable Rd 02649 508-539-3600
Mark Balestracci, prin. Fax 539-3607
Mashpee MS 300/7-8
500 Old Barnstable Rd 02649 508-539-3601
Mark Balestracci, prin. Fax 539-3603

**Mattapan, See Boston**
Boston SD
Supt. — See Boston
Mildred Avenue S 600/3-8
5 Mildred Ave 02126 617-635-1642
Andrew Rollins, prin. Fax 635-1641

**Mattapoisett, Plymouth, Pop. 2,949**
Old Rochester Regional SD 1,200/7-12
135 Marion Rd 02739 508-758-2772
Dr. Douglas White, supt. Fax 758-2802
www.oldrochester.org
Old Rochester Regional HS 700/9-12
135 Marion Rd 02739 508-758-3745
Michael Devoll, prin. Fax 758-3167
Old Rochester Regional JHS 500/7-8
133 Marion Rd 02739 508-758-4928
Kevin Brogioli, prin. Fax 758-6021

**Maynard, Middlesex, Pop. 9,932**
Maynard SD 1,300/PK-12
3-R Tiger Dr 01754 978-897-2222
Dr. Robert Gerardi, supt. Fax 897-4610
www.maynard.k12.ma.us
Maynard HS 300/8-12
1 Tiger Dr 01754 978-897-8891
Charles Caragianes, prin. Fax 897-6089

**Medfield, Norfolk, Pop. 6,407**
Medfield SD 2,900/PK-12
459 Main St Fl 3 02052 508-359-2302
Jeffrey Marsden, supt. Fax 359-9829
www.medfield.net
Blake MS 700/6-8
24 Pound St 02052 508-359-2396
Nathaniel Vaughn, prin. Fax 359-0134
Medfield HS 900/9-12
88R South St 02052 508-359-8385
Robert Parga, prin. Fax 359-2963

---

Montrose S 200/6-12
29 North St 02052 508-359-2423
Dr. Karen E. Bohlin Ed.D., head sch Fax 359-2597

**Medford, Middlesex, Pop. 53,960**
Medford SD 4,800/PK-12
489 Winthrop St 02155 781-393-2442
Roy Belson, supt. Fax 393-2322
www.medford.k12.ma.us
Andrews MS 500/6-8
3000 Mystic Valley Pkwy 02155 781-393-2228
Paul D'Alleva, prin. Fax 395-8128
Curtis-Tufts Alternative S 50/Alt
437 Main St 02155 781-393-2343
Brian Twomey, dir. Fax 393-0699
McGlynn MS 600/6-8
3004 Mystic Valley Pkwy 02155 781-393-2333
Jacob Edwards, prin. Fax 393-5462
Medford HS 1,200/9-12
489 Winthrop St 02155 781-393-2301
John Perella, prin. Fax 395-1468
Medford Vo-Tech HS Vo/Tech
489 Winthrop St 02155 781-393-2260
Heidi Riccio, dir. Fax 393-2293

---

Lawrence Memorial/Regis College Post-Sec.
170 Governors Ave 02155 781-306-6600
St. Clement S 200/K-12
579 Boston Ave 02155 617-393-5600
Robert Chevrier, prin. Fax 396-3230
The Elizabeth Grady School of Esthetics Post-Sec.
34 Salem St 02155 781-395-1971
Tufts University Post-Sec.
520 Boston Ave 02155 617-628-5000

**Medway, Norfolk, Pop. 9,931**
Medway SD 2,000/PK-12
45 Holliston St 02053 508-533-3222
Armand Pires Ph.D., supt. Fax 533-3226
www.medwayschools.org
Medway HS 800/9-12
88 Summer St 02053 508-533-3227
Timothy McCarron, prin. Fax 533-3246
Medway MS 800/5-8
45 Holliston St 02053 508-533-3230
Cari Lynne Perchase, prin. Fax 533-3257

**Melrose, Middlesex, Pop. 26,480**
Melrose SD 3,800/PK-12
360 Lynn Fells Pkwy 02176 781-662-2000
Cyndy Taymore, supt. Fax 979-2149
www.melroseschools.com
Melrose HS 1,000/9-12
360 Lynn Fells Pkwy 02176 781-979-2200
Marianne Farrell, prin. Fax 979-2205
Melrose Veterans Memorial MS 900/6-8
350 Lynn Fells Pkwy 02176 781-979-2100
Brent Conway, prin. Fax 979-2104

**Mendon, Worcester**
Mendon-Upton Regional SD 2,600/PK-12
150 North Ave 01756 508-634-1585
Joseph Maruszczak, supt. Fax 634-1582
mursd.org
Miscoe Hill S 800/5-8
148 North Ave 01756 508-634-1590
Ann Farrell, prin. Fax 634-1576
Other Schools – See Upton

---

Bethany Christian Academy 100/PK-12
15 Cape Rd 01756 508-634-8171

**Methuen, Essex, Pop. 46,662**
Methuen SD 7,000/PK-12
10 Ditson Pl 01844 978-722-6000
Judith Scannell, supt. Fax 722-6002
www.methuen.k12.ma.us
Methuen HS 1,800/9-12
1 Ranger Rd 01844 978-722-6040
Richard Barden, prin. Fax 722-6042

---

Fellowship Christian Academy 100/PK-12
1 Fellowship Way 01844 978-686-9373
Joann Spain, admin. Fax 685-7466
Presentation of Mary Academy 100/9-12
209 Lawrence St 01844 978-682-9391
Rose Maria Redman, prin. Fax 975-3595

**Middleboro, Plymouth, Pop. 7,135**
Middleborough SD 3,300/PK-12
30 Forest St 02346 508-946-2000
Brian Lynch, supt. Fax 946-2004
www.middleboro.k12.ma.us
Middleboro HS 800/9-12
71 E Grove St 02346 508-946-2010
Paul Branagan, prin. Fax 946-8852
Nichols MS 900/6-8
112 Tiger Dr 02346 508-946-2020
Martin Geoghegan, prin. Fax 946-2019

**Milford, Worcester, Pop. 23,757**
Milford SD 4,100/PK-12
31 W Fountain St 01757 508-478-1100
Dr. Robert Tremblay Ed.D., supt. Fax 478-1459
www.milfordpublicschools.com
Milford HS 1,100/9-12
31 W Fountain St 01757 508-478-1110
Carolyn Banach, prin. Fax 478-1460
Milford MS East 300/8-8
45 Main St 01757 508-478-1170
Fax 634-2381

**Millbury, Worcester, Pop. 12,228**
Millbury SD 1,800/PK-12
12 Martin St 01527 508-865-9501
Gregory Myers, supt. Fax 865-0888
www.millburyschools.org
Millbury JSHS 800/7-12
12 Martin St 01527 508-865-5841
Tara Bennett, prin. Fax 865-5845

**Millis, Norfolk, Pop. 4,081**
Millis SD 1,500/PK-12
245 Plain St 02054 508-376-7000
Nancy Gustafson, supt. Fax 376-7020
www.millisps.org
Millis HS 400/9-12
245 Plain St 02054 508-376-7010
Robert Mullaney, prin. Fax 376-7020
Millis MS 400/5-8
245 Plain St 02054 508-376-7014
Maureen Knowlton, prin. Fax 376-7020

**Milton, Norfolk, Pop. 26,216**
Milton SD 3,900/PK-12
25 Gile Rd 02186 617-696-4808
Mary C. Gormley, supt. Fax 696-5099
www.miltonps.org
Milton HS 1,000/9-12
25 Gile Rd 02186 617-696-4470
James Jette, prin. Fax 696-6990
Pierce MS 900/6-8
451 Central Ave 02186 617-696-4568
Dr. Karen Spaulding, prin. Fax 698-2238

---

Curry College Post-Sec.
1071 Blue Hill Ave 02186 617-333-0500
Fontbonne Academy 400/9-12
930 Brook Rd 02186 617-696-3241
Mary Ellen Barnes, head sch Fax 696-7688
Milton Academy 1,000/K-12
170 Centre St 02186 617-898-1798
Todd Bland, hdmstr. Fax 898-1700

**Monson, Hampden, Pop. 2,101**
Monson SD 1,300/PK-12
PO Box 159 01057 413-267-4150
Cheryl Clarke, supt. Fax 267-9168
www.monsonschools.com
Granite Valley MS 500/5-8
21 Thompson St 01057 413-267-4155
Mary Cieplik, prin. Fax 267-4624
Monson Innovation HS 300/9-12
55 Margaret St 01057 413-267-4589
William Metzger, prin. Fax 267-4157

**Montague, Franklin**
Gill-Montague SD
Supt. — See Turners Falls
Great Falls MS 200/6-8
224 Turnpike Rd 01351 413-863-7300
Ann Leonard, prin. Fax 863-7354
Turners Falls HS 300/9-12
222 Turnpike Rd 01351 413-863-7200
Thomas Osborn, prin. Fax 863-7353

**Mount Hermon, Franklin**

---

Northfield Mt. Hermon S 600/9-12
1 Lamplighter Way 01354 413-498-3000
Peter Fayroian, hdmstr. Fax 498-3170

**Nantucket, Nantucket, Pop. 7,268**
Nantucket SD 1,300/PK-12
10 Surfside Rd 02554 508-228-7285
William Cozort, supt. Fax 325-5318
www.npsk.org
Nantucket HS 400/9-12
10 Surfside Rd 02554 508-228-7280
John Buckey, prin. Fax 325-5318
Peirce MS 300/6-8
10 Surfside Rd 02554 508-228-7283
Peter Cohen, prin. Fax 325-7597

**Natick, Middlesex, Pop. 30,700**
Natick SD 4,900/PK-12
13 E Central St 01760 508-647-6500
Dr. Peter Sanchioni, supt. Fax 647-6506
www.natickps.org/
Kennedy MS 600/5-8
165 Mill St 01760 508-647-6650
Andrew Zitoli, prin. Fax 647-6658
Natick HS 1,300/PK-PK, 9-
15 West St 01760 508-647-6600
Brian Harrigan, prin. Fax 651-7372
Wilson MS 900/5-8
22 Rutledge Rd 01760 508-647-6670
Teresa Carney, prin. Fax 647-6678

---

Walnut Hill S for the Arts 300/9-12
12 Highland St 01760 508-653-4312
Antonio Viva, head sch Fax 655-3726

**Needham, Norfolk, Pop. 28,386**
Needham SD 5,400/PK-12
1330 Highland Ave 02492 781-455-0400
Dr. Daniel Gutekanst, supt. Fax 455-0417
www.needham.k12.ma.us/
Pollard MS 800/7-8
200 Harris Ave 02492 781-455-0480
Tamatha Bibbo, prin. Fax 455-0413
Other Schools – See Needham Heights

---

Franklin W. Olin College of Engineering Post-Sec.
Olin Way 02492 781-292-2300
Haddad MS 200/6-8
110 May St 02492 781-449-0133
Jane Abel, prin. Fax 449-8096
St. Sebastians S 400/7-12
1191 Greendale Ave 02492 781-449-5200
William Burke, hdmstr. Fax 449-5630

**Needham Heights, Norfolk**
Needham SD
Supt. — See Needham
Needham HS 1,500/9-12
609 Webster St 02494 781-455-0800
Joseph Barnes, prin. Fax 449-5111

**New Bedford, Bristol, Pop. 86,721**
Greater New Bedford Reg Vo/Tech HSD
1121 Ashley Blvd 02745 508-998-3321
James O'Brien, supt. Fax 995-7268
www.gnbvt.edu
Greater New Bedford Reg. Vo Tech HS Vo/Tech
1121 Ashley Blvd 02745 508-998-3321
Rosanne Franco, prin. Fax 995-7268

New Bedford SD 12,500/PK-12
455 County St 02740 508-997-4511
Dr. Pia Durkin Ph.D., supt. Fax 997-0298
www.newbedfordschools.org
Keith MS 900/6-8
225 Hathaway Blvd 02740 508-997-4511
Dr. Paula Bailey, prin. Fax 996-2040
New Bedford HS 2,500/9-12
230 Hathaway Blvd 02740 508-997-4511
Bernadette Coelho, prin. Fax 991-7483
Normandin MS 1,000/6-8
81 Felton St 02745 508-997-4511
Stephen Farrell, prin. Fax 995-6975
Roosevelt MS 800/6-8
119 Frederick St 02744 508-997-4511
Daniel Bossolt, prin. Fax 997-1198
Trinity Day Academy 50/Alt
181 Hillman St 02740 508-997-4511
Matthew Kravitz, prin. Fax 991-7483
Whaling City Alternative S 100/Alt
455 County St 02740 508-997-4511
Arnold Chamanlal, prin.

---

LaBaron Hairdressing Academy Post-Sec.
281 Union St 02740 508-996-6611
Nazarene Christian Academy 200/PK-12
764 Hathaway Rd 02740 508-992-7944
Susan Helm, prin. Fax 328-9513
Rob Roy Academy Post-Sec.
1872 Acushnet Ave 02746 508-995-8711
St. Luke's Hospital Post-Sec.
101 Page St 02740 508-997-1525
Salter School Post-Sec.
950 Kings Hwy Ste 4 02745 774-328-3500

**Newburyport, Essex, Pop. 17,171**
Newburyport SD 2,100/PK-12
70 Low St 01950 978-465-4456
Susan Viccaro, supt. Fax 462-3495
www.newburyport.k12.ma.us/
Newburyport HS 700/9-12
241 High St 01950 978-465-4440
Michael Parent, prin. Fax 465-2198
Nock MS 500/6-8
70 Low St 01950 978-465-4447
Beth Raucci, prin. Fax 465-4074

**Newton, Middlesex, Pop. 83,100**
Newton SD
Supt. — See Newtonville
Bigelow MS 500/6-8
42 Vernon St 02458 617-552-7800
Todd Harrison, prin. Fax 552-7752
Oak Hill MS 600/6-8
130 Wheeler Rd 02459 617-559-9200
Dr. John Harutunian, prin. Fax 552-5547

---

CATS Academy Boston 200/9-12
575 Washington St 02458 857-400-9700
Dr. James Tracy, head sch Fax 400-9704

Hebrew College Post-Sec.
160 Herrick Rd 02459 617-559-8600
Lasell College Post-Sec.
1844 Commonwealth Ave 02466 617-243-2000
Massachusetts School Professional Psych. Post-Sec.
1 Wells Ave 02459 617-327-6777
Mt. Alvernia HS 200/7-12
790 Centre St 02458 617-969-2260
Eileen McLaughlin, hdmstr. Fax 969-4246
New England School of Acupuncture Post-Sec.
150 California St 02458 617-558-1788
Newton Country Day S 400/5-12
785 Centre St 02458 617-244-4246
Sr. Barbara Rogers, hdmstr. Fax 965-5313

**Newton Center, See Newton**
Newton SD
Supt. — See Newtonville
Brown MS 700/6-8
125 Meadowbrook Rd 02459 617-559-6900
John Jordan, prin. Fax 552-7729
Newton South HS 1,700/9-12
140 Brandeis Rd 02459 617-559-6700
Joel Stembridge, prin. Fax 559-6701

---

Andover Newton Theological School Post-Sec.
210 Herrick Rd 02459 617-964-1100
Mt. Ida College Post-Sec.
777 Dedham St 02459 617-928-4500

**Newtonville, See Newton**
Newton SD 12,100/PK-12
100 Walnut St 02460 617-559-6100
David Fleishman, supt. Fax 559-6101
www.newton.k12.ma.us
Day MS 800/6-8
21 Minot Pl 02460 617-559-9100
Brian Turner, prin. Fax 559-9103
Newton North HS 1,800/9-12
457 Walnut St 02460 617-559-6200
Mark Aronson, prin. Fax 559-6204
Other Schools – See Newton, Newton Center

**Norfolk, Norfolk**
King Philip Regional SD 2,100/7-12
18 King St 02056 508-520-7991
Dr. Elizabeth Zielinski, supt.
www.kingphilip.org
King Philip MS 900/7-8
18 King St 02056 508-541-7324
Dr. Susan Gilson, prin. Fax 541-3467
Other Schools – See Wrentham

**North Adams, Berkshire, Pop. 13,389**
North Adams SD 1,500/PK-12
37 Main St Ste 200 01247 413-776-1458
James E. Montepare, supt. Fax 776-1685
www.napsk12.org/
Drury HS 500/8-12
1130 S Church St 01247 413-662-3240
Amy Meehan, prin. Fax 662-3239

Northern Berkshire Vocational Regnl SD
70 Hodges Crossroads 01247 413-663-5383
James Brosnan, supt. Fax 664-9424
www.mccanntech.org
McCann Technical S Vo/Tech
70 Hodges Crossroads 01247 413-663-5383
Justin R. Kratz, prin. Fax 664-9424

---

C.H. McCann Technical School Post-Sec.
70 Hodges Crossroads 01247 413-663-5383
Massachusetts College of Liberal Arts Post-Sec.
375 Church St 01247 413-662-5000

**Northampton, Hampshire, Pop. 27,865**
Northampton SD 2,700/PK-12
212 Main St Rm 200 01060 413-587-1315
Dr. John Provost, supt. Fax 587-1318
www.northampton-k12.us/
Northampton HS 900/9-12
380 Elm St 01060 413-587-1346
Bryan Lombardi, prin. Fax 587-1374
Other Schools – See Florence

Northampton-Smith SD
80 Locust St 01060 413-587-1414
Jeffrey Peterson, supt. Fax 587-1405
smith.tec.ma.us
Smith Vocational & Agricultural HS Vo/Tech
80 Locust St 01060 413-587-1414
John Kelly, prin. Fax 587-1406

---

Smith College 01063 Post-Sec.
413-584-2700

**North Andover, Essex, Pop. 22,792**
North Andover SD 4,700/PK-12
566 Main St 01845 978-794-1503
Dr. Jennifer Price, supt. Fax 794-0231
www.northandoverpublicschools.com
North Andover HS 1,300/9-12
430 Osgood St 01845 978-794-1711
Carla Scuzzarella, prin. Fax 688-3536
North Andover MS 1,100/6-8
495 Main St 01845 978-794-1870
Joan McQuade, prin. Fax 794-3619

---

Brooks S 400/9-12
1160 Great Pond Rd 01845 978-725-6300
John Packard, head sch Fax 725-6215
Merrimack College Post-Sec.
315 Turnpike St 01845 978-837-5000

**North Attleboro, Bristol, Pop. 16,178**
North Attleborough SD 4,700/PK-12
6 Morse St 02760 508-643-2100
Suzan Cullen, supt. Fax 643-2110
www.naschools.net
North Attleboro HS 1,200/9-12
1 Wilson W Whitty Way 02760 508-643-2115
Craig Juelis, prin. Fax 643-2173
North Attleboro MS 1,200/6-8
564 Landry Ave 02760 508-643-2130
Dr. Victoria Ekk, prin. Fax 643-2134

**Northborough, Worcester, Pop. 6,020**
Northborough-Southborough SD
Supt. — See Southborough
Algonquin Regional HS 1,400/9-12
79 Bartlett St 01532 508-351-7010
Thomas Mead, prin. Fax 393-9226
Melican MS 700/6-8
145 Lincoln St 01532 508-351-7020
Michelle Karb, prin. Fax 351-7006

**North Brookfield, Worcester, Pop. 2,236**
North Brookfield SD 600/PK-12
10 New School Dr 01535 508-867-9821
Dr. Marilyn Tencza, supt. Fax 867-8148
www.nbschools.org
North Brookfield JSHS 200/7-12
10 New School Dr 01535 508-867-7131
William Evans, prin. Fax 867-3496

**North Chelmsford, Middlesex**
Chelmsford SD
Supt. — See Chelmsford
Chelmsford HS 1,600/9-12
200 Richardson Rd 01863 978-251-5111
Stephen Murray, prin. Fax 251-5117

**North Dartmouth, Bristol, Pop. 8,000**
Dartmouth SD
Supt. — See South Dartmouth
Dartmouth MS 1,000/6-8
366 Slocum Rd 02747 508-997-9333
Darren Doane, prin. Fax 999-7720

---

Bishop Stang HS 700/9-12
500 Slocum Rd 02747 508-996-5602
Peter Shaughnessy, prin. Fax 994-6756
University of Massachusetts Dartmouth Post-Sec.
285 Old Westport Rd 02747 508-999-8000

**North Dighton, Bristol**
Dighton-Rehoboth Regional SD 3,100/PK-12
2700 Regional Rd 02764 508-252-5000
Dr. Anthony C. Azar, supt. Fax 252-5024
www.drregional.org
Dighton-Rehoboth Regional HS 900/9-12
2700 Regional Rd 02764 508-252-5025
Kevin Braga, prin. Fax 252-5079
Other Schools – See Dighton, Rehoboth

**North Eastham, Barnstable, Pop. 1,790**
Nauset SD
Supt. — See Orleans
Nauset Regional HS 1,000/9-12
PO Box 1887 02651 508-255-1505
Eduardo MacDonald, prin. Fax 255-9701

**North Easton, Bristol, Pop. 4,400**
Easton SD 3,700/PK-12
PO Box 359 02356 508-230-3200
Dr. Andrew Keough, supt. Fax 238-3563
www.easton.k12.ma.us
Ames HS 1,200/9-12
100 Lothrop St 02356 508-230-3210
Wesley Paul, prin. Fax 238-7325
Easton MS 900/6-8
98 Columbus Ave 02356 508-230-3222
R. Luke Carroll, prin. Fax 230-3102

---

Stonehill College Post-Sec.
320 Washington St 02357 508-565-1000

**Northfield, Franklin, Pop. 1,078**
Pioneer Valley SD 1,100/PK-12
97 F Sumner Turner Rd 01360 413-498-2911
Ruth Miller, supt. Fax 498-0045
sites.google.com/a/pvrsdk12.org/pvrsdhome/
Pioneer Valley Regional JSHS 600/7-12
97 F Sumner Turner Rd 01360 413-498-2931
Bill Wehrli, prin. Fax 498-0184

---

Redemption Christian Academy 50/PK-12
PO Box 183 01360 855-722-1979
John Massey, admin.

**North Quincy, See Quincy**
Quincy SD
Supt. — See Quincy
Atlantic MS 500/6-8
86 Hollis Ave 02171 617-984-8727
Maureen MacNeil, prin. Fax 984-8646
North Quincy HS 1,300/9-12
316 Hancock St 02171 617-984-8745
Robert Shaw, prin. Fax 984-8647

**North Reading, Middlesex, Pop. 12,002**
North Reading SD 2,600/PK-12
Sherman Rd 01864 978-664-7810
Jon Bernard, supt. Fax 664-0252
www.north-reading.k12.ma.us/
North Reading HS 700/9-12
Sherman Rd 01864 978-664-7800
Anthony Loprete, prin. Fax 664-7826
North Reading MS 700/6-8
Sherman Rd 01864 978-664-7806
Catherine O'Connell, prin. Fax 276-0679

**Norton, Bristol, Pop. 1,899**
Norton SD 2,700/PK-12
64 W Main St 02766 508-285-0100
Joseph Baeta, supt. Fax 285-0199
www.norton.k12.ma.us
Norton HS 700/9-12
66 W Main St 02766 508-285-0160
Megan Lafayette, prin. Fax 285-0164
Norton MS 700/6-8
215 W Main St 02766 508-285-0140
Vincent Hayward, prin. Fax 286-9457

---

Legacy Christian Academy 100/PK-12
1 New Taunton Ave 02766 508-952-2997
Katrina Joseph, head sch Fax 952-2977
Wheaton College Post-Sec.
26 E Main St 02766 508-286-8200

**Norwell, Plymouth**
Norwell SD 2,300/PK-12
322 Main St 02061 781-659-8800
Matthew Keegan, supt. Fax 659-8805
www.norwellschools.org
Norwell HS 700/9-12
18 South St 02061 781-659-8810
William Fish, prin. Fax 659-1824
Norwell MS 600/6-8
328 Main St 02061 781-659-8814
Derek Sulc, prin. Fax 659-8822

**Norwood, Norfolk, Pop. 27,997**
Norwood SD 3,500/PK-12
PO Box 67 02062 781-762-6804
James Hayden, supt. Fax 762-0229
www.norwood.k12.ma.us/
Coakley MS 700/6-8
PO Box 67 02062 781-762-7880
Jacqueline Mann, prin. Fax 255-5630
Norwood HS 1,100/9-12
PO Box 67 02062 781-769-2333
Jonathan Bourn, prin. Fax 762-0826

---

FINE Mortuary College Post-Sec.
150 Kerry Pl 02062 781-762-1211
ITT Technical Institute Post-Sec.
333 Providence Hwy 02062 781-278-7200
Universal Technical Institute Post-Sec.
1 Upland Rd Ste 200 02062 781-948-2000

**Oak Bluffs, Dukes**
Martha's Vineyard SD
Supt. — See Vineyard Haven
Martha's Vineyard Regional HS 700/9-12
PO Box 1385 02557 508-693-1033
Gil Traverso, prin. Fax 693-1891

**Orange, Franklin, Pop. 3,955**
Ralph C. Mahar Regional SD 700/7-12
PO Box 680 01364 978-544-2920
Tari Thomas, supt. Fax 544-8383
www.rcmahar.org
Mahar Regional S 700/7-12
PO Box 680 01364 978-544-2542
Scott Hemlin, prin. Fax 544-8383

**Orleans, Barnstable, Pop. 1,586**
Nauset SD 1,500/6-12
78 Eldridge Park Way 02653 508-255-8800
Thomas M. Conrad, supt. Fax 240-2351
www.nausetschools.org
Nauset Regional MS 600/6-8
70 S Orleans Rd 02653 508-255-0016
Dr. Maxine Minkoff, prin. Fax 240-1105
Other Schools – See North Eastham

**Osterville, Barnstable, Pop. 2,911**

---

Cape Cod Academy 300/PK-12
50 Osterville-W Barnstable 02655 508-428-5400
Thomas Trigg, head sch Fax 428-0701

**Oxford, Worcester, Pop. 6,042**
Oxford SD 2,000/PK-12
4 Maple Rd 01540 508-987-6050
Dr. Mark Garceau, supt. Fax 987-6054
www.oxps.org
Oxford HS 500/9-12
495 Main St 01540 508-987-6081
Ross Thibault, prin. Fax 987-6083
Oxford MS 700/5-8
497 Main St 01540 508-987-6074
David Cornacchioli, prin. Fax 987-2588
Project C.O.F.F.E.E. Alt
495 Main St 01540 508-987-6090
David Nugent, prin. Fax 987-6097

**Palmer, Hampden, Pop. 4,069**
Palmer SD 1,600/PK-12
24 Converse St Ste 1 01069 413-283-2650
Dr. Nancy Spitulnik, supt. Fax 283-2655
www.palmerschools.org
Palmer HS 500/8-12
4105 Main St 01069 413-283-6511
Mary Lou Callahan, prin. Fax 283-3476

Pathfinder Vocational-Technical SD
240 Sykes St 01069 413-283-9701
Dr. Gerald Paist, supt. Fax 284-0032
www.pathfindertech.org/
Pathfinder Reg Vocational Technical HS Vo/Tech
240 Sykes St 01069 413-283-9701
Mary Jane Rickson, prin. Fax 284-0032

**Paxton, Worcester**

---

Anna Maria College Post-Sec.
50 Sunset Ln 01612 508-849-3330

**Peabody, Essex, Pop. 50,101**
Peabody SD, 21 Johnson St 01960 6,000/PK-12
Herbert Levine Ph.D., supt. 978-531-1600
www.peabody.k12.ma.us/
Higgins MS 1,400/6-8
1 King St 01960 978-536-4800
Todd Bucey, prin. Fax 536-4810

Peabody Veterans Memorial HS 1,800/9-12
485 Lowell St 01960 978-536-4500
Eric Buckley, prin. Fax 535-9578

---

Bishop Fenwick HS 600/9-12
99 Margin St 01960 978-587-8300
Sr. Catherine Fleming, admin. Fax 587-8309

**Pembroke, Plymouth**
Pembroke SD 3,300/PK-12
72 Pilgrim Rd 02359 781-829-0832
Erin Obey, supt. Fax 826-6957
www.edlinesites.net/pages/PembrokePS
Pembroke Community MS 500/7-8
559 School St 02359 781-293-8627
Donna McGarrigle, prin. Fax 294-0916
Pembroke HS 900/9-12
80 Learning Ln 02359 781-293-9281
Margaret Szostak, prin. Fax 293-2812

**Pepperell, Middlesex, Pop. 2,459**
North Middlesex SD 4,100/PK-12
45 Main St 01463 978-597-8713
Joan Landers, supt. Fax 597-6534
nmrsd.org
Nissitissit MS 600/5-8
33 Chase Ave 01463 978-433-0114
Diane Gleason, prin. Fax 433-0118
Other Schools – See Townsend

**Pittsfield, Berkshire, Pop. 43,503**
Pittsfield SD 6,000/PK-12
269 1st St 01201 413-499-9512
Dr. Jason McCandless, supt. Fax 448-2643
www.pittsfield.net
Herberg MS 600/6-8
501 Pomeroy Ave 01201 413-448-9640
Gina Coleman, prin. Fax 448-9644
Pittsfield HS 900/9-12
300 East St 01201 413-499-9535
Matthew Bishop, prin. Fax 442-2540
Reid MS 600/6-8
950 North St 01201 413-448-9620
Linda Whitacre, prin. Fax 443-1587
Taconic HS 900/9-12
96 Valentine Rd 01201 413-448-9600
John Vosburgh, prin. Fax 499-4835

---

Berkshire Community College Post-Sec.
1350 West St 01201 413-499-4660
Berkshire Medical Center Post-Sec.
725 North St 01201 413-447-2144
Mildred Elley School Post-Sec.
505 East St 01201 413-499-8618
Miss Hall's S 200/9-12
PO Box 1166 01202 413-443-6401
Julia Heaton, head sch Fax 448-2994
St. Joseph Central HS 200/9-12
22 Maplewood Ave 01201 413-447-9121
Dr. Amy Gelinas, prin. Fax 443-7020

**Plymouth, Plymouth, Pop. 7,138**
Plymouth SD 8,000/PK-12
253 S Meadow Rd 02360 508-830-4300
Dr. Gary Maestas, supt. Fax 746-1873
www.plymouth.k12.ma.us
Plymouth Community IS 1,200/6-8
117 Long Pond Rd 02360 508-830-4450
Brian Palladino, prin. Fax 830-4464
Plymouth North HS 1,000/9-12
41 Obery St 02360 508-830-4400
Kathleen McSweeney, prin. Fax 830-4405
Plymouth South HS 1,400/9-12
490 Long Pond Rd 02360 508-224-7512
Patricia Fry, prin. Fax 224-6765
Plymouth South MS 700/5-8
488 Long Pond Rd 02360 508-224-2725
Steven Morgenweck, prin. Fax 224-5660

**Quincy, Norfolk, Pop. 89,796**
Quincy SD 9,200/PK-12
34 Coddington St 02169 617-984-8700
Dr. Richard DeCristofaro, supt. Fax 984-8965
www.quincypublicschools.com
Broad Meadows MS 300/6-8
50 Calvin Rd 02169 617-984-8723
Daniel Gilbert, prin. Fax 984-8834
Central MS 600/6-8
875 Hancock St 02170 617-984-8725
Rick DeCristofaro, prin. Fax 984-8661
Point Webster MS 400/5-8
60 Lancaster St 02169 617-984-6600
Christine Barrett, prin. Fax 984-6609
Quincy HS, 100 Coddington St 02169 1,500/9-12
Lawrence Taglieri, prin. 617-376-3355
Sterling MS 400/5-8
444 Granite St 02169 617-984-8729
John Franceschini, prin. Fax 984-8640
Other Schools – See North Quincy

---

Eastern Nazarene College Post-Sec.
23 E Elm Ave 02170 617-745-3000
Mansfield Beauty School Post-Sec.
200 Parkingway 02169 617-479-1090
Massachusetts School of Barbering Post-Sec.
64 Ross Way 02169 617-770-4444
Quincy College Post-Sec.
1250 Hancock St 02169 617-984-1700
Woodward S 100/6-12
1102 Hancock St 02169 617-773-5610
Carol Andrews, head sch Fax 770-1551

**Randolph, Norfolk, Pop. 30,586**
Randolph SD 2,900/PK-12
40 Highland Ave 02368 781-961-6205
Thomas Anderson, supt. Fax 961-6295
www.randolph.k12.ma.us
Randolph Community MS 800/6-8
225 High St 02368 781-961-6243
Thea Stovell, prin. Fax 961-6286
Randolph HS 800/9-12
70 Memorial Pkwy 02368 781-961-6220
Michael Allen, prin. Fax 961-6235

**Raynham, Bristol, Pop. 2,100**
Bridgewater-Raynham Regional SD
Supt. — See Bridgewater
Raynham MS 700/5-8
420 Titicut Rd 02767 508-977-0504
Richard Florence, prin. Fax 977-0659

**Reading, Middlesex, Pop. 24,477**
Reading SD 4,500/PK-12
82 Oakland Rd 01867 781-944-5800
Dr. John Doherty, supt. Fax 942-9149
reading.k12.ma.us/
Coolidge MS 500/6-8
89 Birch Meadow Dr 01867 781-942-9158
Sarah Marchant, prin. Fax 942-9118
Parker MS 600/6-8
45 Temple St 01867 781-944-1236
Douglas Lyons, prin. Fax 942-9008
Reading Memorial HS 1,300/9-12
62 Oakland Rd 01867 781-944-8200
Adam Bakr, prin. Fax 942-5435

---

Austin Preparatory HS 700/6-12
101 Willow St 01867 781-944-4900
Dr. James Hickey, hdmstr. Fax 944-7530

**Rehoboth, Bristol**
Dighton-Rehoboth Regional SD
Supt. — See North Dighton
Beckwith MS 600/5-8
330R Winthrop St 02769 508-252-5080
Joseph Pirraglia, prin. Fax 252-5082

**Revere, Suffolk, Pop. 50,075**
Revere SD 6,500/PK-12
101 School St 02151 781-286-8226
Dr. Dianne Kelly, supt. Fax 286-8221
www.revereps.mec.edu
Anthony MS 500/6-8
107 Newhall St 02151 781-388-7520
Joanne Willett, prin. Fax 388-7521
Garfield MS 500/6-8
176 Garfield Ave 02151 781-286-8298
Samantha Meier, prin. Fax 286-3557
Revere HS 1,500/9-12
101 School St 02151 781-286-8222
Lourenco Garcia Ed.D., prin. Fax 286-8378
Rumney Marsh Academy 500/6-8
140 American Legion Hwy 02151 781-388-3500
Richard Gallucci, prin. Fax 485-8443
Seacoast HS 100/Alt
15 Everard Ave 02151 781-485-2715
Thomas Misci, prin. Fax 485-2718

**Rochester, Plymouth**
Old Colony Reg Vocational Technical HSD
476 North Ave 02770 508-763-8011
Frank Cote, supt. Fax 763-9821
www.oldcolony.us
Old Colony Reg Vocational Tech HS Vo/Tech
476 North Ave 02770 508-763-8011
Karen Guenette, prin. Fax 763-9821

**Rockland, Plymouth, Pop. 16,123**
Rockland SD 1,900/K-12
34 MacKinlay Way 02370 781-878-3893
John Retchless, supt. Fax 982-1483
rocklandschools.org
Rockland HS 600/9-12
52 MacKinlay Way 02370 781-871-0541
Alan Cron, prin. Fax 878-0158
Rogers MS 600/5-8
100 Taunton Ave 02370 781-878-4341
Elizabeth Bohn, prin. Fax 871-8448

---

Calvary Chapel Academy 100/PK-12
PO Box 409 02370 781-871-1043
Richard Colello, hdmstr. Fax 792-3902

**Rockport, Essex, Pop. 4,922**
Rockport SD 900/PK-12
24 Jerdens Ln 01966 978-546-1200
Robert Liebow, supt. Fax 546-1205
www.rpk12.org
Rockport HS 300/9-12
24 Jerdens Ln 01966 978-546-1234
Greg Bach, prin. Fax 546-1205
Rockport MS 200/6-8
26 Jerdens Ln 01966 978-546-1250
Gregg Bach, prin. Fax 546-1205

**Roslindale, See Boston**
Boston SD
Supt. — See Boston
Irving MS 500/6-8
105 Cummins Hwy 02131 617-635-8072
Karin Kell-Deyo, prin. Fax 635-9363

**Roxbury, See Boston**
Boston SD
Supt. — See Boston
Greater Egleston Community HS 100/9-12
80 School St 02119 617-635-6429
Julie Coles, hdmstr. Fax 635-6469
Hayes S of Music 9-12
55 Malcolm X Blvd 02120 617-635-8973
Gregory Gazzola, dir. Fax 635-6363
Madison Park Technical Vocational HS Vo/Tech
75 Malcolm X Blvd 02120 617-635-8970
Shawn Shackelford, hdmstr. Fax 635-9831
O'Bryant HS of Mathematics & Science 1,300/7-12
55 Malcolm X Blvd 02120 617-635-9932
Nicole Gittens, hdmstr. Fax 635-7769

Timilty MS 700/6-8
205 Roxbury St 02119 617-635-8109
Renee McCall, prin. Fax 635-8115

**Roxbury Crossing, See Boston**

---

Roxbury Community College Post-Sec.
1234 Columbus Ave 02120 617-427-0060

**Rutland, Worcester, Pop. 2,084**
Wachusett Regional SD
Supt. — See Jefferson
Central Tree MS 400/6-8
281 Main St 01543 508-886-0073
Todd Stewart, prin. Fax 886-0141

---

Devereux Center in Massachusetts Post-Sec.
PO Box 219 01543 508-886-4746

**Salem, Essex, Pop. 40,441**
Salem SD 4,600/PK-12
29 Highland Ave 01970 978-740-1212
Margarita Ruiz, supt. Fax 740-3083
www.salemk12.org
Collins MS 600/6-8
29 Highland Ave 01970 978-740-1191
Glenn Burns, prin. Fax 740-1183
Salem HS 1,200/9-12
77 Willson St 01970 978-740-1123
David Angeramo, prin. Fax 740-1110
Salem Preparatory HS 50/9-12
114 Derby St 01970 978-740-1171
Carole Donnelly, prin. Fax 740-1239

---

Salem State University Post-Sec.
352 Lafayette St 01970 978-542-6000

**Sandwich, Barnstable, Pop. 2,933**
Sandwich SD 3,300/PK-12
33 Water St 02563 508-888-1054
Dr. C. Richard Canfield, supt. Fax 888-9505
www.sandwichk12.org
Other Schools – See East Sandwich

**Saugus, Essex, Pop. 26,187**
Saugus SD 2,800/PK-12
23 Main St 01906 781-231-5000
Dr. Matthew Malone, supt. Fax 233-9424
www.saugus.k12.ma.us
Belmonte MS 700/6-8
25 Dow St 01906 781-231-5052
Kerry Robbins, prin. Fax 233-5665
Saugus HS 700/9-12
1 Pierce Memorial Dr 01906 781-231-5027
Michael Hashem, prin. Fax 231-5030

**Scituate, Plymouth, Pop. 5,135**
Scituate SD 3,200/PK-12
606 Chief Justice Cushing 02066 781-545-8759
John McCarthy, supt. Fax 545-6291
www.scituate.k12.ma.us/
Gates IS 500/7-8
327 First Parish Rd 02066 781-545-8760
Ryan Lynch, prin. Fax 545-8767
Scituate HS 900/9-12
606 Chief Justice Cushing 02066 781-545-8750
Robert Wargo, prin. Fax 545-8758

**Seekonk, Bristol, Pop. 13,046**
Seekonk SD 2,100/PK-12
25 Water Ln 02771 508-399-5106
Arlene Bosco, supt. Fax 399-5128
seekonk.sharpschool.com/
Hurley MS 500/6-8
650 Newman Ave 02771 508-761-7570
Dr. William Whalen, prin. Fax 336-9630
Seekonk HS 700/9-12
261 Arcade Ave 02771 508-336-7272
Marcia McGovern, prin. Fax 336-8535

---

MotoRing Technical Training Institute Post-Sec.
1241 Fall River Ave 02771 866-454-6884

**Sharon, Norfolk, Pop. 5,546**
Sharon SD 3,400/K-12
75 Mountain St 02067 781-784-1570
Timothy Farmer, supt. Fax 784-1573
www.sharon.k12.ma.us
Sharon HS 1,200/9-12
181 Pond St 02067 781-784-1554
Dr. Jose Libano Ed.D., prin. Fax 784-1550
Sharon MS 800/6-8
75 Mountain St 02067 781-784-1560
Kevin O'Rourke, prin. Fax 784-8432

**Sheffield, Berkshire**
Southern Berkshire Regional SD 800/PK-12
PO Box 339 01257 413-229-8778
David Hastings, supt. Fax 229-2913
sbrsd.org
Mount Everett Regional HS 400/7-12
PO Box 219 01257 413-229-8734
Glenn Devoti, prin. Fax 229-2044

---

Berkshire S 400/9-12
245 N Undermountain Rd 01257 413-229-8511
Pieter Mulder, head sch Fax 229-1010

**Shelburne Falls, Franklin, Pop. 1,695**
Mohawk Trail SD 1,000/PK-12
24 Ashfield Rd 01370 413-625-0192
Michael Buoniconti, supt. Fax 625-0196
www.mohawkschools.org
Mohawk Trail Regional HS 500/7-12
26 Ashfield Rd 01370 413-625-9811
Lynn Dole, prin. Fax 625-6652

**Shirley, Middlesex, Pop. 1,415**
Ayer Shirley SD
Supt. — See Ayer
Ayer-Shirley MS 400/6-8
1 Hospital Rd 01464 978-772-8600
Roberta Aikey, prin. Fax 425-0474

**Shrewsbury, Worcester, Pop. 25,900**
Shrewsbury SD 5,900/PK-12
100 Maple Ave 01545 508-841-8400
Joseph Sawyer, supt. Fax 841-8490
schools.shrewsbury-ma.gov
Oak MS 900/7-8
45 Oak St 01545 508-841-1200
Ann Jones, prin. Fax 841-1223
Shrewsbury HS 1,600/9-12
64 Holden St 01545 508-841-8800
Todd Bazydlo, prin. Fax 841-8858

---

St. John's HS 1,100/9-12
378 Main St 01545 508-842-8934
Michael Welch, admin. Fax 842-3670

**Somerset, Bristol, Pop. 17,980**
Somerset Berkley Regional SD 1,000/9-12
580 Whetstone Hill Rd 02726 508-324-3100
Jeffrey Schoonover, supt. Fax 324-3118
www.sbregional.org
Somerset Berkley Regional HS 1,000/9-12
625 County St 02726 508-324-3115
David Lanczycki, prin. Fax 324-3118

Somerset SD 1,800/PK-8
580 Whetstone Hill Rd 02726 508-324-3100
Jeffrey Schoonover, supt. Fax 324-3104
www.somersetps.com
Somerset MS 600/6-8
1141 Brayton Ave 02726 508-324-3140
Pauline Camara Ph.D., prin. Fax 324-3145

**Somerville, Middlesex, Pop. 71,913**
Somerville SD 4,900/PK-12
42 Cross St 02145 617-629-5200
Mary Skipper, supt. Fax 666-1130
www.somerville.k12.ma.us
Full Circle HS 100/Alt
8 Bonair St 02145 617-629-5640
Margaret DePasquale, prin. Fax 628-6836
Next Wave JHS 50/Alt
8 Bonair St 02145 617-629-5640
Margaret DePasquale, prin. Fax 628-6837
Somerville HS 1,300/9-12
81 Highland Ave 02143 617-629-5250
John Oteri, hdmstr. Fax 629-4763

---

Lincoln Technical Institute Post-Sec.
5 Middlesex Ave 02145 617-776-3500

**Southborough, Worcester**
Northborough-Southborough SD 4,800/PK-12
53 Parkerville Rd 01772 508-486-5115
Christine Johnson, supt. Fax 486-5123
www.nsboro.k12.ma.us
Trottier MS 500/6-8
49 Parkerville Rd 01772 508-485-2400
Keith Lavoie, prin. Fax 481-1506
Other Schools – See Northborough

---

St. Marks S 300/9-12
25 Marlboro Rd 01772 508-786-6000
John Warren, head sch Fax 786-6109

**South Boston, See Boston**
Boston SD
Supt. — See Boston
Excel HS 700/9-12
95 G St 02127 617-635-9870
Stephanie Sibley, hdmstr. Fax 635-9711

**Southbridge, Worcester, Pop. 13,631**
Southbridge SD 1,700/PK-12
25 Cole Ave 01550 508-764-5415
Timothy Connors, supt. Fax 764-3181
www.southbridge.k12.ma.us
Southbridge MSHS 400/6-12
132 Torrey Rd 01550 508-764-5450
Melissa Earls, prin. Fax 318-1687

**South Dartmouth, Bristol, Pop. 9,850**
Dartmouth SD 3,900/PK-12
8 Bush St 02748 508-997-3391
Dr. Bonny L. Gifford, supt. Fax 991-4184
dartmouthps.schoolfusion.us/
Dartmouth HS 1,100/9-12
555 Bakerville Rd 02748 508-961-2700
John Gould, prin. Fax 910-1410
Other Schools – See North Dartmouth

**South Deerfield, Franklin, Pop. 1,861**
Frontier Regional SD 700/7-12
219 Christian Ln 01373 413-665-1155
Martha Barrett Ed.D., supt. Fax 665-8506
www.frsu38.org
Frontier Regional JSHS 700/7-12
113 N Main St 01373 413-665-2118
Darius Modestow, prin. Fax 665-1518

**South Easton, Bristol**
Southeastern Regional Voc Tech SD
250 Foundry St 02375 508-230-1200
Luis Lopes, supt. Fax 230-1563
www.sersd.org
Southeastern Regional Vo-Tech HS Vo/Tech
250 Foundry St 02375 508-230-1200
David Wheeler, prin. Fax 230-1567

---

Southeastern Technical Institute Post-Sec.
250 Foundry St 02375 508-238-1860

**South Hadley, Hampshire, Pop. 5,400**
South Hadley SD 2,000/PK-12
116 Main St 01075 413-538-5060
Dr. Nicholas D. Young, supt. Fax 532-6284
www.southhadleyschools.org
Smith MS 600/5-8
100 Mosier St 01075 413-538-5074
Paul Plummer, prin. Fax 538-5003
South Hadley HS 600/9-12
153 Newton St 01075 413-538-5063
Diana Bonneville, prin. Fax 532-6538

---

Mt. Holyoke College Post-Sec.
50 College St 01075 413-538-2000

**South Hamilton, Essex, Pop. 2,750**

---

Gordon-Conwell Theological Seminary Post-Sec.
130 Essex St 01982 978-468-7111
Pingree S 300/9-12
537 Highland St 01982 978-468-4415
Dr. Timothy Johnson, head sch Fax 468-3758

**South Lancaster, Worcester, Pop. 1,842**

---

South Lancaster Academy 300/PK-12
PO Box 1129 01561 978-368-8544

**Southwick, Hampden**
Southwick-Tolland-Granville SD 1,800/PK-12
86 Powder Mill Rd 01077 413-569-5391
John Barry, supt. Fax 569-1711
www.stgrsd.org
Southwick-Tolland Regional HS 500/7-12
93 Feeding Hills Rd 01077 413-569-6171
Joseph Turmel, prin. Fax 569-1723

**South Yarmouth, Barnstable, Pop. 10,789**
Dennis-Yarmouth SD 2,500/PK-12
296 Station Ave 02664 508-398-7600
Carol Woodbury, supt. Fax 398-7622
www.dy-regional.k12.ma.us/
Dennis-Yarmouth Regional HS 900/8-12
210 Station Ave 02664 508-398-7636
Kenneth Jenks, prin. Fax 398-7635

**Spencer, Worcester, Pop. 5,615**
Spencer-East Brookfield SD 1,400/PK-12
306 Main St 01562 508-885-8500
Dr. N. Tracy Crowe, supt. Fax 885-8504
www.sebrsd.org
Knox Trail JHS 300/5-8
73 Ash St 01562 508-885-8550
Jodi Bourassa, prin. Fax 885-8557
Prouty HS 500/9-12
302 Main St 01562 508-885-8505
David Bachant, prin. Fax 885-8511

---

Central Mass School of Massage & Therapy Post-Sec.
200 Main St 01562 508-885-0306

**Springfield, Hampden, Pop. 149,577**
Springfield SD 26,700/PK-12
1550 Main St 01103 413-787-7100
Daniel Warwick, supt. Fax 787-6713
www.sps.springfield.ma.us
Balliet MS 100/Alt
111 Seymour Ave 01109 413-787-7284
Chestnut Accelerated MS North 1,000/6-8
355 Plainfield St 01107 413-750-2333
Jason Hynek, prin. Fax 750-2351
Chestnut Accelerated MS South 6-8
355 Plainfield St 01107 413-750-2333
Daniel Sullivan, prin. Fax 750-2351
Chestnut Accelerated MS Talented & Gift 6-8
355 Plainfield St 01107 413-750-2333
Colleen O'Connor, prin. Fax 750-2351
Duggan MS 500/6-9
1015 Wilbraham Rd 01109 413-787-7410
Michael Calvanese, prin. Fax 750-2209
Forest Park MS 500/6-8
46 Oakland St 01108 413-787-7420
Thomas Mazza, prin. Fax 787-7419
Gateway to College at STCC 9-12
1 Armory Sq 01102 413-755-6344
Rhonda Reddick, prin.
Kennedy MS 700/6-8
1385 Berkshire Ave 01151 413-787-7510
Ryan Kelly, prin. Fax 787-7561
Kiley MS 700/6-8
180 Cooley St 01128 413-787-7240
Christopher Sutton, prin. Fax 787-7247
Liberty Preparatory Academy Alt
37 Alderman St 01108 413-750-2484
Putnam Vocational Technical HS Vo/Tech
1300 State St 01109 413-787-7424
George Johnson, prin. Fax 787-7330
South End MS, 36 Margaret St 01105 200/6-8
Cheryl Despirt, prin. 413-750-2442
Springfield Central HS 2,100/9-12
1840 Roosevelt Ave 01109 413-787-7085
Thaddeus Tokarz, prin. Fax 787-7040
Springfield Conservatory of the Arts 6-12
34 Kopernick St 01151 413-787-6914
David Brewster, prin.
Springfield HS Alt
37 Alderman St 01108 413-787-7285
HS of Commerce 1,100/9-12
415 State St 01105 413-787-7220
Diane Bauer, prin. Fax 787-7041
Springfield HS of Science-Tech 1,400/9-12
1250 State St 01109 413-750-2000
Sara Pragluski, prin. Fax 750-2047
Springfield Public Day MS 100/Alt
118 Alden St 01109 413-787-7261
Rhonda Jacobs, prin.
Springfield Renaissance S 700/6-12
1170 Carew St 01104 413-750-2929
Arria Coburn, prin. Fax 750-2978
STEM Middle Academy 300/6-8
60 Alton St 01109 413-787-6750
Kevin Lalime, prin. Fax 787-6952
Van Sickle Academy 1,000/6-8
1170 Carew St 01104 413-750-2887
Matthew Kuzmeskas, prin. Fax 750-2972
Van Sickle International Baccalaureate S 6-8
1170 Carew St 01104 413-750-2887
Daisy Roman-Davis, prin. Fax 750-2972
Adult Education Center Adult
310 State St 01105 413-787-7210
Armando Feliciano, dir.
Other Schools – See Holyoke, Indian Orchard

---

American International College Post-Sec.
1000 State St 01109 413-737-7000
Branford Hall Career Institute Post-Sec.
112 Industry Ave 01104 413-781-2276
Mansfield Beauty School Post-Sec.
266 Bridge St 01103 413-788-7575
Pioneer Valley Christian Academy 300/PK-12
965 Plumtree Rd 01119 413-782-8031
Timothy Duff, hdmstr. Fax 782-8033
Springfield College Post-Sec.
263 Alden St 01109 413-748-3000
Springfield Technical Community College Post-Sec.
PO Box 9000 01102 413-781-7822
Western New England University Post-Sec.
1215 Wilbraham Rd 01119 413-782-3111

**Sterling, Worcester**
Wachusett Regional SD
Supt. — See Jefferson
Chocksett MS 400/5-8
40 Boutelle Rd 01564 978-422-6552
Christopher LaBreck, prin. Fax 422-7720

**Stockbridge, Berkshire**
Berkshire Hills SD 1,300/PK-12
PO Box 617 01262 413-298-4017
Dr. Peter Dillon, supt. Fax 298-4672
www.bhrsd.org
Other Schools – See Great Barrington

---

Berkshire Waldorf HS 50/9-12
14 Pine St 01262 413-298-3800

**Stoneham, Middlesex, Pop. 21,118**
Stoneham SD 2,500/PK-12
149 Franklin St 02180 781-279-3802
Dr. Les Olson, supt. Fax 279-3818
www.stonehamschools.org
Stoneham HS 700/9-12
149 Franklin St 02180 781-279-3810
Donna Cargill, prin. Fax 279-2070
Stoneham MS 600/5-8
101 Central St 02180 781-279-3840
Christopher Banos, prin. Fax 279-3843

---

Edgewood/Greater Boston Academy 200/PK-12
108 Pond St 02180 781-438-4253

**Stoughton, Norfolk, Pop. 27,500**
Stoughton SD 3,800/PK-12
232 Pearl St 02072 781-344-4000
Marguerite C. Rizzi Ed.D., supt. Fax 344-3789
www.stoughtonschools.org/
O'Donnell MS 900/6-8
211 Cushing St 02072 781-344-7002
Matt Colantonio, prin. Fax 297-5263
Stoughton HS 1,100/9-12
232 Pearl St 02072 781-344-7001
Juliette Miller, prin. Fax 341-6041

**Stow, Middlesex**
Nashoba Regional SD
Supt. — See Bolton
Hale MS 300/6-8
55 Hartley Rd 01775 978-897-4788
George King, prin. Fax 897-3631

**Sudbury, Middlesex**
Lincoln-Sudbury SD 1,600/9-12
390 Lincoln Rd 01776 978-443-9961
Bella Wong, supt. Fax 443-8824
www.lsrhs.net
Lincoln-Sudbury Regional HS 1,600/9-12
390 Lincoln Rd 01776 978-443-9961
Bella Wong, prin. Fax 443-8824

Sudbury SD 3,100/PK-8
40 Fairbank Rd Ste C 01776 978-639-3211
Anne Wilson, supt. Fax 443-9001
www.sudbury.k12.ma.us
Curtis MS 1,100/6-8
22 Pratts Mill Rd 01776 978-443-1071
Stephen Lambert, prin. Fax 443-1098

---

Willow Hill S 100/6-12
98 Haynes Rd 01776 978-443-2581
Marilyn G. Reid, head sch Fax 443-7560

**Sutton, Worcester**
Sutton SD 1,600/PK-12
383 Boston Rd 01590 508-581-1600
Theodore Friend, supt. Fax 865-6463
www.suttonschools.net/
Sutton HS 400/9-12
383 Boston Rd 01590 508-581-1640
Ted McCarthy, prin. Fax 917-0063
Sutton MS 400/6-8
383 Boston Rd 01590 508-581-1630
Gerard Goyette, prin. Fax 865-6463

**Swampscott, Essex, Pop. 13,607**
Swampscott SD 2,200/K-12
207 Forest Ave 01907 781-596-8800
Pamela R. H. Angelakis M.Ed., supt. Fax 599-2502
www.swampscott.k12.ma.us
Swampscott HS 700/9-12
200 Essex St 01907 781-596-8830
Edward Rozmiarek Ed.D., prin. Fax 599-2034
Swampscott MS 700/5-8
207 Forest Ave 01907 781-596-8820
Robert Murphy Ed.D., prin. Fax 593-2126

Marian Court College Post-Sec.
35 Littles Point Rd 01907 781-595-6768

**Swansea, Bristol**
Swansea SD 2,000/PK-12
1 Gardners Neck Rd 02777 508-675-1195
Robert Monterio, supt. Fax 672-1040
www.swanseaschools.org
Case HS 600/9-12
70 School St 02777 508-675-7483
Brian McCann, prin. Fax 646-4405
Case JHS 500/6-8
195 Main St 02777 508-675-0116
Robert Silveira, prin. Fax 646-4413

**Taunton, Bristol, Pop. 53,462**
Bristol-Plymouth Regional-Tech SD
207 Hart St 02780 508-823-5151
Alexandre Magalhaes, supt. Fax 880-7287
www.bptech.org
Bristol-Plymouth Regional Technical S Vo/Tech
207 Hart St 02780 508-823-5151
Elizabeth Sullivan, prin. Fax 822-2687

Taunton SD 7,500/PK-12
215 Harris St 02780 508-821-1100
Dr. Julie Hackett, supt. Fax 821-1177
www.tauntonschools.org
Taunton Alternative HS Alt
120 Cohannet St 02780 508-821-1201
Burt Delaney, prin. Fax 821-1177
Taunton HS 2,400/8-12
50 Williams St 02780 508-821-1101
Matt Mattos, prin. Fax 821-1362

Coyle & Cassidy MSHS 600/6-12
2 Hamilton St 02780 508-823-6164
Kathleen St. Laurent, prin. Fax 823-2530
Rob Roy Academy Post-Sec.
1 School St 02780 508-822-1405

**Tewksbury, Middlesex, Pop. 11,000**
Tewksbury SD 3,900/PK-12
139 Pleasant St 01876 978-640-7800
John O'Connor, supt. Fax 640-7804
www.tewksbury.k12.ma.us
Tewksbury Memorial HS 900/9-12
320 Pleasant St 01876 978-640-7825
Kristen Vogel, prin. Fax 640-7829
Wynn MS 700/7-8
1 Griffin Way 01876 978-640-7846
John Weir, prin. Fax 640-7850

Electrology Institute of New England Post-Sec.
1501 Main St Ste 50 01876 800-548-6339
Salter School Post-Sec.
515 Woburn St 01876 978-934-9300

**Townsend, Middlesex, Pop. 1,114**
North Middlesex SD
Supt. — See Pepperell
Hawthorne Brook MS 600/5-8
64 Brookline St 01469 978-597-6914
Stephen Coughlan, prin. Fax 597-0354
North Middlesex Regional HS 1,100/9-12
19 Main St 01469 978-597-8721
Isaac Taylor, prin. Fax 597-0350

**Turners Falls, Franklin, Pop. 4,349**
Franklin County Technical SD
82 Industrial Blvd 01376 413-863-4239
Richard Martin, supt. Fax 863-2816
www.fcts.org
Franklin County Technical HS Vo/Tech
82 Industrial Blvd 01376 413-863-9561
Shawn Rickan, prin. Fax 863-2816

Gill-Montague SD 1,000/PK-12
35 Crocker Ave 01376 413-863-9324
Michael Sullivan, supt. Fax 863-4560
www.gmrsd.org
Other Schools – See Montague

Hallmark Institute of Photography Post-Sec.
PO Box 308 01376 413-863-2478

**Tyngsboro, Middlesex**
Greater Lowell Technical HSD
250 Pawtucket Blvd 01879 978-441-4800
Roger Bourgeois, supt. Fax 441-5353
www.gltech.org
Greater Lowell Technical HS Vo/Tech
250 Pawtucket Blvd 01879 978-441-4807
Jill Davis, prin. Fax 441-5353

Tyngsborough SD 1,900/PK-12
50 Norris Rd 01879 978-649-7488
Donald Ciampa, supt. Fax 649-7199
www.tyngsboroughps.org/
Tyngsborough HS 500/9-12
36 Norris Rd 01879 978-649-7571
Michael Woodlock, prin. Fax 649-6530
Tyngsborough MS 500/6-8
50 Norris Rd 01879 978-649-3115
Mary Alise Herrera, prin. Fax 649-8673

Academy of Notre Dame HS 200/9-12
180 Middlesex Rd 01879 978-649-7611
Sr. Patricia Conner, prin. Fax 649-2909

**Upton, Worcester, Pop. 2,982**
Blackstone Valley Vocational Regional SD
65 Pleasant St 01568 508-529-7758
Dr. Michael F. Fitzpatrick, supt. Fax 529-3079
www.valleytech.k12.ma.us
Blackstone Valley Regional Voc-Tech HS Vo/Tech
65 Pleasant St 01568 508-529-7758
Anthony E. Steele, prin. Fax 529-2403

Mendon-Upton Regional SD
Supt. — See Mendon
Nipmuc Regional HS 700/9-12
90 Pleasant St 01568 508-529-2130
John Clements, prin. Fax 529-2129

**Uxbridge, Worcester, Pop. 3,400**
Uxbridge SD 1,400/PK-12
21 S Main St 01569 508-278-8648
Kevin Carney, supt. Fax 278-8612
uxbridgeschools.com
McCloskey MS 500/6-8
62 Capron St 01569 508-278-8634
Dr. Rich Drolet, prin. Fax 278-8627
Uxbridge HS 500/9-12
300 Quaker Hwy 01569 508-278-8636
Michael Rubin, prin. Fax 278-8627

**Vineyard Haven, Dukes, Pop. 1,950**
Martha's Vineyard SD 1,000/K-12
4 Pine St 02568 508-693-2007
Dr. Matthew D'Andrea, supt. Fax 693-3190
www.mvyps.org
Other Schools – See Oak Bluffs

**Wakefield, Middlesex, Pop. 24,651**
Northeast Metro Vocational SD
100 Hemlock Rd 01880 781-246-0810
Theodore Nickole, supt. Fax 246-4919
northeastmetrotech.com
Northeast Metro Regional Vocational HS Vo/Tech
100 Hemlock Rd 01880 781-246-0810
David DiBarri, prin. Fax 246-4919

Wakefield SD 3,400/PK-12
60 Farm St 01880 781-246-6400
Dr. Kim Smith, supt. Fax 245-9164
www.wakefield.k12.ma.us
Galvin MS 1,100/5-8
525 Main St 01880 781-246-6410
Adam Colantuoni, prin. Fax 224-5009
Wakefield Memorial HS 1,000/9-12
60 Farm St 01880 781-246-6440
Richard Metropolis, prin. Fax 246-4714

Nazareth Academy 100/9-12
27 Cordis St 01880 781-246-7600
Phyllis Morrison, prin. Fax 246-5400

**Walpole, Norfolk, Pop. 5,864**
Norfolk County Agricultural SD
400 Main St 02081 508-668-0268
Suzanne Green, supt. Fax 668-0612
www.norfolkaggie.org
Norfolk County Agricultural HS Vo/Tech
400 Main St 02081 508-668-0268
Dr. Tammy Quinn, prin. Fax 668-0612

Walpole SD 4,000/PK-12
135 School St 02081 508-660-7200
Lincoln Lynch Ed.D., supt. Fax 668-1167
www.walpole.k12.ma.us/
Johnson MS 400/6-8
111 Robbins Rd 02081 508-660-7242
William Hahn, prin. Fax 660-7240
Walpole HS 1,100/9-12
275 Common St 02081 508-660-7257
Stephen Imbusch, prin. Fax 850-7958
Other Schools – See East Walpole

**Waltham, Middlesex, Pop. 59,317**
Waltham SD 5,000/PK-12
617 Lexington St 02452 781-314-5400
Drew Echelson Ed.D., supt. Fax 314-5411
www.walthampublicschools.org
Kennedy MS 600/6-8
655 Lexington St 02452 781-314-5560
John Cawley, prin. Fax 314-5571
McDevitt MS 500/6-8
75 Church St 02452 781-314-5590
Michael Sabin, prin. Fax 314-5601
Waltham HS 1,400/9-12
617 Lexington St 02452 781-314-5440
Gregory DeMeo, prin. Fax 647-0309

Bentley University Post-Sec.
175 Forest St 02452 781-891-2000
Blaine The Beauty Career School Post-Sec.
314 Moody St 02453 781-899-1500
Brandeis University Post-Sec.
415 South St 02453 781-736-2000
Center for Digital Imaging Arts at BU Post-Sec.
282 Moody St 02453 800-808-2342
Chapel Hill-Chauncy Hall S 200/9-12
785 Beaver St 02452 781-314-0800
Lance Conrad, hdmstr. Fax 894-5205
Gann Academy 300/9-12
333 Forest St 02452 781-642-6800
Rabbi Marc Baker, hdmstr. Fax 642-6805
Sodexho Marriott Services Post-Sec.
200 5th Ave 02451 800-926-7429

**Ware, Hampshire, Pop. 6,031**
Ware SD 1,300/PK-12
PO Box 240 01082 413-967-4271
Dr. Marlene DiLeo, supt. Fax 967-9580
www.wareps.org
Ware JSHS 500/7-12
237 West St 01082 413-967-6234
Darren Elwell, prin. Fax 967-9053

**Wareham, Plymouth, Pop. 19,232**
Wareham SD 2,700/PK-12
48 Marion Rd Ste 302 02571 508-291-3500
Kimberly Shaver-Hood, supt. Fax 291-3578
www.warehamps.org
Wareham HS 700/9-12
7 Viking Dr 02571 508-291-3510
Scott Palladino, prin. Fax 291-3577
Wareham MS 700/5-8
4 Viking Dr 02571 508-291-3550
Daniel Minkle, prin. Fax 291-3580
Other Schools – See East Wareham

**Warren, Worcester, Pop. 1,379**
Quaboag Regional SD 1,400/PK-12
PO Box 1538 01083 413-436-9256
Brett Kustigian, supt. Fax 436-9738
www.quaboagrsd.org
Quaboag Regional MSHS 600/7-12
PO Box 909 01083 413-436-5991
Mary Lafreniere, prin. Fax 436-9636

**Watertown, Middlesex, Pop. 30,947**
Watertown SD 2,500/PK-12
30 Common St 02472 617-926-7700
Jean Fitzgerald, supt. Fax 923-1234
www.watertown.k12.ma.us
Watertown HS 700/9-12
50 Columbia St 02472 617-926-7760
Shirley Lundberg, hdmstr. Fax 926-7723
Watertown MS 600/6-8
68 Waverley Ave 02472 617-926-7783
James Carter, prin. Fax 926-5407

Cortiva Institute - Boston Post-Sec.
103 Morse St 02472 617-612-6900
Perkins School for the Blind Post-Sec.
175 N Beacon St 02472 617-972-7285

**Wayland, Middlesex, Pop. 2,500**
Wayland SD 2,700/K-12
PO Box 408 01778 508-358-3763
Paul Stein, supt. Fax 358-7708
www.wayland.k12.ma.us
Wayland HS 900/9-12
264 Old Connecticut Path 01778 508-358-7746
Allyson Mizoguchi, prin. Fax 358-8082
Wayland MS 600/6-8
201 Main St 01778 508-655-6670
Betsy Gavron, prin. Fax 655-2548

**Webster, Worcester, Pop. 11,152**
Webster SD 1,800/PK-12
PO Box 430 01570 508-943-0104
Dr. Barbara Malkas, supt. Fax 943-0315
www.webster-schools.org
Bartlett HS 800/9-12
52 Lake Pkwy 01570 508-943-8552
Steven Knowlton, prin. Fax 949-8274
Webster MS 600/5-8
75 Poland St 01570 508-943-1922
Jennifer Lundwall, prin. Fax 949-2648

**Wellesley, Norfolk, Pop. 27,391**
Wellesley SD 5,000/PK-12
40 Kingsbury St 02481 781-446-6210
David Lussier, supt. Fax 446-6207
www.wellesley.k12.ma.us
Wellesley HS 1,400/9-12
50 Rice St 02481 781-446-6290
Jamie Chisum, prin. Fax 237-6004
Wellesley MS 1,200/6-8
50 Kingsbury St 02481 781-446-6235
Mark Ito, prin. Fax 446-6208

Dana Hall S 500/5-12
45 Dana Rd 02482 781-235-3010
Caroline Erisman, head sch Fax 237-5949
Massachusetts Bay Community College Post-Sec.
50 Oakland St 02481 781-239-3000
Wellesley College Post-Sec.
106 Central St 02481 781-283-1000

**Wendell, Franklin**

Lake Grove School-Maple Valley Post-Sec.
PO Box 767 01379 888-585-9007

**Wenham, Essex, Pop. 4,212**
Hamilton-Wenham SD 2,000/PK-12
5 School St 01984 978-468-5310
Dr. Michael M. Harvey, supt. Fax 468-7889
www.hwschools.net/
Other Schools – See Hamilton

Gordon College Post-Sec.
255 Grapevine Rd 01984 978-927-2300

**West Barnstable, Barnstable, Pop. 1,508**

Cape Cod Community College Post-Sec.
2240 Iyannough Rd 02668 508-362-2131

**Westborough, Worcester, Pop. 3,951**
Westborough SD 3,500/PK-12
45 W Main St 01581 508-836-7700
Amber Bock, supt. Fax 836-7704
westborough.ma.schoolwebpages.com

Gibbons MS 500/7-8
20 Fisher St 01581 508-836-7740
John Foley, prin. Fax 836-7744
Westborough HS 1,100/9-12
90 W Main St 01581 508-836-7720
Brian Callaghan, prin. Fax 836-7723

---

Porter & Chester Institute Post-Sec.
129 Flanders Rd 01581 508-366-0296

**West Boylston, Worcester, Pop. 6,611**
West Boylston SD 1,000/PK-12
125 Crescent St 01583 508-835-2917
Elizabeth Schaper, supt. Fax 835-8992
www.wbschools.com
West Boylston JSHS 500/6-12
125 Crescent St 01583 508-835-4475
Christopher Fournier, prin. Fax 835-3925

---

Salter College Post-Sec.
184 W Boylston St 01583 508-853-1074

**West Bridgewater, Plymouth**
West Bridgewater SD 1,300/PK-12
2 Spring St 02379 508-894-1230
Dr. Patricia Oakley, supt. Fax 894-1232
wbridgewaterschools.org
West Bridgewater MSHS 600/7-12
155 W Center St 02379 508-894-1220
Mark Bodwell, prin. Fax 894-1226

---

New England Baptist Academy 100/PK-12
560 N Main St 02379 508-584-5188

**Westfield, Hampden, Pop. 40,552**
Westfield SD 5,900/PK-12
94 N Elm St Ste 101 01085 413-572-6403
Dr. Suzanne Scallion, supt. Fax 572-6518
www.schoolsofwestfield.org
North MS 700/6-8
350 Southampton Rd 01085 413-572-6441
Katie Ross, prin. Fax 572-1669
South MS 600/6-8
30 W Silver St 01085 413-568-1900
Justin Baker, prin. Fax 572-4892
Westfield HS 1,500/9-12
177 Montgomery Rd 01085 413-572-6466
Dennis Duquette, prin. Fax 572-6346
Westfield Technical Academy Vo/Tech
33 Smith Ave 01085 413-572-6533
Stefan Czaporowski, prin. Fax 572-6542

---

St. Mary's Parish HS 100/9-12
86 Mechanic St 01085 413-568-5692
Nichole Nietsche, head sch Fax 562-3501
Westfield State University Post-Sec.
577 Western Ave 01085 413-572-5300

**Westford, Middlesex**
Nashoba Valley Technical SD
100 Littleton Rd 01886 978-692-4711
Judith Klimkiewicz Ed.D., supt. Fax 392-0570
www.nashobatech.net
Nashoba Valley Technical HS Vo/Tech
100 Littleton Rd 01886 978-692-4711
Denise Pigeon, prin. Fax 392-0570

Westford SD 5,300/PK-12
23 Depot St 01886 978-692-5560
Everett Olsen, supt. Fax 392-4497
westfordk12.us/
Blanchard MS 600/6-8
14 West St 01886 978-692-5582
Timothy Hislop, prin. Fax 692-5598
Stony Brook MS 700/6-8
9 Farmers Way 01886 978-692-2708
Christopher Chew, prin. Fax 692-5391
Westford Academy 1,700/9-12
30 Patten Rd 01886 978-692-5570
James Antonelli, prin. Fax 692-5502

**Westhampton, Hampshire**
Hampshire SD 800/7-12
19 Stage Rd 01027 413-527-7200
Dr. Craig Jurgensen, supt. Fax 529-9497
www.hr-k12.org/
Hampshire Regional JSHS 800/7-12
19 Stage Rd 01027 413-527-7680
Kristen Smidy, prin. Fax 527-1831

**West Newbury, Essex**
Pentucket SD 3,000/PK-12
22 Main St 01985 978-363-2280
Jeffrey Mulqueen, supt. Fax 363-1165
www.prsd.org
Pentucket Regional HS 800/9-12
24 Main St 01985 978-363-5507
John Seymour, prin. Fax 363-2730
Pentucket Regional MS 500/7-8
20 Main St 01985 978-363-2957
Kenneth Kelley, prin. Fax 363-2720

**Weston, Middlesex, Pop. 10,200**
Weston SD 2,400/PK-12
89 Wellesley St 02493 781-786-5200
Dr. John Brackett, supt. Fax 786-5209
www.westonschools.org/
Weston HS 800/9-12
444 Wellesley St 02493 781-786-5800
Anthony Parker, prin. Fax 786-5829
Weston MS 600/6-8
456 Wellesley St 02493 781-786-5600
John Gibbons, prin. Fax 786-5609

---

Blessed John XXIII National Seminary Post-Sec.
558 South Ave 02493 781-899-5500
Cambridge S of Weston 300/9-12
45 Georgian Rd 02493 781-642-8600
Jane Moulding, hdmstr. Fax 398-8344
Regis College Post-Sec.
235 Wellesley St 02493 781-768-7000
Rivers S 500/6-12
333 Winter St 02493 781-235-9300
Edward V. Parsons, head sch Fax 239-3614

**West Peabody, Essex**

---

Covenant Christian Academy 200/PK-12
83 Pine St 01960 978-535-7100
Robert Armstrong, head sch Fax 535-7123

**Westport, Bristol, Pop. 13,852**
Westport Community SD 1,700/PK-12
17 Main Rd 02790 508-636-1140
Dr. Ann Marie Dargon Ed.D., supt. Fax 636-1146
www.westportschools.org
Westport HS 400/9-12
19 Main Rd 02790 508-636-1050
Cheryl Tutalo, prin. Fax 636-1053
Westport JHS 500/7-8
19 Main Rd 02790 508-636-1140
Carolyn Pontes, prin. Fax 636-7413

**West Roxbury, See Boston**
Boston SD
Supt. — See Boston
Ohrenberger S 600/3-8
175 W Boundary Rd 02132 617-635-8157
Naomi Krakow, prin. Fax 635-8163
Urban Science Academy 600/9-12
1205 VFW Pkwy 02132 617-635-8930
Jeff Cook, prin. Fax 635-7895
West Roxbury Academy 700/9-12
1205 VFW Pkwy 02132 617-635-8935
Rudolph Weekes, prin. Fax 635-7912

---

Catholic Memorial HS 700/7-12
235 Baker St 02132 617-469-8000
Richard Chisholm, prin. Fax 325-0888
Roxbury Latin S 300/7-12
101 Saint Theresa Ave 02132 617-325-4920
Kerry Brennan, hdmstr. Fax 325-3585

**West Springfield, Hampden, Pop. 27,989**
West Springfield SD 3,800/PK-12
26 Central St Ste 33 01089 413-263-3290
Michael Richard J.D., supt. Fax 739-8748
www.wsps.org
West Springfield HS 1,200/9-12
425 Piper Rd 01089 413-263-3400
Dr. Vito Perrone, prin. Fax 781-4836
West Springfield MS 900/6-8
31 Middle School Dr 01089 413-263-3406
Peter Gillen, prin. Fax 781-0965

---

Kay Harvey Hairdressing Academy Post-Sec.
11 Central St 01089 413-732-7117

**Westwood, Norfolk, Pop. 12,557**
Westwood SD 3,200/PK-12
220 Nahatan St 02090 781-326-7500
Dr. John Antonucci, supt. Fax 326-8154
www.westwood.k12.ma.us
Thurston MS 800/6-8
850 High St 02090 781-326-7500
Allison Borchers, prin. Fax 326-2709
Westwood HS 900/9-12
200 Nahatan St 02090 781-326-7500
Sean Bevan, prin. Fax 461-8561

---

Xaverian Brothers HS 900/9-12
800 Clapboardtree St 02090 781-326-6392
Br. Daniel Skala, hdmstr. Fax 320-0458

**Weymouth, Norfolk, Pop. 53,900**
Weymouth SD 6,900/PK-12
111 Middle St 02189 781-335-1460
Kenneth Salim, supt. Fax 335-8777
www.weymouthschools.org
Weymouth HS 2,100/9-12
1 Wildcat Way 02190 781-337-7500
Peter Haviland, prin. Fax 340-2568
Other Schools – See East Weymouth

---

South Shore Christian Academy 300/PK-12
45 Broad St 02188 781-331-4340
Dr. Mark Jennings, head sch Fax 331-9956

**Whitinsville, Worcester, Pop. 6,595**
Northbridge SD 2,600/PK-12
87 Linwood Ave 01588 508-234-8156
Dr. Catherine Stickney, supt. Fax 234-8469
www.nps.org/
Northbridge HS 700/9-12
427 Linwood Ave 01588 508-234-6221
Michael Gauthier, prin. Fax 234-0802
Northbridge MS 800/5-8
171 Linwood Ave 01588 508-234-8718
Jennifer Sauter, prin. Fax 234-9718

---

Whitinsville Christian S 500/PK-12
279 Linwood Ave 01588 508-234-8211
Lance Engbers, hdmstr. Fax 234-0624

**Whitman, Plymouth, Pop. 13,240**
Whitman-Hanson SD 4,300/PK-12
610 Franklin St 02382 781-618-7000
Ruth Gilbert-Whitner Ed.D., supt. Fax 618-7099
www.whrsd.k12.ma.us
Whitman-Hanson Regional HS 1,200/9-12
600 Franklin St 02382 781-618-7020
Jeffrey Szymaniak, prin. Fax 618-7099
Whitman MS 600/6-8
100 Corthell Ave 02382 781-618-7035
George Ferro, prin. Fax 618-7091
Other Schools – See Hanson

**Wilbraham, Hampden, Pop. 3,882**
Hampden-Wilbraham SD 3,500/PK-12
621 Main St 01095 413-596-3884
Martin O'Shea, supt. Fax 599-1328
www.hwrsd.org
Minnechaug Regional HS 1,200/9-12
621 Main St 01095 413-596-9011
Stephen Hale, prin. Fax 596-8907
Wilbraham MS 600/6-8
466 Stony Hill Rd 01095 413-596-9061
Noel Pixley, prin. Fax 596-9382
Other Schools – See Hampden

---

Cathedral HS 300/8-12
310 Main St 01095 413-782-5285
John Miller, prin. Fax 782-5065
Wilbraham & Monson Academy 400/6-12
423 Main St 01095 413-596-6811
Brian Easler, head sch Fax 599-1749

**Williamstown, Berkshire, Pop. 4,791**
Mt. Greylock Regional SD / S Union 71 1,200/PK-12
1781 Cold Spring Rd 01267 413-458-9582
Dr. Douglas Dias, supt. Fax 458-2856
www.wlschools.org
Mount Greylock Regional JSHS 600/7-12
1781 Cold Spring Rd 01267 413-458-9582
Mary MacDonald, prin. Fax 458-2856

---

Buxton S 100/9-12
291 South St 01267 413-458-3919
Peter Smith, dir. Fax 458-9427
Williams College 01267 Post-Sec.
413-597-3131

**Wilmington, Middlesex, Pop. 22,011**
Wilmington SD 3,600/PK-12
161 Church St 01887 978-694-6000
Mary DeLai, supt. Fax 694-6005
wpsk12.com
Wilmington HS 1,000/9-12
159 Church St 01887 978-694-6060
Linda Peters, prin. Fax 694-6074
Wilmington MS 900/6-8
25 Carter Ln 01887 978-694-6080
Amy Gerade, prin. Fax 694-6085

---

ITT Technical Institute Post-Sec.
200 Ballardvale St Ste 200 01887 978-658-2636

**Winchendon, Worcester, Pop. 4,143**
Winchendon SD 1,000/PK-12
175 Grove St 01475 978-616-1452
Steven Haddad, supt. Fax 297-5250
www.winchendonk12.org
Murdock Academy for Success Alt
89 Ash St 01475 978-616-1690
Kris Provost, dir. Fax 297-5250
Murdock HS 400/9-12
3 Memorial Dr 01475 978-616-1653
Joshua Romano, prin. Fax 297-5250
Murdock MS 6-8
3 Memorial Dr 01475 978-616-1603
Joseph Mackey, prin. Fax 297-5250

---

Winchendon S 200/9-12
172 Ash St 01475 978-297-1223
John Kerney, hdmstr. Fax 297-0911

**Winchester, Middlesex, Pop. 20,931**
Winchester SD 4,400/PK-12
40 Samoset Rd 01890 781-721-7004
Judith Evans, supt. Fax 721-0016
www.winchester.k12.ma.us
McCall MS 1,000/6-8
458 Main St 01890 781-721-7026
Jorge Goncalves, prin. Fax 721-0886
Winchester HS 1,100/9-12
80 Skillings Rd 01890 781-721-7020
Christine Kelley, prin. Fax 721-7042

**Winthrop, Suffolk, Pop. 18,127**
Winthrop SD 1,900/PK-12
1 Metcalf Sq 02152 617-846-5500
John Macero, supt. Fax 539-0891
www.winthrop.k12.ma.us
Winthrop HS 500/8-12
151 Pauline St 02152 617-846-5505
Matthew Crombie, prin. Fax 539-0535

**Woburn, Middlesex, Pop. 37,207**
Woburn SD 4,800/PK-12
55 Locust St 01801 781-937-8233
Mark Donovan, supt. Fax 937-0668
www.edline.net/pages/WPS
Joyce MS 500/6-8
55 Locust St 01801 781-937-8233
Thomas Qualey, prin. Fax 937-8279
Kennedy MS 600/6-8
41 Middle St 01801 781-937-8230
Carl Nelson, prin. Fax 937-8223
Woburn Memorial HS 1,300/9-12
88 Montvale Ave 01801 781-937-8210
Joseph Finigan, prin. Fax 937-8216

---

Catherine Hinds Institute of Esthetics Post-Sec.
300 Wildwood Ave 01801 781-935-3344
Millenium Training Institute Post-Sec.
600 W Cummings Park # 2550 01801 888-388-9981
New England Tractor Trailer Training Sch Post-Sec.
1600 Osgood St 01815 800-333-2888
Porter & Chester Institute Post-Sec.
8 Presidential Way 01801 781-935-1108

**Woods Hole, Barnstable, Pop. 767**

Woods Hole Oceanographic Institution Post-Sec.
266 Woods Hole Rd 02543 508-289-2252

**Worcester, Worcester, Pop. 175,487**
Massachusetts Academy of Math & Science 100/11-12
85 Prescott St 01605 508-831-5859
Michael Barney, dir. Fax 831-5880
www.massacademy.org/
Massachusetts Academy of Math & Science 100/11-12
85 Prescott St 01605 508-831-5859
Michael Barney, dir. Fax 831-5880

Worcester SD 23,700/PK-12
20 Irving St 01609 508-799-3115
Dr. Melinda Boone, supt. Fax 799-3119
worcesterschools.org
Burncoat HS 1,000/9-12
179 Burncoat St 01606 508-799-3300
William Foley, prin. Fax 799-8206
Burncoat MS 600/7-8
135 Burncoat St 01606 508-799-3390
Lisa Houlihan, prin. Fax 799-8207
Caradonio New Citizens Center Alt
1407A Main St 01603 508-799-3494
Steven Alzamora, prin. Fax 799-3222
Claremont Academy 400/7-12
15 Claremont St 01610 508-799-3077
Ricci Hall, prin. Fax 799-8202
Creamer Center Alt
120 Granite St 01604 508-799-3476
Timothy Whalen, prin. Fax 799-3459
Doherty Memorial HS 1,300/9-12
299 Highland St 01602 508-799-3270
Sally Maloney, prin. Fax 799-3276
Forest Grove MS 900/7-8
495 Grove St 01605 508-799-3420
Mark Williams, prin. Fax 799-8218
North HS 1,200/9-12
140 Harrington Way 01604 508-799-3370
Lisa Dyer, prin. Fax 799-8252
South Community HS 1,300/9-12
170 Apricot St 01603 508-799-3325
Maureen Binienda, prin. Fax 799-8242
Sullivan MS 800/7-8
140 Apricot St 01603 508-799-3350
Dr. Josephine Robertson, prin. Fax 799-8244
University Park Campus S 200/7-12
12 Freeland St 01603 508-799-3591
Daniel St. Louis, prin. Fax 799-8159
Woodward Day S 100/Alt
190 Fremont St 01603 508-799-3513
Angela Moore, dir. Fax 799-3486
Worcester East MS 600/7-8
420 Grafton St 01604 508-799-3430
Dr. Rose Dawkins, prin. Fax 799-8251
Worcester Technical HS Vo/Tech
1 Skyline Dr 01605 508-799-1940
Kyle Brenner, prin. Fax 799-1933

Assumption College Post-Sec.
500 Salisbury St 01609 508-767-7000
Bancroft S 500/PK-12
110 Shore Dr 01605 508-853-2640
James P. Cassidy, head sch Fax 853-7824
Bancroft School of Massage Therapy Post-Sec.
333 Shrewsbury St 01604 508-757-7923
Becker College Post-Sec.
61 Sever St 01609 508-791-9241
Clark University Post-Sec.
950 Main St 01610 508-793-7711
College of the Holy Cross Post-Sec.
1 College St 01610 508-793-2011
Hair in Motion Beauty Academy Post-Sec.
6 Park Ave 01605 508-756-6060
Holy Name Central Catholic HS 600/7-12
144 Granite St 01604 508-753-6371
Edward Reynolds, admin. Fax 831-1287
Nativity S of Worcester 5-8
67 Lincoln St 01605 508-799-0100
Notre Dame Academy 300/9-12
425 Salisbury St 01609 508-757-6200
Sr. Ann Morrison, prin. Fax 757-7200
Quinsigamond Community College Post-Sec.
670 W Boylston St 01606 508-853-2300
Rob Roy Academy Post-Sec.
150 Pleasant St 01609 508-799-2111
St. Mary HS 100/7-12
50 Richland St 01610 508-753-1170
Adam Cormier, prin. Fax 795-0560
St. Peter-Marian Central HS 600/7-12
781 Grove St 01605 508-852-5555
Matthew Sturgis, admin. Fax 852-7238
University of Massachusetts Medical Sch Post-Sec.
55 Lake Ave N 01655 508-856-8989
Worcester Academy 600/6-12
81 Providence St 01604 508-754-5302
Ronald Cino, head sch Fax 792-1471
Worcester Polytechnic Institute Post-Sec.
100 Institute Rd 01609 508-831-5000
Worcester State University Post-Sec.
486 Chandler St 01602 508-929-8000

**Wrentham, Norfolk**
King Philip Regional SD
Supt. — See Norfolk
King Philip Regional HS 1,300/9-12
201 Franklin St 02093 508-384-1000
Dr. Lisa Oliveira, prin.

# MICHIGAN

## MICHIGAN DEPARTMENT OF EDUCATION
**608 W Allegan St, Lansing 48933-1524**
**Telephone 517-373-3324**
**Fax 517-335-4565**
**Website http://www.michigan.gov/mde**

Superintendent of Public Instruction Michael Flanagan

## MICHIGAN BOARD OF EDUCATION
**608 W Allegan St, Lansing 48933-1524**

President John C. Austin

## INTERMEDIATE SCHOOL DISTRICTS (ISD)

Allegan Area ESA
Mark Dobias, supt. 269-673-2161
310 Thomas St, Allegan 49010 Fax 673-2361
www.alleganaesa.org/

Alpena-Montmorency-Alcona ESD
Brian Wilmot, supt. 989-354-3101
2118 US Highway 23 S Fax 356-3385
Alpena 49707
www.amaesd.org

Barry ISD
Richard Franklin, supt. 269-945-9545
535 W Woodlawn Ave Fax 945-2575
Hastings 49058
www.barryisd.org

Bay-Arenac ISD
Deborah Kadish, supt. 989-686-4410
4228 2 Mile Rd, Bay City 48706 Fax 667-3286
www.baisd.net

Berrien RESA
Dr. Kevin Ivers, supt. 269-471-7725
PO Box 364, Berrien Springs 49103 Fax 471-2941
www.berrienresa.org

Branch ISD
Joseph Lopez, supt. 517-279-5730
370 Morse St, Coldwater 49036 Fax 279-5766
www.branch-isd.org

Calhoun ISD
Terance Lunger, supt. 269-781-5141
17111 G Dr N, Marshall 49068 Fax 781-7071
www.calhounisd.org

Charlevoix-Emmet ISD
Jeff Crouse, supt. 231-547-9947
8568 Mercer Rd, Charlevoix 49720 Fax 547-5621
www.charemisd.org

Cheboygan-Otsego-Presque Isle ISD
Mary Vratanina, supt. 231-238-9394
6065 Learning Ln Fax 238-8551
Indian River 49749
www.copesd.org/

Clare-Gladwin RESD
Sheryl Presler, supt. 989-386-3851
4041 E Mannsiding Rd Fax 386-3238
Clare 48617
www.cgresd.net/

Clinton County RESA
Dr. Wayne Petroelje, supt. 989-224-6831
1013 S US Highway 27 Ste A Fax 224-9574
Saint Johns 48879
www.ccresa.org

C.O.O.R. ISD
Greg Bush, supt. 989-275-9555
PO Box 827, Roscommon 48653 Fax 275-5881
www.coorisd.net

Copper Country ISD
George Stockero, supt. 906-482-4250
809 Hecla St, Hancock 49930 Fax 482-1931
www.copperisd.org

Delta-Schoolcraft ISD
Doug Leisenring, supt. 906-786-9300
2525 3rd Ave S, Escanaba 49829 Fax 786-9318
www.dsisd.k12.mi.us

Dickinson-Iron ISD
Wendy Warmuth, supt. 906-779-2690
1074 Pyle Dr, Kingsford 49802 Fax 779-2669
www.diisd.org

Eastern Upper Peninsula ISD
Daniel Reattoir, supt., 315 Armory Pl 906-632-3373
Sault Sainte Marie 49783 Fax 632-1125
www.eup.k12.mi.us

Eaton RESA
Cindy Anderson, supt. 517-543-5500
1790 Packard Hwy Fax 543-6633
Charlotte 48813
www.eatonresa.org

Genesee ISD
Lisa Hagel, supt. 810-591-4400
2413 W Maple Ave, Flint 48507 Fax 591-7570
www.geneseeisd.org

Gogebic-Ontonagon ISD
Bruce F. Mayle, supt. 906-575-3438
PO Box 218, Bergland 49910 Fax 575-3373
www.goisd.org/

Gratiot-Isabella RESD
Jan Amsterburg, supt. 989-875-5101
PO Box 310, Ithaca 48847 Fax 875-7531
www.giresd.net/

Hillsdale ISD
Ronna Steel, supt. 517-437-0990
310 W Bacon St, Hillsdale 49242 Fax 439-4388
www.hillsdale-isd.org

Huron ISD
Joseph Murphy, supt. 989-269-6406
1299 S Thomas Rd Ste 1 Fax 269-9218
Bad Axe 48413
www.huronisd.org

Ingham ISD
Dr. Scott Koenigsknecht, supt. 517-676-1051
2630 W Howell Rd, Mason 48854 Fax 676-1277
www.inghamisd.org

Ionia County ISD
Jason Mellema, supt. 616-527-4900
2191 Harwood Rd, Ionia 48846 Fax 527-4731
www.ioniaisd.org

Iosco RESA
Dana McGrew, supt. 989-362-3006
27 N Rempert Rd Fax 362-9076
Tawas City 48763
www.ioscoresa.net/

Jackson County ISD
Kevin Oxley, supt. 517-768-5200
6700 Browns Lake Rd Fax 787-2026
Jackson 49201
www.jcisd.org

Kalamazoo RESA
David Campbell, supt. 269-250-9200
1819 E Milham Ave, Portage 49002 Fax 250-9205
www.kresa.org

Kent ISD
Ron Caniff, supt., 2930 Knapp St NE 616-364-1333
Grand Rapids 49525 Fax 364-1488
www.kentisd.org

Lapeer County ISD
Steven Zott, supt. 810-664-5917
1996 W Oregon St, Lapeer 48446 Fax 664-1011
www.lcisd.k12.mi.us

Lenawee ISD
Jim Philp, supt. 517-265-2119
4107 N Adrian Hwy, Adrian 49221 Fax 265-9875
www.lisd.us/

Lewis Cass ISD
Robert Colby, supt. 269-445-6204
61682 Dailey Rd, Cassopolis 49031 Fax 445-2981
www.lewiscassisd.org

Livingston ESA
Dan Danosky, supt. 517-546-5550
1425 W Grand River Ave Fax 546-7047
Howell 48843
www.livingstonesa.org/

Macomb ISD
Michael DeVault, supt. 586-228-3300
44001 Garfield Rd Fax 286-1523
Clinton Township 48038
www.misd.net

Manistee ISD
Jeff Jennette, supt. 231-723-4264
772 E Parkdale Ave Fax 398-3036
Manistee 49660
www.manistee.org

Marquette-Alger RESA
Deborah Veiht, supt. 906-226-5100
321 E Ohio St, Marquette 49855 Fax 226-5134
www.maresa.org

Mecosta-Osceola ISD
Dr. Curtis Finch, supt. 231-796-3543
15760 190th Ave Fax 796-3300
Big Rapids 49307
www.moisd.org

Menominee ISD
John Mans, supt. 906-863-5665
1201 41st Ave, Menominee 49858 Fax 863-7776
www.mc-isd.org

Midland County ESA
John Searles, supt. 989-631-5890
3917 Jefferson Ave, Midland 48640 Fax 631-4361
www.midlandesa.org

Monroe County ISD
Stephen McNew, supt. 734-242-5799
1101 S Raisinville Rd Fax 242-0567
Monroe 48161
www.monroeisd.us/

Montcalm Area ISD
Ron Simon, supt. 989-831-5261
PO Box 367, Stanton 48888 Fax 831-8727
www.maisd.com

Muskegon Area ISD
Dr. John Severson, supt. 231-777-2637
630 Harvey St, Muskegon 49442 Fax 767-7299
www.muskegonisd.org

Newaygo County RESA
Lori Clark, supt. 231-924-0381
4747 W 48th St, Fremont 49412 Fax 924-8910
www.ncresa.org

Oakland ISD
Dr. Wanda Cook-Robinson, supt. 248-209-2000
2111 Pontiac Lake Rd Fax 209-2206
Waterford 48328
www.oakland.k12.mi.us

Ottawa Area ISD
Peter Haines, supt. 616-738-8940
13565 Port Sheldon St Fax 738-8946
Holland 49424
www.oaisd.org

Saginaw ISD
Kathy Stewart, supt. 989-399-7473
6235 Gratiot Rd, Saginaw Fax 793-1571
www.sisd.cc

St. Clair County RESA
Dan DeGrow, supt. 810-364-8990
PO Box 1500, Marysville 48040 Fax 364-7474
www.sccresa.org/

St. Joseph County ISD
Barbara Marshall, supt. 269-467-5400
62445 Shimmel Rd Fax 467-4309
Centreville 49032
www.sjcisd.org

Sanilac ISD
Duane Lange Ph.D., supt. 810-648-4700
175 E Aitken Rd, Peck 48466 Fax 648-5784
www.sanilac.k12.mi.us

Shiawassee RESD
David Schulte, supt. 989-743-3471
1025 N Shiawassee St Fax 743-6477
Corunna 48817
www.sresd.org

Traverse Bay Area ISD
Michael Hill, supt. 231-922-6200
1101 Red Dr, Traverse City 49684 Fax 922-6270
www.tbaisd.org

Tuscola ISD
Eugene Pierce, supt. 989-673-2144
1385 Cleaver Rd, Caro 48723 Fax 673-5366
www.tuscolaisd.org/

Van Buren ISD
Jeffrey Mills, supt. 269-674-8091
490 S Paw Paw St Fax 674-8030
Lawrence 49064
www.vbisd.org/

Washtenaw ISD
Scott Menzel, supt. 734-994-8100
PO Box 1406, Ann Arbor 48106 Fax 994-2203
washtenawisd.org

Wayne RESA
Randy Liepa, supt. 734-334-1300
33500 Van Born Rd, Wayne 48184 Fax 334-1760
www.resa.net

West Shore ESD
Randy Howes, supt. 231-757-3716
2130 W US Highway 10 Fax 757-2406
Ludington 49431
www.wsesd.org

Wexford-Missaukee ISD
Jeff Jennette, supt. 231-876-2260
9907 E 13th St, Cadillac 49601 Fax 876-2261
www.wmisd.org

## PUBLIC, PRIVATE AND CATHOLIC SECONDARY SCHOOLS

**Ada, Kent**
Forest Hills SD
Supt. — See Grand Rapids
Central MS 600/7-8
5810 Ada Dr SE 49301 616-493-8750
Glenn Mitcham, prin. Fax 493-8764
Eastern HS 800/9-12
2200 Pettis Ave NE 49301 616-493-8830
Steve Harvey, prin. Fax 493-8839
Eastern MS 400/7-8
2200 Pettis Ave NE 49301 616-493-8850
David Washburn, prin. Fax 493-8839

**Addison, Lenawee, Pop. 592**
Addison Community SD 600/K-12
219 N Comstock St 49220 517-547-6901
Steven Guerra, supt. Fax 547-3838
www.addisonschools.org
Addison HS 300/9-12
219 N Comstock St 49220 517-547-6951
Steven Guerra, supt. Fax 547-3838
Addison MS 100/6-8
219 N Comstock St 49220 517-547-6952
Chad VanSickle, admin. Fax 547-3838

**Adrian, Lenawee, Pop. 20,608**
Adrian SD 3,100/PK-12
785 Riverside Ave Ste 1 49221 517-263-2115
Robert Behnke, supt. Fax 265-5381
www.theadrianmaples.com
Adrian HS 900/9-12
785 Riverside Ave 49221 517-263-2181
Kevin Ohrman, prin. Fax 263-0814
Adrian MS 7-8 500/7-8
615 Springbrook Ave 49221 517-263-0543
Nate Parker, prin. Fax 265-5984
McKinley Education Center 100/Alt
726 Elm St 49221 517-263-1332
Derrick Richards, coord. Fax 263-1385

Lenawee ISD 100/
4107 N Adrian Hwy 49221 517-265-2119
Jim Philp, supt. Fax 265-9875
www.lisd.us/
LISD Tech Center Vo/Tech
1372 N Main St 49221 517-263-2108
Shelley Jusick, prin. Fax 263-9433

Madison SD 1,500/PK-12
3498 Treat Hwy 49221 517-263-0741
Ryan Rowe, supt. Fax 265-5635
www.madisonk12.us
Madison HS 400/9-12
3498 Treat Hwy 49221 517-263-0742
Kristin Thomas, prin. Fax 265-1848
Madison MS 400/6-8
3498 Treat Hwy 49221 517-263-0743
Brad Anschuetz, prin. Fax 265-1848

---

Adrian College Post-Sec.
110 S Madison St 49221 517-265-5161
Fiser's College of Cosmetology Post-Sec.
329 1/2 E Maumee St 49221 517-264-2199
Lenawee Christian S 600/PK-12
111 Wolf Creek Hwy 49221 517-265-7590
Tom Durbin, head sch Fax 265-6558
Siena Heights University Post-Sec.
1247 E Siena Heights Dr 49221 517-263-0731

**Alanson, Emmet, Pop. 721**
Alanson SD 300/K-12
7400 North St 49706 231-548-2261
Dean Paul, supt. Fax 548-2132
www.alansonvikings.net
Alanson HS 100/9-12
7400 North St 49706 231-548-2261
Dean Paul, admin. Fax 548-2132
Alanson MS 100/5-8
7400 North St 49706 231-548-2261
Dean Paul, admin. Fax 548-2165

**Alba, Antrim, Pop. 295**
Alba SD 200/PK-12
PO Box 10 49611 231-584-2000
Douglas Tippett, supt. Fax 584-2001
www.albaschool.org/
Alba S 200/PK-12
PO Box 10 49611 231-584-2000
Rich Satterlee, supt. Fax 584-2001

**Albion, Calhoun, Pop. 8,323**
Marshall SD
Supt. — See Marshall
ECEC/Marshall Alternative HS 100/Alt
14055 26 Mile Rd 49224 517-629-7547
Ben Wallace, dir. Fax 629-7534

---

Albion College Post-Sec.
611 E Porter St 49224 517-629-1000

**Algonac, Saint Clair, Pop. 4,051**
Algonac Community SD 1,900/PK-12
1216 Saint Clair Blvd 48001 810-794-9364
Dr. John Strycker, supt. Fax 794-0040
algonac.k12.mi.us
Algonac JSHS 600/7-12
5200 Taft Rd 48001 810-794-4911
Ryan Melrose, prin. Fax 794-8876

**Allegan, Allegan, Pop. 4,893**
Allegan Area ESA 50/
310 Thomas St 49010 269-673-2161
Mark Dobias, supt. Fax 673-2361
www.alleganaesa.org/
Allegan Co. Area Technical & Educ. Ctr. Alt
2891 116th Ave 49010 269-673-3121
Linda Blankenship, dir. Fax 686-0327
Allegan SD 2,700/PK-12
550 5th St 49010 269-673-5431
Kevin Harness, supt. Fax 673-5463
www.alleganps.org/
Allegan Alternative HS 100/Alt
550 5th St 49010 269-673-5433
Laura Feffer, prin.
Allegan HS 800/9-12
1560 Lincoln Rd 49010 269-673-7002
Jim Mallard, prin. Fax 686-2486
White MS, 3300 115th Ave 49010 600/6-8
James Antoine, prin. 269-673-2241

**Allendale, Ottawa, Pop. 17,229**
Allendale SD 2,400/PK-12
10505 Learning Ln 49401 616-892-5570
Daniel Jonker Ed.D., supt. Fax 895-6690
www.allendale.k12.mi.us
Allendale HS 600/9-12
10760 68th Ave 49401 616-892-5585
Dan Remenap, prin. Fax 895-4280
Allendale MS 500/6-8
7161 Pleasant View Ct 49401 616-892-5595
Rocky Thompson, prin. Fax 895-9111
Allendale New Options 100/Alt
6633 Lake Michigan Dr 49401 616-892-5575
Tamika Henry, prin. Fax 892-4668

---

Grand Valley State University Post-Sec.
1 Campus Dr 49401 616-331-5000

**Allen Park, Wayne, Pop. 27,848**
Allen Park SD 3,700/K-12
9601 Vine Ave 48101 313-827-2100
Dr. John Sturock, supt. Fax 827-2151
www.apps.k12.mi.us
Allen Park HS 1,200/9-12
18401 Champaign Rd 48101 313-827-1200
Janet Wasko, prin. Fax 827-1231
Allen Park MS 900/6-8
8401 Vine Ave 48101 313-827-2200
Mark Lowe, prin. Fax 827-2251
Community S 200/Alt
14700 Moore Ave 48101 313-827-2660
Rebecca Westrate, dir. Fax 827-2661

---

Baker College of Allen Park Post-Sec.
4500 Enterprise Dr 48101 313-425-3700
Cabrini HS 500/9-12
15305 Wick Rd 48101 313-388-0110
James Wasukanis, prin. Fax 388-1876
Inter City Baptist S 300/K-12
4700 Allen Rd 48101 313-928-6900
Jim Hubbard Ed.D., admin. Fax 928-7310
Stautzenberger Institute Post-Sec.
16630 Southfield Rd 48101 313-294-9715

**Alma, Gratiot, Pop. 9,259**
Alma SD 2,200/PK-12
1500 Pine Ave 48801 989-463-3111
Sonia Lark, supt. Fax 466-2943
www.almaschools.net
Alma HS 600/9-12
1500 Pine Ave 48801 989-463-3111
Thomas Torok, prin. Fax 463-2176
Pavlik MS 500/6-8
1700 Pine Ave 48801 989-463-3111
Sandy Rusell, prin. Fax 466-7612

Gratiot-Isabella RESD
Supt. — See Ithaca
Gratiot Technical Education Center Vo/Tech
327 E Center St 48801 989-875-4832
Fax 466-9734

---

Alma College Post-Sec.
614 W Superior St 48801 989-463-7111

**Almont, Lapeer, Pop. 2,651**
Almont Community SD 1,600/K-12
401 Church St 48003 810-798-8561
Joseph Candela, supt. Fax 798-2367
www.almontschools.org
Almont HS 500/9-12
4701 Howland Rd 48003 810-798-8595
Timothy Woelkers, prin. Fax 798-7011
Almont MS 500/5-8
4624 Kidder Rd 48003 810-798-3578
Kimberly VonHiltmayer, prin. Fax 673-9349

**Alpena, Alpena, Pop. 10,337**
Alpena SD 4,000/K-12
2373 Gordon Rd 49707 989-358-5040
Brent Holcomb, supt. Fax 358-5041
www.alpenaschools.com
ACES/Oxbow Adult/Alternative/Comm Educ 200/Alt
700 Pinecrest St 49707 989-358-5170
Michelle Cornish, dir. Fax 358-5175
Alpena HS 1,300/9-12
3303 S 3rd Ave 49707 989-358-5200
Matt Poli, prin. Fax 358-5205
Thunder Bay JHS 1,000/6-8
3500 S 3rd Ave 49707 989-358-5400
Steve Genschaw, prin. Fax 358-5499

---

Alpena Community College Post-Sec.
665 Johnson St 49707 989-356-9021

**Ann Arbor, Washtenaw, Pop. 109,999**
Ann Arbor SD 16,400/PK-12
PO Box 1188 48106 734-994-2200
Dr. Jeanice Swift, supt. Fax 994-2414
www.aaps.k12.mi.us
Clague MS 800/6-8
2616 Nixon Rd 48105 734-994-1976
Che' Carter, prin. Fax 994-1645
Community HS 500/9-12
401 N Division St 48104 734-994-2025
Marci Tuzinsky, dean Fax 994-0042
Forsythe MS 700/6-8
1655 Newport Rd 48103 734-994-1985
Jerry Morrissey, prin. Fax 994-5749
Huron HS 1,600/9-12
2727 Fuller Rd 48105 734-994-2040
Jennifer Hein, prin. Fax 994-2048
Pathways To Success Academic Campus Alt
2800 Stone School Rd 48104 734-997-1237
Tyrone Weeks, prin. Fax 997-1261
Pioneer HS 1,600/9-12
601 W Stadium Blvd 48103 734-994-2120
Tracey Lowder, prin. Fax 994-2198
Scarlett MS 500/6-8
3300 Lorraine St 48108 734-997-1220
Gerald Vazquez, prin. Fax 997-1885
Skyline HS 1,500/9-12
2552 N Maple Rd 48103 734-994-6515
Cory McElmeel, prin. Fax 994-7028
Slauson MS 800/6-8
1019 W Washington St 48103 734-994-2004
Rick Weiler, prin. Fax 994-1681
Tappan MS 700/6-8
2251 E Stadium Blvd 48104 734-994-2011
Jazz Parks, prin. Fax 997-1873

Washtenaw ISD 300/
PO Box 1406 48106 734-994-8100
Scott Menzel, supt. Fax 994-2203
washtenawisd.org
Other Schools – See Ypsilanti

---

Ann Arbor Academy 50/4-12
1153 Oak Valley Dr 48108 734-747-6641
Meredith Schindler M.S., dir. Fax 747-9994
Cleary University Post-Sec.
3601 Plymouth Rd 48105 800-686-1883
Concordia University Post-Sec.
4090 Geddes Rd 48105 734-995-7300
Father Gabriel Richard HS 500/9-12
4333 Whitehall Dr 48105 734-662-0496
Brian Wolcott, prin. Fax 662-4133
Greenhills S 500/6-12
850 Greenhills Dr 48105 734-769-4010
Carl Pelofsky, head sch Fax 769-5029
Michigan Islamic Academy 200/PK-12
2301 Plymouth Rd 48105 734-665-8882
Sr. Fayzeh Madani, prin. Fax 665-9058
Ross Medical Education Center Post-Sec.
4741 Washtenaw Ave 48108 734-434-7320
Steiner S of Ann Arbor 100/9-12
2230 Pontiac Trl 48105 734-669-9394
Sandra Greenstone, admin. Fax 669-9396
University of Michigan-Ann Arbor Post-Sec.
1220 Student Activities Bld 48109 734-764-1817
Washtenaw Community College Post-Sec.
4800 E Huron River Dr 48105 734-973-3300

**Armada, Macomb, Pop. 1,714**
Armada Area SD 2,000/PK-12
74500 Burk St 48005 586-784-2112
Michael Musary, supt. Fax 784-4268
www.armadaschools.org
Armada Continuing Education Center 50/Alt
23211 Prospect Ave 48005 586-784-2400
William Zebelian, prin. Fax 784-9592
Armada HS 700/9-12
23655 Armada Center Rd 48005 586-784-2400
Laurie Wilson, prin. Fax 784-9592
Armada MS 500/6-8
23550 Armada Center Rd 48005 586-784-2500
Todd Schafer, prin. Fax 784-8650
Macomb Academy of Arts & Sciences 100/9-12
23211 Prospect Ave 48005 586-784-2150
William Zebelian, dir. Fax 784-8688

**Ashley, Gratiot, Pop. 562**
Ashley Community SD 300/PK-12
PO Box 6 48806 989-847-4000
Tim Hughes, supt. Fax 847-3500
www.ashleyschools.net/
Ashley HS 100/9-12
PO Box 6 48806 989-847-2514
Traci Gavenda, prin. Fax 847-4204
Ashley MS 100/5-8
PO Box 6 48806 989-846-2514
Traci Gavenda, prin. Fax 847-4204

**Athens, Calhoun, Pop. 1,000**
Athens Area SD
Supt. — See East Leroy
Athens JSHS 300/6-12
300 E Holcomb St 49011 269-729-5414
Joe Huepenbecker, prin. Fax 729-9616

**Atlanta, Montmorency, Pop. 815**
Atlanta Community SD 300/K-12
PO Box 619 49709 989-785-4877
Donald Haskin, supt. Fax 785-2611
www.atlanta.k12.mi.us
Atlanta Community S 300/K-12
PO Box 619 49709 989-785-4877
Donald Haskin, supt. Fax 785-2611

**Attica, Lapeer, Pop. 985**
Lapeer County ISD
Supt. — See Lapeer
Lapeer County ISD Education Center Vo/Tech
690 N Lake Pleasant Rd 48412 810-664-1124
Dale Moore, prin. Fax 724-7600

**Auburn, Bay, Pop. 2,077**
Bay City SD
Supt. — See Bay City

Western HS 1,200/9-12
500 W Midland Rd 48611 989-662-4481
Judy Cox, prin. Fax 662-4413
Western MS 900/6-8
500 W Midland Rd 48611 989-662-4489
Amy Bailey, prin. Fax 662-0185

**Auburn Hills, Oakland, Pop. 20,778**
Avondale SD 3,500/K-12
2940 Waukegan St 48326 248-537-6000
Dr. James V. Schwarz, supt. Fax 537-6005
www.avondale.k12.mi.us
Avondale HS 1,100/9-12
2800 Waukegan St 48326 248-537-6100
Julie Lublin, prin. Fax 537-6105
Other Schools – See Rochester Hills

---

Auburn Hills Christian S 200/PK-12
PO Box 214386 48321 248-373-3399
Scott Wickson, prin. Fax 409-2786
Baker College of Auburn Hills Post-Sec.
1500 University Dr 48326 248-340-0600
Oakland Christian S 700/PK-12
3075 Shimmons Rd 48326 248-373-2700
Roger VanDorp, supt. Fax 373-9255
Oakland Community College Post-Sec.
2900 Featherstone Rd 48326 248-232-4100

**Au Gres, Arenac, Pop. 875**
Au Gres-Sims SD 400/PK-12
PO Box 648 48703 989-876-7150
Jeffrey Collier, supt. Fax 876-6752
www.ags-schools.org
Au Gres-Sims HS 100/9-12
PO Box 648 48703 989-876-7157
Chad Zeien, prin. Fax 876-4684
Au Gres-Sims MS 200/6-8
PO Box 648 48703 989-876-7157
Chad Zeien, prin. Fax 876-4684

**Augusta, Kalamazoo, Pop. 868**
Galesburg-Augusta Community SD
Supt. — See Galesburg
Galesburg-Augusta MS 400/5-8
750 W Van Buren St 49012 269-484-2020
Jeremy Mansfield, prin. Fax 731-4138

**Bad Axe, Huron, Pop. 3,092**
Bad Axe SD 900/K-12
200 N Barrie Rd Ste 100 48413 989-269-9938
Gregory Newland, supt. Fax 269-2739
www.badaxeps.org/
Ascent HS, 200 N Barrie Rd 48413 Alt
Donald Rudolph, prin. 989-269-2737
Bad Axe HS 500/8-12
200 N Barrie Rd 48413 989-269-9593
Kurt Dennis, prin. Fax 269-6947

Huron ISD 100/
1299 S Thomas Rd Ste 1 48413 989-269-6406
Joseph Murphy, supt. Fax 269-9218
www.huronisd.org
Huron Area Technical Center Vo/Tech
1160 S Van Dyke Rd 48413 989-269-9284
Clark Brock, dir. Fax 269-2844

**Baldwin, Lake, Pop. 1,141**
Baldwin Community SD 600/PK-12
525 4th St 49304 231-745-4791
Stiles Simmons, supt. Fax 745-3240
www.baldwin.k12.mi.us
Baldwin HS 200/9-12
525 4th St 49304 231-745-4683
Calvin Patillo, prin. Fax 745-2898
Baldwin JHS 100/7-8
525 4th St 49304 231-745-4683
Calvin Patillo, prin. Fax 745-2898

**Bangor, Van Buren, Pop. 1,809**
Bangor SD 1,200/K-12
801 W Arlington St 49013 269-427-6800
Dennis Paquette, supt. Fax 427-8274
www.bangorvikings.org
Bangor HS 400/9-12
801 W Arlington St 49013 269-427-6844
Wendy Tremblay, prin. Fax 427-6825
Bangor MS 400/5-8
803 W Arlington St 49013 269-427-6824
Michael Dandron, prin. Fax 427-6892

**Baraga, Baraga, Pop. 1,981**
Baraga Area SD 500/K-12
210 Lyons St 49908 906-353-6664
Jennifer Lynn, supt. Fax 353-7454
www.baragaschools.org
Baraga JSHS 300/6-12
210 Lyons St 49908 906-353-6661
Richard Sarau, prin. Fax 353-6662

---

Keweenaw Bay Ojibwa Community College Post-Sec.
PO Box 519 49908 906-353-4600

**Bath, Clinton, Pop. 2,052**
Bath Community SD 1,000/K-12
PO Box 310 48808 517-641-6721
Jake Huffman, supt. Fax 641-6958
www.bathschools.net
Bath HS 300/9-12
PO Box 310 48808 517-641-6724
Matt Dodson, prin. Fax 641-7046
Bath MS 200/6-8
PO Box 310 48808 517-641-6781
Lorenda Jonas, prin. Fax 641-4996

**Battle Creek, Calhoun, Pop. 50,321**
Battle Creek SD 5,300/K-12
3 Van Buren St W 49017 269-965-9500
Kim Parker-DeVauld, supt. Fax 965-9474
www.battlecreekpublicschools.org
Battle Creek Central HS 900/10-12
100 Van Buren St W 49017 269-965-9526
Toni McClenney, prin. Fax 660-5864
Bearcat Success Academy 400/9-9
100 Van Buren St W 49017 269-213-1742
Anita Harvey, prin. Fax 965-9567
Mathematics & Science Center 300/8-12
171 Michigan Ave W 49017 269-965-9440
Susan Buckham, admin. Fax 965-9589
Northwestern MS 500/6-8
176 Limit St, 269-965-9607
Bernard Brown, prin. Fax 965-9525
Battle Creek Adult Education Adult
77 Capital Ave NE 49017 269-965-9514
Shari Jones, admin. Fax 965-9545
Other Schools – See Springfield

Calhoun ISD
Supt. — See Marshall
Calhoun Area Career Center Vo/Tech
475 Roosevelt Ave E 49017 269-968-2271
Tim Staffen, prin. Fax 968-4344

Harper Creek Community SD 2,500/K-12
7454 B Dr N 49014 269-441-6550
Rob Ridgeway, supt. Fax 962-6034
www.harpercreek.net
Harper Creek HS 800/9-12
12677 Beadle Lake Rd 49014 269-441-8450
Matthew Montange, prin. Fax 441-2206
Harper Creek MS 800/5-8
7290 B Dr N 49014 269-441-4750
Kimberly Thayer, prin. Fax 979-4613

Lakeview SD 3,900/K-12
15 Arbor St 49015 269-565-2400
Dave Peterson, supt. Fax 565-2408
www.lakeviewspartans.org
Lakeview HS 1,400/9-12
15060 Helmer Rd S 49015 269-565-3700
Jeffrey Bohl, prin. Fax 565-3708
Lakeview MS 1,300/5-8
300 28th St S 49015 269-565-3900
Michael Norstrom, prin. Fax 565-3908

Pennfield SD 2,100/K-12
8587 Pennfield Rd 49017 269-961-9781
Tim Everett, supt. Fax 961-9799
www.pennfield.net/
Pennfield HS 700/9-12
8587 Pennfield Rd 49017 269-961-9770
Barry Duckham, prin. Fax 441-1274
Pennfield MS 500/6-8
8587 Pennfield Rd 49017 269-961-9784
Michele Herzing, prin. Fax 441-5535

---

Battle Creek Academy 100/K-12
480 Parkway Dr, 269-965-1278
James Davis, prin. Fax 965-3250
Calhoun Christian S 200/PK-12
20 Woodrow Ave S 49015 269-965-5560
Jeralyn Belote, prin. Fax 965-8038
Davenport University Post-Sec.
200 Van Buren St W 49017 269-968-6105
Kambly School/Developmentally Impaired Post-Sec.
1003 North Ave 49017
Kellogg Community College Post-Sec.
450 North Ave 49017 269-965-3931
Robert Miller College Post-Sec.
450 North Ave 49017 269-660-8021
St. Joseph MS 100/6-8
44 25th St N 49015 269-963-4935
Marcy Arnson, prin. Fax 963-0354
St. Philip Catholic Central HS 100/9-12
20 Cherry St 49017 269-963-4503
Vicky Groat, prin. Fax 963-5590
Wright Beauty Academy Post-Sec.
492 Capital Ave SW 49015 269-964-4016

**Bay City, Bay, Pop. 33,947**
Bangor Township SD 2,500/PK-12
3359 E Midland Rd 48706 989-684-8121
Matthew Schmidt, supt. Fax 684-6000
www.bangorschools.org
Glenn HS 900/9-12
3201 Kiesel Rd 48706 989-684-7510
Daniel Decuf, prin. Fax 684-1545
McAuliffe MS 600/6-8
3281 Kiesel Rd 48706 989-686-7640
Kevin Biskup, prin. Fax 686-7633

Bay City SD 8,400/PK-12
910 N Walnut St 48706 989-686-9700
Janet Greif, supt. Fax 686-1047
www.bcschools.net
Central HS 1,500/9-12
1624 Columbus Ave 48708 989-893-9541
Tim Marciniak, prin. Fax 893-0333
Handy MS 1,000/6-8
601 Blend St 48706 989-684-1723
Brian DuFresne, prin. Fax 684-1960
Wenona Center 200/Alt
201 Woodside Ln 48708 989-895-5550
Joe Buggs, prin. Fax 895-6517
Other Schools – See Auburn

Bay-Arenac ISD
4228 2 Mile Rd 48706 989-686-4410
Deborah Kadish, supt. Fax 667-3286
www.baisd.net
Bay-Arenac ISD Career Center Vo/Tech
4155 Monitor Rd 48706 989-686-4770
Linda Englehardt, prin.

---

All Saints Central MSHS 300/6-12
217 S Monroe St 48708 989-892-2533
Brian Campbell, prin. Fax 892-7188
Bayshire Beauty Academy Post-Sec.
917 Saginaw St 48708 989-894-2431

**Bear Lake, Manistee, Pop. 281**
Bear Lake SD 300/K-12
7748 Cody St 49614 231-864-3133
Marlen Cordes, supt. Fax 864-3434
www.bearlake.k12.mi.us
Bear Lake HS 200/6-12
7748 Cody St 49614 231-864-3133
Sarah Harless, prin. Fax 864-3434

**Beaver Island, Charlevoix**
Beaver Island Community SD 100/K-12
37895 Kings Hwy 49782 231-448-2744
Judith Gallagher, supt. Fax 448-2919
www.beaverisland.k12.mi.us
Beaver Island Community S 100/K-12
37895 Kings Hwy 49782 231-448-2744
Riley Justis, prin. Fax 448-2919

**Beaverton, Gladwin, Pop. 1,061**
Beaverton Rural SD 1,300/K-12
PO Box 529 48612 989-246-3000
Susan Wooden, supt. Fax 435-7631
www.brs.cgresd.net
Beaverton JSHS 400/7-12
PO Box 529 48612 989-246-3010
Jeffrey Budge, prin. Fax 246-3366

**Belding, Ionia, Pop. 5,669**
Belding Area SD 2,100/PK-12
850 Hall St 48809 616-794-4700
Sara Shriver, supt. Fax 794-4730
www.bas-k12.org/
Belding HS 700/9-12
850 Hall St 48809 616-794-4900
Brett Zuver, prin. Fax 794-4956
Belding MS 500/6-8
410 Ionia St 48809 616-794-4400
Joel Olson, prin. Fax 794-4420
Belding Adult and Community Education Adult
1975 Orchard St 48809 616-794-4602
Ann VanDusen, prin. Fax 794-4403

**Bellaire, Antrim, Pop. 1,076**
Bellaire SD 500/K-12
204 W Forrest Home Ave 49615 231-533-8141
James Emery, supt. Fax 533-6797
www.bellairepublicschools.com/
Bellaire MSHS 300/6-12
204 W Forrest Home Ave 49615 231-533-8015
James Emery, prin. Fax 533-6797

**Belleville, Wayne, Pop. 3,881**
Van Buren SD 3,700/PK-12
555 W Columbia Ave 48111 734-697-9123
Michael Van Tassel, supt. Fax 697-6385
www.vanburenschools.net
Belleville HS 1,700/9-12
501 W Columbia Ave 48111 734-697-9133
Abdul Madyun, prin. Fax 697-6551
McBride MS 500/7-8
47097 McBride Ave 48111 734-697-9171
John Leroy, prin. Fax 697-6573

**Bellevue, Eaton, Pop. 1,257**
Bellevue Community SD 600/K-12
904 W Capital Ave 49021 269-763-9432
John C. Prescott, supt. Fax 763-3101
www.bellevue-schools.com/
Bellevue HS 300/6-12
576 Love Hwy 49021 269-763-9413
Monica Burger, prin. Fax 763-3955

**Benton Harbor, Berrien, Pop. 9,796**
Benton Harbor Area SD 2,100/PK-12
PO Box 1107 49023 269-605-1000
Gregory Weatherspoon, supt. Fax 605-1043
www.bhas.org
Benton Harbor HS 800/9-12
870 Colfax Ave 49022 269-605-1200
Rodger Tripplett, prin. Fax 605-1203

---

Lake Michigan College Post-Sec.
2755 E Napier Ave 49022 269-927-1000

**Benzonia, Benzie, Pop. 484**
Benzie County Central SD 1,600/K-12
9222 Homestead Rd 49616 231-882-9653
David Micinski, supt. Fax 882-9121
www.benzieschools.net/
Benzie Central HS 500/9-12
PO Box 240 49616 231-882-4497
Larry Haughn, prin. Fax 882-5699
Benzie Central MS 300/7-8
9300 Homestead Rd 49616 231-882-4498
David Clasen, prin. Fax 882-7627

**Berkley, Oakland, Pop. 14,700**
Berkley SD
Supt. — See Oak Park
Anderson MS 600/6-8
3205 Catalpa Dr 48072 248-837-8200
Mike Ross, prin. Fax 546-0696
Berkley HS 1,200/9-12
2325 Catalpa Dr 48072 248-837-8100
Randy Gawel, prin. Fax 544-5860

**Berrien Springs, Berrien, Pop. 1,747**
Berrien Springs SD 2,100/K-12
PO Box 130 49103 269-471-2891
David Eichberg, supt. Fax 471-2590
www.homeoftheshamrocks.org
Berrien Springs Discovery Academy 300/Alt
PO Box 130 49103 269-471-2593
William Bergan, prin. Fax 471-8865
Berrien Springs HS 600/9-12
PO Box 130 49103 269-471-1748
Ryan Pesce, prin. Fax 471-1511
Berrien Springs MS 500/6-8
PO Box 130 49103 269-471-2796
Mitchell Cumings, prin. Fax 471-2590

Andrews Academy 200/9-12
8833 Garland Ave 49104 269-471-3138
Jeannie Leiterman M.A., prin. Fax 471-6368
Andrews University Post-Sec.
8975 US 31 49104 269-471-7771
Griggs University Post-Sec.
8903 US Highway 31 49104 800-782-4769

**Bessemer, Gogebic, Pop. 1,874**
Bessemer City SD 400/PK-12
301 E Sellar St 49911 906-667-0802
David Radovich, supt. Fax 667-0318
www.bessemer.k12.mi.us
Johnston JSHS 200/7-12
100 W Lead St 49911 906-667-0413
Daniel VanderVelden, prin. Fax 667-0320

**Beverly Hills, Oakland, Pop. 10,098**
Birmingham SD 8,100/PK-12
31301 Evergreen Rd 48025 248-203-3000
Dr. Daniel Nerad, supt. Fax 203-3009
www.birmingham.k12.mi.us
Berkshire MS 800/6-8
21707 W 14 Mile Rd 48025 248-203-4702
Jason Clinckscale, prin. Fax 203-4802
Groves HS 1,300/9-12
20500 W 13 Mile Rd 48025 248-203-3530
Cathy Hurley, prin. Fax 203-3636
Other Schools – See Birmingham, Bloomfield Hls

Detroit Country Day MS 400/6-8
22400 Hillview Ln 48025 248-430-1677
Glen Shilling, hdmstr.
Detroit Country Day Upper S 700/9-12
22305 W 13 Mile Rd 48025 248-646-7717
Glen Shilling, hdmstr. Fax 646-2458

**Big Rapids, Mecosta, Pop. 10,347**
Big Rapids SD 1,800/K-12
21034 15 Mile Rd 49307 231-796-2627
Tim Haist, supt. Fax 592-0639
www.brps.org
Big Rapids HS 700/9-12
21175 15 Mile Rd 49307 231-796-7651
Ron Pincumbe, prin. Fax 592-8505
Big Rapids MS 600/5-8
500 N Warren Ave 49307 231-796-9965
Lenore Weaver, prin. Fax 592-3494
New Directions Alternative HS 50/Alt
21485 15 Mile Rd 49307 231-796-3489
Josh Easler, coord. Fax 592-0644

Mecosta-Osceola ISD 100/
15760 190th Ave 49307 231-796-3543
Dr. Curtis Finch, supt. Fax 796-3300
www.moisd.org
Mecosta-Osceola Career Center Vo/Tech
15830 190th Ave 49307 231-796-5805
Mike Miller, prin. Fax 796-0262

Ferris State University Post-Sec.
1201 S State St 49307 231-591-2000

**Birch Run, Saginaw, Pop. 1,524**
Birch Run Area SD 1,800/K-12
12400 Church St 48415 989-624-9307
David Bush, supt. Fax 624-8503
www.birchrunschools.org
Birch Run Early College 11-12
12450 Church St 48415 989-624-9392
Mike Baszler, prin.
Birch Run HS 600/9-12
12450 Church St 48415 989-624-9392
Michael Baszler, prin. Fax 624-8502
Birch Run Progressive HS 100/Alt
12400 Church St 48415 989-624-9392
Mike Baszler, prin. Fax 624-8502
Greene MS 600/5-8
8225 Main St 48415 989-624-5821
Scott Preston, prin. Fax 624-8507

**Birmingham, Oakland, Pop. 19,789**
Birmingham SD
Supt. — See Beverly Hills
Derby MS 800/6-8
1300 Derby Rd 48009 248-203-5003
Celeste Nowacki, prin. Fax 203-4948
Seaholm HS 1,300/9-12
2436 W Lincoln St 48009 248-203-3707
Rachel Guinn, prin. Fax 203-3706

Roeper S 6-12
1051 Oakland Ave 48009 248-203-7300
David Feldman, head sch Fax 203-7310

**Blanchard, Isabella**
Montabella Community SD
Supt. — See Edmore
Montabella JSHS 400/7-12
1324 N County Line Rd 49310 989-427-5175
Shane Riley, prin. Fax 427-5107

**Blissfield, Lenawee, Pop. 3,300**
Blissfield Community SD 1,200/K-12
630 S Lane St 49228 517-486-2205
Jerry Johnson, supt. Fax 486-5701
www.blissfieldschools.us/
Blissfield HS 400/9-12
630 S Lane St 49228 517-486-2148
Steve Gfell, prin. Fax 486-4749
Blissfield MS 300/6-8
1305 Beamer Rd 49228 517-486-4420
Cris Rupp, prin. Fax 486-4758

**Bloomfield Hls, Oakland, Pop. 3,811**
Birmingham SD
Supt. — See Beverly Hills
Birmingham Covington S 700/3-8
1525 Covington Rd, 248-203-4425
Mark Morawski, prin. Fax 203-4433

Bloomfield Hills SD 4,800/PK-12
7273 Wing Lake Rd, 248-341-5400
Robert Glass, supt. Fax 341-5449
www.bloomfield.org
Bloomfield Hills HS 800/9-12
4200 Andover Rd, 248-341-5700
Charles Hollerith, prin. Fax 341-5899
Bloomfield Hills MS 700/5-8
4200 Quarton Rd, 248-341-6000
Randy English, prin. Fax 341-6099
Bowers Academy Alt
1223 E Square Lake Rd, 248-341-5985
Bill Boyle, prin. Fax 341-5998
East Hills MS 500/5-8
2800 Kensington Rd, 248-341-6200
Jason Rubel, prin. Fax 341-6299
International Academy 1,300/9-12
1020 E Square Lake Rd, 248-341-5900
Lynne Gibson, prin. Fax 341-5959
Model HS Alt
4220 Andover Rd, 248-341-5960
Bill Boyle, prin. Fax 341-5999
Other Schools – See West Bloomfield

Academy of the Sacred Heart 400/PK-12
1250 Kensington Rd, 248-646-8900
Sr. Bridget Bearss, hdmstr. Fax 646-4143
Bloomfield Christian School 200/K-12
3570 Telegraph Rd, 248-457-1510
Patsy Hinton, head sch Fax 457-1520
Brother Rice HS 700/9-12
7101 Lahser Rd, 248-833-2000
Br. Michael Segvich, prin. Fax 833-2001
Cranbrook Academy of Art Post-Sec.
PO Box 801, 248-645-3300
Cranbrook S 1,700/PK-12
PO Box 801, 248-645-3000
Arlyce Seibert, dir. Fax 645-3524
Marian HS 500/9-12
7225 Lahser Rd, 248-644-1750
Sr. Lenore Pochelski, pres. Fax 644-6107

**Bloomingdale, Van Buren, Pop. 446**
Bloomingdale SD 1,300/K-12
PO Box 217 49026 269-521-3900
Deb Paquette, supt. Fax 521-3907
www.bdalecards.org/
Bloomingdale HS 300/9-12
PO Box 217 49026 269-521-3910
Rick Reo, prin. Fax 521-3915
Bloomingdale MS 300/6-8
PO Box 217 49026 269-521-3950
Rick Reo, prin. Fax 521-3958

**Boyne City, Charlevoix, Pop. 3,622**
Boyne City SD 1,300/K-12
321 S Park St 49712 231-439-8190
Peter Moss M.A., supt. Fax 439-8195
www.boyne.k12.mi.us
Boyne City HS 400/9-12
1035 Boyne Ave 49712 231-439-8100
Karen Jarema M.A., prin. Fax 439-8194
Boyne City MS 400/5-8
1025 Boyne Ave 49712 231-439-8200
Mike Wilson M.A., prin. Fax 439-8233
Morgan-Shaw S 50/Alt
321 S Park St 49712 231-439-8140
Nicholas McLane, admin. Fax 439-8195

**Boyne Falls, Charlevoix, Pop. 286**
Boyne Falls SD 200/K-12
PO Box 356 49713 231-549-2211
Cynthia Pineda, admin. Fax 549-2922
www.boynefalls.org
Boyne Falls S 200/K-12
PO Box 356 49713 231-549-2211
Cynthia Pineda, admin. Fax 549-2922

**Breckenridge, Gratiot, Pop. 1,316**
Breckenridge Community SD 800/PK-12
PO Box 217 48615 989-842-3182
Kimberly Thompson, supt. Fax 842-3625
breckhuskies.org
Breckenridge AIM S 50/Alt
700 Wright St 48615 989-842-3182
Sheila Pilmore, admin. Fax 842-5761
Breckenridge HS 200/9-12
PO Box 217 48615 989-842-3182
Sheila Pilmore, prin. Fax 842-5761
Breckenridge MS 200/6-8
PO Box 217 48615 989-842-3182
Sheila Pilmore, prin. Fax 842-5761

**Brethren, Manistee, Pop. 407**
Kaleva Norman Dickson SD 600/K-12
4400 Highbridge Rd 49619 231-477-5353
Marlen Cordes, supt. Fax 477-5240
www.knd.k12.mi.us
Brethren HS 200/9-12
4400 Highbridge Rd 49619 231-477-5355
Jakob Veith, prin. Fax 477-5242
Brethren MS 100/7-8
4400 Highbridge Rd 49619 231-477-5354
Jakob Veith, prin. Fax 477-5351

**Bridgeport, Saginaw, Pop. 6,811**
Bridgeport-Spaulding Community SD 1,100/PK-12
PO Box 657 48722 989-777-1770
Carol W. Selby, supt. Fax 777-4720
www.bscs.k12.mi.us
Bridgeport HS 500/9-12
4691 Bearcat Blvd 48722 989-777-3100
Brian McCarthy, prin. Fax 777-6910

**Bridgman, Berrien, Pop. 2,260**
Bridgman SD 1,000/PK-12
9964 Gast Rd 49106 269-466-0271
Shane Peters, supt. Fax 466-0221
www.bridgmanschools.com
Bridgman HS 300/9-12
9964 Gast Rd 49106 269-465-6848
Chris Machiniak, prin. Fax 466-0355
Reed MS 300/5-8
10254 California 49106 269-465-5410
Sam Stine, prin. Fax 466-0393

**Brighton, Livingston, Pop. 7,364**
Brighton Area SD 6,100/K-12
125 S Church St 48116 810-299-4000
Greg Gray, supt. Fax 299-4092
www.brightonk12.com/
Bridge Alternative HS 100/Alt
125 S Church St 48116 810-299-4046
Colleen Deaven, admin.
Brighton HS 2,000/9-12
7878 Brighton Rd 48116 810-299-4100
Gavin Johnson, prin. Fax 299-4111
Scranton MS 1,000/7-8
8415 Maltby Rd 48116 810-299-3700
Mark Wilson, prin. Fax 299-3710

Livingston Christian S 200/PK-12
7669 Brighton Rd 48116 734-878-9818
Theodore Nast, admin.
Ross Medical Education Center Post-Sec.
8110 Murphy Dr 48116 810-227-0160

**Brimley, Chippewa**
Brimley Area SD 500/K-12
7134 S M 221 49715 906-248-3218
Brian Reattoir, supt. Fax 248-3220
brimley.eup.k12.mi.us
Brimley HS 200/7-12
7134 S M 221 49715 906-248-3218
Brian Reattoir, prin. Fax 248-5339

Bay Mills Community College Post-Sec.
12214 W Lakeshore Dr 49715 906-248-3354

**Britton, Lenawee, Pop. 584**
Britton Deerfield SD 700/PK-12
201 College Ave 49229 517-451-4581
Charles Pelham, supt. Fax 451-8595
www.bdschools.us
Britton S 500/PK-12
201 College Ave 49229 517-451-4581
John Eisley, prin. Fax 451-8595

**Bronson, Branch, Pop. 2,313**
Bronson Community SD 1,100/K-12
501 E Chicago St 49028 517-369-3260
Dr. Teresa Belote, supt. Fax 369-2802
www.bronsonschools.org
Bronson JSHS 500/6-12
450 E Grant St 49028 517-369-3230
Wesley McCrea, prin. Fax 369-3506

**Brooklyn, Jackson, Pop. 1,196**
Columbia SD 1,500/PK-12
11775 Hewitt Rd 49230 517-592-6641
Dr. Pamela Campbell, supt. Fax 592-8090
www.myeagles.org
Columbia Central JSHS 500/7-12
11775 Hewitt Rd 49230 517-592-6634
Daniel Hyliard, prin. Fax 592-8909
Other Schools – See Clarklake

**Brown City, Sanilac, Pop. 1,303**
Brown City Community SD 900/PK-12
PO Box 160 48416 810-346-4700
Doug Muxlow, supt. Fax 346-3762
www.bc.k12.mi.us
Brown City JSHS 400/7-12
PO Box 160 48416 810-346-4700
Neil Kohler, prin. Fax 346-2381

**Brownstown, See Flat Rock**
Woodhaven-Brownstown SD
Supt. — See Woodhaven
Maple Grove Alternative HS Alt
24787 Van Horn Rd 48134 734-783-3333
Matt Czajkowski, prin. Fax 783-3342
Woodhaven HS 1,100/10-12
24787 Van Horn Rd 48134 734-783-3333
Matthew Czajkowski, prin. Fax 783-3342

**Buchanan, Berrien, Pop. 4,325**
Buchanan Community SD 1,500/PK-12
401 W Chicago St 49107 269-695-8401
Dr. Andrea Van der Laan, supt. Fax 695-8450
www.buchananschools.com
Buchanan HS 600/8-12
401 W Chicago St 49107 269-695-8403
Stacey DeMaio, prin. Fax 695-8451

**Buckley, Wexford, Pop. 683**
Buckley Community SD 400/K-12
305 S 1st St 49620 231-269-3325
Laurie Walles, supt. Fax 269-3833
www.buckleyschools.com
Buckley Community S 400/K-12
305 S 1st St 49620 231-269-3325
Laurie Walles, prin. Fax 269-3833

**Burr Oak, Saint Joseph, Pop. 822**
Burr Oak Community SD 200/K-12
PO Box 337 49030 269-489-2213
Terry Conklin, supt. Fax 489-5198
burroak.remc12.k12.mi.us
Burr Oak HS 100/5-12
PO Box 337 49030 269-489-5534
Robert Cary, prin. Fax 489-5198

**Burton, Genesee, Pop. 29,312**
Atherton Community SD 500/K-12
3354 S Genesee Rd 48519 810-591-9182
John Ploof, supt. Fax 591-1926
www.athertonschools.org
Atherton JSHS 300/7-12
3354 S Genesee Rd 48519 810-591-9184
Steven Vowles, prin. Fax 591-9180

Bendle SD 1,200/PK-12
3420 Columbine Ave 48529 810-591-2501
John Krolewski, supt. Fax 591-2210
www.bendleschools.org
Bendle HS 400/9-12
2283 E Scottwood Ave 48529 810-591-5103
Scott Williams, prin. Fax 591-2510
Bendle MS 300/6-8
2294 E Bristol Rd 48529 810-591-3385
Pete Gleason, prin. Fax 591-2540

Bentley Community SD 900/K-12
1170 N Belsay Rd 48509 810-591-9100
Rebekah Dupuis, supt. Fax 591-9102
www.bentleyschools.org
Bentley HS 300/9-12
1150 N Belsay Rd 48509 810-591-5811
Brian Eddy, prin. Fax 591-9158
Bentley High School FUSION Academy Alt
1150 N Belsay Rd 48509 810-591-9516
Brian Eddy, prin. Fax 591-9158
Bentley MS 200/6-8
1180 N Belsay Rd 48509 810-591-9043
Brian Eddy, prin. Fax 591-9166

---

Faithway Christian S 100/PK-12
1225 S Center Rd 48509 810-743-0055
Laura Walthers, prin. Fax 743-0033
Genesee Christian S 400/PK-12
1223 S Belsay Rd 48509 810-743-3108
Robert Buchalski, prin. Fax 743-3230
St. Thomas More Academy 100/K-12
6456 E Bristol Rd 48519 810-742-2411

**Byron, Shiawassee, Pop. 573**
Byron Area SD 1,100/K-12
312 W Maple St 48418 810-266-4881
Tricia Murphy-Alderman, supt. Fax 266-5723
www.byron.k12.mi.us
Byron HS 400/9-12
312 W Maple St 48418 810-266-4620
Grant Hegenauer, prin. Fax 266-5010
Byron MS 300/6-8
312 W Maple St 48418 810-266-4422
Grant Hegenauer, prin. Fax 266-4151

**Byron Center, Kent, Pop. 5,750**
Byron Center SD 3,400/PK-12
8542 Byron Center Ave SW 49315 616-878-6100
Daniel Takens, supt. Fax 878-6120
www.bcpsk12.net
Byron Center HS 1,100/9-12
8500 Burlingame Ave SW 49315 616-878-6600
Scott Joseph, prin. Fax 878-6620
Byron Center West MS 500/7-8
8654 Homerich Ave SW 49315 616-878-6500
John Krajewski, prin. Fax 878-6520

---

Zion Christian S 300/PK-12
7555 Byron Center Ave SW 49315 616-878-9472
Todd Hoekstra, admin. Fax 878-9473

**Cadillac, Wexford, Pop. 10,183**
Cadillac Area SD 3,000/K-12
421 S Mitchell St 49601 231-876-5000
Jennifer Brown, supt. Fax 876-5021
www.cadillac.k12.mi.us
Cadillac HS 900/9-12
400 Linden St 49601 231-876-5800
Shaina Squires, prin. Fax 876-5821
Cadillac JHS 400/7-8
500 Chestnut St 49601 231-876-5700
Michael Outman, prin. Fax 876-5721
Cooley Alternative S 100/Alt
221 Granite St 49601 231-876-5900
Dave Champion, prin. Fax 876-5921

Wexford-Missaukee ISD 50/
9907 E 13th St 49601 231-876-2260
Jeff Jennette, supt. Fax 876-2261
www.wmisd.org
Wexford-Missaukee Area Career Tech Vo/Tech
9901 E 13th St 49601 231-876-2200
David Cox, dir. Fax 876-2212

---

Baker College of Cadillac Post-Sec.
9600 E 13th St 49601 231-876-3100
Cadillac Heritage Christian S 100/PK-12
1706 Wright St 49601 231-775-4272
William Goodwill, admin. Fax 775-2999

**Caledonia, Kent, Pop. 1,496**
Caledonia Community SD 4,000/PK-12
9753 Duncan Lake Ave SE 49316 616-891-8185
Randy Rodriguez, supt. Fax 891-9253
www.calschools.org
Caledonia HS 1,300/9-12
9050 Kraft Ave SE 49316 616-891-8129
Brady Lake, prin. Fax 891-7038
Duncan Lake MS 500/6-8
9757 Duncan Lake Ave SE 49316 616-891-1380
Ryan Graham, prin. Fax 891-0833
Glenmor HS 50/Alt
8948 Kraft Ave SE 49316 616-891-8236
Brady Lake, prin. Fax 891-8139
Kraft Meadows MS 500/6-8
9230 Kraft Ave SE 49316 616-891-8649
Steve Uyl, prin. Fax 891-7013

**Calumet, Houghton, Pop. 716**
Calumet-Laurium-Keweenaw SD 1,500/K-12
57070 Mine St 49913 906-337-0311
Darryl Pierce, supt. Fax 337-1406
clkschools.org
Calumet HS 400/9-12
57070 Mine St 49913 906-337-0311
Christopher Davidson, prin. Fax 337-5405
Horizon Alternative HS 50/Alt
57070 Mine St 49913 906-337-4611
Marlene Horton, prin. Fax 337-4614
Washington MS 300/6-8
57070 Mine St 49913 906-337-0311
Michael Steber, prin. Fax 337-5406

**Camden, Hillsdale, Pop. 510**
Camden-Frontier SD 600/K-12
4971 W Montgomery Rd 49232 517-368-5991
Scott Riley, supt. Fax 368-5959
www.cfss.org/
Camden Frontier HS 200/9-12
4971 W Montgomery Rd 49232 517-368-5255
Scott Riley, prin. Fax 368-5959

**Canton, Wayne, Pop. 81,500**
Plymouth-Canton Community SD
Supt. — See Plymouth
Canton HS 2,100/9-12
8415 N Canton Center Rd 48187 734-416-2850
Hal Heard, prin. Fax 416-7531
Discovery MS 1,000/6-8
45083 Hanford Rd 48187 734-416-2880
Roche La Victor, prin. Fax 416-2895
Liberty MS 6-8
46250 Cherry Hill Rd 48187 734-416-7600
James Hunter, prin. Fax 927-0576
Plymouth HS 2,100/9-12
8400 N Beck Rd 48187 734-582-5500
Cheri Steckel, prin. Fax 582-5555
Salem HS 2,000/9-12
46181 Joy Rd 48187 734-416-7800
Kim Villarosa, prin. Fax 416-7791

---

ITT Technical Institute Post-Sec.
1905 S Haggerty Rd 48188 734-397-7800
Michigan Institute of Aviation & Tech Post-Sec.
2955 S Haggerty Rd 48188 734-423-2100
Plymouth Christian Academy 600/PK-12
43065 Joy Rd 48187 734-459-3505
Caryn Huntsman, supt. Fax 459-9997

**Capac, Saint Clair, Pop. 1,866**
Capac Community SD 1,300/PK-12
403 N Glassford St 48014 810-395-3710
Stephen Bigelow, supt. Fax 395-4858
www.capacschools.us
Capac JSHS 500/9-12
541 N Glassford St 48014 810-395-3800
Nicole Kirby, prin. Fax 395-2427
Capac MS 300/6-8
201 N Neeper St 48014 810-395-3750
David Kochan, prin. Fax 395-4098

**Carleton, Monroe, Pop. 2,303**
Airport Community SD 2,400/PK-12
11270 Grafton Rd 48117 734-654-2414
John Krimmel, supt. Fax 654-4014
www.airportschools.com
Airport HS 900/9-12
11330 Grafton Rd 48117 734-654-6208
Chris Lukosavich, prin. Fax 654-3005
Wagar 7/8 MS 600/7-8
11200 Grafton Rd 48117 734-654-6205
Dan Bondy, prin. Fax 654-0057
Other Schools – See Newport

**Carney, Menominee, Pop. 190**
Carney-Nadeau SD 200/PK-12
PO Box 68 49812 906-639-2171
Adam Cocco, supt. Fax 639-2176
www.cnps.us
Carney-Nadeau S 200/PK-12
PO Box 68 49812 906-639-2171
Adam Cocco, supt. Fax 639-2176

**Caro, Tuscola, Pop. 4,185**
Caro Community SD 1,800/K-12
301 N Hooper St 48723 989-673-3160
Michael Joslyn, supt. Fax 673-6248
www.carok12.org
Caro Alternative HS Alt
1205 E Caro Rd 48723 989-673-6845
Kimberly Byington, prin. Fax 673-8554
Caro HS 600/9-12
301 N Hooper St 48723 989-673-3165
Stephan Clark, prin. Fax 673-8707
Caro MS 400/6-8
299 N Hooper St 48723 989-673-3167
JoAnn Nordstrom, prin. Fax 673-1225

Tuscola ISD 200/
1385 Cleaver Rd 48723 989-673-2144
Eugene Pierce, supt. Fax 673-5366
www.tuscolaisd.org/
Tuscola Technology Center Vo/Tech
1401 Cleaver Rd 48723 989-673-5300
Shawn Petri, prin. Fax 673-4228

**Carson City, Montcalm, Pop. 1,086**
Carson City-Crystal Area SD 1,100/K-12
PO Box 780 48811 989-584-3138
Kevin Murphy, supt. Fax 584-3539
www.carsoncity.k12.mi.us
Carson City-Crystal HS 400/9-12
PO Box 780 48811 989-584-3175
Duane Lyons, prin. Fax 584-3043
Carson City-Crystal Upper Elementary MS 400/4-8
PO Box 780 48811 989-584-3903
Ben Brock, prin. Fax 584-3259
Other Schools – See Crystal

**Carsonville, Sanilac, Pop. 513**
Carsonville-Port Sanilac SD 600/K-12
100 N Goetze Rd 48419 810-657-9393
Gale Travis, supt. Fax 657-9060
www.cpsk12.us
Carsonville-Port Sanilac JSHS 200/6-12
100 N Goetze Rd 48419 810-657-9394
Jennifer Richmond, prin. Fax 657-9431
Carsonville-Pt Sanilac Acad Alt Learners 100/Alt
100 N Goetze Rd 48419 810-657-9393
Gale Travis, dir. Fax 657-9060

**Casco, Saint Clair**
Anchor Bay SD 6,200/PK-12
5201 County Line Rd Ste 100 48064 586-725-2861
Leonard Woodside, supt. Fax 727-9059
www.anchorbay.misd.net
Other Schools – See Fair Haven, New Baltimore

**Caseville, Huron, Pop. 766**
Caseville SD 100/K-12
6609 Vine St 48725 989-856-2940
Dr. Kenneth Ewald, supt. Fax 856-3095
www.caseville.k12.mi.us
Caseville S 100/K-12
6609 Vine St 48725 989-856-7192
Dr. Kenneth Ewald, prin. Fax 856-8641

**Cass City, Tuscola, Pop. 2,395**
Cass City SD 800/PK-12
4868 Seeger St 48726 989-872-2200
Jeffrey Hartel, supt. Fax 872-5015
www.casscity.k12.mi.us
Cass City JSHS 400/7-12
4868 Seeger St 48726 989-872-2148
Chad Daniels, prin. Fax 872-2068

**Cassopolis, Cass, Pop. 1,687**
Cassopolis SD 1,000/K-12
725 Center St 49031 269-445-0503
Tracy D. Hertsel, supt. Fax 445-0505
www.cassopolis.k12.mi.us
Beatty JSHS 500/7-12
22721 Diamond Cove St 49031 269-445-0540
Dave VanLue, prin. Fax 445-3112

**Cedar Lake, Montcalm**

---

Great Lakes Adventist Academy 200/9-12
PO Box 68 48812 989-427-5181
Delwin Garcia, prin. Fax 427-5027

**Cedar Springs, Kent, Pop. 3,426**
Cedar Springs SD 3,300/PK-12
204 E Muskegon St 49319 616-696-1204
Dr. Laura VanDuyn Ed.D., supt. Fax 696-3755
www.csredhawks.org
Cedar Springs HS 1,000/9-12
204 E Muskegon St 49319 616-696-1200
Ron Behrenwald, prin. Fax 696-4016
Cedar Springs MS 500/7-8
204 E Muskegon St 49319 616-696-9100
Sue Spahr, prin. Fax 696-3109
New Beginnings HS 100/Alt
204 E Muskegon St 49319 616-696-1203
Stacey Jennette, prin. Fax 696-0296

**Cedarville, Mackinac**
Les Cheneaux Community SD 100/K-12
PO Box 366 49719 906-484-2256
Randy Schaedig, supt. Fax 484-2072
lescheneaux.eup.k12.mi.us/site/default.aspx?PageID=1
Cedarville S 100/K-12
PO Box 366 49719 906-484-2256
Randy Schaedig, prin. Fax 484-2072

**Center Line, Macomb, Pop. 8,060**
Center Line SD 2,600/PK-12
26400 Arsenal 48015 586-510-2000
Eve Kaltz, supt. Fax 510-2019
www.clps.org
Center Line HS 800/9-12
26300 Arsenal 48015 586-510-2100
Benjamin Gurk, prin. Fax 510-2119
Wolfe MS 600/6-8
8640 McKinley 48015 586-510-2300
Amy Maruca, prin. Fax 510-2319

**Central Lake, Antrim, Pop. 931**
Central Lake SD 400/PK-12
PO Box 128 49622 231-544-3141
Benjamin Williams, supt. Fax 544-2903
clps.k12.mi.us
Central Lake JSHS 200/6-12
PO Box 128 49622 231-544-5221
Michele Derenzy, prin. Fax 544-6981

**Centreville, Saint Joseph, Pop. 1,388**
Centreville SD 900/K-12
PO Box 158 49032 269-467-5220
Robert Kuhlman, supt. Fax 467-5214
www.cpschools.org
Centreville HS 300/9-12
PO Box 158 49032 269-467-5210
Dennis Kirby, prin. Fax 467-5214
Centreville JHS 100/7-8
PO Box 158 49032 269-467-5210
Dennis Kirby, prin. Fax 467-5214
Covered Bridge Alternative S 50/Alt
PO Box 158 49032 269-467-5215
Juanita Miller, prin. Fax 467-5227

---

Glen Oaks Community College Post-Sec.
62249 Shimmel Rd 49032 269-467-9945

**Charlevoix, Charlevoix, Pop. 2,468**
Charlevoix SD 700/PK-12
104 E Saint Marys Dr 49720 231-547-3200
Michael Ritter, supt. Fax 547-0556
www.rayder.net

Charlevoix MSHS 400/7-12
5200 Marion Center Rd 49720 231-547-3222
Suzanne Klinger, prin. Fax 547-3245

**Charlotte, Eaton, Pop. 8,946**
Charlotte SD 2,400/K-12
378 State St 48813 517-541-5100
Mark Rosekrans, supt. Fax 541-5105
www.charlottenet.org
Charlotte Early Middle College 9-12
378 State St 48813 517-541-5601
Bill Barnes Ed.D., prin.
Charlotte HS 900/9-12
378 State St 48813 517-541-5600
William Barnes, prin. Fax 541-5625
Charlotte MS 400/7-8
1068 Carlisle Hwy 48813 517-541-5700
Matthew Maitland, prin. Fax 541-5705

**Chassell, Houghton**
Chassell Township SD 300/K-12
PO Box 140 49916 906-483-2132
Fax 487-9045
www.chassellschools.org
Chassell Township S 300/K-12
PO Box 140 49916 906-483-2132
Fax 487-9045

**Cheboygan, Cheboygan, Pop. 4,714**
Cheboygan Area SD 1,900/K-12
PO Box 100 49721 231-627-4436
Mark Dombroski, supt. Fax 627-9105
www.chebschools.org
Cheboygan Area HS 600/8-12
PO Box 100 49721 231-627-7191
Dr. Michele Ackerman, prin. Fax 627-2430
Inverness Academy Alternative Education 100/Alt
PO Box 100 49721 231-627-5613
Christopher Ackerman, dir. Fax 627-4180

**Chelsea, Washtenaw, Pop. 4,865**
Chelsea SD 2,400/PK-12
500 Washington St 48118 734-433-2200
David K. Killips, supt. Fax 433-2218
www.chelsea.k12.mi.us
Beach MS 600/6-8
445 Mayer Dr 48118 734-433-2202
Nick Angel, prin. Fax 433-2212
Chelsea HS 800/9-12
740 N Freer Rd 48118 734-433-2201
Michael Kapolka, prin. Fax 433-2211

**Chesaning, Saginaw, Pop. 2,377**
Chesaning UNSD 1,600/K-12
PO Box 95 48616 989-845-7020
Mike McGough, supt. Fax 845-3722
www.chesaningschools.net
Chesaning MS 500/5-8
431 N 4th St 48616 989-845-7040
Melinda Soule, prin. Fax 845-5335
Chesaning Union HS 500/9-12
850 N 4th St 48616 989-845-2040
Kimberly Vincke, prin. Fax 845-2117

**Chesterfield, Macomb**
L'Anse Creuse SD
Supt. — See Clinton Township
L'Anse Creuse MS East 700/6-8
30300 Hickey Rd 48051 586-493-5200
Nina Davis, prin. Fax 493-5205

**Clare, Clare, Pop. 3,061**
Clare SD 1,500/K-12
201 E State St 48617 989-386-9945
Doniel Pummell, supt. Fax 386-6055
www.clare.k12.mi.us
Clare HS 500/9-12
201 E State St 48617 989-386-7789
Ed Hubel, prin. Fax 386-1236
Clare MS 400/5-8
201 E State St 48617 989-386-9979
Steve Newkirk, prin. Fax 386-4008
Pioneer HS 100/Alt
670 Ann Arbor Trl 48617 989-386-3067
Amanda Emeott, prin. Fax 386-3274

**Clarklake, Jackson, Pop. 400**
Columbia SD
Supt. — See Brooklyn
Columbia Options HS 100/Alt
4460 N Lake Rd 49234 517-529-9400
Ralph Piepkow, prin. Fax 529-4853

**Clarkston, Oakland, Pop. 980**
Clarkston Community SD 8,000/PK-12
6389 Clarkston Rd 48346 248-623-5400
Dr. Rod Rock, supt. Fax 623-5450
www.clarkston.k12.mi.us
Clarkston HS 1,900/10-12
6093 Flemings Lake Rd 48346 248-623-3600
Gary Kaul, prin. Fax 623-3535
Clarkston JHS 1,400/8-9
6595 Waldon Rd 48346 248-623-5600
Adam Kern, prin. Fax 623-5680
Renaissance HS 200/Alt
6558 Waldon Rd 48346 248-623-8060
Christa Fons, prin. Fax 623-4555

Oakland ISD
Supt. — See Waterford
Oakland Technical Campus NW Vo/Tech
8211 Big Lake Rd 48346 248-922-5800
Chuck Locklear, dean Fax 922-5805

---

Everest Collegiate HS & Academy 500/PK-12
5935 Clarkston Rd 48348 248-620-3390
Gregory Reichert, pres. Fax 620-3942

**Clawson, Oakland, Pop. 11,609**
Clawson SD 1,800/K-12
626 Phillips Ave 48017 248-655-4400
Monique Beels, supt. Fax 655-4422
www.clawson.k12.mi.us
Clawson HS 600/9-12
101 John M Ave 48017 248-655-4200
Ryan Sines, prin. Fax 655-4205
Clawson MS 400/6-8
150 John M Ave 48017 248-655-4250
Adam Schihl, prin. Fax 655-4251

---

Academy of Court Reporting Post-Sec.
1055 W Maple Rd 48017 248-435-9030

**Climax, Kalamazoo, Pop. 761**
Climax-Scotts Community SD 600/PK-12
372 S Main St 49034 269-746-2400
Douglas Newington, supt. Fax 746-4374
www.csschools.net
Climax-Scotts Adult/Alternative Educ 100/Alt
372 S Main St 49034 269-746-4250
Douglas Newington, prin. Fax 746-2409
Climax-Scotts JSHS 300/6-12
372 S Main St 49034 269-746-2300
Kimberly Kirshman, prin. Fax 746-4142

**Clinton, Lenawee, Pop. 2,302**
Clinton Community SD 1,200/PK-12
341 E Michigan Ave 49236 517-456-6501
David Pray, supt. Fax 456-4324
www.clinton.k12.mi.us/
Clinton HS 400/9-12
340 E Michigan Ave 49236 517-456-6511
Kevin Beazley, prin. Fax 456-2042
Clinton MS 300/6-8
100 E Franklin St 49236 517-456-6507
Eric Claus, prin. Fax 456-4997

**Clinton Township, Macomb, Pop. 95,648**
Chippewa Valley SD 14,800/K-12
19120 Cass Ave 48038 586-723-2000
Ron Roberts, supt. Fax 723-2001
www.chippewavalleyschools.org
Algonquin MS 600/6-8
19150 Briarwood Ln 48036 586-723-3500
Walter Kozlowski, prin. Fax 723-3501
Chippewa Valley HS 1,800/9-12
18300 19 Mile Rd 48038 586-723-2300
Dr. Jerry Davisson, prin. Fax 723-2336
International Academy of Macomb 9-12
42755 Romeo Plank Rd 48038 586-723-7200
Eric Sturm, prin. Fax 723-7201
Mohegan HS 200/Alt
19230 Cass Ave 48038 586-723-2080
Jim Fields, admin. Fax 723-2051
Wyandot MS 1,000/6-8
39490 Garfield Rd 48038 586-723-4200
Darleen Sims, prin. Fax 723-4201
Other Schools – See Macomb

Clintondale Community SD 2,800/PK-12
35100 Little Mack Ave 48035 586-791-6300
Gregory Green, supt. Fax 791-6786
seatwaitingforyou.com/
Clintondale Continuing Education Center 900/Alt
22280 E Price Dr 48035 586-790-2756
Gregory Green, prin. Fax 790-7620
Clintondale HS 600/9-12
35200 Little Mack Ave 48035 586-791-6300
Meloney Cargill, prin. Fax 790-7645
Clintondale MS 400/6-8
35300 Little Mack Ave 48035 586-791-6300
Ira Hamden, prin. Fax 790-7642

L'Anse Creuse SD 11,500/PK-12
24076 Frederick Pankow Blvd 48036 586-783-6300
Jackie Johnston, supt. Fax 783-6310
www.lc-ps.org
Pankow Center Vo/Tech
24600 Frederick Pankow Blvd 48036 586-783-6570
John Haas, prin. Fax 783-6577
Pellerin Center Adult
24001 Frederick Pankow Blvd 48036 586-783-6420
Jeff Glombowski, prin. Fax 783-6423
Other Schools – See Chesterfield, Harrison Township, Macomb

---

Baker College of Clinton Township Post-Sec.
34950 Little Mack Ave 48035 586-791-6610
Faith Christian S 100/PK-12
23130 Remick Dr 48036 586-783-9630
Jim Hawkins, prin. Fax 783-9628

**Clio, Genesee, Pop. 2,597**
Clio Area SD 3,400/PK-12
430 N Mill St 48420 810-591-0500
Fletcher Spears, supt. Fax 591-0140
www.clioschools.org
Carter MS 1,100/5-8
300 Rogers Ldg 48420 810-591-0503
Neil Bedell, prin. Fax 591-8148
Clio Community HS 100/Alt
420 N Mill St 48420 810-591-4804
John Roark, dir. Fax 591-8193
Clio HS 1,000/9-12
1 Mustang Dr 48420 810-591-1359
Mike Lytle, prin. Fax 591-8169

**Coldwater, Branch, Pop. 10,680**
Branch ISD 100/
370 Morse St 49036 517-279-5730
Joseph Lopez, supt. Fax 279-5766
www.branch-isd.org
Branch Area Career Center Vo/Tech
366 Morse St 49036 517-279-5721
Michael Hoffner, prin. Fax 279-5777

Coldwater Community SD 2,800/PK-12
401 Sauk River Dr 49036 517-279-5910
Terry Boguth, supt. Fax 279-7651
www.coldwaterschools.org
Coldwater HS 800/9-12
275 N Fremont St 49036 517-279-5930
William Milnes, prin. Fax 278-2475
Legg MS 700/6-8
175 Green St 49036 517-279-5940
Julie Slusher, prin. Fax 279-5945

---

School of Creative Hair Design Post-Sec.
470 Marshall St 49036 517-279-2355

**Coleman, Midland, Pop. 1,211**
Coleman Community SD 800/K-12
4823 N Coleman Schools Dr 48618 989-465-6060
Mary Pitchford, supt. Fax 465-9853
www.colemanschools.net
Coleman JSHS 300/7-12
4951 N Lewis Rd 48618 989-465-6171
John Young, prin. Fax 465-9222

**Coloma, Berrien, Pop. 1,456**
Coloma Community SD 1,800/PK-12
PO Box 550 49038 269-468-2424
Pete Bush, supt. Fax 468-2440
www.ccs.coloma.org
Coloma HS 400/9-12
PO Box 550 49038 269-468-2400
David Ehlers, prin. Fax 468-2423
Coloma JHS 300/6-8
PO Box 550 49038 269-468-2405
Peter Olsen, prin. Fax 468-2428

**Colon, Saint Joseph, Pop. 1,152**
Colon Community SD 600/PK-12
400 Dallas St 49040 269-386-2239
Christine Barnes, supt. Fax 432-2577
www.colonschools.org
Colon JSHS 200/7-12
400 Dallas St 49040 269-432-3231
Beth Robb, prin. Fax 432-9851

**Commerce Township, Oakland, Pop. 26,955**
Huron Valley SD
Supt. — See Highland
Oak Valley MS 800/6-8
4200 White Oak Trl 48382 248-684-8101
Michele Butler, prin. Fax 684-8105

Walled Lake Consolidated SD
Supt. — See Walled Lake
Central HS 1,900/9-12
1600 E Oakley Park Rd 48390 248-956-4700
Charles Morgan, prin. Fax 956-4705
Northern HS 1,600/9-12
6000 Bogie Lake Rd 48382 248-956-5300
Greg Diamond, prin. Fax 956-5305
Smart MS 1,000/6-8
8500 Commerce Rd 48382 248-956-3500
Brian Kaplan, prin. Fax 956-3505

**Comstock Park, Kent, Pop. 9,824**
Comstock Park SD 2,300/PK-12
101 School St NE 49321 616-254-5001
Ethan Ebenstein, supt. Fax 784-5404
www.cppschools.com
Comstock Park HS 700/9-12
150 6 Mile Rd NE 49321 616-254-5200
Steve Gough, prin. Fax 785-9835
Mill Creek MS 500/6-8
100 Betty St NE 49321 616-254-5100
August Harju, prin. Fax 785-2464

**Concord, Jackson, Pop. 1,046**
Concord Community SD 800/K-12
PO Box 338 49237 517-524-8850
Al Widner, supt. Fax 524-8613
www.concordschools.net
Concord HS 300/9-12
PO Box 338 49237 517-524-8384
Cheryl Price, prin. Fax 524-6196
Concord MS 200/6-8
PO Box 338 49237 517-524-8854
Matt Lehman, prin. Fax 524-7324

**Constantine, Saint Joseph, Pop. 2,015**
Constantine SD 1,400/K-12
1 Falcon Dr 49042 269-435-8900
Charles Frisbie, supt. Fax 435-8980
www.constps.org
Constantine HS 400/9-12
1 Falcon Dr 49042 269-435-8920
Travis Walker, prin. Fax 435-8981
Constantine MS 300/6-8
260 W 6th St 49042 269-435-8940
Ray Bohm, prin. Fax 435-8982

**Cooks, Delta**
Big Bay de Noc SD 200/PK-12
8928 00.25 Rd 49817 906-644-2773
Mary Brayak, supt. Fax 644-2615
www.bigbayschool.com
Big Bay de Noc S 200/PK-12
8928 00.25 Rd 49817 906-644-2773
DeeDee Thill, prin. Fax 644-2615

**Coopersville, Ottawa, Pop. 4,215**
Coopersville Area SD 2,400/PK-12
198 East St 49404 616-997-3200
Ron Veldman, supt. Fax 997-3214
www.coopersvillebroncos.org/
Coopersville MS 600/6-8
198 East St 49404 616-997-3400
Ryan Pfahler, prin. Fax 997-3414
Coopersville SHS 800/9-12
198 East St 49404 616-997-3500
Brent Hadden, prin. Fax 997-3514

**Corunna, Shiawassee, Pop. 3,446**
Corunna SD 2,200/PK-12
124 N Shiawassee St 48817 989-743-6338
Dave Moore, supt. Fax 743-4474
www.corunna.k12.mi.us
Corunna HS 800/8-12
417 E King St 48817 989-743-3441
Leo Constine, prin. Fax 743-5901

**Covert, Van Buren**
Covert SD 500/PK-12
35323 M 140 Hwy 49043 269-764-3701
Dr. Bobbi Morehead, supt. Fax 764-8598
www.covertps.org
Covert HS 200/9-12
35323 M 140 Hwy 49043 269-764-3730
Yolanda Brunt, prin. Fax 764-3754
Covert MS 100/6-8
35323 M 140 Hwy 49043 269-764-3730
Yolanda Brunt, prin. Fax 764-3754

**Croswell, Sanilac, Pop. 2,419**
Croswell-Lexington SD 2,100/PK-12
5407 Peck Rd 48422 810-679-1000
Julie Western, supt. Fax 679-1005
www.croslex.org
Croswell-Lexington HS 700/9-12
5461 Peck Rd 48422 810-679-1500
Ryan Cayce, prin. Fax 679-1505
Croswell-Lexington MS 700/5-8
5485 Peck Rd 48422 810-679-1400
Mark Benson, prin. Fax 679-1405
Other Schools – See Lexington

**Crystal, Montcalm**
Carson City-Crystal Area SD
Supt. — See Carson City
Carson City-Crystal Alternative Academy Alt
217 Park St 48818 989-584-6927
Devin Pringle, prin. Fax 584-3539

**Crystal Falls, Iron, Pop. 1,443**
Forest Park SD 500/PK-12
801 Forest Pkwy 49920 906-214-4695
Becky Waters, supt. Fax 875-4660
www.fptrojans.org
Forest Park JSHS 300/6-12
801 Forest Pkwy 49920 906-214-4695
Lisa Olson, prin. Fax 875-4660

**Custer, Mason, Pop. 279**
Mason County Eastern SD 400/K-12
18 S Main St 49405 231-757-3733
Paul Shoup, supt. Fax 757-9671
mceschools.com
Mason County Eastern JSHS 200/7-12
18 S Main St 49405 231-757-3733
Paul Shoup, prin. Fax 757-9671

**Dansville, Ingham, Pop. 554**
Dansville SD 900/K-12
PO Box 187 48819 517-623-6120
Amy Hodgson, supt. Fax 623-6719
www.dansville.org
Dansville HS 300/9-12
PO Box 187 48819 517-623-6120
Tania Dupuis, prin. Fax 623-0127
Dansville MS 200/6-8
PO Box 187 48819 517-623-6120
Tania Dupuis, prin. Fax 623-1087

**Davison, Genesee, Pop. 5,081**
Davison Community SD 5,500/K-12
PO Box 319 48423 810-591-0801
Eric Lieske, supt. Fax 591-7813
www.davisonschools.org/
Alternative Education 200/Alt
1250 N Oak Rd 48423 810-591-1020
Christopher Wilson, dean Fax 591-3784
Davison HS 1,500/9-12
1250 N Oak Rd 48423 810-591-3531
Sue Kenkel, prin. Fax 591-3555
Davison MS 900/7-8
600 S Dayton St 48423 810-591-0848
Shelly Fenner-Krasny, prin. Fax 591-2754

---

Faith Baptist S 300/PK-12
7306 E Atherton Rd 48423 810-653-9661
Waterbrook Christian Academy 100/PK-12
8031 E Court St Ste 2B 48423 810-653-9701
Dean Bowen, admin. Fax 412-5700

**Dearborn, Wayne, Pop. 94,259**
Dearborn SD 17,600/PK-12
18700 Audette St 48124 313-827-3020
Dr. Glenn Maleyko, supt. Fax 827-3137
www.dearbornschools.org
Bryant MS 700/6-8
460 N Vernon St 48128 313-827-2900
Andrew Denison, prin. Fax 827-2905
Dearborn HS 1,800/9-12
19501 Outer Dr 48124 313-827-1600
Charles Baughman, prin. Fax 827-1605
Ford Early College HS 200/9-12
5101 Evergreen Rd 48128 313-317-1588
Majed Fadlallah, prin. Fax 317-2585
Ford HS 1,500/9-12
20601 Rotunda Dr 48124 313-827-1500
Scott Casebolt, prin. Fax 827-1505
Fordson HS 2,400/9-12
13800 Ford Rd 48126 313-827-1400
Youssef Mosallam, prin. Fax 827-1405
Salina IS 500/4-8
2623 Salina St 48120 313-827-6600
Jamel Lawera, prin. Fax 827-6605
Smith MS 600/6-8
23851 Yale St 48124 313-827-2800
Sean Fisher, prin. Fax 827-2805
Stout MS 700/6-8
18500 Oakwood Blvd 48124 313-827-4600
Gregory Oke, prin. Fax 827-4605
Woodworth MS 700/6-8
4951 Ternes St 48126 313-827-7100
Maysam Alie-Bazzi, prin. Fax 827-7105
Other Schools – See Dearborn Heights

Westwood Community SD
Supt. — See Dearborn Heights
Westwood Alternative Education 100/Alt
23810 Michigan Ave 48124 313-730-1667
Leslie Simmons, prin. Fax 730-1674

---

Divine Child HS 800/9-12
1001 N Silvery Ln 48128 313-562-1990
Damian Hermann, prin. Fax 562-9361
Everest Institute Post-Sec.
23400 Michigan Ave Ste 200 48124 313-562-4228
Henry Ford Community College Post-Sec.
5101 Evergreen Rd 48128 313-845-9600
ITT Technical Institute Post-Sec.
19855 Outer Dr Ste L10W 48124 313-278-5208
University of Michigan-Dearborn Post-Sec.
4901 Evergreen Rd 48128 313-593-5000

**Dearborn Heights, Wayne, Pop. 56,336**
Crestwood SD 3,300/PK-12
1501 N Beech Daly Rd 48127 313-278-0906
Dr. Laurine VanValkenburg, supt. Fax 278-4774
www.csdm.k12.mi.us/
Crestwood HS 1,200/9-12
1501 N Beech Daly Rd 48127 313-278-0900
John Tafelski, prin. Fax 792-0205
Riverside MS 1,100/5-8
25900 W Warren St 48127 313-274-0140
Dennis Faletti, prin. Fax 792-0201

Dearborn Heights SD 7 1,900/K-12
20629 Annapolis St 48125 313-278-1900
John Fazer, supt. Fax 278-1413
www.district7.net
Annapolis HS 800/9-12
4650 Clippert St 48125 313-278-9870
Dan Scott, prin. Fax 278-1238
Best JHS 800/6-8
22201 Powers Ave 48125 313-278-6200
Jon Znamierowski, prin. Fax 278-2470

Dearborn SD
Supt. — See Dearborn
Berry Career Center Vo/Tech
22586 Ann Arbor Trl 48127 313-827-4800
Winifred Green, prin. Fax 827-4805
Dearborn Ctr for Math Science & Tech Alt
22586 Ann Arbor Trl 48127 313-827-2720
Winifred Green, prin. Fax 827-2725
Dearborn Magnet HS 50/9-12
22586 Ann Arbor Trl 48127 313-827-4800
Winifred Green, prin. Fax 827-4805
Adult & Community Education Adult
22586 Ann Arbor Trl 48127 313-827-1900
Julie Maconochie, coord. Fax 827-1906

Westwood Community SD 2,000/K-12
3335 S Beech Daly St 48125 313-565-1900
Sue Carnell, supt. Fax 565-3162
www.westwood.k12.mi.us
Robichaud HS 400/9-12
3601 Janet St 48125 313-565-8850
James Konrad, prin. Fax 565-0304
Westwood Alternative Education HS North Alt
23914 Ford Rd 48127 313-730-1667
Leslie Simmons, prin. Fax 565-2379
Other Schools – See Dearborn, Inkster

**Decatur, Van Buren, Pop. 1,763**
Decatur SD 900/K-12
110 Cedar St 49045 269-423-6800
Dr. Patrick Creagan, supt. Fax 423-6849
www.raiderpride.org/
Decatur HS 300/9-12
110 Cedar St 49045 269-423-6850
Matthew McLouth, prin. Fax 423-6899
Decatur MS 200/6-8
405 N Phelps St 49045 269-423-6900
Matthew McLouth, prin. Fax 423-6949

Marcellus Community SD
Supt. — See Marcellus
Volinia Outcome Base S 100/Alt
54080 Gards Prairie Rd 49045 269-782-9716
Donald Price, prin. Fax 782-9789

**Deckerville, Sanilac, Pop. 821**
Deckerville Community SD 600/K-12
2633 Black River St 48427 810-376-3615
Tricia Pawlowski, supt. Fax 376-3115
www.deckerville.k12.mi.us
Deckerville Community JSHS 300/7-12
2633 Black River St 48427 810-376-3875
Matt Connelly, prin. Fax 376-3115

**Delton, Barry, Pop. 851**
Delton Kellogg SD 1,400/K-12
327 N Grove St 49046 269-623-1501
Carl Schoessel, supt. Fax 623-1508
dkschools.org
Delton Kellogg HS 500/9-12
10425 Panther Pride 49046 269-623-1522
Lucas Trierweiler, prin. Fax 623-1150
Delton Kellogg MS 500/5-8
6325 Delton Rd 49046 269-623-1542
Mark Martin, prin. Fax 623-1548

**De Tour Village, Chippewa, Pop. 312**
De Tour Area SD 100/K-12
PO Box 429 49725 906-297-2421
Angela Reed, supt. Fax 297-3403
detour.eup.k12.mi.us
De Tour JSHS 100/7-12
PO Box 429 49725 906-297-2011
Angela Reed, supt. Fax 297-3403

**Detroit, Wayne, Pop. 700,219**
Detroit SD 47,700/PK-12
7321 2nd Ave Fl 14 48202 313-873-7450
Lamont Satchel, supt. Fax 873-7433
detroitk12.org
Banks HS, 5020 Cadieux Rd 48224 9-12
Roslyn Fluker, prin. 313-347-7280
Breithaupt Career/Tech S Vo/Tech
9300 Hubbell St 48228 313-866-9550
Charlene Mallory, prin. Fax 866-9605
Carson S for Science & Medicine 100/9-12
571 Mack Ave 48201 313-494-1805
Charles Todd, prin. Fax 494-0992
Cass Technical HS Vo/Tech
2501 2nd Ave 48201 313-263-2000
Lisa Phillips, prin. Fax 263-2001
Clippert Academy 500/5-8
1981 McKinstry St 48209 313-849-5009
Kim Gonzalez, prin. Fax 849-5740
Cody - Academy of Public Leadership 300/9-12
18445 Cathedral St 48228 313-852-6612
Johnathon Matthews, prin. Fax 866-9266
Cody - Detroit Institute of Technology 300/9-12
18445 Cathedral St 48228 313-866-9200
Latoya Hall-King, prin. Fax 866-9266
Cody - Medicine and Community Health Acd 300/9-12
18445 Cathedral St 48228 313-866-9200
Michelle Parker, prin. Fax 866-9266
Communications & Media Arts HS 500/9-12
14771 Mansfield St 48227 313-866-9300
Donya Odom, prin. Fax 866-9304
Crockett Career/Tech S Vo/Tech
571 Mack Ave 48201 313-494-1805
Brenda Belcher, prin. Fax 494-0992
Davis Aerospace Technical HS Vo/Tech
900 Dickerson St 48215 313-822-8820
Ian Diem, prin. Fax 866-5408
Detroit Collegiate Preparatory HS 9-12
2200 W Grand Blvd 48208 313-623-0056
Kenyuano Jones, prin.
Detroit Intl Acad for Young Women 500/K-12
9026 Woodward Ave 48202 313-873-3050
Beverly Hibbler, prin. Fax 873-3088
Detroit Lions Alternative S 100/Alt
10101 E Canfield St 48214 313-852-9677
Cheryl White, prin. Fax 852-9676
Detroit S of Arts 600/9-12
123 Selden St 48201 313-494-6000
Delois Cooke Sprysak, prin. Fax 494-2129
Douglass Academy for Young Men 200/Alt
2001 W Warren Ave 48208 313-596-3555
Berry Greer, prin. Fax 596-3552
East English Village Preparatory Academy 9-12
5020 Cadieux Rd 48224 313-922-5600
Charlene Mallory, prin.
Fisher Magnet Upper Academy 700/5-8
15491 Maddelein St 48205 313-866-7233
Harry Coakley, prin. Fax 866-7329
Golightly Career and Technical Center Vo/Tech
900 Dickerson St 48215 313-822-8820
Nina Graves-Hicks, prin. Fax 866-3131
King HS 1,300/9-12
3200 E Lafayette St 48207 313-494-7373
Dr. Deborah Jenkins, prin. Fax 262-9140
Ludington Magnet MS 400/5-8
19501 Berg Rd 48219 313-494-7577
Allan Cosma, prin. Fax 494-7707
Osborn Academy of Mathematics 300/9-12
11600 E 7 Mile Rd 48205 313-866-0343
Dr. Dennis Myles, prin. Fax 866-0356
Osborn College Preparatory Academy 300/9-12
11600 E 7 Mile Rd 48205 313-866-0343
Senta Ray-Conley, prin. Fax 866-0356
Osborn Evergreen Acad Design & Alt Enrgy 200/9-12
11600 E 7 Mile Rd 48205 313-866-0343
Michael Barclay, prin. Fax 866-0356
Randolph Career and Technical Center Vo/Tech
17101 Hubbell St 48235 313-494-7100
Cynthia Hough, prin. Fax 494-7114
Renaissance HS 1,100/9-12
6565 W Outer Dr 48235 313-416-4600
Anita Williams, prin. Fax 416-4620
Western International HS 1,300/9-12
1500 Scotten St 48209 313-849-4758
Angel Garcia, prin. Fax 849-4695
West Side Academy of Alternative Ed 500/Alt
4701 McKinley St 48208 313-456-8000
Andrea Ford-Ayler, prin. Fax 456-8001
Adult Education Center East Adult
13840 Lappin St 48205 313-579-7109
Leonard Samborski, prin.
Adult Education Center West Adult
16164 Asbury Park 48235 313-852-1089
Dedria Willis, prin.

---

College for Creative Studies Post-Sec.
201 E Kirby St 48202 313-664-7400
Cornerstone S 500/PK-12
6861 E Nevada St 48234 313-892-1860
Ernestine Sanders, pres. Fax 892-1861
Detroit Cristo Rey HS 200/9-12
5679 W Vernor Hwy 48209 313-843-2747
Susan Rowe, prin. Fax 843-2750
Detroit Health Department Post-Sec.
1151 Taylor St 48202 313-876-4090
DMC University Laboratories Post-Sec.
4201 Saint Antoine St 48201 313-745-3053
Dorsey School of Business Post-Sec.
18660 Ford Rd 48228 313-982-3730
Ecumenical Theological Seminary Post-Sec.
2930 Woodward Ave 48201 313-831-5200
Everest Institute Post-Sec.
300 River Place Dr Ste 1000 48207 313-567-5350

Grace Hospital — Post-Sec.
6071 W Outer Dr 48235 — 313-966-3525
Harper Hospital — Post-Sec.
3990 John R St 48201 — 313-745-9375
Henry Ford Hospital — Post-Sec.
2799 W Grand Blvd 48202 — 313-876-1257
Lewis College of Business — Post-Sec.
17370 Meyers Rd 48235 — 313-862-6300
Loyola HS — 200/9-12
15325 Pinehurst St 48238 — 313-861-2407
Wyatt Jones, prin. — Fax 861-4718
Marygrove College — Post-Sec.
8425 W McNichols Rd 48221 — 313-927-1240
Michigan Barber School — Post-Sec.
8988 Grand River Ave # 90 48204 — 313-894-2300
Sacred Heart Major Seminary — Post-Sec.
2701 W Chicago 48206 — 313-883-8500
St. John's Hospital — Post-Sec.
22101 Moross Rd 48236 — 313-343-7531
University of Detroit/Jesuit HS — 900/7-12
8400 S Cambridge Ave 48221 — 313-862-5400
Anthony Trudel, prin. — Fax 862-3299
University of Detroit Mercy — Post-Sec.
4001 W McNichols Rd 48221 — 313-993-1000
Wayne County Community College — Post-Sec.
801 W Fort St 48226 — 313-496-2600
Wayne State University — Post-Sec.
42 W Warren Ave 48201 — 877-978-4636

**De Witt, Clinton, Pop. 4,434**
De Witt SD — 3,000/K-12
PO Box 800, — 517-668-3000
Dr. John Deiter, supt. — Fax 668-3018
www.dewittschools.net/
De Witt HS — 900/9-12
PO Box 800, — 517-668-3100
Jody McKean, prin. — Fax 668-3155
De Witt JHS — 500/7-8
PO Box 800, — 517-668-3200
Keith Cravotta, prin. — Fax 668-3255

**Dexter, Washtenaw, Pop. 3,976**
Dexter Community SD — 3,600/PK-12
7714 Ann Arbor St 48130 — 734-424-4100
Christopher Timmis, supt. — Fax 424-4112
dexterschools.org
Dexter HS — 1,200/9-12
2200 N Parker Rd 48130 — 734-424-4240
Kit Moran, prin. — Fax 424-2747
Mill Creek MS — 600/7-8
7305 Dexter Ann Arbor Rd 48130 — 734-424-4150
Jami Bronson, prin. — Fax 424-4159

**Dollar Bay, Houghton, Pop. 1,072**
Dollar Bay-Tamarack City SD — 300/K-12
PO Box 371 49922 — 906-482-5800
Dr. Jan Quarless Ph.D., supt. — Fax 487-5931
www.dollarbay.k12.mi.us
Dollar Bay JSHS — 100/7-12
PO Box 371 49922 — 906-482-5812
C. Norland, prin. — Fax 487-5940

**Douglas, Allegan, Pop. 1,221**
Saugatuck SD — 600/PK-12
PO Box 818 49406 — 269-857-1444
Rolfe Timmerman Ph.D., supt. — Fax 857-1448
www.saugatuckps.com
Other Schools – See Saugatuck

**Dowagiac, Cass, Pop. 5,518**
Dowagiac UNSD — 2,400/K-12
243 S Front St 49047 — 269-782-4400
Paul Hartsig, supt. — Fax 782-4418
www.dowagiacschools.org
Dowagiac MS — 500/6-8
243 S Front St 49047 — 269-782-4440
Matthew Severin, prin. — Fax 782-4449
Pathfinders Alternative/Adult Education — 100/Alt
243 S Front St 49047 — 269-782-4471
Sara Park, dir. — Fax 782-9748
Union HS — 600/9-12
243 S Front St 49047 — 269-782-4420
Kelly Millin, prin. — Fax 782-9518

---

Southwestern Michigan College — Post-Sec.
58900 Cherry Grove Rd 49047 — 269-782-1000

**Dryden, Lapeer, Pop. 947**
Dryden Community SD — 700/K-12
3866 Rochester Rd 48428 — 810-796-9534
Dr. Gary Richards, supt. — Fax 796-3698
www.dryden.k12.mi.us
Dryden JSHS — 400/7-12
3866 Rochester Rd 48428 — 810-796-2266
Mary Finnigan, prin. — Fax 796-2510

**Dundee, Monroe, Pop. 3,916**
Dundee Community SD — 1,600/PK-12
420 Ypsilanti St 48131 — 734-529-2350
Michael Dodge, supt. — Fax 529-5606
www.dundeecommunityschools.org
Dundee HS — 500/9-12
130 Viking Dr 48131 — 734-529-7008
Bryan Schroeder, prin. — Fax 529-7053
Dundee MS — 500/5-8
420 Ypsilanti St 48131 — 734-529-2350
Charles Fuller, prin. — Fax 529-7380
Riverside Academy — 100/Alt
445 Toledo St 48131 — 734-529-3916
Tom Walentowski, dir. — Fax 529-5593

**Durand, Shiawassee, Pop. 3,411**
Durand Area SD — 1,600/PK-12
310 N Saginaw St 48429 — 989-288-2681
Craig McCrumb, supt. — Fax 288-3553
durand.k12.mi.us/
Durand Area HS — 700/8-12
9575 E Monroe Rd 48429 — 989-288-2684
Dave Zuehlke, prin. — Fax 288-2966

**East China, Saint Clair, Pop. 3,216**
East China SD — 4,600/K-12
1585 Meisner Rd 48054 — 810-676-1000
Dr. Steven Skalka, supt. — Fax 676-1037
www.ecsd.us
Other Schools – See Marine City, Saint Clair

**East Jordan, Charlevoix, Pop. 2,312**
East Jordan SD — 1,000/K-12
PO Box 399 49727 — 231-536-3131
Matt Stevenson, supt. — Fax 536-3310
www.ejps.org
East Jordan HS — 300/7-12
PO Box 399 49727 — 231-536-2259
Tammy Jackson, prin. — Fax 536-3536

**East Lansing, Ingham, Pop. 47,217**
East Lansing SD — 3,400/K-12
501 Burcham Dr 48823 — 517-333-7420
Dr. Robyne Thompson, supt. — Fax 333-7470
www.elps.us
East Lansing HS — 1,100/9-12
509 Burcham Dr 48823 — 517-333-7500
Coby Fletcher, prin. — Fax 333-7559
MacDonald MS — 500/6-8
1601 Burcham Dr 48823 — 517-333-7600
Amy Martin, prin. — Fax 333-5098

---

Douglas J Educational Center — Post-Sec.
331 E Grand River Ave 48823 — 517-351-0746
Michigan State Univ - College of Law — Post-Sec.
648 N Shaw Ln Rm 368 48824 — 517-432-6800
Michigan State University — Post-Sec.
220 Trowbridge Rd 48824 — 517-355-1855

**East Leroy, Calhoun**
Athens Area SD — 600/K-12
4320 K Dr S 49051 — 269-729-5427
Joseph Huepenbecker, supt. — Fax 729-9610
www.athensk12.org
Other Schools – See Athens

**Eastpointe, Macomb, Pop. 31,538**
East Detroit SD — 2,900/K-12
24685 Kelly Rd 48021 — 586-533-3000
Dr. Ryan McLeod, supt. — Fax 533-3025
www.eastdetroit.org
East Detroit HS — 1,200/9-12
15501 Couzens Ave 48021 — 586-533-3700
Scott Johnson, prin. — Fax 533-3709
Kellwood Alternative HS — 100/Alt
23750 David Ave 48021 — 586-533-3900
Samy Chaptini, prin. — Fax 533-3909
Kelly MS — 600/6-8
24701 Kelly Rd 48021 — 586-533-3600
Matthew Karaffa, prin. — Fax 533-3609

**Eaton Rapids, Eaton, Pop. 5,118**
Eaton Rapids SD — 2,400/K-12
912 Greyhound Dr 48827 — 517-663-8155
Dr. William DeFrance, supt. — Fax 663-2236
www.erpsk12.org/
Eaton Rapids HS — 900/9-12
800 State St 48827 — 517-663-2231
Derek Lounds, prin. — Fax 663-5727
Eaton Rapids MS — 600/6-8
815 Greyhound Dr 48827 — 517-663-8151
Therese Lake, prin. — Fax 663-0625
Greyhound Central Performance Academy — Alt
912 Greyhound Dr 48827 — 517-663-3510
Brooke Ballee, prin. — Fax 663-0626

**Eau Claire, Berrien, Pop. 604**
Eau Claire SD — 800/K-12
6190 W Main St 49111 — 269-461-6947
David Gray, supt. — Fax 461-0089
www.eauclaireps.com
Eau Claire Alternative HS — 50/Alt
7450 Hochberger Rd 49111 — 269-461-6997
Shane Lausch, admin.
Eau Claire HS — 200/9-12
7450 Hochberger Rd 49111 — 269-461-6997
Shane Lausch, prin. — Fax 461-0065
Eau Claire MS — 200/6-8
7450 Hochberger Rd 49111 — 269-461-0083
Mike Dandron, prin. — Fax 461-0082

**Eben Junction, Alger**
Superior Central SD — 400/K-12
PO Box 148 49825 — 906-439-5531
William Valima, supt. — Fax 439-5734
superiorcentralschools.org
Superior Central S — 400/K-12
PO Box 148 49825 — 906-439-5532
William Valima, prin. — Fax 439-5243

**Ecorse, Wayne, Pop. 9,214**
Ecorse SD — 1,000/PK-12
27225 W Outer Dr 48229 — 313-294-4750
Thomas E. Parker, supt. — Fax 294-4769
www.eps.k12.mi.us
Ecorse Community HS — 500/8-12
27385 W Outer Dr 48229 — 313-294-4700
Nina Hicks, prin. — Fax 294-4709
Hope Academic Academy — Alt
27225 W Outer Dr 48229 — 313-294-4730
Kenneth McPhaul, head sch — Fax 382-6534

**Edmore, Montcalm, Pop. 1,174**
Montabella Community SD — 800/PK-12
PO Box 349 48829 — 989-427-5148
Shelly Millis, supt. — Fax 427-3828
www.montabella.com
Other Schools – See Blanchard

**Edwardsburg, Cass, Pop. 1,228**
Edwardsburg SD — 2,700/K-12
69410 Section St 49112 — 269-663-3055
Sherman Ostrander, supt. — Fax 663-6485
www.edwardsburgpublicschools.org/
Edwardsburg HS — 800/9-12
69410 Section St 49112 — 269-663-1044
Jeffrey Leslie Ph.D., prin. — Fax 663-8915
Edwardsburg MS — 600/6-8
69410 Section St 49112 — 269-663-1031
James Knoll, prin. — Fax 663-8638

**Elk Rapids, Antrim, Pop. 1,628**
Elk Rapids SD — 1,400/K-12
707 E 3rd St 49629 — 231-264-8692
Stephen Prissel, supt. — Fax 264-6538
www.erschools.com
Cherryland MS — 300/6-8
707 E 3rd St 49629 — 231-264-8991
Terry Starr, prin. — Fax 264-9370
Elk Rapids HS — 500/9-12
308 Meguzee Pt 49629 — 231-264-8108
Michael Travis, prin. — Fax 264-0895
Sunrise Academy — Alt
97 Lake St 49629 — 231-264-5890
Jim Standerfer, prin. — Fax 264-0895

**Ellsworth, Antrim, Pop. 341**
Ellsworth Community SD — 200/PK-12
9467 Park St 49729 — 231-588-2544
Aaron Gaffney, supt. — Fax 588-6183
www.ellsworth.k12.mi.us/
Ellsworth Community S — 200/PK-12
9467 Park St 49729 — 231-588-2544
Aaron Gaffney, admin. — Fax 588-6183

**Elsie, Clinton, Pop. 962**
Ovid-Elsie Area SD — 1,700/PK-12
8989 E Colony Rd 48831 — 989-834-2271
Ryan Cunningham, supt. — Fax 862-5887
www.ovidelsie.org
Ovid-Elsie HS — 600/9-12
8989 E Colony Rd 48831 — 989-834-2271
Jason Tokar, prin. — Fax 862-4463
Ovid-Elsie MS — 300/6-8
8989 E Colony Rd 48831 — 989-834-2271
Randy Barton, prin. — Fax 862-4463

**Engadine, Mackinac**
Engadine Consolidated SD — 300/K-12
W13920 Melville St 49827 — 906-477-6313
Angie McArthur, supt. — Fax 477-6643
www.eup.k12.mi.us/engadine
Engadine Consolidated S — 300/K-12
W13920 Melville St 49827 — 906-477-6351
Kendra Feldhusen, prin. — Fax 477-6643

**Erie, Monroe**
Mason Consolidated SD — 1,200/PK-12
2400 Mason Eagle Dr 48133 — 734-848-5475
Andrew Shaw, supt. — Fax 848-2516
www.eriemason.k12.mi.us
Mason HS — 400/9-12
2400 Mason Eagle Dr 48133 — 734-848-5755
Brandon Bates, prin. — Fax 848-5425
Mason MS — 300/6-8
2400 Mason Eagle Dr 48133 — 734-848-4211
Ben Russow, prin. — Fax 848-0035

**Escanaba, Delta, Pop. 12,293**
Escanaba Area SD — 2,000/PK-12
1500 Ludington St 49829 — 906-786-5411
Michele Lemire, supt. — Fax 786-4469
www.eskymos.com
Escanaba HS — 800/9-12
500 S Lincoln Rd 49829 — 906-786-6521
Darci Griebel, prin. — Fax 786-2166
Escanaba JHS — 7-8
500 S Lincoln Rd 49829 — 906-786-6521
Jude VanDamme, prin.
Other Schools – See Wells

---

Bay de Noc Community College — Post-Sec.
2001 N Lincoln Rd 49829 — 906-786-5802
U.P. Academy of Hair Design — Post-Sec.
1625 Sheridan Rd 49829 — 906-786-5750

**Essexville, Bay, Pop. 3,434**
Essexville-Hampton SD — 1,500/K-12
303 Pine St 48732 — 989-894-9700
Matthew T. Cortez, supt. — Fax 894-9705
www.e-hps.net
Cramer JHS — 400/5-8
313 Pine St 48732 — 989-894-9740
James Glasgow, prin. — Fax 894-9720
Garber HS — 600/9-12
213 Pine St 48732 — 989-894-9710
Barry Kenniston, prin. — Fax 894-9730

**Evart, Osceola, Pop. 1,857**
Evart SD — 900/PK-12
PO Box 917 49631 — 231-734-5594
Howard Hyde, supt. — Fax 734-2931
www.evart.k12.mi.us/
Evart HS — 300/9-12
6221 95th Ave 49631 — 231-734-5551
Dennis Peacock, prin. — Fax 734-4156
Evart MS — 300/5-8
321 N Hemlock St 49631 — 231-734-4222
Jason O'Dell, prin. — Fax 734-3367

**Ewen, Ontonagon**
Ewen-Trout Creek SD — 300/K-12
14312 Airport Rd 49925 — 906-813-0620
Alan Tulppo, supt. — Fax 813-0621
www.etc.k12.mi.us/
Ewen-Trout Creek JSHS — 100/7-12
14312 Airport Rd 49925 — 906-813-0620
Alan Tulppo, supt. — Fax 813-0621

**Fairgrove, Tuscola, Pop. 559**
Akron-Fairgrove SD — 200/K-12
PO Box 319 48733 — 989-693-6163
Stephen Ley, supt. — Fax 693-6560
www.akronfairgrove.org

Akron-Fairgrove JSHS 100/6-12
PO Box 319 48733 989-693-6112
Andrew Beauvais, prin. Fax 693-6160

**Fair Haven, Saint Clair, Pop. 1,505**
Anchor Bay SD
Supt. — See Casco
Anchor Bay HS 1,800/9-12
6319 County Line Rd 48023 586-648-2525
Jack Stanton, prin. Fax 716-8306

**Fairview, Oscoda**
Fairview Area SD 100/K-12
1879 E Miller Rd 48621 989-848-7000
Robert Ricketson, supt. Fax 848-7070
www.fairview.k12.mi.us
Fairview Area S 100/K-12
1879 E Miller Rd 48621 989-848-7009
Robert Ricketson, supt. Fax 848-7070

**Farmington, Oakland, Pop. 10,133**
Farmington SD 11,200/PK-12
32500 Shiawassee Rd 48336 248-489-3349
Dr. George Heitsch, supt. Fax 489-3348
www.farmington.k12.mi.us
Farmington HS 1,200/9-12
32000 Shiawassee Rd 48336 248-489-3455
Julie Kaminski, prin. Fax 489-3474
Other Schools – See Farmington Hills

**Farmington Hills, Oakland, Pop. 77,980**
Farmington SD
Supt. — See Farmington
Dunckel MS 800/7-8
32800 W 12 Mile Rd 48334 248-489-3577
Allen Archer, prin. Fax 489-3590
East MS 900/7-8
25000 Middlebelt Rd 48336 248-489-3601
Ken Sanders, prin. Fax 489-3606
Farmington Central HS 100/Alt
30415 Shiawassee Rd 48336 248-489-3827
Dee Lacy, coord. Fax 489-3380
Harrison HS 1,300/9-12
29995 W 12 Mile Rd 48334 248-489-3499
Jim Anderson, prin. Fax 489-3514
North Farmington HS 1,300/9-12
32900 W 13 Mile Rd 48334 248-785-2005
Joe Greene, prin. Fax 855-2060
Farmington Community S Adult
30415 Shiawassee Rd 48336 248-489-3827
Dee Lacy, prin. Fax 489-3380

West Bloomfield SD
Supt. — See West Bloomfield
Oakland Early College S 200/9-12
27055 Orchard Lake Rd 48334 248-522-3540
Jennifer Newman, hdmstr. Fax 471-9543

---

Dorsey School of Business Post-Sec.
33533 W 12 Mile Rd Ste 152 48331 248-994-0133
Mercy HS 800/9-12
29300 W 11 Mile Rd 48336 248-476-8020
Carolyn Witte, prin. Fax 476-3691
Michigan Sch of Professional Psychology Post-Sec.
26811 Orchard Lake Rd 48334 248-476-1122
Oakland Community College Post-Sec.
27055 Orchard Lake Rd 48334 248-522-3400

**Farwell, Clare, Pop. 865**
Farwell Area SD 1,400/K-12
399 E Michigan St 48622 989-588-9917
Carl Seiter, supt. Fax 588-6440
www.farwellschools.net/
Farwell HS 400/9-12
399 E Michigan St 48622 989-588-9913
Dee Yarger, prin. Fax 588-6041
Farwell MS 500/5-8
500 E Ohio St 48622 989-588-9915
Catheryn Gross, prin. Fax 588-3337

**Felch, Dickinson**
North Dickinson County SD 300/K-12
W6588 State Highway M69 49831 906-542-9281
Angel Inglese, supt. Fax 542-6950
www.go-nordics.com
North Dickinson County S 300/K-12
W6588 State Highway M69 49831 906-542-9281
Angel Inglese, admin. Fax 542-6950

**Fennville, Allegan, Pop. 1,373**
Fennville SD 1,500/PK-12
5 Memorial Dr 49408 269-561-7331
Dirk Weeldreyer, supt. Fax 561-5792
www.fennville.org
Fennville HS 400/9-12
4 Memorial Dr 49408 269-561-7241
Jim Greydanus, prin. Fax 561-6901
Fennville MS 400/6-8
1 Memorial Dr 49408 269-561-7341
Kim Zdybel, prin. Fax 561-2143
Pearl Alternative & Adult Education Ctr 50/Alt
5 Memorial Dr 49408 269-561-2343
Mitch Overway, lead tchr. Fax 561-8630

**Fenton, Genesee, Pop. 11,554**
Fenton Area SD 3,500/PK-12
3100 Owen Rd 48430 810-591-4700
Dr. Timothy Jalkanen, supt. Fax 591-4705
www.fentonschools.org
Fenton HS 1,200/9-12
3200 W Shiawassee Ave 48430 810-591-2600
Mark Suchowski, prin. Fax 591-2605
Schmidt MS 800/6-8
3255 Donaldson Dr 48430 810-591-7700
Heidi Ciesielski, prin. Fax 591-7705

Lake Fenton Community SD 1,900/K-12
11425 Torrey Rd 48430 810-591-4141
Wayne Wright, supt. Fax 591-9866
www.lakefentonschools.org
Lake Fenton MS 400/6-8
11425 Torrey Rd 48430 810-591-2209
Dr. Daniel Ferguson, prin. Fax 591-8475
Other Schools – See Linden

**Ferndale, Oakland, Pop. 19,252**
Ferndale SD 3,700/PK-12
2920 Burdette St 48220 248-586-8651
Blake Prewitt, supt. Fax 586-8655
www.ferndaleschools.org
Ferndale HS 900/9-12
881 Pinecrest Dr 48220 248-548-8600
Roger Smith, prin. Fax 586-8620
Ferndale MS 400/7-8
725 Pinecrest Dr 48220 248-541-1783
Jason Gillespie, prin. Fax 586-8834
University HS 500/9-12
1244 Paxton St 48220 248-586-8846
Jason Beatty, admin. Fax 586-8857
Other Schools – See Oak Park

**Fife Lake, Grand Traverse, Pop. 434**
Forest Area Community SD 600/PK-12
7741 Shippy Rd SW 49633 231-369-4191
Josh Rothwell M.S., supt. Fax 369-4153
www.forestarea.org
Forest Area HS 200/9-12
7741 Shippy Rd SW 49633 231-369-2884
Fred Boss, prin. Fax 369-3646
Forest Area MS 100/5-8
7741 Shippy Rd SW 49633 231-369-2884
Fred Boss, prin. Fax 369-3646

**Flat Rock, Wayne, Pop. 9,628**
Flat Rock Community SD 1,900/K-12
28639 Division St 48134 734-535-6500
Andrew Brodie, supt. Fax 535-6501
www.flatrockschools.org
Flat Rock HS 600/9-12
25600 Seneca St 48134 734-535-6600
Marc Lafayette, prin. Fax 535-6601
Simpson MS 400/6-8
24900 Meadows Ave 48134 734-535-6700
Blaine Armstrong, prin. Fax 535-6701

**Flint, Genesee, Pop. 98,869**
Beecher Community SD 1,700/PK-12
1020 W Coldwater Rd 48505 810-591-9200
Josha Talison Ed.D., supt. Fax 591-9851
www.beecherschools.org/
Tucker MS 400/5-8
G5159 Summit St 48505 810-591-9399
Kevin Brock, prin. Fax 591-6190
Beecher Adult Education Adult
1020 W Coldwater Rd 48505 810-591-9825
Other Schools – See Mount Morris

Carman-Ainsworth Community SD 4,100/K-12
G3475 W Court St 48532 810-591-3700
Dr. Steven Tunnicliff, supt. Fax 591-3323
www.carman.k12.mi.us
Atlantis Alternative S Alt
G-3475 Beveridge Rd 48532 810-591-3700
Wes Mayo, coord. Fax 591-3290
Carman-Ainsworth HS 1,400/9-12
1300 N Linden Rd 48532 810-591-3240
Deborah Davis, prin. Fax 591-3215
Carman-Ainsworth MS 1,100/6-8
1409 W Maple Ave 48507 810-591-3500
Kevin Summey, prin. Fax 591-3594

Flint Community SD 5,500/PK-12
923 E Kearsley St 48503 810-760-1000
Bilal K. Tawwab, supt. Fax 760-7601
www.flintschools.org
Northwestern HS 700/9-12
G2138 W Carpenter Rd 48505 810-760-1780
Timothy Green, prin. Fax 760-6809
Southwestern Classical Academy 500/7-12
1420 W 12th St 48507 810-760-1400
Cheryl Tate, prin. Fax 760-7772
Accelerated Learning Academy Adult
G2138 Carpenter Rd 48505 810-767-8500
Timothy Green, prin. Fax 760-6809

Genesee ISD 1,000/
2413 W Maple Ave 48507 810-591-4400
Lisa Hagel, supt. Fax 591-7570
www.geneseeisd.org
Genessee Career Institute Vo/Tech
2143 W Maple Ave 48507 810-591-4462
Fax 244-1242
Mott Middle College HS 400/Alt
1401 E Court St Ste 1123 48503 810-232-8530
Chery Wagonlander Ed.D., prin. Fax 232-8660
Other Schools – See Grand Rapids

Kearsley Community SD 3,300/PK-12
4396 Underhill Dr 48506 810-591-8000
Patti Yorks, supt. Fax 591-8421
www.kearsleyschools.org
Armstrong MS 800/6-8
6161 Hopkins Rd 48506 810-591-9929
Casey Killingbeck, prin. Fax 591-9944
Kearsley HS 1,100/9-12
4302 Underhill Dr 48506 810-591-9883
Brian Wiskur, prin. Fax 591-9888

Westwood Heights SD 900/PK-12
3223 W Carpenter Rd 48504 810-591-0870
Salli Stevens, supt. Fax 591-0898
www.hamadyhawks.net
Academy West Alternative Education Alt
3400 N Jennings Rd 48504 810-591-0123
Peter Toal, prin. Fax 591-0124

Hamady Community HS 300/9-12
3223 W Carpenter Rd 48504 810-591-0890
Leslie Key, prin. Fax 591-5140
Hamady MS 200/7-8
3223 W Carpenter Rd 48504 810-591-0895
Leslie Key, prin. Fax 591-5140

---

Baker College of Flint Post-Sec.
1050 W Bristol Rd 48507 810-766-4000
Davenport University Post-Sec.
4318 Miller Rd 48507 810-732-9977
Flint Institute of Barbering Post-Sec.
3214 Flushing Rd 48504 810-232-4711
Hurley Medical Center Post-Sec.
701 W 8th Ave 48503 810-257-9237
Kettering University Post-Sec.
1700 University Ave 48504 810-762-9500
Mott Community College Post-Sec.
1401 E Court St 48503 810-762-0200
Powers Catholic HS 500/9-12
1505 W Court St 48503 810-591-4741
Sally Bartos, prin. Fax 591-1794
Ross Medical Education Center Post-Sec.
G3630 Miller Rd Ste D 48507 810-230-1100
University of Michigan-Flint Post-Sec.
303 E Kearsley St 48502 810-762-3300

**Flushing, Genesee, Pop. 8,256**
Flushing Community SD 4,200/PK-12
522 N McKinley Rd 48433 810-591-1180
Timothy Stein, supt. Fax 591-0656
www.flushingschools.org/
Flushing HS 1,400/9-12
5039 Deland Rd 48433 810-591-3770
Jason Melynchek, prin. Fax 591-0693
Flushing MS 700/7-8
8100 Carpenter Rd 48433 810-591-2800
Andrew Schmidt, prin. Fax 591-0148

**Fort Gratiot, Saint Clair, Pop. 8,968**
Port Huron Area SD
Supt. — See Port Huron
Fort Gratiot MS 600/6-8
3985 Keewahdin Rd 48059 810-984-6544
Alycia Shagena, prin. Fax 275-1271

**Fowler, Clinton, Pop. 1,204**
Fowler SD 500/PK-12
PO Box 407 48835 989-593-2296
Neil Hufnagel, supt. Fax 593-2358
www.fowlerschools.net
Fowler HS 200/9-12
PO Box 407 48835 989-593-2250
Neil Hufnagel, prin. Fax 593-2358

**Fowlerville, Livingston, Pop. 2,844**
Fowlerville Community SD 2,900/K-12
7677 W Sharpe Rd Ste A 48836 517-223-6000
Wayne Roedel, supt. Fax 223-6022
www.fowlervilleschools.org
Fowlerville HS 900/9-12
7677 W Sharpe Rd 48836 517-223-6002
Bradford Lusk, prin. Fax 223-6065
Fowlerville JHS 700/6-8
7677 W Sharpe Rd 48836 517-223-6003
Myriah Lillie, prin. Fax 223-6199
Fowlerville Online Learning Academy 50/Alt
7677 W Sharpe Rd 48836 517-223-6236
Grace Damerow, admin. Fax 223-6121

**Frankenmuth, Saginaw, Pop. 4,915**
Frankenmuth SD 1,200/PK-12
525 E Genesee St 48734 989-652-9958
Mary Anne Ackerman, supt. Fax 652-9780
www.frankenmuth.k12.mi.us/
Frankenmuth HS 500/9-12
525 E Genesee St 48734 989-652-9955
JoLynn Clark, prin. Fax 652-7253
Rittmueller MS 300/5-8
965 E Genesee St 48734 989-652-6119
Kristin Hecht, prin. Fax 652-2921

**Frankfort, Benzie, Pop. 1,275**
Frankfort-Elberta Area SD 500/K-12
534 11th St 49635 231-352-4641
Jeffrey Tousley, supt. Fax 352-5066
www.frankfort.k12.mi.us
Frankfort JSHS 200/7-12
534 11th St 49635 231-352-4781
Matt Stapleton, prin. Fax 352-6501

**Fraser, Macomb, Pop. 14,229**
Fraser SD 5,200/PK-12
33466 Garfield Rd 48026 586-439-7000
Dr. David Richards Ph.D., supt. Fax 439-7001
www.fraser.k12.mi.us/
Fraser HS 1,700/9-12
34270 Garfield Rd 48026 586-439-7200
Dr. Michael Lonze, prin. Fax 439-7201
Richards MS 800/7-8
33500 Garfield Rd 48026 586-439-7400
Jessica Carrier, prin. Fax 439-7401

**Freeland, Saginaw, Pop. 6,900**
Freeland Community SD 1,800/K-12
710 Powley Dr 48623 989-695-5527
Matthew Cairy, supt. Fax 695-5789
www.freeland.k12.mi.us
Freeland HS 600/9-12
8250 Webster Rd 48623 989-695-2586
Traci Smith, prin. Fax 695-8022
Freeland MS 300/7-8
8250 Webster Rd 48623 989-692-4032
Renee Wulff, prin. Fax 692-4034

**Fremont, Newaygo, Pop. 4,037**
Fremont SD 2,100/K-12
450 E Pine St 49412 231-924-2350
Ken Haggart, supt. Fax 924-5264
www.fremont.net

Fremont HS 700/9-12
5421 S Warner Ave 49412 231-924-5300
Scott Sherman, prin. Fax 924-9262
Fremont MS 500/6-8
500 Woodrow St 49412 231-924-0230
Kenneth Haggart, prin. Fax 924-9149
Quest HS 100/Alt
350 Cedar St 49412 231-924-0470
Tracy Sanchez, dir. Fax 924-9207

Newaygo County RESA 200/
4747 W 48th St 49412 231-924-0381
Lori Clark, supt. Fax 924-8910
www.ncresa.org
Newaygo County Career-Tech Center Vo/Tech
4645 W 48th St 49412 231-924-8879
Kirk Wyers, dir. Fax 924-7815

**Fruitport, Muskegon, Pop. 1,081**
Fruitport Community SD 2,900/PK-12
3255 Pontaluna Rd 49415 231-865-4100
Bob Szymoniak, supt. Fax 865-3393
www.fruitportschools.net
Fruitport HS 900/9-12
357 N 6th Ave 49415 231-865-3101
Lauren Chesney, prin. Fax 865-6351
Fruitport MS 700/6-8
3113 Pontaluna Rd 49415 231-865-3128
Wendy Somers, prin. Fax 865-4086

---

Calvary Christian S 200/PK-12
5873 Kendra Rd 49415 231-865-2141
Thomas Kapanka, admin. Fax 865-8730

**Galesburg, Kalamazoo, Pop. 1,969**
Galesburg-Augusta Community SD 1,100/PK-12
1076 N 37th St 49053 269-484-2000
Dr. Dania Bazzi, supt. Fax 484-2001
www.g-aschools.org
Galesburg-Augusta HS 300/9-12
1076 N 37th St 49053 269-484-2010
Christie Robinson, prin. Fax 484-2011
Other Schools – See Augusta

**Garden City, Wayne, Pop. 27,153**
Garden City SD 3,300/PK-12
1333 Radcliff St 48135 734-762-8300
Derek Fisher, supt. Fax 762-8530
www.gardencityschools.com
Cambridge HS 500/Alt
28901 Cambridge St 48135 734-762-8430
Debbie Eves, prin. Fax 762-8534
Garden City HS 1,400/9-12
6500 Middlebelt Rd 48135 734-762-8350
Sharon Kollar, prin. Fax 762-8531
Garden City MS 700/7-8
1851 Radcliff St 48135 734-762-8400
Kip O'Leary, prin. Fax 762-8532

**Gaylord, Otsego, Pop. 3,564**
Gaylord Community SD 3,000/K-12
615 S Elm Ave 49735 989-705-3080
Cheryl Wojtas, supt. Fax 732-6029
www.gaylordschools.com
Gaylord HS 1,000/9-12
90 Livingston Blvd 49735 989-731-0969
Christopher Hodges, prin. Fax 731-2585
Gaylord MS 500/7-8
600 E 5th St 49735 989-731-0848
Gerald Belanger, prin. Fax 732-2632

---

St. Mary Cathedral S 300/PK-12
321 N Otsego Ave 49735 989-732-5801
Nicole Hatch, prin. Fax 732-2085

**Genesee, Genesee**
Genesee SD 800/PK-12
PO Box 220 48437 810-591-1650
Kevin Green, supt. Fax 591-1646
www.geneseeschools.org
Genesee JSHS 500/7-12
7347 N Genesee Rd 48437 810-591-1450
Charleen McKeever, prin. Fax 591-0302

**Gibraltar, Wayne, Pop. 4,593**
Gibraltar SD
Supt. — See Woodhaven
Carlson HS 1,200/9-12
30550 W Jefferson Ave 48173 734-379-7100
Jessica Shultz, prin. Fax 379-5444
Shumate MS 900/6-8
30448 W Jefferson Ave 48173 734-379-7600
Els Ferguson, prin. Fax 379-2370

**Gladstone, Delta, Pop. 4,885**
Gladstone Area SD 1,600/K-12
400 S 10th St 49837 906-428-2417
Dr. Jay Kulbertis, supt. Fax 789-8457
www.gladstoneschools.com
Gladstone HS 500/9-12
2100 State Highway M35 49837 906-428-9200
Brady Downey, prin. Fax 789-8312
Gladstone MS 400/6-8
300 S 10th St 49837 906-428-2295
Dave Ballard, prin. Fax 789-8404

**Gladwin, Gladwin, Pop. 2,897**
Gladwin Community SD 1,800/K-12
401 N Bowery Ave 48624 989-426-9255
Rick Seebeck, supt. Fax 426-5981
www.gladwinschools.net
Gladwin Community Alternative HS Alt
1400 N Spring St 48624 989-426-7341
Dave Beyer, prin. Fax 426-6031
Gladwin HS 500/9-12
1400 N Spring St 48624 989-426-7341
Dave Beyer, prin. Fax 426-6031
Gladwin JHS 500/6-8
401 N Bowery Ave 48624 989-426-3808
Mandi Zaborowski, prin. Fax 426-6038

---

Skeels Christian S 100/PK-12
3956 N M 18 48624 989-426-2054
John Shoaf, dir. Fax 426-4411

**Glen Arbor, Leelanau, Pop. 228**

---

Leelanau S 50/9-12
1 Old Homestead Rd 49636 231-334-5800
Matt Ralston, hdmstr. Fax 334-5898

**Gobles, Van Buren, Pop. 803**
Gobles SD 800/K-12
PO Box 412 49055 269-628-5618
Jeff Rehlander, supt. Fax 628-5306
www.gobles.org/
Gobles HS 300/9-12
PO Box 412 49055 269-628-2113
Phil McAndrew, prin. Fax 628-5306
Gobles MS 200/6-8
PO Box 412 49055 269-628-2113
Chris Miller, dean Fax 628-5306

---

Gobles Jr. Academy 50/K-10
32110 6th Ave 49055 269-628-2704
Thomas Coffee, prin. Fax 628-7314

**Goodrich, Genesee, Pop. 1,851**
Goodrich Area SD 2,100/PK-12
8029 Gale Rd 48438 810-591-2250
Michelle Imbrunone, supt. Fax 591-2550
www.goodrich.k12.mi.us
Goodrich HS 700/9-12
8029 Gale Rd 48438 810-591-2251
David St. Aubin, prin. Fax 591-2234
Goodrich MS 600/6-8
7480 Gale Rd 48438 810-591-4210
Kapeka vonKeltz, prin. Fax 636-7879

**Grand Blanc, Genesee, Pop. 8,062**
Grand Blanc Community SD 7,900/PK-12
11920 S Saginaw St 48439 810-591-6000
Dr. Norman M. Abdella, supt. Fax 591-6018
www.grandblancschools.org
Grand Blanc HS 2,000/10-12
12500 Holly Rd 48439 810-591-6638
Dr. Jennifer Hammond, prin. Fax 591-6513
Grand Blanc HS West 9-9
1 Jewett Trl 48439 810-591-6350
Jennifer Hammond, prin. Fax 591-6400
Grand Blanc MS East 1,100/6-8
6100 Perry Rd 48439 810-591-4696
Jodi Kruse, prin. Fax 591-0242
Grand Blanc MS West 1,000/6-8
1515 E Reid Rd 48439 810-591-7309
Jeff Neall, prin. Fax 591-0182

---

Sharps Academy of Hairstyling Post-Sec.
8166 Holly Rd 48439 810-695-6742

**Grand Haven, Ottawa, Pop. 10,239**
Grand Haven Area SD 4,700/PK-12
1415 S Beechtree St 49417 616-850-5000
Andrew Ingall, supt. Fax 850-5010
www.ghaps.org
Central HS 100/Alt
106 S 6th St 49417 616-850-6800
Paul Kunde, prin. Fax 850-6810
Grand Haven HS 1,800/9-12
17001 Ferris St 49417 616-850-6000
Tracy Wilson, prin. Fax 850-6010
Lakeshore MS 400/7-8
900 Cutler St 49417 616-850-6500
Kevin Polston, prin. Fax 850-6510

**Grand Ledge, Eaton, Pop. 7,630**
Grand Ledge SD 5,000/PK-12
220 Lamson St 48837 517-925-5400
Dr. Brian Metcalf, supt. Fax 925-5409
www.glcomets.net/
Grand Ledge HS 1,700/9-12
820 Spring St 48837 517-925-5815
Sara Sutherland, prin. Fax 925-5829
Hayes MS 800/7-8
12620 Nixon Rd 48837 517-925-5680
Dr. Michael Johnson, prin. Fax 925-5730

**Grand Marais, Alger**
Burt Township SD 50/K-12
PO Box 338 49839 906-494-2543
Heidi Homeister, supt. Fax 494-2522
grandmaraisschools.org/
Burt Township S 50/K-12
PO Box 338 49839 906-494-2521
Heidi Homeister, supt. Fax 494-2522

**Grand Rapids, Kent, Pop. 182,274**
East Grand Rapids SD 3,000/K-12
2915 Hall St SE 49506 616-235-3535
Dr. Sara Shubel, supt. Fax 235-6730
www.egrps.org
East Grand Rapids HS 1,000/9-12
2211 Lake Dr SE 49506 616-235-7555
Jennifer Fee, prin. Fax 235-7592
East Grand Rapids MS 700/6-8
2425 Lake Dr SE 49506 616-235-7551
J. Peter Stuursma, prin. Fax 235-7587

Forest Hills SD 10,100/PK-12
6590 Cascade Rd SE 49546 616-493-8800
Daniel Behm, supt. Fax 493-8552
www.fhps.net
Central HS 1,300/9-12
5901 Hall St SE 49546 616-493-8700
Stephen Passinault, prin. Fax 493-8721
Northern HS 1,100/9-12
3801 Leonard St NE 49525 616-493-8600
Jon Gregory, prin. Fax 493-8644
Northern Hills MS 600/7-8
3775 Leonard St NE 49525 616-493-8650
Nancy Susterka, prin. Fax 493-8686
Other Schools – See Ada

Genesee ISD
Supt. — See Flint
Genessee Early College 9-12
509 N Harrison St 49502 810-591-5115
Sandra Morgan-Jones, prin. Fax 591-2503

Grand Rapids SD 14,500/PK-12
PO Box 117 49501 616-819-2000
Teresa Weatherall Neal M.Ed., supt. Fax 819-3480
www.grps.org/
Academy Business Leadership & Entrpnrshp 9-12
421 Fountain St NE 49503 616-819-2310
Mark Frost, prin. Fax 819-2369
Academy of Design and Construction 100/9-12
421 Fountain St NE 49503 616-819-2310
Mark Frost, prin. Fax 819-2369
Academy of Health Science and Technology 9-12
421 Fountain St NE 49503 616-819-2310
Mark Frost, prin. Fax 819-2369
Academy of Modern Engineering 9-12
421 Fountain St NE 49503 616-819-2310
Mark Frost, prin. Fax 819-2369
Alger MS 400/6-8
921 Alger St SE 49507 616-819-6200
Roderick Wade, prin. Fax 819-6201
Burton MS 500/6-8
2133 Buchanan Ave SW 49507 616-819-2269
Lametria Johnson-Eaddy, prin. Fax 819-2282
City MSHS 700/7-12
1720 Plainfield Ave NE 49505 616-819-2380
Michael Pascoe, prin. Fax 819-2496
Grand Rapids Montessori at Central 100/9-12
421 Fountain St NE 49503 616-819-2405
Nikki Jones, prin. Fax 819-2369
Kent Vocational Options Vo/Tech
864 Crahen Ave NE 49525 616-819-2740
Laura Ochoa, prin. Fax 819-2747
Ottawa Hills HS 700/9-12
2055 Rosewood Ave SE 49506 616-819-2900
Rodney Lewis, prin. Fax 819-2877
Public Museum S 6-12
272 Pearl St NW 49504 616-819-3600
Christopher Hanks, prin.
Riverside MS 400/6-8
265 Eleanor St NE 49505 616-819-2969
Donna Boman, prin. Fax 819-2981
Southeast Career Pathways 200/Alt
1356 Jefferson Ave SE 49507 616-819-2666
Stephanie Davis, prin. Fax 819-2941
Union HS 900/9-12
1800 Tremont Blvd NW 49504 616-819-3160
Karl Nelson, prin. Fax 819-3205
University Preparatory Academy 6-12
512 Division Ave S 49503 616-819-1010
Daniel Williams, prin. Fax 819-1011
Westwood MS 400/6-8
1525 Mount Mercy Dr NW 49504 616-819-3322
Arthur Garner, prin. Fax 819-3301

Kelloggsville SD 1,600/PK-12
242 52nd St SE 49548 616-538-7460
Samuel Wright, supt. Fax 532-1597
www.kvilleps.org
54th Street Academy Alt
173 54th St SW 49548 616-531-7433
Scott Gunn, prin. Fax 531-6996
Kelloggsville HS 600/9-12
23 Jean St SW 49548 616-532-1570
Scott Gunn, prin. Fax 532-7780
Kelloggsville MS 500/6-8
4650 Division Ave S 49548 616-532-1575
James Alston, prin. Fax 532-1579

Kenowa Hills SD 3,300/PK-12
2325 4 Mile Rd NW 49544 616-784-2511
Gerald Hopkins M.Ed., supt. Fax 784-8323
khps.org
Kenowa Hills HS 1,100/9-12
3825 Hendershot Ave NW 49544 616-784-2400
Katie Pennington M.Ed., prin. Fax 647-0149
Kenowa Hills MS 700/6-8
3950 Hendershot Ave NW 49544 616-785-3225
Abby Wiseman M.Ed., prin. Fax 784-2404

Kent ISD
2930 Knapp St NE 49525 616-364-1333
Ron Caniff, supt. Fax 364-1488
www.kentisd.org
Kent Career/Technical Center Vo/Tech
1655 E Beltline Ave NE 49525 616-364-8421
John Kraus, prin. Fax 364-9140
Kent Innovation HS 9-12
1655 E Beltline Ave NE 49525 616-363-8010
Kimberly Kimber, prin. Fax 363-8030

Northview SD 3,400/PK-12
4365 Hunsberger Ave NE 49525 616-363-6861
Dr. M Korpak, supt. Fax 363-9609
www.nvps.net
Crossroads MS 500/7-8
4400 Ambrose Ave NE 49525 616-361-3430
Daniel Duba, prin. Fax 363-7868
East Campus HS 200/Alt
3801 E Beltline Ave NE 49525 616-361-7396
Derek Schmidt, prin. Fax 361-7398
Northview HS 1,200/9-12
4451 Hunsberger Ave NE 49525 616-363-4857
Mark Thomas, prin. Fax 361-3494

---

All Saints Academy - MS Campus 100/4-8
1110 4 Mile Rd NE 49525 616-363-7725
Michael Debri, prin. Fax 363-3086
Aquinas College Post-Sec.
1607 Robinson Rd SE 49506 616-632-8900

Calvin College Post-Sec.
3201 Burton St SE 49546 616-526-6000
Calvin Theological Seminary Post-Sec.
3233 Burton St SE 49546 800-388-6034
Catholic Central HS 700/9-12
319 Sheldon Blvd SE 49503 616-233-5899
Greg Deja, prin. Fax 459-0257
Compass College of Cinematic Arts Post-Sec.
41 Sheldon Blvd SE 49503 616-988-1000
Cornerstone University Post-Sec.
1001 E Beltline Ave NE 49525 616-949-5300
Covenant Christian HS 200/9-12
1401 Ferndale Ave SW, 616-453-5048
Rick Noorman, prin. Fax 453-4277
Davenport University Post-Sec.
6191 Kraft Ave SE 49512 616-698-7111
Empire Beauty School Post-Sec.
1735 4 Mile Rd NE 49525 616-363-9853
Empire Beauty School Post-Sec.
455 Standale Plz NW, 616-735-9680
Everest Institute Post-Sec.
1750 Woodworth St NE 49525 616-364-8464
Grace Bible College Post-Sec.
1011 Aldon St SW 49509 616-538-2330
Grand Rapids Adventist Academy 100/K-12
1151 Oakleigh Rd NW 49504 616-791-9797
Burney Culpepper, prin. Fax 791-7242
Grand Rapids Christian HS 900/9-12
2300 Plymouth Ave SE 49506 616-574-5500
Dr. Randy Morris, prin. Fax 241-3141
Grand Rapids Christian MS 400/5-8
2036 Chesaning Dr SE 49506 616-574-6300
Ashanti Bryant, prin. Fax 574-6316
Grand Rapids Community College Post-Sec.
143 Bostwick Ave NE 49503 616-234-4000
ITT Technical Institute Post-Sec.
3518 Plainfield Ave NE 49525 616-365-4800
Kuyper College Post-Sec.
3333 E Beltline Ave NE 49525 800-511-3749
Legacy Christian West Campus 200/5-8
67 68th St SW 49548 616-455-3860
Vince Bonnema M.A., admin. Fax 455-1960
NorthPointe Christian HS 400/6-12
3101 Leonard St NE 49525 616-942-0350
Todd Tolsma, head sch Fax 942-4647
Plymouth Christian HS 200/7-12
965 Plymouth Ave NE 49505 616-454-9481
James Bazen, prin. Fax 454-7243
Puritan Reformed Theological Seminary Post-Sec.
2965 Leonard St NE 49525 616-977-0599
Ross Medical Education Center Post-Sec.
4528 Breton Rd SE 49508 616-698-3075
South Christian HS 700/9-12
160 68th St SW 49548 616-455-3210
George Guichelaar, prin. Fax 455-8840
Spectrum Health Post-Sec.
100 Michigan St NE 49503 616-391-1605
Taratuta School of Truck Driving Post-Sec.
2215 Oak Indstrl Dr NE #212 49505 616-742-9000
Van Andel Institute Graduate School Post-Sec.
333 Bostwick Ave NE 49503 616-234-5708
West Catholic HS 500/9-12
1801 Bristol Ave NW 49504 616-233-5900
Cynthia Kneibel, prin. Fax 453-4320

**Grandville, Kent, Pop. 15,098**
Grandville SD 5,600/PK-12
3839 Prairie St SW 49418 616-254-6570
Roger Bearup, supt. Fax 254-6580
www.grandville.k12.mi.us
Grandville HS 1,900/9-12
4700 Canal Ave SW 49418 616-254-6430
Chris VanderSlice, prin. Fax 254-6462
Grandville MS 900/7-8
3535 Wilson Ave SW 49418 616-254-6610
John Philo, prin. Fax 254-6613

---

Calvin Christian HS 400/9-12
3750 Ivanrest Ave SW 49418 616-538-0990
Thelma Ensink, prin. Fax 538-9930
Calvin Christian MS 7-8
3740 Ivanrest Ave SW 49418 616-531-7400
Thelma Ensink, prin. Fax 531-7402

**Grant, Newaygo, Pop. 889**
Grant SD 2,100/PK-12
148 Elder St 49327 231-834-5621
Jonathan Whan, supt. Fax 834-7146
www.grantps.net
Grant HS 600/9-12
331 E State Rd 49327 231-834-5622
Dan Simon, prin. Fax 834-8043
Grant Learning Center 200/Alt
331 E State Rd 49327 231-834-5639
Jonathan Whan, supt. Fax 834-8111
Grant MS 600/5-8
96 E 120th St 49327 231-834-5910
Lance Jones, prin. Fax 834-9029

**Grass Lake, Jackson, Pop. 1,146**
Grass Lake Community SD 1,300/K-12
899 S Union St 49240 517-522-5540
Brad Hamilton, supt. Fax 522-8195
www.grasslakeschools.com
Grass Lake HS 400/9-12
11500 Warrior Trl 49240 517-522-5570
Brian Thompson, prin. Fax 522-5490
Grass Lake MS 300/6-8
1000 Grass Lake Rd 49240 517-522-5550
Jeanene Satterthwaite, prin. Fax 522-4775

**Grayling, Crawford, Pop. 1,867**
Crawford AuSable SD 1,600/PK-12
1135 N Old 27 49738 989-344-3500
Joseph Powers, supt. Fax 348-6822
www.casdk12.net/
Grayling HS 500/9-12
1135 N Old 27 49738 989-344-3532
Donna Boughner, prin. Fax 348-7799
Grayling MS 400/6-8
500 Spruce St 49738 989-344-3550
Jeffrey Branch, prin. Fax 348-7045

**Greenville, Montcalm, Pop. 8,316**
Greenville SD 3,700/K-12
1414 Chase St 48838 616-754-3686
Peter Haines, supt. Fax 754-5374
www.greenville.k12.mi.us
Greenville HS 1,200/9-12
111 N Hillcrest St 48838 616-754-3681
Jeffrey Wright, prin. Fax 754-1994
Greenville MS 900/6-8
1321 Chase St 48838 616-754-9361
Leigh Acker, prin. Fax 754-2901

**Grosse Ile, Wayne, Pop. 9,781**
Grosse Ile Township SD 1,900/K-12
23276 E River Rd 48138 734-362-2555
Joanne Lelekatch, supt. Fax 362-2594
www.gischools.org/
Grosse Ile HS 700/9-12
7800 Grays Dr 48138 734-362-2400
James Stewart, prin. Fax 362-2496
Grosse Ile MS 500/6-8
23270 E River Rd 48138 734-362-2500
David Tucker, prin. Fax 362-2596

**Grosse Pointe, Wayne, Pop. 5,336**
Grosse Pointe SD 8,300/K-12
389 Saint Clair St 48230 313-432-3000
Dr. Gary Niehaus, supt. Fax 432-3002
www.gpschools.org
Brownell MS 700/6-8
260 Chalfonte Ave 48236 313-432-3900
Dr. Michael Dib, prin. Fax 432-3902
Grosse Pointe North HS 1,400/9-12
707 Vernier Rd 48236 313-432-3200
Kathryn Murray, prin. Fax 432-3202
Grosse Pointe South HS 1,700/9-12
11 Grosse Pointe Blvd 48236 313-432-3500
Moussa Hamka, prin. Fax 432-3502
Parcells MS 700/6-8
20600 Mack Ave 48236 313-432-4600
Daniel Hartley, prin. Fax 432-4602
Pierce MS 600/6-8
15430 Kercheval Ave 48230 313-432-4700
Chris Clark, prin. Fax 432-4702

---

University Liggett S 700/PK-12
1045 Cook Rd 48236 313-884-4444
Joseph P. Healey Ph.D., head sch Fax 884-1775

**Gwinn, Marquette, Pop. 1,874**
Gwinn Area Community SD 900/K-12
50 W State Highway M35 49841 906-346-9283
Thomas Jayne, supt. Fax 346-3616
www.gwinn.k12.mi.us
Gwinn HS 400/9-12
50 W State Highway M35 49841 906-346-9247
Brian Rice, prin. Fax 346-0300
Gwinn MS 200/6-8
50 W State Highway M35 49841 906-346-5914
Brian Rice, prin. Fax 346-0300

**Hale, Iosco**
Hale Area SD 400/K-12
200 W Main St 48739 989-728-7661
Loren Vannest, supt. Fax 728-2406
www.haleschools.net
Hale S 400/K-12
311 N Washington St 48739 989-728-3551
Loren Vannest, prin. Fax 728-9551

**Hamilton, Allegan**
Hamilton Community SD 2,700/PK-12
4815 136th Ave 49419 269-751-5148
David Tebo, supt. Fax 751-7116
www.hamiltonschools.us
Hamilton HS 800/9-12
4911 136th Ave 49419 269-751-5185
Tim Reeves, prin. Fax 751-7670
Hamilton MS 600/5-8
4845 136th Ave 49419 269-751-4436
Rick Frens, prin. Fax 751-8560
Other Schools – See Holland

**Hamtramck, Wayne, Pop. 21,353**
Hamtramck SD 2,700/PK-12
PO Box 12012 48212 313-872-9270
Thomas Niczay, supt. Fax 872-8679
www.hamtramck.k12.mi.us
Hamtramck HS 900/9-12
11410 Charest St 48212 313-892-7505
Terrence George, prin. Fax 892-1990
Horizon Alternative Education 100/Alt
3225 Caniff St 48212 313-893-2355
Kristen Hurt, prin. Fax 893-2294
Kosciuszko MS 400/7-8
2333 Burger St 48212 313-365-4625
Nuo Ivezaj, prin. Fax 365-4760

**Hancock, Houghton, Pop. 4,572**
Copper Country ISD
809 Hecla St 49930 906-482-4250
George Stockero, supt. Fax 482-1931
www.copperisd.org
Career and Technical Education Vo/Tech
110 E Quincy St 49930 906-482-4250
William Rivest, prin. Fax 482-1931
Hancock SD 800/K-12
501 Campus Dr 49930 906-487-5925
Monica Healy, supt. Fax 455-2255
www.hancockpublicschools.org
Hancock Central HS 200/9-12
501 Campus Dr 49930 906-483-2540
Kipp Beaudoin, prin. Fax 483-2539
Hancock MS 200/6-8
501 Campus Dr 49930 906-487-5923
Kipp Beaudoin, prin. Fax 487-5924

---

Finlandia University Post-Sec.
601 Quincy St 49930 906-482-5300

**Harbor Beach, Huron, Pop. 1,671**
Harbor Beach Community SD 500/K-12
402 S 5th St 48441 989-479-3261
Lawrence Kroswek, supt. Fax 479-9881
www.hbpirates.org
Harbor Beach HS 200/9-12
402 S 5th St 48441 989-479-3261
Michael Hugan, prin. Fax 479-9881
Harbor Beach MS 200/5-8
402 S 5th St 48441 989-479-3261
Dr. Tumara Johnston, prin. Fax 479-9881

**Harbor Springs, Emmet, Pop. 1,169**
Harbor Springs SD 900/PK-12
800 S State Rd 49740 231-526-4545
Mark Tompkins, supt. Fax 526-4544
www.harborps.org
Harbor Springs HS 300/9-12
500 N Spring St 49740 231-526-4800
Susan Jacobs, prin. Fax 526-4833
Harbor Springs MS 200/6-8
800 S State Rd 49740 231-526-4700
Wil Cwikiel, prin. Fax 526-4760

---

Harbor Light Christian S 100/PK-12
8333 Clayton Rd 49740 231-347-7859
Gary Urman, head sch Fax 347-7703

**Harper Woods, Wayne, Pop. 13,876**
Harper Woods SD 1,200/PK-12
20225 Beaconsfield St 48225 313-245-3000
Todd Biederwolf, supt. Fax 839-1249
www.hwschools.org
Harper Woods HS 500/9-12
20225 Beaconsfield St 48225 313-245-3084
Schranda Collier, prin. Fax 371-5548
Harper Woods MS 200/7-8
20225 Beaconsfield St 48225 313-245-3000
Heath Filber, prin. Fax 839-4360
Diploma Success Community S Adult
19344 Kelly Rd 48225 313-458-8796
Lawrence Massey, prin. Fax 458-8801

**Harris, Menominee**
Bark River-Harris SD 700/K-12
PO Box 350 49845 906-466-9981
Jason Lockwood, supt. Fax 466-0107
www.brhschools.org/
Bark River-Harris JSHS 300/7-12
PO Box 350 49845 906-466-5321
Darren Bray, prin. Fax 466-2925

**Harrison, Clare, Pop. 2,058**
Harrison Community SD 1,600/K-12
PO Box 529 48625 989-539-7871
Richard T. Foote, supt. Fax 539-7491
www.harrisonschools.com/
Harrison Community Education 50/Alt
PO Box 529 48625 989-539-7194
Jeremy Thomas, dir. Fax 539-4314
Harrison HS 500/9-12
PO Box 529 48625 989-539-7417
Jeremy Thomas, prin. Fax 539-4319
Harrison MS 400/6-8
PO Box 529 48625 989-539-7194
Kelly Pieprzyk, prin. Fax 539-0460

---

Mid-Michigan Community College Post-Sec.
1375 S Clare Ave 48625 989-386-6622

**Harrison Township, Macomb, Pop. 24,685**
L'Anse Creuse SD
Supt. — See Clinton Township
L'Anse Creuse HS 1,700/9-12
38495 LAnse Creuse St 48045 586-783-6400
Stephen Czapski, prin. Fax 783-6408
L'Anse Creuse MS Central 700/6-8
38000 Reimold St 48045 586-783-6430
Andrea Glynn, prin. Fax 783-6437
L'Anse Creuse MS South 500/6-8
34641 Jefferson Ave 48045 586-493-5620
Paul Lasala, prin. Fax 493-5625

**Hart, Oceana, Pop. 2,108**
Hart SD 1,300/PK-12
301 Johnson St W 49420 231-873-6214
Mark Platt, supt. Fax 873-6244
www.hartschools.net
Hart HS 400/9-12
300 Johnson St W 49420 231-873-5691
Matthew McDonald, prin. Fax 873-0586
Hart MS 400/5-8
308 Johnson St W 49420 231-873-6320
Kevin Ackley, prin. Fax 873-0245

**Hartford, Van Buren, Pop. 2,604**
Hartford SD 1,400/PK-12
115 School St 49057 269-621-7000
Andrew Hubbard, supt. Fax 621-3887
www.hpsmi.org/
Hartford Alternative Education 100/Alt
115 School St 49057 269-621-7139
Erik Parker, prin.

Hartford HS 400/9-12
121 School St 49057 269-621-7100
David Janicki, prin. Fax 621-7160
Hartford MS 300/6-8
141 School St 49057 269-621-7200
Joel Messenger, prin. Fax 621-7260

**Hartland, Livingston**
Hartland Consolidated SD
Supt. — See Howell
Hartland HS 1,800/9-12
10635 Dunham Rd 48353 810-626-2200
David Minsker, prin. Fax 626-2201
Hartland MS 900/7-8
3250 Hartland Rd 48353 810-626-2400
Steve Livingway, prin. Fax 626-2401

**Haslett, Ingham, Pop. 18,726**
Haslett SD 2,700/K-12
5593 Franklin St 48840 517-339-8242
Michael Duda, supt. Fax 339-1360
www.haslett.k12.mi.us/
Haslett HS 900/9-12
5450 Marsh Rd 48840 517-339-8249
Bart Wegenke, prin. Fax 339-7353
Haslett MS 600/6-8
1535 Franklin St 48840 517-339-8233
Susan Gillings, prin. Fax 339-4837

**Hastings, Barry, Pop. 7,265**
Hastings Area SD 2,800/PK-12
232 W Grand St 49058 269-948-4400
Dr. Carrie Duits, supt. Fax 948-4425
www.hassk12.org
Hastings HS 900/9-12
520 W South St 49058 269-948-4409
Christopher Macklin, prin. Fax 948-8081
Hastings MS 700/6-8
232 W Grand St 49058 269-948-4404
Christopher Cooley, prin. Fax 945-6101

---

Barry County Christian S 100/K-12
2999 McKeown Rd 49058 269-948-2151
Brandon Strong, admin. Fax 948-2795

**Hazel Park, Oakland, Pop. 15,715**
Hazel Park SD 4,300/PK-12
1620 E Elza Ave 48030 248-658-5200
Amy Kruppe, supt. Fax 544-5443
www.hazelparkschools.org
Hazel Park HS 1,000/9-12
23400 Hughes Ave 48030 248-658-5100
Fax 544-5389
Hazel Park JHS 700/6-8
22770 Highland Ave 48030 248-658-2300
Tammy Scholz, prin. Fax 586-5875
Hazel Park Adult S Adult
420 W 9 Mile Rd 48030 248-658-5600
Michelle LaPorte, prin. Fax 544-5447

**Hemlock, Saginaw, Pop. 1,446**
Hemlock SD 1,200/PK-12
PO Box 260 48626 989-642-5282
Donald Killingbeck, supt. Fax 642-2773
www.hemlockps.com
Hemlock Alternative S 50/Alt
PO Box 260 48626 989-642-5287
Michael Vondette, coord. Fax 642-5109
Hemlock HS 400/9-12
PO Box 260 48626 989-642-5287
Randy Kreger, prin. Fax 642-5109
Hemlock HS Early Middle College 11-12
PO Box 260 48626 989-642-5287
Randy Kreger, prin. Fax 642-2773
Hemlock MS 300/5-8
PO Box 260 48626 989-642-5253
Terry Keyser, prin. Fax 642-8239

**Hermansville, Menominee**
North Central Area SD 400/PK-12
PO Box 159 49847 906-498-7737
Bruce Tapio, supt. Fax 498-2235
www.ncajets.org
Other Schools – See Powers

**Hesperia, Oceana, Pop. 932**
Hesperia Community SD 1,100/K-12
PO Box 338 49421 231-854-6185
Michael Corey, supt. Fax 854-1586
www.hesp.net
Hesperia HS 300/9-12
PO Box 338 49421 231-854-6385
David LaPrairie, prin. Fax 854-6070
Hesperia MS 300/5-8
PO Box 338 49421 231-854-6475
David LaPrairie, prin. Fax 854-6096

**Highland, Oakland**
Huron Valley SD 9,800/PK-12
2390 S Milford Rd 48357 248-684-8000
James Baker, supt. Fax 684-8235
www.hvs.org
Harbor HS 100/Alt
5061 N Duck Lake Rd 48356 248-676-8421
Susan Gallagher, dir. Fax 676-8420
Milford HS 1,500/9-12
2380 S Milford Rd 48357 248-684-8091
Kevin McKenna, prin. Fax 684-8094
Other Schools – See Commerce Township, Milford, White Lake

**Hillman, Montmorency, Pop. 696**
Hillman Community SD 500/K-12
26042 M 32 S 49746 989-742-2908
Jason McElrath, supt. Fax 742-3376
www.hillmanschools.com
Hillman JSHS 200/7-12
26042 M 32 S 49746 989-742-4538
Jason McElrath, prin. Fax 742-4536

**Hillsdale, Hillsdale, Pop. 8,143**
Hillsdale Community SD 1,600/PK-12
30 S Norwood Ave 49242 517-437-4401
Shawn Vondra, supt. Fax 439-4194
www.hillsdaleschools.org
Davis MS 500/5-8
30 N West St 49242 517-439-4326
Erin North, prin. Fax 437-1195
Hillsdale HS 400/9-12
30 S Norwood Ave 49242 517-439-4320
Jeff Terpenning, prin. Fax 437-0377
Horizon Alternative HS Alt
30 S Norwood Ave 49242 517-437-4403
Jeff Terpenning, prin. Fax 437-0377

Hillsdale ISD 50/
310 W Bacon St 49242 517-437-0990
Ronna Steel, supt. Fax 439-4388
www.hillsdale-isd.org
Workforce Development & Tech Center Vo/Tech
279 Industrial Dr 49242 517-437-3729
Kevin Leonard, dir. Fax 437-3743

---

Hillsdale Academy 200/K-12
1 Academy Ln 49242 517-439-8644
Dr. Kenneth Calvert, hdmstr. Fax 607-2794
Hillsdale Beauty College Post-Sec.
64 Waldron St 49242 517-437-4670
Hillsdale College Post-Sec.
33 E College St 49242 517-437-7341

**Holland, Ottawa, Pop. 32,396**
Hamilton Community SD
Supt. — See Hamilton
Pioneer Tech HS 50/Alt
1362 S Point Rdg 49423 616-394-1370
Joy Zomer, lead tchr.

Holland SD 4,100/PK-12
320 W 24th St 49423 616-494-2000
Brian Davis Ph.D., supt. Fax 392-8225
www.hollandpublicschools.org
Holland Early College 8-12
45 E 25th St 49423 616-494-2700
Andrea Mehall, dir. Fax 928-0581
Holland HS 1,500/8-12
600 Van Raalte Ave 49423 616-494-2200
Deb Feenstra, prin. Fax 393-7534
Holland Virtual Tech HS 200/Alt
600 Van Raalte Ave 49423 616-494-2000
Tung Nguyen, dir. Fax 393-7534

Ottawa Area ISD 300/
13565 Port Sheldon St 49424 616-738-8940
Peter Haines, supt. Fax 738-8946
www.oaisd.org
Careerline Tech Center Vo/Tech
13663 Port Sheldon St 49424 616-738-8950
Dave Searles, dir. Fax 738-8956

West Ottawa SD 7,300/K-12
1138 136th Ave 49424 616-738-5700
Thomas K. Martin, supt. Fax 738-5791
www.westottawa.net
Dunes Alternative HS Alt
3600 152nd Ave 49424 616-738-6700
Todd Tulgestke, prin. Fax 738-6791
Harbor Lights MS 1,000/6-8
1024 136th Ave 49424 616-786-1000
Dennis White, prin. Fax 786-1091
Macatawa Bay MS 700/6-8
3700 140th Ave 49424 616-786-2000
Michael Fine, prin. Fax 786-2091
West Ottawa HS 2,300/9-12
3685 Butternut Dr 49424 616-994-5000
Todd Tulgestke, prin. Fax 994-5091

---

Calvary S of Holland 200/PK-12
518 Plasman Ave 49423 616-396-4494
Dr. Joyce DeRidder, dir. Fax 396-0326
Davenport University Post-Sec.
643 S Waverly Rd 49423 616-395-4600
Holland Christian HS 800/9-12
950 Ottawa Ave 49423 616-820-2905
Darryl DeRuiter, prin. Fax 820-2910
Holland Christian MS 200/7-8
850 Ottawa Ave 49423 616-820-3205
Mark Van Dyke, prin. Fax 820-3210
Hope College Post-Sec.
PO Box 9000 49422 616-395-7000
Western Theological Seminary Post-Sec.
101 E 13th St 49423 616-392-8555

**Holly, Oakland, Pop. 5,990**
Holly Area SD 3,400/PK-12
920 Baird St 48442 248-328-3100
David M. Nuss, supt. Fax 328-3145
www.has-k12.org/
Holly HS 1,200/9-12
6161 E Holly Rd 48442 248-328-3200
Peter LoFiego, prin. Fax 328-3211
Holly MS 500/6-8
14470 N Holly Rd 48442 248-328-3400
Dr. Elise Schmidt, prin. Fax 328-3404

---

Adelphian Junior Academy 50/K-10
PO Box 208 48442 248-634-9481
Nancy Danelson, prin. Fax 634-9222

**Holt, Ingham, Pop. 23,336**
Holt SD 5,700/PK-12
5780 Holt Rd 48842 517-694-0401
David G. Hornak, supt. Fax 694-1335
www.hpsk12.net/
EdTrek Alternative Education Center Alt
4610 Spahr St 48842 517-709-3148
Connie Ragnone, coord. Fax 709-3156
Holt HS 1,300/9-12
5885 Holt Rd 48842 517-694-2162
Michael Willard, prin. Fax 699-3451
Holt HS North Campus 500/12-12
5780 Holt Rd 48842 517-694-4370
Michael Willard, prin. Fax 694-8362
Holt JHS 1,000/7-8
1784 Aurelius Rd 48842 517-694-7117
Marshall Perkins, prin. Fax 694-3535

**Holton, Muskegon**
Holton SD 900/PK-12
6500 4th St 49425 231-821-1700
Jason Kennedy, supt. Fax 821-1724
www.holtonschools.com
Holton HS 300/9-12
6477 Syers Rd 49425 231-821-1725
Adam Bayne, prin. Fax 821-1774
Holton MS 200/7-8
6477 Syers Rd 49425 231-821-1775
Adam Bayne, prin. Fax 821-1824

**Homer, Calhoun, Pop. 1,660**
Homer Community SD 1,000/K-12
403 S Hillsdale St 49245 517-568-4463
Robert Wright, supt. Fax 568-4468
www.homerschools.net
Homer HS 300/9-12
403 S Hillsdale St 49245 517-568-4464
Tom Salow, prin. Fax 568-7125
Homer MS 300/5-8
403 S Hillsdale St 49245 517-568-4456
Scott Salow, prin. Fax 568-7125

**Hopkins, Allegan, Pop. 603**
Hopkins SD 1,600/K-12
400 S Clark St 49328 269-793-7261
Gary Wood, supt. Fax 557-7919
www.hpsvikings.org
Hopkins HS 500/9-12
333 S Clark St 49328 269-793-7616
Ken Szczepanski, prin. Fax 557-7919
Hopkins MS 300/6-8
215 S Clark St 49328 269-793-7407
Ken Szczepanski, prin. Fax 557-7919

**Horton, Jackson**
Hanover-Horton SD 1,300/K-12
10400 Moscow Rd 49246 517-563-0100
John Denney, supt. Fax 563-0150
www.hanoverhorton.org/
Hanover-Horton HS 400/9-12
10000 Moscow Rd 49246 517-563-0101
Isaac Cottrell, prin. Fax 563-0155
Hanover-Horton MS 300/6-8
10000 Moscow Rd 49246 517-563-0102
Denise Bergstrom, prin. Fax 563-9140

**Houghton, Houghton, Pop. 7,574**
Houghton-Portage Township SD 1,300/K-12
1603 Gundlach Rd 49931 906-482-0451
Doreen Klingbeil, supt. Fax 487-9764
www.hpts.us
Houghton Central HS 400/9-12
1603 Gundlach Rd 49931 906-482-0450
Patrick Aldrich, prin. Fax 482-5218
Houghton MS 300/6-8
1603 Gundlach Rd 49931 906-482-4871
Julie Filpus, prin. Fax 483-2566

---

Michigan Technological University Post-Sec.
1400 Townsend Dr 49931 906-487-1885

**Houghton Lake, Roscommon, Pop. 3,390**
Houghton Lake Community SD 1,600/PK-12
6001 W Houghton Lake Dr 48629 989-366-2000
Brent Cryderman, supt. Fax 422-6606
www.hlcsk12.net
Houghton Lake HS 700/8-12
4433 W Houghton Lake Dr 48629 989-366-2005
John Winkler, prin. Fax 366-2071

---

Houghton Lake Institute of Cosmetology Post-Sec.
PO Box 669 48629 - -

**Howard City, Montcalm, Pop. 1,777**
Tri County Area SD
Supt. — See Sand Lake
Tri County HS 700/9-12
21338 Kendaville Rd 49329 231-937-4338
Tim Goheen, prin. Fax 937-5684
Tri County MS 600/6-8
21350 Kendaville Rd 49329 231-937-4318
Steve Johnson, prin. Fax 937-6319

**Howell, Livingston, Pop. 9,332**
Hartland Consolidated SD 5,600/K-12
9525 E Highland Rd 48843 810-626-2100
Janet Sifferman, supt. Fax 626-2101
www.hartlandschools.us/
Hartland Alternative Education 100/Alt
9525 E Highland Rd 48843 810-626-2140
Fax 626-2101
Other Schools – See Hartland

Howell SD 8,600/K-12
411 N Highlander Way 48843 517-548-6200
Erin J. MacGregor, supt. Fax 548-6229
www.howellschools.com
Highlander Way MS 1,100/6-8
511 N Highlander Way 48843 517-548-6252
Melanie Post, prin. Fax 545-1455
Howell HS 2,100/10-12
1200 W Grand River Ave 48843 517-540-8300
Jason Schrock, prin. Fax 545-1496
Howell HS Freshman Campus 600/9-9
1400 W Grand River Ave 48843 517-548-6267
Jason Schrock, prin. Fax 545-1439

Parker MS 900/6-8
400 Wright Rd 48843 517-552-4600
Susan Muntz, prin. Fax 552-0106

---

Cleary University - Livingston Campus Post-Sec.
3750 Cleary Dr 48843 800-686-1883

**Hudson, Lenawee, Pop. 2,276**
Hudson Area SD 1,000/K-12
781 N Maple Grove Ave 49247 517-448-8912
Michael Osborne Ph.D., supt. Fax 448-8570
www.hudson.k12.mi.us
Hudson Alternative HS 50/Alt
771 N Maple Grove Ave 49247 517-448-8912
Lance Horwath, prin. Fax 448-8975
Hudson Area HS 300/9-12
771 N Maple Grove Ave 49247 517-448-8912
Lance Horwath, prin. Fax 448-8975
Hudson MS 200/6-8
771 N Maple Grove Ave 49247 517-445-8912
Lance Horwath, prin. Fax 448-8975
Southern MI Ctr for Science & Industry Vo/Tech
550 E Main St 49247 517-448-1413
Dan Rogers, admin. Fax 448-1414

**Hudsonville, Ottawa, Pop. 7,024**
Hudsonville SD 6,000/PK-12
3886 Van Buren St 49426 616-669-1740
Dr. Nicholas Ceglarek, supt. Fax 669-4878
www.hudsonville.k12.mi.us
Baldwin Street MS 800/6-8
3835 Baldwin St 49426 616-669-7750
Fax 669-7755
Hudsonville Freshman Campus 400/9-9
3370 Allen St 49426 616-669-1510
Matt Blood, prin.
Hudsonville HS 1,200/10-12
5037 32nd Ave 49426 616-669-1500
Dave Feenstra, prin. Fax 669-4891
Riley Street MS 600/6-8
2745 Riley St 49426 616-896-1920
Bill Ross, prin. Fax 896-1925

---

Hudsonville Christian MS 300/6-8
3925 Van Buren St 49426 616-669-7487
Mary Broene, prin. Fax 669-2031
Unity Christian HS 700/9-12
5900 48th Ave 49426 616-669-1820
Jerry DeGroot, prin. Fax 669-5760

**Ida, Monroe**
Ida SD 1,500/K-12
3145 Prairie St 48140 734-269-3110
Richard Carsten, supt. Fax 269-2294
www.idaschools.org
Ida HS 500/9-12
3145 Prairie St 48140 734-269-3485
Thomas Dykstra, prin. Fax 269-3495
Ida MS 500/5-8
3143 Prairie St 48140 734-269-2220
Dave Eack, prin. Fax 269-2576

**Imlay City, Lapeer, Pop. 3,545**
Imlay City Community SD 2,200/PK-12
634 W Borland Rd 48444 810-724-2765
Dr. Gary Richards, supt. Fax 724-4307
www.icschools.us
Imlay City HS 600/9-12
1001 Norlin Dr 48444 810-724-9810
Dr. Bill Kalmar, prin. Fax 724-9897
Imlay City MS 500/6-8
495 W 1st St 48444 810-724-9811
Patrick Brown, prin. Fax 724-9896
Venture HS 100/Alt
2061 S Almont Ave 48444 810-724-9814
Dr. Bill Kalmar, dean Fax 724-2315

**Indian River, Cheboygan, Pop. 1,930**
Inland Lakes SD 700/K-12
4363 S Straits Hwy 49749 231-238-6868
Fred Osborn, supt. Fax 238-4181
www.inlandlakes.org
Inland Lakes JSHS 400/6-12
4363 S Straits Hwy 49749 231-238-6868
Melanie Allen, prin. Fax 238-7240

**Inkster, Wayne, Pop. 24,504**
Westwood Community SD
Supt. — See Dearborn Heights
Tomlinson MS 300/7-8
25912 Annapolis St 48141 313-565-3393
Kristen Kajoian, prin. Fax 565-0920

---

Peterson-Warren Academy 100/PK-12
PO Box 888 48141 313-565-5808
Buford Griffith M.Ed., prin. Fax 565-7784

**Interlochen, Grand Traverse, Pop. 574**

---

Interlochen Center for the Arts 500/9-12
PO Box 199 49643 231-276-7200
Matthew Colpitts, dean Fax 276-7885

**Ionia, Ionia, Pop. 11,276**
Ionia County ISD
2191 Harwood Rd 48846 616-527-4900
Jason Mellema, supt. Fax 527-4731
www.ioniaisd.org
Heartlands Institute of Technology Vo/Tech
250 E Tuttle Rd 48846 616-527-6540
Anne Sharkey-Scott, prin. Fax 527-6670

Ionia SD 3,000/PK-12
250 E Tuttle Rd 48846 616-527-9280
Dr. Patricia Batista, supt. Fax 527-8846
www.ioniaschools.org
Ionia HS 900/9-12
250 E Tuttle Rd 48846 616-527-0600
Jack Manciu, prin. Fax 527-8057

Ionia MS 700/6-8
438 Union St 48846 616-527-0040
Cheri Meier, prin. Fax 527-3380
Welch HS 100/Alt
830 Harrison St 48846 616-527-3530
Jonathan Duley, prin. Fax 527-8012

**Iron Mountain, Dickinson, Pop. 7,523**
Iron Mountain SD 900/K-12
217 Izzo-Mariucci Way 49801 906-779-2600
Raphael Rittenhouse, supt. Fax 779-2676
www.imschools.org
Central MS 200/7-8
300 W B St 49801 906-779-2610
Mark Herman, prin. Fax 779-2638
IM-K Community Education Alt
800 E E St 49801 906-779-2660
Julie Wonders, prin. Fax 779-2675
Iron Mountain HS 400/9-12
300 W B St 49801 906-779-2610
Mark Herman, prin. Fax 779-2638

**Iron River, Iron, Pop. 2,984**
West Iron County SD 700/PK-12
601 Garfield Ave 49935 906-265-9218
Christopher Thomson, supt. Fax 265-9736
www.westiron.org
West Iron County JSHS 300/6-12
701 Garfield Ave 49935 906-265-5184
Michael Berutti, prin. Fax 265-9750

**Ironwood, Gogebic, Pop. 5,289**
Ironwood Area SD 800/K-12
650 E Ayer St 49938 906-932-0200
Timothy Kolesar, supt. Fax 932-9915
www.ironwood.k12.mi.us/
Wright K-12 S 400/K-12
650 E Ayer St 49938 906-932-0932
Michelle Kanipes, prin. Fax 932-9915

---

Gogebic Community College Post-Sec.
E4946 Jackson Rd 49938 906-932-4231

**Ishpeming, Marquette, Pop. 6,339**
Ishpeming SD 1 700/PK-12
319 E Division St 49849 906-485-5501
John Summerhill, supt. Fax 485-1422
www.ishpemingschools.com
Ishpeming HS 300/9-12
319 E Division St 49849 906-485-1066
Vicki Lempinen, prin. Fax 485-4750
Ishpeming MS 300/PK-K, 5-8
324 E Pearl St 49849 906-485-1066
Vicki Lempinen, prin. Fax 485-4750

NICE Community SD 1,200/K-12
300 S Westwood Dr 49849 906-485-1021
Bryan DeAugustine, supt. Fax 485-4095
www.nice.k12.mi.us/
Westwood HS 400/9-12
300 S Westwood Dr 49849 906-485-1023
David Boase, prin. Fax 485-1530

**Ithaca, Gratiot, Pop. 2,877**
Gratiot-Isabella RESD
PO Box 310 48847 989-875-5101
Jan Amsterburg, supt. Fax 875-7531
www.giresd.net/
Other Schools – See Alma

Ithaca SD 1,300/PK-12
710 N Union St 48847 989-875-3700
Corinne Netzley, supt. Fax 875-4538
www.ithacaschools.net
Ithaca JSHS 600/7-12
710 N Union St 48847 989-875-3373
Steven Netzley, prin. Fax 875-2500

**Jackson, Jackson, Pop. 31,900**
East Jackson Community SD 1,200/K-12
1404 N Sutton Rd 49202 517-764-2090
Patrick Little, supt. Fax 764-6033
www.eastjacksonschools.org/
East Jackson HS 400/9-12
1566 N Sutton Rd 49202 517-764-1700
Brent Cole, prin. Fax 764-6083
East Jackson MS 200/7-8
1566 N Sutton Rd 49202 517-764-6010
Brent Cole, prin. Fax 764-6081
W-A-Y East Jackson Alt
1404 N Sutton Rd 49202 517-764-2090
Brent Cole, prin. Fax 764-6033

Jackson County ISD 50/
6700 Browns Lake Rd 49201 517-768-5200
Kevin Oxley, supt. Fax 787-2026
www.jcisd.org
Jackson Area Career Center Vo/Tech
6800 Browns Lake Rd 49201 517-768-5100
Patty Horning, prin. Fax 787-2844

Jackson SD 5,800/K-12
522 Wildwood Ave 49201 517-841-2200
Jeffrey Beal, supt. Fax 789-8056
www.jpsk12.org/
Fourth Street Learning Center Alt
2400 4th St 49203 517-841-2300
Jeremy Patterson, prin.
Jackson HS 1,500/9-12
544 Wildwood Ave 49201 517-841-3700
Barbara Baird-Pauli, prin. Fax 768-5910
MS at Parkside 900/6-8
2400 4th St 49203 517-841-2300
Jeremy Patterson, prin. Fax 768-5968
Wilson Academy 400/Alt
310 W Morrell St 49203 517-841-2800
Deven Moore, prin. Fax 783-3582

Napoleon Community SD
Supt. — See Napoleon
Ackerson Lake Community Center 50/Alt
4126 Brooklyn Rd 49201 517-905-5701
Zack Kanaan, admin. Fax 764-0265

Northwest Community SD 2,800/PK-12
6900 Rives Junction Rd 49201 517-817-4700
Geoff Bontrager, supt. Fax 569-2395
www.nwschools.org/
Northwest Alternative HS 100/Alt
6900 Rives Junction Rd 49201 517-517-4702
Paul Scholz, prin. Fax 569-2870
Northwest HS 900/9-12
4200 Van Horn Rd 49201 517-817-4701
Scott Buchler, prin. Fax 569-2935
Northwest Kidder MS 700/6-8
6700 Rives Junction Rd 49201 517-817-4703
Dan Brooks, prin. Fax 569-2931

Vandercook Lake SD 1,300/K-12
1000 E Golf Ave 49203 517-782-9044
Anthony Hollow, supt. Fax 788-3690
www.vandyschools.org
Vandercook Lake JSHS 700/6-12
1000 E Golf Ave 49203 517-782-8167
Mark Schonhard, prin. Fax 782-3730

Western SD
Supt. — See Parma
Woodville Community Center 200/Alt
3950 Catherine St 49203 517-841-8700
Jared Vickers, prin. Fax 841-8807

---

Baker College of Jackson Post-Sec.
2800 Springport Rd 49202 517-788-7800
Jackson Christian MSHS 200/6-12
4200 Lowe Rd 49203 517-783-2658
Todd Barney, prin. Fax 783-4235
Jackson College Post-Sec.
2111 Emmons Rd 49201 517-787-0800
Lumen Christi HS 500/7-12
3483 Spring Arbor Rd 49203 517-787-0630
Christopher Smith, prin. Fax 787-1066

**Jenison, Ottawa, Pop. 16,336**
Jenison SD 4,500/PK-12
8375 20th Ave 49428 616-457-8890
Thomas TenBrink, supt. Fax 457-8898
www.jpsonline.org/
Jenison HS 1,400/9-12
2140 Bauer Rd 49428 616-457-3400
Dr. Brandon Graham, prin. Fax 457-4070
Jenison JHS 700/7-8
8295 20th Ave 49428 616-457-1402
Brett Cataldo, prin. Fax 457-8090

**Johannesburg, Otsego**
Johannesburg-Lewiston Area SD 700/K-12
PO Box 69 49751 989-732-1773
Kathleen Makowski, supt. Fax 732-6556
www.jlas.org
Johannesburg-Lewiston HS 200/9-12
PO Box 69 49751 989-731-4420
Curt Chrencik, prin. Fax 732-6556

**Jonesville, Hillsdale, Pop. 2,240**
Jonesville Community SD 1,500/PK-12
202 Wright St 49250 517-849-9075
Chellie Broesamle, supt. Fax 849-2434
www.jonesvilleschools.org
Jonesville HS 400/9-12
460 Adrian Rd 49250 517-849-9934
Dustin Scharer, prin. Fax 849-2755
Jonesville MS 300/6-8
401 E Chicago St 49250 517-849-3210
Bryan Playford, prin. Fax 849-3213
Phoenix Alternative S 100/Alt
401 E Chicago St 49250 517-849-7304
Eric Swihart, prin. Fax 849-3213

**Kalamazoo, Kalamazoo, Pop. 71,183**
Comstock SD 2,100/PK-12
3010 Gull Rd 49048 269-250-8900
Todd Mora, supt. Fax 250-8901
www.comstockps.org
Comstock Compass HS 300/Alt
3010 Gull Rd 49048 269-250-8930
Jay Birchmeier, prin. Fax 250-8931
Comstock HS 500/9-12
2107 N 26th St 49048 269-250-8700
Josh Cunningham, prin. Fax 250-8701
Comstock Northeast MS 400/5-8
1423 N 28th St 49048 269-250-8600
Kelley Howard, prin. Fax 250-8601

Kalamazoo RESA
Supt. — See Portage
Valley Center S 50/Alt
3122 Lake St 49048 269-388-9494
Fax 382-8546
Youth Opportunities Unlimited Alt
422 E South St 49007 269-349-9676
Karen Carlisle, admin. Fax 349-6852
Young Adult Program Adult
422 E South St 49007 269-250-9602
Deborah Wild, prin. Fax 250-9601

Kalamazoo SD 12,100/K-12
1220 Howard St 49008 269-337-0100
Michael Rice, supt. Fax 337-0149
www.kalamazoopublicschools.com
Alternative Learning Program Alt
3410 Laird Ave 49008 269-337-0540
Tamica Frison, prin. Fax 337-1652
Central HS 1,700/9-12
2432 N Drake Rd 49006 269-337-0300
Valerie Boggan, prin. Fax 337-0391

Hillside MS 600/6-8
1941 Alamo Ave 49006 269-337-0570
Atiba McKissack, prin. Fax 337-1618
Kalamazoo Area Math and Science Center 9-12
600 W Vine St Ste 400 49008 269-337-0004
Dr. Michael Tanoff, prin.
Linden Grove MS 800/6-8
4241 Arboretum Pkwy 49006 269-337-1740
Craig McCane, prin. Fax 337-1614
Maple Magnet MS 800/6-8
922 W Maple St 49008 269-337-0730
Dr. Jeffery Boggan, prin. Fax 337-1633
Milwood Magnet MS 800/6-8
2916 Konkle St 49001 269-337-0670
Craig LeSuer, prin. Fax 337-1628
Norrix HS 1,400/9-12
606 E Kilgore Rd 49001 269-337-0200
Rodney Prewitt, prin. Fax 337-1617
Phoenix HS 200/Alt
1411 Oakland Dr 49008 269-337-0760
Mark Hill, prin. Fax 337-1756
Adult Education Program Adult
714 S Westnedge Ave 49007 269-337-0422
Kim Bell, dir. Fax 337-0490

Parchment SD
Supt. — See Parchment
Barclay Hills Education Center Adult
1125 E Mosel Ave 49004 269-488-1470
Tina Maxwell, prin. Fax 488-1480

---

Davenport University Post-Sec.
4123 W Main St 49006 269-382-2835
Everest Institute Post-Sec.
5177 W Main St 49009 269-381-9616
Heritage Christian Academy 300/PK-12
6312 Quail Run Dr 49009 269-372-1400
Bob Bauman, admin. Fax 372-6018
Kalamazoo Christian HS 300/9-12
2121 Stadium Dr 49008 269-381-2250
B.J. Huizenga, prin. Fax 381-0319
Kalamazoo College Post-Sec.
1200 Academy St 49006 269-337-7000
Kalamazoo Junior Academy 100/K-10
1601 Nichols Rd 49006 269-342-8943
William Crawford, prin. Fax 492-1459
Kalamazoo Valley Community College Post-Sec.
PO Box 4070 49003 269-488-4400
Msgr. Hackett Catholic Prep S 300/9-12
1000 W Kilgore Rd 49008 269-381-2646
Brian Kosmerick, prin. Fax 381-3919
Western Michigan University Post-Sec.
1903 W Michigan Ave 49008 269-387-1000
West Michigan Coll of Barbering & Beauty Post-Sec.
3200 S Westnedge Ave Ste 1 49008 269-381-4424

**Kalkaska, Kalkaska, Pop. 1,989**
Kalkaska SD 1,600/PK-12
315 S Coral St 49646 231-258-9109
Karen Sherwood, supt. Fax 258-4474
www.kpschools.com/
Kalkaska HS 500/9-12
315 S Coral St 49646 231-258-9167
John Sattler, prin. Fax 258-5188
Kalkaska MS 300/6-8
315 S Coral St 49646 231-258-4040
Staci Short, prin. Fax 258-3576
Northside Educational Center 100/Alt
315 S Coral St 49646 231-258-5140
Brian Harbour, prin. Fax 258-4940

**Kent City, Kent, Pop. 1,047**
Kent City Community SD 1,300/PK-12
200 N Clover St 49330 616-678-7714
Mike Weiler, supt. Fax 678-4320
www.kentcityschools.org
Kent City Alternative HS Alt
351 N Main St 49330 616-678-7714
Bill Crane, prin. Fax 678-4320
Kent City HS 400/9-12
351 N Main St 49330 616-678-4210
Bill Crane, prin. Fax 678-4371
Kent City MS 300/6-8
285 N Main St 49330 616-678-4214
Bill Crane, prin. Fax 678-5099

---

Algoma Christian S 200/PK-12
PO Box 220 49330 616-678-7480
Dr. Brian Hazeltine Ed.D., supt. Fax 678-7484

**Kentwood, Kent, Pop. 47,105**
Kentwood SD 8,600/PK-12
5820 Eastern Ave SE 49508 616-455-4400
Michael Zoerhoff, supt. Fax 455-4476
www.kentwoodps.org
Crestwood MS 600/6-8
2674 44th St SE 49512 616-455-1200
Omar Bakri, prin. Fax 455-2338
East Kentwood Freshman Campus HS 800/9-9
6170 Valley Lane Dr SE 49508 616-698-9292
Michele Siderman, prin. Fax 698-0313
East Kentwood HS 2,000/10-12
6230 Kalamazoo Ave SE 49508 616-698-6700
John Keenoy, prin. Fax 698-2384
Pinewood MS 700/6-8
2100 60th St SE 49508 616-455-1224
Gary Harmon, prin. Fax 455-2054
Valleywood MS 700/6-8
1110 50th St SE 49508 616-538-7670
Mindy Westra, prin. Fax 538-9301
Kentwood Community Education Adult
28 60th St SE 49548 616-261-6166
Rick Hatfield, prin. Fax 261-6170

**Kimball, Saint Clair, Pop. 7,247**

---

New Life Christian Academy 200/PK-12
5517 Griswold Rd 48074 810-367-3770
Lee Ann Shimmel, admin. Fax 367-2249

**Kincheloe, Chippewa**
Pickford SD
Supt. — See Pickford
Consolidated Community School Services Alt
4900 W Davis Ct 49788 906-495-7305
Bill Henry, prin. Fax 495-5710

**Kinde, Huron, Pop. 445**
North Huron SD 500/K-12
21 Main St 48445 989-874-4100
Martin Prout, supt. Fax 874-4109
www.nhuron.org
North Huron S 500/K-12
21 Main St 48445 989-874-4101
Tanya Kramer, prin. Fax 874-4129

**Kingsford, Dickinson, Pop. 5,077**
Breitung Township SD 1,700/PK-12
2000 W Pyle Dr 49802 906-779-2650
Craig Allen, supt. Fax 779-7703
www.kingsford.org
Kingsford HS 600/9-12
431 Hamilton Ave 49802 906-779-2670
Lyle Smithson, prin. Fax 779-2883
Kingsford MS 400/6-8
445 Hamilton Ave 49802 906-779-2680
David Holmes, prin. Fax 774-1354

Dickinson-Iron ISD 50/
1074 Pyle Dr 49802 906-779-2690
Wendy Warmuth, supt. Fax 779-2669
www.diisd.org
Dickinson-Iron Tech Educ Center Vo/Tech
300 North Blvd 49802 906-779-2697
Paul Bonsall, prin. Fax 779-2087

**Kingsley, Grand Traverse, Pop. 1,450**
Kingsley Area SD 1,400/K-12
402 Fenton St 49649 231-263-5261
Keith Smith, supt. Fax 263-5282
www.kingsley.k12.mi.us
Kingsley Area HS 500/9-12
402 Fenton St 49649 231-263-5262
Mike Moran, prin. Fax 263-3813
Kingsley Area MS 500/5-8
402 Fenton St 49649 231-263-5262
Vaughn White, prin. Fax 263-4623

**Kingston, Tuscola, Pop. 436**
Kingston Community SD 600/PK-12
5790 State St 48741 989-683-2294
Matt Drake, supt. Fax 683-2081
www.kingstonk12.org
Kingston JSHS 300/7-12
5790 State St 48741 989-683-2550
Matthew Drake, supt. Fax 683-2081

**Laingsburg, Shiawassee, Pop. 1,260**
Laingsburg Community SD 1,200/PK-12
205 S Woodhull Rd 48848 517-651-2705
Matthew Shastal, supt. Fax 651-9075
www.laingsburg.k12.mi.us/
Laingsburg HS 400/9-12
8008 Woodbury Rd 48848 517-651-5091
Brian Doepker, prin. Fax 651-9621
Laingsburg MS 300/6-8
112 High St 48848 517-651-5034
Brandon Woodworth, prin. Fax 651-6213

**Lake City, Missaukee, Pop. 830**
Lake City Area SD 1,100/K-12
PO Box 900 49651 231-839-4333
Kim Blaszak, supt. Fax 839-5219
www.lakecityschools.net
Lake City HS 300/9-12
PO Box 900 49651 231-839-4331
Tim Hejnal, prin. Fax 839-6031
Lake City MS 300/6-8
PO Box 900 49651 231-839-7163
Tim Hejnal, prin. Fax 839-6042

**Lake Leelanau, Leelanau, Pop. 250**

---

St. Mary S 200/PK-12
PO Box 340 49653 231-256-9636
Megan Glynn, prin. Fax 256-7239

**Lake Linden, Houghton, Pop. 992**
Lake Linden-Hubbell SD 500/K-12
601 Calumet St 49945 906-296-6211
Craig Sundblad, supt. Fax 296-0943
www.lakelinden.k12.mi.us
Lake Linden Hubbell JSHS 200/7-12
601 Calumet St 49945 906-296-6681
Craig Sundblad, prin. Fax 296-0219

**Lake Odessa, Ionia, Pop. 1,980**
Lakewood SD
Supt. — See Woodland
Lakewood HS 700/9-12
7223 Velte Rd 48849 616-374-8868
Jay Larner, prin. Fax 374-1477

**Lake Orion, Oakland, Pop. 2,917**
Lake Orion Community SD 7,600/K-12
315 N Lapeer St 48362 248-693-5400
Marion Ginopolis, supt. Fax 693-5464
www.lakeorion.k12.mi.us/
Lake Orion Community HS 2,500/9-12
495 E Scripps Rd 48360 248-693-5420
Stephen Hawley, prin. Fax 693-5459
Scripps MS 700/6-8
385 E Scripps Rd 48360 248-693-5440
Dan Haas, prin. Fax 693-5301

Waldon MS 600/6-8
2509 Waldon Rd 48360 248-391-1100
Randy Groya, prin. Fax 391-5452
Other Schools – See Oakland

---

Lake Orion Baptist S 100/K-12
255 E Scripps Rd 48360 248-693-6203
Tony Bryson, prin. Fax 693-6177

**Lakeview, Montcalm, Pop. 988**
Lakeview Community SD 1,300/PK-12
123 5th St 48850 989-352-7221
Kyle Hamlin, supt. Fax 352-8245
www.lakeviewschools.net
Lakeview HS 600/8-12
9800 Youngman Rd 48850 989-352-7221
Tom Wilcox, prin. Fax 352-6320

**LAnse, Baraga, Pop. 1,920**
L'Anse Area SD 700/K-12
201 N 4th St 49946 906-524-6000
Carrie Meyer, supt. Fax 524-6001
www.lanseschools.org/
L'Anse JSHS 400/6-12
201 N 4th St 49946 906-524-6000
Melissa Scroggs, prin. Fax 524-0345

**Lansing, Ingham, Pop. 108,750**
Lansing SD 9,100/PK-12
519 W Kalamazoo St 48933 517-755-1000
Yvonne Caamal Canul, supt. Fax 755-2009
www.lansingschools.net
Eastern HS 1,200/7-12
220 N Pennsylvania Ave 48912 517-755-1050
Donna Pohl, prin. Fax 755-1059
Everett HS 1,400/7-12
3900 Stabler St 48910 517-755-1080
Susan Cheadle-Holt, prin. Fax 755-1089
Sexton HS 800/7-12
102 Mcpherson Ave 48915 517-755-1070
Sandra Noecker, prin. Fax 755-1079
Woodcreek Achievement Center Alt
4000 Woodcreek Ln 48911 517-755-1700
Carl Word, prin. Fax 755-1709

Waverly Community SD 2,800/PK-12
515 Snow Rd 48917 517-321-7265
Terry Urquhart, supt. Fax 321-8577
www.waverlycommunityschools.net
Waverly HS 1,000/9-12
160 Snow Rd 48917 517-323-3831
Christopher Huff, prin. Fax 323-7714
Waverly MS 500/7-8
620 Snow Rd 48917 517-321-7240
Michael Moreno, prin. Fax 321-5789

---

American Hotel/Lodging Educational Inst Post-Sec.
2113 N High St 48906 800-390-8399
Career Quest Learning Center Post-Sec.
3215 S Pennsylvania Ave 48910 517-318-3330
Davenport University Post-Sec.
220 E Kalamazoo St 48933 517-484-2600
Dorsey School of Business Post-Sec.
6250 S Cedar St Ste 9 48911 517-272-4018
Greater Lansing Adventist S 100/PK-10
5330 W St Joe Hwy 48917 517-321-5565
Judy Shull, prin. Fax 321-5580
Great Lakes Christian College Post-Sec.
6211 W Willow Hwy 48917 517-321-0242
Lansing Catholic Central HS 500/9-12
501 Marshall St 48912 517-267-2100
Doug Moore, prin. Fax 267-2135
Lansing Christian S 600/PK-12
3405 Belle Chase Way 48911 517-882-5779
Wendy Hofman, supt. Fax 882-5849
Lansing Community College Post-Sec.
PO Box 40010 48901 517-483-1957
New Covenant Christian S 100/PK-12
PO Box 80737 48908 517-323-8903
Fred McGlone, prin. Fax 323-0421
Ross Medical Education Center Post-Sec.
4106 W Saginaw Hwy 48917 517-703-9044
Thomas M. Cooley Law School Post-Sec.
PO Box 13038 48901 517-371-5140

**Lapeer, Lapeer, Pop. 8,708**
Lapeer Community SD 4,600/PK-12
250 2nd St 48446 810-667-2401
Matthew Wandrie, supt. Fax 667-2411
www.lapeerschools.org
Lapeer Community HS 100/Alt
1220 Lake Nepessing Rd 48446 810-667-2453
Troy Norman, dir. Fax 667-2412
Lapeer HS 1,100/10-12
933 S Saginaw St 48446 810-667-2418
Douglas Lindsay, prin. Fax 667-2422
Zemmer MS 200/8-9
1920 W Oregon St 48446 810-667-2413
Aaron Shinn, prin. Fax 667-2483

Lapeer County ISD 50/
1996 W Oregon St 48446 810-664-5917
Steven Zott, supt. Fax 664-1011
www.lcisd.k12.mi.us
Other Schools – See Attica

---

Health Enrichment Center Post-Sec.
204 E Nepessing St 48446 810-667-9453

**Lathrup Village, Oakland, Pop. 3,943**
Southfield SD
Supt. — See Southfield
Southfield-Lathrup HS 1,100/9-12
19301 W 12 Mile Rd 48076 248-746-7200
Joseph Spryszak, prin. Fax 746-7488

**Lawrence, Van Buren, Pop. 973**
Lawrence SD 700/PK-12
650 W Saint Joseph St 49064 269-674-8233
Gretchen Gendron, supt. Fax 674-8206
www.lawrencetigers.com
Lawrence JSHS 300/7-12
650 W Saint Joseph St 49064 269-674-8232
Elizabeth Baleja, prin. Fax 674-8206

Van Buren ISD 100/
490 S Paw Paw St 49064 269-674-8091
Jeffrey Mills, supt. Fax 674-8030
www.vbisd.org/
Van Buren Technology Center Vo/Tech
250 South St 49064 269-674-8091
Scott Starkweather, prin. Fax 674-8954

**Lawton, Van Buren, Pop. 1,870**
Lawton Community SD 1,000/PK-12
101 Primary Way 49065 269-624-7901
Christopher Rice M.Ed., supt. Fax 624-6489
www.lawtoncs.org
Lawton Accelerated Academic Center 50/Alt
101 Primary Way 49065 269-624-7542
Tamara Webster M.Ed., admin.
Lawton HS 300/9-12
101 Primary Way 49065 269-624-7840
Tammy Wilson, prin. Fax 624-6554
Lawton MS 300/6-8
101 Primary Way 49065 269-624-7610
Tim Cerven, prin. Fax 624-5206

**Leland, Leelanau, Pop. 377**
Leland SD 400/K-12
PO Box 498 49654 231-256-9857
Jason Stowe, supt. Fax 256-9844
www.lelandpublicschools.com
Leland S 400/K-12
PO Box 498 49654 231-256-9857
Charles Gann, prin. Fax 256-9844

**LeRoy, Osceola, Pop. 252**
Pine River Area SD 800/K-12
17445 Pine River Rd 49655 231-829-3141
Matt Lukshaitis, supt. Fax 829-4410
www.pineriver.org/
Pine River Area MSHS 400/6-12
17445 Pine River Rd 49655 231-829-3841
Kim Miller, prin. Fax 829-5227

**Leslie, Ingham, Pop. 1,824**
Leslie SD 1,300/K-12
4141 Hull Rd 49251 517-589-8200
Jeff Manthei, supt. Fax 589-5340
www.lesliek12.net/
Leslie HS 500/9-12
4141 Hull Rd 49251 517-589-9500
Scott Powers, prin. Fax 589-5720
Leslie MS 400/5-8
400 Kimball St 49251 517-589-8218
Carol Franz, prin. Fax 589-5714

**Lexington, Sanilac, Pop. 1,169**
Croswell-Lexington SD
Supt. — See Croswell
Croswell-Lexington Alternative S 50/Alt
7178 Boynton St 48450 810-679-1500
Damien Pepin, prin.

**Lincoln, Alcona, Pop. 335**
Alcona Community SD 800/PK-12
PO Box 249 48742 989-736-6212
Shawn Thornton, supt. Fax 736-6261
www.alconaschools.net/
Alcona JSHS 400/7-12
PO Box 249 48742 989-736-8534
Daniel O'Connor, prin. Fax 736-8495

**Lincoln Park, Wayne, Pop. 37,338**
Lincoln Park SD 4,400/K-12
1650 Champaign Rd 48146 313-389-0200
Terry Dangerfield, supt. Fax 389-1322
www.lincolnparkpublicschools.com
Lincoln Park HS 1,400/9-12
1701 Champaign Rd 48146 313-389-0234
Jennifer Borg, prin. Fax 383-5738
Lincoln Park MS 700/6-8
2800 Lafayette Blvd 48146 313-389-0757
Daniel Mercer, prin. Fax 389-0761

**Linden, Genesee, Pop. 3,937**
Lake Fenton Community SD
Supt. — See Fenton
Lake Fenton HS 600/9-12
4070 Lahring Rd 48451 810-591-9591
Todd Reynolds, prin. Fax 591-9495

Linden Community SD 3,200/PK-12
7205 Silver Lake Rd 48451 810-591-0980
Russ Ciesielski, supt. Fax 591-5587
www.lindenschools.org
Linden HS 900/9-12
7201 Silver Lake Rd 48451 810-591-0410
Darin Dreasky, prin. Fax 591-8014
Linden MS 700/6-8
15425 Lobdell Rd 48451 810-591-0710
Julie Brown, prin. Fax 591-0155

**Litchfield, Hillsdale, Pop. 1,359**
Litchfield Community SD 300/K-12
210 Williams St 49252 517-542-2388
Dr. Corey Helgesen, supt. Fax 542-2580
www.lcsmi.org
Litchfield JSHS 200/6-12
210 Williams St 49252 517-542-2386
Dr. Corey Helgesen, prin. Fax 542-2703

**Livonia, Wayne, Pop. 95,640**
Clarenceville SD 1,800/PK-12
20210 Middlebelt Rd 48152 248-919-0400
Paul Shepich, supt. Fax 919-0430
www.clarenceville.k12.mi.us
Clarenceville HS 600/9-12
20155 Middlebelt Rd 48152 248-919-0408
Troy Nelson, prin. Fax 919-0438
Clarenceville MS 400/6-8
20210 Middlebelt Rd 48152 248-919-0406
Fax 919-0436

Livonia SD 15,000/PK-12
15125 Farmington Rd 48154 734-744-2500
Andrea Oquist, supt. Fax 744-2571
www.livoniapublicschools.org
Churchill HS 1,900/9-12
8900 Newburgh Rd 48150 734-744-2650
Keith McDonald, prin. Fax 744-2652
Emerson MS 800/7-8
29100 W Chicago St 48150 734-744-2665
Ann Owen, prin. Fax 744-2667
Franklin HS 1,800/9-12
31000 Joy Rd 48150 734-744-2655
Daniel Willenborg, prin. Fax 744-2657
Frost MS 800/7-8
14041 Stark Rd 48154 734-744-2670
Anthony Abbate, prin. Fax 744-2672
Holmes MS 800/7-8
16200 Newburgh Rd 48154 734-744-2675
Eric Stromberg, prin. Fax 744-2677
Livonia Career/Technical Center Vo/Tech
8985 Newburgh Rd 48150 734-744-2816
R. Joseph Anderson, prin. Fax 744-2817
Stevenson HS 2,000/9-12
33500 6 Mile Rd 48152 734-744-2660
Gary Harper, prin. Fax 744-2662
Other Schools – See Westland

Davenport University Post-Sec.
19499 Victor Pkwy 48152 734-943-2800
Ladywood HS 300/9-12
14680 Newburgh Rd 48154 734-591-1544
Tracey Mocon, prin. Fax 591-1545
Madonna University Post-Sec.
36600 Schoolcraft Rd 48150 734-432-5300
Schoolcraft College Post-Sec.
18600 Haggerty Rd 48152 734-462-4400

**Lowell, Kent, Pop. 3,710**
Lowell Area SD 3,800/K-12
300 High St 49331 616-987-2500
Gregory Pratt, supt. Fax 987-2511
www.lowellschools.com/
Lowell HS 1,200/9-12
11700 Vergennes St 49331 616-987-2900
Amy Pallo, prin. Fax 987-2911
Lowell MS 900/6-8
750 Foreman St 49331 616-987-2800
Dan VanderMeulen, prin. Fax 987-2811
Unity Alternative S 50/Alt
300 High St 49331 616-987-2524
Amy Pallo, prin. Fax 987-2511

**Ludington, Mason, Pop. 7,926**
Ludington Area SD 2,300/PK-12
809 E Tinkham Ave 49431 231-845-7303
Andrea D. Large, supt. Fax 843-4930
www.lasd.net
DeJonge MS 500/6-8
706 E Tinkham Ave 49431 231-845-3810
Kristi Zimmerman, prin. Fax 845-3814
Ludington HS 700/9-12
508 N Washington Ave 49431 231-845-3880
Dale Horowski, prin. Fax 845-3881

West Shore ESD 100/
2130 W US Highway 10 49431 231-757-3716
Randy Howes, supt. Fax 757-2406
www.wsesd.org
Other Schools – See Scottville

**Mc Bain, Missaukee, Pop. 651**
McBain Rural Agricultural SD 1,100/PK-12
107 E Maple St 49657 231-825-2165
Steve Brimmer, supt. Fax 825-2119
www.mcbain.org
Mc Bain JSHS 300/7-12
107 E Maple St 49657 231-825-2412
Joel Bronkema, prin. Fax 825-2119

Northern Michigan Christian S 300/PK-12
128 S Martin St 49657 231-825-2492
Dirk Walhout, supt. Fax 825-2371

**Mackinac Island, Mackinac, Pop. 466**
Mackinac Island SD 100/PK-12
PO Box 340 49757 906-847-3377
David Waaso, supt. Fax 847-3773
mackinac.eup.k12.mi.us
Mackinac Island S 100/PK-12
PO Box 340 49757 906-847-3377
David Waaso, admin. Fax 847-3773

**Mackinaw City, Emmet, Pop. 794**
Mackinaw City SD 200/PK-12
609 W Central Ave 49701 231-436-8211
Jeffrey Curth, supt. Fax 436-5434
www.mackcity.k12.mi.us
Mackinaw City S 200/PK-12
609 W Central Ave 49701 231-436-8211
Jeffrey Curth, supt. Fax 436-5434

**Macomb, Macomb, Pop. 22,714**
Chippewa Valley SD
Supt. — See Clinton Township
Dakota HS 1,900/10-12
21051 21 Mile Rd 48044 586-723-2702
Paul Sibley, prin. Fax 723-2701
Iroquois MS 1,100/6-8
48301 Romeo Plank Rd 48044 586-723-3700
Chirs Gardner, prin. Fax 723-3701
Seneca MS 1,400/6-8
47200 Heydenreich Rd 48044 586-723-3900
Todd Distelrath, prin. Fax 723-3901

L'Anse Creuse SD
Supt. — See Clinton Township
L'Anse Creuse HS - North 1,900/9-12
23700 21 Mile Rd 48042 586-493-5270
Greg Dixon, prin. Fax 493-5275
L'Anse Creuse MS North 700/6-8
46201 Fairchild Rd 48042 586-493-5260
Brian Fahning, prin. Fax 493-5265

Lutheran HS North 500/9-12
16825 24 Mile Rd 48042 586-781-9151
John Reincke, prin. Fax 781-8673

**Madison Heights, Oakland, Pop. 28,913**
Lamphere SD 2,800/K-12
31201 Dorchester Ave 48071 248-589-1990
Dale Steen, supt. Fax 589-2618
www.lamphereschools.org
Lamphere HS 800/9-12
610 W 13 Mile Rd 48071 248-589-3943
Gregory Fuller, prin. Fax 589-0240
Page MS 600/6-8
29615 Tawas St 48071 248-589-3428
Douglas Kelley, prin. Fax 545-1870

Madison SD 1,300/K-12
26524 John R Rd 48071 248-399-7800
Randy Seck, supt. Fax 399-2229
www.madisonschools.k12.mi.us/
Madison HS 400/9-12
915 E Eleven Mile Rd 48071 248-548-1800
Dan Gilbertson, prin. Fax 548-9758
Madison Preparatory HS 200/Alt
25601 Couzens Ave 48071 248-543-5465
Leslie Renne-Kegebein, prin. Fax 543-9323
Wilkinson MS 300/6-8
26524 John R Rd 48071 248-399-0455
Angel Abdulahad, prin. Fax 399-1965

Bishop Foley HS 300/9-12
32000 Campbell Rd 48071 248-585-1210
Elizabeth Hubbell, prin. Fax 585-3667
Dorsey School of Business Post-Sec.
30821 Barrington St 48071 248-588-9660
Ross Medical Education Center Post-Sec.
29429 John R Rd 48071 248-548-4389

**Mancelona, Antrim, Pop. 1,339**
Mancelona SD 1,000/PK-12
PO Box 739 49659 231-587-9764
Jeffery DiRosa, supt. Fax 587-9500
www.mancelonaschools.org/
Mancelona HS 300/9-12
PO Box 739 49659 231-587-8551
Larry Rager, prin. Fax 587-5401
Mancelona MS 300/5-8
PO Box 739 49659 231-587-9869
Dr. Tina Frollo, prin. Fax 587-0615

**Manchester, Washtenaw, Pop. 2,074**
Manchester Community SD 1,200/K-12
410 City Rd 48158 734-428-9711
Cherie Vannatter, supt. Fax 428-9188
www.mcs.k12.mi.us
Manchester HS 400/9-12
20500 Dutch Dr 48158 734-428-7333
Dr. Kevin Mowrer, prin. Fax 428-0178
Manchester MS 400/5-8
710 E Main St 48158 734-428-7442
Fax 428-9264

**Manistee, Manistee, Pop. 6,070**
Manistee Area SD 1,300/PK-12
550 Maple St 49660 231-723-3521
Ronald Stoneman, supt. Fax 723-1507
maps.manistee.org
Manistee MSHS 500/7-12
525 12th St 49660 231-723-2547
Julia Raddatz, prin. Fax 398-9277

Manistee Catholic Central S 200/PK-12
1200 US Highway 31 S 49660 231-723-2529
Jason Allen, prin. Fax 723-0669

**Manistique, Schoolcraft, Pop. 2,986**
Manistique Area SD 800/K-12
100 N Cedar St 49854 906-341-4300
Maryann Boddy, supt. Fax 341-2374
www.manistique.k12.mi.us
Manistique Middle & HS 300/6-12
100 N Cedar St 49854 906-341-4300
John Shiner, prin. Fax 341-8473

**Manton, Wexford, Pop. 1,266**
Manton Consolidated SD 900/K-12
105 5th St 49663 231-824-6411
Leonard Morrow, supt. Fax 824-4101
www.mantonschools.org
Manton HS 300/9-12
105 5th St 49663 231-824-6411
Char Siddall, prin. Fax 824-6114
Manton MS 300/5-8
105 5th St 49663 231-824-6401
Ryan Hiller, prin. Fax 824-4121

**Maple City, Leelanau, Pop. 204**
Glen Lake Community SD 800/PK-12
3375 W Burdickville Rd 49664 231-334-3061
Michael Hartigan, supt. Fax 334-6255
www.glenlake.k12.mi.us
Glen Lake JSHS 400/7-12
3375 W Burdickville Rd 49664 231-334-3061
Konrad Molter, prin. Fax 334-6295

**Marcellus, Cass, Pop. 1,184**
Marcellus Community SD — 700/K-12
PO Box 48 49067 — 269-646-7655
Nanette Pauley, supt. — Fax 646-2700
www.marcelluscs.org/
Marcellus JSHS — 300/7-12
PO Box 48 49067 — 269-646-5081
Lynn Wagner, prin. — Fax 646-5021
Other Schools – See Decatur

---

Howardsville Christian S — 200/PK-12
53441 Bent Rd 49067 — 269-646-9367
Dave Nelson, admin. — Fax 646-7006

**Marine City, Saint Clair, Pop. 4,184**
East China SD
Supt. — See East China
Marine City HS — 700/9-12
1085 Ward St 48039 — 810-676-1900
Suzanne Cybulla, prin. — Fax 676-1925
Marine City MS — 500/6-8
6373 King Rd 48039 — 810-676-1201
Catherine Woolman, prin. — Fax 676-1225
Riverview East HS — 100/Alt
6373 King Rd 48039 — 810-676-1280
Nina Reznich, prin. — Fax 676-1285

---

Cardinal Mooney HS — 200/9-12
660 S Water St 48039 — 810-765-8825
Jason Petrella, prin. — Fax 765-7164

**Marion, Osceola, Pop. 863**
Marion SD — 500/K-12
PO Box O 49665 — 231-743-2486
Mort Meier, supt. — Fax 743-2890
www.marion.k12.mi.us
Marion JSHS — 200/6-12
PO Box O 49665 — 231-743-2836
John Russell, prin. — Fax 743-9622

**Marlette, Sanilac, Pop. 1,847**
Marlette Community SD — 1,000/PK-12
6230 Euclid St 48453 — 989-635-7429
Sarah Barratt, supt. — Fax 635-7103
www.marlette.k12.mi.us
Marlette JSHS — 500/7-12
3051 Moore St 48453 — 989-635-4946
Kyle Wood, prin. — Fax 635-5300

**Marquette, Marquette, Pop. 20,996**
Marquette Area SD — 3,000/PK-12
1201 W Fair Ave 49855 — 906-225-4200
William Saunders, supt. — Fax 225-5340
www.mapsnet.org
Bothwell MS — 800/6-8
1200 Tierney St 49855 — 906-225-4262
Dan Gannon, prin. — Fax 225-4229
Marquette Alternative HS at Vandenboom — 100/Alt
1175 Erie Ave 49855 — 906-225-4321
Andrew Crunkleton, admin. — Fax 225-4312
Marquette HS — 1,000/9-12
1203 W Fair Ave 49855 — 906-225-5353
Jonathon Young, prin. — Fax 225-5370

---

Father Marquette MS — 100/5-8
414 W College Ave 49855 — 906-226-7912
Michael Hedges, prin. — Fax 225-9962
Marquette General Hospital — Post-Sec.
420 W Magnetic St 49855 — 906-225-3434
Northern Michigan University — Post-Sec.
1401 Presque Isle Ave 49855 — 906-227-1000

**Marshall, Calhoun, Pop. 6,978**
Calhoun ISD — 400/
17111 G Dr N 49068 — 269-781-5141
Terance Lunger, supt. — Fax 781-7071
www.calhounisd.org
Other Schools – See Battle Creek

Marshall SD — 2,300/PK-12
100 E Green St 49068 — 269-781-1250
Dr. Randy Davis, supt. — Fax 789-1813
www.marshall.k12.mi.us
Marshall HS — 700/9-12
701 N Marshall Ave 49068 — 269-781-1252
Scott Hutchins, prin. — Fax 781-5304
Marshall MS — 500/6-8
100 E Green St 49068 — 269-781-1251
David Turner, prin. — Fax 781-6621
Other Schools – See Albion

**Martin, Allegan, Pop. 398**
Martin SD — 600/PK-12
PO Box 241 49070 — 269-672-7194
Dr. David Harnish, supt. — Fax 672-7116
www.martinpublicschools.org
Martin JSHS — 200/7-12
PO Box 241 49070 — 269-672-5555
Dr. David Harnish, prin. — Fax 672-9263

**Marysville, Saint Clair, Pop. 9,889**
Marysville SD — 2,600/K-12
495 E Huron Blvd 48040 — 810-364-7731
Dr. Shawn Wightman, supt. — Fax 364-3150
www.marysvilleschools.us/
Marysville HS — 800/9-12
555 E Huron Blvd 48040 — 810-364-7161
Bill Farnsworth, prin. — Fax 364-8878
Marysville MS — 600/6-8
400 Collard Dr 48040 — 810-364-6336
Jay Schultz, prin. — Fax 364-4456

St. Clair County RESA — 50/
PO Box 1500 48040 — 810-364-8990
Dan DeGrow, supt. — Fax 364-7474
www.sccresa.org/
Career Technical Center — Vo/Tech
PO Box 1500 48040 — 810-455-1010

**Mason, Ingham, Pop. 8,111**
Ingham ISD — 200/
2630 W Howell Rd 48854 — 517-676-1051
Dr. Scott Koenigsknecht, supt. — Fax 676-1277
www.inghamisd.org
Capital Area Career Center — Vo/Tech
611 Hagadorn Rd 48854 — 517-244-1330
Jeanne Farina, prin. — Fax 676-3602

Mason SD — 3,000/K-12
400 S Cedar St 48854 — 517-676-2484
Ronald Drzewicki, supt. — Fax 676-6058
www.masonk12.net
Mason HS — 1,100/9-12
1001 S Barnes St 48854 — 517-676-9055
Lance Delbridge, prin. — Fax 244-6412
Mason MS — 700/6-8
235 Temple St 48854 — 517-676-6514
Daniel McConeghy, prin. — Fax 676-0287

**Mattawan, Van Buren, Pop. 1,954**
Mattawan Consolidated SD — 3,800/K-12
56720 Murray St 49071 — 269-668-3361
Dr. Robin Buchler, supt. — Fax 668-2372
www.mattawanschools.org
Mattawan HS — 1,200/9-12
56720 Murray St 49071 — 269-668-3361
Tim Eastman, prin. — Fax 668-8245
Mattawan MS — 1,000/6-8
56720 Murray St 49071 — 269-668-3361
Chip Schuman, prin. — Fax 668-3188

**Mayville, Tuscola, Pop. 933**
Mayville Community SD — 700/PK-12
6250 Fulton St 48744 — 989-843-6115
Barry Markwart, supt. — Fax 843-6988
www.mayville.k12.mi.us
Mayville HS — 300/9-12
6250 Fulton St 48744 — 989-843-6115
Barry Markwart, prin. — Fax 843-7208
Mayville MS — 100/7-8
6210 Fulton St 48744 — 989-843-6115
Barry Markwart, prin. — Fax 843-7209

**Melvindale, Wayne, Pop. 10,396**
Melvindale-Northern Allen Park SD — 2,800/K-12
18530 Prospect St 48122 — 313-389-3300
Cora Kelly, supt. — Fax 389-3312
www.melnap.k12.mi.us
Melvindale HS — 900/9-12
18656 Prospect St 48122 — 313-389-3320
Jason Hanna, prin. — Fax 389-2072
Strong MS — 600/6-8
3303 Oakwood Blvd 48122 — 313-389-3330
Donald Fish, prin. — Fax 389-2077

**Memphis, Saint Clair, Pop. 1,172**
Memphis Community SD — 700/PK-12
PO Box 201 48041 — 810-392-2151
Nancy Thomson, supt. — Fax 392-3614
www.memphisk12.org/
Memphis JSHS — 300/6-12
PO Box 201 48041 — 810-392-2186
Brad Gudme, prin. — Fax 392-2083

**Mendon, Saint Joseph, Pop. 857**
Mendon Community SD — 700/K-12
148 Kirby Rd 49072 — 269-496-9940
Roger Rathburn, supt. — Fax 496-8234
www.mendonschools.org
Mendon MSHS — 200/6-12
148 Kirby Rd 49072 — 269-496-8491
Marc Kramer, prin. — Fax 496-8234

**Menominee, Menominee, Pop. 8,500**
Menominee Area SD — 1,500/PK-12
1230 13th St 49858 — 906-863-9951
Terri Mileski, supt. — Fax 863-1171
www.menominee.k12.mi.us
Menominee HS — 500/9-12
2101 18th St 49858 — 906-863-7814
Michael Cattani, prin. — Fax 863-8883
Menominee JHS — 300/7-8
2101 18th St 49858 — 906-863-9929
Alison Granquist, admin. — Fax 863-8883

**Merrill, Saginaw, Pop. 771**
Merrill Community SD — 700/PK-12
431 W Alice St 48637 — 989-643-7261
Sarah Kettelhohn, supt. — Fax 643-5570
saginawmerrill.mi.schoolwebpages.com
Merrill Alternative Education — Alt
431 W Alice St 48637 — 989-643-7231
Todd Barraco, prin. — Fax 643-7942
Merrill HS — 200/9-12
431 W Alice St 48637 — 989-643-7231
Todd Barraco, prin. — Fax 643-7942
Merrill MS — 200/6-8
431 W Alice St 48637 — 989-643-7231
Todd Barraco, prin. — Fax 643-7942

**Mesick, Wexford, Pop. 390**
Mesick Consolidated SD — 700/K-12
PO Box 275 49668 — 231-885-1200
Scott Akom, supt. — Fax 885-1234
www.mesick.org
Mesick JSHS — 300/7-12
PO Box 275 49668 — 231-885-1201
Scott Morey, prin. — Fax 885-2554

**Michigan Center, Jackson, Pop. 4,596**
Michigan Center SD — 1,400/K-12
400 S State St 49254 — 517-764-5778
Scott Koziol, supt. — Fax 764-9607
www.mccardinals.org/
Michigan Center JSHS — 600/7-12
400 S State St 49254 — 517-764-1440
Lisa Falasco, prin. — Fax 764-3346

**Middleton, Gratiot**
Fulton SD — 1,100/PK-12
8060 Ely Hwy 48856 — 989-236-7300
Daymond Grifka, supt. — Fax 236-7660
fultonpirates.net
Fulton Alternative Education — 300/Alt
8060 Ely Hwy 48856 — 989-236-5130
Mike Myers, prin. — Fax 236-7301
Fulton HS — 200/9-12
8060 Ely Hwy 48856 — 989-236-7232
Paul Hungerford, prin. — Fax 236-7628
Fulton MS — 100/7-8
8060 Ely Hwy 48856 — 989-236-7232
Paul Hungerford, prin. — Fax 236-7628

**Middleville, Barry, Pop. 3,261**
Thornapple-Kellogg SD — 3,000/PK-12
10051 Green Lake Rd 49333 — 269-795-5521
Tom Enslen, supt. — Fax 795-5401
www.tkschools.org/
Thornapple-Kellogg HS — 900/9-12
3885 Bender Rd 49333 — 269-795-3394
Tony Petersen, prin. — Fax 795-5492
Thornapple-Kellogg MS — 700/6-8
10375 Green Lake Rd 49333 — 269-795-3349
Brian Balding, prin. — Fax 795-5455

**Midland, Midland, Pop. 41,135**
Bullock Creek SD — 1,900/K-12
1420 S Badour Rd 48640 — 989-631-9022
Shawn Hale, supt. — Fax 631-2882
www.bcreek.k12.mi.us
Bullock Creek HS — 600/9-12
1420 S Badour Rd 48640 — 989-631-2340
Todd Gorsuch, prin. — Fax 835-5467
Bullock Creek MS — 400/6-8
644 S Badour Rd 48640 — 989-631-9260
Curt Moses, prin. — Fax 832-4018

Midland SD — 7,700/K-12
600 E Carpenter St 48640 — 989-923-5001
Michael Sharrow, supt. — Fax 923-5003
www.midlandps.org
Dow HS — 1,300/9-12
3901 N Saginaw Rd 48640 — 989-923-5382
Pam Kastl, prin. — Fax 923-5301
Jefferson MS — 800/6-8
800 W Chapel Ln 48640 — 989-923-5873
Steve Poole, prin. — Fax 923-5800
Midland HS — 1,500/9-12
1301 Eastlawn Dr 48642 — 989-923-5181
Jeff Jaster, prin. — Fax 923-5100
Northeast MS — 800/6-8
1305 E Sugnet Rd 48642 — 989-923-5772
Dirk DeBoer, prin. — Fax 923-5780

---

Calvary Baptist Academy — 500/PK-12
6100 Perrine Rd 48640 — 989-832-3341
David Warren, prin. — Fax 832-7443
Davenport University — Post-Sec.
3555 E Patrick Rd 48642 — 989-835-5588
Midland Christian S — 100/PK-12
4417 W Wackerly St 48640 — 989-835-9881
Eric Robyn, hdmstr. — Fax 835-5201
Northwood University — Post-Sec.
4000 Whiting Dr 48640 — 989-837-4200

**Milan, Monroe, Pop. 5,683**
Milan Area SD — 2,500/K-12
100 Big Red Dr 48160 — 734-439-5050
Bryan Girbach, supt. — Fax 439-5083
www.milanareaschools.org/
Milan HS — 900/9-12
200 Big Red Dr 48160 — 734-439-5000
Ryan McMahon, prin. — Fax 439-5084
Milan MS — 600/6-8
920 North St 48160 — 734-439-5200
Shanna Spickart, prin. — Fax 439-5288

**Milford, Oakland, Pop. 6,058**
Huron Valley SD
Supt. — See Highland
Muir MS — 800/6-8
425 George St 48381 — 248-684-8060
Martin Lindberg, prin. — Fax 684-8068

---

West Highland Christian Academy — 100/K-12
1116 S Hickory Ridge Rd 48380 — 248-887-6698
Kevin Whitted, prin. — Fax 629-4267

**Millington, Tuscola, Pop. 1,059**
Millington Community SD — 1,100/K-12
8780 Dean Dr 48746 — 989-871-5227
Bruce Martin, supt. — Fax 871-5260
www.mcsdistrict.com
Millington Accelerated Learning Center — 50/Alt
8537 Gleason St 48746 — 989-871-5211
Roger Bearss, admin. — Fax 871-5249
Millington JSHS — 500/7-12
8780 Dean Dr 48746 — 989-871-5221
Stephen Bouvy, prin. — Fax 871-5244

**Mio, Oscoda, Pop. 1,791**
Mio-AuSable SD — 600/K-12
1110 W 8th St 48647 — 989-826-2401
James Gendernalik, supt. — Fax 826-2415
www.miok12.net
Mio-AuSable HS — 200/9-12
1110 W 8th St 48647 — 989-826-2481
James Gendernalik, prin. — Fax 826-2416
Mio-AuSable MS — 100/6-8
1110 W 8th St 48647 — 989-826-2481
James Gendernalik, prin. — Fax 826-2416

**Monroe, Monroe, Pop. 20,187**
Jefferson SD — 2,000/K-12
2400 N Dixie Hwy 48162 — 734-289-5550
Craig Haugen, supt. — Fax 289-5574
www.jeffersonschools.org

Jefferson HS 700/9-12
5707 Williams Rd 48162 734-289-5555
David Vensel, prin. Fax 289-5595
Jefferson MS 300/7-8
5102 N Stoney Creek Rd 48162 734-289-5565
Stephen Kinsland, prin. Fax 289-5596

Monroe County ISD 500/
1101 S Raisinville Rd 48161 734-242-5799
Stephen McNew, supt. Fax 242-0567
www.monroeisd.us/
Monroe County Middle College 100/Alt
1101 S Raisinville Rd 48161 734-242-5799
Robert Krueger, prin. Fax 242-0567

Monroe SD 6,300/PK-12
PO Box 733 48161 734-265-3000
Dr. Barry Martin, supt. Fax 265-3001
www.monroe.k12.mi.us
Monroe HS 1,900/9-12
901 Herr Rd 48161 734-265-3400
Sandra Kreps, prin. Fax 265-3401
Monroe MS 900/7-8
503 Washington St 48161 734-265-4000
Cindy Flynn, prin. Fax 265-4001
Orchard Center HS 200/Alt
1750 Oak St 48161 734-265-3700
Chantele Henry, prin. Fax 265-3701

---

Meadow Montessori S 200/PK-12
1670 S Raisinville Rd 48161 734-241-9496
Catharine Calder, head sch Fax 241-0829
Michigan College of Beauty Post-Sec.
1020 S Monroe St 48161 734-241-8877
Monroe County Community College Post-Sec.
1555 S Raisinville Rd 48161 734-242-7300
St. Mary HS 400/9-12
108 W Elm Ave 48162 734-241-7622
Jason Linster, prin. Fax 241-9042
St. Mary MS 200/5-8
151 N Monroe St 48162 734-241-3377
Sheena Zawistowicz, prin. Fax 241-0497

**Montague, Muskegon, Pop. 2,329**
Montague Area SD 1,300/PK-12
4882 Stanton Blvd 49437 231-893-1515
Jeffrey Johnson, supt. Fax 894-6586
www.mapsk12.org
Chisholm MS 300/6-8
4700 Stanton Blvd 49437 231-894-5617
James Perreault, prin. Fax 894-5728
Montague HS 400/9-12
4900 Stanton Blvd 49437 231-894-2661
Kevin Kruger, prin. Fax 893-0609

**Montrose, Genesee, Pop. 1,644**
Montrose Community SD 1,400/PK-12
PO Box 3129 48457 810-591-8800
Dr. Edward Graham Ph.D., supt. Fax 591-7268
www.montroseschools.org
Hill-McCloy HS 400/9-12
PO Box 3129 48457 810-591-8822
Linden Bo Moore, prin. Fax 591-7281
Kuehn-Haven MS 400/5-8
PO Box 3129 48457 810-591-8832
Rhonda Barber, prin. Fax 591-7282
Montrose Choice S 100/Alt
PO Box 3129 48457 810-591-8833
Linden Bo Moore, prin. Fax 591-7289

**Morenci, Lenawee, Pop. 2,192**
Morenci Area SD 700/PK-12
788 Coomer St 49256 517-458-7501
Michael McAran, supt. Fax 458-7821
www.morenci.k12.mi.us
Morenci MSHS 200/5-12
788 Coomer St 49256 517-458-7502
Kimberly Irish, prin. Fax 458-7146

**Morley, Mecosta, Pop. 490**
Morley Stanwood Community SD 1,000/K-12
4700 Northland Dr 49336 231-856-4392
Roger Cole, supt. Fax 856-4180
www.morleystanwood.org
Morley-Stanwood HS 400/9-12
4700 Northland Dr 49336 231-856-4444
James Nelson, prin. Fax 856-7012
Morley-Stanwood MS 300/6-8
4700 Northland Dr 49336 231-856-4550
Kim Colby, prin. Fax 856-0136

**Morrice, Shiawassee, Pop. 914**
Morrice Area SD 500/PK-12
111 E Mason 48857 517-625-3142
William Hath, supt. Fax 625-3866
www.morrice.k12.mi.us
Morrice JSHS 200/7-12
691 Purdy Ln 48857 517-625-3143
William Heath, prin. Fax 625-8935

**Mount Clemens, Macomb, Pop. 15,743**
Mount Clemens Community SD 900/PK-12
167 Cass Ave 48043 586-469-6100
Dr. William Pearson, supt. Fax 461-3799
www.mtcps.org
Mount Clemens HS 400/9-12
155 Cass Ave 48043 586-461-3400
Joseph Gibson, prin. Fax 469-7058
Mount Clemens MS 200/4-8
161 Cass Ave 48043 586-461-3300
James Wagner, prin. Fax 469-7066

**Mount Morris, Genesee, Pop. 2,972**
Beecher Community SD
Supt. — See Flint
Beecher HS 300/9-12
6255 Neff Rd 48458 810-591-9277
Diana Castle, prin. Fax 591-6911

Mount Morris Consolidated SD 2,000/K-12
12356 Walter St 48458 810-591-8760
Tricia Hill, supt. Fax 591-7469
www.mtmorrisschools.org
Johnson HS 600/9-12
8041 Neff Rd 48458 810-591-2370
Andrew Lintz, prin. Fax 591-3410
Mt. Morris Education & Community Center Alt
1000 E Mount Morris St 48458 810-591-4680
Mount Morris MS 500/6-8
12356 Walter St 48458 810-591-7100
Allen Peter, prin. Fax 591-7105

**Mount Pleasant, Isabella, Pop. 25,361**
Beal City SD 600/PK-12
3180 W Beal City Rd 48858 989-644-3901
William Chilman, supt. Fax 644-5847
www.bealcityschools.net
Beal City JSHS 300/7-12
3180 W Beal City Rd 48858 989-644-3944
Jeffrey Jackson, prin. Fax 644-5847
Beal City South Alternative HS Alt
3032 S Winn Rd 48858 989-773-9543
Jerry Ward, prin. Fax 773-9543

Mount Pleasant SD 3,500/K-12
720 N Kinney Ave 48858 989-775-2300
Michael Pung, supt. Fax 775-2309
www.mtpleasant.edzone.net
Mount Pleasant Area Technical Center Vo/Tech
1155 S Elizabeth St 48858 989-775-2210
Mary Kay Voeks, dir. Fax 775-2215
Mount Pleasant HS 1,100/9-12
1155 S Elizabeth St 48858 989-775-2200
Fax 775-2209
Oasis/W-A-Y Alternative Education S 100/Alt
3480 S Isabella Rd 48858 989-775-2290
Stacie Zeien, dir. Fax 772-3165
West IS 500/7-8
440 S Bradley St 48858 989-775-2220
Dana Calkins, prin. Fax 775-2229
Mount Pleasant Comm & Adult Education Adult
3480 S Isabella Rd 48858 989-775-2370
Mary Murphy, dir. Fax 773-2374

Shepherd SD
Supt. — See Shepherd
Odyssey MSHS 100/Alt
3441 S Wise Rd 48858 989-773-9473
Lou Ann Schmidt, prin. Fax 779-0429

---

Central Michigan University Post-Sec.
100 Warriner Hall 48859 989-774-4000
M.J. Murphy Beauty College Post-Sec.
201 W Broadway St 48858 989-772-2339
Sacred Heart Academy 200/7-12
316 E Michigan St 48858 989-772-1457
Mary Kay Yonker, prin. Fax 772-1707
Saginaw Chippewa Tribal College Post-Sec.
2274 Enterprise Dr 48858 989-775-4123

**Munising, Alger, Pop. 2,289**
Munising SD 600/K-12
810 State Highway M28 W 49862 906-387-2251
Pete Kelto, supt. Fax 387-5416
www.mps-up.com
Munising MSHS 300/6-12
810 State Highway M28 W 49862 906-387-2103
Peter Kelto, prin. Fax 387-5686

**Muskegon, Muskegon, Pop. 37,002**
Muskegon Area ISD 200/
630 Harvey St 49442 231-777-2637
Dr. John Severson, supt. Fax 767-7299
www.muskegonisd.org
Muskegon Area Career Tech Center Vo/Tech
200 Harvey St 49442 231-767-3600
Kyle Fiebig, prin. Fax 767-2692

Muskegon Heights SD 1,300/PK-12
2603 Leahy St 49444 231-830-3221
Steve Schiller, admin. Fax 830-3560
www.mhpsnet.org
Other Schools – See Muskegon Heights

Muskegon SD 3,400/PK-12
349 W Webster Ave 49440 231-720-2000
Jon Felske, supt. Fax 720-2050
www.mpsk12.net/
MCEC 200/Alt
571 E Apple Ave 49442 231-720-2530
Brad Perkins, prin. Fax 720-2593
Muskegon HS 1,100/9-12
80 W Southern Ave 49441 231-720-2800
Bradley Perkins, prin. Fax 720-2811
Muskegon MS 200/7-8
1150 Amity Ave 49442 231-720-3000
Paul Kurdziel, prin. Fax 720-3025

Oakridge SD 1,800/PK-12
275 S Wolf Lake Rd 49442 231-788-7100
Tom Livezey, supt. Fax 788-7114
www.oakridgeschools.org
Oakridge HS 500/9-12
5493 Hall Rd 49442 231-788-7300
Jason McVoy, prin. Fax 788-7314
Oakridge MS 300/7-8
251 S Wolf Lake Rd 49442 231-788-7400
Jason McVoy, prin. Fax 788-7414

Orchard View SD 2,400/PK-12
35 S Sheridan Dr 49442 231-760-1300
Jim Nielsen, supt. Fax 760-1323
www.orchardview.org
Orchard View HS 700/9-12
16 N Quarterline Rd 49442 231-760-1400
Dan Bolhuis, prin. Fax 760-1407
Orchard View MS 600/6-8
35 S Sheridan Dr 49442 231-760-1500
Ken Byard, prin. Fax 760-1506

Reeths-Puffer SD 3,700/PK-12
991 W Giles Rd 49445 231-744-4736
Steve Edwards, supt. Fax 744-9497
www.reeths-puffer.org
Reeths-Puffer HS 1,200/9-12
1545 Roberts Rd 49445 231-744-1647
Daniel Beckeman, prin. Fax 744-4796
Other Schools – See North Muskegon

---

Baker College of Muskegon Post-Sec.
1903 Marquette Ave 49442 231-777-5200
Muskegon Catholic Central HS 300/7-12
1145 W Laketon Ave 49441 231-755-2201
Allison Grinnell, prin. Fax 755-8615
Muskegon Community College Post-Sec.
221 S Quarterline Rd 49442 231-773-9131
Ross Medical Education Center Post-Sec.
950 W Norton Ave 49441 231-730-9531
Western Michigan Christian HS 300/7-12
455 E Ellis Rd 49441 231-799-9644
Doug Doty, prin. Fax 798-9018

**Muskegon Heights, Muskegon, Pop. 10,491**
Muskegon Heights SD
Supt. — See Muskegon
Muskegon Heights Academy 300/7-12
2441 Sanford St 49444 231-830-3700
Carla Laws, prin. Fax 830-3534

**Napoleon, Jackson, Pop. 1,230**
Napoleon Community SD 1,500/K-12
PO Box 308 49261 517-536-8667
James Graham, supt. Fax 536-8006
www.napoleonschools.org
Napoleon HS 500/9-12
PO Box 308 49261 517-536-8667
Patrick Dillon, prin. Fax 536-8007
Napoleon MS 400/6-8
PO Box 308 49261 517-536-8667
Chris Adams, prin. Fax 536-8005
Other Schools – See Jackson

**Negaunee, Marquette, Pop. 4,500**
Negaunee SD 1,400/PK-12
101 S Pioneer Ave 49866 906-475-4157
Dan Skewis, supt. Fax 475-5107
www.negauneeschools.org
Negaunee HS 400/9-12
500 W Arch St 49866 906-475-7861
Mark Marana, prin. Fax 475-7989
Negaunee MS 300/5-8
102 W Case St 49866 906-475-7866
Michael McCollum, prin. Fax 475-6408

**Newaygo, Newaygo, Pop. 1,944**
Newaygo SD 1,400/K-12
PO Box 820 49337 231-652-6984
Dr. Peggy Mathis, supt. Fax 652-6505
www.newaygo.net
Newaygo HS 500/9-12
PO Box 820 49337 231-652-1646
Jackie Knight, prin. Fax 652-3500
Newaygo MS 400/5-8
PO Box 820 49337 231-652-1285
Brad Reyburn, prin. Fax 652-9704

**New Baltimore, Macomb, Pop. 11,927**
Anchor Bay SD
Supt. — See Casco
Anchor Bay MS North 1,000/6-8
52805 Ashley Dr 48047 586-725-7373
Robin Stanton, prin. Fax 725-6760
Anchor Bay MS South 500/6-8
48650 Sugarbush Rd 48047 586-949-4510
Phil Latona, prin. Fax 949-4739
Compass Pointe 100/Alt
51510 Industrial Dr 48047 586-716-7862
Robert Tidd, coord. Fax 716-7864

**Newberry, Luce, Pop. 1,471**
Tahquamenon Area SD 600/PK-12
700 Newberry Ave 49868 906-293-3226
Dr. David Barry, supt. Fax 293-3709
www.taschools.org
Newberry HS 300/7-12
700 Newberry Ave 49868 906-293-3243
Clifford Fossitt, prin. Fax 293-3709

**New Boston, Wayne**
Huron SD 2,400/K-12
32044 Huron River Dr 48164 734-782-2441
Richard Naughton, supt. Fax 783-0338
www.huronschools.org
Huron HS 800/9-12
32044 Huron River Dr 48164 734-782-1436
Donovan Rowe, prin. Fax 783-1534
Renton JHS 600/6-8
31578 Huron River Dr 48164 734-782-2483
Kurt Mrocko, prin. Fax 783-0327

**New Buffalo, Berrien, Pop. 1,853**
New Buffalo Area SD 600/K-12
1112 E Clay St 49117 269-469-6010
Mark Westerburg, supt. Fax 469-3315
www.nbas.org/
New Buffalo HS 300/9-12
1112 E Clay St 49117 269-469-6001
Guy Reece, prin. Fax 469-6017
New Buffalo MS 100/6-8
1112 E Clay St 49117 269-469-6003
Wayne Butler, prin. Fax 469-6017

**New Haven, Macomb, Pop. 4,447**
New Haven Community SD 1,200/PK-12
PO Box 482000 48048 586-749-5123
Todd Robinson, supt. Fax 749-6307
newhaven.misd.net/
New Haven HS 300/9-12
PO Box 482000 48048 586-749-5104
Will Timmerman, prin. Fax 749-8460

**New Lothrop, Shiawassee, Pop. 573**
New Lothrop Area SD — 900/PK-12
PO Box 339 48460 — 810-638-5091
Anthony Berthiaume, supt. — Fax 638-7277
www.newlothrop.k12.mi.us
New Lothrop JSHS — 400/7-12
PO Box 339 48460 — 810-638-5054
Stephanie O'Dea, prin. — Fax 638-5057

**Newport, Monroe**
Airport Community SD
Supt. — See Carleton
Niedermeier Center for Education — 100/Alt
8400 Newport South Rd 48166 — 734-654-8694
Matthew Furtney, dir. — Fax 586-3342

---

Lutheran HS South — 100/9-12
8210 N Telegraph Rd 48166 — 734-586-8832
Rev. D. Lee Cullen, prin. — Fax 586-7006

**Niles, Berrien, Pop. 11,170**
Brandywine Community SD — 1,200/PK-12
1830 S 3rd St 49120 — 269-684-7150
Dr. John Jarpe, supt. — Fax 684-8998
www.brandywinebobcats.org
Bell Education Center — 50/Alt
1830 S 3rd St 49120 — 269-683-8805
Michelle Wruble, prin. — Fax 684-8998
Brandywine MSHS — 400/7-12
1700 Bell Rd 49120 — 269-683-4800
Patrick Weckel, prin. — Fax 683-1186

Niles Community SD — 3,800/PK-12
111 Spruce St 49120 — 269-683-0732
Dan Applegate Ed.D., supt. — Fax 684-6337
www.nilesschools.org
Cedar Lane Alternative S — 100/Alt
2301 Niles Buchanan Rd 49120 — 269-684-9554
John Fonash, prin. — Fax 684-9555
Niles HS — 800/9-12
1441 Eagle St 49120 — 269-683-2894
Robin Hadrick, prin. — Fax 684-9516
Niles New Tech Entrepreneurial Academy — 100/9-12
1441 Eagle St 49120 — 269-683-6031
Jerry Holtgren, dir. — Fax 683-1533
Ring Lardner MS — 500/7-8
801 N 17th St 49120 — 269-683-6610
Douglas Langmeyer, prin. — Fax 684-9524
Niles Adult Education — Adult
111 Spruce St 49120 — 269-684-4480
John Fonash, dir. — Fax 684-9548

**North Adams, Hillsdale, Pop. 473**
North Adams-Jerome SD — 400/K-12
4555 Knowles Rd 49262 — 517-287-4214
Carl Christenson, supt. — Fax 287-4722
www.najps.org
North Adams-Jerome JSHS — 300/6-12
4555 Knowles Rd 49262 — 517-287-4214
Tom George, prin. — Fax 287-4722

**North Branch, Lapeer, Pop. 1,023**
North Branch Area SD — 2,400/K-12
PO Box 3620 48461 — 810-688-3570
Thomas English, supt. — Fax 688-7010
www.nbbroncos.net
North Branch HS — 800/9-12
PO Box 3620 48461 — 810-688-3001
Mark Hiltunen, prin. — Fax 688-8057
North Branch MS — 400/7-8
PO Box 3620 48461 — 810-688-4431
Cindy Howe, prin. — Fax 688-4344
Quest HS, PO Box 3620 48461 — Alt
Mark Hiltunen, prin. — 810-688-3570

**North Muskegon, Muskegon, Pop. 3,727**
North Muskegon SD — 1,000/K-12
1600 Mills Ave 49445 — 231-719-4100
Dr. Curt Babcock, supt. — Fax 744-0739
www.nmps.net
North Muskegon HS — 300/9-12
1507 Mills Ave 49445 — 231-719-4110
Heidi Christiansen, prin. — Fax 719-4156
North Muskegon MS — 200/6-8
1507 Mills Ave 49445 — 231-719-4110
Heidi Christiansen, prin. — Fax 719-4156

Reeths-Puffer SD
Supt. — See Muskegon
Reeths-Puffer MS — 600/7-8
1911 W Giles Rd 49445 — 231-744-4721
Jennifer Anderson, prin. — Fax 744-6049

**Northport, Leelanau, Pop. 512**
Northport SD — 200/K-12
PO Box 188 49670 — 231-386-5153
Chris Parker, supt. — Fax 386-9838
www.northportps.org
Northport S — 200/K-12
PO Box 188 49670 — 231-386-5153
Chris Parker, supt. — Fax 386-9838

**Northville, Oakland, Pop. 5,889**
Northville SD — 7,100/K-12
501 W Main St 48167 — 248-349-3400
Mary Gallagher, supt. — Fax 347-6928
www.northvilleschools.org
Hillside MS — 800/6-8
775 N Center St 48167 — 248-344-8493
James Cracraft, prin. — Fax 334-8480
Meads Mill MS — 900/6-8
16700 Franklin Rd, — 248-344-8435
Brad O'Neill, prin. — Fax 334-1830
Northville HS — 2,200/9-12
45700 6 Mile Rd, — 248-344-8420
Anthony Koski, prin. — Fax 344-8497

**Norton Shores, Muskegon, Pop. 23,577**
Mona Shores SD — 3,800/K-12
121 Randall Rd 49441 — 231-780-4751
Greg Helmer, supt. — Fax 780-2099
www.monashores.net
Mona Shores HS — 1,300/9-12
1121 Seminole Rd 49441 — 231-780-4711
Jennifer Bustard, prin. — Fax 780-3634
Mona Shores MS — 900/6-8
1700 Woodside Rd 49441 — 231-759-8506
Doug Ammeraal, prin. — Fax 755-0514

**Norway, Dickinson, Pop. 2,807**
Norway-Vulcan Area SD — 700/PK-12
300 Section St 49870 — 906-563-9552
Louis Steigerwald, supt. — Fax 563-5169
www.norway.k12.mi.us
Norway HS — 200/9-12
300 Section St 49870 — 906-563-9542
Joseph Tinti, prin. — Fax 563-8708
Vulcan MS, 300 Section St 49870 — 200/5-8
Joseph Tinti, prin. — 906-563-9563

**Novi, Oakland, Pop. 54,165**
Novi Community SD — 6,200/K-12
25345 Taft Rd 48374 — 248-449-1200
Dr. Steve Matthews, supt. — Fax 449-1219
www.novi.k12.mi.us
Novi HS — 2,000/9-12
24062 Taft Rd 48375 — 248-449-1500
Nicole Carter, prin. — Fax 449-1519
Novi MS — 1,100/7-8
49000 W 11 Mile Rd 48374 — 248-449-1600
Stephanie Schriner, prin. — Fax 449-1619
Novi Adult Education — Adult
49000 W 11 Mile Rd 48374 — 248-449-1717
Linda Cianferra, prin. — Fax 449-1719

---

Detroit Catholic Central HS — 1,000/9-12
27225 Wixom Rd 48374 — 248-596-3810
Fr. Dennis Noelke, prin. — Fax 596-3811
Franklin Road Christian S — 300/K-12
40800 W 13 Mile Rd 48377 — 248-668-7100
Daniel Robinson, admin. — Fax 668-7101
The Art Institute of Michigan — Post-Sec.
28125 Cabot Dr Ste 120 48377 — 248-675-3800

**Oakland, Oakland**
Lake Orion Community SD
Supt. — See Lake Orion
Oakview MS — 600/6-8
917 Lake George Rd 48363 — 248-693-0321
Sarah Manzo, prin. — Fax 693-5419

**Oak Park, Oakland, Pop. 28,448**
Berkley SD — 4,300/K-12
14700 Lincoln St 48237 — 248-837-8000
Dennis McDavid, supt. — Fax 544-5835
www.berkleyschools.org
Other Schools – See Berkley

Ferndale SD
Supt. — See Ferndale
Center for Advanced Studies & the Arts — 11-12
23561 Rosewood St 48237 — 248-586-8860
Bill James, dir. — Fax 414-6508

Oak Park SD — 3,700/K-12
13900 Granzon St 48237 — 248-336-7700
Dr. Daveda Colbert, supt. — Fax 336-7738
www.oakparkschools.org
NOVA Discipline Academy — 100/Alt
22180 Parklawn St 48237 — 248-336-7650
Derek Faulk, admin.
Oak Park Alternative Education Center — 400/Alt
12901 Albany St 48237 — 248-291-6722
Harry Bautista, prin. — Fax 291-6724
Oak Park Freshman Institute — 500/9-9
22180 Parklawn St 48237 — 248-336-7780
Pam Vermiglio, prin. — Fax 336-7781
Oak Park Preparatory Academy — 500/7-8
22180 Parklawn St 48237 — 248-336-7780
Nickolus South, prin. — Fax 336-7738
Oak Park SHS — 1,000/10-12
13701 Oak Park Blvd 48237 — 248-336-7740
Kwame Stephens, prin. — Fax 336-7758

---

Beth Jacob School for Girls — 300/K-12
14390 W 10 Mile Rd 48237 — 248-544-9070
Lawton Career Institute — Post-Sec.
20820 Greenfield Rd 48237 — 248-569-7559
Yeshiva Gedolah of Greater Detroit — Post-Sec.
24600 Greenfield Rd 48237 — 248-968-3360
Yeshivah Gedolah HS — 100/9-12
24600 Greenfield Rd 48237 — 248-968-3360
Rabbi Mordechai Gold, prin. — Fax 968-8613

**Okemos, Ingham, Pop. 20,807**
Okemos SD — 3,900/K-12
4406 Okemos Rd 48864 — 517-706-5010
Catherine Ash Ph.D., supt. — Fax 349-6235
www.okemosschools.net/
Chippewa MS — 600/7-8
4000 Okemos Rd 48864 — 517-706-4800
Jody Noble, prin. — Fax 347-9824
Okemos HS — 1,300/9-12
2800 Jolly Rd 48864 — 517-706-4900
Christine Sermak, prin. — Fax 351-2850

**Olivet, Eaton, Pop. 1,574**
Olivet Community SD — 1,500/K-12
255 1st St 49076 — 269-749-9129
David Campbell, supt. — Fax 749-9701
www.olivetschools.org
Olivet HS — 500/9-12
255 1st St 49076 — 269-749-3671
Tim Volovsek, prin. — Fax 749-4560
Olivet MS — 600/4-8
255 1st St 49076 — 269-749-9953
Steven Stierley, prin. — Fax 749-9701

---

Olivet College — Post-Sec.
320 S Main St 49076 — 269-749-7000

**Onaway, Presque Isle, Pop. 861**
Onaway Area SD — 700/K-12
4549 M 33 49765 — 989-733-4950
Rod Fullerton, supt. — Fax 733-8612
www.onawayschools.com/
Onaway HS — 200/9-12
4549 M 33 49765 — 989-733-4800
Marty Mix, prin. — Fax 733-4899
Onaway MS — 200/6-8
4549 M 33 49765 — 989-733-4850
Marty Mix, prin. — Fax 733-4899

**Onekama, Manistee, Pop. 404**
Onekama Consolidated SD — 400/K-12
5016 Main St 49675 — 231-889-4251
Kevin Hughes, supt. — Fax 889-3720
ocs.manistee.org
Onekama MSHS — 200/6-12
5016 Main St 49675 — 231-889-5521
Gina Hagen, prin. — Fax 889-9567

**Onsted, Lenawee, Pop. 906**
Onsted Community SD — 1,500/K-12
10109 Slee Rd 49265 — 517-467-2173
Mark Haag, supt. — Fax 467-5600
www.onsted.k12.mi.us
Onsted HS — 500/9-12
10109 Slee Rd 49265 — 517-467-2171
Steve Head, prin. — Fax 467-5602
Onsted MS — 400/6-8
10109 Slee Rd 49265 — 517-467-2168
Damien Hiram, prin. — Fax 467-5603

**Ontonagon, Ontonagon, Pop. 1,473**
Ontonagon Area SD — 200/K-12
701 Parker Ave 49953 — 906-813-0614
James Bobula, supt. — Fax 813-0615
www.oasd.k12.mi.us
Ontonagon Area S — 200/K-12
701 Parker Ave 49953 — 906-813-0614
James Bobula, admin. — Fax 813-0615

**Orchard Lake, Oakland**

---

St. Marys Preparatory HS — 500/9-12
3535 Indian Trl 48324 — 248-683-0530
Cormac Lynn, hdmstr. — Fax 683-1740
SS. Cyril and Methodius Seminary — Post-Sec.
3535 Indian Trl 48324 — 248-683-0310

**Ortonville, Oakland, Pop. 1,423**
Brandon SD — 2,800/PK-12
1025 S Ortonville Rd 48462 — 248-627-1800
Dr. Matthew Outlaw, supt. — Fax 627-4533
www.brandonschooldistrict.org
Brandon HS — 1,200/9-12
1025 S Ortonville Rd 48462 — 248-627-1820
Daniel Stevens, prin. — Fax 627-5628
Brandon MS — 500/7-8
609 S Ortonville Rd 48462 — 248-627-1830
Tina Chambers, prin. — Fax 627-7201

**Oscoda, Iosco, Pop. 877**
Oscoda Area SD — 500/K-12
3550 E River Rd 48750 — 989-739-2033
Scott Moore, supt. — Fax 739-2325
www.oscodaschools.org
Oscoda Area HS — 400/7-12
3550 E River Rd 48750 — 989-739-9121
Terence Allison, prin. — Fax 739-1688

**Otisville, Genesee, Pop. 856**
LakeVille Community SD — 1,600/PK-12
11107 Washburn Rd 48463 — 810-591-3980
Vickie Luoma, supt. — Fax 591-6538
www.lakevilleschools.org/
Lakeville HS — 500/9-12
11107 Washburn Rd 48463 — 810-591-4050
Mary Haslinger, prin. — Fax 591-3961
Lakeville MS — 400/6-8
11107 Washburn Rd 48463 — 810-591-3945
Kelli-Ann Fazer, prin. — Fax 591-6632

**Otsego, Allegan, Pop. 3,879**
Otsego SD — 2,300/PK-12
400 Sherwood St 49078 — 269-692-6066
Jeffrey Haase, supt. — Fax 692-6074
www.otsegops.org
Otsego HS — 700/9-12
550 Washington St 49078 — 269-692-6166
Herve Dardis, prin. — Fax 692-6188
Otsego MS — 500/6-8
540 Washington St 49078 — 269-692-6199
Melissa Koenig, prin. — Fax 692-6228
West Campus HS — 100/Alt
570 Washington St 49078 — 269-692-6166
Herve Dardis, prin. — Fax 692-6188

---

Otsego Christian Academy — 50/PK-10
247 E Allegan St 49078 — 269-694-6738
Lydia Hutchens, admin.

**Ottawa Lake, Monroe**
Whiteford Agricultural SD — 700/K-12
6655 Consear Rd 49267 — 734-856-1443
Valerie Orr, supt. — Fax 854-6463
www.whiteford.k12.mi.us
Whiteford HS — 300/9-12
6655 Consear Rd 49267 — 734-856-1443
Kelli Tuller, prin. — Fax 856-2564
Whiteford MS — 200/6-8
6655 Consear Rd 49267 — 734-856-1443
Kelli Tuller, prin. — Fax 856-2564

**Owendale, Huron, Pop. 236**
Owendale-Gagetown Area SD 200/K-12
7166 E Main St 48754 989-678-4261
Terri Falkenberg, supt. Fax 678-4284
www.owengage.org/
Owendale-Gagetown JSHS 100/6-12
7166 E Main St 48754 989-678-4141
Terri Falkenberg, prin. Fax 678-0920

**Owosso, Shiawassee, Pop. 14,957**
Owosso SD 3,400/PK-12
PO Box 340 48867 989-723-8131
Andrea Tuttle Ed.D., supt. Fax 723-7777
www.owosso.k12.mi.us
Lincoln HS 100/Alt
645 Alger Ave 48867 989-725-2839
Steve Irelan, prin. Fax 729-6706
Owosso HS 1,000/9-12
765 E North St 48867 989-723-8231
Jeff Phillips, prin. Fax 729-5600
Owosso MS 700/6-8
219 N Water St 48867 989-723-3460
Rich Collins, prin. Fax 729-5760

---

Baker College of Owosso Post-Sec.
1020 S Washington St 48867 989-729-3370

**Oxford, Oakland, Pop. 3,399**
Oxford Community SD 5,000/PK-12
10 N Washington St 48371 248-969-5000
Tim Throne, supt. Fax 969-5016
www.oxfordschools.org
Oxford Bridges HS Alt
1420 E Lakeville Rd 48371 248-969-1800
Aletha Vanloozen, prin. Fax 969-1840
Oxford Crossroads Alternative S Alt
810 James Hunt Dr 48371 248-969-1887
Shelly Chapman, admin.
Oxford HS 1,400/9-12
745 N Oxford Rd 48371 248-969-5100
Todd Dunckley, prin. Fax 969-5145
Oxford MS 1,000/6-8
1420 E Lakeville Rd 48371 248-969-1800
Dacia Beazley, prin. Fax 969-1840
Oxford Schools Early College 9-12
176 S Washington St 48371 248-969-5194
Andrew Hulbert, prin. Fax 886-9116

**Painesdale, Houghton**
Adams Township SD 400/K-12
PO Box 37 49955 906-482-0599
Tim Keteri, supt. Fax 487-5999
www.adams.k12.mi.us
Jeffers HS 200/7-12
PO Box 37 49955 906-482-0580
Tim Keteri, admin. Fax 487-5999

**Paradise, Chippewa**
Whitefish Township Community SD 50/K-12
PO Box 58 49768 906-492-3353
Dr. Ann Vayre, supt. Fax 492-3254
whitefish.eup.k12.mi.us/
Whitefish Township S 50/K-12
PO Box 58 49768 906-492-3353
Dr. Ann Vayre, prin. Fax 492-3254

**Parchment, Kalamazoo, Pop. 1,738**
Parchment SD 1,700/PK-12
520 N Orient St 49004 269-488-1050
Matthew Miller, supt. Fax 488-1060
www.parchmentschools.org
Parchment HS 500/9-12
1916 E G Ave 49004 269-488-1100
Scott Karaptian, prin. Fax 488-1110
Parchment MS 400/6-8
307 N Riverview Dr 49004 269-488-1200
George Stamas, prin. Fax 488-1210
Other Schools – See Kalamazoo

**Parma, Jackson, Pop. 755**
Western SD 2,900/PK-12
1400 S Dearing Rd 49269 517-841-8100
Michael Smajda, supt. Fax 841-8801
www.wsdpanthers.org
Western HS 900/9-12
1400 S Dearing Rd 49269 517-841-8200
Susan VanRiper, prin. Fax 841-8282
Western MS 700/6-8
1400 S Dearing Rd 49269 517-841-8300
Ryan Tripp, prin. Fax 841-8803
Other Schools – See Jackson

**Paw Paw, Van Buren, Pop. 3,443**
Paw Paw SD 2,300/K-12
119 Johnson Rd 49079 269-657-8800
Anthony Habra, supt. Fax 657-7292
www.ppps.org
Cedar Street Comm & Family Center Alt
555 Cedar St 49079 269-657-8831
Beth Davis, prin. Fax 657-8836
Michigan Avenue Academy 100/Alt
600 E Michigan Ave 49079 269-657-8831
Beth Davis, prin. Fax 657-7411
Paw Paw HS 700/9-12
30609 E Red Arrow Hwy 49079 269-657-8840
Michael Dahlinger, prin. Fax 655-0009
Paw Paw MS 500/6-8
313 W Michigan Ave 49079 269-657-8870
Jerry McDaniel, prin. Fax 657-5011

**Peck, Sanilac, Pop. 624**
Peck Community SD 500/K-12
222 E Lapeer St 48466 810-378-5171
Ryle Kiser, supt. Fax 378-5116
www.peck.k12.mi.us
Peck JSHS 200/7-12
222 E Lapeer St 48466 810-378-5501
Ryle Kiser, prin. Fax 378-5116

**Pellston, Emmet, Pop. 782**
Pellston SD 600/K-12
172 Park St 49769 231-539-8682
Monique Dean, supt. Fax 539-8838
www.pellstonschools.org/
Pellston MSHS 400/6-12
172 Park St 49769 231-539-8801
Enos Bacon, prin. Fax 539-8110

**Pentwater, Oceana, Pop. 845**
Pentwater SD 300/K-12
600 Park St 49449 231-869-4100
Mary Marshall, supt. Fax 869-4535
www.pentwater.k12.mi.us
Pentwater S 300/K-12
600 Park St 49449 231-869-4100
Mary Marshall, prin. Fax 869-4535

**Perry, Shiawassee, Pop. 2,154**
Perry SD 1,400/PK-12
2665 W Britton Rd 48872 517-625-3108
Mike Foster, supt. Fax 625-6256
www.goperry.org
Perry HS 500/9-12
2555 W Britton Rd 48872 517-625-3104
Don Beck, prin. Fax 625-0012
Perry MS 400/5-8
2775 W Britton Rd 48872 517-625-6196
Matt Schmidtfranz, prin. Fax 625-0120

**Petersburg, Monroe, Pop. 1,129**
Summerfield SD 700/K-12
17555 Ida West Rd 49270 734-279-1035
John Hewitt, supt. Fax 279-1448
www.summerfield.k12.mi.us
Summerfield JSHS 200/7-12
17555 Ida West Rd 49270 734-279-1012
Scott Leach, prin. Fax 279-1018

**Petoskey, Emmet, Pop. 5,571**
Petoskey SD 2,900/K-12
1130 Howard St 49770 231-348-2100
Dr. John Scholten Ed.D., supt. Fax 348-2342
www.petoskeyschools.org
Petoskey HS 1,000/9-12
1500 Hill St 49770 231-348-2160
Mandy Stewart, prin. Fax 348-2214
Petoskey MS 700/6-8
801 Northmen Dr 49770 231-348-2150
Jon Wilcox, prin. Fax 348-2234

---

North Central Michigan College Post-Sec.
1515 Howard St 49770 231-348-6600

**Pickford, Chippewa**
Pickford SD 400/K-12
333 S Pleasant St 49774 906-647-6285
Angela Nettleton, supt. Fax 647-3706
pickford.eup.k12.mi.us/
Pickford S 200/K-12
333 S Pleasant St 49774 906-647-4028
Angela Nettleton, prin. Fax 647-3706
Other Schools – See Kincheloe

**Pigeon, Huron, Pop. 1,203**
Elkton-Pigeon-Bay Port Laker SD 900/PK-12
6136 Pigeon Rd 48755 989-453-4600
Robert Smith, supt. Fax 453-4609
www.lakerschools.org
Laker HS 300/9-12
6136 Pigeon Rd 48755 989-453-4600
Brian Keim, prin. Fax 453-4615
Laker MS 200/6-8
6136 Pigeon Rd 48755 989-453-4600
Brian Keim, prin. Fax 453-4609

**Pinckney, Livingston, Pop. 2,402**
Pinckney Community SD 3,700/K-12
2130 E M 36 48169 810-225-3900
Richard Todd M.A., supt. Fax 225-3905
www.pinckneyschools.org
Pathfinder S 700/7-8
2100 E M 36 48169 810-225-5200
Eric Ray, prin. Fax 225-5205
Pinckney Community HS 1,500/9-12
10255 Dexter Pinckney Rd 48169 810-225-5500
Dr. James Darga, prin. Fax 225-5505

**Pinconning, Bay, Pop. 1,286**
Pinconning Area SD 1,500/PK-12
605 W 5th St 48650 989-308-0500
Michael Vieau, supt. Fax 879-4705
www.pasd.org/
Pinconning Area HS 500/9-12
605 W 5th St 48650 989-308-0503
Tim Hoffman, prin. Fax 879-7258
Pinconning Area MS 300/6-8
605 W 5th St 48650 989-308-0503
Tim Hoffman, prin. Fax 879-7258

**Pittsford, Hillsdale**
Pittsford Area SD 700/K-12
9304 Hamilton Rd 49271 517-523-3481
Deanna Edens, supt. Fax 523-3467
pittsfordk12.org
Pittsford JSHS 300/7-12
9304 Hamilton Rd 49271 517-523-3481
T.G. Cook, prin. Fax 523-2059

**Plainwell, Allegan, Pop. 3,755**
Plainwell Community SD 2,700/PK-12
600 School Dr 49080 269-685-5823
Susan Wakefield, supt. Fax 685-1108
www.plainwellschools.org
Plainwell HS 800/9-12
684 Starr Rd 49080 269-685-9554
Dr. Jeremy Wright, prin. Fax 685-9064
Plainwell MS 600/6-8
720 Brigham St 49080 269-685-5813
Tasia Stamos, prin. Fax 685-2099
Renaissance HS 100/Alt
422 Acorn St 49080 269-685-1573
Tammy Glupker, prin. Fax 685-1564

**Plymouth, Wayne, Pop. 8,997**
Plymouth-Canton Community SD 18,000/PK-12
454 S Harvey St 48170 734-416-2700
Dr. Michael Meissen, supt. Fax 416-4932
www.pccsk12.com
East MS 800/6-8
1042 S Mill St 48170 734-416-4950
Scott Burek, prin. Fax 416-4949
Pioneer MS 900/6-8
46081 Ann Arbor Rd W 48170 734-416-2770
Kevin Rhein, prin. Fax 416-7569
Starkweather Academy 200/Alt
39750 Joy Rd 48170 734-416-4901
Kevin Lane, coord. Fax 416-6031
West MS 900/6-8
44401 W Ann Arbor Trl 48170 734-416-7550
Clinton Smiley, prin. Fax 416-7648
Other Schools – See Canton

---

Metropolitan SDA Jr Academy 50/K-10
15585 N Haggerty Rd 48170 734-420-4044
Craig Morgan, prin. Fax 420-3710
Moody Theological Seminary Post-Sec.
41550 E Ann Arbor Trl 48170 734-207-9581

**Pontiac, Oakland, Pop. 57,635**
Oakland ISD
Supt. — See Waterford
Oakland Technical Campus NE Vo/Tech
1371 N Perry St 48340 248-451-2700
Paul Galbenski, dean Fax 451-2720

Pontiac SD 4,500/PK-12
47200 Woodward Ave 48342 248-451-6800
Kelley Williams, supt. Fax 451-6890
www.pontiac.k12.mi.us
International Technology Academy Vo/Tech
125 W Montcalm St 48342 248-451-7950
Suzanne Kavanaugh, prin. Fax 451-7963
Pontiac HS 1,600/10-12
1051 Arlene Ave 48340 248-451-7300
Burdena Johnson, prin. Fax 451-7321
Pontiac MS 700/7-9
1275 N Perry St 48340 248-451-8010
Shana Jackson, prin. Fax 451-8034

---

Dorsey School of Business Post-Sec.
440 N Telegraph Rd 48341 248-333-1814
Notre Dame Marist Acad - Middle Division 200/6-8
1300 Giddings Rd 48340 248-373-5371
Jill Mistretta, prin. Fax 373-4707
Notre Dame Preparatory HS 700/9-12
1300 Giddings Rd 48340 248-373-5300
Rev. Joseph Hindelang, prin. Fax 373-8024
Oakland County Health Division Post-Sec.
1200 N Telegraph Rd 48341 248-858-1832

**Portage, Kalamazoo, Pop. 44,979**
Kalamazoo RESA 300/
1819 E Milham Ave 49002 269-250-9200
David Campbell, supt. Fax 250-9205
www.kresa.org
Other Schools – See Kalamazoo

Portage SD 8,300/K-12
8107 Mustang Dr 49002 269-323-5000
Mark T. Bielang, supt. Fax 323-5001
www.portageps.org
Northern HS 1,300/9-12
1000 Idaho Ave 49024 269-323-5400
Jim French, prin. Fax 323-5490
North MS 600/6-8
5808 Oregon Ave 49024 269-323-5700
Travis Thomsen, prin. Fax 323-5790
Portage Central HS 1,300/9-12
8135 S Westnedge Ave 49002 269-323-5200
Eric Alburtus, prin. Fax 323-5290
Portage Central MS 700/6-8
8305 S Westnedge Ave 49002 269-323-5600
Chuck Haskin, prin. Fax 323-5690
Portage Community HS Alt
1010 W Milham Ave 49024 269-323-6769
Clint Wagner, prin. Fax 323-6790
West MS 700/6-8
7145 Moorsbridge Rd 49024 269-323-5800
Denny Roehm, prin. Fax 323-5890

---

Chic University of Cosmetology Post-Sec.
6091 Constitution Blvd 49024 269-329-3333
Wright Beauty Academy Post-Sec.
6666 Lovers Ln 49002 269-321-8708

**Port Huron, Saint Clair, Pop. 29,088**
Port Huron Area SD 9,300/PK-12
PO Box 5013 48061 810-984-3101
James Cain, supt. Fax 984-6606
www.phasd.us/
Central MS 900/6-8
200 32nd St 48060 810-984-6533
Bethany Davis, prin. Fax 989-2709
Holland Woods MS 600/6-8
1617 Holland Ave 48060 810-984-6548
Ronnie Belle, prin. Fax 989-2713
Port Huron HS 1,500/9-12
2215 Court St 48060 810-984-2611
Michael Palmer, prin. Fax 984-6559
Port Huron Northern HS 1,400/9-12
1799 Krafft Rd 48060 810-984-2671
Charles Mossett, prin. Fax 984-2747
Harrison Center Adult
55 15th St 48060 810-455-0029
Gloria Henry, prin. Fax 455-0047
Other Schools – See Fort Gratiot

---

Baker College of Port Huron Post-Sec.
3403 Lapeer Rd 48060 810-985-7000
Port Huron Hospital Post-Sec.
1221 Pine Grove Ave 48060 810-987-5000
Ross Medical Education Center Post-Sec.
2887 Krafft Rd Ste 700 48060 810-982-0454
St. Clair County Community College Post-Sec.
PO Box 5015 48061 810-984-3881

**Portland, Ionia, Pop. 3,841**
Portland SD 2,000/K-12
1100 Ionia Rd 48875 517-647-4161
Charles Dumas, supt. Fax 647-2975
portland.schooldesk.net
Portland HS 600/9-12
1100 Ionia Rd 48875 517-647-2981
Christine Rockey, prin. Fax 647-1791
Portland MS 500/6-8
745 Storz St 48875 517-647-2985
Kevin Robydek, prin. Fax 647-2820

---

St. Patrick S 400/PK-12
122 N West St 48875 517-647-7551
Randy Hodge, prin. Fax 647-4545

**Posen, Presque Isle, Pop. 228**
Posen Consolidated SD 9 300/K-12
PO Box 187 49776 989-766-2573
Dr. John Palmer, supt. Fax 766-2519
www.posen.k12.mi.us
Posen Consolidated JSHS 100/7-12
PO Box 187 49776 989-766-2471
Dr. John Palmer, prin. Fax 766-2519

**Potterville, Eaton, Pop. 2,560**
Potterville SD 900/K-12
420 N High St 48876 517-645-2662
Timothy Donahue, supt. Fax 645-0392
www.pps.k12.mi.us
CAP Adult and Alternative Education Alt
420 N High St 48876 517-645-4792
Cathleen Weaver, prin. Fax 645-0390
Potterville HS 300/9-12
422 N High St 48876 517-645-7609
Julie Klomp, prin. Fax 645-0177
Potterville MS 300/5-8
424 N High St 48876 517-645-4777
Nathan Leale, prin. Fax 645-0091

**Powers, Menominee, Pop. 422**
North Central Area SD
Supt. — See Hermansville
North Central JSHS 200/7-12
PO Box 601 49874 906-497-5226
Bruce Tapio, prin. Fax 497-5066

**Quincy, Branch, Pop. 1,637**
Quincy Community SD 1,300/PK-12
1 Educational Pkwy 49082 517-639-7141
Craig Artist, supt. Fax 639-4273
www.quincyschools.org
Quincy HS 400/9-12
18 Colfax St 49082 517-639-9245
David Spalding, prin. Fax 639-3701
Quincy MS 400/5-8
32 Fulton St 49082 517-639-4201
Penny Brockway, prin. Fax 639-3701

**Rapid River, Delta**
Rapid River SD 400/K-12
10070 US Highway 2 49878 906-474-6411
Jay Kulbertis, supt. Fax 474-9903
www.rapidriver.k12.mi.us
Rapid River JSHS 200/6-12
10070 US Highway 2 49878 906-474-6411
William Warning, prin. Fax 474-9883

**Ravenna, Muskegon, Pop. 1,203**
Ravenna SD 1,100/PK-12
12322 Stafford St 49451 231-853-2231
John Van Loon, supt. Fax 853-2193
www.ravennaschools.org
Ravenna HS 300/9-12
2766 S Ravenna Rd 49451 231-853-2218
Steven Anderson, prin. Fax 853-6981
Ravenna MS 300/5-8
2700 S Ravenna Rd 49451 231-853-2268
Mindy Lynch, prin. Fax 853-2629

**Ray, Macomb**

---

Austin Catholic HS 9-12
24125 26 Mile Rd 48096 586-749-7900
Janel Coppens, prin. Fax 749-5217

**Reading, Hillsdale, Pop. 1,073**
Reading Community SD 800/K-12
PO Box 330 49274 517-283-2166
Chuck North, supt. Fax 283-3519
www.readingrangers.org
Owens JSHS 400/7-12
301 Chestnut St 49274 517-283-2142
Kurt Stump, prin. Fax 283-3758

**Redford, Wayne, Pop. 51,100**
Redford Union SD 2,400/K-12
17715 Brady 48240 313-242-6000
Dr. Sarena Shivers, supt. Fax 242-6025
www.redfordu.k12.mi.us
Hilbert MS 700/6-8
26440 Puritan 48239 313-242-4000
Andrew Christopherson, prin. Fax 242-4005
Redford Union HS 1,000/9-12
17711 Kinloch 48240 313-242-4200
Judy Nachman, prin. Fax 242-4205
Veritas Alternative Ed Alt
17715 Brady 48240 313-242-3520
Katy Jain, coord. Fax 242-6060

South Redford SD 3,200/PK-12
26141 Schoolcraft 48239 313-535-4000
Brian Galdes, supt. Fax 535-1059
www.southredford.org
Pierce MS 800/6-8
25605 Orangelawn 48239 313-937-8880
Christine Hofer, prin. Fax 937-9486
SOAR Academic Institute Alt
26255 Schoolcraft 48239 313-535-4000
Matt Daly, coord.
Thurston HS 1,100/9-12
26255 Schoolcraft 48239 313-242-0600
William Simms, prin. Fax 592-0740

---

Concordia Lutheran S - South Campus 50/5-8
9600 Leverne 48239 313-937-2233
David Kusch, prin. Fax 937-2173

**Reed City, Osceola, Pop. 2,371**
Reed City Area SD 1,500/K-12
225 W Church Ave 49677 231-832-2201
Timothy Webster, supt. Fax 832-2202
www.reedcity.k12.mi.us
Reed City HS 500/9-12
225 W Church Ave 49677 231-832-2224
Monty Price, prin. Fax 832-2501
Reed City MS 400/6-8
233 W Church Ave 49677 231-832-6174
Dean McGuire, prin. Fax 832-6180

**Reese, Tuscola, Pop. 1,450**
Reese SD 900/PK-12
PO Box 389 48757 989-868-9864
Keith Wetters, supt. Fax 868-9570
www.reese.k12.mi.us/
Reese HS 400/9-12
PO Box 389 48757 989-868-4191
Brian Galsterer, prin. Fax 868-4091
Reese MS 300/6-8
PO Box 389 48757 989-868-4191
Dave Hurst, prin. Fax 868-4091

**Remus, Mecosta**
Chippewa Hills SD 1,900/PK-12
3226 Arthur Rd 49340 989-967-2000
Dr. Michael Bob Grover, supt. Fax 967-2009
www.chsd.us
Chippewa Hills HS 600/9-12
3226 Arthur Rd 49340 989-967-2100
Michelle Newman, prin. Fax 967-2109
Chippewa Hills IS 300/7-8
3102 Arthur Rd 49340 989-967-2200
Dr. James Russell, prin. Fax 967-2209
Mosaic S 100/Alt
350 E Wheatland Ave 49340 989-967-8150
Dawn Hawley, prin. Fax 967-8385

**Republic, Marquette, Pop. 565**
Republic-Michigamme SD 100/K-12
227 Maple St 49879 906-376-2277
Kevin Luokkala, supt. Fax 376-8299
r-mschool.org
Republic-Michigamme S 100/K-12
227 Maple St 49879 906-376-2277
Kevin Luokkala, supt. Fax 376-8299

**Richland, Kalamazoo, Pop. 729**
Gull Lake Community SD 2,800/PK-12
11775 E D Ave 49083 269-488-5000
Christopher Rundle, supt. Fax 488-5011
www.gulllakecs.org
Gull Lake HS 1,000/9-12
7753 N 34th St 49083 269-488-5020
Don Eastman, prin. Fax 488-5031
Gull Lake MS 700/6-8
9550 M 89 49083 269-488-5040
David Alban, prin. Fax 488-5041

**Richmond, Macomb, Pop. 5,652**
Richmond Community SD 1,700/PK-12
35276 Division Rd 48062 586-727-3565
Brian Walmsley, supt. Fax 727-2098
www.richmond.k12.mi.us
Richmond HS 600/9-12
35320 Division Rd 48062 586-727-3225
Deborah Michon, prin. Fax 727-9072
Richmond MS 500/5-8
35250 Division Rd 48062 586-727-7552
Keith Bartels, prin. Fax 727-2545

**River Rouge, Wayne, Pop. 7,623**
River Rouge SD 1,100/K-12
1460 Coolidge Hwy 48218 313-297-9600
Derrick Coleman, supt. Fax 297-6525
www.riverrougeschools.org
River Rouge HS 500/9-12
1460 Coolidge Hwy 48218 313-297-9600
Michael Mokdad, prin. Fax 297-7322
Sabbath MS 200/6-8
340 Frazier St 48218 313-297-9654
Brandon Cox, prin. Fax 297-5695

**Riverview, Wayne, Pop. 12,365**
Riverview Community SD 2,800/K-12
13425 Colvin St Ste 1, 734-285-9660
Russell Pickell, supt. Fax 285-9822
www.riverviewschools.com
Riverview HS 1,000/9-12
12431 Longsdorf St, 734-285-7361
J.J. Hatzl, prin. Fax 785-6598
Seitz MS 700/6-8
17800 Kennebec St, 734-285-2043
Andrew Zulewski, prin. Fax 285-6649

---

Detroit Business Institute Post-Sec.
19100 Fort St, 734-479-0660
Richard HS 300/9-12
15325 Pennsylvania Rd, 734-284-1875
Joseph Whalen, prin. Fax 284-9304

**Rochester, Oakland, Pop. 12,556**
Rochester Community SD 14,600/K-12
501 W University Dr 48307 248-726-3000
Dr. Robert Shaner, supt. Fax 726-3105
www.rochester.k12.mi.us
Other Schools – See Rochester Hills

---

Oakland University Post-Sec.
2200 N Squirrel Rd 48309 248-370-2100

**Rochester Hills, Oakland, Pop. 69,733**
Avondale SD
Supt. — See Auburn Hills
Avondale Academy 100/Alt
1435 W Auburn Rd 48309 248-537-6600
Taylor Chapman, prin. Fax 537-6605
Avondale MS 800/6-8
1445 W Auburn Rd 48309 248-537-6300
Fax 537-6305
Meadows Learning Center Alt
1435 W Auburn Rd 48309 248-537-6400
Karen Olex, prin. Fax 537-6405

Rochester Community SD
Supt. — See Rochester
ACE Alternative S 100/Alt
1440 John R Rd 48307 248-726-5900
Susan Demeniuk, prin. Fax 726-5905
Adams HS 1,500/9-12
3200 W Tienken Rd 48306 248-726-5200
Kevin Cumming, prin. Fax 726-5205
Hart MS 1,100/6-8
6500 Sheldon Rd 48306 248-726-4500
Allison Roberts, prin. Fax 726-4505
Reuther MS 700/6-8
1430 E Auburn Rd 48307 248-726-4700
Cheryl Gambaro, prin. Fax 726-4705
Rochester HS 1,600/9-12
180 S Livernois Rd 48307 248-726-5400
Neil Deluca, prin. Fax 726-5405
Stony Creek HS 1,700/9-12
575 E Tienken Rd 48306 248-726-5700
Cathryn Skedel Ph.D., prin. Fax 726-5705
Van Hoosen MS 800/6-8
1339 N Adams Rd 48306 248-726-4900
Dan Mooney, prin. Fax 726-4905
West MS 900/6-8
500 Old Perch Rd 48309 248-726-5000
Mike Dillon, prin. Fax 726-5005
RACE Adult
1435 W Auburn Rd 48309 248-726-5950
Sean Lively, admin. Fax 726-5955

---

Holy Family Regional S - South Campus 600/4-8
2633 John R Rd 48307 248-299-3798
Jon Myers, prin. Fax 299-3843
Lutheran HS Northwest 300/9-12
1000 Bagley Dr 48309 248-852-6677
Steve Garrabrant, prin. Fax 852-2667
Rochester College Post-Sec.
800 W Avon Rd 48307 248-218-2000
Rochester Hills Christian S 300/PK-12
3300 S Livernois Rd 48307 248-852-0585
Karen Patton, prin. Fax 852-4757

**Rock, Delta**
Mid Peninsula SD 200/K-12
5055 Saint Nicholas 31st Rd 49880 906-359-4387
Mary F. Brayak, supt. Fax 359-4167
midpen.dsisd.net/
Mid Peninsula S 200/K-12
5055 Saint Nicholas 31st Rd 49880 906-359-4390
Mary F. Brayak, supt. Fax 359-4167

**Rockford, Kent, Pop. 5,617**
Rockford SD 7,500/PK-12
350 N Main St 49341 616-863-6320
Michael Shibler Ph.D., supt. Fax 866-1911
www.rockfordschools.org
East Rockford MS 900/6-8
8615 9 Mile Rd NE 49341 616-863-6140
Mike Ramm, prin. Fax 863-6565
North Rockford MS 900/6-8
397 E Division St 49341 616-863-6300
Lissa Weidenfeller, prin. Fax 866-5998
River Valley Academy 100/Alt
350 N Main St 49341 616-863-6324
Lisa Jacobs, prin. Fax 866-1911
Rockford Freshman Center 600/9-9
4500 Kroes St NE 49341 616-863-6348
Tom Hosford, prin. Fax 866-7134
Rockford HS 1,900/10-12
4100 Kroes St NE 49341 616-863-6030
Daniel Zang, prin. Fax 866-5997

**Rockwood, Wayne, Pop. 3,246**
Gibraltar SD
Supt. — See Woodhaven
Downriver HS 50/Alt
33211 Mccann Rd 48173 734-379-7080
Carol Ellison, prin. Fax 379-7081

**Rogers City, Presque Isle, Pop. 2,809**
Rogers City Area SD 500/K-12
1033 W Huron Ave Ste B 49779 989-734-9100
Lee Sandy, supt. Fax 734-7428
www.rcashurons.org
Rogers City MSHS 300/6-12
1033 W Huron Ave 49779 989-734-9170
David O'Bryant, prin. Fax 734-2969

**Romeo, Macomb, Pop. 3,511**
Romeo Community SD 5,300/PK-12
316 N Main St 48065 586-752-0200
Eric Whitney, supt. Fax 752-0228
www.romeo.k12.mi.us
Romeo HS 1,800/9-12
11091 32 Mile Rd 48065 586-752-0300
Michael Kaufman, prin. Fax 752-0402

Romeo MS 500/6-8
297 Prospect St 48065 586-752-0240
Brad Martz, prin. Fax 752-0256
Other Schools – See Washington

**Romulus, Wayne, Pop. 23,107**
Romulus Community SD 3,300/PK-12
36540 Grant St 48174 734-532-1602
Marjie McAnally, supt. Fax 532-1611
www.romulus.net
Romulus Early College 9-12
9650 Wayne Rd 48174 734-532-1603
Fax 532-1611
Romulus HS 1,000/9-12
9650 Wayne Rd 48174 734-532-1003
Flinnioa Hall, prin. Fax 532-1001
Romulus MS 700/6-8
37300 Wick Rd 48174 734-532-1703
Jason Salhaney, prin. Fax 532-1701

**Roscommon, Roscommon, Pop. 1,048**
C.O.O.R. ISD
PO Box 827 48653 989-275-9555
Greg Bush, supt. Fax 275-5881
www.coorisd.net
C.O.O.R. CTE, PO Box 827 48653 Vo/Tech
Dan Beltz, prin. 989-275-9536

Roscommon Area SD 1,300/PK-12
PO Box 825 48653 989-275-6600
Catherine Erickson, supt. Fax 275-8227
www.rapsk12.net
Roscommon HS 500/8-12
PO Box 825 48653 989-275-6675
Martin Ewald, prin. Fax 275-6681

---

Kirtland Community College Post-Sec.
10775 N Saint Helen Rd 48653 989-275-5000

**Roseville, Macomb, Pop. 46,120**
Roseville Community SD 5,200/K-12
18975 Church St 48066 586-445-5505
John Kment, supt. Fax 771-1772
www.rcs.misd.net
Eastland MS 400/6-8
18700 Frank St 48066 586-445-5702
Jason Bettin, prin. Fax 445-5721
Roseville HS 1,700/9-12
17855 Common Rd 48066 586-445-5542
Peter Hedemark, prin. Fax 445-5654
Roseville MS 600/6-8
16250 Martin Rd 48066 586-445-5605
David Rice, prin. Fax 445-5620

---

Dorsey School of Business Post-Sec.
31542 Gratiot Ave 48066 586-296-3225

**Royal Oak, Oakland, Pop. 56,180**
Oakland ISD
Supt. — See Waterford
Oakland Technical Campus SE Vo/Tech
5055 Delemere Ave 48073 248-288-4020
Amy Gole, dean Fax 288-4071

Royal Oak SD 5,100/PK-12
800 Devillen Ave 48073 248-435-8400
Shawn Lewis-Lakin, supt. Fax 435-6170
www.royaloakschools.org
Churchill Community Education Center 200/Alt
707 Girard Ave 48073 248-588-5050
Melissa Hutchinson, prin. Fax 588-2881
Royal Oak HS 1,500/9-12
1500 Lexington Blvd 48073 248-435-8500
Michael Giromini, prin. Fax 288-8733
Royal Oak MS 1,100/6-8
709 N Washington Ave 48067 248-541-7100
Todd Noonan, prin. Fax 541-0408

---

David Pressley School of Cosmetology Post-Sec.
1127 S Washington Ave 48067 248-548-5090
Oakland Community College Post-Sec.
739 S Washington Ave 48067 248-246-2400
Shrine Catholic HS & Academy 300/7-12
3500 W 13 Mile Rd 48073 248-549-2925
Thomas Oppat, prin. Fax 549-2953
William Beaumont Hospital Post-Sec.
3601 W 13 Mile Rd 48073 248-551-0681

**Rudyard, Chippewa**
Rudyard Area SD 700/PK-12
11185 W 2nd St 49780 906-478-3771
Mark Pavloski, supt. Fax 478-3912
www.rudyard.k12.mi.us
Rudyard JSHS 200/7-12
11185 W 2nd St 49780 906-478-3771
Mike DeYoung, prin. Fax 478-4101

**Saginaw, Saginaw, Pop. 50,106**
Carrollton SD 2,000/PK-12
3211 Carla Dr 48604 989-754-1475
Tim Wilson, supt. Fax 754-1470
www.carrolltonpublicschools.org
Carrollton HS 500/9-12
1235 Mapleridge Rd 48604 989-753-3433
Shawn Thelen, prin. Fax 754-1041
Carrollton MS 400/6-8
3211 Carla Dr 48604 989-753-9704
Marc McKenzie, prin. Fax 754-1470
Omni Alternative HS 200/Alt
479 Shattuck Rd 48604 989-753-3477
Tiffany Peterson, prin. Fax 776-0283

Saginaw ISD 300/
6235 Gratiot Rd, 989-399-7473
Kathy Stewart, supt. Fax 793-1571
www.sisd.cc
Other Schools – See University Center

Saginaw SD 6,700/PK-12
550 Millard St 48607 989-399-6500
Nathaniel McClain Ph.D., supt. Fax 399-6635
www.spsd.net
Hill HS 1,100/8-12
3115 Mackinaw St 48602 989-399-5800
Mit Foley, prin. Fax 399-5815
Saginaw Arts & Sciences Academy 700/6-12
1903 N Niagara St 48602 989-399-5500
Priscilla Arocha-Roby, prin. Fax 399-5515
Saginaw Career Complex Vo/Tech
2102 Weiss St 48602 989-399-6150
Mark Frost, prin. Fax 399-6165
Saginaw HS 700/8-12
3100 Webber St 48601 989-399-6000
Janice Davis, prin. Fax 399-6015
Thompson MS 600/6-8
3021 Court St 48602 989-399-5600
Rachel Reid, prin. Fax 399-5615

Saginaw Township Community SD 5,000/K-12
PO Box 6278 48608 989-797-1800
Douglas Trombley, supt. Fax 797-1801
stcs.org
Heritage HS 1,700/9-12
3465 N Center Rd 48603 989-799-5790
Michael Newman, prin. Fax 799-5159
Mackinaw HS 200/Alt
2775 Shattuck Rd 48603 989-799-8470
Alan Kern, prin. Fax 797-1860
White Pine MS 1,200/6-8
505 N Center Rd, 989-797-1814
Pri Victoria Wandmacher, prin. Fax 797-1859

Swan Valley SD 1,800/K-12
8380 OHern Rd 48609 989-921-3701
Mat McRae, supt. Fax 921-3705
www.swanvalley.k12.mi.us
Swan Valley Adult & Alternative Educ 50/Alt
8400 OHern Rd 48609 989-921-2472
Shelley Hanson, prin. Fax 921-2405
Swan Valley HS 700/9-12
8400 OHern Rd 48609 989-921-2401
Craig Blower, prin. Fax 921-2405
Swan Valley MS 400/6-8
453 Van Wormer Rd 48609 989-921-2601
Jennifer Coppens, prin. Fax 921-2605

---

Community Baptist Christian S 100/PK-12
8331 Gratiot Rd 48609 989-781-2340
Douglas Jackson, prin. Fax 781-1344
Davenport University Post-Sec.
5300 Bay Rd 48604 989-799-7800
Dorsey School of Business Post-Sec.
4390 Bay Rd 48603 989-249-1926
Grace Christian S 100/PK-12
4619 Mackinaw Rd 48603 989-793-2129
Sharon Gamber, prin. Fax 793-2125
Michigan Lutheran Seminary 200/9-12
2777 Hardin St 48602 989-793-1010
Rev. Joel Petermann, pres. Fax 793-4213
Nouvel Catholic Central HS 300/9-12
2555 Wieneke Rd 48603 989-791-4330
John Hoving, prin. Fax 797-6603
Ross Medical Education Center Post-Sec.
4300 Fashion Square # 202 48603 989-791-5192
St. Mary's Medical Center Post-Sec.
800 S Washington Ave 48601 989-776-8176
Valley Lutheran HS 300/9-12
3560 McCarty Rd 48603 989-790-1676
Dr. John Brandt, prin. Fax 790-1680

**Saint Charles, Saginaw, Pop. 2,035**
Saint Charles Community SD 1,200/PK-12
891 W Walnut St 48655 989-865-9961
Michael Decker, supt. Fax 865-6185
www.stccs.org
Saint Charles HS 400/9-12
881 W Walnut St 48655 989-865-9991
Fax 865-8185
Thurston MS 300/6-8
893 W Walnut St 48655 989-865-9927
Fax 865-2429

**Saint Clair, Saint Clair, Pop. 5,422**
East China SD
Supt. — See East China
Saint Clair HS 900/9-12
2200 Clinton Ave 48079 810-676-1700
Ronald Miller, prin. Fax 676-1725
Saint Clair MS 600/6-8
4335 Yankee Rd 48079 810-676-1800
Michael Alley, prin. Fax 676-1825

**Saint Clair Shores, Macomb, Pop. 58,728**
Lake Shore SD 3,500/K-12
28850 Harper Ave 48081 586-285-8480
Christopher Loria, supt. Fax 285-8463
www.lakeshoreschools.org
Kennedy MS 800/6-8
23101 Masonic Blvd 48082 586-285-8800
Patrick Donohue, prin. Fax 285-8804
Lake Shore HS 1,100/9-12
22980 E 13 Mile Rd 48082 586-285-8900
Dr. Joseph DiPonio, prin. Fax 285-8904
North Lake Alternative HS 200/Alt
23340 Elmira St 48082 586-285-8780
Chad Johnson, prin. Fax 285-8783
St. Clair Shores Adult & Comm Education Adult
23055 Masonic 48082 586-285-8880
Gerilyn Whitfield, prin. Fax 285-8881

Lakeview SD 3,700/K-12
27575 Harper Ave 48081 586-445-4000
Karl Paulson, supt. Fax 445-4029
www.lakeview.misd.net
Jefferson MS 1,000/6-8
27900 Rockwood St 48081 586-445-4130
David Lavender, prin. Fax 445-4041
Lakeview HS 1,400/9-12
21100 E 11 Mile Rd 48081 586-445-4045
Brent Case, prin. Fax 445-4072

South Lake SD 2,100/K-12
23101 Stadium Dr 48080 586-435-1600
Pamela Balint, supt. Fax 445-4202
www.solake.org
South Lake HS 700/9-12
21900 E 9 Mile Rd 48080 586-435-1400
Fax 445-4243
South Lake MS 500/6-8
21621 California St 48080 586-435-1300
Michael Bruce, prin. Fax 778-3151

**Saint Ignace, Mackinac, Pop. 2,280**
Saint Ignace Area SD 600/K-12
W429 Portage St 49781 906-643-8145
Donald Gustafson, supt. Fax 643-7873
stignace.eup.k12.mi.us/
Lasalle HS 200/9-12
W443 Portage St 49781 906-643-8800
Gregg Fettig, prin. Fax 643-7696

**Saint Johns, Clinton, Pop. 7,721**
Saint Johns SD 3,200/K-12
501 W Sickles St 48879 989-227-4050
Dedrick Martin, supt. Fax 227-4099
www.sjredwings.org
Saint Johns HS 1,100/9-12
501 W Sickles St 48879 989-227-4100
Mark Palmer, prin. Fax 227-4199
Saint Johns MS 800/6-8
900 W Townsend Rd 48879 989-227-4300
Adel DiOrio, prin. Fax 227-4399
Wilson Center 50/Alt
101 W Cass St 48879 989-227-5200
Dedrick Martin, prin. Fax 227-5299

**Saint Joseph, Berrien, Pop. 8,211**
Saint Joseph SD 2,800/K-12
3275 Lincoln Ave 49085 269-926-3100
Ann Cardon, supt. Fax 429-5042
www.sjschools.org/
Saint Joseph HS 1,000/9-12
2521 Stadium Dr 49085 269-926-3200
Kevin Riggs, prin. Fax 926-3203
Upton MS 600/6-8
800 Maiden Ln 49085 269-926-3400
Chad Mandarino, prin. Fax 926-3403

---

Lake Michigan Catholic HS 200/9-12
915 Pleasant St 49085 269-983-2511
John Berlin, prin. Fax 983-0883
Lake Michigan Catholic MS 100/6-8
915 Pleasant St 49085 269-983-2511
John Berlin, prin. Fax 983-0883
Michigan Lutheran HS 100/9-12
615 E Marquette Woods Rd 49085 269-429-7861
Matthew Herbst, prin. Fax 429-4428
Twin City Beauty College Post-Sec.
2600 Lincoln Ave 49085 269-428-2900

**Saint Louis, Gratiot, Pop. 7,441**
Saint Louis SD 1,100/PK-12
113 E Saginaw St 48880 989-681-2545
Kristi Teall, supt. Fax 681-5894
www.stlouisschools.net
Nurnberger MS 300/6-8
312 Union St 48880 989-681-5155
Shane Brooks, prin. Fax 681-4658
Saint Louis HS 400/9-12
113 E Saginaw St 48880 989-681-2500
Jennifer McKittrick, prin. Fax 681-4535

**Saline, Washtenaw, Pop. 8,661**
Saline Area SD 5,200/PK-12
7265 N Ann Arbor St 48176 734-401-4000
Scot Graden, supt. Fax 401-4098
www.salineschools.com
Saline Alternative HS 100/Alt
7265 Saline Ann Arbor Rd 48176 734-401-4000
Carol Melcher, prin. Fax 401-4098
Saline HS 1,800/9-12
1300 Campus Pkwy 48176 734-401-4200
Julie Helber, prin. Fax 401-4398
Saline MS 1,200/6-8
7190 N Maple Rd 48176 734-401-4600
David Raft, prin. Fax 401-4745

---

Washtenaw Christian Academy 300/PK-12
7200 Moon Rd 48176 734-429-7733
Eric VanDerhoof, head sch Fax 944-8343

**Sand Creek, Lenawee**
Sand Creek Community SD 900/PK-12
6518 Sand Creek Hwy 49279 517-436-3108
Steven Laundra, supt. Fax 436-3143
www.sc-aggies.us
Sand Creek JSHS 400/6-12
6518 Sand Creek Hwy 49279 517-436-3124
Matt Benge, dean Fax 436-3193

**Sand Lake, Montcalm, Pop. 495**
Tri County Area SD 2,500/PK-12
PO Box 79 49343 616-636-5454
Allen Cumings M.A., supt. Fax 636-5677
www.tricountyschools.com
Other Schools – See Howard City

**Sandusky, Sanilac, Pop. 2,651**
Sandusky Community SD 800/PK-12
191 E Pinetree Ln 48471 810-648-3400
Mike Carmean, supt. Fax 648-5113
www.sandusky.k12.mi.us
Sandusky JSHS 300/7-12
191 E Pinetree Ln 48471 810-648-3401
Steve Carlson, prin. Fax 648-3148

**Sanford, Midland, Pop. 854**
Meridian SD 1,400/PK-12
3361 N Meridian Rd 48657 989-687-3200
Craig Carmoney, supt. Fax 687-3222
merps.org
Meridian Early College HS 400/9-12
3303 N Meridian Rd 48657 989-687-3300
Patrick Malley, prin. Fax 687-3309
Meridian JHS 400/5-8
3475 N Meridian Rd 48657 989-687-3360
Kent Boxey, prin. Fax 687-3364

**Saranac, Ionia, Pop. 1,311**
Saranac Community SD 1,100/PK-12
88 Pleasant St 48881 616-642-1400
Richard Geiger, supt. Fax 642-1405
www.saranac.k12.mi.us
Saranac JSHS 600/7-12
150 Pleasant St 48881 616-642-1100
Josh Leader, prin. Fax 642-1105

**Saugatuck, Allegan, Pop. 909**
Saugatuck SD
Supt. — See Douglas
Saugatuck MSHS 300/6-12
401 Elizabeth St 49453 269-857-2133
Timothy Travis, prin. Fax 857-6145

**Sault Sainte Marie, Chippewa, Pop. 13,362**
Sault Sainte Marie Area SD 2,400/PK-12
876 Marquette Ave 49783 906-635-6609
Timothy D. Hall Ed.D., supt. Fax 635-6642
sault.eup.k12.mi.us
Malcolm HS 100/Alt
460 W Spruce St 49783 906-635-6638
Sandy Sawyer, prin. Fax 635-3836
Sault Area Career Center Vo/Tech
904 Marquette Ave 49783 906-635-6652
Jo Anne Lussier, dir. Fax 635-6641
Sault Sainte Marie Area HS 900/9-12
904 Marquette Ave 49783 906-635-6605
Carl McCready, prin. Fax 635-6641
Sault Sainte Marie MS 500/6-8
684 Marquette Ave 49783 906-635-6604
Jessica Rondeau, prin. Fax 635-3841

---

Lake Superior State University Post-Sec.
650 W Easterday Ave 49783 906-632-6841

**Schoolcraft, Kalamazoo, Pop. 1,506**
Schoolcraft Community SD 1,000/PK-12
551 E Lyons St 49087 269-488-7390
Dr. Wayne Stitt, supt. Fax 488-7391
www.schoolcraftschools.org
Schoolcraft HS 400/9-12
551 E Lyons St 49087 269-488-7350
Ric Seager, prin. Fax 488-7364
Schoolcraft MS 300/6-8
551 E Lyons St 49087 269-488-7300
Dave Powers, prin. Fax 488-7303

**Scottville, Mason, Pop. 1,185**
Mason County Central SD 1,500/PK-12
300 W Broadway Ave 49454 231-757-3713
Jeff Mount, supt. Fax 757-5716
mccschools.org
Mason County Central HS 500/9-12
210 W Broadway Ave 49454 231-757-4748
Brad Jacobs, prin. Fax 757-9084
Mason County Central MS 300/6-8
310 W Beryl St 49454 231-757-3724
Mark Olmstead, prin. Fax 757-4820
Mason-Lake Community Educ. Consortium Adult
300 W Broadway Ave 49454 231-757-3713
Elizabeth Stark, dir. Fax 757-5716

West Shore ESD
Supt. — See Ludington
West Shore ESD Career & Technical Educ Vo/Tech
3000 N Stiles Rd 49454 231-843-5976
Lynda Matson, prin. Fax 845-7227

---

West Shore Community College Post-Sec.
3000 N Stiles Rd 49454 231-845-6211

**Sebewaing, Huron, Pop. 1,753**
Unionville-Sebewaing SD 600/PK-12
2203 Wildner Rd 48759 989-883-2360
George Rierson, supt. Fax 883-9021
main.think-usa.org
Unionville-Sebewaing HS 300/9-12
2203 Wildner Rd 48759 989-883-2534
Josh Hahn, prin. Fax 883-9739
Unionville-Sebewaing MS 200/6-8
2203 Wildner Rd 48759 989-883-3140
Josh Hahn, prin.

**Shelby, Oceana, Pop. 2,029**
Shelby SD 1,400/PK-12
525 N State St 49455 231-861-5211
Dan Bauer, supt. Fax 861-5416
www.shelbypublicschools.net
Shelby HS 400/9-12
641 N State St 49455 231-861-4452
Frances Schamber, prin. Fax 861-6867
Shelby MS 300/6-8
525 N State St 49455 231-861-4521
Mark Olmstead, prin. Fax 861-0415

**Shelby Township, Macomb, Pop. 69,500**
Utica Community SD
Supt. — See Sterling Heights
Eisenhower SHS 2,100/10-12
6500 25 Mile Rd 48316 586-797-1300
Nanette Chesney, prin. Fax 797-1301
Malow JHS 1,200/7-9
6400 25 Mile Rd 48316 586-797-3500
Brandon Manzella, prin. Fax 797-3501
Shelby JHS 1,200/7-9
51700 Van Dyke Ave 48316 586-797-3700
Lisa McDill, prin. Fax 797-3701

**Shepherd, Isabella, Pop. 1,488**
Shepherd SD 1,800/K-12
PO Box 219 48883 989-828-5520
Claire Bunker, supt. Fax 828-5679
www.shepherdschools.net
Shepherd HS 500/9-12
100 E Hall St 48883 989-828-6601
Joseph Passalacqua, prin. Fax 828-5452
Shepherd MS 400/6-8
150 E Hall St 48883 989-828-6601
Kelly Miscikoski, prin. Fax 828-6578
Other Schools – See Mount Pleasant

**Sheridan, Montcalm, Pop. 639**

---

Beth Haven Baptist Academy 100/PK-12
1158 W Carson City Rd 48884 989-291-0555
Kevin Crowell, prin. Fax 527-3122

**Sidney, Montcalm**
Montcalm Area ISD
Supt. — See Stanton
Montcalm Area Career Center Vo/Tech
1550 W Sidney Rd 48885 989-225-5708
Celena Mills, prin. Fax 225-5709

---

Montcalm Community College Post-Sec.
2800 College Dr 48885 989-328-2111

**Southfield, Oakland, Pop. 70,027**
Southfield SD 7,300/PK-12
24661 Lahser Rd 48033 248-746-8500
Dr. Lynda Wood, supt. Fax 746-8540
www.southfield.k12.mi.us
Levey MS 500/6-8
25300 W 9 Mile Rd, 248-746-8740
Rita Teague, prin. Fax 746-8718
Southfield HS 1,000/9-12
24675 Lahser Rd, 248-746-8600
Sonia Jackson, prin. Fax 746-8773
Southfield Regional Academic Campus Alt
21705 Evergreen Rd 48075 248-746-0012
Dwayne Eason, prin. Fax 746-0028
Southfield Regional Academic Center 400/Alt
21705 Evergreen Rd 48075 248-746-0012
Dwayne Eason, prin. Fax 746-0028
University HS Academy 300/9-12
24815 Lahser Rd, 248-746-4370
Marcia Williams, dean Fax 746-4374
Other Schools – See Lathrup Village

---

Abcott Institute Post-Sec.
16250 Northland Dr Ste 205 48075 866-532-7699
Akiva Hebrew Day S 300/PK-12
21100 W 12 Mile Rd 48076 248-386-1625
Jordana Wolfson, dir. Fax 386-1632
DeVry University Post-Sec.
26999 Central Park Ste 125 48076 248-213-1610
Everest Institute Post-Sec.
21107 Lahser Rd, 248-799-9933
ITT Technical Institute Post-Sec.
26700 Lahser Rd Ste 100, 248-603-6100
Lawrence Technological University Post-Sec.
21000 W 10 Mile Rd 48075 248-204-4000
Northwestern Technological Institute Post-Sec.
24567 Northwestern Hwy #200 48075 248-358-4006
Oakland Community College Post-Sec.
22322 Rutland Ave 48075 248-233-2700
Providence Hospital Post-Sec.
16001 W 9 Mile Rd 48075 248-424-3000
Southfield Christian S 500/PK-12
28650 Lahser Rd 48034 248-357-3660
Sue Hoffenbacher, supt. Fax 357-5271
Specs Howard School of Broadcast Arts Post-Sec.
19900 W 9 Mile Rd 48075 248-358-9000
Yeshivas Darchei Torah Girls S 300/K-12
21550 W 12 Mile Rd 48076 248-948-1080
Sharon Kahn, prin. Fax 948-1825

**Southgate, Wayne, Pop. 29,584**
Southgate Community SD 3,700/K-12
14600 Dix Toledo Rd 48195 734-246-4600
Leslie Hainrihar, supt. Fax 283-6791
www.sgate.k12.mi.us/
Anderson HS 1,100/9-12
15475 Leroy St 48195 734-246-4611
Dr. Michelle Baker-Herring, prin. Fax 246-7840
Davidson MS 400/6-8
15800 Trenton Rd 48195 734-246-4628
Dennis Kemp, prin. Fax 246-7280
Asher Adult & Community Education Adult
14101 Leroy St 48195 734-246-4633
Mark Carter, dir. Fax 246-7244

---

Dorsey School of Business Post-Sec.
15755 Northline Rd 48195 734-285-5400

**South Haven, Van Buren, Pop. 4,285**
South Haven SD 2,200/PK-12
554 Green St 49090 269-637-0520
Robert Herrera, supt. Fax 637-3025
www.shps.org
Baseline MS 500/6-8
7357 Baseline Rd 49090 269-637-0530
Dr. William Stitt, prin. Fax 639-9689
Career and Early College Academy Vo/Tech
125 Veterans Dr 49090 269-637-0500
Jeremy Burleson, admin. Fax 637-3025
Mohr HS 700/9-12
600 Elkenburg St 49090 269-637-0502
Jerry Sardina, prin. Fax 637-0516

**South Lyon, Oakland, Pop. 11,160**
South Lyon Community SD 7,000/PK-12
345 S Warren St 48178 248-573-8127
Melissa Baker, supt. Fax 437-8686
www.slcs.us
Centennial MS 800/6-8
62500 9 Mile Rd 48178 248-573-8600
Brian Toth, prin. Fax 486-4302
Millennium MS 900/6-8
61526 9 Mile Rd 48178 248-573-8200
Kelly Gallagher, prin. Fax 437-4066
South Lyon East HS 900/9-12
52200 10 Mile Rd 48178 248-573-8700
Dr. David Phillips, prin. Fax 486-4009
South Lyon HS 1,300/9-12
1000 N Lafayette St 48178 248-573-8150
Chad Scaling, prin. Fax 437-0233

**Sparta, Kent, Pop. 4,088**
Sparta Area SD 2,700/PK-12
465 S Union St 49345 616-887-8253
Gordie Nickels, supt. Fax 887-9958
www.spartaschools.org
Sparta HS 900/9-12
475 W Spartan Dr 49345 616-887-8213
Matt Spencer, prin. Fax 887-1264
Sparta MS 600/6-8
480 S State St 49345 616-887-8211
Brad Wood, prin. Fax 887-1080

**Spring Arbor, Jackson, Pop. 2,850**

---

Spring Arbor University Post-Sec.
106 E Main St 49283 517-750-1200

**Springfield, Calhoun, Pop. 5,036**
Battle Creek SD
Supt. — See Battle Creek
Springfield MS 500/6-8
1023 Avenue A, 269-965-9640
William Martin, prin. Fax 962-2486

**Spring Lake, Ottawa, Pop. 2,288**
Spring Lake SD 2,400/K-12
345 Hammond St 49456 616-846-5500
Dennis Furton, supt. Fax 846-9830
www.springlakeschools.org
Spring Lake HS 800/9-12
16140 148th Ave 49456 616-846-5501
Mike Gilchrist, prin. Fax 847-5855
Spring Lake MS 400/7-8
345 Hammond St 49456 616-846-5502
Aaron West, prin. Fax 847-7913

**Springport, Jackson, Pop. 785**
Springport SD 1,000/K-12
PO Box 100 49284 517-857-3495
Randall Cook, supt. Fax 857-4179
springportschools.net
Springport HS 300/9-12
PO Box 100 49284 517-857-3475
Tanya Overweg, prin. Fax 857-4179
Springport MS 200/6-8
PO Box 100 49284 517-857-3475
Chris Kregel, prin. Fax 857-3251

**Standish, Arenac, Pop. 1,487**
Standish-Sterling Community SD 1,700/PK-12
3789 Wyatt Rd 48658 989-846-3670
Darren Kroczaleski, supt. Fax 846-7890
www.standish-sterling.org
Standish-Sterling Central HS 500/9-12
2401 Grove Street Rd 48658 989-846-3660
Mark Williams, prin. Fax 846-3666
Standish-Sterling MS 400/6-8
3789 Wyatt Rd 48658 989-846-4526
Gary Roper, prin. Fax 846-4529

**Stanton, Montcalm, Pop. 1,397**
Central Montcalm SD 1,800/PK-12
PO Box 9 48888 989-831-2000
Amy Meinhardt, supt. Fax 831-2010
www.central-montcalm.org
Central Montcalm HS 600/9-12
PO Box 9 48888 989-831-2100
C. Martin James, prin. Fax 831-2110
Central Montcalm MS 500/6-8
PO Box 9 48888 989-831-2200
Jason Johnston, prin. Fax 831-2210

Montcalm Area ISD 100/
PO Box 367 48888 989-831-5261
Ron Simon, supt. Fax 831-8727
www.maisd.com
Other Schools – See Sidney

**Stephenson, Menominee, Pop. 850**
Stephenson Area SD 500/K-12
PO Box 509 49887 906-753-2221
Stephen Paliewicz, supt. Fax 753-4676
www.stephenson.k12.mi.us
Stephenson JSHS 200/6-12
PO Box 529 49887 906-753-2222
Terry Proos, prin. Fax 753-2326

**Sterling Heights, Macomb, Pop. 126,870**
Utica Community SD 28,200/PK-12
11303 Greendale Dr 48312 586-797-1100
Christine Johns Ed.D., supt. Fax 797-1101
www.uticak12.org/
Bemis JHS 900/7-8
12500 19 Mile Rd 48313 586-797-2500
Thomas Yaw, prin. Fax 797-2501
Davis JHS 900/7-9
11311 Plumbrook Rd 48312 586-797-2700
Brian Shepard, prin. Fax 797-2701
Ford HS 2,000/9-12
11911 Clinton River Rd 48313 586-797-1600
Ken Cucchi, prin. Fax 797-1601

Heritage JHS 600/7-9
37400 Dodge Park Rd 48312 586-797-3100
Scott Waak, prin. Fax 797-3101
Jeanette JHS 800/7-9
40400 Gulliver Dr 48310 586-797-3300
Jared McEvoy, prin. Fax 797-3301
Stevenson SHS 2,000/10-12
39701 Dodge Park Rd 48313 586-797-1900
Steve Pfannes, prin. Fax 797-1901
UCS Alternative Learning Center 200/Alt
7600 18 Mile Rd 48314 586-797-7000
Marc Kay, prin. Fax 797-7001
Other Schools – See Shelby Township, Utica

Warren Consolidated SD
Supt. — See Warren
Career Prep Center Vo/Tech
12200 15 Mile Rd 48312 586-825-2800
Douglas Babcock, prin. Fax 698-4177
Carleton MS 500/6-8
8900 15 Mile Rd 48312 586-825-2590
John Bernia, prin. Fax 698-4286
Flynn Educational Center Alt
2899 Fox Hill Dr 48310 586-825-2900
Paul Yestrepsky, dir. Fax 698-4304
Grissom MS 700/6-8
35701 Ryan Rd 48310 586-825-2560
Mary Ann Figurski, prin. Fax 698-4313
Sterling Heights HS 1,500/9-12
12901 15 Mile Rd 48312 586-825-2700
Craig Miller, prin. Fax 698-4253

---

Parkway Christian S 500/PK-12
14500 Metropolitan Pkwy 48312 586-446-9900
Lila Place, head sch Fax 446-9904

**Stevensville, Berrien, Pop. 1,138**
Lakeshore SD 2,900/PK-12
5771 Cleveland Ave 49127 269-428-1400
Philip Freeman, admin. Fax 428-1574
www.lakeshoreschools.k12.mi.us
Lakeshore HS 900/9-12
5771 Cleveland Ave 49127 269-428-1402
Brad Brunner, prin. Fax 428-1423
Lakeshore MS 700/6-8
1459 W John Beers Rd 49127 269-428-1408
Jason Messenger, prin. Fax 428-1571

**Stockbridge, Ingham, Pop. 1,207**
Stockbridge Community SD 1,500/K-12
305 W Elizabeth St 49285 517-851-7188
Karl Heidrich, supt. Fax 851-8334
panthernet.net
Stockbridge HS 500/8-12
416 N Clinton St 49285 517-851-7770
Rick Cook, prin. Fax 851-9446

**Sturgis, Saint Joseph, Pop. 10,748**
Sturgis SD 3,200/K-12
107 W West St 49091 269-659-1500
Dr. Thomas Langdon, supt. Fax 659-1584
www.sturgisps.org/
Sturgis HS 900/9-12
216 Vinewood Ave 49091 269-659-1515
Ron Ehlers, prin. Fax 659-1532
Sturgis MS 700/6-8
1400 E Lafayette St 49091 269-659-1550
Lauri Schirk, prin. Fax 659-1553
Adult Education Center Adult
107 W West St 49091 269-659-1540
Jill Snyder, prin. Fax 659-1544

---

Lake Area Christian S 50/K-12
63590 Borgert Rd 49091 269-651-5135
Gregory Long, admin. Fax 651-8648

**Suttons Bay, Leelanau, Pop. 604**
Suttons Bay SD 700/PK-12
PO Box 367 49682 231-271-8601
Chris Nelson, supt. Fax 271-8691
www.suttonsbayschools.com
Suttons Bay MSHS 300/6-12
PO Box 367 49682 231-271-8603
Fax 271-8671

**Swartz Creek, Genesee, Pop. 5,666**
Swartz Creek Community SD 3,900/PK-12
8354 Cappy Ln 48473 810-591-2300
Jeff Hall Ed.D., supt. Fax 591-2784
www.swartzcreek.org
Alternative HS 100/Alt
8197 Miller Rd 48473 810-591-4380
Richard Thompson, dean Fax 591-4348
Swartz Creek HS 1,100/9-12
1 Dragon Dr 48473 810-591-1800
Jamie Johnston, prin. Fax 591-1895
Swartz Creek MS 1,000/6-8
8230 Crapo St 48473 810-591-1705
Kevin Klaeren, prin. Fax 591-1712

---

Genesee Academy 200/PK-12
9447 Corunna Rd 48473 810-250-7557
ITT Technical Institute Post-Sec.
6359 Miller Rd 48473 810-628-2500

**Tawas City, Iosco, Pop. 1,814**
Iosco RESA
27 N Rempert Rd 48763 989-362-3006
Dana McGrew, supt. Fax 362-9076
www.ioscoresa.net/
Career & Technical Education Center Vo/Tech
27 N Rempert Rd 48763 989-362-3006
Ronald Stec, dir. Fax 362-6905

Tawas Area SD 1,300/K-12
245 W M 55 48763 989-984-2250
Jeffrey Hutchison, supt. Fax 984-2253
www.tawas.net
Tawas Area HS 600/8-12
255 W M 55 48763 989-984-2100
Eric Diroff, prin. Fax 984-2106

**Taylor, Wayne, Pop. 61,678**
Taylor SD 7,400/PK-12
23033 Northline Rd 48180 734-374-1200
Diane Allen, supt. Fax 287-6083
www.taylorschools.net
Hoover MS 500/7-8
27101 Beverly Rd 48180 313-295-5775
Michelle Tocco, prin. Fax 295-8354
Kennedy HS 1,200/9-12
13505 Kennedy Dr 48180 734-374-1229
Tommie Saylor, prin. Fax 374-1676
Taylor Career & Technical Center Vo/Tech
9601 Westlake St 48180 313-295-5750
Jackie Lancina, prin. Fax 291-1090
Titan Alternative HS 100/Alt
11211 Beech Daly 48180 734-946-6551
Melissa Skopczynski, prin. Fax 946-6590
Truman HS 1,200/9-12
11211 Beech Daly Rd 48180 734-946-6555
Melissa Skopczynski, prin. Fax 946-6590
West MS 700/7-8
10575 William St 48180 313-295-5783
Patricia Kaechele, prin. Fax 291-2203

---

Baptist Park S 200/PK-12
12501 Telegraph Rd 48180 734-287-2720
Roger Cook, admin.
Dorsey School of Business Post-Sec.
23129 Ecorse Rd 48180 313-291-2177
Taylortown School of Beauty Post-Sec.
23129 Ecorse Rd 48180 313-291-2177

**Tecumseh, Lenawee, Pop. 8,429**
Tecumseh SD 2,900/PK-12
212 N Ottawa St 49286 517-424-7318
Dr. Kelly Coffin, supt. Fax 423-3847
tps.k12.mi.us
Tecumseh HS 900/9-12
760 Brown St 49286 517-423-6008
Griff Mills, prin. Fax 423-9644
Tecumseh MS 900/5-8
307 N Maumee St 49286 517-423-1105
Rick Hilderley, prin. Fax 423-1300
Tecumseh Virtual Academy 9-12
760 Brown St 49286 517-424-9951
Craig Freestone, lead tchr. Fax 423-9644

**Tekonsha, Calhoun, Pop. 699**
Tekonsha Community SD 200/K-12
245 S Elm St 49092 517-767-4121
Jeff Kawaski, supt. Fax 767-3465
www.tekonshaschools.org
Tekonsha JSHS 100/K-12
245 S Elm St 49092 517-767-4121
Jeffrey Kawaski, admin. Fax 767-3465

**Temperance, Monroe, Pop. 8,433**
Bedford SD 4,300/K-12
1623 W Sterns Rd 48182 734-850-6000
Mark Kleinhans, supt. Fax 850-6099
www.mybedford.us
Bedford HS 1,600/9-12
8285 Jackman Rd 48182 734-850-6100
Andy Rousselo, prin. Fax 850-6199
Bedford JHS 1,200/6-8
8405 Jackman Rd 48182 734-850-6200
Roderick Hurley, prin. Fax 850-6299

---

State Line Christian S 300/K-12
6320 Lewis Ave 48182 734-847-6773
Joshua Newbold, prin. Fax 847-4968

**Three Oaks, Berrien, Pop. 1,589**
River Valley SD 400/PK-12
15480 Three Oaks Rd 49128 269-756-9541
William Kearney, supt. Fax 756-6631
www.rivervalleyschools.org/
River Valley MSHS 200/6-12
15480 Three Oaks Rd 49128 269-756-9541
Cynthia Ursprung, prin. Fax 756-3007

**Three Rivers, Saint Joseph, Pop. 7,541**
Three Rivers Community SD 2,800/K-12
851 6th Avenue Rd 49093 269-279-1100
Jean Logan, supt. Fax 279-5584
www.trschools.org
Three Rivers HS 800/9-12
700 6th Ave 49093 269-279-1120
Carrie Balk, prin. Fax 273-8014
Three Rivers MS 600/6-8
1101 Jefferson St 49093 269-279-1130
Nikki Nash, prin. Fax 279-1139
Barrows Adult Education Adult
416 Washington St 49093 269-279-9581
Scott Grace, dean Fax 278-5103

**Traverse City, Grand Traverse, Pop. 14,412**
Traverse Bay Area ISD
1101 Red Dr 49684 231-922-6200
Michael Hill, supt. Fax 922-6270
www.tbaisd.org
TBA Career Tech Center Vo/Tech
880 Parsons Rd 49686 231-922-6273
Patrick Lamb, prin. Fax 922-6364

Traverse City Area SD 9,600/PK-12
412 Webster St 49686 231-933-1700
Paul Soma, supt. Fax 933-1721
www.tcaps.net
Traverse City Central HS 1,400/9-12
1150 Milliken Dr 49686 231-933-3500
Rick Vandermolen, prin. Fax 933-3506
Traverse City East MS 900/6-8
1776 3 Mile Rd N 49696 231-933-7300
Colleen Smith, prin. Fax 933-6998
Traverse City HS 200/Alt
3962 3 Mile Rd N 49686 231-933-5860
Lance Morgan, prin. Fax 933-5885
Traverse City West HS 1,700/9-12
5376 N Long Lake Rd 49685 231-933-7500
Joe Esper, prin. Fax 933-7506
Traverse City West MS 1,200/6-8
3950 Silver Lake Rd 49684 231-933-8200
Pam Alfieri, prin. Fax 933-8205

---

Davenport University Post-Sec.
2200 Dendrinos Dr Ste 104 49684 231-995-1740
Munson Medical Center Post-Sec.
1105 6th St 49684 231-935-6501
Northwestern Michigan College Post-Sec.
1701 E Front St 49686 231-995-1000
St. Elizabeth Ann Seton MS 200/6-8
1601 3 Mile Rd N 49696 231-932-4810
Matt Bauman, prin. Fax 932-4814
St. Francis HS 300/9-12
123 E 11th St 49684 231-946-8038
Erick Chittle, prin. Fax 946-1878
Traverse City Christian S 200/PK-12
753 Emerson Rd 49696 231-929-1747
Tony Clymer, admin. Fax 929-1831

**Trenton, Wayne, Pop. 18,620**
Trenton SD 2,600/K-12
2603 Charlton Rd 48183 734-676-8600
Rodney Wakeham, supt. Fax 676-4851
www.trentonschools.com
Arthurs MS 700/6-8
4000 Marian Dr 48183 734-676-8700
Stephanie O'Connor, prin. Fax 676-7364
Trenton HS 900/9-12
2601 Charlton Rd 48183 734-692-4530
Michael Doyle Ed.D., prin. Fax 692-4615

**Troy, Oakland, Pop. 79,352**
Troy SD 11,800/K-12
4400 Livernois Rd 48098 248-823-4000
Dr. Richard Machesky, supt. Fax 823-4013
www.troy.k12.mi.us
Athens HS 1,600/9-12
4333 John R Rd 48085 248-823-2900
Dr. Lara Dixon, prin. Fax 823-2913
Baker MS 700/6-8
1359 Torpey Dr 48083 248-823-4600
Dr. Audra Melton, prin. Fax 823-4613
Boulan Park MS 700/6-8
3570 Northfield Pkwy 48084 248-823-4900
Jo Kwasny, prin. Fax 823-4913
International Academy East 100/9-12
1291 Torpey Dr 48083 248-283-8300
Ryan Brinks, prin. Fax 823-8313
Larson MS 700/6-8
2222 E Long Lake Rd 48085 248-823-4800
Joseph Duda, prin. Fax 823-4813
Niles Community HS 100/Alt
201 W Square Lake Rd 48098 248-823-5100
Debra MacDonald-Linford, prin. Fax 823-5133
Smith MS 700/6-8
5835 Donaldson Dr 48085 248-823-4700
Timothy Fulcher, prin. Fax 823-4713
Troy HS 1,900/9-12
4777 Northfield Pkwy 48098 248-823-2700
Remo Roncone, prin. Fax 823-2713

---

Bethany Christian S 300/K-12
2601 John R Rd 48083 248-689-4821
Philip Fitzgerald, prin. Fax 689-3441
Carnegie Institute Post-Sec.
550 Stephenson Hwy Ste 100 48083 248-589-1078
ITT Technical Institute Post-Sec.
1522 E Big Beaver Rd 48083 248-524-1800
Walsh Coll. Accountancy & Bus. Admin. Post-Sec.
PO Box 7006 48007 248-689-8282

**Twining, Arenac, Pop. 180**
Arenac Eastern SD 200/K-12
PO Box 98 48766 989-867-4234
Darren Kroczaleski, supt. Fax 867-4241
www.arenaceastern.org
Arenac Eastern S 200/K-12
PO Box 98 48766 989-867-4234
Darren Kroczaleski, supt. Fax 867-4241

**Ubly, Sanilac, Pop. 853**
Ubly Community SD 700/K-12
2020 Union St 48475 989-658-8202
Rocky Aldrich, supt. Fax 658-2361
www.ublyschools.org
Ubly HS 300/7-12
2020 Union St 48475 989-658-8554
Steve Noble, prin. Fax 658-2072

**Union City, Branch, Pop. 1,560**
Union City Community SD 1,100/PK-12
430 Saint Joseph St 49094 517-741-8091
Patrick Kreger, supt. Fax 741-5205
www.unioncityschools.org/
Union City HS 400/9-12
430 Saint Joseph St 49094 517-741-8561
Christina Feneley, prin. Fax 741-5205
Union City MS 400/5-8
430 Saint Joseph St 49094 517-741-5381
Brandon Bruce, prin. Fax 741-8513

**University Center, Bay**
Saginaw ISD
Supt. — See Saginaw
Great Lakes Bay Early College 50/10-12
7400 Bay Rd 48710 989-964-2059
Marlene Searles, prin.

---

Delta College Post-Sec.
1961 Delta Rd 48710 989-686-9000
Saginaw Valley State University Post-Sec.
7400 Bay Rd 48710 989-964-4000

**Utica, Macomb, Pop. 4,675**
Utica Community SD
Supt. — See Sterling Heights
Eppler JHS 700/7-9
45461 Brownell St 48317 586-797-2900
Gerard Pantano, prin. Fax 797-2901
Utica SHS 1,400/10-12
47255 Shelby Rd 48317 586-797-2200
Thomas Lietz, prin. Fax 797-2201

**Vanderbilt, Otsego, Pop. 548**
Vanderbilt Area SD 200/K-12
947 Donovan St 49795 989-983-2561
Michelle Kihn, supt. Fax 983-3051
www.vanderbilt.k12.mi.us
Vanderbilt Area S 200/K-12
947 Donovan St 49795 989-983-2561
Michelle Kihn, supt. Fax 983-3051

**Vassar, Tuscola, Pop. 2,631**
Vassar SD 1,100/PK-12
220 Athletic St 48768 989-823-8535
Thomas Palmer, supt. Fax 823-7823
www.vassar.k12.mi.us
Vassar HS 400/9-12
220 Athletic St 48768 989-823-8534
Jason Kiss, prin. Fax 823-7823
Vassar MS 200/6-8
220 Athletic St 48768 989-823-8533
Jason Kiss, prin. Fax 823-7823
Wolverine Alternative Education 100/Alt
1120 Commerce Dr 48768 989-823-9303
Charles Fabbro, prin. Fax 823-3144

**Vermontville, Eaton, Pop. 745**
Maple Valley SD 1,200/PK-12
11014 Nashville Hwy 49096 517-852-9699
Michelle Falcon, supt. Fax 852-5076
mvs.k12.mi.us
Maple Valley JSHS 700/7-12
11090 Nashville Hwy 49096 517-852-9275
Todd Gonser, prin. Fax 852-2283
Maple Valley Pathways HS 50/Alt
11090 Nashville Hwy 49096 517-852-2322
Duska Brumm, prin.

**Vestaburg, Montcalm**
Vestaburg Community SD 700/PK-12
7188 Avenue B 48891 989-268-5353
Brandon Hubbard, supt. Fax 268-5246
www.vcs-k12.net
Vestaburg JSHS 400/7-12
7188 Avenue B 48891 989-268-5343
Brandon Hubbard, prin. Fax 268-5246

**Vicksburg, Kalamazoo, Pop. 2,854**
Vicksburg Community SD 2,500/PK-12
PO Box 158 49097 269-321-1000
Charles Glaes, supt. Fax 321-1055
www.vicksburgcommunityschools.org/
Vicksburg HS 800/9-12
501 E Highway St 49097 269-321-1100
Keevin O'Neill, prin. Fax 321-1155
Vicksburg MS 600/6-8
348 E Prairie St 49097 269-321-1300
Laura Kuhlman, prin. Fax 321-1355
W-A-Y Program Alt
301 S Kalamazoo St 49097 269-321-1020
Steven Fryling, dir. Fax 321-1055

**Wakefield, Gogebic, Pop. 1,831**
Wakefield-Marenisco SD 300/K-12
715 Putnam St 49968 906-224-9421
Catherine Shamion, supt. Fax 224-1771
www.wmschools.org
Wakefield-Marenisco S 300/K-12
715 Putnam St 49968 906-224-7211
Catherine Shamion, supt. Fax 224-1771

**Waldron, Hillsdale, Pop. 534**
Waldron Area SD 100/K-12
13380 Waldron Rd 49288 517-286-6251
Jose Vera, supt. Fax 286-6254
www.wassd.org
Waldron Area S 100/K-12
13380 Waldron Rd 49288 517-286-6251
Jose Vera, admin. Fax 286-6254

**Walkerville, Oceana, Pop. 238**
Walkerville SD 200/PK-12
145 Lathrop St 49459 231-873-4850
Michael Sweet, supt. Fax 873-5615
www.walkerville.k12.mi.us
Walkerville S 100/PK-12
145 Lathrop St 49459 231-873-4850
Michael Sweet, prin. Fax 873-5615

**Walled Lake, Oakland, Pop. 6,836**
Walled Lake Consolidated SD 14,600/PK-12
850 Ladd Rd Bldg D 48390 248-956-2000
Kenneth Gutman M.A., supt. Fax 956-2123
www.wlcsd.org
Geisler MS 800/6-8
46720 W Pontiac Trl 48390 248-956-2900
Sheryl Kennedy Ph.D., prin. Fax 956-2905
Western HS 1,600/9-12
600 Beck Rd 48390 248-956-4400
Joe Bell, prin. Fax 956-4405
Other Schools – See Commerce Township, West Bloomfield, Wixom

**Warren, Macomb, Pop. 130,738**
Fitzgerald SD 2,800/PK-12
23200 Ryan Rd 48091 586-757-1750
Barbara VanSweden, supt. Fax 758-0991
www.fitz.k12.mi.us
Chatterton MS 600/6-8
24333 Ryan Rd 48091 586-757-6650
L. Fournier, prin. Fax 620-6011
Fitzgerald HS 900/9-12
23200 Ryan Rd 48091 586-757-7070
Kimberly Cerrini, prin. Fax 620-6372

Van Dyke SD 2,600/PK-12
23500 Mac Arthur Blvd 48089 586-757-6600
Joseph Pius, supt. Fax 759-9408
www.vdps.net
Lincoln HS 800/9-12
22900 Federal Ave 48089 586-758-8307
Billie Sczepaniak, prin. Fax 758-8304
Lincoln MS 600/6-8
22500 Federal Ave 48089 586-758-8320
Michael Wiltse, prin. Fax 758-8322
Success Academy Alt
23500 Mac Arthur Blvd 48089 586-427-0836
Jennifer Iloff, dir. Fax 759-9408

Warren Consolidated SD 15,500/PK-12
31300 Anita Dr 48093 586-825-2400
Dr. Robert Livernois, supt. Fax 698-4095
www.wcskids.net
Beer MS 700/6-8
3200 Martin Rd 48092 586-574-3175
Annette Lauria, prin. Fax 698-4277
Butcher Educational Center Alt
27500 Cosgrove Dr 48092 586-698-4394
Dr. Catherine Neuhoff, dir. Fax 698-4397
Carter MS 900/6-8
12000 Masonic Blvd 48093 586-825-2620
Amy Hendry, prin. Fax 698-4295
Cousino HS 1,700/9-12
30333 Hoover Rd 48093 586-574-3100
Stephen Bigelow, prin. Fax 698-4204
Warren-Mott HS 1,900/9-12
3131 E 12 Mile Rd 48092 586-574-3250
John Dignan, prin. Fax 698-4226
Other Schools – See Sterling Heights

Warren Woods SD 3,200/PK-12
12900 Frazho Rd 48089 586-439-4400
Stacey Denewith-Fici, supt. Fax 353-0544
warrenwoods.misd.net
Warren Woods Enterprise HS 100/Alt
28600 Suburban Dr 48088 586-439-4407
George Hamblin, prin. Fax 578-9474
Warren Woods MS 800/6-8
13400 E 12 Mile Rd 48088 586-439-4403
Donny Sikora, prin. Fax 574-9830
Warren Woods Tower HS 1,100/9-12
27900 Bunert Rd 48088 586-439-4402
Michael Mackenzie, prin. Fax 445-8013
Warren Woods Adult Education Adult
12900 Frazho Rd 48089 586-439-4408
Kristen Allen, prin. Fax 439-4968

---

Davenport University Post-Sec.
27650 Dequindre Rd 48092 586-558-8700
De La Salle Collegiate HS 800/9-12
14600 Common Rd 48088 586-778-2207
Patrick Adams, prin. Fax 778-6016
Lawton Career Institute Post-Sec.
13877 E 8 Mile Rd 48089 586-777-7344
Macomb Christian S 200/PK-12
28501 Lorraine Ave 48093 586-751-8980
Dr. Margie Baldwin, supt. Fax 751-7946
Macomb Community College Post-Sec.
14500 E 12 Mile Rd 48088 586-445-7999
Regina HS 500/9-12
13900 Masonic Blvd 48088 586-585-0500
Ann Diamond, prin. Fax 585-0507

**Washington, Macomb**
Romeo Community SD
Supt. — See Romeo
Powell MS 700/6-8
62100 Jewell Rd 48094 586-752-0270
Jeffrey LaPerriere, prin. Fax 752-0276
Romeo Engineering and Technology Center Vo/Tech
62300 Jewell Rd 48094 586-752-0245
Natalie Davis, admin. Fax 752-0452

**Waterford, Oakland, Pop. 74,500**
Oakland ISD
2111 Pontiac Lake Rd 48328 248-209-2000
Dr. Wanda Cook-Robinson, supt. Fax 209-2206
www.oakland.k12.mi.us
Other Schools – See Clarkston, Pontiac, Royal Oak, Wixom

Waterford SD 9,200/PK-12
501 N Cass Lake Rd 48328 248-682-7800
Dr. Keith Wunderlich, supt. Fax 706-4888
www.wsdmi.org
Kettering HS 1,600/9-12
2800 Kettering Dr 48329 248-673-1261
Jeffrey Frankowiak, prin. Fax 673-1778
Mason MS 1,300/6-8
3835 W Walton Blvd 48329 248-674-2281
Roger Opsommer, prin. Fax 673-3718
Mott HS 1,600/9-12
1151 Scott Lake Rd 48328 248-674-4134
Jason Riggs, prin. Fax 674-2825
Pierce MS 1,100/6-8
5145 Hatchery Rd 48329 248-674-0331
Yvonne Dixon, prin. Fax 674-4222
Waterford Durant HS 200/Alt
501 N Cass Lake Rd 48328 248-674-3145
Craig Blomquist, prin. Fax 674-6320

---

Michigan College of Beauty Post-Sec.
5620 Dixie Hwy 48329 248-623-9494
Oakdale Academy 200/PK-12
3200 Beacham Dr 48329 248-333-4309
Rachel Greb, head sch Fax 333-7098
Oakland Community College Post-Sec.
7350 Cooley Lake Rd 48327 248-942-3100
Our Lady of the Lakes HS 300/6-12
5495 Dixie Hwy 48329 248-623-0340
Fr. Michael Gawlowski, prin. Fax 623-2274

**Watersmeet, Gogebic, Pop. 416**
Watersmeet Township SD 200/K-12
PO Box 217 49969 906-358-4504
Gerry Pease, supt. Fax 358-4713
www.watersmeet.k12.mi.us/
Watersmeet Township S 200/K-12
PO Box 217 49969 906-358-4504
George Peterson, prin. Fax 358-3036

**Watervliet, Berrien, Pop. 1,689**
Watervliet SD 1,300/PK-12
450 E Red Arrow Hwy 49098 269-463-0300
Kevin Schooley, supt. Fax 463-6809
www.watervlietps.org
Watervliet HS 400/9-12
450 E Red Arrow Hwy 49098 269-463-0730
Dave Armstrong, prin. Fax 463-6809
Watervliet MS 300/6-8
450 E Red Arrow Hwy 49098 269-463-0780
Dave Armstrong, prin. Fax 463-0325

---

Grace Christian S 200/PK-12
325 N M 140 49098 269-463-5545
Todd Zimmerman, head sch Fax 463-5739

**Wayland, Allegan, Pop. 3,998**
Wayland UNSD 2,700/PK-12
850 E Superior St 49348 269-792-2181
Norman Taylor, supt. Fax 792-1615
www.wayland.k12.mi.us
Wayland HS 900/9-12
870 E Superior St 49348 269-792-2254
Thomas Cutler, prin. Fax 792-2116
Wayland Union MS 400/7-8
701 Wildcat Dr 49348 269-792-2306
Carolyn Whyte, prin. Fax 792-1126

**Wayne, Wayne, Pop. 17,081**
Wayne-Westland Community SD
Supt. — See Westland
Franklin MS 900/7-8
33555 Annapolis St 48184 734-419-2400
Stacy Williamson, prin. Fax 595-2401
Wayne Memorial HS 1,800/9-12
3001 4th St 48184 734-419-2200
Kevin Weber, prin. Fax 595-2227

---

Dorsey School of Business Post-Sec.
35005 W Michigan Ave 48184 734-595-1540
Oakwood - Hospital Annapolis Center Post-Sec.
33155 Annapolis St 48184 734-467-4000

**Webberville, Ingham, Pop. 1,262**
Webberville Community SD 500/PK-12
309 E Grand River Rd 48892 517-521-3422
Brian Friddle, supt. Fax 521-4139
www.webbervilleschools.org
Webberville JSHS 200/6-12
309 E Grand River Rd 48892 517-521-3447
Kathy Pierman, prin. Fax 521-4740

**Wells, Delta**
Escanaba Area SD
Supt. — See Escanaba
Escanaba Student Success Center Alt
5775 Main St 49894 906-553-7334
Dan Seder, prin. Fax 553-7335

**West Bloomfield, Oakland, Pop. 67,200**
Bloomfield Hills SD
Supt. — See Bloomfield Hls
West Hills MS 600/4-8
2601 Lone Pine Rd 48323 248-341-6100
Rob Durecka, prin. Fax 341-6199

Walled Lake Consolidated SD
Supt. — See Walled Lake
Walnut Creek MS 1,000/6-8
7601 Walnut Lake Rd 48323 248-956-2400
Sophia Lafayette, prin. Fax 956-2405

West Bloomfield SD 5,500/K-12
5810 Commerce Rd 48324 248-865-6420
Dr. Gerald Hill, supt. Fax 865-6481
www.westbloomfield.k12.mi.us
Abbott MS 700/6-8
3380 Orchard Lake Rd 48324 248-865-3670
Amy Hughes, prin. Fax 865-3671
Orchard Lake MS 800/6-8
6000 Orchard Lake Rd 48322 248-865-4480
Morrison Borders, prin. Fax 865-4481
West Bloomfield HS 1,900/9-12
4925 Orchard Lake Rd 48323 248-865-6720
Patrick Watson, prin. Fax 865-6721
Other Schools – See Farmington Hills

---

Frankel Jewish Academy 200/9-12
6600 W Maple Rd 48322 248-592-5263
Rabbi Eric Grossman, hdmstr. Fax 592-0022
Michigan Jewish Institute Post-Sec.
6890 W Maple Rd 48322 248-414-6900

**West Branch, Ogemaw, Pop. 2,115**
West Branch-Rose City Area SD 2,000/PK-12
PO Box 308 48661 989-343-2000
Philip Mikulski, supt. Fax 343-2006
www.wbrc.k12.mi.us/

Ogemaw Heights HS 800/9-12
PO Box 308 48661 989-343-2020
Jonathan Good, prin. Fax 343-2130
Surline MS 500/5-8
PO Box 308 48661 989-343-2140
Wendy Tuttle, prin. Fax 343-2239

**Westland, Wayne, Pop. 82,217**
Livonia SD
Supt. — See Livonia
Western Wayne Skill Center Vo/Tech
8075 Ritz Ave 48185 734-744-2810
Alphonse DiPaolo, prin. Fax 744-2811

Wayne-Westland Community SD 12,500/PK-12
36745 Marquette St 48185 734-419-2000
Michele Harmala Ph.D., supt. Fax 595-2123
www.wwcsd.net
Ford Career-Technical Center Vo/Tech
36455 Marquette St 48185 734-419-2100
Steven Kay, prin. Fax 595-2127
Glenn HS 2,000/9-12
36105 Marquette St 48185 734-419-2300
David Ingham, prin. Fax 595-2338
Stevenson MS 900/7-8
38501 Palmer Rd 48186 734-419-2350
Adam Martin, prin. Fax 595-2692
Tinkham Alternative Education 50/Alt
450 S Venoy Rd 48186 734-419-2436
Kim Doman, dir. Fax 595-2439
Tinkham Adult and Community Education Adult
450 S Venoy Rd 48186 734-419-2427
Kim Doman, dir. Fax 595-2439
Other Schools – See Wayne

---

Huron Valley Lutheran HS 100/9-12
33740 Cowan Rd 48185 734-525-0160
Daniel Schultz, prin. Fax 525-6717
Lutheran HS Westland 200/9-12
33300 Cowan Rd 48185 734-422-2090
Steven Schwecke, prin. Fax 422-8566
Manthano Christian College Post-Sec.
6420 N Newburgh Rd 48185 734-895-3280

**Westphalia, Clinton, Pop. 918**
Pewamo-Westphalia SD 500/K-12
5101 S Clintonia Rd 48894 989-587-5100
Dr. Garth Cooper, supt. Fax 587-5120
www.pwschools.org
Pewamo-Westphalia MSHS 300/6-12
5101 S Clintonia Rd 48894 989-587-5100
Todd Simmons, prin. Fax 587-3550

**White Cloud, Newaygo, Pop. 1,346**
White Cloud SD 700/K-12
PO Box 1000 49349 231-689-6591
Barry Seabrook, supt. Fax 689-3210
www.whitecloud.net
White Cloud JSHS 300/6-12
PO Box 1000 49349 231-689-1707
Ed Canning, prin. Fax 689-3349

**Whitehall, Muskegon, Pop. 2,657**
Whitehall SD 2,000/PK-12
541 E Slocum St 49461 231-893-1005
Jerry McDowell, supt. Fax 894-6450
www.whitehallschools.net
Whitehall HS 700/9-12
3100 White Lake Dr 49461 231-893-1020
Dale McKenzie, prin. Fax 893-2923
Whitehall MS 500/6-8
401 S Elizabeth St 49461 231-893-1030
Joe Barron, prin. Fax 894-6844

**White Lake, Oakland, Pop. 22,608**
Huron Valley SD
Supt. — See Highland
International Academy West HS 9-12
1630 Bogie Lake Rd 48383 248-676-2735
Nhu Do, prin. Fax 676-2734
Lakeland HS 1,500/9-12
1630 Bogie Lake Rd 48383 248-676-8320
Paul Gmelin, prin. Fax 676-8330
White Lake MS 800/6-8
1450 Bogie Lake Rd 48383 248-684-8004
Kristin Rousseau, prin. Fax 676-8437

**White Pigeon, Saint Joseph, Pop. 1,492**
White Pigeon Community SD 800/K-12
410 Prairie Ave 49099 269-483-7676
Carrie Erlandson, supt. Fax 483-2256
www.wpcschools.org
White Pigeon JSHS 400/6-12
410 Prairie Ave 49099 269-483-7679
Jon Keyer, prin. Fax 483-8742

**Whitmore Lake, Washtenaw, Pop. 6,301**
Whitmore Lake SD 900/PK-12
8845 Main St 48189 734-449-4464
Tom DeKeyser, supt. Fax 449-5336
www.wlps.net/
Whitmore Lake HS 400/7-12
7430 Whitmore Lake Rd 48189 734-449-4461
Tom DeKeyser, prin. Fax 449-5576

**Whittemore, Iosco, Pop. 377**
Whittemore-Prescott Area SD 700/PK-12
PO Box 250 48770 989-756-2500
Joseph Perrera, supt. Fax 756-2278
www.wpas.net
Whittemore-Prescott Area JSHS 300/7-12
PO Box 250 48770 989-756-2400
Bunny Miller, prin. Fax 756-3363

**Williamston, Ingham, Pop. 3,766**
Williamston Community SD 1,900/PK-12
418 Highland St 48895 517-655-4361
Narda Murphy, supt. Fax 655-7500
www.gowcs.net
Williamston HS 600/9-12
3939 Vanneter Rd 48895 517-655-2142
Dr. Jeffrey Thoenes, prin. Fax 655-7501
Williamston MS 500/6-8
3845 Vanneter Rd 48895 517-655-4668
Scott Martin, prin. Fax 655-7502

**Wilson, Menominee, Pop. 1,391**

---

Wilson SDA Academy 50/1-10
N13925 County Road 551 49896 906-639-2566
Emily Gibbs, prin. Fax 639-2566

**Wixom, Oakland, Pop. 13,242**
Oakland ISD
Supt. — See Waterford
Oakland Opportunity Academy Alt
1000 Beck Rd 48393 248-668-5679
Dr. Marlana Krolicki, prin. Fax 668-5670
Oakland Technical Campus SW Vo/Tech
1000 Beck Rd 48393 248-922-5864
Alethia Barnes, dean

Walled Lake Consolidated SD
Supt. — See Walled Lake
Banks MS 900/6-8
1760 Charms Rd 48393 248-956-2200
Brad Paddock, prin. Fax 956-2205

---

St. Catherine of Siena Academy 9-12
28200 Napier Rd 48393 248-946-4848
Karen Ervin, prin. Fax 438-1679
Wixom Christian S 100/PK-12
620 N Wixom Rd 48393 248-624-4362

**Wolverine, Cheboygan, Pop. 234**
Wolverine Community SD 300/K-12
PO Box 219 49799 231-525-8201
Joe Hart, supt. Fax 525-8591
wolverineschools.org
Wolverine HS 200/7-12
PO Box 219 49799 231-525-9050
Stephen Seelye, prin. Fax 525-8251

**Woodhaven, Wayne, Pop. 12,674**
Gibraltar SD 3,700/PK-12
19370 Vreeland Rd 48183 734-379-6350
Amy Conway, supt. Fax 379-6359
www.gibdist.net
Other Schools – See Gibraltar, Rockwood

Woodhaven-Brownstown SD 4,700/K-12
24821 Hall Rd 48183 734-783-3300
Mark Greathead, supt. Fax 783-3316
www.woodhaven.k12.mi.us
Henry MS 800/8-9
24825 Hall Rd 48183 734-362-6100
Molly Mazei, prin. Fax 362-3045
Other Schools – See Brownstown

**Woodland, Barry, Pop. 422**
Lakewood SD 2,000/PK-12
223 W Broadway St 48897 616-374-8043
Randy Fleenor, supt. Fax 374-8858
www.lakewoodps.org
Lakewood MS 500/5-8
8699 Brown Rd 48897 616-374-2400
Kellie Rowland, prin. Fax 374-2424
Other Schools – See Lake Odessa

**Wyandotte, Wayne, Pop. 25,476**
Wyandotte SD 4,700/PK-12
PO Box 130 48192 734-759-5000
Dr. Catherine Cost, supt. Fax 759-6009
www.wyandotte.org
Roosevelt HS 1,300/9-12
540 Eureka Rd 48192 734-759-5000
Thomas Kell, prin. Fax 759-5009
Wilson MS 1,000/6-8
1275 15th St 48192 734-759-5300
Jason Krajewski, prin. Fax 759-5309

**Wyoming, Kent, Pop. 70,258**
Godfrey-Lee SD 1,800/PK-12
1324 Burton St SW 49509 616-241-4722
David Britten, supt. Fax 241-4707
www.godfrey-lee.org/
East Lee Campus 100/Alt
982 Lee St SW 49509 616-241-2661
James Jenson, prin. Fax 241-6764
Lee HS 400/9-12
1335 Lee St SW 49509 616-452-3296
Kathryn Curry, prin. Fax 241-4677
Lee MS 400/6-8
1335 Lee St SW 49509 616-452-3296
Kathryn Curry, prin. Fax 241-4677

Godwin Heights SD 2,500/K-12
15 36th St SW 49548 616-252-2090
William Fetterhoff, supt. Fax 252-2232
www.godwinschools.org
Godwin Heights HS 600/9-12
50 35th St SW 49548 616-252-2050
Chad Conklin, prin. Fax 252-2067
Godwin Heights Learning Center 100/Alt
3529 Division Ave S 49548 616-252-2040
Chad Conklin, dir. Fax 252-2043
Godwin Heights MS 600/5-8
111 36th St SE 49548 616-252-2070
Rinard Pugh, prin. Fax 252-2075

Wyoming SD 3,800/PK-12
3575 Gladiola Ave SW, 616-530-7550
Dr. Thomas Reeder, supt. Fax 530-7557
www.wyoming.k12.mi.us
Wyoming HS 800/10-12
1350 Prairie Pkwy SW 49509 616-530-7580
Nathan Robrahn, prin. Fax 530-7589
Wyoming JHS 700/7-9
2125 Wrenwood St SW, 616-530-7590
Jon Blackburn, prin. Fax 249-7673
Wyoming Community Education Center Adult
3600 Byron Center Ave SW, 616-530-7500
Adrian Lamar, dir. Fax 531-8350

---

ITT Technical Institute Post-Sec.
1980 Metro Ct SW, 616-406-1200
Potter's House HS 100/9-12
2500 Newport St SW, 616-249-8050
Dr. Peter VandeBrake, prin. Fax 249-8555
Tri-Unity Christian HS 200/7-12
2104 44th St SW, 616-532-8827
West Michigan Lutheran HS 100/6-12
601 36th St SW 49509 616-455-2200
Robert Patrick, prin. Fax 455-2211

**Yale, Saint Clair, Pop. 1,919**
Yale SD 2,100/K-12
198 School Dr 48097 810-387-3231
Kenneth Nicholl, supt. Fax 387-4418
www.ypsd.us/
Yale HS 700/9-12
247 School Dr 48097 810-387-3231
Paul Flynn, prin. Fax 387-9108
Yale JHS 500/6-8
198 School Dr 48097 810-387-3231
Brad Dykstra, prin. Fax 387-9207

**Ypsilanti, Washtenaw, Pop. 18,646**
Lincoln Consolidated SD 4,000/PK-12
8970 Whittaker Rd 48197 734-484-7000
Ellen Bonter, supt. Fax 484-1212
www.lincolnk12.org
Lincoln HS 1,300/9-12
7425 Willis Rd 48197 734-484-7004
Nicole Holden, prin. Fax 484-7012
Lincoln MS 1,100/6-8
8744 Whittaker Rd 48197 734-484-7033
Genevieve Bertsos, prin. Fax 484-7088

Washtenaw ISD
Supt. — See Ann Arbor
Washtenaw International HS 100/9-12
510 Emerick St 48198 734-994-8145
Nhu Do, prin. Fax 484-9719

Ypsilanti Community SD 3,700/PK-12
1885 Packard Rd 48197 734-221-1210
Dr. Benjamin Edmondson, supt. Fax 714-1214
www.ycschools.us
AC Tech HS 9-12
2095 Packard Rd 48197 734-221-1001
Justin Jennings, prin. Fax 221-1001
STEMM Academy 9-12
2095 Packard Rd 48197 734-221-1006
Christopher Johnson, prin. Fax 721-1003
Washtenaw International HS 9-12
510 Emerick St 48198 734-994-8145
Nhu Do, prin. Fax 484-9719
Washtenaw International Middle Academy 6-8
510 Emerick St 48198 734-994-8145
Nhu Do, prin. Fax 484-9719
Ypsilanti Community HS 800/9-12
2095 Packard Rd 48197 734-221-1001
Tanya Bowman, prin. Fax 221-1003
Ypsilanti Community MS 400/6-8
235 Spencer Ln 48198 734-221-2200
Aaron Rose, prin. Fax 221-2203
Ypsilanti New Tech HS 200/9-12
2100 Ellsworth Rd 48197 734-221-1500
Scott Snyder M.Ed., prin. Fax 221-1503
Adult Education Adult
1076 Ecorse Rd 48198 734-221-1601
Nathan Moger, dir. Fax 221-1693

---

Calvary Christian Academy 200/K-12
1007 Ecorse Rd 48198 734-482-1990
Cathy White, prin. Fax 484-5118
Eastern Michigan University 48197 Post-Sec.
734-487-1849

**Zeeland, Ottawa, Pop. 5,407**
Zeeland SD 6,000/PK-12
PO Box 110 49464 616-748-3000
Cal De Kuiper, supt. Fax 748-3035
www.zps.org/
Cityside MS 800/6-8
320 E Main Ave 49464 616-748-3200
Sarah Huizenga, prin. Fax 748-3210
Creekside MS 500/6-8
179 W Roosevelt Ave 49464 616-748-3300
Greg Eding, prin. Fax 748-3325
Venture Academy 50/Alt
3333 96th Ave 49464 616-748-4770
Roberta Brown-Parker, dir. Fax 748-1404
Zeeland East HS 1,100/9-12
3333 96th Ave 49464 616-748-3100
Marc VanSoest, prin. Fax 748-3198
Zeeland West HS 800/9-12
3390 100th Ave 49464 616-748-4500
Colleen Johnson, prin. Fax 748-4505

# MINNESOTA

## MN DEPARTMENT OF EDUCATION
## 1500 Highway 36 W, Roseville 55113-4035
## Telephone 651-582-8200
## Website education.state.mn.us

Commissioner of Education   Dr. Brenda Cassellius

## PUBLIC, PRIVATE AND CATHOLIC SECONDARY SCHOOLS

**Ada, Norman, Pop. 1,681**
Ada-Borup SD 2854 — 500/PK-12
604 W Thorpe Ave 56510 — 218-784-5300
Michael Kolness, supt. — Fax 784-3475
www.ada.k12.mn.us
Ada-Borup JSHS — 200/7-12
604 W Thorpe Ave 56510 — 218-784-5300
Michael Kolness, prin. — Fax 784-3475

**Adams, Mower, Pop. 779**
Southland SD 500 — 500/K-12
203 NW 2nd St 55909 — 507-582-3283
Jeff Sampson, supt. — Fax 582-7813
www.isd500.k12.mn.us
Southland HS — 200/9-12
203 NW 2nd St 55909 — 507-582-3568
Keith Fleming, prin. — Fax 582-7813
Southland MS — 100/6-8
203 NW 2nd St 55909 — 507-582-3568
Keith Fleming, prin. — Fax 582-7813

**Adrian, Nobles, Pop. 1,201**
Adrian SD 511 — 600/PK-12
PO Box 40 56110 — 507-483-2266
Roger Graff, supt. — Fax 483-2342
www.isd511.net
Adrian HS — 200/9-12
PO Box 40 56110 — 507-483-2232
Tim Christensen, prin. — Fax 483-2375
Adrian MS — 100/6-8
PO Box 40 56110 — 507-483-2232
Tim Christensen, prin. — Fax 483-2375

**Aitkin, Aitkin, Pop. 2,132**
Aitkin SD 1 — 1,200/PK-12
306 2nd St NW 56431 — 218-927-2115
Bernie Novak, supt. — Fax 927-4234
home.isd1.org
Aitkin Alternative S — Alt
306 2nd St NW 56431 — 218-927-3421
Chad Pederson, prin.
Aitkin HS — 600/7-12
306 2nd St NW 56431 — 218-927-2115
Chad Pederson, prin. — Fax 927-4234

**Albany, Stearns, Pop. 2,533**
Albany SD 745 — 1,400/PK-12
PO Box 40 56307 — 320-845-2171
Greg Johnson, supt. — Fax 845-4017
www.albany.k12.mn.us
Albany JSHS — 500/7-12
PO Box 40 56307 — 320-845-2171
Tim Wege, prin. — Fax 845-4017

**Albert Lea, Freeborn, Pop. 17,797**
Albert Lea SD 241 — 3,200/K-12
211 W Richway Dr 56007 — 507-379-4800
Dr. Mike Funk, supt.
alschools.org
Albert Lea ALC — 100/Alt
211 W Richway Dr 56007 — 507-379-4850
Kathy Niebuhr, admin. — Fax 379-5498
Albert Lea HS — 1,100/8-12
2000 Tiger Ln 56007 — 507-379-5340
Mark Grossklaus, prin. — Fax 379-5498

---

Riverland Community College — Post-Sec.
2200 Riverland Dr 56007 — 507-379-3300

**Albertville, Wright, Pop. 6,921**
Saint Michael-Albertville SD 885 — 4,700/PK-12
11343 50th St NE 55301 — 763-497-3180
Dr. James Behle, supt. — Fax 497-6588
www.stma.k12.mn.us
Saint Michael-Albertville MS West — 900/5-8
11343 50th St NE 55301 — 763-497-4524
Andrew Merfeld, prin. — Fax 497-6566
Other Schools – See Saint Michael

**Alden, Freeborn, Pop. 654**
Alden-Conger SD 242 — 500/PK-12
PO Box 99 56009 — 507-874-3240
Brian Shanks, supt. — Fax 874-2747
www.alden-conger.org
Alden-Conger HS — 200/7-12
PO Box 99 56009 — 507-874-3240
Brian Shanks, supt. — Fax 874-2747

**Alexandria, Douglas, Pop. 10,938**
Alexandria SD 206 — 3,800/PK-12
PO Box 308 56308 — 320-762-2141
Julie Critz, supt. — Fax 762-2765
www.alexandria.k12.mn.us
Alexandria Area HS — 1,400/9-12
4300 Pioneer Rd SE 56308 — 320-762-2142
Chad Duwenhoegger, prin. — Fax 762-7749
Discovery JHS — 900/6-8
510 McKay Ave N 56308 — 320-762-7900
Matt Aker, prin. — Fax 762-8347

---

Alexandria Technical College — Post-Sec.
1601 Jefferson St 56308 — 320-762-0221

**Andover, Anoka, Pop. 30,071**
Anoka-Hennepin SD 11
Supt. — See Anoka
Andover HS — 1,700/9-12
2115 Andover Blvd NW 55304 — 763-506-8400
Becky Brodeur, prin. — Fax 767-3575
Oak View MS — 1,300/6-8
15400 Hanson Blvd NW 55304 — 763-506-5600
Gary Lundeen, prin. — Fax 506-5603

---

Legacy Christian Academy — 500/PK-12
3037 Bunker Lake Blvd NW 55304 — 763-427-4595
Jake Mulvihill, admin. — Fax 427-3398

**Annandale, Wright, Pop. 3,201**
Annandale SD 876 — 1,600/PK-12
PO Box 190 55302 — 320-274-5602
Steve Niklaus, supt. — Fax 274-5978
www.annandale.k12.mn.us
Annandale HS — 500/9-12
PO Box 190 55302 — 320-274-8208
Scot Kerbaugh, prin. — Fax 274-2316
Annandale MS — 400/6-8
PO Box 190 55302 — 320-274-8226
Tim Prom, prin. — Fax 274-5978

**Anoka, Anoka, Pop. 16,703**
Anoka-Hennepin SD 11 — 37,200/K-12
2727 N Ferry St 55303 — 763-506-1000
David Law, supt. — Fax 506-1003
www.anoka.k12.mn.us
Anoka-Hennepin Technical HS — 100/Alt
1255 W Highway 10 55303 — 763-433-4500
Nancy Chave, prin. — Fax 433-4503
Anoka HS — 2,300/9-12
3939 7th Ave 55303 — 763-506-6200
Mike Farley, prin. — Fax 506-6203
Anoka MS of the Arts - Fred Moore Campus — 1,300/7-8
1523 5th Ave 55303 — 763-506-5000
Jerri McGonigal, prin. — Fax 506-6003
Secondary Technical Education Program — Vo/Tech
1353 W Highway 10 55303 — 763-433-4001
Jessica Lipa, dir. — Fax 433-4003
Other Schools – See Andover, Blaine, Champlin, Coon Rapids

---

Anoka Technical College — Post-Sec.
1355 W Highway 10 55303 — 763-576-4700

**Apple Valley, Dakota, Pop. 47,792**
Rosemount-Apple Valley-Eagan ISD 196
Supt. — See Rosemount
Apple Valley HS — 1,800/9-12
14450 Hayes Rd 55124 — 952-431-8200
Steve Degenaar, prin. — Fax 431-8744
Area Learning Center — 200/Alt
5840 149th St W 55124 — 952-431-8720
David Schmitz, coord. — Fax 431-8722
Eastview HS — 2,100/9-12
6200 140th St W 55124 — 952-431-8900
Randall Peterson, prin. — Fax 431-8911
Falcon Ridge MS — 1,100/6-8
12900 Johnny Cake Ridge Rd 55124 — 952-431-8760
Noel Mehus, prin. — Fax 431-8770
School of Enviromental Studies — 400/11-12
12155 Johnny Cake Ridge Rd 55124 — 952-431-8750
Dan Bodette, prin. — Fax 431-8755
Scott Highlands MS — 800/6-8
14011 Pilot Knob Rd 55124 — 952-423-7581
Daniel Wilharber, prin. — Fax 423-7601
Valley MS - S of STEM — 900/6-8
900 Garden View Dr 55124 — 952-431-8300
Dave McKeag, prin. — Fax 431-8313

**Arden Hills, Ramsey, Pop. 9,377**
Mounds View SD 621
Supt. — See Shoreview
Mounds View HS — 1,700/9-12
1900 Lake Valentine Rd 55112 — 651-621-7100
Dr. Jeff Ridlehoover, prin. — Fax 621-7105

**Arlington, Sibley, Pop. 2,206**
Sibley East SD 2310 — 1,200/PK-12
PO Box 1000 55307 — 507-964-2292
James Amsden, supt. — Fax 964-8224
www.sibleyeast.org/
Sibley East SHS — 300/10-12
PO Box 1000 55307 — 507-964-8235
Tim Schellhammer, prin. — Fax 964-8245

Other Schools – See Gaylord

**Ashby, Grant, Pop. 435**
Ashby SD 261 — 200/PK-12
PO Box 30 56309 — 218-747-2257
Allan Jensen, supt. — Fax 747-2289
www.ashby.k12.mn.us
Ashby JSHS — 100/7-12
PO Box 30 56309 — 218-747-2257
Shane Tappe, prin. — Fax 747-2289

---

Destiny Academy — 50/PK-12
27871 140th Ave 56309 — 218-685-4026
Mary Beardsley, admin. — Fax 685-6712

**Aurora, Saint Louis, Pop. 1,668**
Mesabi East SD 2711 — 900/PK-12
601 N 1st St W 55705 — 218-229-3321
Gregg Allen, supt. — Fax 229-3736
www.mesabieast.k12.mn.us/
Mesabi East JSHS — 400/7-12
601 N 1st St W 55705 — 218-229-3321
Erik Erie, prin. — Fax 229-3736

**Austin, Mower, Pop. 24,273**
Austin SD 492 — 4,500/PK-12
401 3rd Ave NW 55912 — 507-460-1900
David Krenz, supt. — Fax 460-1939
www.austin.k12.mn.us
Austin Area Learning Center — 100/Alt
301 3rd St NW 55912 — 507-460-1804
Andrea Malo, dir. — Fax 460-1810
Austin HS — 1,100/9-12
301 3rd St NW 55912 — 507-460-1800
Katie Baskin, prin. — Fax 460-1810
Ellis MS — 1,000/6-8
1700 4th Ave SE 55912 — 507-460-1500
Jason Senne, prin. — Fax 460-1510

---

Pacelli JSHS — 100/6-12
311 4th Ave NW 55912 — 507-437-3278
James Hamburge, pres. — Fax 433-5693
Riverland Community College — Post-Sec.
1900 8th Ave NW 55912 — 507-433-0600

**Babbitt, Saint Louis, Pop. 1,456**
Saint Louis County SD 2142
Supt. — See Virginia
Northeast Range S — 200/PK-12
30 South Dr 55706 — 218-827-3101
Kelly Engman, prin. — Fax 827-3103

**Badger, Roseau, Pop. 364**
Badger SD 676 — 300/PK-12
PO Box 68 56714 — 218-528-3201
Tom Jerome, supt. — Fax 528-3366
www.badger.k12.mn.us/
Badger JSHS — 100/7-12
PO Box 68 56714 — 218-528-3201
Thomas Jerome, prin. — Fax 528-3366

**Bagley, Clearwater, Pop. 1,356**
Bagley SD 162 — 1,000/PK-12
202 Bagley Ave NW 56621 — 218-694-6184
Steve Cairns, supt. — Fax 694-3221
www.bagley.k12.mn.us/
Bagley JSHS — 500/7-12
1130 Main Ave N 56621 — 218-694-3120
Helen Kennedy, prin. — Fax 694-3225

**Barnesville, Clay, Pop. 2,545**
Barnesville SD 146 — 800/PK-12
PO Box 189 56514 — 218-354-2217
Scott Loeslie, supt. — Fax 354-7260
www.barnesville.k12.mn.us/
Barnesville JSHS — 400/7-12
PO Box 189 56514 — 218-354-2228
Bryan Strand, prin. — Fax 354-2305

**Barnum, Carlton, Pop. 583**
Barnum SD 91 — 800/PK-12
3675 County Road 140 55707 — 218-389-6978
David Bottem, supt. — Fax 389-3259
www.barnum.k12.mn.us
Barnum JSHS — 300/7-12
3675 County Road 140 55707 — 218-389-3273
Brian Kazmierczak, prin. — Fax 389-3259

**Barrett, Grant, Pop. 415**
West Central Area SD 2342 — 600/PK-12
301 County Road 2 56311 — 320-528-2650
Patrick Westby, supt. — Fax 528-2279
www.westcentralareaschools.net
West Central Area Secondary S — 300/5-12
301 County Road 2 56311 — 320-528-2520
Nels Onstad, prin. — Fax 528-2609

**Battle Lake, Otter Tail, Pop. 865**
Battle Lake SD 542 500/K-12
402 W Summit St 56515 218-864-5215
Jeff Drake, supt. Fax 864-0919
www.battlelake.k12.mn.us/
Battle Lake JSHS 200/7-12
402 W Summit St 56515 218-864-5215
Jeff Drake, prin. Fax 864-8651

**Baudette, Lake of the Woods, Pop. 1,074**
Lake of the Woods SD 390 500/PK-12
PO Box 310 56623 218-634-2735
Jeff Nelson, supt. Fax 634-2467
lakeofthewoodsschool.org
Lake of the Woods JSHS 200/7-12
PO Box 310 56623 218-634-2510
Brain Novak, prin. Fax 634-2750

**Baxter, Crow Wing, Pop. 7,503**
Brainerd SD 181
Supt. — See Brainerd
Forestview MS 1,900/5-8
12149 Knollwood Dr 56425 218-454-6000
Jonathan Anderson, prin. Fax 454-6687

---

Lake Region Christian S 200/PK-12
7398 Fairview Rd 56425 218-828-1226

**Becker, Sherburne, Pop. 4,467**
Becker SD 726 2,700/PK-12
12000 Hancock St SE 55308 763-261-4502
Dr. Stephen Malone, supt. Fax 261-4559
www.becker.k12.mn.us
Becker HS 800/9-12
12000 Hancock St SE 55308 763-261-4501
Sandra Logrono, prin. Fax 261-4559
Becker MS 700/6-8
12000 Hancock St SE 55308 763-261-6300
Nancy Helmer, prin. Fax 261-6306

**Belgrade, Stearns, Pop. 733**
Belgrade-Brooten-Elrosa SD 2364 700/PK-12
PO Box 339 56312 320-254-8211
Matt Bullard, supt. Fax 254-3784
www.bbejaguars.org
Belgrade-Brooten-Elrosa JSHS 300/7-12
PO Box 339 56312 320-254-8211
Matt Bullard, prin. Fax 254-3784

**Belle Plaine, Scott, Pop. 6,520**
Belle Plaine SD 716 1,600/PK-12
130 S Willow St 56011 952-873-2400
Dr. Kelly Smith, supt. Fax 873-6909
www.belleplaine.k12.mn.us/
Belle Plaine HS 500/9-12
220 S Market St 56011 952-873-2403
Dave Kreft, prin. Fax 378-2420
Belle Plaine JHS 300/7-8
220 S Market St 56011 952-873-2403
Dave Kreft, prin. Fax 378-2420

**Bemidji, Beltrami, Pop. 12,863**
Bemidji SD 31 4,900/PK-12
502 Minnesota Ave NW 56601 218-333-3100
James Hess Ed.D., supt. Fax 333-3129
www.bemidji.k12.mn.us
Bemidji Alternative Education Center 50/Alt
502 Minnesota Ave NW 56601 218-333-3299
Tama Wesely, prin. Fax 759-3462
Bemidji HS 1,400/9-12
502 Minnesota Ave NW 56601 218-444-1600
Brian Stefanich, prin. Fax 444-1630
Bemidji MS 1,100/6-8
502 Minnesota Ave NW 56601 218-333-3215
Drew Hildenbrand, prin. Fax 333-3333
Lumberjack HS 100/Alt
502 Minnesota Ave NW 56601 218-444-1600
Brian Stefanich, prin. Fax 444-1630

---

Bemidji State University Post-Sec.
1500 Birchmont Dr NE 56601 218-755-2001
Northwest Technical College Post-Sec.
905 Grant Ave SE 56601 218-333-6600
Oak Hills Christian College Post-Sec.
1600 Oak Hills Rd SW 56601 218-751-8670

**Benson, Swift, Pop. 3,222**
Benson SD 777 800/PK-12
1400 Montana Ave 56215 320-843-2710
Dennis Laumeyer, supt. Fax 843-2262
www.benson.k12.mn.us
Benson Area Learning Center 50/Alt
1400 Montana Ave 56215 320-843-2710
Jonas Grossman, dir. Fax 843-2262
Benson HS 400/7-12
1400 Montana Ave 56215 320-843-2710
Dennis Laumeyer, prin. Fax 843-2262

**Bertha, Todd, Pop. 494**
Bertha-Hewitt SD 786 400/K-12
PO Box 8 56437 218-924-2500
Eric Koep, supt. Fax 924-3252
www.bertha-hewitt.k12.mn.us
Bertha JSHS 200/7-12
PO Box 8 56437 218-924-2500
Mary Merchant, prin. Fax 924-3252

**Bigfork, Itasca, Pop. 444**
Grand Rapids SD 318
Supt. — See Grand Rapids
Bigfork HS 100/7-12
PO Box 228 56628 218-743-3444
Scott Patrow, prin. Fax 743-3443

**Big Lake, Sherburne, Pop. 9,820**
Big Lake SD 727 3,400/PK-12
501 Minnesota Ave 55309 763-262-2536
Steve Westerberg, supt. Fax 262-2539
www.biglakeschools.org
Big Lake HS 1,000/9-12
501 Minnesota Ave 55309 763-262-2547
Bob Dockendorf, prin. Fax 262-2543
Big Lake MS 800/6-8
601 Minnesota Ave 55309 763-262-2567
Mark Ernst, prin. Fax 262-2563

**Birchdale, Koochiching**
South Koochiching-Rainy River ISD 363
Supt. — See Northome
Indus JSHS 100/7-12
8560 Highway 11 56629 218-634-2425
Michael Underwood, prin. Fax 634-1334

**Blackduck, Beltrami, Pop. 754**
Blackduck SD 32 600/PK-12
PO Box 550 56630 218-835-5200
Wallace Schoeb, supt. Fax 835-4491
www.blackduck.k12.mn.us/
Blackduck HS 300/7-12
PO Box 550 56630 218-835-5210
Joshua Grover, prin. Fax 835-5281

**Blaine, Anoka, Pop. 55,728**
Anoka-Hennepin SD 11
Supt. — See Anoka
Blaine HS 2,900/9-12
12555 University Ave NE 55434 763-506-6500
John Phelps, prin. Fax 506-6503
Roosevelt MS 1,100/6-8
650 125th Ave NE 55434 763-506-5800
Greg Blodgett, prin. Fax 506-5803

Spring Lake Park SD 16
Supt. — See Spring Lake Park
Westwood MS 800/6-8
711 91st Ave NE 55434 763-600-5300
Tom Larson, prin. Fax 600-5313

---

Minnesota School of Business Post-Sec.
3680 Pheasant Ridge Dr NE 55449 763-225-8000
Northside Christian S 100/PK-12
804 131st Ave NE 55434 763-755-3993
Beth Dvorak, admin. Fax 755-4405
Rasmussen College Post-Sec.
3629 95th Ave NE 55014 763-795-4720
Regency Beauty Academy Post-Sec.
1351 113th Ave NE 55434 763-784-9102

**Blooming Prairie, Steele, Pop. 1,975**
Blooming Prairie SD 756 700/PK-12
202 4th Ave NW 55917 507-583-4426
Barry Olson, supt. Fax 583-7952
www.blossoms.k12.mn.us
Blooming Prairie JSHS 300/7-12
202 4th Ave NW 55917 507-583-4426
John Worke, prin. Fax 583-7952

**Bloomington, Hennepin, Pop. 80,538**
Bloomington SD 271 10,300/K-12
1350 W 106th St 55431 952-681-6400
Les Fujitake, supt. Fax 681-6401
www.bloomington.k12.mn.us/
Jefferson HS 1,700/9-12
4001 W 102nd St 55437 952-806-7600
Kevin Groebner, prin. Fax 806-7601
Kennedy HS 1,600/9-12
9701 Nicollet Ave S 55420 952-681-5000
Andrew Beaton, prin. Fax 681-5001
Oak Grove MS 800/6-8
1300 W 106th St 55431 952-681-6600
Brian Ingemann, prin. Fax 681-6601
Olson MS 900/6-8
4551 W 102nd St 55437 952-806-8600
Jeremy Kuhns, prin. Fax 806-8601
Valley View MS 700/6-8
8900 Portland Ave S 55420 952-681-5800
Benjamin Magras, prin. Fax 681-5801

---

Academy College Post-Sec.
1600 W 82nd St Ste 100 55431 952-851-0066
Bethany Academy 200/K-12
4300 W 98th St 55437 952-831-8686
Bruce Maeda, head sch Fax 831-9568
Empire Beauty School Post-Sec.
9749 Lyndale Ave S 55420 952-881-8662
National American University Post-Sec.
7801 Metro Pkwy Ste 200 55425 952-356-3600
Normandale Community College Post-Sec.
9700 France Ave S 55431 952-358-8200
Northwestern Health Sciences University Post-Sec.
2501 W 84th St 55431 952-888-4777
Rasmussen College Post-Sec.
4400 W 78th St Fl 6 55435 952-545-2000

**Blue Earth, Faribault, Pop. 3,328**
Blue Earth Area ISD 2860 1,200/K-12
315 E 6th St 56013 507-526-3188
Evan Gough, supt. Fax 526-2432
www.blueearth.k12.mn.us
Blue Earth HS 400/8-12
1125 N Grove St 56013 507-526-3201
Richard Schneider, prin. Fax 526-3260

**Bluffton, Otter Tail, Pop. 204**

---

SonRise Christian S, PO Box 65 56518 50/PK-12
Cindi Wimer, admin. 218-385-3774

**Braham, Isanti, Pop. 1,757**
Braham SD 314 900/K-12
531 Elmhurst Ave S 55006 320-396-3313
Fax 396-3068
www.braham.k12.mn.us
Braham Area JSHS 400/7-12
531 Elmhurst Ave S 55006 320-396-4444
Mat Lattimore, prin. Fax 396-3068

**Brainerd, Crow Wing, Pop. 13,204**
Brainerd SD 181 6,400/PK-12
804 Oak St 56401 218-454-6900
Robert Gross, supt. Fax 454-5549
www.isd181.org
Brainerd HS 1,500/9-12
702 S 5th St 56401 218-454-6200
Andrea Rusk, prin. Fax 824-6325
Brainerd Learning Center 100/Alt
311 10th Ave NE 56401 218-454-5400
Jessica Haapajoki, prin. Fax 454-5401
Lincoln Education Center 100/Alt
604 S 6th St 56401 218-454-6600
Nancy Anderson, admin. Fax 454-6601
Other Schools – See Baxter

---

Central Lakes College Post-Sec.
501 W College Dr 56401 218-855-8000

**Brandon, Douglas, Pop. 489**
Brandon-Evansville ISD 2908 400/PK-12
PO Box 185 56315 320-524-2263
Mark Westby, supt. Fax 524-2228
www.b-e.k12.mn.us
Brandon-Evansville HS 100/9-12
PO Box 185 56315 320-524-2263
Tom Trisko, prin. Fax 524-2228
Other Schools – See Evansville

**Breckenridge, Wilkin, Pop. 3,345**
Breckenridge SD 846 700/PK-12
810 Beede Ave 56520 218-643-6822
Diane Cordes, supt. Fax 641-4035
www.breckenridge.k12.mn.us
Breckenridge HS 300/9-12
710 13th St N 56520 218-643-2694
Ivan Hirst, prin. Fax 643-5229
Breckenridge MS 100/6-8
810 Beede Ave 56520 218-643-6681
Corinna Erickson, prin. Fax 643-5021

**Brewster, Nobles, Pop. 468**
Round Lake-Brewster SD 200/PK-8
PO Box 309 56119 507-842-5951
Raymond Hassing, supt. Fax 842-5365
www.rlb.mntm.org
Other Schools – See Round Lake

**Brooklyn Center, Hennepin, Pop. 28,921**
Brooklyn Center SD 286 1,700/PK-12
6500 Humboldt Ave N 55430 763-450-3386
Mark Bonine, supt. Fax 560-2647
brooklyncenterschools.org
Brooklyn Center Secondary 700/6-12
6500 Humboldt Ave N 55430 763-561-2120
Carly Jarva, prin. Fax 450-3477
Other Schools – See Minneapolis

---

Minnesota School of Business Post-Sec.
5910 Shingle Creek Pkwy 55430 763-566-7777
National American University Post-Sec.
6200 Shingle Creek Pkwy 130 55430 763-852-7500

**Brooklyn Park, Hennepin, Pop. 73,081**
Osseo Area ISD 279
Supt. — See Maple Grove
Brooklyn MS 800/6-8
7377 Noble Ave N 55443 763-569-7700
Kim Monette, prin. Fax 569-7707
North View Intl Baccalaureate World MS 700/6-8
5869 69th Ave N 55429 763-585-7200
Diana Bledsoe, prin. Fax 585-7210
Osseo Area Learning Center 50/Alt
7300 Boone Ave N 55428 763-391-8890
Jonas Beugen, prin. Fax 391-8895
Park Center Intl Baccalaureate World SHS 1,400/9-12
7300 Brooklyn Blvd 55443 763-569-7600
John Groenke, prin. Fax 569-7606

---

Hennepin Technical College Post-Sec.
9000 Brooklyn Blvd 55445 952-995-1300
Maranatha Christian Academy 700/PK-12
9201 75th Ave N 55428 763-488-7900
Brian Sullivan, admin. Fax 315-7294
North Hennepin Community College Post-Sec.
7411 85th Ave N 55445 763-488-0391
Rasmussen College Post-Sec.
8301 93rd Ave N 55445 763-493-4500

**Browerville, Todd, Pop. 779**
Browerville SD 787 500/PK-12
PO Box 185 56438 320-594-2272
Scott Vedbraaten, supt. Fax 594-8105
www.browerville.k12.mn.us/
Browerville JSHS 300/7-12
PO Box 185 56438 320-594-2272
Patrick Sutlief, prin. Fax 594-8105

**Browns Valley, Traverse, Pop. 577**
Browns Valley SD 801 100/PK-8
PO Box N 56219 320-695-2103
Brenda Reed, supt. Fax 695-2868
www.brownsvalley.k12.mn.us/
Browns Valley MS 50/5-8
PO Box N 56219 320-695-2103
Brenda Reed, supt. Fax 695-2868

**Buffalo, Wright, Pop. 15,192**
Buffalo-Hanover-Montrose SD 5,700/K-12
214 1st Ave NE 55313 763-682-5200
Scott Thielman, supt. Fax 682-8785
www.bhmschools.org
Buffalo Community MS 1,300/6-8
1300 Highway 25 N 55313 763-682-8200
Matt Lubben, prin. Fax 682-8209
Buffalo HS 1,800/9-12
877 Bison Blvd 55313 763-682-8100
Mark Mischke, prin. Fax 682-8118
Phoenix Learning Center 50/Alt
800 8th St NE 55313 763-682-8680
Gretchen Lieb, coord. Fax 682-8681

**Burnsville, Dakota, Pop. 58,440**
Burnsville-Eagan-Savage ISD 191 9,300/K-12
100 River Ridge Ct 55337 952-707-2000
Dr. Joseph M. Gothard, supt. Fax 707-2002
www.isd191.org
Burnsville SHS 2,100/10-12
600 Highway 13 E 55337 952-707-2100
David Helke, prin. Fax 707-2102
Metcalf JHS 600/7-9
2250 Diffley Rd 55337 952-707-2400
Kelly Ronn, prin. Fax 707-2402
Nicollet JHS 600/7-9
400 E 134th St 55337 952-707-2600
Renee Brandner, prin. Fax 707-2602
Other Schools – See Eagan, Savage

Southview Christian S 100/PK-10
15304 County Road 5 55306 952-898-2727
Rayleen Hansen M.A., prin. Fax 898-0457

**Butterfield, Watonwan, Pop. 581**
Butterfield SD 836 200/K-12
PO Box 189 56120 507-956-2771
Lisa Shellum, supt. Fax 956-3431
butterfield.k12.mn.us/
Butterfield JSHS 100/7-12
PO Box 189 56120 507-956-2771
Barry Schmidt, prin. Fax 956-3431

**Byron, Olmsted, Pop. 4,841**
Byron SD 531 1,600/PK-12
1887 2nd Ave NW 55920 507-775-2383
Jeffrey Elstad, supt. Fax 775-2385
www.bears.byron.k12.mn.us
Byron HS 500/9-12
1887 2nd Ave NW 55920 507-775-2301
Steve Willman, prin. Fax 775-2303
Byron MS 500/5-8
601 4th St NW 55920 507-775-2189
Richard Swanson, prin. Fax 775-2825

**Caledonia, Houston, Pop. 2,844**
Caledonia SD 299 700/PK-12
511 W Main St 55921 507-725-3389
Benjamin Barton, supt. Fax 725-3558
www.cps.k12.mn.us/
Caledonia Area HS 300/9-12
825 N Warrior Ave 55921 507-725-3316
Paul DeMorett, prin. Fax 725-3319
Caledonia Area MS 100/6-8
825 N Warrior Ave 55921 507-725-3316
Paul DeMorett, prin. Fax 725-3319

**Cambridge, Isanti, Pop. 7,948**
Cambridge-Isanti SD 911 5,100/PK-12
625A Main St N 55008 763-689-6188
Dr. Raymond Queener, supt. Fax 689-6200
www.cambridge.k12.mn.us
Cambridge-Isanti HS 1,500/9-12
430 8th Ave NW 55008 763-689-6066
Brenda Damiani, prin. Fax 689-6060
Cambridge MS 600/6-8
31374 Xylite St NE 55008 763-552-6300
Charlie Burroughs, prin. Fax 552-6399
Other Schools – See Isanti

Anoka-Ramsey Community College Post-Sec.
300 Spirit River Dr S 55008 763-433-1100
Cambridge Christian S 200/PK-12
2211 Old Main St S 55008 763-689-3806
Scott Thune, supt. Fax 689-3807

**Campbell, Wilkin, Pop. 158**
Campbell-Tintah SD 852 100/PK-12
PO Box 8 56522 218-630-5311
Kyle Edgerton, supt. Fax 630-5881
www.campbell.k12.mn.us
Campbell-Tintah S 100/PK-12
PO Box 8 56522 218-630-5311
Kyle Edgerton, admin. Fax 630-5881

**Canby, Yellow Medicine, Pop. 1,782**
Canby SD 891 500/PK-12
307 1st St W 56220 507-223-2001
Laura Schuster, supt. Fax 223-2011
www.canbymn.org/
Canby JSHS 300/7-12
307 1st St W 56220 507-223-2002
Robert Slaba, prin. Fax 223-2012

Minnesota West Community & Tech College Post-Sec.
1011 1st St W 56220 507-223-7252

**Cannon Falls, Goodhue, Pop. 4,027**
Cannon Falls SD 252 1,100/PK-12
820 Minnesota St E 55009 507-263-6800
Beth Giese, supt. Fax 263-2555
www.cannonfallsschools.com
Cannon Falls Alternative Learning Center 50/Alt
120 State St W 55009 507-263-6800
Tim Hodges, dir. Fax 263-4888
Cannon Falls HS 600/7-12
820 Minnesota St E 55009 507-263-3331
Tim Hodges, prin. Fax 263-2515

**Carlton, Carlton, Pop. 843**
Carlton ISD 93 500/PK-12
PO Box 310 55718 218-384-4225
Peter E. Haapala, supt. Fax 384-3543
www.carlton.k12.mn.us
Carlton JSHS 200/6-12
PO Box 310 55718 218-384-4226
Craig Kotsmith, prin. Fax 384-3607

**Cass Lake, Cass, Pop. 725**
Cass Lake-Bena SD 115 1,100/PK-12
208 Central Ave NW 56633 218-335-2204
Rochelle Johnson, supt. Fax 335-2614
www.clbs.k12.mn.us
Cass Lake ALC 100/Alt
208 Central Ave NW 56633 218-335-6529
Pat Rendle, prin. Fax 335-8826
Cass Lake-Bena HS 200/9-12
15308 State Highway 371 NW 56633 218-335-2203
Bryan Hackbarth, prin. Fax 335-7649
Cass Lake-Bena MS 300/5-8
15314 State Highway 371 NW 56633 218-335-7851
Kevin Wellen, prin. Fax 335-1194

Leech Lake Tribal College Post-Sec.
PO Box 180 56633 218-335-4200

**Center City, Chisago, Pop. 624**

Hazelden Graduate School Post-Sec.
PO Box 11 55012 651-213-4175

**Champlin, Hennepin, Pop. 22,615**
Anoka-Hennepin SD 11
Supt. — See Anoka
Champlin Park HS 2,900/9-12
6025 109th Ave N 55316 763-506-6800
Michael George, prin. Fax 506-6803
Jackson MS 1,900/6-8
6000 109th Ave N 55316 763-506-5200
Thomas Hagerty, prin. Fax 506-5203

**Chanhassen, Carver, Pop. 22,622**
Eastern Carver County SD 112
Supt. — See Chaska
Chanhassen HS 1,500/9-12
2200 Lyman Blvd 55317 952-556-3500
Tim Dorway, prin. Fax 556-3509

**Chaska, Carver, Pop. 23,347**
Eastern Carver County SD 112 9,000/PK-12
11 Peavey Rd 55318 952-556-6100
Dr. Jim Bauck, supt. Fax 556-6109
www.district112.org
Chaska HS 1,200/9-12
545 Pioneer Trl 55318 952-556-7100
David Brecht, prin. Fax 556-7109
Chaska MS East 700/6-8
1600 Park Ridge Dr 55318 952-556-7600
James Bach, prin. Fax 556-7609
Chaska MS West 800/6-8
140 Engler Blvd 55318 952-556-7400
Sheryl Hough, prin. Fax 556-7409
Integrated Arts Academy Alt
11 Peavey Rd 55318 952-556-6201
Jackie Johnston, prin. Fax 556-6109
Pioneer Ridge MS 700/6-8
1085 Pioneer Trl 55318 952-556-7800
Dana Miller, prin. Fax 556-7809
Other Schools – See Chanhassen

Southwest Christian HS 200/9-12
1981 Bavaria Rd 55318 952-556-0040
Dan Beckering, head sch Fax 556-5567

**Chatfield, Fillmore, Pop. 2,758**
Chatfield SD 227 900/PK-12
205 Union St NE 55923 507-867-4210
Edward Harris, supt. Fax 518-0704
www.chatfield.k12.mn.us
Chatfield JSHS 400/7-12
205 Union St NE 55923 507-867-4210
Randy Paulson, prin. Fax 518-0701

**Chisago City, Chisago, Pop. 4,910**

Chisago Lakes Baptist S 100/PK-12
9387 Wyoming Trl 55013 651-257-4587

**Chisholm, Saint Louis, Pop. 4,873**
Chisholm SD 695 700/PK-12
300 3rd Ave SW 55719 218-254-5726
James Varichak, supt. Fax 254-3741
www.chisholm.k12.mn.us
Chisholm HS 300/7-12
301 4th St SW 55719 218-254-5726
Richard Aldrich, prin. Fax 254-1434

**Chokio, Stevens, Pop. 399**
Chokio-Alberta SD 771 100/PK-12
PO Box 68 56221 320-324-7131
Dr. David Baukol, supt. Fax 324-2731
www.chokioalberta.k12.mn.us
Chokio-Alberta S 100/PK-12
PO Box 68 56221 320-324-7131
Tate Jerome, prin. Fax 324-2731

**Circle Pines, Anoka, Pop. 4,828**
Centennial SD 12 6,400/PK-12
4707 North Rd 55014 763-792-6000
Brian Dietz, supt. Fax 792-6050
www.isd12.org
Centennial ALC 100/Alt
4203 Woodland Rd 55014 763-398-2960
Stephanie Miska, dir. Fax 717-4538
Centennial HS 2,100/9-12
4757 North Rd 55014 763-792-5000
Tom Breuning, prin. Fax 792-5050
Other Schools – See Lino Lakes

**Clara City, Chippewa, Pop. 1,350**
MACCRAY SD 2180 700/K-12
PO Box 690 56222 320-847-2154
Brian Koslofsky, supt. Fax 847-3239
www.maccray.k12.mn.us
MACCRAY Alternative Learning 50/Alt
PO Box 690 56222 320-847-3525
Gary Sims, dir. Fax 847-2154
MACCRAY JSHS 300/7-12
PO Box 690 56222 320-847-2154
Melissa Sparks, prin. Fax 847-3239

**Clarissa, Todd, Pop. 674**
Eagle Valley SD 2759 300/PK-12
PO Box 468 56440 218-756-3631
Barry Johnson, supt. Fax 738-6493
www.evps.k12.mn.us
Other Schools – See Eagle Bend

**Clearbrook, Clearwater, Pop. 513**
Clearbrook-Gonvick SD 2311 400/PK-12
16770 Clearwater Lake Rd 56634 218-776-3112
Wayne Olson, supt. Fax 776-3117
www.clearbrook-gonvick.k12.mn.us
Clearbrook-Gonvick JSHS 200/7-12
16770 Clearwater Lake Rd 56634 218-776-3112
Kristil McDonald, prin. Fax 776-3117

**Cleveland, LeSueur, Pop. 714**
Cleveland SD 391 200/PK-12
PO Box 310 56017 507-931-5953
Brian Phillips, supt. Fax 931-9088
cleveland.k12.mn.us/
Cleveland S 200/PK-12
PO Box 310 56017 507-931-5953
Scott Lusk, prin. Fax 931-9088

**Climax, Polk, Pop. 262**
Climax-Shelly SD 592 100/PK-12
PO Box 67 56523 218-857-2385
Norman Baumgarn, supt. Fax 857-3544
www.climax.k12.mn.us
Climax-Shelly S 100/PK-12
PO Box 67 56523 218-857-2385
Nancy Newcomb, prin. Fax 857-3544

**Clinton, Big Stone, Pop. 449**
Clinton-Graceville-Beardsley SD 2888 300/K-12
PO Box 361 56225 320-325-5282
Phil Grant, supt. Fax 325-5509
www.graceville.k12.mn.us
Lismore Colony S 50/K-12
PO Box 361 56225 320-325-5583
Larry Mischke, prin. Fax 325-5509
Other Schools – See Graceville

**Cloquet, Carlton, Pop. 11,711**
Cloquet SD 94 2,300/K-12
302 14th St 55720 218-879-6721
Ken Scarbrough, supt. Fax 879-6724
www.isd94.org
Cloquet Area Alternative Education 100/Alt
302 14th St 55720 218-879-0115
Connie Hyde, prin. Fax 879-6941
Cloquet HS 700/9-12
1000 18th St 55720 218-879-3393
Warren Peterson, prin. Fax 879-6494
Cloquet MS 500/6-8
509 Carlton Ave 55720 218-879-3328
Tom Brenner, prin. Fax 879-4175

Fond du Lac Tribal Community College Post-Sec.
2101 14th St 55720 218-879-0800

**Cokato, Wright, Pop. 2,654**
Dassel-Cokato SD 466 2,300/PK-12
4852 Reardon Ave SW 55321 320-286-4100
Jeff Powers, supt. Fax 286-4101
www.dc.k12.mn.us
Dassel-Cokato Area Learning Center 50/Alt
4852 Reardon Ave SW 55321 320-286-4100
Jon Nelson, dir. Fax 286-4132
Dassel-Cokato HS 600/9-12
4852 Reardon Ave SW 55321 320-286-4100
Dean Jennissen, prin. Fax 286-4201
Dassel-Cokato MS 700/5-8
4852 Reardon Ave SW 55321 320-286-4100
Alisa Johnson, prin. Fax 286-4176

**Cold Spring, Stearns, Pop. 3,975**
Rocori SD 750 2,000/PK-12
534 5th Ave N 56320 320-685-4901
Scott Staska, supt. Fax 685-4906
www.rocori.k12.mn.us/
Rocori ALC, 534 5th Ave N 56320 Alt
Mindi Jenson, admin. 320-685-4904
Rocori HS 800/9-12
534 5th Ave N 56320 320-685-8683
Mark Jenson, prin. Fax 685-4968
Rocori MS 500/6-8
534 5th Ave N 56320 320-685-3296
Mark Jenson, prin. Fax 685-3448

**Coleraine, Itasca, Pop. 1,927**
Greenway SD 316
Supt. — See Marble
Greenway HS 300/5-12
PO Box 520 55722 218-245-1287
Anne Olson, prin. Fax 245-2397

**Collegeville, Stearns**

St. Johns Preparatory S 300/6-12
PO Box 4000 56321 320-363-3321
Matt Reichert, prin. Fax 525-7737
St. John's University Post-Sec.
PO Box 2000 56321 320-363-2011

**Columbia Heights, Anoka, Pop. 18,748**
Columbia Heights SD 13 2,900/PK-12
1440 49th Ave NE 55421 763-528-4500
Kathy Kelly, supt. Fax 571-9203
www.colheights.k12.mn.us
Columbia Academy 600/6-8
900 49th Ave NE 55421 763-586-4701
Mary Bussman, prin. Fax 528-4707
Columbia Heights HS 900/9-12
1400 49th Ave NE 55421 763-528-4600
Joann Karetov, prin. Fax 571-9267

**Comfrey, Brown, Pop. 378**
Comfrey SD 81 200/K-12
305 Ochre St W 56019 507-877-3491
Kirsten Hutchison, supt. Fax 877-3492
www.comfreyps.new.rschooltoday.com
Comfrey JSHS 100/7-12
305 Ochre St W 56019 507-877-3491
Kirsten Hutchison, prin. Fax 877-3492

**Cook, Saint Louis, Pop. 560**
Saint Louis County SD 2142
Supt. — See Virginia
North Woods S 200/PK-12
10248 E Olson Rd 55723 218-666-5221
John Metsa, prin. Fax 666-5223

**Coon Rapids, Anoka, Pop. 59,722**
Anoka-Hennepin SD 11
Supt. — See Anoka
Anoka-Hennepin Regional HS 200/Alt
1313 Coon Rapids Blvd NW 55433 763-506-7400
Nancy Chave, prin. Fax 506-7403
Coon Rapids HS 2,300/9-12
2340 Northdale Blvd NW 55433 763-506-7100
Annette Ziegler, prin. Fax 506-7103
Coon Rapids MS 1,300/6-8
11600 Raven St NW 55433 763-506-4800
Tom Shaw, prin. Fax 506-4803
Northdale MS 1,200/6-8
11301 Dogwood St NW 55448 763-506-5400
Kari Rock, prin. Fax 506-5403
Pathways Adult
11238 Crooked Lake Blvd NW 55433 763-506-7600
Kathy Ferguson, prin. Fax 506-7603

---

Anoka-Ramsey Community College Post-Sec.
11200 Mississippi Blvd NW 55433 763-433-1100

**Cottage Grove, Washington, Pop. 33,853**
South Washington County SD 833 17,400/K-12
7362 E Point Douglas Rd S 55016 651-425-6300
Keith Jacobus Ph.D., supt. Fax 425-6318
www.sowashco.org
Alternative Learning Center 100/Alt
8400 E Point Douglas Rd S 55016 651-425-7000
Mike Mahaffey, prin. Fax 425-7015
Cottage Grove MS 1,100/6-8
9775 Indian Blvd S 55016 651-425-6800
Elise Block, prin. Fax 425-6828
Park HS 1,800/9-12
8040 80th St S 55016 651-425-3700
Kerry Timmerman, prin. Fax 425-3705
Other Schools – See Saint Paul Park, Woodbury

**Cottonwood, Lyon, Pop. 1,201**
Lakeview SD 2167 600/PK-12
PO Box 107 56229 507-423-5164
Chris Fenske, supt. Fax 423-5568
www.lakeview2167.com
Lakeview HS 300/7-12
PO Box 107 56229 507-423-5166
Philip Lienemann, prin. Fax 423-5568

**Cromwell, Carlton, Pop. 231**
Cromwell-Wright SD 95 300/PK-12
PO Box 7 55726 218-644-3737
Dr. Ronald Bratlie, supt. Fax 644-3992
www.cromwellwright.k12.mn.us
Cromwell-Wright JSHS 100/7-12
PO Box 7 55726 218-644-3716
Nathan Libbon, prin. Fax 644-3992

**Crookston, Polk, Pop. 7,779**
Crookston SD 593 1,300/PK-12
402 W Fisher Ave Ste 593 56716 218-281-5313
Chris Bates, supt. Fax 281-3505
www.crookston.k12.mn.us
Crookston HS 500/7-12
402 W Fisher Ave 56716 218-281-2144
Eric Bubna, prin. Fax 281-4709
New Paths Area Learning Center 100/Alt
121 E 3rd St 56716 218-281-5864
Eric Bubna, prin. Fax 281-2386

---

University of Minnesota Crookston Post-Sec.
2900 University Ave 56716 218-281-6510

**Crosby, Crow Wing, Pop. 2,354**
Crosby-Ironton SD 182 1,200/PK-12
711 Poplar St 56441 218-545-8801
Dr. Jamie Skjeveland, supt. Fax 545-8836
www.ci.k12.mn.us
Crosby-Ironton JSHS 500/7-12
711 Poplar St 56441 218-545-8802
James Christenson, prin. Fax 545-8835

**Culver, Saint Louis**
Saint Louis County SD 2142
Supt. — See Virginia
South Ridge S PK-12
8162 Swan Lake Rd 55779 218-345-6789
Andrew Bernard, prin. Fax 345-6790

**Dawson, Lac qui Parle, Pop. 1,527**
Dawson-Boyd SD 378 500/PK-12
848 Chestnut St 56232 320-769-2955
Brad Madsen, supt. Fax 769-4502
dawsonboydschools.org/
Dawson-Boyd JSHS 200/7-12
848 Chestnut St 56232 320-769-2955
Ryan Stotesbery, prin. Fax 769-4502

**Deer River, Itasca, Pop. 888**
Deer River SD 317 900/PK-12
PO Box 307 56636 218-246-2420
Matt Grose, supt. Fax 246-8948
www.isd317.org
Deer River JSHS 400/6-12
PO Box 307 56636 218-246-8241
Lisa Cooney, prin. Fax 246-8717

**Delano, Wright, Pop. 5,379**
Delano SD 879 2,300/PK-12
700 Elm Ave E 55328 763-972-3365
Matthew Schoen, supt. Fax 972-6706
www.delano.k12.mn.us
Delano HS 800/9-12
700 Elm Ave E 55328 763-972-3365
Steven Heil, prin. Fax 972-6706
Delano MS 700/5-8
700 Elm Ave E 55328 763-972-3365
Barry Voight, prin. Fax 972-6876

**Detroit Lakes, Becker, Pop. 8,324**
Detroit Lakes SD 22 2,700/PK-12
PO Box 766 56502 218-847-9271
Doug Froke, supt. Fax 847-9273
www.dlschools.net/
Detroit Lakes ALC 50/Alt
826 Summit Ave 56501 218-847-5687
Peter Sasso-Lundin, prin. Fax 847-9273
Detroit Lakes HS 800/9-12
1301 Roosevelt Ave 56501 218-847-4491
Darren Wolf, prin. Fax 846-1797
Detroit Lakes MS 600/6-8
510 11th Ave 56501 218-847-9228
Michael Suckert, prin. Fax 847-0057

---

MN State Community & Technical College Post-Sec.
900 Highway 34 E 56501 218-846-3700

**Dilworth, Clay, Pop. 3,965**
Dilworth-Glyndon-Felton SD 2164 1,300/PK-12
PO Box 188 56529 218-477-6800
Bryan Thygeson, supt. Fax 477-6807
www.dgf.k12.mn.us
Dilworth-Glyndon-Felton MS 200/6-8
PO Box 188 56529 218-477-6803
Heidi Critchley, prin. Fax 477-6807
Other Schools – See Glyndon

**Dodge Center, Dodge, Pop. 2,647**
Triton SD 2125 1,200/PK-12
813 W Highway St 55927 507-374-2192
Brett Joyce, supt. Fax 374-6524
www.triton.k12.mn.us
Triton HS 300/9-12
813 W Highway St 55927 507-374-6305
Craig Schlichting, prin. Fax 374-2447
Triton MS 200/6-8
813 W Highway St 55927 507-633-8676
Mark Raymond, prin. Fax 633-8673

**Duluth, Saint Louis, Pop. 83,742**
Duluth ISD 709 7,900/PK-12
215 N 1st Ave E 55802 218-336-8700
William Gronseth, supt. Fax 336-8773
www.isd709.org
Area Learning Center 100/Alt
215 N 1st Ave E 55802 218-336-8756
Adrian Norman, prin. Fax 336-8770
Denfeld HS 1,300/9-12
401 N 44th Ave W 55807 218-336-8830
Tonya Sconiers, prin. Fax 336-8844
East HS 1,600/9-12
301 N 40th Ave E 55804 218-336-8845
Laurie Knapp, prin. Fax 336-8859
Lincoln Park MS 500/6-8
3215 W 3rd St 55806 218-336-8880
Brenda Vatthauer, prin. Fax 336-8894
Ordean East MS 800/6-8
2900 E 4th St 55812 218-336-8940
Gina Kleive, prin. Fax 336-8949
Adult Basic Education / GED Adult
215 N 1st Ave E 55802 218-336-8790
Patricia Fleege, admin. Fax 336-8791

---

College of Saint Scholastica Post-Sec.
1200 Kenwood Ave 55811 218-723-6000
Cosmetology Careers Unlimited - Duluth Post-Sec.
121 W Superior St 55802 218-722-7484
Duluth Business University Post-Sec.
4724 Mike Colalillo Dr 55807 218-722-4000
Lake Superior College Post-Sec.
2101 Trinity Rd 55811 218-733-7600
Lakeview Christian Academy 200/PK-12
155 W Central Entrance 55811 218-723-8844
Todd Benson, admin. Fax 722-7850
Marshall S 500/4-12
1215 Rice Lake Rd 55811 218-727-7266
Kevin Breen, head sch Fax 727-1569
University of Minnesota Duluth Post-Sec.
1049 University Dr 55812 218-726-8000

**Eagan, Dakota, Pop. 62,501**
Burnsville-Eagan-Savage ISD 191
Supt. — See Burnsville
Burnsville Alternative HS 200/Alt
2140 Diffley Rd 55122 952-707-4077
Janice Porter, prin. Fax 707-4024

Rosemount-Apple Valley-Eagan ISD 196
Supt. — See Rosemount
Black Hawk MS 900/6-8
1540 Deerwood Dr 55122 651-683-8521
Richard Wendorff, prin. Fax 683-8527
Dakota Hills MS 1,100/6-8
4183 Braddock Trl 55123 651-683-6800
Trevor Johnson, prin. Fax 683-6858
Eagan HS 2,200/9-12
4185 Braddock Trl 55123 651-683-6900
Polly Reikowski, prin. Fax 683-6910

---

Everest Institute Post-Sec.
1000 Blue Gentian Rd 55121 651-688-2145
Rasmussen College Post-Sec.
3500 Federal Dr 55122 651-687-9000
Trinity S at River Ridge 300/7-12
601 River Ridge Pkwy 55121 651-789-2890
Twin Cities Argosy University Post-Sec.
1515 Central Pkwy 55121 888-844-2004

**Eagle Bend, Todd, Pop. 527**
Eagle Valley SD 2759
Supt. — See Clarissa
Eagle Valley JSHS 100/7-12
PO Box 299 56446 218-756-3631
Barry Johnson, admin. Fax 738-6493

**East Grand Forks, Polk, Pop. 8,422**
East Grand Forks SD 595 1,700/PK-12
PO Box 151 56721 218-773-3494
David Pace, supt. Fax 773-7408
www.egf.k12.mn.us/
Central MS 400/6-8
PO Box 151 56721 218-773-1141
Lon Ellingson, prin. Fax 773-9112
East Grand Forks HS 500/9-12
PO Box 151 56721 218-773-2405
Brian Loer, prin. Fax 773-3070

---

Northland Community & Technical College Post-Sec.
2022 Central Ave NE 56721 218-793-2800
Sacred Heart HS 100/7-12
122 3rd St NW 56721 218-773-0230
David Andrys, prin. Fax 773-7042

**Eden Prairie, Hennepin, Pop. 59,499**
Eden Prairie SD 272 9,400/PK-12
8100 School Rd 55344 952-975-7000
Curt Tryggestad Ph.D., supt. Fax 975-7020
www.edenpr.org
Central MS 1,400/7-8
8025 School Rd 55344 952-975-7300
Nathan Swenson, prin. Fax 975-7320
Eden Prairie HS 3,100/9-12
17185 Valley View Rd 55346 952-975-8000
Conn McCartan, prin. Fax 975-8020

---

International School of Minnesota 400/PK-12
6385 Beach Rd 55344 952-918-1800
ITT Technical Institute Post-Sec.
8911 Columbine Rd 55347 952-914-5300

**Eden Valley, Meeker, Pop. 1,031**
Eden Valley-Watkins SD 463 900/PK-12
298 Brooks St N 55329 320-453-2900
Mark Messman, supt. Fax 453-5600
www.evw.k12.mn.us
Eden Valley Secondary S 400/7-12
298 Brooks St N 55329 320-453-2900
Bruce Kiehn, prin. Fax 453-5600

**Edgerton, Pipestone, Pop. 1,174**
Edgerton SD 581 300/PK-12
PO Box 28 56128 507-442-7881
Keith Buckridge, supt. Fax 442-8541
edgertonpublic.com
Edgerton JSHS 200/7-12
PO Box 28 56128 507-442-7881
Brian Gilbertson, prin. Fax 442-8541

---

Southwest Minnesota Christian HS 100/9-12
550 W Elizabeth St 56128 507-442-4471
Darrel Ulferts, prin. Fax 442-5801

**Edina, Hennepin, Pop. 47,052**
Edina SD 273 8,200/K-12
5701 Normandale Rd 55424 952-848-3900
Ric Dressen Ed.D., supt. Fax 848-3901
www.edinaschools.org
Edina SHS 1,900/10-12
6754 Valley View Rd 55439 952-848-3800
Bruce Locklear, prin. Fax 848-3801
South View MS 1,300/6-9
4725 S View Ln 55424 952-848-3700
Beth Russell, prin. Fax 848-3701
Valley View MS 1,300/6-9
6750 Valley View Rd 55439 952-848-3500
Shawn Dudley, prin. Fax 848-3501

---

DeVry University Post-Sec.
7700 France Ave S Ste 575 55435 952-838-1860
Minneapolis Media Institute Post-Sec.
4100 W 76th St 55435 866-701-1310

**Elgin, Wabasha, Pop. 1,079**
Plainview-Elgin-Millville ISD 2899
Supt. — See Plainview
Plainview-Elgin-Millville JHS 200/7-8
70 1st St SE 55932 507-876-2521
Clark Olstad, prin. Fax 876-2110

**Elk River, Sherburne, Pop. 22,557**
Elk River Area SD 728 11,700/K-12
815 Highway 10 55330 763-241-3400
Dr. Mark Bezek, supt. Fax 241-3407
www.elkriver.k12.mn.us
Elk River HS 1,700/9-12
900 School St NW 55330 763-241-3434
Terry Bizal, prin. Fax 241-3421
Salk MS 700/6-8
11970 Highland Rd NW 55330 763-241-3455
Julie Athman, prin. Fax 241-3456
Sand Community HS 100/Alt
1232 School St NW 55330 763-241-3530
Thomas Hoffman, prin. Fax 241-3532
VandenBerge MS 500/6-8
948 Proctor Ave NW 55330 763-241-3450
Marcia Welch, prin. Fax 241-3552
Other Schools – See Rogers, Zimmerman

---

Minnesota School of Business Post-Sec.
11500 193rd Ave NW 55330 763-367-7000

**Ellsworth, Nobles, Pop. 460**
Ellsworth SD 514 100/PK-12
PO Box 8 56129 507-967-2242
John Willey, supt. Fax 967-2588
www.ellsworth.mntm.org

Ellsworth S 100/PK-12
PO Box 8 56129 507-967-2242
John Willey, prin. Fax 963-2588

**Ely, Saint Louis, Pop. 3,405**
ISD 696 500/PK-12
600 E Harvey St 55731 218-365-6166
Alexis Leitgeb, supt. Fax 365-6138
www.ely.k12.mn.us
Ely Memorial HS 200/7-12
600 E Harvey St 55731 218-365-6166
Mary McGrane, prin. Fax 365-6138

---

Vermillion Community College Post-Sec.
1900 E Camp St 55731 218-235-2100

**Erskine, Polk, Pop. 492**
Win-E-Mac SD 2609 400/PK-12
23130 345th St SE 56535 218-687-2236
Randy Bruer, supt. Fax 563-2902
www.win-e-mac.k12.mn.us
Win-E-Mac JSHS 200/7-12
23130 345th St SE 56535 218-687-2236
Kevin McKeever, prin. Fax 563-2902

**Esko, Carlton, Pop. 1,843**
Esko SD 99 1,200/PK-12
PO Box 10 55733 218-879-2969
Aaron Fischer, supt. Fax 879-7490
www.esko.k12.mn.us/
Lincoln JSHS 600/7-12
PO Box 10 55733 218-879-4673
Greg Hexum, prin. Fax 879-7490

**Evansville, Douglas, Pop. 609**
Brandon-Evansville ISD 2908
Supt. — See Brandon
Brandon-Evansville MS 50/6-8
PO Box 40 56326 218-948-2241
Mark Westby, prin. Fax 948-2441

**Eveleth, Saint Louis, Pop. 3,636**
Eveleth-Gilbert SD 2154 1,000/PK-12
801 Jones St 55734 218-744-7700
Jeff Carey, supt. Fax 744-4381
www.isd2154.k12.mn.us
Eveleth-Gilbert SHS 300/9-12
801 Jones St 55734 218-744-7706
Danette Seboe, prin. Fax 744-4381
Other Schools – See Gilbert

---

Mesabi Range Community & Technical Coll. Post-Sec.
PO Box 648 55734 218-741-3095

**Excelsior, Hennepin, Pop. 2,144**
Minnetonka SD 276
Supt. — See Minnetonka
Minnetonka West MS 900/6-8
6421 Hazeltine Blvd 55331 952-401-5300
Dr. Paula Hoff, prin. Fax 401-5350

**Eyota, Olmsted, Pop. 1,965**
Dover-Eyota SD 533 1,200/PK-12
615 South Ave SW 55934 507-545-2125
Michael Carolan, supt. Fax 545-2349
www.desch.org
Dover-Eyota HS 300/9-12
615 South Ave SW 55934 507-545-2631
Todd Rowekamp, prin. Fax 545-2218
Dover-Eyota MS 300/6-8
615 South Ave SW 55934 507-545-2631
Todd Rowekamp, prin. Fax 545-2218

**Fairfax, Renville, Pop. 1,227**
GFW SD 2365
Supt. — See Gibbon
GFW MS 200/5-8
300 2nd Ave SE 55332 507-426-7251
Ralph Fairchild, prin. Fax 426-7425

---

Prairie Lutheran MS 50/5-8
PO Box 130 55332 507-426-7755
Macord Johnson, prin. Fax 426-8372

**Fairmont, Martin, Pop. 10,613**
Fairmont Area SD 2752 1,700/PK-12
714 Victoria St Ste 103 56031 507-238-4234
Joseph Brown, supt. Fax 235-4050
fairmont.k12.mn.us
Fairmont JSHS 800/7-12
900 Johnson St 56031 507-238-4411
Kim Niss, prin. Fax 235-4130

**Faribault, Rice, Pop. 23,011**
Faribault SD 656 3,800/PK-12
2800 1st Ave NW Ste 1 55021 507-333-6000
Todd Sesker, supt. Fax 333-6050
www.faribault.k12.mn.us/
Faribault ALC 100/Alt
PO Box 618 55021 507-333-6187
Margaret Gare, dir. Fax 333-6048
Faribault HS 1,100/9-12
330 9th Ave SW 55021 507-333-6100
Lyle Turtle, prin. Fax 333-6248
Faribault MS 900/6-8
704 17th St SW 55021 507-333-6300
Michael Meihak, prin. Fax 333-6400

---

Bethlehem Academy 300/6-12
105 3rd Ave SW 55021 507-334-3948
Thomas Donlon, prin. Fax 334-3949
Minnesota School for the Deaf Post-Sec.
615 Olof Hanson Dr 55021
Shattuck/St. Marys S 400/6-12
PO Box 218 55021 507-333-1500
Nick Stoneman, pres. Fax 333-1591
South Central College Post-Sec.
1225 3rd St SW 55021 800-422-0391

**Farmington, Dakota, Pop. 20,570**
Farmington SD 192 6,500/PK-12
20655 Flagstaff Ave 55024 651-463-5000
Jay Haugen, supt. Fax 463-5010
www.farmington.k12.mn.us
Boeckman MS 700/6-8
800 Denmark Ave 55024 651-460-1400
Dan Miller, prin. Fax 460-1410
Dodge MS 800/6-8
4200 208th St W 55024 651-460-1500
Chris Bussmann, prin. Fax 460-1510
Farmington HS 1,700/9-12
20655 Flagstaff Ave 55024 651-460-1400
Jason Berg, prin. Fax 460-1410
Special Services Center Alt
510 Walnut St 55024 651-463-5020
Carla Nohr Schulz, dir. Fax 463-5021

---

Christian Life S 200/PK-12
6300 212th St W 55024 651-463-4545
Rev. Darin Kindle, admin. Fax 463-8353

**Fergus Falls, Otter Tail, Pop. 12,946**
Fergus Falls SD 544 2,400/PK-12
601 Randolph Ave 56537 218-998-0544
Gerald Ness, supt. Fax 755-5000
www.isd544.org
Area Learning Center 100/Alt
340 Friberg Ave 56537 218-739-2360
Dean Monke, prin. Fax 755-5000
Kennedy HS 1,200/9-12
601 Randolph Ave 56537 218-998-0544
Dean Monke, prin. Fax 998-3947
Kennedy MS 500/6-8
601 Randolph Ave 56537 218-998-0544
Dean Monke, prin. Fax 755-5000

---

Hillcrest Lutheran Academy 200/7-12
610 Hillcrest Dr 56537 218-739-3371
Jeff Isaac M.Ed., prin. Fax 739-3372
Lutheran Brethren Seminary Post-Sec.
815 W Vernon Ave 56537 218-739-3375
MN State Community & Technical College Post-Sec.
1414 College Way 56537 218-736-1500

**Fertile, Polk, Pop. 831**
Fertile-Beltrami SD 599 500/PK-12
210 S Mill St 56540 218-945-6933
Brian Clarke, supt. Fax 945-6934
fertilebeltrami.k12.mn.us
Fertile-Beltrami JSHS 200/7-12
210 S Mill St 56540 218-945-6953
Nathaniel Messick, prin. Fax 945-6934

**Finlayson, Pine, Pop. 312**
East Central SD 2580 700/PK-12
61085 State Highway 23 55735 320-245-2289
Andy Almos, supt. Fax 245-5453
www.eastcentral.k12.mn.us
East Central Secondary S 300/6-12
61085 State Highway 23 55735 320-245-2289
Stef Youngberg, prin. Fax 245-2448
Other Schools – See Sandstone

**Fisher, Polk, Pop. 434**
Fisher SD 600 300/PK-12
313 Park Ave 56723 218-891-4105
Evan Hanson, supt. Fax 891-4251
www.fisher.k12.mn.us
Fisher JSHS 100/7-12
313 Park Ave 56723 218-891-4905
Evan Hanson, admin. Fax 891-4251

**Floodwood, Saint Louis, Pop. 508**
Floodwood SD 698 300/PK-12
PO Box 287 55736 218-476-2285
Rae Villebrun, supt. Fax 476-2813
www.floodwood.k12.mn.us/
Floodwood HS 100/7-12
PO Box 287 55736 218-476-2285
Rae Villebrun, prin. Fax 476-2813

**Foley, Benton, Pop. 2,576**
Foley SD 51 1,900/PK-12
840 Norman Ave N 56329 320-968-7175
Darrin Strosahl, supt. Fax 968-8608
foley.k12.mn.us
Foley HS 500/9-12
621 Penn St 56329 320-968-7246
Shayne Kusler, prin. Fax 968-8456
Foley MS 700/4-8
840 Norman Ave N 56329 320-968-6251
Brad Kelvington, prin. Fax 968-8608

**Forest Lake, Washington, Pop. 18,070**
Forest Lake SD 831 6,700/PK-12
6100 210th St N 55025 651-982-8100
Dr. Linda Madsen, supt. Fax 982-8114
www.flaschools.org
Area Learning Center 100/Alt
200 4th St SW 55025 651-982-3171
Kelly Tschudy-Lafean, prin. Fax 982-3172
Century JHS 900/7-9
21395 Goodview Ave N 55025 651-982-3000
John-Paul Jacobson, prin. Fax 982-3017
Forest Lake SHS 1,500/10-12
6101 Scandia Trl N 55025 651-982-8400
Dr. Steve Massey, prin. Fax 982-8428
Southwest JHS 700/7-9
943 9th Ave SW 55025 651-982-8700
Scott Geary, prin. Fax 982-8798

**Foreston, Mille Lacs, Pop. 528**

---

Faith Christian S 100/PK-12
11818 160th Ave 56330 320-294-5501
Nate Johnson, admin.

**Fosston, Polk, Pop. 1,489**
Fosston SD 601 600/PK-12
301 1st St E 56542 218-435-6335
Mark Nohner, supt. Fax 435-1663
www.fosston.k12.mn.us
Fosston JSHS 300/7-12
301 1st St E 56542 218-435-1909
Patti Johnson, prin. Fax 435-6340

**Frazee, Becker, Pop. 1,295**
Frazee-Vergas SD 23 900/PK-12
305 N Lake St 56544 218-334-3181
Terry S. Karger, supt. Fax 334-3182
www.frazee.k12.mn.us/
Frazee HS 400/7-12
305 N Lake St 56544 218-334-3181
Rob Nudell, prin. Fax 334-4696

**Fridley, Anoka, Pop. 26,152**
Fridley SD 14 2,900/K-12
6000 Moore Lake Dr W 55432 763-502-5000
Dr. Peggy Flathmann, supt. Fax 502-5040
www.fridley.k12.mn.us
Fridley HS 900/9-12
6000 Moore Lake Dr W 55432 763-502-5600
Renee Van Gorp, prin. Fax 502-5640
Fridley MS 800/5-8
6100 Moore Lake Dr W 55432 763-502-5400
Matthew Boucher, prin. Fax 502-5440
Fridley Moore Lake Area Learning Center 100/Alt
6085 7th St NE 55432 763-502-5165
Dr. Robert Smith, prin. Fax 502-5140

---

Al-Amal S PK-12
1401 Gardena Ave NE 55432 763-571-8886
Calvin Christian HS 100/9-12
755 73rd Ave NE 55432 763-531-1732
Wendell Schaap, prin. Fax 531-8075
Totino-Grace HS 800/9-12
1350 Gardena Ave NE 55432 763-571-9116
Cheri Broadhead, prin. Fax 571-9118

**Fulda, Murray, Pop. 1,307**
Fulda SD 505 300/PK-12
410 N College Ave 56131 507-425-2514
Luther Onken, supt. Fax 425-2001
www.fps.mntm.org
Fulda JSHS 200/7-12
410 N College Ave 56131 507-425-2514
Gregg Slaathaug, prin. Fax 425-2001

**Gaylord, Sibley, Pop. 2,288**
Sibley East SD 2310
Supt. — See Arlington
Sibley East JHS 300/7-9
PO Box 356 55334 507-237-3315
Steve Harter, prin. Fax 237-3300

**Gibbon, Sibley, Pop. 764**
GFW SD 2365 800/PK-12
323 E 11th St 55335 507-834-9813
Tami Martin, supt. Fax 834-6264
www.gfw.k12.mn.us
Other Schools – See Fairfax, Winthrop

**Gilbert, Saint Louis, Pop. 1,775**
Eveleth-Gilbert SD 2154
Supt. — See Eveleth
Eveleth-Gilbert JHS 200/7-8
Summit St 55741 218-744-7770
Brian Hake, prin. Fax 744-4381

**Glencoe, McLeod, Pop. 5,593**
Glencoe-Silver Lake SD 2859 1,700/PK-12
1621 16th St E 55336 320-864-2499
Chris Sonju, supt. Fax 864-6320
www.gsl.k12.mn.us
Glencoe-Silver Lake HS 600/9-12
1621 16th St E 55336 320-864-2400
Paul Sparby, prin. Fax 864-6475
Lincoln JHS 300/PK-PK, 7-
1621 16th St E 55336 320-864-2456
Dan Svoboda, prin. Fax 864-2475

**Glenville, Freeborn, Pop. 641**
Glenville-Emmons SD 2886 300/K-12
PO Box 38 56036 507-448-2889
Jerry Reshetar, supt. Fax 448-2836
www.geschools.com
Glenville-Emmons JSHS 200/7-12
230 5th St SE 56036 507-448-2889
Jeff Tietje, prin. Fax 448-2836

**Glenwood, Pope, Pop. 2,537**
Minnewaska SD 2149 900/PK-12
25122 State Highway 28 56334 320-239-4820
Greg Schmidt, supt. Fax 239-1360
www.minnewaska.k12.mn.us
Minnewaska Area HS 300/7-12
25122 State Highway 28 56334 320-239-4800
Pat Falk, prin. Fax 239-1362

**Glyndon, Clay, Pop. 1,373**
Dilworth-Glyndon-Felton SD 2164
Supt. — See Dilworth
Dilworth-Glyndon-Felton HS 400/9-12
513 Parke Ave S 56547 218-477-6804
Matt Naugle, prin. Fax 477-6808

**Golden Valley, Hennepin, Pop. 19,843**

---

Breck S 1,100/PK-12
123 Ottawa Ave N 55422 763-381-8100
Edward Kim, hdmstr. Fax 381-8288

**Goodhue, Goodhue, Pop. 1,166**
Goodhue SD 253 600/PK-12
510 3rd Ave 55027 651-923-4447
Michael Redmond, supt. Fax 923-4036
www.goodhue.k12.mn.us

Goodhue JSHS 300/7-12
510 3rd Ave 55027 651-923-4447
Mike Harvey, prin. Fax 923-4036

**Goodridge, Pennington, Pop. 132**
Goodridge SD 561 200/K-12
PO Box 195 56725 218-378-4133
Galen Clow, supt. Fax 378-4142
www.goodridge.k12.mn.us/
Goodridge JSHS 100/7-12
PO Box 195 56725 218-378-4133
Becky Carlson, prin. Fax 378-4142

**Graceville, Big Stone, Pop. 577**
Clinton-Graceville-Beardsley SD 2888
Supt. — See Clinton
Clinton-Graceville-Beardsley HS 200/7-12
PO Box 398 56240 320-748-7233
Larry Mischke, prin. Fax 748-7159

**Granada, Martin, Pop. 302**
Granada - Huntley - East Chain SD 2536 200/PK-12
PO Box 17 56039 507-447-2211
Dale Brandsoy, supt. Fax 447-2214
www.ghec.k12.mn.us
Granada - Huntley - East Chain JSHS 100/7-12
PO Box 17 56039 507-447-2211
Dale Brandsoy, supt. Fax 447-2214

**Grand Marais, Cook, Pop. 1,315**
Cook County SD 166 300/K-12
101 W 5th St 55604 218-387-2271
Beth Schwarz, supt. Fax 387-1093
www.cookcountyschools.org/
Cook County MSHS 200/6-12
101 W 5th St 55604 218-387-2273
Adam Nelson, prin. Fax 387-9746

**Grand Meadow, Mower, Pop. 1,132**
Grand Meadow SD 495 400/PK-12
PO Box 68 55936 507-754-5318
Jerry Reshetar, supt. Fax 754-5608
www.gm.k12.mn.us/
Grand Meadow HS 100/9-12
PO Box 68 55936 507-754-5310
Paul Besel, prin. Fax 754-5608
Grand Meadow MS 100/5-8
PO Box 68 55936 507-754-5310
Paul Besel, prin. Fax 754-5608

**Grand Rapids, Itasca, Pop. 10,671**
Grand Rapids SD 318 3,900/PK-12
820 NW 1st Ave 55744 218-327-5700
Dr. Bruce Thomas, supt. Fax 327-5702
www.isd318.org
Elkington MS 900/5-8
1000 NE 8th Ave 55744 218-327-5800
Brent Brunetta, prin. Fax 327-5801
Grand Rapids Area Learning Center 100/Alt
409 SE 13th St 55744 218-999-9930
Matt Dass, prin.
Grand Rapids HS 1,100/9-12
800 NW Conifer Dr 55744 218-327-5760
Mark Schroeder, prin. Fax 327-5761
Itaskin Education Center 50/Alt
1880 River Rd 55744 218-322-4129
Fax 327-2921
Middle Area Learning Center 100/Alt
1000 NE 8th Ave 55744 218-326-5800
Brent Brunetta, prin. Fax 326-5701
Northland Education Center 50/Alt
510 SE 13th St 55744 218-327-2570
Other Schools – See Bigfork

---

Itasca Community College Post-Sec.
1851 E US Highway 169 55744 218-322-2300

**Granite Falls, Yellow Medicine, Pop. 2,841**
Yellow Medicine East SD 2190 800/K-12
450 9th Ave 56241 320-564-4081
Dr. Rick Clark, supt. Fax 564-4781
isd2190.org/
Yellow Medicine East HS 400/6-12
450 9th Ave 56241 320-564-4083
Ryan Luft, prin. Fax 564-4782

---

Minnesota West Community & Tech College Post-Sec.
1593 11th Ave 56241 320-564-5000

**Greenbush, Roseau, Pop. 717**
Greenbush-Middle River SD 2683 400/PK-12
PO Box 70 56726 218-782-2231
Tom Jerome, supt. Fax 782-3141
www.middleriver.k12.mn.us/
Greenbush-Middle River HS 100/9-12
PO Box 70 56726 218-782-2232
Eldon Sparby, prin. Fax 782-2165
Other Schools – See Middle River

**Grove City, Meeker, Pop. 630**
ACGC SD 2396 600/K-12
27250 Minnesota Highway 4 56243 320-857-2271
Sherri Broderius, admin. Fax 857-2989
www.acgc.k12.mn.us
ACGC JSHS 400/5-12
27250 Minnesota Highway 4 56243 320-857-2276
Sherri Broderius, prin. Fax 857-2937

**Grygla, Marshall, Pop. 220**
Grygla SD 447 200/PK-12
PO Box 18 56727 218-294-6155
Galen Clow, supt. Fax 294-6766
www.grygla.k12.mn.us/
Grygla JSHS 100/7-12
PO Box 18 56727 218-294-6155
Jamie Lunsetter, prin. Fax 294-6766

**Hallock, Kittson, Pop. 976**
Kittson Central SD 2171 200/PK-12
PO Box 670 56728 218-843-3682
Bob Jaszczak, supt. Fax 843-2856
www.kittson.k12.mn.us
Kittson Central S 200/PK-12
PO Box 670 56728 218-843-3682
Bob Jaszczak, prin. Fax 843-2856

**Halstad, Norman, Pop. 582**
Norman County West SD 2527 300/PK-12
PO Box 328 56548 218-456-2151
Kevin Hedstrom, supt. Fax 456-2193
www.ncw.k12.mn.us
Norman County West JSHS 100/7-12
PO Box 328 56548 218-456-2151
Kevin Hedstrom, prin. Fax 456-2193

**Hancock, Stevens, Pop. 763**
Hancock SD 768 300/K-12
PO Box 367 56244 320-392-5622
Loren Hacker, supt. Fax 392-5156
hancock.k12.mn.us
Hancock JSHS 100/7-12
PO Box 367 56244 320-392-5622
Tim Pahl, prin. Fax 392-5156

**Harmony, Fillmore, Pop. 1,010**
Fillmore Central SD 2198
Supt. — See Preston
Fillmore Central HS 200/7-12
PO Box 599 55939 507-886-6464
Heath Olstad, prin. Fax 886-6642

**Hastings, Dakota, Pop. 21,783**
Hastings SD 200 4,600/K-12
1000 11th St W 55033 651-480-7000
Tim Collins, supt. Fax 480-7001
www.hastings.k12.mn.us
Hastings Area Learning Center Alt
213 Ramsey St 55033 651-480-7690
Dan Branby, prin. Fax 438-9082
Hastings HS 1,500/9-12
200 General Sieben Dr 55033 651-480-7470
Mike Johnson, prin. Fax 480-7474
Hastings MS 1,400/5-8
1000 11th St W 55033 651-480-7060
Mark Zuzek, prin. Fax 480-7066

**Hawley, Clay, Pop. 2,037**
Hawley SD 150 900/K-12
PO Box 608 56549 218-483-4647
Phil Jensen, supt. Fax 483-3510
www.hawley.k12.mn.us/
Hawley JSHS 400/7-12
PO Box 608 56549 218-483-3555
Mike Martin, prin. Fax 483-4802
Spring Prairie S 50/K-12
PO Box 608 56549 218-483-3316
Chris Ellingson, prin. Fax 483-4638

**Hayfield, Dodge, Pop. 1,321**
Hayfield SD 203 800/PK-12
9 6th Ave SE 55940 507-477-3235
Belinda Selfors, supt. Fax 477-3230
hayfield.k12.mn.us
Hayfield JSHS 300/7-12
9 6th Ave SE 55940 507-477-3235
John Howe, prin. Fax 477-3230

**Hector, Renville, Pop. 1,148**
Buffalo Lake-Hector-Stewart SD 2159 600/PK-12
PO Box 307 55342 320-848-2233
Robert Doetsch, supt. Fax 848-2401
www.blhsd.org
Buffalo Lake-Hector-Stewart JSHS 300/6-12
PO Box 307 55342 320-848-2233
David Hansen, prin. Fax 848-2401

**Hendricks, Lincoln, Pop. 712**
Hendricks SD 402 100/PK-12
PO Box 137 56136 507-275-3116
Bruce Houck, supt. Fax 275-3150
www.hendrickspublicschools.org
Hendricks S 100/PK-12
PO Box 137 56136 507-275-3115
Dale Weegman, prin. Fax 275-3150

**Henning, Otter Tail, Pop. 795**
Henning SD 545 400/PK-12
500 School Ave 56551 218-583-2927
Dean Krogstad, supt. Fax 583-2312
www.henning.k12.mn.us
Henning JSHS 200/7-12
500 School Ave 56551 218-583-2927
Thomas Williams, prin. Fax 583-2312

**Herman, Grant, Pop. 435**
Herman-Norcross SD 264 100/K-12
PO Box 288 56248 320-677-2291
Rick Bleichner, supt. Fax 677-2412
herman.mn.schoolwebpages.com
Herman JSHS 50/7-12
PO Box 288 56248 320-677-2291
Rick Bleichner, prin. Fax 677-2412

**Hermantown, Saint Louis, Pop. 9,290**
Hermantown SD 700 2,100/PK-12
4307 Ugstad Rd 55811 218-729-9313
Brad Johnson, supt. Fax 729-9315
www.hermantown.k12.mn.us
Hermantown HS 700/9-12
4335 Hawk Circle Dr 55811 218-729-8874
John Muenich, prin. Fax 729-0180
Hermantown MS 800/4-8
4289 Ugstad Rd 55811 218-729-6690
Kerry Juntunen, prin. Fax 729-9890

**Hibbing, Saint Louis, Pop. 16,076**
Hibbing SD 701 2,400/K-12
800 E 21st St 55746 218-208-0848
Brad Johnson, supt. Fax 208-0866
www.hibbing.k12.mn.us
Hibbing HS 1,100/7-12
800 E 21st St 55746 218-208-0841
Mike Finco, prin. Fax 208-0856

---

Cosmetology Careers Unlimited - Hibbing Post-Sec.
2534 E Beltline 55746 218-263-8354
Hibbing Community College Post-Sec.
1515 E 25th St 55746 218-262-7200
Victory Christian Academy 100/PK-12
206 E 39th St 55746 218-262-6550
Jo Terska, admin.

**Hill City, Aitkin, Pop. 617**
Hill City SD 2 300/PK-12
500 Ione Ave 55748 218-697-2394
Dean Yocum, supt. Fax 697-2594
www.hillcity.k12.mn.us/
Hill City JSHS 100/7-12
500 Ione Ave 55748 218-697-2394
Dean Yocum, prin. Fax 697-2594

**Hills, Rock, Pop. 678**
Hills-Beaver Creek SD 671 400/PK-12
PO Box 547 56138 507-962-3240
Todd Holthaus, supt. Fax 962-3238
www.hbcpatriots.com
Hills-Beaver Creek JSHS 200/6-12
PO Box 547 56138 507-962-3240
Todd Holthaus, admin. Fax 962-3238

**Hinckley, Pine, Pop. 1,722**
Hinckley-Finlayson SD 2165 1,000/PK-12
PO Box 308 55037 320-384-6277
Rob Prater, supt. Fax 384-6135
www.hf.k12.mn.us/
Hinckley-Finlayson HS 400/7-12
PO Box 308 55037 320-384-6132
Brian Masterson, prin. Fax 384-6135

**Holdingford, Stearns, Pop. 699**
Holdingford SD 738 1,000/PK-12
PO Box 250 56340 320-746-2196
Eric Williams, supt. Fax 746-2274
www.edline.net/pages/Holdingford_Public_Schools
Holdingford JSHS 500/7-12
PO Box 250 56340 320-746-2221
Brian Silbernick, prin. Fax 746-9959

**Hopkins, Hennepin, Pop. 17,010**
Hopkins SD 270 7,000/K-12
1001 Highway 7 55305 952-988-4000
John Schultz, supt. Fax 988-4020
www.hopkins.k12.mn.us
Other Schools – See Minnetonka

---

Blake S 1,400/PK-12
110 Blake Rd S 55343 952-988-3400
Dr. Anne Stavney, head sch Fax 988-3455

**Houston, Winona, Pop. 978**
Houston SD 294 2,200/PK-12
306 W Elm St 55943 507-896-5323
Krin Abraham, supt. Fax 896-3452
www.houston.k12.mn.us
Houston JSHS 200/7-12
306 W Elm St 55943 507-896-5323
Todd Lundberg, prin. Fax 896-4665

**Howard Lake, Wright, Pop. 1,947**
Howard Lake-Waverly-Winsted SD 2687 1,000/PK-12
PO Box 708 55349 320-543-3521
Brad Sellner, supt. Fax 543-3590
www.hlww.k12.mn.us
Howard Lake MS 300/5-8
PO Box 708 55349 320-543-3501
Jim Schimelpfenig, prin. Fax 543-3590
Howard Lake-Waverly-Winsted HS 300/9-12
PO Box 708 55349 320-543-4600
Jason Mix, prin. Fax 543-4601

**Hutchinson, McLeod, Pop. 14,005**
Hutchinson SD 423 2,900/PK-12
30 Glen St NW 55350 320-587-2860
Daron VanderHeiden, supt. Fax 587-4590
www.hutch.k12.mn.us
Crow River ALC 100/Alt
1200 Roberts Rd SW 55350 320-587-2151
Michael Scott, prin. Fax 587-8217
Hutchinson HS 800/9-12
1200 Roberts Rd SW 55350 320-587-2151
Patrick Walsh, prin. Fax 587-8217
Hutchinson MS 600/6-8
1365 S Grade Rd SW 55350 320-587-2854
Todd Grina, prin. Fax 587-2857

---

Maplewood Academy 100/9-12
700 Main St N 55350 320-587-2830
Ridgewater College-Hutchinson Campus Post-Sec.
2 Century Ave SE 55350 320-234-8500

**International Falls, Koochiching, Pop. 6,261**
International Falls SD 361 1,000/PK-12
1515 11th St 56649 218-283-2571
Kevin Grover, supt. Fax 283-8104
www.isd361.k12.mn.us
Falls HS 600/7-12
1515 11th St 56649 218-283-2571
Tim Everson, prin. Fax 283-2384

---

Rainy River Community College Post-Sec.
1501 Highway 71 56649 218-285-7722

**Inver Grove Heights, Dakota, Pop. 33,073**
Inver Grove Heights Community ISD 199 3,600/PK-12
2990 80th St E 55076 651-306-7800
Dr. Deirdre Wells, supt. Fax 306-7295
www.invergrove.k12.mn.us
Inver Grove Heights MS 900/6-8
8167 Cahill Ave 55076 651-306-7200
Jodi Wendel, prin. Fax 306-7152
Simley HS 1,100/9-12
2920 80th St E 55076 651-306-7000
Gerald Sakala, prin. Fax 306-7016

Inver Hills Community College — Post-Sec.
2500 80th St E 55076 — 651-450-3000

**Iron, Saint Louis, Pop. 85**
Saint Louis County SD 2142
Supt. — See Virginia
Cherry S — 200/PK-12
3943 Tamminen Rd 55751 — 218-258-8991
Scott Hall, prin. — Fax 258-8993

**Isanti, Isanti, Pop. 5,155**
Cambridge-Isanti SD 911
Supt. — See Cambridge
Isanti MS — 400/6-8
201 Centennial Dr 55040 — 763-691-8600
Randy Pauly, prin. — Fax 691-8662
Minnesota Center S — 100/6-8
201 Centennial Dr 55040 — 763-691-8676
Randy Pauly, prin. — Fax 691-8677

**Isle, Mille Lacs, Pop. 739**
Isle SD 473 — 500/K-12
PO Box 25 56342 — 320-676-3146
Dean Kapsner, supt. — Fax 676-3966
www.isle.k12.mn.us
Isle Area Learning Center — 50/Alt
PO Box 25 56342 — 320-676-3721
Jean Novak, coord. — Fax 676-3062
Isle JSHS — 200/7-12
PO Box 25 56342 — 320-676-3101
Bryan Brown, prin. — Fax 676-1034

**Jackson, Jackson, Pop. 3,254**
Jackson County Central SD 2895 — 1,200/PK-12
PO Box 119 56143 — 507-847-3608
Todd Meyer, supt. — Fax 847-3078
www.jccschools.com/
Jackson County Central HS — 300/9-12
PO Box 119 56143 — 507-847-5310
Larry Traetow, prin. — Fax 847-3078
Other Schools – See Lakefield

Minnesota West Community & Tech College — Post-Sec.
401 West St 56143 — 507-847-7920

**Janesville, Waseca, Pop. 2,234**
Janesville-Waldorf-Pemberton SD 2835 — 600/PK-12
PO Box 389 56048 — 507-234-5181
Bill Adams, supt. — Fax 234-5796
www.jwp.k12.mn.us
Janesville-Waldorf-Pemberton HS — 300/6-12
PO Box 389 56048 — 507-234-5181
Kevin Babcock, prin. — Fax 234-5796

**Jordan, Scott, Pop. 5,361**
Jordan SD 717 — 1,700/PK-12
500 Sunset Dr 55352 — 952-492-6200
Matthew Helgerson, supt. — Fax 492-4445
www.jordan.k12.mn.us
Jordan HS — 500/9-12
600 Sunset Dr 55352 — 952-492-4400
Barb McNulty, prin. — Fax 492-4425
Jordan MS — 500/5-8
500 Sunset Dr 55352 — 952-492-2332
Lance Chambers, prin. — Fax 492-4450

**Karlstad, Kittson, Pop. 759**
Tri-County SD 2358 — 200/PK-12
PO Box 178 56732 — 218-436-2261
Dave Sorgaard, supt. — Fax 436-2263
www.tricounty.k12.mn.us
Tri-County HS — 100/7-12
PO Box 178 56732 — 218-436-2374
Nick Amb, dean — Fax 436-3422

**Kasson, Dodge, Pop. 5,864**
Kasson-Mantorville SD 204 — 2,200/PK-12
101 16th St NE 55944 — 507-634-1100
Mark D. Matuska, supt. — Fax 634-6661
www.komets.k12.mn.us
Kasson-Mantorville HS — 600/9-12
101 16th St NE 55944 — 507-634-2961
Jerry Reker, prin. — Fax 634-4745
Kasson-Mantorville MS — 700/5-8
1400 5th Ave NE 55944 — 507-634-4030
Alan Hodge, prin. — Fax 634-6485

**Kelliher, Beltrami, Pop. 261**
Kelliher SD 36 — 100/PK-12
PO Box 259 56650 — 218-647-8286
Tim Lutz, supt. — Fax 647-8660
www.kelliherschools.org
Kelliher S — 100/PK-12
PO Box 259 56650 — 218-647-8286
Mary Lundin, admin. — Fax 647-3110

**Kenyon, Goodhue, Pop. 1,804**
Kenyon-Wanamingo SD 2172
Supt. — See Wanamingo
Kenyon-Wanamingo HS — 300/9-12
400 6th St 55946 — 507-789-6186
Matt Ryan, prin. — Fax 789-6188
Kenyon-Wanamingo MS — 100/7-8
400 6th St 55946 — 507-789-6186
Matt Ryan, prin. — Fax 789-6188

**Kerkhoven, Swift, Pop. 759**
Kerkhoven-Murdock-Sunburg SD 775 — 600/PK-12
PO Box 168 56252 — 320-264-1411
Martin Heidelberger, supt. — Fax 264-1410
www.kms.k12.mn.us
Kerkhoven JSHS — 300/7-12
PO Box 168 56252 — 320-264-1412
Ted Brown, prin. — Fax 264-1410

**Kimball, Stearns, Pop. 750**
Kimball SD 739 — 700/PK-12
PO Box 368 55353 — 320-398-5585
Jim Wagner, supt. — Fax 398-5595
www.kimball.k12.mn.us/
Kimball JSHS — 300/7-12
PO Box 368 55353 — 320-398-7700
Erik Widvey, prin. — Fax 398-7733

**La Crescent, Houston, Pop. 4,750**
La Crescent-Hokah SD 300 — 1,300/PK-12
703 S 11th St 55947 — 507-895-4484
Ron Wilke, supt. — Fax 895-8560
www.isd300.k12.mn.us
Bluff Country Learning Options — 50/Alt
1301 Lancer Blvd 55947 — 507-895-4474
Steve Smith, prin.
La Crescent HS — 500/9-12
1301 Lancer Blvd 55947 — 507-895-4481
Rick Wolter, prin. — Fax 895-4490
La Crescent MS — 400/5-8
1301 Lancer Blvd 55947 — 507-895-4474
Steve Smith, prin. — Fax 895-8597

**Lake City, Wabasha, Pop. 4,995**
Lake City SD 813 — 1,200/PK-12
PO Box 454 55041 — 651-345-2198
Erick Enger, supt. — Fax 345-3709
www.lake-city.k12.mn.us
Lincoln JSHS — 600/7-12
PO Box 454 55041 — 651-345-4553
Greg Berge, prin. — Fax 345-5894

**Lake Crystal, Blue Earth, Pop. 2,527**
Lake Crystal Wellcome Memorial SD 2071 — 800/PK-12
PO Box 160 56055 — 507-726-2323
Tom Farrell, supt. — Fax 726-2334
www.isd2071.k12.mn.us
Lake Crystal Wellcome Memorial HS — 400/7-12
PO Box 160 56055 — 507-726-2110
Brian Hansen, prin. — Fax 726-2283

**Lake Elmo, Washington, Pop. 7,919**
Stillwater Area SD 834
Supt. — See Stillwater
Oak-Land JHS — 900/7-9
820 Manning Ave N 55042 — 651-351-8500
Andy Fields, prin. — Fax 351-8505

Rasmussen College — Post-Sec.
8565 Eagle Point Cir 55042 — 651-259-6600

**Lakefield, Jackson, Pop. 1,687**
Jackson County Central SD 2895
Supt. — See Jackson
Jackson County Central MS — 300/6-8
PO Box 338 56150 — 507-662-6625
Chris Naumann, prin. — Fax 662-5083

**Lake Park, Becker, Pop. 774**
Lake Park Audubon ISD 2889 — 600/K-12
PO Box 479 56554 — 218-238-5914
Dale Hogie, supt. — Fax 201-0886
www.lakeparkaudubon.com
Lake Park Audubon JSHS — 300/7-12
PO Box 479 56554 — 218-238-5916
Kevin Ricke, prin. — Fax 201-0886

**Lakeville, Dakota, Pop. 54,640**
Lakeville Area SD 194 — 10,900/K-12
8670 210th St W 55044 — 952-232-2000
Dr. Lisa Snyder, supt. — Fax 469-6054
www.isd194.k12.mn.us
Century MS — 900/6-8
18610 Ipava Ave 55044 — 952-232-2300
Christopher Endicott, prin. — Fax 469-6103
Kenwood Trail MS — 800/6-8
19455 Kenwood Trl 55044 — 952-232-3800
Kate Eisenthal, prin. — Fax 469-3508
Lakeville Area Learning Center — 100/Alt
20950 Howland Ave W 55044 — 952-232-2080
Clifford Skagen, prin. — Fax 469-7171
Lakeville North HS — 1,800/9-12
19600 Ipava Ave 55044 — 952-232-3600
Marne Berkvam, prin. — Fax 469-3367
Lakeville South HS — 1,900/9-12
21135 Jacquard Ave 55044 — 952-232-3300
John Braun, prin. — Fax 469-8383
McGuire MS — 900/6-8
21220 Holyoke Ave 55044 — 952-232-2200
Joshua Alexander, prin. — Fax 469-7224

Glory Academy — 50/PK-12
25170 Dodd Blvd 55044 — 952-985-3659
Rev. Cheryl Engelman, prin.
Minnesota School of Business — Post-Sec.
17685 Juniper Path 55044 — 952-892-9000

**Lamberton, Redwood, Pop. 817**
Red Rock Central SD 2884 — 400/PK-12
PO Box 278 56152 — 507-752-7361
Bruce Olson, supt. — Fax 752-6133
www.rrcnet.org
Red Rock Central HS — 200/5-12
PO Box 278 56152 — 507-752-7361
Phil Goetstouwers, prin. — Fax 752-6133

**Lancaster, Kittson, Pop. 340**
Lancaster SD 356 — 200/PK-12
401 Central Ave S 56735 — 218-762-5400
Steven Swiontek, supt. — Fax 762-5512
www.lancaster.k12.mn.us/
Lancaster JSHS — 100/7-12
401 Central Ave S 56735 — 218-762-5400
Steven Swiontek, admin. — Fax 762-5512

**Lanesboro, Fillmore, Pop. 743**
Lanesboro SD 229 — 300/PK-12
100 Kirkwood St E 55949 — 507-467-2229
Jeff Boggs, supt. — Fax 467-3026
www.lanesboro.k12.mn.us
Lanesboro JSHS — 100/7-12
100 Kirkwood St E 55949 — 507-467-2229
Brett Clarke, prin. — Fax 467-3026

**Laporte, Hubbard, Pop. 104**
Laporte SD 306 — 300/PK-12
315 Main St W 56461 — 218-224-2288
Harvey Johnson, supt. — Fax 224-2905
www.laporte.k12.mn.us
Laporte JSHS — 100/7-12
315 Main St W 56461 — 218-224-2288
Kim Goodwin, prin. — Fax 224-2905

**Le Roy, Mower, Pop. 926**
Le Roy-Ostrander SD 499 — 300/PK-12
PO Box 1000 55951 — 507-324-5743
Jeff Sampson, supt. — Fax 324-5149
www.leroy.k12.mn.us
Le Roy-Ostrander JSHS — 100/7-12
PO Box 1000 55951 — 507-324-5741
Aaron Hungerholt, prin. — Fax 324-5149

**Lester Prairie, McLeod, Pop. 1,714**
Lester Prairie SD 424 — 400/PK-12
131 Hickory St N 55354 — 320-395-2521
Jeremy Schmidt, supt. — Fax 395-4204
www.lp.k12.mn.us
Lester Prairie JSHS — 200/6-12
131 Hickory St N 55354 — 320-395-2521
Nathaniel Boyer, prin. — Fax 395-4204

**Le Sueur, LeSueur, Pop. 4,019**
Le Sueur-Henderson SD 2397 — 700/PK-12
115 1/2 N 5th St Ste 200 56058 — 507-665-4600
Brian Gersich, supt. — Fax 665-6858
www.isd2397.org
Alternative Learning Center — 50/Alt
901 Ferry St 56058 — 507-665-5800
Kevin Enerson, prin. — Fax 665-4187
Le Sueur-Henderson MSHS — 300/6-12
901 Ferry St 56058 — 507-665-5800
Kevin Enerson, prin. — Fax 665-6012

**Lewiston, Winona, Pop. 1,612**
Lewiston-Altura SD 857 — 800/PK-12
100 County Road 25 55952 — 507-523-2191
Jeff Apse, supt. — Fax 523-3460
www.lewalt.k12.mn.us
Lewiston-Altura HS — 400/7-12
100 County Road 25 55952 — 507-523-2191
Mitch Schiltz, prin. — Fax 523-2286

**Lindstrom, Chisago, Pop. 4,380**
Chisago Lakes SD 2144 — 3,400/PK-12
13750 Lake Blvd 55045 — 651-213-2000
Joe Thimm, supt. — Fax 213-2050
chisagolakes.mn.schoolwebpages.com
Chisago Lakes HS — 1,100/9-12
13750 Lake Blvd 55045 — 651-213-2500
David Ertl, prin. — Fax 213-2550
Chisago Lakes MS — 800/6-8
13750 Lake Blvd 55045 — 651-213-2400
Jodi Otte, prin. — Fax 213-2051

**Lino Lakes, Anoka, Pop. 19,895**
Centennial SD 12
Supt. — See Circle Pines
Centennial MS — 1,500/6-8
399 Elm St 55014 — 763-792-5400
Robert Stevens, prin. — Fax 792-5450

**Litchfield, Meeker, Pop. 6,688**
Litchfield SD 465 — 1,700/PK-12
307 E 6th St Ste 100 55355 — 320-693-2444
Dan Frazier, supt. — Fax 593-6528
www.litchfield.k12.mn.us
Litchfield HS — 500/9-12
901 N Gilman Ave 55355 — 320-693-2424
Patrick Devine, prin. — Fax 593-3308
Litchfield MS — 400/5-8
340 E 10th St 55355 — 320-693-2441
Patrick Devine, prin. — Fax 593-3485

**Little Canada, Ramsey, Pop. 9,560**
Roseville Area SD 623
Supt. — See Roseville
Roseville Area MS — 800/7-8
15 County Road B2 E 55117 — 651-482-5280
Dr. Tyrone Brookins, prin. — Fax 482-5299

**Little Falls, Morrison, Pop. 8,197**
Little Falls SD 482 — 2,400/PK-12
1001 5th Ave SE 56345 — 320-632-2002
Stephen Jones, supt. — Fax 632-2012
www.lfalls.k12.mn.us
Little Falls Community HS — 800/9-12
1001 5th Ave SE 56345 — 320-616-2200
Tim Bjorge, prin. — Fax 616-2210
Little Falls Community MS — 500/6-8
1000 1st Ave NE 56345 — 320-616-4200
Wade Mathers, prin. — Fax 616-4210

Mary of Lourdes MS — 100/5-8
205 3rd St NW 56345 — 320-632-6742
Maria Heymans-Becker, prin. — Fax 632-3556

**Littlefork, Koochiching, Pop. 646**
Littlefork-Big Falls SD 362 — 200/PK-12
700 Main St 56653 — 218-278-6614
Christopher Bachmeier, supt. — Fax 278-6615
www.isd362.k12.mn.us
Littlefork-Big Falls S — 200/PK-12
700 Main St 56653 — 218-278-6614
Christopher Bachmeier, prin. — Fax 278-6615

**Long Lake, Hennepin, Pop. 1,729**
Orono SD 278 — 2,700/K-12
685 N Old Crystal Bay Rd 55356 — 952-449-8300
Dr. Karen Orcutt, supt. — Fax 449-8399
www.orono.k12.mn.us
Orono HS — 900/9-12
795 N Old Crystal Bay Rd 55356 — 952-449-8400
Dave Benson, prin. — Fax 449-8449
Orono MS — 700/6-8
800 N Old Crystal Bay Rd 55356 — 952-449-8450
Dr. Patricia Wroten, prin. — Fax 449-8453

**Long Prairie, Todd, Pop. 3,383**
Long Prairie-Grey Eagle SD 2753 800/PK-12
205 2nd St S 56347 320-732-2194
Jon Kringen, supt. Fax 732-3791
www.lpge.k12.mn.us/
Long Prairie-Grey Eagle HS 300/7-12
510 9th St NE 56347 320-732-2194
Paul Weinzierl, prin. Fax 732-6470

**Luverne, Rock, Pop. 4,679**
Luverne SD 2184 1,200/PK-12
709 N Kniss Ave 56156 507-283-8088
Gary Fisher, supt. Fax 283-9681
www.isd2184.net/
Luverne Alternative Program 50/Alt
709 N Kniss Ave 56156 507-283-0075
Gary Fisher, prin. Fax 283-9681
Luverne HS 400/9-12
709 N Kniss Ave 56156 507-283-4491
Ryan Johnson, prin. Fax 283-9681
Luverne MS 300/6-8
709 N Kniss Ave 56156 507-283-4491
Ryan Johnson, prin. Fax 283-9681

**Lyle, Mower, Pop. 544**
Lyle SD 497 200/PK-12
700 E 2nd St 55953 507-325-4146
Jennifer Backer, supt. Fax 325-4611
www.lyle.k12.mn.us
Lyle HS 100/6-12
700 E 2nd St 55953 507-325-2201
Melanie Jiskra, prin. Fax 325-4611

**Mabel, Fillmore, Pop. 777**
Mabel-Canton SD 238 300/PK-12
316 W Fillmore 55954 507-493-5423
Jennifer Backer, supt. Fax 493-5425
www.mabelcanton.k12.mn.us/
Mabel-Canton JSHS 100/7-12
316 W Fillmore 55954 507-493-5422
Michelle Weidemann, admin. Fax 493-5425

**Mc Gregor, Aitkin, Pop. 390**
McGregor ISD 4 400/PK-12
PO Box 160 55760 218-768-2111
Paul Grams, supt. Fax 768-3901
www.mcgregor.k12.mn.us
McGregor JSHS 200/7-12
PO Box 160 55760 218-768-2111
Robert Staska, prin. Fax 768-3802

**Madelia, Watonwan, Pop. 2,301**
Madelia SD 837 500/PK-12
320 Buck Ave SE 56062 507-642-3232
Brian Grenell, supt. Fax 642-3622
www.madelia.k12.mn.us
Madelia JSHS 200/7-12
320 Buck Ave SE 56062 507-642-3232
Allan Beyer, prin. Fax 642-3622

**Madison, Lac qui Parle, Pop. 1,527**
Lac qui Parle Valley SD 2853 800/PK-12
2860 291st Ave 56256 320-752-4800
Renae Tostenson, supt. Fax 752-4401
www.lqpv.org
Lac qui Parle Valley HS 400/7-12
2860 291st Ave 56256 320-752-4800
Scott Sawatzky, prin. Fax 752-4401

**Mahnomen, Mahnomen, Pop. 1,108**
Mahnomen SD 432 600/PK-12
PO Box 319 56557 218-935-2211
Jeff Bisek, supt. Fax 935-5921
www.mahnomen.k12.mn.us/
Mahnomen Area Learning Center 50/Alt
PO Box 319 56557 218-935-2346
Sandra Haddeland, dir. Fax 935-5921
Mahnomen JSHS 300/7-12
PO Box 319 56557 218-935-2213
Brian Michaelson, prin. Fax 935-5921

---

White Earth Tribal and Community College Post-Sec.
124 1st St SW 56557 218-935-0417

**Mahtomedi, Washington, Pop. 7,538**
Mahtomedi SD 832 3,300/PK-12
1520 Mahtomedi Ave 55115 651-407-2000
Dr. Mark Larson, supt. Fax 407-2025
www.mahtomedi.k12.mn.us
Mahtomedi HS 1,200/9-12
8000 75th St N 55115 651-762-5800
Kathe Nickleby, prin. Fax 762-5825
Mahtomedi MS 800/6-8
8100 75th St N 55115 651-407-2200
Dr. Mike Neubeck, prin. Fax 407-2225

**Mankato, Blue Earth, Pop. 38,565**
Mankato SD 77 7,400/K-12
PO Box 8741 56002 507-387-1868
Sheri Allen, supt. Fax 387-4257
www.isd77.org
Central Freedom S 50/Alt
110 Fulton St 56001 507-387-2794
Kathleen Johnson, prin. Fax 387-7737
Central HS 100/Alt
110 Fulton St 56001 507-387-3047
Kathy Johnson, prin. Fax 387-7737
Mankato East HS 900/9-12
2600 Hoffman Rd 56001 507-387-5671
Jeff Dahline, prin. Fax 387-7927
Mankato East JHS 500/7-8
2600 Hoffman Rd 56001 507-345-6625
Stephen Rustad, prin. Fax 387-2890
Mankato West HS 1,100/9-12
1351 S Riverfront Dr 56001 507-387-3461
Dave Lutz, prin. Fax 345-1502
Other Schools – See North Mankato

---

Bethany Lutheran College Post-Sec.
700 Luther Dr 56001 507-344-7000
Loyola HS 200/9-12
145 Good Counsel Dr 56001 507-388-2997
Samuel Cotton, prin. Fax 388-3081
Loyola IS Fitzgerald Campus 200/4-8
110 N 5th St 56001 507-388-9344
William Schumacher, prin. Fax 388-2750
Minnesota State University Mankato Post-Sec.
309 Wigley Administrtn Ctr 56001 800-722-0544
Rasmussen College Post-Sec.
130 Saint Andrews Dr 56001 507-625-6556

**Maple Grove, Hennepin, Pop. 60,235**
Osseo Area ISD 279 20,400/PK-12
11200 93rd Ave N 55369 763-391-7000
Kate Maguire, supt. Fax 391-7070
www.district279.org
Maple Grove HS 1,700/9-12
9800 Fernbrook Ln N 55369 763-391-8700
Bart Becker, prin. Fax 391-8701
Maple Grove MS 1,600/6-8
7000 Hemlock Ln N 55369 763-315-7600
Lisa Hartman, prin. Fax 315-7601
Other Schools – See Brooklyn Park, Osseo

---

Heritage Christian Academy 500/PK-12
15655 Bass Lake Rd 55311 763-463-2200
Tonya Scott, pres. Fax 463-2299

**Maple Lake, Wright, Pop. 2,037**
Maple Lake SD 881 1,000/PK-12
PO Box 760 55358 320-963-3171
Mark Redemske, supt. Fax 963-3170
www.maplelake.k12.mn.us
Maple Lake JSHS 500/7-12
PO Box 820 55358 320-963-3171
David J. Hansen, prin. Fax 963-3170

**Mapleton, Blue Earth, Pop. 1,738**
Maple River SD 2135 1,100/PK-12
PO Box 515 56065 507-524-3918
Dan Anderson, supt. Fax 524-4882
www.isd2135.k12.mn.us/
Maple River HS 300/9-12
PO Box 515 56065 507-524-3918
Todd Griepentrog, prin. Fax 524-4919
Maple River MS 300/6-8
PO Box 515 56065 507-524-3918
Todd Griepentrog, prin. Fax 524-3638

**Maplewood, Ramsey, Pop. 37,068**
North St. Paul-Maplewood-Oakdale SD 622
Supt. — See North Saint Paul
Glenn MS 800/6-8
1560 County Road B E 55109 651-748-6300
Jill Miklausich, prin. Fax 748-6391
Harmony Learning Center 100/Alt
1961 County Road C E 55109 651-748-6200
Sue Bartling, admin. Fax 748-7486
Maplewood MS 800/6-8
2410 Holloway Ave E 55109 651-748-6500
Kevin Wolff, prin. Fax 748-6591

---

Hill-Murray HS 800/7-12
2625 Larpenteur Ave E 55109 651-777-1376
David Meyer, prin. Fax 748-2444

**Marble, Itasca, Pop. 685**
Greenway SD 316 600/PK-12
201 Kate St 55764 218-247-7306
Mark Adams, supt. Fax 245-6612
www.isd316.org
Other Schools – See Coleraine

**Marshall, Lyon, Pop. 13,459**
Marshall SD 413 2,200/K-12
401 S Saratoga St 56258 507-537-6924
Scott Monson, supt. Fax 537-6931
www.marshall.k12.mn.us
Marshall HS 800/9-12
400 Tiger Dr 56258 507-537-6920
Brian Jones, prin. Fax 537-6933
Marshall MS 500/5-8
401 S Saratoga St 56258 507-537-6938
Mary Kay Thomas, prin. Fax 537-6942
MA-TEC 100/Alt
305 S 2nd St 56258 507-537-6210
Michelle Noriega, prin. Fax 537-7609

---

Southwest Minnesota State University Post-Sec.
1501 State St 56258 507-537-7678

**Mayer, Carver, Pop. 1,725**

---

Mayer Lutheran HS 200/9-12
305 5th St NE 55360 952-657-2251
Kevin Wilaby, prin. Fax 657-2344

**Mazeppa, Wabasha, Pop. 837**
Zumbrota-Mazeppa SD 2805 900/PK-12
343 3rd Ave NE 55956 507-732-1400
Gary Anger, supt. Fax 732-1401
www.zmschools.us/
Other Schools – See Zumbrota

**Medford, Steele, Pop. 1,228**
Medford ISD 763 900/PK-12
750 2nd Ave SE 55049 507-214-6300
Rick Dahlman, supt. Fax 451-6474
www.medford.k12.mn.us
Medford JSHS 400/7-12
750 2nd Ave SE 55049 507-214-6302
Chris Ovrebo, prin. Fax 451-6474

**Melrose, Stearns, Pop. 3,582**
Melrose SD 740 1,300/PK-12
546 5th Ave NE 56352 320-256-5160
Tom Rich, supt. Fax 256-4311
isd740org.weebly.com
Melrose HS 500/9-12
546 5th Ave NE 56352 320-256-5160
Chad Doetkott, prin. Fax 256-4639
Melrose MS 400/6-8
546 5th Ave NE 56352 320-256-5160
Randy Bergquist, prin. Fax 256-4311

**Menahga, Wadena, Pop. 1,296**
Menahga SD 821 800/PK-12
PO Box 160 56464 218-564-4141
Mary Klamm, supt. Fax 564-5401
www.menahga.k12.mn.us
Menahga JSHS 300/7-12
PO Box 160 56464 218-564-4141
Daniel Stifter, prin. Fax 564-5401

**Mendota Heights, Dakota, Pop. 10,905**
West St. Paul-Mendota Hts-Eagan SD 197 4,500/PK-12
1897 Delaware Ave 55118 651-403-7000
Dr. Nancy Allen-Mastro, supt. Fax 403-7010
isd197.org
Friendly Hills MS 600/5-8
701 Mendota Heights Rd 55120 651-403-7600
Chris Hiti, prin. Fax 403-7610
Sibley HS 1,400/9-12
1897 Delaware Ave 55118 651-403-7100
Dr. Ron Monson, prin. Fax 403-7110
Other Schools – See West Saint Paul

---

Convent of the Visitation S 600/PK-12
2455 Visitation Dr 55120 651-683-1700
Dawn Nichols, head sch Fax 454-7144
Le Cordon Bleu College of Culinary Arts Post-Sec.
1315 Mendota Heights Rd 55120 651-675-4700
St. Thomas Academy 700/7-12
949 Mendota Heights Rd 55120 651-454-4570
Michael Mohs, hdmstr. Fax 454-4574
Sanford-Brown College Post-Sec.
1345 Mendota Heights Rd 55120 651-905-3400

**Middle River, Marshall, Pop. 301**
Greenbush-Middle River SD 2683
Supt. — See Greenbush
Greenbush-Middle River JHS 100/6-8
PO Box 130 56737 218-222-3310
Sharon Schultz, prin. Fax 222-3314

**Milaca, Mille Lacs, Pop. 2,899**
Milaca SD 912 1,900/PK-12
500 Highway 23 W 56353 320-982-7210
Tim Truebenbach, supt. Fax 982-7179
www.milaca.k12.mn.us/
Milaca ALC 50/Alt
305 3rd Ave NW 56353 320-982-7249
Steve Hammero, prin. Fax 982-7290
Milaca HS 800/7-12
500 Highway 23 W 56353 320-982-7206
Damian Patnode, prin. Fax 983-3566

**Milroy, Redwood, Pop. 251**
Milroy SD 635 100/PK-8
PO Box 10 56263 507-336-2563
Wade McKittrick, supt. Fax 336-2568
www.milroy.k12.mn.us
Milroy JHS 50/7-8
PO Box 10 56263 507-336-2563
Heidi Sachariason, prin. Fax 336-2568

**Minneapolis, Hennepin, Pop. 368,444**
Brooklyn Center SD 286
Supt. — See Brooklyn Center
Brooklyn Center Academy Alt
5910 Shingle Creek Pkwy #1A 55430 612-450-3383
Randy Koch, prin. Fax 561-1966

Minneapolis SD 1 32,100/PK-12
1250 W Broadway Ave 55411 612-668-0000
Michael Goar, supt. Fax 668-0195
www.mpls.k12.mn.us
Anthony MS 900/6-8
5757 Irving Ave S 55419 612-668-3240
Mai Chang Vue, prin. Fax 668-3250
Anwatin MS 500/6-8
256 Upton Ave S 55405 612-668-2450
Steve Flucas, prin. Fax 668-2460
Broadway Alternative HS 100/Alt
3017 E 31st St 55406 612-668-4700
Padmini Udupa, dir. Fax 668-4710
Edison HS 800/9-12
700 22nd Ave NE 55418 612-668-1300
Carla Steinbach, prin. Fax 668-1320
Field Community MS 500/5-8
4645 4th Ave S 55419 612-668-3640
VaNita Miller, prin. Fax 668-3661
Fine Arts Interdisciplinary Resource S 500/K-12
10 S 10th St 55403 612-668-1060
Kevin Bennett, prin.
Franklin MS 6-8
1501 Aldrich Ave N 55411 612-668-2600
Karon Cunningham, prin. Fax 668-2649
Henry HS 1,100/9-12
4320 Newton Ave N 55412 612-668-2000
Yusuf Abdullah, prin. Fax 668-1993
Lake Harriet Community Upper ES 700/4-8
4912 Vincent Ave S 55410 612-668-3310
Walter Schleisman, prin. Fax 668-3320
Lake Nokomis S - Keewaydin Campus 300/3-8
5209 30th Ave S 55417 612-668-4670
Martha Spriggs, prin. Fax 668-4680
MPS Metro St. Joseph's S 100/Alt
1121 E 46th St 55407 612-668-4782
Kristi Ward, admin. Fax 668-1422
North Academy of Arts & Communication 9-12
1500 James Ave N 55411 612-668-1700
Shawn Harris-Berry, prin. Fax 668-1770
Northeast MS 500/6-8
2955 Hayes St NE 55418 612-668-1500
Vernon Rowe, prin. Fax 668-1510
Olson MS 300/6-8
1607 51st Ave N 55430 612-668-1640
Steve Emerson, prin. Fax 668-1650
Ramsey MS 100/6-8
1 W 49th St 55419 612-668-4040
Amy Janecek, prin. Fax 668-4050

Roosevelt HS 800/9-12
4029 28th Ave S 55406 612-668-4800
Michael Bradley, prin. Fax 668-4810
Sanford MS 600/6-8
3524 42nd Ave S 55406 612-668-4900
Emily Palmer, prin. Fax 668-4910
South HS 1,800/9-12
3131 19th Ave S 55407 612-668-4300
Ray Aponte, prin. Fax 668-4310
Southwest HS 1,700/9-12
3414 W 47th St 55410 612-668-3030
Bill Smith, prin. Fax 668-3080
Stadium View S 50/Alt
510 Park Ave 55415 612-348-7740
Rhonda Larkin, prin. Fax 596-9989
Washburn HS 1,200/9-12
201 W 49th St 55419 612-668-3400
Rhonda Dean, prin. Fax 668-3410
Wellstone International HS 100/Alt
3328 Elliot Ave 55407 612-668-5115
Aimee Fearing, prin. Fax 668-5140
Adult Continuing Education Adult
2225 E Lake St 55407 612-668-3800
Fax 668-3805

---

Art Institutes International Minnesota Post-Sec.
15 S 9th St 55402 612-332-3361
Art Instruction Schools Post-Sec.
3400 Technology Dr 55418 800-801-6940
Augsburg College Post-Sec.
2211 Riverside Ave 55454 612-330-1000
Aveda Institute Post-Sec.
400 Central Ave SE 55414 612-378-7404
Bais Yaakov HS of the Twin Cities 50/9-12
4221 Sunset Blvd 55416 952-915-9117
Bethany College of Missions Post-Sec.
6820 Auto Club Rd 55438 952-944-2121
Blake S - Northrop Campus 500/9-12
511 Kenwood Pkwy 55403 952-988-3700
Dr. Anne Stavney, head sch Fax 988-3705
Capella University Post-Sec.
225 S 6th St Fl 9 55402 888-227-3552
Cristo Rey Jesuit HS 300/9-12
2924 4th Ave S 55408 612-545-9700
Jeb Myers, pres. Fax 276-0142
De La Salle HS 700/9-12
1 De La Salle Dr 55401 612-676-7600
James Benson, prin. Fax 362-9641
Dunwoody College of Technology Post-Sec.
818 Dunwoody Blvd 55403 612-374-5800
Globe University Post-Sec.
80 S 8th St Ste 51 55402 612-455-3000
Hennepin County Medical Center Post-Sec.
701 Park Ave 55415 612-347-2352
Herzing University Post-Sec.
5700 W Broadway Ave 55428 763-535-3000
Institute of Production and Recording Post-Sec.
300 1st Ave N Ste 500 55401 612-375-1900
ITT Technical Institute Post-Sec.
6120 Earle Brown Dr Ste 100 55430 763-549-5900
Minneapolis College of Art & Design Post-Sec.
2501 Stevens Ave 55404 612-874-3700
Minneapolis Community and Tech College Post-Sec.
1501 Hennepin Ave 55403 612-659-6000
Minneapolis VA Medical Center Post-Sec.
1 Veterans Dr 55417 612-725-2000
Minnehaha Academy 400/9-12
3100 W River Pkwy 55406 612-729-8321
Dr. Donna Harris, pres. Fax 728-7787
North Central University Post-Sec.
910 Elliot Ave 55404 612-343-4400
North Memorial Medical Center Post-Sec.
3300 Oakdale Ave N 55422 763-520-5200
Sanford-Brown College Post-Sec.
5951 Earle Brown Dr 55430 763-279-2400
Summit Academy OIC Post-Sec.
935 Olson Memorial Hwy 55405 612-377-0150
University of Minnesota Twin Cities Post-Sec.
231 Pillsbury Dr SE 55455 612-625-2008
Walden University Post-Sec.
100 Washington Ave S # 900 55401 612-338-7224
Woodcrest Baptist Academy 100/PK-12
6875 University Ave NE 55432 763-571-6410
Loren Isaacs, admin. Fax 571-3978

**Minneota, Lyon, Pop. 1,386**
Minneota SD 414 400/K-12
PO Box 98 56264 507-872-6532
Dan Deitte, supt. Fax 872-5172
www.minneotaschools.org/
Minneota JSHS 200/7-12
PO Box 98 56264 507-872-6175
Jeremy Frie, prin. Fax 872-6494

**Minnetonka, Hennepin, Pop. 48,748**
Hopkins SD 270
Supt. — See Hopkins
Hopkins HS 1,800/10-12
2400 Lindbergh Dr 55305 952-988-4500
Patty Johnson, prin. Fax 988-4716
Hopkins North JHS 900/7-9
10700 Cedar Lake Rd 55305 952-988-4800
Becky Melville, prin. Fax 988-4869
Hopkins West JHS 800/7-9
3830 Baker Rd 55305 952-988-4400
Shirley Gregoire, prin. Fax 988-4477

Minnetonka SD 276 9,000/K-12
5621 County Road 101 55345 952-401-5000
Dr. Dennis Peterson, supt. Fax 401-5083
www.minnetonka.k12.mn.us
Minnetonka East MS 1,000/6-8
17000 Lake Street Ext 55345 952-401-5200
Pete Dymit, prin. Fax 401-5268
Minnetonka HS 2,900/9-12
18301 Highway 7 55345 952-401-5700
Jeff Erickson, prin. Fax 401-5709
Other Schools – See Excelsior

**Minnetrista, Hennepin, Pop. 6,316**
Westonka SD 277 2,200/PK-12
5901 Sunnyfield Rd E 55364 952-491-8000
Kevin Borg, supt. Fax 491-8012
www.westonka.k12.mn.us
Other Schools – See Mound

**Montevideo, Chippewa, Pop. 5,317**
Montevideo SD 129 1,300/PK-12
2001 William Ave 56265 320-269-8833
Dr. Luther Heller, supt. Fax 269-8834
www.montevideoschools.com
Montevideo HS 500/8-12
1501 William Ave 56265 320-269-6446
Bruce Bergeson, prin. Fax 321-8960

**Montgomery, LeSueur, Pop. 2,910**
Tri-City United ISD 2905 1,600/PK-12
101 2nd St NE Ste 3 56069 507-364-8100
Teri Preisler, supt. Fax 364-8103
www.tcu2905.us
Tri-City United HS 300/9-12
700 4th St NW 56069 507-364-8111
Alan Fitterer, prin. Fax 364-8410

**Monticello, Wright, Pop. 12,521**
Monticello SD 882 4,000/PK-12
302 Washington St 55362 763-272-2000
James Johnson, supt. Fax 272-2009
www.monticello.k12.mn.us
Monticello HS 1,200/9-12
5225 School Blvd 55362 763-272-3000
Joel Lundin, prin. Fax 272-3009
Monticello MS 1,000/6-8
800 E Broadway St 55362 763-272-2100
Jeff Scherber, prin. Fax 272-2109
Turning Point 100/Alt
407 E 7th St 55362 763-272-3200
Joel Lundin, prin. Fax 272-3209

**Moorhead, Clay, Pop. 37,202**
Moorhead Area SD 152 5,600/K-12
2410 14th St S 56560 218-284-3330
Lynne Kovash Ed.D., supt. Fax 284-3332
www.moorheadschools.org/
Horizon MS 1,200/6-8
3601 12th Ave S 56560 218-284-7300
Jeremy Larson Ed.D., prin. Fax 284-7333
Moorhead HS 1,500/9-12
2300 4th Ave S 56560 218-284-2300
Dave Lawrence, prin. Fax 284-2333
Red River Area Learning Center 100/Alt
1100 32nd Ave S 56560 218-284-2200
Deb Pender-Tilleraas, dir. Fax 284-2233

---

Concordia College Post-Sec.
901 8th St S 56562 218-299-4000
Globe University Post-Sec.
2777 34th St S 56560 218-422-1000
MN State Community & Technical College Post-Sec.
1900 28th Ave S 56560 218-299-6500
Minnesota State University Moorhead Post-Sec.
1104 7th Ave S 56563 218-477-4000
Park Christian S 300/K-12
300 17th St N 56560 218-236-0500
Kent Hannestad, pres. Fax 236-7301
Rita's Moorhead Beauty College Post-Sec.
1024 Center Ave 56560 218-236-7201

**Moose Lake, Carlton, Pop. 2,729**
Moose Lake SD 97 700/PK-12
PO Box 489 55767 218-485-4435
Bob Indihar, supt. Fax 485-8110
www.mooselake.k12.mn.us
Moose Lake JSHS 300/7-12
PO Box 489 55767 218-485-4622
Billie Jo Steen, prin. Fax 485-8681

**Mora, Kanabec, Pop. 3,511**
Mora SD 332 1,700/PK-12
400 Maple Ave E 55051 320-679-6200
Craig Schultz, supt. Fax 679-6209
www.mora.k12.mn.us
Mora Alternative Learning Center 50/Alt
400 Maple Ave E 55051 320-679-6250
Karen Felger, coord.
Mora HS 800/7-12
400 Maple Ave E 55051 320-679-6220
Brent Nelson, prin. Fax 679-6238

**Morgan, Redwood, Pop. 873**
Cedar Mountain SD 2754 500/K-12
PO Box 188 56266 507-249-5990
Robert Tews, supt. Fax 249-3149
www.cms.mntm.org/
Cedar Mountain JSHS 300/6-12
PO Box 188 56266 507-249-5888
Jeremy Schultz, prin. Fax 249-3149

**Morris, Stevens, Pop. 5,158**
Morris SD 769 1,000/PK-12
201 S Columbia Ave 56267 320-589-4840
Richard Lahn, supt. Fax 585-2208
www.morris.k12.mn.us
Morris Area HS 500/9-12
201 S Columbia Ave 56267 320-589-4400
Bill Kehoe, prin. Fax 589-3203
Morris Area JHS 200/6-8
201 S Columbia Ave 56267 320-589-4400
Bill Kehoe, prin. Fax 589-3203

---

University of Minnesota Morris Post-Sec.
600 E 4th St 56267 320-589-6035

**Morristown, Rice, Pop. 973**
Waterville-Elysian-Morristown SD 2143
Supt. — See Waterville
Waterville-Elysian-Morristown JHS 100/7-8
PO Box 278 55052 507-685-4222
Anna Braam, prin. Fax 685-2420

**Motley, Morrison, Pop. 649**
Staples-Motley ISD 2170
Supt. — See Staples
Motley-Staples MS 300/6-8
132 1st Ave N 56466 218-352-6315
Thomas Riitters, prin. Fax 352-6508

**Mound, Hennepin, Pop. 8,930**
Westonka SD 277
Supt. — See Minnetrista
Mound-Westonka HS 900/8-12
5905 Sunnyfield Rd E 55364 952-491-8100
Mark McIlmoyle, prin. Fax 491-8103

**Mounds View, Ramsey, Pop. 11,818**
Mounds View SD 621
Supt. — See Shoreview
Edgewood MS 500/6-8
5100 Edgewood Dr 55112 651-621-6600
Penny Howard, prin. Fax 621-6605

**Mountain Iron, Saint Louis, Pop. 2,818**
Mountain Iron-Buhl SD 712 500/PK-12
5720 Marble Ave 55768 218-735-8271
John Klarich, supt. Fax 735-8244
www.mib.k12.mn.us
Mountain Iron-Buhl JSHS 200/7-12
5720 Marble Ave 55768 218-735-8271
Angie Williams, prin. Fax 735-8217

**Mountain Lake, Cottonwood, Pop. 2,081**
Mountain Lake SD 173 500/PK-12
PO Box 400 56159 507-427-2325
William Strom, supt. Fax 427-3047
www.mountainlake.k12.mn.us
Mountain Lake JSHS 200/7-12
PO Box 400 56159 507-427-2325
Pamela Anderson, prin. Fax 427-3047

---

Mountain Lake Christian S 100/PK-12
PO Box 478 56159 507-427-2010
Michael James, admin. Fax 427-3123

**Nashwauk, Itasca, Pop. 964**
Nashwauk-Keewatin SD 319 500/PK-12
400 2nd St 55769 218-885-1280
Lance Northey, supt.
www.isd319.org
Nashwauk-Keewatin JSHS 200/7-12
400 2nd St 55769 218-885-1280
Derek Gabardi, prin. Fax 885-2910

**Nevis, Hubbard, Pop. 379**
Nevis SD 308 300/PK-12
PO Box 138 56467 218-652-3500
Gregg Parks, supt. Fax 652-3505
www.nevis.k12.mn.us
Nevis S 300/PK-12
PO Box 138 56467 218-652-3500
John Strom, prin. Fax 652-3505

**New Brighton, Ramsey, Pop. 20,903**
Mounds View SD 621
Supt. — See Shoreview
Area Learning Center 100/Alt
2574 Highway 10 55112 651-621-6200
Julie Wikelius, prin. Fax 621-6205
Highview MS 700/6-8
2300 7th St NW 55112 651-621-6700
Sheila Eller, prin. Fax 621-6705
Irondale HS 1,600/9-12
2425 Long Lake Rd 55112 651-621-6800
Eric Nelson, prin. Fax 621-6805

---

United Theological Seminary/Twin Cities Post-Sec.
3000 5th St NW 55112 651-633-4311

**Newfolden, Marshall, Pop. 366**
Marshall County Central SD 441 400/K-12
PO Box 189 56738 218-874-8530
Jeffrey Lund, supt. Fax 874-8581
www.newfolden.k12.mn.us/
Marshall County Central HS 200/7-12
PO Box 189 56738 218-874-7225
Ryan Johnson, prin. Fax 874-8581

**New Hope, Hennepin, Pop. 19,669**
Robbinsdale SD 281 11,800/K-12
4148 Winnetka Ave N 55427 763-504-8000
Aldo Sicoli, supt. Fax 504-8979
www.rdale.org
Robbinsdale Cooper HS 1,900/9-12
8230 47th Ave N 55428 763-504-8500
Christina Hester, prin. Fax 504-8531
Other Schools – See Plymouth, Robbinsdale

**New London, Kandiyohi, Pop. 1,247**
New London-Spicer SD 345 1,400/K-12
101 4th Ave SW 56273 320-354-2252
Paul Carlson, supt. Fax 354-9001
nls.k12.mn.us
New London ALP Alt
101 4th Ave SW 56273 320-354-2252
Kevin Acquard, prin. Fax 354-9001
New London-Spicer HS 500/9-12
101 4th Ave SW 56273 320-354-2252
Kevin Acquard, prin. Fax 354-9001
New London-Spicer MS 400/5-8
101 4th Ave SW 56273 320-354-2252
Trish Perry, prin. Fax 354-4244

**New Prague, Scott, Pop. 7,228**
New Prague Area SD 721 3,800/PK-12
410 Central Ave N 56071 952-758-1700
Tim Dittberner, supt. Fax 758-1799
www.npaschools.org
New Prague Alternative Learning Center Alt
405 1st Ave NW 56071 952-758-1746
Lisa Ruedy-Decker, admin.
New Prague HS 1,200/9-12
221 12th St NE 56071 952-758-1200
Lonnie Seifert, prin. Fax 758-1299

New Prague MS 900/6-8
721 Central Ave N 56071 952-758-1400
Brad Gregor, prin. Fax 758-1499

**New Richland, Waseca, Pop. 1,198**
NRHEG SD 2168 1,000/PK-12
306 Ash Ave S 56072 507-465-3205
Dale Carlson, supt. Fax 465-8633
nrheg.k12.mn.us/pages/NRHEG
NRHEG HS 400/6-12
306 Ash Ave S 56072 507-465-3205
David Bunn, prin. Fax 465-8633

**New Ulm, Brown, Pop. 13,436**
New Ulm ISD 88 2,000/PK-12
15 N State St 56073 507-359-8414
Jeff Bertrang, supt. Fax 359-8406
www.newulm.k12.mn.us
New Ulm HS 900/7-12
414 S Payne St 56073 507-359-8420
Mark Bergmann, prin. Fax 359-8432

---

Cathedral HS 200/7-12
600 N Washington St 56073 507-354-4511
Robert Brandl, prin. Fax 354-5711
Martin Luther College Post-Sec.
1995 Luther Ct 56073 507-354-8221
Minnesota Valley Lutheran HS 200/9-12
45638 561st Ave 56073 507-354-6851
Tim Plath, prin. Fax 354-6854

**New York Mills, Otter Tail, Pop. 1,166**
New York Mills SD 553 700/PK-12
PO Box 218 56567 218-385-4201
Blaine Novak, supt. Fax 385-2551
www.nymills.k12.mn.us
New York Mills JSHS 300/7-12
PO Box 218 56567 218-385-4211
Michelle Young-Lecoustre, prin. Fax 385-2551

**Nicollet, Nicollet, Pop. 1,085**
Nicollet SD 507 100/K-12
PO Box 108 56074 507-232-3411
Jack Eustice, supt. Fax 232-3536
www.isd507.k12.mn.us
Nicollet S 100/K-12
PO Box 108 56074 507-232-3411
Jennifer Baumgartner, prin. Fax 232-3536

**North Branch, Chisago, Pop. 9,994**
North Branch Area ISD 138 3,200/PK-12
PO Box 370 55056 651-674-1000
Dr. Deb Henton Ed.D., supt. Fax 674-1010
www.isd318.org
North Branch Area HS 1,000/9-12
PO Box 370 55056 651-674-1500
Coleman McDonough, prin. Fax 674-1510
North Branch Area Learning Center 50/Alt
PO Box 370 55056 651-674-1506
Glen Stevens, dir. Fax 674-1510
North Branch Area MS 1,000/5-8
PO Box 370 55056 651-674-1300
Todd Tetzlaff, prin. Fax 674-1310

**Northfield, Rice, Pop. 19,624**
Northfield SD 659 3,800/K-12
1400 Division St S 55057 507-663-0600
L. Chris Richardson Ph.D., supt. Fax 663-0611
www.nfld.k12.mn.us
Longfellow S 100/Alt
201 Orchard St S 55057 507-645-1200
Mary Hanson, admin. Fax 645-1250
Northfield Area Learning Center 100/Alt
201 Orchard St S 55057 507-645-1201
Daryl Kehler, prin. Fax 645-1250
Northfield HS 1,200/9-12
1400 Division St S 55057 507-663-0630
Joel Leer, prin. Fax 645-3455
Northfield MS 900/6-8
2200 Division St S 55057 507-663-0650
Greg Gelineau, prin. Fax 663-0660

---

Carleton College Post-Sec.
1 N College St 55057 507-222-4000
Laura Baker School Post-Sec.
211 Oak St 55057 507-645-8866
St. Olaf College Post-Sec.
1520 Saint Olaf Ave 55057 507-786-2222

**North Mankato, Nicollet, Pop. 13,239**
Mankato SD 77
Supt. — See Mankato
Dakota Meadows MS 600/6-8
1900 Howard Dr W 56003 507-387-5077
Carmen Strahan, prin. Fax 387-1119

---

South Central College Post-Sec.
1920 Lee Blvd 56003 507-389-7200

**Northome, Koochiching, Pop. 196**
South Koochiching-Rainy River ISD 363 400/K-12
PO Box 465 56661 218-897-5275
Jim Muckenhirn, supt. Fax 897-5280
www.northome.k12.mn.us
Northome JSHS 100/7-12
PO Box 465 56661 218-897-5275
Judd Wheatley, prin. Fax 897-5280
Other Schools – See Birchdale

**Northrop, Martin, Pop. 227**

---

Luther HS 100/9-12
PO Box 228 56075 507-436-5249
Paul Steinhaus, prin. Fax 436-5240

**North Saint Paul, Ramsey, Pop. 11,176**
North St. Paul-Maplewood-Oakdale SD 622 10,400/K-12
2520 12th Ave E 55109 651-748-7622
Christine Osorio, supt. Fax 748-7413
www.isd622.org/
North HS 1,900/9-12
2416 11th Ave E 55109 651-748-6000
Greg Nelson, prin. Fax 748-6091
Other Schools – See Maplewood, Oakdale

**Norwood Young America, Carver, Pop. 3,521**
Central ISD 108 1,000/PK-12
PO Box 247 55368 952-467-7000
Brian Corlett, supt. Fax 467-7003
raiders.central.k12.mn.us
Central HS 300/9-12
PO Box 247 55368 952-467-7100
Tom Erickson, prin. Fax 467-7103
Central MS 200/6-8
PO Box 247 55368 952-467-7200
Ron Erpenbach, prin. Fax 467-7203

**Oakdale, Washington, Pop. 26,751**
North St. Paul-Maplewood-Oakdale SD 622
Supt. — See North Saint Paul
Skyview Community MS 800/6-8
1100 Heron Ave N 55128 651-702-8000
Joe Slavin, prin. Fax 702-8091
Tartan HS 1,800/9-12
828 Greenway Ave N 55128 651-702-8600
Adam Ehrmantraut, prin. Fax 702-8799

**Ogilvie, Kanabec, Pop. 366**
Ogilvie SD 333 600/PK-12
333 School Dr 56358 320-272-5000
Kathy Belsheim, supt. Fax 272-5072
www.ogilvie.k12.mn.us
Ogilvie JSHS 300/7-12
333 School Dr 56358 320-272-5000
Suzanne Davis, prin. Fax 272-5072

**Okabena, Jackson, Pop. 186**
Heron Lake-Okabena SD 330 400/PK-12
PO Box 97 56161 507-853-4507
Fax 853-4642
www.ssc.mntm.org
Heron Lake-Okabena HS 200/7-12
PO Box 97 56161 507-853-4507
Paul Bang, prin. Fax 853-4642

**Oklee, Red Lake, Pop. 424**
Red Lake County Central ISD 2906 400/PK-12
PO Box 100 56742 218-796-5136
James Guetter, supt. Fax 796-5139
www.rlcc2906.org
Red Lake County Central HS 200/7-12
PO Box 100 56742 218-796-5136
Randy Pederson, prin. Fax 796-5139

**Olivia, Renville, Pop. 2,461**
BOLD SD 2534 700/K-12
701 9th St S 56277 320-523-1031
John Dotson, supt. Fax 523-2399
www.bold.k12.mn.us
BOLD JSHS 400/7-12
701 9th St S 56277 320-523-1031
Brian Gauer, prin. Fax 523-5410

**Onamia, Mille Lacs, Pop. 845**
Onamia SD 480 600/K-12
35465 125th Ave 56359 320-532-4174
Bert Strassburg, supt. Fax 532-4658
www.onamia.k12.mn.us
Kokesh Area Learning Center 50/Alt
35465 125th Ave 56359 320-532-6831
Fax 532-4658
Onamia JSHS 300/7-12
35465 125th Ave 56359 320-532-4174
Jason Vold, prin. Fax 532-4974

**Ortonville, Big Stone, Pop. 1,887**
Ortonville SD 2903 300/PK-12
200 Trojan Dr 56278 320-839-6181
Jeffrey Taylor, supt. Fax 839-3708
www.ortonville.k12.mn.us
Ortonville S 300/PK-12
200 Trojan Dr 56278 320-839-6181
Jeff Taylor, supt. Fax 839-2499

**Osakis, Douglas, Pop. 1,728**
Osakis SD 213 700/PK-12
PO Box X 56360 320-859-2191
Joe Broderick, supt. Fax 859-2835
www.osakis.k12.mn.us
Osakis JSHS 400/5-12
PO Box X 56360 320-859-2191
Tim Roggenbuck, prin. Fax 859-2835

**Osseo, Hennepin, Pop. 2,385**
Osseo Area ISD 279
Supt. — See Maple Grove
Osseo HS 1,500/9-12
317 2nd Ave NW 55369 763-391-8500
Michael Lehan, prin. Fax 391-8501
Osseo MS 1,200/6-8
10223 93rd Ave N 55369 763-391-8800
Brian Chance, prin. Fax 391-8801

**Owatonna, Steele, Pop. 25,301**
Owatonna SD 761 4,700/K-12
515 W Bridge St 55060 507-444-8600
Peter Grant, supt. Fax 444-8688
www.owatonna.k12.mn.us
Owatonna Alternative Learning Ctr 100/Alt
130 E Vine St 55060 507-444-8000
Melodee Hoffner, prin.
Owatonna HS 1,500/9-12
333 E School St 55060 507-444-8810
Mark Randall, prin. Fax 444-8999
Owatonna JHS 700/7-8
500 15th St NE 55060 507-444-8710
Jason Hunt, prin. Fax 444-8799

**Parkers Prairie, Otter Tail, Pop. 1,009**
Parkers Prairie ISD 547 500/PK-12
PO Box 46 56361 218-338-6011
Thomas Ames, supt. Fax 338-4077
www.isd547.com
Parkers Prairie JSHS 300/7-12
PO Box 46 56361 218-338-6011
Carey Johnson, prin. Fax 338-4077

**Park Rapids, Hubbard, Pop. 3,639**
Park Rapids SD 309 1,500/PK-12
301 Huntsinger Ave 56470 218-237-6500
Lance Bagstad, supt. Fax 237-6519
www.parkrapids.k12.mn.us
Century MS 500/5-8
501 Helten Ave 56470 218-237-6300
Joleen DeLaHunt, prin. Fax 237-6349
Park Rapids Area HS 400/9-12
401 Huntsinger Ave 56470 218-237-6400
Jeff Johnson, admin. Fax 237-6401

**Paynesville, Stearns, Pop. 2,410**
Paynesville SD 741 800/PK-12
217 W Mill St 56362 320-243-3410
Robert Huot, supt. Fax 243-7525
www.paynesvilleschools.com/
Paynesville MSHS 300/6-12
795 Business 23 W 56362 320-243-3761
Lorie Floura, prin. Fax 243-4534

**Pelican Rapids, Otter Tail, Pop. 2,413**
Pelican Rapids SD 548 900/PK-12
PO Box 642 56572 218-863-5910
Deborah Wanek, supt. Fax 863-5915
www.pelicanrapids.k12.mn.us
Pelican Rapids Alt Learning Center Alt
PO Box 642 56572 218-863-5910
Jacob Richter, prin.
Pelican Rapids JSHS 400/7-12
PO Box 642 56572 218-863-5910
Brian Korf, prin. Fax 863-5915

**Pequot Lakes, Crow Wing, Pop. 2,149**
Pequot Lakes SD 186 1,500/PK-12
30805 Olson St 56472 218-568-4996
Chris Lindholm, supt. Fax 568-5259
www.isd186.org
Pequot Lakes HS 500/9-12
30805 Olson St 56472 218-568-9210
Chip Rankin, prin. Fax 568-9250
Pequot Lakes MS 400/5-8
30805 Olson St 56472 218-568-9357
Michael O'Neil, prin. Fax 568-9202

**Perham, Otter Tail, Pop. 2,944**
Perham-Dent SD 549 1,400/PK-12
200 5th St SE 56573 218-346-4501
Mitch Anderson, supt. Fax 346-4506
www.perham.k12.mn.us
Perham Area Learning Center 50/Alt
520 1st Ave S 56573 218-346-6502
Jace Hennagir, dir. Fax 346-4506
Perham HS 500/9-12
200 5th St SE 56573 218-346-6500
Ehren Zimmerman, prin. Fax 346-6504
Prairie Lakes Education Center Alt
480 Coney St W 56573 218-346-1700
Fax 346-1704
Prairie Wind MS 500/5-8
480 Coney St W 56573 218-346-1700
Scott Bjerke, prin. Fax 346-1704

**Peterson, Fillmore, Pop. 199**
Rushford-Peterson SD 239
Supt. — See Rushford
Rushford-Peterson MS 200/6-8
PO Box 8 55962 507-875-2238
Angela Shepard, prin. Fax 875-2316

**Pierz, Morrison, Pop. 1,383**
Pierz SD 484 1,100/PK-12
112 Kamnic St 56364 320-468-6458
George Weber, supt. Fax 468-6408
www.pierz.k12.mn.us
Healy JSHS 600/7-12
112 Kamnic St 56364 320-468-6458
Karrie Boser, prin. Fax 468-6408

**Pillager, Cass, Pop. 463**
Pillager SD 116 900/PK-12
323 E 2nd St 56473 218-746-2100
Michael Malmberg, supt. Fax 746-4236
www.isd116.org
Pillager HS 9-12
323 E 2nd St S 56473 218-746-2117
Shannon Hunstad, prin. Fax 746-3406
Pillager MS 400/5-8
323 E 2nd St 56473 218-746-2112
Scott Doss, prin. Fax 746-3406

**Pine City, Pine, Pop. 3,072**
Pine City SD 578 1,600/K-12
1400 Main St S 55063 320-629-4010
Wayne Gilman, supt. Fax 629-4070
www.isd578.org
Pine City Area Learning Center 50/Alt
1400 Main St S 55063 320-629-4040
Troy Anderson, prin. Fax 629-3571
Pine City JSHS 700/7-12
1400 Main St S 55063 320-629-4112
Troy Anderson, prin. Fax 629-4105

---

Pine Technical College Post-Sec.
900 4th St SE 55063 320-629-5100

**Pine Island, Goodhue, Pop. 3,224**
Pine Island SD 255 700/PK-12
PO Box 398 55963 507-356-4849
Tammy Berg-Beniak, supt. Fax 356-8827
www.pineisland.k12.mn.us
Pine Island HS 300/5-12
PO Box 398 55963 507-356-4849
Jeff Horton, prin. Fax 356-4130

**Pine River, Cass, Pop. 928**
Pine River-Backus SD 2174 — 900/PK-12
PO Box 610 56474 — 218-587-4720
Catherine Bettino, supt. — Fax 587-4120
www.prbschools.org
Pine River Area Learning Center — 100/Alt
PO Box 610 56474 — 218-587-3131
Sue Peet, dir. — Fax 587-3130
Pine River-Backus HS — 400/7-12
PO Box 610 56474 — 218-587-4425
Andrew Forbort, prin. — Fax 587-3108

**Pipestone, Pipestone, Pop. 4,229**
Pipestone Area SD 2689 — 1,100/PK-12
1401 7th St SW 56164 — 507-825-5861
Jim Lentz, supt. — Fax 825-6718
pas.k12.mn.us
Pipestone HS — 300/9-12
1401 7th St SW 56164 — 507-825-5861
Cory Strasser, prin. — Fax 825-6729
Pipestone MS — 300/5-8
1401 7th St SW 56164 — 507-825-5861
Cory Strasser, prin. — Fax 825-6729

Minnesota West Community & Tech College — Post-Sec.
1314 N Hiawatha Ave 56164 — 507-825-6800

**Plainview, Wabasha, Pop. 3,322**
Plainview-Elgin-Millville ISD 2899 — 1,500/PK-12
500 W Broadway 55964 — 507-534-3651
Gary Kuphal, supt. — Fax 534-3907
www.pem.k12.mn.us/
Plainview-Elgin-Millville HS — 500/9-12
500 W Broadway 55964 — 507-534-3128
Bill Ihrke, prin. — Fax 534-0174
Other Schools – See Elgin

**Plymouth, Hennepin, Pop. 69,055**
Robbinsdale SD 281
Supt. — See New Hope
Plymouth MS — 1,300/6-8
10011 36th Ave N 55441 — 763-504-7100
Bruce Beidelman, prin. — Fax 504-7131
Robbinsdale Armstrong HS — 2,000/9-12
10635 36th Ave N 55441 — 763-504-8800
David Dahl, prin. — Fax 504-8831

Wayzata SD 284 — 10,300/PK-12
210 County Road 101 N 55447 — 763-745-5000
Dr. Chace B. Anderson, supt. — Fax 745-5091
www.wayzata.k12.mn.us
Wayzata Central MS — 1,000/6-8
305 Vicksburg Ln N 55447 — 763-745-6000
Clark Doten, prin. — Fax 745-6091
Wayzata East MS — 800/6-8
12000 Ridgemount Ave W 55441 — 763-745-6200
Paul Paetzel, prin. — Fax 745-6291
Wayzata HS — 3,200/9-12
4955 Peony Ln N, — 763-745-6600
Scott Gengler, prin. — Fax 745-6691
Other Schools – See Wayzata

Central Baptist Theological Seminary — Post-Sec.
900 Forestview Ln N 55441 — 763-417-8250
Minnesota School of Business — Post-Sec.
1455 County Road 101 N 55447 — 763-476-2000
Providence Academy — 900/PK-12
15100 Schmidt Lake Rd, — 763-258-2500
Dr. Todd Flanders, hdmstr. — Fax 258-2501
West Lutheran HS — 200/9-12
3350 Harbor Ln N 55447 — 763-509-9378
Adam Wiechmann, prin. — Fax 509-0861

**Preston, Fillmore, Pop. 1,314**
Fillmore Central SD 2198 — 600/PK-12
PO Box 50 55965 — 507-765-3845
Richard Keith, supt. — Fax 765-3636
www.fillmorecentral.k12.mn.us/
Other Schools – See Harmony

**Princeton, Mille Lacs, Pop. 4,614**
Princeton SD 477 — 3,400/PK-12
706 1st St 55371 — 763-389-2422
Dr. Julia Espe, supt. — Fax 389-9142
www.princeton.k12.mn.us
Princeton HS — 1,000/9-12
807 8th Ave S 55371 — 763-389-4101
Barbara Muckenhirn, prin. — Fax 389-5816
Princeton MS — 800/6-8
1100 4th Ave N 55371 — 763-389-6704
Dan Voce, prin. — Fax 389-6737

**Prinsburg, Kandiyohi, Pop. 492**

Central Minnesota Christian S — 300/PK-12
PO Box 98 56281 — 320-978-8700
Peter Van Der Puy, supt. — Fax 978-6797

**Prior Lake, Scott, Pop. 22,273**
Prior Lake - Savage Area SD 719 — 7,100/K-12
4540 Tower St SE 55372 — 952-226-0000
Teri Staloch, supt. — Fax 226-0059
www.priorlake-savage.k12.mn.us
Bridges Area Learning Center — Alt
15875 Franklin Trl SE 55372 — 952-226-0840
Dave Brown, dean — Fax 226-9724
Hidden Oaks MS — 900/6-8
15855 Fish Point Rd SE 55372 — 952-226-0700
Sasha Kuznetsov, prin. — Fax 226-0749
Twin Oaks MS — 800/6-8
15860 Fish Point Rd SE 55372 — 952-226-0500
Dr. Dan Edwards, prin. — Fax 226-0549
Other Schools – See Savage

**Proctor, Saint Louis, Pop. 3,021**
Proctor SD 704 — 1,800/PK-12
131 9th Ave 55810 — 218-628-4934
John Engelking, supt. — Fax 628-4937
www.proctor.k12.mn.us
Jedlicka MS — 400/6-8
131 9th Ave 55810 — 218-628-4926
Tim Rohweder, prin. — Fax 628-4932
Proctor HS — 500/9-12
131 9th Ave 55810 — 218-628-4926
Tim Rohweder, prin. — Fax 628-4931

**Randolph, Dakota, Pop. 430**
Randolph SD 195 — 600/PK-12
PO Box 38 55065 — 507-263-2151
Michael Kelley, supt. — Fax 645-5950
www.randolph.k12.mn.us
Randolph JSHS — 300/7-12
PO Box 38 55065 — 507-263-2151
Benjamin Fisher, prin. — Fax 645-5950

**Redlake, Beltrami, Pop. 1,719**
Red Lake SD 38 — 1,200/PK-12
PO Box 499 56671 — 218-679-3353
Anne Lundquist Ed.D., supt. — Fax 679-2321
www.redlake.k12.mn.us
Red Lake Alternative Learning Center — 50/Alt
PO Box 499 56671 — 218-679-3353
Jason Stanoch, prin. — Fax 679-2321
Red Lake HS — 300/9-12
PO Box 499 56671 — 218-679-3353
Jason Stanoch, prin. — Fax 679-2717
Red Lake MS — 200/6-8
PO Box 499 56671 — 218-679-2700
Susan Ninham, prin. — Fax 679-2733

**Red Lake Falls, Red Lake, Pop. 1,407**
Red Lake Falls SD 630 — 400/PK-12
PO Box 399 56750 — 218-253-2139
Jim Guetter, supt. — Fax 253-2135
www.redlakefalls.k12.mn.us
LaFayette JSHS — 200/7-12
PO Box 399 56750 — 218-253-2163
Brad Kennett, prin. — Fax 253-4480

**Red Wing, Goodhue, Pop. 16,138**
Red Wing SD 256 — 2,800/K-12
2451 Eagle Ridge Dr 55066 — 651-385-4500
Karsten Anderson, supt. — Fax 385-4510
www.rwps.org
Red Wing HS — 1,100/8-12
2451 Eagle Ridge Dr 55066 — 651-385-4600
Todd Herber, prin. — Fax 385-4610
Tower View Alternative HS — 100/Alt
154 Tower View Dr 55066 — 651-388-8963
Dr. Beth Borgen, prin. — Fax 385-8619

Minnesota State College Southeast Tech. — Post-Sec.
308 Pioneer Rd 55066 — 651-385-6300

**Redwood Falls, Redwood, Pop. 5,083**
Redwood Area SD 2897 — 1,100/PK-12
100 George Ramseth Dr 56283 — 507-644-3531
Rick Ellingworth, supt. — Fax 644-3057
www.redwoodareaschools.com
Redwood Valley Alternative S — Alt
100 George Ramseth Dr 56283 — 507-644-3531
Robin Beske, dir. — Fax 644-3057
Redwood Valley HS — 400/9-12
100 George Ramseth Dr 56283 — 507-644-3511
Rick Jorgenson, prin. — Fax 644-3057
Redwood Valley MS — 300/5-8
100 George Ramseth Dr 56283 — 507-644-3521
Nicole Lydick, prin. — Fax 644-3057

**Remer, Cass, Pop. 366**
Northland Community SD 118 — 400/PK-12
316 Main St E Rm 200 56672 — 218-566-2351
Tim Mayclin, supt. — Fax 566-2053
www.isd118.k12.mn.us
Northland HS — 200/7-12
316 Main St E Rm 300 56672 — 218-566-2352
Clayton Lindner, prin. — Fax 566-3199

**Renville, Renville, Pop. 1,277**
Renville County West SD 2890 — 200/K-12
PO Box 338 56284 — 320-329-8362
Michelle Mortensen, supt. — Fax 329-3271
www.rcw.k12.mn.us
Renville County West S — 200/K-12
PO Box 338 56284 — 320-329-8368
Rich Schrupp, prin. — Fax 329-8191

**Richfield, Hennepin, Pop. 34,223**
Richfield SD 280 — 4,000/K-12
7001 Harriet Ave 55423 — 612-798-6000
Steven Unowsky, supt. — Fax 798-6057
www.richfield.k12.mn.us
Central Education Center — Alt
7145 Harriet Ave 55423 — 612-243-3001
Lisa Rahn, admin.
Richfield HS — 1,200/9-12
7001 Harriet Ave 55423 — 612-798-6100
Jason Wenschlag, prin. — Fax 798-6127
Richfield MS — 900/6-8
7461 Oliver Ave S 55423 — 612-798-6400
Brian Zambreno, prin. — Fax 798-6427

Academy of Holy Angels — 700/9-12
6600 Nicollet Ave 55423 — 612-798-2600
Heidi Foley, prin. — Fax 798-2610
Adler Graduate School — Post-Sec.
1550 E 78th St 55423 — 612-861-7554
Blessed Trinity S - Nicollet Campus — 100/4-8
6720 Nicollet Ave 55423 — 612-869-5200
Patrick O'Keefe, prin. — Fax 767-2191
Minnesota School of Business — Post-Sec.
1401 W 76th St Ste 500 55423 — 612-861-2000

**Robbinsdale, Hennepin, Pop. 13,450**
Robbinsdale SD 281
Supt. — See New Hope
Robbinsdale MS — 1,300/6-8
3730 Toledo Ave N 55422 — 763-504-4800
George Nolan, prin. — Fax 504-4831

**Rochester, Olmsted, Pop. 104,165**
Rochester ISD 535 — 14,600/PK-12
615 7th St SW 55902 — 507-328-3000
Michael Munoz, supt. — Fax 328-4212
www.rochester.k12.mn.us
Adams MS — 1,000/6-8
1525 31st St NW 55901 — 507-328-5700
Kim McDonald, prin. — Fax 280-4726
Century HS — 1,300/9-12
2525 Viola Rd NE 55906 — 507-328-5100
Chris Fogarty, prin. — Fax 328-5045
Friedell MS — 400/6-8
1200 S Broadway 55904 — 507-328-5650
Monica Bowler, prin. — Fax 328-5635
Kellogg MS, 503 17th St NE 55906 — 900/6-8
Dwight Jennings, prin. — 507-328-5800
Marshall HS — 1,600/9-12
1510 14th St NW 55901 — 507-328-5400
Tim Limberg, prin. — Fax 328-5295
Mayo HS, 1420 11th Ave SE 55904 — 1,600/9-12
Tom Olson, prin. — 507-328-5500
Rochester Area Learning Center — 100/Alt
37 Woodlake Dr SE 55904 — 507-328-4373
Gordon Ziebart, prin.
Willow Creek MS — 1,000/6-8
2425 11th Ave SE 55904 — 507-328-5900
Nancy Denzer, prin. — Fax 328-5905
Hawthorne Adult Literacy Center — Adult
700 4th Ave SE 55904 — 507-328-4440
Julie Nigon, admin. — Fax 287-2643

Crossroads College — Post-Sec.
920 Mayowood Rd SW 55902 — 507-288-4563
Lourdes HS — 500/9-12
2800 19th St NW 55901 — 507-289-3991
Dr. Joseph O'Toole, prin. — Fax 289-4008
Mayo Graduate School — Post-Sec.
200 1st St SW 55905 — 507-538-1160
Mayo Medical School — Post-Sec.
200 1st St SW 55905 — 507-538-4897
Mayo School of Health Sciences — Post-Sec.
200 1st St SW Bldg 11 55905 — 507-284-3678
Minnesota School of Business — Post-Sec.
2521 Pennington Dr NW 55901 — 507-536-9500
Rochester Community & Technical College — Post-Sec.
851 30th Ave SE 55904 — 507-285-7210
St. John the Evangelist S — 300/5-8
424 W Center St 55902 — 507-282-5248
Erin Widman, prin. — Fax 282-1343
St. Mary's Hospital/Mayo Medical Center — Post-Sec.
1216 2nd St NW 55901 — 507-255-5221
Schaeffer Academy — 400/K-12
2700 Schaeffer Ln NE 55906 — 507-286-1050
Keith E. Phillips, hdmstr. — Fax 282-3823
University of Minnesota Rochester — Post-Sec.
111 S Broadway Ste 300 55904 — 800-947-0117

**Rockford, Wright, Pop. 4,215**
Rockford Area ISD 883 — 1,600/PK-12
6051 Ash St 55373 — 763-477-9165
Paul Durand, supt. — Fax 477-5833
www.rockford.k12.mn.us
Rockford HS — 500/9-12
7600 County Road 50 55373 — 763-477-5846
Dr. Matthew Scheidler, prin. — Fax 477-6123
Rockford MS Center for Environmental Std — 300/5-8
6051 Ash St 55373 — 763-477-5831
Amy Denneson, prin. — Fax 477-5832

**Rogers, Hennepin, Pop. 8,439**
Elk River Area SD 728
Supt. — See Elk River
Rogers HS — 1,300/9-12
21000 141st Ave N 55374 — 763-274-3140
Jason Paurus, prin. — Fax 274-3141
Rogers MS — 1,000/6-8
20855 141st Ave N 55374 — 763-241-3550
Mark Huss, prin. — Fax 241-3518

**Roseau, Roseau, Pop. 2,615**
Roseau SD 682 — 1,200/PK-12
509 3rd St NE 56751 — 218-463-1471
Larry Guggisberg, supt. — Fax 463-3243
www.roseau.k12.mn.us/
Roseau JSHS — 600/7-12
509 3rd St NE 56751 — 218-463-2770
Dave Reaves, prin. — Fax 463-3658

**Rosemount, Dakota, Pop. 21,334**
Rosemount-Apple Valley-Eagan ISD 196 — 26,900/K-12
3455 153rd St W 55068 — 651-423-7700
Jane Berenz, supt. — Fax 423-7633
www.district196.org
Rosemount HS — 2,200/9-12
3335 142nd St W 55068 — 651-423-7501
John Wollersheim, prin. — Fax 423-7511
Rosemount MS — 1,200/6-8
3135 143rd St W 55068 — 651-423-7570
Mary Thompson, prin. — Fax 423-7664
Other Schools – See Apple Valley, Eagan

Dakota Co. Technical College — Post-Sec.
1300 145th St E 55068 — 651-423-8301
First Baptist S — 200/PK-12
14400 Diamond Path W 55068 — 651-423-2272

**Roseville, Ramsey, Pop. 32,857**
Roseville Area SD 623 — 6,700/K-12
1251 County Road B2 W 55113 — 651-635-1600
Dr. Aldo Sicoli, supt. — Fax 635-1659
www.isd623.org
Fairview Alternative HS — 100/Alt
1910 County Road B W 55113 — 651-604-3800
Laura Freer, prin. — Fax 604-3801
Roseville Area HS — 2,100/9-12
1240 County Road B2 W 55113 — 651-635-1660
Dr. Jenny Loeck, prin. — Fax 635-1699
Other Schools – See Little Canada

American Academy of Acupuncture — Post-Sec.
1925 County Road B2 W 55113 — 651-631-0204
Concordia Academy — 300/9-12
2400 Dale St N 55113 — 651-484-8429
Dr. Tim Berner, prin. — Fax 484-0594
Minneapolis Business College — Post-Sec.
1711 County Road B W 55113 — 651-636-7406
National American University — Post-Sec.
1550 Highway 36 W 55113 — 651-855-6300

**Rothsay, Wilkin, Pop. 493**
Rothsay SD 850 — 100/PK-12
2040 County Road 52 56579 — 218-867-2117
Warren Schmidt, supt. — Fax 867-2376
www.rothsay.k12.mn.us
Rothsay S — 100/PK-12
2040 County Road 52 56579 — 218-867-2116
Staci Allmaras, prin. — Fax 867-2376

**Round Lake, Nobles, Pop. 376**
Round Lake-Brewster SD
Supt. — See Brewster
Round Lake-Brewster MS — 50/7-8
445 Harrison St 56167 — 507-945-8123
Raymond Hassing, prin. — Fax 945-8124

**Royalton, Morrison, Pop. 1,237**
Royalton SD 485 — 800/PK-12
120 S Hawthorn St 56373 — 320-584-4000
Dr. Jon Ellerbusch, supt. — Fax 584-4249
www.royalton.k12.mn.us
Royalton JSHS — 300/7-12
120 S Hawthorn St 56373 — 320-584-4000
Joel Swenson, prin. — Fax 584-4242

**Rush City, Chisago, Pop. 3,060**
Rush City SD 139 — 900/PK-12
PO Box 566 55069 — 320-358-4855
Teresa Dupre, supt. — Fax 358-1351
www.rushcity.k12.mn.us
Rush City HS — 400/7-12
PO Box 566 55069 — 320-358-4795
Brent Stavig, prin. — Fax 358-1261

**Rushford, Fillmore, Pop. 1,721**
Rushford-Peterson SD 239 — 600/PK-12
PO Box 627 55971 — 507-864-7785
Charles Ehler, supt. — Fax 864-2085
www.r-pschools.com
Rushford-Peterson HS — 200/9-12
PO Box 627 55971 — 507-864-7786
Jake Timm, prin. — Fax 864-2085
Other Schools – See Peterson

**Russell, Lyon, Pop. 338**
R T R ISD 2902
Supt. — See Tyler
R T R MS — 100/6-8
PO Box 310 56169 — 507-823-4371
James Burns, prin. — Fax 823-4657

**Saint Anthony, Hennepin, Pop. 8,057**
Saint Anthony-New Brighton SD 282 — 1,800/PK-12
3303 33rd Ave NE 55418 — 612-706-1000
William Robert Laney, supt. — Fax 706-1020
www.stanthony.k12.mn.us
Saint Anthony MS — 400/6-8
3303 33rd Ave NE 55418 — 612-706-1032
Renee Corneille, prin. — Fax 706-1040
Saint Anthony Village HS — 700/9-12
3303 33rd Ave NE 55418 — 612-706-1102
Wayne Terry, prin. — Fax 706-1140

**Saint Bonifacius, Hennepin, Pop. 2,257**

Crown College — Post-Sec.
8700 College View Dr 55375 — 952-446-4100

**Saint Charles, Winona, Pop. 3,695**
Saint Charles SD 858 — 1,000/PK-12
600 E 6th St 55972 — 507-932-4420
Mark Roubinek, supt. — Fax 932-4700
www.scschools.net
Saint Charles HS — 500/7-12
600 E 6th St 55972 — 507-932-4420
Dr. Ben Bernard, prin. — Fax 932-4700

**Saint Clair, Blue Earth, Pop. 859**
Saint Clair SD 75 — 600/PK-12
PO Box 99 56080 — 507-245-3501
Tom Bruels, supt. — Fax 245-3517
www.stclair.new.rschooltoday.com
Saint Clair JSHS — 300/7-12
PO Box 99 56080 — 507-245-3027
Dustin Bosshart, prin. — Fax 245-3517

**Saint Cloud, Stearns, Pop. 64,343**
Saint Cloud Area SD 742 — 9,300/PK-12
1000 44th Ave N 56303 — 320-253-9333
Willie Jett, supt. — Fax 529-4343
www.isd742.org
Apollo HS — 1,200/9-12
1000 44th Ave N 56303 — 320-253-1600
Adam Holm, prin. — Fax 253-8475
North JHS — 700/6-8
1212 29th Ave N 56303 — 320-251-2159
Brenda Blackmore, prin. — Fax 251-7350
Saint Cloud ALC — 300/Alt
809 12th St N 56303 — 320-251-4963
Al Johnson, prin. — Fax 251-4173
South JHS — 800/6-8
1120 15th Ave S 56301 — 320-251-1322
Jason Harris, prin. — Fax 251-2911
Technical HS — 1,400/9-12
233 12th Ave S 56301 — 320-252-2231
Charles Eisenreich, prin. — Fax 252-0257

Cathedral HS — 600/7-12
PO Box 1579 56302 — 320-251-3421
Lynn Grewing, prin. — Fax 253-5576
Model College of Hair Design — Post-Sec.
201 8th Ave S 56301 — 320-253-4222
Rasmussen College — Post-Sec.
226 Park Ave S 56301 — 320-251-5600
Saint Cloud Christian S — 200/K-12
430 3rd Ave NE 56304 — 320-252-8182
Jim Daniels, admin. — Fax 656-9678
St. Cloud Hospital — Post-Sec.
1406 6th Ave N 56303 — 320-255-5666
St. Cloud State University — Post-Sec.
720 4th Ave S 56301 — 320-308-0121
St. Cloud Technical & Community College — Post-Sec.
1540 Northway Dr 56303 — 320-308-5000

**Saint Francis, Anoka, Pop. 7,077**
Saint Francis SD 15 — 5,100/K-12
4115 Ambassador Blvd NW 55070 — 763-753-7040
Troy Ferguson, supt. — Fax 753-4693
www.isd15.org
Crossroads S & Vocational Center — 100/Alt
4111 Ambassador Blvd NW 55070 — 763-753-7120
Scott Manni, prin. — Fax 753-1385
Saint Francis HS — 1,700/9-12
3325 Bridge St NW 55070 — 763-213-1500
Douglas Austin, prin. — Fax 213-1693
Saint Francis MS — 1,200/6-8
23026 Ambassador Blvd NW 55070 — 763-213-8500
Bobbi Hume, prin. — Fax 753-3821
Community Education — Adult
4115 Ambassador Blvd NW 55070 — 763-753-7041
Troy Ferguson, dir. — Fax 753-4693

**Saint James, Watonwan, Pop. 4,579**
Saint James SD 840 — 1,100/PK-12
PO Box 509 56081 — 507-375-5974
Becky Cselovszki, supt. — Fax 375-7143
www.stjames.k12.mn.us
Saint James JSHS — 600/6-12
1001 10th Ave N 56081 — 507-375-3381
Karla Beck, prin. — Fax 375-4371

**Saint Joseph, Stearns, Pop. 6,430**

College of Saint Benedict — Post-Sec.
37 College Ave S 56374 — 320-363-5011

**Saint Louis Park, Hennepin, Pop. 43,914**
Saint Louis Park SD 283 — 4,300/K-12
6425 W 33rd St 55426 — 952-928-6000
Robert Metz, supt. — Fax 928-6020
www.slpschools.org
Saint Louis Park HS — 1,400/9-12
6425 W 33rd St 55426 — 952-928-6100
Joann Karetov, prin. — Fax 928-6113
Saint Louis Park MS — 900/6-8
2025 Texas Ave S 55426 — 952-928-6300
Les Bork, prin. — Fax 928-6383

Anthem College — Post-Sec.
5100 Gamble Dr Ste 200 55416 — 952-417-2200
Benilde-St. Margarets HS — 1,200/7-12
2501 Highway 100 S 55416 — 952-927-4176
Dr. Sue Skinner, prin. — Fax 920-8889
Groves Academy — 200/1-12
3200 Highway 100 S 55416 — 952-920-6377
Health System Minnesota/Methodist Hosp. — Post-Sec.
6500 Excelsior Blvd 55426 — 952-993-3601

**Saint Michael, Wright, Pop. 16,153**
Saint Michael-Albertville SD 885
Supt. — See Albertville
Saint Michael-Albertville HS — 1,400/9-12
5800 Jamison Ave NE 55376 — 763-497-2192
Bob Driver, prin. — Fax 497-6590
Saint Michael-Albertville MS East — 5-8
4862 Naber Ave NE 55376 — 763-497-2655
Jennifer Kelly, prin. — Fax 497-6591

**Saint Paul, Ramsey, Pop. 275,178**
Saint Paul SD 625 — 31,500/PK-12
360 Colborne St 55102 — 651-767-8100
Valeria Silva, supt. — Fax 293-8586
www.spps.org
Battle Creek MS — 700/6-8
2121 N Park Dr 55119 — 651-293-8960
Tyrone Brookins, prin. — Fax 293-8866
Central HS — 2,200/9-12
275 Lexington Pkwy N 55104 — 651-744-4900
Mary Mackbee, prin. — Fax 293-5433
Como Park HS — 1,500/9-12
740 Rose Ave W 55117 — 651-293-8800
Theresa Neal, prin. — Fax 293-8806
Creative Arts HS — 100/6-12
65 Kellogg Blvd E 55101 — 651-292-3480
Dr. Valerie Littles-Butler, prin. — Fax 292-3484
Farnsworth Aerospace Magnet MS — 600/5-8
1000 Walsh St 55106 — 651-293-8880
Hamilton Bell, prin. — Fax 293-8888
Harding HS — 2,000/9-12
1540 6th St E 55106 — 651-793-4700
Doug Revsbeck, prin. — Fax 293-8912
Highland Park HS — 1,400/9-12
1015 Snelling Ave S 55116 — 651-293-8940
Dr. Winston Tucker, prin. — Fax 293-8939
Highland Park MS — 800/6-8
975 Snelling Ave S 55116 — 651-293-8950
Charlene Hoff, prin. — Fax 293-8953
Humboldt MSHS — 800/6-12
30 Baker St E 55107 — 651-293-8600
Mike Sodomka, prin. — Fax 293-8605
Johnson HS — 1,600/9-12
1349 Arcade St 55106 — 651-293-8890
Micheal Thompson, prin. — Fax 293-8895
LEAP HS — 200/Alt
631 Albert St N 55104 — 651-228-7706
Rose Santos, prin. — Fax 228-7711
Linwood Monroe Arts Plus MS — 500/4-8
810 Palace Ave 55102 — 651-293-8690
Bryan Bass, prin. — Fax 293-8699
Murray MS — 700/6-8
2200 Buford Ave 55108 — 651-293-8740
Kirk Morris, prin. — Fax 293-8742
Open World Learning Community S — 200/6-12
640 Humboldt Ave 55107 — 651-293-8670
Dave Gundale, prin. — Fax 293-5308
Parks HS — 200/Alt
1212 University Ave W 55104 — 651-744-1212
Traci Gauer, prin. — Fax 744-1208
Parkway Montessori MS — 400/6-8
1363 Bush Ave 55106 — 651-744-1000
Timothy Hoffman, prin. — Fax 744-1001
Ramsey MS — 500/6-8
1700 Summit Ave 55105 — 651-293-8860
Dr. Teresa Vibar, prin. — Fax 298-1587
Washington Technology Magnet MSHS — 1,500/6-12
1495 Rice St 55117 — 651-293-8830
Mike McCollor, prin. — Fax 228-4331
Evening HS — Adult
1212 University Ave W 55104 — 651-744-1210
Sharon Eichten, prin. — Fax 744-1208

Bethel Seminary — Post-Sec.
3949 Bethel Dr 55112 — 651-638-6288
Bethel University — Post-Sec.
3900 Bethel Dr 55112 — 651-638-6400
Christ's Household of Faith S — 200/PK-12
355 Marshall Ave 55102 — 651-265-3400
Concordia University-St. Paul — Post-Sec.
275 Syndicate St N 55104 — 651-641-8278
Cretin-Derham Hall HS — 1,300/9-12
550 Albert St S 55116 — 651-690-2443
Mona Passman, prin. — Fax 696-3394
Empire Beauty School — Post-Sec.
1905 Suburban Ave 55119 — 651-209-6930
Hamline University — Post-Sec.
1536 Hewitt Ave 55104 — 651-523-2800
Luther Seminary — Post-Sec.
2481 Como Ave 55108 — 800-588-4373
Macalester College — Post-Sec.
1600 Grand Ave 55105 — 651-696-6000
McNally Smith College of Music — Post-Sec.
19 Exchange St E 55101 — 651-291-0177
Metropolitan State University — Post-Sec.
700 7th St E 55106 — 651-793-1300
Mounds Park Academy — 600/PK-12
2051 Larpenteur Ave E 55109 — 651-777-2555
Dr. Bill Hudson, head sch — Fax 777-8633
Northwestern College — Post-Sec.
3003 Snelling Ave N 55113 — 651-631-5100
St. Agnes S — 500/K-12
530 Lafond Ave 55103 — 651-925-8700
James Morehead, prin. — Fax 925-8708
Saint Catherine University — Post-Sec.
2004 Randolph Ave 55105 — 651-690-6000
St. Paul Academy & Summit S — 600/6-12
1712 Randolph Ave 55105 — 651-698-2451
Bryn Roberts, head sch — Fax 698-6787
St. Paul College — Post-Sec.
235 Marshall Ave 55102 — 651-846-1600
St. Paul Preparatory S — 9-12
380 Jackson St Ste 100 55101 — 651-288-4606
John Belpedio, prin. — Fax 288-4616
University of St. Thomas — Post-Sec.
2115 Summit Ave 55105 — 651-962-5000
William Mitchell College of Law — Post-Sec.
875 Summit Ave 55105 — 651-227-9171

**Saint Paul Park, Washington, Pop. 5,176**
South Washington County SD 833
Supt. — See Cottage Grove
Oltman MS — 700/6-8
1020 3rd St 55071 — 651-425-3500
Becky Schroeder, prin. — Fax 425-3555

Hope Christian Academy — 100/PK-12
920 Holley Ave Ste 2 55071 — 651-459-6438
Randy Krussow, prin. — Fax 769-2108

**Saint Peter, Nicollet, Pop. 11,009**
Saint Peter SD 508 — 1,600/PK-12
100 Lincoln Dr 56082 — 507-934-5703
Dr. Paul Peterson, supt. — Fax 934-2805
www.stpeterschools.org
Saint Peter MSHS — 500/7-12
100 Lincoln Dr 56082 — 507-934-4210
Paul Preimesberger, prin. — Fax 934-4783

Gustavus Adolphus College — Post-Sec.
800 W College Ave 56082 — 507-933-8000

**Sandstone, Pine, Pop. 2,776**
East Central SD 2580
Supt. — See Finlayson
Crossroads Learning Center — 50/Alt
130 Oriole St E Ste 2 55072 — 320-216-4155
Stef Youngberg, dir. — Fax 216-4170

Harvest Christian S — 100/PK-12
PO Box 646 55072 — 320-245-5330
Jack Allen, admin. — Fax 245-5330

**Sartell, Stearns, Pop. 15,661**
Sartell-St. Stephen SD 748 — 3,700/K-12
212 3rd Ave N 56377 — 320-656-3715
Jeff Schwiebert, supt. — Fax 656-3765
www.sartell.k12.mn.us
Sartell HS — 1,000/9-12
748 7th St N 56377 — 320-656-0748
Brenda Steve, prin. — Fax 656-5296
Sartell MS — 1,200/5-8
627 3rd Ave N 56377 — 320-253-2200
Julie Tripp, prin. — Fax 253-1403

**Sauk Centre, Stearns, Pop. 4,294**
Sauk Centre SD 743 — 1,000/PK-12
903 State Rd 56378 — 320-352-2284
Dan Brooks, supt. — Fax 352-3404
www.isd743.k12.mn.us

Sauk Centre Secondary S 500/7-12
903 State Rd 56378 320-352-2856
Sheila Flatau, prin. Fax 352-3404

**Sauk Rapids, Benton, Pop. 12,559**
Sauk Rapids-Rice SD 47 3,900/PK-12
1833 Osauka Rd 56379 320-253-4703
Dr. Daniel Bittman, supt. Fax 255-1914
www.isd47.org
Sauk Rapids-Rice HS 1,200/9-12
1835 Osauka Rd 56379 320-253-4700
Erich Martens, prin. Fax 258-1717
Sauk Rapids-Rice MS 900/6-8
901 1st St S 56379 320-654-9073
Nate Rudolph, prin. Fax 259-8909
Hillside ECFE & ABE Adult
30 4th Ave S 56379 320-255-8910
Julie Midas, dir. Fax 258-1197

**Savage, Scott, Pop. 26,220**
Burnsville-Eagan-Savage ISD 191
Supt. — See Burnsville
Eagle Ridge JHS 800/7-9
13955 Glendale Rd 55378 952-707-2800
Don Leake, prin. Fax 707-2802

Prior Lake - Savage Area SD 719
Supt. — See Prior Lake
Prior Lake HS 2,300/9-12
7575 150th St W 55378 952-226-8600
Dave Lund, prin. Fax 226-8649

**Sebeka, Wadena, Pop. 700**
Sebeka SD 820 500/PK-12
PO Box 249 56477 218-837-5101
Dave Fjeldheim, supt. Fax 837-5967
www.sebeka.k12.mn.us
Sebeka JSHS 300/7-12
PO Box 249 56477 218-837-5101
Dave Fjeldheim, prin. Fax 837-5967

**Shakopee, Scott, Pop. 36,163**
Shakopee SD 720 6,600/K-12
505 Holmes St S 55379 952-496-5000
Dr. Rod Thompson, supt. Fax 496-5056
www.shakopee.k12.mn.us
East JHS 600/7-9
1137 Marschall Rd 55379 952-496-5702
Jim Miklausich, prin. Fax 496-5715
Shakopee SHS 1,500/10-12
100 17th Ave W 55379 952-496-5152
Ben Kusch, prin. Fax 496-5155
Tokata Learning Center Alt
1110 Shakopee Town Sq 55379 952-496-5982
Eric Serbus, prin. Fax 496-5985
West JHS 1,000/7-9
200 10th Ave E 55379 952-496-5752
Lori Link, prin. Fax 496-5755

---

Minnesota School of Business Post-Sec.
1200 Shakopee Town Sq 55379 952-345-1200

**Sherburn, Martin, Pop. 1,125**
Martin County West SD 2448 600/K-12
105 E 5th St 56171 507-764-2330
Allison Schmidt, supt. Fax 764-2335
www.martin.k12.mn.us
Martin County West JSHS 300/7-12
16 W 5th St 56171 507-764-4661
David Traetow, prin. Fax 764-4681

**Shoreview, Ramsey, Pop. 24,520**
Mounds View SD 621 9,900/K-12
350 Highway 96 W 55126 651-621-6000
Dan Hoverman, supt. Fax 621-6046
www.moundsviewschools.org
Chippewa MS 900/6-8
5000 Hodgson Rd 55126 651-621-6400
Rob Reetz, prin. Fax 621-6405
Other Schools – See Arden Hills, Mounds View, New Brighton

**Silver Bay, Lake, Pop. 1,866**
Lake Superior SD 381
Supt. — See Two Harbors
Kelley JSHS 200/7-12
137 Banks Blvd 55614 218-226-4437
Joe Nicklay, prin. Fax 226-4860

**Slayton, Murray, Pop. 2,140**
Murray County Central SD 2169 800/PK-12
2420 28th St 56172 507-836-6183
Luther Onken, supt. Fax 836-6375
www.mcc.mntm.org
Murray County Central JSHS 300/7-12
2420 28th St 56172 507-836-6184
Joe Meyer, prin. Fax 836-6375

**Sleepy Eye, Brown, Pop. 3,585**
Sleepy Eye SD 84 600/PK-12
400 4th Ave SW 56085 507-794-7903
John Cselovszki, supt. Fax 794-5404
www.sleepyeyeschools.com
Sleepy Eye JSHS 300/7-12
400 4th Ave SW 56085 507-794-7904
Shane Laffen, prin. Fax 794-5404

---

St. Mary JSHS 200/7-12
104 Saint Marys St NW 56085 507-794-4121
Andrew Bach, prin. Fax 794-4841

**South Saint Paul, Dakota, Pop. 19,660**
South St. Paul SD 6 3,300/PK-12
104 5th Ave S 55075 651-457-9400
Dr. Dave Webb, supt. Fax 457-9485
www.sspps.org
Community Learning Center 100/Alt
151 6th St E 55075 651-450-9966
Nick Falde, dir. Fax 306-3666
South Saint Paul HS 1,400/6-12
700 2nd St N 55075 651-457-9408
Chuck Ochocki, prin. Fax 457-9455

**Springfield, Brown, Pop. 2,141**
Springfield SD 85 600/PK-12
12 Burns Ave 56087 507-723-4283
Keith Kottke, supt. Fax 723-6407
www.springfield.mntm.org/
Springfield JSHS 300/7-12
12 Burns Ave 56087 507-723-4288
Pat Moriarty, prin. Fax 723-4447

**Spring Grove, Houston, Pop. 1,322**
Spring Grove SD 297 300/K-12
PO Box 626 55974 507-498-3221
Rachel Udstuen, supt. Fax 498-3470
www.springgrove.k12.mn.us
Spring Grove JSHS 100/7-12
PO Box 626 55974 507-498-3223
Nancy Gulbranson, prin. Fax 498-3470

**Spring Lake Park, Anoka, Pop. 6,217**
Spring Lake Park SD 16 4,400/K-12
1415 81st Ave NE 55432 763-600-5000
Dr. Jeff Ronneberg, supt. Fax 600-5582
www.springlakeparkschools.org
Lighthouse S 1-12
7925 Able St NE 55432 763-600-5200
Mike Callahan, admin. Fax 600-5213
Spring Lake Park HS 1,300/9-12
1100 81st Ave NE 55432 763-600-5100
Jane Stevenson, prin. Fax 600-5113
Other Schools – See Blaine

---

Empire Beauty School Post-Sec.
8205 University Ave NE 55432 - -

**Spring Valley, Fillmore, Pop. 2,458**
Kingsland SD 2137 600/PK-12
705 N Section Ave 55975 507-346-7276
John McDonald, supt. Fax 346-7278
www.kingsland.k12.mn.us
Kingsland JSHS 300/7-12
705 N Section Ave 55975 507-346-7276
Jim Hecimovich, prin. Fax 346-7278

**Staples, Todd, Pop. 2,930**
Staples-Motley ISD 2170 1,300/PK-12
202 Pleasant Ave NE 56479 218-894-5400
Mary Klamm, supt. Fax 894-1828
www.isd2170.k12.mn.us/
Staples-Motley HS 400/9-12
401 Centennial Ln 56479 218-894-2431
Michael Schmidt, prin. Fax 894-2434
Other Schools – See Motley

---

Central Lakes College Post-Sec.
1830 Airport Rd 56479 218-894-5100

**Stephen, Marshall, Pop. 657**
Stephen-Argyle Central SD 2856 400/PK-12
PO Box 68 56757 218-478-3315
Chris Mills, supt. Fax 478-3537
www.sac.k12.mn.us/
Stephen JSHS 200/7-12
PO Box 68 56757 218-478-3314
Mark Kroulik, prin. Fax 478-3537

**Stewartville, Olmsted, Pop. 5,872**
Stewartville SD 534 1,900/PK-12
440 6th Ave SW 55976 507-533-1438
Dr. David Thompson, supt. Fax 533-4012
www.ssd.k12.mn.us
Stewartville HS 500/9-12
440 6th Ave SW 55976 507-533-1600
Steve Gibbs, prin. Fax 533-4143
Stewartville MS 400/6-8
440 6th Ave SW 55976 507-533-1666
Steven Gibbs, prin. Fax 533-1021

**Stillwater, Washington, Pop. 17,911**
Stillwater Area SD 834 8,100/K-12
1875 Greeley St S 55082 651-351-8301
Tom Nelson, supt. Fax 351-8380
www.stillwater.k12.mn.us
St. Croix Valley ALC 100/Alt
5640 Memorial Ave N 55082 651-351-8464
Kristen Hauge, prin. Fax 351-8465
Stillwater Area SHS 2,000/10-12
5701 Stillwater Blvd N 55082 651-351-8040
Robert Bach, prin. Fax 351-8049
Stillwater JHS 1,100/7-9
523 Marsh St W 55082 651-351-6905
Chuck Ochocki, prin. Fax 351-6999
Other Schools – See Lake Elmo

**Swanville, Morrison, Pop. 348**
Swanville SD 486 400/PK-12
PO Box 98 56382 320-547-5100
Gene Harthan, supt. Fax 547-2576
www.swanville.k12.mn.us/
Molly Creek ALC 50/Alt
PO Box 98 56382 320-547-9930
Michelle Peterson, lead tchr. Fax 547-2576
Swanville JSHS 200/7-12
PO Box 98 56382 320-547-5100
Sheryl Johnson, prin. Fax 547-2576

**Thief River Falls, Pennington, Pop. 8,403**
Thief River Falls SD 564 2,000/PK-12
230 LaBree Ave S 56701 218-681-8711
Laine Larson, supt. Fax 681-2905
www.trf.k12.mn.us
Franklin MS 500/6-8
300 Spruce Ave S 56701 218-681-8813
Bob Wayne, prin. Fax 681-4771
Lincoln HS 600/9-12
101 Knight Ave S 56701 218-681-7432
Shane Zutz, prin. Fax 681-4510
Northwest Area Learning Center 50/Alt
230 LaBree Ave S 56701 218-681-8711
Loren Leake, dir. Fax 681-4686

---

Northland Community & Technical College Post-Sec.
1101 Highway 1 E 56701 218-683-8800
St. John Lutheran S 50/PK-10
15671 158th St NE 56701 218-681-7753
John Folland, prin.

**Tracy, Lyon, Pop. 2,129**
Tracy SD 2904 800/PK-12
934 Pine St 56175 507-629-5500
Chad Anderson, supt. Fax 629-5507
tracy.k12.mn.us
Tracy JSHS 400/7-12
934 Pine St 56175 507-629-5500
Kathy VonDracek, prin. Fax 629-5507

**Truman, Martin, Pop. 1,111**
Truman SD 458 300/K-12
PO Box 276 56088 507-776-2111
Dr. Virginia Dahlstrom, supt. Fax 776-3379
www.truman.k12.mn.us
Truman JSHS 100/7-12
PO Box 276 56088 507-776-2111
Mark Nass, prin. Fax 776-3379

**Twin Valley, Norman, Pop. 807**
Norman County East SD 2215 300/PK-12
PO Box 420 56584 218-584-5151
Mark Lundin, supt. Fax 584-5170
nce.k12.mn.us/
Norman County East HS 200/7-12
PO Box 420 56584 218-584-5151
Mark Lundin, prin. Fax 584-5170

**Two Harbors, Lake, Pop. 3,693**
Lake Superior SD 381 1,400/PK-12
1640 Highway 2 55616 218-834-8201
Dr. Bill Crandall, supt. Fax 834-8239
www.isd381.k12.mn.us
Two Harbors JSHS 600/6-12
1640 Highway 2 Ste 100 55616 218-834-8201
Jay Belcastro, prin. Fax 834-5513
Other Schools – See Silver Bay

**Tyler, Lincoln, Pop. 1,129**
R T R ISD 2902 600/PK-12
PO Box 659 56178 507-247-5913
Bruce Houck, supt. Fax 247-3876
www.rtrschools.org
R T R HS 200/9-12
PO Box 659 56178 507-247-5911
Dan Bettin, prin. Fax 247-3876
Other Schools – See Russell

**Ulen, Clay, Pop. 535**
Ulen-Hitterdal SD 914 300/K-12
PO Box 389 56585 218-596-8853
Todd Cameron, supt. Fax 596-8610
www.ulenhitterdal.k12.mn.us
Ulen-Hitterdal JSHS 100/7-12
PO Box 389 56585 218-596-8853
Kent Henrickson, prin. Fax 596-8610

**Underwood, Otter Tail, Pop. 340**
Underwood SD 550 600/PK-12
100 Southern Ave E 56586 218-826-6101
Dr. Jeremiah Olson, supt. Fax 826-6310
www.underwood.k12.mn.us
Underwood JSHS 300/7-12
100 Southern Ave E 56586 218-826-6102
John Hamann, prin. Fax 826-6310

**Upsala, Morrison, Pop. 425**
Upsala SD 487 400/PK-12
PO Box 190 56384 320-573-2174
Gery Arndt, supt. Fax 573-2173
www.upsala.k12.mn.us/
Upsala JSHS 200/7-12
PO Box 190 56384 320-573-2176
Vern Capelle, prin. Fax 573-2173

**Verndale, Wadena, Pop. 586**
Verndale SD 818 500/PK-12
411 SW Brown St 56481 218-445-5184
Paul Brownlow, supt. Fax 445-5185
www.verndale.k12.mn.us
Verndale JSHS 200/7-12
411 SW Brown St 56481 218-445-5184
Thomas Ritters, prin. Fax 445-5185

**Victoria, Carver, Pop. 7,244**

---

Holy Family HS 500/9-12
8101 Kochia Ln 55386 952-443-4659
Kathie Brown, prin. Fax 443-1822

**Virginia, Saint Louis, Pop. 8,491**
Saint Louis County SD 2142 600/PK-12
1701 N 9th Ave 55792 218-749-8130
Steven Sallee, supt. Fax 749-8133
isd2142.net
Other Schools – See Babbitt, Cook, Culver, Iron

Virginia SD 706 1,600/PK-12
411 S 5th Ave 55792 218-742-3901
Deron Stender, supt. Fax 742-3960
vmps.org
Virginia Secondary S 800/7-12
411 S 5th Ave 55792 218-742-3916
Laverne Hakly, prin. Fax 741-8522

---

Mesabi Range Community & Technical Coll. Post-Sec.
1001 Chestnut St W 55792 218-741-3095

**Wabasha, Wabasha, Pop. 2,493**
Wabasha-Kellogg SD 811 600/PK-12
2113 Hiawatha Dr E 55981 651-565-3559
Jim Freihammer, supt. Fax 565-2769
www.wabasha-kellogg.k12.mn.us/
Wabasha-Kellogg JSHS 300/7-12
2113 Hiawatha Dr E 55981 651-565-3559
Rob Stewart, prin. Fax 565-2769

**Wabasso, Redwood, Pop. 691**
Wabasso SD 640 400/PK-12
PO Box 69 56293 507-342-5114
Wade McKittrick, supt. Fax 342-5203
isd640.org
Wabasso JSHS 200/7-12
PO Box 69 56293 507-342-5114
Wade McKittrick, supt. Fax 342-5203

**Waconia, Carver, Pop. 10,592**
Waconia SD 110 3,400/PK-12
512 Industrial Blvd 55387 952-442-0600
Patrick Devine, supt. Fax 442-0609
www.waconia.k12.mn.us
Clearwater MS 1,100/5-8
1650 Community Dr 55387 952-442-0650
Shane Clausen, prin. Fax 442-0659
Waconia HS 1,000/9-12
1400 Community Dr 55387 952-442-0670
Mark Fredericksen, prin. Fax 442-0679

**Wadena, Wadena, Pop. 4,023**
Wadena-Deer Creek SD 2155 1,000/PK-12
600 Colfax Ave SW 56482 218-632-2155
Lee Westrum, supt. Fax 632-2199
www.wdc2155.k12.mn.us
Wadena-Deer Creek MSHS 400/5-12
600 Colfax Ave SW 56482 218-632-2300
Tyler Church, prin. Fax 632-2399

MN State Community & Technical College Post-Sec.
405 Colfax Ave SW 56482 218-631-7800

**Waite Park, Stearns, Pop. 6,543**

Minnesota School of Business Post-Sec.
1201 2nd St S 56387 320-257-2000
Regency Beauty Institute Post-Sec.
110 2nd St S 56387 320-251-0500

**Walker, Cass, Pop. 910**
Walker-Hackensack-Akeley SD 113 800/PK-12
PO Box 4000 56484 218-547-1311
Dave Endicott, supt. Fax 547-4298
www.wha.k12.mn.us
Walker-Hackensack-Akeley HS 300/7-12
PO Box 4000 56484 218-547-4210
Dave Wineburner, prin. Fax 547-4297

**Wanamingo, Goodhue, Pop. 1,081**
Kenyon-Wanamingo SD 2172 700/PK-12
225 3rd Ave 55983 507-789-7000
Jeff Pesta, supt. Fax 789-7032
www.kw.k12.mn.us
Other Schools – See Kenyon

**Warren, Marshall, Pop. 1,554**
Warren-Alvarado-Oslo SD 2176 400/PK-12
224 E Bridge Ave 56762 218-745-5393
Lon Jorgensen, supt. Fax 745-5886
www.wao.k12.mn.us
Warren-Alvarado-Oslo JSHS 200/7-12
224 E Bridge Ave 56762 218-745-4646
Wade Johnson, prin. Fax 745-7658

**Warroad, Roseau, Pop. 1,740**
Warroad SD 690 1,100/PK-12
510 Cedar Ave NW 56763 218-386-1472
Craig Oftedahl, supt. Fax 386-1909
www.warroad.k12.mn.us
Border Area Learning Center 50/Alt
510 Cedar Ave NW 56763 218-386-3385
Maureen Stodgell, dir. Fax 386-1909
Warroad JSHS 500/7-12
510 Cedar Ave NW 56763 218-386-1820
Brad Nash, prin. Fax 386-1909

**Waseca, Waseca, Pop. 9,257**
Waseca SD 829 1,500/PK-12
501 Elm Ave E 56093 507-835-2500
Thomas Lee, supt. Fax 835-1161
www.waseca.k12.mn.us
Waseca Alternative Learning Center 50/Alt
501 Elm Ave E 56093 507-835-5588
John Sakellario, coord. Fax 835-1724
Waseca JSHS 600/7-12
1717 2nd St NW 56093 507-835-5470
Jeanne Swanson, prin. Fax 835-1724

**Watertown, Carver, Pop. 4,128**
Watertown-Mayer SD 111 1,600/PK-12
1001 Highway 25 Shls NW 55388 952-955-0480
Ron Wilke, supt. Fax 955-0481
www.wm.k12.mn.us
Watertown-Mayer HS 500/9-12
1001 Highway 25 Shls NW 55388 952-955-0600
Bob Hennen, prin. Fax 955-0601
Watertown-Mayer MS 400/6-8
1001 Highway 25 Shls NW 55388 952-955-0400
Nick Guertin, prin. Fax 955-0481

**Waterville, LeSueur, Pop. 1,853**
Waterville-Elysian-Morristown SD 2143 900/PK-12
500 Paquin St E 56096 507-362-4432
Joel Whitehurst, supt. Fax 362-4561
www.wem.k12.mn.us/
Waterville-Elysian-Morristown HS 300/9-12
500 Paquin St E 56096 507-362-4431
John Kaplan, prin. Fax 362-4561
Other Schools – See Morristown

**Waubun, Mahnomen, Pop. 324**
Waubun-Ogema-White Earth SD 435 600/PK-12
PO Box 98 56589 218-473-6171
Lisa Weber, supt. Fax 473-6191
www.waubun.k12.mn.us
Waubun JSHS 300/7-12
PO Box 98 56589 218-473-6173
Eric Martinez, prin. Fax 473-6190

**Wayzata, Hennepin, Pop. 3,646**
Wayzata SD 284
Supt. — See Plymouth
Wayzata West MS 700/6-8
149 Barry Ave N 55391 952-745-6400
Susan Sommerfeld, prin. Fax 745-6491

**Wells, Faribault, Pop. 2,325**
United South Central SD 2134 600/PK-12
PO Box 312 56097 507-553-3134
Dr. Jerry Jensen, supt. Fax 553-5929
www.usc.k12.mn.us
United South Central JSHS 300/7-12
PO Box 312 56097 507-553-5819
Kelly Schlaak, prin. Fax 553-5929

**Westbrook, Cottonwood, Pop. 737**
Westbrook-Walnut Grove SD 2898 500/PK-12
PO Box 129 56183 507-274-5450
Loy Woelber, supt. Fax 274-6113
www.walnut.mntm.org/
Westbrook-Walnut Grove JHHS 200/7-12
PO Box 129 56183 507-274-5450
William Richards, prin. Fax 858-2329

**West Saint Paul, Dakota, Pop. 19,105**
West St. Paul-Mendota Hts-Eagan SD 197
Supt. — See Mendota Heights
Heritage MS 700/5-8
121 Butler Ave W 55118 651-403-7400
Karen Allen, prin. Fax 403-7410

St. Croix Lutheran MSHS 500/6-12
1200 Oakdale Ave 55118 651-455-1521
Todd Russ, pres. Fax 451-3968

**Wheaton, Traverse, Pop. 1,408**
Wheaton Area SD 803 400/PK-12
1700 3rd Ave S 56296 320-563-8283
Daniel Posthumus, supt. Fax 563-4218
www.wheaton.k12.mn.us
Wheaton JSHS 200/6-12
1700 3rd Ave S 56296 320-563-8282
Martin Lanter, prin. Fax 563-4218

**White Bear Lake, Ramsey, Pop. 23,270**
White Bear Lake Area SD 624 7,600/PK-12
4855 Bloom Ave 55110 651-407-7500
Dr. Michael Lovett, supt. Fax 407-7566
www.isd624.org
Central MS 900/6-8
4857 Bloom Ave 55110 651-653-2888
Dr. Noel Schmidt, prin. Fax 653-2885
Sunrise Park MS 700/6-8
2399 Cedar Ave 55110 651-653-2700
Dr. Bob McDowell, prin. Fax 653-2716
White Bear Lake Area HS - North Campus 1,200/9-10
5045 Division Ave 55110 651-653-2920
Donald Bosch, prin. Fax 653-2630
White Bear Lake Area HS - South Campus 1,200/11-12
3551 McKnight Rd N 55110 651-773-6200
Timothy Wald, prin. Fax 773-6215
White Bear Lake Area Learning Center 200/Alt
2449 Orchard Ln 55110 651-773-6400
Gretchen Harriman, admin. Fax 773-6402

Century College Post-Sec.
3300 Century Ave N 55110 651-779-3200

**Willmar, Kandiyohi, Pop. 19,385**
Willmar SD 347 4,000/K-12
611 5th St SW 56201 320-231-8500
Dr. Jeffrey Holm, supt. Fax 231-1061
www.willmar.k12.mn.us
Willmar Area Learning Center 100/Alt
512 8th St SW 56201 320-214-6692
Linda Bahe, coord. Fax 235-5352
Willmar HS 1,200/9-12
2701 30th St NE 56201 320-231-8300
Paul Schmitz, prin. Fax 231-8460
Willmar MS 800/6-8
201 Willmar Ave SE 56201 320-214-6000
Mark Miley, prin. Fax 235-1254

Community Christian S 200/PK-12
1300 19th Ave SW 56201 320-235-0592
John Chapin, admin. Fax 235-0620
Rice Memorial Hospital Post-Sec.
301 Becker Ave SW 56201 320-231-4530
Ridgewater College Post-Sec.
PO Box 1097 56201 320-222-5200

**Willow River, Pine, Pop. 405**
Willow River SD 577 400/PK-12
PO Box 66 55795 218-372-3131
Scott Anderson, supt. Fax 372-3132
www.willowriver.k12.mn.us
Willow River JSHS 200/5-12
PO Box 66 55795 218-372-3131
Matt Hosmer, prin. Fax 372-3132

**Windom, Cottonwood, Pop. 4,585**
Windom SD 177 900/K-12
PO Box 177 56101 507-831-6901
Wayne Wormstadt, supt. Fax 831-6919
www.windom.k12.mn.us
Windom Area HS 300/9-12
PO Box 177 56101 507-831-6910
Jake Tietje, prin. Fax 831-6909
Windom MS 300/4-8
PO Box 177 56101 507-831-6910
Jake Tietje, prin. Fax 831-6909

**Winona, Winona, Pop. 27,243**
Winona Area SD 861 3,200/PK-12
903 Gilmore Ave 55987 507-494-0861
Dr. Stephen West, supt. Fax 494-0863
www.winona.k12.mn.us
Winona ALC 100/Alt
1299 W 3rd St 55987 507-494-1460
Mark Winter, dir. Fax 494-1465
Winona HS 1,100/9-12
901 Gilmore Ave 55987 507-494-1504
Ryan Jensen, prin. Fax 494-1501
Winona MS 900/5-8
1570 Homer Rd 55987 507-494-1000
Mark Anderson, prin. Fax 494-1002

Cotter HS 300/9-12
1115 W Broadway St 55987 507-453-5000
Oscar Uribe, prin. Fax 453-5006
Cotter JHS 100/7-8
1115 W Broadway St 55987 507-453-5000
Oscar Uribe, dir. Fax 453-5006
Hope Lutheran HS 50/9-12
253 Liberty St 55987 507-474-7799
Rocky Sandcork, admin. Fax 452-8992
Minnesota State College Southeast Tech. Post-Sec.
PO Box 409 55987 507-453-2700
St. Mary's University of Minnesota Post-Sec.
700 Terrace Hts 55987 507-452-4430
Winona State University Post-Sec.
PO Box 5838 55987 507-457-5000

**Winsted, McLeod, Pop. 2,341**

Holy Trinity HS 100/7-12
PO Box 38 55395 320-485-2182
Wesley Kapping, prin. Fax 485-4283

**Winthrop, Sibley, Pop. 1,386**
GFW SD 2365
Supt. — See Gibbon
GFW HS 300/9-12
1001 N Cottonwood St 55396 507-647-5382
Nathaniel Boyer, prin. Fax 647-4329

**Woodbury, Washington, Pop. 60,529**
South Washington County SD 833
Supt. — See Cottage Grove
East Ridge HS 1,700/9-12
4200 Pioneer Dr 55129 651-425-2300
James Smokrovich, prin. Fax 425-2305
Lake MS 1,100/6-8
3133 Pioneer Dr 55125 651-425-6400
Molly Roeske, prin. Fax 425-6428
Woodbury HS 1,800/9-12
2665 Woodlane Dr 55125 651-425-4400
Sarah Sorenson-Wagner, prin. Fax 425-4411
Woodbury MS 900/6-8
1425 School Dr 55125 651-425-4500
Kari Lopez, prin. Fax 425-4567

Globe University Post-Sec.
8089 Globe Dr 55125 651-730-5100
New Life Academy 700/PK-12
6758 Bailey Rd 55129 651-459-4121
Cade Lambert, head sch Fax 459-6194

**Worthington, Nobles, Pop. 12,573**
Worthington SD 518 2,600/PK-12
1117 Marine Ave 56187 507-372-2172
John Landgaard, supt. Fax 372-2174
www.isd518.net
Worthington Area Learning Center 100/Alt
117 11th Ave 56187 507-372-1322
Nate Hanson, prin. Fax 372-1361
Worthington HS 700/9-12
1211 Clary St 56187 507-376-6121
Josh Noble, prin. Fax 372-4304
Worthington MS 700/5-8
1401 Crailsheim Dr 56187 507-376-4174
Jeff Luke, prin. Fax 372-1424

Minnesota West Community & Tech College Post-Sec.
1450 Collegeway 56187 507-372-3400

**Wrenshall, Carlton, Pop. 390**
Wrenshall SD 100 300/PK-12
207 Pioneer Dr 55797 218-384-4274
Dr. Kimberly Belcastro, supt. Fax 384-4293
www.wrenshall.k12.mn.us
Wrenshall JSHS 200/7-12
207 Pioneer Dr 55797 218-384-4274
Sue Frank, prin. Fax 384-4293

**Zimmerman, Sherburne, Pop. 5,145**
Elk River Area SD 728
Supt. — See Elk River
Zimmerman MSHS 600/6-12
25900 4th St W 55398 763-241-3505
Marco Voce, prin. Fax 241-3506

**Zumbrota, Goodhue, Pop. 3,200**
Zumbrota-Mazeppa SD 2805
Supt. — See Mazeppa
Zumbrota-Mazeppa HS 300/9-12
705 Mill St 55992 507-732-7395
Dave Anderson, prin. Fax 732-4511
Zumbrota-Mazeppa MS 200/7-8
705 Mill St 55992 507-732-7395
Dave Anderson, prin. Fax 324-4511

# MISSISSIPPI

## MISSISSIPPI DEPARTMENT OF EDUCATION
**PO Box 771, Jackson 39205**
**Telephone 601-359-1750**
**Fax 601-359-3242**
**Website http://www.mde.k12.ms.us**

Superintendent of Education Lynn J. House Ph.D

## MISSISSIPPI BOARD OF EDUCATION
**PO Box 771, Jackson 39205**

Chairperson Dr. O. Wayne Gann

## PUBLIC, PRIVATE AND CATHOLIC SECONDARY SCHOOLS

**Aberdeen, Monroe, Pop. 5,561**
Aberdeen SD 1,000/PK-12
PO Box 607 39730 662-369-4682
John Mac Curlee, admin. Fax 369-0987
www.asdms.us
Aberdeen HS 500/9-12
PO Box 607 39730 662-369-8933
Cloyd Garth, prin. Fax 369-6004
Shivers MS 200/6-8
PO Box 607 39730 662-369-6241
Russell Greene, prin. Fax 369-3207

Monroe County SD
Supt. — See Amory
Monroe Co. Career and Technical Center Vo/Tech
50057 Airport Rd 39730 662-369-7845
Steve Cantrell, dir. Fax 369-9607

**Ackerman, Choctaw, Pop. 1,499**
Choctaw County SD 1,300/PK-12
PO Box 398 39735 662-285-4022
Stewart Beard, supt. Fax 285-4049
www.choctaw.k12.ms.us/
Choctaw County Career & Technology Ctr Vo/Tech
PO Box 775 39735 662-285-4160
Ronda Huffman, prin. Fax 285-4199
Choctaw County HS 400/7-12
393 E Main St 39735 662-285-4101
Shane Burton, prin. Fax 285-4149

**Amory, Monroe, Pop. 7,262**
Amory SD 1,800/K-12
PO Box 330 38821 662-256-5991
Tony Cook, supt. Fax 256-6302
www.amoryschools.com/
Amory Career and Technical Center Vo/Tech
PO Box 330 38821 662-256-7601
Andy Cantrell, dir. Fax 256-1649
Amory HS 500/9-12
1006 Sam Haskell Cir 38821 662-256-5753
Ken Byars, prin. Fax 256-5754
Amory MS 400/6-8
700 2nd Ave N 38821 662-256-5658
David Poss, prin. Fax 256-6304

Monroe County SD 2,200/K-12
PO Box 209 38821 662-257-2176
Scott Cantrell, supt. Fax 257-2181
www.mcsd.us
Advanced Learning Center 10-12
52251 Highway 25 S 38821 662-256-2495
Jeff Brooks, prin. Fax 256-2731
Hatley S 1,000/K-12
60286 Hatley Rd 38821 662-256-4563
Van Pearson, prin. Fax 256-5626
Other Schools – See Aberdeen, Hamilton, Smithville

**Anguilla, Sharkey, Pop. 721**
South Delta SD
Supt. — See Rolling Fork
South Delta MS 200/6-8
PO Box 487 38721 662-873-6535
Mark Beechem, prin. Fax 873-6073

**Arcola, Washington, Pop. 359**

---

Deer Creek S 200/PK-12
PO Box 376 38722 662-827-5165

**Ashland, Benton, Pop. 566**
Benton County SD 1,200/K-12
PO Box 247 38603 662-224-6252
Jack Gadd, supt. Fax 224-3607
www.benton.k12.ms.us
Ashland HS 100/9-12
PO Box 187 38603 662-224-6247
Dr. Lakimberly Hobson, prin. Fax 224-3614
Ashland MS 100/6-8
PO Box 368 38603 662-224-6485
Rosie Ladd, prin. Fax 224-3609
Benton County Regional Vocational Center Vo/Tech
PO Box 754 38603 662-224-3108
Merri Gadd, dir. Fax 224-3629
Other Schools – See Hickory Flat

**Avon, Washington**
Western Line SD 2,000/PK-12
PO Box 50 38723 662-335-7186
Larry Green, supt. Fax 378-2285
www.westernline.org
Riverside HS 400/7-12
PO Box 80 38723 662-335-4527
Donald Coleman, prin. Fax 334-1797
Other Schools – See Greenville

**Baldwyn, Lee, Pop. 3,256**
Baldwyn SD 800/K-12
107 W Main St 38824 662-365-1000
Jason McKay, supt. Fax 365-1003
www.baldwynschools.com
Baldwyn HS 300/9-12
512 N Fourth St 38824 662-365-1020
Jeff Palmer, prin. Fax 365-1028
Baldwyn MS 300/5-8
452 N Fourth St 38824 662-365-1015
Danny Ramsey, prin. Fax 365-1029

**Bassfield, Jefferson Davis, Pop. 253**
Jefferson Davis County SD
Supt. — See Prentiss
Bassfield JSHS 300/7-12
PO Box 370 39421 601-943-5391
John Daley, prin. Fax 943-5790

**Batesville, Panola, Pop. 7,385**
South Panola SD 4,500/PK-12
209 Boothe St 38606 662-563-9361
Tim Wilder, supt. Fax 563-6077
www.spsd.k12.ms.us
Batesville JHS 900/6-8
507 Tiger Dr 38606 662-563-4503
Charles Stevenson, prin. Fax 563-6038
South Panola Alternative S Alt
507 Tiger Dr 38606 662-563-3706
Patricia Gleeton, dir. Fax 563-9666
South Panola HS 1,100/9-12
601 Tiger Dr 38606 662-563-4756
Rodney Flowers, prin. Fax 563-8993

---

North Delta S 400/PK-12
330 Green Wave Ln 38606 662-563-4536

**Bay Saint Louis, Hancock, Pop. 9,056**
Bay St. Louis-Waveland SD 1,500/K-12
200 N 2nd St 39520 228-467-6621
Dr. Rebecca Ladner, supt. Fax 467-1230
www.bwsd.org/
Bay HS 500/9-12
750 Blue Meadow Rd 39520 228-467-6611
Dr. Amy Coyne, prin. Fax 466-0883
Bay-Waveland MS 400/6-8
600 Pine St 39520 228-463-0315
Dr. Cherie Labat, prin. Fax 463-2681

---

Our Lady Academy 200/7-12
222 S Beach Blvd 39520 228-467-7048
Tiffany Lindmark, prin. Fax 467-1666
St. Stanislaus College Prep S 400/7-12
304 S Beach Blvd 39520 228-467-9057
Patrick McGrath, prin. Fax 466-2972

**Bay Springs, Jasper, Pop. 1,763**
West Jasper Consolidated SD 1,500/K-12
PO Box 610 39422 601-764-2280
Warren Woodrow, supt. Fax 764-4490
wjsd-mississippi.schoolloop.com/
Bay Springs HS 200/9-12
PO Box 389 39422 601-764-4151
James Raborn, prin. Fax 764-6445
Bay Springs MS 300/5-8
PO Box 587 39422 601-764-3378
Tracy Adcock, prin. Fax 764-2329
Other Schools – See Stringer

---

Sylva-Bay Academy 300/PK-12
PO Box J 39422 601-764-2157

**Belden, Lee**
Lee County SD
Supt. — See Tupelo
Belden Center Alt
4677 Endville Rd 38826 662-842-2050
Pam Blissard, prin.

---

Tupelo Christian Preparatory S 500/PK-12
5440 Endville Rd 38826 662-844-8604
Brian Benscoter, hdmstr. Fax 823-6972

**Belmont, Tishomingo, Pop. 2,002**
Tishomingo County Special Municipal SD
Supt. — See Iuka
Belmont S 1,000/K-12
9 School Dr 38827 662-454-7924
Van Roberts, prin. Fax 454-7611

**Belzoni, Humphreys, Pop. 2,229**
Humphreys County SD 1,400/K-12
PO Box 678 39038 662-247-6000
Elliot Wheeler, supt. Fax 247-6004
www.humphreyscountyschools.com
Humphreys County HS 500/9-12
PO Box 658 39038 662-247-6040
Kathleen Turner, prin. Fax 247-6044
Humphreys JHS 300/6-8
PO Box 678 39038 662-247-6050
Arnesser Moore, prin. Fax 247-6054
Randle Career and Technical Ctr Vo/Tech
PO Box 672 39038 662-247-6030
Jimmie Hurst, prin. Fax 247-6034

---

Humphreys Academy 100/K-12
PO Box 179 39038 662-247-1572

**Benoit, Bolivar, Pop. 477**
West Bolivar SD
Supt. — See Rosedale
Brooks S 300/PK-12
PO Box 8 38725 662-742-3257
Barbara Flore, prin. Fax 742-3493

**Benton, Yazoo**

---

Benton Academy 200/PK-12
PO Box 308 39039 662-673-9722

**Biloxi, Harrison, Pop. 42,823**
Biloxi Public SD 5,100/PK-12
PO Box 168 39533 228-374-1810
Arthur McMillan, supt. Fax 435-6289
www.biloxischools.net
Biloxi HS 1,500/9-12
1845 Richard Dr 39532 228-435-6105
Marcus Boudreaux, prin. Fax 435-6353
Biloxi JHS 1,100/6-8
1424 Father Ryan Ave 39530 228-435-1421
Scott Powell, prin. Fax 435-1426

Harrison County SD
Supt. — See Gulfport
D'Iberville HS 1,200/9-12
15625 Lamey Bridge Rd 39540 228-392-2678
Cheryle Broadus, prin. Fax 392-7807

---

Cedar Lake Christian Academy 200/PK-12
11555 Cedar Lake Rd 39532 228-392-6279
St. Patrick HS 500/7-12
18300 Saint Patrick Rd 39532 228-702-0500
J. Renee McDaniel, prin. Fax 702-0511
Virginia College Post-Sec.
920 Cedar Lake Rd 39532 228-546-9100

**Blue Mountain, Tippah, Pop. 901**
South Tippah SD
Supt. — See Ripley
Blue Mountain S 300/K-12
408 W Mill St 38610 662-685-4706
Brad Pounders, prin. Fax 685-4706

---

Blue Mountain College Post-Sec.
PO Box 160 38610 662-685-4771

**Blue Springs, Union, Pop. 228**
Union County SD
Supt. — See New Albany

East Union S 800/K-12
1548 Highway 9 S 38828 662-534-6920
Ray Kennedy, prin. Fax 534-6542

**Bogue Chitto, Lincoln, Pop. 518**
Lincoln County SD
Supt. — See Brookhaven
Bogue Chitto S 600/K-12
385 Monticello St 39629 601-734-2723
Mickey Myers, prin. Fax 734-6020

**Bolton, Hinds, Pop. 565**
Hinds County SD
Supt. — See Raymond
Main Street Restart S Alt
130 Champion Hill Rd 39041 601-866-2642
Kim Davenport, prin. Fax 866-4414

**Booneville, Prentiss, Pop. 8,634**
Booneville SD 1,300/K-12
201 N 1st St 38829 662-728-2171
Todd English, supt. Fax 728-4940
boonevilleschools.org
Booneville HS 400/9-12
300 W George E Allen Dr # B 38829 662-728-5445
Terry King, prin. Fax 728-2953
Booneville MS 400/5-8
300 W George E Allen Dr # B 38829 662-728-5843
Brad Mixon, prin. Fax 728-2427

Prentiss County SD 2,000/K-12
PO Box 179 38829 662-728-4911
Randle Downs, supt. Fax 728-2000
www.prentiss.k12.ms.us/
Jumpertown S 300/K-12
717 Highway 4 W 38829 662-728-6378
Anthony Michael, prin. Fax 728-9420
Prentiss County Vocational Technical S Vo/Tech
302 W George E Allen Dr 38829 662-728-9259
Kim Green, dir. Fax 728-9259
Thrasher S 400/K-12
167 County Road 1040 38829 662-728-5233
Jason Potts, prin. Fax 728-8107
Other Schools – See New Site, Wheeler

Northeast Mississippi Community College Post-Sec.
101 Cunningham Blvd 38829 662-728-7751

**Brandon, Rankin, Pop. 21,524**
Rankin County SD 18,700/K-12
PO Box 1359 39043 601-825-5590
Dr. Lynn Weathersby, supt. Fax 825-2618
www.rcsd.ms
Brandon HS 1,500/9-12
3090 Highway 18 39042 601-825-2261
Buddy Bailey, prin. Fax 591-1037
Brandon MS 1,300/6-8
408 S College St 39042 601-825-5998
Dr. Charles Frazier, prin. Fax 825-8402
Learning Center Alt
200 School Rd 39042 601-824-0334
Harry Hill, prin. Fax 825-2988
Other Schools – See Florence, Flowood, Pelahatchie, Puckett, Richland, Sandhill

**Brookhaven, Lincoln, Pop. 12,389**
Brookhaven SD 2,900/K-12
PO Box 540 39602 601-833-6661
Ben Cox, supt. Fax 833-4154
www.brookhavenschools.org
Alexander JHS 400/7-8
713 Beauregard St 39601 601-833-7549
Rod Henderson, prin. Fax 835-5467
Brookhaven HS 800/9-12
PO Box 532 39602 601-833-4498
David Martin, prin. Fax 823-3792
Brookhaven Technical Center Vo/Tech
325 E Court St 39601 601-833-8335
Jackie Martin, dir. Fax 835-3985
Mullins S Alt
711 Martin Luther King Dr 39601 601-833-7479
Janee Harrison, prin. Fax 823-6598

Lincoln County SD 3,000/K-12
PO Box 826 39602 601-835-0011
Terry Brister, supt. Fax 833-3030
lcsd.k12.ms.us/
Enterprise S 800/K-12
1601 Highway 583 SE 39601 601-833-7284
Shannon Eubanks, prin. Fax 835-1261
Star S 800/K-12
1880 Highway 550 NW 39601 601-833-3473
Robin Case, prin. Fax 833-1254
West Lincoln S 700/K-12
948 Jackson Liberty Dr SW 39601 601-833-4600
Jason Case, prin. Fax 833-9909
Other Schools – See Bogue Chitto

Brookhaven Academy 500/PK-12
943 Brookway Blvd Ext 39601 601-833-4041
Julie Wright, hdmstr. Fax 833-1846

**Brooklyn, Forrest**
Forrest County Agricultural HSD
215 Old Highway 49 E 39425 601-582-4102
Billy Ellzey, supt. Fax 545-9483
www.forrestcountyahs.com
Forrest County Agricultural HS Vo/Tech
215 Old Highway 49 E 39425 601-582-4741
Charles Johnson, prin. Fax 545-9031

**Bruce, Calhoun, Pop. 1,918**
Calhoun County SD
Supt. — See Pittsboro
Bruce HS 400/7-12
PO Box 248 38915 662-983-3350
Michael Gillespie, prin. Fax 983-3356

**Byhalia, Marshall, Pop. 1,278**
Marshall County SD
Supt. — See Holly Springs
Byhalia HS 500/9-12
278 Highway 309 N 38611 662-838-2206
William Johnson, prin. Fax 838-2218
Byhalia MS 400/6-8
172 Highway 309 N 38611 662-838-2591
Landon Pollard, prin. Fax 838-5141

**Caledonia, Lowndes, Pop. 1,021**
Lowndes County SD
Supt. — See Columbus
Caledonia HS 500/9-12
111 Confederate Dr 39740 662-356-2001
Dr. Andy Stevens, prin. Fax 356-2036
Caledonia MS 500/6-8
105 Confederate Dr 39740 662-356-2042
Karen Pittman, prin. Fax 356-2045

**Calhoun City, Calhoun, Pop. 1,755**
Calhoun County SD
Supt. — See Pittsboro
Calhoun Career and Technical Center Vo/Tech
PO Box 1573 38916 662-628-1143
Kyle Clark, admin. Fax 628-1123
Calhoun City HS 200/9-12
PO Box 559 38916 662-628-5112
Mike Ray, prin. Fax 628-6240
Calhoun City MS 200/5-8
PO Box 1546 38916 662-628-1890
Stacia Parker, prin. Fax 628-1896

**Camden, Madison**
Madison County SD
Supt. — See Ridgeland
Jackson HS 300/9-12
2000 Loring Rd 39045 662-468-2531
Bertram Goodloe, prin. Fax 468-2748

**Canton, Madison, Pop. 13,125**
Canton SD 3,400/K-12
403 Lincoln St 39046 601-859-4110
Ike Haynes, supt. Fax 859-4023
www.cantonschools.net
Canton Career Center Vo/Tech
487 N Union Street Ext 39046 601-859-3984
W.K. Luckett, dir. Fax 859-1115
Canton Educational Services Center Alt
529 Mace St 39046 601-859-5010
Jacqueline Griffin, prin. Fax 859-5011
Canton HS 900/9-12
634 Finney Rd 39046 601-859-5325
Timothy Chambers, prin. Fax 859-2554
Nichols MS 700/6-8
529 Mace St 39046 601-859-3741
Tina Manning, prin. Fax 859-6561
Porter MS 6-8
Finney Rd 39046 601-407-1819
Michael Ellis, prin. Fax 407-1401

Madison County SD
Supt. — See Ridgeland
Simmons MS 200/6-8
820 Sulphur Springs Rd 39046 601-855-2406
Kelvin Griffin, prin. Fax 859-7615

Canton Academy 300/K-12
PO Box 116 39046 601-859-5231

**Carriere, Pearl River**
Pearl River County SD 3,000/K-12
7441 Highway 11 39426 601-798-7744
Alan Lumpkin, supt. Fax 798-3527
www.prc.k12.ms.us/
Pearl River Central Alternative Educ Alt
461 Burgetown Rd 39426 601-798-6852
Lori Burkett, dir. Fax 799-4355
Pearl River Central HS 900/9-12
7407 Highway 11 39426 601-798-1986
Stacy Baudoin, prin. Fax 798-0068
Pearl River Central MS 700/6-8
7391 Highway 11 39426 601-798-5654
Missy Holston, prin. Fax 798-2822

**Carrollton, Carroll, Pop. 190**
Carroll County SD 1,000/K-12
PO Box 256 38917 662-237-9276
Billy Joe Ferguson, supt. Fax 237-9703
www.ccsd.ms
Other Schools – See North Carrollton

Carroll Academy 300/PK-12
PO Box 226 38917 662-237-6858

**Carson, Jefferson Davis**
Jefferson Davis County SD
Supt. — See Prentiss
Davis County Voc-Tech Center Vo/Tech
PO Box 70 39427 601-792-5005
Dr. Thomas Johnson, dir. Fax 792-2511

**Carthage, Leake, Pop. 5,025**
Leake County SD 2,600/K-12
PO Box 478 39051 601-267-4579
Patrick Posey, supt. Fax 267-5283
www.leakesd.org
Leake Central HS 600/9-12
704 N Jordan St 39051 601-267-7713
Bruce Burns, prin. Fax 267-3738
Leake Central JHS 400/6-8
801 Martin Luther King Dr 39051 601-267-8909
Peggy Marble, prin. Fax 267-5902
Leake County Career & Technical Center Vo/Tech
703 N West St 39051 601-267-8442
Glenda Holleyman, prin. Fax 267-5150
Other Schools – See Walnut Grove

Infinity Career College Post-Sec.
305B Highway 16 W 39051 601-267-3678

**Centreville, Wilkinson, Pop. 1,683**
Wilkinson County SD
Supt. — See Woodville
Winans MS 300/6-8
PO Box 610 39631 601-645-0008
Melvin Craige, prin. Fax 645-0170

Centreville Academy 400/K-12
PO Box 70 39631 601-645-5912

**Charleston, Tallahatchie, Pop. 2,183**
East Tallahatchie Consolidated SD 1,300/PK-12
411 E Chestnut St 38921 662-647-5524
Dr. Ben Kennedy, supt. Fax 647-3720
www.etsd.k12.ms.us
Charleston HS 400/9-12
411 E Chestnut St 38921 662-647-5359
Scotty Collins, prin. Fax 647-3724
Charleston MS 300/5-8
411 E Chestnut St 38921 662-647-2115
James Harrison, prin. Fax 647-2380

Strider Academy 100/K-12
3698 MS Highway 32 Central 38921 662-647-5833

**Clarksdale, Coahoma, Pop. 17,884**
Clarksdale Municipal SD 2,400/PK-12
PO Box 1088 38614 662-627-8500
Dennis Dupree, supt. Fax 627-8542
www.cmsd.k12.ms.us/
Clarksdale HS 600/10-12
PO Box 1088 38614 662-627-8530
Dr. Manika Kemp, prin. Fax 627-8549
Higgins MS 200/7-8
PO Box 1088 38614 662-627-8550
Valarie Davis, prin. Fax 627-8543
Keen Vocational Center Vo/Tech
PO Box 1088 38614 662-627-8580
Kenisha Shelton, dir. Fax 627-8582
Stampley 9th Grade Academy 200/9-9
PO Box 1088 38614 662-627-8570
Herbert Smith, prin. Fax 627-7143

Coahoma Agricultural HSD 300/9-12
3240 Friars Point Rd 38614 662-621-4258
Dr. Valmadge Towner, supt. Fax 624-4315
cahs.k12.ms.us
Coahoma Agricultural HS 300/9-12
3240 Friars Point Rd 38614 662-624-8045
Braxton Stowe M.D., prin. Fax 621-4672

Coahoma County SD 1,400/K-12
PO Box 820 38614 662-624-5448
Pauline Rhoads, supt. Fax 624-5512
www.coahoma.k12.ms.us
Coahoma County JSHS 500/7-12
1535 Lee Dr 38614 662-627-7378
Tony Young, prin. Fax 627-4516

Coahoma Community College Post-Sec.
3240 Friars Point Rd 38614 662-627-2571
Lee Academy 400/PK-12
415 Lee Dr 38614 662-627-7891
Tommy Gunn, admin. Fax 627-7896

**Cleveland, Bolivar, Pop. 12,236**
Cleveland SD 3,200/PK-12
305 Merritt Dr 38732 662-843-3529
Jacquelyn Thigpen Ed.D., supt. Fax 843-9731
www.cleveland.k12.ms.us
Cleveland Career Development & Tech Ctr. Vo/Tech
601 3rd St 38732 662-843-8818
Monica Mitchell, dir. Fax 545-4612
Cleveland HS 500/9-12
300 W Sunflower Rd 38732 662-843-2460
Steven Craddock, prin. Fax 843-2455
East Side HS 300/9-12
601 Lucy Seaberry Blvd 38732 662-843-2338
Dr. Randy Grierson, prin. Fax 843-1900
Green JHS 400/7-8
305 N Bolivar Ave 38732 662-843-2456
Archie Mitchell, prin. Fax 843-6820
Robinson Achievement Center Alt
607 3rd St 38732 662-846-6478
Dianne Hill, prin. Fax 846-7125
Smith MS 200/7-8
715 S Martin Luther King Dr 38732 662-843-4355
L'Kenna Whitehead, prin. Fax 843-7334

Bayou Academy 400/PK-12
PO Box 417 38732 662-843-3708
Dr. David Granville, hdmstr. Fax 843-9618
Delta State University Post-Sec.
1003 W Sunflower Rd 38733 662-846-3000

**Clinton, Hinds, Pop. 24,956**
Clinton SD 4,600/K-12
PO Box 300 39060 601-924-7533
Phillip Burchfield Ed.D., supt. Fax 924-6345
www.clintonpublicschools.com
Clinton Alternative S Alt
PO Box 300 39060 601-925-4027
Kelly Heather, prin. Fax 925-8156
Clinton Career Complex Vo/Tech
715 Lakeview Dr 39056 601-924-0247
Brett Robinson, dir. Fax 924-1168
Clinton HS 1,000/10-12
401 Arrow Dr 39056 601-924-5656
Anthony Goins, prin. Fax 924-4622
Clinton JHS 700/7-8
711 Lakeview Dr 39056 601-924-0619
Dr. Bill Hardin, prin. Fax 924-7703
Sumner Hill JHS 400/9-9
400 W Northside Dr 39056 601-924-5510
John Wallace, prin. Fax 924-4182

Clinton Christian Academy — 200/PK-12
PO Box 330 39060 — 601-910-5990
Mississippi College — Post-Sec.
200 W College St 39058 — 601-925-3000
Mount Salus Christian S — 100/K-12
1580 Clinton Raymond Rd 39056 — 601-924-5863

**Coffeeville, Yalobusha, Pop. 891**
Coffeeville SD — 600/PK-12
96 Mississippi St 38922 — 662-675-8941
Eddie Anderson Ph.D., supt. — Fax 675-5004
www.coffeevilleschools.org/
Coffeeville HS — 200/8-12
96 Mississippi St 38922 — 662-675-8904
Joey Cooley, prin. — Fax 675-8905

**Coldwater, Tate, Pop. 1,663**
Tate County SD
Supt. — See Senatobia
Coldwater Attendence Center — 500/K-12
340 Darnell St 38618 — 662-622-5561
Cedrick Jackson, prin. — Fax 622-7253
Independence HS — 600/7-12
3184 Highway 305 38618 — 662-233-4691
Melody Carter, prin. — Fax 233-2214
Senatobia/Tate Vocational-Technical Ctr — Vo/Tech
165 W Central Ave 38618 — 662-622-5142
Richard Hartley, dir. — Fax 622-7005

**Collins, Covington, Pop. 2,566**
Covington County SD — 3,000/K-12
PO Box 1269 39428 — 601-765-4457
Clay Anglin, supt. — Fax 765-4102
www.cov.k12.ms.us
Carver MS — 300/5-8
PO Box 757 39428 — 601-765-4908
Cedric Collins, prin. — Fax 765-4100
Collins HS — 300/9-12
PO Box 1479 39428 — 601-765-3203
Brian Bagwell, prin. — Fax 765-4116
Covington County Alternative S — 50/Alt
PO Box 1269 39428 — 601-765-1465
Jake Kyzar, prin. — Fax 765-4102
Covington County Vocational Ctr — Vo/Tech
PO Box 1268 39428 — 601-765-8253
Cecil Easterling, dir. — Fax 765-6360
Other Schools – See Mount Olive, Seminary

**Collinsville, Lauderdale, Pop. 1,932**
Lauderdale County SD
Supt. — See Meridian
West Lauderdale HS — 600/9-12
9916 W Lauderdale Rd 39325 — 601-737-2277
Kevin Cheatham, prin. — Fax 737-2377
West Lauderdale MS — 700/5-8
9916 W Lauderdale Rd 39325 — 601-737-8689
Ben Alexander, prin. — Fax 737-5145

**Columbia, Marion, Pop. 6,495**
Columbia SD — 1,800/K-12
613 Bryan Ave 39429 — 601-736-2366
Marietta James Ed.D., supt. — Fax 736-2653
www.columbiaschools.org
Columbia HS — 500/9-12
1009 Broad St 39429 — 601-736-5334
Sheila Burbridge, prin. — Fax 731-1068
Jefferson MS — 400/6-8
611 Owens St 39429 — 601-736-2786
Raymond Powell, prin. — Fax 731-3762

Marion County SD — 2,300/PK-12
1010 Highway 13 N Ste 2 39429 — 601-736-7193
Craig Robbins, supt. — Fax 736-6274
www.marionk12.org
East Marion JSHS — 400/7-12
527 E Marion School Rd 39429 — 601-736-3006
John Taylor, prin. — Fax 736-8215
Loftin Career and Technology Ctr — Vo/Tech
1140 Highway 13 S 39429 — 601-736-6095
Dr. Jan Sears, dir. — Fax 731-2077
Other Schools – See Foxworth

Columbia Academy — 600/K-12
1548 Highway 98 E 39429 — 601-736-6418

**Columbus, Lowndes, Pop. 23,393**
Columbus Municipal SD — 3,600/PK-12
PO Box 1308 39703 — 662-241-7400
Dr. Philip Hickman, supt. — Fax 241-7453
www.columbuscityschools.org
CMSD Alternative S — Alt
924 20th St N 39701 — 662-241-7250
Tamela Barr, dir. — Fax 241-7252
Columbus HS — 1,200/9-12
215 Hemlock St 39702 — 662-241-7200
Undray Scott, prin. — Fax 241-7205
Columbus MS — 1,000/6-8
175 Highway 373 39705 — 662-241-7300
Karus Jamison, prin. — Fax 241-7305
McKellar Technology Center — Vo/Tech
810 N Browder St 39702 — 662-241-7290
Christopher Bray, dir. — Fax 241-7293

Lowndes County SD — 4,900/PK-12
1053 Highway 45 S 39701 — 662-244-5000
Lynn Wright, supt. — Fax 244-5043
www.lowndes.k12.ms.us/
Lowndes County Alternative S — Alt
1380 Motley Rd 39701 — 662-244-5060
Charles Jackson, prin. — Fax 327-4857
New Hope HS — 700/9-12
3419 New Hope Rd 39702 — 662-244-4701
Matthew Smith, prin. — Fax 244-4725
New Hope MS — 600/6-8
462 Center Rd 39702 — 662-244-4740
Sam Allison, prin. — Fax 244-4758
West Lowndes HS — 200/7-12
644 S Frontage Rd 39701 — 662-328-1369
Cynthia McMath, prin. — Fax 327-3353

Other Schools – See Caledonia

Heritage Academy — 500/K-12
625 Magnolia Ln 39705 — 662-327-5272
Mississippi University for Women — Post-Sec.
1100 College St 39701 — 662-329-4750

**Como, Panola, Pop. 1,273**
North Panola SD
Supt. — See Sardis
North Panola Career & Technical Center — Vo/Tech
601 Railroad St 38619 — 662-526-5804
Lakeldra Pride, dir. — Fax 526-5868
North Panola JHS — 400/6-8
200 Lewers Dr 38619 — 662-526-5938
Valeree Ellis-Barnes, prin. — Fax 526-5990

**Corinth, Alcorn, Pop. 14,398**
Alcorn SD — 3,500/PK-12
PO Box 1420 38835 — 662-286-5591
Gina Rogers Smith, supt. — Fax 286-7766
www.alcorn.k12.ms.us
Alcorn Alternative S — Alt
2101 Norman Rd 38834 — 662-284-3359
Randy Holt, admin. — Fax 284-4950
Alcorn Career & Technology Center — Vo/Tech
2101 Norman Rd 38834 — 662-286-7727
Rodney Hopper, admin. — Fax 286-5674
Biggersville JSHS — 200/7-12
571 Highway 45 38834 — 662-286-3542
Chad Lindamood, admin. — Fax 286-3023
Kossuth HS — 500/9-12
15 County Road 604 38834 — 662-286-3653
Travis Smith, admin. — Fax 286-3507
Kossuth MS — 500/5-8
17 County Road 604 38834 — 662-286-7093
Samuel Roberts, admin. — Fax 286-6837
Other Schools – See Glen

Corinth SD — 1,700/PK-12
1204 N Harper Rd 38834 — 662-287-2425
Edward Lee Childress Ed.D., supt. — Fax 286-1885
www.corinth.k12.ms.us
Corinth HS — 500/9-12
1310 N Harper Rd 38834 — 662-286-1000
Dane Aube, prin. — Fax 286-1003
Corinth MS — 300/5-8
1000 E 5th St 38834 — 662-286-1261
Nathan Hall, prin. — Fax 287-0296

ICS The Wright Beauty College — Post-Sec.
2077 Highway 72 E Anx 38834 — 662-287-0944

**Crystal Springs, Copiah, Pop. 5,021**
Copiah County SD
Supt. — See Hazlehurst
Crystal Springs HS — 400/9-12
201 Newton St 39059 — 601-892-4791
Bill Broadhead, prin. — Fax 892-2071
Crystal Springs MS — 600/4-8
2092 S Pat Harrison Dr 39059 — 601-892-2722
Donald Regan, prin. — Fax 892-9949

**Decatur, Newton, Pop. 1,826**
Newton County SD — 1,900/K-12
15305 Highway 15 39327 — 601-635-2317
J.O. Amis, supt. — Fax 635-4025
www.newton.k12.ms.us
East Central Alternative S — Alt
15305 Highway 15 39327 — 601-635-2118
Sal LaBue, prin. — Fax 635-5659
Newton Co. Career and Technical Center — Vo/Tech
15935 Highway 15 N 39327 — 601-635-4138
Ken Stringer, dir. — Fax 635-4024
Newton County HS — 1,000/6-12
16255 Highway 503 39327 — 601-635-2718
Shane Phillips, prin. — Fax 635-4045

East Central Community College — Post-Sec.
PO Box 129 39327 — 601-635-2111
Newton County Academy — 200/PK-12
PO Box 25 39327 — 601-635-2756

**De Kalb, Kemper, Pop. 1,156**
Kemper County SD — 1,100/PK-12
PO Box 219 39328 — 601-743-2657
Jackie Pollock, supt. — Fax 743-9297
kemper.k12.ms.us
Kemper County HS — 500/7-12
PO Box 429 39328 — 601-743-5292
Calvin Melton, prin. — Fax 743-5952
Stennis Vocational Complex — Vo/Tech
PO Box 549 39328 — 601-743-5226
Monica Westerfield, dir. — Fax 743-2351

Kemper Academy — 100/PK-12
149 Walnut Ave 39328 — 601-743-2232

**D'Iberville, Harrison, Pop. 9,203**
Harrison County SD
Supt. — See Gulfport
D'Iberville MS — 700/4-8
3320 Warrior Dr 39540 — 228-392-1746
Dana Trochessett, prin. — Fax 392-9948

**Drew, Sunflower, Pop. 1,923**
Sunflower County Consolidated SD
Supt. — See Indianola
Drew Hunter MS — 100/6-8
10 Swoope Rd 38737 — 662-745-8940
Brenda Singleton, prin. — Fax 745-8529

North Sunflower Academy — 100/K-12
148 Academy Rd 38737 — 662-756-4573

**Durant, Holmes, Pop. 2,658**
Durant SD — 500/K-12
5 W Madison St 39063 — 662-653-3175
Edwin Robinson, supt. — Fax 653-6151
durant.k12.ms.us
Durant S — 500/K-12
PO Box 669 39063 — 662-653-3429
Aleen Benson, prin. — Fax 653-3472

**Ecru, Pontotoc, Pop. 882**
Pontotoc County SD
Supt. — See Pontotoc
North Pontotoc HS — 500/9-12
8324 Highway 15 N 38841 — 662-489-5612
Roger Smith, prin. — Fax 489-2985
North Pontotoc MS — 200/7-8
8324 Highway 15 N 38841 — 662-489-2479
roger smith, prin. — Fax 489-7068

**Ellisville, Jones, Pop. 4,419**
Jones County SD — 8,300/K-12
5204 Highway 11 N 39437 — 601-649-5201
Thomas Parker, supt. — Fax 649-1613
www.jones.k12.ms.us/
South Jones JSHS — 1,200/7-12
313 Anderson St 39437 — 601-477-8451
Larry Johnson, prin. — Fax 477-3505
Other Schools – See Laurel

Jones County Junior College — Post-Sec.
900 S Court St 39437 — 601-477-4000

**Enterprise, Clarke, Pop. 526**
Enterprise SD — 1,000/PK-12
503 S River Rd 39330 — 601-659-7965
Rita Windham, supt. — Fax 659-3254
www.esd.k12.ms.us/
Enterprise HS — 300/9-12
501 S River Rd 39330 — 601-659-4435
Mike Weathers, prin. — Fax 659-3274
Enterprise MS — 300/5-8
105 Short St 39330 — 601-659-7722
Steven Gunn, prin. — Fax 659-7722

**Ethel, Attala, Pop. 416**
Attala County SD
Supt. — See Kosciusko
Ethel JSHS — 300/7-12
PO Box 340 39067 — 662-674-5673
James Wood, prin. — Fax 674-5817

**Eupora, Webster, Pop. 2,169**
Webster County SD — 1,800/PK-12
95 Clark Ave 39744 — 662-258-5921
Jack Treloar, supt. — Fax 258-3134
www.webstercountyschools.org
Eupora HS — 400/7-12
65 Clark Ave 39744 — 662-258-4041
Laci Knight, prin. — Fax 258-4716
Webster County Career & Technology Ctr — Vo/Tech
605 Hall Rd 39744 — 662-258-8206
Phil Ferguson, dir. — Fax 258-6769
Other Schools – See Maben

**Falkner, Tippah, Pop. 510**
North Tippah SD
Supt. — See Tiplersville
Falkner JSHS — 200/7-12
20350 Highway 15 38629 — 662-837-7892
Jennifer Stroupe, prin. — Fax 837-8800

**Fayette, Jefferson, Pop. 1,609**
Jefferson County SD — 1,300/PK-12
PO Box 157 39069 — 601-786-3721
Tracy M. Cook, supt. — Fax 786-8441
www.jcpsd.net
Jefferson County Career & Technical Ctr — Vo/Tech
205 Industrial Park Rd 39069 — 601-786-3642
Cleveland Moore, dir. — Fax 786-2271
Jefferson County HS — 400/9-12
2277 Main St 39069 — 601-786-3919
David Day, prin. — Fax 786-6002
Jefferson County JHS — 100/7-8
468 Highway 33 39069 — 601-786-3900
LaRondrial Barnes, prin. — Fax 786-2273

**Flora, Madison, Pop. 1,878**

Tri-County Academy — 300/PK-12
PO Box K 39071 — 601-879-8517
Mark Johnson, hdmstr. — Fax 879-3373

**Florence, Rankin, Pop. 4,112**
Rankin County SD
Supt. — See Brandon
Florence HS — 700/9-12
232 Highway 469 N 39073 — 601-845-2205
Tony Martin, prin. — Fax 845-3752
Florence MS — 600/6-8
PO Box 159 39073 — 601-845-2862
Jessica Hodges, prin. — Fax 845-2114
McLaurin JSHS — 600/7-12
130 Tiger Dr 39073 — 601-845-2247
Scott Rimes, prin. — Fax 845-1170

**Flowood, Rankin, Pop. 7,724**
Rankin County SD
Supt. — See Brandon
Northwest Rankin HS — 1,600/9-12
5805 Highway 25 39232 — 601-992-2242
Ben Stein, prin. — Fax 992-6005
Northwest Rankin MS — 1,400/6-8
1 Paw Print Pl 39232 — 601-992-1329
Jacob McEwen, prin. — Fax 992-1347

Hartfield Academy — 400/PK-12
1240 Luckney Rd 39232 — 601-992-5333
Rick Burslem, hdmstr. — Fax 992-5320

**Forest, Scott, Pop. 5,620**
Forest Municipal SD 1,500/K-12
325 Cleveland St 39074 601-469-3250
Dr. Joseph White, supt. Fax 469-3101
www.forest.k12.ms.us/
Forest HS 400/9-12
511 Cleveland St 39074 601-469-3255
Kim Shoemaker, prin. Fax 469-8250
Hawkins MS 500/5-8
803 E Oak St 39074 601-469-1474
Harry Bates, prin. Fax 469-8251

Scott County SD 3,700/K-12
100 E First St 39074 601-469-3861
Fax 469-3874
www.scott.k12.ms.us
Forest/Scott County Career & Tech Ctr Vo/Tech
521 Cleveland St 39074 601-469-2913
Timmy Fanguy, dir. Fax 469-2917
Scott Central S 900/K-12
2415 Old Jackson Rd 39074 601-469-4883
Ben Lundy, prin. Fax 469-3746
Other Schools – See Lake, Morton, Sebastopol

**Foxworth, Marion, Pop. 592**
Marion County SD
Supt. — See Columbia
West Marion JSHS 600/7-12
2 W Marion St 39483 601-736-6381
Ellie Rich, prin. Fax 731-7937

**Fulton, Itawamba, Pop. 3,914**
Itawamba County SD 3,000/PK-12
605 S Cummings St 38843 662-862-2159
Michael Nanney, supt. Fax 862-4713
www.itawamba.k12.ms.us/
Itawamba Agricultural HS 600/9-12
11900 Highway 25 S 38843 662-862-3104
Trae Wiygul, prin. Fax 862-5494
Itawamba Career & Technical Center Vo/Tech
200 Vo Tech Rd 38843 662-862-3137
Gary Hamm, prin. Fax 862-3138
Other Schools – See Mantachie, Tremont

---

Itawamba Community College Post-Sec.
602 W Hill St 38843 662-862-8000

**Gallman, Copiah**

---

Copiah Educational Foundation 700/PK-12
PO Box 125 39077 601-892-3770
Paul Hayles, hdmstr. Fax 892-6222

**Gautier, Jackson, Pop. 18,202**
Pascagoula-Gautier SD
Supt. — See Pascagoula
Gautier HS 900/9-12
4307 Gautier Vancleave Rd 39553 228-522-8783
Al Sparkman, prin. Fax 522-8788
Gautier MS 400/7-8
1920 Graveline Rd 39553 228-522-8806
Christy Reimsnyder, prin. Fax 522-8813

**Glen, Alcorn, Pop. 409**
Alcorn SD
Supt. — See Corinth
Alcorn Central HS 400/9-12
8 County Road 254 38846 662-286-8720
Brandon Quinn, admin. Fax 286-8720
Alcorn Central MS 400/5-8
8A County Road 254 38846 662-286-3674
Brian Phelps, admin. Fax 286-6712

**Goodman, Holmes, Pop. 1,376**

---

Holmes Community College Post-Sec.
PO Box 369 39079 662-472-2312

**Greenville, Washington, Pop. 34,233**
Greenville SD 5,800/PK-12
PO Box 1619 38702 662-334-7000
Dr. Leeson Taylor, supt. Fax 334-7021
www.gvillepublicschooldistrict.com
Coleman MS 700/6-8
400 Dr Martin L King Blvd 38701 662-334-7036
Dianne Zanders, prin. Fax 334-7040
Darling Achievement Center 50/Alt
242 S Broadway St 38701 662-334-7040
Charles Brady, prin. Fax 334-7023
Greenville HS 1,200/10-12
419 E Robert Shaw St 38701 662-334-7063
Xavier Hodo, prin. Fax 334-7060
Greenville Technical Center Vo/Tech
350 S Raceway Rd 38703 662-334-7170
Sherry Jackson, dir. Fax 334-2848
Solomon Magnet S 600/6-8
556 Bowman Blvd 38701 662-334-7050
Michael Dean, prin. Fax 334-7053
Weston 9th Grade Academy 400/9-9
901 Archer St 38701 662-334-7080
Willie Goins, prin. Fax 334-7091

Western Line SD
Supt. — See Avon
O'Bannon HS 400/7-12
PO Box 5816 38704 662-335-2637
Derrick Cook, prin. Fax 334-1689

---

Delta Beauty College Post-Sec.
697 Delta Pl 38701 662-332-0587
Greenville Christian S 200/PK-12
2064 Greenville Christian 38701 662-332-0946
St. Joseph Catholic S 200/7-12
1501 V F W Rd 38701 662-378-9711
Paul Artman, prin. Fax 378-3496
Washington S 700/PK-12
1605 E Reed Rd 38703 662-334-4096

**Greenwood, LeFlore, Pop. 15,124**
Greenwood SD 2,800/PK-12
PO Box 1497 38935 662-453-4231
Dr. Montelle Greene, supt. Fax 455-7409
www.greenwood.k12.ms.us/
Greenwood Alternative S Alt
410 Main St 38930 662-455-8989
Kenneth Pulley, dir. Fax 455-7433
Greenwood Career and Technical Ctr Vo/Tech
616 Sycamore Ave 38930 662-455-7414
David Taylor, dir. Fax 455-8979
Greenwood HS 700/9-12
1209 Garrard Ave 38930 662-455-7450
Dr. Lorita Harris, prin. Fax 455-7468
Greenwood MS 400/7-8
1200 Garrard Ave 38930 662-455-3661
Chiqueta Daniels, prin. Fax 455-5559

Leflore County SD 2,700/PK-12
1901 Highway 82 W 38930 662-453-8566
Robert Strebeck, supt. Fax 459-7265
www.leflorecountyschools.org
Elzy HS 600/9-12
604 Elzy Ave 38930 662-453-3394
Joe Griffin, prin. Fax 459-7266
Elzy JHS 400/6-8
604 Elzy Ave 38930 662-453-9677
Barren Cleark, prin. Fax 455-0139
Leflore County Career & Tech Educ Ctr Vo/Tech
PO Box 1158 38935 662-453-7706
Charles Streeter, dir. Fax 453-7733
Other Schools – See Itta Bena

---

Pillow Academy 800/PK-12
69601 Highway 82 W 38930 662-453-1266

**Grenada, Grenada, Pop. 12,980**
Grenada SD 4,100/K-12
PO Box 1940 38902 662-226-1606
Dr. David Daigneault, supt. Fax 226-7994
www.gsd.k12.ms.us/
Grenada Enrichment and Transition Center Alt
809 Tie Plant Rd 38901 662-226-3311
Dr. Tina Herrington, prin. Fax 226-8388
Grenada HS 1,100/9-12
1875 Fairground Rd 38901 662-226-8844
Jerry Williams, prin. Fax 227-6109
Grenada MS 1,000/6-8
28 Jones Rd 38901 662-226-5135
Lyle Williams, prin. Fax 227-6106
Grenada Vocational Complex Vo/Tech
2035 Jackson Ave 38901 662-226-5969
Dr. Cliff Craven, prin. Fax 226-5992

---

Academy of Hair Design #1 Post-Sec.
2003B Commerce St 38901 662-226-2462
Kirk Academy 300/PK-12
PO Box 1008 38902 662-226-2791

**Gulfport, Harrison, Pop. 66,180**
Gulfport SD 5,800/K-12
2001 Pass Rd 39501 228-865-4600
Glen East, supt. Fax 865-1918
www.gulfportschools.org/
Bayou View MS 800/6-8
212 43rd St 39507 228-865-4633
Dean Scarbrough, prin. Fax 867-1967
Gulfport Central MS 600/6-8
1310 42nd Ave 39501 228-870-1035
Dr. Mike Battle, prin. Fax 870-1041
Gulfport HS 1,500/9-12
100 Perry St 39507 228-896-7525
Michael Lindsey, prin. Fax 896-8281
Gulfport Vocational Annex S Vo/Tech
100 Perry St 39507 228-896-6011
David Fava, dir. Fax 896-7686
Learning Center Alt
1215 Church St 39507 228-897-6045
Tim Bellipanni, prin. Fax 897-6053

Harrison County SD 13,700/K-12
11072 Highway 49 39503 228-539-6500
Henry Arledge, supt. Fax 539-6507
www.harrison.k12.ms.us/
Harrison Central HS 1,500/9-12
15600 School Rd 39503 228-832-2610
Averie Bush, prin. Fax 832-7433
Harrison County Alternative S Alt
11072 Highway 49 39503 228-539-5956
Joycelyn Moody, prin. Fax 539-5959
Harrison County Vocational Complex Vo/Tech
15600 School Rd 39503 228-832-6652
Russell Clark, prin. Fax 539-5965
North Gulfport 8th Grade S 400/8-8
4715 Illinois Ave 39501 228-864-8944
Regina Watts Lewis, prin. Fax 863-7326
West Harrison HS 1,100/9-12
10399 County Farm Rd 39503 228-539-8900
Sherry Washburn, prin. Fax 539-8910
Other Schools – See Biloxi, D'Iberville

---

Blue Cliff College Post-Sec.
12251 Bernard Pkwy 39503 228-896-9727
Chris' Beauty College Post-Sec.
1265 Pass Rd 39501 228-864-2920
Christian Collegiate Academy 300/PK-12
12200 Dedeaux Rd 39503 228-832-4585
Infinity Career College Post-Sec.
319 Pass Rd 39507 228-864-4663
Miller-Motte Technical College Post-Sec.
12121 Highway 49 39503 228-273-3400

**Guntown, Lee, Pop. 2,042**
Lee County SD
Supt. — See Tupelo
Guntown MS 800/6-8
PO Box 8 38849 662-348-8800
Steven Havens, prin. Fax 348-8810

**Hamilton, Monroe, Pop. 450**
Monroe County SD
Supt. — See Amory
Hamilton S 700/K-12
40201 Hamilton Rd 39746 662-343-8307
Tim Dickerson, prin. Fax 343-5813

**Hattiesburg, Forrest, Pop. 45,409**
Forrest County SD 2,300/K-12
400 Forrest St 39401 601-545-6055
Brian Freeman, supt. Fax 545-6054
www.forrest.k12.ms.us/
North Forrest JSHS 300/7-12
693 Eatonville Rd 39401 601-545-9304
Jennifer Riels, prin. Fax 545-9318

Hattiesburg SD 4,300/PK-12
PO Box 1569 39403 601-582-5078
James Q. Bacchus, supt. Fax 582-6666
www.hattiesburgpsd.com
Bethune Alternative Center Alt
610 Dumas Ave 39401 601-584-6311
Dr. Vanessa Lofton, prin. Fax 583-7322
Burger MS 600/7-8
174 WSF Tatum Drive Ext 39401 601-582-0536
Dr. Robert Williams, prin. Fax 582-0572
Hattiesburg HS 1,200/9-12
301 Hutchinson Ave 39401 601-544-0811
C. Jermaine Brown, prin. Fax 544-8946

Lamar County SD
Supt. — See Purvis
Oak Grove HS 1,500/9-12
5198 Old Highway 11 39402 601-264-7232
Helen Price, prin. Fax 264-0160
Oak Grove MS 1,300/6-8
2543 Old Highway 24 39402 601-264-4634
Patrick Gray, prin. Fax 264-0160

---

Antonelli College Post-Sec.
1500 N 31st Ave 39401 601-583-4100
Forrest General Hospital Post-Sec.
6051 U S Highway 49 39401 601-288-4201
Hattiesburg Radiology Group Post-Sec.
5000 W 4th St 39402 601-288-4241
Presbyterian Christian S 1,000/PK-12
221 Bonhomie Rd 39401 601-582-4956
Sacred Heart S 700/PK-12
608 Southern Ave 39401 601-583-8683
Brian McCrory, prin. Fax 583-8684
University of Southern Mississippi Post-Sec.
118 College Dr 39406 601-266-1000
William Carey University Post-Sec.
498 Tuscan Ave 39401 601-318-6051

**Hazlehurst, Copiah, Pop. 3,977**
Copiah County SD 2,700/K-12
254 W Gallatin St 39083 601-894-1341
Rickey Clopton, supt. Fax 894-2634
www.copiah.ms/
Other Schools – See Crystal Springs, Wesson

Hazlehurst CSD 1,500/PK-12
119 Robert McDaniel Dr 39083 601-894-1152
John Sullivan, admin. Fax 894-3170
www.hazlehurst.k12.ms.us
Hazlehurst HS 400/9-12
101 S Haley St 39083 601-894-2489
Dr. Thaddeus Peters, prin. Fax 894-3120
Hazlehurst MS 500/5-8
112 School Dr 39083 601-894-3463
Lisa Davis, prin. Fax 894-5939

**Heidelberg, Jasper, Pop. 716**
East Jasper Consolidated SD 1,000/K-12
PO Box E 39439 601-787-3281
Dr. Gwendolyn Page, supt. Fax 787-3410
www.eastjasper.k12.ms.us
Heidelberg HS 300/9-12
PO Box M 39439 601-787-3414
Bufus Ellis, prin. Fax 787-3416
Heidelberg JHS 200/7-8
PO Box M 39439 601-787-3665
Ashley Green, prin. Fax 787-3045

---

Heidelberg Academy 200/PK-12
PO Box Q 39439 601-787-4589

**Hernando, DeSoto, Pop. 13,952**
DeSoto County SD 30,500/PK-12
5 E South St 38632 662-429-5271
Milton Kuykendall, supt. Fax 429-4198
www.desotocountyschools.org
Hernando HS 1,100/9-12
805 Dilworth Ln 38632 662-429-4170
Freddie Joseph, prin. Fax 429-6269
Hernando MS 900/6-8
700 Dilworth Ln 38632 662-429-4154
Rob Chase, prin. Fax 429-4189
Other Schools – See Horn Lake, Lake Cormorant, Olive Branch, Southaven

**Hickory Flat, Benton, Pop. 592**
Benton County SD
Supt. — See Ashland
Hickory Flat S 700/K-12
26 Rebel Dr 38633 662-333-7731
Barry Goolsby, prin. Fax 333-4127

**Hollandale, Washington, Pop. 2,691**
Hollandale SD 700/K-12
PO Box 128 38748 662-827-2276
Angela Johnson, supt. Fax 827-5261
www.hollandalesd.org
Simmons JSHS 300/7-12
PO Box 428 38748 662-827-2228
Shiquita Brown, prin. Fax 827-2231

**Holly Springs, Marshall, Pop. 7,662**
Holly Springs SD 1,300/PK-12
840 Highway 178 E 38635 662-252-2183
Dr. Irene Walton Turnage, supt. Fax 252-7718
www.hssd.k12.ms.us
Holly Springs Career & Technical Center Vo/Tech
410 E Falconer Ave 38635 662-252-2071
Cravin Turnage, dir. Fax 252-7719
Holly Springs HS 400/9-12
165 N Walthall St 38635 662-252-4371
Marcus Autry, prin. Fax 252-7720
Holly Springs JHS 200/7-8
325 E Falconer Ave 38635 662-252-7737
Letashia White, prin. Fax 252-7751

Marshall County SD 3,100/K-12
122 S Spring St 38635 662-252-4271
Jerry Moore, supt. Fax 252-5129
www.marshallcountysd.org/
Byers HS 200/9-12
4178 Highway 72 38635 662-851-7826
Dante Thornton, prin. Fax 851-4027
Byers MS, 4178 Highway 72 38635 200/6-8
Equan Ashe, prin. 662-851-7826
Other Schools – See Byhalia, Potts Camp

---

Infinity Career College Post-Sec.
960 Highway 4 E 38635 662-252-2600
Marshall Academy 300/PK-12
100 Academy Dr 38635 662-252-3449
Rust College Post-Sec.
150 Rust Ave 38635 662-252-8000

**Horn Lake, DeSoto, Pop. 25,611**
DeSoto County SD
Supt. — See Hernando
Desoto County Alternative Center Alt
6870 Center St E 38637 662-253-0017
Jay Baird, prin. Fax 253-0013
Horn Lake HS 1,300/9-12
3360 Church Rd 38637 662-393-5273
Andy Orr, prin. Fax 393-5275
Horn Lake MS 1,100/6-8
6125 Hurt Rd 38637 662-393-7443
Nick Toungett, prin. Fax 342-5039

---

Delta Technical College Post-Sec.
6550 Interstate Dr # D 38637 662-280-1443

**Houlka, Chickasaw, Pop. 621**
Chickasaw County SD 600/PK-12
PO Box 480 38850 662-568-3333
Dr. Betsy Collums, supt. Fax 568-2993
chickasaw.k12.ms.us/
Houlka S 600/PK-12
510 Griffin Ave 38850 662-568-2772
William Cotton, prin. Fax 568-7931

**Houston, Chickasaw, Pop. 3,580**
Houston SD 1,800/K-12
PO Box 351 38851 662-456-3332
Dr. Steve Coker, supt. Fax 456-5259
www.houston.k12.ms.us
Houston HS 500/9-12
PO Box 568 38851 662-456-3320
Buz Boyer, prin. Fax 456-3527
Houston MS 400/6-8
PO Box 192 38851 662-456-5174
Tony Horton, prin. Fax 456-2254
Houston Vocational Center Vo/Tech
PO Box 608 38851 662-456-3748
Beverly James, dir. Fax 456-5172

**Indianola, Sunflower, Pop. 10,634**
Sunflower County Consolidated SD 1,900/K-12
PO Box 70 38751 662-887-4919
Dr. Debra Dace, supt. Fax 887-7051
www.sunflower.k12.ms.us
Gentry HS 500/10-12
801 BB King Rd 38751 662-884-1240
Randy Ball, prin. Fax 887-7410
Indianola Academic Achievement Center Alt
300 Jefferson St 38751 662-884-1278
Earl Liddell, prin. Fax 887-3038
Indianola Career & Technical Center Vo/Tech
801 BB King Rd 38751 662-884-6000
Rosalind Johnson, dir. Fax 887-7087
Merritt MS 500/7-9
705 Kinlock Rd 38751 662-884-1270
Martha Jackson, prin. Fax 887-5247
Other Schools – See Drew, Inverness, Moorhead, Ruleville

---

Indianola Academy 500/PK-12
PO Box 967 38751 662-887-2025
Restoration Ministries Christian Academy 100/PK-12
PO Box 1001 38751 662-887-2040
Rev. Richard Jenkins, admin. Fax 887-2040

**Inverness, Sunflower, Pop. 1,017**
Sunflower County Consolidated SD
Supt. — See Indianola
Ruleville Central HS 300/9-12
PO Box 228 38753 662-756-4757
Dr. Cassandra Winters, prin. Fax 265-0027

**Itta Bena, LeFlore, Pop. 2,046**
Leflore County SD
Supt. — See Greenwood
Leflore County HS 500/7-12
PO Box 564 38941 662-254-7762
Michael Tardy, prin. Fax 254-7530

---

Mississippi Valley State University Post-Sec.
14000 Highway 82 W 38941 662-254-9041

**Iuka, Tishomingo, Pop. 2,992**
Tishomingo County Special Municipal SD 3,200/K-12
1620 Paul Edmondson Dr 38852 662-423-3206
Christie Holly, supt. Fax 424-9820
www.tishomingo.k12.ms.us
Iuka MS 300/5-8
507 W Quitman St 38852 662-423-3316
Roy Lawson, prin. Fax 423-2426
Tishomingo County HS 600/9-12
701 Highway 72 38852 662-423-7300
Jackie Beals, prin. Fax 423-7307
Other Schools – See Belmont, Tishomingo

**Jackson, Hinds, Pop. 172,074**
Jackson SD 28,800/PK-12
PO Box 2338 39225 601-960-8700
Dr. Cedrick Gray, supt. Fax 960-8713
www.jackson.k12.ms.us
Bailey APAC MS 200/6-8
1900 N State St 39202 601-960-5343
Christi Hollingshead, prin. Fax 592-2496
Blackburn MS 400/6-8
1311 W Pearl St 39203 601-960-5329
Valerie Bradley, prin. Fax 360-2601
Brinkley MS 400/6-8
3535 Albermarle Rd 39213 601-987-3573
Larry Armstrong, prin. Fax 987-3746
Callaway HS 1,100/9-12
601 Beasley Rd 39206 601-987-3535
William Trammell, prin. Fax 987-3729
Capital City Alternative S Alt
2221 Boling St 39213 601-713-2376
Dr. Falanda Addison, prin. Fax 987-3727
Cardozo MS 600/6-8
3180 McDowell Road Ext 39204 601-346-5635
Eliza Lee, prin. Fax 373-0286
Chastain MS 800/6-8
4650 Manhattan Rd 39206 601-987-3550
Anthony Moore, prin. Fax 987-4930
Forest Hill HS 1,300/9-12
2607 Raymond Rd 39212 601-371-4313
Dr. Kimberly Warfield, prin. Fax 371-4379
Hardy MS 500/6-8
545 Ellis Ave 39209 601-960-5362
Antonius Caldwell, prin. Fax 360-2686
Hill HS 1,200/9-12
2185 Fortune St 39204 601-960-5354
Bobby Brown, prin. Fax 360-2625
Jackson Career Development Center Vo/Tech
2703 First Ave 39209 601-960-5322
Dr. Brenda Jackson, prin. Fax 960-5411
Kirksey MS, 5677 Highland Dr 39206 400/6-8
Dr. Edward Buck, prin. 601-987-8360
Lanier HS 700/9-12
833 Maple St 39203 601-960-5369
Eric Johnson, prin. Fax 960-4047
Murrah HS 1,400/9-12
1400 Murrah Dr 39202 601-960-5380
Kennieth Green, prin. Fax 360-2622
Northwest Jackson MS 600/6-8
7020 Highway 49 N 39213 601-987-3609
Chinelo Evans, prin. Fax 987-4975
Peeples MS 600/6-8
2940 Belvedere Dr 39212 601-346-5660
David Herndon, prin. Fax 371-4722
Powell MS 600/6-8
3655 Livingston Rd 39213 601-987-3580
Justin Green, prin. Fax 987-3583
Provine HS 1,000/9-12
2400 Robinson St 39209 601-960-5393
Laketia Marshall-Thomas, prin. Fax 360-2606
Rowan MS 200/6-8
136 E Ash St 39202 601-960-5349
Dr. Shimelle Mayers, prin. Fax 960-4046
Siwell Road MS 700/6-8
1983 N Siwell Rd 39209 601-923-2550
Marnetta McIntyre, prin. Fax 923-2570
Whitten MS 700/6-8
210 Daniel Lake Blvd 39212 601-371-4309
Victor Ellis, prin. Fax 371-4728
Wingfield HS 1,000/9-12
1985 Scanlon Dr 39204 601-371-4350
Dr. Willie Killins, prin. Fax 371-4734

---

Academy of Hair Design #3 Post-Sec.
1815 Terry Rd 39204 601-372-9800
Antonelli College Post-Sec.
2323 Lakeland Dr 39232 601-362-9991
Belhaven University Post-Sec.
1500 Peachtree St 39202 601-968-5940
Christ Missionary & Industrial S 200/PK-12
3910 Main St 39213 601-366-6413
Education Center S 200/K-12
PO Box 55509 39296 601-982-2812
Healthcare Institute of Jackson Post-Sec.
405 Briarwood Dr Ste 110 39206 601-956-3940
Hillcrest Christian S 500/K-12
4060 S Siwell Rd 39212 601-372-0149
Jackson Academy 1,200/PK-12
PO Box 14978 39236 601-362-9676
Dr. Pat Taylor, hdmstr. Fax 364-5722
Jackson Preparatory S 800/6-12
3100 Lakeland Dr 39232 601-939-8611
Jason Walton Ph.D., head sch Fax 936-4068
Jackson State University Post-Sec.
1440 J R Lynch St 39217 601-979-2100
Magnolia College of Cosmetology Post-Sec.
4725 I 55 N 39206 601-362-6940
Millsaps College Post-Sec.
1701 N State St 39210 601-974-1000
Mississippi Baptist Medical Center Post-Sec.
1225 N State St 39202 601-968-5130
Mississippi School for the Blind Post-Sec.
1252 Eastover Dr 39211 601-984-8000
Mississippi School for the Deaf Post-Sec.
1253 Eastover Dr 39211 601-984-8001
Reformed Theological Seminary Post-Sec.
5422 Clinton Blvd 39209 601-923-1600
St. Dominic-Jackson Memorial Hospital Post-Sec.
969 Lakeland Dr 39216 601-364-6935
Traxler School of Hair Post-Sec.
2845 Suncrest Dr 39212 601-371-0226
University of Mississippi Medical Center Post-Sec.
2500 N State St 39216 601-984-1000
Virginia College Post-Sec.
5841 Ridgewood Rd 39211 601-977-0960
Wesley Biblical Seminary Post-Sec.
787 E Northside Dr 39206 601-366-8880

**Kilmichael, Montgomery, Pop. 698**
Montgomery County SD
Supt. — See Winona
Montgomery County HS 200/7-12
PO Box 278 39747 662-262-5535
Lewis Zeigler, prin. Fax 262-4218

**Kiln, Hancock, Pop. 2,194**
Hancock County SD 4,900/K-12
17304 Highway 603 39556 228-255-0376
Alan Dedeaux, supt. Fax 255-0378
www.hancock.k12.ms.us
Hancock County Career Technical Center Vo/Tech
7180 Stennis Airport Rd 39556 228-467-3568
Dr. Rick Saucier, dir. Fax 466-4944
Hancock HS 1,200/9-12
7084 Stennis Airport Rd 39556 228-467-2251
Tara Ladner, prin. Fax 467-2689
Hancock MS 1,000/6-8
7070 Stennis Airport Rd 39556 228-467-1889
Dr. Jessical Taylor, prin. Fax 467-2812

**Kosciusko, Attala, Pop. 7,358**
Attala County SD 1,100/PK-12
100 Courthouse Ste 3 39090 662-289-2801
Bryan Weaver, supt. Fax 289-2804
www.attala.k12.ms.us/
Kosciusko-Attala County Voc Complex Vo/Tech
450 Highway 12 E 39090 662-289-2689
Fax 289-2701
Other Schools – See Ethel, Sallis

Kosciusko SSD 2,300/K-12
229 W Washington St 39090 662-289-4771
Tony McGee, supt. Fax 289-1177
www.ksd.k12.ms.us/
Kosciusko HS 600/9-12
229 W Washington St 39090 662-289-2424
Jonathan Carnes, prin. Fax 289-8767
Kosciusko JHS 600/6-8
229 W Washington St 39090 662-289-3737
Roger Hill, prin. Fax 289-1177

**Lake, Newton, Pop. 321**
Scott County SD
Supt. — See Forest
Lake HS 200/9-12
24442 Highway 80 39092 601-775-3248
Lee Killen, prin. Fax 775-3861
Lake MS 200/5-8
1770 E Scott Rd 39092 601-775-3614
Nancy Butler, prin. Fax 775-8830

**Lake Cormorant, DeSoto**
DeSoto County SD
Supt. — See Hernando
Lake Cormorant HS 800/9-12
10201 Star Landing Rd 38641 662-996-3060
Rhonda Guice, prin. Fax 996-2520
Lake Cormorant MS 700/6-8
3203 Wilson Mill Rd 38641 662-781-0778
Jeff Morgan, prin. Fax 781-0688

**Laurel, Jones, Pop. 18,408**
Jones County SD
Supt. — See Ellisville
Jones County Career & Tech Center Vo/Tech
2409 Moose Dr 39440 601-425-2378
Patsy Reon, prin. Fax 425-2349
Northeast Jones JSHS 1,000/7-12
68 Northeast Dr 39443 601-425-2347
Cooper Pope, prin. Fax 649-1736
Pine Belt Educational Center Alt
923B Sawmill Rd 39440 601-428-8080
Mike Moore, prin.
West Jones JSHS 1,300/7-12
254 Springhill Rd 39443 601-729-8144
Lynn Lyon, prin. Fax 729-8148

Laurel SD 3,000/PK-12
PO Box 288 39441 601-649-6391
Dr. Chuck Benigno, supt. Fax 649-6398
www.laurelschools.org
Laurel HS 700/9-12
1100 W 12th St 39440 601-649-4145
Carl Day, prin. Fax 426-2347
Laurel MS 700/6-8
1600 Grandview Dr 39440 601-428-5312
Leah McCullum, prin. Fax 426-6775

---

Laurel Christian S 500/PK-12
PO Box 8425 39441 601-649-4190
Mississippi College of Beauty Culture Post-Sec.
732 Sawmill Rd 39440 601-428-7127
Southeastern Baptist College Post-Sec.
4229 Highway 15 N 39440 601-426-6346

**Leakesville, Greene, Pop. 893**
Greene County SD 2,100/PK-12
PO Box 1329 39451 601-394-2364
Richard Fleming, supt. Fax 394-5542
www.greene.k12.ms.us/
Greene County HS 600/9-12
4336 High School Rd 39451 601-394-5290
Scott Bray, prin. Fax 394-4878

Greene County Vo-Tech Complex Vo/Tech
173 Vo Tech Rd 39451 601-394-2973
Dr. Tom Wallace, dir. Fax 394-5953
Leakesville JHS 400/5-8
620 Main St 39451 601-394-2495
Monica Edwards, prin. Fax 394-5690

**Learned, Hinds, Pop. 92**

Rebul Academy 100/PK-12
5257 Learned Rd 39154 601-885-6802

**Leland, Washington, Pop. 4,449**
Leland SD 900/PK-12
408 4th St 38756 662-686-5000
Malcolm Brown, supt. Fax 686-5029
leland.schoolfusion.us/
Leland HS 300/9-12
404 E 3rd St 38756 662-686-5020
Donnie Hollins, prin. Fax 686-5027
Leland School Park 300/5-8
200 Milam St 38756 662-686-5017
Monroe Golden, prin. Fax 686-5042
Leland Vocational Center Vo/Tech
E Deer Creek Dr 38756 662-686-5025
Kermit McAdory, dir. Fax 686-5024

**Lexington, Holmes, Pop. 1,722**
Holmes County SD 3,100/PK-12
PO Box 630 39095 662-834-2175
Powell Rucker, supt. Fax 834-9060
www.holmes.k12.ms.us
Holmes County Career & Technical Center Vo/Tech
77 Kickernick St 39095 662-834-3052
Fax 834-3053
Holmes County Central HS 400/9-12
9479 Brozville Rd 39095 662-834-2172
Elbert Smith, prin. Fax 834-2709
Other Schools – See Tchula

Central Holmes Christian S 300/PK-12
130 Robert E Lee Dr 39095 662-834-3011
Mike Sumlin, hdmstr. Fax 834-1011

**Liberty, Amite, Pop. 726**
Amite County SD 800/K-12
PO Box 378 39645 601-657-4361
Scotty Whittington, supt. Fax 657-4291
www.amite.k12.ms.us/
Amite County HS 300/7-12
PO Box 328 39645 601-657-8920
Celdric McDowell, prin. Fax 657-4044
Amite County Vocational Educational S Vo/Tech
PO Box 770 39645 601-657-8081
Augustus Russ, dir. Fax 657-8098

Amite School Center 200/K-12
1604 Old McComb Liberty Rd 39645 601-657-8896

**Long Beach, Harrison, Pop. 14,545**
Long Beach SD 2,900/K-12
19148 Commission Rd 39560 228-864-1146
Carrolyn Hamilton, supt. Fax 863-3196
www.lbsdk12.com
Long Beach HS 900/9-12
300 E Old Pass Rd 39560 228-863-6945
Peter Dabbs, prin. Fax 864-8961
Long Beach MS 500/7-8
204 N Cleveland Ave 39560 228-864-3370
Dr. Tim Holland, prin. Fax 867-1789

**Lorman, Jefferson**

Alcorn State University Post-Sec.
1000 Alcorn Dr 39096 601-877-6100

**Louisville, Winston, Pop. 6,587**
Louisville Municipal SD 2,700/PK-12
PO Box 909 39339 662-773-3411
Ken McMullan, supt. Fax 773-4013
louisville.k12.ms.us/
Eiland MS 200/6-8
508 Camille Ave 39339 662-773-9001
Jawana Young, prin. Fax 773-4016
Louisville HS 500/9-12
200 Ivy Ave 39339 662-773-3431
Hilute Hudson, prin. Fax 773-4017
Waiya S 500/K-12
13937 Highway 397 39339 662-773-6770
Belinda Swart, prin. Fax 773-6764
Winston-Louisville Career & Tech Center Vo/Tech
204 Ivy Ave 39339 662-773-6152
James Webb, dir. Fax 773-9572
Other Schools – See Noxapater

Grace Christian S 100/PK-12
173 McLeod Rd 39339 662-773-8524
James Gregory, hdmstr. Fax 773-4308
Winston Academy 500/PK-12
PO Box 545 39339 662-773-3569

**Lucedale, George, Pop. 2,907**
George County SD 4,100/PK-12
5152 Main St 39452 601-947-6993
Debbie Harrell, supt. Fax 947-8805
www.gcsd.us
George County HS 1,100/9-12
9284 Old 63 S 39452 601-947-3116
Wade Whitney, prin. Fax 947-1076
George County MS 700/7-8
330 Church St 39452 601-947-3106
Kiley Hughes, prin. Fax 947-6004

**Lumberton, Lamar, Pop. 2,065**
Lumberton SD 700/K-12
107 E 10th Ave 39455 601-796-2441
Dr. Linda Smith, supt. Fax 796-2051
www.lumberton.k12.ms.us/
Lumberton HS 200/9-12
7920 US Highway 11 39455 601-796-2451
John Barnes, prin. Fax 796-7907

Bass Memorial Academy 100/9-12
6433 U S Highway 11 39455 601-794-8561

**Maben, Webster, Pop. 864**
Webster County SD
Supt. — See Eupora
East Webster HS 400/7-12
195 Old Cumberland Rd 39750 662-263-5321
Bill Brand, prin. Fax 263-4518

**Mc Comb, Pike, Pop. 12,696**
McComb SD 2,800/PK-12
PO Box 868 39649 601-684-4661
Cederick Ellis Ph.D., supt. Fax 249-4732
www.mccomb.k12.ms.us
Business & Technology Complex Vo/Tech
1003 Virginia Ave 39648 601-684-5288
Robert Biggs, dir. Fax 249-2454
Denman JHS 400/7-8
1211 Louisiana Ave 39648 601-684-2387
James Brown, prin. Fax 249-3564
McComb HS 700/9-12
310 7th St 39648 601-684-5678
Robert Lamkin, prin. Fax 249-4737
Summit Learning Center Adult
411A Saint Augustine Ave 39648 601-684-4306
Alvin Hogan, dir. Fax 684-4308

Parklane Academy 900/K-12
1115 Parklane Dr 39648 601-684-8113
SW Mississippi Regional Medical Center Post-Sec.
PO Box 1307 39649 601-249-1807

**Macon, Noxubee, Pop. 2,760**
Noxubee County SD 1,900/PK-12
PO Box 540 39341 662-726-4527
Kevin Jones Ed.D., supt. Fax 726-2809
www.noxcnty.k12.ms.us
Liddell MS 500/5-8
PO Box 229 39341 662-726-4880
Wendi Dancy-Clark, prin. Fax 726-5044
Noxubee County HS 500/9-12
PO Box 490 39341 662-726-4428
Dr. Hattie Thomas, prin. Fax 726-5048
Noxubee County Vocational Center Vo/Tech
PO Box 266 39341 662-726-4225
Dr. Annie Snow, dir. Fax 726-2804
Other Schools – See Shuqualak

Central Academy 100/PK-12
PO Box 231 39341 662-726-4817

**Madden, Leake**

Leake Academy 600/PK-12
PO Box 128 39109 601-267-4461

**Madison, Madison, Pop. 23,961**
Madison County SD
Supt. — See Ridgeland
Germantown HS 600/9-12
200 Calhoun Pkwy 39110 601-859-6150
Wesley Quick, prin. Fax 859-6075
Germantown MS 600/6-8
202 Calhoun Pkwy 39110 601-859-0376
Chris Perritt, prin. Fax 859-1302
Madison Central HS 1,300/10-12
1417 Highland Colony Pkwy 39110 601-856-7121
Austin Brown, prin. Fax 853-2712
Madison County Academic Options Center Alt
300 Industrial Dr S 39110 601-859-0367
Bill Lenington, prin. Fax 859-0374
Madison County Career & Tech Center Vo/Tech
142 Calhoun Pkwy 39110 601-859-6847
Aimee Brown Ph.D., dir. Fax 859-0372
Madison MS 1,400/6-8
1365 Mannsdale Rd 39110 601-605-4171
Dee Walsh, prin. Fax 853-2254
Scott S 400/9-9
200 Crawford St 39110 601-605-0054
Sean Brewer, prin. Fax 898-5017

ITT Technical Institute Post-Sec.
382 Galleria Pkwy Ste 100 39110 601-607-4500
Madison Ridgeland Academy 900/PK-12
7601 Old Canton Rd 39110 601-856-4455
Termie Land, head sch Fax 853-3835
St. Joseph Catholic S 500/7-12
PO Box 2027 39130 601-898-4800
Cathy Cook, prin. Fax 898-4689

**Magee, Simpson, Pop. 4,347**
Simpson County SD
Supt. — See Mendenhall
Magee HS 500/9-12
501 Choctaw St E 39111 601-849-2263
Debra Ware, prin. Fax 849-6201
Magee MS 600/5-8
413 Choctaw St E Ste 100 39111 601-849-3334
Dr. Rasheda Bell, prin. Fax 849-6130
Simpson County Achievement Center Alt
177 Simpson Highway 149 39111 601-849-6135
Fax 849-6137

**Magnolia, Pike, Pop. 2,410**
South Pike SD 1,900/K-12
250 W Bay St 39652 601-783-0430
Dr. Estes Taplin, supt. Fax 783-6733
www.southpike.org
South Pike Career & Technical Center Vo/Tech
252 W Bay St 39652 601-783-0438
Billy Passman, dir. Fax 783-3491
South Pike HS 500/9-12
205 W Myrtle St 39652 601-783-0420
LeDewayne Harris, prin. Fax 783-4179
South Pike JHS 300/7-8
222 W Myrtle St 39652 601-783-0425
LaDewayne Harris, prin. Fax 783-2272

**Mantachie, Itawamba, Pop. 1,139**
Itawamba County SD
Supt. — See Fulton
Mantachie HS 7-12
PO Box 38 38855 662-282-4276
Jeff Credille, prin. Fax 282-4270

**Marks, Quitman, Pop. 1,725**
Quitman County SD 1,200/K-12
PO Box E 38646 662-326-7046
Dr. Brenda Hobson, supt. Fax 326-3694
www.qcschools.org
Palmer HS 300/9-12
PO Box 350 38646 662-326-5191
Kegi Wells, prin. Fax 326-8918
Quitman County MS 400/5-8
PO Box 290 38646 662-326-6871
Nanette Reed, prin. Fax 326-6300
Quitman County Vocational HS Vo/Tech
PO Box 117 38646 662-326-8427
Cynthia Washington, dir. Fax 326-8430

Delta Academy 200/PK-12
PO Box 70 38646 662-326-8164

**Meadville, Franklin, Pop. 448**
Franklin County SD 1,200/PK-12
PO Box 605 39653 601-384-2340
Ray Carlock, supt. Fax 384-2393
www.franklincountyschoolsms.com
Franklin County Career & Technical Ctr Vo/Tech
PO Box 155 39653 601-384-5889
Terry Moffett, prin. Fax 384-5578
Franklin County HS 400/9-12
PO Box 666 39653 601-384-2965
Marion Bilbo, prin. Fax 384-2498
Franklin County MS 200/7-8
236 Edison St S 39653 601-384-2441
Chris Kent, prin. Fax 384-2085

**Mendenhall, Simpson, Pop. 2,477**
Simpson County SD 4,200/K-12
111 Education Ln 39114 601-847-8000
Glenn Harris, supt. Fax 847-8001
www.simpson.k12.ms.us
Mendenhall HS 600/9-12
207 Circle Dr 39114 601-847-2411
Robert Sanders, prin. Fax 847-8002
Mendenhall JHS 500/5-8
733 Dixie Ave 39114 601-847-2296
Kirby Craft, prin. Fax 847-7175
Simpson County Technical Center Vo/Tech
3415 Simpson Highway 49 39114 601-847-4000
George Huffman, prin. Fax 847-8011
Other Schools – See Magee

Simpson County Academy 500/K-12
124 Academy Cir 39114 601-847-1394

**Meridian, Lauderdale, Pop. 40,816**
Lauderdale County SD 6,300/PK-12
PO Box 5498 39302 601-693-1683
Randy Hodges, supt. Fax 485-1748
www.lauderdale.k12.ms.us
Clarkdale HS 300/9-12
7000 Highway 145 39301 601-693-4463
Cheryl Thomas, prin. Fax 693-6329
Clarkdale MS 300/5-8
7000 Highway 145 39301 601-693-4463
Dr. Angie McHenry, prin. Fax 693-4463
Northeast Lauderdale HS 600/9-12
702 Briarwood Rd 39305 601-679-8523
Steve Nelson, prin. Fax 679-7515
Northeast MS 700/5-8
7763 Highway 39 39305 601-483-3532
Billy Burnham, prin. Fax 485-0846
Southeast HS 400/9-12
2362 Long Creek Rd 39301 601-483-5501
Tim Moore, prin. Fax 483-6347
Southeast MS 400/5-8
2535 Old Highway 19 SE 39301 601-485-5751
Marcus Irby, prin. Fax 485-2302
Other Schools – See Collinsville

Meridian SD 6,100/PK-12
1019 25th Ave 39301 601-483-6271
Dr. Alvin Taylor, supt. Fax 484-4917
www.mpsd.k12.ms.us
Carver MS 400/6-8
900 44th Ave 39307 601-484-4482
Tommy Branch, prin. Fax 484-3011
Collins Career & Tech Center Vo/Tech
2640 24th Ave 39305 601-483-3331
Terry Moore, dir. Fax 484-5173
Magnolia MS 400/6-8
1350 24th St 39301 601-484-4060
Angela McQuarley, prin. Fax 484-5179
Marion Park Complex Alt
2815 25th St 39301 601-484-4977
Beverly Pennington, dir. Fax 482-6286
Meridian HS 1,600/9-12
2320 32nd St 39305 601-482-3191
Victor Hubbard, prin. Fax 483-5502
Northwest MS 500/6-8
4400 32nd St 39307 601-484-4094
Jackie McFarland, prin. Fax 484-5180

Calvary Christian S 50/PK-12
3917 7th St 39307 601-483-2305
Final Touch Beauty School Post-Sec.
5700 N Hills St 39307 601-485-7733

Lamar S 500/PK-12
544 Lindley Rd 39305 601-482-1345
Leigh Ann Ballou, hdmstr. Fax 482-7202
Meridian Community College Post-Sec.
910 Highway 19 N 39307 601-483-8241
Russell Christian Academy 400/PK-12
1844D Highway 11 And 80 39301 601-484-5888

**Mississippi State, Oktibbeha, Pop. 3,939**

---

Mississippi State University Post-Sec.
PO Box J 39762 662-325-2323

**Mize, Smith, Pop. 339**
Smith County SD
Supt. — See Raleigh
Mize S 800/K-12
PO Box 187 39116 601-733-2242
Chuck Jones, prin. Fax 733-9649

**Monticello, Lawrence, Pop. 1,561**
Lawrence County SD 2,100/K-12
346 Thomas E Jolly Dr W 39654 601-587-2506
Tammy Fairburn, supt. Fax 587-2221
www.lawrence.k12.ms.us
Lawrence County HS 600/9-12
PO Box 488 39654 601-587-4910
Darrell Turner, prin. Fax 587-5001
Lawrence County Technology & Career Ctr Vo/Tech
PO Box 578 39654 601-587-9346
Cindy Williamson, dir. Fax 587-2980
Paige MS 400/5-8
1570 W Broad St 39654 601-587-2128
Cassie Bridges, prin. Fax 587-7178

**Mooreville, Lee, Pop. 646**
Lee County SD
Supt. — See Tupelo
Mooreville HS 400/9-12
PO Box 60 38857 662-842-6859
Lee Bruce, prin. Fax 841-5988
Mooreville MS 400/6-8
PO Box 60 38857 662-680-4894
Roman Doty, prin. Fax 680-4896

**Moorhead, Sunflower, Pop. 2,399**
Sunflower County Consolidated SD
Supt. — See Indianola
Moorhead MS 100/6-8
PO Box 749 38761 662-246-5680
Tanya Rodges, prin. Fax 246-5080

---

Mississippi Delta Community College Post-Sec.
PO Box 668 38761 662-246-6322

**Morton, Scott, Pop. 3,416**
Scott County SD
Supt. — See Forest
Jack Upper MS 400/5-8
PO Box 500 39117 601-732-6977
Marsha Purvis, prin. Fax 732-2242
Morton HS 400/9-12
238 E Fourth Ave 39117 601-732-6210
Dr. William Shaw, prin. Fax 732-8086

**Moss Point, Jackson, Pop. 13,562**
Jackson County SD
Supt. — See Vancleave
East Central HS 800/9-12
21700 Slider Rd 39562 228-588-7000
James Hughey, prin. Fax 588-7045
East Central MS 700/6-8
5404 Hurley Wade Rd 39562 228-588-7009
R. L. Watson, prin. Fax 588-7043

Moss Point SD 1,700/PK-12
4924 Church St 39563 228-475-0691
Maggie Griffin Ph.D., supt. Fax 474-3302
www.mosspointschools.org/
Career & Technical Center Vo/Tech
4924 Church St 39563 228-475-1455
Dr. Durand Payton, dir.
Magnolia MS 400/6-8
4924 Church St 39563 228-475-1429
David Maxwell, prin. Fax 475-2684
Moss Point Alternative Learning Center Alt
4924 Church St 39563 228-475-3543
Janice Thomas, prin. Fax 474-3395
Moss Point HS 800/9-12
4924 Church St 39563 228-475-5721
Jeff Mumford, prin. Fax 474-3305

**Mound Bayou, Bolivar, Pop. 1,532**
North Bolivar Consolidated SD 600/K-12
201 Green St 38762 662-741-2555
Johnnie Vick, supt. Fax 741-2726
www.nbcsd.k12.ms.us
Kennedy Memorial HS 300/7-12
204 N Edwards Ave 38762 662-741-2510
Dr. Wanda Stringer, prin. Fax 741-2246
Other Schools – See Shelby

**Mount Olive, Covington, Pop. 971**
Covington County SD
Supt. — See Collins
Mt. Olive S 500/K-12
PO Box 309 39119 601-797-3939
O'Tonya Walker, prin. Fax 797-3980

**Myrtle, Union, Pop. 482**
Union County SD
Supt. — See New Albany
Myrtle S 700/K-12
1008 Hawk Ave 38650 662-988-2416
Nancy Yates, prin. Fax 988-2001
West Union S 600/K-12
1610 State Road 30 W 38650 662-534-6745
Russell Taylor, prin. Fax 534-6716

**Natchez, Adams, Pop. 15,630**
Natchez-Adams SD 3,400/PK-12
10 Homochitto St 39120 601-445-2800
Dr. Frederick Hill, supt. Fax 445-2818
www.natchez.k12.ms.us
Fallin Career & Technology Center Vo/Tech
315 Sgt Prentiss Dr 39120 601-445-2902
Daisy West, prin. Fax 445-2967
Freshman Academy 300/9-9
208 Pilgrim Blvd 39120 601-445-2941
Virginia Cowart, admin. Fax 445-2498
Morgantown Arts Academy 200/6-8
101 Cottage Home Dr 39120 601-445-2917
Tawanna Thornton, admin. Fax 445-2912
Morgantown College Prep 100/6-8
101 Cottage Home Dr 39120 601-445-2917
Orisha Mims, admin. Fax 445-2912
Morgantown Leadership Academy S 300/6-8
101 Cottage Home Dr 39120 601-445-2917
Nekeshia Collins, prin. Fax 445-2912
Natchez Early College 100/9-10
319 Sgt Prentiss Dr 39120 601-445-2865
Kesha Campbell, admin. Fax 445-2870
Natchez HS 700/10-12
319 Sgt Prentiss Dr 39120 601-445-2864
Dr. Willis Smith, prin. Fax 445-2870

---

Adams County Christian S 400/PK-12
300 Chinquapin Ln 39120 601-442-1422
Cathedral S 700/PK-12
701 N Dr ML King Jr St 39120 601-442-2531
Patrick Sanguinetti, prin. Fax 442-0960
Copiah-Lincoln Community College Post-Sec.
11 Co Lin Cir 39120 601-442-9111
Trinity Episcopal Day S 300/PK-12
1 Mallan G Morgan Dr 39120 601-442-5424
Les Hegwood, hdmstr. Fax 442-3216

**Nettleton, Itawamba, Pop. 1,982**
Nettleton SD 1,200/K-12
PO Box 409 38858 662-963-2151
Michael Cates, supt. Fax 963-7407
www.nettletonschools.com/
Nettleton HS 400/9-12
PO Box 409 38858 662-963-2306
Billy Tacker, prin. Fax 963-7407
Nettleton JHS 200/6-8
PO Box 409 38858 662-963-7400
Marshall Johnson, prin. Fax 963-1525

**New Albany, Union, Pop. 7,897**
New Albany SD 2,100/PK-12
301 State Highway 15 N 38652 662-534-1800
Jackie Ford, supt. Fax 534-3608
www.newalbany.k12.ms.us
New Albany HS 600/9-12
201 State Highway 15 N 38652 662-534-1805
Lance Evans, prin. Fax 534-1817
New Albany MS 500/6-8
400 Apple St 38652 662-534-1820
Damon Ladner Ph.D., prin. Fax 534-1819
New Albany/S. Tippah/Union Co. Alt S Alt
915 Denmill Rd 38652 662-538-4100
Minerva Graham, dir. Fax 538-4102
New Albany Vocational Complex Vo/Tech
203 State Highway 15 N 38652 662-534-1810
John Ferrell, dir. Fax 534-1811

Union County SD 2,700/K-12
PO Box 939 38652 662-534-1960
Ken Basil, supt. Fax 534-1961
www.union.k12.ms.us
Ingomar S 600/K-12
1384 County Road 101 38652 662-534-2680
Mark Grubbs, prin. Fax 534-3624
Other Schools – See Blue Springs, Myrtle

**New Augusta, Perry, Pop. 638**
Perry County SD 1,200/K-12
PO Box 137 39462 601-964-3211
Dr. Scott Dearman, supt. Fax 964-8204
www.perry.k12.ms.us/
Perry Central HS 400/9-12
PO Box 139 39462 601-964-3235
Titus Hines, prin. Fax 964-8273
Perry County Vocational Tech Center Vo/Tech
PO Box 138 39462 601-964-8282
Rex Buckhaults, admin. Fax 964-8562

**New Site, Prentiss**
Prentiss County SD
Supt. — See Booneville
New Site HS 300/9-12
1020 Highway 4 E 38859 662-728-5205
Ronald Clark, prin. Fax 728-1965

**Newton, Newton, Pop. 3,349**
Newton Municipal SD 1,000/K-12
205 School St 39345 601-683-2451
Dr. Virginia Young, supt. Fax 683-7131
www.nmsd.k12.ms.us
Newton HS 300/9-12
PO Box 150 39345 601-683-2232
Vicky Hood, prin. Fax 683-6808
Newton Municipal Career Center Vo/Tech
203 W First St 39345 601-683-6338
Tracy Dearing, prin. Fax 683-2283
Pilate MS 300/5-8
521 E Church St 39345 601-683-3926
Tammy Bell, prin. Fax 683-7139

**North Carrollton, Carroll, Pop. 470**
Carroll County SD
Supt. — See Carrollton
George HS 300/9-12
PO Box 398 38947 662-237-4701
Joey Carpenter, prin. Fax 237-4522
George MS 300/6-8
PO Box 398 38947 662-237-4701
Coretta Green, prin. Fax 237-9742

**Noxapater, Winston, Pop. 468**
Louisville Municipal SD
Supt. — See Louisville
Noxapater S 400/K-12
220 W Alice St 39346 662-724-4241
Chet Wilkes, prin. Fax 724-4240

**Ocean Springs, Jackson, Pop. 17,087**
Jackson County SD
Supt. — See Vancleave
St. Martin HS 1,100/9-12
11300 Yellow Jacket Rd 39564 228-875-8418
Dina Holland, prin. Fax 875-8426
St. Martin MS 900/6-8
10800 Yellow Jacket Rd 39564 228-818-4833
Stephanie Gruich, prin. Fax 818-0198

Ocean Springs SD 4,500/K-12
PO Box 7002 39566 228-875-7706
Dr. Bonita Coleman-Potter, supt. Fax 875-7708
www.ossdms.org/
Keys Alternative Education Center Alt
PO Box 7002 39566 228-872-0031
Jon Wilson, prin. Fax 875-7745
Ocean Springs HS 1,600/9-12
PO Box 7002 39566 228-875-0333
Vickie Tiblier, prin. Fax 875-7404
Ocean Springs MS 900/7-8
PO Box 7002 39566 228-872-6210
Adele Register, prin. Fax 872-9850

---

Day Spa Career College Post-Sec.
3900 Bienville Blvd 39564 228-875-4809

**Okolona, Chickasaw, Pop. 2,664**
Okolona SSD 600/K-12
411 W Main St 38860 662-447-2353
Dexter Green, supt. Fax 447-9955
okolona.k12.ms.us
Okolona JSHS 300/5-12
404 Winter St 38860 662-447-2362
Christopher Hill, prin. Fax 447-3306
Okolona Vocational Complex Vo/Tech
605 N Church St 38860 662-447-3331
Amy Anderson, dir. Fax 447-2721

**Olive Branch, DeSoto, Pop. 33,067**
DeSoto County SD
Supt. — See Hernando
Center Hill HS 800/9-12
13250 Kirk Rd 38654 662-890-2490
Doug Payne, prin. Fax 890-2458
Center Hill MS 700/6-8
8756 Forest Hill Irene Ln 38654 662-892-6800
Jacob Stripling, prin. Fax 892-6810
Desoto County Career Tech East Vo/Tech
8890 Deerfield Dr 38654 662-893-0855
Beth Turner, prin. Fax 893-0853
Lewisburg HS 700/9-12
1755 Craft Rd 38654 662-890-6708
Chris Fleming, prin. Fax 890-6202
Lewisburg MS 600/6-8
1711 Craft Rd 38654 662-892-5050
Brad Meadows, prin. Fax 892-5060
Olive Branch HS 1,100/9-12
9366 E Sandidge Rd 38654 662-893-3344
Allyson Killough, prin. Fax 893-3353
Olive Branch MS 900/6-8
6530 Blocker St 38654 662-895-4610
Jerry Floate, prin. Fax 895-7358

**Oxford, Lafayette, Pop. 18,701**
Lafayette County SD 2,600/PK-12
100 Commodore Dr 38655 662-234-3271
Dr. Adam Pugh, supt. Fax 236-3019
www.gocommodores.org
Lafayette HS 700/9-12
160 Commodore Dr 38655 662-234-3614
Glenn Kitchens, prin. Fax 234-3856
Lafayette MS 600/6-8
102 Commodore Dr 38655 662-234-1664
Chad Chism, prin. Fax 232-8736
Oxford/Lafayette School of Applied Tech Vo/Tech
134 Highway 7 S 38655 662-234-9469
Marybeth Lowrey, prin. Fax 236-2496

Oxford SD 3,700/PK-12
224 Bramlett Blvd 38655 662-234-3541
Brian Harvey, supt. Fax 232-2862
www.oxfordsd.org
Oxford HS 900/9-12
101 Charger Loop 38655 662-234-1562
W. Bradley Roberson, prin. Fax 232-1862
Oxford Learning Center Alt
399 N 5th St 38655 662-234-3588
Kathy Howington, prin. Fax 236-1052
Oxford MS 900/7-8
222 Bramlett Blvd 38655 662-234-2288
Audra Rester, prin. Fax 236-7337

---

Regents S of Oxford 200/PK-12
14 County Road 130 38655 662-232-1945

**Pascagoula, Jackson, Pop. 22,125**
Pascagoula-Gautier SD 6,000/K-12
PO Box 250 39568 228-938-6491
Wayne Rodolfich, supt. Fax 938-6528
www.psd.ms
College & Career Technical Institute Vo/Tech
2602 Market St 39567 228-938-6579
Thomas Brooks, dir. Fax 938-6597
Colmer MS 600/7-8
3112 Eden St 39581 228-938-6473
Dr. Myrick Nicks, prin. Fax 938-6593
Opportunity Center Alt
1520 Tucker Ave 39567 228-938-6222
Melissa DeAngelo, prin. Fax 938-6210

Pascagoula HS 1,100/9-12
1716 Tucker Ave 39567 228-938-6443
Anthony Herbert, prin. Fax 938-6445
Other Schools – See Gautier

---

Resurrection Catholic MSHS 200/7-12
520 Watts Ave 39567 228-762-3353
Kay McKenna, prin. Fax 769-1226

**Pass Christian, Harrison, Pop. 4,509**
Pass Christian SD 1,700/K-12
6457 Kiln Delisle Rd 39571 228-255-6200
Beth John, supt. Fax 255-6204
www.pc.k12.ms.us/
Pass Christian HS 500/9-12
720 W North St 39571 228-452-2008
Robyn Killebrew, prin. Fax 452-6128
Pass Christian MS 400/6-8
280 W Second St 39571 228-452-5220
Joe Nelson, prin. Fax 452-9616

**Pearl, Rankin, Pop. 24,692**
Pearl SD 3,800/K-12
3375 Highway 80 E 39208 601-932-7921
Dr. Raymond Morgigno, supt. Fax 932-7929
www.pearl.k12.ms.us/
Pearl HS 1,000/9-12
500 Pirates Cv 39208 601-932-7931
Dr. Lundy Brantley, prin. Fax 932-7992
Pearl JHS 900/6-8
200 Mary Ann Dr 39208 601-932-7952
Dr. Jessica Broome, prin. Fax 932-7998

---

Academy of Hair Design #4 Post-Sec.
3167 Highway 80 E 39208 601-939-4441
Park Place Christian Academy 400/PK-12
201 Park Place Dr 39208 601-939-6229
Ted Poore, head sch Fax 939-3276

**Pelahatchie, Rankin, Pop. 1,321**
Rankin County SD
Supt. — See Brandon
Pelahatchie JSHS 300/7-12
PO Box 569 39145 601-854-8135
Dr. Bryan Marshall, prin. Fax 854-8638

---

East Rankin Academy 800/PK-12
PO Box 509 39145 601-854-5691
Robert Gates M.Ed., hdmstr. Fax 854-5893

**Perkinston, Stone**

---

Mississippi Gulf Coast Community College Post-Sec.
PO Box 548 39573 601-928-5211

**Petal, Forrest, Pop. 10,310**
Petal SD 4,000/K-12
115 E Central Ave 39465 601-545-3002
Dr. Matthew L. Dillon, supt. Fax 584-4700
www.petalschools.com
Petal HS 1,100/9-12
1145 Highway 42 39465 601-583-3538
Steven Hampton, prin. Fax 545-1229
Petal MS 600/7-8
203 Highway 42 39465 601-584-6301
Michael Hogan, prin. Fax 584-4716

**Pheba, Clay**

---

Hebron Christian S 100/PK-12
6230 Henryville Rd 39755 662-494-7513

**Philadelphia, Neshoba, Pop. 7,347**
Neshoba County SD 3,300/K-12
401 E Beacon St Ste 102 39350 601-656-3752
Tommy Dearing, supt. Fax 656-3789
www.neshoba.k12.ms.us/
Neshoba Central HS 900/9-12
1125 Golf Course Rd 39350 601-656-3654
John Bowen, prin. Fax 656-1588
Neshoba Central MS 800/6-8
1000 Saint Francis Dr 39350 601-656-4636
Dr. Kenyon Barron, prin. Fax 389-2989

Philadelphia SD 1,200/K-12
248 Byrd Ave N 39350 601-656-2955
Fax 656-3141
www.phillytornadoes.com
Philadelphia HS 300/9-12
248 Byrd Ave N 39350 601-656-2672
Jason Gentry, prin. Fax 656-2273
Philadelphia MS 200/7-8
248 Byrd Ave N 39350 601-656-6439
Stacie Collins, prin. Fax 656-5328

**Picayune, Pearl River, Pop. 10,684**
Picayune SD 3,400/K-12
706 Goodyear Blvd 39466 601-798-3230
Dean Shaw, supt. Fax 798-1742
www.pcu.k12.ms.us/
Center for Alternative Education Alt
900 Third St 39466 601-799-0684
Daphnie Beebe, prin. Fax 799-0325
Picayune JHS 600/7-8
702 Goodyear Blvd 39466 601-798-5449
James Williams, prin. Fax 799-4715
Picayune Memorial HS 900/9-12
800 Fifth Ave 39466 601-798-1380
Kent Kirkland, prin. Fax 798-4705
PMHS Career & Technology Center Vo/Tech
600 Goodyear Blvd 39466 601-798-7601
Christie Pinero, prin. Fax 799-4711

**Piney Woods, Rankin**

---

Piney Woods S 100/9-12
PO Box 57 39148 601-845-2214

**Pittsboro, Calhoun, Pop. 200**
Calhoun County SD 2,500/PK-12
119 W Main St 38951 662-412-3152
Mike Moore, supt. Fax 412-3157
www.calhoun.k12.ms.us/
Other Schools – See Bruce, Calhoun City, Vardaman

---

Calhoun Academy 200/PK-12
10 County Road 406 38951 662-412-2084

**Plantersville, Lee, Pop. 1,140**
Lee County SD
Supt. — See Tupelo
Plantersville MS 300/5-8
PO Box 29 38862 662-842-4690
Rodney Spears, prin. Fax 791-0491

**Pontotoc, Pontotoc, Pop. 5,537**
Pontotoc CSD 2,300/K-12
140 Education Dr 38863 662-489-3336
Karen Tutor, supt. Fax 489-7932
www.pontotoc.k12.ms.us
Pontotoc HS 700/9-12
123 N Main St 38863 662-489-1275
Paul Henry, prin. Fax 489-5255
Pontotoc JHS 400/7-8
132 N Main St 38863 662-489-8360
Phil Webb, prin. Fax 489-8947

Pontotoc County SD 3,100/PK-12
285 Highway 15 S 38863 662-489-3932
Kenneth Roye, supt. Fax 489-3922
www.pcsd.k12.ms.us/
Pontotoc Ridge Career & Technolog Center Vo/Tech
354 Ridge Dr 38863 662-489-1826
Phil Ryan, dir. Fax 489-0704
South Pontotoc HS 400/9-12
1523 S Pontotoc Rd 38863 662-489-5925
Tim West, prin. Fax 489-8598
South Pontotoc MS 400/6-8
1523 S Pontotoc Rd 38863 662-489-5925
Jimmy Flake, prin. Fax 489-6252
Other Schools – See Ecru

**Poplarville, Pearl River, Pop. 2,824**
Poplarville SSD 2,000/PK-12
302 Julia St 39470 601-795-8477
Carl Merritt, supt. Fax 795-0712
www.poplarvilleschools.org/
Poplarville Career Development Center Vo/Tech
9 Career Center Cir 39470 601-795-8343
Marlene Cole, prin. Fax 795-1353
Poplarville HS 600/9-12
1 Hornet Dr 39470 601-795-8424
Jonathan Will, prin. Fax 795-1345
Poplarville MS 500/6-8
6 Spirit Dr 39470 601-795-1350
Heidi Dillon, prin. Fax 795-1351

---

Pearl River Community College Post-Sec.
101 Highway 11 N 39470 601-403-1000

**Port Gibson, Claiborne, Pop. 1,561**
Claiborne County SD 1,700/PK-12
404 Market St 39150 601-437-4232
Dr. Earl Watkins Ph.D., supt. Fax 437-3036
www.claiborne.k12.ms.us/
Claiborne Co. Voc Educational Complex Vo/Tech
PO Box 47 39150 601-437-3800
Norma Thompson-Lewis, dir. Fax 437-3099
Port Gibson HS 500/9-12
159 Old Highway 18 39150 601-437-4190
Eddwin Smith, prin. Fax 437-3803
Port Gibson MS 400/6-8
PO Box 567 39150 601-437-4251
Marvin Harvey, prin. Fax 437-3099

**Potts Camp, Marshall, Pop. 520**
Marshall County SD
Supt. — See Holly Springs
Potts Camp HS 200/9-12
7050 Church St 38659 662-333-6354
Noah Hamilton, prin. Fax 333-7023
Potts Camp MS 200/4-8
7050 Church St 38659 662-333-6354
Leigh Anne Sanderson, prin.

**Prentiss, Jefferson Davis, Pop. 1,069**
Jefferson Davis County SD 1,700/K-12
PO Box 1197 39474 601-792-4267
John Daley, supt. Fax 792-2251
www.jdcsd.com
Prentiss JSHS 500/7-12
PO Box 1168 39474 601-792-4646
Pete Howell, prin. Fax 792-8149
Other Schools – See Bassfield, Carson

---

Prentiss Christian S 300/K-12
PO Box 1287 39474 601-792-8549

**Puckett, Rankin, Pop. 315**
Rankin County SD
Supt. — See Brandon
Puckett HS 400/7-12
PO Box 40 39151 601-825-5742
Robert Crain, prin. Fax 825-9838

**Purvis, Lamar, Pop. 2,145**
Lamar County SD 9,100/K-12
PO Box 609 39475 601-794-1030
Tess Smith, supt. Fax 794-1012
www.lamarcountyschools.org
Jefferson-Todd Alternative Education Ctr Alt
449 Brown St 39475 601-794-8121
Bryan Stewart, prin. Fax 794-2005
Lamar County Vo-Tech Center Vo/Tech
41 College Dr 39475 601-794-8298
Tina Byrd, prin. Fax 794-1026

Purvis HS 500/9-12
PO Box 1089 39475 601-794-2708
Brad Skeen, prin. Fax 794-2150
Purvis MS 400/6-8
PO Box 549 39475 601-794-1068
Frank Bunnell, prin. Fax 794-1069
Other Schools – See Hattiesburg, Sumrall

---

Lamar Christian S 300/PK-12
62 Purvis Oloh Rd 39475 601-794-0016

**Quitman, Clarke, Pop. 2,307**
Quitman SD 2,000/PK-12
104 E Franklin St 39355 601-776-2186
Fax 776-1051
www.quitmanschools.org
Clarke County Vocational Center Vo/Tech
910 N Archusa Ave 39355 601-776-5219
Mark Hudson, dir. Fax 776-5219
Quitman HS 500/9-12
210 S Jackson Ave 39355 601-776-3341
Michael McDonald, prin. Fax 776-6136
Quitman JHS 500/6-8
501 W Lynda St 39355 601-776-6243
John James, prin. Fax 776-1288

**Raleigh, Smith, Pop. 1,457**
Smith County SD 2,900/K-12
PO Box 308 39153 601-782-4296
Nick Hillman, supt. Fax 782-9895
smithcountyschools.net
Raleigh HS 600/7-12
491 Magnolia Dr 39153 601-782-4261
Miles Butler, prin. Fax 782-4359
Smith County Career Center Vo/Tech
469 Magnolia Dr 39153 601-782-4211
Hollis Blackwell, dir. Fax 782-9842
Other Schools – See Mize, Taylorsville

**Raymond, Hinds, Pop. 1,915**
Hinds County SD 6,200/PK-12
13192 Highway 18 39154 601-857-5222
Dr. Delesicia Martin, supt. Fax 857-8548
www.hinds.k12.ms.us/
Carver MS 200/6-8
PO Box 47 39154 601-857-5006
Shakinna Patterson, prin. Fax 857-4935
Hinds County Career Center Vo/Tech
PO Box 789 39154 601-857-5536
Patricia Ashmore, prin. Fax 857-2212
Raymond HS 600/9-12
14050 Highway 18 39154 601-857-8016
Shakinna Patterson, prin. Fax 857-2007
Other Schools – See Bolton, Terry

---

Central Hinds Academy 400/K-12
2894 Raymond Bolton Rd 39154 601-857-5568
Hinds Community College Post-Sec.
PO Box 1100 39154 601-857-5261

**Richland, Rankin, Pop. 6,844**
Rankin County SD
Supt. — See Brandon
Richland HS 900/7-12
1202 Highway 49 S 39218 601-939-5144
Richard Sutton, prin. Fax 939-7631

**Richton, Perry, Pop. 1,058**
Richton SD 700/K-12
PO Box 568 39476 601-788-6581
Dr. Noal Cochran, supt. Fax 788-9391
www.richtonschools.com
Richton JSHS 300/7-12
PO Box 568 39476 601-788-9608
Daniel Henley, prin. Fax 788-6390

**Ridgeland, Madison, Pop. 23,769**
Madison County SD 11,400/PK-12
476 Highland Colony Pkwy 39157 601-879-3000
Dr. Ronnie McGehee, supt. Fax 879-3039
www.madison-schools.com/
Olde Towne MS 700/6-8
210 Sunnybrook Rd 39157 601-898-8730
Tim Dowdy, prin. Fax 853-8108
Ridgeland HS 900/9-12
586 Sunnybrook Rd 39157 601-898-5023
Eric Brooks, prin. Fax 853-7822
Other Schools – See Camden, Canton, Madison

---

Delta Technical College Post-Sec.
113 Marketridge Dr 39157 601-206-5200
St. Andrew's Episcopal S 700/5-12
370 Old Agency Rd 39157 601-853-6000
Dr. George Penick, head sch Fax 853-6001

**Ripley, Tippah, Pop. 5,308**
South Tippah SD 2,700/K-12
402 Greenlee Dr 38663 662-837-7156
Frank Campbell, supt. Fax 837-1362
www.stippah.k12.ms.us/
Pine Grove S 600/K-12
3510A County Road 600 38663 662-837-7789
Clint Stroupe, prin. Fax 837-8179
Ripley HS 500/9-12
720 S Clayton St 38663 662-837-7583
George Buchanan, prin. Fax 837-0118
Ripley MS 600/5-8
718 S Clayton St 38663 662-837-7959
James Storey, prin. Fax 837-0251
Tippah Career & Technology Center Vo/Tech
PO Box 533 38663 662-837-9798
Tony Elliott, dir. Fax 837-8833
Other Schools – See Blue Mountain

---

Foster's Cosmetology College Post-Sec.
PO Box 66 38663 662-837-9334

**Rolling Fork, Sharkey, Pop. 2,129**
South Delta SD 1,000/PK-12
PO Box 219 39159 662-873-4302
Sammie Ivy, supt. Fax 873-6114
www.southdelta.k12.ms.us/
South Delta HS 300/9-12
303 Parkway Ave 39159 662-873-4308
Arian Dorsey, prin. Fax 873-6106
South Delta Vocational S Vo/Tech
285 Maple St 39159 662-873-2029
Beverly Wilson, prin. Fax 873-4194
Other Schools – See Anguilla

---

Sharkey Issaquena Academy 200/K-12
272 Academy Dr 39159 662-873-4241

**Rosedale, Bolivar, Pop. 1,864**
West Bolivar SD 800/PK-12
PO Box 189 38769 662-759-3525
Henry Phillips, supt. Fax 759-6795
www.wbsd.k12.ms.us
Barnes Vocational Center Vo/Tech
PO Box 160 38769 662-759-3791
Raymond Russell, dir. Fax 759-6795
West Bolivar HS 300/9-12
PO Box 398 38769 662-759-3346
Joseph Griffin, prin. Fax 759-0039
West Bolivar MS 200/5-8
PO Box 159 38769 662-759-3743
Dr. Nehru Brown, prin. Fax 759-6795
Other Schools – See Benoit, Shaw

**Ruleville, Sunflower, Pop. 2,980**
Sunflower County Consolidated SD
Supt. — See Indianola
Ruleville MS 200/6-8
250 Oscar St 38771 662-756-4698
Zinnia Wince, prin. Fax 756-4902

**Sallis, Attala, Pop. 134**
Attala County SD
Supt. — See Kosciusko
Mc Adams JSHS 200/7-12
6315 Attala Road 4167 39160 662-289-3838
Jackie Sandifer, prin. Fax 289-7181

**Saltillo, Lee, Pop. 4,701**
Lee County SD
Supt. — See Tupelo
Saltillo HS 900/9-12
PO Box 460 38866 662-869-5466
Tim DeVaughn, prin. Fax 869-7229

**Sandhill, Rankin**
Rankin County SD
Supt. — See Brandon
Pisgah HS 400/7-12
PO Box 70 39161 601-829-2825
Dr. Norman Session, prin. Fax 829-1753

**Sarah, Tate**
Tate County SD
Supt. — See Senatobia
Strayhorn HS 300/7-12
86 Mustang Dr 38665 662-562-9246
John Shows, prin. Fax 562-9249

**Sardis, Panola, Pop. 1,686**
North Panola SD 1,600/K-12
470 Highway 51 N 38666 662-487-2305
Cedric Richardson, supt. Fax 487-2050
www.northpanolaschools.org
North Panola HS 400/9-12
500 Highway 51 N 38666 662-487-1070
Braxton Stowe, prin. Fax 487-2052
Other Schools – See Como

**Scooba, Kemper, Pop. 727**

---

East Mississippi Community College Post-Sec.
PO Box 158 39358 662-476-8442

**Sebastopol, Scott, Pop. 272**
Scott County SD
Supt. — See Forest
Sebastopol Attendance Center 600/K-12
PO Box 86 39359 601-625-8654
Lorie Lundy, prin. Fax 625-9426

**Seminary, Covington, Pop. 314**
Covington County SD
Supt. — See Collins
Seminary HS 400/9-12
PO Box 34 39479 601-722-3220
Brad Skeen, prin. Fax 722-9543
Seminary MS 400/5-8
PO Box 34 39479 601-722-4510
John Chancelor, prin. Fax 722-4463

**Senatobia, Tate, Pop. 8,076**
Senatobia Municipal SD 1,900/K-12
104 McKie St 38668 662-562-4897
Jay Foster, supt. Fax 562-4996
www.senatobiaschools.com
Senatobia JSHS 800/7-12
221 Warrior Dr 38668 662-562-4230
Bradley Roberson, prin. Fax 562-6659
Tate County Optional Learning Center Alt
403 W Gilmore St 38668 662-562-5193
Robert Downing, prin. Fax 562-4996

Tate County SD 2,800/K-12
107 Court St 38668 662-562-5861
Daryl Scoggin, supt. Fax 562-8516
www.tcsd.k12.ms.us
Other Schools – See Coldwater, Sarah

---

Infinity Career College Post-Sec.
562 W Main St Ste B 38668 662-562-8010

Magnolia Heights S 600/PK-12
1 Chiefs Dr 38668 662-562-4491
Dr. Marvin Lishman Ph.D., admin. Fax 562-0386
Northwest Mississippi Community College Post-Sec.
4975 Highway 51 N 38668 662-562-3200

**Shannon, Lee, Pop. 1,726**
Lee County SD
Supt. — See Tupelo
Shannon HS 600/9-12
PO Box 8 38868 662-767-9566
Bill Rosenthal, prin. Fax 767-2847
Shannon MS 300/6-8
232 E Cherry St 38868 662-767-3986
Barry Woods, prin. Fax 767-9981

**Shaw, Bolivar, Pop. 1,947**
West Bolivar SD
Supt. — See Rosedale
Shaw HS 200/9-12
PO Box 510 38773 662-754-2611
L'Kenna Whitehead, prin. Fax 754-4418

**Shelby, Bolivar, Pop. 2,225**
North Bolivar Consolidated SD
Supt. — See Mound Bayou
Broad Street HS 200/9-12
PO Box 149 38774 662-398-4040
Tommy Molden, prin. Fax 398-5900
Shelby MS 200/5-8
PO Box 28 38774 662-398-4020
Fredrick Ford, prin. Fax 398-4039

**Shuqualak, Noxubee, Pop. 499**
Noxubee County SD
Supt. — See Macon
Reed Resource Center 100/Alt
PO Box 29 39361 662-793-4544
Holli Jenkins-Chandler, prin. Fax 793-4793

**Smithville, Monroe, Pop. 930**
Monroe County SD
Supt. — See Amory
Smithville S 500/K-12
60017 Highway 23 38870 662-651-4276
Chad O'Brian, prin. Fax 651-4163

**Southaven, DeSoto, Pop. 48,244**
DeSoto County SD
Supt. — See Hernando
Desoto Central HS 1,500/9-12
2911 Central Pkwy 38672 662-536-3612
Cory Uselton, prin. Fax 536-3623
Desoto Central MS 1,200/6-8
2611 Central Pkwy 38672 662-349-6660
Duane Case, prin. Fax 349-1045
DeSoto County Career Tech West Vo/Tech
847 Rasco Rd W 38671 662-393-6211
Paul Chrestman, prin. Fax 393-5708
Southaven HS 1,800/9-12
735 Rasco Rd W 38671 662-393-9300
Shane Jones, prin. Fax 996-1574
Southaven MS 1,500/6-8
899 Rasco Rd W 38671 662-280-0422
Levi Williams, prin. Fax 280-3613

---

Northpoint Christian S 1,100/PK-12
7400 Getwell Rd 38672 662-349-3096
David Manley, pres. Fax 349-4962

**Starkville, Oktibbeha, Pop. 23,580**
Starkville-Oktibbeha SD 3,300/PK-12
401 Greensboro St 39759 662-324-4050
Dr. Lewis Holloway, supt. Fax 324-4068
www.starkvillesd.com/
Armstrong MS 900/6-8
303 McKee St 39759 662-324-4070
Timothy Bourne, prin. Fax 324-4075
Millsaps Career & Tech Center Vo/Tech
803 Louisville St 39759 662-324-4170
Ray New, prin. Fax 324-4103
Overstreet S Alt
307 S Jackson St 39759 662-324-4090
Lisa Thompson, dir. Fax 324-4162
Starkville HS 1,000/9-12
603 Yellow Jacket Dr 39759 662-324-4130
David Baggett, prin. Fax 324-4128

---

Starkville Academy 700/PK-12
505 Academy Rd 39759 662-323-7814
Starkville Christian S 200/PK-12
303 Lynn Ln 39759 662-323-7453
Rev. Randall Witbeck, prin. Fax 323-7571

**Steens, Lowndes**

---

Columbus Christian Academy 300/PK-12
6405 Military Rd 39766 662-328-7888
Sandra White, admin. Fax 328-7750

**Stringer, Jasper**
West Jasper Consolidated SD
Supt. — See Bay Springs
Stringer S 600/K-12
PO Box 1068 39481 601-428-5508
Jay Arrington, prin. Fax 426-6760

**Summit, Pike, Pop. 1,702**
North Pike SD 2,400/K-12
1036 Jaguar Trl 39666 601-276-2216
Dennis Penton, supt. Fax 276-3666
npsd.k12.ms.us/
North Pike HS 600/9-12
1022 Jaguar Trl 39666 601-276-2175
Scott Hallmark, prin. Fax 276-2720
North Pike MS 800/5-8
2034 Highway 44 NE 39666 601-684-3283
Janice Samuels, prin. Fax 684-3269

---

Southwest Mississippi Community College Post-Sec.
1156 College Dr 39666 601-276-2000

**Sumner, Tallahatchie, Pop. 316**
West Tallahatchie SD
Supt. — See Webb
North Delta Alternative S Alt
300 Jennings St 38957 662-375-8392
Sherry T. Ellington, prin. Fax 375-0069

**Sumrall, Lamar, Pop. 1,412**
Lamar County SD
Supt. — See Purvis
Sumrall HS 500/9-12
PO Box 187 39482 601-758-4730
Sheila Kribbs, prin. Fax 758-0512
Sumrall MS 400/6-8
1217 Highway 42 39482 601-758-4416
Terry Smith, prin. Fax 758-4148

**Taylorsville, Smith, Pop. 1,344**
Smith County SD
Supt. — See Raleigh
Taylorsville HS 400/6-12
PO Box 8 39168 601-785-6942
Jeff Duvall, prin. Fax 785-9711

**Tchula, Holmes, Pop. 2,088**
Holmes County SD
Supt. — See Lexington
Holmes County Learning Center Alt
32 School St 39169 662-235-5638
Fax 235-5639

**Terry, Hinds, Pop. 1,052**
Hinds County SD
Supt. — See Raymond
Byram MS 1,000/6-8
2009 Byram Bulldog Blvd 39170 601-372-4597
LaQuanta Nelson, prin. Fax 346-2383
Terry HS 1,300/9-12
235 W Beasley St 39170 601-878-5905
Anthony Goins, prin. Fax 878-2782

**Tiplersville, Tippah**
North Tippah SD 1,300/K-12
PO Box 65 38674 662-223-4384
Junior Wooten, supt. Fax 223-5379
www.ntippah.k12.ms.us
Other Schools – See Falkner, Walnut

**Tishomingo, Tishomingo, Pop. 335**
Tishomingo County Special Municipal SD
Supt. — See Iuka
Tishomingo County Alternative S Alt
1421 Highway 25 N 38873 662-438-6864
Nancy Parker, prin. Fax 424-9820
Tishomingo County Vocational Center Vo/Tech
1421 Highway 25 38873 662-438-6689
John Taylor, dir. Fax 438-6777

**Tougaloo, Hinds**

---

Tougaloo College Post-Sec.
500 W County Line Rd 39174 601-977-7700

**Tremont, Itawamba, Pop. 462**
Itawamba County SD
Supt. — See Fulton
Tremont Attendance Center 300/K-12
320 School Loop Dr 38876 662-652-3391
Brady Ramey, prin. Fax 652-3994

**Tunica, Tunica, Pop. 1,021**
Tunica County SD 2,200/PK-12
PO Box 758 38676 662-363-2811
Dr. Margie Pulley, supt. Fax 363-3061
www.tunicak12.org
Rosa Fort HS 500/9-12
PO Box 997 38676 662-363-1343
Derrick Dace, prin. Fax 363-4222
TCS Alternative S Alt
PO Box 997 38676 662-363-1343
Willie Bolden, prin. Fax 363-4222
Tunica MS 500/6-8
PO Box 967 38676 662-363-4224
Glen Newson, prin. Fax 357-1058
Williams Career and Technical Ctr Vo/Tech
PO Box 2618 38676 662-363-2051
Dianne Daley, dir. Fax 363-2052

---

Tunica Academy 200/PK-12
PO Box 966 38676 662-363-1051

**Tupelo, Lee, Pop. 34,140**
Lee County SD 7,000/K-12
1280 College View St 38804 662-841-9144
Jimmy Weeks, supt. Fax 680-6012
www.leecountyschools.us/
Other Schools – See Belden, Guntown, Mooreville, Plantersville, Saltillo, Shannon

Tupelo SD 7,400/PK-12
PO Box 557 38802 662-841-8850
Dr. Gearl Loden, supt. Fax 841-8887
www.tupeloschools.com/
Tupelo HS 2,100/9-12
4125 Golden Wave Dr 38801 662-841-8970
Jason Harris, prin. Fax 841-8987
Tupelo MS 1,000/7-8
1009 Varsity Dr 38801 662-840-8780
Dr. Kristy Luse, prin. Fax 840-1831

---

Creations College of Cosmetology Post-Sec.
PO Box 2635 38803 662-844-9264
North Mississippi Medical Center Post-Sec.
830 S Gloster St 38801 662-841-3136

**Tylertown, Walthall, Pop. 1,598**
Walthall County SD 2,300/K-12
814A Morse Ave 39667 601-876-3401
Cynthia Magee, supt. Fax 876-6982
www.wcsd.k12.ms.us
Dexter S 200/K-12
927 Highway 48 E 39667 601-876-3985
Allen Dyess, prin. Fax 876-5410
Salem S 500/K-12
881 Highway 27 N 39667 601-876-2580
Charles Boyd, prin. Fax 876-4155
Tylertown JSHS 700/7-12
204 High School Rd 39667 601-876-3370
Dr. Ronald Morgan, prin. Fax 876-3122
Walthall County Career & Tech Center Vo/Tech
803 Ball Ave 39667 601-222-1500
Wade Carney, dir. Fax 222-1506

**Union, Newton, Pop. 1,954**
Union SD 1,000/PK-12
PO Box 445 39365 601-774-9579
Ray Perry, supt. Fax 774-0600
www.unioncity.k12.ms.us/
Union HS 200/9-12
101 Forest St 39365 601-774-8257
Brett Rigby, prin. Fax 774-9600
Union MS 300/5-8
115 James St 39365 601-774-5303
Tyler Hansford, prin. Fax 774-9607

**University, Lafayette, Pop. 4,155**

---

University of Mississippi Post-Sec.
PO Box 1848 38677 662-915-7211

**Vancleave, Jackson, Pop. 5,787**
Jackson County SD 9,200/K-12
PO Box 5069 39565 228-826-1757
Dr. Barry Amacker, supt. Fax 826-3393
www.jcsd.k12.ms.us/
Jackson County Technology Center Vo/Tech
12425 Highway 57 39565 228-826-5944
Diane Novak, dir. Fax 826-4209
Vancleave HS 700/9-12
12424 Highway 57 39565 228-826-4701
Anthony Gruich, prin. Fax 826-5066
Vancleave MS 600/6-8
4725 Bull Dog Ln 39565 228-826-5902
Jill Davis, prin. Fax 826-1421
Other Schools – See Moss Point, Ocean Springs

**Vardaman, Calhoun, Pop. 1,309**
Calhoun County SD
Supt. — See Pittsboro
Vardaman HS 300/7-12
PO Box 193 38878 662-682-7574
Porter Casey, prin. Fax 682-7743

**Vicksburg, Warren, Pop. 23,676**
Vicksburg Warren SD 8,500/PK-12
1500 Mission 66 39180 601-638-5122
Chad Shealy, supt. Fax 631-2819
www.vwsd.k12.ms.us/
Academy of Innovation 7-8
1315 Grove St 39183 601-636-2539
Jason McKellar, prin. Fax 631-2856
Vicksburg HS 1,100/9-12
3701 Drummond St 39180 601-636-2914
Deowarski McDonald, prin. Fax 631-2885
Vicksburg JHS 600/7-8
1533 Baldwin Ferry Rd 39180 601-636-1966
LeAndrew Drake, prin. Fax 631-2830
Warren Central HS 1,100/9-12
1000 Highway 27 39180 601-638-3372
Eric Green, prin. Fax 631-2937
Warren Central JHS 700/7-8
1630 Baldwin Ferry Rd 39180 601-638-3981
Cedric Magee, prin. Fax 631-2839

---

Porters Chapel Academy 200/K-12
3460 Porters Chapel Rd 39180 601-638-3733
Vicksburg Catholic S-St. Aloysius 300/7-12
1900 Grove St 39183 601-636-2256
Dr. Buddy Strickland, prin. Fax 631-0430

**Walnut, Tippah, Pop. 762**
North Tippah SD
Supt. — See Tiplersville
Walnut S 500/K-12
280 Commerce Ave 38683 662-223-6471
Joe McCoy, prin. Fax 223-5275

**Walnut Grove, Leake, Pop. 1,907**
Leake County SD
Supt. — See Carthage
Leake County HS 300/7-12
PO Box 159 39189 601-253-2393
Sammie McLaurin, prin. Fax 253-0100

**Water Valley, Yalobusha, Pop. 3,370**
Water Valley SD 1,200/K-12
PO Box 788 38965 662-473-1203
Fax 473-1225
www.wvsd.k12.ms.us
Water Valley JSHS 500/7-12
PO Box 647 38965 662-473-2468
Dr. Glenn Kitchens, prin. Fax 473-1444

**Waynesboro, Wayne, Pop. 4,998**
Wayne County SD 3,500/K-12
810 Chickasawhay St 39367 601-735-4871
Ben Graves, supt. Fax 735-4872
www.wayne.k12.ms.us
Wayne County Career and Technical Center Vo/Tech
800 Collins St 39367 601-735-5036
Bobby Jones, prin. Fax 735-6326
Wayne County HS 1,000/9-12
1325 Azalea Dr 39367 601-735-2851
Dr. Cathy Davis, prin. Fax 735-1389
Waynesboro MS 500/5-8
155 Wayne St 39367 601-735-3159
Tyrone Marshall, prin. Fax 735-6316

---

Wayne Academy 300/K-12
46 Joe Jordan Dr 39367 601-735-2921

**Webb, Tallahatchie, Pop. 557**
West Tallahatchie SD 800/K-12
PO Box 129 38966 662-375-9291
Eddie McCord, supt. Fax 375-9294
www.wtsd.k12.ms.us
West Tallahatchie HS 400/7-12
PO Box 130 38966 662-375-8829
Christopher Furdge, prin. Fax 375-7402
Other Schools – See Sumner

**Wesson, Copiah, Pop. 1,907**
Copiah County SD
Supt. — See Hazlehurst
Wesson S 1,100/K-12
1048 Grove St 39191 601-643-2221
Marilyn Phillips, prin. Fax 643-2458

---

Copiah-Lincoln Community College Post-Sec.
PO Box 649 39191 601-643-5101

**West Point, Clay, Pop. 11,257**
West Point SD 3,200/PK-12
PO Box 656 39773 662-494-4242
Burnell McDonald, supt. Fax 494-8605
www.westpoint.k12.ms.us/
Fifth Street JHS 500/7-8
620 5th St 39773 662-494-2191
Richard Bryant, prin. Fax 494-2432
West Point Career and Technology Center Vo/Tech
1253 E Church Hill Rd 39773 662-494-6176
Patrick Ray, prin. Fax 495-2426
West Point HS 1,000/9-12
950 S Eshman Ave 39773 662-494-5083
Jermaine Taylor, prin. Fax 494-0969
West Point Learning Center Alt
1399 Highway 45 N Alt 39773 662-494-6202
Fax 495-6202

---

Gibson's Barber & Beauty College Post-Sec.
PO Box 990 39773 662-494-5444
Oak Hill Academy 400/PK-12
800 N Eshman Ave 39773 662-494-5043
Dr. Cathy Davis, hdmstr. Fax 494-0487

**Wheeler, Prentiss**
Prentiss County SD
Supt. — See Booneville
Wheeler S 200/K-12
318 County Road 5011 38880 662-365-2629
Todd Swinney, prin. Fax 365-2535

**Wiggins, Stone, Pop. 4,345**
Stone County SD 2,700/K-12
214 Critz St N 39577 601-928-7247
Gwen Miller, supt. Fax 928-5122
www.stone.k12.ms.us
Stone HS 700/9-12
400 Border Ave E 39577 601-928-5492
Diane Roberts, prin. Fax 928-6874
Stone MS 700/6-8
532 Central Ave E 39577 601-928-4876
Dr. Shauna Breland, prin. Fax 928-6440

---

Gateway Christian Academy 100/PK-12
908 Frontage Dr W 39577 601-528-5454
Dr. Eugene Anderson, admin. Fax 928-3973

**Winona, Montgomery, Pop. 5,020**
Montgomery County SD 300/K-12
PO Box 687 38967 662-283-4533
Michael Hood, supt. Fax 283-4584
www.mcsdms.net
Other Schools – See Kilmichael

Winona SD 1,100/K-12
218 Fairground St 38967 662-283-3731
Dr. Teresa Jackson, supt. Fax 283-1003
www.winonaschools.net
Winona Career and Technical Center Vo/Tech
300 N Applegate St 38967 662-283-3601
Lance VanHorn, prin. Fax 283-9807
Winona HS 500/7-12
301 Fairground St 38967 662-283-1244
Charlie Parkerson, prin. Fax 283-4267

---

Winona Christian S 300/PK-12
1014 S Applegate St 38967 662-283-1169
Jimmy Pittman, hdmstr. Fax 283-3333

**Woodville, Wilkinson, Pop. 1,088**
Wilkinson County SD 1,300/PK-12
PO Box 785 39669 601-888-3582
Timothy Scott, supt. Fax 888-3133
wilkinsoncounty.schoolinsites.com/
King Vocational Complex Vo/Tech
PO Box 1193 39669 601-888-4394
Kimberly Jackson, prin. Fax 888-4740
Wilkinson County HS 300/9-12
522 Pinckneyville Rd 39669 601-888-4228
Ougrett Brumfield, prin. Fax 888-4736
Other Schools – See Centreville

---

Wilkinson County Christian Academy 300/K-12
2420 US Highway 61 S 39669 601-888-4313

**Yazoo City, Yazoo, Pop. 11,345**
Yazoo City Municipal SD 2,400/PK-12
1133 Calhoun Ave 39194 662-746-2125
Dr. Lucille Lovette, supt. Fax 746-9210
www.yazoocity.k12.ms.us/
Woolfolk MS 600/5-8
209 E Fifth St 39194 662-746-2904
Michael Johnson Ed.D., prin. Fax 746-8609
Yazoo City Alternative S Alt
1318 Grand Ave 39194 662-746-0985
Georgia Ingram Ed.D., prin.
Yazoo City HS 700/9-12
1825 Dr Mrtn Lthr Kng Jr Dr 39194 662-746-2378
Lawrence Hudson, prin. Fax 746-3779
Yazoo City Vocational Center Vo/Tech
1825 Dr Mrtn Lthr Kng Jr Dr 39194 662-746-7642
Gregg Giles, dir. Fax 746-0991

Yazoo County SD 1,700/K-12
94 Panther Dr 39194 662-746-4672
Rebecca Fisher, supt. Fax 746-9270
www.yazoo.k12.ms.us
Yazoo County HS 500/9-12
191 Panther Dr 39194 662-746-1492
Jana Bardwell, prin. Fax 746-1593
Yazoo County MS 300/6-8
116 Panther Dr 39194 662-746-1596
Gloria W. Jamison, prin. Fax 746-1616

---

Manchester Academy 400/PK-12
2132 Gordon Ave 39194 662-746-5913

# MISSOURI

**MISSOURI DEPARTMENT OF EDUCATION**
**PO Box 480, Jefferson City 65102-0480**
**Telephone 573-751-4212**
**Fax 573-751-1179**
**Website http://www.dese.mo.gov**

Commissioner of Education Chris Nicastro

**MISSOURI BOARD OF EDUCATION**
**PO Box 480, Jefferson City 65102-0480**

President Peter Herschend

## PUBLIC, PRIVATE AND CATHOLIC SECONDARY SCHOOLS

**Adrian, Bates, Pop. 1,663**
Adrian R-III SD 700/PK-12
PO Box 98 64720 816-297-2710
Don Lile, supt. Fax 297-2980
www.adrian.k12.mo.us
Adrian JSHS 400/6-12
PO Box 98 64720 816-297-4460
Abe Lewis, prin. Fax 297-4598

**Advance, Stoddard, Pop. 1,340**
Advance R-IV SD 400/PK-12
201 E School St 63730 573-722-3581
Dr. Stan Seiler, supt. Fax 722-9886
www.advance.k12.mo.us
Advance JSHS 200/7-12
201 E School St 63730 573-722-3584
Shana Kight, prin. Fax 722-5479

**Albany, Gentry, Pop. 1,720**
Albany R-III SD 400/PK-12
101 W Jefferson St 64402 660-726-3911
Erin Oligschlaeger, supt. Fax 726-5841
www.albany.k12.mo.us
Albany HS 100/9-12
101 W Jefferson St 64402 660-726-3912
Dallas Giedd, prin. Fax 726-5841
Albany MS 100/6-8
101 W Jefferson St 64402 660-726-3912
Dallas Giedd, prin. Fax 726-5841

**Alma, Lafayette, Pop. 395**
Santa Fe R-X SD 400/K-12
PO Box 197 64001 660-674-2238
Dr. Rhoda Barnett, supt. Fax 674-2239
santafechiefs.k12.mo.us
Santa Fe HS 200/7-12
PO Box 197 64001 660-674-2236
Tom Burton, prin. Fax 674-2760

**Alton, Oregon, Pop. 847**
Alton R-IV SD 700/K-12
RR 2 Box 2180 65606 417-778-7216
Dr. Eric Allen, supt. Fax 778-6394
www.alton.k12.mo.us/
Alton HS 400/7-12
RR 2 Box 2180 65606 417-778-7215
Joby Steele, prin. Fax 778-7851

**Amoret, Bates, Pop. 185**
Miami R-I SD 200/K-12
7638 NW State Route J 64722 660-267-3480
Dr. Steven Beckett, supt. Fax 267-3630
www.miamir1.net
Miami JSHS 100/7-12
7638 NW State Route J 64722 660-267-3484
Dr. Daniel Johnson, prin. Fax 267-3630

**Anderson, McDonald, Pop. 1,900**
McDonald County R-I SD 3,600/PK-12
100 Mustang Dr 64831 417-845-3321
Dr. Mark Stanton, supt. Fax 845-6972
mcdonaldr1.net
Anderson MS 200/7-8
135 Mustang Dr 64831 417-845-1805
Ken Anders, prin. Fax 845-7406
McDonald County HS 1,000/9-12
100 Mustang Dr 64831 417-845-3322
Greg Leach, prin. Fax 845-8467
Other Schools – See Noel, Pineville

**Annapolis, Iron, Pop. 343**
South Iron R-I SD 300/PK-12
210 School St 63620 573-598-4241
Donald Wakefield, supt. Fax 598-4210
www.sipanthers.k12.mo.us
South Iron JSHS 200/7-12
210 School St 63620 573-598-4241
Joseph Jackson, prin. Fax 598-4210

**Appleton City, Saint Clair, Pop. 1,108**
Appleton City R-II SD 300/K-12
408 W 4th St 64724 660-476-2161
Steven Beckett, supt. Fax 476-5564
www.appletoncity.k12.mo.us
Appleton City HS 200/6-12
408 W 4th St 64724 660-476-2118
James Gurney, prin. Fax 476-5564

**Archie, Cass, Pop. 1,157**
Archie R-V SD 600/PK-12
302 W State Route A 64725 816-293-5312
Jeff Kramer, supt. Fax 293-5712
www.archie.k12.mo.us
Archie JSHS 300/7-12
302 W State Route A 64725 816-293-5312
Jeff Kramer, prin. Fax 293-5712

**Arnold, Jefferson, Pop. 20,546**
Fox C-6 SD 11,300/PK-12
745 Jeffco Blvd 63010 636-296-8000
Dr. Jim Wipke, supt. Fax 282-5170
www.fox.k12.mo.us
Fox HS 1,800/9-12
751 Jeffco Blvd 63010 636-296-5210
Dr. Kevin Rossiter, prin. Fax 282-6980
Fox MS 500/7-8
743 Jeffco Blvd 63010 636-296-5077
Aaron Wilken, prin. Fax 282-5171
Ridgewood MS 500/7-8
1401 Ridgewood School Rd 63010 636-282-1459
Jamie Cavato, prin. Fax 282-5193
Other Schools – See Barnhart, Imperial

---

ITT Technical Institute Post-Sec.
1930 Meyer Drury Dr 63010 636-464-6600
Metro Business College Post-Sec.
2132 Tenbrook Rd 63010 636-296-9300

**Ash Grove, Greene, Pop. 1,452**
Ash Grove R-IV SD 600/PK-12
100 N Maple Ln 65604 417-751-2534
Dr. Kyle Collins, supt. Fax 751-2283
www.ashgrove.k12.mo.us
Ash Grove JSHS 400/7-12
100 N Maple Ln 65604 417-751-2330
Christopher Thompson, prin. Fax 751-2889

**Ashland, Boone, Pop. 3,660**
Southern Boone County R-I SD 1,500/PK-12
PO Box 168 65010 573-657-2147
Christopher Felmlee, supt. Fax 657-5513
ashland.k12.mo.us
Southern Boone County HS 500/9-12
PO Box 168 65010 573-657-2144
Dale Van Deven, prin. Fax 657-9035
Southern Boone County MS 300/6-8
PO Box 168 65010 573-657-2146
Kevin Kiley, prin. Fax 657-5519

**Atlanta, Macon, Pop. 377**
Atlanta C-3 SD 200/K-12
600 S Atterberry St 63530 660-239-4212
William Perkins, supt. Fax 239-4205
www.atlanta.k12.mo.us/
Atlanta JSHS 100/7-12
600 S Atterberry St 63530 660-239-4211
Josh Brummit, prin. Fax 239-4205

**Aurora, Lawrence, Pop. 7,398**
Aurora R-VIII SD 2,100/PK-12
409 W Locust St 65605 417-678-3373
Dr. Travis Shaw, supt. Fax 678-4043
www.aurorar8.org
Aurora HS 600/9-12
305 W Prospect St 65605 417-678-3355
Kevin Kultgen, prin. Fax 678-2905
Aurora JHS 300/7-8
500 W Olive St 65605 417-678-3630
Dr. Allison Murphy-Pope, prin. Fax 678-2487

**Ava, Douglas, Pop. 2,954**
Ava R-I SD 1,400/PK-12
PO Box 338 65608 417-683-4717
Dr. Nancy Lawler, supt. Fax 683-6329
www.avaschools.k12.mo.us/
Ava HS 500/9-12
PO Box 338 65608 417-683-5747
Teresa Nash, prin. Fax 683-2306
Ava MS 400/5-8
PO Box 338 65608 417-683-3835
Aaron Dalton, prin. Fax 683-9101

---

Ava Victory Academy 100/PK-12
PO Box 608 65608 417-683-6630

**Bakersfield, Ozark, Pop. 240**
Bakersfield R-IV SD 400/PK-12
PO Box 38 65609 417-284-7333
Dr. Amy Britt, supt. Fax 284-7335
www.bakersfield.k12.mo.us
Bakersfield JSHS 200/6-12
PO Box 38 65609 417-284-7333
Troy Wiesner, prin. Fax 284-7335

**Ballwin, Saint Louis, Pop. 29,903**
Parkway C-2 SD
Supt. — See Chesterfield
Parkway South HS 1,900/9-12
801 Hanna Rd 63021 314-415-7700
Dr. Patrice Aitch, prin. Fax 415-7712
Parkway West HS 1,200/9-12
14653 Clayton Rd 63011 314-415-7500
Dr. Jeremy Mitchell, prin. Fax 415-7534

Rockwood R-VI SD
Supt. — See Eureka
Crestview MS 1,200/6-8
16025 Clayton Rd 63011 636-207-2520
Dr. Nisha Patel, prin. Fax 207-2529
Lafayette HS 2,000/9-12
17050 Clayton Rd 63011 636-733-4100
John Shaughnessy, prin. Fax 458-7219
Selvidge MS 700/6-8
235 New Ballwin Rd 63021 636-207-2622
Dr. Michael Anselmo, prin. Fax 207-2632

---

Grabber School of Hair Design Post-Sec.
14557 Manchester Rd 63011 636-227-4440

**Barnard, Nodaway, Pop. 221**
South Nodaway County R-IV SD 200/PK-12
209 Morehouse St 64423 660-652-3221
Johnnie Silkett, supt. Fax 652-3411
www.southnodaway.k12.mo.us/
South Nodaway JSHS 100/7-12
209 Morehouse St 64423 660-652-3727
Ethan Sickles, prin. Fax 652-3411

**Barnhart, Jefferson, Pop. 5,631**
Fox C-6 SD
Supt. — See Arnold
Antonia MS 6-8
6798 Saint Lukes Church Rd 63012 636-282-6970
Joe Willis, prin. Fax 282-6971

**Bell City, Stoddard, Pop. 438**
Bell City R-II SD 200/K-12
25254 Walnut St 63735 573-733-4444
Matthew Asher, supt. Fax 733-4114
www.bellcity.k12.mo.us/
Bell City JSHS 100/7-12
25254 Walnut St 63735 573-733-4444
Lincoln Scherer, prin. Fax 733-4114

**Belle, Maries, Pop. 1,518**
Maries County R-II SD 800/K-12
PO Box 819 65013 573-859-3800
Dr. Patrick Call, supt. Fax 859-3883
www.mariesr2.org
Belle HS 200/9-12
PO Box 819 65013 573-859-6114
Danielle Tuepker, prin. Fax 859-6122
Other Schools – See Bland

**Belton, Cass, Pop. 22,497**
Belton SD 124 5,100/PK-12
110 W Walnut St 64012 816-489-7000
Dr. Andrew Underwood, supt. Fax 489-7005
www.beltonschools.org
Belton HS 1,000/10-12
801 W North Ave 64012 816-489-7500
Dr. Fred Skretta, prin. Fax 489-7505
Belton MS/Freshman Center 700/7-9
107 Pirate Pkwy 64012 816-348-1040
Dr. Jean Selby, prin. Fax 348-1595

---

Heartland Christian S 100/PK-12
810 S Cedar St 64012 816-331-1000
Claire Baker, prin. Fax 322-2782

**Benton, Scott, Pop. 855**
Scott County R-IV SD 1,000/PK-12
4035 State Highway 77 63736 573-545-3541
Fara Jones, supt. Fax 545-3929
sites.google.com/a/kellyhawks.org/kellyhawks
Kelly HS 300/9-12
4035 State Highway 77 63736 573-545-3541
Dan Hecht, prin. Fax 545-4485
Scott County MS 200/6-8
4035 State Highway 77 63736 573-545-3541
Kari Bickings, prin. Fax 545-4386

**Berkeley, Saint Louis, Pop. 8,830**
Ferguson-Florissant R-II SD
Supt. — See Florissant
Berkeley MS 300/7-8
8300 Frost Ave 63134 314-524-3883
Sharleta Williams, prin. Fax 524-3885

---

Vatterott College - NorthPark Post-Sec.
8580 Evans Ave 63134 314-264-1000

**Bernie, Stoddard, Pop. 1,930**
Bernie R-XIII SD 500/PK-12
516 W Main Ave 63822 573-293-5333
Doug Ruck, supt. Fax 293-5731
www.bernie.k12.mo.us
Bernie JSHS 300/7-12
516 W Main Ave 63822 573-293-5334
Miller Gavin, prin. Fax 293-6124

**Bethany, Harrison, Pop. 3,262**
South Harrison County R-II SD 900/PK-12
PO Box 445 64424 660-425-8044
Dennis Eastin, supt. Fax 425-7050
www.shr2.k12.mo.us
North Central Career Center Vo/Tech
PO Box 445 64424 660-425-2196
Billy Pottorff, dir. Fax 425-2197
South Harrison County R-II HS 300/9-12
PO Box 445 64424 660-425-8051
Mark Forster, prin. Fax 425-7447
South Harrison County R-II MS 6-8
PO Box 445 64424 660-425-8051
Shane Jones, prin. Fax 425-7447

**Bevier, Macon, Pop. 711**
Bevier C-4 SD 200/K-12
400 Bloomington St 63532 660-773-6611
Joan Patrick, supt. Fax 773-6955
bevierc-4.com
Bevier HS 100/9-12
400 Bloomington St 63532 660-773-5213
Jason Martie, prin. Fax 773-6964

**Billings, Christian, Pop. 1,023**
Billings R-IV SD 400/PK-12
118 W Mount Vernon Rd 65610 417-744-2623
Cynthia Brandt, supt. Fax 744-4545
www.billings.k12.mo.us
Billings HS 200/7-12
118 W Mount Vernon Rd 65610 417-744-2551
Roger Cavener, prin. Fax 744-4545

**Bismarck, Saint Francois, Pop. 1,531**
Bismarck R-V SD 600/PK-12
PO Box 257 63624 573-734-6111
Charles Hasty, supt. Fax 734-2957
www.bismarckr5.org
Bismarck JSHS 200/6-12
PO Box 257 63624 573-734-6111
Jason King, prin. Fax 734-2957

**Black, Reynolds**
Lesterville R-IV SD
Supt. — See Lesterville
Lesterville Ranch Campus 50/Alt
525 County Road 816 63625 573-269-4207
Mary Balderas, prin. Fax 269-4277

**Bland, Gasconade, Pop. 534**
Maries County R-II SD
Supt. — See Belle
Maries County MS 200/5-8
PO Box 10 65014 573-646-3912
Kristin Williams, prin. Fax 646-3148

**Bloomfield, Stoddard, Pop. 1,925**
Bloomfield R-XIV SD 700/PK-12
505 Court St 63825 573-568-4564
Toni Hill, supt. Fax 568-4565
www.bps14.org
Bloomfield HS 200/9-12
505 Court St 63825 573-568-2146
Dustin Hicks, prin. Fax 568-2147
Bloomfield MS 200/6-8
505 Court St 63825 573-568-4283
Louis Bell, prin. Fax 568-4286

**Blue Eye, Stone, Pop. 163**
Blue Eye R-V SD 700/PK-12
PO Box 105 65611 417-779-5332
Dan Ray, supt. Fax 779-2151
www.blueeye.k12.mo.us
Blue Eye HS 200/9-12
PO Box 105 65611 417-779-5331
Ben Johnson, prin. Fax 779-2151
Blue Eye MS 200/5-8
PO Box 105 65611 417-779-4299
Craig Linson, prin. Fax 779-4526

**Blue Springs, Jackson, Pop. 51,123**
Blue Springs R-IV SD 14,100/K-12
1801 NW Vesper St 64015 816-224-1300
Dr. James Finley, supt. Fax 224-1310
www.bssd.net
Blue Springs Freshman Center 1,200/9-9
2103 NW Vesper St 64015 816-224-1325
Brandon Martin, prin. Fax 224-1344
Blue Springs HS 1,700/10-12
2000 NW Ashton Dr 64015 816-229-3459
Robert Jerome, prin. Fax 229-1025
Blue Springs South HS 1,400/10-12
1200 SE Adams Dairy Pkwy 64014 816-224-1315
Dr. Charles Belt, prin. Fax 224-1324
Brittany Hill MS 800/6-8
2701 NW 1st St 64014 816-224-1700
Dallas Truex, prin. Fax 224-1704
Kinder MS 800/6-8
3930 S R D Mize Rd 64015 816-224-1330
Steve Goddard, prin. Fax 224-1309
Moreland Ridge MS 1,000/6-8
900 SW Bishop Dr 64015 816-224-1800
Kevin Grover, prin. Fax 224-1805
Valley View HS Alt
5000 NW Valley View Rd 64015 816-224-4388
Charles Weber, prin. Fax 224-1374
Other Schools – See Lees Summit

---

House of Heavilin Beauty College Post-Sec.
2000 SW State Route 7 64014 816-229-9000
Plaza Heights Christian Academy 200/PK-12
1500 SW Clark Rd 64015 816-228-0670
Chuck Lawson, admin. Fax 229-4092

**Bolivar, Polk, Pop. 10,153**
Bolivar R-I SD 2,900/PK-12
524 W Madison St 65613 417-326-5291
Dr. Jason Dial, supt. Fax 326-3562
www.bolivarschools.org
Bolivar HS 800/9-12
1401 Highway D 65613 417-326-5228
Dr. David Geurin, prin. Fax 326-4325
Bolivar MS 600/6-8
604 W Jackson St 65613 417-326-3811
Dr. Shane Dublin, prin. Fax 326-8277

---

Bolivar Technical College Post-Sec.
2001 W Broadway St Ste 2 65613 417-777-5062
Southwest Baptist University Post-Sec.
1600 University Ave 65613 417-328-5281

**Bonne Terre, Saint Francois, Pop. 6,797**
North St. Francois County R-I SD 3,200/PK-12
300 Berry Rd 63628 573-431-3300
Dr. Yancy Poorman, supt. Fax 358-2377
www.ncsd.k12.mo.us/
North St. Francois County HS 900/9-12
7151 Raider Rd 63628 573-431-3300
Lance Sprenkel, prin. Fax 358-0021
Unitec Career Center Vo/Tech
7163 Raider Rd 63628 573-358-2271
Larry Kekec, dir. Fax 358-3577
Other Schools – See Desloge

**Boonville, Cooper, Pop. 8,135**
Boonville R-I SD 1,500/K-12
736 Main St 65233 660-882-7474
Mark Ficken, supt. Fax 882-5721
www.boonville.k12.mo.us/
Boonslick Technical Education Center Vo/Tech
1694 W Ashley Rd 65233 660-882-5306
Cody Bashore, dir. Fax 882-3269
Boonville HS 500/9-12
1690 W Ashley Rd 65233 660-882-7426
Timothy Edwards, prin. Fax 882-3368
Elliott MS 300/6-8
700 Main St 65233 660-882-6649
Frederick Smith, prin. Fax 882-8646

**Bosworth, Carroll, Pop. 302**
Bosworth R-V SD 100/PK-12
102 E Eldridge St 64623 660-534-7311
Lachrissa Smith, supt. Fax 534-7409
www.bosworthr-v.k12.mo.us/
Bosworth JSHS 50/7-12
102 E Eldridge St 64623 660-534-7311
Natalie Ikenberry, prin. Fax 534-7409

**Bourbon, Crawford, Pop. 1,624**
Crawford County R-I SD 1,000/PK-12
1444 S Old Highway 66 65441 573-732-4426
Patricia Thompson, supt. Fax 732-4545
www.warhawks.k12.mo.us
Bourbon HS 300/9-12
1500 S Old Highway 66 65441 573-732-5615
Dena Smith, prin. Fax 732-4407
Bourbon MS 300/5-8
363 Jost St 65441 573-732-4424
Brian Witt, prin. Fax 732-4425

**Bowling Green, Pike, Pop. 5,265**
Bowling Green R-I SD 1,300/K-12
700 W Adams St 63334 573-324-5441
J.W. Brandt, supt. Fax 324-2439
www.bgschools.k12.mo.us
Bowling Green HS 400/9-12
700 W Adams St 63334 573-324-5341
Brock Bailey, prin. Fax 324-3011
Bowling Green MS 300/6-8
700 W Adams St 63334 573-324-2181
Kimberlee Pafford, prin. Fax 324-3292

**Bradleyville, Taney, Pop. 84**
Bradleyville R-I SD 200/PK-12
PO Box 20 65614 417-796-2288
Joe Combs Ed.D., supt. Fax 796-2289
Bradleyville JSHS 100/7-12
PO Box 20 65614 417-796-2288
Scott Ewing M.Ed., prin. Fax 796-2289

**Branson, Taney, Pop. 10,302**
Branson R-IV SD 4,400/PK-12
1756 Bee Creek Rd 65616 417-334-6541
Dr. Doug Hayter, supt. Fax 332-2510
www.branson.k12.mo.us
Branson HS 1,400/9-12
935 Buchanan Rd 65616 417-334-6511
Chip Arnette, prin. Fax 335-4889
Branson JHS 700/7-8
263 Buccaneer Dr 65616 417-334-3087
Bryan Bronn, prin. Fax 336-3913

**Brashear, Adair, Pop. 264**
Adair County R-II SD 200/K-12
205 W Dewey St 63533 660-323-5272
Shelly Shipman, supt. Fax 323-5250
brashear.k12.mo.us
Adair County R-II HS 100/7-12
205 W Dewey St 63533 660-323-5272
Brent Doolin, prin. Fax 323-5250

**Braymer, Caldwell, Pop. 864**
Braymer C-4 SD 300/PK-12
400 Bobcat Ave 64624 660-645-2284
Don Regan, supt. Fax 645-2780
www.braymerbobcats.org
Braymer JSHS 100/7-12
400 Bobcat Ave 64624 660-645-2284
Mitchel Barnes, prin. Fax 645-2780

**Breckenridge, Caldwell, Pop. 364**
Breckenridge R-I SD 100/PK-12
400 W Colfax St 64625 660-644-5715
Brent Skinner, supt. Fax 644-5710
Breckenridge HS 50/7-12
400 W Colfax St 64625 660-644-5715
Brent Skinner, prin. Fax 644-5710

**Brentwood, Saint Louis, Pop. 7,905**
Brentwood SD 800/PK-12
1201 Hanley Industrial Ct 63144 314-962-4507
David Faulkner, supt. Fax 962-7302
www.brentwoodmoschools.org
Brentwood HS 200/9-12
2221 High School Dr 63144 314-962-3837
Dr. Edward M. Johnson, prin. Fax 963-3166
Brentwood MS 200/6-8
9127 White Ave 63144 314-962-8238
Dr. Andrew Loiterstein, prin. Fax 968-8724

---

Missouri College Post-Sec.
1405 S Hanley Rd 63144 314-768-7800

**Brighton, Polk**
Pleasant Hope R-VI SD
Supt. — See Pleasant Hope
Pleasant Hope Ranch S 100/4-12
5545 N Highway 13 65617 417-376-3000
Gloria Bailey, dir. Fax 376-3575

**Bronaugh, Vernon, Pop. 241**
Bronaugh R-VII SD 200/PK-12
527 E 6th St 64728 417-922-3211
Dr. David Copeland, supt. Fax 922-3308
www.bronaughschools.net
Bronaugh JSHS 100/7-12
527 E 6th St 64728 417-922-3211
Jordan Dickey, prin. Fax 922-3308

**Brookfield, Linn, Pop. 4,463**
Brookfield R-III SD 1,100/PK-12
124A N Pershing Dr 64628 660-258-7443
Dr. Paul Barger, supt. Fax 258-4711
www.brookfield.k12.mo.us
Brookfield HS 300/9-12
124 N Pershing Dr 64628 660-258-7242
Vicki Enyart, prin. Fax 258-2871
Brookfield MS 300/5-8
126 N Pershing Dr 64628 660-258-7335
Melinda Wilbeck, prin. Fax 258-2190
Linn County Area Career Tech Center Vo/Tech
122 N Pershing Dr 64628 660-258-2682
Carey Smith, dir. Fax 258-3875

**Broseley, Butler**
Twin Rivers R-X SD 1,000/K-12
PO Box 146 63932 573-328-4321
Jeremy Siebert, supt. Fax 328-1070
www.tr10.us
Twin Rivers HS 300/9-12
PO Box 146 63932 573-328-4730
Misty Lovelace, prin. Fax 328-1511

**Brunswick, Chariton, Pop. 841**
Brunswick R-II SD 300/PK-12
1008 County Rd 65236 660-548-3550
Robert Kottman, supt. Fax 548-3029
www.brunswick.k12.mo.us
Brunswick JSHS 100/7-12
1008 County Rd 65236 660-548-3771
Cara Engelbrecht, prin. Fax 548-3072

**Bucklin, Linn, Pop. 465**
Bucklin R-II SD 100/PK-12
26832 Highway 129 64631 660-695-3555
Stephen Coulson, supt. Fax 695-3345
www.bucklin.k12.mo.us/
Bucklin R-II S 100/PK-12
26832 Highway 129 64631 660-695-3225
Nicole Head, prin. Fax 695-3345

**Buffalo, Dallas, Pop. 3,038**
Dallas County R-I SD 1,800/K-12
309 W Commercial St 65622 417-345-2222
Dr. Tim Ryan, supt. Fax 345-8446
www.bisonpride.us
Buffalo HS 600/9-12
500 W Main St 65622 417-345-2223
Teresa Mabary, prin. Fax 345-8495

Buffalo MS 500/5-8
926 Truman Rd 65622 417-345-2335
Jeremie akins, prin. Fax 345-5968
Other Schools – See Louisburg

**Bunceton, Cooper, Pop. 348**
Cooper County R-IV SD 200/K-12
500 E Main St 65237 660-427-5347
John Thompson, supt. Fax 427-5348
www.bunceton.k12.mo.us
Bunceton JSHS 100/7-12
500 E Main St 65237 660-427-5415
Chris Kendrick, prin. Fax 427-5348

**Bunker, Reynolds, Pop. 405**
Bunker R-III SD 300/K-12
PO Box 365 63629 573-689-2507
John Eaton, supt. Fax 689-1268
www.bunkerr3.k12.mo.us/
Bunker JSHS 100/7-12
PO Box 365 63629 573-689-2211
Rob Harlow, prin. Fax 689-2011

**Burlington Junction, Nodaway, Pop. 533**
West Nodaway R-I SD 200/PK-12
PO Box 260 64428 660-725-4613
Nancy Greeley, supt. Fax 725-4300
www.wnrockets.com/
West Nodaway JSHS 100/6-12
PO Box 260 64428 660-725-3317
Shannon Nolte, prin. Fax 725-4300

**Butler, Bates, Pop. 4,155**
Ballard R-II SD 200/K-12
10247 NE State Route 18 64730 816-297-2656
John Siebeneck, supt. Fax 297-4002
www.ballardr2.net
Ballard JSHS 100/7-12
10247 NE State Route 18 64730 816-297-2656
Samie Hill, prin. Fax 297-4002

Butler R-V SD 1,000/PK-12
420 S Fulton St 64730 660-679-0653
Darin Carter, supt. Fax 200-3010
www.butlerr5.org/
Butler JSHS 400/7-12
420 S Fulton St 64730 660-679-6121
Heath Oates, prin. Fax 679-4378

**Cabool, Texas, Pop. 2,104**
Cabool R-IV SD 800/PK-12
1025 Rogers Ave 65689 417-962-3153
Dr. Wesley Davis, supt. Fax 962-5043
www.cabool.k12.mo.us
Cabool HS 200/9-12
1025 Rogers Ave 65689 417-962-3153
Brad Shockley, prin. Fax 962-5663
Cabool MS 200/5-8
1025 Rogers Ave 65689 417-962-3153
Cheryl Manning, prin. Fax 962-5043

**Cadet, Washington**
Kingston SD K-14 700/K-12
10047 Diamond Rd 63630 573-438-4982
Alex McCaul, supt. Fax 438-8813
www.kingston.k12.mo.us
Kingston HS 200/9-12
10047 Diamond Rd 63630 573-438-4982
Bryce Wilson, prin. Fax 438-1212
Kingston MS 200/6-8
10047 Diamond Rd 63630 573-438-4982
Bryce Wilson, prin. Fax 438-1212

**Cainsville, Harrison, Pop. 285**
Cainsville R-I SD 100/PK-12
PO Box 108 64632 660-893-5213
Richard Smith, supt. Fax 893-5713
cainsville.k12.mo.us
Cainsville JSHS 50/7-12
PO Box 108 64632 660-893-5214
Kristi Reeder, prin. Fax 893-5713

**Cairo, Randolph, Pop. 287**
Northeast Randolph County R-IV SD 400/PK-12
301 W Martin St 65239 660-263-2788
Darren Rapert, supt. Fax 263-5735
www.ner4schools.org
Northeast JSHS 200/6-12
301 W Martin St 65239 660-263-2788
Greg Taylor, prin. Fax 263-5735

**Caledonia, Washington, Pop. 130**
Valley R-VI SD 300/K-12
1 Viking Dr 63631 573-779-3446
Brad Crocker, supt. Fax 779-3505
www.valleyschooldistrict.org
Valley JSHS 200/7-12
1 Viking Dr 63631 573-779-3515
Michael Silvy, prin. Fax 779-3346

**Calhoun, Henry, Pop. 463**
Calhoun R-VIII SD 100/K-12
409 S College St 65323 660-694-3422
Gene Hay, supt. Fax 694-3501
calhoun.k12.mo.us
Calhoun JSHS 100/7-12
409 S College St 65323 660-694-3412
Scott Calhoun, prin. Fax 694-3941

**California, Moniteau, Pop. 4,221**
Moniteau County R-I SD 1,300/PK-12
211 S Owen St Ste B 65018 573-796-2145
Dwight Sanders, supt. Fax 796-6123
www.californiak12.org/
California HS 400/9-12
1501 W Buchanan St 65018 573-796-4911
Sean Kirksey, prin. Fax 796-4503
California MS 300/6-8
211 S Owen St 65018 573-796-2146
Matt Abernathy, prin. Fax 796-8257

**Camdenton, Camden, Pop. 3,647**
Camdenton R-III SD 4,300/PK-12
PO Box 1409 65020 573-346-9213
Dr. Tim Hadfield, supt. Fax 346-9211
camdentonschools.schoolwires.net/
Camdenton HS 1,400/9-12
PO Box 1409 65020 573-346-9232
Brett Thompson, prin. Fax 346-9238
Camdenton MS 600/7-8
PO Box 1409 65020 573-346-9257
Dr. Paula Brown, prin. Fax 346-9288
Lake Career & Technical Center Vo/Tech
PO Box 1409 65020 573-346-9260
Jackie Jenkins, dir. Fax 346-9284

**Cameron, Clinton, Pop. 9,834**
Cameron R-I SD 1,800/PK-12
423 N Chestnut St 64429 816-632-2170
Dr. Matt Robinson, supt. Fax 632-2612
www.cameron.k12.mo.us
Cameron HS 500/9-12
1022 S Chestnut St 64429 816-632-2129
Wiegers Mark, prin. Fax 632-1634
Cameron Veterans MS 500/6-8
1015 S Park 64429 816-632-2185
Jay Albright, prin. Fax 632-3752

**Campbell, Dunklin, Pop. 1,968**
Campbell R-II SD 600/PK-12
801 S State Highway 53 63933 573-246-2133
Jay Thornton, supt. Fax 246-3212
www.campbell.k12.mo.us
Campbell JSHS 300/7-12
801 S State Highway 53 63933 573-246-2576
Daren Ellsworth, prin. Fax 246-2890

**Canton, Lewis, Pop. 2,342**
Canton R-V SD 500/PK-12
200 S 4th St 63435 573-288-5216
W.A. Anderson, supt. Fax 288-5442
www.canton.k12.mo.us
Canton JSHS 200/7-12
200 S 4th St 63435 573-288-5216
Jesse Uhlmeyer, prin. Fax 288-5442

---

Culver-Stockton College Post-Sec.
1 College Hl 63435 573-288-6000

**Cape Girardeau, Cape Girardeau, Pop. 37,082**
Cape Girardeau SD 63 4,200/PK-12
301 N Clark St 63701 573-335-1867
Dr. James Welker, supt. Fax 335-1820
www.capetigers.com
Cape Girardeau Career & Technology Ctr Vo/Tech
1080 S Silver Springs Rd 63703 573-334-0826
Rich Payne, dir. Fax 334-5930
Central Academy Alt
301 N Spring St 63701 573-335-5939
Scott McMullen, admin. Fax 335-6041
Central HS 1,200/9-12
1000 S Silver Springs Rd 63703 573-335-8228
Chris Kase, prin. Fax 334-1114
Central JHS 600/7-8
205 Caruthers St 63701 573-334-2923
Carla Fee, prin. Fax 332-8746

---

Cape Girardeau Career & Technical School Post-Sec.
1080 S Silver Springs Rd 63703 573-334-0826
Eagle Ridge Christian S 100/PK-12
4210 State Highway K 63701 573-339-1335
Janice Margrabe, admin. Fax 339-1390
Metro Business College Post-Sec.
1732 N Kings Highway St 63701 573-334-9181
Notre Dame Regional HS 600/9-12
265 Notre Dame Dr 63701 573-335-6772
Br. David Migliorino, prin. Fax 335-3458
Southeast Hospital College of Nursing Post-Sec.
2001 William St # 2 63703 573-334-6825
Southeast Missouri State University Post-Sec.
1 University Plz 63701 573-651-2000

**Cardwell, Dunklin, Pop. 704**
Southland C-9 SD 400/PK-12
500 S Main St 63829 573-654-3574
Kim Campbell, supt. Fax 654-3575
southland.k12.mo.us
Southland JSHS 100/7-12
500 S Main St 63829 573-654-3531
Johnny McMinn, prin. Fax 654-3534

**Carl Junction, Jasper, Pop. 7,264**
Carl Junction R-I SD 3,400/PK-12
206 S Roney St 64834 417-649-7026
Dr. Phillip Cook, supt. Fax 649-6594
www.cjr1.org
Carl Junction HS 900/9-12
206 S Roney St 64834 417-649-7081
David Pyle, prin. Fax 649-5791
Carl Junction JHS 500/7-8
206 S Roney St 64834 417-649-7246
Scott Sawyer, prin. Fax 649-0022
Carl Junction Satellite 50/Alt
206 S Roney St 64834 417-347-7895
Cindy Jackson, dir. Fax 649-7895

**Carrollton, Carroll, Pop. 3,737**
Carrollton R-VII SD 1,000/PK-12
103 E 9th St 64633 660-542-2769
Dr. Jon Oetinger, supt. Fax 542-3416
www.trojans.k12.mo.us/
Carrollton Area Career Center Vo/Tech
305 E 10th St 64633 660-542-0000
David Reinke, dir. Fax 542-0600
Carrollton HS 300/9-12
300 E 9th St 64633 660-542-1276
Todd Park, prin. Fax 542-1903
Carrollton MS 300/5-8
300 E 9th St 64633 660-542-3472
Brent Dobbins, prin. Fax 542-3169

**Carthage, Jasper, Pop. 14,047**
Carthage R-IX SD 4,500/PK-12
710 Lyon St 64836 417-359-7000
Dr. Sean Smith, supt. Fax 359-7004
www.carthagetigers.org
Carthage HS 1,200/9-12
2600 S River St 64836 417-359-7020
Matt Huntley, prin. Fax 359-7037
Carthage JHS 600/7-8
714 S Main St 64836 417-359-7050
Jenny Bogle, prin. Fax 359-7057
Carthage Technical Center North Campus Vo/Tech
609 S River St 64836 417-359-7095
Gregg Wolf, dir. Fax 359-7419
Carthage Technical Center South Campus Vo/Tech
1100 E Airport Dr 64836 417-359-7026
Wolf Gregg, dir. Fax 359-7098

**Caruthersville, Pemiscot, Pop. 6,073**
Caruthersville SD 18 1,300/PK-12
1711 Ward Ave 63830 573-333-6100
J.J. Bullington, supt. Fax 333-6108
www.cps18.org
Caruthersville HS 300/9-12
1708 Ward Ave 63830 573-333-6110
Dr. Roger Alsup, prin. Fax 333-6117
Caruthersville MS 300/6-8
1705 Ward Ave 63830 573-333-6120
Stephanie McGraw, prin. Fax 333-1835

**Cassville, Barry, Pop. 3,224**
Cassville R-IV SD 1,900/PK-12
1501 Main St 65625 417-847-2221
Dr. Richard Asbill, supt. Fax 847-4009
cassville.k12.mo.us/
Cassville HS 600/9-12
1501 Main St 65625 417-847-3137
Jeff Swadley, prin. Fax 847-5111
Cassville MS 400/6-8
1501 Main St 65625 417-847-3136
Jimmie Barton, prin. Fax 847-3156

**Cedar Hill, Jefferson, Pop. 1,703**
Northwest R-I SD
Supt. — See High Ridge
Northwest HS 2,100/9-12
6005 Cedar Hill Rd 63016 636-274-0555
Brad Snell, prin. Fax 274-2076

**Center, Ralls, Pop. 502**
Ralls County R-II SD 700/PK-12
21622 Highway 19 63436 573-267-3397
Deanette Jarman, supt. Fax 267-3538
rallsr2.k12.mo.us/
Twain HS 200/9-12
21622 Highway 19 63436 573-267-3397
Mike Boedeker, prin. Fax 267-3538
Twain JHS 200/6-8
21622 Highway 19 63436 573-267-3397
Delores Woodhurst, prin. Fax 267-3538

**Centerview, Johnson, Pop. 266**
Johnson County R-VII SD 600/PK-12
92 NW State Route 58 64019 660-656-3316
Dr. Julie Dill, supt. Fax 656-3633
www.crestridge.org
Crest Ridge HS 200/7-12
92 NW State Route 58 64019 660-656-3391
Marlon Dyer, prin. Fax 656-3633

**Centralia, Boone, Pop. 3,976**
Centralia R-VI SD 1,400/PK-12
1399 E Highway 22 Ste B 65240 573-682-3561
Darin Ford, supt. Fax 682-2181
www.centralia.k12.mo.us
Boren MS 300/6-8
110 N Jefferson St 65240 573-682-2617
Vincent Matlick, prin. Fax 682-1500
Centralia HS 400/9-12
849 S Jefferson St 65240 573-682-3508
Matt Smith, prin. Fax 682-2749

---

Sunnydale Adventist Academy 100/9-12
6818 Audrain Road 9139 65240 573-682-2164

**Chadwick, Christian**
Chadwick R-I SD 200/PK-12
PO Box 274 65629 417-634-3588
Dana Comstock, supt. Fax 634-2668
www.chadwick.k12.mo.us/
Chadwick JSHS 100/7-12
PO Box 274 65629 417-634-3588
David Aldrich, contact Fax 634-4040

**Chaffee, Scott, Pop. 2,925**
Chaffee R-II SD 600/PK-12
517 W Yoakum Ave 63740 573-887-3532
Ken Latham, supt. Fax 887-3926
chaffee.k12.mo.us
Chaffee JSHS 300/7-12
517 W Yoakum Ave 63740 573-887-3226
Brad Blackman, prin. Fax 887-3926

**Chamois, Osage, Pop. 395**
Osage County R-I SD 200/K-12
614 S Poplar St 65024 573-763-5666
Michael Bumgarner, supt. Fax 763-5686
www.chamois.k12.mo.us
Chamois JSHS 100/7-12
614 S Poplar St 65024 573-763-5393
Bradley Strobel, prin. Fax 763-5686

**Charleston, Mississippi, Pop. 5,882**
Charleston R-I SD 1,000/PK-12
PO Box 39 63834 573-683-3776
Tony Watkins, supt. Fax 683-2909
charleston.k12.mo.us
Charleston HS 300/9-12
PO Box 39 63834 573-683-3761
Kathy Browning, prin. Fax 683-2907

Charleston MS 200/6-8
PO Box 39 63834 573-683-3346
Sarah Spain, prin. Fax 683-2930

**Chesterfield, Saint Louis, Pop. 46,860**
Parkway C-2 SD 17,400/PK-12
455 N Woods Mill Rd 63017 314-415-8100
Dr. Keith Marty, supt. Fax 415-8009
www.parkwayschools.net
Parkway Central HS 1,300/9-12
369 N Woods Mill Rd 63017 314-415-7900
Tim McCarthy, prin. Fax 415-7913
Parkway Central MS 900/6-8
471 N Woods Mill Rd 63017 314-415-7800
Dr. Michael Baugus, prin. Fax 415-7834
Parkway West MS 900/6-8
2312 Baxter Rd 63017 314-415-7400
Anne Miller, prin. Fax 415-7409
Other Schools – See Ballwin, Creve Coeur, Manchester

Rockwood R-VI SD
Supt. — See Eureka
Marquette HS 2,200/9-12
2351 Clarkson Rd 63017 636-891-6000
Dr. Greg Mathison, prin. Fax 537-4319

---

Barat Academy 200/9-12
17815 Wild Horse Creek Rd 63005 636-300-5500
Debra Watson, pres. Fax 300-5501
Logan College of Chiropractic Post-Sec.
1851 Schoettler Rd 63017 800-533-9210
Missouri Torah Institute 50/9-12
1809 Clarkson Rd 63017 636-778-1897
Rabbi Dovid Goldman, prin. Fax 778-1899
St. Joseph's Institute for the Deaf Post-Sec.
1809 Clarkson Rd 63017 636-532-3211
Westminster Christian Academy 900/7-12
800 Maryville Centre Dr 63017 314-997-2900
Dr. Thomas Stoner, head sch Fax 997-2903

**Chilhowee, Johnson, Pop. 315**
Chilhowee R-IV SD 100/PK-12
101 Highway 2 64733 660-678-2511
Troy Marnholtz, supt. Fax 678-5711
www.chilhowee.k12.mo.us
Chilhowee JSHS 100/7-12
101 Highway 2 64733 660-678-4511
Jennifer Corson, prin. Fax 678-5711

**Chillicothe, Livingston, Pop. 9,375**
Chillicothe R-II SD 1,900/K-12
PO Box 530 64601 660-646-4566
Dr. Roger Barnes, supt. Fax 646-6508
www.chillicotheschools.org/
Chillicothe HS 600/9-12
2801 Hornet Rd 64601 660-646-0700
Brian Sherrow, prin. Fax 646-7106
Chillicothe MS 400/6-8
1529 Calhoun St 64601 660-646-1916
Steve Haley, prin. Fax 646-5065
Grand River Tech S Vo/Tech
1200 Fair St 64601 660-646-3414
Jayme Caughron, prin. Fax 646-3568

---

Chillicothe Beauty Academy Post-Sec.
505 Elm St 64601 660-646-4198

**Clarksville, Pike, Pop. 436**
Pike County R-III SD 500/PK-12
28176 Highway WW 63336 573-242-3546
Mark Harvey, supt. Fax 485-2393
www.cloptonhawks.com
Clopton JSHS 200/7-12
28176 Highway WW 63336 573-242-3546
Larry Lagemann, prin. Fax 485-2393
Other Schools – See Eolia

**Clarkton, Dunklin, Pop. 1,265**
Clarkton C-4 SD 300/PK-12
PO Box 637 63837 573-448-3712
Delane Beckwith, supt. Fax 448-5182
www.clarktonschools.org/
Clarkton JSHS 100/7-12
PO Box 637 63837 573-448-3712
Paul Lynch, prin. Fax 448-3226

**Clayton, Saint Louis, Pop. 15,572**
Clayton SD 2,800/PK-12
2 Mark Twain Cir 63105 314-854-6000
Dr. Sharmon Wilkinson, supt. Fax 854-6093
www.claytonschools.net
Clayton HS 800/9-12
1 Mark Twain Cir 63105 314-854-6600
Dr. Dan Gutchewsky, prin. Fax 854-6793
Wydown MS 600/6-8
6500 Wydown Blvd 63105 314-854-6400
Dr. Jamie Jordan, prin. Fax 854-6491

**Cleveland, Cass, Pop. 645**
Midway R-I SD 500/K-12
5801 E State Route 2 64734 816-250-2994
Gordon Myers, supt. Fax 899-2823
www.midwayk12.net
Midway JSHS 200/7-12
5801 E State Route 2 64734 816-250-2994
Doug Dahman, prin. Fax 899-2823

**Clever, Christian, Pop. 2,109**
Clever R-V SD 400/PK-12
103 S Public Ave 65631 417-743-4800
Steve Carvajal, supt. Fax 743-4802
www.clever.k12.mo.us
Clever HS 300/9-12
6800 State Highway 14 W 65631 417-743-4830
Robert Parker, prin. Fax 743-4832

**Clifton Hill, Randolph, Pop. 111**
Westran R-I SD
Supt. — See Huntsville
Westran MS 200/6-8
622 Harlan St 65244 660-261-4511
Mike Aulbur, prin. Fax 261-4292

**Climax Springs, Camden, Pop. 124**
Climax Springs R-IV SD 200/PK-12
119 Nort Dr 65324 573-347-3905
Nathan Barb, supt. Fax 347-9931
www.csprings.k12.mo.us
Climax Springs JSHS 100/7-12
119 Nort Dr 65324 573-347-2351
Mary Gerriets, prin. Fax 347-2394

**Clinton, Henry, Pop. 8,864**
Clinton SD 124 1,800/PK-12
701 S 8th St 64735 660-885-2237
Craig Eaton, supt. Fax 885-7033
clinton.k12.mo.us
Clinton HS 600/9-12
701 S 8th St 64735 660-885-2247
Dr. Bryan Pettengill, prin. Fax 885-2012
Clinton MS 400/6-8
701 S 8th St 64735 660-885-3353
Ashlee Holmes, prin. Fax 885-4826
Clinton Technical S Vo/Tech
701 S 8th St 64735 660-885-6101
Jacob Fowler, dir. Fax 885-6789

**Cole Camp, Benton, Pop. 1,108**
Cole Camp R-I SD 700/PK-12
500 S Keeney St 65325 660-668-4427
Dr. Tim Roling, supt. Fax 668-4703
colecamp.schoolwires.net
Cole Camp HS 200/9-12
500 S Keeney St 65325 660-668-3751
Brandon Harding, prin. Fax 668-4703
Cole Camp MS 200/5-8
500 S Keeney St 65325 660-668-3502
Tyler Clark, prin. Fax 668-4703

**Columbia, Boone, Pop. 105,254**
Columbia SD 93 16,200/PK-12
1818 W Worley St 65203 573-214-3400
Dr. Peter Stiepleman, supt. Fax 214-3401
www.cpsk12.org
Battle HS 9-12
7575 E Saint Charles Rd 65202 573-214-3300
Dr. Kim Presko, prin. Fax 214-3301
Columbia Area Career Ctr Vo/Tech
4203 S Providence Rd 65203 573-214-3800
Randy Gooch, dir. Fax 214-3801
Douglass HS 200/Alt
310 N Providence Rd 65203 573-214-3680
Dr. Eryca Neville, prin. Fax 214-3681
Gentry MS 800/6-8
4200 Bethel St 65203 573-214-3240
Dr. Jeff Beiswinger, prin. Fax 214-3241
Hickman HS 1,900/9-12
1104 N Providence Rd 65203 573-214-3000
Eric Johnson, prin. Fax 214-3057
Jefferson MS 400/6-8
713 Rogers St 65201 573-214-3210
Dr. Greg Caine, prin. Fax 214-3211
Lange MS 900/6-8
2201 Smiley Ln 65202 573-214-3250
Dr. Bernard Solomon, prin. Fax 214-3251
Oakland MS 400/6-8
3405 Oakland Pl 65202 573-214-3220
Helen Porter, prin. Fax 214-3221
Rock Bridge HS 1,800/9-12
4303 S Providence Rd 65203 573-214-3100
Dr. Jennifer Rukstad, prin. Fax 214-3109
Smithton MS 900/6-8
3600 W Worley St 65203 573-214-3260
Edward Schumaker, prin. Fax 214-3261
West MS 400/6-8
401 Clinkscales Rd 65203 573-214-3230
Dr. Connie Dewey, prin. Fax 214-3231

---

Bryan University Post-Sec.
3215 Lemone Industrial Blvd 65201 573-777-5550
Christian Fellowship S 300/PK-12
4600 Christian Fellowship 65203 573-445-8565
Dr. Rick Mueller, admin. Fax 445-8564
Columbia Beauty Academy Post-Sec.
503 E Nifong Blvd 65201 573-445-6611
Columbia College Post-Sec.
1001 Rogers St 65216 573-875-8700
Columbia Independent S 400/PK-12
1801 N Stadium Blvd 65202 573-777-9250
Adam Dube, head sch Fax 777-9251
Jerry's School of Hairstyling Post-Sec.
1001 Royal Birkdale Dr 65203 573-449-7527
Stephens College Post-Sec.
1200 E Broadway 65215 800-876-7207
Tolton HS 9-12
3351 E Gans Rd 65201 573-445-7700
Kristie Wolfe, prin. Fax 445-7703
University of Missouri Post-Sec.
228 Jesse Hall 65211 573-882-2121

**Conception, Nodaway, Pop. 209**

---

Conception Seminary College Post-Sec.
PO Box 502 64433 660-944-3105

**Conception Junction, Nodaway, Pop. 198**
Jefferson C-123 SD 200/PK-12
37614 US Highway 136 64434 660-944-2316
Tim Jermain, supt. Fax 944-2315
Jefferson JSHS 100/7-12
37614 US Highway 136 64434 660-944-2316
Tim Jermain, supt. Fax 944-2315

**Concordia, Lafayette, Pop. 2,425**
Concordia R-II SD 500/PK-12
PO Box 879 64020 660-463-7235
Mary Beth Scherer, supt. Fax 463-1326
www.concordia.k12.mo.us
Concordia JSHS 300/7-12
PO Box 879 64020 660-463-2246
Brandon Figg, prin. Fax 463-4081

---

St. Paul Lutheran HS 200/9-12
PO Box 719 64020 660-463-2238
Rev. Paul Mehl, dir. Fax 463-7621

**Conway, Laclede, Pop. 768**
Laclede County R-I SD 800/K-12
726 W Jefferson Ave 65632 417-589-2951
Dr. Tanya Vest, supt. Fax 589-3202
www.lacledecountyr1.com
Conway HS 300/7-12
726 W Jefferson Ave 65632 417-589-2941
Ricky Lowrance, prin. Fax 589-2500

**Cooter, Pemiscot, Pop. 468**
Cooter R-IV SD 300/K-12
PO Box 218 63839 573-695-3312
William Crowder, supt. Fax 695-3073
cooter.k12.mo.us
Cooter JSHS 200/7-12
PO Box 218 63839 573-695-4972
Clay Snider, prin. Fax 695-3073

**Cottleville, Saint Charles, Pop. 3,037**

---

Patsy & Rob's Academy of Beauty Post-Sec.
5065 Highway N 63304 636-447-0650
St. Charles Community College Post-Sec.
4601 Mid Rivers Mall Dr 63376 636-922-8000

**Craig, Holt, Pop. 248**
Craig R-III SD 50/K-12
402 N Ward St 64437 660-683-5351
Michael Leach, supt. Fax 683-5769
www.craigr3school.com
Craig R-III S 50/K-12
402 N Ward St 64437 660-683-5431
Ken Grove, prin. Fax 683-5769

**Crane, Stone, Pop. 1,443**
Crane R-III SD 500/PK-12
PO Box 405 65633 417-723-5300
Dr. Chris Johnson, supt. Fax 723-5551
www.crane.k12.mo.us
Crane HS 200/7-12
PO Box 405 65633 417-723-5300
Grant Stock, prin. Fax 723-8598

**Creighton, Cass, Pop. 347**
Sherwood Cass R-VIII SD 900/PK-12
PO Box 98 64739 660-499-2834
Dr. Tim Gallagher, supt. Fax 499-2624
sites.google.com/a/sherwoodk12.net/sherwood/home
Sherwood HS 300/9-12
PO Box 98 64739 660-499-2239
William Stackhouse, prin. Fax 499-2258
Sherwood MS 200/6-8
PO Box 98 64739 660-499-2239
Brenda Koch, prin. Fax 499-2585

**Creve Coeur, Saint Louis, Pop. 17,490**
Parkway C-2 SD
Supt. — See Chesterfield
Fern Ridge HS 100/Alt
13157 N Olive Spur Rd 63141 314-415-6900
Michelle Howren, coord. Fax 415-6912
Parkway Northeast MS 900/6-8
181 Coeur De Ville Dr 63141 314-415-7100
Kashina Bell, prin. Fax 415-7113
Parkway North HS 1,500/9-12
12860 Fee Fee Rd, Saint Louis MO 63146
314-415-7600
Dr. Jenny Marquart, prin. Fax 415-7614

**Crocker, Pulaski, Pop. 1,094**
Crocker R-II SD 600/PK-12
PO Box 488 65452 573-736-5000
Gary Doerhoff, supt. Fax 736-5924
www.crockerschools.org
Crocker JSHS 200/7-12
PO Box 488 65452 573-736-5000
Heath Waters, prin. Fax 736-2801

**Crystal City, Jefferson, Pop. 4,757**
Crystal City SD 47 700/K-12
1100 Mississippi Ave 63019 636-937-4411
Philip Harrison, supt. Fax 937-2512
www.crystal.k12.mo.us/
Crystal City HS 300/9-12
1100 Mississippi Ave 63019 636-937-2005
Matthew Holdinghausen, prin. Fax 937-2075

---

National Academy of Beauty Arts Post-Sec.
137 Twin City Mall 63019 636-931-7100

**Cuba, Crawford, Pop. 3,311**
Crawford County R-II SD 1,500/K-12
1 Wildcat Pride Dr 65453 573-885-2534
Johnny Thompson, supt. Fax 885-3900
www.cuba.k12.mo.us/
Cuba HS 400/9-12
1 Wildcat Pride Dr 65453 573-885-2534
Jonathan Earnhart, prin. Fax 885-7726
Cuba MS 400/5-8
1 Wildcat Pride Dr 65453 573-885-2534
Marie Shoemaker, prin. Fax 885-6278

**Curryville, Pike, Pop. 217**

---

Pike County Christian S 50/K-12
PO Box 96 63339 573-324-2700
Frank Welch, admin. Fax 324-2700

**Dadeville, Dade, Pop. 228**
Dadeville R-II SD | 100/K-12
PO Box 188 65635 | 417-995-2201
Matt Bushey, supt. | Fax 995-2110
bearcats.dadeville.k12.mo.us
Dadeville JSHS | 100/6-12
PO Box 188 65635 | 417-995-2201
Cassy Farmer, prin. | Fax 995-2110

**Dearborn, Platte, Pop. 488**
North Platte County R-I SD | 600/PK-12
212 W 6th St 64439 | 816-450-3511
Karl Matt, supt. | Fax 992-8727
www.nppanthers.org
North Platte HS | 200/9-12
212 W 6th St 64439 | 816-450-3344
Michelle Johnson, prin. | Fax 992-8955
North Platte JHS | 100/7-8
212 W 6th St 64439 | 816-450-3350
Michelle Johnson, prin. | Fax 992-3665

**Deepwater, Henry, Pop. 430**
Lakeland R-III SD | 400/PK-12
12530 Lakeland School Dr 64740 | 417-644-2223
Mitch Towne, supt. | Fax 644-2316
www.lakeland.k12.mo.us
Lakeland JSHS | 200/7-12
12530 Lakeland School Dr 64740 | 417-644-2223
Adam Collins, prin. | Fax 644-2316

**Deering, Pemiscot, Pop. 130**
Delta C-7 SD | 200/K-12
PO Box 297 63840 | 573-757-6648
Kenny Copley, supt. | Fax 757-9691
www.deltac7.k12.mo.us
Delta C-7 JSHS | 100/7-12
PO Box 297 63840 | 573-757-6611
Nathan Baker, prin. | Fax 757-9691

**De Kalb, Buchanan, Pop. 219**
Buchanan County R-IV SD | 300/PK-12
702 Main St 64440 | 816-685-3160
Travis Dittemore, supt. | Fax 685-3203
www.bcr4.k12.mo.us/
De Kalb JSHS | 200/7-12
702 Main St 64440 | 816-685-3211
Brian Hansen, prin. | Fax 685-3156

**Delta, Cape Girardeau, Pop. 421**
Delta R-V SD | 300/PK-12
PO Box 787 63744 | 573-794-2500
Nathan Crowden, supt. | Fax 794-2504
www.deltar5schools.com
Delta JSHS | 100/7-12
PO Box 787 63744 | 573-794-2511
James Gloth, prin. | Fax 794-2504

**Desloge, Saint Francois, Pop. 4,987**
North St. Francois County R-I SD
Supt. — See Bonne Terre
North County MS | 500/7-8
406 E Chestnut St 63601 | 573-431-3300
Brenda Hampton, prin. | Fax 431-5203

**De Soto, Jefferson, Pop. 6,303**
Desoto SD 73 | 3,000/PK-12
610 Vineland School Rd 63020 | 636-586-1000
Dr. Trisha Burkeen, supt. | Fax 586-1009
www.desoto.k12.mo.us
De Soto HS | 900/9-12
815 Amvets Dr 63020 | 636-586-1050
Mike Rickermann, prin. | Fax 586-1059
De Soto JHS | 400/7-8
731 Amvets Dr 63020 | 636-586-1030
Alex Mahn, prin. | Fax 586-1039

**Dexter, Stoddard, Pop. 7,773**
Dexter R-XI SD | 2,100/PK-12
1031 Brown Pilot Ln 63841 | 573-614-1000
Mitchell D. Wood, supt. | Fax 614-1002
dexter.k12.mo.us/
Dexter HS | 600/9-12
1101 W Grant St 63841 | 573-614-1030
Dan Pollock, prin. | Fax 614-1032
Hill MS | 500/6-8
1107 Brown Pilot Ln 63841 | 573-614-1010
Scott Kruse, prin. | Fax 614-1012

**Diamond, Newton, Pop. 880**
Diamond R-IV SD | 900/K-12
PO Box 68 64840 | 417-325-5186
Dr. Mike Mabe, supt. | Fax 325-5338
www.diamondwildcats.org/
Diamond HS | 300/9-12
PO Box 68 64840 | 417-325-5188
Brian Lee, prin. | Fax 325-5331
Diamond MS | 300/5-8
PO Box 68 64840 | 417-325-5336
Chris Gold, prin. | Fax 325-5333

**Dixon, Pulaski, Pop. 1,508**
Dixon R-I SD | 1,100/PK-12
106 W 4th St 65459 | 573-759-7163
Duane Doyle, supt. | Fax 759-2506
www.dixonr1.com
Dixon HS | 300/9-12
106 W 4th St 65459 | 573-759-7163
Brian Foerster, prin. | Fax 759-3625
Dixon MS | 300/6-8
106 W 4th St 65459 | 573-759-7163
Mark Parker, prin. | Fax 759-6627

**Doniphan, Ripley, Pop. 1,976**
Doniphan R-I SD | 1,500/PK-12
309 Pine St 63935 | 573-996-3667
Dr. Jennifer Snyder, supt. | Fax 996-5865
www.doniphanr1.k12.mo.us
Current River Career Center | Vo/Tech
301 E Spring St 63935 | 573-996-3667
Dustin Braschler, dir. | Fax 996-7838
Doniphan HS | 500/9-12
5 Ball Park Rd 63935 | 573-996-3667
Mike Jones, prin. | Fax 996-3739
Doniphan MS | 300/5-8
651 E Summit St 63935 | 573-996-3667
Gaylon Justus, prin. | Fax 996-4525

**Dora, Ozark**
Dora R-III SD | 300/PK-12
613 County Road 379 65637 | 417-261-2346
Steve Richards, supt. | Fax 261-2673
www.dora.org
Dora JSHS | 200/7-12
613 County Road 379 65637 | 417-261-2263
Rick Luna, prin. | Fax 261-2673

**Drexel, Bates, Pop. 952**
Drexel R-IV SD | 300/K-12
PO Box 860 64742 | 816-657-4715
Bill Johnston, supt. | Fax 657-4798
www.drexel.k12.mo.us/
Drexel HS | 100/7-12
PO Box 860 64742 | 816-619-2287
Dennis Bolton, prin. | Fax 657-4798

**Eagleville, Harrison, Pop. 315**
North Harrison R-III SD | 200/PK-12
12023 Fir St 64442 | 660-867-5222
Rick Johnson, supt. | Fax 867-5263
www.nhr3.net
North Harrison County JSHS | 100/7-12
12023 Fir St 64442 | 660-867-5221
Mike Schmidli, prin. | Fax 867-5263

**Earth City, Saint Louis**

---

Everest College | Post-Sec.
3420 Rider Trl S 63045 | 314-739-7333
ITT Technical Institute | Post-Sec.
3640 Corporate Trail Dr 63045 | 314-298-7800
Midwest Institute - Earth City | Post-Sec.
4260 Shoreline Dr 63045 | 314-344-4440

**Easton, Buchanan, Pop. 228**
East Buchanan County C-1 SD
Supt. — See Gower
East Buchanan MS | 200/6-8
301 N County Park Rd 64443 | 816-473-2451
David Elms, prin. | Fax 473-2604

**East Prairie, Mississippi, Pop. 3,146**
East Prairie R-II SD | 1,100/PK-12
PO Box 10 63845 | 573-649-3562
C.A. Counts, supt. | Fax 649-5455
eastprairie.org/
East Prairie HS | 300/9-12
PO Box 10 63845 | 573-649-3564
Steve Douglas, prin. | Fax 649-3208
East Prairie JHS | 200/7-8
210 E Washington St 63845 | 573-649-9368
Amanda Dean, prin. | Fax 649-9370

**Edina, Knox, Pop. 1,171**
Knox County R-I SD | 500/PK-12
RR 3 Box 59 63537 | 660-397-2228
Andy Turgeon, supt. | Fax 397-3998
www.knox.k12.mo.us/
Knox County JSHS | 300/6-12
RR 3 Box 59 63537 | 660-397-2231
Brian Brown, prin. | Fax 397-3282

**Eldon, Miller, Pop. 4,478**
Eldon R-I SD | 1,900/PK-12
112 S Pine St 65026 | 573-392-8000
Matt Davis, supt. | Fax 392-8080
www.eldon.k12.mo.us/
Eldon Career Center | Vo/Tech
112 S Pine St 65026 | 573-392-8060
Kelli Englebrecht, dir. | Fax 392-9154
Eldon HS | 600/9-12
101 S Pine St 65026 | 573-392-8010
Kris Harwood, prin. | Fax 392-5057
Eldon MS | 300/7-8
1400 N Grand Ave 65026 | 573-392-8020
Shaun Fischer, prin. | Fax 392-9151

**El Dorado Springs, Cedar, Pop. 3,534**
El Dorado Springs R-II SD | 1,200/PK-12
901 S Grand Ave 64744 | 417-876-3112
Mark Koca, supt. | Fax 876-2128
www.eldo.k12.mo.us/
El Dorado Springs HS | 400/9-12
901 S Grand Ave 64744 | 417-876-3112
David Hedrick, prin. | Fax 876-2128
El Dorado Springs MS | 300/6-8
901 S Grand Ave 64744 | 417-876-3112
Brad Steward, prin. | Fax 876-2128

---

El Dorado Christian S | 100/PK-12
1600 S Ohio St 64744 | 417-876-2201
Amy Castor, prin. | Fax 876-4913

**Ellington, Reynolds, Pop. 979**
Southern Reynolds County R-II SD | 500/PK-12
1 School St 63638 | 573-663-3591
Dr. Mike Redlich, supt. | Fax 663-2412
www.ellington.k12.mo.us/
Southern Reynolds County HS | 200/7-12
1 School St 63638 | 573-663-2291
Dr. Tim Hager, prin. | Fax 663-2155

**Ellsinore, Carter, Pop. 444**
East Carter County R-II SD | 800/PK-12
24 S Herren Ave 63937 | 573-322-5625
Dr. Richard Sullivan, supt. | Fax 322-8586
www.ecarter.k12.mo.us
East Carter County R-II HS | 200/9-12
24 S Herren Ave 63937 | 573-322-5653
Robert Eudaley, prin. | Fax 322-5720
East Carter County R-II MS | 200/6-8
24 S Herren Ave 63937 | 573-322-5420
Theresa Kearbey, prin. | Fax 322-5420

**Elsberry, Lincoln, Pop. 1,898**
Elsberry R-II SD | 800/PK-12
PO Box 106 63343 | 573-898-5554
Dr. Tim Reller, supt. | Fax 898-3140
www.elsberryschools.com
Cannon MS | 200/5-8
PO Box 106 63343 | 573-898-5554
Jason Miller, prin. | Fax 898-5825
Elsberry HS | 200/9-12
PO Box 106 63343 | 573-898-5554
Steve Hill, prin. | Fax 898-9132

**Eminence, Shannon, Pop. 585**
Eminence R-I SD | 300/PK-12
PO Box 730 65466 | 573-226-3251
Charles James, supt. | Fax 226-3250
www.redwingsk12.org/
Eminence JSHS | 100/7-12
PO Box 730 65466 | 573-226-3252
James McBride, prin. | Fax 226-3211

**Eolia, Pike, Pop. 513**
Pike County R-III SD
Supt. — See Clarksville
Pike-Lincoln Technical Center | Vo/Tech
342 Vo Tech Rd 63344 | 573-485-2900
Martin Hanley, dir. | Fax 485-2388

**Essex, Stoddard, Pop. 469**
Richland R-I SD | 300/K-12
24456 State Highway 114 63846 | 573-283-5332
Frank Killian, supt. | Fax 283-5798
www.richland.k12.mo.us/
Richland JSHS | 100/7-12
24456 State Highway 114 63846 | 573-283-5332
Cynthia Rhodes, prin. | Fax 283-5798

**Eugene, Cole, Pop. 159**
Cole County R-V SD | 700/PK-12
14803 Highway 17 65032 | 573-498-4000
Dawna Burrow, supt. | Fax 498-4090
www.coler-v.k12.mo.us
Eugene JSHS | 400/7-12
14803 Highway 17 65032 | 573-498-4001
Brian Dickerson, prin. | Fax 498-4091

**Eureka, Saint Louis, Pop. 10,033**
Rockwood R-VI SD | 22,500/PK-12
111 E North St 63025 | 636-733-2000
Dr. Eric Knost, supt. | Fax 938-2251
www.rockwood.k12.mo.us
Eureka HS | 2,000/9-12
4525 Highway 109 63025 | 636-733-3100
Charles Crouther, prin. | Fax 938-2411
Individualized Learning Center | Alt
500 N Central Ave 63025 | 636-733-2100
Matthew Dieckhaus, admin. | Fax 938-2346
Other Schools – See Ballwin, Chesterfield, Fenton, Glencoe

**Everton, Dade, Pop. 310**
Everton R-III SD | 100/K-12
211 E School St 65646 | 417-535-2221
Dr. Karl Janson, supt. | Fax 535-4105
www.evertontigers.org
Everton HS | 50/9-12
211 E School St 65646 | 417-535-2221
Heather Harden, prin. | Fax 535-4105
Everton MS | 6-8
211 E School St 65646 | 417-535-2221
Heather Harden, prin. | Fax 535-4105

**Excelsior Springs, Clay, Pop. 10,839**
Excelsior Springs SD 40 | 2,900/PK-12
PO Box 248 64024 | 816-630-9200
Dr. David Lawrence, supt. | Fax 630-9203
www.essd40.com
Excelsior Springs Career Ctr | Vo/Tech
PO Box 248 64024 | 816-630-9240
Dr. Chris Lake, dir. | Fax 630-9245
Excelsior Springs HS | 800/9-12
PO Box 248 64024 | 816-630-9210
John Newell, prin. | Fax 630-9227
Excelsior Springs MS | 600/6-8
PO Box 248 64024 | 816-630-9230
Chris Hubbuch, prin. | Fax 630-9236
Excelsior Springs Technical HS | 100/Alt
PO Box 248 64024 | 816-630-5501
Tom Mayfield, prin. | Fax 637-1806

---

Martinez School of Cosmetology | Post-Sec.
248 1/2 E Broadway St 64024 | 816-630-3900

**Exeter, Barry, Pop. 762**
Exeter R-VI SD | 400/K-12
101 Locust St 65647 | 417-835-2922
Dr. Ernest Raney, supt. | Fax 835-3201
www.exeter.k12.mo.us/
Exeter HS | 100/9-12
101 Locust St 65647 | 417-835-3745
Robert Taylor, prin. | Fax 835-3201

**Fairfax, Atchison, Pop. 634**
Fairfax R-III SD | 200/PK-12
500 E Main St 64446 | 660-686-2421
Michael Garrett, supt. | Fax 686-2848
www.fairfaxk12mo.us/
Fairfax JSHS | 100/7-12
500 E Main St 64446 | 660-686-2851
Dustin Barnes, prin. | Fax 686-3436

**Fair Grove, Greene, Pop. 1,384**
Fair Grove R-X SD | 1,100/PK-12
PO Box 367 65648 | 417-759-2233
Mike Bell, supt. | Fax 759-7150
www.fairgrove.k12.mo.us

Fair Grove HS 300/9-12
PO Box 367 65648 417-759-2554
Chris Stallings, prin. Fax 759-7685
Fair Grove MS 400/5-8
PO Box 367 65648 417-759-2556
Marc Green, prin. Fax 759-9053

**Fair Play, Polk, Pop. 467**
Fair Play R-II SD 400/PK-12
301 N Walnut St 65649 417-654-2231
Renee Sagaser, supt. Fax 654-5028
www.fairplay.k12.mo.us/
Fair Play JSHS 200/7-12
301 N Walnut St 65649 417-654-2232
Randy Lightfoot, prin. Fax 654-3503

**Farmington, Saint Francois, Pop. 16,061**
Farmington R-VII SD 4,000/PK-12
PO Box 570 63640 573-701-1300
Matthew R. Ruble, supt. Fax 701-1309
www.fsdknights.com
Farmington HS 1,200/9-12
1 Black Knight Dr 63640 573-701-1310
Dr. Nathan Hostetler, prin. Fax 701-1329
Farmington MS 600/7-8
506 S Fleming St 63640 573-701-1330
Dr. Dorothy Winslow, prin. Fax 701-1339
Midwest Learning Center 50/Alt
PO Box 570 63640 573-701-1395
Jerry Will, lead tchr. Fax 701-1388

---

Mineral Area Regional Medical Center Post-Sec.
1212 Weber Rd 63640 573-756-4581
National Academy of Beauty Arts Post-Sec.
670 Walton Dr 63640 573-756-2730
St. Paul Lutheran HS 50/9-12
4337 Showplace Dr 63640 573-756-1099
Andy Sherril, prin.

**Faucett, Buchanan**
Mid-Buchanan County R-V SD 700/K-12
3221 State Route H SE 64448 816-238-1646
John James, supt. Fax 238-4150
www.midbuchanan.k12.mo.us
Mid-Buchanan JSHS 300/7-12
3221 State Route H SE 64448 816-238-1646
Dave Rapp, prin. Fax 238-2484

**Fayette, Howard, Pop. 2,632**
Fayette R-III SD 500/PK-12
705 Lucky St 65248 660-248-2153
Dr. Tamara Kimball, supt. Fax 248-3702
www.fayette.k12.mo.us/
Fayette HS 200/9-12
510 N Cleveland St 65248 660-248-2124
Corey Felten, prin. Fax 248-2120

---

Central Methodist University Post-Sec.
411 Central Methodist Sq 65248 660-248-3391

**Fenton, Saint Louis, Pop. 3,976**
Rockwood R-VI SD
Supt. — See Eureka
Rockwood South MS 1,000/6-8
1628 Hawkins Rd 63026 636-861-7723
Laurie Birkenmeier, prin. Fax 861-7730
Rockwood Summit HS 1,300/9-12
1780 Hawkins Rd 63026 636-891-6800
Renee Trotier, prin. Fax 861-7717

---

Anthem College Post-Sec.
645 Gravois Bluffs Blvd 63026 888-852-7272
Brown Mackie College Post-Sec.
2 Soccer Park Rd 63026 636-651-3290
Midwest Institute Post-Sec.
964 S Highway Dr 63026 314-965-8363
St. Louis College of Health Careers Post-Sec.
1297 N Highway Dr 63026 636-529-0000

**Ferguson, Saint Louis, Pop. 20,785**

---

St. Louis Community College Post-Sec.
3400 Pershall Rd 63135 314-513-4200

**Festus, Jefferson, Pop. 11,379**
Festus R-VI SD 3,000/K-12
1515 Midmeadow Ln 63028 636-937-4920
Dr. Link Luttrell, supt. Fax 937-8525
www.festus.k12.mo.us
Festus HS 900/9-12
501 Westwind Dr 63028 636-937-5410
Allen Diana, prin. Fax 937-8048
Festus MS 500/7-8
1717 W Main St 63028 636-937-5417
Tina Thebeau, prin. Fax 937-4171

Jefferson County R-VII SD 1,000/PK-12
1250 Dooling Hollow Rd 63028 636-937-7940
Clint D. Johnston, supt. Fax 937-9189
www.jr7.k12.mo.us/
Danby-Rush Tower MS 200/6-8
1250 Dooling Hollow Rd 63028 636-937-9188
Cynthia Holdinghausen, admin. Fax 937-9189
Jefferson County HS 200/9-12
7 Blue Jay Way 63028 636-933-6900
David Haug, prin. Fax 933-2663

---

St. Pius X HS 300/9-12
1030 Saint Pius Dr 63028 636-931-7488
Karen DeCosty, prin. Fax 931-3519

**Florissant, Saint Louis, Pop. 50,980**
Ferguson-Florissant R-II SD 12,300/PK-12
1005 Waterford Dr 63033 314-506-9000
Dr. Joseph Davis, supt. Fax 506-9010
www.fergflor.org
Cross Keys MS 900/7-8
14205 Cougar Dr 63033 314-506-9700
LINDA MILLER, prin. Fax 506-9701
McCluer HS 1,300/9-12
1896 S New Florissant Rd 63031 314-506-9400
Jane Crawford, prin. Fax 506-9401
McCluer North HS 1,700/9-12
705 Waterford Dr 63033 314-506-9200
Dr. ANDREW CROLEY, prin. Fax 506-9201
Student Support Center 200/Alt
1555 Derhake Rd 63033 314-839-5959
Mark Weller, prin. Fax 839-7536
Other Schools – See Berkeley, Saint Louis

Hazelwood SD 17,800/PK-12
15955 New Halls Ferry Rd 63031 314-953-5000
Dr. Ingrid Clark-Jackson, supt. Fax 953-5085
www.hazelwoodschools.org
Hazelwood Central HS 2,000/9-12
15875 New Halls Ferry Rd 63031 314-953-5400
Audrey Lee, prin. Fax 953-5413
Hazelwood Central MS 700/6-8
13450 Old Jamestown Rd 63033 314-953-7400
Steve Richards, prin. Fax 953-7413
Hazelwood North MS 800/6-8
4420 Vaile Ave 63034 314-953-7500
Crystal Reiter, prin. Fax 953-7513
Hazelwood Northwest MS 800/6-8
1605 Shackelford Rd 63031 314-953-5500
Nicole Huffman, prin. Fax 953-5513
Other Schools – See Hazelwood, Saint Louis

Special SD of St. Louis County
Supt. — See Saint Louis
North Technical HS Vo/Tech
1700 Derhake Rd 63033 314-989-7600
James Hieger, prin. Fax 989-7665

---

North County Christian S 300/PK-12
845 Dunn Rd 63031 314-972-6227
Dr. Greg Clark, admin. Fax 972-6220
St. Louis Christian College Post-Sec.
1360 Grandview Dr 63033 314-837-6777
Urshan Graduate School of Theology Post-Sec.
704 Howdershell Rd 63031 314-921-9290

**Fordland, Webster, Pop. 792**
Fordland R-III SD 600/PK-12
1230 School St 65652 417-738-2296
Chris Ford, supt. Fax 767-4483
www.fordland.k12.mo.us
Fordland HS 200/9-12
1248 School St 65652 417-738-2212
Doug Fields, prin. Fax 767-2240
Fordland MS 100/6-8
1230 School St 65652 417-738-2119
Vanessa Criger, prin. Fax 767-4483

**Forsyth, Taney, Pop. 2,219**
Forsyth R-III SD 1,200/PK-12
PO Box 187 65653 417-546-6384
Dr. Jeff Mingus, supt. Fax 546-2204
www.forsythpanthers.org
Forsyth HS 400/9-12
PO Box 187 65653 417-546-6383
Christian Meier, prin. Fax 546-5987
Forsyth MS 400/5-8
PO Box 187 65653 417-546-6382
Dr. Sandra Goss, prin. Fax 546-6943

**Fredericktown, Madison, Pop. 3,947**
Fredericktown R-I SD 1,900/PK-12
704 E Highway 72 63645 573-783-2570
Brett Reutzel, supt. Fax 783-7045
www.fpsk12.org/
Fredericktown HS 600/9-12
805 E Highway 72 63645 573-783-3628
Shannon Henson, prin. Fax 783-8224
Fredericktown MS 500/6-8
805A E Highway 72 63645 573-783-6555
Kenneth Lunsford, prin. Fax 783-8079

**Fulton, Callaway, Pop. 12,513**
Fulton SD 58 2,100/K-12
2 Hornet Dr 65251 573-590-8000
Dr. Jacque Cowherd, supt. Fax 590-8090
www.fulton58.org
Fulton HS 600/9-12
1 Hornet Dr 65251 573-590-8100
Chris Mincher, prin. Fax 590-8190
Fulton MS 500/6-8
403 E 10th St 65251 573-590-8200
Beth Houf, prin. Fax 590-8290

---

Kingdom Christian Academy 200/PK-12
650 E 8th St 65251 573-642-2117
Paulette Eichman M.Ed., admin. Fax 642-2022
Missouri School for the Deaf Post-Sec.
505 E 5th St 65251 573-592-4000
Westminster College Post-Sec.
501 Westminster Ave 65251 573-642-3361
William Woods University Post-Sec.
1 University Ave 65251 573-642-2251

**Gainesville, Ozark, Pop. 761**
Gainesville R-V SD 600/PK-12
422 Bulldog Dr 65655 417-679-4260
Joe Donley, supt. Fax 679-4270
gainesville.mo.schoolwebpages.com
Gainesville HS 300/7-12
422 Bulldog Dr 65655 417-679-4200
Aaron Dalton, prin. Fax 679-4270

**Galena, Stone, Pop. 437**
Galena R-II SD 500/PK-12
PO Box 286 65656 417-357-6027
Daniel Humble, supt. Fax 357-0058
www.galena.k12.mo.us/
Galena JSHS 200/7-12
PO Box 286 65656 417-357-6618
Bob Baker, prin. Fax 357-8444

**Gallatin, Daviess, Pop. 1,762**
Gallatin R-V SD 700/PK-12
602 S Olive St 64640 660-663-2171
Dr. Bryan Copple, supt. Fax 663-2559
gallatin.k12.mo.us
Gallatin JSHS 300/7-12
602 S Olive St 64640 660-663-2171
Stan Coulson, prin. Fax 663-2559

**Galt, Grundy, Pop. 246**
Grundy County R-V SD 200/K-12
PO Box 6 64641 660-673-6511
Robert Deaver, supt. Fax 673-6523
Grundy County JSHS 100/7-12
PO Box 6 64641 660-673-6511
Randy Huffman, prin. Fax 673-6523

**Garden City, Cass, Pop. 1,626**

---

Training Center Christian S 50/PK-12
PO Box 200 64747 816-773-8367
Judy Williams, supt. Fax 862-6052

**Gideon, New Madrid, Pop. 1,088**
Gideon SD 37 300/PK-12
PO Box 227 63848 573-448-3911
Dr. James Breece, supt. Fax 448-5197
gideon.k12.mo.us/
Gideon JSHS 100/7-12
PO Box 227 63848 573-448-3471
Keenan Buchanan, prin. Fax 448-3868

**Gilman City, Daviess, Pop. 381**
Gilman City R-IV SD 100/PK-12
141 Lindsey Ave 64642 660-876-5221
Roger Alley, supt. Fax 876-5553
www.gilman.k12.mo.us
Gilman City JSHS 50/7-12
141 Lindsey Ave 64642 660-876-5221
Brent Mitchell, prin. Fax 876-5553

**Gladstone, Clay, Pop. 24,544**
North Kansas City SD 74
Supt. — See Kansas City
Antioch MS 900/6-8
2100 NE 65th St 64118 816-321-5260
Dr. Stephanie Schnoebelen, prin. Fax 321-5261

---

Paris II Educational Center Post-Sec.
6840 N Oak Trfy 64118 816-468-6666

**Glasgow, Howard, Pop. 1,085**
Glasgow SD 300/PK-12
860 Randolph St 65254 660-338-2012
Michael Reynolds, supt. Fax 338-2610
Glasgow JSHS 100/7-12
860 Randolph St 65254 660-338-2012
Sonya Fuemmeler, prin. Fax 338-2610

**Glencoe, Saint Louis**
Rockwood R-VI SD
Supt. — See Eureka
LaSalle Springs MS 900/6-8
3300 Highway 109 63038 636-938-2425
Deborah Brandt, prin. Fax 938-2434
Rockwood Valley MS 800/6-8
1220 Babler Park Dr 63038 636-458-7324
Dr. Karen Hedrick, prin. Fax 458-7325
Wildwood MS 800/6-8
17401 Manchester Rd 63038 636-458-7360
Dr. Allison Klouse, prin. Fax 458-7372

**Golden City, Barton, Pop. 757**
Golden City R-III SD 200/PK-12
1208 Walnut St 64748 417-537-4900
Steven Brigham, supt. Fax 537-8717
Golden City JSHS 100/7-12
1208 Walnut St 64748 417-537-8311
Jason Kramer, prin. Fax 537-8717

**Gower, Buchanan, Pop. 1,511**
East Buchanan County C-1 SD 700/K-12
100 Smith St 64454 816-424-6466
Paul Mensching, supt. Fax 424-3511
www.ebs.k12.mo.us/
East Buchanan HS 200/9-12
100 Smith St 64454 816-424-6460
Douglas Miller, prin. Fax 424-6410
Other Schools – See Easton

**Graham, Nodaway, Pop. 171**
Nodaway-Holt R-VII SD 200/PK-12
318 S Taylor St 64455 660-939-2137
Karma Coleman, supt. Fax 939-2200
www.nodholt.k12.mo.us
Nodaway-Holt JSHS 100/7-12
318 S Taylor St 64455 660-939-2135
Terry Petersen, prin. Fax 939-2201

**Grain Valley, Jackson, Pop. 12,604**
Grain Valley R-V SD 3,400/PK-12
PO Box 304 64029 816-847-5006
Dr. Roy Moss Ph.D., supt. Fax 229-4831
www.gvr5.net
Grain Valley HS 900/9-12
PO Box 304 64029 816-847-5000
Dr. Jeremy Plowman Ph.D., prin. Fax 847-5002
Grain Valley North MS 6-8
PO Box 304 64029 816-994-4800
Theresa Nelson, prin. Fax 994-4899
Grain Valley South MS 600/6-8
PO Box 304 64029 816-229-3499
Jeff Scalfaro, prin. Fax 847-5017

**Granby, Newton, Pop. 2,075**
East Newton County R-VI SD 1,600/PK-12
22808 E Highway 86 64844 417-472-6231
Todd McCrackin, supt. Fax 472-3500
www.eastnewton.org

East Newton HS — 500/9-12
22876 E Highway 86 64844 — 417-472-6238
Scott Charlton, prin. — Fax 472-7129

**Grandview, Jackson, Pop. 23,651**
Grandview C-4 SD — 3,800/PK-12
13015 10th St 64030 — 816-316-5000
Dr. Ralph Teran, supt. — Fax 316-5050
www.grandviewc4.net
C.A.I.R. — Alt
1001 Main St 64030 — 816-316-5150
Derek Jordan, prin. — Fax 316-5995
Grandview HS — 1,000/9-12
2300 High Grove Rd 64030 — 816-316-5800
Jennifer Price, prin. — Fax 316-5898
Grandview MS — 600/6-8
12650 Manchester Ave 64030 — 816-316-5600
Jacqueline Spencer, prin. — Fax 316-5699

---

Grandview Christian S — 100/K-12
12340 Grandview Rd 64030 — 816-767-8630
Nita Tripp, prin. — Fax 763-5029

**Grant City, Worth, Pop. 858**
Worth County R-III SD — 300/PK-12
510 East Ave 64456 — 660-564-3389
Matt Martz, supt. — Fax 564-2193
wc.k12.mo.us
Worth County JSHS — 200/7-12
510 East Ave 64456 — 660-564-2218
Jonathan Adwell, prin. — Fax 564-2193

**Green City, Sullivan, Pop. 647**
Green City R-I SD — 300/PK-12
301 Northeast St 63545 — 660-874-4128
Donnie Campbell, supt. — Fax 874-4515
www.greencity.k12.mo.us/
Green City JSHS — 100/7-12
301 Northeast St 63545 — 660-874-4127
Laura Olmstead, prin. — Fax 874-5010

**Greenfield, Dade, Pop. 1,342**
Greenfield R-IV SD — 500/PK-12
410 College St 65661 — 417-637-5321
Jeffery Davis, supt. — Fax 637-5805
www.greenfieldwildcats.org
Greenfield JSHS — 200/7-12
410 College St 65661 — 417-637-5328
John Hinsley, prin. — Fax 637-5805

**Green Ridge, Pettis, Pop. 466**
Green Ridge R-VIII SD — 400/K-12
PO Box 70 65332 — 660-527-3315
Cara Easter, supt. — Fax 527-3299
greenridge.k12.mo.us
Green Ridge JSHS — 200/7-12
PO Box 70 65332 — 660-527-3315
Rodney Edington, prin. — Fax 527-3299

**Greenville, Wayne, Pop. 503**
Greenville R-II SD — 800/PK-12
PO Box 320 63944 — 573-224-3844
Dr. Todd Porter, supt. — Fax 224-3412
bears.k12.mo.us
Greenville HS — 200/9-12
PO Box 320 63944 — 573-224-3618
Rick Rainwater, prin. — Fax 224-3580
Greenville JHS — 100/7-8
PO Box 320 63944 — 573-224-3833
Rick Rainwater, prin. — Fax 224-3580

**Hale, Carroll, Pop. 409**
Hale R-I SD — 200/PK-12
PO Box 248 64643 — 660-565-2417
Clinton Heussner, supt. — Fax 565-2418
haleschooldistrict.com
Hale JSHS — 100/7-12
PO Box 248 64643 — 660-565-2417
Hollie Burnside, prin. — Fax 565-2418

**Half Way, Polk, Pop. 165**
Halfway R-III SD — 300/K-12
2150 Highway 32 65663 — 417-445-2351
Tim Boatwright, supt. — Fax 445-2026
www.halfwayschools.org
Halfway JSHS — 100/7-12
2150 Highway 32 65663 — 417-445-2211
Tammy Highley, prin. — Fax 445-3330

**Hallsville, Boone, Pop. 1,463**
Hallsville R-IV SD — 1,400/PK-12
421 Hwy 124 E 65255 — 573-696-5512
John Robertson, supt. — Fax 696-3606
www.hallsville.org/
Hallsville HS — 400/9-12
421 Hwy 124 E 65255 — 573-696-5512
Scott Daly, prin. — Fax 696-1482
Hallsville MS — 300/6-8
421 Hwy 124 E 65255 — 573-696-5512
Clinton Hague, prin. — Fax 696-7238

**Hamilton, Caldwell, Pop. 1,790**
Hamilton R-II SD — 700/K-12
PO Box 130 64644 — 816-583-2134
Troy Ford, supt. — Fax 583-2139
www.hamilton.k12.mo.us/
Hamilton MS — 200/6-8
PO Box 130 64644 — 816-583-2173
Dave Richman, prin. — Fax 583-2686
Penney HS — 200/9-12
PO Box 130 64644 — 816-583-2136
Tim Schieber, prin. — Fax 583-2319

**Hannibal, Marion, Pop. 17,465**
Hannibal SD 60 — 3,700/PK-12
4650 McMasters Ave 63401 — 573-221-1258
Susan Johnson, supt. — Fax 221-2994
www.hannibal.k12.mo.us
Hannibal Career & Technical Center — Vo/Tech
4550 McMasters Ave 63401 — 573-221-4430
Roger McGregor, dir. — Fax 221-7971
Hannibal HS — 1,000/9-12
4500 Mcmasters Ave 63401 — 573-221-2733
Ted Sampson, prin. — Fax 221-9511
Hannibal MS — 800/6-8
4700 Mcmasters Ave 63401 — 573-221-5840
Matt Nimmo, prin. — Fax 221-7779

---

Hannibal Area Voc. Technical School — Post-Sec.
4550 McMasters Ave 63401 — 573-221-4430
Hannibal-LaGrange University — Post-Sec.
2800 Palmyra Rd 63401 — 573-221-3675

**Hardin, Ray, Pop. 565**
Hardin-Central C-2 SD — 200/PK-12
PO Box 548 64035 — 660-398-4394
Micheal Cohron, supt. — Fax 398-4396
www.hardin-central.org
Hardin-Central JSHS — 100/7-12
PO Box 548 64035 — 660-398-4394
Rodney Clodfelter, prin. — Fax 398-4396

**Harrisburg, Boone, Pop. 260**
Harrisburg R-VIII SD — 500/K-12
1000 S Harris St 65256 — 573-875-5604
Lynn Proctor, supt. — Fax 875-8877
www.harrisburg.k12.mo.us
Harrisburg HS — 200/9-12
801 S Harris St 65256 — 573-875-5602
Steve Combs, prin. — Fax 443-1559
Harrisburg MS — 100/6-8
233 S Harris St 65256 — 573-817-5857
Troy Lentz, prin. — Fax 875-8936

**Harrisonville, Cass, Pop. 9,864**
Harrisonville R-IX SD — 2,700/PK-12
503 S Lexington St 64701 — 816-380-2727
Frank Dahman, supt. — Fax 380-3134
www.harrisonvilleschools.org
Cass Career Center — Vo/Tech
1600 E Elm St 64701 — 816-380-3253
Jeanette Miller, dir. — Fax 884-3179
Harrisonville HS — 900/9-12
1504 E Elm St 64701 — 816-380-3273
Jason Eggers, prin. — Fax 380-5853
Harrisonville MS — 600/6-8
601 S Highland Dr 64701 — 816-380-7654
Chris Grantham, prin. — Fax 884-5733

---

Harrisonville Christian S West Campus — 100/5-8
1202 S Commercial St 64701 — 816-884-6499
Al Sancken, prin. — Fax 887-2093

**Hartville, Wright, Pop. 610**
Hartville R-II SD — 800/PK-12
PO Box 460 65667 — 417-741-7676
Mark Piper, supt. — Fax 741-7746
www.hartville.k12.mo.us
Hartville JSHS — 300/7-12
PO Box 460 65667 — 417-741-7676
Scott Keith, prin. — Fax 741-7746

**Hayti, Pemiscot, Pop. 2,893**
Hayti R-II SD — 600/PK-12
PO Box 469 63851 — 573-359-6500
Mitchell Fisher, supt. — Fax 359-6502
haytir2.com
Hayti HS — 200/9-12
PO Box 469 63851 — 573-359-6500
Jackie Johnson, prin. — Fax 359-6504
Wallace MS — 100/5-8
PO Box 469 63851 — 573-359-6500
Doug White, prin. — Fax 359-6254

Pemiscot County Special SD
1317 State Highway 84 63851 — 573-359-0021
Sandra Manley, supt. — Fax 359-6525
Pemiscot County Career & Tech Center — Vo/Tech
1317 State Highway 84 63851 — 573-359-2601
Stanley Templeton, dir. — Fax 359-1317

**Hazelwood, Saint Louis, Pop. 25,088**
Hazelwood SD
Supt. — See Florissant
Hazelwood West HS — 2,300/9-12
1 Wildcat Ln 63042 — 314-953-5800
Dennis Newell, prin. — Fax 953-5813
Hazelwood West MS — 800/6-8
12834 Missouri Bottom Rd 63042 — 314-953-5800
Lisa Ostrowski, prin. — Fax 953-5813

**Herculaneum, Jefferson, Pop. 3,429**
Dunklin R-V SD — 1,600/K-12
497 Joachim Ave 63048 — 636-479-5200
Stan Stratton, supt. — Fax 479-6208
www.dunklin.k12.mo.us
Herculaneum HS — 400/9-12
1 Black Cat Dr 63048 — 636-479-5200
Dr. John Crabtree, prin. — Fax 479-2050
Senn-Thomas MS — 300/6-8
200 Senn Tomas Dr 63048 — 636-479-5200
Brian Johnson, prin. — Fax 479-7219

**Hermann, Gasconade, Pop. 2,399**
Gasconade County R-I SD — 1,000/K-12
170 Blue Pride Dr 65041 — 573-486-2116
Dr. Tracey Hankins, supt. — Fax 486-3032
www.hermann.k12.mo.us
Hermann HS — 400/9-12
176 Bearcat Xing 65041 — 573-486-5425
Gary Leimkuehler, prin. — Fax 486-3058
Hermann MS — 300/4-8
164 Blue Pride Dr 65041 — 573-486-3121
Chip Stutzman, prin. — Fax 486-5106

**Hermitage, Hickory, Pop. 457**
Hermitage R-IV SD — 300/PK-12
PO Box 327 65668 — 417-745-6418
William Vest, supt. — Fax 745-6475
www.hermitage.k12.mo.us/
Hermitage HS — 100/9-12
PO Box 327 65668 — 417-745-6417
Krissy Friedman, prin. — Fax 745-6475
Hermitage MS — 100/6-8
PO Box 327 65668 — 417-745-6417
Krissy Friedman, prin. — Fax 745-6475

**Higbee, Randolph, Pop. 552**
Higbee R-VIII SD — 200/K-12
PO Box 128 65257 — 660-456-7277
Darrell Treece, supt. — Fax 456-7278
www.higbeeschool.com/
Higbee JSHS — 100/7-12
PO Box 128 65257 — 660-456-7206
Christopher Stockhorst, prin. — Fax 456-7207

**Higginsville, Lafayette, Pop. 4,706**
Lafayette County C-1 SD — 1,000/PK-12
805 W 31st St 64037 — 660-584-3631
David Figg, supt. — Fax 584-2622
www.huskers.k12.mo.us
Lafayette County HS — 300/9-12
807a W 31st St 64037 — 660-584-3661
Todd Whitney, prin. — Fax 584-8666
Lafayette County MS — 200/6-8
807b W 31st St 64037 — 660-584-7161
Gary Wheeler, prin. — Fax 584-6080

**Highlandville, Christian, Pop. 898**
Spokane R-VII SD — 800/PK-12
167 Kentling Ave 65669 — 417-443-2200
Daryl Bernskoetter, supt. — Fax 443-2205
www.spokane.k12.mo.us
Other Schools – See Spokane

**High Ridge, Jefferson, Pop. 4,270**
Northwest R-I SD — 6,300/PK-12
2843 Community Ln 63049 — 636-677-3473
Dr. Paul Ziegler, supt. — Fax 677-5480
www.nwr1.k12.mo.us/
Woodridge MS — 600/6-8
2109 Gravois Rd 63049 — 636-677-3577
Kim Quentin, prin. — Fax 677-5581
Other Schools – See Cedar Hill, House Springs

**Hillsboro, Jefferson, Pop. 2,784**
Grandview R-II SD — 800/K-12
11470 State Road C 63050 — 636-944-3941
Matt Zoph, supt. — Fax 944-5239
www.grandviewr2.com
Grandview HS — 300/9-12
11470 State Road C 63050 — 636-944-3390
Matthew Zoph, prin. — Fax 944-3515
Grandview MS — 200/6-8
11470 State Road C 63050 — 636-944-3931
James Keeling, prin. — Fax 944-5239

Hillsboro R-III SD — 3,600/K-12
5 Ridgewood Dr 63050 — 636-789-0060
Aaron Cornman Ph.D., supt. — Fax 789-3216
www.hsdr3.org
Hillsboro Alternative S — 50/Alt
10486 Business 21 63050 — 636-789-0000
Melissa Hildebrand, prin. — Fax 789-2773
Hillsboro HS — 1,100/9-12
123 Leon Hall Pkwy 63050 — 636-789-0010
Cathleen Freeman, prin. — Fax 789-3211
Hillsboro JHS — 600/7-8
12 Hawk Dr 63050 — 636-789-0020
Heath Allison, prin. — Fax 789-3212

---

Christian Outreach S — 50/PK-12
4450 Outreach Dr 63050 — 636-797-3466
Steve Miller, prin.
Jefferson College — Post-Sec.
1000 Viking Dr 63050 — 636-797-3000

**Holcomb, Dunklin, Pop. 633**
Holcomb R-III SD — 600/PK-12
PO Box 190 63852 — 573-792-3113
Ashley McMillian, supt. — Fax 792-3118
www.holcombschools.com
Holcomb JSHS — 300/7-12
PO Box 190 63852 — 573-792-3362
Matthew Hodges, prin. — Fax 792-3631

**Holden, Johnson, Pop. 2,201**
Holden R-III SD — 1,400/PK-12
1612 S Main St 64040 — 816-732-5568
Wade Schroeder, supt. — Fax 732-4336
www.holdenschools.org
Holden HS — 400/9-12
1901 S Main St 64040 — 816-732-5523
Ginger Jones, prin. — Fax 732-4142
Holden MS — 400/6-8
301 Eagle Dr 64040 — 816-732-4125
Dr. Mike Hough, prin. — Fax 732-2009

**Hollister, Taney, Pop. 4,346**
Hollister R-V SD — 1,200/PK-12
1914 State Highway BB 65672 — 417-243-4005
Dr. Brian Wilson, supt. — Fax 334-2663
www.hollister.k12.mo.us/
Hollister HS — 500/9-12
2112 State Highway BB 65672 — 417-243-4045
Travis Graham, prin. — Fax 334-2240
Hollister MS — 300/6-8
1798 State Highway BB 65672 — 417-243-4035
Shawn Page, prin. — Fax 334-6482

---

Trinity Christian Academy — 100/PK-12
119 Myrtle Ave 65672 — 417-334-7084
Holly Gregory, prin. — Fax 334-1794

**Hopkins, Nodaway, Pop. 530**
North Nodaway County R-VI SD — 300/PK-12
705 E Barnard St 64461 — 660-778-3411
James Simmelink, supt. — Fax 778-3210
www.nnr6.org/

North Nodaway County JSHS 100/6-12
705 E Barnard St 64461 660-778-3315
Timothy Conn, prin. Fax 778-3210

**Hornersville, Dunklin, Pop. 654**
Senath-Hornersville C-8 SD
Supt. — See Senath
Senath-Hornersville MS 300/5-8
601 School St 63855 573-737-2455
Jared Gurley, prin. Fax 737-2456

**House Springs, Jefferson**
Northwest R-I SD
Supt. — See High Ridge
Valley MS 900/6-8
4300 Gravois Rd 63051 636-671-3470
Barbara Gilcrease, prin. Fax 671-0948

**Houston, Texas, Pop. 2,038**
Houston R-I SD 1,100/PK-12
423 W Pine St 65483 417-967-3024
Scott Dill, supt. Fax 967-4887
www.houston.k12.mo.us
Houston HS 400/9-12
423 W Pine St 65483 417-967-3024
Charlie Malam, prin. Fax 967-3669
Houston MS 200/6-8
423 W Pine St 65483 417-967-3024
Terry Mayfield, prin. Fax 967-5481

---

Texas County Techical College Post-Sec.
6915 Highway 63 65483 417-967-5466

**Hughesville, Pettis, Pop. 182**
Pettis County R-V SD 300/K-12
16215 Highway H 65334 660-827-0772
Sharee Norfleet, supt. Fax 827-7162
www.northwest.k12.mo.us
Northwest JSHS 200/7-12
16215 Highway H 65334 660-827-0774
David Dawson, prin. Fax 827-7162

**Humansville, Polk, Pop. 1,030**
Humansville R-IV SD 400/K-12
300 N Oak St 65674 417-754-2535
Tammy Erwin, supt. Fax 754-8565
www.humansville.k12.mo.us
Humansville HS 200/7-12
300 N Oak St 65674 417-754-2219
Steve Gallivan, prin. Fax 754-8565

**Hume, Bates, Pop. 331**
Hume R-VIII SD 200/PK-12
9163 SW 2nd St 64752 660-643-7411
David Quick, supt. Fax 643-7506
www.humer8.k12.mo.us
Hume JSHS 100/7-12
9163 SW 2nd St 64752 660-643-7411
Kirk Hart, prin. Fax 643-7506

**Huntsville, Randolph, Pop. 1,540**
Westran R-I SD 700/PK-12
228 Huntsville Ave 65259 660-277-4429
Dr. Kelly Shelby, supt. Fax 277-4420
westran.k12.mo.us/
Westran HS 200/9-12
601 Hornet Ln 65259 660-277-4415
Michael Nagel, prin. Fax 277-4644
Other Schools – See Clifton Hill

**Hurley, Stone, Pop. 177**
Hurley R-I SD 200/K-12
PO Box 248 65675 417-369-3271
Dr. Doug Arnold, supt. Fax 369-2212
www.hurley.k12.mo.us/
Hurley JSHS 100/6-12
PO Box 248 65675 417-369-3271
Joey Little, prin. Fax 369-2202

**Iberia, Miller, Pop. 730**
Iberia R-V SD 700/PK-12
201 Pemberton Dr 65486 573-793-6818
Thomas Gotsch, supt. Fax 793-6821
www.iberia.k12.mo.us/
Iberia HS 300/7-12
201 Pemberton Dr 65486 573-793-2228
Tara Luttrell, prin. Fax 793-2946

**Imperial, Jefferson, Pop. 4,673**
Fox C-6 SD
Supt. — See Arnold
Seckman HS 1,800/9-12
2800 Seckman Rd 63052 636-282-1485
Don Grimshaw, prin. Fax 282-5177
Seckman MS 500/7-8
2840 Seckman Rd 63052 636-296-5707
Dr. Tammy Cardona, prin. Fax 296-5707

Windsor C-1 SD 3,000/K-12
6208 US Highway 61/67 63052 636-464-4400
Joel Holland Ed.D., supt. Fax 464-4454
windsorc1sd.schoolwires.com/
Windsor HS 900/9-12
6208 US Highway 61/67 63052 636-464-4429
David Gilmore, prin. Fax 464-4456
Windsor MS 700/6-8
6208 US Highway 61/67 63052 636-464-4417
Karl Shininger, prin. Fax 464-4473

**Independence, Jackson, Pop. 113,065**
Fort Osage R-I SD 4,800/PK-12
2101 N Twyman Rd 64058 816-650-7000
Jason Snodgrass, supt. Fax 650-3888
www.fortosage.net
Career & Technology Center Vo/Tech
2101 N Twyman Rd 64058 816-650-7180
Mike Pantleo, dir. Fax 650-7195
Ft. Osage HS 1,500/9-12
2101 N Twyman Rd 64058 816-650-7030
Scott Moore, prin. Fax 650-7088
Lewis and Clark Academy Alt
2101 N Twyman Rd 64058 816-650-7708
Kim Hawley, prin. Fax 650-7712
Osage Trail MS 800/7-8
2101 N Twyman Rd 64058 816-650-7151
Robbie Shepherd, prin. Fax 650-7152

Independence SD 30 14,300/PK-12
201 N Forest Ave 64050 816-521-5300
Dr. Dale Herl, supt. Fax 521-5680
www.isdschools.org
Bingham MS 600/6-8
1716 S Speck Rd 64057 816-521-5490
Brett Playter, prin. Fax 521-5631
Bridger MS 900/6-8
18200 E State Route 78 64057 816-521-5375
Dr. Janet Richards, prin. Fax 521-5632
Chrisman HS 1,500/9-12
1223 N Noland Rd 64050 816-521-5355
Mike Becker, prin. Fax 521-5606
Independence Academy 100/Alt
600 W Mechanic Ave 64050 816-521-5505
Rebecca Bressman, prin. Fax 521-5613
Nowlin MS 700/6-8
2800 S Hardy Ave 64052 816-521-5380
Cristin Nowak, prin. Fax 521-5633
Pioneer Ridge MS 900/6-8
1656 S Speck Rd 64057 816-521-5385
Michael Estes, prin. Fax 521-5630
Truman HS 1,600/9-12
3301 S Noland Rd 64055 816-521-5350
Pam Boatright, prin. Fax 521-5604
Van Horn HS 700/9-12
1109 S Arlington Ave 64053 816-521-5360
Patrick Layden, prin. Fax 521-5610

---

Graceland University Post-Sec.
1401 W Truman Rd 64050 816-833-0524
Independence College of Cosmetology Post-Sec.
815 W 23rd St 64055 816-252-4247
Metropolitan Community Coll - Blue River Post-Sec.
20301 E State Route 78 64057 816-604-6500
National American University Post-Sec.
3620 Arrowhead Ave 64057 816-353-4554

**Ironton, Iron, Pop. 1,442**
Arcadia Valley R-II SD 1,000/PK-12
750 Park Dr 63650 573-546-9700
Jim Carver Ed.D., supt. Fax 546-7314
www.avr2.org
Arcadia Valley Career Tech Vo/Tech
650 Park Dr 63650 573-546-9700
Steve Pursley, dir. Fax 546-6956
Arcadia Valley HS 300/9-12
520 Park Dr 63650 573-546-9700
Brian Beard, prin. Fax 546-3934
Arcadia Valley MS 300/5-8
550 Park Dr 63650 573-546-9700
Kent Huddleston, prin. Fax 546-7304

**Jackson, Cape Girardeau, Pop. 13,577**
Jackson R-II SD 4,900/PK-12
614 E Adams St 63755 573-243-9501
John Link, supt. Fax 243-9503
www.jacksonr2schools.com
Hawkins JHS 700/8-9
210 N West Ln 63755 573-243-9533
Cory Crosnoe, prin. Fax 243-9584
Jackson SHS 1,100/10-12
315 S Missouri St 63755 573-243-9513
Vince Powell, prin. Fax 243-9524

---

Saxony Lutheran HS 200/9-12
2004 Saxony Ln 63755 573-204-7555
Mark Ruark, prin. Fax 204-7445

**Jameson, Daviess, Pop. 124**
North Daviess R-III SD 100/PK-12
413 E 2nd St 64647 660-828-4123
Terry Mayfield, supt. Fax 828-4122
northdaviess.webs.com
North Daviess JSHS 50/7-12
413 E 2nd St 64647 660-828-4123
Daniel Street, prin. Fax 828-4122

**Jamesport, Daviess, Pop. 506**
Tri-County R-VII SD 200/K-12
904 W Auberry Grv 64648 660-684-6118
David Probasco, supt. Fax 684-6218
Tri-County HS 100/7-12
904 W Auberry Grv 64648 660-684-6116
Tinna Croy, prin. Fax 684-6218

**Jamestown, Moniteau, Pop. 378**
Jamestown C-1 SD 200/K-12
222 School St 65046 660-849-2141
Ellen Ash, supt. Fax 849-2600
www.jamestown.k12.mo.us
Jamestown C-I JSHS 100/7-12
222 School St 65046 660-849-2141
Steven McDannold, prin. Fax 849-2600

**Jasper, Jasper, Pop. 913**
Jasper County R-V SD 500/K-12
201 W Mercer St 64755 417-394-2416
Rick Stark, supt. Fax 394-2394
www.jasper.k12.mo.us/
Jasper County JSHS 200/7-12
201 W Mercer St 64755 417-394-2511
Christina Hess, prin. Fax 394-9977

**Jefferson City, Cole, Pop. 42,185**
Jefferson City SD 8,900/PK-12
315 E Dunklin St 65101 573-659-3000
Larry Linthacum, supt. Fax 659-3807
www.jcschools.us
Jefferson City HS 1,900/10-12
609 Union St 65101 573-659-3050
Dr. P. Jeffrey Dodson, prin. Fax 659-3153
Jefferson MS 900/6-8
1201 Fairgrounds Rd 65109 573-659-3250
Bray David, prin. Fax 659-3259
Lewis and Clark MS 900/6-8
325 Lewis and Clark Dr 65101 573-659-3200
Sherri Thomas, prin. Fax 659-3209
Nichols Career Center Vo/Tech
605 Union St 65101 573-659-3100
Sharon Longan, dir. Fax 659-3154
Simonsen Ninth Grade Center 700/9-9
501 E Miller St 65101 573-659-3125
Ben Meldrum, admin. Fax 659-7362

---

Helias Catholic HS 800/9-12
1305 Swifts Hwy 65109 573-635-6139
Sr. Jean Dietrich, prin. Fax 635-5615
Lincoln University Post-Sec.
820 Chestnut St 65101 573-681-5000
Merrell Univ of Beauty Arts & Science Post-Sec.
1101 Southwest Blvd Ste R 65109 573-635-4433
Metro Business College Post-Sec.
210 El Mercado Plz 65109 573-635-6600
Nichols Career Center Post-Sec.
605 Union St 65101 573-659-3100

**Jennings, Saint Louis, Pop. 14,545**
Jennings SD 2,600/PK-12
2559 Dorwood Dr 63136 314-653-8000
Dr. Tiffany Anderson, supt. Fax 653-8030
www.jenningsk12.org
Jennings HS 800/9-12
8850 Cozens Ave 63136 314-653-8100
Dayle Burgdorf, prin. Fax 653-8102
Jennings JHS 400/7-8
8831 Cozens Ave 63136 314-653-8150
Melba Davis, prin. Fax 653-8168

**Joplin, Jasper, Pop. 48,394**
Joplin R-VIII SD 7,100/PK-12
PO Box 128 64802 417-625-5200
Dr. Norm Ridder, supt. Fax 625-5210
www.joplinschools.org
East MS 500/6-8
PO Box 128 64802 417-625-5280
James Sexson, prin. Fax 625-5284
Franklin Tech S Vo/Tech
PO Box 128 64802 417-625-5260
David Rockers, dir. Fax 625-5266
Joplin HS 2,100/9-12
PO Box 128 64802 417-625-5230
Dr. Kerry Sachetta, prin. Fax 625-5238
North MS 500/6-8
PO Box 128 64802 417-625-5270
Brandon Eggleston, prin. Fax 625-5273
South MS 600/6-8
PO Box 128 64802 417-625-5250
Stephen Gilbreth, prin. Fax 625-5256

---

College Heights Christian S 500/PK-12
4311 Newman Rd 64801 417-782-4114
Nelson Horton, supt. Fax 659-9092
Franklin Technology - MSSU Post-Sec.
3950 Newman Rd 64801 417-659-4400
Jefferson Independent Day S 300/PK-12
3401 Newman Rd 64801 417-781-5124
McAuley Catholic HS 100/9-12
930 S Pearl Ave 64801 417-624-9320
Gene Koester, prin. Fax 626-8334
Messenger College Post-Sec.
300 E 50th St 64804 417-624-7070
Missouri Southern State University Post-Sec.
3950 Newman Rd 64801 417-625-9300
New Dimensions School of Hair Design Post-Sec.
705 Illinois Ave Ste 12 64801 417-782-2875
Ozark Christian College Post-Sec.
1111 N Main St 64801 417-626-1234
St. John's Regional Medical Center Post-Sec.
2727 Mc Clelland Blvd 64804 417-781-2727
St. Peter MS 100/6-8
931 Byers Ave 64801 417-624-5605
Greg Emory, prin. Fax 624-6254
Vatterott College - Joplin Post-Sec.
809 Illinois Ave 64801 417-781-5633
Wichita Technical Institute - Joplin Post-Sec.
1715 N Range Line Rd 64801 417-206-9115

**Kahoka, Clark, Pop. 2,063**
Clark County R-I SD 1,000/PK-12
427 W Chestnut St 63445 660-727-2377
Ritchie Kracht, supt. Fax 727-2035
www.clarkcounty.k12.mo.us/
Clark County HS 300/9-12
680 E Main St 63445 660-727-2205
Jason Harper, prin. Fax 727-2245
Clark County MS 200/6-8
384 N Jefferson St 63445 660-727-3319
Jason Church, prin. Fax 727-3363

---

Shiloh Christian S 50/K-12
RR 1 Box 68A 63445 573-853-4430
Ken Penfield, admin. Fax 853-4432

**Kansas City, Jackson, Pop. 447,224**
Center SD 58 2,500/PK-12
8701 Holmes Rd 64131 816-349-3300
Dr. Sharon Nibbelink, supt. Fax 349-3431
www.center.k12.mo.us
Center Alternative S Alt
8434 Paseo Blvd 64131 816-349-3662
Melissa Dorris, prin. Fax 349-3667
Center HS 700/9-12
8715 Holmes Rd 64131 816-349-3330
Joe Gunderson, prin. Fax 349-3427
Center MS 500/6-8
326 E 103rd St 64114 816-612-4000
Linda Williams, prin. Fax 612-4053

Hickman Mills C-I SD 4,400/PK-12
9000 Old Santa Fe Rd 64138 816-316-7000
Dr. Dennis Carpenter, supt. Fax 316-7020
www.hickmanmills.org
Hickman Mills Freshman Center 400/9-9
9010 Old Santa Fe Rd 64138 816-316-7300
Venita Truman, prin. Fax 316-8009
Ruskin HS 500/10-12
7000 E 111th St Ste 46 64134 816-316-7400
Dawn Smith, prin. Fax 316-7475
Smith-Hale MS 500/7-8
8925 Longview Rd 64134 816-316-7700
Elizabeth Woods, prin. Fax 316-7704

Kansas City SD 33 14,500/PK-12
1211 McGee St 64106 816-418-7000
Stephen Green, supt. Fax 418-7766
www.kcpublicschools.org/
African-Centered College Prep Academy 400/7-12
3500 E Meyer Blvd 64132 816-418-1028
Carl Robinson, prin.
Central Academy of Excellence 800/8-12
3221 Indiana Ave 64128 816-418-2000
Larry Gray, prin. Fax 418-2027
East HS 1,100/7-12
1924 Van Brunt Blvd 64127 816-418-3125
Thomas Herrera, prin. Fax 418-3130
Lincoln College Prep HS 900/6-12
2111 Woodland Ave 64108 816-418-3000
Joseph Hesman, prin. Fax 418-3015
Manual Career & Tech Center Vo/Tech
1215 E Truman Rd 64106 816-418-5200
Jack Bitzenburg, prin. Fax 418-5220
Northeast HS 1,000/7-12
415 Van Brunt Blvd 64124 816-418-3300
Douglas Bolden, prin. Fax 418-3310
Paseo Academy of Fine & Performing Arts 500/7-12
4747 Flora Ave 64110 816-418-2275
Dennis Walker, prin. Fax 418-2300
Southwest Early College Campus 1,000/7-12
6512 Wornall Rd 64113 816-418-1800
Archie Brown, prin. Fax 418-1837
Success Academy at Anderson Alt
1601 Forest Ave 64108 816-418-5300
James Kilgore, prin. Fax 418-5323

North Kansas City SD 74 19,200/PK-12
2000 NE 46th St 64116 816-321-5000
Paul Kinder Ed.D., supt. Fax 321-5005
www.nkcschools.org
Career & Technical Education Vo/Tech
1950 NE 46th St 64116 816-321-6425
Dr. Renee Freers, dir.
Eastgate MS 700/6-8
4700 NE Parvin Rd 64117 816-321-5270
Dr. Chris McCann, prin. Fax 321-5271
Maple Park MS 800/6-8
5300 N Bennington Ave 64119 816-321-5280
Brian Van Batavia, prin. Fax 321-5281
New Mark MS 1,000/6-8
515 NE 106th St 64155 816-321-5290
Terri Sherry, prin. Fax 321-5291
Northgate MS 800/6-8
2117 NE 48th St 64118 816-321-5300
P.J. McGinnis, prin. Fax 321-5301
Oak Park HS 1,400/9-12
825 NE 79th Ter 64118 816-321-5320
Mark Maus, prin. Fax 321-5321
Staley HS 1,400/9-12
2800 NE Shoal Creek Pkwy 64156 816-321-5330
Clark Mershon, prin. Fax 321-5331
Winnetonka HS 1,300/9-12
5815 NE 48th St 64119 816-321-5340
Matt Lindsey, prin. Fax 321-5341
Other Schools – See Gladstone, North Kansas City

Park Hill SD 11,300/PK-12
7703 NW Barry Rd 64153 816-359-4000
Dr. Jeanette Cowherd, supt. Fax 359-4049
www.parkhill.k12.mo.us
Congress MS 900/7-8
8150 N Congress Ave 64152 816-359-4230
Dr. Timothy Todd, prin. Fax 359-4219
Jones Education Center 50/Alt
7642 N Green Hills Rd 64151 816-359-4510
Dr. Lance Miller, prin. Fax 359-4519
Lakeview MS 700/7-8
6720 NW 64th St 64151 816-359-4220
Larry Smith, prin. Fax 359-4229
Park Hill HS 1,800/9-12
7701 NW Barry Rd 64153 816-359-4110
Dr. J. Bradford Kincheloe, prin. Fax 359-4119
Other Schools – See Riverside

Platte County R-III SD
Supt. — See Platte City
Barry S 600/3-8
2001 NW 87th Ter 64154 816-436-9623
Merri Beth Means, prin. Fax 468-6046

Raytown C-2 SD
Supt. — See Raytown
Raytown MS 800/6-8
4900 Pittman Rd 64133 816-268-7360
Dr. Georgetta May, prin. Fax 268-7365

---

Achieve Test Prep Post-Sec.
2300 Main St Fl 9 64108 816-399-4556
Anthem College Post-Sec.
9001 State Line Rd 64114 888-852-7272
ARAMARK Healthcare Support Services SW Post-Sec.
1000 Carondelet Dr 64114 816-943-2146
Archbishop O'Hara HS 400/9-12
9001 James A Reed Rd 64138 816-763-4800
John O'Connor, prin. Fax 763-0156
Aviation Institute of Maintenance Post-Sec.
4100 Raytown Rd 64129 816-753-9920
Avila University Post-Sec.
11901 Wornall Rd 64145 816-942-8400
Barstow S 700/PK-12
11511 State Line Rd 64114 816-942-3255
Shane Foster, head sch Fax 942-3227
Blue Ridge Christian S 200/PK-12
8524 Blue Ridge Blvd 64138 816-358-0950
Larry Becker, prin. Fax 358-1138
Calvary Bible College & Theological Sem Post-Sec.
15800 Calvary Rd 64147 816-322-0110
City Vision College Post-Sec.
3101 Troost Ave Ste 200 64109 816-960-2008
Concorde Career College Post-Sec.
3239 Broadway St 64111 816-531-5223
Cristo Rey Kansas City HS 400/9-12
211 W Linwood Blvd 64111 816-457-6044
Kathleen Hanlon, pres. Fax 457-6046
DeVry University Post-Sec.
11224 Holmes Rd 64131 816-943-7300
DeVry University Post-Sec.
1100 Main St Ste 118 64105 816-221-1300
Everest College Post-Sec.
1740 W 92nd St 64114 816-423-8600
Grantham University Post-Sec.
7200 NW 86th St 64153 800-955-2527
Heritage College Post-Sec.
1200 E 104th St Ste 300 64131 816-942-5474
House of Heavilin Beauty College Post-Sec.
5720 Troost Ave 64110 816-523-2471
Islamic S of Greater Kansas City 300/PK-12
8505 E 99th St 64134 816-763-0322
ITT Technical Institute Post-Sec.
9150 E 41st Ter 64133 816-276-1400
Kansas City Academy 50/6-12
7933 Main St 64114 816-444-5225
Kansas City Art Institute Post-Sec.
4415 Warwick Blvd 64111 816-472-4852
KC Univ. of Medicine and Biosciences Post-Sec.
1750 Independence Ave 64106 816-654-7000
L'Ecole Culinaire Post-Sec.
310 Ward Pkwy 64112 866-205-2521
Lutheran HS of Kansas City 100/9-12
12411 Wornall Rd 64145 816-241-5478
Dr. Cary Stelmachowicz Ed.D., admin. Fax 876-2069
Metropolitan Comm College - Penn Valley Post-Sec.
3201 Southwest Traffic Way 64111 816-604-5000
Metropolitan Community Coll - Bus & Tech Post-Sec.
1775 Universal Ave 64120 816-604-1000
Metropolitan Community Coll-Maple Woods Post-Sec.
2601 NE Barry Rd 64156 816-604-3000
Midwestern Baptist Theological Seminary Post-Sec.
5001 N Oak Trfy 64118 816-414-3700
Nazarene Theological Seminary Post-Sec.
1700 E Meyer Blvd 64131 816-268-5400
Northland Christian S 200/PK-12
4214 NW Cookingham Rd 64164 816-548-2222
Richard Rice, supt. Fax 533-6914
Notre Dame De Sion HS 400/9-12
10631 Wornall Rd 64114 816-942-3282
Natalie McDonough, prin. Fax 942-4052
Pembroke Hill S - Ward Pkwy Campus 700/6-12
400 W 51st St 64112 816-936-1200
Dr. Steven J. Bellis, head sch Fax 936-1208
Pinnacle Career Institute Post-Sec.
1001 E 101st Ter Ste 325 64131 816-331-5700
Pinnacle Career Institute Post-Sec.
11500 N Ambassador Dr # 221 64153 816-270-5300
Research College of Nursing Post-Sec.
2525 E Meyer Blvd 64132 816-995-2800
Research Medical Center Post-Sec.
2316 E Meyer Blvd 64132 816-276-4101
Rockhurst HS 1,100/9-12
9301 State Line Rd 64114 816-363-2036
Gregory Harkness, prin. Fax 363-3764
Rockhurst University Post-Sec.
1100 Rockhurst Rd 64110 816-501-4000
St. Luke's College of Health Sciences Post-Sec.
624 Westport Rd 64111 816-932-6700
St. Paul School of Theology Post-Sec.
5123 E Truman Rd 64127 816-483-9600
St. Pius X HS 400/9-12
1500 NE 42nd Ter 64116 816-453-3450
Joseph Monachino, prin. Fax 452-7099
St. Teresa Academy 600/9-12
5600 Main St 64113 816-501-0011
Barbara McCormick M.S., prin. Fax 523-0232
Strayer University Post-Sec.
10450 Holmes Rd Ste 100 64131 816-489-4500
Truman Medical Center Post-Sec.
2301 Holmes St 64108 816-556-3153
University of Missouri - Kansas City Post-Sec.
5100 Rockhill Rd 64110 816-235-1000
Vatterott College - Kansas City Post-Sec.
4131 N Corrington Ave 64117 816-861-1000

**Kearney, Clay, Pop. 8,257**
Kearney R-I SD 3,700/K-12
1002 S Jefferson St 64060 816-628-4116
Dr. Bill Nicely, supt. Fax 628-4074
www.ksdr1.net
Kearney HS 900/10-12
715 E 19th St 64060 816-628-4585
David Schwarzenbach, prin. Fax 628-3383
Kearney JHS 600/8-9
2215 S Campus St 64060 816-628-2650
Andy Gustafson, prin. Fax 628-1938

**Kennett, Dunklin, Pop. 10,740**
Kennett SD 39 2,200/PK-12
510 College Ave 63857 573-717-1100
Chris Wilson, supt. Fax 717-1016
www.kennett.k12.mo.us
Kennett Career & Technology Center Vo/Tech
1400 W Washington St 63857 573-717-1123
Terry Bruce, dir. Fax 717-1386
Kennett HS 600/9-12
1400 W Washington St 63857 573-717-1120
David Gilmore, prin. Fax 717-1016
Kennett MS 500/6-8
510 College Ave 63857 573-717-1105
Ward Billings, prin. Fax 717-1106

**Keytesville, Chariton, Pop. 471**
Keytesville R-III SD 200/PK-12
27247 Highway 5 65261 660-288-3787
Tracy Bottoms, supt. Fax 288-3110
keytesville.k12.mo.us
Keytesville R-III HS 100/7-12
27247 Highway 5 65261 660-288-3767
Bottoms Tracy, prin. Fax 288-3110

**King City, Gentry, Pop. 1,004**
King City R-I SD 300/PK-12
PO Box 189 64463 660-535-4319
Danny Johnson, supt. Fax 535-4765
www.kingcityschools.org
King City JSHS 100/7-12
PO Box 189 64463 660-535-4319
Dottie Stoll, prin. Fax 535-4765

**Kingdom City, Callaway, Pop. 127**
North Callaway County R-I SD 1,100/PK-12
2690 Thunderbird Dr 65262 573-386-2214
Dr. Bryan Thomsen, supt. Fax 386-2169
nc.k12.mo.us
North Callaway HS 400/9-12
2700 Thunderbird Dr 65262 573-386-2211
Matt Boyer, prin. Fax 386-2403

**Kingsville, Johnson, Pop. 264**
Kingsville R-I SD 100/K-12
PO Box 7 64061 816-597-3422
Kevin Coleman, supt. Fax 597-3702
kingsville.k12.mo.us
Kingsville S 100/K-12
PO Box 7 64061 816-597-3422
Lorna Warren, prin. Fax 597-3702

**Kirbyville, Taney, Pop. 203**
Kirbyville R-VI SD 300/K-8
6225 E State Highway 76 65679 417-337-8913
Carless Osbourn, supt. Fax 348-0794
www.kirbyville.k12.mo.us/
Kirbyville MS 200/4-8
6225 E State Highway 76 65679 417-348-0444
Amy Burton, prin. Fax 348-0525

**Kirksville, Adair, Pop. 17,170**
Kirksville R-III SD 2,700/PK-12
1901 E Hamilton St 63501 660-665-7774
Dr. Damon Kizzire, supt. Fax 626-1448
www.kirksville.k12.mo.us
Kirksville Area Technical Center Vo/Tech
1103 Cottage Grove Ave 63501 660-665-2865
Sheryl Ferguson, prin. Fax 626-1477
Kirksville HS 800/9-12
1300 Cottage Grove Ave 63501 660-665-4631
Randy Mikel, prin. Fax 626-1439
Matthew MS 500/6-8
1515 Cottage Grove Ave 63501 660-665-3793
Dr. Michael Mitchell, prin. Fax 626-1418

---

Kirksville Coll. of Osteopathic Medicine Post-Sec.
800 W Jefferson St 63501 660-626-2237
School of Health Management Post-Sec.
800 W Jefferson St 63501 877-626-5577
Still Univ MO Sch of Dentistry & Oral Hl Post-Sec.
800 W Jefferson St 63501 866-626-2878
Truman State University Post-Sec.
100 E Normal Ave 63501 660-785-4000

**Kirkwood, Saint Louis, Pop. 27,112**
Kirkwood R-VII SD 5,100/PK-12
11289 Manchester Rd 63122 314-213-6101
Dr. Tom Williams, supt. Fax 984-0002
www.kirkwoodschools.org
Kirkwood HS 1,700/9-12
801 W Essex Ave 63122 314-213-6110
Dr. Michael Havener, prin. Fax 984-4412
Nipher MS 600/6-8
700 S Kirkwood Rd 63122 314-213-6180
Dr. Michele Condon, prin. Fax 213-6178
North Kirkwood MS 600/6-8
11287 Manchester Rd 63122 314-213-6170
Tim Cochran, prin. Fax 213-6177

---

St. Louis Community College - Meramec Post-Sec.
11333 Big Bend Rd 63122 314-984-7500

**Knob Noster, Johnson, Pop. 2,592**
Knob Noster R-VIII SD 1,400/PK-12
401 E Wimer St 65336 660-563-3186
Dr. Kristee Lorenz, supt. Fax 563-3026
www.knobnoster.k12.mo.us
Knob Noster HS 400/9-12
504 S Washington Ave 65336 660-563-2283
Connie Morris, prin. Fax 563-3384
Knob Noster MS 300/5-8
211 E Wimer St 65336 660-563-2260
Ronald Franklin, prin. Fax 563-3274

**Koshkonong, Oregon, Pop. 200**
Oregon-Howell R-III SD 200/K-12
100 School St 65692 417-867-5601
Seth Bryant, supt. Fax 867-3757
Koshkonong HS 100/9-12
100 School St 65692 417-867-5601
David Miller, prin. Fax 867-3757

**Laddonia, Audrain, Pop. 512**
Community R-VI SD 300/PK-12
35063 Highway BB 63352 855-708-7567
Cheryl Mack, supt. Fax 492-6268
www.cr6.net/
Community HS 200/6-12
35063 Highway BB 63352 855-708-7567
Bob Curtis, prin. Fax 492-6407

**Lake Ozark, Camden, Pop. 1,563**
School of the Osage R-II SD 1,900/PK-12
PO Box 1960 65049 573-365-4091
Dr. Brent Depee', supt. Fax 365-5748
www.osage.k12.mo.us
Other Schools – See Osage Beach

**Lake Saint Louis, Saint Charles, Pop. 14,381**
Wentzville R-IV SD
Supt. — See Wentzville
Liberty HS 9-12
2275 Sommers Rd 63367 636-561-0075
Edgar Nelson, prin. Fax 561-0058

**Lamar, Barton, Pop. 4,398**
Lamar R-I SD 1,400/PK-12
202 W 7th St 64759 417-682-3527
Dr. Zach Harris, supt. Fax 682-6013
www.lamar.k12.mo.us
Lamar Career & Technical Center Vo/Tech
202 W 7th St 64759 417-682-3384
Dr. Scott Nolting, dir. Fax 682-3420
Lamar HS 400/9-12
202 W 7th St 64759 417-682-5571
Jennifer Beem, prin. Fax 681-0328
Lamar MS 300/6-8
202 W 7th St 64759 417-682-3548
Alan Ray, prin. Fax 682-4409

**La Monte, Pettis, Pop. 1,113**
La Monte R-IV SD 400/PK-12
301 S Washington St 65337 660-347-5439
Joan Twidwell, supt. Fax 347-5467
lamonte.k12.mo.us/
La Monte JSHS 200/7-12
301 S Washington St 65337 660-347-5439
Jana Fleckenstine, prin. Fax 347-5467

**La Plata, Macon, Pop. 1,336**
La Plata R-II SD 300/PK-12
201 W Moore St 63549 660-332-7001
Dr. Craig Noah, supt. Fax 332-7929
laplata.k12.mo.us
La Plata JSHS 200/7-12
201 W Moore St 63549 660-332-7001
Andy Jackson, prin. Fax 332-7656

**Laquey, Pulaski**
Laquey R-V SD 700/PK-12
PO Box 130 65534 573-765-3716
Randy Caffey, supt. Fax 765-4052
www.laquey.k12.mo.us/
Laquey R-V HS 200/9-12
PO Box 130 65534 573-765-4051
Eric Shaw, prin. Fax 765-5608
Laquey R-V MS 200/6-8
PO Box 130 65534 573-765-3129
Jamie Roberts, prin. Fax 765-4086

**Lathrop, Clinton, Pop. 2,052**
Lathrop R-II SD 900/K-12
700 East St 64465 816-528-7500
Chris Fine, supt. Fax 528-7514
lathropschools.com
Lathrop HS 200/9-12
102 N School Dr 64465 816-528-7400
Robert Bowers, prin. Fax 528-7456
Lathrop MS 200/6-8
612 Center St 64465 816-528-7600
Andy McNeely, prin. Fax 528-7646

**Lawson, Ray, Pop. 2,441**
Lawson R-XIV SD 1,200/PK-12
PO Box 157 64062 816-580-7277
Roger Schmitz, supt. Fax 296-7723
lawsoncardinals.org/
Lawson HS 400/9-12
PO Box 157 64062 816-580-7270
Scott Harrold, prin. Fax 296-3048
Lawson MS 400/5-8
PO Box 157 64062 816-580-7279
Tammy Dunn, prin. Fax 296-3164

**Leadwood, Saint Francois, Pop. 1,274**
West St. Francois County R-IV SD 1,000/PK-12
1124 Main St 63653 573-562-7535
Stacy Stevens, supt. Fax 562-7510
westco.k12.mo.us/
West County MS 200/6-8
1124 Main St 63653 573-562-7544
Kevin Coffman, prin. Fax 562-2714
Other Schools – See Park Hills

**Lebanon, Laclede, Pop. 14,144**
Lebanon R-III SD 4,700/PK-12
1310 E Route 66 65536 417-532-9141
Dr. Duane Widhalm, supt. Fax 532-9492
www.lebanon.k12.mo.us
Lebanon Alternative S Alt
1015 N Jefferson Ave 65536 417-533-3824
Scott Williamson, dir.
Lebanon JHS 700/7-8
500 N Adams Ave 65536 417-532-9121
Tom Merriott, prin. Fax 533-3805
Lebanon SHS 1,400/9-12
777 Brice St 65536 417-532-9144
Kevin Lowery, prin. Fax 532-3386
Lebanon Technology Career Center Vo/Tech
757 Brice St 65536 417-532-5494
Keith Davis, dir. Fax 532-4510

**Lees Summit, Jackson, Pop. 89,308**
Blue Springs R-IV SD
Supt. — See Blue Springs
Delta Woods MS 800/6-8
4401 NE Lakewood Way 64064 816-795-5830
Steven Cook, prin. Fax 795-5839

Lee's Summit R-VII SD 17,800/PK-12
301 NE Tudor Rd 64086 816-986-1000
Dr. David McGehee, supt. Fax 986-1170
www.lsr7.org
Campbell MS 900/7-8
1201 NE Colbern Rd 64086 816-986-3175
Dr. Sherri Lewis, prin. Fax 986-3245
Lee's Summit HS 1,800/9-12
400 SE Blue Pkwy 64063 816-986-2000
Dr. John Faulkenberry, prin. Fax 986-2095
Lee's Summit North HS 2,000/9-12
901 NE Douglas St 64086 816-986-3000
Dr. Jeff Meisenheimer, prin. Fax 986-3170
Lee's Summit West HS 1,700/9-12
2600 SW Ward Rd 64082 816-986-4000
Dr. David Sharp, prin. Fax 986-4115
Pleasant Lea MS 900/7-8
630 SW Persels Rd 64081 816-986-1175
Janette Miller, prin. Fax 986-1225
Summit Lakes MS 1,000/7-8
3500 SW Windemere Dr 64082 816-986-1375
Dr. David Carlson, prin. Fax 986-1435
Summit Ridge Academy Alt
2620 SW Ward Rd 64082 816-986-4120
Burt Whaley, prin. Fax 986-4135
Summit Technology Academy Vo/Tech
777 NW Blue Pkwy 64086 816-524-3366
Elaine Metcalf, prin. Fax 524-1436

---

Metropolitan Community Coll - Longview Post-Sec.
500 SW Longview Rd 64081 816-604-2000
Summit Christian Academy 700/PK-12
1500 SW Jefferson St 64081 816-525-1480
Linda Harrelson, head sch Fax 525-5402

**Leeton, Johnson, Pop. 557**
Leeton R-X SD 300/PK-12
500 N Main St 64761 660-653-2301
Susan Crooks, supt. Fax 653-4315
www.leeton.k12.mo.us/
Leeton HS 100/9-12
500 N Main St 64761 660-653-4314
Bryan Himes, prin. Fax 653-4315
Leeton MS 100/6-8
500 N Main St 64761 660-653-4314
Bryan Himes, prin. Fax 653-4315

**Leopold, Bollinger**
Leopold R-III SD 200/K-12
PO Box 39 63760 573-238-2211
Keenan Kinder, supt. Fax 238-9868
www.leopold.k12.mo.us
Leopold JSHS 100/7-12
PO Box 39 63760 573-238-2211
Matt Britt, prin. Fax 238-9868

**Lesterville, Reynolds**
Lesterville R-IV SD 300/PK-12
PO Box 120 63654 573-637-2201
Earlene Fox, supt. Fax 637-2279
www.lesterville.k12.mo.us/
Lesterville JSHS 100/7-12
PO Box 120 63654 573-637-2201
James Watts, prin. Fax 637-2279
Other Schools – See Black

**Lewistown, Lewis, Pop. 532**
Lewis County C-1 SD 1,000/PK-12
21504 State Highway 6 63452 573-209-3217
John French, supt. Fax 209-3318
www.lewis.k12.mo.us
Highland JSHS 500/7-12
21504 State Highway 6 63452 573-209-3215
Alan Koch, prin. Fax 209-3469

**Lexington, Lafayette, Pop. 4,541**
Lexington R-V SD 900/PK-12
2323 High School Dr Ste A 64067 660-259-4369
Dr. Dan Hoehn, supt. Fax 259-4992
www.lexington.k12.mo.us
Lexington HS 300/9-12
2309 Aull Ln 64067 660-259-4391
Moore Travis, prin. Fax 259-2166
Lexington MS 300/5-8
1111 S 24th St 64067 660-259-4611
Anneliese Gould, prin. Fax 259-2538
Lex La-Ray Tech Ctr Vo/Tech
2323 High School Dr 64067 660-259-2264
Sarrah Dobson, dir. Fax 259-6262

---

Wentworth Military Academy Post-Sec.
1880 Washington Ave 64067 800-962-7682
Wentworth Military Academy 100/9-12
1880 Washington Ave 64067 660-259-2221
Col. Michael Lierman, pres. Fax 259-2064

**Liberal, Barton, Pop. 739**
Liberal R-II SD 500/PK-12
PO Box 38 64762 417-843-5115
William Harvey, supt. Fax 843-6698
www.liberal.k12.mo.us/
Liberal HS 100/9-12
PO Box 38 64762 417-843-2125
Anthony Robertson, prin. Fax 843-2403
Liberal MS 100/6-8
PO Box 38 64762 417-843-6033
Nicole Ruddick, prin. Fax 843-2403

**Liberty, Clay, Pop. 28,451**
Liberty SD 53 9,800/PK-12
8 Victory Ln 64068 816-736-5300
Dr. Jeremy Tucker, supt. Fax 736-5306
www.liberty.k12.mo.us
Discovery MS 400/6-8
800 Midjay Dr 64068 816-736-7300
Dr. Julie Moore, prin. Fax 736-7306
Heritage MS 400/6-8
600 W Kansas St 64068 816-736-5380
Scott Carr, prin. Fax 736-5384

Liberty Academy Alt
8 Victory Ln 64068 816-736-5470
Dr. Robert Cordell, dir. Fax 736-5471
Liberty HS 1,500/9-12
200 Blue Jay Dr 64068 816-736-5340
April Adams, prin. Fax 736-5345
Liberty MS 800/6-8
1500 S Withers Rd 64068 816-736-5410
Dan Weakley, prin. Fax 736-5415
Liberty North HS 9-12
1000 NE 104th St 64068 816-736-5500
Martin Jacobs, prin. Fax 736-5535
South Valley MS 900/6-8
1000 Midjay Dr 64068 816-736-7180
Jill Mullen, prin. Fax 736-7185

---

William Jewell College Post-Sec.
500 College Hl 64068 816-781-7700

**Licking, Texas, Pop. 3,111**
Licking R-VIII SD 900/PK-12
125 College Ave 65542 573-674-2911
Dr. John Hood, supt. Fax 674-4064
www.licking.k12.mo.us/
Licking JSHS 400/7-12
125 College Ave 65542 573-674-2711
Grant Crow, prin. Fax 674-2142

**Lincoln, Benton, Pop. 1,178**
Lincoln R-II SD 500/K-12
PO Box 39 65338 660-547-3514
Kevin Smith, supt. Fax 547-3729
www.lincoln.k12.mo.us/
Lincoln JSHS 200/7-12
PO Box 39 65338 660-547-3514
Marc Spunaugle, prin. Fax 547-3729

**Linn, Osage, Pop. 1,447**
Osage County R-II SD 600/PK-12
1212 E Main St 65051 573-897-4200
Shawn Poyser, supt. Fax 897-3768
www.linn.k12.mo.us
Linn JSHS 300/6-12
1212 E Main St 65051 573-897-4216
Dr. Melinda Aholt, prin. Fax 897-4570

---

Linn State Technical College Post-Sec.
1 Technology Dr 65051 573-897-5000

**Lockwood, Dade, Pop. 928**
Lockwood R-I SD 300/PK-12
400 W 4th St 65682 417-232-4513
Bill Rogers, supt. Fax 232-4187
www.lockwoodschools.org/
Lockwood HS 100/9-12
400 W 4th St 65682 417-232-4513
Clay Lasater, prin. Fax 232-4187

**Lone Jack, Jackson, Pop. 1,030**
Lone Jack C-6 SD 500/PK-12
313 S Bynum Rd 64070 816-697-3539
Bryan Prewitt, supt. Fax 566-3128
www.lonejackc6.net
Lone Jack JSHS 300/7-12
313 S Bynum Rd 64070 816-697-2215
Matthew Tarwater, prin. Fax 566-3128

**Louisburg, Dallas, Pop. 116**
Dallas County R-I SD
Supt. — See Buffalo
Dallas County Career Center Vo/Tech
PO Box 100 65685 417-752-3491
Debby Dryer, admin. Fax 752-3493

**Louisiana, Pike, Pop. 3,291**
Louisiana R-II SD 700/PK-12
3321 Georgia St 63353 573-754-4261
Dr. Todd Smith, supt. Fax 754-4319
louisianarii.org
Louisiana HS 200/9-12
3321 Georgia St 63353 573-754-6181
Derrick Branstetter, prin. Fax 754-5964
Louisiana MS 100/6-8
3321 Georgia St 63353 573-754-5340
Chuck Tophinke, prin. Fax 754-5377

**Ludlow, Livingston, Pop. 131**
Southwest Livingston County R-I SD 200/PK-12
4944 Highway DD 64656 660-738-4433
Cinthia Barnes, supt. Fax 738-4441
www.southwestr1.org/
Southwest Livingston County JSHS 100/7-12
4944 Highway DD 64656 660-738-4433
Lucas Lewis, prin. Fax 738-4115

**Macks Creek, Camden, Pop. 238**
Macks Creek R-V SD 300/PK-12
245 State Rd N 65786 573-363-5909
Joshua Phillips, supt. Fax 363-0127
mcreek.k12.mo.us
Macks Creek JSHS 100/7-12
245 State Rd N 65786 573-363-5911
Doug Kempker, prin. Fax 363-5981

**Macon, Macon, Pop. 5,339**
Macon County R-I SD 1,400/PK-12
702 N Missouri St 63552 660-385-5719
Dr. Charles Stockton, supt. Fax 385-7179
www.macon.k12.mo.us
Family Literacy Center Alt
204 Crescent Dr 63552 660-385-2061
Shandra Clark, dir. Fax 385-5893
Macon Area Vocational Technical S Vo/Tech
702 N Missouri St 63552 660-385-2158
Peter Claas, dir. Fax 385-3667
Macon County HS 400/9-12
702 N Missouri St 63552 660-385-5748
Jeffrey Haley, prin. Fax 385-2746

Macon County MS 300/6-8
702 N Missouri St 63552 660-385-2189
Dustin Fanning, prin. Fax 385-7230

**Madison, Monroe, Pop. 551**
Madison C-3 SD 200/PK-12
309 S Thomas St 65263 660-291-5115
Lesa Rapert, supt. Fax 291-5006
www.madison.k12.mo.us
Madison JSHS 100/7-12
309 S Thomas St 65263 660-291-4515
Shane Stocks, prin. Fax 291-5006

**Malden, Dunklin, Pop. 4,199**
Malden R-I SD 1,100/PK-12
505 Burkhart St 63863 573-276-5794
Kenneth Cook, supt. Fax 276-5796
www.malden.k12.mo.us/
Malden JSHS 400/7-12
505 Burkhart St 63863 573-276-4546
Jeri Hardy, prin. Fax 276-4548

**Malta Bend, Saline, Pop. 249**
Malta Bend R-V SD 100/K-12
PO Box 10 65339 660-595-2371
John Angelhow, supt. Fax 595-2430
mbtigers.weebly.com
Malta Bend JSHS 50/7-12
PO Box 10 65339 660-595-2371
Angelhow John, prin. Fax 595-2430

**Manchester, Saint Louis, Pop. 17,723**
Parkway C-2 SD
Supt. — See Chesterfield
Parkway South MS 600/6-8
760 Woods Mill Rd 63011 314-415-7200
Amy Branson, prin. Fax 415-7213
Parkway Southwest MS 600/6-8
701 Wren Ave 63021 314-415-7300
Dr. Craig Maxwell, prin. Fax 415-7334

---

Heritage Classical Christian Academy 50/7-12
625 Meramec Station Rd 63021 636-394-8063
Jason Wood, dir. Fax 394-8067
Kennedy HS 300/9-12
500 Woods Mill Rd 63011 636-227-5900
Mary Hey, prin. Fax 227-0298

**Mansfield, Wright, Pop. 1,287**
Mansfield R-IV SD 800/PK-12
316 W Ohio St 65704 417-924-8458
Dr. Nathan Moore, supt. Fax 924-3427
www.mansfieldschool.net
Mansfield HS 200/9-12
315 W Ohio St 65704 417-924-3236
Richard Wylie, prin. Fax 924-8789
Mansfield JHS 200/6-8
316 W Ohio St 65704 417-924-8625
Gary Greene, prin. Fax 924-8789

**Maplewood, Saint Louis, Pop. 7,766**
Maplewood Richmond Heights SD 1,200/PK-12
7539 Manchester Rd 63143 314-644-4400
Karen I. Hall, supt. Fax 781-3160
www.mrhschools.net
Maplewood Richmond Heights HS 300/9-12
7539 Manchester Rd 63143 314-644-4401
Kevin Grawer, prin. Fax 644-3681
Maplewood Richmond Heights MS 100/7-8
7539 Manchester Rd 63143 314-644-4406
Dr. Dittrich Michael, prin. Fax 781-4629

**Marble Hill, Bollinger, Pop. 1,464**
Woodland R-IV SD 900/K-12
RR 5 Box 3210 63764 573-238-3343
Daniel Schlief, supt. Fax 238-2153
www.woodland.k12.mo.us/
Woodland HS 300/9-12
RR 5 Box 3210 63764 573-238-2663
Shawn Kinder, prin. Fax 238-0186
Woodland MS 300/5-8
RR 5 Box 3210 63764 573-238-2656
Brian Hukel, prin. Fax 238-0133

**Marceline, Linn, Pop. 2,210**
Marceline R-V SD 600/PK-12
400 E Santa Fe Ave 64658 660-376-3371
Dr. Gabe Edgar Ed.D., supt. Fax 376-6001
www.marcelineschools.org
Marceline HS 200/9-12
314 E Santa Fe Ave 64658 660-376-2411
Matt Finch, prin. Fax 376-6016
Marceline MS 100/6-8
314 E Santa Fe Ave 64658 660-376-2411
Matt Finch, prin. Fax 376-6016

**Marionville, Lawrence, Pop. 2,171**
Marionville R-IX SD 800/PK-12
PO Box 409 65705 417-258-7755
Dr. Larry Brown, supt. Fax 258-2564
www.marionville.us/
Marionville HS 200/9-12
PO Box 409 65705 417-258-2521
Mark Estep, prin. Fax 258-7637
Marionville MS 200/6-8
PO Box 409 65705 417-258-2531
Shane Moseman, prin. Fax 258-2564

**Marquand, Madison, Pop. 203**
Marquand-Zion R-VI SD 200/K-12
205 E Morley 63655 573-783-3388
Scott Blake, supt. Fax 783-3067
mz.k12.mo.us
Marquand-Zion JSHS 100/7-12
205 E Morley 63655 573-783-3388
Scott Blake, prin. Fax 783-3067

**Marshall, Saline, Pop. 12,591**
Marshall SD 2,400/K-12
860 W Vest St 65340 660-886-7414
Dr. Carol Maher, supt. Fax 886-5641
www.marshallschools.com/
Bueker MS 700/5-8
565 S Odell Ave 65340 660-886-6833
Lance Tobin, prin. Fax 886-7529
Marshall HS 700/9-12
805 S Miami Ave 65340 660-886-2244
Royal Peterson, prin. Fax 886-2669
Saline County Career Ctr Vo/Tech
900 W Vest St 65340 660-886-6958
Derek Lark, dir. Fax 886-3092

---

Missouri Valley College Post-Sec.
500 E College St 65340 660-831-4000

**Marshfield, Webster, Pop. 6,529**
Marshfield R-I SD 3,000/PK-12
170 State Highway DD 65706 417-859-2120
Mark Mayo, supt. Fax 859-2193
marshfieldbluejays.org/
Marshfield HS 900/9-12
370 State Highway DD 65706 417-859-2120
Jeff Curley, prin. Fax 859-7756
Marshfield JHS 700/6-8
660 N Locust St 65706 417-859-2120
Doug Summers, prin. Fax 859-4970

**Maryland Heights, Saint Louis, Pop. 26,834**
Pattonville R-3 SD
Supt. — See Saint Ann
Pattonville Heights MS 500/6-8
195 Fee Fee Rd 63043 314-213-8033
Scot Mosher, prin. Fax 213-8633
Pattonville HS 1,800/9-12
2497 Creve Coeur Mill Rd 63043 314-213-8051
Joe Dobrinic Ed.D., prin. Fax 213-8651

---

Anthem College Post-Sec.
13723 Riverport Dr Ste 103 63043 888-852-7272

**Maryville, Nodaway, Pop. 11,837**
Maryville R-II SD 1,400/PK-12
1429 S Munn Ave 64468 660-562-3255
Larry Linthacum, supt. Fax 562-4113
www.maryville.k12.mo.us/
Maryville HS 400/9-12
1503 S Munn Ave 64468 660-562-3511
Thom Alvarez, prin. Fax 562-4822
Maryville MS 400/5-8
525 W South Hills Dr 64468 660-562-3244
Kevin Pitts, prin. Fax 562-4138
Northwest Technical S Vo/Tech
1515 S Munn Ave 64468 660-562-3022
Jeremy Ingraham, dir. Fax 562-2010

---

Northwest Missouri State University Post-Sec.
800 University Dr 64468 660-562-1212

**Maysville, DeKalb, Pop. 1,100**
Maysville R-I SD 600/K-12
PO Box 68 64469 816-449-2308
Robert Smith, supt. Fax 449-5678
www.maysville.k12.mo.us
Maysville JSHS 300/7-12
PO Box 68 64469 816-449-2154
Alan Hutchcraft, prin. Fax 449-5610

**Meadville, Linn, Pop. 461**
Meadville R-IV SD 300/K-12
PO Box 217 64659 660-938-4111
Ron Holcer, supt. Fax 938-4100
Meadville JSHS 100/7-12
PO Box 217 64659 660-938-4112
Ronald Holcer, prin. Fax 938-4100

**Memphis, Scotland, Pop. 1,807**
Scotland County R-I SD 600/PK-12
438 W Lovers Ln 63555 660-465-8531
Ryan Bergeson, supt. Fax 465-8636
scotland.k12.mo.us/
Scotland County JSHS 300/7-12
606 W Lovers Ln 63555 660-465-8901
Kirk Stott, prin. Fax 465-7715

**Mendon, Chariton, Pop. 171**
Northwestern R-I SD 200/PK-12
PO Box 43 64660 660-272-3201
Ron Garber, supt. Fax 272-3419
www.northwestern.k12.mo.us
Northwestern HS 100/7-12
PO Box 43 64660 660-272-3201
Eric Hoyt, prin. Fax 272-3738

**Mercer, Mercer, Pop. 315**
North Mercer County R-III SD 200/PK-12
PO Box 648 64661 660-382-4214
Dan Owens, supt. Fax 382-4239
www.northmercer.k12.mo.us
Mercer JSHS 100/7-12
PO Box 648 64661 660-382-4214
Kim Palmer, prin. Fax 382-4239

**Mexico, Audrain, Pop. 11,278**
Mexico SD 59 2,400/PK-12
2101 Lakeview Rd 65265 573-581-3773
Kevin Freeman, supt. Fax 581-1794
www.mexicoschools.net
Hart Career Center Vo/Tech
905 N Wade St 65265 573-581-5684
Chris Denham, dir. Fax 581-7084
Mexico Education Center Alt
905 N Wade St 65265 573-581-5529
Chris Denham, dir. Fax 581-1794
Mexico HS 800/9-12
639 N Wade St 65265 573-581-4296
Dr. Terry Robinson, prin. Fax 581-3788
Mexico MS 500/6-8
1200 W Boulevard St 65265 573-581-4664
Deb Haag, prin. Fax 581-8440

---

Missouri Military Academy 200/6-12
204 N Grand St 65265 573-581-1776
Charles McGeorge, pres. Fax 581-0081

**Milan, Sullivan, Pop. 1,949**
Milan C-2 SD 700/PK-12
373 S Market St 63556 660-265-4414
Dr. Ben Yocom, supt. Fax 265-4315
www.milan.k12.mo.us/
Milan HS 200/9-12
373 S Market St 63556 660-265-4415
Michael Hostetter, prin. Fax 265-4315
Milan MS 200/5-8
373 S Market St 63556 660-265-4421
Erik Logan, prin. Fax 265-4315

**Miller, Lawrence, Pop. 697**
Miller R-II SD 500/K-12
110 W 6th St 65707 417-452-3515
Dr. Dustin Storm, supt. Fax 452-2709
www.millerschools.org/
Miller JSHS 200/7-12
110 W 6th St 65707 417-452-3271
Charles Marcum, prin. Fax 452-2310

---

Round Grove Christian Academy 100/PK-12
877 Highway UU 65707 417-452-2324
Tammy McCanless, admin. Fax 452-2573

**Moberly, Randolph, Pop. 13,647**
Moberly SD 2,300/K-12
926 Kwix Rd 65270 660-269-2600
Gena McCluskey, supt. Fax 269-2611
moberly.k12.mo.us/
Moberly Area Technical Center Vo/Tech
1623 Gratz Brown St 65270 660-269-2690
Mike Barner, dir. Fax 269-2692
Moberly HS 700/9-12
1625 Gratz Brown St 65270 660-269-2660
Zach McMains, prin. Fax 263-5977
Moberly MS 500/6-8
920 Kwix Rd 65270 660-269-2680
Wes Land, prin. Fax 269-8519
North Central Regional Alt. S Alt
200 Porter St 65270 660-269-8800
Debbie Young, dir. Fax 269-8576

---

Central Christian College of the Bible Post-Sec.
911 E Urbandale Dr 65270 660-263-3900
Moberly Area Community College Post-Sec.
101 College Ave 65270 660-263-4110

**Mokane, Callaway, Pop. 182**
South Callaway County R-II SD 800/PK-12
10135 State Road C 65059 573-676-5225
Kevin Hillman, supt. Fax 676-5134
www.sc.k12.mo.us/
South Callaway HS 300/9-12
10135 State Road C 65059 573-676-5225
Heather Helsel, prin. Fax 676-5132
South Callaway MS 200/6-8
10135 State Road C 65059 573-676-5216
Gary Bonsall, prin. Fax 676-5347

**Monett, Barry, Pop. 8,746**
Monett R-I SD 2,400/PK-12
900 E Scott St 65708 417-235-7422
Dr. Brad Hanson, supt. Fax 235-1415
monett.schoolfusion.us/
Monett HS 600/9-12
1 David Sippy Dr 65708 417-235-5445
David Steward, prin. Fax 235-7884
Monett MS 400/7-8
710 9th St 65708 417-235-6228
Dr. Jonathan Apostol, prin. Fax 235-3278
Scott Regional Tech Center Vo/Tech
2 David Sippy Dr 65708 417-235-7022
David Miller, dir. Fax 235-8270

**Monroe City, Monroe, Pop. 2,481**
Monroe City R-I SD 700/PK-12
401 US Highway 24/36 E 63456 573-735-4631
James Masters, supt. Fax 735-2413
monroe.k12.mo.us/
Monroe City MS 200/5-8
430 N Washington St 63456 573-735-4742
Joshua Klusmeyer, prin. Fax 735-2413
Monroe City R-I HS 200/9-12
401 US Highway 24/36 E 63456 573-735-4626
Ryan Watson, prin. Fax 735-2413

**Montgomery City, Montgomery, Pop. 2,792**
Montgomery County R-II SD 1,300/PK-12
418 N Highway 19 63361 573-564-2278
Michael Gray, supt. Fax 782-8700
www.mc-wildcats.org
Montgomery County HS 400/9-12
394 N Highway 19 63361 573-564-2278
Chris Redmon, prin. Fax 782-8701
Montgomery County MS 300/6-8
418 N Highway 19 63361 573-564-2278
Madonna Pund, prin. Fax 782-8702

**Montrose, Henry, Pop. 383**
Montrose R-XIV SD 100/K-12
307 E 2nd St 64770 660-693-4812
Denise Fast, supt. Fax 693-4594
www.montrose.k12.mo.us
Montrose R-XIV HS 50/9-12
307 E 2nd St 64770 660-693-4812
Denise Fast, admin. Fax 693-4594

**Morrisville, Polk, Pop. 377**
Marion C. Early R-V SD 500/PK-12
5309 S Main Ave 65710 417-376-2255
Eric Kurre, supt. Fax 376-3243
www.mceonline.net
Early HS 200/9-12
5309 S Main Ave 65710 417-376-2216
Dr. Joel Carey, prin. Fax 376-7622
Early JHS 200/6-8
5309 S Main Ave 65710 417-376-2216
Dr. Joel Carey, prin. Fax 376-7622

**Moscow Mills, Lincoln, Pop. 2,430**
Lincoln County R-III SD
Supt. — See Troy
Ninth Grade Center 500/9-9
80 Elm Tree Rd 63362 636-366-4450
Dr. Chris Chaney, prin. Fax 366-4451

**Mound City, Holt, Pop. 1,154**
Mound City R-II SD 200/PK-12
708 Nebraska St 64470 660-442-3737
Kenneth Eaton, supt. Fax 442-5941
mndcty.k12.mo.us
Mound City HS 100/9-12
708 Nebraska St 64470 660-442-5429
Korey Miles, prin. Fax 442-3154

**Mountain Grove, Wright, Pop. 4,721**
Mountain Grove R-III SD 1,400/K-12
PO Box 806 65711 417-926-3177
Jim Dickey, supt. Fax 926-4564
www.mg.k12.mo.us
Mountain Grove HS 400/9-12
PO Box 806 65711 417-926-3177
Marcia Stumpff, prin. Fax 926-1702
Mountain Grove MS 400/5-8
PO Box 806 65711 417-926-3177
Lori Golden, prin. Fax 926-1673
Ozark Mountain Technical Center Vo/Tech
PO Box 806 65711 417-926-3177
J.T. Hale, dir. Fax 926-6858

**Mountain View, Howell, Pop. 2,694**
Mountain View-Birch Tree R-III SD 1,300/PK-12
PO Box 464 65548 417-934-2020
Dr. Don Christensen, supt. Fax 934-5404
mvbt.k12.mo.us
Liberty HS 400/9-12
PO Box 464 65548 417-934-2020
John Daniels, prin. Fax 934-1329
Liberty MS 300/6-8
PO Box 464 65548 417-934-2020
Dr. Walt Belcher, prin. Fax 934-1329

**Mount Vernon, Lawrence, Pop. 4,491**
Mt. Vernon R-V SD 1,500/K-12
731 S Landrum St 65712 417-466-7573
James Cruzan, supt. Fax 466-7058
www.mtvernon.k12.mo.us
Mount Vernon HS 500/9-12
400 W Highway 174 65712 417-466-7526
Scott Cook, prin. Fax 466-4307
Mount Vernon MS 300/6-8
731 S Landrum St 65712 417-466-3137
Robert Senninger, prin. Fax 466-7058

**Myrtle, Oregon**
Couch R-I SD 200/PK-12
RR 91 Box 1187 65778 417-938-4211
Allen Moss, supt. Fax 938-4267
www.couch.k12.mo.us/
Couch JSHS 200/7-12
RR 91 Box 1187 65778 417-938-4212
Sherry McMasters, prin. Fax 938-4267

**Naylor, Ripley, Pop. 602**
Naylor R-II SD 400/K-12
101 Batten St 63953 573-399-2505
Terry Arnold, supt. Fax 399-2874
naylor.k12.mo.us
Naylor JSHS 200/7-12
RR 2 Box 512 63953 573-399-2506
Terry Arnold, prin. Fax 399-2388

**Neelyville, Butler, Pop. 467**
Neelyville R-IV SD 600/PK-12
PO Box 8 63954 573-989-3813
Bradley Hagood, supt. Fax 989-3434
www.neelyville.k12.mo.us
Neelyville JSHS 300/7-12
PO Box 8 63954 573-989-3815
Justin Dobbins, prin. Fax 989-6322

**Neosho, Newton, Pop. 11,282**
Neosho R-V SD 4,500/PK-12
418 Fairground Rd 64850 417-451-8600
Dan Decker, supt. Fax 451-8604
www.neoshopublicschools.net
Neosho HS 1,200/9-12
511 S Neosho Blvd 64850 417-451-8670
Darren Cook, prin. Fax 451-8605
Neosho JHS 300/7-8
511 S Neosho Blvd 64850 417-451-8660
Dr. Jenifer Cryer, prin. Fax 451-8687

---

Crowder College Post-Sec.
601 Laclede Ave 64850 417-451-3223
Neosho Beauty College Post-Sec.
116 N Wood St 64850 417-451-7216
Neosho Christian S 100/PK-12
903 W South St 64850 417-451-1941
Lowell McInturff M.Ed., supt. Fax 451-4059
Ozark Christian Academy 50/K-12
PO Box 786 64850 417-451-1100
Joyce Prihoda, prin. Fax 451-2059

**Nevada, Vernon, Pop. 8,266**
Nevada R-V SD 2,900/PK-12
811 W Hickory St 64772 417-448-2000
Dr. Tyson Beshore, supt. Fax 448-2006
www.nevada.k12.mo.us
Nevada HS 800/9-12
800 W Hickory St 64772 417-448-2020
Gerald Whalen, prin. Fax 448-1923
Nevada MS 600/6-8
900 N Olive St 64772 417-448-2040
Geoff Stewart, prin. Fax 448-2048
Nevada Regional Tech-Center Vo/Tech
900 W Ashland St 64772 417-448-2090
Dr. Phillip Witt, dir. Fax 448-2092

---

Cottey College Post-Sec.
1000 W Austin Blvd 64772 417-667-8181

**Newark, Knox, Pop. 88**

---

Heartland Christian College Post-Sec.
500 New Creation Rd N 63458 660-284-4800

**New Bloomfield, Callaway, Pop. 652**
New Bloomfield R-III SD 700/PK-12
307 Redwood Dr 65063 573-491-3700
David Tramel, supt. Fax 491-3772
www.nb.k12.mo.us
New Bloomfield JSHS 400/6-12
307 Redwood Dr 65063 573-491-3700
Jeremy Davidson, prin. Fax 491-3696

**Newburg, Phelps, Pop. 466**
Newburg R-II SD 500/PK-12
PO Box C 65550 573-762-9653
Dr. Lynne Reed, supt. Fax 762-3040
www.newburg.k12.mo.us
Newburg JSHS 200/7-12
PO Box C 65550 573-762-2331
Steve Guffey, prin. Fax 762-0140

**New Cambria, Macon, Pop. 195**
Macon County R-IV SD 100/K-12
PO Box 70 63558 660-226-5615
John Dunham, supt. Fax 226-5618
www.mcr4.k12.mo.us/
Macon County JSHS 100/7-12
PO Box 70 63558 660-226-5615
Zach Bruner, prin. Fax 226-5618

**New Franklin, Howard, Pop. 1,064**
New Franklin R-I SD 500/PK-12
412 W Broadway 65274 660-848-2141
Dr. David Haggard, supt. Fax 848-2226
www.nfranklin.k12.mo.us/
New Franklin MSHS 200/6-12
412 W Broadway 65274 660-848-2314
Benji Dorson, prin. Fax 848-3071

**New Haven, Franklin, Pop. 2,057**
New Haven SD 500/K-12
100 Park Dr 63068 573-237-3231
Kyle Kruse, supt. Fax 237-5959
www.newhavenschools.org
New Haven HS 200/9-12
100 Park Dr 63068 573-237-2629
Josh Hoener, prin. Fax 237-5959
New Haven MS 100/7-8
100 Park Dr 63068 573-237-2900
Josh Hoener, prin. Fax 237-5959

**New Madrid, New Madrid, Pop. 3,072**
New Madrid County R-I SD 1,500/PK-12
310 US Highway 61 63869 573-688-2161
Dr. Cindy Amick, supt. Fax 688-2169
www.newmadridco.k12.mo.us/
Central HS 400/9-12
310 US Highway 61 63869 573-688-2165
Gerald Murphy, prin. Fax 688-2169
Central MS 300/6-8
308 US Highway 61 63869 573-688-2176
Thomas Drummond, prin. Fax 688-2245
New Madrid R-I Tech Skills Center Vo/Tech
310 US Highway 61 63869 573-688-2161
John Garner, dir. Fax 688-2169

**Newtown, Sullivan, Pop. 178**
Newtown-Harris R-III SD 100/PK-12
306 N Main St 64667 660-794-2245
William Copple, supt. Fax 794-2730
www.nhtigers.k12.mo.us/
Newtown-Harris JSHS 50/7-12
306 N Main St 64667 660-794-2245
Misty Foster, prin. Fax 794-2730

**Niangua, Webster, Pop. 404**
Niangua R-V SD 300/PK-12
301 Rumsey St 65713 417-473-6101
Thomas Bransfield, supt. Fax 473-6124
www.nianguaschools.com
Niangua JSHS 100/7-12
301 Rumsey St 65713 417-473-6101
Thomas Bransfield, prin. Fax 473-6124

**Nixa, Christian, Pop. 18,653**
Nixa SD 5,300/PK-12
301 S Main St 65714 417-875-5400
Dr. Stephen Kleinsmith, supt. Fax 449-3190
www.nixapublicschools.net
Nixa HS 1,700/9-12
514 S Nicholas Rd 65714 417-724-3500
Mark McGehee, prin. Fax 724-3515
Nixa JHS 900/7-8
205 North St 65714 417-875-5430
Dr. Lori Wilson, prin. Fax 875-5426
SCORE Learning Center Alt
1398 W Mount Vernon St 65714 417-724-4080
Cheryl Huson, prin. Fax 724-4088

**Noel, McDonald, Pop. 1,745**
McDonald County R-I SD
Supt. — See Anderson
Noel ES 400/3-8
318 Sulphur St 64854 417-475-3302
Tim Kilby, prin. Fax 475-6516

**Norborne, Carroll, Pop. 697**
Norborne R-VIII SD 200/PK-12
PO Box 192 64668 660-593-3319
Dr. Roger Feagan, supt. Fax 593-3657
www.norborneschools.com/
Norborne HS 100/6-12
PO Box 192 64668 660-593-3319
Roger Stone, prin. Fax 593-3657

**Normandy, Saint Louis, Pop. 4,907**
Normandy Schools Collaborative
Supt. — See Saint Louis
Normandy MS 1,000/7-8
7855 Natural Bridge Rd 63121 314-493-0500
Andrew Miller, prin. Fax 493-0560

**North Kansas City, Clay, Pop. 4,094**
North Kansas City SD 74
Supt. — See Kansas City
North Kansas City HS 1,500/9-12
620 E 23rd Ave 64116 816-321-5310
Dr. Dan Wartick, prin. Fax 321-5311

---

North Kansas City Hospital Post-Sec.
2800 Clay Edwards Dr 64116 816-691-2000

**Norwood, Wright, Pop. 654**
Norwood R-I SD 400/K-12
675 N Hawk St 65717 417-746-4101
Shannon Crain, supt. Fax 746-9950
www.norwood.k12.mo.us/
Norwood HS 200/6-12
675 N Hawk St 65717 417-746-4101
Kevin Johnson, prin. Fax 746-9950

**Novinger, Adair, Pop. 454**
Adair County R-I SD 300/K-12
600 Rombauer Ave 63559 660-488-6411
Rick Roberts, supt. Fax 488-5400
www.novinger.k12.mo.us
Adair County JSHS 100/7-12
600 Rombauer Ave 63559 660-488-6411
Robin Carter, prin. Fax 488-5400

**Oak Grove, Jackson, Pop. 7,672**
Oak Grove R-VI SD 2,000/PK-12
601 SE 12th St 64075 816-690-4156
Freddie Doherty, supt. Fax 690-3031
www.oakgrove.k12.mo.us
Oak Grove HS 700/9-12
605 SE 12th St 64075 816-690-4152
Adam Salmon, prin. Fax 690-5666
Oak Grove MS 500/6-8
401 SE 12th St 64075 816-690-4154
Tracy Kemp, prin. Fax 690-3976

**Oak Ridge, Cape Girardeau, Pop. 236**
Oak Ridge R-VI SD 300/K-12
PO Box 10 63769 573-266-3218
Dr. Gerald Landewee, supt. Fax 266-0133
www.oakridger6schools.com
Oak Ridge JSHS 200/7-12
PO Box 10 63769 573-266-3630
Allan Horrell, prin. Fax 266-0133

**Odessa, Lafayette, Pop. 5,180**
Odessa R-VII SD 2,000/K-12
701 S 3rd St 64076 816-633-5316
Robert Brinkley, supt. Fax 633-8582
www.odessa.k12.mo.us/
Odessa HS 600/9-12
713 S 3rd St 64076 816-633-5533
Buffie McConville, prin. Fax 633-7506
Odessa MS 500/6-8
607 S 5th St 64076 816-633-1500
Kendra Malizzi, prin. Fax 633-7101

**O Fallon, Saint Charles, Pop. 77,920**
Ft. Zumwalt R-II SD 18,800/K-12
555 E Terra Ln 63366 636-240-2072
Dr. Bernard DuBray, supt. Fax 272-1059
www.fz.k12.mo.us
Fort Zumwalt Hope HS 100/Alt
307 W Pitman St 63366 636-379-5300
Ryan Bishop, prin. Fax 379-5909
Ft. Zumwalt North HS 1,400/9-12
1230 Tom Ginnever Ave 63366 636-272-4447
Joe Sutton, prin. Fax 272-6124
Ft. Zumwalt North MS 1,000/6-8
210 Virgil St 63366 636-281-2356
Dr. Tim Jamieson, prin. Fax 281-0005
Ft. Zumwalt West HS 2,100/9-12
1251 Turtle Creek Dr 63366 636-379-0300
Neil Berry, prin. Fax 281-0202
Ft. Zumwalt West MS 1,500/6-8
150 Waterford Crossing Dr, 636-272-6690
Jennifer Hecktor, prin. Fax 272-6361
Other Schools – See Saint Peters

Wentzville R-IV SD
Supt. — See Wentzville
Frontier MS 1,200/6-8
9233 Highway DD, 636-625-1026
Dr. Kelly Mcclain, prin. Fax 625-1094

---

Living Word Christian MSHS 500/6-12
1145 Tom Ginnever Ave 63366 636-978-1680
Keith Currivean, supt. Fax 978-5024
St. Dominic HS 700/9-12
31 Saint Dominic Dr 63366 636-240-8303
Janet Eaton, prin. Fax 240-9884

**Oran, Scott, Pop. 1,284**
Oran R-III SD — 400/K-12
PO Box 250 63771 — 573-262-2330
Mitchell Wood, supt. — Fax 262-2330
www.oran.k12.mo.us
Oran HS — 200/7-12
PO Box 250 63771 — 573-262-3345
Adam Friga, prin. — Fax 262-2289

**Oregon, Holt, Pop. 851**
South Holt County R-I SD — 300/PK-12
201 S Barbour St 64473 — 660-446-2282
Bob Ottman, supt. — Fax 446-2312
www.southholtr1.com
South Holt County JSHS — 100/7-12
201 S Barbour St 64473 — 660-446-3454
Rachel Peek, prin. — Fax 446-2312

**Orrick, Ray, Pop. 827**
Orrick R-XI SD — 400/PK-12
100 Kirkham St 64077 — 816-770-0094
Aerin O'Dell, supt. — Fax 496-3829
www.orrick.k12.mo.us
Orrick JSHS — 200/7-12
100 Kirkham St 64077 — 816-770-3327
Scott Archibald, prin. — Fax 496-3829

**Osage Beach, Miller, Pop. 4,299**
School of the Osage R-II SD
Supt. — See Lake Ozark
Osage HS — 500/9-12
636 Highway 42 65065 — 573-348-0115
Mike Williams, prin. — Fax 348-9774
Osage MS — 500/6-8
635 Highway 42 65065 — 573-552-8326
Tony Slack, prin. — Fax 552-8322

**Osborn, DeKalb, Pop. 422**
Osborn R-0 SD — 100/K-12
275 Clinton Ave 64474 — 816-675-2217
Richard Goin, supt. — Fax 675-2222
www.osbornwildcats.org
Osborn JSHS — 100/7-12
275 Clinton Ave 64474 — 816-675-2217
Derek Brady, prin. — Fax 675-2222

**Osceola, Saint Clair, Pop. 924**
Osceola SD — 500/PK-12
76 SE Highway WW 64776 — 417-646-8143
Danny DeWitt, supt. — Fax 646-8075
www.osceola.k12.mo.us
Osceola JSHS — 200/7-12
76 SE Highway WW 64776 — 417-646-8144
Dustin Schubert, prin. — Fax 646-8549

**Otterville, Cooper, Pop. 446**
Otterville R-VI SD — 200/K-12
101 W Georgetown St 65348 — 660-366-4391
Matt Unger, supt. — Fax 366-4293
www.ottervillervi.k12.mo.us
Otterville JSHS — 100/7-12
101 W Georgetown St 65348 — 660-366-4621
Kim Oelrichs, prin. — Fax 366-4293

**Overland, Saint Louis, Pop. 15,614**
Ritenour SD
Supt. — See Saint Louis
Ritenour HS — 1,800/9-12
9100 Saint Charles Rock Rd 63114 — 314-493-6105
Gary Spiller, prin. — Fax 429-6725
Ritenour MS — 600/6-8
2500 Marshall Ave 63114 — 314-493-6250
Kenneth Roumpos, prin. — Fax 429-6726

**Owensville, Gasconade, Pop. 2,647**
Gasconade County R-II SD — 1,900/PK-12
PO Box 536 65066 — 573-437-2177
Dr. Chuck Garner, supt. — Fax 437-5808
www.owensville.k12.mo.us
Owensville HS — 600/9-12
PO Box 536 65066 — 573-437-2174
Jeff Jacques, prin. — Fax 437-7174
Owensville MS — 400/6-8
PO Box 536 65066 — 573-437-2172
Teresa Schulte, prin. — Fax 437-6704

**Ozark, Christian, Pop. 17,472**
Ozark R-VI SD — 5,400/K-12
PO Box 166 65721 — 417-582-5900
Dr. Kevin Patterson, supt. — Fax 582-5960
www.ozark.k12.mo.us
Ozark HS — 1,600/9-12
PO Box 166 65721 — 417-582-5901
Dr. Sam Taylor, prin. — Fax 582-5944
Ozark JHS — 800/7-8
PO Box 166 65721 — 417-582-4701
Jim Hubbard, prin. — Fax 582-4714

**Pacific, Franklin, Pop. 6,911**
Meramec Valley R-III SD — 3,300/PK-12
126 N Payne St 63069 — 636-271-1400
Randy George, supt. — Fax 271-1406
www.mvr3.k12.mo.us/
Pacific HS — 1,000/9-12
425 Indian Warpath Dr 63069 — 636-271-1414
Tom Sauvage, prin. — Fax 271-1420
Riverbend S — 200/8-8
2085 Highway N 63069 — 636-271-1481
Ketina Armstrong, prin. — Fax 271-1485

**Palmyra, Marion, Pop. 3,541**
Palmyra R-I SD — 1,200/K-12
PO Box 151 63461 — 573-769-2066
Eric Churchwell, supt. — Fax 769-4218
www.palmyra.k12.mo.us
Palmyra HS — 400/9-12
PO Box 151 63461 — 573-769-2067
Kenneth Holstine, prin. — Fax 769-1013
Palmyra MS — 400/5-8
PO Box 151 63461 — 573-769-2174
Michael Kirt Malone, prin. — Fax 769-4227

**Paris, Monroe, Pop. 1,208**
Paris R-II SD — 500/PK-12
740 Cleveland St 65275 — 660-327-4112
Chris Johnson, supt. — Fax 327-4290
paris.k12.mo.us/site/
Paris HS — 200/9-12
25686 Business Highway 24 65275 — 660-327-4111
Chris Willingham, prin. — Fax 327-6220
Paris JHS — 100/7-8
25678 Business Highway 24 65275 — 660-327-4563
Chris Willingham, prin. — Fax 327-4782

**Park Hills, Saint Francois, Pop. 8,642**
Central R-III SD — 2,000/PK-12
200 High St 63601 — 573-431-2616
Dr. Desmond Mayberry, supt. — Fax 431-2107
www.centralr3.org
Central HS — 600/9-12
116 Rebel Dr 63601 — 573-431-2616
Brad Coleman, prin. — Fax 431-0700
Central MS — 500/6-8
801 Columbia St 63601 — 573-431-2616
Mike Harlow, prin. — Fax 431-5393

West St. Francois County R-IV SD
Supt. — See Leadwood
West County HS — 300/9-12
768 Highway M 63601 — 573-562-7521
Eric Moyers, prin. — Fax 562-7554

---

Mineral Area College — Post-Sec.
PO Box 1000 63601 — 573-431-4593

**Parkville, Platte, Pop. 5,415**

---

Park University — Post-Sec.
8700 NW River Park Dr 64152 — 816-741-2000

**Patton, Bollinger**
Meadow Heights R-II SD — 500/K-12
RR 5 Box 2365 63662 — 573-866-0060
Andrew B. Comstock, supt. — Fax 866-3240
Meadow Heights JSHS — 300/7-12
RR 5 Box 2365 63662 — 573-866-2924
Mitchell Nanney, prin. — Fax 866-2219

**Pattonsburg, Daviess, Pop. 346**
Pattonsburg R-II SD — 200/PK-12
PO Box 200 64670 — 660-367-2111
Troy Clawson, supt. — Fax 367-4205
www.pattonsburg.k12.mo.us
Pattonsburg JSHS — 100/7-12
PO Box 200 64670 — 660-367-2111
Chris Hodge, prin. — Fax 367-4205

**Peculiar, Cass, Pop. 4,532**
Raymore-Peculiar R-II SD — 6,500/PK-12
PO Box 789 64078 — 816-892-1300
Dr. Kari Monsees, supt. — Fax 892-1380
www.raypec.k12.mo.us
Raymore-Peculiar Academy — 400/Alt
PO Box 789 64078 — 816-892-1530
Jim Brown, prin. — Fax 892-1529
Raymore-Peculiar HS — 1,800/9-12
PO Box 789 64078 — 816-892-1400
Steven Miller, prin. — Fax 892-1401
Other Schools – See Raymore

**Perryville, Perry, Pop. 8,127**
Perry County SD 32 — 2,300/K-12
326 College St 63775 — 573-547-7500
Scott Ireland, supt. — Fax 547-8572
www.perryville.k12.mo.us
Perry County MS — 700/5-8
326 College St 63775 — 573-547-7500
Velda Haertling, prin. — Fax 547-1962
Perryville Area Career Center — Vo/Tech
326 College St 63775 — 573-547-7500
Craig Hayden, dir. — Fax 517-0396
Perryville HS — 800/9-12
326 College St 63775 — 573-547-7500
Rich Thomas, prin. — Fax 517-0592

---

St. Vincent JSHS — 200/7-12
210 S Waters St 63775 — 573-547-2560
Dr. Patricia Hensley, head sch — Fax 547-1722

**Philadelphia, Marion**
Marion County R-II SD — 200/PK-12
2905 Highway D 63463 — 573-439-5913
Dianna Hoenes, supt. — Fax 439-5914
www.marion.k12.mo.us/
Marion County JSHS — 100/7-12
2905 Highway D 63463 — 573-439-5913
Dianna Hoenes, supt. — Fax 439-5914

**Piedmont, Wayne, Pop. 1,960**
Clearwater R-I SD — 1,000/PK-12
RR 4 Box 1004 63957 — 573-223-7426
Deborah Hand, supt. — Fax 223-2932
Clearwater HS — 300/9-12
RR 4 Box 1004 63957 — 573-223-4524
Teresa Smith, prin. — Fax 223-3208
Clearwater MS — 300/5-8
RR 4 Box 1004 63957 — 573-223-7724
Michael Keller, prin. — Fax 223-3117

---

Lighthouse Christian Academy — 50/6-12
PO Box 100 63957 — 573-223-2025
Larry Musgrave, pres. — Fax 223-2105

**Pierce City, Lawrence, Pop. 1,276**
Pierce City R-VI SD — 700/PK-12
300 N Myrtle St 65723 — 417-476-2555
Dr. Russell Moreland, supt. — Fax 476-5213
www.pcschools.net
Pierce City HS — 200/9-12
300 N Myrtle St 65723 — 417-476-2515
Steve Garner, prin. — Fax 476-3516
Pierce City MS — 200/5-8
300 N Myrtle St 65723 — 417-476-2842
Russ Moreland, prin. — Fax 476-5405

**Pilot Grove, Cooper, Pop. 759**
Pilot Grove C-4 SD — 300/PK-12
107 School St 65276 — 660-834-6915
Ashley Groepper, supt. — Fax 834-6925
www.pilotgrove.k12.mo.us
Pilot Grove HS — 100/9-12
107 School St 65276 — 660-834-4415
Randall Glenn, prin. — Fax 834-4401
Pilot Grove MS — 50/7-8
107 School St 65276 — 660-834-4415
Randall Glenn, prin. — Fax 834-4401

**Pineville, McDonald, Pop. 780**
McDonald County R-I SD
Supt. — See Anderson
Pineville ES — 300/3-8
202 E 8th St 64856 — 417-223-4346
Tamra Kester, prin. — Fax 223-4195

**Plato, Texas, Pop. 109**
Plato R-V SD — 700/PK-12
PO Box A 65552 — 417-458-3333
Dan Chappell, supt. — Fax 458-4706
www.plato.k12.mo.us/
Plato HS — 300/6-12
PO Box A 65552 — 417-458-4980
Justin Copley, prin. — Fax 458-4706

**Platte City, Platte, Pop. 4,565**
Platte County R-III SD — 3,700/PK-12
998 Platte Falls Rd 64079 — 816-858-5420
Dr. Mike Reik, supt. — Fax 858-5593
www.plattecountyschooldistrict.com/
Northland Career Center — Vo/Tech
1801 Branch St 64079 — 816-858-5505
Brian Noller, dir. — Fax 858-3278
Platte City MS — 600/6-8
900 Pirate Dr 64079 — 816-858-2036
Dr. Chris Miller, prin. — Fax 858-3748
Platte County HS — 1,000/9-12
1501 Branch St 64079 — 816-858-2822
Dr. Chad Sayre, prin. — Fax 858-5140
Other Schools – See Kansas City

**Plattsburg, Clinton, Pop. 2,263**
Clinton County R-III SD — 800/PK-12
800 W Frost St 64477 — 816-539-2183
Dr. Marcus Stucker, supt. — Fax 539-2412
ccr3.k12.mo.us
Clinton County R-III MS — 200/6-8
800 W Frost St 64477 — 816-539-3920
Danny Knapp, prin. — Fax 539-2412
Plattsburg HS — 300/9-12
800 W Frost St 64477 — 816-539-2184
Zach Mcmains, prin. — Fax 539-3315

**Pleasant Hill, Cass, Pop. 7,996**
Pleasant Hill R-III SD — 2,200/PK-12
318 Cedar St 64080 — 816-540-3161
Dr. Wesley Townsend, supt. — Fax 540-5135
www.pleasanthillschools.com
Pleasant Hill HS — 700/9-12
1 Rooster Way 64080 — 816-540-3111
Dr. Paul Canaan, prin. — Fax 987-6084
Pleasant Hill MS — 300/7-8
1301 E Myrtle St 64080 — 816-540-2149
Jenny Daniel, prin. — Fax 987-2017

**Pleasant Hope, Polk, Pop. 604**
Pleasant Hope R-VI SD — 1,000/PK-12
PO Box 387 65725 — 417-267-2850
Kelly Lowe, supt. — Fax 267-4373
www.phr6.org
Pleasant Hope HS — 300/9-12
PO Box 387 65725 — 417-267-2271
Brent Offerdahl, prin. — Fax 267-5007
Pleasant Hope MS — 300/5-8
PO Box 387 65725 — 417-267-7701
Michael Smith, prin. — Fax 267-9221
Other Schools – See Brighton

**Point Lookout, Taney**

---

College of the Ozarks — Post-Sec.
PO Box 17 65726 — 417-334-6411

**Polo, Caldwell, Pop. 552**
Polo R-VII SD — 400/K-12
300 W School St 64671 — 660-354-2326
Donald Wilburn, supt. — Fax 354-2910
polo.k12.mo.us/
Polo HS — 100/9-12
300 W School St 64671 — 660-354-2524
Kyle Ross, prin. — Fax 354-2738
Polo MS — 100/5-8
300 W School St 64671 — 660-354-2200
Monica Palmer, prin. — Fax 354-3162

**Poplar Bluff, Butler, Pop. 16,562**
Poplar Bluff R-I SD — 5,100/PK-12
1110 N Westwood Blvd 63901 — 573-785-7751
Chris Hon, supt. — Fax 785-0336
www.poplarbluffschools.net
Poplar Bluff HS — 1,400/9-12
1300 Victory Ln 63901 — 573-785-6471
Michael Kiehne, prin. — Fax 785-6471
Poplar Bluff JHS — 800/7-8
550 N Westwood Blvd 63901 — 573-785-5602
Bob Case, prin. — Fax 785-5004
Technical Career Center — Vo/Tech
3203 Oak Grove Rd 63901 — 573-785-2248
Charles Kinsey, prin. — Fax 785-4168

---

Three Rivers Community College — Post-Sec.
2080 Three Rivers Blvd 63901 — 573-840-9600

**Portageville, New Madrid, Pop. 3,162**
Portageville SD 800/PK-12
904 King Ave 63873 573-379-3855
Michael Allred, supt. Fax 379-5817
www.portageville.k12.mo.us
Portageville HS 200/9-12
904 King Ave 63873 573-379-3819
Jeff Bullock, prin. Fax 379-5817
Portageville MS 200/6-8
902 King Ave 63873 573-379-3853
Barry Branscum, prin. Fax 379-5817

**Potosi, Washington, Pop. 2,627**
Potosi R-III SD 2,400/PK-12
400 N Mine St 63664 573-438-5485
Randy Davis, supt. Fax 438-5487
www.potosir3.org/
Evans MS 400/7-8
303 S Lead St 63664 573-438-2101
Dan Beckwith, prin. Fax 438-4635
Potosi HS 700/9-12
1 Trojan Dr 63664 573-438-2156
Dr. Shawn Mccue, prin. Fax 438-2269

**Prairie Home, Cooper, Pop. 279**
Prairie Home R-V SD 200/K-12
301 Highway 87 65068 660-841-5296
Dr. Steven Barnes, supt. Fax 841-5513
www.prairiehome.k12.mo.us
Prairie Home HS 100/7-12
301 Highway 87 65068 660-841-5296
Patrick Tray, prin. Fax 841-5513

**Princeton, Mercer, Pop. 1,164**
Princeton R-V SD 400/PK-12
1008 E Coleman St 64673 660-748-3490
Jerry Girdner, supt. Fax 748-3212
www.tigertown.k12.mo.us
Princeton JSHS 200/7-12
1008 E Coleman St 64673 660-748-3490
Tamie Miller, prin. Fax 748-4018

**Purdin, Linn, Pop. 189**
Linn County R-I SD 100/PK-12
PO Box 130 64674 660-244-5045
Ryan Livingston, supt. Fax 244-5025
www.linnr1.k12.mo.us
Linn County R-1 S 100/PK-12
PO Box 130 64674 660-244-5035
Candi Gray, prin. Fax 244-5025

**Purdy, Barry, Pop. 1,081**
Purdy R-II SD 600/K-12
PO Box 248 65734 417-442-3216
Dr. Steven Chancellor, supt. Fax 442-3963
www.purdyk12.com
Purdy HS 200/9-12
PO Box 248 65734 417-442-3215
Matthew Gower, prin. Fax 442-3632
Purdy MS 200/5-8
PO Box 248 65734 417-442-7066
Janet Boys, prin. Fax 442-7067

**Puxico, Stoddard, Pop. 867**
Puxico R-VIII SD 800/PK-12
481 N Bedford St 63960 573-222-3762
Dr. Kyle Dare, supt. Fax 222-3137
www.puxico.k12.mo.us
Mingo/Puxico Technical HS Vo/Tech
481 N Bedford St 63960 573-222-2675
Jason Hill, prin. Fax 222-3137
Puxico HS 200/9-12
481 N Bedford St 63960 573-222-3175
Cindy Crabb, prin. Fax 222-2375
Puxico JHS 200/6-8
481 N Bedford St 63960 573-222-3058
Jason Hill, prin. Fax 222-6373

**Queen City, Schuyler, Pop. 595**
Schuyler County R-I SD 700/PK-12
1170 Highway 63 63561 660-766-2204
Robert Amen, supt. Fax 766-2400
www.schuyler.k12.mo.us
Schuyler County R-I HS 300/7-12
1170 Highway 63 63561 660-766-2424
Kyle Windy, prin. Fax 766-2646

**Ravenwood, Nodaway, Pop. 439**
Northeast Nodaway County R-V SD 200/PK-12
PO Box 206 64479 660-937-3112
Jeff Mehlenbacher Ed.D., supt. Fax 937-3110
nen.k12.mo.us
Northeast Nodaway HS 100/7-12
PO Box 206 64479 660-937-3125
Linda Mattson, prin. Fax 937-3110

**Raymore, Cass, Pop. 18,776**
Raymore-Peculiar R-II SD
Supt. — See Peculiar
Raymore-Peculiar East MS 1,000/7-8
17509 E State Route 58 64083 816-388-4000
David Mitchell, prin. Fax 388-4001

---

House of Heavilin Beauty College Post-Sec.
800 W Foxwood Dr 64083 816-767-8000

**Raytown, Jackson, Pop. 28,561**
Raytown C-2 SD 8,400/PK-12
6608 Raytown Rd 64133 816-268-7000
Dr. Allan Markley, supt. Fax 268-7019
www.raytownschools.org/
Herndon Career Center Vo/Tech
11501 E State Route 350 64138 816-268-7140
Cheryl Reichert, dir. Fax 268-7149
Raytown Alternative S Alt
10750 E State Route 350 64138 816-268-7180
Lori Forte, prin. Fax 268-7185
Raytown Central MS 600/6-8
10601 E 59th St 64133 816-268-7050
Dr. Jaime Sadich, prin. Fax 268-7055
Raytown HS 1,400/9-12
6019 Blue Ridge Blvd 64133 816-268-7300
Dr. Chad Bruton, prin. Fax 268-7315
Raytown South HS 1,200/9-12
8211 Sterling Ave 64138 816-268-7330
Dr. Kevin Overfelt, prin. Fax 268-7345
Raytown South MS 600/6-8
8401 E 83rd St 64138 816-268-7380
Carl Calcara, prin. Fax 268-7385
Other Schools – See Kansas City

**Reeds Spring, Stone, Pop. 896**
Reeds Spring R-IV SD 2,000/PK-12
20281 State Highway 413 65737 417-272-8173
Dr. Michael Mason, supt. Fax 272-8656
www.wolves.k12.mo.us
Gibson Technical Center Vo/Tech
386 W State Highway 76 65737 417-272-3271
Nick Thieman, dir. Fax 272-1529
New Horizons Alternative S Alt
386 W State Highway 76 65737 417-272-3271
Nick Thieman, dir. Fax 272-1529
Reeds Spring HS 600/9-12
20277 State Highway 413 65737 417-272-8171
Dr. Isaac Sooter, prin. Fax 272-1481
Reeds Spring MS 300/7-8
21016 Main St 65737 417-272-8245
Travis Kite, prin. Fax 272-8490

**Republic, Greene, Pop. 14,495**
Republic R-III SD 4,800/PK-12
518 N Hampton Ave 65738 417-732-3605
Chance Wistrom, supt. Fax 732-3609
www.republicschools.org
Republic HS 1,200/9-12
4370 S Repmo Dr 65738 417-732-3650
Tyler Overstreet Ed.D., prin. Fax 732-3659
Republic MS 1,000/6-8
1 Tiger Dr 65738 417-732-3640
Tonia Herbold, prin. Fax 732-3649

**Rich Hill, Bates, Pop. 1,356**
Rich Hill R-IV SD 400/K-12
703 N 3rd St 64779 417-395-2418
Jeff Blackford, supt. Fax 395-2407
www.richhill.k12.mo.us/
Rich Hill HS 200/7-12
703 N 3rd St 64779 417-395-4191
Brian Gillis, prin. Fax 395-2407

**Richland, Pulaski, Pop. 1,803**
Richland R-IV SD 600/PK-12
714 E Jefferson Ave 65556 573-765-3241
Tony Hermann, supt. Fax 765-5552
www.richlandbears.us
Richland HS 200/9-12
714 E Jefferson Ave 65556 573-765-3711
Doug Smith, prin. Fax 765-5552
Richland JHS 100/7-8
714 E Jefferson Ave 65556 573-765-3711
Doug Smith, prin. Fax 765-5552

**Richmond, Ray, Pop. 5,691**
Richmond R-XVI SD 1,600/PK-12
1017 E Main St 64085 816-776-6912
Dr. Mike Aytes, supt. Fax 776-5554
richmond.k12.mo.us
Richmond HS 400/9-12
451 E South St 64085 816-776-2226
John Parker, prin. Fax 776-8748
Richmond MS 400/6-8
715 S Wellington St 64085 816-776-5841
Trey Cavanan, prin. Fax 776-2788

**Ridgeway, Harrison, Pop. 462**
Ridgeway R-V SD 100/PK-12
305 Main St 64481 660-872-6813
Brenda Dougan, supt. Fax 872-6230
Ridgeway JSHS 50/7-12
305 Main St 64481 660-872-6813
Tim Conn, prin. Fax 872-6230

**Risco, New Madrid, Pop. 338**
Risco R-II SD 200/K-12
PO Box 17 63874 573-396-5568
Amy Baker, supt. Fax 396-5503
www.risco.k12.mo.us/
Risco JSHS 100/7-12
PO Box 17 63874 573-396-5568
Ronald Cross, prin. Fax 396-5503

**Riverside, Platte, Pop. 2,836**
Park Hill SD
Supt. — See Kansas City
Park Hill South HS 1,600/9-12
4500 NW River Park Dr 64150 816-359-4120
Dr. Dale Longenecker, prin. Fax 359-4129

**Rock Port, Atchison, Pop. 1,303**
Rock Port R-II SD 300/K-12
600 S Nebraska St 64482 660-744-6298
Craig Walker, supt. Fax 744-5539
rockport.k12.mo.us
Rock Port JSHS 200/7-12
600 S Nebraska St 64482 660-744-6296
Jonnie Kemerling, prin. Fax 744-5539

**Rogersville, Greene, Pop. 3,000**
Logan-Rogersville R-VIII SD 2,200/PK-12
100 E Front St 65742 417-753-2891
Dr. Shawn B. Randles, supt. Fax 753-3063
logrog.net/
Logan-Rogersville HS 700/9-12
4700 S State Highway 125 65742 417-753-2813
Dr. Teresa McKenzie, prin. Fax 753-3960
Logan-Rogersville MS 300/7-8
8225 E Farm Road 174 65742 417-753-2896
Toby Kite, prin. Fax 753-3182

**Rolla, Phelps, Pop. 19,067**
Rolla SD 31 4,000/PK-12
500A Forum Dr 65401 573-458-0100
Dr. Aaron Zalis, supt. Fax 458-0105
rolla.k12.mo.us
Rolla JHS 600/8-9
1360 Soest Rd 65401 573-458-0130
Monica Fulton, prin. Fax 458-0135
Rolla SHS 1,000/10-12
900 Bulldog Run 65401 573-458-0140
Dr. Jim Pritchett, prin. Fax 458-0147
Rolla Technical Center Vo/Tech
500 Forum Dr 65401 573-458-0160
Keith McCarthy, dir. Fax 458-0164
Rolla Technical Institute Vo/Tech
1304 E 10th St 65401 573-458-0150
Lucas Chapman, dir. Fax 458-0155

---

Metro Business College Post-Sec.
1202 E State Route 72 65401 573-364-8464
Missouri University of Science & Tech Post-Sec.
1870 Miner Cir 65409 573-341-4111
Salem College of Hairstyling Post-Sec.
1051 Kingshighway St Ste 1 65401 573-368-3136

**Rosendale, Andrew, Pop. 143**
North Andrew County R-VI SD 400/K-12
9120 Highway 48 64483 816-567-2965
Jim Shultz, supt. Fax 567-2096
northandrew.org
North Andrew HS 100/9-12
9120 Highway 48 64483 816-567-2525
Jason Tolen, prin. Fax 567-2096
North Andrew MS 100/6-8
9120 Highway 48 64483 816-567-2525
Jason Tolen, prin. Fax 567-2096

**Russellville, Cole, Pop. 799**
Cole County R-I SD 600/PK-12
13600 Route C 65074 573-782-3534
Jerry Hobbs, supt. Fax 782-3545
www.cole.k12.mo.us
Cole County R-I HS 200/9-12
13600 Route C 65074 573-782-3313
Heath Waters, prin. Fax 782-3262
Cole County R-I MS 100/6-8
13600 Route C 65074 573-782-4915
Elaine Buschjost, prin. Fax 782-3775

**Saint Albans, Franklin**

---

Fulton S at St. Albans 100/PK-12
PO Box 78 63073 636-458-6688

**Saint Ann, Saint Louis, Pop. 12,679**
Pattonville R-3 SD 5,600/PK-12
11097 Saint Charles Rock Rd 63074 314-213-8500
Dr. Michael Fulton, supt. Fax 213-8601
psdr3.org
Holman MS 600/6-8
11055 Saint Charles Rock Rd 63074 314-213-8032
Teisha Ashford, prin. Fax 213-8632
Other Schools – See Maryland Heights

Ritenour SD
Supt. — See Saint Louis
Hoech MS 800/6-8
3312 Ashby Rd 63074 314-493-6200
Dr. Timothy Streicher, prin. Fax 426-3837

---

American Trade School Post-Sec.
3925 Industrial Dr 63074 314-423-1900
Patsy & Rob's Academy of Beauty Post-Sec.
18 Northwest Plz 63074 314-298-8808

**Saint Charles, Saint Charles, Pop. 64,512**
Francis Howell R-III SD 19,800/PK-12
4545 Central School Rd 63304 636-851-4000
Dr. Pam Sloan, supt. Fax 851-4093
www.fhsdschools.org
Barnwell MS 800/6-8
1035 Jungs Station Rd 63303 636-851-4100
David Eckhoff, prin. Fax 851-4095
Heritage Landing Alternative Program Alt
1400 Gettysburg Lndg 63303 636-851-5300
Anthony Haan, prin. Fax 851-4130
Hollenbeck MS 600/6-8
4555 Central School Rd 63304 636-851-5400
Woody Borgschulte, prin. Fax 851-4132
Howell Central HS 1,900/9-12
5199 Highway N 63304 636-851-4600
Dr. Sonny Arnel, prin. Fax 851-4111
Howell HS 1,800/9-12
7001 S Highway 94 63304 636-851-4700
Dave Wedlock, prin. Fax 851-4116
Howell North HS 1,900/9-12
2549 Hackmann Rd 63303 636-851-4900
Andrew Downs, prin. Fax 851-6199
Howell Union HS 100/Alt
1405 Highway D 63304 636-851-5000
Krisandra Worley, prin. Fax 851-4127
Saeger MS 700/6-8
5201 Highway N 63304 636-851-5600
Brian Schick, prin. Fax 851-4138
Other Schools – See Weldon Spring

Orchard Farm R-V SD 1,300/PK-12
2115 Highway V 63301 636-250-5000
Dr. Thomas Muzzey, supt. Fax 250-5444
www.ofsd.k12.mo.us
Orchard Farm HS 400/9-12
2175 Highway V 63301 636-250-5400
Brian Smith, prin. Fax 250-5425
Orchard Farm MS 300/6-8
2192 Highway V 63301 636-250-5300
Keith Klostermann, prin. Fax 250-5306

St. Charles R-VI SD 5,200/PK-12
400 N 6th St 63301 636-443-4000
Dr. Jeff Marion, supt. Fax 443-4001
www.stcharles.k12.mo.us
Hardin MS 800/7-8
1950 Elm St 63301 636-443-4300
Dr. Ed Gettemeier, prin. Fax 443-4301
Lewis & Clark Career Center Vo/Tech
2400 Zumbehl Rd 63301 636-443-4950
Kathy Frederking, dir. Fax 443-4951
St. Charles HS 900/9-12
725 N Kingshighway St 63301 636-443-4100
Jeff Walker, prin. Fax 443-4101
St. Charles West HS 700/9-12
3601 Droste Rd 63301 636-443-4200
Dr. Kim Fitterling, prin. Fax 443-4201
Success Campus Alternative S Alt
1600 Waverly St 63301 636-443-4890
Dr. Christine Jarus, prin. Fax 443-4891

---

Duchesne HS 500/9-12
2550 Elm St 63301 636-946-6767
Fritz Long, prin. Fax 946-6267
Lewis & Clark Career Center Post-Sec.
2400 Zumbehl Rd 63301 636-443-4950
Lindenwood University Post-Sec.
209 S Kingshighway St 63301 636-949-2000
Missouri Tech Post-Sec.
1690 Country Club Dr 63303 636-573-9300
The Art Institute of Saint Louis Post-Sec.
1520 S 5th St Ste 107 63303 636-688-3010
Vatterott College - St. Charles Post-Sec.
3550 W Clay St 63301 636-940-4100

**Saint Clair, Franklin, Pop. 4,665**

St. Clair R-XIII SD 2,200/K-12
905 Bardot St 63077 636-629-3500
Dr. Michael Murphy, supt. Fax 629-4466
www.stcmo.org
Saint Clair HS 700/9-12
1015 High School Dr 63077 636-629-3500
Michael Hunter, prin. Fax 629-1979
Saint Clair JHS 500/6-8
925 High School Dr 63077 636-629-3500
Eric Lause, prin. Fax 629-1363

**Sainte Genevieve, Sainte Genevieve, Pop. 4,356**

St. Genevieve County R-II SD 1,900/K-12
375 N 5th St 63670 573-883-4500
Jeffrey Lindsey, supt. Fax 883-5957
www.sgdragons.org
Sainte Genevieve HS 600/9-12
715 Washington St 63670 573-883-4500
Chris Hoehne, prin. Fax 883-5957
Sainte Genevieve MS 500/6-8
211 N 5th St 63670 573-883-4500
Paul Taylor, prin. Fax 883-5957

---

Valle Catholic HS 100/9-12
40 N 4th St 63670 573-883-7496
Dr. Mark Gilligan, prin. Fax 883-9142

**Saint Elizabeth, Miller, Pop. 334**

St. Elizabeth R-IV SD 100/PK-12
PO Box 68 65075 573-493-2246
Toni Taylor, supt. Fax 493-2380
www.ste.k12.mo.us
Saint Elizabeth S 100/PK-12
PO Box 68 65075 573-493-2246
Crintina Wald, prin. Fax 493-2380

**Saint James, Phelps, Pop. 4,150**

St. James R-I SD 1,800/PK-12
122 E Scioto St 65559 573-265-2300
Joy Tucker, supt. Fax 265-6126
www.stjschools.org/
St. James HS 500/9-12
101 E Scioto St 65559 573-265-2300
Jo Stammers, prin. Fax 265-3652
St. James MS 400/6-8
1 Tiger Dr 65559 573-265-2300
Kaaren Lepper, prin. Fax 265-6302

**Saint John, Saint Louis, Pop. 6,331**

Ritenour SD
Supt. — See Saint Louis
Ritenour Adult Learning Center Adult
8762 Saint Charles Rock Rd 63114 314-426-7900
Javonda Quinn, dir. Fax 429-4348

**Saint Joseph, Buchanan, Pop. 74,914**

St. Joseph SD 11,800/PK-12
925 Felix St 64501 816-671-4000
Dr. Fred Czerwonka, supt. Fax 671-4470
www.sjsd.k12.mo.us
Benton HS 900/9-12
5655 S 4th St 64504 816-671-4030
Beery Johnson, prin. Fax 671-4036
Bode MS 500/7-8
720 N Noyes Blvd 64506 816-671-4050
Roberta Dias, prin. Fax 671-4473
Central HS 1,600/9-12
2602 Edmond St 64501 816-671-4080
Deborah Stephens, prin. Fax 671-4474
Colgan Alternative Resource Center 300/Alt
3510 Frederick Ave 64506 816-671-4072
Jeremy Burright, dir. Fax 671-4022
Hillyard Technical Center Vo/Tech
3434 Faraon St 64506 816-671-4170
Dennis Merritt, dir. Fax 671-4479
Lafayette HS 900/9-12
412 E Highland Ave 64505 816-671-4220
Dr. Tyran Sumy, prin. Fax 671-4480
Robidoux MS 400/7-8
4212 Saint Joseph Ave 64505 816-671-4350
Precious Kurth, prin. Fax 671-4487
Spring Garden MS 400/7-8
5802 S 22nd St 64503 816-671-4380
Dr. Lara Gilpin, prin. Fax 671-4489
Truman MS 500/7-8
3227 Olive St Ste 45 64507 816-671-4400
Jason Callaway, prin. Fax 671-4491
Webster Learning Center Alt
1211 N 18th St 64501 816-671-4020
Fax 671-4471

---

American Business and Technology Univ Post-Sec.
1018 W Saint Maartens Dr 64506 816-279-7000
Bishop Le Blond HS 200/9-12
3529 Frederick Ave 64506 816-279-1629
Dr. Solon Haynes, prin. Fax 279-5488
Missouri Western State University Post-Sec.
4525 Downs Dr 64507 816-271-4200
St. Joseph Christian S 300/PK-12
5401 Gene Field Rd 64506 816-279-1555
Dr. Jason Tindol, supt. Fax 279-4574
Vatterott College - Saint Joseph Post-Sec.
3709 N Belt Hwy 64506 816-558-7500

**Saint Louis, Saint Louis, Pop. 312,138**

Affton SD 101 2,400/PK-12
8701 MacKenzie Rd 63123 314-638-8770
Dr. Steve Brotherton, supt. Fax 631-2548
www.afftonschools.net
Affton HS 800/9-12
8309 MacKenzie Rd 63123 314-638-6330
Dr. Susan Jackson, prin. Fax 633-5990
Rogers MS 500/6-8
7550 MacKenzie Rd 63123 314-351-9679
Jason Buck, prin. Fax 351-6381

Bayless SD 1,500/PK-12
4530 Weber Rd 63123 314-256-8600
Ronald J. Tucker, supt. Fax 544-6315
baylessk12.org
Bayless HS 500/9-12
4532 Weber Rd 63123 314-256-8660
Patrick McEvoy, prin. Fax 544-6315
Bayless JHS 200/6-8
4530 Weber Rd 63123 314-256-8690
Doug Harness, prin. Fax 544-6315

Ferguson-Florissant R-II SD
Supt. — See Florissant
Ferguson MS 600/7-8
701 January Ave 63135 314-506-9600
KATHERINE CHAMBERS, prin. Fax 506-9601
McCluer South - Berkeley HS 600/9-12
201 Brotherton Ln 63135 314-506-9800
Steven Lawler, prin. Fax 506-9801

Hancock Place SD 1,600/PK-12
9417 S Broadway 63125 314-544-1300
Dr. Kevin Carl, supt. Fax 631-3752
hancock.k12.mo.us
Hancock Place HS 500/9-12
229 W Ripa Ave 63125 314-544-1200
Dr. Shelly Vogler, prin. Fax 544-6427
Hancock Place MS 300/6-8
243 W Ripa Ave 63125 314-544-6423
Thomas Dittrich, prin. Fax 544-6470

Hazelwood SD
Supt. — See Florissant
Hazelwood East HS 1,400/9-12
11300 Dunn Rd 63138 314-953-5600
Yolander Pittman, prin. Fax 953-5613
Hazelwood East MS 500/6-8
1865 Dunn Rd 63138 314-953-5700
Dr. Gary Jansen, prin. Fax 953-5713
Hazelwood Southeast MS 700/6-8
918 Prigge Rd 63138 314-953-7700
Chauncey Granger, prin. Fax 953-7713

Ladue SD 3,900/PK-12
9703 Conway Rd 63124 314-994-7080
Dr. Donna Jahnke, supt. Fax 994-0441
www.ladueschools.net
Ladue MS 900/6-8
9701 Conway Rd 63124 314-993-3900
Greg Baber, prin. Fax 997-8736
Watkins HS 1,200/9-12
1201 S Warson Rd 63124 314-993-6447
Brad Griffith, prin. Fax 994-1467

Lindbergh R-VIII SD 5,400/PK-12
4900 S Lindbergh Blvd 63126 314-729-2480
Dr. Jim Simpson, supt. Fax 729-2482
www.lindberghschools.ws/
Lindbergh HS 2,000/9-12
5000 S Lindbergh Blvd 63126 314-729-2410
Dr. Andrew Croley, prin. Fax 729-2412
Sperreng MS 700/6-8
12111 Tesson Ferry Rd 63128 314-729-2420
Mark Eggers, prin. Fax 729-2422
Truman MS 700/6-8
12225 Eddie and Park Rd 63127 314-729-2470
Dr. Tara Sparks, prin. Fax 729-2472

Mehlville R-IX SD 10,600/PK-12
3120 Lemay Ferry Rd 63125 314-467-5000
Dr. Chris Gaines, supt. Fax 467-5099
www.mehlvilleschooldistrict.com
Bernard MS 700/6-8
1054 Forder Rd 63129 314-467-6600
Lori Sullivan, prin. Fax 467-6699
Buerkle MS 600/6-8
623 Buckley Rd 63125 314-467-6800
Jim Kern, prin. Fax 467-6899
Mehlville HS 1,900/9-12
3200 Lemay Ferry Rd 63125 314-467-6000
Dr. Denise Swanger, prin. Fax 467-6099
Oakville HS 1,800/9-12
5557 Milburn Rd 63129 314-467-7000
Jan Kellerman, prin. Fax 467-7099
Oakville MS 700/6-8
5950 Telegraph Rd 63129 314-467-7400
Mike Salsman, prin. Fax 467-7499
Washington MS 600/6-8
5165 Ambs Rd 63128 314-467-7600
Adam Smith, prin. Fax 467-7699

Normandy Schools Collaborative 3,800/PK-12
3855 Lucas and Hunt Rd 63121 314-493-0400
Dr. Charles Pearson, supt. Fax 493-0475
www.normandysd.org
Normandy HS 1,000/9-12
6701 Saint Charles Rock Rd 63133 314-493-0600
Derrick Mitchell, prin. Fax 493-0668
Other Schools – See Normandy

Ritenour SD 6,100/PK-12
2420 Woodson Rd 63114 314-493-6010
Dr. Christopher Kilbride, supt. Fax 426-7144
www.ritenour.k12.mo.us
Other Schools – See Overland, Saint Ann, Saint John

Riverview Gardens SD 6,100/PK-12
1370 Northumberland Dr 63137 314-869-2505
Dr. Scott Spurgeon, supt. Fax 388-6002
www.rgsd.k12.mo.us
Central MS 800/6-8
9800 Patricia Barkalow Dr 63137 314-867-2603
Chaketa Riddle, prin. Fax 388-6028
Riverview Gardens HS 1,400/9-12
1218 Shepley Dr 63137 314-869-4700
Darius Kirk, prin. Fax 388-6020
Westview MS 600/6-8
1950 Nemnich Rd 63136 314-867-0410
Valeska Hill, prin. Fax 388-6055

Special SD of St. Louis County 2,700/10-12
12110 Clayton Rd 63131 314-989-8100
Don Bohannon, supt. Fax 989-8440
www.ssdmo.org/
South Technical HS Vo/Tech
12721 W Watson Rd 63127 314-989-7400
Jacob Lohse, prin. Fax 989-7503
Other Schools – See Florissant

St. Louis City SD 25,800/PK-12
801 N 11th St 63101 314-231-3720
Dr. Kelvin Adams, supt. Fax 345-2661
www.slps.org/
Beaumont HS 300/9-12
3836 Natural Bridge Ave 63107 314-533-2410
Terrell Henderson, prin. Fax 244-1712
Busch MS of Character & Athletics 300/6-8
5910 Clifton Ave 63109 314-352-1043
Robert Lescher, prin. Fax 244-1729
Carnahan HS of the Future 400/9-12
4041 S Broadway 63118 314-457-0582
LaTasha Jones, prin. Fax 457-9741
Carr Lane Visual & Performing Art MS 500/6-8
1004 N Jefferson Ave 63106 314-231-0413
Cornelius Green, prin. Fax 244-1733
Central Visual and Performing Arts HS 400/9-12
3125 S Kingshighway Blvd 63139 314-771-2772
Dr. Amy Phillips, prin. Fax 771-0135
Cleveland NJROTC Academy 300/9-12
4939 Kemper Ave 63139 314-776-1301
Susan Viviano, prin. Fax 244-1747
Collegiate S of Medicine and Bioscience 9-12
450 Des Peres Ave 63112 314-696-2290
Chip Clatto, prin. Fax 244-1790
Compton-Drew ILC MS 500/6-8
5130 Oakland Ave 63110 314-652-9282
Nicole Holland, prin. Fax 244-1756
Fanning MS Community Education Center 400/6-8
3417 Grace Ave 63116 314-772-1038
June Berry, prin. Fax 244-1766
Fresh Start Academy Alt
4248 Cottage Ave 63113 314-531-2220
Debra Powell-Childress, prin. Fax 244-1930
Gateway MST Prep S 500/6-8
1200 N Jefferson Ave 63106 314-241-2295
Aisha Grace, prin. Fax 241-7698
Gateway STEM HS 1,200/9-12
5101 McRee Ave 63110 314-776-3300
Dr. Elizabeth Bender, prin. Fax 776-8267
Langston MS 300/6-8
5511 Wabada Ave 63112 314-383-2908
Lanetra Thomas, prin. Fax 385-4632
Long MS Community Education Center 300/6-8
5028 Morganford Rd 63116 314-481-3440
Brenda Smith, prin. Fax 481-7329
McKinley Classical Junior Academy 200/6-8
2156 Russell Blvd 63104 314-773-0027
Earl Williams, prin. Fax 771-9749
McKinley Classical Leadership Academy 100/9-12
2156 Russell Blvd 63104 314-773-0027
Earl Williams, prin. Fax 244-1834
Metro Academic & Classical HS 300/9-12
4015 McPherson Ave 63108 314-534-3894
Wilfred Moore Ph.D., prin. Fax 531-4894
Miller Career Academy Vo/Tech
1000 N Grand Blvd 63106 314-371-0394
Michael Brown, prin. Fax 371-1311
Northwest Academy of Law 300/9-12
5140 Riverview Blvd 63120 314-385-4774
Valerie Carter-Thomas, prin. Fax 385-3651
Nottingham CAJT Vo/Tech
4915 Donovan Ave 63109 314-481-4095
Brian O'Connor, prin. Fax 244-1730
Roosevelt HS 900/9-12
3230 Hartford St 63118 314-776-6040
Crystal Gale, prin. Fax 244-1861
Soldan International Studies HS 600/9-12
918 Union Blvd 63108 314-367-9222
Dr. Thomas Cason, prin. Fax 367-1898
Stevens Center for Academic Development 200/6-8
1033 Whittier St 63113 314-533-8550
Dr. Kacy Seals, prin. Fax 533-0306
Sumner Magnet HS 500/9-12
4248 Cottage Ave 63113 314-371-1048
Isaiah McHellen, prin. Fax 531-9852

Vashon HS 800/9-12
3035 Cass Ave 63106 314-533-9487
Joseph Williams, prin. Fax 533-7540
Yeatman-Liddell MS 300/7-9
4265 Athlone Ave 63115 314-261-8132
Dr. Leslie Bonner, prin. Fax 389-4613

Webster Groves SD
Supt. — See Webster Groves
Hixson MS 700/7-8
630 S Elm Ave 63119 314-963-6450
Dr. Stacie Smith, prin. Fax 918-4624

---

Achieve Test Prep Post-Sec.
1810 Craig Rd Ste 213 63146 314-288-0702
Aquinas Institute of Theology Post-Sec.
23 S Spring Ave 63108 314-256-8800
Bishop DuBourg HS 500/9-12
5850 Eichelberger St 63109 314-832-3030
Bridget Timoney, prin. Fax 832-0529
Block Yeshiva HS 50/9-12
1146 N Warson Rd 63132 314-872-8701
Brookes Bible Institute Post-Sec.
3465 S Grand Blvd 63118 314-773-0083
Burroughs S 600/7-12
755 S Price Rd 63124 314-993-4040
Andy Abbott, head sch Fax 993-6458
Cardinal Ritter College Prep HS 300/9-12
701 N Spring Ave 63108 314-446-5500
Michael Blackshear, prin. Fax 446-5570
Chamberlain College of Nursing Post-Sec.
11830 Westline Indtrl # 106 63146 314-991-6200
Chaminade College Preparatory S 800/6-12
425 S Lindbergh Blvd 63131 314-993-4400
Philip Rone, prin. Fax 993-4403
Christian Academy of Greater St. Louis 100/PK-12
11050 N Warson Rd 63114 314-429-7070
Christian Brothers College HS 900/9-12
1850 De La Salle Dr 63141 314-985-6100
Br. David Poos, prin. Fax 985-6115
Concordia Seminary Post-Sec.
801 Seminary Pl 63105 314-505-7000
Cor Jesu Academy 600/9-12
10230 Gravois Rd 63123 314-842-1546
Sr. Kathleen Coonan, prin. Fax 842-6061
Court Reporting Institute Post-Sec.
7730 Carondelet Ave Ste 400 63105 888-208-6780
Covenant Theological Seminary Post-Sec.
12330 Conway Rd 63141 800-264-8064
Crossroads College Preparatory S 200/7-12
500 De Baliviere Ave 63112 314-367-8085
Dr. Jason Heisserer, head sch Fax 367-9711
De Smet Jesuit HS 1,000/9-12
233 N New Ballas Rd 63141 314-567-3500
Dr. Ronald Rebore, prin. Fax 567-1519
DeVry University Post-Sec.
11830 Westline Indstrl #100 63146 866-831-3882
DVA Medical Center Post-Sec.
1 Jefferson Barracks Rd 63125 314-894-6631
Elaine Steven Beauty College Post-Sec.
10420 W Florissant Ave 63136 314-868-8196
ex'treme Institute by Nelly Post-Sec.
800 N 3rd St 63102 888-669-0633
Fontbonne University Post-Sec.
6800 Wydown Blvd 63105 314-862-3456
Goldfarb School of Nursing Barnes-Jewish Post-Sec.
4483 Duncan Ave 63110 314-454-7055
Harris-Stowe State University Post-Sec.
3026 Laclede Ave 63103 314-340-3300
Healing Arts Center Post-Sec.
10073 Manchester Rd Ste 100 63122 314-647-8080
Hickey College Post-Sec.
940 W Port Plz Ste 101 63146 314-434-2212
IHM Health of EMS Post-Sec.
2500 Abbott Pl 63143 314-768-1234
IHM Health Studies Center Post-Sec.
3663 Lindell Blvd 63108 314-768-1000
Incarnate Word Academy 400/9-12
2788 Normandy Dr 63121 314-725-5850
Molly Grumich, prin. Fax 725-2308
Jefferson S 100/7-12
4100 S Lindbergh Blvd 63127 314-843-4151
Dr. Elizabeth Holekamp, head sch Fax 843-3527
Kenrick School of Theology Post-Sec.
5200 Glennon Dr 63119 314-792-6100
L'Ecole Culinaire Post-Sec.
9811 S 40 Dr 63124 314-587-2433
Logos S 100/6-12
9137 Old Bonhomme Rd 63132 314-997-7002
Dr. Kathleen Boyd-Fenger, head sch Fax 997-6848
Loyola Academy 100/6-8
3851 Washington Blvd 63108 314-531-9091
Paul Bozdech, prin. Fax 531-3603
Lutheran HS North 300/9-12
5401 Lucas and Hunt Rd 63121 314-389-3100
Tim Brackman, prin. Fax 389-3103
Lutheran HS South 500/9-12
9515 Tesson Ferry Rd 63123 314-631-1400
Brian Ryherd, prin. Fax 631-7762
Lutheran School of Nursing Post-Sec.
3547 S Jefferson Ave 63118 314-577-5850
Marian MS 100/5-8
4130 Wyoming St 63116 314-771-7674
Christy Toben, prin. Fax 771-7679
Mary Institute/St. Louis Country Day S 1,200/PK-12
101 N Warson Rd 63124 314-995-7367
Lisa Lyle, head sch Fax 995-7470
Maryville University of St. Louis Post-Sec.
650 Maryville University Dr 63141 314-529-9300
Miller Bais Yaakov HS 50/9-12
700 N and South Rd 63130 314-863-9230
Missouri Baptist University Post-Sec.
1 College Park Dr 63141 314-434-1115
Missouri School for the Blind Post-Sec.
3815 Magnolia Ave 63110 314-776-4320
National Academy of Beauty Arts Post-Sec.
157 Concord Plz 63128 314-842-3616

Nerinx Hall HS 600/9-12
530 E Lockwood Ave 63119 314-968-1505
Jane Kosash, prin. Fax 968-0604
Notre Dame HS 200/9-12
320 E Ripa Ave 63125 314-544-1015
Sr. Michelle Emmerich, prin. Fax 544-8003
Parks College of St. Louis University Post-Sec.
3450 Lindell Blvd 63103 314-977-8203
Principia S 500/PK-12
13201 Clayton Rd 63131 314-434-2100
Travis Brantingham, prin. Fax 275-3583
Providence Classical Christian Academy 100/K-12
5293 S Lindbergh Blvd 63126 314-842-6846
Jonathan Mattull, hdmstr.
Ranken Technical College Post-Sec.
4431 Finney Ave 63113 314-371-0236
Rosati-Kain HS 400/9-12
4389 Lindell Blvd 63108 314-533-8513
Elizabeth Goodwin, prin. Fax 533-1618
St. John Vianney HS 600/9-12
1311 S Kirkwood Rd 63122 314-965-4853
Dr. Timothy Dilg, prin. Fax 965-1950
St. Joseph's Academy 600/9-12
2307 S Lindbergh Blvd 63131 314-394-4300
Dr. Diane Cooper, prin. Fax 965-9114
St. Louis College of Health Careers Post-Sec.
909 S Taylor Ave 63110 314-652-0300
St. Louis College of Pharmacy Post-Sec.
4588 Parkview Pl 63110 314-367-8700
St. Louis Community College- Forest Park Post-Sec.
5600 Oakland Ave 63110 314-644-9100
St. Louis Hair Academy Post-Sec.
3701 Kossuth Ave 63107 314-533-3125
St. Louis Priory S 400/7-12
500 S Mason Rd 63141 314-434-3690
Fr. Gregory Mohrmann, hdmstr. Fax 576-7088
St. Louis University Post-Sec.
221 N Grand Blvd 63103 800-758-3678
St. Louis University HS 1,100/9-12
4970 Oakland Ave 63110 314-531-0330
Dr. John Moran, prin. Fax 531-3441
St. Mary's HS 300/9-12
4701 S Grand Blvd 63111 314-481-8400
Kevin Hacker, prin. Fax 481-3670
Stevens Institute of Business & Arts Post-Sec.
1521 Washington Ave 63103 800-871-0949
Strayer University Post-Sec.
1600 S Brentwood Blvd # 300 63144 314-817-9100
Tower Grove Christian S 200/PK-12
4257 Magnolia Ave 63110 314-776-6473
Michael Gregory, admin. Fax 776-4867
Trinity Catholic HS 300/9-12
1720 Redman Rd 63138 314-741-1333
Nancy Lydon, prin. Fax 741-1335
University of Missouri - Saint Louis Post-Sec.
1 University Blvd 63121 314-516-5000
Ursuline Academy 600/9-12
341 S Sappington Rd 63122 314-984-2800
Dr. Mark Michalski, prin. Fax 966-3396
Villa Duchesne/Oak Hill JSHS 400/7-12
801 S Spoede Rd 63131 314-432-2021
Sr. Donna Collins, prin. Fax 432-0199
Visitation Academy 600/PK-12
3020 N Ballas Rd 63131 314-625-9100
Mary Ellen Schraeder, prin. Fax 432-7210
Washington University in St. Louis Post-Sec.
1 Brookings Dr 63130 314-935-5000
Webster University Post-Sec.
470 E Lockwood Ave 63119 314-968-6900
Whitfield S 400/6-12
175 S Mason Rd 63141 314-434-5141
John Delautre, head sch Fax 434-6193

**Saint Peters, Saint Charles, Pop. 51,692**
Ft. Zumwalt R-II SD
Supt. — See O Fallon
DuBray MS 900/6-8
100 DuBray Dr 63376 636-279-7979
Michael Anderson, prin. Fax 278-4749
Ft. Zumwalt East HS 1,300/9-12
600 First Executive Ave 63376 636-477-2400
Brian Bishop, prin. Fax 926-3345
Ft. Zumwalt South HS 1,400/9-12
8050 Mexico Rd 63376 636-978-1212
Dr. Kevin Keltner, prin. Fax 980-1745
Ft. Zumwalt South MS 1,000/6-8
300 Knaust Rd 63376 636-281-0776
Dr. Monte Massey, prin. Fax 281-0006

---

Le Cordon Bleu College of Culinary Arts Post-Sec.
7898 Veterans Memorial Pkwy 63376 866-863-2061
Lutheran HS of St. Charles County 300/9-12
5100 Mexico Rd 63376 636-928-5100
Jon Bernhardt, prin. Fax 928-8451

**Salem, Dent, Pop. 4,859**
Salem R-80 SD 1,300/PK-12
1409 W Rolla Rd 65560 573-729-6642
John McColloch, supt. Fax 729-8493
www.salem.k12.mo.us/
Salem HS 600/9-12
1400 Tiger Pride Dr 65560 573-729-6642
John Smith, prin. Fax 729-7408
Salem MS 200/6-8
1400 Tiger Pride Dr 65560 573-729-6642
Kerry Roberts, prin. Fax 729-2720

**Salisbury, Chariton, Pop. 1,601**
Salisbury R-IV SD 400/K-12
1000 S Maple Ave 65281 660-388-6699
Todd Willhite, supt. Fax 388-6753
www.salisbury.k12.mo.us/
Salisbury JSHS 200/7-12
1000 S Maple Ave 65281 660-388-6442
Ryan Taylor, prin. Fax 388-5651

**Sarcoxie, Jasper, Pop. 1,304**
Sarcoxie R-II SD 800/K-12
101 S 17th St 64862 417-548-3134
Dr. Kevin Goddard, supt. Fax 548-6165
www.sarcoxie.k12.mo.us/
Sarcoxie JSHS 400/6-12
101 S 17th St 64862 417-548-2153
Philip Lewis, prin. Fax 548-7193

**Savannah, Andrew, Pop. 5,020**
Savannah R-III SD 2,300/K-12
408 W Market St 64485 816-324-3144
Dr. David Brax, supt. Fax 324-5594
www.savannahr3.com
Savannah HS 700/9-12
701 State Rte E 64485 816-324-3128
Zac Coughlin, prin. Fax 324-6536
Savannah MS 600/6-8
10500 State Route T 64485 816-324-3126
Leisa Blair, prin. Fax 324-6397

**Scott City, Scott, Pop. 4,518**
Scott City R-I SD 900/K-12
3000 Main St 63780 573-264-2381
Diann Ulmer, supt. Fax 264-2206
scschools.k12.mo.us/
Scott City HS 300/9-12
3000 Main St 63780 573-264-2138
Michael Johnson, prin. Fax 264-2608
Scott City MS 200/5-8
3000 Main St 63780 573-264-2139
Michael Umfleet, prin. Fax 264-2599

**Sedalia, Pettis, Pop. 20,824**
Sedalia SD 200 4,000/PK-12
2806 Matthew Dr 65301 660-829-6450
Bradley Pollitt, supt. Fax 827-8938
www.sedalia200.org
Smith-Cotton HS 1,000/9-12
2010 Tiger Pride Blvd 65301 660-851-5300
Wade Norton, prin. Fax 851-5393
Smith-Cotton JHS 300/6-8
312 E Broadway Blvd 65301 660-829-6300
Jason Curry, prin. Fax 829-6409

---

American College of Hair Design Post-Sec.
125 Duke Rd 65301 660-827-3295
Sacred Heart HS 100/PK-12
416 W 3rd St 65301 660-827-3800
Dr. Gary Manning, prin. Fax 827-3806
State Fair Community College Post-Sec.
3201 W 16th St 65301 660-530-5800

**Senath, Dunklin, Pop. 1,752**
Senath-Hornersville C-8 SD 900/PK-12
PO Box 370 63876 573-738-2669
Larry Wood, supt. Fax 738-9845
www.shs.k12.mo.us/
Senath-Hornersville HS 200/9-12
PO Box 370 63876 573-738-2661
Chad Morgan, prin. Fax 738-3481
Other Schools – See Hornersville

**Seneca, Newton, Pop. 2,214**
Seneca R-VII SD 1,300/PK-12
914 Frisco St 64865 417-776-3426
Jim Cummins, supt. Fax 776-2177
www.seneca.k12.mo.us
Seneca HS 500/9-12
914 Frisco St 64865 417-776-3926
Wellington Ng, prin. Fax 776-1878
Seneca JHS 200/7-8
914 Frisco St 64865 417-776-3911
John Whitehead, prin. Fax 776-2673

**Seymour, Webster, Pop. 1,885**
Seymour R-II SD 800/PK-12
416 E Clinton Ave 65746 417-935-2287
Bruce Denney, supt. Fax 935-4060
www.seymourschool.net
Seymour HS 200/9-12
625 E Clinton Ave 65746 417-935-4508
Wilbanks Brian, prin. Fax 935-4539
Seymour MS 200/6-8
501 E Clinton Ave 65746 417-935-4626
Brian Bell, prin. Fax 935-2848

**Shelbina, Shelby, Pop. 1,695**
Shelby County R-IV SD 600/PK-12
4154 Highway 36 63468 573-588-4961
Tim Maddex, supt. Fax 588-2490
www.cardinals.k12.mo.us
South Shelby MSHS 200/6-12
4154 Highway 36 63468 573-588-4163
Deacon Windsor, prin. Fax 588-2490

**Shelbyville, Shelby, Pop. 547**
North Shelby SD 300/PK-12
3071 Highway 15 63469 573-633-2410
Kim Gaines, supt. Fax 633-2138
www.nshelby.k12.mo.us
North Shelby JSHS 100/7-12
3071 Highway 15 63469 573-633-2410
Kerri Greenwell, prin. Fax 633-2138

**Sheldon, Vernon, Pop. 525**
Sheldon R-VIII SD 200/PK-12
100 E Gene Lathrop Dr 64784 417-884-5113
Tim Judd, supt. Fax 884-5331
www.sheldon.k12.mo.us
Sheldon JSHS 100/7-12
100 E Gene Lathrop Dr 64784 417-884-5111
Jason Irwin, prin. Fax 884-5331

**Sikeston, Scott, Pop. 16,008**
Scott County Central SD 400/PK-12
20794 US Highway 61 63801 573-471-2686
Alvin McFerren, supt. Fax 471-2029
scottcentral.k12.mo.us

Scott County Central JSHS 200/7-12
20794 US Highway 61 63801 573-471-2001
John-Mark Jones M.Ed., prin. Fax 471-2004

Sikeston R-6 SD 3,500/K-12
1002 Virginia St 63801 573-472-2581
Thomas Williams, supt. Fax 472-2584
www.sikeston.k12.mo.us
Sikeston 7th and 8th Grade Center 500/7-8
1002 Virginia St 63801 573-471-1720
Frank Staple, prin. Fax 472-8884
Sikeston Career & Technology Center Vo/Tech
1002 Virginia St 63801 573-471-5442
Chad King, dir. Fax 472-8861
Sikeston HS 1,000/9-12
1002 Virginia St 63801 573-472-8850
Seth Harrell, prin. Fax 472-8857

---

Christian Academy 100/PK-12
103 E Kathleen St 63801 573-481-0216
Kevin Self, admin. Fax 481-9485

**Silex, Lincoln, Pop. 187**
Silex R-I SD 400/K-12
PO Box 46 63377 573-384-5227
Elaine Henderson, supt. Fax 384-5996
www.silex.k12.mo.us
Silex JSHS 200/7-12
PO Box 46 63377 573-384-5227
Dr. Bruce Werkmeister, prin. Fax 384-5996

**Slater, Saline, Pop. 1,827**
Slater SD 400/PK-12
515 Elm St 65349 660-529-2278
Dr. Terry Lorenz, supt. Fax 529-2279
www.slaterpublicschools.net
Slater HS 100/9-12
515 Elm St 65349 660-529-3133
Dr. Terry Lorenz, prin. Fax 529-3134

**Smithton, Pettis, Pop. 561**
Smithton R-VI SD 600/K-12
505 S Myrtle Ave 65350 660-343-5316
Matt Teeter Ed.D., supt. Fax 343-5389
smithton.k12.mo.us
Smithton HS 300/7-12
505 S Myrtle Ave 65350 660-343-5318
Jonathan Petersen M.S., prin. Fax 343-5389
Smithton MS 5-8
505 S Myrtle Ave 65350 660-343-5316
Brandon Wallace, prin. Fax 343-5389

**Smithville, Clay, Pop. 8,290**
Smithville R-II SD 2,400/PK-12
655 S Commercial Ave 64089 816-532-0406
Dr. Todd Schuetz, supt. Fax 532-4192
www.smithvilleschooldistrict.net
Smithville HS 700/9-12
645 S Commercial Ave 64089 816-532-0405
Dr. Rudy Papenfuhs, prin. Fax 532-4193
Smithville MS 600/6-8
675 S Commercial Ave 64089 816-532-1122
Matt Teeter, prin.

**Sparta, Christian, Pop. 1,734**
Sparta R-III SD 800/PK-12
PO Box 160 65753 417-634-4284
Dr. Jeffrey Hyatt, supt. Fax 634-3156
www.sparta.k12.mo.us/
Sparta HS 200/9-12
PO Box 160 65753 417-634-3224
Aaron Gerla, prin. Fax 634-0091
Sparta MS 200/5-8
PO Box 160 65753 417-634-5518
Valentine Rocky, prin. Fax 634-3426

**Spokane, Christian, Pop. 175**
Spokane R-VII SD
Supt. — See Highlandville
Spokane HS 200/9-12
PO Box 218 65754 417-443-3502
Mike Morelock, prin. Fax 443-7714
Spokane MS 200/6-8
PO Box 220 65754 417-443-3506
Pamila Rowe, prin. Fax 443-2069

**Springfield, Greene, Pop. 154,799**
Springfield R-XII SD 24,600/PK-12
1359 E Saint Louis St 65802 417-523-0000
Dr. John Jungmann, supt. Fax 523-0391
www.springfieldpublicschoolsmo.org/
Carver MS 800/6-8
3325 W Battlefield St 65807 417-888-2510
Dr. Dan O'Reilly, prin. Fax 888-2514
Central HS 1,700/6-12
423 E Central St 65802 417-523-9600
Lisa Anderson, prin. Fax 523-9695
Cherokee MS 800/6-8
420 E Farm Road 182 65810 417-523-7200
William Powers, prin. Fax 523-7295
Glendale HS 1,300/9-12
2727 S Ingram Mill Rd 65804 417-523-8900
Dr. Natalie Cauldwell, prin. Fax 523-8995
Hickory Hills MS 500/6-8
4650 E State Highway YY 65802 417-523-7100
Sarah Odom, prin. Fax 523-7195
Hillcrest HS 1,100/9-12
3319 N Grant Ave 65803 417-523-8000
Garry Moore, prin. Fax 523-8095
Jarrett MS 500/6-8
840 S Jefferson Ave 65806 417-523-6600
Rob Kroll, prin. Fax 523-6695
Kickapoo HS 1,700/9-12
3710 S Jefferson Ave 65807 417-523-8500
Kelly Allison, prin. Fax 523-8595
OTC Middle College Alt
1001 E Chestnut Expy 65802 417-447-7500
Jackie Jenkins, prin.
Parkview HS 1,400/9-12
516 W Meadowmere St 65807 417-523-9200
Eric Ramsey, prin. Fax 523-9295
Pershing MS 700/6-8
2120 S Ventura Ave 65804 417-523-2400
Dr. Pam Holmes, prin. Fax 523-2495
Pipkin MS 600/6-8
1215 N Boonville Ave 65802 417-523-6000
Dr. Tim Zeigler, prin. Fax 523-6195
Pleasant View MS 300/6-8
2210 E State Highway AA 65803 417-523-2100
Donna Aldrich, prin. Fax 523-2395
Reed MS 500/6-8
2000 N Lyon Ave 65803 417-523-6300
Dr. Debbie Grega, prin. Fax 523-6395
Study Alternative Center Alt
2343 W Olive St 65802 417-523-6400
Justin Dickenson, coord.
Westport MS 6-8
415 S Golden Ave 65802 417-523-3100
Jeff Wilcox, prin. Fax 523-3195

---

Baptist Bible College Post-Sec.
628 E Kearney St 65803 800-228-5754
Bryan University Post-Sec.
4255 S Nature Center Way 65804 417-862-5700
Cox College Post-Sec.
1423 N Jefferson Ave 65802 417-269-3401
Drury University Post-Sec.
900 N Benton Ave 65802 417-873-7879
Evangel University Post-Sec.
1111 N Glenstone Ave 65802 417-865-2811
Everest College Post-Sec.
1010 W Sunshine St 65807 417-864-7220
Global University Post-Sec.
1211 S Glenstone Ave 65804 417-862-9533
Greenwood Laboratory S 400/K-12
901 S National Ave, 417-836-5124
ITT Technical Institute Post-Sec.
3216 S National Ave 65807 417-877-4800
Missouri College of Cosmetology North Post-Sec.
2555 W Kearney St 65803 417-866-2786
Missouri State University Post-Sec.
901 S National Ave, 417-836-5000
New Covenant Academy 300/PK-12
3304 S Cox Ave 65807 417-887-9848
Matthew Searson, admin. Fax 887-2419
Ozarks Technical Community College Post-Sec.
1001 E Chestnut Expy 65802 417-447-7500
Professional Massage Training Center Post-Sec.
229 E Commercial St 65803 417-863-7682
Rockbridge Seminary Post-Sec.
3111 E Battlefield St 65804 866-931-4300
St. John's Regional Health Center Post-Sec.
1235 E Cherokee St 65804 417-885-2845
St. John's School of Nursing Post-Sec.
4431 S Fremont Ave 65804 417-885-2098
School of Professional Psychology Post-Sec.
2885 W Battlefield St 65807 417-823-3477
Southwest Baptist University Post-Sec.
4431 S Fremont Ave 65804 417-820-2069
Springfield Catholic HS 300/9-12
2340 S Eastgate Ave 65809 417-887-8817
Jeanne Skahan, prin. Fax 885-1165
Springfield SDA S 50/K-10
704 S Belview Ave 65802 417-862-0833
Summit Prep S of Southwest Missouri 100/PK-12
2155 W Chesterfield Blvd 65807 417-869-8077
Rob Gronniger, head sch Fax 869-8087
Vatterott College - Springfield Post-Sec.
3850 S Campbell Ave 65807 417-831-8116

**Stanberry, Gentry, Pop. 1,181**
Stanberry R-II SD 300/PK-12
610 N Park St 64489 660-783-2136
Dr. Adam Willard, supt. Fax 783-2177
www.sr2.k12.mo.us
Stanberry JSHS 100/7-12
610 N Park St 64489 660-783-2163
Lisa Craig, prin. Fax 783-2177

**Steele, Pemiscot, Pop. 2,134**
South Pemiscot County R-V SD 700/PK-12
611 Beasley Rd 63877 573-695-4426
Chris Moore, supt. Fax 695-4427
www.southpemiscot.com
South Pemiscot HS 300/7-12
611 Beasley Rd 63877 573-695-3342
Glenn Carter, prin. Fax 695-7461

**Steelville, Crawford, Pop. 1,631**
Steelville R-III SD 900/PK-12
PO Box 339 65565 573-775-2175
Mike Whittaker, supt. Fax 775-2179
steelville.k12.mo.us
Steelville HS 300/9-12
PO Box 339 65565 573-775-2144
Tana Booker, prin. Fax 775-5050
Steelville MS 300/5-8
PO Box 339 65565 573-775-2176
John Bunch, prin. Fax 775-2591

**Stewartsville, DeKalb, Pop. 741**
Stewartsville C-2 SD 200/K-12
902 Buchanan St 64490 816-669-3792
Paul Perry, supt. Fax 669-8125
www.stewartsville.k12.mo.us
Stewartsville JSHS 100/7-12
902 Buchanan St 64490 816-669-3258
Chris Gagnon, prin. Fax 669-8125

**Stockton, Cedar, Pop. 1,789**
Stockton R-I SD 1,100/K-12
PO Box 190 65785 417-276-5143
Shannon Snow, supt. Fax 276-3765
www.stockton.k12.mo.us/
Stockton HS 300/9-12
PO Box 190 65785 417-276-8806
Michael Postlewait, prin. Fax 276-8584
Stockton MS 400/5-8
PO Box 190 65785 417-276-5141
Robert Bolte, prin. Fax 276-6389

**Stoutland, Laclede, Pop. 192**
Stoutland R-II SD 500/PK-12
7584 State Road T 65567 417-286-3711
Eric Cooley, supt. Fax 286-3153
www.stoutlandschools.com
Stoutland JSHS 200/7-12
7584 State Road T 65567 417-286-3711
Tami Bobbitt, prin. Fax 286-3981

**Stover, Morgan, Pop. 1,079**
Morgan County R-I SD 500/PK-12
701 N Oak St 65078 573-377-2217
Dr. Steve Weinhold, supt. Fax 377-2211
mcr1.stovermo.com/
Morgan County R-I HS 200/7-12
701 N Oak St 65078 573-377-2218
Michael Marriott, prin. Fax 377-2952

**Strafford, Greene, Pop. 2,311**
Strafford R-VI SD 1,200/K-12
201 W McCabe St 65757 417-736-7000
John Collins, supt. Fax 736-7016
straffordschools.net
Strafford HS 400/9-12
201 W McCabe St 65757 417-736-7000
Brett Soden, prin. Fax 736-7020
Strafford MS 400/6-8
211 W McCabe St 65757 417-736-7000
Marcia Chadwell, prin. Fax 736-7019

**Sturgeon, Boone, Pop. 864**
Sturgeon R-V SD 400/PK-12
210 W Patton St 65284 573-687-3515
Shawn Schultz, supt. Fax 687-2116
www.sturgeon.k12.mo.us/
Sturgeon HS 100/9-12
210 W Patton St 65284 573-687-3512
Becky Shafer, prin. Fax 687-3441
Sturgeon MS 100/5-8
210 W Patton St 65284 573-687-2155
Brandee Brown, prin. Fax 687-1226

**Sullivan, Franklin, Pop. 7,019**
Sullivan SD 2,200/PK-12
138 Taylor St 63080 573-468-5171
Dr. Thomas Allen, supt. Fax 468-7720
www.sullivaneagles.org
Sullivan HS 800/9-12
1073 E Vine St 63080 573-468-5181
Dr. Jennifer Schmidt, prin. Fax 860-3524
Sullivan MS 400/6-8
1156 Elmont Rd 63080 573-468-5191
Dill Kim, prin. Fax 860-2326

**Summersville, Texas, Pop. 492**
Summersville R-II SD 400/PK-12
PO Box 198 65571 417-932-4045
Merlyn Johnson, supt. Fax 932-5360
www.sville.k12.mo.us
Summersville JSHS 200/7-12
PO Box 198 65571 417-932-4929
Jon Johnson, prin. Fax 932-4178

**Sunset Hills, Saint Louis, Pop. 8,388**

---

Vatterott College - Sunset Hills Post-Sec.
12900 Maurer Industrial Dr 63127 314-843-4200

**Sweet Springs, Saline, Pop. 1,457**
Sweet Springs R-VII SD 500/PK-12
600 E Marshall St 65351 660-335-4860
Donna Wright, supt. Fax 335-4378
sweetsprings.k12.mo.us/
Sweet Springs JSHS 200/7-12
600 E Marshall St 65351 660-335-6341
David Honeycutt, prin. Fax 335-6379

**Tarkio, Atchison, Pop. 1,576**
Tarkio R-I SD 300/K-12
312 S 11th St 64491 660-736-4161
Dr. Patrick Martin, supt. Fax 736-4546
tarkio.k12.mo.us
Tarkio JSHS 200/7-12
312 S 11th St 64491 660-736-4118
Patrick Martin, prin. Fax 736-4546

**Thayer, Oregon, Pop. 2,197**
Thayer R-II SD 700/PK-12
401 E Walnut St 65791 417-264-4600
Tonya Woods, supt. Fax 264-4608
thayer.k12.mo.us/
Thayer JSHS 300/7-12
401 E Walnut St 65791 417-264-4600
Marc Pitts, prin. Fax 264-4608

**Theodosia, Ozark, Pop. 239**
Lutie R-VI SD 200/K-12
5802 US Highway 160 65761 417-273-4274
Scot Young, supt. Fax 273-4171
lutieschool.org
Lutie JSHS 100/6-12
5802 US Highway 160 65761 417-273-4274
Stephen Fox, prin. Fax 273-4171

**Tina, Carroll, Pop. 154**
Tina-Avalon R-II SD 200/PK-12
11896 Highway 65 64682 660-622-4211
Jana Holcer, supt. Fax 622-4210
tinaavalon.k12.mo.us/
Tina-Avalon JSHS 100/7-12
11896 Highway 65 64682 660-622-4212
Shelly Rex, prin. Fax 622-4210

**Tipton, Moniteau, Pop. 3,237**
Tipton R-VI SD 600/K-12
305 US Highway 50 E 65081 660-433-5520
Scott Jarvis, supt. Fax 433-5241
tipton.k12.mo.us/

Tipton HS 300/7-12
305 US Highway 50 E 65081 660-433-5528
Allee Ellen, prin. Fax 433-2419

**Trenton, Grundy, Pop. 5,941**
Trenton R-IX SD 1,300/K-12
1607 Normal St 64683 660-359-3994
Becky Albrecht, supt. Fax 359-3995
www.trentonr9.k12.mo.us/
Trenton HS 400/9-12
1415 Oklahoma Ave 64683 660-359-2291
Daniel Wiebers, prin. Fax 359-4073
Trenton MS 400/5-8
1417 Oklahoma Ave 64683 660-359-4328
Dustin Jenkerson, prin. Fax 359-6554

---

North Central Missouri College Post-Sec.
1301 Main St 64683 660-359-3948

**Troy, Lincoln, Pop. 10,315**
Lincoln County R-III SD 6,200/PK-12
951 W College St 63379 636-462-6098
Dr. Mark S. Penny, supt. Fax 462-6099
www.troy.k12.mo.us
Buchanan HS 1,400/10-12
1190 Old Cap Au Gris Rd 63379 636-462-5148
Dr. Jerry Raines, prin. Fax 462-5149
New Horizons HS Alt
41 Clonts Field Dr 63379 636-462-4967
Barb Hatcher, prin. Fax 462-4968
Troy MS 1,400/6-8
713 W College St 63379 636-462-4937
Dr. Briscoe Kelly, prin. Fax 462-4938
Other Schools – See Moscow Mills

**Tuscumbia, Miller, Pop. 203**
Miller County R-III SD 200/K-12
PO Box 1 65082 573-369-2375
Jason Price, supt. Fax 369-2833
www.tuscumbialions.k12.mo.us
Tuscumbia HS 100/9-12
PO Box 1 65082 573-369-2375
Randy Gum, prin. Fax 369-2833

**Union, Franklin, Pop. 10,024**
Union R-XI SD 3,000/K-12
PO Box 440 63084 636-583-8626
Steve Bryant, supt. Fax 583-2403
union.k12.mo.us
Union HS 900/9-12
PO Box 440 63084 636-583-2513
Doug Cuneio, prin. Fax 583-4203
Union MS 400/7-8
PO Box 440 63084 636-583-5855
Ty Crain, prin. Fax 583-6156

---

East Central College Post-Sec.
1964 Prairie Dell Rd 63084 636-584-6500

**Union Star, DeKalb, Pop. 430**
Union Star R-II SD 200/K-12
6132 NW State Route Z 64494 816-593-2294
Rick Calloway, supt. Fax 593-4427
www.usr2.com
Union Star JSHS 100/6-12
6132 NW State Route Z 64494 816-593-2294
Chris Turpin, prin. Fax 593-4427

**Unionville, Putnam, Pop. 1,843**
Putnam County R-I SD 700/PK-12
803 S 20th St 63565 660-947-3361
Dr. Heath Halley Ed.D., supt. Fax 947-2912
www.putnamcountyr1.net
Putnam County R-1 HS 200/9-12
803 S 20th St 63565 660-947-2481
Jeremy Watt, prin. Fax 947-2912
Putnam County R-1 MS 200/6-8
802 S 18th St 63565 660-947-3237
Andrew Garber, prin. Fax 947-2912

**University City, Saint Louis, Pop. 34,413**
School District of University City 3,100/PK-12
8136 Groby Rd 63130 314-290-4000
Joylynn Pruitt, supt.
www.ucityschools.org
Brittany Woods MS 700/6-8
8125 Groby Rd 63130 314-290-4280
Jamie Jordan, prin. Fax 997-1786
Lieberman Learning Center Alt
8136 Groby Rd 63130 314-290-4330
Chris Blumenhorst, prin. Fax 432-4478
University City HS 900/9-12
7401 Balson Ave 63130 314-290-4100
Michael Maclin, prin. Fax 290-4120

**Urbana, Hickory, Pop. 412**
Hickory County R-I SD 500/K-12
RR 1 Box 838 65767 417-993-4241
Dr. Mark Beem, supt. Fax 993-4269
www.skylineschools.info
Skyline HS 200/7-12
RR 1 Box 838 65767 417-993-4226
Randall Dougherty, prin. Fax 993-5947

**Valley Park, Saint Louis, Pop. 6,786**
Valley Park SD 1,100/PK-12
1 Main St 63088 636-923-3500
Dr. David Knes, supt. Fax 861-1002
www.vp.k12.mo.us
Valley Park HS 300/9-12
1 Main St 63088 636-923-3613
Dr. Matt Bailey, prin. Fax 225-0542
Valley Park MS 200/6-8
1 Main St 63088 636-923-3624
Dr. Tad Savage, prin. Fax 225-1529

**Van Buren, Carter, Pop. 813**
Van Buren R-I SD 500/PK-12
PO Box 550 63965 573-323-4281
Sonia Kuessner, supt. Fax 323-4297
www.vanburen.k12.mo.us
Van Buren HS 300/7-12
PO Box 550 63965 573-323-4295
Mark Wood, prin. Fax 323-4295

**Vandalia, Audrain, Pop. 3,832**
Van-Far R-I SD 600/PK-12
2200 W US Highway 54 63382 573-594-6111
Stephen Hunter, supt. Fax 594-2878
www.vf.k12.mo.us
Van-Far JSHS 300/7-12
2200 W US Highway 54 63382 573-594-6442
Cindy Mckee-Pirch, prin. Fax 594-3054

**Verona, Lawrence, Pop. 608**
Verona R-VII SD 400/K-12
PO Box 7 65769 417-498-2274
Tony L. Simmons, supt. Fax 498-6590
verona.k12.mo.us
Verona JSHS 200/7-12
PO Box 7 65769 417-498-6775
Terry Winton, prin. Fax 498-6045

**Versailles, Morgan, Pop. 2,421**
Morgan County R-II SD 1,400/PK-12
913 W Newton St 65084 573-378-4231
Dr. Joyce Ryerson, supt. Fax 378-5714
www.mcr2.k12.mo.us/
Morgan County HS 400/9-12
913 W Newton St 65084 573-378-4697
Chris Marshall, prin. Fax 378-2704
Morgan County MS 300/6-8
913 W Newton St 65084 573-378-5432
Travis Troyer, prin. Fax 378-6610

**Viburnum, Iron, Pop. 688**
Iron County C-4 SD 400/K-12
35 Highway 49 65566 573-244-5422
Dr. Blane Keel, supt. Fax 244-5424
www.ironc4.k12.mo.us
Viburnum JSHS 200/7-12
35 Highway 49 65566 573-244-5521
Clay LaRue, prin. Fax 244-3410

**Vienna, Maries, Pop. 605**
Maries County R-I SD 500/PK-12
PO Box 218 65582 573-422-3304
Joseph Dunlap, supt. Fax 422-3185
www.mariesr1.k12.mo.us
Vienna HS 300/7-12
PO Box 218 65582 573-422-3363
Ian Murray, prin. Fax 422-3185

**Villa Ridge, Franklin, Pop. 2,605**

---

Crosspoint Christian S 100/PK-12
PO Box 100 63089 636-742-5380
Bob Templeton, admin. Fax 742-5917

**Walker, Vernon, Pop. 266**
Northeast Vernon County R-I SD 300/PK-12
216 E Leslie Ave 64790 417-465-2221
Charles Naas, supt. Fax 465-2388
www.nevcknights.org
Northeast Vernon County R-I HS 100/7-12
216 E Leslie Ave 64790 417-465-2221
Chris Hudson, prin. Fax 465-2388

**Walnut Grove, Greene, Pop. 659**
Walnut Grove R-V SD 300/K-12
PO Box 187 65770 417-788-2543
Gwenda Barton, supt. Fax 788-1254
www.wgtigers.com
Walnut Grove JSHS 100/7-12
PO Box 187 65770 417-788-2543
Rory Henry, prin. Fax 788-1254

**Wardell, Pemiscot, Pop. 423**
North Pemiscot County R-I SD 200/K-12
PO Box 38 63879 573-628-3471
Terry Hamilton, supt. Fax 628-3472
www.northpem.k12.mo.us
North Pemiscot County JSHS 100/6-12
PO Box 38 63879 573-628-3465
Bill Hoffmann, prin. Fax 628-3418

**Wardsville, Cole, Pop. 1,489**
Blair Oaks R-II SD 1,100/K-12
6124 Falcon Ln 65101 573-636-2020
Dr. James Jones, supt. Fax 636-2202
www.blairoaks.k12.mo.us
Blair Oaks HS 400/9-12
6124 Falcon Ln 65101 573-635-8514
Gary Verslues, prin. Fax 635-6327
Blair Oaks MS 300/5-8
6124 Falcon Ln 65101 573-634-2053
Julia Gampher, prin. Fax 636-3509

**Warrensburg, Johnson, Pop. 18,253**
Warrensburg R-VI SD 2,900/PK-12
PO Box 638 64093 660-747-7823
Dr. Scott Patrick, supt. Fax 747-9615
www.warrensburgr6.org
Reese S Alt
301 W Market St 64093 660-747-2496
Leslie Brown, dir. Fax 747-2579
Warrensburg Area Career Center Vo/Tech
205 S Ridgeview Dr 64093 660-747-2283
Rusty Sproat, dir. Fax 747-3778
Warrensburg HS 1,000/9-12
1411 S Ridgeview Dr 64093 660-747-2262
Simone Dillingham, prin. Fax 747-8731
Warrensburg MS 700/6-8
640 E Gay St 64093 660-747-5612
Jim Elliott, prin. Fax 747-8779

---

University of Central Missouri Post-Sec.
PO Box 800 64093 660-543-4111

**Warrenton, Warren, Pop. 7,746**
Warren County R-III SD 3,000/PK-12
385 W Veterans Memorial Dr 63383 636-456-6901
Dr. James Chandler, supt. Fax 456-7687
www.warrencor3.org
Black Hawk MS 700/6-8
300 Kuhl Ave 63383 636-456-6903
Lisa Pirrung, prin. Fax 456-1445
Warrenton HS 900/9-12
803 Pinckney St 63383 636-456-6902
Nicholas Heggemann, prin. Fax 456-5771

**Warsaw, Benton, Pop. 2,107**
Warsaw R-IX SD 1,300/PK-12
PO Box 248 65355 660-438-7120
Scott Downing, supt. Fax 438-5028
www.warsaw.k12.mo.us/
Boise MS 400/6-8
PO Box 1750 65355 660-438-9079
Dr. Eric Findley, prin. Fax 438-2209
Warsaw HS 400/9-12
PO Box 248 65355 660-438-7351
Randy Luebbert, prin. Fax 438-3749

**Washburn, Barry, Pop. 418**
Southwest R-V SD 800/PK-12
529 E Pineville Rd 65772 417-826-5410
Robert Walker, supt. Fax 826-5603
www.swr5.k12.mo.us
Southwest HS 300/9-12
529 E Pineville Rd 65772 417-826-5413
Tosha Watson, prin. Fax 826-5603
Southwest MS 200/5-8
529 E Pineville Rd 65772 417-826-5050
Beverly Bonner, prin. Fax 826-5603

**Washington, Franklin, Pop. 13,819**
Washington SD 4,100/PK-12
220 Locust St 63090 636-231-2000
Dr. Lori VanLeer, supt. Fax 239-3315
www.washington.k12.mo.us
Four Rivers Career Center Vo/Tech
1978 Image Dr 63090 636-231-2100
Randy Kosark, dir. Fax 239-0791
Washington HS 1,400/9-12
600 Blue Jay Dr 63090 636-231-2200
Dr. Frank Wood, prin. Fax 231-2165
Washington MS 600/7-8
401 E 14th St 63090 636-231-2300
Ron Millheiser, prin. Fax 231-2305

---

St. Francis Borgia Regional HS 500/9-12
1000 Borgia Dr 63090 636-239-7871
Kevin Mabie, prin. Fax 239-1198

**Waynesville, Pulaski, Pop. 4,531**
Waynesville R-VI SD 5,500/PK-12
200 Fleetwood Dr 65583 573-842-2097
Dr. Brian Henry, supt. Fax 433-2968
waynesville.k12.mo.us
Waynesville Career Center Vo/Tech
400 GW Ln 65583 573-842-2500
Dr. Pattison Traci, dir. Fax 842-2402
Waynesville HS 1,700/9-12
200 GW Ln 65583 573-842-2400
Courtney Long, prin. Fax 842-2401
Waynesville MS 900/7-8
1001 Historic 66 W 65583 573-842-2550
John Fluhrer, prin. Fax 842-2559

---

Central College of Cosmetology Post-Sec.
PO Box 463 65583 573-336-3888

**Weaubleau, Hickory, Pop. 411**
Weaubleau R-III SD 300/PK-12
509 N Center St 65774 417-428-3317
Eric Wilken, supt. Fax 428-3521
www.weaubleau.k12.mo.us/
Weaubleau HS 200/7-12
509 N Center St 65774 417-428-3368
Rodney Delmont, prin. Fax 428-3004

**Webb City, Jasper, Pop. 10,693**
Webb City R-VII SD 4,100/PK-12
411 N Madison St 64870 417-673-6000
Anthony Rossetti, supt. Fax 673-6007
www.wcr7.org
Webb City HS 1,200/9-12
621 N Madison St 64870 417-673-6010
Tim Davied, prin. Fax 673-6017
Webb City JHS 600/7-8
807 W 1st St 64870 417-673-6030
Angie Broadus, prin. Fax 673-6037

**Webster Groves, Saint Louis, Pop. 22,645**
Webster Groves SD 4,500/PK-12
400 E Lockwood Ave 63119 314-961-1233
Dr. Sarah Riss, supt. Fax 963-6411
www.webster.k12.mo.us
Webster Groves HS 1,300/9-12
100 Selma Ave 63119 314-963-6400
Dr. Jon Clark, prin. Fax 963-6483
Other Schools – See Saint Louis

---

Eden Theological Seminary Post-Sec.
475 E Lockwood Ave 63119 314-961-3627
Holy Cross Academy Annunciation S 50/6-8
16 W Glendale Rd 63119 314-961-7712
Janet Dolan, prin. Fax 961-2157

**Weldon Spring, Saint Charles, Pop. 5,401**
Francis Howell R-III SD
Supt. — See Saint Charles
Bryan MS 900/6-8
605 Independence Rd 63304 636-851-5800
Mark Delaney, prin. Fax 851-6208

Howell MS 800/6-8
825 OFallon Rd 63304 636-851-4800
Ted Huff, prin. Fax 851-4121

**Wellington, Lafayette, Pop. 797**
Wellington-Napoleon R-IX SD 400/K-12
800 Highway 131 64097 816-934-2531
Jeff Ruskey, supt. Fax 934-8649
www.wntigers.net
Wellington-Napoleon JSHS 200/6-12
800 Highway 131 64097 816-240-2621
Mindy Hampton, prin. Fax 934-8649

**Wellsville, Montgomery, Pop. 1,206**
Wellsville Middletown R-I SD 400/PK-12
900 Burlington St 63384 573-684-2428
Pete Nasir, supt. Fax 684-2018
wmr1.k12.mo.us/
Wellsville-Middleton JSHS 200/7-12
900 Burlington St 63384 573-684-2017
Darin Sehlke, prin. Fax 684-2018

**Wentzville, Saint Charles, Pop. 28,539**
Wentzville R-IV SD 12,300/K-12
1 Campus Dr 63385 636-327-3800
Dr. Curtis Cain, supt. Fax 327-8611
www.wentzville.k12.mo.us
Holt HS 1,700/9-12
600 Campus Dr 63385 636-327-3876
Shane Schlueter, prin. Fax 327-3953
Timberland HS 1,900/9-12
559 E Highway N 63385 636-327-3988
Kyle Lindquist, prin. Fax 327-3922
Wentzville MS 1,100/6-8
405 Campus Dr 63385 636-327-3815
Dr. Kelly Mantz, prin. Fax 327-3954
Wentzville South MS 800/6-8
561 E Highway N 63385 636-327-3928
Scott Swift, prin. Fax 327-3955
Other Schools – See Lake Saint Louis, O Fallon

---

Midwest University Post-Sec.
851 Parr Rd 63385 636-327-4645

**Weston, Platte, Pop. 1,614**
West Platte County R-II SD 600/PK-12
1103 Washington St 64098 816-640-2236
John Rinehart, supt. Fax 386-2104
www.wpsd.net
West Platte County JSHS 300/7-12
935 Washington St 64098 816-640-2292
Dr. Logan Lightfoot, prin. Fax 386-2293

**Westphalia, Osage, Pop. 382**
Osage County R-III SD 800/K-12
PO Box 37 65085 573-455-2375
Joe Scott, supt. Fax 455-9884
www.fatimacomets.org
Fatima JSHS 500/7-12
PO Box 37 65085 573-455-2550
Chuck Woody, prin. Fax 455-9884

**West Plains, Howell, Pop. 11,780**
West Plains R-VII SD 2,600/PK-12
305 Valley View Dr 65775 417-256-6150
Dr. John Mulford, supt. Fax 256-8616
wpr7.schoolwires.net
South Central Career Center Vo/Tech
407 W Thornburgh St 65775 417-256-6152
Jim Laughary, dir. Fax 256-5786
West Plains HS 1,200/9-12
602 E Olden St 65775 417-256-6150
Jack Randolph, prin. Fax 256-8908
West Plains MS 600/5-8
730 E Olden St 65775 417-256-6150
Lenny Eagleman, prin. Fax 256-8907

---

Missouri State University - West Plains Post-Sec.
128 Garfield Ave 65775 417-255-7255

**Wheatland, Hickory, Pop. 358**
Wheatland R-II SD 300/PK-12
PO Box 68 65779 417-282-6433
David McQuerter, supt. Fax 282-5733
sites.google.com/a/wheatland.k12.mo.us/district/
Wheatland JSHS 100/7-12
PO Box 68 65779 417-282-5833
Matt Gunter, prin. Fax 282-5733

**Wheaton, Barry, Pop. 680**
Wheaton R-III SD 500/PK-12
PO Box 249 64874 417-652-3914
Dr. Lance Massey, supt. Fax 652-7355
www.wheatonbulldogs.org/
Wheaton JSHS 200/7-12
PO Box 249 64874 417-652-7249
Traci Mitchell, prin. Fax 652-7355

**Wildwood, Saint Louis, Pop. 35,007**

---

Living Water Academy 100/PK-10
17770 Mueller Rd 63038 636-821-2308
Thomas Keller, head sch Fax 779-0011
Saint Louis Community College - Wildwood Post-Sec.
2645 Generations Dr 63040 636-422-2000

**Willard, Greene, Pop. 5,200**
Willard R-II SD 4,300/PK-12
500 Kime St 65781 417-742-2584
Dr. Kent Medlin, supt. Fax 742-2586
www.willardschools.net
Willard HS 1,300/9-12
515 E Jackson St 65781 417-742-3524
Curt Graves, prin. Fax 742-3667
Willard MS 700/7-8
205 S Miller Rd 65781 417-742-2588
Amy Sims, prin. Fax 742-3505

**Willow Springs, Howell, Pop. 2,140**
Willow Springs R-IV SD 1,300/PK-12
215 W 4th St 65793 417-469-3260
Derrick Hutsell, supt. Fax 469-5127
www.willowspringsschool.com/
Willow Springs HS 400/9-12
215 W 4th St 65793 417-469-2114
Jimalee James, prin. Fax 469-2507
Willow Springs MS 400/5-8
215 W 4th St 65793 417-469-3211
Philip Pietroburgo, prin. Fax 469-1229

**Windsor, Henry, Pop. 2,866**
Henry County R-I SD 700/PK-12
210 North St 65360 660-647-3533
Kevin Sandlin, supt. Fax 647-2711
henrycountyr1.k12.mo.us
Windsor JSHS 300/7-12
210 North St 65360 660-647-3106
Cindy Hawkins, prin. Fax 647-3218

**Winfield, Lincoln, Pop. 1,383**
Winfield R-IV SD 1,500/K-12
701 W Elm St 63389 636-668-8188
Nancy Baker, supt. Fax 668-8641
www.winfield.k12.mo.us
Winfield HS 500/9-12
701 W Elm St 63389 636-668-8130
Eric Alderson, prin. Fax 566-6455
Winfield MS 300/6-8
701 W Elm St 63389 636-668-8001
Tom McCracken, prin. Fax 668-6044

**Winona, Shannon, Pop. 1,311**
Winona R-III SD 500/PK-12
PO Box 248 65588 573-325-8101
Scott Lindsey, supt. Fax 325-8447
www.winonar3.org
Winona HS 200/9-12
PO Box 248 65588 573-325-8101
Gilbert Miley, prin. Fax 325-4700

**Winston, Daviess, Pop. 258**
Winston R-VI SD 200/PK-12
PO Box 38 64689 660-749-5331
Brian Robinson, supt. Fax 749-5432
www.winston.k12.mo.us
Winston JSHS 100/7-12
PO Box 38 64689 660-749-5456
Chris Gagnon, prin. Fax 749-5432

**Wright City, Warren, Pop. 3,037**
Wright City R-II SD 1,500/PK-12
90 Bell Rd 63390 636-745-7200
David Buck, supt. Fax 745-3613
www.wrightcity.k12.mo.us/
Wright City HS 500/9-12
520 Westwoods Rd 63390 636-745-7500
Shawn Brown, prin. Fax 745-7518
Wright City MS 300/6-8
100 Bell Rd 63390 636-745-7300
Douglas Smith, prin. Fax 745-7304

---

Liberty Christian Academy 100/PK-12
PO Box 514 63390 636-745-0388
Beverly Wilgus, admin. Fax 745-0390

**Zalma, Bollinger, Pop. 122**
Zalma R-V SD 200/K-12
HC 2 Box 184 63787 573-722-5504
Darryl Sauer, supt. Fax 722-9870
www.zalma.k12.mo.us/
Zalma JSHS 100/7-12
HC 2 Box 184 63787 573-722-3320
Gerard Vandeven, prin. Fax 722-9870

# MONTANA

**MONTANA OFFICE OF PUBLIC INSTRUCTION**
**PO Box 202501, Helena 59620-2501**
**Telephone 406-444-3095**
**Fax 406-444-2893**
**Website opi.mt.gov**

State Superintendent of Public Instruction    Denise Juneau

**MONTANA BOARD OF EDUCATION**
**PO Box 200601, Helena 59620-0601**

Chairperson    Patty Myers

## COUNTY SUPERINTENDENTS OF SCHOOLS

Beaverhead County Office of Education
Linda Marsh, supt. 406-683-3737
2 S Pacific St Ste 7, Dillon 59725 Fax 683-3769
Big Horn County Office of Education
Sandy Watts, supt. 406-665-9823
PO Box 908, Hardin 59034 Fax 665-9823
Blaine County Office of Education
Terry Brockie, supt. 406-357-3270
PO Box 819, Chinook 59523 Fax 357-2199
Broadwater County Office of Education
Douglas Ellis, supt. 406-266-9215
515 Broadway St, Townsend 59644 Fax 266-3674
Carbon County Office of Education
Jerry Scott, supt. 406-446-1301
PO Box 116, Red Lodge 59068 Fax 446-9155
Carter County Office of Education
Marilyn Hutchinson, supt. 406-775-8721
PO Box 352, Ekalaka 59324 Fax 775-8703
Cascade County Office of Education
Patricia Boyle, supt. 406-454-6776
121 4th St N Ste 1A Fax 454-6778
Great Falls 59401
www.cascadecountymt.gov
Chouteau County Office of Education
Rick Cook, supt. 406-622-3242
PO Box 459, Fort Benton 59442 Fax 622-3028
Custer County Office of Education
Doug Ellingson, supt. 406-874-3421
1010 Main St, Miles City 59301 Fax 874-3452
Daniels County Office of Education
Joan Bjarko, supt. 406-487-2651
PO Box 67, Scobey 59263 Fax 487-5432
Dawson County Office of Education
Steve Engebretson, supt. 406-377-3963
207 W Bell St, Glendive 59330 Fax 377-2022
Deer Lodge County Office of Education
Michael O'Rourke, supt. 406-563-9178
800 Main St, Anaconda 59711 Fax 563-5476
Fallon County Office of Education
Don Dilworth, supt. 406-778-8182
PO Box 846, Baker 59313 Fax 778-2048
Fergus County Office of Education
Rhonda Long, supt. 406-535-3136
712 W Main St, Lewistown 59457 Fax 535-2819
Flathead County Office of Education
Jack Eggensperger, supt. 406-758-5720
935 1st Ave W, Kalispell 59901 Fax 758-5850
Gallatin County Office of Education
Mary Ellen Fitzgerald, supt. 406-582-3090
311 W Main St Rm 107 Fax 582-3093
Bozeman 59715
Garfield County Office of Education
Jessica McWilliams, supt. 406-557-6115
PO Box 28, Jordan 59337 Fax 557-6115
Glacier County Office of Education
Darryl Omsberg, supt. 406-873-2295
1210 E Main St, Cut Bank 59427 Fax 873-9103
www.glaciercountygov.com
Golden Valley County Office of Education
Craig Mattheis, supt. 406-568-2342
107 Kemp St, Ryegate 59074 Fax 568-2428

Granite County Office of Education
Vicki Harding, supt. 406-859-7024
PO Box 9, Philipsburg 59858 Fax 859-3817
Hill County Office of Education
Diane McLean, supt. 406-265-5481
315 4th St, Havre 59501 Fax 265-5487
Jefferson County Office of Education
Garry Pace, supt. 406-225-4114
PO Box H, Boulder 59632 Fax 225-4149
Judith Basin County Office of Education
Julie Peevey, supt. 406-566-2277
PO Box 307, Stanford 59479 Fax 566-2211
Lake County Office of Education
Gale Decker, supt. 406-883-7262
106 4th Ave E, Polson 59860 Fax 883-7283
www.lakemt.gov/
Lewis & Clark County Office of Education
Katrina Chaney, supt. 406-447-8344
316 N Park Ave Ste 221 Fax 447-8398
Helena 59623
www.lccountymt.gov/education
Liberty County Office of Education
Kathy Armstrong, supt. 406-759-5216
PO Box 684, Chester 59522 Fax 759-5996
Lincoln County Office of Education
Ron Higgins, supt. 406-283-2450
418 Mineral Ave, Libby 59923 Fax 283-2453
Madison County Office of Education
Pam Birkeland, supt. 406-843-4217
PO Box 247, Virginia City 59755 Fax 843-5261
McCone County Office of Education
Jackie Becker, supt. 406-485-3590
PO Box 180, Circle 59215 Fax 485-2689
Meagher County Office of Education
Helen Hanson, supt., PO Box 354 406-547-3612
White Sulphur Springs 59645 Fax 547-3388
Mineral County Office of Education
Mary Yarnall, supt. 406-822-3529
PO Box 100, Superior 59872 Fax 822-3579
Missoula County Office of Education
Erin Lipkind, supt. 406-258-3349
438 W Spruce St, Missoula 59802 Fax 258-3973
Musselshell County Office of Education
Kathryn Pfister, supt. 406-323-1470
506 Main St, Roundup 59072 Fax 323-3303
Park County Office of Education
Ed Barich, supt., 414 E Callender St 406-222-4148
Livingston 59047 Fax 222-4199
Petroleum County Office of Education
Pamela Bevis, supt. 406-429-5551
PO Box 226, Winnett 59087 Fax 429-6328
Phillips County Office of Education
Vivian Taylor, supt. 406-654-2010
PO Box 138, Malta 59538 Fax 654-1213
Pondera County Office of Education
Jo Stone, supt. 406-271-4055
20 4th Ave SW Ste 307 Fax 271-4070
Conrad 59425
Powder River County Office of Education
Charlotte Miller, supt. 406-436-2488
PO Box 718, Broadus 59317 Fax 436-2151

Powell County Office of Education
Jules Waber, supt. 406-846-9719
409 Missouri Ave Fax 846-3891
Deer Lodge 59722
Prairie County Office of Education
Jamie Smith, supt. 406-635-5577
PO Box 566, Terry 59349 Fax 635-5576
Ravalli County Office of Education
Regina Plettenberg, supt. 406-375-6522
215 S 4th St Ste B, Hamilton 59840 Fax 375-6554
Richland County Office of Education
Gail Anne Staffanson, supt. 406-433-1608
201 W Main St, Sidney 59270 Fax 433-3731
Roosevelt County Office of Education
Jeri Toavs, supt. 406-653-6266
400 2nd Ave S, Wolf Point 59201 Fax 653-6203
Rosebud County Office of Education
Joby Parker, supt. 406-346-2537
PO Box 407, Forsyth 59327 Fax 346-7319
Sanders County Office of Education
Kathy McEldery, supt. 406-826-4288
PO Box 519, Plains 59859 Fax 826-4299
Sheridan County Office of Education
June Johnson, supt. 406-765-3403
100 W Laurel Ave Fax 765-2609
Plentywood 59254
Silver Bow County Office of Education
Cathy Maloney, supt. 406-497-6215
155 W Granite St, Butte 59701 Fax 497-6328
Stillwater County Office of Education
Judy Martin, supt. 406-322-8057
PO Box 1139, Columbus 59019 Fax 322-1118
Sweet Grass County Office of Education
Susan Metcalf, supt. 406-932-5147
PO Box 1310, Big Timber 59011 Fax 932-5112
Teton County Office of Education
Diane Inbody, supt. 406-466-2907
PO Box 610, Choteau 59422 Fax 466-2138
www.tetoncomt.org/supofschools
Toole County Office of Education
Boyd Jackson, supt. 406-424-8322
226 1st St S, Shelby 59474 Fax 424-8321
toolecountymt.gov
Treasure County Office of Education
Tamara Kimball, supt. 406-342-5545
PO Box 429, Hysham 59038 Fax 342-5445
Valley County Office of Education
Lynne Nyquist, supt. 406-228-6226
501 Court Sq Ste 2 Fax 228-9027
Glasgow 59230
Wheatland County Office of Education
Susan Beley, supt. 406-632-4816
PO Box 637, Harlowton 59036 Fax 632-4880
Wibaux County Office of Education
Patricia Zinda, supt. 406-796-2481
PO Box 199, Wibaux 59353 Fax 796-2625
Yellowstone County Office of Education
Max Lenington, supt. 406-256-6933
PO Box 35022, Billings 59107 Fax 256-6930
www.co.yellowstone.mt.gov/

## PUBLIC, PRIVATE AND CATHOLIC SECONDARY SCHOOLS

**Absarokee, Stillwater, Pop. 1,134**
Absarokee SD 300/PK-12
327 S Woodard Ave 59001 406-328-4583
Dustin Sturm, supt. Fax 328-4077
www.absarokee.k12.mt.us/
Absarokee HS 100/9-12
327 S Woodard Ave 59001 406-328-4583
Dustin Sturm, prin. Fax 328-4077
Absarokee MS 50/7-8
327 S Woodard Ave 59001 406-328-4583
Dustin Sturm, prin. Fax 328-4077

**Alberton, Mineral, Pop. 415**
Alberton SD 100/PK-12
PO Box 330 59820 406-722-4413
Clay Acker, supt. Fax 722-3040
Alberton HS 50/9-12
PO Box 330 59820 406-722-3381
Kyle Fisher, prin. Fax 722-3040
Alberton MS 50/7-8
PO Box 330 59820 406-722-4413
Kyle Fisher, prin. Fax 722-3040

**Anaconda, Deer Lodge, Pop. 9,095**
Anaconda SD 1,100/PK-12
1410 W Park Ave 59711 406-563-6361
Dr. Tom Darnell, supt. Fax 563-7763
www.anacondaschools.org/
Anaconda HS 400/9-12
515 Main St 59711 406-563-5269
Paul Furthmyre, prin. Fax 563-5260
Moody JHS 200/6-8
219 E 3rd St 59711 406-563-6242
Sue Meredith, prin. Fax 563-5093

**Arlee, Lake, Pop. 605**
Arlee SD 400/K-12
72220 Fyant St 59821 406-726-3216
Dave Whitesell, supt. Fax 360-8531
www.arleeschools.org
Arlee HS 100/9-12
72220 Fyant St 59821 406-726-3216
James Taylor, prin. Fax 726-3940
Arlee JHS 100/7-8
72220 Fyant St 59821 406-726-3216
James Taylor, prin. Fax 726-3940

**Ashland, Rosebud, Pop. 799**
Ashland ESD 100/PK-8
PO Box 17 59003 406-784-2568
Steve Henderson, supt. Fax 784-6138
Ashland MS 50/7-8
PO Box 17 59003 406-784-2568
Stephen Henderson, prin. Fax 784-6138

St. Labre Catholic HS 100/9-12
PO Box 216 59003 406-784-4564
Trivian Rides The Bear, prin. Fax 784-4565
St. Labre Catholic MS 200/5-8
PO Box 216 59003 406-784-4567
Jack Gion, prin. Fax 784-4565

**Augusta, Lewis and Clark, Pop. 305**
Augusta SD 100/PK-12
PO Box 307 59410 406-562-3384
Larry Markuson, supt. Fax 562-3898
Augusta HS 50/9-12
PO Box 307 59410 406-562-3384
Larry Markuson, prin. Fax 562-3898
Augusta MS 50/7-8
PO Box 307 59410 406-562-3384
Larry Markuson, prin. Fax 562-3898

**Bainville, Roosevelt, Pop. 202**
Bainville SD 100/PK-12
PO Box 177 59212 406-769-2321
Renee Rasmussen, supt. Fax 769-3291
www.bainvilleschool.k12.mt.us
Bainville HS 50/9-12
PO Box 177 59212 406-769-2321
Rhiannon Beery, prin. Fax 769-3291
Bainville MS 50/7-8
PO Box 177 59212 406-769-2321
Rhiannon Beery, prin. Fax 769-3291

**Baker, Fallon, Pop. 1,723**
Baker SD 400/PK-12
PO Box 659 59313 406-778-3574
Donald Schillinger, supt. Fax 778-2785
www.baker.k12.mt.us/
Baker HS 100/9-12
PO Box 659 59313 406-778-3329
David Breitbach, prin. Fax 778-2785
Baker JHS 100/7-8
PO Box 659 59313 406-778-3329
David Breitbach, prin. Fax 778-2785

**Belfry, Carbon, Pop. 215**
Belfry SD 50/PK-12
PO Box 210 59008 406-664-3319
Jason Olson, supt. Fax 664-3274
belfrybats.org
Belfry HS 50/9-12
PO Box 210 59008 406-664-3319
Jason Olson, prin. Fax 664-3274
Belfry MS 50/7-8
PO Box 210 59008 406-664-3319
Jason Olson, prin. Fax 664-3274

**Belgrade, Gallatin, Pop. 7,233**
Belgrade SD 2,400/PK-12
PO Box 166 59714 406-924-2006
Candy Lubansky, supt. Fax 388-0122
www.bsd44.org
Belgrade HS 800/9-12
303 N Hoffman St 59714 406-924-2513
Russ McDaniel, prin. Fax 388-4633
Belgrade MS 500/5-8
410 Triple Crown St 59714 406-924-2258
Julie Mickolio, prin. Fax 388-8894

**Belt, Cascade, Pop. 585**
Belt SD 300/PK-12
PO Box 197 59412 406-277-3351
Kathleen Prody, supt. Fax 277-4466
www.beltschool.com
Belt HS 100/9-12
PO Box 197 59412 406-277-3351
Kyle Paulson, prin. Fax 277-4466
Belt MS 50/6-8
PO Box 197 59412 406-277-3351
Kyle Paulson, prin. Fax 277-4466

**Bigfork, Flathead, Pop. 4,196**
Bigfork SD 800/K-12
PO Box 188 59911 406-837-7400
Matt Jensen, supt. Fax 837-7407
www.bigforkschools.org
Bigfork HS 300/9-12
PO Box 188 59911 406-837-7420
Alan Robbins, prin. Fax 837-7245
Bigfork MS 100/7-8
PO Box 188 59911 406-837-7412
Brenda Clarke, prin. Fax 837-7438

Swan River ESD 200/K-8
1205 Swan Hwy 59911 406-837-4528
Marc Bunker, prin. Fax 837-4055
www.swanriverschool.org
Swan River MS 50/7-8
1205 Swan Hwy 59911 406-837-4528
Marc Bunker, prin. Fax 837-4055

**Big Sandy, Chouteau, Pop. 583**
Big Sandy SD 200/PK-12
PO Box 570 59520 406-378-2502
Brad Moore, supt. Fax 378-2275
www.bigsandy.k12.mt.us
Big Sandy HS 100/9-12
PO Box 570 59520 406-378-2502
Brad Moore, prin. Fax 378-2275
Big Sandy JHS 50/7-8
PO Box 570 59520 406-378-2502
Brad Moore, prin. Fax 378-2275

**Big Sky, Gallatin, Pop. 2,277**
Big Sky SD
Supt. — See Gallatin Gateway
Lone Peak HS 50/9-12
PO Box 161280 59716 406-995-4281
Alexander Ide, prin. Fax 995-2161

Big Sky Discovery Academy 50/PK-12
PO Box 161548 59716 406-993-2008
Brenda Yahraes, dir.

**Big Timber, Sweet Grass, Pop. 1,599**
Big Timber ESD 300/PK-8
PO Box 887 59011 406-932-5939
Mark Ketcham, supt. Fax 932-4069
www.bigtimber-gs.k12.mt.us
Big Timber MS 100/7-8
PO Box 887 59011 406-932-5939
Mark Ketcham, prin. Fax 932-4069

Sweet Grass County HSD 200/9-12
PO Box 886 59011 406-932-5993
Alvin Buerkle, supt. Fax 932-5982
www.sgchs.com/
Sweet Grass County HS 200/9-12
PO Box 886 59011 406-932-5993
Matt Kleinsasser, prin. Fax 932-5982

**Billings, Yellowstone, Pop. 101,668**
Billings SD 15,800/PK-12
415 N 30th St 59101 406-281-5065
Terry Bouck, supt. Fax 281-6179
www.billingsschools.org/
Billings HS 1,700/9-12
425 Grand Ave 59101 406-281-5400
Dennis Holmes, prin. Fax 281-6174
Billings West HS 2,000/9-12
2201 Saint Johns Ave 59102 406-281-5600
David Cobb, prin. Fax 655-3100
Career Center Vo/Tech
3723 Central Ave 59102 406-281-5340
Scott Anderson, dir. Fax 655-3096
Castle Rock MS 700/7-8
1441 Governors Blvd 59105 406-281-5800
Nikki Hofmann, prin. Fax 254-1116
James MS 500/6-8
1200 30th St W 59102 406-281-6100
Reece Kalfell, prin. Fax 281-6178
Lewis & Clark MS 600/6-8
1315 Lewis Ave 59102 406-281-5900
Steve Pomroy, prin. Fax 281-6177
Riverside MS 500/6-8
3700 Madison Ave 59101 406-281-6000
Kevin Kirkman, prin. Fax 255-3534
Skyview HS 1,500/9-12
1775 High Sierra Blvd 59105 406-281-5200
Debra Black, prin. Fax 255-3507
Adult & Basic Education Adult
415 N 30th St 59101 406-281-5001
Brian Kroll, dir. Fax 281-6827

Canyon Creek ESD 200/PK-8
3139 Duck Creek Rd 59101 406-656-4471
Brent Lipp, supt. Fax 655-1031
www.canyoncreekschool.org
Canyon Creek MS 50/7-8
3139 Duck Creek Rd 59101 406-656-4471
Brent Lipp, prin. Fax 655-1031

Elder Grove ESD 300/K-8
1532 S 64th St W 59106 406-656-2893
Justin Klebe, supt. Fax 651-4346
www.eldergrove.k12.mt.us/
Elder Grove MS 100/6-8
1532 S 64th St W 59106 406-656-2893
Nathan Schmitz, prin. Fax 651-4346

Elysian ESD 200/PK-8
6416 Elysian Rd 59101 406-656-4101
Bob Whalen, supt. Fax 656-9941
elysianschool.org
Elysian MS 50/7-8
6416 Elysian Rd 59101 406-656-4101
Barbara Frank, prin. Fax 656-9941

Lockwood ESD 1,200/PK-8
1932 US Highway 87 E 59101 406-252-6022
Tobin Novasio, supt. Fax 259-2502
www.lockwoodschool.org/
Lockwood MS 400/6-8
1932 US Highway 87 E 59101 406-259-0154
Gordon Klasna, prin. Fax 259-3832

Billings Central Catholic HS 300/9-12
3 Broadwater Ave 59101 406-245-6651
Sheldon Hanser, prin. Fax 259-3124
Billings Christian S 100/PK-12
4519 Grand Ave 59106 406-656-9484
Paul Waggoner, prin. Fax 655-4880
City College MSU Billings Post-Sec.
3803 Central Ave 59102 406-247-3000
Montana State University - Billings Post-Sec.
1500 University Dr 59101 406-657-2011
Rocky Mountain College Post-Sec.
1511 Poly Dr 59102 800-877-6259
SAGE Technical Service Truck Driving Sch Post-Sec.
3044 Hesper Rd 59102 800-545-4546
St. Francis Upper S 200/6-8
205 N 32nd St 59101 406-259-5037
Jim Stanton, prin. Fax 259-7981
St. Vincent's Hospital & Health Center Post-Sec.
PO Box 35200 59107 406-657-7102

**Bonner, Missoula, Pop. 1,669**
Bonner ESD 300/PK-8
PO Box 1004 59823 406-258-6151
Fax 258-6153
www.bonner.k12.mt.us
Bonner MS 100/7-8
PO Box 1004 59823 406-258-6151
Fax 258-6153
Potomac ESD 100/PK-8
29750 Potomac Rd 59823 406-244-5581
Fax 244-5840
www.potomacschoolmontana.us/
Potomac MS 50/7-8
29750 Potomac Rd 59823 406-244-5581
David Allen, prin. Fax 244-5840

**Boulder, Jefferson, Pop. 1,141**
Boulder ESD 200/PK-8
PO Box 1346 59632 406-225-3316
Maria Pace, supt. Fax 225-9218
www.bgs.k12.mt.us/
Boulder MS 50/7-8
PO Box 1346 59632 406-225-3316
Maria Pace, prin. Fax 225-9218

Jefferson HSD 200/9-12
PO Box 838 59632 406-225-3740
Tim Norbeck, supt. Fax 225-3289
www.jhs.k12.mt.us
Jefferson HS 200/9-12
PO Box 838 59632 406-225-3317
Daryl Mikesell, prin. Fax 225-3289

**Box Elder, Hill, Pop. 80**
Box Elder SD 400/PK-12
PO Box 205 59521 406-352-4195
Darin Hannum, supt. Fax 352-3830
www.boxelder.k12.mt.us
Box Elder HS 100/9-12
PO Box 205 59521 406-352-4195
Jeremy MacDonald, prin. Fax 352-3830
Box Elder MS 100/7-8
PO Box 205 59521 406-352-4195
Jeremy MacDonald, prin. Fax 352-3830

Rocky Boy SD 600/PK-12
81 Mission Taylor Rd 59521 406-395-4291
Voyd St. Pierre, supt. Fax 395-4829
www.rockyboy.k12.mt.us
Rocky Boy HS 100/9-12
81 Mission Taylor Rd 59521 406-395-4270
Lewis Reese, prin. Fax 395-4829
Rocky Boy MS 100/7-8
81 Mission Taylor Rd 59521 406-395-4270
Lewis Reese, prin. Fax 395-4829

Stone Child College Post-Sec.
8294 Upper Box Elder Rd 59521 406-395-4875

**Bozeman, Gallatin, Pop. 36,568**
Anderson ESD 200/PK-8
10040 Cottonwood Rd 59718 406-587-1305
Scott McDowell, supt. Fax 587-2501
www.andersonmt.org/
Anderson MS 50/7-8
10040 Cottonwood Rd 59718 406-587-1305
Scott McDowlell, prin. Fax 587-2501

Bozeman SD 5,400/PK-12
404 W Main St 59715 406-522-6000
Robert Watson, supt. Fax 522-6065
www.bsd7.org
Bozeman HS 1,800/9-12
205 N 11th Ave 59715 406-522-6200
Kevin Conwell, prin. Fax 522-6222
Chief Joseph MS 600/6-8
4255 Kimberwicke St 59718 406-522-6300
Brian Ayers, prin. Fax 522-6306
Hyalite MS 100/6-8
3600 W Babcock St 59718 406-582-6800
Mike Van Buren, prin. Fax 582-6850
Sacajawea MS 600/6-8
3525 S 3rd Rd 59715 406-522-6470
Gordon Grissom, prin. Fax 522-6474

LaMotte ESD 100/PK-8
841 Bear Canyon Rd 59715 406-586-2838
Fax 585-8626
www.lamotteschool.com
LaMotte MS 50/7-8
841 Bear Canyon Rd 59715 406-586-2838
LeeAnn Burke, supt. Fax 585-8626

Monforton ESD 300/PK-8
6001 Monforton School Rd 59718 406-586-1557
Darren Strauch, supt. Fax 587-5049
www.monfortonschool.org/
Monforton MS 50/7-8
6001 Monforton School Rd 59718 406-586-1557
Darren Strauch, supt. Fax 587-5049

Academy of Cosmetology Post-Sec.
133 W Mendenhall St 59715 406-587-1265
Headwaters Academy 50/6-8
418 W Garfield St 59715 406-585-9997
Joseph Stefani, head sch Fax 585-9992
Heritage Christian S 200/K-12
4310 Durston Rd 59718 406-587-9311
Gerry Goede, admin. Fax 587-1838
Montana Bible College Post-Sec.
3625 S 19th Ave 59718 406-586-3585
Montana State University Post-Sec.
PO Box 172190 59717 406-994-0211
Mt. Ellis Academy 100/9-12
3641 Bozeman Trail Rd 59715 406-587-5178
Petra Academy 100/PK-12
4720 Classical Way 59718 406-582-8165
Craig Dunham, hdmstr. Fax 556-8777

**Bridger, Carbon, Pop. 700**
Bridger SD 200/PK-12
429 W Park Ave 59014 406-662-3588
Bill Phillips, supt. Fax 662-3076
www.bridgerscouts.org
Bridger HS 100/9-12
429 W Park Ave 59014 406-662-3533
Jim Goltz, prin. Fax 662-3076

Bridger MS — 50/7-8
106 N 4th St 59014 — 406-662-3588
Jim Goltz, prin. — Fax 662-3520

**Broadus, Powder River, Pop. 457**

Broadus SD — 200/PK-12
PO Box 500 59317 — 406-436-2658
Jim Hansen, supt. — Fax 436-2660
www.broadus.net/

Powder River County District HS — 100/7-12
PO Box 500 59317 — 406-436-2658
Rosalie Lunby, prin. — Fax 436-2660

**Broadview, Yellowstone, Pop. 191**

Broadview SD — 100/PK-12
PO Box 147 59015 — 406-667-2337
Rob Osborne, supt. — Fax 667-2195
www.broadviewschools.org

Broadview HS — 50/9-12
PO Box 147 59015 — 406-667-2337
Rob Osborne, supt. — Fax 667-2195

Broadview MS — 50/7-8
PO Box 147 59015 — 406-667-2337
Rob Osborne, supt. — Fax 667-2195

**Brockton, Roosevelt, Pop. 255**

Brockton SD — 100/PK-12
PO Box 198 59213 — 406-786-3311
Francis J. LaBounty, supt. — Fax 786-3377
www.brockton.k12.mt.us/

Brockton HS — 50/9-12
PO Box 198 59213 — 406-786-3311
Francis J. LaBounty, supt. — Fax 786-3377

Gilligan MS — 50/7-8
PO Box 198 59213 — 406-786-3311
Francis LaBounty, supt. — Fax 786-3377

**Browning, Glacier, Pop. 998**

Browning SD — 1,900/PK-12
PO Box 610 59417 — 406-338-2715
John P. Rouse, supt. — Fax 338-3200
www.bps.k12.mt.us

Browning HS — 500/9-12
PO Box 610 59417 — 406-338-2745
Shawn Clark, prin. — Fax 338-2844

Browning MS — 300/7-8
PO Box 610 59417 — 406-338-2725
Julie Hayes, prin. — Fax 338-5320

---

Blackfeet Community College — Post-Sec.
PO Box 819 59417 — 406-338-5441

De LaSalle Blackfeet S — 100/4-8
PO Box 1489 59417 — 406-338-5290
Br. Dale Mooney, admin. — Fax 338-7900

**Butte, Silver Bow, Pop. 32,958**

Butte SD — 4,200/PK-12
111 N Montana St 59701 — 406-533-2500
Judy Jonart, supt. — Fax 533-2525
www.butte.k12.mt.us

Butte HS — 1,300/9-12
401 S Wyoming St 59701 — 406-533-2200
John Metz, prin. — Fax 533-2277

East MS — 700/7-8
2600 Grand Ave 59701 — 406-533-2600
Larry Driscoll, prin. — Fax 533-2670

---

Butte Academy of Beauty Culture — Post-Sec.
303 W Park St 59701 — 406-723-8565

Butte Central HS — 100/9-12
9 S Idaho St 59701 — 406-782-6761
Kevin St. John, prin. — Fax 723-3873

Highlands College of Montana Tech — Post-Sec.
25 Basin Creek Rd 59701 — 406-496-3707

Montana Tech of the University of MT — Post-Sec.
1300 W Park St 59701 — 406-496-4101

**Cascade, Cascade, Pop. 673**

Cascade SD — 300/K-12
PO Box 529 59421 — 406-468-9383
Justin Barnes, supt. — Fax 468-2212
www.cascade.k12.mt.us

Cascade HS — 100/9-12
PO Box 529 59421 — 406-468-9383
Kevin Sukut, prin. — Fax 468-2212

Cascade JHS — 50/7-8
PO Box 529 59421 — 406-468-9383
Kevin Sukut, prin. — Fax 468-2212

**Charlo, Lake, Pop. 328**

Charlo SD — 300/PK-12
PO Box 10 59824 — 406-644-2206
Thom Peck, supt. — Fax 644-2400
www.charlo.k12.mt.us/

Charlo HS — 100/9-12
PO Box 10 59824 — 406-644-2206
Steve Love, prin. — Fax 644-2400

Charlo MS — 50/7-8
PO Box 10 59824 — 406-644-2206
Steve Love, prin. — Fax 644-2400

**Chester, Liberty, Pop. 830**

Chester-Joplin-Inverness SD — 300/PK-12
PO Box 550 59522 — 406-759-5108
Thad Kaiser, supt. — Fax 759-5867
www.cji.k12.mt.us

Chester-Joplin-Inverness HS — 100/9-12
PO Box 550 59522 — 406-759-5108
Pam Graff, prin. — Fax 759-5867

Chester-Joplin-Inverness MS — 50/7-8
PO Box 550 59522 — 406-759-5108
Pam Graff, prin. — Fax 759-5867

**Chinook, Blaine, Pop. 1,183**

Chinook SD — 400/PK-12
PO Box 1059 59523 — 406-357-2628
Jay Eslick, supt. — Fax 357-2238
www.chinookschools.org

Chinook HS — 100/9-12
PO Box 1059 59523 — 406-357-2236
Matt Molyneaux, prin. — Fax 357-2238

Chinook MS — 100/7-8
PO Box 1059 59523 — 406-357-2237
Matt Molyneaux, prin. — Fax 357-2238

**Choteau, Teton, Pop. 1,646**

Choteau SD — 400/PK-12
204 7th Ave NW 59422 — 406-466-5303
Lynn Utterback, supt. — Fax 466-5305
www.choteauschools.net

Choteau HS — 200/9-12
204 7th Ave NW 59422 — 406-466-5303
Nate Achenbach, prin. — Fax 466-5305

Choteau MS — 100/7-8
204 7th Ave NW 59422 — 406-466-5303
Nate Achenbach, prin. — Fax 466-5305

**Circle, McCone, Pop. 606**

Circle SD — 200/PK-12
PO Box 99 59215 — 406-485-2545
Gary Fisher, supt. — Fax 485-2332
circleschools.k12.mt.us

Circle HS — 100/9-12
PO Box 99 59215 — 406-485-3600
Gary Fisher, prin. — Fax 485-2332

Redwater MS — 50/7-8
PO Box 99 59215 — 406-485-2140
Helen Murphy, prin. — Fax 485-2332

**Clancy, Jefferson, Pop. 1,638**

Clancy ESD — 300/PK-8
PO Box 209 59634 — 406-933-5575
Bruce Dunkle, supt. — Fax 933-5715
www.clancy.k12.mt.us/

Clancy MS — 100/7-8
PO Box 209 59634 — 406-933-5575
Bruce Dunkle, prin. — Fax 933-5715

Montana City ESD — 400/K-8
11 McClellan Creek Rd 59634 — 406-442-6779
Tony Kloker, supt. — Fax 443-8875
montanacity.schoolwires.com

Montana City MS — 100/6-8
11 McClellan Creek Rd 59634 — 406-442-6779
Daryl Mikesell, prin. — Fax 443-8875

**Clinton, Missoula, Pop. 1,018**

Clinton ESD — 200/PK-8
PO Box 250 59825 — 406-825-3113
Tom Stack, supt. — Fax 825-3114
www.clintoncougars.com

Clinton MS — 50/7-8
PO Box 250 59825 — 406-825-3113
Julie Espinosa, prin. — Fax 825-3114

**Clyde Park, Park, Pop. 288**

Shields Valley SD — 200/PK-12
405 1st St E 59018 — 406-578-2535
Erik Wilkerson, supt. — Fax 578-2176
www.shieldsvalleyschools.org/

Shields Valley HS — 100/9-12
405 1st St E 59018 — 406-686-4621
Greg Sager, prin. — Fax 686-4937

Shields Valley MS — 50/7-8
405 1st St E 59018 — 406-686-4621
Greg Sager, prin. — Fax 686-4937

**Colstrip, Rosebud, Pop. 2,118**

Colstrip SD — 600/PK-12
PO Box 159 59323 — 406-748-4699
Bob Lewandowski, supt. — Fax 748-2268
colstripschools.org

Brattin MS — 200/6-8
PO Box 159 59323 — 406-748-4699
Sherry Foote, prin. — Fax 748-3143

Colstrip HS — 200/9-12
PO Box 159 59323 — 406-748-4699
Mark Ator, prin. — Fax 748-2517

**Columbia Falls, Flathead, Pop. 4,562**

Columbia Falls SD — 1,900/K-12
PO Box 1259 59912 — 406-892-6550
Steven Bradshaw, supt. — Fax 892-6552
www.sd6.k12.mt.us

Columbia Falls HS — 700/9-12
PO Box 1259 59912 — 406-892-6500
Scott Gaiser, prin. — Fax 892-6583

Columbia Falls JHS — 300/6-8
PO Box 1259 59912 — 406-892-6530
Dave Wick, prin. — Fax 892-6528

Deer Park ESD — 100/PK-8
2105 Middle Rd 59912 — 406-892-5388
Fax 892-3504
www.deerpark.k12.mt.us

Deer Park MS — 50/7-8
2105 Middle Rd 59912 — 406-892-5388
Dan Block, prin. — Fax 892-3504

**Columbus, Stillwater, Pop. 1,857**

Columbus SD — 700/PK-12
433 N 3rd St 59019 — 406-322-5373
Allan Sipes, supt. — Fax 322-5028
www.columbus.k12.mt.us

Columbus HS — 200/9-12
433 N 3rd St 59019 — 406-322-5373
George McKay, prin. — Fax 322-5028

Columbus MS — 100/6-8
415 N 3rd St 59019 — 406-322-5375
Ron Osborne, prin. — Fax 322-5376

**Conrad, Pondera, Pop. 2,522**

Conrad SD — 500/PK-12
215 S Maryland St 59425 — 406-278-5521
Dr. Donald Mathis, supt. — Fax 278-3630
www.conradschools.org

Conrad HS — 200/9-12
308 S Illinois St 59425 — 406-278-3285
Ken Larson, prin. — Fax 278-3806

Utterback MS — 100/6-8
201 S Maryland St 59425 — 406-278-3227
Tara Thielman, prin. — Fax 278-3228

**Corvallis, Ravalli, Pop. 945**

Corvallis SD — 1,300/PK-12
PO Box 700 59828 — 406-961-4211
Tim Johnson, supt. — Fax 961-5144
www.corvallis.k12.mt.us

Corvallis HS — 500/9-12
PO Box 700 59828 — 406-961-3201
Jason Wirt, prin. — Fax 961-4894

Corvallis JHS — 200/7-8
PO Box 700 59828 — 406-961-3007
Rich Durgin, prin. — Fax 961-5144

**Crow Agency, Big Horn, Pop. 1,597**

---

Little Big Horn College — Post-Sec.
PO Box 370 59022 — 406-638-3100

**Culbertson, Roosevelt, Pop. 690**

Culbertson SD — 300/PK-12
PO Box 459 59218 — 406-787-6246
Larry Crowder, supt. — Fax 787-6244
www.culbertsonschool.com

Culbertson HS — 100/9-12
PO Box 459 59218 — 406-787-6241
Mike Olson, prin. — Fax 787-6244

Culbertson MS — 50/7-8
PO Box 459 59218 — 406-787-6241
Mike Olson, prin. — Fax 787-6244

**Custer, Yellowstone, Pop. 158**

Custer SD — 100/K-12
PO Box 69 59024 — 406-856-4117
Dr. David Perkins, supt. — Fax 856-4206
www.custerschools.org

Custer HS — 50/9-12
PO Box 69 59024 — 406-856-4117
Dr. David Perkins, supt. — Fax 856-4206

Custer MS — 50/7-8
PO Box 69 59024 — 406-856-4117
Dr. David Perkins, supt. — Fax 856-4206

**Cut Bank, Glacier, Pop. 2,736**

Cut Bank SD — 600/PK-12
101 3rd Ave SE 59427 — 406-873-2229
Wade Johnson, supt. — Fax 873-4691
www.cutbankschools.net

Cut Bank HS — 200/9-12
101 3rd Ave SE 59427 — 406-873-5629
Peter Hamilton, prin. — Fax 873-4691

Cut Bank MS — 100/6-8
101 3rd Ave SE 59427 — 406-873-4421
Gail Hofstad, prin. — Fax 873-4691

**Darby, Ravalli, Pop. 697**

Darby SD — 300/PK-12
209 School Dr 59829 — 406-821-3841
Loyd Rennaker, supt. — Fax 821-4977
www.darby.k12.mt.us/

Darby HS — 100/9-12
209 School Dr 59829 — 406-821-3252
Jennifer Burdette, prin. — Fax 821-4977

Darby MS — 100/7-8
209 School Dr 59829 — 406-821-3252
Jennifer Burdette, prin. — Fax 821-4977

**Deer Lodge, Powell, Pop. 3,077**

Deer Lodge ESD — 400/PK-8
444 Montana Ave 59722 — 406-846-1553
Rodney Simpson, supt. — Fax 846-1599

Duvall MS — 100/7-8
444 Montana Ave 59722 — 406-846-1684
Rick Chrisman, prin. — Fax 846-1599

Powell County HSD — 300/9-12
709 Missouri Ave 59722 — 406-846-2757
Rick Duncan, supt. — Fax 846-2759
www.pchs.dl.k12.mt.us

Powell County HS — 300/9-12
709 Missouri Ave 59722 — 406-846-2757
Kerry Glisson, prin. — Fax 846-2759

**Denton, Fergus, Pop. 253**

Denton SD — 100/K-12
PO Box 1048 59430 — 406-567-2270
Gerald Krenzke, supt. — Fax 567-2559
www.denton.k12.mt.us/

Denton HS — 50/9-12
PO Box 1048 59430 — 406-567-2270
Gerald Krenzke, supt. — Fax 567-2559

Denton JHS — 50/7-8
PO Box 1048 59430 — 406-567-2270
Gerald Krenzke, supt. — Fax 567-2559

**Dillon, Beaverhead, Pop. 4,039**

Beaverhead County HSD — 300/9-12
104 N Pacific St 59725 — 406-683-2361
Fred Chouinard, supt. — Fax 683-5263
bchsmt.schoolwires.com

Beaverhead County HS — 300/9-12
104 N Pacific St 59725 — 406-683-2361
Fred Chouinard, supt. — Fax 683-5263

Dillon ESD — 600/PK-8
22 Cottom Dr 59725 — 406-683-4311
Glen Johnson, supt. — Fax 683-4312
www.dillonelem.k12.mt.us/

Dillon MS — 200/6-8
14 Cottom Dr 59725 — 406-683-2368
Randy Shipman, prin. — Fax 683-2369

---

University of Montana Western — Post-Sec.
710 S Atlantic St 59725 — 406-683-7331

**Dixon, Sanders, Pop. 184**
Dixon ESD 100/PK-8
PO Box 10 59831 406-246-3566
Crista Anderson, admin. Fax 246-3379
dixonschool.net
Dixon MS 50/7-8
PO Box 10 59831 406-246-3566
Crista Anderson, prin. Fax 246-3379

**Dodson, Phillips, Pop. 121**
Dodson SD 100/PK-12
PO Box 278 59524 406-383-4361
Debbie Combs, supt. Fax 383-4489
www.dodson.k12.mt.us
Dodson HS 50/9-12
PO Box 278 59524 406-383-4361
Debbie Combs, supt. Fax 383-4489
Dodson MS 50/7-8
PO Box 278 59524 406-383-4362
Debbie Combs, supt. Fax 383-4489

**Drummond, Granite, Pop. 304**
Drummond SD 200/K-12
PO Box 349 59832 406-288-3281
Bryan Kott, supt. Fax 288-3299
Drummond HS 100/9-12
PO Box 349 59832 406-288-3281
Bryan Kott, prin. Fax 288-3299
Drummond MS 50/7-8
PO Box 349 59832 406-288-3281
Bryan Kott, prin. Fax 288-3299

**Dutton, Teton, Pop. 311**
Dutton/Brady SD 100/PK-12
101 2nd St NE 59433 406-476-3424
D.K. Brooks, supt. Fax 476-3342
duttonbradyps.schoolwires.net
Dutton/Brady HS 50/9-12
101 2nd St NE 59433 406-476-3424
D.K. Brooks, prin. Fax 476-3342
Dutton/Brady MS 50/7-8
101 2nd St NE 59433 406-476-3201
D.K. Brooks, prin. Fax 476-3342

**East Helena, Lewis and Clark, Pop. 1,919**
East Helena ESD 1,100/PK-8
PO Box 1280 59635 406-227-7700
Ron Whitmoyer, supt. Fax 227-5534
www.ehps.k12.mt.us
East Valley MS 400/6-8
PO Box 1280 59635 406-227-7740
Dan Rispens, prin. Fax 227-9730

Helena Christian S 200/PK-12
3384 Canyon Ferry Rd 59635 406-442-3821
Mike Dellwo, prin. Fax 442-0341

**Ekalaka, Carter, Pop. 327**
Ekalaka SD 100/PK-12
PO Box 458 59324 406-775-8601
Allison Hardin, supt. Fax 775-8766
www.ekalaka.net
Carter County HS 50/9-12
PO Box 458 59324 406-775-8767
Allison Hardin, prin. Fax 775-8766
Ekalaka MS 50/7-8
PO Box 458 59324 406-775-8767
Allison Hardin, prin. Fax 775-8766

**Ennis, Madison, Pop. 828**
Ennis SD 300/PK-12
PO Box 517 59729 406-682-4258
John Overstreet, supt. Fax 682-7751
www.ennisschools.org
Ennis HS 100/9-12
PO Box 517 59729 406-682-4258
John Sullivan, prin. Fax 682-7751
Ennis MS 50/7-8
PO Box 517 59729 406-682-4237
Brian Hilton, prin. Fax 682-7752

**Eureka, Lincoln, Pop. 1,015**
Eureka SD 800/PK-12
PO Box 2000 59917 406-297-5650
Jim Mepham, supt. Fax 297-2644
www.lchigh.net
Eureka MS 200/5-8
PO Box 2000 59917 406-297-5600
Trevor Utter, prin. Fax 297-5653
Lincoln County HS 300/9-12
PO Box 2000 59917 406-297-5700
Joel Graves, prin. Fax 297-5714

**Fairfield, Teton, Pop. 690**
Fairfield SD 300/K-12
PO Box 399 59436 406-467-2103
Les Meyer, supt. Fax 467-2554
www.fairfield.k12.mt.us/
Fairfield HS 100/9-12
PO Box 399 59436 406-467-2528
Dustin Gordon, prin. Fax 467-2554
Fairfield MS 100/7-8
PO Box 399 59436 406-467-2425
Dustin Gordon, prin. Fax 467-2554

Greenfield ESD 100/PK-8
590 Mt Highway 431 59436 406-467-2433
Fax 467-3138

Greenfield MS 50/7-8
590 Mt Highway 431 59436 406-467-2433
Paul Wilson, prin. Fax 467-3138

**Fairview, Richland, Pop. 832**
Fairview SD 300/PK-12
PO Box 467 59221 406-742-5265
Luke Kloker, supt. Fax 742-3336
fschool.org
Fairview HS 100/9-12
PO Box 467 59221 406-742-5265
Rick Miller, prin. Fax 742-3336
Fairview MS 50/7-8
PO Box 467 59221 406-742-5265
Mark Thompson, prin. Fax 742-8265

**Florence, Ravalli, Pop. 755**
Florence-Carlton SD 800/PK-12
5602 Old US Highway 93 59833 406-273-6751
Bud Scully, supt.
www.florence.k12.mt.us
Florence-Carlton HS 300/9-12
5602 Old US Highway 93 59833 406-273-6301
Audrey Backus, prin. Fax 273-2643
Florence-Carlton MS 100/7-8
5602 Old US Highway 93 59833 406-273-0587
Audrey Backus, prin. Fax 273-0545

**Forsyth, Rosebud, Pop. 1,757**
Forsyth SD 400/PK-12
PO Box 319 59327 406-346-2796
Dinny Bennett, supt. Fax 346-7455
www.forsyth.k12.mt.us
Forsyth HS 100/9-12
PO Box 319 59327 406-346-2796
Shelly Weight, prin. Fax 346-9219
Forsyth JHS 100/7-8
PO Box 319 59327 406-346-2796
Shelly Weight, prin. Fax 346-9219

**Fort Benton, Chouteau, Pop. 1,439**
Ft. Benton SD 300/PK-12
PO Box 399 59442 406-622-5691
Jory Thompson, supt. Fax 622-5691
fortbentonschools.weebly.com
Fort Benton HS 100/9-12
PO Box 399 59442 406-622-3213
Jory Thompson, prin. Fax 622-5691
Fort Benton JHS 50/7-8
PO Box 399 59442 406-622-3213
Christopher Scott Gragg, prin. Fax 622-5691

**Frazer, Valley, Pop. 360**
Frazer SD 100/PK-12
PO Box 488 59225 406-695-2241
Corrina Guardipee-Hall, supt. Fax 695-2243
www.frazer.k12.mt.us
Frazer HS 50/9-12
PO Box 488 59225 406-695-2241
Corrina Hall, admin. Fax 695-2243
Frazer MS 50/7-8
PO Box 488 59225 406-695-2241
Corrina Hall, admin. Fax 695-2243

**Frenchtown, Missoula, Pop. 1,780**
Frenchtown SD 1,000/PK-12
PO Box 117 59834 406-626-2600
Randy Cline, supt. Fax 626-2605
www.ftsd.org
Frenchtown HS 400/9-12
PO Box 117 59834 406-626-2670
Jacob Haynes, prin. Fax 626-2676
Frenchtown MS 200/7-8
PO Box 117 59834 406-626-2650
Mark McMurray, prin. Fax 626-2654

**Froid, Roosevelt, Pop. 181**
Froid SD 100/K-12
PO Box 218 59226 406-766-2343
Felecia Kleven M.Ed., supt. Fax 766-2206
Froid HS 50/9-12
PO Box 218 59226 406-766-2342
Felecia Kleven M.Ed., prin. Fax 766-2206
Froid MS 50/7-8
PO Box 218 59226 406-766-2342
Felecia Kleven M.Ed., prin. Fax 766-2206

**Fromberg, Carbon, Pop. 437**
Fromberg SD 100/PK-12
319 School St 59029 406-668-7611
Teri Harris, supt. Fax 668-7669
frombergpublicschools.com
Fromberg HS 50/9-12
319 School St 59029 406-668-7315
Teri Harris, admin. Fax 668-7669
Fromberg MS 50/7-8
319 School St 59029 406-668-7315
Teri Harris, admin. Fax 668-7669

**Gallatin Gateway, Gallatin, Pop. 845**
Big Sky SD 200/PK-12
45465 Gallatin Rd 59730 406-995-4281
Dr. Dustin Shipman, supt. Fax 995-2161
www.bssd72.org
Ophir MS 50/5-8
45465 Gallatin Rd 59730 406-995-4281
Alexander Ide, prin. Fax 995-2161
Other Schools – See Big Sky

Gallatin Gateway ESD 200/PK-8
PO Box 265 59730 406-763-4415
Kim DeBruycker, supt. Fax 763-4886
www.gallatingatewayschool.com
Gallatin Gateway MS 50/7-8
PO Box 265 59730 406-763-4415
Kim DeBruycker, prin. Fax 763-4886

**Gardiner, Park, Pop. 871**
Gardiner SD 200/PK-12
510 Stone St 59030 406-848-7563
J.T. Stroder, supt. Fax 848-0606
www.gardinerpublicschools.org
Gardiner HS 100/9-12
510 Stone St 59030 406-848-7261
Mike Baer, prin. Fax 848-9489
Gardiner MS 50/7-8
510 Stone St 59030 406-848-7563
Mike Baer, prin. Fax 848-9489

**Geraldine, Chouteau, Pop. 255**
Geraldine SD 100/PK-12
PO Box 347 59446 406-737-4371
Chad Fordyce, supt. Fax 737-4478
www.geraldine.k12.mt.us/
Geraldine HS 50/9-12
PO Box 347 59446 406-737-4371
Chad Fordyce, prin. Fax 737-4478
Geraldine MS 50/7-8
PO Box 347 59446 406-737-4371
Chad Fordyce, prin. Fax 737-4478

**Geyser, Judith Basin, Pop. 87**
Geyser SD 58 100/PK-12
PO Box 70 59447 406-735-4368
Dale Bernard, supt. Fax 735-4452
www.geyser.k12.mt.us
Geyser HS 50/9-12
PO Box 70 59447 406-735-4368
Dale Bernard, admin. Fax 735-4452
Geyser MS 50/7-8
PO Box 70 59447 406-735-4368
Dale Bernard, admin. Fax 735-4452

**Glasgow, Valley, Pop. 3,170**
Glasgow SD 800/PK-12
PO Box 28 59230 406-228-2406
Robert Connors, supt. Fax 228-2407
www.glasgow.k12.mt.us/
Glasgow HS 200/9-12
PO Box 28 59230 406-228-2485
Shawnda Zahara-Harris, prin. Fax 228-4061
Glasgow MS 100/7-8
PO Box 28 59230 406-228-2485
Shawnda Zahara-Harris, prin. Fax 228-4061

**Glendive, Dawson, Pop. 4,857**
Glendive SD 1,100/PK-12
PO Box 701 59330 406-377-5293
Ross Farber, supt. Fax 377-6212
www.glendiveschools.com
Dawson County HS 300/9-12
PO Box 701 59330 406-377-5265
Wade Murphy, prin. Fax 377-8206
Washington MS 300/6-8
PO Box 701 59330 406-377-2356
Willie Thibault, prin. Fax 377-2357

Dawson Community College Post-Sec.
300 College Dr 59330 406-377-3396

**Grass Range, Fergus, Pop. 109**
Grass Range SD #27 100/PK-12
PO Box 58 59032 406-428-2122
Darrell Sanborn, supt. Fax 428-2235
www.grps.k12.mt.us
Grass Range HS 50/9-12
PO Box 58 59032 406-428-2341
Darrell Sanborn, supt. Fax 428-2235
Grass Range MS 50/7-8
PO Box 58 59032 406-428-2122
Darrell Sanborn, supt. Fax 428-2235

**Great Falls, Cascade, Pop. 56,542**
Great Falls SD 10,500/K-12
PO Box 2429 59403 406-268-6001
Tammy Lacey, supt. Fax 268-6002
www.gfps.k12.mt.us
East MS 800/7-8
4040 Central Ave 59405 406-268-6500
Paul Furthmyre, prin. Fax 268-6524
Great Falls HS 1,600/9-12
1900 2nd Ave S 59405 406-268-6250
Heather Hoyer, prin. Fax 268-6256
North MS 700/7-8
2601 8th St NE 59404 406-268-6525
Brad Barringer, prin. Fax 268-6575
Paris Gibson Education Center 300/Alt
2400 Central Ave 59401 406-268-6600
Drew Uecker, prin. Fax 268-6603
Russell HS 1,500/9-12
228 17th Ave NW 59404 406-268-6100
Kerry Parsons, prin. Fax 268-6109

Benefits Health Care-West Campus Post-Sec.
PO Box 5013 59403 406-727-3333
Dahl's College of Beauty Post-Sec.
718 Central Ave 59401 406-454-3453
Foothills Community Christian S 200/PK-12
2210 5th Ave N 59401 406-452-5276
Janelle Lund, prin. Fax 452-8606
Great Falls Central Catholic HS 100/9-12
2800 18th Ave S 59405 406-216-3344
Vickie Donisthorpe, prin. Fax 216-3343
Great Falls College Montana State Univ Post-Sec.
2100 16th Ave S 59405 406-771-4300
Montana School for the Deaf and Blind Post-Sec.
3911 Central Ave 59405 406-771-6000
University of Great Falls Post-Sec.
1301 20th St S 59405 800-856-9544

**Hamilton, Ravalli, Pop. 4,256**
Hamilton SD 1,600/PK-12
217 Daly Ave 59840 406-363-2280
Tom Korst, supt. Fax 363-1843
www.hsd3.org
Hamilton HS 600/9-12
327 Fairgrounds Rd 59840 406-375-6060
Dan Kimzey, prin. Fax 375-6076
Hamilton MS 400/6-8
209 S 5th St 59840 406-363-2121
Marlin Lewis, prin. Fax 363-7032

**Hardin, Big Horn, Pop. 3,345**
Hardin SD 17-H & 1 1,800/PK-12
401 Park Rd 59034 406-665-9300
Dennis Gerke, supt. Fax 665-9338
www.hardin.k12.mt.us

Hardin HS 500/9-12
702 N Terry Ave 59034 406-665-6300
Rob Hankins, prin. Fax 665-1909
Hardin MS 400/6-8
611 5th St W 59034 406-665-6350
Scott Brokaw, prin. Fax 665-1409

**Harlem, Blaine, Pop. 770**
Harlem SD 500/PK-12
PO Box 339 59526 406-353-2289
Rhonda Baker, supt. Fax 353-2674
www.harlem-hs.k12.mt.us
Harlem HS 200/9-12
PO Box 339 59526 406-353-2287
John Salois, prin. Fax 353-2339
Harlem MS 100/7-8
PO Box 339 59526 406-353-2287
John Salois, prin. Fax 353-2339

---

Aaniiih Nakoda College Post-Sec.
PO Box 159 59526 406-353-2607

**Harlowton, Wheatland, Pop. 971**
Harlowton SD 300/PK-12
PO Box 288 59036 406-632-4822
Andrew Begger, supt. Fax 632-4416
www.harlowton.k12.mt.us
Harlowton HS 100/9-12
PO Box 288 59036 406-632-4324
Gregg Wasson, prin. Fax 632-4416
Hillcrest MS 50/7-8
PO Box 288 59036 406-632-4361
Gregg Wasson, prin. Fax 632-4416

**Harrison, Madison, Pop. 137**
Harrison SD 100/K-12
PO Box 7 59735 406-685-3428
Fred Hofman, supt. Fax 685-3420
sites.google.com/a/harrison.k12.mt.us/hhswildcats/
Harrison HS 50/9-12
PO Box 7 59735 406-685-3428
Fred Hofman, admin. Fax 685-3430
Harrison MS 50/7-8
PO Box 7 59735 406-685-3428
Fred Hofman, admin. Fax 685-3430

**Havre, Hill, Pop. 8,979**
Havre SD 1,900/K-12
PO Box 7791 59501 406-265-4356
Andy Carlson, supt. Fax 265-8460
www.havre.k12.mt.us/
Havre HS 600/9-12
PO Box 7791 59501 406-265-6731
Craig Mueller, prin. Fax 265-3217
Havre MS 400/6-8
1441 11th St W 59501 406-265-9613
Dustin Kraske, prin. Fax 265-4414

---

Montana State University - Northern Post-Sec.
PO Box 7751 59501 406-265-3700

**Hays, Blaine, Pop. 831**
Hays-Lodge Pole SD 200/PK-12
PO Box 110 59527 406-673-3120
Margaret Campbell, supt. Fax 673-3294
www.hays.schoolaccess.net/HLP%20Home%20Page.html
Hays-Lodge Pole HS 100/9-12
PO Box 110 59527 406-673-3120
Amy Snow, prin. Fax 673-3415
Hays-Lodge Pole MS 50/7-8
PO Box 110 59527 406-673-3120
Amy Snow, prin. Fax 673-3274

**Heart Butte, Pondera, Pop. 576**
Heart Butte SD 200/PK-12
PO Box 259 59448 406-338-3344
Robin Kratz, supt. Fax 338-5832
www.heartbutteschool.com
Heart Butte HS 50/9-12
PO Box 259 59448 406-338-3344
Dr. Charle Smith, prin. Fax 338-5832
Heart Butte MS 50/7-8
PO Box 259 59448 406-338-2200
Dr. Charle Smith, prin. Fax 338-5832

**Helena, Lewis and Clark, Pop. 27,530**
Helena SD 8,000/K-12
55 S Rodney St 59601 406-324-2001
Kent Kultgen, supt. Fax 324-2035
www.helena.k12.mt.us
Anderson MS 1,000/6-8
1200 Knight St 59601 406-324-2800
Bruce Campbell, prin. Fax 324-2801
Capital HS 1,400/9-12
100 Valley Dr 59601 406-324-2500
Brett Zanto, prin. Fax 324-2501
Helena HS 1,600/9-12
1300 Billings Ave 59601 406-324-2200
Steve Thennis, prin. Fax 324-2201
Helena MS 700/6-8
1025 N Rodney St 59601 406-324-1000
Josh McKay, prin. Fax 324-1001
Project for Alternative Learning Alt
815 Front St 59601 406-324-1630
Stephanie Thennis, prin. Fax 324-1631

---

Carroll College Post-Sec.
1601 N Benton Ave 59625 406-447-4300
Helena College University of Montana Post-Sec.
1115 N Roberts St 59601 406-447-6900
St. Andrew's S 200/K-12
PO Box 231 59624 406-449-3201
Donna Smillie, prin. Fax 449-0129

**Highwood, Chouteau, Pop. 174**
Highwood SD 100/PK-12
160 West St S 59450 406-733-2081
Becky Aaring, supt. Fax 733-2671
www.highwood.k12.mt.us
Highwood HS 50/9-12
160 West St S 59450 406-733-2081
Jane Suberg, prin. Fax 733-2671
Highwood MS 50/6-8
160 West St S 59450 406-733-2081
Jane Suberg, prin. Fax 733-2671

**Hinsdale, Valley, Pop. 212**
Hinsdale SD 100/PK-12
PO Box 398 59241 406-364-2314
Julie Gaffney, supt. Fax 364-2205
Hinsdale HS 50/9-12
PO Box 398 59241 406-364-2314
Julie Gaffney, admin. Fax 364-2205
Hinsdale MS 50/7-8
PO Box 398 59241 406-364-2314
Julie Gaffney, admin. Fax 364-2205

**Hobson, Judith Basin, Pop. 215**
Hobson SD 100/PK-12
PO Box 410 59452 406-423-5483
Colby Fitzgerald, supt. Fax 423-5260
www.hobson.k12.mt.us/
Hobson HS 50/9-12
PO Box 410 59452 406-423-5483
Fax 423-5260
Hobson MS 50/7-8
PO Box 410 59452 406-423-5483
Fax 423-5260

**Hot Springs, Sanders, Pop. 493**
Hot Springs SD 200/PK-12
PO Box 1005 59845 406-741-3285
Kevin Meredith, supt. Fax 741-3287
Hot Springs HS 100/9-12
PO Box 1005 59845 406-741-2962
Chris Clairmont, prin. Fax 741-3287
Hot Springs MS 50/7-8
PO Box 1005 59845 406-741-2962
Chris Clairmont, prin. Fax 741-3287

**Hysham, Treasure, Pop. 299**
Hysham SD 100/PK-12
PO Box 272 59038 406-342-5237
Larry Fink, supt. Fax 342-5257
www.hysham.k12.mt.us
Hysham HS 50/9-12
PO Box 272 59038 406-342-5237
Larry Fink, prin. Fax 342-5257
Hysham MS 50/7-8
PO Box 272 59038 406-342-5237
Larry Fink, prin. Fax 342-5257

**Joliet, Carbon, Pop. 592**
Joliet SD 400/PK-12
PO Box 590 59041 406-962-3541
Jeff Bermes, supt. Fax 962-3958
www.jolietschools.org/
Joliet HS 100/9-12
PO Box 590 59041 406-962-3541
Marilyn Vukonich, prin. Fax 962-3958
Joliet MS 100/7-8
PO Box 590 59041 406-962-3541
Marilyn Vukonich, prin. Fax 962-3958

**Jordan, Garfield, Pop. 342**
Jordan SD 200/PK-12
PO Box 409 59337 406-557-2259
Nathan Olson, supt. Fax 557-2778
jordanpublicschools.org
Garfield County HS 100/9-12
PO Box 409 59337 406-557-2259
Nathan Olson, supt. Fax 557-2778
Jordan MS 50/7-8
PO Box 409 59337 406-557-2259
Nathan Olson, supt. Fax 557-2778

**Judith Gap, Wheatland, Pop. 125**
Judith Gap SD 50/PK-12
PO Box 67 59453 406-473-2211
Annette Hart, supt. Fax 473-2250
www.judithgap.k12.mt.us/
Judith Gap HS 50/9-12
PO Box 67 59453 406-473-2211
Annette Hart, supt. Fax 473-2250
Judith Gap MS 50/7-8
PO Box 67 59453 406-473-2211
Annette Hart, supt. Fax 473-2250

**Kalispell, Flathead, Pop. 19,453**
Cayuse Prairie ESD 200/PK-8
897 Lake Blaine Rd 59901 406-756-4560
Amy Piazzola, supt. Fax 756-4570
cayuseprairie.com
Cayuse Prairie MS 50/7-8
897 Lake Blaine Rd 59901 406-756-4560
Amy Piazzola, prin. Fax 756-4570

Evergreen ESD 800/PK-8
18 W Evergreen Dr 59901 406-751-1111
Dr. Laurie Barron, supt. Fax 752-2307
www.evergreensd50.com
Evergreen JHS 200/5-8
18 W Evergreen Dr 59901 406-751-1131
Kim Anderson, prin. Fax 751-1134

Fair-Mont-Egan ESD 200/PK-8
797 Fairmont Rd 59901 406-755-7072
Christine Anthony, admin. Fax 755-7077
www.fmemontana.net
Fair-Mont-Egan MS 50/7-8
797 Fairmont Rd 59901 406-755-7072
Christine Schmidt-Anthon, prin. Fax 755-7077

Helena Flats SD 15 200/K-8
1000 Helena Flats Rd 59901 406-257-2301
Dan Anderson, supt. Fax 257-2304
helenaflats.org
Helena Flats MS 100/7-8
1000 Helena Flats Rd 59901 406-257-2301
Dan Anderson, prin. Fax 257-2304

Kalispell SD 5,700/PK-12
233 1st Ave E 59901 406-751-3400
Mark Flatau, supt. Fax 751-3416
www.sd5.k12.mt.us
Flathead HS 1,500/9-12
644 4th Ave W 59901 406-751-3500
Peter Fusaro, prin. Fax 751-3505
Glacier HS 1,300/9-12
375 Wolfpack Way 59901 406-758-8600
Callie Langohr, prin. Fax 758-8602
Kalispell MS 1,000/6-8
205 Northwest Ln 59901 406-751-3800
Tryg Johnson, prin. Fax 751-3805

Smith Valley ESD 200/K-8
2901 US Highway 2 W 59901 406-756-4535
Laili Komenda, admin. Fax 756-4534
www.smithvalleyschool.org
Smith Valley MS 50/7-8
2901 US Highway 2 W 59901 406-756-4535
Laili Komenda, prin. Fax 756-4534

West Valley ESD 500/PK-8
2290 Farm To Market Rd 59901 406-755-7239
Cal Ketchum, supt. Fax 755-7300
www.westvalleyschool.com
West Valley MS 100/6-8
2290 Farm To Market Rd 59901 406-755-7239
Carrie Burnham, prin. Fax 755-7300

---

Flathead Valley Community College Post-Sec.
777 Grandview Dr 59901 406-756-3822
Stillwater Christian S 300/PK-12
255 FFA Dr 59901 406-752-4400
Daniel Makowski, head sch Fax 755-4061

**Kila, Flathead, Pop. 375**
Kila ESD 200/PK-8
PO Box 40 59920 406-257-2428
Fax 755-6663
www.kilaschool.com/
Kila MS 50/7-8
PO Box 40 59920 406-257-2428
Jason Christy, prin. Fax 755-6663

**Lambert, Richland**
Lambert SD 100/PK-12
PO Box 260 59243 406-774-3333
Tyler Arlint, supt. Fax 774-3335
Lambert HS 50/9-12
PO Box 260 59243 406-774-3333
Kara Triplett, admin. Fax 774-3335
Lambert MS 50/7-8
PO Box 260 59243 406-774-3333
Kara Triplett, admin. Fax 774-3335

**Lame Deer, Rosebud, Pop. 2,025**
Lame Deer SD 500/PK-12
PO Box 96 59043 406-477-6305
William Parker, supt. Fax 477-6535
www.lamedeer.k12.mt.us/
Lame Deer HS 100/9-12
PO Box 96 59043 406-477-8900
Fax 477-8906
Lame Deer MS 100/7-8
PO Box 96 59043 406-477-8900
Fax 477-8906

---

Chief Dull Knife College Post-Sec.
PO Box 98 59043 406-477-6215

**Laurel, Yellowstone, Pop. 6,588**
Laurel SD 1,900/PK-12
410 Colorado Ave 59044 406-628-8623
Tim Bronk, supt. Fax 628-8625
www.laurel.k12.mt.us
Laurel HS 600/9-12
203 E 8th St 59044 406-628-7911
Edward Norman, prin. Fax 628-3558
Laurel MS 600/5-8
725 Washington Ave 59044 406-628-6919
Patrick Cates, prin. Fax 628-3350

**Lavina, Golden Valley, Pop. 177**
Lavina SD 100/PK-12
PO Box 290 59046 406-636-2761
Steven Schwartz, supt. Fax 636-4911
www.edline.net/pages/lavina_k-12_schools
Lavina HS 50/9-12
PO Box 290 59046 406-636-2761
Steven Schwartz, prin. Fax 636-4911
Lavina MS 50/7-8
PO Box 290 59046 406-636-2761
Steven Schwartz, prin. Fax 636-4911

**Lewistown, Fergus, Pop. 5,800**
Lewistown SD 1,200/PK-12
215 7th Ave S 59457 406-535-8777
Jason Butcher, supt. Fax 535-7292
www.lewistown.k12.mt.us
Fergus HS 400/9-12
215 7th Ave S 59457 406-535-2321
Jerry Feller, prin. Fax 535-3835
Lewistown JHS 200/7-8
215 7th Ave S 59457 406-535-5419
Tim Majerus, prin. Fax 535-2300

**Libby, Lincoln, Pop. 2,579**
Libby SD 1,000/PK-12
724 Louisiana Ave 59923 406-293-8811
Craig Barringer, supt. Fax 293-8812
www.libbyschools.org

Libby JSHS 400/7-12
150 Education Way 59923 406-293-8802
Ruth VanWorth-Rogers, prin. Fax 293-3927

**Lima, Beaverhead, Pop. 213**
Lima SD 100/PK-12
PO Box 186 59739 406-276-3571
Dr. W. Blair Wilding, supt. Fax 276-3495
www.lima.k12.mt.us
Lima HS 50/9-12
PO Box 186 59739 406-276-3571
Dr. W. Blair Wilding, supt. Fax 276-3495
Lima JHS 50/7-8
PO Box 186 59739 406-276-3571
Dr. W. Blair Wilding, supt. Fax 276-3495

**Lincoln, Lewis and Clark, Pop. 993**
Lincoln SD 100/PK-12
PO Box 39 59639 406-362-4201
Kathy Heisler, supt. Fax 362-4030
www.lincolnlynx.com
Lincoln HS 100/9-12
PO Box 39 59639 406-362-4201
Laurie Maughan, prin. Fax 362-4030
Lincoln MS 50/7-8
PO Box 39 59639 406-362-4201
Laurie Maughan, prin. Fax 362-4030

**Livingston, Park, Pop. 6,921**
Arrowhead ESD 75 100/K-8
1489 E River Rd 59047 406-333-4359
Jan Cahill, supt. Fax 333-4975
arrowheadk8.org
Arrowhead MS 50/7-8
1489 E River Rd 59047 406-333-4359
Leah Shannon, lead tchr. Fax 333-4975

Livingston SD 1,400/K-12
132 S B St 59047 406-222-0861
Rich Moore Ph.D., supt. Fax 222-7323
www.livingston.k12.mt.us
Park HS 500/9-12
102 View Vista Dr 59047 406-222-0448
Lynne Scalia, prin. Fax 222-9404
Sleeping Giant MS 300/6-8
301 View Vista Dr 59047 406-222-3292
Lisa Rosburg, prin. Fax 222-3512

Pine Creek ESD 50/PK-8
2575 E River Rd 59047 406-222-0059
Fax 222-0059
pinecreekschool.com
Pine Creek MS 50/7-8
2575 E River Rd 59047 406-222-0059
Leah Shannon, lead tchr. Fax 222-0059

**Lodge Grass, Big Horn, Pop. 414**
Lodge Grass SD 300/PK-12
PO Box 810 59050 406-639-2304
Victoria Falls Down M.Ed., supt. Fax 639-2388
www.lodgegrass.k12.mt.us
Lodge Grass HS 100/9-12
PO Box 810 59050 406-639-2702
Curtis Brien M.Ed., prin. Fax 639-2066
Lodge Grass MS 50/7-8
PO Box 810 59050 406-639-2702
Curtis Brien M.Ed., prin. Fax 639-2066

**Lolo, Missoula, Pop. 3,815**
Lolo ESD 500/PK-8
11395 US Highway 93 S 59847 406-273-0451
Dr. Michael Magone, supt. Fax 273-2628
www.lolo.k12.mt.us
Lolo MS 200/5-8
11395 US Highway 93 S 59847 406-273-0451
Shawna Kientz M.Ed., prin. Fax 273-2628

Woodman ESD 50/K-8
18470 Lolo Creek Rd 59847 406-273-6770
Fax 273-6659
Woodman MS 50/7-8
18470 Lolo Creek Rd 59847 406-273-6770
Jeanine Fillinger, admin. Fax 273-6659

**Lustre, Valley**

---

Lustre Christian HS 50/9-12
294 Lustre Rd 59225 406-392-5735
Wes Young, admin. Fax 392-5765

**Malta, Phillips, Pop. 1,893**
Malta SD 500/PK-12
PO Box 670 59538 406-654-1871
Kris Kuehn, supt. Fax 654-2205
www.malta.k12.mt.us/
Malta HS 200/9-12
PO Box 670 59538 406-654-2002
Scott King, prin. Fax 654-2226
Malta JHS 100/6-8
PO Box 670 59538 406-654-2225
Shawn Bleth, prin. Fax 654-2226

**Manhattan, Gallatin, Pop. 1,493**
Manhattan SD 500/PK-12
PO Box 425 59741 406-284-6460
Jim Notaro, supt. Fax 284-6853
www.manhattan.k12.mt.us
Manhattan HS 200/9-12
PO Box 425 59741 406-284-3341
Bob Moore, prin. Fax 284-3104
Manhattan MS 100/7-8
PO Box 425 59741 406-284-3250
Scott Schumacher, prin. Fax 284-4122

---

Manhattan Christian S 300/PK-12
8000 Churchill Rd 59741 406-282-7261
Patrick DeJong, supt. Fax 282-7701

**Marion, Flathead, Pop. 853**
Marion ESD 100/K-8
205 Gopher Ln 59925 406-854-2333
Cherie Stobie, prin. Fax 854-2690
www.marionschoolmt.com
Marion MS 50/7-8
205 Gopher Ln 59925 406-854-2333
Cherie Stobie, prin. Fax 854-2690

**Medicine Lake, Sheridan, Pop. 215**
Medicine Lake SD 100/PK-12
PO Box 265 59247 406-789-2211
Tiffani Anderson, supt. Fax 789-2213
www.medicinelake.k12.mt.us/
Medicine Lake HS 50/9-12
PO Box 265 59247 406-789-2211
Tiffani Anderson, supt. Fax 789-2213
Medicine Lake MS 50/7-8
PO Box 265 59247 406-789-2211
Tiffani Anderson, supt. Fax 789-2213

**Melstone, Musselshell, Pop. 96**
Melstone SD 100/PK-12
PO Box 97 59054 406-358-2352
Kelly Haaland, supt. Fax 358-2346
Melstone HS 50/9-12
PO Box 97 59054 406-358-2352
Kelly Haaland, prin. Fax 358-2346
Melstone MS 50/7-8
PO Box 97 59054 406-358-2352
Kelly Haaland, prin. Fax 358-2346

**Miles City, Custer, Pop. 8,282**
Miles City SD 1,500/PK-12
1604 Main St 59301 406-234-3840
Keith Campbell, supt. Fax 234-3147
www.milescity.k12.mt.us
Custer County District HS 500/9-12
20 S Center Ave 59301 406-234-4920
Jamie Ogolin, prin. Fax 234-4923
Washington MS 200/7-8
210 N 9th St 59301 406-234-2084
Derrick Tvedt, prin. Fax 234-7403

---

Miles Community College Post-Sec.
2715 Dickinson St 59301 406-874-6100

**Missoula, Missoula, Pop. 65,061**
DeSmet ESD 100/PK-8
6355 Padre Ln 59808 406-549-4994
Shelley Andes, admin. Fax 549-6731
www.desmet.k12.mt.us
DeSmet MS 50/7-8
6355 Padre Ln 59808 406-549-4994
Shelley Andres, prin. Fax 549-6731

Hellgate ESD 1,300/PK-8
2385 Flynn Ln 59808 406-728-5626
Dr. Doug Reisig, supt. Fax 728-5636
www.hellgate.k12.mt.us
Hellgate MS 400/6-8
2385 Flynn Ln 59808 406-721-2452
Jamie Courville, prin. Fax 728-0967

Missoula SD 1 8,500/K-12
215 S 6th St W 59801 406-728-2400
Alex Apostle, supt. Fax 542-4009
www.mcpsmt.org
Big Sky HS 1,000/9-12
3100 South Ave W 59804 406-728-2401
Brian Fortmann, prin. Fax 549-4616
Hellgate HS 1,300/9-12
900 S Higgins Ave 59801 406-728-2402
Lisa Hendrix, prin. Fax 728-2496
Meadow Hill MS 500/6-8
4210 S Reserve St 59803 406-542-4045
Christina Stevens, prin. Fax 721-4418
Porter MS 500/6-8
2510 W Central Ave 59804 406-542-4060
Julie Robitaille, prin. Fax 542-4098
Sentinel HS 1,200/9-12
901 South Ave W 59801 406-728-2403
Tom Blakely, prin. Fax 329-5959
Washington MS 600/6-8
645 W Central Ave 59801 406-542-4085
Paul Johnson, prin. Fax 721-7346
Willard Alternative Learning Center Alt
901 S 6th St W 59801 406-542-4073
Jane Bennett, prin. Fax 327-6965
Other Schools – See Seeley Lake

Target Range ESD 400/PK-8
4095 South Ave W 59804 406-549-9239
Dr. Corey Austin, supt. Fax 728-8841
www.target.k12.mt.us
Target Range MS 100/6-8
4095 South Ave W 59804 406-549-9239
Barbara Droessler, prin. Fax 728-8841

---

Loyola Sacred Heart HS 200/9-12
320 Edith St 59801 406-549-6101
Kathy Schneider, prin. Fax 542-1432
Missoula College University of Montana Post-Sec.
909 South Ave W 59801 406-243-7882
Modern Beauty School Post-Sec.
2700 Paxson St Ste G 59801 406-721-1800
St. Patrick Hospital Post-Sec.
PO Box 4587 59806 406-543-7271
University of Montana Post-Sec.
32 Campus Dr 59812 406-243-0211
Valley Christian S 200/PK-12
2526 Sunset Ln 59804 406-549-0482
Anthony Baugher, head sch Fax 549-5047

**Moore, Fergus, Pop. 188**
Moore SD 100/PK-12
509 Highland Ave 59464 406-374-2231
Denise Chrest, supt. Fax 374-2490
www.moore.k12.mt.us
Moore HS 50/9-12
509 Highland Ave 59464 406-374-2231
Denise Chrest, admin. Fax 374-2490
Moore MS 50/7-8
509 Highland Ave 59464 406-374-2231
Denise Chrest, admin. Fax 374-2490

**Nashua, Valley, Pop. 284**
Nashua SD 100/PK-12
PO Box 170 59248 406-746-3411
Jennifer Cunningham, supt. Fax 746-3458
www.nashua.k12.mt.us
Nashua HS 50/9-12
PO Box 170 59248 406-746-3411
Jennifer Cunningham, supt. Fax 746-3458
Nashua MS 50/7-8
PO Box 170 59248 406-746-3411
Jennifer Cunningham, supt. Fax 746-3458

**Noxon, Sanders, Pop. 210**
Noxon SD 200/PK-12
300 Noxon Ave 59853 406-847-2442
Joshua Patterson, supt. Fax 847-2232
noxonschools.com
Noxon HS 100/9-12
300 Noxon Ave 59853 406-847-2442
Rik Rewerts, prin. Fax 847-2232
Noxon MS 50/7-8
300 Noxon Ave 59853 406-847-2442
Rik Rewerts, prin. Fax 847-2232

**Opheim, Valley, Pop. 83**
Opheim SD 50/PK-12
PO Box 108 59250 406-762-3214
Tony Warren, supt. Fax 762-3348
sites.google.com/site/opheimschool/Home
Opheim HS 50/9-12
PO Box 108 59250 406-762-3214
Tony Warren, prin. Fax 762-3348
Opheim MS 50/7-8
PO Box 108 59250 406-762-3214
Tony Warren, prin. Fax 762-3348

**Pablo, Lake, Pop. 2,090**

---

Salish Kootenai College Post-Sec.
PO Box 70 59855 406-275-4800

**Park City, Stillwater, Pop. 973**
Park City SD 400/PK-12
PO Box 278 59063 406-633-2350
Dan Grabowska, supt. Fax 633-2913
parkcityschools.org
Park City HS 100/9-12
PO Box 278 59063 406-633-2350
Jared Delaney, prin. Fax 633-2913
Park City MS 100/7-8
PO Box 278 59063 406-633-2350
Jared Delaney, prin. Fax 633-2913

**Philipsburg, Granite, Pop. 808**
Philipsburg SD 200/PK-12
PO Box 400 59858 406-859-3232
Mike Cutler, supt. Fax 859-3674
pburg.k12.mt.us
Granite HS 100/9-12
PO Box 400 59858 406-859-3232
Mike Cutler, prin. Fax 859-3674
Philipsburg MS 50/7-8
PO Box 400 59858 406-859-3232
Mike Cutler, prin. Fax 859-3674

**Plains, Sanders, Pop. 1,024**
Plains SD 500/PK-12
PO Box 549 59859 406-826-8600
Thomas Chisholm, supt. Fax 826-4439
www.plainsschools.net/
Plains HS 200/9-12
PO Box 549 59859 406-826-8600
Larry McDonald, prin. Fax 826-4439
Plains MS 100/7-8
PO Box 549 59859 406-826-8600
Jim Holland, prin. Fax 826-4439

**Plentywood, Sheridan, Pop. 1,706**
Plentywood SD 400/PK-12
100 E Laurel Ave 59254 406-765-1803
Joe Bennett, supt. Fax 765-1195
www.plentywood.k12.mt.us/
Plentywood HS 100/9-12
100 E Laurel Ave 59254 406-765-1803
Matt Torix, prin. Fax 765-1195
Plentywood MS 100/7-8
100 E Laurel Ave 59254 406-765-1803
Rob Pedersen, prin. Fax 765-1195

**Plevna, Fallon, Pop. 160**
Plevna SD 100/PK-12
PO Box 158 59344 406-772-5666
Jule Walker, supt. Fax 772-5548
www.plevna.k12.mt.us/
Plevna HS 50/9-12
PO Box 158 59344 406-772-5666
Jule Walker, prin. Fax 772-5548
Plevna MS 50/7-8
PO Box 158 59344 406-772-5666
Jule Walker, prin. Fax 772-5548

**Polson, Lake, Pop. 4,155**
Polson SD 1,700/PK-12
111 4th Ave E 59860 406-883-6355
Dr. Linda E. Reksten, supt. Fax 883-6345
www.polson.k12.mt.us
Polson HS 500/9-12
111 4th Ave E 59860 406-883-6351
Rex Weltz, prin. Fax 883-6330
Polson MS 300/7-8
111 4th Ave E 59860 406-883-6335
Jesse Yarbrough, prin. Fax 883-6334

Mission Valley Christian Academy 100/K-12
38907 Mt Highway 35 59860 406-883-6858
Chris Bumgarner, dir. Fax 883-6858

**Poplar, Roosevelt, Pop. 787**
Poplar SD 700/PK-12
PO Box 458 59255 406-768-6602
James Baldwin, supt. Fax 768-6800
www.poplar.k12.mt.us
Poplar HS 200/9-12
PO Box 458 59255 406-768-6830
Dwain Haggard, prin. Fax 768-6803
Poplar JHS 100/5-8
PO Box 458 59255 406-768-6730
Glen Hageman, prin. Fax 768-6802

Fort Peck Community College Post-Sec.
PO Box 398 59255 406-768-6300

**Power, Teton, Pop. 174**
Power SD 100/PK-12
PO Box 155 59468 406-463-2251
Loren Dunk, supt. Fax 463-2360
www.power.k12.mt.us/
Power HS 100/9-12
PO Box 155 59468 406-463-2251
Loren Dunk, prin. Fax 463-2360
Power MS 50/7-8
PO Box 155 59468 406-463-2251
Loren Dunk, prin. Fax 463-2360

**Pryor, Big Horn, Pop. 610**
Pryor SD 100/PK-12
PO Box 229 59066 406-259-7329
D McGee, supt. Fax 245-8938
Plenty Coups HS 50/9-12
PO Box 229 59066 406-259-7329
Dan McGee, prin. Fax 245-8938
Pryor MS 50/7-8
PO Box 229 59066 406-259-7329
Dan McGee, prin. Fax 245-8938

**Ramsay, Silver Bow**
Ramsay ESD 100/K-8
PO Box 105 59748 406-782-5470
Fax 723-8905
Ramsay MS 50/7-8
PO Box 105 59748 406-782-5470
Maury Cook, prin. Fax 723-8905

**Rapelje, Stillwater**
Rapelje SD 100/K-12
PO Box 89 59067 406-663-2215
Jerry Thompson, supt. Fax 663-2299
www.rapelje.k12.mt.us/
Rapelje HS 50/9-12
PO Box 89 59067 406-663-2215
Jerry Thompson, admin. Fax 663-2299
Rapelje MS 50/7-8
PO Box 89 59067 406-663-2215
Jerry Thompson, admin. Fax 663-2299

**Red Lodge, Carbon, Pop. 2,091**
Red Lodge SD 500/PK-12
PO Box 1090 59068 406-446-2110
John Fitzgerald, supt. Fax 446-2037
redlodge.schoolwires.com/
Red Lodge HS 200/9-12
PO Box 1090 59068 406-446-1903
Rex Ternan, prin. Fax 446-3953
Roosevelt JHS 100/6-8
PO Box 1090 59068 406-446-2110
Jason Reimer, prin. Fax 446-3975

**Reed Point, Stillwater, Pop. 186**
Reed Point SD 100/K-12
PO Box 338 59069 406-326-2245
Michael Ehinger, supt. Fax 326-2339
www.reedpoint.k12.mt.us/
Reed Point HS 50/9-12
PO Box 338 59069 406-326-2245
Michael Ehinger, supt. Fax 326-2339
Reed Point MS 50/7-8
PO Box 338 59069 406-326-2245
Michael Ehinger, supt. Fax 326-2339

**Richey, Dawson, Pop. 177**
Richey SD 100/PK-12
PO Box 60 59259 406-773-5680
Maureen Simonson, supt. Fax 773-5554
www.richey.k12.mt.us/
Richey HS 50/9-12
PO Box 60 59259 406-773-5523
Maureen Simonson, prin. Fax 773-5554
Richey MS 50/7-8
PO Box 60 59259 406-773-5680
Maureen Simonson, prin. Fax 773-5554

**Roberts, Carbon, Pop. 354**
Roberts SD 100/K-12
PO Box 78 59070 406-445-2421
Alexander Ator, supt. Fax 445-2506
www.roberts.k12.mt.us
Roberts HS 50/9-12
PO Box 78 59070 406-445-2421
Elliott Crump, prin. Fax 445-2506
Roberts MS 50/7-8
PO Box 78 59070 406-445-2421
Elliott Crump, prin. Fax 445-2506

**Ronan, Lake, Pop. 1,691**
Ronan SD 1,300/PK-12
421 Andrew St NW 59864 406-676-3390
Andrew Holmlund, supt. Fax 676-3392
www.ronank12.edu/
Ronan HS 300/9-12
421 Andrew St NW 59864 406-676-3390
Kevin Kenelty, prin. Fax 676-3330
Ronan MS 300/5-8
421 Andrew St NW 59864 406-676-3390
Mark Johnston, prin. Fax 676-2852

**Rosebud, Rosebud, Pop. 111**
Rosebud SD 100/PK-12
PO Box 38 59347 406-347-5353
Matt Kleinsasser, supt. Fax 347-5544
www.rhs12.com
Rosebud HS 50/9-12
PO Box 38 59347 406-347-5353
Matt Kleinsasser, prin. Fax 347-5544
Rosebud MS 50/7-8
PO Box 38 59347 406-347-5353
Matt Kleinsasser, prin. Fax 347-5544

**Roundup, Musselshell, Pop. 1,766**
Roundup SD 600/PK-12
700 3rd St W 59072 406-323-1507
Chad Sealey, supt. Fax 323-1927
www.roundup.k12.mt.us
Roundup HS 200/9-12
525 6th Ave W 59072 406-323-2402
Dana Quenzer, prin. Fax 323-1583
Roundup MS 100/7-8
525 6th Ave W 59072 406-323-2402
Dana Quenzer, prin. Fax 323-1583

**Roy, Fergus, Pop. 108**
Roy SD 50/K-12
PO Box 9 59471 406-464-2511
Steve Picard, supt. Fax 464-2561
www.roy.k12.mt.us
Roy HS 50/9-12
PO Box 9 59471 406-464-2511
Steve Picard, prin. Fax 464-2561
Roy MS 50/7-8
PO Box 9 59471 406-464-2511
Steve Picard, prin. Fax 464-2561

**Rudyard, Hill, Pop. 252**
North Star SD 200/K-12
PO Box 129 59540 406-355-4481
Bart Hawkins, supt. Fax 355-4532
www.northstar.k12.mt.us
North Star HS 50/9-12
PO Box 129 59540 406-355-4481
Bart Hawkins, prin. Fax 355-4532
North Star MS 50/7-8
PO Box 129 59540 406-355-4481
Bart Hawkins, prin. Fax 355-4532

**Ryegate, Golden Valley, Pop. 241**
Ryegate SD 100/K-12
PO Box 129 59074 406-568-2211
Park A. Hook, supt. Fax 568-2528
Ryegate HS 50/9-12
PO Box 129 59074 406-568-2211
Park A. Hook, supt. Fax 568-2528
Ryegate MS 50/7-8
PO Box 129 59074 406-568-2211
Park A. Hook, supt. Fax 568-2528

**Saco, Phillips, Pop. 189**
Saco SD 100/PK-12
PO Box 298 59261 406-527-3531
Gordon Hahn, supt. Fax 527-3479
www.sacoschools.k12.mt.us
Saco HS 50/9-12
PO Box 298 59261 406-527-3531
Gordon Hahn, prin. Fax 527-3479
Saco MS 50/7-8
PO Box 298 59261 406-527-3531
Gordon Hahn, prin. Fax 527-3479

**Saint Ignatius, Lake, Pop. 774**
St. Ignatius SD 500/PK-12
PO Box 1540 59865 406-745-3811
Jason Sargent, supt. Fax 745-4421
www.stignatiusschools.org
St. Ignatius HS 200/9-12
PO Box 1540 59865 406-745-3811
Shawn Hendrickson, prin. Fax 745-4060
St. Ignatius MS 100/6-8
PO Box 1540 59865 406-745-3811
Shawn Hendrickson, prin. Fax 745-4060

**Saint Regis, Mineral, Pop. 301**
Saint Regis SD 200/PK-12
PO Box 280 59866 406-649-2311
Judy McKay, supt. Fax 649-2271
sites.google.com/a/stregis.k12.mt.us/stregisschool/
Saint Regis HS 50/9-12
PO Box 280 59866 406-649-2311
Brent Nice, prin. Fax 649-2788
Saint Regis MS 50/7-8
PO Box 280 59866 406-649-2311
Brent Nice, prin. Fax 649-2788

**Sand Coulee, Cascade, Pop. 209**
Centerville SD 200/PK-12
PO Box 100 59472 406-736-5123
John McGee, supt. Fax 736-5210
www.centerville.k12.mt.us/
Centerville HS 100/9-12
PO Box 100 59472 406-736-5167
Michael Taylor, prin. Fax 736-5210
Centerville MS 50/7-8
PO Box 100 59472 406-736-5167
Michael Taylor, prin. Fax 736-5210

**Savage, Richland**
Savage SD 100/PK-12
PO Box 110 59262 406-776-2317
Lynne Peterson, supt. Fax 776-2260
www.savagepublicschool.com
Savage HS 50/9-12
PO Box 110 59262 406-776-2317
Lynne Peterson, prin. Fax 776-2260
Savage MS 50/7-8
PO Box 110 59262 406-776-2317
Lynne Peterson, prin. Fax 776-2260

**Scobey, Daniels, Pop. 996**
Scobey SD 300/PK-12
PO Box 10 59263 406-487-2202
Dave Selvig, supt. Fax 487-2204
Scobey HS 100/9-12
PO Box 10 59263 406-487-2202
Bryan Pechtl, prin. Fax 487-2204
Scobey MS 50/7-8
PO Box 10 59263 406-487-2202
Bryan Pechtl, prin. Fax 487-2204

**Seeley Lake, Missoula, Pop. 1,625**
Missoula SD 1
Supt. — See Missoula
Seeley-Swan HS 100/9-12
PO Box 416 59868 406-677-2224
Kathleen Pecora, prin. Fax 677-2949

Seeley Lake ESD 34 200/PK-8
PO Box 840 59868 406-677-2265
Chris Stout, supt. Fax 677-2264
www.sleonline.org
Seeley Lake MS 50/7-8
PO Box 840 59868 406-677-2265
Chris Stout, prin. Fax 677-2264

**Shelby, Toole, Pop. 3,316**
Shelby SD 500/PK-12
1010 Oilfield Ave 59474 406-434-2622
Elliott Crump, supt. Fax 434-2959
www.shelbypublicschools.org/
Shelby HS 200/9-12
1001 Valley St 59474 406-424-8910
Phil French, prin. Fax 434-7273
Shelby MS 100/7-8
1001 Valley St 59474 406-424-8910
Phil French, prin. Fax 434-7273

**Shepherd, Yellowstone, Pop. 501**
Shepherd SD 800/PK-12
PO Box 8 59079 406-373-5461
Dan Jamieson, supt. Fax 373-5284
www.shepherd.k12.mt.us/
Shepherd HS 300/9-12
PO Box 8 59079 406-373-5300
Kenneth Poepping, prin. Fax 373-5342
Shepherd MS 100/6-8
PO Box 8 59079 406-373-5873
Richard Hash, prin. Fax 373-5648

**Sheridan, Madison, Pop. 623**
Sheridan SD 200/K-12
PO Box 586 59749 406-842-5302
Micheal Wetherbee, supt. Fax 842-5391
www.sheridan.k12.mt.us/
Sheridan HS 100/9-12
PO Box 586 59749 406-842-5401
Micheal Wetherbee, prin. Fax 842-5856
Sheridan MS 50/7-8
PO Box 586 59749 406-842-5302
Micheal Wetherbee, prin. Fax 842-5391

**Sidney, Richland, Pop. 5,107**
Sidney SD 900/PK-12
200 3rd Ave SE 59270 406-433-4080
Dr. Daniel Farr Ed.D., supt. Fax 433-4358
www.sidney.k12.mt.us/
Sidney HS 400/9-12
200 3rd Ave SE 59270 406-433-2330
Sue Andersen, prin. Fax 433-2481
Sidney MS 300/6-8
200 3rd Ave SE 59270 406-433-4050
Kelly Johnson, prin. Fax 433-4052

**Simms, Cascade, Pop. 343**
Sun River Valley SD 200/PK-12
PO Box 380 59477 406-264-5110
Dave Marzolf, supt. Fax 264-5189
www.srvs.k12.mt.us
Simms HS 100/7-12
PO Box 380 59477 406-264-5110
Dave Marzolf, prin. Fax 264-5189

**Somers, Flathead, Pop. 1,095**
Somers ESD 600/PK-8
315 School Addition Rd 59932 406-857-3661
Paul Jenkins, supt. Fax 857-3144
www.somersdist29.org
Somers MS 200/6-8
315 School Addition Rd 59932 406-857-3661
Lori Schieffer, prin. Fax 857-3144

**Stanford, Judith Basin, Pop. 400**
Stanford SD 100/PK-12
PO Box 506 59479 406-566-2265
Nancy Coleman, supt. Fax 566-2772
www.stanford.k12.mt.us/
Stanford HS 50/9-12
PO Box 506 59479 406-566-2265
Nancy Coleman, supt. Fax 566-2772
Stanford MS 50/7-8
PO Box 506 59479 406-566-2265
Nancy Coleman, prin. Fax 566-2772

**Stevensville, Ravalli, Pop. 1,781**
Lone Rock ESD 300/K-8
1112 Three Mile Creek Rd 59870 406-777-3314
Dr. Roger Samples, supt. Fax 777-2770
www.lonerockschool.org/
Lone Rock MS 100/7-8
1112 Three Mile Creek Rd 59870 406-777-3314
Angie Williams, prin. Fax 777-2770

Stevensville SD 1,000/PK-12
300 Park St 59870 406-777-5481
Bob Moore, supt. Fax 258-1246
www.stevensvilleschool.net/
Stevensville HS 400/9-12
300 Park St 59870 406-777-5481
Brian Gum, prin. Fax 258-1243
Stevensville JHS 100/7-8
300 Park St 59870 406-777-5533
Brian Gum, prin. Fax 258-1242

**Sunburst, Toole, Pop. 361**
Sunburst SD 2 300/K-12
PO Box 710 59482 406-937-2811
Tim Tharp, supt. Fax 937-2828
www.sunburstschools.net/
Sunburst HS 100/9-12
PO Box 710 59482 406-937-2811
Tim Tharp, prin. Fax 937-2828
Sunburst MS 50/7-8
PO Box 710 59482 406-937-2816
Dan Nau, prin. Fax 937-4444

**Superior, Mineral, Pop. 795**
Superior SD 300/PK-12
PO Box 400 59872 406-822-3600
Scott Kinney, supt. Fax 822-3601
www.superior.k12.mt.us
Superior HS 100/9-12
PO Box 400 59872 406-822-4851
Allan Labbe, prin. Fax 822-4396
Superior MS 50/7-8
PO Box 400 59872 406-822-4851
Allan Labbe, prin. Fax 822-4396

**Terry, Prairie, Pop. 589**
Terry SD 100/PK-12
PO Box 187 59349 406-635-5533
Casey Klasna, supt. Fax 635-5705
www.terry.k12.mt.us/
Terry HS 100/9-12
PO Box 187 59349 406-635-5533
Casey Klasna, prin. Fax 635-5705
Terry MS 50/7-8
PO Box 187 59349 406-635-5595
Casey Klasna, prin. Fax 635-5705

**Thompson Falls, Sanders, Pop. 1,286**
Thompson Falls SD 500/PK-12
PO Box 129 59873 406-827-3323
Jason Slater, supt. Fax 827-3020
www.thompsonfalls.net
Thompson Falls HS 200/9-12
PO Box 129 59873 406-827-3561
Don Jensen, prin. Fax 827-9463
Thompson Falls MS 100/7-8
PO Box 129 59873 406-827-3593
Len Dorscher, prin. Fax 827-0306

**Three Forks, Gallatin, Pop. 1,859**
Three Forks SD 500/PK-12
212 E Neal St 59752 406-285-3224
Dr. Robert DoBell, supt. Fax 285-3503
www.tfschools.com
Three Forks HS 200/9-12
210 E Neal St 59752 406-285-3224
Justin Helvik, prin. Fax 285-3503
Three Forks MS 100/7-8
210 E Neal St 59752 406-285-3224
Justin Helvik, prin. Fax 285-3503

**Townsend, Broadwater, Pop. 1,847**
Townsend SD 700/PK-12
201 N Spruce St 59644 406-441-3454
Erik Wilkerson, supt. Fax 441-3457
townsendps.schoolwires.com
Broadwater HS 200/9-12
201 N Spruce St 59644 406-441-3430
Sheri Heavrin, prin. Fax 441-3466
Townsend MS 100/7-8
201 N Spruce St 59644 406-441-3431
Brad Racht, prin. Fax 441-3475

**Trout Creek, Sanders, Pop. 235**
Trout Creek SD 100/PK-8
4 School Ln 59874 406-827-3629
Daisy Carlsmith, admin. Fax 827-4185
www.troutcreekeagles.org
Trout Creek MS 50/7-8
4 School Ln 59874 406-827-3629
Daisy Carlsmith, lead tchr. Fax 827-4185

**Troy, Lincoln, Pop. 913**
Troy SD 400/PK-12
PO Box 867 59935 406-295-4606
Dr. Jacob Francom, supt. Fax 295-4802
troymtk-12.us/
Troy HS 100/9-12
PO Box 867 59935 406-295-4520
Dr. Jacob Francom, prin. Fax 295-5371
Troy MS 100/7-8
PO Box 867 59935 406-295-4520
Dr. Jacob Francom, prin. Fax 295-5371

**Turner, Blaine, Pop. 56**
Turner SD 100/K-12
PO Box 40 59542 406-379-2315
Rita Chvilicek, supt. Fax 379-2398
www.turner.k12.mt.us
Turner HS 50/9-12
PO Box 40 59542 406-379-2219
Rita Chvilicek, supt. Fax 379-2398
Turner MS 50/7-8
PO Box 40 59542 406-379-2219
Rita Chvilicek, supt. Fax 379-2398

**Twin Bridges, Madison, Pop. 367**
Twin Bridges SD 300/PK-12
PO Box 419 59754 406-684-5657
Chad Johnson, supt. Fax 684-5656
www.twinbridges.k12.mt.us
Twin Bridges HS 100/9-12
PO Box 419 59754 406-684-5657
Chad Johnson, prin. Fax 684-5656
Twin Bridges MS 50/7-8
PO Box 419 59754 406-684-5613
Brian Smith, prin. Fax 684-5656

**Ulm, Cascade, Pop. 714**
Ulm ESD 100/PK-8
PO Box 189 59485 406-866-3313
Fax 866-3209
Ulm MS 50/7-8
PO Box 189 59485 406-866-3313
Lori Brown-Chauvet, prin. Fax 866-3209

**Valier, Pondera, Pop. 489**
Valier SD 200/PK-12
PO Box 528 59486 406-279-3613
Brent Nice, supt. Fax 279-3764
valier.k12.mt.us
Valier HS 100/9-12
PO Box 528 59486 406-279-3613
Matthew Hauk, prin. Fax 279-3764
Valier MS 50/7-8
PO Box 508 59486 406-279-3314
Jackie Christiaens, prin. Fax 279-3510

**Vaughn, Cascade, Pop. 628**
Vaughn ESD 100/PK-8
PO Box 279 59487 406-965-2231
Jan Cahill, supt. Fax 965-3703
www.vaughnschool.com
Vaughn MS 50/7-8
PO Box 279 59487 406-965-2231
Jan Cahill, admin. Fax 965-3703

**Victor, Ravalli, Pop. 724**
Victor SD 300/PK-12
425 4th Ave 59875 406-642-3221
Lance Pearson, supt. Fax 642-3446
www.victor.k12.mt.us/
Victor HS 100/9-12
425 4th Ave 59875 406-642-3221
Danny Johnston, prin. Fax 642-3446
Victor MS 100/6-8
425 4th Ave 59875 406-642-3221
Danny Johnston, prin. Fax 642-3446

**Westby, Sheridan, Pop. 166**
Westby SD 100/PK-12
PO Box 109 59275 406-385-2225
Tony Holecek, supt. Fax 385-2430
www.westbyschool.k12.mt.us/
Westby HS 50/9-12
PO Box 109 59275 406-385-2225
Tony Holecek, prin. Fax 385-2430
Westby MS 50/7-8
PO Box 109 59275 406-385-2225
Tony Holecek, prin. Fax 385-2430

**West Yellowstone, Gallatin, Pop. 1,235**
West Yellowstone SD 200/PK-12
PO Box 460 59758 406-646-7617
Mary Margaret Williams, supt. Fax 646-7232
www.westyellowstone.k12.mt.us
West Yellowstone HS 100/9-12
PO Box 460 59758 406-646-7617
Mary Margaret Williams, prin. Fax 646-7232
West Yellowstone MS 50/7-8
PO Box 460 59758 406-646-7617
Mary Margaret Williams, prin. Fax 646-7232

**Whitefish, Flathead, Pop. 6,250**
Olney-Bissell ESD 100/PK-8
5955 Farm To Market Rd 59937 406-862-2828
Fax 862-2838
Bissell MS 50/7-8
5955 Farm to Market Rd 59937 406-862-2828
Lona Everett, prin. Fax 862-2838

Whitefish SD 1,600/PK-12
600 2nd St E 59937 406-862-8640
Heather Davis Schmidt, supt. Fax 862-1507
whitefishschools.com
Whitefish HS 500/9-12
600 2nd St E 59937 406-862-8600
Kerry Drown, prin. Fax 862-2586
Whitefish Independent HS Alt
600 2nd St E 59937 406-862-8688
Jill Rocksund, prin. Fax 862-8689
Whitefish MS 500/5-8
600 2nd St E 59937 406-862-8650
Josh Branstetter, prin. Fax 862-8664

**Whitehall, Jefferson, Pop. 1,005**
Whitehall SD 400/PK-12
PO Box 1109 59759 406-287-3455
John Sullivan, supt. Fax 287-3843
whitehall.schoolwires.com/
Whitehall HS 100/9-12
PO Box 1109 59759 406-287-3862
Britt McLean, prin. Fax 287-3843
Whitehall JHS 100/7-8
PO Box 1109 59759 406-287-3882
Nate Lant, prin. Fax 287-5508

**White Sulphur Springs, Meagher, Pop. 922**
White Sulphur Springs SD 200/PK-12
PO Box C 59645 406-547-3751
Larry Markuson, supt. Fax 547-3922
www.whitesulphur.k12.mt.us/
White Sulphur Springs HS 100/9-12
PO Box C 59645 406-547-3351
Tom Vail, prin. Fax 547-2407
White Sulphur Springs MS 50/7-8
PO Box C 59645 406-547-3351
Tom Vail, prin. Fax 547-2407

**Whitewater, Phillips, Pop. 62**
Whitewater SD 100/PK-12
PO Box 46 59544 406-674-5418
Darin Cummings, supt. Fax 674-5460
www.whitewater.k12.mt.us
Whitewater HS 50/9-12
PO Box 46 59544 406-674-5417
Darin Cummings, prin. Fax 674-5460
Whitewater MS 50/7-8
PO Box 46 59544 406-674-5417
Darin Cummings, prin. Fax 674-5460

**Wibaux, Wibaux, Pop. 582**
Wibaux SD 100/PK-12
121 F St N 59353 406-796-2474
Terry Quintus, supt. Fax 796-2259
wibauxschools.net
Wibaux HS 50/9-12
121 F St N 59353 406-795-2474
Terry Quintus, prin. Fax 795-2259
Wibaux JHS 50/7-8
121 F St N 59353 406-796-2474
Janet Huisman, prin. Fax 796-2259

**Willow Creek, Gallatin, Pop. 206**
Willow Creek SD 100/PK-12
PO Box 189 59760 406-285-6991
Bonnie Lower, supt. Fax 285-6923
www.willowcreek.k12.mt.us
Willow Creek HS 50/9-12
PO Box 189 59760 406-285-6991
Bonnie Lower, prin. Fax 285-6923
Willow Creek MS 50/7-8
PO Box 189 59760 406-285-6991
Bonnie Lower, prin. Fax 285-6923

**Winifred, Fergus, Pop. 207**
Winifred SD 50/PK-12
PO Box 109 59489 406-462-5420
Fax 462-5477
www.winifred.k12.mt.us
Winifred S 50/PK-12
PO Box 109 59489 406-462-5420
Kelli Carlson, prin. Fax 462-5477

**Winnett, Petroleum, Pop. 182**
Winnett SD 100/PK-12
PO Box 167 59087 406-429-2251
Don Johnson, supt. Fax 429-7631
Winnett HS 50/9-12
PO Box 167 59087 406-429-2251
Don Johnson, admin. Fax 429-7631
Winnett MS 50/7-8
PO Box 167 59087 406-429-2251
Don Johnson, admin. Fax 429-7631

**Wolf Point, Roosevelt, Pop. 2,478**
Frontier ESD 100/PK-8
6996 Roy St 59201 406-653-7083
Christine Eggar, supt. Fax 653-2508
www.wolfpoint.k12.mt.us
Frontier MS 50/7-8
6996 Roy St 59201 406-653-2501
Jeff Whitmus, admin. Fax 653-2508

Wolf Point SD 900/PK-12
213 6th Ave S 59201 406-653-2361
Gary Scott, supt. Fax 653-3405
wolfpoint.k12.mt.us
Wolf Point HS 200/9-12
213 6th Ave S 59201 406-653-1200
Kime Hanks, prin. Fax 653-3104
Wolf Point JHS 100/7-8
213 6th Ave S 59201 406-653-1200
Kime Hanks, prin. Fax 653-3104

**Worden, Yellowstone, Pop. 573**
Huntley Project SD 800/PK-12
1477 Ash St 59088 406-967-2540
Wes Coy, supt. Fax 967-3059
www.huntley.k12.mt.us/
Huntley Project HS 200/9-12
1477 Ash St 59088 406-967-2540
Mark Wandle, prin. Fax 967-2589
Huntley Project MS 100/7-8
1477 Ash St 59088 406-967-2540
Frank Hollowell, prin. Fax 967-3054

**Wyola, Big Horn, Pop. 212**
Wyola ESD 100/PK-8
PO Box 66 59089 406-343-2722
Linda Brien, supt. Fax 343-5901
www.wyola.k12.mt.us
Wyola MS 50/7-8
PO Box 66 59089 406-343-2722
Linda Brien, prin. Fax 343-5901

# NEBRASKA

## NEBRASKA DEPARTMENT OF EDUCATION
**PO Box 94987, Lincoln 68509-4987**
**Telephone 402-471-2295**
**Fax 402-471-0117**
**Website http://www.education.ne.gov/**

Commissioner of Education Dr. Scott Swisher

## NEBRASKA BOARD OF EDUCATION
**PO Box 94987, Lincoln 68509-4987**

President Jim Scheer

### EDUCATIONAL SERVICE UNITS (ESU)

ESU 1
Robert Uhing, admin. 402-287-2061
211 10th St, Wakefield 68784 Fax 287-2065
www.esu1.org/
ESU 2
Dr. Ted DeTurk Ed.D., admin. 402-721-7710
PO Box 649, Fremont 68026 Fax 721-7712
www.esu2.org/
ESU 3
Dr. Dan Schnoes, admin. 402-597-4800
6949 S 110th St, La Vista 68128 Fax 597-4808
www2.esu3.org/esu3/
ESU 4
Jon Fisher, admin. 402-274-4354
919 16th St, Auburn 68305 Fax 274-4356
www.esu4.org/
ESU 5
Brian Gegg, admin. 402-223-5277
900 W Court St, Beatrice 68310 Fax 223-5279
www.esu5.org/
ESU 6
Dr. Dan Shoemake, admin. 800-327-0091
210 5th St, Milford 68405 Fax 761-3279
www.esu6.org/
ESU 7
Larianne Polk, admin. 402-564-5753
2657 44th Ave, Columbus 68601 Fax 563-1121
ww2.esu7.org
ESU 8
Bill Mowinkel, admin. 402-887-5041
PO Box 89, Neligh 68756 Fax 887-4604
www.esu8.org/
ESU 9
Kraig Lofquist, admin. 402-463-5611
PO Box 2047, Hastings 68902 Fax 463-9555
home.site.esu9.org
ESU 10
Wayne Bell, admin. 308-237-5927
PO Box 850, Kearney 68848 Fax 237-5920
www.esu10.org/
ESU 11
Paul Tedesco, admin. 308-995-6585
PO Box 858, Holdrege 68949 Fax 995-6587
www.esu11.org/
ESU 13
Dr. Jeff West, admin. 308-635-3696
4215 Avenue I, Scottsbluff 69361 Fax 635-0680
www.esu13.org/
ESU 15
Paul Calvert, admin. 308-334-5160
PO Box 398, Trenton 69044 Fax 334-5581
www.esu15.org
ESU 16
Margene Beatty, admin. 308-284-8481
PO Box 915, Ogallala 69153 Fax 284-8483
www.esu16.org/
ESU 17
Dennis Radford, admin. 402-387-1420
207 N Main St, Ainsworth 69210 Fax 387-1028
www.esu17.org/
ESU 18
Steve Joel Ed.D., supt. 402-436-1000
PO Box 82889, Lincoln 68501 Fax 436-1620
www.lps.org/
ESU 19
Julia Allen, admin. 402-557-2265
3215 Cuming St, Omaha 68131 Fax 557-2499
esu19.org/

### PUBLIC, PRIVATE AND CATHOLIC SECONDARY SCHOOLS

**Adams, Gage, Pop. 572**
Freeman SD 400/PK-12
PO Box 259 68301 402-988-2525
Randy Page, supt. Fax 988-3475
www.freemanpublicschools.org/
Freeman JSHS 200/7-12
PO Box 259 68301 402-988-2525
Bob Michl, prin. Fax 988-3475

**Ainsworth, Brown, Pop. 1,710**
Ainsworth SD 500/PK-12
PO Box 65 69210 402-387-2333
Darrell Peterson, supt. Fax 387-0525
www.ainsworthschools.org/
Ainsworth HS 200/9-12
PO Box 65 69210 402-387-2082
Richard Gilson, prin. Fax 387-0525
Ainsworth MS 100/5-8
PO Box 65 69210 402-387-2082
Sarah Williams, prin. Fax 387-0525

**Albion, Boone, Pop. 1,646**
Boone Central SD 500/K-12
PO Box 391 68620 402-395-2134
Cory Worrell, supt. Fax 395-2137
www.boonecentral.esu7.org/
Boone Central HS 200/9-12
PO Box 391 68620 402-395-2134
Erik Kravig, prin. Fax 395-2137
Other Schools – See Petersburg

**Allen, Dixon, Pop. 375**
Allen Consolidated SD 200/K-12
PO Box 190 68710 402-635-2484
Michael Pattee, supt. Fax 635-2331
www.allenschools.org/
Allen JSHS 100/7-12
PO Box 190 68710 402-635-2484
Lana Oswald, prin. Fax 635-2331

**Alliance, Box Butte, Pop. 8,339**
Alliance SD 1,600/K-12
1604 Sweetwater Ave 69301 308-762-5475
Troy Unzicker, supt. Fax 762-8249
apschools.schoolfusion.us
Alliance HS 500/9-12
1604 Sweetwater Ave 69301 308-762-3359
George Clear, prin. Fax 762-7683
Alliance MS 400/5-8
1604 Sweetwater Ave 69301 308-762-3079
Troy Mach, prin. Fax 762-7302

---

Western Nebraska Community College Post-Sec.
1750 Sweetwater Ave 69301 308-763-2000

**Alma, Harlan, Pop. 1,129**
Alma SD 300/K-12
PO Box 170 68920 308-928-2131
Jon Davis, supt. Fax 928-2763
almacardinals.org
Alma JSHS 100/7-12
PO Box 170 68920 308-928-2131
Galen Kronhofman, prin. Fax 928-2763

**Amherst, Buffalo, Pop. 248**
Amherst SD 300/K-12
PO Box 8 68812 308-826-3131
Tom Moore, supt. Fax 826-4865
amherst.k12.ne.us/
Amherst JSHS 100/7-12
PO Box 8 68812 308-826-3131
Roger Thomsen, prin. Fax 826-4865

**Ansley, Custer, Pop. 440**
Ansley SD 200/PK-12
PO Box 370 68814 308-935-1121
Dave Mroczek, supt. Fax 935-9103
ansleynebraska.org
Ansley JSHS 100/7-12
PO Box 370 68814 308-935-1121
Lance Bristol, prin. Fax 935-9103

**Arapahoe, Furnas, Pop. 1,013**
Arapahoe SD 300/K-12
PO Box 360 68922 308-962-5458
Charles Curnyn, supt. Fax 962-7481
Arapahoe HS 100/7-12
PO Box 360 68922 308-962-5458
Bob Braithwait, prin. Fax 962-7481

**Arcadia, Valley, Pop. 309**
Arcadia SD 100/PK-12
PO Box 248 68815 308-789-6522
Dave Mroczek Ed.D., supt. Fax 789-6214
www.arcadiapublicschools.org/
Arcadia JSHS 100/7-12
PO Box 248 68815 308-789-6522
Dave Mroczek Ed.D., admin. Fax 789-6214

**Arlington, Washington, Pop. 1,239**
Arlington SD 500/K-12
PO Box 580 68002 402-478-4173
Lynn Johnson, supt. Fax 478-4176
www.apseagles.org
Arlington JSHS 300/7-12
PO Box 580 68002 402-478-4171
Andrew Farber, prin. Fax 478-4176

**Arnold, Custer, Pop. 592**
Arnold SD 100/K-12
PO Box 399 69120 308-848-2226
Dawn Lewis, supt. Fax 848-2201
blog.arnold.k12.ne.us
Arnold JSHS 100/7-12
PO Box 399 69120 308-848-2226
Joel Morgan, prin. Fax 848-2201

**Arthur, Arthur, Pop. 117**
Arthur County SD 100/K-12
PO Box 145 69121 308-764-2253
Barry Schaeffer, supt. Fax 764-2206
www.arthurcountywolves.org
Arthur County JSHS 50/7-12
PO Box 145 69121 308-764-2253
Barry Schaeffer, supt. Fax 764-2206

**Ashland, Saunders, Pop. 2,429**
Ashland-Greenwood SD 800/PK-12
1842 Furnas St 68003 402-944-2128
Dr. Zach Kassebaum, supt. Fax 944-3310
www.agps.org/
Ashland-Greenwood HS 300/9-12
1842 Furnas St 68003 402-944-2114
Brad Jacobsen, prin. Fax 944-2116
Ashland-Greenwood MS 100/6-8
1842 Furnas St 68003 402-944-2114
Brad Jacobsen, prin. Fax 944-2116

**Atkinson, Holt, Pop. 1,242**
West Holt SD 400/K-12
PO Box 457 68713 402-925-2848
Paul Pistulka, supt. Fax 925-2177
www.westholtps.org
West Holt HS 200/7-12
PO Box 457 68713 402-925-2848
Kevin Young, prin. Fax 925-2177

**Auburn, Nemaha, Pop. 3,425**
Auburn SD 800/PK-12
1713 J St 68305 402-274-4830
Kevin Reiman, supt. Fax 274-5227
www.auburnpublicschools.org/
Auburn HS 300/9-12
1713 J St 68305 402-274-4328
Vernon Golladay, prin. Fax 274-5434
Auburn MS 200/6-8
1713 J St 68305 402-274-4027
Vernon Golladay, prin. Fax 274-4147

**Aurora, Hamilton, Pop. 4,447**
Aurora SD 1,200/PK-12
300 L St 68818 402-694-6923
Damon McDonald, supt. Fax 694-5097
aurorahuskies.us
Aurora HS 400/9-12
300 L St 68818 402-694-6968
Douglas Kittle, prin. Fax 694-2573
Aurora MS 300/6-8
300 L St 68818 402-694-6915
Kenneth Thiele, prin. Fax 694-3815

**Axtell, Kearney, Pop. 718**
Axtell Community SD 200/K-12
PO Box 97 68924 308-743-2415
Steven Wickham, supt. Fax 743-2417
axtell.k12.ne.us
Axtell HS 100/9-12
PO Box 97 68924 308-743-2415
Bill Gilbreath, prin. Fax 743-2417
Axtell MS 5-8
PO Box 97 68924 308-743-2415
Bill Gilbreath, prin. Fax 743-2417

**Bancroft, Cuming, Pop. 482**
Bancroft-Rosalie SD 300/K-12
PO Box 129 68004 402-648-3336
Jon Cerny, supt. Fax 648-3338
www.bancroft-rosalie.org/
Bancroft JSHS 100/7-12
PO Box 129 68004 402-648-3336
Mike Sjuts, prin. Fax 648-3338

**Bartlett, Wheeler, Pop. 117**
Wheeler Central SD 100/PK-12
PO Box 68 68622 308-654-3273
Gary Klahn, supt. Fax 654-3237
www.wbroncs.org
Wheeler Central JSHS 100/7-12
PO Box 68 68622 308-654-3273
Gary Klahn, prin. Fax 654-3237

**Bartley, Red Willow, Pop. 282**
Southwest SD 179 300/PK-12
PO Box 187 69020 308-692-3223
Robert Porter, supt. Fax 692-3221
www.swpschools.org/
Southwest JSHS 100/7-12
PO Box 187 69020 308-692-3223
Matt Springer, prin. Fax 692-3221

**Bassett, Rock, Pop. 618**
Rock County SD 200/K-12
PO Box 448 68714 402-684-3411
Thomas Becker, supt. Fax 684-3671
Rock County HS 100/7-12
PO Box 448 68714 402-684-3411
Steve Camp, prin. Fax 684-3671

**Battle Creek, Madison, Pop. 1,202**
Battle Creek SD 400/K-12
PO Box 100 68715 402-675-6905
Jay Bellar, supt. Fax 675-1038
bcps.esu8.org/
Battle Creek JSHS 200/7-12
PO Box 100 68715 402-675-3705
Jeff Heimes, prin. Fax 675-1038

**Bayard, Morrill, Pop. 1,198**
Bayard SD 400/PK-12
PO Box 607 69334 308-586-1325
Travis Miller, supt. Fax 586-1638
www.bayardpublicschools.org/
Bayard JSHS 200/7-12
PO Box 607 69334 308-586-1700
Thomas Perlinski, prin. Fax 586-1638

**Beatrice, Gage, Pop. 12,303**
Beatrice SD 2,100/PK-12
320 N 5th St 68310 402-223-1500
Pat Nauroth, supt. Fax 223-1509
www.beatricepublicschools.org
Beatrice HS 700/9-12
600 Orange Blvd 68310 402-223-1515
Jason Sutter, prin. Fax 223-1510
Beatrice MS 500/6-8
215 N 5th St 68310 402-223-1545
John Jarosh, prin. Fax 223-1547
Compass Learning Community Alt
2920 E Court St 68310 402-223-1500
Jason Sutter, prin.

---

Joseph's College of Beauty Post-Sec.
618 Court St 68310 402-223-3588
Southeast Community College Post-Sec.
4771 W Scott Rd 68310 402-228-3468

**Bellevue, Sarpy, Pop. 48,571**
Bellevue SD 9,800/PK-12
2600 Arboretum Dr 68005 402-293-4000
Frank Harwood, supt. Fax 293-5002
www.bellevuepublicschools.org
Bellevue East HS 1,500/9-12
1401 High School Dr 68005 402-293-4150
Brad Stueve, prin. Fax 293-4259
Bellevue West HS 1,700/9-12
1501 Thurston Ave 68123 402-293-4040
Kevin Rohlfs, prin. Fax 293-4149
Fontenelle MS 500/7-8
701 Kayleen Dr 68005 402-293-4360
Doug Schaefer, prin. Fax 293-4450
Lewis & Clark MS 500/7-8
13502 S 38th St 68123 402-898-8760
Dr. Mike Smith, prin. Fax 898-9018
Mission MS 400/7-8
2202 Washington St 68005 402-293-4260
Dr. Jenny Powell, prin. Fax 293-4350

---

Bellevue University Post-Sec.
1000 Galvin Rd S 68005 402-293-2000
Cornerstone Christian S 100/K-12
3704 370 Plz 68123 402-292-1030
Teri Lynn Schrag M.Ed., admin. Fax 884-1725
Gross HS 400/9-12
7700 S 43rd St 68147 402-734-2000
John Schultz, prin. Fax 734-4270

**Benkelman, Dundy, Pop. 937**
Dundy County-Straton SD 300/PK-12
PO Box 586 69021 308-423-2738
James Kent, supt. Fax 423-2711
204.234.184.9
Dundy County Stratton HS 100/9-12
PO Box 586 69021 308-423-2738
Adam Fette, prin. Fax 423-2711

**Bennington, Douglas, Pop. 1,439**
Bennington SD 1,500/K-12
PO Box 309 68007 402-238-3044
Dr. Terry Haack, supt. Fax 238-2185
www.benningtonschools.org
Bennington JSHS 500/7-12
PO Box 309 68007 402-238-2447
Matthew Blomenkamp, prin. Fax 238-2950

**Bertrand, Phelps, Pop. 742**
Bertrand SD 200/K-12
PO Box 278 68927 308-472-3427
Dr. Dennis Shipp, supt. Fax 472-3429
Bertrand JSHS 100/7-12
PO Box 278 68927 308-472-3427
Shaun Kidder, prin. Fax 472-3429

**Big Springs, Deuel, Pop. 393**
South Platte SD 200/K-12
PO Box 457 69122 308-889-3674
David Spencer, supt. Fax 889-3523
www.southplatteschools.com
South Platte HS 100/7-12
PO Box 457 69122 308-889-3622
Seth Ford, prin. Fax 889-3523

**Blair, Washington, Pop. 7,886**
Blair Community SD 2,300/PK-12
PO Box 288 68008 402-426-2610
Rex Pfeil, supt. Fax 426-3110
www.blairschools.org/
Blair HS 700/9-12
PO Box 288 68008 402-426-4941
Thomas Anderson, prin. Fax 426-4949
Otte Blair MS 600/6-8
PO Box 288 68008 402-426-3678
Chris Stogdill, prin. Fax 426-1788

**Bloomfield, Knox, Pop. 1,011**
Bloomfield SD 200/PK-12
PO Box 308 68718 402-373-4800
Robert Marks, supt. Fax 373-2712
www.bloomfieldschools.net/
Bloomfield JSHS 100/7-12
PO Box 308 68718 402-373-4800
Shane Alexander, prin. Fax 373-2712

**Blue Hill, Webster, Pop. 925**
Blue Hill SD 300/K-12
PO Box 217 68930 402-756-2085
Joel Ruybalid, supt. Fax 756-2086
www.bluehillschools.org/
Blue Hill JSHS 200/7-12
PO Box 217 68930 402-756-3043
Rodney Olson, prin. Fax 756-3044

**Boys Town, Douglas, Pop. 727**

---

Boys Town HS 300/9-12
13727 Flanagan Blvd 68010 402-498-1800

**Brady, Lincoln, Pop. 425**
Brady SD 200/K-12
PO Box 68 69123 308-584-3317
Russell Finken, supt. Fax 584-3725
www.bradyschools.org
Brady JSHS 100/7-12
PO Box 68 69123 308-584-3317
Dana Reinke, prin. Fax 584-3725

**Brainard, Butler, Pop. 330**
East Butler SD 300/K-12
PO Box 36 68626 402-545-2081
Sam Stecher, supt. Fax 545-2023
www.ebutlertigers.org
Brainard JSHS 200/7-12
PO Box 36 68626 402-545-2081
Michael Eldridge, prin. Fax 545-2023

**Bridgeport, Morrill, Pop. 1,536**
Bridgeport SD 63 500/K-12
PO Box 430 69336 308-262-1470
Chuck Lambert, supt. Fax 262-1284
www.bridgeportschools.org
Bridgeport JSHS 200/7-12
PO Box 430 69336 308-262-0346
Matt Asche, prin. Fax 262-1284

**Broken Bow, Custer, Pop. 3,500**
Broken Bow SD 700/PK-12
323 N 7th Ave 68822 308-872-6821
Tom Bailey, supt. Fax 872-2751
www.bbps.org
Broken Bow HS 200/9-12
323 N 7th Ave 68822 308-872-2475
Rusty Kluender, prin. Fax 872-6296
Broken Bow JHS 100/7-8
323 N 7th Ave 68822 308-872-6441
Rusty Kluender, prin. Fax 872-2528

**Bruning, Thayer, Pop. 279**
Bruning-Davenport USD
Supt. — See Davenport
Bruning-Davenport HS 100/9-12
PO Box 70 68322 402-353-4685
Erik Sokol, prin. Fax 353-4445

**Burwell, Garfield, Pop. 1,207**
Burwell SD 400/PK-12
PO Box 670 68823 308-346-4150
Daniel Bird, supt. Fax 346-5430
www.burwellpublicschools.org/
Burwell JSHS 200/7-12
PO Box 670 68823 308-346-4150
David Owen, prin. Fax 346-5430

**Cairo, Hall, Pop. 780**
Centura SD 500/PK-12
PO Box 430 68824 308-485-4258
Julie Otero, supt. Fax 485-4780
www.centura.k12.ne.us/
Centura JSHS 200/7-12
PO Box 430 68824 308-485-4258
Tammy Holcomb, prin. Fax 485-4780

**Callaway, Custer, Pop. 533**
Callaway SD 200/K-12
PO Box 280 68825 308-836-2272
Dawn Lewis, supt. Fax 836-2771
callawaypublicschools.org
Callaway JSHS 100/7-12
PO Box 280 68825 308-836-2272
Jane Brown, prin. Fax 836-2771

**Cambridge, Furnas, Pop. 1,055**
Cambridge SD 300/K-12
PO Box 100 69022 308-697-3322
Robert Gregory, supt. Fax 697-4880
cambridge.k12.ne.us/
Cambridge JSHS 200/7-12
PO Box 100 69022 308-697-3322
Jarod Albers, prin. Fax 697-4880

**Cedar Bluffs, Saunders, Pop. 604**
Cedar Bluffs SD 200/PK-12
PO Box 66 68015 402-628-2060
Harlan Ptomey, supt. Fax 628-2108
www.cedarbluffsschools.org/
Cedar Bluffs HS 100/9-12
PO Box 66 68015 402-628-2080
Kevin Janssen, prin. Fax 628-2108
Cedar Bluffs MS 100/6-8
PO Box 66 68015 402-628-2080
Kevin Janssen, admin. Fax 628-2108

**Cedar Rapids, Boone, Pop. 382**
Riverside SD 100/PK-12
408 W Dayton St 68627 308-358-0640
Dr. Joan Carraher, supt. Fax 358-0211
www.riversideps.org
Cedar Rapids MSHS 100/6-12
408 W Dayton St 68627 308-358-0640
Christopher Kuncl, prin. Fax 358-0211

**Central City, Merrick, Pop. 2,899**
Central City SD 700/PK-12
PO Box 57 68826 308-946-3055
Jeff Jensen, supt. Fax 946-3149
www.centralcityschoolsne.org
Central City HS 200/9-12
PO Box 57 68826 308-946-3086
Shawn McDiffett, prin. Fax 946-2954
Central City MS 200/5-8
PO Box 57 68826 308-946-3056
Holee Hanke, prin. Fax 946-2124

---

Nebraska Christian S 200/PK-12
1847 Inskip Ave 68826 308-946-3836
Joshua Cumpston, admin. Fax 946-3837

**Chadron, Dawes, Pop. 5,665**
Chadron SD 900/K-12
602 E 10th St 69337 308-432-0700
Dr. Caroline Winchester, supt. Fax 432-0702
www.chadronschools.org/
Chadron HS 300/9-12
901 Cedar St 69337 308-432-0707
Jerry Mack, prin. Fax 432-0723
Chadron MS 300/5-8
551 E 6th St 69337 308-432-0708
Nichlas Dressel, prin. Fax 432-0720

Pine Ridge Job Corps
Supt. — None
Pine Ridge Job Corps Vo/Tech
15710 Highway 385 69337 308-432-8650
Brian Kizer, prin. Fax 432-8655

---

Chadron State College Post-Sec.
1000 Main St 69337 308-432-6000

**Chambers, Holt, Pop. 268**
Chambers SD 100/K-12
PO Box 218 68725 402-482-5233
Justin Frederick, supt. Fax 482-5234
chambers.esu8.org/
Chambers JSHS 100/7-12
PO Box 218 68725 402-482-5233
Justin Frederick, prin. Fax 482-5234

**Chappell, Deuel, Pop. 921**
Creek Valley SD 300/K-12
PO Box 608 69129 308-874-2911
Ron Howard, supt. Fax 874-2602
creekvalleystorm.com
Creek Valley HS 100/9-12
PO Box 608 69129 308-874-3310
Patrick Ningen, prin. Fax 874-2604
Other Schools – See Lodgepole

**Clarks, Merrick, Pop. 363**
High Plains Community SD
Supt. — See Polk
High Plains MS 100/6-8
PO Box 205 68628 308-548-2216
Karyee LeSuer, prin. Fax 548-2120

**Clarkson, Colfax, Pop. 655**
Clarkson SD 100/K-12
PO Box 140 68629 402-892-3454
Rich Lemburg, supt. Fax 892-3455
www.clarksonpublicschools.org
Clarkson S 100/K-12
PO Box 140 68629 402-892-3454
Rich Lemburg, prin. Fax 892-3455

**Clearwater, Antelope, Pop. 413**
Nebraska USD 1
Supt. — See Orchard
Clearwater/Orchard S — 100/PK-12
PO Box 38 68726 — 402-485-2505
Mike Sanne, prin. — Fax 485-2634

**Cody, Cherry, Pop. 150**
Cody-Kilgore SD — 100/K-12
PO Box 216 69211 — 402-823-4190
Clarence Chessmore, supt. — Fax 823-4275
www.cody-kilgore.com
Cody-Kilgore JSHS — 100/7-12
PO Box 216 69211 — 402-823-4190
Clarence Chessmore, prin. — Fax 823-4275

**Coleridge, Cedar, Pop. 470**
Laurel-Concord-Coleridge SD
Supt. — See Laurel
Laurel-Concord-Coleridge MS — 5-8
PO Box 37 68727 — 402-283-4844
Stephanie Petersen, prin. — Fax 283-4230

**Columbus, Platte, Pop. 21,922**
Columbus SD — 3,600/K-12
PO Box 947 68602 — 402-563-7000
Dr. Troy Loeffelholz, supt. — Fax 563-7005
www.columbuspublicschools.org
Columbus HS — 1,100/9-12
2200 26th St 68601 — 402-563-7050
Steve Woodside, prin. — Fax 563-7058
Columbus MS — 800/6-8
2410 16th St 68601 — 402-563-7060
Amy Haynes, prin. — Fax 563-7068

Lakeview Community SD — 600/K-12
3744 83rd St 68601 — 402-563-2345
Russ Freeman, supt. — Fax 564-5209
www.lakeviewcs.esu7.org
Lakeview JSHS — 300/7-12
3744 83rd St 68601 — 402-563-2345
Steve Borer, prin. — Fax 564-5209

---

Central Community College — Post-Sec.
PO Box 1027 68602 — 402-564-7132
Scotus Central Catholic JSHS — 400/7-12
1554 18th Ave 68601 — 402-564-7165
Wayne Morfeld, pres. — Fax 564-6004

**Cook, Johnson, Pop. 316**
Johnson County Central SD
Supt. — See Tecumseh
Johnson County Central MS — 100/6-8
PO Box 255 68329 — 402-864-4181
Rich Bacon, prin. — Fax 864-2074

**Cozad, Dawson, Pop. 3,959**
Cozad Community SD — 1,000/PK-12
1910 Meridian Ave 69130 — 308-784-2745
Joel Applegate, supt. — Fax 784-2784
www.cozadschools.net
Cozad Alternative Ed Center — Alt
1910 Meridian Ave 69130 — 308-784-2745
Fax 784-2784
Cozad HS — 300/9-12
1710 Meridian Ave 69130 — 308-784-2744
William Beckenhauer, prin. — Fax 784-2728
Cozad MS — 200/6-8
1810 Meridian Ave 69130 — 308-784-2746
Brian Regelin, prin. — Fax 784-2606

**Crawford, Dawes, Pop. 968**
Crawford SD — 200/PK-12
908 5th St 69339 — 308-665-1537
Dick Lesher, supt. — Fax 665-1909
www.cpsrams.org/
Crawford JSHS — 100/7-12
908 5th St 69339 — 308-665-1531
Christopher Geary, prin. — Fax 665-1483

**Creighton, Knox, Pop. 1,135**
Creighton SD — 300/K-12
PO Box 10 68729 — 402-358-3663
Jeff Jensen, supt. — Fax 358-3804
creighton.esu1.org/
Creighton Community JSHS — 200/4-12
PO Box 10 68729 — 402-358-3663
Greg Wilmes, prin. — Fax 358-3804

**Crete, Saline, Pop. 6,858**
Crete SD — 1,600/PK-12
920 Linden Ave 68333 — 402-826-5855
Kyle McGowan, supt. — Fax 826-5120
www.creteschools.com
Crete HS — 500/9-12
1500 E 15th St 68333 — 402-826-5811
Tim Conway, prin. — Fax 826-2701
Crete MS — 500/5-8
1700 Glenwood Ave 68333 — 402-826-5844
Steve Teget, prin. — Fax 826-7789

---

Doane College — Post-Sec.
1014 Boswell Ave 68333 — 402-826-2161

**Crofton, Knox, Pop. 722**
Crofton Community SD — 300/K-12
PO Box 429 68730 — 402-388-2440
Randall Anderson, supt. — Fax 388-4265
www.croftonschools.com/
Crofton JSHS — 200/7-12
PO Box 429 68730 — 402-388-2440
Todd Strom, prin. — Fax 388-4265

**Curtis, Frontier, Pop. 926**
Medicine Valley SD — 200/K-12
PO Box 9 69025 — 308-367-4106
Alan Garey, supt. — Fax 367-4108
www.mvraiders.org/
Medicine Valley JSHS — 100/7-12
PO Box 9 69025 — 308-367-4106
Steven Gleisberg, prin. — Fax 367-4108

---

University of Nebraska NE Coll of Tech — Post-Sec.
404 E 7th St 69025 — 308-367-4124

**Dalton, Cheyenne, Pop. 312**
Leyton SD — 200/K-12
PO Box 297 69131 — 308-377-2303
Gregory Brenner, supt. — Fax 377-2304
www.leytonwarriors.org
Leyton HS — 100/9-12
PO Box 297 69131 — 308-377-2303
James McGown, prin. — Fax 377-2304

**Davenport, Thayer, Pop. 289**
Bruning-Davenport USD — 200/PK-12
PO Box 190 68335 — 402-364-2225
Dr. Trudy Clark, supt. — Fax 364-2477
www.bruningdavenport.org/
Bruning-Davenport MS — 50/5-8
PO Box 190 68335 — 402-364-2225
Erik Sokol, prin. — Fax 364-2477
Other Schools – See Bruning

**David City, Butler, Pop. 2,884**
David City SD — 700/PK-12
750 D St 68632 — 402-367-4590
Chad Denker, supt. — Fax 367-3479
www.davidcitypublicschools.org/
David City JSHS — 300/7-12
750 D St 68632 — 402-367-3187
Cortney Couch, prin. — Fax 367-3479

---

Aquinas HS — 300/6-12
PO Box 149 68632 — 402-367-3175
David McMahon, prin. — Fax 367-3176

**Daykin, Jefferson, Pop. 166**
Meridian SD — 200/K-12
PO Box 190 68338 — 402-446-7265
Randall Kort, supt. — Fax 446-7246
www.meridianmustangs.org
Meridian JSHS — 100/7-12
PO Box 190 68338 — 402-446-7265
Harold Scott, prin. — Fax 446-7246

**Deshler, Thayer, Pop. 745**
Deshler SD — 200/K-12
PO Box 547 68340 — 402-365-7272
Dr. Al Meier, supt. — Fax 365-7560
www.deshlerpublicschools.org
Deshler JSHS — 100/7-12
PO Box 547 68340 — 402-365-7272
Jack Waite, prin. — Fax 365-7560

**De Witt, Saline, Pop. 509**
Tri County SD — 400/K-12
72520 Highway 103 68341 — 402-683-2037
Randy Schlueter, supt. — Fax 683-2116
www.tricountyschools.org
Tri County JSHS — 200/7-12
72520 Highway 103 68341 — 402-683-2015
Matthew Uher, prin. — Fax 683-2116

**Doniphan, Hall, Pop. 824**
Doniphan-Trumbull SD — 500/K-12
PO Box 300 68832 — 402-845-2282
Kirk Russell, supt. — Fax 845-6688
www.dtcardinals.org
Doniphan-Trumbull JSHS — 200/7-12
PO Box 300 68832 — 402-845-6531
Brent Breckner, prin. — Fax 845-6688

**Dorchester, Saline, Pop. 580**
Dorchester SD — 200/K-12
PO Box 7 68343 — 402-946-2781
Mitch Kubicek, supt. — Fax 946-6271
www.dorchesterschool.org
Dorchester JSHS — 100/7-12
PO Box 7 68343 — 402-946-2781
Adrian Allen, prin. — Fax 946-6271

**Dunning, Blaine, Pop. 103**
Sandhills SD — 100/K-12
PO Box 29 68833 — 308-538-2224
Dale Hafer, supt. — Fax 538-2228
blog.sandhills.k12.ne.us/
Dunning JSHS — 100/7-12
PO Box 29 68833 — 308-538-2224
Dale Hafer, prin. — Fax 538-2228

**Elba, Howard, Pop. 212**
Elba SD — 100/PK-12
PO Box 100 68835 — 308-863-2228
William Porter, supt. — Fax 863-2329
www.elba.k12.ne.us
Elba JSHS — 50/7-12
PO Box 100 68835 — 308-863-2228
William Porter, supt. — Fax 863-2329

**Elgin, Antelope, Pop. 656**
Elgin SD — 100/K-12
PO Box 399 68636 — 402-843-2455
Daniel Polk, supt. — Fax 843-2475
www.elgineagles.org
Elgin HS — 100/9-12
PO Box 399 68636 — 402-843-2457
Greg Wemhoff, prin. — Fax 843-2475

---

Pope John XXIII Central Catholic HS — 100/7-12
PO Box 179 68636 — 402-843-5325
Betty Getzfred, prin. — Fax 843-2297

**Elkhorn, Douglas, Pop. 8,192**
Elkhorn SD — 4,500/PK-12
20650 Glenn St 68022 — 402-289-2579
Steve Baker, supt. — Fax 289-2585
www.elkhornweb.org/
Elkhorn HS — 700/9-12
1401 Veterans Dr 68022 — 402-289-4239
Dan Radicia, prin. — Fax 289-4383
Elkhorn MS — 600/6-8
3200 N 207th Plz 68022 — 402-289-2428
Deb Garrison, prin. — Fax 289-1639
Elkhorn Valley View MS — 6-8
1313 S 208th St 68022 — 402-289-0362
Chad Soupir, prin.
Other Schools – See Omaha

---

Mt. Michael Benedictine HS — 200/9-12
22520 Mount Michael Rd 68022 — 402-289-2541
Dr. David Peters, head sch — Fax 289-4539

**Elm Creek, Buffalo, Pop. 896**
Elm Creek SD — 300/PK-12
PO Box 490 68836 — 308-856-4300
Dean Tickle, supt. — Fax 856-4907
elmcreekschools.org
Elm Creek JSHS — 200/7-12
PO Box 490 68836 — 308-856-4300
Jason Sullivan, prin. — Fax 856-4907

**Elwood, Gosper, Pop. 693**
Elwood SD — 200/K-12
PO Box 107 68937 — 308-785-2491
Daren Hatch, supt. — Fax 785-2322
elwood.k12.ne.us
Elwood JSHS — 100/7-12
PO Box 107 68937 — 308-785-2491
Kyle Hemmerling, prin. — Fax 785-2322

**Emerson, Dakota, Pop. 834**
Emerson-Hubbard SD — 300/K-12
PO Box 9 68733 — 402-695-2621
David Jones, supt. — Fax 695-2622
www.emersonhubbardschools.org
Emerson-Hubbard JSHS — 100/7-12
PO Box 9 68733 — 402-695-2636
Mark Koch, prin. — Fax 695-2637

**Eustis, Frontier, Pop. 399**
Eustis-Farnam SD — 200/K-12
PO Box 9 69028 — 308-486-3991
Steve Sampy, supt. — Fax 486-5350
www.efknights.org
Eustis-Farnam HS — 100/7-12
PO Box 9 69028 — 308-486-3991
Nick Hodge, prin. — Fax 486-5659

**Ewing, Holt, Pop. 385**
Ewing SD — 100/K-12
PO Box 98 68735 — 402-626-7235
Dr. Alberta Moore, supt. — Fax 626-7236
ewing.ne.schoolwebpages.com
Ewing JSHS — 100/7-12
PO Box 98 68735 — 402-626-7235
Greg Appleby, prin. — Fax 626-7236

**Exeter, Fillmore, Pop. 589**
Exeter-Milligan SD — 200/PK-12
PO Box 139 68351 — 402-266-5911
Paul Sheffield, supt. — Fax 266-4811
www.emwolves.org/
Exeter-Milligan JSHS — 100/7-12
PO Box 139 68351 — 402-266-5911
Lindley Schlueter, prin. — Fax 266-4811

**Fairbury, Jefferson, Pop. 3,893**
Fairbury SD — 1,000/PK-12
703 K St 68352 — 402-729-6104
Frederick Helmink, supt. — Fax 729-6392
www.fairburyjeffs.org/
Fairbury JSHS — 400/7-12
1501 9th St 68352 — 402-729-6116
Jeff Vetter, prin. — Fax 729-6275

**Fairfield, Clay, Pop. 385**
South Central Nebraska Unified SD — 600/PK-12
30671 Highway 14 68938 — 402-726-2151
Dr. Randall Gilson, supt. — Fax 726-2208
www.southcentralunified.org
Sandy Creek JSHS — 200/7-12
30671 Highway 14 68938 — 402-726-2151
Jason Searle, prin. — Fax 726-2208
Other Schools – See Nelson

**Fairmont, Fillmore, Pop. 560**
Fillmore Central SD
Supt. — See Geneva
Fillmore Central MS — 200/5-8
PO Box 157 68354 — 402-268-3411
Steven Adkisson, prin. — Fax 268-3491

**Falls City, Richardson, Pop. 4,224**
Falls City SD — 900/PK-12
PO Box 129 68355 — 402-245-2825
Dr. Tim Heckenlively, supt. — Fax 245-2022
www.fctigers.org/
Falls City HS — 300/9-12
1400 Fulton St 68355 — 402-245-2116
Gale Dunkhas, prin. — Fax 245-5050
Falls City MS — 200/6-8
PO Box 129 68355 — 402-245-3455
Rick Johnson, prin. — Fax 245-2022

---

Sacred Heart S — 200/K-12
1820 Fulton St 68355 — 402-245-4151
Doug Goltz, prin. — Fax 245-5217

**Firth, Lancaster, Pop. 580**
Norris SD 160 — 2,100/PK-12
25211 S 68th St 68358 — 402-791-0000
Dr. John Skretta, supt. — Fax 791-0025
www.norris160.org
Norris HS — 600/9-12
25211 S 68th St 68358 — 402-791-0010
Ryan Ruhl, prin. — Fax 791-0027
Norris MS — 600/5-8
25211 S 68th St 68358 — 402-791-0020
MaryJo Rupert, prin. — Fax 791-0029

**Fort Calhoun, Washington, Pop. 895**
Fort Calhoun SD — 600/K-12
PO Box 430 68023 — 402-468-5591
Donald Johnson, supt. — Fax 468-5593
www.fortcalhounschools.org/

Fort Calhoun JSHS 300/7-12
PO Box 430 68023 402-468-5591
Jerry Green, prin. Fax 468-5593

**Franklin, Franklin, Pop. 993**
Franklin SD 300/K-12
1001 M St 68939 308-425-6283
Dr. Candace Conradt, supt. Fax 425-6553
fpsflyers.org
Franklin JSHS 200/7-12
1001 M St 68939 308-425-6283
Adam Boettcher, prin. Fax 425-6553

**Fremont, Dodge, Pop. 26,088**
Fremont SD 3,900/PK-12
130 E 9th St 68025 402-727-3000
Mark Shepard, supt. Fax 727-3002
www.fpsweb.org
Fremont HS 1,400/9-12
1750 N Lincoln Ave 68025 402-727-3050
Chuck Story, prin. Fax 727-3033
Fremont Learning Center 100/Alt
130 E 9th St 68025 402-727-3180
Lea Adler, lead tchr. Fax 727-3085
Fremont MS 600/7-8
540 Johnson Rd 68025 402-727-3100
Scott Jensen, prin. Fax 727-3963

---

Archbishop Bergan JSHS 200/7-12
545 E 4th St 68025 402-721-9683
Dan Koenig, prin. Fax 721-5366
Midland University Post-Sec.
900 N Clarkson St 68025 800-642-8382

**Friend, Saline, Pop. 1,022**
Friend SD 300/K-12
PO Box 67 68359 402-947-2781
David Kraus, supt. Fax 947-2026
www.friendbulldogs.org
Friend JSHS 200/7-12
PO Box 67 68359 402-947-2781
Ben Dempsey, prin. Fax 947-2026

**Fullerton, Nance, Pop. 1,303**
Fullerton SD 200/K-12
PO Box 520 68638 308-536-2431
Jeffrey Anderson, supt. Fax 536-2432
Fullerton HS 100/9-12
PO Box 520 68638 308-536-2431
Pat Larsen, prin. Fax 536-2432

**Geneva, Fillmore, Pop. 2,199**
Fillmore Central SD 500/K-12
1410 L St 68361 402-759-4955
Mark Norvell, supt. Fax 759-4038
www.fillmorecentral.org
Fillmore Central HS 200/9-12
1410 L St 68361 402-759-3141
James Rose, prin. Fax 759-4038
Other Schools – See Fairmont

**Genoa, Nance, Pop. 992**
Twin River SD 500/K-12
PO Box 640 68640 402-993-2274
David Patton, supt. Fax 993-7718
www.twinriverschools.org
Twin River JSHS 200/7-12
PO Box 640 68640 402-993-2911
Terry Gray, prin. Fax 993-7718

**Gering, Scotts Bluff, Pop. 8,397**
Gering SD 2,000/PK-12
1519 10th St 69341 308-436-3125
Bob Hastings, supt. Fax 436-4301
www.geringschools.net
Gering Freshman Academy 9-9
800 Q St 69341 308-436-4255
Kraig Weyrich, prin.
Gering JHS 300/7-8
800 Q St 69341 308-436-3123
Dora Olivares, prin. Fax 436-6010
Gering SHS 500/10-12
1500 U St 69341 308-436-3121
Eldon Hubbard, prin. Fax 436-4214

**Gibbon, Buffalo, Pop. 1,809**
Gibbon SD 600/K-12
PO Box 790 68840 308-468-6555
Larry Witt, supt. Fax 468-5164
www.gibbonpublic.org
Gibbon JSHS 300/7-12
PO Box 790 68840 308-468-5721
Loreda Miller, prin. Fax 468-5164

**Giltner, Hamilton, Pop. 348**
Giltner SD 200/K-12
PO Box 160 68841 402-849-2238
Larry Lambert, supt. Fax 849-2440
www.giltner.k12.ne.us/
Giltner JSHS 100/7-12
PO Box 160 68841 402-849-2238
Kurt Polt, prin. Fax 849-2440

**Gordon, Sheridan, Pop. 1,571**
Gordon-Rushville SD 700/PK-12
PO Box 530 69343 308-282-1322
Merrell Nelsen, supt. Fax 282-2207
www.grmustangs.org
Gordon-Rushville HS 200/9-12
PO Box 530 69343 308-282-1322
Lori Liggett, prin. Fax 282-2207
Other Schools – See Rushville

**Gothenburg, Dawson, Pop. 3,547**
Gothenburg SD 900/K-12
1322 Avenue I 69138 308-537-3651
Michael Teahon, supt. Fax 537-3965
www.gothenburgswedes.org
Gothenburg JSHS 400/7-12
1322 Avenue I 69138 308-537-3651
Randy Evans, prin. Fax 537-3965

**Grand Island, Hall, Pop. 47,867**
Grand Island SD 9,200/PK-12
PO Box 4904 68802 308-385-5900
Robert Winter Ed.D., supt. Fax 385-5949
www.gips.org
Barr MS 800/6-8
602 W Stolley Park Rd 68801 308-385-5875
Brian Kort, prin. Fax 385-5880
Grand Island HS 2,100/9-12
2124 N Lafayette Ave 68803 308-385-5950
Jeff Gilbertson, prin. Fax 385-5966
Success Academy Alt
1912 N Lafayette Ave 68803 308-385-5885
Kenneth Defrank, dir. Fax 385-5608
Walnut MS 800/6-8
1600 N Custer Ave 68803 308-385-5990
Rod Foley, prin. Fax 385-5992
Westridge MS 400/6-8
4111 W 13th St 68803 308-385-5886
Brad Wolfe, prin. Fax 385-5003

Northwest SD 1,400/PK-12
2710 N North Rd 68803 308-385-6398
Matthew Fisher, supt. Fax 385-6393
www.ginorthwest.org
Northwest HS 700/9-12
2710 N North Rd 68803 308-385-6394
Tim Krupicka, prin. Fax 385-6393

---

Central Catholic MSHS 300/6-12
1200 Ruby Ave 68803 308-384-2440
Steve Osborn, prin. Fax 389-3274
Central Community College Post-Sec.
PO Box 4903 68802 308-398-4222
Heartland Lutheran HS 100/9-12
3900 W Husker Hwy 68803 308-385-3900
Curtis Wudtke, prin. Fax 381-7415
Joseph's College of Beauty Post-Sec.
305 W 3rd St 68801 308-381-8848

**Grant, Perkins, Pop. 1,163**
Perkins County SD 400/K-12
PO Box 829 69140 308-352-4735
Phillip Picquet, supt. Fax 352-4769
www.perkinscountyschools.org
Perkins County HS 100/9-12
PO Box 829 69140 308-352-4735
Dean Friedel, prin. Fax 352-4769
Other Schools – See Madrid

**Greeley, Greeley, Pop. 461**
Central Valley SD 200/PK-12
PO Box 160 68842 308-428-3145
Amy Malander, supt. Fax 428-5395
www.centralvps.org
Central Valley JSHS 100/7-12
PO Box 160 68842 308-428-3145
Todd Beck, prin. Fax 428-5395

**Gretna, Sarpy, Pop. 4,403**
Gretna SD 3,300/PK-12
11717 S 216th St 68028 402-332-3265
Dr. Kevin Riley, supt. Fax 332-5833
www.gretnadragons.org
Gretna HS 800/9-12
11717 S 216th St 68028 402-332-3936
Roger Miller, prin. Fax 332-4119
Gretna MS 700/6-8
11717 S 216th St 68028 402-332-3048
Harvey Birky, prin. Fax 332-2931

**Hampton, Hamilton, Pop. 420**
Hampton SD 200/PK-12
458 5th St 68843 402-725-3117
Holly Herzberg, supt. Fax 725-3334
www.hamptonhawks.us
Hampton JSHS 100/7-12
458 5th St 68843 402-725-3116
Tim Huls, prin. Fax 725-3334

**Harrisburg, Banner, Pop. 96**
Banner County SD 200/K-12
PO Box 5 69345 308-436-5263
Lana Sides, supt. Fax 436-5252
www.bannercountyschool.org
Banner County JSHS 100/7-12
PO Box 5 69345 308-436-5263
Heath Johnson, prin. Fax 436-5252

**Harrison, Sioux, Pop. 247**
Sioux County SD 100/K-12
PO Box 38 69346 308-668-2415
Dr. Brett Gies, supt. Fax 668-2260
www.siouxcountyschools.org
Sioux County HS 50/9-12
PO Box 38 69346 308-668-2415
Barry Swisher, prin. Fax 668-2260

**Hartington, Cedar, Pop. 1,550**
Hartington - Newcastle SD 300/PK-12
PO Box 75 68739 402-254-3947
Randall Anderson, supt. Fax 254-3945
hartington.esu1.org/
Hartington - Newcastle JSHS 100/7-12
PO Box 75 68739 402-254-3947
A.J. Johnson, prin. Fax 254-3945

---

Cedar Catholic JSHS 200/7-12
PO Box 15 68739 402-254-3906
Terry Kathol, prin. Fax 254-3976

**Harvard, Clay, Pop. 1,002**
Harvard SD 300/K-12
PO Box 100 68944 402-772-2171
Michael Derr, supt. Fax 772-2204
Harvard JSHS 100/6-12
PO Box 100 68944 402-772-2171
Brent Williamson, prin. Fax 772-2204

**Hastings, Adams, Pop. 24,622**
Adams Central SD 800/K-12
PO Box 1088 68902 402-463-3285
Shawn Scott, supt. Fax 463-6344
adamscentral.us
Adams Central JSHS 500/7-12
PO Box 1088 68902 402-463-3285
David Barrett, prin. Fax 463-6344

Hastings SD 3,600/PK-12
1924 W A St 68901 402-461-7500
Craig Kautz, supt. Fax 461-7509
www.hastingspublicschools.org/
Hastings HS 1,000/9-12
1100 W 14th St 68901 402-461-7550
Jay Opperman, prin. Fax 461-7535
Hastings MS 800/6-8
201 N Marian Rd 68901 402-461-7520
David Essink, prin. Fax 461-7650

---

Central Community College Post-Sec.
PO Box 1024 68902 402-463-9811
Hastings College Post-Sec.
PO Box 269 68902 402-463-2402
Joseph's College of Beauty Post-Sec.
828 W 2nd St 68901 402-463-1357
Mary Lanning Healthcare Radiology Sch Post-Sec.
715 N Saint Joseph Ave 68901 402-461-5177
St. Cecilia MSHS 300/6-12
521 N Kansas Ave 68901 402-462-2105
Fr. Lee Jirovsky, prin. Fax 462-2106

**Hayes Center, Hayes, Pop. 214**
Hayes Center SD 100/K-12
PO Box 8 69032 308-286-5600
Ron Howard, supt. Fax 286-5629
www.hccardinals.org
Hayes Center JSHS 100/7-12
PO Box 8 69032 308-286-5600
Ron Howard, prin. Fax 286-5629

**Hay Springs, Sheridan, Pop. 560**
Hay Springs SD 100/PK-12
PO Box 280 69347 308-638-4434
Jason Cline, supt. Fax 638-7500
hshawks.com
Hay Springs HS 50/9-12
PO Box 280 69347 308-638-4434
Jason Cline, prin. Fax 638-7500
Hay Springs MS 50/6-8
PO Box 280 69347 308-638-4434
Jason Cline, prin. Fax 638-7500

**Hebron, Thayer, Pop. 1,566**
Thayer Central Community SD 400/K-12
PO Box 9 68370 402-768-6117
Drew Harris, supt. Fax 768-6110
www.thayercentral.org/
Thayer Central HS 200/7-12
PO Box 9 68370 402-768-6117
Tom Kiburz, prin. Fax 768-6110

**Hemingford, Box Butte, Pop. 793**
Hemingford SD 400/PK-12
PO Box 217 69348 308-487-3328
Casper Ningen, supt. Fax 487-5215
www.hemingfordschools.org/
Hemingford JSHS 200/7-12
PO Box 217 69348 308-487-3328
Peggy Foster, prin. Fax 487-5215

**Henderson, York, Pop. 988**
Heartland Community SD 300/K-12
1501 Front St 68371 402-723-4434
Brad Best, supt. Fax 723-4431
www.heartlandschools.org/
Heartland Community JSHS 100/7-12
1501 Front St 68371 402-723-4434
Tim Carr, prin. Fax 723-4431

**Hershey, Lincoln, Pop. 650**
Hershey SD 500/PK-12
PO Box 369 69143 308-368-5572
Jane Davis, supt. Fax 368-5570
www.hpspanthers.org
Hershey JSHS 200/7-12
PO Box 369 69143 308-368-5573
Jeff Steinbeck, prin. Fax 368-5571

**Hildreth, Franklin, Pop. 376**
Wilcox-Hildreth SD
Supt. — See Wilcox
Wilcox-Hildreth MS 100/6-8
613 Nelson St 68947 308-938-2415
Justin Patterson, prin. Fax 938-5335

**Holdrege, Phelps, Pop. 5,459**
Holdrege SD, PO Box 2002 68949 1,100/K-12
Todd Hilyard, supt. 308-995-8663
www.holdregedusters.org
Holdrege HS, PO Box 2002 68949 300/9-12
Robert Drews, prin. 308-995-6558
Holdrege MS, PO Box 2002 68949 400/5-8
Angie Girard, prin. 308-995-5421

**Homer, Dakota, Pop. 542**
Homer Community SD 400/PK-12
PO Box 340 68030 402-698-2377
Cheryll Malcom, supt. Fax 698-2379
www.homerknights.org
Homer JSHS 200/7-12
PO Box 340 68030 402-698-2377
Randy Pirner, prin. Fax 698-2379

**Hooper, Dodge, Pop. 820**
Logan View SD 300/K-12
2163 County Road G 68031 402-654-3317
Jeremy Klein, supt. Fax 654-3699
www.loganview.org/
Logan View JSHS 300/7-12
2163 County Road G 68031 402-654-3317
Rochelle Clausen, prin. Fax 654-3699

**Howells, Colfax, Pop. 557**
Howells-Dodge SD 200/K-12
PO Box 159 68641 402-986-1621
Jeffrey Walburn, supt. Fax 986-1261
www.howellsdodgeschools.org
Howells JSHS 100/7-12
PO Box 159 68641 402-986-1621
Dirk Coon, prin. Fax 986-1261

**Humboldt, Richardson, Pop. 874**
Humboldt Table Rock Steinauer SD 70 400/PK-12
810 Central Ave 68376 402-862-2235
Clinton Kimbrough, supt. Fax 862-3135
www.htrstitans.net
Humboldt Table Rock Steinauer HS 100/9-12
810 Central Ave 68376 402-862-2151
Lisa Othmer, prin. Fax 862-2152
Other Schools – See Table Rock

**Humphrey, Platte, Pop. 758**
Humphrey SD 67 200/PK-12
PO Box 278 68642 402-923-1230
Greg Sjuts, supt. Fax 923-1235
www.humphrey.esu7.org
Humphrey JSHS 100/7-12
PO Box 278 68642 402-923-1230
Nic Simonson, prin. Fax 923-1235

---

St. Francis S 200/PK-12
PO Box 277 68642 402-923-0818
Jennifer Dunn, prin. Fax 923-1590

**Hyannis, Grant, Pop. 178**
Hyannis Area SD 100/K-12
PO Box 286 69350 308-458-2202
Troy Unzicker, supt. Fax 458-2227
www.disteleven.org
Hyannis JSHS 100/7-12
PO Box 286 69350 308-458-2202
Bruce Parish, prin. Fax 458-2227

**Imperial, Chase, Pop. 2,057**
Chase County SD 600/K-12
PO Box 577 69033 308-882-4304
Dr. Brad Schoeppey, supt. Fax 882-5629
chasecountyschools.org
Chase County HS 300/7-12
PO Box 577 69033 308-882-4304
Michael Sorensen, prin. Fax 882-5629

**Johnson, Nemaha, Pop. 325**
Johnson-Brock SD 300/K-12
PO Box 186 68378 402-868-5235
Jeffrey Kochler, supt. Fax 868-4785
www.johnsonbrock.esu6.org/
Johnson JSHS 100/7-12
PO Box 186 68378 402-868-5235
Peyton Lewis, prin. Fax 868-4785

**Kearney, Buffalo, Pop. 30,426**
Kearney SD 5,100/PK-12
310 W 24th St 68845 308-698-8000
Virginia Moon, supt. Fax 698-8001
www.kearneypublicschools.org
Horizon MS 600/6-8
915 W 35th St 68845 308-698-8120
Kipp Petersen, prin. Fax 698-8143
Kearney HS 1,400/9-12
3610 6th Ave 68845 308-698-8060
Dr. Jay Dostal, prin. Fax 698-8061
Sunrise MS 500/6-8
4611 N Ave 68847 308-698-8150
Jeff Ganz, prin. Fax 698-8152

---

Joseph's of Kearney Sch of Hair Design Post-Sec.
2213 Central Ave 68847 308-234-6594
Kearney Catholic HS 300/6-12
PO Box 1866 68848 308-234-2610
Terrence Torson, prin. Fax 234-4986
University of Nebraska at Kearney Post-Sec.
905 W 25th St 68849 308-865-8526

**Kenesaw, Adams, Pop. 876**
Kenesaw SD 200/K-12
PO Box 129 68956 402-752-3215
Robby Thompson, supt. Fax 752-3579
www.kenesawschools.org/
Kenesaw JSHS 100/7-12
PO Box 129 68956 402-752-3215
Rodney Richardson, prin. Fax 752-3579

**Kimball, Kimball, Pop. 2,447**
Kimball SD 500/PK-12
901 S Nadine St 69145 308-235-2188
Marshall Lewis, supt. Fax 235-3269
kimball.k12.ne.us/
Kimball JSHS 200/7-12
901 S Nadine St 69145 308-235-4861
Eugene Hanks, prin. Fax 235-4128

**Laurel, Cedar, Pop. 959**
Laurel-Concord-Coleridge SD 200/K-12
PO Box 8 68745 402-256-3133
Randall Klooz, supt. Fax 256-9465
www.lccschool.org
Laurel-Concord-Coleridge HS 100/7-12
PO Box 8 68745 402-256-3731
Jay Vance, prin. Fax 256-9465
Other Schools – See Coleridge

**La Vista, Sarpy, Pop. 15,366**
Papillion-La Vista SD
Supt. — See Papillion
La Vista JHS 700/7-8
7900 Edgewood Blvd 68128 402-898-0436
Patrice Zalesky, prin. Fax 898-0442

**Leigh, Colfax, Pop. 404**
Leigh Community SD 200/K-12
PO Box 98 68643 402-487-3301
Dr. Michael Montgomery Ed.D., supt. Fax 487-3341
www.esu7.org/~leiweb/
Leigh JSHS 100/7-12
PO Box 98 68643 402-487-2228
Jarred Royal, prin. Fax 487-2607

**Lewiston, Pawnee, Pop. 68**
Lewiston SD 200/K-12
306 Tiger Ave 68380 402-865-4675
Rick Kentfield, supt. Fax 865-4875
www.lewistonschool.org/
Lewiston JSHS 100/7-12
306 Tiger Ave 68380 402-865-4675
Fred Ivey, prin. Fax 865-4875

**Lexington, Dawson, Pop. 10,140**
Lexington SD 2,900/PK-12
PO Box 890 68850 308-324-4681
John Hakonson Ed.D., supt. Fax 324-2528
www.lexschools.org
Lexington HS 800/9-12
705 W 13th St 68850 308-324-4691
Kyle Hoehner, prin. Fax 324-7224
Lexington MS 600/6-8
1100 N Washington St 68850 308-324-2349
Scott West, prin. Fax 324-6612

**Lincoln, Lancaster, Pop. 251,784**
Lincoln SD 36,200/PK-12
PO Box 82889 68501 402-436-1000
Stephen Joel Ed.D., supt. Fax 436-1084
www.lps.org/
Arts & Humanities Focus Program 9-12
643 S 25th St 68510 402-436-1785
Dr. Pat Hunter-Pirtle, prin. Fax 458-3281
Bryan Community S 100/Alt
300 S 48th St 68510 402-436-1308
Dr. Mindy Roberts, prin. Fax 458-3208
Culler MS 500/6-8
5201 Vine St 68504 402-436-1210
Gary Czapla, prin. Fax 458-3210
Dawes MS 600/6-8
5130 Colfax Ave 68504 402-436-1211
Angela Plugge, prin. Fax 458-3211
Goodrich MS 600/6-8
4600 Lewis Ave 68521 402-436-1213
Kelly Schrad, prin. Fax 458-3213
Irving MS 900/6-8
2745 S 22nd St 68502 402-436-1214
Dr. Susette Taylor, prin. Fax 458-3214
Lefler MS 600/6-8
1100 S 48th St 68510 402-436-1215
Jessie Carlson, prin. Fax 458-3215
Lincoln East HS 1,400/9-12
1000 S 70th St 68510 402-436-1302
Susan Cassata, prin. Fax 436-1325
Lincoln HS 1,600/9-12
2229 J St 68510 402-436-1301
Mark Larson, prin. Fax 458-1540
Lincoln Northeast HS 1,400/9-12
2635 N 63rd St 68507 402-436-1303
Kurt Glathar, prin. Fax 436-1345
Lincoln North Star HS 1,900/9-12
5801 N 33rd St 68504 402-436-1305
Vann Price, prin. Fax 436-1054
Lincoln Southeast HS 2,000/9-12
2930 S 37th St 68506 402-436-1304
Brent Toalson, prin. Fax 436-1357
Lincoln Southwest HS 1,900/9-12
7001 S 14th St 68512 402-436-1306
Mike Gillotti, prin. Fax 436-1085
Lux MS 900/6-8
7800 High St 68506 402-436-1220
Duane Dohmen, prin. Fax 458-3292
Mickle MS 700/6-8
2500 N 67th St 68507 402-436-1216
Gene Thompson, prin. Fax 458-3216
Park MS 700/6-8
855 S 8th St 68508 402-436-1212
Ryan Zabawa, prin. Fax 458-3212
Pound MS 800/6-8
4740 S 45th St 68516 402-436-1217
Dr. Christopher Deibler, prin. Fax 458-3217
Schoo MS 800/6-8
700 Penrose Dr 68521 402-436-1222
Bill Schulenberg, prin. Fax 458-3222
Science Focus Program 9-12
1222 S 27th St 68502 402-436-1780
Dr. Pat Hunter-Pirtle, prin. Fax 458-3280
Scott MS 900/6-8
2200 Pine Lake Rd 68512 402-436-1218
Dave Knudsen, prin. Fax 458-3218

---

Bryan College of Health Sciences Post-Sec.
5035 Everett St 68506 402-481-3801
College of Hair Design Post-Sec.
304 S 11th St 68508 402-477-4040
College of Hair Design - East Post-Sec.
9000 Andermatt Dr 68526 402-477-4040
College View Academy 200/PK-12
5240 Calvert St 68506 402-483-1181
Joseph's College of Beauty Post-Sec.
2637 O St 68510 402-435-2333
Kaplan University Post-Sec.
1821 K St 68508 402-474-5315
Lincoln Christian S 600/PK-12
5801 S 84th St 68516 402-488-8888
Rodney Zach, admin. Fax 488-6617
Lincoln Lutheran MSHS 400/6-12
1100 N 56th St 68504 402-467-5404
Scott Ernstmeyer, dir. Fax 467-5405
Lincoln Pius X HS 1,100/9-12
6000 A St 68510 402-488-0931
Thomas Korta, prin. Fax 488-1061
Myotherapy Institute Post-Sec.
4001 Pioneer Woods Dr 68506 402-421-7410
Nebraska Wesleyan University Post-Sec.
5000 Saint Paul Ave 68504 402-466-2371
Parkview Christian S 200/PK-12
4400 N 1st St 68521 402-474-8309
Southeast Community College Post-Sec.
8800 O St 68520 402-471-3333
Union College Post-Sec.
3800 S 48th St 68506 402-486-2600
University of Nebraska Post-Sec.
14th & R Sts 68588 402-472-7211

**Lindsay, Platte, Pop. 253**

---

Holy Family S 100/PK-12
PO Box 158 68644 402-428-3455
Andy Bishop, prin. Fax 428-3231

**Litchfield, Sherman, Pop. 262**
Litchfield SD 100/K-12
PO Box 167 68852 308-446-2244
Scott Maline, supt. Fax 446-2244
blog.litchfield.k12.ne.us
Litchfield JSHS 100/7-12
PO Box 167 68852 308-446-2244
Jeffrey Smith, prin. Fax 446-2244

**Lodgepole, Cheyenne, Pop. 315**
Creek Valley SD
Supt. — See Chappell
Creek Valley MS 100/5-8
PO Box 158 69149 308-483-5252
Tessa Fraass, prin. Fax 483-5251

**Loomis, Phelps, Pop. 377**
Loomis SD 200/K-12
PO Box 250 68958 308-876-2111
Nicole Hardwick, supt. Fax 876-2372
loomiswolves.org
Loomis JSHS 100/7-12
PO Box 250 68958 308-876-2111
Sam Dunn, prin. Fax 876-2372

**Louisville, Cass, Pop. 1,086**
Louisville SD 500/K-12
PO Box 489 68037 402-234-3585
Gregory Shepard, supt. Fax 234-2141
www.lpslions.org
Louisville HS 200/9-12
PO Box 489 68037 402-234-3585
Brett Schwartz, prin. Fax 234-2141
Louisville MS 100/6-8
PO Box 489 68037 402-234-3585
Brett Schwartz, prin. Fax 234-2141

**Loup City, Sherman, Pop. 1,023**
Loup City SD 300/K-12
PO Box 628 68853 308-745-0120
Blake Dahlberg, supt. Fax 745-0130
blog.loupcity.k12.ne.us
Loup City HS 100/7-12
PO Box 628 68853 308-745-0548
Blake Dahlberg, prin. Fax 745-0130

**Lynch, Boyd, Pop. 241**
Lynch SD 100/K-12
PO Box 98 68746 402-569-2081
Ted Hillman, supt. Fax 569-2091
lynch.esu8.org/
Lynch JSHS 100/7-12
PO Box 98 68746 402-569-2081
Ted Hillman, prin. Fax 569-2091

**Lyons, Burt, Pop. 845**
Lyons-Decatur Northeast SD 300/PK-12
PO Box 526 68038 402-687-2363
Fred Hansen, supt. Fax 687-2472
www.lyonsdecaturschools.org/
Northeast JSHS 100/7-12
PO Box 526 68038 402-687-2349
Derek Lahm, prin. Fax 687-2472

**Mc Cook, Red Willow, Pop. 7,616**
Mc Cook SD 1,500/PK-12
700 W 7th St 69001 308-345-2510
Grant Norgaard, supt. Fax 345-2511
www.mccookbison.org/
Mc Cook HS 500/9-12
600 W 7th St 69001 308-345-5422
Jerome Smith, prin. Fax 345-5477
Mc Cook JHS 300/6-8
800 W 7th St 69001 308-345-6940
Chad Lyons, prin. Fax 345-6941
Mc Cook Learning Center 50/Alt
404 W 7th St 69001 308-345-5631
Jeff Gross, prin. Fax 345-6134

---

McCook Community College Post-Sec.
1205 E 3rd St 69001 308-345-8100

**Mc Cool Junction, York, Pop. 409**
Mc Cool Junction SD 200/K-12
PO Box 278 68401 402-724-2231
Curtis Cogswell, supt. Fax 724-2232
www.mccool.esu6.org/
Mc Cool Junction JSHS 100/7-12
PO Box 278 68401 402-724-2231
Dade McDonald, prin. Fax 724-2232

**Macy, Thurston, Pop. 1,021**
UMO N HO N Nation SD 500/PK-12
PO Box 280 68039 402-837-5622
Tom Carlstrom, supt. Fax 837-5245
omahanation.ne.schoolinsites.com
UMO N HO N Nation HS 100/9-12
PO Box 280 68039 402-837-5622
Broderick Steed, prin. Fax 837-5245
UMO N HO N Nation MS 100/6-8
PO Box 280 68039 402-837-5622
Broderick Steed, prin. Fax 837-5245

---

Nebraska Indian Community College Post-Sec.
PO Box 428 68039 402-494-2311

**Madison, Madison, Pop. 2,422**
Madison SD 500/PK-12
PO Box 450 68748 402-454-3336
Alan Ehlers, supt. Fax 454-2238
madison.esu8.org/

Madison HS 200/9-12
PO Box 450 68748 402-454-3336
Jim Crilly, prin. Fax 454-2238
Madison MS 100/6-8
PO Box 450 68748 402-454-3336
Andrew Offner, prin. Fax 454-2238

**Madrid, Perkins, Pop. 231**
Perkins County SD
Supt. — See Grant
Perkins County JHS 100/6-8
501 S Ford Ave 69150 308-326-4201
Terry Prante, prin. Fax 326-4231

**Malcolm, Lancaster, Pop. 378**
Malcolm SD 500/K-12
10004 NW 112th St 68402 402-796-2151
Ryan Terwilliger, supt. Fax 796-2178
www.malcolmschools.org
Malcolm JSHS 200/7-12
10002 NW 112th St 68402 402-796-2151
Greg Adams, prin. Fax 796-2189

**Maxwell, Lincoln, Pop. 309**
Maxwell SD 300/PK-12
PO Box 188 69151 308-582-4585
Todd Rhodes, supt. Fax 582-4584
www.maxwellschools.org
Maxwell JSHS 100/7-12
PO Box 188 69151 308-582-4585
Aubrey Boucher, prin. Fax 582-4584

**Maywood, Frontier, Pop. 257**
Maywood SD 200/K-12
PO Box 46 69038 308-362-4223
Trent Benjamin, supt. Fax 362-4454
www.maywoodtigers.org
Maywood JSHS 100/7-12
PO Box 46 69038 308-362-4223
Jason Brown, prin. Fax 362-4454

**Mead, Saunders, Pop. 567**
Mead SD 200/K-12
PO Box 158 68041 402-624-2745
Dr. Dale Rawson, supt. Fax 624-2001
www.meadpublicschools.org/
Mead JSHS 100/7-12
PO Box 158 68041 402-624-3435
P.J. Quinn, prin. Fax 624-2069

**Merna, Custer, Pop. 361**
Anselmo-Merna SD 100/K-12
PO Box 68 68856 308-643-2224
Jason Mundorf, supt. Fax 643-2243
a-mps.fesdev.org/
Anselmo-Merna S 100/K-12
PO Box 68 68856 308-643-2224
Darrin Max, prin. Fax 643-2243

**Milford, Seward, Pop. 2,066**
Milford SD 700/PK-12
PO Box C 68405 402-761-3321
Kevin Wingard, supt. Fax 761-3322
www.milfordpublicschools.org/
Milford JSHS 300/7-12
PO Box C 68405 402-761-2525
Brandon Mowinkel, prin. Fax 761-2663

---

Southeast Community College Post-Sec.
600 State St 68405 402-761-2131

**Minatare, Scotts Bluff, Pop. 808**
Minatare SD 200/PK-12
PO Box 425 69356 308-783-1232
Tim Cody, supt. Fax 783-1050
www.edline.net/pages/Minatare_Public_Schools
Minatare JSHS 100/7-12
PO Box 425 69356 308-783-1733
Kyle Metzger, prin. Fax 783-2982

**Minden, Kearney, Pop. 2,907**
Minden SD 800/PK-12
PO Box 301 68959 308-832-2440
Melissa Wheelock, supt. Fax 832-2567
minden.k12.ne.us
Jones MS 300/4-8
PO Box 301 68959 308-832-2338
John Osgood, prin. Fax 832-3236
Minden HS 200/9-12
PO Box 301 68959 308-832-2254
Don Hosick, prin. Fax 832-1892

**Mitchell, Scotts Bluff, Pop. 1,691**
Mitchell SD 700/PK-12
1819 19th Ave 69357 308-623-1707
Katherine Urbanek, supt. Fax 623-1330
www.mpstigers.com
Mitchell JSHS 300/7-12
1819 19th Ave 69357 308-623-1707
Heath Peters, prin. Fax 623-1330

**Morrill, Scotts Bluff, Pop. 916**
Morrill SD 400/PK-12
PO Box 486 69358 308-247-3414
Joseph Sherwood, supt. Fax 247-2196
www.mpslions.org
Morrill JSHS 200/7-12
PO Box 486 69358 308-247-2149
Tom Peacock, prin. Fax 247-2196

**Mullen, Hooker, Pop. 506**
Mullen SD 200/K-12
PO Box 127 69152 308-546-2223
Mark Sievering, supt. Fax 546-2209
spssailors.org/esu16/esu16/ESU_16_School_Websites.html
Mullen JSHS 100/7-12
PO Box 127 69152 308-546-2223
Michael Kvanvig, prin. Fax 546-2209

**Murdock, Cass, Pop. 236**
Elmwood-Murdock SD 400/K-12
300 Wyoming St 68407 402-867-2341
Daniel Novak, supt. Fax 867-2009
www.elm.esu3.org
Elmwood-Murdock JSHS 200/7-12
300 Wyoming St 68407 402-867-2341
Tim Allemang, prin. Fax 867-2009

**Murray, Cass, Pop. 456**
Conestoga SD 600/PK-12
PO Box 184 68409 402-235-2992
Beth Johnsen, supt. Fax 227-2992
www.conestogacougars.org/
Conestoga JSHS 300/7-12
PO Box 40 68409 402-235-2271
David Friedli, prin. Fax 235-2421
Other Schools – See Nehawka

**Nebraska City, Otoe, Pop. 7,192**
Nebraska City SD 1,400/PK-12
215 N 12th St 68410 402-873-6033
Dr. Jeffrey Edwards, supt. Fax 873-6030
www.nebcityps.org
Nebraska City HS 400/9-12
141 Steinhart Park Rd 68410 402-873-3360
Brian Hoover, prin. Fax 873-3831
Nebraska City MS 300/6-8
909 1st Corso 68410 402-873-5591
Craig Taylor, prin. Fax 873-5641

---

Lourdes Central S 200/6-12
412 2nd Ave 68410 402-873-6154
Fr. Mark Cyza, prin. Fax 873-3154
Nebraska School for Visually Handicapped Post-Sec.
PO Box 129 68410

**Nehawka, Cass, Pop. 204**
Conestoga SD
Supt. — See Murray
Conestoga Alternative S Alt
PO Box 187 68413 402-227-2935
Fax 227-2945

**Neligh, Antelope, Pop. 1,591**
Neligh-Oakdale SD 400/PK-12
PO Box 149 68756 402-887-4166
Kimberly Lingenfelter, supt. Fax 887-5322
Neligh-Oakdale JSHS 200/7-12
PO Box 149 68756 402-887-4166
George Loofe, prin. Fax 887-5322

**Nelson, Nuckolls, Pop. 480**
South Central Nebraska Unified SD
Supt. — See Fairfield
Lawrence/Nelson JSHS 100/7-12
PO Box 368 68961 402-225-3371
Craig McLey, prin. Fax 225-5431

**Newman Grove, Madison, Pop. 715**
Newman Grove SD 200/K-12
PO Box 370 68758 402-447-2721
Mikal Shalikow, supt. Fax 447-2445
newman.esu8.org
Newman Grove JSHS 100/7-12
PO Box 370 68758 402-447-6294
Darrell Barnes, prin. Fax 447-2445

**Niobrara, Knox, Pop. 360**
Niobrara SD 100/K-12
PO Box 310 68760 402-857-3323
Margaret Sandoz, supt. Fax 857-3877
www.niobraraschools.org
Niobrara JSHS 100/5-12
PO Box 310 68760 402-857-3322
Angie Guenther, prin. Fax 857-3716

Santee SD 200/K-12
206 Frazier Ave E 68760 402-857-2741
Tom Carlstrom, supt. Fax 857-2743
santeeweb.esu1.org
Santee HS 50/9-12
206 Frazier Ave E 68760 402-857-2741
Tony Hoffman, prin. Fax 857-2743

**Norfolk, Madison, Pop. 23,882**
Norfolk SD 3,900/PK-12
PO Box 139 68702 402-644-2500
Jami Jo Thompson, supt. Fax 644-2506
www.norfolkpublicschools.org/
Alternatives for Success 50/Alt
PO Box 139 68702 402-844-3515
Fax 844-3515
Norfolk JHS 500/7-8
PO Box 139 68702 402-644-2516
Michael Hart, prin. Fax 644-2519
Norfolk SHS 1,200/9-12
PO Box 139 68702 402-644-2529
Jason Luhr, prin. Fax 644-2538

---

Joseph's College of Beauty Post-Sec.
202 W Madison Ave 68701 402-371-3358
Keystone Christian Academy 50/PK-12
715 W Madison Ave 68701 402-371-3531
Sharon Lotz, admin. Fax 371-4824
Lutheran HS Northeast 100/9-12
2010 N 37th St 68701 402-379-3040
Paul Leckband, prin. Fax 379-8340
Norfolk Catholic JSHS 300/7-12
2300 W Madison Ave 68701 402-371-2784
Jeff Bellar, prin. Fax 379-2929
Northeast Community College Post-Sec.
PO Box 469 68702 402-371-2020

**North Bend, Dodge, Pop. 1,172**
North Bend Central SD 500/K-12
PO Box 160 68649 402-652-3268
Dan Endorf, supt. Fax 652-8348
www.nbtigers.org/
North Bend Central JSHS 200/7-12
PO Box 160 68649 402-652-3268
Brenda Petersen, prin. Fax 652-8348

**North Platte, Lincoln, Pop. 24,455**
North Platte SD 4,200/PK-12
PO Box 1557 69103 308-535-7100
Ron Hanson, supt. Fax 535-5300
www.nppsd.org
Adams MS 700/6-8
1200 McDonald Rd 69101 308-535-7112
Vikki Carlson, prin. Fax 535-5309
Learning Center 50/Alt
1400 N Madison Ave 69101 308-535-5311
James Ayres, prin. Fax 535-5311
Madison MS 200/6-8
1400 N Madison Ave 69101 308-535-7126
Danny McMurtry, prin. Fax 535-5303
North Platte HS 1,100/9-12
1220 W 2nd St 69101 308-535-7105
James Ayres, prin. Fax 535-7111

---

Joseph's College of Beauty Post-Sec.
1620 E 4th St 69101 308-532-4664
Mid-Plains Community College Post-Sec.
601 W State Farm Rd 69101 308-535-3600
North Platte Community College Post-Sec.
1101 Halligan Dr 69101 308-535-3600
St. Patrick JSHS 200/7-12
PO Box 970 69103 308-532-1874
Mark Skillstad, prin. Fax 532-8015

**Oakland, Burt, Pop. 1,227**
Oakland Craig SD 400/K-12
309 N Davis Ave 68045 402-685-5661
Jeffery Smith, supt. Fax 685-5697
www.ocknights.org
Oakland Craig HS 100/9-12
309 N Davis Ave 68045 402-685-5661
Rusty Droescher, prin. Fax 685-5697
Oakland Craig JHS 100/7-8
309 N Davis Ave 68045 402-685-5661
Rusty Droescher, prin. Fax 685-5697

**Odell, Gage, Pop. 299**
Diller-Odell SD 200/K-12
PO Box 188 68415 402-766-4171
Michael Meyerle, supt. Fax 766-4211
www.dillerodell.org/
Diller-Odell JSHS 100/7-12
PO Box 188 68415 402-766-4210
Christopher Prososki, prin. Fax 766-4211

**Ogallala, Keith, Pop. 4,669**
Ogallala SD 900/PK-12
801 E O St 69153 308-284-4060
Carl Dietz, supt. Fax 284-3981
www.opsd.org/
Ogallala HS 300/9-12
602 E G St 69153 308-284-4029
Greg Pavlik, prin. Fax 284-3869

**Omaha, Douglas, Pop. 399,005**
Elkhorn SD
Supt. — See Elkhorn
Elkhorn Grandview MS 6-8
17801 Grand Ave 68116 402-289-9399
Mike Tomjack, prin. Fax 289-9499
Elkhorn Ridge MS 300/6-8
17880 Marcy St 68118 402-334-9302
Kevin Riggert, prin. Fax 334-9378
Elkhorn South HS 900/9-12
20303 Blue Sage Pkwy 68130 402-289-0616
Mark Kalvoda, prin. Fax 289-1523

Millard SD 22,100/PK-12
5606 S 147th St 68137 402-715-8200
Dr. James Sutfin, supt. Fax 715-8409
www.mpsomaha.org
Andersen MS 800/6-8
15404 Adams St 68137 402-715-8440
Jeff Alfrey, prin. Fax 715-8410
Beadle MS 1,000/6-8
18201 Jefferson St 68135 402-715-6100
John Southworth, prin. Fax 715-6140
Horizon HS 100/Alt
5300 George B Lake Pkwy, 402-715-8470
Angie Craft, prin. Fax 715-6196
Kiewit MS 900/6-8
15650 Howard St 68118 402-715-1470
Marshall Smith, prin. Fax 715-1490
Millard Central MS 800/6-8
12801 L St 68137 402-715-8225
Beth Fink, prin. Fax 715-8574
Millard North HS 2,500/9-12
1010 S 144th St 68154 402-715-1365
Brian Begley, prin. Fax 715-1336
Millard North MS 800/6-8
2828 S 139th St 68144 402-715-1280
Scott Ingwerson, prin. Fax 715-1275
Millard South HS 2,100/9-12
14905 Q St 68137 402-715-8268
Heidi Weaver, prin. Fax 715-6160
Millard West HS 2,300/9-12
5710 S 176th Ave 68135 402-715-6000
Greg Tiemann, prin. Fax 715-6060
Russell MS 900/6-8
5304 S 172nd St 68135 402-715-8500
Teresa Perkins, prin. Fax 715-8368

Omaha SD 47,800/PK-12
3215 Cuming St 68131 402-557-2222
Mark Evans, supt. Fax 557-2019
www.ops.org
Accelere 9-12
2606 Hamilton St 68131 402-898-1568
Benson Magnet HS 1,500/9-12
5120 Maple St 68104 402-557-3000
Anita Harkins, prin. Fax 557-3039
Beveridge Magnet MS 800/7-8
1616 S 120th St 68144 402-557-4000
Dr. David Lavender, prin. Fax 557-4009
Blackburn Alternative S Alt
2606 Hamilton St 68131 402-344-3385
Fred Marisett, dir. Fax 344-3724

Bryan HS 1,700/9-12
4700 Giles Rd 68157 402-557-3100
Robert Aranda, prin. Fax 557-3139
Bryan MS 700/7-8
8210 S 42nd St 68147 402-557-4100
Darren Rasmussen, prin. Fax 557-4129
Buffet Magnet MS 700/5-8
14101 Larimore Ave 68164 402-561-6160
Dr. Rony Ortega, prin. Fax 561-6170
Burke HS 2,100/9-12
12200 Burke Blvd 68154 402-557-3200
Dr. Deborah Frison, prin. Fax 557-3239
Career Center Vo/Tech
3230 Burt St 68131 402-557-3700
Timothy Hoffman, dir. Fax 557-2629
Central HS 2,600/9-12
124 N 20th St 68102 402-557-3300
Dr. Ed Bennett, prin. Fax 557-3339
Davis MS 6-8
8050 N 129th Ave 68142 402-561-6130
Dan Bartels, prin. Fax 933-9131
Hale MS 400/7-8
6143 Whitmore St 68152 402-557-4200
Darin Williams, prin. Fax 557-4229
King Science Magnet MS 400/5-8
3720 Florence Blvd 68110 402-557-3720
Steve Eubanks, prin. Fax 557-4459
Lewis & Clark MS 700/7-8
6901 Burt St 68132 402-557-4300
Dr. Lisa Sterba, prin. Fax 557-4309
Marrs Magnet MS 600/5-8
5619 S 19th St 68107 402-557-4400
Bryan Dunne, prin. Fax 557-4429
McMillan Magnet MS 600/7-8
3802 Redick Ave 68112 402-557-4500
Dr. Jeaneen Talbott, prin. Fax 557-4509
Monroe MS 500/7-8
5105 Bedford Ave 68104 402-557-4600
Boris Moore, prin. Fax 557-4609
Morton Magnet MS 700/5-8
4606 Terrace Dr 68134 402-557-4700
Matt Brandl, prin. Fax 557-4709
Norris MS 800/7-8
2235 S 46th St 68106 402-557-4800
David Alati, prin. Fax 557-4809
Omaha North Magnet HS 2,000/9-12
4410 N 36th St 68111 402-557-3400
Gene Haynes, prin. Fax 557-3439
Omaha Northwest Magnet HS 1,300/9-12
8204 Crown Point Ave 68134 402-557-3500
Thomas Lee, prin. Fax 557-3539
Omaha South Magnet HS 2,200/9-12
4519 S 24th St 68107 402-557-3600
Ruben Cano, prin. Fax 557-3639
Parrish S Alt
4469 Farnam St 68131 402-554-8460
Dr. Bonnie Perry-Adams, prin. Fax 554-1639

Westside Community SD 5,900/PK-12
909 S 76th St 68114 402-390-2100
Dr. Blane McCann Ph.D., supt. Fax 390-2120
www.westside66.org
Westside Career Center Vo/Tech
3534 S 108th St 68144 402-390-8214
Jenni Allen, admin. Fax 390-8212
Westside HS 1,900/9-12
8701 Pacific St 68114 402-343-2600
Maryanne Ricketts, prin. Fax 343-2608
Westside MS 900/7-8
8601 Arbor St 68124 402-390-6464
Russ Olsen, prin. Fax 390-6454

---

Alegent Health School of Radiologic Tech Post-Sec.
7500 Mercy Rd 68124 402-398-5527
Bishop Clarkson Memorial Hospital Post-Sec.
4350 Dewey Ave 68105 402-552-3203
Brownell-Talbot S 500/PK-12
400 N Happy Hollow Blvd 68132 402-556-3772
Dr. Kristi Gibbs, head sch Fax 553-2994
Capitol School of Hairstyling - West Post-Sec.
10803 John Galt Blvd 68137 402-333-3329
Clarkson College Post-Sec.
101 S 42nd St 68131 402-552-3100
College of Saint Mary Post-Sec.
7000 Mercy Rd 68106 402-399-2400
Concordia Lutheran JSHS 300/7-12
15656 Fort St 68116 402-445-4000
Matthew Korte, prin. Fax 965-9310
Creighton Preparatory S 1,000/9-12
7400 Western Ave 68114 402-393-1190
John Naatz, prin. Fax 393-0620
Creighton University Post-Sec.
2500 California Plz 68178 402-280-2700
Duchesne Academy 300/9-12
3601 Burt St 68131 402-558-3800
Laura Hickman, prin. Fax 558-0051
Grace University Post-Sec.
1311 S 9th St 68108 402-449-2800
Immanuel Medical Center Post-Sec.
6901 N 72nd St 68122 402-572-2270
ITT Technical Institute Post-Sec.
1120 N 103rd Plz Ste 200 68114 402-331-2900
Jesuit Academy 100/4-8
2311 N 22nd St 68110 402-346-4464
Troy Wharton, prin. Fax 341-1817
Kaplan University Post-Sec.
5425 N 103rd St 68134 402-431-6100
Marian HS 700/9-12
7400 Military Ave 68134 402-571-2618
Susan Sullivan, prin. Fax 571-2978
Mercy HS 400/9-12
1501 S 48th St 68106 402-553-9424
Sarah Regan, prin. Fax 553-0394
Metropolitan Community College Post-Sec.
PO Box 3777 68103 402-738-4500
Metropolitan Community College- Ft Omaha Post-Sec.
PO Box 3777 68103 402-457-2700
Metropolitan Community Coll- Elkhorn Vly Post-Sec.
PO Box 3777 68103 402-289-1200
Montessori International S of the Plains 50/7-12
7001 Oak St 68106 402-614-9074
Nebraska Methodist College Post-Sec.
720 N 87th St 68114 402-354-7000
Omaha Christian Academy 300/PK-12
10244 Wiesman Dr 68134 402-399-9565
Dr. Victor Fordyce Ed.D., supt. Fax 399-0248
Omaha School of Massage Therapy Post-Sec.
9748 Park Dr 68127 402-331-3694
Roncalli HS 400/9-12
6401 Sorensen Pkwy 68152 402-571-7670
Paul Hans, prin. Fax 571-3216
Skutt Catholic HS 700/9-12
3131 S 156th St 68130 402-333-0818
Rob Meyers, prin. Fax 333-1790
The Creative Center Post-Sec.
10850 Emmet St 68164 402-898-1000
Universal College of Healing Arts Post-Sec.
8702 N 30th St 68112 402-556-4456
University of Nebraska Medical Center Post-Sec.
987020 Nebraska Medical Ctr 68198 402-559-4000
University of Nebraska Omaha Post-Sec.
6001 Dodge St 68182 402-554-2800
Vatterott College - Omaha Post-Sec.
11818 I St 68137 402-891-9411
Wright Career College Post-Sec.
3000 S 84th St 68124 913-381-2577
Xenon International Academy Post-Sec.
8516 Park Dr 68127 402-393-2933

**O Neill, Holt, Pop. 3,676**
O'Neill SD 700/PK-12
PO Box 230 68763 402-336-3775
Amy Shane, supt. Fax 336-4890
www.oneillpublicschools.org
O'Neill JSHS 300/7-12
PO Box 230 68763 402-336-1544
Corey Fisher, prin. Fax 336-1105

---

St. Mary S 300/PK-12
326 E Benton St 68763 402-336-4455
Cody Havranek, prin. Fax 336-1281

**Orchard, Antelope, Pop. 377**
Nebraska USD 1 200/PK-12
PO Box 248 68764 402-893-2068
Dale Martin, supt. Fax 893-2065
neunified1.esu8.org/
Other Schools – See Clearwater, Verdigre

**Ord, Valley, Pop. 2,094**
Ord SD 500/K-12
320 N 19th St 68862 308-728-5013
Jason Alexander, supt. Fax 728-5108
www.ordps.org
Ord JSHS 200/7-12
1800 K St 68862 308-728-3241
Mark Hagge, prin. Fax 728-5108

**Osceola, Polk, Pop. 874**
Osceola SD 300/K-12
PO Box 198 68651 402-747-3121
Steve Rinehart, supt. Fax 747-3041
www.edline.net/pages/Osceola_Public_School/
Osceola HS 100/9-12
PO Box 198 68651 402-747-3121
Dale Maynard, prin. Fax 747-3041
Osceola MS 100/6-8
PO Box 198 68651 402-747-3121
Dale Maynard, prin. Fax 747-3041

**Oshkosh, Garden, Pop. 869**
Garden County SD 200/PK-12
PO Box 230 69154 308-772-3242
Dr. Paula Sissel, supt. Fax 772-3039
www.gardencountyschools.org/
Garden County HS 100/7-12
PO Box 230 69154 308-772-3242
Jason Spady, prin. Fax 772-3039

**Osmond, Pierce, Pop. 774**
Osmond SD 200/K-12
PO Box 458 68765 402-748-3777
David Hamm, supt. Fax 748-3210
www.osmondtigers.org
Osmond JSHS 100/7-12
PO Box 458 68765 402-748-3777
Michael Brown, prin. Fax 748-3210

**Overton, Dawson, Pop. 592**
Overton SD 300/PK-12
PO Box 310 68863 308-987-2424
Mark Aten, supt. Fax 987-2349
www.ovr.esu10.k12.ne.us/
Overton JSHS 100/7-12
PO Box 310 68863 308-987-2424
Brian Fleischman, prin. Fax 987-2349

**Oxford, Furnas, Pop. 773**
Southern Valley SD 400/K-12
43739 Highway 89 68967 308-868-2222
Darren Tobey, supt. Fax 868-2223
sites.google.com/a/sveagles.org/southern-valley
Southern Valley JSHS 200/7-12
43739 Highway 89 68967 308-868-2222
Darren Tobey, prin. Fax 868-2223

**Palmer, Merrick, Pop. 470**
Palmer SD 300/PK-12
PO Box 248 68864 308-894-3065
Dr. Joel Bohlken, supt. Fax 894-8245
www.palmertigers.org
Palmer JSHS 100/7-12
PO Box 248 68864 308-894-3065
Dr. Joel Bohlken, supt. Fax 894-8245

**Palmyra, Otoe, Pop. 536**
Palmyra OR 1 SD 400/K-12
PO Box 130 68418 402-780-5327
Robert Hanger, supt. Fax 780-5328
www.districtor1.org/
Palmyra JSHS 200/7-12
PO Box 130 68418 402-780-5327
David Bottrell, prin. Fax 780-5328

**Papillion, Sarpy, Pop. 18,478**
Papillion-La Vista SD 10,300/PK-12
420 S Washington St 68046 402-537-6200
Andrew Rikli, supt. Fax 537-6216
www.paplv.org
Ideal S Alt
1104 Applewood Dr 68046 402-898-0485
Jim Larson, prin. Fax 898-0486
Papillion JHS 700/7-8
423 S Washington St 68046 402-898-0424
Brent Holder, prin. Fax 898-0430
Papillion-La Vista HS 1,500/9-12
402 E Centennial Rd 68046 402-898-0400
Melissa Jabens, prin. Fax 898-0415
Papillion-La Vista South HS 1,600/9-12
10799 Highway 370 68046 402-829-4600
Melissa Jabens, prin. Fax 827-1330
Other Schools – See La Vista

---

Nebraska Christian College Post-Sec.
12550 S 114th St 68046 402-935-9400

**Pawnee City, Pawnee, Pop. 861**
Pawnee City SD 300/K-12
PO Box 393 68420 402-852-2988
Stephen Grizzle, supt. Fax 852-2993
www.pawneecityschool.com
Pawnee City JSHS 100/7-12
PO Box 393 68420 402-852-2988
Donald Jacobs, prin. Fax 852-2993

**Paxton, Keith, Pop. 521**
Paxton Consolidated SD 200/K-12
PO Box 368 69155 308-239-4283
Delbert Dack, supt. Fax 239-4359
www.paxtonschools.org
Paxton JSHS 100/7-12
PO Box 368 69155 308-239-4283
Sheri Chittenden, prin. Fax 239-4359

**Pender, Thurston, Pop. 991**
Pender SD 400/PK-12
609 Whitney St 68047 402-385-3244
Jason Dolliver, supt. Fax 385-3342
www.penderschools.org/
Pender JSHS 200/7-12
609 Whitney St 68047 402-385-3244
Eric Miller, prin. Fax 385-3342

**Peru, Nemaha, Pop. 853**

---

Peru State College Post-Sec.
PO Box 10 68421 402-872-3815

**Petersburg, Boone, Pop. 329**
Boone Central SD
Supt. — See Albion
Boone Central MS 100/6-8
PO Box 240 68652 402-386-5302
Jimmy Feeney, prin. Fax 386-5464

**Pierce, Pierce, Pop. 1,757**
Pierce SD 700/K-12
201 N Sunset St 68767 402-329-4677
Kendall Steffensen, supt. Fax 329-4678
www.piercepublic.org/
Pierce JSHS 300/7-12
201 N Sunset St 68767 402-329-6217
Mark Brahmer, prin. Fax 329-4678

**Pilger, Stanton, Pop. 343**
Wisner-Pilger SD
Supt. — See Wisner
Wisner-Pilger MS 100/7-8
350 E 2nd St 68768 402-396-3566
Mark Porter, prin. Fax 396-3566

**Plainview, Pierce, Pop. 1,240**
Plainview SD 300/K-12
PO Box 638 68769 402-582-4993
Richard Alt, supt. Fax 582-4665
www.plainviewschools.org/
Plainview JSHS 200/7-12
PO Box 638 68769 402-582-4991
Patty Novicki, prin. Fax 582-4665

**Plattsmouth, Cass, Pop. 6,376**
Plattsmouth SD 1,900/PK-12
1912 E Highway 34 68048 402-296-3361
Dr. Richard Hasty, supt. Fax 296-2667
www.pcsd.org
Plattsmouth HS 500/9-12
1916 E Highway 34 68048 402-296-3322
Jeffery Wiles, prin. Fax 296-3342
Plattsmouth MS 500/5-8
1724 8th Ave 68048 402-296-3174
Mark Smith, prin. Fax 296-2910

**Pleasanton, Buffalo, Pop. 340**
Pleasanton SD 300/PK-12
PO Box 190 68866 308-388-2041
Ronald Wymore, supt. Fax 388-5502
pleasantonbulldogs.org
Pleasanton JSHS 100/7-12
PO Box 190 68866 308-388-2041
James Westland, prin. Fax 388-5502

**Polk, Polk, Pop. 321**
High Plains Community SD 200/K-12
PO Box 29 68654 402-765-2271
Philip Mahan Ed.D., supt. Fax 765-2272
www.hpcstorm.org
High Plains HS 100/9-12
PO Box 29 68654 402-765-3331
Cameron Hudson, prin. Fax 765-3332
Other Schools – See Clarks

**Ponca, Dixon, Pop. 947**
Ponca SD 400/K-12
PO Box 568 68770 402-755-5700
Joan Reznicek, supt. Fax 755-5773
www.poncaschool.org
Ponca JSHS 200/7-12
PO Box 568 68770 402-755-5701
Michelle Rinas, prin. Fax 755-5773

**Potter, Cheyenne, Pop. 337**
Potter-Dix SD 200/K-12
PO Box 189 69156 308-879-4434
Kevin Thomas, supt. Fax 879-4566
www.pdcoyotes.com
Potter-Dix JSHS 100/7-12
PO Box 189 69156 308-879-4434
Greg Morris, prin. Fax 879-4566

**Ralston, Douglas, Pop. 5,872**
Ralston SD 3,100/PK-12
8545 Park Dr 68127 402-331-4700
Dr. Mark Adler, supt. Fax 331-4843
www.ralstonschools.org/
Ralston HS 900/9-12
8969 Park Dr 68127 402-331-7373
Steve Schrad, prin. Fax 898-3511
Ralston MS 400/7-8
8202 Lakeview St 68127 402-331-4701
Andy Parizek, prin. Fax 331-5376

**Randolph, Cedar, Pop. 943**
Randolph SD 45 300/PK-12
PO Box 755 68771 402-337-0252
Jeffrey Hoesing, supt. Fax 337-0235
www.randolphpublic.org/
Randolph JSHS 100/7-12
PO Box 755 68771 402-337-0252
Dennis Bazata, prin. Fax 337-0235

**Ravenna, Buffalo, Pop. 1,347**
Ravenna SD 400/PK-12
PO Box 8400 68869 308-452-3249
Dr. Ken Schroeder, supt. Fax 452-3172
www.ravennabluejays.org
Ravenna JSHS 200/7-12
PO Box 8400 68869 308-452-3249
Craig McLey, prin. Fax 452-3172

**Raymond, Lancaster, Pop. 163**
Raymond Central SD 600/K-12
1800 W Agnew Rd 68428 402-785-2615
Paul Hull, supt. Fax 785-2097
www.rcentral.org
Raymond JSHS 300/7-12
1800 W Agnew Rd 68428 402-785-2685
Kolin Haecker, prin. Fax 785-7070

**Red Cloud, Webster, Pop. 1,006**
Red Cloud Community SD 200/K-12
334 N Cherry St 68970 402-746-3413
Brian Hof, supt. Fax 746-3690
www.redcloud.k12.ne.us/
Washington JSHS 100/7-12
121 W 7th Ave 68970 402-746-2818
Tom Borders, prin. Fax 746-2817

**Rising City, Butler, Pop. 373**
Shelby-Rising City SD
Supt. — See Shelby
Shelby-Rising City MS 6-8
PO Box 160 68658 402-542-2216
William Curry, prin. Fax 542-2265

**Roseland, Adams, Pop. 235**
Silver Lake SD 200/K-12
PO Box 8 68973 402-756-6611
Mel Crowe, supt. Fax 756-6613
www.silverlakemustangs.org
Silver Lake JSHS 100/7-12
PO Box 8 68973 402-756-6611
Kenneth Mahoney, prin. Fax 756-6613

**Rushville, Sheridan, Pop. 866**
Gordon-Rushville SD
Supt. — See Gordon
Gordon-Rushville MS 100/6-8
PO Box 590 69360 308-327-2491
Jeanne Hensley, prin. Fax 327-2504

**Saint Edward, Boone, Pop. 704**
Saint Edward SD 100/K-12
PO Box C 68660 402-678-2282
Kevin Lyons, supt. Fax 678-2284
stedwardpublicschools.schoolinsites.com
Saint Edward JSHS 100/7-12
PO Box C 68660 402-678-2282
Kevin Lyons, prin. Fax 678-2284

**Saint Paul, Howard, Pop. 2,270**
Saint Paul SD 500/K-12
PO Box 325 68873 308-754-4433
John Poppert, supt. Fax 754-5374
www.stpaulpublicschools.org/
Saint Paul JSHS 200/7-12
PO Box 325 68873 308-754-4433
Jennifer Hagen, prin. Fax 754-5374

**Sargent, Custer, Pop. 524**
Sargent SD 200/K-12
PO Box 366 68874 308-527-4119
Wayne Ruppert, supt. Fax 527-3332
blog.sargent.k12.ne.us
Sargent JSHS 100/7-12
PO Box 366 68874 308-527-4119
Cory Grint, prin. Fax 527-3332

**Schuyler, Colfax, Pop. 6,165**
Schuyler Community SD 900/PK-12
401 Adam St 68661 402-352-2421
Dr. Daniel Hoesing, supt. Fax 352-5552
schuylercommunityschools.org
Schuyler Alternative Education 50/Alt
697 Road 16 68661 402-352-2755
Stephen Grammer, admin. Fax 352-2755
Schuyler Central HS 400/9-12
401 Adam St 68661 402-352-3527
Stephen Grammer, prin. Fax 352-5552
Schuyler MS 300/6-8
200 W 10th St 68661 402-352-5514
Michelle Burton, prin. Fax 352-2644

**Scottsbluff, Scotts Bluff, Pop. 14,885**
Scottsbluff SD 2,900/PK-12
1722 1st Ave 69361 308-635-6200
Rick Myles, supt. Fax 635-6217
www.sbps.net/
Bluffs MS 700/6-8
23rd and Broadway 69361 308-635-6270
Andrew Dick, prin. Fax 635-6271
Scottsbluff HS 800/9-12
313 E 27th St 69361 308-635-6230
Michael Halley, prin. Fax 635-6240

---

Regional West Medical Center Post-Sec.
4021 Avenue B 69361 308-635-3711
Western Nebraska Community College Post-Sec.
1601 E 27th St 69361 308-635-3606

**Scribner, Dodge, Pop. 841**
Scribner-Snyder SD 200/K-12
PO Box L 68057 402-664-2568
Ginger Meyer, supt. Fax 664-2708
www.sstrojans.org
Scribner-Snyder JSHS 100/7-12
PO Box L 68057 402-664-2567
Brad Stithem, prin. Fax 664-2407

**Seward, Seward, Pop. 6,883**
Seward SD 1,400/PK-12
410 South St 68434 402-643-2941
Greg Barnes, supt. Fax 643-4986
www.sewardpublicschools.org
Seward HS 500/9-12
532 Northern Heights Dr 68434 402-643-2988
John Schwartz, prin. Fax 643-2599
Seward MS 400/5-8
2401 Karol Kay Blvd 68434 402-643-2986
Kirk Gottschalk, prin. Fax 643-6686

---

Concordia University Post-Sec.
800 N Columbia Ave 68434 402-643-3651
Saint Gregory the Great Seminary Post-Sec.
800 Fletcher Rd 68434 402-643-4052

**Shelby, Polk, Pop. 707**
Shelby-Rising City SD 300/K-12
PO Box 218 68662 402-527-5946
Chester Kay, supt. Fax 527-5133
www.shelby.esu7.org
Shelby-Rising City HS 100/9-12
PO Box 218 68662 402-527-5946
Troy Holmberg, prin. Fax 527-5133
Other Schools – See Rising City

**Shelton, Buffalo, Pop. 1,053**
Shelton SD 300/K-12
PO Box 610 68876 308-647-6742
Brian Redinger, supt. Fax 647-5233
www.sheltonbulldogs.org
Shelton JSHS 100/7-12
PO Box 610 68876 308-647-5459
John Vanderbeek, prin. Fax 647-5233

**Shickley, Fillmore, Pop. 338**
Shickley SD 50/PK-12
PO Box 407 68436 402-627-3375
Bryce Jorgenson, supt. Fax 627-2003
www.shickleypublicschool.com
Shickley S 50/PK-12
PO Box 407 68436 402-627-3375
Derek Ippensen, prin. Fax 627-2003

**Sidney, Cheyenne, Pop. 6,700**
Sidney SD 1,200/PK-12
1101 21st Ave 69162 308-254-5855
Jay Ehler, supt. Fax 254-5756
www.sidneyraiders.org
Sidney HS 300/9-12
1101 21st Ave 69162 308-254-5893
Chris Arent, prin. Fax 254-5992
Sidney MS 200/7-8
1101 21st Ave 69162 308-254-5853
Brandon Ross, prin. Fax 254-1130

---

Western Nebraska Community College Post-Sec.
371 College Dr 69162 308-254-5450

**South Sioux City, Dakota, Pop. 13,178**
South Sioux City SD 3,600/K-12
PO Box 158 68776 402-494-2425
Dr. Vernon Fisher, supt. Fax 494-3916
www.ssccardinals.org/
South Sioux City HS 1,100/9-12
3301 G St 68776 402-494-2433
Ed Akins, prin. Fax 494-2464
South Sioux City MS 800/6-8
3625 G St 68776 402-494-3061
Tom McGuire, prin. Fax 494-8427

**Spalding, Greeley, Pop. 485**

---

Spalding Academy 100/K-12
PO Box 310 68665 308-497-2103
Amy McKay, prin. Fax 497-2105

**Spencer, Boyd, Pop. 452**
West Boyd SD 200/K-12
PO Box 109 68777 402-589-1333
Duane Lechtenberg, supt. Fax 589-2041
www.westboyd.com/
West Boyd - Spencer Attendance Center 100/5-12
PO Box 109 68777 402-589-1333
Duane Lechtenberg, prin. Fax 589-1142

**Springfield, Sarpy, Pop. 1,494**
Springfield Platteview Community SD 1,000/PK-12
14801 S 108th St 68059 402-592-1300
Brett Richards, supt. Fax 597-8551
www.springfieldplatteview.org
Platteview Central JHS 200/7-8
14801 S 108th St 68059 402-339-5052
Darin Johnson, prin. Fax 339-3166
Platteview HS 300/9-12
14801 S 108th St 68059 402-339-3606
Angela Simpson, prin. Fax 339-3751

**Springview, Keya Paha, Pop. 242**
Keya Paha County SD 100/K-12
PO Box 219 68778 402-497-3501
Geraldine Erickson, supt. Fax 497-4321
keyapahacountyschools.org/
Keya Paha County HS 50/7-12
PO Box 219 68778 402-497-3501
Lucas Wroblewski, prin. Fax 497-4321

**Stanton, Stanton, Pop. 1,562**
Stanton Community SD 400/K-12
PO Box 749 68779 402-439-2233
Michael J. Sieh Ed.D., supt. Fax 439-2270
www.scs-ne.org/
Stanton MSHS 200/7-12
PO Box 749 68779 402-439-2250
David Cunningham, prin. Fax 439-2270

**Stapleton, Logan, Pop. 305**
Stapleton SD 200/PK-12
PO Box 128 69163 308-636-2252
Clayton Waddle, supt. Fax 636-2618
Stapleton JSHS 100/7-12
PO Box 128 69163 308-636-2252
Clayton Waddle, prin. Fax 636-2618

**Sterling, Johnson, Pop. 476**
Sterling SD 200/K-12
PO Box 39 68443 402-866-4761
Ryan Knippelmeyer, supt. Fax 866-4771
www.sterlingjets.org
Sterling HS 100/9-12
PO Box 39 68443 402-866-4761
Ryun Theobald, prin. Fax 866-4771
Sterling MS 50/6-8
PO Box 39 68443 402-866-4761
Ryun Theobald, prin. Fax 866-4771

**Stromsburg, Polk, Pop. 1,155**
Cross County Community SD 400/PK-12
PO Box 525 68666 402-764-5521
Brent Hollinger, supt. Fax 764-8294
crosscountyschools.com/
Cross County MSHS 200/6-12
PO Box 525 68666 402-764-5521
Bobby Kelley, prin. Fax 764-8294

**Stuart, Holt, Pop. 586**
Stuart SD 200/K-12
PO Box 99 68780 402-924-3302
Robert Hanzlik, supt. Fax 924-3676
stuart.esu8.org/
Stuart JSHS 100/7-12
PO Box 99 68780 402-924-3302
Robert Hanzlik, prin. Fax 924-3676

**Sumner, Dawson, Pop. 234**
Sumner-Eddyville-Miller SD 200/K-12
PO Box 126 68878 308-752-2925
Dr. Cynthia Wendell, supt. Fax 752-2600
www.semmustangs.org
SEM JSHS 100/7-12
PO Box 126 68878 308-752-2925
William Schmidt, supt. Fax 752-2600

**Superior, Nuckolls, Pop. 1,929**
Superior SD 300/K-12
PO Box 288 68978 402-879-3258
Charles Isom, supt. Fax 879-3022
Superior JSHS 200/7-12
PO Box 288 68978 402-879-3257
Robert Cook, prin. Fax 879-3022

**Sutherland, Lincoln, Pop. 1,283**
Sutherland SD 400/PK-12
PO Box 217 69165 308-386-4656
Dan Keyser, supt. Fax 386-2426
www.spssailors.org/
Sutherland JSHS 200/7-12
PO Box 217 69165 308-386-4656
Dustin Mitchell, prin. Fax 386-2426

**Sutton, Clay, Pop. 1,500**
Sutton SD 400/PK-12
PO Box 590 68979 402-773-5569
Dana Wiseman, supt. Fax 773-5578
www.suttonpublicschool.org
Sutton JSHS 200/7-12
PO Box 590 68979 402-773-4303
Brandy Thompson, prin. Fax 773-5578

**Syracuse, Otoe, Pop. 1,933**
Syracuse-Dunbar-Avoca SD 500/PK-12
PO Box P 68446 402-269-2381
Bradley Buller, supt. Fax 269-3028
www.sdarockets.org/
Syracuse HS 200/9-12
PO Box P 68446 402-269-2381
Joy Stilmock, prin. Fax 269-3028
Syracuse MS 100/4-8
PO Box P 68446 402-269-2388
Tim Farley, prin. Fax 269-2402

**Table Rock, Pawnee, Pop. 267**
Humboldt Table Rock Steinauer SD 70
Supt. — See Humboldt
Humboldt Table Rock Steinauer MS 100/4-8
PO Box F 68447 402-839-2085
Kari Cover, prin. Fax 839-2088

**Taylor, Loup, Pop. 190**
Loup County SD 100/K-12
PO Box 170 68879 308-942-6115
Wayne Ruppert, supt. Fax 942-6248
blog.loupcounty.k12.ne.us/school/
Loup County JSHS 100/7-12
PO Box 170 68879 308-942-6115
Ken Sheets, prin. Fax 942-6248

**Tecumseh, Johnson, Pop. 1,665**
Johnson County Central SD 500/PK-12
PO Box 338 68450 402-335-3320
Jack Moles, supt. Fax 335-3346
www.jccentral.org
Johnson County Central HS 100/9-12
PO Box 338 68450 402-335-3328
Rick Lester, prin. Fax 335-3346
Other Schools – See Cook

**Tekamah, Burt, Pop. 1,725**
Tekamah-Herman SD 600/PK-12
112 N 13th St 68061 402-374-2157
Brandon Lavaley, supt. Fax 374-2155
www.tekamah.esu2.org/
Tekamah JSHS 200/7-12
112 N 13th St 68061 402-374-2156
Daniel Gross, prin. Fax 374-2155

**Thedford, Thomas, Pop. 188**
Thedford SD 100/PK-12
PO Box 248 69166 308-645-2230
Henry Eggert, supt. Fax 645-2618
thedfordschools.org/thedfordschools.org/Thedford_Home
Thedford HS 100/7-12
PO Box 248 69166 308-645-2614
Jim York, prin. Fax 645-2618

**Tilden, Madison, Pop. 942**
Elkhorn Valley SD 300/PK-12
PO Box 430 68781 402-368-5301
Keith Leckron, supt. Fax 368-5338
www.elkhornvalleyschools.org
Elkhorn Valley JSHS 100/7-12
PO Box 430 68781 402-368-5301
Darin Hahne, prin. Fax 368-5338

**Trenton, Hitchcock, Pop. 557**
Hitchcock County SD 300/PK-12
PO Box 368 69044 308-334-5575
Mike Apple, supt. Fax 334-5381
www.hcfalcons.org/
Hitchcock County HS 100/7-12
PO Box 368 69044 308-334-5575
Mike Apple, prin. Fax 334-5381

**Tryon, McPherson, Pop. 153**
McPherson County SD 100/K-12
PO Box 38 69167 308-587-2262
Lorrie Miller, supt. Fax 587-2571
www.mcstryon.org
McPherson County HS 50/9-12
PO Box 38 69167 308-587-2262
Debra Brownfield, prin. Fax 587-2571

**Utica, Seward, Pop. 859**
Centennial SD 400/PK-12
PO Box 187 68456 402-534-2291
Tim DeWaard, supt. Fax 534-2291
www.centennialbroncos.org
Centennial JSHS 200/7-12
PO Box 187 68456 402-534-2321
Colin Bargen, prin. Fax 534-2291

**Valentine, Cherry, Pop. 2,652**
Valentine SD 600/K-12
431 N Green St 69201 402-376-1780
Jamie Isom, supt. Fax 376-2736
www.valentinecommunityschools.org/
Valentine HS 200/9-12
431 N Green St 69201 402-376-2730
Andy Cronin, prin. Fax 376-2736
Valentine MS 100/6-8
239 N Wood St 69201 402-376-3367
Jeff Sayer, prin. Fax 376-3386

**Valley, Douglas, Pop. 1,851**
Douglas County West Community SD 700/K-12
PO Box 378 68064 402-359-2583
Melissa Poloncic, supt. Fax 359-4371
www.dcwest.org/
Douglas County West HS 200/9-12
PO Box 378 68064 402-359-2121
Jim Knott, prin. Fax 359-2893
Other Schools – See Waterloo

**Verdigre, Knox, Pop. 565**
Nebraska USD 1
Supt. — See Orchard
Verdigre S 50/PK-12
201 S 3rd St 68783 402-668-2275
Chuck Kucera, prin. Fax 668-2276

**Waco, York, Pop. 233**

---

Nebraska Lutheran HS 100/9-12
203 Kendall St 68460 402-728-5236
Mark Otte, prin. Fax 728-5433

**Wahoo, Saunders, Pop. 4,441**
Wahoo SD 900/PK-12
2201 N Locust St 68066 402-443-3051
Galen Boldt, supt. Fax 443-4731
www.wahooschools.org/
Wahoo HS 300/9-12
2201 N Locust St 68066 402-443-4332
Jason Libal, prin. Fax 443-4731
Wahoo MS 200/6-8
2201 N Locust St 68066 402-443-3101
John Harris, prin. Fax 443-4731

---

Bishop Neumann Central HS 300/7-12
202 S Linden St 68066 402-443-4151
Fr. Jeremy Hazuka, prin. Fax 443-5551

**Wakefield, Dixon, Pop. 1,440**
Wakefield SD 400/PK-12
PO Box 330 68784 402-287-2012
Mark Bejot, supt. Fax 287-2014
www.wakefieldschools.org/
Wakefield JSHS 200/7-12
PO Box 330 68784 402-287-2012
Jason Heitz, prin. Fax 287-2014

**Wallace, Lincoln, Pop. 360**
Wallace SD 65 R 200/K-12
151 N Wallace Rd 69169 308-387-4323
Thomas Sandberg, supt. Fax 387-4322
whs.esu16.org
Wallace JSHS 100/7-12
151 N Wallace Rd 69169 308-387-4323
Shari Goodenberger, prin. Fax 387-4322

**Walthill, Thurston, Pop. 761**
Walthill SD 300/K-12
PO Box 3C 68067 402-846-5432
Ed Stansberry, supt. Fax 846-5029
walthweb.esu1.org/
Walthill JSHS 100/7-12
PO Box 3C 68067 402-846-5432
Joseph Ross, prin. Fax 846-5029

**Waterloo, Douglas, Pop. 837**
Douglas County West Community SD
Supt. — See Valley
Douglas County West MS 200/5-8
800 N Front St 68069 402-779-2646
Jeremy Travis, prin. Fax 779-2534

**Wauneta, Chase, Pop. 575**
Wauneta-Palisade SD 100/K-12
PO Box 368 69045 308-394-5700
Randy Geier, supt. Fax 394-5962
www.waunetapalisadeschools.org
Wauneta-Palisade HS 100/9-12
PO Box 368 69045 308-394-5650
Roger Reikofski, prin. Fax 394-5962
Wauneta Palisade MS 50/7-8
PO Box 368 69045 308-394-5650
Roger Reikofski, prin. Fax 394-5962

**Wausa, Knox, Pop. 629**
Wausa SD 200/K-12
PO Box 159 68786 402-586-2255
Robert Marks Ed.D., supt. Fax 586-2406
wausaweb.esu1.org/
Wausa JSHS 100/7-12
PO Box 159 68786 402-586-2255
Bradley Hoesing, prin. Fax 586-2406

**Waverly, Lancaster, Pop. 3,253**
Waverly SD 145 1,800/K-12
PO Box 426 68462 402-786-2321
Dr. Bill Heimann, supt. Fax 786-2799
www.dist145schools.org/
Waverly HS 600/9-12
PO Box 426 68462 402-786-2765
Ryan Ricenbaw, prin. Fax 786-2799
Waverly MS 400/6-8
PO Box 426 68462 402-786-2348
Ross Ricenbaw, prin. Fax 786-2782

**Wayne, Wayne, Pop. 5,585**
Wayne SD 400/K-12
611 W 7th St 68787 402-375-3150
Mark Lenihan, supt. Fax 375-5251
www.wayneschools.org
Wayne JSHS 300/7-12
611 W 7th St 68787 402-375-3150
Mark Hanson, prin. Fax 375-5251

---

Wayne State College Post-Sec.
1111 Main St 68787 402-375-7000

**Weeping Water, Cass, Pop. 1,042**
Weeping Water SD 400/PK-12
PO Box 206 68463 402-267-2445
Dr. Ken Heinz, supt. Fax 267-5217
www.weepingwaterps.org/
Weeping Water HS 200/6-12
PO Box 206 68463 402-267-2445
Gary Wockenfuss, prin. Fax 267-5217

**West Point, Cuming, Pop. 3,356**
West Point SD 600/PK-12
1200 E Washington St 68788 402-372-5860
Gary Cooper, supt. Fax 372-5458
www.wpcadets.org/
West Point-Beemer JSHS 200/7-12
1200 E Washington St 68788 402-372-5546
Daniel Weddle, prin. Fax 372-2252

---

Guardian Angels/Central Catholic HS 200/7-12
419 E Decatur St 68788 402-372-5326
Kate Hagemann, prin. Fax 372-5327

**Wilber, Saline, Pop. 1,843**
Wilber-Clatonia SD 600/PK-12
PO Box 487 68465 402-821-2266
Ray Collins, supt. Fax 821-3013
www.wilber-clatonia.org
Wilber-Clatonia JSHS 300/7-12
PO Box 487 68465 402-821-2508
Mark Fritch, prin. Fax 821-3013

**Wilcox, Kearney, Pop. 354**
Wilcox-Hildreth SD 200/K-12
PO Box 190 68982 308-478-5265
Dan Ingwersen, supt. Fax 478-5260
whfalcons.org
Wilcox-Hildreth HS 100/9-12
PO Box 190 68982 308-478-5265
Justin Patterson, prin. Fax 478-5260
Other Schools – See Hildreth

**Winnebago, Thurston, Pop. 756**
Winnebago SD 500/K-12
PO Box KK 68071 402-878-2224
Dan Fehringer, supt. Fax 878-2472
winnebago.esu1.org/
Winnebago HS 100/7-12
PO Box KK 68071 402-878-2224
Chris Bernard, prin. Fax 878-2472

---

Little Priest Tribal College Post-Sec.
PO Box 270 68071 402-878-2380

**Winside, Wayne, Pop. 419**
Winside SD 200/PK-12
203 Crawford St 68790 402-286-4466
Michael Shoff, supt. Fax 286-4466
www.winsidewildcats.org
Winside JSHS 100/7-12
203 Crawford St 68790 402-286-4465
Sarah Remm, prin. Fax 286-4466

**Wisner, Cuming, Pop. 1,154**
Wisner-Pilger SD 400/K-12
PO Box 580 68791 402-529-3249
Chad Boyer, supt. Fax 529-3477
www.wisnerpilger.org/
Wisner HS 200/9-12
PO Box 580 68791 402-529-3249
Christopher Uttecht, prin. Fax 529-3477
Other Schools – See Pilger

**Wood River, Hall, Pop. 1,319**
Wood River Rural SD 500/K-12
PO Box 518 68883 308-583-2249
James Haley, supt. Fax 583-2395
www.woodriver.k12.ne.us/
Wood River Rural HS 200/9-12
PO Box 518 68883 308-583-2249
Terry Zessin, prin. Fax 583-2395
Wood River Rural MS 100/6-8
PO Box 518 68883 308-583-2249
Terry Zessin, prin. Fax 583-2395

**Wymore, Gage, Pop. 1,431**
Southern SD 1 400/K-12
PO Box 237 68466 402-645-3326
Gene Haddix, supt. Fax 645-8049
www.southernschools.org
Southern JSHS 200/7-12
PO Box 237 68466 402-645-3326
Jeff Murphy, prin. Fax 645-8049

**Wynot, Cedar, Pop. 165**
Wynot SD 100/K-12
PO Box 157 68792 402-357-2121
Jeff Messersmith, supt. Fax 357-2524
www.wynotpublicschools.org
Wynot HS 100/9-12
PO Box 157 68792 402-357-2121
Richard Higgins, prin. Fax 357-2524
Wynot MS 50/5-8
PO Box 157 68792 402-357-2121
Richard Higgins, prin. Fax 357-2524

**York, York, Pop. 7,673**
York SD 1,200/PK-12
1715 N Delaware Ave 68467 402-362-6655
Mike Lucas, supt. Fax 362-6943
www.yorkpublic.org/
York HS 400/9-12
1005 Duke Dr 68467 402-362-6655
Mitch Bartholomew, prin. Fax 362-2994
York MS 300/6-8
1730 N Delaware Ave 68467 402-362-6655
Kenny Loosvelt, prin. Fax 362-6831

---

York College Post-Sec.
1125 E 8th St 68467 402-363-5600

**Yutan, Saunders, Pop. 1,169**
Yutan SD 400/K-12
1200 2nd St 68073 402-625-2243
Kevin Johnson, supt. Fax 625-2812
www.teacherweb.com/NE/YutanPublicSchools/Home/sdhp1.aspx
Yutan JSHS 200/7-12
1200 2nd St 68073 402-625-2241
Timothy McNamara, prin. Fax 625-2812

# NEVADA

## NEVADA DEPARTMENT OF EDUCATION
**700 E Fifth St, Carson City 89701-5096**
**Telephone 775-687-9200**
**Fax 775-687-9101**
**Website http://www.doe.nv.gov/**

Superintendent of Instruction Dale Erquiaga

## NEVADA BOARD OF EDUCATION
**700 E Fifth St, Carson City 89701-5096**

President Stavan Corbett

## PUBLIC, PRIVATE AND CATHOLIC SECONDARY SCHOOLS

**Alamo, Lincoln, Pop. 1,045**
Lincoln County SD
Supt. — See Panaca
Pahranagat Valley JSHS 100/7-12
PO Box 298 89001 775-725-3321
Mike Strong, prin. Fax 725-3334

**Austin, Lander, Pop. 191**
Lander County SD
Supt. — See Battle Mountain
Austin S 50/K-12
PO Box 160 89310 775-964-2467
Michelle Caramella, lead tchr. Fax 964-1206

**Battle Mountain, Lander, Pop. 3,594**
Lander County SD 1,100/PK-12
PO Box 1300 89820 775-635-2886
Jim Squibb, supt. Fax 635-5347
www.lander.k12.nv.us
Battle Mountain HS 400/9-12
PO Box 1330 89820 775-635-5436
Collin Belnap, prin. Fax 635-5459
Lemaire JHS 200/6-8
PO Box 1360 89820 775-635-8114
Dr. Toby Melver, prin. Fax 635-8803
Other Schools – See Austin

**Beatty, Nye, Pop. 983**
Nye County SD
Supt. — See Tonopah
Beatty HS 100/9-12
PO Box 806 89003 775-553-2595
Gary Flood, prin. Fax 553-2887

**Boulder City, Clark, Pop. 14,662**
Clark County SD
Supt. — See Las Vegas
Boulder City HS 700/9-12
1101 5th St 89005 702-799-8200
Amy Wagner, prin. Fax 799-8230
Garrett MS 500/6-8
1200 Avenue G 89005 702-799-8290
Jamey Hood, prin. Fax 799-8252

**Caliente, Lincoln, Pop. 1,102**
Lincoln County SD
Supt. — See Panaca
Bastian HS 100/7-12
PO Box 1088 89008 775-726-3140
Dr. Ken Higbee, prin. Fax 726-3371

**Carlin, Elko, Pop. 2,339**
Elko County SD
Supt. — See Elko
Carlin S 100/K-12
PO Box 730 89822 775-754-6317
Janice Alexander, prin. Fax 754-2175

**Carson City, Carson City, Pop. 54,098**
Carson City SD 7,700/K-12
PO Box 603 89702 775-283-2000
Richard Stokes, supt. Fax 283-2090
www.carsoncityschools.com
Carson HS 2,100/9-12
1111 N Saliman Rd 89701 775-283-1600
Tasha Fuson, prin. Fax 283-1790
Carson MS 1,200/6-8
1140 W King St 89703 775-283-2800
Dan Sadler, prin. Fax 283-2890
Eagle Valley MS 600/6-8
4151 E Fifth St 89701 775-283-2600
Lee Conley, prin. Fax 283-2690
Pioneer HS 200/Alt
202 E Corbett St 89706 775-283-1300
Jason Zona, prin. Fax 283-1390

---

Carson City Beauty Academy Post-Sec.
1851 S Roop St Ste 100 89701 775-885-9853
Sierra Lutheran HS 100/9-12
3601 Romans Rd 89705 775-267-1921
Rev. Juls Clausen, prin. Fax 267-6580
Western Nevada College Post-Sec.
2201 W College Pkwy 89703 775-445-3000

**Dayton, Lyon, Pop. 8,727**
Lyon County SD
Supt. — See Yerington
Dayton HS 700/9-12
335 Dayton Valley Rd 89403 775-246-6240
Steve Henderson, prin. Fax 246-6245
Dayton IS 600/6-8
315 Dayton Valley Rd 89403 775-246-6250
Kevin Kranjcec, prin. Fax 246-6253

**Dyer, Esmeralda, Pop. 249**

---

Deep Springs College Post-Sec.
HC 72 Box 45001 89010 760-872-2000

**Elko, Elko, Pop. 17,970**
Elko County SD 8,600/K-12
PO Box 1012 89803 775-738-5196
Jeff Zander, supt. Fax 738-5857
www.ecsdnv.net
Adobe MS 700/7-8
3375 Jennings Way 89801 775-738-3375
Colby Corbitt, prin. Fax 738-3860
Elko HS 1,300/9-12
987 College Ave 89801 775-738-7281
Tim Wickersham, prin. Fax 738-9616
Adult HS Adult
PO Box 1012 89803 775-753-2233
Jack French, dir. Fax 753-2257
Other Schools – See Carlin, Jackpot, Owyhee, Spring Creek, Wells, West Wendover

---

Great Basin College Post-Sec.
1500 College Pkwy 89801 775-738-8493

**Ely, White Pine, Pop. 4,185**
White Pine County SD 1,400/K-12
1135 Avenue C 89301 775-289-4851
Bob Dolezal, supt. Fax 289-3999
www.whitepine.k12.nv.us
White Pine HS 400/9-12
1800 Bobcat Dr 89301 775-289-4811
Adam Young, prin. Fax 289-1542
White Pine MS 300/6-8
844 Aultman St 89301 775-289-4841
Sharyl Allen, prin. Fax 289-1565
Other Schools – See Lund

**Eureka, Eureka, Pop. 600**
Eureka County SD 200/K-12
PO Box 249 89316 775-237-5373
Dr. Greg Wieman, supt. Fax 237-5014
www.eureka.k12.nv.us
Eureka County JSHS 100/7-12
PO Box 237 89316 775-237-5361
Dan Wold, prin. Fax 237-5113

**Fallon, Churchill, Pop. 8,201**
Churchill County SD 3,600/PK-12
690 S Maine St 89406 775-423-5184
Dr. Sandra Sheldon, supt. Fax 423-0583
www.churchill.k12.nv.us
Churchill County HS 1,300/9-12
1222 S Taylor St 89406 775-423-2181
Kevin Lords, prin. Fax 423-8968
Churchill County MS 600/7-8
650 S Maine St 89406 775-423-7701
Scott Meihack, prin. Fax 423-8010

**Fernley, Lyon, Pop. 18,657**
Lyon County SD
Supt. — See Yerington
Fernley HS 1,000/9-12
1300 US Highway 95A S 89408 775-575-3400
Kent Jones, prin. Fax 575-3406
Silverland MS 500/7-8
1100 Jasmine Ln 89408 775-575-1575
Ryan Cross, prin. Fax 575-1566
Fernley Adult Education Center Adult
1300 US Highway 95A S 89408 775-575-3409
Carol King, coord. Fax 575-3399

**Gabbs, Nye, Pop. 259**
Nye County SD
Supt. — See Tonopah
Gabbs S 50/PK-12
PO Box 147 89409 775-285-2692
David Dispensa, prin. Fax 285-2381

**Gardnerville, Douglas, Pop. 5,526**
Douglas County SD
Supt. — See Minden
Carson Valley MS 800/7-9
1477 US Highway 395 N 89410 775-782-2265
Bob Been, prin. Fax 782-7341
Pau-Wa-Lu MS 600/7-9
701 Long Valley Rd, 775-265-6100
Keith Lewis, prin. Fax 265-1653

**Gerlach, Washoe, Pop. 206**
Washoe County SD
Supt. — See Reno
Gerlach S 50/K-12
555 E Sunset Blvd 89412 775-557-2326
Rick Taylor, prin. Fax 557-2587

**Hawthorne, Mineral, Pop. 3,168**
Mineral County SD 300/PK-12
PO Box 1540 89415 775-945-2403
Chris Schultz, supt. Fax 945-3709
www.mineral.k12.nv.us
Hawthorne JHS 100/7-8
PO Box 938 89415 775-945-3332
Michael Domagala, prin. Fax 945-3371
Mineral County HS 100/9-12
PO Box 938 89415 775-945-3332
Michael Domagala, prin. Fax 945-3371

**Henderson, Clark, Pop. 247,241**
Clark County SD
Supt. — See Las Vegas
Basic Academy of International Studies 2,400/9-12
400 Palo Verde Dr 89015 702-799-8000
David Bechtel, prin. Fax 799-8966
Brown JHS 800/6-8
307 Cannes St 89015 702-799-8900
Wendy Phelps, prin. Fax 799-3511
Burkholder MS 800/6-8
355 W Van Wagenen St 89015 702-799-8080
Jessie Phee, prin. Fax 799-8088
College of Southern Nevada HS-South 100/11-12
700 College Dr, 702-651-3080
Barbara Collins, prin. Fax 651-3075
Coronado HS 3,000/9-12
1001 Coronado Center Dr 89052 702-799-6800
Mike Piccininni, prin. Fax 799-6839
Foothill HS 2,600/9-12
800 College Dr, 702-799-3500
Joseph Caruso, prin. Fax 799-3524

Greenspun JHS 1,300/6-8
140 N Valle Verde Dr 89074 702-799-0920
Jacqueline Carducci, prin. Fax 799-0925
Green Valley HS 2,800/9-12
460 N Arroyo Grande Blvd 89014 702-799-0950
Kent Roberts, prin. Fax 799-0717
Liberty HS 2,100/9-12
3700 Liberty Heights Ave 89052 702-799-2270
Derek Bellow, prin. Fax 799-6858
Mannion MS 1,800/6-8
155 E Paradise Hills Dr, 702-799-3020
David Erbach, prin. Fax 799-3501
Miller MS 1,700/6-8
2400 Cozy Hill Cir 89052 702-799-2260
Nicole Lehman-Donadio, prin. Fax 799-1309
Webb MS 1,800/6-8
2200 Reunion Ave 89052 702-799-1305
Paula Naegle, prin. Fax 799-1310
White MS 1,400/6-8
1661 Galleria Dr 89014 702-799-0777
Andrea Katona, prin. Fax 799-7690

Calvary Chapel Green Vlly Christian Acad 100/K-12
2615 W Horizon Ridge Pkwy 89052 702-456-2422
DeVry University Post-Sec.
2490 Paseo Verde Pkwy #150 89074 702-933-9700
Euphoria Inst of Beauty Arts & Sciences Post-Sec.
11041 S Eastern Ave Ste 112 89052 702-932-8111
Everest College Post-Sec.
170 N Stephanie St 89074 702-567-1920
Green Valley Christian S 600/PK-12
711 N Valle Verde Ct 89014 702-454-4056
Deborah Ingalls, prin. Fax 454-6275
Henderson International S 400/PK-12
1165 Sandy Ridge Ave 89052 702-818-2100
ITT Technical Institute Post-Sec.
168 N Gibson Rd 89014 702-558-5404
Lake Mead Christian Academy 600/PK-12
540 E Lake Mead Pkwy 89015 702-565-5831
Gayle Blakeley, admin. Fax 566-6206
Nevada State College Post-Sec.
1125 Nevada State Dr, 702-992-2000
Roseman University of Health Sciences Post-Sec.
11 Sunset Way 89014 702-990-4433
Sanford-Brown College Post-Sec.
2495 Village View Dr 89074 702-990-0150
The Art Institute of Las Vegas Post-Sec.
2350 Corporate Cir 89074 702-369-9944

**Incline Village, Washoe, Pop. 8,627**
Washoe County SD
Supt. — See Reno
Incline HS 300/9-12
499 Village Blvd 89451 775-832-4260
Leslie Hermann, prin. Fax 832-4208
Incline MS 200/6-8
931 Southwood Blvd 89451 775-832-4220
Leslie Hermann, prin. Fax 832-4210

Sierra Nevada College-Lake Tahoe Post-Sec.
999 Tahoe Blvd 89451 775-831-1314

**Indian Springs, Clark, Pop. 947**
Clark County SD
Supt. — See Las Vegas
Indian Springs S 100/K-12
PO Box 1088 89018 702-799-0932
Brian Wiseman, prin. Fax 879-3142

**Jackpot, Elko, Pop. 1,175**
Elko County SD
Supt. — See Elko
Jackpot S 100/K-12
PO Box 463 89825 775-755-2374
Brian Messmer, prin. Fax 755-2291

**Las Vegas, Clark, Pop. 562,567**
Clark County SD 304,900/PK-12
5100 W Sahara Ave 89146 702-799-5000
Pat Skorkowsky, supt. Fax 799-5125
www.ccsd.net/
Advanced Technologies Academy 1,100/9-12
2501 Vegas Dr 89106 702-799-7870
Deborah Kral, prin. Fax 799-0656
Arbor View HS 2,700/9-12
7500 Whispering Sands Dr 89131 702-799-6660
Kevin McPartlin, prin. Fax 799-6669
Bailey MS 1,300/6-8
2500 N Hollywood Blvd 89156 702-799-4811
Gregory Cole, prin. Fax 799-4807
Becker MS 1,400/6-8
9151 Pinewood Hills Dr 89134 702-799-4460
Amy Smith, prin. Fax 799-4470
Biltmore Continuation S 200/Alt
801 Veterans Memorial Dr 89101 702-799-7880
Michael Englert, prin. Fax 799-7889
Bonanza HS 2,000/9-12
6665 Del Rey Ave 89146 702-799-4000
Neddy Alvarez, prin. Fax 799-4078
Brinley MS 900/6-8
2480 Maverick St 89108 702-799-4550
Fax 799-4549
Burk Horizon/Southwest Sunset HS 200/Alt
4560 W Harmon Ave 89103 702-799-8150
Gina Piccolo, prin. Fax 799-1207
Cadwallader MS 1,500/6-8
7775 Elkhorn Rd 89131 702-799-6692
Mindi Martinez, prin. Fax 799-4536
Canarelli MS 1,800/6-8
7808 S Torrey Pines Dr 89139 702-799-1340
Monica Lang, prin. Fax 799-5715
Cannon JHS 900/6-8
5850 Euclid St 89120 702-799-5600
Warren McKay, prin. Fax 799-5644
Cashman MS 1,500/6-8
4622 W Desert Inn Rd 89102 702-799-5880
Misti Taton, prin. Fax 799-5947
Centennial HS 3,000/9-12
10200 Centennial Pkwy 89149 702-799-3440
Trent Day, prin. Fax 799-3443
Chaparral HS 2,300/9-12
3850 Annie Oakley Dr 89121 702-799-7580
Lolo James, prin. Fax 799-0776
Cimarron-Memorial HS 2,500/9-12
2301 N Tenaya Way 89128 702-799-4400
Lori Sarabyn, prin. Fax 799-4425
Clark HS 2,900/9-12
4291 Pennwood Ave 89102 702-799-5800
Jillyn Pendleton, prin. Fax 799-5813
College of Southern Nevada HS-West 200/11-12
6375 W Charleston Blvd 89146 702-651-5030
Barbara Collins, prin. Fax 651-5035
Cortney JHS 1,200/6-8
5301 E Hacienda Ave 89122 702-799-2400
David Rose, prin. Fax 799-2407
Cowan Behavior JSHS 100/Alt
5300 E Russell Rd 89122 702-799-6380
Belinda Marentic, prin. Fax 799-6388
Cowan Sunset Southeast High School 100/Alt
5300 E Russell Rd 89122 702-799-6370
Anita Williams, prin. Fax 799-6377
Del Sol HS 2,000/9-12
3100 E Patrick Ln 89120 702-799-6830
Gregory Misel, prin. Fax 799-2235
Desert Oasis HS 2,100/9-12
6600 W Erie Ave 89141 702-799-6881
Arthur Adams, prin. Fax 799-6888
Desert Pines HS 2,200/9-12
3800 Harris Ave 89110 702-799-2196
Isaac Stein, prin. Fax 799-2198
Durango HS 2,200/9-12
7100 W Dewey Dr 89113 702-799-5850
Nathan Miller, prin. Fax 799-5855
East Career & Technical Academy Vo/Tech
6705 Vegas Valley Dr 89142 702-799-8888
Glenda Goetting, prin. Fax 799-8899
Eldorado HS 1,700/9-12
1139 Linn Ln 89110 702-799-7200
David Wilson, prin. Fax 799-7255
Escobedo MS 1,200/6-8
9501 Echelon Point Dr 89149 702-799-4560
Stefanie Machin, prin. Fax 799-4568
Faiss MS 1,300/6-8
9525 W Maule Ave 89148 702-799-6850
Joseph Petrie, prin. Fax 799-6852
Fertitta MS 1,400/6-8
9905 W Mesa Vista Ave 89148 702-799-1900
Lisa Burkhead, prin. Fax 799-5688
Fremont Professional Development MS 900/6-8
1100 E Saint Louis Ave 89104 702-799-5558
Ann Schiller, prin. Fax 799-5566
Garside JHS 1,100/6-8
300 S Torrey Pines Dr 89107 702-799-4245
Scarlett Perryman, prin. Fax 799-4296
Gibson MS 1,100/6-8
3900 W Washington Ave 89107 702-799-4700
Jennifer Messinger, prin. Fax 799-4705
Global Community HS 200/Alt
3801 E Washington Ave 89110 702-799-8850
Gerald Bustamante, prin. Fax 799-8898
Guinn MS 800/6-8
4150 S Torrey Pines Dr 89103 702-799-5900
Georgia Taton, prin. Fax 799-5905
Harney MS 1,800/6-8
1580 S Hollywood Blvd 89142 702-799-3240
Susan Echols, prin. Fax 799-3286
Hyde Park MS 1,700/6-8
900 Hinson St 89107 702-799-4260
Anna Belknap, prin. Fax 799-0348
Johnson JHS 1,200/6-8
7701 Ducharme Ave 89145 702-799-4480
George Anas, prin. Fax 799-4497
Keller MS 1,200/6-8
301 N Fogg St 89110 702-799-3220
Karen Smallwood, prin. Fax 799-3226
Knudson MS 1,300/6-8
2400 Atlantic St 89104 702-799-7470
Monica Cortez, prin. Fax 799-0157
Las Vegas Academy of the Arts 1,700/9-12
315 S 7th St 89101 702-799-7800
Scott Walker, prin. Fax 799-7807
Las Vegas HS 2,900/9-12
6500 E Sahara Ave 89142 702-799-0180
Debbie Brockett, prin. Fax 799-0192
Lawrence JHS 1,400/6-8
4410 S Juliano Rd 89147 702-799-2540
Bevelyn Smothers, prin. Fax 799-2563
Leavitt MS 1,500/6-8
4701 Quadrel St 89129 702-799-4699
Keith Wipperman, prin. Fax 799-4528
Lied MS 1,300/6-8
5350 W Tropical Pkwy 89130 702-799-4620
Kelly O'Rourke, prin. Fax 799-4626
Mack MS 1,300/6-8
4250 Karen Ave 89121 702-799-2005
Roxanne Kelley, prin. Fax 799-2412
Martin MS 1,400/6-8
200 N 28th St 89101 702-799-7922
Mary Hafner, prin. Fax 799-7959
Molasky JHS 1,400/6-8
7801 W Gilmore Ave 89129 702-799-3400
Daron Heilman, prin. Fax 799-3407
Monaco MS 1,200/6-8
1870 N Lamont St 89115 702-799-3670
Lisa Medina, prin. Fax 799-3202
Morris Behavior JSHS 100/Alt
3801 E Washington Ave 89110 702-855-7820
Gerald Bustamante, prin. Fax 855-7879
Morris Sunset E HS 100/Alt
3801 E Washington Ave 89110 702-799-8880
Stacey White, prin. Fax 799-8898
Northwest Career & Technical Academy 1,900/9-12
8200 W Tropical Pkwy 89149 702-799-4640
Fax 799-4644
O'Callaghan MS 1,500/6-8
1450 Radwick Dr 89110 702-799-7340
Scott Fligor, prin. Fax 799-8870
Orr MS 900/6-8
1562 E Katie Ave 89119 702-799-5573
George Leavens, prin. Fax 799-0297
Palo Verde HS 2,700/9-12
333 S Pavilion Center Dr 89144 702-799-1450
Darren Sweikert, prin. Fax 799-1455
Peterson Behavior JSHS 100/Alt
10250 Centennial Pkwy 89149 702-799-6610
Michael Sharapan, prin. Fax 799-6604
Rancho HS 2,900/9-12
1900 Searles Ave 89101 702-799-7000
James Kuzma, prin. Fax 799-8316
Robison MS 1,100/6-8
825 Marion Dr 89110 702-799-7300
Elena Baker, prin. Fax 799-7302
Rogich MS 1,700/6-8
235 N Pavilion Center Dr 89144 702-799-6040
Susan Harrison, prin. Fax 799-6094
Saville MS 1,500/6-8
8101 N Torrey Pines Dr 89131 702-799-3460
Sean Davis, prin. Fax 799-4511
Sawyer MS 1,300/6-8
5450 Redwood St 89118 702-799-5980
Joy Lea, prin. Fax 799-5969
Schofield MS 1,300/6-8
8625 Spencer St 89123 702-799-2290
Terri Knepp, prin. Fax 799-5717
Shadow Ridge HS 2,300/9-12
5050 Brent Ln 89131 702-799-6699
Travis Warnick, prin. Fax 799-4698
Sierra Vista HS 2,100/9-12
8100 W Robindale Rd 89113 702-799-6820
John Anzalone, prin. Fax 799-6847
Silverado HS 2,300/9-12
1650 Silver Hawk Ave 89123 702-799-5790
Robert Mars, prin. Fax 799-5744
Silvestri JHS 1,600/6-8
1055 E Silverado Ranch Blvd, 702-799-2240
Merry Sillitoe, prin. Fax 799-2247
South Continuation HS 100/Alt
1905 Atlantic St 89104 702-799-2070
Thomas Gerbracht, prin. Fax 799-2089
Southeast Career Tech Academy Vo/Tech
5710 Mountain Vista St 89120 702-799-7500
Kerry Pope, prin. Fax 799-2007
Southwest Behavior JSHS 100/Alt
6480 Fairbanks Rd 89103 702-799-5904
Caryl Suzuki, prin. Fax 799-1294
Southwest Career & Tech Academy Vo/Tech
7050 W Shelbourne Ave 89113 702-799-5766
Donna Levy, prin. Fax 799-5751
Spring Mountain JSHS 100/Alt
PO Box 252 89125 702-455-5555
Daniel Triana, prin. Fax 382-6035
Spring Valley HS 2,100/9-12
3750 S Buffalo Dr 89147 702-799-2580
Tam Larnerd, prin. Fax 799-1288
Sunrise Mountain HS 2,500/9-12
2575 Los Feliz St 89156 702-799-7207
Fax 799-7212
Tarkanian MS 1,300/6-8
5800 W Pyle Ave 89141 702-799-6801
Eric Johnson, prin. Fax 799-6805

Valley HS 2,900/9-12
2839 Burnham Ave, 702-799-5450
Ramona Esparza, prin. Fax 799-1074
Veterans Tribute Career Technical Acad 700/9-12
2531 Vegas Dr 89106 702-799-4710
Tammy Bofelli, prin. Fax 799-4722
Von Tobel MS 1,200/6-8
2436 N Pecos Rd 89115 702-799-7280
Jaime Ditto, prin. Fax 799-7286
West Career & Technical Academy 1,000/9-12
11945 W Charleston Blvd 89135 702-799-4340
Amy Dockter-Rozar, prin. Fax 799-4355
Western HS 2,100/9-12
4601 W Bonanza Rd 89107 702-799-4080
RoAnn Triana, prin. Fax 799-4104
West Prep S 1,300/K-12
2050 Saphire Stone Ave 89106 702-799-3120
Danny Eichelberger, prin. Fax 799-1858
Woodbury MS 900/6-8
3875 E Harmon Ave 89121 702-799-7660
Greg Snelling, prin. Fax 799-0805
Other Schools – See Boulder City, Henderson, Indian Springs, Laughlin, Mesquite, North Las Vegas, Overton, Sandy Valley

---

Academy of Hair Design Post-Sec.
5191 W Charleston Blvd #150 89146 702-878-1185
Adelson Educational Campus 500/PK-12
9700 Hillpointe Rd 89134 702-255-4500
Paul Schiffman, head sch Fax 255-7232
American Heritage Academy 100/PK-12
6126 S Sandhill Rd 89120 702-949-5614
American Institute of Medical Sonography Post-Sec.
5450 W Sahara Ave Ste 320 89146 702-369-4216
Anthem Institute Post-Sec.
2320 S Rancho Dr 89102 702-385-6700
Associated Pathologist Laboratories Post-Sec.
4230 Burnham Ave 89119 702-733-7866
Bishop Gorman HS 1,300/9-12
5959 S Hualapai Way 89148 702-732-1945
Kevin Kiefer, prin. Fax 732-2856
Calvary Chapel Christian S 600/PK-12
7175 W Oquendo Rd 89113 702-248-8879
Rick Martin Ed.D., supt. Fax 220-8694
Carrington College Post-Sec.
5740 S Eastern Ave Ste 140 89119 702-514-3236
College of Southern Nevada Post-Sec.
6375 W Charleston Blvd 89146 702-651-5000
Desert Torah Academy 200/PK-12
1312 Vista Dr 89102 702-259-1000
Euphoria Inst of Beauty Arts & Sciences Post-Sec.
6578 N Decatur Blvd Ste 200 89131 702-360-8111
Euphoria Inst of Beauty Arts & Sciences Post-Sec.
9340 W Sahara Ave Ste 205 89117 702-341-8111
Faith Lutheran MSHS 1,400/6-12
2015 S Hualapai Way 89117 702-804-4400
Dr. Steven Buuck Ph.D., admin. Fax 804-4488
Institute of Professional Careers Post-Sec.
4472 S Eastern Ave 89119 702-734-9900
Kaplan College Post-Sec.
3535 W Sahara Ave 89102 702-368-2338
Le Cordon Bleu College of Culinary Arts Post-Sec.
1451 Center Crossing Rd 89144 702-365-7690
Liberty Baptist Academy 200/K-12
6501 W Lake Mead Blvd 89108 702-647-4522
John Shorer, admin. Fax 647-8083
Marinello School of Beauty Post-Sec.
5001 E Bonanza Rd Ste 110 89110 702-796-6200
Meadows S 900/PK-12
8601 Scholar Ln 89128 702-254-1610
Jeremy Gregersen, head sch Fax 254-2452
Montessori Visions Academy 100/PK-12
3551 E Sunset Rd 89120 702-451-9801
Lori Bossy M.Ed., dir. Fax 451-0049
Mountain View Christian S 500/PK-12
3900 E Bonanza Rd 89110 702-452-1300
Dr. Crystal McClanahan, supt. Fax 452-0499
Northwest Career College Post-Sec.
7398 Smoke Ranch Rd 89128 702-254-7577
Pima Medical Institute Post-Sec.
3333 E Flamingo Rd 89121 702-458-9650
Southern Nevada Univ of Cosmetology Post-Sec.
3315 E Russell Rd Ste A4 89120 702-458-6333
Spring Valley Christian Academy 50/K-12
7570 Peace Way 89147 702-873-3216
Trinity International S 100/6-12
4141 Meadows Ln 89107 702-732-3957
Maria Cochrane, admin. Fax 784-0192
University of Nevada Las Vegas Post-Sec.
4505 S Maryland Pkwy 89154 702-895-3011
Word of Life Christian Academy 300/PK-12
3520 N Buffalo Dr 89129 702-645-1180
Rev. Kelly Marchello, prin. Fax 396-0293

**Laughlin, Clark, Pop. 7,092**
Clark County SD
Supt. — See Las Vegas
Laughlin MSHS 400/6-12
1900 Cougar Dr 89029 702-298-1996
Dawn Estes, prin. Fax 298-5493

**Lovelock, Pershing, Pop. 1,824**
Pershing County SD 700/K-12
PO Box 389 89419 775-273-7819
Russell Fecht, supt. Fax 273-2668
www.pershing.k12.nv.us
Pershing County HS 200/9-12
PO Box 990 89419 775-273-2625
Thomas R. Brooks, prin. Fax 273-2163
Pershing County MS 200/6-8
PO Box 1020 89419 775-273-1200
Cindy Plummer, prin. Fax 273-3191

**Lund, White Pine, Pop. 277**
White Pine County SD
Supt. — See Ely
Lund JSHS 50/7-12
PO Box 129 89317 775-238-5200
Alan Hedges, prin. Fax 238-0208

**Mc Dermitt, Humboldt, Pop. 172**
Humboldt County SD
Supt. — See Winnemucca
Mc Dermitt JSHS 50/7-12
PO Box 98 89421 775-532-8761
Doc Welter, prin. Fax 532-8017

**Mesquite, Clark, Pop. 15,069**
Clark County SD
Supt. — See Las Vegas
Hughes MS 600/6-8
550 Hafen Ln 89027 702-346-3250
Maurice Perkins, prin. Fax 346-3095
Virgin Valley HS 700/9-12
820 Valley View Dr 89027 702-346-2780
Clifford Hughes, prin. Fax 346-7265

**Minden, Douglas, Pop. 2,948**
Douglas County SD 6,100/K-12
1638 Mono Ave 89423 775-782-5134
Lisa Noonan Ed.D., supt. Fax 782-3162
www.dcsd.k12.nv.us
ASPIRE Academy Alt
1680 Bently Pkwy S 89423 775-392-1475
Michelle Trujillo, prin.
Douglas HS 1,300/10-12
1670 State Route 88 89423 775-782-5136
Marty Swisher, prin. Fax 782-7039
Other Schools – See Gardnerville, Zephyr Cove

**North Las Vegas, Clark, Pop. 207,375**
Clark County SD
Supt. — See Las Vegas
Bridger MS 1,400/6-8
2505 N Bruce St 89030 702-799-7185
Deanna Jaskolski, prin. Fax 799-7074
Canyon Springs HS 2,600/9-12
350 E Alexander Rd 89032 702-799-1870
Ronnie Guerzon, prin. Fax 799-1876
Cheyenne HS 2,200/9-12
3200 W Alexander Rd 89032 702-799-4830
Zachary Robbins, prin. Fax 799-4856
College of Southern Nevada HS-East 100/11-12
3200 E Cheyenne Ave 89030 702-651-4070
Barbara Collins, prin. Fax 651-4627
Cram MS 1,500/6-8
1900 W Deer Springs Way 89084 702-799-7020
Gary Bugash, prin. Fax 799-8346
Findlay MS 1,500/6-8
333 W Tropical Pkwy 89031 702-799-3160
Brenda Caszatt, prin. Fax 799-3169
Jeffrey Behavior JSHS 100/Alt
602 W Brooks Ave 89030 702-799-8375
Fax 799-8369
Johnston MS 1,400/6-8
5855 Lawrence St, 702-799-7001
Demetrius Johnson, prin. Fax 799-7010
Legacy HS 2,900/9-12
150 W Deer Springs Way 89084 702-799-1777
Kenneth Sobaszek, prin. Fax 799-1701
Mojave HS 2,000/9-12
5302 Goldfield St 89031 702-799-0432
Antonio Rael, prin. Fax 799-0437
Sedway MS 1,400/6-8
3465 Engelstad St 89032 702-799-3880
Chareece Sheppard, prin. Fax 799-1785
Smith MS 900/6-8
1301 E Tonopah Ave 89030 702-799-7080
Brett Booth, prin. Fax 799-7195
Swainston MS 1,200/6-8
3500 W Gilmore Ave 89032 702-799-4860
Lori Desiderato, prin. Fax 799-4806
Desert Rose Adult HS Adult
444 W Brooks Ave 89030 702-799-6240
Sandra Ransel, prin. Fax 799-0397

---

American Institute of Trucking Post-Sec.
4020 E Lone Mountain Rd, 702-508-9659
ITT Technical Institute Post-Sec.
3825 W Cheyenne Ave Ste 600 89032 702-240-0967
University Baptist Academy 100/K-12
3770 W Washburn Rd 89031 702-732-3385

**Overton, Clark**
Clark County SD
Supt. — See Las Vegas
Lyon MS 400/6-8
179 S Andersen St 89040 702-397-8610
K. Paul, prin. Fax 397-2754
Moapa Valley HS 500/9-12
PO Box 278 89040 702-397-2611
Roderick Adams, prin. Fax 397-2892

**Owyhee, Elko, Pop. 941**
Elko County SD
Supt. — See Elko
Owyhee S 100/K-12
PO Box 100 89832 775-757-3400
Steve Cook, prin. Fax 757-3663

**Pahrump, Nye, Pop. 35,299**
Nye County SD
Supt. — See Tonopah
Clarke MS 1,000/6-8
4201 N Blagg Rd 89060 775-727-5546
Tim Wombaker, prin. Fax 727-7104
Pahrump Valley HS 1,300/9-12
501 E Calvada Blvd 89048 775-727-7737
Chris Brockman, prin. Fax 727-7722
Pathways Innovative Education 100/Alt
484 West St 89048 775-751-6822
Karen Hills, prin. Fax 751-6829

**Panaca, Lincoln, Pop. 955**
Lincoln County SD 900/K-12
PO Box 118 89042 775-728-4471
Steve Hansen, supt. Fax 728-4435
lcsdnv.com
Lincoln County HS 200/9-12
PO Box 268 89042 775-728-4481
Marty Soderborg, prin. Fax 728-4484
Meadow Valley MS 100/7-8
PO Box 567 89042 775-728-4655
Cody Christensen, prin. Fax 728-4302
Other Schools – See Alamo, Caliente

**Reno, Washoe, Pop. 217,361**
State Supported Schools
Supt. — None
Davidson Academy of Nevada 100/5-12
PO Box 9119 89507 775-682-5800
Colleen Harsin, dir. Fax 682-5801

Washoe County SD 63,200/PK-12
PO Box 30425 89520 775-348-0200
Traci Davis, supt. Fax 348-0304
www.washoeschools.net
Academy of Arts Careers and Technology Vo/Tech
380 Edison Way 89502 775-327-3920
Robert Sullivan, prin. Fax 861-4415
Billinghurst MS 700/7-8
6685 Chesterfield Ln 89523 775-746-5870
Sheri-Lyn Cutler, prin. Fax 746-5875
Clayton Pre-AP Academy 600/7-8
1295 Wyoming Ave 89503 775-746-5860
Bruce Meissner, prin. Fax 746-5864
Cold Springs MS 800/5-8
18235 Cody Ct, 775-677-5433
Roberta Duval, prin. Fax 677-5439
Damonte Ranch HS 1,400/9-12
10500 Rio Wrangler Pkwy, 775-851-5656
Denise Hausauer, prin. Fax 851-5663
Depoali MS 1,200/6-8
9300 Wilbur May Pkwy, 775-852-6700
Juliana Annand, prin. Fax 852-6701
Galena HS 1,400/9-12
3600 Butch Cassidy Dr 89511 775-851-5630
Tom Brown, prin. Fax 851-5607
Hare Occupational Center Vo/Tech
350 Hunter Lake Dr 89509 775-857-4947
Hug HS 1,400/9-12
2880 Sutro St 89512 775-333-5300
Lauren Ford-Baxter, prin. Fax 333-5312
McQueen HS 1,800/9-12
6055 Lancer St 89523 775-746-5880
Sue Denning, prin. Fax 747-6883
North Valleys HS 2,200/9-12
1470 E Golden Valley Rd 89506 775-677-5499
Jeana Curtis, prin. Fax 677-5497
O'Brien STEM Academy 700/7-8
10500 Stead Blvd 89506 775-677-5420
Mary Basso, prin. Fax 677-5423
Pine MS 800/7-8
4800 Neil Rd 89502 775-689-2550
Brad Boudreau, prin. Fax 689-2539
Reno HS 1,600/9-12
395 Booth St 89509 775-333-5050
Kris Hackbusch, prin. Fax 333-5058
Swope MS 700/7-8
901 Keele Dr 89509 775-333-5330
George Brown, prin. Fax 333-5083
Traner MS 500/7-8
1700 Carville Dr 89512 775-333-5130
Chad Lindeen, prin. Fax 333-5135
Truckee Meadows Community College HS 200/11-12
7000 Dandini Blvd 89512 775-674-7660
Susan Mayes-Smith, admin. Fax 674-7931

Vaughn MS 500/7-8
1200 Bresson Ave 89502 775-333-5160
Dr. Ginny Knowles, prin. Fax 333-5118
Washoe Innovations HS 700/Alt
777 W 2nd St 89503 775-333-5150
Taylor Harper, prin. Fax 333-5122
Washoe Inspire Academy 100/Alt
1155 Corporate Blvd 89502 775-857-3181
Josh Rosenbloom, admin. Fax 857-3182
Wooster HS 1,700/9-12
1331 E Plumb Ln 89502 775-333-5100
Leah Keuscher, prin. Fax 333-5108
Washoe Adult HS Adult
1301 Cordone Ave 89502 775-337-9939
Fax 333-5324
Other Schools – See Gerlach, Incline Village, Sparks

---

Bishop Manogue HS 600/9-12
110 Bishop Manogue Dr 89511 775-336-6000
Rick Harris, prin. Fax 336-6015
Carrington College Post-Sec.
5580 Kietzke Ln 89511 775-335-1714
Church Academy 50/1-12
1205 N McCarran Blvd 89512 775-329-5848
Dan Moriarty, admin. Fax 329-3360
Morrison University Post-Sec.
10315 Professional Cir #201, 888-852-7272
Sage Ridge S 200/5-12
2515 Crossbow Ct 89511 775-852-6222
Norman Colb, head sch Fax 852-6228
Sierra Nevada HS 600/9-12
14175 Mount Charleston St 89506 775-789-0951
Truckee Meadows Community College Post-Sec.
7000 Dandini Blvd 89512 775-673-7000
University of Nevada Reno Post-Sec.
1664 N Virginia St 89557 775-784-1110

**Round Mountain, Nye**
Nye County SD
Supt. — See Tonopah
Round Mountain JSHS 100/6-12
PO Box 1427 89045 775-377-2690
James Fitch, prin. Fax 377-1239

**Sandy Valley, Clark, Pop. 1,978**
Clark County SD
Supt. — See Las Vegas
Sandy Valley S 100/K-12
HC 31 Box 111 89019 702-799-0935
Christopher Lounsbery, prin. Fax 723-1802

**Silver Springs, Lyon, Pop. 5,112**
Lyon County SD
Supt. — See Yerington
Silver Stage HS 300/9-12
3755 W Spruce Ave 89429 775-577-5071
Patrick Peters, prin. Fax 577-5079

**Smith, Lyon, Pop. 1,033**
Lyon County SD
Supt. — See Yerington
Smith Valley S 200/K-12
20 Day Ln 89430 775-465-2332
Kathy Bomba-Edgerton, prin. Fax 465-2681

**Sparks, Washoe, Pop. 87,304**
Washoe County SD
Supt. — See Reno
Dilworth MS 600/7-8
255 Prater Way 89431 775-353-5740
Laura Peterson, prin. Fax 353-5584
Mendive MS 1,000/7-8
1900 Whitewood Dr 89434 775-353-5990
Brandon Bringhurst, prin. Fax 353-5994
Reed HS 2,000/9-12
1350 Baring Blvd 89434 775-353-5700
Mary Vesco, prin. Fax 353-5708
Shaw MS 1,200/7-8
600 Eagle Canyon Dr, 775-425-7777
Gina Leonhard, prin. Fax 425-7779
Spanish Springs HS 2,400/9-12
1065 Eagle Canyon Dr, 775-425-7733
Tammy Hart, prin. Fax 425-7735
Sparks HS 1,200/9-12
820 15th St 89431 775-353-5550
Kevin Carroll, prin. Fax 353-5514
Sparks MS 600/7-8
2275 18th St 89431 775-353-5770
Stacey Ting-Senini, prin. Fax 353-5585

---

Career College of Northern Nevada Post-Sec.
1421 Pullman Dr 89434 775-856-2266
Excel Christian S 100/PK-12
850 Baring Blvd 89434 775-356-9995
Lisa Cross, admin. Fax 356-9527
Milan Institute Post-Sec.
950 Industrial Way 89431 775-348-7200

**Spring Creek, Elko, Pop. 12,111**
Elko County SD
Supt. — See Elko
Spring Creek HS 900/9-12
14550 Lamoille Hwy 89815 775-753-5575
Keith Walz, prin. Fax 753-5956
Spring Creek MS 700/6-8
14650 Lamoille Hwy 89815 775-777-1688
Tim Giere, prin. Fax 777-1738

**Tonopah, Nye, Pop. 2,418**
Nye County SD 5,200/PK-12
PO Box 113 89049 775-482-6258
Dale Norton, supt. Fax 482-8573
www.nye.k12.nv.us
Tonopah HS 200/9-12
PO Box 1349 89049 775-482-3698
Alvin Eiseman, prin. Fax 482-3635
Other Schools – See Beatty, Gabbs, Pahrump, Round Mountain

**Virginia City, Storey, Pop. 832**
Storey County SD 400/PK-12
PO Box C 89440 775-847-0983
Dr. Robert Slaby, supt. Fax 847-0989
www.storey.k12.nv.us
Virginia City HS 100/9-12
PO Box C 89440 775-847-0992
Richard Schrank, prin. Fax 847-0994
Virginia City MS 100/6-8
PO Box C 89440 775-847-0980
Todd Hess, prin. Fax 847-0913

**Wells, Elko, Pop. 1,257**
Elko County SD
Supt. — See Elko
Wells S 100/K-12
PO Box 338 89835 775-752-3837
Chris McAnany, prin. Fax 752-2470

**West Wendover, Elko, Pop. 4,333**
Elko County SD
Supt. — See Elko
West Wendover JSHS 300/7-12
PO Box 3830 89883 775-664-3940
Craig Kyllonen, prin. Fax 664-3944

**Winnemucca, Humboldt, Pop. 7,277**
Humboldt County SD 3,400/K-12
310 E 4th St 89445 775-623-8100
Dr. David Jensen, supt. Fax 623-8102
www.humboldt.k12.nv.us
Leighton Hall Alt
310 E 4th St 89445 775-623-6382
Ray Parks, prin. Fax 623-6386
Lowry HS 1,000/9-12
5375 Kluncy Canyon Rd 89445 775-623-8130
Ray Parks, prin. Fax 623-8185
Winnemucca JHS 500/7-8
451 Reinhart St 89445 775-623-8120
Janet Kennedy, prin. Fax 623-8208
Other Schools – See Mc Dermitt

**Yerington, Lyon, Pop. 2,993**
Lyon County SD 7,300/PK-12
25 E Goldfield Ave 89447 775-463-6800
Wayne Workman, supt. Fax 463-6808
www.lyoncsd.org
Yerington HS 400/9-12
114 Pearl St 89447 775-463-6822
Duane Mattice, prin. Fax 463-6828
Yerington IS 400/5-8
215 Pearl St 89447 775-463-6833
Sean Moyle, prin. Fax 463-6840
Other Schools – See Dayton, Fernley, Silver Springs, Smith

**Zephyr Cove, Douglas, Pop. 557**
Douglas County SD
Supt. — See Minden
Whittell HS 200/7-12
PO Box 677 89448 775-588-2446
Crespin Esquivel, prin. Fax 588-2443

# NEW HAMPSHIRE

## NEW HAMPSHIRE DEPT. OF EDUCATION
**101 Pleasant St, Concord 03301-3852**
**Telephone 603-271-3494**
**Fax 603-271-1953**
**Website http://www.education.nh.gov/**

Commissioner of Education Virginia Barry

## NEW HAMPSHIRE BOARD OF EDUCATION
**101 Pleasant St, Concord 03301-3852**

Chairperson Tom Raffio

### SCHOOL ADMINISTRATIVE UNITS (SAU)

SAU 1
Brendan Minnihan, supt. 603-924-3336
106 Hancock Rd Fax 924-6707
Peterborough 03458
www.conval.edu/

SAU 2
Mary Ellen Ormond, supt. 603-279-7947
103 Main St Ste 2, Meredith 03253 Fax 279-3044
www.sau2.k12.nh.us/

SAU 3
Corinne Cascadden, supt. 603-752-6500
183 Hillside Ave, Berlin 03570 Fax 752-2528
www.sau3.org/

SAU 4
Stacy Buckley, supt. 603-744-5555
20 N Main St, Bristol 03222 Fax 744-6659
www.sau4.org

SAU 5
Dr. James Morse, supt. 603-868-5100
36 Coe Dr, Durham 03824 Fax 868-6668
www.orcsd.org

SAU 6
Dr. Middleton McGoodwin Ed.D., supt. 603-543-4200
165 Broad St, Claremont 03743 Fax 543-4244
www.sau6.org

SAU 7
Robert Mills, supt. 603-237-5571
21 Academy St, Colebrook 03576 Fax 237-5126
www.sau7.org

SAU 8
Terri Forsten, supt. 603-225-0811
38 Liberty St, Concord 03301 Fax 226-2187
www.concordnhschools.net

SAU 9
Kevin Richard, supt. 603-447-8368
176A Main St, Conway 03818 Fax 447-8497
www.sau9.org

SAU 10
Dr. Laura Nelson, supt. 603-432-1210
18 S Main St, Derry 03038 Fax 432-1264
www.sau10.org

SAU 11
Dr. Elaine Arbour, supt. 603-516-6800
61 Locust St Ste 409, Dover 03820 Fax 516-6809
www.dover.k12.nh.us

SAU 12
Dr. Nathan Greenberg, supt. 603-432-6920
268C Mammoth Rd Fax 425-1049
Londonderry 03053
www.londonderry.org

SAU 13
Louis Goscinski, supt. 603-323-5088
881A Tamworth Rd Fax 323-5093
Tamworth 03886
sau13.weebly.com

SAU 14
Valerie McKenney, supt. 603-679-5402
213 Main St, Epping 03042 Fax 679-1237
www.sau14.org

SAU 15
Dr. Charles Littlefield, supt. 603-622-3731
90 Farmer Rd, Hooksett 03106 Fax 669-4352
www.sau15.net

SAU 16
Michael Morgan, supt. 603-775-8653
30 Linden St, Exeter 03833 Fax 775-8673
www.sau16.org/

SAU 17
Dr. Brian Blake, supt. 603-642-3688
178 Main St, Kingston 03848 Fax 642-7885
web.sau17.org

SAU 18
Daniel LeGallo, supt. 603-934-3108
119 Central St, Franklin 03235 Fax 934-3462
www.franklin.k12.nh.us

SAU 19
Brian Balke, supt. 603-497-4818
11 School St, Goffstown 03045 Fax 497-8425
www.goffstown.k12.nh.us

SAU 20
Paul Bousquet, supt. 603-466-3632
123 Main St, Gorham 03581 Fax 466-3870
www.sau20.org/

SAU 21
Robert Sullivan Ed.D., supt. 603-926-8992
2 Alumni Dr, Hampton 03842 Fax 926-5157
www.sau21.org/sau

SAU 23
Laurie Melanson, supt. 603-787-2113
2975 Dartmouth College Hwy Fax 787-2118
North Haverhill 03774
www.sau23.org

SAU 24
Dr. Lorraine Tacconi-Moore, supt. 603-428-3269
258 Western Ave, Henniker 03242 Fax 428-6545
www.sau24.org

SAU 25
Eric McGee, supt. 603-472-3755
103 County Rd, Bedford 03110 Fax 472-2567
www.sau25.net/

SAU 26
Marjorie Chiafery, supt. 603-424-6200
36 McElwain St, Merrimack 03054 Fax 424-6229
www.merrimack.k12.nh.us

SAU 27
James O'Neill, supt. 603-578-3570
1 Highlander Ct, Litchfield 03052 Fax 578-1267
www.litchfieldsd.org

SAU 28
Dr. Amanda Lecaroz, supt. 603-635-1145
59A Marsh Rd, Pelham 03076 Fax 635-1283
www.pelhamsd.org

SAU 29
Robert Malay, supt. 603-357-9002
193 Maple Ave, Keene 03431 Fax 357-9012
www.sau29.org

SAU 30
Terri Forsten, supt. 603-524-5710
PO Box 309, Laconia 03247 Fax 528-8442
www2.laconiaschools.org/sau/

SAU 31
Dr. Michael Martin, supt. 603-659-5020
186A Main St, Newmarket 03857 Fax 659-5022
www.newmarket.k12.nh.us

SAU 32
Frank Perotti, supt. 603-469-3442
92 Bonner Rd, Meriden 03770 Fax 469-3985
www.plainfieldschool.org

SAU 33
Ellen Small, supt. 603-895-4299
43 Harriman Hill Rd Fax 895-0147
Raymond 03077
www.sau33.com

SAU 34
Dr. Robert Hassett, supt. 603-464-4466
PO Box 2190, Deering 03244 Fax 464-4053
www.hdsd.org

SAU 35
Pierre Couture, supt. 603-444-3925
260 Cottage St Ste C Fax 444-6299
Littleton 03561
www.sau35.k12.nh.us

SAU 36
Marion Anastasia, supt. 603-837-9363
14 King Sq, Whitefield 03598 Fax 837-2326
www.sau36.org

SAU 37
Dr. Debra Livingston, supt. 603-624-6300
195 McGregor St Ste 201 Fax 624-6337
Manchester 03102
www.mansd.org

SAU 39
Peter Warburton, supt. 603-673-2690
PO Box 849, Amherst 03031 Fax 672-1786
www.sau39.org

SAU 40
Robert Marquis, supt. 603-673-2202
100 West St, Milford 03055 Fax 673-2237
milfordk12.org

SAU 41
Andrew Corey, supt. 603-324-5999
4 Lund Ln, Hollis 03049 Fax 465-3933
www.sau41.org

SAU 42
Mark Conrad, supt. 603-966-1000
PO Box 687, Nashua 03061 Fax 594-4350
www.nashua.edu

SAU 43
Cindy Gallagher, supt. 603-863-3540
9 Depot St Ste 2, Newport 03773 Fax 863-5368
www.sau43.org

SAU 44
Robert Gadomski, supt. 603-942-1290
23 Mountain Ave Unit A Fax 942-1295
Northwood 03261
www.sau44.org

SAU 45
Susan Noyes M.Ed., supt. 603-476-5247
PO Box 419 Fax 476-8009
Moultonborough 03254
sau45.org

SAU 46
Mark MacLean, supt. 603-753-6561
105 Community Dr Fax 753-6023
Penacook 03303
sau46.mvsd.k12.nh.us

SAU 47
Reuben Duncan, supt. 603-532-8100
81 Fitzgerald Dr Unit 2 Fax 532-8165
Jaffrey 03452
www.sau47.org

SAU 48
Mark Halloran, supt. 603-536-1254
47 Old Ward Bridge Rd Fax 536-3545
Plymouth 03264
sau48.org

SAU 49
Kathleen Cuddy-Egbert, supt. 603-569-1658
PO Box 190, Wolfeboro Falls 03896 Fax 569-6983
www.govwentworth.k12.nh.us

SAU 50
Salvatore Petralia, supt. 603-422-9572
48 Post Rd, Greenland 03840 Fax 422-9575
www.sau50.org

SAU 51
Dr. John Freeman, supt. 603-435-5526
23 Oneida St Unit 1 Fax 435-5331
Pittsfield 03263
pittsfield-nh.com/sau/district-2/district

SAU 52
Stephen Zadravec, supt. 603-431-5080
1 Junkins Ave Unit 402 Fax 431-6753
Portsmouth 03801
www.cityofportsmouth.com/school/

SAU 53
Patty Sherman, supt. 603-485-5188
267 Pembroke St, Pembroke 03275 Fax 485-9529
www.sau53.org

SAU 54
Michael Hopkins, supt. 603-332-3678
150 Wakefield St Ste 8 Fax 335-7367
Rochester 03867
www.rochesterschools.com

SAU 55
Dr. Earl Metzler, supt. 603-382-6119
30 Greenough Rd, Plaistow 03865 Fax 382-3334
www.timberlane.net/sau/

SAU 56
Jeni Mosca, supt. 603-692-4450
51 W High St, Somersworth 03878 Fax 692-9100
www.sau56.org

SAU 57
Michael Delahanty, supt. 603-893-7040
38 Geremonty Dr, Salem 03079 Fax 893-7080
www.sau57.org

SAU 58
Dr. Carl Ladd, supt. 603-636-1437
15 Preble St, Groveton 03582 Fax 636-6102
www.sau58.org

SAU 59
Dr. Tammy Davis, supt. 603-286-4116
433 W Main St, Northfield 03276 Fax 286-7402
www.winnisquam.k12.nh.us/Sau/index.htm

SAU 60
Lorraine Landry, supt. 603-826-7756
159 East St, Charlestown 03603 Fax 826-4430
www.sau60.org

SAU 61
Steve Welford, supt. 603-755-2627
60 Charles St, Farmington 03835 Fax 755-9334
www.sau61.org

SAU 62
Patrick Andrew, supt. 603-632-5563
PO Box 789, Enfield 03748 Fax 632-4181
www.mascoma.k12.nh.us
SAU 63
Christine Tyrie, supt. 603-654-8088
PO Box 1149, Wilton 03086 Fax 654-6691
www.sau63.org
SAU 64
Michael Tursi, supt. 603-652-0262
18 Commerce Way, Milton 03851 Fax 652-0250
www.sau64.org
SAU 65
Winfried Feneberg, supt. 603-526-2051
114 Cougar Ct, New London 03257 Fax 526-2145
www.kearsarge.org
SAU 66
Steven Chamberlin, supt. 603-746-5186
204 Maple St, Contoocook 03229 Fax 746-5714
www.hopkintonschools.org
SAU 67
Dr. Dean Cascadden, supt. 603-224-4728
32 White Rock Hill Rd, Bow 03304 Fax 224-4111
www.bownet.org
SAU 68
Judith McGann, supt. 603-745-2051
PO Box 846, Lincoln 03251 Fax 745-2352
www.lin-wood.org
SAU 70
Franklyn Bass, supt. 603-643-6050
41 Lebanon St Ste 2 Fax 643-3073
Hanover 03755
www.sau70.org/
SAU 71
Dr. Michele Munson, supt. 603-863-2420
29 School Rd, Lempster 03605 Fax 863-2451
www.sau71.org
SAU 72
Dr. Maureen Ward, supt. 603-875-7890
252 Suncook Valley Rd Fax 875-0391
Alton 03809
www.alton.k12.nh.us
SAU 73
Kent Hemingway, supt. 603-527-9215
2 Belknap Mountain Rd Fax 527-9216
Gilford 03249
www.sau73.org/
SAU 74
Gail Kushner, supt. 603-664-2715
77 Ramsdell Ln, Barrington 03825 Fax 664-2609
www.sau74.org

SAU 75
Jacqueline Guillette, supt. 603-863-9689
300 Route 10 S, Grantham 03753 Fax 863-9684
www.gvshawks.org/sau-75
SAU 76
Dr. Michael Harris, supt. 603-795-4431
PO Box 117, Lyme 03768 Fax 795-9407
www.lymeschool.org
SAU 77
Dr. Jean Richards, admin. 603-638-2800
PO Box 130, Monroe 03771 Fax 638-2031
www.monroeschool77.com
SAU 78
Brenda Needham, supt. 603-353-2170
10 School Dr, Orford 03777 Fax 353-2189
www.rivendellschool.org
SAU 79
John Fauci, supt. 603-267-9097
9 Currier Hill Rd, Gilmanton 03237 Fax 267-9498
www.gilmanton.k12.nh.us
SAU 80
Maria Dreyer, supt. 603-267-9223
58 School St, Belmont 03220 Fax 267-9225
www.sau80.org
SAU 81
Bryan Lane, supt. 603-886-1235
20 Library St, Hudson 03051 Fax 886-1236
www.sau81.org
SAU 82
Dr. Darrell Lockwood, supt. 603-887-3621
22 Murphy Dr, Chester 03036 Fax 887-4961
www.chesteracademy.org/
SAU 83
Betsey Cox-Buteau, supt. 603-895-6903
5 Hall Rd Unit 1, Fremont 03044 Fax 895-6905
www.sau83.org
SAU 84
David Bickford, supt. 603-444-5215
65 Maple St, Littleton 03561 Fax 444-3015
www.littletonschools.org/
SAU 85
Russell Holden, supt. 603-763-4627
70 Lower Main St, Sunapee 03782 Fax 763-4718
www.sunapeeschools.org
SAU 86
John Fauci, supt., PO Box 250 603-435-1510
Center Barnstead 03225 Fax 435-1511
www.barnstead.k12.nh.us
SAU 87
Ruthann Goguen, supt. 603-721-0160
16 School St, Greenville 03048 Fax 721-0175
www.sau.mascenic.org

SAU 88
Joanne Roberts, supt. 603-790-8500
20 Seminary Hl Fax 790-8310
West Lebanon 03784
www.sau88.net
SAU 89
James McCormick, supt. 603-878-2962
13 Darling Hill Rd, Mason 03048 Fax 878-3439
mason.sau89.org
SAU 90
Kathleen Murphy, supt. 603-926-4560
6 Marston Way, Hampton 03842 Fax 926-5070
www.sau90.org/
SAU 91
Kenneth Dassau, supt. 603-209-3315
1 Village Rd, Surry 03431
SAU 92
Patricia Bassett, supt. 603-336-5728
PO Box 27, Hinsdale 03451 Fax 336-5731
www.hnhsd.org
SAU 93
Lisa Witte, supt. 603-352-6955
600 Old Homestead Hwy Fax 358-6708
Swanzey 03446
www.mrsd.org
SAU 94
James Lewis, supt. 603-239-8061
PO Box 46, Winchester 03470 Fax 239-7593
www.wnhsd.org
SAU 95
Winfried Feneberg, supt. 603-425-1976
19 Haverhill Rd, Windham 03087 Fax 425-1719
www.sau95.org
SAU 96
Kenneth Dassau, supt. 603-209-3315
PO Box 111, Sullivan 03445
SAU 97
Kathleen Vizard, supt. 603-356-5535
91 Samuel Hale Dr Fax 356-5535
Hales Location 03860
SAU 98
Jennifer Fish, supt. 603-246-3321
136 County Farm Rd Fax 246-8117
West Stewartstown 03597
SAU 201
David Smith, hdmstr. 603-942-5531
907 1st NH Tpke Fax 942-7537
Northwood 03261
www.coebrown.org
SAU 202
Griffin Morse, hdmstr. 603-437-5200
5 Pinkerton St, Derry 03038 Fax 432-5328
www.pinkertonacademy.net
SAU 301
Robert Cullison, supt. 603-875-8600
242 Suncook Valley Rd Fax 875-8200
Alton 03809
www.pmhschool.com

## PUBLIC, PRIVATE AND CATHOLIC SECONDARY SCHOOLS

**Allenstown, Merrimack**
Allenstown SD
Supt. — See Pembroke
Dupont MS 100/5-8
10 1/2 School St 03275 603-485-4474
Mark Dangora, prin. Fax 485-1806

**Alstead, Cheshire**
Fall Mountain Regional SD
Supt. — See Charlestown
Vilas MS 100/5-8
82 Mechanic St 03602 603-835-6351
Gail Rowe, prin. Fax 835-2052

**Alton, Belknap, Pop. 499**
Prospect Mountain SD 500/9-12
242 Suncook Valley Rd 03809 603-875-3800
Robert L. Cullison M.Ed., supt. Fax 875-8200
www.pmhschool.com
Prospect Mountain HS 500/9-12
242 Suncook Valley Rd 03809 603-875-3800
James Fitzpatrick, prin. Fax 875-8200

**Amherst, Hillsborough, Pop. 612**
Amherst SD 1,500/K-8
PO Box 849 03031 603-673-2690
Peter Warburton, supt. Fax 672-1786
www.sau39.org
Amherst MS 800/5-8
PO Box 966 03031 603-673-8944
Porter Dodge, prin. Fax 673-6774

Souhegan Cooperative SD 900/9-12
PO Box 849 03031 603-673-2690
Peter Warburton, supt. Fax 672-1786
www.sau39.org
Souhegan Cooperative HS 900/9-12
PO Box 1152 03031 603-673-9940
Rob Scully, prin. Fax 673-0318

**Andover, Merrimack**

---

Proctor Academy 400/9-12
PO Box 500 03216 603-735-6000
Michael Henriques, head sch Fax 735-5129

**Antrim, Hillsborough, Pop. 1,376**
Contoocook Valley SD
Supt. — See Peterborough
Great Brook MS 300/5-8
16 School St 03440 603-588-6630
James Elder, prin. Fax 588-3207

**Barrington, Strafford**
Barrington SD 900/PK-8
77 Ramsdell Ln 03825 603-664-2715
Gail Kushner, supt. Fax 664-2609
www.sau74.org
Barrington MS 400/5-8
51 Haley Dr 03825 603-664-2127
Terrence Leatherman, prin. Fax 664-5739

**Bedford, Hillsborough**
Bedford SD 4,400/PK-12
103 County Rd 03110 603-472-3755
Eric McGee, supt. Fax 472-2567
www.sau25.net/
Bedford HS 1,300/9-12
47 Nashua Rd Unit B 03110 603-310-9000
William Hagen, prin. Fax 472-3024
Lurgio MS 700/7-8
47 Nashua Rd Unit A 03110 603-310-9100
Edward Joyce, prin. Fax 472-5090

---

Michael's School of Hair Design Post-Sec.
79 S River Rd Ste 6 03110 603-668-4300

**Belmont, Belknap, Pop. 1,272**
Shaker Regional SD 1,400/PK-12
58 School St 03220 603-267-9223
Maria Dreyer, supt. Fax 267-9225
www.sau80.org
Belmont HS 500/9-12
255 Seavey Rd 03220 603-267-6525
Dan Clary, prin. Fax 267-5962
Belmont MS 400/5-8
38 School St 03220 603-267-9220
Aaron Pope, prin. Fax 267-9228

**Berlin, Coos, Pop. 9,890**
Berlin SD 1,200/K-12
183 Hillside Ave 03570 603-752-6500
Corinne Cascadden, supt. Fax 752-2528
www.sau3.org/
Berlin HS 400/9-12
550 Willard St 03570 603-752-4122
Kevin Carpenter, prin. Fax 752-8566
Berlin MS 200/6-8
200 State St 03570 603-752-5311
Daniel Record, prin. Fax 752-8580
Berlin Regional Vocational Center Vo/Tech
550 Willard St 03570 603-752-4122
Roland Pinette, coord. Fax 752-8566

---

White Mountains Community College Post-Sec.
2020 Riverside Dr 03570 603-752-1113

**Bethlehem, Grafton, Pop. 962**
Profile SD
Supt. — See Littleton
Profile HS 200/9-12
691 Profile Rd 03574 603-823-7411
Kyle Jacobs, prin. Fax 823-7490
Profile JHS 100/7-8
691 Profile Rd 03574 603-823-7411
Kyle Jacobs, prin. Fax 823-7490

---

White Mountain S 100/9-12
371 W Farm Rd 03574 603-444-2928
Dr. Timothy Breen Ph.D., head sch Fax 444-1258

**Bow, Merrimack**
Bow SD 1,400/PK-12
55 Falcon Way 03304 603-224-4728
Dr. Dean Cascadden, supt. Fax 224-4111
www.bownet.org
Bow HS 500/9-12
55 Falcon Way 03304 603-228-2210
Dr. John House-Myers, prin. Fax 228-2212
Bow Memorial S 500/5-8
20 Bow Center Rd 03304 603-225-3212
Adam Osburn, prin. Fax 228-2228

**Bristol, Grafton, Pop. 1,657**
Newfound Area SD 1,300/PK-12
20 N Main St 03222 603-744-5555
Stacy Buckley, supt. Fax 744-6659
www.sau4.org
Newfound Memorial MS 300/6-8
155 N Main St 03222 603-744-8162
Eric Chase, prin. Fax 744-8037
Newfound Regional HS 400/9-12
150 Newfound Rd 03222 603-744-6006
Paul Hoiriis, prin. Fax 744-2526

**Canaan, Grafton, Pop. 511**
Mascoma Valley Regional SD
Supt. — See Enfield
Indian River S 400/5-8
45 Royal Rd 03741 603-632-4357
Kevin Towle, prin. Fax 632-4262
Mascoma Valley Regional HS 400/9-12
27 Royal Rd 03741 603-632-4308
James Collins, prin. Fax 632-5419

---

Cardigan Mountain S 200/6-9
62 Alumni Dr 03741 603-523-4321
David McCusker, hdmstr. Fax 523-7227

**Candia, Rockingham**

Remington HS 50/9-12
PO Box 473 03034 603-483-5664
Jeffrey Philbrick, hdmstr. Fax 483-4811

**Charlestown, Sullivan, Pop. 1,173**
Fall Mountain Regional SD 1,700/PK-12
159 East St 03603 603-826-7756
Lorraine Landry, supt. Fax 826-4430
www.sau60.org
Charlestown MS 200/6-8
307 Main St 03603 603-826-7711
Paula Southard-Stevens, prin. Fax 826-3102
Other Schools – See Alstead, Langdon, Walpole

**Claremont, Sullivan, Pop. 13,132**
Claremont SD 1,900/PK-12
165 Broad St 03743 603-543-4200
Dr. Middleton McGoodwin Ed.D., supt. Fax 543-4244
www.sau6.org
Claremont MS 400/6-8
107 South St 03743 603-543-4250
Paulette Fitzgerald, prin. Fax 543-4289
Stevens HS 600/9-12
175 Broad St 03743 603-543-4220
Patricia Barry, prin. Fax 542-2805
Sugar River Valley Regional Technical Ct Vo/Tech
175 Broad St 03743 603-543-4291
Joel Schneid, dir. Fax 543-4296

Claremont Christian Academy 100/K-12
97 Maple Ave 03743 603-542-8759
Mark Pomeroy, dir. Fax 542-8759
River Valley Community College Post-Sec.
1 College Dr 03743 603-542-7744

**Colebrook, Coos, Pop. 1,376**
Colebrook SD 400/PK-12
21 Academy St 03576 603-237-5571
Robert Mills, supt. Fax 237-5126
www.colebrook.sau7.org
Colebrook Academy 100/9-12
13 Academy St 03576 603-237-4280
Mark Fiorentino, prin. Fax 237-5717

Pittsburg SD 100/PK-12
21 Academy St 03576 603-237-5571
Robert Mills, supt. Fax 237-5126
www.sau7.org
Other Schools – See Pittsburg

**Concord, Merrimack, Pop. 41,988**
Concord SD 4,400/PK-12
38 Liberty St 03301 603-225-0811
Terri Forsten, supt. Fax 226-2187
www.concordnhschools.net
Concord HS 1,800/9-12
170 Warren St 03301 603-225-0800
Gene Connolly, prin. Fax 223-2054
Concord Regional Technical Center Vo/Tech
170 Warren St 03301 603-225-0800
Steve Rothenberg, admin. Fax 223-2050
Rundlett MS 1,000/6-8
144 South St 03301 603-225-0862
Thomas Sica, prin. Fax 226-3288

Bishop Brady HS 400/9-12
25 Columbus Ave 03301 603-224-7418
Andrea Elliot, prin. Fax 228-6664
Concord Academy of Hair Design Post-Sec.
20 S Main St 03301 603-224-2211
Concord Christian Academy 200/PK-12
37 Regional Dr 03301 603-228-8888
Dr. David Johnson, hdmstr. Fax 226-9696
Granite State College Post-Sec.
25 Hall St 03301 603-228-3000
NHTI - Concord's Community College Post-Sec.
31 College Dr 03301 603-271-6484
St. Paul's S 500/9-12
325 Pleasant St 03301 603-229-4600
Michael Hirschfeld, head sch Fax 225-0487
Trinity Christian S 200/PK-12
80 Clinton St 03301 603-225-5410
Michael Kingsley, prin. Fax 225-3235
University of New Hampshire Sch of Law Post-Sec.
2 White St 03301 603-228-1541

**Contoocook, Merrimack, Pop. 1,432**
Hopkinton SD 1,000/PK-12
204 Maple St 03229 603-746-5186
Steven Chamberlin, supt. Fax 746-5714
www.hopkintonschools.org
Hopkinton HS 300/9-12
297 Park Ave 03229 603-746-4167
Christopher Kelley, prin. Fax 746-5109
Hopkinton MS 200/7-8
297 Park Ave 03229 603-746-4167
Christopher Kelley, prin. Fax 746-5109

**Conway, Carroll, Pop. 1,799**
Conway SD 1,900/K-12
176A Main St 03818 603-447-8368
Kevin Richard, supt. Fax 447-8497
www.sau9.org
Kennett MS 300/7-8
176 Main St 03818 603-447-6364
Jocelyn Judge, prin. Fax 447-6842
Other Schools – See North Conway

**Deering, Hillsborough**
Hillsboro-Deering Cooperative SD 1,300/PK-12
78 School St 03244 603-464-4466
Dr. Robert Hassett, supt. Fax 464-4053
www.hdsd.org
Other Schools – See Hillsborough

**Derry, Rockingham, Pop. 21,640**
Derry Cooperative SD 3,600/PK-8
18 S Main St 03038 603-432-1210
Dr. Laura Nelson, supt. Fax 432-1264
www.sau10.org
Hood MS 800/6-8
5 Hood Rd 03038 603-432-1224
Austin Garofalo, prin. Fax 432-1227
West Running Brook MS 600/6-8
1 W Running Brook Ln 03038 603-432-1250
Leslie Saucier, prin. Fax 432-1243

Pinkerton Academy 3,100/9-12
5 Pinkerton St 03038 603-437-5200
Griffin Morse, hdmstr. Fax 432-5328
www.pinkertonacademy.org
Pinkerton Academy 3,100/9-12
5 Pinkerton St 03038 603-437-5200
Griffin Morse, hdmstr. Fax 432-5328

**Dover, Strafford, Pop. 29,321**
Dover SD 4,100/PK-12
61 Locust St Ste 409 03820 603-516-6800
Dr. Elaine Arbour, supt. Fax 516-6809
www.dover.k12.nh.us
Dover HS 1,400/9-12
25 Alumni Dr 03820 603-516-6900
Peter Driscoll, prin. Fax 516-6926
Dover MS 1,100/5-8
16 Daley Dr 03820 603-516-7200
Kimberly Lyndes, prin. Fax 516-5747
Dover Regional Career Technical Center Vo/Tech
25 Alumni Dr 03820 603-516-6978
Louise Paradis, dir. Fax 516-6975

Portsmouth Christian Academy 600/PK-12
20 Seaborne Dr 03820 603-742-3617
Dr. John Engstrom, head sch Fax 750-0490
St. Thomas Aquinas HS 600/9-12
197 Dover Point Rd 03820 603-742-3206
Kevin Collins, prin. Fax 749-7822

**Dublin, Cheshire**

Dublin S 100/9-12
PO Box 522 03444 603-563-8584
Bradford Bates, head sch Fax 563-7121

**Durham, Strafford, Pop. 10,187**
Oyster River Cooperative SD 2,000/K-12
36 Coe Dr 03824 603-868-5100
Dr. James Morse Ed.D., supt. Fax 868-6668
www.orcsd.org
Oyster River HS 700/9-12
55 Coe Dr 03824 603-868-2375
Todd Allen, prin. Fax 868-2049
Oyster River MS 600/5-8
1 Coe Dr 03824 603-868-2155
Jay Richard, prin. Fax 868-3469

University of New Hampshire Post-Sec.
105 Main St 03824 603-862-1234

**Enfield, Grafton, Pop. 1,510**
Mascoma Valley Regional SD 1,300/PK-12
PO Box 789 03748 603-632-5563
Patrick Andrew, supt. Fax 632-4181
www.mascoma.k12.nh.us/
Other Schools – See Canaan

**Epping, Rockingham, Pop. 1,654**
Epping SD 1,000/PK-12
213 Main St 03042 603-679-5402
Valerie McKenney, supt. Fax 679-1237
www.sau14.org
Epping HS 300/9-12
21 Academy St 03042 603-679-5472
Kyle Repucci, prin. Fax 679-2966
Epping MS 200/6-8
33 Prescott Rd 03042 603-679-2544
Brian Ernest, prin. Fax 679-5514

**Exeter, Rockingham, Pop. 9,087**
Exeter Region Cooperative SD 3,100/6-12
30 Linden St 03833 603-775-8653
Michael Morgan, supt. Fax 775-8673
www.sau16.org/
Exeter HS 1,700/9-12
1 Blue Hawk Dr 03833 603-775-8400
James Tremblay, prin. Fax 395-2499
Seacoast School of Tech Vo/Tech
40 Linden St 03833 603-775-8461
Margaret Callahan, prin. Fax 775-8983
Other Schools – See Stratham

Phillips Exeter Academy 1,000/9-12
20 Main St 03833 603-772-4311
Lisa MacFarlane, prin. Fax 777-4384

**Farmington, Strafford, Pop. 3,815**
Farmington SD 1,400/PK-12
60 Charles St 03835 603-755-2627
Steve Welford, supt. Fax 755-9334
www.sau61.org
Farmington HS 400/9-12
40 Thayer Dr 03835 603-755-2811
Matthew Jozokos, prin. Fax 755-3252
Wilson Memorial MS 600/4-8
51 School St 03835 603-755-2181
Richard Hartford, prin. Fax 755-9473

**Franklin, Merrimack, Pop. 8,346**
Franklin SD 1,300/PK-12
119 Central St 03235 603-934-3108
Daniel LeGallo, supt. Fax 934-3462
www.sau18.org
Franklin HS 400/9-12
119 Central St 03235 603-934-5441
Richard Towne, prin. Fax 934-7445
Franklin MS 400/5-8
200 Sanborn St 03235 603-934-5828
Kevin Barbour, prin. Fax 934-2432

**Gilford, Belknap**
Gilford SD 1,300/K-12
2 Belknap Mountain Rd 03249 603-527-9215
Kent Hemingway, supt. Fax 527-9216
www.sau73.org/
Gilford HS 500/9-12
88 Alvah Wilson Rd 03249 603-524-7135
Anthony Sperazzo, prin. Fax 524-3867
Gilford MS 300/5-8
72 Alvah Wilson Rd 03249 603-527-2460
Peter Sawyer, prin. Fax 527-2461

**Goffstown, Hillsborough, Pop. 14,621**
Goffstown SD 2,900/PK-12
11 School St 03045 603-497-4818
Brian Balke, supt. Fax 497-8425
www.goffstown.k12.nh.us
Goffstown HS 1,200/9-12
27 Wallace Rd 03045 603-497-4841
Frank McBride, prin. Fax 497-5257
Mountain View MS 900/5-8
41 Lauren Ln 03045 603-497-8288
Wendy Hastings, prin. Fax 497-4987

**Gorham, Coos, Pop. 1,579**
Gorham Randolph Shelburne Cooperative SD 400/K-12
123 Main St 03581 603-466-3632
Paul Bousquet, supt. Fax 466-3870
www.sau20.org/
Gorham HS 200/9-12
120 Main St 03581 603-466-2776
David Backler, prin. Fax 466-3111
Gorham MS 100/6-8
120 Main St 03581 603-466-2776
David Backler, prin. Fax 466-3111

**Greenland, Rockingham**
Rye SD 500/K-8
48 Post Rd 03840 603-422-9572
Salvatore Petralia, supt. Fax 422-9575
www.sau50.org
Other Schools – See Rye

**Greenville, Hillsborough, Pop. 1,101**
Mascenic Regional SD 900/PK-12
16 School St 03048 603-721-0160
Ruthann Goguen, supt. Fax 721-0175
www.sau.mascenic.org
Other Schools – See New Ipswich

**Groveton, Coos, Pop. 1,110**
Northumberland SD 300/K-12
15 Preble St 03582 603-636-1437
Dr. Carl Ladd, supt. Fax 636-6102
www.sau58.org
Groveton HS 200/6-12
65 State St 03582 603-636-1619
Michael Kelley, prin. Fax 636-9752

**Hampstead, Rockingham**
Hampstead SD
Supt. — See Plaistow
Hampstead MS 400/5-8
28 School St 03841 603-329-6743
Maria Di Nola, prin. Fax 329-4120

**Hampton, Rockingham, Pop. 9,556**
Hampton SD 1,200/PK-8
6 Marston Way 03842 603-926-4560
Kathleen Murphy, supt. Fax 926-5070
www.sau90.org
Hampton Academy 400/6-8
29 Academy Ave 03842 603-926-2000
David O'Connor, prin. Fax 926-1855

Seabrook SD 700/PK-8
2 Alumni Dr 03842 603-926-8992
Robert Sullivan Ed.D., supt. Fax 926-5157
www.sau21.org/sau
Other Schools – See Seabrook

Winnacunnet Cooperative SD 1,200/9-12
2 Alumni Dr 03842 603-926-8992
Robert Sullivan Ed.D., supt. Fax 926-5157
www.sau21.org/sau
Winnacunnet HS 1,200/9-12
1 Alumni Dr 03842 603-926-3395
William McGowan, prin. Fax 926-5418

**Hampton Falls, Rockingham**

Heronfield Academy 100/6-8
356 Exeter Rd 03844 603-772-9093
Martha Shepardson-Killam, head sch

**Hanover, Grafton, Pop. 8,321**
Dresden SD 1,200/6-12
41 Lebanon St Ste 2 03755 603-643-6050
Dr. Franklyn Bass, supt. Fax 643-3073
www.sau70.org/
Hanover HS 800/9-12
41 Lebanon St Ste 1 03755 603-643-3431
Justin Campbell, prin. Fax 643-0661
Richmond MS 400/6-8
63 Lyme Rd 03755 603-643-6040
Michael Lepene, prin. Fax 643-0662

Dartmouth College 03755 Post-Sec.
603-646-1110

**Henniker, Merrimack, Pop. 1,723**
John Stark Regional SD 800/9-12
258 Western Ave 03242 603-428-3269
Dr. Lorraine Tacconi-Moore, supt. Fax 428-6545
www.sau24.org
Other Schools – See Weare

Weare SD 1,100/PK-8
258 Western Ave 03242 603-428-3269
Dr. Lorraine Tacconi-Moore, supt. Fax 428-6545
www.sau24.org
Other Schools – See Weare

---

New England College Post-Sec.
98 Bridge St 03242 603-428-2211

**Hillsborough, Hillsborough, Pop. 1,929**
Hillsboro-Deering Cooperative SD
Supt. — See Deering
Hillsboro-Deering HS 400/9-12
12 Hillcat Dr 03244 603-464-1130
James O'Rourke, prin. Fax 464-4028
Hillsboro-Deering MS 300/6-8
6 Hillcat Dr 03244 603-464-1120
Marc Peterson, prin. Fax 464-5759

**Hinsdale, Cheshire, Pop. 1,534**
Hinsdale SD 600/PK-12
PO Box 27 03451 603-336-5728
Patricia Bassett, supt. Fax 336-5731
www.hnhsd.org
Hinsdale HS 200/9-12
49 School St 03451 603-336-5984
Ann Freitag, prin. Fax 336-7497
Hinsdale MS 100/6-8
49 School St 03451 603-336-5984
Ann Freitag, prin. Fax 336-7497

**Holderness, Grafton**

---

Holderness S 300/9-12
33 Chapel Ln 03245 603-536-1257
Phillip Peck, head sch Fax 536-1267

**Hollis, Hillsborough**
Hollis-Brookline Cooperative SD 1,300/7-12
4 Lund Ln 03049 603-324-5999
Andrew Corey, supt. Fax 465-3933
www.sau41.org
Hollis-Brookline HS 900/9-12
24 Cavalier Ct 03049 603-465-2269
Richard Barnes, prin. Fax 465-2485
Hollis-Brookline MS 400/7-8
25 Main St 03049 603-324-5997
Robert Thompson, prin. Fax 465-7523

**Hooksett, Merrimack, Pop. 4,079**
Hooksett SD 1,500/PK-8
90 Farmer Rd 03106 603-622-3731
Dr. Charles Littlefield, supt. Fax 669-4352
www.sau15.net
Cawley MS 500/6-8
89 Whitehall Rd 03106 603-518-5047
Matthew Benson, prin. Fax 518-5086

**Hopkinton, Merrimack**

---

Beech Hill S, 20 Beech Hill Rd 03229 50/6-8
Rick Johnson, head sch 603-715-5129

**Hudson, Hillsborough, Pop. 7,236**
Hudson SD 3,600/PK-12
20 Library St 03051 603-886-1235
Bryan Lane, supt. Fax 886-1236
www.sau81.org
Alvirne HS 1,400/9-12
200 Derry Rd 03051 603-886-1260
Steven Beals, prin. Fax 595-1525
Hudson Memorial MS 1,000/6-8
1 Memorial Dr 03051 603-886-1240
Keith Bowen, prin. Fax 883-1252
Palmer Vocational Tech Center Vo/Tech
200 Derry Rd 03051 603-886-1260
Karen Worthen, dir. Fax 595-1529

---

Continental Academie of Hair Design Post-Sec.
PO Box 370 03051 603-889-1614

**Jaffrey, Cheshire, Pop. 2,700**
Jaffrey-Rindge Cooperative SD 1,600/PK-12
81 Fitzgerald Dr Unit 2 03452 603-532-8100
Reuben Duncan, supt. Fax 532-8165
www.sau47.org
Conant HS 500/9-12
3 Conant Way 03452 603-532-8131
Lawrence Pimental, prin. Fax 532-8102
Jaffrey-Rindge MS 400/6-8
1 Conant Way 03452 603-532-8122
Robert Clark, prin. Fax 532-8124

**Keene, Cheshire, Pop. 23,106**
Keene SD 3,400/PK-12
193 Maple Ave 03431 603-357-9002
Robert Malay, supt. Fax 357-9012
www.sau29.org
Cheshire Career Center Vo/Tech
43 Arch St 03431 603-352-0640
Lisa Danley, prin. Fax 357-9061
Keene HS 1,600/9-12
43 Arch St 03431 603-352-0640
James Logan, prin. Fax 357-1512
Keene MS 600/6-8
167 Maple Ave 03431 603-357-9020
Dorothy Frazier, prin. Fax 357-9045

---

Antioch University New England Post-Sec.
40 Avon St 03431 800-553-8920
Keene Beauty Academy Post-Sec.
800 Park Ave 03431 603-357-3736
Keene State College Post-Sec.
229 Main St 03435 603-352-1909
Monadnock Waldorf S 200/PK-12
98 S Lincoln St 03431 603-357-4442
Tari Steinrueck, dir. Fax 357-2955

**Kingston, Rockingham**
Sanborn Regional SD 1,800/PK-12
17 Danville Rd 03848 603-642-3688
Dr. Brian Blake, supt. Fax 642-7885
sau17.org
Sanborn Regional HS 700/9-12
17 Danville Rd 03848 603-642-3341
Brian Stack, prin. Fax 642-6947
Other Schools – See Newton

**Laconia, Belknap, Pop. 15,741**
Laconia SD 2,000/PK-12
PO Box 309 03247 603-524-5710
Dr. Phil McCormack, supt. Fax 528-8442
www2.laconiaschools.org
Huot Technical Center Vo/Tech
345 Union Ave 03246 603-528-8693
David Warrender, prin. Fax 524-5711
Laconia HS 600/9-12
345 Union Ave 03246 603-524-3350
James McCollum, prin. Fax 528-8683
Laconia MS 500/6-8
150 McGrath St 03246 603-524-4632
Chris Ennis, prin. Fax 528-8675

---

Empire Beauty School Post-Sec.
556 Main St 03246 603-524-8777
Laconia Christian Academy 100/PK-12
1386 Meredith Center Rd 03246 603-524-3250
Rick Duba, head sch Fax 524-3285
Lakes Region Community College Post-Sec.
379 Belmont Rd 03246 603-524-3207

**Langdon, Sullivan**
Fall Mountain Regional SD
Supt. — See Charlestown
Fall Mountain Regional HS 600/9-12
134 Fmrhs Rd 03602 603-835-6318
Thomas Ronning, prin. Fax 835-6254
Fall Mountain Regional Vocational Center Vo/Tech
134 Fmrhs Rd 03602 603-826-7756
Lorraine Landry, prin. Fax 835-6254

**Lebanon, Grafton, Pop. 12,877**
Lebanon SD
Supt. — See West Lebanon
Lebanon HS 700/9-12
195 Hanover St 03766 603-448-2055
Tom Marshall, prin. Fax 448-0605
Lebanon MS 300/5-8
3 Moulton Ave 03766 603-448-3056
Martha Langill, prin. Fax 448-0616

---

Lebanon College Post-Sec.
15 Hanover St 03766 603-448-2445
Upper Valley Teacher Institute Post-Sec.
194 Dartmouth College Hwy 03766 603-678-4888

**Lincoln, Grafton, Pop. 991**
Lincoln-Woodstock Cooperative SD 100/K-12
PO Box 846 03251 603-745-2051
Judith McGann, supt. Fax 745-2351
www.lin-wood.org
Lin-Wood S 100/K-12
72 Linwood Dr 03251 603-745-2214
Robert Nelson, prin. Fax 745-6797

**Lisbon, Grafton, Pop. 967**
Lisbon Regional SD
Supt. — See Littleton
Lisbon Regional S 100/K-12
24 Highland Ave 03585 603-838-5506
Jacqueline Daniels, prin. Fax 838-5012

**Litchfield, Hillsborough**
Litchfield SD 1,500/PK-12
1 Highlander Ct 03052 603-578-3570
James L. O'Neill, supt. Fax 578-1267
www.litchfieldsd.org
Campbell HS 500/9-12
1 Highlander Ct 03052 603-546-0300
Laura Rothhaus, prin. Fax 546-0310
Litchfield MS 500/5-8
19 McElwain Dr 03052 603-424-0566
Thomas Lecklider, prin. Fax 424-1296

**Littleton, Grafton, Pop. 4,350**
Lisbon Regional SD 100/K-12
260 Cottage St Ste C 03561 603-444-3925
Pierre Couture, supt. Fax 444-6299
www.sau35.k12.nh.us
Other Schools – See Lisbon

Littleton SD 800/K-12
65 Maple St 03561 603-444-5215
David Bickford, supt. Fax 444-3015
www.littletonschools.org
Bronson JHS 100/7-8
159 Oak Hill Ave 03561 603-444-5601
Joanne Melanson, prin. Fax 444-3009
Gallen Career & Technical Center Vo/Tech
140 High St 03561 603-444-5186
Alan Smith, dir. Fax 444-0167
Littleton HS 300/9-12
159 Oak Hill Ave 03561 603-444-5601
Joanne Melanson, prin. Fax 444-3009

Profile SD 300/7-12
260 Cottage St Ste C 03561 603-444-3925
Pierre Couture, supt. Fax 444-6299
www.sau35.k12.nh.us
Other Schools – See Bethlehem

**Londonderry, Rockingham, Pop. 10,903**
Londonderry SD 4,800/PK-12
268C Mammoth Rd 03053 603-432-6920
Dr. Nathan Greenberg, supt. Fax 425-1049
www.londonderry.org
Londonderry HS 1,700/9-12
295 Mammoth Rd 03053 603-432-6941
Jason Parent, prin. Fax 425-1022
Londonderry MS 1,200/6-8
313 Mammoth Rd 03053 603-432-6925
Richard Zacchilli, prin. Fax 432-0714

**Manchester, Hillsborough, Pop. 107,082**
Manchester SD 15,500/PK-12
195 McGregor St Ste 201 03102 603-624-6300
Dr. Debra Livingston, supt. Fax 624-6337
www.mansd.org
Hillside MS 900/6-8
112 Reservoir Ave 03104 603-624-6352
Brendan McCafferty, prin. Fax 628-6049
Manchester Central HS 2,200/9-12
207 Lowell St 03104 603-624-6363
John Vaccarezza, prin. Fax 624-6376
Manchester Memorial HS 2,000/9-12
1 Crusader Way 03103 603-624-6378
Arthur Adamakos, prin. Fax 628-6009
Manchester School of Technology Vo/Tech
530 S Porter St 03103 603-624-6490
Karen White, prin. Fax 628-6146
Manchester West HS 1,300/9-12
9 Notre Dame Ave 03102 603-624-6384
Christopher Motika, prin. Fax 628-6153
McLaughlin MS 800/6-8
290 S Mammoth Rd 03109 603-628-6247
William Krantz, prin. Fax 628-6274
Parkside MS 700/6-8
75 Parkside Ave 03102 603-624-6356
Forrest Ransdell, prin. Fax 624-6355
Southside MS 800/6-8
140 S Jewett St 03103 603-624-6359
Jennifer Gillis, prin. Fax 624-6361

---

Derryfield S 400/6-12
2108 River Rd 03104 603-669-4524
Mary Halpin Carter Ph.D., head sch Fax 641-9521
Holy Family Academy 100/7-12
49 Ashland St 03104 603-644-7247
Mark Gillis, head sch Fax 644-1004
Manchester Community College Post-Sec.
1066 Front St 03102 603-206-8000
Mount Washington College Post-Sec.
3 Sundial Ave 03103 603-668-6660
Mount Zion Christian S 100/PK-12
132 Titus Ave 03103 603-606-7930
Robert Carter, hdmstr. Fax 606-7935
New England EMS Institute Post-Sec.
1 Elliot Way 03103 603-628-2220
New Hampshire Institute of Art Post-Sec.
148 Concord St 03104 603-623-0313
St. Anselm College Post-Sec.
100 Saint Anselms Dr 03102 603-641-7000
St. Joseph Regional JHS 100/7-8
148 Belmont St 03103 603-624-4811
Denis Mailloux, prin. Fax 624-6670
Salter School of Nursing & Allied Health Post-Sec.
670 N Commercial St Ste 403 03101 603-622-8400
Southern New Hampshire University Post-Sec.
2500 N River Rd 03106 800-668-1249
Trinity HS 400/9-12
581 Bridge St 03104 603-668-2910
Denis Mailloux, prin. Fax 668-2913
University of New Hampshire Post-Sec.
400 Commercial St 03101 603-641-4321

**Meredith, Belknap, Pop. 1,695**
Inter-Lakes Cooperative SD 1,100/PK-12
103 Main St Ste 2 03253 603-279-7947
Mary Ellen Ormond, supt. Fax 279-3044
www.interlakes.org/
Inter-Lakes HS 400/9-12
1 Laker Ln 03253 603-279-6162
Patricia Kennelly, prin. Fax 279-5302
Inter-Lakes MS 300/5-8
1 Laker Ln 03253 603-279-5312
Everett Bennett, prin. Fax 279-5310

**Meriden, Sullivan**

---

Kimball Union Academy 300/9-12
PO Box 188 03770 603-469-2000
Michael Schafer, hdmstr. Fax 469-2033

**Merrimack, Hillsborough, Pop. 22,156**
Merrimack SD 4,100/PK-12
36 McElwain St 03054 603-424-6200
Marjorie Chiafery, supt. Fax 424-6229
www.merrimack.k12.nh.us
Merrimack HS 1,400/9-12
38 McElwain St 03054 603-424-6204
Kenneth Johnson, prin. Fax 424-6230
Merrimack MS 600/7-8
31 Madeline Bennett Ln 03054 603-424-6289
Adam Caragher, prin. Fax 423-1109

---

South Merrimack Christian Academy 300/PK-12
517 Boston Post Rd 03054 603-880-6832
Brian Burbach, hdmstr. Fax 598-7085
Thomas More College of Liberal Arts Post-Sec.
6 Manchester St 03054 603-880-8308

**Milford, Hillsborough, Pop. 8,681**
Milford SD 2,700/PK-12
100 West St 03055 603-673-2202
Robert Marquis, supt. Fax 673-2237
milfordk12.org
Milford Applied Technology Center Vo/Tech
100 West St 03055 603-673-4201
Don Jalbert, dir. Fax 673-4202
Milford HS 900/9-12
100 West St 03055 603-673-4201
Bradford Craven Ph.D., prin. Fax 673-4201

Milford MS 600/6-8
33 Osgood Rd 03055 603-673-5221
Anthony DeMarco, prin. Fax 673-5221

**Milton, Strafford, Pop. 560**
Milton SD 600/K-12
18 Commerce Way 03851 603-652-0262
Michael Tursi, supt. Fax 652-0250
www.sau64.org
Nute HS 200/9-12
22 Elm St 03851 603-652-4591
Scott Currier, prin. Fax 652-9926
Nute JHS 100/6-8
22 Elm St 03851 603-652-4591
Scott Currier, prin. Fax 652-9926

**Moultonborough, Carroll**
Moultonborough SD 600/PK-12
PO Box 419 03254 603-476-5247
Susan Noyes, supt. Fax 476-8009
sau45.org
Moultonborough Academy 100/7-8
PO Box 228 03254 603-476-5517
Andrew Coppinger, prin. Fax 476-5153
Moultonborough Academy 200/9-12
PO Box 228 03254 603-476-5517
Andrew Coppinger, prin. Fax 476-5153

**Nashua, Hillsborough, Pop. 84,540**
Nashua SD 11,900/PK-12
PO Box 687 03061 603-966-1000
Mark Conrad, supt. Fax 594-4350
www.nashua.edu
Elm Street MS 1,100/6-8
117 Elm St 03060 603-594-4322
Michael Fredereickson, prin. Fax 594-4370
Fairgrounds MS 700/6-8
27 Cleveland St 03060 603-594-4393
Sharon Coffey, prin. Fax 594-4355
Nashua HS North 1,800/9-12
8 Titan Way 03063 603-589-6400
Marianne Busteed, prin. Fax 589-6449
Nashua HS South 2,000/9-12
36 Riverside Dr 03062 603-589-4311
Keith Richard, prin. Fax 589-8722
Pennichuck MS 700/6-8
207 Manchester St 03064 603-594-4308
Lynne Joseph, prin. Fax 594-4413

---

Bishop Guertin HS 900/9-12
194 Lund Rd 03060 603-889-4107
Jason Strinste, prin. Fax 889-0701
Daniel Webster College Post-Sec.
20 University Dr 03063 800-325-6876
Nashua Catholic Regional JHS 200/7-8
6 Bartlett Ave 03064 603-883-6707
Glenda McFadden, prin. Fax 594-8955
Nashua Christian Academy 200/PK-12
55 Franklin St 03064 603-889-8892
Christine Urban, hdmstr. Fax 821-7451
Nashua Community College Post-Sec.
505 Amherst St 03063 603-882-6923
Rivier University Post-Sec.
420 S Main St 03060 603-888-1311
St. Joseph School of Nursing Post-Sec.
5 Woodward Ave 03060 603-594-2567

**New Hampton, Belknap, Pop. 350**

---

New Hampton S 300/9-12
70 Main St 03256 603-677-3400
Andrew Menke, head sch Fax 677-3482

**New Ipswich, Hillsborough**
Mascenic Regional SD
Supt. — See Greenville
Boynton MS 400/5-8
500 Turnpike Rd 03071 603-878-4800
John MacArthur, prin. Fax 878-0525
Mascenic Regional HS 400/9-12
175 Turnpike Rd 03071 603-878-1113
Tom Marshall, prin. Fax 878-3344

**New London, Merrimack, Pop. 1,397**
Kearsarge Regional SD 1,900/PK-12
114 Cougar Ct 03257 603-526-2051
Winfried Feneberg, supt.
www.kearsarge.org
Other Schools – See North Sutton

---

Colby-Sawyer College Post-Sec.
541 Main St 03257 603-526-3000

**Newmarket, Rockingham, Pop. 5,181**
Newmarket SD 800/PK-12
186A Main St 03857 603-659-5020
Dr. Michael Martin, supt. Fax 659-5022
www.newmarket.k12.nh.us
Newmarket JSHS 300/6-12
213 S Main St 03857 603-659-3271
Christopher Andriski, prin. Fax 659-5304

**Newport, Sullivan, Pop. 4,688**
Newport SD 1,000/PK-12
247 N Main St 03773 603-865-9701
Dr. Cynthia Gallagher, supt. Fax 865-9707
www.sau43.org
Newport HS 400/9-12
245 N Main St 03773 603-863-2414
Linda Sutton, prin. Fax 863-0887
Newport MS 200/7-8
245 N Main St 03773 603-863-2414
Linda Sutton, prin. Fax 863-0887
Sugar River Valley Reg Voc Ctr Vo/Tech
243 N Main St 03773 603-863-3759
Jennifer Haskins, dir. Fax 863-7104

**Newton, Rockingham**
Sanborn Regional SD
Supt. — See Kingston
Sanborn Regional MS 400/6-8
31A W Main St 03858 603-382-6226
Alexander Rutherford, prin. Fax 382-9771

**North Conway, Carroll, Pop. 2,311**
Conway SD
Supt. — See Conway
Kennett HS 800/9-12
409 Eagles Way 03860 603-356-4343
Cornelius Moylan, prin. Fax 356-4391
Mt. Washington Vly Career/Technical Ctr Vo/Tech
409 Eagles Way 03860 603-356-4370
Richard Biche, dir. Fax 356-4373

**North Haverhill, Grafton**
Haverhill Cooperative SD 800/PK-12
2975 Dartmouth College Hwy 03774 603-787-2113
Dr. Donald LaPlante, supt. Fax 787-2118
www.sau23.org
Haverhill Cooperative MS 300/4-8
175 Morrill Dr 03774 603-787-2100
Robert Phillips, prin. Fax 787-6117
Other Schools – See Woodsville

**North Sutton, Merrimack**
Kearsarge Regional SD
Supt. — See New London
Kearsage Regional HS 600/9-12
PO Box 182 03260 603-927-4261
Robert Bennett, prin.
Kearsarge Regional MS 500/6-8
PO Box 269 03260 603-927-2100
Stephen Paterson, prin.

**Northwood, Rockingham**
Coe-Brown Northwood Academy 700/9-12
907 1st NH Tpke 03261 603-942-5531
David Smith, hdmstr. Fax 942-7537
www.coebrown.org
Coe-Brown Northwood Academy 700/9-12
907 1st NH Tpke 03261 603-942-5531
David Smith, hdmstr. Fax 942-7537

**Orford, Grafton**
Rivendell Interstate SD 400/PK-12
10 School Dr 03777 603-353-2170
Brenda Needham, supt. Fax 353-2189
www.rivendellschool.org
Rivendell Academy 200/7-12
2972 Route 25A 03777 603-353-4321
Keri Gelenian, prin. Fax 353-4414

**Pelham, Hillsborough**
Pelham SD 2,100/PK-12
59A Marsh Rd 03076 603-635-1145
Amanda Lecaroz, supt. Fax 635-1283
www.pelhamsd.org
Pelham HS 600/9-12
85 Marsh Rd 03076 603-635-2115
Dr. Dorothy Mohr, prin. Fax 635-3994
Pelham Memorial MS 600/6-8
59 Marsh Rd 03076 603-635-2321
Stephen Secor, prin. Fax 635-2369

**Pembroke, Merrimack, Pop. 6,561**
Allenstown SD 400/PK-8
267 Pembroke St 03275 603-485-5188
Patty Sherman, supt. Fax 485-9529
www.sau53.org
Other Schools – See Allenstown

Pembroke SD 1,700/K-12
267 Pembroke St 03275 603-485-5188
Patty Sherman, supt. Fax 485-9529
www.sau53.org
Pembroke Academy 900/9-12
209 Academy Rd 03275 603-485-7881
Paul Famulari, prin. Fax 485-1824
Three Rivers MS 400/5-8
243 Academy Rd 03275 603-485-9539
Jonathan Marston, prin. Fax 485-1829

**Penacook, See Concord**
Merrimack Valley SD 2,700/PK-12
105 Community Dr 03303 603-753-6561
Mark MacLean, supt. Fax 753-6023
www.mvsdpride.org
Merrimack Valley HS 900/9-12
106 Village St 03303 603-753-4311
David Miller, prin. Fax 753-6423
Merrimack Valley MS 600/6-8
14 Allen St 03303 603-753-6336
Patricia Severance, prin. Fax 753-8107

**Peterborough, Hillsborough, Pop. 3,075**
Contoocook Valley SD 2,500/PK-12
106 Hancock Rd 03458 603-924-3336
Dr. Brendan Minnihan, supt. Fax 924-6707
www.conval.edu
ConVal Regional HS 900/9-12
184 Hancock Rd 03458 603-924-3869
Brian Pickering, prin. Fax 924-9176
Region 14 Applied Technology Center Vo/Tech
184 Hancock Rd 03458 603-924-3869
Fax 924-9176
South Meadow MS 500/5-8
108 Hancock Rd 03458 603-924-7105
Anne O'Bryant, prin. Fax 924-2064
Other Schools – See Antrim

**Pittsburg, Coos**
Pittsburg SD
Supt. — See Colebrook
Pittsburg HS 50/9-12
12 School St 03592 603-538-6536
Heather Zybas, prin. Fax 538-6996

**Pittsfield, Merrimack, Pop. 1,547**
Pittsfield SD 600/PK-12
23 Oneida St Unit 1 03263 603-435-5526
Dr. John Freeman, supt. Fax 435-5331
pittsfield-nh.com/sau
Pittsfield HS 200/9-12
23 Oneida St 03263 603-435-6701
Danielle Harvey, prin. Fax 435-7087
Pittsfield MS 100/7-8
23 Oneida St 03263 603-435-6701
Danielle Harvey, prin. Fax 435-7087

**Plainfield, Sullivan, Pop. 204**

---

Estabrook Christian S 50/K-10
1050 Route 12A 03781 603-675-2455
Ellen Busl M.Ed., prin.

**Plaistow, Rockingham**
Hampstead SD 900/PK-8
30 Greenough Rd 03865 603-382-6119
Dr. Earl Metzler, supt. Fax 382-3334
www.hampstead.k12.nh.us
Other Schools – See Hampstead

Timberlane Regional SD 4,100/PK-12
30 Greenough Rd 03865 603-382-6119
Dr. Earl Metzler, supt. Fax 382-3334
www.timberlane.net/
Timberlane Regional HS 1,400/9-12
36 Greenough Rd 03865 603-382-6541
Donald Woodworth, prin. Fax 382-8086
Timberlane Regional MS 1,000/6-8
44 Greenough Rd 03865 603-382-7131
Michael Hogan, prin. Fax 382-2781

**Plymouth, Grafton, Pop. 4,412**
Pemi-Baker Regional SD 700/9-12
47 Old Ward Bridge Rd 03264 603-536-1254
Mark Halloran, supt. Fax 536-3545
www.pemibaker.org
Plymouth Applied Technology Center Vo/Tech
86 Old Ward Bridge Rd 03264 603-536-1444
Randy Cleary, prin. Fax 536-9086
Plymouth Regional HS 700/9-12
86 Old Ward Bridge Rd 03264 603-536-1444
Bruce Parsons, prin. Fax 536-9086

---

Plymouth State University Post-Sec.
17 High St 03264 603-535-5000

**Portsmouth, Rockingham, Pop. 20,315**
Portsmouth SD 2,700/PK-12
1 Junkins Ave Unit 402 03801 603-431-5080
Steve Zadravec, supt. Fax 431-6753
www.cityofportsmouth.com/school/
Portsmouth Career-Tech Center 19 Vo/Tech
50 Andrew Jarvis Dr 03801 603-436-7100
Diane Canada, dir. Fax 436-6793
Portsmouth HS 1,100/9-12
50 Andrew Jarvis Dr 03801 603-436-7100
Mary Lyons, prin. Fax 427-2320
Portsmouth MS 500/6-8
155 Parrott Ave 03801 603-436-5781
Phillip Davis, prin. Fax 427-2326

---

Great Bay Community College Post-Sec.
320 Corporate Dr 03801 603-427-7600
Portsmouth Beauty School of Hair Design Post-Sec.
140 Congress St 03801 603-436-7775

**Raymond, Rockingham, Pop. 2,815**
Raymond SD 1,400/PK-12
43 Harriman Hill Rd 03077 603-895-4299
Ellen Small M.Ed., supt. Fax 895-0147
www.sau33.com/
Gove MS 500/5-8
1 Stephen K Batchelder Pkwy 03077 603-895-3394
Robert Bickford, prin. Fax 895-9856
Raymond HS 400/9-12
45 Harriman Hill Rd 03077 603-895-6616
Steven Woodward, prin. Fax 895-1582

**Rindge, Cheshire**

---

Franklin Pierce University Post-Sec.
40 University Dr 03461 603-899-4000

**Rochester, Strafford, Pop. 29,277**
Rochester SD 4,400/PK-12
150 Wakefield St Ste 8 03867 603-332-3678
Michael Hopkins, supt. Fax 335-7367
www.rochesterschools.com
Carlson Academy 100/Alt
150 Wakefield St Ste 8 03867 603-332-3678
Kathy Dubois, dir. Fax 335-7367
Creteau Regional Technology Center Vo/Tech
140 Wakefield St 03867 603-332-0757
Sean Peschel, dir. Fax 335-7365
Rochester MS 900/6-8
47 Brock St 03867 603-332-4090
Adam Houghton, prin. Fax 332-9384
Spaulding HS 1,400/9-12
130 Wakefield St 03867 603-332-0757
Peter Weaver, prin. Fax 330-0251

**Rye, Rockingham**
Rye SD
Supt. — See Greenland
Rye JHS 200/6-8
501 Washington Rd 03870 603-964-5591
Christopher Pollet, prin. Fax 964-3881

**Salem, Rockingham, Pop. 27,400**
Salem SD 4,300/PK-12
38 Geremonty Dr 03079 603-893-7040
Dr. Michael Delahanty, supt. Fax 893-7080
www.sau57.org

Center for Career & Technical Education — Vo/Tech
44 Geremonty Dr 03079 — 603-893-7069
Chris Dodge, prin. — Fax 898-0208
Salem HS — 1,500/9-12
44 Geremonty Dr 03079 — 603-893-7069
Tracy Collyer, prin. — Fax 893-7087
Woodbury MS — 1,100/6-8
206 Main St 03079 — 603-893-7055
Brad St. Laurent, prin. — Fax 898-0634

**Seabrook, Rockingham**
Seabrook SD
Supt. — See Hampton
Seabrook MS — 300/5-8
236 Walton Rd 03874 — 603-474-9221
Leslie Shepard, prin. — Fax 474-8020

**Somersworth, Strafford, Pop. 11,470**
Somersworth SD — 1,300/PK-12
51 W High St 03878 — 603-692-4450
Jeni Mosca, supt. — Fax 692-9100
www.sau56.org/somersworth-school-district/home
Somersworth Career Technical Center — Vo/Tech
18 Cemetery Rd 03878 — 603-692-2242
Katelyn Carrington, dean — Fax 692-9116
Somersworth HS — 600/9-12
11 Memorial Dr 03878 — 603-692-2431
Sharon Lampros, prin. — Fax 692-7326
Somersworth MS — 400/6-8
7 Memorial Dr 03878 — 603-692-2126
Dana Hilliard, prin. — Fax 692-9101

---

Empire Beauty School — Post-Sec.
362 Route 108 03878 — 603-692-1515
Tri-City Christian Academy — 300/PK-12
150 W High St 03878 — 603-692-2093
Paul Edgar, admin. — Fax 692-6305

**Stratham, Rockingham**
Exeter Region Cooperative SD
Supt. — See Exeter
Cooperative MS — 1,400/6-8
100 Academic Way 03885 — 603-775-8700
William Furbush, prin. — Fax 775-0151

**Sunapee, Sullivan**
Sunapee SD — 500/K-12
70 Lower Main St 03782 — 603-763-4627
Russell Holden, supt. — Fax 763-4718
www.sunapeeschools.org
Sunapee HS — 200/9-12
10 North Rd 03782 — 603-763-5615
Sean Moynihan, prin. — Fax 763-3055
Sunapee MS — 100/6-8
10 North Rd 03782 — 603-763-5615
Sean Moynihan, prin. — Fax 763-3055

---

Mount Royal Academy — 100/PK-12
PO Box 362 03782 — 603-763-9010
Derek Tremblay, hdmstr. — Fax 763-5390

**Swanzey, Cheshire**
Monadnock Regional SD — 1,800/PK-12
600 Old Homestead Hwy 03446 — 603-352-6955
Lisa Spencer, supt. — Fax 358-6708
www.mrsd.org
Monadnock Regional HS — 600/9-12
580 Old Homestead Hwy 03446 — 603-352-6575
Linda Kalloger, prin. — Fax 355-1209
Monadnock Regional MS — 300/7-8
580 Old Homestead Hwy 03446 — 603-352-6575
Linda Kalloger, prin. — Fax 357-6520

**Tilton, Belknap, Pop. 3,081**
Winnisquam Regional SD — 1,500/PK-12
433 W Main St 03276 — 603-286-4116
Dr. Tammy Davis, supt. — Fax 286-7402
www.winnisquam.k12.nh.us
Winnisquam Regional HS — 500/9-12
435 W Main St 03276 — 603-286-4531
Tom Laliberte, prin. — Fax 286-2006
Winnisquam Regional MS — 300/6-8
76 Winter St 03276 — 603-286-7143
Robert Seaward, prin. — Fax 286-7410

---

Tilton S — 200/9-12
30 School St 03276 — 603-286-4342
Peter Saliba, head sch — Fax 286-3137

**Walpole, Cheshire, Pop. 595**
Fall Mountain Regional SD
Supt. — See Charlestown
Walpole MS — 100/5-8
PO Box 549 03608 — 603-756-4728
Samuel Jacobs, prin. — Fax 756-3343

**Warner, Merrimack, Pop. 440**

---

College of St. Mary Magdalen — Post-Sec.
511 Kearsarge Mountain Rd 03278 — 603-456-2656

**Weare, Hillsborough**
John Stark Regional SD
Supt. — See Henniker
Stark Regional HS — 800/9-12
618 N Stark Hwy 03281 — 603-529-7675
Christopher Corkery, prin. — Fax 529-4646

Weare SD
Supt. — See Henniker
Weare MS — 500/5-8
16 East Rd 03281 — 603-529-7555
Mark Willis, prin. — Fax 529-0464

**West Lebanon, See Lebanon**
Lebanon SD — 1,500/PK-12
20 Seminary Hl 03784 — 603-790-8500
Joanne Roberts, supt. — Fax 790-8310
www.sau88.net
Other Schools – See Lebanon

---

New England School of Hair Design — Post-Sec.
12 Interchange Dr 03784 — 603-298-5199

**Whitefield, Coos, Pop. 1,128**
White Mountains Regional SD — 1,300/PK-12
14 King Sq 03598 — 603-837-9363
Dr. Marion Anastasia, supt. — Fax 837-2326
www.sau36.org
White Mountains Regional HS — 400/9-12
PO Box 338 03598 — 603-837-2528
Michael Berry, prin. — Fax 837-3811
White Mountains Reg/Voc HS — Vo/Tech
PO Box 338 03598 — 603-837-2528
Lisa Perras, dir. — Fax 837-3811

**Wilton, Hillsborough, Pop. 1,150**
Wilton-Lyndeborough Cooperative SD — 600/PK-12
PO Box 1149 03086 — 603-654-8088
Dr. Christine Tyrie Ed.D., supt. — Fax 654-6691
www.sau63.org
Wilton-Lyndeborough Cooperative MSHS — 200/6-12
57 School Rd 03086 — 603-654-6123
Brian Bagley, prin. — Fax 654-2104

---

High Mowing S — 100/9-12
222 Isaac Frye Hwy 03086 — 603-654-2391
Rea Taylor Gill, dir. — Fax 654-6588

**Windham, Rockingham**
Windham SD — 2,600/PK-12
19 Haverhill Rd 03087 — 603-425-1976
Dr. Winfried Feneberg, supt. — Fax 425-1719
www.sau95.org
Windham HS — 700/9-12
64 London Bridge Rd 03087 — 603-537-2400
Robert Dawson, prin. — Fax 537-2499
Windham MS — 600/6-8
112 Lowell Rd Ste A 03087 — 603-893-2636
Patricia Wons, prin. — Fax 870-9007

**Wolfeboro, Carroll, Pop. 2,811**
Governor Wentworth Regional SD — 2,400/PK-12
140 Pine Hill Rd 03894 — 603-569-1658
Kathleen Cuddy-Egbert, supt. — Fax 569-6983
www.govwentworth.k12.nh.us
Kingswood Regional HS — 800/9-12
396 S Main St 03894 — 603-569-2055
Guy Donnelly, prin. — Fax 569-8104
Kingswood Regional MS — 400/7-8
404 S Main St 03894 — 603-569-3689
Suzanne Onufry, prin. — Fax 569-8113
Lakes Region Technology Center — Vo/Tech
384 S Main St 03894 — 603-569-4361
B. Farr, prin. — Fax 569-9243

---

Brewster Academy — 400/9-12
80 Academy Dr 03894 — 603-569-1600
Dr. Craig Gemmell, head sch — Fax 569-7199

**Woodsville, Grafton, Pop. 1,115**
Haverhill Cooperative SD
Supt. — See North Haverhill
Woodsville HS — 300/9-12
9 High St 03785 — 603-747-2781
Robert Jones, prin. — Fax 747-2766

# NEW JERSEY

## NEW JERSEY DEPARTMENT OF EDUCATION
**PO Box 500, Trenton 08625**
**Telephone 609-292-4469**
**Fax 609-777-4099**
**Website http://www.state.nj.us/education**

Commissioner of Education  Chris Cerf

## NEW JERSEY BOARD OF EDUCATION
**PO Box 500, Trenton 08625-0500**

President  Arcelio Aponte

### COUNTY SUPERINTENDENTS OF SCHOOLS

Atlantic County Office of Education
Dr. Richard Stepura, supt. 609-625-0004
6260 Old Harding Hwy Ste 1 Fax 625-6539
Mays Landing 08330
www.aclink.org/education/

Bergen County Office of Education
Norah Peck, supt. 201-336-6875
1 Bergen County Plz Rm 350 Fax 336-6880
Hackensack 07601

Burlington County Office of Education
Todd Flora, supt. 609-265-5060
PO Box 6000, Westampton 08060 Fax 265-5922
www.co.burlington.nj.us/553/Superintendent-of-Schools

Camden County Office of Education
Dr. Lovell Pugh-Bassett, supt. 856-401-2400
PO Box 200, Blackwood 08012 Fax 401-2410
www.camdencounty.com/education

Cape May County Office of Education
Dr. Richard Stepura, supt. 609-465-1283
4 Moore Rd Fax 465-2094
Cape May Court House
www.capemaycountygov.net/

Cumberland County Office of Education
Dr. Richard Stepura, supt. 856-451-0211
19 Landis Ave, Bridgeton 08302 Fax 455-9523
www.co.cumberland.nj.us/

Essex County Office of Education
Joseph Zarra, supt. 973-621-2750
60 Nelson Pl, Newark 07102 Fax 621-1603

Gloucester County Office of Education
Ave Altersitz, supt. 856-686-8370
254 County House Rd Fax 423-5296
Clarksboro 08020
gloucester-web.civicasoft.com/depts/s/sos/default.asp

Hudson County Office of Education
Monica Tone, supt. 201-369-5290
595 Newark Ave, Jersey City 07306 Fax 369-5288
www.hcstonline.org/main/hcdoe/Home.aspx

Hunterdon County Office of Education
Juan Torres, supt. 908-788-1414
PO Box 2900, Flemington 08822 Fax 788-1457
www.co.hunterdon.nj.us/schools.htm

Mercer County Office of Education
Dr. Laura Morana, supt. 609-588-5877
1075 Old Trenton Rd Fax 588-5878
Trenton 08690
nj.gov/counties/mercer/departments/schools/index.html

Middlesex County Office of Education
Dr. Laura Morana, supt. 732-249-2900
1460 Livingston Ave Fax 296-0683
North Brunswick 08902

Monmouth County Office of Education
Dr. Lester Richens, supt. 732-431-7810
4000 Kozloski Rd, Freehold 07728 Fax 776-7237

Morris County Office of Education
Roger Jinks, supt. 973-285-8332
PO Box 900, Morristown 07963 Fax 285-8341

Ocean County Office of Education
Todd Flora, supt. 732-929-2078
212 Washington St Fax 506-5336
Toms River 08753
www.co.ocean.nj.us/ocschools/

Passaic County Office of Education
Robert Davis, supt. 973-569-2110
501 River St, Paterson 07524 Fax 754-0241

Salem County Office of Education
Peggy Nicolosi, supt. 856-339-8611
110 5th St Ste 900, Salem 08079 Fax 935-6290
www.salemcountynj.gov/departments/schools/

Somerset County Office of Education
Juan Torres, supt. 908-541-5700
PO Box 3000, Somerville 08876 Fax 722-6902
www.co.somerset.nj.us/schools/

Sussex County Office of Education
Dr. Rosalie Lamonte, supt. 973-579-6996
262 White Lake Rd, Sparta 07871 Fax 579-6476
www.sussex.nj.us/Cit-e-Access/webpage.cfm?TID=7&TPID=1560

Union County Office of Education
Roger Jinks, supt. 908-654-9860
300 North Ave E, Westfield 07090 Fax 654-9869

Warren County Office of Education
Dr. Rosalie Lamonte, supt. 908-689-0497
1501 State Route 57 W Fax 689-1457
Washington 07882
www.co.warren.nj.us/edu.html

### PUBLIC, PRIVATE AND CATHOLIC SECONDARY SCHOOLS

**Aberdeen, Monmouth, Pop. 17,038**
Matawan-Aberdeen Regional SD 3,800/PK-12
1 Crest Way 07747 732-705-4000
Joseph Majka J.D., supt.
www.marsd.org
Matawan Regional HS 1,100/9-12
450 Atlantic Ave 07747 732-705-5200
Michele Ruscavage, prin. Fax 566-2404
Other Schools – See Cliffwood

Monmouth County Vocational SD
Supt. — See Freehold
Aberdeen Vocational S Vo/Tech
450 Atlantic Ave 07747 732-566-5599
Denise Kebeck, prin. Fax 566-2392

**Absecon, Atlantic, Pop. 8,239**
Absecon CSD 800/K-8
800 Irelan Ave 08201 609-641-5375
Dr. Theresa DeFranco, supt. Fax 641-8692
www.abseconschools.org
Attales MS 300/5-8
800 Irelan Ave Ste 1 08201 609-641-5375
Andrew Weber, prin. Fax 641-8692

---

Holy Spirit HS 600/9-12
500 S New Rd 08201 609-646-3000
Susan Dennen, prin. Fax 646-1770

**Adelphia, Monmouth**

---

Talmudical Academy of New Jersey Post-Sec.
Route 524 07710 732-431-1600
Talmudical Academy of NJ 100/9-12
PO Box 7 07710 732-431-1600

**Allamuchy, Warren, Pop. 77**
Allamuchy Township SD 700/PK-8
PO Box J 07820 908-852-1894
Joseph Flynn, supt. Fax 852-9816
www.aes.k12.nj.us
Allamuchy S 300/3-8
PO Box J 07820 908-852-1894
Jennifer Chickey, prin. Fax 852-9816

**Allendale, Bergen, Pop. 6,407**
Allendale SD 900/PK-8
100 Brookside Ave 07401 201-327-2020
Michael Barcadepone Ed.D., supt. Fax 785-9735
www.allendalek8.com
Brookside MS 500/4-8
100 Brookside Ave 07401 201-327-2020
Bruce Winkelstein, prin. Fax 825-6553

Northern Highlands Regional HSD 1,400/9-12
298 Hillside Ave 07401 201-327-8700
Scot Beckerman, supt. Fax 327-5274
www.northernhighlands.org
Northern Highlands Regional HS 1,400/9-12
298 Hillside Ave 07401 201-327-8700
Joseph Occhino, prin. Fax 327-3370

**Allentown, Monmouth, Pop. 1,798**
Upper Freehold Regional SD 2,300/PK-12
27 High St 08501 609-259-7292
Dr. Richard Fitzpatrick, supt. Fax 259-0881
www.ufrsd.net
Allentown HS 1,200/9-12
27 High St 08501 609-259-2160
Connie Embley, prin. Fax 259-0390
Stone Bridge MS 500/5-8
27 High St 08501 609-259-7369
Stefanie Negro, prin. Fax 208-1411

**Annandale, Hunterdon, Pop. 1,653**
North Hunterdon/Voorhees Regional HSD 2,900/9-12
1445 State Route 31 S 08801 908-735-2846
Dr. Frank Helies, supt. Fax 735-6914
www.nhvweb.net
North Hunterdon HS 1,800/9-12
1445 State Route 31 S 08801 908-735-5191
Richard Bergacs, prin. Fax 735-6447
Other Schools – See Glen Gardner

**Asbury, Hunterdon, Pop. 273**
Bethlehem Township SD 500/K-8
940 Iron Bridge Rd 08802 908-537-4044
Dr. Edward Keegan, admin. Fax 537-4309
www.btschools.org
Hoppock MS 200/6-8
280 Asbury West Portal Rd 08802 908-479-6336
Jane Smith, prin. Fax 479-1021

**Asbury Park, Monmouth, Pop. 15,693**
Asbury Park SD 1,800/PK-12
603 Mattison Ave Ste 3 07712 732-776-2606
Dr. Lamont Repollet, supt. Fax 774-8067
www.asburypark.k12.nj.us
Asbury Park HS 400/9-12
1003 Sunset Ave 07712 732-776-2638
Reginald Mirthil, prin. Fax 776-3119
Asbury Park MS 400/6-8
1200 Bangs Ave 07712 732-776-2559
Dr. Antonio Lewis, prin. Fax 776-7503

Monmouth County Vocational SD
Supt. — See Freehold
Culinary Education Center Vo/Tech
101 Drury Ln 07712 732-988-3299
Michael Sirianni, prin. Fax 776-8096

**Atco, Camden**
Winslow Township SD 4,700/PK-12
40 Cooper Folly Rd 08004 856-767-2850
Dr. H. Major Poteat, supt. Fax 767-4782
www.winslow-schools.com
Winslow Township HS 1,400/9-12
10 Cooper Folly Rd 08004 856-767-1850
Kurtis Marella, prin. Fax 767-5670
Winslow Township MS 800/7-8
30 Cooper Folly Rd 08004 856-767-7222
Stella Nwanguma, prin. Fax 767-5411

**Atlantic City, Atlantic, Pop. 38,716**
Atlantic City SD 6,100/PK-12
1300 Atlantic Ave 08401 609-343-7200
Paul Spaventa, supt. Fax 345-3268
www.acboe.org
Atlantic City HS 2,100/9-12
1400 N Albany Ave 08401 609-343-7300
Charles Wilson, prin. Fax 343-7345

**Audubon, Camden, Pop. 8,746**
Audubon SD 1,400/PK-12
350 Edgewood Ave 08106 856-547-7695
Steven C. Crispin, supt. Fax 546-8550
www.audubonschools.org/
Audubon JSHS 800/7-12
350 Edgewood Ave 08106 856-547-7695
J. Robert Buchs, prin. Fax 547-4073

**Avalon, Cape May, Pop. 1,326**
Avalon SD 100/5-8
235 32nd St 08202 609-967-7544
Stacey Tracy, supt. Fax 967-3109
www.avesnj.org/
Avalon ES 100/5-8
235 32nd St 08202 609-967-7544
Stacey Tracy, supt. Fax 967-3109

**Avenel, Middlesex, Pop. 16,588**
Woodbridge Township SD
Supt. — See Woodbridge

Avenel MS 600/6-8
85 Woodbine Ave 07001 732-586-5622
Joseph Short, prin. Fax 574-0573

**Barnegat, Ocean, Pop. 2,775**
Barnegat Township SD 3,100/PK-12
550 Barnegat Blvd N 08005 609-698-5800
Karen Wood, supt. Fax 698-6638
www.barnegatschools.com
Barnegat HS 1,000/9-12
180 Bengal Blvd 08005 609-660-7510
Steve Nichol, prin. Fax 660-7598
Brackman MS 700/6-8
600 Barnegat Blvd N 08005 609-698-5880
John Fiorentino, prin. Fax 698-7965

**Barrington, Camden, Pop. 6,884**
Barrington Borough SD 600/PK-8
311 Reading Ave 08007 856-547-8467
Anthony Arcodia, supt. Fax 547-5533
www.barringtonschools.net/
Woodland MS 200/5-8
1 School Ln 08007 856-547-8402
Fax 522-1248

---

Castle Academy 200/PK-12
500 Clements Bridge Rd 08007 856-546-5901

**Basking Ridge, Somerset, Pop. 4,000**
Bernards Township SD 5,500/K-12
101 Peachtree Rd 07920 908-204-2600
Nick Markarian, supt. Fax 766-7641
www.bernardsboe.com/
Annin MS 1,400/6-8
70 Quincy Rd 07920 908-204-2610
Karen Hudock, prin. Fax 204-0244
Ridge HS 1,800/9-12
268 S Finley Ave 07920 908-204-2585
Frank Howlett, prin. Fax 204-2582

---

Pingry S 700/7-12
131 Martinsville Rd 07920 908-647-5555
Nathaniel Conard, hdmstr. Fax 647-3703

**Bayonne, Hudson, Pop. 61,671**
Bayonne SD 8,900/PK-12
669 Avenue A 07002 201-858-5800
Dr. Patricia L. McGeehan Ed.D., supt. Fax 858-6289
www.bboed.org
Bayonne HS 2,400/9-12
667 Avenue A 07002 201-858-5900
Richard Baccarella, prin. Fax 858-6263

---

Bayonne Hospital School of Nursing Post-Sec.
29 E 29th St 07002 201-339-9656
Marist HS 400/9-12
1241 Kennedy Blvd 07002 201-437-4544
Alice Miesnik, head sch Fax 437-6013
Yeshiva Gedola of Bayonne 100/9-12
747 Avenue C 07002 201-339-7187

**Bayville, Ocean**
Central Regional SD 1,900/7-12
509 Forest Hills Pkwy 08721 732-269-1100
Dr. T. Parlapanides, supt. Fax 237-8872
www.centralreg.k12.nj.us
Central Regional HS 1,300/9-12
509 Forest Hills Pkwy 08721 732-269-1100
Dr. Douglas Corbett, prin. Fax 269-7723
Central Regional MS 700/7-8
509 Forest Hills Pkwy 08721 732-269-1100
Dr. Joseph Firetto, prin. Fax 269-7723

**Beachwood, Ocean, Pop. 10,934**
Toms River Regional SD
Supt. — See Toms River
Toms River IS South 1,000/6-8
1675 Pinewald Rd 08722 732-505-3900
Paul Gluck, prin. Fax 818-7512

**Belleville, Essex, Pop. 36,300**
Belleville SD 4,200/PK-12
102 Passaic Ave 07109 973-450-3500
Dr. Richard Tomko, supt. Fax 450-3504
www.bellevilleschools.org
Belleville HS 1,500/9-12
100 Passaic Ave 07109 973-450-3500
Russell Pagano, prin. Fax 450-3196
Belleville MS 600/6-8
279 Washington Ave 07109 973-450-3500
Shana Wright, prin. Fax 450-5001

---

Eastern International College Post-Sec.
251 Washington Ave 07109 973-751-9051

**Bellmawr, Camden, Pop. 11,414**
Bellmawr Borough SD 1,100/PK-8
256 Anderson Ave 08031 856-931-3620
Annette Castiglione, supt. Fax 931-9326
bellmawrschools.org
Bell Oaks MS 500/5-8
256 Anderson Ave 08031 856-931-6273
Anthony Farinelli, prin. Fax 931-9326

**Belmar, Monmouth, Pop. 5,731**

---

Mesivta Keser Torah Post-Sec.
503 11th Ave 07719 732-367-4259
Mesivta Keser Torah 50/9-12
503 11th Ave 07719 732-681-5656
St. Rose HS 500/9-12
607 7th Ave 07719 732-681-2858
Sr. Kathy Nace, prin. Fax 280-2745

**Belvidere, Warren, Pop. 2,652**
Belvidere SD 800/K-12
809 Oxford St 07823 908-475-6600
Christopher Carrubba, supt. Fax 475-6619
www.belvideresd.org
Belvidere HS 500/9-12
809 Oxford St 07823 908-475-4025
Edward Lazzara, prin. Fax 475-1685

Oxford Street MS 200/4-8
807 Oxford St 07823 908-475-4001
Sebastian Powell, prin. Fax 475-6619

**Bergenfield, Bergen, Pop. 26,177**
Bergenfield SD 3,200/PK-12
225 W Clinton Ave 07621 201-385-8801
Dr. Michael Kuchar, supt. Fax 384-2914
www.bergenfield.org/
Bergenfield HS 1,200/9-12
80 S Prospect Ave 07621 201-385-8600
James Fasano, prin. Fax 439-0978
Brown MS 800/6-8
130 S Washington Ave 07621 201-385-8847
Shane Biggins, prin. Fax 385-0219

**Berkeley Heights, Union, Pop. 11,980**
Berkeley Heights SD 2,700/PK-12
345 Plainfield Ave 07922 908-464-1718
Judith Rattner, supt. Fax 464-1728
www.bhpsnj.org/
Columbia MS 600/6-8
345 Plainfield Ave 07922 908-464-1600
Frank Geiger, prin. Fax 464-0017
Livingston HS 1,000/9-12
175 Watchung Blvd 07922 908-464-3100
Robert Nixon, prin. Fax 464-7508

**Bernardsville, Somerset, Pop. 7,613**
Somerset Hills SD 2,000/PK-12
25 Olcott Ave 07924 908-204-1930
Dr. Frances Wood, supt. Fax 953-0699
www.shsd.org/
Bernards HS 800/9-12
25 Olcott Ave 07924 908-204-1930
Scott Neigel, prin. Fax 766-8223
Bernardsville MS 600/5-8
141 Seney Dr 07924 908-204-1916
Dr. John B. Alfieri, prin. Fax 953-2184

**Blackwood, Camden, Pop. 4,485**
Black Horse Pike Regional SD 3,900/9-12
580 Erial Rd 08012 856-227-4106
Dr. Brian Repici, supt. Fax 227-6835
www.bhprsd.org
Highland HS 1,100/9-12
450 Erial Rd 08012 856-227-4100
Elizabeth Petitte, prin. Fax 227-3619
Other Schools – See Erial, Runnemede

Gloucester Township SD 6,700/PK-8
17 Erial Rd 08012 856-227-1400
John Bilodeau, supt. Fax 228-1422
www.gloucestertownshipschools.org/
Glen Landing MS 800/6-8
85 Little Gloucester Rd 08012 856-227-3534
Suzanne Schultes, prin. Fax 228-5260
Lewis MS 600/6-8
875 Erial Rd 08012 856-227-8400
Theodore Otten, prin. Fax 228-5130
Other Schools – See Sicklerville

---

Camden County College Post-Sec.
PO Box 200 08012 856-227-7200

**Blairstown, Warren**
North Warren Regional SD 1,000/7-12
PO Box 410 07825 908-362-9342
Sarah Bilotti Ed.D., supt. Fax 362-8744
www.northwarren.org
North Warren Regional MSHS 1,000/7-12
PO Box 410 07825 908-362-8211
Louis Melchor, prin. Fax 362-7353

---

Blair Academy 400/9-12
PO Box 600 07825 908-362-6121
Christopher Fortunato J.D., admin. Fax 362-7945

**Bloomfield, Essex, Pop. 48,200**
Bloomfield Township SD 5,800/PK-12
155 Broad St 07003 973-680-8500
Salvatore Goncalves, supt. Fax 680-8274
www.bloomfield.k12.nj.us
Bloomfield HS 1,800/9-12
160 Broad St 07003 973-680-8600
Christopher Jennings, prin. Fax 680-8684
Bloomfield MS 900/7-8
60 Huck Rd 07003 973-680-8620
Alla Vayda-Manzo, prin. Fax 338-6523

Essex County Vocational Technical SD
Supt. — See Newark
Essex Co. Vocational Tech - Bloomfield Vo/Tech
209 Franklin St 07003 973-412-2226
Eric Love, prin. Fax 412-2096

---

Bloomfield College Post-Sec.
467 Franklin St 07003 973-748-9000
Concorde School of Hair Design Post-Sec.
15 Ward St 07003 973-680-0099

**Bloomingdale, Passaic, Pop. 7,587**
Bloomingdale SD 600/PK-8
225 Glenwild Ave 07403 973-838-3282
Mario Cardinale, supt. Fax 838-8898
www.bloomingdaleschools.org
Bergen MS 300/5-8
225 Glenwild Ave 07403 973-838-4835
Frank Verducci, prin. Fax 283-1893

**Bogota, Bergen, Pop. 7,987**
Bogota SD 1,100/PK-12
1 Henry C Luthin Pl 07603 201-441-4800
Dr. Letizia Pantoliano, supt. Fax 489-5759
www.bogotaboe.com
Bogota JSHS 500/7-12
2 Henry C Luthin Pl 07603 201-441-4808
Linda Gatusso, prin. Fax 441-4849

**Boonton, Morris, Pop. 8,097**
Boonton SD 900/PK-12
434 Lathrop Ave 07005 973-335-3994
Joseph C. Luongo, supt. Fax 335-8281
www.boontonschools.org
Boonton HS 600/9-12
306 Lathrop Ave 07005 973-335-9700
Jacalyn Richardson, prin. Fax 402-5135

**Bordentown, Burlington, Pop. 3,853**
Bordentown Regional SD 2,100/K-12
318 Ward Ave 08505 609-298-0025
Edward Forsthoffer, supt. Fax 298-2515
www.bordentown.k12.nj.us
Bordentown Regional HS 600/9-12
318 Ward Ave 08505 609-298-0025
Robert Walder, prin. Fax 291-0347
Bordentown Regional MS 500/6-8
50 Dunns Mill Rd 08505 609-298-0674
Sam Tola, prin. Fax 291-1929

**Bound Brook, Somerset, Pop. 10,250**
Bound Brook Borough SD 1,500/PK-12
111 W Union Ave 08805 732-652-7920
Dr. Daniel Gallagher, supt. Fax 271-9097
www.bbrook.org
Bound Brook HS 500/9-12
111 W Union Ave 08805 732-652-7950
Edward Smith, prin. Fax 356-6445
Community MS 6-8
120 E Second St 08805 732-852-1130
Dr. Joseph Santicerma, prin.

**Branchburg, Somerset**
Branchburg Township SD 1,700/PK-8
240 Baird Rd 08876 908-722-3335
Rebecca Gensel, supt. Fax 526-6144
www.branchburg.k12.nj.us
Branchburg Central MS 600/6-8
220 Baird Rd 08876 908-526-1415
Matthew Barbosa, prin. Fax 526-7486

---

Raritan Valley Community College Post-Sec.
118 Larmington Rd 08876 908-526-1200

**Brick, Ocean, Pop. 78,300**
Brick Township SD 9,400/PK-12
101 Hendrickson Ave 08724 732-785-3000
Dr. Richard Caldes, supt. Fax 840-9089
www.brickschools.org/
Brick Township HS 1,500/9-12
346 Chambersbridge Rd 08723 732-262-2500
Dennis Filippone, prin. Fax 920-5907
Brick Township Memorial HS 1,800/9-12
2001 Lanes Mill Rd 08724 732-785-3090
Jennifer Joseph, prin. Fax 458-2748
Lake Riviera MS 1,000/6-8
171 Beaverson Blvd 08723 732-785-3000
Dr. Alyce Anderson, prin. Fax 477-0392
Veteran's Memorial MS 1,200/6-8
105 Hendrickson Ave 08724 732-785-3000
Renee Kotsianas, prin. Fax 458-9777

Ocean County Vocational SD
Supt. — See Toms River
Ocean County Voc-Tech S - Brick Vo/Tech
350 Chambersbridge Rd 08723 732-286-5670
Lynn Sauer, prin. Fax 920-0108

---

Capri Institute of Hair Design Post-Sec.
268 Brick Blvd 08723 732-920-3600
Star Career Academy Post-Sec.
150 Brick Blvd 08723 732-451-9710

**Bridgeton, Cumberland, Pop. 24,883**
Bridgeton SD 4,700/PK-12
PO Box 657 08302 856-455-8030
Dr. Thomasina Jones, supt. Fax 455-0176
www.bridgeton.k12.nj.us/
Bridgeton HS 800/9-12
111 N West Ave 08302 856-455-8030
Penny Britt, prin. Fax 455-0486
ExCEL S 6-8
398 N Pearl St 08302 856-455-8030
Isaias Garza, lead tchr. Fax 451-0328

Cumberland County Technical SD
601 Bridgeton Ave 08302 856-451-9000
Dr. Dina Elliott, supt. Fax 453-1118
www.cumberland.tec.nj.us
Cumberland Co. Technical Education Ctr Vo/Tech
601 Bridgeton Ave 08302 856-451-9000
Patrick Cruet, prin. Fax 453-1118

Cumberland Regional SD 1,300/9-12
65 Love Ln 08302 856-451-9400
William Stonis, supt. Fax 455-9750
www.crhsd.org/
Cumberland Regional HS 1,300/9-12
90 Silver Lake Rd 08302 856-451-9400
Ralph Aiello, prin. Fax 455-8514

---

Cumberland Co. Tech. Education Center Post-Sec.
601 Bridgeton Ave 08302 856-451-9000
Devereux New Jersey Center for Autism Post-Sec.
198 Roadstown Rd 08302 856-599-6411

**Bridgewater, Somerset, Pop. 36,400**
Bridgewater-Raritan Regional SD
Supt. — See Martinsville
Bridgewater-Raritan HS 2,900/9-12
PO Box 6569 08807 908-231-8660
Dr. Mark Morrell, prin. Fax 231-0467
Bridgewater-Raritan MS 1,400/7-8
PO Box 6933 08807 908-231-8661
Nancy Iatesta, prin. Fax 575-0847

Somerset County Vocational SD
PO Box 6350 08807 — 908-526-8900
Chrys Harttraft, supt. — Fax 704-0784
www.scvths.org/
Somerset County Vo-Tech HS — Vo/Tech
PO Box 6350 08807 — 908-526-8900
Diane Ziegler, prin. — Fax 704-0784

**Brigantine, Atlantic, Pop. 9,281**
Brigantine CSD — 800/PK-8
PO Box 947 08203 — 609-266-7671
Brian M. Pruitt, supt. — Fax 266-4748
www.brigantineschools.org/
Brigantine North MS — 300/5-8
PO Box 947 08203 — 609-266-3603
Kathleen Fox, prin. — Fax 266-7062

**Brookside, Morris**
Mendham Township SD — 800/K-8
PO Box 510 07926 — 973-543-7107
Dr. Salvatore Constantino, supt. — Fax 543-5537
www.mendhamtwp.org
Mendham Township MS — 400/5-8
PO Box 510 07926 — 973-543-2505
Dr. Patrick Ciccone, prin. — Fax 543-0701

**Budd Lake, Morris, Pop. 8,814**
Mt. Olive Township SD
Supt. — See Flanders
Mt. Olive MS — 1,100/6-8
160 Wolfe Rd 07828 — 973-691-4006
Susan Breton-Miranda, prin. — Fax 691-4029

**Buena, Atlantic, Pop. 4,524**
Buena Regional SD — 1,700/PK-12
PO Box 309 08310 — 856-697-0800
John DeStefano, supt. — Fax 697-4963
www.buena.k12.nj.us
Buena Regional HS — 800/9-12
125 Weymouth Rd 08310 — 856-697-2400
Moses White, prin. — Fax 697-4701
Buena Regional MS — 500/6-8
175 Weymouth Rd 08310 — 856-697-0100
Karen Santoro, prin. — Fax 697-9580

**Burlington, Burlington, Pop. 9,602**
Burlington CSD — 1,700/PK-12
518 Locust Ave 08016 — 609-387-5874
Dr. Patricia Doloughty, supt. — Fax 386-6971
www.burlington-nj.net
Burlington City JSHS — 700/7-12
100 Blue Devil Way 08016 — 609-387-5800
James Flynn, prin. — Fax 387-4287

Burlington Township SD — 4,000/PK-12
PO Box 428 08016 — 609-387-3955
Dr. Mary Ann Bell, supt. — Fax 239-2192
www.burltwpsch.org
BTMS @ Springside — 1,000/6-8
1600 Burlington Byp 08016 — 609-699-4021
Lawrence Penny, prin. — Fax 699-4022
Burlington Township HS — 1,300/9-12
610 Fountain Ave 08016 — 609-387-1713
Phillip Brownridge, prin. — Fax 387-0439

---

Doane Academy — 200/PK-12
350 Riverbank 08016 — 609-386-3500
George Sanderson, hdmstr. — Fax 386-5878
Institute of Logistical Management — Post-Sec.
PO Box 427 08016 — 609-747-1515
Life Center Academy — 300/PK-12
2045 Columbus Rd 08016 — 609-499-2100
Dr. Bryan Sanders, hdmstr. — Fax 499-4905

**Butler, Morris, Pop. 7,440**
Butler SD — 1,100/K-12
38 Bartholdi Ave 07405 — 973-492-2000
Dr. Alexander Anemone, supt. — Fax 492-1016
www.butlerboe.org
Butler HS — 500/9-12
38 Bartholdi Ave 07405 — 973-492-2000
Martin Wall, prin. — Fax 492-8672
Butler MS — 300/5-8
30 Pearl Pl 07405 — 973-492-2079
Jamie Manco, prin. — Fax 492-9774

Morris County Vocational SD
Supt. — See Denville
Academy for Law & Public Safety — Vo/Tech
Bartholdi Ave 07405 — 973-492-2000

**Caldwell, Essex, Pop. 7,489**
Caldwell-West Caldwell SD
Supt. — See West Caldwell
Cleveland MS — 600/6-8
36 Academy Rd 07006 — 973-228-9115
James Brown, prin. — Fax 228-7471

---

Caldwell College — Post-Sec.
120 Bloomfield Ave 07006 — 973-618-3000
Mt. St. Dominic Academy — 300/9-12
3 Ryerson Ave 07006 — 973-226-0660
Sr. Frances Sullivan, head sch — Fax 226-2693

**Califon, Hunterdon, Pop. 1,050**
Hunterdon Co. Educational Services Comm.
Supt. — See Lebanon
ESC Academy Tewksbury Campus — 50/Alt
37 Hoffmans Crossing Rd 07830 — 908-439-3703
Lou Johnson, dir. — Fax 439-3701

Lebanon Township SD — 700/PK-8
70 Bunnvale Rd 07830 — 908-638-4521
Jason R. Kornegay, supt. — Fax 638-5511
www.lebtwpk8.org
Woodglen MS — 300/5-8
70 Bunnvale Rd 07830 — 908-638-4111
Michael Rubright, prin. — Fax 638-8418

Tewksbury Township SD — 700/PK-8
173 County Road 517 07830 — 908-439-2010
Monica Rowland, supt. — Fax 439-2655
www.tewksburyschools.org
Old Turnpike MS — 400/5-8
171 County Road 517 07830 — 908-439-2010
Michael Ryder, prin. — Fax 439-3160

**Camden, Camden, Pop. 76,282**
Camden CSD — 11,600/PK-12
201 N Front St 08102 — 856-966-2040
Paymon Rouhanifard, supt. — Fax 966-2138
www.camden.k12.nj.us
Brimm Medical Arts HS — 200/9-12
1626 Copewood St 08103 — 856-966-2500
Herbert Simons, prin. — Fax 966-2489
Camden HS — 600/9-12
1700 Park Blvd 08103 — 856-966-5100
Scott Shanklin, prin. — Fax 966-4756
Creative Arts Morgan Village Academy — 400/6-12
990 Morgan St 08104 — 856-966-8955
Davida Coe-Brockington, prin. — Fax 964-9759
MetEast HS — 100/9-12
1656 Kaighns Ave 08103 — 856-966-8950
Timothy Jenkins, prin. — Fax 966-2388
Wilson HS — 800/9-12
3100 Federal St 08105 — 856-966-5300
Keith Miles, prin. — Fax 966-4755
Riggs Adult Learning Center — Adult
1656 Kaighns Ave 08103 — 856-966-5223
Timothy Jenkins, prin. — Fax 541-8671

---

Cooper Hospital/Univ Medical Center — Post-Sec.
1 Cooper Plz # 217 08103 — 856-342-2416
Our Lady of Lourdes School of Nursing — Post-Sec.
1600 Haddon Ave 08103 — 856-757-3729
Rowan University — Post-Sec.
200 N Broadway 08102 — 856-361-2900
Rutgers-The State University of N.J. — Post-Sec.
303 Cooper St 08102 — 856-225-1766
West Jersey Health System — Post-Sec.
1000 Atlantic Ave 08104 — 856-342-4600

**Cape May, Cape May, Pop. 3,525**
Lower Cape May Regional SD — 1,500/7-12
687 Route 9 08204 — 609-884-3475
Chris Kobik, supt. — Fax 884-0546
lcmrschooldistrict.com
Lower Cape May Regional HS — 1,000/9-12
687 Route 9 08204 — 609-884-3475
Larry Ziemba, prin. — Fax 884-0546
Teitelman MS — 500/7-8
687 Route 9 08204 — 609-884-3475
Greg Lasher, prin. — Fax 884-0546

**Cape May Court House, Cape May, Pop. 5,227**
Cape May County Technical SD
188 Crest Haven Rd, — 609-465-2161
Dr. Nancy M. Hudanich, supt. — Fax 465-3069
www.capemaytech.com
Cape May County Tech HS — Vo/Tech
188 Crest Haven Rd, — 609-465-2161
Michael Adams, prin. — Fax 465-4504
Cape May County Tech Evening HS — Adult
188 Crest Haven Rd, — 609-465-2161

Dennis Township SD — 600/PK-8
601 Hagan Rd, — 609-861-2821
Mark Miller, supt. — Fax 861-1833
dennistwpschools.org
Other Schools – See Dennisville

Middle Township SD — 2,600/PK-12
216 S Main St, — 609-465-1800
David Salvo, supt. — Fax 463-1979
www.middletwp.k12.nj.us
Middle Township HS — 900/9-12
300 E Atlantic Ave, — 609-465-1852
Frank Riggitano, prin. — Fax 465-3415
Middle Township MS 4 — 500/6-8
300 E Pacific Ave, — 609-465-1834
Toni Lehmen, prin. — Fax 465-5524

---

Burdette Tomlin Memorial Hospital — Post-Sec.
2 Stone Harbor Blvd, — 609-463-2180
Cape Christian Academy — 100/PK-12
10 Oyster Rd, — 609-465-4132
John Spriggs, admin. — Fax 465-0170
Cape May County Technical Institute — Post-Sec.
188 Crest Haven Rd, — 609-465-2161

**Carneys Point, Salem, Pop. 7,250**
Penns Grove-Carneys Point Regional SD
Supt. — See Penns Grove
Penns Grove HS — 600/9-12
334 Harding Hwy 08069 — 856-299-6300
Jocelyn Brown, prin. — Fax 299-5192

---

Salem Community College — Post-Sec.
460 Hollywood Ave 08069 — 856-299-2100

**Carteret, Middlesex, Pop. 22,279**
Carteret Borough SD — 3,600/PK-12
599 Roosevelt Ave 07008 — 732-541-8960
Kevin Ahearn, supt. — Fax 541-0433
www.carteretschools.org
Carteret HS — 1,000/9-12
199 Washington Ave 07008 — 732-541-8960
David Salvatore, prin. — Fax 969-4004
Carteret MS — 900/6-8
300 Carteret Ave 07008 — 732-541-8960
Mary Spiga, prin. — Fax 541-0483

**Cedar Grove, Essex, Pop. 12,053**
Cedar Grove Township SD — 1,600/K-12
520 Pompton Ave 07009 — 973-239-1550
Michael Fetherman, supt. — Fax 239-2994
www.cgschools.org
Cedar Grove HS — 400/9-12
90 Rugby Rd 07009 — 973-239-6400
Richard Mangili, prin. — Fax 857-9833
Cedar Grove Memorial MS — 500/5-8
500 Ridge Rd 07009 — 973-239-5233
Nicholas DeCorte, prin.

**Chatham, Morris, Pop. 8,814**
School District of the Chathams — 4,000/K-12
58 Meyersville Rd 07928 — 973-457-2520
Dr. Michael LaSusa, supt. — Fax 457-2481
www.chatham-nj.org
Chatham HS — 1,100/9-12
255 Lafayette Ave 07928 — 973-457-2505
Darren Groh, prin. — Fax 635-8670
Chatham MS — 1,000/6-8
480 Main St 07928 — 973-457-2506
Jill Gihorski, prin. — Fax 457-2492

**Cherry Hill, Camden, Pop. 70,100**
Cherry Hill SD — 11,200/K-12
PO Box 5015 08034 — 856-429-5600
Dr. Joseph Meloche, supt. — Fax 354-1864
www.chclc.org
Beck MS — 900/6-8
950 Cropwell Rd 08003 — 856-424-4505
Dr. Dennis Perry, prin. — Fax 424-8602
Carusi MS — 900/6-8
315 Roosevelt Dr 08002 — 856-667-1220
John Cafagna, prin. — Fax 779-0613
Cherry Hill HS - East — 2,000/9-12
1750 Kresson Rd 08003 — 856-424-2222
Lawyer Chapman, prin. — Fax 424-0637
Cherry Hill HS - West — 1,500/9-12
2101 Chapel Ave W 08002 — 856-663-8006
Kwame Morton, prin. — Fax 663-5746
Malberg Alternative HS — 50/Alt
45 Ranoldo Ter 08034 — 856-427-4311
James Riordan, prin. — Fax 427-0017
Rosa International MS — 800/6-8
485 Browning Ln 08003 — 856-616-8787
George Guy, prin. — Fax 616-0904

---

Anthem Institute — Post-Sec.
2100 Route 38 08002 — 856-755-4800
Camden Catholic HS — 700/9-12
300 Cuthbert Blvd 08002 — 856-663-2247
Heather Crisci, prin. — Fax 661-0632
Empire Beauty School — Post-Sec.
2100 State Highway #38 08002 — 856-667-8887
Harris School of Business — Post-Sec.
1 Mall Dr Ste 700 08002 — 856-662-5300
Kings Christian S — 300/PK-12
5 Carnegie Plz 08003 — 856-489-6720
John Walsh, prin. — Fax 489-6727

**Chester, Morris, Pop. 1,618**
Chester SD — 1,300/K-8
50 North Rd 07930 — 908-879-7373
Dr. Christina Van Woert, supt. — Fax 879-5887
www.chester-nj.org
Black River MS — 500/6-8
133 North Rd 07930 — 908-879-6363
Robert Mullen, prin. — Fax 879-9085

West Morris Regional HSD — 2,700/9-12
10 S Four Bridges Rd 07930 — 908-879-6404
Michael Ben-David, supt. — Fax 879-8861
www.wmrhsd.org
West Morris Central HS — 1,400/9-12
259 Bartley Rd 07930 — 908-879-5212
Stephen Ryan, prin. — Fax 879-2741
Other Schools – See Mendham

**Chesterfield, Burlington**

---

Meadow View Junior Academy — 50/K-10
241 Bordentown Chstrfeld Rd, — 609-298-1122

**Cinnaminson, Burlington, Pop. 14,583**
Cinnaminson Township SD — 1,600/PK-12
PO Box 224 08077 — 856-829-7600
Dr. Salvatore Illuzzi, supt. — Fax 786-9618
www.cinnaminson.com
Cinnaminson HS — 600/9-12
1197 Riverton Rd 08077 — 856-829-7770
Darlene Llewellyn, prin. — Fax 829-7777
Cinnaminson MS — 400/6-8
312 N Fork Landing Rd 08077 — 856-786-8012
Frank Goulburn, prin. — Fax 786-1860

**Clark, Union, Pop. 14,629**
Clark Township SD — 2,200/PK-12
365 Westfield Ave 07066 — 732-574-9600
Edward Grande, supt. — Fax 574-1456
www.clarkschools.org
Johnson HS — 800/9-12
365 Westfield Ave 07066 — 732-382-0910
Richard Delmonaco, prin. — Fax 382-5957
Kumpf MS — 500/6-8
59 Mildred Ter 07066 — 732-381-0400
Jennifer Feeley, prin. — Fax 381-0262

---

Mother Seton Regional HS — 300/9-12
Valley Rd 07066 — 732-382-1952
Joan Barron, admin. — Fax 382-4725

**Clayton, Gloucester, Pop. 7,923**
Clayton SD — 1,300/PK-12
350 E Clinton St 08312 — 856-881-8700
David Lindenmuth, supt. — Fax 863-8196
claytonps.org
Clayton HS — 300/9-12
55 Pop Kramer Blvd 08312 — 856-881-8701
Fax 863-0808
Clayton MS — 300/6-8
55 Pop Kramer Blvd 08312 — 856-881-8702
Nikolaos Koutsogiannis, prin. — Fax 863-0808

**Cliffside Park, Bergen, Pop. 22,965**
Cliffside Park SD — 2,600/PK-12
525 Palisade Ave 07010 — 201-313-2310
Michael Romagnino, supt. — Fax 943-7050
www.cliffsidepark.edu

Cliffside Park HS 1,000/9-12
64 Riverview Ave 07010 201-313-2370
Lawrence Pinto, prin. Fax 313-7961

**Cliffwood, Monmouth, Pop. 1,500**
Matawan-Aberdeen Regional SD
Supt. — See Aberdeen
Matawan Aberdeen MS 800/6-8
469 Matawan Ave 07721 732-705-5400
Cory Radisch, prin. Fax 765-0894

**Clifton, Passaic, Pop. 82,465**
Clifton SD, 745 Clifton Ave 07013 10,500/K-12
Richard Tardalo, supt. 973-470-2300
www.clifton.k12.nj.us
Clifton HS 3,200/9-12
333 Colfax Ave 07013 973-470-2312
Anthony Orlando, prin. Fax 458-9290
Columbus MS 1,200/6-8
350 Piaget Ave 07011 973-470-2360
Evelyn Sherman, prin. Fax 470-2365
Wilson MS 1,300/6-8
1400 Van Houten Ave 07013 973-470-2348
Maria Caiafa-Romeo, prin. Fax 470-2607

Garfield SD
Supt. — See Garfield
Garfield Auxiliary MSHS 100/Alt
43 Clifton Ave 07011 973-272-7465
Dr. Charles Bonanno, prin. Fax 253-5696

American Institute Post-Sec.
346 Lexington Ave 07011 973-340-9500
Capri Institute of Hair Design Post-Sec.
1595 Main Ave 07011 973-772-4610
Dover Business College Post-Sec.
600 Getty Ave 07011 973-546-0123
Mesivta of Clifton 100/9-12
338 Delawanna Ave 07014 973-779-4800
Star Career Academy Post-Sec.
1231 Main Ave 07011 973-928-1700

**Clinton, Hunterdon, Pop. 2,686**
Clinton Township SD
Supt. — See Lebanon
Clinton Township MS 500/7-8
34 Grayrock Rd 08809 908-238-9141
Judith Hammond, prin. Fax 238-9376

**Closter, Bergen, Pop. 8,270**
Closter SD 1,100/PK-8
340 Homans Ave 07624 201-768-3001
Joanne Newberry, supt. Fax 768-1903
www.closterschools.org
Tenakill MS 600/5-8
275 High St 07624 201-768-1332
Joanne Newberry, prin. Fax 784-0726

**Collingswood, Camden, Pop. 13,647**
Collingswood Borough SD 1,800/PK-12
200 Lees Ave 08108 856-962-5700
Dr. Scott Oswald, supt. Fax 962-5723
www.collingswood.k12.nj.us/
Collingswood HS 700/9-12
424 W Collings Ave 08108 856-962-5701
Matthew Genna, prin. Fax 962-5565
Collingswood MS 400/6-8
414 W Collings Ave 08108 856-962-5702
Dr. John McMullin, prin. Fax 962-5751

**Colonia, Middlesex, Pop. 17,529**
Woodbridge Township SD
Supt. — See Woodbridge
Colonia HS 1,300/9-12
180 East St 07067 732-726-7060
Kenneth Pace, prin. Fax 574-2575
Colonia MS 600/6-8
100 Delaware Ave 07067 732-396-7000
Cynthia Lagunovich, prin. Fax 574-0772

**Colts Neck, Monmouth**
Colts Neck Township SD 1,200/PK-8
70 Conover Rd 07722 732-946-0055
MaryJane Garibay Ed.D., supt. Fax 858-8583
www.coltsneckschools.org
Cedar Drive MS 500/6-8
73 Cedar Dr 07722 732-946-0055
Colin Rigby, prin. Fax 462-4108

Freehold Regional HSD
Supt. — See Englishtown
Colts Neck HS 1,400/9-12
59 Five Points Rd 07722 732-761-0190
Daniel Simon, prin. Fax 761-0193

**Columbus, Burlington**
Northern Burlington County Regional SD 1,900/7-12
160 Mansfield Rd E 08022 609-298-3900
Dr. James Sarruda, supt. Fax 298-3154
www.nburlington.com
Northern Burlington County Regional HS 1,200/9-12
160 Mansfield Rd E 08022 609-298-3900
Sally Lopez, prin. Fax 298-8563
Northern Burlington County Regional JHS 700/7-8
180 Mansfield Rd E 08022 609-298-3900
Andrew Kearns Ed.D., prin. Fax 291-1563

**Convent Station, Morris**

Academy of St. Elizabeth 200/9-12
PO Box 297 07961 973-290-5202
Lynn Burek, prin. Fax 290-5335

**Cranbury, Middlesex, Pop. 2,142**

Gentle Healing School of Massage Post-Sec.
1274 S River Rd 08512 609-409-2700

**Cranford, Union, Pop. 22,624**
Cranford Township SD 3,600/K-12
132 Thomas St 07016 908-709-6202
Dr. Gayle Carrick Ed.D., supt. Fax 272-7735
www.cranfordschools.org
Cranford HS 1,100/9-12
201 W End Pl 07016 908-709-6272
Kathleen McCabe, prin. Fax 276-6552
Orange Avenue S 700/3-8
901 Orange Ave 07016 908-709-6257
Kevin Deacon, prin. Fax 272-3025

Union County College Post-Sec.
1033 Springfield Ave 07016 908-709-7000

**Cream Ridge, Monmouth**

New Jersey United Christian Academy 100/6-12
73 Holmes Mill Rd 08514 609-738-2121
Tim Costello, prin. Fax 738-2151

**Cresskill, Bergen, Pop. 8,463**
Cresskill SD 1,700/K-12
1 Lincoln Dr 07626 201-227-7791
Michael Burke, supt. Fax 567-7976
www.cboek12.org
Cresskill HS 600/9-12
1 Lincoln Dr 07626 201-567-7791
Alison Angrisani, prin. Fax 567-0028
Cresskill MS 400/6-8
1 Lincoln Dr 07626 201-227-7791
Fax 567-0028

**Delanco, Burlington, Pop. 3,316**
Delanco Township SD 400/K-8
1301 Burlington Ave 08075 856-461-1905
Joseph Mersinger, supt. Fax 461-1627
www.delanco.com
Walnut Street MS 100/6-8
411 Walnut St 08075 856-461-0874
Joseph Mersinger, admin. Fax 461-6903

**Delran, Burlington, Pop. 13,178**
Delran Township SD 2,800/PK-12
52 Hartford Rd 08075 856-461-6800
Brian Brotschul, supt. Fax 461-6125
www.delranschools.org/
Delran HS 800/9-12
50 Hartford Rd 08075 856-461-6100
Daniel Finkle, prin. Fax 764-6177
Delran MS 700/6-8
905 S Chester Ave 08075 856-461-8822
Joseph Miller, prin. Fax 461-0311

Holy Cross Academy 600/9-12
5035 Route 130 08075 856-461-5400
Dennis Guida, prin. Fax 461-0323

**Demarest, Bergen, Pop. 4,792**
Demarest SD 700/K-8
568 Piermont Rd 07627 201-768-6060
Michael Fox, supt. Fax 767-9122
demarestsd.schoolwires.net/
Demarest MS 300/5-8
568 Piermont Rd 07627 201-768-6060
Dr. Emily Codey, prin. Fax 768-9122

Northern Valley Regional HSD 2,400/9-12
162 Knickerbocker Rd 07627 201-768-2200
Dr. Geoffrey Gordon, supt. Fax 768-9488
www.nvnet.org
Northern Valley Regional HS 1,100/9-12
150 Knickerbocker Rd 07627 201-768-3200
James Santana, prin. Fax 768-5438
Other Schools – See Old Tappan

Academy of the Holy Angels 600/9-12
315 Hillside Ave 07627 201-768-7822
Jennifer Moran, prin. Fax 768-6933

**Dennisville, Cape May**
Dennis Township SD
Supt. — See Cape May Court House
Dennis Township ES 400/4-8
PO Box 363 08214 609-861-2821
Dr. Joseph LaRosa, prin. Fax 861-5229

**Denville, Morris, Pop. 13,812**
Denville Township SD 1,800/PK-8
400 Morris Ave Ste 279 07834 973-983-6530
Steven Forte, supt. Fax 784-4778
www.denville.org
Valleyview MS 700/6-8
320 Diamond Spring Rd 07834 973-983-6535
Paul Iantosca, prin. Fax 627-0632

Morris County Vocational SD
400 E Main St 07834 973-627-4600
Scott Moffitt, supt. Fax 627-6979
www.mcvts.org
Morris County School of Technology Vo/Tech
400 E Main St 07834 973-627-4600
Lynne Jackson, prin. Fax 627-4958
Other Schools – See Butler, Rockaway

Morris Catholic HS 400/9-12
200 Morris Ave 07834 973-627-6660
Robert Loia, prin. Fax 627-4351

**Deptford, Gloucester**
Deptford Township SD 4,200/PK-12
2022 Good Intent Rd 08096 856-232-2700
Dr. Charles Ford Jr, supt. Fax 227-7473
www.deptford.k12.nj.us
Deptford Township HS 1,000/9-12
575 Fox Run Rd 08096 856-232-2713
Melvin Allen, prin. Fax 374-9145
Other Schools – See Sewell

**Dover, Morris, Pop. 17,974**
Dover Town SD 2,900/PK-12
100 Grace St 07801 973-989-2000
Robert Becker, supt. Fax 989-1662
district.dover-nj.org
Dover HS 800/9-12
100 Grace St 07801 973-989-2010
Delvis Rodriguez, prin. Fax 989-1662
Dover MS 400/7-8
302 E McFarlan St 07801 973-989-2040
Robert Franks, prin. Fax 361-2117

Dover Business College Post-Sec.
1 W Blackwell St 07801 973-285-8400
Joe Kubert Sch of Cartoon & Graphic Arts Post-Sec.
37 Myrtle Ave 07801 973-361-1327

**Dumont, Bergen, Pop. 17,212**
Dumont SD 2,600/PK-12
25 Depew St 07628 201-387-1600
Emanuele Triggiano, supt. Fax 387-0259
www.dumontnj.org
Dumont HS 900/9-12
101 New Milford Ave 07628 201-387-3000
James Wichmann, prin. Fax 387-8461

**Dunellen, Middlesex, Pop. 7,100**
Dunellen SD 1,100/PK-12
400 High St 08812 732-968-3226
Pio Pennisi, supt. Fax 968-3513
www.dunellenschools.org
Dunellen HS 300/9-12
411 1st St 08812 732-968-0885
Paul Lynch, prin. Fax 968-3138
Lincoln MS 300/6-8
400 Dunellen Ave 08812 732-968-0885
Robert Altmire, prin. Fax 424-1359

**East Brunswick, Middlesex, Pop. 47,400**
East Brunswick Township SD 8,100/PK-12
760 State Route 18 08816 732-613-6700
Victor Valeski, supt. Fax 698-9871
www.ebnet.org
Churchill JHS 1,500/8-9
18 Norton Rd 08816 732-613-6800
Mark Sutor, prin. Fax 257-0087
East Brunswick HS 2,200/10-12
380 Cranbury Rd 08816 732-613-6904
Dr. Michael Vinella, prin. Fax 254-1938

Middlesex County Vocational SD
PO Box 1070 08816 732-257-3300
Brian Loughlin, supt. Fax 257-9388
www.mcvts.net
East Brunswick Vocational HS Vo/Tech
PO Box 1070 08816 732-254-8700
Jeffrey Bicsko, prin. Fax 613-9608
Other Schools – See Edison, Perth Amboy, Piscataway, Woodbridge

**East Hanover, Morris, Pop. 9,926**
East Hanover Township SD 1,100/PK-8
20 School Ave 07936 973-887-2112
Dr. Scott Rubin, supt. Fax 887-2773
www.easthanoverschools.org/
East Hanover MS 400/6-8
477 Ridgedale Ave 07936 973-887-8810
Stacie Costello, prin. Fax 887-5079

Hanover Park Regional HSD 1,500/9-12
75 Mount Pleasant Ave 07936 973-887-0320
Carol Grossi, supt. Fax 887-9247
www.hpreg.org
Hanover Park HS 800/9-12
63 Mount Pleasant Ave 07936 973-887-0300
Thomas Callanan, prin. Fax 515-7680
Other Schools – See Whippany

**East Orange, Essex, Pop. 62,841**
East Orange SD 7,500/PK-12
199 4th Ave 07017 973-266-5760
Dr. Gloria Scott, supt. Fax 678-4865
www.eastorange.k12.nj.us
East Orange Campus HS 1,300/10-12
344 Prospect St 07017 973-266-7300
Jose Aviles, prin. Fax 266-7368
East Orange Campus STEM Academy 200/6-12
129 Renshaw Ave 07017 973-266-5900
Dr. Nicholas Del Tufo, prin. Fax 266-3473
Fresh Start Academy Alt
74 Halsted St 07018 973-266-5640
Dr. Neville Matadin, admin. Fax 673-1374
Tyson Comm MSHS Prfrmg/Fine Arts 800/6-12
35 Winans St 07017 973-414-8600
Anita Champagne, prin. Fax 395-3888

Ahlus Sunnah S 100/PK-12
215 N Oraton Pkwy 07017 973-672-4121
Best Care Training Institute Post-Sec.
68 S Harrison St 07017 973-673-3900
National Career Institute Post-Sec.
134 Evergreen Pl Fl 2 07018 973-678-3901

**East Rutherford, Bergen, Pop. 8,757**
Carlstadt-East Rutherford Regional HSD 500/9-12
120 Paterson Ave 07073 201-935-3007
Louise Clarke, supt. Fax 935-5639
www.bectonhs.org/
Becton Regional HS 500/9-12
120 Paterson Ave 07073 201-935-3007
Dario Sforza, prin. Fax 935-5639

East Rutherford SD 800/PK-8
100 Uhland St 07073 201-804-3100
Joseph Abate, supt. Fax 804-3131
www.erboe.net/
Faust MS 300/5-8
100 Uhland St 07073 201-804-3100
Regina Barrale, prin. Fax 804-3131

**East Windsor, Mercer, Pop. 22,353**
East Windsor Regional SD
Supt. — See Hightstown
Kreps MS 1,200/6-8
5 Kent Ln 08520 609-443-7767
Lori Emmerson, prin. Fax 443-8972

**Eatontown, Monmouth, Pop. 12,304**
Eatontown SD 1,000/PK-8
5 Grant Ave 07724 732-542-1310
Scott T. McCue, supt. Fax 578-0017
www.eatontown.org

Memorial MS 200/7-8
7 Grant Ave 07724 732-542-5013
Jay Medlin, prin. Fax 389-1364

**Edgewater Park, Burlington, Pop. 8,388**
Edgewater Park Township SD 800/PK-8
25 Washington Ave 08010 609-877-2124
Dr. Roy Rakszawski, supt. Fax 877-4235
edgewaterparksd.org
Ridgeway MS 300/5-8
300 Delanco Rd 08010 609-871-3434
Ronald Trampe, prin. Fax 871-2434

**Edison, Middlesex, Pop. 99,500**
Edison Township SD 13,900/PK-12
312 Pierson Ave 08837 732-452-4900
Dr. Richard O'Malley, supt. Fax 452-4993
www.edison.k12.nj.us
Adams MS 800/6-8
1081 New Dover Rd 08820 732-452-2920
Joan Valentine, prin. Fax 452-2922
Edison HS 2,000/9-12
50 Boulevard of Eagles 08817 732-650-5200
Charles Ross, prin. Fax 650-5259
Hoover MS 800/6-8
174 Jackson Ave 08837 732-452-2940
Brian McGrath, prin. Fax 452-2950
Jefferson MS 700/6-8
450 Division St 08817 732-650-5290
Antoinette Emden, prin. Fax 652-5295
Stevens HS 2,200/9-12
855 Grove Ave 08820 732-452-2800
Gail Pawlikowski, prin. Fax 452-2863
Wilson MS 900/6-8
50 Woodrow Wilson Dr 08820 732-452-2870
Patricia Cotoia, prin. Fax 452-2876

Middlesex County Vocational SD
Supt. — See East Brunswick
Academy of Math Sci & Engineering/Tech Vo/Tech
100 Technology Dr 08837 732-452-2600
Dr. Linda Russo, prin. Fax 906-8421

---

Bishop George Ahr HS 900/9-12
1 Tingley Ln 08820 732-549-1108
Sr. Donna Trukowski, prin. Fax 494-2229
Lincoln Technical Institute Post-Sec.
1697 Oak Tree Rd 08820 732-548-8798
Middlesex County College Post-Sec.
2600 Woodbridge Ave 08837 732-548-6000
PC AGE Career Institute Post-Sec.
145 Talmadge Rd Ste 19 08817 732-287-3622
Rabbi Jacob Joseph School Post-Sec.
1 Plainfield Ave 08817 732-985-6533
Rabbi Jacob Joseph S 100/9-12
1 Plainfield Ave 08817 732-985-6533
Wardlaw-Hartridge S 400/PK-12
1295 Inman Ave 08820 908-754-1882
Andrew Webster, hdmstr. Fax 754-9678

**Egg Harbor City, Atlantic, Pop. 4,134**
Egg Harbor City SD 500/PK-8
730 Havana Ave 08215 609-965-1034
Adrienne Shulby, supt. Fax 965-6719
www.ehcs.k12.nj.us
Egg Harbor City Community S 200/4-8
730 Havana Ave 08215 609-965-1034
Jack Griffith, prin. Fax 965-4742

Greater Egg Harbor Regional HSD
Supt. — See Mays Landing
Cedar Creek HS 600/9-12
1701 New York Ave 08215 609-593-3560
James Reina, prin. Fax 593-3570

---

Pilgrim Academy 300/PK-12
PO Box 322 08215 609-965-2866
Christopher Storr, hdmstr. Fax 965-3379

**Egg Harbor Township, Atlantic**
Egg Harbor Township SD 7,600/PK-12
13 Swift Ave 08234 609-646-7911
Dr. Scott McCartney, supt. Fax 383-8749
www.eht.k12.nj.us
Alder Avenue MS 800/6-8
25 Alder Ave 08234 609-383-3366
Joseph Marinelli, prin. Fax 383-1492
Eagle Academy Alt
3517 Bargaintown Rd 08234 609-926-1235
Earl Smith, dir. Fax 926-1095
Egg Harbor Township HS 2,500/9-12
24 High School Dr 08234 609-653-0100
Terry Charlton, prin. Fax 927-8844
Fernwood Avenue MS 1,000/6-8
4034 Fernwood Ave 08234 609-383-3355
James Battersby, prin. Fax 383-0628

---

Atlantic Christian S 400/PK-12
391 Zion Rd 08234 609-653-1199
Karen Oblen, head sch Fax 653-1435
Star Career Academy Post-Sec.
3003 English Creek Ave #212 08234 609-407-2999
Trocki Hebrew Academy 50/PK-12
6814 Black Horse Pike 08234 609-383-8484

**Elizabeth, Union, Pop. 122,789**
Elizabeth SD 22,500/PK-12
500 N Broad St 07208 908-436-5000
Olga Hugelmeyer, supt. Fax 436-6133
www.epsnj.org
Dwyer Technology Academy 800/9-12
123 Pearl St 07202 908-436-6565
Diana Pinto-Gomez, prin.
Edison Career & Technical Academy 600/9-12
625 Summer St 07202 908-436-6800
Fatimah Bey, prin. Fax 436-6780
Elizabeth HS 300/9-12
447 Richmond St 07202 908-436-5870
Michael Cummings, admin. Fax 436-5861
Halsey Leadership Academy 900/9-12
641 South St 07202 908-436-6600
Jeffrey Roszkowski, prin.
Hamilton Preparatory Academy 900/9-12
310 Cherry St 07208 908-436-6100
George Mikros, prin. Fax 436-6082
Jefferson Arts Academy 800/9-12
27 Martin Luther King Plz 07201 908-436-6767
Michael Ojeda, prin. Fax 436-6733

---

Benedictine Academy 200/9-12
840 N Broad St 07208 908-352-0670
James Sarto, prin. Fax 352-0698
Drake College of Business Post-Sec.
125 Broad St 07201 908-352-5509
Elizabeth General Medical Center School Post-Sec.
925 E Jersey St 07201 908-965-7390
Jewish Educational Center - Bruriah HS 400/7-12
35 North Ave 07208 908-355-4850
Rav Teitz Mesivta Academy 200/6-12
330 Elmora Ave 07208 908-355-4850
St. Mary of the Assumption HS 200/9-12
237 S Broad St 07202 908-352-4350
David Evans, prin. Fax 352-2359
Union County College Post-Sec.
40 W Jersey St Fl 8 07202 908-965-6000
Yeshivas Be'er Yitzchok Post-Sec.
1391 North Ave 07208 908-354-6057

**Elmwood Park, Bergen, Pop. 19,032**
Elmwood Park SD 2,400/PK-12
60 E 53rd St 07407 201-796-8700
Anthony Grieco, supt. Fax 703-9337
www.epps.org
Memorial HS 800/9-12
375 River Dr 07407 201-796-8700
David Warner, prin. Fax 797-1405
Memorial MS 600/6-8
375 River Dr 07407 201-796-8700
Corinne DiMartino, prin. Fax 797-1405

**Elwood, Atlantic, Pop. 1,395**
Mullica Township SD 700/PK-8
PO Box 318 08217 609-561-3868
Dr. Thomas Baruffi, supt. Fax 561-7133
www.mullica.k12.nj.us
Mullica Township MS 300/5-8
PO Box 318 08217 609-561-3868
Matt Mazzoni, prin. Fax 561-7133

**Emerson, Bergen, Pop. 7,299**
Emerson SD 1,200/PK-12
131 Main St 07630 201-262-3875
Brian Gatens, supt. Fax 599-4160
www.emersonschools.org
Emerson JSHS 500/7-12
131 Main St 07630 201-262-4447
Brian Hutchinson, prin. Fax 262-1041

**Englewood, Bergen, Pop. 26,555**
Englewood CSD 2,800/PK-12
274 Knickerbocker Rd 07631 201-862-6000
Michelle James, supt. Fax 569-6099
www.epsd.org
Dismus MS 400/7-8
325 Tryon Ave 07631 201-862-6025
Lamarr Thomas, prin. Fax 833-9103
Morrow HS 1,000/9-12
274 Knickerbocker Rd 07631 201-862-6039
Peter Elbert, prin. Fax 833-9620

---

Dwight-Englewood S 900/PK-12
315 E Palisade Ave 07631 201-569-9500
Dr. Rodney DeJarnett, head sch Fax 569-1676
Englewood Hospital & Medical Center Post-Sec.
350 Engle St 07631 201-894-3002
Yeshiva Ohr Simcha of Englewood 50/9-12
101 W Forest Ave 07631 201-816-1800

**Englewood Cliffs, Bergen, Pop. 5,175**
Englewood Cliffs SD 400/PK-8
143 Charlotte Pl 07632 201-567-7292
Robert Kravitz, supt. Fax 567-2738
www.englewoodcliffs.org
Upper S 200/3-8
143 Charlotte Pl 07632 201-567-6151
Robert Kravitz, prin. Fax 541-8672

---

St. Peter's University Post-Sec.
Hudson Terrace 07632 201-761-7480

**Englishtown, Monmouth, Pop. 1,825**
Freehold Regional HSD 11,400/9-12
11 Pine St 07726 732-792-7300
Charles Sampson, supt. Fax 446-9126
www.frhsd.com
Manalapan HS 2,000/9-12
20 Church Ln 07726 732-792-7200
Dr. Adam Angelozzi, prin. Fax 446-4981
Other Schools – See Colts Neck, Farmingdale, Freehold, Marlboro

Manalapan-Englishtown Regional SD 5,000/PK-8
54 Main St 07726 732-786-2500
John Marciante Ph.D., supt. Fax 786-2542
www.mers.k12.nj.us
Other Schools – See Manalapan

**Erial, Camden, Pop. 2,500**
Black Horse Pike Regional SD
Supt. — See Blackwood
Timber Creek Regional HS 1,400/9-12
501 Jarvis Rd 08081 856-232-9703
Mae Robinson, prin. Fax 232-5267

---

Divers Academy International Post-Sec.
1500 Liberty Pl 08081 856-404-6100

**Ewing, Mercer, Pop. 36,000**
Ewing Township SD 3,500/PK-12
2099 Pennington Rd 08618 609-538-9800
Michael Nitti, supt. Fax 538-0041
www.ewing.k12.nj.us
Ewing HS 1,100/9-12
900 Parkway Ave 08618 609-538-9800
Rodney Logan Ed.D., prin. Fax 882-8172
Fisher MS 900/6-8
1325 Lower Ferry Rd 08618 609-538-9800
Barbara Brower, prin. Fax 637-9753

---

College of New Jersey Post-Sec.
2000 Pennington Rd 08618 609-771-1855
Villa Victoria Academy - Upper 100/9-12
376 W Upper Ferry Rd 08628 609-882-1700
Sr. Lesley Draper, prin. Fax 882-8421

**Fairfield, Essex, Pop. 7,615**
Essex Regional Educ Services Commission 50/6-12
369 Passaic Ave 07004 973-405-6262
Fax 405-6555
www.eresc.com
Essex Campus Academy 50/Alt
369 Passaic Ave 07004 973-575-0469
David Pinkney, prin. Fax 575-0136
Other Schools – See Newark, Passaic

---

StenoTech Career Institute Post-Sec.
20 Just Rd 07004 888-783-6685

**Fair Haven, Monmouth, Pop. 6,047**
Fair Haven Borough SD 900/PK-8
224 Hance Rd 07704 732-747-2294
Nelson Ribon, supt. Fax 747-7441
www.fairhaven.edu
Knollwood MS 500/4-8
224 Hance Rd 07704 732-747-0320
Kevin Davis, prin. Fax 747-7441

**Fair Lawn, Bergen, Pop. 32,055**
Fair Lawn SD 4,400/PK-12
37-01 Fair Lawn Ave 07410 201-794-5500
Bruce Watson, supt. Fax 797-9296
www.fairlawnschools.org/
Fair Lawn HS 1,500/9-12
14-00 Berdan Ave 07410 201-794-5450
James Marcella, prin. Fax 794-8107
Jefferson MS 700/6-8
35-01 Morlot Ave 07410 201-703-2240
Sherrie Galofaro, prin. Fax 475-9185
Memorial MS 400/6-8
12-00 1st St 07410 201-794-5470
Scott Helfand, prin. Fax 703-2237

---

Artistic Academy of Hair Design Post-Sec.
21 S Broadway 07410 201-794-3502

**Fairview, Bergen, Pop. 13,423**
Fairview SD 1,100/PK-8
130 Hamilton Ave 07022 201-943-0201
David Sleppin, supt. Fax 941-1195
fairviewps.org
Lincoln S 600/4-8
140 Anderson Ave 07022 201-943-0560
Lea Turro, prin. Fax 943-7154

**Farmingdale, Monmouth, Pop. 1,307**
Freehold Regional HSD
Supt. — See Englishtown
Howell HS 2,400/9-12
405 Squankum Yellowbrook Rd 07727 732-919-2131
Jeremy Braverman, prin. Fax 919-1964

Howell Township SD 6,100/PK-8
200 Squankum Yellowbrook Rd 07727 732-751-2480
Joseph Isola, supt. Fax 919-1060
www.howell.k12.nj.us
Howell Township MS North 800/6-8
501 Squankum Yellowbrook Rd 07727 732-919-0095
Paul Farley, prin. Fax 919-1008
Other Schools – See Howell

**Flanders, Morris, Pop. 1,200**
Mt. Olive Township SD 4,500/K-12
227 US Highway 206 Ste 10 07836 973-691-4000
Larrie Reynolds Ph.D., supt. Fax 691-4022
www.mtoliveboe.org
Mt. Olive HS 1,400/9-12
18 Corey Rd 07836 973-927-2208
Kevin Stansberry, prin. Fax 927-2204
Other Schools – See Budd Lake

**Flemington, Hunterdon, Pop. 4,482**
Flemington-Raritan Regional SD 3,500/PK-8
50 Court St 08822 908-284-7561
Maryrose Caulfield, supt. Fax 284-7514
www.frsd.k12.nj.us/
Case MS 800/7-8
301 Case Blvd 08822 908-284-5100
Robert Castellano, prin. Fax 284-5144

Hudson County Schools of Technology
Supt. — See North Bergen
Hunterdon County Adult S Vo/Tech
8 Bartles Corner Rd Ste 2 08822 201-778-1119
Christina Shockley, dir.

Hunterdon Central Regional SD 3,100/9-12
84 State Route 31 08822 908-782-5727
Christina Steffner, supt. Fax 284-7138
www.hcrhs.k12.nj.us
Hunterdon Central Regional HS 3,100/9-12
84 State Route 31 08822 908-782-5727
Suzanne Cooley, prin. Fax 284-7138

Hunterdon County Vocational SD
8 Bartles Corner Rd Ste 2 08822 908-788-1119
Dr. Kimberly Metz, supt. Fax 806-4839
www.hcpolytech.org
Hunterdon County Vocational S - Bartles Vo/Tech
8 Bartles Corner Rd 08822 908-788-1119
Dan Kerr, prin. Fax 806-4839
Hunterdon County Vocational S - Central Vo/Tech
10 Junction Rd 08822 908-284-1444
Dan Kerr, prin. Fax 284-9824
Other Schools – See Frenchtown

**Florence, Burlington, Pop. 4,260**
Florence Township SD — 1,500/K-12
201 Cedar St 08518 — 609-499-4600
Donna Ambrosius, supt. — Fax 499-9679
www.florence.k12.nj.us
Florence Township Memorial HS — 400/9-12
1050 Cedar Ln 08518 — 609-499-4620
John Cogan, prin. — Fax 499-3424
Riverfront S — 600/4-8
500 E Front St 08518 — 609-499-4647
Rosario Casiano, prin. — Fax 499-8356

**Florham Park, Morris, Pop. 11,496**
Florham Park SD — 1,000/PK-8
PO Box 39 07932 — 973-822-3880
Dr. Melissa Varley, supt. — Fax 822-0716
www.fpks.org
Ridgedale MS — 300/6-8
71 Ridgedale Ave 07932 — 973-822-3855
Peter Christ, prin. — Fax 822-7963

**Fords, Middlesex, Pop. 14,870**
Woodbridge Township SD
Supt. — See Woodbridge
Fords MS — 700/6-8
100 Fanning St 08863 — 732-596-4200
James Parry, prin. — Fax 417-2159

**Forked River, Ocean, Pop. 5,199**
Lacey Township SD
Supt. — See Lanoka Harbor
Lacey Township MS — 700/7-8
660 Denton Ave 08731 — 609-242-2100
Jason King, prin. — Fax 242-2114

**Fort Lee, Bergen, Pop. 34,777**
Fort Lee SD — 3,500/PK-12
2175 Lemoine Ave Fl 6 07024 — 201-585-4612
Kenneth Rota, supt. — Fax 585-7997
www.flboe.com
Cole MS — 500/7-8
467 Stillwell Ave 07024 — 201-585-4660
Robert Daniello, prin. — Fax 585-1688
Fort Lee HS — 1,000/9-12
3000 Lemoine Ave 07024 — 201-585-4675
Dr. Lauren Glynn, prin. — Fax 585-2296

**Franklin Lakes, Bergen, Pop. 10,458**
Franklin Lakes SD — 1,300/PK-8
490 Pulis Ave 07417 — 201-891-1856
Dr. Lydia Furnari, supt. — Fax 891-9333
www.franklinlakes.k12.nj.us
Franklin Avenue MS — 500/6-8
755 Franklin Ave 07417 — 201-891-0202
Joseph Keiser, prin. — Fax 848-5190

Ramapo Indian Hills Regional HSD
Supt. — See Oakland
Ramapo HS — 1,100/9-12
331 George St 07417 — 201-891-1500
Dr. Louis Moore, prin. — Fax 891-6844

**Franklinville, Gloucester**
Delsea Regional SD — 1,600/7-12
242 Fries Mill Rd 08322 — 856-694-0100
Dr. Piera Gravenor, supt. — Fax 694-4417
www.delsearegional.us/
Delsea Regional HS — 1,100/9-12
PO Box 405 08322 — 856-694-0100
Paul Berardelli, prin. — Fax 694-2046
Delsea Regional MS — 500/7-8
PO Box 405 08322 — 856-694-0100
Jill Bryfogle, prin. — Fax 694-4417

**Freehold, Monmouth, Pop. 11,870**
Freehold Borough SD — 1,400/PK-8
280 Park Ave 07728 — 732-761-2100
Rocco Tomazic Ed.D., supt. — Fax 462-8954
www.freeholdboro.k12.nj.us
Freehold IS — 400/6-8
280 Park Ave 07728 — 732-761-2156
Ronnie Dougherty, prin. — Fax 761-2181

Freehold Regional HSD
Supt. — See Englishtown
Freehold Borough HS — 1,500/9-12
2 Robertsville Rd 07728 — 732-431-8360
Linda Jewell, prin. — Fax 577-8228
Freehold Township HS — 2,200/9-12
281 Elton Adelphia Rd 07728 — 732-431-8460
Elizabeth Higley, prin. — Fax 780-5314

Freehold Township SD — 4,100/PK-8
384 W Main St 07728 — 732-866-8400
Ross Kasun Ed.D., supt. — Fax 761-1809
www.freeholdtwp.k12.nj.us/
Barkalow MS — 800/6-8
498 Stillwells Corner Rd 07728 — 732-431-4403
John Soviero, prin. — Fax 294-5560
Eisenhower MS — 800/6-8
279 Burlington Rd 07728 — 732-431-3910
Dianne Brethauer, prin. — Fax 294-7180

Monmouth County Vocational SD
PO Box 5033 07728 — 732-431-7942
Timothy McCorkell, supt. — Fax 409-6736
www.mcvsd.org
Biotechnology HS — Vo/Tech
5000 Kozloski Rd 07728 — 732-431-6443
Linda Eno, prin. — Fax 409-6736
Freehold Vocational S — Vo/Tech
21 Robertsville Rd 07728 — 732-462-7570
Anthony Villane, prin. — Fax 294-0569
Monmouth County Career Center — Vo/Tech
1000 Kozloski Rd 07728 — 732-431-3773
Thomas Sansevero, prin. — Fax 409-7292
Other Schools – See Aberdeen, Asbury Park, Hazlet, Highlands, Keyport, Lincroft, Long Branch, Middletown, Neptune, Tinton Falls, Wall

**Frenchtown, Hunterdon, Pop. 1,362**
Delaware Valley Regional HSD — 700/9-12
19 Senator Stout Rd 08825 — 908-996-2727
Daria Wasserbach, supt. — Fax 996-4527
www.dvrhs.org
Delaware Valley Regional HS — 700/9-12
19 Senator Stout Rd 08825 — 908-996-2131
Adrienne Olcott, prin. — Fax 996-6653

Hunterdon County Vocational SD
Supt. — See Flemington
Hunterdon Co. Computer Science Academy — Vo/Tech
19 Senator Stout Rd 08825 — 908-788-1119
Jessica Cangelosi-Hade, dir. — Fax 284-1391

**Galloway, Atlantic**
Galloway Township SD — 3,200/PK-8
101 S Reeds Rd 08205 — 609-748-1250
Annette Giaquinto Ed.D., supt. — Fax 748-1796
www.gtps.k12.nj.us
Galloway Township MS — 800/7-8
100 S Reeds Rd 08205 — 609-748-1250
Paula Junker, prin. — Fax 748-8926

Greater Egg Harbor Regional HSD
Supt. — See Mays Landing
Absegami HS — 1,800/9-12
201 S Wrangleboro Rd 08205 — 609-652-1372
Jeri-Lynn Gatto Ed.D., prin. — Fax 652-0139

---

Richard Stockton College of New Jersey — Post-Sec.
101 Vera King Farris Dr 08205 — 609-652-1776

**Garfield, Bergen, Pop. 30,041**
Garfield SD — 4,400/PK-12
34 Outwater Ln 07026 — 973-340-5000
Nicholas Perrapato, supt. — Fax 340-4620
www.garfield.k12.nj.us/
Garfield HS — 1,000/9-12
500 Palisade Ave 07026 — 973-340-5010
Dora D'Amico, prin. — Fax 546-8430
Garfield MS — 900/6-8
175 Lanza Ave 07026 — 973-272-7020
Anna Sciacca, prin. — Fax 340-1767
Other Schools – See Clifton

**Gibbstown, Gloucester, Pop. 3,693**
Greenwich Township SD — 500/PK-8
415 Swedesboro Rd 08027 — 856-224-4920
Thomas Schulte, supt. — Fax 224-5761
www.greenwich.k12.nj.us
Nehaunsey MS — 200/5-8
415 Swedesboro Rd 08027 — 856-224-4920
Alisa Whitcraft, prin. — Fax 224-5765

**Gillette, Morris**
Long Hill Township SD — 900/PK-8
759 Valley Rd 07933 — 908-647-1200
John Petrelli, supt. — Fax 647-1200
www.longhill.org
Other Schools – See Stirling

**Gladstone, Somerset, Pop. 2,086**

---

Gill St. Bernard's S — 700/PK-12
PO Box 604 07934 — 908-234-1611
Sid Rowell, hdmstr. — Fax 234-1712

**Glassboro, Gloucester, Pop. 18,158**
Glassboro SD — 1,800/PK-12
560 Bowe Blvd 08028 — 856-652-2700
Dr. Mark Silverstein, supt. — Fax 881-0884
www.glassboroschools.us
Glassboro HS — 500/9-12
550 Bowe Blvd 08028 — 856-652-2700
Dr. Danielle Sneathen, prin. — Fax 307-1189
Glassboro IS — 300/7-8
202 Delsea Dr N 08028 — 856-652-2700
Kriston Matthews, prin. — Fax 881-3751

---

Rowan University — Post-Sec.
201 Mullica Hill Rd 08028 — 856-256-4000

**Glen Gardner, Hunterdon, Pop. 1,684**
North Hunterdon/Voorhees Regional HSD
Supt. — See Annandale
Voorhees HS — 1,100/9-12
256 County Road 513 08826 — 908-638-6116
Ronald Peterson, prin. — Fax 638-8689

**Glen Ridge, Essex, Pop. 7,336**
Glen Ridge SD — 1,600/PK-12
12 High St 07028 — 973-429-8302
Dirk Phillips, supt. — Fax 429-5750
www.glenridge.org
Glen Ridge HS — 700/7-12
200 Ridgewood Ave 07028 — 973-429-8303
Fax 429-3531

**Glen Rock, Bergen, Pop. 11,424**
Glen Rock SD — 2,400/K-12
620 Harristown Rd 07452 — 201-445-7700
Dr. Paula Valenti, supt. — Fax 389-5019
www.glenrocknj.org
Glen Rock HS — 700/9-12
600 Harristown Rd 07452 — 201-445-7700
John Arlotta, prin. — Fax 389-5015
Glen Rock MS — 600/6-8
400 Hamilton Ave 07452 — 201-445-7700
Edward Thompson, prin. — Fax 389-5042

**Gloucester City, Camden, Pop. 11,306**
Gloucester City SD — 1,900/PK-12
520 Cumberland St 08030 — 856-456-7000
Joseph Rafferty, supt. — Fax 742-8815
www.gcsd.k12.nj.us
Gloucester City JSHS — 800/7-12
1300 Market St 08030 — 856-456-7000
Sean Gorman, prin. — Fax 456-2348
Gloucester City Adult HS — Adult
1300 Market St 08030 — 856-456-7000
Victoria Ernst, prin. — Fax 742-8570

---

Gloucester Catholic HS — 700/7-12
333 Ridgeway St 08030 — 856-456-4400
Edward Beckett, prin. — Fax 456-0506
P.B. Cosmetology Education Centre — Post-Sec.
110 Monmouth St 08030 — 856-456-4927

**Great Meadows, Warren, Pop. 303**
Great Meadows Regional SD — 800/K-8
PO Box 74 07838 — 908-637-6576
David C. Mango, supt. — Fax 637-6356
www.gmrsd.com
Great Meadows Regional MS — 300/6-8
273 US Highway 46 07838 — 908-637-4584
Israel Marmolejos, prin. — Fax 637-4492

**Green Brook, Somerset**
Green Brook Township SD — 900/PK-8
132 Jefferson Ave 08812 — 732-968-1171
Kevin Carroll, supt. — Fax 968-1869
www.gbtps.org
Green Brook MS — 600/4-8
132 Jefferson Ave 08812 — 732-968-1051
James Bigsby, prin. — Fax 752-1086

**Hackensack, Bergen, Pop. 42,163**
Bergen County Vocational Technical SD
Supt. — See Paramus
Bergen County Academies — Vo/Tech
200 Hackensack Ave 07601 — 201-343-6000
Russell Davis, prin. — Fax 996-6955
Bergen Co. Adult & Continuing Education — Adult
200 Hackensack Ave 07601 — 201-343-6000
Paul Castiglia, prin.

Hackensack SD — 4,400/PK-12
191 2nd St 07601 — 201-646-7830
Karen Lewis, supt. — Fax 646-7827
www.hackensackschools.org
Hackensack HS — 1,700/9-12
135 1st St 07601 — 201-646-7900
James Montesano, prin. — Fax 646-7922
Hackensack MS — 1,300/5-8
360 Union St 07601 — 201-646-7842
Corey Jones, prin. — Fax 646-7840

---

Academy of Massage Therapy — Post-Sec.
321 Main St 07601 — 201-568-3220
Center for Allied Health & Nursing Educ — Post-Sec.
387 Main St 07601 — 201-489-5836
Eastwick College — Post-Sec.
250 Moore St 07601 — 201-488-9400
Hackensack Univ Medical Center — Post-Sec.
30 Prospect Ave 07601 — 201-996-2000
Parisian Academy — Post-Sec.
21 Passaic St 07601 — 201-487-2203

**Hackettstown, Warren, Pop. 9,581**
Hackettstown SD — 1,800/PK-12
PO Box 465 07840 — 908-852-2800
David C. Mango, supt. — Fax 852-0286
www.hackettstown.org
Hackettstown HS — 900/9-12
701 Warren St 07840 — 908-852-8150
Matthew Scanlon, prin. — Fax 852-6214
Hackettstown MS — 400/5-8
500 Washington St 07840 — 908-852-8554
William Thompson, prin. — Fax 850-6544

---

Centenary College — Post-Sec.
400 Jefferson St 07840 — 908-852-1400

**Haddonfield, Camden, Pop. 11,436**
Haddonfield Borough SD — 2,400/PK-12
1 Lincoln Ave 08033 — 856-429-7510
Dr. Richard Perry, supt. — Fax 429-6015
www.haddonfield.k12.nj.us
Haddonfield Memorial HS — 700/9-12
401 Kings Hwy E 08033 — 856-429-3960
Chuck Klaus, prin. — Fax 795-8910
Haddonfield MS — 600/6-8
5 Lincoln Ave 08033 — 856-429-5851
Dennis Moroldo, prin. — Fax 429-2006

---

Paul VI HS — 1,100/9-12
901 Hopkins Rd Ste B 08033 — 856-858-4900
Sr. Marianne McCann, prin. — Fax 858-6832

**Haddon Heights, Camden, Pop. 7,379**
Haddon Heights SD — 1,300/PK-12
316A 7th Ave 08035 — 856-547-1412
Michael Adams, supt. — Fax 547-3868
hhsd.k12.nj.us
Haddon Heights JSHS — 800/7-12
301 2nd Ave 08035 — 856-547-1920
Ron Corn, prin. — Fax 547-6808

---

Baptist Regional S — 200/K-12
300 Station Ave 08035 — 856-547-2996
Lynn Conahan, admin. — Fax 547-6584

**Haledon, Passaic, Pop. 8,172**
Passaic County Manchester Regional HSD — 800/9-12
70 Church St 07508 — 973-389-2820
Dr. Michael Wanko, supt. — Fax 956-8805
www.mrhs.net
Manchester Regional HS — 800/9-12
70 Church St 07508 — 973-389-2820
Dr. Richard Ney, prin. — Fax 956-8805

**Hamburg, Sussex, Pop. 3,209**
Hardyston Township SD — 700/PK-8
183 Wheatsworth Rd 07419 — 973-823-7000
Dr. Richard Corbett, supt. — Fax 823-7010
www.htps.org
Hardyston MS — 300/5-8
183 Wheatsworth Rd 07419 — 973-823-7000
Dr. Richard Corbett, prin. — Fax 823-7011

Wallkill Valley Regional SD — 700/9-12
10 Grumm Rd 07419 — 973-827-4100
Robert Walker, supt. — Fax 827-8318
www.wallkill.k12.nj.us
Wallkill Valley Regional HS — 700/9-12
10 Grumm Rd 07419 — 973-827-4100
Robert Walker, prin. — Fax 827-8318

**Hamilton, Mercer**
Hamilton Township SD 11,800/PK-12
90 Park Ave 08690 609-631-4100
Thomas Ficarra, supt. Fax 631-4103
www.hamilton.k12.nj.us
Crockett MS 800/6-8
2631 Kuser Rd 08691 609-631-4149
Roger Bigos, prin. Fax 631-4116
Grice MS 900/6-8
901 Whitehorse Hamilton Sq 08610 609-631-4152
David Innocenzi, prin. Fax 631-4119
Hamilton East-Steinert HS 1,500/9-12
2900 Klockner Rd 08690 609-631-4150
Frank Ingargiola, prin. Fax 631-4117
Hamilton North-Nottingham HS 1,300/9-12
1055 Klockner Rd 08619 609-631-4161
Michael Giambelluca, prin. Fax 631-4129
Hamilton West-Watson HS 1,300/9-12
2720 S Clinton Ave 08610 609-631-4168
Jeff Hudanish, prin. Fax 631-4137
Reynolds MS 1,000/6-8
2145 Yrdvll Hamilton Squ Rd 08690 609-631-4162
P. Landolfi-Collins, prin. Fax 631-4130
Accredited Evening HS Adult
90 Park Ave 08690 609-631-4100
Steven Bollar, prin. Fax 631-4106

---

Trenton Catholic Academy - Upper 200/9-12
175 Leonard Ave 08610 609-586-3705
Timothy Lynch, prin. Fax 586-6584

**Hammonton, Atlantic, Pop. 14,622**
Hammonton SD 3,200/PK-12
566 Old Forks Rd 08037 609-567-7000
Dr. Dan Blachford, supt. Fax 561-3567
www.hammontonps.org/
Hammonton HS 1,300/9-12
566 Old Forks Rd 08037 609-567-7000
Thomas Ramsay, prin. Fax 567-5985
Hammonton MS 800/6-8
75 N Liberty St 08037 609-567-7007
Michael Nolan, prin. Fax 561-3974

---

St. Joseph HS 400/9-12
328 Vine St 08037 609-561-8700
Lynn Domenico, prin. Fax 561-8701

**Hampton, Hunterdon, Pop. 1,385**
Union Township SD 500/PK-8
165 Perryville Rd 08827 908-735-5511
Jeffrey Bender, supt. Fax 735-6657
www.uniontwpschool.org
Union Township MS 200/5-8
165 Perryville Rd 08827 908-735-5511
Frances Suchovic, prin. Fax 735-6657

**Harrison, Hudson, Pop. 13,212**
Harrison SD 2,000/K-12
501 Hamilton St 07029 973-483-4627
Frederick Confessore Ed.D., supt. Fax 484-7484
www.harrisonschools.org
Harrison HS 600/9-12
800 Hamilton St 07029 973-482-5050
Matthew Weber, prin. Fax 412-8729
Washington MS 400/6-8
1 N 5th St 07029 973-483-2285
Donna McBride, prin. Fax 482-3625

**Hasbrouck Heights, Bergen, Pop. 11,674**
Hasbrouck Heights SD 1,700/PK-12
379 Boulevard 07604 201-288-6150
Dr. Matthew Helfant, supt. Fax 288-0289
www.hhschools.org
Hasbrouck Heights HS 500/9-12
365 Boulevard 07604 201-393-8164
Linda Simmons, prin. Fax 288-2083
Hasbrouck Heights MS 400/6-8
365 Boulevard 07604 201-393-8164
Joseph Mastropietro, prin. Fax 288-2083

**Haskell, See Wanaque**

---

Institute for Therapeutic Massage Post-Sec.
1069 Ringwood Ave Ste 315 07420 973-839-6131

**Hawthorne, Passaic, Pop. 18,585**
Hawthorne SD 2,100/K-12
445 Lafayette Ave 07506 973-427-1300
Richard Spirito, supt. Fax 427-1757
www.hawthorne.k12.nj.us
Hawthorne HS 700/9-12
160 Parmelee Ave 07506 973-423-6415
Daniel LaGrone, prin. Fax 423-6422
Lincoln MS 400/6-8
230 Hawthorne Ave 07506 973-423-6460
Erin Devor, prin. Fax 427-5393

---

Hawthorne Christian Academy 400/PK-12
2000 State Rt 208 07506 973-423-3331
David Seidman, head sch Fax 238-1718
Roman Academy of Beauty Culture Post-Sec.
431 Lafayette Ave 07506 973-423-2223

**Hazlet, Monmouth, Pop. 21,976**
Hazlet Township SD 3,200/PK-12
421 Middle Rd 07730 732-264-8402
Dr. Bernard Bragen, supt. Fax 264-1599
www.hazlet.org
Hazlet MS 500/7-8
1639 Union Ave 07730 732-264-0940
Christine McCoid, prin. Fax 264-0571
Raritan HS 1,000/9-12
419 Middle Rd 07730 732-264-8411
William Smith, prin. Fax 264-3214

Monmouth County Vocational SD
Supt. — See Freehold
Hazlet Vocational S Vo/Tech
417 Middle Rd 07730 732-264-4995
Denise Kebeck, prin. Fax 264-3846

**Hibernia, Morris, Pop. 200**
Rockaway Township SD 2,400/K-8
PO Box 500 07842 973-627-8200
Dr. Greg McGann, supt. Fax 627-7968
www.rocktwp.org
Other Schools – See Rockaway

**High Bridge, Hunterdon, Pop. 3,609**
High Bridge SD 400/PK-8
50 Thomas St 08829 908-638-4103
Dr. Gregory Hobaugh, supt. Fax 638-4211
www.hbschools.org
High Bridge MS 100/5-8
50 Thomas St 08829 908-638-4101
Dr. Gregory Hobaugh, prin. Fax 638-4211

**Highland Park, Middlesex, Pop. 13,661**
Highland Park SD 1,400/PK-12
435 Mansfield St 08904 732-572-2400
Fax 393-1174
www.hpschools.net
Highland Park HS 400/9-12
102 N 5th Ave 08904 732-572-2400
Michael Lassiter, prin. Fax 819-7041
Highland Park MS 300/6-8
330 Wayne St 08904 732-572-2400
Fax 819-7041

---

Reenas Bais Yaakov 100/9-12
1131 Raritan Ave 08904 732-985-5646
Chaya Eidelman, prin. Fax 985-5660

**Highlands, Monmouth, Pop. 4,929**
Henry Hudson Regional SD 400/7-12
1 Grand Tour 07732 732-872-0900
Dr. Susan Compton, supt. Fax 872-1315
www.henryhudsonreg.k12.nj.us
Hudson Regional JSHS 400/7-12
1 Grand Tour 07732 732-872-0900
Lenore Kingsmore, prin. Fax 708-1409

Monmouth County Vocational SD
Supt. — See Freehold
Marine Academy of Science & Technology Vo/Tech
305 Mast Way 07732 732-291-0995
Earl Moore, prin. Fax 291-9367

**Hightstown, Mercer, Pop. 5,390**
East Windsor Regional SD 4,900/PK-12
25A Leshin Ln 08520 609-443-7717
Dr. Thomas Gialanella, supt. Fax 443-7704
www.eastwindsorregionalschools.com
Hightstown HS 1,400/9-12
25 Leshin Ln 08520 609-443-7738
Dennis Vinson, prin. Fax 443-7880
Other Schools – See East Windsor

---

Peddie S 600/9-12
201 S Main St 08520 609-944-7500
Peter Quinn, hdmstr. Fax 944-7901

**Hillsborough, Somerset**
Hillsborough Township SD 7,100/PK-12
379 S Branch Rd 08844 908-431-6600
Dr. Jorden Schiff, supt. Fax 369-8286
www.htps.us
Hillsborough HS 2,400/9-12
466 Raider Blvd 08844 908-431-6600
Karen Bingert, prin. Fax 874-3762
Hillsborough MS 1,100/7-8
260 Triangle Rd 08844 908-431-6600
Dr. Joseph Trybulski, prin. Fax 874-3492

**Hillsdale, Bergen, Pop. 10,123**
Hillsdale SD 1,400/PK-8
32 Ruckman Rd 07642 201-664-4512
Kevin Brentnall, supt. Fax 664-9049
www.hillsdaleschools.com
White MS 700/5-8
120 Magnolia Ave 07642 201-664-0286
Donald Bergamini, prin. Fax 664-2715

Pascack Valley Regional HSD
Supt. — See Montvale
Pascack Valley HS 1,200/9-12
200 Piermont Ave 07642 201-358-7060
Thomas DeMaio, prin. Fax 358-7102

**Hillside, Union, Pop. 21,044**
Hillside Township SD 2,900/PK-12
195 Virginia St 07205 908-352-7664
Dr. Frank Deo, supt. Fax 282-5831
www.hillsidek12.org
Hillside HS 700/9-12
1085 Liberty Ave 07205 908-352-7664
Dr. Christine Sidwa, prin. Fax 352-4246
Krumbiegel MS 600/6-8
145 Hillside Ave 07205 908-352-7664
Juan Leonardo, prin. Fax 282-5840

**Hoboken, Hudson, Pop. 49,047**
Hoboken SD, 158 4th St 07030 1,500/PK-12
Dr. Christine Johnson, supt. 201-356-3600
www.hoboken.k12.nj.us
Hoboken JSHS 600/7-12
900 Clinton St 07030 201-356-3700
Robin Piccapietra, prin. Fax 356-3704

---

Cortiva Institute - Hoboken Post-Sec.
2 Hudson Pl Ste 2 07030 201-215-6440
Hudson S 200/5-12
601 Park Ave 07030 201-659-8335
Suellen Newman, dir. Fax 222-3669
Stevens Institute of Technology Post-Sec.
Castle Point on Hudson 07030 201-216-5000

**Holmdel, Monmouth**
Holmdel Township SD 3,100/K-12
65 McCampbell Rd 07733 732-946-1800
Barbara Duncan, supt. Fax 946-1875
www.holmdelschools.org
Holmdel HS 1,000/9-12
36 Crawfords Corner Rd 07733 732-946-1832
William Loughran, prin. Fax 946-0093
Satz MS 500/7-8
24 Crawfords Corner Rd 07733 732-946-1808
Arthur Howard, prin. Fax 834-0089

---

St. John Vianney HS 1,000/9-12
540A Line Rd 07733 732-739-0800
Steven DiMezza, prin. Fax 739-0843

**Hopatcong, Sussex, Pop. 14,950**
Hopatcong Borough SD 1,900/K-12
PO Box 1029 07843 973-398-8800
Cynthia Randina, supt. Fax 398-1961
www.hopatcongschools.org/
Hopatcong HS 600/9-12
PO Box 1029 07843 973-398-8803
Lewis Benfatti, prin. Fax 398-9048
Hopatcong MS 400/6-8
PO Box 1029 07843 973-398-8804
Emil Binotto, prin. Fax 398-4184

**Howell, Monmouth**
Howell Township SD
Supt. — See Farmingdale
Howell Township MS South 800/6-8
1 Kuzminski Way 07731 732-836-1327
Thomas Feaster, prin. Fax 836-0698

---

Yeshivas Emek Hatorah 100/9-12
395 Kent Rd 07731 732-367-1289

**Irvington, Essex, Pop. 60,600**
Irvington Township SD 6,100/PK-12
1 University Pl 07111 973-399-6800
Dr. Neely Hackett, supt. Fax 372-3724
www.irvington.k12.nj.us
Blue Knights Academy Alt
255 Myrtle Ave 07111 973-399-6879
Hubert Chase, prin.
Irvington HS 1,400/9-12
1253 Clinton Ave 07111 973-399-6897
Sandra Boone-Gibbs, prin. Fax 371-7045
Union Avenue MS 700/6-8
427 Union Ave 07111 973-399-6885
Muller Pierre, prin. Fax 371-0957
University MS 700/6-8
255 Myrtle Ave 07111 973-399-6879
Andrea Tucker, prin. Fax 351-1025

**Iselin, Middlesex, Pop. 18,174**
Woodbridge Township SD
Supt. — See Woodbridge
Iselin MS 600/6-8
900 Woodruff St 08830 732-602-8450
Kelly Cilento, prin. Fax 750-4861
Kennedy Memorial HS 1,400/9-12
200 Washington Ave 08830 732-602-8650
Michael Cilento, prin. Fax 634-1112

---

Sanford-Brown Institute Post-Sec.
675 US Highway 1 S Fl 2 08830 732-623-5740

**Jackson, Ocean, Pop. 800**
Jackson Township SD 9,200/PK-12
151 Don Connor Blvd 08527 732-833-4600
Dr. Stephen Genco, supt. Fax 833-4609
www.jacksonsd.org
Goetz MS 1,300/6-8
835 Patterson Rd 08527 732-833-4610
Dr. Faith Lessig, prin. Fax 833-4749
Jackson Liberty HS 1,300/9-12
125 N Hope Chapel Rd 08527 732-833-4700
Maureen Butler, prin. Fax 415-7099
Jackson Memorial HS 1,700/9-12
101 Don Connor Blvd 08527 732-833-4670
Kevin DiEugenio, prin. Fax 833-4629
McAuliffe MS 1,000/6-8
35 S Hope Chapel Rd 08527 732-833-4701
Debra Phillips, prin. Fax 833-4729

Ocean County Vocational SD
Supt. — See Toms River
Ocean County Voc-Tech S - Jackson Vo/Tech
850 Toms River Rd 08527 732-286-5665
Lillian Zavattieri, prin. Fax 928-0490

**Jamesburg, Middlesex, Pop. 5,804**
Jamesburg SD 700/PK-8
13 Augusta St 08831 732-521-0303
Brian Betze, supt. Fax 521-1267
www.jamesburg.org
Breckwedel MS 200/6-8
13 Augusta St 08831 732-521-0303
Chad Donahue, prin. Fax 521-1267

**Jersey City, Hudson, Pop. 239,244**
Hudson County Schools of Technology
Supt. — See North Bergen
Academy of Technology Design Vo/Tech
525 Montgomery St 07302 201-631-6300
Barbara Mendolla, admin.
County Prep HS Vo/Tech
525 Montgomery St 07302 201-631-6302
Barbara Mendolla, prin.
Explore 2000 Vo/Tech
180 9th St 07302 201-631-6396
Amy Lin-Rodriguez, prin. Fax 369-5562

Jersey City SD 26,200/PK-12
346 Claremont Ave 07305 201-915-6202
Dr. Marcia Lyles, supt. Fax 915-6084
www.jcboe.org/
Academy I 400/Alt
209 Bergen Ave 07305 201-915-6500
Grace Moriarty, prin. Fax 435-9224
Conwell MS 800/6-8
107 Bright St 07302 201-946-5740
Joanna Veloz, prin. Fax 209-1293
Dickinson HS 2,300/9-12
2 Palisade Ave 07306 201-714-4400
Dr. Frederick Williams, prin. Fax 792-2292

Ferris HS 1,500/9-12
35 Colgate St 07302 201-915-6660
Jaime Morales, prin. Fax 451-6067
Infinity Institute 100/6-12
193 Old Bergen Rd 07305 201-915-1404
Treniere Dobson, prin. Fax 433-9456
Innovation HS 100/9-10
239 Bergen Ave 07305 201-915-1504
Frank Iannucci, admin. Fax 369-6935
Liberty HS 200/Alt
299 Sip Ave 07306 201-714-4373
Monica Grazilla, prin. Fax 369-3714
Lincoln HS 800/9-12
60 Crescent Ave 07304 201-915-6700
Cheryl Richardson-Evans, prin. Fax 435-4493
McNair Academic HS 700/9-12
123 Coles St 07302 201-418-7618
Edward Slattery, prin. Fax 792-1498
Nolan MS 400/6-8
88 Gates Ave 07305 201-915-6570
Francine Luce, prin. Fax 369-3749
Snyder HS 900/9-12
239 Bergen Ave 07305 201-915-6600
Yvonne Waller, prin. Fax 435-5019
Williams MS 700/6-8
222 Laidlaw Ave 07306 201-714-8342
Edwin Rivera, prin. Fax 659-6457

---

Anthem Institute Post-Sec.
40 Journal Sq 07306 201-876-3800
Christ Hospital School of Nursing Post-Sec.
176 Palisade Ave 07306 201-795-8360
Christ Hospital School of Radiography Post-Sec.
176 Palisade Ave 07306 201-795-8246
Eastern International College Post-Sec.
684 Newark Ave 07306 201-216-9901
Full Will of God Christian Academy 50/K-12
84 Martin Luther King Jr Dr 07305 201-433-6278
Roberta Glee-Stevens M.P., prin. Fax 938-1481
Hudson Catholic Regional HS 400/9-12
790 Bergen Ave 07306 201-332-5970
Richard Garibell, prin. Fax 332-6373
Hudson County Community College Post-Sec.
70 Sip Ave 07306 201-714-7100
Natural Motion Institute of Hair Design Post-Sec.
2800 John F Kennedy Blvd 07306 201-659-0303
New Jersey City University Post-Sec.
2039 John F Kennedy Blvd 07305 201-200-2000
PC AGE Career Institute Post-Sec.
2815 John F Kennedy Blvd #3 07306 201-761-0144
St. Anthony HS 200/9-12
175 8th St 07302 201-653-5143
Chad Broussard, head sch Fax 653-8120
St. Dominic Academy 500/9-12
2572 John F Kennedy Blvd 07304 201-434-5938
Barbara Griffin, head sch Fax 434-2603
St. Peter Preparatory S 1,000/9-12
144 Grand St 07302 201-434-4400
James DeAngelo, prin. Fax 547-2341
St. Peter's University Post-Sec.
2641 John F Kennedy Blvd 07306 201-761-6000
The Institute for Health Education Post-Sec.
600 Pavonia Ave Ste 1 07306 201-217-1113

**Keansburg, Monmouth, Pop. 9,873**
Keansburg Borough SD 1,600/PK-12
100 Palmer Pl 07734 732-787-2007
Gerald North, supt. Fax 495-6714
www.keansburg.k12.nj.us
Bolger MS 400/5-8
100 Palmer Pl 07734 732-787-2007
John Niesz, prin. Fax 495-7906
Keansburg HS 400/9-12
140 Port Monmouth Rd 07734 732-787-2007
Michelle Derpich, prin. Fax 495-5401

**Kearny, Hudson, Pop. 39,579**
Kearny SD 5,900/PK-12
172 Midland Ave 07032 201-955-5000
Patricia Blood, supt. Fax 955-0544
www.kearnyschools.com
Kearny HS 1,700/9-12
336 Devon St 07032 201-955-5050
Linda Rocco, prin. Fax 998-9653
Lincoln MS 400/7-8
121 Beech St 07032 201-955-5095
Robert Zika, prin. Fax 997-2590

---

Kearny Christian Academy 100/PK-12
22 Wilson Ave 07032 201-998-0788

**Kenilworth, Union, Pop. 7,800**
Kenilworth SD 1,300/PK-12
426 Boulevard 07033 908-276-5936
Dr. Scott Taylor, supt. Fax 709-7315
www.kenilworthschools.com
Brearley MSHS 700/7-12
401 Monroe Ave 07033 908-931-9696
Brian Luciani, prin. Fax 931-1618

---

Capri Institute of Hair Design Post-Sec.
660 N Michigan Ave 07033 908-964-1330

**Keyport, Monmouth, Pop. 7,124**
Keyport SD 900/PK-12
370 Broad St 07735 732-212-6100
Dr. Lisa Savoia, supt. Fax 212-6125
www.kpsdschools.org
Keyport HS 400/9-12
351 Broad St 07735 732-212-6100
Michael Waters, prin. Fax 212-6145

Monmouth County Vocational SD
Supt. — See Freehold
Keyport Vocational S Vo/Tech
280 Atlantic St 07735 732-739-0592
Denise Kebeck, prin. Fax 739-1470

**Kinnelon, Morris, Pop. 10,145**
Kinnelon Borough SD 2,100/PK-12
109 Kiel Ave 07405 973-838-1418
Diane DiGiuseppe, supt. Fax 838-5527
kinnelonpublicschools.org/
Kinnelon HS 700/9-12
121 Kinnelon Rd 07405 973-838-5500
Gary Suda, prin. Fax 838-0261
Miller MS 500/6-8
117 Kiel Ave 07405 973-838-5250
Mark Mongon, prin. Fax 283-0390

**Lake Hopatcong, Morris, Pop. 3,000**
Jefferson Township SD 3,200/PK-12
31 State Route 181 07849 973-663-5780
Joseph Kraemer, supt. Fax 663-2790
www.jefftwp.org/
Other Schools – See Oak Ridge

**Lakehurst, Ocean, Pop. 2,552**
Ocean County Vocational SD
Supt. — See Toms River
Ocean County Voc-Tech S - Navy Lakehurst Vo/Tech
PO Box 1125 08733 732-286-5678
Karen Homiek, prin. Fax 657-4500
Performing Arts Academy Vo/Tech
Hangar One NAVAIR 08733 732-286-5678

**Lakewood, Ocean, Pop. 53,516**
Lakewood Township SD 3,600/PK-12
1771 Madison Ave Ste B 08701 732-364-2400
Laura Winters, supt. Fax 905-3687
www.lakewoodpiners.org
Lakewood HS 1,000/9-12
855 Somerset Ave 08701 732-905-3502
Marcy Marshall, prin. Fax 905-0895
Lakewood MS 600/6-8
755 Somerset Ave 08701 732-905-3600
Richard Goldstein, prin. Fax 905-3695

---

Achieve Test Prep Post-Sec.
1072 Madison Ave 08701 732-719-2353
Bais Kaila Torah Prep HS 300/9-12
PO Box 952 08701 732-370-4300
Bais Medrash Toras Chesed Post-Sec.
901 Monmouth Ave 08701 732-364-1220
Bais Shaindel HS 500/9-12
685 River Ave 08701 732-363-7074
Bais Yaakov HS 400/9-12
277 James St 08701 732-370-8200
Beth Medrash Govoha Post-Sec.
617 6th St 08701 732-367-1060
Calvary Academy 300/PK-12
1133 E County Line Rd 08701 732-363-3633
Suzanne Bruno M.Ed., head sch Fax 363-7337
Georgian Court University Post-Sec.
900 Lakewood Ave 08701 732-987-2200
Lakewood Cheder S 7-8
520 James St 08701 732-370-6460
Lakewood Cheder S Bais Faga 1,300/3-8
350 Courtney Rd 08701 732-363-5070
Mesivta Keren HaTorah 100/9-12
PO Box 1004 08701 732-942-7300
Mesivta of Lakewood 400/8-12
415 6th St 08701 732-905-8370
Oros Bais Yaakov 200/9-12
50 Lapsley Ln 08701 732-370-6049
Yeshiva Bais Aharon 50/9-12
1430 14th St 08701 732-367-7604
Yeshiva Chayei Olam 100/9-12
14 11th St E 08701 732-363-1267
Yeshiva Gedola Ohr HaTalmud 50/9-12
PO Box 826 08701 732-364-7062
Yeshivas Bais Pinchos 100/9-12
1951 New Central Ave 08701 732-367-2880
Yeshiva Toras Chaim Post-Sec.
1027 Ridge Ave 08701 732-414-2834
Yeshiva Toras Chaim 9-12
999 Ridge Ave 08701 732-414-2834
Yeshiva Yesodei Hatorah Post-Sec.
2 Yesodei Ct 08701 732-370-3360

**Lambertville, Hunterdon, Pop. 3,873**
South Hunterdon Regional SD 400/PK-12
301 Mt Airy Harbourton Rd 08530 609-397-2060
Dr. Louis Muenker, supt. Fax 397-2366
shrsd.org
South Hunterdon Regional HS 400/7-12
301 Mt Airy Harbourton Rd 08530 609-397-2060
Mark Collins, prin. Fax 397-2366

**Lanoka Harbor, Ocean**
Lacey Township SD 4,300/PK-12
200 Western Blvd 08734 609-971-2000
Dr. Sandra Anthony, supt. Fax 242-9406
www.laceyschools.org
Lacey Township HS 1,400/9-12
73 Haines St 08734 609-971-2020
James Handschuch, prin. Fax 242-0873
Other Schools – See Forked River

**Laurel Springs, Camden, Pop. 1,884**

---

Empire Beauty School Post-Sec.
1305 Blackwood Clementon Rd 08021 856-435-8100

**Lawrenceville, Mercer, Pop. 3,814**
Lawrence Township SD 4,000/PK-12
2565 Princeton Pike 08648 609-671-5500
Crystal Edwards Ed.D., supt. Fax 883-4225
www.ltps.org
Lawrence HS 1,200/9-12
2525 Princeton Ave 08648 609-671-5510
David Adam, prin. Fax 671-3411
Lawrence MS 600/7-8
2455 Princeton Pike 08648 609-671-5520
Mindy Milavsky, prin. Fax 671-3421

---

Fortis Institute Post-Sec.
2572 US Highway 1 Ste 100 08648 609-512-2560
Lawrenceville S 800/9-12
PO Box 6008 08648 609-896-0400
Steve Murray, hdmstr. Fax 895-2217
Notre Dame HS 1,300/9-12
601 Lawrence Rd 08648 609-882-7900
Mary Liz Ivins, prin. Fax 882-5723
Rider University Post-Sec.
2083 Lawrenceville Rd 08648 609-896-5000

**Lebanon, Hunterdon, Pop. 1,334**
Clinton Township SD 1,600/PK-8
PO Box 362 08833 908-236-7235
Dr. Drucilla Clark, supt. Fax 236-6358
www.ctsd.k12.nj.us
Other Schools – See Clinton

Hunterdon Co. Educational Services Comm. 50/7-12
51 Sawmill Rd 08833 908-439-4280
Marie Kisch, supt. Fax 439-2270
www.hcesc.com
Other Schools – See Califon

**Leonardo, Monmouth, Pop. 2,725**
Middletown Township SD 9,700/PK-12
834 Leonardville Rd Fl 2 07737 732-671-3850
Dr. William George, supt. Fax 615-9351
mtps.schoolwires.net
Bayshore MS 700/6-8
834 Leonardville Rd 07737 732-291-1380
Michael Scarano, prin.
Other Schools – See Middletown, Port Monmouth

---

Trinity Hall 50/9-12
900 Leonardville Rd 07737 732-291-1297
Mary Sciarrillo, head sch Fax 291-2623

**Leonia, Bergen, Pop. 8,727**
Leonia SD 1,700/PK-12
570 Grand Ave 07605 201-302-5200
Joanne Megargee, supt. Fax 947-4782
www.leoniaschools.org
Leonia HS 600/9-12
100 Christie Heights St 07605 201-302-5200
Dr. Edward Bertolini, prin. Fax 461-8957
Leonia MS 500/6-8
500 Broad Ave 07605 201-302-5200
Dr. Nicholas Bernice, prin. Fax 461-1510

**Lincoln Park, Morris, Pop. 10,363**
Lincoln Park Borough SD 800/PK-8
92 Ryerson Rd 07035 973-696-5500
James Grube, supt. Fax 696-9273
www.lincolnparkboe.org
Lincoln Park MS 300/5-8
90 Ryerson Rd 07035 973-696-5520
Michael Meyer, prin. Fax 872-8930

**Lincroft, Monmouth, Pop. 6,069**
Monmouth County Vocational SD
Supt. — See Freehold
High Technology HS Vo/Tech
PO Box 119 07738 732-842-8444
Kevin Bals, prin. Fax 219-9418

---

Brookdale Community College Post-Sec.
765 Newman Springs Rd 07738 732-224-2345
Christian Brothers Academy 1,000/9-12
850 Newman Springs Rd 07738 732-747-1959
R. Ross Fales, prin. Fax 747-1643

**Linden, Union, Pop. 39,711**
Linden SD 5,600/PK-12
2 E Gibbons St 07036 908-486-2800
Danny Robertozzi Ed.D., supt. Fax 486-6331
www.linden.k12.nj.us
Linden HS 1,700/9-12
121 W Saint Georges Ave 07036 908-486-5432
Yelena Horre, prin. Fax 486-3242
McManus MS 700/6-8
300 Edgewood Rd 07036 908-486-7751
Kcyronne Zahir, prin. Fax 587-0607
Soehl MS 600/6-8
300 E Henry St 07036 908-486-0550
Joseph Picaro, prin. Fax 486-3478

---

Sinai Christian Academy 100/PK-12
2301 Grier Ave 07036 908-486-2006
Kathleen Salardino, prin. Fax 925-9258
Yeshiva Gedolah Zichron Leyma Post-Sec.
1000 Orchard Ter 07036 908-587-0502

**Lindenwold, Camden, Pop. 17,154**
Lindenwold SD 2,300/PK-12
801 Egg Harbor Rd 08021 856-783-0276
Lori Moore, supt. Fax 435-5887
www.lindenwold.k12.nj.us/
Lindenwold HS 500/9-12
801 Egg Harbor Rd 08021 856-741-0320
Peter Brandt, prin. Fax 741-0350
Lindenwold MS 700/5-8
40 White Horse Ave 08021 856-346-3330
Kasha Giddins, prin. Fax 346-0554

**Linwood, Atlantic, Pop. 6,996**
Linwood CSD 900/PK-8
51 Belhaven Ave 08221 609-926-6700
Dr. Marianne W. Gaffney Ed.D., supt. Fax 926-6705
www.linwoodschools.org
Belhaven MS 400/5-8
51 Belhaven Ave 08221 609-926-6700
Frank Rudnesky Ed.D., prin. Fax 926-6705

Mainland Regional HSD 1,400/9-12
1301 Oak Ave 08221 609-927-4151
Dr. Robert Previti, supt. Fax 927-1942
www.mainlandregional.net
Mainland Regional HS 1,400/9-12
1301 Oak Ave 08221 609-927-4151
Mark Marrone, prin. Fax 927-1942

---

Harris School of Business Post-Sec.
1201 New Rd Ste 226 08221 609-927-4310

**Little Egg Harbor Township, Ocean, Pop. 13,333**
Ocean County Vocational SD
Supt. — See Toms River
Ocean County Center for Culinary Arts Vo/Tech
261 Country Club Blvd 08087 609-296-2137
Gary MacDonald, prin.

Pinelands Regional SD 1,700/7-12
PO Box 248, 609-296-3106
Dr. Robert Blake, supt. Fax 294-9519
www.prsdnj.org
Pinelands Regional HS 800/10-12
PO Box 248, 609-296-3106
Thomas Normile, prin. Fax 296-6905
Pinelands Regional JHS 800/7-9
PO Box 248, 609-296-3106
Frank Pschorr, prin. Fax 296-2626

**Little Falls, Passaic, Pop. 11,294**
Little Falls Township SD 800/K-8
560 Main St 07424 973-812-9512
Dr. Tracey Marinelli, supt. Fax 256-6542
www.lfnjschools.org
Little Falls MS 1 400/5-8
32 Stevens Ave 07424 973-256-1033
Philip Ligus, prin. Fax 785-4857

Passaic Valley Regional HSD 1 1,400/9-12
100 E Main St 07424 973-890-2500
Dr. Terrance Brennan, supt. Fax 890-0512
www.pvhs.k12.nj.us
Passaic Valley Regional HS 1,400/9-12
100 E Main St 07424 973-890-2500
Ray Rotella, supt. Fax 890-0512

**Little Silver, Monmouth, Pop. 5,876**
Little Silver Borough SD 800/PK-8
124 Willow Dr 07739 732-741-2188
Dr. Carolyn Kossack, supt. Fax 741-3644
www.littlesilverschools.org
Markham Place MS 300/5-8
95 Markham Pl 07739 732-741-7112
Eric Platt, prin. Fax 741-3562

Red Bank Regional HSD 1,200/9-12
101 Ridge Rd 07739 732-842-8000
Thomas Pagano, supt. Fax 842-8504
www.rbrhs.org
Red Bank Regional HS 1,200/9-12
101 Ridge Rd 07739 732-842-8000
Risa Clay, prin. Fax 842-4868

**Livingston, Essex, Pop. 27,500**
Livingston SD 5,600/PK-12
11 Foxcroft Dr 07039 973-535-8000
Ernest Palestis, supt. Fax 535-1254
www.livingston.org
Heritage MS 900/7-8
20 Foxcroft Dr 07039 973-535-8000
Jennifer Wirt, prin. Fax 597-9492
Livingston HS 1,800/9-12
30 Robert H Harp Dr 07039 973-535-8000
Mark Stern, prin. Fax 994-4297

---

Kushner Yeshiva HS 200/9-12
110 S Orange Ave 07039 973-437-8000
Newark Academy 600/6-12
91 S Orange Ave 07039 973-992-7000
Donald Austin, hdmstr. Fax 992-8962
St. Barnabas Medical Center Post-Sec.
94 Old Short Hills Rd 07039 973-533-5628

**Lodi, Bergen, Pop. 23,608**
Lodi SD 3,200/PK-12
8 Hunter St 07644 973-778-4620
Frank Quatrone, supt. Fax 778-6393
www.lodi.k12.nj.us
Jefferson MS 700/6-8
75 1st St 07644 973-478-8662
Robert Sciolaro, prin. Fax 478-0358
Lodi HS 900/9-12
99 Putnam St 07644 973-478-6100
Frank D'Amico, prin. Fax 478-4012

---

Felician College Post-Sec.
262 S Main St 07644 201-559-6000
Immaculate Conception HS 200/9-12
258 S Main St 07644 973-773-2400
Joseph Azzolino, prin. Fax 614-0893

**Logan, Gloucester**
Logan Township SD 800/PK-8
110 School Ln 08085 856-467-5133
Patricia Haney, supt. Fax 467-9012
www.logan.k12.nj.us
Logan MS 400/6-8
110 School Ln 08085 856-467-5133
Heather Moran, prin. Fax 467-9012

**Long Branch, Monmouth, Pop. 29,197**
Long Branch SD 5,200/PK-12
540 Broadway 07740 732-571-2868
Michael Salvatore, supt. Fax 229-0797
www.longbranch.k12.nj.us
Long Branch HS 1,100/9-12
404 Indiana Ave 07740 732-229-7300
Vincent Muscillo, prin. Fax 229-2825
Long Branch MS 900/6-8
350 Indiana Ave 07740 732-229-5533
Michael Viturello, prin. Fax 229-4894

Monmouth County Vocational SD
Supt. — See Freehold
Academy of Law & Public Safety Vo/Tech
255 W End Ave 07740 732-229-3019
Joseph Diver, prin. Fax 229-5727

---

Ma'or Yeshiva HS for Boys 100/9-12
250 Park Ave 07740 732-222-4797
Monmouth Medical Center Post-Sec.
300 2nd Ave 07740 732-222-5200

**Long Valley, Morris, Pop. 1,859**
Washington Township SD 2,500/PK-8
53 W Mill Rd 07853 908-876-4172
Jeffrey Mohre, supt. Fax 876-9392
www.wtschools.org
Long Valley MS 900/6-8
51 W Mill Rd 07853 908-876-3434
Mark Ippolito, prin. Fax 876-3436

**Lumberton, Burlington**
Lumberton Township SD 1,600/K-8
33 Municipal Dr 08048 609-267-1406
Joseph Langowski, supt. Fax 267-0002
www.lumberton.k12.nj.us/
Lumberton MS 600/6-8
30 Dimsdale Dr 08048 609-265-0123
Pete DeFeo, prin. Fax 265-0476

**Lyndhurst, Bergen, Pop. 18,262**
Lyndhurst Township SD 1,600/PK-12
420 Fern Ave 07071 201-438-5683
James Corino, supt. Fax 896-2118
www.lyndhurstschools.net
Jefferson S 100/4-8
336 Lake Ave 07071 201-896-2065
Joseph Vastola, prin. Fax 933-3112
Lincoln S 200/4-8
281 Ridge Rd 07071 201-438-5683
Michael Rizzo, prin. Fax 438-5786
Lyndhurst HS 700/9-12
400 Weart Ave 07071 201-896-2100
Laura Vuono, prin. Fax 896-2088
Roosevelt S 300/4-8
530 Stuyvesant Ave 07071 201-896-2068
Joseph DeCorso, prin. Fax 933-3143

**Madison, Morris, Pop. 15,563**
Madison SD 2,400/PK-12
359 Woodland Rd 07940 973-593-3100
Dr. Michael Rossi, supt. Fax 301-2170
www.madisonpublicschools.org
Madison HS 800/9-12
170 Ridgedale Ave 07940 973-593-3117
Greg Robertson, prin. Fax 593-3141
Madison JHS 500/6-8
285 Main St 07940 973-593-3149
Nicole Sherrin, prin. Fax 966-1908

---

Drew University Post-Sec.
36 Madison Ave 07940 973-408-3000
Fairleigh Dickinson University Post-Sec.
285 Madison Ave 07940 973-443-8500

**Mahwah, Bergen, Pop. 17,905**
Mahwah Township SD 3,200/PK-12
60 Ridge Rd 07430 201-762-2400
C. Lauren Schoen, supt. Fax 529-1287
www.mahwah.k12.nj.us
Mahwah HS 1,000/9-12
50 Ridge Rd 07430 201-762-2300
John Pascale, prin. Fax 512-0949
Ramapo Ridge MS 800/6-8
150 Ridge Rd 07430 201-762-2380
Brian Miller, prin. Fax 529-6790

---

Lincoln Technical Institute Post-Sec.
70 McKee Dr 07430 201-529-1414
National Tax Training School Post-Sec.
PO Box 767 07430 800-914-8138
Ramapo College of New Jersey Post-Sec.
505 Ramapo Valley Rd 07430 201-684-7500

**Manahawkin, Ocean, Pop. 2,289**
Ocean County Vocational SD
Supt. — See Toms River
Ocean County Voc-Tech S - MATES Vo/Tech
195 Cedar Bridge Rd 08050 609-978-8439
Alison Carroll, prin. Fax 978-8540

Southern Regional SD 3,000/7-12
105 Cedar Bridge Rd 08050 609-597-9481
Craig Henry, supt. Fax 978-0298
www.srsd.net
Southern Regional HS 1,000/9-10
600 N Main St 08050 609-597-9481
Eric Wilhelm, prin. Fax 978-5375
Southern Regional HS 1,000/11-12
90 Cedar Bridge Rd 08050 609-597-9481
Eric Wilhelm, prin. Fax 978-5357
Southern Regional MS 1,000/7-8
75 Cedar Bridge Rd 08050 609-597-9481
Lorraine Airey, prin. Fax 978-8209

**Manalapan, Monmouth**
Manalapan-Englishtown Regional SD
Supt. — See Englishtown
Manalapan-Englishtown MS 1,300/7-8
155 Millhurst Rd 07726 732-786-2650
Robert Williams, prin. Fax 786-2660

**Manasquan, Monmouth, Pop. 5,870**
Manasquan SD 1,700/PK-12
169 Broad St 08736 732-528-8800
Dr. Frank Kasyan, supt. Fax 223-6286
www.manasquanschools.org
Manasquan HS 1,000/9-12
167 Broad St 08736 732-528-8820
Richard Coppola, prin. Fax 528-0316

**Manchester, Ocean**
Manchester Township SD
Supt. — See Whiting
Manchester Township HS 1,100/9-12
101 S Colonial Dr 08759 732-657-2121
Dennis Adams, prin. Fax 657-2781
Manchester Township MS 600/6-8
2759 Ridgeway Rd 08759 732-657-1717
Nancy Driber, prin. Fax 657-0326

**Manville, Somerset, Pop. 10,188**
Manville Borough SD 1,200/K-12
410 Brooks Blvd 08835 908-231-8500
Anne Facendo, supt. Fax 707-3963
www.manvilleschools.org
Batcho IS, 100 N 13th Ave 08835 300/6-8
Michael Magliacano, prin. 908-231-8521
Manville HS 400/9-12
1100 Brooks Blvd 08835 908-231-6806
Dr. James Brunn, prin. Fax 231-8532

**Maple Shade, Burlington, Pop. 19,211**
Maple Shade Township SD 1,800/K-12
170 Frederick Ave 08052 856-779-1750
Beth Norcia, supt. Fax 779-1054
www.mapleshade.org
Maple Shade JSHS 700/7-12
180 Frederick Ave 08052 856-779-2880
Scott Arnauer, prin. Fax 779-8849

**Maplewood, Essex, Pop. 21,756**
South Orange-Maplewood SD 6,400/PK-12
525 Academy St 07040 973-762-5600
James Memoli, supt. Fax 378-9464
www.somsd.k12.nj.us
Columbia HS 1,800/9-12
17 Parker Ave 07040 973-762-5600
Elizabeth Aaron, prin. Fax 378-7607
Maplewood MS 800/6-8
7 Burnett St 07040 973-378-7660
Louis Brown, prin. Fax 378-5247
Other Schools – See South Orange

**Margate City, Atlantic, Pop. 6,302**
Margate City SD 500/PK-8
8103 Winchester Ave 08402 609-822-2080
John DiNicola, supt. Fax 822-3399
www.margateschools.org
Tighe MS 200/5-8
7804 Amherst Ave 08402 609-822-2353
Audrey Becker, prin. Fax 822-8456

**Marlboro, Monmouth**
Freehold Regional HSD
Supt. — See Englishtown
Marlboro HS 1,900/9-12
95 N Main St 07746 732-617-8393
Shaun Boylan, prin. Fax 972-6615

Marlboro Township SD 5,100/PK-8
1980 Township Dr 07746 732-972-2000
Dr. Eric Hibbs, supt. Fax 972-2003
www.marlboro.k12.nj.us
Marlboro MS 1,100/6-8
355 County Road 520 07746 732-972-2100
Patricia Nieliwocki, prin. Fax 972-6765
Other Schools – See Morganville

**Marlton, Burlington, Pop. 9,983**
Evesham Township SD 4,500/PK-8
25 S Maple Ave 08053 856-983-1800
John Scavelli, supt. Fax 983-2939
www.evesham.k12.nj.us
DeMasi MS 800/6-8
199 Evesboro Medford Rd 08053 856-988-0777
Irene Romanelli, prin. Fax 596-1571
Marlton MS 800/6-8
150 Tomlinson Mill Rd 08053 856-988-0684
Gary Hoffman, prin. Fax 988-9327

Lenape Regional HSD
Supt. — See Shamong Township
Cherokee HS 2,200/9-12
120 Tomlinson Mill Rd 08053 856-983-5140
Donna Charlesworth, prin. Fax 596-6495

---

Achieve Test Prep Post-Sec.
1 Eves Dr 08053 609-529-8589
ITT Technical Institute Post-Sec.
9000 Lincoln Dr E Ste 100 08053 856-396-3500
The School of Court Reporting Post-Sec.
1002 Lincoln Dr W Ste F 08053 856-988-0800

**Martinsville, Somerset, Pop. 11,795**
Bridgewater-Raritan Regional SD 8,700/PK-12
836 Newmans Ln 08836 908-685-2777
Dr. Victor Hayek, supt. Fax 231-8496
www.brrsd.k12.nj.us
Other Schools – See Bridgewater

**Matawan, Monmouth, Pop. 8,609**
Old Bridge Township SD 8,200/K-12
4207 Highway 516 07747 732-566-1000
David Cittadino, supt.
www.oldbridgeadmin.org
McDermott Grade Nine Center 9-9
4206 Highway 516 07747 732-290-3887
Timothy Dolan, prin. Fax 566-1497
Old Bridge HS 2,300/10-12
4209 Highway 516 07747 732-290-3900
Vincent Sasso, prin. Fax 566-1263
Other Schools – See Old Bridge

**Mays Landing, Atlantic, Pop. 2,098**
Atlantic County Vocational SD
5080 Atlantic Ave 08330 609-625-2249
Dr. Philip Guenther, supt. Fax 625-2876
Atlantic County Alternative HS Alt
1450 19th St 08330 609-625-2249
Atlantic County Institute of Technology Vo/Tech
5080 Atlantic Ave 08330 609-625-2249
Ronald DeFelice, prin. Fax 625-0707

Greater Egg Harbor Regional HSD 3,100/9-12
1824 Dr Dennis Foreman Dr 08330 609-625-1456
John Keenan, supt. Fax 625-0045
www.gehrhsd.net
Oakcrest HS 1,200/9-12
1824 Dr Dennis Foreman Dr 08330 609-909-2600
Joseph Carruth, prin. Fax 625-0872
Other Schools – See Egg Harbor City, Galloway

Hamilton Township SD 3,000/PK-8
1876 Dr Dennis Foreman Dr 08330 609-476-6300
Michelle Cappelluti Ed.D., supt. Fax 625-4847
www.hamiltonschools.org
Davies MS 1,000/6-8
1876 Dr Dennis Foreman Dr 08330 609-476-6242
Stephen Santilli, prin.

Atlantic Cape Community College Post-Sec.
5100 Black Horse Pike 08330 609-343-5000

**Maywood, Bergen, Pop. 9,373**
Maywood SD 900/PK-8
452 Maywood Ave 07607 201-845-9114
Michael Jordan, supt. Fax 845-7146
www.maywoodschools.org
Maywood Avenue MS 500/4-8
452 Maywood Ave 07607 201-845-9110
Michael Jordan, prin. Fax 291-1917

**Medford, Burlington**
Burlington Co. Institute of Tech SD
Supt. — See Mount Holly
Burlington Co. Institute of Technology Vo/Tech
10 Hawkin Rd 08055 609-654-0200
Mike Parker, prin. Fax 654-1081

Lenape Regional HSD
Supt. — See Shamong Township
Lenape HS 1,900/9-12
235 Hartford Rd 08055 609-654-5111
Anthony Cattani, prin. Fax 953-6779
Shawnee HS 1,600/9-12
600 Tabernacle Rd 08055 609-654-7544
Matthew Campbell, prin. Fax 654-5611

Medford Township SD 2,900/PK-8
137 Hartford Rd 08055 609-654-6416
Joseph Del Rossi Ed.D., supt. Fax 654-7436
www.medford.k12.nj.us/
Medford Township Memorial MS 700/7-8
55 Mill St 08055 609-654-7707
Shawn Ryan, prin. Fax 654-7297

**Medford Lakes, Burlington, Pop. 4,117**
Medford Lakes Borough SD 500/PK-8
44 Neeta Tr 08055 609-654-5155
Anthony V. Dent, supt. Fax 714-0235
www.medford-lakes.k12.nj.us
Neeta S 300/3-8
44 Neeta Trl 08055 609-654-5155
Anthony Dent, admin. Fax 953-8258

**Mendham, Morris, Pop. 4,930**
Mendham Borough SD 700/PK-8
12 Hilltop Rd 07945 973-543-4251
Mitzi N. Morillo, supt. Fax 543-2805
www.mendhamboro.org
Mountain View MS 300/5-8
100 Dean Rd 07945 973-543-7075
Charles Seipp, prin. Fax 543-7993

West Morris Regional HSD
Supt. — See Chester
West Morris Mendham HS 1,400/9-12
65 E Main St 07945 973-543-2501
Michael Matyas, prin. Fax 543-6950

Assumption College for Sisters Post-Sec.
350 Bernardsville Rd 07945 973-543-6528

**Metuchen, Middlesex, Pop. 13,256**
Metuchen SD 1,900/PK-12
16 Simpson Pl 08840 732-321-8700
Vincent Caputo, supt. Fax 321-6567
www.metuchenschools.org
Edgar MS 600/5-8
49 Brunswick Ave 08840 732-321-8770
Katherine Glutz, prin. Fax 452-0571
Metuchen HS 600/9-12
400 Grove Ave 08840 732-321-8743
Bruce Peragallo, prin. Fax 549-6415

St. Joseph HS 800/9-12
145 Plainfield Rd 08840 732-549-7600
John Anderson, prin. Fax 549-0664

**Middlesex, Middlesex, Pop. 13,451**
Middlesex Borough SD 2,000/PK-12
300 John F Kennedy Dr 08846 732-317-6000
Dr. Linda Madison Ed.D., supt. Fax 317-6006
www.middlesex.k12.nj.us
Mauger MS 800/4-8
Fisher Ave 08846 732-317-6000
Jason Sirna, prin. Fax 317-6002
Middlesex HS 600/9-12
300 John F Kennedy Dr 08846 732-317-6000
Joseph Sabato, prin. Fax 317-6008

**Middletown, Monmouth, Pop. 24,000**
Middletown Township SD
Supt. — See Leonardo
Middletown HS North 1,500/9-12
63 Tindall Rd 07748 732-706-6061
Patricia Cartier, prin. Fax 706-6067
Middletown HS South 1,400/9-12
900 Nutswamp Rd 07748 732-706-6111
Patrick Rinella, prin. Fax 706-8058
Thompson MS 900/6-8
1001 Middletown Lincroft Rd 07748 732-671-2212
Matthew Kirkpatrick, prin.

Monmouth County Vocational SD
Supt. — See Freehold
Middletown Vocational S Vo/Tech
2 Swartzel Dr 07748 732-671-0650
Joseph Diver, prin. Fax 671-7455

Mater Dei Prep HS 300/9-12
538 Church St 07748 732-671-9100
James Hauenstein, prin. Fax 671-9214

**Midland Park, Bergen, Pop. 7,021**
Midland Park Borough SD 800/PK-12
250 Prospect St 07432 201-444-1400
Dr. Marie Cirasella Ed.D., supt. Fax 444-3051
www.mpsnj.org
Midland Park JSHS 500/7-12
250 Prospect St 07432 201-444-7400
Nicholas Capuano, prin. Fax 444-0352

**Millburn, Essex, Pop. 18,630**
Millburn Township SD 4,800/PK-12
434 Millburn Ave 07041 973-376-3600
Dr. Christine Burton, supt. Fax 912-9396
www.millburn.org
Millburn HS, 462 Millburn Ave 07041 1,500/9-12
Dr. William Miron, prin. 973-564-7130
Millburn MS 1,100/6-8
25 Old Short Hills Rd 07041 973-379-2600
Michael Cahill, prin. Fax 912-0939

Milburn School for Hearing Handicapped Post-Sec.
Spring & Willow Sts 07041 973-376-9439

**Millstone Township, Monmouth**
Millstone Township SD 1,100/PK-8
5 Dawson Ct, 732-786-0950
Scott Feder, supt. Fax 792-0951
www.millstone.k12.nj.us/
Millstone Township MS 400/6-8
5 Dawson Ct, 732-786-0950
Christopher Huss, prin. Fax 786-0953

**Milltown, Middlesex, Pop. 6,830**
Milltown SD 600/K-8
80 Violet Ter 08850 732-214-2365
Dr. Stephanie Brown, supt. Fax 214-2376
www.milltownps.org
Kilmer S 300/4-8
21 W Church St 08850 732-214-2370
William Veit, prin. Fax 214-2378

**Millville, Cumberland, Pop. 27,693**
Millville SD 5,800/PK-12
PO Box 5010 08332 856-293-2000
Dr. David Gentile, supt. Fax 293-9852
mps.millvillenj.gov
Alternative S Alt
200 N Wade Blvd 08332 856-327-6058
Fax 825-2543
Lakeside MS 1,100/6-8
2 N Sharp St 08332 856-293-2420
Steve Price, prin. Fax 825-7588
Memorial HS 700/9-10
504 E Broad St 08332 856-327-6072
Stephanie Derose, prin. Fax 825-4480
Millville SHS 1,200/10-12
200 N Wade Blvd 08332 856-327-6040
Kathleen Procopio, prin. Fax 293-1342

**Monmouth Junction, Middlesex, Pop. 2,829**
South Brunswick Township SD
Supt. — See North Brunswick
Crossroads North MS 1,100/6-8
635 Georges Rd 08852 732-329-4191
Mark Daniels, prin. Fax 329-1905
Crossroads South MS 1,100/6-8
195 Major Rd 08852 732-329-4633
Bonnie Capes, prin. Fax 329-1906
South Brunswick HS 2,800/9-12
750 Ridge Rd 08852 732-329-4044
Peter Varela, prin. Fax 274-1237

Noor-Ul-Iman S 500/PK-12
4137 US Highway 1 08852 732-329-1800

**Monroe Township, Middlesex**
Monroe Township SD 5,500/PK-12
423 Buckelew Ave 08831 732-521-2111
Dr. Michael Kozak, supt. Fax 521-2719
www.monroe.k12.nj.us
Monroe Township HS 1,800/9-12
200 Schoolhouse Rd 08831 732-521-2882
Robert Goodall, prin. Fax 521-2976
Monroe Township MS 1,400/6-8
1629 Perrineville Rd 08831 732-521-6042
Chari Chanley, prin. Fax 521-2846

**Montclair, Essex, Pop. 39,200**
Montclair SD 6,000/K-12
22 Valley Rd 07042 973-509-4000
Ron Bolandi, supt. Fax 509-0586
www.montclair.k12.nj.us
Glenfield MS 700/6-8
25 Maple Ave 07042 973-509-4172
Joseph Putrino, prin. Fax 509-4179
Montclair HS 1,900/9-12
100 Chestnut St 07042 973-509-4100
James Earle, prin. Fax 509-4098
Renaissance MS 200/6-8
176 N Fullerton Ave 07042 973-509-5741
Dr. Barbara Weller, prin. Fax 509-5752
Other Schools – See Upper Montclair

Eastern School of Acupuncture Post-Sec.
427 Bloomfield Ave Ste 301 07042 973-746-8717
Immaculate Conception HS 200/9-12
33 Cottage Pl 07042 973-744-7445
Joann Degnan, prin. Fax 744-3926
Lacordaire Academy 100/9-12
155 Lorraine Ave 07043 973-744-1156
Brian Morgan, head sch Fax 783-9521
Montclair Kimberley Academy 400/4-8
201 Valley Rd 07042 973-746-9800
Thomas Nammack, hdmstr. Fax 509-7950
Montclair Kimberley Academy - Upper S 400/9-12
201 Valley Rd 07042 973-783-8300
Thomas Nammack, hdmstr. Fax 744-4051
Montclair State University Post-Sec.
1 Normal Ave 07043 973-655-4000
Mountainside Hospital Post-Sec.
1 Bay Ave 07042 973-429-6850

**Montvale, Bergen, Pop. 7,749**
Montvale SD 1,100/PK-8
47 Spring Valley Rd 07645 201-391-1662
Dr. Darren Petersen, supt. Fax 391-8935
www.montvalek8.org
Fieldstone MS 500/5-8
47 Spring Valley Rd 07645 201-391-9000
Erik Parks, prin. Fax 391-8935

Pascack Valley Regional HSD 2,000/9-12
46 Akers Ave 07645 201-358-7004
P. Erik Gundersen, supt. Fax 505-4858
www.pascack.k12.nj.us
Pascack Hills HS 800/9-12
225 W Grand Ave 07645 201-358-7020
Glenn de Marrais, prin. Fax 358-7019
Other Schools – See Hillsdale

St. Joseph Regional HS 500/9-12
40 Chestnut Ridge Rd 07645 201-391-3300
Barry Donnelly, prin. Fax 391-8073

**Montville, Morris, Pop. 15,600**
Montville Township SD 4,100/K-12
86 River Rd 07045 973-331-7100
Dr. Rene Rovtar, supt. Fax 316-4640
montville.net
Lazar MS 1,000/6-8
123 Changebridge Rd 07045 973-331-7100
Sharon Carr, prin. Fax 331-9279
Montville Township HS 1,400/9-12
100 Horseneck Rd 07045 973-331-7100
Douglas Sanford, prin.

Trinity Christian S 200/K-12
160 Changebridge Rd 07045 973-334-1785
Douglas Prol, head sch Fax 334-9282

**Moorestown, Burlington, Pop. 13,242**
Moorestown Township SD 4,000/K-12
803 N Stanwick Rd 08057 856-778-6600
Timothy Rehm, supt. Fax 235-0961
www.mtps.com
Allen III MS 700/7-8
801 N Stanwick Rd 08057 856-778-6620
Matthew Keith, prin. Fax 727-9309
Moorestown HS 1,400/9-12
350 Bridgeboro Rd 08057 856-778-6610
Andrew Seibel, prin. Fax 722-8983

Lincoln Technical Institute Post-Sec.
308 W Route 38 Ste 2 08057 856-722-9333
Moorestown Friends S 700/PK-12
110 E Main St 08057 856-235-2900
Laurence Van Meter, head sch Fax 235-6684

**Morganville, Monmouth, Pop. 4,962**
Marlboro Township SD
Supt. — See Marlboro
Marlboro Memorial MS 1,100/6-8
71 Nolan Rd 07751 732-972-7115
John Pacifico, prin. Fax 972-7118

**Morris Plains, Morris, Pop. 5,456**
Morris Plains SD 600/PK-8
500 Speedwell Ave 07950 973-538-1650
Mark Maire, supt. Fax 540-1983
morrisplains.schoolwires.net
Borough MS 400/3-8
500 Speedwell Ave 07950 973-538-1650
Andrew Kramar, prin. Fax 538-8367

Parsippany-Troy Hills Township SD
Supt. — See Parsippany
Parsippany Hills HS 1,100/9-12
20 Rita Dr 07950 973-682-2815
Michael DiSanto, prin. Fax 682-2855

**Morristown, Morris, Pop. 18,125**
Morris SD 4,200/K-12
31 Hazel St 07960 973-292-2300
Mackey Pendergrast, supt. Fax 292-2057
www.morrisschooldistrict.org
Frelinghuysen MS 1,000/6-8
10 Jean St 07960 973-292-2200
Joseph Uglialoro, prin. Fax 292-2458
Morristown HS 1,400/9-12
50 Early St 07960 973-292-2000
Mark Manning, prin. Fax 539-5573

College of Saint Elizabeth Post-Sec.
2 Convent Rd 07960 973-290-4000
Delbarton S 600/7-12
230 Mendham Rd 07960 973-538-3231
Br. Paul Diveny, hdmstr. Fax 538-8836
Morristown-Beard S 500/6-12
70 Whippany Rd 07960 973-539-3032
Peter Caldwell, hdmstr. Fax 539-1590
Morristown Memorial Hospital Post-Sec.
100 Madison Ave 07960 973-971-5177
Rabbinical College of America Post-Sec.
226 Sussex Ave 07960 973-267-9404
Villa Walsh Academy 300/7-12
455 Western Ave 07960 973-538-3680
Sr. Patricia Pompa, prin. Fax 538-6733

**Mountain Lakes, Morris, Pop. 4,079**
Mountain Lakes SD 1,600/K-12
400 Boulevard 07046 973-334-8280
Dr. Anne Mucci, supt. Fax 334-2316
www.mlschools.org
Briarcliff MS 300/6-8
93 Briarcliff Rd 07046 973-334-0342
Bryan Fleming, prin. Fax 334-6857
Mountain Lakes HS 700/9-12
96 Powerville Rd 07046 973-334-8400
Jeremy Davies, prin. Fax 334-3550

**Mountainside, Union, Pop. 6,605**
Mountainside SD 800/PK-8
1497 Woodacres Dr 07092 908-232-3232
Dr. Nancy Lubarsky, admin. Fax 232-1743
www.mountainsideschools.org
Deerfield ES 500/3-8
302 Central Ave 07092 908-232-8828
Kimberly Richards, prin. Fax 232-7338

**Mount Arlington, Morris, Pop. 4,979**
Mount Arlington SD 400/PK-8
446 Howard Blvd 07856 973-770-7140
Jane Mullins Jameson, supt. Fax 398-3614
www.mtarlingtonk8.org/
Mount Arlington MS 200/3-8
235 Howard Blvd 07856 973-398-4400
Jeffrey Grillo, prin. Fax 398-5726

**Mount Ephraim, Camden, Pop. 4,636**
Mount Ephraim Borough SD 400/PK-8
225 W Kings Hwy 08059 856-931-7807
Leslie Koller, supt. Fax 931-5831
mtephraimschools.org/
Kershaw MS 200/5-8
125 S Black Horse Pike 08059 856-931-1634
Michael Hunter, prin. Fax 931-5831

**Mount Holly, Burlington, Pop. 10,639**
Burlington Co. Institute of Tech SD
695 Woodlane Rd 08060 609-267-4226
Dr. Christopher Manno, supt. Fax 267-9788
www.bcit.cc/
Burlington Co. Institute of Tech Evening Vo/Tech
695 Woodlane Rd 08060 609-267-4226
Patrick Cruet, prin.
Burlington Co. Institute of Technology Vo/Tech
695 Woodlane Rd 08060 609-267-4226
Joseph Venuto, prin. Fax 267-3752
Other Schools – See Medford

Mount Holly Township SD 900/PK-8
331 Levis Dr 08060 609-267-7108
James DiDonato, supt. Fax 702-9082
www.mtholly.k12.nj.us
Holbein MS 300/6-8
333 Levis Dr 08060 609-267-7200
Carolyn McDonald, prin. Fax 702-9775

Rancocas Valley Regional HSD 2,000/9-12
520 Jacksonville Rd 08060 609-267-0830
Christopher Heilig, supt. Fax 702-0167
www.rvrhs.com/
Rancocas Valley Regional HS 2,000/9-12
520 Jacksonville Rd 08060 609-267-0830
Christopher Heilig, supt. Fax 702-0167

---

Burlington County Inst. of Technology Post-Sec.
695 Woodlane Rd 08060 609-267-4226

**Mount Laurel, Burlington**
Burlington County Special Services SD
Supt. — See Westampton
Burlington County Alternative HS Alt
1000 Briggs Rd 08054 609-261-5600
Russell McLemore, prin.

Mount Laurel Township SD 4,000/K-8
330 Mount Laurel Rd 08054 856-235-3387
Dr. Sharon Vitella, supt. Fax 235-1837
www.mtlaurelschools.org
Harrington MS 1,000/7-8
514 Mount Laurel Rd 08054 856-234-1610
Kathleen Haines, prin. Fax 222-9754

**Mullica Hill, Gloucester, Pop. 3,933**
Clearview Regional HSD 2,400/7-12
420 Cedar Rd 08062 856-223-2765
John Horchak, supt. Fax 478-0409
www.clearviewregional.edu
Clearview Regional HS 1,500/9-12
625 Breakneck Rd 08062 856-223-2790
Keith Brook, prin. Fax 478-6705
Clearview Regional MS 900/7-8
595 Jefferson Rd 08062 856-223-2740
Robin Bazzel, prin. Fax 223-9068

**Neptune, Monmouth, Pop. 4,773**
Monmouth County Vocational SD
Supt. — See Freehold
Monmouth Co. Acad of Allied Health & Sci Vo/Tech
2325 Heck Ave 07753 732-775-0058
Paul Mucciarone, prin. Fax 775-6646

Neptune Township SD 4,000/PK-12
60 Neptune Blvd 07753 732-776-2000
Tami Crader, supt. Fax 897-7595
www.neptune.k12.nj.us/
Neptune HS 1,300/9-12
55 Neptune Blvd 07753 732-776-2200
Richard Allen, prin. Fax 776-2253
Neptune MS 800/6-8
2300 Heck Ave 07753 732-776-2200
Dr. Mark Alfone, prin. Fax 776-2254

---

Jersey Shore Medical Center Post-Sec.
1945 State Route 33 07753 732-776-4603

**Newark, Essex, Pop. 268,973**
Essex County Vocational Technical SD
60 Nelson Pl 1 North 07102 973-412-2050
Dr. James M. Pedersen, supt. Fax 412-2100
www.essextech.org
Essex Co. Vocational Tech - N 13th St Vo/Tech
300 N 13th St 07107 973-412-2203
Patricia Clark-Jeter, prin. Fax 412-2098
Essex Co. Vocational Tech - Newark Tech Vo/Tech
91 W Market St 07103 973-412-2204
Oge Denis, prin. Fax 412-2094
Other Schools – See Bloomfield, West Caldwell

Essex Regional Educ Services Commission
Supt. — See Fairfield
Sojourn HS Alt
80 Duryea St 07103 973-484-4858
Dr. Jacqueline Young, prin. Fax 268-3511

Newark SD 36,800/PK-12
2 Cedar St 07102 973-733-7333
Christopher Cerf, supt. Fax 733-6834
www.nps.k12.nj.us
American History HS 300/9-12
74 Montgomery St 07103 973-733-6903
Robert Gregory, prin. Fax 456-7086
Arts HS 600/9-12
550 Martin Luther King Jr 07102 973-733-7391
Lynn Jackson, prin. Fax 483-5524
Bard HS Early College 100/9-12
321 Bergen St 07103 973-733-8353
John Weinstein, prin.
Barringer Academy of Arts & Humanities 9-12
90 Parker St 07104 973-268-5106
Dr. Crystal Breedlove, prin. Fax 268-5033
Barringer S.T.E.A.M. HS 1,200/9-12
90 Parker St 07104 973-268-5125
Angela Mincy, prin. Fax 268-5322
Central HS 600/9-12
246 18th Ave 07108 973-733-6897
Sharnee Brown, prin. Fax 733-8212
Eagle Academy Alt
279 Chancellor Ave 07112 973-733-7165
Vaughn Thompson, prin.
East Side HS 1,400/9-12
238 Van Buren St 07105 973-465-4900
Dr. Mario Santos, prin. Fax 465-4936
Fast Track Success Academy 200/Alt
200 Washington St 07102 973-733-8765
Mark Comesanas, prin.
Girls Academy of Newark 6-12
279 Chancellor Ave 07112 973-733-6403
Tanishia Williams, prin.
Newark Leadership Academy 100/9-12
301 W Kinney St 07103 973-733-6773
Gabriele Kuriloff, prin.
Newark Vocational S Vo/Tech
403 S Orange Ave 07103 973-733-7018
Larry Ramkissoon, prin. Fax 792-6018
Science Park MSHS 800/7-12
260 Norfolk St 07103 973-733-8689
Lamont Thomas, prin. Fax 733-8236
Shabazz HS 700/9-12
80 Johnson Ave 07108 973-733-6760
Brad Haggerty, prin. Fax 792-6514
Technology HS Vo/Tech
187 Broadway 07104 973-481-5962
Edwin Reyes, prin. Fax 497-5786
University JSHS 500/7-12
55 Clinton Pl 07108 973-351-2010
Regina Sharpe, prin. Fax 424-4447
Weequahic HS 600/9-12
279 Chancellor Ave 07112 973-705-3900
Lisa McDonald, prin. Fax 923-4095
West Side HS 900/9-12
403 S Orange Ave 07103 973-733-6977
Fax 733-8941

---

Berkeley College Post-Sec.
536 Broad St 07102 973-642-3888
Christ the King Preparatory S 300/9-12
239 Woodside Ave 07104 973-483-0033
Rev. Gregory Gebbia, prin. Fax 481-0693
Drake College of Business Post-Sec.
800 Broad St 07102 973-645-1333
Essex County College Post-Sec.
303 University Ave 07102 973-877-3000
New Community Workforce Development Ctr. Post-Sec.
201 Bergen St 07103 973-824-6484
New Jersey Institute of Technology Post-Sec.
University Heights 07102 973-596-3000
New Testament S 50/PK-12
511 Orange St 07107 973-268-1310
Mollie Haynes, admin. Fax 268-1310
Pillar College Post-Sec.
60 Park Pl Ste 701 07102 973-803-5000
Rutgers-The State University of N.J. Post-Sec.
249 University Ave 07102 973-353-5568
St. Benedict Preparatory S 600/7-12
520 Martin Luther King Jr 07102 973-643-4800
Rev. Edwin Leahy, hdmstr. Fax 643-6922
St. Vincent Academy 300/9-12
228 W Market St 07103 973-622-1613
Sr. June Favata, dir. Fax 622-1128
Seton Hall University School of Law Post-Sec.
1 Newark Ctr 07102 973-642-8500
Star Career Academy Post-Sec.
550 Broad St 07102 973-639-0789

**New Brunswick, Middlesex, Pop. 54,229**
New Brunswick SD 6,900/PK-12
PO Box 2683 08903 732-745-5300
Aubrey Johnson, supt. Fax 745-5459
www.nbps.k12.nj.us
New Brunswick HS 1,400/9-12
1000 Somerset St 08901 732-745-5300
Janene Rodriguez, prin. Fax 214-1215
New Brunswick MS 1,100/6-8
1125 Livingston Ave 08901 732-745-5300
Jeremiah Clifford, prin. Fax 565-7630
Adult HS Adult
268 Baldwin St 08901 732-846-5300
Timothy TImberlake, prin. Fax 745-5325

---

New Brunswick Theological Seminary Post-Sec.
17 Seminary Pl 08901 732-247-5241
Rutgers-The State University of N.J. Post-Sec.
57 US Highway 1 08901 732-445-4636

**New Egypt, Ocean, Pop. 2,476**
Plumsted Township SD 1,600/PK-12
117 Evergreen Rd 08533 609-758-6800
Stephanie Bilenker Ed.D., supt. Fax 758-6808
www.newegypt.us
New Egypt HS 500/9-12
117 Evergreen Rd 08533 609-758-6800
Eugene Mosley, prin. Fax 758-5683
New Egypt MS 500/6-8
115 Evergreen Rd 08533 609-758-6800
Andrea Caldes, prin. Fax 758-5538

**Newfield, Gloucester, Pop. 1,534**

---

Our Lady of Mercy Academy 100/9-12
1001 Main Rd 08344 856-697-2008
Sr. Grace Scandale, prin. Fax 697-2887

**New Milford, Bergen, Pop. 16,071**
New Milford SD 2,000/K-12
145 Madison Ave 07646 201-261-2952
Michael Polizzi, supt. Fax 261-8018
www.newmilfordschools.org
New Milford HS 600/9-12
1 Snyder Cir 07646 201-262-0172
Louis Manuppelli, prin. Fax 262-4445
Owens MS 500/6-8
470 Marion Ave 07646 201-265-8661
James DeLalla, prin. Fax 265-5680

**New Providence, Union, Pop. 12,002**
New Providence SD 2,000/PK-12
356 Elkwood Ave 07974 908-464-9050
David Miceli Ed.D., supt. Fax 464-9041
www.npsd.k12.nj.us
New Providence HS 600/9-12
35 Pioneer Dr 07974 908-464-4700
Lauren Zirpoli, prin. Fax 464-8556
New Providence MS 300/7-8
35 Pioneer Dr 07974 908-464-9161
Jay Richter, prin. Fax 464-5927

**Newton, Sussex, Pop. 7,865**
Andover Regional SD 500/K-8
707 Limecrest Rd 07860 973-383-3746
Anthony Macerino, supt. Fax 579-3972
www.andoverregional.org
Long Pond S 300/5-8
707 Limecrest Rd 07860 973-940-1234
T. Jon Sinclair, prin. Fax 579-2690

Kittatinny Regional SD 1,100/7-12
77 Halsey Rd 07860 973-383-1800
Craig Hutcheson, supt. Fax 383-6218
www.krhs.net
Kittatinny Regional JSHS 1,100/7-12
77 Halsey Rd 07860 973-383-1800
Christian Angelillo, prin. Fax 383-4392

Newton SD 1,500/PK-12
57 Trinity St 07860 973-383-1900
Dr. G. Kennedy Greene, supt. Fax 383-5378
www.newtonnj.org
Halsted Street MS 200/6-8
59 Halsted St 07860 973-383-7440
Kristi Greene, prin. Fax 383-7432
Newton HS 800/9-12
44 Ryerson Ave 07860 973-383-7573
Jeff Waldron, prin. Fax 383-1153

---

Sussex County Community College Post-Sec.
1 College Hill Rd 07860 973-300-2100

**North Arlington, Bergen, Pop. 15,146**
North Arlington SD 1,600/PK-12
222 Ridge Rd 07031 201-991-6800
Dr. Oliver Stringham, supt. Fax 991-1656
www.narlington.k12.nj.us
North Arlington HS 500/9-12
222 Ridge Rd 07031 201-991-6800
Stephen Yurchack, prin. Fax 991-0188
North Arlington MS 300/6-8
45 Beech St 07031 201-991-6800
Nicole Russo, prin. Fax 246-0703

---

Queen of Peace HS 500/9-12
191 Rutherford Pl 07031 201-998-8227
John Tonero, prin. Fax 998-3040

**North Bergen, Hudson, Pop. 59,000**
Hudson County Schools of Technology
8511 Tonnelle Ave 07047 201-662-6700
Frank Gargiulo, supt.
www.hcstonline.org
High Tech HS Vo/Tech
2000 85th St 07047 201-662-6801
Dr. Joseph Giammarella, prin. Fax 854-4129
Knowledge Advanced Skills Vo/Tech
2000 85th St 07047 201-662-6804
Dr. Joseph Giammarella, prin.
Other Schools – See Flemington, Jersey City

North Bergen SD 7,400/PK-12
7317 Kennedy Blvd 07047 201-868-1000
Dr. George Solter, supt. Fax 295-2747
www.northbergen.k12.nj.us/
North Bergen HS 2,400/9-12
7417 Kennedy Blvd 07047 201-295-2800
Paschal Tennaro, prin. Fax 295-2873

**North Brunswick, Middlesex, Pop. 37,400**
North Brunswick Township SD 5,800/PK-12
PO Box 6016 08902 732-289-3000
Dr. Brian Zychowski, supt. Fax 297-8567
www.nbtschools.org
Linwood MS 1,300/6-8
25 Linwood Pl 08902 732-289-3600
Dr. Raymond Tucholski, prin. Fax 247-7033
North Brunswick Township HS 1,700/9-12
98 Raider Rd 08902 732-289-3700
Peter Clark, prin. Fax 821-8342

South Brunswick Township SD 8,700/PK-12
231 Black Horse Ln 08902 732-297-7800
Dr. Gerard Jellig, supt. Fax 297-8456
www.sbschools.org
Other Schools – See Monmouth Junction

---

Anthem Institute — Post-Sec.
651 US Highway 1 08902 — 732-448-2600
DeVry University — Post-Sec.
630 US Highway 1 08902 — 732-729-3960

**North Caldwell, Essex, Pop. 6,124**
West Essex Regional SD — 1,600/7-12
65 W Greenbrook Rd 07006 — 973-228-1200
Barbara Longo, supt. — Fax 228-0559
www.westex.org
West Essex HS — 1,000/9-12
65 W Greenbrook Rd 07006 — 973-228-1200
Caesar Diliberto, prin. — Fax 364-1872
West Essex MS — 600/7-8
65 W Greenbrook Rd 07006 — 973-228-1200
Vee Popat, prin. — Fax 228-5852

**Northfield, Atlantic, Pop. 8,484**
Northfield CSD — 1,000/K-8
2000 New Rd 08225 — 609-407-4000
Robert Garguilo, supt. — Fax 646-0608
northfield.groupfusion.net
Northfield Community MS — 500/5-8
2000 New Rd 08225 — 609-407-4008
Glenn Robbins, prin. — Fax 641-2646

**North Haledon, Passaic, Pop. 8,332**
North Haledon SD — 700/PK-8
201 Squawbrook Rd 07508 — 973-427-8993
Nicholas Coffaro, supt. — Fax 427-4357
www.nhschools.net
High Mountain MS — 300/5-8
515 High Mountain Rd 07508 — 973-427-1220
Giovanni Giancaspro M.A., prin. — Fax 427-7685

---

Eastern Christian HS — 300/9-12
50 Oakwood Ave 07508 — 973-427-0900
Ruth Kuder, prin. — Fax 427-3716
Mary Help of Christians Academy — 200/8-12
659 Belmont Ave 07508 — 973-790-6200
Sr. Marisa DeRose, prin. — Fax 790-6125

**North Plainfield, Somerset, Pop. 21,559**
North Plainfield Borough SD — 3,100/PK-12
33 Mountain Ave 07060 — 908-769-6060
Dr. James McLaughlin, supt. — Fax 755-5490
www.nplainfield.org
Alternative HS — Alt
12 Harrison Ave 07060 — 908-769-6090
John Tarnofsky, prin. — Fax 769-6116
North Plainfield HS — 1,500/7-12
34 Wilson Ave 07060 — 908-769-6000
Dr. Jerard Stephenson, prin. — Fax 769-6032

---

Robert Fiance Beauty School — Post-Sec.
121 Watchung Ave 07060 — 908-754-4247

**Nutley, Essex, Pop. 27,400**
Nutley SD — 3,700/K-12
315 Franklin Ave 07110 — 973-661-8798
Russell Lazovick, supt. — Fax 320-8476
www.nutleyschools.org
Nutley HS — 1,200/9-12
300 Franklin Ave 07110 — 973-661-8832
Denis Williams, prin. — Fax 661-3664
Walker MS — 600/7-8
325 Franklin Ave 07110 — 973-661-8871
Tracy Egan, prin. — Fax 661-3775

---

Abundant Life Academy — 400/PK-12
390 Washington Ave 07110 — 973-667-9700
John Kuebler, head sch — Fax 667-1278
Eastwick College — Post-Sec.
103 Park Ave 07110 — 973-661-0600

**Oakhurst, Monmouth, Pop. 3,965**
Ocean Township SD — 3,800/PK-12
163 Monmouth Rd 07755 — 732-531-5600
Dr. James Stefankiewicz, supt. — Fax 531-3874
www.oceanschools.org
Ocean Township HS — 1,200/9-12
550 W Park Ave 07755 — 732-531-5650
Kelly Weldon, prin. — Fax 571-4009
Other Schools – See Ocean

**Oakland, Bergen, Pop. 12,608**
Oakland SD — 1,700/K-8
315 Ramapo Valley Rd 07436 — 201-337-6156
Dr. Gina Coffaro, supt. — Fax 405-1237
www.oaklandschoolsnj.org
Valley MS — 600/6-8
71 Oak St 07436 — 201-337-8185
Gregg Desiderio, prin. — Fax 337-7089

Ramapo Indian Hills Regional HSD — 2,300/9-12
131 Yawpo Ave 07436 — 201-416-8100
Beverly MacKay, supt. — Fax 416-8123
www.rih.org
Indian Hills HS — 1,200/9-12
97 Yawpo Ave 07436 — 201-337-0100
Joseph Collins, prin. — Fax 337-1031
Other Schools – See Franklin Lakes

---

Barnstable Academy — 100/5-12
8 Wright Way 07436 — 201-651-0200

**Oak Ridge, Passaic**
Jefferson Township SD
Supt. — See Lake Hopatcong
Jefferson Township HS — 1,000/9-12
1010 Weldon Rd 07438 — 973-697-3535
Karl Mundi, prin. — Fax 208-8409
Jefferson Township MS — 800/6-8
1000 Weldon Rd 07438 — 973-697-1980
Kevin Lipton, prin. — Fax 697-1348

**Ocean, Monmouth, Pop. 26,700**
Ocean Township SD
Supt. — See Oakhurst
Ocean Township IS — 1,300/5-8
1200 W Park Ave 07712 — 732-531-5630
Larry Kostula, prin. — Fax 493-1891

---

Concorde School of Hair Design — Post-Sec.
1458 State Route 35 07712 — 732-918-0505
Deal Yeshiva — 300/K-12
1515 Logan Rd 07712 — 732-663-1717
Hillel Yeshiva HS — 200/9-12
1027 Deal Rd 07712 — 732-493-0420
Ilan HS — 100/9-12
1200 Roseld Ave 07712 — 732-517-1111

**Ocean City, Cape May, Pop. 11,545**
Ocean City SD — 2,000/K-12
501 Atlantic Ave Ste 1 08226 — 609-399-5150
Dr. Kathleen Taylor, supt. — Fax 399-4656
www.oceancityschools.org/
Ocean City HS — 1,200/9-12
501 Atlantic Ave 08226 — 609-399-1290
Matthew Jamison, prin. — Fax 399-1966
Ocean City IS — 500/4-8
1801 Bay Ave 08226 — 609-399-5611
Geoffrey Haines, prin. — Fax 398-7089

**Oceanport, Monmouth, Pop. 5,763**
Oceanport Borough SD — 600/PK-8
29 Wolfhill Ave 07757 — 732-542-0683
Thomas Farrell, supt.
www.oceanport.k12.nj.us
Maple Place MS — 300/5-8
2 Maple Pl 07757 — 732-229-0267
Matthew Howell, prin. — Fax 229-0961

**Old Bridge, Middlesex, Pop. 23,304**
Old Bridge Township SD
Supt. — See Matawan
Salk MS — 1,000/6-8
155 W Greystone Rd 08857 — 732-360-4519
William Rezes, prin. — Fax 251-1690
Sandburg MS — 1,200/6-8
3439 Highway 516 08857 — 732-360-4400
Martha Simon, prin. — Fax 360-9676

---

Calvary Christian S — 300/PK-12
123 White Oak Ln 08857 — 732-479-0700
Yeshiva Tiferes Naftoli of Central NJ — 50/9-12
8998 State Route 18 08857 — 732-446-5841

**Old Tappan, Bergen, Pop. 5,680**
Northern Valley Regional HSD
Supt. — See Demarest
Northern Valley Regional HS — 1,300/9-12
100 Central Ave 07675 — 201-784-1600
Bruce Sabatini, prin. — Fax 768-7724

Old Tappan SD — 800/K-8
277 Old Tappan Rd 07675 — 201-664-1421
Danielle DaGiau, supt. — Fax 664-4418
oldtappanschools.org
DeWolf MS — 400/5-8
275 Old Tappan Rd 07675 — 201-664-1475
Justin O'Neill, prin. — Fax 664-8101

**Oradell, Bergen, Pop. 7,880**
River Dell Regional SD
Supt. — See River Edge
River Dell Regional HS — 1,100/9-12
55 Pyle St 07649 — 201-599-7240
Lorraine Brooks, prin. — Fax 599-2294

---

Bergen Catholic HS — 700/9-12
1040 Oradell Ave 07649 — 201-261-1844
Timothy McElhinney, prin. — Fax 599-9507

**Orange, Essex, Pop. 33,300**
Orange Township SD — 3,600/PK-12
451 Lincoln Ave 07050 — 973-677-4000
Ronald Lee, supt. — Fax 677-0486
www.orange.k12.nj.us
Career & Innovation Academy of Orange — Vo/Tech
123 Cleveland St 07050 — 973-677-4000
Erica Stewart, prin.
Orange HS — 700/10-12
400 Lincoln Ave 07050 — 973-677-4050
Jason Belton, prin. — Fax 677-4069
Orange Preparatory Academy — 300/7-9
400 Central Ave 07050 — 973-677-4135
Aretha Malloy, prin. — Fax 677-2439

**Palisades Park, Bergen, Pop. 19,390**
Palisades Park SD — 1,400/PK-12
410 2nd St 07650 — 201-947-3550
Joseph Cirillo, supt. — Fax 947-4079
www.palpkschools.org/
Palisades Park HS — 500/8-12
1 Veterans Plz 07650 — 201-941-1100
Nicholas Cipriano, prin. — Fax 947-1280

**Palmyra, Burlington, Pop. 7,223**
Palmyra Borough SD — 900/PK-12
301 Delaware Ave 08065 — 856-786-9300
Brian McBride, supt. — Fax 829-9638
palmyraschools.com
Palmyra HS — 400/7-12
311 W 5th St 08065 — 856-786-9400
Kenneth Holloway, prin. — Fax 786-3014

**Paramus, Bergen, Pop. 25,735**
Bergen County Vocational Technical SD
327 E Ridgewood Ave 07652 — 201-343-6000
Dr. Howard Lerner, supt. — Fax 225-9182
bcts.bergen.org
Applied Technology HS — Vo/Tech
400 Paramus Rd 07652 — 201-343-6000
Andrea Sheridan, prin.
Bergen County Technical HS - Paramus — Vo/Tech
285 Pascack Rd 07652 — 201-343-6000
Fax 996-6935
Other Schools – See Hackensack, Teterboro

Paramus SD — 3,900/K-12
145 Spring Valley Rd 07652 — 201-261-7800
Michele Robinson, supt. — Fax 261-5861
www.paramusschools.org/ppsd/
East Brook MS — 600/5-8
190 Spring Valley Rd 07652 — 201-261-7800
Thomas LoBue, prin. — Fax 262-1541
Paramus HS — 1,300/9-12
99 E Century Rd 07652 — 201-261-7800
Raymond Kiem, prin. — Fax 261-3833
West Brook MS — 700/5-8
560 Roosevelt Blvd 07652 — 201-261-7800
Carla Alvarez, prin. — Fax 652-0376

---

Bergen Community College — Post-Sec.
400 Paramus Rd 07652 — 201-447-7100
Berkeley College — Post-Sec.
64 E Midland Ave 07652 — 201-967-9667
Capri Institute of Hair Design — Post-Sec.
615 Winters Ave 07652 — 201-599-0880
DeVry University — Post-Sec.
81 E State Rt 4 Ste 102 07652 — 201-556-2840
Frisch S — 600/9-12
120 W Century Rd 07652 — 201-267-9100
Lincoln Technical Institute — Post-Sec.
240 Bergen Town Ctr 07652 — 201-845-6868
Paramus Catholic HS — 1,500/9-12
425 Paramus Rd 07652 — 201-445-6465
James Vail, pres. — Fax 445-3952

**Park Ridge, Bergen, Pop. 8,566**
Park Ridge SD — 1,200/PK-12
85 Pascack Rd 07656 — 201-573-6000
Dr. Robert Gamper, supt. — Fax 391-6511
www.parkridge.k12.nj.us
Park Ridge HS — 500/7-12
2 Park Ave 07656 — 201-573-6000
Troy Lederman, prin. — Fax 930-4874

**Parlin, Middlesex**
Sayreville SD
Supt. — See South Amboy
Sayreville MS — 1,200/6-8
800 Washington Rd 08859 — 732-525-5288
Donna Jakubik, prin. — Fax 727-5621
Sayreville War Memorial HS — 1,700/9-12
820 Washington Rd 08859 — 732-525-5253
James Brown, prin. — Fax 316-0720

**Parsippany, Morris, Pop. 51,000**
Parsippany-Troy Hills Township SD — 6,900/PK-12
PO Box 52 07054 — 973-263-7250
Scott Rixford, supt. — Fax 263-7230
www.pthsd.k12.nj.us
Brooklawn MS — 800/6-8
250 Beachwood Rd 07054 — 973-428-7551
Dr. Natalie Betz, prin. — Fax 781-0309
Central MS — 800/6-8
1620 US Highway 46 07054 — 973-263-7125
Gary Borges, prin. — Fax 402-1579
Parsippany HS — 1,000/9-12
309 Baldwin Rd 07054 — 973-263-7001
Dr. Denis Mulroony, prin. — Fax 263-7347
Other Schools – See Morris Plains

---

Anthem Institute — Post-Sec.
959 US Highway 46 07054 — 888-852-7272
Parsippany Christian S — 200/PK-12
PO Box 5365 07054 — 973-539-7012
David Detwiler, admin. — Fax 539-2527

**Passaic, Passaic, Pop. 69,000**
Essex Regional Educ Services Commission
Supt. — See Fairfield
Essex HS — Adult
188 1st St 07055 — 973-815-1389
Charles Johnson, prin. — Fax 815-1635

Passaic CSD — 12,300/PK-12
PO Box 388 07055 — 973-470-5500
Pablo Munoz, supt. — Fax 470-8984
www.passaicschools.org/
Lincoln MS — 1,600/7-8
291 Lafayette Ave 07055 — 973-470-5504
Fawzi Naji, prin. — Fax 470-5128
Passaic HS — 2,400/9-12
170 Paulison Ave 07055 — 973-470-5600
Francisco Velez, prin. — Fax 470-5135

Passaic Co. Education Services Comm.
Supt. — See Wayne
Hope Academy — 100/Alt
266 Harrison St 07055 — 973-928-1509
Irene LeFebvre Ed.D., dir. — Fax 928-1505

---

Bais Yaakov of Passaic HS — 200/9-12
181 Pennington Ave 07055 — 973-365-0100
Baila Stern, prin. — Fax 365-0570
Collegiate S — 100/PK-12
22 Kent Ct 07055 — 973-777-1714
Mesivta Tiferes Rav Zvi Aryeh Zemel — 100/9-12
15 Temple Pl 07055 — 973-594-9001

**Paterson, Passaic, Pop. 143,991**
Paterson SD — 21,200/PK-12
90 Delaware Ave 07503 — 973-321-1000
Dr. Donnie Evans, supt. — Fax 321-0470
www.paterson.k12.nj.us
Academy of Gifted & Talented — 4-8
200 Presidential Blvd 07522 — 973-321-0280
Nancy Castro, prin. — Fax 321-0287
Alternative MS (STRIVE) — Alt
13 Wagaraw Blvd 07508 — 973-321-0096
Mirva Rivera, prin.
Bosco Technology Academy — 300/7-8
202 Union Ave 07502 — 973-321-0580
Wendy Munoz, prin. — Fax 321-0587
Destiny Academy — Alt
47 State St 07501 — 973-321-2392
Jalyn Lyde, prin. — Fax 321-2396

Eastside HS Operations 9-12
150 Park Ave 07501 973-321-2487
Zatiti Moody, prin. Fax 321-0517
Eastside HS S of Culinary Arts Hosp Trsm 600/9-12
150 Park Ave 07501 973-321-2489
Edgar Nieves, prin. Fax 321-0517
Eastside HS S of Government/Public Admin 600/9-12
150 Park Ave 07501 973-321-2488
Karen Johnson, prin. Fax 321-0517
Eastside HS S of Information and Tech 600/9-12
150 Park Ave 07501 973-321-2490
Vivian Gaines, prin. Fax 321-0517
HARP Academy 300/9-12
175 Main St 07505 973-321-0560
Kelli White, admin. Fax 321-0565
International HS 400/9-12
200 Grand St 07501 973-321-2280
Robina Puryear-Castro, prin. Fax 321-2283
Kennedy HS Academy of Arch & Const Trade 400/9-12
127 Preakness Ave 07522 973-321-0504
Dewitt Evering, admin. Fax 321-0507
Kennedy HS Academy of Bus Tech Mktg 500/9-12
127 Preakness Ave 07522 973-321-0505
Pamela Powell, admin. Fax 321-0507
Kennedy HS Academy of Sci Tech Eng Math 600/9-12
127 Preakness Ave 07522 973-321-0507
Nicholas Vancheri, prin. Fax 321-0507
Kennedy HS Acad of Education & Training 9-12
127 Preakness Ave 07522 973-321-2461
Maryanne Perrotta, admin. Fax 321-0507
Kennedy HS Operations 9-12
127 Preakness Ave 07522 973-321-0500
David Cozart, prin. Fax 321-0507
Morgan Academy of Trans & Engineering 100/9-12
200 Grand St 07501 973-321-2540
Stanley Sumter, admin. Fax 321-2547
New Roberto Clemente S 300/6-8
482 Market St 07501 973-321-0240
Hector Montes, prin. Fax 321-0247
PANTHER Academy 200/9-12
201 Memorial Dr 07505 973-321-2290
Gregg Festa, admin. Fax 321-2297
Parks HS of Fine & Performing Arts 200/9-12
413 12th Ave 07514 973-321-0520
Jalyn Lyde, prin. Fax 321-0527
Paterson City S 7 200/5-8
106 Ramsey St 07501 973-321-0070
Rebecca Cecala, prin. Fax 321-0077
Paterson City S 11 100/4-8
350 Market St 07501 973-321-0110
Carlos Ortiz, prin. Fax 321-0117
YES Academy 50/Alt
45 Smith St 07505 973-321-0570
Nicole Payne, prin. Fax 321-0577
Silk City 2000 Academy/Adult S Adult
151 Ellison St 07505 973-321-0760
Dr. Sebastian Calabria, prin. Fax 321-0767
Other Schools – See Prospect Park

---

HoHoKus Sch of Trade/Technical Sciences Post-Sec.
634 Market St 07513 800-646-9353
Passaic County Community College Post-Sec.
1 College Blvd 07505 973-684-6868

**Paulsboro, Gloucester, Pop. 5,820**
Paulsboro SD 1,100/PK-12
662 N Delaware St 08066 856-423-2222
Dr. Laurie Bandlow, supt. Fax 423-4602
www.paulsboro.k12.nj.us
Paulsboro HS 500/9-12
670 N Delaware St 08066 856-423-2222
Paul Morina, prin. Fax 423-8915
Paulsboro JHS 200/7-8
670 N Delaware Ave 08066 856-423-2222
Mildred Tolbert, prin. Fax 423-8915

**Pemberton, Burlington, Pop. 1,373**
Pemberton Township SD 4,300/PK-12
PO Box 228 08068 609-893-8141
Dr. Tony Trongone, supt. Fax 894-0933
www.pemberton.k12.nj.us
Fort/Newcomb MS 1,000/6-8
301 Fort Dix Rd 08068 609-893-8141
Keith Swaney, prin. Fax 894-9287
Pemberton Township HS 1,000/9-12
148 Arneys Mount Rd 08068 609-893-8141
Ida Smith, prin. Fax 894-0804

---

Burlington County College Post-Sec.
601 Pemberton Brown Mill Rd 08068 609-894-9311

**Pennington, Mercer, Pop. 2,560**
Hopewell Valley Regional SD 3,700/PK-12
425 S Main St 08534 609-737-4000
Dr. Thomas A. Smith, supt. Fax 737-1418
www.hvrsd.org/
Central HS 1,200/9-12
259 Pennington Titusville 08534 609-737-4003
Michael Daher, prin. Fax 737-1581
Timberlane MS 1,000/6-8
51 Timberlane Dr 08534 609-737-4004
Rosetta Treece, prin. Fax 737-2718

Mercer County Technical SD
Supt. — See Trenton
Sypek Center Vo/Tech
129 Bull Run Rd 08534 609-737-9785
Mary Smith Jones, prin. Fax 737-3951

---

Pennington S 500/6-12
112 W Delaware Ave 08534 609-737-1838
Dr. William Hawkey, hdmstr. Fax 737-2851

**Pennsauken, Camden, Pop. 35,900**
Camden County Technical Schools
Supt. — See Sicklerville
Camden County Technical S - Pennsauken Vo/Tech
6008 Browning Rd 08109 856-663-1040
Gregory Cappello, prin. Fax 655-8011

Pennsauken Township SD 4,800/PK-12
1695 Hylton Rd 08110 856-662-8505
Jame F. Chapman Ed.D., supt. Fax 663-5865
www.pennsauken.net
Pennsauken HS 1,400/9-12
800 Hylton Rd 08110 856-662-8500
Tameka Matthews, prin. Fax 910-2612
Phifer MS 700/7-8
8201 Park Ave 08109 856-662-8511
Thomas Honeyman, prin. Fax 486-1422

---

Bishop Eustace Prep S 700/9-12
5552 Marlton Pike 08109 856-662-2160
Cyril Bleistine, prin. Fax 662-0025
Omega Institute Post-Sec.
7050 Kaighns Ave 08109 856-663-4299

**Penns Grove, Salem, Pop. 4,982**
Penns Grove-Carneys Point Regional SD 2,300/PK-12
100 Iona Ave 08069 856-299-4250
Dr. Zenaida Cobian, supt. Fax 299-5226
pgcpschools.org
Penns Grove MS 500/6-8
351 E Maple Ave 08069 856-299-0576
Dr. Luis Amberths, prin. Fax 299-4378
Other Schools – See Carneys Point

**Pennsville, Salem, Pop. 11,771**
Pennsville Township SD 1,800/PK-12
30 Church St 08070 856-540-6200
Dr. Michael Brodzik, supt. Fax 678-7565
www.psdnet.org/
Pennsville Memorial HS 500/9-12
110 S Broadway 08070 856-540-6220
Matthew McFarland, prin. Fax 678-2715
Pennsville MS 500/6-8
4 William Penn Ave 08070 856-540-6240
Sheila Burris, prin. Fax 678-2908

---

Salem County Christian Academy 200/PK-12
104 Sparks Ave 08070 856-678-9464
Mike Tardive, admin. Fax 678-3696

**Perth Amboy, Middlesex, Pop. 50,388**
Middlesex County Vocational SD
Supt. — See East Brunswick
Perth Amboy Vocational HS Vo/Tech
457 High St 08861 732-376-6300
Robert Fuller, prin. Fax 376-6391

Perth Amboy SD 10,000/PK-12
178 Barracks St 08861 732-376-6200
Dr. David Roman, supt. Fax 826-1644
www.paps.net
McGinnis MS 1,300/5-8
271 State St 08861 732-376-6040
Dr. Melissa Espana-Rodriguez, prin. Fax 376-6047
Perth Amboy HS 2,200/9-12
300 Eagle Ave 08861 732-376-6030
Dr. Gene Mosley, prin. Fax 376-6275
Shull MS 1,400/5-8
380 Hall Ave 08861 732-376-6060
Michael Heidelberg, prin. Fax 376-6067
Perth Amboy Adult HS Adult
178 Barracks St 08861 732-376-6240
Dr. Luis Ortega, prin. Fax 376-6245

---

Perth Amboy Catholic Upper S 100/4-8
500 State St 08861 732-826-1598
Sr. Mary Rebecca Piatek, prin. Fax 826-7063
Raritan Bay Medical Center Post-Sec.
530 New Brunswick Ave 08861 732-324-5232
Robert Fiance Beauty Academy Post-Sec.
312 State St 08861 732-442-6007
Universal Training Institute Post-Sec.
174 Jefferson St 08861 732-826-0155

**Petersburg, See Woodbine**
Upper Township SD 1,400/PK-8
525 Perry Rd 08270 609-628-3500
Vincent Palmieri, supt. Fax 628-2002
upperschools.org/
Upper Township MS 500/6-8
525 Perry Rd 08270 609-628-3500
Jeffery Leek, prin. Fax 628-3506

**Phillipsburg, Warren, Pop. 14,597**
Lopatcong Township SD 900/PK-8
263 State Route 57 08865 908-859-0800
Rainie Roncoroni, supt. Fax 213-1339
www.lopatcongschool.org
Lopatcong MS 400/5-8
321 Stonehenge Dr 08865 908-213-2955
Jeanene Dutt, prin. Fax 213-0373

Phillipsburg SD 3,500/PK-12
445 Marshall St 08865 908-454-3400
George M. Chando, supt. Fax 213-2424
www.pburgsd.net/
Phillipsburg Alternative HS Alt
20 Fairview Ave 08865 908-213-2688
Kyle Rovi, dir. Fax 213-2708
Phillipsburg Alternative Learning S Alt
445 Marshall St 08865 908-213-2651
Kyle Rovi, dir. Fax 454-2479
Phillipsburg HS 1,600/9-12
200 Hillcrest Blvd 08865 908-454-6551
Janice Trent, prin. Fax 213-2427
Phillipsburg MS 500/6-8
525 Warren St 08865 908-454-5577
Raffaele LaForgia, prin. Fax 213-2546

**Pilesgrove, Salem**
Salem County Vocational Technical SD
880 Route 45 08098 856-769-0101
John Swain, supt. Fax 769-3602
www.scvts.org/
Salem County Career & Technical HS Vo/Tech
880 Route 45 08098 856-769-0101
Jason Helder, prin. Fax 769-4214

**Pine Hill, Camden, Pop. 9,944**
Pine Hill Borough SD 1,700/PK-12
1003 Turnerville Rd 08021 856-783-6900
Dr. Kenneth Koczur, supt. Fax 783-2955
www.pinehill.k12.nj.us
Overbrook HS 600/9-12
1200 Turnerville Rd 08021 856-767-8000
Adam Lee, prin. Fax 767-3082
Pine Hill MS 300/6-8
1100 Turnerville Rd 08021 856-210-0200
Kathleen Klemick, prin. Fax 210-0195

**Piscataway, Middlesex, Pop. 48,900**
Middlesex County Vocational SD
Supt. — See East Brunswick
Piscataway Vocational HS Vo/Tech
21 Suttons Ln 08854 732-985-0717
Joseph Armstead, prin. Fax 985-7717

Piscataway Township SD 7,000/PK-12
PO Box 1332 08855 732-572-2289
Teresa Rafferty, supt. Fax 777-1361
www.piscatawayschools.org/
Conackamack MS 400/6-8
5205 Witherspoon St 08854 732-699-1577
Donna White, prin. Fax 699-0118
Piscataway Township HS 2,200/9-12
100 Behmer Rd 08854 732-981-0700
Jason Lester, prin. Fax 981-1985
Quibbletown MS 600/6-8
99 Academy St 08854 732-752-0444
William Gonzalez, prin. Fax 752-5798
Schor MS 600/6-8
243 N Randolphville Rd 08854 732-752-4457
Richard Hueston, prin. Fax 424-9445

---

An-Noor Academy 300/PK-12
220 Centennial Ave 08854 732-667-5300
Dr. Hassan Elannani, prin. Fax 410-7857
Lake Nelson SDA S 100/PK-10
555 S Randolphville Rd 08854 732-981-0626
StenoTech Career Institute Post-Sec.
262 Old New Brunswick Rd 08854 732-562-1200
Timothy Christian S 500/K-12
2008 Ethel Rd 08854 732-985-0300
Dr. Hubert Hartzler, head sch Fax 985-8008

**Pitman, Gloucester, Pop. 8,890**
Pitman SD 1,500/PK-12
420 Hudson Ave 08071 856-589-2145
Dr. Patrick McAleer, supt. Fax 582-5465
www.pitman.k12.nj.us
Pitman HS 400/9-12
225 Linden Ave 08071 856-589-2121
Dr. Cherie Lombardo, prin. Fax 589-8855
Pitman MS 400/6-8
138 E Holly Ave 08071 856-589-0636
Bud Wrigley, prin. Fax 589-2289

**Pittsgrove, Salem**
Pittsgrove Township SD 1,500/PK-12
1076 Almond Rd 08318 856-358-3094
Henry Bermann, supt. Fax 358-6020
www.pittsgrove.org
Pittsgrove Township MS 400/6-8
1082 Almond Rd 08318 856-358-8529
Priscilla Ocasio-Jimenez, prin. Fax 358-2686
Schalick HS 600/9-12
718 Centerton Rd 08318 856-358-2054
Yvette Dubois, prin. Fax 358-7063

**Pittstown, Hunterdon**
Alexandria Township SD 500/PK-8
557 County Road 513 08867 908-996-6811
Dr. Matthew Jennings, supt. Fax 996-7029
www.alexandriaschools.org
Alexandria MS 300/4-8
557 County Road 513 08867 908-996-6811
Joy Dominic, prin. Fax 996-7963

**Plainfield, Union, Pop. 48,849**
Plainfield SD 5,700/PK-12
1200 Myrtle Ave 07063 908-731-4335
Anna Belin-Pyles, supt. Fax 731-4336
www.plainfieldnjk12.org
Hubbard MS 200/6-8
661 W 8th St 07060 908-731-4320
Kwame Asante, prin. Fax 731-4315
Maxson MS 300/6-8
920 E 7th St 07062 908-731-4310
Reginald Davenport, prin. Fax 731-4306
Obama Acad for Academic & Civic Dvlpmnt 100/Alt
1200 Myrtle Ave 07063 908-731-4270
Deitria Smith-Snead, prin.
Plainfield Academy for the Arts 200/7-12
1700 W Front St 07063 908-731-4421
Angela Bento, prin.
Plainfield HS 1,300/9-12
950 Park Ave 07060 908-731-4390
Willie Worley, prin. Fax 731-4394

---

Koinonia Academy 200/PK-12
1040 Plainfield Ave 07060 908-668-9002
Muhlenberg - Snyder Schools Post-Sec.
Park Avenue And Randolph Rd 07061 908-668-2400
Union County College Post-Sec.
232 E 2nd St 07060 908-412-3599

**Plainsboro, Middlesex**
West Windsor-Plainsboro Regional SD
Supt. — See West Windsor
Community MS 1,100/6-8
95 Grovers Mill Rd 08536 609-716-5300
Dr. Shauna Carter, prin. Fax 716-5333
West Windsor-Plainsboro HS North 1,600/9-12
90 Grovers Mill Rd 08536 609-716-5100
Jonathan Dauber, prin. Fax 716-5142

**Pleasantville, Atlantic, Pop. 19,789**
Pleasantville SD 2,900/PK-12
PO Box 960 08232 609-383-6800
Dr. Leonard Fitts, supt. Fax 677-8101
www.pps-nj.us/

Pleasantville HS 700/9-12
701 Mill Rd 08232 609-383-6900
Kelvin Cherry, prin. Fax 383-9934
Pleasantville MS 600/6-8
801 Mill Rd 08232 609-383-6800
Stephen Townsend, prin. Fax 677-0852

Shore Beauty School Post-Sec.
103 W Washington Ave 08232 609-645-3635

**Point Pleasant, Ocean, Pop. 18,265**
Point Pleasant Borough SD 2,900/PK-12
2100 Panther Path 08742 732-701-1900
Vincent Smith, supt. Fax 892-8403
www.pointpleasant.k12.nj.us/
Memorial MS 700/6-8
808 Laura Herbert Dr 08742 732-701-1900
Gary Floyd, prin. Fax 892-0984
Point Pleasant Borough HS 900/9-12
808 Laura Herbert Dr 08742 732-701-1900
Kurtis Karcich, prin. Fax 892-1252

**Pt Pleas Bch, Ocean, Pop. 4,621**
Point Pleasant Beach SD 900/PK-12
299 Cooks Ln 08742 732-899-8840
Renae LaPrete, supt. Fax 899-1730
ptbeach.com
Point Pleasant Beach HS 400/9-12
700 Trenton Ave 08742 732-899-1817
Terri King, prin. Fax 899-1145

**Pompton Lakes, Passaic, Pop. 10,956**
Pompton Lakes SD 1,600/K-12
237 Van Ave 07442 973-835-4334
Dr. Paul Amoroso, supt. Fax 835-1748
www.plps-k12.org
Lakeside MS 400/6-8
316 Lakeside Ave 07442 973-835-2221
Jake Herninko, prin. Fax 835-8088
Pompton Lakes HS 600/9-12
44 Lakeside Ave 07442 973-835-7100
Vincent Przybylinski, prin. Fax 835-1054

**Pompton Plains, Morris**
Pequannock Township SD 2,200/PK-12
538 Newark Pompton Tpke 07444 973-616-6040
Maria Nuccetelli, supt. Fax 616-6043
www.pequannock.org
Pequannock Township HS 700/9-12
85 Sunset Rd 07444 973-616-6000
Brett Charleston, prin. Fax 616-6029
Pequannock Valley MS 600/6-8
493 Newark Pompton Tpke 07444 973-616-6050
Richard Hayzler, prin. Fax 616-8370

Chancellor Academy 100/6-12
PO Box 338 07444 973-835-4989
Kevin McNaught, dir. Fax 835-0768
Netherlands Reformed Christian S 200/PK-12
164 Jacksonville Rd 07444 973-628-7400
John VanDerBrink, prin. Fax 628-0461

**Port Monmouth, Monmouth, Pop. 3,791**
Middletown Township SD
Supt. — See Leonardo
Thorne MS, 70 Murphy Rd 07758 800/6-8
Thomas Olausen, prin. 732-787-1220

**Port Norris, Cumberland, Pop. 1,319**
Commercial Township SD 600/PK-8
1308 North Ave 08349 856-785-0840
Daniel Dooley Ed.D., supt. Fax 785-2354
www.commercial.k12.nj.us
Port Norris MS 200/6-8
6812 Brown St 08349 856-785-1611
Daniel Dooley, prin. Fax 785-2556

**Pottersville, Hunterdon**

Purnell S 100/9-12
PO Box 500 07979 908-439-2154
Dr. Jeffrey Beedy, head sch Fax 439-2090

**Princeton, Mercer, Pop. 11,896**
Princeton SD 3,300/PK-12
25 Valley Rd 08540 609-806-4220
Steve Cochrane, supt. Fax 806-4221
www.princetonk12.org
Princeton HS 1,400/9-12
151 Moore St 08540 609-806-4280
Gary Snyder, prin. Fax 806-4281
Witherspoon MS 700/6-8
217 Walnut Ln 08540 609-806-4270
Jason Burr, prin. Fax 806-4271

Achieve Test Prep Post-Sec.
100 Overlook Ctr 08540 609-964-0772
American Boychoir S 50/4-8
PO Box 7468 08543 609-924-5858
Hun S of Princeton 600/6-12
176 Edgerstoune Rd 08540 609-921-7600
Jonathan Brougham, hdmstr.
Princeton Day S 900/PK-12
PO Box 75 08542 609-924-6700
Paul Stellato, head sch Fax 924-8944
Princeton Theological Seminary Post-Sec.
PO Box 821 08542 609-921-8300
Princeton University 08544 Post-Sec.
609-258-3000
Raritan Valley Flying School Post-Sec.
41 Airpark Rd 08540 609-921-3100
Stuart Country Day S 400/K-12
1200 Stuart Rd 08540 609-921-2330
Dr. Patty Fagin, hdmstr. Fax 497-0784

**Princeton Junction, Mercer, Pop. 2,407**
West Windsor-Plainsboro Regional SD
Supt. — See West Windsor
Grover MS 1,100/6-8
10 Southfield Rd 08550 609-716-5250
Lamont Thomas, prin. Fax 716-5270

Wilberforce S 100/PK-12
99 Clarksville Rd 08550 609-924-6111
Howe Whitman, hdmstr. Fax 924-6995

**Prospect Park, Passaic, Pop. 5,739**
Paterson SD
Supt. — See Paterson
Great Falls Academy 100/9-12
13 Wagaraw Blvd 07508 973-321-2380
Andre McCollum, prin. Fax 321-2387

**Rahway, Union, Pop. 26,740**
Rahway SD 3,500/PK-12
1138 Kline Pl 07065 732-396-1000
Christine Salcito, supt. Fax 396-1391
www.rahway.net
Rahway HS 1,100/9-12
1012 Madison Ave 07065 732-396-1090
John Farinella, prin. Fax 396-2630
Rahway MS 600/7-8
1138 Kline Pl 07065 732-396-1025
Alan Johnson, prin. Fax 396-2633

**Ramsey, Bergen, Pop. 14,315**
Ramsey SD 2,900/PK-12
266 E Main St 07446 201-785-2300
Matthew Murphy Ed.D., supt. Fax 934-6623
www.ramsey.k12.nj.us
Ramsey HS 1,000/9-12
256 E Main St 07446 201-785-2300
Dr. Michael Thumm, prin. Fax 818-2656
Smith MS 700/6-8
2 Monroe St 07446 201-785-2313
Stacie Poelstra, prin. Fax 785-2320

Don Bosco Prep HS 900/9-12
492 N Franklin Tpke 07446 201-327-8003
John Stanczak, prin. Fax 327-3397
Eastwick College Post-Sec.
10 S Franklin Tpke 07446 201-327-8877

**Randolph, Morris, Pop. 19,974**
Randolph Township SD 5,100/PK-12
25 Schoolhouse Rd 07869 973-361-0808
David Browne Ed.D., supt. Fax 361-2405
www.rtnj.org
Randolph HS 1,600/9-12
511 Millbrook Ave 07869 973-361-2400
Debbie Iosso, prin. Fax 361-1661
Randolph MS 1,300/6-8
507 Millbrook Ave 07869 973-366-8700
Dennis Copeland Ed.D., prin. Fax 361-6501

County College of Morris Post-Sec.
214 Center Grove Rd 07869 973-328-5000

**Red Bank, Monmouth, Pop. 11,983**
Red Bank Borough SD 1,000/PK-8
76 Branch Ave 07701 732-758-1500
Dr. Jared Rumage, supt. Fax 212-1356
www.rbb.k12.nj.us
Red Bank MS 400/4-8
101 Harding Rd 07701 732-758-1500
Maria Iozzi, prin. Fax 758-1518

Red Bank Catholic HS 1,100/9-12
112 Broad St 07701 732-747-1774
Robert Abatemarco, prin. Fax 747-1936

**Richland, Atlantic**

St. Augustine Prep S 700/9-12
PO Box 279 08350 856-697-2600
Kevin Burke, prin. Fax 697-8389

**Ridgefield, Bergen, Pop. 10,875**
Ridgefield SD 1,400/1-12
555 Chestnut St 07657 201-945-9236
Dr. Frank Romano, supt. Fax 945-7830
www.ridgefieldschools.com
Ridgefield Memorial HS 500/9-12
555 Walnut St 07657 201-945-4455
Dr. Tamika DePass, prin. Fax 945-3505
Slocum/Skewes ES 500/3-8
650 Prospect Ave 07657 201-943-4299
John Coviello, prin. Fax 943-9527

**Ridgefield Park, Bergen, Pop. 12,530**
Ridgefield Park SD 2,100/PK-12
712 Lincoln Ave 07660 201-641-0800
John Richardson, supt. Fax 641-2203
www.rpps.net
Ridgefield Park JSHS 1,200/7-12
1 Ozzie Nelson Dr 07660 201-440-1440
James Donohue, prin. Fax 641-6861

**Ridgewood, Bergen, Pop. 24,497**
Ridgewood Village SD 5,600/PK-12
49 Cottage Pl 07450 201-670-2700
Dr. Daniel Fishbein, supt. Fax 670-2668
www.ridgewood.k12.nj.us
Franklin MS 700/6-8
335 N Van Dien Ave 07450 201-670-2780
Anthony Orsini, prin. Fax 670-3382
Ridgewood HS 1,700/9-12
627 E Ridgewood Ave 07450 201-670-2800
Dr. Thomas Gorman, prin. Fax 444-7008
Washington MS 700/6-8
155 Washington Pl 07450 201-670-2790
Dr. Katie Kashmanian, prin. Fax 670-3290

Valley Hospital Post-Sec.
223 N Van Dien Ave 07450 201-447-8002

**Ringwood, Passaic, Pop. 11,996**
Ringwood SD 900/K-8
121 Carletondale Rd 07456 973-962-7028
Jeffrey Feifer, supt. Fax 962-9211
www.ringwoodschools.org/
Ryerson MS 400/6-8
130 Valley Rd 07456 973-962-7063
Paul Scutti, prin. Fax 962-6905

**River Edge, Bergen, Pop. 11,204**
River Dell Regional SD 1,700/7-12
230 Woodland Ave 07661 201-599-7206
Patrick Fletcher, supt. Fax 261-3809
www.riverdell.org/
River Dell MS 600/7-8
230 Woodland Ave 07661 201-599-7250
Richard Freedman, prin. Fax 599-2202
Other Schools – See Oradell

**Riverside, Burlington, Pop. 7,974**
Riverside Township SD 1,400/PK-12
112 E Washington St 08075 856-461-1255
Robin A. Ehrich, supt. Fax 461-5168
www.riverside.k12.nj.us
Riverside HS 400/9-12
112 E Washington St 08075 856-461-1255
Todd Pae, prin. Fax 461-7277
Riverside MS 300/6-8
112 E Washington St 08075 856-461-1255
Michael W. Mongon, prin. Fax 461-0182

**River Vale, Bergen, Pop. 9,410**
River Vale SD 1,300/K-8
609 Westwood Ave 07675 201-358-4000
Rory McCourt, supt. Fax 358-8319
www.rivervaleschools.com/
Holdrum MS 500/6-8
393 Rivervale Rd 07675 201-358-4016
James Cody, prin. Fax 358-8427

**Robbinsville, Mercer, Pop. 2,974**
Robbinsville SD 2,800/PK-12
155 Robbinsville Edinburg 08691 609-632-0910
Steven Mayer, supt. Fax 371-7964
www.robbinsville.k12.nj.us
Pond Road MS 1,100/5-8
150 Pond Rd 08691 609-632-0940
Paul Gizzo, prin. Fax 918-9011
Robbinsville HS 900/9-12
155 Robbinsville Edinburg 08691 609-632-0950
Molly Avery, prin. Fax 371-7961

**Rockaway, Morris, Pop. 6,360**
Morris County Vocational SD
Supt. — See Denville
Academy for Math Science & Engineering Vo/Tech
520 W Main St 07866 973-664-2301

Morris Hills Regional SD 2,700/9-12
48 Knoll Dr 07866 973-664-2291
James Jencarelli, supt. Fax 627-6588
mhrd.org
Morris Hills HS 1,100/9-12
520 W Main St 07866 973-664-2309
Todd Toriello, prin. Fax 983-7461
Morris Knolls HS 1,600/9-12
50 Knoll Dr 07866 973-664-2200
Ryan MacNaughton, prin. Fax 586-3550
Morris Hills Adult HS Adult
50 Knoll Dr 07866 973-664-2232
Scott Gambale, coord. Fax 586-3550

Rockaway Borough SD 600/PK-8
103 E Main St 07866 973-625-8600
Mark Schwarz, supt. Fax 625-7355
www.rockboro.org/
Jefferson MS, 95 E Main St 07866 400/4-8
Stephanie Bonaparte, prin. 973-625-8603

Rockaway Township SD
Supt. — See Hibernia
Copeland MS 900/6-8
100 Lake Shore Dr 07866 973-627-2465
F. Scott Allshouse, prin. Fax 983-1843

**Roselle, Union, Pop. 20,670**
Roselle Borough SD 2,300/PK-12
710 Locust St 07203 908-298-2040
Dr. Kevin West, supt. Fax 298-3353
www.roselleschools.org
Clark HS 800/9-12
122 E 6th Ave 07203 908-298-2004
Rashon Mickens, prin. Fax 259-0782
Wilday JHS 300/7-8
400 Brooklawn Ave 07203 908-298-2066
Dr. Josue Falaise, prin. Fax 298-2068

Roselle Catholic HS 500/9-12
350 Raritan Rd 07203 908-245-2350
Thomas Berrios, prin. Fax 241-3869

**Roselle Park, Union, Pop. 13,111**
Roselle Park SD 1,900/K-12
510 Chestnut St 07204 908-245-1197
Pedro Garrido, supt. Fax 245-1226
www.rpsd.org/
Roselle Park HS 600/9-12
185 W Webster Ave 07204 908-241-4550
Sarah Costa, prin. Fax 245-6609
Roselle Park MS 500/6-8
57 W Grant Ave 07204 908-245-1634
Kathleen Carlin, prin. Fax 245-7491

**Rumson, Monmouth, Pop. 7,054**
Rumson Borough SD 1,000/PK-8
60 Forrest Ave 07760 732-842-4747
Dr. John Bormann, supt. Fax 842-4877
www.rumsonschool.org/
Forrestdale MS 600/4-8
60 Forrest Ave 07760 732-842-0383
Jennifer Gibbons, prin. Fax 219-9458

Rumson-Fair Haven Regional HSD 900/9-12
74 Ridge Rd 07760 732-842-1597
Dr. Peter Righi, supt. Fax 741-1712
www.rumsonfairhaven.org
Rumson-Fair Haven Regional HS 900/9-12
74 Ridge Rd 07760 732-842-1597
Tracy Handerhan, prin. Fax 741-1712

**Runnemede, Camden, Pop. 8,357**
Black Horse Pike Regional SD
Supt. — See Blackwood

Triton HS 1,500/9-12
250 Schubert Ave 08078 856-939-4500
Melissa Sheppard, prin. Fax 939-4724

Runnemede Borough SD 800/PK-8
505 W 3rd Ave 08078 856-931-5365
Mark Iannucci, supt. Fax 931-4446
www.runnemedeschools.org/
Volz MS, 505 W 3rd Ave 08078 500/PK-PK, 4-
Steve Pili, prin. 856-931-5353

**Rutherford, Bergen, Pop. 17,647**
Rutherford SD, 176 Park Ave 07070 2,500/K-12
John Hurley, supt. 201-438-7675
www.rutherfordschools.org
Pierrepont S 500/4-8
70 E Pierrepont Ave 07070 201-438-7675
Joan Carrion, prin. Fax 842-0452
Rutherford HS 800/9-12
56 Elliott Pl 07070 201-438-7675
Frank Morano, prin. Fax 438-7293
Union S 500/4-8
359 Union Ave 07070 201-438-7675
Kurt Schweitzer, prin. Fax 804-8248

St. Mary HS 300/9-12
64 Chestnut St 07070 201-933-5220
Richard Bayhan, prin. Fax 933-0834
Yeshivas Mesillah 6-8
185 Montross Ave 07070 201-372-0020

**Saddle Brook, Bergen, Pop. 13,296**
Saddle Brook Township SD 1,700/K-12
355 Mayhill St 07663 201-843-2880
Dr. Richard Katz, supt. Fax 843-0216
www.saddlebrookschools.org/
Saddle Brook MSHS 800/7-12
355 Mayhill St Ste 1 07663 201-843-2880
John Lawlor, prin. Fax 843-4305

**Saddle River, Bergen, Pop. 3,086**

Saddle River Day S 300/PK-12
147 Chestnut Ridge Rd 07458 201-327-4050
Eileen Lambert, head sch Fax 327-6161

**Salem, Salem, Pop. 4,985**
Salem CSD 1,200/PK-12
205 Walnut St 08079 856-935-3800
Dr. Amiot Michel, supt. Fax 935-6977
www.salemnj.org
Salem HS 400/9-12
219 Walnut St 08079 856-935-3900
John Mulhorn, prin. Fax 935-3288
Salem MS 400/3-8
51 New Market St 08079 856-935-2700
Pascale DeVilme, prin. Fax 935-2284

Salem County Special Services SD
Supt. — See Woodstown
Alternative S Alt
SCC Davidow Hall Rm 122, 856-351-2238
Frank Maurer, prin.

**Scotch Plains, Union, Pop. 21,160**
Scotch Plains-Fanwood SD 5,400/PK-12
2280 Evergreen Ave 07076 908-232-6161
Dr. Margaret Hayes, supt. Fax 889-1769
www.spfk12.org
Park MS 900/5-8
580 Park Ave 07076 908-322-4445
Lisa Rebimbas, prin. Fax 561-5929
Scotch Plains-Fanwood HS 1,500/9-12
667 Westfield Rd 07076 908-889-8600
Dr. David Heisey, prin. Fax 889-8254
Terrill MS 900/5-8
1301 Terrill Rd 07076 908-322-5215
Dr. Kevin Holloway, prin. Fax 322-6813

Union Co. Educational Services Comm SD
Supt. — See Westfield
Hillcrest Academy North Campus 100/Alt
2630 Plainfield Ave 07076 908-233-9366
John Marquet, prin. Fax 301-9093

Union County Vocational-Technical SD
1776 Raritan Rd 07076 908-889-8288
Peter A. Capodice, supt. Fax 889-4336
www.ucvts.tec.nj.us
Academy for Allied Health Sciences Vo/Tech
1776 Raritan Rd 07076 908-889-8288
Walter Smolenski, prin. Fax 889-4734
Academy for Information Technology Vo/Tech
1776 Raritan Rd 07076 908-889-8288
Colleen Gialanella, prin. Fax 889-6831
Academy for Performing Arts Vo/Tech
1776 Raritan Rd 07076 908-889-8288
Kelly Douglas-Jackson, prin. Fax 889-1666
Union County Magnet HS Vo/Tech
1776 Raritan Rd 07076 908-889-8288
Paul Rafalowski, prin. Fax 889-3196
Union County Vo-Tech HS Vo/Tech
1776 Raritan Rd 07076 908-889-8288
Jeffrey Lerner, prin. Fax 889-4399

Union Catholic Regional HS 800/9-12
1600 Martine Ave 07076 908-889-1600
Sr. Percylee Hart, prin. Fax 889-7867

**Seabrook, Cumberland, Pop. 1,405**
Upper Deerfield Township SD 800/PK-8
1369 Highway 77 08302 856-455-2267
Dr. Peter Koza Ed.D., supt. Fax 453-7077
www.udts.org
Woodruff MS 300/6-8
1385 Highway 77 08302 856-455-2267
Dr. Peter Koza Ed.D., prin. Fax 453-7077

**Secaucus, Hudson, Pop. 15,983**
Secaucus SD 2,100/PK-12
PO Box 1496 07096 201-974-2004
Robert Presuto, supt. Fax 974-1911
www.sboe.us

Secaucus HS 600/9-12
11 Millridge Rd 07094 201-974-2033
Dr. Robert Berckes, prin. Fax 974-0026
Secaucus MS 300/7-8
11 Millridge Rd 07094 201-974-2022
Robert Valente, prin. Fax 974-2006

**Sewell, Gloucester**
Deptford Township SD
Supt. — See Deptford
Monongahela MS 600/7-8
890 Bankbridge Rd 08080 856-415-9540
Arthur Dietz, prin. Fax 464-9284

Gloucester County Vocational SD
1360 Tanyard Rd 08080 856-468-1445
Michael Dicken, supt. Fax 468-3397
www.gcit.org
Gloucester Co. Institute of Technology Vo/Tech
1360 Tanyard Rd 08080 856-468-1445
James Dundee, prin. Fax 468-1035
Adult Regional HS Adult
1360 Tanyard Rd 08080 856-468-1445

Washington Township SD 8,000/PK-12
206 E Holly Ave 08080 856-589-6644
Thomas Flemming, supt. Fax 582-1918
www.wtps.org
Bunker Hill MS 700/6-8
372 Pitman Downer Rd 08080 856-881-7007
Dr. Mark Ebner, prin. Fax 881-5414
Chestnut Ridge MS 600/6-8
641 Hurffville Crosskeys Rd 08080 856-582-3535
James Barnes, prin. Fax 589-0683
Orchard Valley MS 600/6-8
238 Pitman Downer Rd 08080 856-582-5353
Stevan Gregor, prin. Fax 589-0197
Washington Township HS 2,600/9-12
519 Hurffville Crosskeys Rd 08080 856-589-8500
Joseph Bollendorf, prin. Fax 218-0991

Gloucester County Christian S 400/PK-12
151 Golf Club Rd 08080 856-589-1665
Gloucester County College Post-Sec.
1400 Tanyard Rd 08080 856-468-5000

**Shamong Township, Burlington, Pop. 5,765**
Lenape Regional HSD 6,900/9-12
93 Willow Grove Rd 08088 609-268-2000
Dr. Carol Birnbohm, supt. Fax 268-6642
www.lrhsd.org/
Other Schools – See Marlton, Medford, Tabernacle

Shamong Township SD 900/K-8
295 Indian Mills Rd 08088 609-268-0120
Christine Vespe Ed.D., supt. Fax 268-1229
www.ims.k12.nj.us
Indian Mills Memorial MS 400/5-8
295 Indian Mills Rd 08088 609-268-0440
Timothy Carroll, prin. Fax 268-1229

**Sicklerville, Camden**
Camden County Technical Schools
343 Berlin Cross Keys Rd 08081 856-767-7000
Patricia Fitzgerald, supt. Fax 767-3589
www.ccts.info
Camden County Technical S - Gloucester Vo/Tech
343 Berlin Cross Keys Rd 08081 856-767-7000
Bonnie Durante, prin. Fax 767-3638
Other Schools – See Pennsauken

Gloucester Township SD
Supt. — See Blackwood
Mullen MS 1,100/6-8
1400 Sicklerville Rd 08081 856-875-8777
Timothy Trow, prin. Fax 875-0902

Technical Institute of Camden County Post-Sec.
343 Berlin Cross Keys Rd 08081 856-767-7000

**Skillman, Somerset, Pop. 236**
Montgomery Township SD 4,900/PK-12
1014 Route 601 08558 609-466-7600
Nancy Gartenberg, supt. Fax 466-0944
www.mtsd.k12.nj.us
Montgomery HS 1,700/9-12
1016 Route 601 08558 609-466-7602
Paul Popadiuk, prin. Fax 466-0243
Montgomery Upper MS 900/7-8
375 Burnt Hill Rd 08558 609-466-7604
Cory Delgado, prin. Fax 874-7045

**Somerdale, Camden, Pop. 5,010**
Sterling HSD 900/9-12
801 W Preston Ave Ste B 08083 856-784-1287
Mark Napoleon, supt. Fax 435-1530
www.sterling.k12.nj.us
Sterling HS 900/9-12
501 S Warwick Rd 08083 856-784-1333
Mark Napoleon, prin. Fax 784-7661

**Somerset, Somerset, Pop. 21,468**
Franklin Township SD 7,500/PK-12
1755 Amwell Rd 08873 732-873-2400
Dr. John Ravally, supt.
www.franklinboe.org
Franklin HS 2,000/9-12
500 Elizabeth Ave 08873 732-302-4200
Thomas DiGanci, prin. Fax 302-4212
Franklin MS 1,000/7-8
415 Francis St 08873 732-249-6410
RaShawn Adams, prin. Fax 246-0770

Rutgers Preparatory S 700/PK-12
1345 Easton Ave 08873 732-545-5600
Dr. Steven Loy, hdmstr. Fax 214-1819

**Somers Point, Atlantic, Pop. 10,546**

Shore Memorial Hospital Post-Sec.
Shore Rd 08244 609-653-3545

**Somerville, Somerset, Pop. 11,787**
Somerville Borough SD 2,100/PK-12
51 W Cliff St 08876 908-218-4100
Dr. Timothy Purnell, supt. Fax 526-9668
www.somervillenjk12.org
Somerville HS 1,100/9-12
222 Davenport St 08876 908-218-4108
Gerard Foley, prin. Fax 707-0971
Somerville MS 200/6-8
51 W Cliff St 08876 908-218-4107
Georgette Boulegeris, prin. Fax 575-9526

Immaculata HS 800/9-12
240 Mountain Ave 08876 908-722-0200
Jean Kline, prin. Fax 218-7765

**South Amboy, Middlesex, Pop. 8,493**
Sayreville SD 5,400/K-12
150 Lincoln St 08879 732-525-5200
Dr. Richard Labbe, supt. Fax 727-5769
www.sayrevillek12.net/
Other Schools – See Parlin

South Amboy SD 1,000/PK-12
240 John St 08879 732-525-2100
Frank Alfano, supt. Fax 727-0730
www.sapublicschools.com
South Amboy MSHS 400/6-12
200 Gvrnr Hrold G Hffmn Plz 08879 732-316-7669
Dr. Patrick McCabe, prin. Fax 721-0054

Raritan Bay Catholic Preparatory S 300/PK-12
301 2nd St 08879 732-721-0834
Joseph Conry, prin. Fax 316-0326

**Southampton, Burlington**
Southampton Township SD 800/K-8
177 Main St 08088 609-859-2256
Michael Harris, supt. Fax 859-1542
www.southampton.k12.nj.us
Southampton Township MS 3 300/6-8
100 Warrior Way 08088 609-859-2256
Jennifer Horner, prin. Fax 801-0754

**South Orange, Essex, Pop. 16,390**
South Orange-Maplewood SD
Supt. — See Maplewood
South Orange MS 700/6-8
70 N Ridgewood Rd 07079 973-378-2772
Joseph Uglialoro, prin. Fax 378-2775

Seton Hall University Post-Sec.
400 S Orange Ave 07079 973-761-9000

**South Plainfield, Middlesex, Pop. 22,711**
South Plainfield SD 3,500/K-12
125 Jackson Ave 07080 908-754-4620
Johanna Ruberto Ed.D., supt. Fax 822-2453
www.spboe.org
South Plainfield HS 1,200/9-12
200 Lake St 07080 908-754-4620
James Pedersen, prin. Fax 756-7659
South Plainfield MS 600/7-8
2201 Plainfield Ave 07080 908-754-4620
Kevin Hajduk, admin. Fax 791-1152

Avtech Institute of Technology Post-Sec.
50 Cragwood Rd Ste 350 07080 908-222-2833
Central Career School Post-Sec.
126 Corporate Blvd 07080 908-412-8600
Everest Institute Post-Sec.
5000 Hadley Rd Ste 100 07080 908-222-9300
Lincoln Technical Institute Post-Sec.
901 Hadley Rd 07080 800-305-3487

**South River, Middlesex, Pop. 15,456**
South River SD 2,200/PK-12
15 Montgomery St 08882 732-613-4000
Michael Pfister, supt. Fax 613-4756
www.srivernj.org
South River HS 600/9-12
11 Montgomery St 08882 732-613-4014
Kamila Buffalino, prin. Fax 613-4044
South River MS 500/6-8
3 Montgomery St 08882 732-613-4073
Lisa Wargo, prin. Fax 698-9305

**Sparta, Sussex, Pop. 15,157**
Sparta Township SD 3,400/PK-12
18 Mohawk Ave 07871 973-729-7886
Dennis Tobin, supt. Fax 729-0576
www.sparta.org
Sparta HS 1,200/9-12
70 W Mountain Rd 07871 973-729-6191
Janet Ferraro Ed.D., prin. Fax 729-3258
Sparta MS 900/6-8
350 Main St 07871 973-729-3151
Michael Gregory, prin. Fax 729-0573

Sussex County Technical SD
105 N Church Rd 07871 973-383-6700
Gus Modla, supt. Fax 383-4272
www.sussex.tec.nj.us
Sussex County Technical S Vo/Tech
105 N Church Rd 07871 973-383-6700
Gus Modla, prin. Fax 383-4272

Pope John XXIII HS 900/9-12
28 Andover Rd 07871 973-729-6125
Thomas Costello, prin. Fax 729-3487
Veritas Christian Academy 100/9-12
385 Houses Corner Rd 07871 973-579-6333
Sean Bevier, admin. Fax 579-6293

**Spotswood, Middlesex, Pop. 8,141**
Spotswood SD 1,800/PK-12
105 Summerhill Rd 08884 732-723-2200
Scott Rocco, supt. Fax 251-7666
www.spotswood.k12.nj.us
Spotswood HS 700/9-12
105 Summerhill Rd 08884 732-723-2202
Thomas Calder, prin. Fax 251-7666

Spotswood Memorial MS 400/6-8
115 Summerhill Rd 08884 732-723-2227
Christine Smith, prin. Fax 251-7666

**Springfield, Union, Pop. 13,420**
Springfield SD 2,100/PK-12
PO Box 210 07081 973-376-1025
Michael Davino, supt. Fax 912-9229
www.springfieldschools.com
Dayton HS 600/9-12
139 Mountain Ave 07081 973-376-1025
Elizabeth Cresci, prin. Fax 376-4570
Gaudineer MS 500/6-8
75 S Springfield Ave 07081 973-376-1025
Timothy Kielty, prin. Fax 376-3259

**Stanhope, Sussex, Pop. 3,550**
Byram Township SD 1,000/K-8
12 Mansfield Dr 07874 973-347-1047
Bryan Hensz, supt. Fax 347-9001
www.byramschools.org
Byram IS 500/5-8
12 Mansfield Dr 07874 973-347-1047
John Fritzky, prin. Fax 691-7780

Lenape Valley Regional HSD 700/9-12
PO Box 578 07874 973-347-7600
Paul DiRupo, supt. Fax 691-0164
www.lvhs.org
Lenape Valley Regional HS 700/9-12
PO Box 578 07874 973-347-7600
Thomas Claeys, prin. Fax 347-2536

**Stewartsville, Warren, Pop. 346**
Greenwich Township SD 900/PK-8
101 Wyndham Farm Blvd 08886 908-859-2022
Maria Eppolite, supt. Fax 859-4522
www.gtsd.net
Stewartsville MS 300/6-8
642 S Main St 08886 908-859-2023
Stephanie Snyder, prin. Fax 859-4522

**Stirling, Morris**
Long Hill Township SD
Supt. — See Gillette
Central MS 400/6-8
90 Central Ave 07980 908-647-2311
George Villar, prin. Fax 647-0610

**Stratford, Camden, Pop. 6,903**
Stratford Borough SD 800/PK-8
111 Warwick Rd 08084 856-783-2555
Thomas Attanasi, supt. Fax 784-8486
www.stratford.k12.nj.us
Yellin MS 400/4-8
111 Warwick Rd 08084 856-783-1094
David Ricci, prin. Fax 309-0304

**Succasunna, Morris, Pop. 9,054**
Roxbury Township SD 4,000/PK-12
42 N Hillside Ave 07876 973-584-6099
Dr. Patrick Tierney, supt. Fax 252-1434
www.roxbury.org
Eisenhower MS 700/7-8
47 Eyland Ave 07876 973-584-2973
Dominick Miller, prin. Fax 584-4529
Roxbury HS 1,500/9-12
1 Bryant Dr 07876 973-584-7699
Jeffrey Swanson, prin. Fax 584-7584

American Christian S 200/PK-12
126 S Hillside Ave 07876 973-584-6616
Kristen Brennan, head sch Fax 584-0686

**Summit, Union, Pop. 21,055**
Summit CSD 4,000/PK-12
14 Beekman Ter 07901 908-918-2100
Mr. June Chang, supt. Fax 273-3656
www.summit.k12.nj.us
Summit HS 1,100/9-12
125 Kent Place Blvd 07901 908-273-1494
Paul Sears, prin. Fax 273-2832
Summit MS 1,000/6-8
272 Morris Ave 07901 908-273-1190
Matt Block, prin. Fax 273-8320

Kent Place S 600/PK-12
42 Norwood Ave 07901 908-273-0900
Susan Bosland, head sch Fax 273-9390
Oak Knoll S of the Holy Child 600/K-12
44 Blackburn Rd 07901 908-522-8100
Timothy Saburn, head sch Fax 277-1838
Oratory Preparatory S 300/7-12
1 Beverly Rd 07901 908-273-1084
Robert Costello, head sch Fax 273-5505

**Sussex, Sussex, Pop. 2,089**
High Point Regional SD 1,100/9-12
299 Pidgeon Hill Rd 07461 973-875-3101
Dr. Scott D. Ripley Ed.D., supt. Fax 875-0904
www.hpregional.org
High Point Regional HS 1,100/9-12
299 Pidgeon Hill Rd 07461 973-875-3101
Jonathan Tallamy, prin. Fax 875-2756

Sussex-Wantage Regional SD 1,200/PK-8
27 Bank St 07461 973-875-3175
Dr. Jeanne Apryasz, supt. Fax 875-7175
www.swregional.org
Sussex MS 400/6-8
10 Loomis Ave 07461 973-875-4138
Shane Schwarz, prin. Fax 875-6790

**Tabernacle, Burlington**
Lenape Regional HSD
Supt. — See Shamong Township
Seneca HS 1,200/9-12
110 Carranza Rd 08088 609-268-4600
Jeffrey Spector, prin. Fax 268-4635

Tabernacle Township SD 800/K-8
132 New Rd 08088 609-268-0153
George Rafferty, supt. Fax 268-1006
www.tabschools.org
Olson MS 400/5-8
132 New Rd 08088 609-268-0153
Susan Grosser, prin. Fax 268-1006

**Teaneck, Bergen, Pop. 39,500**
Teaneck SD 3,600/PK-12
1 Merrison St 07666 201-833-5510
Barbara Pinsak, supt. Fax 837-9468
www.teaneckschools.org/
Franklin MS 500/5-8
1315 Taft Rd 07666 201-833-5450
Dr. Lennox Small, prin. Fax 862-2465
Jefferson MS 600/5-8
655 Teaneck Rd 07666 201-833-5471
Angela Davis, prin. Fax 833-3983
Teaneck HS 1,300/9-12
100 Elizabeth Ave 07666 201-833-5400
Dennis Heck, prin. Fax 833-5403

Fairleigh Dickinson University Post-Sec.
1000 River Rd 07666 201-692-2000
Holy Name Hospital School of Nursing Post-Sec.
690 Teaneck Rd 07666 201-833-3005
Ma'ayanot Yeshiva HS for Girls 300/9-12
1650 Palisade Ave 07666 201-833-4307
Rachel Feldman, admin. Fax 833-0816
Torah Academy of Bergen County 300/9-12
1600 Queen Anne Rd 07666 201-837-7696

**Tenafly, Bergen, Pop. 14,170**
Tenafly SD 3,600/K-12
500 Tenafly Rd 07670 201-816-4500
Lynn Trager, supt. Fax 816-4521
www.tenafly.k12.nj.us
Tenafly HS 1,200/9-12
19 Columbus Dr 07670 201-816-6600
Dr. James Morrison, prin. Fax 871-9184
Tenafly MS 800/6-8
10 Sunset Ln 07670 201-816-4900
Dr. John Fabbo, prin. Fax 569-0327

**Teterboro, Bergen, Pop. 61**
Bergen County Vocational Technical SD
Supt. — See Paramus
Bergen County Technical HS - Teterboro Vo/Tech
504 State Rt 46 07608 201-343-6000
David Tankard, prin. Fax 996-6925

Teterboro School of Aeronautics Post-Sec.
80 Moonachie Ave 07608 201-288-6300

**Tinton Falls, Monmouth, Pop. 17,575**
Monmouth County Vocational SD
Supt. — See Freehold
CLASS Academy Alt
537 Tinton Ave 07724 732-542-5455
Paul Christopher, prin. Fax 544-8018

Monmouth Regional HSD 1,000/9-12
1 Norman J Field Way 07724 732-542-1170
Dr. Andrew Teeple, supt. Fax 542-5815
www.monmouthregional.net
Monmouth Regional HS 1,000/9-12
1 Norman J Field Way 07724 732-542-1170
Corey Radisch, prin. Fax 542-5815

Monmouth-Ocean Ed. Serv. Comm. SD 50/6-12
900 Hope Rd, 732-695-7800
Christopher Rooney, supt.
www.moesc.org
Regional Alternative S 50/Alt
100 Tornillo Way Ste 1, 732-389-5555
Kimberly Brucale, prin. Fax 542-0302

Tinton Falls SD 1,500/K-8
658 Tinton Ave 07724 732-460-2400
John Russo, supt. Fax 542-1158
www.tfs.k12.nj.us
Tinton Falls MS 500/6-8
674 Tinton Ave 07724 732-542-0775
Mary Ehid, prin. Fax 542-8723

Ranney S 800/PK-12
235 Hope Rd 07724 732-542-4777
Dr. John Griffith, head sch Fax 544-1629

**Toms River, Ocean, Pop. 87,576**
Ocean County Vocational SD
137 Bey Lea Rd 08753 732-240-6414
William Hoey, supt. Fax 505-8929
www.ocvts.org
Ocean County Voc-Tech S - Toms River Vo/Tech
1299 Old Freehold Rd 08753 732-473-3100
Jo-Ann Price, prin. Fax 349-9788
Other Schools – See Brick, Jackson, Lakehurst, Little Egg Harbor Township, Manahawkin, Waretown

Toms River Regional SD 16,100/K-12
1144 Hooper Ave 08753 732-505-5510
David Healy, supt. Fax 505-9330
www.trschools.com
Toms River HS - East 1,700/9-12
1225 Raider Way 08753 732-505-5666
Patrick Thomas, prin. Fax 270-0909
Toms River HS - North 2,300/9-12
1245 Old Freehold Rd 08753 732-505-5702
James Ricotta, prin. Fax 341-6249
Toms River HS - South 1,500/9-12
55 Hyers St 08753 732-505-5738
Leonard Stanziano, prin. Fax 341-1321
Toms River IS East 1,400/6-8
1519 Hooper Ave 08753 732-505-5777
Bryan Madigan, prin. Fax 286-1290
Toms River IS North 1,400/6-8
150 Intermediate North Way 08753 732-505-5800
Lynn Fronzak, prin. Fax 286-1291
Other Schools – See Beachwood

American Institution Post-Sec.
2363 Lakewood Rd 08755 973-340-9500
Donovan Catholic HS 1,000/9-12
711 Hooper Ave 08753 732-349-8801
Dr. Edward Gere, prin. Fax 349-8956
Ocean County College Post-Sec.
PO Box 2001 08754 732-255-0400

**Totowa, Passaic, Pop. 10,662**
Totowa SD 1,000/PK-8
10 Crews St 07512 973-956-0010
Dr. Vincent Varcadipane, supt. Fax 956-9859
www.totowa.k12.nj.us
Washington Park MS 600/3-8
10 Crews St 07512 973-956-0010
Patricia Capitelli, prin. Fax 389-2270

**Trenton, Mercer, Pop. 83,491**
Mercer County Technical SD
1085 Old Trenton Rd 08690 609-586-2129
Dr. Kimberly J. Schneider, supt. Fax 586-8966
www.mcts.edu
Assunpink Center Vo/Tech
1085 Old Trenton Rd 08690 609-586-5144
Sharon Nemeth, prin. Fax 586-1709
Health Careers Center Vo/Tech
1070 Klockner Rd 08619 609-587-7640
Fax 587-3304
Adult Evening S Adult
1085 Old Trenton Rd 08690 609-586-5146
Fax 586-1709
Other Schools – See Pennington

Trenton SD 5,700/PK-12
108 N Clinton Ave 08609 609-656-4900
Dr. Francisco Duran, supt. Fax 989-2682
www.trenton.k12.nj.us
Dunn MS 200/6-8
401 Dayton St 08611 609-656-4700
Madeline Roman, prin. Fax 989-1478
Hedgepeth-Williams MS 200/6-8
301 Gladstone Ave 08629 609-656-4760
Adrienne Hill, prin. Fax 989-2544
Kilmer MS 100/6-8
1300 Stuyvesant Ave 08618 609-656-4800
Paula Bethea, prin. Fax 989-2927
Munoz-Rivera MS 6-8
400 N Montgomery St 08618 609-656-4840
Bernadette Trapp, prin. Fax 656-2149
Trenton Central HS - Chambers 900/9-12
544 Chestnut Ave 08611 609-278-7260
Hope Grant, prin. Fax 989-2940
Trenton Central HS - West 300/9-12
1001 W State St 08618 609-656-4770
Mark Hoppe, prin. Fax 989-2925
Daylight/Twilight HS Adult
501 Edgewood Ave 08618 609-656-4850
Shenette Gray, prin. Fax 777-9490

Destiny Christian Academy 50/9-9
210 Genesee St 08611 609-273-4651
Dr. Adekemi Bankole, dir. Fax 695-5345
Harris School of Business Post-Sec.
3620 Quakerbridge Rd 08619 609-586-9104
Helene Fuld Medical Center Post-Sec.
750 Brunswick Ave 08638 609-394-3174
Marie Katzenbach School for the Deaf Post-Sec.
PO Box 535 08625 609-530-3100
Mercer Medical Center Post-Sec.
PO Box 1658 08607 609-394-4050
St. Francis Medical Center Post-Sec.
601 Hamilton Ave 08629 609-599-5000
Thomas Edison State College Post-Sec.
101 W State St 08608 609-984-1100

**Union, Union, Pop. 55,000**
Township of Union SD 7,400/PK-12
2369 Morris Ave 07083 908-851-3000
Gregory Tatum, supt. Fax 851-9688
www.twpunionschools.org
Burnet MS 1,000/6-8
1000 Caldwell Ave 07083 908-851-6490
Raymond Salvatore, prin. Fax 687-2645
Kawameeh MS 700/6-8
490 David Ter 07083 908-851-6570
Jason Malanda, prin. Fax 687-5741
Union HS 2,300/9-12
2350 N 3rd St 07083 908-851-6500
Ben Kloc, prin. Fax 687-5204

European Academy of Cosmetology Post-Sec.
1126 Morris Ave 07083 908-686-4422
Healthcare Training Institute Post-Sec.
1969 Morris Ave 07083 908-851-7711
Kean University Post-Sec.
1000 Morris Ave 07083 908-737-5326
Lincoln Technical Institute Post-Sec.
2299 Vauxhall Rd 07083 908-964-7800

**Union City, Hudson, Pop. 65,896**
Union City SD 8,300/PK-12
3912 32nd St 07087 201-348-5851
Silvia Abbato, supt. Fax 330-1736
www.union-city.k12.nj.us
Emerson MS 700/6-8
318 18th St 07087 201-348-5900
Mike Cirone, prin. Fax 864-2262
Marti Freshman Academy 500/9-9
1800 Summit Ave 07087 201-348-5400
Rudy Baez, prin. Fax 345-5405
Union City HS 2,000/10-12
2500 Kennedy Blvd 07087 201-330-8678
John Bennetti, prin. Fax 330-8736
Union Hill MS 600/7-8
3808 Hudson Ave 07087 201-348-5808
Victoria Dickson, prin. Fax 867-4205
Adult Learning Center Adult
400 38th St 07087 201-348-5658
Ryan Lewis, prin. Fax 348-5659

---

Mesivta Sanz Hudson County S — 300/K-12
3400 New York Ave 07087 — 201-867-8690
Miftaahul Uloom Academy — 200/PK-12
501 15th St 07087 — 201-223-9920
Rising Star Academy — 100/PK-12
4613 Cottage Pl 07087 — 201-758-5590

**Upper Montclair, Essex, Pop. 11,116**
Montclair SD
Supt. — See Montclair
Mt. Hebron MS — 500/6-8
173 Bellevue Ave 07043 — 973-509-4220
Dr. Jill Sack, prin. — Fax 509-4218

**Upper Saddle River, Bergen, Pop. 8,104**
Upper Saddle River SD — 1,300/PK-8
395 W Saddle River Rd 07458 — 201-961-6500
Dr. Monica Browne, supt. — Fax 934-4923
www.usrschoolsk8.com
Cavallini MS — 500/6-8
392 W Saddle River Rd 07458 — 201-961-6400
James McCusker, prin. — Fax 236-9662

**Ventnor City, Atlantic, Pop. 10,474**
Ventnor City SD — 900/PK-8
400 N Lafayette Ave 08406 — 609-487-7900
Eileen Johnson, supt. — Fax 822-0150
www.veccnj.org/
Ventnor MS — 400/5-8
400 N Lafayette Ave 08406 — 609-487-7900
Robert Baker, prin. — Fax 823-4036

**Vernon, Sussex**
Vernon Township SD — 3,700/PK-12
PO Box 99 07462 — 973-764-2900
Arthur DiBenedetto, supt. — Fax 764-0033
www.vtsd.com
Glen Meadow MS — 600/7-8
PO Box 516 07462 — 973-764-8981
Dr. Pauline Anderson, prin. — Fax 764-3295
Vernon Township HS — 1,300/9-12
PO Box 800 07462 — 973-764-2960
Timothy Dunnigan, prin. — Fax 764-2961

**Verona, Essex, Pop. 13,597**
Verona SD — 2,100/K-12
121 Fairview Ave 07044 — 973-571-2029
Rui Dionisio, supt. — Fax 571-6779
www.veronaschools.org
Verona HS — 600/9-12
151 Fairview Ave 07044 — 973-571-6750
Glenn Cesa, prin. — Fax 571-6765
Whitehorne MS — 700/5-8
600 Bloomfield Ave 07044 — 973-571-6751
Yvette McNeal, prin. — Fax 571-6767

**Vineland, Cumberland, Pop. 59,740**
Vineland CSD — 9,200/PK-12
625 E Plum St 08360 — 856-794-6700
Dr. Mary Gruccio, supt. — Fax 794-9464
www.vineland.org
Landis MS — 500/6-8
61 W Landis Ave 08360 — 856-794-6925
Melanie Beck, prin. — Fax 507-8763
Rossi MS — 500/6-8
2572 Palermo Ave 08361 — 856-794-6961
Tammy Monahan, prin. — Fax 507-8786
Veterans Memorial MS — 500/6-8
424 S Main Rd 08360 — 856-794-6918
Hope Johnson, prin. — Fax 507-8759
Vineland HS North — 1,400/9-10
3010 E Chestnut Ave 08361 — 856-794-6800
Dr. Thomas McCann, prin. — Fax 507-8781
Vineland HS South — 1,200/11-12
2880 E Chestnut Ave 08361 — 856-794-6800
Dr. Thomas McCann, prin. — Fax 507-8751
Wallace MS — 400/6-8
688 N Mill Rd 08360 — 856-362-8887
Dr. Juanita Davis, prin. — Fax 362-8980

---

Achieve Test Prep — Post-Sec.
313 W Landis Ave 08360 — 856-457-3881
Cumberland Christian S — 400/PK-12
1100 W Sherman Ave 08360 — 856-696-1600
David R. Hobbs, hdmstr. — Fax 696-0631
Cumberland County College — Post-Sec.
PO Box 1500 08362 — 856-691-8600

**Voorhees, Camden, Pop. 946**
Eastern Camden County Regional HSD — 1,000/9-12
PO Box 2500 08043 — 856-784-4441
Dr. Harold Melleby, supt. — Fax 627-7894
www.eccrsd.us
Eastern HS — 1,000/9-12
PO Box 2500 08043 — 856-784-4441
Robert Tull, prin. — Fax 784-1322

Voorhees Township SD — 3,100/PK-8
329 Route 73 08043 — 856-751-8446
Raymond Brosel, supt. — Fax 751-3666
www.voorhees.k12.nj.us/
Voorhees MS — 1,100/6-8
1000 Holly Oak Dr 08043 — 856-795-2025
Robert Rossi, prin. — Fax 795-4611

---

Harris School of Business — Post-Sec.
401 White Horse Rd Ste 200 08043 — 856-309-3701
Rizzieri Aveda School — Post-Sec.
8200 Town Center Blvd 08043 — 856-988-8600

**Waldwick, Bergen, Pop. 9,513**
Waldwick SD — 1,500/PK-12
155 Summit Ave 07463 — 201-445-3131
Dr. Paul D. Casarico, supt. — Fax 445-0584
www.waldwick.k12.nj.us/
Waldwick HS — 500/9-12
155 Wyckoff Ave 07463 — 201-652-9000
Kevin Carroll, prin. — Fax 652-5053
Waldwick MS — 400/6-8
155 Wyckoff Ave 07463 — 201-652-9000
Michael J. Meyers, prin. — Fax 652-5053

---

Waldwick SDA S — 100/PK-12
70 Wyckoff Ave 07463 — 201-652-6078

**Wall, Monmouth, Pop. 5,201**
Monmouth County Vocational SD
Supt. — See Freehold
Communications HS of Monmouth Co. — Vo/Tech
1740 New Bedford Rd 07719 — 732-681-1010
James Gleason, prin. — Fax 681-6780

Wall Township SD — 3,800/PK-12
1620 18th Ave 07719 — 732-556-2000
Cheryl Dyer, supt. — Fax 556-2101
www.wall.k12.nj.us
Wall HS — 1,200/9-12
1630 18th Ave 07719 — 732-556-2000
Rosaleen Sirchio, prin. — Fax 556-2104
Wall IS — 1,000/6-8
2801 Allaire Rd 07719 — 732-556-2500
Erin Embon, prin. — Fax 556-2535

---

Cortiva Institute - Wall — Post-Sec.
1985 State Route 34 07719 — 732-282-0100

**Wallington, Bergen, Pop. 11,200**
Wallington SD — 1,100/K-12
32 Pine St 07057 — 973-777-4421
James Albro, supt. — Fax 614-9391
www.wboe.org
Wallington JSHS — 500/7-12
234 Main Ave 07057 — 973-777-0808
Fred Fromfield, prin. — Fax 777-1434

**Wanaque, Passaic, Pop. 10,935**
Lakeland Regional HSD — 1,100/9-12
205 Conklintown Rd 07465 — 973-835-1900
Hugh Beattie, supt. — Fax 835-2834
www.lakeland.k12.nj.us
Lakeland Regional HS — 1,100/9-12
205 Conklintown Rd 07465 — 973-835-1900
Dr. Matthew Certo, prin. — Fax 835-6369

**Waretown, Ocean, Pop. 1,552**
Ocean County Vocational SD
Supt. — See Toms River
Ocean County Voc-Tech S - Waretown — Vo/Tech
423 Wells Mill Rd 08758 — 609-286-5660
Thomas McInerney, prin. — Fax 693-1514

**Warren, Somerset**
Warren Township SD — 2,000/K-8
213 Mount Horeb Rd 07059 — 732-753-5300
Dr. Elizabeth Nastus, supt. — Fax 560-8801
www.warrentboe.org
Warren MS — 800/6-8
100 Old Stirling Rd 07059 — 908-753-5300
Robert Comba, prin. — Fax 753-4789

Watchung Hills Regional SD — 2,100/9-12
108 Stirling Rd 07059 — 908-647-4800
Elizabeth Jewett, supt. — Fax 647-4852
www.whrhs.org
Watchung Hills Regional HS — 2,100/9-12
108 Stirling Rd 07059 — 908-647-4800
Dr. George Alexis, prin. — Fax 647-4852

**Washington, Warren, Pop. 6,336**
Warren County Vocational SD
1500 State Route 57 W 07882 — 908-689-0122
Robert F. Glowacky, supt. — Fax 689-9598
www.wctech.org
Warren County Technical S — Vo/Tech
1500 State Route 57 W 07882 — 908-689-0122
Robert F. Glowacky, admin. — Fax 689-7699

Warren Hills Regional HSD — 1,800/7-12
89 Bowerstown Rd 07882 — 908-689-3143
Dr. Gary Bowen, supt. — Fax 689-4814
www.warrenhills.org
Warren Hills Regional HS — 1,200/9-12
41 Jackson Valley Rd 07882 — 908-689-3050
Earl Clymer, prin. — Fax 689-9640
Warren Hills Regional MS — 600/7-8
64 Carlton Ave 07882 — 908-689-0750
Patricia Hetrick, prin. — Fax 689-3663

---

Warren County Community College — Post-Sec.
475 State Route 57 W 07882 — 908-835-9222

**Washington Township, Bergen, Pop. 9,245**
Westwood Regional SD — 2,000/K-12
701 Ridgewood Rd 07676 — 201-664-0880
Dr. Raymond Gonzalez, supt. — Fax 664-7642
www.wwrsd.org
Westwood Regional JSHS — 900/8-12
701 Ridgewood Rd 07676 — 201-664-0880
Scott Cascone, prin. — Fax 722-1542

---

Immaculate Heart Academy — 800/9-12
500 Van Emburgh Ave 07676 — 201-445-6800
Patricia Molloy, prin. — Fax 445-7416

**Watchung, Somerset, Pop. 5,662**
Watchung Borough SD — 700/PK-8
1 Dr Parenty Way 07069 — 908-755-8121
Dr. Barbara Resko, supt. — Fax 755-6946
www.watchungschools.com
Valley View MS — 300/5-8
50 Valleyview Rd 07069 — 908-755-4422
Mary Nunn, prin. — Fax 755-4035

---

Mt. St. Mary Academy — 400/9-12
1645 US Highway 22 07069 — 908-757-0108
Sr. Lisa Gambacorto, dir. — Fax 756-5751

**Wayne, Passaic, Pop. 55,000**
Passaic Co. Education Services Comm. — 100/7-12
45 Reinhardt Rd 07470 — 973-614-8585
Diana Lobosco, supt. — Fax 614-1334
www.pcesc.org
Preakness Academy — Alt
1006 Hamburg Tpke 07470 — 973-832-4097
Fax 614-1334

Other Schools – See Passaic

Passaic County Technical Inst SD
45 Reinhardt Rd 07470 — 973-790-6000
Diana Lobosco, supt.
www.pcti.tec.nj.us
Passaic County Technical Institute — Vo/Tech
45 Reinhardt Rd 07470 — 973-389-4259
Dr. Michael Parent, prin. — Fax 389-2049
Passaic County Adult HS — Adult
45 Reinhardt Rd 07470 — 973-389-4101
John DePalma, admin.

Wayne Township SD — 8,300/PK-12
50 Nellis Dr 07470 — 973-633-3000
Dr. Mark Toback, supt. — Fax 628-8058
www.wayneschools.com
Schuyler-Colfax MS — 800/6-8
1500 Hamburg Tpke 07470 — 973-633-3130
Aimee Toth, prin. — Fax 633-3195
Washington MS — 600/6-8
68 Lenox Rd 07470 — 973-633-3140
Jack Leonard, prin. — Fax 633-7590
Wayne Hills HS — 1,300/9-12
272 Berdan Ave 07470 — 973-317-2000
Maureen Weir, prin. — Fax 633-2589
Wayne MS — 700/6-8
201 Garside Ave 07470 — 973-389-2120
David Aulenbach, prin. — Fax 389-2130
Wayne Valley HS — 1,500/9-12
551 Valley Rd 07470 — 973-633-3067
Kenneth Palczewski, prin. — Fax 633-3082

---

Achieve Test Prep — Post-Sec.
40 Galesi Dr 07470 — 973-321-3217
De Paul Catholic HS — 900/9-12
1512 Alps Rd 07470 — 973-694-3702
Kenneth Jennings, prin. — Fax 633-5381
Fortis Institute — Post-Sec.
201 Willowbrook Blvd 07470 — 973-837-1818
William Paterson University — Post-Sec.
300 Pompton Rd 07470 — 973-720-2000

**Weehawken, Hudson, Pop. 12,385**
Weehawken Township SD — 1,200/PK-12
53 Liberty Pl 07086 — 201-422-6120
John Fitzsimons, supt.
www.weehawken.k12.nj.us
Weehawken JSHS — 400/7-12
53 Liberty Pl 07086 — 201-422-6130
Dr. Steven Spinosa, prin.

**Westampton, Burlington, Pop. 60,004**
Burlington County Special Services SD — 50/10-12
20 Pioneer Blvd 08060 — 609-261-5600
Dr. Christopher Manno, supt. — Fax 261-5967
www.bcsssd.k12.nj.us
Other Schools – See Mount Laurel

Westampton Township SD — 900/PK-8
700 Rancocas Rd 08060 — 609-267-2053
Virginia Grossman, supt. — Fax 267-2760
www.westamptonschools.org
Westampton MS — 400/PK-PK, 5-
700 Rancocas Rd 08060 — 609-267-2722
Matthew Andris, prin. — Fax 702-9017

**West Berlin, Camden, Pop. 3,000**
Berlin Township SD — 600/PK-8
225 Grove Ave 08091 — 856-767-9480
Dr. Edythe Austermuhl Ed.D., supt. — Fax 767-8235
www.btwpschools.org
Eisenhower MS — 300/4-8
235 Grove Ave 08091 — 856-767-9480
Marilyn Bright, prin. — Fax 767-7992

**West Caldwell, Essex, Pop. 10,422**
Caldwell-West Caldwell SD — 2,500/K-12
104 Gray St 07006 — 973-228-6979
Dr. James Heinegg, supt. — Fax 228-8716
www.cwcboe.org/
Caldwell HS — 800/9-12
265 Westville Ave 07006 — 973-228-6981
James Devlin, prin. — Fax 228-1116
Other Schools – See Caldwell

Essex County Vocational Technical SD
Supt. — See Newark
Essex Co. Vocational Tech - W Caldwell — Vo/Tech
620 Passaic Ave 07006 — 973-412-2205
Ayisha Ingram-Robinson, prin. — Fax 412-2090

---

Essex County College — Post-Sec.
730 Bloomfield Ave 07006 — 973-877-6590

**West Deptford, Gloucester, Pop. 19,380**
West Deptford Township SD — 2,900/PK-12
675 Grove Rd 08066 — 856-848-4300
Kevin Kitchenman, supt. — Fax 845-5743
www.wdeptford.k12.nj.us/
West Deptford HS — 900/9-12
1600 Crown Point Rd, — 856-848-6110
Dr. Brian Gismondi, prin. — Fax 845-5774
West Deptford MS — 1,000/5-8
675 Grove Rd 08066 — 856-848-1200
Christine Trampe, prin. — Fax 848-2325

**Westfield, Union, Pop. 29,789**
Union Co. Educational Services Comm SD — 100/9-12
45 Cardinal Dr 07090 — 908-233-9317
Terry Foppert, supt. — Fax 233-7432
www.ucesc.org/
Hillcrest Academy South Campus — 100/Alt
1571 Lamberts Mill Rd 07090 — 908-654-8558
Dr. Jason Balsamello, prin. — Fax 233-2954
Other Schools – See Scotch Plains

Westfield SD 6,200/PK-12
302 Elm St 07090 908-789-4400
Dr. Margaret Dolan, supt. Fax 789-4192
www.westfieldnjk12.org
Edison IS 800/6-8
800 Rahway Ave 07090 908-789-4470
Matthew Bolton, prin. Fax 789-1506
Roosevelt IS 700/6-8
301 Clark St 07090 908-789-4560
Stewart Carey, prin. Fax 789-4193
Westfield HS 1,800/9-12
550 Dorian Rd 07090 908-789-4500
Peter Renwick, prin. Fax 789-4230

**West Long Branch, Monmouth, Pop. 8,009**
Shore Regional HSD 700/9-12
132 State Route 36 07764 732-222-9300
Thomas Farrell, supt. Fax 222-8849
www.shoreregional.org
Shore Regional HS 700/9-12
132 State Route 36 07764 732-222-9300
Vincent DalliCardillo, prin. Fax 222-8849

West Long Branch SD 600/PK-8
135 Locust Ave 07764 732-222-5900
Thomas Farrell, supt. Fax 222-9325
www.wlbschools.com
Antonides S 400/5-8
135 Locust Ave 07764 732-222-5900
Michael Fiorillo, prin. Fax 222-8154

---

Monmouth University Post-Sec.
400 Cedar Ave 07764 732-571-3400

**West Milford, Passaic, Pop. 26,600**
West Milford Township SD 3,700/PK-12
46 Highlander Dr 07480 973-697-1700
Anthony Riscica, supt. Fax 697-8351
www.wmtps.org
Macopin MS 600/7-8
70 Highlander Dr 07480 973-697-5691
Mary Reinhold, prin. Fax 697-0301
West Milford HS 1,200/9-12
67 Highlander Dr 07480 973-697-1701
Fred Hessler, prin. Fax 208-0912

**Westmont, Camden, Pop. 5,500**
Haddon Township SD 1,800/PK-12
500 Rhoads Ave 08108 856-869-7700
Bonnie Edwards, supt. Fax 854-7792
www.haddontwpschools.com/
Haddon Township HS 500/9-12
406 Memorial Ave 08108 856-869-7750
Gary O'Brien, prin. Fax 869-7764
Rohrer MS 400/6-8
101 MacArthur Blvd 08108 856-869-7750
Dr. Patricia Schwab, prin. Fax 869-7772

**West New York, Hudson, Pop. 49,199**
West New York SD 7,600/PK-12
6028 Broadway 07093 201-553-4000
Clara Brito Herrera, supt. Fax 865-2725
www.wnyschools.net
Memorial HS 1,700/9-12
5501 Park Ave 07093 201-553-4110
Scott Wohlrab, prin. Fax 864-2151
West New York MS 900/7-8
201 57th St 07093 201-563-4160
Patrick Gagliardi, prin. Fax 863-6698

---

Robert Fiance Beauty School Post-Sec.
5518 Bergenline Ave 07093 201-866-4000

**West Orange, Essex, Pop. 45,500**
West Orange SD 6,400/PK-12
179 Eagle Rock Ave 07052 973-669-5400
Jeffrey Rutzky, supt. Fax 669-1432
www.woboe.org
Liberty MS 500/7-8
1 Kelly Dr 07052 973-243-2007
Robert Klemt, prin. Fax 243-2743
Roosevelt MS 400/7-8
36 Gilbert Pl 07052 973-669-5373
Lionel Hush, prin. Fax 243-9807
West Orange HS 2,000/9-12
51 Conforti Ave 07052 973-669-5301
Hayden Moore, prin. Fax 669-1260

---

Golda Och Academy 300/6-12
1418 Pleasant Valley Way 07052 973-602-3600
Seton Hall Preparatory HS 1,000/9-12
120 Northfield Ave 07052 973-325-6624
Rev. Michael Kelly, pres. Fax 325-6652

**Westville, Gloucester, Pop. 4,234**

---

St. John of God Community Services Post-Sec.
1145 Delsea Dr 08093 856-848-4700

**West Windsor, Mercer**
West Windsor-Plainsboro Regional SD 9,500/K-12
PO Box 505 08550 609-716-5000
David Aderhold Ed.D., supt. Fax 716-5012
www.ww-p.org
West Windsor-Plainsboro HS South 1,600/9-12
346 Clarksville Rd 08550 609-716-5050
Dennis Lepold, prin. Fax 716-5092
Other Schools – See Plainsboro, Princeton Junction

---

Mercer County Community College Post-Sec.
1200 Old Trenton Rd 08550 609-586-4800
Mercer County Community College Post-Sec.
1200 Old Trenton Rd 08550 609-586-4800

**Wharton, Morris, Pop. 6,390**
Wharton Borough SD 700/K-8
137 E Central Ave 07885 973-361-2592
Christopher Herdman, supt. Fax 895-2187
www.wbps.org/
MacKinnon MS 300/6-8
137 E Central Ave 07885 973-361-1253
Patrick Ketch, prin. Fax 361-4805

**Whippany, Morris**
Hanover Park Regional HSD
Supt. — See East Hanover
Whippany Park HS 700/9-12
165 Whippany Rd 07981 973-887-3004
John Manning, prin. Fax 887-0451

Hanover Township SD 1,500/K-8
61 Highland Ave 07981 973-515-2404
Robert Mooney, supt. Fax 540-1023
www.hanovertwpschools.com/
Memorial JHS 600/6-8
61 Highland Ave 07981 973-515-2427
Michael Wasko, prin. Fax 515-2481

---

Abundant Life Christian S 100/PK-12
43 S Jefferson Rd 07981 973-888-2083
Yolanda Garris, prin. Fax 463-9677

**White House Station, Hunterdon, Pop. 2,066**
Readington Township SD 1,900/PK-8
PO Box 807 08889 908-534-2195
Dr. Barbara Sargent, supt. Fax 349-3042
www.readington.k12.nj.us
Readington MS 700/6-8
PO Box 700 08889 908-534-2113
Sharon Moffat, prin. Fax 534-6802

**Whiting, Ocean**
Manchester Township SD 3,000/K-12
121 Route 539 08759 732-350-5900
David Trethaway, supt. Fax 350-0436
www.manchestertwp.org
Other Schools – See Manchester

**Wildwood, Cape May, Pop. 5,246**
Wildwood CSD 800/PK-12
4300 Pacific Ave 08260 609-522-7922
J. Kenyon Kummings, supt. Fax 523-1014
www.edline.net/pages/Wildwood_PSD
Wildwood HS 300/9-12
4300 Pacific Ave 08260 609-522-7922
Philip Schaffer, prin. Fax 522-7914
Wildwood MS 100/6-8
4300 Pacific Ave 08260 609-522-7922
Fax 522-7914

---

Wildwood Catholic HS 200/9-12
1500 Central Ave 08260 609-522-7257
Fr. Joseph Wallace, pres. Fax 522-2453

**Williamstown, Gloucester, Pop. 15,255**
Monroe Township SD 5,700/PK-12
75 E Academy St 08094 856-629-6400
Charles Earling, supt. Fax 262-2499
www.monroetwp.k12.nj.us
Williamstown HS 1,800/9-12
700 N Tuckahoe Rd 08094 856-262-8200
Jill DelConte, prin. Fax 262-0869
Williamstown MS 1,900/5-8
561 Clayton Rd 08094 856-629-7444
Dana Mericle, prin. Fax 875-6757

**Willingboro, Burlington, Pop. 32,400**
Willingboro Township SD 4,000/PK-12
440 Beverly Rancocas Rd 08046 609-835-8600
Dr. Ronald G. Taylor, supt. Fax 835-3880
www.willingboroschools.org/
Memorial MS 900/6-8
451 Van Sciver Pkwy 08046 609-835-8700
Ellis Brown, prin. Fax 835-1457
Willingboro Alternative Education Alt
56 Brooklawn Dr 08046 609-835-8950
Dr. Alicia Turner-Biddle, prin.
Willingboro HS 900/9-12
20 S John F Kennedy Way 08046 609-835-8800
Kimberly Ash, prin. Fax 835-8877

---

Strayer University Post-Sec.
300 Willingboro Way # 125 08046 609-835-6000

**Woodbridge, Middlesex, Pop. 18,933**
Middlesex County Vocational SD
Supt. — See East Brunswick
Acad for Allied Health & Biomed Science Vo/Tech
1 Convery Blvd 07095 732-634-5858
Michael Fanelli, prin. Fax 632-7073

Woodbridge Township SD 12,500/PK-12
PO Box 428 07095 732-750-3200
Dr. Robert Zega, supt. Fax 750-3493
www.woodbridge.k12.nj.us
Woodbridge HS 1,400/9-12
25 Samuel Lupo Pl 07095 732-602-8600
Glenn Lottmann, prin. Fax 602-8612
Woodbridge MS 400/6-8
525 Barron Ave 07095 732-602-8690
Dr. John Crowe, prin. Fax 855-0326
Other Schools – See Avenel, Colonia, Fords, Iselin

---

Achieve Test Prep Post-Sec.
1480 US Highway 9 N 07095 732-750-2321
Berkeley College Post-Sec.
430 Rahway Ave 07095 732-750-1800

**Woodbury, Gloucester, Pop. 9,869**
Woodbury SD 1,400/PK-12
25 N Broad St 08096 856-853-0123
Joseph Jones, supt. Fax 853-0704
www.woodburysch.com
Woodbury JSHS 700/6-12
25 N Broad St 08096 856-853-0123
Eder Joseph, prin. Fax 853-2684

**Woodbury Heights, Gloucester, Pop. 3,021**
Gateway Regional SD 900/7-12
775 Tanyard Rd, 856-848-8172
Shannon Whalen Ed.D., supt. Fax 848-2049
www.gatewayhs.com
Gateway Regional MSHS 900/7-12
775 Tanyard Rd, 856-848-8200
Jeff Pierro, prin. Fax 251-9813

**Woodcliff Lake, Bergen, Pop. 5,674**
Woodcliff Lake SD 800/PK-8
134 Woodcliff Ave 07677 201-930-5600
Lauren Barbelet, supt. Fax 930-0488
www.woodcliff-lake.com
Woodcliff MS 300/6-8
134 Woodcliff Ave 07677 201-930-5600
Robert Lombardy, prin. Fax 391-7932

**Woodland Park, Passaic**
Woodland Park SD 1,000/K-8
853 McBride Ave, 973-317-7700
Dr. Michele R. Pillari, supt. Fax 317-7773
wpschools.org
Memorial MS 500/5-8
15 Memorial Dr, 973-317-7750
Charles Silverstein, prin. Fax 317-7753

---

Berkeley College Post-Sec.
44 Rifle Camp Rd, 973-278-5400

**Wood Ridge, Bergen, Pop. 7,540**
Wood-Ridge SD 800/PK-12
540 Windsor Rd 07075 201-933-6777
Nicholas Cipriano, supt. Fax 804-9204
www.wood-ridgeschools.org
Wood-Ridge JSHS 400/7-12
258 Hackensack St 07075 201-933-6777
Russell Petrocelli, prin. Fax 939-1195

**Woodstown, Salem, Pop. 3,420**
Salem County Special Services SD 50/6-12
PO Box 126 08098 856-769-0101
John Swain, supt. Fax 769-3202
www.scsssd.org/
Other Schools – See Salem

Woodstown-Pilesgrove Regional SD 1,600/PK-12
135 East Ave 08098 856-769-0144
Thomas Coleman, supt. Fax 769-4549
www.woodstown.org
Woodstown HS 700/9-12
140 East Ave 08098 856-769-0144
Dr. Scott Hoopes, prin. Fax 769-4102
Woodstown MS 300/6-8
15 Lincoln Ave 08098 856-769-0144
Allison Pessolano, prin. Fax 769-3872

**Woolwich, Gloucester**
Kingsway Regional SD 2,000/7-12
213 Kings Hwy 08085 856-467-3300
Dr. James Lavender, supt. Fax 467-5382
www.krsd.org
Kingsway Regional HS 1,200/9-12
201 Kings Hwy 08085 856-467-3300
Craig Stephenson, prin. Fax 241-1932
Kingsway Regional MS 900/7-8
203 Kings Hwy 08085 856-467-3300
Brian Tonelli, prin. Fax 467-2703

**Wyckoff, Bergen, Pop. 15,372**
Wyckoff Township SD 2,200/PK-8
241 Morse Ave 07481 201-848-5700
Richard Kuder, supt. Fax 848-5695
www.wyckoffps.org/
Eisenhower MS 800/6-8
344 Calvin Ct 07481 201-848-5750
Christopher Iasiello, prin. Fax 848-5682

---

Eastern Christian MS 200/5-8
518 Sicomac Ave 07481 201-891-3663
Daniel Lazor, prin.

# NEW MEXICO

**NEW MEXICO PUBLIC EDUCATION DEPARTMENT**
**300 Don Gaspar Ave, Santa Fe 87501-2786**
**Telephone 505-827-5800**
**Fax 505-827-6696**
**Website http://www.sde.state.nm.us**

Secretary of Education Hanna Skandara

**NEW MEXICO PUBLIC EDUCATION COMMISSION**
**300 Don Gaspar Ave, Santa Fe 87501-2744**

Chairperson Andrew Garrison

## REGIONAL EDUCATION COOPS (REC) & REGIONAL CENTER COOPS (RCC)

Central REC 5
Maria Jaramillo, dir. 505-889-3412
PO Box 37440, Albuquerque 87176 Fax 889-3422
www.crecnm.org/

High Plains REC 3
Stephen Aguirre, dir. 575-445-7090
101 N 2nd St, Raton 87740 Fax 445-7663
hprec.com

Northeast REC 4
Dr. Jim Abreu, dir. 505-426-2262
PO Box 927, Las Vegas 87701 Fax 454-1473
www.rec4.com

Northwest REC 2
Dr. Kim Mizell, dir. 575-756-1274
PO Box 113, Chama 87520 Fax 756-1278
www.nwrec2.org

Pecos Valley REC 8
David Willden, dir. 575-748-6100
PO Box 155, Artesia 88211 Fax 748-6160
www.pvrec8.com/

REC 6
Scott McMath, dir. 575-562-4455
1500 S Avenue K, Portales 88130 Fax 562-4460
www.rec6.net

REC 7
Belinda Morris, dir. 575-393-0755
315 E Clinton St, Hobbs 88240 Fax 393-0249
hobbsschools.net/department/regional_education_cooperative_7

REC 9
Sean Wootton, dir. 575-257-2368
237 Service Rd, Ruidoso 88345 Fax 257-2141
rec9nm.org

Southwest REC 10
Vicki Chavez, dir. 575-546-5951
310 W Elm St, Deming 88030 Fax 546-5994
www.swrecnm.org

## PUBLIC, PRIVATE AND CATHOLIC SECONDARY SCHOOLS

**Alamogordo, Otero, Pop. 29,463**

Alamogordo SD 6,100/PK-12
PO Box 650 88311 575-812-6000
Adrianne Salas, supt. Fax 812-6003
www.aps4kids.org

Academy Del Sol 200/10-12
PO Box 650 88311 575-812-5500
Pamela Engstom, prin. Fax 812-5503

Alamogordo HS 1,600/9-12
PO Box 650 88311 575-812-6500
George Heaton, prin. Fax 812-6503

Chaparral MS 700/6-8
PO Box 650 88311 575-812-6300
Robbi Coker, prin. Fax 812-6303

Mountain View MS 500/6-8
PO Box 650 88311 575-812-6400
Moises Cardiel, prin. Fax 812-6403

Other Schools – See Holloman AFB

---

Legacy Christian Academy 100/PK-12
3001 Thunder Rd 88310 575-434-0352
Cindy McKee, dir. Fax 434-0352

New Mexico School Visually Handicapped Post-Sec.
1900 N White Sands Blvd 88310 575-437-3505

New Mexico State University Post-Sec.
2400 Scenic Dr 88310 575-439-3600

Olympian University of Cosmetology Post-Sec.
1810 10th St 88310 575-437-2221

**Albuquerque, Bernalillo, Pop. 534,167**

Albuquerque SD 92,400/PK-12
PO Box 25704 87125 505-880-3700
Dr. Brad Winter, supt. Fax 872-8855
ww2.aps.edu

Adams MS 800/6-8
5401 Glenrio Rd NW 87105 505-831-0400
Modesta Hernandez, prin. Fax 836-7760

Albuquerque HS 1,600/9-12
800 Odelia Rd NE 87102 505-843-6400
Tim McCorkle, prin. Fax 848-9432

Atrisco Heritage Academy 2,300/9-12
10800 Dennis Chavez Blvd SW 87121 505-243-1458
Antonio Gonzales, prin. Fax 873-1041

Career Enrichment Ctr Vo/Tech
807 Mountain Rd NE 87102 505-247-3658
Patrick Arguelles, prin. Fax 848-9421

Carter MS 1,200/6-8
8901 Bluewater Rd NW 87121 505-833-7540
Amy Mahr, prin. Fax 833-7559

Cibola HS 1,900/9-12
1510 Ellison Dr NW 87114 505-897-0110
Pam Meyer, prin. Fax 897-4251

Cleveland MS 700/6-8
6910 Natalie Ave NE 87110 505-881-9227
Susan Labarge, prin. Fax 881-9441

College and Career HS 9-12
525 Buena Vista Dr SE 87106 505-224-4880
Elizabeth Abeyta, prin. Fax 224-4898

Del Norte HS 1,200/9-12
5323 Montgomery Blvd NE 87109 505-883-7222
Jo Sloan, prin. Fax 880-3965

Desert Ridge MS 1,000/6-8
8400 Barstow St NE 87122 505-857-9282
Troy Hughes, prin. Fax 857-0201

Eisenhower MS 900/6-8
11001 Camero Ave NE 87111 505-292-2530
Kathy Alexander, prin. Fax 291-6884

Eldorado HS 1,900/9-12
11300 Montgomery Blvd NE 87111 505-296-4871
Martin Sandoval, prin. Fax 291-6809

Freedom HS 200/Alt
5200 Cutler Ave NE 87110 505-884-6012
Esther Keeton, prin. Fax 880-3979

Garfield STEM S 300/6-8
3501 6th St NW 87107 505-344-1647
David Lynch, prin. Fax 344-6562

Grant MS 700/6-8
1111 Easterday Dr NE 87112 505-299-2113
Paul Roney, prin. Fax 291-6881

Harrison MS 900/6-8
3912 Isleta Blvd SW 87105 505-877-1279
Kevin Cummings, prin. Fax 877-6797

Hayes MS 400/6-8
1100 Texas St NE 87110 505-265-7741
Antoinette Valenzuela, prin. Fax 260-6108

Highland HS 1,600/9-12
4700 Coal Ave SE 87108 505-265-3711
Marco Harris, prin. Fax 348-8503

Hillerman MS 1,000/6-8
8101 Rainbow Blvd NW 87114 505-792-0698
Renee Salazar, prin. Fax 792-2322

Hoover MS 700/6-8
12015 Tivoli Ave NE Ste A 87111 505-298-6896
Robert Abney, prin. Fax 291-6883

Jackson MS 600/6-8
10600 Indian School Rd NE 87112 505-299-7377
Tracy Straub, prin. Fax 291-6877

Jefferson MS 900/6-8
712 Girard Blvd NE 87106 505-255-8691
Shawn Morris, prin. Fax 268-2334

Johnson MS 1,000/6-8
6811 Taylor Ranch Rd NW 87120 505-898-1492
Mike Bachicha, prin. Fax 898-7150

Kennedy MS 500/6-8
721 Tomasita St NE 87123 505-298-6701
Ed Bortot, prin. Fax 291-6879

La Cueva HS 1,900/9-12
7801 Wilshire Ave NE 87122 505-823-2327
Dana Richardson, prin. Fax 857-0177

Madison MS 800/6-8
3501 Moon St NE 87111 505-299-4735
Andrew Legant, prin. Fax 323-9512

Manzano HS 1,800/9-12
12200 Lomas Blvd NE 87112 505-559-2200
Dr. Karen Webb, prin. Fax 291-6854

McKinley MS 600/6-8
4500 Comanche Rd NE 87110 505-881-9390
Vernon Martinez, prin. Fax 880-3968

Monroe MS 1,000/6-8
6100 Paradise Blvd NW 87114 505-897-0101
Jane Sichler, prin. Fax 897-2371

Nex+Gen Academy 200/9-12
5325 Montgomery Blvd NE 87109 505-878-6400
Amy Milazzo, prin.

Polk MS 400/6-8
2220 Raymac Rd SW 87105 505-877-6444
Michelle Armijo, prin. Fax 877-1618

Pyle MS 700/6-8
1820 Valdora Rd SW 87105 505-877-3770
Ryan Homistek, prin. Fax 873-8540

Rio Grande HS 1,500/9-12
2300 Arenal Rd SW 87105 505-873-0220
Amanda De Bell, prin. Fax 873-8523

Sandia HS 1,900/9-12
7801 Candelaria Rd NE 87110 505-294-1511
Scott Elder, prin. Fax 291-6878

School on Wheels 100/Alt
129 Hartline Ave SW 87105 505-243-2395
Stan Pena, prin. Fax 243-5180

Taylor MS 600/6-8
8200 Guadalupe Trl NW 87114 505-898-3666
Sandra Patterson, prin. Fax 897-5165

Truman MS 1,300/6-8
9400 Benavides Rd SW 87121 505-836-3030
Michele Torres, prin. Fax 836-7745

Valley HS 1,400/9-12
1505 Candelaria Rd NW 87107 505-345-9021
Anthony Griego, prin. Fax 761-8429

Van Buren MS 600/6-8
700 Louisiana Blvd SE 87108 505-268-3833
Jeri Heileman, prin. Fax 260-6104

Vision Quest Alternative MS 50/Alt
5401 Glenrio Rd NW 87105 505-352-0343
Adele Evans, prin. Fax 352-0343

Volcano Vista HS 2,200/9-12
8100 Rainbow Blvd NW 87114 505-890-0343
Valerie Atencio, prin. Fax 792-4805

Washington MS 500/6-8
1101 Park Ave SW 87102 505-764-2000
Angela Rodriguez, prin. Fax 764-2022

West Mesa HS 1,600/9-12
6701 Fortuna Rd NW 87121 505-831-6993
Mark Garcia, prin. Fax 836-7756

Wilson MS 500/6-8
1138 Cardenas Dr SE 87108 505-268-3961
Ann Piper, prin. Fax 260-2000

Other Schools – See Los Ranchos, Tijeras

---

Albuquerque Academy 1,100/6-12
6400 Wyoming Blvd NE 87109 505-828-3200
Andrew Watson, head sch Fax 828-3320

Aveda Institute New Mexico Post-Sec.
1816 Central Ave SW 87104 505-294-5333

Bosque S 500/6-12
4000 Learning Rd NW 87120 505-898-6388
William B. Handmaker, head sch Fax 922-0392

Brookline College Post-Sec.
4201 Central Ave NW Ste J 87105 505-880-2877

Brown Mackie College Post-Sec.
10500 Copper Ave NE 87123 505-559-5200

Calvary Christian Academy 100/PK-12
12820 Indian School Rd NE 87112 505-842-8681
Nicole Craner, admin. Fax 842-8746

Carrington College Post-Sec.
1001 Menaul Blvd NE 87107 505-254-7777

Central New Mexico Community College Post-Sec.
525 Buena Vista Dr SE 87106 505-224-3000

DeWolff Coll of Hairstyling\Cosmetology Post-Sec.
1500 Eubank Blvd NE 87112 505-296-4100

Evangel Christian Academy 200/PK-12
4501 Montgomery Blvd NE 87109 505-883-4674

Graceway Christian Academy 100/PK-12
1621 Arizona St NE 87110 505-262-0969
Dr. John Adams, supt. Fax 717-1467

Hope Christian S 1,400/PK-12
8005 Louisiana Blvd NE 87109 505-822-8868
Tom Morris, dir. Fax 822-8260
Hope Connection S 100/6-12
4700 Eubank Blvd NE 87111 505-237-0844
Hope Lucero, dir. Fax 237-0110
ITT Technical Institute Post-Sec.
5100 Masthead St NE 87109 505-828-1114
Menaul S 200/6-12
301 Menaul Blvd NE 87107 505-345-7727
Lindsey Gilbert, head sch Fax 344-2517
National American University Post-Sec.
4775 Indian Sch Rd NE #200 87110 505-348-3700
National American University Post-Sec.
10131 Coors Blvd NW Ste I1 87114 800-895-9904
New Life Baptist Academy 200/PK-12
6900 Los Volcanes Rd NW 87121 505-352-2628
Olympian University of Cosmetology Post-Sec.
6300 San Mateo Blvd NE # J 87109 505-765-1044
Pima Medical Institute Post-Sec.
4400 Cutler Ave NE 87110 505-881-1234
St. Pius X HS 800/9-12
5301 Saint Josephs Dr NW 87120 505-831-8400
Barbara Rothweiler, prin. Fax 831-8413
Sandia Preparatory S 700/6-12
532 Osuna Rd NE 87113 505-338-3000
Bill Sinfield, head sch Fax 338-3099
Southwest Acupuncture College Post-Sec.
7801 Academy Rd NE 87109 505-888-8898
Southwestern Indian Polytechnic Inst. Post-Sec.
9169 Coors Blvd NW 87120 505-346-2347
Southwest University of Visual Arts Post-Sec.
5000 Marble Ave NE 87110 505-254-7575
Universal Therapeutic Massage Institute Post-Sec.
3410 Aztec Rd NE 87107 505-888-0020
University of New Mexico Post-Sec.
PO Box 4895 87196 505-277-0111
University of Phoenix-NM Division Post-Sec.
5700 Pasadena Ave NE 87113 505-821-4800
Victory Christian S 100/K-12
220 El Pueblo Rd NW 87114 505-898-3060
Glenn Frey, supt. Fax 898-6690

**Animas, Hidalgo, Pop. 225**
Animas SD 200/PK-12
PO Box 85 88020 575-548-2299
Loren Cushman, supt. Fax 548-2388
www.animask12.net
Animas HS 100/7-12
PO Box 90 88020 575-548-2296
Loren Cushman, prin. Fax 548-2388

**Anthony, Dona Ana, Pop. 9,342**
Gadsden ISD
Supt. — See Sunland Park
Alta Vista Early College HS 300/9-12
PO Box 70 88021 575-882-6400
Rosa Hood, prin. Fax 882-6420
Desert Pride Academy 300/Alt
PO Box 70 88021 575-882-0142
Don Smelser, prin. Fax 882-4926
Gadsden HS 1,600/9-12
6301 Highway 28 88021 575-882-6300
Hector Giron, prin. Fax 882-2370
Gadsden MS 800/7-8
1301 Washington St 88021 575-882-2372
Veronica Quinones, prin. Fax 882-5227

**Anton Chico, Guadalupe, Pop. 188**
Santa Rosa Consolidated SD
Supt. — See Santa Rosa
Anton Chico MS 50/6-8
PO Box 169 87711 575-427-6038
Joseph Salas, prin. Fax 427-4246

**Artesia, Eddy, Pop. 11,178**
Artesia SD 3,700/PK-12
1106 W Quay Ave 88210 575-746-3585
Dr. Crit Caton, supt. Fax 746-6232
www.bulldogs.org
Artesia HS 700/10-12
1006 W Richardson Ave 88210 575-746-9816
Scotty Stall, prin. Fax 746-4365
Artesia Park JHS 600/8-9
1508 W Cannon Ave 88210 575-746-9892
Cody Skinner, prin. Fax 746-4462

**Aztec, San Juan, Pop. 6,640**
Aztec Municipal SD 3,300/PK-12
1118 W Aztec Blvd 87410 505-334-9474
Kirk Carpenter, supt. Fax 334-9861
www.aztecschools.com
Aztec HS 1,000/9-12
500 E Chaco St 87410 505-334-9414
Warman Hall, prin. Fax 599-4387
Koogler MS 700/6-8
455 N Light Plant Rd 87410 505-334-6102
Jessica Sledzinski, prin. Fax 599-4385
Vista Nueva HS 50/Alt
315 S Ash St Ste 100 87410 505-334-3831
Rocky Torres, prin. Fax 334-1427

**Bayard, Grant, Pop. 2,310**
Cobre Consolidated SD 1,300/PK-12
PO Box 1000 88023 575-537-4010
Robert Mendoza, supt. Fax 537-5455
www.cobre.k12.nm.us
Cobre HS 400/9-12
PO Box 749 88023 575-537-4020
Frank Quarrell, prin. Fax 537-5503
Snell MS 200/7-8
PO Box 729 88023 575-537-4030
Christopher Rottman, prin. Fax 537-3022

**Belen, Valencia, Pop. 7,165**
Belen Consolidated SD 4,500/PK-12
520 N Main St 87002 505-966-1000
Ron Marquez, supt. Fax 966-1050
www.beleneagles.org
Belen HS 1,200/9-12
520 N Main St 87002 505-966-1300
Rodney Wright, prin. Fax 966-1350
Belen Infinity HS 100/Alt
520 N Main St 87002 505-966-1500
Mary Batista, prin. Fax 966-1550
Belen MS 600/7-8
520 N Main St 87002 505-966-1600
Kim Ortiz, prin. Fax 966-1650

**Bernalillo, Sandoval, Pop. 8,231**
Bernalillo SD 2,400/PK-12
560 S Camino Del Pueblo 87004 505-867-2317
Allan Tapia, supt. Fax 867-7850
www.bernalillo-schools.org
Bernalillo HS 900/9-12
250 Isidora Sanchez 87004 505-867-2388
Keith Cowan, prin. Fax 867-7826
Bernalillo MS 400/6-8
485 Camino don Tomas 87004 505-867-3309
Jacque Mangham, prin. Fax 867-7819

**Bloomfield, San Juan, Pop. 7,953**
Bloomfield SD 3,000/PK-12
325 N Bergin Ln 87413 505-632-4300
Dr. Kim Mizell, supt. Fax 632-4371
www.bsin.k12.nm.us
Bloomfield HS 800/9-12
520 N 1st St 87413 505-634-3400
Chad Burkholder, prin. Fax 634-3413
Brown Secondary S 100/Alt
924 S Bloomfield Blvd 87413 505-634-3940
Robert Lopez, prin. Fax 634-3950
Mesa Alta JHS 500/7-8
329 N Bergin Ln 87413 505-632-8021
Adam Benavidez, prin. Fax 634-3872

**Capitan, Lincoln, Pop. 1,465**
Capitan Municipal SD 500/K-12
PO Box 278 88316 575-354-8500
Shirley Crawford, supt. Fax 354-8505
www.capitantigers.org
Capitan HS 200/9-12
PO Box 278 88316 575-354-8503
Jimmie Mace, prin. Fax 354-8508
Capitan MS 100/6-8
PO Box 278 88316 575-354-8502
Jimmie Mace, prin. Fax 354-8507

**Carlsbad, Eddy, Pop. 25,808**
Carlsbad Municipal SD 5,800/K-12
408 N Canyon St 88220 575-234-3300
Gary Perkowski, supt. Fax 234-3367
www.carlsbadnmschools.com
Carlsbad HS 1,600/9-12
408 N Canyon St 88220 575-234-3319
Mark Driskell, prin. Fax 234-3393
Carlsbad IS @ P.R. Leyva Campus 800/7-8
408 N Canyon St 88220 575-234-3318
Stephanie West, prin. Fax 234-3452
Early College HS 9-12
408 N Canyon St 88220 575-234-9415
Peter McWain, prin.

---

Eddy County Beauty College Post-Sec.
1115 W Mermod St 88220 575-885-4545
New Mexico State University Post-Sec.
1500 University Dr 88220 575-234-9200

**Carrizozo, Lincoln, Pop. 975**
Carrizozo Municipal SD 100/PK-12
PO Box 99 88301 575-648-2346
Ricky Espinoza, supt. Fax 648-2216
www.carrizozoschools.org
Carrizozo MSHS 50/7-12
PO Box 99 88301 575-648-2346
Ricky Espinoza, prin. Fax 648-3255

**Casa Blanca, Cibola**
Grants-Cibola County SD
Supt. — See Grants
Laguna Acoma JSHS 300/7-12
PO Box 689 87007 505-285-2670
Tom Trujillo, prin. Fax 552-7184

**Chaparral, Dona Ana, Pop. 14,528**
Gadsden ISD
Supt. — See Sunland Park
Chaparral HS 1,100/9-12
800 S County Line Dr, 575-824-6700
Mark Rupcich, prin. Fax 824-5081
Chaparral MS 600/7-8
290 E Lisa Dr, 575-824-4847
Marti Muela, prin. Fax 824-4045

**Cimarron, Colfax, Pop. 1,000**
Cimarron Municipal SD 300/K-12
125 N Collison Ave 87714 575-376-2445
Adan Estrada, supt. Fax 376-2442
cimarronschools.org
Cimarron HS 100/9-12
125 N Collison Ave 87714 575-376-2241
Letitia Martinez, prin. Fax 376-2428
Cimarron MS 50/5-8
125 N Collison Ave 87714 575-376-2512
Bonnie Lightfoot, prin. Fax 376-2217
Other Schools – See Eagle Nest

**Clayton, Union, Pop. 2,951**
Clayton Municipal SD 500/PK-12
323 S 5th St 88415 575-374-9611
Dr. Nelda Isaacs, supt. Fax 374-9881
www.claytonschools.us
Clayton HS 200/9-12
323 S 5th St 88415 575-374-2596
Marvin Martin, prin. Fax 374-6012
Clayton JHS 100/7-8
323 S 5th St 88415 575-374-9543
Kitty Martin, prin. Fax 374-9469

**Cliff, Grant, Pop. 288**
Silver Consolidated SD
Supt. — See Silver City
Cliff JSHS 100/7-12
PO Box 9 88028 575-535-2051
Dean Spurgeon, prin. Fax 535-2054

**Cloudcroft, Otero, Pop. 659**
Cloudcroft Municipal SD 300/PK-12
PO Box 198 88317 575-601-4416
Travis Dempsey, supt. Fax 235-1668
www.cmsbears.org
Cloudcroft HS 100/9-12
PO Box 198 88317 575-601-4416
Tana Daugherty, prin. Fax 405-0833

**Clovis, Curry, Pop. 36,950**
Clovis Municipal SD 8,800/PK-12
PO Box 19000 88102 575-769-4300
Jody Balch, supt. Fax 769-4333
www.clovis-schools.org/
Choices Alternative HS Alt
1900 Thornton St 88101 575-769-4859
Todd Morris, prin. Fax 769-4857
Clovis Freshman Academy 600/9-9
1400 Cameo St 88101 575-769-4400
Diana Russell, prin. Fax 769-4403
Clovis HS 1,700/10-12
1900 N Thornton St 88101 575-769-4350
Wayne Marshall, prin. Fax 769-4366
Gattis MS 6-8
5100 N Thornton St 88101 575-769-4305
Tandee Delk, prin. Fax 935-5103
Marshall MS 600/6-8
100 Commerce Way 88101 575-769-4410
Jay Brady, prin. Fax 769-4413
Yucca MS 600/6-8
1500 Sycamore St 88101 575-769-4420
Loran Hill, prin. Fax 769-4421

---

Clovis Christian Schools - West Campus 50/9-12
PO Box 608 88102 575-763-5311
Dr. Ladona Clayton, supt. Fax 763-4469
Clovis Community College Post-Sec.
417 Schepps Blvd 88101 575-769-2811

**Corona, Lincoln, Pop. 169**
Corona Municipal SD 100/PK-12
PO Box 258 88318 575-849-1911
Travis Lightfoot, supt. Fax 849-2026
www.cpscardinals.org
Corona HS 50/7-12
PO Box 258 88318 575-849-1911
Rick Cogdill, prin. Fax 849-2026

**Corrales, Sandoval, Pop. 8,197**

---

Sandia View Academy 50/9-12
65 Sandia View Ln 87048 505-898-0717
Gary Brown, prin. Fax 897-7053

**Crownpoint, McKinley, Pop. 2,253**
Gallup-McKinley County SD
Supt. — See Gallup
Crownpoint HS 300/9-12
PO Box 700 87313 505-721-1600
James Reed, prin. Fax 721-1699
Crownpoint MS 100/6-8
PO Box 1110 87313 505-786-5663
Michael Cubacub, prin. Fax 721-5499

---

Navajo Technical College Post-Sec.
PO Box 849 87313 505-786-4100

**Cuba, Sandoval, Pop. 717**
Cuba ISD 500/PK-12
PO Box 70 87013 575-289-3211
Tony Archuleta, supt. Fax 289-3314
cuba.k12.nm.us/
Cuba HS 300/9-12
PO Box 70 87013 575-289-3211
Archie Jacquez, prin. Fax 289-3314
Cuba MS 100/6-8
PO Box 70 87013 575-289-3211
Lynn Vasquez, prin. Fax 289-3314

**Deming, Luna, Pop. 14,749**
Deming SD 5,300/PK-12
1001 S Diamond Ave 88030 575-546-8841
Dr. Daniel Lere, supt. Fax 546-8517
www.demingps.org
Deming HS 1,500/9-12
1100 S Nickel St 88030 575-546-2678
Janean Garney, prin. Fax 544-0918
Red Mountain MS 800/7-8
2100 Highway 418 SW 88030 575-546-0668
Robin Parnell, prin. Fax 546-9263

**Des Moines, Union, Pop. 140**
Des Moines Municipal SD 100/K-12
PO Box 38 88418 575-278-2611
Mark Chandler, supt. Fax 278-2617
www.desmoines.k12.nm.us/
Des Moines JSHS 50/7-12
PO Box 38 88418 575-278-2611
Kodi Sumpter, prin. Fax 278-2617

**Dexter, Chaves, Pop. 1,260**
Dexter Consolidated SD 1,000/PK-12
PO Box 159 88230 575-734-5420
Lesa Dodd, supt. Fax 734-6813
www.dexterdemons.org
Dexter HS 300/9-12
PO Box 159 88230 575-734-5420
Craig DeYoung, prin. Fax 734-6709
Dexter MS 200/6-8
PO Box 159 88230 575-734-5414
Chanda Crandall, prin. Fax 734-6811

**Dora, Roosevelt, Pop. 133**
Dora Consolidated SD 300/PK-12
PO Box 327 88115 575-477-2216
Steve Barron, supt. Fax 477-2464
www.doraschools.com
Dora JSHS 100/7-12
PO Box 327 88115 575-477-2216
Brandon Hays, prin. Fax 477-2464

**Dulce, Rio Arriba, Pop. 2,716**
Dulce ISD 600/K-12
PO Box 547 87528 575-759-3225
Tom Savage, supt. Fax 759-3533
www.dulceschools.com/
Dulce JSHS 200/7-12
PO Box 547 87528 575-759-2959
Manuel Valdez, prin. Fax 759-3535

**Eagle Nest, Colfax, Pop. 289**
Cimarron Municipal SD
Supt. — See Cimarron
Eagle Nest MS 100/5-8
225 Lake St 87718 575-377-6991
Fax 377-3646

**Edgewood, Santa Fe, Pop. 3,663**
Moriarty-Edgewood SD
Supt. — See Moriarty
Edgewood MS 300/6-8
17 Venus Rd W 87015 505-832-5880
Todd Bibiano, prin. Fax 281-7210

**Elida, Roosevelt, Pop. 195**
Elida Municipal SD 100/K-12
PO Box 8 88116 575-274-6211
Jim Daugherty, supt. Fax 274-6213
www.elidaschools.net/
Elida JSHS 100/7-12
PO Box 8 88116 575-274-6211
Larry Gregory, prin. Fax 274-6213

**El Rito, Rio Arriba, Pop. 781**

---

Northern New Mexico Community College Post-Sec.
PO Box 160 87530 575-581-4110

**Espanola, Rio Arriba, Pop. 10,179**
Espanola SD 4,400/PK-12
714 Calle Don Diego 87532 505-753-2254
Bobbie Gutierrez, supt. Fax 747-3514
www.k12espanola.org
Espanola Valley HS 1,000/9-12
714 Calle Don Diego 87532 505-753-7357
Elizabeth Lucero, prin. Fax 753-6177
Vigil MS 600/7-8
714 Calle Don Diego 87532 505-753-1348
Julie Gutierrez, prin. Fax 747-3083

---

Northern New Mexico College Post-Sec.
921 N Paseo De Onate 87532 505-747-2100
Victory Christian Academy 50/K-12
PO Box 540 87532 505-753-0039

**Estancia, Torrance, Pop. 1,626**
Estancia Municipal SD 800/PK-12
PO Box 68 87016 505-384-2001
Audie Brown, supt. Fax 384-2015
www.estancia.k12.nm.us
Estancia HS 200/9-12
PO Box 68 87016 505-384-2002
Theresa Hough, prin. Fax 384-2015
Estancia MS 100/7-8
PO Box 68 87016 505-384-2003
Theresa Hough, prin. Fax 384-2015

**Eunice, Lea, Pop. 2,893**
Eunice SD 600/PK-12
PO Box 129 88231 575-394-2524
Dwain Haynes, supt. Fax 394-3006
www.eunice.org/
Caton MS 100/6-8
PO Box 129 88231 575-394-3338
Christy Boyd, prin. Fax 394-3661
Eunice HS 200/9-12
PO Box 129 88231 575-394-2332
Gary Frazier, prin. Fax 394-3140

**Farmington, San Juan, Pop. 44,787**
Farmington Municipal SD 10,700/PK-12
PO Box 5850 87499 505-324-9840
Eugene Schmidt, supt. Fax 599-8806
district.fms.k12.nm.us
Farmington HS 1,400/9-12
2200 N Sunset Ave 87401 505-324-0352
Tim Kienitz, prin. Fax 599-8832
Heights MS 700/6-8
3700 College Blvd 87402 505-599-8611
Nathan Pierantoni, prin. Fax 599-8673
Hermosa MS 600/6-8
312 E Apache St 87401 505-599-8612
Mark Harris, prin. Fax 599-8681
Mesa View MS 600/6-8
4451 Wildflower Mesa Dr 87401 505-599-8622
Kim Salazar, prin. Fax 599-8646
Piedra Vista HS 1,300/9-12
5700 College Blvd 87402 505-599-8880
Dave Golden, prin. Fax 599-8891
Rocinante HS 200/Alt
3250 E 30th St 87402 505-599-8627
Bob Rank, prin. Fax 599-8731
Tibbetts MS 500/6-8
3500 Twin Peaks Blvd 87401 505-599-8613
Karen Brown, prin. Fax 599-8675

---

Grace Baptist Academy 100/PK-12
2200 Sullivan Ave 87401 505-325-7802
San Juan College Post-Sec.
4601 College Blvd 87402 505-326-3311

**Floyd, Roosevelt, Pop. 133**
Floyd Municipal SD 200/PK-12
PO Box 65 88118 575-478-2211
Damon Terry, supt. Fax 478-2811
www.floydbroncos.com
Floyd HS 100/9-12
PO Box 65 88118 575-478-2211
Damon Terry, prin. Fax 478-2811
Floyd MS 100/5-8
PO Box 65 88118 575-478-2211
Damon Terry, prin. Fax 478-2811

**Fort Sumner, DeBaca, Pop. 1,008**
Fort Sumner Municipal SD 300/PK-12
PO Box 387 88119 575-355-7734
Freda Daugherty, supt. Fax 355-7716
www.ftsumnerk12.com
Fort Sumner HS 100/9-12
PO Box 387 88119 575-355-2231
Sean Wootton, prin. Fax 355-7663
Fort Sumner MS 100/6-8
PO Box 387 88119 575-355-2231
Sean Wootton, prin. Fax 355-7663

**Gallina, Rio Arriba, Pop. 280**
Jemez Mountain SD 200/K-12
PO Box 230 87017 575-638-5419
Dr. Manuel Medrano, supt. Fax 638-5571
www.jmsk12.com/
Coronado MSHS 100/6-12
PO Box 230 87017 575-638-5549
Donna Manuelito, prin. Fax 638-5571

**Gallup, McKinley, Pop. 21,028**
Gallup-McKinley County SD 12,000/PK-12
PO Box 1318 87305 505-722-1000
Frank Chiapetti, supt. Fax 721-1199
www.gmcs.k12.nm.us
Chief Manuelito MS 600/6-8
1325 Rico St 87301 505-721-5600
Steve Wargo, prin. Fax 721-5699
Gallup Central HS 200/Alt
325 Marguerite St 87301 505-721-2400
John Overheim, prin. Fax 721-2499
Gallup HS 1,100/9-12
1055 Rico St 87301 505-721-2500
Kim Orr, prin. Fax 721-2556
Gallup MS 400/6-8
1001 S Grandview Dr 87301 505-721-2700
Carrie Lovato, prin. Fax 721-2799
Kennedy MS 700/6-8
600 S Boardman Ave 87301 505-721-3100
Roberta Tayah, prin. Fax 721-3199
Miyamura HS 1,100/9-12
680 Boardman Ave 87301 505-721-1900
Jack McFarland, prin. Fax 721-1999
Other Schools – See Crownpoint, Navajo, Pueblo Pintado, Ramah, Thoreau, Tohatchi

---

University of New Mexico - Gallup Post-Sec.
705 Gurley Ave 87301 505-863-7500

**Grady, Curry, Pop. 103**
Grady Municipal SD 100/PK-12
PO Box 71 88120 575-357-2192
Ted Trice, supt. Fax 357-2000
www.gradyschool.com/
Grady HS 50/9-12
PO Box 71 88120 575-357-2192
Alicia Rush, prin. Fax 357-2000
Grady MS 50/6-8
PO Box 71 88120 575-357-2192
Alicia Rush, prin. Fax 357-2000

**Grants, Cibola, Pop. 9,030**
Grants-Cibola County SD 3,600/PK-12
PO Box 8 87020 505-285-2600
Dr. Marc Space, supt. Fax 285-2628
www.gccs.cc/
Grants HS 900/9-12
500 Mountain Rd 87020 505-285-2651
Alton Autrey, prin. Fax 285-2661
Los Alamitos MS 500/7-8
1100 Mount Taylor Ave 87020 505-285-2683
Joan Gilmore, prin. Fax 285-2692
Other Schools – See Casa Blanca

---

New Mexico State University Post-Sec.
1500 N 3rd St 87020 505-287-6678

**Hagerman, Chaves, Pop. 1,250**
Hagerman Municipal SD 400/PK-12
PO Box B 88232 575-752-3254
Ricky Williams, supt. Fax 752-3255
bobcat.net
Hagerman HS 100/9-12
PO Box B 88232 575-752-3283
Mark Lovas, prin. Fax 752-3306
Hagerman MS 100/6-8
PO Box B 88232 575-752-2002
Mark Lovas, prin. Fax 752-0241

**Hatch, Dona Ana, Pop. 1,642**
Hatch Valley SD 1,300/K-12
PO Box 790 87937 575-267-8200
Linda Hale, supt. Fax 267-8202
www.hatchschools.net
Hatch Valley HS 400/9-12
PO Box 790 87937 575-267-8230
Carmen Garcia, prin. Fax 267-8235
Hatch Valley MS 300/6-8
PO Box 790 87937 575-267-8250
Daniel Montoya, prin. Fax 267-8255

**Hobbs, Lea, Pop. 33,769**
Hobbs Municipal SD 8,100/PK-12
PO Box 1030 88241 575-433-0100
T.J. Parks, supt. Fax 433-0142
www.hobbsschools.net
Freshman HS 600/9-9
1401 E Sanger St 88240 575-433-0300
Dawni Nelson, prin. Fax 433-1109
Heizer MS 6-8
101 E Stanolind Rd 88240 575-433-1100
Rene Cantu, prin. Fax 433-1101
Highland MS 700/6-8
2500 N Jefferson St 88240 575-433-1200
Ron Haggerton, prin. Fax 433-1203
Hobbs Alternative Learning Center 100/Alt
PO Box 1030 88241 575-433-0226
Lorna Jackson, prin. Fax 433-0229
Hobbs HS 1,700/10-12
800 N Jefferson St 88240 575-433-0200
Zeke Kaney, prin. Fax 433-0203
Houston MS 600/6-8
300 N Houston St 88240 575-433-1300
Donna Jones, prin. Fax 433-1303

---

New Mexico Junior College Post-Sec.
1 Thunderbird Cir 88240 505-392-4510
University of the Southwest Post-Sec.
6610 N Lovington Hwy 88240 575-392-6561
Veritas Classical Christian Academy K-12
PO Box 2844 88241 575-942-4664
Lori Bova, admin.

**Holloman AFB, Otero, Pop. 2,857**
Alamogordo SD
Supt. — See Alamogordo
Holloman MS 200/6-8
381 1st St 88330 575-812-6200
Maria Showalter, prin. Fax 812-6203

**Hondo, Lincoln**
Hondo Valley SD 200/K-12
PO Box 55 88336 575-653-4411
Andrea Nieto, supt. Fax 653-4414
www.hondoschools.org
Hondo HS 100/7-12
PO Box 55 88336 575-653-4411
Craig Washnok, prin. Fax 653-4414

**House, Quay, Pop. 68**
House Municipal SD 100/K-12
PO Box 673 88121 575-279-7353
Lecil Richards, supt. Fax 279-6201
www.houseschools.net
House JSHS 50/7-12
PO Box 673 88121 575-279-7353
Lecil Richards, prin. Fax 279-6201
Learning Center Alt
PO Box 673 88121 575-279-7322
Lecil Richards, prin. Fax 279-6093

**Jal, Lea, Pop. 2,030**
Jal SD 300/PK-12
PO Box 1386 88252 575-395-2101
Brian Snider, supt. Fax 395-2146
www.jalnm.org
Jal JSHS 100/7-12
PO Box 1386 88252 575-395-2277
Elaine O'Neal, prin. Fax 395-3177

**Jemez Pueblo, Sandoval, Pop. 1,783**
Jemez Valley SD 500/PK-12
8501 Highway 4 87024 575-834-7391
Dr. Susan Wilkinson-Davis, supt. Fax 834-7394
www.jvps.org
Jemez Valley HS 100/9-12
8501 Highway 4 87024 575-834-7392
Scott Meihack, prin. Fax 834-7676
Jemez Valley MS 100/6-8
8501 Highway 4 87024 575-834-3315
Deneen Bair, prin. Fax 834-3311

**Kirtland, San Juan, Pop. 7,619**
Central Consolidated SD 22
Supt. — See Shiprock
Kirtland Central HS 800/9-12
550 Road 6100 87417 505-598-5881
Shawna Becenti, prin. Fax 598-9712
Kirtland MS 500/7-8
538 Road 6100 87417 505-598-6114
Randy Mason, prin. Fax 598-9562

**Lake Arthur, Chaves, Pop. 422**
Lake Arthur Municipal SD 100/PK-12
PO Box 98 88253 575-365-2000
Michael Grossman, supt. Fax 365-2002
www.la-panthers.org/
Lake Arthur HS 50/9-12
PO Box 98 88253 575-365-2000
Dale Ballard, prin. Fax 365-2002
Lake Arthur MS 50/6-8
PO Box 98 88253 575-365-2000
Dale Ballard, prin. Fax 365-2002

**Las Cruces, Dona Ana, Pop. 96,217**
Las Cruces SD 24,900/PK-12
505 S Main St Ste 249 88001 575-527-5800
Stan Rounds, supt. Fax 527-5972
lcps.k12.nm.us
Arrowhead Park Early College HS 9-12
505 S Main St Ste 249 88001 575-527-9540
Jennifer Amis, prin.
Camino Real MS 600/6-8
505 S Main St Ste 249 88001 575-527-6030
Ralph Ramos, prin. Fax 527-6031
Centennial HS 9-12
505 S Main St Ste 249 88001 575-527-9330
Michael Montoya, prin. Fax 527-9331
Las Cruces HS 2,300/9-12
505 S Main St Ste 249 88001 575-527-9400
Jed Hendee, prin. Fax 527-9767
Lynn MS 700/6-8
505 S Main St Ste 249 88001 575-527-9445
Mary Nunez, prin. Fax 527-9454

Mayfield HS 2,200/9-12
505 S Main St Ste 249 88001 575-527-9415
Eric Fraass, prin. Fax 527-9420
Mesa MS 700/6-8
505 S Main St Ste 249 88001 575-527-9510
Gabe Jacquez, prin. Fax 527-9511
Mesilla Valley Alternative MS Alt
505 S Main St Ste 249 88001 575-527-6059
Dennis Padilla, prin.
Onate HS 2,100/9-12
505 S Main St Ste 249 88001 575-527-9430
James Schapekahm, prin. Fax 527-9444
Picacho MS 800/6-8
505 S Main St Ste 249 88001 575-527-9455
Fred Montalvo, prin. Fax 527-9459
Sierra MS 900/6-8
505 S Main St Ste 249 88001 575-527-9640
Maryester Garza, prin. Fax 527-9768
Vista MS 700/6-8
505 S Main St Ste 249 88001 575-527-9465
Wendi Hammond, prin. Fax 527-9470
Zia MS 800/6-8
505 S Main St Ste 249 88001 575-527-9475
Heather Kingery, prin. Fax 527-9479
Other Schools – See Mesilla, White Sands

---

Las Cruces Catholic S 300/PK-12
1331 N Miranda St 88005 575-526-2517
Connie Limon, prin. Fax 524-0544
Mesilla Valley Christian S 400/PK-12
3850 Stern Dr 88001 575-525-8515
Dr. John Foreman, supt. Fax 526-2713
New Mexico State Univ. Dona Ana Branch Post-Sec.
2800 Sonoma Ranch Blvd 88011 575-527-7500
New Mexico State University Post-Sec.
PO Box 30001 88003 575-646-0111
Olympian University of Cosmetology Post-Sec.
1460 Missouri Ave # 5 88001 575-523-7181
Vista College Post-Sec.
850 N Telshor Blvd Ste F 88011 866-442-4197

**Las Vegas, San Miguel, Pop. 13,609**
Las Vegas City SD 1,800/PK-12
901 Douglas Ave 87701 505-454-5700
Dr. Ruben Cordova, supt. Fax 454-5712
cybercardinal.com
Memorial MS 400/6-8
901 Douglas Ave 87701 505-454-5710
Monica Montoya, prin. Fax 454-2753
Robertson HS 500/9-12
901 Douglas Ave 87701 505-454-5770
Mike Yara, prin. Fax 454-2707

West Las Vegas SD 1,500/K-12
179 Bridge St 87701 505-426-2300
Gene Parsons, supt. Fax 426-2318
www.wlvs.k12.nm.us
West Las Vegas HS 500/9-12
179 Bridge St 87701 505-426-2500
John Bustos, prin. Fax 426-2501
West Las Vegas MS 300/6-8
179 Bridge St 87701 505-426-2541
Julianna Trujillo, prin. Fax 426-2542
W Las Vegas Schools Family Partnership 100/Alt
179 Bridge St 87701 505-426-2535
Anna Valdez, prin. Fax 426-2526
Other Schools – See Ribera

---

Luna Community College Post-Sec.
366 Luna Dr 87701 505-454-2500
New Mexico Highlands University Post-Sec.
PO Box 9000 87701 505-425-7511

**La Union, Dona Ana, Pop. 1,103**

---

Calvary West Christian HS 50/9-12
7048 McNutt Rd 88021 575-589-1433
Elizabeth Gonzales, admin.

**Logan, Quay, Pop. 1,034**
Logan Municipal SD 300/PK-12
PO Box 67 88426 575-487-2252
Dennis Roch, supt. Fax 487-9479
www.loganschool.net
Logan HS 100/9-12
PO Box 67 88426 575-487-2252
Craig Terry, prin. Fax 487-9479
Logan MS 100/6-8
PO Box 67 88426 575-487-2252
Craig Terry, prin. Fax 487-9479

**Lordsburg, Hidalgo, Pop. 2,787**
Lordsburg Municipal SD 500/PK-12
PO Box 430 88045 575-542-9361
Randy Piper, supt. Fax 542-9364
www.lmsed.org
Dugan-Tarango MS 100/7-8
1352 Hardin St 88045 575-542-9806
Leo Garcia, prin. Fax 542-9811
Lordsburg HS 200/9-12
501 W 4th St 88045 575-542-3782
Randall Houk, prin. Fax 542-3712

**Los Alamos, Los Alamos, Pop. 11,762**
Los Alamos SD 3,500/PK-12
PO Box 90 87544 505-663-2222
Dr. Kurt Steinhaus, supt. Fax 663-3247
www.laschools.net
Los Alamos HS 1,100/9-12
1300 Diamond Dr 87544 505-663-2510
Deborah Belew-Nyquist, prin. Fax 662-6846
Los Alamos MS 600/7-8
2101 Hawk Dr 87544 505-663-2375
Rex Kilburn, prin. Fax 662-4270

---

University of New Mexico - Los Alamos Post-Sec.
4000 University Dr 87544 505-662-5919

**Los Lunas, Valencia, Pop. 14,610**
Los Lunas SD 8,000/PK-12
PO Box 1300 87031 505-865-9636
Dana Sanders, supt. Fax 865-7766
www.llschools.net
Century Alternative HS 100/Alt
PO Box 1300 87031 505-866-2453
Eliseo Aguirre, prin. Fax 866-8064
Los Lunas HS 1,300/9-12
PO Box 1300 87031 505-865-4646
Dan Padilla, prin. Fax 565-2847
Los Lunas MS 800/7-8
PO Box 1300 87031 505-865-7273
Susana Stanojevic, prin. Fax 865-9742
Valencia HS 1,000/9-12
PO Box 1300 87031 505-565-8755
Darian Jaramillo, prin. Fax 565-8762
Valencia MS 500/7-8
PO Box 1300 87031 505-865-1750
Yvonne Tabet, prin. Fax 866-8921

---

University of New Mexico - Valencia Post-Sec.
280 La Entrada Rd 87031 505-925-8500

**Los Ranchos, Bernalillo**
Albuquerque SD
Supt. — See Albuquerque
Taft MS 500/6-8
620 Schulte Rd NW, 505-344-4389
Steve Scully, prin. Fax 761-8440

**Loving, Eddy, Pop. 1,402**
Loving Municipal SD 600/PK-12
PO Box 98 88256 575-745-2000
Dr. Ann Lynn McIlroy, supt. Fax 745-2002
www.lovingschools.com
Loving HS 200/9-12
PO Box 98 88256 575-745-2020
Lee White, prin. Fax 745-2002
Loving MS 200/6-8
PO Box 98 88256 575-745-2050
Israel Carrera, prin. Fax 745-2052

**Lovington, Lea, Pop. 10,904**
Lovington Municipal SD 3,400/PK-12
18 W Washington Ave 88260 575-739-2200
LeAnne Gandy, supt. Fax 739-2205
www.lovingtonschools.net/
Freshman Academy 200/9-9
701 W Avenue K 88260 575-739-2260
Michael Michaleson, prin. Fax 739-2261
Lovington SHS 500/10-12
701 W Avenue K 88260 575-739-2230
Michael Michaleson, prin. Fax 739-2242
New Hope Alternative HS 100/Alt
601 N 5th St 88260 575-739-2416
John Moore, prin. Fax 739-2417
Taylor MS 500/7-8
700 S 11th St 88260 575-739-2435
Lori Brattain, prin. Fax 739-2438

**Magdalena, Socorro, Pop. 910**
Magdalena Municipal SD 400/PK-12
PO Box 24 87825 575-854-2241
Mike Chambers, supt. Fax 854-2531
www.magdalena.k12.nm.us
Magdalena HS 100/9-12
PO Box 629 87825 575-854-2241
Fax 854-2294
Magdalena MS 100/6-8
PO Box 629 87825 575-854-2241
Fax 854-2294

**Maxwell, Colfax, Pop. 243**
Maxwell Municipal SD 100/PK-12
PO Box 275 87728 575-375-2371
Kristen Forrester, supt. Fax 375-2375
www.maxwellp12.com/
Maxwell HS 50/9-12
PO Box 275 87728 575-375-2371
Pagan Roueche, prin. Fax 375-2375
Maxwell MS 50/7-8
PO Box 275 87728 575-375-2371
Pagan Roueche, prin. Fax 375-2375

**Melrose, Curry, Pop. 637**
Melrose SD 200/PK-12
PO Box 275 88124 575-253-4269
Jamie Widner, supt. Fax 253-4291
www.melroseschools.org
Melrose JSHS 100/7-12
PO Box 275 88124 575-253-4267
Dickie Roybal, prin. Fax 253-4291

**Mesilla, Dona Ana, Pop. 2,164**
Las Cruces SD
Supt. — See Las Cruces
Rio Grande Preparatory HS 100/Alt
2355 Avenida de Mesilla 88046 575-527-6058
Kathryn Davis, prin. Fax 527-9736

**Montezuma, San Miguel**

---

United World College USA 200/11-12
PO Box 248 87731 505-454-4245
Dr. Mukul Kumar, pres. Fax 454-4274

**Mora, Mora, Pop. 656**
Mora ISD 500/K-12
PO Box 179 87732 575-387-3101
Dora Romero, supt. Fax 387-3111
mora.k12.nm.us
Garcia MS 100/6-8
PO Box 687 87732 575-387-3128
Danny Chavez, prin. Fax 387-3126
Mora HS 200/9-12
PO Box 180 87732 575-387-3122
Danny Chavez, prin. Fax 387-3121

**Moriarty, Torrance, Pop. 1,873**
Moriarty-Edgewood SD 2,600/PK-12
PO Box 2000 87035 505-832-4471
Tom Sullivan, supt. Fax 832-4472
www.mesd.us
Moriarty HS 1,000/9-12
PO Box 2000 87035 505-832-4254
Doug Wine, prin. Fax 832-5989
Moriarty MS 200/6-8
PO Box 2000 87035 505-832-6200
Robert Adams, prin. Fax 832-5919
Other Schools – See Edgewood

**Mosquero, Harding, Pop. 93**
Mosquero Municipal SD 50/K-12
PO Box 258 87733 575-673-2271
Bill Ward, supt. Fax 673-2305
www.mosquero.net
Mosquero JSHS 50/7-12
PO Box 258 87733 575-673-2271
Bill Ward, prin. Fax 673-2305

**Mountainair, Torrance, Pop. 908**
Mountainair SD 200/PK-12
PO Box 456 87036 505-847-2333
Ron Hendrix, supt. Fax 847-2843
mps-nm.schoolloop.com
Mountainair HS 100/6-12
PO Box 456 87036 505-847-2211
Eliza Romero, prin. Fax 847-2843

**Navajo, McKinley, Pop. 1,626**
Gallup-McKinley County SD
Supt. — See Gallup
Navajo MS 100/6-8
PO Box 1287 87328 505-777-2390
Mary Ann Sherman, prin. Fax 721-5399
Navajo Pine HS 100/9-12
PO Box 1286 87328 505-777-2288
Mary Ann Sherman, prin. Fax 721-3699

**Newcomb, San Juan, Pop. 335**
Central Consolidated SD 22
Supt. — See Shiprock
Newcomb HS 200/9-12
PO Box 7927 87455 505-696-3417
Tamara Allison, prin. Fax 696-3265
Newcomb MS 200/6-8
PO Box 7927 87455 505-696-3434
Dr. J. Kaibah Begay, prin. Fax 696-3430

**Ojo Caliente, Taos**
Mesa Vista Consolidated SD 400/PK-12
PO Box 309 87549 575-583-2645
Ernesto Valdez, supt. Fax 583-2815
www.mesavista.org
Mesa Vista MSHS 100/7-12
PO Box 50 87549 575-583-2275
Gina Terrazas, prin. Fax 583-9133

**Pecos, San Miguel, Pop. 1,378**
Pecos ISD 600/PK-12
PO Box 368 87552 505-757-4700
Fred Trujillo, supt. Fax 757-8721
www.pecos.k12.nm.us
Pecos HS 200/9-12
PO Box 368 87552 505-757-4720
Claire Lazar, prin. Fax 757-2772
Pecos MS 100/6-8
PO Box 368 87552 505-757-4620
Claire Lazar, prin. Fax 757-2561

**Penasco, Taos, Pop. 584**
Penasco ISD 400/K-12
PO Box 520 87553 575-587-2502
Darlene Ulibarri, supt. Fax 587-2513
phs-pisd-nm.schoolloop.com
Penasco HS 100/9-12
PO Box 520 87553 575-587-2502
Marvin MacAuley, prin. Fax 587-9908
Penasco MS 100/7-8
PO Box 520 87553 575-587-2502
Marvin MacAuley, prin. Fax 587-9910

**Portales, Roosevelt, Pop. 12,080**
Portales Municipal SD 2,800/PK-12
501 S Abilene Ave 88130 575-356-7000
Johnnie S. Cain, supt. Fax 356-4377
www.portalesschools.com
Portales HS 800/9-12
201 S Knoxville St 88130 575-356-7015
Melvin Nusser, prin. Fax 356-8082
Portales JHS 500/7-8
700 E 3rd St 88130 575-356-7045
Steve Harris, prin. Fax 359-0826

---

Eastern New Mexico University Post-Sec.
1500 S Avenue K 88130 575-562-1011

**Pueblo Pintado, McKinley, Pop. 187**
Gallup-McKinley County SD
Supt. — See Gallup
Tse' Yi Gai HS 100/9-12
118 Counselor Rd 87013 505-721-5500
Brian Staples, prin. Fax 721-5599

**Quemado, Catron, Pop. 224**
Quemado ISD 100/K-12
PO Box 128 87829 575-773-4700
David Lackey, supt. Fax 773-4717
www.quemadoschools.org
Quemado JSHS 100/7-12
PO Box 128 87829 575-773-4700
Don Goodman, prin. Fax 773-4717

**Questa, Taos, Pop. 1,751**
Questa ISD 400/PK-12
PO Box 440 87556 575-586-0421
Valerie Trujillo, supt. Fax 586-0531
www.qisd-nm.schoolloop.com

Questa JSHS 100/7-12
PO Box 529 87556 575-586-1604
Hector Cavazos, prin. Fax 586-2282

**Ramah, McKinley, Pop. 354**
Gallup-McKinley County SD
Supt. — See Gallup
Ramah MSHS 200/6-12
PO Box 849 87321 505-783-4211
Rick Hall, prin. Fax 721-3699

**Ranchos de Taos, Taos, Pop. 2,481**

---

University of New Mexico - Taos Post-Sec.
1157 County Road 110 87557 575-737-6200

**Raton, Colfax, Pop. 6,809**
Raton SD 1,300/PK-12
1550 Tiger Cir 87740 575-445-9111
Dr. M. Neil Trerhune, supt. Fax 445-5641
www.ratonschools.org
Raton HS 400/7-12
1535 Tiger Cir 87740 575-445-3541
Duncan Ware, prin. Fax 445-2237

**Rehoboth, McKinley**

---

Rehoboth Christian S 400/PK-12
PO Box 41 87322 505-863-4412
Dr. Franklin Freeland, supt. Fax 863-2185

**Reserve, Catron, Pop. 285**
Reserve ISD 200/K-12
PO Box 350 87830 575-533-6242
Bill Green, supt. Fax 533-6900
www.reserveschools.com
Reserve JSHS 100/7-12
PO Box 350 87830 575-533-6242
Cindy Shellhorn, prin. Fax 533-6900

**Ribera, San Miguel, Pop. 415**
West Las Vegas SD
Supt. — See Las Vegas
Valley MS 50/6-8
PO Box 519 87560 505-426-2581
Cathy Lucero, prin. Fax 426-2582

**Rio Rancho, Sandoval, Pop. 85,293**
Rio Rancho SD 16,900/PK-12
500 Laser Rd NE 87124 505-896-0667
Dr. V. Sue Cleveland, supt. Fax 896-0662
www.rrps.net
Cleveland HS 2,200/9-12
4800 Laban Rd NE, 505-938-0300
Scott Affentranger, prin. Fax 338-3474
Eagle Ridge MS 900/6-8
800 Fruta Rd NE 87124 505-892-6630
Sarah Poutsch, prin. Fax 892-6909
Independence HS 200/Alt
421 Quantum Rd NE 87124 505-338-4658
Myra Roosevelt, prin. Fax 892-9742
Lincoln MS 1,000/6-8
2287 Lema Rd SE 87124 505-892-1100
Debby Morrell, prin. Fax 892-9728
Mountain View MS 900/6-8
4101 Montreal Loop NE, 505-867-0711
Julie Arnold, prin. Fax 867-7901
Rio Rancho HS 2,400/9-12
301 Loma Colorado Blvd NE 87124 505-896-5600
Richard Von Ancken, prin. Fax 896-5901
Rio Rancho MS 1,200/6-8
1600 Loma Colorado Blvd NE, 505-891-5335
Lynda Kitts, prin. Fax 896-6761

**Roswell, Chaves, Pop. 47,742**
Roswell ISD 10,100/PK-12
PO Box 1437 88202 575-627-2500
Tom Burrris, supt. Fax 627-2512
www.risd.k12.nm.us
Berrendo MS 700/6-8
800 Marion Richards Rd 88201 575-627-2775
Susan Martin, prin. Fax 625-8248
Goddard HS 1,100/9-12
701 E Country Club Rd 88201 575-627-4800
Brian Luck, prin. Fax 627-4856
Mesa MS 400/6-8
1601 E Bland St 88203 575-627-2800
Jennifer Cole, prin. Fax 625-8263
Mountain View MS 500/6-8
312 E Mountain View Rd 88203 575-627-2825
Glenda Leonard, prin. Fax 625-8260
Roswell HS 1,300/9-12
500 W Hobbs St 88203 575-637-3200
Ruben Bolanos, prin. Fax 637-3268
Sierra MS 600/6-8
615 S Sycamore Ave 88203 575-627-2850
Kevin Summers, prin. Fax 625-8283
University HS 200/Alt
25 W Martin St 88203 575-627-2750
Porter Cutrell, prin. Fax 625-8278

---

Aladdin Beauty College Post-Sec.
108 S Union Ave 88203 575-623-6331
Eastern New Mexico University Post-Sec.
PO Box 6000 88202 575-624-7000
Gateway Christian S 300/PK-12
PO Box 1642 88202 575-622-9710
Rick Rapp, admin. Fax 622-9739
New Mexico Military Institute Post-Sec.
101 W College Blvd 88201 575-622-6250
New Mexico Military Institute 400/9-12
101 W College Blvd 88201 575-624-8001
Dr. Jerry Grizzle Ph.D., pres. Fax 624-8025
Valley Christian Academy 200/PK-12
1500 S Main St 88203 575-627-1500

**Roy, Harding, Pop. 234**
Roy Municipal SD 50/PK-12
PO Box 430 87743 575-485-2242
Nino Esquibel, supt. Fax 485-2497
www.royschools.org
Roy JSHS 50/7-12
PO Box 430 87743 575-485-2242
Fax 485-2497

**Ruidoso, Lincoln, Pop. 7,928**
Ruidoso Municipal SD 2,100/PK-12
200 Horton Cir 88345 575-257-4051
Dr. George Bickert, supt. Fax 257-4150
www.ruidososchools.org/
Ruidoso HS 600/9-12
200 Horton Cir 88345 575-258-4910
Pauline Staski, prin. Fax 258-3516
Ruidoso MS 500/6-8
200 Horton Cir 88345 575-630-7800
Anna Addis, prin. Fax 258-5809

**San Jon, Quay, Pop. 209**
San Jon Municipal SD 100/PK-12
PO Box 5 88434 575-576-2466
Colin Taylor, supt. Fax 576-2772
www.sanjonschools.com/
San Jon HS 50/9-12
PO Box 5 88434 575-576-2466
Fax 576-2772
San Jon MS 50/6-8
PO Box 5 88434 575-576-2466
Fax 576-2772

**Santa Fe, Santa Fe, Pop. 66,849**

Pojoaque Valley SD 1,900/PK-12
1574 State Road 502 87506 505-455-2282
Dr. Melville Morgan, supt. Fax 455-7152
pvs.k12.nm.us/
Pojoaque Valley HS 700/9-12
1574 State Road 502 87506 505-455-2234
Jennifer Baca, prin. Fax 455-3471
Pojoaque Valley MS 300/7-8
1574 State Road 502 87506 505-455-2238
Vera Trujillo, prin. Fax 455-3392

Santa Fe SD 13,400/PK-12
610 Alta Vista St 87505 505-467-2000
Dr. Joel Boyd, supt. Fax 995-3300
www.sfps.info
Academy at Larragoite 100/Alt
1604 Agua Fria St 87505 505-467-1900
Dr. Cynthia Sanchez, prin. Fax 995-3394
Capital HS 1,100/9-12
4851 Paseo Del Sol 87507 505-467-1000
Channell Wilson-Segura, prin. Fax 995-3311
Capshaw MS 500/7-8
351 W Zia Rd 87505 505-467-4300
Laura Jeffery, prin. Fax 989-5439
De Vargas MS 500/7-8
1720 Llano St 87505 505-467-3300
Marc Ducharme, prin. Fax 995-3307
Mandela International Magnet S 50/7-8
1720 Llano St 87505 505-467-2000
Tony Gerlicz, prin.
Ortiz MS 800/6-8
4164 S Meadows Rd 87507 505-467-2300
Steve Baca, prin. Fax 989-5597
Santa Fe HS 1,500/9-12
2100 Yucca St 87505 505-467-2400
Mary Massey, prin. Fax 467-2992

---

Adventist Academy of Santa Fe K-10
PO Box 28327 87592 505-954-1845
Desert Academy 200/6-12
7300 Old Santa Fe Trl 87505 505-992-8284
Terry Passalacqua, hdmstr. Fax 992-8270
Institute of American Indian Arts Post-Sec.
83 Avan NU PO 87508 505-424-2300
New Mexico School for the Deaf Post-Sec.
1060 Cerrillos Rd 87505 505-827-6739
St. John's College Post-Sec.
1160 Camino De Cruz Blanca 87505 505-984-6000
St. Michael's HS 700/7-12
100 Siringo Rd 87505 505-983-7353
Sam Govea, prin. Fax 982-8722
Santa Fe Community College Post-Sec.
6401 S Richards Ave 87508 505-428-1000
Santa Fe Preparatory S 300/7-12
1101 Camino De Cruz Blanca 87505 505-982-1829
James Leonard, hdmstr. Fax 982-2897
Santa Fe University of Art and Design Post-Sec.
1600 Saint Michaels Dr 87505 505-473-6011
Sante Fe Waldorf S 200/PK-12
26 Puesta Del Sol 87508 505-983-9727
Southwest Acupuncture College Post-Sec.
1622 Galisteo St 87505 505-438-8884
Southwestern College Post-Sec.
3960 San Felipe Rd 87507 505-471-5756

**Santa Rosa, Guadalupe, Pop. 2,827**
Santa Rosa Consolidated SD 600/PK-12
344 S 4th St 88435 575-472-3171
Richard Perea, supt. Fax 472-5609
www.srlions.com
Santa Rosa HS 200/9-12
717 S 3rd St 88435 575-472-3422
Martin Madrid, prin. Fax 472-3169
Santa Rosa MS 100/6-8
116 Camino de Vida 88435 575-472-3633
Lee Vega, prin. Fax 472-0663
Other Schools – See Anton Chico

**Santa Teresa, Dona Ana, Pop. 4,240**
Gadsden ISD
Supt. — See Sunland Park
Santa Teresa HS 1,300/9-12
100 Airport Rd 88008 575-589-5300
Nicholas Wohlgemuth, prin. Fax 589-5311
Santa Teresa MS 700/7-8
4800 McNutt Rd 88008 575-874-7200
Rosa Lovelace, prin. Fax 589-2780

---

Anamarc College Post-Sec.
2660 Airport Rd 88008 575-589-3158

**Shiprock, San Juan, Pop. 8,162**
Central Consolidated SD 22 6,400/PK-12
PO Box 1199 87420 505-368-4984
Donald Levinski, supt. Fax 368-5232
www.ccsdnm.org
Career Prep HS 100/Alt
PO Box 3514 87420 505-368-4980
Stacie Gallaher, prin. Fax 368-5703
Shiprock HS 600/9-12
PO Box 3578 87420 505-368-5161
Rick Edwards, prin. Fax 368-5796
Tse' Bit'ai MS 500/6-8
PO Box 1703 87420 505-368-4741
Max Perez, prin. Fax 368-5105
Other Schools – See Kirtland, Newcomb

**Silver City, Grant, Pop. 10,166**
Silver Consolidated SD 3,000/PK-12
2810 N Swan St 88061 575-956-2000
Lon Streib, supt. Fax 956-2039
www.silverschools.org
La Plata MS 700/6-8
3500 N Silver St 88061 575-956-2060
Wayne Mendonca, prin. Fax 956-2098
Opportunity HS 100/Alt
600 E 32nd St 88061 575-956-2140
Jason Ping, prin. Fax 956-2149
Silver HS 700/9-12
3200 N Silver St 88061 575-956-2158
Beth Lougee, prin. Fax 388-2927
Other Schools – See Cliff

---

Western New Mexico University Post-Sec.
PO Box 680 88062 575-538-6011

**Socorro, Socorro, Pop. 8,907**
Socorro Consolidated SD 1,900/K-12
700 Franklin St 87801 575-835-0300
Dr. Randall Earwood, supt. Fax 835-1682
www.socorro.k12.nm.us/
Sarracino MS 400/6-8
1425 El Camino Real St 87801 575-835-0283
Manual Molina, prin. Fax 835-0360
Socorro HS 500/9-12
1200 Michigan St 87801 575-835-0700
Susan Comiskey, admin. Fax 835-0704

---

New Mexico Institute Mining & Technology Post-Sec.
801 Leroy Pl 87801 575-835-5434

**Springer, Colfax, Pop. 1,037**
Springer Municipal SD 100/K-12
PO Box 308 87747 575-483-3432
Eddie King, supt. Fax 483-2387
www.springerschools.org
Springer HS 100/7-12
PO Box 308 87747 575-483-3464
Sherie Montoya, prin. Fax 483-3970

**Sunland Park, Dona Ana, Pop. 14,071**
Gadsden ISD 14,100/PK-12
4950 McNutt Rd 88063 575-882-6200
Efren Yturralde, supt. Fax 882-6229
www.gisd.k12.nm.us
Other Schools – See Anthony, Chaparral, Santa Teresa

---

International School Post-Sec.
PO Box 1919 88063 800-743-1414

**Taos, Taos, Pop. 5,592**
Taos Municipal SD 2,500/PK-12
310 Camino De La Placita 87571 575-758-5200
Dr. Lillian Torrez, supt. Fax 758-5298
www.taosschools.org/
Taos HS 700/9-12
134 Cervantes St 87571 575-751-8000
Robert Trujillo, prin. Fax 751-8001
Taos MS 500/6-8
235 Paseo Del Canon E 87571 575-737-6000
Alfred Cordova, prin. Fax 737-6001

---

National College of Midwifery Post-Sec.
209 State Road 240 87571 575-758-8914

**Tatum, Lea, Pop. 793**
Tatum Municipal SD 300/PK-12
PO Box 685 88267 575-398-4455
Buddy Little, supt. Fax 398-8220
www.tatumschools.org/
Tatum JSHS 100/7-12
PO Box 685 88267 575-398-4555
Greg Slover, prin. Fax 398-4450

**Texico, Curry, Pop. 1,118**
Texico Municipal SD 500/PK-12
PO Box 237 88135 575-482-3801
Robert Brown, supt. Fax 482-3650
www.texicoschools.com
Texico HS 200/9-12
PO Box 237 88135 575-482-3305
Dee Rae Timberlake, prin. Fax 482-3650
Texico MS 100/6-8
PO Box 237 88135 575-482-9520
Beth Thornton, prin. Fax 482-3650

**Thoreau, McKinley, Pop. 1,831**
Gallup-McKinley County SD
Supt. — See Gallup

Thoreau HS 400/9-12
PO Box 969 87323 505-721-4500
Dominic Romero, prin. Fax 721-4599
Thoreau MS 200/6-8
PO Box 787 87323 505-721-4600
Moni Short, prin. Fax 721-4699

**Tierra Amarilla, Rio Arriba, Pop. 379**
Chama Valley ISD 300/PK-12
PO Box 10 87575 575-588-7285
Anthony Casados, supt. Fax 588-7860
www.chamaschools.org
Escalante MSHS 100/7-12
PO Box 157 87575 575-588-7201
Gilbert Martinez, prin. Fax 588-7911

**Tijeras, Bernalillo, Pop. 534**
Albuquerque SD
Supt. — See Albuquerque
Roosevelt MS 400/6-8
11799 S Highway 14 87059 505-281-3316
Cee Kay Nation, prin. Fax 281-5120

**Tohatchi, McKinley, Pop. 799**
Gallup-McKinley County SD
Supt. — See Gallup
Tohatchi HS 300/9-12
PO Box 248 87325 505-733-2206
Craig Robinson, prin. Fax 721-4899
Tohatchi MS 200/6-8
PO Box 322 87325 505-721-4900
Anthony Morrison, prin. Fax 721-4999

**Truth or Consequences, Sierra, Pop. 6,359**
Truth or Consequences Municipal SD 1,400/PK-12
180 N Date St 87901 575-894-8150
Dr. Craig Cummins, supt. Fax 894-7532
www.torcschools.net
Hot Springs HS 400/9-12
180 N Date St 87901 575-894-8350
Patti Nesbitt, prin. Fax 894-0471
Truth or Consequences MS 300/6-8
180 N Date St 87901 575-894-8380
Dr. Renee Garcia, prin. Fax 894-0606

---

AppleTree Education Center 100/PK-12
1300 S Broadway St 87901 575-894-5646

**Tucumcari, Quay, Pop. 5,279**
Tucumcari SD 1,100/PK-12
700 W Amarosa 88401 575-461-3910
Aaron McKinney, supt. Fax 461-3554
tucumcarischools.com
Tucumcari HS 300/9-12
1001 S 7th St 88401 575-461-3830
Nicole Lesley, prin. Fax 461-3769
Tucumcari MS 200/6-8
909 S 5th St 88401 575-461-2310
Roberta Segura, prin. Fax 461-8610

---

Mesalands Community College Post-Sec.
911 S 10th St 88401 575-461-4413

**Tularosa, Otero, Pop. 2,782**
Tularosa Municipal SD 900/K-12
504 1st St 88352 575-585-8800
Brenda Vigil, supt. Fax 585-4439
www.tularosa.k12.nm.us
Tularosa HS 300/9-12
504 1st St 88352 575-585-8866
John J. Marrujo, prin. Fax 585-8112
Tularosa MS 100/7-8
504 1st St 88352 575-585-8803
Bobbie Grace, prin. Fax 585-4739

**Vaughn, Guadalupe, Pop. 444**
Vaughn Municipal SD 100/PK-12
PO Box 489 88353 575-584-2283
Dr. Elliott McDaniel, supt. Fax 584-2355
www.vaughn.k12.nm.us/
Vaughn JSHS 100/7-12
PO Box 489 88353 575-584-2283
Elliott McDaniel, prin. Fax 584-2355

**Wagon Mound, Mora, Pop. 312**
Wagon Mound SD 100/K-12
PO Box 158 87752 575-666-3000
Albert Martinez, supt. Fax 666-9001
www.wm.k12.nm.us
Wagon Mound JSHS 50/7-12
PO Box 158 87752 575-666-3001
Albert Martinez, supt. Fax 666-9001

**White Sands, Dona Ana, Pop. 1,564**
Las Cruces SD
Supt. — See Las Cruces
White Sands MS 100/6-8
1 Viking Dr 88002 575-674-1241
Tom Bulger, prin. Fax 674-1515

**Zuni, McKinley, Pop. 5,857**
Zuni SD 1,300/PK-12
PO Box A 87327 505-782-5511
Hayes A. Lewis, supt. Fax 782-5505
www.zpsd.org
Twin Buttes HS 100/9-12
PO Box 680 87327 505-782-4446
Florence Acque, prin. Fax 782-4944
Zuni HS 300/9-12
PO Box 550 87327 505-782-4451
Terri Sebastian, prin. Fax 782-5551
Zuni MS 200/6-8
PO Box E 87327 505-782-5561
Ophelia Barber, prin. Fax 782-5563

# NEW YORK

## NEW YORK EDUCATION DEPARTMENT

**89 Washington Ave, Albany 12234**
**Telephone 518-474-3852**
**Fax 518-473-4909**
**Website http://www.nysed.gov**

Commissioner of Education John King

## NEW YORK BOARD OF REGENTS

**89 Washington Ave, Albany 12234-1000**

Chancellor Merryl Tisch

## BOARDS OF COOPERATIVE EDUCATIONAL SERVICES (BOCES)

Broome-Deleware-Tioga BOCES
Allen Buyck, supt. 607-766-3802
435 Glenwood Rd Fax 763-3691
Binghamton 13905
www.btboces.org/

Capital Region BOCES
Dr. Charles Dedrick, supt. 518-862-4900
900 Watervliet Shaker Rd Fax 862-4903
Albany 12205
www.capregboces.org

Cattaraugus/Allegany/Erie/Wyoming BOCES
Lynda Quick, supt. 585-376-8246
1825 Windfall Rd, Olean 14760 Fax 376-8452
www.caboces.org

Cayuga/Onondaga BOCES
William Speck, supt. 315-253-0361
1879 W Genesee Street Rd Fax 252-6493
Auburn 13021
cayboces.org

Champlain Valley Educational Services
Dr. Mark Davey, supt. 518-561-0100
PO Box 455, Plattsburgh 12901 Fax 562-1471
www.cves.org/

Ctr for Instruction Technology & Innovtn
Christopher Todd, supt. 315-963-4222
179 County Route 64 Fax 963-4475
Mexico 13114
www.oswegoboces.org

Delaware/Chenango/Madison/Otsego BOCES
Bill Tammaro, supt. 607-335-1233
6678 County Road 32 Fax 334-9848
Norwich 13815
www.dcmoboces.com

Dutchess BOCES
Dr. John Pennoyer, supt. 845-486-4800
5 Boces Rd, Poughkeepsie 12601 Fax 486-4981
www.dcboces.org

Eastern Suffolk BOCES
Dean Lucera, supt. 631-687-3006
201 S Service Rd Fax 289-2529
Patchogue 11772
www.esboces.org

Erie 1 BOCES
Lynda Quick, supt., 355 Harlem Rd 716-821-7001
West Seneca 14224 Fax 821-7242
www.erie1boces.org

Erie 2-Chautauqua-Cattaraugus BOCES
Dr. David O'Rourke, supt. 716-549-4454
8685 Erie Rd, Angola 14006 Fax 549-5181
www.e2ccb.org

Franklin-Essex-Hamilton BOCES
Stephen Shafer, supt. 518-483-6420
PO Box 28, Malone 12953 Fax 483-2178
www.fehb.org/

Genesee Valley BOCES
Kevin MacDonald, supt. 585-658-7900
80 Munson St, Le Roy 14482 Fax 344-7910
www.gvboces.org

Greater Southern Tier BOCES
Kevin MacDonald, supt. 607-654-2283
9579 Vocational Dr Fax 654-2302
Painted Post 14870
www.gstboces.org

Hamilton-Fulton-Montgomery BOCES
Dr. Patrick Michel, supt. 518-736-4300
2755 State Highway 67 Fax 736-4301
Johnstown 12095
www.hfmboces.org

Herkimer-Fulton-Hamilton-Otsego BOCES
Mark Vivacqua, supt. 315-867-2023
352 Gros Blvd, Herkimer 13350 Fax 867-2002
www.herkimer-boces.org

Jefferson-Lewis-Hmltn-Hrkmr-Oneida BOCES
Stephen Todd, supt. 315-779-7010
20104 State Route 3 Fax 779-7009
Watertown 13601
www.boces.com

Madison-Oneida BOCES
Jacklin Starks, supt. 315-361-5510
PO Box 168, Verona 13478 Fax 361-5517
www.moboces.org

Monroe 1 BOCES
Daniel White, supt. 585-383-2200
41 OConnor Rd, Fairport 14450 Fax 383-6404
www.monroe.edu/

Monroe 2 BOCES
JoAnne Antonacci, supt. 585-352-2400
3599 Big Ridge Rd Fax 352-2442
Spencerport 14559
www.monroe2boces.org

Nassau BOCES
Dr. James Langlois, supt. 516-396-2200
PO Box 9195, Garden City 11530 Fax 997-8742
www.nassauboces.org

Oneida-Herkimer-Madison BOCES
Howard Mettelman, supt. 315-793-8561
PO Box 70, New Hartford 13413 Fax 793-8541
www.oneida-boces.org/

Onondaga-Cortland-Madison BOCES
Jody Manning, supt. 315-433-2602
PO Box 4754, Syracuse 13221 Fax 434-9347
www.ocmboces.org

Orange-Ulster BOCES
William Hecht, supt. 845-291-0100
53 Gibson Rd, Goshen 10924 Fax 291-0118
www.ouboces.org/

Orleans-Niagara BOCES
Dr. Clark Godshall, supt. 800-836-7510
4232 Shelby Basin Rd Fax 798-1317
Medina 14103
www.onboces.org

Otsego-Northern Catskills BOCES
Nicholas Savin, supt. 607-588-6291
PO Box 382, Stamford 12167 Fax 588-6098
www.oncboces.org

Putnam Northern Westchester BOCES
Dr. James Langlois, supt. 914-248-2300
200 BOCES Dr Fax 248-2308
Yorktown Heights 10598
www.pnwboces.org

Questar III BOCES
Dr. James Baldwin, supt. 518-477-8771
10 Empire State Blvd Fax 477-9833
Castleton on Hudson 12033
www.questar.org

Rockland BOCES
Dr. Mary Marsico, supt. 845-627-4701
65 Parrott Rd, West Nyack 10994 Fax 624-1764
www.rocklandboces.org/

St. Lawrence-Lewis BOCES
Thomas Burns, supt. 315-386-4504
PO Box 231, Canton 13617 Fax 386-2099
www.sllboces.org

Southern Westchester BOCES
Dr. Harold Coles, supt. 914-937-3820
17 Berkley Dr, Rye Brook 10573 Fax 937-7850
www.swboces.org

Sullivan County BOCES
Lawrence Thomas, supt. 845-295-4000
6 Wierk Ave, Liberty 12754 Fax 292-8694
www.scboces.org

Tompkins-Seneca-Tioga BOCES
Dr. Jeffrey Matteson, supt. 607-257-1551
555 Warren Rd, Ithaca 14850 Fax 257-2825
www.tstboces.org/

Ulster BOCES
Dr. Charles Khoury, supt. 845-255-3040
175 State Route 32 N Fax 255-7942
New Paltz 12561
www.ulsterboces.org/

Washington-Srtg-Warren-Hmltn-Essex BOCES
James Dexter, supt. 518-746-3310
1153 Burgoyne Ave Ste 2 Fax 746-3319
Fort Edward 12828
wswheboces.org

Wayne-Finger Lakes BOCES
Scott Bischoping, supt. 315-332-7284
131 Drumlin Ct, Newark 14513 Fax 332-7425
www.wflboces.org

Western Suffolk BOCES
Maureen Donahue-Whitney, admin. 631-549-4900
507 Deer Park Rd, Dix Hills 11746 Fax 623-4996
www.wsboces.org/

## PUBLIC, PRIVATE AND CATHOLIC SECONDARY SCHOOLS

**Accord, Ulster, Pop. 551**
Rondout Valley Central SD 1,500/K-12
PO Box 9 12404 845-687-2400
Rosario Agostaro, supt. Fax 687-9577
www.rondout.k12.ny.us
Rondout Valley HS 700/9-12
PO Box 9 12404 845-687-2400
Robert Cook, prin. Fax 687-7665
Rondout Valley JHS 300/7-8
PO Box 9 12404 845-687-2400
Charles Tadduni, prin. Fax 687-8980

**Adams, Jefferson, Pop. 1,752**
South Jefferson Central SD
Supt. — See Adams Center
Clarke MS 500/6-8
11060 US Route 11 13605 315-232-4531
Tom O'Brien, prin. Fax 232-4620
South Jefferson HS 600/9-12
11060 US Route 11 13605 315-232-4531
Karen Denny, prin. Fax 232-3728

**Adams Center, Jefferson, Pop. 1,533**
South Jefferson Central SD 1,900/K-12
13180 US Route 11 13606 315-583-6104
Mary Beth Denny, supt. Fax 583-6381
www.spartanpride.org
Other Schools – See Adams

**Addison, Steuben, Pop. 1,744**
Addison Central SD 1,100/PK-12
7 Cleveland Dr 14801 607-359-2244
Joseph DioGuardi, supt. Fax 359-2246
www.addisoncsd.org/
Addison MSHS 400/8-12
1 Colwell St 14801 607-359-2241
Jennifer Crane, prin. Fax 359-3443

**Afton, Chenango, Pop. 818**
Afton Central SD 500/K-12
PO Box 5 13730 607-639-8229
Elizabeth Briggs, supt. Fax 639-1801
www.aftoncsd.org

Afton JSHS 300/6-12
PO Box 5 13730 607-639-8223
David Glover, prin. Fax 639-8257

**Airmont, Rockland, Pop. 8,483**

---

Mesifta Beth Shraga S 100/9-12
28 N Saddle River Rd, 845-356-1980
Monsey Beis Chaya Mushka 100/9-12
27 S Monsey Rd, 845-634-7400
Rabbinical College Beth Shraga Post-Sec.
28 N Saddle River Rd, 845-356-1980
Toras Chaim 50/9-12
1 Regina Rd, 845-352-9126

**Akron, Erie, Pop. 2,833**
Akron Central SD 1,500/K-12
47 Bloomingdale Ave 14001 716-542-5010
Kevin Shanley, supt. Fax 542-5018
www.akronschools.org

Akron HS 500/9-12
47 Bloomingdale Ave 14001 716-542-5030
Joseph Lucenti, prin. Fax 542-5018

Akron MS 400/6-8
47 Bloomingdale Ave 14001 716-542-5040
Joseph Caprio, prin. Fax 542-5018

**Albany, Albany, Pop. 94,773**

CSD of Albany 8,300/PK-12
1 Academy Park 12207 518-475-6000
M. Vanden Wyngaard Ph.D., supt. Fax 475-6009
www.albanyschools.org

Abrookin Career & Tech Center Vo/Tech
99 Kent St 12206 518-475-6400
Fax 475-6402

Albany HS 2,200/9-12
700 Washington Ave 12203 518-475-6200
Dale Getto, prin. Fax 475-6202

Alternative Learning Center Alt
50 Lark St 12210 518-475-6525
Sophia Newell, prin. Fax 475-6527

Hackett MS 600/6-8
45 Delaware Ave 12202 518-475-6475
Michael Paolino, prin. Fax 475-6477

Myers MS 700/6-8
100 Elbel Ct 12209 518-475-6425
Kimberly Wilkins Ed.D., prin. Fax 475-6427

West Hill MS 6-8
395 Elk St 12206 518-475-6900
Kandie Antonetti, prin. Fax 475-6902

South Colonie Central SD 5,200/PK-12
102 Loralee Dr 12205 518-869-3576
Jonathan Buhner, supt. Fax 869-6517
www.southcolonieschools.org

Colonie Central HS 1,700/9-12
1 Raider Blvd 12205 518-459-1220
Christopher Robilotti, prin. Fax 459-8524

Lisha Kill MS 700/5-8
68 Waterman Ave 12205 518-456-2306
David Wetzel, prin. Fax 452-8165

Sand Creek MS 800/5-8
329 Sand Creek Rd 12205 518-459-1333
Thomas Nicholson, prin. Fax 459-1404

---

Academy of the Holy Names 300/6-12
1075 New Scotland Rd 12208 518-438-7895
Mary Ann Vigliante, prin. Fax 438-7368

Albany Academies 500/PK-12
135 Academy Rd 12208 518-429-2300
Dr. Douglas North Ph.D., head sch Fax 427-7016

Albany Academy for Girls 400/PK-12
140 Academy Rd 12208 518-429-2300
Dr. Douglas North Ph.D., head sch Fax 463-5096

Albany College of Pharmacy & Health Sci Post-Sec.
106 New Scotland Ave 12208 888-203-8010

Albany Law School Post-Sec.
80 New Scotland Ave 12208 518-445-2311

Albany Medical College Post-Sec.
47 New Scotland Ave Code 3 12208 518-262-5521

Bishop Maginn HS 100/9-12
75 Park Ave 12202 518-463-2247
Christopher Signor, prin. Fax 463-9880

Branford Hall Career Institute Post-Sec.
500 New Karner Rd 12205 518-456-4464

Bryant & Stratton College Post-Sec.
1259 Central Ave 12205 518-437-1802

Center for Natural Wellness School Post-Sec.
3 Cerone Commercial Dr 12205 518-489-4026

Christian Brothers Academy 400/6-12
12 Airline Dr 12205 518-452-9809
James Schlegel, prin. Fax 452-9804

College of Saint Rose Post-Sec.
432 Western Ave 12203 800-637-8556

Excelsior College Post-Sec.
7 Columbia Cir 12203 518-464-8500

ITT Technical Institute Post-Sec.
13 Airline Dr 12205 518-452-9300

Maimonides Hebrew Day S 100/PK-12
404 Partridge St 12208 518-453-9363

Maria College of Albany Post-Sec.
700 New Scotland Ave 12208 518-438-3111

Memorial Hospital School of Nursing Post-Sec.
600 Northern Blvd 12204 518-471-3260

Mildred Elley School Post-Sec.
855 Central Ave 12206 518-786-0855

Orlo School of Hair Design & Cosmetology Post-Sec.
232 N Allen St 12206 518-459-7832

SUNY at Albany Post-Sec.
1400 Washington Ave 12222 518-442-3300

The New School of Radio & Television Post-Sec.
7 Harriman Campus Rd 12206 518-438-7682

**Albertson, Nassau, Pop. 5,037**

Herricks UFD
Supt. — See New Hyde Park

Herricks MS 1,000/6-8
7 Hilldale Dr 11507 516-305-8600
Joan Keegan, prin. Fax 248-3281

**Albion, Orleans, Pop. 5,876**

Albion Central SD 2,100/PK-12
324 East Ave 14411 585-589-2056
Michael Bonnewell, supt. Fax 589-2059
www.albionk12.org/

Bergerson MS, 254 East Ave 14411 500/6-8
Daniel Monacelli, prin. 585-589-2020

D'Amico HS, 302 East Ave 14411 700/9-12
Leslie Stauss, prin. 585-589-2040

**Alden, Erie, Pop. 2,590**

Alden Central SD 1,700/K-12
13190 Park St 14004 716-937-9116
Adam Stoltman, supt. Fax 937-7132
www.aldenschools.org

Alden HS 600/9-12
13190 Park St 14004 716-937-9116
Kevin Ryan, prin. Fax 937-1740

Alden MS 700/4-8
13250 Park St 14004 716-937-9116
Steven Smith, prin. Fax 937-3563

**Alexander, Genesee, Pop. 501**

Alexander Central SD 900/PK-12
3314 Buffalo St 14005 585-591-1551
Kathleen Maerten, supt. Fax 591-2257
www.alexandercsd.org

Alexander MSHS 500/6-12
3314 Buffalo St 14005 585-591-1551
Shannon Whitcombe, prin. Fax 591-1098

**Alexandria Bay, Jefferson, Pop. 1,066**

Alexandria Central SD 600/PK-12
34 Bolton Ave 13607 315-482-9971
Kyle Faulkner, supt. Fax 482-9973
www.alexandriacentral.org

Alexandria Central JSHS 300/7-12
34 Bolton Ave 13607 315-482-5113
Julie Ludwig, prin. Fax 482-9973

**Alfred, Allegany, Pop. 4,085**

---

Alfred State College Post-Sec.
10 Upper College Dr 14802 800-425-3733

Alfred University Post-Sec.
1 Saxon Dr 14802 607-871-2111

**Allegany, Cattaraugus, Pop. 1,807**

Allegany-Limestone Central SD 1,200/PK-12
3131 Five Mile Rd 14706 716-375-6600
Dr. Karen Geelan, supt. Fax 375-6629
alcsny.org

Allegany-Limestone HS 400/9-12
3131 Five Mile Rd 14706 716-375-6600
Dean Mesi, prin. Fax 375-6630

Allegany-Limestone MS 300/6-8
3131 Five Mile Rd 14706 716-375-6600
Cory Pecorella, prin. Fax 375-6630

**Almond, Allegany, Pop. 460**

Alfred-Almond Central SD 600/PK-12
6795 State Route 21 14804 607-276-6500
Richard Calkins, supt. Fax 276-6556
www.aacs.wnyric.org

Alfred-Almond JSHS 300/7-12
6795 State Route 21 14804 607-276-6555
Susan Bain-Lucey, prin. Fax 276-6556

**Amenia, Dutchess, Pop. 935**

Webutuck Central SD 800/PK-12
PO Box 405 12501 845-373-4100
James Gratto, supt. Fax 373-4102
www.webutuckschools.org/

Brooks IS 300/4-8
PO Box 405 12501 845-373-4114
Jennifer Chason, prin. Fax 373-4126

Webutuck HS 200/9-12
PO Box 405 12501 845-373-4106
Ken Sauer, prin. Fax 373-8529

---

Kildonan S 100/1-12
425 Morse Hill Rd 12501 845-373-8111
Kevin Pendergast, hdmstr. Fax 373-9793

**Amherst, Erie, Pop. 45,800**

Amherst Central SD 2,900/K-12
55 Kings Hwy 14226 716-362-3000
Dr. Laura Chabe, supt. Fax 362-3022
amherstschools.org

Amherst Central HS 800/9-12
4301 Main St 14226 716-362-8100
Gregory Pigeon, prin. Fax 836-4972

Amherst MS 700/6-8
55 Kings Hwy 14226 716-362-7100
John Griesmer, prin. Fax 836-0193

Sweet Home Central SD 3,400/PK-12
1901 Sweet Home Rd 14228 716-250-1402
Anthony Day, supt. Fax 250-1374
www.sweethomeschools.org

Sweet Home HS 1,200/9-12
1901 Sweet Home Rd 14228 716-250-1200
Joleen Reinholz, prin. Fax 250-1362

Sweet Home MS 800/6-8
4150 Maple Rd 14226 716-250-1450
Marty Pizur, prin. Fax 250-1490

---

Daemen College Post-Sec.
4380 Main St 14226 716-839-8225

**Amityville, Suffolk, Pop. 9,408**

Amityville UFD, 150 Park Ave 11701 3,000/PK-12
Dr. Mary Kelly, supt. 631-565-6019
www.amityvilleufsd.org/

Amityville Memorial HS 700/10-12
250 Merrick Rd 11701 631-565-6100
Dr. Mary DeRose, prin.

Miles MS, 501 Route 110 11701 700/7-9
Edward Plaia, prin. 631-565-6200

---

Bethesda SDA Junior Academy 50/PK-10
76 Parkway Ave 11701 631-842-3321

Branford Hall Career Institute Post-Sec.
1100 Broadway 11701 631-608-9113

Island Drafting & Technical Institute Post-Sec.
128 Broadway 11701 631-691-8733

**Amsterdam, Montgomery, Pop. 18,256**

Broadalbin-Perth Central SD
Supt. — See Broadalbin

Broadalbin-Perth MS 400/6-8
1870 County Highway 107 12010 518-954-2700
Wayne Bell, prin. Fax 954-2709

Greater Amsterdam SD 3,500/PK-12
PO Box 309 12010 518-843-3180
Thomas Perillo, supt. Fax 842-0012
www.gasd.org

Amsterdam HS 1,100/9-12
140 Saratoga Ave 12010 518-843-4932
Fax 843-5432

Lynch Literacy Academy 800/6-8
55 Brandt Pl 12010 518-843-3716
Fred Hutchinson, prin. Fax 843-6287

**Andes, Delaware, Pop. 250**

Andes Central SD 100/PK-12
PO Box 248 13731 845-676-3167
Dr. Robert Chakar, supt. Fax 676-3181
www.andescentralschool.org

Andes Central S 100/PK-12
PO Box 248 13731 845-676-3166
Dr. Robert Chakar, supt. Fax 676-3181

**Andover, Allegany, Pop. 1,032**

Andover Central SD 300/PK-12
PO Box G 14806 607-478-8491
Lawrence Spangenburg, supt. Fax 478-8833
www.andovercsd.org/

Andover S 300/PK-12
PO Box G 14806 607-478-8491
Jon Morris, prin. Fax 478-8833

**Angola, Erie, Pop. 2,096**

Lake Shore Central SD 2,600/K-12
959 Beach Rd 14006 716-549-2300
James E. Przepasniak, supt. Fax 549-6407
www.lakeshorecsd.org

Lake Shore MS 700/6-8
8855 Erie Rd 14006 716-926-2400
Erich Reidell, prin. Fax 549-4374

Lake Shore SHS 900/9-12
959 Beach Rd 14006 716-926-2301
JulieAnn Hoerner, prin. Fax 549-4033

**Annandale on Hudson, Dutchess**

---

Bard College Post-Sec.
PO Box 5000 12504 845-758-6822

**Ardsley, Westchester, Pop. 4,379**

Ardsley UFD 2,000/K-12
500 Farm Rd 10502 914-295-5500
Dr. Lauren Allan, supt. Fax 295-5976
www.ardsleyschools.org

Ardsley HS 700/9-12
300 Farm Rd 10502 914-295-5800
Rudy Arietta, prin. Fax 295-5977

Ardsley MS 600/5-8
700 Ashford Ave 10502 914-295-5600
Dr. Jo Anne Januzzi, prin. Fax 295-5677

**Argyle, Washington, Pop. 303**

Argyle Central SD 600/K-12
5023 State Route 40 12809 518-638-8243
Jan Jehring, supt. Fax 638-6373
www.argylecsd.org

Argyle Central JSHS 300/7-12
5023 State Route 40 12809 518-638-8243
Susan Passaro, prin. Fax 638-6373

**Arkport, Steuben, Pop. 839**

Arkport Central SD 500/K-12
35 East Ave 14807 607-295-7471
Dr. Glenn Niles, supt. Fax 295-7473
www.arkportcsd.org

Arkport Central S 500/K-12
35 East Ave 14807 607-295-7471
Caitlin Dewey, prin. Fax 295-7473

**Armonk, Westchester, Pop. 4,278**

Byram Hills Central SD 2,600/K-12
10 Tripp Ln 10504 914-273-4082
Dr. William Donohue, supt. Fax 273-2516
www.byramhills.org

Byram Hills HS 900/9-12
12 Tripp Ln Ste 1 10504 914-273-9200
Christopher Borsari, prin. Fax 273-2067

Crittenden MS 700/6-8
10 MacDonald Ave 10504 914-273-4250
Dr. H. Evan Powderly, prin. Fax 273-4618

**Astoria, See New York**

NYC Department of Education
Supt. — See New York

Academy for New Americans 200/6-8
3014 30th St 11102 718-932-5876
Betty Cartagena, prin. Fax 932-5990

IS 10 900/6-8
4511 31st Ave 11103 718-278-7054
Clemente Lopes, prin. Fax 274-1578

Baccalaureate S for Global Education 400/7-12
3412 36th Ave 11106 718-361-5275
Kelly Johnson, prin. Fax 361-5395

Long Island City HS 3,300/9-12
1430 Broadway 11106 718-545-7095
Vivian Selenikas, prin. Fax 545-2980

Sinatra HS 800/9-12
3512 35th Ave 11106 718-361-9920
Donna Finn, prin. Fax 361-9995

---

Empire Beauty School Post-Sec.
3815 Broadway 11103 718-726-8383

St. Demetrios Greek American S 400/4-12
3003 30th Dr 11102 718-728-1754

St. John's Prep HS 800/9-12
2121 Crescent St 11105 718-721-7200
William Higgins, prin. Fax 545-9385

**Athol Springs, Erie**

---

St. Francis HS 500/9-12
4129 Lake Shore Rd 14010 716-627-1200
Thomas Braunscheidel, prin. Fax 627-4610

**Attica, Wyoming, Pop. 2,513**
Attica Central SD 1,500/K-12
3338 E Main Street Rd 14011 585-591-0400
Bryce Thompson, supt. Fax 591-2681
www.atticacsd.org
Attica HS 500/9-12
3338 E Main Street Rd 14011 585-591-0400
Josh Andsley, prin. Fax 591-4484
Attica MS 500/5-8
3338 E Main Street Rd 14011 585-591-0400
Paul Clark, prin. Fax 591-4496

**Auburn, Cayuga, Pop. 26,874**
Auburn CSD 4,200/K-12
78 Thornton Ave 13021 315-255-8800
Jeffrey Pirozzolo, supt. Fax 255-8855
district.auburn.cnyric.org
Auburn HS 1,300/9-12
250 Lake Ave 13021 315-255-8300
Brian Morgan, prin. Fax 255-8357
Auburn JHS 700/7-8
191 Franklin St 13021 315-255-8480
David Oliver, prin. Fax 255-8495

---

Cayuga Community College Post-Sec.
197 Franklin St 13021 315-255-1743

**Aurora, Cayuga, Pop. 708**
Southern Cayuga Central SD 300/PK-12
2384 State Route 34B 13026 315-364-7211
Patrick Jensen, supt. Fax 364-7863
www.southerncayuga.org
Southern Cayuga JSHS 200/7-12
2384 State Route 34B 13026 315-364-7111
Luke Carnicelli, prin. Fax 364-8207

---

Wells College Post-Sec.
170 Main St 13026 315-364-3264

**Averill Park, Rensselaer, Pop. 1,668**
Averill Park Central SD 3,200/K-12
146 Gettle Rd Ste 1 12018 518-674-7050
Dr. James D. Hoffman, supt. Fax 674-3802
www.averillpark.k12.ny.us/
Algonquin MS 800/6-8
333 NY Highway 351 12018 518-674-7100
Robert Messia, prin. Fax 674-0671
Averill Park HS 1,100/9-12
146 Gettle Rd 12018 518-674-7000
Michelle Tsao, prin. Fax 674-7046

**Avoca, Steuben, Pop. 933**
Avoca Central SD 500/K-12
PO Box G 14809 607-566-2221
Richard Yochem, supt. Fax 566-2398
www.avocacsd.org/
Avoca Central S 500/K-12
PO Box G 14809 607-566-2221
Matthew Pfleegor, prin. Fax 566-8384

**Avon, Livingston, Pop. 3,354**
Avon Central SD 1,000/K-12
191 Clinton St 14414 585-226-2455
Bruce Amey, supt. Fax 226-8202
www.avoncsd.org
Avon HS 300/9-12
245 Clinton St 14414 585-226-2455
Barbara Zelazny, prin. Fax 226-8202
Avon MS 300/5-8
191 Clinton St 14414 585-226-2455
Jennifer Miller, prin. Fax 226-8202

**Babylon, Suffolk, Pop. 11,970**
Babylon UFD 1,700/K-12
50 Railroad Ave 11702 631-893-7925
Linda J. Rozzi, supt. Fax 893-7935
www.babylonschools.org
Babylon JSHS 800/7-12
50 Railroad Ave 11702 631-893-7910
Al Cirone, prin. Fax 893-7936

**Bainbridge, Chenango, Pop. 1,346**
Bainbridge-Guilford Central SD 800/PK-12
18 Juliand St 13733 607-967-6321
Dr. Don Wheeler, supt. Fax 967-4231
www.bgcsd.org
Bainbridge-Guilford HS 400/7-12
18 Juliand St 13733 607-967-6323
William Zakrajsek, prin. Fax 967-4231

**Baldwin, Nassau, Pop. 23,329**
Baldwin UFD 4,700/K-12
960 Hastings St 11510 516-377-9271
Dr. Shari Camhi, supt. Fax 377-9421
www.baldwinschools.org/
Baldwin HS 1,700/9-12
841 Ethel T Kloberg Dr 11510 516-377-9204
Susan Knors, prin. Fax 377-9208
Baldwin MS 1,200/6-8
3211 Schreiber Pl 11510 516-377-9321
Timothy Maher, prin. Fax 377-9432

**Baldwinsville, Onondaga, Pop. 7,290**
Baldwinsville Central SD 5,700/K-12
29 E Oneida St 13027 315-638-6043
Dr. David S. Hamilton, supt. Fax 638-6041
www.bville.org
Baker HS 1,400/10-12
29 E Oneida St 13027 315-638-6008
Robert Edwards, prin. Fax 638-6150
Durgee JHS 900/8-9
29 E Oneida St 13027 315-638-6086
Bonnie VanBenschoten, prin. Fax 638-6168

---

Baldwinsville Christian Academy 100/PK-12
7312 Van Buren Rd 13027 315-638-1069
Ric Auwarter, admin. Fax 638-4207

**Ballston Spa, Saratoga, Pop. 5,283**
Ballston Spa Central SD 4,200/K-12
70 Malta Ave 12020 518-884-7195
Joseph Dragone Ph.D., supt. Fax 884-7101
www.bscsd.org
Ballston Spa HS 1,300/9-12
220 Ballston Ave 12020 518-884-7150
Kristi Jensen, prin. Fax 884-7199
Ballston Spa MS 1,000/6-8
210 Ballston Ave 12020 518-884-7200
Pamela Motler, prin. Fax 884-7234

---

John Pauls Hair Nails & Skin Care Inst Post-Sec.
2144 Saratoga Ave 12020 518-583-3700

**Bardonia, Rockland, Pop. 4,047**

---

Albertus Magnus HS 500/9-12
798 Route 304 10954 845-623-8842
Joseph Troy, pres. Fax 623-0009

**Barker, Niagara, Pop. 527**
Barker Central SD 900/PK-12
1628 Quaker Rd 14012 716-795-3832
Dr. Roger Klatt, supt. Fax 795-3394
barkercsd.net
Barker JSHS 500/7-12
1628 Quaker Rd 14012 716-795-3201
Bradley Pritchard, prin. Fax 795-3911

**Barrytown, Dutchess**

---

Unification Theological Seminary Post-Sec.
30 Seminary Dr 12507 845-752-3000

**Batavia, Genesee, Pop. 15,019**
Batavia CSD 1,600/PK-12
260 State St 14020 585-343-2480
Christopher J. Dailey, supt. Fax 344-8204
www.bataviacsd.org
Batavia HS 700/9-12
260 State St 14020 585-343-2480
Scott Wilson, prin. Fax 344-8609
Batavia MS 500/5-8
96 Ross St 14020 585-343-2480
Sandra Griffin, prin. Fax 344-8626

---

Continental School of Beauty Culture Post-Sec.
215 Main St 14020 585-344-0886
Genesee Community College Post-Sec.
1 College Rd 14020 585-343-0055
New York State School for the Blind Post-Sec.
2A Richmond Ave 14020
Notre Dame HS 200/9-12
73 Union St 14020 585-343-2783
Wade Bianco, prin. Fax 343-7323

**Bath, Steuben, Pop. 5,678**
Bath Central SD 1,600/PK-12
25 Ellas Ave 14810 607-776-3301
Joseph L. Rumsey, supt. Fax 776-5021
www.bathcsd.org
Haverling HS 500/9-12
25 Ellas Ave 14810 607-776-4107
Randy Brzezinski, prin. Fax 776-5021
Lyon MS 500/4-8
25 Ellas Ave 14810 607-776-2170
Michael Siebert, prin. Fax 776-1470

**Bayport, Suffolk, Pop. 8,813**
Bayport-Blue Point UFD 2,500/K-12
189 Academy St 11705 631-472-7860
Vincent Butera Ed.D., supt. Fax 472-7873
www.bbpschools.org/
Bayport-Blue Point HS 800/9-12
200 Snedecor Ave 11705 631-472-7800
Dr. Gaurav Passi, prin. Fax 472-7814
Young MS 600/6-8
602 Sylvan Ave 11705 631-472-7820
Nichole Cush, prin. Fax 472-7849

**Bay Shore, Suffolk, Pop. 25,685**
Bay Shore UFD 5,800/K-12
75 Perkal St 11706 631-968-1100
Dr. Karen Salmon, supt. Fax 968-4131
www.bayshoreschools.org
Bay Shore HS 1,900/9-12
155 3rd Ave 11706 631-968-1157
Robert Pashkin, prin. Fax 968-2332
Bay Shore MS 1,400/6-8
393 Brook Ave 11706 631-968-1210
Dr. LaQuita Outlaw, prin. Fax 968-2342

Brentwood UFD
Supt. — See Brentwood
West MS 800/6-8
2030 Udall Rd 11706 631-434-2371
Felicia Thomas-Williams, prin. Fax 242-3992

**Bayside, See New York**
NYC Department of Education
Supt. — See New York
Bayside HS 3,300/9-12
3224 Corporal Kennedy St 11361 718-229-7600
Michael Athy, prin. Fax 423-9566
MS 158 1,100/6-8
4635 Oceania St 11361 718-423-8100
Marie Nappi, prin. Fax 423-8135
Bell Academy 300/6-8
1825 212th St 11360 718-428-0587
David Abbott, prin. Fax 428-0237

---

CUNY Queensborough Community College Post-Sec.
22205 56th Ave, Oakland Gardens NY 11364
718-631-6262

**Beacon, Dutchess, Pop. 15,060**
Beacon CSD 3,300/PK-12
10 Education Dr 12508 845-838-6900
Dr. Barbara Walkley, supt. Fax 838-6905
www.beaconcityk12.org
Beacon HS 1,000/9-12
101 Matteawan Rd 12508 845-838-6900
Dr. Joannes Sieverding, prin. Fax 838-0796
Rombout MS 700/6-8
84 Matteawan Rd 12508 845-838-6900
Brian Soltish, prin. Fax 231-0474

**Beaver Falls, Lewis**
Beaver River Central SD 900/K-12
9508 Artz Rd 13305 315-346-1211
Leueen Smithling, supt. Fax 346-6775
www.brcsd.org
Beaver River HS 300/9-12
9508 Artz Rd 13305 315-346-1211
Rebecca Dunckel-King, prin. Fax 346-6775
Beaver River MS 200/6-8
9508 Artz Rd 13305 315-346-1211
Christine LaBare, prin. Fax 346-6775

**Bedford, Westchester, Pop. 1,810**
Bedford Central SD 4,300/K-12
632 S Bedford Rd 10506 914-241-6000
John Chambers, supt. Fax 241-6004
www.bcsdny.org
Fox Lane HS 1,300/9-12
PO Box 390 10506 914-241-6085
Dr. Joel Adelberg, prin. Fax 241-6064
Other Schools – See Mount Kisco

---

Rippowam Cisqua S 200/5-9
PO Box 488 10506 914-244-1250
Colm MacMahon, hdmstr. Fax 244-1245

**Bedford Hills, Westchester, Pop. 2,942**

---

Yeshiva & Mesivta Ohel Shmuel 50/11-12
165 Haines Rd Stop 1 10507 914-241-2700

**Belfast, Allegany, Pop. 823**
Belfast Central SD 400/PK-12
1 King St 14711 585-365-9940
Judy May, supt. Fax 365-2648
www.belfast.wnyric.org
Belfast Central S 400/PK-12
1 King St 14711 585-365-8285
Michael Roche, prin. Fax 365-2648

**Belle Harbor, Queens**

---

Mercaz Hatorah of Belle Harbor 100/9-12
505 Beach 129th St, 718-474-3064

**Bellerose, Queens, Pop. 1,168**
NYC Department of Education
Supt. — See New York
HS of Teaching Liberal Arts & Science 1,200/9-12
7420 Commonwealth Blvd 11426 718-736-7100
Jae Hyun-Cho, dir. Fax 736-7117

**Belleville, Jefferson, Pop. 225**
Belleville Henderson Central SD 500/PK-12
PO Box 158 13611 315-846-5826
Rick Moore, supt. Fax 846-5617
www.bhpanthers.org
Belleville Henderson Central S 500/PK-12
PO Box 158 13611 315-846-5121
Scott Storey, prin. Fax 846-5617

**Bellmore, Nassau, Pop. 16,044**
Bellmore-Merrick Central HSD
Supt. — See North Merrick
Grand Avenue MS 900/7-8
2301 Grand Ave 11710 516-992-1100
Carlo Conte, prin. Fax 679-5068
Kennedy HS 1,300/9-12
3000 Bellmore Ave 11710 516-992-1400
Lorraine Poppe, prin. Fax 826-0526
Mepham HS 1,400/9-12
2401 Camp Ave 11710 516-992-1500
Michael Harrington, prin. Fax 785-7590

**Bellport, Suffolk, Pop. 2,050**
South Country Central SD
Supt. — See East Patchogue
Bellport MS 1,000/6-8
35 Kreamer St 11713 631-730-1657
Travis Davey, prin. Fax 286-4460

**Belmont, Allegany, Pop. 950**
Genesee Valley Central SD 600/PK-12
1 Jaguar Dr 14813 585-268-7900
Dr. Brian Schmitt, supt. Fax 268-7990
www.genvalley.org
Genesee Valley HS 200/7-12
1 Jaguar Dr 14813 585-268-7900
Brian LeBaron, prin. Fax 268-7990

**Bemus Point, Chautauqua, Pop. 360**
Bemus Point Central SD 800/PK-12
PO Box 468 14712 716-386-2375
Michael Mansfield, supt. Fax 386-2376
www.bemusptcsd.org
Maple Grove JSHS 400/6-12
PO Box 468 14712 716-386-2855
Julie Verdonik, prin. Fax 386-2376

**Bergen, Genesee, Pop. 1,158**
Byron-Bergen Central SD 800/PK-12
6917 W Bergen Rd 14416 585-494-1220
Casey Kosiorek, supt. Fax 494-2613
www.bbschools.org/
Byron-Bergen JSHS 400/7-12
6917 W Bergen Rd 14416 585-494-1220
Dr. Aaron Johnson, prin. Fax 494-2613

**Berne, Albany**
Berne-Knox-Westerlo Central SD 800/K-12
1738 Helderberg Trl 12023 518-872-1293
Dr. Timothy Mundell, supt. Fax 872-2031
www.bkwschools.org
Berne-Knox-Westerlo JSHS 400/7-12
1738 Helderberg Trl 12023 518-872-1482
Marna McMorris, prin. Fax 872-2083

**Bethpage, Nassau, Pop. 16,246**
Bethpage UFD 3,000/K-12
10 Cherry Ave 11714 516-644-4000
Terrence Clark, supt. Fax 931-8783
www.bethpagecommunity.com/Schools/
Bethpage HS 1,000/9-12
10 Cherry Ave 11714 516-644-4100
Michael Spence, prin. Fax 937-6076
Kennedy MS 700/6-8
500 Broadway 11714 516-644-4200
Kevin Fullerton, prin. Fax 937-0540

Plainedge UFD
Supt. — See North Massapequa
Plainedge MS 800/6-8
200 Stewart Ave 11714 516-992-7650
Anthony DeRiso, prin. Fax 992-7645

Briarcliffe College Post-Sec.
1055 Stewart Ave 11714 516-918-3600

**Binghamton, Broome, Pop. 45,574**
Binghamton CSD 5,200/PK-12
PO Box 2126 13902 607-762-8100
Dr. Marion H. Martinez, supt. Fax 762-8112
www.binghamtonschools.org
Binghamton HS 1,600/9-12
31 Main St 13905 607-762-8200
Roxie Oberg, prin. Fax 762-6072
East MS 600/6-8
167 E Frederick St 13904 607-762-8300
Lori Czeitner, prin. Fax 762-8398
West MS 700/6-8
W Middle Ave 13905 607-763-8400
Michael Holly, prin. Fax 763-8429

Chenango Forks Central SD 1,600/PK-12
1 Gordon Dr 13901 607-648-7543
Lloyd Peck, supt. Fax 648-7560
www.cforks.org
Chenango Forks HS 500/9-12
1 Gordon Dr 13901 607-648-7544
John Hillis, prin. Fax 648-7568
Chenango Forks MS 400/6-8
1 Gordon Dr 13901 607-648-7576
Lorraine Pourby, prin. Fax 648-2767

Chenango Valley Central SD 1,800/PK-12
221 Chenango Bridge Rd 13901 607-762-6800
David Gill, supt. Fax 762-6890
www.cvcsd.stier.org/
Chenango Valley HS 500/9-12
221 Chenango Bridge Rd 13901 607-762-6900
Terrence Heller, prin. Fax 779-4777
Chenango Valley MS 300/7-8
221 Chenango Bridge Rd 13901 607-762-6902
Eric Attleson, prin. Fax 779-4784

Binghamton University SUNY Post-Sec.
4400 Vestal Pkwy 13902 607-777-2000
Broome Community College Post-Sec.
PO Box 1017 13902 607-778-5000
Ridley-Lowell Business & Technical Inst. Post-Sec.
116 Front St 13905 607-724-2941
Seton Catholic Central HS 400/7-12
70 Seminary Ave 13905 607-723-5307
Fax 723-4601

**Blauvelt, Rockland, Pop. 5,591**
South Orangetown Central SD 3,400/K-12
160 Van Wyck Rd 10913 845-680-1050
Harry LeFevre, supt. Fax 680-1900
www.socsd.org
South Orangetown MS 800/6-8
160 Van Wyck Rd 10913 845-680-1100
Karen Tesik, prin. Fax 680-1905
Other Schools – See Orangeburg

**Bloomfield, Ontario, Pop. 1,335**
Bloomfield Central SD 1,000/PK-12
45 Maple Ave Ste A 14469 585-657-6121
Michael Midey, supt. Fax 657-6060
www.bloomfieldcsd.org
Bloomfield HS 300/9-12
1 Oakmount Ave 14469 585-657-6121
Nancy Gerstner, prin. Fax 657-4771
Bloomfield MS 200/6-8
1 Oakmount Ave 14469 585-657-6121
Nancy Gerstner, prin. Fax 657-4771

**Bohemia, Suffolk, Pop. 10,114**
Connetquot Central SD 6,500/K-12
780 Ocean Ave 11716 631-244-2215
Lynda Adams, supt. Fax 589-0683
www.ccsdli.org
Connetquot HS 2,100/9-12
190 7th St 11716 631-244-2226
Gregory Murtha, prin. Fax 244-2287
Other Schools – See Oakdale, Ronkonkoma

Branford Hall Career Institute Post-Sec.
565 Johnson Ave 11716 631-471-9100

**Boiceville, Ulster**
Onteora Central SD 1,400/K-12
PO Box 300 12412 845-657-6383
Dr. Phyllis McGill, supt. Fax 657-8742
onteora.schoolwires.com/
Onteora HS 500/9-12
PO Box 300 12412 845-657-2373
Lance Edelman, prin. Fax 657-8430
Onteora MS 200/7-8
PO Box 300 12412 845-657-2373
Jennifer O'Connor, prin. Fax 657-7763

**Bolivar, Allegany, Pop. 1,040**
Bolivar-Richburg Central SD 900/PK-12
100 School St 14715 585-928-2561
John Marshall, supt. Fax 928-2411
www.brcs.wnyric.org
Bolivar-Richburg JSHS 400/6-12
100 School St 14715 585-928-2561
Christopher Parker, prin. Fax 928-1368

**Bolton Landing, Warren, Pop. 501**
Bolton Central SD 200/PK-12
PO Box 120 12814 518-644-2400
Michael Graney, supt. Fax 644-2124
www.boltoncsd.org
Bolton Central S 200/PK-12
PO Box 120 12814 518-644-2400
Michele French, prin. Fax 644-2124

**Boonville, Oneida, Pop. 2,065**
Adirondack Central SD 1,300/PK-12
110 Ford St 13309 315-942-9200
Edward Niznik, supt. Fax 942-5522
www.adirondackcsd.org
Adirondack HS 400/9-12
8181 State Route 294 13309 315-942-9250
Heidi Smith, prin. Fax 942-9254
Adirondack MS 300/6-8
8181 State Route 294 13309 315-942-9202
Mark Trabucco, prin. Fax 942-9211

**Bradford, Schuyler**
Bradford Central SD 300/PK-12
2820 State Route 226 14815 607-583-4616
Fax 583-4013
www.bradfordcsd.org
Bradford Central S 300/PK-12
2820 State Route 226 14815 607-583-4616
Mary Ordway, prin. Fax 583-4013

**Brasher Falls, Saint Lawrence, Pop. 656**
Brasher Falls Central SD 1,000/PK-12
PO Box 307 13613 315-389-5131
Robert Stewart, supt. Fax 389-5245
bfcsd.org
St. Lawrence Central HS 300/9-12
PO Box 307 13613 315-389-5131
Tracy Davison, prin. Fax 389-5245
St. Lawrence Central MS 300/5-8
PO Box 307 13613 315-389-5131
Christoper Rose, prin. Fax 389-4185

**Breesport, Chemung, Pop. 625**

Twin Tiers Christian Academy 100/7-12
PO Box K 14816 607-739-3619
Cary Shaw, admin. Fax 739-3619

**Brentwood, Suffolk, Pop. 59,660**
Brentwood UFD 16,900/PK-12
52 3rd Ave 11717 631-434-2323
Joseph Bond, supt. Fax 273-6575
www.bufsd.org/
Brentwood Freshman Center 1,100/9-9
33 Leahy Ave 11717 631-434-2541
Jerry Cheng, prin. Fax 434-2549
Brentwood SHS 3,800/10-12
2 6th Ave 11717 631-434-2204
Richard Loeschner, prin. Fax 434-2206
East MS 1,000/6-8
70 Hilltop Dr 11717 631-434-2473
John Callan, prin. Fax 434-2171
North MS 1,000/6-8
350 Wicks Rd 11717 631-434-2356
Matthew Gengler, prin. Fax 952-9249
South MS 900/6-8
785 Candlewood Rd 11717 631-434-2341
Bergre Escobores Ed.D., prin. Fax 434-2560
Other Schools – See Bay Shore

Long Island University Post-Sec.
100 2nd Ave 11717 631-273-5112
Suffolk County Community College Grant Post-Sec.
1001 Crooked Hill Rd 11717 631-851-6700

**Brewster, Putnam, Pop. 2,362**
Brewster Central SD 2,800/K-12
30 Farm To Market Rd 10509 845-279-8000
Dr. Timothy Conway, supt. Fax 279-3510
www.brewsterschools.org
Brewster HS 1,200/9-12
50 Foggintown Rd 10509 845-279-5051
Dr. Joseph Castagnola, prin. Fax 279-6730
Wells MS 800/6-8
570 Route 312 10509 845-279-3702
Michelle Gosh, prin. Fax 279-7634

**Briarcliff Manor, Westchester, Pop. 7,748**
Briarcliff Manor UFD 1,600/K-12
45 Ingham Rd 10510 914-941-8880
James Kaishian, supt. Fax 941-2177
www.briarcliffschools.org
Briarcliff Manor HS 600/9-12
444 Pleasantville Rd 10510 914-769-6299
Debora French, prin. Fax 769-2509
Briarcliff MS 400/6-8
444 Pleasantville Rd 10510 914-769-6343
Susan Howard, prin. Fax 769-6375

**Bridgehampton, Suffolk, Pop. 1,736**
Bridgehampton UFD 200/PK-12
PO Box 3021 11932 631-537-0271
Dr. Lois Favre, supt. Fax 537-9038
www.bridgehampton.k12.ny.us/
Bridgehampton S 200/PK-12
PO Box 3021 11932 631-537-0271
Dr. Lois Favre, prin. Fax 537-0443

**Broadalbin, Fulton, Pop. 1,305**
Broadalbin-Perth Central SD 1,800/PK-12
20 Pine St 12025 518-954-2500
Stephen Tomlinson, supt. Fax 954-2509
www.bpcsd.org
Broadalbin-Perth HS 600/9-12
100 Bridge St 12025 518-954-2600
Margaret Blowers, prin. Fax 954-2609
Other Schools – See Amsterdam

**Brockport, Monroe, Pop. 8,227**
Brockport Central SD 3,700/K-12
40 Allen St 14420 585-637-1810
Lesli Myers Ed.D., supt. Fax 637-0165
www.bcs1.org
Brockport HS 1,300/9-12
40 Allen St 14420 585-637-1877
Dana Boshnack, prin. Fax 637-1867
Oliver MS 900/6-8
40 Allen St 14420 585-637-1860
Melody Martinez-Davis, prin. Fax 637-1869

SUNY College at Brockport Post-Sec.
350 New Campus Dr 14420 585-395-2211

**Brocton, Chautauqua, Pop. 1,467**
Brocton Central SD 600/K-12
138 W Main St 14716 716-792-9121
John Hertlein, supt. Fax 792-9965
www.broctoncsd.org
Brocton MSHS 300/6-12
138 W Main St 14716 716-792-2190
Jason Delcamp, prin. Fax 792-2246

**Bronx, See New York**
NYC Department of Education
Supt. — See New York
Academy for Language and Technology 300/9-12
1700 Macombs Rd 10453 718-731-0219
Jose Vinales, prin. Fax 731-2031
Academy for Personal Leadership 300/6-8
120 E 184th St 10468 718-220-3139
Angelo Ledda, prin. Fax 220-6018
Academy of Applied Math & Technology 300/6-8
345 Brook Ave 10454 718-292-3883
Vincent Gassetto, prin. Fax 292-4473
Academy of Public Relations 300/6-8
778 Forest Ave 10456 718-665-8866
Amy Andino, prin. Fax 401-0051
Acad for Scholarship & Entrepreneurship 600/6-12
921 E 228th St 10466 718-696-3840
Zenobia White, prin. Fax 696-3841
Accion Academy 200/6-8
1825 Prospect Ave 10457 718-294-0514
Nikole Booker, prin. Fax 294-3869
Addams Academic Careers HS Vo/Tech
900 Tinton Ave 10456 718-292-4513
Joel DiBartolomeo, prin. Fax 292-1947
Archimedes Academy 500/6-12
456 White Plains Rd 10473 718-617-5046
Miriam Lazar, prin. Fax 617-7395
Astor Collegiate Academy 500/9-12
925 Astor Ave 10469 718-944-3418
Sandra Burgos, prin. Fax 944-3638
Baychester MS 100/6-8
3750 Baychester Ave 10466 718-547-1890
Shawn Mangar, prin. Fax 547-1895
Belmont Preparatory HS 400/9-12
500 E Fordham Rd 10458 718-733-4559
Stephen Gumbs, prin. Fax 295-3655
Blueprint MS 100/6-8
1111 Pugsley Ave 10472 718-822-2780
Tyneka Harrington, prin. Fax 822-2279
Bronck Academy 300/6-8
400 E Fordham Rd 10458 718-365-2502
Brenda Gonzalez, prin. Fax 365-3892
Bronx Academy for Software Engineering 100/9-10
2474 Crotona Ave 10458 718-733-6024
Benjamin Grossman, prin. Fax 733-6429
Bronx Academy of Health Careers 500/9-12
800 E Gun Hill Rd 10467 718-696-3340
Dawn Santiago, prin. Fax 696-3380
Bronx Aerospace Academy 400/9-12
800 E Gun Hill Rd 10467 718-696-6010
Erika Hurtado, prin. Fax 696-6030
Bronx Arena HS 100/Alt
1440 Story Ave 10473 718-860-5060
Ty Cesene, prin. Fax 860-5058
Bronx Bridges HS 200/9-12
1980 Lafayette Ave 10473 718-829-2984
Pablo Villavicencio, prin. Fax 829-2987
Bronx Career and College Preparatory HS Vo/Tech
800 Home St 10456 718-542-4011
Kizhaya Roberts, prin. Fax 542-4377
Bronx Center for Science & Mathematics 400/9-12
1363 Fulton Ave 10456 718-992-7089
Edward Tom, prin. Fax 590-1052
Bronx Collaborative HS 100/9-10
100 W Mosholu Pkwy S 10468 718-543-1023
Brett Schneider, prin. Fax 543-1029
Bronx Collegiate Academy 400/9-12
240 E 172nd St 10457 718-410-4077
D. White, prin. Fax 293-9567
Bronx Community HS 200/Alt
1980 Lafayette Ave 10473 718-892-1026
Flora Greenaway, prin. Fax 892-6941
Bronx Compass HS 9-12
1980 Lafayette Ave 10473 718-828-1206
Stacy McCoy, prin.
Bronxdale HS 100/9-12
925 Astor Ave 10469 718-944-3655
Carolyne Quintana, prin. Fax 944-3662

Bronx Dance Academy 300/6-8
3617 Bainbridge Ave 10467 718-515-0410
Sandra Sanchez, prin. Fax 515-0345

Bronx Design and Construction Academy 100/9-12
333 E 151st St 10451 718-402-7690
Matthew Williams, prin. Fax 402-4216

Bronx Early College Academy 500/6-12
250 E 164th St 10456 718-681-8287
Yvette Rivera, prin. Fax 681-8650

Bronx Engineering & Technology Academy 400/9-12
99 Terrace View Ave Rm 544 10463 718-563-6678
Karalyne Sperling, prin. Fax 741-5263

Bronx Envision Academy 100/9-12
1619 Boston Rd 10460 718-589-1590
Emily Shu, prin. Fax 589-1595

Bronx Green MS 400/6-8
2441 Wallace Ave 10467 718-325-6593
Charles Johnson, prin. Fax 325-3625

Bronx Guild HS 300/9-12
1980 Lafayette Ave 10473 718-597-1587
Sam Decker, prin. Fax 597-1371

Bronx Haven HS 100/Alt
333 E 151st St 10451 718-292-3638
Lucinda Mendez, prin. Fax 292-6065

Bronx Health Sciences HS 400/9-12
750 Baychester Ave 10475 718-862-4406
Miriam Rivas, prin. Fax 862-4410

HS for Contemporary Arts 500/9-12
800 E Gun Hill Rd 10467 718-944-5610
Francisco Sanchez, prin. Fax 944-5650

HS for Energy and Technology 9-12
2474 Crotona Ave 10458 718-733-3080
Ignazio Accardi, prin.

HS for Language and Innovation 100/9-12
925 Astor Ave 10469 718-944-3625
Julie Nariman, prin. Fax 944-3641

Bronx HS for Law & Community Service 400/9-12
500 E Fordham Rd 10458 718-733-5274
Michael Barakate, prin. Fax 295-3631

HS for Teaching & Professions 500/9-12
2780 Reservoir Ave 10468 718-329-7380
Jason Maass, prin. Fax 365-7984

HS for Violin & Dance 300/9-12
1110 Boston Rd 10456 718-842-0687
Franklin Sim, prin. Fax 589-9849

Bronx HS for Visual Arts 500/9-12
2040 Antin Pl 10462 718-319-5160
G. Jones, prin. Fax 319-5165

Bronx HS for Writing & Communication 400/9-12
800 E Gun Hill Rd 10467 718-944-5660
Terri Grey, prin. Fax 944-5690

HS of American Studies 400/9-12
2925 Goulden Ave 10468 718-329-2144
Alessandro Weiss, prin. Fax 329-0792

Bronx HS of Business 400/9-12
240 E 172nd St 10457 718-410-4060
Vincent Rodriguez, prin. Fax 992-5760

HS of Computers & Technology 500/9-12
800 E Gun Hill Rd 10467 718-696-3930
Bruce Abramowitz, prin. Fax 696-3950

Bronx HS of Science 3,000/9-12
75 W 205th St 10468 718-817-7700
Jean Donahue, prin. Fax 733-7951

HS of World Cultures 400/9-12
1300 Boynton Ave 10472 718-860-8120
Dr. Ramon Namnum, prin. Fax 893-7152

IS 117 700/6-8
1865 Morris Ave 10453 718-583-7750
Delise Jones, prin. Fax 583-7658

IS 129 600/6-8
2055 Mapes Ave 10460 718-933-5976
Raymond Granda, prin. Fax 933-8132

IS 181 700/6-8
800 Baychester Ave 10475 718-904-5600
Christopher Warnock, prin. Fax 904-5620

IS 190 200/6-8
1550 Crotona Park E 10460 718-620-9423
Diana Santiago, prin. Fax 620-9927

IS 206 400/5-8
2280 Aqueduct Ave 10468 718-584-1570
David Neering, prin. Fax 584-7928

IS 219 400/6-8
3630 3rd Ave 10456 718-681-7093
Dominic Cipollone, prin. Fax 681-7324

IS 224 400/6-8
345 Brook Ave 10454 718-665-9804
Sojourner Welch, prin. Fax 665-0078

IS 229 200/6-8
275 Harlem River Park Brg 10453 718-583-6266
Dr. Ezra Matthias, prin. Fax 583-6325

IS 232 500/6-8
1700 Macombs Rd 10453 718-583-7007
Neifi Acosta, prin. Fax 583-4864

IS 254 400/6-8
2452 Washington Ave 10458 718-220-8700
Antonio Pozo, prin. Fax 220-4881

IS 303 300/6-8
1700 Macombs Rd 10453 718-583-5466
Patricia Bentley, prin. Fax 583-2463

IS 313 500/6-10
1600 Webster Ave 10457 718-583-1736
Earl Brathwaite, prin. Fax 299-5559

IS 318 400/6-8
1919 Prospect Ave 10457 718-294-8504
Maria Lopez, prin. Fax 901-0778

IS 339 700/6-8
1600 Webster Ave 10457 718-583-6767
Kim Outerbridge, prin. Fax 583-0281

Bronx International HS 400/9-12
1110 Boston Rd 10456 718-620-1053
Joaquin Vega, prin. Fax 620-1056

JHS 22 700/6-8
270 E 167th St 10456 718-681-6850
Edgar Lin, prin. Fax 681-6895

JHS 80 600/6-8
149 E Mosholu Pkwy N 10467 718-405-6300
Emmanuel Polanco, prin. Fax 405-6324

JHS 98 400/6-8
1619 Boston Rd 10460 718-589-8200
Claralee Irobunda, prin. Fax 589-8179

JHS 118 1,200/6-8
577 E 179th St 10457 718-584-2330
Elizabeth Lawrence, prin. Fax 584-7763

JHS 123 500/6-8
1025 Morrison Ave 10472 718-328-2105
Tyra Williams, prin. Fax 328-8561

JHS 125 600/6-8
1111 Pugsley Ave 10472 718-822-5186
Rudolph Rupnarain, prin. Fax 239-3121

JHS 127 700/6-8
1560 Purdy St 10462 718-892-8600
Harry Sherman, prin. Fax 892-8300

JHS 131 800/6-8
885 Bolton Ave 10473 718-991-7490
Monique Mason, prin. Fax 328-6705

JHS 144 900/6-8
2545 Gunther Ave 10469 718-379-7400
Jeremy Cavinoff, prin. Fax 320-7135

JHS 145 500/5-8
1000 Teller Ave 10456 718-681-7219
David McIntosh, prin. Fax 681-6913

JHS 151 300/6-8
250 E 156th St 10451 718-292-0260
Socorro Rivera, prin. Fax 292-5704

JHS 162 500/6-8
600 Saint Anns Ave 10455 718-292-0880
Angel Fani, prin. Fax 292-5735

Bronx Lab S 500/9-12
800 E Gun Hill Rd 10467 718-696-3700
Sarah Marcy, prin. Fax 696-3730

Bronx Latin S 400/6-12
800 Home St 10456 718-991-6349
Annette Fiorentino, prin. Fax 991-6627

Bronx Leadership Academy 700/9-12
1710 Webster Ave 10457 718-299-4274
Kenneth Gaskins, prin. Fax 299-4707

Bronx Leadership Academy II 400/9-12
730 Concourse Vlg W 10451 718-292-7171
Katherine Callaghan, prin. Fax 292-2355

Bronx Mathematics Preparatory S 300/6-8
456 White Plains Rd 10473 718-542-5063
Anya Munce, prin. Fax 542-5236

MS 101 500/6-8
2750 Lafayette Ave 10465 718-829-6372
Jared Rosoff, prin. Fax 829-6594

MS 142 600/6-8
3750 Baychester Ave 10466 718-231-0100
Louisa Palmer, prin. Fax 231-3046

MS 180 800/6-8
700 Baychester Ave 10475 718-904-5650
Frank Uzzo, prin. Fax 904-5655

MS 203 300/6-8
339 Morris Ave 10451 718-292-1052
William Hewlett, prin. Fax 292-5765

MS 223 500/6-8
360 E 145th St 10454 718-292-8627
Ramon Gonzalez, prin. Fax 292-7435

MS 301 300/6-8
890 Cauldwell Ave 10456 718-585-2950
Benjamin Basile, prin. Fax 401-2567

MS 302 700/6-8
681 Kelly St 10455 718-292-6070
Liza Ortiz, prin. Fax 401-2958

MS 390 400/6-8
1930 Andrews Ave 10453 718-583-5501
Robert Mercedes, prin. Fax 583-5556

Bronx MSHS for Medical Science 500/6-12
240 E 172nd St 10457 718-410-4040
William Quintana, prin. Fax 992-4129

Bronx Park MS 6-8
2441 Wallace Ave 10467 718-652-6090

Bronx Regional HS 300/Alt
1010 Rev James A Polite Ave 10459 718-991-2020
Colin Thomas, prin. Fax 617-0257

Bronx River HS 100/9-12
3000 E Tremont Ave 10461 718-904-4210
Gregory Fucheck, prin. Fax 904-4209

S for Tourism and Hospitality 9-12
900 Tinton Ave 10456 718-401-4214
Brian Condon, prin.

Bronx S Law Government & Justice 800/6-12
244 E 163rd St 10451 718-410-3430
Meisha Ross-Porter, prin. Fax 410-3950

Bronx S of Law & Finance 400/9-12
99 Terrace View Ave Rm 804 10463 718-561-0113
Jessica Goring, prin. Fax 561-0595

Bronx S of Young Leaders 400/6-8
40 W Tremont Ave 10453 718-583-4146
Serapha Cruz, prin. Fax 583-4292

Bronx Studio S 500/6-12
928 Simpson St 10459 718-893-5158
David Vazquez, prin. Fax 893-5982

Bronx Theatre HS 400/9-12
99 Terrace View Ave Rm 716 10463 718-329-2902
Charles Gallo, prin. Fax 329-0433

Bronxwood Preparatory Academy 400/9-12
921 E 228th St 10466 718-696-3820
Janet Gallardo, prin. Fax 696-3821

Bronx Writing Academy 500/6-8
270 E 167th St 10456 718-293-9048
Kamar Samuels, prin. Fax 293-9748

Chaifetz Transfer HS 200/Alt
778 Forest Ave 10456 718-402-2429
Anne Fennelly, prin. Fax 402-3120

Cinema S 200/9-12
1551 E 172nd St 10472 718-620-2560
Keisha Warner, prin. Fax 620-2561

Clinton HS 4,200/9-12
100 W Mosholu Pkwy S 10468 718-543-1000
Santiago Taveras, prin. Fax 548-0036

Collegiate Institute of Math & Science 500/9-12
925 Astor Ave 10469 718-944-3635
Frederick Nelson, prin. Fax 652-3525

Community S for Social Justice 300/9-12
350 Gerard Ave 10451 718-402-8481
Sue-Ann Rosch, prin. Fax 402-8650

Comprehensive Model S Project-MS 327 400/6-9
1501 Jerome Ave 10452 718-861-0852
Manuel Ramirez, prin. Fax 993-2990

Cornerstone Academy for Social Action MS 300/6-8
3441 Steenwick Ave 10475 718-794-7970
Jamaal Bowman, prin. Fax 794-7981

Creston Academy 400/6-8
125 E 181st St 10453 718-367-5035
Pamela Edwards, prin. Fax 367-5176

Crotona Academy HS 100/Alt
639 Saint Anns Ave 10455 718-402-8378
Anthony Harris, prin. Fax 402-8446

Crotona International HS 100/9-12
2474 Crotona Ave 10458 718-561-8701
Jesseca Long, prin. Fax 561-8707

Cruz Bronx HS of Music 400/9-12
2780 Reservoir Ave 10468 718-329-8550
Jerrod Mabry, prin. Fax 329-8559

Curie HS 500/9-12
120 W 231st St 10463 718-432-6491
Rodney Fisher, prin. Fax 796-7051

Discovery HS 500/9-12
2780 Reservoir Ave 10468 718-733-3872
Rolando Rivera, prin. Fax 733-3621

Dodge Career & Technology HS Vo/Tech
2474 Crotona Ave 10458 718-584-2700
Frank Giaimo, prin. Fax 584-7490

Douglas Academy V 200/6-8
2111 Crotona Ave 10457 718-561-1617
Deborah Cimini, prin. Fax 561-2184

Douglass Academy III 500/8-12
3630 3rd Ave 10456 718-538-9726
Rahesha Amon, prin. Fax 538-9796

Dreamyard Preparatory S 300/9-12
240 E 172nd St 10457 718-410-4242
Alicia Wargo, prin. Fax 410-4312

Eagle Academy for Young Men 500/9-12
4143 3rd Ave 10457 718-466-8000
Jonathan Foy, prin. Fax 466-8090

East Bronx Academy for the Future 600/6-12
1716 Southern Blvd 10460 718-861-8641
Sarah Scrogin, prin. Fax 861-8634

East Fordham Academy for the Arts 300/6-8
120 E 184th St 10468 718-220-4185
Tanicia Rivera, prin. Fax 220-5976

Emolior Academy 200/6-8
1970 W Farms Rd 10460 718-842-2670
Derick Spaulding, prin. Fax 842-2857

English Language Learners Academy 300/9-12
99 Terrace View Ave 10463 718-220-1889
Norma Vega, prin. Fax 220-8758

Entrada Academy 300/6-8
977 Fox St 10459 718-378-1649
Jazmin Rivera-Polanco, prin. Fax 378-4707

Eximius College Preparatory Academy 400/9-12
1363 Fulton Ave 10456 718-992-7154
Jonathan Daly, prin. Fax 590-1081

Explorations Academy 400/9-12
1619 Boston Rd 10460 718-893-6173
Susana Hernandez, prin. Fax 893-6439

Fordham HS for the Arts 400/9-12
500 E Fordham Rd 10458 718-733-4656
Iris Blige, prin. Fax 295-3605

Fordham Leadership Academy 400/9-12
500 E Fordham Rd 10458 718-733-5024
Maryann Tucker, prin. Fax 295-3674

Foreign Langugage Academy\Global Study 300/9-12
470 Jackson Ave 10455 718-585-4024
Leba Augone, prin. Fax 585-4239

Forward School of Creative Writing 200/6-8
3710 Barnes Ave 10467 718-652-0519
Magdalen Neyra, prin. Fax 652-0428

Gateway S of Environmental Research 500/9-12
1980 Lafayette Ave 10473 718-824-9327
Lucille Dimeglio, prin. Fax 824-4368

Giordano MS 1,000/6-8
2502 Lorillard Pl 10458 718-584-1660
Anna Maria Giordano, prin. Fax 584-7968

Globe S for Environmental Research 400/6-8
3710 Barnes Ave 10467 718-994-1395
Rashaunda Shaw, prin. Fax 994-1316

Gompers Career & Technical HS Vo/Tech
455 Southern Blvd 10455 718-665-0950
Joyce Kittrell, prin. Fax 292-3164

Hamer Freedom HS 500/9-12
1021 Jennings St 10460 718-861-0521
Nancy Mann, prin. Fax 861-0619

Hamer MS 300/6-8
1001 Jennings St 10460 718-860-2707
Lorraine Chanon, prin. Fax 860-3212

Health Opportunities HS 600/9-12
350 Gerard Ave 10451 718-401-1826
Julie McHedlishvili, prin. Fax 401-1632

HERO HS 100/9-10
455 Southern Blvd 10455 718-585-8013
Kristin Garcia, prin. Fax 585-8019

Highbridge Green S 100/6-8
200 W 167th St 10452 718-410-5770
Kyle Brillante, prin. Fax 410-5779

Hostos-Lincoln Academy 500/6-12
600 Saint Anns Ave 10455 718-402-5640
Nick Paarlberg, prin. Fax 518-4321

Hunts Point S 400/6-8
730 Bryant Ave 10474 718-328-1972
Sonya Johnson, prin. Fax 328-7330

Institute for Law and Public Policy 400/9-12
1440 Story Ave 10473 718-860-5110
Grismaldy Laboy-Wilson, prin. Fax 860-5081

In-Tech Academy 1,100/6-12
2975 Tibbett Ave 10463 718-432-4300
Yvette Allen, prin. Fax 432-4310

International Community HS 400/9-12
345 Brook Ave 10454 718-665-4128
Berena Cabarcas, prin. Fax 665-4547

International S for Liberal Arts 600/6-12
2780 Reservoir Ave 10468 718-329-8570
Francine Cruz, prin. Fax 329-8572
KAPPA 400/5-8
3630 3rd Ave 10456 718-590-5455
Sheri Warren, prin. Fax 681-4266
KAPPA 300/9-12
500 E Fordham Rd 10458 718-933-1247
Panorea Panagiosoulis, prin. Fax 933-1568
KAPPA III S 200/6-8
2055 Mapes Ave 10460 718-561-3580
Elisa Alvarez, prin. Fax 561-3719
Kelly HS 400/9-12
965 Longwood Ave 10459 718-860-1242
Charlette Pope, prin. Fax 860-1934
Kingsbridge International HS 500/9-12
2780 Reservoir Ave 10468 718-329-8580
Ronald Foreman, prin. Fax 329-8582
Leadership Institute 200/9-12
1701 Fulton Ave 10457 718-299-7490
Marta Colon, prin.
Lehman HS 3,600/9-12
3000 E Tremont Ave 10461 718-904-4200
R. Lobianco, prin. Fax 904-4285
Levin HS for Media & Communications 400/9-12
240 E 172nd St 10457 718-992-3709
Nasib Hoxha, prin. Fax 992-4170
Marble Hill HS for International Studies 500/9-12
99 Terrace View Ave Rm 822 10463 718-561-0973
Kirsten Larson, prin. Fax 561-5612
Metropolitan HS 300/9-12
1180 Rev James A Polite Ave 10459 718-991-4634
Andrea Riley, prin. Fax 542-7294
Metropolitan Soundview HS 9-12
1300 Boynton Ave 10472 718-860-8240
Michael Lanaghan, prin. Fax 860-8232
Millenium Art Academy 500/9-12
1980 Lafayette Ave 10473 718-824-0978
Herman Guy, prin. Fax 824-0963
Monroe Academy for Visual Arts & Design 500/9-12
1300 Boynton Ave 10472 718-860-8160
Richard Massel, prin. Fax 860-8110
Morris Academy for Collaborative Studies 400/9-12
1110 Boston Rd 10456 718-542-3700
Matthew Mazzarol, prin. Fax 542-3958
Mott Hall Bronx HS 300/9-12
1595 Bathgate Ave 10457 718-466-6800
Kathryn Malloy, prin. Fax 466-6801
Mott Hall Community S 300/6-8
650 Hollywood Ave 10465 718-829-3254
Juana Rosario, prin. Fax 829-3859
Mott Hall III 400/6-8
580 Crotona Park S 10456 718-842-6138
Jorisis Stupart, prin. Fax 842-6348
Mott Hall V 500/6-12
1551 E 172nd St 10472 718-620-8160
Peter Oroszlany, prin. Fax 620-8161
Mott Haven Community HS 9-12
455 Southern Blvd 10455 718-665-8512
Helene Spadaccini, prin.
Mott Haven Village Prep HS 400/9-12
701 Saint Anns Ave 10455 718-402-0571
Melanie Williams, prin. Fax 665-2363
Neruda Academy 300/9-12
1980 Lafayette Ave 10473 718-824-1682
David Liu, prin. Fax 824-1663
New Directions Secondary S 100/6-8
240 E 172nd St 10457 718-410-4343
James Waslawski, prin. Fax 410-4101
New Explorers HS 400/9-12
730 Concourse Vlg W 10451 718-292-4150
Jake Hobson, prin. Fax 292-5887
New Millenium Business Academy 200/6-8
1000 Teller Ave 10456 718-588-8308
Dorald Bastian, prin. Fax 681-6913
New S for Leadership and Journalism 600/6-8
120 W 231st St 10463 718-601-2869
Dolores Peterson, prin. Fax 601-2867
New World HS 400/9-12
921 E 228th St 10466 718-696-3800
Fausto Salazar, prin. Fax 696-3801
One World MS 100/6-8
3750 Baychester Ave 10466 718-515-6780
Patricia Wynne, prin. Fax 515-6785
Pan American International HS 400/9-12
1300 Boynton Ave 10472 718-991-7238
Bridgit Bye, prin. Fax 991-7872
Pantoja Preparatory Academy 400/6-12
1980 Lafayette Ave 10473 718-824-3152
Nancy Diaz, prin. Fax 824-3543
Patri MS 600/6-8
2225 Webster Ave 10457 718-584-1295
Gracela Abadia, prin. Fax 584-1358
Peace & Diversity Academy 200/9-12
1180 Rev James A Polite Ave 10459 718-991-1855
Andrew Turay, prin. Fax 991-2998
Pelham Academy of Academics 300/6-8
2441 Wallace Ave 10467 718-881-3136
Anthony Rivera, prin. Fax 881-3413
Pelham Gardens MS 6-8
2545 Gunther Ave 10469 718-794-9750
Pelham Lab HS 100/9-10
3000 E Tremont Ave 10461 718-904-5090
Jason Wagner, prin. Fax 904-5099
Pelham Preparatory Academy 500/9-12
925 Astor Ave 10469 718-944-3401
Carlos Santiago, prin. Fax 944-3479
PULSE HS 200/Alt
560 E 179th St 10457 718-294-0230
Carol Wiggins, prin. Fax 584-7809
Renaissance HS of Musical Theater 500/9-12
3000 E Tremont Ave 10461 718-430-6390
Maria Herrera, prin. Fax 430-6308
Riverdale/Kingsbridge Academy 1,300/6-12
660 W 237th St 10463 718-796-8516
Lori O'Mara, prin. Fax 796-8657

Rucker S of Community Research 300/9-12
965 Longwood Ave 10459 718-860-1053
Sharif Rucker, prin. Fax 860-1321
Schomburg Satellite Academy 200/Alt
1010 Rev James A Polite Ave 10459 718-542-2700
Marsha Vernon, prin. Fax 589-3710
School for Excellence HS 400/9-12
1110 Boston Rd 10456 718-860-1385
Carmen Brown, prin. Fax 860-4882
School for Inquiry & Social Justice 300/6-8
1025 Morrison Ave 10472 718-860-4181
Andrea Cyprys, prin. Fax 860-4163
School of Diplomacy 400/6-8
3710 Barnes Ave 10467 718-994-1028
Sean Licata, prin.
School of Performing Arts 300/6-8
977 Fox St 10459 718-589-4844
Maiysha Etienne, prin. Fax 589-7998
Schuylerville Preparatory HS 100/9-12
3000 E Tremont Ave 10461 718-904-4200
Roberto Ossorio, prin. Fax 935-4209
Science and Technology Academy 400/6-8
250 E 164th St 10456 718-293-4017
Dr. Patrick Awosogba, prin. Fax 293-7396
Smith Career and Tech HS Vo/Tech
333 E 151st St 10451 718-993-5000
Evan Schwartz, prin. Fax 292-1944
Soundview Acad for Culture & Scholarship 300/6-8
885 Bolton Ave 10473 718-991-4027
William Frackelton, prin. Fax 991-4807
South Bronx Academy for Applied Media 300/6-8
778 Forest Ave 10456 718-401-0059
Roshone Ault, prin. Fax 401-0577
South Bronx Preparatory HS 600/6-12
360 E 145th St 10454 718-292-2211
Ellen Flanagan, prin. Fax 292-2172
Theatre Arts Production Company S 500/6-12
2225 Webster Ave 10457 718-584-0832
Ron Link, prin. Fax 584-5102
Truman HS 1,700/9-12
750 Baychester Ave 10475 718-904-5400
Keri Alfano, prin. Fax 904-5502
University Heights HS 300/9-12
701 Saint Anns Ave 10455 718-292-0578
Hazel Roseboro, prin. Fax 292-4276
Urban Assembly Academy Civic Engagement 200/6-8
650 Hollywood Ave 10465 718-822-0126
Mary Sheppard, prin. Fax 822-1049
Urban Assembly Bronx Academy of Letters 600/6-12
339 Morris Ave 10451 718-401-4891
Jeffrey Garrett, prin. Fax 401-6626
Urban Assembly Math & Science MSHS 600/6-12
1595 Bathgate Ave 10457 718-466-7800
David Krulwich, prin. Fax 466-7801
Urban Assembly S for Careers in Sports 500/9-12
730 Concourse Vlg W 10451 718-292-7110
Johanny Garcia, prin. Fax 993-1567
Urban Assembly S Wildlife Conservation 400/6-12
2024 Mohegan Ave 10460 718-991-2695
Mark Ossenheimer, prin. Fax 991-2980
Urban Institute of Mathematics 300/6-8
650 Hollywood Ave 10465 718-823-6042
Jennifer Joynt, prin. Fax 823-6347
Urban Science Academy 400/5-8
1000 Teller Ave 10456 718-588-8221
Patrick Kelly, prin. Fax 588-8263
Validus Preparatory Academy 400/9-12
1595 Bathgate Ave 10457 718-466-4000
Javier Ocampo, prin. Fax 466-4001
West Bronx Academy for the Future 600/6-12
500 E Fordham Rd 10458 718-563-7139
Wilper Morales, prin. Fax 563-7362
Westchester Square Academy 9-12
3000 E Tremont Ave 10461 718-904-5050
Sara Dingledy, prin.
Wings Academy 500/9-12
1122 E 180th St 10460 718-597-1751
Tuwanna Williams Gray, prin. Fax 931-8366
Womans Academy of Excellence 400/9-12
456 White Plains Rd 10473 718-542-0740
Arnette Crocker, prin. Fax 542-0841
World View HS 100/9-12
100 W Mosholu Pkwy S 10468 718-601-0391
Martin Hernandez, prin. Fax 601-0821
Young Scholars Academy 400/6-8
3710 Barnes Ave 10467 718-325-5834
Jeanette Vargas, prin. Fax 325-5676
Young Womens Leadership S of the Bronx 6-8
1865 Morris Ave 10453 718-731-2590
Lemarie Laureano, prin.

---

Academy of Mt. St. Ursula 400/9-12
330 Bedford Park Blvd 10458 718-364-5353
Sr. Jean Marie Humphries, prin. Fax 364-2354
All Hallows HS 700/9-12
111 E 164th St 10452 718-293-4545
Sean Sullivan, prin. Fax 410-8298
Aquinas HS 600/9-12
685 E 182nd St 10457 718-367-2113
Sr. Catherine Rose Quigley, prin. Fax 295-5864
Bronx Lebanon Hospital Center Post-Sec.
1650 Grand Concourse 10457 718-518-1800
Cardinal Hayes HS 900/9-12
650 Grand Concourse 10451 718-292-6100
William Lessa, prin. Fax 292-9178
Cardinal Spellman HS 1,400/9-12
1 Cardinal Spellman Pl 10466 718-881-8000
Daniel O'Keefe, prin. Fax 515-6615
CUNY Bronx Community College Post-Sec.
2155 University Ave 10453 718-289-5100
CUNY Hostos Community College Post-Sec.
500 Grand Concourse 10451 718-518-4444
CUNY Lehman College Post-Sec.
250 Bedford Park Blvd W 10468 718-960-8000
Ethical Culture Fieldston S 400/6-12
3901 Fieldston Rd 10471 718-329-7300
Dr. Damian Fernandez Ph.D., head sch Fax 329-7305

Fordham Preparatory HS 900/9-12
441 E Fordham Rd 10458 718-367-7500
Robert Gomprecht, prin. Fax 367-7598
Fordham University Post-Sec.
441 E Fordham Rd 10458 718-817-1000
Hope Academy of the Bronx 5-8
2206 Andrews Ave 10453 347-762-2463
Naomi Woodmansee, head sch
Lavelle School/Blind-Visually Impaired Post-Sec.
E 221 St & Paulding Ave 10469
Mann S 1,700/PK-12
231 W 246th St 10471 718-432-4000
Dr. Thomas M. Kelly, head sch Fax 548-2089
Monroe College Post-Sec.
2501 Jerome Ave 10468 718-933-6700
Monsignor Scanlan HS 500/9-12
915 Hutchinson River Pkwy 10465 718-430-0100
Peter Doran, prin. Fax 892-8845
Montefiore Medical Center Post-Sec.
111 E 210th St 10467 718-920-4001
Mt. St. Michael Academy 800/6-12
4300 Murdock Ave 10466 718-515-6400
Br. Steve Schlitte, prin. Fax 994-7729
New York Institute for Special Education Post-Sec.
999 Pelham Pkwy N 10469 718-519-7000
Our Saviour Lutheran S 200/PK-12
1734 Williamsbridge Rd 10461 718-792-5665
Rev. Paul Sauer, admin. Fax 409-3877
Preston HS 600/9-12
2780 Schurz Ave 10465 718-863-9134
Jane Grendell, prin. Fax 863-6125
Riverdale Country S 800/6-12
5250 Fieldston Rd 10471 718-549-8810
Dominic Randolph, hdmstr. Fax 519-2795
St. Barnabas HS 200/9-12
425 E 240th St 10470 718-325-8800
Sr. Joan Faraone, prin. Fax 325-8820
St. Catharine Academy 700/9-12
2250 Williamsbridge Rd 10469 718-882-2882
Sr. Ann Welch, prin. Fax 231-9099
St. Ignatius Academy 100/6-8
740 Manida St 10474 718-861-9084
Richard Darrell, prin. Fax 861-9096
St. Raymond Girls Academy 400/9-12
1725 Castle Hill Ave 10462 718-824-4220
Sr. Mary Ann D'Antonio, prin. Fax 829-3571
St. Raymond HS for Boys 800/9-12
2151 Saint Raymonds Ave 10462 718-824-5050
Br. Daniel Gardner, prin. Fax 863-8808
Salanter Akiba Riverdale HS 500/9-12
503 W 259th St 10471 718-548-2727
SUNY Maritime College Post-Sec.
6 Pennyfield Ave 10465 718-409-7200
Veterans Affairs Medical Center Post-Sec.
130 W Kingsbridge Rd 10468 718-579-1640
Yeshiva of the Telshe Alumni Post-Sec.
4904 Independence Ave 10471 718-601-3523

**Bronxville, Westchester, Pop. 6,193**
Bronxville UFD 1,500/K-12
177 Pondfield Rd 10708 914-395-0500
Dr. David Quattrone, supt. Fax 337-7109
www.bronxville.k12.ny.us
Bronxville HS 400/9-12
177 Pondfield Rd 10708 914-395-0500
Ann Meyer, prin. Fax 395-0513
Bronxville MS 400/6-8
177 Pondfield Rd 10708 914-395-0500
Dr. Thomas Wilson, prin. Fax 771-6223

---

Concordia College Post-Sec.
171 White Plains Rd 10708 914-337-9300
Sarah Lawrence College Post-Sec.
1 Mead Way 10708 914-337-0700

**Brookfield, Madison**
Brookfield Central SD 200/PK-12
PO Box 60 13314 315-899-3323
James Plows, supt. Fax 899-8902
www.brookfieldcsd.org
Brookfield Central S 200/PK-12
PO Box 60 13314 315-899-3323
Carrie Smith, prin. Fax 899-8902

**Brookhaven, Suffolk, Pop. 3,414**
South Country Central SD
Supt. — See East Patchogue
Bellport HS 1,300/9-12
205 Beaver Dam Rd 11719 631-730-1575
Tim Hogan, prin. Fax 286-5336

**Brooklyn, See New York**
NYC Department of Education
Supt. — See New York
Academy for College Preparation 600/6-12
911 Flatbush Ave 11226 718-564-2566
Doris Unger, prin. Fax 564-2567
Academy for Conservation & Environment 300/9-12
6565 Flatlands Ave 11236 718-968-4101
Eugene Mazzola, prin. Fax 968-4296
Academy for Environmental Leadership 400/9-12
400 Irving Ave 11237 718-381-7100
Nilda Gomez-Katz, prin. Fax 628-6965
Academy for Health Careers 100/9-12
150 Albany Ave 11213 718-773-0128
Deonne Martin, prin. Fax 773-0648
Academy for Young Writers 400/9-12
1065 Elton St 11239 718-688-7230
Courtney Winkfield, prin. Fax 688-7236
Academy of Hospitality & Tourism 300/9-12
911 Flatbush Ave 11226 718-564-2580
Adam Brier, prin. Fax 564-2581
Academy of Innovative Technology 500/9-12
999 Jamaica Ave 11208 718-827-2469
Cynthia Fowlkes, prin. Fax 827-4013
Academy of Urban Planning 400/9-12
400 Irving Ave 11237 718-381-7100
Kyleema Norman, prin. Fax 418-0314

Acorn Community HS 700/9-12
561 Grand Ave 11238 718-789-2258
Andrea Piper, dir. Fax 789-2260

All City Leadership Academy 300/6-12
321 Palmetto St 11237 718-246-6500
Elvis Estevez, prin. Fax 381-9680

Arts & Media Preparatory Academy 300/9-12
905 Winthrop St 11203 718-773-3908
Deb Glauner, prin. Fax 773-7274

Aspirations Diploma Plus HS 300/Alt
1495 Herkimer St 11233 718-498-5257
Shermila Bharat, prin. Fax 498-7170

Automotive HS Vo/Tech
50 Bedford Ave 11222 718-218-9301
Catherina Lafergola, prin. Fax 599-4351

Banneker Academy 900/9-12
77 Clinton Ave 11205 718-797-3702
Deonca Renee, prin. Fax 797-3862

Barton HS Vo/Tech
901 Classon Ave 11225 718-636-4900
Dr. Richard Forman, prin. Fax 857-3688

Bedford Academy HS 400/9-12
1119 Bedford Ave 11216 718-398-3061
Adofo Muhammad, prin. Fax 636-3819

Bedford - Stuyvesant Prep HS 100/Alt
832 Marcy Ave 11216 718-622-4310
Darryl Rascoe, prin. Fax 398-4381

Boys & Girls HS 1,600/9-12
1700 Fulton St 11213 718-467-1700
Bernard Gassaway, prin. Fax 221-0645

Brooklyn Academy HS 200/Alt
832 Marcy Ave 11216 718-638-4235
Charon Hall, prin. Fax 638-0051

Brooklyn Academy of Global Finance 200/9-12
125 Stuyvesant Ave 11221 718-574-3126
Dannielle Darbee, prin. Fax 574-3681

Brooklyn Acad of Science & Environment 500/9-12
883 Classon Ave 11225 718-230-6363
Veronica Peterson, prin. Fax 230-6370

Brooklyn Bridge Academy 200/Alt
6565 Flatlands Ave 11236 718-968-1689
Max Paul, prin. Fax 968-1678

Brooklyn College Academy 600/7-12
350 Coney Island Ave 11218 718-951-5941
Nick Mazzarella, prin. Fax 951-4441

Brooklyn Collegiate S 500/7-12
2021 Bergen St 11233 718-922-1145
Amote Sias, prin. Fax 922-2347

Brooklyn Community HS of Arts & Media 500/9-12
300 Willoughby Ave 11205 718-230-5748
James O'Brien, prin. Fax 230-3050

Brooklyn Democracy Academy 200/Alt
985 Rockaway Ave 11212 718-342-6348
Andrew Brown, prin. Fax 342-6708

Brooklyn Frontiers HS 100/9-12
112 Schermerhorn St 11201 718-722-4727
Alona Cohen Ph.D., prin. Fax 722-7919

Brooklyn Generation S 300/9-12
6565 Flatlands Ave 11236 718-968-4200
Lydia Bomani, prin. Fax 444-5419

HS for Civil Rights 400/9-12
400 Pennsylvania Ave 11207 718-922-6289
Michael Steele, prin. Fax 922-7253

HS for Global Citizenship 300/9-12
883 Classon Ave 11225 718-230-6300
Michelle Rochon, prin. Fax 230-6301

Brooklyn HS for Law & Technology 400/9-12
1396 Broadway 11221 718-919-1256
Michael Prayor, prin. Fax 852-4593

HS for Medical Professions 500/9-12
1600 Rockaway Pkwy 11236 718-290-8700
Pauline O'Brien, prin. Fax 290-8705

HS for Public Service 400/9-12
600 Kingston Ave 11203 718-756-5325
Ben Shuldiner, prin. Fax 363-3206

HS for Service & Learning 400/9-12
911 Flatbush Ave 11226 718-564-2551
Peter Fabianski, prin. Fax 564-2552

Brooklyn HS for the Arts 700/9-12
345 Dean St 11217 718-855-2412
Margaret Berman, prin. Fax 852-8734

HS for Youth & Community Development 400/9-12
911 Flatbush Ave 11226 718-564-2470
Mary Prendergast, prin. Fax 564-2471

HS Innovation in Advertising 300/9-12
1600 Rockaway Pkwy 11236 718-290-8760
Adaleza Michelena, prin. Fax 290-8766

Brooklyn HS Leadership Community Service 200/Alt
300 Willoughby Ave 11205 718-638-3062
Georgia Kouriampalis, prin. Fax 638-3404

HS of Enterprise - Business & Tech 1,000/9-12
850 Grand St 11211 718-387-2800
Holger Carrillo, prin. Fax 387-2748

HS of Sports Management 400/9-12
2630 Benson Ave 11214 718-333-7650
Robin Pitts, prin. Fax 333-7675

HS of Telecommunications Arts & Tech 1,300/9-12
350 67th St 11220 718-759-3400
Xhenete Shepard, prin. Fax 759-3490

Brooklyn Institute For Liberal Arts 9-12
600 Kingston Ave 11203 718-221-1097
Ann-Marie Henry-Stephens, prin.

IS 30 400/6-8
7002 4th Ave 11209 718-491-5684
Carol Heeraman, prin. Fax 491-0071

IS 68 900/6-8
956 E 82nd St 11236 718-241-4800
Merve Williams, prin. Fax 241-5582

IS 96 800/6-8
99 Avenue P 11204 718-236-1344
Erin Lynch, prin. Fax 236-2397

IS 98 1,200/6-8
1401 Emmons Ave 11235 718-891-9005
Maria Timo, prin. Fax 646-7250

IS 136 500/6-8
4004 4th Ave 11232 718-965-3333
Eric Sackler, prin. Fax 965-9567

IS 171 900/5-8
528 Ridgewood Ave 11208 718-647-0111
Indira Mota, prin. Fax 827-5834

IS 211 700/6-8
1001 E 100th St 11236 718-251-4411
Carolyn James, prin. Fax 241-2503

IS 228 800/6-8
228 Avenue S 11223 718-375-7635
Dominick D'Angelo, prin. Fax 376-1209

IS 281 1,200/6-8
8787 24th Ave 11214 718-996-6706
Maria Bender, prin. Fax 996-4186

IS 285 900/6-8
5909 Beverley Rd 11203 718-451-2200
Frederick Underwood, prin. Fax 451-0229

IS 303 600/6-8
501 West Ave 11224 718-996-0100
Carmen Amador, prin. Fax 996-3785

IS 318 1,600/6-8
101 Walton St 11206 718-782-0589
Leander Windley, prin. Fax 384-7715

IS 340 300/6-8
227 Sterling Pl 11238 718-857-5516
Jean Williams, prin. Fax 230-5479

IS 347 500/5-8
35 Starr St 11221 718-821-4248
John Barbella, prin. Fax 821-1332

IS 349 500/6-8
35 Starr St 11221 718-418-6389
Rogelio Parris, prin. Fax 418-6146

IS 364 400/6-8
1426 Freeport Loop 11239 718-642-3007
Dale Kelly, prin. Fax 642-8516

IS 381 400/6-8
1599 E 22nd St 11210 718-252-0058
Mary Harrington, prin. Fax 252-0035

IS 392 300/5-8
104 Sutter Ave 11212 718-498-2491
Ingrid Joseph, prin. Fax 346-2804

Brooklyn International HS 400/9-12
49 Flatbush Avenue Ext 11201 718-643-9315
Pamela Taranto, prin. Fax 643-9516

JHS 14 600/6-8
2424 Batchelder St 11235 718-743-0220
Teri Ahearn, prin. Fax 769-8632

JHS 50 400/6-8
183 S 3rd St 11211 718-387-4184
Denise Jamison, prin. Fax 302-2320

JHS 57 200/6-8
125 Stuyvesant Ave 11221 718-574-2357
Celeste Douglas, prin. Fax 453-0577

JHS 62 1,300/6-8
700 Cortelyou Rd 11218 718-941-5450
Barry Kevorkian, prin. Fax 693-7433

JHS 78 1,100/6-8
1420 E 68th St 11234 718-763-4701
Anthony Cusumano, prin. Fax 251-3439

JHS 88 1,000/6-8
544 7th Ave 11215 718-788-4482
Ailene Altman-Mitchell, prin. Fax 768-0213

JHS 162 500/6-8
1390 Willoughby Ave 11237 718-821-4860
Barbara DeMartino, prin. Fax 821-1728

JHS 166 400/6-8
800 Van Siclen Ave 11207 718-649-0765
Maria Ortega, prin. Fax 927-2172

JHS 201 1,500/6-8
8010 12th Ave 11228 718-833-9363
Robert Ciulla, prin. Fax 836-1786

JHS 218 600/6-8
370 Fountain Ave 11208 718-647-9050
Lisa Ann Hermann, prin. Fax 827-5839

JHS 220 1,300/6-8
4812 9th Ave 11220 718-633-8200
Loretta Witek, prin. Fax 871-7466

JHS 223 700/6-8
4200 16th Ave 11204 718-438-0155
Andrew Frank, prin. Fax 871-7477

JHS 227 1,300/6-8
6500 16th Ave 11204 718-256-8218
Edwin Hernandez, prin. Fax 234-6204

JHS 234 1,900/6-8
1875 E 17th St 11229 718-645-1334
Susan Schaeffer, prin. Fax 645-7759

JHS 259 1,500/6-8
7305 Fort Hamilton Pkwy 11228 718-833-1000
Janice Geary, prin. Fax 833-3419

JHS 278 1,100/6-8
1925 Stuart St 11229 718-375-3523
Debra Garofalo, prin. Fax 998-7324

JHS 291 600/6-8
231 Palmetto St 11221 718-574-0361
Jacqueline Rosado, prin. Fax 574-1360

JHS 292 800/6-8
301 Vermont St 11207 718-498-6562
Gloria Nandan, prin. Fax 345-3327

JHS 302 900/6-8
350 Linwood St 11208 718-647-9500
Lisa Linder, prin. Fax 827-3294

JHS 383 800/5-8
1300 Greene Ave 11237 718-574-0390
Jeanette Smith, prin. Fax 574-1366

Brooklyn Lab S 400/9-12
999 Jamaica Ave 11208 718-235-3592
Renel Piton, prin. Fax 235-4028

Brooklyn Latin S 500/9-12
223 Graham Ave 11206 718-366-0154
Gina Mautschke, prin. Fax 381-3012

MS 35 200/6-8
272 MacDonough St 11233 718-574-2345
Jackie Charles-Marcus, prin. Fax 452-1273

MS 51 1,100/6-8
350 5th Ave 11215 718-369-7603
Lenore Berner, prin. Fax 499-4948

MS 61 1,100/6-8
400 Empire Blvd 11225 718-774-1002
Shannon Burton, prin. Fax 467-4335

MS 113 900/6-8
300 Adelphi St 11205 718-834-6734
Dawnique Daughtry, prin. Fax 596-2802

MS 246 600/6-8
72 Veronica Pl 11226 718-282-5230
Bently Warrington, prin. Fax 284-6429

MS 266 200/6-8
62 Park Pl 11217 718-857-2291
Glenda Esperance, prin. Fax 857-2347

MS 267 300/6-8
800 Gates Ave 11221 718-574-2318
Patricia King, prin. Fax 574-2320

MS 582 300/6-8
207 Bushwick Ave 11206 718-456-8218
Brian Walsh, prin. Fax 456-8220

MS 584 200/6-8
130 Rochester Ave 11213 718-604-1380
Gilleyan Hargrove, prin. Fax 604-3784

MS 596 200/6-8
300 Willoughby Ave 11205 718-230-3273
Amy Rodriguez, prin. Fax 230-0173

MS for Academic and Social Excellence 200/6-8
1224 Park Pl 11213 718-774-0105
Andrea Whitehurst, prin. Fax 774-0298

MS for Art and Philosophy 400/6-8
1084 Lenox Rd 11212 718-342-7563
Neil McNeill, prin. Fax 342-8131

MS of Marketing & Legal Studies 400/6-8
905 Winthrop St 11203 718-773-7343
Jameela Horton-Ball, prin. Fax 773-7946

Brooklyn Preparatory HS 400/9-12
257 N 6th St 11211 718-486-2550
Noah Lansner, prin. Fax 486-2505

Brooklyn S for Collaborative Studies 700/6-12
610 Henry St 11231 718-923-4750
Priscilla Chan, prin. Fax 923-4730

Brooklyn S for Global Studies 400/6-12
284 Baltic St 11201 718-694-9741
Dawn Meconi, prin. Fax 694-9745

Brooklyn School for Math and Research 50/9-12
400 Irving Ave 11237 718-381-7100
Perry Rainey, prin. Fax 381-9897

Brooklyn S for Music & Theater 400/9-12
883 Classon Ave 11225 718-230-6250
Pamela Dorcely, prin. Fax 230-6262

S of Business Finance Entrepreneurship 200/6-8
125 Stuyvesant Ave 11221 718-602-3271
Anne Malcom, prin. Fax 602-3274

Brooklyn Science and Engineering Academy 6-8
5404 Tilden Ave 11203 718-935-9439
Angela Defilippis, prin.

Brooklyn Studio Secondary S 900/6-12
8310 21st Ave 11214 718-266-5032
Andrea Ciliotta, prin. Fax 266-5093

Brooklyn Technical HS 5,300/9-12
29 Fort Greene Pl 11217 718-804-6400
Randy Asher, prin. Fax 260-9245

Brooklyn Theatre Arts HS 400/9-12
6565 Flatlands Ave 11236 718-968-1072
David Ward, prin. Fax 968-1065

Brownsville Academy HS 200/Alt
1150 E New York Ave 11212 718-778-7305
Katwona Warren, prin. Fax 778-7385

Brownsville Collaborative MS 6-8
85 Watkins St 11212 718-495-1202
Stacy Walsh, prin.

Bushwick Community HS 400/Alt
231 Palmetto St 11221 718-443-3083
Llermi Gonzalez, prin. Fax 443-4757

Bushwick HS for Social Justice 400/9-12
400 Irving Ave 11237 718-381-7100
Lucas Cooke, prin. Fax 418-0192

Bushwick Leaders HS 500/9-12
797 Bushwick Ave 11221 718-919-4212
Catherine Reilly, prin. Fax 574-1103

Campos Secondary S 800/6-12
215 Heyward St 11206 718-302-7900
Eric Fraser, prin. Fax 302-7979

Carson HS for Coastal Studies 500/9-12
521 West Ave 11224 718-265-0329
Ed Wilensky, prin. Fax 372-2514

Cobble Hill S of American Studies 700/9-12
347 Baltic St 11201 718-403-9544
Annamaria Mule, prin. Fax 403-9553

Conselyea Preparatory S 500/6-8
208 N 5th St 11211 718-486-6211
Maria Masullo, prin. Fax 486-6771

Cultural Academy for Arts and Sciences 300/9-12
5800 Tilden Ave 11203 718-968-6630
Diane Varano, prin. Fax 968-6635

Cypress Hills Collegiate Preparatory S 400/9-12
999 Jamaica Ave 11208 718-647-1672
Any Yager, prin. Fax 647-6719

Dewey HS 2,200/9-12
50 Avenue X 11223 718-373-6400
Kathleen Elvin, prin. Fax 266-4385

Douglas Academy IV 400/7-12
1014 Lafayette Ave 11221 718-574-2820
Elvin Crespo, prin. Fax 574-2821

Douglas Academy VII HS 400/9-12
226 Bristol St 11212 718-485-3789
Tamika Matheson, prin. Fax 922-2761

Douglass Academy VIII MS 300/6-8
1400 Pennsylvania Ave 11239 718-642-4305
Yolanda Martin, prin. Fax 642-4537

Eagle Academy for Young Men II 300/6-10
1137 Herkimer St 11233 718-495-0863
Rashad Meade, prin. Fax 732-2129

East Brooklyn Community HS 200/9-12
9517 Kings Hwy 11212 718-927-6880
Patrick McGillicuddy, prin. Fax 927-6885

East Flatbush Community Research S 300/6-8
905 Winthrop St 11203 718-773-3059
Daveida Daniel, prin. Fax 773-3827

East NY Family Academy 400/6-12
2057 Linden Blvd 11207 718-927-0012
Anthony Yard, prin. Fax 927-0411

East New York MS of Excellence 200/6-8
605 Shepherd Ave 11208 718-257-4061
Malik Small, prin. Fax 257-4738
Ebbets Field MS 300/6-8
46 McKeever Pl 11225 718-941-5097
Margaret Baker, prin. Fax 284-7973
EBC-HS for Public Service 600/9-12
1155 Dekalb Ave 11221 718-452-3440
Shawn Brown, prin. Fax 452-3603
Edmonds Learning Center II 200/6-8
430 Howard Ave 11233 718-467-0306
Michele Luard, prin. Fax 953-0682
El Puente Academy for Peace & Justice 200/Alt
250 Hooper St 11211 718-387-1125
Wanda Vazquez, prin. Fax 387-4229
Ericsson MS 300/6-8
424 Leonard St 11222 718-782-2527
Marcos Bausch, prin. Fax 302-2319
Essence MS 200/6-8
590 Sheffield Ave 11207 718-272-8371
Jermaine Lewis, prin. Fax 272-8372
Evergreen MS for Urban Exploration 200/6-8
125 Covert St 11207 718-455-0180
Lauren Reiss, prin. Fax 455-4381
Evers Preparatory S 1,100/6-12
1186 Carroll St 11225 718-703-5400
Dr. Michael Wiltshire, prin. Fax 703-5600
Expeditionary Learning S for Comm Leader 200/9-12
2630 Benson Ave 11214 718-333-7700
David O'Hara, prin. Fax 333-7725
FDNY S for Fire & Life Safety 400/9-12
400 Pennsylvania Ave 11207 718-922-0389
James Anderson, prin. Fax 922-0593
Fort Greene Preparatory Academy 200/6-8
100 Clermont Ave 11205 718-254-9401
Paula Lettiere, prin. Fax 254-9407
Ft. Hamilton HS 4,300/9-12
8301 Shore Rd 11209 718-748-1537
Kaye Houlihan, prin. Fax 836-3955
Foundations Academy 100/9-12
70 Tompkins Ave 11206 718-302-5092
Neil Monheit, prin. Fax 599-1369
Gibran International Academy 50/8-9
362 Schermerhorn St 11217 718-237-2502
Winston Hamann, prin. Fax 488-1724
Goldstein - Sciences HS 1,000/9-12
1830 Shore Blvd 11235 718-368-8500
Scott Hughes, prin. Fax 368-8555
Gotham Professional Arts Academy 300/9-12
265 Ralph Ave 11233 718-455-0746
Alexander White, prin. Fax 574-3971
Grady Career & Tech HS Vo/Tech
25 Brighton 4th Rd 11235 718-332-5000
Tarah Montalbano, prin. Fax 332-2544
Green S Academy for Environmental Career 400/9-12
223 Graham Ave 11206 718-599-1207
Cara Tait, prin. Fax 387-7945
Highland Park Community S 6-8
528 Ridgewood Ave 11208 718-935-3614
Jamilah Seifullah, prin.
Hudde IS 1,000/6-8
2500 Nostrand Ave 11210 718-253-3700
Gina Votinelli, prin. Fax 253-0356
International Arts & Business HS 400/9-12
600 Kingston Ave 11203 718-467-7400
Angelo Marra, prin. Fax 604-3029
International HS at Lafayette 300/9-12
2630 Benson Ave 11214 718-333-7860
Jon Harriman, prin. Fax 333-7861
International HS at Prospect Heights 400/9-12
883 Classon Ave 11225 718-230-6333
Nedda DeCastro, prin. Fax 230-6322
It Takes a Village Academy 400/9-12
5800 Tilden Ave 11203 718-629-2307
Marina Vinitskaya, prin. Fax 629-6162
James MS of Science 200/6-8
76 Riverdale Ave 11212 718-498-5276
Drew Goodman, prin. Fax 498-5361
KAPPA V S, 985 Rockaway Ave 11212 200/6-8
Thomas Mullin, prin. 718-922-4690
Kingsborough Early College S 500/6-12
2630 Benson Ave 11214 718-333-7850
Connie Hamilton, prin. Fax 333-7875
Liberation Diploma Plus 200/9-12
2865 W 19th St 11224 718-946-6812
April Leong, prin. Fax 946-6825
Life Academy HS for Film and Music 200/9-12
2630 Benson Ave 11214 718-333-7750
Lisa Farraiola, prin. Fax 333-7775
Lincoln HS 2,600/9-12
2800 Ocean Pkwy 11235 718-333-7400
Ari Hoogenboom, prin. Fax 946-5035
Lyons Community S 500/6-12
223 Graham Ave 11206 718-782-0918
Taeko Onishi, prin. Fax 782-5283
Madiba Prep MS 6-8
1014 Lafayette Ave 11221 718-574-2804
Sharon Stephens, prin.
Madison HS 3,100/9-12
3787 Bedford Ave 11229 718-758-7200
Jodie Cohen, prin. Fax 758-7341
Mandela HS, 1700 Fulton St 11213 9-12
Tabari Bomani, prin. 718-935-3604
Math & Science Exploratory S 500/6-8
345 Dean St 11217 718-330-9328
Dawn Valle, prin. Fax 330-0944
Maxwell Career and Technical HS Vo/Tech
145 Pennsylvania Ave 11207 718-345-9100
Jocelyn Babette, prin. Fax 345-5470
McAuliffe S 900/6-8
1171 65th St 11219 718-236-3394
Justin Berman, prin. Fax 236-3638
McKinney S of the Arts 400/6-12
101 Park Ave 11205 718-834-6760
Michael Walker, prin. Fax 834-6776
Metropolitan Diploma Plus HS 200/Alt
985 Rockaway Ave 11212 718-342-6249
Meri Yallowitz, prin. Fax 342-6329

Midwood HS 3,900/9-12
2839 Bedford Ave 11210 718-724-8500
Michael McDonnell, prin. Fax 724-8515
Millennium Brooklyn HS 100/9-12
237 7th Ave 11215 718-832-4333
Lisa Gioe, prin. Fax 499-2126
Mott Hall Bridges MS 100/6-8
210 Chester St 11212 718-345-6912
Nadia Lopez, prin. Fax 345-6918
Mott Hall IV, 1137 Herkimer St 11233 200/6-8
Dr. Thomas McBryde, prin. 718-485-5240
Multicultural HS 400/9-12
999 Jamaica Ave 11208 718-827-2796
Alexandra Hernandez, prin. Fax 827-3970
Murrow HS 3,900/9-12
1600 Avenue L 11230 718-258-9283
Allen Barge, prin. Fax 252-2611
New Heights MS 6-8
790 E New York Ave 11203 718-467-4501
Jessica Luciano, prin.
New Horizons S 200/6-8
317 Hoyt St 11231 718-330-9227
Deanna Sinito, dir. Fax 330-9251
New Utrecht HS 3,200/9-12
1601 80th St 11214 718-232-2500
Maureen Goldfarb, prin. Fax 259-5526
New Voices S of Academic & Creative Arts 500/6-8
330 18th St 11215 718-965-0390
Frank Giordano, prin. Fax 965-0603
Olympus Academy 200/Alt
755 E 100th St 11236 718-272-1926
P.J. Murray, prin. Fax 272-5713
Origins HS 100/9-12
3000 Avenue X 11235 718-891-0037
John Banks, prin. Fax 891-0047
Parkside Preparatory Academy 400/6-8
655 Parkside Ave 11226 718-462-6992
Adrienne Spencer, prin. Fax 284-7717
Park Slope Collegiate S 400/6-12
237 7th Ave 11215 718-832-4300
Jill Bloomberg, prin. Fax 788-8127
Pathways in Technology Early College HS 100/9-12
150 Albany Ave 11213 718-221-1593
Rashid Davis, prin. Fax 221-1781
Performing Arts & Technology HS 400/9-12
400 Pennsylvania Ave 11207 718-922-0762
Reginald Richardson, prin. Fax 922-0953
Perkins Academy Vo/Tech
50 Bedford Ave 11222 718-388-7721
Kevin Bryant, prin. Fax 388-7793
Professional Pathways HS 100/9-12
3000 Avenue X 11235 718-332-6290
David Decamp, prin. Fax 332-6296
Progress HS 1,100/9-12
850 Grand St 11211 718-387-0228
William Jusino, prin. Fax 782-0911
Research and Service HS 100/9-12
1700 Fulton St 11213 718-804-6800
Allison Farrington, prin. Fax 804-6801
Roosevelt HS 3,100/9-12
5800 20th Ave 11204 718-621-8800
Steven Demarco, prin. Fax 232-9513
Satellite East 200/6-8
344 Monroe St 11216 718-789-4251
Kim McPherson, prin. Fax 789-4823
Satellite West MS 100/6-8
209 York St 11201 718-834-6774
Sylvia Harris, prin. Fax 834-2979
School for Classics 300/9-12
370 Fountain Ave 11208 718-277-1069
Janice Ross, prin. Fax 277-1873
School for Democracy & Leadership 400/6-12
600 Kingston Ave 11203 718-771-4865
James Olearchek, prin. Fax 771-5847
School for Human Rights 400/6-12
600 Kingston Ave 11203 718-771-4793
Michael Alexander, prin. Fax 771-4815
School for International Studies 500/6-12
284 Baltic St 11201 718-330-9390
Jillian Juman, prin. Fax 875-7522
School for Legal Studies 800/9-12
850 Grand St 11211 718-387-2800
Monica Ortiz, prin. Fax 387-3281
School of Integrated Learning 300/6-8
1224 Park Pl 11213 718-774-0362
Monique Campbell, prin. Fax 774-0521
Science and Medicine MS 300/6-8
965 E 107th St 11236 718-688-6400
Ingrid Thomas-Clark, prin. Fax 688-6401
Science Skills Center HS 500/9-12
49 Flatbush Avenue Ext 11201 718-243-9413
Dahilia McGregor, prin. Fax 243-9399
Science Technology & Research HS 500/6-12
911 Flatbush Ave 11226 718-564-2540
Dr. Eric Blake, prin. Fax 564-2541
Secondary S for Journalism 300/8-12
237 7th Ave 11215 718-832-4201
Eileen Coppola, prin. Fax 832-0273
Secondary S for Law 500/8-12
237 7th Ave 11215 718-832-4250
Oneatha Swinton, prin. Fax 499-3947
Sheepshead Bay HS 1,900/9-12
3000 Avenue X 11235 718-332-2003
John Omahoney, prin. Fax 648-9349
South Brooklyn Community HS 100/9-12
173 Conover St 11231 718-237-8902
Jean Foley, dir. Fax 422-1927
Spring Creek Community S 6-12
1065 Elton St 11239 718-935-3605
Christina Koza, prin.
Stroud MS 200/6-8
750 Classon Ave 11238 718-638-3067
Tricia Delauney, prin. Fax 638-3515
Sunset Park HS 1,000/9-12
153 35th St 11232 718-840-1900
Corinne Vinal, prin. Fax 840-1925

Sunset Park Prep MS 500/6-8
4004 4th Ave 11232 718-965-3331
Jennifer Spalding, prin. Fax 965-3330
Teachers Preparatory HS 600/6-12
226 Bristol St 11212 718-498-2605
Carmen Simon, prin. Fax 345-8069
Transit Tech HS Vo/Tech
1 Wells St 11208 718-647-5204
Marlon Bynum, prin. Fax 647-4458
Twain Gifted & Talented S 1,300/6-8
2401 Neptune Ave 11224 718-266-0814
Karen Ditolla, prin. Fax 266-1693
Upper S @ PS 25 200/6-8
787 Lafayette Ave 11221 718-574-6032
Ativia Sandusky, prin. Fax 602-2357
Urban Action Academy 300/9-12
1600 Rockaway Pkwy 11236 718-290-8720
Steve Dorcely, prin. Fax 290-8721
Urban Assembly Institute Math & Science 500/6-12
283 Adams St 11201 718-260-2300
Kiri Soares, prin. Fax 260-2301
Urban Assembly S Collaborty Healthcare 9-12
999 Jamaica Ave 11208 718-935-3505
Kevin Bradley, prin.
Urban Assembly S for Criminal Justice 400/6-12
4200 16th Ave 11204 718-438-3893
Mariela Graham, prin. Fax 438-3527
Urban Assembly S for Law & Justice 400/9-12
283 Adams St 11201 718-858-1160
Suzette Dyer, prin. Fax 858-4733
Urban Assembly S for Music & Art 400/9-12
49 Flatbush Avenue Ext 11201 718-858-0249
Paul Thompson, prin. Fax 858-0492
Urban Assembly S for Urban Environment 100/6-8
70 Tompkins Ave 11206 718-599-0371
Kourtney Boyd, prin. Fax 388-0872
Victory Collegiate HS 300/9-12
6565 Flatlands Ave 11236 718-968-1530
Marcel Deans, prin. Fax 968-1526
WATCH HS 400/9-12
400 Pennsylvania Ave 11207 718-922-0650
Claudette Christie, prin. Fax 922-0709
W.E.B. DuBois Academic HS 200/9-12
402 Eastern Pkwy 11225 718-773-7765
Catherine Hartnett, prin. Fax 773-7849
West Brooklyn Community HS 200/10-12
1053 41st St 11219 718-686-1444
Gloria Rosario, prin. Fax 686-1189
Westinghouse Career & Tech HS Vo/Tech
105 Johnson St 11201 718-625-6130
Janine Kieran, prin. Fax 596-9434
Williamsburg HS Architecture & Design 500/9-12
257 N 6th St 11211 718-388-1260
Gill Cornell, prin. Fax 486-2580
Williamsburg Preparatory S 600/9-12
257 N 6th St 11211 718-302-2306
Michael Shadrick, prin. Fax 302-3726
Young Womens Leadership S of Brooklyn 200/6-12
325 Bushwick Ave 11206 718-387-5641
Talana Bradley, prin.

---

Access Careers Post-Sec.
25 Elm Pl Ste 201 11201 718-643-9060
Adelphi Academy of Brooklyn 100/PK-12
8515 Ridge Blvd 11209 718-238-3308
Al-Noor S 600/PK-12
675 4th Ave 11232 718-768-7181
ASA Inst of Business & Computer Tech Post-Sec.
81 Willoughby St 11201 718-522-9073
Bais Brocha Stolin Karlin 500/PK-12
4314 10th Ave 11219 718-853-1222
Bais Esther S 300/PK-12
1353 50th St 11219 718-436-1234
Bais Rochel HS 900/9-12
68 Harrison Ave 11211 718-963-9287
Bais Rochel S of Boro Park 400/K-12
5301 14th Ave 11219 718-438-7822
Bais Ruchel D'Satmar 3-12
84 Sandford St 11205 718-422-0375
Bais Sarah Girls S 900/PK-12
6101 16th Ave 11204 718-871-7571
Bais Tziporah S 400/PK-12
1449 39th St 11218 718-436-8336
Bais Yaakov Academy 900/PK-12
1213 Elm Ave 11230 718-339-4747
Faigie Selengut, prin. Fax 998-5766
Bais Yaakov Adas Yereim 500/PK-12
563 Bedford Ave 11211 718-302-7500
D. Ausch, prin. Fax 384-5885
Bais Yaakov Adas Yereim 300/PK-12
1169 43rd St 11219 718-435-5111
Bais Yaakov D'Chassidei Gur 500/PK-12
1975 51st St 11204 718-338-5600
Bais Yaakov D'Rav Meir HS 9-12
98 Lawrence Ave 11230 718-633-1232
Bay Ridge Preparatory S 400/K-12
8101 Ridge Blvd 11209 718-833-9090
Dr. Charles Fasano, head sch Fax 833-6680
Be'er Hagolah Institutes 500/K-12
671 Louisiana Ave 11239 718-642-6800
Beikvei Hatzoin S 200/PK-12
31 Division Ave 11249 718-486-6363
Beis Chaya Mushka 200/PK-12
1505 Carroll St 11213 718-756-0770
Beis Frima Chinuch Ctr 300/PK-10
1377 42nd St 11219 718-972-7666
Rabbi Steve Frankel, dir. Fax 972-0975
Beit Yaakov Orot Sarah 50/9-12
1123 Avenue N 11230 718-627-3158
Aviva Ben-Haim, prin. Fax 627-3101
Belz Girls S 1,100/PK-12
600 McDonald Ave 11218 718-871-0500
Berkeley Carroll S 500/5-12
181 Lincoln Pl 11217 718-534-6550
Robert Vitalo, head sch Fax 398-3640
Beth Chana S 300/1-12
712 Bedford Ave 11206 718-935-1845

Beth HaMedrash Shaarei Yosher Post-Sec.
4102 16th Ave # 10 11204 718-854-2290
Beth Hamedrash Shaarei Yosher 100/9-12
4102 16th Ave 11204 718-854-2290
Beth Hatalmud Rabbinical College Post-Sec.
2127 82nd St 11214 718-259-2525
Beth Jacob HS 600/9-12
4420 15th Ave 11219 718-851-2255
D. Wolf, prin. Fax 435-3736
Beth Rivkah HS 500/9-12
310 Crown St 11225 718-735-0400
Bet Medrash Gadol Ateret Post-Sec.
901 Quentin Rd 11223 347-394-1036
Bet Yaakov Ateret Torah HS 200/9-12
2166 Coney Island Ave 11223 718-382-7002
Bishop Kearney HS 600/9-12
2202 60th St 11204 718-236-6363
Elizabeth Guglielmo, prin. Fax 236-7784
Bishop Loughlin Memorial HS 700/9-12
357 Clermont Ave 11238 718-857-2700
Edward Bolan, prin. Fax 398-4227
Bnos Menachem S for Girls 600/PK-12
739 E New York Ave 11203 718-493-1100
Rabbi Zalman Wilhelm, admin. Fax 493-4836
Bnos Yaakov Educational Center 600/1-12
62 Harrison Ave 11211 718-387-7905
Bnos Yaakov Pupa 900/PK-12
1402 40th St 11218 718-851-0316
Bnos Yisroel Viznitz S 500/PK-12
12 Franklin Ave 11249 718-330-0222
Eva Rozman, prin. Fax 858-7387
Bnos Zion of Bobov 1,400/PK-12
5000 14th Ave 11219 718-438-3080
Brooklyn Amity S 200/PK-12
3867 Shore Pkwy 11235 718-891-6100
Brooklyn Friends S 800/PK-12
375 Pearl St 11201 718-852-1029
Dr. Larry Weiss, head sch Fax 643-4868
Brooklyn Hospital Post-Sec.
121 Dekalb Ave 11201 718-250-8005
Brooklyn Jesuit Prep S 100/5-8
560 Sterling Pl 11238 718-638-5884
Brian Chap, prin. Fax 228-6324
Brooklyn Law School Post-Sec.
250 Joralemon St 11201 718-625-2200
Career & Educational Consultants Post-Sec.
270 Flatbush Avenue Ext 11201 718-858-8500
Career Institute of Health & Technology Post-Sec.
340 Flatbush Avenue Ext 11201 718-422-1212
Central Yeshiva Tomchei Tmimim Lubavitz Post-Sec.
841 Ocean Pkwy 11230 718-434-0784
Charles Stuart School of Locksmithing Post-Sec.
1420 Kings Hwy 11229 718-339-2640
Chatzar Hakodesh Sanz-Klausenberg 700/PK-12
4511 14th Ave 11219 718-436-1248
Christian Heritage Academy 300/PK-12
1100 E 42nd St 11210 718-377-5682
Cope Institute Post-Sec.
4006 18th Ave 11218 718-506-0500
Cristo Rey Brooklyn HS 9-12
710 E 37th St 11203 718-455-3555
Richard Reyes, prin. Fax 455-3556
CUNY Brooklyn College Post-Sec.
2900 Bedford Ave 11210 718-951-5000
CUNY Kingsborough Community College Post-Sec.
2001 Oriental Blvd 11235 718-368-5000
CUNY Medgar Evers College Post-Sec.
1650 Bedford Ave 11225 718-270-4900
CUNY New York City College of Technology Post-Sec.
300 Jay St 11201 718-260-5000
Darkei Noam Rabbinical College Post-Sec.
2822 Avenue J 11210 718-338-6464
EDP School of Computer Programming Post-Sec.
1601 Voorhies Ave 11235 718-332-6469
Educational Institute Oholei Torah 400/9-12
667 Eastern Pkwy 11213 718-363-0019
Elite HS 50/9-12
2115 Benson Ave 11214 718-373-0960
Followers of Jesus S 50/1-12
3065 Atlantic Ave 11208 718-235-5493
James Gochnauer, prin. Fax 484-1477
Fontbonne Hall Academy 500/9-12
9901 Shore Rd 11209 718-748-2244
Mary Ann Spicijaric, prin. Fax 745-3841
Gamla College Post-Sec.
1213 Elm Ave 11230 718-339-4747
Gerer Mesivta Bais Yisroel 100/9-12
5407 16th Ave 11204 718-854-8777
Hair Design Institute at Fifth Avenue Post-Sec.
6711 5th Ave 11220 718-745-1000
Harma Religious Institute Yeshiva HS 200/12-12
30 Lancaster Ave 11223 718-743-3141
Institute of Design and Construction Post-Sec.
141 Willoughby St 11201 718-855-3661
Kehilath Yakov Rabbinical Seminary Post-Sec.
638 Bedford Ave 11249 718-963-1212
Learning Institute for Beauty Sciences Post-Sec.
2384 86th St 11214 718-373-2400
Lev Bais Yaakov S 400/PK-12
3574 Nostrand Ave 11229 718-332-6000
Rabbi Samuel Deutsch, dir. Fax 332-8868
Long Island University Post-Sec.
1 University Plz 11201 718-488-1000
Lubavitcher S Chabad 100/PK-12
841 Ocean Pkwy 11230 718-434-0795
Machon Bais Yaakov S 300/9-12
1683 42nd St 11204 718-972-7900
Machzikei Hadath Rabbinical College Post-Sec.
5407 16th Ave 11204 718-854-8777
Magen David Yeshiva HS 500/9-12
7801 Bay Pkwy 11214 718-331-4002
Rabbi Saul Zucker, prin. Fax 331-2174
Manhattan School of Computer Technology Post-Sec.
931 Coney Island Ave 11230 212-349-9768
Masores Bais Yaakov S 800/PK-12
1395 Ocean Ave 11230 718-692-2424
Merkaz Bnos - Career Institute Post-Sec.
2115 Benson Ave 11214 718-234-4000

Merkaz Bnos HS 100/9-12
1400 W 6th St 11204 718-259-5600
Mesivta Eastern Parkway Rabbinical Sem. Post-Sec.
510 Dahill Rd 11218 718-438-1002
Mesivta Eitz Chaim S 300/9-12
1577 48th St 11219 718-438-2018
Mesivta Imrei Yosef Spinka 400/9-12
1460 56th St 11219 718-851-1600
Mesivta Lev Bonim 100/9-12
8700 Avenue K 11236 718-444-5996
Mesivta Nachlas Yakov of Adas Yereim 100/9-12
185 Wilson St 11211 718-388-1751
Mesivta Nesivos Hatalmud 8-12
PO Box 190432 11219 718-972-0804
Rabbi Samuel Wolner, admin. Fax 972-6633
Mesivta of Manhattan Beach 50/9-11
59 W End Ave 11235 718-368-1333
Mesivta Sholom Shachne 100/9-12
129 Elmwood Ave 11230 718-252-6333
Mesivta Tiferes Elimelech S 200/9-12
4407 12th Ave 11219 718-854-3062
Mesivta Torah Vodaath Seminary Post-Sec.
425 E 9th St 11218 718-941-8000
Mesivta Veretzky 100/9-12
1102 Avenue L 11230 718-258-3888
Mesivta Yeshiva Rabbi Chaim Berlin 200/9-12
1585 Coney Island Ave 11230 718-377-8400
Rabbi Yosef Landsberg, prin. Fax 377-5883
Mesivta Zichron Eliezer S 50/9-12
1543 E 9th St 11230 718-336-9629
Mikdash Shelomo HS 50/8-12
1532 E 10th St 11230 718-382-1152
Mirrer Yeshiva Central Institute Post-Sec.
1795 Ocean Pkwy 11223 718-645-0536
Mirrer Yeshiva Mesivta HS 200/9-12
1795 Ocean Pkwy 11223 718-375-0771
Mosdos Chasidei Square 300/K-12
1373 43rd St 11219 718-436-2550
Nazareth Regional HS 400/9-12
475 E 57th St 11203 718-763-1100
Providentia Quiles, prin. Fax 629-5382
Nefesh Academy 100/PK-12
2005 E 17th St 11229 718-627-4463
Sandra Newhouse, prin.
New York Methodist Hospital Post-Sec.
1401 Kings Hwy 11229 718-780-3706
Packer Collegiate Institute 1,000/PK-12
170 Joralemon St 11201 718-250-0222
Dr. Bruce Dennis, hdmstr. Fax 875-1363
Poly Prep Country Day S 700/5-12
9216 7th Ave 11228 718-836-9800
David Harman, hdmstr. Fax 921-5112
Polytechnic Institute of New York Univ. Post-Sec.
6 Metrotech Ctr 11201 718-260-3600
Pratt Institute Post-Sec.
200 Willoughby Ave 11205 718-636-3600
Prospect Park Bnos Leah HS 300/9-12
1604 Avenue R 11229 718-376-4400
Rabbinical Academy Mesivta Rabbi Chaim Post-Sec.
1605 Coney Island Ave 11230 718-377-0777
Rabbinical Coll. Bobovr Yeshiva Bnei Zn. Post-Sec.
1577 48th St 11219 718-438-2018
Rabbinical College Ch' San Sofer Post-Sec.
1876 50th St 11204 718-236-1171
Rabbinical College Ohr Shimon Yisroel Post-Sec.
215 Hewes St 11211 718-855-4092
Rabbinical College Ohr Yisroel Post-Sec.
8800 Seaview Ave 11236 718-633-4715
Rabbinical Seminary Adas Yereim Post-Sec.
185 Wilson St 11211 718-388-1751
Rabbinical Seminary M'Kor Chaim Post-Sec.
1571 55th St 11219 718-851-0183
St. Ann's S 1,100/PK-12
129 Pierrepont St 11201 718-522-1660
Vincent Tompkins, hdmstr. Fax 522-2599
St. Edmund Preparatory HS 700/9-12
2474 Ocean Ave 11229 718-743-6100
John Lorenzetti, prin. Fax 743-5243
St. Francis College Post-Sec.
180 Remsen St 11201 718-522-2300
St. Joseph HS 300/9-12
80 Willoughby St 11201 718-624-3618
Sr. Joan Gallagher, prin. Fax 624-2792
St. Joseph's College New York Post-Sec.
245 Clinton Ave 11205 718-940-5300
St. Saviour HS 200/9-12
588 6th St 11215 718-768-4406
Sr. Valeria Belanger, prin. Fax 369-2688
Shalsheles Bais Yaakov S 100/1-12
4421 15th Ave 11219 718-436-1122
Sinai Academy 50/9-12
2025 79th St 11214 718-256-7400
Soille Bais Yaakov HS 100/9-12
2600 Ocean Ave 11229 718-769-8160
SUNY Downstate Medical Center Post-Sec.
450 Clarkson Ave 11203 718-270-1000
Talmudical Seminary of Bobov Post-Sec.
5120 New Utrecht Ave 11219 718-854-8700
Talmudical Seminary Oholei Torah Post-Sec.
667 Eastern Pkwy 11213 718-774-5050
Talmud Torah Imrei Chaim 600/PK-12
1824 53rd St 11204 718-234-2000
Tichon Bnot Rachel HS 100/9-12
1950 E 7th St 11223 718-382-1555
Rachel Pinto, admin. Fax 376-2488
Tomer Dvora HS 300/9-12
5801 16th Ave 11204 718-633-4125
Torah Academy HS of Brooklyn 50/9-12
2066 E 9th St 11223 718-339-8844
Torah Temimah Talmudical Seminary Post-Sec.
507 Ocean Pkwy 11218 718-853-8500
United Lubavitcher Yeshiva 100/9-12
PO Box 130347 11213 718-735-6607
United Talmudical Academy 400/7-9
1346 53rd St 11219 718-438-7038
United Talmudical Seminary Post-Sec.
191 Rodney St 11211 718-963-9770

Xaverian HS 1,000/9-12
7100 Shore Rd 11209 718-836-7100
Kevin McCormack, admin. Fax 836-7114
Yeshiva and Kollel Harbotzas Torah Post-Sec.
1049 E 15th St 11230 718-692-0208
Yeshiva & Mesivta Torah Temimah 600/PK-12
555 Ocean Pkwy 11218 718-853-8500
Yeshiva Beis Meir 200/9-12
1327 38th St 11218 718-437-5844
Yeshiva Chanoch Lenaar 50/8-12
876 Eastern Pkwy 11213 718-774-8456
Yeshiva Chemdas Yisroel Kerem 200/10-12
1149 38th St 11218 718-686-5500
Yeshiva Ch'san Sofer - Mesivta M'shmuel 500/PK-12
1876 50th St 11204 718-236-1171
Yeshiva Darchai Menachem 100/4-12
432 Rutland Rd 11203 718-953-2919
Yeshiva Derech Chaim Post-Sec.
1573 39th St 11218 718-438-5476
Yeshiva Derech HaTorah 300/PK-10
2810 Nostrand Ave 11229 718-258-4441
Yeshiva Farm Settlement S 400/K-12
194 Division Ave 11211 914-387-0422
Yeshiva Gedolah Bais Yisroel Post-Sec.
2002 Avenue J 11210 718-258-7400
Yeshiva Gedolah Imrei Yosef D'Spinka Post-Sec.
1466 56th St 11219 718-851-8721
Yeshiva Gedolah of Midwood 100/11-12
201 Avenue F 11218 718-853-2400
Yeshiva Gedolah Ohr Yisrael Post-Sec.
2899 Nostrand Ave 11229 718-382-8702
Yeshiva Imrei Yoseph Spinka 200/K-12
5801 15th Ave 11219 718-851-1600
Yeshiva Karlin Stolin Post-Sec.
1818 54th St 11204 718-232-7800
Yeshiva Kehilath Yaakov 700/PK-10
183 Wilson St Ste 136 11211 718-486-7934
Yeshiva Ketana of Bensonhurst 200/PK-10
2025 67th St 11204 718-236-4100
Yeshiva Ketana Toldos Yaakov 100/9-12
87 Heyward St 11206 718-852-0502
Yeshiva Machzikei Hadas Belz 1,100/PK-12
1601 42nd St 11204 718-436-4445
Yeshiva Mesivta Arugath Habosem 400/K-12
40 Lynch St 11206 718-237-4500
Yeshiva Mesivta Karlin Stolin 600/PK-12
1818 54th St 11204 718-232-7800
Yeshiva Mesivta Tiferes Yisroel S 700/K-12
1271 E 35th St 11210 718-258-9006
David Schonbrun, prin. Fax 258-9055
Yeshiva Mikdash Melech Post-Sec.
1326 Ocean Pkwy 11230 718-339-1090
Yeshiva Minchas Eluzar S 50/9-12
4706 14th Ave 11219 718-438-7633
Yeshiva Nesivos Chaim 50/9-12
221 Avenue F 11218 718-633-4760
Yeshiva of Brooklyn-Girls 700/PK-12
1470 Ocean Pkwy 11230 718-376-3775
Yeshiva of Flatbush Joel Braverman HS 600/9-12
1609 Avenue J 11230 718-377-1100
Rabbi Raymond Harari, hdmstr. Fax 258-0933
Yeshiva of Machzikai Hadas Post-Sec.
1301 47th St 11219 718-853-2442
Yeshiva of Nitra Rabbinical College Post-Sec.
194 Division Ave 11211 718-387-0422
Yeshiva R'tzahd S 400/5-8
8700 Avenue K 11236 718-444-5996
Yeshivas Boyan Tiferes Mordechai Shlomo 200/PK-12
1205 44th St 11219 718-435-6060
Yeshiva Sholom Shachna Post-Sec.
401 Elmwood Ave 11230 718-252-6333
Yeshivas Novominsk Post-Sec.
1690 60th St 11204 718-438-2727
Yeshivas Novominsk-Kol Yehuda 200/9-12
1690 60th St 11204 718-438-2727
Yeshivas Tiferes Avos 50/9-12
1960 Schenectady Ave 11234 718-252-0801
Yeshivas Vyelipol HS 100/9-12
860 E 27th St 11210 718-951-1800
Yehuda Rubin, prin. Fax 951-3414
Yeshivat Ateret Torah 1,600/PK-12
901 Quentin Rd 11223 718-375-7100
Yeshiva Tiferes Shmiel D'Aleksander 100/9-12
PO Box 190738 11219 718-633-5952
Yeshiva Toldos Yitzchok Bnei Mordechai 500/K-10
1413 45th St 11219 718-633-4802
Yeshiva Toras Emes Kamenitz 500/PK-12
1904 Avenue N 11230 718-375-0900
Rabbi Fischel Engelberg, prin. Fax 376-4661
Yeshivat Or Hatorah S 100/9-12
2119 Homecrest Ave 11229 718-645-4645
Yeshivat Shaare Torah Boys S 100/PK-12
1202 Avenue P 11229 718-645-6676
Yeshivat Shaare Torah Girls HS 100/9-12
1768 Ocean Ave 11230 718-382-4000
Sarah Wadler, prin. Fax 382-7999
Yeshiva Yesode Hatorah 100/9-12
620 Bedford Ave 11249 718-802-1613
Zvi Dov Roth Academy 100/6-12
3300 Kings Hwy 11234 718-677-5100

**Brookville, Nassau, Pop. 3,435**

Long Island Lutheran Middle & HS 600/6-12
131 Brookville Rd 11545 516-626-1700
Dr. Andrew Grove, head sch Fax 622-7459
Long Island University Post-Sec.
720 Northern Blvd 11548 516-299-2000

**Brushton, Franklin, Pop. 466**

Brushton-Moira Central SD 700/PK-12
758 County Route 7 12916 518-529-8942
Donna Andre, supt. Fax 529-6062
www.bmcsd.org
Brushton-Moira Central HS 400/7-12
758 County Route 7 12916 518-529-7342
Todd LaPage, prin. Fax 529-6062

**Buffalo, Erie, Pop. 254,867**
Buffalo CSD 30,700/PK-12
712 City Hall 14202 716-816-3500
Dr. Kriner Cash, supt. Fax 851-3535
www.buffaloschools.org
Public HS 195 900/5-12
186 E North St 14204 716-816-4230
Dr. William Kresse, prin. Fax 888-7145
Public HS 200 700/9-12
2885 Main St 14214 716-816-4250
Bert Stevenson, prin. Fax 838-7490
Public HS 204 500/9-12
370 Lafayette Ave 14213 716-816-4340
Denise Clarke, prin. Fax 888-7096
Public HS 205 800/9-12
51 Ontario St 14207 716-816-4360
Ella Dunne, prin. Fax 871-6046
Public HS 206 800/9-12
150 Southside Pkwy 14220 716-816-4828
Theresa Schuta, prin. Fax 828-4905
Public HS 212 400/9-12
320 Porter Ave 14201 716-816-4380
Florence Krieter, prin. Fax 888-7181
Public HS 301 Vo/Tech
400 Kensington Ave 14214 716-816-4450
Charlene Watson, prin. Fax 838-7546
Public HS 302 400/9-12
70 W Chippewa St 14202 716-816-3018
James Weimer, prin. Fax 851-3017
Public HS 304 1,000/9-12
256 S Elmwood Ave 14201 716-816-3888
Sabatino Cimato, prin. Fax 851-3890
Public HS 305 Vo/Tech
1500 Elmwood Ave 14207 716-816-4480
Crystal Barton, prin. Fax 897-6073
Public HS 307 500/9-12
820 Northampton St 14211 716-816-4520
Casey Young, prin. Fax 897-8130
Public HS 353 Alt
370 Lafayette Ave 14213 716-816-4340
Teena Jackson, prin.
Public HS 357 Alt
820 Northampton St 14211 716-816-4520
Michael Mogavero, prin.
Public HS 415 9-12
2885 Main St 14214 716-816-4010
Susan Doyle, prin. Fax 851-3868
Public JSHS 131 7-12
425 S Park Ave 14204 716-816-3270
Michael Mogavero, prin. Fax 851-3761
Public JSHS 197 400/5-12
101 Hertel Ave 14207 716-816-4500
Todd Miklas, prin. Fax 871-6007
Public MS 66 400/5-8
780 Parkside Ave 14216 716-816-3440
Shanie Keelean, prin. Fax 838-7448
Public MSHS 192 800/5-12
450 Masten Ave 14209 716-816-4220
Jody Covington, prin. Fax 888-7136
Public MSHS 198 500/5-12
110 14th St 14213 716-816-4300
Carlos Alvarez, prin. Fax 851-3863
Public S 156 600/5-12
319 Suffolk St 14215 716-816-4330
Michael Gruber, prin. Fax 838-7530

Kenmore-Tonawanda UFSD 7,200/K-12
1500 Colvin Blvd 14223 716-874-8400
Dawn F. Mirand, supt. Fax 874-8621
www.ktufsd.org
Franklin MS 500/6-8
540 Parkhurst Blvd 14223 716-874-8404
Kevin Kruger, prin. Fax 874-8480
Hoover MS 600/6-8
249 Thorncliff Rd 14223 716-874-8405
Carmelina Persico, prin. Fax 874-8470
Kenmore West HS 1,400/9-12
33 Highland Pkwy 14223 716-874-8401
Dean Johnson, prin. Fax 874-8527
Other Schools – See Kenmore, Tonawanda

---

Bishop Timon-St. Jude HS 300/9-12
601 McKinley Pkwy 14220 716-826-3610
Thomas Sullivan, prin. Fax 824-5833
Bryant & Stratton College Post-Sec.
465 Main St Ste 400 14203 716-884-9120
Buffalo Academy of the Sacred Heart 400/9-12
3860 Main St 14226 716-834-2101
Jennifer Demert, head sch Fax 834-2944
Buffalo Seminary 200/9-12
205 Bidwell Pkwy 14222 716-885-6780
Jody Douglass, hdmstr. Fax 885-6785
Canisius College Post-Sec.
2001 Main St 14208 716-883-7000
Canisius HS 800/9-12
1180 Delaware Ave 14209 716-882-0466
Andrea Tyrpak-Endres, prin. Fax 883-1870
Continental School of Beauty Culture Post-Sec.
326 Kenmore Ave 14223 716-833-5016
Darul-Uloom Al Madania 200/PK-10
182 Sobieski St 14212 716-892-2606
D'Youville College Post-Sec.
320 Porter Ave 14201 716-829-8000
Erie Community College City Post-Sec.
121 Ellicott St 14203 716-842-2770
Medaille College Post-Sec.
18 Agassiz Cir 14214 716-880-2000
Mt. Mercy Academy 300/9-12
88 Red Jacket Pkwy 14220 716-825-8796
Margaret Staszak, prin. Fax 825-0976
Nardin Academy 500/K-12
135 Cleveland Ave 14222 716-881-6262
Rebecca Reeder, prin. Fax 881-0086
National Tractor Trailer School Post-Sec.
175 Katherine St 14210 716-849-6887
Nativity Miguel MS 100/5-8
21 Davidson Ave 14215 716-836-5188
Fr. Edward Durkin, prin. Fax 836-5189
New York Institute of Massage Post-Sec.
PO Box 645 14231 716-633-0355
Nichols S 600/5-12
1250 Amherst St 14216 716-332-6300
Bill Clough, head sch Fax 875-2169
St. Mary's School for the Deaf Post-Sec.
2253 Main St 14214
Salvatore Sch of Hospitality & Business Post-Sec.
6681 Transit Rd 14221 716-827-4300
SUNY Buffalo State College Post-Sec.
1300 Elmwood Ave 14222 716-878-4000
SUNY Educational Opportunity Center Post-Sec.
465 Washington St 14203 716-849-6725
Trocaire College Post-Sec.
360 Choate Ave 14220 716-826-1200
University at Buffalo SUNY Post-Sec.
12 Capen Hall 14260 716-645-2000
Villa Maria College of Buffalo Post-Sec.
240 Pine Ridge Rd 14225 716-896-0700

**Burnt Hills, Saratoga**
Burnt Hills-Ballston Lake Central SD
Supt. — See Glenville
Burnt Hills-Ballston Lake HS 1,100/9-12
88 Lake Hill Rd 12027 518-399-9141
Timothy Brunson, prin. Fax 399-4341
O'Rourke MS 800/6-8
173 Lake Hill Rd 12027 518-399-9141
Colleen Wolff, prin. Fax 384-2588

**Burt, Niagara**
Newfane Central SD 1,800/PK-12
6048 Godfrey Rd 14028 716-778-6850
Dr. Bruce Fraser, supt. Fax 778-6852
www.newfane.wnyric.org
Other Schools – See Newfane

**Cairo, Greene, Pop. 1,375**
Cairo-Durham Central SD 1,100/PK-12
PO Box 780 12413 518-622-8534
Anthony Taibi, supt. Fax 622-9566
www.cairodurham.org
Cairo-Durham HS 500/9-12
PO Box 598 12413 518-622-8543
Matthew Ward, prin. Fax 622-8857
Cairo-Durham MS 300/6-8
PO Box 1139 12413 518-622-0490
Nathan Farrell, prin. Fax 622-0493

**Caledonia, Livingston, Pop. 2,169**
Caledonia-Mumford Central SD 900/PK-12
PO Box 150 14423 585-538-3400
Robert Molisani, supt. Fax 538-3450
www.cal-mum.org
Caledonia-Mumford HS 300/9-12
PO Box 150 14423 585-538-3483
Merritt Holly, prin. Fax 538-3470
Caledonia-Mumford MS 200/6-8
PO Box 150 14423 585-538-3482
Paul Estabrooks, prin. Fax 538-3430

**Cambridge, Washington, Pop. 1,844**
Cambridge Central SD 900/K-12
58 S Park St 12816 518-677-8527
Vincent Canini, supt. Fax 677-3889
www.cambridgecsd.org
Cambridge HS 400/7-12
24 S Park St 12816 518-677-8527
Tammy Silvernell, prin. Fax 677-3246

**Camden, Oneida, Pop. 2,211**
Camden Central SD 2,300/PK-12
51 3rd St 13316 315-245-4075
Mary Lynne Szczerba, supt. Fax 245-1622
www.camdenschools.org
Camden HS 700/9-12
55 Oswego St 13316 315-245-3168
Heather Wieland, prin. Fax 245-4173
Camden MS 500/5-8
32 Union St 13316 315-245-0080
Mary Walker, prin. Fax 245-0083

**Camillus, Onondaga, Pop. 1,196**
West Genesee Central SD 4,900/K-12
300 Sanderson Dr 13031 315-487-4562
Dr. Christopher Brown, supt. Fax 487-2999
www.westgenesee.org
Camillus MS 500/6-8
5525 Ike Dixon Rd 13031 315-672-3159
Beth Lozier, prin. Fax 672-3309
West Genesee HS 1,700/9-12
5201 W Genesee St 13031 315-487-4592
Dr. Barry Copeland, prin. Fax 487-4582
West Genesee MS 700/6-8
500 Sanderson Dr 13031 315-487-4615
Stephen Dunham, prin. Fax 487-4618

**Campbell, Steuben, Pop. 695**
Campbell-Savona Central SD 900/PK-12
8455 County Route 125 14821 607-527-9800
Kathleen Hagenbuch, supt. Fax 527-9863
www.cscsd.org
Campbell-Savona JSHS 400/7-12
8455 County Route 125 14821 607-527-9800
Lisa Hawken, prin. Fax 527-9862

**Canaan, Columbia**
Berkshire UFD 100/7-12
13640 State Route 22 12029 518-781-3500
Bruce Potter, supt. Fax 781-4890
www.berkshirefarm.org
Berkshire JSHS 100/Alt
13640 State Route 22 12029 518-781-3500
Michael Mitchell, prin. Fax 781-4890

**Canajoharie, Montgomery, Pop. 2,208**
Canajoharie Central SD 1,000/PK-12
136 Scholastic Way 13317 518-673-6302
Deborah Grimshaw, supt. Fax 673-3177
www.canajoharieschools.org
Canajoharie HS 300/9-12
136 Scholastic Way 13317 518-673-6330
Rebecca Gleason, prin. Fax 673-3177
Canajoharie MS 200/6-8
25 School District Rd 13317 518-673-6320
Mark Rauch, prin. Fax 673-5557

**Canandaigua, Ontario, Pop. 10,383**
Canandaigua CSD 3,700/PK-12
143 N Pearl St 14424 585-396-3700
Lynne H. Erdle, supt. Fax 396-7306
www.canandaiguaschools.org/
Canandaigua Academy 1,200/9-12
435 East St 14424 585-396-3800
Vernon Tenney, prin. Fax 396-3806
Canandaigua MS 800/6-8
215 Granger St 14424 585-396-3850
John Arthur, prin. Fax 396-3863

---

Finger Lakes Community College Post-Sec.
3325 Marvin Sands Dr 14424 585-394-3500

**Canaseraga, Allegany, Pop. 544**
Canaseraga Central SD 300/PK-12
PO Box 230 14822 607-545-6421
Chad Groff, supt. Fax 545-6265
www.ccsdny.org/
Canaseraga S 300/PK-12
PO Box 230 14822 607-545-6421
Chad Groff, supt. Fax 545-6265

**Canastota, Madison, Pop. 4,723**
Canastota Central SD 1,500/K-12
120 Roberts St 13032 315-697-2025
June Clarke, supt. Fax 697-6368
www.canastotacsd.org
Canastota JSHS 700/7-12
101 Roberts St 13032 315-697-2003
Molly Mecca, prin. Fax 697-6314

---

USC The Business College Post-Sec.
PO Box 462 13032 315-697-8200

**Candor, Tioga, Pop. 840**
Candor Central SD 800/K-12
PO Box 145 13743 607-659-5010
Jeffrey Kisloski, supt. Fax 659-7112
candor.org
Candor JSHS 400/7-12
PO Box 145 13743 607-659-5020
Wayne Aman, prin. Fax 659-4692

**Canisteo, Steuben, Pop. 2,260**
Canisteo-Greenwood Central SD 1,000/PK-12
84 Greenwood St 14823 607-698-4225
Jeremy Palotti, supt. Fax 698-2833
www.cg.wnyric.org
Canisteo-Greenwood HS 300/9-12
84 Greenwood St 14823 607-698-4225
Michael Wright, prin. Fax 698-9125
Canisteo-Greenwood MS 300/5-8
120 Greenwood St 14823 607-698-4225
Paul Cone, prin. Fax 698-2244

**Canton, Saint Lawrence, Pop. 6,213**
Canton Central SD 1,200/PK-12
99 State St 13617 315-386-8561
William Gregory, supt. Fax 386-1323
www.ccsdk12.org/
McKenney MS 400/5-8
99 State St 13617 315-386-8561
Viola Schmid-Doyle, prin. Fax 386-1323
Williams HS 400/9-12
99 State St 13617 315-386-8561
Henry D. Dominy, prin. Fax 386-1323

---

St. Lawrence University Post-Sec.
23 Romoda Dr 13617 315-229-5011
SUNY Canton Post-Sec.
34 Cornell Dr 13617 315-386-7011

**Carle Place, Nassau, Pop. 4,914**
Carle Place UFD 1,400/K-12
168 Cherry Ln 11514 516-622-6442
David J. Flatley, supt. Fax 622-6447
www.cps.k12.ny.us
Carle Place MSHS 700/7-12
168 Cherry Ln 11514 516-622-6431
Thomas DePaola, prin. Fax 622-6587

**Carmel, Putnam, Pop. 4,800**
Carmel Central SD
Supt. — See Patterson
Carmel HS 1,500/9-12
30 Fair St 10512 845-225-8441
Lou Riolo, prin. Fax 228-2308
Fischer MS 1,400/5-8
281 Fair St 10512 845-228-2300
John Piscitella, prin. Fax 228-2304

**Carthage, Jefferson, Pop. 3,663**
Carthage Central SD 3,400/K-12
25059 Woolworth St 13619 315-493-5000
Peter Turner, supt. Fax 493-5069
www.carthagecsd.org
Carthage HS 1,000/9-12
36500 State Route 26 13619 315-493-5030
Joseph Sedita, prin. Fax 493-5039
Carthage MS 1,000/5-8
21986 Cole Rd 13619 315-493-5020
Kylie Buker, prin. Fax 493-5029

**Castleton on Hudson, Rensselaer, Pop. 1,464**
Schodack Central SD · 1,000/K-12
1216 Maple Hill Rd 12033 · 518-732-2297
Robert Horan, supt. · Fax 732-7710
www.schodack.k12.ny.us/
Maple Hill HS · 400/9-12
1216 Maple Hill Rd 12033 · 518-732-7701
Ron Agostinoni, prin. · Fax 732-0494
Maple Hill MS · 200/6-8
1477 S Schodack Rd 12033 · 518-732-7736
James Derby, prin. · Fax 732-0493

**Cato, Cayuga, Pop. 516**
Cato-Meridian Central SD · 1,100/PK-12
2851 State Route 370 13033 · 315-626-3439
W. Noel Patterson, supt. · Fax 626-2888
www.catomeridian.org/
Cato-Meridian HS · 300/9-12
2851 State Route 370 13033 · 315-626-3317
Danielle Mahoney, prin. · Fax 626-2551
Cato-Meridian MS · 300/5-8
2851 State Route 370 13033 · 315-626-3319
Sean Gleason, prin. · Fax 626-2327

**Catskill, Greene, Pop. 3,926**
Catskill Central SD · 1,600/PK-12
343 W Main St 12414 · 518-943-4696
Kathleen Farrell Ph.D., supt. · Fax 943-7116
www.catskillcsd.org
Catskill HS · 500/9-12
341 W Main St 12414 · 518-943-2300
William Ball, prin. · Fax 943-1451
Catskill MS · 400/6-8
345 W Main St 12414 · 518-943-5665
Marielena Davis, prin. · Fax 943-3001

**Cattaraugus, Cattaraugus, Pop. 997**
Cattaraugus-Little Valley Central SD · 800/PK-12
25 N Franklin St 14719 · 716-257-5293
Jon Peteson, supt. · Fax 257-5298
www.cattlv.wnyric.org/
Cattaraugus-Little Valley HS · 300/8-12
25 N Franklin St 14719 · 716-257-3483
Tony Giannicchi, prin. · Fax 257-5108

**Cazenovia, Madison, Pop. 2,807**
Cazenovia Central SD · 1,600/K-12
31 Emory Ave 13035 · 315-655-1317
Matthew Reilly, supt. · Fax 655-1375
www.caz.cnyric.org
Cazenovia JSHS · 700/8-12
31 Emory Ave 13035 · 315-655-1314
Eric Knuth, prin. · Fax 655-1371

---

Cazenovia College 13035 · Post-Sec.
800-654-3210

**Cedarhurst, Nassau, Pop. 6,500**
Lawrence UFD
Supt. — See Lawrence
Lawrence HS · 900/9-12
2 Reilly Rd 11516 · 516-295-8000
Dr. Jennifer Lagnado, prin. · Fax 295-2754

---

Hebrew Academy of Five Towns HS · 300/9-12
635 Central Ave 11516 · 516-569-3807
Shulamith S for Girls · 500/PK-12
305 Cedarhurst Ave 11516 · 516-564-1500

**Centereach, Suffolk, Pop. 31,131**
Middle Country Central SD · 10,500/PK-12
8 43rd St 11720 · 631-285-8005
Dr. Roberta Gerold, supt. · Fax 738-2719
www.mccsd.net
Centereach HS · 1,600/9-12
14 43rd St 11720 · 631-285-8100
Thomas Bell, prin. · Fax 285-8101
Dawnwood MS · 1,200/6-8
10 43rd St 11720 · 631-285-8200
Kristine Leonard, prin. · Fax 285-8201
Selden MS · 1,200/6-8
22 Jefferson Ave 11720 · 631-285-8400
Jonathan Singer, prin. · Fax 285-8401
Other Schools – See Selden

---

Our Savior New American S · 200/PK-12
140 Mark Tree Rd 11720 · 631-588-2757
Dolores Reade, prin. · Fax 588-2617

**Center Moriches, Suffolk, Pop. 7,447**
Center Moriches UFD · 1,600/K-12
529 Main St 11934 · 631-878-0052
Russell Stewart, supt. · Fax 878-4326
www.cmschools.org
Center Moriches HS · 600/9-12
311 Frowein Rd 11934 · 631-878-0092
Edward Casswell, prin. · Fax 878-1796
Center Moriches MS · 400/6-8
311 Frowein Rd 11934 · 631-878-2519
Melissa Bates, prin. · Fax 878-0362

**Central Islip, Suffolk, Pop. 33,583**
Central Islip UFD · 6,500/PK-12
50 Wheeler Rd 11722 · 631-348-5112
Dr. Craig Carr, supt. · Fax 348-0366
www.cischools.org
Central Islip HS · 1,800/9-12
85 Wheeler Rd 11722 · 631-348-5078
Catherine Vereline, prin. · Fax 342-0161
Mulligan MS · 1,000/6-8
1 Broadway Ave 11722 · 631-348-5042
Dr. Tracy Hudson, prin. · Fax 348-5164
Reed MS · 900/7-8
200 Half Mile Rd 11722 · 631-348-5066
Brett MacMonigle, prin. · Fax 348-5159

**Central Square, Oswego, Pop. 1,828**
Central Square Central SD · 4,200/K-12
642 S Main St 13036 · 315-668-4220
Joseph Menard, supt. · Fax 676-4437
www.cssd.org
Central Square MS · 1,000/6-8
248 US Route 11 13036 · 315-668-4269
Concetta Galvan, prin. · Fax 668-8410
Moore HS · 1,400/9-12
44 School Dr 13036 · 315-668-4231
Jeffrey King, prin. · Fax 668-4346

**Central Valley, Orange, Pop. 1,929**
Monroe-Woodbury Central SD · 7,100/K-12
278 Route 32 10917 · 845-460-6200
Elsie Rodriguez, supt. · Fax 460-6080
www.mw.k12.ny.us
Monroe-Woodbury HS · 2,300/9-12
155 Dunderberg Rd 10917 · 845-460-7000
David Bernsley, prin. · Fax 460-7090
Monroe-Woodbury MS · 1,700/6-8
199 Dunderberg Rd 10917 · 845-460-6400
John Kaste, prin. · Fax 460-6044

**Champlain, Clinton, Pop. 1,086**
Northeastern Clinton Central SD · 1,300/K-12
103 State Route 276 12919 · 518-298-8242
Lisa Grenville, supt. · Fax 298-4293
www.nccscougar.org
Northeastern Clinton HS · 500/9-12
103 State Route 276 12919 · 518-298-8638
Stephen Gratto, prin. · Fax 298-4293
Northeastern Clinton MS · 300/6-8
103 State Route 276 12919 · 518-298-8681
Thomas Brandell, prin. · Fax 298-4293

**Chappaqua, Westchester, Pop. 1,404**
Chappaqua Central SD · 4,100/K-12
PO Box 21 10514 · 914-238-7200
Dr. Lyn Mckay, supt. · Fax 238-7231
www.ccsd.ws
Bell MS · 700/5-8
50 Senter St 10514 · 914-238-7202
Martin Fitzgerald, prin. · Fax 238-2085
Greeley HS · 1,300/9-12
70 Roaring Brook Rd 10514 · 914-738-7201
Robert Rhodes, prin.
Seven Bridges MS · 600/5-8
PO Box 22 10514 · 914-238-7203
Michael Kirsch, prin. · Fax 666-7306

**Chateaugay, Franklin, Pop. 824**
Chateaugay Central SD · 500/K-12
PO Box 904 12920 · 518-497-6420
Loretta Fowler, supt. · Fax 497-3170
www.chateaugaycsd.org
Chateaugay JSHS · 300/7-12
PO Box 904 12920 · 518-497-6611
Lori Tourville, prin. · Fax 497-3170

**Chatham, Columbia, Pop. 1,720**
Chatham Central SD · 1,200/K-12
50 Woodbridge Ave 12037 · 518-392-1501
Cheryl Nuciforo, supt. · Fax 392-2413
www.chathamcentralschools.com
Chatham HS · 500/9-12
50 Woodbridge Ave 12037 · 518-392-4142
John Thorsen, prin. · Fax 392-0908
Chatham MS · 300/6-8
50 Woodbridge Ave 12037 · 518-392-1560
Amy Potter, prin. · Fax 392-1559

**Chaumont, Jefferson, Pop. 611**
Lyme Central SD · 300/PK-12
PO Box 219 13622 · 315-649-2417
Cammy Morrison, supt. · Fax 649-2663
www.lymecsd.org
Lyme Central S · 300/PK-12
PO Box 219 13622 · 315-649-2417
Barry Davis, prin. · Fax 649-2663

**Chazy, Clinton, Pop. 555**
Chazy Central UFD · 500/K-12
609 Miner Farm Rd 12921 · 518-846-7135
John Fairchild, supt. · Fax 846-8322
www.chazy.org
Chazy Central Rural JSHS · 200/7-12
609 Miner Farm Rd 12921 · 518-846-7135
John Fairchild, prin. · Fax 846-8322

**Cheektowaga, Erie, Pop. 74,096**
Cheektowaga Central SD · 2,000/PK-12
3600 Union Rd 14225 · 716-686-3606
Dennis Kane, supt. · Fax 681-5232
www.cheektowagacentral.org
Cheektowaga Central HS · 600/9-12
3600 Union Rd 14225 · 716-686-3602
Scott Zipp, prin. · Fax 686-3619
Cheektowaga Central MS · 500/6-8
3600 Union Rd 14225 · 716-686-3660
Gretchen Sukdola, prin. · Fax 686-3669

Cheektowaga-Maryvale UFD · 2,200/PK-12
1050 Maryvale Dr 14225 · 716-631-7407
Joseph D'Angelo, supt. · Fax 635-4699
www.maryvaleufsd.org
Maryvale HS · 700/9-12
1050 Maryvale Dr 14225 · 716-631-7481
Tom Stack, prin. · Fax 631-7404
Maryvale MS · 500/6-8
1050 Maryvale Dr 14225 · 716-631-7425
Jeff Richards, prin. · Fax 631-7499

Cheektowago-Sloan UFD
Supt. — See Sloan
Kennedy HS · 500/9-12
305 Cayuga Creek Rd 14227 · 716-891-6407
Kevin Kazmierczak, prin. · Fax 270-0160
Kennedy MS · 300/6-8
305 Cayuga Creek Rd 14227 · 716-897-7300
Gretchen Cercone, prin. · Fax 892-2624

Cleveland Hill UFD · 1,400/PK-12
105 Mapleview Dr 14225 · 716-836-7200
Jon MacSwan, supt. · Fax 836-0675
www.clevehill.wnyric.org/
Cleveland Hill HS · 400/9-12
105 Mapleview Dr 14225 · 716-836-7200
Jill Sherman, prin. · Fax 836-7741
Cleveland Hill MS · 300/6-8
105 Mapleview Dr 14225 · 716-836-7200
Andrea Kersten, prin. · Fax 836-7741

**Cherryplain, Rensselaer**
Berlin Central SD · 600/PK-12
17400 Route 22 12040 · 518-658-2690
Dr. Stephen Young, supt. · Fax 658-3822
www.berlincentral.org/
Berlin Central JSHS · 300/6-12
17400 Route 22 12040 · 518-658-2515
Dr. Cathie Allain, prin. · Fax 658-2535

**Cherry Valley, Otsego, Pop. 511**
Cherry Valley-Springfield Central SD · 500/PK-12
PO Box 485 13320 · 607-264-3265
Timothy Ryan, supt. · Fax 264-3458
www.cvscs.org
Cherry Valley-Springfield JSHS · 300/6-12
PO Box 485 13320 · 607-264-3265
Lauren Crisman, prin. · Fax 264-3458

**Chester, Orange, Pop. 3,852**
Chester UFD · 1,000/K-12
64 Hambletonian Ave 10918 · 845-469-5052
Sean Michel, supt. · Fax 469-2377
chesterufsd.org
Chester Academy · 600/6-12
64 Hambletonian Ave 10918 · 845-469-2231
Denis Petrilak, prin. · Fax 469-3547

**Chestertown, Warren, Pop. 671**
North Warren Central SD · 500/PK-12
6110 State Route 8 12817 · 518-494-3015
Margaret Brady, supt. · Fax 494-2929
www.northwarren.k12.ny.us
North Warren Central S · 500/PK-12
6110 State Route 8 12817 · 518-494-3015
Theresa Andrew, prin. · Fax 494-2929

**Chestnut Ridge, Rockland, Pop. 7,763**
East Ramapo Central SD
Supt. — See Spring Valley
Chestnut Ridge MS · 500/7-8
892 Chestnut Ridge Rd 10977 · 845-577-6300
Maria Vergez, prin. · Fax 426-1063

---

Green Meadow Waldorf S · 400/PK-12
307 Hungry Hollow Rd 10977 · 845-356-2514
Bill Pernice, admin. · Fax 356-2921

**Chittenango, Madison, Pop. 5,016**
Chittenango Central SD · 2,100/K-12
1732 Fyler Rd 13037 · 315-687-2850
Michael Schiedo, supt. · Fax 687-2841
www.chittenangoschools.org
Chittenango HS · 700/9-12
150 Genesee St 13037 · 315-687-2900
Derek Sajnog, prin. · Fax 687-2924
Chittenango MS · 500/5-8
1732 Fyler Rd 13037 · 315-687-2800
Thomas Piatti, prin. · Fax 687-2801

**Churchville, Monroe, Pop. 1,935**
Churchville-Chili Central SD · 4,000/K-12
139 Fairbanks Rd 14428 · 585-293-1800
Loretta Orologio, supt. · Fax 293-1013
www.cccsd.org
Churchville-Chili MS · 1,300/5-8
139 Fairbanks Rd 14428 · 585-293-4541
Giulio Bosco, prin. · Fax 293-4516
Churchville-Chili SHS · 1,000/10-12
5786 Buffalo Rd 14428 · 585-293-4540
Bill Geraci, prin. · Fax 293-4508
9th Grade Academy · 300/9-9
137 Fairbanks Rd 14428 · 585-293-4546
Mary Leach, admin. · Fax 293-4521

**Cicero, Onondaga**
North Syracuse Central SD
Supt. — See North Syracuse
Cicero-North Syracuse SHS · 2,200/10-12
6002 State Route 31 13039 · 315-218-4100
Bob Gaetano, prin. · Fax 218-4185

**Cincinnatus, Cortland**
Cincinnatus Central SD · 400/K-12
2809 Cincinnatus Rd 13040 · 607-863-4069
Steven Hubbard, supt. · Fax 863-4109
www.cc.cnyric.org/
Cincinnatus HS · 200/7-12
2809 Cincinnatus Rd 13040 · 607-863-3200
Dr. Karen Genzel, prin. · Fax 863-4559

**Circleville, Orange, Pop. 1,350**
Pine Bush Central SD
Supt. — See Pine Bush
Circleville MS · 600/6-8
PO Box 143 10919 · 845-744-2031
Lisa Hankinson, prin. · Fax 361-3811

**Clarence, Erie, Pop. 2,634**
Clarence Central SD · 4,900/K-12
9625 Main St 14031 · 716-407-9100
Geoffrey Hicks, supt. · Fax 407-9126
www.clarenceschools.org
Clarence HS · 1,600/9-12
9625 Main St 14031 · 716-407-9020
Kenneth Smith, prin. · Fax 407-9061
Clarence MS · 1,200/6-8
10150 Greiner Rd 14031 · 716-407-9200
Robert Moore, prin. · Fax 407-9229

**Clayton, Jefferson, Pop. 1,959**
Thousand Islands Central SD 1,000/K-12
8481 County Route 9 13624 315-686-5594
Frank House, supt. Fax 686-5511
www.1000islandsschools.org
Thousand Islands HS 300/9-12
8481 Country Route 9 13624 315-686-5594
Joseph Gilfus, prin. Fax 654-5039
Thousand Islands MS 300/6-8
8487 County Route 9 13624 315-686-5594
Michael Bashaw, prin. Fax 654-5038

**Clifton Park, Saratoga**
Shenendehowa Central SD 9,700/K-12
5 Chelsea Pl 12065 518-881-0600
Dr. L. Oliver Robinson, supt. Fax 371-9393
www.shenet.org/
Acadia MS 800/6-8
970 Route 146 Ste 54 12065 518-881-0450
Jonathan Burns, prin. Fax 371-3981
Gowana MS 800/6-8
970 Route 146 Ste 55 12065 518-881-0460
Robin Gawrys, prin. Fax 383-1490
Koda MS 800/6-8
970 Route 146 Ste 59 12065 518-881-0470
Sean Gnat, prin. Fax 383-1532
Shenendehowa HS 2,200/9-12
970 Route 146 12065 518-881-0310
Donald Flynt, prin. Fax 383-1670

**Clifton Springs, Ontario, Pop. 2,111**
Phelps-Clifton Springs Central SD 1,400/K-12
1490 State Route 488 14432 315-548-6420
Jamie Farr, supt. Fax 548-6429
www.midlakes.org
Midlakes MSHS 600/7-12
1554 State Route 488 14432 315-548-6300
Frank Bai-Rossi, prin. Fax 548-6319

**Climax, Greene**

---

Grapeville Christian S 100/K-12
2416 County Route 26 12042 518-966-5037
Rebecca Chmielewski, prin. Fax 966-5498

**Clinton, Oneida, Pop. 1,917**
Clinton Central SD 1,400/K-12
75 Chenango Ave 13323 315-557-2253
Dr. Stephen Grimm, supt. Fax 853-8727
www.ccs.edu
Clinton HS 500/9-12
75 Chenango Ave 13323 315-557-2233
Matthew Lee, prin. Fax 853-1424
Clinton MS 300/6-8
75 Chenango Ave 13323 315-557-2260
Shaun Carney, prin. Fax 853-8727

---

Hamilton College Post-Sec.
198 College Hill Rd 13323 315-859-4011

**Clinton Corners, Dutchess**

---

Upton Lake Christian S 100/K-12
PO Box 63 12514 845-266-3497
Dietlind Hoiem, admin. Fax 266-3828

**Clintonville, Clinton**
Au Sable Valley Central SD 1,200/K-12
1273 Route 9N 12924 518-834-2845
Paul Savage, supt. Fax 834-2843
www.avcs.org
Au Sable Valley HS 400/9-12
1490 Route 9N 12924 518-834-2800
Javier Perez, prin. Fax 834-2847
Au Sable Valley MS 200/7-8
1490 Route 9N 12924 518-834-2800
Philip Mero, prin. Fax 834-2847

**Clyde, Wayne, Pop. 2,017**
Clyde-Savannah Central SD 700/PK-12
215 Glasgow St 14433 315-902-3000
Michael Hayden, supt. Fax 923-2560
www.clydesavannah.org/
Clyde-Savannah HS 300/9-12
215 Glasgow St 14433 315-902-3050
Dr. Craig Pawlak, prin. Fax 923-7906
Clyde-Savannah MS 200/6-8
215 Glasgow St 14433 315-902-3200
Jennifer Kelly, prin. Fax 923-2560

**Clymer, Chautauqua**
Clymer Central SD 400/PK-12
8672 E Main St 14724 716-355-4444
Bert Lictus, supt. Fax 355-2200
www.clymercsd.org
Clymer Central S 400/PK-12
8672 E Main St 14724 716-355-4444
Edward Bailey, prin. Fax 355-4467

**Cobleskill, Schoharie, Pop. 4,593**
Cobleskill-Richmondville Central SD 1,900/K-12
155 Washington Ave 12043 518-234-4032
Carl Mummenthey, supt. Fax 234-7721
www.crcs.k12.ny.us
Golding MS 400/6-8
193 Golding Dr 12043 518-234-8368
Scott McDonald, prin. Fax 234-1018
Other Schools – See Richmondville

---

SUNY at Cobleskill Post-Sec.
State Route 7 12043 518-255-5011

**Cohoes, Albany, Pop. 15,737**
Cohoes CSD 1,900/K-12
7 Bevan St 12047 518-237-0100
Jennifer Spring Ed.D., supt. Fax 237-2912
www.cohoes.org
Cohoes HS 600/9-12
1 Tiger Cir 12047 518-237-9100
Joseph Rajczak, prin. Fax 238-0169
Cohoes MS 400/6-8
7 Bevan St 12047 518-237-4131
Daniel Martinelli, prin. Fax 237-2253
Page Avenue S, 21 Page Ave 12047 Alt
Erin Hill, prin. 518-237-0990

**Cold Spring, Putnam, Pop. 1,981**
Haldane Central SD 900/K-12
15 Craigside Dr 10516 845-265-9254
Diana Bowers, supt. Fax 265-9213
www.haldaneschool.org
Haldane HS 300/9-12
15 Craigside Dr 10516 845-265-9254
Brian Alm, prin. Fax 265-3510

**Cold Spring Harbor, Suffolk, Pop. 5,024**
Cold Spring Harbor Central SD 2,000/K-12
75 Goose Hill Rd 11724 631-367-5900
Judith Wilansky Ed.D., supt. Fax 367-3108
www.csh.k12.ny.us
Cold Spring Harbor JSHS 1,000/7-12
82 Turkey Ln 11724 631-367-6900
Jay Matuk, prin. Fax 692-8016

---

Watson School of Biological Sciences Post-Sec.
1 Bungtown Rd 11724 516-367-6890

**College Point, See New York**

---

St. Agnes Academic HS 300/9-12
1320 124th St 11356 718-353-6276
Susan Nicoletti, prin. Fax 353-6068

**Colton, Saint Lawrence, Pop. 343**
Colton-Pierrepont Central SD 300/PK-12
4921 State Highway 56 13625 315-262-2100
Joseph Kardash, supt. Fax 262-2644
www.cpcs.us/
Colton-Pierrepont Central S 300/PK-12
4921 State Highway 56 13625 315-262-2100
James Nee, prin. Fax 262-2644

**Commack, Suffolk, Pop. 35,739**
Commack UFD
Supt. — See East Northport
Commack HS, 1 Scholar Ln 11725 2,500/9-12
Catherine Nolan, prin. 631-912-2100
Commack MS 1,800/6-8
700 Vanderbilt Pkwy 11725 631-858-3500
Anthony Davidson, prin.

---

Long Island Business Institute Post-Sec.
6500 Jericho Tpke Ste 202 11725 631-499-7100

**Congers, Rockland, Pop. 8,213**

---

Rockland Country Day S 100/PK-12
34 Kings Hwy 10920 845-268-6802
Kimberly Morcate, head sch Fax 268-4644

**Conklin, Broome**
Susquehanna Valley Central SD 1,600/K-12
PO Box 200 13748 607-775-0170
Roland Doig, supt. Fax 775-4575
www.svsabers.org
Stank MS 400/6-8
PO Box 225 13748 607-775-0303
Natalie Brubaker, prin. Fax 775-9142
Susquehanna Valley HS 600/9-12
PO Box 275 13748 607-775-0304
David Daniels, prin. Fax 775-9126

**Cooperstown, Otsego, Pop. 1,834**
Cooperstown Central SD 600/K-12
39 Linden Ave 13326 607-547-8181
C.J. Hebert, supt. Fax 547-5100
www.cooperstowncs.org/
Cooperstown JSHS 500/7-12
39 Linden Ave 13326 607-547-8181
Michael Cring, prin. Fax 547-5100

**Copenhagen, Lewis, Pop. 796**
Copenhagen Central SD 500/PK-12
PO Box 30 13626 315-688-4411
Dr. Scott Connell, supt. Fax 688-2001
www.ccsknights.org/
Copenhagen Central S 500/PK-12
PO Box 30 13626 315-688-4411
Nadine O'Shaughnessy, prin. Fax 688-2001

**Copiague, Suffolk, Pop. 22,652**
Copiague UFD 4,700/K-12
2650 Great Neck Rd 11726 631-842-4015
Charles Leunig, supt. Fax 841-4614
www.copiague.k12.ny.us/
Copiague MS 1,100/6-8
2650 Great Neck Rd 11726 631-842-4011
Andrew Lagnado, prin. Fax 841-4630
O'Connell - Copiague HS 1,400/9-12
1100 Dixon Ave 11726 631-842-4010
Jeanette Altruda, prin. Fax 841-4642

**Corfu, Genesee, Pop. 702**
Pembroke Central SD 1,000/PK-12
PO Box 308 14036 585-599-4525
Matthew Calderon, supt. Fax 599-4213
www.pembroke.k12.ny.us
Pembroke JSHS 500/7-12
PO Box 308 14036 585-599-4525
Dr. Nathan Work, prin. Fax 599-4213

**Corinth, Saratoga, Pop. 2,505**
Corinth Central SD 1,100/K-12
105 Oak St 12822 518-654-2601
Dr. Daniel Starr, supt. Fax 654-6266
www.corinthcsd.com/
Corinth HS 400/9-12
105 Oak St 12822 518-654-9005
Brian Testani, prin. Fax 654-6132
Corinth MS 300/6-8
105 Oak St 12822 518-654-9005
Lisa Meade, prin. Fax 654-2129

**Corning, Steuben, Pop. 10,950**
Corning CSD
Supt. — See Painted Post
Corning - Painted Post HS 800/9-12
201 Cantigney St 14830 607-654-2988
Robin Sheehan, prin. Fax 654-2907
Corning - Painted Post HS Learning Ctr 50/Alt
1 Academic Dr 14830 607-962-9283
Frank Barber, prin.

---

Alternative S for Math & Science 100/6-8
PO Box 114 14830 607-962-0011
Linda Cole, head sch Fax 962-4866
Corning Christian Academy 200/PK-12
11 Aisne St 14830 607-962-4220
Richard Cornfield, admin. Fax 962-4410
Corning Community College Post-Sec.
1 Academic Dr 14830 607-962-9011

**Cornwall, Orange, Pop. 11,270**
Cornwall Central SD
Supt. — See Cornwall on Hudson
Cornwall Central MS 1,000/5-8
122 Main St 12518 845-534-8009
Kate Polumbo, prin. Fax 534-7809

**Cornwall on Hudson, Orange, Pop. 2,955**
Cornwall Central SD 3,400/K-12
24 Idlewild Ave 12520 845-534-8009
Neal S. Miller, supt. Fax 534-9032
www.cornwallschools.com
Other Schools – See Cornwall, New Windsor

---

New York Military Academy 100/7-12
78 Academy Ave 12520 845-534-3710
William Beard, supt. Fax 534-7121
Storm King S 200/8-12
314 Mountain Rd 12520 845-534-7892
Jonathan Lamb, head sch Fax 534-4128

**Corona, See New York**
NYC Department of Education
Supt. — See New York
HS for Arts & Business 800/9-12
10525 Horace Harding Expy 11368 718-271-8383
Ana Bruakov, prin. Fax 271-7196
IS 61 2,300/6-8
9850 50th Ave 11368 718-760-3233
Joseph Lisa, prin. Fax 760-5220

**Cortland, Cortland, Pop. 18,830**
Cortland Enlarged CSD 2,600/K-12
1 Valley View Dr 13045 607-758-4100
Michael J. Hoose, supt. Fax 758-4128
www.cortlandschools.org
Cortland JSHS 1,200/7-12
8 Valley View Dr 13045 607-758-4100
Joseph Mack, prin. Fax 758-4119

---

Cortland Christian Academy 100/PK-12
15 West Rd 13045 607-756-5838
Craig Miller, admin. Fax 756-7716
SUNY College at Cortland Post-Sec.
PO Box 2000 13045 607-753-2011

**Cortlandt Manor, See Peekskill**
Hendrick Hudson Central SD
Supt. — See Montrose
Blue Mountain MS 600/6-8
7 Furnace Woods Rd 10567 914-257-5700
John Owens, prin. Fax 257-5701

Lakeland Central SD
Supt. — See Shrub Oak
Panas HS 1,000/9-12
300 Croton Ave 10567 914-739-2823
Keith Yi, prin. Fax 739-3545

---

Ohr Hameir Seminary Tifereth Israel HS 100/9-12
141 Furnace Woods Rd 10567 914-736-1500
Ohr HaMeir Theological Seminary Post-Sec.
141 Furnace Woods Rd 10567 914-736-1500

**Coxsackie, Greene, Pop. 2,765**
Coxsackie-Athens Central SD 1,500/K-12
24 Sunset Blvd 12051 518-731-1710
Randall Squier, supt. Fax 731-1729
www.cacsd.org
Coxsackie-Athens HS 500/9-12
24 Sunset Blvd 12051 518-731-1800
Heath Quiles, prin. Fax 731-1809
Coxsackie-Athens MS 400/5-8
24 Sunset Blvd 12051 518-731-1850
David Proper, prin. Fax 731-1859

**Craryville, Columbia**
Taconic Hills Central SD 1,200/PK-12
73 County Route 11A 12521 518-325-2800
Dr. Neil Howard, supt.
www.taconichills.k12.ny.us/
Taconic Hills JSHS 500/7-12
73 County Route 11A 12521 518-325-2840
James Buhrmaster, prin. Fax 325-2845

**Cross River, Westchester**
Katonah-Lewisboro UFD
Supt. — See South Salem
Jay HS 1,200/9-12
60 N Salem Rd 10518 914-763-7200
Jess Godin, prin. Fax 763-7494

Jay MS 900/6-8
40 N Salem Rd 10518 914-763-7500
Rich Leprine, prin. Fax 763-7665

**Croton on Hudson, Westchester, Pop. 7,883**
Croton-Harmon UFD 1,700/K-12
10 Gerstein St 10520 914-271-4713
Dr. Edward Fuhrman, supt. Fax 271-8685
www.chufsd.org
Croton-Harmon HS 600/9-12
36 Old Post Rd S 10520 914-271-2147
Alan Capasso, prin. Fax 271-6643
Van Cortlandt MS 500/5-8
3 Glen Pl 10520 914-271-2191
Dr. Barbara Ulm, prin. Fax 271-6618

**Crown Point, Essex**
Crown Point Central SD 300/PK-12
PO Box 35 12928 518-597-4200
Shari Brannock, supt. Fax 597-4121
cpcsteam.org/
Crown Point Central S 300/PK-12
PO Box 35 12928 518-597-3285
Tara Spaulding, prin. Fax 597-4121

**Cuba, Allegany, Pop. 1,561**
Cuba-Rushford Central SD 800/K-12
5476 Route 305 14727 585-968-2650
Carlos Gildemeister, supt. Fax 968-2651
www.crcs.wnyric.org/
Cuba-Rushford HS 300/9-12
5476 Route 305 14727 585-968-2650
Carrie Bold, prin. Fax 968-2651
Cuba-Rushford MS 200/6-8
5476 Route 305 14727 585-968-2650
Andrew Rantz, prin. Fax 968-2651

**Cutchogue, Suffolk, Pop. 3,330**
Mattituck-Cutchogue UFD 1,300/1-12
385 Depot Ln 11935 631-298-4242
Dr. Anne Smith, supt. Fax 298-8573
www.mufsd.com/cms/
Other Schools – See Mattituck

**Dannemora, Clinton, Pop. 3,874**
Saranac Central SD 1,500/K-12
32 Emmons St 12929 518-565-5600
Jonathan Parks, supt. Fax 565-5617
www.saranac.org
Other Schools – See Saranac

**Dansville, Livingston, Pop. 4,671**
Dansville Central SD 1,500/K-12
284 Main St 14437 585-335-4000
Dr. Paul Alioto, supt. Fax 335-4002
www.dansvillecsd.org
Dansville HS 700/7-12
282 Main St 14437 585-335-4010
Michael Falzoi, prin. Fax 335-4080

**Davenport, Delaware**
Charlotte Valley Central SD 400/PK-12
15611 State Highway 23 13750 607-278-5511
James Harter, supt. Fax 278-5900
www.charlottevalleycs.org
Charlotte Valley S 400/PK-12
15611 State Highway 23 13750 607-278-5511
James Harter, supt. Fax 278-5900

**Deer Park, Suffolk, Pop. 27,209**
Deer Park UFD 4,100/PK-12
1881 Deer Park Ave 11729 631-274-4000
Eva Demyen, supt. Fax 242-6762
www.deerparkschools.org/
Deer Park HS 1,400/9-12
1 Falcon Pl 11729 631-274-4100
James Cummings, prin. Fax 254-0237
Frost MS 1,000/6-8
450 Half Hollow Rd 11729 631-274-4200
Dr. Eliana Levey, prin. Fax 242-0035

**De Kalb Junction, Saint Lawrence, Pop. 515**
Hermon-DeKalb Central SD 400/PK-12
709 E DeKalb Rd 13630 315-347-3442
Mark White, supt. Fax 347-3817
www.hdcsk12.org
Hermon-DeKalb Central S 400/PK-12
709 E DeKalb Rd 13630 315-347-3442
Megan Foster, prin. Fax 347-3817

**Delanson, Schenectady, Pop. 371**
Duanesburg Central SD 700/K-12
133 School Rd 12053 518-895-2279
Christine Crowley, supt. Fax 895-2626
www.duanesburg.org/
Duanesburg JSHS 300/6-12
163 School Rd 12053 518-895-2355
Leslie Wehner, prin. Fax 895-9971

**Delhi, Delaware, Pop. 3,025**
Delaware Academy Central SD at Delhi 600/K-12
2 Sheldon Dr 13753 607-746-1300
Jason D. Thomson, supt. Fax 746-6028
www.delhischools.org
Delaware Academy MSHS 200/6-12
2 Sheldon Dr 13753 607-746-1300
Laurie Alberti, prin. Fax 746-1324

---

SUNY Delhi Post-Sec.
2 Main St 13753 607-746-4000

**Delmar, Albany, Pop. 8,360**
Bethlehem Central SD 4,900/K-12
700 Delaware Ave 12054 518-439-7098
Jody Monroe, supt. Fax 475-0352
bcsd.k12.ny.us
Bethlehem Central HS 1,700/9-12
700 Delaware Ave 12054 518-439-4921
Scott Landry, prin. Fax 439-2837
Bethlehem Central MS 1,200/6-8
332 Kenwood Ave 12054 518-439-7460
Mike Klugman, prin. Fax 475-0092

**Depew, Erie, Pop. 15,147**
Depew UFD 2,000/K-12
5201 S Transit Rd 14043 716-686-5105
Jeffrey Rabey, supt. Fax 686-5101
www.depewschools.org/
Depew HS 600/9-12
5201 Transit Rd 14043 716-686-5095
Carol Townsend, prin. Fax 686-5094
Depew MS 500/6-8
5201 Transit Rd 14043 716-686-5050
Joseph D'Amato, prin. Fax 686-5057

**Deposit, Delaware, Pop. 1,641**
Deposit Central SD 600/PK-12
171 2nd St 13754 607-467-5380
Ed Shirkey, supt. Fax 467-5535
www.depositcsd.org/
Deposit MSHS 300/7-12
171 2nd St 13754 607-467-2197
Theresa Rajner, prin. Fax 467-5504

**DeRuyter, Madison, Pop. 552**
De Ruyter Central SD 400/PK-12
711 Railroad St 13052 315-852-3400
Charles Walters, supt. Fax 852-3446
www.deruytercentral.org/
De Ruyter Central JSHS 200/6-12
711 Railroad St 13052 315-852-3400
Dr. Sarah Stack Feinberg, prin. Fax 852-3404

**De Witt, Onondaga, Pop. 8,244**
Jamesville-DeWitt Central SD 2,800/K-12
PO Box 606 13214 315-445-8304
Dr. Alice Kendrick, supt. Fax 445-8477
www.jamesvilledewitt.org
Jamesville-DeWitt HS 900/9-12
PO Box 606 13214 315-445-8340
Paul Gasparini, prin. Fax 445-8307
Other Schools – See Jamesville

**Dexter, Jefferson, Pop. 1,036**
General Brown Central SD 1,500/K-12
PO Box 500 13634 315-779-2300
Cammy Morrison, supt. Fax 639-6916
www.gblions.org
Brown JSHS 700/7-12
17643 Cemetery Rd 13634 315-779-2300
Tina Heckman, prin. Fax 639-3444

**Dix Hills, Suffolk, Pop. 26,364**
Half Hollow Hills Central SD 9,500/K-12
525 Half Hollow Rd 11746 631-592-3000
Kelly Fallon, supt. Fax 592-3900
www.hhh.k12.ny.us
Candlewood MS 1,000/6-8
1200 Carlls Straight Path 11746 631-592-3300
Andrew Greene, prin. Fax 592-3921
Half Hollow Hills HS East 1,800/9-12
50 Vanderbilt Pkwy 11746 631-592-3100
Dr. Jeffery Woodberry, prin. Fax 592-3907
Half Hollow Hills HS West 1,400/9-12
375 Wolf Hill Rd 11746 631-592-3200
Dr. Michael Catapano, prin. Fax 592-3923
Other Schools – See Melville

---

Five Towns College Post-Sec.
305 N Service Rd 11746 631-656-2110
Upper Room Christian S 200/K-12
722 Deer Park Rd 11746 631-242-5359

**Dobbs Ferry, Westchester, Pop. 10,650**
Dobbs Ferry UFD 1,400/K-12
505 Broadway 10522 914-693-1506
Dr. Lisa Brady, supt. Fax 693-1787
www.dfsd.org
Dobbs Ferry HS 400/9-12
505 Broadway 10522 914-693-7645
John Falino, prin. Fax 693-5227
Dobbs Ferry MS 300/6-8
505 Broadway 10522 914-693-7640
Patrick Mussolini, prin. Fax 693-5229

Greenburgh-North Castle UFD 100/7-12
71 Broadway 10522 914-231-8620
Dr. Edward Placke, supt. Fax 693-8030
greenburghnorthcastleschools.com/
Other Schools – See New Windsor

---

Masters S 600/5-12
49 Clinton Ave 10522 914-479-6400
Dr. Maureen Fonseca, hdmstr. Fax 693-1230
Mercy College Post-Sec.
555 Broadway 10522 800-637-2969

**Dolgeville, Herkimer, Pop. 2,188**
Dolgeville Central SD 700/PK-12
38 Slawson St 13329 315-429-3155
Christine Reynolds, supt. Fax 429-8473
www.dolgeville.org
Dolgeville Central MS 300/5-8
38 Slawson St 13329 315-429-3155
Crystal Chrisman, prin. Fax 429-8473
Green HS 300/9-12
38 Slawson St 13329 315-429-3155
Timothy Jenny, prin. Fax 429-8473

**Dover Plains, Dutchess, Pop. 1,293**
Dover UFD 1,500/K-12
2368 Route 22 12522 845-877-5700
Michael Tierney, supt. Fax 877-5766
www.doverschools.org
Dover HS 500/9-12
2368 Route 22 12522 845-877-5750
Daniel Doherty, prin. Fax 877-5759
Dover MS 400/6-8
2368 Route 22 12522 845-877-5740
Patricia Rizzo, prin. Fax 877-5749

**Downsville, Delaware, Pop. 606**
Downsville Central SD 300/PK-12
PO Box J 13755 607-363-2100
John Evans, supt. Fax 363-2105
www.dcseagles.org
Downsville Central S 300/PK-12
PO Box J 13755 607-363-2111
Timothy McNamara, prin. Fax 363-2105

**Dryden, Tompkins, Pop. 1,854**
Dryden Central SD 1,100/PK-12
PO Box 88 13053 607-844-5361
Sandra Sherwood, supt. Fax 844-4733
dcsd-ny.schoolloop.com
Dryden HS 500/9-12
PO Box 88 13053 607-844-8694
Brett Fingland, prin. Fax 844-9004
Dryden MS 400/6-8
PO Box 88 13053 607-844-8694
John Birmingham, prin. Fax 844-5174

---

Tompkins Cortland Community College Post-Sec.
PO Box 139 13053 607-844-8211

**Dundee, Yates, Pop. 1,714**
Dundee Central SD 700/PK-12
55 Water St 14837 607-243-5533
Kelly Houck, supt. Fax 243-7912
www.dundeecs.org
Dundee JSHS 400/7-12
55 Water St 14837 607-243-5534
Chris Arnold, prin. Fax 243-7912

**Dunkirk, Chautauqua, Pop. 12,328**
Dunkirk CSD 2,000/K-12
620 Marauder Dr 14048 716-366-9300
Gary Cerne, supt. Fax 366-9399
www.dunkirkcsd.org
Dunkirk HS 600/9-12
75 W 6th St 14048 716-366-9300
Steve O'Brien, prin. Fax 366-0321
Dunkirk MS 400/6-8
525 Eagle St 14048 716-366-9300
Rocco Vallone, prin. Fax 366-9357

**East Amherst, Erie**
Williamsville Central SD 10,300/K-12
PO Box 5000 14051 716-626-8000
Dr. Scott Martzloff, supt. Fax 626-8089
www.williamsvillek12.org
Casey MS 700/5-8
105 Casey Rd 14051 716-626-8585
Francis McGreevy, prin. Fax 626-8562
Transit MS 1,000/5-8
8730 Transit Rd 14051 716-626-8701
Daniel Walh, prin. Fax 626-8796
Williamsville East HS 1,100/9-12
151 Paradise Rd 14051 716-626-8404
Scott Taylor, prin. Fax 626-8408
Other Schools – See Williamsville

**East Aurora, Erie, Pop. 6,180**
East Aurora UFD 1,900/K-12
430 Main St 14052 716-687-2302
Brian Russ, supt. Fax 652-8581
eastauroraschools.org/
East Aurora HS 700/9-12
1003 Center St 14052 716-687-2505
Dr. James Hoagland, prin. Fax 687-2552
East Aurora MS 600/5-8
430 Main St 14052 716-687-2453
Mark Mambretti, prin. Fax 652-8581

---

Christ the King Seminary Post-Sec.
PO Box 607 14052 716-652-8900

**Eastchester, Westchester, Pop. 19,285**
Eastchester UFD 3,000/K-12
580 White Plains Rd 10709 914-793-6130
Dr. Walter Moran, supt. Fax 793-9006
district.eastchesterschools.org
Eastchester HS 900/9-12
2 Stewart Pl 10709 914-793-6130
Dr. Jeffrey Capuano, prin. Fax 793-9000
Eastchester MS 700/6-8
550 White Plains Rd 10709 914-793-6130
Scott Wynne, prin. Fax 793-1699

Tuckahoe UFD 1,100/K-12
65 Siwanoy Blvd 10709 914-337-6600
Dr. Barbara Nuzzi, supt. Fax 337-3072
www.tuckahoeschools.org
Tuckahoe HS 300/9-12
65 Siwanoy Blvd 10709 914-337-5376
Bart Linehan Ed.D., prin. Fax 337-5168
Tuckahoe MS 200/6-8
65 Siwanoy Blvd 10709 914-337-5376
Dr. Ellen McDonnell, prin. Fax 337-5236

**East Elmhurst, See New York**
NYC Department of Education
Supt. — See New York
IS 227 1,600/5-8
3202 Junction Blvd 11369 718-335-7500
William Fahey, prin. Fax 779-7186

---

Monsignor McClancy Memorial HS 500/9-12
7106 31st Ave 11370 718-898-3800
James Castrataro, prin. Fax 898-3929

**East Greenbush, Rensselaer, Pop. 4,416**
East Greenbush Central SD 4,300/K-12
29 Englewood Ave 12061 518-207-2500
Angela Nagle Ph.D., supt. Fax 477-4833
www.egcsd.org

Columbia HS	1,500/9-12
962 Luther Rd 12061	518-207-2000
John Sawchuk, prin.	Fax 207-2009
Goff MS	900/6-8
35 Gilligan Rd 12061	518-207-2430
Matthew Sloane, prin.	Fax 477-2667

**East Hampton, Suffolk, Pop. 1,079**
East Hampton UFD	1,800/K-12
4 Long Ln 11937	631-329-4100
Richard Burns, supt.	Fax 324-0109
www.ehufsd.org
East Hampton HS	900/9-12
2 Long Ln 11937	631-329-4130
Adam Fine, prin.	Fax 329-4210
East Hampton MS	300/6-8
76 Newtown Ln 11937	631-329-4116
Dr. Charles Soriano, prin.	Fax 329-4187

---

Ross S	300/7-12
18 Goodfriend Dr 11937	631-907-5000
Patty Lein, head sch	Fax 329-6830

**East Meadow, Nassau, Pop. 37,572**
East Meadow UFD
Supt. — See Westbury
East Meadow HS	1,600/9-12
101 Carman Ave 11554	516-228-5331
Richard Howard, prin.	Fax 228-5339
Woodland MS	1,200/6-8
690 Wenwood Dr 11554	516-564-6523
James Lethbridge, prin.	Fax 564-6519

**East Moriches, Suffolk, Pop. 5,179**
East Moriches UFD	700/K-8
9 Adelaide Ave 11940	631-878-0162
Dr. Charles Russo, supt.	Fax 878-0186
emoschools.org/
East Moriches MS	300/5-8
9 Adelaide Ave 11940	631-878-0162
Michael Carlson, prin.	Fax 874-0096

**East Northport, Suffolk, Pop. 19,969**
Commack UFD	7,400/K-12
480 Clay Pitts Rd 11731	631-912-2000
Dr. Donald James, supt.	Fax 912-2240
www.commack.k12.ny.us
Other Schools – See Commack

Northport-East Northport UFD
Supt. — See Northport
East Northport MS	700/6-8
1075 5th Ave 11731	631-262-6770
Pasquale DeStefano, prin.	Fax 262-6773

**East Patchogue, Suffolk, Pop. 22,129**
South Country Central SD	4,500/PK-12
189 N Dunton Ave 11772	631-730-1510
Dr. Joseph Giani, supt.	Fax 286-6394
www.southcountry.org
Other Schools – See Bellport, Brookhaven

---

Victory Christian Academy	100/PK-12
1343 Montauk Hwy 11772	631-654-9284

**East Rochester, Monroe, Pop. 6,434**
East Rochester UFD	1,200/PK-12
222 Woodbine Ave 14445	585-248-6302
Richard Stutzman, supt.	Fax 586-3254
www.erschools.org
East Rochester JSHS	500/7-12
200 Woodbine Ave 14445	585-248-6350
Casey van Harssel, prin.	Fax 248-6383

**East Rockaway, Nassau, Pop. 9,736**
East Rockaway UFD	1,300/K-12
443 Ocean Ave 11518	516-887-8300
Lisa J. Ruiz, supt.	Fax 887-8308
www.eastrockawayschools.org
East Rockaway JSHS	600/7-12
443 Ocean Ave 11518	516-887-8300
Joseph Spero, prin.	Fax 887-8308

**East Setauket, See Setauket**
Three Village Central SD
Supt. — See Stony Brook
Melville HS	1,800/10-12
380 Old Town Rd 11733	631-730-4900
Alan Baum, prin.	Fax 730-4901

**East Syracuse, Onondaga, Pop. 2,961**
East Syracuse Minoa Central SD	3,500/PK-12
407 Fremont Rd 13057	315-434-3000
Dr. Donna DeSiato, supt.	Fax 434-3020
www.esmschools.org
East Syracuse Minoa Central HS	1,100/9-12
6400 Fremont Rd 13057	315-434-3300
Grenardo Avellino, prin.	Fax 434-3335
Pine Grove MS	700/7-8
6318 Fremont Rd 13057	315-434-3050
Doug Mohorter, prin.	Fax 434-3070

---

Bishop Grimes JSHS	400/7-12
6653 Kirkville Rd 13057	315-437-0356
David Wheeler, prin.	Fax 437-0358

**Eden, Erie, Pop. 3,494**
Eden Central SD	1,600/PK-12
3150 Schoolview Rd 14057	716-992-3629
Sandra Anzalone, supt.	Fax 992-3656
www.edencsd.org/
Eden JSHS	800/7-12
3150 Schoolview Rd 14057	716-992-3641
Jeff Cervoni, prin.	Fax 992-3652

**Edmeston, Otsego, Pop. 650**
Edmeston Central SD	500/PK-12
PO Box 5129 13335	607-965-8931
Brian Hunt, supt.	Fax 965-8942
edmestoncentralschool.net
Edmeston Central S	500/PK-12
PO Box 5129 13335	607-965-8931
Christine Nichols, prin.	Fax 965-8942

**Elba, Genesee, Pop. 668**
Elba Central SD	500/PK-12
PO Box 370 14058	585-757-9967
Keith Palmer, supt.	Fax 757-2713
www.elbacsd.org
Elba JSHS	200/7-12
PO Box 370 14058	585-757-9967
Dr. Chris Salinas, prin.	Fax 757-6683

**Eldred, Sullivan**
Eldred Central SD	700/PK-12
PO Box 249 12732	845-456-1100
Robert M. Dufour, supt.	Fax 557-3672
www.eldred.k12.ny.us/
Eldred Central JSHS	300/7-12
PO Box 249 12732	845-456-1100
Scott Krebs, prin.	Fax 557-3672

**Elizabethtown, Essex**
Elizabethtown-Lewis Central SD	300/K-12
PO Box 158 12932	518-873-6371
Scott Osborne, supt.	Fax 873-9552
elcsd.org
Elizabethtown-Lewis Central S	300/K-12
PO Box 158 12932	518-873-6371
Scott Osborne, prin.	Fax 873-9552

**Ellenburg Depot, Clinton**
Northern Adirondack Central SD	900/K-12
PO Box 164 12935	518-594-7060
Laura Marlow, supt.	Fax 594-7255
www.nacs1.org/
Northern Adirondack MSHS	500/6-12
PO Box 164 12935	518-594-3962
Michael Loughman, prin.	Fax 594-7255

**Ellenville, Ulster, Pop. 3,954**
Ellenville Central SD	1,600/PK-12
28 Maple Ave 12428	845-647-0100
Lisa Wiles, supt.	Fax 647-0105
www.ecs.k12.ny.us
Ellenville HS	500/9-12
28 Maple Ave 12428	845-647-0123
Carl Pabon, prin.	Fax 647-5972
Ellenville MS	400/6-8
28 Maple Ave 12428	845-647-0126
Angela Urbina, prin.	Fax 647-0230

**Ellicottville, Cattaraugus, Pop. 371**
Ellicottville Central SD	500/PK-12
5873 Route 219 S 14731	716-699-2368
Mark Ward, supt.	Fax 699-6017
www.ellicottvillecentral.com/
Ellicottville MSHS	300/7-12
5873 Route 219 S 14731	716-699-2316
Robert Miller, prin.	Fax 699-5423

**Elma, Erie**
Iroquois Central SD	2,500/K-12
PO Box 32 14059	716-652-3000
Douglas Scofield, supt.	Fax 652-9305
www.iroquoiscsd.org
Iroquois HS	900/9-12
PO Box 32 14059	716-652-3000
Dennis Kenney, prin.	Fax 995-2440
Iroquois MS	600/6-8
PO Box 32 14059	716-652-3000
Ross Esslinger, prin.	Fax 995-2335

**Elmhurst, See New York**
NYC Department of Education
Supt. — See New York
Civic Leadership Academy	400/9-12
4510 94th St 11373	718-271-1487
Phuong Nguyen, prin.	Fax 271-3408
IS 5	1,500/6-9
5040 Jacobus St 11373	718-205-6788
Kelly Nepogoda, prin.	Fax 429-6518
International HS for Health Sciences	100/9-12
4801 90th St 11373	718-595-8600
Carl Finney, prin.	Fax 595-8605
Maspeth HS	9-12
5440 74th St 11373	718-803-7100
Khurshid Mutakabbir, prin.	Fax 803-7105
Newtown HS	2,500/9-12
4801 90th St 11373	718-595-8400
John Ficalora, prin.	Fax 699-8584
Pan American International HS	400/9-12
4510 94th St 11373	718-271-3602
Minerva Zanca, prin.	Fax 271-4041
VOYAGES Preparatory S	200/9-12
4510 94th St 11373	718-271-7851
Nicholas Bleiberg, prin.	Fax 271-8549

---

Cathedral Preparatory Seminary	200/9-12
5625 92nd St 11373	718-592-6800
Richie Diaz, prin.	Fax 592-5574
Jewish Institute of Queens	400/PK-12
6005 Woodhaven Blvd 11373	718-426-9369

**Elmira, Chemung, Pop. 27,883**
Elmira CSD	4,700/PK-12
951 Hoffman St 14905	607-735-3000
Hillary Austin, supt.	Fax 735-3009
www.elmiracityschools.com
Davis Academy	800/9-12
933 Hoffman St 14905	607-735-3100
Christopher Krantz, prin.	Fax 735-3109
Davis MS	500/7-8
610 Lake St 14901	607-735-3400
John Wood, prin.	Fax 735-3409
Elmira HS	1,100/9-12
777 S Main St 14904	607-735-3200
Christopher Krantz, prin.	Fax 735-3209

---

Arnot-Ogden Medical Center	Post-Sec.
600 Roe Ave 14905	607-737-4289
Arnot-Ogden Medical Center	Post-Sec.
600 Roe Ave 14905	607-737-4153
Elmira Business Institute	Post-Sec.
303 N Main St 14901	800-843-1812
Elmira Christian Academy	100/PK-12
235 E Miller St 14904	607-734-7195
Martin Douglass, prin.	Fax 734-7195
Elmira College	Post-Sec.
1 Park Pl 14901	607-735-1800
Notre Dame HS	200/9-12
1400 Maple Ave 14904	607-734-2267
Sr. Nancy Kelly, prin.	Fax 737-8903

**Elmira Heights, Chemung, Pop. 4,011**
Elmira Heights Central SD	1,000/K-12
2083 College Ave 14903	607-734-7114
Mary Beth Fiore, supt.	Fax 734-7134
www.heightsschools.com
Cohen MS	200/6-8
100 Robinwood Ave 14903	607-734-5078
Dawn Hanrahan, prin.	Fax 734-9382
Edison HS	300/9-12
2083 College Ave 14903	607-733-5604
Thomas Boyanowski, prin.	Fax 737-7976

**Elmont, Nassau, Pop. 32,024**
Sewanhaka Central HSD
Supt. — See Floral Park
Elmont Memorial HS	1,900/7-12
555 Ridge Rd 11003	516-488-9200
Kevin Dougherty, prin.	Fax 488-5560

**Elmsford, Westchester, Pop. 4,549**
Elmsford UFD	900/PK-12
98 S Goodwin Ave 10523	914-592-6632
Joseph Ricca, supt.	Fax 592-2181
www.elmsd.org
Hamilton JSHS	400/7-12
98 S Goodwin Ave 10523	914-592-7311
Marc Baiocco, prin.	Fax 592-2881

**Elwood, Suffolk, Pop. 11,032**
Elwood UFD
Supt. — See Greenlawn
Elwood/John H. Glenn HS	800/9-12
478 Elwood Rd 11731	631-266-5410
Dr. James Ruck, prin.	Fax 368-5038
Elwood MS	600/6-8
478 Elwood Rd 11731	631-266-5420
Dr. Hugh Gigante, prin.	Fax 266-3987

**Endicott, Broome, Pop. 12,995**
Union-Endicott Central SD	4,000/K-12
1100 E Main St 13760	607-757-2111
Dr. Suzanne McLeod, supt.	Fax 757-2809
www.uek12.org
Snapp MS	900/6-8
101 S Loder Ave 13760	607-757-2156
Catherine Kacyvenski, prin.	Fax 658-7117
Union-Endicott HS	1,300/9-12
1200 E Main St 13760	607-757-2181
Steven DiStefano, prin.	Fax 757-2592

**Endwell, Broome, Pop. 11,248**
Maine-Endwell Central SD	2,500/K-12
712 Farm To Market Rd 13760	607-754-1400
Jason R. Van Fossen, supt.	Fax 754-1650
www.me.stier.org/
Maine-Endwell HS	800/9-12
750 Farm To Market Rd 13760	607-748-8070
Thomas Burkhardt, prin.	Fax 786-8209
Maine-Endwell MS	600/6-8
1119 Farm To Market Rd 13760	607-786-8271
Richard Otis, prin.	Fax 786-5137

**Fabius, Onondaga, Pop. 352**
Fabius-Pompey Central SD	800/K-12
1211 Mill St 13063	315-683-5301
Timothy Ryan, supt.	Fax 683-5827
www.fabiuspompey.org
Fabius-Pompey MSHS	500/6-12
1211 Mill St 13063	315-683-5811
Kevin Linck, prin.	Fax 683-5569

**Fairport, Monroe, Pop. 5,283**
Fairport Central SD	6,400/K-12
38 W Church St 14450	585-421-2000
Dr. William Cala, supt.	Fax 421-3421
www.fairport.org
Brown MS	800/6-8
665 Ayrault Rd 14450	585-421-2065
David Dunn, prin.	Fax 421-2136
Fairport HS	1,600/10-12
1 Dave Paddock Way 14450	585-421-2100
Joseph Fantigrossi, prin.	Fax 421-4645
Minerva-Deland JHS	500/9-9
140 Hulburt Rd 14450	585-421-2030
Pam Ciranni, prin.	Fax 421-1985
Perrin MS	700/6-8
85 Potter Pl 14450	585-421-2080
Brett Provenzano, prin.	Fax 421-2097

**Falconer, Chautauqua, Pop. 2,402**
Falconer Central SD	1,300/PK-12
2 East Ave N 14733	716-665-6624
Stephen Penhollow, supt.	Fax 665-9265
www.falconerschools.org
Falconer MSHS	700/6-12
2 East Ave N 14733	716-665-6624
Jeffrey Jordan, prin.	Fax 665-9265

**Fallsburg, Sullivan**
Fallsburg Central SD	1,400/PK-12
PO Box 124 12733	845-434-5884
Dr. Ivan Katz, supt.	Fax 434-8346
www.fallsburgcsd.net/

Fallsburg HS 600/7-12
PO Box 124 12733 845-434-6800
Michael Williams, prin. Fax 434-0418

**Farmingdale, Nassau, Pop. 8,087**
Farmingdale UFD 6,000/K-12
50 Van Cott Ave 11735 516-752-6510
John Lorentz, supt.
www.farmingdaleschools.org
Farmingdale HS 2,000/9-12
150 Lincoln St 11735 516-752-6600
Glen Zakian, prin. Fax 454-6196
Howitt MS 1,400/6-8
70 Van Cott Ave 11735 516-752-6519
Luis Pena, prin. Fax 752-2004

---

Farmingdale State College SUNY Post-Sec.
2350 Broadhollow Rd 11735 631-420-2000

**Farmingville, Suffolk, Pop. 15,238**
Sachem Central SD
Supt. — See Ronkonkoma
Sachem HS East 2,300/9-12
177 Granny Rd 11738 631-716-8200
Louis Antonetti, prin. Fax 716-8207

**Far Rockaway, See New York**
NYC Department of Education
Supt. — See New York
Academy of Medical Technology 500/6-12
821 Bay 25th St 11691 718-471-3571
Jose Merced, prin. Fax 471-0314
Douglass Academy VI HS 400/9-12
821 Bay 25th St 11691 718-471-2154
Carlston Gray, prin. Fax 471-2890
MS 53 400/6-8
1045 Nameoke St 11691 718-471-6900
Shawn Rux, prin. Fax 471-6955
KAPPA VI 300/6-8
821 Bay 25th St 11691 718-471-6934
Gary Dumornay, prin. Fax 471-6938
Queens HS for Info. Research & Tech. 300/9-12
821 Bay 25th St 11691 718-868-2978
Magaly Hicks, prin. Fax 868-1653
Village Academy 300/6-8
1045 Nameoke St 11691 718-471-6042
Doris Lee, prin. Fax 471-6243

---

Beis Medrash Heichal Dovid Post-Sec.
211 Beach 17th St 11691 718-868-2300
Global Business Institute Post-Sec.
1931 Mott Ave 11691 718-327-2220
Mesivta Chaim Shlomo S 300/9-12
211 Beach 17th St 11691 718-868-2300
Tichon Meir Moshe S 100/9-12
613 Beach 9th St 11691 718-327-6645
Torah Academy HS for Girls 300/9-12
636 Lanett Ave 11691 718-327-1300
Yeshiva Darchei Torah S 1,600/PK-12
257 Beach 17th St 11691 718-868-2300
Rabbi Yehuda Harbater, dir. Fax 868-4450
Yeshiva of Far Rockaway Post-Sec.
802 Hicksville Rd 11691 718-327-7600
Yeshiva of Far Rockaway S 200/9-12
802 Hicksville Rd 11691 718-327-7600
Yeshiva Zichron Aryeh Post-Sec.
1213 Bay 25th St 11691 516-295-5700

**Fayetteville, Onondaga, Pop. 4,326**
Fayetteville-Manlius Central SD
Supt. — See Manlius
Wellwood MS 700/5-8
700 S Manlius St 13066 315-692-1300
Melissa Corbin, prin. Fax 692-1049

**Fillmore, Allegany, Pop. 603**
Fillmore Central SD 700/K-12
104 W Main St 14735 585-567-2251
Ravo Root, supt. Fax 567-2541
www.fillmorecsd.org
Fillmore Central S 700/K-12
104 W Main St 14735 585-567-2289
Michael Dodge, prin. Fax 567-2541

**Fishers Island, Suffolk, Pop. 231**
Fishers Island UFD 100/PK-12
78 Greenwood Rd Ste 600 06390 631-788-7444
Karen Goodwin, supt. Fax 788-5562
www.fischool.com
Fishers Island S 100/PK-12
78 Greenwood Rd Ste 600 06390 631-788-7444
Karen Goodwin, prin. Fax 788-5532

**Fleetwood, See Mount Vernon**

---

Montfort Academy 50/9-12
125 E Birch St 10552 914-699-7090
David Petrillo Ph.D., head sch Fax 699-7150

**Floral Park, Nassau, Pop. 15,623**
NYC Department of Education
Supt. — See New York
Altman MS 1,000/6-8
8114 257th St 11004 718-831-4000
Jeffrey Slivko, prin. Fax 831-4008

Sewanhaka Central HSD 8,300/7-12
77 Landau Ave 11001 516-488-9800
Dr. Ralph Ferrie, supt. Fax 488-7738
www.sewanhaka.k12.ny.us/
Floral Park Memorial HS 1,400/7-12
210 Locust St 11001 516-488-9300
Dr. Kathleen Sottile, prin. Fax 394-5079
Sewanhaka HS 1,600/7-12
500 Tulip Ave 11001 516-488-9600
Debra Lidowsky, prin. Fax 488-9215
Other Schools – See Elmont, Franklin Square, New Hyde Park

**Florida, Orange, Pop. 2,798**
Florida UFD 800/K-12
PO Box 757 10921 845-651-3095
Diane Munro, supt. Fax 651-6801
www.floridaufsd.org
Seward Institute 500/6-12
PO Box 757 10921 845-651-4038
Michael Rheaume, prin. Fax 651-7166

**Flushing, See New York**
NYC Department of Education
Supt. — See New York
Bowne HS 3,600/9-12
6325 Main St 11367 718-263-1919
Howie Kwait, prin. Fax 575-4069
East-West S of International Studies 600/6-12
4621 Colden St 11355 718-353-0009
Benjamin Sherman, prin. Fax 353-3772
Flushing HS 3,100/9-12
3501 Union St 11354 718-888-7500
Dr. James Brown, prin. Fax 886-4255
IS 25 900/6-8
3465 192nd St 11358 718-961-3480
Maryellen Beirne, prin. Fax 358-1563
IS 237 1,200/6-8
4621 Colden St 11355 718-353-6464
Judith Freidman, prin. Fax 460-6427
IS 250 400/6-8
15840 76th Rd 11366 718-591-9000
Tara Mrwik, prin. Fax 591-2340
Flushing International HS 400/9-12
14480 Barclay Ave 11355 718-463-2348
Lara Evangelista, prin. Fax 463-3514
JHS 185 1,300/6-8
14726 25th Dr 11354 718-445-3232
Theresa Mshar, prin. Fax 359-5352
JHS 189 800/6-8
14480 Barclay Ave 11355 718-359-6676
Cindy Diaz-Burgos, prin. Fax 358-0155
JHS 216 1,300/6-8
6420 175th St 11365 718-358-2005
Reginald Landeau, prin. Fax 358-2070
Harris HS 1,100/9-12
14911 Melbourne Ave 11367 718-575-5580
Anthony Barbetta, prin. Fax 575-1366
Kennedy Community HS 700/9-12
7540 Parsons Blvd 11366 718-969-5510
Beshir Abdellatif, prin. Fax 969-5524
Lewis HS 4,100/9-12
5820 Utopia Pkwy 11365 718-281-8200
David Marmor, prin. Fax 746-2017
North Queens Community HS 200/9-12
14125 77th Rd 11367 718-380-1650
Winston McCarthy, prin. Fax 380-2189
Queens Academy HS 400/10-12
13811 35th Ave 11354 718-463-3111
Vasilios Manolios, prin. Fax 886-5015
Queens HS for Language Studies 100/9-12
3501 Union St 11354 718-888-7530
Melanie Lee, prin. Fax 888-7526
Veritas Academy 100/9-12
3501 Union St 11354 718-888-7520
Cheryl Quatrano, prin. Fax 888-7524
World Journalism Preparatory S 600/6-12
3465 192nd St 11358 718-461-2219
Cynthia Schneider, prin. Fax 461-2633

---

CUNY Queens College Post-Sec.
6530 Kissena Blvd 11367 718-997-5000
Holy Cross HS 900/9-12
2620 Francis Lewis Blvd 11358 718-886-7250
Edward Burns, prin. Fax 886-7257
Long Island Business Institute Post-Sec.
13618 39th Ave 11354 718-939-5100
Mesivta Yesodei Yeshurun 100/9-12
14151 71st Ave 11367 718-261-4738
New York Medical Career Training Center Post-Sec.
3609 Main St Fl 5 11354 718-460-4340
Rabbinical Seminary Chofetz Chaim HS 100/9-12
7601 147th St 11367 718-263-1445
Rabbinical Seminary of America Post-Sec.
7601 147th St 11367 718-268-4700
Vaughn College of Aeronautics and Tech Post-Sec.
8601 23rd Ave 11369 718-429-6600
Windsor S 200/7-12
37-02 Main St Fl 4 11354 718-359-8300
James Seery, prin. Fax 359-1876

**Fonda, Montgomery, Pop. 787**
Fonda-Fultonville Central SD 1,400/PK-12
PO Box 1501 12068 518-853-4415
Thomas Ciaccio, supt. Fax 853-4461
www.fondafultonvilleschools.org
Fonda-Fultonville HS 500/9-12
PO Box 1501 12068 518-853-3182
Aaron Grady, prin. Fax 853-1239
Fonda-Fultonville MS 400/5-8
PO Box 1501 12068 518-853-4747
David Zadoorian, prin. Fax 853-4498

**Forest Hills, See New York**
NYC Department of Education
Supt. — See New York
Forest Hills HS 3,800/9-12
6701 110th St 11375 718-268-3137
Saul Gootnick, prin. Fax 793-7850
JHS 190 1,000/6-8
6817 Austin St 11375 718-830-4970
Marilyn Grant, prin. Fax 830-3566
Metropolitan Expeditionary Learning S 200/6-12
9130 Metropolitan Ave 11375 718-286-3500
Daman McCord, prin. Fax 286-3501
Queens Metropolitan HS 400/9-12
9130 Metropolitan Ave 11375 718-286-3600
Gregory Dutton, prin. Fax 286-3601

---

ACE Computer Training Center Post-Sec.
10919 72nd Rd Ste 4F 11375 718-575-3223
Bramson ORT College Post-Sec.
6930 Austin St 11375 718-261-5800
Emerging Technologies Institute Post-Sec.
11616 Queens Blvd Ste 200 11375 718-261-1272
Ezra Academy 100/7-12
11945 Union Tpke 11375 718-263-5500
Kew-Forest S 200/PK-12
11917 Union Tpke 11375 718-268-4667
Mark Fish, hdmstr. Fax 268-9121

**Forestville, Chautauqua, Pop. 686**
Forestville Central SD 500/K-12
12 Water St 14062 716-965-2742
Dr. Whitney Vantine, supt. Fax 965-2117
www.forestville.com
Forestville Central JSHS 300/7-12
4 Academy St 14062 716-965-2711
Patrick Moses, prin. Fax 965-2102

**Fort Ann, Washington, Pop. 482**
Fort Ann Central SD 500/K-12
1 Catherine St 12827 518-639-5594
William Scott, supt. Fax 639-8911
www.fortannschool.org
Fort Ann S 500/K-12
1 Catherine St 12827 518-639-5594
Dan Ward, prin. Fax 639-8911

**Fort Covington, Franklin**
Salmon River Central SD 1,600/PK-12
637 County Route 1 12937 518-358-6610
Jane Collins, supt. Fax 358-3492
www.srk12.org/
Salmon River HS 400/9-12
637 County Route 1 12937 518-358-6620
Mike Warden, prin. Fax 358-9787
Salmon River MS 400/6-8
637 County Route 1 12937 518-358-6650
Michael Warden, prin. Fax 358-6510

**Fort Edward, Washington, Pop. 3,335**
Fort Edward UFD 500/PK-12
220 Broadway 12828 518-747-4594
Jeffery Ziegler, supt. Fax 747-6543
www.fortedward.org
Fort Edward S 500/PK-12
220 Broadway 12828 518-747-4529
Thomas McGurl, prin. Fax 747-6543

Hudson Falls Central SD 2,300/PK-12
1153 Burgoyne Ave 12828 518-747-2121
Mark Doody, supt. Fax 747-0951
www.hfcsd.org
Other Schools – See Hudson Falls

**Fort Montgomery, Orange, Pop. 1,512**
Highland Falls Ft. Montgomery Central SD 900/PK-12
21 Morgan Farm Rd 10922 845-446-9575
Frank Sheboy, supt. Fax 446-3321
www.hffmcsd.org
O'Neill HS 500/9-12
21 Morgan Rd 10922 845-446-4914
Louis Trombetta, prin. Fax 446-2123
Other Schools – See Highland Falls

**Fort Plain, Montgomery, Pop. 2,284**
Fort Plain Central SD 800/PK-12
25 High St 13339 518-993-4000
Douglas Burton, supt. Fax 993-3393
www.fortplain.org
Fort Plain JSHS 400/7-12
1 West St 13339 518-993-4000
Deborah Larrabee, prin. Fax 993-2897

**Frankfort, Herkimer, Pop. 2,561**
Frankfort-Schuyler Central SD 800/K-12
605 Palmer St 13340 315-894-5083
Robert Reina, supt. Fax 895-7011
www.frankfort-schuyler.org
Frankfort-Schuyler Central MSHS 400/6-12
605 Palmer St 13340 315-895-7461
John Bubb, prin. Fax 895-4032

**Franklin, Delaware, Pop. 368**
Franklin Central SD 300/PK-12
PO Box 888 13775 607-829-3551
Gordon Daniels, supt. Fax 829-2101
www.franklincsd.org
Franklin Central S 300/PK-12
PO Box 888 13775 607-829-3551
Julie Bergman, prin. Fax 829-2101

**Franklin Square, Nassau, Pop. 28,887**
Sewanhaka Central HSD
Supt. — See Floral Park
Carey HS 1,800/7-12
230 Poppy Ave 11010 516-539-9400
Valerie Angelillo, prin. Fax 538-1791

Valley Stream Central HSD
Supt. — See Valley Stream
Valley Stream North HS 1,200/7-12
750 Herman Ave 11010 516-564-5510
Clifford Odell, prin. Fax 564-5539

**Franklinville, Cattaraugus, Pop. 1,715**
Franklinville Central SD 700/PK-12
31 N Main St 14737 716-676-8029
Michelle Spasiano, supt. Fax 676-8041
tbafcs.org
Franklinville JSHS 300/7-12
31 N Main St 14737 716-676-8060
Jennifer Cappelletti, prin. Fax 676-8042

**Fredonia, Chautauqua, Pop. 11,103**
Fredonia Central SD 1,600/PK-12
425 E Main St 14063 716-679-1581
Paul DiFonzo, supt. Fax 679-1555
www.fredonia.wnyric.org
Fredonia HS 500/9-12
425 E Main St 14063 716-679-1581
Todd Crandall, prin. Fax 672-8687

Fredonia MS 500/5-8
425 E Main St 14063 716-679-1581
Andrew Ludwig, prin. Fax 672-2686

---

SUNY at Fredonia Post-Sec.
280 Central Ave 14063 716-673-3111

**Freeport, Nassau, Pop. 41,960**
Freeport UFD 6,600/PK-12
235 N Ocean Ave 11520 516-867-5200
Dr. Kishore Kuncham, supt. Fax 623-4759
www.freeportschools.org
Dodd MS 900/7-8
25 Pine St 11520 516-867-5280
Johane Ligonde, prin. Fax 379-6794
Freeport HS 2,100/9-12
50 S Brookside Ave 11520 516-867-5300
Linda Carter, prin. Fax 379-7592

---

De LaSalle S 100/5-8
87 Pine St 11520 516-379-8660
Kathleen Boniello, prin. Fax 379-8806

**Fresh Meadows, See New York**
NYC Department of Education
Supt. — See New York
Queens S of Inquiry 600/6-12
15840 76th Rd 11366 718-380-6929
Meredith Inbal, prin. Fax 380-6809

---

St. Francis Preparatory HS 2,600/9-12
6100 Francis Lewis Blvd 11365 718-423-8810
Patrick McLaughlin, prin. Fax 504-7668

**Frewsburg, Chautauqua, Pop. 1,879**
Frewsburg Central SD 900/PK-12
PO Box 690 14738 716-569-7041
Danielle O'Connor, supt. Fax 569-7050
www.frewsburgcsd.org/
Frewsburg JSHS 400/7-12
PO Box 690 14738 716-569-7055
Scott Cooper, prin. Fax 569-7050

**Friendship, Allegany, Pop. 1,208**
Friendship Central SD 400/PK-12
46 W Main St 14739 585-973-3534
Judy May, supt. Fax 973-2023
www.friendship.wnyric.org/
Friendship Central S 400/PK-12
46 W Main St 14739 585-973-3311
Judy May, supt. Fax 973-2023

**Fulton, Oswego, Pop. 11,719**
Fulton CSD 3,600/K-12
167 S 4th St 13069 315-593-5510
William Lynch, supt. Fax 598-6351
www.fulton.cnyric.org/
Bodley HS 1,100/9-12
6 Gillard Dr 13069 315-593-5400
Donna Parkhurst, prin. Fax 593-5427
Fulton JHS 600/7-8
129 Curtis St 13069 315-593-5440
Ryan Lanigan, prin. Fax 593-5459

**Gainesville, Wyoming, Pop. 228**
Letchworth Central SD 900/K-12
5550 School Rd 14066 585-493-5450
Julia Reed, supt. Fax 493-2762
www.letchworth.k12.ny.us
Letchworth HS 300/9-12
5550 School Rd 14066 585-493-2571
Matthew Wilkins, prin. Fax 493-2762
Letchworth MS 300/5-8
5550 School Rd 14066 585-493-2592
Paul Rogers, prin. Fax 493-2762

**Galway, Saratoga, Pop. 200**
Galway Central SD 900/K-12
5317 Sacandaga Rd 12074 518-882-1033
Shannon Shine, supt. Fax 882-5250
www.galwaycsd.org
Galway JSHS 500/7-12
5317 Sacandaga Rd 12074 518-882-1033
Michael Healey, prin. Fax 882-5250

**Garden City, Nassau, Pop. 22,129**
Garden City UFD 4,000/K-12
56 Cathedral Ave 11530 516-478-1000
Dr. Robert Feirsen, supt. Fax 294-5631
www.gardencity.k12.ny.us
Garden City HS 1,200/9-12
170 Rockaway Ave 11530 516-478-2000
Nanine McLaughlin, prin. Fax 294-2639
Garden City MS 1,000/6-8
98 Cherry Valley Ave 11530 516-478-3000
Dr. Peter Osroff, prin. Fax 294-0732

---

Adelphi University Post-Sec.
PO Box 701 11530 516-877-3000
Career Institute of Health & Technology Post-Sec.
400 Oak St Ste 104 11530 516-877-1225
Nassau Community College Post-Sec.
1 Education Dr 11530 516-572-7501
Sanford-Brown Institute Post-Sec.
711 Stewart Ave Ste 2 11530 516-247-2900
Waldorf S of Garden City 300/PK-12
225 Cambridge Ave 11530 516-742-3434
Susan Braun, admin. Fax 742-3457

**Garden City Park, Nassau, Pop. 7,612**
Mineola UFD
Supt. — See Mineola
Mineola HS 800/9-12
10 Armstrong Rd 11040 516-237-2600
Edward Escobar, prin. Fax 739-4765

**Garnerville, See West Haverstraw**
North Rockland Central SD 5,200/K-12
65 Chapel St 10923 845-942-3000
Ileana Eckert, supt. Fax 942-3175
www.nrcsd.org
Other Schools – See Thiells

**Geneseo, Livingston, Pop. 7,881**
Geneseo Central SD 900/K-12
4050 Avon Rd 14454 585-243-3450
Timothy Hayes, supt. Fax 243-9481
www.geneseocsd.org/
Geneseo MSHS 500/6-12
4050 Avon Rd 14454 585-243-3450
Michael Salatel, prin. Fax 243-9481

---

SUNY at Geneseo Post-Sec.
1 College Cir 14454 585-245-5000

**Geneva, Ontario, Pop. 12,783**
Geneva CSD 2,200/PK-12
400 W North St 14456 315-781-0400
Trina Smith Newton, supt. Fax 781-4193
www.genevacsd.org
Geneva HS 700/9-12
101 Carter Rd 14456 315-781-0402
Greg Baker, prin. Fax 781-0695
Geneva MS 500/6-8
101 Carter Rd 14456 315-781-0404
Robert Smith, prin. Fax 781-0694

---

Finger Lakes Health College of Nursing Post-Sec.
196 North St 14456 315-787-4000
Hobart & William Smith Colleges Post-Sec.
300 Pulteney St 14456 315-781-3000

**Germantown, Columbia**
Germantown Central SD 600/K-12
123 Main St 12526 518-537-6280
Susan Brown, supt. Fax 537-6283
www.germantowncsd.org
Germantown Central HS 300/7-12
123 Main St 12526 518-537-6281
Karol Harlow, prin. Fax 537-6893

**Getzville, Erie, Pop. 2,300**

---

Bryant & Stratton College Post-Sec.
3650 Millersport Hwy 14068 716-625-6300
ITT Technical Institute Post-Sec.
PO Box 327 14068 716-689-2200

**Ghent, Columbia, Pop. 556**

---

Hawthorne Valley Waldorf S 200/PK-12
330 County Route 21C 12075 518-672-7092

**Gilbertsville, Otsego, Pop. 397**
Gilbertsville-Mount Upton Central SD 400/PK-12
693 State Highway 51 13776 607-783-2207
Glenn Hamilton, supt. Fax 783-2254
www.gmucsd.org/
Gilbertsville-Mount Upton JSHS 300/6-12
693 State Highway 51 13776 607-783-2207
Annette Hammond, prin. Fax 783-2254

**Gilboa, Schoharie**
Gilboa-Conesville Central SD 400/PK-12
132 Wyckoff Rd 12076 607-588-7541
Ruth Reeve, supt. Fax 588-6820
www.gilboa-conesville.k12.ny.us/
Gilboa-Conesville Central S 400/PK-12
132 Wyckoff Rd 12076 607-588-7541
Thomas Santacross, prin. Fax 588-6820

**Glen Cove, Nassau, Pop. 26,520**
Glen Cove CSD 3,200/PK-12
150 Dosoris Ln 11542 516-801-7010
Maria Rianna, supt. Fax 801-7019
www.glencove.k12.ny.us
Finley MS 700/6-8
1 Forest Ave 11542 516-801-7510
Nelson Iocolano, prin. Fax 801-7519
Glen Cove HS 1,000/9-12
150 Dosoris Ln 11542 516-801-7610
Roseann Cirnigliaro, prin. Fax 801-7619

---

Webb Institute Post-Sec.
298 Crescent Beach Rd 11542 516-671-2213

**Glendale, See New York**
NYC Department of Education
Supt. — See New York
IS 119 800/6-8
7401 78th Ave 11385 718-326-8261
Dr. Jeanne Fagan, prin. Fax 456-9523

**Glen Head, Nassau, Pop. 4,626**
North Shore Central SD
Supt. — See Sea Cliff
North Shore HS 900/9-12
450 Glen Cove Ave 11545 516-277-7000
Albert Cousins, prin. Fax 277-7001
North Shore MS 700/6-8
505 Glen Cove Ave 11545 516-277-7300
Marc Ferris, prin. Fax 277-7301

**Glens Falls, Warren, Pop. 14,415**
Glens Falls CSD 2,100/PK-12
15 Quade St 12801 518-792-1212
Paul Jenkins, supt. Fax 792-1538
www.gfsd.org
Glens Falls HS 800/9-12
10 Quade St 12801 518-792-6564
Mark Stratton, prin. Fax 743-1164
Glens Falls MS 600/5-8
20 Quade St 12801 518-793-3418
Christopher Reed, prin. Fax 793-4888

---

Adirondack Beauty School Post-Sec.
108 Dix Ave 12801 518-745-1646
Glens Falls Hospital Post-Sec.
100 Park St 12801 518-792-3151

**Glenville, Schenectady**
Burnt Hills-Ballston Lake Central SD 3,200/K-12
50 Cypress Dr 12302 518-399-9141
Patrick McGrath, supt. Fax 399-1882
www.bhbl.org
Other Schools – See Burnt Hills

**Gloversville, Fulton, Pop. 15,362**
Gloversville CSD 3,100/PK-12
234 Lincoln St 12078 518-775-5700
Michael Vanyo, supt. Fax 725-8793
www.gloversvilleschools.org
Gloversville HS 900/9-12
199 Lincoln St 12078 518-775-5710
Dr. Richard DeMallie, prin. Fax 773-3674
Gloversville MS 700/6-8
234 Lincoln St 12078 518-775-5720
Mark Batty, prin. Fax 773-9865

**Goshen, Orange, Pop. 5,361**
Goshen Central SD 2,900/K-12
227 Main St 10924 845-615-6720
Daniel Connor, supt. Fax 615-6725
www.gcsny.org
Goshen Central HS 900/9-12
222 Scotchtown Rd 10924 845-615-6100
Kurtis Kotes, prin. Fax 615-6116
Hooker MS 700/6-8
41 Lincoln Ave 10924 845-615-6300
William Rolon, prin. Fax 615-6310

---

Burke Catholic HS 400/9-12
80 Fletcher St 10924 845-294-5481
John Dolan, prin. Fax 294-7957

**Gouverneur, Saint Lawrence, Pop. 3,883**
Gouverneur Central SD 1,500/PK-12
133 E Barney St 13642 315-287-4870
Lauren French, supt. Fax 287-4736
www.gcsk12.org
Gouverneur HS 500/9-12
113 E Barney St 13642 315-287-1900
Cory Wood, prin. Fax 287-7963
Gouverneur MS 400/6-8
113 E Barney St 13642 315-287-1903
Steven Coffin, prin. Fax 287-2666

**Gowanda, Cattaraugus, Pop. 2,660**
Gowanda Central SD 1,300/PK-12
10674 Prospect St 14070 716-532-3325
James Klubek, supt. Fax 995-2154
www.gowcsd.com
Gowanda HS 400/9-12
10674 Prospect St 14070 716-532-3325
Dr. Robert Anderson, prin. Fax 995-2108
Gowanda MS 400/5-8
10674 Prospect St 14070 716-532-3325
David Smith, prin. Fax 995-2127

**Grahamsville, Sullivan**
Tri-Valley Central SD 1,200/PK-12
34 Moore Hill Rd 12740 845-985-2296
Thomas Palmer, supt. Fax 985-0310
www.trivalleycsd.org
Tri-Valley Secondary S 500/7-12
34 Moore Hill Rd 12740 845-985-2296
Robert Peters, prin. Fax 985-7903

**Grand Island, Erie**
Grand Island Central SD 3,100/PK-12
1100 Ransom Rd 14072 716-773-8800
Teresa Lawrence Ph.D., supt.
www.grandislandschools.org
Connor MS 800/6-8
1100 Ransom Rd 14072 716-773-8830
John Fitzpatrick, prin. Fax 773-8983
Grand Island HS 1,000/9-12
1100 Ransom Rd 14072 716-773-8820
Daniel Quartley, prin. Fax 773-8951

**Granville, Washington, Pop. 2,523**
Granville Central SD 1,200/PK-12
58 Quaker St 12832 518-642-1051
Mark Bessen, supt. Fax 642-2491
www.granvillecsd.org
Granville JSHS 700/7-12
58 Quaker St 12832 518-642-1051
Camille Harrelson, prin. Fax 642-4544

**Great Neck, Nassau, Pop. 9,663**
Great Neck UFD 6,500/PK-12
345 Lakeville Rd 11020 516-441-4001
Dr. Teresa Prendergast, supt. Fax 441-4994
www.greatneck.k12.ny.us
Great Neck South MS 800/6-8
349 Lakeville Rd 11020 516-441-4600
Dr. James Welsch, prin. Fax 441-4690
Miller Great Neck North HS 1,000/9-12
35 Polo Rd 11023 516-441-4700
Bernard Kaplan, prin. Fax 441-4795
Sherman Great Neck North MS 700/6-8
77 Polo Rd 11023 516-441-4500
Gerald Cozine, prin. Fax 773-4841
Shine Great Neck South HS 1,300/9-12
341 Lakeville Rd 11020 516-441-4800
Susan Elliott, prin. Fax 773-8279
Village S 50/Alt
614 Middle Neck Rd 11023 516-441-4900
Stephen Goldberg, prin. Fax 441-4909

---

North Shore Hebrew Academy 200/6-8
26 Old Mill Rd 11023 516-487-9163

**Greene, Chenango, Pop. 1,564**
Greene Central SD 1,100/K-12
40 S Canal St 13778 607-656-4161
Jonathan Retz, supt. Fax 656-9362
www.greenecsd.org
Greene HS 400/9-12
40 S Canal St 13778 607-656-4161
James Walters, prin. Fax 656-8872
Greene MS 300/6-8
40 S Canal St 13778 607-656-4161
Timothy Calice, prin. Fax 656-4520

**Green Island, Albany, Pop. 2,545**
Green Island UFD 300/K-12
171 Hudson Ave 12183 518-273-1422
Dr. Michael Mugits, supt. Fax 270-0818
www.greenisland.org
Heatly S 300/K-12
171 Hudson Ave 12183 518-273-1422
Erin Peteani, prin. Fax 270-0818

**Greenlawn, Suffolk, Pop. 13,492**
Elwood UFD 2,500/K-12
100 Kenneth Ave 11740 631-266-5400
Peter Scordo, supt. Fax 368-2338
www.elwood.k12.ny.us
Other Schools – See Elwood

Harborfields Central SD 3,500/K-12
2 Oldfield Rd 11740 631-754-5320
Diana Todaro, supt. Fax 261-0068
www.harborfieldscsd.net
Harborfields HS 1,100/9-12
98 Taylor Ave 11740 631-754-5360
Dr. Rory Manning, prin. Fax 754-3751
Oldfield MS 900/6-8
2 Oldfield Rd 11740 631-754-5310
Joanne Giordano, prin. Fax 754-2677

**Greenport, Suffolk, Pop. 2,155**
Greenport UFD 600/K-12
720 Front St 11944 631-477-1950
David Gamberg, supt. Fax 593-8951
www.gufsd.org/
Greenport JSHS 300/7-12
720 Front St 11944 631-477-1950
Leonard Skuggevik, prin. Fax 593-8954

**Greenville, Greene, Pop. 9,528**
Greenville Central SD 1,300/K-12
4982 State Route 81 12083 518-966-5070
Cheryl Dudley, supt.
www.greenville.k12.ny.us
Greenville HS 400/9-12
4976 State Route 81 12083 518-966-5070
Todd Hilgendorff, prin.
Greenville MS 300/6-8
4976 State Route 81 12083 518-966-5070
Brian Reeve, prin.

**Greenwich, Washington, Pop. 1,754**
Greenwich Central SD 1,000/K-12
10 Gray Ave 12834 518-692-9542
Mark Fish, supt. Fax 692-9547
www.greenwichcsd.org
Greenwich JSHS 500/7-12
10 Gray Ave 12834 518-692-9542
George Niesz, prin. Fax 692-8503

**Groton, Tompkins, Pop. 2,324**
Groton Central SD 700/PK-12
400 Peru Rd 13073 607-898-5301
James Abrams, supt. Fax 898-4647
www.grotoncs.org
Groton JSHS 300/6-12
400 Peru Rd 13073 607-898-5803
Laura Norris, prin. Fax 898-4555

**Guilderland, Albany**
Guilderland Central SD
Supt. — See Guilderland Center
Farnsworth MS 1,200/6-8
6072 State Farm Rd 12084 518-456-6010
Mary Summermatter, prin. Fax 456-3747

**Guilderland Center, Albany**
Guilderland Central SD 5,000/K-12
PO Box 18 12085 518-456-6200
Dr. Marie Wiles, supt. Fax 456-1152
www.guilderlandschools.org
Guilderland HS 1,700/9-12
PO Box 37 12085 518-861-8591
Thomas Lutsic, prin. Fax 861-5874
Other Schools – See Guilderland

**Hadley, Saratoga, Pop. 1,003**

King's S 200/PK-12
6087 State Route 9N 12835 518-654-6230

**Hamburg, Erie, Pop. 9,357**
Frontier Central SD 5,000/K-12
5120 Orchard Ave 14075 716-926-1700
Dr. Bret Apthorpe, supt. Fax 926-1776
www.frontier.wnyric.org
Frontier HS 1,600/9-12
4432 Bay View Rd 14075 716-926-1720
Jeffrey Sortisio, prin. Fax 646-2195
Frontier MS 1,200/6-8
2751 Amsdell Rd 14075 716-926-1730
Ryan Sikorski, prin. Fax 646-2207

Hamburg Central SD 3,900/PK-12
5305 Abbott Rd 14075 716-646-3220
Michael Cornell, supt. Fax 646-3209
www.hamburgschools.org
Hamburg HS 1,200/9-12
4111 Legion Dr 14075 716-646-3300
Michael Gallagher, prin. Fax 646-3028
Hamburg MS 900/6-8
360 Division St 14075 716-646-3250
Jennifer Giallella, prin. Fax 646-6380

Hilbert College Post-Sec.
5200 S Park Ave 14075 716-649-7900
Immaculata Academy 200/9-12
5138 S Park Ave 14075 716-649-6161
Jill Monaco, prin. Fax 646-1782

**Hamilton, Madison, Pop. 4,131**
Hamilton Central SD 600/PK-12
47 W Kendrick Ave 13346 315-824-6300
Dr. Patrick Curtin, supt. Fax 824-6314
www.hamiltoncentral.org
Hamilton JSHS 300/6-12
47 W Kendrick Ave 13346 315-824-6320
William Dowsland, prin. Fax 824-6314

Colgate University Post-Sec.
13 Oak Dr 13346 315-228-1000
New Life Christian S 100/PK-12
1528 River Rd 13346 315-824-2625
Todd Slabaugh, prin. Fax 824-5102

**Hammond, Saint Lawrence, Pop. 278**
Hammond Central SD 300/PK-12
PO Box 185 13646 315-324-5931
Karen Carswell, supt. Fax 324-6057
hammond.sllboces.org
Hammond Central S 300/PK-12
PO Box 185 13646 315-324-5931
Kathleen Cruikshank, prin. Fax 324-6057

**Hammondsport, Steuben, Pop. 654**
Hammondsport Central SD 500/K-12
8272 Main Street Ext 14840 607-569-5200
Kyle Bower, supt. Fax 569-5212
www.hammondsportcsd.org
Hammondsport JSHS 300/7-12
8272 Main Street Ext 14840 607-569-5200
Tad Rounds, prin. Fax 569-5212

**Hampton Bays, Suffolk, Pop. 13,462**
Hampton Bays UFD 1,700/PK-12
86 Argonne Rd E 11946 631-723-2100
Lars Clemensen, supt. Fax 723-2109
www.hbschools.us
Hampton Bays HS 600/9-12
88 Argonne Rd E 11946 631-723-2110
Chris Richardt, prin. Fax 723-2120
Hampton Bays MS 600/5-8
70 Ponquogue Ave 11946 631-723-4700
Dennis Schug, prin. Fax 723-4900

**Hancock, Delaware, Pop. 1,014**
Hancock Central SD 400/PK-12
67 Education Ln 13783 607-637-1301
Dr. Terrance Dougherty, supt. Fax 637-2512
hancock.stier.org
Hancock JSHS 200/5-12
67 Education Ln 13783 607-637-1306
Brenton Taylor, prin. Fax 637-2512

**Hannibal, Oswego, Pop. 547**
Hannibal Central SD 1,500/PK-12
928 Cayuga St 13074 315-564-8100
Edmund Backus, supt. Fax 564-7263
www.hannibalcsd.org
Hannibal HS 500/9-12
928 Cayuga St 13074 315-564-8130
Stephen Dunn, prin. Fax 564-7973
Kenney MS 500/5-8
928 Cayuga St 13074 315-564-8120
Dee Froio, prin. Fax 564-7509

**Harpursville, Broome**
Harpursville Central SD 900/PK-12
PO Box 147 13787 607-693-8101
Kathleen Wood, supt. Fax 693-1480
www.hcs.stier.org/
Harpursville JSHS 400/7-12
PO Box 147 13787 607-693-8105
Michael Rullo, prin. Fax 693-1480

**Harrison, Westchester, Pop. 26,975**
Harrison Central SD 3,500/K-12
50 Union Ave 10528 914-630-3021
Dr. Louis Wool, supt. Fax 835-5893
www.harrisoncsd.org
Harrison HS 1,000/9-12
255 Union Ave 10528 914-630-3095
Steven Siciliano, prin. Fax 835-5471
Klein MS 900/6-8
50 Union Ave 10528 914-630-3033
Scott Fried, prin. Fax 777-1346

**Harrisville, Lewis, Pop. 623**
Harrisville Central SD 400/PK-12
14371 Pirate Ln 13648 315-543-2707
Robert Finster, supt. Fax 543-2360
www.hcsk12.org
Harrisville JSHS 200/7-12
14371 Pirate Ln 13648 315-543-2920
Eric Luther, prin. Fax 543-2360

**Hartford, Washington**
Hartford Central SD 500/PK-12
4704 State Route 149 12838 518-632-5931
Andrew Cook, supt. Fax 632-5231
www.hartfordcsd.org
Hartford MSHS 300/6-12
4704 State Route 149 12838 518-632-5923
Brian George, prin. Fax 632-5231

**Hartsdale, Westchester, Pop. 5,198**
Greenburgh Central SD 1,700/PK-12
475 W Hartsdale Ave 10530 914-761-6000
Dr. Tahira DuPree Chase, supt. Fax 761-2354
www.greenburghcsd.org
Woodlands HS 500/9-12
475 W Hartsdale Ave 10530 914-761-6052
Matthew Smith, prin. Fax 761-6951
Woodlands MS 200/7-8
475 W Hartsdale Ave 10530 914-761-6052
Fax 686-0445

Maria Regina HS 600/9-12
500 W Hartsdale Ave 10530 914-761-3300
Valerie Reidy, prin. Fax 761-0860
Solomon Schechter S of Westchester 500/6-12
555 W Hartsdale Ave 10530 914-948-8333
Michael Kay Ph.D., hdmstr. Fax 948-7979

**Hastings on Hudson, Westchester, Pop. 7,663**
Greenburgh-Graham UFD 200/1-12
1 S Broadway 10706 914-478-1106
Amy Goodman, supt. Fax 478-0904
www.greenburgh-graham.org
King HS 100/9-12
1 S Broadway 10706 914-478-1106
Paul Tobin, prin. Fax 478-2321

Hastings-on-Hudson UFD 1,600/K-12
27 Farragut Ave 10706 914-478-2900
Dr. Roy Montesano, supt. Fax 478-6209
www.hohschools.org
Farragut MS 500/5-8
27 Farragut Ave 10706 914-478-6230
Gail Kipper, prin. Fax 478-6314
Hastings HS 500/9-12
1 Mount Hope Blvd 10706 914-478-6250
Louis Adipietro, prin. Fax 478-7842

**Hauppauge, Suffolk, Pop. 20,653**
Hauppauge UFD 4,000/K-12
PO Box 6006 11788 631-265-3630
Patricia Sullivan-Kriss, supt. Fax 265-9546
www.hauppauge.k12.ny.us
Hauppauge HS 1,400/9-12
PO Box 6006 11788 631-761-8302
Christine O'Connor, prin. Fax 979-0926
Hauppauge MS 1,000/6-8
PO Box 6006 11788 631-761-8230
Maryann Fletcher, prin. Fax 265-9546

Learning Institute for Beauty Sciences Post-Sec.
544 Route 111 11788 631-724-0440

**Hempstead, Nassau, Pop. 52,895**
Hempstead UFD 5,600/PK-12
185 Peninsula Blvd 11550 516-434-4000
Susan Johnson, supt. Fax 292-9471
www.hempsteadschools.org
Hempstead HS 900/9-12
201 President St 11550 516-434-4200
Dr. Stephen Strachan, prin. Fax 292-7770
Schultz MS 1,200/6-8
70 Greenwich St 11550 516-434-4300
Noel Rios, prin. Fax 483-2549

Uniondale UFD
Supt. — See Uniondale
Lawrence Road MS 700/6-8
50 Lawrence Rd 11550 516-918-1500
Dexter Hodge, prin. Fax 565-5023

Crescent S 200/PK-12
130 Front St 11550 516-292-1787
Franklin Career Institute Post-Sec.
91 N Franklin St 11550 516-481-4444
Hofstra University Post-Sec.
100 Hofstra University 11549 516-463-6600
Learning Institute for Beauty Sciences Post-Sec.
173A Fulton Ave 11550 516-483-6259
Sacred Heart Academy 900/9-12
47 Cathedral Ave 11550 516-483-7383
Sr. Joanne Forker, prin. Fax 483-1016

**Henrietta, Monroe**
Rush-Henrietta Central SD 5,500/K-12
2034 Lehigh Station Rd 14467 585-359-5012
Dr. J. Kenneth Graham, supt. Fax 359-5045
www.rhnet.org
Ninth Grade Academy 400/9-9
2000 Lehigh Station Rd 14467 585-359-5550
Kerry Macko, prin. Fax 359-5559
Roth MS 800/6-8
4000 E Henrietta Rd 14467 585-359-5108
Denise Zeh, prin. Fax 359-5164
Rush-Henrietta HS 1,300/10-12
1799 Lehigh Station Rd 14467 585-359-5208
Beth Patton, prin. Fax 359-5290
Other Schools – See West Henrietta

**Herkimer, Herkimer, Pop. 7,636**
Herkimer Central SD 1,200/K-12
801 W German St 13350 315-866-2230
Robert Miller, supt. Fax 866-2234
www.herkimercsd.org
Herkimer JSHS 500/7-12
801 W German St 13350 315-866-2230
Mary Tomaso, prin. Fax 866-8595

Herkimer County Community College Post-Sec.
100 Reservoir Rd 13350 315-866-0300

**Hermon, Saint Lawrence, Pop. 418**
Edwards-Knox Central SD 600/PK-12
2512 County Route 24 13652 315-562-8130
George F. Merritt, supt. Fax 562-2477
www.ekcsk12.org
Edwards-Knox JSHS 300/7-12
2512 County Route 24 13652 315-562-8131
Amy Sykes, prin. Fax 562-8139

**Heuvelton, Saint Lawrence, Pop. 711**
Heuvelton Central SD 500/PK-12
PO Box 375 13654 315-344-2414
Susan Todd, supt. Fax 344-2349
heuvelton.schoolfusion.us
Heuvelton Central S 500/PK-12
PO Box 375 13654 315-344-2414
Jesse Coburn, prin. Fax 344-2349

**Hewlett, Nassau, Pop. 6,722**
Hewlett-Woodmere UFD
Supt. — See Woodmere
Hewlett HS, 60 Everit Ave 11557 1,000/9-12
Theodore Fulton, prin. 516-792-4100
Woodmere MS 700/6-8
1170 Peninsula Blvd 11557 516-792-4368
Albert Bauer, prin.

---

Abraham HS for Girls 300/9-12
291 Meadowview Ave 11557 516-374-7195

**Hicksville, Nassau, Pop. 40,674**
Hicksville UFD 5,200/PK-12
200 Division Ave 11801 516-733-2105
Dr. Carl Bonuso, supt. Fax 733-6584
www.hicksvillepublicschools.com
Hicksville HS 1,700/9-12
180 Division Ave 11801 516-733-2201
Raymond Williams, prin. Fax 733-6626
Hicksville MS 1,200/6-8
215 Jerusalem Ave 11801 516-733-2261
Mara Jorisch, prin. Fax 733-6528

---

Holy Trinity Diocesan HS 1,400/9-12
98 Cherry Ln 11801 516-433-2900
Gene Fennell, prin. Fax 433-2827

**Highland, Ulster, Pop. 5,534**
Highland Central SD 1,800/K-12
320 Pancake Hollow Rd 12528 845-691-1000
Deborah Haab, supt. Fax 691-1039
www.highland-k12.org/
Highland HS 600/9-12
320 Pancake Hollow Rd 12528 845-691-1020
Pete Harris, prin. Fax 691-1038
Highland MS 400/6-8
71 Main St 12528 845-691-1080
Daniel Seyler-Wetzel, prin. Fax 691-1083

**Highland Falls, Orange, Pop. 3,773**
Highland Falls Ft. Montgomery Central SD
Supt. — See Fort Montgomery
Highland Falls MS 200/3-8
PO Box 287 10928 845-446-4761
Chris Fiorentino, prin. Fax 446-0858

**Hillburn, Rockland, Pop. 844**
Ramapo Central SD 4,500/K-12
45 Mountain Ave 10931 845-357-7783
Douglas Adams, supt. Fax 357-5707
www.ramapocentral.org
Other Schools – See Suffern

---

Mesivta Ohr Naftoli 100/9-12
275 Route 17 10931 845-357-5609

**Hilton, Monroe, Pop. 5,826**
Hilton Central SD 4,400/PK-12
225 West Ave 14468 585-392-1000
David Dimbleby, supt. Fax 392-1038
www.hilton.k12.ny.us
Hilton HS 1,400/9-12
400 East Ave 14468 585-392-1000
Brian Bartalo, prin. Fax 392-1052
Williams MS 700/7-8
200 School Ln 14468 585-392-1000
Tim Dobbertin, prin. Fax 392-1054

**Hinsdale, Cattaraugus**
Hinsdale Central SD 400/PK-12
3701 Main St 14743 716-557-2227
Larry Ljungberg, supt. Fax 557-2259
www.hinsdalebobcats.org
Hinsdale Central S 400/PK-12
3701 Main St 14743 716-557-2227
Laurie Cuddy, prin. Fax 557-2259

**Holbrook, Suffolk, Pop. 26,920**
Sachem Central SD
Supt. — See Ronkonkoma
Seneca MS 800/6-8
850 Main St 11741 631-471-1850
Gemma Salvia, prin. Fax 471-1849

**Holland, Erie, Pop. 1,197**
Holland Central SD 700/PK-12
103 Canada St 14080 716-537-8200
Cathy Fabiatos, supt. Fax 537-8203
www.holland.wnyric.org
Holland JSHS 300/7-12
103 Canada St 14080 716-537-8221
Carl Guidotti, prin. Fax 537-8233

**Holland Patent, Oneida, Pop. 456**
Holland Patent Central SD 1,500/PK-12
9601 Main St 13354 315-865-7200
Kathleen Davis Ed.D., supt. Fax 865-4057
www.hpschools.org
Holland Patent Central HS 500/9-12
9601 Main St 13354 315-865-8154
Russell Stevener, prin. Fax 865-4069
Holland Patent MS 400/6-8
9601 Main St 13354 315-865-8152
J. Andrew Massoud, prin. Fax 865-7243

**Holley, Orleans, Pop. 1,790**
Holley Central SD 1,200/PK-12
3800 N Main Street Rd 14470 585-638-6316
Robert D'Angelo, supt. Fax 638-7409
www.holleycsd.org
Holley JSHS 600/7-12
3800 N Main Street Rd 14470 585-638-6335
Susan Cory, prin. Fax 638-7925

**Hollis, See New York**
NYC Department of Education
Supt. — See New York
Cambria Heights Academy 100/9-12
18804 91st Ave 11423 718-776-2815
Melissa Menake, prin. Fax 776-2818
IS 238 1,600/6-8
8815 182nd St 11423 718-297-9821
Peter Leddy, prin. Fax 658-5288

---

Wang Yeshiva University HS for Girls 300/9-12
8686 Palo Alto St 11423 718-479-8550

**Holtsville, Suffolk, Pop. 19,502**
Sachem Central SD
Supt. — See Ronkonkoma
Sagamore MS 800/6-8
57 Division St 11742 631-696-8600
Andrew Larson, prin. Fax 696-8620
Sequoya MS 1,000/6-8
750 Waverly Ave 11742 631-207-7100
Frank Panasci, prin. Fax 207-7115

**Homer, Cortland, Pop. 3,225**
Homer Central SD 2,000/K-12
PO Box 500 13077 607-749-7241
Nancy Ruscio, supt. Fax 749-2312
www.homercentral.org
Homer HS 700/9-12
PO Box 500 13077 607-749-7246
Doug VanEtten, prin. Fax 749-2312
Homer JHS 400/6-8
PO Box 500 13077 607-749-1230
Tom Turck, prin. Fax 749-1238

**Honeoye, Ontario, Pop. 571**
Honeoye Central SD 700/K-12
PO Box 170 14471 585-229-4125
David C. Bills, supt. Fax 229-5633
www.honeoye.org
Honeoye MSHS 400/6-12
PO Box 170 14471 585-229-5171
Mike Mead, prin. Fax 229-4879

**Honeoye Falls, Monroe, Pop. 2,631**
Honeoye Falls-Lima Central SD 2,400/K-12
20 Church St 14472 585-624-7000
Gene Mancuso, supt. Fax 624-7003
www.hflcsd.org/
Honeoye Falls-Lima HS 800/9-12
83 East St 14472 585-624-7051
David Roth, prin. Fax 624-7118
Honeoye Falls-Lima MS 600/6-8
619 Quaker Meeting House Rd 14472 585-624-7100
Shawn Williams, prin. Fax 624-7121

**Hoosick, Rensselaer**

---

Hoosac S 100/8-12
PO Box 9 12089 518-686-7331
Dean Foster, hdmstr. Fax 686-3370

**Hoosick Falls, Rensselaer, Pop. 3,451**
Hoosick Falls Central SD 1,200/PK-12
PO Box 192 12090 518-686-7012
Kenneth Facin, supt. Fax 686-9060
www.hoosickfallscsd.org/
Hoosick Falls HS 600/7-12
PO Box 192 12090 518-686-7321
Stacy Vadney, prin. Fax 686-7452

**Hopewell Junction, Dutchess, Pop. 354**
Wappingers Central SD 11,900/K-12
25 Corporate Park Dr 12533 845-298-5000
Jose Carrion, supt. Fax 298-5041
www.wappingersschools.org
Jay HS 2,200/9-12
2012 Route 52 12533 845-897-6700
Dwight Bonk, prin. Fax 897-6719
Other Schools – See Wappingers Falls

**Hornell, Steuben, Pop. 8,357**
Hornell CSD 1,600/K-12
25 Pearl St 14843 607-324-1302
Douglas Wyant, supt. Fax 324-4060
www.hornellcityschools.com
Hornell JHS 400/7-8
134 Seneca St 14843 607-324-1303
Theodore Illi, prin. Fax 324-3421
Hornell SHS 400/9-12
134 Seneca St 14843 607-324-1303
Fax 324-3702

---

St. James Mercy Hospital Post-Sec.
411 Canisteo St 14843 607-324-3900

**Horseheads, Chemung, Pop. 6,375**
Horseheads Central SD 4,200/PK-12
1 Raider Ln 14845 607-739-5601
Thomas Douglas, supt. Fax 795-2405
www.horseheadsdistrict.com/
Horseheads HS 1,300/9-12
401 Fletcher St 14845 607-795-2500
Karen Donahue, prin. Fax 795-2505
Horseheads MS 700/7-8
950 Sing Sing Rd 14845 607-739-6357
Ronald Holloway, prin. Fax 795-2525

**Houghton, Allegany, Pop. 1,665**

---

Houghton Academy 100/7-12
9790 Thayer St 14744 585-567-8115
John Nelson, head sch Fax 567-8048
Houghton College Post-Sec.
1 Willard Ave 14744 585-567-9200

**Hudson, Columbia, Pop. 6,373**
Hudson CSD 2,000/PK-12
215 Harry Howard Ave 12534 518-828-4360
Maria J. Suttmeier, supt. Fax 697-8777
www.hudsoncityschooldistrict.com/
Columbia-Greene Partnership Academy Alt
364 Warren St 12534 518-781-3500
Thomas Gavin, prin.
Hudson HS 600/9-12
215 Harry Howard Ave 12534 518-828-4132
Antonio Abitabile, prin. Fax 697-8418
Hudson JHS 300/7-8
215 Harry Howard Ave 12534 518-828-4360
Derek Reardon, prin. Fax 697-8522

---

Columbia-Greene Community College Post-Sec.
4400 State Route 23 12534 518-828-4181

**Hudson Falls, Washington, Pop. 7,173**
Hudson Falls Central SD
Supt. — See Fort Edward
Hudson Falls HS 700/9-12
80 E La Barge St 12839 518-747-2121
James Bennefield, prin. Fax 746-9033
Hudson Falls MS 500/6-8
131 Notre Dame St 12839 518-747-2121
Todd Gonyeau, prin. Fax 746-2790

**Huntington, Suffolk, Pop. 17,836**
Huntington UFD
Supt. — See Huntington Station
Finley MS 700/7-8
20 Greenlawn Rd 11743 631-673-2020
John Amato, prin. Fax 425-4746
Huntington HS 1,200/9-12
188 Oakwood Rd 11743 631-673-2003
Dr. Carmela Leonardi, prin. Fax 425-4730

**Huntington Station, Suffolk, Pop. 32,344**
Huntington UFD 4,300/K-12
50 Tower St 11746 631-673-2038
James Polansky, supt. Fax 423-3447
www.hufsd.edu/
Other Schools – See Huntington

South Huntington UFD 5,500/K-12
60 Weston St 11746 631-812-3070
Dr. David P. Bennardo, supt. Fax 812-3075
www.shufsd.org
Stimson MS 900/7-8
401 Oakwood Rd 11746 631-812-3700
Edwin Smith, prin. Fax 812-3737
Whitman HS 1,800/9-12
301 W Hills Rd 11746 631-812-3800
John Murphy, prin. Fax 812-3838

---

St. Anthony HS 2,500/9-12
275 Wolf Hill Rd 11747 631-271-2020
Br. Gary Cregan, prin. Fax 547-6820

**Hurley, Ulster, Pop. 3,401**

---

Coleman HS 200/9-12
430 Hurley Ave 12443 845-338-2750
James Lyons, prin. Fax 338-0250

**Hyde Park, Dutchess, Pop. 1,897**
Hyde Park Central SD 3,700/K-12
PO Box 2033 12538 845-229-4000
Dr. Greer Rychcik, supt. Fax 229-4056
www.hpcsd.org
Haviland MS 900/6-8
PO Box 721 12538 845-229-4030
Eric Shaw, prin. Fax 229-2475
Other Schools – See Staatsburg on Hudson

---

Culinary Institute of America Post-Sec.
1946 Campus Dr 12538 845-452-9600

**Ilion, Herkimer, Pop. 7,948**
Central Valley Central SD 1,200/PK-12
111 Frederick St 13357 315-894-9934
Richard Hughes, supt. Fax 894-2716
www.cvalleycsd.org
Central Valley Academy 500/9-12
111 Frederick St 13357 315-895-7471
Renee Rudd, prin. Fax 894-5255
Other Schools – See Mohawk

**Indian Lake, Hamilton**
Indian Lake Central SD 100/PK-12
6345 Nys Route 30 12842 518-648-5024
Mark Brand, supt. Fax 648-6346
www.ilcsd.org
Indian Lake Central S 100/PK-12
6345 Nys Route 30 12842 518-648-5024
David Snide, prin. Fax 648-6346

**Irvington, Westchester, Pop. 6,319**
Irvington UFD 1,700/K-12
6 Dows Ln 10533 914-591-8500
Dr. Kristopher Harrison, supt. Fax 591-3064
www.irvingtonschools.org
Irvington HS 600/9-12
40 N Broadway 10533 914-591-8648
David Cohen, prin. Fax 591-6714
Irvington MS 400/6-8
40 N Broadway 10533 914-591-9494
David Sottile, prin. Fax 591-8535

**Island Park, Nassau, Pop. 4,586**
Island Park UFD 700/K-8
150 Trafalgar Blvd 11558 516-434-2600
Dr. Rosmarie T. Bovino, supt. Fax 431-7550
www.ips.k12.ny.us
Island Park/Lincoln Orens MS 300/5-8
150 Trafalgar Blvd 11558 516-434-2630
Vincent Randazzo, prin. Fax 431-7550

**Islip, Suffolk, Pop. 18,391**
Islip UFD 3,200/K-12
215 Main St 11751 631-650-8210
Susan Schnebel, supt. Fax 650-8218
www.islipufsd.org/
Islip HS 1,200/9-12
2508 Union Blvd 11751 631-650-8305
Michael Mosca, prin. Fax 650-8308
Islip MS 800/6-8
211 Main St 11751 631-650-8505
Dr. Timothy Martin, prin. Fax 650-8508

**Islip Terrace, Suffolk, Pop. 5,327**
East Islip UFD 4,400/PK-12
1 Craig B Gariepy Ave 11752 631-224-2000
Linda Rozzi, supt. Fax 581-1617
www.eischools.org
East Islip HS 1,600/9-12
1 Redmen St 11752 631-224-2100
William Brennen, prin. Fax 581-4410
East Islip MS 1,000/6-8
100 Redmen St 11752 631-224-2170
Mark Bernard, prin. Fax 859-3745

**Ithaca, Tompkins, Pop. 28,833**
Ithaca CSD 5,500/PK-12
400 Lake St 14850 607-274-2101
Dr. Luvelle Brown, supt. Fax 274-2271
www.icsd.k12.ny.us
Boynton MS 600/6-8
1601 N Cayuga St 14850 607-274-2241
Joseph Dhara, prin. Fax 274-2357
De Witt MS 500/6-8
560 Warren Rd 14850 607-257-3222
Mac Knight, prin. Fax 266-3502
Ithaca HS 1,400/9-12
1401 N Cayuga St 14850 607-274-2145
Jarett Powers, prin. Fax 277-3061
Lehman Alternative Community S 300/Alt
111 Chestnut St 14850 607-274-2183
Diane Carruthers, prin. Fax 274-2351

---

Cornell University Post-Sec.
410 Thurston Ave 14850 607-255-2000
Ithaca College Post-Sec.
953 Danby Rd 14850 607-274-3011

**Jackson Heights, See New York**
NYC Department of Education
Supt. — See New York
IS 145 2,000/6-8
3334 80th St 11372 718-457-1242
Delores Beckham, prin. Fax 335-0601
IS 230 1,000/6-8
7310 34th Ave 11372 718-335-7648
Ronald Zirin, prin. Fax 335-7513

---

Garden S 300/PK-12
3316 79th St 11372 718-335-6363
Dr. Richard Marotta, hdmstr. Fax 565-1169
Plaza College Post-Sec.
7409 37th Ave 11372 718-779-1430

**Jamaica, See New York**
NYC Department of Education
Supt. — See New York
Basie MS 800/6-8
13325 Guy R Brewer Blvd 11434 718-723-6200
Omotayo Cineus, prin. Fax 527-1675
Business/Computer Applications S 400/9-12
20701 116th Ave 11411 718-978-2807
Lynne Callender, prin. Fax 978-3402
Edison Career & Tech HS Vo/Tech
16565 84th Ave 11432 718-297-6580
Moses Ojeda, prin. Fax 658-0365
Emerson S 100/6-8
10835 167th St 11433 718-657-4801
Jakub Lau, prin. Fax 657-4807
Franklin HS Finance & Info Technology 9-12
20701 116th Ave 11411 718-276-0150
Carla Theodorou, prin. Fax 276-4725
Hillcrest HS 3,100/9-12
16005 Highland Ave 11432 718-658-5407
David Morrison, prin. Fax 739-5137
Hillside Arts & Letters Academy 100/9-12
16701 Gothic Dr 11432 718-658-1249
Matthew Ritter, prin. Fax 658-1613
Humanities & the Arts Magnet HS 500/9-12
20701 116th Ave 11411 718-978-2135
Rosemarie O'Mard, prin. Fax 978-2309
Institute for Health Professions 100/9-12
20701 116th Ave 11411 718-723-7301
Gareth Robinson, prin. Fax 723-7306
Jamaica Gateway to the Sciences 9-12
16701 Gothic Dr 11432 718-480-2689
Caren Taylor, prin. Fax 480-2697
HS for Community Leadership 100/9-12
16701 Gothic Dr 11432 718-558-9801
Carlos Borrero, prin. Fax 558-9807
HS for Law Enforcement & Public Safety 500/9-12
11625 Guy R Brewer Blvd 11434 718-977-4800
Laura Van Deren, dir. Fax 977-4802
JHS 8 700/6-8
10835 167th St 11433 718-739-6883
Angela Green, prin. Fax 526-2727
JHS 217 1,700/6-8
8505 144th St 11435 718-657-1120
Patrick Burns, prin. Fax 291-3668
Law 400/9-12
20701 116th Ave 11411 718-978-6432
Donna White, prin. Fax 978-6749
Martin HS 1,000/9-12
15610 Baisley Blvd 11434 718-528-2920
Gillian Smith, prin. Fax 276-1846
Math Science Research & Tech Magnet HS 400/9-12
20701 116th Ave 11411 718-978-1837
Jose Cruz, prin. Fax 978-2063
Queens Collegiate HS 500/6-12
16701 Gothic Dr 11432 718-658-4016
Jaime Dubei, prin. Fax 658-5149
Queens Gateway to the Health Sciences 800/6-12
16020 Goethals Ave 11432 718-969-3155
Judy Henry, prin. Fax 969-3552
Queens HS for Science 400/9-12
9450 159th St 11433 718-657-3181
Lenneen Gibson, prin. Fax 657-2579
Queens Satellite HS for Opportunity Alt
16202 Hillside Ave 11432 718-657-3920
Mark Melkonian, prin. Fax 658-2309
Redwood MS 6-8
13325 Guy R Brewer Blvd 11434 718-276-4540
Lisa Reiter, prin.
Voyages Prep - South Queens 100/9-12
15610 Baisley Blvd 11434 718-276-1946
Christopher Losurdo, prin. Fax 276-2784
York Early College Academy 500/6-12
10835 167th St 11433 718-262-8547
Deborah Burnett, prin. Fax 558-4257
Young Womens Leadership S 500/6-12
15091 87th Rd 11432 718-725-0402
Mala Panday, prin. Fax 725-0390

---

Al-Iman S 100/PK-12
8989 Van Wyck Expy 11435 718-297-6520
Allen School Post-Sec.
16318 Jamaica Ave 11432 888-620-6745
Archbishop Molloy HS 1,500/9-12
8353 Manton St 11435 718-441-2100
Br. Thomas Schady, prin. Fax 849-8251
CUNY York College Post-Sec.
9420 Guy R Brewer Blvd 11451 718-262-2000
Jon Louis School of Beauty Post-Sec.
9114 Merrick Blvd 11432 718-658-6240
Louis Academy 900/9-12
17621 Wexford Ter 11432 718-297-2120
Sr. Kathleen McKinney, prin. Fax 739-0037
New York Automotive & Diesel Institute Post-Sec.
17818 Liberty Ave 11433 718-658-0006
St. John's University Post-Sec.
8000 Utopia Pkwy 11439 718-990-2000

**Jamestown, Chautauqua, Pop. 30,116**
Jamestown CSD 4,600/PK-12
197 Martin Rd 14701 716-483-4420
Tim O. Mains, supt. Fax 483-4421
www.jamestown.wnyric.org
Jamestown HS 1,300/9-12
350 E 2nd St 14701 716-483-3470
Mike McElrath Ph.D., prin. Fax 483-4399
Jefferson MS 400/5-8
195 Martin Rd 14701 716-483-4411
Carm Proctor, prin. Fax 483-4273
Persell MS 500/5-8
375 Baker St 14701 716-483-4406
Philip Cammarata, prin. Fax 483-4417
Washington MS 500/5-8
159 Buffalo St 14701 716-483-4413
Melissa Emerson, prin. Fax 483-4268

Southwestern Central SD 1,500/PK-12
600 Hunt Rd 14701 716-484-1136
Maureen Donahue, supt. Fax 484-1139
swcs.wnyric.org
Southwestern HS 400/9-12
600 Hunt Rd 14701 716-664-6273
Michael Cipolla, prin. Fax 484-1167
Southwestern MS 400/6-8
600 Hunt Rd 14701 716-664-6270
Richard Rybicki, prin. Fax 487-0855

---

Bethel Baptist Christian Academy 100/K-12
200 Hunt Rd 14701 716-484-7420
Mike Stormont, chrpsn. Fax 484-0087
Jamestown Business College Post-Sec.
PO Box 429 14702 716-664-5100
Jamestown Community College Post-Sec.
PO Box 20 14702 716-338-1000
Woman's Christian Assoc. Hospital Post-Sec.
207 Foote Ave 14701 716-664-8110

**Jamesville, Onondaga**
Jamesville-DeWitt Central SD
Supt. — See De Witt
Jamesville-DeWitt MS 900/5-8
6280 Randall Rd 13078 315-445-8360
Thomas A. Eldridge, prin. Fax 445-8421

**Jasper, Steuben**
Jasper-Troupsburg Central SD 600/PK-12
PO Box 81 14855 607-792-3675
Wendell Binley, supt. Fax 792-3749
www.jtcsd.org
Jasper-Troupsburg JSHS 300/7-12
PO Box 81 14855 607-792-3675
Christopher Parker, prin. Fax 792-3749

**Jefferson, Schoharie**
Jefferson Central SD 300/K-12
1332 State Route 10 12093 607-652-7821
Brian Corey, supt. Fax 652-7806
www.jeffersoncs.org
Jefferson Central S 300/K-12
1332 State Route 10 12093 607-652-7821
Brian Corey, admin. Fax 652-7806

**Jeffersonville, Sullivan, Pop. 355**
Sullivan West Central SD 1,200/PK-12
PO Box 308 12748 845-482-4610
Dr. Nancy Hackett, supt. Fax 482-3022
www.swcsd.org/
Other Schools – See Lake Huntington

**Jericho, Nassau, Pop. 13,391**
Jericho UFD 3,000/K-12
99 Old Cedar Swamp Rd 11753 516-203-3600
Henry Grishman, supt. Fax 933-2047
www.jerichoschools.org
Jericho HS 1,200/9-12
99 Old Cedar Swamp Rd 11753 516-203-3610
Joan Rosenberg, prin. Fax 681-2895
Jericho MS 700/6-8
99 Old Cedar Swamp Rd 11753 516-203-3620
Donald Gately, prin. Fax 681-8984

**Johnson City, Broome, Pop. 14,676**
Johnson City Central SD 2,600/K-12
666 Reynolds Rd 13790 607-763-1230
Mary Kay Frys, supt. Fax 729-2767
www.jcschools.com
Johnson City HS 700/9-12
666 Reynolds Rd 13790 607-763-1256
Kimberly Beukema, prin. Fax 763-1211
Johnson City MS 600/6-8
601 Columbia Dr 13790 607-763-1240
Joseph Guccia, prin. Fax 763-1297

---

Davis College Post-Sec.
400 Riverside Dr 13790 607-729-1581
United Health Services Hospital Post-Sec.
33-57 Harrison St 13790 607-763-6000

**Johnstown, Fulton, Pop. 8,615**
Johnstown CSD 1,900/PK-12
1 Sir Bills Cir Ste 101 12095 518-762-4611
Robert DeLilli, supt. Fax 762-6379
www.johnstownschools.org/
Jansen Avenue S 9-12
305 Jansen Ave 12095 518-762-9119
Scott Hale, admin.
Johnstown HS 700/9-12
1 Sir Bills Cir 12095 518-762-4661
Michael Beatty, prin. Fax 736-1489
Knox JHS 300/7-8
400 S Perry St 12095 518-762-3711
Michael Satterlee, prin. Fax 762-2775

---

Fulton-Montgomery Community College Post-Sec.
2805 State Highway 67 12095 518-736-3622

**Jordan, Onondaga, Pop. 1,356**
Jordan-Elbridge Central SD 1,300/PK-12
PO Box 902 13080 315-689-8500
James Froio, supt. Fax 689-0084
www.jecsd.org
Jordan-Elbridge HS 500/9-12
PO Box 901 13080 315-689-8510
Mary Madonna, prin. Fax 689-1985
Jordan-Elbridge MS 300/5-8
PO Box 1150 13080 315-689-8520
David Shafer, prin. Fax 689-6524

**Jordanville, Herkimer**

---

Holy Trinity Orthodox Seminary Post-Sec.
PO Box 36 13361 315-858-0945

**Katonah, Westchester, Pop. 1,654**

---

Harvey S 300/6-12
260 Jay St 10536 914-232-3161
Barry Fenstermacher, hdmstr. Fax 232-6034

**Keene Valley, Essex**
Keene Central SD 200/K-12
PO Box 67 12943 518-576-4555
Daniel Mayberry, supt. Fax 576-4599
www.keenecentralschool.org
Keene Central S 200/K-12
PO Box 67 12943 518-576-4555
Daniel J. Mayberry, supt. Fax 576-4599

**Kendall, Orleans**
Kendall Central SD 800/K-12
1932 Kendall Rd 14476 585-659-2741
Julie Christensen, supt. Fax 659-8903
www.kendallschools.org
Kendall JSHS 400/7-12
16887 Roosevelt Hwy 14476 585-659-2706
Carol D'Agostino, prin. Fax 659-8988

**Kenmore, Erie, Pop. 15,148**
Kenmore-Tonawanda UFSD
Supt. — See Buffalo
Kenmore MS 600/6-8
155 Delaware Rd 14217 716-874-8403
Elaine Thomas, prin. Fax 874-8650

---

Mt. St. Mary Academy 300/9-12
3756 Delaware Ave 14217 716-877-1358
Dawn Riggie, prin. Fax 877-0548
St. Joseph Collegiate Institute 700/9-12
845 Kenmore Ave 14223 716-874-4024
Br. Christopher Belleman, prin. Fax 874-4956

**Keuka Park, Yates, Pop. 1,126**

---

Keuka College Post-Sec.
141 Central Ave 14478 315-279-5000

**Kew Garden Hills, See New York**

---

Shaarey B'nos Chayil - Shevach HS 200/9-12
7509 Main St, 718-263-0525
Rochelle Hirtz, prin. Fax 263-3759

**Kew Gardens, See New York**

---

Yeshiva Shaar Hatorah-Grodno 100/9-12
11706 84th Ave 11418 718-846-1940

**Kings Park, Suffolk, Pop. 17,098**
Kings Park Central SD 3,800/K-12
180 Lawrence Rd 11754 631-269-3310
Dr. Timothy Eagen, supt. Fax 269-0750
www.kpcsd.org
Kings Park HS 1,200/9-12
200 Route 25A 11754 631-269-3345
Lino Bracco, prin. Fax 269-7472
Rogers MS 1,000/6-8
97 Old Dock Rd 11754 631-269-3369
Fax 269-3282

**Kings Point, Nassau, Pop. 4,807**

United States Merchant Marine Academy Post-Sec.
300 Steamboat Rd 11024 516-726-5800

**Kingston, Ulster, Pop. 22,973**
Kingston CSD 5,800/PK-12
61 Crown St 12401 845-339-3000
Dr. Paul Padalino, supt. Fax 339-2249
www.kingstoncityschools.org/
Bailey MS 800/6-8
Merilina Ave Ext 12401 845-943-3940
Julie Linton, prin. Fax 338-6312
Kingston HS 2,100/9-12
403 Broadway 12401 845-331-1970
Kirk Reinhardt, prin. Fax 331-1628
Other Schools – See Lake Katrine

Gloden Hall Health Care Center Post-Sec.
Golden Hill Dr 12401 845-339-4540

**Lackawanna, Erie, Pop. 17,629**
Lackawanna CSD 1,800/PK-12
245 S Shore Blvd 14218 716-827-6767
Anne Spadone, supt. Fax 827-6710
www.lackawannaschools.org
Lackawanna HS 600/9-12
550 Martin Rd 14218 716-827-6727
Bruce Axelson, prin. Fax 827-6724
Lackawanna MS 200/7-8
550 Martin Rd 14218 716-827-6704
Matthew McKenna, prin. Fax 827-6784

**La Fargeville, Jefferson, Pop. 577**
La Fargeville Central SD 600/PK-12
PO Box 138 13656 315-658-2241
Travis Hoover, supt. Fax 658-4223
www.lafargevillecsd.org
La Fargeville Central HS 300/7-12
PO Box 138 13656 315-658-2241
Steven Newcombe, prin. Fax 658-4223

**La Fayette, Onondaga**
La Fayette Central SD 900/PK-12
5955 US Route 20 13084 315-677-9728
Laura Lavine, supt. Fax 677-3372
www.lafayetteschools.org
Big Picture S Alt
5940 Feather Dr 13084 315-504-1000
Susan Osborn, prin. Fax 504-1004
La Fayette JSHS 400/7-12
3122 US Route 11 13084 315-677-3131
James Chupaila, prin. Fax 677-5507

**Lagrangeville, Dutchess**
Arlington Central SD 9,400/K-12
144 Todd Hill Rd 12540 845-486-4460
Dr. Brendan Lyons, supt. Fax 486-4457
www.arlingtonschools.org
Arlington HS 3,300/9-12
1157 Route 55 12540 845-486-4860
Paul Fanuele, prin. Fax 486-4879
Lagrange MS 900/6-8
110 Stringham Rd 12540 845-486-4880
Eric Schetter, prin. Fax 486-8863
Union Vale MS 900/6-8
1657 E Noxon Rd 12540 845-223-8600
Scott Wood, prin. Fax 223-8610

**Lake George, Warren, Pop. 894**
Lake George Central SD 900/K-12
381 Canada St 12845 518-668-5456
Patrick Dee, supt. Fax 668-2285
www.lkgeorge.org
Lake George JSHS 500/7-12
381 Canada St 12845 518-668-5452
Francis Cocozza, prin. Fax 668-2285

**Lake Grove, Suffolk, Pop. 11,039**

Lake Grove School Post-Sec.
PO Box 712 11755 888-585-9007

**Lake Huntington, Sullivan**
Sullivan West Central SD
Supt. — See Jeffersonville
Sullivan West JSHS 600/7-12
PO Box 309 12752 845-932-8401
Margaret Tenbus, prin. Fax 932-8425

**Lake Katrine, Ulster, Pop. 2,330**
Kingston CSD
Supt. — See Kingston
Miller MS 700/6-8
65 Fording Place Rd 12449 845-943-3941
Jo Burruby, prin. Fax 382-6069

**Lake Luzerne, Warren, Pop. 1,220**
Hadley-Luzerne Central SD 800/PK-12
PO Box 200 12846 518-696-2378
Paul Berry, supt. Fax 696-5884
www.hlcs.org
Hadley-Luzerne JSHS 300/6-12
PO Box 200 12846 518-696-2112
Beecher Baker, prin. Fax 696-2356

**Lake Placid, Essex, Pop. 2,496**
Lake Placid Central SD 700/K-12
50 Cummings Rd 12946 518-523-2475
Dr. Roger Carania, supt. Fax 523-4971
www.lpcsd.org
Lake Placid JSHS 400/6-12
34 School St 12946 518-523-2474
Dana Wood, prin. Fax 523-2896

Mountain Lake Children's Residence Post-Sec.
386 River Rd 12946 888-585-9007
North Country S 100/4-9
4382 Cascade Rd 12946 518-523-9329
David Hochschartner, head sch Fax 523-4858
Northwood S 200/9-12
PO Box 1070 12946 518-523-3357
Edward Good, hdmstr. Fax 523-3405

**Lake Ronkonkoma, Suffolk, Pop. 19,855**
Sachem Central SD
Supt. — See Ronkonkoma
Sachem HS North 2,300/9-12
212 Smith Rd 11779 631-471-1400
Patricia Trombetta, prin. Fax 471-1408
Samoset MS 900/6-8
51 School St 11779 631-471-1700
James Horan, prin. Fax 471-1706

**Lancaster, Erie, Pop. 10,243**
Lancaster Central SD 5,900/K-12
177 Central Ave 14086 716-686-3201
Dr. Michael Vallely, supt. Fax 686-3350
www.lancasterschools.org
Lancaster HS 2,000/9-12
1 Forton Dr 14086 716-686-3250
Cesar Marchioli, prin. Fax 686-3347
Lancaster MS 1,000/7-8
148 Aurora St 14086 716-686-3220
Peter Kruszynski, prin. Fax 686-3223

St. Mary HS 400/9-12
142 Laverack Ave 14086 716-683-4824
Rebecca Kranz, prin. Fax 683-4996

**Lansing, Tompkins, Pop. 3,411**
Lansing Central SD 1,100/K-12
284 Ridge Rd 14882 607-533-3020
Chris Pettograsso, supt. Fax 533-3602
www.lcsd.k12.ny.us/
Lansing HS 400/9-12
300 Ridge Rd 14882 607-533-3020
Colleen Ledley, prin. Fax 533-4612
Lansing MS 400/5-8
6 Ludlowville Rd 14882 607-533-3020
Jeffrey Evener, prin. Fax 533-3543

**Larchmont, Westchester, Pop. 5,760**
Mamaroneck UFD
Supt. — See Mamaroneck
Hommocks MS 1,100/6-8
10 Hommocks Rd 10538 914-220-3300
Seth Weitzman, prin. Fax 220-3315

**Latham, Albany, Pop. 10,131**
North Colonie Central SD 5,400/K-12
91 Fiddlers Ln 12110 518-785-8591
D. Joseph Corr, supt. Fax 785-5504
www.northcolonie.org
Shaker HS 2,000/9-12
445 Watervliet Shaker Rd 12110 518-785-5511
Richard Murphy, prin. Fax 783-5905
Shaker JHS 900/7-8
475 Watervliet Shaker Rd 12110 518-785-1341
Dr. Russell Moore, prin. Fax 783-8877

John Paolo's Exteme Beauty Institute Post-Sec.
638 Columbia St Ext Ste 1 12110 518-783-0808

**Laurelton, See New York**
NYC Department of Education
Supt. — See New York
Collaborative Arts MS 200/6-8
14500 Springfield Blvd 11413 718-977-6181
Tammy Holloway, prin.
Community Voices MS 100/6-8
14500 Springfield Blvd 11413 718-977-6180
Tamra Collins, prin. Fax 977-6182

**Laurens, Otsego, Pop. 259**
Laurens Central SD 300/K-12
PO Box 301 13796 607-432-2050
Romona Wenck, supt. Fax 432-4388
laurenscs.org
Laurens Central S 300/K-12
PO Box 301 13796 607-432-2050
Bill Dorritie, prin. Fax 432-4388

**Lawrence, Nassau, Pop. 6,454**
Lawrence UFD 3,000/PK-12
PO Box 477 11559 516-295-7030
Gary Schall, supt. Fax 239-7164
www.lawrence.org
Lawrence MS 900/5-8
195 Broadway 11559 516-295-7000
Willis Perry, prin. Fax 295-7196
Other Schools – See Cedarhurst

Hebrew Academy of Five Towns Rockaway MS 300/6-8
44 Frost Ln 11559 516-569-6352
Mesivta Ateres Yaakov HS 200/9-12
131 Washington Ave 11559 516-374-6465
Rambam Mesivta 200/9-12
15 Frost Ln 11559 516-371-5824
Shor Yoshuv Rabbinical College Post-Sec.
1 Cedarlawn Ave 11559 516-239-9002

**Le Roy, Genesee, Pop. 4,322**
Le Roy Central SD 1,300/PK-12
2 Trigon Park 14482 585-768-8133
Kim Cox, supt. Fax 768-8929
www.leroycsd.org
Le Roy JSHS 600/7-12
9300 S Street Rd 14482 585-768-8131
Tim McArdle, prin. Fax 768-8929

**Levittown, Nassau, Pop. 51,176**
Island Trees UFD 2,500/K-12
74 Farmedge Rd 11756 516-520-2100
Dr. Charles Murphy, supt. Fax 520-2113
www.islandtrees.org
Island Trees HS 800/9-12
59 Straight Ln 11756 516-520-2135
Nicholas Grande, prin. Fax 520-9199
Island Trees Memorial MS 700/5-8
45 Wantagh Ave 11756 516-520-2157
Dr. Roger Bloom, prin. Fax 520-2168

Levittown UFD 7,300/K-12
150 Abbey Ln 11756 516-434-7020
Dr. Tonie McDonald, supt. Fax 520-8314
www.levittownschools.com
Division Avenue HS 1,100/9-12
120 Division Ave 11756 516-434-7150
Joan Lorelli, prin. Fax 520-8364
MacArthur HS 1,400/9-12
3369 N Jerusalem Rd 11756 516-434-7225
Joseph Sheehan, prin. Fax 520-8466
Salk MS 900/6-8
3359 N Jerusalem Rd 11756 516-434-7350
John Zampaglione, prin. Fax 520-8479
Wisdom Lane MS 800/6-8
120 Center Ln 11756 516-434-7300
John Avena, prin. Fax 520-8380

Hunter Business School Post-Sec.
3601 Hempstead Tpke 11756 516-796-1000

**Liberty, Sullivan, Pop. 4,273**
Liberty Central SD 1,600/PK-12
115 Buckley St 12754 845-292-6990
Dr. William Silver Ed.D., supt. Fax 292-1164
www.libertyk12.org
Liberty HS 500/9-12
125 Buckley St 12754 845-292-5400
Jack Strassman, prin. Fax 292-7262
Liberty MS 400/5-8
145 Buckley St 12754 845-292-5400
Jack Strassman, prin. Fax 292-5691

**Lido Beach, Nassau, Pop. 2,865**
Long Beach CSD 4,000/K-12
235 Lido Blvd 11561 516-897-2000
David Weiss, supt. Fax 897-2107
www.lbeach.org
Long Beach HS 1,300/9-12
322 Lagoon Dr W 11561 516-897-2012
William Stroud, prin. Fax 897-2052
Long Beach MS 900/6-8
239 Lido Blvd 11561 516-897-2166
Paul Romanelli, prin. Fax 897-2145

**Lima, Livingston, Pop. 2,111**

Lima Christian S 200/K-12
1574 Rochester St 14485 585-624-3841
Todd Steltz, prin. Fax 624-8293

**Lincolndale, Westchester, Pop. 1,500**
Somers Central SD
Supt. — See Somers
Somers HS 1,000/9-12
PO Box 640 10540 914-248-8585
Mark Bayer, prin. Fax 248-8186

Ives S 100/7-11
PO Box 600 10540 914-248-7474

**Lindenhurst, Suffolk, Pop. 26,920**
Lindenhurst UFD 6,500/K-12
PO Box 621 11757 631-867-3000
Daniel Giordano, supt. Fax 867-3008
www.lindenhurstschools.org
Lindenhurst HS 2,200/9-12
300 Charles St 11757 631-867-3700
Christopher Gitz, prin. Fax 867-3708
Lindenhurst MS 1,600/6-8
350 S Wellwood Ave 11757 631-867-3500
Frank Naccarato, prin. Fax 867-3508

**Lisbon, Saint Lawrence**
Lisbon Central SD 600/PK-12
6866 County Route 10 13658 315-393-4951
Erin Woods, supt. Fax 393-7666
lisboncs.schoolwires.com
Lisbon Central S 600/PK-12
6866 County Route 10 13658 315-393-4951
Eric Burke, prin. Fax 393-7666

**Little Falls, Herkimer, Pop. 4,870**
Little Falls CSD 1,100/K-12
15 Petrie St 13365 315-823-1470
Louis Patrei, supt. Fax 823-0321
www.lfcsd.org
Little Falls HS 400/9-12
1 High School Rd 13365 315-823-1167
Bart Tooley, prin. Fax 823-1209
Little Falls MS 300/6-8
1 High School Rd 13365 315-823-4300
Brian Coleman, prin. Fax 823-3920

**Little Neck, See New York**
NYC Department of Education
Supt. — See New York
JHS 67 900/6-8
5160 Marathon Pkwy 11362 718-423-8138
Zoi McGrath, prin. Fax 423-8281

**Liverpool, Onondaga, Pop. 2,310**
Liverpool Central SD 6,700/K-12
195 Blackberry Rd 13090 315-622-7900
Dr. Mark F. Potter, supt. Fax 622-7115
www.liverpool.k12.ny.us
Chestnut Hill MS 300/7-8
204 Saslon Park Dr 13088 315-453-0245
Michael Baroody, prin. Fax 453-0278
Liverpool HS 1,700/10-12
4338 Wetzel Rd 13090 315-453-1500
Douglas Lawrence, prin. Fax 453-1246
Liverpool MS 300/7-8
720 7th St 13088 315-453-0258
Joseph Mussi, prin. Fax 453-0281
Ninth Grade Annex 9-9
4340 Wetzel Rd 13090 315-453-1275
Judy Campolieta, prin. Fax 453-1247
Soule Road MS 500/7-8
8340 Soule Rd 13090 315-453-1283
Amanda Caldwell, prin. Fax 453-1286

---

Bryant & Stratton College Post-Sec.
8687 Carling Rd 13090 315-652-6500
ITT Technical Institute Post-Sec.
235 Greenfield Pkwy 13088 315-461-8000
National Tractor Trailer School Post-Sec.
4650 Buckley Rd 13088 315-451-2430

**Livingston Manor, Sullivan, Pop. 1,201**
Livingston Manor Central SD 500/PK-12
PO Box 947 12758 845-439-4400
Dr. Deborah Fox, supt. Fax 439-4717
lmcs.k12.ny.us
Livingston Manor JSHS 200/7-12
PO Box 947 12758 845-439-4400
Sandra Johnson, prin. Fax 439-4717

**Livonia, Livingston, Pop. 1,405**
Livonia Central SD 1,800/PK-12
PO Box E 14487 585-346-4000
Matthew Cole, supt. Fax 346-6145
www.livoniacsd.org
Livonia HS 600/9-12
PO Box E 14487 585-346-4040
Karen Bennett, prin. Fax 346-9605
Livonia MS 400/6-8
PO Box E 14487 585-346-4050
Chuck D'Imperio, prin. Fax 346-6835

**Loch Sheldrake, Sullivan**

---

SUNY Sullivan County Community College Post-Sec.
112 College Rd 12759 845-434-5750

**Lockport, Niagara, Pop. 20,480**
Lockport CSD 4,700/K-12
130 Beattie Ave 14094 716-478-4800
Michelle T. Bradley, supt. Fax 478-4863
www.lockportschools.org
Lockport HS 1,600/9-12
250 Lincoln Ave 14094 716-478-4450
Frank Movalli, prin. Fax 478-4498
Lockport HS West at Charlotte Cross Alt
319 West Ave 14094 716-478-4626
Russell Buckley, prin. Fax 478-4634
North Park JHS 800/7-8
160 Passaic Ave 14094 716-478-4700
Ryan Schoenfeld, prin. Fax 478-4705

Starpoint Central SD 2,700/K-12
4363 Mapleton Rd 14094 716-210-2352
Dr. C. Douglas Whelan, supt. Fax 210-2355
www.starpointcsd.org/
Starpoint HS 900/9-12
4363 Mapleton Rd 14094 716-210-2300
Gil Licata, prin. Fax 210-2334
Starpoint MS 600/6-8
4363 Mapleton Rd 14094 716-210-2200
James Bryer, prin. Fax 210-2233

**Locust Valley, Nassau, Pop. 3,370**
Locust Valley Central SD 2,200/K-12
22 Horse Hollow Rd 11560 516-277-5000
Dr. Anna Hunderfund, supt. Fax 277-5098
www.lvcsd.k12.ny.us/
Locust Valley HS 700/9-12
99 Horse Hollow Rd 11560 516-277-5100
Dr. Kieran McGuire, prin. Fax 277-5108
Locust Valley MS 600/6-8
99 Horse Hollow Rd 11560 516-277-5200
H. Thomas Hogan, prin. Fax 277-5208

---

Friends Academy 700/PK-12
270 Duck Pond Rd 11560 516-676-0393
William Morris, hdmstr. Fax 393-4276
Portledge S 400/PK-12
355 Duck Pond Rd 11560 516-750-3100
Simon Owen-Williams, head sch Fax 674-7063

**Long Beach, Nassau, Pop. 32,689**

---

Eisman Community S 100/9-12
2 W Park Ave Ste 2 11561 516-889-2332
Mesivta of Long Beach 100/9-12
205 W Beech St 11561 516-255-4700
Rabbinical College of Long Island Post-Sec.
205 W Beech St 11561 516-255-4700

**Long Island City, See New York**
NYC Department of Education
Supt. — See New York
Academy for Careers in TV & Film 400/9-12
1-50 51st Ave 11101 718-609-3330
Edgar Rodriguez, prin.
Academy of American Studies 700/9-12
2804 41st Ave 11101 718-361-8786
William Bassell, prin. Fax 361-8832
Academy of Finance & Enterprise 400/9-12
3020 Thomson Ave 11101 718-389-3623
Victoria Armano, prin. Fax 389-3724
Aviation Career & Technical HS Vo/Tech
4530 36th St 11101 718-361-2032
Deno Charalambous, prin. Fax 784-8654
Bard HS Early College II 500/9-12
3020 Thomson Ave 11101 718-361-3133
Valerie Thomson, prin. Fax 361-6742
Bryant HS 2,900/9-12
4810 31st Ave 11103 718-721-5404
Namita Dwarka, prin. Fax 728-3478
Energy Tech HS 100/9-12
3641 28th St 11106 718-472-0536
Hope Barter, prin. Fax 472-0490
Hunters Point Community MS 100/6-8
1-50 51st Ave 11101 718-609-3300
Sarah Goodman, prin. Fax 609-3319
Information Technology HS 900/9-12
2116 44th Rd 11101 718-937-4270
Joseph Reed, dir. Fax 937-5236
International HS at Laguardia College 500/9-12
4535 Van Dam St 11101 718-392-3433
John Starkey, prin. Fax 392-3443
HS of Applied Communication 400/9-12
3020 Thomson Ave 11101 718-389-3163
Daniel Korb, prin. Fax 389-3427
IS 141 1,100/6-8
3711 21st Ave 11105 718-278-6403
Miranda Pavlou, prin. Fax 278-2884
IS 204 700/6-8
3641 28th St 11106 718-937-1463
Yvonne Leimsider, prin. Fax 937-7964
Middle College HS 500/9-12
4535 Van Dam St 11101 718-392-3330
Linda Siegmund, prin. Fax 392-3315
Newcomers HS 900/9-12
2801 41st Ave 11101 718-937-6005
Orlando Sarmiento, prin. Fax 937-6316
Queens Vocational HS Vo/Tech
3702 47th Ave 11101 718-937-3010
Melissa Burg, prin. Fax 392-8397
Riverview S K-12
1-50 51st Ave 11101 718-609-3320
Susan McNulty, prin. Fax 609-3322
Shanker S for Visual & Performing Arts 500/6-8
3151 21st St 11106 718-274-8316
Alexander Angueira, prin. Fax 278-6512
Wagner HS 600/7-12
4707 30th Pl 11101 718-472-5671
Peggy Ann Jayne, prin. Fax 472-9117
Young Womens Leadership S 500/6-12
2315 Newtown Ave 11102 718-267-2839
Laura Mitchell, prin. Fax 728-0218

---

Apex Technical School Post-Sec.
2402 Queens Plz S 11101 212-645-3300
Berk Trade and Business School Post-Sec.
3309 Queens Blvd Fl 2 11101 718-729-0909
CUNY LaGuardia Community College Post-Sec.
31-10 Thompson Ave 11101 718-482-7200
Evangel Christian S 500/PK-12
3921 Crescent St 11101 718-937-9600
Rev. Robert Johansson, hdmstr. Fax 937-1613
New York School for Medical Dental Asst. Post-Sec.
3310 Queens Blvd 11101 718-793-2330

**Long Lake, Hamilton, Pop. 541**
Long Lake Central SD 100/PK-12
PO Box 217 12847 518-624-2147
Donald Carlisle, supt. Fax 624-3896
www.longlakecsd.org
Long Lake Central S 100/PK-12
PO Box 217 12847 518-624-2147
Donald Carlisle, prin. Fax 624-3896

**Loudonville, Albany, Pop. 10,822**

---

Loudonville Christian S 300/PK-12
374 Loudon Rd 12211 518-434-6051
Kathryn Hills M.Ed., admin. Fax 935-2258
Siena College Post-Sec.
515 Loudon Rd 12211 518-783-2300

**Lowville, Lewis, Pop. 3,442**
Lowville Central SD 1,400/K-12
7668 N State St 13367 315-376-9000
Cheryl Steckly, supt. Fax 376-1933
www.lowvilleacademy.org
Lowville HS 400/9-12
7668 N State St 13367 315-376-9015
Daniel Cushing, prin. Fax 376-9016
Lowville MS 300/6-8
7668 N State St 13367 315-376-9010
Scott Exford, prin. Fax 376-9011

**Lynbrook, Nassau, Pop. 19,147**
Lynbrook UFD 2,800/K-12
111 Atlantic Ave 11563 516-887-0253
Melissa Burak, supt. Fax 887-3263
www.lynbrookschools.org
Lynbrook HS 900/9-12
9 Union Ave 11563 516-887-0200
Joseph Rainis, prin. Fax 887-8079
Lynbrook North MS 300/6-8
529 Merrick Rd 11563 516-887-0282
Sean Fallon, prin. Fax 887-0286
Lynbrook South MS 400/6-8
333 Union Ave 11563 516-887-0266
Margaret Ronai Ed.D., prin. Fax 887-0268

**Lyndonville, Orleans, Pop. 823**
Lyndonville Central SD 700/PK-12
PO Box 540 14098 585-765-3101
Jason Smith, supt. Fax 765-2106
www.lyndonvillecsd.org/
Webber MSHS 300/7-12
PO Box 540 14098 585-765-3162
Aaron Slack Ed.D., prin. Fax 765-2106

**Lyons, Wayne, Pop. 3,527**
Lyons Central SD 700/K-12
10 Clyde Rd 14489 315-946-2200
Denise Dzikowski, supt. Fax 946-2205
www.lyonscsd.org
Lyons MSHS 300/7-12
10 Clyde Rd 14489 315-946-2220
Nelson Kise, prin. Fax 946-2221

**Mc Graw, Cortland, Pop. 1,031**
Mc Graw Central SD 500/K-12
10 W Academy St 13101 607-836-3636
Mary Curcio, supt. Fax 836-3635
www.mcgrawschools.org
Mc Graw JSHS 300/6-12
10 W Academy St 13101 607-836-3601
Mark Dimorier, prin. Fax 836-3635

**Madison, Madison, Pop. 304**
Madison Central SD 400/K-12
7303 State Route 20 13402 315-893-1878
Perry Dewey, supt. Fax 893-7111
www.madisoncentralny.org
Madison Central S 400/K-12
7303 State Route 20 13402 315-893-1878
Larry Nichols, prin. Fax 893-7111

**Madrid, Saint Lawrence, Pop. 751**
Madrid-Waddington Central SD 800/PK-12
PO Box 67 13660 315-322-5746
Lynn Roy, supt. Fax 322-4462
www.mwcsk12.org
Madrid-Waddington JSHS 400/6-12
PO Box 67 13660 315-322-5746
Eric Burke, prin. Fax 322-4462

**Mahopac, Putnam, Pop. 8,268**
Mahopac Central SD 4,600/K-12
179 E Lake Blvd 10541 845-628-3415
Dennis Creedon Ed.D., supt. Fax 628-5502
www.mahopac.k12.ny.us
Mahopac HS 1,700/9-12
421 Baldwin Place Rd 10541 845-628-3256
Adam Pease, prin. Fax 628-4380
Mahopac MS 1,200/6-8
425 Baldwin Place Rd 10541 845-621-1330
Vincent DiGrandi, prin. Fax 628-5847

**Malone, Franklin, Pop. 5,853**
Malone Central SD 2,300/PK-12
PO Box 847 12953 518-483-7800
Jerry Griffin, supt. Fax 483-3071
www.malonecsd.org
Franklin Academy HS 800/9-12
42 Huskie Ln 12953 518-483-7807
Brandon Pelkey, prin. Fax 483-7813
Malone MS 500/6-8
15 Francis St 12953 518-483-7801
James Knight, prin. Fax 483-9497

**Malverne, Nassau, Pop. 8,420**
Malverne UFD 1,500/K-12
301 Wicks Ln 11565 516-887-6405
Dr. James Hunderfund, supt. Fax 596-2910
www.malverne.k12.ny.us
Herber MS 400/6-8
75 Ocean Ave 11565 516-887-6444
Steven Gilhuley, prin. Fax 596-0525
Malverne HS 600/9-12
80 Ocean Ave 11565 516-887-6420
Dr. Vincent Romano, prin. Fax 887-6479

**Mamaroneck, Westchester, Pop. 18,587**
Mamaroneck UFD 5,100/PK-12
1000 W Boston Post Rd 10543 914-220-3000
Dr. Robert Shaps Ed.D., supt. Fax 220-3010
www.mamkschools.org
Mamaroneck HS 1,500/9-12
1000 W Boston Post Rd 10543 914-220-3100
Elizabeth Clain, prin. Fax 220-3115
Other Schools – See Larchmont

Rye Neck UFD 1,200/K-12
310 Hornidge Rd 10543 914-777-5200
Dr. Peter Mustich, supt. Fax 777-5201
www.ryeneck.k12.ny.us/
Rye Neck HS 400/9-12
300 Hornidge Rd 10543 914-777-5200
Dr. Barbara Ferraro, prin. Fax 777-4801
Rye Neck MS 400/5-8
300 Hornidge Rd 10543 914-777-5200
Dr. Eric Lutinski, prin. Fax 777-4701

---

French-American S of NY 900/PK-12
525 Fenimore Rd 10543 914-250-0400
Joel Peinado, hdmstr.
Westchester Hebrew HS 100/9-12
856 Orienta Ave 10543 914-698-0806

**Manhasset, Nassau, Pop. 7,968**
Manhasset UFD 3,200/K-12
200 Memorial Pl 11030 516-267-7700
Charles Cardillo, supt. Fax 627-1618
www.manhasset.k12.ny.us
Manhasset HS 900/9-12
200 Memorial Pl 11030 516-267-7600
Dean Schlanger, prin. Fax 627-4604
Manhasset MS 600/7-8
200 Memorial Pl 11030 516-267-7500
Dean Schlanger, prin. Fax 627-8157

---

Elmezzi Graduate School of Molecular Med Post-Sec.
350 Community Dr 11030 516-562-3405
St. Mary HS 700/9-12
51 Clapham Ave 11030 516-627-2711
Jonathan Kramer, prin. Fax 627-3209

**Manlius, Onondaga, Pop. 4,642**
Fayetteville-Manlius Central SD 4,400/K-12
8199 E Seneca Tpke 13104 315-692-1200
Dr. Craig Tice, supt. Fax 692-1227
www.fmschools.org
Eagle Hill MS 700/5-8
4645 Enders Rd 13104 315-692-1400
Maureen McCrystal, prin. Fax 692-1046
Fayetteville-Manlius HS 1,600/9-12
8201 E Seneca Tpke 13104 315-692-1900
Raymond Kilmer, prin. Fax 692-1028
Other Schools – See Fayetteville

**Manorville, Suffolk, Pop. 14,172**
Eastport-South Manor Central SD 3,700/K-12
149 Dayton Ave 11949 631-801-3013
Mark Nocero, supt. Fax 874-6750
www.esmonline.org
Eastport/South Manor JSHS 1,800/7-12
543 Moriches Middle Isle Rd 11949 631-801-3250
Salvatore Alaimo, prin. Fax 874-6787

**Marathon, Cortland, Pop. 912**
Marathon Central SD 700/PK-12
PO Box 339 13803 607-849-3117
Rebecca Stone, supt. Fax 849-3305
www.marathonschools.org/
Marathon JSHS 400/7-12
PO Box 339 13803 607-849-3251
Fax 849-3305

**Marcellus, Onondaga, Pop. 1,781**
Marcellus Central SD 1,900/K-12
2 Reed Pkwy 13108 315-673-6000
Dr. Craig Tice, supt. Fax 673-1727
marcellusschools.org
Driver MS 800/4-8
2 Reed Pkwy 13108 315-673-6200
Janet O'Mara, prin. Fax 673-1727
Marcellus HS 600/9-12
1 Mustang Hl 13108 315-673-6300
John Durkee, prin. Fax 673-0312

**Marcy, Oneida, Pop. 8,685**
Whitesboro Central SD
Supt. — See Whitesboro
Whitesboro HS 1,100/9-12
6000 State Route 291 13403 315-266-3200
Jeff Kuhn, prin. Fax 266-3223

**Margaretville, Delaware, Pop. 595**
Margaretville Central SD 400/K-12
PO Box 319 12455 845-586-2647
Robert Chakar Ed.D., supt. Fax 586-2949
www.margaretvillecs.org
Margaretville Central S 400/K-12
PO Box 319 12455 845-586-2647
Colin Clark, prin. Fax 586-2949

**Marion, Wayne, Pop. 1,490**
Marion Central SD 800/K-12
4034 Warner Rd 14505 315-926-2300
Kathryn Wegman, supt. Fax 926-5797
www.marioncs.org/
Marion JSHS 400/7-12
4034 Warner Rd 14505 315-926-4228
Duane Perry, prin. Fax 926-3114

**Marlboro, Ulster, Pop. 3,611**
Marlboro Central SD
Supt. — See Milton
Marlboro Central HS 700/9-12
50 Cross Rd 12542 845-236-5810
Roseanne Collins-Judon, prin. Fax 236-2638
Marlboro MS 500/6-8
1375 Route 9W 12542 845-236-5840
Debra Clinton, prin. Fax 236-3634

**Maspeth, See New York**
NYC Department of Education
Supt. — See New York
IS 73 1,500/6-8
7002 54th Ave 11378 718-639-3817
Camillo Turriciano, prin. Fax 429-5162

---

Luther S 200/9-12
6002 Maspeth Ave 11378 718-894-4000
Randal Gast, dir. Fax 894-1469

**Massapequa, Nassau, Pop. 21,527**
Massapequa UFD 7,800/K-12
4925 Merrick Rd 11758 516-308-5000
Lucille Iconis, supt.
www.msd.k12.ny.us
Berner MS, 50 Carman Mill Rd 11758 1,300/7-8
Jason Esposito, prin. 516-308-5700
Massapequa HS 2,000/10-12
4925 Merrick Rd 11758 516-308-5900
Dr. Barbara Williams, prin.
Massapequa HS Ames Campus 600/9-9
198 Baltimore Ave 11758 516-308-5800
Patrick DiClemente, prin.

Plainedge UFD
Supt. — See North Massapequa
Plainedge HS 1,000/9-12
241 Wyngate Dr 11758 516-992-7550
Robert Amster, prin. Fax 992-7545

**Massena, Saint Lawrence, Pop. 10,748**
Massena Central SD 2,800/PK-12
84 Nightengale Ave 13662 315-764-3700
William Flynn, supt. Fax 764-3701
www.mcs.k12.ny.us
Leary JHS 500/7-8
84 Nightengale Ave 13662 315-764-3720
Burton Peck, prin. Fax 764-3723
Massena HS 800/9-12
84 Nightengale Ave 13662 315-764-3710
Steven Barlow, prin. Fax 764-3719

**Mastic Beach, Suffolk, Pop. 12,605**
William Floyd UFD 8,900/K-12
240 Mastic Beach Rd 11951 631-874-1100
Dr. Paul Casciano, supt. Fax 281-3047
www.wfsd.k12.ny.us
Floyd HS 2,900/9-12
240 Mastic Beach Rd 11951 631-874-1699
Barbara Butler, prin. Fax 874-1540
Paca MS 1,000/6-8
338 Blanco Dr 11951 631-874-1414
Fax 874-1561
Other Schools – See Moriches

**Mattituck, Suffolk, Pop. 4,155**
Mattituck-Cutchogue UFD
Supt. — See Cutchogue
Mattituck-Cutchogue JSHS 800/7-12
15125 Main Rd 11952 631-298-8460
Shawn Petretti, prin. Fax 298-8544

**Mayfield, Fulton, Pop. 827**
Mayfield Central SD 1,000/PK-12
27 School St 12117 518-661-8207
A. Paul Scott, supt. Fax 661-7666
www.mayfieldcsd.org
Mayfield JSHS 500/7-12
27 School St 12117 518-661-8200
Dr. Christopher Wojeski, prin. Fax 661-7666

**Mayville, Chautauqua, Pop. 1,698**
Chautauqua Lake Central SD 800/PK-12
100 N Erie St 14757 716-753-5808
Benjamin Spitzer, supt. Fax 753-5813
www.clake.org
Chautauqua Lake Central Secondary S 400/7-12
100 N Erie St 14757 716-753-5882
Joshua Liddell, prin. Fax 753-5886

**Mechanicville, Saratoga, Pop. 5,096**
Mechanicville CSD 1,300/K-12
25 Kniskern Ave 12118 518-664-5727
Dr. Michael J. McCarthy, supt. Fax 514-2101
www.mechanicville.org
Mechanicville JSHS 700/6-12
25 Kniskern Ave 12118 518-664-9888
Kevin Kolakowski, prin. Fax 514-2107

**Medford, Suffolk, Pop. 23,778**
Patchogue-Medford UFD
Supt. — See Patchogue
Oregon MS, 109 Oregon Ave 11763 600/6-9
Bryan Lake, prin. 631-687-6800
Patchogue-Medford HS 2,000/10-12
181 Buffalo Ave 11763 631-687-6500
Randy Rusielewicz Ed.D., prin.

---

Hunter Business School Post-Sec.
3247 Route 112 Ste 3 11763 631-736-7360

**Medina, Orleans, Pop. 5,905**
Medina Central SD 1,000/PK-12
1 Mustang Dr 14103 585-798-2700
Jeffrey Evoy, supt. Fax 798-5676
www.medinacsd.org
Medina HS 600/8-12
2 Mustang Dr 14103 585-798-2700
Mark Kruzynski, prin. Fax 798-2787

**Melville, Suffolk, Pop. 18,680**
Half Hollow Hills Central SD
Supt. — See Dix Hills
West Hollow MS 1,500/6-8
250 Old East Neck Rd 11747 631-592-3400
Milton Strong, prin. Fax 592-3922

---

SBI Campus Post-Sec.
320 S Service Rd 11747 631-370-3300

**Merrick, Nassau, Pop. 21,879**
Bellmore-Merrick Central HSD
Supt. — See North Merrick
Calhoun HS 1,400/9-12
1786 State St 11566 516-992-1300
Nicole Hollings, prin. Fax 867-7390
Merrick Avenue MS 900/7-8
1870 Merrick Ave 11566 516-992-1200
Taryn Johnson, prin. Fax 867-6391

---

Grace Christian Academy 100/K-12
36 Smith St 11566 516-379-2223
Stephen Schultz, hdmstr. Fax 771-8063

**Mexico, Oswego, Pop. 1,597**
Mexico Central SD 2,200/PK-12
16 Fravor Rd Ste A 13114 315-963-8400
Sean Bruno, supt. Fax 963-5801
www.mexicocsd.org
Mexico HS 700/9-12
3338 Main St 13114 315-963-8400
Donald Root, prin. Fax 963-8887
Mexico MS 700/5-8
16 Fravor Rd 13114 315-963-8400
Kim Holliday, prin. Fax 963-3848

**Middleburgh, Schoharie, Pop. 1,471**
Middleburgh Central SD 800/PK-12
PO Box 606 12122 518-827-3625
Michele Weaver, supt. Fax 827-6632
www.middleburgh.k12.ny.us
Middleburgh JSHS 300/7-12
PO Box 850 12122 518-827-3600
Lorianne Petrosino, prin. Fax 827-5192

**Middle Island, Suffolk, Pop. 10,280**
Longwood Central SD 8,900/K-12
35 Yaphank Middle Island Rd 11953 631-345-2172
Dr. Michael Lonergan, supt. Fax 345-2166
www.longwood.k12.ny.us
Longwood HS 2,800/9-12
100 Longwood Rd 11953 631-345-9200
Dr. Maria Castro, prin. Fax 345-9279
Longwood JHS 1,300/7-8
198 Longwood Rd 11953 631-345-2701
Adam Dewitt, prin. Fax 345-9281

**Middleport, Niagara, Pop. 1,807**
Royalton-Hartland Central SD 1,500/PK-12
54 State St 14105 716-735-2000
Dr. Roger Klatt, supt. Fax 735-2036
www.royhart.org
Royalton-Hartland HS 500/9-12
54 State St 14105 716-735-2000
Gary Bell, prin. Fax 735-2046
Royalton-Hartland MS 500/5-8
78 State St 14105 716-735-2000
John Fisgus, prin. Fax 735-2056

**Middletown, Orange, Pop. 27,256**
Middletown CSD 6,000/K-12
223 Wisner Ave 10940 845-326-1193
Dr. Kenneth Eastwood, supt. Fax 326-1225
www.middletowncityschools.org/
Middletown HS 2,100/9-12
24 Gardner Ave Ext 10940 845-326-1600
Jessica Turner, admin. Fax 326-1605
Monhagen MS 800/6-8
555 County Highway 78 10940 845-326-1700
Tracey Sorrentino, prin. Fax 326-1701
Twin Towers MS 800/6-8
112 Grand Ave 10940 845-326-1650
Gordon Dean, prin. Fax 326-1651

---

Beauty School of Middletown Post-Sec.
225 Dolson Ave Ste 100 10940 845-343-2171
Harmony Christian S 200/PK-12
1790 Route 211 E 10941 845-692-5353
SUNY Orange County Community College Post-Sec.
115 South St 10940 845-344-6222

**Middle Village, See New York**

---

Christ the King Regional HS 900/9-12
6802 Metropolitan Ave 11379 718-366-7400
Peter Mannarino, prin. Fax 366-1165

**Milford, Otsego, Pop. 406**
Milford Central SD 400/K-12
PO Box 237 13807 607-286-7721
Peter Livshin, supt. Fax 286-7879
www.schoolworld.milfordcentral.org
Milford Central S 400/K-12
PO Box 237 13807 607-286-3349
Michael Miller, prin. Fax 286-7879

**Millbrook, Dutchess, Pop. 1,439**
Millbrook Central SD 1,100/K-12
PO Box AA 12545 845-677-4200
Philip D'Angelo, supt. Fax 677-4206
www.millbrookcsd.org/
Millbrook HS, PO Box AA 12545 400/9-12
Julie Roberts, prin. 845-677-2510
Millbrook MS 300/6-8
PO Box AA 12545 845-677-4210
Dr. Phyllis Amori, prin. Fax 677-6913

---

Millbrook S 300/9-12
131 Millbrook School Rd 12545 845-677-8261
Drew Casertano, hdmstr. Fax 677-8598

**Miller Place, Suffolk, Pop. 12,218**
Miller Place UFD 3,000/K-12
7 Memorial Dr 11764 631-474-2700
Dr. Marianne Higuera, supt. Fax 474-0686
www.millerplace.k12.ny.us
Miller Place HS 1,000/9-12
15 Memorial Dr 11764 631-474-2723
Kevin Slavin, prin. Fax 474-1734
North Country Road MS 700/6-8
191 N Country Rd 11764 631-474-2710
Matthew Clark, prin. Fax 474-5178

**Mill Neck, Nassau, Pop. 979**

Mill Neck Lutheran School Post-Sec.
Frost Mill Rd B12 11765

**Millwood, Westchester, Pop. 1,000**

---

Yeshiva Kehilath Yaakov 50/11-12
PO Box 501 10546 914-762-3010

**Milton, Ulster, Pop. 1,389**
Marlboro Central SD 1,400/K-12
21 Milton Tpke Ste 100 12547 845-236-8000
Michael Brooks, supt. Fax 795-5904
www.marlboroschools.org
Other Schools – See Marlboro

**Mineola, Nassau, Pop. 18,445**
Mineola UFD 2,400/PK-12
121 Jackson Ave 11501 516-237-2000
Dr. Michael Nagler, supt. Fax 237-2008
www.mineola.k12.ny.us
Mineola MS 400/6-8
200 Emory Rd 11501 516-237-2500
Matthew Gaven, prin. Fax 739-4129
Other Schools – See Garden City Park

---

Chaminade HS 1,700/9-12
340 Jackson Ave 11501 516-742-5555
Br. Joseph Bellizzi, prin. Fax 742-1989
NY College Traditional Chinese Medicine Post-Sec.
155 1st St 11501 516-739-1545
Winthrop University Hospital Post-Sec.
259 1st St 11501 516-663-2201

**Mohawk, Herkimer, Pop. 2,697**
Central Valley Central SD
Supt. — See Ilion
Jarvis MS 100/5-8
28 Grove St 13407 315-866-2620
Melissa Hoskey, prin. Fax 867-2909

**Monroe, Orange, Pop. 8,240**
Greenwood Lake UFD 500/K-8
1247 Lakes Rd 10950 845-782-8678
Dr. Christine Ackerman, supt. Fax 782-8582
www.gwlufsd.org/
Greenwood Lake MS 300/4-8
1247 Lakes Rd 10950 845-782-8678
Matthew Lawrence, prin. Fax 782-2004

Kiryas Joel Village UFSD 50/PK-12
48 Bakertown Rd Ste 401 10950 845-782-2300
Joel Petlin, supt. Fax 782-4176
Kiryas Joel Village S 50/PK-12
1 Dinev Ct 10950 845-782-7510
Jehudah Halpern, prin. Fax 782-5849

---

Bnei Yoel S 300/PK-12
PO Box 255, 845-783-8036
UTA Mesivta of Kiryas Joel Post-Sec.
PO Box 2009, 845-783-9901
UTA of Kiryas Joel 5,800/K-12
PO Box 477, 845-783-5800

**Monsey, Rockland, Pop. 18,318**

---

Ateres Bais Yaakov 300/PK-12
236 Cherry Ln 10952 845-368-2200
Rabbi Aaron Fink, dean Fax 368-2210
Bais Malka Girls S of Belz 500/PK-12
PO Box 977 10952 845-354-9500
Bais Shifra Miriam S 300/K-12
PO Box 682 10952 845-356-0061
Bais Yaakov HS of Spring Valley 400/9-12
11 Smolley Dr 10952 845-356-3113
Bais Yaakov of Ramapo HS 100/9-12
16 Hershel Ter 10952 845-356-0580
Gitty Kramer, admin. Fax 356-0584
Beth Medrash Meor Yitzchok Post-Sec.
65 Dykstras Way E 10952 845-426-3488
Beth Rochel School for Girls 1,000/K-12
145 Saddle River Rd 10952 845-352-5000
Bnos Yisroel Girls S of Viznitz 1,400/1-12
1 School Ter 10952 845-731-3700
Kol Yaakov Torah Center Post-Sec.
29 W Maple Ave 10952 845-425-3863
Mesivta Yesodei Yisroel 50/9-12
51 Carlton Rd 10952 845-425-2520
Mesivta Ziev Hatorah 50/9-12
PO Box 814 10952 845-426-6868
Monsey Academy for Girls 50/9-12
27 Remsen Ave 10952 845-918-1220
Ohr Somayach Monsey Post-Sec.
244 Route 306 10952 845-425-1370
Yeshiva and Kolel Bais Medrash Elyon Post-Sec.
73 Main St 10952 845-356-7064
Yeshiva Beth David S 600/PK-12
PO Box 136 10952 845-352-3100
Rabbi Aron Bayer, prin. Fax 352-0153
Yeshiva D'Monsey Rabbinical College Post-Sec.
2 Roman Blvd 10952 845-426-3276
Yeshiva Gedolah Bais Yisroel 50/12-12
4 Solond Rd 10952 845-258-7400
Yeshiva Gedolah Kesser Torah Post-Sec.
28 Cedar Ln 10952 845-406-4308
Yeshiva Gedola of South Monsey 100/9-12
260 Saddle River Rd 10952 845-356-4030
Yeshiva Ohel Torah 9-12
91 College Rd 10952 845-371-3740
Yeshiva Shaar Ephraim S 200/9-12
PO Box 253 10952 845-426-3110
Rabbi Yehuda Oshry, prin. Fax 425-4721
Yeshivath Viznitz Post-Sec.
PO Box 446 10952 845-731-3700
Yeshiva Viznitz 2,500/PK-12
15 Elyon Rd 10952 845-356-1010

**Montgomery, Orange, Pop. 3,752**
Valley Central SD 4,400/K-12
944 State Route 17K 12549 845-457-2400
Richard M. Hooley Ed.D., supt. Fax 457-4319
www.vcsd.k12.ny.us
Valley Central HS 1,500/9-12
1175 State Route 17K 12549 845-457-2400
Jayme Ginda-Baxter, prin. Fax 457-4056
Valley Central MS 1,100/6-8
1189 State Route 17K 12549 845-457-2400
Ned Hayes, prin. Fax 457-4008

**Monticello, Sullivan, Pop. 6,485**
Monticello Central SD 3,100/K-12
237 Forestburgh Rd 12701 845-794-7700
Daniel Teplesky, supt. Fax 794-7710
www.monticelloschools.net
Kaiser MS 700/6-8
45 Breakey Ave 12701 845-796-3058
Nichole Horler, prin. Fax 796-3099
Monticello HS 900/9-12
39 Breakey Ave 12701 845-794-8840
Lori Orestano-James, prin. Fax 794-8133

**Montrose, Westchester, Pop. 2,689**
Hendrick Hudson Central SD 2,600/K-12
61 Trolley Rd 10548 914-257-5100
Joseph Hochreiter, supt. Fax 257-5121
www.henhudschools.org/
Hendrick Hudson HS 800/9-12
2166 Albany Post Rd 10548 914-257-5800
James Mackin, prin. Fax 257-5801
Other Schools – See Cortlandt Manor

**Moravia, Cayuga, Pop. 1,274**
Moravia Central SD 900/K-12
PO Box 1189 13118 315-497-2670
Michelle Brantner, supt. Fax 497-2260
www.moraviaschool.org/
Moravia JSHS 500/6-12
PO Box 1189 13118 315-497-2670
Greg Jenne, prin. Fax 497-3852

**Moriches, Suffolk, Pop. 2,802**
William Floyd UFD
Supt. — See Mastic Beach
Floyd MS 1,100/6-8
630 Moriches Middle Island 11955 631-874-5505
Carolyn Schick, prin. Fax 878-7690

**Morris, Otsego, Pop. 573**
Morris Central SD 400/PK-12
PO Box 40 13808 607-263-6102
Matthew Sheldon, supt. Fax 263-2483
morriscs.org
Morris Central S 400/PK-12
PO Box 40 13808 607-263-6100
Katharine Smith, prin. Fax 263-2483

**Morristown, Saint Lawrence, Pop. 395**
Morristown Central SD 400/PK-12
PO Box 217 13664 315-375-8814
Douglas H. McQueer, supt. Fax 375-8604
mcsd.schoolfusion.us/
Morristown Central S 400/PK-12
PO Box 217 13664 315-375-8814
David Doe, prin. Fax 375-8604

**Morrisville, Madison, Pop. 2,159**
Morrisville-Eaton Central SD 700/PK-12
PO Box 990 13408 315-684-9300
Michael Drahos, supt. Fax 684-9399
www.m-ecs.org
Morrisville-Eaton MSHS 300/7-12
PO Box 990 13408 315-684-9121
Christopher Brewer, prin. Fax 684-7033

---

SUNY at Morrisville Post-Sec.
PO Box 901 13408 315-684-6000

**Mountain Dale, Sullivan, Pop. 200**

---

Yeshiva Zichron Mayir 12-12
5 Ronald Tawil Way 12763 845-434-5328

**Mount Kisco, Westchester, Pop. 10,701**
Bedford Central SD
Supt. — See Bedford
Fox Lane MS 1,000/6-8
S Bedford Rd 10549 914-241-6126
Anne Marie Berardi, prin. Fax 241-6129

**Mount Morris, Livingston, Pop. 2,942**
Mount Morris Central SD 500/K-12
30 Bonadonna Ave 14510 585-658-2568
Gregory Bump, supt. Fax 658-4814
www.mtmorriscsd.org
Mount Morris JSHS 200/7-12
30 Bonadonna Ave 14510 585-658-3333
Becky Chenaille, prin. Fax 658-4814

**Mount Sinai, Suffolk, Pop. 11,989**
Mount Sinai UFD 2,500/K-12
118 N Country Rd 11766 631-870-2550
Gordon Brosdal, supt. Fax 473-0905
www.mtsinai.k12.ny.us
Mount Sinai HS 800/9-12
1 Gertrude Goodman Dr 11766 631-870-2800
Robert Grable, prin. Fax 928-3668
Mount Sinai MS 800/5-8
114 N Country Rd 11766 631-870-2700
Peter Pramataris, prin. Fax 928-3129

**Mount Vernon, Westchester, Pop. 64,673**
Mount Vernon CSD 8,100/PK-12
165 N Columbus Ave 10553 914-358-2400
Dr. Kenneth R. Hamilton, supt. Fax 665-6077
www.mtvernoncsd.org
Davis MS 800/7-8
350 Gramatan Ave 10552 914-665-5120
Joshua Whitham, prin. Fax 665-5128
Mandela-Zollicoffer Alternative HS 200/Alt
250 Gramatan Ave 10550 914-358-2720
Ralph Burts, prin. Fax 665-5086
Mount Vernon HS 1,300/9-12
100 California Rd 10552 914-665-5300
Ronald Gonzalez, prin. Fax 665-5281
Thornton HS 700/9-12
121 S 6th Ave 10550 914-358-2740
Sharon Bradley, prin. Fax 358-2792
Turner MS 400/7-8
624 S 3rd Ave 10550 914-665-5150
Dr. Jonathan Brown, prin. Fax 665-5152

---

Montefiore School of Nursing Post-Sec.
53 Valentine St 10550 914-361-6472
Westchester School of Beauty Culture Post-Sec.
6 Gramatan Ave 10550 914-699-2344

**Munnsville, Madison, Pop. 470**
Stockbridge Valley Central SD 500/K-12
PO Box 732 13409 315-495-4400
Michael Sandore, supt. Fax 495-4492
www.stockbridgevalley.org
Stockbridge Valley Central S 500/K-12
PO Box 732 13409 315-495-4550
Gina Terzini, prin. Fax 495-4492

**Nanuet, Rockland, Pop. 17,600**
Nanuet UFD 2,300/K-12
101 Church St 10954 845-627-9888
Dr. Mark McNeill, supt. Fax 624-5338
www.nanuetsd.org
Barr MS 700/7-8
143 Church St 10954 845-627-4040
Roger Guccione, prin. Fax 624-3138
Nanuet HS 700/9-12
103 Church St 10954 845-627-9804
Dr. Vin Carella, prin. Fax 624-5520

---

Capri Cosmetology Learning Center Post-Sec.
251 W Route 59 10954 845-623-6339

**Naples, Ontario, Pop. 1,024**
Naples Central SD 800/PK-12
136 N Main St 14512 585-374-7900
Matthew Frahm, supt. Fax 374-5859
www.naples.k12.ny.us
Naples HS 400/7-12
136 N Main St 14512 585-374-7905
Justin Stuck, prin. Fax 374-5859

**Nedrow, Onondaga, Pop. 2,167**
Onondaga Central SD 1,000/PK-12
4466 S Onondaga Rd 13120 315-552-5000
Rob Price, supt. Fax 492-4650
www.ocs.cnyric.org
Onondaga JSHS 400/7-12
4479 S Onondaga Rd 13120 315-552-5020
Timothy Mumford, prin. Fax 552-5027

**Nesconset, Suffolk, Pop. 13,284**
Smithtown Central SD
Supt. — See Smithtown
Great Hollow MS 1,000/6-8
150 Southern Blvd 11767 631-382-2800
John Scomillio, prin. Fax 382-2807

**Newark, Wayne, Pop. 8,894**
Newark Central SD 2,100/PK-12
100 E Miller St Ste 5 14513 315-332-3217
Matthew Cook, supt. Fax 332-3523
www.newarkcsd.org
Newark HS 600/9-12
625 Peirson Ave 14513 315-332-3242
Thomas Roote, prin. Fax 332-3567
Newark MS 500/6-8
701 Peirson Ave 14513 315-332-3295
Teresa Prinzi, prin. Fax 332-3584

**Newark Valley, Tioga, Pop. 980**
Newark Valley Central SD 1,200/K-12
PO Box 547 13811 607-642-3221
Ryan Dougherty, supt. Fax 642-8821
www.nvcs.stier.org/
Newark Valley HS 500/8-12
68 Wilson Creek Rd 13811 607-642-8665
Diane Arbes, prin. Fax 642-5292

**New Berlin, Chenango, Pop. 1,014**
Unadilla Valley Central SD 900/PK-12
PO Box F 13411 607-847-7500
Robert Mackey, admin. Fax 847-6924
www.uvstorm.org
Unadilla Valley Secondary S 200/6-12
PO Box F 13411 607-847-7500
Franklin Johnson, prin. Fax 847-8045

**Newburgh, Orange, Pop. 28,122**
Newburgh Enlarged CSD 12,200/PK-12
124 Grand St 12550 845-563-3500
Dr. Roberto Padilla, supt. Fax 563-3501
www.newburghschools.org
Newburgh Free Academy 3,400/9-12
201 Fullerton Ave 12550 845-563-5400
Matteo Doddo, prin. Fax 563-5405
Newburgh Free Academy North 700/9-12
301 Robinson Ave 12550 845-563-8400
Matteo Doddo, prin. Fax 563-8409
South MS 900/6-8
33 Monument St 12550 845-563-7000
Michael Ragusa, prin. Fax 563-7019
Other Schools – See New Windsor

---

Cronin Presentation Academy 100/5-8
69 Bay View Ter 12550 845-567-0708
Sr. Yliana Hernandez, prin. Fax 567-0709
Mt. St. Mary College Post-Sec.
330 Powell Ave 12550 845-561-0800

**New City, Rockland, Pop. 32,957**
Clarkstown Central SD 8,900/K-12
62 Old Middletown Rd 10956 845-639-6418
Dr. J. Thomas Morton Ed.D., supt. Fax 639-6488
www.ccsd.edu
Clarkstown North HS 1,500/9-12
151 Congers Rd 10956 845-639-6504
Harry Leonardatos, prin. Fax 638-6916
Other Schools – See West Nyack

**Newcomb, Essex**
Newcomb Central SD 100/PK-12
PO Box 418 12852 518-582-3341
Clark Hults, supt. Fax 582-2163
www.newcombcsd.org
Newcomb Central S 100/PK-12
PO Box 418 12852 518-582-3341
Clark Hults, prin. Fax 582-2163

**Newfane, Niagara, Pop. 3,772**
Newfane Central SD
Supt. — See Burt
Newfane HS 600/9-12
6273 Charlotteville Rd 14108 716-778-6551
Dr. Andres Arroyo, prin. Fax 778-6590
Newfane MS 600/5-8
6273 Charlotteville Rd 14108 716-778-6452
Thomas Adams, prin. Fax 778-6460

**Newfield, Tompkins**
Newfield Central SD 900/PK-12
247 Main St 14867 607-564-9955
Dr. Cheryl Thomas, supt. Fax 564-0055
www.newfieldschools.org

Newfield HS 300/9-12
247 Main St 14867 607-564-9955
Robin Hawk, prin. Fax 564-3624
Newfield MS 200/6-8
247 Main St 14867 607-564-9955
Catherine Griggs, prin. Fax 564-3403

**New Hartford, Oneida, Pop. 1,828**
New Hartford Central SD 2,600/K-12
33 Oxford Rd 13413 315-624-1218
Robert Nole, supt. Fax 724-8940
www.newhartfordschools.org
New Hartford SHS 600/10-12
33 Oxford Rd 13413 315-624-1214
Jennifer Spring, prin. Fax 738-9209
Perry JHS 700/7-9
9499 Weston Rd 13413 315-738-9300
Keith Levatino, prin. Fax 738-9349

**New Hyde Park, Nassau, Pop. 9,473**
Herricks UFD 3,900/K-12
999 Herricks Rd 11040 516-305-8900
Dr. John Bierwirth, supt. Fax 248-3108
www.herricks.org/
Herricks HS 1,400/9-12
100 Shelter Rock Rd 11040 516-305-8700
Dr. Jane Modoono, prin. Fax 248-3282
Other Schools – See Albertson

Sewanhaka Central HSD
Supt. — See Floral Park
New Hyde Park Memorial HS 1,700/7-12
500 Leonard Blvd 11040 516-488-9500
Dr. Richard Faccio, prin. Fax 488-9506

**New Lebanon, Columbia**
New Lebanon Central SD 500/K-12
14665 State Route 22 12125 518-794-9016
Leslie Whitcomb, supt. Fax 766-5574
www.newlebanoncsd.org
New Lebanon JSHS 200/7-12
14665 State Route 22 12125 518-794-7600
Matthew Klafehn, prin. Fax 766-6265

---

Darrow S 100/9-12
110 Darrow Rd 12125 518-794-6000
Simon Holzapfel, head sch Fax 794-7065

**New Paltz, Ulster, Pop. 6,646**
New Paltz Central SD 2,200/K-12
196 Main St 12561 845-256-4020
Maria Rice, supt. Fax 256-4025
www.newpaltz.k12.ny.us
New Paltz Central HS 700/9-12
196 Main St 12561 845-256-4100
Barbara Clinton, prin. Fax 256-4109
New Paltz MS 500/6-8
196 Main St 12561 845-256-4200
Dr. Richard Wiesenthal, prin. Fax 256-4209

---

SUNY College at New Paltz Post-Sec.
1 Hawk Dr 12561 845-257-7869

**Newport, Herkimer, Pop. 637**
West Canada Valley Central SD 700/K-12
PO Box 360 13416 315-845-6800
D.J. Shepardson, supt. Fax 845-8652
www.westcanada.org
West Canada Valley JSHS 400/7-12
PO Box 360 13416 315-845-6800
Frank Sutliff, prin. Fax 845-8652

**New Rochelle, Westchester, Pop. 75,662**
New Rochelle CSD 10,700/PK-12
515 North Ave 10801 914-576-4300
Dr. Brian G. Osborne, supt. Fax 632-4144
www.nred.org
Leonard MS 1,200/6-8
25 Gerada Ln 10804 914-576-4339
John Barnes, prin. Fax 576-4784
New Rochelle HS 3,300/9-12
265 Clove Rd 10801 914-576-4502
Reginald Richardson, prin. Fax 576-4284
Young MS 1,100/6-8
270 Centre Ave 10805 914-576-4360
Dr. Anthony Bongo, prin. Fax 632-2738

---

College of New Rochelle Post-Sec.
29 Castle Pl 10805 914-654-5000
Iona College Post-Sec.
715 North Ave 10801 914-633-2000
Iona Preparatory S 800/9-12
255 Wilmot Rd 10804 914-632-0714
Edward O'Neill, prin. Fax 632-9760
Salesian HS 500/9-12
148 E Main St 10801 914-632-0248
John Flaherty, prin. Fax 632-5426
Thornton-Donovan S 200/K-12
100 Overlook Cir 10804 914-632-8836
Ursuline HS 800/6-12
1354 North Ave 10804 914-636-3950
Carol Killebrew, prin. Fax 636-3949

**New Square, Rockland, Pop. 6,907**

---

Avir Yaakov Girl's S 1,200/K-12
15 Roosevelt Ave 10977 845-354-0874

**New Windsor, Orange, Pop. 8,717**
Cornwall Central SD
Supt. — See Cornwall on Hudson
Cornwall Central HS 1,200/9-12
10 Dragon Dr 12553 845-534-8009
Lynn Imperato, prin. Fax 565-2754

Greenburgh-North Castle UFD
Supt. — See Dobbs Ferry
Kaplan Career Academy Alt
623 Blooming Grove Tpke 12553 845-522-8460
Jason Gerard, prin. Fax 522-8456

Newburgh Enlarged CSD
Supt. — See Newburgh
Heritage MS 1,000/6-8
405 Union Ave 12553 845-563-3750
Raul Rodriguez, prin. Fax 563-3759

**New York, New York, Pop. 7,965,821**
NYC Department of Education 962,600/PK-12
52 Chambers St 10007 718-935-2000
Carmen Farina, chncllr.
schools.nyc.gov/
Academy for Social Action 400/6-12
509 W 129th St 10027 212-234-3102
Rhokeisha Ford, prin. Fax 234-8597
Academy for Software Engineering 9-12
40 Irving Pl 10003 – Seung Yu, prin. 212-253-3299
American Sign Language S 200/9-12
223 E 23rd St 10010 917-326-6668
Watfa Shama, prin. Fax 326-6688
Art & Design HS 1,300/9-12
231 E 56th St 10022 212-752-4340
Eric Strauss, prin. Fax 752-4945
Baldwin S 200/Alt
351 W 18th St 10011 212-627-2812
Brady Smith, prin. Fax 627-9803
Ballet Tech / S for Dance 200/4-8
890 Broadway Fl 3 10003 212-254-1803
Roy O'Neill, prin. Fax 477-5048
Bard HS Early College 600/9-12
525 E Houston St 10002 212-995-8479
Michael Lerner, prin. Fax 777-4702
Baruch College Campus HS 400/9-12
55 E 25th St 10010 212-683-7440
Alicia Katz, prin. Fax 683-7338
Beacon HS 1,200/9-12
530 W 44th St 10036 212-465-4230
Ruth Lacey, prin. Fax 465-4235
Bergtraum HS 2,100/9-12
411 Pearl St 10038 212-964-9610
Lottie Almonte, prin. Fax 732-6622
Bread & Roses Integrated Arts HS 500/9-12
6 Edgecombe Ave 10030 212-926-4152
Dr. Rodney Lofton, prin. Fax 926-4317
Business of Sports S 300/9-12
439 W 49th St 10019 212-246-2183
Joshua Solomon, prin. Fax 246-2913
Cascade HS 200/Alt
198 Forsyth St 10002 646-654-1261
Paul Rotondo, prin. Fax 654-1742
Central Park East HS 400/9-12
1573 Madison Ave 10029 212-860-5929
Bennett Lieberman, prin. Fax 860-2938
Chelsea Career & Technical Education HS Vo/Tech
131 Avenue of the Americas 10013 212-925-1080
Brian Rosenblum, prin. Fax 941-7934
Choir Academy of Harlem 300/6-12
2005 Madison Ave 10035 212-289-6227
Dr. Melissa Vaughan, prin. Fax 289-4195
City As School HS 600/Alt
16 Clarkson St 10014 212-337-6800
Alan Cheng, prin. Fax 337-6875
City College Academy of the Arts 600/6-12
4600 Broadway 10040 212-567-3164
Bernadette Drysdale, prin. Fax 567-3958
City Knoll MS, 525 W 44th St 10036 6-8
Victoria Armas, prin. 718-935-3649
Coalition S for Social Change 300/Alt
2351 1st Ave 10035 212-831-5153
John Sullivan, prin. Fax 831-5951
Collaborative Academy of Science 200/6-8
220 Henry St 10002 212-227-0762
Judith DeLosSantos, prin. Fax 577-9785
College Academy 600/9-12
549 Audubon Ave 10040 212-927-1841
Peter Sloman, prin. Fax 927-2388
Columbia Secondary S 500/6-12
425 W 123rd St 10027 212-666-1278
Miriam Nightengale, prin. Fax 666-3805
Community Action S - MS 258 200/6-8
154 W 93rd St 10025 212-678-5888
John Curry, prin. Fax 961-1613
Community Health Academy of the Heights 500/6-12
504 W 158th St 10032 212-342-6600
Mark House, prin.
Douglas Academy 1,500/6-12
2581 7th Ave 10039 212-491-4107
Joseph Gates, prin. Fax 491-4414
Douglass Academy II 400/6-12
215 W 114th St 10026 212-865-9260
Osei Owusu-Afriyie, prin. Fax 865-9281
East Side Community HS 600/6-12
420 E 12th St 10009 212-460-8467
Mark Federman, prin. Fax 260-9657
East Side MS 400/6-8
331 E 91st St 10128 212-360-0114
David Getz, prin. Fax 360-0121
Esperanza Preparatory Academy 200/6-8
240 E 109th St 10029 212-722-6507
Wendy Mercedes, prin. Fax 722-6717
Essex Street Academy 300/9-12
350 Grand St 10002 212-475-4773
Erin Carstensen, prin. Fax 674-2058
Facing History S 400/9-12
525 W 50th St 10019 212-757-2680
Dana Panagot, prin. Fax 757-2156
Food & Finance HS 400/9-12
525 W 50th St 10019 212-586-2943
Roger Turgeon, prin. Fax 586-4205
Forsyth Satellite Academy 9-12
198 Forsyth St 10002 212-677-8900
Ingrid Haynes, prin. Fax 260-3063

Global Learning Collaborative 400/9-12
145 W 84th St 10024 212-877-1103
Karla Chiluiza, prin. Fax 877-1138
Global Neighborhood Secondary S 200/6-8
240 E 109th St 10029 212-289-4204
Luis Genao, prin. Fax 289-4301
Global Technology Preparatory S 200/6-8
160 E 120th St 10035 212-722-1395
David Baiz, prin. Fax 722-5864
Gramercy Arts HS 500/9-12
40 Irving Pl 10003 212-253-7076
Susan DiCicco, prin. Fax 253-8095
Grange MS 6-8
500 W 138th St 10031 212-281-6184
Benjamin Lev, prin. Fax 234-4903
Green HS of Teaching 600/9-12
26 Broadway 10004 646-826-8174
Nigel Pugh, prin. Fax 826-8175
Harbor Heights MS 200/6-8
306 Fort Washington Ave 10033 212-568-6052
Monica Klehr, prin. Fax 568-7959
Harlem Renaissance HS 200/9-12
22 E 128th St 10035 212-996-3795
Nadv Ziemer, prin. Fax 996-4354
Harvest Collegiate HS 9-12
34 W 14th St 10011 212-242-3384
Catherine Burch, prin.
Health Professions & Human Services HS 1,800/9-12
345 E 15th St 10003 212-780-9175
Robert Gentile, prin. Fax 979-7261
Henry Street S for International Studies 400/6-12
220 Henry St 10002 212-406-9411
Christine Loughlin, prin. Fax 406-9417
Heritage S 300/9-12
1680 Lexington Ave 10029 212-828-2858
Dyanand Sugrim, prin. Fax 828-2861
Hudson HS of Learning Technologies 200/9-12
351 W 18th St 10011 212-488-3330
Nancy Amling, prin. Fax 488-3335
Humanities Preparatory S 200/9-12
351 W 18th St 10011 212-929-4433
Jeannie Ferrari, prin. Fax 929-4445
Independence HS 400/Alt
850 10th Ave 10019 212-262-8067
Ron Smolkin, prin. Fax 262-8110
Innovation Diploma Plus 200/Alt
145 W 84th St 10024 212-724-2039
Daniel Storchan, prin. Fax 724-2765
Institute for Collaborative Education 500/6-12
345 E 15th St 10003 212-475-7972
Peter Karp, prin. Fax 475-0459
International HS at Union Square 200/9-12
40 Irving Pl 10003 212-533-2560
Daniel Walsh, prin. Fax 228-2946
Inwood Early College for Health and Info 9-12
650 Academy St 10034 212-567-1394
Samona Tait, prin. Fax 567-1825
Irving HS 1,000/9-12
40 Irving Pl 10003 212-674-5000
Sarah Hernandez, prin. Fax 673-9569
KAPPA IV S 200/6-8
6 Edgecombe Ave 10030 212-690-4963
Juan Vives, prin. Fax 690-8056
Kennedy-Onassis HS 700/9-12
120 W 46th St 10036 212-391-0041
Edward Demeo, prin. Fax 391-1293
La Guardia HS 2,600/9-12
100 Amsterdam Ave 10023 212-496-0700
Dr. Lisa Mars, prin. Fax 724-5748
Landmark HS 400/9-12
351 W 18th St 10011 212-647-7410
Caron Pinkus, prin. Fax 647-7416
Lazarus HS 300/Alt
100 Hester St 10002 212-925-5017
Melody Kellogg, prin. Fax 925-5920
Leadership & Public Service HS 600/9-12
90 Trinity Pl 10006 212-346-0007
Philip Santos, prin. Fax 346-0612
Legacy S for Integrated Studies 300/9-12
34 W 14th St 10011 212-645-1980
Arleen Liquori, prin. Fax 645-2596
Liberty HS 400/Alt
250 W 18th St 10011 212-691-0934
Rhonda Huegel, prin. Fax 727-1369
Life Science Secondary S 700/6-12
320 E 96th St 10128 212-348-1694
Genevieve Stanislaus, prin. Fax 348-4293
Lower East Side Prep S 600/Alt
145 Stanton St 10002 212-505-6366
Martha Polin, prin. Fax 260-0813
Lower Manhattan Arts Academy 300/9-12
350 Grand St 10002 212-505-0143
John Wenk, prin. Fax 674-8021
Lower Manhattan Community MS 300/6-8
26 Broadway 10004 646-826-8100
Kelly McGuire, prin. Fax 826-8101
Luperon HS of Science & Math 500/9-12
501 W 165th St 10032 212-928-1202
Juan Villar, prin. Fax 928-1309
Manhattan Academy for Arts & Language 200/9-12
111 E 33rd St 10016 212-576-0502
Siv Boletsis, prin. Fax 576-0518
Manhattan Bridges HS 500/9-12
525 W 50th St 10019 212-757-5274
Mirza Sanchez-Medina, prin. Fax 757-5411
Manhattan Business Academy 300/9-12
351 W 18th St 10011 212-647-1983
Karen Polsonetti, prin. Fax 647-1989
Manhattan Center for Science/Math 1,600/9-12
260 Pleasant Ave 10029 212-876-4639
Jose Jimenez, prin. Fax 996-5946
Manhattan Early Coll S for Advertising 9-12
411 Pearl St 10038 718-935-3477
Matthew Tossman, prin.
Manhattan/Hunter Science HS 500/9-12
122 Amsterdam Ave 10023 212-501-1235
Kevin Froner, prin. Fax 501-1171

Manhattan International HS 300/9-12
317 E 67th St, 212-517-6728
Gladys Rodriguez, prin. Fax 517-7147
Manhattan Theatre Lab HS 400/9-12
122 Amsterdam Ave 10023 212-362-2075
Lisa Ostrom, prin. Fax 362-9031
Manhattan Village Academy 400/9-12
43 W 22nd St 10010 212-242-8752
Hector Geager, prin. Fax 242-7630
Marshall Academy 600/6-12
200 W 135th St 10030 212-283-8055
Sean Davenport, prin. Fax 283-8109
Marte Valle HS 400/9-12
145 Stanton St 10002 212-473-8152
Jannett Bailey, prin. Fax 475-7588
Mather Building Arts & Craftsmanship HS 100/9-12
439 W 49th St 10019 212-225-0998
Larry Gabbard, prin. Fax 225-0996
McCourt HS 200/9-12
145 W 84th St 10024 212-362-2015
Danielle Salzberg, prin. Fax 362-5926
Milk HS 100/9-12
2 Astor Pl 10003 212-477-1555
Daphne Perrini, prin. Fax 674-8650
Millenium HS 600/9-12
75 Broad St 10004 212-825-9008
Colin McEvoy, prin. Fax 825-9095
Mott Hall HS 400/9-12
6 Edgecombe Ave 10030 212-690-5501
Altagracia Villalona, prin. Fax 690-5047
Mott Hall II 300/6-8
234 W 109th St 10025 212-678-2960
Marlon Lowe, prin. Fax 222-0560
Mott Hall S 300/6-8
71 Convent Ave 10027 212-281-5028
Marva Picou, prin. Fax 491-3451
Murray Hill Academy 200/9-12
111 E 33rd St 10016 212-696-0195
Anita Felix, prin. Fax 696-2498
New Design HS 400/9-12
350 Grand St 10002 212-475-4148
Scott Conti, prin. Fax 674-2128
New Design MS 6-8
625 W 133rd St 10027 212-281-6339
Francesca Pisa, prin. Fax 281-6674
New Explorations Science Tech/Math S 1,600/K-12
111 Columbia St 10002 212-677-5190
Dr. Olga Livanis, prin. Fax 260-8124
Newton MS for Science Math Tech 400/6-8
260 Pleasant Ave 10029 212-860-6006
Lisa Nelson, prin. Fax 987-4197
HS for Arts Imagination & Inquiry 400/9-12
122 Amsterdam Ave 10023 212-799-4064
Stephen Noonan, prin. Fax 799-4171
HS for Dual Language & Asian Studies 400/9-12
350 Grand St 10002 212-475-4097
Li Yan, prin. Fax 674-1392
HS for Environmental Studies 1,400/9-12
444 W 56th St 10019 212-262-8113
Shirley Matthews, prin. Fax 262-0702
HS for Excellence and Innovation 200/9-12
650 Academy St 10034 212-569-1022
Tyona Washington, prin. Fax 569-1190
HS for Health Careers & Science 700/9-12
549 Audubon Ave 10040 212-927-1841
Javier Trejo, prin. Fax 927-2179
HS for Language and Diplomacy 200/9-12
40 Irving Pl 10003 212-253-2480
Amber Najmi-Shadid, prin. Fax 253-2539
HS for Law Advocacy & Community Justice 500/9-12
122 Amsterdam Ave 10023 212-501-1201
Doreen Conwell, prin. Fax 501-1195
HS for Law & Public Service 700/9-12
549 Audubon Ave 10040 212-927-2380
Nicholas Politis, prin. Fax 781-9516
HS for Math Science Engineering 400/9-12
240 Convent Ave 10031 212-281-6490
Crystal Bonds, prin. Fax 281-6918
HS for Media & Communications 600/9-12
549 Audubon Ave 10040 212-927-1841
Ronni Michelen, prin. Fax 927-2326
HS of Arts & Technology 600/9-12
122 Amsterdam Ave 10023 212-501-1198
Anne Geiger, prin. Fax 441-3693
HS of Economic & Finance 800/9-12
100 Trinity Pl 10006 212-346-0708
Michael Stanzione, prin. Fax 346-0712
HS of Fashion Industries 1,600/9-12
225 W 24th St 10011 212-255-1235
Daryl Blank, prin. Fax 255-4756
HS of Graphic Communication Arts 1,400/9-12
439 W 49th St 10019 212-245-5925
Brendon Lyons, prin. Fax 265-1552
HS of Hospitality Management 400/9-12
525 W 50th St 10019 212-586-1819
Matthew Corallo, prin. Fax 586-2713
IS 218 300/6-8
4600 Broadway 10040 212-567-2322
June Barnett, prin. Fax 569-7421
IS 286 200/6-8
509 W 129th St 10027 212-690-5972
Melisha Jackman, prin. Fax 694-4124
IS 289 300/6-8
201 Warren St 10282 212-571-9268
Zeynep Ozkan, prin. Fax 587-6610
IS 528 300/6-8
180 Wadsworth Ave 10033 212-740-4900
Kristy Dela Cruz, prin. Fax 781-7302
JHS 13 200/6-8
1573 Madison Ave 10029 212-860-8935
Jacob Michelman, prin. Fax 860-5933
JHS 52 600/6-8
650 Academy St 10034 212-567-9162
Sal Fernandez, prin. Fax 942-4952
JHS 54 800/6-8
103 W 107th St 10025 212-678-2861
Dr. Elana Elster, prin. Fax 316-0883

JHS 104 1,100/6-8
330 E 21st St 10010 212-674-4545
Rosemarie Gaetani, prin. Fax 477-2205
JHS 143 600/6-8
511 W 182nd St 10033 212-927-7739
Lakisha Luke, prin. Fax 781-5539
JHS 167 1,200/6-8
220 E 76th St 10021 212-535-8610
Kaye Kerr, prin. Fax 472-9385
MS 131 500/6-8
100 Hester St 10002 212-219-1204
Phyllis Tam, prin. Fax 925-6386
MS 224 200/6-8
410 E 100th St 10029 212-860-6047
Liliana Sarro, prin. Fax 410-0678
MS 243 200/5-8
100 W 84th St 10024 212-799-1477
Elaine Schwartz, prin. Fax 579-9728
MS 245 400/6-8
100 W 77th St 10024 917-441-0873
Henry Zymeck, prin. Fax 678-5908
MS 247 200/6-8
32 W 92nd St 10025 212-799-2653
Claudia Aguirre, prin. Fax 579-2407
MS 250 200/6-8
735 W End Ave 10025 212-866-6313
Novella Bailey, dir. Fax 678-5295
MS 255 400/6-8
319 E 19th St 10003 212-614-8785
Rhonda Perry, prin. Fax 614-0095
MS 256 200/6-8
154 W 93rd St 10025 212-222-2857
Brian Zager, prin. Fax 531-0586
MS 260 300/6-8
425 W 33rd St 10001 212-695-9114
Jonathan Levin, prin. Fax 695-9611
MS 319 600/6-8
21 Jumel Pl 10032 212-923-3827
Ysidro Abreu, prin. Fax 923-3676
MS 322 500/6-8
4600 Broadway 10040 212-304-0853
Erica Zigelman, prin. Fax 567-3016
MS 324 400/6-8
21 Jumel Pl 10032 212-923-4057
Janet Heller, prin. Fax 923-4626
MS 326 300/6-8
401 W 164th St 10032 917-521-1875
Sharon Weissbrot, prin. Fax 521-1750
MS 328 400/6-8
401 W 164th St 10032 917-521-2508
Olga Quiles, prin. Fax 521-7797
NYC iSchool 400/9-12
131 Avenue of the Americas 10013 917-237-7300
Isora Bailey, prin. Fax 219-0743
NYC Lab HS for Collaborative Studies 600/9-12
333 W 17th St 10011 212-691-6119
Brooke Jackson, prin. Fax 691-2147
NYC Lab MS for Collaborative Studies 600/6-8
333 W 17th St 10011 212-691-6119
Megan Adams, prin. Fax 691-6219
NYC Museum S 400/9-12
333 W 17th St 10011 212-675-6206
Darlene Miller, dir. Fax 675-6524
Pace HS 400/9-12
100 Hester St 10002 212-334-4663
Yvette Sy, prin. Fax 334-4919
Park East HS 300/9-12
230 E 105th St 10029 212-831-1517
Kevin McCarthy, prin. Fax 348-6097
Professional Performing Arts HS 500/6-12
328 W 48th St 10036 212-247-8652
Keith Ryan, prin. Fax 247-7514
Quest to Learn S 200/6-9
351 W 18th St 10011 212-488-3645
Elisa Aragon, prin.
Randolph HS 1,200/9-12
443 W 135th St 10031 212-926-0113
David Fanning, prin. Fax 281-2726
Renaissance School of the Arts 200/6-8
319 E 117th St 10035 212-534-6072
Tammy Pate-Spears, prin. Fax 534-7418
Repertory Company HS for Theatre Arts 200/9-12
123 W 43rd St 10036 212-382-1875
Manuel Urena, prin. Fax 382-2306
Reynolds West Side HS 600/Alt
140 W 102nd St 10025 212-678-7300
Jean McTavish, prin. Fax 678-7380
Roosevelt HS 500/9-12
411 E 76th St 10021 212-772-1220
Demitri Saliani, prin. Fax 772-1440
Satellite Academy 200/Alt
120 W 30th St 10001 646-674-2800
Steve Zbaida, prin.
School for Global Leaders 300/6-8
145 Stanton St 10002 212-260-5375
Carry Chan, prin. Fax 260-7386
School of the Future 700/6-12
127 E 22nd St 10010 212-475-8086
Stacy Goldstein, admin. Fax 475-9273
Stuyvesant HS 3,300/9-12
345 Chambers St 10282 212-312-4800
Jie Zhang, prin. Fax 587-3874
Talent Unlimited HS 500/9-12
317 E 67th St, 212-737-1530
Linda Hamil, prin. Fax 737-2863
Technology Arts & Sciences Studio 200/6-8
185 1st Ave 10003 212-982-1836
George Morgan, prin. Fax 982-0528
Tompkins Square MS 400/6-8
600 E 6th St 10009 212-995-1430
Sonhando Estwick, prin. Fax 979-1341
Union Square Academy for Health Science 9-12
40 Irving Pl 10003 212-253-3110
Bernardo Ascona, prin.
Unity Center for Urban Technologies 200/9-12
111 E 33rd St 10016 212-576-0530
Fausto DeLaRosa, prin. Fax 576-0562

University Neighborhood HS 400/9-12
200 Monroe St 10002 212-962-4341
Elizabeth Collins, prin. Fax 267-5611
University Nieghborhood MS 100/6-8
220 Henry St 10002 212-267-5701
Laura Peynado, prin. Fax 349-8224
Urban Academy Laboratory HS 200/9-12
317 E 67th St, 212-570-5284
Adam Grumbach, prin. Fax 570-5366
Urban Assembly Academy Government & Law 300/9-12
350 Grand St 10002 212-505-0745
David Glasner, prin. Fax 674-8021
Urban Assembly for Media Studies HS 400/9-12
122 Amsterdam Ave 10023 212-501-1110
Cordelia Veve, prin. Fax 580-0156
Urban Assembly Gateway S for Technology 9-12
439 W 49th St 10019 212-246-1041
April McCoy, prin. Fax 246-2654
Urban Assembly Inst for New Technologies 200/6-8
509 W 129th St 10027 212-690-5977
Jeffrey Chetirko, prin. Fax 690-5980
Urban Assembly Maker Academy 9-12
411 Pearl St 10038 718-935-3442
Luke Bauer, prin.
Urban Assembly New York Harbor S Vo/Tech
10 South St Slip 7 10004 212-458-0800
Edward Biedermann, prin. Fax 458-0801
Urban Assembly S Design & Construction 400/9-12
525 W 50th St 10019 212-586-0981
Mathew Willoughby, prin. Fax 586-1731
Urban Assembly S for Emergency Mgmt 100/9-12
411 Pearl St 10038 212-245-4670
Rodolfo Elizondo, prin. Fax 246-4669
Urban Assembly S for Global Commerce 100/9-10
2005 Madison Ave 10035 212-831-5201
Erin Gehant, prin. Fax 831-5206
Urban Assembly S for Green Careers 300/9-12
145 W 84th St 10024 212-787-1189
Kerry Decker, prin. Fax 787-1455
Urban Assembly S for Performing Arts 400/9-12
509 W 129th St 10027 212-234-4631
Fia Davis, prin. Fax 234-4975
Urban Assembly S of Business 400/9-12
26 Broadway 10004 212-668-0169
Patricia Minaya, prin. Fax 668-0635
Vanguard HS 400/9-12
317 E 67th St, 212-517-5175
William Klann, prin. Fax 517-5334
Wadleigh Arts HS 500/6-12
215 W 114th St 10026 212-749-5800
Tyee Chin, prin. Fax 749-6463
Washington Hts. Expeditionary Learning S 600/6-12
511 W 182nd St 10033 212-781-0524
Brett Kimmel, prin. Fax 781-0742
West Prep Academy 200/6-8
150 W 105th St 10025 212-362-1674
Carland Washington, prin. Fax 362-2794
Yorkville East MS 6-8
1458 York Ave, 917-432-5413
Christina Riggio, prin. Fax 432-5418
Young Womens Leadership HS 400/6-12
105 E 106th St 10029 212-289-7593
Dr. Althea Bradshaw-Tyson, prin. Fax 289-7728
Manhattan Comprehensive Night & Day HS Adult
240 2nd Ave 10003 212-353-2010
Michael Toice, prin. Fax 353-1673
Other Schools – See Astoria, Bayside, Bellerose, Bronx, Brooklyn, Corona, East Elmhurst, Elmhurst, Far Rockaway, Floral Park, Flushing, Forest Hills, Fresh Meadows, Glendale, Hollis, Jackson Heights, Jamaica, Laurelton, Little Neck, Long Island City, Maspeth, Oakland Gardens, Ozone Park, Queens Village, Rego Park, Richmond Hill, Ridgewood, Rockaway Park, Saint Albans, South Ozone Park, Springfield Gardens, Staten Island, Whitestone, Woodside

---

ABI School of Barbering and Cosmetology Post-Sec.
252 W 29th St 10001 212-290-2289
Achieve Test Prep Post-Sec.
5 Penn Plz Ste 1975 10001 917-267-0711
AMDA College & Conservatory Post-Sec.
211 W 61st St 10023 212-787-5300
American Academy McAllister Institute Post-Sec.
619 W 54th St Fl 2 10019 212-757-1190
American Academy of Dramatic Arts Post-Sec.
120 Madison Ave 10016 800-463-8990
American University in Cairo Post-Sec.
420 5th Ave Fl 3 10018 212-730-8800
Avenues: The World S 700/PK-12
259 10th Ave 10001 212-524-9000
Dr. Robert Mattoon, head sch Fax 664-0701
Bank Street College of Education Post-Sec.
610 W 112th St 10025 212-875-4400
Barnard College Post-Sec.
3009 Broadway 10027 212-854-5262
Bellevue Hospital Center Post-Sec.
462 1st Ave 10016 212-561-4132
Berkeley College Post-Sec.
3 E 43rd St 10017 212-986-4343
Birch Wathen Lenox S 600/K-12
210 E 77th St, 212-861-0404
Frank J. Carnabuci, hdmstr. Fax 879-3388
Boricua College Post-Sec.
3755 Broadway 10032 212-694-1000
Brearley S 700/K-12
610 E 83rd St 10028 212-744-8582
Jane Fried, hdmstr. Fax 472-8020
Browning S 400/K-12
52 E 62nd St, 212-838-6280
Dr. Stephen Clement, hdmstr. Fax 355-5602
Calhoun S 500/2-12
433 W End Ave 10024 212-497-6500
Steven Nelson, admin. Fax 497-6530
Cathedral HS 600/9-12
350 E 56th St 10022 212-688-1545
Maria Spagnuolo, prin. Fax 754-2024

Chapin S 700/K-12
100 E End Ave 10028 212-744-2335
Patricia Hayot Ph.D., hdmstr. Fax 535-8138
Christie's Education Post-Sec.
11 W 42nd St Fl 8 10036 212-355-1501
Collegiate S 600/K-12
260 W 78th St 10024 212-812-8500
Lee Levison, hdmstr. Fax 812-8524
Columbia Grammar & Preparatory S 1,300/PK-12
5 W 93rd St 10025 212-749-6200
Dr. Richard Soghoian, hdmstr. Fax 865-4278
Columbia University Post-Sec.
2960 Broadway 10027 212-854-1754
Connelly Center for Education 100/5-8
220 E 4th St 10009 212-982-2287
Shalonda Gutierrez, prin. Fax 982-0547
Convent of the Sacred Heart S 700/PK-12
1 E 91st St 10128 212-722-4745
Dr. Joseph Ciancaglini, hdmstr. Fax 996-1784
Cooper Union Post-Sec.
30 Cooper Sq 10003 212-353-4100
County Univ. Sch. of Dental & Oral Surg. Post-Sec.
630 W 168th St 10032
Cristo Rey HS 400/9-12
112 E 106th St 10029 212-996-7000
William Ford, prin. Fax 427-7444
CUNY Bernard M. Baruch College Post-Sec.
1 Bernard Baruch Way 10010 646-312-1000
CUNY Borough/Manhattan Comm. College Post-Sec.
199 Chambers St 10007 212-220-8000
CUNY City College Post-Sec.
160 Convent Ave 10031 212-650-7000
CUNY Graduate Center Post-Sec.
365 5th Ave 10016 212-817-7000
CUNY Hunter College Post-Sec.
695 Park Ave, 212-772-4000
CUNY John Jay College Criminal Justice Post-Sec.
524 W 59th St 10019 212-237-8000
CUNY Stella & Charles Guttman Comm Coll Post-Sec.
50 W 40th St 10018 646-313-8000
Dalton S 1,300/K-12
108 E 89th St 10128 212-423-5200
Ellen Stein, hdmstr. Fax 423-5259
De La Salle Academy 100/6-8
332 W 43rd St 10036 212-316-5840
Br. Brian Carty, pres. Fax 316-5998
DeVry University Post-Sec.
180 Madison Ave Ste 900 10016 212-312-4300
Dominican Academy 200/9-12
44 E 68th St, 212-744-0195
Sr. Barbara Kane, prin. Fax 744-0375
Dwight S 800/PK-12
291 Central Park W 10024 212-724-6360
Dianne Drew, head sch Fax 874-4232
East Harlem S 200/4-8
309 E 103rd St 10029 212-876-8775
Fashion Institute of Technology Post-Sec.
227 W 27th St 10001 212-217-7999
Friends Seminary 700/K-12
222 E 16th St 10003 212-979-5030
Robert Lauder, prin. Fax 979-5034
Fusion Academy 6-12
460 Park Ave S 10016 212-326-9522
Heather Brookman, head sch
Gateway MS 100/6-8
211 W 61st St 10023 212-777-5966
Carolyn Salzman, head sch Fax 777-5794
Gemological Institute of America Post-Sec.
270 Madison Ave Fl 2 10016 800-366-8519
General Theological Seminary Post-Sec.
440 W 21st St 10011 212-243-5150
Global Business Institute Post-Sec.
145 E 125th St 10035 212-663-1500
Globe Institute of Technology Post-Sec.
500 7th Ave 10018 212-349-4330
Grace Church HS 9-12
46 Cooper Sq 10034 212-475-5610
George Davison, head sch
Hebrew Union College Post-Sec.
1 W 4th St 10012 212-674-5300
Helene Fuld College of Nursing Post-Sec.
24 E 120th St Ste 3 10035 212-616-7200
Heschel HS 300/9-12
20 W End Ave 10023 212-246-7717
Ariela Dubler, head sch Fax 246-7686
Heschel MS 100/6-8
30 W End Ave 10023 212-595-7087
Ariela Dubler, head sch Fax 489-1990
Hewitt S 500/K-12
45 E 75th St 10021 212-288-1919
Joan Lonergan, hdmstr. Fax 472-7531
Hunter College Campus S 300/K-12
71 E 94th St 10128 212-860-1291
Dean Ketchum, dir. Fax 722-6693
Icahn School of Medicine at Mount Sinai Post-Sec.
1 Gustave L Levy Pl 10029 212-241-6500
IDEAL S and Academy 100/PK-12
314 W 91st St 10024 212-769-1699
Dr. Tim Burns, head sch Fax 769-1698
Institute of Audio Research Post-Sec.
64 University Pl 10003 212-677-7580
Jewish Theological Seminary of America Post-Sec.
3080 Broadway 10027 212-678-8000
Juilliard School Post-Sec.
60 Lincoln Center Plz 10023 212-799-5000
Keller Graduate School Post-Sec.
120 W 45th St Fl 6 10036 212-556-0002
LaSalle Academy 300/9-12
215 E 6th St 10003 212-475-8940
Br. William Johnson, prin. Fax 529-3598
La Scuola d'Italia Guglielmo Marconi S 200/PK-12
12 E 96th St 10128 212-369-3290
Learning Institute for Beauty Sciences Post-Sec.
22 W 34th St 10001 212-695-4555
Leman Manhattan Preparatory S 500/PK-12
41 Broad St 10004 212-232-0266
Drew Alexander, hdmstr. Fax 232-0284

Lia Schorr Inst of Cosmetic Skin Care Post-Sec.
686 Lexington Ave 10022 212-486-9541
LIM College Post-Sec.
12 E 53rd St 10022 212-752-1530
Lookstein MS 200/5-8
114 E 85th St 10028 212-774-8040
Lookstein Upper S 500/9-12
60 E 78th St, 212-774-8070
Louis Gerstner Graduate Sch Biomed Sci Post-Sec.
1275 York Ave Ste 441, 646-888-6639
Loyola HS 200/9-12
980 Park Ave 10028 212-288-3522
Kristin Ross, prin. Fax 861-1021
LREI Little Red School House & Irwin HS 400/PK-12
272 6th Ave 10014 212-477-5316
Philip Kassen, dir. Fax 677-9159
Lycee Francais De New York 1,300/PK-12
505 E 75th St 10021 212-369-1400
Sean Lynch, hdmstr. Fax 439-4200
Lyceum Kennedy French American S 200/PK-12
225 E 43rd St 10017 212-681-1877
Dominique Velociter, head sch Fax 681-1922
Make-Up Designory Post-Sec.
375 W Broadway 10012 212-925-9250
Mandl School College of Allied Health Post-Sec.
254 W 54th St Fl 9 10019 212-247-3434
Manhattan HS for Girls 200/9-12
154 E 70th St 10021 212-737-6800
Manhattan Institute Post-Sec.
255 5th Ave 10016 347-220-8181
Manhattan Institute of Management Post-Sec.
110 William St Fl 3 10038 646-389-0947
Manhattan School of Music Post-Sec.
120 Claremont Ave 10027 212-749-2802
Marymount Manhattan College Post-Sec.
221 E 71st St 10021 212-517-0400
Marymount S 600/PK-12
1026 5th Ave 10028 212-744-4486
Concepcion Alvar, hdmstr. Fax 744-0163
Mesivta Tifereth Jerusalem of America Post-Sec.
1417 E Broadway 10002 212-964-2830
Mesivta Tifereth Jerusalem S 200/K-12
145 E Broadway 10002 212-964-2830
Metropolitan College of New York Post-Sec.
431 Canal St 10013 212-343-1234
Micropower Career Institute Post-Sec.
137 W 25th St 10001 212-279-2550
Mildred Elley School Post-Sec.
25 Broadway Fl 16 10004 212-380-9004
New York Academy of Art Post-Sec.
111 Franklin St 10013 212-966-0300
New York Career Institute Post-Sec.
11 Park Pl Fl 4 10007 212-962-0002
New York College of Podiatric Medicine Post-Sec.
53 E 124th St 10035 212-410-8000
New York Eye & Ear Infirmary Post-Sec.
310 E 14th St 10003 212-979-4375
New York Institute of Photography Post-Sec.
211 E 43rd St Ste 2402 10017 212-867-8260
New York Inst. of English and Business Post-Sec.
248 W 35th St 10001 212-725-9400
New York International Beauty School Post-Sec.
500 8th Ave Rm 803 10018 212-868-7171
New York Law School Post-Sec.
185 W Broadway 10013 212-431-2100
New York Presbyterian Hospital Post-Sec.
525 E 68th St, 212-746-4000
New York School of Interior Design Post-Sec.
170 E 70th St 10021 212-472-1500
New York Theological Seminary Post-Sec.
475 Riverside Dr Ste 500 10115 212-870-1211
New York University Post-Sec.
70 Washington Sq S 10012 212-998-1212
Nightingale-Bamford S 600/K-12
20 E 92nd St 10128 212-289-5020
Paul Burke, head sch Fax 876-1045
Northeastern Academy 100/9-12
532 W 215th St 10034 212-569-4800
Notre Dame HS 300/9-12
327 W 13th St 10014 212-620-5575
Jaclyn Brilliant, prin. Fax 620-0432
Pace University Post-Sec.
1 Pace Plz 10038 212-346-1200
Pacific College of Oriental Medicine Post-Sec.
915 Broadway Fl 2 10010 212-982-3456
Phillips Beth Israel School of Nursing Post-Sec.
776 Ave of Americas Fl 4 10001 212-614-6110
Professional Business College Post-Sec.
408 Broadway Fl 2 10013 212-226-7300
Professional Children's S 200/6-12
132 W 60th St 10023 212-582-3116
Dr. James Dawson, head sch Fax 956-3295
Rabbi Isaac Elchanan Theological Sem. Post-Sec.
515 W 185th St 10033 646-592-4455
Regis HS 500/9-12
55 E 84th St 10028 212-288-1100
Dr. Gary Tocchet, prin. Fax 794-1221
Relay Graduate School of Education Post-Sec.
40 W 20th St Fl 7 10011 212-228-1888
Richard Gilder Graduate School Post-Sec.
Central Park W at 79th St 10024 212-769-5055
Rockefeller University Post-Sec.
1230 York Ave, 212-327-8000
SAE Institute of Technology Post-Sec.
218 W 18th St Fl 4 10011 212-944-9121
St. George Academy HS 100/9-12
215 E 6th St 10003 212-473-3323
Rev. Peter Shyshka, prin. Fax 534-0819
St. Jean Baptiste HS 300/9-12
173 E 75th St 10021 212-288-1645
Sr. Maria Cassano, prin. Fax 288-6540
St. Thomas Choir S 50/3-8
202 W 58th St 10019 212-247-3311
Fr. Charles Wallace, hdmstr. Fax 247-3393
St. Vincent Ferrer HS 500/9-12
151 E 65th St, 212-535-4680
Sr. Gail Morgan, prin. Fax 988-3455

St. Vincent's Hospital & Medical Center Post-Sec.
153 W 11th St 10011 212-604-7500
Sanford-Brown Institute Post-Sec.
120 E 16th St Fl 4 10003 646-313-4510
School for the Deaf Post-Sec.
225 E 23rd St 10010
School of Visual Arts Post-Sec.
209 E 23rd St 10010 212-592-2000
Sheffield School of Interior Design Post-Sec.
211 E 43rd St 10017 212-661-7270
Sotheby's Institute of Art Post-Sec.
570 Lexington Ave Fl 6 10022 212-517-3929
Spanish-American Institute Post-Sec.
215 W 43rd St 10036 212-840-7111
Spence S, 22 E 91st St 10128 700/K-12
Bodie Brizendine, head sch 212-289-5940
Star Career Academy Post-Sec.
154 W 14th St 10011 212-675-6655
Steiner Upper S 100/7-12
15 E 78th St, 212-879-1101
Dr. William Macatee Ed.D., admin. Fax 794-1554
Stevenson S, 24 W 74th St 10023 50/7-12
Douglas Herron M.A., admin. 212-787-6400
Studio Jewelers Post-Sec.
32 E 31st St 10016 212-686-1944
SUNY College of Optometry Post-Sec.
33 W 42nd St 10036 212-938-4000
Swedish Institute College of Health Sci Post-Sec.
226 W 26th St Fl 5 10001 212-924-5900
Teachers College of Columbia University Post-Sec.
525 W 120th St 10027 212-678-3000
Technical Career Institute Post-Sec.
320 W 31st St 10001 212-594-4000
The Art Institute of New York City Post-Sec.
218 W 40th St Ste 232 10018 212-226-5500
The Institute of Culinary Education Post-Sec.
50 W 23rd St 10010 212-847-0711
The International Culinary Center Post-Sec.
462 Broadway 10013 888-324-2433
The King's College Post-Sec.
56 Broadway 10004 212-659-7200
The New School Post-Sec.
66 W 12th St 10011 212-229-5600
Touro College Post-Sec.
27 W 23rd St 10010 212-463-0400
Transfiguration ES 200/4-8
37 Saint James Pl 10038 212-267-9289
Dr. Patrick Taharally, prin. Fax 227-0065
Trevor Day S 400/6-12
1 W 88th St 10024 212-426-3360
Scott Reisinger, hdmstr. Fax 873-8520
Trinity S 1,000/K-12
139 W 91st St 10024 212-932-6814
John Allman, head sch Fax 799-3417
Tri-State College of Acupuncture Post-Sec.
80 8th Ave Ste 400 10011 212-242-2255
Ultrasound Diagnostic School Post-Sec.
120 E 16th St Fl 2 10003 212-645-9116
Union Theological Seminary Post-Sec.
3041 Broadway 10027 212-662-7100
United Nations International S 1,500/K-12
2450 FDR Dr 10010 212-684-7400
Jane Camblin, dir. Fax 684-1382
Weill Cornell Medical College Post-Sec.
1300 York Ave, 212-746-5454
Wood Tobe-Coburn School Post-Sec.
8 E 40th St 10016 212-686-9040
Xavier HS 1,000/9-12
30 W 16th St 10011 212-924-7900
Michael LiVigni, hdmstr. Fax 924-0303
Yeshiva Rabbi S.R. Hirsch 400/PK-12
91 Bennett Ave 10033 212-568-6200
Yeshiva University Post-Sec.
500 W 185th St 10033 212-960-5400
Yeshiva University HS for Boys 300/9-12
2540 Amsterdam Ave 10033 212-960-5337
Rabbi Michael Taubes, admin. Fax 960-0027
York Prep S 300/6-12
40 W 68th St 10023 212-362-0400

**New York Mills, Oneida, Pop. 3,298**

New York Mills UFD 600/K-12
1 Marauder Blvd 13417 315-768-8127
Kathy Houghton, supt. Fax 768-3521
www.newyorkmills.org
New York Mills JSHS 300/7-12
1 Marauder Blvd 13417 315-768-8124
Michael Spost, prin. Fax 768-3397

**Niagara Falls, Niagara, Pop. 48,343**

Niagara Falls CSD 6,800/PK-12
630 66th St 14304 716-286-4205
Cynthia Bianco, supt. Fax 286-4283
www.nfschools.net/
Gaskill Preparatory S 500/7-8
910 Hyde Park Blvd 14301 716-278-5820
Sheila Smith, prin. Fax 278-5829
La Salle Preparatory S 500/7-8
7436 Buffalo Ave 14304 716-278-5880
James Spanbauer, prin. Fax 278-5899
Niagara Falls HS 1,900/9-12
4455 Porter Rd 14305 716-278-5800
Robert Bradley, prin. Fax 286-7964

Niagara-Wheatfield Central SD 4,200/PK-12
6700 Schultz St 14304 716-215-3003
Daniel Ljiljanich, supt. Fax 215-3039
www.nwcsd.k12.ny.us
Other Schools – See Sanborn

---

Cheryl Fell's School of Business Post-Sec.
2541 Military Rd 14304 716-297-2750
Niagara Catholic JSHS 100/7-12
520 66th St 14304 716-283-8771
Ronald Buggs, prin. Fax 283-8774

**Niagara University, Niagara**

---

Niagara University — Post-Sec.
PO Box 2011 14109 — 716-285-1212

**North Babylon, Suffolk, Pop. 17,252**
North Babylon UFD — 4,800/K-12
5 Jardine Pl 11703 — 631-620-7000
Glen Eschbach, supt. — Fax 321-3295
www.northbabylonschools.net
Moses MS — 1,200/6-8
250 Phelps Ln 11703 — 631-620-7300
Kathleen Hartnett, prin. — Fax 587-2619
North Babylon HS — 1,600/9-12
1 Phelps Ln 11703 — 631-620-7100
Jonathan Klomp, prin. — Fax 321-3327

**North Collins, Erie, Pop. 1,203**
North Collins Central SD — 600/PK-12
2045 School St 14111 — 716-337-0101
Joan Thomas, supt. — Fax 337-3457
www.northcollins.com
North Collins JSHS — 300/7-12
2045 School St 14111 — 716-337-0101
Erich Ploetz, prin. — Fax 337-3457

**North Creek, Warren, Pop. 613**
Johnsburg Central SD — 300/K-12
165 Main St 12853 — 518-251-2814
Michael Markwica, supt. — Fax 251-2562
www.johnsburgcsd.org
Johnsburg Central S — 300/K-12
165 Main St 12853 — 518-251-3504
Nadeen Kearney, prin. — Fax 251-2562

**North Massapequa, Nassau, Pop. 17,762**
Plainedge UFD — 3,300/K-12
241 Wyngate Dr 11758 — 516-992-7455
Dr. Edward Salina, supt. — Fax 992-7446
www.plainedgeschools.org
Other Schools – See Bethpage, Massapequa

**North Merrick, Nassau, Pop. 12,143**
Bellmore-Merrick Central HSD — 5,900/7-12
1260 Meadowbrook Rd 11566 — 516-992-1000
John DeTommaso, supt. — Fax 623-0151
www.bellmore-merrick.k12.ny.us
Other Schools – See Bellmore, Merrick

**Northport, Suffolk, Pop. 7,346**
Northport-East Northport UFD — 6,200/K-12
PO Box 210 11768 — 631-262-6604
Robert L. Banzer, supt. — Fax 262-6607
web.northport.k12.ny.us/
Northport HS — 2,100/9-12
154 Laurel Hill Rd 11768 — 631-262-6652
Irene McLaughlin, prin. — Fax 262-6736
Northport MS — 800/6-8
11 Middleville Rd 11768 — 631-262-6750
Timothy Hoss, prin. — Fax 262-6793
Other Schools – See East Northport

---

Northport VA Medical Center — Post-Sec.
79 Middleville Rd 11768 — 631-261-4400

**North Salem, Westchester**
North Salem Central SD — 1,300/K-12
230 June Rd 10560 — 914-669-5414
Dr. Kenneth Freeston, supt. — Fax 669-8753
www.northsalemschools.org
North Salem MSHS — 700/6-12
230 June Rd 10560 — 914-669-5414
Dr. Patricia Cyganovich, prin. — Fax 669-5663

**North Syracuse, Onondaga, Pop. 6,697**
North Syracuse Central SD — 9,300/PK-12
5355 W Taft Rd 13212 — 315-218-2100
Annette Speach, supt. — Fax 218-2185
www.nscsd.org
North Syracuse JHS — 1,400/8-9
5353 W Taft Rd 13212 — 315-218-3600
Constance Turose, prin. — Fax 218-3685
Other Schools – See Cicero

**North Tonawanda, Niagara, Pop. 31,199**
North Tonawanda CSD — 3,400/K-12
176 Walck Rd 14120 — 716-807-3500
Gregory Woytila, supt. — Fax 807-3525
www.ntschools.org
North Tonawanda HS — 1,300/9-12
405 Meadow Dr 14120 — 716-807-3600
James Fisher, prin. — Fax 807-3639
North Tonawanda MS — 600/7-8
1500 Vanderbilt Ave 14120 — 716-807-3700
Gregory Burgess, prin. — Fax 807-3701

---

Christian Academy of Western New York — 100/PK-12
789 Gilmore Ave 14120 — 716-433-1652
Patricia Poeller, admin.

**Northville, Fulton, Pop. 1,084**
Northville Central SD — 500/PK-12
PO Box 608 12134 — 518-863-7000
Dr. Leslie Ford, supt. — Fax 863-7011
northvillecsd.org
Northville MSHS — 300/6-12
PO Box 608 12134 — 518-863-7000
Kyle McFarland, prin. — Fax 863-7011

**Norwich, Chenango, Pop. 7,042**
Norwich CSD — 2,000/PK-12
89 Midland Dr 13815 — 607-334-1600
Gerard O'Sullivan, supt. — Fax 336-8652
www.norwichcsd.org
Norwich HS — 600/9-12
89 Midland Dr 13815 — 607-334-1600
Kermit Moyer, prin. — Fax 334-6680
Norwich MS — 500/6-8
89 Midland Dr 13815 — 607-334-1600
Scott Ryan, prin. — Fax 334-6210

**Norwood, Saint Lawrence, Pop. 1,621**
Norwood-Norfolk Central SD — 1,000/PK-12
7852 State Highway 56 13668 — 315-353-6631
James Cruikshank, supt. — Fax 353-2467
www.nncsk12.org/
Norwood HS — 300/9-12
7852 State Highway 56 13668 — 315-353-6631
Robin Fetter, prin. — Fax 353-2480
Norwood-Norfolk MS — 300/5-8
7852 State Highway 56 13668 — 315-353-6631
Jon Sovay, prin.

**Nunda, Livingston, Pop. 1,354**
Keshequa Central SD — 800/PK-12
PO Box 517 14517 — 585-468-2900
Tom Cox, supt. — Fax 468-3814
www.keshequa.org
Keshequa HS — 200/9-12
PO Box 517 14517 — 585-468-2900
Peter Reynolds, prin. — Fax 468-5493
Keshequa MS — 200/7-8
PO Box 517 14517 — 585-468-2900
Peter Reynolds, prin. — Fax 468-5493

**Nyack, Rockland, Pop. 6,636**
Nyack UFD — 2,900/K-12
13A Dickinson Ave 10960 — 845-353-7000
James Montesano Ed.D., supt. — Fax 353-7019
www.nyackschools.com
Nyack MS — 600/6-8
98 S Highland Ave 10960 — 845-353-7200
Kevin Brentnall, prin. — Fax 353-0506
Other Schools – See Upper Nyack

---

Alliance Theological Seminary — Post-Sec.
350 N Highland Ave 10960 — 845-353-2020
Nyack College — Post-Sec.
1 S Boulevard 10960 — 845-358-1710

**Oakdale, Suffolk, Pop. 7,925**
Connetquot Central SD
Supt. — See Bohemia
Oakdale-Bohemia Road MS — 800/6-8
60 Oakdale Bohemia Rd 11769 — 631-244-2268
Susanne Bailey, prin. — Fax 563-6167

---

Dowling College — Post-Sec.
150 Idle Hour Blvd 11769 — 631-244-3000

**Oakfield, Genesee, Pop. 1,789**
Oakfield-Alabama Central SD — 800/PK-12
7001 Lewiston Rd 14125 — 585-948-5211
Mark Alexander, supt. — Fax 948-9362
www.oahornets.org
Oakfield-Alabama MSHS — 400/7-12
7001 Lewiston Rd 14125 — 585-948-5211
Lynn Muscarella, prin. — Fax 948-9362

**Oakland Gardens, See New York**
NYC Department of Education
Supt. — See New York
Cardozo HS — 3,900/9-12
5700 223rd St 11364 — 718-279-6500
Gerald Martori, prin. — Fax 631-7880
JHS 74 — 900/6-8
6115 Oceania St 11364 — 718-631-6800
Anthony Armstrong, prin. — Fax 631-6899

**Oceanside, Nassau, Pop. 31,810**
Oceanside UFD — 5,800/PK-12
145 Merle Ave 11572 — 516-678-1215
Phyllis Harrington, supt. — Fax 678-7503
www.oceansideschools.org
Castleton Academy HS — 100/Alt
145 Merle Ave 11572 — 516-678-7593
Dorie Ciulla, prin. — Fax 678-7594
Oceanside HS — 1,900/9-12
3160 Skillman Ave 11572 — 516-678-7526
Geraldine DeCarlo, prin. — Fax 678-6790
Oceanside MS — 900/7-8
186 Alice Ave 11572 — 516-678-8518
Allison Glickman-Rogers, prin. — Fax 594-2365

---

Hochstim School of Radiography — Post-Sec.
PO Box 9007 11572 — 516-763-2030

**Odessa, Schuyler, Pop. 582**
Odessa-Montour Central SD — 800/PK-12
300 College Ave 14869 — 607-594-3341
Christopher Wood, supt. — Fax 594-3976
www.omschools.org
Odessa-Montour JSHS — 400/7-12
300 College Ave 14869 — 607-594-3341
Almon McCarty, prin. — Fax 594-3438

**Ogdensburg, Saint Lawrence, Pop. 10,977**
Ogdensburg CSD — 1,500/PK-12
1100 State St 13669 — 315-393-0900
Timothy Vernsey, supt. — Fax 393-2767
www.ogdensburgk12.org/
Ogdensburg Free Academy — 700/7-12
1100 State St 13669 — 315-393-0900
Cynthia Tuttle, prin. — Fax 393-7412

**Old Forge, Herkimer, Pop. 747**
Town of Webb UFD — 300/K-12
PO Box 38 13420 — 315-369-3222
Rex Germer, supt. — Fax 369-6216
www.towschool.org
Town of Webb S — 300/K-12
PO Box 38 13420 — 315-369-3222
John Swick, prin. — Fax 369-6216

**Old Westbury, Nassau, Pop. 4,556**
East Williston UFD — 1,800/K-12
11 Bacon Rd 11568 — 516-333-1630
Dr. Elaine Kanas, supt. — Fax 333-1937
www.ewsdonline.org/
Wheatley HS, 11 Bacon Rd 11568 — 800/8-12
Dr. Sean Feeney, prin. — 516-333-7804

Westbury UFD — 4,400/PK-12
2 Hitchcock Ln 11568 — 516-876-5016
Dr. Mary A. Lagnado, supt. — Fax 876-5181
www.westburyschools.org
Westbury HS — 1,200/9-12
1 Post Rd 11568 — 516-876-5047
Manuel Arias, prin. — Fax 876-5079
Other Schools – See Westbury

---

New York Institute of Technology — Post-Sec.
PO Box 8000 11568 — 516-686-1000
SUNY College at Old Westbury — Post-Sec.
PO Box 210 11568 — 516-876-3000

**Olean, Cattaraugus, Pop. 14,023**
Olean CSD — 1,800/PK-12
410 W Sullivan St 14760 — 716-375-8018
Dr. Colleen Taggerty, supt. — Fax 375-8047
www.oleanschools.org
Olean HS — 600/8-12
410 W Sullivan St 14760 — 716-375-8010
Barbara Lias, prin. — Fax 375-8048

---

Archbishop Walsh Academy — 100/9-12
208 N 24th St 14760 — 585-372-8122
Thomas Manko, prin. — Fax 372-6707
Continental School of Beauty Culture — Post-Sec.
517 N Barry St 14760 — 716-372-5095
Jamestown Community College- Cattaraugus — Post-Sec.
PO Box 5901 14760 — 716-376-7500

**Olmstedville, Essex**
Minerva Central SD — 100/K-12
PO Box 39 12857 — 518-251-2000
Timothy Farrell, supt. — Fax 251-2395
www.minervasd.org/
Minerva Central S — 100/K-12
PO Box 39 12857 — 518-251-2000
Heidi Kelly, prin. — Fax 251-2395

**Oneida, Madison, Pop. 11,232**
Oneida CSD — 2,100/PK-12
PO Box 327 13421 — 315-363-2550
Ronald Spadafora, supt. — Fax 363-6728
www.oneidacsd.org/
Oneida HS — 700/9-12
560 Seneca St 13421 — 315-363-6901
Brian Gallagher, prin. — Fax 366-0619
Other Schools – See Wampsville

**Oneonta, Otsego, Pop. 13,601**
Oneonta CSD — 1,600/PK-12
31 Center St 13820 — 607-433-8200
Joseph Yelich, supt. — Fax 433-8290
oneontacsd.org
Oneonta HS — 600/9-12
130 East St 13820 — 607-433-8243
Thomas Brindley, prin. — Fax 433-8204
Oneonta MS — 300/7-8
130 East St 13820 — 607-433-8262
Kevin Johnson, prin. — Fax 433-8203

---

Hartwick College — Post-Sec.
PO Box 4020 13820 — 607-431-4000
Lighthouse Christian Academy — 50/PK-12
12 Grove St 13820 — 607-432-2031
Chris Cleveland, admin. — Fax 432-3403
SUNY College at Oneonta — Post-Sec.
108 Ravine Pkwy 13820 — 607-436-3500
USC The Business College — Post-Sec.
17 Elm St 13820 — 607-432-7003

**Ontario Center, Wayne**
Wayne Central SD — 2,300/K-12
PO Box 155 14520 — 315-524-1000
John Carlevatti, supt. — Fax 524-1049
www.wayne.k12.ny.us
Armstrong MS — 500/6-8
PO Box 155 14520 — 315-524-1080
Pamela Tatro, prin. — Fax 524-1119
Beneway HS — 800/9-12
PO Box 155 14520 — 315-524-1050
Michael Pullen, prin. — Fax 524-1079

**Orangeburg, Rockland, Pop. 4,499**
South Orangetown Central SD
Supt. — See Blauvelt
Tappan Zee HS — 1,100/9-12
15 Dutch Hill Rd 10962 — 845-680-1600
Dr. Jennifer Amos, prin. — Fax 680-1950

---

Dominican College of Blauvelt — Post-Sec.
470 Western Hwy 10962 — 845-359-7800
Long Island University-Hudson Grad Ctr — Post-Sec.
70 Route 340 10962 — 845-359-7200

**Orchard Park, Erie, Pop. 3,209**
Orchard Park Central SD
Supt. — See West Seneca
Orchard Park HS — 1,600/9-12
4040 Baker Rd 14127 — 716-209-6242
Jonathan Wolf, prin. — Fax 209-6451
Orchard Park MS — 1,300/6-8
60 S Lincoln Ave 14127 — 716-209-6227
David Lilleck, prin. — Fax 209-6338

---

Bryant & Stratton College — Post-Sec.
200 Red Tail 14127 — 716-677-9500
Erie Community College South — Post-Sec.
4041 Southwestern Blvd 14127 — 716-648-5400

**Oriskany, Oneida, Pop. 1,381**
Oriskany Central SD — 700/K-12
PO Box 539 13424 — 315-768-2058
Gregory Kelahan, supt. — Fax 768-1733
www.oriskanycsd.org

Oriskany JSHS 300/7-12
PO Box 539 13424 315-768-2063
Eric Knuth, prin. Fax 768-4496

**Ossining, Westchester, Pop. 24,636**
Ossining UFD 4,500/PK-12
190 Croton Ave 10562 914-941-7700
Raymond Sanchez, supt. Fax 941-7291
www.ossiningufsd.org/
Dorner MS 900/6-8
Van Cortlandt Ave 10562 914-762-5740
Regina Cellio, prin. Fax 762-5246
Ossining HS 1,300/9-12
29 S Highland Ave 10562 914-762-5760
Joshua Mandel, prin. Fax 762-4011

**Oswego, Oswego, Pop. 17,912**
Oswego CSD 3,900/K-12
120 E 1st St Ste 1 13126 315-341-2000
Benjamin Halsey, supt. Fax 341-2910
www.oswego.org
Oswego HS 1,300/9-12
2 Buccaneer Blvd 13126 315-341-2200
Fax 341-2920
Oswego MS 600/7-8
100 Mark Fitzgibbons Dr 13126 315-341-2300
Mary Fierro, prin. Fax 341-2390

---

SUNY at Oswego Post-Sec.
7060 State Route 104 13126 315-312-2500

**Otego, Otsego, Pop. 991**
Unatego Central SD 800/K-12
2641 State Highway 7 13825 607-988-5038
Dr. David S. Richards, supt. Fax 988-1039
www.unatego.org
Unatego HS 300/9-12
2641 State Highway 7 13825 607-988-5098
Julie Lambiaso, prin. Fax 988-1050
Unatego MS 200/6-8
2641 State Highway 7 13825 607-988-5036
Patricia Hoyt, prin. Fax 988-5058

**Ovid, Seneca, Pop. 592**
South Seneca Central SD 800/PK-12
7263 Main St 14521 607-869-9636
Stephen Zielinski, supt. Fax 532-8540
www.southseneca.com
South Seneca HS 200/9-12
7263 Main St 14521 607-869-9636
John Steedle, prin. Fax 869-9553
South Seneca MS 200/6-8
7263 Main St 14521 607-869-9636
John Steedle, prin. Fax 532-9553

**Owego, Tioga, Pop. 3,824**
Owego-Apalachin Central SD 2,200/PK-12
36 Talcott St 13827 607-687-6224
Dr. William Russell, supt. Fax 687-6313
www.oacsd.org
Owego-Apalachin MS 500/5-8
3 Sheldon Guile Blvd 13827 607-687-6248
Thomas Beatty, prin. Fax 687-6593
Owego Free Academy 700/9-12
1 Sheldon Guile Blvd 13827 607-687-6230
Heath Georgia, prin. Fax 687-6244

**Oxford, Chenango, Pop. 1,425**
Oxford Academy & Central SD 800/PK-12
PO Box 192 13830 607-843-2025
Shawn Bissetta, supt. Fax 843-3241
www.oxac.org
Oxford Academy HS 300/9-12
PO Box 192 13830 607-843-2025
Janet Laytham, prin. Fax 843-3231
Oxford Academy MS 200/5-8
PO Box 192 13830 607-843-2025
Kathleen Hansen, prin. Fax 843-3241

**Oyster Bay, Nassau, Pop. 6,598**
Oyster Bay-East Norwich Central SD 1,600/PK-12
1 McCouns Ln 11771 516-624-6505
Dr. Laura Seinfeld, supt. Fax 624-6520
obenschools.org
Oyster Bay JSHS 700/7-12
150 E Main St 11771 516-624-6524
Dr. Dennis O'Hara, prin. Fax 624-6684

---

St. Dominic HS 400/9-12
110 Anstice St 11771 516-922-4888
Dr. Denise Smith, prin. Fax 922-4898

**Ozone Park, See New York**
NYC Department of Education
Supt. — See New York
Adams HS 3,300/9-12
10101 Rockaway Blvd 11417 718-322-0500
Daniel Scanlon, prin. Fax 738-9077
Goddard HS of Communication Arts & Tech. 600/9-12
13830 Lafayette St 11417 718-848-8357
Joseph Birgeles, prin. Fax 848-8579
HS for Construction Engineering & Arch 900/9-12
9406 104th St 11416 718-846-6280
Lakesha Gordon, prin. Fax 846-6283
JHS 202 1,100/6-8
13830 Lafayette St 11417 718-848-0001
William Fitzgerald, prin. Fax 848-8082
JHS 210 2,000/6-8
9311 101st Ave 11416 718-845-5942
Rosalyn Allman-Manning, prin. Fax 845-4037
MS 137 2,000/6-8
10915 98th St 11417 718-659-0471
Laura Mastrogiovanni, prin. Fax 659-4594

**Painted Post, Steuben, Pop. 1,780**
Corning CSD 5,100/K-12
165 Charles St 14870 607-936-3704
Michael Ginalski, supt. Fax 654-2735
www.corningareaschools.com
Corning - Painted Post MS 1,100/6-8
35 Victory Hwy 14870 607-654-2966
Richard Kimble, prin. Fax 654-2908
Other Schools – See Corning

**Palmyra, Wayne, Pop. 3,491**
Palmyra-Macedon Central SD 2,000/K-12
151 Hyde Pkwy 14522 315-597-3401
Dr. Robert Ike, supt. Fax 597-3898
www.palmaccsd.org
Palmyra-Macedon HS 700/9-12
151 Hyde Pkwy 14522 315-597-3420
Andrew Wahl, prin. Fax 597-3425
Palmyra-Macedon MS 500/6-8
163 Hyde Pkwy 14522 315-597-3450
Darcy Smith, prin. Fax 597-3460

---

East Palmyra Christian S 100/PK-12
2023 E Palmyra Port Gibson 14522 315-597-4400
Keith Vanderzwan, prin. Fax 597-9717

**Panama, Chautauqua, Pop. 475**
Panama Central SD 600/PK-12
41 North St 14767 716-782-2455
Bert Lictus, supt. Fax 782-4674
www.pancent.org
Panama Central S 300/7-12
41 North St 14767 716-782-2455
Stephanie Lackie, prin. Fax 782-4674

**Parish, Oswego, Pop. 445**
Altmar-Parish-Williamstown Central SD 800/PK-12
PO Box 97 13131 315-625-5251
Anita Murphy, supt. Fax 625-7952
www.apw.cnyric.org
Altmar-Parish-Williamstown JSHS 400/7-12
PO Box 97 13131 315-625-5222
James Heffron, prin. Fax 625-4638

**Parishville, Saint Lawrence, Pop. 641**
Parishville-Hopkinton Central SD 500/PK-12
PO Box 187 13672 315-265-4642
Darin Saiff, supt. Fax 268-1309
phcs.neric.org
Parishville-Hopkinton JSHS 200/7-12
PO Box 187 13672 315-265-4642
Robert Stewart, prin. Fax 268-1309

**Patchogue, Suffolk, Pop. 11,620**
Patchogue-Medford UFD 7,400/PK-12
241 S Ocean Ave 11772 631-687-6300
Michael Hynes, supt.
www.pmschools.org
Saxton MS 700/6-9
121 Saxton St 11772 631-687-6700
Manuel Sanzone, prin. Fax 687-6740
South Ocean MS 500/6-9
225 S Ocean Ave 11772 631-687-6600
Timothy Piciullo, prin.
Other Schools – See Medford

---

Briarcliffe College Post-Sec.
225 W Main St 11772 631-654-5300
St. Joseph's College New York Post-Sec.
155 W Roe Blvd 11772 631-687-5100

**Patterson, Putnam**
Carmel Central SD 4,500/K-12
PO Box 296 12563 845-878-2094
Andy Irvin, supt. Fax 878-2566
www.carmelschools.org
Other Schools – See Carmel

**Paul Smiths, Franklin, Pop. 664**

---

Paul Smith's College Post-Sec.
PO Box 265 12970 518-327-6227

**Pavilion, Genesee, Pop. 644**
Pavilion Central SD 700/PK-12
7014 Big Tree Rd 14525 585-584-3115
Kenneth Ellison, supt. Fax 584-3421
www.pavilioncsd.org
Pavilion JSHS 400/6-12
7014 Big Tree Rd 14525 585-584-3070
Dr. Sheila Eigenbrod, prin. Fax 584-3421

**Pawling, Dutchess, Pop. 2,332**
Pawling Central SD 1,300/K-12
515 Route 22 12564 845-855-4600
Dr. William M. Ward, supt. Fax 855-4659
www.pawlingschools.org
Pawling HS 400/9-12
30 Wagner Dr 12564 845-855-4620
Helen Callan, prin. Fax 855-4621
Pawling MS 400/5-8
80 Wagner Dr 12564 845-855-4653
Allan Lipsky, prin. Fax 855-4131

---

Trinity-Pawling S 300/7-12
700 Route 22 12564 845-855-3100
Archibald Smith, hdmstr. Fax 855-3816

**Pearl River, Rockland, Pop. 15,720**
Pearl River UFD 2,600/K-12
135 W Crooked Hill Rd 10965 845-620-3900
Marco Pochintesta, supt. Fax 620-3927
www.pearlriver.org
Pearl River HS 1,000/8-12
275 E Central Ave 10965 845-620-3800
Michael Murphy, prin. Fax 620-3852

---

Iona College Rockland Graduate Center Post-Sec.
PO Box 1522 10965 845-620-1350

**Peekskill, Westchester, Pop. 22,929**
Peekskill CSD 3,000/PK-12
1031 Elm St 10566 914-737-3300
Dr. Lorenzo Licopoli, supt. Fax 737-3912
www.peekskillcsd.org
Peekskill HS 900/9-12
1072 Elm St 10566 914-737-0201
Cassandra Hyacinthe, prin. Fax 737-2550
Peekskill MS 600/6-8
212 Ringgold St 10566 914-737-4542
Jamal Lewis, prin. Fax 737-3253

---

Northern Westchester Sch of Hairdressing Post-Sec.
19 Bank St 10566 914-739-8400

**Pelham, Westchester, Pop. 6,710**
Pelham UFD 2,800/K-12
18 Franklin Pl 10803 914-738-3434
Dr. Peter Giarrizzo, supt. Fax 738-7223
www.pelhamschools.org
Pelham Memorial HS 800/9-12
575 Colonial Ave 10803 914-738-8110
Jeannine Clark, prin. Fax 738-8122
Pelham MS 700/6-8
28 Franklin Pl 10803 914-738-8190
Dr. Robert Roelle, prin. Fax 738-8132

**Penfield, Monroe, Pop. 30,219**
Penfield Central SD
Supt. — See Rochester
Bay Trail MS 1,100/6-8
1760 Scribner Rd 14526 585-249-6450
Winton Buddington, prin. Fax 248-0735
Penfield HS 1,500/9-12
25 High School Dr 14526 585-249-6700
Dr. Leslie Maloney Ed.D., prin. Fax 248-2810

---

Finney S 200/K-12
2070 Five Mile Line Rd 14526 585-387-3770
Michael VanLeeuwen, pres. Fax 387-3771

**Penn Yan, Yates, Pop. 5,081**
Penn Yan Central SD 1,600/PK-12
1 School Dr 14527 315-536-3371
Howard Dennis, supt. Fax 536-0068
www.pycsd.org
Penn Yan Academy 600/9-12
305 Court St 14527 315-536-4408
David Pullen, prin. Fax 536-0341
Penn Yan MS 400/6-8
515 Liberty St 14527 315-536-3366
Kelley Johnson, prin. Fax 536-7769

**Perry, Wyoming, Pop. 3,633**
Perry Central SD 900/PK-12
33 Watkins Ave 14530 585-237-0270
Daryl McLaughlin, supt. Fax 237-6172
www.perry.k12.ny.us
Perry JSHS 300/7-12
33 Watkins Ave 14530 585-237-0270
Rebecca Belkota, admin. Fax 237-6350

**Peru, Clinton, Pop. 1,580**
Peru Central SD 1,100/K-12
PO Box 68 12972 518-643-6000
Dr. Patrick Brimstein, supt. Fax 643-2043
www.perucsd.org
Peru JSHS 600/7-12
PO Box 68 12972 518-643-6400
Christopher Mazzella, prin. Fax 643-6438

**Philadelphia, Jefferson, Pop. 1,192**
Indian River Central SD 4,200/PK-12
32735 County Route 29 Ste B 13673 315-642-3441
James Kettrick, supt. Fax 642-3738
www.ircsd.org
Indian River HS 1,000/9-12
32925 US Route 11 13673 315-642-3427
Troy Decker, prin. Fax 642-5658
Indian River MS 800/6-8
32735 County Route 29 Ste A 13673 315-642-0125
Nancy Taylor-Schmitt, prin. Fax 642-0802

**Phoenix, Oswego, Pop. 2,343**
Phoenix Central SD 1,800/K-12
116 Volney St 13135 315-695-1555
Judy Belfield, supt. Fax 695-1201
www.phoenixcsd.org
Birdlebough HS 600/9-12
552 Main St 13135 315-695-1631
Gregory Molloy, prin. Fax 695-1618
Dillon MS 500/6-8
116 Volney St 13135 315-695-1521
Susan Anderson, prin. Fax 695-1523

**Pine Bush, Orange, Pop. 1,744**
Pine Bush Central SD 5,700/PK-12
PO Box 700 12566 845-744-2031
Joan M. Carbone, supt. Fax 744-6189
www.pinebushschools.org
Crispell MS 700/6-8
PO Box 780 12566 845-744-2031
John Boyle, prin. Fax 744-2261
Pine Bush HS 1,900/9-12
PO Box 670 12566 845-744-2031
Aaron Hopmayer, prin. Fax 744-3488
Other Schools – See Circleville

---

AEF Chapel Field S 100/PK-12
211 Fleury Rd 12566 845-778-1881

**Pine Plains, Dutchess, Pop. 1,324**
Pine Plains Central SD 1,100/K-12
2829 Church St 12567 518-398-7181
Dr. Martin Handler Ed.D., supt. Fax 398-6592
www.ppcsd.org
Stissing Mountain HS 400/9-12
2829 Church St 12567 518-398-7181
Tara Grieb, prin. Fax 398-6592

Stissing Mountain MS 300/6-8
2829 Church St 12567 518-398-7181
James DiDonna, prin. Fax 398-6592

**Pittsford, Monroe, Pop. 1,344**
Pittsford Central SD 5,900/K-12
75 Barker Rd 14534 585-267-1000
Michael Pero, supt. Fax 267-1088
www.pittsfordschools.org
Barker Road MS 700/6-8
75 Barker Rd 14534 585-267-1800
Shana Cutaia, prin. Fax 385-5960
Calkins Road MS 700/6-8
1899 Calkins Rd 14534 585-267-1900
Joshua Walker, prin. Fax 264-0053
Pittsford-Mendon HS 1,000/9-12
472 Mendon Rd 14534 585-267-1600
Karl Thielking, prin. Fax 267-1679
Pittsford Sutherland HS 1,000/9-12
55 Sutherland St 14534 585-267-1100
Brian Weller, prin. Fax 381-7687

**Plainview, Nassau, Pop. 25,853**
Plainview-Old Bethpage Central SD 4,900/K-12
106 Washington Ave 11803 516-434-3000
Dr. Lorna R. Lewis, supt. Fax 937-6303
www.pobschools.org
Mattlin MS 800/5-8
100 Washington Ave 11803 516-434-3250
Christopher Donarummo, prin. Fax 937-6431
Plainview-Old Bethpage/JFK HS 1,500/9-12
50 Kennedy Dr 11803 516-434-3125
James Murray, prin. Fax 937-6433
Plainview-Old Bethpage MS 800/5-8
121 Central Park Rd 11803 516-434-3308
Alice Bowman, prin. Fax 349-4777

**Plattsburgh, Clinton, Pop. 19,572**
Plattsburgh CSD 1,900/PK-12
49 Broad St 12901 518-957-6002
James Short, supt. Fax 561-6605
www.plattscsd.org/
Plattsburgh HS 600/9-12
1 Clifford Dr 12901 518-561-7500
Glenn Hurlock, prin. Fax 561-1895
Stafford MS 400/6-8
15 Broad St 12901 518-563-6800
Jamie Labarge, prin. Fax 563-8520

---

Champlain Valley Physicians Hospital Post-Sec.
75 Beekman St 12901 518-561-2000
New Life Christian Academy 50/PK-10
164 Prospect Ave 12901 518-563-2842
Rev. James Miller, admin. Fax 563-8331
Seton Catholic Central JSHS 100/7-12
206 New York Rd 12903 518-561-4031
Catherine Russell, prin. Fax 563-1193
SUNY Clinton Community College Post-Sec.
136 Clinton Point Dr 12901 518-562-4200
SUNY College at Plattsburgh Post-Sec.
101 Broad St 12901 518-564-2000

**Pleasantville, Westchester, Pop. 6,927**
Pleasantville UFD 1,800/K-12
60 Romer Ave 10570 914-741-1400
Mary Fox-Alter, supt. Fax 741-1499
www.pleasantvilleschools.com
Pleasantville HS 600/9-12
60 Romer Ave 10570 914-741-1420
Joseph Palumbo, prin. Fax 741-2546
Pleasantville MS 600/5-8
40 Romer Ave 10570 914-741-1450
Vivian Ossowski, prin. Fax 741-1476

**Poland, Herkimer, Pop. 505**
Poland Central SD 600/PK-12
PO Box 8 13431 315-826-7900
Laura Dutton, supt. Fax 826-7516
www.polandcs.org
Poland JSHS 300/6-12
PO Box 8 13431 315-826-7900
Fax 826-7516

**Port Byron, Cayuga, Pop. 1,272**
Port Byron Central SD 1,000/K-12
30 Maple Ave 13140 315-776-5728
Neil O'Brien, supt. Fax 776-4050
pbcschools.org
West HS 500/7-12
30 Maple Ave 13140 315-776-5728
James Wood, prin. Fax 776-4050

**Port Chester, Westchester, Pop. 28,517**
Port Chester-Rye UFD 4,200/K-12
PO Box 246 10573 914-934-7900
Dr. Edward Kliszus, supt. Fax 934-0727
www.portchesterschools.org
Port Chester HS 1,200/9-12
1 Tamarack Rd 10573 914-934-7950
Dr. Mitchell Combs, prin. Fax 934-2998
Port Chester MS 900/6-8
113 Bowman Ave 10573 914-934-7930
Patrick Swift, prin. Fax 934-7886

**Port Henry, Essex, Pop. 1,181**
Moriah Central SD 1,100/PK-12
39 Viking Ln 12974 518-546-3301
William Larrow, supt. Fax 546-7895
www.moriahk12.org/
Moriah JSHS 300/7-12
39 Viking Ln 12974 518-546-3301
Alison Burch, prin. Fax 546-7895

**Port Jefferson, Suffolk, Pop. 7,650**
Port Jefferson UFD 1,300/PK-12
550 Scraggy Hill Rd 11777 631-791-4500
Dr. Kenneth Bossert, supt. Fax 476-4409
www.portjeffschools.org
Port Jefferson MS 300/6-8
350 Old Post Rd 11777 631-791-4400
Antonio Santana, prin. Fax 476-4430
Vandermuelen HS 400/9-12
350 Old Post Rd 11777 631-791-4400
Dr. Matthew Murphy, prin. Fax 476-4408

**Port Jefferson Station, Suffolk, Pop. 7,762**
Comsewogue SD 3,600/K-12
290 Norwood Ave 11776 631-474-8100
Joseph Rella, supt. Fax 474-3568
www.comsewogue.k12.ny.us
Comsewogue HS 1,300/9-12
565 Bicycle Path 11776 631-474-8178
Joseph Coniglione, prin. Fax 474-8175
Kennedy MS 800/6-8
200 Jayne Blvd 11776 631-474-8160
Michael Fama, prin. Fax 474-8176

**Port Jervis, Orange, Pop. 8,515**
Port Jervis CSD 2,900/K-12
9 Thompson St 12771 845-858-3100
Thomas Bongiovi, supt. Fax 856-1885
www.pjschools.org
Port Jervis HS 900/9-12
10 Route 209 12771 845-858-3100
Andrew Marotta, prin. Fax 858-2895
Port Jervis MS 500/7-8
118 E Main St 12771 845-858-3100
Jean Lain, prin. Fax 858-2893

**Portville, Cattaraugus, Pop. 993**
Portville Central SD 1,000/PK-12
PO Box 790 14770 585-933-6000
Thomas Simon, supt. Fax 933-6774
www.portville.wnyric.org/
Portville JSHS 400/7-12
PO Box 790 14770 585-933-6705
Lawrence Welty, prin. Fax 933-6774

**Port Washington, Nassau, Pop. 15,596**
Port Washington UFD 5,000/K-12
100 Campus Dr 11050 516-767-5000
Dr. Kathleen Mooney, supt. Fax 767-5007
www.portnet.org
Schreiber HS 1,600/9-12
101 Campus Dr 11050 516-767-5800
Ira Pernick, prin. Fax 767-5807
Weber MS 1,200/6-8
52 Campus Dr 11050 516-767-5500
Christopher Shields, prin. Fax 767-5507

**Potsdam, Saint Lawrence, Pop. 9,246**
Potsdam Central SD 1,400/PK-12
29 Leroy St 13676 315-265-2000
Joann Chambers, supt. Fax 265-2048
www.potsdam.k12.ny.us
Kingston MS 400/5-8
29 Leroy St 13676 315-265-2000
Mark Bennett, prin. Fax 265-8103
Potsdam HS 400/9-12
29 Leroy St 13676 315-265-2000
Fax 265-8134

---

Clarkson University Post-Sec.
8 Clarkson Ave 13676 315-268-6400
SUNY College at Potsdam Post-Sec.
44 Pierrepont Ave 13676 315-267-2000

**Pottersville, Warren, Pop. 420**

---

Word of Life Bible Institute Post-Sec.
PO Box 129 12860 518-494-4723

**Poughkeepsie, Dutchess, Pop. 31,635**
Poughkeepsie CSD 4,100/K-12
11 College Ave 12603 845-451-4900
Dr. Nicole Williams, supt. Fax 451-4955
www.poughkeepsieschools.org/
Poughkeepsie HS 1,200/9-12
70 Forbus St 12603 845-451-4850
Phee Simpson, prin. Fax 451-4853
Poughkeepsie MS 1,000/6-8
55 College Ave 12603 845-451-4800
David Scott, prin. Fax 451-4836

Spackenkill UFD 1,300/K-12
15 Croft Rd 12603 845-463-7800
Dr. Lois Powell Ed.D., supt. Fax 463-7804
www.spackenkillschools.org/
Spackenkill HS 500/9-12
112 Spackenkill Rd 12603 845-463-7810
Steven Malkischer, prin. Fax 463-7826
Todd MS 400/6-8
11 Croft Rd 12603 845-463-7830
Dan Doherty, prin. Fax 463-7832

---

Dutchess Community College Post-Sec.
53 Pendell Rd 12601 845-431-8000
Faith Christian Academy 300/PK-12
25 Golf Club Ln 12601 845-462-0266
Alexander Averin, hdmstr. Fax 462-1561
Marist College Post-Sec.
3399 North Rd 12601 845-575-3000
Oakwood Friends S 100/6-12
22 Spackenkill Rd 12603 845-462-4200
Chad Cianfrani, head sch Fax 462-4251
Our Lady of Lourdes HS 700/9-12
131 Boardman Rd 12603 845-463-0400
Catherine Merryman, prin. Fax 463-0174
Poughkeepsie Day S 300/PK-12
260 Boardman Rd 12603 845-462-7600
Josie Holford, head sch Fax 462-7603
Ridley-Lowell Business & Technical Inst. Post-Sec.
26 S Hamilton St 12601 845-471-0330
Tabernacle Christian Academy 100/K-12
155 Academy St 12601 845-454-2792
Timothy Hostetter, prin. Fax 483-0926

Vassar College Post-Sec.
124 Raymond Ave 12604 845-437-7000

**Prattsburgh, Steuben, Pop. 649**
Prattsburg Central SD 500/PK-12
1 Academy St 14873 607-522-3795
Jeffrey Black, supt. Fax 522-6221
www.prattsburghcsd.org/
Prattsburg Central S 500/PK-12
1 Academy St 14873 607-522-3795
Kory Bay, supt. Fax 522-6221

**Pulaski, Oswego, Pop. 2,352**
Pulaski Central SD 900/PK-12
2 Hinman Rd 13142 315-298-5188
Brian Hartwell, supt. Fax 298-4390
www.pacs.cnyric.org
Pulaski HS 300/9-12
4624 Salina St 13142 315-298-5103
Fax 298-2371
Pulaski MS 300/6-8
4624 Salina St 13142 315-298-6001
Michael Bateson, prin. Fax 298-2371

**Purchase, See Harrison**

---

Keio Academy of New York 300/9-12
3 College Rd 10577 914-694-4825
Fumihiko Kono, hdmstr. Fax 694-4830
Long Island University Post-Sec.
735 Anderson Hill Rd 10577 914-831-2700
Manhattanville College Post-Sec.
2900 Purchase St 10577 914-694-2200
SUNY Purchase College Post-Sec.
735 Anderson Hill Rd 10577 914-251-6000

**Putnam Valley, Putnam**
Putnam Valley Central SD 1,800/K-12
146 Peekskill Hollow Rd 10579 845-528-8143
Dr. Fran Wills, supt. Fax 528-0274
www.pvcsd.org
Putnam Valley HS 600/9-12
146 Peekskill Hollow Rd 10579 845-526-7847
Sandra Intrieri, prin. Fax 528-4456
Putnam Valley MS 600/5-8
142 Peekskill Hollow Rd 10579 845-528-8101
Edward Hallisey, prin. Fax 528-8145

**Queensbury, Warren**
Queensbury UFD 3,500/K-12
429 Aviation Rd 12804 518-824-5600
Dr. Douglas Huntley, supt. Fax 793-4476
www.queensburyschool.org/
Queensbury HS 1,200/9-12
409 Aviation Rd 12804 518-824-4626
Damian Switzer, prin. Fax 824-4680
Queensbury MS 800/6-8
455 Aviation Rd 12804 518-824-3610
Richard Keys, prin. Fax 824-3682

---

SUNY Adirondack Post-Sec.
640 Bay Rd 12804 518-743-2200

**Queens Village, See New York**
NYC Department of Education
Supt. — See New York
Business Technology Early College HS 9-12
23017 Hillside Ave 11427 718-216-3613
Hoa Tu, prin. Fax 216-3616
Nuzzi IS 1,100/6-8
21310 92nd Ave 11428 718-465-0651
Karleen Comrie, prin. Fax 264-1246
Van Buren HS 2,400/9-12
23017 Hillside Ave 11427 718-776-4728
Sam Sochet, prin. Fax 217-6287

**Randolph, Cattaraugus, Pop. 1,268**
Randolph Central SD 1,000/PK-12
18 Main St 14772 716-358-7005
Kimberly Moritz, supt. Fax 358-7072
www.randolphcsd.org/
Randolph JSHS 500/7-12
18 Main St 14772 716-358-7007
Laurie Sanders, prin. Fax 358-7072

**Ravena, Albany, Pop. 3,205**
Ravena-Coeymans-Selkirk Central SD 2,000/PK-12
15 Mountain Rd 12143 518-756-5200
Robert Libby, supt. Fax 767-2644
www.rcscsd.org
Ravena-Coeymans-Selkirk HS 600/9-12
2025 US Route 9W 12143 518-756-5200
Thomas Diacetis, prin. Fax 756-3534
Ravena-Coeymans-Selkirk MS 500/5-8
2025 US Route 9W 12143 518-756-5200
Pam Black, prin. Fax 756-1988

**Red Creek, Wayne, Pop. 530**
Red Creek Central SD 900/K-12
PO Box 190 13143 315-754-2010
David Sholes, supt. Fax 754-8169
www.rccsd.org
Red Creek HS 300/9-12
PO Box 190 13143 315-754-2040
Timothy Gaffney, prin. Fax 754-2068
Red Creek MS 200/6-8
PO Box 190 13143 315-754-2070
Matthew Vanorman, prin. Fax 754-2077

**Red Hook, Dutchess, Pop. 1,942**
Red Hook Central SD 2,100/K-12
9 Mill Rd 12571 845-758-2241
Paul Finch Ed.D., supt. Fax 758-3366
www.redhookcentralschools.org/
Linden Avenue MS 500/6-8
65 W Market St 12571 845-758-2241
Dr. Katie Zahedi, prin. Fax 758-0688
Red Hook HS 700/9-12
103 W Market St 12571 845-758-2241
Roy Paisley, prin. Fax 758-0482

Devereux Center in New York | Post-Sec.
40 Devereux Way 12571 | 845-758-1899

**Rego Park, See New York**
NYC Department of Education
Supt. — See New York
JHS 157 | 1,200/6-9
6355 102nd St 11374 | 718-830-4910
Vincent Suraci, prin. | Fax 830-4993

Metropolitan Learning Institute | Post-Sec.
9777 Queens Blvd Ste 900 11374 | 718-897-0482
Midrash L'man Achai | 100/7-12
9730 Queens Blvd 11374 | 718-544-4875
Rabbi Shmuel Kleinman, prin.
St. Paul's School of Nursing | Post-Sec.
9777 Queens Blvd 11374 | 718-357-0500

**Remsen, Oneida, Pop. 502**
Remsen Central SD | 400/PK-12
PO Box 406 13438 | 315-831-3797
William Crankshaw, supt. | Fax 831-2172
www.remsencsd.org
Remsen JSHS | 200/7-12
PO Box 406 13438 | 315-831-3851
Dale Turner, prin. | Fax 831-2172

**Rensselaer, Rensselaer, Pop. 9,055**
Rensselaer CSD | 1,100/PK-12
25 Van Rensselaer Dr 12144 | 518-465-7509
Sally Ann Shields, supt. | Fax 436-0479
www.rcsd.k12.ny.us
Rensselaer JSHS | 400/7-12
25 Van Rensselaer Dr 12144 | 518-436-8561
Karen Urbanski, prin. | Fax 436-8563

Doane Stuart S | 300/PK-12
199 Washington Ave 12144 | 518-465-5222
Pamela Clarke, head sch | Fax 465-5230

**Retsof, Livingston, Pop. 330**
York Central SD | 800/K-12
PO Box 102 14539 | 585-243-1730
Dr. Daniel Murray, supt. | Fax 243-5269
www.yorkcsd.org/
York MSHS | 400/7-12
PO Box 102 14539 | 585-243-1730
David Sylvester, prin. | Fax 243-5269

**Rhinebeck, Dutchess, Pop. 2,623**
Rhinebeck Central SD | 1,200/K-12
PO Box 351 12572 | 845-871-5520
Joseph Phelan, supt. | Fax 876-4276
www.rhinebeckcsd.org/
Bulkeley MS | 300/6-8
PO Box 351 12572 | 845-871-5500
John Kemnitzer, prin. | Fax 871-5553
Rhinebeck HS | 400/9-12
PO Box 351 12572 | 845-871-5500
Dr. Edwin Davenport, prin. | Fax 876-8755

**Richfield Springs, Otsego, Pop. 1,252**
Richfield Springs Central SD | 500/PK-12
PO Box 631 13439 | 315-858-0610
Frank D. Myers, supt. | Fax 858-2440
www.richfieldcsd.org
Richfield Springs Central S | 500/PK-12
PO Box 631 13439 | 315-858-0610
Therijo Climenhaga, prin. | Fax 858-2440

**Richmond Hill, See New York**
NYC Department of Education
Supt. — See New York
Epic HS - North | 9-12
9425 117th St, S Richmond Hl NY 11419
David Weinberg, prin. | 718-935-3597
Richmond Hill HS | 2,500/9-12
8930 114th St 11418 | 718-846-3335
Neil Ganesh, prin. | Fax 847-0980

Yeshiva Shaar HaTorah - Grodno | Post-Sec.
8396 117th St 11418 | 718-846-1940

**Richmondville, Schoharie, Pop. 910**
Cobleskill-Richmondville Central SD
Supt. — See Cobleskill
Cobleskill-Richmondville HS | 600/9-12
1353 State Route 7 12149 | 518-234-3565
Melissa Ausfeld, prin. | Fax 234-1018

**Ridgewood, See New York**
NYC Department of Education
Supt. — See New York
Cleveland HS | 2,000/9-12
2127 Himrod St 11385 | 718-381-9600
Denise Vittor, prin. | Fax 417-8457
IS 77 | 1,100/6-8
976 Seneca Ave 11385 | 718-366-7120
Joseph Miller, prin. | Fax 456-9512
IS 93 | 1,300/6-8
6656 Forest Ave 11385 | 718-821-4882
Edward Santos, prin. | Fax 456-9521

Midway Paris Beauty School | Post-Sec.
5440 Myrtle Ave 11385 | 718-418-2790

**Riverdale, See New York**

College of Mount Saint Vincent | Post-Sec.
6301 Riverdale Ave 10471 | 718-405-3267
Manhattan College | Post-Sec.
4513 Manhattan College Pkwy 10471 | 718-862-8000
Yeshiva of Telshe Alumni | 100/9-12
4904 Independence Ave 10471 | 718-601-3523
Yeshiva Ohavei Torah of Riverdale | 100/9-12
450 W 250th St 10471 | 718-432-2600

**Riverhead, Suffolk, Pop. 12,979**
Riverhead Central SD | 5,000/K-12
700 Osborn Ave 11901 | 631-369-6700
Nancy Carney, supt. | Fax 369-6816
www.riverhead.net
Riverhead HS | 1,500/9-12
700 Harrison Ave 11901 | 631-369-6723
Charles Regan, prin. | Fax 369-5164
Riverhead MS | 700/7-8
600 Harrison Ave 11901 | 631-369-6759
Andrea Pekar, prin. | Fax 369-6829

Central Suffolk Hospital | Post-Sec.
1300 Roanoke Ave 11901 | 631-548-6000
Long Island University | Post-Sec.
121 Speonk Riverhead Rd 11901 | 631-287-8010
McGann-Mercy HS | 500/7-12
1225 Ostrander Ave 11901 | 631-727-5900
Carl Semmler, prin. | Fax 369-7328
Suffolk County Community College | Post-Sec.
121 Speonk Riverhead Rd 11901 | 631-548-2500

**Rochester, Monroe, Pop. 203,996**
Brighton Central SD | 3,500/K-12
2035 Monroe Ave 14618 | 585-242-5200
Dr. Kevin McGowan, supt. | Fax 242-5164
www.bcsd.org
Brighton HS | 1,200/9-12
1150 Winton Rd S 14618 | 585-242-5000
Thomas Hall, prin. | Fax 242-7364
Twelve Corners MS | 800/6-8
2643 Elmwood Ave 14618 | 585-242-5100
Rob Thomas, prin. | Fax 242-2540

East Irondequoit Central SD | 3,000/K-12
600 Pardee Rd 14609 | 585-339-1210
Susan Allen, supt. | Fax 339-1219
www.eastiron.org
East Irondequoit MS | 700/6-8
155 Densmore Rd 14609 | 585-339-1400
Lori Garsin, prin. | Fax 339-1409
Eastridge HS | 1,000/9-12
2350 E Ridge Rd 14622 | 585-339-1450
Mary Grow, prin. | Fax 339-1459

Gates-Chili Central SD | 4,200/K-12
3 Spartan Way 14624 | 585-247-5050
Kimberle Ward, supt. | Fax 340-1072
www.gateschili.org
Gates-Chili HS | 1,500/9-12
1 Spartan Way 14624 | 585-247-5050
Timothy Clasgens, prin. | Fax 340-5518
Gates-Chili MS | 1,000/6-8
2 Spartan Way 14624 | 585-247-5050
Dr. Lisa Buckshaw, prin. | Fax 340-5532

Greece Central SD | 10,500/PK-12
750 Maiden Ln 14615 | 585-966-2000
Kathleen Graupman, supt. | Fax 581-8203
www.greece.k12.ny.us
Arcadia HS | 1,100/9-12
120 Island Cottage Rd 14612 | 585-966-3000
Lesley Flick, prin. | Fax 966-3039
Arcadia MS | 900/6-8
130 Island Cottage Rd 14612 | 585-966-3300
Linda Pickering, prin. | Fax 966-3339
Athena HS | 1,200/9-12
800 Long Pond Rd 14612 | 585-966-4000
David Richardson, prin. | Fax 966-4039
Athena MS | 800/6-8
800 Long Pond Rd 14612 | 585-966-8800
Jason Fulkerson, prin. | Fax 966-4039
Odyssey Academy | 800/Alt
750 Maiden Ln 14615 | 585-966-5500
Toyia Wilson, prin. | Fax 966-5539
Olympia HS | 1,000/9-12
1139 Maiden Ln 14615 | 585-966-5000
Christina Sloane, prin. | Fax 966-5039

Penfield Central SD | 4,500/K-12
2590 Atlantic Ave 14625 | 585-249-5700
Dr. Thomas K. Putnam Ed.D., supt. | Fax 248-8412
www.penfield.edu
Other Schools – See Penfield

Rochester CSD | 26,700/PK-12
131 W Broad St 14614 | 585-262-8100
Dr. Bolgen Vargas, supt. | Fax 262-8381
www.rcsdk12.org
All City HS | 1,000/Alt
175 Martin St 14605 | 585-458-2110
Armando Ramirez, prin. | Fax 277-0077
Charlotte HS | 600/10-12
4115 Lake Ave 14612 | 585-663-7070
Michael Allen, prin. | Fax 621-0275
East HS | 1,700/6-12
1801 E Main St 14609 | 585-288-3130
Anibal Soler, prin. | Fax 654-1066
Edison Career and Technology HS | 400/9-12
655 Colfax St 14606 | 585-324-9700
Brad Zilliox, prin.
Integrated Arts & Technology HS | 200/7-12
950 Norton St 14621 | 585-324-3750
Kevin Klein, prin.
Leadership Academy for Young Men | 100/7-12
4115 Lake Ave 14612 | 585-324-7760
Wakili Moore, prin.
Monroe HS | 1,200/7-12
180 Ridgeway Ave 14615 | 585-232-1530
Vicma Ramos, prin. | Fax 262-8965
Northeast College HS | 300/9-12
940 Fernwood Park 14609 | 585-324-9273
Dr. Linus Guillory, prin.
Northwest JHS at Douglass | 500/7-8
940 Fernwood Park 14609 | 585-324-9289
Barbara Fagan-Zelazny, prin.
Rochester Early College International HS | 200/9-12
200 Genesee St 14611 | 585-324-9010
Sandra Jordan, prin.

School of the Arts | 1,100/7-12
45 Prince St 14607 | 585-242-7682
Brenda Pacheco, prin. | Fax 256-6580
School Without Walls Commencement Acad | 300/9-12
480 Broadway 14607 | 585-546-6732
Idonia Owens, prin. | Fax 262-8947
Vanguard Collegiate HS | 200/9-12
950 Norton St 14621 | 585-324-3760
Bonnie Atkins, prin.
Wilson Magnet HS Commencement Academy | 1,100/9-12
501 Genesee St 14611 | 585-328-3440
Uma Mehta, prin. | Fax 464-6153
World of Inquiry S 58 | 500/K-12
200 University Ave 14605 | 585-325-6170
Sheelarani Webster, prin. | Fax 262-8964

West Irondequoit Central SD | 3,700/K-12
321 List Ave 14617 | 585-342-5500
Jeffrey Crane, supt. | Fax 266-1556
www.westirondequoit.org
Dake MS | 600/7-8
350 Cooper Rd 14617 | 585-342-2140
Matthew Schrage, prin. | Fax 336-3034
Irondequoit HS | 1,300/9-12
260 Cooper Rd 14617 | 585-336-2914
Douglas Lauf, prin. | Fax 336-2929

Allendale Columbia S | 300/PK-12
519 Allens Creek Rd 14618 | 585-381-4560
Michael Gee, head sch | Fax 383-1191
Aquinas Institute | 900/6-12
1127 Dewey Ave 14613 | 585-254-2020
Theodore Mancini, prin. | Fax 254-7401
Bishop Kearney HS | 500/6-12
125 Kings Hwy S 14617 | 585-342-4000
| Fax 342-4694
Bryant & Stratton College | Post-Sec.
854 Long Pond Rd 14612 | 585-720-0660
Bryant & Stratton College | Post-Sec.
1225 Jeffson Rd 14623 | 585-292-5627
Colgate Rochester Crozer Divinity School | Post-Sec.
1100 Goodman St S 14620 | 585-271-1320
Continental School | Post-Sec.
633 Jefferson Rd 14623 | 585-272-8060
David Hochstein School of Music & Dance | Post-Sec.
50 Plymouth Ave N 14614 | 585-454-4596
Destiny Christian S | 100/PK-12
1876 Elmwood Ave 14620 | 585-473-1680
Lavonda Lofton, prin. | Fax 473-2112
Everest Institute | Post-Sec.
1630 Portland Ave 14621 | 585-266-0430
Harley S | 500/PK-12
1981 Clover St 14618 | 585-442-1770
Ward Ghory Ed.D., head sch | Fax 442-5758
McQuaid Jesuit HS | 800/6-12
1800 Clinton Ave S 14618 | 585-473-1130
Adam Baber, prin. | Fax 256-6171
Monroe Community College | Post-Sec.
1000 E Henrietta Rd 14623 | 585-292-2000
Nazareth College of Rochester | Post-Sec.
4245 East Ave 14618 | 585-389-2525
Northeastern Seminary | Post-Sec.
2265 Westside Dr 14624 | 585-594-6800
Northstar Christian Academy | 300/PK-12
332 Spencerport Rd 14606 | 585-429-5530
Onondaga School of Therapeutic Massage | Post-Sec.
302 Goodman St N Ste 200 14607 | 585-241-0070
Ora Academy | 50/9-12
139 Winton Rd S 14610 | 585-271-8711
Rabbi Eliezer Lehrer, hdmstr. | Fax 271-8158
Our Lady of Mercy HS | 700/6-12
1437 Blossom Rd 14610 | 585-288-7120
Terence Quinn, prin. | Fax 288-7966
Roberts Wesleyan College | Post-Sec.
2301 Westside Dr 14624 | 585-594-6000
Rochester General Hospital | Post-Sec.
1425 Portland Ave 14621 | 585-338-4430
Rochester Institute of Technology | Post-Sec.
1 Lomb Memorial Dr 14623 | 585-475-2411
Rochester School for the Deaf | Post-Sec.
1545 Saint Paul St 14621 | 585-544-1240
St. Bernard's Sch of Theology & Ministry | Post-Sec.
120 French Rd 14618 | 585-271-3657
St. John Fisher College | Post-Sec.
3690 East Ave 14618 | 585-385-8000
Shear Ego Intl School of Hair Design | Post-Sec.
525 Titus Ave 14617 | 585-342-0070
Siena Catholic Academy | 300/6-8
2617 East Ave 14610 | 585-381-1220
Martin Kilbridge, prin. | Fax 381-1223
Talmudical Institute of Upstate New York | Post-Sec.
769 Park Ave 14607 | 585-473-2810
Talmudical Institute of Upstate New York | 50/9-12
769 Park Ave 14607 | 585-473-2810
University of Rochester | Post-Sec.
500 Joseph C Wilson Blvd 14627 | 585-275-2121

**Rockaway Park, See New York**
NYC Department of Education
Supt. — See New York
Channel View S for Research | 600/6-12
10000 Beach Channel Dr 11694 | 718-634-1970
Patricia Tubridy, prin. | Fax 634-2896
Rockaway Collegiate HS | 9-12
10000 Beach Channel Dr 11694 | 718-634-3031
Carol Ying, prin. | Fax 634-3043
Rockaway Park HS for Environmental Sust | 100/9-12
10000 Beach Channel Dr 11694 | 718-318-6170
Jennifer Connolly, prin. | Fax 318-6176
Scholars Academy | 1,100/6-12
320 Beach 104th St 11694 | 718-474-6918
Brian O'Connell, prin. | Fax 945-8958
Waterside S for Leadership | 200/6-8
190 Beach 110th St 11694 | 718-634-1128
Linda Munro, prin. | Fax 634-1185

**Rockville Centre, Nassau, Pop. 23,734**
Rockville Centre UFD 3,500/K-12
128 Shepherd St 11570 516-255-8957
Dr. William H. Johnson, supt. Fax 255-8810
www.rvcschools.org
South Side HS 1,100/9-12
140 Shepherd St 11570 516-255-8944
John Murphy, prin. Fax 766-7934
South Side MS 800/6-8
67 Hillside Ave 11570 516-255-8976
Shelagh McGinn, prin. Fax 763-0914

Mercy Medical Center Post-Sec.
PO Box 9024 11571 516-705-2525
Molloy College Post-Sec.
PO Box 5002 11571 516-323-4000

**Rocky Point, Suffolk, Pop. 13,836**
Rocky Point UFD 3,300/K-12
90 Rocky Point Yaphank Rd 11778 631-744-1600
Dr. Michael Ring, supt. Fax 849-7557
www.rockypointschools.org
Rocky Point HS 1,000/9-12
82 Rocky Point Yaphank Rd 11778 631-744-1604
John DeBenedetto, prin. Fax 591-0220
Rocky Point MS 800/6-8
76 Rocky Point Yaphank Rd 11778 631-744-1603
Scott O'Brien Ed.D., prin. Fax 886-0000

**Rome, Oneida, Pop. 32,943**
Rome CSD 5,200/PK-12
409 Bell Rd S 13440 315-338-6500
Jeffrey P. Simons, supt. Fax 334-7409
www.romecsd.org
Rome Free Academy 1,600/9-12
95 Dart Cir 13441 315-334-7203
Mark Benson, prin. Fax 334-7236
Strough MS 800/7-8
801 Laurel St 13440 315-338-5201
Tracy O'Rourke, prin. Fax 334-7465

New York State School for the Deaf Post-Sec.
401 Turin St 13440

**Romulus, Seneca, Pop. 400**
Romulus Central SD 400/PK-12
5705 State Route 96 14541 866-810-0345
Martin Rotz, supt. Fax 869-5961
www.rcs.k12.ny.us
Romulus Central HS 200/7-12
5705 State Route 96 14541 866-810-0345
Lynn Rhone, prin. Fax 869-5961

**Ronkonkoma, Suffolk, Pop. 18,816**
Connetquot Central SD
Supt. — See Bohemia
Ronkonkoma MS 700/6-8
501 Peconic St 11779 631-467-6000
Charles Morea, prin. Fax 467-6003

Sachem Central SD 14,400/K-12
51 School St 11779 631-471-1336
James Nolan, supt. Fax 471-1341
www.sachem.edu
Other Schools – See Farmingville, Holbrook, Holtsville, Lake Ronkonkoma

**Roosevelt, Nassau, Pop. 15,891**
Roosevelt UFD 2,600/PK-12
240 Denton Pl 11575 516-345-7000
Dr. Deborah Wortham, supt. Fax 345-7326
www.rooseveltufsd.org
Roosevelt HS 800/9-12
1 Wagner Ave 11575 516-345-7200
Shawn Farnum, prin. Fax 345-7290
Roosevelt MS 400/7-8
335 E Clinton Ave 11575 516-345-7700
Nateasha McVea, prin. Fax 345-7791

**Roscoe, Sullivan, Pop. 539**
Roscoe Central SD 300/PK-12
PO Box 429 12776 607-498-4126
John Evans, supt. Fax 498-5609
www.roscoe.k12.ny.us
Roscoe Central S 300/PK-12
PO Box 429 12776 607-498-4126
Janice Phillips, prin. Fax 498-6015

**Roslyn, Nassau, Pop. 2,718**
Roslyn UFD 3,300/PK-12
PO Box 367 11576 516-801-5000
Dr. Dan Brenner, supt. Fax 801-5008
www.roslynschools.org
Other Schools – See Roslyn Heights

Mesivta of Roslyn 50/9-12
2 Shelter Rock Rd 11576 516-877-2131

**Roslyn Heights, Nassau, Pop. 6,383**
Roslyn UFD
Supt. — See Roslyn
Roslyn HS 1,100/9-12
475 Round Hill Rd 11577 516-801-5100
Scott Andrews, prin. Fax 801-5108
Roslyn MS 800/6-8
375 Locust Ln 11577 516-801-5200
Jack Palmadesso, prin. Fax 801-5208

**Roxbury, Delaware**
Roxbury Central SD 300/PK-12
53729 State Highway 30 12474 607-326-4151
Thomas O'Brien, supt. Fax 326-4154
www.roxburycs.org
Roxbury Central S 300/PK-12
53729 State Highway 30 12474 607-326-4151
Fax 326-4154

**Rushville, Ontario, Pop. 661**
Marcus Whitman Central SD 1,200/K-12
4100 Baldwin Rd 14544 585-554-4848
Jeramy Clingerman, supt. Fax 554-4882
www.mwcsd.org
Whitman HS 400/9-12
4100 Baldwin Rd 14544 585-554-6441
Jennifer Taft, prin. Fax 554-5201
Whitman MS 300/6-8
4100 Baldwin Rd 14544 585-554-6442
Clayton Cole, prin. Fax 554-3414

**Rye, Westchester, Pop. 15,489**
Rye CSD 3,200/K-12
411 Theodore Fremd Ste 100S 10580 914-967-6100
Dr. Frank Alvarez, supt. Fax 967-6957
www.ryeschools.org/
Rye HS 900/9-12
1 Parsons St 10580 914-967-6100
Patricia Taylor, prin. Fax 967-4380
Rye MS 800/6-8
3 Parsons St 10580 914-967-6100
Dr. Ann Edwards, prin. Fax 921-6189
Rye S of Leadership Alt
324 Midland Ave 10580 914-760-1462
Jennifer Fall, dir.

Rye Country Day S 900/PK-12
Cedar St 10580 914-967-1417
Scott Nelson, hdmstr. Fax 967-1418
School of the Holy Child 300/5-12
2225 Westchester Ave 10580 914-967-5622
William Hambleton, head sch Fax 967-7210

**Rye Brook, Westchester, Pop. 9,207**
Blind Brook-Rye UFD 1,500/K-12
390 N Ridge St 10573 914-937-3600
Jonathan Ross Ed.D., supt. Fax 937-5871
www.blindbrook.org
Blind Brook HS 400/9-12
840 King St 10573 914-937-3600
Patricia Lambert, prin. Fax 937-4509
Blind Brook MS 400/6-8
840 King St 10573 914-937-3600
Todd Richard, prin. Fax 937-4509

**Sackets Harbor, Jefferson, Pop. 1,431**
Sackets Harbor Central SD 500/K-12
PO Box 290 13685 315-646-3575
Frederick Hall, supt. Fax 646-1038
www.sacketspatriots.org
Sackets Harbor Central S 500/K-12
PO Box 290 13685 315-646-3575
Jennifer Gaffney, prin. Fax 646-1038

**Sag Harbor, Suffolk, Pop. 2,139**
Sag Harbor UFD 1,000/PK-12
200 Jermain Ave 11963 631-725-5300
Catherine Barber-Graves, supt. Fax 725-5330
www.sagharborschools.org
Pierson MSHS 500/6-12
200 Jermain Ave 11963 631-725-5302
Jeff Nichols, prin. Fax 725-5314

**Saint Albans, See New York**
NYC Department of Education
Supt. — See New York
Pathways College Preparatory S 600/6-12
10989 204th St 11412 718-454-4957
Kimberly Mitchell, prin. Fax 454-4892
IS 192 600/6-8
10989 204th St 11412 718-479-5540
Harriett Diaz, prin. Fax 217-4645

**Saint Bonaventure, Cattaraugus, Pop. 2,013**

St. Bonaventure University Post-Sec.
3261 W State Rd 14778 716-375-2000

**Saint James, Suffolk, Pop. 13,215**
Smithtown Central SD
Supt. — See Smithtown
Nesaquake MS 800/6-8
479 Edgewood Ave 11780 631-382-5100
Kevin Simmons, prin. Fax 382-5107
Smithtown HS East 1,800/9-12
10 School St 11780 631-382-2700
Edwin Thompson, prin. Fax 382-2707

Knox S 100/6-12
541 Long Beach Rd 11780 631-686-1600
Kristen B. Tillona, head sch Fax 686-1650

**Saint Johnsville, Montgomery, Pop. 1,719**
Oppenheim-Ephratah-St. Jhnsvll Cntrl SD 600/PK-12
44 Center St 13452 518-568-2011
David Halloran, supt. Fax 568-2797
www.oesj.org
Oppenheim-Ephratah-St. Johnsville JSHS 100/7-12
44 Center St 13452 518-568-2011
David Slater, prin. Fax 568-2797

**Saint Regis Falls, Franklin, Pop. 456**
Saint Regis Falls Central SD 300/PK-12
PO Box 309 12980 518-856-9421
Alan Tessier, supt. Fax 856-0142
stregisfallscsd.org/
Saint Regis Falls S 300/PK-12
PO Box 309 12980 518-856-9421
Marc Czadzeck, prin. Fax 856-0142

**Salamanca, Cattaraugus, Pop. 5,605**
Salamanca City Central SD 1,000/PK-12
50 Iroquois Dr 14779 716-945-2400
Robert Breidenstein, supt. Fax 945-3964
www.salamancany.org/
Salamanca JSHS 400/7-12
50 Iroquois Dr 14779 716-945-2404
Charles Crist, prin. Fax 945-5983

**Salem, Washington, Pop. 930**
Salem Central SD 500/K-12
PO Box 517 12865 518-854-7855
Dr. David GLover, supt. Fax 854-3957
salemcsd.org/
Salem JSHS 300/7-12
PO Box 517 12865 518-854-7600
Jared Davis, prin. Fax 854-3957

**Sanborn, Niagara, Pop. 1,620**
Niagara-Wheatfield Central SD
Supt. — See Niagara Falls
Niagara-Wheatfield HS 1,300/9-12
2292 Saunders Settlement Rd 14132 716-215-3100
Tim Carter, prin. Fax 215-3125
Town MS 900/6-8
2292 Saunders Settlement Rd 14132 716-215-3150
Dr. Laura Palka, prin. Fax 215-3160

SUNY Niagara County Community College Post-Sec.
3111 Saunders Settlement Rd 14132 716-614-6200

**Sandy Creek, Oswego, Pop. 769**
Sandy Creek Central SD 900/PK-12
PO Box 248 13145 315-387-3445
Stewart Amell, supt. Fax 387-2196
www.sccs.cnyric.org/
Sandy Creek HS 300/9-12
PO Box 248 13145 315-387-3445
Maureen Shiel, prin. Fax 387-2196
Sandy Creek MS 200/6-8
PO Box 248 13145 315-387-3445
Carolyn Shirley, prin. Fax 387-2196

**Saranac, Clinton**
Saranac Central SD
Supt. — See Dannemora
Saranac HS 600/9-12
PO Box 8 12981 518-565-5800
Steven Grenville, prin. Fax 565-5809
Saranac MS 300/6-8
PO Box 8 12981 518-565-5700
Katie McNeil, prin. Fax 565-5706

**Saranac Lake, Franklin, Pop. 5,317**
Saranac Lake Central SD 1,300/K-12
79 Canaras Ave 12983 518-891-5460
Diane Fox, supt. Fax 891-5140
saranaclakecs.org
Saranac Lake HS 500/9-12
79 Canaras Ave 12983 518-891-4450
Joshua Dann, prin. Fax 891-6813
Saranac Lake MS 300/6-8
79 Canaras Ave 12983 518-891-4221
Bruce VanWeelden, prin. Fax 891-6615

SUNY North Country Community College Post-Sec.
PO Box 89 12983 518-891-2915

**Saratoga Springs, Saratoga, Pop. 26,062**
Saratoga Springs CSD 6,600/K-12
3 Blue Streak Blvd 12866 518-583-4700
Michael Piccirillo, supt. Fax 584-6624
www.saratogaschools.org
Maple Ave MS 1,700/6-8
515 Maple Ave 12866 518-587-4551
Stuart Byrne, prin. Fax 587-5759
Saratoga Springs HS 2,000/9-12
1 Blue Streak Blvd 12866 518-587-6690
Brett Miller, prin. Fax 583-1671

Saratoga Central Catholic HS 200/6-12
247 Broadway 12866 518-587-7070
Steve Lombard, prin. Fax 587-0678
Skidmore College Post-Sec.
815 N Broadway 12866 518-580-5000
SUNY Empire State College Post-Sec.
2 Union Ave 12866 518-587-2100
Waldorf S of Saratoga Springs 200/PK-12
122 Regent St 12866 518-587-0549

**Saugerties, Ulster, Pop. 3,876**
Saugerties Central SD 2,400/K-12
PO Box A 12477 845-247-6550
Seth Turner, supt. Fax 246-8364
www.saugerties.k12.ny.us
Saugerties JSHS 1,000/7-12
PO Box A 12477 845-247-6650
Thomas Averill, prin. Fax 246-4312

Woodstock Day S 200/PK-12
1430 Glasco Tpke 12477 845-246-3744
Dr. James Handlin, hdmstr. Fax 246-0053

**Sauquoit, Oneida**
Sauquoit Valley Central SD 1,000/K-12
2601 Oneida St 13456 315-839-6311
Ronald Wheelock, supt. Fax 839-5352
www.svcsd.org
Sauquoit Valley HS 400/9-12
2601 Oneida St 13456 315-839-6316
Zane Mahar, prin. Fax 839-6397
Sauquoit Valley MS 200/6-8
2601 Oneida St 13456 315-839-6371
Peter Madden, prin. Fax 839-6390

**Sayville, Suffolk, Pop. 16,715**
Sayville UFD 3,200/K-12
99 Greeley Ave 11782 631-244-6510
Dr. Walter Schartner, supt. Fax 244-6504
www.sayvilleschools.org
Sayville MS 700/6-8
291 Johnson Ave 11782 631-244-6650
Thomas Murray, prin. Fax 244-6655
Other Schools – See West Sayville

**Scarsdale, Westchester, Pop. 16,786**
Edgemont UFD 1,900/K-12
300 White Oak Ln 10583 914-472-7768
Dr. Victoria S. Kniewel, supt. Fax 472-6846
www.edgemont.org/
Edgemont JSHS 900/7-12
200 White Oak Ln 10583 914-725-1500
Devan Ganeshananthan, prin. Fax 725-1057

Scarsdale UFD 4,700/K-12
2 Brewster Rd Ste 2 10583 914-721-2410
Dr. Thomas Hagerman, supt. Fax 722-2822
www.scarsdaleschools.k12.ny.us
Scarsdale HS 1,400/9-12
1057 Post Rd 10583 914-721-2450
Kenneth Bonamo, prin. Fax 721-2549
Scarsdale MS 1,200/6-8
134 Mamaroneck Rd 10583 914-721-2600
Michael McDermott, prin. Fax 721-2655

**Schaghticoke, Rensselaer, Pop. 588**
Hoosic Valley Central SD 1,100/K-12
2 Pleasant Ave 12154 518-753-4450
Amy Goodell, supt. Fax 753-7665
www.hoosicvalley.k12.ny.us
Hoosic Valley JSHS 400/7-12
1548 State Route 67 12154 518-753-4432
G. Michael Apostol, prin. Fax 753-7491

**Schenectady, Schenectady, Pop. 59,889**
Mohonasen Central SD 2,900/K-12
2072 Curry Rd 12303 518-356-8200
Dr. Kathleen Spring, supt. Fax 356-8247
www.mohonasen.org
Draper MS 700/6-8
2070 Curry Rd 12303 518-356-8350
Debra Male, prin. Fax 356-8359
Mohonasen HS 1,000/9-12
2072 Curry Rd 12303 518-356-8300
David Collins, prin. Fax 356-8309

Niskayuna Central SD 4,100/K-12
1239 Van Antwerp Rd 12309 518-377-4666
Dr. Cosimo Tangorra Ed.D., supt. Fax 377-4074
www.niskyschools.org
Iroquois MS 600/6-8
2495 Rosendale Rd 12309 518-377-2233
Vicki Wyld, prin. Fax 377-2219
Niskayuna HS 1,400/9-12
1626 Balltown Rd 12309 518-382-2511
John Rickert, prin. Fax 382-2539
Van Antwerp MS 400/6-8
2253 Story Ave 12309 518-370-1243
Luke Rakoczy, prin. Fax 370-4610

Schalmont Central SD 1,900/K-12
4 Sabre Dr 12306 518-355-9200
Carol Pallas, supt. Fax 355-9203
www.schalmont.org
Schalmont HS 600/9-12
1 Sabre Dr 12306 518-355-6110
Imran Abbasi, prin. Fax 355-8720
Schalmont MS 600/5-8
2 Sabre Dr 12306 518-355-6255
Fax 355-5329

Schenectady CSD 8,800/PK-12
108 Education Dr 12303 518-370-8100
Laurence Spring, supt. Fax 370-8173
www.schenectady.k12.ny.us
Mont Pleasant MS 600/7-8
1121 Forest Rd 12303 518-370-8160
Kiante Jones, prin. Fax 881-3562
Schenectady HS 2,700/9-12
1445 The Plz 12308 518-881-2044
Diane Wilkinson, prin. Fax 881-3802
Steinmetz Career and Leadership Academy 9-12
880 Oakwood Ave 12303 518-881-2030
Gregory Fields, prin. Fax 881-3602

---

Mid-America Baptist Theological Seminary Post-Sec.
2810 Curry Rd 12303 518-355-4000
Modern Welding School Post-Sec.
1842 State St 12304 518-374-1216
Notre Dame-Bishop Gibbons HS 300/6-12
2600 Albany St 12304 518-393-3131
Peter Fusco, prin. Fax 370-3817
SUNY Schenectady County Community Coll. Post-Sec.
78 Washington Ave 12305 518-381-1200
The Belanger School of Nursing Post-Sec.
650 McClellan St 12304 518-243-4471
Troy School of Beauty Culture Post-Sec.
101 Deanna Ct 12309 518-273-7741
Union College Post-Sec.
807 Union St 12308 518-388-6000
Union Graduate College Post-Sec.
80 Nott Ter 12308 518-631-9900

**Schenevus, Otsego, Pop. 543**
Schenevus Central SD 400/K-12
159 Main St 12155 607-638-5530
Thomas Jennings, supt. Fax 638-5600
www.schenevuscs.org/
Schenevus Central S 400/K-12
159 Main St 12155 607-638-5881
Coleen Lewis, prin. Fax 638-5600

**Schoharie, Schoharie, Pop. 912**
Schoharie Central SD 800/K-12
PO Box 430 12157 518-295-6600
Kathryn Gerbino, supt. Fax 295-8178
www.schoharie.k12.ny.us
Schoharie JSHS 400/7-12
PO Box 430 12157 518-295-6601
Stacey DeLaney, prin. Fax 295-8161

**Schroon Lake, Essex, Pop. 817**
Schroon Lake Central SD 200/K-12
PO Box 338 12870 518-532-7164
Stephen Gratto, supt. Fax 532-0284
www.schroonschool.org
Schroon Lake Central S 200/K-12
PO Box 338 12870 518-532-7164
Stephen Gratto, prin. Fax 532-0284

**Schuylerville, Saratoga, Pop. 1,376**
Schuylerville Central SD 1,700/K-12
14 Spring St 12871 518-695-3255
Ryan Sherman Ed.D., supt. Fax 695-6491
www.schuylervilleschools.org
Schuylerville HS 600/9-12
14 Spring St 12871 518-695-3255
Matthew Sickles, prin. Fax 695-3103
Schuylerville MS 500/6-8
14 Spring St 12871 518-695-3255
Mary Kate Elsworth, prin. Fax 695-6491

**Scio, Allegany, Pop. 604**
Scio Central SD 400/PK-12
3968 Washington St 14880 585-593-5076
Gregory L. Hardy, supt. Fax 593-3468
scio.schooltools.us/
Scio Central S 400/PK-12
3968 Washington St 14880 585-593-5510
Nancy Sampson, prin. Fax 593-0653

**Scotia, Schenectady, Pop. 7,607**
Scotia-Glenville Central SD 2,700/K-12
900 Preddice Pkwy 12302 518-382-1215
Susan Swartz, supt. Fax 386-4336
www.sgcsd.net
Scotia-Glenville HS 900/9-12
1 Tartan Way 12302 518-382-1231
Peter Bednarek, prin. Fax 386-4303
Scotia-Glenville MS 600/6-8
10 Prestige Pkwy 12302 518-382-1263
Robert Cosmer, prin. Fax 386-4303

---

Mekeel Christian Academy 300/PK-12
36-38 Sacandaga Rd 12302 518-370-4272
W. Chad Bowman, head sch Fax 370-4778

**Scottsville, Monroe, Pop. 1,964**
Wheatland-Chili Central SD 700/K-12
13 Beckwith Ave 14546 585-889-6246
Dr. Deborah Leh, supt. Fax 889-6284
www.wheatland.k12.ny.us
Wheatland-Chili MSHS 400/6-12
940 North Rd 14546 585-889-6245
Eric Windover, prin. Fax 889-6217

**Sea Cliff, Nassau, Pop. 4,948**
North Shore Central SD 2,800/K-12
112 Franklin Ave 11579 516-277-7800
Dr. Edward Melnick, supt. Fax 277-7801
www.northshoreschools.org
Other Schools – See Glen Head

**Seaford, Nassau, Pop. 15,154**
Seaford UFD 2,500/K-12
1600 Washington Ave 11783 516-592-4000
Brian Conboy, supt. Fax 592-4049
www.seaford.k12.ny.us
Seaford HS 800/9-12
1575 Seamans Neck Rd 11783 516-592-4300
Scott Bersin, prin. Fax 592-4399
Seaford MS 600/6-8
3940 Sunset Ave 11783 516-592-4200
Dan Smith, prin. Fax 592-4299

**Selden, Suffolk, Pop. 19,540**
Middle Country Central SD
Supt. — See Centereach
Newfield HS 1,700/9-12
145 Marshall Dr 11784 631-285-8300
Scott Graviano, prin. Fax 285-8301

---

SUNY Suffolk County Community College Post-Sec.
533 College Rd 11784 631-451-4000

**Seneca Falls, Seneca, Pop. 6,593**
Seneca Falls Central SD 1,300/K-12
PO Box 268 13148 315-568-5500
Robert McKeveny, supt. Fax 712-0535
www.sfcs.k12.ny.us/
Mynderse Academy 400/9-12
105 Troy St 13148 315-568-5500
Andrew Doell, prin. Fax 712-0523
Seneca Falls MS 300/6-8
95 Troy St 13148 315-568-5500
Kevin Rhinehart, prin. Fax 712-0524

---

New York Chiropractic College Post-Sec.
2360 State Route 89 13148 315-568-3000

**Setauket, Suffolk, Pop. 15,248**
Three Village Central SD
Supt. — See Stony Brook
Gelinas JHS 900/7-9
25 Mud Rd 11733 631-730-4700
William Bernhard, prin. Fax 730-4706

**Sharon Springs, Schoharie, Pop. 550**
Sharon Springs Central SD 300/K-12
PO Box 218 13459 518-284-2266
Patterson Green, supt. Fax 284-9033
www.sharonsprings.org/
Sharon Springs Central S 300/K-12
PO Box 218 13459 518-284-2267
Patterson Green, prin. Fax 284-9075

**Shelter Island, Suffolk, Pop. 1,316**
Shelter Island UFD 200/K-12
PO Box 2015 11964 631-749-0302
Leonard Skuggevik, supt. Fax 749-1262
www.shelterisland.k12.ny.us
Shelter Island S 200/K-12
PO Box 2015 11964 631-749-0302
Leonard Skuggevik, supt. Fax 749-1262

**Sherburne, Chenango, Pop. 1,358**
Sherburne-Earlville Central SD 1,400/K-12
15 School St 13460 607-674-7300
Eric Schnabl, supt. Fax 674-9742
secsd.org
Sherburne-Earlville HS 500/9-12
13 School St 13460 607-674-7380
Julie Thompson, prin. Fax 674-7368
Sherburne-Earlville MS 300/6-8
13 School St 13460 607-674-7350
Jolene Emhof, prin. Fax 674-7392

**Sherman, Chautauqua, Pop. 717**
Sherman Central SD 400/PK-12
PO Box 950 14781 716-761-6122
Kaine Kelly, supt. Fax 761-6119
www.sherman.wnyric.org
Sherman HS 200/7-12
PO Box 950 14781 716-761-6121
Michael Ginestre, prin. Fax 761-6119

**Shoreham, Suffolk, Pop. 528**
Shoreham-Wading River Central SD 2,600/K-12
250B Route 25A 11786 631-821-8100
Dr. Steven Cohen, admin. Fax 929-3001
www.swrschools.org
Prodell MS 600/6-8
100 Randall Rd 11786 631-821-8212
Dr. Linda Anthony, prin. Fax 821-8275
Shoreham-Wading River HS 800/9-12
250A Route 25A 11786 631-821-8264
Dan Holtzman, prin. Fax 821-8162

**Shortsville, Ontario, Pop. 1,429**
Manchester-Shortsville Central SD 900/PK-12
1506 State Route 21 14548 585-289-3964
Charlene Harvey, supt. Fax 289-6660
www.redjacket.org
Red Jacket HS 300/9-12
1506 State Route 21 14548 585-289-3966
James Niedermeier, prin. Fax 289-4755
Red Jacket MS 200/6-8
1506 State Route 21 14548 585-289-3967
Sarah Shainfeld, prin. Fax 289-8715

**Shrub Oak, Westchester, Pop. 1,970**
Lakeland Central SD 6,000/K-12
1086 E Main St 10588 914-245-1700
Dr. George Stone, supt. Fax 245-1589
www.lakelandschools.org
Lakeland HS 1,100/9-12
1349 E Main St 10588 914-528-0600
Lorrie Yurish, prin. Fax 528-0521
Other Schools – See Cortlandt Manor, Yorktown Heights

**Sidney, Delaware, Pop. 3,846**
Sidney Central SD 1,000/K-12
95 W Main St 13838 607-563-2135
William Christensen, supt. Fax 563-2386
www.sidneycsd.org
Sidney JSHS 400/7-12
95 W Main St 13838 607-561-7703
Eben Bullock, prin. Fax 563-1800

**Silver Creek, Chautauqua, Pop. 2,618**
Silver Creek Central SD 1,000/PK-12
1 Dickinson St 14136 716-934-2603
Delia Bonenberger, admin. Fax 934-7983
www.silvercreek.wnyric.org/
Silver Creek HS 300/9-12
1 Dickinson St 14136 716-934-2603
James Lauria, prin. Fax 934-2103
Silver Creek MS 200/6-8
1 Dickinson St 14136 716-934-2603
Eleanor Payne, prin. Fax 934-3760

**Sinclairville, Chautauqua, Pop. 578**
Cassadaga Valley Central SD 1,000/PK-12
PO Box 540 14782 716-962-5155
Charles Leichner, supt. Fax 962-5976
cvweb.wnyric.org
Cassadaga Valley HS 400/9-12
PO Box 540 14782 716-962-8581
Josh Gilevski, prin. Fax 962-5788
Cassadega Valley MS 200/6-8
PO Box 540 14782 716-962-8581
Josh Gilevski, prin. Fax 962-5788

**Skaneateles, Onondaga, Pop. 2,428**
Skaneateles Central SD 1,500/K-12
55 East St 13152 315-291-2221
Kenneth Slentz, supt. Fax 685-0347
www.skanschools.org
Skaneateles HS 500/9-12
49 E Elizabeth St 13152 315-291-2231
Gregory Santoro, prin. Fax 291-2250
Skaneateles MS 400/6-8
35 East St 13152 315-291-2241
Gary Gerst, prin. Fax 291-2267

**Slate Hill, Orange**
Minisink Valley Central SD 4,300/K-12
PO Box 217 10973 845-355-5100
John Latini, supt. Fax 355-5119
www.minisink.com
Minisink Valley HS 1,500/9-12
PO Box 217 10973 845-355-5150
Kenneth Hauck, prin. Fax 355-5198
Minisink Valley MS 1,000/6-8
PO Box 217 10973 845-355-5200
Michael Giardina, prin. Fax 355-5205

**Sleepy Hollow, Westchester, Pop. 9,977**
Tarrytown UFD 2,800/PK-12
200 N Broadway 10591 914-631-9404
Dr. Daniel McCann, supt. Fax 332-6283
www.tufsd.org

Sleepy Hollow HS 900/9-12
210 N Broadway 10591 914-631-8838
Carol Conklin-Spillane, prin. Fax 332-6219
Sleepy Hollow MS 600/6-8
210 N Broadway 10591 914-332-6275
Elizabeth Lopez, prin. Fax 332-6546

**Sloan, Erie, Pop. 3,611**
Cheektowago-Sloan UFD 1,500/PK-12
166 Halstead Ave 14212 716-891-6402
Andrea Galenski, supt. Fax 891-6435
www.sloanschools.org
Other Schools – See Cheektowaga

**Smithtown, Suffolk, Pop. 27,100**
Smithtown Central SD 10,200/K-12
26 New York Ave 11787 631-382-2000
James J. Grossane Ed.D., supt. Fax 382-2010
www.smithtown.k12.ny.us
Accompsett MS 800/6-8
660 Meadow Rd 11787 631-382-2300
Paul McNeil, prin. Fax 382-2307
Smithtown HS West 1,700/9-12
100 Central Rd 11787 631-382-2905
John Coady, prin. Fax 382-2910
Other Schools – See Nesconset, Saint James

---

Smithtown Christian S 500/PK-12
1 Higbie Dr 11787 631-265-3334
Rev. Roger Erdvig M.Ed., supt. Fax 265-1079

**Snyder, Erie**

---

Park S of Buffalo 300/PK-12
4625 Harlem Rd 14226 716-839-1242
Christopher Lauricella, hdmstr. Fax 839-2014

**Sodus, Wayne, Pop. 1,754**
Sodus Central SD 1,200/PK-12
PO Box 220 14551 315-483-5201
Martin Cox, supt. Fax 483-4755
www.soduscsd.org
Sodus JSHS 400/7-12
PO Box 220 14551 315-483-5285
Eugene Hoskins, prin. Fax 483-6168

**Solvay, Onondaga, Pop. 6,416**
Solvay UFD 1,500/K-12
103 3rd St 13209 315-468-1111
Lawrence Wright, supt. Fax 468-2755
www.solvayschools.org
Solvay HS 600/9-12
600 Gertrude Ave 13209 315-468-2551
Jay Tinklepaugh, prin. Fax 484-1404
Other Schools – See Syracuse

**Somers, Westchester**
Somers Central SD 3,100/K-12
250 Route 202 10589 914-277-2400
Dr. Raymond Blanch, supt. Fax 277-2409
www.somersschools.org/
Somers MS 500/6-8
250 Route 202 10589 914-277-3399
Jeffrey Getman, prin. Fax 277-2236
Other Schools – See Lincolndale

---

Kennedy HS 600/9-12
54 Route 138 10589 914-232-5061
Rev. Mark Vaillancourt Ph.D., prin. Fax 232-3416

**Southampton, Suffolk, Pop. 3,057**
Southampton UFD 1,600/PK-12
70 Leland Ln 11968 631-591-4500
Dr. Scott Farina, supt. Fax 287-2870
www.southamptonschools.org
Southampton HS 600/9-12
141 Narrow Ln 11968 631-591-4600
Dr. Brian Zahn, prin. Fax 283-6313
Southampton IS 400/5-8
70 Leland Ln 11968 631-591-4700
Timothy Frazier, prin. Fax 283-6899

**South Dayton, Chautauqua, Pop. 607**
Pine Valley Central SD 600/PK-12
7755 Route 83 14138 716-988-3293
Scott Payne, supt. Fax 988-3243
www.pval.org
Pine Valley Central JSHS 300/7-12
7827 Route 83 14138 716-988-3276
Paul Mihalko, prin. Fax 988-3139

**South Fallsburg, Sullivan, Pop. 2,810**

---

Yeshivath Zichron Moshe Post-Sec.
PO Box 580 12779 845-434-5240
Zichron Moshe S 50/PK-12
PO Box 580 12779 845-434-5240

**South Glens Falls, Saratoga, Pop. 3,492**
South Glens Falls Central SD 3,200/PK-12
6 Bluebird Rd 12803 518-793-9617
Michael Patton, supt. Fax 761-0723
www.sgfcsd.org
South Glens Falls HS 1,000/9-12
42 Merritt Rd 12803 518-792-9987
Carla Biviano, prin. Fax 792-5412
Winch MS 800/6-8
99 Hudson St 12803 518-792-5891
Tim Dawkins, prin. Fax 793-9505

**South Kortright, Delaware**
South Kortright Central SD 400/PK-12
PO Box 113 13842 607-538-9111
Patricia Norton-White, supt. Fax 538-9205
www.skcs.org/pages/South_Kortright_Central_School
South Kortright Central S 400/PK-12
PO Box 113 13842 607-538-9111
Krislynn Dengler, prin. Fax 538-9205

**Southold, Suffolk, Pop. 5,696**
Southold UFD 900/K-12
PO Box 470 11971 631-765-5400
David Gamberg, supt. Fax 765-5086
www.southoldufsd.com
Southold JSHS 400/7-12
PO Box 470 11971 631-765-5081
William Galati, prin. Fax 765-5086

**South Otselic, Chenango**
Otselic Valley Central SD 200/K-12
PO Box 161 13155 315-653-7218
Richard Hughes, supt. Fax 653-7500
www.ovcs.org/
Otselic Valley S 200/K-12
PO Box 161 13155 315-653-7218
Daniel Henner, prin. Fax 653-7500

**South Ozone Park, See New York**
NYC Department of Education
Supt. — See New York
Epic HS - South 9-9
12110 Rockaway Blvd 11420 718-935-3643
Darius Mensah, prin.
Hawtree Creek MS 100/6-8
12110 Rockaway Blvd 11420 718-659-3792
M. Hussey, prin. Fax 659-3798
JHS 226 1,300/6-8
12110 Rockaway Blvd 11420 718-843-2260
Rushell White, prin. Fax 835-6317

---

Al-Ihsan Academy 400/PK-12
PO Box 200215 11420 718-322-3154

**South Salem, Westchester**
Katonah-Lewisboro UFD 3,600/K-12
1 Shady Ln 10590 914-763-7000
John Goetz, supt. Fax 763-7035
www.klschooldistrict.org/
Other Schools – See Cross River

**Sparkill, Rockland, Pop. 1,536**

---

St. Thomas Aquinas College Post-Sec.
125 Route 340 10976 845-398-4000

**Spencer, Tioga, Pop. 744**
Spencer-Van Etten Central SD 900/PK-12
PO Box 307 14883 607-589-7100
Dr. Joseph Morgan, supt. Fax 589-3010
www.svecsd.org/
Spencer-Van Etten HS 300/9-12
PO Box 307 14883 607-589-7140
Melissa Jewell, prin. Fax 589-3010
Spencer-Van Etten MS 300/5-8
PO Box 369 14883 607-589-7120
Eric Knolles, prin. Fax 589-3020

---

North Spencer Christian Academy 100/PK-12
721 Ithaca Rd 14883 607-589-6366
Rev. Steve Barrows, admin. Fax 589-4455

**Spencerport, Monroe, Pop. 3,553**
Spencerport Central SD 3,800/K-12
71 Lyell Ave 14559 585-349-5000
Michael Crumb, supt. Fax 349-5011
www.spencerportschools.org
Cosgrove MS 900/6-8
2749 Spencerport Rd 14559 585-349-5300
Ned Dale, prin. Fax 349-5346
Spencerport HS 1,300/9-12
2707 Spencerport Rd 14559 585-349-5200
Sean McCabe, prin. Fax 349-5266

**Springfield Gardens, See New York**
NYC Department of Education
Supt. — See New York
Carver HS for the Sciences 500/9-12
14310 Springfield Blvd 11413 718-525-6439
Dr. Janice Sutton, prin. Fax 525-6482
Excelsior Preparatory HS 400/9-12
14310 Springfield Blvd 11413 718-525-6507
Lillie Lucas, prin. Fax 525-6276
Preparatory Academy for Writers 500/6-12
14310 Springfield Blvd 11413 718-949-8405
Charles Anderson, prin. Fax 525-8495
Queens Preparatory Academy 400/9-12
14310 Springfield Blvd 11413 718-712-2304
Tashon Haywood, prin. Fax 712-3273
Queens United MS 100/6-8
22902 137th Ave 11413 718-723-3501
Richard Roder, prin. Fax 723-3507
IS 59 700/6-8
13255 Ridgedale St 11413 718-527-3501
Carleton Gordon, prin. Fax 276-1364

**Spring Valley, Rockland, Pop. 30,786**
East Ramapo Central SD 7,100/K-12
105 S Madison Ave 10977 845-577-6000
Dr. Joel Klein, supt. Fax 577-6168
www.eram.k12.ny.us
Ramapo HS 1,400/9-12
400 Viola Rd 10977 845-577-6400
Sherrill Murray-Lazarus, prin. Fax 426-1124
Spring Valley HS 1,200/9-12
361 W Route 59 10977 845-577-6500
Karen Pinel, prin. Fax 426-1127
Other Schools – See Chestnut Ridge, Suffern

---

Bais Malka HS of Belz 100/9-12
111 Union Rd 10977 845-371-0020
Bais Yaakov D'Rav Hirsch 200/9-12
235 N Main St 10977 845-371-6750
Be'er Yaakov Talmudic Seminary Post-Sec.
12 Jefferson Ave 10977 845-362-3053
Bnos Esther Pupa 300/PK-12
246 N Main St 10977 845-371-1220
Mesivta Shaarei Arazim 100/9-12
52 S Main St 10977 845-426-6401
Sunbridge Institute Post-Sec.
285 Hungry Hollow Rd 10977 845-425-0055
United Talmudical Academy 1,700/K-12
89 S Main St 10977 845-425-0392
Yidel Spitzer, admin. Fax 352-7253
Yeshiva Avir Yaakov 3,100/PK-12
766 N Main St 10977 845-362-6600
Yeshiva Bais Hachinuch 100/3-8
50A S Main St Ste 8 10977 845-354-3805
Yeshiva Degel Hatorah 300/K-12
111 Maple Ave 10977 845-356-4610
Yeshiva Tzoin Yosef-Pupa 400/PK-12
15 Widman Ct 10977 845-371-1220
Yeshiva Zichron Yaakov 50/9-12
720 Union Rd 10977 845-362-4990

**Springville, Erie, Pop. 4,257**
Springville-Griffith Inst. Central SD 2,000/K-12
307 Newman St 14141 716-592-3230
Sylvia Root, supt. Fax 592-3209
www.springvillegi.org/
Griffith Institute HS 700/9-12
290 N Buffalo St 14141 716-592-3202
Vincent Vanderlip, prin. Fax 592-3297
Griffith Institute MS 500/6-8
267 Newman St 14141 716-592-3203
Michael Retzlaff, prin. Fax 592-3268

**Staatsburg on Hudson, Dutchess, Pop. 372**
Hyde Park Central SD
Supt. — See Hyde Park
Roosevelt HS 1,400/9-12
156 S Cross Rd 12580 845-229-4020
Rick Pardy, prin. Fax 229-4029

**Stamford, Delaware, Pop. 1,103**
Stamford Central SD 400/K-12
1 River St 12167 607-652-7301
Dr. Glen Huot, supt. Fax 652-3446
www.stamfordcs.org
Stamford Central S 400/K-12
1 River St 12167 607-652-7301
Ruth Ehrets, prin. Fax 652-3446

**Star Lake, Saint Lawrence, Pop. 799**
Clifton-Fine Central SD 300/PK-12
11 Hall Ave 13690 315-848-3333
Regina Yeo, supt. Fax 848-3350
www.cliftonfine.org
Clifton-Fine JSHS 100/7-12
11 Hall Ave 13690 315-848-3333
Susan Shene, prin. Fax 848-3350

**Staten Island, See New York**
NYC Department of Education
Supt. — See New York
Concord HS 200/Alt
109 Rhine Ave 10304 718-447-1274
Ron Gorsky, prin. Fax 442-6276
CSI HS for International Studies 500/9-12
100 Essex Dr 10314 718-370-6900
Joseph Canale, prin. Fax 370-6915
Curtis HS 2,500/9-12
105 Hamilton Ave 10301 718-390-1800
Aurelia Curtis, prin. Fax 556-4800
Eagle Academy for Young Men 6-8
101 Warren St 10304 718-935-3472
Jermaine Cameron, prin.
Marsh Ave S for Expeditionary Learning 400/6-8
100 Essex Dr 10314 718-370-6850
Cara DeAngelo, prin. Fax 370-6860
McCown Expeditionary Learning S 400/9-12
100 Essex Dr 10314 718-370-6950
Traci Frey, prin. Fax 370-6960
McKee Career and Technical HS Vo/Tech
290 Saint Marks Pl 10301 718-420-2600
Sharon Henry, prin. Fax 981-8776
New Dorp HS 2,600/9-12
465 New Dorp Ln 10306 718-667-8686
Deirdre DeAngelis, prin. Fax 987-4889
Petrides S 1,300/K-12
715 Ocean Ter 10301 718-815-0186
Joanne Buckheit, prin. Fax 815-9638
Port Richmond HS 2,100/9-12
85 Saint Josephs Ave 10302 718-420-2100
Tim Gannon, prin. Fax 981-6203
IS 2 1,000/6-8
333 Midland Ave 10306 718-987-5336
Adrienne Stallone, prin. Fax 987-6937
IS 7 1,200/6-8
1270 Huguenot Ave 10312 718-697-8488
Dr. Nora DeRosa, prin. Fax 967-0809
IS 24 1,400/6-8
225 Cleveland Ave 10308 718-982-4700
Lenny Santamaria, prin. Fax 356-5834
IS 27 1,100/6-8
11 Clove Lake Pl 10310 718-981-8800
Tracey Kornish, prin. Fax 815-4677
IS 34 1,100/6-8
528 Academy Ave 10307 718-477-4500
John Boyle, prin. Fax 227-4074
IS 49 900/6-8
101 Warren St 10304 718-727-6040
Linda Hill, prin. Fax 876-8207
IS 51 900/6-8
20 Houston St 10302 718-981-0502
Nicholas Mele, prin. Fax 815-3957
IS 61 1,300/6-8
445 Castleton Ave 10301 718-727-8481
Susan Tronolone, prin. Fax 447-2112
IS 72 1,500/6-8
33 Ferndale Ave 10314 718-698-5757
Peter Macellari, prin. Fax 761-5928
IS 75 1,300/6-8
455 Huguenot Ave 10312 718-356-0130
Kenneth Zapata, prin. Fax 984-5302
Staten Island Tech HS Vo/Tech
485 Clawson St 10306 718-667-3222
Mark Erlenwein, prin. Fax 987-5872

Tottenville HS 3,900/9-12
100 Luten Ave 10312 718-668-8800
Joseph Scarmato, prin. Fax 317-0962
Wagner HS 3,100/9-12
1200 Manor Rd 10314 718-698-4200
Gary Giordano, prin. Fax 698-5213

---

Career School of New York Post-Sec.
350 Saint Marks Pl 10301 718-420-6440
CUNY College of Staten Island Post-Sec.
2800 Victory Blvd 10314 718-982-2000
Monsignor Farrell HS 900/9-12
2900 Amboy Rd 10306 718-987-2900
Msgr. Edmund Whalen, prin. Fax 987-4241
Moore Catholic HS 600/9-12
100 Merrill Ave 10314 718-761-9200
Dr. Joseph Fusco, prin. Fax 982-7779
Notre Dame Academy 400/9-12
134 Howard Ave 10301 718-447-8878
Kathryn Jaenicke, prin. Fax 447-2926
St. John Villa Academy 500/9-12
25 Landis Ave 10305 718-442-6240
Barbara Logan, prin. Fax 447-6729
St. Joseph by the Sea HS 400/9-12
5150 Hylan Blvd 10312 718-984-6500
Fr. Michael Reilly, prin. Fax 984-6503
St. Joseph Hill Academy 500/9-12
850 Hylan Blvd 10305 718-447-1374
Angela Ferrando, prin. Fax 447-3041
St. Pauls School of Nursing Post-Sec.
2 Teleport Dr Ste 203 10311 718-818-6470
St. Peter's Boys HS 600/9-12
200 Clinton Ave 10301 718-447-1676
John Fodera, prin. Fax 447-4027
St. Vincent's Medical Center Post-Sec.
355 Bard Ave 10310 718-876-2413
Sisters of Charity Medical Center Post-Sec.
75 Vanderbilt Ave 10304 718-818-6470
Staten Island Academy 300/PK-12
715 Todt Hill Rd 10304 718-987-8100
Albert Cauz, head sch Fax 979-7641
Wagner College Post-Sec.
1 Campus Rd 10301 718-390-3100
Yeshiva & Mesvita of Staten Island 100/9-12
1870 Drumgoole Rd E 10309 718-356-4323

**Stillwater, Saratoga, Pop. 1,707**
Stillwater Central SD 1,100/PK-12
1068 Hudson Ave 12170 518-373-6100
Dr. Stan Maziejka, supt. Fax 664-9134
www.scsd.org/
Stillwater HS 400/9-12
1068 Hudson Ave 12170 518-373-6100
Mario Fernandez, prin. Fax 664-1832
Stillwater MS 300/6-8
1068 Hudson Ave 12170 518-373-6100
Patti Morris, prin. Fax 664-1832

**Stone Ridge, Ulster, Pop. 1,136**

---

SUNY Ulster Post-Sec.
491 Cottekill Rd 12484 845-687-5000

**Stony Brook, Suffolk, Pop. 13,574**
Three Village Central SD 7,200/K-12
100 Suffolk Ave 11790 631-730-4000
Cheryl Pedisich, supt. Fax 474-7784
www.threevillagecsd.org
Murphy JHS 1,000/7-9
351 Oxhead Rd 11790 631-730-4800
Vincent Vizzo, prin. Fax 730-4801
Other Schools – See East Setauket, Setauket

---

Stony Brook S 300/7-12
1 Chapman Pkwy 11790 631-751-1800
Joshua Crane B.D., head sch Fax 751-3449
SUNY at Stony Brook Post-Sec.
118 Administration 11794 631-632-6000

**Stottville, Columbia, Pop. 1,324**

---

Faith Christian Academy 100/K-11
PO Box 89 12172 518-828-4119

**Suffern, Rockland, Pop. 10,548**
East Ramapo Central SD
Supt. — See Spring Valley
Pomona MS 600/7-8
101 Pomona Rd 10901 845-577-6200
Christine Alfonso, prin. Fax 577-6245

Ramapo Central SD
Supt. — See Hillburn
Suffern HS 1,500/9-12
49 Viola Rd 10901 845-357-3800
Patrick Breen, prin. Fax 357-5035
Suffern MS 1,100/6-8
80 Hemion Rd 10901 845-357-7400
Brian Fox, prin. Fax 357-4563

---

Salvation Army College Officer Training Post-Sec.
201 Lafayette Ave 10901 845-368-7200
SUNY Rockland Community College Post-Sec.
145 College Rd 10901 845-574-4000
Yeshiva Ohr Reuven 100/9-12
259 Grandview Ave 10901 845-362-8362
Yeshiva Shaarei Torah 100/9-12
91 Carlton Rd W 10901 845-352-3431
Yeshiva Shaarei Torah of Rockland Post-Sec.
91 Carlton Rd W 10901 845-352-3431

**Syosset, Nassau, Pop. 18,544**
Syosset Central SD, 99 Pell Ln 11791 6,500/K-12
Dr. Thomas Rogers, supt. 516-364-5600
www.syossetschools.org
South Woods MS, 99 Pell Ln 11791 800/6-8
Michelle Burget, prin. 516-364-5621
Syosset HS, 70 Southwoods Rd 11791 2,200/9-12
Dr. Giovanni Durante, prin. 516-364-5675
Thompson MS, 98 Ann Dr 11791 800/6-8
James Kassebaum, prin. 516-364-5760

---

New York College of Health Professions Post-Sec.
6801 Jericho Tpke 11791 800-922-7337
Our Lady of Mercy Academy 500/9-12
815 Convent Rd 11791 516-921-1047
Lisa Harrison, prin. Fax 921-3634
Star Career Academy Post-Sec.
125 Michael Dr 11791 516-364-4344

**Syracuse, Onondaga, Pop. 138,722**
Solvay UFD
Supt. — See Solvay
Solvay MS 500/4-8
299 Bury Dr 13209 315-487-7061
Diane Hagemann, prin. Fax 484-1444

Syracuse CSD 19,000/K-12
1025 Erie Blvd W 13204 315-435-4161
Sharon Contreras, supt. Fax 435-4015
www.syracusecityschools.com/
Clary MS 400/6-8
100 Amidon Dr 13205 315-435-4411
Daniel Straub, prin. Fax 435-5832
Corcoran HS 1,300/9-12
919 Glenwood Ave 13207 315-435-4321
Jennifer King-Reese, prin. Fax 435-4024
Danforth MS 500/6-8
309 W Brighton Ave 13205 315-435-4535
Dr. Ronardo Reeves, prin. Fax 435-6208
Elmcrest S Alt
960 Salt Springs Rd 13224 315-435-6244
Debra Mastropaolo, prin. Fax 435-6246
Expeditionary Learning S 100/6-8
4942 S Salina St 13205 315-435-6416
Kevin Burns, prin. Fax 435-4880
Fowler HS 1,100/9-12
227 Magnolia St 13204 315-435-4376
Lynelle Francis, prin. Fax 435-6313
Grant MS 600/6-8
2400 Grant Blvd 13208 315-435-4433
Pamela Odom, prin. Fax 435-4856
Henninger HS 1,600/9-12
600 Robinson St 13206 315-435-4343
Robert DiFlorio, prin. Fax 435-6277
Institute of Technology at Syracuse Cntr Vo/Tech
258 E Adams St 13202 315-435-4300
Donna Formica, prin. Fax 435-5816
Lincoln MS 500/6-8
1613 James St 13203 315-435-4450
Rebecca Groat, prin. Fax 435-4455
Nottingham HS 1,200/9-12
3100 E Genesee St 13224 315-435-4380
David Maynard, prin. Fax 435-4177
Westside Academy at Blodgett 400/6-8
312 Oswego St 13204 315-435-4386
Alton Hicks, prin. Fax 435-4539
Johnson Adult & Continuing Education Ctr Adult
573 E Genesee St 13202 315-435-4135
John Dittmann, prin. Fax 435-5875

Westhill Central SD 1,700/K-12
400 Walberta Rd 13219 315-426-3218
Casey Barduhn, supt. Fax 488-6411
www.westhillschools.org/
Onondaga Hill MS 600/5-8
4860 Onondaga Rd 13215 315-426-3400
Mark Bednarski, prin. Fax 492-0156
Westhill HS 600/9-12
4501 Onondaga Blvd 13219 315-426-3100
Lee Roscoe, prin. Fax 475-0319

---

Bishop Ludden JSHS 300/7-12
815 Fay Rd 13219 315-468-2591
Brenda Reichert, admin. Fax 468-0097
Bryant & Stratton College Post-Sec.
953 James St 13203 315-472-6603
Christian Brothers Academy 700/7-12
6245 Randall Rd 13214 315-446-5960
Br. Joseph Jozwiak, prin. Fax 446-3393
Crouse Hospital College of Nursing Post-Sec.
736 Irving Ave 13210 315-470-7481
Faith Heritage S 300/PK-12
3740 Midland Ave 13205 315-469-7777
Neal Capone, head sch Fax 492-7440
Le Moyne College Post-Sec.
1419 Salt Springs Rd 13214 315-445-4100
Living Word Academy 200/PK-12
6101 Court Street Rd 13206 315-437-6744
Manlius Pebble Hill S 500/PK-12
5300 Jamesville Rd 13214 315-446-2452
Jim Dunaway, head sch Fax 446-2620
Onondaga School of Therapeutic Massage Post-Sec.
719 E Genesee St 13210 315-424-1159
Phillips Hairstyling Institute Post-Sec.
709 E Genesee St 13210 315-422-9656
St. Joseph's Hospital College of Nursing Post-Sec.
206 Prospect Ave 13203 315-448-5040
SUNY College Environ. Science - Forestry Post-Sec.
1 Forestry Dr 13210 315-470-6500
SUNY Onondaga Community College Post-Sec.
4585 W Seneca Tpke 13215 315-498-2622
SUNY Upstate Medical University Post-Sec.
750 E Adams St 13210 315-464-5540
Syracuse University 13244 Post-Sec.
315-443-1870

**Tannersville, Greene, Pop. 531**
Hunter-Tannersville Central SD 400/PK-12
PO Box 1018 12485 518-589-5400
Dr. Patrick Sweeney, supt. Fax 589-5403
www.htcsd.org/
Tannersville MSHS 200/7-12
PO Box 1018 12485 518-589-5880
Dr. Adeline Basil, prin. Fax 589-7071

**Tarrytown, Westchester, Pop. 11,035**

---

Hackley S 800/K-12
293 Benedict Ave 10591 914-366-2642
Walter Johnson, hdmstr. Fax 366-2636

**Thiells, Rockland, Pop. 4,970**
North Rockland Central SD
Supt. — See Garnerville
Fieldstone MS 600/7-8
100 Fieldstone Dr 10984 845-942-7900
Anthony Zollo, prin. Fax 942-7910
North Rockland HS 1,900/9-12
106 Hammond Rd 10984 845-942-3300
Michael Gill, prin. Fax 942-3365

**Thornwood, Westchester, Pop. 3,718**
Mount Pleasant Central SD 2,000/K-12
825 Westlake Dr 10594 914-769-5500
Dr. Susan Guiney, supt. Fax 769-3733
www.mtplcsd.org
Westlake HS 600/9-12
825 Westlake Dr 10594 914-769-8311
Keith Schenker, prin. Fax 769-0596
Westlake MS 500/6-8
825 Westlake Dr 10594 914-769-8540
Dr. Robert Hendrickson, prin. Fax 769-8550

**Ticonderoga, Essex, Pop. 3,342**
Ticonderoga Central SD 800/K-12
5 Calkins Pl 12883 518-585-7400
John McDonald, supt. Fax 585-2682
www.ticonderogak12.org
Ticonderoga HS 300/9-12
5 Calkins Pl 12883 518-585-7400
John Donohue, prin. Fax 585-4076
Ticonderoga MS 200/6-8
116 Alexandria Ave 12883 518-585-7400
John Perrault, prin. Fax 585-2716

**Tioga Center, Tioga**
Tioga Central SD 1,000/K-12
PO Box 241 13845 607-687-8000
Scot Taylor, supt. Fax 687-8007
www.tiogacentral.org
Tioga HS 300/9-12
PO Box 241 13845 607-687-8001
Margo Martin, prin. Fax 687-8010
Tioga MS 300/5-8
PO Box 241 13845 607-687-8004
Willard Cook, prin. Fax 687-6910

**Tonawanda, Erie, Pop. 14,988**
Kenmore-Tonawanda UFSD
Supt. — See Buffalo
Kenmore East HS 1,100/9-12
350 Fries Rd 14150 716-874-8402
Patrick Heyden, prin. Fax 874-8443

Tonawanda CSD 1,300/PK-12
100 Hinds St 14150 716-694-7784
James Newton, supt. Fax 695-8738
www.tonawandacsd.org
Tonawanda MSHS 1,000/6-12
600 Fletcher St 14150 716-694-7660
Jessica Lyons, prin. Fax 743-8839

---

Cardinal O'Hara HS 200/9-12
39 Ohara Rd 14150 716-695-2600
Mary Holzerland, prin. Fax 692-8697
MarJon School of Beauty Culture Post-Sec.
1154 Niagara Falls Blvd 14150 716-836-6240

**Troy, Rensselaer, Pop. 48,315**
Brunswick Central SD 1,300/K-12
3992 State Highway 2 12180 518-279-4600
Dr. Angelina Maloney, supt. Fax 279-1918
www.brittonkill.k12.ny.us
Tamarac MSHS 800/6-12
3992 State Highway 2 12180 518-279-4600
Richard Pogue, prin. Fax 279-3888

Lansingburgh Central SD 2,400/PK-12
576 5th Ave 12182 518-233-6850
Cynthia DeDominick, supt. Fax 235-7436
www.lansingburgh.org
Knickerbacker MS 600/6-8
320 7th Ave 12182 518-233-6811
Michael Harkin, prin. Fax 238-2518
Lansingburgh HS 800/9-12
320 7th Ave 12182 518-233-6806
Frank Macri, prin. Fax 233-6826

Troy CSD 4,000/PK-12
475 1st St 12180 518-328-5052
John Carmello, supt. Fax 271-5229
www.troycsd.org
Public S 12, 475 1st St 12180 500/Alt
James Canfield, dir. 518-328-5083
Troy HS 1,300/9-12
1950 Burdett Ave 12180 518-328-5401
Joseph Mariano, prin. Fax 274-2341
Troy MS 500/6-8
1976 Burdett Ave 12180 518-328-5301
Brian Dunn, prin. Fax 274-8160

---

Catholic Central HS 500/7-12
625 7th Ave 12182 518-235-7100
Christopher Bott, prin. Fax 237-1796
La Salle Institute 400/6-12
174 Williams Rd 12180 518-283-2500
Br. Carl Malacalza, prin. Fax 283-6265
Redemption Christian Academy 100/PK-12
PO Box 753 12181 518-272-6679
Rensselaer Polytechnic Institute Post-Sec.
110 8th St 12180 518-276-6000
Samaritan Hospital School of Nursing Post-Sec.
2215 Burdett Ave 12180 518-271-3285

SUNY Hudson Valley Community College Post-Sec.
80 Vandenburgh Ave 12180 518-629-4822
The Sage Colleges Post-Sec.
65 1st St 12180 518-244-2000
Willard S 300/9-12
285 Pawling Ave 12180 518-833-1300
Trudy Hall, hdmstr. Fax 833-1800

**Trumansburg, Tompkins, Pop. 1,761**
Trumansburg Central SD 1,100/K-12
100 Whig St 14886 607-387-7551
Michael McGuire, supt. Fax 387-2807
www.tburg.k12.ny.us
Dickerson HS 400/9-12
100 Whig St 14886 607-387-7551
Jon Koeng, prin. Fax 387-2807
Doig MS 300/5-8
100 Whig St 14886 607-387-7551
Joshua Hunkele, prin. Fax 387-2807

**Tully, Onondaga, Pop. 852**
Tully Central SD 1,000/K-12
20 State St 13159 315-696-6204
Robert Hughes, supt. Fax 883-1343
www.tullyschools.org
Tully JSHS 500/7-12
20 State St 13159 315-696-6235
Mary Ann Murphy, prin. Fax 696-6237

**Tupper Lake, Franklin, Pop. 3,639**
Tupper Lake Central SD 800/PK-12
294 Hosley Ave 12986 518-359-3371
Seth McGowan, supt. Fax 359-7862
www.tupperlakecsd.net/
Tupper Lake MSHS 400/7-12
25 Chaney Ave 12986 518-359-3322
Matthew Southwick, prin. Fax 359-7862

**Turin, Lewis, Pop. 232**
South Lewis Central SD 900/PK-12
PO Box 10 13473 315-348-2500
Douglas Premo, supt. Fax 348-2510
www.southlewis.org
South Lewis HS 300/9-12
PO Box 40 13473 315-348-2520
Chad Luther, prin. Fax 348-2510
South Lewis MS 200/5-8
PO Box 70 13473 315-348-2570
Judith Duppert, prin. Fax 348-2510

**Tuxedo Park, Orange, Pop. 598**
Tuxedo UFD 600/K-12
PO Box 2002 10987 845-351-4799
Nancy Teed, supt. Fax 351-5296
www.tuxedoufsd.org
Baker HS 400/7-12
PO Box 2002 10987 845-351-4786
Arthur Schouten, prin. Fax 351-4823

**Uniondale, Nassau, Pop. 24,253**
Uniondale UFD 6,300/PK-12
933 Goodrich St 11553 516-560-8800
Dr. William Lloyd, supt. Fax 292-2659
www.uniondaleschools.org
Turtle Hook MS 700/6-8
975 Jerusalem Ave 11553 516-918-1300
Dr. Donald Humphrey, prin. Fax 505-2533
Uniondale HS 2,100/9-12
933 Goodrich St 11553 516-560-8831
Dr. Florence Simmons, prin. Fax 564-8464
Other Schools – See Hempstead

---

Hebrew Academy of Nassau County 400/7-12
215 Oak St 11553 516-538-8161
Institute of Allied Medical Professions Post-Sec.
333 Earle Ovington Ste 305 11553 516-450-3110
Kellenberg Memorial HS 2,600/6-12
1400 Glenn Curtiss Blvd 11553 516-292-0200
Br. Kenneth Hoagland, prin. Fax 292-0877

**Union Springs, Cayuga, Pop. 1,182**
Union Springs Central SD 900/K-12
239 Cayuga St 13160 315-889-4101
Linda Rice, supt. Fax 889-4108
www.uscsd.info/
Union Springs MSHS 400/7-12
239 Cayuga St 13160 315-889-4110
Charles Walker, prin. Fax 889-4118

---

Union Springs Academy 100/9-12
PO Box 524 13160 315-889-7314

**Upper Nyack, Rockland, Pop. 2,003**
Nyack UFD
Supt. — See Nyack
Nyack HS 900/9-12
360 Christian Herald Rd 10960 845-353-7100
Nicole Saieva, prin. Fax 353-7119

**Utica, Oneida, Pop. 60,287**
Utica CSD 8,500/K-12
106 Memorial Pkwy 13501 315-792-2210
Bruce Karam, supt. Fax 792-2200
www.uticacsd.org/
Donovan MS 700/6-8
1701 Noyes St 13502 315-792-2006
Ann Marie Palladino, prin. Fax 792-2077
Kennedy MS 700/6-8
500 Deerfield Dr E 13502 315-792-2088
Joshua Gifford, prin. Fax 792-2084
Proctor HS 2,600/9-12
1203 Hilton Ave 13501 315-368-6400
Steven Falchi, prin. Fax 223-4896

---

Faxton-St. Luke's Healthcare Post-Sec.
PO Box 479 13503 315-624-6136
Mohawk Valley Community College Post-Sec.
1101 Sherman Dr 13501 315-792-5400

Notre Dame JSHS 300/7-12
2 Notre Dame Ln 13502 315-724-5118
Sr. Anna Mae Collins, prin. Fax 724-9460
Pratt MWP Post-Sec.
310 Genesee St 13502 800-755-8920
St. Elizabeth College of Nursing Post-Sec.
2215 Genesee St 13501 315-798-8144
SUNY Institute of Technology Utica/Rome Post-Sec.
100 Seymour Rd 13502 315-792-7500
USC The Business College Post-Sec.
201 Bleecker St 13501 315-733-2300
Utica College Post-Sec.
1600 Burrstone Rd 13502 315-792-3111

**Valatie, Columbia, Pop. 1,798**
Ichabod Crane Central SD 1,800/K-12
PO Box 820 12184 518-758-7575
George Zini, supt. Fax 758-7579
www.ichabodcrane.org/
Crane HS 700/9-12
PO Box 820 12184 518-758-7575
Craig Shull, prin. Fax 758-2181
Crane MS 400/6-8
PO Box 820 12184 518-758-7575
Tim Farley, prin. Fax 758-1405

**Valhalla, Westchester, Pop. 3,081**
Valhalla UFD 1,500/K-12
316 Columbus Ave 10595 914-683-5040
Dr. Brenda Myers, supt. Fax 683-5075
www.valhallaschools.org/
Valhalla HS 400/9-12
300 Columbus Ave 10595 914-683-5014
Jonathan Thomas, prin. Fax 683-5003
Valhalla MS 400/6-8
300 Columbus Ave 10595 914-683-5011
Roberto Trigosso, prin. Fax 683-5003

---

New York Medical College Post-Sec.
40 Sunshine Cottage Rd 10595 914-594-4000
SUNY Westchester Community College Post-Sec.
75 Grasslands Rd 10595 914-606-6600

**Valley Stream, Nassau, Pop. 36,423**
Valley Stream Central HSD 4,700/7-12
1 Kent Rd 11580 516-872-5601
Dr. Bill Heidenreich, supt. Fax 872-5658
www.vschsd.org
Valley Stream Central HS 1,100/10-12
135 Fletcher Ave 11580 516-561-4410
Dr. Joseph Pompilio, prin. Fax 561-4490
Valley Stream Memorial JHS 1,000/7-9
320 Fletcher Ave 11580 516-872-7710
Anthony Mignella, prin. Fax 872-7711
Valley Stream South HS 1,300/7-12
150 Jedwood Pl 11581 516-791-0310
Maureen Henry, prin. Fax 791-0305
Other Schools – See Franklin Square

---

Business Informatics Center Post-Sec.
134 S Central Ave 11580 516-561-0050
Valley Stream Christian Academy 200/K-12
12 E Fairview Ave 11580 516-561-6122
Leslie Fowley, supt. Fax 284-7191

**Van Hornesville, Herkimer**
Van Hornesville-Owen D. Young Central SD 200/K-12
PO Box 125 13475 315-858-0729
Christopher Groves, supt. Fax 858-2019
Young Central S 200/K-12
PO Box 125 13475 315-858-0729
Christopher Groves, supt. Fax 858-2019

**Verona, Oneida, Pop. 837**
Vernon-Verona-Sherrill Central SD 2,000/PK-12
PO Box 128 13478 315-829-2520
Martha Group, supt. Fax 829-4949
www.vvsschools.org
Vernon-Verona-Sherrill HS 700/9-12
PO Box 128 13478 315-829-7446
Andy Brown, prin. Fax 829-4465
Vernon-Verona-Sherrill MS 300/7-8
PO Box 128 13478 315-829-7444
Carrie Hodkinson, prin. Fax 829-5966

**Vestal, Broome, Pop. 5,000**
Vestal Central SD 3,600/K-12
201 Main St 13850 607-757-2241
Mark LaRoach, supt. Fax 757-2227
www.vestal.k12.ny.us/
Vestal HS 1,200/9-12
205 Woodlawn Dr 13850 607-757-2281
Catherine Hepler, prin. Fax 757-2301
Vestal MS 900/6-8
600 S Benita Blvd 13850 607-757-2331
Ann Marie Loose, prin. Fax 757-2229

---

Elmira Business Institute Post-Sec.
4100 Vestal Rd 13850 607-729-8915
Ross Corners Christian Academy 100/PK-12
2101 Owego Rd 13850 607-748-3301
Toby Wyse, admin. Fax 748-3301

**Victor, Ontario, Pop. 2,645**
Victor Central SD 4,400/PK-12
953 High St 14564 585-924-3252
Dr. Dawn Santiago-Marullo, supt. Fax 742-7090
www.victorschools.org
Victor HS 1,200/9-12
953 High St 14564 585-924-3252
Yvonne O'Shea, prin. Fax 924-9536
Victor JHS 700/7-8
953 High St 14564 585-924-3252
Carl Christensen, prin. Fax 924-9535

**Voorheesville, Albany, Pop. 2,770**
Voorheesville Central SD 1,200/K-12
432 New Salem Rd 12186 518-765-3313
Brian Hunt, supt. Fax 765-2751
vcsd.neric.org/
Bouton HS 400/9-12
432 New Salem Rd 12186 518-765-3314
Patrick Corrigan, prin. Fax 765-5547
Voorheesville MS 300/6-8
432 New Salem Rd 12186 518-765-3314
Jennifer Drautz, prin. Fax 765-3842

**Wallkill, Ulster, Pop. 2,258**
Wallkill Central SD 3,300/K-12
PO Box 310 12589 845-895-7100
Kevin Castle, supt. Fax 895-3630
www.wallkillcsd.k12.ny.us
Borden MS 500/7-8
PO Box 310 12589 845-895-7175
Marjorie Anderson, prin. Fax 895-8036
Wallkill HS 1,200/9-12
PO Box 310 12589 845-895-7150
Michael Rydell, prin. Fax 895-8003

**Walton, Delaware, Pop. 3,059**
Walton Central SD 1,400/PK-12
47-49 Stockton Ave 13856 607-865-4116
Roger Clough, supt. Fax 865-8568
www.waltoncsd.org
Mack MS 200/6-8
47-49 Stockton Ave 13856 607-865-4116
Robert Knushke, prin. Fax 865-8568
O'Neill HS 300/9-12
47-49 Stockton Ave 13856 607-865-4116
Robert Knushke, prin. Fax 865-6130

**Walworth, Wayne**
Gananda Central SD 1,100/K-12
1500 Dayspring Rdg 14568 315-986-3521
Dr. Shawn Van Scoy, supt. Fax 986-2003
www.gananda.org
Gananda MS 300/6-8
1500 Dayspring Rdg 14568 315-986-3521
Matthew Mahoney, prin. Fax 986-1927
Gananda / Ruben A. Cirillo HS 400/9-12
1500 Dayspring Rdg 14568 315-986-3521
Kelly Van Laeken, prin. Fax 986-1761

**Wampsville, Madison, Pop. 531**
Oneida CSD
Supt. — See Oneida
Shortell MS 400/7-8
PO Box 716 13163 315-363-1050
Todd Widrick, prin. Fax 366-0622

**Wantagh, Nassau, Pop. 18,699**
Wantagh UFD 3,400/K-12
3301 Beltagh Ave 11793 516-781-8000
Maureen Goldberg, supt. Fax 781-6076
www.wantaghschools.org
Wantagh HS 1,200/9-12
3297 Beltagh Ave 11793 516-679-6402
Dr. Carolyn Breivogel, prin. Fax 679-6432
Wantagh MS 900/6-8
3299 Beltagh Ave 11793 516-679-6350
Dawn Matrochano, prin. Fax 679-6311

**Wappingers Falls, Dutchess, Pop. 5,339**
Wappingers Central SD
Supt. — See Hopewell Junction
Ketcham HS 1,900/9-12
99 Myers Corners Rd 12590 845-298-5100
G. Thomas Stella, prin. Fax 298-5099
Orchard View Alternative HS 50/Alt
167 Myers Corners Rd 12590 845-298-5000
Kenneth Haskins, prin.
Van Wyck JHS 1,500/6-8
6 Hillside Lake Rd 12590 845-227-1700
Steve Shuchat, prin. Fax 227-1748
Wappingers Falls JHS 900/7-8
30 Major MacDonald Way 12590 845-298-5200
Terrence Thompson, prin. Fax 298-5156

**Warrensburg, Warren, Pop. 3,071**
Warrensburg Central SD 800/K-12
103 Schroon River Rd 12885 518-623-2861
John Goralski, supt. Fax 623-2436
www.wcsd.org
Warrensburg JSHS 400/7-12
103 Schroon River Rd 12885 518-623-2862
Doug Duell, prin. Fax 623-5089

**Warsaw, Wyoming, Pop. 3,438**
Warsaw Central SD 1,000/K-12
153 W Buffalo St 14569 585-786-8000
Joseph Englebert, supt. Fax 786-8008
www.warsaw.k12.ny.us
Warsaw MSHS 500/6-12
81 W Court St 14569 585-786-8000
Christopher Swiatek, prin. Fax 786-3193

**Warwick, Orange, Pop. 6,603**
Warwick Valley Central SD 3,500/K-12
PO Box 595 10990 845-987-3000
Dr. David Leach, supt. Fax 986-1408
www.warwickvalleyschools.com
Warwick Valley HS 1,500/9-12
PO Box 595 10990 845-987-3050
Dr. Larry Washington, prin. Fax 987-8982
Warwick Valley MS 1,000/5-8
PO Box 595 10990 845-987-3100
Cindy Leandro, prin. Fax 986-6942

**Washingtonville, Orange, Pop. 5,806**
Washingtonville Central SD 4,400/K-12
52 W Main St 10992 845-497-4000
Roberta Greene, supt. Fax 496-2330
www.ws.k12.ny.us
Washingtonville HS 1,500/9-12
54 W Main St 10992 845-497-4000
Brian Connolly, prin. Fax 496-2212

Washingtonville MS 1,000/6-8
38 W Main St 10992 845-497-4000
Teresa Thompson, prin. Fax 496-2099

**Waterford, Saratoga, Pop. 1,958**
Waterford-Halfmoon UFD 800/K-12
125 Middletown Rd 12188 518-237-0800
Patrick Pomerville, supt. Fax 237-7335
www.whufsd.org
Waterford-Halfmoon HS 400/7-12
125 Middletown Rd 12188 518-237-0800
Christopher Scanlan, prin. Fax 237-7335

**Waterloo, Seneca, Pop. 5,097**
Waterloo Central SD 1,600/K-12
109 Washington St 13165 315-539-1500
Terry MacNabb, supt. Fax 539-1504
www.waterloocsd.org
Waterloo HS 600/9-12
96 Stark St 13165 315-539-1550
Susan Burgess, prin. Fax 539-1536
Waterloo MS 400/6-8
65 Center St 13165 315-539-1540
Vincent Vitale, prin. Fax 539-1534

**Watertown, Jefferson, Pop. 26,112**
Watertown CSD 4,100/K-12
1351 Washington St 13601 315-785-3700
Terry Fralick, supt. Fax 785-6855
www.watertowncsd.org
Case MS 600/7-8
1237 Washington St 13601 315-785-3870
Terry Gonseth, prin. Fax 785-3731
Watertown HS 1,200/9-12
1335 Washington St 13601 315-785-3800
Leslie Atkinson, prin. Fax 785-3733

---

Faith Fellowship Christian S 200/PK-12
131 Moore Ave 13601 315-782-9342
Immaculate Heart Central JSHS 300/7-12
1316 Ives St 13601 315-788-4670
Lisa Parsons, prin. Fax 788-4672
Jefferson Community College Post-Sec.
1220 Coffeen St 13601 315-786-2200
Samaritan Medical Center Post-Sec.
830 Washington St 13601 315-785-4000

**Waterville, Oneida, Pop. 1,551**
Waterville Central SD 800/PK-12
381 Madison St 13480 315-841-3900
Charles Chafee, supt. Fax 841-3939
www.watervillecsd.org
Waterville JSHS 400/7-12
381 Madison St 13480 315-841-3800
Matt St. Peter, prin. Fax 841-3838

**Watervliet, Albany, Pop. 9,992**
Watervliet CSD 1,300/K-12
1245 Hillside Dr 12189 518-629-3200
Dr. Lori Caplan, supt. Fax 629-3265
vliet.neric.org/
Watervliet JSHS 700/7-12
1245 Hillside Dr 12189 518-629-3300
Ryan Groat, prin. Fax 273-4772

**Watkins Glen, Schuyler, Pop. 1,826**
Watkins Glen Central SD 1,100/PK-12
303 12th St 14891 607-535-3220
Thomas Phillips, supt. Fax 535-4629
www.wgcsd.org
Watkins Glen Central JSHS 400/7-12
301 12th St 14891 607-535-3210
Kai D'Alleva, prin. Fax 535-3262

**Waverly, Tioga, Pop. 4,388**
Waverly Central SD 1,700/PK-12
15 Frederick St 14892 607-565-2841
Dr. Randy Richards, supt. Fax 565-4997
www.waverlyschools.com/
Waverly HS 500/9-12
1 Frederick St 14892 607-565-8101
Ashlee Hunt, prin. Fax 565-4997
Waverly MS 400/6-8
1 Frederick St 14892 607-565-3410
Paul Vesci, prin. Fax 565-4997

**Wayland, Steuben, Pop. 1,852**
Wayland-Cohocton Central SD 1,500/PK-12
2350 State Route 63 14572 585-728-2211
Michael Wetherbee, supt. Fax 728-3566
www.wccsk12.org
Wayland-Cohocton HS 500/9-12
2350 State Route 63 14572 585-728-2366
William Whyte, prin. Fax 728-2425
Wayland-Cohocton MS 400/5-8
2350 State Route 63 14572 585-728-2551
Eileen Feinman, prin. Fax 728-3556

**Webster, Monroe, Pop. 5,251**
Webster Central SD 8,600/K-12
119 South Ave 14580 585-216-0000
Carmen Gumina, supt. Fax 265-6561
www.websterschools.org
Spry MS 1,000/6-8
119 South Ave 14580 585-265-6500
James Baehr, prin. Fax 265-6512
Thomas HS 1,400/9-12
800 Five Mile Line Rd 14580 585-670-8000
Glenn Widor, prin. Fax 671-1884
Webster Schroeder HS 1,500/9-12
875 Ridge Rd 14580 585-670-5000
David Paddock, prin. Fax 671-8681
Willink MS 1,000/6-8
900 Publishers Pkwy 14580 585-670-1030
Jim Gindling, prin. Fax 671-1978

---

Webster Christian S 200/PK-12
675 Holt Rd 14580 585-872-5150
Keith Bell, admin. Fax 872-5932

**Weedsport, Cayuga, Pop. 1,803**
Weedsport Central SD 800/K-12
2821 E Brutus Street Rd 13166 315-834-6637
Shaun O'Connor, supt.
www.weedsport.org
Weedsport JSHS 400/6-12
2821 E Brutus Street Rd 13166 315-834-6652
Carrie Widrick, prin. Fax 834-8693

**Wells, Hamilton**
Wells Central SD 200/PK-12
PO Box 300 12190 518-924-6000
Thomas Sincavage, supt. Fax 924-9246
wellscsd.com/
Wells Central S 200/PK-12
PO Box 300 12190 518-924-6000
Thomas Sincavage, supt. Fax 924-9246

**Wellsville, Allegany, Pop. 4,622**
Wellsville Central SD 1,300/PK-12
126 W State St 14895 585-596-2170
Kimberly Mueller, supt. Fax 596-2177
www.wellsvilleschools.org
Wellsville HS 400/9-12
126 W State St 14895 585-596-2188
Jeff White, prin. Fax 596-2180
Wellsville MS 300/6-8
126 W State St 14895 585-596-2144
Mary Ellen O'Connell, prin. Fax 596-2142

**West Babylon, Suffolk, Pop. 42,432**
West Babylon UFD 4,300/K-12
10 Farmingdale Rd 11704 631-376-7000
Dr. Yiendhy Farrelly, supt. Fax 376-7019
www.wbschools.org
West Babylon HS 1,400/9-12
500 Great East Neck Rd 11704 631-376-7101
Dr. Ellice Vassallo, prin. Fax 376-7119
West Babylon JHS 1,000/6-8
200 Old Farmingdale Rd 11704 631-376-7201
Scott Payne, prin. Fax 376-7209

---

Commercial Driver Training School Post-Sec.
600 Patton Ave 11704 631-249-1330

**Westbury, Nassau, Pop. 14,820**
East Meadow UFD 7,200/K-12
718 The Plain Rd 11590 516-478-5776
Leon Campo, supt. Fax 478-5779
www.eastmeadow.k12.ny.us
Clarke HS 800/9-12
740 Edgewood Dr 11590 516-876-7451
Timothy Voels, prin. Fax 876-7416
Clarke MS 600/6-8
740 Edgewood Dr 11590 516-876-7401
Stacy Breslin, prin. Fax 876-7407
Other Schools – See East Meadow

Westbury UFD
Supt. — See Old Westbury
Westbury MS 900/6-8
455 Rockland St 11590 516-876-5082
David Zimbler, prin. Fax 876-5141

**West Chazy, Clinton, Pop. 516**
Beekmantown Central SD 2,000/PK-12
37 Eagle Way 12992 518-563-8250
Daniel W. Mannix, supt. Fax 563-8132
www.bcsdk12.org
Beekmantown HS 600/9-12
37 Eagle Way 12992 518-563-8787
Justin Gardner, prin. Fax 563-8789
Beekmantown MS 500/6-8
37 Eagle Way 12992 518-563-8690
Amy Campbell, prin. Fax 563-8691

**Westfield, Chautauqua, Pop. 3,195**
Westfield Central SD 700/K-12
203 E Main St 14787 716-326-2151
David Davison, supt. Fax 326-2195
www.wacs.wnyric.org/
Westfield HS 300/9-12
203 E Main St 14787 716-326-2151
Ivana Hite, prin. Fax 326-2157
Westfield MS 200/6-8
203 E Main St 14787 716-326-2151
Ivana Hite, prin. Fax 326-2157

**Westhampton Beach, Suffolk, Pop. 1,702**
Westhampton Beach UFD 1,800/K-12
340 Mill Rd 11978 631-288-3800
Mike Radday, supt. Fax 288-8351
www.westhamptonbeach.k12.ny.us
Westhampton Beach HS 1,000/9-12
49 Lilac Rd 11978 631-288-3800
Christopher Herr, prin. Fax 288-3915
Westhampton Beach MS 400/6-8
340 Mill Rd 11978 631-288-3800
Charisse Miller, prin. Fax 288-5496

**West Hempstead, Nassau, Pop. 18,467**
West Hempstead UFD 2,200/K-12
252 Chestnut St 11552 516-390-3100
John Hogan, supt. Fax 489-1776
www.whufsd.com/
West Hempstead HS 900/9-12
400 Nassau Blvd 11552 516-390-3214
Daniel Rehman, prin. Fax 489-1769
West Hempstead MS 500/6-8
450 Nassau Blvd 11552 516-390-3160
Teresa Grossane, prin. Fax 489-8946

**West Henrietta, Monroe**
Rush-Henrietta Central SD
Supt. — See Henrietta
Burger MS 500/6-8
639 Erie Station Rd 14586 585-359-5308
Greg Lane, prin. Fax 359-5333
Vollmer Alternative Center 100/Alt
159 Telephone Rd 14586 585-359-5520
Curt Diesenberg, dir. Fax 359-5523

**West Islip, Suffolk, Pop. 28,075**
West Islip UFD 4,500/K-12
100 Sherman Ave 11795 631-893-3200
Bernadette Burns, supt. Fax 893-3212
www.wi.k12.ny.us
Beach Street MS 600/6-8
17 Beach St 11795 631-893-3310
Andrew O'Farrell, prin. Fax 893-3318
Udall Road MS 600/6-8
900 Udall Rd 11795 631-893-3290
Daniel Marquardt, prin. Fax 893-3301
West Islip HS 1,800/9-12
1 Lions Path 11795 631-893-3250
Dr. Anthony Bridgeman, prin. Fax 893-3318

---

St. John the Baptist Diocesan HS 1,700/9-12
1170 Montauk Hwy 11795 631-587-8000
Nan Doherty, prin. Fax 587-8996

**Westmoreland, Oneida, Pop. 420**
Westmoreland Central SD 1,000/K-12
PO Box 430 13490 315-557-2614
Rocco Migliori, supt. Fax 853-4602
www.westmorelandschool.org
Westmoreland HS 300/9-12
PO Box 430 13490 315-557-2616
Joshua Saxton, prin. Fax 557-2672
Westmoreland MS 300/5-8
PO Box 430 13490 315-557-2618
Eric Coriale, prin. Fax 557-2760

**West Nyack, Rockland, Pop. 3,385**
Clarkstown Central SD
Supt. — See New City
Clarkstown South HS 1,500/9-12
31 Demarest Mill Rd 10994 845-624-3400
Debra Tarantino, prin. Fax 623-5470
Festa MS 2,200/6-8
30 Parrott Rd 10994 845-624-3484
Kevin Horan, prin. Fax 634-5874

**West Point, Orange, Pop. 6,475**

---

United States Military Academy Post-Sec.
646 Swift Rd 10996 845-938-4041

**Westport, Essex, Pop. 508**
Westport Central SD 200/K-12
25 Sisco St 12993 518-962-8244
Cynthia Ford-Johnston, supt. Fax 962-4571
www.westportcs.org
Westport Central S 200/K-12
25 Sisco St 12993 518-962-8244
Adam Facteau, prin. Fax 962-4571

**West Sayville, Suffolk, Pop. 4,972**
Sayville UFD
Supt. — See Sayville
Sayville HS 1,100/9-12
20 Brook St 11796 631-244-6600
Ronald Hoffer, prin. Fax 244-6779

**West Seneca, Erie, Pop. 44,393**
Orchard Park Central SD 5,100/K-12
2240 Southwestern Blvd 14224 716-209-6200
Matthew McGarrity, supt. Fax 209-6353
www.opschools.org
Other Schools – See Orchard Park

West Seneca Central SD 6,800/PK-12
1397 Orchard Park Rd 14224 716-677-3101
Dr. Mark J. Crawford, supt. Fax 677-3104
www.wscschools.org/
East MS 400/5-8
1445 Center Rd 14224 716-677-3530
Sharon Loughran, prin. Fax 674-1046
West MS 600/6-8
395 Center Rd 14224 716-677-3500
Matthew Bystrak, prin. Fax 675-6134
West Seneca East HS 900/9-12
4760 Seneca St 14224 716-677-3300
Jonathan Cervoni, prin. Fax 677-2933
West Seneca West HS 1,400/9-12
3330 Seneca St 14224 716-677-3350
John Brinker, prin. Fax 674-3551

---

Continental School of Beauty Culture Post-Sec.
1050 Union Rd 14224 716-675-8205
West Seneca Christian S 100/PK-12
511 Union Rd 14224 716-674-1820
Orlando Buria Ph.D., admin. Fax 674-4894

**West Valley, Cattaraugus, Pop. 518**
West Valley Central SD 300/PK-12
PO Box 290 14171 716-942-3293
Eric Lawton, supt. Fax 942-3440
www.wvalley.wnyric.org
West Valley Central S 300/PK-12
PO Box 290 14171 716-942-3293
Daniel Amodeo, prin. Fax 942-3440

**West Winfield, Herkimer, Pop. 820**
Mount Markham CSD 1,200/K-12
500 Fairground Rd 13491 315-822-2824
Shawn Bissetta, supt. Fax 822-6162
www.mmcsd.org
Mount Markham HS 400/9-12
500 Fairground Rd 13491 315-822-2900
Russell Kissinger, prin. Fax 822-3486
Mount Markham MS 400/5-8
500 Fairground Rd 13491 315-822-2870
Dawn Yerkie, prin. Fax 822-6125

**Whitehall, Washington, Pop. 2,580**
Whitehall Central SD 700/K-12
87 Buckley Rd 12887 518-499-1772
Elizabeth Legault, supt. Fax 499-1759
www.railroaders.net

Whitehall JSHS 300/7-12
87 Buckley Rd 12887 518-499-1770
Kelly McHugh, prin. Fax 499-1759

**White Plains, Westchester, Pop. 55,780**
White Plains CSD 6,900/K-12
5 Homeside Ln 10605 914-422-2000
Timothy Connors, supt. Fax 422-2024
www.wpcsd.k12.ny.us
White Plains HS 2,100/9-12
550 North St 10605 914-422-2182
Ellen Doherty, prin. Fax 422-2196
White Plains MS - Eastview Campus 6-8
350 Main St 10601 914-422-2223
Joseph Cloherty, prin. Fax 422-2222
White Plains MS - Highlands Campus 1,500/6-8
128 Grandview Ave 10605 914-422-2092
Ernest Spatafore, prin. Fax 422-2273

---

Academy of Our Lady of Good Counsel HS 300/9-12
52 N Broadway 10603 914-949-0178
Sr. Laura Donovan, prin. Fax 682-3531
Archbishop Stepinac HS 600/9-12
950 Mamaroneck Ave 10605 914-946-4800
Paul Carty, prin. Fax 684-2591
Berkeley College Post-Sec.
99 Church St 10601 914-694-1122
German International S New York 300/PK-12
50 Partridge Rd 10605 914-948-6513
Music Conservatory of Westchester Post-Sec.
216 Central Ave 10606 914-761-3715
New York School for the Deaf Post-Sec.
555 Knollwood Rd 10603
Sanford-Brown Institute Post-Sec.
333 Westchester Ave 10604 914-874-2500
The College of Westchester Post-Sec.
325 Central Ave 10606 914-948-4442

**Whitesboro, Oneida, Pop. 3,727**
Whitesboro Central SD 3,400/K-12
65 Oriskany Blvd 13492 315-266-3300
David Langone, supt. Fax 768-9730
www.wboro.org
Whitesboro MS 500/7-8
75 Oriskany Blvd 13492 315-266-3100
John Egresits, prin. Fax 768-9770
Other Schools – See Marcy

**Whitestone, See New York**
NYC Department of Education
Supt. — See New York
JHS 194 1,100/6-8
15460 17th Ave 11357 718-746-0818
Jennifer Miller, prin. Fax 746-7618

---

Lincoln Technical Institute Post-Sec.
1530 Petracca Pl 11357 718-640-9800

**Whitesville, Allegany**
Whitesville Central SD 300/K-12
692 Main St 14897 607-356-3301
Laurie Sanders, supt. Fax 356-3598
www.whitesvillesd.org
Whitesville Central S 300/K-12
692 Main St 14897 607-356-3301
Tammy Emery, prin. Fax 356-3598

**Whitney Point, Broome, Pop. 945**
Whitney Point Central SD 1,500/PK-12
PO Box 249 13862 607-692-8202
Patricia Follette, supt. Fax 692-4434
www.wpcsd.org
Tioughnioga Riverside Academy 600/4-8
PO Box 249 13862 607-692-8232
Laura Chestnut, prin. Fax 692-8283
Whitney Point HS 400/9-12
PO Box 249 13862 607-692-8201
Bruce Tytler, prin. Fax 692-8256

**Williamson, Wayne, Pop. 2,435**
Williamson Central SD 1,100/K-12
PO Box 900 14589 315-589-9661
Dr. Gregory Macaluso, supt. Fax 589-7611
www.williamsoncentral.org
Williamson HS 400/9-12
PO Box 900 14589 315-589-9621
Kathryn Avery, prin. Fax 589-8310
Williamson MS 300/5-8
PO Box 900 14589 315-589-9665
John Fulmer, prin. Fax 589-8314

**Williamsville, Erie, Pop. 5,229**
Williamsville Central SD
Supt. — See East Amherst
Heim MS 600/5-8
175 Heim Rd 14221 716-626-8600
Jeffrey Jachlewski, prin. Fax 626-8626
Mill MS 900/5-8
505 Mill St 14221 716-626-8300
Michael Calandra, prin. Fax 626-8326
Williamsville North HS 1,300/9-12
1595 Hopkins Rd 14221 716-626-8505
Gary Collichio, prin. Fax 626-8597
Williamsville South HS 1,000/9-12
5950 Main St 14221 716-626-8200
Keith Boardman, prin. Fax 626-8207

---

Christian Central Academy 400/K-12
39 Academy St 14221 716-634-4821
Thad Gaebelein, hdmstr. Fax 634-5851
Erie Community College North Post-Sec.
6205 Main St 14221 716-634-0800
Leon Studio One School of Hair Design Post-Sec.
5221 Main St 14221 716-631-3878

**Williston Park, Nassau, Pop. 7,170**

---

Schechter S of Long Island 6-12
6 Cross St 11596 516-539-3700

**Willsboro, Essex, Pop. 740**
Willsboro Central SD 300/PK-12
PO Box 180 12996 518-963-4456
Stephen Broadwell, supt. Fax 963-7577
www.willsborocsd.org/
Willsboro Central S 300/PK-12
PO Box 180 12996 518-963-4456
Stephen Broadwell, prin. Fax 963-7577

**Wilson, Niagara, Pop. 1,249**
Wilson Central SD 1,400/PK-12
PO Box 648 14172 716-751-9341
Dr. Michael Wendt, supt. Fax 751-6556
www.wilson.wnyric.org/
Wilson HS 400/9-12
PO Box 648 14172 716-751-9341
Daniel Johnson, prin. Fax 751-9597
Wilson MS 300/6-8
PO Box 648 14172 716-751-9341
Scott Benton, prin. Fax 751-9597

**Windham, Greene, Pop. 359**
Windham-Ashland-Jewett Central SD 400/K-12
PO Box 429 12496 518-734-3400
John Wiktorko, supt. Fax 734-6050
www.wajcs.org/
Windham-Ashland Central S 400/K-12
PO Box 429 12496 518-734-3400
Kerry Overbaugh, prin. Fax 734-6050

**Windsor, Broome, Pop. 903**
Windsor Central SD 1,700/PK-12
1191 State Route 79 13865 607-655-8216
Jason Andrews, supt. Fax 655-3553
www.windsor-csd.org
Windsor Central HS 600/9-12
1191 State Route 79 13865 607-655-8250
Jeffrey Salasny, prin. Fax 655-3622
Windsor MS 400/6-8
213 Main St 13865 607-655-8247
Kevin Strahley, prin. Fax 655-3760

**Wolcott, Wayne, Pop. 1,683**
North Rose-Wolcott Central SD 1,300/PK-12
11631 Salter Colvin Rd 14590 315-594-3141
Stephan Vigliotti, supt. Fax 594-2352
www.nrwcs.org
North Rose-Wolcott HS 400/9-12
11631 Salter Colvin Rd 14590 315-594-3141
Paul Benz, prin. Fax 594-6235
North Rose-Wolcott MS 400/5-8
5957 New Hartford St 14590 315-594-3141
Mark Mathews, prin. Fax 594-3120

**Woodbourne, Sullivan**

---

Hamesivta 50/9-12
Hasbrouck Rd 12788 845-369-3360

**Woodmere, Nassau, Pop. 17,006**
Hewlett-Woodmere UFD 3,000/PK-12
1 Johnson Pl 11598 516-792-4800
Dr. Ralph Marino, supt. Fax 374-8185
www.hewlett-woodmere.net
Other Schools – See Hewlett

---

Davis Renov Stahler Yeshiva HS for Boys 300/9-12
700 Ibsen St 11598 516-295-7700
Lawrence Woodmere Academy 300/PK-12
336 Woodmere Blvd 11598 516-374-9000
Alan Bernstein, hdmstr. Fax 374-4707

**Woodside, See New York**
NYC Department of Education
Supt. — See New York
IS 125 1,600/5-8
4602 47th Ave 11377 718-937-0320
Judy Mittler, prin. Fax 361-2451

---

Greater New York Academy 200/9-12
4132 58th St 11377 718-639-1752
Razi S 300/PK-12
5511 Queens Blvd 11377 718-779-0711

**Worcester, Otsego, Pop. 1,097**
Worcester Central SD 400/PK-12
198 Main St 12197 607-397-8785
William Diamond, supt. Fax 397-8464
www.worcestercs.org
Worcester Central S 400/PK-12
198 Main St 12197 607-397-8785
Elizabeth Fallo, prin. Fax 397-9454

**Wyandanch, Suffolk, Pop. 11,382**
Wyandanch UFD 2,100/PK-12
1445 Straight Path 11798 631-870-0400
Dr. Mary Jones, supt. Fax 870-0404
www.wufsd.net/
Olive MS 400/6-8
140 Garden City Ave 11798 631-870-0525
Kester Hodge, prin. Fax 870-0533
Wyandanch Memorial HS 500/9-12
54 S 32nd St 11798 631-870-0450
Paul Sibblies, prin. Fax 870-0459

**Yonkers, Westchester, Pop. 192,139**
Yonkers CSD 23,800/PK-12
1 Larkin Ctr 10701 914-376-8000
Dr. Michael Yazurlo, supt. Fax 376-8062
www.yonkerspublicschools.org
Gorton HS 1,100/9-12
100 Shonnard Pl 10703 914-376-8350
Gail Joyner-White, prin. Fax 376-8377
Lincoln HS 1,200/9-12
375 Kneeland Ave 10704 914-376-8400
Ian Sherman, prin. Fax 376-8414
Palisade Preparatory S 500/7-12
201 Palisade Ave 10703 914-376-8177
Dr. Michelle Yazurlo, prin. Fax 376-8484
Riverside HS 1,000/9-12
565 Warburton Ave 10701 914-376-8425
Dr. Don Solimene, prin. Fax 376-8475
Roosevelt HS - Early College Studies 700/9-12
631 Tuckahoe Rd 10710 914-376-8118
Ed DeChent, prin. Fax 793-4971
Saunders Trades & Tech HS 1,200/9-12
183 Palmer Rd 10701 914-376-8150
Steve Mazzola, prin. Fax 376-8154
Yonkers Montessori Academy 1,200/PK-12
160 Woodlawn Ave 10704 914-376-8540
Dr. Eileen Rivera-Shapiro, prin. Fax 376-8552
Yonkers MSHS 1,200/7-12
150 Rockland Ave 10705 914-376-8191
Jane Wermuth, prin. Fax 376-4856
Pathways to Success Adult
75 Riverdale Ave 10701 914-376-8600
Sanah Naber, prin. Fax 376-0541

---

Cochran School of Nursing Post-Sec.
967 N Broadway 10701 914-964-4296
Sacred Heart HS 400/9-12
34 Convent Ave 10703 914-965-3114
Rev. Maurice Moreau, head sch Fax 965-4510
St. Joseph's Seminary Post-Sec.
201 Seminary Ave 10704 914-968-6200
St. Vladimir's Orthodox Theological Sem. Post-Sec.
575 Scarsdale Rd 10707 914-961-8313

**Yorkshire, Cattaraugus, Pop. 1,167**
Yorkshire-Pioneer Central SD 2,400/K-12
PO Box 579 14173 716-492-9300
Chuck J. Rinaldi Ed.D., supt. Fax 492-9360
www.pioneerschools.org
Pioneer HS 800/9-12
PO Box 639 14173 716-492-9334
Mark Schultz, prin. Fax 492-9350
Pioneer MS 800/5-8
PO Box 619 14173 716-492-9371
Melissa Prorok, prin. Fax 492-9417

**Yorktown Heights, Westchester, Pop. 1,760**
Lakeland Central SD
Supt. — See Shrub Oak
Lakeland-Copper Beech MS 1,400/6-8
3401 Old Yorktown Rd 10598 914-245-1885
Robert Bergmann, prin. Fax 245-1259

Yorktown Central SD 3,700/K-12
2725 Crompond Rd 10598 914-243-8000
Dr. Ralph Napolitano, supt. Fax 243-8002
www.yorktown.org/
Strang MS 900/6-8
2701 Crompond Rd 10598 914-243-8100
Linda Grimm, prin. Fax 243-0016
Yorktown HS 1,300/9-12
2727 Crompond Rd 10598 914-243-8050
Joseph DeGennaro, prin. Fax 245-9256

**Youngstown, Niagara, Pop. 1,918**
Lewiston-Porter Central SD 2,200/K-12
4061 Creek Rd 14174 716-754-8281
Chris Roser, supt. Fax 754-2755
www.lew-port.com
Lewiston-Porter HS 700/9-12
4061 Creek Rd 14174 716-286-7262
Paul Casseri, prin. Fax 286-7852
Lewiston-Porter MS 500/6-8
4061 Creek Rd 14174 716-286-7201
Dean Ramirez, prin. Fax 286-7204

# NORTH CAROLINA

## NORTH CAROLINA DEPT. PUBLIC INSTRUCTION
**301 N Wilmington St, Raleigh 27601-1058**
**Telephone 919-807-3300**
**Fax 919-807-3445**
**Website http://www.dpi.state.nc.us**

Superintendent of Public Instruction June Atkinson

## NORTH CAROLINA BOARD OF EDUCATION
**301 N Wilmington St, Raleigh 27601-1058**

Chairperson William Harrison

## PUBLIC, PRIVATE AND CATHOLIC SECONDARY SCHOOLS

**Aberdeen, Moore, Pop. 6,182**
Moore County SD
Supt. — See Carthage
Southern MS 800/6-8
717 Johnson St 28315 910-693-1550
Shelia Gilliard, prin. Fax 693-1544

**Advance, Davie, Pop. 1,117**
Davie County SD
Supt. — See Mocksville
Ellis MS 500/6-8
144 William Ellis Dr 27006 336-998-2007
Alicia Holman, prin. Fax 998-6249

**Ahoskie, Hertford, Pop. 4,982**
Hertford County SD
Supt. — See Winton
Hertford County Early College HS 100/9-12
109 Community College Rd 27910 252-332-7788
Bryan Ruffin, prin. Fax 332-3605
Hertford County HS 700/9-12
1500 1st St W 27910 252-332-4096
James Futrell, prin. Fax 332-6176

---

Ahoskie Christian S 200/PK-12
500 Kiwanis St 27910 252-332-2764
Elaine Pool, prin. Fax 332-2492
Ridgecroft S 300/PK-12
PO Box 1008 27910 252-332-2964
Roanoke-Chowan Community College Post-Sec.
109 Community College Rd 27910 252-862-1200

**Albemarle, Stanly, Pop. 15,632**
Stanly County SD 8,000/PK-12
1000 N 1st St Ste 4 28001 704-961-3000
Dr. Terry Griffin, supt. Fax 961-3099
www.stanlycountyschools.org
Albemarle HS 500/9-12
311 Park Ridge Rd 28001 704-961-3000
Douglas Kilgore, prin. Fax 961-3099
Albemarle MS 400/6-8
1811 Badin Rd 28001 704-961-3400
Beverly Pennington, prin. Fax 961-3499
Stanly Academy Learning Center 50/Alt
1121 Austin St 28001 704-961-4500
Shannon Batchelor, prin. Fax 961-4599
Stanly Early College HS 200/9-12
141 College Dr 28001 704-991-0128
Anne Faulkenberry, dean Fax 991-0109
Other Schools – See Locust, New London, Norwood, Oakboro

---

Stanly Community College Post-Sec.
141 College Dr 28001 704-982-0121

**Andrews, Cherokee, Pop. 1,715**
Cherokee County SD
Supt. — See Murphy
Andrews HS 300/9-12
50 High School Dr 28901 828-321-5415
Lisa Anderson, prin. Fax 321-3986
Andrews MS 200/6-8
2750 Business 19 28901 828-321-5762
Andy Pyle, prin. Fax 321-2009

**Angier, Harnett, Pop. 4,289**
Harnett County SD
Supt. — See Lillington
Harnett Central HS 1,400/9-12
2911 Harnett Central Rd 27501 919-639-6161
Chris Mace, prin. Fax 639-3642
Harnett Central MS 1,300/6-8
2529 Harnett Central Rd 27501 919-639-6000
Linwood Smith, prin. Fax 639-9617

**Apex, Wake, Pop. 36,623**
Wake County SD
Supt. — See Cary
Apex Friendship HS 9-12
7801 Humie Olive Rd 27502 919-694-0500
Matt Wight, prin.
Apex HS 2,400/9-12
1501 Laura Duncan Rd 27502 919-387-2208
Dr. Diann Kearney, prin. Fax 387-3023
Apex MS 1,100/6-8
400 E Moore St 27502 919-387-2181
Allen Ellzey, prin. Fax 387-2203
Lufkin Road MS 1,000/6-8
1002 Lufkin Rd, 919-387-4465
Karen Sinders, prin. Fax 363-1095
Middle Creek HS 1,900/9-12
123 Middle Creek Park Ave, 919-773-3838
Wade Martin, prin. Fax 773-3880
Salem MS 1,100/6-8
6150 Old Jenks Rd, 919-363-1870
Elaine Hofmann, prin. Fax 363-1876
West Lake MS 1,300/6-8
4600 W Lake Rd, 919-662-2900
Anne Adkins, prin. Fax 662-2906

**Arden, Buncombe**
Buncombe County SD
Supt. — See Asheville
Valley Springs MS 500/6-8
224 Long Shoals Rd 28704 828-654-1785
Eddie Burchfiel, prin. Fax 654-1789

---

Christ S 200/8-12
500 Christ School Rd 28704 828-684-6232
Paul Krieger, hdmstr. Fax 684-2745

**Asheboro, Randolph, Pop. 24,567**
Asheboro CSD 4,700/PK-12
PO Box 1103 27204 336-625-5104
Dr. Terry Worrell, supt. Fax 625-9238
www.asheboro.k12.nc.us
Asheboro HS 1,300/9-12
1221 S Park St 27203 336-625-6185
Dr. Brian Toth, prin. Fax 625-9320
North Asheboro MS 500/6-8
1861 N Asheboro School Rd 27203 336-672-1900
Candace Call, prin. Fax 672-6267
South Asheboro MS 600/6-8
523 W Walker Ave 27203 336-629-4141
Charlie Lyons, prin. Fax 629-3761

Randolph County SD 18,500/PK-12
2222 S Fayetteville St # C 27205 336-318-6100
Dr. Stephen Gainey, supt. Fax 318-6155
www.randolph.k12.nc.us
Randolph Early College HS 300/9-12
629 Industrial Park Ave 27205 336-625-1137
April Thompson, prin. Fax 625-3186
Southwestern Randolph HS 1,200/9-12
1641 Hopewell Friends Rd 27205 336-381-7747
Shon Hildreth, prin. Fax 381-7743
Southwestern Randolph MS 600/6-8
1509 Hopewell Friends Rd 27205 336-381-3900
Michael Crider, prin. Fax 381-3905
Other Schools – See Climax, Liberty, Ramseur, Randleman, Trinity

---

Fayetteville Street Christian S 200/PK-12
151 W Pritchard St 27203 336-629-1383
David Jeffreys, admin. Fax 629-0067
Neighbors Grove Christian Academy 100/K-12
1928 N Fayetteville St 27203 336-672-1147
Randy Haithcock, admin. Fax 672-5500
Randolph Community College Post-Sec.
629 Industrial Park Ave 27205 336-633-0200

**Asheville, Buncombe, Pop. 81,334**
Asheville CSD 3,800/PK-12
85 Mountain St 28801 828-350-7000
Dr. Pamela Baldwin, supt. Fax 255-5131
www.ashevillecityschools.net
Asheville HS 1,000/9-12
419 Mcdowell St 28803 828-350-2500
Joyce Best, prin. Fax 255-5316
Asheville MS 800/6-8
197 S French Broad Ave 28801 828-350-6200
Cynthia Sellinger, prin. Fax 255-5311
School of Inquiry and Life Sciences 200/9-12
419 McDowell St 28803 828-350-2700
David Robinson, prin. Fax 255-5119

Buncombe County SD 24,000/K-12
175 Bingham Rd 28806 828-255-5921
Dr. Tony Baldwin, supt. Fax 255-5923
www.buncombe.k12.nc.us
Buncombe County Early College S 200/9-12
340 Victoria Rd 28801 828-232-4123
Bonnie Johnston, prin. Fax 232-4165
Buncombe County Middle College HS 100/Alt
340 Victoria Rd 28801 828-232-4123
Bonnie Johnston, prin. Fax 232-4165
Erwin HS 1,300/9-12
60 Lees Creek Rd 28806 828-232-4251
Dr. Jim Brown, prin. Fax 251-2893
Erwin MS 700/7-8
20 Erwin Hills Rd 28806 828-232-4264
Joel Hathaway, prin. Fax 253-4267
Nesbitt Discovery Academy 9-10
175 Bingham Rd 28806 828-271-4521
Nathan Alison, prin.
Reynolds HS 1,400/9-12
1 Rocket Dr 28803 828-298-2500
Doris Sellers, prin. Fax 298-2002
Reynolds MS 600/6-8
2 Rocket Dr 28803 828-298-7484
Jamie Johnson, prin. Fax 298-7503
Roberson HS 1,500/9-12
250 Overlook Rd 28803 828-654-1765
Amy Rhoney, prin. Fax 654-1768
Other Schools – See Arden, Black Mountain, Candler, Fletcher, Swannanoa, Weaverville

---

Asheville Buncombe Technical Comm. Coll. Post-Sec.
340 Victoria Rd 28801 828-254-1921
Asheville S 300/9-12
360 Asheville School Rd 28806 828-254-6345
Archibald Montgomery, hdmstr. Fax 252-8666
Carolina Day S 700/PK-12
1345 Hendersonville Rd 28803 828-274-0757
Kirk Duncan, head sch Fax 274-0756
Daoist Traditions Coll of Chinese Med Post-Sec.
382 Montford Ave 28801 828-225-3993
North Asheville Christian S 100/PK-12
20 Reynolds Mountain Blvd 28804 828-645-8053
Susie Hepler, admin. Fax 645-4542
South College - Asheville Post-Sec.
140 Sweeten Creek Rd 28803 828-398-2500
Temple Baptist S 100/PK-12
985 1/2 Patton Ave 28806 828-252-3712
University of North Carolina Post-Sec.
1 University Hts 28804 828-251-6600
Warren Wilson College Post-Sec.
PO Box 9000 28815 828-298-3325

**Ayden, Pitt, Pop. 4,853**
Pitt County SD
Supt. — See Greenville
Ayden-Grifton HS 700/9-12
7653 NC 11 S 28513 252-746-4183
Marty Baker, prin. Fax 746-2120
Ayden MS 300/6-8
192 3rd St 28513 252-746-3672
Dr. Jeff Theus, prin. Fax 746-9923

**Bailey, Nash, Pop. 561**
Nash-Rocky Mount SD
Supt. — See Nashville
Southern Nash HS 1,300/9-12
6446 Southern Nash High Rd 27807 252-451-8520
Dr. Mark Cockrell, prin. Fax 478-5953

**Bakersville, Mitchell, Pop. 450**
Mitchell County SD 1,900/K-12
72 Ledger School Rd 28705 828-766-2220
Dr. Richard Spurling, supt. Fax 766-2221
www.mcsnc.org
Bowman MS 200/5-8
410 S Mitchell Ave 28705 828-766-3370
Fax 688-6002
Mitchell HS 600/9-12
416 Ledger School Rd 28705 828-766-3400
Mark Woody, prin. Fax 688-4847
Other Schools – See Spruce Pine

**Banner Elk, Avery, Pop. 1,011**

---

Lees-McRae College — Post-Sec.
PO Box 128 28604 — 828-898-5241

**Barco, Currituck**
Currituck County SD
Supt. — See Currituck
Currituck County HS — 1,000/9-12
4203 Caratoke Hwy 27917 — 252-453-0014
Renee Dowdy, prin. — Fax 453-0017
Currituck County MS — 400/6-8
4263 Caratoke Hwy 27917 — 252-453-2171
Claire King, prin. — Fax 453-0019

**Battleboro, Edgecombe, Pop. 559**
Edgecombe County SD
Supt. — See Tarboro
Phillips MS — 200/6-8
4371 Battleboro Leggett Rd 27809 — 252-446-2031
Donita Gregory, prin. — Fax 446-1629

Nash-Rocky Mount SD
Supt. — See Nashville
Red Oak MS — 900/6-8
3170 Red Oak Battleboro Rd 27809 — 252-462-2000
Margaret Sharpe, prin. — Fax 451-5510

**Bayboro, Pamlico, Pop. 1,250**
Pamlico County SD — 1,400/PK-12
507 Anderson Dr 28515 — 252-745-4171
Lisa Jackson, supt. — Fax 745-4172
www.pamlico.k12.nc.us
Pamlico County HS — 500/9-12
601 Main St 28515 — 252-745-3151
Chris Meadows, prin. — Fax 745-3153
Pamlico County MS — 300/6-8
15526 NC Highway 55 28515 — 252-745-4061
Jeremy Johnson, prin. — Fax 745-5583

**Bear Creek, Chatham**
Chatham County SD
Supt. — See Pittsboro
Chatham Central HS — 400/9-12
14950 NC 902 Hwy 27207 — 919-837-2251
Mitch Stensland, prin. — Fax 837-2975

**Beaufort, Carteret, Pop. 3,948**
Carteret County SD — 8,600/PK-12
107 Safrit Dr 28516 — 252-728-4583
Dr. Daniel Novey, supt. — Fax 728-3028
www.carteretcountyschools.org
Beaufort MS — 300/6-8
100 Carraway Dr 28516 — 252-728-4520
Dr. Cathy Tomon, prin. — Fax 728-3392
East Carteret HS — 500/9-12
3263 US Highway 70 E 28516 — 252-728-3514
April Lilley, prin. — Fax 728-3487
Other Schools – See Morehead City, Newport, Smyrna

**Belhaven, Beaufort, Pop. 1,666**

---

Pungo Christian Academy — 200/PK-12
983 W Main St 27810 — 252-943-2678

**Belmont, Gaston, Pop. 9,916**
Gaston County SD
Supt. — See Gastonia
Belmont MS — 700/6-8
110 N Central Ave 28012 — 704-825-9619
Susan Redmond, prin. — Fax 825-6951
Cramer HS — 9-12
101 Lakewood Rd 28012 — 704-866-5700
Audrey Devine, prin. — Fax 825-8950
South Point HS — 1,300/9-12
906 S Point Rd 28012 — 704-825-3351
Gary Ford, prin. — Fax 825-2820

---

Belmont Abbey College — Post-Sec.
100 Belmont Mount Holly Rd 28012 — 888-222-0110

**Benson, Johnston, Pop. 3,270**
Johnston County SD
Supt. — See Smithfield
Benson MS — 400/5-8
1600 N Wall St 27504 — 919-894-3889
Ron Anthony, prin. — Fax 894-1551
McGee's Crossroads MS — 800/6-8
13353 NC Highway 210 27504 — 919-894-6003
Sheila Singleton, prin. — Fax 894-6007
West Johnston HS — 1,600/9-12
5935 Raleigh Rd 27504 — 919-934-7333
Paula Coates, prin. — Fax 934-6906

**Bessemer City, Gaston, Pop. 5,262**
Gaston County SD
Supt. — See Gastonia
Bessemer City HS — 500/9-12
119 Yellow Jacket Rd 28016 — 704-836-9601
James Montgomery, prin. — Fax 629-2775
Bessemer City MS — 600/6-8
525 Ed Wilson Rd 28016 — 704-836-9602
Dr. Rebecca Wilson, prin. — Fax 629-4501

**Bethel, Pitt, Pop. 1,573**
Pitt County SD
Supt. — See Greenville
North Pitt HS — 1,000/9-12
5659 NC Highway 11 N 27812 — 252-825-0054
Dr. Lionel Kato, prin. — Fax 825-1310

**Beulaville, Duplin, Pop. 1,278**
Duplin County SD
Supt. — See Kenansville
East Duplin HS — 900/9-12
394 N NC 111 Hwy 28518 — 910-298-4535
Scott Ballard, prin. — Fax 298-2021

**Biscoe, Montgomery, Pop. 1,683**
Montgomery County SD
Supt. — See Troy
East MS — 500/6-8
1834 US Highway 220 Alt S 27209 — 910-428-3278
Della Ingram, prin. — Fax 428-1279
East Montgomery HS — 600/9-12
157 Eagle Ln 27209 — 910-428-9641
Heather Seawell, prin. — Fax 428-1197

**Black Mountain, Buncombe, Pop. 7,683**
Buncombe County SD
Supt. — See Asheville
Owen HS — 800/9-12
99 Lake Eden Rd 28711 — 828-686-3852
Margaret Turner, prin. — Fax 686-8442

**Bladenboro, Bladen, Pop. 1,726**
Bladen County SD
Supt. — See Elizabethtown
Bladenboro MS — 400/5-8
910 S Main St 28320 — 910-863-3232
Randi Harrelson, prin. — Fax 863-4683
West Bladen HS — 800/9-12
1600 NC 410 Hwy 28320 — 910-862-2130
Wesley Floyd, prin. — Fax 862-3328

**Boiling Springs, Cleveland, Pop. 4,581**

---

Gardner-Webb University — Post-Sec.
PO Box 997 28017 — 704-406-4000

**Bolivia, Brunswick, Pop. 139**
Brunswick County SD — 12,200/PK-12
35 Referendum Dr NE 28422 — 910-253-2900
Leslie K. Tubb, supt. — Fax 253-2983
www.bcswan.net
Brunswick County Academy — 100/Alt
1109 Old Ocean Hwy 28422 — 910-754-9593
Marcia Heady, prin. — Fax 754-9594
Brunswick County Early College HS — 300/9-12
60 College Rd NE 28422 — 910-754-8565
Dr. Cheryl Skaggs, prin. — Fax 754-8567
Other Schools – See Leland, Shallotte, Southport, Supply

**Boone, Watauga, Pop. 16,843**
Watauga County SD — 4,600/PK-12
PO Box 1790 28607 — 828-264-7190
Dr. Scott Elliott, supt. — Fax 264-7196
www.watauga.k12.nc.us
Watauga HS — 1,400/9-12
300 Go Pioneers Dr 28607 — 828-264-2407
Marshall Gasperson, prin. — Fax 264-9030

---

Appalachian State University — Post-Sec.
Asu Sta 28608 — 828-262-2000

**Boonville, Yadkin, Pop. 1,215**
Yadkin County SD
Supt. — See Yadkinville
Starmount HS — 700/9-12
2516 Longtown Rd 27011 — 336-468-2891
Cody Hemric, prin. — Fax 468-6434
Starmount MS — 400/7-8
2626 Longtown Rd 27011 — 336-468-6833
Rick Swaim, prin. — Fax 468-6838

**Bostic, Rutherford, Pop. 382**
Rutherford County SD
Supt. — See Forest City
East Rutherford MS — 700/6-8
259 E Church St 28018 — 828-245-3750
Jo Oliver, prin. — Fax 245-1491

**Brevard, Transylvania, Pop. 7,401**
Transylvania County SD — 3,500/K-12
225 Rosenwald Ln 28712 — 828-884-6173
Dr. Jeff McDaris, supt. — Fax 884-9524
www.tcsnc.org
Brevard HS — 700/9-12
609 Country Club Rd 28712 — 828-884-4103
Jennifer Anderson, prin. — Fax 885-7355
Brevard MS — 600/6-8
400 Fisher Rd 28712 — 828-884-2091
Jeff Bailey, prin. — Fax 883-3150
Davidson River S — 100/Alt
970 Ecusta Rd 28712 — 828-884-9567
Donna Wilde, prin. — Fax 862-5347
Other Schools – See Rosman

---

Brevard College — Post-Sec.
1 Brevard College Dr 28712 — 828-883-8292

**Browns Summit, Guilford**
Guilford County SD
Supt. — See Greensboro
Brown Summit MS — 200/6-8
4720 E NC Highway 150 27214 — 336-656-0432
Deborah Mott, prin. — Fax 656-0439

**Bryson City, Swain, Pop. 1,399**
Swain County SD — 2,000/PK-12
PO Box 2340 28713 — 828-488-3129
Sam Pattillo, supt. — Fax 488-8510
www.swain.k12.nc.us
Swain County HS — 600/9-12
1415 Fontana Rd 28713 — 828-488-2152
Mark Sale, prin. — Fax 488-0523
Swain County MS — 500/PK-PK, 6-
135 Arlington Ave 28713 — 828-488-3480
Brandon Suttn, prin. — Fax 488-0949

**Buies Creek, Harnett, Pop. 2,881**

---

Campbell University — Post-Sec.
PO Box 567 27506 — 910-893-1200

**Bunn, Franklin, Pop. 340**
Franklin County SD
Supt. — See Louisburg
Bunn HS — 900/9-12
PO Box 146 27508 — 919-496-3975
Robin Faulkner, prin. — Fax 496-6943
Bunn MS — 700/6-8
4742 NC 39 Hwy S 27508 — 919-496-7700
Roosevelt Alston, prin. — Fax 496-1404

**Burgaw, Pender, Pop. 3,819**
Pender County SD — 8,000/PK-12
925 Penderlea Hwy 28425 — 910-259-2187
Dr. Terri Cobb, supt. — Fax 259-0133
www.pendercountyschools.net/
Burgaw MS — 200/6-8
500 S Wright St 28425 — 910-259-0149
Darren Lafon, prin. — Fax 259-0150
Pender Early College HS — 200/8-12
100 Industrial Dr 28425 — 910-259-7925
Dr. Edith Skipper, prin. — Fax 259-7174
Pender HS — 600/9-12
5380 NC Highway 53 W 28425 — 910-259-0162
Anthony Baker, prin. — Fax 259-0166
West Pender MS — 200/6-8
10750 NC Highway 53 W 28425 — 910-283-5626
Keith Whitaker, prin. — Fax 283-9537
Other Schools – See Hampstead, Rocky Point

**Burlington, Alamance, Pop. 49,060**
Alamance-Burlington SD — 22,700/PK-12
1712 Vaughn Rd 27217 — 336-570-6060
Dr. William Harrison, supt. — Fax 570-6218
www.abss.k12.nc.us
Broadview MS — 700/6-8
2229 Broadview Dr 27217 — 336-570-6195
Brie Butler, prin. — Fax 570-6202
Career and Technical Education Center — Vo/Tech
2550 Buckingham Rd 27217 — 336-570-6092
Darrell Thomas, prin. — Fax 570-6093
Cummings HS — 900/9-12
2200 N Mebane St 27217 — 336-570-6100
Emmet Alexander, prin. — Fax 570-6107
Turrentine MS — 900/6-8
1710 Edgewood Ave 27215 — 336-570-6150
Brian Williams, prin. — Fax 570-6210
Williams HS — 1,200/9-12
1307 S Church St 27215 — 336-570-6161
Dr. Joe Ferrelll, prin. — Fax 570-6214
Other Schools – See Elon, Graham, Mebane

---

Burlington Christian Academy — 700/PK-12
621 E 6th St 27215 — 336-227-0288
Michael Brown, admin. — Fax 570-1314
Burlington Day S — 200/PK-12
1615 Greenwood Ter 27215 — 336-228-0296
Ronnie Wall, head sch — Fax 226-6249

**Burnsville, Yancey, Pop. 1,680**
Yancey County SD — 2,400/K-12
PO Box 190 28714 — 828-682-6101
Dr. Tony Tipton Ed.D., supt. — Fax 682-7110
www.yanceync.net
Cane River MS — 300/6-8
1128 Cane River School Rd 28714 — 828-682-2202
Alton Robinson, prin. — Fax 682-3754
East Yancey MS — 300/6-8
285 Georges Fork Rd 28714 — 828-682-2281
Angie Anglin, prin. — Fax 682-3513
Mountain Heritage HS — 700/9-12
PO Box 70 28714 — 828-682-6103
Kevin Huskins, prin. — Fax 682-4287

**Butner, Granville, Pop. 7,466**
Granville County SD
Supt. — See Oxford
Butner-Stem MS — 500/6-8
501 E D St 27509 — 919-575-9429
Lauren Allen, prin. — Fax 575-5894

**Buxton, Dare, Pop. 1,259**
Dare County SD
Supt. — See Nags Head
Cape Hatteras S of Coastal Studies — 300/6-12
PO Box 948 27920 — 252-995-5730
Beth Rooks, prin. — Fax 995-6161

**Camden, Camden, Pop. 580**
Camden County SD — 1,900/PK-12
174 NC Highway 343 N 27921 — 252-335-0831
Melvin Hawkins, supt. — Fax 331-2300
www.camden.k12.nc.us
Camden County HS — 400/9-12
103 US Highway 158 W 27921 — 252-338-0114
Billie Berry, prin. — Fax 331-6792
Camden MS — 300/7-8
248 Scotland Rd 27921 — 252-338-3349
Ernest Cooley, prin. — Fax 331-2253
CamTech HS — 200/9-12
103 US Highway 158 W Ste A 27921 — 252-335-7219
Amber Davis, prin. — Fax 335-4219

**Cameron, Moore, Pop. 274**
Moore County SD
Supt. — See Carthage
New Century MS — 500/6-8
1577 Union Church Rd 28326 — 910-947-1301
Tracy Metcalf, prin. — Fax 947-1227
Union Pines HS — 1,200/9-12
1981 Union Church Rd 28326 — 910-947-5511
Robin Lea, prin. — Fax 947-5117

**Candler, Buncombe**
Buncombe County SD
Supt. — See Asheville
Enka HS — 1,300/9-12
475 Enka Lake Rd 28715 — 828-670-5000
Edwin Spivey, prin. — Fax 670-5007
Enka MS — 1,100/6-8
390 Asbury Rd 28715 — 828-670-5010
Leland Blankenship, prin. — Fax 670-5015

---

Mt. Pisgah Academy — 100/9-12
75 Academy Dr 28715 — 828-667-2535

**Canton, Haywood, Pop. 4,165**
Haywood County SD
Supt. — See Waynesville

Canton MS 600/6-8
60 Penland St 28716 828-646-3467
Todd Barbee, prin. Fax 646-3478
Pisgah HS 1,100/9-12
1 Black Bear Dr 28716 828-646-3440
Greg Bailey, prin. Fax 648-8618

**Carrboro, Orange, Pop. 19,067**
Chapel Hill-Carrboro CSD
Supt. — See Chapel Hill
Carrboro HS 900/9-12
201 Rock Haven Rd 27510 919-918-2200
LaVerne Mattocks, prin. Fax 918-2507

**Carthage, Moore, Pop. 2,154**
Moore County SD 12,200/PK-12
PO Box 1180 28327 910-947-2976
Robert Grimesey, supt. Fax 947-3011
www.ncmcs.org
Community Learning Center @ Pinckney 50/Alt
160 Pinckney Rd 28327 910-947-2603
Shaun Krencicki, prin. Fax 947-2404
Crain's Creek MS 6-8
4631 Union Church Rd 28327 910-245-3796
Rose Cooper, prin. Fax 245-7312
Other Schools – See Aberdeen, Cameron, Robbins, Southern Pines, West End

**Cary, Wake, Pop. 131,955**
Wake County SD 140,400/PK-12
5625 Dillard Dr 27518 919-431-7400
Dr. Jim Merrill, supt.
www.wcpss.net
Cary HS 2,300/9-12
638 Walnut St 27511 919-460-3549
Jacob Bryant, prin. Fax 460-3573
Davis Drive MS 1,200/6-8
2101 Davis Dr 27519 919-387-3033
Rick Williams, prin. Fax 387-3039
East Cary MS 700/6-8
1111 SE Maynard Rd 27511 919-466-4377
Nikia Davis, prin. Fax 466-4388
Green Hope HS 2,000/9-12
2500 Carpenter Upchurch Rd 27519 919-380-3700
Karen Summers, prin. Fax 380-3712
Mills Park MS 1,300/6-8
441 Mills Park Dr 27519 919-466-1500
Robert Smith, prin. Fax 466-1522
Panther Creek HS 2,500/9-12
6770 McCrimmon Pkwy 27519 919-463-8656
Dr. Camille Hedrick, prin. Fax 463-8666
Reedy Creek MS 1,000/6-8
930 Reedy Creek Rd 27513 919-460-3504
Hilton Evans, prin. Fax 460-3391
West Cary MS 700/6-8
1000 Evans Rd 27513 919-460-3528
Robert James, prin. Fax 460-3540
Other Schools – See Apex, Fuquay Varina, Garner, Holly Springs, Knightdale, Raleigh, Rolesville, Wake Forest, Wendell, Zebulon

---

Cary Academy 700/6-12
1500 N Harrison Ave 27513 919-677-3873
Michael Ehrhardt Ed.D., head sch Fax 677-4002
Cary Christian S 800/K-12
1330 Old Apex Rd 27513 919-303-2560
Dell Cook, admin. Fax 367-7558
Hopewell Academy 50/6-12
101 Preston Executive Dr 27513 919-481-2123
ITT Technical Institute Post-Sec.
5520 Dillard Dr Ste 100 27518 919-233-2520
Miller-Motte College Post-Sec.
2205 Walnut St 27518 919-532-7171
Shepherds Theological Seminary Post-Sec.
6051 Tryon Rd 27518 919-573-5350

**Cashiers, Jackson, Pop. 156**
Jackson County SD
Supt. — See Sylva
Blue Ridge Early College 100/7-12
95 Bobcat Dr 28717 828-743-2646
Adam Holt, prin. Fax 743-5320

**Castle Hayne, New Hanover, Pop. 1,182**
New Hanover County SD
Supt. — See Wilmington
Holly Shelter MS 700/6-8
3921 Roger Haynes Dr 28429 910-602-4046
Jayne Kiker, prin. Fax 602-4045
Wilmington Early College HS 200/9-12
4500 Blue Clay Rd 28429 910-362-7789
Ivy Murrain, prin. Fax 362-7424

**Catawba, Catawba, Pop. 599**
Catawba County SD
Supt. — See Newton
Bandys HS 900/9-12
5040 E Bandys Xrd 28609 828-241-3171
Angela Williams, prin. Fax 241-9402

**Cerro Gordo, Columbus, Pop. 201**
Columbus County SD
Supt. — See Whiteville
West Columbus HS 500/9-12
PO Box 130 28430 910-654-6111
Jeffrey Greene, prin. Fax 654-4082

**Chadbourn, Columbus, Pop. 1,832**
Columbus County SD
Supt. — See Whiteville
Chadbourn MS 200/6-8
801 W Smith St 28431 910-654-4300
Georgia Spaulding, prin. Fax 654-6809

**Chapel Hill, Orange, Pop. 55,802**
Chapel Hill-Carrboro CSD 11,900/PK-12
750 S Merritt Mill Rd 27516 919-967-8211
Dr. Tom Forcella, supt. Fax 933-4560
www.chccs.k12.nc.us
Chapel Hill HS 1,400/9-12
1709 High School Rd 27516 919-929-2106
Sulura Jackson, prin. Fax 929-2455
East Chapel Hill HS 1,400/9-12
500 Weaver Dairy Rd 27514 919-969-2482
Eileen Tully, prin. Fax 969-2492
Grey Culbreth MS 700/6-8
225 Culbreth Rd 27516 919-929-7161
Beverly Rudolph, prin. Fax 969-2412
McDougle MS 700/6-8
900 Old Fayetteville Rd 27516 919-933-1556
Bob Bales, prin. Fax 969-2433
Phillips MS 600/6-8
606 N Estes Dr 27514 919-929-2188
Tomeka Ward-Satterfield, prin. Fax 969-2477
Phoenix Academy HS 50/Alt
750 S Merritt Mill Rd 27516 919-918-2300
John Williams, prin. Fax 933-4560
Smith MS 700/6-8
9201 Seawell School Rd 27516 919-918-2145
Phil Holmes, prin. Fax 918-2079
Other Schools – See Carrboro

Chatham County SD
Supt. — See Pittsboro
Pollard MS 500/6-8
185 Granite Mill Blvd 27516 919-969-0070
LaShonda Hester, prin.

---

Emerson Waldorf S 200/PK-12
6211 New Jericho Rd 27516 919-967-1858
Christina Wise, admin. Fax 967-2732
University of North Carolina 27599 Post-Sec.
919-962-2211
University of North Carolina Hospitals Post-Sec.
101 Manning Dr 27514 919-966-5111

**Charlotte, Mecklenburg, Pop. 715,605**
Charlotte/Mecklenburg County SD 130,000/PK-12
PO Box 30035 28230 980-343-6270
Ann Clark, supt. Fax 343-7135
www.cms.k12.nc.us/
Albemarle Road MS 1,000/6-8
6900 Democracy Dr 28212 980-343-6420
Toni Perry, prin. Fax 343-6501
Berry Academy of Technology 1,500/9-12
1430 Alleghany St 28208 980-343-5992
Terra Kennedy, prin. Fax 343-5994
Biotechnolgy Health & Public Admin @ OHS 400/9-12
4301 Sandy Porter Rd Ste E 28273 980-343-1110
Angela Bozeman, prin. Fax 343-1114
Carmel MS 1,100/6-8
5001 Camilla Dr 28226 980-343-6705
Mark Angerer, prin. Fax 343-6749
Cato Middle College HS 200/11-12
8120 Grier Rd 28215 980-343-1452
Alicisa Johnson, prin. Fax 343-1453
Charlotte Engineering Early College 9-12
9000 Robert Snyder Rd 28262 980-343-9898
Will Leach, prin. Fax 343-2517
Cochrane Collegiate Academy 600/6-12
6200 Starhaven Dr 28215 980-343-6460
Rachel Corn, prin. Fax 343-6521
Community House MS 1,500/6-8
9500 Community House Rd 28277 980-343-0689
Jamie Brooks, prin. Fax 343-0691
Coulwood MS 800/6-8
500 Kentberry Dr 28214 980-343-6090
Janet Moss, prin. Fax 343-6142
East Mecklenburg HS 1,700/9-12
6800 Monroe Rd 28212 980-343-6430
Richard Parker, prin. Fax 343-6437
Eastway MS 900/6-8
1501 Norland Rd 28205 980-343-6410
Mary Webb, prin. Fax 343-6406
Garinger HS 700/9-12
1100 Eastway Dr 28205 980-343-6450
Kelly Gwaltney, prin. Fax 343-1475
Graham MS 1,400/6-8
1800 Runnymede Ln 28211 980-343-5810
Robert Folk, prin. Fax 343-5868
Harding University HS 1,800/9-12
2001 Alleghany St 28208 980-343-6007
Eric Ward, prin. Fax 343-1767
Hawthorne Academy of Health Science 9-12
2300 W Sugar Creek Rd 28262 980-343-6011
Diann Weston, prin. Fax 343-5609
Independence HS 2,000/9-12
1967 Patriot Dr 28227 980-343-6900
Amy Dellinger, prin. Fax 343-6907
Kell HS 2,400/9-12
10220 Ardrey Kell Rd 28277 980-343-0860
David Switzer, prin. Fax 343-0862
Kennedy MS 600/6-8
4000 Gallant Ln 28273 980-343-5540
Kevin Sudimack, prin. Fax 343-5412
King MS 800/6-8
500 Bilmark Ave 28213 980-343-0698
Jennifer Dean, prin. Fax 343-0700
Leadership & Development @ Olympic 400/9-12
4301 Sandy Porter Rd Ste C 28273 980-343-1104
Monique Hicks, prin. Fax 343-1108
Mallard Creek HS 2,200/9-12
3825 Johnston Oehler Rd 28269 980-343-1341
Kevin Garay, prin. Fax 343-1342
Martin MS 1,100/6-8
7800 IBM Dr 28262 980-343-5382
Tonya Faison, prin. Fax 343-5135
Math Engineering Tech/Science S @ OHS 500/9-12
4301 Sandy Porter Rd Ste B 28273 980-343-1101
LeDaun Pratt, prin. Fax 343-1105
McClintock MS 700/6-8
1925 Rama Rd 28212 980-343-6425
Paul Williams, prin. Fax 343-6509
Military & Global Leadrshp Acad @ Davis K-12
3351 Griffith St 28203 980-343-0006
Ann Laszewski, prin. Fax 343-1735
Myers Park HS 2,800/9-12
2400 Colony Rd 28209 980-343-5800
Mark Bosco, prin. Fax 343-5803
Northridge MS 900/6-8
7601 the Plz 28215 980-343-5015
Vince Golden, prin. Fax 343-5174
Northwest S of the Arts 1,000/6-12
1415 Beatties Ford Rd 28216 980-343-5500
Melody Sears, prin. Fax 343-5593
Performance Learning Center 100/Alt
2300 W Sugar Creek Rd 28262 980-343-1118
Tracey Pickard, prin. Fax 343-1117
Piedmont IB MS 1,000/6-8
1241 E 10th St 28204 980-343-5435
Jackie Barone, prin. Fax 343-5557
Providence HS 2,000/9-12
1800 Pineville Matthews Rd 28270 980-343-5390
Tracey Harrill, prin. Fax 343-3956
Quail Hollow MS 900/6-8
2901 Smithfield Church Rd 28210 980-343-3620
Rachael Neill, prin. Fax 343-3622
Randolph MS 1,100/6-8
4400 Water Oak Rd 28211 980-343-6700
Brian Bambauer, prin. Fax 343-6741
Ranson MS 1,100/6-8
5850 Statesville Rd 28269 980-343-6800
Erica Jordan-Thomas, prin. Fax 343-6796
Renaissance S @ Olympic 500/9-12
4301 Sandy Porter Rd Ste D 28273 980-343-1107
Tamara Hines, prin. Fax 343-1111
Ridge Road MS 1,300/6-8
7260 Highland Creek Pkwy 28269 980-344-3410
Jametta Martin-Tanner, prin. Fax 343-1835
Robinson MS 1,100/6-8
5925 Ballantyne Commons Pky 28277 980-343-6944
Mike Miliote, prin. Fax 343-6947
Sedgefield MS 500/6-8
2700 Dorchester Pl 28209 980-343-5840
Erik Turner, prin. Fax 343-5862
South Charlotte MS 900/6-8
8040 Strawberry Ln 28277 980-343-3670
Lisa Bailes, prin. Fax 343-3725
South Mecklenburg HS 2,400/9-12
8900 Park Rd 28210 980-343-3600
Dr. Maureen Furr, prin. Fax 343-3607
Southwest MS 1,400/6-8
13624 Steele Creek Rd 28273 980-343-5006
Barry Blair, prin. Fax 343-3239
TEAM HS @ Olympic 9-12
4301 Sandy Porter Rd Ste A 28273 980-343-1113
Erik Olejarczyk, prin. Fax 343-1102
Turning Point Academy 200/Alt
2400 Carmine St 28206 980-343-5231
Valoria Burch, prin. Fax 343-0924
Vance HS 1,800/9-12
7600 IBM Dr 28262 980-343-5284
Kit Rea, prin. Fax 343-5286
West Charlotte HS 1,700/9-12
2219 Senior Dr 28216 980-343-6060
Tamisha Barnes-Jones, prin. Fax 343-6049
West Mecklenburg HS 1,800/9-12
7400 Tuckaseegee Rd 28214 980-343-6080
Casey Jones, prin. Fax 343-6079
Whitewater MS 900/6-8
10201 Running Rapids Rd 28214 980-344-3400
Beth Thompson, prin. Fax 344-1814
Other Schools – See Cornelius, Huntersville, Matthews, Mint Hill

---

Art Institute of Charlotte Post-Sec.
2110 Water Ridge Pkwy 28217 704-357-8020
Back Creek Christian Academy 200/PK-10
1827 Back Creek Church Rd 28213 704-549-4101
Janet Ballard, head sch Fax 548-1152
Brisbane Academy Preparatory S 100/PK-12
5901 Statesville Rd 28269 704-598-5208
British International S of Charlotte 100/PK-10
7000 Endhaven Ln 28277 704-341-3236
Adam Stevens, prin.
Brookstone College of Business Post-Sec.
10125 Berkeley Place Dr 28262 704-547-8600
Carolina School of Broadcasting Post-Sec.
3435 Performance Rd 28214 704-395-9272
Carolinas College of Health Sciences Post-Sec.
PO Box 32861 28232 704-355-5043
Central Piedmont Community College Post-Sec.
PO Box 35009 28235 704-330-2722
Charlotte Catholic HS 1,400/9-12
7702 Pineville Matthews Rd 28226 704-543-1127
Kurt Telford, prin. Fax 543-1217
Charlotte Christian S 1,000/PK-12
7301 Sardis Rd 28270 704-366-5657
Charlotte Country Day S 1,600/PK-12
1440 Carmel Rd 28226 704-943-4500
Mark Reed, hdmstr. Fax 943-4536
Charlotte Latin S 1,400/PK-12
9502 Providence Rd 28277 704-846-1100
Arch McIntosh, hdmstr. Fax 846-1712
Charlotte School of Law Post-Sec.
2145 Suttle Ave 28208 704-971-8500
Charlotte United Christian Academy 100/PK-12
7640 Wallace Rd 28212 704-537-0331
Dr. Hank Corcoran, head sch Fax 537-0568
Countryside Montessori S 200/1-12
9026 Mallard Creek Rd 28262 704-503-6000
Crosland S 100/K-12
5146 Parkway Plaza Blvd 28217 704-365-5490
Dr. Sean Preston, head sch Fax 365-3240
DeVry University Post-Sec.
2015 Ayrsley Town Blvd #109 28273 704-362-2345
Dudley Beauty College Post-Sec.
1950 John McDonald Ave 28216 704-392-2564
ECPI University Post-Sec.
4800 Airport Center Pkwy 28208 704-399-1010
Hairstyling Institute of Charlotte Post-Sec.
209B S Kings Dr 28204 704-334-5511
Hickory Grove Christian S 1,000/K-12
6050 Hickory Grove Rd 28215 704-531-4008
Wanda Royal, prin. Fax 531-3509
Holy Trinity Catholic MS 900/6-8
3100 Park Rd 28209 704-527-7822
Kevin Parks, prin. Fax 525-7288
ITT Technical Institute Post-Sec.
4135 Southstream Blvd # 200 28217 704-423-3100

ITT Technical Institute Post-Sec.
10926 David Taylor Dr # 100 28262 704-548-2300
Johnson & Wales University Post-Sec.
801 W Trade St 28202 980-598-1000
Johnson C. Smith University Post-Sec.
100 Beatties Ford Rd 28216 704-378-1000
Kaplan College Post-Sec.
6070 E Independence Blvd 28212 704-567-3700
King's College Post-Sec.
322 Lamar Ave 28204 704-372-0266
Mercy School of Nursing Post-Sec.
701 Forest Point Cir Ste B 28273 704-512-2010
New Life Theological Seminary Post-Sec.
3117 Whiting Ave 28205 704-334-6882
Northside Christian Academy 500/PK-12
333 Jeremiah Blvd 28262 704-599-9015
Tony Fajardo, hdmstr. Fax 921-1384
Presbyterian Hospital Post-Sec.
PO Box 33549 28233 704-384-4141
Providence Day S 1,500/PK-12
5800 Sardis Rd 28270 704-887-6000
Dr. Glyn Cowlishaw, head sch Fax 887-7042
Queens University of Charlotte Post-Sec.
1900 Selwyn Ave 28274 704-337-2200
Reformed Theological Seminary Post-Sec.
2101 Carmel Rd 28226 704-366-5066
Southeastern Institute Post-Sec.
5250 77 Center Dr Ste 100 28217 704-527-4979
Trinity Christian Preparatory S 100/8-12
7516 E Independence Ste 100 28227 704-569-1900
Doug Corwin, head sch Fax 569-1999
United Faith Christian Academy 300/PK-12
8617 Providence Rd 28277 704-541-1742
Windy Woodall, head sch Fax 540-7926
Universal College of Beauty Post-Sec.
1701 W Trade St 28216 704-333-6969
University of North Carolina Post-Sec.
9201 University City Blvd 28223 704-687-2000
Victory Christian Center S 300/PK-12
1501 Carrier Dr 28216 704-391-7339
Michael Pratt, prin. Fax 391-0494

**Cherryville, Gaston, Pop. 5,683**
Gaston County SD
Supt. — See Gastonia
Chavis MS 500/6-8
103 S Chavis Dr 28021 704-836-9606
Justin Beam, prin. Fax 435-6168
Cherryville HS 600/9-12
313 Ridge Ave 28021 704-836-9605
Kevin Doran, prin. Fax 435-4989

**China Grove, Rowan, Pop. 3,516**
Rowan-Salisbury County SD
Supt. — See Salisbury
Carson HS 1,200/9-12
290 Kress Venture Rd 28023 704-855-7297
Angelo DelliSanti, prin. Fax 857-3485
China Grove MS 600/6-8
1013 N Main St 28023 704-857-7038
Dennis Hobbs, prin. Fax 857-6650
South Rowan HS 1,000/9-12
1655 Patterson St 28023 704-857-1161
Kelly Withers, prin. Fax 855-1420

**Chocowinity, Beaufort, Pop. 806**
Beaufort County SD
Supt. — See Washington
Chocowinity MS 500/5-8
3831 US Highway 17 S 27817 252-946-6191
Michelle Warren, prin. Fax 975-3812
Southside HS 400/9-12
5700 NC Highway 33 E 27817 252-940-1881
Dale Cole, prin. Fax 940-1888

---

Unity Christian Academy 50/K-12
1501 Haw Branch Rd 27817 252-946-5083
Kenneth Leys, admin. Fax 946-2707

**Claremont, Catawba, Pop. 1,328**
Catawba County SD
Supt. — See Newton
Bunker Hill HS 900/9-12
4675 Oxford School Rd 28610 828-241-3355
Dr. Jeff Isenhour, prin. Fax 241-9401
Mill Creek MS 400/7-8
1041 Shiloh Rd 28610 828-241-2711
Maria Ballard, prin. Fax 241-2743
River Bend MS 600/7-8
4670 Oxford School Rd 28610 828-241-2754
Chip Cathey, prin. Fax 241-2820

**Clarkton, Bladen, Pop. 821**
Bladen County SD
Supt. — See Elizabethtown
Clarkton MS of Discovery 400/6-8
PO Box 127 28433 910-647-6531
Stephanie Ensminger, prin. Fax 647-6671

**Clayton, Johnston, Pop. 15,821**
Johnston County SD
Supt. — See Smithfield
Clayton HS 1,600/9-12
600 S Fayetteville St 27520 919-553-4064
Clint Eaves, prin. Fax 553-2563
Clayton MS 800/6-8
490 Guy Rd 27520 919-553-5811
Jocell Flores, prin. Fax 553-6978
Cleveland HS 900/9-12
1892 Polenta Rd 27520 919-934-2455
Anne Meredith, prin. Fax 934-2414
Riverwood MS 1,000/6-8
204 Athletic Club Blvd, 919-359-2769
Phillip Lee, prin. Fax 359-1519

---

Southside Christian S 100/PK-12
2028 Orton Rd 27520 919-553-7652
Chad Jewett, admin. Fax 553-5077

**Clemmons, Forsyth, Pop. 18,375**
Winston-Salem/Forsyth SD
Supt. — See Winston Salem
West Forsyth HS 2,000/9-12
1735 Lewisville Clemmons Rd 27012 336-712-4400
Charles McAninch, prin. Fax 712-4416

**Climax, Guilford**
Randolph County SD
Supt. — See Asheboro
Providence Grove HS 800/9-12
5555 Mack Lineberry Rd 27233 336-685-0728
Dr. Brad Walston, prin. Fax 685-0731

**Clinton, Sampson, Pop. 8,488**
Clinton CSD 3,100/PK-12
300 Westover Rd 28328 910-592-3132
Dr. Stuart Blount, supt. Fax 592-2011
www.clinton.k12.nc.us
Clinton HS 800/9-12
340 Indian Town Rd 28328 910-592-2067
Dr. Steven Miller, prin. Fax 299-5164
Sampson MS 700/6-8
1201 W Elizabeth St 28328 910-592-3327
Greg Dirks, prin. Fax 592-6185

Sampson County SD 8,300/PK-12
PO Box 439 28329 910-592-1401
Dr. Eric Bracy, supt. Fax 590-2445
www.sampson.k12.nc.us
Sampson Early College HS 200/9-12
PO Box 318 28329 910-592-8081
Susan Westerbeek, prin. Fax 592-8048
Union MS 500/6-8
455 River Rd 28328 910-592-4547
Lynn Prescott, prin. Fax 592-4211
Other Schools – See Dunn, Newton Grove, Roseboro, Rose Hill, Salemburg

---

Sampson Community College Post-Sec.
PO Box 318 28329 910-592-8081

**Clyde, Haywood, Pop. 1,216**
Haywood County SD
Supt. — See Waynesville
Central Haywood HS 100/Alt
3215 Broad St 28721 828-627-9944
Jeff Haney, prin. Fax 627-0709
Haywood Early College HS 100/9-12
185 Freedlander Dr 28721 828-565-4000
Doris Greene, prin. Fax 565-4074

---

Haywood Christian Academy 100/PK-12
1400 Old Clyde Rd 28721 828-627-0229
Msgr. Blake Stanbery, hdmstr. Fax 880-8447
Haywood Community College Post-Sec.
185 Freedlander Dr 28721 828-627-4500

**Columbia, Tyrrell, Pop. 886**
Tyrrell County SD 600/PK-12
PO Box 328 27925 252-796-1121
Dr. Michael Dunsmore, supt. Fax 796-1492
www.tyrrell.k12.nc.us
Columbia Early College HS 200/9-12
PO Box 419 27925 252-796-8161
Marcia Manning, prin. Fax 796-0143
Columbia MS 100/6-8
PO Box 839 27925 252-796-0369
T.J. Worrell, prin. Fax 796-3639

**Columbus, Polk, Pop. 981**
Polk County SD 2,400/PK-12
PO Box 638 28722 828-894-3051
William Miller, supt. Fax 894-8153
www.polkschools.org
Polk County Early College HS 50/9-12
1545 NC 108 Hwy E 28722 828-894-2525
Mary Greene, dir. Fax 894-2971
Polk County HS 700/9-12
1681 NC 108 Hwy E 28722 828-894-2525
Mary Feagan, prin. Fax 894-2093
Other Schools – See Mill Spring

**Concord, Cabarrus, Pop. 77,521**
Cabarrus County SD 27,000/PK-12
PO Box 388 28026 704-786-6191
Dr. Chris Lowder, supt. Fax 786-6141
www.cabarrus.k12.nc.us
Cabarrus County Opportunity S 100/Alt
120 Marsh Ave NW 28025 704-793-1736
Beverly Mack, prin. Fax 788-6158
Cabarrus-Kannapolis Early College HS 200/9-12
1531 Trinity Church Rd 28027 704-260-0227
Vance Fishback, prin. Fax 260-0229
Central Cabarrus HS 1,100/9-12
505 Highway 49 S 28025 704-786-0125
Andrew Crook, prin. Fax 920-7164
Concord HS 1,100/9-12
481 Burrage Rd NE 28025 704-786-4161
Carla Black, prin. Fax 782-7539
Concord MS 900/6-8
1500 Gold Rush Dr 28025 704-786-4121
Carrie Tulbert, prin. Fax 782-8632
Cox Mill HS 1,200/9-12
1355 Cox Mill Rd 28027 704-788-6700
Todd Smith, prin. Fax 788-1112
Fries MS 400/6-9
133 Stonecrest Cir SW 28027 704-788-4140
Dr. Kristi Bullock, prin. Fax 784-2086
Griffin MS 900/6-9
7650 Griffins Gate Dr SW 28025 704-455-4700
Kristy Bullock, prin. Fax 454-4780
Harris Road MS 1,000/6-8
1251 Patriot Plantation 28027 704-782-2002
Raymond Aldridge, prin. Fax 262-4298
Northwest Cabarrus HS 1,100/9-12
5130 NW Cabarrus Dr 28027 704-788-4111
Mike Jolley, prin. Fax 723-4114
Northwest Cabarrus MS 900/6-8
5140 NW Cabarrus Dr 28027 704-788-4135
Kenna Eyster-Terrill, prin. Fax 784-2649
Performance Learning Center 100/Alt
133 Stonecrest Cir SW 28027 704-795-7074
Dr. James Williams, prin. Fax 795-5994
Robinson HS 1,500/9-12
300 Pitts School Rd SW 28027 704-788-4500
Gregory Hall, prin. Fax 723-4352
Winkler MS 900/6-9
4501 Weddington Rd NW 28027 704-786-2000
Dr. Mary Roth, prin. Fax 786-2002
Other Schools – See Harrisburg, Mount Pleasant

---

Cabarrus College of Health Sciences Post-Sec.
401 Medical Park Dr 28025 704-403-1555
Cannon S 900/PK-12
5801 Poplar Tent Rd 28027 704-786-8171
Matthew Gossage, hdmstr. Fax 788-7779
CFA Academy 600/K-12
154 Warren C Coleman Blvd N 28027 704-793-4750
Covenant Classical S 200/PK-12
3200 Patrick Henry Dr NW 28027 704-792-1854
Empire Beauty School Post-Sec.
10075 Weddington Road Ext 28027 800-575-5983

**Connelly Sprngs, Burke**
Burke County SD
Supt. — See Morganton
East Burke HS 1,000/9-12
3695 E Burke Blvd, 828-397-5541
Phil Smith, prin. Fax 397-7652
East Burke MS 800/6-8
3519 Miller Bridge Rd, 828-397-7446
Shane Mace, prin. Fax 397-1086

**Conover, Catawba, Pop. 8,005**
Newton-Conover CSD
Supt. — See Newton
Newton-Conover MS 600/6-8
873 Northern Dr NW 28613 828-464-4221
Rosanna Whisnant, prin. Fax 464-5238

---

Tri-City Christian S 200/PK-12
PO Box 1690 28613 828-465-0475
Keith Thomas, admin. Fax 466-3749

**Conway, Northampton, Pop. 825**
Northampton County SD
Supt. — See Jackson
Conway MS 400/5-8
400 E Main St 27820 252-585-0312
Oliver Holley, prin. Fax 585-0335
Northampton County HS 400/9-12
750 NCHS Rd 27820 252-585-0627
Chanda Battle, prin. Fax 585-9019

**Cornelius, Mecklenburg, Pop. 24,533**
Charlotte/Mecklenburg County SD
Supt. — See Charlotte
Bailey MS 1,300/6-8
11900 Bailey Rd 28031 980-343-1068
Chad Thomas, prin. Fax 343-1069
Hough HS 2,000/9-12
12420 Bailey Rd 28031 980-344-0514
Dr. Laura Rosenbach, prin. Fax 343-2215

**Cramerton, Gaston, Pop. 4,105**
Gaston County SD
Supt. — See Gastonia
Cramerton MS 900/6-8
601 Cramer Mountain Rd 28032 704-836-9603
Bryan Denton, prin. Fax 824-0228

---

Cramerton Christian Academy 300/K-12
426 Woodlawn Ave 28032 704-824-2840

**Creedmoor, Granville, Pop. 4,037**
Granville County SD
Supt. — See Oxford
Granville Early College HS 100/9-12
1552 S Campus Dr 27522 919-528-5583
Jackie Harris, prin. Fax 528-5584
Hawley MS 700/6-8
2173 Brassfield Rd 27522 919-528-0091
Frank Wiggins, prin. Fax 528-0051
South Granville HS of Health & Life Sci 400/9-12
701 N Crescent Dr 27522 919-528-5532
Lisa Tusa, prin. Fax 528-5575
South Granville HS of ITL 400/9-12
701 N Crescent Dr 27522 919-528-5533
Kathy Fuerst, prin. Fax 528-5577

**Creswell, Washington, Pop. 268**
Washington County SD
Supt. — See Plymouth
Creswell JSHS 100/6-12
PO Box 188 27928 252-797-4766
Sharon Cherry, prin. Fax 797-4651

**Cullowhee, Jackson, Pop. 6,135**

---

Western Carolina University Post-Sec.
University Dr 28723 828-227-7211

**Currituck, Currituck**
Currituck County SD 3,700/PK-12
2958 Caratoke Hwy 27929 252-232-2223
Allison Osmon, supt. Fax 232-3655
www.currituck.k12.nc.us
Knapp Early College HS 200/9-12
2966 Caratoke Hwy 27929 252-232-3107
Stephen Basnight, prin. Fax 232-3923
Other Schools – See Barco, Moyock

**Dallas, Gaston, Pop. 4,415**
Gaston County SD
Supt. — See Gastonia
Friday MS 700/6-8
1221 Ratchford Dr 28034 704-922-5297
Crystal Houser, prin. Fax 922-9841
Gaston Early College HS 9-12
201 Highway 321 S 28034 704-922-2405
Sheila Wyont, prin. Fax 922-7456

North Gaston HS 1,100/9-12
1133 Ratchford Dr 28034 704-922-5285
Judy Moore, prin. Fax 922-7486

Gaston College Post-Sec.
201 Highway 321 S 28034 704-922-6200

**Danbury, Stokes, Pop. 189**
Stokes County SD 7,000/PK-12
PO Box 50 27016 336-593-8146
Ronnie Mendenhall, supt. Fax 593-2041
www.stokes.k12.nc.us
North Stokes HS 500/9-12
1350 N Stokes School Rd 27016 336-593-8134
Nathan Rasey, prin. Fax 593-8882
Other Schools – See King, Lawsonville, Walnut Cove

**Davidson, Mecklenburg, Pop. 10,776**

Davidson College Post-Sec.
PO Box 7171 28035 704-894-2000
Davidson Day S 500/PK-12
750 Jetton St 28036 704-237-5200
Gene Bratek, head sch Fax 896-5535
Lake Norman Christian S 100/K-12
PO Box 4267 28036 704-987-9811
Dr. Wes Johnston, head sch Fax 896-5875

**Deep Run, Lenoir**
Lenoir County SD
Supt. — See Kinston
South Lenoir HS 800/9-12
3355 Old Hwy 11 28525 252-568-6161
James Saint-Amand, prin. Fax 568-6015

**Delco, Columbus, Pop. 332**
Columbus County SD
Supt. — See Whiteville
Acme-Delco MS 200/6-8
PO Box 40 28436 910-655-3200
Christy Brown, prin. Fax 655-6865

**Denton, Davidson, Pop. 1,618**
Davidson County SD
Supt. — See Lexington
South Davidson HS 400/9-12
14956 S NC Highway 109 27239 336-242-5700
Mike Lawson, prin. Fax 242-5702
South Davidson MS 400/6-8
14954 S NC Highway 109 27239 336-242-5705
Kim Dixon, prin. Fax 242-5707

**Denver, Lincoln, Pop. 2,276**
Lincoln County SD
Supt. — See Lincolnton
East Lincoln HS 900/9-12
6471 Highway 73 28037 704-736-1860
Samantha Campbell, prin. Fax 483-6751
North Lincoln MS 700/6-8
1503 Amity Church Rd 28037 704-736-0262
Dr. Misha Rogers, prin. Fax 736-9812

**Dobson, Surry, Pop. 1,569**
Surry County SD 7,800/PK-12
PO Box 364 27017 336-386-8211
Dr. Travis Reeves, supt. Fax 386-4279
www.surry.k12.nc.us/
Central MS 700/6-8
PO Box 768 27017 336-386-4018
Bill Goins, prin. Fax 386-4371
Surry Central HS 800/9-12
PO Box 8 27017 336-386-8842
Celia Hodges, prin. Fax 386-4424
Surry Early College HS of Design 300/9-12
630 S Main St 27017 336-386-3621
Kevin Via, prin. Fax 386-3629
Other Schools – See Mount Airy, Pilot Mountain

Surry Community College Post-Sec.
630 S Main St 27017 336-386-8121

**Drexel, Burke, Pop. 1,832**
Burke County SD
Supt. — See Morganton
Hallyburton Academy 100/Alt
PO Box 3238 28619 828-437-4184
Rob Ford, prin. Fax 437-0655

**Dublin, Bladen, Pop. 329**

Bladen Community College Post-Sec.
PO Box 266 28332 910-879-5500

**Dudley, Wayne**
Wayne County SD
Supt. — See Goldsboro
Brogden MS 500/5-8
3761 US 117 Alt 28333 919-705-6010
Sylvester Townsend, prin. Fax 705-6000
Southern Wayne HS 1,000/9-12
124 Walter Fulcher Rd 28333 919-705-6060
Dr. John Boldt, prin. Fax 731-5982

**Dunn, Harnett, Pop. 9,078**
Harnett County SD
Supt. — See Lillington
Coats-Erwin MS 600/6-8
2833 NC Highway 55 E 28334 910-230-0300
Whit Bradham, prin. Fax 230-0306
Dunn MS 400/6-8
1301 Meadow Lark Rd 28334 910-892-1017
Dr. Janet Doffermyre, prin. Fax 892-7923

Sampson County SD
Supt. — See Clinton
Midway MS 600/6-8
1115 Roberts Grove Rd 28334 910-567-5879
John Goode, prin. Fax 567-5131

Dream Big Christian Academy PK-12
1409 S Clinton Ave 28334 910-891-5100
Jeanine Page, prin. Fax 891-5110
Heritage Bible College Post-Sec.
PO Box 1628 28335 910-892-3178

**Durham, Durham, Pop. 223,352**
Durham County SD 31,400/PK-12
PO Box 30002 27702 919-560-2000
Dr. Bert L'Homme, supt. Fax 560-2422
www.dpsnc.net
Brogden MS 700/6-8
1001 Leon St 27704 919-560-3906
Latonya Smith, prin. Fax 560-3957
Carrington MS 1,200/6-8
227 Milton Rd 27712 919-560-3916
Holly Emmanuel, prin. Fax 560-3522
City of Medicine Academy 300/9-12
200 Wisteria Ave 27704 919-560-2001
Jackie Tobias, prin. Fax 477-3128
Clement Early College HS 400/9-12
1801 Fayetteville St 27707 919-560-2696
Gloria Woods-Weaks, prin. Fax 560-2698
Durham S of the Arts 1,500/6-12
401 N Duke St 27701 919-560-3926
David Hawks, prin. Fax 560-2217
Githens MS 1,000/6-8
4800 Old Chapel Hill Rd 27707 919-560-3966
Tonya Williams, prin. Fax 560-3454
Hillside HS 1,300/9-12
3727 Fayetteville St 27707 919-560-3925
Dr. William Logan, prin. Fax 560-2312
Hillside New Tech HS 300/9-12
3727 Fayetteville St 27707 919-560-9183
Tounya Wright, prin. Fax 560-3686
Holton Career & Resource Center Vo/Tech
401 N Driver St 27703 919-560-2219
Danny Gilford, prin. Fax 237-5669
Jordan HS 1,800/9-12
6806 Garrett Rd 27707 919-560-3912
Dr. Kerry Chisnall, prin. Fax 560-2620
Lakeview S 100/Alt
3507 Dearborn Dr 27704 919-560-2520
Jeffery Dockery, prin. Fax 560-2446
Lakewood Montessori S 200/6-8
2119 Chapel Hill Rd 27701 919-560-2894
Patricia Geter, prin. Fax 237-7388
Lowes Grove MS 600/6-8
4418 S Alston Ave 27713 919-560-3946
Tekeisha Mitchell, prin. Fax 560-2102
Lucas MS 6-8
923 Snow Hill Rd 27712 919-560-3843
Tom Seckler, prin. Fax 471-0072
Middle College HS at DTCC 100/11-12
1616 Cooper St Bldg Newton 27703 919-536-7203
Dr. Charles Nolan, prin. Fax 536-7294
Neal MS 600/6-8
201 Baptist Rd 27704 919-560-3955
Michael Fuga, prin. Fax 560-3451
Northern HS 1,400/9-12
117 Tom Wilkinson Rd 27712 919-560-3956
Matthew Hunt, prin. Fax 479-3001
Performance Learning Center 200/Alt
401 N Driver St 27703 919-560-9190
Danny Gilfort, prin. Fax 560-2214
Riverside HS 1,800/9-12
3218 Rose of Sharon Rd 27712 919-560-3965
Joel County, prin. Fax 560-3798
Rogers-Herr MS 600/6-8
911 W Cornwallis Rd 27707 919-560-3970
Kecia Rogers, prin. Fax 560-2439
School for Creative Studies 6-12
5001 Red Mill Rd 27704 919-560-3535
Renee Price Trapp, prin. Fax 477-9189
Shepard MS 500/6-8
2401 Dakota St 27707 919-560-3938
Ericka Boone, prin. Fax 560-3945
Southern HS of Energy and Sustainability 1,000/9-12
800 Clayton Rd 27703 919-560-3968
Jerome Leathers, prin. Fax 560-2445

Apex School of Theology Post-Sec.
1701 TW Alexander Dr 27703 919-572-1625
Art Institute of Raleigh - Durham Post-Sec.
410 Blackwell St Ste 200 27701 919-317-3050
Camelot Academy 100/K-12
809 Proctor St 27707 919-688-3040
Thelma Decarlo-Glynn, dir. Fax 682-4320
Carolina Friends S 500/PK-12
4809 Friends School Rd 27705 919-383-6602
Mike Hanas, prin. Fax 383-6009
Cresset Christian Academy 200/PK-12
3707 Garrett Rd 27707 919-489-2655
Greg Hardy, admin. Fax 354-8009
Duke University 27708 Post-Sec.
919-684-8111
Durham Academy 400/5-8
3116 Academy Rd 27707 919-489-9118
Jon Meredith, dir. Fax 489-9110
Durham Academy 400/9-12
3601 Ridge Rd 27705 919-489-6569
Lee Hark, dir. Fax 489-7356
Durham Technical Community College Post-Sec.
1637 E Lawson St 27703 919-536-7200
Fellowship Baptist Academy 100/PK-12
515 Southerland St 27703 919-596-9331
ITT Technical Institute Post-Sec.
3518 Westgate Dr Ste 150 27707 919-401-1400
Liberty Christian S 200/K-12
3864 Guess Rd 27705 919-471-5522
Mt. Zion Christian Academy 200/K-12
3519 Fayetteville St 27707 919-688-4245
Peggy McIlwain, prin. Fax 688-2201
North Carolina Central University Post-Sec.
1801 Fayetteville St 27707 919-560-6100
Trinity S of Durham & Chapel Hill 500/PK-12
4011 Pickett Rd 27705 919-402-8262
Dr. Peter T. Denton, hdmstr. Fax 402-0762

**East Bend, Yadkin, Pop. 604**
Yadkin County SD
Supt. — See Yadkinville
Forbush HS 900/9-12
1525 Falcon Rd 27018 336-961-4644
Dr. Eddie Karriker, prin. Fax 961-2575
Forbush MS 600/7-8
1431 Falcon Rd 27018 336-961-6360
Kelly Mabe, prin. Fax 961-6370

**East Flat Rock, Henderson, Pop. 4,872**
Henderson County SD
Supt. — See Hendersonville
East Henderson HS 1,000/9-12
150 Eagle Pride Dr 28726 828-697-4768
Scott Rhodes, prin. Fax 698-6123
Flat Rock MS 800/6-8
191 Preston Ln 28726 828-697-4775
Jeff Roper, prin. Fax 698-6124

**Eden, Rockingham, Pop. 15,244**
Rockingham County SD 13,600/PK-12
511 Harrington Hwy 27288 336-627-2600
Dr. Rodney Shotwell, supt. Fax 627-2660
www.rock.k12.nc.us
Holmes MS 800/6-8
211 N Pierce St 27288 336-623-9791
Elliott Miller, prin. Fax 627-0075
Morehead HS 1,000/9-12
134 N Pierce St 27288 336-627-7731
Al Royster, prin. Fax 623-5462
Other Schools – See Madison, Mayodan, Reidsville, Wentworth

**Edenton, Chowan, Pop. 4,952**
Edenton-Chowan County SD 2,400/PK-12
PO Box 206 27932 252-482-4436
Dr. Rob Jackson, supt. Fax 482-7309
www.ecps.k12.nc.us
Holmes HS 700/9-12
PO Box 409 27932 252-482-8426
Steve Wood, prin. Fax 482-2010
Other Schools – See Tyner

**Efland, Orange, Pop. 722**
Orange County SD
Supt. — See Hillsborough
Gravelly Hill MS 500/6-8
4819 W Ten Rd 27243 919-732-8126
Eric Yarbrough, prin. Fax 245-4055

**Elizabeth City, Pasquotank, Pop. 18,282**
Elizabeth City/Pasquotank County SD 6,100/PK-12
1200 Halstead Blvd 27909 252-335-2981
Dr. Larry Cartner, supt. Fax 335-0974
www.ecpps.k12.nc.us
Elizabeth City MS 700/6-8
1066 Northside Rd 27909 252-335-2974
Timothy Worrell, prin. Fax 335-1751
Northeastern HS 900/9-12
963 Oak Stump Rd 27909 252-335-2932
Ron Payne, prin. Fax 335-1005
Pasquotank County HS 800/9-12
1064 Northside Rd 27909 252-337-6880
Amy Fyffe, prin. Fax 337-6890
River Road MS 700/6-8
1701 River Rd 27909 252-333-1454
LeVar Mizelle, prin. Fax 331-1339
Trigg Community HS 100/Alt
1004 Parkview Dr 27909 252-335-1765
Ainslie Jones, prin. Fax 337-6740

Albemarle S 200/PK-12
1210 US Highway 17 S 27909 252-338-0883
Dr. Holly Glenn, prin. Fax 338-1222
College of the Albemarle Post-Sec.
PO Box 2327 27906 252-335-0821
Elizabeth City SDA S 50/6-8
1117 US Highway 17 S 27909 252-335-0343
Elizabeth City State University Post-Sec.
1704 Weeksville Rd 27909 252-335-3400
Mid Atlantic Christian University Post-Sec.
715 N Poindexter St 27909 252-334-2000
Victory Christian S 200/PK-12
684 Old Hertford Hwy 27909 252-264-2011

**Elizabethtown, Bladen, Pop. 3,534**
Bladen County SD 5,400/PK-12
PO Box 37 28337 910-862-4136
Robert Taylor, supt. Fax 862-4277
www.bladen.k12.nc.us/
East Bladen HS 700/9-12
5600 NC Highway 87 E 28337 910-645-2500
Jason Wray, prin. Fax 645-2509
Elizabethtown MS 400/5-8
PO Box 639 28337 910-862-4071
Elizabeth Cole, prin. Fax 862-7426
Other Schools – See Bladenboro, Clarkton, Tar Heel

**Elkin, Surry, Pop. 3,953**
Elkin CSD 1,200/PK-12
202 W Spring St 28621 336-835-3135
Dr. Randy Bledsoe, supt. Fax 835-3376
www.elkin.k12.nc.us
Elkin HS 400/9-12
334 Elk Spur St 28621 336-835-3858
Joel Hoyle, prin. Fax 835-3253
Elkin MS 200/7-8
300 Elk Spur St 28621 336-835-3175
Pam Colbert, prin. Fax 835-1427

**Elk Park, Avery, Pop. 449**
Avery County SD
Supt. — See Newland
Cranberry MS 200/6-8
6230 N US Highway 19E 28622 828-733-2932
Matthew Bentley, prin. Fax 733-6863

**Ellerbe, Richmond, Pop. 1,027**
Richmond County SD
Supt. — See Hamlet

Ellerbe MS 200/6-8
128 W Ballard St 28338 910-652-3231
Melvin Ingram, prin. Fax 652-3106

**Elm City, Wilson, Pop. 1,289**
Wilson County SD
Supt. — See Wilson
Elm City MS 500/6-8
215 Church St E 27822 252-236-4148
Robert Pope, prin. Fax 236-3754

**Elon, Alamance, Pop. 9,262**
Alamance-Burlington SD
Supt. — See Burlington
Western Alamance HS 1,200/9-12
1731 N NC Highway 87 27244 336-538-6020
Todd Stephan, prin. Fax 538-6014
Western Alamance MS 900/6-8
2100 Eldon Dr 27244 336-538-6010
Gregory Holland, prin. Fax 538-6012

---

Elon University Post-Sec.
2700 Campus Box 27244 336-278-2000

**Enfield, Halifax, Pop. 2,522**
Halifax County SD
Supt. — See Halifax
Enfield MS 400/6-8
13723 Highway 481 27823 252-445-5455
Teicher Patterson, prin. Fax 445-3866

**Erwin, Harnett, Pop. 4,318**
Harnett County SD
Supt. — See Lillington
Triton HS 1,400/9-12
215 Maynard Lake Rd 28339 910-897-8121
Chip Mangum, prin. Fax 897-3148

---

Cape Fear Christian Academy 300/PK-12
138 Erwin Chapel Rd 28339 910-897-5423
Karen Parker, hdmstr. Fax 897-2150

**Fair Bluff, Columbus, Pop. 944**
Columbus County SD
Supt. — See Whiteville
Columbus Career & Coll Acad - Fair Bluff 9-12
685 Academy St 28439 910-649-7622
Nicky Hobbs, prin. Fax 649-6506

**Fairmont, Robeson, Pop. 2,595**
Robeson County SD
Supt. — See Lumberton
Fairgrove MS 300/4-8
1953 Fairgrove Rd 28340 910-628-8290
Charles Locklear, prin. Fax 628-6181
Fairmont HS 700/9-12
5419 Old Stage Rd 28340 910-628-6727
Ronald Prater, prin. Fax 628-0652
Fairmont MS 400/5-8
402 Iona St 28340 910-628-4363
John Brooks, prin. Fax 628-0335

**Falcon, Cumberland, Pop. 249**

---

Falcon Christian Academy 50/6-12
PO Box 39 28342 910-980-1065
Renee McLamb, head sch Fax 980-1161

**Farmville, Pitt, Pop. 4,617**
Pitt County SD
Supt. — See Greenville
Farmville Central HS 800/9-12
PO Box 209 27828 252-753-5138
Brad Johnston, prin. Fax 753-7873
Farmville MS 600/6-8
3914 Grimmersburg St 27828 252-753-2116
Paul Briney, prin. Fax 753-7995

**Fayetteville, Cumberland, Pop. 191,875**
Cumberland County SD 51,900/PK-12
PO Box 2357 28302 910-678-2300
Dr. Frank Till, supt. Fax 678-2339
www.ccs.k12.nc.us
Abbott MS 900/6-8
590 Winding Creek Rd 28305 910-323-2201
Scott Pope, prin. Fax 485-0841
Britt HS 1,900/9-12
7403 Rockfish Rd 28306 910-429-2800
Denise Garison, prin. Fax 429-2810
Byrd HS 1,300/9-12
1624 Ireland Dr 28304 910-484-8121
Dan Krumanocker, prin. Fax 323-4127
Byrd MS 700/7-8
1616 Ireland Dr 28304 910-483-3101
Zoletta Taylor, prin. Fax 483-3741
Cape Fear HS 1,600/9-12
4762 Clinton Rd, 910-483-0191
Lee Spruill, prin. Fax 483-1679
Chesnutt MS 600/6-8
2121 Skibo Rd 28314 910-867-9147
Tonjai Robertson, prin. Fax 868-3695
Cross Creek Early College HS 200/9-12
1200 Murchison Rd 28301 910-672-1499
Patsy Patrick, prin. Fax 672-1590
Cumberland International Early College S 100/9-12
1200 Murchison Rd 28301 910-672-2830
Lavette McMillan, prin. Fax 672-2849
Griffin MS 1,200/6-8
5551 Fisher Rd 28304 910-424-7678
Tommy Dent, prin. Fax 424-7602
Howard Health & Life Sciences HS 200/9-12
1608 Camden Rd 28306 910-485-1634
Joy Williams, prin. Fax 483-5754
Jeralds MS 600/6-8
2517 Ramsey St 28301 910-822-2570
Maria Pierce-Ford, prin. Fax 822-1534
Jones Alternative S Alt
225 B St 28301 910-483-5434
Sandra Braxton, prin. Fax 323-3159
Lewis Chapel MS 900/6-8
2150 Skibo Rd 28314 910-864-1407
Sheldon Harvey, prin. Fax 864-8298
Massey Hill Classical HS 400/9-12
1062 Southern Ave 28306 910-485-8761
Tonya Higgins, prin. Fax 485-7950
New Century International MS 6-8
7455 Century Cir 28306 910-487-2001
Tonya Page, prin. Fax 487-2009
Pine Forest HS 1,600/9-12
525 Andrews Rd 28311 910-488-2384
David Culberth, prin. Fax 488-0790
Pine Forest MS 800/6-8
6901 Ramsey St 28311 910-488-2711
Bill Starks, prin. Fax 630-2357
Ramsey Street Alternative HS 50/Alt
117 Quincy St 28301 910-437-5829
Reggie Pinkney, prin. Fax 437-5121
Ross Classical JSHS 700/6-12
3200 Ramsey St 28301 910-488-8415
Thomas Hatch, prin. Fax 488-6209
Sanford HS 1,400/9-12
2301 Fort Bragg Rd 28303 910-484-1151
Robert Guzman, prin. Fax 484-7203
Seventy-First Academy of Arts HS 1,700/9-12
6764 Raeford Rd 28304 910-867-3116
Myron Williams, prin. Fax 867-1445
Seventy-First Classical MS 500/6-8
6830 Raeford Rd 28304 910-864-0092
Patricia Ramos, prin. Fax 487-8547
Smith HS 1,200/9-12
1800 Seabrook Rd 28301 910-483-0153
Melody Chalmers, prin. Fax 483-7696
Westover HS 1,100/9-12
277 Bonanza Dr 28303 910-864-0190
Thomas Benson, prin. Fax 864-5924
Westover MS 700/6-8
275 Bonanza Dr 28303 910-864-0813
La'Shanda Carver-Moore, prin. Fax 864-7906
Wilkins HS 200/Alt
1429 Skibo Rd 28303 910-864-5438
Vernon Lowery, prin. Fax 868-1777
Williams MS 1,200/6-8
4644 Clinton Rd, 910-483-8222
Steven Morris, prin. Fax 483-4831
Other Schools – See Hope Mills, Spring Lake

---

Bal-Perazim Christian Academy 50/PK-12
4921 Bragg Blvd 28303 910-487-4220
Morris Braxton D.D.S., head sch Fax 864-3451
Berean Baptist Academy 400/PK-12
518 Glensford Dr 28314 910-868-2511
Carolina College of Biblical Studies Post-Sec.
817 S McPherson Church Rd 28303 910-323-5614
Cornerstone Christian Academy 200/PK-12
3000 Scotty Hill Rd 28303 910-867-1166
Fayetteville Academy 400/PK-12
3200 Cliffdale Rd 28303 910-868-5131
Ray Quesnel, head sch Fax 868-7351
Fayetteville Beauty College Post-Sec.
3442 Bragg Blvd 28303 910-487-0227
Fayetteville Christian S 600/PK-12
1422 Ireland Dr 28304 910-483-3905
Tammi Peters, head sch Fax 483-6966
Fayetteville State University Post-Sec.
1200 Murchison Rd 28301 910-672-1111
Fayetteville Technical Community College Post-Sec.
PO Box 35236 28303 910-678-8400
Freedom Christian Academy 300/PK-12
3130 Gillespie St 28306 910-485-7777
Joan Dayton M.Ed., head sch Fax 485-7757
Grace College of Divinity Post-Sec.
5117 Cliffdale Rd 28314 910-221-2224
Harvest Preparatory Academy 50/PK-12
PO Box 2391 28302 910-483-6838
Dr. Rosa Herman, admin. Fax 433-2364
Liberty Christian Academy 300/PK-12
6548 Rockfish Rd 28306 910-424-1205
Duncan Edge, prin. Fax 424-8049
Methodist University Post-Sec.
5400 Ramsey St 28311 910-630-7000
Miller-Motte College Post-Sec.
3725 Ramsey St 28311 910-354-1900
Mitchell's Hairstyling Academy Post-Sec.
222 Tallywood Shopping Ctr 28303 910-485-6310
Northwood Temple Academy 400/PK-12
4200 Ramsey St 28311 910-822-7711
Lisa Till, supt. Fax 488-7299
Trinity Christian S of Academics 200/K-12
3727 Rosehill Rd 28311 910-488-6779
Village Christian Academy 800/K-12
908 S McPherson Church Rd 28303 910-483-5500
Dr. Gene Hales, supt. Fax 483-5335

**Flat Rock, Henderson, Pop. 3,091**
Henderson County SD
Supt. — See Hendersonville
Henderson County Early College HS 200/9-12
120 Alumni Way 28731 828-697-4561
Beth Caudle, prin. Fax 697-4564

---

Blue Ridge Community College Post-Sec.
180 W Campus Dr 28731 828-694-1700

**Fletcher, Henderson, Pop. 7,049**
Buncombe County SD
Supt. — See Asheville
Cane Creek MS 700/6-8
570 Lower Brush Creek Rd 28732 828-628-0824
Karen Barnhill, prin. Fax 628-9833

---

Fletcher Academy 200/9-12
PO Box 5440 28732 828-209-6800
Veritas Christian Academy 400/PK-12
17 Cane Creek Rd 28732 828-681-0546
Kay Belknap, hdmstr. Fax 681-0547

**Forest City, Rutherford, Pop. 7,281**
Rutherford County SD 8,700/PK-12
382 W Main St 28043 828-288-2200
Dr. Janet Mason, supt. Fax 288-2490
www.rcsnc.org/
Chase HS 800/9-12
1603 Chase High Rd 28043 828-245-7668
Kevin Bradley, prin. Fax 248-3584
Chase MS 700/6-8
840 Chase High Rd 28043 828-247-1044
La'Ronda Whiteside, prin. Fax 247-0551
East Rutherford HS 800/9-12
PO Box 668 28043 828-245-6424
Brad Teague, prin. Fax 247-0039
Rutherford Opportunity Center Alt
140 Old Caroleen Rd 28043 828-248-5294
Tim Torvinen, prin. Fax 248-5297
Other Schools – See Bostic, Rutherfordton, Spindale

**Four Oaks, Johnston, Pop. 1,883**
Johnston County SD
Supt. — See Smithfield
Four Oaks MS 600/6-8
1475 Boyette Rd 27524 919-963-4022
David Cobb, prin. Fax 963-4123
South Johnston HS 1,200/9-12
10381 US Highway 301 S 27524 919-894-3146
Eddie Price, prin. Fax 894-3229

**Franklin, Macon, Pop. 3,786**
Macon County SD 3,700/K-12
1202 Old Murphy Rd 28734 828-524-3314
Dr. Chris Baldwin, supt. Fax 524-5938
www.macon.k12.nc.us
Franklin HS 1,000/9-12
100 Panther Dr 28734 828-524-6467
Barry Woody, prin. Fax 524-0684
Macon Early College HS 100/9-12
77 Siler Farm Rd 28734 828-369-7331
Todd Gibbs, prin. Fax 349-9692
Macon MS 600/7-8
1345 Wells Grove Rd 28734 828-524-3766
Scot Maslin, prin. Fax 349-3900
Union Academy 100/Alt
158 Union School Rd 28734 828-369-1277
Diane Cotton, prin. Fax 524-2859
Other Schools – See Highlands, Topton

---

Trimont Christian Academy 200/PK-12
98 Promise Ln 28734 828-369-6756

**Franklinton, Franklin, Pop. 1,988**
Franklin County SD
Supt. — See Louisburg
Franklinton HS 900/9-12
910 Cedar Creek Rd 27525 919-494-2332
Russell Holloman, prin. Fax 494-5140
Franklinton MS 6-8
3 N Main St 27525 919-494-2971
Fax 494-1625

**Fremont, Wayne, Pop. 1,228**
Wayne County SD
Supt. — See Goldsboro
Norwayne MS 1,100/6-8
1394 Norwayne School Rd 27830 919-242-3414
Mario Re, prin. Fax 242-3418

**Fuquay Varina, Wake, Pop. 17,531**
Wake County SD
Supt. — See Cary
Fuquay-Varina HS 2,000/9-12
201 Bengal Dr 27526 919-557-2511
Jonathan Enns, prin. Fax 557-2512
Fuquay-Varina MS 900/6-8
109 N Ennis St 27526 919-557-2727
William Chavis, prin. Fax 557-2732

---

Hilltop Christian S 300/K-12
10212 Fayetteville Rd 27526 919-552-5612
Travis Moots, prin. Fax 552-3189

**Garner, Wake, Pop. 25,256**
Johnston County SD
Supt. — See Smithfield
Cleveland MS 1,100/6-8
2323 Cornwallis Rd 27529 919-553-7500
Kendrick Byrd, prin. Fax 553-7798

Wake County SD
Supt. — See Cary
East Garner MS 1,300/6-8
6301 Jones Sausage Rd 27529 919-662-2339
Elena Ashburn, prin. Fax 662-2357
Garner Magnet HS 2,300/9-12
2101 Spring Dr 27529 919-662-2398
Carter Hillman, prin. Fax 662-2397
North Garner MS 1,000/6-8
720 Powell Dr 27529 919-662-2434
Gregory Butler, prin. Fax 662-5637

**Gaston, Northampton, Pop. 1,141**
Northampton County SD
Supt. — See Jackson
Gaston MS 400/5-8
152 Hurricane Dr 27832 252-537-1910
Martha Paige, prin. Fax 537-9028

**Gastonia, Gaston, Pop. 70,333**
Gaston County SD 31,300/PK-12
PO Box 1397 28053 704-866-6100
Jeffrey Booker, supt. Fax 866-6321
www.gaston.k12.nc.us/
Ashbrook HS 1,300/9-12
2222 S New Hope Rd 28054 704-866-6600
Joey Clinton, prin. Fax 866-6203
Forestview HS 1,300/9-12
5545 Union Rd 28056 704-861-2625
Chad Carper, prin. Fax 853-3323

Grier MS 700/6-8
1622 E Garrison Blvd 28054 704-836-9604
Loretta Reed, prin. Fax 866-6116
Highland School of Technology 600/9-12
1600 N Morris St 28052 704-810-8816
Denise McLean, prin. Fax 866-6105
Huss HS 1,000/9-12
1518 Edgefield Ave 28052 704-866-6610
Torben Ross, prin. Fax 866-6103
Southwest MS 800/6-8
1 Roadrunner Dr 28052 704-866-6290
Rebecca Huffstetler, prin. Fax 866-6293
Warlick Academy 100/Alt
1316 Spencer Mountain Rd 28054 704-824-3012
Curt Hovis, prin. Fax 824-0918
York Chester MS 400/6-8
601 S Clay St 28052 704-866-6297
Amy Holbrook, prin. Fax 866-6319
Other Schools – See Belmont, Bessemer City, Cherryville, Cramerton, Dallas, Lowell, Mount Holly, Stanley

---

Gaston Christian S 800/PK-12
1625 Lowell Bethesda Rd 28056 704-349-5020
Dr. Marc Stout, hdmstr. Fax 349-5029
Gaston Day S 500/PK-12
2001 Gaston Day School Rd 28056 704-864-7744
Dr. Richard Rankin, hdmstr. Fax 865-3813

**Gatesville, Gates, Pop. 318**
Gates County SD 1,900/PK-12
PO Box 125 27938 252-357-1113
Dr. Barry Williams, supt. Fax 357-0207
coserver.gates.k12.nc.us/
Central MS 400/6-8
362 US Highway 158 W 27938 252-357-0470
James Woods, prin. Fax 357-1319
Gates County HS 600/9-12
88 US Highway 158 W 27938 252-357-0720
Tammi Ward, prin. Fax 357-2058

**Gibsonville, Guilford, Pop. 6,318**
Guilford County SD
Supt. — See Greensboro
Eastern Guilford HS 1,200/9-12
415 Peeden Dr 27249 336-449-6311
Marilyn Foley, prin. Fax 449-7392
Eastern MS 1,000/6-8
435 Peeden Dr 27249 336-449-4255
Christopher Tolliver, prin. Fax 449-0728

**Goldsboro, Wayne, Pop. 35,562**
Wayne County SD 19,900/PK-12
PO Box 1797 27533 919-731-5900
Dr. Steven Taylor, supt. Fax 705-6199
www.waynecountyschools.org
Dillard MS 600/5-8
1101 Devereaux St 27530 919-580-9360
Sonja Emerson, prin. Fax 736-1121
Eastern Wayne HS 1,100/9-12
1135 E New Hope Rd 27534 919-751-7120
Eugene Byrd, prin. Fax 751-7107
Eastern Wayne MS 600/6-8
3518 Central Heights Rd 27534 919-751-7110
Catherine Fulcher, prin. Fax 751-7114
Goldsboro HS 500/9-12
901 Beech St 27530 919-731-5930
Brian Weeks, prin. Fax 731-5914
Grantham MS 5-8
3093 S US Highway 13 27530
Lisa Tart, prin.
Greenwood MS 600/5-8
3209 E Ash St 27534 919-751-7100
Rolanda Best, prin. Fax 751-7201
Rosewood HS 500/9-12
900 Rosewood Rd 27530 919-705-6050
Karen Rogers, prin. Fax 705-6055
Rosewood MS 400/6-8
541 NC 581 Hwy S 27530 919-736-5050
Freda Allen, prin. Fax 736-5055
Wayne Early Middle College HS 300/9-12
3000 Wayne Memorial Dr 27534 919-739-7070
Lee Johnson, prin. Fax 581-1011
Wayne MSHS Academy 100/Alt
801 Lionel St 27530 919-580-3608
Carole Battle, prin. Fax 731-5495
Wayne S of Engineering 300/6-12
700 N Herman St 27530 919-734-0070
Gary Hales, prin. Fax 731-0072
Other Schools – See Dudley, Fremont, Mount Olive, Pikeville, Seven Springs

---

Faith Christian Academy 300/PK-12
1200 W Grantham St 27530 919-734-8701
Mitchell's Hairstyling Academy Post-Sec.
1021 N Spence Ave 27534 919-778-8200
Wayne Christian S 500/PK-12
1201 Patetown Rd 27530 919-735-5605
Dr. Ashley Shook, admin. Fax 735-5229
Wayne Community College Post-Sec.
PO Box 8002 27533 919-735-5151
Wayne Country Day S 300/PK-12
480 Country Day Rd 27530 919-736-1045

**Graham, Alamance, Pop. 13,906**
Alamance-Burlington SD
Supt. — See Burlington
Alamance-Burlington Middle College HS 100/9-12
PO Box 8000 27253 336-506-4001
Bonnie Roane, prin. Fax 506-4004
Graham HS 800/9-12
903 Trollinger Rd 27253 336-570-6440
Charlotte Holmes, prin. Fax 570-6446
Graham MS 600/6-8
311 E Pine St 27253 336-570-6460
Patrick Hosey, prin. Fax 570-6464
Ray Street Academy Alt
609 Ray St 27253 336-570-6643
Michael Bayless, prin. Fax 570-6353

Southern Alamance HS 1,400/9-12
631 Southern High School Rd 27253 336-570-6400
Teresa Faucette, prin. Fax 570-6404
Southern Alamance MS 900/6-8
771 Southern High School Rd 27253 336-570-6500
Heather Ward, prin. Fax 570-6504

---

Alamance Christian S 300/PK-12
PO Box 838 27253 336-578-0318
Dr. Robert Hodges, supt. Fax 578-7200
Alamance Community College Post-Sec.
PO Box 8000 27253 336-578-2002

**Granite Falls, Caldwell, Pop. 4,669**
Caldwell County SD
Supt. — See Lenoir
Caldwell County Gateway S 50/Alt
1889 Dudley Shoals Rd 28630 828-396-8373
Michael Wyant, prin. Fax 396-7960
Granite Falls MS 700/6-8
90 N Main St 28630 828-396-2341
Bill Schreiber, prin. Fax 396-7072

**Grantsboro, Pamlico, Pop. 679**

---

Pamlico Community College Post-Sec.
PO Box 185 28529 252-249-1851

**Greensboro, Guilford, Pop. 263,264**
Guilford County SD 73,700/PK-12
PO Box 880 27402 336-370-8100
Maurice Green, supt. Fax 370-8299
www.gcsnc.com
Academy at Lincoln 800/4-8
1016 Lincoln St 27401 336-370-3471
Anita Stewart, prin. Fax 370-3480
Academy at Smith 200/9-12
2225 S Holden Rd 27407 336-316-5866
Lance Stokes, prin. Fax 316-5869
Allen MS 700/6-8
1108 Glendale Dr 27406 336-294-7325
Sheila Gorham, prin. Fax 294-7315
Aycock MS 600/6-8
811 Cypress St 27405 336-370-8110
Keisha Brown, prin. Fax 370-8044
Dudley HS 1,400/9-12
1200 Lincoln St 27401 336-370-8130
Rodney Wilds, prin. Fax 370-8979
Early College at Guilford 200/9-12
5608 W Friendly Ave 27410 336-316-2860
Linda Kidd, prin. Fax 316-2858
Greenboro Middle College HS 100/11-12
815 W Market St 27401 336-370-8300
Cheri Keels, prin. Fax 370-8918
Grimsley HS 1,700/9-12
801 Westover Ter 27408 336-370-8180
W. Charles Blanchard, prin. Fax 370-8194
Guilford MS 700/6-8
320 Lindley Rd 27410 336-316-5833
Patrice Brown, prin. Fax 316-5837
Hairston MS 600/6-8
3911 Naco Rd 27401 336-370-8250
Calvin Freeman, prin. Fax 370-8153
Henderson Newcomers S 200/Alt
411 Friendway Rd 27410 336-316-5883
Candice Bailey, prin. Fax 316-7092
High School Ahead Academy 100/Alt
1401 Summit Ave 27405 336-294-7640
Michelle Hayes, prin. Fax 294-7643
Jackson MS 400/6-8
2200 Ontario St 27403 336-294-7350
Katrinka Brown, prin. Fax 294-7316
Kernodle MS 1,000/6-8
3600 Drawbridge Pkwy 27410 336-545-3717
Thea McHam, prin. Fax 545-3714
Kiser MS 1,000/6-8
716 Benjamin Pkwy 27408 336-370-8240
Gerald O'Donnell, prin. Fax 370-8248
Mendenhall MS 900/6-8
205 Willoughby Blvd 27408 336-545-2000
Marshall Matson, prin. Fax 545-2004
Middle College HS @ Bennett 100/9-12
722 Gorrell St 27401 336-517-1832
Esther Coble, prin. Fax 517-2120
Middle College HS @ GTCC Greensboro 9-12
3505 E Wendover Ave 27405 336-375-2466
Rodney Boone, prin. Fax 375-2469
Middle College HS @ NC A&T 100/9-12
1601 E Market St 27411 336-691-0941
Marcus Gause, prin. Fax 691-0952
Middle College HS @ UNCG 50/9-12
1408 Walker Ave 27412 336-334-3662
Angela Polk-Jones, prin. Fax 334-5503
Northern HS 1,300/9-12
7101 Spencer Dixon Rd 27455 336-643-8449
William Laine, prin. Fax 644-2589
Northern MS 900/6-8
616 Simpson Calhoun Rd 27455 336-605-3342
Ashley Triplett, prin. Fax 643-8435
Northwest HS 1,900/9-12
5240 NW School Rd 27409 336-605-3300
Ralph Kitley, prin. Fax 605-3314
Northwest MS 1,000/6-8
5300 NW School Rd 27409 336-605-3333
Richard Thomae, prin. Fax 605-3325
Page HS 1,900/9-12
201 Alma Pinnix Dr 27405 336-370-8200
Patrice Faison, prin. Fax 370-8219
SCALE - Greensboro 50/Alt
116 Pisgah Church Rd 27455 336-545-2031
Russell Woodward, prin. Fax 545-2035
Smith HS 1,200/9-12
2407 S Holden Rd 27407 336-294-7300
Donevin Hoskins, prin. Fax 294-7313
Southeast HS 1,400/9-12
4530 SE School Rd 27406 336-674-4300
Dr. James Seagraves, prin. Fax 674-4290
Southeast MS 1,000/6-8
4825 Woody Mill Rd 27406 336-674-4280
Karen Burress, prin. Fax 674-4276

Southern HS 1,100/9-12
5700 Drake Rd 27406 336-674-4250
Debbra Kraszeski, prin. Fax 674-4254
Southern MS 700/6-8
5747 Drake Rd 27406 336-674-4266
Karen Ellis, prin. Fax 674-4278
STEM Early College at NC A&T 9-12
402 Laurel St 27411 336-370-8580
Jamisa Williams, prin. Fax 274-7167
Twilight HS 100/Alt
116 Pisgah Church Rd 27455 336-282-6797
Pandora Bell, prin.
Weaver Academy 300/9-12
300 S Spring St 27401 336-370-8282
Johncarlos Miller, prin. Fax 370-8287
Western HS 1,300/9-12
409 Friendway Rd 27410 336-316-5800
Pete Kashubara, prin. Fax 316-5813
Other Schools – See Browns Summit, Gibsonville, High Point, Jamestown, Mc Leansville

---

American Hebrew Academy 200/9-12
4334 Hobbs Rd 27410 336-217-7100
Glenn Drew, dir. Fax 217-7011
Bennett College Post-Sec.
900 E Washington St 27401 336-273-4431
Brookstone College of Business Post-Sec.
424 Gallimore Dairy Rd St A 27409 336-668-2627
Caldwell Academy 700/PK-12
2900 Horse Pen Creek Rd 27410 336-665-1161
Sam Cox, head sch Fax 665-1178
Carolina Graduate School of Divinity Post-Sec.
PO Box 7148 27417 336-315-8660
ECPI University Post-Sec.
7802 Airport Center Dr 27409 336-665-1400
Greensboro College Post-Sec.
815 W Market St 27401 336-272-7102
Greensboro Day S 900/PK-12
5401 Lawndale Dr 27455 336-288-8590
Mark Hale, head sch Fax 282-2905
Guilford College Post-Sec.
5800 W Friendly Ave 27410 336-316-2000
Hope Academy, PO Box 10616 27404 5-8
Dayna Carr, admin. 336-303-0436
Leon's Beauty School Post-Sec.
1305 Coliseum Blvd 27403 336-274-4601
Moses H. Cone Memorial Hospital Post-Sec.
1200 N Elm St 27401 336-574-7881
New Garden Friends S 300/PK-12
1128 New Garden Rd 27410 336-299-0964
Steve Blanchard, head sch Fax 292-0347
Noble Academy 100/K-12
3310 Horse Pen Creek Rd 27410 336-282-7044
Linda Hale, head sch Fax 282-2048
North Carolina A&T State University Post-Sec.
1601 E Market St 27411 336-334-7500
Shining Light Academy 200/PK-12
4530 W Wendover Ave 27409 336-299-9688
Bill Smith, prin. Fax 299-6126
University of North Carolina Post-Sec.
PO Box 26170 27402 336-334-5000
Vandalia Christian S 700/PK-12
3919 Pleasant Garden Rd 27406 336-379-8380
Dr. Mark Weatherford, admin. Fax 379-8671
Virginia College Post-Sec.
3740 S Holden Rd 27406 336-398-5400

**Greenville, Pitt, Pop. 82,822**
Pitt County SD 22,900/PK-12
1717 W 5th St 27834 252-830-4200
Dr. Ethan Lenker, supt. Fax 830-4239
www.pitt.k12.nc.us/
Aycock MS 700/6-8
1325 Red Banks Rd 27858 252-756-4181
Janarde Cannon, prin. Fax 756-2408
Conley HS 1,400/9-12
2006 Worthington Rd 27858 252-756-3440
Don Marr, prin. Fax 756-3028
Eppes MS 600/6-8
1100 S Elm St 27858 252-757-2160
Charlie Langley, prin. Fax 757-2163
Hope MS 700/6-8
2995 Mills Rd 27858 252-355-7071
Jennifer Poplin, prin. Fax 355-6055
Rose HS 1,600/9-12
600 W Arlington Blvd 27834 252-321-3640
Monica Jacobson, prin. Fax 321-3653
Wellcome MS 400/6-8
3101 N Memorial Dr 27834 252-752-5938
Maurice Harris, prin. Fax 752-1685
Other Schools – See Ayden, Bethel, Farmville, Winterville

---

East Carolina University Post-Sec.
1000 E 5th St 27858 252-328-6131
Greenville Christian Academy 300/PK-12
1621 Greenville Blvd SW 27834 252-756-0939
Mike Lopez, prin. Fax 756-5532
John Paul II Catholic HS 9-12
PO Box 4431 27836 252-215-1224
John Donohue, prin. Fax 225-0212
Miller-Motte College Post-Sec.
1021 WH Smith Blvd Ste 102 27834 252-215-2000
Mitchell's Hairstyling Academy Post-Sec.
426 E Arlington Blvd 27858 252-756-3050
Oakwood S 300/PK-12
4000 MacGregor Downs Rd 27834 252-931-0760
Robert Peterson, hdmstr. Fax 931-0964
Pitt Community College Post-Sec.
PO Box 7007 27835 252-493-7200
Trinity Christian S 400/PK-12
3111 Golden Rd 27858 252-758-0037

**Halifax, Halifax, Pop. 232**
Halifax County SD 3,900/PK-12
PO Box 468 27839 252-583-5111
Dr. Elease Frederick, supt. Fax 583-1474
www.halifax.k12.nc.us/

Southeast Halifax HS 500/9-12
16683 NC Highway 125 27839 252-445-2027
Ann Davis, prin. Fax 445-3463
Other Schools – See Enfield, Littleton

Weldon CSD
Supt. — See Weldon
Weldon MS 200/5-8
4489 US Highway 301 27839 252-536-2571
Andre Stewart, prin. Fax 536-3485

**Hallsboro, Columbus, Pop. 457**
Columbus County SD
Supt. — See Whiteville
Hallsboro MS 200/6-8
PO Box 248 28442 910-646-4192
Adam Thompson, prin. Fax 646-5072

**Hamlet, Richmond, Pop. 6,381**
Richmond County SD 7,200/PK-12
PO Box 1259 28345 910-582-5860
Cindy Goodman Ed.D., supt. Fax 582-7921
www.richmond.k12.nc.us
Hamlet MS 600/6-8
1406 Mcdonald Ave 28345 910-582-7903
Jim Butler, prin. Fax 582-5730
Richmond County 9th Grade Academy 600/9-9
804 County Home Rd 28345 910-582-7800
Pam Patterson, prin. Fax 582-7804
Richmond Early College HS 100/9-12
1042 W Hamlet Ave 28345 910-410-1922
Tonya Waddell, prin.
Other Schools – See Ellerbe, Rockingham

Richmond Community College Post-Sec.
PO Box 1189 28345 910-410-1700

**Hampstead, Pender, Pop. 4,028**
Pender County SD
Supt. — See Burgaw
Topsail HS 1,100/9-12
245 N Saint Johns Church Rd 28443 910-270-2755
Michael Hodges, prin. Fax 270-9290
Topsail MS 800/6-8
17445 US Highway 17 N 28443 910-270-2612
Christopher Madden, prin. Fax 270-3190

**Harrells, Sampson, Pop. 202**

Harrells Christian Academy 400/K-12
PO Box 88 28444 910-532-4575
Kevin Kunst, hdmstr. Fax 532-2958

**Harrisburg, Cabarrus, Pop. 11,315**
Cabarrus County SD
Supt. — See Concord
Hickory Ridge HS 1,400/9-12
7321 Raging Ridge Rd 28075 704-454-7300
Michelle Cline, prin. Fax 454-7330
Hickory Ridge MS 1,100/6-8
7336 Raging Ridge Rd 28075 704-455-1331
Elizabeth Snyder, prin. Fax 455-1338

Charlotte Islamic Academy 200/K-12
8810 Hickory Ridge Rd 28075 704-537-1772

**Havelock, Craven, Pop. 19,878**
Craven County SD
Supt. — See New Bern
Early College EAST HS 9-12
104 Middle School Ln 28532 252-444-5194
Allan Quinn, prin. Fax 444-5129
Havelock HS 1,200/9-12
101 Webb Blvd 28532 252-444-5112
Jeffrey Murphy, prin. Fax 444-5112
Havelock MS 500/6-8
102 High School Dr 28532 252-444-5125
Tabari Wallace, prin. Fax 444-5129
Tucker Creek MS 500/6-8
200 Sermons Blvd 28532 252-444-7200
Angie Franks, prin. Fax 444-7206

**Hayesville, Clay, Pop. 309**
Clay County SD 1,400/PK-12
154 Yellow Jacket Dr 28904 828-389-8513
Dr. Mark Leek, supt. Fax 389-3437
www.clayschools.org/
Hayesville HS 400/9-12
205 Yellow Jacket Dr 28904 828-389-6532
Mickey Noe, prin. Fax 389-6251
Hayesville MS 400/5-8
135 School Dr 28904 828-389-9924
Justin Clapsaddle, prin. Fax 389-1706

**Hays, Wilkes, Pop. 1,835**
Wilkes County SD
Supt. — See North Wilkesboro
North Wilkes HS 700/9-12
2986 Traphill Rd 28635 336-957-8601
Lisa Joines, prin. Fax 957-4787

**Henderson, Vance, Pop. 15,184**
Vance County SD 6,900/PK-12
PO Box 7001 27536 252-492-2127
Dr. Anthony D. Jackson, supt. Fax 438-6119
www.vcs.k12.nc.us
Eaton-Johnson MS 800/6-8
500 N Beckford Dr 27536 252-438-5017
Dr. Brad Jones, prin. Fax 738-0250
Henderson MS 800/6-8
219 Charles St 27536 252-492-0054
Dr. John Hargrove, prin. Fax 430-8588
Northern Vance HS 1,000/9-12
293 Warrenton Rd 27537 252-492-6041
Dr. Larry Webb, prin. Fax 492-7878
Southern Vance HS 800/9-12
925 Garrett Rd 27537 252-430-6000
Stephanie Ayscue, prin. Fax 430-0308
STEM Early HS 300/6-8
293 Warrenton Rd 27537 252-738-2260
Rey Horner, prin. Fax 738-2261

Vance County Early College HS 200/9-12
PO Box 917 27536 252-738-3580
Michael Bullard, prin. Fax 438-3128
Western Vance Secondary S 100/Alt
2785 Poplar Creek Rd 27537 252-438-8407
Clarence Hicks, prin. Fax 438-4957

Crossroads Christian S 200/PK-12
PO Box 249 27536 252-431-1333
Jonathan Capps, hdmstr. Fax 431-0333
Kerr-Vance Academy 500/PK-12
700 Vance Academy Rd 27537 252-492-0018
Vance-Granville Community College Post-Sec.
PO Box 917 27536 252-492-2061
Victory Christian S 100/K-12
PO Box 592 27536 252-492-6079

**Hendersonville, Henderson, Pop. 12,877**
Henderson County SD 13,400/K-12
414 4th Ave W 28739 828-697-4733
David L. Jones, supt. Fax 697-5541
www.hendersoncountypublicschoolsnc.org
Apple Valley MS 900/6-8
43 Fruitland Rd 28792 828-697-4545
Melanie Adams, prin. Fax 698-6119
Balfour Education Center 100/Alt
2529 Asheville Hwy 28791 828-697-4629
Kent Parent, prin. Fax 698-6130
Hendersonville HS 700/9-12
1 Bearcat Blvd 28791 828-697-4802
W. Robert Wilkins, prin. Fax 698-6126
Hendersonville MS 500/6-8
825 N Whitted St 28791 828-697-4800
Luke Manuel, prin. Fax 698-6127
North Henderson HS 1,000/9-12
35 Fruitland Rd 28792 828-697-4500
John Shepard, prin. Fax 698-6129
Rugby MS 900/6-8
3345 Haywood Rd 28791 828-891-6566
Scott Moore, prin. Fax 891-6589
West Henderson HS 1,100/9-12
3600 Haywood Rd 28791 828-891-6571
R. Dean Jones, prin. Fax 891-6590
Other Schools – See East Flat Rock, Flat Rock

**Hertford, Perquimans, Pop. 2,119**
Perquimans County SD 1,800/PK-12
PO Box 337 27944 252-426-5741
Dr. Dwayne Stallings, supt. Fax 426-4913
www.pcs.k12.nc.us
Perquimans County HS 500/9-12
PO Box 398 27944 252-426-5778
Chante Jordan, prin. Fax 426-7614
Other Schools – See Winfall

**Hickory, Catawba, Pop. 39,263**
Catawba County SD
Supt. — See Newton
Arndt MS 700/7-8
3350 34th Street Dr NE 28601 828-256-9545
Lee Miller, prin. Fax 256-6748
Catawba Valley Early College HS 300/9-12
2550 US Highway 70 SE 28602 828-485-2980
Heather Benfield, prin. Fax 485-2981
St. Stephens HS 1,200/9-12
3205 34th Street Dr NE 28601 828-256-9841
Jeff Taylor, prin. Fax 256-7159

Hickory CSD 4,500/PK-12
432 4th Ave SW 28602 828-322-2855
Robbie Adell Ed.D., supt. Fax 322-1834
www.hickoryschools.net
Grandview MS 500/6-8
451 Catawba Valley Blvd 28602 828-328-2289
Dr. Vanessa Howerton, prin. Fax 328-2992
Hickory Career and Arts Magnet HS 200/6-12
409 8th Ave NE 28601 828-328-6738
Teresa Carroll, prin. Fax 328-8539
Hickory HS 1,000/9-12
1234 3rd St NE 28601 828-322-5860
Dr. Ann Stalnaker, prin. Fax 326-7101
Northview MS 600/6-8
302 28th Ave NE 28601 828-327-6300
Stephanie Dischiavi, prin. Fax 327-6367

Catawba Valley Community College Post-Sec.
2550 US Highway 70 SE 28602 828-327-7000
Hickory Christian Academy 400/K-12
3260 6th Street Dr NW 28601 828-324-5405
Lenoir-Rhyne College Post-Sec.
625 7th Ave NE 28601 828-328-1741
Tabernacle Christian S 100/PK-12
1225 29th Avenue Dr NE 28601 828-324-9936
University Christian HS 100/9-12
602 7th Ave NE 28601 828-855-2995

**Hiddenite, Alexander, Pop. 532**
Alexander County SD
Supt. — See Taylorsville
East Alexander MS 700/6-8
1285 White Plains Rd 28636 828-632-7565
Dr. Lisa Harrington, prin. Fax 632-4508

**Highlands, Macon, Pop. 908**
Macon County SD
Supt. — See Franklin
Highlands S 400/K-12
PO Box 940 28741 828-526-2147
Brian Jetter, prin. Fax 526-0615

**High Point, Guilford, Pop. 102,180**
Guilford County SD
Supt. — See Greensboro
Academy at HP Central 100/9-12
700 Chestnut Dr 27262 336-885-7905
Howard Stimpson, prin. Fax 885-7927
Andrews HS 800/9-12
1920 McGuinn Dr 27265 336-819-2800
David Miller, prin. Fax 887-5585

Ferndale MS 900/6-8
701 Ferndale Blvd 27262 336-819-2855
Quincy Williams, prin. Fax 885-2854
High Point Central HS 1,400/9-12
801 Ferndale Blvd 27262 336-819-2825
Bryan Johnson, prin. Fax 819-2991
Middle College HS @ GTCC High Point 100/9-12
901 S Main St 27260 336-819-4111
Lance Sockwell, prin. Fax 819-4116
Penn-Griffin School for the Arts 600/6-12
825 E Washington Dr 27260 336-819-2870
Dr. Shelley Nixon-Greene, prin. Fax 889-4841
Pruett SCALE Academy Alt
900 W English Rd 27262 336-878-5380
Joseph Stone, prin. Fax 889-7625
Southwest HS 1,400/9-12
4364 Barrow Rd 27265 336-819-2970
George Alan Parker, prin. Fax 454-5175
Southwest MS 1,100/6-8
4368 Barrow Rd 27265 336-819-2985
Kerrie Douglas, prin. Fax 454-4015
Welborn Academy of Science & Technology 500/6-8
1710 McGuinn Dr 27265 336-819-2880
N. Brewington-McCormick, prin. Fax 819-2879

Hayworth Christian S 100/PK-12
1696 Westchester Dr 27262 336-882-3126
Vicki Beale, admin.
High Point Christian Academy 700/PK-12
800 Phillips Ave 27262 336-841-8702
Keith Curlee, head sch Fax 841-8850
High Point University Post-Sec.
833 Montlieu Ave 27262 336-841-9000
ITT Technical Institute Post-Sec.
4050 Piedmont Pkwy 27265 336-819-5900
Laurel University Post-Sec.
1215 Eastchester Dr 27265 336-887-3000
Piedmont S 100/K-10
815 Old Mill Rd 27265 336-883-0992
Tim Montgomery, head sch Fax 883-4752
Tri-City Christian Academy 100/PK-12
8000 Clinard Farms Rd 27265 336-665-9822
Wesleyan Christian Academy 1,000/PK-12
1917 N Centennial St 27262 336-884-3333
Dr. Rob Brown, head sch Fax 884-8232
Westchester Country Day S 400/PK-12
2045 N Old Greensboro Rd 27265 336-869-2128
Cobb Atkinson, head sch Fax 869-6685

**Hillsborough, Orange, Pop. 5,962**
Orange County SD 7,300/K-12
200 E King St 27278 919-732-8126
Dr. Todd Wirt, supt. Fax 732-8120
www.orange.k12.nc.us
Cedar Ridge HS 1,100/9-12
1125 New Grady Brown Sch Rd 27278 919-245-4000
Heather Blackmon, prin. Fax 245-4010
Orange HS 1,200/9-12
500 Orange High School Rd 27278 919-732-6133
Jason Johnson, prin. Fax 644-7699
Partnership Academy S 50/Alt
1006 Storey Ln 27278 919-245-4030
Paige Marsh, prin. Fax 245-4035
Stanback MS 600/6-8
3700 NC Highway 86 S 27278 919-644-3200
Jeff Rachlin, prin. Fax 644-3226
Stanford MS 600/6-8
308 Orange High School Rd 27278 919-732-6121
Anne Purcell, prin. Fax 732-6910
Other Schools – See Efland

**Hobgood, Halifax, Pop. 346**

Hobgood Academy 200/PK-12
201 S Beech St 27843 252-826-4116
Dr. Teresa Byrum, hdmstr. Fax 826-2265

**Holly Ridge, Onslow, Pop. 1,230**
Onslow County SD
Supt. — See Jacksonville
Dixon HS 700/9-12
160 Dixon School Rd 28445 910-347-2958
Vikki Childress, prin. Fax 347-3932
Dixon MS 600/6-8
200 Dixon School Rd 28445 910-347-2738
Leigh Bizzell, prin. Fax 347-4399

**Holly Springs, Wake, Pop. 24,092**
Wake County SD
Supt. — See Cary
Holly Grove MS 1,100/6-8
1401 Avent Ferry Rd 27540 919-567-4177
Kenneth Proulx, prin. Fax 567-4159
Holly Ridge MS 1,000/6-8
950 Holly Springs Rd 27540 919-577-1335
Emily Mountford, prin. Fax 577-1379
Holly Springs HS 2,100/9-12
5329 Cass Holt Rd 27540 919-577-1444
Brian Pittman, prin. Fax 577-1742

**Hope Mills, Cumberland, Pop. 14,573**
Cumberland County SD
Supt. — See Fayetteville
Grays Creek HS 1,300/9-12
5301 Celebration Dr 28348 910-424-8589
Vernon Aldridge, prin. Fax 424-7411
Grays Creek MS 1,000/6-8
5151 Celebration Dr 28348 910-483-4124
Lisa Stewart, prin. Fax 483-5296
Hope Mills MS 700/6-8
4975 Cameron Rd 28348 910-425-5106
Cherie Graham, prin. Fax 423-5887
South View HS 1,800/9-12
4184 Elk Rd 28348 910-425-8181
Brian Edkins, dir. Fax 425-2962
South View MS 800/6-8
4100 Elk Rd 28348 910-424-3131
Janet Kehoe, prin. Fax 424-2402

**Hubert, Onslow**
Onslow County SD
Supt. — See Jacksonville
Onslow County Learning Center — Alt
PO Box 158 28539 — 910-326-2305
Felicia Walton, dir. — Fax 326-2208

**Hudson, Caldwell, Pop. 3,744**
Caldwell County SD
Supt. — See Lenoir
Caldwell County Career Center HS — Vo/Tech
2857 Hickory Blvd 28638 — 828-759-4640
Brian Suddreth, prin. — Fax 759-4672
Caldwell Early College HS — 300/9-12
2859 Hickory Blvd 28638 — 828-759-4636
Candis Hagaman, prin. — Fax 759-4666
Hudson MS — 800/6-8
291 Pine Mountain Rd 28638 — 828-728-4281
Julia Knight, prin. — Fax 726-8157
South Caldwell HS — 1,500/9-12
7035 Spartan Dr 28638 — 828-396-2188
Michael Peake, prin. — Fax 396-5929

---

Caldwell Community Coll. & Tech. Inst. — Post-Sec.
2855 Hickory Blvd 28638 — 828-726-2200
Harris Chapel Christian Academy — 50/PK-12
1444 Cajah Mountain Rd 28638 — 828-728-3721
Heritage Christian S — 100/K-12
239 Mount Herman Rd 28638 — 828-726-0055

**Huntersville, Mecklenburg, Pop. 45,893**
Charlotte/Mecklenburg County SD
Supt. — See Charlotte
Alexander MS — 800/6-8
12201 Hambright Rd 28078 — 980-343-3830
Angela Richardson, prin. — Fax 343-3851
Bradley MS — 1,200/6-8
13345 Beatties Ford Rd 28078 — 980-343-5750
Penny Presley, prin. — Fax 343-5743
Hopewell HS — 1,700/9-12
11530 Beatties Ford Rd 28078 — 980-343-5988
J. Dino Gisiano, prin. — Fax 343-5990
North Mecklenburg HS — 1,600/9-12
11201 Old Statesville Rd 28078 — 980-343-3840
Sonya McInnis, prin. — Fax 343-3845

---

Christ the King HS — 9-12
2011 Crusader Way 28078 — 704-799-4400
Brendan Keane, prin. — Fax 799-4404
Phoenix Montessori Academy — 100/PK-12
12340 Mt Holly Huntersville 28078 — 704-892-7536
SouthLake Christian Academy — 900/PK-12
13820 Hagers Ferry Rd 28078 — 704-949-2200
David Rowles, head sch — Fax 949-2203

**Indian Trail, Union, Pop. 32,854**
Union County SD
Supt. — See Monroe
Porter Ridge HS — 1,400/9-12
2839 Ridge Rd 28079 — 704-292-7662
Dr. Bashawn Harris, prin. — Fax 296-9733
Porter Ridge MS — 1,300/6-8
2827 Ridge Rd 28079 — 704-225-7555
Lee Casey, prin. — Fax 226-9844
Sun Valley MS — 1,200/6-8
1409 Wesley Chapel Rd 28079 — 704-296-3009
Vicki Merritt, prin. — Fax 296-3045

---

Central Academy at Lake Park — 200/K-12
3624 Lake Park Rd 28079 — 704-882-6267
Dr. Terry Moffitt, head sch — Fax 882-4651
Metrolina Christian Academy — 1,000/PK-12
PO Box 1460 28079 — 704-882-3375
Richard Calloway, head sch — Fax 882-0631

**Iron Station, Lincoln, Pop. 736**
Lincoln County SD
Supt. — See Lincolnton
East Lincoln MS — 700/6-8
4137 Highway 73 28080 — 704-732-0761
Heather Myers, prin. — Fax 732-4456

**Jackson, Northampton, Pop. 512**
Northampton County SD — 2,300/PK-12
PO Box 158 27845 — 252-534-1371
Dr. Monica Smith-Woofter, supt. — Fax 534-4631
www.northampton.k12.nc.us
Other Schools – See Conway, Gaston

**Jacksonville, Onslow, Pop. 67,399**
Onslow County SD — 24,300/PK-12
PO Box 99 28541 — 910-455-2211
Rick Stout, supt. — Fax 455-3027
www.onslow.k12.nc.us
Hunters Creek MS — 800/6-8
4040 Hunters Trl 28546 — 910-353-2147
Jocelyn Cassidy, prin. — Fax 353-7939
Jacksonville Commons MS — 800/6-8
315 Commons Dr S 28546 — 910-346-6888
Gail Pylant, prin. — Fax 938-1682
Jacksonville HS — 1,100/9-12
1021 Henderson Dr 28540 — 910-989-2048
Donna Lynch, prin. — Fax 989-2046
New Bridge MS — 500/6-8
401 New Bridge St 28540 — 910-346-5144
Chris Barnes, prin. — Fax 346-5402
Northside HS — 900/9-12
365 Commons Dr S 28546 — 910-455-4868
Maria Johnson, prin. — Fax 455-4987
Northwoods Park MS — 700/6-8
904 Sioux Dr 28540 — 910-347-1202
Angela Garland, prin. — Fax 347-0713
Southwest HS — 700/9-12
1420 Burgaw Hwy 28540 — 910-455-4888
Tim Foster, prin. — Fax 455-3949
Southwest MS — 500/6-8
3000 Furia Dr 28540 — 910-455-1105
Steve Clark, prin. — Fax 455-4082
White Oak HS — 1,000/9-12
1001 Piney Green Rd 28546 — 910-455-1541
Jane Dennis, prin. — Fax 938-2302
Other Schools – See Holly Ridge, Hubert, Richlands, Swansboro

---

Cheveux School Hair Design and Hairport — Post-Sec.
4781 Gum Branch Rd Ste 1 28540 — 910-455-5767
Coastal Carolina Community College — Post-Sec.
444 Western Blvd 28546 — 910-455-1221
Jacksonville Christian Academy — 300/K-12
919 Gum Branch Rd 28540 — 910-347-2358
Rev. Larry Haggard, prin. — Fax 347-3138
Living Water Christian S — 300/PK-12
3980 Gum Branch Rd 28540 — 910-938-7017
Miller-Motte College — Post-Sec.
1291 Hargett St Ste A 28540 — 910-478-4300

**Jamestown, Guilford, Pop. 3,331**
Guilford County SD
Supt. — See Greensboro
Jamestown MS — 1,100/6-8
301 Haynes Rd 27282 — 336-819-2100
Trent Vernon, prin. — Fax 454-6734
Middle College HS @ GTCC - Jamestown — 100/9-12
601 High Point Rd 27282 — 336-819-2957
Loretta Rowland-Kitley, prin. — Fax 819-2961
Ragsdale HS — 1,300/9-12
1000 Lucy Ragsdale Rd 27282 — 336-454-7400
James Gibson, prin. — Fax 454-4001

---

Guilford Technical Community College — Post-Sec.
PO Box 309 27282 — 336-334-4822

**Jefferson, Ashe, Pop. 1,599**
Ashe County SD — 3,300/PK-12
PO Box 604 28640 — 336-246-7175
Dr. Todd Holden, supt. — Fax 246-7609
www.ashe.k12.nc.us/
Other Schools – See Warrensville, West Jefferson

**Kannapolis, Cabarrus, Pop. 41,850**
Kannapolis CSD — 5,400/PK-12
100 Denver St 28083 — 704-938-1131
Dr. Pam Cain, supt. — Fax 933-6370
www.kcs.k12.nc.us
Brown HS — 1,400/9-12
415 E 1st St 28083 — 704-932-6125
Todd Parker, prin. — Fax 933-1862
Kannapolis MS — 800/7-8
1445 Oakwood Ave 28081 — 704-932-4102
Bridgette Reese, prin. — Fax 932-4104

---

Franklin Heights Christian Academy — 100/K-12
526 Wright Ave 28083 — 704-933-8348
Suzan Lambert, head sch — Fax 932-9470

**Kenansville, Duplin, Pop. 849**
Duplin County SD — 9,400/PK-12
315 N Main St 28349 — 910-296-1521
Dr. Austin Obasohan, supt. — Fax 296-1396
www.duplinschools.net
Duplin Early College HS — 100/9-12
212 James Sprunt Dr 28349 — 910-296-1136
Tanya Smith, prin. — Fax 296-0348
Smith MS — 400/6-8
PO Box 369 28349 — 910-296-0309
Gary Brown, prin. — Fax 296-0086
Other Schools – See Beulaville, Mount Olive, Rose Hill, Teachey, Warsaw

---

James Sprunt Community College — Post-Sec.
PO Box 398 28349 — 910-296-2400

**Kenly, Johnston, Pop. 1,330**
Johnston County SD
Supt. — See Smithfield
North Johnston HS — 700/9-12
PO Box 339 27542 — 919-284-2031
Tim Harrell, prin. — Fax 284-6224

**Kernersville, Forsyth, Pop. 22,718**
Winston-Salem/Forsyth SD
Supt. — See Winston Salem
East Forsyth HS — 1,900/9-12
2500 W Mountain St 27284 — 336-703-6735
Rodney Bass, prin. — Fax 727-8546
East Forsyth MS — 800/6-8
810 Bagley Rd 27284 — 336-703-6765
Dossie Poteat, prin. — Fax 607-8531
Glenn HS — 1,600/9-12
1600 Union Cross Rd 27284 — 336-771-4500
Brad Craddock, prin. — Fax 771-4507
Kernersville MS — 800/6-8
110 Brown Rd 27284 — 336-703-4255
Pam Helms, prin. — Fax 996-1966
Southeast MS — 1,200/6-8
1200 Old Salem Rd 27284 — 336-703-4219
Stephanie Gentry, prin. — Fax 996-0148

---

Bishop McGuiness HS — 500/9-12
1725 NC Highway 66 S 27284 — 336-564-1010
George Repass, prin. — Fax 564-1060
Dudley Cosmetology University — Post-Sec.
900 E Mountain St 27284 — 336-996-2030
First Christian Academy — 200/PK-12
1130 N Main St 27284 — 336-996-1660
Bonnie McDaniel, prin. — Fax 996-6511
Triad Baptist Christian Academy — 200/PK-11
1175 S Main St 27284 — 336-996-7573
Dennis Roberts, admin. — Fax 996-9791

**Kill Devil Hills, Dare, Pop. 6,558**
Dare County SD
Supt. — See Nags Head
First Flight HS — 800/9-12
100 Veterans Dr 27948 — 252-449-7000
Arty Tillett, prin. — Fax 449-7004
First Flight MS — 600/6-8
109 Veterans Dr 27948 — 252-441-8888
Tim Albert, prin. — Fax 441-7694

**King, Stokes, Pop. 6,843**
Stokes County SD
Supt. — See Danbury
Chestnut Grove MS — 800/6-8
2185 Chestnut Grove Rd 27021 — 336-983-2106
David Durham, prin. — Fax 983-2725
Meadowbrook Academy — 50/Alt
817 Meadowbrook Dr 27021 — 336-985-3224
David Hicks, prin. — Fax 985-3568
West Stokes HS — 1,000/9-12
1400 Priddy Rd 27021 — 336-983-2099
Kevin Spainhour, prin. — Fax 983-6076

---

Calvary Christian S — 200/PK-12
748 Spainhour Rd 27021 — 336-983-3743

**Kings Mountain, Cleveland, Pop. 10,130**
Cleveland County SD
Supt. — See Shelby
Kings Mountain HS — 1,300/9-12
500 Phifer Rd 28086 — 704-476-8330
Ronny Funderburke, prin. — Fax 734-1723
Kings Mountain MS — 700/7-8
1000 Phifer Rd 28086 — 704-476-8340
David Smith, prin. — Fax 734-5615

---

Grace Christian Academy — 100/PK-12
260 Range Rd 28086 — 704-734-0509

**Kinston, Lenoir, Pop. 21,394**
Lenoir County SD — 9,300/PK-12
PO Box 729 28502 — 252-527-1109
Dr. Steve Mazingo, supt. — Fax 527-6884
www.lenoir.k12.nc.us
Kinston HS — 900/9-12
2601 N Queen St 28501 — 252-527-8067
Angela Bryant, prin. — Fax 527-4090
Lenior County Learning Academy — 50/Alt
2529 Cedar Dell Ln 28504 — 252-527-4264
Diane Heath, prin. — Fax 527-7631
Lenoir County Early College HS — 200/9-12
231 Hwy 58 S 28504 — 252-233-6870
Nicholas Harvey, prin. — Fax 233-6879
Rochelle MS — 500/6-8
301 N Rochelle Blvd 28501 — 252-527-4290
Maya Swinson, prin. — Fax 527-6498
Woodington MS — 700/6-8
4939 Hwy 258 S 28504 — 252-527-9570
Pam Heath, prin. — Fax 527-3883
Other Schools – See Deep Run, La Grange

---

Arendell Parrott Academy — 800/PK-12
PO Box 1297 28503 — 252-522-4222
Dr. Bert Bright, hdmstr. — Fax 522-0672
Bethel Christian Academy — 300/PK-12
1936 Banks School Rd 28504 — 252-522-4636
Douglas K. Phillips M.A., admin. — Fax 523-7290
Lenoir Community College — Post-Sec.
PO Box 188 28502 — 252-527-6223
Lenoir Memorial Hospital — Post-Sec.
100 Airport Rd 28501 — 252-522-7797

**Knightdale, Wake, Pop. 11,083**
Wake County SD
Supt. — See Cary
Knightdale HS — 1,700/9-12
100 Bryan Chalk Ln 27545 — 919-217-5350
Dr. James Argent, prin. — Fax 217-5356

**La Grange, Lenoir, Pop. 2,845**
Lenoir County SD
Supt. — See Kinston
Frink MS — 600/6-8
102 Martin Luther King Jr 28551 — 252-566-3326
Tina Letchworth, prin. — Fax 566-4027
North Lenoir HS — 1,000/9-12
2400 Institute Rd 28551 — 252-527-9184
Gil Respess, prin. — Fax 527-8672

**Lake Waccamaw, Columbus, Pop. 1,463**
Columbus County SD
Supt. — See Whiteville
East Columbus HS — 500/9-12
PO Box 401 28450 — 910-646-4094
Bobby Vaughan, prin. — Fax 646-3779

**Landis, Rowan, Pop. 3,094**
Rowan-Salisbury County SD
Supt. — See Salisbury
Corriher-Lipe MS — 500/6-8
214 W Rice St 28088 — 704-857-7946
Tonya German, prin. — Fax 855-2670

**Lasker, Northampton, Pop. 119**

---

Northeast Academy — 200/PK-12
210 E Church St 27845 — 252-539-2461

**Laurel Hill, Scotland, Pop. 1,230**
Scotland County SD
Supt. — See Laurinburg
Carver MS — 500/6-8
18601 Fieldcrest Rd 28351 — 910-462-4669
Dr. Amber Alford-Watkins, prin. — Fax 462-4674

**Laurinburg, Scotland, Pop. 15,644**
Scotland County SD — 5,200/PK-12
322 S Main St 28352 — 910-276-1138
Dr. Ronald Hargrave, supt. — Fax 277-4310
www.scotland.k12.nc.us
Scotland Early College S — 200/9-12
1700 Dogwood Mile St 28352 — 910-277-3951
Patrick Peed, prin. — Fax 277-5020
Scotland HS — 1,600/9-12
1000 W Church St 28352 — 910-276-7370
Greg Batten, prin. — Fax 277-4444

Shaw Academy 200/Alt
18700 Old Wire Rd 28352 910-273-0611
Araunah James, prin. Fax 277-4319
Spring Hill MS 400/6-8
22801 Airbase Rd 28352 910-369-0590
Brent Smith, prin. Fax 369-0595
Other Schools – See Laurel Hill

Christ the Cornerstone Academy 50/K-12
10401 McColl Rd 28352 910-277-0077
Billy Storms, admin. Fax 277-8682
St. Andrews University Post-Sec.
1700 Dogwood Mile St 28352 910-277-5555
Scotland Christian Academy 200/PK-12
10300 McColl Rd 28352 910-276-7722

**Lawndale, Cleveland, Pop. 596**
Cleveland County SD
Supt. — See Shelby
Burns HS 1,100/9-12
307 E Stagecoach Trl 28090 704-476-8335
Dr. Chris Blanton, prin. Fax 538-3895
Burns MS 900/6-8
215 Shady Grove Rd 28090 704-476-8223
Mickey Morehead, prin. Fax 538-3944

**Lawsonville, Stokes**
Stokes County SD
Supt. — See Danbury
Piney Grove MS 300/6-8
3415 Piney Grove Church Rd 27022 336-593-4000
Steve Hall, prin. Fax 593-4003

**Leland, Brunswick, Pop. 13,291**
Brunswick County SD
Supt. — See Bolivia
Leland MS 800/6-8
927 Old Fayetteville Rd NE 28451 910-371-3030
Patricia Underwood, prin. Fax 371-0647
North Brunswick HS 900/9-12
114 Scorpion Dr 28451 910-371-2261
Paul Price, prin. Fax 371-0879

**Lenoir, Caldwell, Pop. 17,882**
Caldwell County SD 12,400/PK-12
1914 Hickory Blvd SW 28645 828-728-8407
Dr. Steve Stone, supt. Fax 728-0012
www.caldwellschools.com
Gamewell MS 600/6-8
3210 Gamewell School Rd 28645 828-754-6204
Anna Crooke, prin. Fax 754-6278
Hibriten HS 900/9-12
1350 Panther Trl SE 28645 828-758-7376
David Colwell, prin. Fax 758-9708
Lenoir MS 500/6-8
1366 Wildcat Trl 28645 828-758-2500
Lisa Vaughn, prin. Fax 758-1570
West Caldwell HS 900/9-12
300 W Caldwell Dr 28645 828-758-5583
Andy Puhl, prin. Fax 754-2783
Other Schools – See Granite Falls, Hudson

**Lewisville, Forsyth, Pop. 12,465**

Forsyth Country Day S 800/PK-12
PO Box 549 27023 336-945-3151
Vincent Stumpo Ph.D., hdmstr. Fax 945-2907

**Lexington, Davidson, Pop. 18,479**
Davidson County SD 20,000/PK-12
PO Box 2057 27293 336-249-8181
Dr. Lory Morrow, supt. Fax 249-1062
www.davidson.k12.nc.us
Central Davidson HS 1,000/9-12
2747 NC Highway 47 27292 336-357-2920
Valerie Feezor, prin. Fax 357-5175
Central Davidson MS 800/6-8
2591 NC Highway 47 27292 336-357-2310
Sloan Denny, prin. Fax 357-5965
Davidson County HS 100/Alt
2061 E Holly Grove Rd 27292 336-242-1459
Ronda Fletcher, prin. Fax 242-1465
North Davidson HS 1,500/9-12
7227 Old US Highway 52 27295 336-731-8431
Angie Kiger, prin. Fax 731-2642
North Davidson MS 1,200/6-8
333 Critcher Dr 27295 336-731-2331
Amy Hyatt, prin. Fax 731-2328
Tyro MS 600/6-8
2946 Michael Rd 27295 336-853-7795
Debbie Hege, prin. Fax 853-7357
West Davidson HS 800/9-12
200 Dragon Dr 27295 336-853-8082
Billy Hunt, prin. Fax 853-7315
Yadkin Valley Regional Career Academy Vo/Tech
2065 E Holly Grove Rd 27292 336-242-5820
Jonathan Brown, prin. Fax 242-5774
Other Schools – See Denton, Thomasville, Winston Salem

Lexington CSD 3,100/1-12
1010 Fair St 27292 336-242-1527
Richard Kriesky, supt. Fax 249-3206
lexcs.org
Lexington HS 800/9-12
26 Penry St 27292 336-242-1574
Monique Curry, prin. Fax 242-1285
Lexington MS 700/6-8
100 W Hemstead St 27292 336-242-1557
Sharolyn Harry-Chisholm, prin. Fax 242-1372

Davidson County Community College Post-Sec.
PO Box 1287 27293 336-249-8186
Sheets Memorial Christian S 300/PK-12
307 Holt St 27292 336-249-4224
Steven Weer, admin. Fax 249-6985
Union Grove Christian S 400/PK-12
2295 Union Grove Rd 27295 336-764-3105
Peter Steinhaus, admin. Fax 764-8657

**Liberty, Randolph, Pop. 2,592**
Randolph County SD
Supt. — See Asheboro
Northeastern Randolph MS 700/6-8
3493 Ramseur Julian Rd 27298 336-622-5808
Dana Albright-Johnson, prin. Fax 622-5868

**Lillington, Harnett, Pop. 3,141**
Harnett County SD 19,500/PK-12
PO Box 1029 27546 910-893-8151
Stanley Williams, supt. Fax 893-4279
www.harnett.k12.nc.us/
STAR Academy 100/Alt
PO Box 1029 27546 910-893-4072
Ron Avery, prin. Fax 893-3421
Western Harnett HS 1,300/9-12
10637 NC 27 W 27546 919-499-5113
Chris Pearson, prin. Fax 499-1537
Western Harnett MS 1,100/6-8
11135 NC 27 W 27546 919-499-4497
Walter McPherson, prin. Fax 499-1788
Other Schools – See Angier, Dunn, Erwin, Sanford, Spring Lake

**Lincolnton, Lincoln, Pop. 10,295**
Lincoln County SD 11,900/PK-12
PO Box 400 28093 704-732-2261
Dr. Sherry Hoyle, supt. Fax 736-4321
www.lincoln.k12.nc.us
Asbury S 50/Alt
221 Salem Church Rd 28092 704-736-4766
Marybeth Avery, prin. Fax 736-4183
Lincoln County School of Technology Vo/Tech
1 Timpken Dr 28092 704-732-4084
Dr. Cale Sain, prin. Fax 735-8292
Lincolnton HS 900/9-12
803 N Aspen St 28092 704-735-3089
Heath Belcher, prin. Fax 736-4234
Lincolnton MS 700/6-8
2361 Startown Rd 28092 704-735-1120
Dana Ayers, prin. Fax 732-6811
North Lincoln HS 1,000/9-12
2737 Lee Lawing Rd 28092 704-736-1969
Mitch Sherrill M.A., prin. Fax 736-1966
West Lincoln HS 1,000/9-12
172 Shoal Rd 28092 704-736-9453
Brian Clary, prin. Fax 276-2004
West Lincoln MS 700/6-8
260 Shoal Rd 28092 704-276-1760
Dr. Timothy Bean, prin. Fax 276-2293
Other Schools – See Denver, Iron Station

**Littleton, Halifax, Pop. 660**
Halifax County SD
Supt. — See Halifax
Northwest HS 600/9-12
8492 NC Highway 48 27850 252-586-4125
Mark Barfield, prin. Fax 586-6240

**Locust, Stanly, Pop. 2,907**
Stanly County SD
Supt. — See Albemarle
West Stanly MS 500/6-8
339 Running Creek Church Rd 28097 704-961-3600
Danny Poplin, prin. Fax 961-3699

Carolina Christian S 300/PK-12
PO Box 399 28097 704-888-4332
Marvin Retzer, hdmstr. Fax 888-4492

**Louisburg, Franklin, Pop. 3,311**
Franklin County SD 8,700/PK-12
53 W River Rd 27549 919-496-2600
Dr. Lisa Martin, supt. Fax 496-2104
www.fcschools.net
Franklin County Early College HS 100/9-12
8150 NC 56 Hwy 27549 919-496-1055
James Harris, prin. Fax 496-1033
Louisburg HS 600/9-12
201 Allen Ln 27549 919-496-3725
Freda Clifton, prin. Fax 496-2505
Terrell Lane MS 400/6-8
101 Terrell Ln 27549 919-496-1855
Fax 496-1370
Other Schools – See Bunn, Franklinton, Youngsville

Louisburg College Post-Sec.
501 N Main St 27549 919-496-2521

**Lowell, Gaston, Pop. 3,488**
Gaston County SD
Supt. — See Gastonia
Holbrook MS 800/6-8
418 S Church St 28098 704-836-9607
Jessica Steiner, prin. Fax 824-4529

**Lucama, Wilson, Pop. 1,093**
Wilson County SD
Supt. — See Wilson
Springfield MS 500/6-8
5551 Wiggins Mill Rd 27851 252-237-4250
Pattie Barnes, prin. Fax 239-1686

**Lumber Bridge, Robeson, Pop. 94**
Hoke County SD
Supt. — See Raeford
Sandy Grove MS 600/6-8
300 Chason Rd 28357 910-875-3559
Tommy Jacobs, prin. Fax 875-3632

**Lumberton, Robeson, Pop. 21,026**
Robeson County SD 24,800/PK-12
410 Caton Rd 28360 910-671-6000
Dr. Johnny Hunt, supt. Fax 671-6024
www.robeson.k12.nc.us
Early College HS 200/9-12
5170 N Fayetteville Rd 28360 910-737-5232
Shelia Gasque, prin. Fax 737-5231
Littlefield MS 800/4-8
9674 NC Highway 41 N 28358 910-671-6065
Kendall Hamilton, prin. Fax 671-6068
Lumberton HS 2,100/9-12
3901 Fayetteville Rd 28358 910-671-6050
Larry Obeda, prin. Fax 671-4399
Lumberton JHS 600/7-8
82 Marion Rd 28358 910-735-2108
Erika McComb, prin. Fax 671-4350
Robeson County Career Center Vo/Tech
1339 Hilly Branch Rd 28360 910-671-6095
Mark Smith, prin. Fax 671-6097
Other Schools – See Fairmont, Maxton, Orrum, Pembroke, Red Springs, Rowland, Saint Pauls

Antioch Christian Academy 300/K-12
5071 Old Whiteville Rd 28358 910-735-1011
Robeson Community College Post-Sec.
PO Box 1420 28359 910-272-3700

**Mc Leansville, Guilford, Pop. 1,014**
Guilford County SD
Supt. — See Greensboro
Northeast HS 1,100/9-12
6700 Mcleansville Rd 27301 336-375-2500
Fabby Williams, prin. Fax 375-2520
Northeast MS 900/6-8
6720 Mcleansville Rd 27301 336-375-2525
Jamie King, prin. Fax 375-2534

**Madison, Rockingham, Pop. 2,190**
Rockingham County SD
Supt. — See Eden
Western Rockingham MS 700/6-8
915 Ayersville Rd 27025 336-548-2168
Duane Hensley, prin. Fax 548-1799

**Maiden, Catawba, Pop. 3,281**
Catawba County SD
Supt. — See Newton
Maiden HS 800/9-12
600 W Main St 28650 828-428-8197
Rob Bliss, prin. Fax 428-8341
Maiden MS 500/7-8
518 N C Ave 28650 828-428-2326
Nan VanHoy, prin. Fax 428-5389

**Manteo, Dare, Pop. 1,400**
Dare County SD
Supt. — See Nags Head
Dare County Alternative S 50/Alt
205 N Highway 64/264 27954 252-473-3141
Fax 473-1638
Manteo HS 500/9-12
829 Wingina St 27954 252-473-5841
John Luciano, prin. Fax 473-2263
Manteo MS 300/6-8
1000 US Highway 64 and 264 27954 252-473-5549
Teresa Twyne, prin. Fax 473-2612

**Marion, McDowell, Pop. 7,708**
McDowell County SD 6,800/PK-12
PO Box 130 28752 828-652-4535
Mark Garrett, supt. Fax 659-2238
www.mcdowell.k12.nc.us/
Alternative Education Center Alt
176 Lukin St 28752 828-652-1040
Tracy Widmann, dir. Fax 652-9840
East McDowell MS 600/6-8
676 State St 28752 828-652-7711
Charles Gaffigan, prin. Fax 652-1469
McDowell Early College 200/9-12
54 College Dr 28752 828-659-0411
Lisa Robinson, prin. Fax 659-0469
McDowell HS 1,300/9-12
600 McDowell High Dr 28752 828-652-7920
Edwin Spivey, prin. Fax 652-1101
West McDowell MS 700/6-8
346 W McDowell Jr High Sch 28752 828-652-3390
Dr. Donna Gardner, prin. Fax 659-1964

McDowell Technical Community College Post-Sec.
54 College Dr 28752 828-652-6021
New Manna Christian S 100/K-12
PO Box 1085 28752 828-652-7729

**Marshall, Madison, Pop. 859**
Madison County SD 2,500/K-12
5738 US 25/70 Hwy 28753 828-649-9276
Ronald Wilcox Ed.D., supt. Fax 649-9334
www.madisonk12.net
Madison HS 600/9-12
5740 US 25/70 Hwy 28753 828-649-2876
Steve Bowlin, prin. Fax 649-0104
Madison MS 600/6-8
95 Upper Brush Creek Rd 28753 828-649-2269
Lisa Gosnell, prin. Fax 649-9015
Other Schools – See Mars Hill

**Mars Hill, Madison, Pop. 1,829**
Madison County SD
Supt. — See Marshall
Madison Early College HS 100/9-12
PO Box 999 28754 828-689-9552
David Robinson, prin. Fax 689-9644

Mars Hill College Post-Sec.
PO Box 370 28754 866-642-4968

**Marshville, Union, Pop. 2,366**
Union County SD
Supt. — See Monroe
East Union MS 800/6-8
6010 W Marshville Blvd 28103 704-290-1540
Anne Radke, prin. Fax 624-9302
Forest Hills HS 900/9-12
100 Forest Hills School S 28103 704-233-4001
Dr. Kevin Plue, prin. Fax 233-4003

**Matthews, Mecklenburg, Pop. 26,705**
Charlotte/Mecklenburg County SD
Supt. — See Charlotte

Butler HS 2,100/9-12
1810 Matthews Mint Hill Rd 28105 980-343-6300
John LeGrand, prin. Fax 343-6315
Crestdale MS 1,000/6-8
940 Sam Newell Rd 28105 980-343-5755
Kathleen Richert, prin. Fax 343-5761
Levine Middle College HS 9-12
2728 Campus Ridge Rd 28105 980-343-9437
Joseph Burch, prin. Fax 343-2432
Mint Hill MS 1,300/6-8
11501 Idlewild Rd 28105 980-343-5439
Steve Drye, prin. Fax 343-5442

Union County SD
Supt. — See Monroe
Weddington HS 1,300/9-12
4901 Weddington Rd 28104 704-708-5530
Jonathan Bowers, prin. Fax 708-6218
Weddington MS 1,100/6-8
5903 Deal Rd 28104 704-814-9772
Marcus Leake, prin. Fax 814-9775

---

Arborbrook Christian Academy 100/K-12
4823 Waxhaw Indian Trail Rd 28104 704-821-9952
Joy Fisk, head sch
Bible Baptist Christian S 200/PK-12
2724 Margaret Wallace Rd 28105 704-535-1694
Carmel Christian S 600/K-12
1145 Pineville Matthews Rd 28105 704-849-9723
Jack Kelley, head sch Fax 847-9908
Covenant Day S 800/PK-12
800 Fullwood Rd 28105 704-847-2385
Mark Davis, hdmstr. Fax 708-6137
Empire Beauty School Post-Sec.
11032 E Independence Blvd 28105 800-575-5983
Grace Academy 300/K-12
PO Box 2553 28106 704-234-0292
Southern Evangelical Seminary Post-Sec.
3000 Tilley Morris Rd 28105 704-847-5600

**Maxton, Robeson, Pop. 2,397**
Robeson County SD
Supt. — See Lumberton
Townsend MS 200/5-8
105 Carolina St 28364 910-844-5086
Eric Sanders, prin. Fax 844-4292

**Mayodan, Rockingham, Pop. 2,444**
Rockingham County SD
Supt. — See Eden
McMichael HS 1,000/9-12
6845 NC Highway 135 27027 336-427-5165
Duane Whittaker, prin. Fax 427-5776

**Mebane, Alamance, Pop. 11,146**
Alamance-Burlington SD
Supt. — See Burlington
Eastern Alamance HS 1,100/9-12
4040 Mebane Rogers Rd 27302 919-563-5991
Dave Ebert, prin. Fax 563-6114
Hawfields MS 700/6-8
1951 S NC Highway 119 27302 919-563-5303
Greg Hook, prin. Fax 563-1351
Woodlawn MS 600/6-8
3970 Mebane Rogers Rd 27302 919-563-3222
Andrew Brehler, prin. Fax 563-6807

**Merry Hill, Bertie**

---

Lawrence Academy 300/PK-12
PO Box 70 27957 252-482-4748

**Micro, Johnston, Pop. 438**
Johnston County SD
Supt. — See Smithfield
North Johnston MS 600/6-8
PO Box 69 27555 919-284-3374
Jarvis Ellis, prin. Fax 284-3399

**Millers Creek, Wilkes, Pop. 2,085**
Wilkes County SD
Supt. — See North Wilkesboro
West Wilkes HS 700/9-12
6598 Boone Trl 28651 336-973-4503
Wayne Sheperd, prin. Fax 973-7323

---

Millers Creek Christian S 200/PK-12
PO Box 559 28651 336-838-2517
April Huffman, prin. Fax 838-2546

**Mill Spring, Polk**
Polk County SD
Supt. — See Columbus
Polk County MS 500/6-8
321 Wolverine Trl 28756 828-894-2215
Hank Utz, prin. Fax 894-0191

**Mint Hill, Mecklenburg, Pop. 22,306**
Charlotte/Mecklenburg County SD
Supt. — See Charlotte
Northeast MS 800/6-8
5960 Brickstone Dr 28227 980-343-6920
Alicia McCree, prin. Fax 343-3264
Rocky River HS 1,700/9-12
10505 Clear Creek Cmmrc Dr 28227 980-344-0409
Brandy Nelson, prin. Fax 343-2135

**Misenheimer, Stanly, Pop. 712**

---

Pfeiffer University Post-Sec.
48380 US Highway 52 28109 800-338-2060

**Mocksville, Davie, Pop. 4,904**
Davie County SD 6,400/PK-12
220 Cherry St 27028 336-751-5921
Dr. Darrin Hartness, supt. Fax 751-9013
www.davie.k12.nc.us
Central Davie Academy 50/Alt
160 Campbell Rd 27028 336-751-5712
Beth Weatherman, prin. Fax 751-5719
Davie County Early College HS 200/9-12
1211 Salisbury Rd 27028 336-753-0888
Denise Absher, prin. Fax 753-1192
Davie County HS 1,700/9-12
1200 Salisbury Rd 27028 336-751-5905
Doyle Nicholson, prin. Fax 751-4597
North Davie MS 500/6-8
497 Farmington Rd 27028 336-998-5555
Mary Foster, prin. Fax 998-7233
South Davie MS 500/6-8
700 Hardison St 27028 336-751-5941
Melissa Lynch, prin. Fax 751-5656
Other Schools – See Advance

**Monroe, Union, Pop. 32,321**
Union County SD 39,100/PK-12
400 N Church St 28112 704-296-0766
Dr. Mary Ellis, supt. Fax 282-2171
www.ucps.k12.nc.us
Central Academy of Technology and Arts 9-12
600 Brewer Dr 28112 704-296-3088
Dr. Kim Fisenne, prin. Fax 296-3090
Monroe HS 900/9-12
1 High School Dr 28112 704-296-3130
Dr. Mike Harvey, prin. Fax 296-3138
Monroe MS 900/6-8
601 E Sunset Dr 28112 704-296-3120
Steven Wray, prin. Fax 296-3122
Parkwood HS 900/9-12
3220 Parkwood School Rd 28112 704-764-2900
Stephanie McManus, prin. Fax 764-2907
Parkwood MS 700/6-8
3219 Parkwood School Rd 28112 704-764-2910
Dr. Jeff Kraftson, prin. Fax 764-2914
Piedmont HS 1,100/9-12
3006 Sikes Mill Rd 28110 704-753-2810
Dr. Jonathan Tyson, prin. Fax 753-2817
Piedmont MS 1,000/6-8
2816 Sikes Mill Rd 28110 704-753-2840
Tracy Strickland, prin. Fax 753-2846
Sun Valley HS 1,400/9-12
5211 Old Charlotte Hwy 28110 704-296-3020
Dr. Shaun Poole, prin. Fax 296-3029
Union County Early College HS 300/9-12
4209A Old Charlotte Hwy 28110 704-290-1565
Tim Conner, prin. Fax 282-0956
Other Schools – See Indian Trail, Marshville, Matthews, Waxhaw

---

Shining Light Baptist Academy 100/PK-12
2541 Old Charlotte Hwy 28110 704-283-1480
Tabernacle Christian S 200/K-12
2900 Walkup Ave 28110 704-283-4395

**Montreat, Buncombe, Pop. 715**

---

Montreat College Post-Sec.
PO Box 1267 28757 800-622-6968

**Mooresville, Iredell, Pop. 32,023**
Iredell-Statesville SD
Supt. — See Statesville
Brawley MS 700/6-8
132 Swift Arrow Dr 28117 704-664-4430
Jimmie Dancy, prin. Fax 664-9846
Lake Norman HS 2,000/9-12
186 Doolie Rd 28117 704-799-8555
Keith Gentle, prin. Fax 799-1512
Lakeshore MS 600/6-8
244 Lakeshore School Dr 28117 704-799-0187
Brian Foster, prin. Fax 663-6431
Mount Mourne IB S 500/6-9
1431 Mecklenburg Hwy 28115 704-892-4711
Dr. Boen Nutting, prin. Fax 892-3804

Mooresville Graded SD 5,600/PK-12
305 N Main St 28115 704-658-2530
Dr. Mark Edwards, supt. Fax 663-3005
www.mgsd.k12.nc.us
Mooresville HS 1,600/9-12
659 E Center Ave 28115 704-658-2580
Michael Royal, prin. Fax 664-4381
Mooresville MS 900/7-8
233 Kistler Farm Rd 28115 704-658-2720
Dr. Carrie Tulbert, prin. Fax 664-5101
Woods Adv Tech / Arts Center Vo/Tech
574 W McLelland Ave 28115 704-658-2500
Devry Gibbs, prin. Fax 664-5102

---

Liberty Preparatory Christian Academy 100/K-12
246 Blume Rd 28117 704-660-3933
Amie Weir, admin. Fax 496-6168
NASCAR Technical Institute Post-Sec.
220 Byers Creek Rd 28117 704-658-1950
Woodlawn S 200/K-12
135 Woodlawn School Loop 28115 704-895-8653
Bob Shirley, head sch Fax 782-1836

**Moravian Falls, Wilkes, Pop. 1,870**
Wilkes County SD
Supt. — See North Wilkesboro
Central Wilkes MS 700/6-8
3541 S NC Highway 16 28654 336-667-7453
Jeffrey Johnson, prin. Fax 667-5825

**Morehead City, Carteret, Pop. 8,439**
Carteret County SD
Supt. — See Beaufort
Bridges S 50/Alt
140 Vashti Dr 28557 252-808-3040
Dr. Mary Keel, prin. Fax 726-5245
Morehead City MS 500/6-8
400 Barbour Rd 28557 252-726-1126
Al Roberson, prin. Fax 726-4980
West Carteret HS 1,200/9-12
4700 Country Club Rd 28557 252-726-1176
Carolyn Heller, prin. Fax 726-6290

---

Carteret Community College Post-Sec.
3505 Arendell St 28557 252-222-6000

**Morganton, Burke, Pop. 16,462**
Burke County SD 13,500/PK-12
PO Box 989 28680 828-439-4312
Larry Putnam, supt. Fax 439-4314
www.burke.k12.nc.us
Burke Middle College HS 100/11-12
1001 Burkemont Ave 28655 828-448-3175
Jonathan Clontz, prin. Fax 442-6172
Freedom HS 1,200/9-12
511 Independence Blvd 28655 828-433-1310
Mike Swan, prin. Fax 439-8420
Johnson MS 500/6-8
701 Lenoir Rd 28655 828-430-7340
Jeana Gallagher, prin. Fax 430-4801
Liberty MS 600/6-8
529 Enola Rd 28655 828-437-1330
Mike Holden, prin. Fax 432-2124
Patton HS 1,000/9-12
701 Enola Rd 28655 828-433-3000
Wendi Barber, prin. Fax 433-3001
Table Rock MS 600/6-8
1585 NC 126 28655 828-437-5212
Felicia Simmons, prin. Fax 439-5702
Other Schools – See Connelly Sprngs, Drexel, Valdese

---

North Carolina School for the Deaf Post-Sec.
517 W Fleming Dr 28655 828-433-2971
Western Piedmont Community College Post-Sec.
1001 Burkemont Ave 28655 828-438-6000

**Morrisville, Wake, Pop. 17,983**

---

DeVry University Post-Sec.
1600 Perimeter Park Dr #100 27560 919-463-1380
The Chef's Acadmey Post-Sec.
2001 Carrington Mill Blvd 27560 919-246-9394

**Mount Airy, Surry, Pop. 10,205**
Mt. Airy CSD 1,700/PK-12
130 Rawley Ave 27030 336-786-8355
Dr. Gregory Little, supt. Fax 786-7553
www.mtairy.k12.nc.us
Mount Airy HS 600/9-12
1011 N South St 27030 336-789-5147
Dr. Sandy George, prin. Fax 719-2341
Mount Airy MS 400/6-8
249 Hamburg St 27030 336-789-9021
Susan Bunch, prin. Fax 789-6074

Surry County SD
Supt. — See Dobson
Gentry MS 400/6-8
1915 W Pine St 27030 336-786-4155
Paige Badgett, prin. Fax 786-6863
Meadowview MS 400/6-8
1282 Mckinney Rd 27030 336-789-0276
Denny Barr, prin. Fax 789-0449
North Surry HS 900/9-12
2440 W Pine St 27030 336-789-5055
Neil Atkins, prin. Fax 786-8630

---

Northern Hospital of Surry County Post-Sec.
PO Box 1101 27030 336-719-7124

**Mount Gilead, Montgomery, Pop. 1,163**
Montgomery County SD
Supt. — See Troy
West MS 500/6-8
129 NC Highway 109 S 27306 910-572-9378
Ellen Jones, prin. Fax 572-2114
West Montgomery HS 600/9-12
147 Warrior Rd 27306 910-439-6191
Benjamin Brown, prin. Fax 439-4600

**Mount Holly, Gaston, Pop. 13,424**
Gaston County SD
Supt. — See Gastonia
East Gaston HS 1,500/9-12
1744 Lane Rd 28120 704-827-7251
Cristi Bostic, prin. Fax 827-5974
Mount Holly MS 800/6-8
124 S Hawthorne St 28120 704-827-4811
Jennifer Reep, prin. Fax 822-1049

**Mount Olive, Wayne, Pop. 4,528**
Duplin County SD
Supt. — See Kenansville
North Duplin JSHS 500/7-12
1388 W NC 403 Hwy 28365 919-658-3051
Anthony Jones, prin. Fax 658-9971

Wayne County SD
Supt. — See Goldsboro
Mount Olive MS 500/5-8
309 Wooten St 28365 919-658-7320
Tammy Keel, prin. Fax 658-7325

---

Mt. Olive College Post-Sec.
634 Henderson St 28365 919-658-2502

**Mount Pleasant, Cabarrus, Pop. 1,645**
Cabarrus County SD
Supt. — See Concord
Mount Pleasant HS 900/9-12
700 Walker Rd 28124 704-436-9321
Jon Lachance, prin. Fax 436-3179
Mount Pleasant MS 700/6-9
8325 Highway 49 N 28124 704-436-9302
Timothy Farra, prin. Fax 436-6112

**Mount Ulla, Rowan**
Rowan-Salisbury County SD
Supt. — See Salisbury
West Rowan HS 1,100/9-12
8050 NC Highway 801 28125 704-278-9233
Dr. Jamie Durant, prin. Fax 278-9733

**Moyock, Currituck, Pop. 3,696**
Currituck County SD
Supt. — See Currituck

Moyock MS 600/6-8
216 Survey Rd 27958 252-435-2566
Phil Walls, prin. Fax 435-2576

**Murfreesboro, Hertford, Pop. 2,786**
Hertford County SD
Supt. — See Winton
Hertford County MS 500/7-8
1850 NC Highway 11 27855 252-398-4091
Jamie Gillepsie, prin. Fax 398-5570

---

Chowan University Post-Sec.
1 University Pl 27855 252-398-6500

**Murphy, Cherokee, Pop. 1,590**
Cherokee County SD 3,500/PK-12
911 Andrews Rd 28906 828-837-2722
Dr. Jeana Hardin, supt. Fax 837-5799
www.cherokee.k12.nc.us
Hiwassee Dam HS 200/9-12
267 Blue Eagle Cir 28906 828-644-5916
Tom Graham, prin. Fax 644-9463
Mountain Youth S 50/Alt
4533 Martins Creek Rd 28906 828-837-6775
Arnold Mathews, prin. Fax 837-7979
Murphy HS 500/9-12
234 High School Cir 28906 828-837-2426
Boyd Shields, prin. Fax 837-2555
Murphy MS 300/6-8
65 Middle School Dr 28906 828-837-0160
Barry McClure, prin. Fax 837-5814
Tri-County Early College HS 100/9-12
4600 E US Highway 64 Alt 28906 828-835-4298
Alissa Cheek, prin. Fax 835-4319
Other Schools – See Andrews

---

Murphy Adventist Christian S 50/PK-12
1584 Old Ranger Rd 28906 828-837-5857
Tri-County Community College Post-Sec.
21 Campus Cir 28906 828-837-6810

**Nags Head, Dare, Pop. 2,716**
Dare County SD 5,000/PK-12
PO Box 1508 27959 252-480-8888
Dr. Sue Burgess, supt. Fax 480-8889
www.dare.k12.nc.us
Other Schools – See Buxton, Kill Devil Hills, Manteo

**Nakina, Columbus**
Columbus County SD
Supt. — See Whiteville
Nakina MS 200/6-8
9822 Seven Creeks Hwy 28455 910-642-8301
Wendell Duncan, prin. Fax 642-3287

**Nashville, Nash, Pop. 5,285**
Nash-Rocky Mount SD 16,700/PK-12
930 Eastern Ave 27856 252-459-5220
Dr. Anthony Jackson, supt. Fax 459-6403
www.nrms.k12.nc.us
Nash Central MS 600/6-8
1638 S 1st St 27856 252-937-9065
Marquis Spell, prin. Fax 459-5297
Other Schools – See Bailey, Battleboro, Rocky Mount, Spring Hope

**New Bern, Craven, Pop. 28,922**
Craven County SD 14,900/PK-12
3600 Trent Rd 28562 252-514-6300
Dr. Lane Mills, supt. Fax 514-6351
www.craven.k12.nc.us
Craven Early College HS 200/9-12
800 College Ct 28562 252-637-5706
Todd Bradley, prin. Fax 637-4459
Fields MS 600/6-8
2000 Dr M L King Jr Blvd 28560 252-514-6438
Thomasine Hassell, prin. Fax 514-6443
MacDonald MS 900/6-8
3127 Elizabeth Ave 28562 252-514-6450
Nancy Gaskill, prin. Fax 514-6456
New Bern HS 1,800/9-12
4200 Academic Dr 28562 252-514-6400
Jerry Simmons, prin. Fax 514-6412
West Craven MS 800/6-8
515 NW Craven Middle School 28562 252-514-6488
Francis Altman, prin. Fax 514-6491
Other Schools – See Havelock, Vanceboro

---

Calvary Baptist Church S 200/PK-12
PO Box 1089 28563 252-633-5410
Robert Tucker, prin. Fax 633-4340
Craven Community College Post-Sec.
800 College Ct 28562 252-638-7200
Epiphany S of Global Studies 300/K-12
2201 Henderson Ave 28560 252-638-0122
Dr. Dwight Carlblom, hdmstr. Fax 288-5723

**Newland, Avery, Pop. 690**
Avery County SD 2,300/PK-12
PO Box 1360 28657 828-733-6006
David Burleson, supt. Fax 733-8943
www.averyschools.net
Avery County HS STEM Academy 200/9-12
401 High School Rd 28657 828-733-0151
Dr. Todd Griffin, prin. Fax 733-1742
Avery County HS Viking Academy 200/9-12
401 High School Rd 28657 828-733-0151
Dr. Monet Samuelson, prin. Fax 733-1742
Avery MS 300/6-8
PO Box 729 28657 828-733-0145
Ricky Ward, prin. Fax 733-3506
Blue Ridge Academy 50/Alt
102 Old Montezuma Rd 28657 828-733-0145
Ricky Ward, prin. Fax 733-3506
Other Schools – See Elk Park

**New London, Stanly, Pop. 599**
Stanly County SD
Supt. — See Albemarle

North Stanly HS 600/9-12
40206 US Highway 52 N 28127 704-961-4600
Joy Hathcock, prin. Fax 961-4699
North Stanly MS 50/6-8
36605 Old Salisbury Rd 28127 704-961-3700
Anne Watson, prin. Fax 961-3799

**Newport, Carteret, Pop. 4,038**
Carteret County SD
Supt. — See Beaufort
Broad Creek MS 600/6-8
2382 Highway 24 28570 252-247-3135
Sarah Weinhold, prin. Fax 247-5114
Croatan HS 900/9-12
3355 Highway 24 28570 252-393-7022
Joseph Poletti, prin. Fax 393-1223
Newport MS 500/6-8
500 E Chatham St 28570 252-223-3482
Chris Yeomans, prin. Fax 223-4914

---

Gramercy Christian S 200/K-12
8170 Highway 70 28570 252-223-5199
Kirk Nielsen, hdmstr. Fax 223-2359

**Newton, Catawba, Pop. 12,714**
Catawba County SD 17,300/PK-12
PO Box 1010 28658 828-464-8333
Dr. Dan Brigman, supt. Fax 464-0925
www.catawbaschools.net/
Foard HS 1,100/9-12
3407 Plateau Rd 28658 704-462-1496
Chris Gibbs, prin. Fax 462-1988
Jacobs Fork MS 600/7-8
3431 Plateau Rd 28658 704-462-1827
Kim Jordan, prin. Fax 462-1600
Other Schools – See Catawba, Claremont, Hickory, Maiden

Newton-Conover CSD 2,900/K-12
605 N Ashe Ave 28658 828-464-3191
Dr. David Stegall, supt. Fax 466-0063
www.nccs.k12.nc.us
Discovery HS 9-12
301 W 18th St 28658 828-464-2631
John Robinson, prin. Fax 464-5891
Newton-Conover HS 700/9-12
338 W 15th St 28658 828-465-0920
Chris Penley, prin. Fax 464-1412
Other Schools – See Conover

**Newton Grove, Sampson, Pop. 561**
Sampson County SD
Supt. — See Clinton
Hobbton HS 500/9-12
12201 Hobbton Hwy 28366 910-594-0242
Jennifer Daughtry, prin. Fax 594-1115
Hobbton MS 500/6-8
12081 Hobbton Hwy 28366 910-594-1420
Jeff Bradshaw, prin. Fax 594-0049
Midway HS 700/9-12
15274 Spiveys Corner Hwy 28366 910-567-6664
Monty Strickland, prin. Fax 567-5989

**North Wilkesboro, Wilkes, Pop. 4,150**
Wilkes County SD 10,500/PK-12
613 Cherry St 28659 336-667-1121
Dr. Marty Hemric, supt. Fax 667-5971
www.wilkescountyschools.org
North Wilkes MS 600/6-8
2776 Yellow Banks Rd 28659 336-696-2724
David Johnson, prin. Fax 696-4183
Other Schools – See Hays, Millers Creek, Moravian Falls, Ronda, Wilkesboro

---

Wilkes Regional Medical Center Post-Sec.
PO Box 609 28659 336-651-8433

**Norwood, Stanly, Pop. 2,351**
Stanly County SD
Supt. — See Albemarle
South Stanly HS 500/9-12
40488 S Stanly School Rd 28128 704-961-4100
Tanya Crisco, prin. Fax 961-4199
South Stanly MS 400/6-8
12492 Cottonville Rd 28128 704-961-5700
Damon Rhodes, prin. Fax 961-5799

**Oakboro, Stanly, Pop. 1,840**
Stanly County SD
Supt. — See Albemarle
West Stanly HS 900/9-12
306 E Red Cross Rd 28129 704-961-5200
Kimberly Page, prin. Fax 961-5299

**Oak Ridge, Guilford, Pop. 6,114**

---

Oak Ridge Military Academy 100/7-12
PO Box 498 27310 336-643-4131
Dr. Dan Nobles, pres. Fax 643-1797

**Ocracoke, Hyde, Pop. 942**
Hyde County SD
Supt. — See Swanquarter
Ocracoke S 200/PK-12
PO Box 189 27960 252-928-3251
Walt Padgett, prin. Fax 928-5380

**Olin, Iredell**
Iredell-Statesville SD
Supt. — See Statesville
North Iredell HS 1,200/9-12
156 Raider Rd 28660 704-876-4191
Teresa Hays, prin. Fax 876-3241
North Iredell MS 700/6-8
2467 Jennings Rd 28660 704-876-4802
Robert Sipes, prin. Fax 876-6190

**Orrum, Robeson, Pop. 91**
Robeson County SD
Supt. — See Lumberton

Orrum MS 400/5-8
PO Box 129 28369 910-628-6285
Cynthia Lewis, prin. Fax 628-8408

**Oxford, Granville, Pop. 8,335**
Granville County SD 8,200/PK-12
PO Box 927 27565 919-693-4613
Dr. Dorwin Howard, supt. Fax 693-7391
www.gcs.k12.nc.us/
Center for Innovative Learning Alt
3144 Webb School Rd 27565 919-690-2300
Helen Lindsey, prin. Fax 690-2301
Granville Magnet S 6-12
204 Taylor St 27565 919-690-2317
Chris Ham, prin. Fax 690-2318
Northern Granville MS 500/6-8
3144 Webb School Rd 27565 919-693-1483
Ashley Lewis, prin. Fax 693-1716
Potter MS 400/6-8
200 Taylor St 27565 919-693-3914
Sherrie Burns, prin. Fax 693-2896
Webb HS 700/9-12
3200 Webb School Rd 27565 919-693-2521
Reginald Brooks, prin. Fax 693-2589
Webb HS of Health & Life Sciences 300/9-12
3200 Webb School Rd 27565 919-693-6411
Angela Salisbury, prin. Fax 693-6079
Other Schools – See Butner, Creedmoor, Stem

**Pantego, Beaufort, Pop. 178**

---

Terra Ceia Christian S 100/K-12
4428 Christian School Rd 27860 252-943-2485
Vern Parsons, prin. Fax 944-0458

**Pembroke, Robeson, Pop. 2,870**
Robeson County SD
Supt. — See Lumberton
Pembroke MS 800/6-8
PO Box 1148 28372 910-522-5013
Darlene Cummings, prin. Fax 522-1562
Swett HS 1,700/9-12
PO Box 1210 28372 910-521-3253
Clyde Leviner, prin. Fax 521-2956

---

University of North Carolina Post-Sec.
PO Box 1510 28372 910-521-6000

**Pfafftown, Forsyth**
Winston-Salem/Forsyth SD
Supt. — See Winston Salem
Reagan HS 1,700/9-12
3750 Transou Rd 27040 336-703-6776
Frank Martin, prin. Fax 922-1752

**Pikeville, Wayne, Pop. 673**
Wayne County SD
Supt. — See Goldsboro
Aycock HS 1,100/9-12
PO Box 159 27863 919-242-3400
Dr. Earl Moore, prin. Fax 242-6994

**Pilot Mountain, Surry, Pop. 1,458**
Surry County SD
Supt. — See Dobson
East Surry HS 600/9-12
801 W Main St 27041 336-368-2251
Lorrie Sawyers, prin. Fax 368-3035
Pilot Mountain MS 500/6-8
543 Old Westfield Rd 27041 336-368-2641
Tracey Lewis, prin. Fax 368-3935

**Pinehurst, Moore, Pop. 12,981**

---

Sandhills Community College Post-Sec.
3395 Airport Rd 28374 910-692-6185

**Pinetops, Edgecombe, Pop. 1,369**
Edgecombe County SD
Supt. — See Tarboro
South Edgecombe MS 400/6-8
230 Pinetops Crisp Rd 27864 252-827-5083
Kevin Cutler, prin. Fax 827-2811
SouthWest Edgecombe HS 900/9-12
5912 NC 43 N 27864 252-827-5016
Craig Harris, prin. Fax 827-2815

**Pinetown, Beaufort, Pop. 155**
Beaufort County SD
Supt. — See Washington
Northside HS 400/9-12
7868 Free Union Church Rd 27865 252-943-6341
Charles Clark, prin. Fax 943-6344

**Pittsboro, Chatham, Pop. 3,666**
Chatham County SD 8,100/PK-12
PO Box 128 27312 919-542-3626
Dr. Derrick D. Jordan, supt. Fax 542-1380
www.chatham.k12.nc.us
Horton MS 400/5-8
PO Box 639 27312 919-542-2303
Mattie Smith, prin. Fax 542-7099
Northwood HS 1,100/9-12
310 Northwood School Rd 27312 919-542-4181
Dr. Justin Bartholomew, prin. Fax 542-4934
Other Schools – See Bear Creek, Chapel Hill, Siler City

**Plymouth, Washington, Pop. 3,841**
Washington County SD 1,700/PK-12
802 Washington St 27962 252-793-5171
Dr. Delilah Jackson, supt. Fax 793-5062
www.wcsnc.org
Plymouth HS 500/9-12
800 E Main St 27962 252-793-3031
Ivry Cheeks, prin. Fax 793-3986
Other Schools – See Creswell, Roper

**Polkton, Anson, Pop. 3,338**
Anson County SD
Supt. — See Wadesboro

Anson County Early College HS 100/9-12
680 Highway 74 W 28135 704-272-5395
Carri Decker, prin. Fax 272-6155

---

South Piedmont Community College Post-Sec.
PO Box 126 28135 704-272-5300

**Princeton, Johnston, Pop. 1,179**
Johnston County SD
Supt. — See Smithfield
Princeton MSHS 900/6-12
PO Box 38 27569 919-936-5011
W. Kirk Denning, prin. Fax 936-2962

**Raeford, Hoke, Pop. 4,467**
Hoke County SD 8,900/PK-12
PO Box 370 28376 910-875-4106
Dr. Freddie Williamson, supt. Fax 875-3362
www.hcs.k12.nc.us
East Hoke MS 900/6-8
4702 Fayetteville Rd 28376 910-875-5048
Michelle Creammer, prin. Fax 875-9307
Hoke County HS 1,800/9-12
505 S Bethel Rd 28376 910-875-2156
Roger Edwards, prin. Fax 904-1644
SandHoke Early College HS 200/9-12
1110 E Central Ave 28376 910-878-5806
Colleen Pegram, prin. Fax 878-5807
Turlington JSHS 50/Alt
116 W Prospect Ave 28376 910-875-2583
Krista Friedrich, prin. Fax 875-3012
West Hoke MS 900/6-8
200 NC Highway 211 28376 910-875-3411
Mary McLeod, prin. Fax 875-0332
Other Schools – See Lumber Bridge

**Raleigh, Wake, Pop. 395,376**
Wake County SD
Supt. — See Cary
Athens Drive HS 2,000/9-12
1420 Athens Dr 27606 919-233-4050
Dr. James Hedrick, prin. Fax 233-4054
Broughton HS 2,200/9-12
723 Saint Marys St 27605 919-856-7810
Stephen Mares, prin. Fax 856-7822
Carnage MS 1,200/6-8
1425 Carnage Dr 27610 919-856-7600
Pamela Johnson, prin. Fax 856-7619
Carroll MS 700/6-8
4520 Six Forks Rd 27609 919-881-1370
Elizabeth MacWilliams, prin. Fax 881-5016
Centennial MS 600/6-8
1900 Main Campus Dr 27606 919-233-4217
Katie McMillan, prin. Fax 233-4268
Daniels MS 1,200/6-8
2816 Oberlin Rd 27608 919-881-4860
Dr. Elizabeth Battle, prin. Fax 881-1418
Dillard Drive MS 1,200/6-8
5200 Dillard Dr 27606 919-233-4228
Shejuanna Rodgers, prin. Fax 854-1615
Durant Road MS 1,500/6-8
10401 Durant Rd 27614 919-870-4098
Nancy Allen, prin. Fax 518-0021
East Millbrook MS 1,200/6-8
3801 Spring Forest Rd 27616 919-850-8755
Andrew Livengood, prin. Fax 850-8770
East Wake MS 1,000/6-8
2700 Old Milburnie Rd 27604 919-266-8500
Rebecca Beaulieu, prin. Fax 266-8506
Enloe HS 2,600/9-12
128 Clarendon Cres 27610 919-856-7918
Scott Lyons, prin. Fax 856-7917
Leesville Road HS 2,200/9-12
8410 Pride Way 27613 919-870-4250
Dr. Anthony Muttillo, prin. Fax 870-4287
Leesville Road MS 1,200/6-8
8406 Pride Way 27613 919-870-4141
Cynthia Kremer, prin. Fax 870-4166
Ligon MS 1,100/6-8
706 E Lenoir St 27601 919-856-7929
Gretta Dula, prin. Fax 856-3745
Malone College & Career Academy 9-12
2200 S Wilmington St 27603 919-856-8119
Dr. Ashlie Thompson, prin. Fax 856-8158
Martin MS 1,100/6-8
1701 Ridge Rd 27607 919-881-4970
Lacey Peckham, prin. Fax 881-5017
Millbrook HS 2,600/9-12
2201 Spring Forest Rd 27615 919-850-8787
Dana King, prin. Fax 850-8803
Moore Square Museums MS 500/6-8
301 S Person St 27601 919-664-5737
Dr. Jackie Jordan, prin. Fax 856-8194
Mt. Vernon MS 100/Alt
5418 Chapel Hill Rd 27607 919-233-4313
Robert Gupton, prin. Fax 233-4006
Phillips HS 200/Alt
1923 Milburnie Rd 27610 919-856-7710
Daniel Colvin, prin. Fax 856-7763
River Oaks MS 50/Alt
4700 New Bern Ave 27610 919-231-5600
Sharon Floyd, prin. Fax 231-5607
Sanderson HS 2,000/9-12
5500 Dixon Dr 27609 919-881-4800
Gregory Decker, prin. Fax 881-5006
Southeast Raleigh HS 1,700/9-12
2600 Rock Quarry Rd 27610 919-856-2800
Candis Jones, prin. Fax 856-2827
Wake Early College of Health & Sciences 200/9-12
2901 Holston Ln 27610 919-212-5800
Lisa Cummings, prin. Fax 212-5810
Wakefield HS 2,500/9-12
2200 Wakefield Pines Dr 27614 919-562-3600
Malik Bazzell, prin. Fax 562-3623
Wakefield MS 1,200/6-8
2300 Wakefield Pines Dr 27614 919-562-3500
James Sposato, prin. Fax 562-3527
Wake STEM Early College HS 9-12
715 Barbour Dr 27603 919-515-2255
David Schwenker, prin. Fax 515-2157
Wake Young Mens Leadership Academy 6-12
567 E Hargett St 27601 919-664-5644
Ian Soloman, prin. Fax 664-5657
Wake Young Womens Leadership Academy 6-12
303 Ashe Ave 27606 919-508-9088
Carla Jernigan-Baker, prin. Fax 508-9091
West Millbrook MS 1,000/6-8
8115 Strickland Rd 27615 919-870-4050
Kelly Aman, prin. Fax 870-4064

---

Cardinal Gibbons HS 1,200/9-12
1401 Edwards Mill Rd 27607 919-834-1625
Jason Curtis, prin. Fax 834-9771
ECPI University Post-Sec.
4101 Doie Cope Rd 27613 919-571-0057
Friendship Christian S 300/PK-12
5510 Falls of Neuse Rd 27609 919-872-2133
Ric Nelson, head sch Fax 872-7451
GRACE Christian HS 200/7-12
1101 Buck Jones Rd 27606 919-747-2020
Mandy Gill, prin. Fax 747-2021
Living Arts College @ Sch of Comm Arts Post-Sec.
3000 Wakefield Crossing Dr 27614 919-488-8500
Meredith College Post-Sec.
3800 Hillsborough St 27607 919-760-8600
Miller-Motte College Post-Sec.
3901 Capital Blvd Ste 151 27604 919-723-2820
Neuse Christian Academy 200/K-12
7600 Falls of Neuse Rd 27615 919-844-6496
Penny Hill, admin. Fax 861-6819
North Carolina State University Post-Sec.
PO Box 7001 27695 919-515-2011
North Raleigh Christian Academy 1,500/PK-12
7300 Perry Creek Rd 27616 919-573-7900
Dr. S.L. Sherrill, supt. Fax 573-7901
Raleigh Christian Academy 300/PK-12
2110 Trawick Rd 27604 919-872-2215
Ravenscroft S 1,200/PK-12
7409 Falls of Neuse Rd 27615 919-847-0900
Doreen Kelly, hdmstr. Fax 847-7952
St. Augustine's University Post-Sec.
1315 Oakwood Ave 27610 919-516-4000
St. David's S 600/PK-12
3400 White Oak Rd 27609 919-782-3331
Kevin Lockerbie, hdmstr. Fax 571-3330
St. Mary's S 200/9-12
900 Hillsborough St 27603 919-424-4000
Dr. Monica Gillespie, head sch Fax 424-4122
Shaw University Post-Sec.
118 E South St 27601 919-546-8200
Strayer University Post-Sec.
8701 Wadford Dr 27616 919-878-9900
Trinity Academy of Raleigh 400/PK-12
10224 Baileywick Rd 27613 919-786-0114
Matthew Breazeale, prin. Fax 786-0621
Upper Room Christian Academy 100/PK-12
3330 Idlewood Village Dr 27610 919-829-6250
John Amanchukwu, dir. Fax 829-6193
Wake Christian Academy 900/K-12
5500 Wake Academy Dr 27603 919-772-6264
Mike Woods M.A., head sch Fax 779-0948
Wake Technical Community College Post-Sec.
9101 Fayetteville Rd 27603 919-866-5000
William Peace University Post-Sec.
15 E Peace St 27604 919-508-2000
Word of God Christian Academy 200/K-12
3000 Rock Quarry Rd 27610 919-834-8200
A Pittman, prin. Fax 899-3640

**Ramseur, Randolph, Pop. 1,657**
Randolph County SD
Supt. — See Asheboro
Eastern Randolph HS 800/9-12
390 Eastern Randolph Rd 27316 336-824-2351
Edwina Ashworth, prin. Fax 824-6164
Southeastern Randolph MS 800/6-8
5302 Foushee Rd 27316 336-824-6700
Michelle Ford, prin. Fax 824-6705

---

Faith Christian S 300/PK-12
5449 Brookhaven Rd 27316 336-824-4156

**Randleman, Randolph, Pop. 4,054**
Randolph County SD
Supt. — See Asheboro
Randleman HS 900/9-12
4396 Tigers Den Rd 27317 336-498-2682
Dennis Hamilton, prin. Fax 498-2609
Randleman MS 800/5-8
800 High Point St 27317 336-498-2606
Tracy Dawes, prin. Fax 498-8015

**Red Springs, Robeson, Pop. 3,362**
Robeson County SD
Supt. — See Lumberton
Red Springs HS 800/9-12
509 N Vance St 28377 910-843-4211
Larry Brooks, prin. Fax 843-2825
Red Springs MS 500/5-8
302 W 2nd Ave 28377 910-843-3883
Karen Brooks-Floyd, prin. Fax 843-3765

---

MacDonald Academy 100/PK-12
200 N College St 28377 910-843-4995

**Reidsville, Rockingham, Pop. 14,244**
Rockingham County SD
Supt. — See Eden
Reidsville HS 900/9-12
1901 S Park Dr 27320 336-349-6361
Mary Ann Mitchell, prin. Fax 349-3205
Reidsville MS 600/6-8
1903 S Park Dr 27320 336-342-4726
Erselle Young, prin. Fax 342-9434
Rockingham County HS 1,100/9-12
180 High School Rd 27320 336-634-3220
Richie Weaver, prin. Fax 342-7794
Rockingham County MS 900/6-8
182 High School Rd 27320 336-616-0073
Moriah Dollarhite, prin. Fax 616-0870
S.C.O.R.E Center 50/Alt
401 Moss St 27320 336-634-3209
Curtis Gore, prin. Fax 634-3260

---

Community Baptist S 200/PK-12
509 Triangle Rd 27320 336-342-5991
Gene Carwile, admin. Fax 342-7180

**Richlands, Onslow, Pop. 1,464**
Onslow County SD
Supt. — See Jacksonville
Richlands HS 1,100/9-12
PO Box 218 28574 910-324-4191
Darin Cloninger, prin. Fax 324-6688
Trexler MS 900/6-8
PO Box 188 28574 910-324-4414
Lynn Jackson, prin. Fax 324-3963

**Roanoke Rapids, Halifax, Pop. 15,565**
Roanoke Rapids CSD 3,100/PK-12
536 Hamilton St 27870 252-519-7100
Dr. John Parker, supt. Fax 519-7195
www.rrgsd.org
Chaloner MS 700/6-8
2100 Virginia Ave 27870 252-519-7600
Jeff White, prin. Fax 519-7695
Roanoke Rapids HS 800/9-12
800 Hamilton St 27870 252-519-7200
Tammie Williams, prin. Fax 519-7295

---

Halifax Academy 400/PK-12
1400 Three Bridges Rd 27870 252-537-8527
Robert Hurley, hdmstr. Fax 308-0555

**Robbins, Moore, Pop. 1,085**
Moore County SD
Supt. — See Carthage
Elise MS 200/6-8
180 W Elm St 27325 910-948-2421
Seth Powers, prin. Fax 948-4112
North Moore HS 600/9-12
PO Box 9 27325 910-464-3105
Jenny Purvis, prin. Fax 464-6016

**Robbinsville, Graham, Pop. 615**
Graham County SD 1,200/PK-12
52 Moose Branch Rd 28771 828-479-3413
Angela Knight, supt. Fax 479-9844
www.graham.k12.nc.us
Robbinsville HS 400/9-12
301 Sweetwater Rd 28771 828-479-9830
David Matheson, prin. Fax 479-9859
Robbinsville MS 200/7-8
301 Sweetwater Rd Ste B 28771 828-479-9840
Kevin White, prin. Fax 479-9847

**Robersonville, Martin, Pop. 1,478**
Martin County SD
Supt. — See Williamston
South Creek HS 400/9-12
21077 NC Highway 903 27871 252-795-4081
Phillip Hagen, prin. Fax 795-4187
South Creek MS 400/6-8
21230 NC Highway 903 27871 252-795-3910
Jan Wagner, prin. Fax 795-3890

**Rockingham, Richmond, Pop. 9,384**
Richmond County SD
Supt. — See Hamlet
Ashley Chapel Educational Center 100/Alt
377 Mizpah Rd 28379 910-997-9797
Susan Brigman, prin. Fax 997-8170
Richmond SHS 1,400/10-12
PO Box 1748 28380 910-997-9812
Keith McKenzie, prin. Fax 997-9816
Rockingham MS 700/6-8
415 Wall St 28379 910-997-9827
Dr. Wendy Jordan, prin. Fax 997-9859
Rohanen MS 300/6-8
252 School St 28379 910-997-9839
Hal Shuler, prin. Fax 997-8172

---

Temple Christian S 100/K-12
165 Airport Rd 28379 910-997-3179

**Rockwell, Rowan, Pop. 2,077**

---

Rockwell Christian S 100/K-12
PO Box 609 28138 704-279-8854

**Rocky Mount, Edgecombe, Pop. 56,654**
Edgecombe County SD
Supt. — See Tarboro
West Edgecombe MS 400/6-8
6301 Nobles Mill Pond Rd 27801 252-446-2030
Fax 446-1592

Nash-Rocky Mount SD
Supt. — See Nashville
Edwards MS 700/6-8
720 Edwards St 27803 252-937-9025
Chris Sivills, prin. Fax 446-5527
Nash Central HS 1,200/9-12
4279 Nash Central High Rd 27804 252-451-2860
Gail Powers, prin. Fax 451-1279
Nash-Rocky Mount Early College HS 200/9-12
530 N Old Carriage Rd 27804 252-451-2890
Chris Catalano, prin. Fax 443-0068
Northern Nash HS 1,200/9-12
4230 Green Hills Rd 27804 252-937-9040
Chad Thompson, prin. Fax 443-5448
Parker MS 400/6-8
1500 E Virginia St 27801 252-937-9060
Gary Major, prin. Fax 446-5756
Rocky Mount HS 1,200/9-12
1400 Bethlehem Rd 27803 252-937-9050
Leon Farrow, prin. Fax 443-6686
Rocky Mount MS 6-8
841 Nash St 27804 252-462-2010
Ann Mitchell, prin. Fax 459-5220

Tar River Academy | Alt
224 S Pearl St 27804 | 252-451-2875
John Milliner-Williams, prin. | Fax 985-4336

---

Faith Christian S | 400/PK-12
1333 Faith Christian Dr 27803 | 252-443-3700
Dr. Edward Bunn, head sch | Fax 443-2456
Nash Community College | Post-Sec.
522 N Old Carriage Rd 27804 | 252-443-4011
North Carolina Wesleyan College | Post-Sec.
3400 N Wesleyan Blvd 27804 | 252-985-5100
Rocky Mount Academy | 400/PK-12
1313 Avondale Ave 27803 | 252-443-4126
Beth Covolo, head sch | Fax 937-7922

**Rocky Point, Pender, Pop. 1,566**
Pender County SD
Supt. — See Burgaw
Cape Fear MS | 500/6-8
1886 NC Highway 133 28457 | 910-602-3334
Greg Goble, prin. | Fax 602-3036
Trask HS | 700/9-12
14328 NC Highway 210 28457 | 910-602-6810
Dr. Tosha Diggs, prin. | Fax 602-6662

**Rolesville, Wake, Pop. 3,697**
Wake County SD
Supt. — See Cary
Rolesville HS, 1099 E Young St 27571 | 9-12
Ericka Lucas, prin. | 919-554-6303
Rolesville MS | 6-8
4700 Burlington Mills Rd 27571 | 919-570-2260
Dhedra Lassiter, prin. | Fax 570-2270

---

Thales Academy of Rolesville JSHS | 100/6-12
1201 Granite Falls Blvd 27571 | 919-435-2715
Melissa Edwards, admin. | Fax 453-0484

**Ronda, Wilkes, Pop. 410**
Wilkes County SD
Supt. — See North Wilkesboro
East Wilkes HS | 600/9-12
13315 Elkin Highway 268 28670 | 336-651-7200
Dr. Jodi Weatherman, prin. | Fax 835-9298
East Wilkes MS | 400/6-8
2202 Macedonia Church Rd 28670 | 336-651-4300
Ramona Hemric, prin. | Fax 957-8734

**Roper, Washington, Pop. 608**
Washington County SD
Supt. — See Plymouth
Washington County Union MS | 300/6-8
37 E Mill Pond Rd 27970 | 252-793-2835
Dianne Stokes, prin. | Fax 793-4411

**Roseboro, Sampson, Pop. 1,167**
Sampson County SD
Supt. — See Clinton
Roseboro-Salemburg MS | 400/6-8
PO Box 976 28382 | 910-525-4764
Sheila Peterson, prin. | Fax 525-3471

---

Mintz Christian Academy | 100/K-12
2741 Mintz Rd 28382 | 910-564-6221
Joy McDowell, prin. | Fax 564-6510

**Rose Hill, Duplin, Pop. 1,619**
Duplin County SD
Supt. — See Kenansville
Charity MS | 500/6-8
PO Box 70 28458 | 910-289-3323
Janice Wynn, prin. | Fax 289-2064

Sampson County SD
Supt. — See Clinton
Union HS | 500/9-12
1189 Kader Merritt Rd 28458 | 910-532-6300
Julie Hunter, prin. | Fax 532-6350

**Rosman, Transylvania, Pop. 567**
Transylvania County SD
Supt. — See Brevard
Rosman HS | 400/9-12
749 Pickens Hwy 28772 | 828-862-4284
Jason Ormsby, prin. | Fax 885-5572
Rosman MS | 300/6-8
2770 Old Rosman Hwy 28772 | 828-862-4286
Greg Carter, prin. | Fax 885-5573

**Rowland, Robeson, Pop. 1,020**
Robeson County SD
Supt. — See Lumberton
Rowland MS | 200/6-8
408 W Chapel St 28383 | 910-422-3983
Benita Tillman, prin. | Fax 422-8369
South Robeson HS | 500/9-12
3268 S Robeson Rd 28383 | 910-422-3987
Dr. Christopher Clark, prin. | Fax 422-3221

**Roxboro, Person, Pop. 8,217**
Person County SD | 4,800/PK-12
304 S Morgan St Ste 25 27573 | 336-599-2191
Danny Holloman, supt. | Fax 599-2194
www.person.k12.nc.us
Northern MS | 500/6-8
1935 Carver Dr, | 336-599-6344
Chris Tomasic, prin. | Fax 598-9207
Person County Learning Academy | Alt
361 Virgilina Rd 27573 | 336-322-1021
Joan Kister, dir. | Fax 322-1029
Person HS | 1,400/9-12
1010 Ridge Rd 27573 | 336-599-8321
Arthur Fleming, prin. | Fax 599-6583
Southern MS | 600/6-8
209 Southern Middle School 27573 | 336-599-6995
Dr. Jonte Hill, prin. | Fax 503-0587

---

Piedmont Community College | Post-Sec.
PO Box 1197 27573 | 336-599-1181

**Rutherfordton, Rutherford, Pop. 4,144**
Rutherford County SD
Supt. — See Forest City
R-S Central HS | 900/9-12
641 US 221 Hwy N 28139 | 828-287-3304
Phil Rogers, prin. | Fax 286-2024
R-S MS | 700/6-8
545 Charlotte Rd 28139 | 828-286-4461
Dr. Keith Silver, prin. | Fax 286-4882

**Saint Pauls, Robeson, Pop. 1,997**
Robeson County SD
Supt. — See Lumberton
Saint Pauls HS | 900/9-12
648 N Old Stage Rd 28384 | 910-865-4177
Hoyt McCormick, prin. | Fax 865-3736
Saint Pauls MS | 500/6-8
526 W Shaw St 28384 | 910-865-4070
Isabel Jones, prin. | Fax 865-1599

**Salemburg, Sampson, Pop. 427**
Sampson County SD
Supt. — See Clinton
Lakewood HS | 500/9-12
245 Lakewood School Rd 28385 | 910-525-5171
Kevin Hunter, prin. | Fax 525-3344

**Salisbury, Rowan, Pop. 33,082**
Rowan-Salisbury County SD | 20,000/PK-12
PO Box 2349 28145 | 704-636-7500
Lynn Moody, supt. | Fax 630-6129
www.rss.k12.nc.us
East Rowan HS | 1,100/9-12
175 Saint Luke Church Rd 28146 | 704-279-5232
Julie Erdie, prin. | Fax 279-4549
Erwin MS | 1,000/6-8
170 Saint Luke Church Rd 28146 | 704-279-7265
Rick Vanhoy, prin. | Fax 279-7954
Henderson Independent HS | 50/Alt
1215 N Main St 28144 | 704-639-3103
Lennetta Bartley, prin. | Fax 639-3118
Knox MS | 600/6-8
1625 W Park Rd 28144 | 704-633-2922
Latoya D. & Michael W., prin. | Fax 638-3538
Rowan County Early College S | 200/9-12
PO Box 1595 28145 | 704-216-3873
David Miller, prin. | Fax 216-2942
Salisbury HS | 900/9-12
500 Lincolnton Rd 28144 | 704-636-1221
Luke Brown, prin. | Fax 639-3029
Southeast MS | 800/6-8
1570 Peeler Rd 28146 | 704-638-5561
Jennifer Lentz, prin. | Fax 638-5719
West Rowan MS | 700/6-8
5925 Statesville Blvd 28147 | 704-633-4775
Derek McCoy, prin. | Fax 633-3157
Other Schools – See China Grove, Landis, Mount Ulla, Spencer

---

Catawba College | Post-Sec.
2300 W Innes St 28144 | 800-228-2922
Hood Theological Seminary | Post-Sec.
1810 Lutheran Synod Dr 28144 | 704-636-7611
Livingstone College | Post-Sec.
701 W Monroe St 28144 | 704-216-6000
North Hills Christian S | 300/PK-12
2970 W Innes St 28144 | 704-636-3005
Maria Lowder, dir. | Fax 636-3597
Rowan-Cabarrus Community College | Post-Sec.
1333 Jake Alexander Blvd S 28146 | 704-216-7222

**Sanford, Lee, Pop. 27,645**
Harnett County SD
Supt. — See Lillington
Highland MS | 300/6-8
345 Highland School Rd 27332
Brian Graham, prin.

Lee County SD | 9,900/PK-12
PO Box 1010 27331 | 919-774-6226
Andy Bryan Ed.D., supt. | Fax 776-0443
www.lee.k12.nc.us
Bragg Street Academy | 100/Alt
504 Bragg St 27330 | 919-775-2686
Jolanda Jordan, prin. | Fax 774-1429
East Lee MS | 700/6-8
1337 Broadway Rd 27332 | 919-776-8441
Shannon Shuey, prin. | Fax 774-7451
Lee County HS | 1,400/9-12
1708 Nash St 27330 | 919-776-7541
Kenna Wilson, prin. | Fax 718-7170
Lee Early College | 300/9-12
1105 Kelly Dr 27330 | 919-718-7259
Robert Biehl, prin. | Fax 718-7519
SanLee MS | 800/6-8
2309 Tramway Rd 27332 | 919-708-7227
Betsy Bridges, prin. | Fax 718-2875
Southern Lee HS | 1,100/9-12
2301 Tramway Rd 27332 | 919-718-2400
Chris Dossenbach, prin. | Fax 718-2410
West Lee MS | 700/6-8
3301 Wicker St 27330 | 919-775-7351
Melvin Marshall, prin. | Fax 776-3694

---

Central Carolina Community College | Post-Sec.
1105 Kelly Dr 27330 | 919-775-5401
Grace Christian S | 300/K-12
PO Box 1408 27331 | 919-774-4415
William Carver, hdmstr. | Fax 718-6777
Lee Christian S | 400/PK-12
3220 Keller Andrews Rd 27330 | 919-708-5115
Dr. Stephen Coble, prin. | Fax 708-6933

**Selma, Johnston, Pop. 5,974**
Johnston County SD
Supt. — See Smithfield
Selma MS | 400/5-8
1533 US Highway 301 N 27576 | 919-965-2555
John Bell, prin. | Fax 202-0116

**Seven Springs, Wayne, Pop. 109**
Wayne County SD
Supt. — See Goldsboro
Spring Creek HS | 1,000/9-12
4340 Indian Springs Rd 28578 | 919-751-7160
Steve Clingan, prin. | Fax 751-7202
Spring Creek MS | 5-8
3579 S NC Highway 111 28578
T. Kevin Smith, prin.

**Shallotte, Brunswick, Pop. 3,616**
Brunswick County SD
Supt. — See Bolivia
Shallotte MS | 600/6-8
225 Village Rd SW 28470 | 910-754-6882
Marie LaBoy, prin. | Fax 754-3108
West Brunswick HS | 1,400/9-12
550 Whiteville Rd NW 28470 | 910-754-4338
Brockton Ahrens, prin. | Fax 754-3110

**Shannon, Robeson, Pop. 263**

---

Native American Bible College | Post-Sec.
PO Box 248 28386 | 910-843-5304

**Shelby, Cleveland, Pop. 19,999**
Cleveland County SD | 15,700/PK-12
400 W Marion St 28150 | 704-476-8000
Dr. Stephen Fisher, supt. | Fax 476-8300
www.clevelandcountyschools.org
Cleveland Early College HS | 200/9-12
137 S Post Rd 28152 | 704-669-4710
Titus Hopper, prin. | Fax 669-4715
Crest HS | 1,200/9-12
800 Old Boiling Springs Rd 28152 | 704-476-8331
Holly Robinson, prin. | Fax 482-1187
Crest MS | 1,000/6-8
315 Beaver Dam Church Rd 28152 | 704-476-8221
Dr. Amy Jones, prin. | Fax 487-0378
Shelby HS | 900/9-12
230 E Dixon Blvd 28152 | 704-476-8325
David Allen, prin. | Fax 487-2869
Shelby MS | 400/7-8
1480 S DeKalb St 28152 | 704-476-8328
Dr. Dustin Bridges, prin. | Fax 487-2889
Turning Point Academy | 100/Alt
409 W Sumter St 28150 | 704-476-8399
Michelle Twiggs, prin. | Fax 476-8316
Other Schools – See Kings Mountain, Lawndale

---

Cleveland Community College | Post-Sec.
137 S Post Rd 28152 | 704-669-6000

**Siler City, Chatham, Pop. 7,749**
Chatham County SD
Supt. — See Pittsboro
Chatham MS | 400/5-8
2025 S 2nd Avenue Ext 27344 | 919-663-2414
Chad Morgan, prin. | Fax 663-2871
Jordan-Matthews HS | 800/9-12
910 E Cardinal St 27344 | 919-742-2916
Tripp Crayton, prin. | Fax 742-2201
SAGE Academy | 100/Alt
501 M L King Jr Blvd 27344 | 919-663-5899
Bobby Dixon, prin. | Fax 663-3827

**Smithfield, Johnston, Pop. 10,815**
Johnston County SD | 30,600/PK-12
PO Box 1336 27577 | 919-934-6031
Dr. Edward Croom, supt. | Fax 934-2586
www.johnston.k12.nc.us
Johnston County Early College Academy | 100/9-12
PO Box 1336 27577 | 919-464-2314
Brandon Garland, prin. | Fax 464-2315
Johnston County Middle College HS | 100/10-12
PO Box 1336 27577 | 919-464-2303
Barretta Haynes, prin. | Fax 464-2300
Smithfield MS | 700/6-8
1455 Buffalo Rd 27577 | 919-934-4696
Jennifer Moore, prin. | Fax 934-7552
Smithfield-Selma HS | 1,300/9-12
700 E Booker Dairy Rd 27577 | 919-934-5191
Stephen Baker, prin. | Fax 934-3001
South Campus Community S | 50/Alt
PO Box 1336 27577 | 919-934-6481
Ersaleen Creech, prin. | Fax 938-3555
Other Schools – See Benson, Clayton, Four Oaks, Garner, Kenly, Micro, Princeton, Selma, Wendell

---

Johnston Community College | Post-Sec.
PO Box 2350 27577 | 919-934-3051

**Smyrna, Carteret**
Carteret County SD
Supt. — See Beaufort
Down East MS | 200/6-8
174 Marshallberg Rd 28579 | 252-729-2301
Richard Paylor, admin.

**Snow Hill, Greene, Pop. 1,577**
Greene County SD | 2,500/PK-12
301 Kingold Blvd 28580 | 252-747-3425
Dr. Patrick Miller, supt. | Fax 747-5942
www.gcsedu.org/
Greene Central HS | 800/9-12
140 School Dr 28580 | 252-747-3814
Patrick Greene, prin. | Fax 747-5972
Greene County MS | 800/6-8
485 Middle School Rd 28580 | 252-747-8191
Diane Blackman, prin. | Fax 747-2484
Greene Early College HS | 100/9-12
818 Hwy 91 28580 | 252-747-9044
Rodney McNeill, prin. | Fax 747-9046

**Southern Pines, Moore, Pop. 12,175**
Moore County SD
Supt. — See Carthage
Pinecrest HS | 2,100/9-12
250 Voit Gilmore Rd 28387 | 910-692-6554
Dr. Thomas Ferrell, prin. | Fax 692-0606

Calvary Christian S 100/PK-12
400 S Bennett St 28387 910-692-8311
O'Neal S 400/PK-12
PO Box 290 28388 910-692-6920
John Elmore, head sch Fax 692-6930
Sandhills Classical Christian S 100/PK-10
PO Box 2600 28388 910-695-1874
Dr. Alan Marshall, head sch Fax 401-1335

**Southport, Brunswick, Pop. 2,791**
Brunswick County SD
Supt. — See Bolivia
South Brunswick HS 1,100/9-12
280 Cougar Rd 28461 910-845-2204
Dr. Vicky Snyder, prin. Fax 845-8974
South Brunswick MS 800/6-8
100 Cougar Rd 28461 910-845-2771
David Ruth, prin. Fax 845-8972

**Sparta, Alleghany, Pop. 1,751**
Alleghany County SD 1,600/PK-12
85 Peachtree St 28675 336-372-4345
Dr. Kim Mattox, supt. Fax 372-4204
www.alleghany.k12.nc.us
Alleghany HS 400/9-12
404 Trojan Ave 28675 336-372-4554
Christopher Barnes, prin. Fax 372-2680

**Spencer, Rowan, Pop. 3,207**
Rowan-Salisbury County SD
Supt. — See Salisbury
North Rowan HS 700/9-12
300 N Whitehead Ave 28159 704-636-4420
Fateama Fulmore, prin. Fax 639-3033
North Rowan MS 500/6-8
512 Charles St 28159 704-639-3018
Alexis Cowan, prin. Fax 639-3099

**Spindale, Rutherford, Pop. 4,228**
Rutherford County SD
Supt. — See Forest City
Rutherford Early College HS 200/9-12
PO Box 804 28160 828-395-1464
Jeremiah McCluney, prin. Fax 288-0285

Isothermal Community College Post-Sec.
PO Box 804 28160 828-286-3636
Word of Faith Christian S 100/K-12
207 Old Flynn Rd 28160 828-286-3772

**Spring Hope, Nash, Pop. 1,294**
Nash-Rocky Mount SD
Supt. — See Nashville
Southern Nash MS 1,100/6-8
5301 S NC Highway 581 27882 252-937-9020
Carina Bryant, prin. Fax 478-4861

**Spring Lake, Cumberland, Pop. 11,305**
Cumberland County SD
Supt. — See Fayetteville
Spring Lake MS 500/6-8
612 Spring Ave 28390 910-497-1175
Masa Kinsey-Shipp, prin. Fax 497-1598

Harnett County SD
Supt. — See Lillington
Overhills HS 1,700/9-12
2495 Ray Rd 28390 910-436-1436
Cicily McCrimmon, prin. Fax 436-0413
Overhills MS 1,100/6-8
2711 Ray Rd 28390 910-436-0009
Tina Tasker, prin. Fax 436-0948

**Spruce Pine, Mitchell, Pop. 2,151**
Mitchell County SD
Supt. — See Bakersville
Harris MS 300/6-8
121 Harris St 28777 828-766-3340
Brandon Birchfield, prin. Fax 765-1595
Mayland Early College HS 100/9-12
200 Mayland Ln 28777 828-765-7351
Martha Dayton, prin. Fax 765-0728

Altapass Christian S 50/PK-12
3631 Altapass Hwy 28777 828-765-0660
Mayland Community College Post-Sec.
PO Box 547 28777 828-765-7351
Tri County Christian S 50/K-12
207 Pinebridge Ave 28777 828-765-2969
Teresa Young, prin. Fax 765-0569

**Stanley, Gaston, Pop. 3,517**
Gaston County SD
Supt. — See Gastonia
Stanley MS 500/6-8
317 Hovis Rd 28164 704-836-9600
George Conner, prin. Fax 263-0993

**Stantonsburg, Wilson, Pop. 782**
Wilson County SD
Supt. — See Wilson
Speight MS 400/6-8
5514 Old Stantonsburg Rd 27883 252-238-3983
Valerie Budd, prin. Fax 238-2104

**Statesville, Iredell, Pop. 24,072**
Iredell-Statesville SD 21,100/K-12
PO Box 911 28687 704-924-2029
Brady Johnson, supt. Fax 871-2834
www.iss.k12.nc.us
Collaborative College for Technology 200/9-12
500 W Broad St 28677 704-978-5450
Teri Hutchens, prin. Fax 878-3330
East Iredell MS 500/6-8
590 Chestnut Grove Rd 28625 704-872-4666
Dr. Tonya Houpe, prin. Fax 873-6602
Monticello S 100/Alt
435 Monticello Rd 28625 704-872-5297
Mark Grega, prin. Fax 924-8814
Northview IB S 400/6-9
625 N Carolina Ave 28677 704-873-7354
Sheila Jenkins, prin. Fax 873-6149
Pressly S 100/Alt
222 Knox St 28677 704-872-7606
Dr. Stacy Williams, prin. Fax 838-0839
South Iredell HS 1,100/9-12
299 Old Mountain Rd 28677 704-528-4536
Tim Ivey, prin. Fax 528-0882
Statesville HS 1,100/9-12
474 N Center St 28677 704-873-3491
Dr. Beth Bradley, prin. Fax 878-6195
Statesville MS 400/6-8
321 Clegg St 28677 704-872-2135
Ericia Turner, prin. Fax 871-9279
Visual & Performing Arts HS 200/9-12
474 N Center St 28677 704-978-0034
Alicia Eller, prin. Fax 978-0035
West Iredell HS 1,000/9-12
213 Warrior Dr 28625 704-873-2181
Gordon Palmer, prin. Fax 873-0356
West Iredell MS 700/6-8
303 Watermelon Rd 28625 704-873-2887
David Ivey, prin. Fax 881-0582
Other Schools – See Mooresville, Olin, Troutman

Crossroads Christian S of Statesville 50/K-12
1950 Salisbury Hwy 28677 704-871-1515
Anne W. Wooten, admin.
Mitchell Community College Post-Sec.
500 W Broad St 28677 704-878-3200
Southview Christian S 100/K-12
625 Wallace Springs Rd 28677 704-872-9554
Statesville Christian S 200/K-12
1210 Museum Rd 28625 704-873-9511
Mark Earwood, head sch Fax 873-0841

**Stem, Granville, Pop. 446**
Granville County SD
Supt. — See Oxford
Granville Central HS 600/9-12
2043 Sanders Rd 27581 919-528-5530
Brian Mathis, prin. Fax 528-5574

**Sugar Grove, Watauga**

Jung Tao School of Chinese Medicine Post-Sec.
207 Dale Adams Rd 28679 828-297-4181

**Supply, Brunswick**
Brunswick County SD
Supt. — See Bolivia
Cedar Grove MS 500/6-8
750 Grove Trl SW 28462 910-846-3400
Michael Hobbs, prin. Fax 846-3401

Brunswick Community College Post-Sec.
PO Box 30 28462 910-755-7300

**Swannanoa, Buncombe, Pop. 4,465**
Buncombe County SD
Supt. — See Asheville
Community HS 200/Alt
235 Old US 70 Hwy 28778 828-686-7734
Clifford Owens, prin. Fax 686-7834
Owen MS 600/6-8
730 Old US 70 Hwy 28778 828-686-7739
Heidi Von Dohlen, prin. Fax 686-7938

Asheville Christian Academy 500/PK-12
PO Box 1089 28778 828-581-2200
Dr. William George, head sch Fax 581-2218

**Swanquarter, Hyde, Pop. 313**
Hyde County SD 600/PK-12
PO Box 217 27885 252-926-3281
Dr. Randolph Latimore, supt. Fax 926-3083
www.hyde.k12.nc.us/
Hyde County Early College HS 200/6-12
20346 US Highway 264 27885 252-926-0221
M.D. Coleman, prin. Fax 926-0224
Other Schools – See Ocracoke

**Swansboro, Onslow, Pop. 2,580**
Onslow County SD
Supt. — See Jacksonville
Swansboro HS 1,000/9-12
161 Queens Creek Rd 28584 910-326-4300
Christine Andre, prin. Fax 326-1674
Swansboro MS 800/6-8
1240 W Corbett Ave 28584 910-326-3601
Brendan Gartner, prin. Fax 326-5848

**Sylva, Jackson, Pop. 2,551**
Jackson County SD 3,600/PK-12
398 Hospital Rd 28779 828-586-2311
Dr. Michael Murray, supt. Fax 586-5450
www.jcps.k12.nc.us
Jackson County Early College 100/9-12
447 College Dr 28779 828-339-4235
Rebecca Ensley, prin.
School of Alternatives 100/Alt
3770 Skyland Dr 28779 828-586-4328
Kristopher Reis, prin. Fax 586-2490
Smoky Mountain HS 800/9-12
100 Smoky Mountain Dr 28779 828-586-2177
Jake Buchanan, prin. Fax 586-2374
Other Schools – See Cashiers

Southwestern Community College Post-Sec.
447 College Dr 28779 828-339-4000

**Tabor City, Columbus, Pop. 2,463**
Columbus County SD
Supt. — See Whiteville
South Columbus HS 800/9-12
40 Stallion Dr 28463 910-653-4073
Eddie Beck, prin. Fax 653-9461
Tabor City MS 200/6-8
701 W 6th St 28463 910-653-3637
Dianna Bellamy, prin. Fax 653-2093

**Tarboro, Edgecombe, Pop. 11,342**
Edgecombe County SD 7,300/PK-12
PO Box 7128 27886 252-641-2600
John Farrelly, supt. Fax 641-5714
www.ecps.us/
Edgecombe Early College HS 100/9-12
2009 W Wilson St 27886 252-823-5166
Matt Smith, prin. Fax 823-2053
North Edgecombe HS 400/9-12
7589 NC Highway 33 NW 27886 252-823-3562
Brian Hopkins, prin. Fax 823-7847
Pattillo MS 600/6-8
PO Box 609 27886 252-823-3812
Lauren Prudenti, prin. Fax 641-5706
Tarboro HS 700/9-12
1400 W Howard Ave 27886 252-823-4284
Robert Batts, prin. Fax 823-0862
Other Schools – See Battleboro, Pinetops, Rocky Mount

Edgecombe Community College Post-Sec.
2009 W Wilson St 27886 252-823-5166

**Tar Heel, Bladen, Pop. 115**
Bladen County SD
Supt. — See Elizabethtown
Tar Heel MS 400/5-8
PO Box 128 28392 910-862-2475
Kimbrie Esters, prin. Fax 872-5599

**Taylorsville, Alexander, Pop. 2,066**
Alexander County SD 5,500/PK-12
700 Liledoun Rd 28681 828-632-7001
Dr. Jennifer Hefner, supt. Fax 632-8862
www.alexander.k12.nc.us
Alexander Central HS 1,700/9-12
223 School Dr 28681 828-632-7063
Doug Rhoney, prin. Fax 632-5387
West Alexander MS 600/6-8
85 Bulldog Ln 28681 828-495-4611
Dr. Chad Maynor, prin. Fax 495-3527
Other Schools – See Hiddenite

**Teachey, Duplin, Pop. 375**
Duplin County SD
Supt. — See Kenansville
Wallace-Rose Hill HS 500/9-12
602 High School Rd 28464 910-285-7501
M.D. Guthrie, prin. Fax 285-1116

**Thomasville, Davidson, Pop. 26,312**
Davidson County SD
Supt. — See Lexington
Brown MS 800/6-8
1140 Kendall Mill Rd 27360 336-475-8845
Christa DiBonaventura, prin. Fax 475-3842
Davidson Early College HS 100/9-12
297 DCCC Rd 27360 336-242-5686
Melissa Glover, prin. Fax 242-5688
East Davidson HS 1,000/9-12
1408 Lake Rd 27360 336-476-4814
Scott Dalton, prin. Fax 476-2982
Ledford HS 1,200/9-12
140 Jesse Green Rd 27360 336-769-9671
Chris Johnston, prin. Fax 769-0650
Ledford MS 1,000/6-8
3954 N NC Highway 109 27360 336-476-4816
Tabitha Broadway, prin. Fax 476-1479

Thomasville CSD 2,500/PK-12
400 Turner St 27360 336-474-4200
Dr. Maria Pitre-Martin, supt. Fax 475-0356
www.tcs.k12.nc.us
Thomasville HS 700/9-12
410 Unity St 27360 336-474-4250
Deboy Beamon, prin. Fax 476-7430
Thomasville MS 600/6-8
400 Unity St 27360 336-474-4120
Kevin Leake, prin. Fax 472-5081

**Topton, Macon**
Macon County SD
Supt. — See Franklin
Nantahala S 100/K-12
213 Winding Stairs Rd 28781 828-321-4388
James Bryan, prin. Fax 321-4834

**Trenton, Jones, Pop. 270**
Jones County SD 1,200/PK-12
320 W Jones St 28585 252-448-2531
Dr. Michael Bracy, supt. Fax 448-1394
www.jonesnc.net
Jones HS 300/9-12
1490 NC Highway 58 S 28585 252-448-2451
Michael White, prin. Fax 448-1034
Jones MS 200/7-8
190 Old New Bern Rd 28585 252-448-3956
Tremaine Young, prin. Fax 448-1044

**Trinity, Randolph, Pop. 6,568**
Randolph County SD
Supt. — See Asheboro
Archdale-Trinity MS 900/7-8
PO Box 232 27370 336-431-2589
Todd Beane, prin. Fax 431-1809
Trinity HS 700/9-12
5746 Trinity High School Dr 27370 336-861-6870
Larry Chappell, prin. Fax 861-8613
Uwharrie MS 400/6-8
1463 Pleasant Union Rd 27370 336-241-3900
Jeff Moss, prin. Fax 241-3904
Wheatmore HS 800/9-12
3678 Finch Farm Rd 27370 336-476-1500
Eric Johnson, prin. Fax 476-1520

**Troutman, Iredell, Pop. 2,323**
Iredell-Statesville SD
Supt. — See Statesville

Career Academy and Technical School 9-12
350 Old Murdock Rd 28166 704-978-2791
Larry Rogers, prin. Fax 978-2792
Troutman MS 400/6-8
305 Rumple St 28166 704-528-5137
Bryan Paslay, prin. Fax 528-4006

**Troy, Montgomery, Pop. 3,135**
Montgomery County SD 4,300/PK-12
PO Box 427 27371 910-576-6511
Dr. Dale Ellis, supt. Fax 576-2044
www.montgomery.k12.nc.us
Montgomery Learning Academy 50/Alt
310 S Main St 27371 910-572-1161
Tim Addis, prin. Fax 572-2362
Other Schools – See Biscoe, Mount Gilead

---

Montgomery Community College Post-Sec.
1011 Page St 27371 910-576-6222
Wescare Christian Academy 100/K-12
1368 NC Hwy 134 N 27371 910-572-2270
Fax 572-2257

**Tyner, Chowan**
Edenton-Chowan County SD
Supt. — See Edenton
Chowan MS 500/6-8
2845 Virginia Rd 27980 252-221-4131
John Lassiter, prin. Fax 221-8033

**Valdese, Burke, Pop. 4,425**
Burke County SD
Supt. — See Morganton
Draughn HS 800/9-12
709 Lovelady Rd NE 28690 828-879-4200
Pat Draughn, prin. Fax 879-4201
Heritage MS 600/6-8
1951 Enon Rd 28690 828-874-0731
Heidi Bristol, prin. Fax 879-6330

**Vanceboro, Craven, Pop. 972**
Craven County SD
Supt. — See New Bern
West Craven HS 1,000/9-12
2600 Streets Ferry Rd 28586 252-244-3200
Karen Barrow, prin. Fax 244-3207

**Wadesboro, Anson, Pop. 5,742**
Anson County SD 3,700/PK-12
320 Camden Rd 28170 704-694-4417
Michael Freeman, supt. Fax 694-7479
www.ansonschools.org/
Anson Academy 100/Alt
514 N Washington St 28170 704-272-5407
Preston Waddell, prin. Fax 993-2435
Anson HS 800/9-12
96 Anson High School Rd 28170 704-694-9301
Charles Murphy, prin. Fax 694-4570
Anson MS 500/7-8
832 US Highway 52 N 28170 704-694-3945
Josh McLaurin, prin. Fax 694-5209
Anson New Technology HS 100/9-12
118 W Ashe St 28170 704-694-7447
Chris Stinson, prin. Fax 994-3675
Other Schools – See Polkton

**Wake Forest, Wake, Pop. 29,480**
Wake County SD
Supt. — See Cary
Heritage HS 9-12
1150 Forestville Rd 27587 919-570-5600
Mark Savage, prin. Fax 570-5650
Heritage MS 1,500/6-8
3400 Rogers Rd 27587 919-562-6204
Christopher McCabe, prin. Fax 562-6227
Wake Forest HS 2,100/9-12
420 Stadium Dr 27587 919-554-8611
Patti Hamler, prin. Fax 554-8617
Wake Forest MS 1,100/6-8
1800 S Main St 27587 919-554-8440
Stacey Weddle, prin. Fax 554-8435

---

Southeastern Baptist Theological Sem. Post-Sec.
PO Box 1889 27588 919-761-2100

**Walkertown, Forsyth, Pop. 4,605**
Winston-Salem/Forsyth SD
Supt. — See Winston Salem
Walkertown HS 9-12
5240 Sullivantown Rd 27051 336-703-4151
Jay Jones, prin.
Walkertown MS 700/6-8
5240 Sullivantown Rd 27051 336-703-4154
Piper Hendrix, prin. Fax 595-1372

**Walnut Cove, Stokes, Pop. 1,407**
Stokes County SD
Supt. — See Danbury
Southeastern Stokes MS 500/6-8
1044 N Main St 27052 336-591-4371
Rhonda Jackson, prin. Fax 591-8164
South Stokes HS 700/9-12
1100 S Stokes High Dr 27052 336-994-2995
Wayne Duggins, prin. Fax 994-2608
Stokes Early College HS 100/9-12
1165 Dodgetown Rd 27052 336-593-5402
Misti Holloway, prin. Fax 593-2501

**Warrensville, Ashe**
Ashe County SD
Supt. — See Jefferson
Ashe County MS 600/7-8
PO Box 259 28693 336-384-3591
Dustin Farmer, prin. Fax 384-2112

**Warrenton, Warren, Pop. 855**
Warren County SD 2,600/PK-12
PO Box 110 27589 252-257-3184
Dr. Ray Spain, supt. Fax 257-5357
www.warrenk12nc.org/
Warren County HS 500/9-12
149 Campus Dr 27589 252-257-4413
Darrell Richardson, prin. Fax 257-1019
Warren County MS 600/6-8
118 Campus Dr 27589 252-257-3751
Joyce Mahomes, prin. Fax 257-4532
Warren Early College HS 100/9-12
PO Box 110 27589 252-738-3598
Tracey Neal, prin. Fax 257-5357
Warren New Tech HS 200/9-12
219 US Highway 158 Byp 27589 252-257-3767
Dr. Chandra Sledge, prin. Fax 257-1266

**Warsaw, Duplin, Pop. 3,022**
Duplin County SD
Supt. — See Kenansville
Kenan HS 600/9-12
1241 NC Highway 24 50 28398 910-293-4218
Michael Holton, prin. Fax 293-6744
Warsaw MS 200/6-8
738 W College St 28398 910-293-7997
Pamela Murray, prin. Fax 293-7397

**Washington, Beaufort, Pop. 9,614**
Beaufort County SD 7,200/PK-12
321 Smaw Rd 27889 252-946-6593
Dr. Don Phipps, supt. Fax 946-3255
www.beaufort.k12.nc.us
Beaufort County Early College HS 200/9-12
5337 US Highway 264 E 27889 252-940-6227
Emily Pake, prin. Fax 975-2752
Beaufort Co. Education Technical Center 50/Alt
820 N Bridge St 27889 252-946-5382
Jeremiah Jackson, prin. Fax 946-7964
Jones MS 800/6-8
4105 Market Street Ext 27889 252-946-0874
Tracey Nixon, prin. Fax 946-7604
Washington HS 1,000/9-12
400 Slatestone Rd 27889 252-946-0858
Misty Walker, prin. Fax 946-9633
Other Schools – See Chocowinity, Pinetown

---

Beaufort County Community College Post-Sec.
PO Box 1069 27889 252-946-6194

**Waxhaw, Union, Pop. 9,622**
Union County SD
Supt. — See Monroe
Cuthbertson HS 1,100/9-12
1400 Cuthbertson Rd 28173 704-296-0105
Dr. Kimberly Schroeder, prin. Fax 843-3565
Cuthbertson MS 1,100/6-8
1520 Cuthbertson Rd 28173 704-296-0107
Kevin Nesteruk, prin. Fax 243-1673
Marvin Ridge HS 1,400/9-12
2825 Crane Rd 28173 704-290-1520
Donna Cook, prin. Fax 243-0012
Marvin Ridge MS 1,300/6-8
2831 Crane Rd 28173 704-290-1510
Dr. Jay Jones, prin. Fax 243-0153
South Providence Alternative S 100/Alt
500 S Providence St 28173 704-290-1580
Willie Howard, prin. Fax 843-5708

**Waynesville, Haywood, Pop. 9,753**
Haywood County SD 7,600/K-12
1230 N Main St 28786 828-456-2400
Anne Garrett, supt. Fax 456-2438
www.haywood.k12.nc.us
Bethel MS 300/6-8
630 Sonoma Rd 28786 828-646-3442
Shawn Parris, prin. Fax 648-6259
Tuscola HS 1,000/9-12
564 Tuscola School Rd 28786 828-456-2408
Travis Collins, prin. Fax 456-2434
Waynesville MS 1,000/6-8
495 Brown Ave 28786 828-456-2403
Trevor Putnam, prin. Fax 452-7905
Other Schools – See Canton, Clyde

**Weaverville, Buncombe, Pop. 3,037**
Buncombe County SD
Supt. — See Asheville
North Buncombe HS 1,100/9-12
890 Clarks Chapel Rd 28787 828-645-4221
Jack Evans, prin. Fax 645-4367
North Buncombe MS 600/7-8
51 N Buncombe School Rd 28787 828-645-7944
Sherry Barnette, prin. Fax 645-2509

---

Timbersong Academy 100/4-12
531 Upper Flat Creek Rd 28787 828-645-1919
Bryan Tomes, dir. Fax 219-7006

**Weldon, Halifax, Pop. 1,616**
Weldon CSD 1,100/PK-12
301 Mulberry St 27890 252-536-4821
Dr. Anitra Wells, supt. Fax 536-3062
district.weldoncityschools.org
Roanoke Valley Early College HS 100/8-12
100 College Dr Bldg 600 27890 252-536-6382
Dr. Michael Butler, prin. Fax 536-3062
Weldon HS 200/9-12
415 County Rd 27890 252-536-4829
Michelle Burton, prin. Fax 536-0168
Other Schools – See Halifax

---

Halifax Community College Post-Sec.
PO Box 809 27890 252-536-4221

**Wendell, Wake, Pop. 5,709**
Johnston County SD
Supt. — See Smithfield
Archer Lodge MS 900/6-8
740 Wendell Rd 27591 919-553-0714
Betsy Huddleston, prin. Fax 553-8540
Corinth Holders HS 1,000/9-12
6875 Applewhite Rd 27591 919-365-4306
Charles Ferrell, prin. Fax 365-4344
Wake County SD
Supt. — See Cary
East Wake HS 1,200/9-12
5101 Rolesville Rd 27591 919-365-2625
Stacey Alston, prin. Fax 365-2658
Wendell MS 1,100/6-8
3409 NC 97 Hwy 27591 919-365-1667
Robert Morrison, prin. Fax 365-1686

**Wentworth, Rockingham, Pop. 2,774**
Rockingham County SD
Supt. — See Eden
Rockingham County Early College HS 200/9-12
310 Wrenn Memorial Rd 27375 336-342-4261
Diane Hill, prin. Fax 349-9986

---

Rockingham Community College Post-Sec.
PO Box 38 27375 336-342-4261

**West End, Moore**
Moore County SD
Supt. — See Carthage
West Pine MS 800/6-8
144 Archie Rd 27376 910-673-1464
Robin Calcutt, prin. Fax 673-1272

**West Jefferson, Ashe, Pop. 1,280**
Ashe County SD
Supt. — See Jefferson
Ashe County HS 900/9-12
PO Box 450 28694 336-846-2400
Jason Krider, prin. Fax 846-2411

**Whiteville, Columbus, Pop. 5,303**
Columbus County SD 6,200/PK-12
PO Box 729 28472 910-642-5168
Alan Faulk, supt. Fax 640-1010
www.columbus.k12.nc.us/
Columbus Career & College Acad - SCC 9-12
PO Box 151 28472 910-642-7141
Nicky Hobbs, prin. Fax 642-7693
Other Schools – See Cerro Gordo, Chadbourn, Delco, Fair Bluff, Hallsboro, Lake Waccamaw, Nakina, Tabor City

Whiteville CSD 2,300/PK-12
107 W Walter St 28472 910-642-4116
Charles Garland, supt. Fax 642-0564
www.whiteville.k12.nc.us
Central MS 500/6-8
310 S Mrtn Lthr King Jr Ave 28472 910-642-3546
Chris Burton, prin. Fax 642-7484
North Whiteville Academy 50/Alt
310 S Martin Luther King Jr 28472 910-914-4161
Susan Smith, dir. Fax 914-4164
Whiteville HS 700/9-12
413 N Lee St 28472 910-914-4189
Jes Sealey, prin. Fax 914-4186

---

Carolina Adventist Academy 50/K-10
PO Box 1937 28472 910-640-0855
Columbus Christian Academy 200/K-12
PO Box 1100 28472 910-642-6196
Southeastern Community College Post-Sec.
PO Box 151 28472 910-642-7141

**Wilkesboro, Wilkes, Pop. 3,340**
Wilkes County SD
Supt. — See North Wilkesboro
West Wilkes MS 600/6-8
1677 N NC Highway 16 28697 336-651-4381
Pam Huffman, prin. Fax 973-7423
Wilkes Central HS 900/9-12
1179 Moravian Falls Rd 28697 336-667-5277
Michelle Shepherd, prin. Fax 667-2091
Wilkes Early College HS 200/9-12
1328 S Collegiate Dr # 800 28697 336-838-6247
Dion Stocks, prin. Fax 838-6198

---

Wilkes Community College Post-Sec.
PO Box 120 28697 336-838-6100

**Williamston, Martin, Pop. 5,452**
Martin County SD 3,300/PK-12
300 N Watts St 27892 252-792-1575
Dr. Ron Melchiorre, supt. Fax 792-1965
martin.sharpschool.net/
Riverside HS 9-12
1260 Godwin Dr 27892 252-792-7881
James Guard, prin. Fax 809-4807
Riverside MS 400/6-8
2920 US Highway 17 27892 252-792-1111
Ronald Byrd, prin. Fax 792-6644
Other Schools – See Robersonville

---

Martin Community College Post-Sec.
1161 Kehukee Park Rd 27892 252-792-1521

**Wilmington, New Hanover, Pop. 104,394**
New Hanover County SD 24,800/PK-12
6410 Carolina Beach Rd 28412 910-763-5431
Dr. Tim Markley, supt. Fax 254-4479
www.nhcs.net
Ashley HS 1,800/9-12
555 Halyburton Memorial Pky 28412 910-790-2360
Jackson Norvell, prin. Fax 790-2356
Bear Early College HS 200/9-12
630 MacMillan Ave N 28403 910-350-1387
Philip Sutton, prin. Fax 350-1392
Hoggard HS 1,700/9-12
4305 Shipyard Blvd 28403 910-350-2072
Dr. Steve Sullivan, prin. Fax 350-2066
Laney HS 1,900/9-12
2700 N College Rd 28405 910-350-2089
Allen O'Briant, prin. Fax 350-2083
Mosley Performance Learning Center 50/Alt
3702 Princess Place Dr 28405 910-251-6161
Adrian Pearson, prin. Fax 251-6022

Murray MS 800/6-8
655 Halyburton Memorial Pky 28412 910-790-2363
Patrick McCarty, prin. Fax 790-2351
Myrtle Grove MS 800/6-8
901 Piner Rd 28409 910-350-2100
Sam Highsmith, prin. Fax 350-2104
New Hanover HS 1,600/9-12
1307 Market St 28401 910-251-6100
James McAdams, prin. Fax 251-6114
Noble MS 700/6-8
6520 Market St 28405 910-350-2112
Wade Smith, prin. Fax 350-2109
Roland-Grise MS 900/6-8
4412 Lake Ave 28403 910-350-2136
Dr. Sherry Pinto, prin. Fax 350-2133
Trask MS 800/6-8
2900 N College Rd 28405 910-350-2142
Sharon Dousharm, prin. Fax 350-2144
Virgo MS 200/6-8
813 Nixon St 28401 910-251-6150
Eric Irizarry, prin. Fax 251-6055
Williston MS 800/6-8
401 S 10th St 28401 910-815-6906
Dr. Jerry Oates, prin. Fax 815-6904
Other Schools – See Castle Hayne

---

Cape Fear Academy 600/PK-12
3900 S College Rd 28412 910-791-0287
Donald Berger, head sch Fax 791-0290
Cape Fear Community College Post-Sec.
411 N Front St 28401 910-362-7000
Coastal Christian HS 200/9-12
1150 the Kings Hwy 28409 910-395-9995
Brenda McCombie, admin. Fax 395-9901
College of Wilmington Post-Sec.
3500 Oleander Dr Ste 1111 28403 910-763-4418
Miller-Motte College Post-Sec.
5000 Market St 28405 910-392-4660
New Hanover Regional Medical Center Post-Sec.
2131 S 17th St 28401 910-343-7074
University of North Carolina Post-Sec.
601 S College Rd 28403 910-962-3000
Wilmington Christian Academy 800/PK-12
1401 N College Rd 28405 910-791-4248

**Wilson, Wilson, Pop. 48,488**
Wilson County SD 12,400/PK-12
PO Box 2048 27894 252-399-7700
Sean Bulson, supt. Fax 399-2776
www.wilsonschoolsnc.net
Beddingfield HS 900/9-12
4510 Old Stantonsburg Rd 27893 252-399-7880
F.T. Franks, prin. Fax 399-7850
Daniels Learning Center 50/Alt
723 Elvie St S 27893 252-399-7900
Leon Dupree, prin. Fax 399-7892
Darden MS 400/6-8
1665 Lipscomb Rd E 27893 252-206-4973
Steve Hunter, prin. Fax 206-1508
Fike HS 1,100/9-12
500 Harrison Dr N 27893 252-399-7905
Mark Holley, prin. Fax 399-7893
Forest Hills MS 600/6-8
1210 Forest Hills Rd NW 27896 252-399-7913
Cheryl Baggett, prin. Fax 399-7894
Hunt HS 1,300/9-12
4559 Lamm Rd SW 27893 252-399-7930
Eddie Doll, prin. Fax 399-7897
Toisnot MS 500/6-8
1301 Corbett Ave N 27893 252-399-7973
Ronnia Cockrell, prin. Fax 399-7749
Wilson Early College Academy 100/9-12
PO Box 4305 27893 252-246-1418
Nelson Johnston, prin. Fax 246-1430
Other Schools – See Elm City, Lucama, Stantonsburg

---

Barton College Post-Sec.
PO Box 5000 27893 252-399-6300
Community Christian S 300/PK-12
5160 Packhouse Rd 27896 252-399-1376
Eastern North Carolina Sch. for the Deaf Post-Sec.
1311 US Highway 301 S 27893 252-237-2450
Greenfield S 300/PK-12
3351 NC Highway 42 W 27893 252-237-8046
Mitchell's Hairstyling Academy Post-Sec.
2620 Forest Hills Rd #A 27893 252-243-3158
Wilson Christian Academy 500/PK-12
PO Box 3818 27895 252-237-8064
Wilson Community College Post-Sec.
PO Box 4305 27893 252-291-1195

**Windsor, Bertie, Pop. 3,573**
Bertie County SD 2,900/PK-12
PO Box 10 27983 252-794-6000
Elaine White, supt. Fax 794-9727
www.bertie.k12.nc.us
Bertie Academy 100/Alt
819 Governors Rd 27983 252-794-2358
Antonio Hoggard, prin.
Bertie Early College HS 100/9-12
819B Governors Rd 27983 252-794-2150
Calvin Moore, prin. Fax 794-3407
Bertie HS 600/9-12
715 US Highway 13 N 27983 252-794-3034
Rickey Eley, prin. Fax 794-1932
Bertie MS 600/6-8
652 US Highway 13 N 27983 252-794-2143
William Peele, prin. Fax 794-4024
Bertie STEM HS 200/9-12
715 US Highway 13 N 27983 252-794-5820
Daphne Williams, prin. Fax 794-5815

---

Bethel Assembly Christian Academy 200/PK-12
105 Askewville Bryant St 27983 252-794-4034

**Winfall, Perquimans, Pop. 587**
Perquimans County SD
Supt. — See Hertford
Perquimans County MS 400/6-8
PO Box 39 27985 252-426-7355
Andrea Greene, prin. Fax 426-1424

**Wingate, Union, Pop. 3,424**

---

Wingate University Post-Sec.
220 N Camden Rd 28174 704-233-8000

**Winston Salem, Forsyth, Pop. 225,143**
Davidson County SD
Supt. — See Lexington
Oak Grove MS 6-8
1771 Hoy Long Rd 27107 336-474-8250
Dan Shamblen, prin. Fax 474-8257

Winston-Salem/Forsyth SD 51,100/PK-12
PO Box 2513 27102 336-727-2816
Dr. Beverly Emory, supt. Fax 661-6572
wsfcs.k12.nc.us
Atkins Academic & Technology HS 300/9-12
3605 Old Greensboro Rd 27101 336-703-6754
Joe Childers, prin. Fax 748-3565
Career Center Vo/Tech
910 Highland Ct 27101 336-727-8181
Chris Nichols, prin. Fax 727-7607
Carver HS 700/9-12
3545 Carver School Rd 27105 336-727-2987
Travis Taylor, prin. Fax 727-8211
Clemmons MS 900/6-8
3785 Fraternity Church Rd 27127 336-703-4217
Sandra Hunter, prin. Fax 774-4678
Early College of Forsyth County 9-12
2100 Silas Creek Pkwy 27103 336-757-3290
Frances Cook, prin. Fax 734-7467
Flat Rock MS, 4648 Ebert Rd 27127 900/6-8
Becky Hodges, prin. 336-703-6762
Forsyth Middle College HS 100/9-12
2100 Silas Creek Pkwy 27103 336-734-7437
William Wynn, prin.
Hanes Magnet MS 1,100/6-8
2355 Pleasant St 27107 336-703-4171
Fax 727-3207
Jefferson MS 1,200/6-8
3500 Sally Kirk Rd 27106 336-703-4222
Brad Royal, prin. Fax 774-4635
Kennedy HS 50/9-12
890 E 11th St 27101 336-703-4143
Sean Gaillard, prin. Fax 727-8559
Kingswood S 50/Alt
1001 Reynolda Rd 27104 336-703-4128
Roderick Dupree, prin.
Main Street Academy Alt
2700 S Main St 27127 336-703-4185
Ronald Travis, prin. Fax 771-4706
Meadowlark MS 1,000/6-8
301 Meadowlark Dr 27106 336-703-4228
Joey Hearl, prin. Fax 922-1745
Mineral Springs MS 500/6-8
4559 Ogburn Ave 27105 336-703-6733
Danyelle Parker, prin. Fax 661-4857
Mt. Tabor HS 1,600/9-12
342 Petree Rd 27106 336-703-6700
Ed Weiss, prin. Fax 774-4606
North Forsyth HS 1,200/9-12
5705 Shattalon Dr 27105 336-661-4880
Melita Wise, prin. Fax 661-4869
Northwest MS 900/6-8
5501 Murray Rd 27106 336-703-4161
Alfreda Smith, prin. Fax 924-5128
Paisley IB Magnet MS 800/6-10
1400 Grant Ave 27105 336-703-4168
Dr. Gary Cone, prin. Fax 727-8315
Parkland HS 1,400/9-12
1600 Brewer Rd 27127 336-771-4700
Spencer Hardy, prin. Fax 771-4703
Philo-Hill Magnet MS 300/6-8
410 Haverhill St 27127 336-703-4165
Kenyatta Bennett, prin. Fax 771-4737
Reynolds HS 1,700/9-12
301 N Hawthorne Rd 27104 336-703-4145
Leslie Alexander, prin. Fax 727-2053
Wiley MS 500/6-8
1400 W Northwest Blvd 27104 336-727-2378
Lisa Bodenheimer, prin. Fax 727-8412
Winston-Salem Preparatory Academy 400/6-12
1215 N Cameron Ave 27101 336-703-6732
Richard Watts, prin. Fax 727-2931
Other Schools – See Clemmons, Kernersville, Pfafftown, Walkertown

---

Calvary Baptist Day S 700/PK-12
5000 Country Club Rd 27104 336-765-5546
Richard Hardee, head sch Fax 714-5577
Carolina Christian College Post-Sec.
PO Box 777 27102 336-774-0900
Forsyth Technical Community College Post-Sec.
2100 Silas Creek Pkwy 27103 336-723-0371
Gospel Light Christian S 400/PK-12
4940 Gospel Light Church Rd 27101 336-722-6100
Living Arts Institute Post-Sec.
1100 S Stratford Rd 27103 336-774-7600
Piedmont Baptist College & Graduate Sch Post-Sec.
420 S Broad St 27101 336-725-8344
Salem Academy 200/9-12
500 E Salem Ave 27101 336-721-2643
Karl Sjolund, head sch Fax 917-5340
Salem Baptist Christian S 300/PK-12
429 S Broad St 27101 336-725-6113
Martha Drake, hdmstr. Fax 725-8455
Salem College Post-Sec.
601 S Church St 27101 800-327-2536
University of NC School of the Arts Post-Sec.
1533 S Main St 27127 336-770-3399
Wake Forest University Post-Sec.
1834 Wake Forest Rd 27109 336-758-5000
Winston-Salem Barber School Post-Sec.
1531 Silas Creek Pkwy 27127 336-724-1459
Winston-Salem State University Post-Sec.
601 S Mrtn Lther King Jr Dr 27110 336-750-2000

**Winterville, Pitt, Pop. 9,094**
Pitt County SD
Supt. — See Greenville
Cox MS 800/6-8
2657 Church St 28590 252-756-3105
Tracy Cole, prin. Fax 756-1081
Pitt County Schools Early College 100/9-12
1986 Pitt Tech Rd 28590 252-493-7821
Wynn Whittington, prin.
South Central HS 1,600/9-12
570 W Forlines Rd 28590 252-321-3232
Julie Cary, prin. Fax 321-7909

---

Christ Covenant S 200/K-11
4889 Old Tar Rd 28590 252-756-3002
Robert Lee, head sch Fax 756-4072

**Winton, Hertford, Pop. 760**
Hertford County SD 3,200/PK-12
PO Box 158 27986 252-358-1761
Dr. Michael Perry, supt. Fax 358-4745
www.hertford.k12.nc.us
Brown HS 50/Alt
102 C S Brown Dr 27986 252-358-2852
Keisha Peele, prin. Fax 358-0121
Other Schools – See Ahoskie, Murfreesboro

**Yadkinville, Yadkin, Pop. 2,941**
Yadkin County SD 5,900/PK-12
121 Washington St 27055 336-679-2051
Dr. Todd Martin, supt. Fax 679-4013
www.yadkin.k12.nc.us
Yadkin Early College HS 200/9-12
121 Washington St 27055 336-679-4600
Tracy Kimmer, prin. Fax 679-3210
Yadkin Success Academy 100/Alt
733 E Main St 27055 336-679-4888
Mary Catherine Berry, prin. Fax 679-6623
Other Schools – See Boonville, East Bend

**Yanceyville, Caswell, Pop. 1,971**
Caswell County SD 2,900/PK-12
PO Box 160 27379 336-694-4116
Dr. Brock Womble, supt. Fax 694-5154
www.caswell.k12.nc.us/
Bartlett Yancey HS 800/9-12
PO Box 190 27379 336-694-4212
JoAnna Gwynn, prin. Fax 694-5285
Dillard MS 700/6-8
255 Hatchett Rd 27379 336-694-4941
Emily Buchanan, prin. Fax 694-6353

**Youngsville, Franklin, Pop. 1,142**
Franklin County SD
Supt. — See Louisburg
Cedar Creek MS 800/6-8
2228 Cedar Creek Rd 27596 919-554-4848
Dr. Laverne Daniels, prin. Fax 570-5143

---

American Institute of Applied Science Post-Sec.
100 Hunter Pl 27596 919-554-2500

**Zebulon, Wake, Pop. 4,340**
Wake County SD
Supt. — See Cary
Zebulon MS 600/6-8
1000 Shepard School Rd 27597 919-404-3630
Stephanie Smith, prin. Fax 404-3651

# NORTH DAKOTA

**NORTH DAKOTA DEPT. OF PUBLIC INSTRUCTION**
**600 E Boulevard Ave, Bismarck 58505-0601**
**Telephone 701-328-2260**
**Fax 701-328-2461**
**Website http://www.dpi.state.nd.us**
Superintendent of Public Instruction Kirsten Baesler

**NORTH DAKOTA BOARD OF EDUCATION**
**600 E Boulevard Ave, Bismarck 58505-0601**

## COUNTY SUPERINTENDENTS OF SCHOOLS

Adams County Office of Education
Patricia Carroll, supt. 701-567-4363
PO Box 589, Hettinger 58639 Fax 567-2910
Barnes County Office of Education
Beth Didier, supt. 701-845-6666
230 4th St NW Rm 202 Fax 845-8548
Valley City 58072
Benson County Office of Education
Lucia Jacobson, supt. 701-473-5370
PO Box 347, Minnewaukan 58351 Fax 473-5571
Billings County Office of Education
Marcia Lamb, supt. 701-623-4377
PO Box 168, Medora 58645 Fax 623-4896
Bottineau County Office of Education
Ann Monson, supt. 701-228-2035
314 5th St W Ste 11 Fax 228-3658
Bottineau 58318
Bowman County Office of Education
Christine Septon, supt. 701-523-3665
PO Box 380, Bowman 58623 Fax 523-3428
Burke County Office of Education
Jeanine Jensen, supt. 701-377-2861
PO Box 310, Bowbells 58721 Fax 377-2020
Burleigh County Office of Education
Mike Heilman, supt. 701-323-4074
806 N Washington St
Bismarck 58501
www.co.burleigh.nd.us
Cass County Office of Education
Mike Montplaisir, supt. 701-241-5600
PO Box 2806, Fargo 58108
www.casscountynd.gov
Cavalier County Office of Education
Lisa Gellner, supt. 701-256-2229
901 3rd St Ste 15, Langdon 58249 Fax 256-2546
Dickey County Office of Education
Deborah Anderson, supt. 701-349-3249
PO Box 148, Ellendale 58436 Fax 349-4639
Divide County Office of Education
Dr. Sherlock Hirning, supt. 701-965-6313
PO Box G, Crosby 58730 Fax 965-6004
www.divide-co.k12.nd.us
Dunn County Office of Education
Tracey Dolezal, supt. 701-573-4448
205 Owens St, Manning 58642 Fax 573-4444
Eddy County Office of Education
Tracy Henningsgard, supt. 701-947-2434
524 Central Ave Fax 947-2279
New Rockford 58356
Emmons County Office of Education
Kayla Hendrickson, supt. 701-254-4417
PO Box 776, Linton 58552 Fax 254-4802
Foster County Office of Education
Jolette Scheen, supt. 701-652-2441
PO Box 104, Carrington 58421 Fax 652-2173
Golden Valley County Office of Education
Ceil Stedman, supt. 701-872-4331
PO Box 67, Beach 58621 Fax 872-4383
www.goldenvalleycounty.org

Grand Forks County Office of Education
David Godfread, supt. 701-795-2777
5216 Chestnut St Fax 795-2770
Grand Forks 58201
Grant County Office of Education
Kelly Bachmeier, supt. 701-622-3263
210 2nd Ave W, Carson 58529 Fax 622-3717
Griggs County Office of Education
Ardis Oettle, supt. 701-797-2411
PO Box 511, Cooperstown 58425 Fax 797-3587
Hettinger County Office of Education
Sheila Steiner, supt. 701-824-2500
336 Pacific Ave, Mott 58646 Fax 824-2717
Kidder County Office of Education
Angela Haverkamp, supt. 701-475-2632
PO Box 66, Steele 58482 Fax 475-2202
La Moure County Office of Education
Mike Johnson, supt. 701-883-5301
PO Box 128, LaMoure 58458 Fax 883-4240
Logan County Office of Education
Gary Schumacher, supt. 701-754-2756
PO Box 7, Napoleon 58561 Fax 754-2270
McHenry County Office of Education
Maxine Rognlien, supt. 701-537-5642
407 Main St S, Towner 58788 Fax 537-5969
www.mchenrycountynd.com
McIntosh County Office of Education
Coreen Schumacher, supt. 605-380-6813
PO Box 290, Ashley 58413 Fax 288-3671
McKenzie County Office of Education
Carol Kieson, supt. 701-444-3456
201 5th St NW Unit 503 Fax 444-4113
Watford City 58854
www.mckenziecounty.net
McLean County Office of Education
Lori Foss, supt. 701-462-8541
PO Box 1108, Washburn 58577 Fax 462-3542
Mercer County Office of Education
Gontran Langowski, supt. 701-748-3300
1021 Arthur St, Stanton 58571 Fax 748-3301
Morton County Office of Education
Dale Ekstrom, supt. 701-667-3315
210 2nd Ave NW, Mandan 58554 Fax 667-3348
www.co.morton.nd.us/
Mountrail County Office of Education
Stephanie Pappa, supt. 701-628-2145
PO Box 69, Stanley 58784 Fax 628-3975
Nelson County Office of Education
Sharon Young, supt. 701-247-2472
210 B Ave W, Lakota 58344 Fax 247-2943
Oliver County Office of Education
Judith Hintz, supt. 701-794-8721
PO Box 188, Center 58530 Fax 794-3476
Pembina County Office of Education
Linda Schlittenhard, supt. 701-265-4231
301 Dakota St W Unit 11 Fax 265-4876
Cavalier 58220

Pierce County Office of Education
Karin Fursather, supt. 701-776-5225
240 2nd St SE Ste 6, Rugby 58368 Fax 776-5707
Ramsey County Office of Education
Lisa Diseth, supt. 701-662-7023
524 4th Ave NE, Devils Lake 58301 Fax 662-7049
Ransom County Office of Education
Suzanne Anderson, supt. 701-683-6117
PO Box 112, Lisbon 58054
Renville County Office of Education
LeAnn Pollman, supt. 701-756-6301
PO Box 68, Mohall 58761 Fax 756-6391
Richland County Office of Education
Harris Bailey, supt. 701-642-7702
418 2nd Ave N Ofc 15 Fax 642-7701
Wahpeton 58075
Rolette County Office of Education
Valerie McCloud, supt. 701-477-5665
PO Box 939, Rolla 58367 Fax 477-6339
Sargent County Office of Education
Pam Maloney, supt. 701-724-6241
355 Main St S Ste 1, Forman 58032 Fax 724-6244
Sheridan County Office of Education
Shirley Murray, supt. 701-363-2205
PO Box 439, Mc Clusky 58463 Fax 363-2953
Sioux County Office of Education
Barb Hettich, supt. 701-854-3481
PO Box L, Fort Yates 58538 Fax 854-3854
Slope County Office of Education
Jacqueline Kathrein, supt. 701-879-6277
PO Box MM, Amidon 58620 Fax 879-6278
Stark County Office of Education
Kay Haag, supt. 701-456-7630
PO Box 130, Dickinson 58602 Fax 456-7634
Steele County Office of Education
Tasha Krueger, supt. 701-524-2110
PO Box 275, Finley 58230 Fax 524-1715
Stutsman County Office of Education
Casey Bradley, supt. 701-252-9035
511 2nd Ave SE Ste 102 Fax 251-1603
Jamestown 58401
Towner County Office of Education
Wayne Lingen, supt. 701-968-4346
PO Box 603, Cando 58324 Fax 968-4342
Traill County Office of Education
Rebecca Braaten, supt. 701-636-4458
PO Box 429, Hillsboro 58045 Fax 636-5418
Walsh County Office of Education
Kris Molde, supt. 701-352-2851
600 Cooper Ave, Grafton 58237 Fax 352-3340
Ward County Office of Education
Jodi Johnson, supt. 701-857-6495
PO Box 5005, Minot 58702 Fax 857-6424
Wells County Office of Education
Janell Rudel, supt. 701-547-3521
700 Railway St N Ste 37 Fax 547-3719
Fessenden 58438
Williams County Office of Education
Patti Ogurchak, supt. 701-577-4580
PO Box 2047, Williston 58802 Fax 577-4535

## PUBLIC, PRIVATE AND CATHOLIC SECONDARY SCHOOLS

**Alexander, McKenzie, Pop. 220**
Alexander SD 2 100/K-12
PO Box 66 58831 701-828-3334
Leslie Bieber, supt. Fax 828-3134
www.alexander.k12.nd.us/
Alexander HS 50/7-12
PO Box 66 58831 701-828-3335
Leslie Bieber, prin. Fax 828-3134

**Ashley, McIntosh, Pop. 736**
Ashley SD 9 100/PK-12
703 W Main St 58413 701-288-3456
Fax 288-3457
www.ashley.k12.nd.us/
Ashley HS 100/7-12
703 W Main St 58413 701-288-3456
Jason Schmidt, prin. Fax 288-3457

**Beach, Golden Valley, Pop. 1,013**
Beach SD 3 300/K-12
PO Box 368 58621 701-872-4161
Larry Helvik, supt. Fax 872-3801
www.beach.k12.nd.us
Beach JSHS 200/7-12
PO Box 368 58621 701-872-4161
Brandt Gaugler, prin. Fax 872-3801

**Belcourt, Rolette, Pop. 2,055**
Belcourt SD 7 1,600/K-12
PO Box 440 58316 701-477-6471
Dr. Lana DeCoteau, supt. Fax 477-6470
www.belcourt.k12.nd.us
Turtle Mountain Community HS 600/9-12
PO Box 440 58316 701-477-6471
Melvin Laducer, prin. Fax 477-8821
Turtle Mountain Community MS 400/6-8
PO Box 440 58316 701-477-6471
Louis Dauphinais, prin. Fax 477-3973

---

Turtle Mountain Community College Post-Sec.
PO Box 340 58316 701-477-7862

**Belfield, Stark, Pop. 793**
Belfield SD 13 200/K-12
PO Box 97 58622 701-575-4275
Wade Northrop, supt. Fax 575-8533
www.belfield.k12.nd.us/
Belfield JSHS 100/7-12
PO Box 97 58622 701-575-4275
Wade Northrop, prin. Fax 575-8533

**Berthold, Ward, Pop. 449**
Lewis and Clark SD 161 400/PK-12
PO Box 185 58718 701-453-3484
Brian Nelson, supt. Fax 453-3488
www.lewisandclark.k12.nd.us/

Berthold HS 100/7-12
PO Box 185 58718 701-453-3484
Margaret Person, prin. Fax 453-3488
Other Schools – See Makoti

**Beulah, Mercer, Pop. 3,078**
Beulah SD 27 700/K-12
204 5th St NW 58523 701-873-2237
Fax 873-5273
www.beulah.k12.nd.us
Beulah HS 200/9-12
204 5th St NW 58523 701-873-2261
Kevin Hoherz, prin. Fax 873-5273
Beulah MS 200/5-8
1700 Central Ave N 58523 701-873-4325
Stacy Murschel, prin. Fax 873-2844

**Binford, Griggs, Pop. 183**
Midkota SD 7 100/K-12
PO Box 38 58416 701-676-2511
Gilbert Black, supt. Fax 676-2510
www.midkotaschools.com
Other Schools – See Glenfield

**Bismarck, Burleigh, Pop. 60,375**
Bismarck SD 1 9,600/PK-12
806 N Washington St 58501 701-323-4000
Tamara Uselman, supt. Fax 355-4001
www.bismarckschools.org
Bismarck Career & Technical Center Vo/Tech
1221 College Dr 58501 701-323-4340
Dale Hoerauf, prin. Fax 323-4345
Bismarck HS 1,300/9-12
800 N 8th St 58501 701-323-4800
David Wisthoff, prin. Fax 323-4805
Century HS 1,200/9-12
1000 E Century Ave 58503 701-323-4900
Steve Madler, prin. Fax 323-4905
Horizon MS 600/6-8
500 Ash Coulee Dr 58503 701-323-4550
Tabby Rabenberg, prin. Fax 323-4555
Legacy HS 9-12
806 N Washington St 58501 701-323-4850
Tom Schmidt, prin. Fax 323-4855
Simle MS 600/6-8
1215 N 19th St 58501 701-323-4600
Russ Riehl, prin. Fax 323-4605
South Central Alternative S 100/Alt
406 S Anderson St 58504 701-323-4520
Joe Kalvoda, prin. Fax 323-4525
Wachter MS 500/6-8
1107 S 7th St 58504 701-323-4650
Lee Ziegler, prin. Fax 323-4655
Adult Learning Center Adult
1500 Edwards Ave Rm 220 58501 701-323-4530
Dale Hoerauf, prin. Fax 323-4477

---

Bismarck State College Post-Sec.
PO Box 5587 58506 701-224-5400
Dakota Adventist Academy 50/9-12
15905 Sheyenne Cir 58503 701-258-9000
Light of Christ Academy 200/7-8
1025 N 2nd St 58501 701-223-4114
Carmen Cain, prin. Fax 223-8629
Medcenter One Health System Post-Sec.
222 N 7th St 58501 701-222-5413
Rasmussen College Post-Sec.
1701 E Century Ave 58503 701-530-9600
R.D. Hairstyling College Post-Sec.
1320 Tacoma Ave 58504 701-223-8804
St. Alexius Medical Center Post-Sec.
PO Box 5510 58506 701-224-7600
St. Marys Central HS 300/9-12
1025 N 2nd St 58501 701-223-4113
Carmen Cain, prin. Fax 223-8629
Shiloh Christian S 400/PK-12
1915 Shiloh Dr 58503 701-221-2104
Travis Jordan, supt. Fax 224-8221
United Tribes Technical College Post-Sec.
3315 University Dr 58504 701-255-3285
University of Mary Post-Sec.
7500 University Dr 58504 701-255-7500

**Bottineau, Bottineau, Pop. 2,163**
Bottineau SD 1 600/K-12
301 Brander St 58318 701-228-2266
Jason Kersten, supt. Fax 228-2021
www.bottineau.k12.nd.us/
Bottineau JSHS 300/7-12
301 Brander St 58318 701-228-2266
Joel Bickford, prin. Fax 228-2021

---

Dakota College at Bottineau Post-Sec.
105 Simrall Blvd 58318 701-228-2277

**Bowbells, Burke, Pop. 335**
Bowbells SD 14 100/K-12
PO Box 279 58721 701-377-2396
Celeste Thingvold, supt. Fax 377-2399
www.bowbells.k12.nd.us
Bowbells HS 50/7-12
PO Box 279 58721 701-377-2396
Celeste Thingvold, supt. Fax 377-2399

**Bowman, Bowman, Pop. 1,641**
Bowman County SD 1 400/K-12
PO Box H 58623 701-523-3283
Tony Duletski, supt. Fax 523-3849
www.bowman.k12.nd.us
Bowman HS 100/9-12
PO Box H 58623 701-523-3283
Wayne Olson, prin. Fax 523-3849

**Buxton, Traill, Pop. 323**
Central Valley SD 3 100/K-12
1556 Highway 81 NE 58218 701-847-2220
Jeremy Brandt, supt. Fax 847-2407
www.centralvalleynd.com
Central Valley S 100/K-12
1556 Highway 81 NE 58218 701-847-2220
Frank Justin, prin. Fax 847-2407

**Cando, Towner, Pop. 1,101**
North Star SD 10 300/PK-12
PO Box 489 58324 701-968-4416
Jeff Hagler, supt. Fax 968-4418
www.northstar.k12.nd.us//index.html
North Star HS 100/9-12
PO Box 489 58324 701-968-4416
Nancy Reiser, prin. Fax 968-4418

**Carrington, Foster, Pop. 2,050**
Carrington SD 49 500/PK-12
PO Box 48 58421 701-652-3136
Dr. Brian Duchscherer, supt. Fax 652-1243
www.carrington.k12.nd.us/
Carrington JSHS 300/7-12
PO Box 48 58421 701-652-3136
David Nowatzki, prin. Fax 652-1243

**Casselton, Cass, Pop. 2,310**
Central Cass SD 17 800/K-12
802 5th St N 58012 701-347-5352
Mark Weston, supt. Fax 347-5354
www.central-cass.k12.nd.us/
Central Cass HS 300/9-12
802 5th St N 58012 701-347-5352
Chris Kittleson, prin. Fax 347-5354
Central Cass MS 200/6-8
802 5th St N 58012 701-347-5352
Nikki Wixo, prin. Fax 347-5354

**Cavalier, Pembina, Pop. 1,278**
Cavalier SD 6 400/K-12
PO Box 410 58220 701-265-8417
Jeff Manley, supt. Fax 265-8106
www.cavalierschool.org
Cavalier HS 100/9-12
PO Box 410 58220 701-265-8417
Sandy Laxdal, prin. Fax 265-8106

**Center, Oliver, Pop. 569**
Center-Stanton SD 1 200/K-12
PO Box 248 58530 701-794-8778
Curt Pierce, supt. Fax 794-3659
www.center.k12.nd.us/
Center-Stanton HS 100/7-12
PO Box 248 58530 701-794-8778
Tracy Peterson, prin. Fax 794-3659

**Colfax, Richland, Pop. 121**
Richland SD 44 300/K-12
PO Box 49 58018 701-372-3713
Les Dale, supt. Fax 372-3718
www.richland.k12.nd.us
Richland JSHS 100/7-12
PO Box 49 58018 701-372-3713
Bruce Anderson, prin. Fax 372-3718

**Cooperstown, Griggs, Pop. 983**
Griggs County Central SD 18 200/K-12
1207 Foster Ave NE 58425 701-797-3114
Wade Faul, supt. Fax 797-3130
www.griggs-co.k12.nd.us/
Griggs County Central HS 100/9-12
1207 Foster Ave NE 58425 701-797-3114
Travis Jordan, admin. Fax 797-3130

**Crosby, Divide, Pop. 1,064**
Divide County SD 1 300/PK-12
PO Box G 58730 701-965-6313
Dr. Sherlock Hirning, supt. Fax 965-6004
www.divide-co.k12.nd.us/
Divide County JSHS 100/7-12
PO Box G 58730 701-965-6392
Russell McKenna, prin. Fax 965-6942

**Crystal, Pembina, Pop. 137**
Valley-Edinburg SD 118
Supt. — See Edinburg
Valley-Edinburg ES 100/5-8
PO Box 129 58222 701-657-2163
Andrew Currie, prin. Fax 657-2150

**Des Lacs, Ward, Pop. 201**
United SD 7 600/PK-12
PO Box 117 58733 701-725-4334
Clarke Ranum, supt. Fax 725-4375
www.united.k12.nd.us/
Des Lacs Burlington HS 200/9-12
PO Box 117 58733 701-725-4334
Clarke Ranum, prin. Fax 725-4375

**Devils Lake, Ramsey, Pop. 6,910**
Devils Lake SD 1 1,600/PK-12
1601 College Dr N 58301 701-662-7640
Scott Privratsky, supt. Fax 662-7646
www.dlschools.org/
Central MS 500/5-8
325 7th St NE 58301 701-662-7664
Jared Schlenker, prin. Fax 662-7649
Devils Lake HS 500/9-12
1601 College Dr N 58301 701-662-1200
Ryan Hanson, prin. Fax 662-1208
Lake Area Career & Technology Center Vo/Tech
205 16th St NW 58301 701-662-7650
Christa Brodina, dir. Fax 662-7658

---

Lake Region State College Post-Sec.
1801 College Dr N 58301 701-662-1600

**Dickinson, Stark, Pop. 17,565**
Dickinson SD 1 2,800/PK-12
444 4th St W 58601 701-456-0002
Dr. Douglas Sullivan, supt. Fax 456-0035
www.dpsnd.org
Dickinson HS 800/9-12
979 13th Ave W 58601 701-456-0030
Ron Dockter, prin. Fax 456-0019
Hagen JHS 400/7-8
402 4th St W 58601 701-456-0020
Marcus Lewton, prin. Fax 456-0044
Southwest Community HS Adult
1173 3rd Ave W Ste 37 58601 701-456-0042
Jay Hepperle, prin. Fax 456-0042

---

Dickinson State University Post-Sec.
291 Campus Dr 58601 701-483-2507
Trinity HS 200/7-12
PO Box 1177 58602 701-483-6081
Steve Glasser, pres. Fax 483-1450

**Drake, McHenry, Pop. 270**
Drake SD 57 100/7-12
PO Box 256 58736 701-465-3732
Steven Heim, supt. Fax 465-3634
Drake/Anamoose HS 100/7-12
PO Box 256 58736 701-465-3732
Travis Engen, prin. Fax 465-3634

**Drayton, Pembina, Pop. 819**
Drayton SD 19 100/PK-12
108 S 5th St 58225 701-454-3324
Hy Schlieve, supt. Fax 454-3485
www.drayton.k12.nd.us/
Drayton JSHS 100/7-12
108 S 5th St 58225 701-454-3324
Dean Ralston, prin. Fax 454-3485

**Dunseith, Rolette, Pop. 742**
Dunseith SD 1 400/K-12
PO Box 789 58329 701-244-0480
Pat Brenden, supt. Fax 244-5129
www.dunseith.k12.nd.us/
Dunseith HS 200/7-12
PO Box 789 58329 701-244-5249
David Sjol, prin. Fax 244-9708

**Edgeley, LaMoure, Pop. 562**
Edgeley SD 3 200/K-12
PO Box 37 58433 701-493-2292
Richard Diegel, supt. Fax 493-2411
www.edgeley.k12.nd.us/
Edgeley HS 100/7-12
PO Box 37 58433 701-493-2292
Todd Kosel, prin. Fax 493-2411

**Edinburg, Walsh, Pop. 192**
Valley-Edinburg SD 118 100/K-12
PO Box 6 58227 701-993-8312
Mitch Jorgensen, supt. Fax 993-8313
www.edinburg.k12.nd.us
Valley-Edinburg HS 100/9-12
PO Box 6 58227 701-993-8312
Brandon Laxdal, prin. Fax 993-8313
Other Schools – See Crystal

**Edmore, Ramsey, Pop. 179**
Edmore SD 2 100/K-12
PO Box 188 58330 701-644-2281
Francis Schill, supt. Fax 644-2222
www.edmore.k12.nd.us
Edmore HS 100/7-12
PO Box 188 58330 701-644-2281
Matt Ford, prin. Fax 644-2222

**Elgin, Grant, Pop. 638**
Elgin - New Leipzig SD 49 100/K-12
PO Box 70 58533 701-584-2374
Martin Schock, supt. Fax 584-3018
www.elgin.k12.nd.us
Grant County HS 100/7-12
PO Box 70 58533 701-584-2374
Terry Bentz, prin. Fax 584-3018

**Ellendale, Dickey, Pop. 1,371**
Ellendale SD 40 300/K-12
PO Box 400 58436 701-349-3232
Jeff Fastnacht, supt. Fax 349-3447
www.ellendale.k12.nd.us
Ellendale JSHS 100/7-12
PO Box 400 58436 701-349-3232
Matthew Herman, prin. Fax 349-3447

---

Trinity Bible College Post-Sec.
50 6th Ave S 58436 701-349-3621

**Enderlin, Ransom, Pop. 884**
Enderlin Area SD 24 300/K-12
410 Bluff St 58027 701-437-2240
Tom Rettig, supt. Fax 437-2242
www.enderlin.k12.nd.us/
Enderlin Area HS 200/7-12
410 Bluff St 58027 701-437-2240
Timothy Michaelson, prin. Fax 437-2242

**Fairmount, Richland, Pop. 360**
Fairmount SD 18 100/K-12
PO Box 228 58030 701-474-5469
Ron Stahlecker, supt. Fax 474-5862
www.fairmount.k12.nd.us/
Fairmount HS 100/7-12
PO Box 228 58030 701-474-5469
Jay Townsend, prin. Fax 474-5862

**Fargo, Cass, Pop. 103,464**
Fargo SD 1 9,400/K-12
415 4th St N 58102 701-446-1000
Dr. Jeff Schatz, supt. Fax 446-1200
www.fargo.k12.nd.us
Davies HS 1,100/9-12
7150 25th St S 58104 701-446-5600
Troy Cody, prin. Fax 446-5910
Discovery MS 900/6-8
1717 40th Ave S 58104 701-446-3300
Dr. Linda Davis, prin. Fax 446-3599
Eielson MS 800/6-8
1601 13th Ave S 58103 701-446-1700
Brad Larson, prin. Fax 446-1799

Fargo North HS 1,000/9-12
801 17th Ave N 58102 701-446-2400
Andrew Dahlen, prin. Fax 446-2799
Fargo South HS 800/9-12
1840 15th Ave S 58103 701-446-2000
Dr. Todd Bertsch, prin. Fax 446-2399
Franklin MS 700/6-8
1420 8th St N 58102 701-446-3600
John Nelson, prin. Fax 446-3899
Wilson HS 100/Alt
1305 9th Ave S 58103 701-446-2800
David Burkman, prin. Fax 446-2899
Evaluation & Training Center Adult
424 9th Ave S 58103 701-241-4858
Scott Burtsfield, dir. Fax 241-4896

---

Josef's School of Hair Design Post-Sec.
627 NP Ave N 58102 701-235-0011
Moler Barber College of HairStyling Post-Sec.
16 8th St S 58103 701-232-6773
North Dakota State University Post-Sec.
PO Box 6050 58108 701-231-8011
Oak Grove Lutheran HS 300/6-12
124 N Terrace N 58102 701-237-0210
Darrin Roach, prin. Fax 297-1993
Rasmussen College Post-Sec.
4012 19th Ave S 58103 701-277-3889
Shanley HS 300/9-12
5600 25th St S 58104 701-893-3200
Sarah Crary, prin. Fax 893-3277
Sullivan MS 200/6-8
5600 25th St S 58104 701-893-3200
Leon Knodel, prin. Fax 893-3277

**Fessenden, Wells, Pop. 475**
Fessenden-Bowdon SD 25 100/PK-12
PO Box 67 58438 701-547-3296
Nancy Bollingberg, supt. Fax 547-3125
fessenden-bowdon.k12.nd.us
Fessenden-Bowdon HS 50/9-12
PO Box 67 58438 701-547-3296
Warren Strand, prin. Fax 547-3125

**Finley, Steele, Pop. 440**
Finley-Sharon SD 19 100/K-12
PO Box 448 58230 701-524-2420
Jeff Larson, supt. Fax 524-2588
www.finleysharonschool.com
Finley-Sharon HS 100/7-12
PO Box 448 58230 701-524-2420
Neil Race, supt. Fax 524-2588

**Flasher, Morton, Pop. 229**
Flasher SD 39 200/K-12
PO Box 267 58535 701-597-3355
Judy Zins, supt. Fax 597-3781
www.flasher.k12.nd.us
Flasher HS 100/7-12
PO Box 267 58535 701-597-3355
Christina Reynolds, prin. Fax 597-3781

**Fordville, Walsh, Pop. 211**
Fordville-Lankin SD 5 50/K-12
PO Box 127 58231 701-229-3297
Michael O'Brien, supt. Fax 229-3231
www.fordville-lankin.k12.nd.us/
Fordville Lankin HS 50/7-12
PO Box 127 58231 701-229-3297
Michael O'Brien, prin. Fax 229-3231

**Forman, Sargent, Pop. 501**
Sargent Central SD 6 200/PK-12
575 5th St SW 58032 701-724-3205
Michael Campbell, supt. Fax 724-3559
www.sargent.k12.nd.us
Sargent Central HS 100/7-12
575 5th St SW 58032 701-724-3205
Steve Thompson, prin. Fax 724-3559

**Fort Totten, Benson, Pop. 1,233**
Fort Totten SD 30 100/9-12
PO Box 239 58335 701-766-1400
Jeff Olson, supt. Fax 766-1475
Four Winds Community HS 100/9-12
PO Box 239 58335 701-766-1400
John Lohnes, prin. Fax 766-1475

---

Cankdeska Cikana Community College Post-Sec.
PO Box 269 58335 701-766-4415

**Fort Yates, Sioux, Pop. 181**
Fort Yates SD 4 200/6-8
9189 Highway 24 58538 701-854-2142
Linda Lawrence, admin. Fax 854-7488
Fort Yates MS 200/6-8
9189 Highway 24 58538 701-854-3819
Tomi Kuntz, prin. Fax 854-7467

---

Sitting Bull College Post-Sec.
9299 Highway 24 58538 701-854-8000

**Gackle, Logan, Pop. 308**
Gackle-Streeter SD 56 100/K-12
PO Box 375 58442 701-485-3692
Duke Larson, supt. Fax 485-3620
www.gacklestreeter.k12.nd.us/
Gackle-Streeter HS 50/7-12
PO Box 375 58442 701-485-3692
Kurt Hayes, prin. Fax 485-3620

**Garrison, McLean, Pop. 1,428**
Garrison SD 51 300/PK-12
PO Box 249 58540 701-463-2818
Steve Brannan, supt. Fax 463-2067
www.garrison.k12.nd.us/
Garrison JSHS 200/7-12
PO Box 249 58540 701-463-2818
Jim Upgren, prin. Fax 463-2067

**Glenburn, Renville, Pop. 368**
Glenburn SD 26 300/K-12
PO Box 138 58740 701-362-7426
David Wisthoff, supt. Fax 362-7349
www.glenburn.k12.nd.us/
Glenburn HS 100/7-12
PO Box 138 58740 701-362-7426
Larry Derr, prin. Fax 362-7349

**Glenfield, Foster, Pop. 91**
Midkota SD 7
Supt. — See Binford
Midkota HS 100/7-12
PO Box 98 58443 701-785-2126
Gilbert Black, prin. Fax 785-2226

**Glen Ullin, Morton, Pop. 794**
Glen Ullin SD 48 100/K-12
PO Box 548 58631 701-348-3590
John Barry, supt. Fax 348-3084
www.glen-ullin.k12.nd.us
Glen Ullin HS 100/9-12
PO Box 548 58631 701-348-3590
Peter Remboldt, prin. Fax 348-3084

**Goodrich, Sheridan, Pop. 98**
Goodrich SD 16 50/K-12
PO Box 159 58444 701-884-2469
Rodney Scherbenske, supt. Fax 884-2496
Goodrich HS 50/7-12
PO Box 159 58444 701-884-2469
Rodney Scherbenske, prin. Fax 884-2496

**Grafton, Walsh, Pop. 4,231**
Grafton SD 3 800/K-12
1548 School Rd 58237 701-352-1930
Jack Maus, supt. Fax 352-1943
www.grafton.k12.nd.us/
Grafton Central MS 200/5-8
1548 School Rd 58237 701-352-1930
Michael Kaiser, prin. Fax 352-1120
Grafton HS 300/9-12
1548 School Rd 58237 701-352-1930
Darren Albrecht, prin. Fax 352-1943
North Valley Area Career & Tech Vo/Tech
1540 School Rd 58237 701-352-3705
Mark Wagner, dir. Fax 352-3170

**Grand Forks, Grand Forks, Pop. 51,662**
Grand Forks SD 1 6,800/K-12
PO Box 6000 58206 701-746-2200
Dr. Larry P. Nybladh, supt. Fax 772-7739
www.gfschools.org
Central HS 900/9-12
115 N 4th St 58203 701-746-2375
Buck Kasowski, prin. Fax 746-2387
Community Alternative HS 100/Alt
500 Stanford Rd 58203 701-795-2777
Terry Bohan, prin. Fax 795-2770
Red River HS 1,100/9-12
2211 17th Ave S 58201 701-746-2400
Kris Arason, prin. Fax 746-2406
Schroeder MS 500/6-8
800 32nd Ave S 58201 701-746-2330
Catherine Gillach, prin. Fax 746-2332
South MS 500/6-8
1999 47th Ave S 58201 701-746-2345
Nancy Dutot, prin. Fax 746-2355
Valley MS 400/6-8
2100 5th Ave N 58203 701-746-2360
Barry Lentz, prin. Fax 746-2363

---

Josef's School of Hair Design Post-Sec.
2011 S Washington St 58201 701-772-2728
North Dakota School for the Blind Post-Sec.
500 Stanford Rd 58203
University of North Dakota Post-Sec.
264 Centennial Dr 58202 701-777-3000

**Granville, McHenry, Pop. 241**
TGU SD 60
Supt. — See Towner
TGU Granville HS 100/7-12
210 6th St SW 58741 701-728-6641
Tonya Hunskor, prin. Fax 728-6386

**Grenora, Williams, Pop. 241**
Grenora SD 99 100/K-12
PO Box 38 58845 701-694-2711
Troy Walters, supt. Fax 694-2717
www.grenora.k12.nd.us/
Grenora HS 50/7-12
PO Box 38 58845 701-694-2711
Troy Walters, prin. Fax 694-2717

**Gwinner, Sargent, Pop. 749**
North Sargent SD 3 200/K-12
PO Box 289 58040 701-678-2492
Randall Cale, supt. Fax 678-2311
www.northsargent.k12.nd.us
North Sargent HS 100/7-12
PO Box 289 58040 701-678-2492
Randal Brockman, prin. Fax 678-2311

**Halliday, Dunn, Pop. 185**
Halliday SD 19 50/K-12
PO Box 188 58636 701-938-4391
William Colter, supt. Fax 938-4373
www.halliday.k12.nd.us/
Halliday HS 50/9-12
PO Box 188 58636 701-938-4391
William Colter, prin. Fax 938-4373

**Hankinson, Richland, Pop. 903**
Hankinson SD 8 300/K-12
PO Box 220 58041 701-242-7516
Chad Benson, supt. Fax 242-7434
www.hankinson.k12.nd.us/
Hankinson HS 100/7-12
PO Box 220 58041 701-242-7138
Kent Dennis, prin. Fax 242-7434

**Harvey, Wells, Pop. 1,771**
Harvey SD 38 400/K-12
811 Burke Ave 58341 701-324-2265
Daniel Stutlien, supt. Fax 324-4414
www.harvey.k12.nd.us/
Harvey HS 100/7-12
200 North St E 58341 701-324-2267
Justin Stanley, prin. Fax 324-2424

**Hatton, Traill, Pop. 763**
Hatton Eielson SD 7 200/K-12
PO Box 200 58240 701-543-3455
Kevin Rogers, supt. Fax 543-3459
www.hatton.k12.nd.us/
Hatton Eielson HS 100/7-12
PO Box 200 58240 701-543-3455
Lucas Soine, prin. Fax 543-3459

**Hazelton, Emmons, Pop. 234**
Hazelton-Moffit-Braddock SD 6 100/K-12
PO Box 209 58544 701-782-6231
Tracy Hanzal, supt. Fax 782-6245
www.hmb.k12.nd.us/
Hazelton-Moffit-Braddock HS 50/7-12
PO Box 209 58544 701-782-6231
Tracy Hanzal, prin. Fax 782-6245

**Hazen, Mercer, Pop. 2,396**
Hazen SD 3 500/PK-12
PO Box 487 58545 701-748-2345
Michael Ness, supt. Fax 748-2342
www.hazen.k12.nd.us
Hazen HS 200/9-12
PO Box 487 58545 701-748-2345
Matthew Norby, prin. Fax 748-2342
Hazen MS 100/7-8
PO Box 487 58545 701-748-6649
Ed Boger, prin. Fax 748-6650

**Hebron, Morton, Pop. 732**
Hebron SD 13 200/K-12
PO Box Q 58638 701-878-4442
Kevin Nelson, supt. Fax 878-4345
www.hebron.k12.nd.us/
Hebron HS 100/7-12
PO Box Q 58638 701-878-4442
Stephanie Hochhalter, prin. Fax 878-4345

**Hettinger, Adams, Pop. 1,214**
Hettinger SD 13 300/PK-12
PO Box 1188 58639 701-567-4502
Larry Sebastian, supt. Fax 567-5094
www.hettinger.k12.nd.us
Hettinger HS 100/7-12
PO Box 1188 58639 701-567-4502
Greg Johnson, prin. Fax 567-5094

**Hillsboro, Traill, Pop. 1,587**
Hillsboro SD 9 400/PK-12
PO Box 579 58045 701-636-4360
Paula Pederson, supt. Fax 636-4362
www.hillsborok12.com
Hillsboro JSHS 200/7-12
PO Box 579 58045 701-636-4360
Terry Baesler, prin. Fax 636-4362

**Hope, Steele, Pop. 258**
Hope SD 10 100/7-12
PO Box 100 58046 701-945-2473
Jeffrey Watts, supt. Fax 945-2511
www.hope-page.k12.nd.us/
Hope-Page HS 100/7-12
PO Box 100 58046 701-945-2473
Dale Krueger, prin. Fax 945-2511

**Hunter, Cass, Pop. 255**
Northern Cass SD 97 500/K-12
16021 18th St SE 58048 701-874-2322
Dr. Cory Steiner, supt. Fax 874-2422
www.northerncass.k12.nd.us
Northern Cass HS 200/7-12
16021 18th St SE 58048 701-874-2322
Ryan Lyson, prin. Fax 874-2422

**Inkster, Grand Forks, Pop. 47**
Midway SD 128 200/PK-12
3202 33rd Ave NE, 701-869-2432
Dr. Roger Abbe Ed.D., supt. Fax 869-2688
www.midwayk12.org
Midway HS 100/9-12
3202 33rd Ave NE, 701-869-2432
George Lee, prin. Fax 869-2688

**Jamestown, Stutsman, Pop. 15,252**
Jamestown SD 1 2,100/PK-12
PO Box 269 58402 701-252-1950
Robert Lech, supt. Fax 251-2011
www.jamestown.k12.nd.us
Jamestown HS 700/9-12
PO Box 269 58402 701-952-4003
William Nold, prin. Fax 252-8580
Jamestown MS 500/6-8
PO Box 269 58402 701-252-0317
Ryan Harty, prin. Fax 252-3310
James Valley Area Vo-Tech Center Vo/Tech
PO Box 269 58402 701-252-8841
John Lynch, prin. Fax 252-3646

---

University of Jamestown Post-Sec.
6000 College Ln 58405 701-252-3467

**Kenmare, Ward, Pop. 1,084**
Kenmare SD 28 300/K-12
PO Box 667 58746 701-385-4996
Duane Mueller, supt. Fax 385-4390
www.kenmare.k12.nd.us/
Kenmare JSHS 100/7-12
PO Box 667 58746 701-385-4996
Angela Madsen, prin. Fax 385-4390

**Kensal, Stutsman, Pop. 163**
Kensal SD 19 — 50/K-12
803 1st Ave 58455 — 701-435-2484
Tom Tracy, supt. — Fax 435-2486
www.kensal.k12.nd.us/
Kensal HS — 50/7-12
803 1st Ave 58455 — 701-435-2484
Matthew Lokemoen, prin. — Fax 435-2486

**Killdeer, Dunn, Pop. 734**
Killdeer SD 16 — 400/PK-12
PO Box 579 58640 — 701-764-5877
Gary Wilz, supt. — Fax 764-5648
www.killdeer.k12.nd.us
Killdeer HS — 200/7-12
PO Box 579 58640 — 701-764-5877
Karter Kleeman, prin. — Fax 764-5648

**Kindred, Cass, Pop. 678**
Kindred SD 2 — 600/K-12
255 Dakota St 58051 — 701-428-3177
Steve Hall, supt. — Fax 428-3149
www.kindred.k12.nd.us/
Kindred HS — 300/7-12
255 Dakota St 58051 — 701-428-3177
Kent Packer, prin. — Fax 428-3149

**Kulm, LaMoure, Pop. 352**
Kulm SD 7 — 100/PK-12
PO Box G 58456 — 701-647-2303
Tami Kramlich, supt. — Fax 647-2304
www.kulmschools.com
Kulm JSHS — 100/7-12
PO Box G 58456 — 701-647-2303
Derrick Bopp, prin. — Fax 647-2457

**Lakota, Nelson, Pop. 665**
Lakota SD 66 — 200/K-12
PO Box 388 58344 — 701-247-2992
Joe Harder, supt. — Fax 247-2910
www.lakota.k12.nd.us
Lakota JSHS — 100/7-12
PO Box 388 58344 — 701-247-2992
Joe Harder, prin. — Fax 247-2910

**LaMoure, LaMoure, Pop. 884**
La Moure SD 8 — 300/K-12
PO Box 656 58458 — 701-883-5396
Mitch Carlson, supt. — Fax 883-5144
www.lamoure.k12.nd.us/
La Moure JSHS — 100/7-12
PO Box 656 58458 — 701-883-5397
Andrew DelaBarre, prin. — Fax 883-5144

**Langdon, Cavalier, Pop. 1,855**
Langdon Area SD 23 — 400/PK-12
715 14th Ave 58249 — 701-256-5291
Rich Rogers, supt. — Fax 256-2606
lhs.utma.com/
Langdon Area JSHS — 200/7-12
715 14th Ave 58249 — 701-256-5291
Daryl Timian, prin. — Fax 256-2606

**Larimore, Grand Forks, Pop. 1,320**
Larimore SD 44 — 400/PK-12
PO Box 769 58251 — 701-343-2366
Dr. Roger Abbe, supt. — Fax 343-2908
www.larimorek12.org
Larimore JSHS — 200/7-12
PO Box 769 58251 — 701-343-2366
Fax 343-2908

**Leeds, Benson, Pop. 425**
Leeds SD 6 — 200/PK-12
PO Box 189 58346 — 701-466-2461
Robert Bubach, supt. — Fax 466-2422
leedsdistrict.new.rschooltoday.com
Leeds JSHS — 100/9-12
PO Box 189 58346 — 701-466-2461
Robert Bubach, prin. — Fax 466-2422

**Lidgerwood, Richland, Pop. 649**
Lidgerwood SD 28 — 200/PK-12
PO Box 468 58053 — 701-538-7341
Doug Jacobson, supt. — Fax 538-4483
www.lidgerwood.k12.nd.us/
Lidgerwood HS — 100/7-12
PO Box 468 58053 — 701-538-7341
Jeremy Popp, prin. — Fax 538-4483

**Lignite, Burke, Pop. 154**
Burke Central SD 36 — 100/K-12
PO Box 91 58752 — 701-933-2821
Sherry Lalum, supt. — Fax 933-2823
www.burkecentral.k12.nd.us
Burke Central HS — 50/7-12
PO Box 91 58752 — 701-933-2821
Erika Landro, prin. — Fax 933-2823

**Linton, Emmons, Pop. 1,084**
Linton SD 36 — 300/PK-12
PO Box 970 58552 — 701-254-4138
Alan Bjornson, supt. — Fax 254-4313
www.linton.k12.nd.us
Linton HS — 100/9-12
PO Box 970 58552 — 701-254-4717
Alan Bjornson, prin. — Fax 254-4313

**Lisbon, Ransom, Pop. 2,132**
Lisbon SD 19 — 600/K-12
PO Box 593 58054 — 701-683-4106
Steven Johnson, supt. — Fax 683-4414
www.lisbon.k12.nd.us/
Lisbon HS — 200/9-12
PO Box 593 58054 — 701-683-4106
Patrick Adair, prin. — Fax 683-4414
Lisbon MS — 200/5-8
PO Box 593 58054 — 701-683-4108
Elinor Meckle, prin. — Fax 683-4111

**Mc Clusky, Sheridan, Pop. 368**
McClusky SD 19 — 100/K-12
PO Box 499 58463 — 701-363-2470
Dr. Cheri Poitra, supt. — Fax 363-2239
mcclusky.nd.schoolwebpages.com/
McClusky JSHS — 50/7-12
PO Box 499 58463 — 701-363-2470
Daniel Klemisch, prin. — Fax 363-2239

**Maddock, Benson, Pop. 380**
Maddock SD 9 — 200/K-12
PO Box 398 58348 — 701-438-2531
Kimberly Anderson, supt. — Fax 438-2620
Maddock HS — 100/9-12
PO Box 398 58348 — 701-438-2531
Kimberly Anderson, prin. — Fax 438-2620

**Makoti, Ward, Pop. 149**
Lewis and Clark SD 161
Supt. — See Berthold
North Shore HS — 100/7-12
PO Box 127 58756 — 701-726-5591
Lori Ostrem, prin. — Fax 726-5701

**Mandan, Morton, Pop. 18,009**
Mandan SD 1 — 3,300/K-12
901 Division St NW 58554 — 701-751-6500
Dr. Mike Bitz, supt. — Fax 751-6674
www.mandan.k12.nd.us
Brave Center Academy — Alt
901 Division St NW 58554 — 701-751-6500
Perry Just, prin. — Fax 751-6674
Mandan HS — 1,000/9-12
905 8th Ave NW 58554 — 701-751-6501
Mark Andresen, prin. — Fax 751-6675
Mandan MS — 800/6-8
2901 12th Ave NW 58554 — 701-751-6502
Ryan Leingang, prin. — Fax 751-6682

Marmot SD — 200/K-12
701 16th Ave SW 58554 — 701-328-6707
Penny Veit-Hetletved, supt. — Fax 328-6651
Marmot HS, 701 16th Ave SW 58554 — 100/9-12
Michelle Hoechst, prin. — 701-667-1445

**Mandaree, McKenzie, Pop. 592**
Mandaree SD 36 — 200/PK-12
PO Box 488 58757 — 701-759-3311
Carolyn Bluestone, supt. — Fax 759-3493
www.mandaree.k12.nd.us/
Mandaree HS — 50/9-12
PO Box 488 58757 — 701-759-3311
Lance Jackson, prin. — Fax 759-3112

**Marion, LaMoure, Pop. 131**
Litchville-Marion SD 46 — 100/PK-12
PO Box 159 58466 — 701-669-2262
Steven Larson, supt. — Fax 669-2316
www.litchville-marion.k12.nd.us/
Litchville-Marion JSHS — 100/7-12
PO Box 159 58466 — 701-669-2261
Marc Ritteman, prin. — Fax 669-2316

**Max, McLean, Pop. 324**
Max SD 50 — 200/K-12
PO Box 297 58759 — 701-679-2685
Pat Windish, supt. — Fax 679-2245
www.max.k12.nd.us/
Max HS — 100/7-12
PO Box 297 58759 — 701-679-2685
Robert Randel, prin. — Fax 679-2245

**Mayville, Traill, Pop. 1,819**
May-Port CG SD 14 — 500/K-12
900 Main St W 58257 — 701-788-2281
Michael Bradner, supt. — Fax 788-2959
www.mayportcg.com/
Mayville-Portland CG HS — 200/9-12
900 Main St W 58257 — 701-788-2281
Scott Ulland, prin. — Fax 788-2959
Mayville-Portland CG MS — 100/6-8
900 Main St W 58257 — 701-788-2281
Jeffrey Houdek, prin. — Fax 788-2959

---

Mayville State University — Post-Sec.
330 3rd St NE 58257 — 800-437-4104

**Medina, Stutsman, Pop. 298**
Medina SD 3 — 100/PK-12
PO Box 547 58467 — 701-486-3121
Brian Christopherson, supt. — Fax 486-3138
www.medina.k12.nd.us/
Medina JSHS — 100/7-12
PO Box 547 58467 — 701-486-3121
Brian Christopherson, admin. — Fax 486-3138

**Milnor, Sargent, Pop. 648**
Milnor SD 2 — 200/K-12
PO Box 369 58060 — 701-427-5237
Diann Aberle M.Ed., supt. — Fax 427-5304
www.milnor.k12.nd.us/
Milnor HS — 100/7-12
PO Box 369 58060 — 701-427-5237
Christopher Larson, prin. — Fax 427-5304
Sundale Colony S — 50/K-10
PO Box 369 58060 — 701-427-5237
Diann Aberle M.Ed., supt. — Fax 427-5304

**Minnewaukan, Benson, Pop. 217**
Minnewaukan SD 5 — 200/K-12
4675 Highway 281 58351 — 701-473-5306
Jean Callahan, supt. — Fax 473-5420
www.minnewaukan.k12.nd.us/
Minnewaukan S — 200/K-12
4675 Highway 281 58351 — 701-473-5306
Jean Callahan, prin. — Fax 473-5420

**Minot, Ward, Pop. 39,893**
Minot SD 1 — 6,800/PK-12
215 2nd St SE 58701 — 701-857-4400
Dr. Mark Vollmer, supt. — Fax 857-4432
www.minot.k12.nd.us/
Central Campus HS — 1,000/9-10
215 1st St SE 58701 — 701-857-4660
Keith Altendorf, prin. — Fax 857-4636
Hill MS — 700/6-8
1000 6th St SW 58701 — 701-857-4477
Michael Arlien, prin. — Fax 857-4479
Magic City Campus HS — 900/11-12
1100 11th Ave SW 58701 — 701-857-4500
Scott Faul, prin. — Fax 857-4521
Ramstad MS — 500/6-8
1215 36th Ave NW 58703 — 701-857-4466
Ione Sautner, prin. — Fax 857-4464
Souris River Campus Alternative HS — 100/Alt
1510 University Ave W 58703 — 701-857-4496
Ned Strand, prin. — Fax 857-4508
Minot Adult Learning Center — Adult
1609 4th Ave NW 58703 — 701-857-4488
Fax 857-4489

Other Schools – See Minot AFB

---

Bishop Ryan S — 400/PK-12
316 11th Ave NW 58703 — 701-852-4004
Darwin Routledje, prin. — Fax 839-4651
Headquarters Academy of Hair Design — Post-Sec.
108 Main St S 58701 — 701-852-8329
Minot State University — Post-Sec.
500 University Ave W 58707 — 701-858-3000
Our Redeemer's Christian S — 300/PK-12
700 16th Ave SE 58701 — 701-839-0772
Charles Strand, admin. — Fax 858-0994
Trinity Medical Center — Post-Sec.
3 Burdick Expy 58701 — 701-857-5000

**Minot AFB, Ward, Pop. 5,179**
Minot SD 1
Supt. — See Minot
Memorial MS — 100/7-8
1 Rocket Rd 58704 — 701-727-3300
Thomas Holtz, prin. — Fax 727-3303

**Minto, Walsh, Pop. 603**
Minto SD 20 — 200/PK-12
200 4th St 58261 — 701-248-3479
Linda Lutovsky, supt. — Fax 248-3001
www.minto.k12.nd.us/
Minto HS — 100/7-12
200 4th St 58261 — 701-248-3479
Shane Robinson, prin. — Fax 248-3001

**Mohall, Renville, Pop. 775**
Mohall-Lansford-Sherwood SD 1 — 300/PK-12
PO Box 187 58761 — 701-756-6660
Kelly Taylor, supt. — Fax 756-6549
www.mls.k12.nd.us//index.html
MLS - Mohall HS — 200/7-12
PO Box 187 58761 — 701-756-6660
Allen Oberlander, prin. — Fax 756-6549

**Montpelier, Stutsman, Pop. 87**
Montpelier SD 14 — 100/PK-12
214 7th Ave 58472 — 701-489-3348
Jerry Waagen, supt. — Fax 489-3349
www.montpelier.k12.nd.us
Montpelier HS — 100/7-12
214 7th Ave 58472 — 701-489-3348
Timothy Godfrey, prin. — Fax 489-3349

**Mott, Hettinger, Pop. 709**
Mott-Regent SD 1 — 200/K-12
205 Dakota Ave 58646 — 701-824-2795
Myron Schweitzer, supt. — Fax 824-2249
mott.nd.schoolwebpages.com/
Mott / Regent HS — 100/7-12
205 Dakota Ave 58646 — 701-824-2795
Adam Hill, prin. — Fax 824-2249

**Munich, Cavalier, Pop. 209**
Munich SD 19 — 100/PK-12
PO Box 39 58352 — 701-682-5321
Dr. Charles Dunlop, supt. — Fax 682-5323
www.munich.k12.nd.us/
Munich HS — 50/9-12
PO Box 39 58352 — 701-682-5321
Daniel Ludrigson, prin. — Fax 682-5323

**Napoleon, Logan, Pop. 791**
Napoleon SD 2 — 300/K-12
PO Box 69 58561 — 701-754-2244
John Jankowski, supt. — Fax 754-2233
www.napoleon.k12.nd.us/
Napoleon HS — 100/7-12
PO Box 69 58561 — 701-754-2244
John Jankowski, prin. — Fax 754-2233

**Newburg, Bottineau, Pop. 110**
Newburg - United SD 54 — 100/PK-12
PO Box 427 58762 — 701-272-6151
Jason Kertsen, supt. — Fax 272-6117
www.newburg.k12.nd.us/
Newburg United HS — 50/7-12
PO Box 427 58762 — 701-272-6151
Bob Beaudrie, prin. — Fax 272-6117

**New England, Hettinger, Pop. 588**
New England SD 9 — 200/K-12
PO Box 307 58647 — 701-579-4160
Kelly Koppinger, supt. — Fax 579-4462
www.new-england.k12.nd.us
New England HS — 100/7-12
PO Box 307 58647 — 701-579-4160
Lawrence Lechler, prin. — Fax 579-4462

**New Rockford, Eddy, Pop. 1,375**
New Rockford-Sheyenne SD 2 300/K-12
437 1st Ave N 58356 701-947-5036
Jill Louters, supt. Fax 947-2195
www.newrockford-sheyenne.k12.nd.us
New Rockford-Sheyenne HS 200/7-12
437 1st Ave N 58356 701-947-5036
Natalie Becker, prin. Fax 947-2195

**New Salem, Morton, Pop. 936**
New Salem-Almont SD 49 300/PK-12
PO Box 378 58563 701-843-7610
Michael Severson, supt. Fax 843-7011
www.newsalem.k12.nd.us/
New Salem-Almont HS 200/7-12
PO Box 378 58563 701-843-7610
Michael Gilbertson, prin. Fax 843-7011

**New Town, Mountrail, Pop. 1,853**
New Town SD 1 700/K-12
PO Box 700 58763 701-627-3650
Marc Bluestone, supt. Fax 627-3689
www.new-town.k12.nd.us/
New Town HS 200/9-12
PO Box 700 58763 701-627-3658
John Gartner, prin. Fax 627-3689
New Town MS 200/6-8
PO Box 700 58763 701-627-3660
Andy Decoteau, prin. Fax 627-3689

---

Fort Berthold Community College Post-Sec.
PO Box 490 58763 701-627-4738

**Northwood, Grand Forks, Pop. 931**
Northwood SD 129 200/K-12
420 Trojan Rd 58267 701-587-5221
Keith Arneson, supt. Fax 587-5423
www.northwoodk12.com
Northwood HS 100/7-12
420 Trojan Rd 58267 701-587-5221
Daniel Azure, prin. Fax 587-5423

**Oakes, Dickey, Pop. 1,836**
Oakes SD 41 500/PK-12
804 Main Ave 58474 701-742-3234
Joshua Johnson, supt. Fax 742-2812
www.oakes.k12.nd.us
Oakes JSHS 200/7-12
804 Main Ave 58474 701-742-3234
Dawn Osborn, prin. Fax 742-2812
Other Schools – See Wahpeton

**Park River, Walsh, Pop. 1,393**
Park River Area SD 8 300/K-12
PO Box 240 58270 701-284-7164
Kirk Ham, supt. Fax 284-7936
www.parkriver.k12.nd.us/
Park River HS 100/7-12
PO Box 240 58270 701-284-7164
Aaron Schramm, prin. Fax 284-7936

**Parshall, Mountrail, Pop. 852**
Parshall SD 3 300/PK-12
PO Box 158 58770 701-862-3129
Dr. John Weidner, supt. Fax 862-3801
www.parshall.k12.nd.us
Parshall JSHS 100/7-12
PO Box 158 58770 701-862-3129
Mark Grueneich, prin. Fax 862-3801

**Pembina, Pembina, Pop. 576**
North Border SD 100
Supt. — See Walhalla
North Border Pembina HS 50/9-12
155 S 3rd St 58271 701-825-6261
Lee Beattie, prin. Fax 825-6645
North Border Pembina MS 50/7-8
155 S 3rd St 58271 701-825-6261
Lee Beattie, prin. Fax 825-6645

**Petersburg, Nelson, Pop. 192**
Dakota Prairie SD 1 300/K-12
PO Box 37 58272 701-345-8233
Janet Edlund, supt. Fax 345-8251
www.dakotaprairie.k12.nd.us/
Dakota Prairie HS 100/7-12
PO Box 37 58272 701-345-8233
Jay Slade, prin. Fax 345-8251

**Pingree, Stutsman, Pop. 59**
Pingree-Buchanan SD 10 200/K-12
111 Lincoln Ave 58476 701-252-5563
Daren Christianson, supt. Fax 252-2245
www.pingree.k12.nd.us/
Pingree Buchanan JSHS 100/7-12
111 Lincoln Ave 58476 701-252-5563
Daren Christianson, prin. Fax 252-2245

**Powers Lake, Burke, Pop. 279**
Powers Lake SD 27 100/K-12
PO Box 346 58773 701-464-5432
Marlyn Vatne, supt. Fax 464-5435
www.powerslake.k12.nd.us/
Powers Lake JSHS 100/7-12
PO Box 346 58773 701-464-5432
Susan Gunderson, prin. Fax 464-5435

**Ray, Williams, Pop. 585**
Nesson SD 2 200/K-12
PO Box 564 58849 701-568-3301
Benjamin Schafer, supt. Fax 568-3302
www.ray.k12.nd.us
Ray HS 100/7-12
PO Box 564 58849 701-568-3301
Arley Larson, prin. Fax 568-3302

**Richardton, Stark, Pop. 528**
Richardton-Taylor SD 34 300/K-12
PO Box 289 58652 701-974-2111
Brent Bautz, supt. Fax 974-2161
www.richardton-taylor.k12.nd.us
Richardton-Taylor HS 100/7-12
PO Box 289 58652 701-974-2111
Russell Ziegler, prin. Fax 974-2161

**Rolette, Rolette, Pop. 566**
Rolette SD 29 100/K-12
PO Box 97 58366 701-246-3595
Wade Sherwin, supt. Fax 246-3452
www.rolettepublicschools.com
Rolette JSHS 50/7-12
PO Box 97 58366 701-246-3595
Katie Crofutt, prin. Fax 246-3452

**Rolla, Rolette, Pop. 1,226**
Mt. Pleasant SD 4 200/PK-12
201 5th St NE 58367 701-477-3151
Kevin Baumgarn, supt. Fax 477-5001
www.rolla.k12.nd.us
Mt. Pleasant HS 100/7-12
201 5th St NE 58367 701-477-3151
Randy Loing, prin. Fax 477-5001

**Rugby, Pierce, Pop. 2,841**
Rugby SD 5 600/PK-12
1123 S Main Ave 58368 701-776-5201
Michael McNeff, supt. Fax 776-5091
www.rugby.k12.nd.us/
North Central Area Career & Tech Ctr Vo/Tech
1123 S Main Ave 58368 701-776-7208
Kathy McCracken, dir. Fax 776-5091
Rugby JSHS 300/7-12
1123 S Main Ave 58368 701-776-5201
Jared Blikre, prin. Fax 776-5091

**Saint John, Rolette, Pop. 309**
Saint John SD 3 400/K-12
PO Box 200 58369 701-477-5651
Donald Davis, supt. Fax 477-8195
www.stjohn.k12.nd.us
Saint John HS 100/9-12
PO Box 200 58369 701-477-5651
Charles Anderson, prin. Fax 477-8195

**Saint Thomas, Pembina, Pop. 330**
Saint Thomas SD 43 100/K-12
PO Box 150 58276 701-257-6424
Darren Albrecht, supt. Fax 257-6461
www.stthomas.k12.nd.us
Saint Thomas HS 50/7-12
PO Box 150 58276 701-257-6424
David Hanson, prin. Fax 257-6461

**Sawyer, Ward, Pop. 354**
Sawyer SD 16 100/K-12
25 1st Ave SW 58781 701-624-5167
George Duenas, admin. Fax 624-5482
www.sawyer.k12.nd.us
Sawyer HS 100/7-12
25 1st Ave SW 58781 701-624-5167
George Duenas, prin. Fax 624-5482

**Scranton, Bowman, Pop. 279**
Scranton SD 33 100/K-12
PO Box 126 58653 701-275-8897
John Pretzer, supt. Fax 275-6221
www.scrantonpublicschool.homestead.com/
Scranton HS 100/7-12
PO Box 126 58653 701-275-8266
John Pretzer, prin. Fax 275-6221

**Selfridge, Sioux, Pop. 151**
Selfridge SD 8 100/K-12
PO Box 45 58568 701-422-3353
James Gross, supt. Fax 422-3348
Selfridge HS 50/7-12
PO Box 45 58568 701-422-3353
James Gross, prin. Fax 422-3348

**Solen, Sioux, Pop. 73**
Solen SD 3 200/K-12
PO Box 128 58570 701-445-3331
Justin Fryer, supt. Fax 445-3323
Solen HS 100/7-12
PO Box 128 58570 701-445-3331
Jeffrey Brandt, prin. Fax 445-3323

**South Heart, Stark, Pop. 298**
South Heart SD 9 200/PK-12
PO Box 159 58655 701-677-5671
Calvin Dean, supt. Fax 677-5616
www.southheart.k12.nd.us/
South Heart HS 100/7-12
PO Box 159 58655 701-677-5671
Scott Jung, prin. Fax 677-5616

**Stanley, Mountrail, Pop. 1,448**
Stanley SD 2 600/K-12
PO Box 10 58784 701-628-3811
Tim Holte, supt. Fax 628-3358
www.stanley.k12.nd.us/
Stanley JSHS 300/7-12
PO Box 10 58784 701-628-2342
Jim Swegarden, prin. Fax 628-3358

**Starkweather, Ramsey, Pop. 114**
Starkweather SD 44 100/PK-12
PO Box 45 58377 701-292-4381
Tony Grubb, supt. Fax 292-5714
www.starkweather.k12.nd.us/
Starkweather HS 50/7-12
PO Box 45 58377 701-292-4381
Tony Grubb, prin. Fax 292-5714

**Steele, Kidder, Pop. 715**
Kidder County SD 1 400/K-12
PO Box 380 58482 701-475-2243
Ken Miller, supt. Fax 475-2737
www.steele-dawson.k12.nd.us/
Steele-Dawson HS 200/7-12
PO Box 380 58482 701-475-2243
Darnell Schmidt, prin. Fax 475-2737
Other Schools – See Tappen

**Strasburg, Emmons, Pop. 408**
Strasburg SD 15 100/K-12
PO Box 308 58573 701-336-2667
Mark Mindt, prin. Fax 336-7490
www.strasburg.k12.nd.us/
Strasburg JSHS 100/7-12
PO Box 308 58573 701-336-2667
Mark Mindt, prin. Fax 336-7490

**Surrey, Ward, Pop. 914**
Surrey SD 41 400/PK-12
PO Box 40 58785 701-839-8867
Kevin Klassen, supt. Fax 838-8822
www.surrey.k12.nd.us
Surrey HS 200/7-12
PO Box 40 58785 701-838-3282
David Gerding, prin. Fax 838-1262

**Tappen, Kidder, Pop. 197**
Kidder County SD 1
Supt. — See Steele
Tappen HS 50/9-12
PO Box 127 58487 701-327-4256
David Goetz, prin. Fax 327-4255

**Thompson, Grand Forks, Pop. 982**
Thompson SD 61 400/K-12
424 3rd St 58278 701-599-2765
John Maus, supt. Fax 599-2819
www.tps-k12.org
Thompson HS 200/7-12
424 3rd St 58278 701-599-2765
John Maus, supt. Fax 599-2819

**Tioga, Williams, Pop. 1,208**
Tioga SD 15 300/K-12
PO Box 279 58852 701-664-2333
Carolyn Eide, supt. Fax 664-3356
www.tioga.k12.nd.us
Tioga HS 200/7-12
PO Box 279 58852 701-664-3606
Brodie Odegaard, prin. Fax 664-3356

**Tower City, Cass, Pop. 251**
Maple Valley SD 4 200/K-12
PO Box 168 58071 701-749-2570
Dr. Brian Wolf, supt. Fax 749-2313
www.maple-valley.k12.nd.us/
Maple Valley HS 100/7-12
PO Box 168 58071 701-749-2570
Wayne Samson, prin. Fax 749-2313

**Towner, McHenry, Pop. 528**
TGU SD 60 300/PK-12
PO Box 270 58788 701-537-5414
Debby Marshall, supt. Fax 537-5413
www.granville.k12.nd.us
TGU Towner HS 50/9-12
PO Box 270 58788 701-537-5414
Erik Sveet, prin. Fax 537-5413
Other Schools – See Granville

**Trenton, Williams**
Eight Mile SD 6 200/K-12
PO Box 239 58853 701-774-8221
Stephen Cascaden, supt. Fax 774-8040
www.eight-mile.k12.nd.us
Eight Mile HS 100/9-12
PO Box 239 58853 701-774-8221
Steve Morben, prin. Fax 774-8040

**Turtle Lake, McLean, Pop. 570**
Turtle Lake - Mercer SD 72 200/K-12
PO Box 160 58575 701-448-2365
Dick Schaffan, supt. Fax 448-2368
www.tlm.k12.nd.us/
Turtle Lake Mercer HS 100/7-12
PO Box 160 58575 701-448-2365
Daren Kurle, prin. Fax 448-2368

**Underwood, McLean, Pop. 762**
Underwood SD 8 200/PK-12
PO Box 100 58576 701-442-3201
Brandt Dick, supt. Fax 442-3274
sites.google.com/a/underwoodschool.org/ups/
Underwood HS 100/7-12
PO Box 100 58576 701-442-3201
Lee Weisgarber, prin. Fax 442-3274

**Valley City, Barnes, Pop. 6,490**
Valley City SD 2 1,100/PK-12
460 Central Ave N 58072 701-845-0483
Dean Koppelman, supt. Fax 845-4109
www.valley-city.k12.nd.us
Sheyenne Valley Area Career & Tech Ctr. Vo/Tech
801 Valley Ave SE 58072 701-845-0256
Jeffrey Bopp, prin. Fax 845-0003
Valley City HS 400/9-12
460 Central Ave N 58072 701-845-0483
Kristi Brandt, prin. Fax 845-2762
Valley City JHS 200/7-8
460 Central Ave N 58072 701-845-0483
Dan Larson, prin. Fax 845-2762

---

Valley City State University Post-Sec.
101 College St SW 58072 800-532-8641

**Velva, McHenry, Pop. 1,077**
Velva SD 1 400/K-12
PO Box 179 58790 701-338-2022
Dave Schoch, supt. Fax 338-2023
www.velva.k12.nd.us
Velva HS 200/7-12
PO Box 179 58790 701-338-2022
Kelly Mogen, prin. Fax 338-2023

**Wahpeton, Richland, Pop. 7,637**
Oakes SD 41
Supt. — See Oakes

SE Rgn Career & Tech-Oakes Ctr Vo/Tech
2101 9th St N 58075 701-642-8701
Dan Rood, dir. Fax 642-3811

Wahpeton SD 37 1,200/PK-12
PO Box 10 58074 701-642-6741
Rick Jacobson, supt. Fax 642-4908
www.wahpeton.k12.nd.us
SE Region Career & Tech-Wahpeton Ctr Vo/Tech
2101 9th St N 58075 701-642-8701
Dan Rood, dir. Fax 642-3811
Wahpeton HS 400/9-12
PO Box 10 58074 701-642-2604
Ned Clooten, prin. Fax 642-1330
Wahpeton MS 300/6-8
PO Box 10 58074 701-642-6687
Beverly Jacobson, prin. Fax 642-5622

---

North Dakota State College of Science Post-Sec.
800 6th St N 58076 800-342-4325

**Walhalla, Pembina, Pop. 969**
North Border SD 100 400/K-12
PO Box 558 58282 701-549-3751
Dr. Paul Stremick, supt. Fax 549-3753
www.northborder.k12.nd.us
North Border Walhalla HS 100/9-12
PO Box 558 58282 701-549-3751
Jeff Carpenter, prin. Fax 549-3753
Other Schools – See Pembina

**Warwick, Benson, Pop. 65**
Warwick SD 29 300/PK-12
210 4th Ave 58381 701-294-2561
Dean Dauphinais, supt. Fax 294-2626
www.warwick.k12.nd.us
Warwick HS 100/7-12
210 4th Ave 58381 701-294-2561
Tara Thomas, prin. Fax 294-2626

**Washburn, McLean, Pop. 1,238**
Washburn SD 4 300/K-12
PO Box 280 58577 701-462-3228
Brad Rinas, supt. Fax 462-3561
sites.google.com/site/washburnk12/
Washburn HS 100/7-12
PO Box 280 58577 701-462-3221
Glen Weinmann, prin. Fax 462-3561

**Watford City, McKenzie, Pop. 1,714**
McKenzie County SD 1 700/K-12
PO Box 589 58854 701-444-3626
Steven Holen, supt. Fax 444-6345
www.watford-city.k12.nd.us/
Watford City JSHS 300/7-12
PO Box 589 58854 701-444-3624
Terry Vanderpan, prin. Fax 444-3612

---

Johnson Corners Christian Academy 50/K-12
11008 Highway 23 58854 701-675-2359
Adrian Timmons, admin. Fax 675-2357

**West Fargo, Cass, Pop. 25,407**
West Fargo SD 6 7,800/PK-12
207 Main Ave W 58078 701-356-2000
Dr. David Flowers, supt. Fax 356-2009
www.west-fargo.k12.nd.us
Cheney MS 1,400/6-8
825 17th Ave E 58078 701-356-2090
Don Lennon, prin. Fax 356-2099
Community HS Alt
109 3rd St E 58078 701-356-2008
Dr. Thomas Gravel, prin. Fax 234-9305
Liberty MS 700/6-8
801 36th Ave E 58078 701-356-2671
Michelle Weber, prin. Fax 356-2679
Sheyenne HS 600/9-12
800 40th Ave E 58078 701-356-2160
Dr. Greg Grooters, prin. Fax 356-2169
West Fargo HS 1,500/9-12
801 9th St E 58078 701-356-2050
Dr. Jennifer Fremstad, prin. Fax 356-2060

**Westhope, Bottineau, Pop. 415**
Westhope SD 17 100/K-12
PO Box 406 58793 701-245-6444
John Gruenberg, supt. Fax 245-6418
www.westhope.k12.nd.us/
Westhope HS 100/7-12
PO Box 406 58793 701-245-6444
John Gruenberg, supt. Fax 245-6418

**Williston, Williams, Pop. 14,321**
New SD 8 200/K-8
111 7th Ave W 58801 701-572-6359
Rob Turner, supt. Fax 572-9311
www.district8.k12.nd.us/
Stoney Creek MS 100/6-8
111 7th Ave W 58801 701-572-3579
Steven Guglich, prin. Fax 572-2731

Williston SD 1 2,800/K-12
PO Box 1407 58802 701-572-1580
Dr. Viola LaFontaine, supt. Fax 572-3547
www.williston.k12.nd.us
Del Easton Alternative HS 50/Alt
PO Box 1407 58802 701-572-0967
Audrey Larson, prin.
Williston HS 800/9-12
PO Box 1407 58802 701-572-0967
Jason Germundson, prin. Fax 572-5449
Williston MS 400/7-8
PO Box 1407 58802 701-572-5618
Duane Noeske, prin. Fax 774-3109

---

Williston State College Post-Sec.
1410 University Ave 58801 701-774-4200

Williston Trinity Christian S 200/PK-12
2419 9th Ave W 58801 701-774-9056
Cory Fleck, prin. Fax 774-3158

**Wilton, McLean, Pop. 705**
Wilton SD 1 200/PK-12
PO Box 249 58579 701-734-6559
Barbara Kady, supt. Fax 734-6944
www.wilton.k12.nd.us
Wilton HS 100/7-12
PO Box 249 58579 701-734-6331
Andrew Jordan, prin. Fax 734-6944

**Wimbledon, Barnes, Pop. 210**
Barnes County North SD 7 300/PK-12
PO Box 255 58492 701-646-6202
Mark Lindahl, supt. Fax 646-6566
www.barnescountynorth.k12.nd.us/
Barnes County North S 300/PK-12
PO Box 255 58492 701-646-6202
Joan Klein, prin. Fax 646-6566

**Wing, Burleigh, Pop. 148**
Wing SD 28 100/K-12
PO Box 130 58494 701-943-2319
Dr. John Tufte, supt. Fax 943-2318
www.wing.k12.nd.us
Wing HS 50/7-12
PO Box 130 58494 701-943-2319
Dr. John Tufte, prin. Fax 943-2318

**Wishek, McIntosh, Pop. 999**
Wishek SD 19 200/PK-12
PO Box 247 58495 701-452-2892
Shawn Kuntz, supt. Fax 452-4273
www.wishek.k12.nd.us
Wishek JSHS 100/7-12
PO Box 247 58495 701-452-2892
Yvonne Engelhart, prin. Fax 452-4273

**Wolford, Pierce, Pop. 36**
Wolford SD 1 50/K-12
401 3rd Ave SW 58385 701-583-2387
Larry Zavada, supt. Fax 583-2519
www.wolford.k12.nd.us/
Wolford HS 50/7-12
401 3rd Ave SW 58385 701-583-2387
Joel Braaten, prin. Fax 583-2519

**Wyndmere, Richland, Pop. 423**
Wyndmere SD 42 200/K-12
PO Box 190 58081 701-439-2287
Chris Swenson, supt. Fax 439-2804
Wyndmere HS 100/7-12
PO Box 190 58081 701-439-2287
Scott Strenge, prin. Fax 439-2804

**Zeeland, McIntosh, Pop. 86**
Zeeland SD 4 100/K-12
PO Box 2 58581 701-423-5429
Corbley Ogren, supt. Fax 423-5465
www.zeeland.k12.nd.us/
Zeeland HS 50/7-12
PO Box 2 58581 701-423-5429
Corbley Ogren, prin. Fax 423-5465

# OHIO

## OHIO DEPARTMENT OF EDUCATION
## 25 S Front St, Columbus 43215-4183
## Telephone 877-644-6338
## Website http://www.ode.state.oh.us

Superintendent of Public Instruction Dr. Richard Ross

## OHIO BOARD OF EDUCATION
## 25 S Front St, Columbus 43215-4176

President Debe Terhar

### EDUCATIONAL SERVICE CENTERS (ESC)

Allen County ESC
Dr. Dean Wittwer, supt. 419-222-1836
1920 Slabtown Rd, Lima 45801 Fax 224-0718
www.allencountyesc.org/

Ashtabula County ESC
John Rubesich, supt. 440-576-9023
4200 State Rd, Ashtabula 44004 Fax 576-3065
www.acesc.k12.oh.us

Athens-Meigs Counties ESC
Ricky Edwards, supt. 740-797-0064
PO Box 40, Chauncey 45719 Fax 797-0070
www.athensmeigs.org

Auglaize County ESC
Ann Harvey, supt. 419-738-3422
1045 Dearbaugh Ave Ste 2 Fax 738-1267
Wapakoneta 45895
www.auglaizeesc.org

Brown County ESC
James Frazier, supt. 937-378-6118
9231 Hamer Rd Fax 378-4286
Georgetown 45121
brown.k12.oh.us

Butler County ESC
Jon Graft, supt. 513-887-3710
400 N Erie Hwy Ste A Fax 887-3709
Hamilton 45011
www.bcesc.org

Clark County ESC
Dan Bennett Ph.D., supt. 937-325-7671
25 W Pleasant St Fax 325-9915
Springfield 45506
www.clarkesc.org/

Clermont County ESC
Jeff Weir, supt. 513-735-8300
2400 Clermont Center Dr Fax 735-8371
Batavia 45103
www.ccesc.org/

Columbiana County ESC
Anna Vaughn, supt. 330-424-9591
38720 Saltwell Rd, Lisbon 44432 Fax 424-9481
www.ccesc.k12.oh.us/

Darke County ESC
Michael Gray, supt. 937-548-4915
5279 Education Dr Fax 548-8920
Greenville 45331
www.darke.k12.oh.us

East Central Ohio ESC
Kevin Spears, supt., 834 E High Ave 330-308-9939
New Philadelphia 44663 Fax 308-0964
www.ecoesc.org

ESC of Central Ohio
Dr. Tom Goodney, supt. 614-445-3750
2080 Citygate Dr, Columbus 43219 Fax 445-3767
www.escofcentralohio.org

ESC of Cuyahoga County
Dr. Robert Mengerink, supt. 216-524-3000
6393 Oak Tree Blvd Fax 524-3683
Independence 44131
www.esc-cc.org/

ESC of Lake Erie West
Sandra C. Frisch, supt. 419-245-4150
2275 Collingwood Blvd Fax 245-4186
Toledo 43620
www.esclakeeriewest.org

ESC of Lorain County
Greg Ring, supt. 440-324-5777
1885 Lake Ave, Elyria 44035 Fax 324-7355
www.loraincountyesc.org

ESC of Medina County
William Koran, supt. 330-723-6393
124 W Washington St Fax 723-0573
Medina 44256
www.medina-esc.org/

Fairfield County ESC
Marie Ward, supt. 740-653-3193
955 Liberty Dr, Lancaster 43130 Fax 653-4053
faircoesc.org/

Gallia-Vinton Counties ESC
Dr. Denise Shockley, supt. 740-245-0593
PO Box 178, Rio Grande 45674 Fax 245-0596
www.galliavintonesc.org

Geauga County ESC
Matthew Galemmo, supt. 440-279-1700
470 Center St Bldg 2 Fax 286-7106
Chardon 44024
www.geaugaesc.org

Greene County ESC
Terry Graves-Strieter, supt. 937-767-1303
360 E Enon Rd Fax 767-1025
Yellow Springs 45387
www.greeneesc.org

Hamilton County ESC
David Distel, supt. 513-674-4251
11083 Hamilton Ave Fax 742-5525
Cincinnati 45231
www.hcesc.org/

Hancock County ESC
Larry Busdeker, supt. 419-422-7525
7746 County Road 140 Fax 422-8766
Findlay 45840
hancockesc.org

Jefferson County ESC
George Ash, supt. 740-283-3347
2023 Sunset Blvd Fax 283-2709
Steubenville 43952
www.jcesc.k12.oh.us

Knox County ESC
Timm Mackley, supt. 740-393-6767
308 Martinsburg Rd Fax 393-6812
Mount Vernon 43050
www.kcesc.org

Lake County ESC
Dr. Brian Bontempo, supt. 440-350-2563
382 Blackbrook Rd Fax 350-2566
Painesville 44077
www.esc-lc.org/

Lawrence County ESC
Dr. James Payne, supt. 740-532-4223
111 S 4th St, Ironton 45638 Fax 532-7226
www.lawrencecountyesc.com

Licking County ESC
Dr. Nelson McCray, supt. 740-349-6084
145 N Quentin Rd, Newark 43055 Fax 349-6107
www.lcesc.org/

Madison-Champaign ESC
Dr. Daniel Kaffenbarger, supt. 937-484-1557
1512 S US Highway 68 J100 Fax 484-1571
Urbana 43078
www.mccesc.k12.oh.us

Mahoning County ESC
Ronald Iarussi, supt. 330-965-7828
100 DeBartolo Pl Ste 220 Fax 965-7902
Youngstown 44512
www.mahoningesc.org/

Mercer County ESC
Shelly Vaughn, supt. 419-586-6628
441 E Market St, Celina 45822 Fax 586-3377
www.mercercountyesc.org/

Miami County ESC
Tom Dunn, supt. 937-339-5100
2000 W Stanfield Rd, Troy 45373 Fax 339-3256
www.miami.k12.oh.us/

Mid-Ohio ESC
Linda Keller, supt. 419-774-5520
890 W 4th St Ste 100 Fax 774-5523
Mansfield 44906
www.moesc.net/

Midwest Regional ESC
Heather O'Donnell, supt. 937-599-5195
121 S Opera St Fax 599-1959
Bellefontaine 43311
www.mresc.org

Montgomery County ESC
Frank DePalma, supt. 937-225-4598
200 S Keowee St, Dayton 45402 Fax 496-7426
www.mcesc.org/

Muskingum Valley ESC
David Branch, supt. 740-452-4518
205 N 7th St, Zanesville 43701 Fax 455-6702
www.mvesc.org

North Central Ohio ESC
Dr. James Lahoski, supt. 419-447-2927
928 W Market St Ste A, Tiffin 44883 Fax 447-2825
www.ncoesc.org/

North Point ESC
Doug Crooks, supt. 419-627-3900
1210 E Bogart Rd, Sandusky 44870 Fax 627-3999
www.npesc.org

Northwest Ohio ESC
Kerri Gearhart, supt. 567-444-4800
205 Nolan Pkwy, Archbold 43502 Fax 444-4802
www.nwoesc.org

Ohio Valley ESC
Chris Keylor, supt. 740-439-3558
128 E 8th St, Cambridge 43725 Fax 439-0012
www.ovesc.k12.oh.us

Pickaway County ESC
Tyrus Ankrom, supt. 740-474-7529
2050 Stoneridge Dr Fax 474-7251
Circleville 43113
pickawayesc.org/

Portage County ESC
Joseph Iacano, supt. 330-297-1436
326 E Main St, Ravenna 44266 Fax 297-1113
www.portage-esc.org

Preble County ESC
Kevin Turner, supt. 937-456-1187
597 Hillcrest Dr, Eaton 45320 Fax 456-3253
www.preblecountyesc.org

Putnam County ESC
Dr. Jan Osborn, supt. 419-523-5951
124 Putnam Pkwy, Ottawa 45875 Fax 523-6126
putnam.noacsc.org/

Ross-Pike Counties ESC
Steve Martin, supt. 740-702-3120
475 Western Ave Ste E Fax 702-3123
Chillicothe 45601
rpesd.org

South Central Ohio ESC
Lowell Howard, supt. 740-354-7761
522 Glenwood Ave Fax 353-1882
New Boston 45662
www.scoesc.org

Southern Ohio ESC
Anthony Long, supt. 937-382-6921
3321 Airborne Rd Fax 383-3171
Wilmington 45177
www.southernohioesc.org

Stark County ESC
Joe Chaddock, supt. 330-492-8136
2100 38th St NW, Canton 44709 Fax 492-6381
www.starkcountyesc.org/

Summit County ESC
Joseph Iacano, supt. 330-945-5600
420 Washington Ave Ste 200 Fax 920-1734
Cuyahoga Falls 44221
www.cybersummit.org/

Tri-County ESC
Deborah Williams, supt. 330-345-6771
741 Winkler Dr, Wooster 44691 Fax 345-7622
www.youresc.k12.oh.us/

Trumbull County ESC
Michael Hanshaw, supt. 330-505-2800
6000 Youngstown Warren Rd Fax 505-2814
Niles 44446
www.trumbull.k12.oh.us

Warren County ESC
Tom Isaacs, supt. 513-695-2900
1879 Deerfield Rd, Lebanon 45036 Fax 695-2961
www.warrencountyesc.com/

Western Buckeye ESC
Brian Gerber, supt. 419-399-4711
PO Box 176, Paulding 45879 Fax 399-3346
www.wbesc.org/

Wood County ESC
Kyle Kanuckel, supt. 419-354-9010
1867 N Research Dr Fax 354-1146
Bowling Green 43402
www.wcesc.org/

## PUBLIC, PRIVATE AND CATHOLIC SECONDARY SCHOOLS

**Aberdeen, Brown, Pop. 1,615**
Ripley-Union-Lewis-Huntington Local SD
Supt. — See Ripley
Ripley-Union-Lewis-Huntington MS 300/5-8
2300 Rains Eitel Rd 45101 937-795-8001
Chris Smith, prin. Fax 795-8035

**Ada, Hardin, Pop. 5,849**
Ada EVD 900/K-12
725 W North Ave 45810 419-634-6421
Dr. Suzanne Darmer, supt. Fax 634-0311
www.adabulldogs.org
Ada JSHS 400/7-12
725 W North Ave 45810 419-634-2746
Robin VanBuskirk, prin. Fax 634-4153

---

Ohio Northern University Post-Sec.
525 S Main St 45810 419-772-2000

**Akron, Summit, Pop. 192,922**
Akron CSD 21,800/K-12
70 N Broadway St 44308 330-761-1661
David James, supt. Fax 761-3225
www.akronschools.com
Akron Alternative Academy 300/Alt
77 W Thornton St 44311 330-761-1609
Rebecca Green-Pallotta, admin. Fax 761-1349
Akron Early College HS 300/9-12
225 S Main St 44325 330-972-6450
Cheryl Connelly, prin. Fax 972-5305
Akron Opportunity Center 100/Alt
77 W Thornton St 44311 330-761-1604
Rebecca Green-Pallotta, prin. Fax 761-1344
Buchtel HS 700/7-12
1040 Copley Rd 44320 330-761-7945
Norma James, prin. Fax 761-7947
East Community Learning Center 1,100/7-12
80 Brittain Rd 44305 330-761-7920
Vyrone Finney, prin. Fax 784-1859
Ellet HS 1,100/9-12
309 Woolf Ave 44312 330-794-4120
Michelle Marquess-Kearns, prin. Fax 794-4130
Firestone HS 1,200/9-12
333 Rampart Ave 44313 330-873-3315
Kenya Harrington, prin. Fax 873-3318
Garfield HS 900/9-12
435 N Firestone Blvd 44301 330-773-6831
Frank Kalain, prin. Fax 773-3403
Hyre Community Learning Center 800/6-8
2385 Wedgewood Dr 44312 330-761-7930
James Retton, prin. Fax 761-7932
Innes Community Learning Center 600/6-8
1999 East Ave 44314 330-761-7900
Kathryn Rodocker, prin. Fax 848-5212
Jennings Community Learning Center 600/6-8
227 E Tallmadge Ave 44310 330-761-2002
Rochelle Brown-Hall, prin. Fax 761-2611
Kenmore HS 800/9-12
2140 13th St SW 44314 330-848-4141
Byron Hopkins, prin. Fax 848-5270
Kent MS 600/6-8
1445 Hammel St 44306 330-773-7631
Anthony Lane, prin. Fax 773-6442
Litchfield MS 600/6-8
630 Mull Ave 44313 330-873-3330
Dyan Floyd, prin. Fax 873-3347
Miller South S for Visual & Perform Arts 500/4-8
1055 East Ave 44307 330-761-1765
Dawn Wilson, prin. Fax 761-1764
National Inventors Hall of Fame S - STEM 400/5-8
199 S Broadway St 44308 330-761-3195
Amanda Morgan, prin. Fax 761-5576
North HS 700/9-12
985 Gorge Blvd 44310 330-761-2665
Rachel Tecca, prin. Fax 761-2661
STEM HS 9-12
123 S Forge St 44308 330-761-7965
Larry Johnson, prin. Fax 761-7966
Evening HS Adult
435 N Firestone Blvd 44301 330-773-2417
Minnie Carter-Page, coord. Fax 773-3403

Coventry Local SD 2,000/K-12
2910 S Main St 44319 330-644-8489
Russell Chaboudy, supt. Fax 644-0159
www.coventryschools.org/
Coventry HS 800/9-12
3089 Manchester Rd 44319 330-644-3004
Neal Kopp, prin. Fax 644-4222
Coventry MS 600/5-8
3257 Cormany Rd 44319 330-644-2232
Tina Norris, prin. Fax 644-0331

Manchester Local SD 1,400/K-12
6075 Manchester Rd 44319 330-882-6926
Dr. James Robinson, supt. Fax 882-0013
www.panthercountry.org/
Manchester HS 500/9-12
437 W Nimisila Rd 44319 330-882-3291
James France, prin. Fax 882-5642
Manchester MS 500/5-8
760 W Nimisila Rd 44319 330-882-3812
James Miller, prin. Fax 882-2013

Springfield Local SD 2,300/K-12
2410 Massillon Rd 44312 330-798-1111
Chuck Sincere, supt. Fax 798-1161
www.springfieldspartans.org/
Springfield HS 700/7-12
1880 Canton Rd 44312 330-798-1002
Shaun Morgan, admin. Fax 798-1162

---

Akron General Medical Center Post-Sec.
1 Akron General Ave 44307 330-846-6548
Archbishop Hoban HS 800/9-12
1 Holy Cross Blvd 44306 330-773-6658
Dr. Mary Anne Beiting, prin. Fax 773-9100
Brown Mackie College Post-Sec.
755 White Pond Dr Ste 101 44320 330-869-3600
Children's Hospital & Medical Center Post-Sec.
1 Perkins Sq 44308 330-379-8293
Cooperative Medical Technology Program Post-Sec.
1 Perkins Sq 44308 330-543-8720
Gerber Akron Beauty School Post-Sec.
1915 W Market St Ste 800 44313 330-867-6200
Herzing University Akron Post-Sec.
1600 S Arlington St Ste 100 44306 330-724-1600
ITT Technical Institute Post-Sec.
3428 W Market St 44333 330-865-8600
Mogadore Christian Academy 50/1-12
3603 Carper Ave 44312 330-628-8482
Mark Marion, prin. Fax 628-2677
National Institute of Massotherapy Post-Sec.
3681 Manchester Rd Ste 304 44319 330-867-1996
Ohio College of Massotherapy Post-Sec.
225 Heritage Woods Dr 44321 330-665-1084
Our Lady of the Elms MSHS 200/7-12
1375 W Exchange St 44313 330-867-0880
Dr. Cynthia Wilhite, prin. Fax 864-6488
St. Vincent-St. Mary HS 700/9-12
15 N Maple St 44303 330-253-9113
Sandra Wilkes, hdmstr. Fax 996-0020
University of Akron Post-Sec.
302 Buchtel Mall 44325 330-972-7111

**Albany, Athens, Pop. 825**
Alexander Local SD 1,200/PK-12
6091 Ayers Rd 45710 740-698-8831
Lindy Douglas, supt. Fax 698-2038
www.alexanderschools.org/
Alexander JSHS 400/6-12
6125 School Rd 45710 740-698-8831
Frank Doudna, prin. Fax 698-3614

**Alliance, Stark, Pop. 21,573**
Alliance CSD 2,900/PK-12
200 Glamorgan St 44601 330-821-2100
Jeffery Talbert, supt. Fax 821-0202
www.alliancecityschools.org
Alliance HS 900/9-12
400 Glamorgan St 44601 330-829-2245
Shawn Jackson, prin. Fax 823-4920
Alliance MS 600/6-8
3205 S Union Ave 44601 330-829-2254
Jason Dixon, prin. Fax 823-0872

Marlington Local SD 2,400/K-12
10320 Moulin Ave NE 44601 330-823-7458
Joe Knoll, supt. Fax 823-7759
www.marlingtonlocal.org
Marlington HS 800/9-12
10450 Moulin Ave NE 44601 330-823-1300
Sam Pepper, prin. Fax 829-1986
Marlington MS 600/6-8
10325 Moulin Ave NE 44601 330-823-7566
Nick Evanich, prin. Fax 823-7594

---

University of Mount Union Post-Sec.
1972 Clark Ave 44601 800-992-6682

**Amanda, Fairfield, Pop. 725**
Amanda-Clearcreek Local SD 1,600/K-12
328 E Main St 43102 740-969-7250
David Gaul, supt. Fax 969-7620
www.amanda.k12.oh.us
Amanda-Clearcreek HS 500/9-12
328 E Main St 43102 740-969-7251
Kimberly Radulovich, prin. Fax 969-7669
Amanda-Clearcreek MS 400/6-8
328 E Main St 43102 740-969-7252
Patricia Haughn, prin. Fax 969-7638

**Amherst, Lorain, Pop. 11,868**
Amherst EVD 3,300/PK-12
185 Forest St 44001 440-988-4406
Steven Sayers, supt. Fax 988-4413
www.amherst.k12.oh.us
Amherst JHS 700/7-8
548 Milan Ave 44001 440-988-0324
Ryan Coleman, prin. Fax 988-0328
Steele HS 1,400/9-12
450 Washington St 44001 440-988-4433
Michael May, prin. Fax 988-5087

**Andover, Ashtabula, Pop. 1,129**
Pymatuning Valley Local SD 1,300/K-12
PO Box 1180 44003 440-293-6488
Mike Candela, supt. Fax 293-7654
www.pvschools.k12.oh.us/
Pymatuning Valley HS 400/9-12
PO Box 1180 44003 440-293-6263
Daniel Jackson, prin. Fax 293-7214
Pymatuning Valley MS 400/5-8
PO Box 1180 44003 440-293-6981
Andrew Kuthy, prin. Fax 293-7237

**Anna, Shelby, Pop. 1,544**
Anna Local SD 1,200/K-12
PO Box 169 45302 937-394-2011
Andrew Bixler, supt. Fax 394-7658
www.anna.k12.oh.us
Anna HS 300/9-12
PO Box 169 45302 937-394-2011
Rick Russell, prin. Fax 394-7658
Anna MS 300/6-8
PO Box 169 45302 937-394-2011
Cynthia Endsley, prin. Fax 394-7658

**Ansonia, Darke, Pop. 1,168**
Ansonia Local SD 700/K-12
PO Box 279 45303 937-337-4000
James Atchley, supt. Fax 337-9520
www.ansonia.k12.oh.us/
Ansonia HS 200/9-12
PO Box 279 45303 937-337-5591
Stephen Garman, prin. Fax 337-9520
Ansonia MS 100/7-8
PO Box 279 45303 937-337-5591
Stephen Garman, prin. Fax 337-9520

**Antwerp, Paulding, Pop. 1,725**
Antwerp Local SD 600/K-12
303 S Harrmann Rd 45813 419-258-5421
Martin Miller, supt. Fax 258-4041
www.antwerpschools.org
Antwerp Local HS 200/9-12
303 S Harrmann Rd 45813 419-258-5421
Michael Bute, prin. Fax 258-4041
Antwerp Local MS 100/6-8
303 S Harrmann Rd 45813 419-258-5421
Michael Bute, prin. Fax 258-4041

**Apple Creek, Wayne, Pop. 1,169**
Southeast Local SD 1,500/PK-12
9048 Dover Rd 44606 330-698-3001
James J. Ritchie, supt. Fax 698-5000
www.southeast.k12.oh.us
Lea MS 200/7-8
9130 Dover Rd 44606 330-698-3151
Erich Riebe, prin. Fax 698-1922
Waynedale HS 300/9-12
9050 Dover Rd 44606 330-698-3071
Richard Roth, prin. Fax 698-1432

**Arcadia, Hancock, Pop. 583**
Arcadia Local SD 500/K-12
19033 State Route 12 44804 419-894-6431
Bruce Kidder, supt. Fax 894-6970
www.arcadia.noacsc.org
Arcadia JSHS 200/7-12
19033 State Route 12 44804 419-894-6431
Bill Dobbins, prin. Fax 894-6970

**Arcanum, Darke, Pop. 2,116**
Arcanum Butler Local SD 1,000/PK-12
2011 Trojan Ave 45304 937-692-5174
John Stephens, supt. Fax 692-5959
www.arcanum-butler.k12.oh.us
Arcanum HS 200/9-12
2011 Trojan Ave 45304 937-692-5174
Jason Stephan, prin. Fax 692-8865
Butler MS 300/5-8
2011 Trojan Ave 45304 937-692-5174
Marcus Bixler, prin. Fax 692-8865

Franklin Monroe Local SD 700/K-12
8639 Oakes Rd 45304 937-947-1212
Jeffrey Patrick, supt. Fax 947-1372
www.franklin-monroe.k12.oh.us/
Franklin Monroe JSHS 300/6-12
8591 Oakes Rd 45304 937-947-1328
Jason Wood, prin. Fax 947-1371

**Archbold, Fulton, Pop. 4,305**
Archbold Area Local SD 1,200/PK-12
600 Lafayette St 43502 419-446-2728
Aaron Rex, supt. Fax 445-8536
www.archbold.k12.oh.us
Archbold HS 400/9-12
600 Lafayette St 43502 419-445-5579
Royal Short, prin. Fax 445-8536
Archbold MS 400/5-8
306 Stryker St 43502 419-446-2726
Matthew Shields, prin. Fax 445-8402

Four County Career Center SD
22900 State Route 34 43502 419-267-3331
Tim Meister, supt. Fax 267-2345
www.fourcounty.net
Four County Career Center Vo/Tech
22900 State Route 34 43502 419-267-3331
Rick Bachman, supt. Fax 267-2345

---

Northwest State Community College Post-Sec.
22600 State Route 34 43502 419-267-5511

**Arlington, Hancock, Pop. 1,451**
Arlington Local SD 600/K-12
336 S Main St 45814 419-365-5121
Kevin Haught, supt. Fax 365-1282
www.noacsc.org/hancock/ag
Arlington JSHS 300/7-12
336 S Main St 45814 419-365-5122
Nate Sorg, prin. Fax 365-1282

**Ashland, Ashland, Pop. 20,088**
Ashland CSD 3,100/K-12
PO Box 160 44805 419-289-1117
Douglas Marrah, supt. Fax 289-9534
www.ashlandcityschools.org/
Ashland HS 1,000/9-12
1440 King Rd 44805 419-289-7968
Thomas Marquette, prin. Fax 289-8218
Ashland MS 500/7-8
345 Cottage St 44805 419-289-7966
Matt White, prin. Fax 289-2303

Ashland County-West Holmes JVSD
1783 State Route 60 44805 419-289-3313
Michael McDaniel, supt. Fax 289-3729
www.acwhcc.org
Ashland Co. - West Holmes JVS Career Ctr Vo/Tech
1783 State Route 60 44805 419-289-3313
Rodney Cheyney, prin. Fax 289-3729

Crestview Local SD 1,200/K-12
1575 State Route 96 44805 419-895-1700
L. Randall Dunlap, supt. Fax 895-1733
www.crestviewschools.net
Crestview HS 300/9-12
1575 State Route 96 44805 419-895-1700
Shannon Sprang, prin. Fax 895-3103
Crestview MS 500/4-8
1575 State Route 96 44805 419-895-1700
Eric Yetter, prin. Fax 895-1733

Mapleton Local SD 900/K-12
635 County Road 801 44805 419-945-2188
Joseph Morabito, supt. Fax 945-8133
www.mapleton.k12.oh.us/
Mapleton HS 300/9-12
1 Mountie Dr 44805 419-945-2188
Joseph Morabito, prin. Fax 945-8166
Mapleton MS 200/6-8
1 Mountie Dr 44805 419-945-2188
Andrew Mangun, prin. Fax 945-8167

---

Ashland County-West Holmes Career Center Post-Sec.
1783 State Route 60 44805 419-289-3313
Ashland University Post-Sec.
401 College Ave 44805 419-289-4142

**Ashtabula, Ashtabula, Pop. 18,304**
Ashtabula Area CSD 2,800/PK-12
2630 W 13th St 44004 440-992-1200
Patrick Colucci, supt. Fax 992-1209
www.aacs.net
Lakeside HS 1,000/9-12
6600 Sanborn Rd 44004 440-993-2522
Donald Rapose, prin. Fax 993-2647
Lakeside JHS 600/7-8
6620 Sanborn Rd 44004 440-993-2618
Kathleen Reichert, prin. Fax 992-2647

Buckeye Local SD 1,800/K-12
3436 Edgewood Dr 44004 440-998-4411
Thomas Diringer, supt. Fax 992-8369
www.buckeyeschools.info/
Braden MS 400/6-8
3436 Edgewood Dr 44004 440-998-0550
Bill Billington, prin.
Edgewood HS 600/9-12
2428 Blake Rd 44004 440-997-5301
Timothy Neal, prin. Fax 998-6143

---

Kent State University at Ashtabula Post-Sec.
3300 Lake Rd W 44004 440-964-3322
St. John S 200/K-12
7911 Depot Rd 44004 440-997-5531
Nicholas Perkoski, prin. Fax 998-1661

**Ashville, Pickaway, Pop. 4,045**
Teays Valley Local SD 3,700/PK-12
385 Circleville Ave 43103 740-983-5000
Robin Halley, supt. Fax 983-4158
www.tvsd.us/
Teays Valley East MS 600/6-8
655 Viking Way 43103 740-983-5000
Shannon Helser, prin. Fax 983-5037
Teays Valley HS 1,000/9-12
3887 State Route 752 43103 740-983-5000
John Keel, prin. Fax 983-5074
Other Schools – See Commercial Point

**Athens, Athens, Pop. 23,284**
Athens CSD
Supt. — See The Plains
Athens MS 400/7-8
51 W State St 45701 740-593-7107
Kara Bolin, prin. Fax 594-6506

---

Ohio University Post-Sec.
1 Ohio University 45701 740-593-1000

**Attica, Seneca, Pop. 880**
Seneca East Local SD 800/K-12
13343 E US Highway 224 44807 419-426-7041
Laura Kagy, supt. Fax 426-5514
www.seneca-east.k12.oh.us/
Seneca East JSHS 300/7-12
13343 E US Highway 224 44807 419-426-3312
Don Vogt, prin. Fax 426-5400

**Atwater, Portage, Pop. 754**
Waterloo Local SD 1,200/K-12
1464 Industry Rd 44201 330-947-2664
Shawn Braman, supt. Fax 947-2847
www.viking.portage.k12.oh.us
Waterloo HS 400/9-12
1464 Industry Rd 44201 330-947-2124
Lori Sandel, prin. Fax 947-1911
Waterloo MS 300/6-8
1464 Industry Rd 44201 330-947-0033
Aaron Walker, prin. Fax 947-4073

**Aurora, Portage, Pop. 15,422**
Aurora CSD 2,700/PK-12
102 E Garfield Rd 44202 330-562-6106
Pat Ciccantelli, supt. Fax 562-4892
www.aurora-schools.org
Aurora HS 1,000/9-12
109 W Pioneer Trl 44202 330-562-3501
Paul Milcetich, prin. Fax 954-2810
Harmon MS 700/6-8
130 Aurora Hudson Rd 44202 330-562-3375
Mark Abramovich, prin. Fax 562-4796

**Austinburg, Ashtabula, Pop. 512**

---

Grand River Academy 100/8-12
3042 College St 44010 440-275-2811
Tim Viands, head sch Fax 275-1825

**Austintown, Mahoning, Pop. 31,500**

---

Hair Academy Post-Sec.
6000 Mahoning Ave 44515 330-792-6504

**Avon, Lorain, Pop. 20,897**
Avon Local SD 4,000/K-12
35573 Detroit Rd 44011 440-937-4680
Michael Laub, supt. Fax 937-4688
www.avonlocalschools.org/
Avon HS 1,000/9-12
37545 Detroit Rd 44011 440-934-6171
Kristina Buller, prin. Fax 934-5450
Avon MS 600/7-8
3445 Long Rd 44011 440-934-3800
Dr. Craig Koehler, prin. Fax 934-3803

**Avon Lake, Lorain, Pop. 22,318**
Avon Lake CSD 3,700/K-12
175 Avon Belden Rd 44012 440-933-6210
Robert Scott, supt. Fax 933-6711
www.avonlakecityschools.org
Avon Lake HS 1,200/9-12
175 Avon Belden Rd 44012 440-933-6290
Dr. Brad Cocco Ph.D., prin. Fax 930-2798
Learwood MS 600/7-8
340 Lear Rd 44012 440-933-8142
Vishtasp Nuggud, prin. Fax 933-8406

**Bainbridge, Ross, Pop. 838**
Paint Valley Local SD 1,000/K-12
7454 US Highway 50 W 45612 740-634-2826
Timothy Winland, supt. Fax 634-2890
paintvalleylocalschools.org
Paint Valley HS 300/9-12
7454 US Highway 50 W 45612 740-634-3582
Casey Smith, prin. Fax 634-3518
Paint Valley MS 300/7-8
7454 US Highway 50 W 45612 740-634-3454
Heather Bowles, prin. Fax 634-3459

**Baltimore, Fairfield, Pop. 2,921**
Liberty Union-Thurston Local SD 1,400/K-12
1108 S Main St 43105 740-862-4171
Todd Osborn, supt. Fax 862-2015
www.libertyunion.org
Liberty Union HS 400/9-12
500 W Washington St 43105 740-862-4107
Matt Gallatin, prin. Fax 862-4100
Liberty Union MS 500/5-8
994 S Main St 43105 740-862-4126
Tim Turner, prin. Fax 862-0239

**Barberton, Summit, Pop. 25,978**
Barberton CSD 1,700/K-12
479 Norton Ave 44203 330-753-1025
Patti Cleary, supt. Fax 848-0884
www.barbertonschools.org
Barberton HS 1,300/9-12
555 Barber Rd 44203 330-753-1084
Jeff Ramnytz, prin. Fax 848-5517
Barberton MS 1,100/5-8
477 4th St NW 44203 330-745-9950
Joyce Walker, prin. Fax 745-9962

**Barnesville, Belmont, Pop. 4,130**
Barnesville EVD 1,100/PK-12
210 W Church St 43713 740-425-3615
Randy Lucas, supt. Fax 425-5000
www.barnesville.k12.oh.us/
Barnesville HS 300/9-12
910 Shamrock Dr 43713 740-425-3617
Micah Fuchs, prin. Fax 425-9254
Barnesville MS 400/5-8
970 Shamrock Dr 43713 740-425-3116
Julie Erwin, prin. Fax 425-9204

---

Olney Friends S 100/9-12
61830 Sandy Ridge Rd 43713 740-425-3655
Charlie Szumilas, head sch Fax 425-3202

**Bascom, Seneca, Pop. 390**
Hopewell-Loudon Local SD 900/K-12
PO Box 400 44809 419-937-2216
Rodney Russell, supt. Fax 937-2516
www.hlschool.org
Hopewell-Loudon Local JSHS 400/7-12
PO Box 400 44809 419-937-2804
Billy Dobbins, prin. Fax 937-2516

**Batavia, Clermont, Pop. 1,482**
Batavia Local SD 2,000/PK-12
2400 Clermont Center Dr 45103 513-732-2343
Keith Millard, supt. Fax 732-3221
www.bataviaschools.org
Batavia HS 500/9-12
1 Bulldog Pl 45103 513-732-2341
Felicia Grooms, prin. Fax 732-9740
Batavia MS 600/5-8
800 Bauer Ave 45103 513-732-9534
Steve Brokamp, prin. Fax 732-3696

Clermont Northeastern Local SD 1,600/K-12
2792 US Highway 50 45103 513-625-5478
Michael Brandt, supt. Fax 625-6080
www.cneschools.org
Clermont Northeastern HS 500/9-12
5327 Hutchinson Rd 45103 513-625-1211
T.J. Glassmeyer, prin. Fax 625-3328
Clermont Northeastern MS 400/6-8
2792 US Highway 50 45103 513-625-1211
Kendra Young, prin. Fax 625-3325

West Clermont Local SD
Supt. — See Cincinnati
Amelia HS 1,100/9-12
1351 Clough Pike 45103 513-947-7400
Stephanie Walker, prin. Fax 753-2419
Amelia MS 1,000/6-8
1341 Clough Pike 45103 513-947-7500
Norbert Martini, prin. Fax 753-7851

---

University of Cincinnati Post-Sec.
4200 Clermont College Dr 45103 513-732-5200

**Bath, Summit**
Revere Local SD
Supt. — See Richfield
Revere HS 900/9-12
3420 Everett Rd 44210 330-659-6111
Phil King, prin. Fax 659-6407
Revere MS 700/6-8
PO Box 339 44210 330-666-4155
Judy Myers, prin. Fax 659-3795

**Bay Village, Cuyahoga, Pop. 15,468**
Bay Village CSD 2,500/K-12
377 Dover Center Rd 44140 440-617-7300
Clinton Keener, supt. Fax 617-7301
www.bayvillageschools.com
Bay HS 800/9-12
29230 Wolf Rd 44140 440-617-7400
Jason Martin, prin. Fax 617-7401
Bay MS 800/5-8
27725 Wolf Rd 44140 440-617-7600
Sean McAndrews, prin. Fax 617-7601

**Beachwood, Cuyahoga, Pop. 11,798**
Beachwood CSD 1,600/PK-12
24601 Fairmount Blvd 44122 216-464-2600
Robert Hardis, supt. Fax 292-2340
www.beachwoodschools.org/
Beachwood HS 600/9-12
25100 Fairmount Blvd 44122 216-831-2080
Dr. Edward Klein, prin. Fax 292-4169
Beachwood MS 400/6-8
2860 Richmond Rd 44122 216-831-0355
Paul Chase, prin. Fax 831-1891

---

Fuchs Mizrachi S 400/PK-12
26600 Shaker Blvd 44122 216-932-0220
Rabbi Barry Kislowicz Ed.D., head sch Fax 932-0345

**Beallsville, Monroe, Pop. 400**
Switzerland of Ohio Local SD
Supt. — See Woodsfield
Beallsville JSHS 200/7-12
PO Box 262 43716 740-926-1302
Rebecca Hilverding, prin. Fax 926-1394

**Beaver, Pike, Pop. 431**
Eastern Local SD 800/PK-12
1170 Tile Mill Rd 45613 740-226-4851
Neil Leist, supt. Fax 226-1331
www.ep.k12.oh.us
Eastern HS 200/9-12
1170 Tile Mill Rd 45613 740-226-1544
Matt Hines, prin. Fax 226-6322
Eastern MS 200/6-8
1170 Tile Mill Rd 45613 740-226-1544
Matt Hines, prin. Fax 226-6322

**Beavercreek, Greene, Pop. 44,171**
Beavercreek CSD 7,000/PK-12
3040 Kemp Rd 45431 937-426-1522
Dr. William McGlothlin, supt. Fax 429-7517
www.beavercreek.k12.oh.us/
Ankeney MS 900/6-8
4085 Shakertown Rd 45430 937-429-7567
Sharma Nachlinger, prin. Fax 429-7685
Beavercreek HS 2,400/9-12
2660 Dayton Xenia Rd 45434 937-429-7547
Marian West, prin. Fax 429-7546
Other Schools – See Xenia

**Bedford, Cuyahoga, Pop. 12,768**
Bedford CSD 3,500/PK-12
475 Northfield Rd 44146 440-439-1500
Dr. Andrea Celico Ph.D., supt. Fax 439-4850
www.bedford.k12.oh.us
Bedford HS 1,200/9-12
481 Northfield Rd 44146 440-439-4848
Samuel Vawters, prin. Fax 439-4627
Other Schools – See Bedford Heights

**Bedford Heights, Cuyahoga, Pop. 10,538**
Bedford CSD
Supt. — See Bedford
Heskett MS 600/7-8
5771 Perkins Rd 44146 440-439-4450
Virginia Golden, prin. Fax 786-3572

**Bellaire, Belmont, Pop. 4,190**
Bellaire Local SD 1,200/K-12
340 34th St 43906 740-676-1826
Tony Scott, supt. Fax 671-6002
www.bellaire.k12.oh.us
Bellaire HS 300/9-12
349 35th St 43906 740-676-3652
Kevin Roseberry, prin. Fax 671-6004
Bellaire MS 400/5-8
54555 Neffs Bellaire Rd 43906 740-676-1635
Derrick McAfee, prin. Fax 676-3014

---

St. John Central HS 100/9-12
3625 Guernsey St 43906 740-676-4932
Dr. Thomes E. Graham, prin. Fax 676-4934

**Bellbrook, Greene, Pop. 6,854**
Bellbrook-Sugarcreek Local SD 2,600/K-12
3757 Upper Bellbrook Rd 45305 937-848-5001
Dr. Keith St. Pierre, supt. Fax 848-5018
www.sugarcreek.k12.oh.us
Bellbrook HS 900/9-12
3737 Upper Bellbrook Rd 45305 937-848-3737
Christopher Baker, prin. Fax 848-5016

Bellbrook MS 600/6-8
3600 Feedwire Rd 45305 937-848-2141
Jenness Sigman, prin. Fax 848-2152

**Bellefontaine, Logan, Pop. 12,899**
Bellefontaine CSD 2,400/K-12
820 Ludlow Rd 43311 937-593-9060
Brad Hall, supt. Fax 599-1346
www.bellefontaine.k12.oh.us/
Bellefontaine HS 800/9-12
555 E Lake Ave 43311 937-593-0545
Bill Badenhop, prin. Fax 593-0575
Bellefontaine MS 600/6-8
1201 Ludlow Rd 43311 937-593-9010
Shanel Henry, prin. Fax 593-9030

Benjamin Logan Local SD 1,700/K-12
4740 County Road 26 43311 937-593-9211
David Harmon, supt. Fax 599-4059
www.benlogan.k12.oh.us
Logan HS 500/9-12
6609 State Route 47 E 43311 937-592-1666
Mark Butler, prin. Fax 599-4061
Logan MS 600/5-8
4626 County Road 26 43311 937-599-2386
Jeff McPheron, prin. Fax 599-4062

Ohio Hi-Point Career Ctr SD
2280 State Route 540 43311 937-599-3010
Jeffrey Price, supt. Fax 599-2318
www.ohiohipoint.com
Ohio Hi-Point Career Center Vo/Tech
2280 State Route 540 43311 937-599-3010
Shelly Swaney, dir. Fax 599-2318

---

Calvary Christian S 200/PK-12
1140 Rush Ave 43311 937-599-6847
Paul Green, admin. Fax 599-4879

**Bellevue, Huron, Pop. 8,079**
Bellevue CSD 2,000/PK-12
125 North St 44811 419-484-5000
Kim Schubert, supt. Fax 483-0723
www.bellevueschools.org
Bellevue HS 600/9-12
200 Oakland Ave 44811 419-484-5070
Nate Artino, prin. Fax 483-7157
Bellevue MS 500/6-8
1035 Castalia St 44811 419-484-5060
John Bollinger, prin. Fax 484-5096

**Bellville, Richland, Pop. 1,888**
Clear Fork Valley Local SD 1,800/K-12
92 Hines Ave 44813 419-886-3855
Janice Wyckoff, supt. Fax 886-2237
www.clearfork.k12.oh.us
Clear Fork HS 600/9-12
987 State Route 97 E 44813 419-886-2601
Brian Brown, prin. Fax 886-4749
Clear Fork MS 400/6-8
987 State Route 97 E 44813 419-886-3111
Jennifer Klaus, prin. Fax 886-4749

**Belmont, Belmont, Pop. 449**
Union Local SD 1,500/PK-12
66779 Belmont Morristown Rd 43718 740-782-1978
Robert Porter, supt. Fax 782-1212
www.ulschools.com
Union Local HS 400/9-12
66779 Belmont Morristown Rd 43718 740-782-1181
Robert Mascolino, prin. Fax 782-1346
Union Local MS 400/6-8
66859 Belmont Morristown Rd 43718 740-782-1388
Michael Saffell, prin. Fax 782-1474

**Beloit, Mahoning, Pop. 960**
West Branch Local SD 1,800/K-12
14277 S Main St 44609 330-938-9324
Dr. Douglas Phillips, supt. Fax 938-6815
www.westbranch.k12.oh.us
West Branch HS 700/9-12
14277 S Main St 44609 330-938-2183
Brian Coffee, prin. Fax 938-4444
West Branch MS 500/5-8
14409 Beloit Snodes Rd 44609 330-938-4300
Roger Kitzmiller, prin. Fax 938-4301

**Belpre, Washington, Pop. 6,292**
Belpre CSD 900/K-12
2014 Rockland Ave 45714 740-423-9511
Dwight Dunn, supt. Fax 423-3050
www.belpre.k12.oh.us
Belpre JSHS 400/7-12
612 3rd St 45714 740-423-3000
Dennis Eichinger, prin. Fax 423-3003

**Berea, Cuyahoga, Pop. 18,699**
Berea CSD 3,700/PK-12
390 Fair St 44017 216-898-8300
Michael Sheppard, supt. Fax 898-8551
www.berea.k12.oh.us
Berea-Midpark HS 800/10-12
165 E Bagley Rd 44017 216-898-8900
Vincenzo Ruggiero, prin. Fax 898-8558
Other Schools – See Middleburg Heights

---

Baldwin-Wallace University Post-Sec.
275 Eastland Rd 44017 440-826-2900

**Berlin, Holmes, Pop. 892**
East Holmes Local SD 1,800/K-12
6108 County Road 77 44610 330-893-2610
James Ritchie, supt. Fax 893-2838
www.eastholmes.k12.oh.us
Hiland JSHS 400/7-12
PO Box 275 44610 330-893-2626
Matthew Johnson, prin. Fax 893-3570
Other Schools – See Charm

**Berlin Center, Mahoning**
Western Reserve Local SD 800/K-12
13850 W Akron Canfield Rd 44401 330-547-4100
Jeffrey Zatchok, supt. Fax 547-9302
www.westernreserve.k12.oh.us
Western Reserve S 800/K-12
13850 W Akron Canfield Rd 44401 330-547-4100
Jeffrey Zatchok, admin. Fax 547-9302

**Berlin Heights, Erie, Pop. 698**
Edison Local SD
Supt. — See Milan
Edison MS 600/4-8
20 Center St 44814 419-588-2078
Cory Smith, prin. Fax 588-3212

**Bethel, Clermont, Pop. 2,658**
Bethel-Tate Local SD 1,800/K-12
675 W Plane St 45106 513-734-2271
Melissa Kircher, supt. Fax 734-4792
www.betheltate.org
Bethel-Tate HS 500/9-12
3420 State Route 125 45106 513-734-2271
Keith Hickman, prin. Fax 734-1355
Bethel-Tate MS 400/6-8
649 W Plane St 45106 513-734-2271
Christen Davis, prin. Fax 734-0888

U.S. Grant JVSD
718 W Plane St 45106 513-734-6222
Lisa Tuttle-Huff, supt. Fax 734-4758
www.grantcareer.com
Grant Career Center Vo/Tech
718 W Plane St 45106 513-734-6222
Barry L. Daulton, prin. Fax 734-4758

**Beverly, Washington, Pop. 1,285**
Fort Frye Local SD 1,000/K-12
PO Box 1149 45715 740-984-2497
Stephanie Starcher, supt. Fax 984-8784
www.fortfrye.k12.oh.us
Ft. Frye JSHS 400/7-12
PO Box 1089 45715 740-984-2376
Andrew Schob, prin. Fax 984-4361

**Bexley, Franklin, Pop. 12,740**
Bexley CSD 2,100/K-12
348 S Cassingham Rd 43209 614-231-7611
Dr. Michael Johnson, supt. Fax 231-8448
www.bexleyschools.org
Bexley HS 700/9-12
326 S Cassingham Rd 43209 614-231-4591
Dr. Harley Williams, prin. Fax 338-2087
Bexley MS 300/7-8
300 S Cassingham Rd 43209 614-237-4277
Dr. Harley Williams, prin. Fax 338-2090

**Bidwell, Gallia**
Gallia County Local SD
Supt. — See Patriot
River Valley HS 400/9-12
8785 State Route 160 45614 740-446-2926
Timothy Edwards, prin. Fax 446-7382
River Valley MS 400/6-8
8779 State Route 160 45614 740-446-8399
O. Ed Moore, prin. Fax 441-3038

**Blanchester, Clinton, Pop. 4,195**
Blanchester Local SD 1,700/PK-12
951 Cherry St 45107 937-783-3523
Dean D. Lynch, supt. Fax 783-2990
www.blan.org
Blanchester HS 500/9-12
953 Cherry St 45107 937-783-2461
Rick Hosler, prin. Fax 783-5666
Blanchester MS 400/6-8
955 Cherry St 45107 937-783-3642
Joel King, prin. Fax 783-3477

**Bloomdale, Wood, Pop. 675**
Elmwood Local SD 1,300/PK-12
7650 Jerry City Rd 44817 419-655-2583
Tony Borton, supt. Fax 655-3995
www.elmwood.k12.oh.us
Elmwood HS 400/9-12
7650 Jerry City Rd 44817 419-655-2583
Tom Bentley, prin. Fax 655-2153
Elmwood MS 400/5-8
7650 Jerry City Rd 44817 419-655-2583
Roger Frank, prin. Fax 655-2153

**Bloomingdale, Jefferson, Pop. 200**
Jefferson County JVSD
1509 County Road 22A 43910 740-264-5545
Dr. Todd Phillipson, supt. Fax 264-3144
www.jcjvs.k12.oh.us
Jefferson County Vocational S Vo/Tech
1509 County Road 22A 43910 740-264-5545
Dr. Todd Phillipson, supt. Fax 264-3144

**Blue Ash, Hamilton, Pop. 11,860**

---

University of Cincinnati Post-Sec.
9555 Plainfield Rd 45236 513-745-5600

**Bluffton, Allen, Pop. 4,072**
Bluffton EVD 1,100/K-12
102 S Jackson St 45817 419-358-5901
Gregory Denecker, supt. Fax 358-4871
www.blufftonschools.org
Bluffton HS 300/9-12
106 W College Ave 45817 419-358-7941
Michael Minnig, prin. Fax 358-6586
Bluffton MS 300/6-8
116 S Jackson St 45817 419-358-7961
Kyle Leatherman, prin. Fax 358-4871

---

Bluffton University Post-Sec.
1 University Dr 45817 419-358-3000

**Botkins, Shelby, Pop. 1,145**
Botkins Local SD 300/K-12
404 E State St 45306 937-693-4241
Connie Schneider, supt. Fax 693-2557
www.botkins.k12.oh.us
Botkins S 300/K-12
404 E State St 45306 937-693-4241
Ryan Loy, prin. Fax 693-2557

**Bowerston, Harrison, Pop. 397**
Conotton Valley Union Local SD
Supt. — See Sherrodsville
Conotton Valley HS 200/PK-K, 5-1
7205 Cumberland Rd SW 44695 740-269-2711
Jerry Herman, prin. Fax 269-4405

**Bowling Green, Wood, Pop. 29,467**
Bowling Green CSD 2,600/PK-12
137 Clough St 43402 419-352-3576
Francis Scruci, supt. Fax 352-1701
www.bgcs.k12.oh.us
Bowling Green HS 900/9-12
530 W Poe Rd 43402 419-354-0100
Jeffrey Dever, prin. Fax 354-1839
Bowling Green MS 500/6-8
1079 Fairview Ave 43402 419-354-0200
Gary Keller, prin. Fax 353-1958

---

Bowling Green Christian Academy 200/PK-12
1165 Haskins Rd 43402 419-354-2422
Wendie Cuckler, prin. Fax 354-0232
Bowling Green State University Post-Sec.
110 McFall Ctr 43403 419-372-2531

**Bradford, Darke, Pop. 1,831**
Bradford EVD 500/K-12
760 Railroad Ave 45308 937-448-2770
Kenneth Miller, supt. Fax 448-2493
www.bradford.k12.oh.us
Bradford JSHS 300/6-12
750 Railroad Ave 45308 937-448-2719
Chris Abke, prin. Fax 448-2742

**Brecksville, Cuyahoga, Pop. 13,500**
Brecksville-Broadview Heights CSD 4,200/PK-12
6638 Mill Rd 44141 440-740-4000
Scot Prebles, supt. Fax 740-4004
www.bbhcsd.org
Other Schools – See Broadview Heights

Cuyahoga Valley Career Ctr SD
8001 Brecksville Rd 44141 440-526-5200
Dr. Celena Roebuck, supt. Fax 746-8298
www.cvccworks.edu
Cuyahoga Valley Career Center Vo/Tech
8001 Brecksville Rd 44141 440-526-5200
Mike Hall, prin. Fax 746-8299

---

Stautzenberger College Post-Sec.
8001 Katherine Blvd 44141 440-838-1999

**Bridgeport, Belmont, Pop. 1,773**
Bridgeport EVD 800/PK-12
55781 National Rd 43912 740-635-1713
Zachary Shutler, supt. Fax 635-6003
www.bevs.k12.oh.us/
Bridgeport HS 200/9-12
55707 Industrial Dr 43912 740-635-0853
Rob Zitzelsberger, prin. Fax 635-6008
Bridgeport MS 200/5-8
55707 Industrial Dr 43912 740-635-0853
Anne Haverty, prin. Fax 635-6003

**Bristolville, Trumbull**
Bristol Local SD 700/K-12
PO Box 260 44402 330-889-3882
Christopher Dray, supt. Fax 889-2529
www.bristol.k12.oh.us
Bristol HS 300/7-12
PO Box 260 44402 330-889-2621
Timothy Fairfield, prin. Fax 889-2529

**Broadview Heights, Cuyahoga, Pop. 19,168**
Brecksville-Broadview Heights CSD
Supt. — See Brecksville
Brecksville-Broadview Heights HS 1,600/9-12
6380 Mill Rd 44147 440-740-4700
Joseph Mueller, prin. Fax 740-4704
Brecksville-Broadview Heights MS 1,000/6-8
6376 Mill Rd 44147 440-740-4400
Todd Rings, prin. Fax 740-4404

---

Vatterott College Post-Sec.
5025 E Royalton Rd 44147 440-526-1660

**Brookfield, Trumbull**
Brookfield Local SD 1,100/K-12
614 Bedford Rd SE 44403 330-448-4930
Tim Saxton, supt. Fax 448-5026
www.brookfield.k12.oh.us
Brookfield HS 400/9-12
614 Bedford Rd SE 44403 330-448-3001
Velina Taylor, prin. Fax 448-8016
Brookfield MS 400/5-8
614 Bedford Rd SE 44403 330-448-3003
Shari Baxter, prin. Fax 448-5028

**Brooklyn, Cuyahoga, Pop. 10,955**
Brooklyn CSD 1,200/PK-12
9200 Biddulph Rd 44144 216-485-8100
Dr. Mark Gleichauf, supt. Fax 485-8118
www.brooklyn.k12.oh.us
Brooklyn HS 500/8-12
9200 Biddulph Rd 44144 216-485-8162
Antoinette Hostetler, prin. Fax 485-8124

**Brookville, Montgomery, Pop. 5,844**
Brookville Local SD 1,400/K-12
75 June Pl 45309 937-833-2181
Timothy Hopkins, supt. Fax 833-2787
www.brookvilleschools.org
Brookville HS 400/9-12
1 Blue Pride Dr 45309 937-833-6761
Christopher Bronner, prin. Fax 833-6302
Brookville IS 600/4-8
2 Blue Pride Dr 45309 937-833-6731
Amy Anyanwu, prin. Fax 833-6756

**Brunswick, Medina, Pop. 33,855**
Brunswick CSD 7,300/PK-12
3643 Center Rd 44212 330-225-7731
Michael Mayell, supt. Fax 273-0507
www.bcsoh.org
Brunswick HS 2,200/9-12
3581 Center Rd 44212 330-225-7731
Michael Draves, prin. Fax 225-0507
Edwards MS 500/6-8
1497 Pearl Rd 44212 330-225-7731
Heidi Armentrout, prin. Fax 273-0507
Visintainer MS 600/6-8
1459 Pearl Rd 44212 330-225-7731
Brian Sharosky, prin. Fax 273-0507
Willetts MS 700/6-8
1045 Hadcock Rd 44212 330-225-7731
Brian Miller, prin. Fax 273-0507

**Bryan, Williams, Pop. 8,426**
Bryan CSD 1,900/PK-12
1350 Fountain Grove Dr 43506 419-636-6973
Diana Savage, supt. Fax 633-6280
www.bryan.k12.oh.us
Bryan HS 600/9-12
150 S Portland St 43506 419-636-4536
Steve Alspaugh, prin. Fax 633-6281
Bryan MS 700/4-8
1301 Center St 43506 419-636-6766
Chad Bassett, prin. Fax 633-6282

---

Fountain City Christian S 50/K-12
PO Box 150 43506 419-636-2333
Troy Cummins, admin. Fax 636-2888

**Bucyrus, Crawford, Pop. 12,227**
Bucyrus CSD 1,600/PK-12
170 Plymouth St 44820 419-562-4045
Kevin Kimmel, supt. Fax 562-3990
bucyrusschools.org
Bucyrus HS 400/9-12
900 W Perry St 44820 419-562-7721
Dr. Mark Burke, prin. Fax 562-7819
Bucyrus MS 300/6-8
455 Redman Way 44820 419-562-0003
John Massara, admin. Fax 562-7819

Wynford Local SD 1,200/PK-12
3288 Holmes Center Rd 44820 419-562-7828
Steve Mohr, supt. Fax 562-7825
www.wynford.k12.oh.us
Wynford HS 200/9-12
3288 Holmes Center Rd 44820 419-562-7828
Jeffrey Holbrook, prin. Fax 562-7825
Wynford JHS 200/7-8
3288 Holmes Center Rd 44820 419-562-7828
Chris Solis, prin. Fax 562-7825

**Burton, Geauga, Pop. 1,446**
Berkshire Local SD 1,000/PK-12
PO Box 364 44021 440-834-3380
Douglas DeLong, supt.
www.berkshire.k12.oh.us
Berkshire JSHS, PO Box 365 44021 500/7-12
Stephen Reedy, prin. 440-834-3380

---

Kent State University-Geauga Campus Post-Sec.
14111 Claridon Troy Rd 44021 440-834-4187

**Byesville, Guernsey, Pop. 2,409**
Rolling Hills Local SD
Supt. — See Cambridge
Meadowbrook HS 500/9-12
58615 Marietta Rd 43723 740-685-2566
Keith Arnold, prin. Fax 685-2797
Meadowbrook MS 400/6-8
58607 Marietta Rd 43723 740-685-2561
William Spence, admin. Fax 685-2628

**Cadiz, Harrison, Pop. 3,237**
Belmont-Harrison Area JVSD
Supt. — See Saint Clairsville
Harrison Career Center Vo/Tech
82500 Cadiz Jewett Rd 43907 740-942-2148
Larry Bossell, lead tchr. Fax 695-4866

Harrison Hills CSD 1,200/PK-12
730 Peppard Ave 43907 740-942-7800
Dana Snider, supt. Fax 942-7808
www.hhcsd.org/
Harrison Central JSHS 600/7-12
440 E Market St 43907 740-942-7700
Brent Ripley, prin. Fax 942-7705

**Caldwell, Noble, Pop. 1,727**
Caldwell EVD 700/K-12
516 Fairground St 43724 740-732-5637
Darren Cook, supt. Fax 732-7303
www.caldwell.k12.oh.us/
Caldwell HS, 516 Fairground St 43724 200/9-12
Devvon Dettra, prin. 740-732-5634

**Caledonia, Marion, Pop. 572**
River Valley Local SD 2,000/K-12
197 Brocklesby Rd 43314 740-725-5400
James Peterson, supt. Fax 725-5499
www.rivervalley.k12.oh.us
River Valley HS 500/9-12
4280 Marion Mount Gilead Rd 43314 740-725-5800
David Coleman, prin. Fax 725-5899
River Valley MS 500/6-8
4334 Marion Mount Gilead Rd 43314 740-725-5700
Donald Gliebe, prin. Fax 725-5799

**Cambridge, Guernsey, Pop. 10,324**
Cambridge CSD 2,200/K-12
6111 Fairdale Dr 43725 740-439-5021
Dennis Dettra, supt. Fax 439-3796
www.cambridge.k12.oh.us/
Cambridge HS 600/9-12
1401 Deerpath Dr 43725 740-435-1100
Margaret Wilcox, prin. Fax 435-1101
Cambridge MS 600/6-8
1400 Deerpath Dr 43725 740-435-1140
Duane Poland, prin. Fax 435-1141

Rolling Hills Local SD 1,700/K-12
60851 Southgate Rd 43725 740-432-5370
Ryan Caldwell, supt. Fax 432-6523
www.rollinghills.k12.oh.us
Other Schools – See Byesville

**Camden, Preble, Pop. 2,033**
Preble Shawnee Local SD 1,400/PK-12
124 Bloomfield St 45311 937-452-1283
David Ulrich, supt. Fax 452-3926
www.preble-shawnee.k12.oh.us
Preble Shawnee JSHS 600/7-12
5495 Somers Gratis Rd 45311 937-787-3541
Dianna Whitis, prin. Fax 787-3664

**Campbell, Mahoning, Pop. 8,033**
Campbell CSD 1,200/K-12
280 6th St 44405 330-799-8777
Matthew Bowen, supt. Fax 799-0875
www.campbell.k12.oh.us
Memorial HS 500/8-12
280 6th St 44405 330-799-1515
Jacquelyn Hampton, prin. Fax 799-6390

**Canal Fulton, Stark, Pop. 5,390**
Northwest Local SD 2,000/K-12
2309 Locust St S 44614 330-854-2291
Dr. Michael Shreffler, supt. Fax 854-3591
www.northwest.sparcc.org/
Northwest HS 600/9-12
8580 Erie Ave NW 44614 330-854-2205
Eric Bornstine, prin. Fax 854-2030
Northwest MS 500/6-8
8614 Erie Ave NW 44614 330-854-3303
Larry Tausch, prin. Fax 854-5883

**Canal Winchester, Franklin, Pop. 6,995**
Canal Winchester Local SD 3,500/K-12
100 Washington St 43110 614-837-4533
James Sotlar, supt. Fax 833-2165
www.cwls.us
Canal Winchester HS 1,000/9-12
300 Washington St 43110 614-833-2157
Kirk Henderson, prin. Fax 833-2163
Canal Winchester MS 900/6-8
7155 Parkview Dr 43110 614-833-2151
Tracie Lees, prin. Fax 833-2173

---

Harvest Preparatory S 500/PK-12
PO Box 400 43110 614-382-1111
Dr. Kenneth Grunden, prin. Fax 837-9591

**Canfield, Mahoning, Pop. 7,448**
Canfield Local SD 2,900/K-12
100 Wadsworth St 44406 330-533-3303
Alex Geordan, supt. Fax 533-6827
www.canfieldschools.net/
Canfield HS 900/9-12
100 Cardinal Dr 44406 330-533-5507
Michael Moldovan, prin. Fax 533-1919
Canfield Village MS 1,000/5-8
42 Wadsworth St 44406 330-533-4019
Judd Rubin, prin. Fax 702-7064

Mahoning County Career & Technical Ctr
7300 N Palmyra Rd 44406 330-729-4000
Dr. Ronald Iarussi, supt. Fax 729-4050
www.mahoningctc.com
Mahoning County Career & Technical Ctr Vo/Tech
7300 N Palmyra Rd 44406 330-729-4000
Jane Hogan, dir. Fax 729-4015

South Range Local SD 1,200/K-12
11300 Columbiana Canfield 44406 330-549-5226
Dennis J. Dunham, supt. Fax 549-4740
www.southrange.k12.oh.us/
South Range HS 400/9-12
11300 Columbiana Canfield 44406 330-549-2163
Stephen Rohan, prin. Fax 549-4083
South Range MS 400/5-8
11300 Columbiana Canfield 44406 330-549-4071
Daniel Szolek, prin. Fax 549-4073

**Canton, Stark, Pop. 69,508**
Canton CSD 6,900/PK-12
305 McKinley Ave NW 44702 330-438-2500
Adrian Allison, supt. Fax 430-4230
www.ccsdistrict.org
Altitude Academy @ Crenshaw 400/6-8
2525 19th St NE 44705 330-454-7717
Tiffany Joseph, prin. Fax 588-2120
Choices Alternative S 200/Alt
401 14th St SE 44707 330-451-3300
Timothy Henderson, prin. Fax 451-3301
College and Career Readiness Academy 700/6-8
1400 Broad Ave NW 44708 330-456-1963
Jeanne McNeal, prin. Fax 456-8121
Compton Learning Center 50/Alt
401 14th St SE 44707 330-456-1189
Tim Henderson, prin. Fax 580-2404
Early College Academy @ Souers 6-8
2800 13th St SW 44710 330-438-2736
Amy Conn, prin. Fax 580-3540
Early College HS 9-12
231 McKinley Ave NW 44702 330-458-3950
Ken Brunner, prin. Fax 458-3980
McKinley HS 1,600/9-12
2323 17th St NW 44708 330-438-2712
Ruth Zitnik, prin. Fax 580-2712
STEAMM Academy @ Hartford 200/6-8
1824 3rd St SE 44707 330-453-6012
David Thompson, prin. Fax 453-5096
Timken HS 1,000/9-12
521 Tuscarawas St W 44702 330-438-2602
Corey Grubbs, prin. Fax 580-3508

Canton Local SD 2,200/PK-12
4526 Ridge Ave SE 44707 330-484-8010
Stephen Milano, supt. Fax 484-8032
www.cantonlocal.org
Canton South HS 800/9-12
600 Faircrest St SE 44707 330-484-8000
Jeffrey Moore, prin. Fax 484-8013
Faircrest Memorial MS 700/5-8
616 Faircrest St SW 44706 330-484-8015
Gay Welker, prin. Fax 484-8033

Plain Local SD 6,000/K-12
901 44th St NW 44709 330-492-3500
Brent May, supt. Fax 493-5542
www.plainlocal.org/
Glenoak HS 2,000/9-12
1801 Schneider St NE 44721 330-491-3800
Tamiko Hatcher, prin. Fax 491-3801
Oakwood MS 900/7-8
2300 Schneider St NE 44721 330-491-3790
Brian Matthews, prin. Fax 491-3791

---

Aultman College Nursing and Health Sci Post-Sec.
2600 6th St SW 44710 330-363-6347
Brown Mackie College Post-Sec.
4300 Munson St NW 44718 330-494-1214
Central Catholic HS 400/9-12
4824 Tuscarawas St W 44708 330-478-2131
David Oates, prin. Fax 478-6086
Heritage Christian S 300/PK-12
2107 6th St SW 44706 330-452-8271
Karla Robinson M.Ed., admin. Fax 452-0672
Malone University Post-Sec.
2600 Cleveland Ave NW 44709 330-471-8100
National Beauty College Post-Sec.
4642 Cleveland Ave NW 44709 330-499-9444
National College Post-Sec.
4736 Dressler Rd NW 44718 330-492-5300
Timken Mercy Medical Center Post-Sec.
1320 Mercy Dr NW 44708 330-489-1001

**Cardington, Morrow, Pop. 2,023**
Cardington-Lincoln Local SD 1,100/K-12
121 Nichols St 43315 419-864-3691
Brian Petrie, supt. Fax 864-0946
www.cardington.k12.oh.us
Cardington-Lincoln HS 300/9-12
349 Chesterville Ave 43315 419-864-2691
Joseph Mills, prin. Fax 864-9515
Cardington-Lincoln JHS 200/7-8
349 Chesterville Ave 43315 419-864-0609
Joseph Mills, prin. Fax 864-3168

**Carey, Wyandot, Pop. 3,640**
Carey EVD 800/K-12
357 E South St 43316 419-396-7922
Michael Wank, supt. Fax 396-3158
careyevs.schoolwires.com/
Carey JSHS 400/7-12
357 E South St 43316 419-396-7638
Peter Cole, prin. Fax 396-3158

**Carlisle, Warren, Pop. 4,885**
Carlisle Local SD 1,700/K-12
724 Fairview Dr 45005 937-746-0710
Larry Hook, supt. Fax 746-0438
www.carlisleindians.org
Carlisle HS 400/9-12
250 Jamaica Rd 45005 937-746-4481
Bradley Potter, prin. Fax 746-6578
Chamberlain MS 400/6-8
720 Fairview Dr 45005 937-746-3227
Daniel Turner, prin. Fax 746-0519

**Carroll, Fairfield, Pop. 510**
Bloom-Carroll Local SD 1,600/K-12
PO Box 338 43112 614-837-6560
Lynn Landis, supt. Fax 756-4221
www.bloomcarroll.net
Bloom-Carroll HS 500/9-12
5240 Plum Rd 43112 740-756-4317
Shawn Haughn, prin. Fax 756-9525
Bloom-Carroll MS 400/5-8
PO Box 338 43112 740-756-9231
Cynthia Freeman, prin. Fax 756-7466

Eastland-Fairfield Career & Technical SD
Supt. — See Groveport
Fairfield Career Center Vo/Tech
3985 Coonpath Rd 43112 614-837-9443
Shelley Groves, dir. Fax 837-9447

**Carrollton, Carroll, Pop. 3,218**
Carrollton EVD 2,300/PK-12
252 3rd St NE 44615 330-627-2181
David Quattrochi, supt. Fax 627-2182
www.carrolltonschools.org
Bell-Herron MS 600/6-8
252 3rd St NE 44615 330-627-7188
Matthew Nicholas, prin. Fax 627-8429
Carrollton HS 700/9-12
252 3rd St NE 44615 330-627-2134
David Davis, prin. Fax 627-8103

**Casstown, Miami, Pop. 267**
Miami East Local SD 1,200/K-12
3825 N State Route 589 45312 937-335-7505
Dr. Todd Rappold, supt. Fax 335-6309
www.miamieast.k12.oh.us
Miami East HS 300/9-12
3925 N State Route 589 45312 937-335-7070
Todd Gentis, prin. Fax 440-9581
Miami East JHS 300/6-8
4025 N State Route 589 45312 937-335-5439
Allen Mack, prin. Fax 332-7927

**Castalia, Erie, Pop. 846**
Margaretta Local SD 1,200/PK-12
305 S Washington St 44824 419-684-5322
Daniel Schroer, supt. Fax 684-9003
www.margarettaschooldistrict.com
Margaretta JSHS 700/6-12
209 Lowell St 44824 419-684-5351
Rodney Smith, prin. Fax 684-5632

Firelands Christian Academy 50/K-12
3809 Maple Ave 44824 419-684-8642
Rusty Yost, prin. Fax 684-5378

**Cedarville, Greene, Pop. 3,956**
Cedar Cliff Local SD 600/K-12
PO Box 45 45314 937-766-6000
Dr. Chad Mason, supt. Fax 766-4717
www.cedarcliffschools.org
Cedarville MSHS 400/7-12
PO Box 45 45314 937-766-1871
Chad Haemmerle, prin. Fax 766-5211

Cedarville University Post-Sec.
251 N Main St 45314 937-766-2211

**Celina, Mercer, Pop. 10,225**
Celina CSD 2,300/K-12
585 E Livingston St 45822 419-586-8300
Dr. Ken Schmiesing, supt. Fax 586-7046
www.celinaschools.org
Celina HS 900/9-12
715 E Wayne St 45822 419-586-8300
Phil Metz, prin. Fax 584-0307
Celina MS 500/7-8
615 Holly St 45822 419-586-8300
Ann Esselstein, prin. Fax 586-9166

Mercer County ESC
441 E Market St 45822 419-586-6628
Shelly Vaughn, supt. Fax 586-3377
www.mercercountyesc.org/
Mercer County Alternative HS Alt
441 E Market St 45822 419-584-0186

Wright State University Post-Sec.
7600 Lake Campus Dr 45822 419-586-0300

**Centerburg, Knox, Pop. 1,748**
Centerburg Local SD 1,100/K-12
119 S Preston St 43011 740-625-6346
Mike Hebenthal, supt. Fax 625-9939
www.centerburgschools.org/
Centerburg HS 300/9-12
3782 Columbus Rd 43011 740-625-6055
Ryan Gallwitz, prin. Fax 625-5799
Centerburg MS 300/6-8
3782 Columbus Rd 43011 740-625-6055
Ryan Gallwitz, prin. Fax 625-5799

**Centerville, Montgomery, Pop. 23,528**
Centerville CSD 8,300/PK-12
111 Virginia Ave 45458 937-433-8841
Dr. Tom Henderson Ph.D., supt. Fax 438-6057
www.centerville.k12.oh.us
Centerville HS 2,900/9-12
500 E Franklin St 45459 937-439-3500
Jon Wesney, prin. Fax 439-3574
Magsig MS 600/6-8
192 W Franklin St 45459 937-433-0965
Stacey Westendorf, prin. Fax 433-5256
Tower Heights MS 600/6-8
195 N Johanna Dr 45459 937-434-0383
Clint Freese, prin. Fax 434-3033
Other Schools – See Dayton

Fortis College Post-Sec.
555 E Alex Bell Rd 45459 937-433-3410
Spring Valley Academy 300/K-12
1461 E Spring Valley Pike 45458 937-433-0790
Darren Wilkins, prin. Fax 433-0914

**Chagrin Falls, Cuyahoga, Pop. 4,089**
Chagrin Falls EVD 2,000/PK-12
400 E Washington St 44022 440-247-4363
Robert Hunt, supt. Fax 247-5883
www.chagrinschools.org
Chagrin Falls HS 600/9-12
400 E Washington St 44022 440-247-2072
Steven Ast, prin. Fax 247-2071
Chagrin Falls MS 300/7-8
342 E Washington St 44022 440-247-4746
David Wessel, prin. Fax 247-4855

Kenston Local SD 2,900/PK-12
17419 Snyder Rd 44023 440-543-9677
Nancy Santilli, supt. Fax 543-8634
www.kenstonlocal.com
Kenston HS 1,000/9-12
9500 Bainbridge Rd 44023 440-543-9821
Jeremy McDevitt, prin. Fax 543-9021
Kenston MS 800/6-8
17425 Snyder Rd 44023 440-543-8241
Patricia Brockway, prin. Fax 543-4851

English Nanny and Governess School Post-Sec.
37 S Franklin St 44022 440-247-0600

**Chardon, Geauga, Pop. 5,091**
Chardon Local SD 3,100/K-12
428 North St 44024 440-285-4052
Michael Hanlon, supt. Fax 285-7229
www.chardon.k12.oh.us
Chardon HS 1,100/9-12
151 Chardon Ave 44024 440-285-4057
Andrew Fetchik, prin. Fax 285-9463
Chardon MS 700/6-8
424 North St 44024 440-285-4062
Douglas Higham, prin. Fax 286-0461

Notre Dame-Cathedral Latin HS 700/9-12
13000 Auburn Rd 44024 440-286-6226
Joseph Waler, prin. Fax 286-7199

**Charm, Holmes**
East Holmes Local SD
Supt. — See Berlin
Wise ES, PO Box 159 44617 100/5-8
Jon Wilson, prin. 330-893-2505

**Chesapeake, Lawrence, Pop. 736**
Chesapeake Union EVD 1,400/K-12
10183 County Road 1 45619 740-867-3135
Jerry McConnell, supt. Fax 867-3136
www.peake.k12.oh.us
Chesapeake HS 400/9-12
10181 County Road 1 45619 740-867-5958
Christopher Smith, prin. Fax 867-1130
Chesapeake MS 400/5-8
10335 County Road 1 45619 740-867-3972
Ty Johnson, prin. Fax 867-1120

Lawrence County JVSD
11627 State Route 243 45619 740-867-6641
Stephen Dodgion, supt. Fax 867-1317
www.collins-cc.edu/
Collins Career Center Vo/Tech
11627 State Route 243 45619 740-867-6641
Stephen Dodgion, supt. Fax 867-1317

Collins Career Center Post-Sec.
11627 State Route 243 45619 740-867-6641

**Chesterland, Geauga, Pop. 2,498**
West Geauga Local SD 2,200/K-12
8615 Cedar Rd 44026 440-729-5900
Dr. Rich Markwardt, supt. Fax 729-5939
www.westg.org
West Geauga HS 900/9-12
13401 Chillicothe Rd 44026 440-729-5950
Jay Bishop, prin. Fax 729-5959
West Geauga MS 500/6-8
8611 Cedar Rd 44026 440-729-5940
James Kish, prin. Fax 729-5909

**Chillicothe, Ross, Pop. 21,171**
Chillicothe CSD 2,600/K-12
425 Yoctangee Pkwy 45601 740-775-4250
Jon Saxton, supt. Fax 775-4270
www.ccsd.us/
Chillicothe HS 800/9-12
421 Yoctangee Pkwy 45601 740-702-2287
Jeffrey Fisher, prin. Fax 773-1097
Chillicothe MS Site 1 500/7-8
381 Yoctangee Pkwy 45601 740-773-2241
Aaron Brown, prin. Fax 774-9482

Huntington Local SD 1,200/K-12
188 Huntsman Rd 45601 740-663-5892
Keith Stevenson, supt. Fax 663-6078
www.huntsmen.org
Huntington HS 300/9-12
188 Huntsman Rd 45601 740-663-2230
Nathan Caplinger, prin. Fax 663-5042
Huntington MS 300/6-8
188 Huntsman Rd 45601 740-663-6079
Alice Kellough, prin. Fax 663-6080

Pickaway-Ross County JVSD
895 Crouse Chapel Rd 45601 740-642-1200
Dennis Franks, supt. Fax 642-1399
www.pickawayross.com
Pickaway-Ross Career & Technology Center Vo/Tech
895 Crouse Chapel Rd 45601 740-642-1200
Shara Cochenour, prin. Fax 642-1399

Southeastern Local SD 1,200/K-12
2003 Lancaster Rd 45601 740-774-2003
Brian Justice, supt. Fax 774-1687
www.sepanthers.k12.oh.us/
Southeastern HS 300/9-12
2003 Lancaster Rd 45601 740-774-2003
Leonard Steyer, prin. Fax 774-1684
Southeastern MS 400/5-8
2003 Lancaster Rd 45601 740-774-2003
Zachary Pfeifer, prin. Fax 774-1684

Union-Scioto Local SD 2,000/PK-12
1565 Egypt Pike 45601 740-773-4102
Matt Thornsberry, supt. Fax 775-2852
www.unioto.org
Unioto HS 600/9-12
14193 Pleasant Valley Rd 45601 740-773-4105
James Osborne, prin. Fax 774-9158
Unioto MS 300/6-8
160 Moundsville Rd 45601 740-773-5211
Wilma Gillott, prin. Fax 772-2974

Zane Trace Local SD 1,500/K-12
946 State Route 180 45601 740-775-1355
Jerry Mowery, supt. Fax 773-0249
www.zanetrace.org
Zane Trace HS 500/9-12
946 State Route 180 45601 740-775-1809
Todd Holdren, prin. Fax 775-1301
Zane Trace MS 500/5-8
946 State Route 180 45601 740-773-5842
Bret Mavis, prin. Fax 773-9998

Daymar College Post-Sec.
1410 Industrial Dr 45601 740-774-6300
Ohio University Post-Sec.
PO Box 629 45601 740-774-7200
Recording Workshop Post-Sec.
455 Massieville Rd 45601 740-663-1000

**Cincinnati, Hamilton, Pop. 289,429**
Cincinnati CSD, PO Box 5381 45201 28,200/PK-12
Mary Ronan, supt. 513-363-0000
www.cps-k12.org
Aiken HS - New Tech 400/7-12
5641 Belmont Ave 45224 513-363-6700
Melissa Votaw, prin. Fax 363-6720
Clark Montessori JSHS 700/7-12
3030 Erie Ave 45208 513-363-7100
John Spieser, prin. Fax 363-7120
Dater JSHS 700/7-12
2146 Ferguson Rd 45238 513-363-7200
Stephen Sippel, prin. Fax 363-7220
Gamble Montessori HS 300/7-12
2700 Felicity Pl 45211 513-363-2600
Jack Jose, prin. Fax 363-2620
Hughes STEM HS 200/7-12
2515 Clifton Ave 45219 513-363-7400
Kathy Wright, prin. Fax 363-7420
Oyler S 700/PK-12
2121 Hatmaker St 45204 513-363-4100
Amy Randolph, prin. Fax 363-4120
Riverview East Academy 600/PK-12
3555 Kellogg Ave 45226 513-363-3400
Charlene Myers, prin. Fax 363-3420
School for Creative & Performing Arts 1,400/K-12
108 W Central Pkwy 45202 513-363-8000
Steve Brokamp, prin. Fax 363-8020
Shroder JSHS 600/7-12
5030 Duck Creek Rd 45227 513-363-6900
Larry Williams, prin. Fax 363-6920
Taft Information Technology HS 600/7-12
420 Ezzard Charles Dr 45214 513-363-8200
Michael Turner, prin. Fax 363-8220
Walnut Hills JSHS 2,400/7-12
3250 Victory Pkwy 45207 513-363-8400
Jeff Brokamp, prin. Fax 363-8420
Western Hills University HS 700/7-12
2144 Ferguson Rd 45238 513-363-8900
Donald Jump, prin. Fax 363-8920
Withrow University JSHS 900/7-12
2488 Madison Rd 45208 513-363-9200
Paul Daniels, prin. Fax 363-9220
Woodward Career Technical HS Vo/Tech
7005 Reading Rd 45237 513-363-9300
Shauna Murphy, prin. Fax 363-9320

Deer Park Community CSD 1,200/K-12
4131 Matson Ave 45236 513-891-0222
Jeff Langdon, supt. Fax 891-2930
www.deerparkcityschools.org
Deer Park JSHS 500/7-12
8351 Plainfield Rd 45236 513-891-0010
Dr. Stace Orso, prin. Fax 891-3845

Finneytown Local SD 1,400/K-12
8916 Fontainebleau Ter 45231 513-728-3700
Tyrone Olverson, supt. Fax 931-0986
www.finneytown.org
Finneytown Secondary Campus 700/7-12
8916 Fontainebleau Ter 45231 513-931-0712
Sally Thurman, prin. Fax 728-7230

Forest Hills Local SD 7,400/PK-12
7550 Forest Rd 45255 513-231-3600
Thomas D. Durbin, supt. Fax 231-3830
www.foresthills.edu
Anderson HS 1,200/9-12
7560 Forest Rd 45255 513-232-2772
Michael Overbey, prin. Fax 232-3146
Nagel MS 1,100/7-8
1500 Nagel Rd 45255 513-474-5407
John Vander Meer, prin. Fax 474-5584
Turpin HS 1,100/9-12
2650 Bartels Rd 45244 513-232-7770
David Spencer, prin. Fax 232-9047

Great Oaks Institute of Technology
110 Great Oaks Dr 45241 513-771-8840
Harry Snyder, supt. Fax 771-6575
www.greatoaks.com/
Diamond Oaks CDC Vo/Tech
6375 Harrison Ave 45247 513-574-1300
Dan Rush, prin. Fax 574-3953
Scarlet Oaks CDC Vo/Tech
300 Scarlet Oaks Dr 45241 513-771-8810
Joe Moon, prin. Fax 771-4928
Other Schools – See Milford, Wilmington

Indian Hill EVD 2,000/K-12
6855 Drake Rd 45243 513-272-4500
Dr. Mark Miles, supt. Fax 272-4756
indianhillschools.org
Indian Hill HS 700/9-12
6865 Drake Rd 45243 513-272-4550
Dr. Antonio Shelton, prin. Fax 272-4557
Indian Hill MS 500/6-8
6845 Drake Rd 45243 513-272-4642
Bridgette Ridley, prin. Fax 272-4690

Madeira CSD 1,500/PK-12
7465 Loannes Dr 45243 513-985-6070
Stephen Kramer, supt. Fax 985-6072
www.madeiracityschools.org
Madeira HS 400/9-12
7465 Loannes Dr 45243 513-891-8222
David Kennedy, prin. Fax 985-6089
Madeira MS 400/5-8
6612 Miami Ave 45243 513-561-5555
Tom Olson, prin. Fax 272-4145

Mariemont CSD 1,600/K-12
2 Warrior Way 45227 513-272-7500
Steve Estepp, supt. Fax 527-3436
www.mariemontschools.org
Mariemont HS 400/9-12
1 Warrior Way 45227 513-272-7600
Jim Renner, prin. Fax 527-5991
Mariemont JHS 300/7-8
3847 Southern Ave 45227 513-272-7300
Molly Connaughton, prin. Fax 527-3432

Mt. Healthy CSD
Supt. — See Mount Healthy
Mt. Healthy HS 800/9-12
8101 Hamilton Ave 45231 513-729-0130
Michael Howton, prin. Fax 728-4695
Mt. Healthy JHS 500/7-8
8101 Hamilton Ave 45231 513-742-0666
Michael Howton, prin. Fax 742-2797

North College Hill CSD 1,500/PK-12
1731 Goodman Ave 45239 513-931-8181
Gary Gellert, supt. Fax 728-4774
www.nchcityschools.org
North College Hill HS 400/9-12
1620 W Galbraith Rd 45239 513-728-4783
Ann Brinkley, prin. Fax 728-4784
North College Hill MS 500/5-8
1624 W Galbraith Rd 45239 513-728-4785
Michelle Garton, prin. Fax 728-4786

Northwest Local SD 7,900/PK-12
3240 Banning Rd 45239 513-923-1000
Todd Bowling, supt. Fax 923-3644
www.nwlsd.org
Colerain HS 1,900/9-12
8801 Cheviot Rd 45251 513-385-6424
Kristilynn Turney, prin. Fax 741-5032
Colerain MS 600/6-8
4700 Poole Rd 45251 513-385-8490
Libby Styles, prin. Fax 385-6685
Northwest HS 1,000/9-12
10761 Pippin Rd 45231 513-851-7300
Susan Smith, prin. Fax 742-6376
Pleasant Run MS 800/6-8
11770 Pippin Rd 45231 513-851-2400
David Maine, prin. Fax 851-7071
White Oak MS 800/6-8
3130 Jessup Rd 45239 513-741-4300
Dustin Gehring, prin. Fax 741-0717

Oak Hills Local SD 7,800/K-12
6325 Rapid Run Rd 45233 513-574-3200
Todd Yohey, supt. Fax 598-2947
ohlsd.us
Bridgetown MS 600/6-8
3900 Race Rd 45211 513-574-3511
Adam Taylor, prin. Fax 574-6689
Delhi MS 600/6-8
5280 Foley Rd 45238 513-922-8400
Scott Toon, prin. Fax 922-8472
Oak Hills HS 2,500/9-12
3200 Ebenezer Rd 45248 513-922-2300
John Stoddard, prin. Fax 922-4900
Rapid Run MS 600/6-8
6345 Rapid Run Rd 45233 513-467-0300
Travis Hunt, prin. Fax 467-0333

Princeton CSD 5,300/PK-12
3900 Cottingham Dr 45241 513-864-1000
Dr. Thomas Tucker, supt. Fax 864-1008
www.princetonschools.net
Princeton Community MS 1,100/6-8
200 Viking Way 45246 513-864-2000
Maureen Durham, prin. Fax 864-2091
Princeton HS 1,600/9-12
11080 Chester Rd 45246 513-864-1500
Charles Ogden, prin. Fax 864-1591

Sycamore Community CSD 5,300/PK-12
5959 Hagewa Dr 45242 513-686-1700
Frank Forsthoefel, supt. Fax 791-4873
www.sycamoreschools.org
Sycamore HS 1,800/9-12
7400 Cornell Rd 45242 513-686-1770
Douglas Mader, prin. Fax 489-7425
Sycamore JHS 800/7-8
5757 Cooper Rd 45242 513-686-1760
Traci Rea, prin. Fax 891-3162

West Clermont Local SD 8,500/K-12
4350 Aicholtz Rd 45245 513-943-5000
Dr. Keith Kline, supt. Fax 752-6158
www.westcler.k12.oh.us
Glen Este HS 1,200/9-12
4342 Glen Este Wthmsvlle Rd 45245 513-947-7600
Robert Walker, prin. Fax 943-7090
Glen Este MS 1,000/6-8
4342 Glen Este Wthmsvlle Rd 45245 513-947-7700
Lori Crowe, prin. Fax 753-3462
Other Schools – See Batavia

Winton Woods CSD 3,600/PK-12
1215 W Kemper Rd 45240 513-619-2300
Anthony G. Smith, supt. Fax 619-2309
www.wintonwoods.org
Academy of Global Studies @ Winton Woods 200/9-12
1231 W Kemper Rd 45240 513-619-2420
Eric Martin, prin. Fax 619-2417
Winton Woods Alternative Education Alt
8 Enfield St 45218 513-619-2389
Brenda Hodges-Davis, admin.
Winton Woods HS 1,100/9-12
1231 W Kemper Rd 45240 513-619-2420
Eric Martin, prin. Fax 619-2417
Winton Woods MS 500/7-8
147 Farragut Rd 45218 513-619-2440
Doug Sanker, prin. Fax 619-2452

---

Aldersgate Christian Academy 100/K-12
1810 Young St 45202 513-763-6655
William Marshall, prin. Fax 763-6643
Antonelli College Post-Sec.
124 E 7th St 45202 513-241-4338
Archbishop McNicholas HS 600/9-12
6536 Beechmont Ave 45230 513-231-3500
Patricia Beckert, prin. Fax 231-1351
Art Academy of Cincinnati Post-Sec.
1212 Jackson St 45202 513-562-6262
Art Institute of Ohio - Cincinnati Post-Sec.
8845 Governors Hill Dr #100 45249 513-833-2400
Athenaeum of Ohio Post-Sec.
6616 Beechmont Ave 45230 513-231-2223
Bacon HS 400/9-12
4320 Vine St 45217 513-641-1300
Steven Schad, prin. Fax 641-0498
Beckfield College Post-Sec.
225 Pictoria Dr Ste 200 45246 513-671-1920
Brown Mackie College Post-Sec.
1011 Glendale Milford Rd 45215 513-771-2424
Christ College of Nursing & Heath Sci Post-Sec.
2139 Auburn Ave 45219 513-585-2401
Cincinnati Christian University Post-Sec.
2700 Glenway Ave 45204 513-244-8100
Cincinnati College of Mortuary Science Post-Sec.
645 W North Bend Rd 45224 888-377-8433
Cincinnati Country Day S 800/PK-12
6905 Given Rd 45243 513-561-7298
Dr. Robert Macrae, hdmstr. Fax 527-7600
Cincinnati Hills Christian Academy HS 500/9-12
11525 Snider Rd 45249 513-247-0900
Dr. Dean Nicholas, prin. Fax 247-0982
Cincinnati Hills Christian Academy MS 400/5-8
11300 Snider Rd 45249 513-247-0900
Randy Brunk, head sch Fax 247-9362
Cincinnati State Technical & Comm Coll Post-Sec.
3520 Central Pkwy 45223 513-569-1500
College of Mount Saint Joseph Post-Sec.
5701 Delhi Rd 45233 513-244-4200
DePaul Cristo Rey HS 100/9-12
1133 Clifton Hills Ave 45220 513-861-0600
Andrew Farfsing, prin.
DeVry University Post-Sec.
8800 Governors Hill Dr #100 45249 513-583-5000
Elder HS 900/9-12
3900 Vincent Ave 45205 513-921-3744
Thomas Otten, prin. Fax 921-8123
Fortis College Post-Sec.
11499 Chester Rd Ste 200 45246 513-771-2795
God's Bible School and College Post-Sec.
1810 Young St 45202 513-721-7944
Good Samaritan Coll of Nursing/Alld Hlth Post-Sec.
375 Dixmyth Ave 45220 513-862-2743
Hebrew Union College Post-Sec.
3101 Clifton Ave 45220 513-221-1875
International Academy of Hair Design Post-Sec.
8419 Colerain Ave 45239 513-741-4777
La Salle HS 700/9-12
3091 N Bend Rd 45239 513-741-3000
Thomas Luebbe, prin. Fax 741-2666
Marinello-Eastern Hills Academy Post-Sec.
7681 Beechmont Ave 45255 513-231-8621
McAuley HS 600/9-12
6000 Oakwood Ave 45224 513-681-1800
Daniel Minelli, prin. Fax 681-1802
Miami Valley Christian Academy 300/PK-12
6830 School St 45244 513-272-6822
Greg Beasley, head sch Fax 272-3711
Moeller HS 900/9-12
9001 Montgomery Rd 45242 513-791-1680
Blane Collison, prin. Fax 792-3343
Moler-Hollywood Beauty Academy Post-Sec.
6142 Montgomery Rd 45213 513-621-5262
Mother of Mercy HS 500/9-12
3036 Werk Rd 45211 513-661-2740
David Mueller, prin. Fax 661-1842
National College Post-Sec.
6871 Steger Dr 45237 513-761-1291
Ohio Center for Broadcasting Post-Sec.
6703 Madison Rd 45227 513-271-6060
Ohio Mid-Western College Post-Sec.
10765 Reading Rd 45241 513-429-1990
Purcell-Marian HS 400/9-12
2935 Hackberry St 45206 513-751-1230
Veronica Murphy, prin. Fax 751-1395
Ross Inst of Medical & Dental Technology Post-Sec.
11590 Century Blvd Ste 210 45246 513-851-8500
St. Rita School for the Deaf Post-Sec.
1720 Glendale Milford Rd 45215 513-771-7600
St. Ursula Academy 700/9-12
1339 E Mcmillan St 45206 513-961-3410
Craig Maliborski, prin. Fax 961-3856
St. Xavier HS 1,500/9-12
600 W North Bend Rd 45224 513-761-7600
Terrence Tyrrell, prin. Fax 842-1610
Seton HS 600/9-12
3901 Glenway Ave 45205 513-471-2600
Karen White, prin. Fax 471-0529
Seven Hills S Hillsdale Campus 500/6-12
5400 Red Bank Rd 45227 513-728-2400
Christopher Garten, hdmstr. Fax 728-2409
Sevenstar Academy 2,200/6-12
3630 Park 42 Dr 45241 513-612-1029
Dr. R. Mark Beadle, admin. Fax 618-3334
Summit Country Day S 1,100/PK-12
2161 Grandin Rd 45208 513-871-4700
Richard Wilson, prin. Fax 871-6558
The AIC College of Design Post-Sec.
1171 E Kemper Rd 45246 513-751-1206
Tri County Beauty College Post-Sec.
111 W Kemper Rd 45246 513-671-8340
Union Institute and University Post-Sec.
440 E McMillan St 45206 513-861-6400
University of Cincinnati Post-Sec.
2600 Clifton Ave 45220 513-556-6000
Ursuline Academy 700/9-12
5535 Pfeiffer Rd 45242 513-791-5791
Thomas Barhorst, prin. Fax 791-5802
Western Hills Sch of Beauty & Hair Dsgn. Post-Sec.
6490 Glenway Ave 45211 513-574-3818
Xavier University Post-Sec.
3800 Victory Pkwy 45207 513-745-3000

**Circleville, Pickaway, Pop. 13,083**

Circleville CSD 1,800/PK-12
388 Clark Dr 43113 740-474-4340
Kirk McMahon, supt. Fax 474-6600
www.circlevillecityschools.org/
Circleville HS 600/9-12
380 Clark Dr 43113 740-474-4846
Chris Thornsley, prin. Fax 474-3987
Everts MS 500/6-8
360 Clark Dr 43113 740-474-2345
Kevin Fox, prin. Fax 477-6384

Logan Elm Local SD 1,700/PK-12
9579 Tarlton Rd 43113 740-474-7501
Tim Williams, supt. Fax 477-6525
www.loganelmschools.com/
Logan Elm HS 600/9-12
9575 Tarlton Rd 43113 740-474-7503
Nate Smith, prin. Fax 477-3592
McDowell-Exchange JHS 300/7-8
9579 Tarlton Rd 43113 740-474-7538
Marsha Waidelich, prin. Fax 474-8539

---

Ohio Christian University Post-Sec.
1476 Lancaster Pike 43113 740-474-8896

**Clarksville, Clinton, Pop. 544**

Clinton-Massie Local SD 1,900/K-12
2556 Lebanon Rd 45113 937-289-2471
Dr. David Baits, supt. Fax 289-3313
www.clinton-massie.k12.oh.us
Clinton-Massie HS 500/9-12
2556 Lebanon Rd 45113 937-289-2109
Barrett Swope, prin. Fax 289-7019
Clinton-Massie MS 400/6-8
2556 Lebanon Rd 45113 937-289-2932
Barrett Swope, prin. Fax 289-8100

**Clayton, Montgomery, Pop. 12,864**

Miami Valley Career Technology Ctr SD
6800 Hoke Rd 45315 937-837-7781
Nicholas Weldy, supt. Fax 837-5318
www.mvctc.com
Miami Valley Career Tech Center Vo/Tech
6800 Hoke Rd 45315 937-837-7781
Fax 837-1594

Other Schools – See Dayton

Northmont CSD
Supt. — See Englewood
Northmont HS 1,600/9-12
4916 National Rd 45315 937-832-6000
George Caras, prin. Fax 832-6001
Northmont MS 900/7-8
4810 National Rd 45315 937-832-6500
Jarrod Brumbaugh, prin. Fax 832-6501

**Cleveland, Cuyahoga, Pop. 388,662**

Cleveland Municipal SD 37,100/PK-12
1111 Superior Ave E 44114 216-838-0000
Eric Gordon, admin. Fax 436-5144
clevelandmetroschools.org
Adams Academy 1,200/9-12
3817 Martin Luther King Jr 44105 216-491-5700
Damon Holmes, prin. Fax 295-4645
Addams Business Careers Center 400/8-12
2373 E 30th St 44115 216-623-8900
Ann McGhee, prin. Fax 621-3910
Bard HS Early College 9-12
11801 Worthington Ave 44111 216-838-9704
Dumaine Williams, prin.
Cleveland Early College HS 200/9-12
2075 Stokes Blvd 44106 216-229-0200
Carol Lockhart, prin. Fax 229-0087
Cleveland HS for the Digital Arts 9-12
1440 Lakeside Ave 44114 216-838-9650
John Buzzard, prin.
Cleveland S of Architecture & Design 300/9-12
2075 Stokes Blvd 44106 216-229-0100
Tianna Maxey, prin. Fax 229-0072
Cleveland S of Science & Medicine 400/9-12
2075 Stokes Blvd 44106 216-229-0070
Edward Weber, prin. Fax 339-3242
Cleveland S of the Arts @ Harry Davis 600/6-12
10700 Churchill Ave 44106 216-791-2496
Kendra Holloway, prin. Fax 421-7689
Collinwood Comprehensive HS 11-12
15210 Saint Clair Ave 44110 216-268-6052
Mary Miller, prin. Fax 268-6057
Collinwood New Tech 9-10
15210 Saint Clair Ave 44110 216-268-6125
Maria Carlson, prin. Fax 268-6057
Design Lab-Early College @ Health Career 9-12
1740 E 32nd St 44114 216-621-5064
Eric Juli, prin.
E3gle Academy 9-9
13604 Christine Ave 44105 216-838-5150
Margaret Schauer, prin.
East Technical Community Wrap Around 9-12
2439 E 55th St 44104 216-432-4554
Paul Hoover, prin. Fax 431-4631
East Technical Engineering & Science 700/9-12
2439 E 55th St 44104 216-432-4558
Temujin Taylor, prin. Fax 431-4631
Facing History New Tech HS @ Mooney 9-9
3213 Montclair Ave 44109 216-838-8600
Marc Engoglia, prin. Fax 838-8610
Ginn Academy 200/9-12
655 E 162nd St 44110 216-531-4466
Nicholas Petty, prin. Fax 531-2874

Glenville Career & College Readiness 11-12
650 E 113th St 44108 216-268-6000
Jackie Bell, prin. Fax 541-7666
Glenville Health Exercise Sports Academy 9-10
650 E 113th St 44108 216-268-6000
Fax 541-7666
Glenville Ninth Grade Academy 9-9
650 E 113th St 44108 216-268-6000
Jackie Bell, prin. Fax 541-7666
Hayes HS 600/9-12
4600 Detroit Ave 44102 216-631-1528
Phillip Schwenk, prin. Fax 634-2175
Health Career Academy - MLK Campus 300/9-12
1651 E 71st St 44103 216-431-6858
Fax 431-5180
High Tech Academy 9-12
2900 Community College Ave 44115 216-987-3549
Stacy Hutchinson, prin. Fax 987-4397
Jefferson Intl Newcomers Academy 300/PK-12
3145 W 46th St 44102 216-404-5100
Marisol Burgos, prin. Fax 404-5492
Kennedy HS 800/11-12
17100 Harvard Ave 44128 216-921-1450
Maryum Sims, prin. Fax 295-2455
Law & Municipal Careers Academy - MLK 300/9-12
1651 E 71st St 44103 216-431-6858
Latonia Davis, prin. Fax 431-5180
Lincoln West International Studies HS 1,100/9-12
3202 W 30th St 44109 216-631-1505
Irene Javier, prin. Fax 634-2403
Marshall 9th Grade Academy @ Hawthorne 9-9
3575 W 130th St 44111 216-889-4000
Lisa Williams-Locklear, prin.
Marshall HS 1,100/9-12
13501 Terminal Ave 44135 216-858-6000
Tiffiany James, prin. Fax 476-4458
MC2 STEM Cleveland State University 400/11-12
1740 E 32nd St 44114 216-838-8500
Feowyn MacKinnon, prin.
MC2 STEM GE Lighting S 10-10
1975 Noble Rd Bldg 336 44112 216-744-1512
Feowyn MacKinnon, head sch
MC2 STEM Great Lakes Science Center 9-9
601 Erieside Ave 44114 216-858-1267
Feowyn MacKinnon, prin. Fax 858-1264
Morgan S of Science 300/9-12
4016 Woodbine Ave 44113 216-281-6188
Fax 634-2113
New Tech East @ East Technical 100/9-12
2439 E 55th St 44104 216-361-3116
Corether Johnson, prin. Fax 361-3282
New Tech West @ Max Hayes 9-12
4600 Detroit Ave 44102 216-281-1030
Erin Frew, prin. Fax 281-1055
PACT, 13604 Christine Ave 44105 9-12
Richard Reynolds, prin. 216-838-5200
Rhodes HS 1,300/9-12
5100 Biddulph Ave 44144 216-459-4200
Dr. Charlene Hilliard, prin. Fax 459-3133
School of One @ Nathaniel Hawthorne 9-12
3575 W 130th St 44111 216-659-4049
Wayne Marok, prin.
SuccessTech Academy 200/10-12
1440 Lakeside Ave E 44114 216-523-8463
Sara Kidner, prin. Fax 523-8464
Young Academy 300/2-12
17900 Harvard Ave 44128 216-283-5220
Karen Byron-Johnson, prin. Fax 295-3547
Other Schools – See Newburgh Heights

---

Benedictine HS 300/9-12
2900 Martin Luther King Jr 44104 216-421-2080
Michael Brunovsky, prin. Fax 421-0107
Bridge Builders Academy for Girls 100/6-8
4620 Ammon Rd 44143 216-225-7471
Tandy Hicks, head sch
Bryant & Stratton College Post-Sec.
3121 Euclid Ave 44115 216-771-1700
Case Western Reserve University Post-Sec.
10900 Euclid Ave 44106 216-368-2000
Chamberlain College of Nursing Post-Sec.
6700 Euclid Ave Ste 201 44103 216-361-6005
Cleveland Central Catholic HS 500/9-12
6550 Baxter Ave 44105 216-441-4700
Sr. Allison Gusdanovic, prin. Fax 441-8353
Cleveland Clinic Center Allied Health Post-Sec.
9500 Euclid Ave 44195 216-986-4312
Cleveland Institute Dental Medical Asst. Post-Sec.
2450 Prospect Ave E 44115 216-241-2930
Cleveland Institute of Art Post-Sec.
11141 East Blvd 44106 216-421-7000
Cleveland Institute of Electronics Post-Sec.
1776 E 17th St 44114 216-781-9400
Cleveland Institute of Music Post-Sec.
11021 East Blvd 44106 216-791-5000
Cleveland State University Post-Sec.
2121 Euclid Ave 44115 216-687-2000
Cleveland Veterans Affairs Medical Ctr Post-Sec.
10701 East Blvd 44106 216-421-3028
Cuyahoga Community College Post-Sec.
2900 Community College Ave 44115 800-954-8742
Fairview General Hospital Post-Sec.
18101 Lorain Ave 44111 216-476-7000
John Carroll University Post-Sec.
1 John Carroll Blvd 44118 216-397-1886
Meridia Health System Post-Sec.
17325 Euclid Ave 44112 440-446-8260
MetroHealth Medical Center Post-Sec.
2500 Metrohealth Dr 44109 216-459-5700
Notre Dame College Post-Sec.
4545 College Rd 44121 216-381-1680
Ohio Center for Broadcasting Post-Sec.
9885 Rockside Rd Ste 160 44125 216-503-5900
Ohio Technical College Post-Sec.
1374 E 51st St 44103 216-881-1700
Remington College Post-Sec.
14445 Broadway Ave 44125 216-475-7520

St. Ignatius HS 1,500/9-12
1911 W 30th St 44113 216-651-0222
Dan Bradesca, prin. Fax 961-2564
St. Joseph Academy 700/9-12
3470 Rocky River Dr 44111 216-251-6788
Jeff Sutliff, prin. Fax 251-5809
St. Luke's Medical Center Post-Sec.
2351 E 22nd St 44115 216-368-7000
St. Martin de Porres HS 500/9-12
6111 Lausche Ave 44103 216-881-1689
Gary Sardon, prin. Fax 881-8303
Southwest General Hospital Post-Sec.
18697 Bagley Rd 44130 440-816-6801
Villa Angela-St. Joseph HS 300/9-12
18491 Lake Shore Blvd 44119 216-481-8414
David Csank, prin. Fax 486-1035

**Cleveland Heights, Cuyahoga, Pop. 44,828**
Cleveland Hts - University Hts CSD
Supt. — See University Heights
Monticello MS 400/6-8
3665 Monticello Blvd 44121 216-371-6520
Deborah Moore, prin. Fax 397-5967
Roxboro MS 500/6-8
2400 Roxboro Rd 44106 216-371-7440
Patrick McNichols, prin. Fax 397-3857

---

Beaumont HS 400/9-12
3301 N Park Blvd 44118 216-321-2954
Mary Whelan, prin. Fax 321-3947
Hebrew Academy of Cleveland 600/PK-12
1860 S Taylor Rd 44118 216-321-5838
Lutheran HS East 100/9-12
3565 Mayfield Rd 44118 216-382-6100
Chris Steinmann, prin. Fax 382-6119
Mosdos Ohr HaTorah S - Boys 200/PK-12
1508 Warrensville Center Rd 44121 216-382-6248
Esther Greenberger, prin. Fax 382-4585
Mosdos Ohr HaTorah S - Girls 400/PK-12
1700 S Taylor Rd 44118 216-321-1547
Fax 321-7505

**Cleves, Hamilton, Pop. 3,191**
Three Rivers Local SD 500/PK-12
401 N Miami Ave 45002 513-941-6400
Craig Hockenberry, supt. Fax 941-1102
www.threeriversschools.org
Taylor HS 500/9-12
56 Cooper Ave 45002 513-467-3200
Megan Rivet, prin. Fax 467-0138
Taylor MS 5-8
56 Cooper Ave 45002 513-467-3500
Matthew Haws, prin. Fax 467-0053

**Clyde, Sandusky, Pop. 6,212**
Clyde-Green Springs EVD 2,300/K-12
106 S Main St 43410 419-547-0588
David Stubblebine, supt. Fax 547-8644
www.clyde.k12.oh.us
Clyde HS 700/9-12
1015 Race St 43410 419-547-9511
Joe Webb, prin. Fax 547-7593
McPherson MS 500/6-8
4230 Limerick Rd 43410 419-547-9150
Rachael Aldrich, prin. Fax 547-9173

**Coal Grove, Lawrence, Pop. 2,141**
Dawson-Bryant Local SD 1,100/K-12
222 Lane St 45638 740-532-6451
Steve Easterling, supt. Fax 533-6019
db.k12.oh.us
Dawson-Bryant HS 300/9-12
1 Hornet Ln 45638 740-532-6345
Dean Mader, prin. Fax 533-6013
Dawson-Bryant MS 300/6-8
1 Hornet Ln 45638 740-533-6008
Michael Eicher, prin. Fax 533-6002

**Coldwater, Mercer, Pop. 4,401**
Coldwater EVD 1,400/K-12
310 N 2nd St 45828 419-678-2611
Jason Wood, supt. Fax 678-3100
cw.noacsc.org
Coldwater HS 500/9-12
310 N 2nd St 45828 419-678-4821
Jason Hemmelgarn, prin. Fax 678-3100
Coldwater MS 400/5-8
310 N 2nd St 45828 419-678-3331
Dan Pohlman, prin. Fax 678-3100

**Collins, Huron, Pop. 625**
Western Reserve Local SD 1,200/K-12
3765 State Route 20 44826 419-660-8508
Rodge Wilson, supt. Fax 660-8429
www.western-reserve.org
Western Reserve HS 400/9-12
3841 State Route 20 44826 419-668-8470
Lisa Border, prin. Fax 663-5916
Western Reserve MS 200/7-8
3841 State Route 20 44826 419-668-1924
Lisa Border, prin. Fax 663-2521

**Columbiana, Columbiana, Pop. 6,337**
Columbiana EVD 900/PK-12
700 Columbiana Waterford Rd 44408 330-482-5352
Donald Mook, supt. Fax 482-5361
www.columbiana.k12.oh.us
Columbiana HS 300/9-12
700 Columbiana Waterford Rd 44408 330-482-3818
Lance Hostetler, prin. Fax 482-5360
South Side MS 300/5-8
720 Columbiana Waterford Rd 44408 330-482-5354
David Buzzard, prin. Fax 482-6332

Crestview Local SD 1,200/K-12
44100 Crestview Rd Ste A 44408 330-482-5526
John Dilling, supt. Fax 482-5367
www.crestviewlocal.k12.oh.us/
Crestview HS 300/9-12
44100 Crestview Rd Ste B 44408 330-482-4744
Lynda Dickson, prin. Fax 482-5369
Crestview MS 400/5-8
44100 Crestview Rd Ste C 44408 330-482-4648
Jeff Richardson, prin. Fax 482-5374

---

Heartland Christian S 400/PK-12
28 Pittsburgh St 44408 330-482-2331
Eric Hosler, admin. Fax 482-2413

**Columbia Station, Lorain**
Columbia Local SD 1,000/K-12
25796 Royalton Rd 44028 440-236-5008
Graig Bansek, supt. Fax 236-8817
www.columbia.k12.oh.us/
Columbia HS 300/9-12
14168 W River Rd 44028 440-236-5001
Sean Lynch, prin. Fax 236-3081
Columbia MS 300/5-8
13646 W River Rd 44028 440-236-5741
Andy Gibson, prin. Fax 236-9274

**Columbus, Franklin, Pop. 762,045**
Columbus CSD 47,400/PK-12
270 E State St 43215 614-365-5000
Dan Good Ph.D., supt. Fax 365-5689
www.ccsoh.us
Africentric Early College S 600/6-12
300 E Livingston Ave 43215 614-365-8675
William Anderson, prin. Fax 365-8908
Arts Impact MS at Everett 500/6-8
680 Jack Gibbs Blvd 43215 614-365-5558
Leon Leavell, prin. Fax 365-5561
Beechcroft HS 700/9-12
6100 Beechcroft Rd 43229 614-365-5364
Monique Jacquet, prin. Fax 365-6963
Briggs HS 1,000/9-12
2555 Briggs Rd 43223 614-365-5915
Marcy Drafts, prin. Fax 365-6964
Buckeye MS 500/6-8
2950 Parsons Ave 43207 614-365-5417
Derick Vickroy, prin. Fax 365-5895
Centennial HS 800/9-12
1441 Bethel Rd 43220 614-365-5491
Frances Hershey, prin. Fax 365-6967
Champion MS 200/6-8
284 N 22nd St 43203 614-365-6082
Stephanie Bland, prin. Fax 365-6080
Columbus Alternative HS 600/Alt
2632 McGuffey Rd 43211 614-365-6006
Sharee Wells, prin. Fax 365-6300
Columbus City Prep S for Boys 200/6-8
3450 Medway Ave 43213 614-365-6166
Michael Owens, prin. Fax 365-6164
Columbus City Prep S for Girls 300/6-8
1390 Bryden Rd 43205 614-365-6113
Stephanie Patton, prin. Fax 365-6112
Columbus Downtown HS 100/9-12
364 S 4th St 43215 614-365-2283
Cheryl Watson, dir. Fax 365-2287
Columbus Global Academy @ Brookhaven 400/6-12
4077 Karl Rd 43224 614-365-8472
Kimberly Normand, prin.
Columbus North International S 300/7-12
100 E Arcadia Ave 43202 614-365-4054
Kenton Lee, prin. Fax 365-8582
Dominion MS 500/6-8
330 E Dominion Blvd 43214 614-365-6020
Dorothy Flanagan, prin. Fax 365-6018
East HS 600/9-12
1500 E Broad St 43205 614-365-6096
Ernest Wood, prin. Fax 365-6966
Eastmoor Academy HS 800/9-12
417 S Weyant Ave 43213 614-365-6158
Brian Morton, prin. Fax 365-6960
Fort Hayes Arts and Academics S 700/9-12
546 Jack Gibbs Blvd 43215 614-365-6681
Milton Ruffin, prin. Fax 365-5620
Fort Hayes Career Center Vo/Tech
546 Jack Gibbs Blvd 43215 614-365-6681
Milton Ruffin, dir. Fax 365-8582
Hilltonia MS 600/6-8
2345 W Mound St 43204 614-365-5937
Donna LeBeau, prin. Fax 365-8015
Independence HS 700/9-12
5175 Refugee Rd 43232 614-365-5372
Ernest West, prin. Fax 365-8286
Johnson Park MS 400/6-8
1130 S Waverly St 43227 614-365-6501
Nicole Edwards, prin. Fax 365-8698
Linden-McKinley STEM HS 800/7-12
1320 Duxberry Ave 43211 614-365-5583
Christopher Rhorer, prin. Fax 365-6968
Marion-Franklin HS 800/9-12
1265 Koebel Rd 43207 614-365-5432
Danielle Woods, prin. Fax 365-6625
Medina MS 400/6-8
1425 Huy Rd 43224 614-365-6050
Charmaine Tinker, prin. Fax 365-8136
Mifflin HS 600/9-12
3245 Oak Spring St 43219 614-365-5466
Duane Bland, prin. Fax 365-6628
Mifflin MS 500/6-8
3000 Agler Rd 43219 614-365-5474
Bao Lam, prin. Fax 365-5477
Northland HS 1,000/9-12
1919 Northcliff Dr 43229 614-365-5342
Timothy Donahue, prin. Fax 365-6479
Ridgeview MS 500/6-8
4241 Rudy Rd 43214 614-365-5506
Natalie James, prin. Fax 365-5505

Sherwood MS 500/6-8
1400 Shady Lane Rd 43227 614-365-5393
Kevin Freeman, prin. Fax 365-8351
South HS 500/9-12
1160 Ann St 43206 614-365-5541
Edmund Baker, prin. Fax 365-5538
Walnut Ridge HS 700/9-12
4841 E Livingston Ave 43227 614-365-5400
Todd Walker, prin. Fax 365-5662
Wedgewood MS 500/6-8
3800 Briggs Rd 43228 614-365-5947
Vince Coleman, prin. Fax 365-5950
West HS 800/9-12
179 S Powell Ave 43204 614-365-5956
Jason Johnson, prin. Fax 365-6970
Westmoor MS 500/6-8
3001 Valleyview Dr 43204 614-365-5974
Paul Bailey, prin. Fax 365-6705
Whetstone HS 1,000/9-12
4405 Scenic Dr 43214 614-365-6060
Janet Routzong, prin. Fax 365-6971
Woodward Park MS 900/6-8
5151 Karl Rd 43229 614-365-5354
Diane Agnes, prin. Fax 365-5357
Yorktown MS 400/6-8
5600 E Livingston Ave 43232 614-365-5408
Ronnie Brown, prin. Fax 365-5411

Grandview Heights CSD 800/PK-12
1587 W 3rd Ave 43212 614-485-4015
Andy Culp, supt. Fax 481-3648
www.ghcsd.org
Edison Intermediate/Larson MS 200/4-8
1240 Oakland Ave 43212 614-481-4100
Tracie Lees, prin. Fax 481-3628
Grandview Heights HS 300/9-12
1587 W 3rd Ave 43212 614-485-4000
Ken Chaffin, prin. Fax 481-3648

Groveport Madison Local SD
Supt. — See Groveport
Groveport Madison MS North 400/6-8
5474 Sedalia Dr 43232 614-837-5508
Brandy Grieves, prin. Fax 833-2033

Hamilton Local SD 3,000/PK-12
775 Rathmell Rd 43207 614-491-8044
William J. Morrison, supt. Fax 491-8323
www.hamiltonrangers.org
Hamilton MS 500/7-8
755 Rathmell Rd 43207 614-491-8044
Jeffrey Endres, prin. Fax 491-0260
Hamilton Township HS 800/9-12
1105 Rathmell Rd 43207 614-491-8044
Dr. James Miller, prin. Fax 492-1495

Hilliard CSD 15,500/K-12
2140 Atlas St 43228 614-921-7000
John Marschhausen Ph.D., supt. Fax 921-7001
www.hilliardschools.org
Other Schools – See Hilliard

South-Western CSD
Supt. — See Grove City
Finland MS 700/7-8
1825 Finland Ave 43223 614-801-3600
Lori Balough, prin. Fax 278-6334
Franklin Heights HS 1,200/9-12
1001 Demorest Rd 43204 614-801-3200
Timothy Donahue, prin. Fax 278-6303
Norton MS 500/7-8
215 Norton Rd 43228 614-801-3700
Tresa Davis, prin. Fax 870-5528

Worthington CSD
Supt. — See Worthington
McCord MS 500/7-8
1500 Hard Rd 43235 614-450-4000
Michael Kuri, prin. Fax 883-3560
Worthington Kilbourne HS 1,200/9-12
1499 Hard Rd 43235 614-450-6400
Angie Adrean, prin. Fax 450-6560

---

American Inst. of Alternative Medicine Post-Sec.
6685 Doubletree Ave 43229 614-825-6255
American School of Technology Post-Sec.
2100 Morse Rd 43229 614-436-4820
Arthur James Cancer Hospital Post-Sec.
300 W 10th Ave 43210 614-293-5485
Bexley Seabury Post-Sec.
583 Sheridan Ave 43209 614-231-3095
Bishop Hartley HS 700/9-12
1285 Zettler Rd 43227 614-237-5421
Mike Winters, prin. Fax 237-3809
Bishop Ready HS 400/9-12
707 Salisbury Rd 43204 614-276-5263
Celene Seamen, prin. Fax 276-5116
Bishop Watterson HS 1,000/9-12
99 E Cooke Rd 43214 614-268-8671
Marian Hutson, prin. Fax 268-0551
Bradford School Post-Sec.
2469 Stelzer Rd 43219 614-416-6200
Capital University Post-Sec.
1 College and Main 43209 614-236-6011
Chamberlain College of Nursing Post-Sec.
1350 Alum Creek Dr 43209 614-252-8890
Columbus College of Art and Design Post-Sec.
60 Cleveland Ave 43215 614-224-9101
Columbus School for Girls 600/PK-12
56 S Columbia Ave 43209 614-252-0781
Jennifer Ciccarelli, hdmstr. Fax 252-0571
Columbus State Community College Post-Sec.
550 E Spring St 43215 614-287-5353
Columbus Torah Academy 200/K-12
181 Noe Bixby Rd 43213 614-864-0299
Rabbi Samuel Levine, head sch Fax 864-2119
Cristo Rey Columbus HS 9-12
400 E Town St 43215 614-223-9261
Dr. Cathy Thomas, prin.

DeVry University Post-Sec.
1350 Alum Creek Dr 43209 614-253-7291
DeVry University Post-Sec.
8800 Lyra Dr Ste 120 43240 614-854-7500
Felbry College School of Nursing Post-Sec.
6055 Cleveland Ave 43231 614-781-1085
Franklin University Post-Sec.
201 S Grant Ave 43215 614-797-4700
ITT Technical Institute Post-Sec.
4717 Hilton Corporate Dr 43232 614-868-2000
Miami-Jacobs Career College Post-Sec.
150 E Gay St Fl 15 43215 614-221-7770
Mt. Carmel College of Nursing Post-Sec.
127 S Davis Ave 43222 614-234-5800
National College Post-Sec.
5665 Forest Hills Blvd 43231 614-212-2800
Nationwide Beauty Academy Post-Sec.
5300 Westpointe Plaza Dr 43228 614-921-9109
Ohio Business College Post-Sec.
4525 Trueman Blvd 43026 800-954-4274
Ohio Center for Broadcasting Post-Sec.
5330 E Main St Ste 200 43213 614-655-5250
Ohio Dominican University Post-Sec.
1216 Sunbury Rd 43219 614-251-4500
Ohio School for the Deaf Post-Sec.
500 Morse Rd 43214
Ohio State College of Barber Styling Post-Sec.
4614 E Broad St 43213 614-868-1015
Ohio State Sch of Cosmetology Northland Post-Sec.
4390 Karl Rd 43224 614-263-1861
Ohio State School for the Blind Post-Sec.
5220 N High St 43214
Ohio State School of Cosmetology East Post-Sec.
1720 E Broad St 43203 614-868-1601
Ohio State University Post-Sec.
154 W 12th Ave 43210 614-292-6446
Ohio State University Hospitals Post-Sec.
450 W 10th Ave 43210 614-293-5555
Pontifical College Josephinum Post-Sec.
7625 N High St 43235 614-885-5585
St. Charles Preparatory S 600/9-12
2010 E Broad St 43209 614-252-6714
Jim Lower, prin. Fax 251-6800
St. Francis De Sales HS 800/9-12
4212 Karl Rd 43224 614-267-7808
Dan Garrick, prin. Fax 265-3375
Spa School Post-Sec.
5050 N High St 43214 614-888-1092
Tree of Life Christian S - Northridge 400/6-12
935 Northridge Rd 43224 614-263-2688
Dr. Todd Marrah Ph.D., supt. Fax 263-6450
Trinity Lutheran Seminary Post-Sec.
2199 E Main St 43209 614-235-4136
Valor Christian College Post-Sec.
PO Box 800 43216 800-940-9422
Wellington S 700/PK-12
3650 Reed Rd 43220 614-457-7883
Robert Brisk, head sch Fax 442-3286

**Columbus Grove, Putnam, Pop. 2,103**
Columbus Grove Local SD 900/K-12
201 W Cross St 45830 419-659-2639
George Verhoff, supt. Fax 659-5134
cg.noacsc.org
Columbus Grove HS 300/9-12
201 W Cross St 45830 419-659-2156
Brian Best, prin. Fax 659-5134
Columbus Grove MS 300/5-8
201 W Cross St 45830 419-659-2631
Brad Calvelage, prin. Fax 659-5134

**Commercial Point, Pickaway, Pop. 1,557**
Teays Valley Local SD
Supt. — See Ashville
Teays Valley West MS 400/6-8
200 Grove Run Rd 43116 740-983-5000
Michael Kauffeld, prin. Fax 983-5040

**Concord, Lake**
Auburn Vocational SD
8221 Auburn Rd 44077 440-357-7542
Margaret Lynch, supt. Fax 357-0310
www.auburncc.org
Auburn Career Center Vo/Tech
8140 Auburn Rd 44077 440-357-7542
Jeff Slavkovsky, prin. Fax 357-0310

---

Hershey Montessori S 200/PK-10
10229 Prouty Rd 44077 440-357-0918
Paula Leigh-Doyle, head sch Fax 357-9096

**Conneaut, Ashtabula, Pop. 12,629**
Conneaut Area CSD 1,800/PK-12
230 Gateway Ave Ste B 44030 440-593-7200
Michael Notar, supt. Fax 593-6253
www.cacsk12.org
Conneaut HS 500/9-12
381 Mill St 44030 440-593-7210
Dawn Zappitelli, prin. Fax 593-6899
Conneaut MS 400/6-8
230 Gateway Ave 44030 440-593-7240
Joel Taylor, prin. Fax 593-6289

**Continental, Putnam, Pop. 1,147**
Continental Local SD 300/K-12
5211 State Route 634 45831 419-596-3671
Joel Mengerink, supt. Fax 596-3861
www.continentalpirates.org
Continental JSHS 100/7-12
5211 State Route 634 45831 419-596-3871
Joel Mengerink, prin. Fax 596-2651

**Convoy, Van Wert, Pop. 1,077**
Crestview Local SD 1,000/K-12
531 E Tully St 45832 419-749-9100
Michael Estes, supt. Fax 749-4235
www.crestviewknights.com/

Crestview HS 300/9-12
531 E Tully St 45832 419-749-9100
Michael Biro, prin. Fax 749-4235
Crestview MS 300/7-8
531 E Tully St 45832 419-749-9100
David Bowen, prin. Fax 749-2484

**Copley, Summit, Pop. 11,130**
Copley-Fairlawn CSD 3,300/PK-12
3797 Ridgewood Rd 44321 330-664-4800
Brian Poe, supt. Fax 664-4811
www.copley-fairlawn.org
Copley-Fairlawn MS 1,100/5-8
1531 S Cleveland Massillon 44321 330-664-4875
Kathleen Ashcroft, prin. Fax 664-4912
Copley HS 1,100/9-12
3807 Ridgewood Rd 44321 330-664-4822
Michael Coury, prin. Fax 664-4951

**Corning, Perry, Pop. 572**
Southern Local SD 700/K-12
10397 State Route 155 SE 43730 740-394-2426
Greg Holbert, supt. Fax 394-2083
www.spsd.k12.oh.us
Miller HS 300/7-12
10397 State Route 155 SE 43730 740-394-2426
Lisa Love, prin. Fax 394-2083

**Cortland, Trumbull, Pop. 7,046**
Lakeview Local SD 1,800/K-12
300 Hillman Dr 44410 330-637-8741
Robert Wilson, supt. Fax 282-4260
www.lakeviewlocal.org
Lakeview HS 700/8-12
300 Hillman Dr 44410 330-637-4921
Richard Stevens, prin. Fax 638-8812

Maplewood Local SD 800/K-12
2414 Greenville Rd 44410 330-637-7506
Perry Nicholas, supt. Fax 637-6616
www.maplewood.k12.oh.us/
Maplewood HS 200/9-12
2414 Greenville Rd 44410 330-637-8466
Gordon Hitchcock, prin. Fax 637-0496
Maplewood MS 300/5-8
4174 Greenville Rd 44410 330-924-2431
Elizabeth Goerig, prin. Fax 924-5151

**Coshocton, Coshocton, Pop. 11,049**
Coshocton CSD 700/PK-12
1207 Cambridge Rd 43812 740-622-1901
Dr. David Hire, supt. Fax 623-5803
www.coshoctonredskins.com/
Coshocton JSHS 700/7-12
1205 Cambridge Rd 43812 740-622-9433
Grant Fauver, prin. Fax 623-0774

Coshocton County JVSD
23640 Airport Rd 43812 740-622-0211
Deborah Kapp-Salupo, supt. Fax 623-4651
www.coshoctoncareers.org
Coshocton County Career Center Vo/Tech
23640 Airport Rd 43812 740-622-0211
Eddie Dovenbarger, prin. Fax 623-4651

---

Coshocton Christian S 100/PK-12
23891 Airport Rd 43812 740-622-5052
Stanley Zurowski, prin. Fax 622-9244

**Covington, Miami, Pop. 2,556**
Covington EVD 800/K-12
25 N Grant St 45318 937-473-2249
Gene Gooding, supt. Fax 473-3730
www.covington.k12.oh.us
Covington HS 200/9-12
807 Chestnut St 45318 937-473-3746
Josh Long, prin. Fax 473-3435
Covington MS 200/6-8
25 N Grant St 45318 937-473-2833
Matt Pond, prin. Fax 473-8189

**Craig Beach, Mahoning, Pop. 1,144**

---

TDDS Technical Institute Post-Sec.
PO Box 506 44429 330-538-2216

**Crestline, Crawford, Pop. 4,534**
Colonel Crawford Local SD
Supt. — See North Robinson
Crawford IS 200/6-8
5444 Crestline Rd 44827 419-562-7529
April Bond, prin. Fax 562-3319

Crestline EVD 400/PK-12
401 Heiser Ct 44827 419-683-3647
Noreen Mullens, supt. Fax 683-2330
www.crestline.k12.oh.us
Crestline HS 300/7-12
435 Oldfield Rd 44827 419-683-3647
David Mounts, prin. Fax 683-9063

**Creston, Wayne, Pop. 2,138**
Norwayne Local SD 1,200/PK-12
350 S Main St 44217 330-435-6382
Karen O'Hare, supt. Fax 435-4633
www.norwayne.net
Norwayne HS 400/9-12
350 S Main St 44217 330-435-6384
Douglas Zimmerly, prin. Fax 435-4633
Norwayne MS 300/6-8
350 S Main St 44217 330-435-1195
Kevin Leatherman, prin. Fax 435-4633

**Crooksville, Perry, Pop. 2,512**
Crooksville EVD 1,100/PK-12
4065 School Dr 43731 740-982-7040
Matt Sheridan, supt. Fax 982-3551
www.crooksville.k12.oh.us
Crooksville HS 400/9-12
4075 Ceramic Way 43731 740-982-7015
Kevin Smith, prin. Fax 982-3086

Crooksville MS 300/5-8
12400 Tunnel Hill Rd 43731 740-982-7010
John Toeller, prin. Fax 982-5087

**Crown City, Gallia, Pop. 412**
Gallia County Local SD
Supt. — See Patriot
South Gallia MSHS 200/6-12
55 Rebel Dr 45623 740-256-1054
Scot West, prin. Fax 256-6399

**Cuyahoga Falls, Summit, Pop. 48,868**
Cuyahoga Falls CSD 5,000/K-12
PO Box 396 44222 330-926-3800
Dr. Todd Nichols, supt. Fax 920-1074
www.cfalls.org
Bolich MS 700/6-8
2630 13th St 44223 330-926-3801
Michael Miller, prin. Fax 920-3737
Cuyahoga Falls HS 1,600/9-12
2300 4th St 44221 330-926-3808
Allison Bogdan, prin. Fax 916-6013
Roberts MS 500/6-8
3333 Charles St 44221 330-926-3809
James Holzapfel, prin. Fax 920-3748

---

Cuyahoga Valley Christian Academy 900/7-12
4687 Wyoga Lake Rd 44224 330-929-0575
Dr. Matt Koons, hdmstr. Fax 929-0156
Fortis College Post-Sec.
2545 Bailey Rd 44221 330-923-9959
Walsh Jesuit HS 1,000/9-12
4550 Wyoga Lake Rd 44224 330-929-4205
Mark Hassman, prin. Fax 929-9749

**Cuyahoga Heights, Cuyahoga, Pop. 635**
Cuyahoga Heights Local SD 900/PK-12
4820 E 71st St 44125 216-429-5700
Thomas Evans, supt. Fax 341-3737
www.cuyhts.org
Cuyahoga Heights HS 300/9-12
4820 E 71st St 44125 216-429-5707
William Young, prin. Fax 429-5706
Cuyahoga Heights MS 200/6-8
4840 E 71st St 44125 216-429-5757
William Young, prin. Fax 429-5735

**Dalton, Wayne, Pop. 1,798**
Dalton Local SD 300/PK-12
PO Box 514 44618 330-828-2267
James R. Saxer, supt. Fax 828-2800
www.dalton.k12.oh.us
Dalton Local HS 300/9-12
PO Box 514 44618 330-828-2261
Nathan Stutz, prin. Fax 828-2904

**Danville, Knox, Pop. 1,035**
Danville Local SD 600/K-12
PO Box 30 43014 740-599-6116
Dan Harper, supt. Fax 599-5417
www.danvilleschools.org
Danville HS 200/9-12
PO Box 30 43014 740-599-6116
Ed Honabarger, prin. Fax 599-5418
Danville MS 100/6-8
PO Box 30 43014 740-599-6116
Matthew Proper, dir. Fax 599-5904

**Dayton, Montgomery, Pop. 137,548**
Centerville CSD
Supt. — See Centerville
Watts MS 800/6-8
7056 McEwen Rd 45459 937-434-0370
Brian Miller, prin. Fax 434-2907

Dayton CSD 14,400/PK-12
115 S Ludlow St 45402 937-542-3000
Lori Ward, supt. Fax 542-3188
www.dps.k12.oh.us
Belmont HS 800/7-12
2615 Wayne Ave 45420 937-542-6460
Melanie Walter, prin. Fax 542-6461
Dunbar Early College HS 600/9-12
1400 Albritton Dr 45417 937-542-6760
Crystal Phillips, prin. Fax 542-6761
Longfellow Academy 200/Alt
245 Salem Ave 45406 937-542-6910
Marlayna Randolph, dir. Fax 542-6911
Marshall HS 700/9-12
4447 Hoover Ave 45417 937-542-6610
Sharon Goins, prin. Fax 542-6611
Meadowdale HS 600/9-12
3873 Whitestone Ct 45416 937-542-7030
Brian McKnight, prin. Fax 542-7031
Ponitz Career Center Vo/Tech
741 Washington St 45402 937-542-7180
Ray Caruthers, prin. Fax 542-7181
Stivers S for the Arts 900/7-12
1313 E 5th St 45402 937-542-7380
Erin Dooley, prin. Fax 542-7381
Wogaman S 200/5-8
920 McArthur Ave 45417 937-542-5890
Renaldo O'Neal, prin. Fax 542-5891

Jefferson Township Local SD 400/K-12
2625 S Union Rd 45417 937-835-5682
Dr. Richard Gates, supt. Fax 835-5955
www.jeffersontwp.k12.oh.us/
Jefferson HS 200/7-12
2701 S Union Rd 45417 937-295-5691
Walter Sledge, prin. Fax 835-5693

Mad River Local SD 3,600/PK-12
801 Old Harshman Rd 45431 937-259-6606
Chad Wyen, supt. Fax 259-6607
www.madriverschools.org
Mad River MS 500/7-8
1801 Harshman Rd 45424 937-237-4265
Laurie Plank, prin. Fax 237-4273

Stebbins HS 1,100/9-12
1900 Harshman Rd 45424 937-237-4250
Brad Holt, prin. Fax 237-4262

Miami Valley Career Technology Ctr SD
Supt. — See Clayton
Miami Valley Career Tech Alternative S Alt
1133 S Edwin C Moses Blvd 45417 937-226-1741
Jay Byrne, prin. Fax 226-1788

Montgomery County ESC
200 S Keowee St 45402 937-225-4598
Frank DePalma, supt. Fax 496-7426
www.mcesc.org/
Montgomery County Learning Ctr West Alt
3500 Kettering Blvd 45439 937-253-4178
Jeff Ochs, dir. Fax 259-5764

Northridge Local SD 1,000/K-12
2011 Timber Ln 45414 937-278-5885
David Jackson, supt. Fax 276-8351
www.northridgeschools.org/
Northridge HS 500/7-12
2251 Timber Ln 45414 937-275-7469
Tim Whitestone, prin. Fax 275-8434

---

Bishop Leibold Consolidated S East 300/4-8
6666 Springboro Pike 45449 937-434-9343
Kim Harnett, prin. Fax 436-3048
Carousel Beauty College Post-Sec.
125 E 2nd St 45402 937-223-3572
Carroll HS 800/9-12
4524 Linden Ave 45432 937-253-8188
Matthew Sableski, prin. Fax 258-7001
Chaminade-Julienne HS 600/9-12
505 S Ludlow St 45402 937-461-3740
John Marshall, prin. Fax 461-6256
Creative Images-Matrix Design Academy Post-Sec.
7535 Poe Ave 45414 937-454-1200
DeVry University Post-Sec.
3610 Pentagon Blvd Ste 100 45431 937-320-3200
East Dayton Christian S 500/PK-12
999 Spinning Rd 45431 937-252-5400
Stacie Auvil, prin. Fax 258-4099
International College of Broadcasting Post-Sec.
6 S Smithville Rd 45431 937-258-8251
ITT Technical Institute Post-Sec.
3325 Stop 8 Rd 45414 937-264-7700
Kaplan College Post-Sec.
2800 E River Rd 45439 937-294-6155
Miami-Jacobs Career College Post-Sec.
110 N Patterson Blvd 45402 937-222-7337
Miami Valley Hospital Post-Sec.
1 Wyoming St 45409 937-223-6192
Miami Valley S 500/PK-12
5151 Denise Dr 45429 937-434-4444
Jay Scheurle, hdmstr. Fax 434-1033
Sinclair Community College Post-Sec.
444 W 3rd St 45402 800-315-3000
United Theological Seminary Post-Sec.
4501 Denlinger Rd 45426 937-529-2201
University of Dayton Post-Sec.
300 College Park Ave 45469 937-229-1000
Wright State University Post-Sec.
3640 Colonel Glenn Hwy 45435 937-775-3333

**Defiance, Defiance, Pop. 16,265**
Ayersville Local SD 800/K-12
28046 Watson Rd 43512 419-395-1111
Don Diglia, supt. Fax 395-9990
www.ayersville.org
Ayersville JSHS 400/7-12
28046 Watson Rd 43512 419-395-1111
Jeremy Kuhlman, prin. Fax 395-2566

Defiance CSD 2,500/K-12
629 Arabella St 43512 419-782-0070
Michael Struble, supt. Fax 782-4395
www.defiancecityschools.org
Defiance HS 700/9-12
1755 Palmer Dr 43512 419-784-2777
Robert Morton, prin. Fax 784-0102
Defiance MS 600/6-8
629 Arabella St 43512 419-782-0050
Richard Peters, prin. Fax 782-0060

Northeastern Local SD 1,100/K-12
5921 Domersville Rd 43512 419-497-3461
James Roach, supt. Fax 497-3401
www.tinora.org
Tinora HS 300/9-12
5921 Domersville Rd 43512 419-497-2621
Christopher Lake, prin. Fax 497-3401
Tinora JHS 200/7-8
5921 Domersville Rd 43512 419-497-2361
G. Kent Adams, prin. Fax 497-3401

---

Defiance College Post-Sec.
701 N Clinton St 43512 419-784-4010

**De Graff, Logan, Pop. 1,275**
Riverside Local SD 700/K-12
2096 County Road 24 S 43318 937-585-5981
Scott Mann, supt. Fax 585-4599
www.riverside.k12.oh.us
Riverside JSHS 300/7-12
2096 County Road 24 S 43318 937-585-5981
Kelly Kauffman, prin. Fax 585-4599

**Delaware, Delaware, Pop. 33,899**
Buckeye Valley Local SD 1,900/PK-12
679 Coover Rd 43015 740-369-8735
Andrew Miller, supt. Fax 363-7654
www.buckeyevalley.k12.oh.us
Buckeye Valley HS 700/9-12
901 Coover Rd 43015 740-363-1349
Jim Albanese, prin. Fax 363-9380
Buckeye Valley MS 600/5-8
683 Coover Rd 43015 740-363-6626
Brian Baker, prin. Fax 363-4483

Delaware Area Career Center
4565 Columbus Pike 43015 740-548-0708
Mary Beth Freeman, supt. Fax 548-0710
www.delawareareacc.org
Delaware Area Career Center North Campus Vo/Tech
1610 State Route 521 43015 740-363-1993
Tom Marchetti, dir. Fax 362-6461
Delaware Area Career Center South Campus Vo/Tech
4565 Columbus Pike 43015 740-548-0708
Kris Lucas, prin. Fax 548-0710
Delaware Area Career Ctr Adult Education Adult
4565 Columbus Pike 43015 740-201-3206
Scott Palmer, prin. Fax 549-1397

Delaware CSD 5,000/PK-12
248 N Washington St 43015 740-833-1100
Paul Craft, supt. Fax 833-1149
www.dcs.k12.oh.us
Dempsey MS 700/7-8
599 Pennsylvania Ave 43015 740-833-1800
Julie German-Murrey, prin. Fax 833-1899
Hayes HS 1,300/9-12
289 Euclid Ave 43015 740-833-1010
Ric Stranges, prin. Fax 833-1099

---

Delaware Christian S 300/PK-12
45 Belle Ave 43015 740-363-8425
John Stubblefield, admin. Fax 203-2117
Methodist Theological School in Ohio Post-Sec.
3081 Columbus Pike 43015 740-363-1146
Ohio Wesleyan University Post-Sec.
61 S Sandusky St 43015 740-368-2000

**Delphos, Allen, Pop. 7,017**
Delphos CSD 1,100/K-12
234 N Jefferson St 45833 419-692-2509
Kevin Wolfe, supt. Fax 692-2653
www.delphoscityschools.org
Jefferson HS 300/9-12
901 Wildcat Ln 45833 419-695-1786
John Edinger, prin. Fax 692-2287
Jefferson MS 300/6-8
227 N Jefferson St 45833 419-695-2523
Doug Westrick, prin. Fax 692-2302

---

St. John HS 300/9-12
515 E 2nd St 45833 419-692-5371
Adam Lee, prin. Fax 879-6874

**Delta, Fulton, Pop. 3,070**
Pike-Delta-York Local SD 1,200/K-12
504 Fernwood St 43515 419-822-3391
Ted Haselman, supt. Fax 822-4478
www.pdys.org
Pike-Delta-York HS 400/9-12
605 Taylor St 43515 419-822-8247
Martin Friess, prin. Fax 822-2826
Pike-Delta-York MS 400/5-8
1101 Panther Pride Dr 43515 419-822-9118
Douglas Ford, prin. Fax 822-8490

**Dennison, Tuscarawas, Pop. 2,624**
Claymont CSD 2,100/PK-12
201 N 3rd St 44621 740-922-5478
John Rocchi, supt. Fax 922-7325
www.claymontschools.org
Other Schools – See Uhrichsville

**Diamond, Portage**
Southeast Local SD
Supt. — See Ravenna
Southeast MS 500/6-8
8540 Tallmadge Rd 44412 330-654-1950
Michelle Hiser, prin. Fax 654-9110

**Dillonvale, Jefferson, Pop. 660**
Buckeye Local SD 1,700/PK-12
6899 State Route 150 43917 740-769-7395
Mark Miller, supt. Fax 769-2361
buckeye.omeresa.net/
Other Schools – See Rayland

**Dola, Hardin, Pop. 136**
Hardin Northern Local SD 500/K-12
11589 State Route 81 45835 419-759-2331
Dr. Jeff Price Ed.D., supt. Fax 759-2581
www.hardinnorthern.org
Hardin Northern JSHS 200/7-12
11589 State Route 81 45835 419-759-3515
Joe Hoelzle, prin. Fax 759-2581

**Dover, Tuscarawas, Pop. 12,639**
Dover CSD 2,600/PK-12
219 W 6th St 44622 330-364-1906
Carla Birney, supt. Fax 343-7070
www.dovertornadoes.com
Dover HS 800/9-12
520 N Walnut St 44622 330-364-7148
Teresa Alberts, prin. Fax 364-7142
Dover MS 700/6-8
2131 N Wooster Ave 44622 330-364-7121
Jack Edwards, prin. Fax 364-7127

**Doylestown, Wayne, Pop. 3,018**
Chippewa Local SD 1,400/K-12
56 N Portage St 44230 330-658-6368
Sandy Stebly, supt. Fax 658-5842
www.chippewa.k12.oh.us
Chippewa HS 400/9-12
100 Valley View Rd 44230 330-658-2011
Shawn Braman, prin. Fax 658-3339
Chippewa MS 400/5-8
257 High St 44230 330-658-2214
Steven Watkins, prin. Fax 658-5842

**Dresden, Muskingum, Pop. 1,503**
Tri-Valley Local SD 3,000/K-12
36 E Muskingum Ave 43821 740-754-1442
Mark Neal, supt. Fax 754-6400
www.tvschools.org
Tri-Valley HS 900/9-12
46 E Muskingum Ave 43821 740-754-2921
Chad Shawger, prin. Fax 754-6409
Tri-Valley MS 500/7-8
1360 Main St 43821 740-754-3531
Patrick Hopkins, prin. Fax 754-1879

**Dublin, Franklin, Pop. 40,967**
Dublin CSD 14,200/PK-12
7030 Coffman Rd 43017 614-764-5913
Dr. Todd Hoadley, supt. Fax 761-5856
www.dublinschools.net
Davis MS 900/6-8
2400 Sutter Pkwy 43016 614-761-5820
Tracey Deagle, prin. Fax 761-5893
Dublin Coffman HS 1,800/9-12
6780 Coffman Rd 43017 614-764-5900
Mike Ulring, prin. Fax 764-5925
Dublin Jerome HS 1,300/9-12
8300 Hyland Croy Rd 43016 614-873-7377
Dustin Miller, prin. Fax 873-7340
Dublin Scioto HS 1,200/9-12
4000 Hard Rd 43016 614-717-2464
Robert Scott, prin. Fax 717-2484
Grizzell MS 700/6-8
8705 Avery Rd 43017 614-798-3569
Corinne Evans, prin. Fax 761-6514
Karrer MS 800/6-8
7245 Tullymore Dr 43016 614-873-0459
Mark Mousa, prin. Fax 873-1492
Sells MS 900/6-8
150 W Bridge St 43017 614-764-5919
Matt Sachtleben, prin. Fax 764-5923

**Duncan Falls, Muskingum, Pop. 873**
Franklin Local SD 2,100/PK-12
PO Box 428 43734 740-674-5203
Sharon McDermott, supt. Fax 674-5214
www.franklinlocalschools.org
Philo HS 500/9-12
4000 Millers Ln 43734 740-674-4355
Troy Dawson, prin. Fax 674-5202
Other Schools – See Philo

**East Canton, Stark, Pop. 1,566**
Osnaburg Local SD 900/PK-12
310 Browning Ct N 44730 330-488-1609
Todd Boggs, supt. Fax 488-4001
ecweb.sparcc.org
East Canton HS 300/9-12
310 Browning Ct N 44730 330-488-0316
Andrew Mangun, prin. Fax 488-4015
East Canton MS 200/6-8
310 Browning Ct N 44730 330-488-0316
Gregory Dente, prin. Fax 488-4015

**East Cleveland, Cuyahoga, Pop. 17,585**
East Cleveland CSD 3,100/PK-12
1843 Stanwood Rd 44112 216-268-6600
Myrna Corley, supt. Fax 268-6676
www.east-cleveland.k12.oh.us
Heritage MS 400/7-8
14410 Terrace Rd 44112 216-268-6610
Gilda Roberts, prin. Fax 268-6676
Shaw HS 1,200/9-12
15320 Euclid Ave 44112 216-268-6500
Diane Hunsbarger, prin. Fax 268-6676

---

Huron School of Nursing Post-Sec.
13951 Terrace Rd 44112 216-761-7996

**Eastlake, Lake, Pop. 18,364**
Lake County ESC
Supt. — See Painesville
Lake Academy Alt
503 Vegas Dr 44095 440-942-7401
Bill Kermavner, dir. Fax 942-1790

Willoughby-Eastlake CSD
Supt. — See Willoughby
Eastlake MS 500/6-8
35972 Lake Shore Blvd 44095 440-942-5696
Michael Chokshi, prin. Fax 918-8973
North HS 1,400/9-12
34041 Stevens Blvd 44095 440-975-3666
Jennifer Chauby, prin. Fax 975-3671

---

Bryant & Stratton College Post-Sec.
35350 Curtis Blvd Ste 100 44095 440-510-1112

**East Liverpool, Columbiana, Pop. 10,871**
Beaver Local SD 1,900/K-12
46088 Bell School Rd 43920 330-385-6831
Louis Ramunno, supt. Fax 386-8711
www.beaver.k12.oh.us/
Beaver Local HS 600/9-12
46088 Bell School Rd 43920 330-386-8700
Thomas Cunningham, prin. Fax 386-8720
Beaver Local MS 600/5-8
46088 Bell School Rd 43920 330-386-8707
Connie Shive, prin. Fax 382-0317

East Liverpool CSD 2,200/K-12
810 W 8th St 43920 330-385-7132
Melissa Watson, supt. Fax 382-7673
www.elcsd.k12.oh.us
East Liverpool HS 600/9-12
100 Maine Blvd 43920 330-386-8750
Randy Taylor, prin. Fax 386-8753
East Liverpool JHS 300/7-8
100 Maine Blvd 43920 330-386-8750
Randy Taylor, prin. Fax 386-8753

---

American Spirit Academy 100/PK-12
46682 Florence St 43920 330-385-5588
Susan Mackall, hdmstr. Fax 385-1267
Kent State University-East Liverpool Post-Sec.
400 E 4th St 43920 330-385-3805
Ohio Valley College of Technology Post-Sec.
15258 State Route 170 43920 330-385-1070

**East Palestine, Columbiana, Pop. 4,696**
East Palestine CSD 1,100/PK-12
200 W North Ave 44413 330-426-4191
Traci Hostetler, supt. Fax 426-9592
www.myepschools.org
East Palestine HS 300/9-12
360 W Grant St 44413 330-426-9401
Chris Neifer, prin. Fax 426-5105
East Palestine MS 300/5-8
320 W Grant St 44413 330-426-9451
James Rook, prin. Fax 426-5118

**Eaton, Preble, Pop. 8,276**
Eaton Community SD 2,200/K-12
306 Eaton Lewisburg Rd 45320 937-456-1107
Barbara Curry, supt. Fax 472-1057
www.eaton.k12.oh.us
Eaton HS 600/9-12
600 Hillcrest Dr 45320 937-456-1141
Scott Couch, prin. Fax 456-1143
Eaton MS 500/6-8
814 Camden Rd 45320 937-456-2286
Derek Flatter, prin. Fax 456-9687

**Edgerton, Williams, Pop. 1,997**
Edgerton Local SD 600/PK-12
111 E River St 43517 419-298-2112
Andy Morr, supt. Fax 298-1322
www.edgerton.k12.oh.us/
Edgerton HS 300/7-12
111 E River St 43517 419-298-2331
Roger Cade, prin. Fax 298-1322

**Edon, Williams, Pop. 823**
Edon Northwest Local SD 400/K-12
802 W Indiana St 43518 419-272-3213
Dr. John Granger, supt. Fax 272-2240
www.edon.k12.oh.us/
Edon Northwest HS 200/7-12
802 W Indiana St 43518 419-272-3113
Anthony Stevens, prin. Fax 272-2240

**Elida, Allen, Pop. 1,868**
Elida Local SD 2,100/K-12
4380 Sunnydale St 45807 419-331-4155
Joel Hatfield, supt. Fax 331-1656
home.elida.k12.oh.us
Elida HS 700/9-12
401 E North St 45807 419-331-4115
Darren Sharp, prin. Fax 339-3523
Elida MS 600/5-8
4500 Sunnydale St 45807 419-331-2505
Douglas Drury, prin. Fax 331-6822

**Elmore, Ottawa, Pop. 1,392**
Woodmore Local SD 1,100/PK-12
349 Rice St 43416 419-862-1060
Linda Bringman, supt. Fax 862-1951
www.woodmore.k12.oh.us
Woodmore HS 500/9-12
633 Fremont St 43416 419-862-2721
James Kieper, prin. Fax 862-3835
Other Schools – See Woodville

**Elyria, Lorain, Pop. 52,588**
Elyria CSD 6,400/PK-12
42101 Griswold Rd 44035 440-284-8000
Dr. Thomas Jama, supt. Fax 284-0678
www.elyriaschools.org
Early College HS 9-12
1005 Abbe Rd N 44035 440-366-4720
Dianne Quinn, prin.
Eastern Heights MS 500/6-8
528 Garford Ave 44035 440-284-8015
Dr. Kimberly Benetto, prin. Fax 323-0827
Elyria HS 1,900/9-12
601 Middle Ave 44035 440-284-8300
Dr. Tim Brown, prin. Fax 323-2543
Northwood MS 500/6-8
700 Gulf Rd 44035 440-284-8016
Michael Basinski, prin. Fax 284-1546
Westwood MS 500/6-8
42350 Adelbert St 44035 440-284-8017
Theresa Lengel, prin. Fax 284-1055

---

Elyria Catholic HS 400/9-12
725 Gulf Rd 44035 440-365-1821
Amy Butler, prin. Fax 365-7536
First Baptist Christian S 100/PK-12
11400 Lagrange Rd 44035 440-458-5185
Tim Spickler, admin. Fax 458-8717
Lorain County Community College Post-Sec.
1005 Abbe Rd N 44035 440-365-5222
Open Door Christian S 500/PK-12
8287 W Ridge Rd 44035 440-322-6386
Denver Daniel, head sch Fax 284-6033

**Englewood, Montgomery, Pop. 13,133**
Northmont CSD 5,200/PK-12
4001 Old Salem Rd 45322 937-832-5000
Dr. Sarah Zatik, supt. Fax 832-5001
www.northmontschools.com/
Other Schools – See Clayton

**Enon, Clark, Pop. 2,391**
Greenon Local SD 1,800/PK-12
500 S Xenia Dr 45323 937-864-1202
Bradley Silvus, supt. Fax 864-2470
www.greenon.k12.oh.us
Other Schools – See Springfield

**Etna, Licking, Pop. 1,187**
Southwest Licking Local SD
Supt. — See Pataskala
Watkins Memorial HS 1,100/9-12
8868 Watkins Rd SW, 740-927-3846
Ben Richards, prin. Fax 964-0088
Watkins MS 900/6-8
8808 Watkins Rd SW, 740-927-5767
Ryan Brown, prin. Fax 927-2337

**Euclid, Cuyahoga, Pop. 47,840**
Euclid CSD 5,000/PK-12
651 E 222nd St 44123 216-261-2900
Keith Bell, supt. Fax 261-3120
www.euclidschools.org
Euclid Central MS 600/6-8
20701 Euclid Ave 44117 216-797-5300
Michael Mennel, prin. Fax 797-5333
Euclid HS 2,100/9-12
711 E 222nd St 44123 216-797-7800
Angela Terella, prin. Fax 797-7900
Forest Park MS 700/6-8
27000 Elinore Ave 44132 216-797-4700
Tina Hardaway, prin. Fax 797-4710

**Fairborn, Greene, Pop. 31,321**
Fairborn CSD 4,500/PK-12
306 E Whittier Ave 45324 937-878-3961
Dave Scarberry, supt. Fax 879-8180
www.fairborn.k12.oh.us
Baker MS 900/6-8
200 Lincoln Dr 45324 937-878-4681
Deb Hauberg, prin. Fax 879-8193
Fairborn HS 1,100/9-12
900 E Dayton Yellow Springs 45324 937-879-3611
Eugene Lolli, prin. Fax 879-8190

---

Hondros College Post-Sec.
1810 Successful Dr 45324 937-879-1940

**Fairfield, Butler, Pop. 41,547**
Fairfield CSD 9,600/PK-12
4641 Bach Ln 45014 513-829-6300
Paul Otten, supt. Fax 829-0148
www.fairfieldcityschools.com
Fairfield Freshman HS 700/9-9
5050 Dixie Hwy 45014 513-829-8300
Larissa Smith, prin. Fax 829-4733
Fairfield MS 1,600/7-8
1111 Nilles Rd 45014 513-829-4433
Dr. Lincoln Butts, prin. Fax 829-6480
Fairfield SHS 2,100/10-12
8800 Holden Blvd 45014 513-942-2999
Billy Smith, prin. Fax 942-3288

---

Moler-Hollywood Beauty Academy Post-Sec.
5951 Boymel Dr Ste S 45014 513-874-5116

**Fairport Harbor, Lake, Pop. 3,058**
Fairport Harbor EVD 500/K-12
329 Vine St 44077 440-354-5400
Domenic Paolo, supt. Fax 354-5426
www.fairport.k12.oh.us/
Fairport Harding JSHS 300/6-12
329 Vine St 44077 440-354-3592
Thomas Fazekas, prin. Fax 354-5426

**Fairview Park, Cuyahoga, Pop. 16,640**
Fairview Park CSD 1,800/PK-12
21620 Mastick Rd 44126 440-331-5500
William Wagner, supt. Fax 356-3545
www.fairviewparkschools.org
Fairview HS 600/9-12
4507 W 213th St 44126 440-356-3500
Brannon Sheets, prin. Fax 356-3529
Mayer MS 200/6-8
21200 Campus Dr 44126 440-356-3510
Brannon Sheets, prin. Fax 895-2191

---

Fairview Academy Post-Sec.
22610 Lorain Rd 44126 440-734-5555

**Farmersville, Montgomery, Pop. 991**
Valley View Local SD
Supt. — See Germantown
Valley View JHS 300/7-8
202 Jackson St 45325 937-696-2591
Nichole Thomas, prin. Fax 696-1007

**Fayette, Fulton, Pop. 1,278**
Fayette Local SD 400/K-12
400 E Gamble Rd 43521 419-237-2573
Erik Belcher, supt. Fax 237-3125
www.fayettesch.org
Fayette JSHS 200/7-12
400 E Gamble Rd 43521 419-237-2114
Jon Molter, prin. Fax 237-4306

**Fayetteville, Brown, Pop. 329**
Fayetteville-Perry Local SD 900/PK-12
551 S Apple St 45118 513-875-2423
James Brady, supt. Fax 875-2703
www.fp.k12.oh.us
Fayetteville-Perry HS 300/9-12
501 S Apple St 45118 513-875-3520
David Tatman, prin. Fax 875-4512
Fayetteville-Perry MS 200/6-8
521 S Apple St 45118 513-875-2829
David Tatman, prin. Fax 875-4200

**Felicity, Clermont, Pop. 815**
Felicity-Franklin Local SD 1,000/PK-12
PO Box 619 45120 513-876-2113
David Gibson, supt. Fax 876-2519
www.felicityschools.org/
Felicity-Franklin Local HS 300/9-12
PO Box 619 45120 513-876-2111
Brad Ellis, prin. Fax 876-2560

Felicity-Franklin Local MS 300/5-8
PO Box 619 45120 513-876-2662
Joe Pfeffer, prin. Fax 876-2848

**Findlay, Hancock, Pop. 40,536**
Findlay CSD 4,600/PK-12
1100 Broad Ave 45840 419-425-8212
Edward Kurt, supt. Fax 425-8203
www.findlaycityschools.org
Donnell MS, 301 Baldwin Ave 45840 800/6-8
Don Williams, prin. 419-425-8370
Findlay HS 2,000/9-12
1200 Broad Ave 45840 419-425-8279
Craig Kupferberg, prin. Fax 427-5448
Glenwood MS 400/6-8
1715 N Main St 45840 419-425-8373
David Alvarado, prin. Fax 427-5455
Millstream Career Center Vo/Tech
1150 Broad Ave 45840 419-425-8293
Chris Renn, prin. Fax 420-7199

Hancock County ESC
7746 County Road 140 45840 419-422-7525
Larry Busdeker, supt. Fax 422-8766
hancockesc.org
Hancock Alternative Opportunity HS Alt
7746 County Road 140 45840 419-422-7525
Randy Ward, admin. Fax 422-8766

Liberty-Benton Local SD 1,300/K-12
9190 County Road 9 45840 419-422-8526
James Kanable, supt. Fax 422-5108
www.liberty-benton.org
Liberty-Benton HS 400/9-12
9190 County Road 9 45840 419-424-5351
Brenda Frankart, prin. Fax 424-5352
Liberty Benton MS 300/6-8
9190 County Road 9 45840 419-422-9166
Bruce Otley, prin. Fax 420-9237

---

Brown Mackie College Post-Sec.
1700 Fostoria Ave Ste 100 45840 419-423-2211
Owens Community College Post-Sec.
3200 Bright Rd 45840 567-661-7000
University of Findlay Post-Sec.
1000 N Main St 45840 800-548-0932
Winebrenner Theological Seminary Post-Sec.
950 N Main St 45840 419-434-4200

**Fort Jennings, Putnam, Pop. 485**
Jennings Local SD 400/K-12
PO Box 98 45844 419-286-2238
Nicholas Langhals, supt. Fax 286-2240
jennings.noacsc.org/
Fort Jennings JSHS 200/7-12
PO Box 98 45844 419-286-2238
Nicholas Langhals, prin. Fax 286-2240

**Fort Loramie, Shelby, Pop. 1,478**
Fort Loramie Local SD 800/K-12
PO Box 26 45845 937-295-3931
Daniel Holland, supt. Fax 295-2758
www.loramie.k12.oh.us/
Fort Loramie JSHS 400/7-12
PO Box 290 45845 937-295-3342
Kreg Hollenbacher, prin. Fax 295-2758

**Fort Recovery, Mercer, Pop. 1,410**
Fort Recovery Local SD 1,100/PK-12
PO Box 604 45846 419-375-4139
Justin Firks, supt. Fax 375-1058
www.fortrecoveryschools.org
Fort Recovery HS 300/9-12
PO Box 604 45846 419-375-4111
Jeffrey Hobbs, prin. Fax 375-2039
Fort Recovery MS 200/4-8
865 Sharpsburg Rd 45846 419-375-2815
Matthew Triplett, prin. Fax 375-1126

**Fostoria, Seneca, Pop. 12,940**
Fostoria CSD 1,900/PK-12
1001 Park Ave 44830 419-435-8163
Andrew Sprang, supt. Fax 436-4109
www.fostoriaschools.org/
Fostoria JSHS 700/7-12
1001 Park Ave 44830 419-436-4110
Drew Bauman, prin. Fax 436-4118

---

St. Wendelin S 300/PK-12
533 N Countyline St 44830 419-435-8144
Cathy Krupp, prin. Fax 436-4042

**Frankfort, Ross, Pop. 1,038**
Adena Local SD 1,200/PK-12
3367 County Road 550 45628 740-998-4633
Peter Ruby, supt. Fax 998-4632
adena.k12.oh.us/
Adena HS 300/9-12
3367 County Road 550 45628 740-998-2313
Craig Kerns, prin. Fax 998-2317
Adena MS 300/6-8
3367 County Road 550 45628 740-998-2313
Lisa Wayland, prin. Fax 998-2317

**Franklin, Warren, Pop. 11,585**
Franklin CSD 2,900/K-12
150 E 6th St 45005 937-746-1699
Michael Sander, supt. Fax 743-8620
www.franklincityschools.com
Franklin HS 800/9-12
750 E 4th St 45005 937-743-8610
James McFarland, prin. Fax 743-8625
Franklin JHS 500/7-8
136 E 6th St 45005 937-743-8630
Jeremy Ward, prin. Fax 743-8635

---

Bishop Fenwick HS 500/9-12
4855 State Route 122 45005 513-423-0723
Andrew Barczak, prin. Fax 420-8690

Middletown Christian S 600/PK-12
3011 Union Rd 45005 513-423-4542
Brian Williams, supt. Fax 261-6841

**Franklin Furnace, Scioto, Pop. 1,641**
Green Local SD 400/PK-12
4070 Gallia Pike 45629 740-354-9221
Jodi Armstrong, supt. Fax 355-8975
www.green.k12.oh.us
Green JSHS 200/7-12
4057 Gallia Pike 45629 740-354-9150
Joseph Emnett, prin. Fax 355-4094

**Fredericktown, Knox, Pop. 2,475**
Fredericktown Local SD 900/K-12
117 Columbus Rd 43019 740-694-2956
Matthew W. Chrispin, supt. Fax 694-0956
www.fredericktownschools.com
Fredericktown MSHS 300/6-12
111 Stadium Dr 43019 740-694-2726
Douglas Potts, prin. Fax 694-1294

**Freeport, Harrison, Pop. 360**

---

Antrim Mennonite S 50/K-12
20360 Cadiz Rd 43973 740-489-5161
Titus Lapp, prin.

**Fremont, Sandusky, Pop. 16,145**
Fremont CSD 3,800/K-12
500 W State St Ste A 43420 419-332-6454
Dr. Traci McCaudy, supt. Fax 334-5454
www.fremontschools.net
Fremont MS 600/6-8
1250 North St 43420 419-332-5569
Anthony Walker, prin. Fax 334-5494
Fremont Ross SHS 1,100/9-12
1100 North St 43420 419-332-8221
Gracy Hinojosa-Lloyd, prin. Fax 334-5450

Vanguard-Sentinel JVSD
1306 Cedar St 43420 419-332-2626
Gregory Edinger, supt. Fax 334-4308
www.vscc.k12.oh.us/
Vanguard Career Center Vo/Tech
1306 Cedar St 43420 419-332-2626
Clay Frye, dir. Fax 334-5692
Other Schools – See Tiffin

---

Bishop Hoffman HS 200/9-12
702 Croghan St 43420 419-332-9947
Tim Cullen, supt. Fax 332-4945
Terra State Community College Post-Sec.
2830 Napoleon Rd 43420 419-334-8400

**Gahanna, Franklin, Pop. 32,425**
Gahanna-Jefferson CSD 7,000/PK-12
160 S Hamilton Rd 43230 614-471-7065
Scott Schmidt, supt. Fax 478-5568
www.gahannaschools.org
Gahanna MS East 600/6-8
730 Clotts Rd 43230 614-478-5550
Brad Barboza, prin. Fax 478-5544
Gahanna MS South 600/6-8
349 Shady Spring Dr 43230 614-337-3730
Robin Murdock, prin. Fax 337-3734
Gahanna MS West 600/6-8
350 N Stygler Rd 43230 614-478-5570
Aaron Winner, prin. Fax 337-3771
Lincoln HS 2,200/9-12
380 Granville St 43230 614-478-5500
Robert Dodd, prin. Fax 337-3769

---

Columbus Academy 1,100/PK-12
4300 Cherry Bottom Rd 43230 614-475-2311
Melissa Soderberg, admin. Fax 475-0396
Everest Institute Post-Sec.
825 Tech Center Dr 43230 614-322-3414
Gahanna Christian Academy 500/PK-12
817 N Hamilton Rd 43230 614-471-9270
Rev. Gary Johnston, supt. Fax 471-9201

**Galena, Delaware, Pop. 644**
Olentangy Local SD
Supt. — See Lewis Center
Berkshire MS 800/6-8
2869 S 3 Bs and K Rd 43021 740-657-5200
Carla Baker, prin. Fax 657-5299

**Galion, Crawford, Pop. 10,395**
Galion CSD 1,800/PK-12
470 Portland Way N 44833 419-468-3432
Dr. Mark Stefanik, supt. Fax 468-4333
www.galionschools.org
Galion HS 400/9-12
472 Portland Way N 44833 419-468-6500
Ronald Williams, prin. Fax 468-4333
Galion MS 400/6-8
474 Portland Way N 44833 419-468-3134
Jennifer Allerding, prin. Fax 468-4333

Northmor Local SD 1,100/K-12
5247 County Road 29 44833 419-946-8861
Chad Redmon Ed.D., supt. Fax 947-6255
www.northmor.k12.oh.us
Northmor HS 500/7-12
7819 State Route 19 44833 419-946-3946
Benji Bethea, prin. Fax 947-7545

**Gallipolis, Gallia, Pop. 3,534**
Gallipolis CSD 2,200/PK-12
61 State St 45631 740-446-3211
Roger Mace, supt. Fax 446-6433
www.gc.k12.oh.us
Alternative S, 340 4th Ave 45631 50/Alt
Jared Denney, prin. 740-446-3214
Gallia Academy HS 600/9-12
2855 Centenary Rd 45631 740-446-3212
Josh Donley, prin. Fax 446-3436
Gallia Academy MS 500/6-8
340 4th Ave 45631 740-446-3214
Craig Wright, prin. Fax 446-2493

---

Gallipolis Career College Post-Sec.
1176 Jackson Pike # 312 45631 740-446-4367
Gallipolis State Institute 45631 Post-Sec.
Ohio Valley Christian S 100/PK-12
1100 4th Ave 45631 740-446-0374
Patrick O'Donnell, admin. Fax 446-3961

**Galloway, Franklin**
South-Western CSD
Supt. — See Grove City
Westland HS 1,600/9-12
146 Galloway Rd 43119 614-851-7000
John Rathburn, prin. Fax 870-5531

**Gambier, Knox, Pop. 2,300**

---

Kenyon College Post-Sec.
1 Kenyon College 43022 740-427-5000

**Garfield Heights, Cuyahoga, Pop. 28,281**
Garfield Heights CSD 3,800/K-12
5640 Briarcliff Dr 44125 216-475-8100
Terrance Olszewski, supt. Fax 475-1824
www.garfieldheightscityschools.com
Garfield Heights HS 1,300/9-12
4900 Turney Rd 44125 216-662-2800
Tammy Hager, prin. Fax 271-6183
Garfield Heights MS 900/6-8
12000 Maple Leaf Dr 44125 216-475-8105
Christopher Sauer, prin. Fax 475-8146

---

Archbishop Lyke S - St. Timothy Campus 100/5-8
4351 E 131st St 44105 216-581-3517
Margarete Smith, prin. Fax 581-6204
Trinity HS 300/9-12
12425 Granger Rd 44125 216-581-1644
Linda Bacho, prin. Fax 581-9348

**Garrettsville, Portage, Pop. 2,303**
James A. Garfield Local SD 1,500/PK-12
10235 State Route 88 44231 330-527-4336
Ted A. Lysiak, supt. Fax 527-5941
garfield.sparcc.org/
Garfield HS 400/9-12
10233 State Route 88 44231 330-527-4341
Michael Dobran, prin. Fax 527-5636
Garfield MS 200/7-8
10231 State Route 88 44231 330-527-2151
Jennifer Mulhern, prin. Fax 527-2601

**Gates Mills, Cuyahoga, Pop. 2,236**

---

Gilmour Academy 700/PK-12
34001 Cedar Rd 44040 440-473-8090
Br. Robert Lavelle, hdmstr. Fax 473-8010
Hawken S 400/9-12
PO Box 8002 44040 440-423-4446
D. Scott Looney, head sch Fax 423-2960

**Geneva, Ashtabula, Pop. 6,134**
Geneva CSD 2,600/PK-12
135 S Eagle St 44041 440-466-4831
Eric Kujala, supt. Fax 466-0908
www.genevaschools.org/
Geneva HS 800/9-12
1301 S Ridge Rd E 44041 440-466-4831
Doug Wetherholt, prin. Fax 466-8547
Geneva MS 600/6-8
839 Sherman St 44041 440-466-4831
Steve Candela, prin. Fax 466-5692

---

SPIRE Independent S 400/9-12
5201 Spire Cir 44041 440-466-1002

**Genoa, Ottawa, Pop. 2,309**
Genoa Area Local SD 1,000/K-12
2810 N Genoa Clay Center Rd 43430 419-855-7741
Michael Ferguson, supt. Fax 855-4030
www.genoaschools.com
Genoa Area HS 400/9-12
2980 N Genoa Clay Center Rd 43430 419-855-7741
Cari Buehler, prin. Fax 855-7739
Genoa Area MS 300/6-8
2950 N Genoa Clay Center Rd 43430 419-855-7741
Kevin Katafias, prin. Fax 855-7784

**Georgetown, Brown, Pop. 4,266**
Georgetown EVD 1,000/PK-12
1043 Mount Orab Pike 45121 937-378-3730
Christopher Burrows, supt. Fax 378-2219
www.gtown.k12.oh.us/
Georgetown JSHS 500/7-12
987 Mount Orab Pike 45121 937-378-6730
Jerry Underwood, prin. Fax 378-2442

Southern Hills JVSD
9193 Hamer Rd 45121 937-378-6131
Kevin Kratzer, supt. Fax 378-4577
www.shctc.k12.oh.us
Southern Hills Career & Technical Center Vo/Tech
9193 Hamer Rd 45121 937-378-6131
Guy Hopkins, prin. Fax 378-4863

**Germantown, Montgomery, Pop. 5,508**
Valley View Local SD 1,900/PK-12
59 Peffley St 45327 937-855-6581
Richard Earley, supt. Fax 855-0266
www.valleyview.k12.oh.us
Valley View HS 600/9-12
6027 Frmrsvll Germantn Pike 45327 937-855-4116
Todd Kozarec, prin. Fax 855-4739
Other Schools – See Farmersville

Germantown Christian S 100/PK-12
9440 Eby Rd 45327 937-855-7334
Rhonda Jerman, prin. Fax 855-7746

**Gibsonburg, Sandusky, Pop. 2,557**
Gibsonburg EVD 1,100/PK-12
301 S Sunset Ave 43431 419-637-2479
Tim Murray, supt. Fax 637-3029
www.gibsonburg.k12.oh.us/
Gibsonburg HS 300/9-12
740 S Main St 43431 419-637-2873
Fax 637-2046
Gibsonburg MS 200/6-8
740 S Main St 43431 419-637-7954
Fax 637-2046

**Girard, Trumbull, Pop. 9,767**
Girard CSD 1,700/K-12
100 W Main St Ste 2 44420 330-545-2596
David Cappuzzello, supt. Fax 545-2597
www.girardcityschools.org/
Girard HS 500/9-12
1244 Shannon Rd 44420 330-545-5431
William Ryser, prin. Fax 545-5440
Girard JHS 300/7-8
1244 Shannon Rd 44420 330-545-5431
Louise Mason, prin. Fax 545-5440

**Glouster, Athens, Pop. 1,756**
Trimble Local SD 700/PK-12
1 Tomcat Dr 45732 740-767-4444
Scott Christman, supt. Fax 767-4901
trimble.k12.oh.us
Trimble HS 200/9-12
1 Tomcat Dr 45732 740-767-3434
Matt Curtis, prin. Fax 767-4901
Trimble MS 100/6-8
18500 Jacksonville Rd 45732 740-767-2810
Roger Nott, prin. Fax 767-9523

**Gnadenhutten, Tuscarawas, Pop. 1,282**
Indian Valley Local SD 1,800/K-12
PO Box 171 44629 740-254-4334
Gary Wentworth, supt. Fax 254-9271
www.ivschools.org/
Indian Valley HS 500/9-12
PO Box 130 44629 740-254-4262
Robert Clarke, prin. Fax 254-4911
Other Schools – See Tuscarawas

**Goshen, Clermont**
Goshen Local SD 2,500/PK-12
6694 Goshen Rd 45122 513-722-2222
Darrell Edwards, supt. Fax 722-3767
www.goshenlocalschools.org
Goshen HS 700/9-12
6707 Goshen Rd 45122 513-722-2227
Nick Inabnitt, prin. Fax 722-2247
Goshen MS 600/6-8
6692 Goshen Rd 45122 513-722-2226
Mark Edwards, prin. Fax 722-2246

**Grafton, Lorain, Pop. 6,573**
Midview Local SD 2,700/K-12
13050 Durkee Rd 44044 440-748-5353
Scott Goggin, supt. Fax 748-5395
www.midviewk12.org
Midview HS 1,000/9-12
38199 Capel Rd 44044 440-748-2124
Thomas Faska, prin. Fax 748-5277
Midview MS 500/7-8
12865 Grafton Rd 44044 440-748-2122
John Brown, prin. Fax 748-0411

**Granville, Licking, Pop. 5,563**
Granville EVD 2,500/K-12
PO Box 417 43023 740-587-8101
Jeffrey Brown, supt. Fax 683-7730
www.granvilleschools.org
Granville HS 800/9-12
248 New Burg St 43023 740-587-8105
Matt Durst, prin. Fax 587-8195
Granville MS 400/7-8
210 New Burg St 43023 740-587-8104
Lisa Sealover-Ormond, prin. Fax 587-8194

Denison University Post-Sec.
100 W College St 43023 740-587-0810
Granville Christian Academy 300/K-12
1820 Newark Granville Rd 43023 740-587-4423
Tim Barrett, supt. Fax 587-4776

**Greenfield, Highland, Pop. 4,562**
Greenfield EVD 2,100/K-12
200 N 5th St 45123 937-981-2152
James Wills, supt. Fax 981-4395
greenfield.k12.oh.us
Greenfield MS 500/6-8
200 N 5th St 45123 937-981-2197
Wendy Callewaert, prin. Fax 981-0417
McClain HS 600/9-12
200 N 5th St 45123 937-981-7731
Jason Potts, prin. Fax 981-4395

**Greenville, Darke, Pop. 13,080**
Greenville CSD 2,700/K-12
215 W 4th St 45331 937-548-3185
Douglas Fries, supt. Fax 548-6943
www.greenville.k12.oh.us
Greenville HS 900/9-12
100 Greenwave Way 45331 937-548-4188
Jeffrey Cassell, prin. Fax 548-3082
Greenville JHS 400/7-8
131 Central Ave 45331 937-548-3202
Christian Mortensen, prin. Fax 548-3315

**Greenwich, Huron, Pop. 1,472**
South Central Local SD 800/PK-12
3305 Greenwich Angling Rd 44837 419-752-3815
Dr. Martha Hasselbusch, supt. Fax 752-0182
www.south-central.org
South Central HS 200/9-12
3305 Greenwich Angling Rd 44837 419-752-3354
Wayne Hinkle, prin. Fax 752-6927
South Central JHS 200/5-8
3291 Greenwich Angling Rd 44837 419-752-0011
Dennis Blanchard, prin. Fax 752-8705

**Grove City, Franklin, Pop. 34,836**
South-Western CSD 20,400/PK-12
3805 Marlane Dr 43123 614-801-3000
Dr. Bill Wise, supt. Fax 871-2781
www.swcs.us
Brookpark MS 600/7-8
2803 Southwest Blvd 43123 614-801-3500
Holly Carr, prin. Fax 871-6512
Central Crossing HS 1,600/9-12
4500 Big Run South Rd 43123 614-801-6500
Dr. Jill Burke, prin. Fax 801-6690
Grove City HS 1,900/9-12
4750 Hoover Rd 43123 614-801-3300
Michael Starner, prin. Fax 871-6563
Jackson MS 600/7-8
2271 Holton Rd 43123 614-801-3800
Daniel Boland, prin. Fax 801-3818
Pleasant View MS 800/7-8
7255 Kropp Rd 43123 614-801-3900
Brett Harmon, prin. Fax 870-5530
South-Western Career Academy Vo/Tech
4750 Big Run South Rd 43123 614-801-3400
James Marion, prin. Fax 801-6138
Other Schools – See Columbus, Galloway

Grove City Christian S 700/K-12
4750 Hoover Rd 43123 614-875-3000
Rebecca Jeffries, prin. Fax 875-8933
Harrison College Post-Sec.
3880 Jackpot Rd 43123 614-539-8800

**Groveport, Franklin, Pop. 5,240**
Eastland-Fairfield Career & Technical SD
4300 Amalgamated Pl 43125 614-836-4530
Bonnie Hopkins, supt. Fax 836-0203
www.eastland-fairfield.com
Eastland Career Center Vo/Tech
4465 S Hamilton Rd 43125 614-836-5725
Nelson Karshner, dir. Fax 836-4525
Adult Workforce Development Adult
4300 Amalgamated Pl Ste 100 43125 614-836-4541
Elaine Anadell, coord. Fax 836-0203
Other Schools – See Carroll

Groveport Madison Local SD 5,500/K-12
5940 Clyde Moore Dr 43125 614-492-2520
Bruce Hoover, supt. Fax 492-2532
www.gocruisers.org
Groveport Madison HS 1,500/9-12
4475 S Hamilton Rd 43125 614-836-4964
Aric Thomas, prin. Fax 836-4690
Groveport Madison MS Central 500/6-8
751 Main St 43125 614-836-4957
Neil Britton, prin. Fax 836-4999
Groveport Madison MS South 500/6-8
4400 Glendenning Dr 43125 614-836-4953
Darren Fillman, prin. Fax 836-4956
Other Schools – See Columbus

Eastland Career Center Post-Sec.
4465 S Hamilton Rd 43125 614-836-5725
Madison Christian S 500/PK-12
3565 Bixby Rd 43125 614-497-3456
Christina Jones, prin. Fax 497-3057

**Hamilton, Butler, Pop. 60,903**
Butler Technology/Career Development SD
3603 Hamilton Middletown Rd 45011 513-868-1911
Bill Miller, supt. Fax 868-9348
www.butlertech.org
Lee Career Technology Center Vo/Tech
3603 Hamilton Middletown Rd 45011 513-868-6300
Rick Pate, prin. Fax 868-1701
Options Arts Academy Alt
101 S Monument Ave 45011 513-863-8898
Fax 863-8865
Other Schools – See Monroe

Hamilton CSD 9,700/PK-12
PO Box 627 45012 513-887-5000
Tony Orr, supt. Fax 868-4473
hamiltoncityschools.com
Garfield MS 800/7-8
250 N Fair Ave 45011 513-887-5035
Brandon Stanfill, prin. Fax 887-4700
Hamilton Freshman HS 700/9-9
2260 NW Washington Blvd 45013 513-896-3400
Jeffrey Miller, prin. Fax 896-3402
Hamilton HS 1,900/10-12
1165 Eaton Ave 45013 513-868-7700
John Wilhelm, prin. Fax 887-4810
Wilson MS 700/7-8
714 Eaton Ave 45013 513-887-5170
Sheryl Burk, prin. Fax 887-5068

New Miami Local SD 700/K-12
600 Seven Mile Ave 45011 513-863-0833
Jonathan Graft, supt. Fax 863-0497
www.new-miami.k12.oh.us
New Miami HS 200/9-12
600 Seven Mile Ave 45011 513-863-4917
Trish Duebber, prin. Fax 896-3956
New Miami MS 200/6-8
600 Seven Mile Ave 45011 513-863-4917
Aileen Ernst, prin. Fax 863-3956

Ross Local SD 2,800/PK-12
3371 Hamilton Cleves Rd 45013 513-863-1253
Gregory Young, supt. Fax 863-6250
www.rossrams.com
Ross HS 900/9-12
3601 Hamilton Cleves Rd 45013 513-863-1252
Brian Martin, prin. Fax 863-8340
Ross MS 900/5-8
3425 Hamilton Cleves Rd 45013 513-863-1251
Christopher Saylor, prin. Fax 863-0066

Badin HS 500/9-12
571 Hamilton New London Rd 45013 513-863-3993
Brian Pendergest, prin. Fax 785-2844
Cincinnati Christian Schools - JSHS Cmps 400/7-12
7474 Morris Rd 45011 513-892-8500
Donna Hempelmann, prin. Fax 892-0516
Miami University-Hamilton Campus Post-Sec.
1601 University Blvd 45011 513-785-3000

**Hamler, Henry, Pop. 573**
Patrick Henry Local SD 1,000/PK-12
6900 State Route 18 43524 419-274-5451
Thomas L. Taylor, supt. Fax 274-1641
www.phpatriots.org
Henry HS 300/9-12
6900 State Route 18 43524 419-274-3015
Josh Biederstedt, prin. Fax 274-1641
Henry MS 300/5-8
E050 County Road 7 43524 419-274-3431
Kyle Lacy, prin. Fax 274-1641

**Hammondsville, Jefferson**
Edison Local SD 1,200/PK-12
14890 State Route 213 43930 330-532-3199
Bill Beattie, supt. Fax 532-2860
www.edisonlocal.k12.oh.us/
Other Schools – See Richmond

**Hannibal, Monroe, Pop. 405**
Switzerland of Ohio Local SD
Supt. — See Woodsfield
River HS 200/9-12
PO Box 37 43931 740-483-1358
Carl Trifonoff, prin. Fax 483-2321

**Hanoverton, Columbiana, Pop. 408**
United Local SD 1,300/K-12
8143 State Route 9 44423 330-223-1521
William Young, supt. Fax 223-2363
www.united.k12.oh.us
United JSHS 600/7-12
8143 State Route 9 44423 330-223-7102
William Young, prin. Fax 223-2363

**Harrison, Hamilton, Pop. 9,812**
Southwest Local SD 3,400/K-12
230 S Elm St 45030 513-367-4139
Chris Brown, supt. Fax 367-2287
www.southwestschools.org
Harrison HS 1,000/9-12
9860 West Rd 45030 513-367-4169
Davis Baker, prin. Fax 367-7251
Harrison MS 600/7-8
9830 West Rd 45030 513-367-4831
Christian Tracy, prin. Fax 367-0370

**Harrod, Allen, Pop. 415**
Allen East Local SD 1,100/PK-12
9105 Harding Hwy 45850 419-648-3333
Mel Rentschler, supt. Fax 648-5282
www.ae.k12.oh.us
Allen East HS 500/7-12
9105 Harding Hwy 45850 419-648-3333
Keith Baumgartner, prin. Fax 649-8900

**Hartville, Stark, Pop. 2,894**
Lake Local SD
Supt. — See Uniontown
Lake MS 800/6-8
511 Market Ave SW 44632 330-877-4290
Brian Reed, prin. Fax 877-1384

Lake Center Christian S 600/PK-12
12893 Kaufman Ave NW 44632 330-877-2049
Dr. Joseph Beeson, supt. Fax 877-2040

**Haviland, Paulding, Pop. 213**
Wayne Trace Local SD 900/PK-12
4915 US Route 127 45851 419-662-5171
Stephen Arnold, supt. Fax 662-3037
www.waynetrace.org
Wayne Trace JSHS 400/7-12
4915 US Route 127 45851 419-399-4100
Phil Noffsinger, prin. Fax 622-3037

**Heath, Licking, Pop. 10,088**
Heath CSD 1,600/K-12
107 Lancaster Dr 43056 740-522-2816
Trevor Thomas, supt. Fax 522-4697
www.heath.k12.oh.us/
Heath HS 500/9-12
300 Licking View Dr 43056 740-788-3300
Ellis Booth, prin. Fax 788-3322
Heath MS 400/6-8
310 Licking View Dr 43056 740-788-3200
Jeffrey Hempleman, prin. Fax 788-3209

**Hebron, Licking, Pop. 2,293**
Lakewood Local SD 2,000/K-12
PO Box 70 43025 740-928-5878
Mary Andrews, supt. Fax 928-3152
www.lakewoodlocal.k12.oh.us/
Lakewood HS 600/9-12
PO Box 70 43025 740-928-4526
Scott Coffey, prin. Fax 928-3731
Lakewood MS 500/6-8
PO Box 70 43025 740-928-8330
Andrew Bowman, prin. Fax 928-5627

**Hicksville, Defiance, Pop. 3,540**
Hicksville EVD 900/PK-12
958 E High St 43526 419-542-7665
Keith Countryman, supt. Fax 542-8534
www.hicksvilleschools.org/
Hicksville JSHS 400/7-12
958 E High St 43526 419-542-7636
Jeff Slattery, prin. Fax 542-8534

**Highland Heights, Cuyahoga, Pop. 8,256**

ATS Institute of Technology Post-Sec.
325 Alpha Park 44143 440-449-1700

**Highland Hills, Cuyahoga, Pop. 1,115**

Cuyahoga Community College Post-Sec.
4250 Richmond Rd 44122 800-954-8742

**Hilliard, Franklin, Pop. 27,909**
Hilliard CSD
Supt. — See Columbus
Hilliard Bradley HS 1,500/9-12
2800 Walker Rd 43026 614-921-7400
Mindy Mordarski, prin. Fax 921-7401
Hilliard Darby HS 1,400/9-12
4200 Leppert Rd 43026 614-921-7300
Joyce Brickley, prin. Fax 921-7301
Hilliard Davidson HS 1,700/9-12
5100 Davidson Rd 43026 614-921-7200
Aaron Cookson, prin. Fax 921-7201
Hilliard Heritage MS 700/7-8
5670 Scioto Darby Rd 43026 614-921-7500
Dawn Sayre, prin. Fax 921-7501
Hilliard Memorial MS 800/7-8
5600 Scioto Darby Rd 43026 614-921-7600
Barry Bay, prin. Fax 921-7601
Hilliard Weaver MS 800/7-8
4600 Avery Rd 43026 614-921-7700
Craig Vroom, prin. Fax 921-7701

ITT Technical Institute Post-Sec.
3781 Park Mill Run Dr 43026 614-771-4888

**Hillsboro, Highland, Pop. 6,439**
Hillsboro CSD 2,600/PK-12
39 Willetsville Pike 45133 937-393-3475
James Smith, supt. Fax 393-5841
www.hcs-k12.org
Hillsboro HS 700/9-12
550 US Highway 62 45133 937-393-3485
Jason Snively, prin. Fax 393-5842
Hillsboro MS 600/6-8
550 US Highway 62 45133 937-393-9877
Kathy Hoop, prin. Fax 393-5843

Hillsboro Christian Academy 100/K-12
8230 US Highway 50 45133 937-393-8422
Connie Sears, admin. Fax 393-4963
Southern State Community College Post-Sec.
100 Hobart Dr 45133 937-393-3431

**Hiram, Portage, Pop. 1,376**

Agape Christian Academy 50/6-12
17791 Claridon Troy Rd 44234 440-834-1705
Russell Gifford, admin. Fax 834-1708
Hiram College Post-Sec.
PO Box 67 44234 330-569-3211

**Holgate, Henry, Pop. 1,102**
Holgate Local SD 400/K-12
801 Joe E Brown Ave 43527 419-264-5141
Kelly Meyers, supt. Fax 264-1965
www.holgateschools.org
Holgate JSHS 200/6-12
801 Joe E Brown Ave 43527 419-264-2521
Casey Hemmelgarn, prin. Fax 264-1965

**Holland, Lucas, Pop. 1,746**
Springfield Local SD 3,900/K-12
6900 Hall St 43528 419-867-5600
Dr. Michael D. O'Shea, supt. Fax 867-5700
www.springfieldlocalschools.net
Springfield HS 1,000/9-12
1470 S Mccord Rd 43528 419-867-5633
Rhonda Jemison, prin. Fax 867-5618
Springfield MS 1,000/6-8
7001 Madison Ave 43528 419-867-5644
Jeff Pendry, prin. Fax 867-5732

**Houston, Shelby**
Hardin-Houston Local SD 900/PK-12
5300 Houston Rd 45333 937-295-3010
Larry Claypool, supt. Fax 295-3737
www.houston.k12.oh.us
Houston JSHS 400/7-12
5300 Houston Rd 45333 937-295-3010
Ryan Maier, prin. Fax 295-3737

**Howard, Knox, Pop. 239**
East Knox Local SD 500/K-12
23201 Coshocton Rd 43028 740-599-7493
Stephen Larcomb, supt. Fax 599-5863
www.ekschools.com
East Knox JSHS 300/7-12
23227 Coshocton Rd 43028 740-599-7000
Lisa Brown, prin. Fax 599-2922

**Hubbard, Trumbull, Pop. 7,784**
Hubbard EVD 2,000/K-12
108 Orchard Ave 44425 330-534-1921
Raymond W. Soloman, supt. Fax 534-0522
www.hubbard.k12.oh.us/
Hubbard HS 700/9-12
350 Hall Ave 44425 330-534-1921
Brandilyn Gough, prin. Fax 534-6191
Hubbard MS 600/5-8
250 Hall Ave 44425 330-534-1921
Brian Hoffman, prin. Fax 534-6191

**Huber Heights, Montgomery, Pop. 36,793**
Huber Heights CSD 5,300/PK-12
5954 Longford Rd 45424 937-237-6300
Susan Gunnell, supt. Fax 237-6307
www.huberheightscityschools.org/
Wayne HS 1,900/9-12
5400 Chambersburg Rd 45424 937-233-6431
Reva Cosby, prin. Fax 237-6321
Weisenborn JHS 500/7-8
6061 Troy Pike 45424 937-237-6350
Brent Carey, prin. Fax 237-7491

Carousel of Miami Valley Beauty College Post-Sec.
7809 Waynetowne Blvd 45424 937-233-8818

**Hudson, Summit, Pop. 21,988**
Hudson CSD 4,700/PK-12
2400 Hudson Aurora Rd 44236 330-653-1200
Phillip Herman, supt. Fax 653-1474
www.hudson.k12.oh.us
Hudson HS 1,600/9-12
2500 Hudson Aurora Rd 44236 330-653-1416
Brian Wilch, prin. Fax 653-1481
Hudson MS 1,200/6-8
77 N Oviatt St 44236 330-653-1316
Dr. Kim Cockley, prin. Fax 653-1368

Western Reserve Academy 400/9-12
115 College St 44236 330-650-4400
Christopher Burner, head sch Fax 650-9754

**Hunting Valley, Cuyahoga, Pop. 696**

University S 400/9-12
2785 Som Center Rd 44022 216-831-2200
Benjamin Rein, hdmstr. Fax 831-0402

**Huntsburg, Geauga**

Hershey Montessori S 50/7-9
11530 Madison Rd 44046 440-636-6290
Paula Leigh-Doyle, prin. Fax 636-5665

**Huron, Erie, Pop. 7,058**
Huron CSD 1,500/PK-12
712 Cleveland Rd E 44839 419-433-1234
Dennis Muratori, supt. Fax 433-7095
www.huronhs.com
Huron HS 500/9-12
710 Cleveland Rd W 44839 419-433-1234
Scott Matheny, prin. Fax 433-2339
McCormick JHS 200/7-8
325 Ohio St 44839 419-433-1234
Chad Carter, prin. Fax 433-8427

Bowling Green State University Post-Sec.
1 University Dr 44839 419-433-5560

**Independence, Cuyahoga, Pop. 7,078**
Independence Local SD 1,100/PK-12
7733 Stone Rd 44131 216-642-5850
Benjamin Hegedish, supt. Fax 642-3482
www.independence.k12.oh.us
Independence HS 400/9-12
6001 Archwood Rd 44131 216-642-5860
William McGuinness, prin. Fax 642-5886
Independence MS 300/5-8
6111 Archwood Rd 44131 216-642-5865
Kevin Jakub, prin. Fax 520-7002

Miami-Jacobs Career College Post-Sec.
6400 Rockside Rd 44131 216-834-1400

**Ironton, Lawrence, Pop. 10,894**
Ironton CSD 1,500/K-12
105 S 5th St 45638 740-532-4133
William Nance, supt. Fax 532-2314
www.tigertown.com
Ironton HS 400/9-12
1701 S 7th St 45638 740-532-3911
Joseph Rowe, prin. Fax 533-6027
Ironton MS 300/6-8
302 Delaware St 45638 740-532-3347
Toben Schreck, prin. Fax 532-3077

Rock Hill Local SD 1,400/PK-12
2325 County Road 26 Unit A 45638 740-532-7030
Wesley Hairston, supt. Fax 532-7043
rockhill.org
Rock Hill HS 300/9-12
2415 County Road 26 45638 740-533-7012
Glenn Hopper, prin. Fax 533-7015
Rock Hill MS 300/6-8
2171 County Road 26 45638 740-532-7026
Darrell Humphreys, prin. Fax 532-7028

Ohio University Southern Campus Post-Sec.
1804 Liberty Ave 45638 740-533-4600
St. Joseph Central HS 100/7-12
912 S 6th St 45638 740-532-0485
Paul Mollett, prin. Fax 532-3699

**Irwin, Union**

Rosedale Bible College Post-Sec.
2270 Rosedale Rd 43029 740-857-1311

**Jackson, Jackson, Pop. 6,292**
Jackson CSD 2,400/K-12
450 Vaughn St 45640 740-286-6442
Phil Howard, supt. Fax 286-6445
www.jcs.k12.oh.us
Jackson HS 700/9-12
500 Vaughn St 45640 740-286-7575
Joseph Hemsley, prin. Fax 286-8197
Jackson MS 600/6-8
21 Tropic St 45640 740-286-7586
Mark Broermann, prin. Fax 286-8637

Christian Life Academy 100/PK-12
10595 Chillicothe Pike 45640 740-286-1234
Melissa Boggs, admin. Fax 286-0234
Daymar College Post-Sec.
980 E Main St 45640 740-286-1554

**Jackson Center, Shelby, Pop. 1,444**
Jackson Center Local SD 400/PK-12
PO Box 849 45334 937-596-6053
William Reichert, supt. Fax 596-6490
www.jackson-center.k12.oh.us
Jackson Center JSHS 200/4-12
PO Box 849 45334 937-596-6149
William Reichert, prin. Fax 596-6490

**Jamestown, Greene, Pop. 1,954**
Greeneview Local SD 1,200/PK-12
4 S Charleston Rd 45335 937-675-2728
Isaac Seevers, supt. Fax 675-6807
www.greeneview.k12.oh.us
Greeneview MS 500/5-8
4990 Cottonville Rd 45335 937-675-9391
Mary Minear, prin. Fax 675-6866
Greenview HS 400/9-12
4710 Cottonville Rd 45335 937-675-9711
Brian Masser, prin. Fax 675-6805

**Jefferson, Ashtabula, Pop. 3,086**
Ashtabula County JVSD
1565 State Route 167 44047 440-576-6015
Dr. Jerome Brockway, supt. Fax 576-6502
atech.edu
A-Tech Vo/Tech
1565 State Route 167 44047 440-576-6015
Paul Brockett, prin. Fax 576-6502

Jefferson Area Local SD 1,900/K-12
121 S Poplar St 44047 440-576-9180
John Montanaro, supt. Fax 576-9876
www.jalsd.org
Jefferson Area HS 600/9-12
207 W Mulberry St 44047 440-576-4731
Jeremy Huber, prin. Fax 576-7344
Jefferson Area JHS 300/7-8
207 W Mulberry St 44047 440-576-1736
Richard Hoyson, prin. Fax 576-3082

**Jeromesville, Ashland, Pop. 562**
Hillsdale Local SD 1,000/K-12
485 Township Road 1902 44840 419-368-8231
Steve Dickerson, supt. Fax 368-7504
www.hillsdale.k12.oh.us/
Hillsdale HS 300/9-12
485 Township Road 1902 44840 419-368-6841
Kevin Reidy, prin. Fax 368-7504
Hillsdale MS 300/5-8
PO Box 57 44840 419-368-4911
Tim Keib, prin. Fax 368-3613

**Johnstown, Licking, Pop. 4,591**
Johnstown-Monroe Local SD 1,600/K-12
441 S Main St 43031 740-967-6846
Dale Dickson, supt. Fax 967-1106
www.johnstown.k12.oh.us/
Adams MS 400/6-8
80 W Maple St 43031 740-967-8766
Michael Carr, prin. Fax 967-0051
Johnstown-Monroe HS 500/9-12
401 S Oregon St 43031 740-967-2721
Derick Busenburg, prin. Fax 967-1140

Northridge Local SD 1,300/K-12
6097 Johnstown Utica Rd 43031 740-967-6631
Dr. Chris Briggs, supt. Fax 967-5022
www.northridge.k12.oh.us
Northridge HS 400/9-12
6066 Johnstown Utica Rd 43031 740-967-6651
Amy Anderson, prin. Fax 967-6958
Northridge MS 300/6-8
6066 Johnstown Utica Rd 43031 740-967-6671
Jason Brasno, prin. Fax 967-7083

**Kalida, Putnam, Pop. 1,534**
Kalida Local SD 600/K-12
PO Box 269 45853 419-532-3534
Karl Lammers, supt. Fax 532-2277
www.kalida.k12.oh.us
Kalida JSHS 300/6-12
PO Box 269 45853 419-532-3529
Chris Pfahler, prin. Fax 532-3582

**Kansas, Sandusky, Pop. 179**
Lakota Local SD 1,000/PK-12
5200 County Road 13 44841 419-986-6650
Jon Detwiler, supt. Fax 986-6651
www.lakota-sandusky.k12.oh.us
Lakota HS 300/9-12
5200 County Road 13 44841 419-986-6620
Sherry Sprow, prin. Fax 986-6621
Lakota MS 300/5-8
5200 County Road 13 44841 419-986-6630
Charles Tackett, prin. Fax 986-6631

**Kelleys Island, Erie, Pop. 311**
Kelleys Island Local SD 50/PK-12
PO Box 349 43438 419-746-2730
Phillip Thiede, supt. Fax 746-2271
www.kelleys.k12.oh.us/
Kelleys Island S 50/PK-12
PO Box 349 43438 419-746-2730
Phillip Thiede, supt. Fax 746-2271

**Kent, Portage, Pop. 28,086**
Kent CSD — 3,600/PK-12
321 N Depeyster St 44240 — 330-676-7600
George Joseph, supt. — Fax 677-6166
www.kentschools.net
Roosevelt HS — 1,400/9-12
1400 N Mantua St 44240 — 330-673-9595
Dennis Love, prin. — Fax 673-9217
Stanton MS — 800/6-8
1175 Hudson Rd 44240 — 330-673-6693
Anthony Horton, prin. — Fax 673-1561

Kent State University — Post-Sec.
PO Box 5190 44242 — 330-672-3000
Northcoast Medical Training Academy — Post-Sec.
1832 St Rd 59 44240 — 330-678-6600

**Kenton, Hardin, Pop. 8,149**
Kenton CSD — 1,900/PK-12
222 W Carrol St 43326 — 419-673-0775
Jennifer Penczarski, supt. — Fax 673-3180
www.kentoncityschools.org
Kenton HS — 500/9-12
200 Harding Ave 43326 — 419-673-1286
Chad Thrush, prin. — Fax 675-5200
Kenton MS — 400/7-8
300 Oriental St 43326 — 419-673-1237
Kirk Cameron, prin. — Fax 673-1626

**Kettering, Montgomery, Pop. 55,018**
Kettering CSD — 7,700/PK-12
3750 Far Hills Ave 45429 — 937-499-1430
Scott Inskeep, supt. — Fax 499-1465
www.ketteringschools.org
Kettering-Fairmont HS — 2,300/9-12
3301 Shroyer Rd 45429 — 937-499-1601
D. Tyler Alexander, prin. — Fax 499-1661
Kettering MS — 1,000/6-8
3000 Glengarry Dr 45420 — 937-499-1550
Hank Jackoby, prin. — Fax 499-1598
Van Buren MS — 700/6-8
3775 Shroyer Rd 45429 — 937-499-1800
Jeff Blakley, prin. — Fax 499-1820

Archbishop Alter HS — 700/9-12
940 E David Rd 45429 — 937-434-4434
Lourdes Lambert, prin. — Fax 434-0507
Carousel Beauty College — Post-Sec.
3076 Woodman Dr 45420 — 937-298-5752
Kettering College — Post-Sec.
3737 Southern Blvd 45429 — 937-395-8601
National College — Post-Sec.
1837 Woodman Center Dr 45420 — 937-299-9450
School of Advertising Art — Post-Sec.
1725 E David Rd 45440 — 877-300-9866

**Kidron, Wayne, Pop. 938**

Central Christian S — 300/PK-12
PO Box 9 44636 — 330-857-7311
Joyce Taylor, prin. — Fax 857-7331

**Kings Mills, Warren, Pop. 1,300**
Kings Local SD — 3,900/K-12
1797 King Ave 45034 — 513-398-8050
Tim Ackermann, supt. — Fax 229-7590
www.kingslocal.net/
Kings HS — 1,100/9-12
5500 Columbia Rd 45034 — 513-398-8050
Doug Leist, prin. — Fax 459-2941
Kings JHS — 600/7-8
5620 Columbia Rd 45034 — 513-398-8050
Nicole Huelsman, prin. — Fax 459-2951

**Kinsman, Trumbull**
Joseph Badger Local SD — 900/PK-12
7119 State Route 7 44428 — 330-876-2800
Dr. David Bair, supt. — Fax 876-2811
www.joseph-badger.k12.oh.us/
Badger HS — 300/9-12
7119 State Route 7 44428 — 330-876-2820
Edwin Baldwin, prin. — Fax 876-2821
Badger MS — 300/5-8
7119 State Route 7 44428 — 330-876-2840
Edwin Baldwin, prin. — Fax 876-2841

**Kirtland, Lake, Pop. 6,804**
Kirtland Local SD — 1,200/K-12
9252 Chillicothe Rd 44094 — 440-256-3311
Stephen G. Barrett, supt. — Fax 256-3831
www.kirtlandschools.org
Kirtland HS — 400/9-12
9150 Chillicothe Rd 44094 — 440-256-3366
Dr. Lynn Campbell, prin. — Fax 256-1042
Kirtland MS — 300/6-8
9152 Chillicothe Rd 44094 — 440-256-3358
Scott A. Amstutz, prin. — Fax 256-3928

Lakeland Community College — Post-Sec.
7700 Clocktower Dr 44094 — 440-525-7000

**LaGrange, Lorain, Pop. 2,072**
Keystone Local SD — 1,500/K-12
531 Opportunity Way 44050 — 440-355-2424
Franco Gallo, supt. — Fax 355-4465
www.keystonelocalschools.org/
Keystone HS — 500/9-12
580 Opportunity Way 44050 — 440-355-2400
James Kohler, prin. — Fax 355-6017
Keystone MS — 400/6-8
501 Opportunity Way 44050 — 440-355-2200
Toni Filut, prin. — Fax 355-6678

**Lakeside, Ottawa, Pop. 691**
Danbury Local SD — 500/PK-12
9451 E Harbor Rd 43440 — 419-798-5185
Daniel Parent, supt. — Fax 798-2260
www.danbury.k12.oh.us
Danbury HS — 100/9-12
9451 E Harbor Rd 43440 — 419-798-4037
Michael Cole, prin. — Fax 798-2262
Danbury MS — 200/5-8
9451 E Harbor Rd 43440 — 419-798-2258
Joseph Miller, prin. — Fax 798-2259

**Lakewood, Cuyahoga, Pop. 50,830**
Lakewood CSD — 5,800/K-12
1470 Warren Rd 44107 — 216-529-4000
Jeffrey Patterson, supt. — Fax 228-8327
www.lakewoodcityschools.org
Garfield MS — 600/6-8
13114 Detroit Ave 44107 — 216-529-4241
Mark Walter, prin. — Fax 529-4146
Harding MS — 700/6-8
16601 Madison Ave 44107 — 216-529-4261
Joseph Niemantsverdriet, prin. — Fax 529-4708
Lakewood HS — 1,800/9-12
14100 Franklin Blvd 44107 — 216-529-4028
Keith Ahearn, prin. — Fax 529-4459

Lakewood College — Post-Sec.
12900 Lake Ave Ste 3A 44107 — 800-517-0857
St. Edward HS — 900/9-12
13500 Detroit Ave 44107 — 216-221-3776
Frank O'Linn, prin. — Fax 221-4609
Virginia Marti College of Art & Design — Post-Sec.
11724 Detroit Ave 44107 — 216-221-8584

**Lancaster, Fairfield, Pop. 38,140**
Fairfield Union Local SD — 1,700/K-12
6417 Cincinnati Zanesvll NE 43130 — 740-536-7384
Wyvonna Broughton, supt. — Fax 536-9132
www.fairfieldunion.org
Fairfield Union HS — 600/9-12
6675 Cincinnati Zansvll NE 43130 — 740-536-7306
Brian Verde, prin. — Fax 536-7911
Rushville MS — 700/5-8
6409 Cincinnati Zanesvll NE 43130 — 740-536-7249
Chris Walton, prin. — Fax 536-7211

Lancaster CSD — 5,900/PK-12
345 E Mulberry St 43130 — 740-687-7300
Steven Wigton, supt. — Fax 687-7303
www.lancaster.k12.oh.us
Ewing JHS — 700/6-8
825 E Fair Ave 43130 — 740-687-7347
Steve Poston, prin. — Fax 687-3446
Lancaster HS — 1,600/9-12
1312 Granville Pike 43130 — 740-681-7500
Jack Greathouse, prin. — Fax 681-7505
Sherman JHS — 700/6-8
701 Union St 43130 — 740-687-7344
Scott Burre, prin. — Fax 687-3443

Daymar College — Post-Sec.
1579 Victor Rd NW 43130 — 740-687-6126
Fairfield Christian Academy — 600/PK-12
1965 N Columbus St 43130 — 740-654-2889
Craig Carpenter, supt. — Fax 654-7689
Fisher Catholic HS — 300/9-12
1803 Granville Pike 43130 — 740-654-1231
Sean Kenney, pres. — Fax 654-1233
Ohio University — Post-Sec.
1570 Granville Pike 43130 — 740-654-6711

**Latham, Pike**
Western Local SD — 800/K-12
PO Box 130 45646 — 740-493-3113
Brock Brewster, supt. — Fax 493-2065
www.westernlocalschools.com/
Western JSHS — 300/7-12
PO Box 130 45646 — 740-493-2514
Carrie Gast, prin. — Fax 493-8513

**Leavittsburg, Trumbull, Pop. 1,932**
LaBrae Local SD — 1,500/K-12
1001 N Leavitt Rd 44430 — 330-898-0800
Anthony J. Calderone, supt. — Fax 898-6112
www.labrae.school
LaBrae HS — 400/9-12
1001 N Leavitt Rd 44430 — 330-898-0800
Jeffrey Starkey, prin. — Fax 898-7808
LaBrae MS — 400/6-8
1001 N Leavitt Rd 44430 — 330-898-0800
Martin Kelly, prin. — Fax 898-7808

**Lebanon, Warren, Pop. 19,670**
Lebanon CSD — 5,400/PK-12
700 Holbrook Ave 45036 — 513-934-5770
Mark North, supt. — Fax 932-5906
www.lebanonschools.org
Lebanon HS — 1,500/9-12
1916 Drake Rd 45036 — 513-934-5100
Scott Butler, prin. — Fax 933-2150
Lebanon JHS — 900/7-8
160 Miller Rd 45036 — 513-934-5300
Jason Enix, prin. — Fax 932-9436

Warren County ESC
1879 Deerfield Rd 45036 — 513-695-2900
Tom Isaacs, supt. — Fax 695-2961
www.warrencountyesc.com/
Lazares Alternative S — Alt
3527 N State Route 48 45036 — 513-695-2994
Mike Bidwell, prin. — Fax 695-1836

Warren County JVSD
3525 N State Route 48 45036 — 513-932-5677
Margaret Hess, supt. — Fax 934-0121
www.mywccc.org/
Warren County Career Center — Vo/Tech
3525 N State Route 48 45036 — 513-932-5677
Margaret Hess, supt. — Fax 932-3810

**Leesburg, Highland, Pop. 1,294**
Fairfield Local SD — 900/K-12
11611 State Route 771 45135 — 937-780-2221
William Garrett, supt. — Fax 780-6900
www.fairfield-highland.k12.oh.us
Fairfield HS — 200/9-12
11611 State Route 771 45135 — 937-780-2966
Stephen Hackett, prin. — Fax 780-2841
Fairfield MS — 300/5-8
11611 State Route 771 45135 — 937-780-2977
Stephen Hackett, prin. — Fax 780-2841

**Leetonia, Columbiana, Pop. 1,931**
Leetonia EVD — 700/K-12
450 Walnut St 44431 — 330-427-6594
Robert Mehno, supt. — Fax 427-1136
www.leetonia.k12.oh.us
Leetonia HS — 200/9-12
450 Walnut St 44431 — 330-427-2115
Troy Radinsky, prin. — Fax 427-6904
Leetonia MS — 300/5-8
450 Walnut St 44431 — 330-427-2444
Troy Radinsky, prin. — Fax 427-2549

**Leipsic, Putnam, Pop. 2,076**
Leipsic Local SD — 600/K-12
232 Oak St 45856 — 419-943-2165
Greg Williamson, supt. — Fax 943-4331
www.lp.noacsc.org
Leipsic HS — 400/6-12
232 Oak St 45856 — 419-943-2164
Brian Bennett, prin. — Fax 943-2185

**Lewisburg, Preble, Pop. 1,788**
Tri-County North Local SD — 900/K-12
PO Box 40 45338 — 937-962-2671
William Derringer, supt. — Fax 962-4731
tricounty.oh.schoolwebpages.com/
Tri-County North HS — 200/9-12
PO Box 610 45338 — 937-962-2675
Doug Dunham, prin. — Fax 833-4860
Tri-County North MS — 300/6-8
PO Box 699 45338 — 937-962-2631
Joseph Finkbine, prin. — Fax 833-4860

**Lewis Center, Delaware, Pop. 300**
Olentangy Local SD — 15,600/PK-12
814 Shanahan Rd Ste 100 43035 — 740-657-4050
Dr. Mark Raiff, supt. — Fax 657-4099
www.olentangy.k12.oh.us
Olentangy HS — 1,300/9-12
675 Lewis Center Rd 43035 — 740-657-4100
Thomas McDonnell, prin. — Fax 657-4199
Olentangy Orange HS — 1,300/9-12
2840 E Orange Rd 43035 — 740-657-5100
Kathryne McFarland, prin. — Fax 657-5199
Olentangy Orange MS — 700/6-8
2680 E Orange Rd 43035 — 740-657-5300
Scott Cunningham, prin. — Fax 657-5399
Olentangy Shanahan MS — 800/6-8
814 Shanahan Rd 43035 — 740-657-4300
Joshua McDaniels, prin. — Fax 657-4398
Other Schools – See Galena, Powell

**Lewistown, Logan, Pop. 220**
Indian Lake Local SD — 1,700/K-12
6210 State Route 235 N 43333 — 937-686-8601
Patrick O'Donnell, supt. — Fax 686-8421
www.indianlake.k12.oh.us
Indian Lake HS — 500/9-12
6210 State Route 235 N 43333 — 937-686-8851
Rob Underwood, prin. — Fax 686-0024
Indian Lake MS — 600/5-8
8920 County Road 91 43333 — 937-686-8833
Melissa Mefford, prin. — Fax 686-8993

**Lexington, Richland, Pop. 4,768**
Lexington Local SD — 2,500/K-12
103 Clever Ln 44904 — 419-884-2132
J. Michael Ziegelhofer, supt. — Fax 884-3129
www.lexington.k12.oh.us
Lexington HS — 800/9-12
103 Clever Ln 44904 — 419-884-1111
Jeremy Secrist, prin. — Fax 884-2340
Lexington JHS — 400/7-8
90 Frederick St 44904 — 419-884-2112
Taylor Gerhardt, prin. — Fax 884-0134

**Liberty Center, Henry, Pop. 1,169**
Liberty Center Local SD — 800/PK-12
PO Box 434 43532 — 419-533-5011
Tod Hug, supt. — Fax 533-5036
www.libertycenterschools.org
Liberty Center HS — 400/9-12
PO Box 434 43532 — 419-533-6641
Larry Black, prin. — Fax 533-6108
Liberty Center MS — 400/5-8
PO Box 434 43532 — 419-533-0020
Dr. Marcia Rozevink, admin. — Fax 533-1021

**Liberty Twp, Butler**
Lakota Local SD — 16,700/PK-12
5572 Princeton Rd 45011 — 513-874-5505
Dr. Karen Mantia, supt. — Fax 644-1167
www.lakotaonline.com
Lakota East Freshman HS — 9-9
7630 Bethany Rd 45044 — 513-588-7700
Jennifer Ulland, prin. — Fax 759-2024
Lakota East HS — 1,900/10-12
6840 Lakota Ln 45044 — 513-755-7211
Suzanna Davis, prin. — Fax 759-8633
Lakota Plains JHS — 700/7-8
5500 Princeton Rd 45011 — 513-644-1130
Kim Wade, prin. — Fax 644-1135
Liberty JHS — 900/7-8
7055 Dutchland Pkwy 45044 — 513-777-4420
Eric Bauman, prin. — Fax 777-7950
Other Schools – See West Chester

**Lima, Allen, Pop. 37,107**
Allen County ESC
1920 Slabtown Rd 45801 419-222-1836
Dr. Dean Wittwer, supt. Fax 224-0718
www.allencountyesc.org/
Allen County Alternative HS Alt
1920 Slabtown Rd 45801 419-222-1836
Mitch Black, admin. Fax 222-2107

Apollo JVSD
3325 Shawnee Rd 45806 419-998-2908
Judy Wells, supt. Fax 998-2929
www.apollocareercenter.com
Apollo Career Center Vo/Tech
3325 Shawnee Rd 45806 419-998-2908
Doug Bodey, dir. Fax 998-2929

Bath Local SD 1,800/K-12
2650 Bible Rd 45801 419-221-0807
Dale Lewellen, supt. Fax 221-0983
www.bathwildcats.org
Bath HS 500/9-12
2850 Bible Rd 45801 419-221-0366
Richard Gross, prin. Fax 221-0766
Bath MS 600/5-8
2700 Bible Rd 45801 419-221-1839
Bradley Clark, prin. Fax 221-2431

Lima CSD 3,200/PK-12
755 Saint Johns Ave 45804 419-996-3400
Jill Ackerman, supt. Fax 996-3401
www.limacityschools.org
Lima HS 300/9-12
1 Spartan Way 45801 419-996-3000
Alison VanGorder, prin. Fax 996-3001
Lima West MS 400/7-8
503 N Cable Rd 45805 419-996-3150
Thomas Winkler, prin. Fax 996-3151

Perry Local SD 900/K-12
2770 E Breese Rd 45806 419-221-2770
Omer Schroeder, supt. Fax 224-6215
mycommodores.org
Perry HS 300/7-12
2770 E Breese Rd 45806 419-221-2773
Nicholas Weingart, prin. Fax 224-6215

Shawnee Local SD 2,500/K-12
3255 Zurmehly Rd 45806 419-998-8031
Michael Lamb, supt. Fax 998-8050
www.limashawnee.com
Shawnee HS 700/9-12
3333 Zurmehly Rd 45806 419-998-8000
Tony Cox, prin. Fax 998-8026
Shawnee MS 800/5-8
3235 Zurmehly Rd 45806 419-998-8057
Judy Gephart, prin. Fax 222-6572

---

Institute of Therapeutic Massage Post-Sec.
311 E Market St Fl 3 45801 419-523-9580
James A. Rhodes State Coll Post-Sec.
4240 Campus Dr 45804 419-995-8020
Liberty Christian S 50/PK-12
801 Bellefontaine Ave 45801 419-229-6266
Br. Nadine Wagner, admin. Fax 229-6266
Lima Central Catholic HS 300/9-12
720 S Cable Rd 45805 419-222-4276
Kathleen Herpich, prin. Fax 222-6933
Ohio State Beauty Academy Post-Sec.
1760 N Eastown Rd 45807 419-229-7896
Ohio State University-Lima Campus Post-Sec.
4240 Campus Dr 45804 419-995-8600
Temple Christian S 200/PK-12
982 Brower Rd 45801 419-227-1644
Dr. Dewitt H. Powell Ph.D., supt. Fax 227-6635
University of Northwestern Ohio Post-Sec.
1441 N Cable Rd 45805 419-998-3120

**Lisbon, Columbiana, Pop. 2,802**
Columbiana County JVSD
9364 State Route 45 44432 330-424-9561
Willard Adkins, supt. Fax 424-9719
www.ccctc.k12.oh.us/
Columbiana County Joint Vocational SHS Vo/Tech
9364 State Route 45 44432 330-424-9561
Jonathan Ludwig, prin. Fax 424-9719

Lisbon EVD 1,000/PK-12
317 N Market St 44432 330-424-7714
Joseph Siefke, supt. Fax 424-0135
www.lisbon.k12.oh.us/
Anderson JSHS 500/6-12
260 W Pine St 44432 330-424-3215
Keith Edenfield, prin. Fax 424-1004

**Lockland, Hamilton, Pop. 3,333**
Lockland Local SD 600/PK-12
210 N Cooper Ave 45215 513-563-5000
Dr. Matt Bishop, supt. Fax 563-9611
www.locklandschools.org
Lockland HS 100/9-12
249 W Forrer St 45215 513-563-5000
Karen Chicketti, prin. Fax 733-0800
Lockland MS 100/7-8
249 W Forrer St 45215 513-563-5000
Karen Chicketti, prin. Fax 733-0800

**Lodi, Medina, Pop. 2,720**
Cloverleaf Local SD 2,700/PK-12
8525 Friendsville Rd 44254 330-948-2500
Daryl Kubilus, supt. Fax 948-1034
www.cloverleaflocal.org/
Cloverleaf HS 900/9-12
8525 Friendsville Rd 44254 330-721-3526
Jamie Lormeau, prin. Fax 721-3559
Other Schools – See Seville

**Logan, Hocking, Pop. 7,087**
Logan-Hocking Local SD 3,900/PK-12
2019 E Front St 43138 740-385-8517
Stephen Stirn, supt. Fax 385-3683
www.lhsd.k12.oh.us
Logan HS 1,000/9-12
14470 State Route 328 43138 740-385-2069
James Robinson, prin. Fax 385-9564
Logan-Hocking MS 1,300/5-8
1 Middleschool Dr 43138 740-385-8764
Chad Grow, prin. Fax 385-9547

**London, Madison, Pop. 9,615**
London CSD 2,400/PK-12
380 Elm St 43140 740-852-5700
Dr. Lou Kramer, supt. Fax 845-3282
www.london.k12.oh.us/
London HS 500/9-12
336 Elm St 43140 740-852-5705
Chad Eisler, prin. Fax 852-3284
London MS 500/6-8
270 Keny Blvd 43140 740-852-5701
Adelle Faulkner, prin. Fax 845-1279

Madison-Plains Local SD 800/K-12
55 Linson Rd 43140 740-852-0290
Tim Dettwiller, supt. Fax 852-5895
www.mplsd.org/
Madison-Plains HS 400/9-12
800 Linson Rd 43140 740-852-0364
Matthew Unger, prin. Fax 852-3046
Madison-Plains JHS 200/6-8
803 Linson Rd 43140 740-852-1707
Dr. Matt Unger, prin. Fax 852-6351

**Lorain, Lorain, Pop. 62,074**
Clearview Local SD 1,700/K-12
4700 Broadway 44052 440-233-5412
Jerome Davis M.Ed., supt. Fax 233-6034
www.clearviewschools.org
Clearview HS 500/9-12
4700 Broadway 44052 440-233-6313
Noeleen Rothacker, prin. Fax 233-6311
Durling MS 500/5-8
100 N Ridge Rd W 44053 440-233-6869
Laura Manning, prin. Fax 233-6204

Lorain CSD 5,300/PK-12
2350 Pole Ave 44052 440-233-2271
Jeffrey Graham, supt. Fax 282-9151
www.lorainschools.org
Credit Recovery Academy Alt
2321 Fairless Dr 44055 440-277-7261
Nikole Davis, prin. Fax 277-5566
Longfellow MS 300/7-8
305 Louisiana Ave 44052 440-288-1002
Christine Miller, prin. Fax 288-1149
Lorain HS 1,900/9-12
2270 E 42nd St 44055 440-277-1176
Stephen Sturgill, prin. Fax 277-1163
New Beginnings Academy 200/Alt
3200 Clinton Ave 44055 440-277-8157
Paul Williams, prin. Fax 277-7354
Wilson MS 300/7-8
2700 Washington Ave 44052 440-246-1020
Michael Scott, prin. Fax 246-1016

---

Northern Institute of Cosmetology Post-Sec.
667 Broadway 44052 440-244-4282

**Lore City, Guernsey, Pop. 322**
East Guernsey Local SD
Supt. — See Old Washington
Buckeye Trail HS 300/9-12
65555 Wintergreen Rd 43755 740-489-5005
William Hartmeyer, prin. Fax 489-9839
Buckeye Trail MS 300/6-8
65553 Wintergreen Rd 43755 740-489-5100
William Hartmeyer, prin. Fax 489-9049

**Loudonville, Ashland, Pop. 2,623**
Loudonville-Perrysville EVD 900/PK-12
210 E Main St 44842 419-994-3912
John E. Miller M.Ed., supt. Fax 994-5528
www.lpschools.k12.oh.us
Loudonville JSHS 300/7-12
421 Campus Ave 44842 419-994-4101
John Lance, prin. Fax 994-3485

**Louisville, Stark, Pop. 9,114**
Louisville CSD 2,500/PK-12
407 E Main St 44641 330-875-1666
Michele Shaffer, supt. Fax 875-7603
www.leopard.sparcc.org
Louisville HS 1,000/9-12
1201 S Nickelplate St 44641 330-875-1438
Kenneth Faye, prin. Fax 875-7671
Louisville MS 700/6-8
1300 S Chapel St 44641 330-875-5597
Jason Orin, prin. Fax 875-7620

---

Good Shepherd S 50/1-12
PO Box 169 44641 330-935-0623
Rev. Gary Spencer, admin. Fax 935-0700
St. Thomas Aquinas HS 300/6-12
2121 Reno Dr 44641 330-875-1631
Joseph Vagedes, prin. Fax 875-8469

**Loveland, Hamilton, Pop. 11,848**
Loveland CSD 4,700/PK-12
757 S Lebanon Rd 45140 513-683-5600
Charles Hilliker Ph.D., supt. Fax 683-5697
www.lovelandschools.org/
Loveland HS 1,400/9-12
1 Tiger Trl 45140 513-683-1920
Christopher Kloesz, prin. Fax 677-7952
Loveland MS 800/7-8
801 S Lebanon Rd 45140 513-683-3100
Christopher Burke, prin. Fax 677-7986

**Lowellville, Mahoning, Pop. 1,148**
Lowellville Local SD 600/K-12
52 Rocket Pl 44436 330-536-6318
Eugene Thomas, supt. Fax 536-8221
www.lowellville.k12.oh.us/
Lowellville JSHS 300/7-12
52 Rocket Pl 44436 330-536-8426
Christine Sawicki, prin. Fax 536-8468

**Lucas, Richland, Pop. 605**
Lucas Local SD 500/PK-12
84 Lucas North Rd 44843 419-892-2338
Daniel Freund, supt. Fax 892-1138
www.lucascubs.org
Lucas HS 200/8-12
5 1st Ave 44843 419-892-2338
Eric Teague, prin. Fax 892-1138

**Lucasville, Scioto, Pop. 2,738**
Scioto County Career Technical Center
951 Vern Riffe Dr 45648 740-259-5522
Stan Jennings, supt. Fax 259-1553
www.sciototech.org
Scioto County Career Technical Center Vo/Tech
951 Vern Riffe Dr 45648 740-259-5522
Stan Jennings, supt. Fax 259-1553

Valley Local SD 1,000/K-12
1821 State Route 728 45648 740-259-3115
Fax 259-2314
www.valleyindians.net
Valley HS 300/9-12
1821 State Route 728 45648 740-259-5551
Jane Thayer, prin. Fax 259-2314
Valley MS, 393 Indian Dr 45648 300/5-8
Aaron Franke, prin. 740-259-2651

**Lynchburg, Highland, Pop. 1,486**
Lynchburg-Clay Local SD 1,200/PK-12
PO Box 515 45142 937-364-2338
Brett Justice, supt. Fax 364-2339
www.lynchclay.k12.oh.us
Lynchburg-Clay HS 400/9-12
6762 State Route 134 45142 937-364-2250
Linda Hatten, prin. Fax 364-6133
Lynchburg-Clay MS 300/6-8
8250 State Route 134 45142 937-364-2811
Casey Smith, prin. Fax 364-2159

**Lyndhurst, Cuyahoga, Pop. 13,838**
South Euclid-Lyndhurst CSD 4,100/K-12
5044 Mayfield Rd 44124 216-691-2000
Linda Reid, supt. Fax 691-2298
www.sel.k12.oh.us
Brush HS 1,600/9-12
4875 Glenlyn Rd 44124 216-691-2065
Karl Williamson, prin. Fax 691-2064
Memorial JHS 600/7-8
1250 Professor Rd 44124 216-691-2141
Kathybel Ortiz, prin. Fax 691-2159

---

Cleveland Institute Dental Medical Asst. Post-Sec.
5564 Mayfield Rd 44124 440-473-6273
Inner State Beauty School Post-Sec.
5150 Mayfield Rd 44124 440-442-4500

**Mc Arthur, Vinton, Pop. 1,685**
Vinton County Local SD 2,300/PK-12
307 W High St 45651 740-596-5218
Rick Brooks, supt. Fax 596-3142
www.vinton.k12.oh.us/
Vinton County HS 600/9-12
63910 US Highway 50 45651 740-596-5258
Kevin Waddell, prin. Fax 596-3003
Vinton County MS 500/6-8
63780 Locker Plant Rd 45651 740-596-5243
Jeremy Ward, prin. Fax 596-3815

**Mc Comb, Hancock, Pop. 1,624**
Mc Comb Local SD 800/PK-12
328 S Todd St 45858 419-293-3979
Meri Skilliter, supt. Fax 293-2412
www.noacsc.org/hancock/mb
Mc Comb Local HS 200/9-12
328 S Todd St 45858 419-293-3853
Jeremy Herr, prin. Fax 293-3107
Mc Comb Local MS 100/7-8
328 S Todd St 45858 419-293-3855
Jeremy Herr, lead tchr. Fax 293-2412

**Mc Connelsville, Morgan, Pop. 1,738**
Morgan Local SD 2,100/PK-12
PO Box 509 43756 740-962-2782
Lori Snyder-Lowe, supt. Fax 962-4931
www.mlsd.k12.oh.us/
Morgan HS 600/9-12
800 Raider Dr 43756 740-962-2944
Anita Eldridge, prin. Fax 962-6005
Morgan JHS 300/7-8
820 Junior Raider Dr 43756 740-962-2833
Timothy Hopkins, prin. Fax 962-3389

**Mc Dermott, Scioto, Pop. 428**
Northwest Local SD 1,600/PK-12
800 Mohawk Dr 45652 740-259-5558
A. Todd Jenkins, supt. Fax 259-3476
www.northwest.k12.oh.us
Northwest HS 400/9-12
914 Mohawk Dr 45652 740-259-2366
Rick Scarberry, prin. Fax 259-8544
Northwest MS 400/6-8
692 Mohawk Dr 45652 740-259-2528
Gregory Tipton, prin. Fax 259-5731

**Mc Donald, Trumbull, Pop. 3,227**
McDonald Local SD 900/K-12
600 Iowa Ave 44437 330-530-8051
Robert Rostan, supt. Fax 530-7041
www.mcdonald.k12.oh.us

McDonald JSHS 400/7-12
600 Iowa Ave 44437 330-530-8051
Gary Carkido, prin. Fax 530-7034

**Macedonia, Summit, Pop. 11,001**
Nordonia Hills CSD
Supt. — See Northfield
Nordonia HS 1,400/9-12
8006 S Bedford Rd 44056 330-468-4601
Casey Wright, prin. Fax 468-0045

**Mc Guffey, Hardin, Pop. 491**
Upper Scioto Valley Local SD 600/K-12
PO Box 305 45859 419-757-3231
Dennis L. Recker, supt. Fax 757-0135
usv.k12.oh.us
Upper Scioto Valley HS 200/9-12
PO Box 305 45859 419-757-3231
Craig Hurley, prin. Fax 757-0135
Upper Scioto Valley MS 100/7-8
PO Box 305 45859 419-757-3231
Craig Hurley, prin. Fax 757-0135

**Madison, Lake, Pop. 3,130**
Madison Local SD 2,700/PK-12
1956 Red Bird Rd 44057 440-428-2166
Angela Smith, supt. Fax 428-9379
www.madisonschools.net
Madison HS 1,100/9-12
3100 Burns Rd 44057 440-428-2161
William Fisher, prin. Fax 428-2165
Madison MS 800/6-8
6079 Middle Ridge Rd 44057 440-428-1196
Thomas Brady, prin. Fax 428-9389

**Magnolia, Stark, Pop. 965**
Sandy Valley Local SD 1,100/PK-12
5362 State Route 183 NE 44643 330-866-3339
David Fischer, supt. Fax 866-5238
cardweb.stark.k12.oh.us/
Sandy Valley MSHS 400/6-12
5130 State Route 183 NE 44643 330-866-9371
Matthew Whitted, prin. Fax 866-2490

**Maineville, Warren, Pop. 962**
Little Miami Local SD 3,300/PK-12
7247 Zoar Rd 45039 513-899-2264
Gregory Power, supt. Fax 899-3244
www.littlemiamischools.com
Other Schools – See Morrow

**Malvern, Carroll, Pop. 1,175**
Brown Local SD 700/K-12
401 W Main St 44644 330-863-1170
Connie Griffin, supt. Fax 863-1172
www.brownlocalschools.com/
Malvern HS 200/9-12
401 W Main St 44644 330-863-1355
Scott Bowling, prin. Fax 863-1366
Malvern MS 200/6-8
401 W Main St 44644 330-863-1355
Scott Bowling, prin. Fax 863-1915

**Manchester, Adams, Pop. 1,976**
Manchester Local SD 900/PK-12
130 Wayne Frye Dr 45144 937-549-4777
Dr. Charles Shreve, supt. Fax 549-4744
www.mlsd.us
Manchester HS 300/7-12
130 Wayne Frye Dr 45144 937-549-4777
James Wilkins, prin. Fax 549-2872

**Mansfield, Richland, Pop. 46,379**
Madison Local SD 3,100/PK-12
1379 Grace St 44905 419-589-2600
Lee Kaple, supt. Fax 589-3653
www.mlsd.net/
Madison Comprehensive HS 900/9-12
600 Esley Ln 44905 419-589-2112
Rob Peterson, prin. Fax 589-2533
Madison MS 500/5-8
1419 Grace St 44905 419-522-0471
Jonathan Muro, prin. Fax 522-1463

Mansfield CSD 3,100/PK-12
PO Box 1448 44901 419-525-6400
Brian Garverick, supt. Fax 525-6415
www.tygerpride.com
Mansfield HS 900/9-12
124 N Linden Rd 44906 419-525-6369
Jose Hernandez, prin. Fax 524-2210
Mansfield Integrated Learning Center 100/Alt
176 Hedges St 44902 419-525-6305
Robert Singleton, prin. Fax 525-6387
Mansfield MS 400/7-8
124 N Linden Rd 44906 419-525-6307
Jason Goings, prin. Fax 525-6306

---

Mansfield Christian S 600/PK-12
500 Logan Rd 44907 419-756-5651
Dr. Cy Smith, supt. Fax 756-7470
North Central State College Post-Sec.
2441 Kenwood Cir 44906 419-755-4800
Ohio State University-Mansfield Campus Post-Sec.
1760 University Dr 44906 419-755-4011
St. Peter HS 300/7-12
104 W 1st St 44902 419-524-0979
Michael Wasiniak, prin. Fax 524-3336
Temple Christian S 200/PK-12
752 Stewart Rd N 44905 419-589-9707
Paul Baird, prin. Fax 589-7213

**Mantua, Portage, Pop. 1,029**
Crestwood Local SD 2,000/PK-12
4565 W Prospect St 44255 330-357-8206
David Toth, supt. Fax 274-3710
www.crestwoodschools.org
Crestwood HS 700/9-12
10919 Main St 44255 330-357-8201
David McMahon, prin. Fax 274-3150
Crestwood MS 500/6-8
10880 John Edward Dr 44255 330-357-8202
Julie Schmidt, prin. Fax 274-3705

**Maple Heights, Cuyahoga, Pop. 22,680**
Maple Heights CSD 3,800/PK-12
5740 Lawn Ave 44137 216-587-6100
Dr. Charles Keenan, supt. Fax 518-2674
www.mapleschools.com/
Maple Heights HS 1,200/9-12
5445 West Blvd 44137 216-438-6400
Aaron Newman, prin.
Milkovich MS 900/6-8
19800 Stafford Ave 44137 216-438-6000
Susan Harvey, prin. Fax 587-4523

**Marengo, Morrow, Pop. 330**
Highland Local SD 1,800/K-12
6506 State Route 229 43334 419-768-2206
Bill Dodds, supt. Fax 768-3115
www.highland.k12.oh.us/
Highland HS 500/9-12
1300 State Route 314 43334 419-768-3101
Nate Huffman, prin. Fax 768-3560
Highland MS 400/6-8
6506 State Route 229 43334 419-768-2781
Matthew Bradley, prin. Fax 768-2742

**Maria Stein, Mercer**
Marion Local SD 900/K-12
7956 State Route 119 45860 419-925-4294
Michael Pohlman, supt. Fax 925-0212
marionlocal.org
Marion Local HS 300/9-12
1901 State Route 716 45860 419-925-4597
Timothy Goodwin, prin. Fax 925-5111

**Marietta, Washington, Pop. 13,848**
Marietta CSD 2,800/K-12
111 Academy Dr 45750 740-374-6500
William Hampton, supt. Fax 374-6506
mariettacityschools.k12.oh.us
Marietta HS 800/9-12
208 Davis Ave 45750 740-374-6540
Chad Rinard, prin. Fax 376-2462
Marietta MS 700/6-8
242 N 7th St 45750 740-374-6530
Brittany Schob, prin. Fax 374-6531

Washington County JVSD
21740 State Route 676 45750 740-373-2766
Dennis Blatt, supt. Fax 373-9026
www.thecareercenter.net
Washington County Career Center Vo/Tech
21740 State Route 676 45750 740-373-2766
Dennis Blatt, supt. Fax 373-9026

---

Marietta College Post-Sec.
215 5th St 45750 740-376-4000
Memorial Hospital Post-Sec.
401 Matthew St 45750 740-374-1412
Valley Beauty School Post-Sec.
113 Wildwood Dr 45750 740-373-3617
Washington State Community College Post-Sec.
710 Colegate Dr 45750 740-374-8716

**Marion, Marion, Pop. 36,113**
Elgin Local SD 800/K-12
1239 Keener Rd S 43302 740-382-1101
Bruce Gast, supt. Fax 382-1672
www.elginschools.org
Elgin HS 400/9-12
1150 Keener Rd S 43302 740-223-4300
Chad Cunningham, prin. Fax 223-4310
Elgin MS 200/6-8
1200 Keener Rd S 43302 740-223-4300
Michael Malcom, prin. Fax 223-4310

Marion CSD 4,500/PK-12
420 Presidential Dr Ste B 43302 740-387-3300
Gary Barber, supt. Fax 223-4400
www.marioncityschools.org
Grant MS 1,000/6-8
420 Presidential Dr 43302 740-223-4900
Adam Kunkle, prin. Fax 223-4820
Harding HS 1,000/9-12
1500 Harding Hwy E 43302 740-223-4700
Kirk Koennecke, prin. Fax 223-4705

Pleasant Local SD 1,200/K-12
1107 Owens Rd W 43302 740-389-4476
Dr. John Bruno, supt. Fax 389-6985
www.pleasant.treca.org
Pleasant HS 400/9-12
1101 Owens Rd W 43302 740-389-2389
Fax 389-3904
Pleasant MS 300/6-8
3507 Smeltzer Rd 43302 740-389-5167
Lane Warner, prin. Fax 389-5111

Tri-Rivers Career Center
2222 Marion Mount Gilead Rd 43302 740-389-4681
Charles Speelman, supt. Fax 389-2963
www.tririvers.com
Tri-Rivers Career Center Vo/Tech
2222 Marion Mount Gilead Rd 43302 740-389-4681
Larry Hickman, dir. Fax 389-2963

---

Marion General Hospital Post-Sec.
1000 McKinley Park Blvd 43302 740-383-8700
Marion Technical College Post-Sec.
1467 Mount Vernon Ave 43302 740-389-4636
Ohio State University at Marion Post-Sec.
1465 Mount Vernon Ave 43302 740-389-6786

**Martins Ferry, Belmont, Pop. 6,765**
Martins Ferry CSD 1,500/K-12
5001 Ayers Lime Stone Rd 43935 740-633-1732
Dirk Fitch, supt. Fax 633-5666
www.mfcsd.k12.oh.us
Martins Ferry HS 400/9-12
5000 Ayers Lime Stone Rd 43935 740-633-0684
Jeffery Oberdick, prin. Fax 635-6103
Martins Ferry MS 500/5-8
5000 Ayers Lime Stone Rd 43935 740-633-9741
Michael Delatore, prin. Fax 635-6107

**Marysville, Union, Pop. 21,701**
Marysville EVD 5,300/K-12
1000 Edgewood Dr 43040 937-578-6100
Diane Mankins, supt. Fax 578-6113
www.marysville.k12.oh.us
Bunsold MS 900/7-8
14198 State Route 4 43040 937-578-6400
Michelle Kaffenbarger, prin. Fax 578-6413
Marysville HS 1,600/9-12
800 Amrine Mill Rd 43040 937-578-6200
Thomas Cochran, prin. Fax 578-6213
Marysville STEM Early College HS 9-12
833 N Maple St 43040 937-578-7300
Kathy McKinniss, prin. Fax 578-7313

**Mason, Warren, Pop. 30,202**
Mason CSD 10,100/PK-12
211 N East St 45040 513-398-0474
Dr. Gail Kist, supt. Fax 398-4554
www.masonohioschools.com
Mason HS 3,200/9-12
6100 S Mason Montgomery Rd 45040 513-398-5025
Melinda McCarty-Stewart, prin. Fax 336-6823
Mason MS 1,800/7-8
6370 S Mason Montgomery Rd 45040 513-398-9035
Tonya McCall, prin. Fax 459-0904

---

Mars Hill Academy 300/K-12
4230 Aero Dr 45040 513-770-3223
Dr. James Albritton, hdmstr. Fax 770-3443

**Massillon, Stark, Pop. 31,305**
Jackson Local SD 5,800/K-12
7602 Fulton Dr NW 44646 330-830-8000
Chris DiLoreto, supt. Fax 830-8008
jackson.stark.k12.oh.us
Jackson HS 1,900/9-12
7600 Fulton Dr NW 44646 330-837-3501
Monica Myers, prin. Fax 830-8069
Jackson Memorial MS 1,500/6-8
7355 Mudbrook Rd NW 44646 330-830-8034
Paul Salvino, prin. Fax 830-8068

Massillon CSD 3,400/PK-12
930 17th St NE 44646 330-830-3900
Richard Goodright, supt. Fax 830-0953
www.massillonschools.org
Massillon JHS 600/7-8
250 29th St NW 44647 330-830-3902
Vincent Lindsey, prin. Fax 830-3952
Washington HS 1,200/9-12
1 Paul E Brown Dr SE 44646 330-830-3901
Brad Warner, prin. Fax 830-1954

Perry Local SD 4,900/PK-12
4201 13th St SW 44646 330-477-8121
Marty Bowe, supt. Fax 478-6184
www.perrylocal.org/
Edison MS 700/7-8
4201 13th St SW 44646 330-478-6167
Diane Kittelberger, prin. Fax 477-4612
Perry HS 1,600/9-12
3737 13th St SW 44646 330-477-3486
Jason Conrad, prin. Fax 478-6180

Stark County Area JVSD
2800 Richville Dr SE 44646 330-832-9856
Cynthia Smythe, dir. Fax 832-9850
www.drage.stark.k12.oh.us
Drage Career-Technical Center Vo/Tech
2800 Richville Dr SE 44646 330-832-9856
Daniel Murphy, dir. Fax 832-9850

Tuslaw Local SD 900/PK-12
1835 Manchester Ave NW 44647 330-837-7813
Alan Osler, supt. Fax 837-7804
www.tuslaw.sparcc.org/
Tuslaw HS 400/9-12
1847 Manchester Ave NW 44647 330-837-7800
Melissa Marconi, prin. Fax 837-6016
Tuslaw MS 500/5-8
1723 Manchester Ave NW 44647 330-837-7807
David Ryder, prin. Fax 837-6015

**Maumee, Lucas, Pop. 14,100**
Maumee CSD 2,600/K-12
716 Askin St 43537 419-893-3200
Gregory Smith, supt. Fax 891-5387
www.maumee.k12.oh.us
Gateway MS 600/6-8
900 Gibbs St 43537 419-893-3386
Angela Rose, prin. Fax 893-2263
Maumee HS 800/9-12
1147 Saco St 43537 419-893-8778
Matthew Dick, prin. Fax 893-5621

---

ITT Technical Institute Post-Sec.
1656 Henthorne Dr Ste B 43537 419-861-6500
Professional Skills Institute Post-Sec.
1505 Holland Rd 43537 419-720-6670
Stautzenberger College Post-Sec.
1796 Indian Wood Cir 43537 419-866-0261

**Mayfield, Cuyahoga, Pop. 3,423**
Mayfield CSD
Supt. — See Mayfield Heights
Mayfield HS 2,000/9-12
6116 Wilson Mills Rd 44143 440-995-6900
Jeffrey Legan, prin. Fax 995-6805

**Mayfield Heights, Cuyahoga, Pop. 18,836**
Mayfield CSD 4,600/K-12
1101 SOM Center Rd 44124 440-995-6800
Dr. Keith Kelly, supt. Fax 995-7205
www.mayfieldschools.org
CEVEC Vo/Tech
1111 Som Center Rd 44124 440-995-7450
Robert Ross, prin. Fax 646-1117
Mayfield MS 900/6-8
1123 SOM Center Rd 44124 440-995-7800
Paul Destino, prin. Fax 449-1413
Other Schools – See Mayfield

**Mechanicsburg, Champaign, Pop. 1,610**
Mechanicsburg EVD 900/K-12
60 High St 43044 937-834-2453
Danielle Prohaska, supt. Fax 834-3954
www.mechanicsburg.k12.oh.us
Mechanicsburg HS 400/9-12
60 High St 43044 937-834-2453
Paul Hershberger, prin. Fax 834-7103
Mechanicsburg MS, 60 High St 43044 200/6-8
Marlo Schipfer, admin. 937-834-2453

**Medina, Medina, Pop. 26,154**
Buckeye Local SD 2,300/PK-12
3044 Columbia Rd 44256 330-722-8257
Dr. Brian Williams, supt. Fax 722-5793
www.buckeyeschools.org
Buckeye HS 600/9-12
3084 Columbia Rd 44256 330-722-8257
Gabriel Tudor, prin. Fax 723-5606
Buckeye JHS 400/7-8
3024 Columbia Rd 44256 330-722-8257
Daniel Flood, prin. Fax 725-2413

Highland Local SD 3,200/PK-12
3880 Ridge Rd 44256 330-239-1901
Catherine Aukerman, supt. Fax 239-2456
www.highlandschools.org
Highland HS 1,000/9-12
4150 Ridge Rd 44256 330-239-1901
Dana Addis, prin. Fax 239-7385
Highland MS 800/6-8
3880 Ridge Rd 44256 330-239-1901
Rob Henry, prin. Fax 239-7388

Medina CSD 7,300/PK-12
739 Weymouth Rd 44256 330-725-8831
David Knight, supt. Fax 636-3006
www.medinabees.org
Claggett MS 1,000/6-8
420 E Union St 44256 330-636-3600
Paul Worsencroft, prin. Fax 725-9349
Evolve Academy 50/Alt
222 S Broadway St 44256 330-336-4213
Peg Hufnagel, dir.
Medina HS 2,100/9-12
777 E Union St 44256 330-636-3200
Jeffrey Harrison, prin. Fax 764-3521
Root MS 800/6-8
333 W Sturbridge Dr 44256 330-636-3500
Bryan Farson, prin. Fax 764-1471

Medina County JVSD
1101 W Liberty St 44256 330-725-8461
Steven Chrisman M.Ed., supt. Fax 725-5870
www.mcjvs.edu
Medina County Career Center Vo/Tech
1101 W Liberty St 44256 330-725-8461
Tresa Goodwin M.Ed., prin. Fax 725-5870

---

Hamrick School Post-Sec.
1156 Medina Rd 44256 330-239-2229
Medina Christian Academy 200/PK-12
3646 Medina Rd 44256 330-725-3227
Paige Donahoe, prin. Fax 725-7762
Medina County Career Center Post-Sec.
1101 W Liberty St 44256 330-725-8461

**Mentor, Lake, Pop. 46,722**
Mentor EVD 8,100/K-12
6451 Center St 44060 440-255-4444
Matthew Miller, supt. Fax 255-4622
www.mentorschools.net
Memorial MS 700/6-8
8979 Mentor Ave 44060 440-974-2250
Adam Dudziak, prin. Fax 974-2259
Mentor HS 2,700/9-12
6477 Center St 44060 440-974-5300
William Wade, prin. Fax 974-5216
Ridge MS 500/6-8
7860 Johnnycake Ridge Rd 44060 440-974-5400
Ericka Blackburn, prin. Fax 974-5285
Shore MS 700/6-8
5670 Hopkins Rd 44060 440-257-8750
Douglas Baker, prin. Fax 257-8761

---

Brown Aveda Institute Post-Sec.
8816 Mentor Ave 44060 440-255-9494
Cleveland Institute Dental Medical Asst. Post-Sec.
5733 Hopkins Rd 44060 440-946-9530
Lake Catholic HS 800/9-12
6733 Reynolds Rd 44060 440-578-1020
Robert Kumazec, prin. Fax 974-9087

**Metamora, Fulton, Pop. 623**
Evergreen Local SD 1,200/K-12
14544 County Road 6 43540 419-644-3521
James Wyse, supt. Fax 644-6070
www.evergreen.k12.oh.us
Evergreen HS 400/9-12
14544 County Road 6 43540 419-644-2951
Joshua Clark, prin. Fax 644-6070
Evergreen MS 300/6-8
14544 County Road 6 43540 419-644-2331
Joseph Zabowski, prin. Fax 644-9203

**Miamisburg, Montgomery, Pop. 19,876**
Miamisburg CSD 4,300/PK-12
540 Park Ave 45342 937-866-3381
Dr. David Vail, supt. Fax 865-5250
www.miamisburgcityschools.org
Miamisburg HS 1,500/9-12
1860 Belvo Rd 45342 937-866-0771
Craig Morris, prin. Fax 865-5267
Miamisburg MS 6-8
8668 Miamisburg Springboro 45342 937-865-0011
Kelly Thomas, prin. Fax 865-0114

---

Dayton Barber College Post-Sec.
2741 Lyons Rd Ste C 45342 937-222-9101
Dayton Christian S 1,000/PK-12
9391 Washington Church Rd 45342 937-291-7201
Richard Anglin, pres. Fax 291-7202

**Middleburg Heights, Cuyahoga, Pop. 15,799**
Berea CSD
Supt. — See Berea
Middleburg Heights JHS 300/7-9
7000 Paula Dr 44130 216-676-8400
Paul Kish, prin. Fax 676-2070

Polaris JVSD
7285 Old Oak Blvd 44130 440-891-7600
Bob Timmons, supt. Fax 243-3952
www.polaris.edu
Polaris Career Center Vo/Tech
7285 Old Oak Blvd 44130 440-891-7600
Gerald Lanning, prin. Fax 243-3952

**Middlefield, Geauga, Pop. 2,651**
Cardinal Local SD 1,300/K-12
PO Box 188 44062 440-632-0261
Scott Hunt Ed.D., supt. Fax 632-5886
www.cardinalschools.org
Cardinal HS 400/9-12
PO Box 7 44062 440-632-0264
Jeremy Hunter, prin. Fax 632-1734
Cardinal MS 300/5-8
PO Box 879 44062 440-632-0263
Dr. Jennifer Sabol, prin. Fax 632-0294

**Middleport, Meigs, Pop. 2,488**

---

Mid Valley Christian S 100/PK-12
500 N 2nd Ave 45760 740-992-6249
Melissa Dailey, admin. Fax 992-6249

**Middletown, Butler, Pop. 47,397**
Madison Local SD 1,200/PK-12
1324 Middletown Eaton Rd 45042 513-420-4750
Curtis Philpot, supt. Fax 420-4781
www.madisonmohawks.org/
Madison JSHS 500/7-12
5797 W Alexandria Rd 45042 513-420-4760
Justin Smith, prin. Fax 420-4914

Middletown CSD 6,300/PK-12
1 Donham Plz Fl 4 45042 513-423-0781
Samuel Ison, supt. Fax 420-4579
www.middletowncityschools.com
Middleton MS 800/7-8
1415 Girard Ave 45044 513-420-4528
Michael Valenti, prin. Fax 420-4527
Middletown HS 1,700/9-12
601 N Breiel Blvd 45042 513-420-4500
Carmela Cotter, prin. Fax 420-4648

---

Carousel Beauty College Post-Sec.
633 S Breiel Blvd 45044 513-422-2962
Miami University-Middletown Campus Post-Sec.
4200 N University Blvd 45042 513-727-3200
Middletown Regional Hospital Post-Sec.
PO Box 428810 45042 513-420-5100

**Milan, Erie, Pop. 1,356**
EHOVE JVSD
316 Mason Rd W 44846 419-499-4663
Sharon Mastroianni, supt. Fax 499-4076
www.ehove.net
EHOVE Career Center Vo/Tech
316 Mason Rd W 44846 419-499-4663
Erika Beckman, prin. Fax 499-4076

Edison Local SD 1,600/PK-12
140 S Main St 44846 419-499-3000
Thomas Roth, supt. Fax 499-4859
www.edisonchargers.org/
Edison HS 500/9-12
2603 State Route 113 E 44846 419-499-4652
Jeffrey Goodwin, prin. Fax 499-2035
Other Schools – See Berlin Heights

**Milford, Clermont, Pop. 6,599**
Great Oaks Institute of Technology
Supt. — See Cincinnati
Live Oaks CDC Vo/Tech
5956 Buckwheat Rd 45150 513-575-1900
Dan Cox, prin. Fax 575-0805

Milford EVD 6,500/PK-12
777 Garfield Ave 45150 513-831-1314
Dr. Robert Farrell, supt. Fax 831-3208
www.milfordschools.org
Milford HS 1,800/9-12
1 Eagles Way 45150 513-831-2990
Josh Kauffman, prin. Fax 831-9714
Milford JHS 1,000/7-8
5735 Pleasant Hill Rd 45150 513-831-1900
Rob Dunn, prin. Fax 248-3451

---

St. Andrew/St. Elizabeth Ann Seton S 200/6-8
555 Main St 45150 513-831-5277
Thomas Devolve, prin. Fax 831-8436

**Milford Center, Union, Pop. 776**
Fairbanks Local SD 1,000/K-12
11158 State Route 38 43045 937-349-3731
Robert Humble, supt. Fax 349-8885
www.fairbanks.k12.oh.us
Fairbanks HS 300/9-12
11158 State Route 38 43045 937-349-3721
Tom Montgomery, prin. Fax 349-2011
Fairbanks MS 200/6-8
11158 State Route 38 43045 937-349-6841
Thomas Montgomery, prin. Fax 349-2013

**Millbury, Wood, Pop. 1,191**
Lake Local SD 1,100/PK-12
28090 Lemoyne Rd 43447 419-661-6690
Jim Witt, supt. Fax 661-6678
www.lakeschools.org
Lake HS 400/8-12
28080 Lemoyne Rd 43447 419-661-6640
Lee Herman, prin. Fax 661-6650

**Miller City, Putnam, Pop. 137**
Miller City-New Cleveland Local SD 500/K-12
PO Box 38 45864 419-876-3172
Kerry Johnson, supt. Fax 876-3849
www.mcncschools.org
Miller City-New Cleveland HS 100/9-12
PO Box 38 45864 419-876-3173
Kerry Johnson, prin. Fax 876-2020
Miller City-New Cleveland MS 100/6-8
PO Box 38 45864 419-876-3174
Dustin Pester, prin. Fax 876-2020

**Millersburg, Holmes, Pop. 2,985**
West Holmes Local SD 2,400/K-12
28 W Jackson St 44654 330-674-3546
William Sterling, supt. Fax 674-1177
www.westholmes.k12.oh.us
West Holmes HS 700/9-12
10909 State Route 39 44654 330-674-6085
Aaron Kaufman, prin. Fax 674-0818
West Holmes MS 600/6-8
10901 State Route 39 44654 330-674-4761
Jeff Woods, prin. Fax 674-2311

---

Gospel Haven Academy 100/K-12
6871 State Route 241 44654 330-674-0752
Galen Kauffman, prin. Fax 674-0752

**Millersport, Fairfield, Pop. 1,033**
Walnut Township Local SD 600/K-12
11850 Lancaster St 43046 740-467-2802
Randall Cotner, supt. Fax 467-3494
www.walnuttsd.org
Millersport JSHS 300/7-12
11850 Lancaster St 43046 740-467-2929
Jeff Stought, prin. Fax 467-3494

**Mineral Ridge, Trumbull, Pop. 3,840**
Weathersfield Local SD 600/K-12
3750 Main St 44440 330-652-0287
Damon Dohar, supt. Fax 544-7476
www.weathersfield.k12.oh.us/
Mineral Ridge HS 300/7-12
1334 Seaborn St 44440 330-652-1451
Robert Martinko, prin. Fax 505-9374

**Minerva, Stark, Pop. 3,671**
Minerva Local SD 1,800/K-12
406 East St 44657 330-868-4332
Gary Chaddock, supt. Fax 868-4731
minerva.web1.schoolpointe.com/
Minerva HS 600/9-12
501 Almeda Ave 44657 330-868-4134
Brett Yeagley, prin. Fax 868-5973
Minerva MS 500/6-8
600 E Line St 44657 330-868-4497
Scott Cassidy, prin. Fax 868-3144

**Minford, Scioto, Pop. 684**
Minford Local SD 1,500/K-12
PO Box 204 45653 740-820-3896
Barbara Dever, supt. Fax 820-3334
www.minfordfalcons.net
Minford HS 400/9-12
PO Box 204 45653 740-820-3445
Jeffrey Pica, prin. Fax 820-4484
Minford MS 600/4-8
PO Box 204 45653 740-820-2181
Dennis Evans, prin. Fax 820-2191

**Mingo Junction, Jefferson, Pop. 3,405**
Indian Creek Local SD
Supt. — See Wintersville
Indian Creek MS 300/5-8
2379 Wilson Ave 43938 740-282-0834
Dr. Holly Minch-Hick, prin. Fax 282-3092

**Minster, Auglaize, Pop. 2,793**
Minster Local SD 600/K-12
50 E 7th St 45865 419-628-3397
Brenda Boeke, supt. Fax 628-2482
www.minsterschools.org
Minster JSHS 400/7-12
100 E 7th St 45865 419-628-2324
Michael Lee, prin. Fax 628-2495

**Mogadore, Summit, Pop. 3,799**
Field Local SD 2,300/K-12
2900 State Route 43 44260 330-673-2659
David Heflinger, supt. Fax 673-0270
www.fieldlocalschools.org
Field HS 700/9-12
2900 State Route 43 44260 330-673-9591
Michael Harris, prin. Fax 677-2520
Field MS, 1379 Saxe Rd 44260 600/6-8
Susan Blake, prin. 330-673-4176

Mogadore Local SD 700/K-12
1 S Cleveland Ave 44260 330-628-9946
Dr. Christina Dinklocker, supt. Fax 628-6661
www.mogadore.net
Mogadore JSHS 200/7-12
130 S Cleveland Ave 44260 330-628-9943
Russ Swartz, prin. Fax 628-6657

**Monclova, Lucas**

Monclova Christian Academy 200/K-12
7819 Monclova Rd 43542 419-866-7630
Neil Black, prin. Fax 868-1062

**Monroe, Butler, Pop. 12,294**
Butler Technology/Career Development SD
Supt. — See Hamilton
Natural Science Center Vo/Tech
640 Hamilton Lebanon Rd E 45050 513-539-0818
Fax 539-1129

Monroe Local SD 2,000/PK-12
500 Yankee Rd 45050 513-539-2536
Dr. Philip Cagwin, supt. Fax 539-2648
www.monroelocalschools.com/
Monroe JSHS 600/7-12
220 Yankee Rd 45050 513-539-8471
Dr. Brian Powderly, prin. Fax 539-8474

**Monroeville, Huron, Pop. 1,379**
Monroeville Local SD 600/K-12
101 West St 44847 419-465-2610
G. Ralph Moore, supt. Fax 465-4263
www.monroevilleschools.org/
Monroeville JSHS 300/7-12
101 West St 44847 419-465-2531
James Kaczor, prin. Fax 465-4580

**Montpelier, Williams, Pop. 4,026**
Montpelier EVD 1,000/PK-12
PO Box 193 43543 419-485-6700
Jamison Grime, supt. Fax 485-4318
www.montpelier-k12.org
Montpelier JSHS 400/7-12
PO Box 193 43543 419-485-6703
Su Thorop, prin. Fax 485-3487

**Morral, Marion, Pop. 394**
Ridgedale Local SD 700/K-12
3103 Hillman Ford Rd 43337 740-382-6065
Robert Britton, supt. Fax 383-6538
www.ridgedale.k12.oh.us/
Ridgedale JSHS 400/6-12
3165 Hillman Ford Rd 43337 740-382-6065
Brian Napper, prin. Fax 387-8525

**Morrow, Warren, Pop. 1,164**
Little Miami Local SD
Supt. — See Maineville
Little Miami HS 900/9-12
3001 E US Highway 22 and 3 45152 513-899-3781
Catherine Trevathan, prin. Fax 899-4912
Little Miami JHS 300/7-8
5290 Morrow Cozaddale Rd 45152 513-899-3408
Ryan Cherry, prin. Fax 899-2048

**Mount Blanchard, Hancock, Pop. 482**
Riverdale Local SD 800/K-12
20613 State Route 37 45867 419-694-4994
Eric Hoffman, supt. Fax 694-6465
www.riverdale.k12.oh.us
Riverdale HS 300/9-12
20613 State Route 37 45867 419-694-2211
Terry Huffman, prin. Fax 694-5008
Riverdale MS 200/6-8
20613 State Route 37 45867 419-694-2211
Terry Huffman, prin. Fax 694-5008

**Mount Gilead, Morrow, Pop. 3,594**
Mt. Gilead EVD 1,300/PK-12
145 N Cherry St 43338 419-946-1646
Jeffrey Thompson, supt. Fax 946-3651
www.mgschools.org
Mount Gilead HS 300/9-12
338 W Park Ave 43338 419-947-6065
Debra Clauss, prin. Fax 946-3263
Mount Gilead MS 300/6-8
324 W Park Ave 43338 419-947-9517
Alan Keesee, prin. Fax 947-9518

Gilead Christian S South Campus 50/7-12
3613 Township Road 115 43338 419-946-5990
Gary W. Miller, admin. Fax 946-1103

**Mount Healthy, Hamilton, Pop. 5,926**
Mt. Healthy CSD 1,400/K-12
7615 Harrison Ave 45231 513-729-0077
Reva Cosby, supt. Fax 728-4692
www.mthcs.org
Other Schools – See Cincinnati

**Mount Orab, Brown, Pop. 3,635**
Western Brown Local SD 3,200/PK-12
524 W Main St 45154 937-444-2044
Raegan White, supt. Fax 444-4303
www.wb.k12.oh.us
Mount Orab MS 700/5-8
472 W Main St 45154 937-444-2529
Sabrina Armstrong, prin. Fax 444-4268
Western Brown HS 800/9-12
476 W Main St 45154 937-444-2544
Heather Cooper, prin. Fax 444-4355

**Mount Vernon, Knox, Pop. 16,729**
Knox County JVSD
306 Martinsburg Rd 43050 740-397-5820
Kathy Greenich, supt. Fax 397-7040
www.knoxcc.org
Knox County Career Center Vo/Tech
306 Martinsburg Rd 43050 740-397-5820
Kathy Greenich, admin. Fax 397-7040

Mt. Vernon CSD 3,900/PK-12
300 Newark Rd 43050 740-397-7422
William Seder, supt. Fax 397-5949
www.mvcsd.us/
Mount Vernon HS 1,000/9-12
300 Martinsburg Rd 43050 740-393-5900
Kathy Kasler, prin. Fax 397-6018
Mount Vernon MS 900/6-8
298 Martinsburg Rd 43050 740-392-6867
Gary Hankins, prin. Fax 392-3369

Christian Star Academy 50/K-12
7 E Sugar St 43050 740-393-0251
Suzanne Feasel, admin. Fax 393-0067
Knox County Career Center Post-Sec.
306 Martinsburg Rd 43050 740-397-5820
Mt. Vernon Nazarene University Post-Sec.
800 Martinsburg Rd 43050 740-392-6868

**Mount Victory, Hardin, Pop. 626**
Ridgemont Local SD 500/PK-12
560 Taylor St W 43340 937-354-2441
Emmy Beeson, supt. Fax 354-2194
www.ridgemont.k12.oh.us
Ridgemont JSHS 200/7-12
560 Taylor St W 43340 937-354-2141
Jill Stover, prin. Fax 354-5099

**Mowrystown, Highland, Pop. 359**
Bright Local SD 600/PK-12
PO Box 299 45155 937-442-3114
Ted Downing, supt. Fax 442-6655
www.brightlocalschools.com
Whiteoak JSHS 200/7-12
PO Box 299 45155 937-442-2241
Michael Roades, prin. Fax 442-2111

**Munroe Falls, Summit, Pop. 4,951**
Stow-Munroe Falls CSD
Supt. — See Stow
Kimpton MS 800/7-8
380 N River Rd 44262 330-689-5288
Susan Palchesko, prin. Fax 686-4718

**Napoleon, Henry, Pop. 8,677**
Napoleon Area CSD 1,900/K-12
701 Briarheath Ave Ste 108 43545 419-599-7015
Dr. Stephen R. Fogo, supt. Fax 599-7035
www.napoleonareaschools.org/
Napoleon JSHS 600/7-12
701 Briarheath Ave Ste 123 43545 419-599-1050
Ryan Wilde, prin. Fax 599-8537

**Navarre, Stark, Pop. 1,939**
Fairless Local SD 1,600/K-12
11885 Navarre Rd SW 44662 330-767-3577
Broc Bidlack, supt. Fax 767-3298
www.falcon.stark.k12.oh.us/
Fairless HS 500/9-12
11885 Navarre Rd SW 44662 330-767-3444
Dr. Larry Chambliss, prin. Fax 767-3447
Fairless MS 400/6-8
11836 Navarre Rd SW 44662 330-767-4293
Theodore George, prin. Fax 767-3807

**Nelsonville, Athens, Pop. 5,295**
Nelsonville-York CSD 1,300/PK-12
2 Buckeye Dr 45764 740-753-4441
Charles McClelland, supt. Fax 753-1968
www.nelsonvilleyork.k12.oh.us/
Nelsonville-York HS 400/9-12
1 Buckeye Dr 45764 740-753-4441
Elise Stephan, prin. Fax 753-1420
Nelsonville-York MS 200/7-8
3 Buckeye Dr 45764 740-753-4441
Thomas Taggart, prin. Fax 753-9450

Tri-County Career Center
15676 State Route 691 45764 740-753-3511
William Wittman, supt. Fax 753-5376
www.tricountyhightech.com
Tri-County Career Center Vo/Tech
15676 State Route 691 45764 740-753-3511
Connie Altier, prin. Fax 753-5132
Tri-County Adult Career Center Adult
15676 State Route 691 45764 740-753-5464
Ron Cassidy, dir. Fax 753-5129

Hocking College Post-Sec.
3301 Hocking Pkwy 45764 740-735-3591

**New Albany, Franklin, Pop. 7,553**
New Albany - Plain Local SD 4,400/K-12
55 N High St 43054 614-855-2040
April Domine, supt. Fax 855-2043
www.napls.us
New Albany HS 1,200/9-12
7600 Fodor Rd 43054 614-413-8300
Dwight Carter, prin. Fax 413-8301
New Albany MS 1,100/6-8
6600 E Dublin Granville Rd 43054 614-413-8500
Elizabeth Gonda, prin. Fax 413-8501

**Newark, Licking, Pop. 46,372**
Career & Technology Educational Ctr SD
150 Price Rd 43055 740-364-2832
Joyce Malainy, supt. Fax 364-2815
www.c-tec.edu/
Career & Technology Educational Center Vo/Tech
150 Price Rd 43055 740-364-2832
Thomas Gamertsfelder, dir. Fax 364-2815

Licking Valley Local SD 2,000/K-12
1379 Licking Valley Rd 43055 740-763-3525
David Hile, supt. Fax 763-0471
www.lickingvalley.k12.oh.us/
Licking Valley HS 600/9-12
100 Hainsview Dr 43055 740-763-3721
Wes Weaver, prin. Fax 763-0847

Licking Valley MS 500/6-8
1379 Licking Valley Rd 43055 740-763-3396
Scott Beery, prin. Fax 763-2612

Newark CSD 6,200/PK-12
621 Mount Vernon Rd 43055 740-670-7000
Douglas Ute, supt. Fax 670-7009
www.newarkcityschools.org
Heritage MS 500/6-8
600 Arlington Ave 43055 740-670-7110
Brent Fickes, prin. Fax 670-7119
Liberty MS 500/6-8
1055 Evans Blvd 43055 740-670-7320
Diane Henry, prin. Fax 670-7329
Newark HS 1,400/9-12
314 Granville St 43055 740-670-7400
Thomas Bowman, prin. Fax 670-7409
Wilson MS 400/6-8
805 W Church St 43055 740-670-7120
John Davis, prin. Fax 670-7129

Central Ohio Technical College Post-Sec.
1179 University Dr 43055 740-366-9494
Newark Catholic HS 200/9-12
1 Green Wave Dr 43055 740-344-3594
Beth Hill, prin. Fax 344-0421
Ohio State University at Newark Post-Sec.
1179 University Dr 43055 740-366-3321

**New Boston, Scioto, Pop. 2,223**
New Boston Local SD 400/PK-12
1 Glenwood Tiger Trl 45662 740-456-4559
Melinda Burnside, supt. Fax 456-6402
www.newboston.k12.oh.us
Glenwood HS 200/7-12
1 Glenwood Tiger Trl 45662 740-456-4559
Donald Stapleton, prin. Fax 456-6402

Daymar College Post-Sec.
3879 Rhodes Ave 45662 740-456-4124

**New Bremen, Auglaize, Pop. 2,950**
New Bremen Local SD 900/K-12
901 E Monroe St 45869 419-629-8606
Dr. Andrea Townsend, supt. Fax 629-0115
www.newbremenschools.org
New Bremen HS 300/9-12
901 E Monroe St 45869 419-629-8606
Brian Pohl, prin. Fax 629-0115

**Newburgh Heights, Cuyahoga, Pop. 2,102**
Cleveland Municipal SD
Supt. — See Cleveland
Washington Park Environmental Studies 200/9-12
3875 Washington Park Blvd 44105 216-482-2671
Donald Strinka, prin. Fax 441-8038

**Newbury, Geauga**
Newbury Local SD 600/K-12
14775 Auburn Rd 44065 440-564-5501
Michelle Mrakovich, supt. Fax 564-9460
www.newburyschools.org/
Newbury JSHS 300/6-12
14775 Auburn Rd 44065 440-564-2281
Michael Chaffee, prin. Fax 564-9788

**New Carlisle, Clark, Pop. 5,735**
Tecumseh Local SD 3,100/K-12
9760 W National Rd 45344 937-845-3576
Norm Glismann, supt. Fax 845-4453
www.tecumseh.k12.oh.us
Tecumseh HS 1,000/9-12
9830 W National Rd 45344 937-845-4500
Ivan Gehret, prin. Fax 845-4547
Tecumseh MS 800/6-8
10000 W National Rd 45344 937-845-4465
Brian Dixon, prin. Fax 845-4484

**Newcomerstown, Tuscarawas, Pop. 3,763**
Newcomerstown EVD 1,100/PK-12
702 S River St 43832 740-498-8373
Jeffrey Staggs, supt. Fax 498-8375
www.nctschools.org
Newcomerstown HS 300/9-12
659 Beaver St 43832 740-498-5111
Matthew Fockler, prin. Fax 498-4994
Newcomerstown MS 200/6-8
325 W State St 43832 740-498-8151
Jason Peoples, prin. Fax 498-4991

**New Concord, Muskingum, Pop. 2,459**
East Muskingum Local SD 2,100/K-12
13505 John Glenn School Rd 43762 740-826-7655
Jill Sheridan, supt. Fax 826-7194
www.east-muskingum.k12.oh.us
East Muskingum MS 500/6-8
13120 John Glenn School Rd 43762 740-826-7631
Trent Cubbison, prin. Fax 826-4392
Glenn HS 600/9-12
13115 John Glenn School Rd 43762 740-826-7641
Steve Brooks, prin. Fax 826-3039

Muskingum University Post-Sec.
163 Stormont St 43762 740-826-8211

**New Knoxville, Auglaize, Pop. 875**
New Knoxville Local SD 400/K-12
PO Box 476 45871 419-753-2431
Kim Waterman, supt. Fax 753-2333
www.nkrangers.org
New Knoxville HS 100/7-12
PO Box 476 45871 419-753-2431
Jenny Fledderjohann, prin. Fax 753-2333

**New Lebanon, Montgomery, Pop. 3,918**
New Lebanon Local SD 1,100/K-12
320 S Fuls Rd 45345 937-687-1301
Dr. Greg Williams, supt. Fax 687-7321
www.newlebanonschools.org

Dixie HS 300/9-12
300 S Fuls Rd 45345 937-687-1366
Brad Wolgast, prin. Fax 687-7074
Dixie MS 300/5-8
200 S Fuls Rd 45345 937-687-3508
Dr. Gary Schomburg, prin. Fax 687-7705

**New Lexington, Perry, Pop. 4,679**
New Lexington CSD 1,800/K-12
1605 Airport Rd 43764 740-342-4133
Casey Coffey, supt. Fax 342-6051
www.nlpanthers.org
New Lexington HS 500/9-12
2547 Panther Dr NE 43764 740-342-3528
James Young, prin. Fax 342-4765
New Lexington MS 400/6-8
2549 Panther Dr NE 43764 740-342-4128
Annette Losco, prin. Fax 342-6071

**New London, Huron, Pop. 2,415**
New London Local SD 900/PK-12
2 Wildcat Dr 44851 419-929-8433
Bradley Romano, supt. Fax 929-4108
www.nlschools.org
New London HS 300/9-12
1 Wildcat Dr 44851 419-929-1586
Cosetta Adkins, prin. Fax 929-9513
New London MS 200/6-8
1 Wildcat Dr 44851 419-929-5409
Cosetta Adkins, prin. Fax 929-9513

**New Madison, Darke, Pop. 886**
Tri-Village Local SD 700/K-12
PO Box 31 45346 937-996-6261
Josh Sagester, supt. Fax 996-5537
www.tri-village.k12.oh.us
Tri-Village JSHS 300/7-12
PO Box 31 45346 937-996-1511
Lee Morris, prin. Fax 996-0307

**New Matamoras, Washington, Pop. 879**
Frontier Local SD 600/K-12
44870 State Route 7 45767 740-865-3473
Bruce Kidder, supt. Fax 865-2010
www.flsd.k12.oh.us
Frontier MSHS 200/7-12
44870 State Route 7 45767 740-865-3441
William Creighton, prin. Fax 865-2011

**New Middletown, Mahoning, Pop. 1,611**
Springfield Local SD 1,100/K-12
PO Box 549 44442 330-542-2929
Debra Mettee, supt. Fax 542-9453
Springfield HS 300/9-12
11335 Youngstown Pittsburgh 44442 330-542-3626
Anthony DeFelice, prin. Fax 542-9453
Springfield IS 300/5-8
11333 Youngstown Pittsburgh 44442 330-542-3624
David Malone, prin. Fax 542-2159

**New Paris, Preble, Pop. 1,607**
National Trail Local SD 1,000/K-12
6940 Oxford Gettysburg Rd 45347 937-437-3333
Jeff Parker, supt. Fax 437-7865
www.nationaltrail.k12.oh.us/
National Trail HS 300/9-12
6940 Oxford Gettysburg Rd 45347 937-437-3333
Bob Fischer, prin. Fax 437-8270
National Trail MS 300/5-8
6940 Oxford Gettysburg Rd 45347 937-437-3333
Mark Wiseman, prin. Fax 437-7306

**New Philadelphia, Tuscarawas, Pop. 17,008**
Buckeye JVSD
545 University Dr NE 44663 330-339-2288
Bob Alsept, supt. Fax 339-5159
buckeyecareercenter.org
Buckeye Career Center Vo/Tech
545 University Dr NE 44663 330-339-2288
Jay Davis, prin. Fax 339-5159

New Philadelphia CSD 2,900/PK-12
248 Front Ave SW 44663 330-364-0600
David Brand, supt. Fax 364-9310
www.npschools.org
New Philadelphia HS 800/9-12
343 Ray Ave NW 44663 330-364-0644
Eric Jurkovic, prin. Fax 364-0633
Welty MS 600/6-8
315 4th St NW 44663 330-364-0645
Carl McCrory, prin. Fax 364-0677

---

Kent State University- Tuscarawas Campus Post-Sec.
330 University Dr NE 44663 330-339-3391
Tuscarawas Central Catholic HS 200/7-12
777 3rd St NE 44663 330-343-3302
Scott Power, prin. Fax 343-6388

**New Richmond, Clermont, Pop. 2,535**
New Richmond EVD 2,300/K-12
212 Market St 45157 513-553-2616
Adam Bird, supt. Fax 553-6431
www.nrschools.org
New Richmond HS 600/9-12
1131 Bethel New Richmond Rd 45157513-553-3191
Mark Bailey, prin. Fax 553-2531
New Richmond MS 400/7-8
1135 Bethel New Richmond Rd 45157513-553-3161
Court Lilly, prin. Fax 553-6412

**New Riegel, Seneca, Pop. 248**
New Riegel Local SD 400/K-12
44 N Perry St 44853 419-595-2256
Elaine Nye, supt. Fax 595-2901
newriegelschools.org
New Riegel JSHS 200/7-12
44 N Perry St 44853 419-595-2256
David Rombach, prin. Fax 595-2901

**Newton Falls, Trumbull, Pop. 4,737**
Newton Falls EVD 1,000/K-12
909 1/2 Milton Blvd 44444 330-872-5445
Paul Woodard, supt. Fax 872-3351
www.newton-falls.k12.oh.us/
Falls Learning Academy Alt
907 Milton Blvd 44444 330-872-5121
John Crowder, prin.
Newton Falls HS 400/9-12
907 Milton Blvd 44444 330-872-5121
John Crowder, prin. Fax 872-3351
Newton Falls JHS 200/7-8
907 1/2 Milton Blvd 44444 330-872-0695
Angellina Berilla, admin. Fax 872-8327

**New Washington, Crawford, Pop. 962**
Buckeye Central Local SD 700/K-12
938 S Kibler St 44854 419-492-2864
Mark Robinson, supt. Fax 492-2039
www.bcbucks.org
Buckeye Central HS 200/9-12
938 S Kibler St 44854 419-492-2266
Jay Zeiter, prin. Fax 492-2039
Buckeye Central MS 200/5-8
938 S Kibler St 44854 419-492-1035
Jay Zeiter, prin. Fax 492-2039

**Niles, Trumbull, Pop. 18,878**
Niles CSD 2,100/K-12
309 N Rhodes Ave 44446 330-989-5095
Ann Marie Thigpen, supt. Fax 989-5096
www.nilescityschools.org/
McKinley HS 700/9-12
616 Dragon Dr 44446 330-652-9968
Mark Lucas, prin. Fax 505-0755
Niles MS 600/6-8
411 Brown St 44446 330-652-5656
Samuel Reigle, prin. Fax 652-9158

---

ETI Technical College of Niles Post-Sec.
2076 Youngstown Warren Rd 44446 330-652-9919
Raphael's School of Beauty Culture Post-Sec.
1324 Youngstown Warren Rd 44446 330-652-1559
Victory Christian S 100/K-12
2053 Pleasant Valley Rd 44446 330-539-9827
Colleen McCullough, prin. Fax 539-9828

**North Baltimore, Wood, Pop. 3,396**
North Baltimore Local SD 700/K-12
201 S Main St 45872 419-257-3531
Ryan Delaney, supt. Fax 257-2008
www.nbls.org/
North Baltimore HS 200/9-12
2012 Tiger Dr 45872 419-257-3464
Dr. Bob Falkenstein, prin. Fax 257-2008
North Baltimore MS 100/7-8
2012 Tiger Dr 45872 419-257-3464
Dr. Bob Falkenstein, prin. Fax 257-2008

**North Bloomfield, Trumbull**
Bloomfield-Mespo Local SD 300/K-12
2077 Park West Rd 44450 440-685-4711
Russell McQuaide, supt. Fax 685-4751
www.bloomfield-mespo.org/
Bloomfield MSHS 100/6-12
2077 Park West Rd 44450 440-685-4711
Steven Kobus, prin. Fax 685-4751

**North Canton, Stark, Pop. 17,236**
North Canton CSD 3,900/PK-12
525 7th St NE 44720 330-497-5600
Michael Hartenstein, supt. Fax 497-5618
www.northcantonschools.org
Hoover HS 1,800/9-12
525 7th St NE 44720 330-497-5620
Anthony Pallija, prin. Fax 497-5606
North Canton MS 1,100/6-8
605 Fair Oaks Ave SW 44720 330-497-5635
Linnea Olbon, prin. Fax 497-5659

---

Kent State University Stark Campus Post-Sec.
6000 Frank Ave NW 44720 330-499-9600
Stark State College Post-Sec.
6200 Frank Ave NW 44720 330-494-6170
Walsh University Post-Sec.
2020 E Maple St 44720 330-490-7090

**North Eaton, Lorain**

---

Christian Community S 100/K-12
35716 Royalton Rd 44044 440-748-6224
Rick Willis, hdmstr. Fax 748-1007

**Northfield, Summit, Pop. 3,593**
Nordonia Hills CSD 3,900/K-12
9370 Olde 8 Rd 44067 330-467-0580
Joseph Clark, supt. Fax 468-0152
www.nordoniaschools.org
Nordonia MS 600/7-8
73 Leonard Ave 44067 330-467-0584
Ryan Durr, prin. Fax 468-6719
Other Schools – See Macedonia

**North Jackson, Mahoning**
Jackson-Milton Local SD 800/K-12
13910 Mahoning Ave 44451 330-538-3232
Kirk Baker, supt. Fax 538-6297
www.jacksonmilton.k12.oh.us/
Jackson-Milton HS 300/9-12
13910 Mahoning Ave 44451 330-538-3308
David Vega, prin. Fax 538-0821
Jackson-Milton MS 100/7-8
13910 Mahoning Ave 44451 330-538-3308
David Vega, prin. Fax 538-0821

**North Lewisburg, Union, Pop. 1,449**
Triad Local SD 1,000/K-12
7920 Brush Lake Rd 43060 937-826-4961
Chris Piper, supt. Fax 826-3281
www.triad.k12.oh.us
Triad HS 300/9-12
8099 Brush Lake Rd 43060 937-826-3771
Kyle Huffman, prin. Fax 826-2002
Triad MS 300/5-8
7941 Brush Lake Rd 43060 937-826-3071
Duane Caudill, prin. Fax 826-1000

**North Olmsted, Cuyahoga, Pop. 32,229**
North Olmsted CSD 3,900/PK-12
27425 Butternut Ridge Rd 44070 440-779-3576
Michael Zalar Ph.D., supt. Fax 779-3505
www.northolmstedschools.org
North Olmsted HS 1,400/9-12
5755 Burns Rd 44070 440-779-8825
Jeffrey Stanton, prin. Fax 777-2216
North Olmsted MS 700/7-8
26855 Lorain Rd 44070 440-779-8503
Tom Dreiling, prin. Fax 779-8510

---

Remington College Post-Sec.
26350 Brookpark Rd 44070 440-777-2560

**North Randall, Cuyahoga, Pop. 1,013**

---

PowerSport Institute Post-Sec.
21210 Emery Rd 44128 216-587-5000

**North Ridgeville, Lorain, Pop. 29,069**
North Ridgeville CSD 4,000/K-12
5490 Mills Creek Ln 44039 440-327-4444
James Powell, supt. Fax 327-9774
www.nrcs.k12.oh.us
North Ridgeville HS 1,100/9-12
34600 Bainbridge Rd 44039 440-327-1992
Tom Szendrey, prin. Fax 327-4056
North Ridgeville MS 900/6-8
35895 Center Ridge Rd 44039 440-353-1180
Amy Peck, prin. Fax 353-1144

---

Lake Ridge Academy 400/K-12
37501 Center Ridge Rd 44039 440-327-1175
Carol Klimas, pres. Fax 327-3641

**North Robinson, Crawford, Pop. 201**
Colonel Crawford Local SD 700/PK-12
PO Box 7 44856 419-562-4666
Todd Martin, supt. Fax 562-3304
www.cck12.org
Crawford HS 300/9-12
PO Box 7 44856 419-562-4666
Jake Bruner, prin. Fax 562-3304
Other Schools – See Crestline

**North Royalton, Cuyahoga, Pop. 30,115**
North Royalton CSD 4,700/1-12
6579 Royalton Rd 44133 440-237-8800
Greg Gurka, supt. Fax 582-7336
www.northroyaltonsd.org
North Royalton HS 1,600/9-12
14713 Ridge Rd 44133 440-582-7801
Sean Osborne, prin. Fax 582-7337
North Royalton MS 1,500/5-8
14709 Ridge Rd 44133 440-582-9120
Jeffrey Cicerchi, prin. Fax 582-7229

**Northwood, Wood, Pop. 5,174**
Northwood Local SD 900/PK-12
500 Lemoyne Rd 43619 419-691-3888
Gregory Clark, supt. Fax 697-2470
www.northwoodschools.org
Northwood HS 400/7-12
700 Lemoyne Rd 43619 419-691-4651
Jason Kozina, prin. Fax 691-2846

**Norton, Summit, Pop. 11,968**
Norton CSD 2,600/PK-12
4128 Cleveland Massillon Rd 44203 330-825-0863
David Dunn, supt. Fax 825-0929
www.norton.k12.oh.us
Norton HS 800/9-12
4108 Cleveland Massillon Rd 44203 330-825-7300
Ryan Shanor, prin. Fax 825-4275
Norton MS 800/5-8
3390 Cleveland Massillon Rd 44203 330-825-5607
Joyce Gerber, prin. Fax 825-1461

**Norwalk, Huron, Pop. 16,729**
Norwalk CSD 2,900/PK-12
134 Benedict Ave 44857 419-668-2779
George Fisk, supt. Fax 663-3302
www.norwalktruckers.net
Norwalk HS 800/9-12
350 Shady Lane Dr 44857 419-660-6500
Brad Cooley, prin. Fax 668-4719
Norwalk MS 500/7-8
64 Christie Ave 44857 419-668-8370
Corey Ream, prin. Fax 668-6622

---

Norwalk Catholic - St. Paul JSHS 300/7-12
93 E Main St 44857 419-668-3005
James Tokarsky, prin. Fax 668-6417

**Norwood, Hamilton, Pop. 18,788**
Norwood CSD 1,800/PK-12
2132 Williams Ave 45212 513-924-2500
Robert Amodio, supt. Fax 396-6420
www.norwoodschools.org
Norwood HS 500/9-12
2020 Sherman Ave 45212 513-924-2800
Bradley Winterod, prin. Fax 396-5559
Norwood MS 300/7-8
2060 Sherman Ave 45212 513-924-2700
Katherine Sabo, prin. Fax 396-5537

---

Cornerstone Christian Academy 50/PK-12
PO Box 12824 45212 513-351-7900
Dr. Phyllis Wilson, dir. Fax 351-7900
ITT Technical Institute Post-Sec.
4750 Wesley Ave 45212 513-531-8300

**Oak Harbor, Ottawa, Pop. 2,732**
Benton Carroll Salem Local SD 1,300/K-12
11685 W State Route 163 43449 419-898-6210
Dr. Guy Parmigian, supt. Fax 898-4303
www.bcssd.com
Oak Harbor HS 500/8-12
11661 W State Route 163 43449 419-898-6216
Cheryl Schell, prin. Fax 898-0116

**Oak Hill, Jackson, Pop. 1,527**
Oak Hill Union Local SD 1,300/PK-12
205 Western Ave 45656 740-682-7595
Michael A. McCoy, supt. Fax 682-6998
www.oakhill.k12.oh.us
Oak Hill MSHS 700/6-12
5063 State Route 93 45656 740-682-7055
Randall Layton, prin. Fax 682-6075

**Oakwood, Paulding, Pop. 604**
Oakwood CSD 2,100/PK-12
20 Rubicon Rd 45409 937-297-5332
Kyle Ramey Ed.D., supt. Fax 297-5345
www.oakwoodschools.org
Oakwood HS 700/9-12
1200 Far Hills Ave 45419 937-297-5325
Paul Waller, prin. Fax 297-5348
Oakwood JHS 300/7-8
1200 Far Hills Ave 45419 937-297-5328
Daniel Weckstein, prin. Fax 297-7807

**Oberlin, Lorain, Pop. 7,787**
Firelands Local SD
Supt. — See South Amherst
Firelands HS 600/9-12
10643 Vermilion Rd 44074 440-965-4255
Robert Maver, prin. Fax 965-5296

Lorain County JVSD
15181 State Route 58 44074 440-774-1051
Dr. Glenn Faircloth, supt. Fax 774-2144
www.lcjvs.com/
Burton Vocational Center HS Vo/Tech
15181 State Route 58 44074 440-774-1051
Jill Petitti, prin. Fax 774-6421

Oberlin CSD 1,100/PK-12
153 N Main St 44074 440-774-1458
Dr. David H. Hall, supt. Fax 774-4492
www.oberlinschools.net
Langston MS 300/6-8
150 N Pleasant St 44074 440-775-7961
Chris Frank, prin. Fax 776-4520
Oberlin HS 300/9-12
281 N Pleasant St 44074 440-774-1295
William Baylis, prin. Fax 774-5099

---

Oberlin College Post-Sec.
101 N Professor St 44074 440-775-8121

**Old Fort, Seneca, Pop. 185**
Old Fort Local SD 500/K-12
7635 N County Rd 51 44861 419-992-4291
Stephen Anway, supt. Fax 992-4293
www.old-fort.k12.oh.us/
Old Fort JSHS 200/7-12
7635 N County Rd 51 44861 419-992-4291
Sonia Herman, prin. Fax 992-4293

**Old Washington, Guernsey, Pop. 277**
East Guernsey Local SD 1,100/K-12
PO Box 128 43768 740-489-5190
Adam Pittis, supt. Fax 489-9813
www.eguernsey.k12.oh.us
Other Schools – See Lore City

**Olmsted Falls, Cuyahoga, Pop. 8,919**
Olmsted Falls CSD 3,800/PK-12
PO Box 38010 44138 440-427-6000
Dr. Jim Lloyd, supt. Fax 427-6010
www.ofcs.net
Olmsted Falls HS 1,200/9-12
26939 Bagley Rd 44138 440-427-6100
Holly Schafer, prin. Fax 427-6110
Olmsted Falls MS 900/6-8
27045 Bagley Rd 44138 440-427-6200
Mark Kurz, prin. Fax 427-6210

**Ontario, Richland, Pop. 6,103**
Ontario Local SD 1,300/PK-12
457 Shelby Ontario Rd, 419-747-4311
Lisa Carmichael, supt. Fax 747-6859
www.ontarioschools.org
Ontario HS 500/9-12
467 Shelby Ontario Rd, 419-529-3969
Chris Smith, prin. Fax 529-5649
Ontario MS 400/6-8
447 Shelby Ontario Rd, 419-529-5507
Sue Weirich, prin. Fax 529-7058

**Oregon, Lucas, Pop. 20,036**
Oregon CSD 3,800/K-12
5721 Seaman Rd 43616 419-693-0661
Hal Gregory, supt. Fax 698-6016
www.oregoncityschools.org
Clay HS 1,200/9-12
5665 Seaman Rd 43616 419-693-0665
James Jurski, prin. Fax 698-6047
Fassett JHS 500/7-8
3025 Starr Ave 43616 419-693-0455
Rebecca Bihn, prin. Fax 698-6048

---

Cardinal Stritch HS 200/9-12
3225 Pickle Rd 43616 419-693-0465
Tim Malone, prin. Fax 697-2816

St. Charles Hospital Post-Sec.
2600 Navarre Ave 43616 419-698-7341
Toledo Academy of Beauty Culture - East Post-Sec.
3341 Navarre Ave 43616 419-693-7257

**Orrville, Wayne, Pop. 8,182**
Orrville CSD 1,500/PK-12
815 N Ella St 44667 330-682-4651
James Ritchie, supt. Fax 682-0073
www.orrville.k12.oh.us
Orrville HS 400/9-12
841 N Ella St 44667 330-682-4661
David Sovacool, prin. Fax 682-4662
Orrville MS 500/5-8
801 Mineral Springs St 44667 330-682-1791
David Sovacool, prin. Fax 682-2743

---

Kingsway Christian S 100/PK-12
11138 Old Lincoln Way E 44667 330-683-0012
Keith Fuller M.Ed., prin. Fax 683-0017
University of Akron-Wayne College Post-Sec.
1901 Smucker Rd 44667 330-683-2010

**Orwell, Ashtabula, Pop. 1,614**
Grand Valley Local SD 1,400/K-12
111 W Grand Valley Ave # A 44076 440-437-6260
Dr. William Nye, supt. Fax 437-1025
www.grand-valley.k12.oh.us
Grand Valley HS 400/9-12
111 W Grand Valley Ave # C 44076 440-437-6260
Douglas Hitchcock, prin. Fax 437-1025
Grand Valley MS 500/5-8
111 W Grand Valley Ave # D 44076 440-437-6260
Roberta Cozad, prin. Fax 437-1025

**Ottawa, Putnam, Pop. 4,436**
Ottawa-Glandorf Local SD 1,400/K-12
630 Glendale Ave 45875 419-523-5261
Don Horstman, supt. Fax 523-5978
www.ottawaglandorf.org
Ottawa-Glandorf HS 500/9-12
630 Glendale Ave 45875 419-523-5702
Jayson Selgo, prin. Fax 523-6346

**Ottawa Hills, Lucas, Pop. 4,439**
Ottawa Hills Local SD 1,000/K-12
3600 Indian Rd, 419-536-6371
Dr. Kevin Miller, supt. Fax 534-5380
www.ottawahillsschools.org/
Ottawa Hills JSHS 500/7-12
2532 Evergreen Rd, 419-534-5376
Ben McMurray, prin. Fax 534-5384

**Ottoville, Putnam, Pop. 974**
Ottoville Local SD 400/K-12
PO Box 248 45876 419-453-3356
Scott Mangas, supt. Fax 453-3367
www.ottovilleschools.org
Ottoville JSHS 200/7-12
PO Box 248 45876 419-453-3358
Jon Thorbahn, prin. Fax 453-3367

**Oxford, Butler, Pop. 20,904**
Talawanda CSD 3,000/PK-12
131 W Chestnut St 45056 513-273-3333
Kelly Spivey, supt. Fax 273-3113
www.talawanda.net/
Talawanda HS 900/9-12
5301 University Park Blvd 45056 513-273-3200
Tom York, prin. Fax 273-3203
Talawanda MS 700/6-8
4030 Oxford Reily Rd 45056 513-273-3300
Mike Malone, prin. Fax 273-3303

---

Miami University Post-Sec.
501 E High St 45056 513-529-1809

**Painesville, Lake, Pop. 18,851**
Lake County ESC
382 Blackbrook Rd 44077 440-350-2563
Dr. Brian Bontempo, supt. Fax 350-2566
www.esc-lc.org/
Other Schools – See Eastlake

Painesville City Local SD 3,500/PK-12
58 Jefferson St 44077 440-392-5060
John Shepard, supt. Fax 392-5089
www.pcls.net
Harvey HS 800/9-12
200 W Walnut Ave 44077 440-392-5110
Van McWreath, prin. Fax 392-5119
Heritage MS 600/6-8
135 Cedarbrook Dr 44077 440-392-5250
Melissa DeAngelis, prin. Fax 392-5259

Riverside Local SD 4,800/K-12
585 Riverside Dr 44077 440-352-0668
James Kalis, supt. Fax 639-1959
www.riversidelocalschools.com
Riverside JSHS 1,800/8-12
585 Riverside Dr 44077 440-352-3341
Peter Hliatzos, prin. Fax 352-0695

---

Lake Erie College Post-Sec.
391 W Washington St 44077 440-296-1856

**Pandora, Putnam, Pop. 1,146**
Pandora-Gilboa Local SD 500/K-12
410 Rocket Rdg 45877 419-384-3227
Todd Schmutz, supt. Fax 384-3230
www.pg.noacsc.org
Pandora-Gilboa HS 200/9-12
410 Rocket Rdg 45877 419-384-3225
Jeffrey Wise, prin. Fax 384-3230
Pandora-Gilboa MS 200/5-8
410 Rocket Rdg 45877 419-384-3225
Jodi Schroeder, prin. Fax 384-3230

**Parma, Cuyahoga, Pop. 80,516**
Parma CSD 10,100/PK-12
5311 Longwood Ave 44134 440-842-5300
Carl Hilling, supt. Fax 885-8304
www.parmacityschools.org
Normandy HS 1,200/8-12
2500 W Pleasant Valley Rd 44134 440-885-2400
Dr. Debora Vanek, prin. Fax 885-2402
Parma HS 1,500/8-12
6285 W 54th St 44129 440-885-2300
Dr. Chad Coffman, prin. Fax 888-0358
Other Schools – See Parma Heights

---

Bryant & Stratton College Post-Sec.
12955 Snow Rd 44130 216-265-3151
Padua Franciscan HS 800/9-12
6740 State Rd 44134 440-845-2444
David Stec, prin. Fax 845-5710
Parma Community General Hospital Post-Sec.
7007 Powers Blvd 44129 440-743-3000

**Parma Heights, Cuyahoga, Pop. 20,381**
Parma CSD
Supt. — See Parma
Valley Forge HS 1,500/8-12
9999 Independence Blvd 44130 440-885-2330
Janine Andrzejewski, prin. Fax 885-8412

---

Cuyahoga Community College Post-Sec.
11000 W Pleasant Valley Rd 44130 800-954-8742
Holy Name HS 700/9-12
6000 Queens Hwy 44130 440-886-0300
Shelbrey Blanc, prin. Fax 886-1267

**Pataskala, Licking, Pop. 14,629**
Licking Heights Local SD 3,000/K-12
6539 Summit Rd SW 43062 740-927-6926
Dr. Philip Wagner, supt. Fax 927-9043
www.licking-heights.k12.oh.us/
Licking Heights Central MS 800/6-8
6565 Summit Rd SW 43062 740-927-3365
Terrance Hubbard, prin. Fax 927-5845
Licking Heights HS 800/9-12
4000 Mink St SW 43062 740-927-9046
Ken Kraemer, prin. Fax 927-3197

Southwest Licking Local SD 3,700/K-12
927 South St Unit A 43062 740-927-3941
Robert Jennell, supt. Fax 927-4648
www.swl.k12.oh.us
Other Schools – See Etna

---

Liberty Christian Academy 300/PK-12
10447 Refugee Rd SW 43062 740-964-2211
LaVonne McIlrath, admin. Fax 964-2311

**Patriot, Gallia**
Gallia County Local SD 2,100/PK-12
4836 State Route 325 45658 740-379-9085
Jude Meyers, supt. Fax 379-9135
gallialocal.org
Other Schools – See Bidwell, Crown City

**Paulding, Paulding, Pop. 3,557**
Paulding EVD 1,500/PK-12
405 N Water St 45879 419-399-4656
William Hanak, supt. Fax 399-2404
www.pauldingschools.org/
Paulding HS 400/9-12
405 N Water St 45879 419-399-4656
Todd Harmon, prin. Fax 399-2404
Paulding MS 300/6-8
405 N Water St 45879 419-399-4656
Chris Etzler, prin. Fax 399-2404

Western Buckeye ESC
PO Box 176 45879 419-399-4711
Brian Gerber, supt. Fax 399-3346
www.wbesc.org/
ACE Academy Alt
PO Box 176 45879 419-399-4649

**Peebles, Adams, Pop. 1,762**
Adams County/Ohio Valley Local SD
Supt. — See West Union
Peebles HS 500/7-12
25719 State Route 41 45660 937-587-2681
Timothy Davis, prin. Fax 587-5236

**Pemberville, Wood, Pop. 1,357**
Eastwood Local SD 1,500/K-12
4800 Sugar Ridge Rd 43450 419-833-6411
William Welker, supt. Fax 833-4915
www.eastwoodschools.org
Eastwood HS 500/9-12
4900 Sugar Ridge Rd 43450 419-833-3611
Jeffrey Hill, prin. Fax 833-6014
Eastwood MS 500/5-8
4800 Sugar Ridge Rd 43450 419-833-6011
John Obrock, prin. Fax 833-7454

**Peninsula, Summit, Pop. 560**
Woodridge Local SD 2,000/K-12
4411 Quick Rd 44264 330-928-9074
Walter Davis, supt. Fax 928-1542
www.woodridge.k12.oh.us/
Woodridge HS 700/9-12
4440 Quick Rd 44264 330-929-3191
Joel Morgan, prin. Fax 928-5036
Woodridge MS 500/6-8
4451 Quick Rd 44264 330-928-7420
Jesse Hosford, prin. Fax 928-5645

**Pepper Pike, Cuyahoga, Pop. 5,884**
Orange CSD 2,200/PK-12
32000 Chagrin Blvd 44124 216-831-8600
Dr. Edwin Holland, supt. Fax 831-8029
www.orangeschools.org

Brady MS 500/6-8
32000 Chagrin Blvd 44124 216-831-8600
Brian Frank, prin. Fax 839-1335
Orange HS 800/9-12
32000 Chagrin Blvd 44124 216-831-8581
Dr. Paul Lucas, prin. Fax 831-2595

---

Ursuline College Post-Sec.
2550 Lander Rd 44124 440-449-4200

**Perry, Lake, Pop. 1,647**
Perry Local SD 1,400/K-12
4325 Manchester Rd 44081 440-259-9200
Jack Thompson Ph.D., supt. Fax 259-3607
www.perry-lake.org
Perry HS 600/9-12
1 Success Blvd 44081 440-259-9300
Todd Porcello, prin. Fax 259-9290
Perry MS 400/5-8
2 Learning Ln 44081 440-259-9500
Robert Knisely, prin. Fax 259-5149

**Perrysburg, Wood, Pop. 20,359**
Penta Career Center
9301 Buck Rd 43551 419-666-1120
Ron Matter, supt. Fax 666-6049
www.pentacareercenter.org
Penta Career Center Vo/Tech
9301 Buck Rd 43551 419-666-1120
Jeffrey Kurtz, prin. Fax 666-6049

Perrysburg SD 4,600/K-12
140 E Indiana Ave 43551 419-874-9131
Thomas Hosler, supt. Fax 872-8820
www.perrysburgschools.net
Perrysburg HS 1,300/9-12
13385 Roachton Rd 43551 419-874-3181
Dr. Michael Short, prin. Fax 872-8813
Perrysburg JHS 1,100/6-8
550 E South Boundary St 43551 419-874-9193
Brent Swartzmiller, prin. Fax 872-8812

---

Healing Arts Institute Post-Sec.
340 3 Meadows Dr 43551 419-874-4496

**Pettisville, Fulton, Pop. 497**
Pettisville Local SD 500/PK-12
PO Box 53001 43553 419-446-2705
Dr. Stephen Switzer, supt. Fax 445-2992
pettisvilleschools.org
Pettisville JSHS 300/7-12
PO Box 53001 43553 419-446-2705
Michael Lane, prin. Fax 445-2992

**Philo, Muskingum, Pop. 726**
Franklin Local SD
Supt. — See Duncan Falls
Philo JHS 500/6-8
PO Box 178 43771 740-674-5210
Robert Preston, prin. Fax 674-5217

**Pickerington, Fairfield, Pop. 17,708**
Pickerington Local SD 10,200/K-12
90 N East St 43147 614-833-2110
Valerie Thompson Ph.D., supt. Fax 833-2143
www.pickerington.k12.oh.us
Pickerington HS Central 1,600/9-12
300 Opportunity Way 43147 614-548-1800
Stacy Tennenbaum, prin. Fax 548-1810
Pickerington HS North 1,700/9-12
7800 Refugee Rd 43147 614-830-2700
Mark Ulbrich, prin. Fax 833-3660
Pickerington Lakeview JHS 900/7-8
12445 Ault Rd 43147 614-830-2200
Pam Bertke, prin. Fax 834-3267
Pickerington Ridgeview STEM JHS 800/7-8
130 Hill Rd S 43147 614-548-1700
Susan Caudill, prin. Fax 548-1710

---

Eagle Prep Academy PK-12
6810 Blacklick Eastern Rd 43147 614-833-0515
Amanda Grady, head sch Fax 834-1443

**Piketon, Pike, Pop. 2,150**
Pike County Area JVSD
PO Box 577 45661 740-289-2721
Eric Meredith, supt. Fax 289-4243
www.pikectc.org
Riffe Career Technology Center Vo/Tech
PO Box 577 45661 740-289-2721
Shon Tackett, dir. Fax 289-2527

Scioto Valley Local SD 1,300/K-12
PO Box 600 45661 740-289-4456
Dr. Todd Burkitt, supt. Fax 289-3065
www.piketon.k12.oh.us/
Piketon JSHS 500/7-12
1414 Piketon Rd 45661 740-289-2254
Jeffrey Reuter, prin. Fax 289-1514

**Pioneer, Williams, Pop. 1,360**
North Central Local SD 600/PK-12
400 E Baubice St 43554 419-737-2392
Kenneth Boyer, supt. Fax 737-3361
www.northcentralschool.org
North Central JSHS 300/7-12
400 E Baubice St 43554 419-737-2366
Timothy Rettig, prin. Fax 737-2531

**Piqua, Miami, Pop. 19,922**
Piqua CSD 3,500/K-12
719 E Ash St 45356 937-773-4321
Richard Hanes, supt. Fax 778-4518
www.piqua.org
Piqua HS 1,000/9-12
1 Indian Trl 45356 937-773-6314
Anthony Lyons, prin. Fax 778-4514
Piqua JHS 600/7-8
1 Tomahawk Trl 45356 937-778-2997
Jeff Clark, prin. Fax 773-3574

Upper Valley JVSD
8811 Career Dr 45356 937-778-1980
Dr. Nancy Luce, supt. Fax 778-0103
www.uppervalleycc.org
Upper Valley Career Center Vo/Tech
8811 Career Dr 45356 937-778-1980
Jason Haak, dir. Fax 778-4677

---

Edison State Community College Post-Sec.
1973 Edison Dr 45356 937-778-8600

**Plain City, Madison, Pop. 4,160**
Jonathan Alder Local SD 2,200/PK-12
9200 US Highway 42 S 43064 614-873-5621
Gary Chapman, supt. Fax 873-8462
www.alder.k12.oh.us
Alder HS 600/9-12
9200 US Highway 42 S 43064 614-873-4642
Phil Harris, prin. Fax 873-4252
Alder JHS 300/7-8
6440 Kilbury Huber Rd 43064 614-873-4635
Jonathan Hayes, prin. Fax 873-0845

Tolles Career & Technical Center
7877 US Highway 42 S 43064 614-873-4666
Kimberly Wilson, supt. Fax 873-8761
www.tollestech.com
Tolles Career & Technical Center Vo/Tech
7877 US Highway 42 S 43064 614-873-4666
Jackie Kuffel, dir. Fax 873-6909

---

Shekinah Christian S 100/K-12
10040 Lafayette Plain City 43064 614-873-3130
Brice Kaufmann, dir. Fax 873-3699

**Pleasant Hill, Miami, Pop. 1,191**
Newton Local SD 600/K-12
PO Box 803 45359 937-676-2002
Pat McBride, supt. Fax 676-2054
www.newton.k12.oh.us/
Newton JSHS 300/7-12
PO Box 803 45359 937-676-2002
Danielle Davis, prin. Fax 676-2397

**Pleasant Plain, Warren, Pop. 153**

---

Village Christian S 200/4-12
PO Box 48 45162 513-877-2125
Barry Boverie, admin. Fax 877-2145

**Plymouth, Huron, Pop. 1,844**
Plymouth-Shiloh Local SD 700/K-12
365 Sandusky St 44865 419-687-4733
James Metcalf, supt. Fax 687-1541
plymouth.schoolwires.com/plymouth/site/
Plymouth HS 200/9-12
400 Trux St 44865 419-687-8200
Amanda Mahon, prin. Fax 687-8175
Shiloh MS 200/6-8
400 Trux St 44865 419-687-8200
Bradley Turson, prin. Fax 687-8175

**Poland, Mahoning, Pop. 2,537**
Poland Local SD 2,200/K-12
3199 Dobbins Rd 44514 330-757-7000
David Janofa, supt. Fax 757-2390
www.polandbulldogs.com/
Poland MS 400/7-8
47 College St 44514 330-757-7003
Mark Covell, prin. Fax 757-2390
Poland Seminary HS 800/9-12
3199 Dobbins Rd 44514 330-757-7018
Kevin Snyder, prin. Fax 757-2390

**Pomeroy, Meigs, Pop. 1,809**
Meigs Local SD 1,800/K-12
41765 Pomeroy Pike 45769 740-992-2153
Rusty Bookman, supt. Fax 992-7814
www.meigslocalschools.org/
Meigs HS 500/9-12
42091 Pomeroy Pike 45769 740-992-2158
Steven Ohlinger, prin. Fax 992-5839
Meigs MS 400/6-8
42353 Charles Chancey Dr 45769 740-992-3058
Vickie Jones, prin. Fax 992-6952

**Port Clinton, Ottawa, Pop. 5,954**
Port Clinton CSD 1,700/K-12
811 Jefferson St 43452 419-732-2102
Patrick Adkins, supt. Fax 734-4527
www.pccsd.net/
Port Clinton HS 500/9-12
821 Jefferson St 43452 419-734-2147
Gary Steyer, prin. Fax 734-4276
Port Clinton MS 400/6-8
807 Jefferson St 43452 419-734-4448
Carrie Sanchez, prin. Fax 734-4440

**Portsmouth, Scioto, Pop. 19,655**
Clay Local SD 200/PK-12
44 Clay High St 45662 740-354-6645
Anthony Mantell, supt. Fax 354-5746
clay.k12.oh.us/
Clay MSHS 200/6-12
44 Clay High St 45662 740-354-6644
William Warnock, prin. Fax 354-6105

Portsmouth CSD 2,000/PK-12
724 Findlay St 45662 740-354-5663
Gary Dutey, supt. Fax 355-4496
www.portsmouthtrojans.org
Portsmouth JSHS 700/7-12
1225 Gallia St 45662 740-353-2398
Amy Hughes, prin. Fax 354-3494

---

Notre Dame JSHS 200/7-12
2220 Sunrise Ave 45662 740-353-0719
Kathy Milligan, prin. Fax 353-2526

Paramount Beauty Academy Post-Sec.
PO Box 1444 45662 740-353-2436
Shawnee State University Post-Sec.
940 2nd St 45662 740-351-4778

**Powell, Delaware, Pop. 11,313**
Olentangy Local SD
Supt. — See Lewis Center
Olentangy Hyatts MS 700/6-8
6885 Sawmill Pkwy 43065 740-657-5400
Derrick Gilliam, prin. Fax 657-5499
Olentangy Liberty HS 1,600/9-12
3584 Home Rd 43065 740-657-4200
William Warfield, prin. Fax 657-4299
Olentangy Liberty MS 800/6-8
7940 Liberty Rd N 43065 740-657-4400
Nancy Freese, prin. Fax 657-4499

---

Village Academy 300/PK-12
284 S Liberty St 43065 614-841-0050
Susan Lasley, head sch Fax 841-0501

**Proctorville, Lawrence, Pop. 565**
Fairland Local SD 1,700/K-12
228 Private Drive 10010 45669 740-886-3100
Roni Hayes, supt. Fax 886-7253
fairland.k12.oh.us/
Fairland HS 400/9-12
812 County Road 411 45669 740-886-3250
Chad Belville, prin. Fax 886-6738
Fairland MS 400/6-8
7875 County Road 107 45669 740-886-3200
Aaron Lewis, prin. Fax 886-5125

**Put in Bay, Ottawa, Pop. 138**
Put-in-Bay Local SD 100/K-12
PO Box 659 43456 419-285-3614
Steven Poe, supt. Fax 285-2137
www.put-in-bay.k12.oh.us
Put-in-Bay JSHS 50/7-12
PO Box 659 43456 419-285-3614
Steven Poe, supt. Fax 285-2137

**Racine, Meigs, Pop. 665**
Southern Local SD 700/K-12
920 Elm St 45771 740-949-2669
Anthony Deem, supt. Fax 949-3309
www.southernlocalmeigs.org/
Southern HS 200/9-12
920 Elm St 45771 740-949-2611
Daniel Otto, prin. Fax 949-2456

**Ravenna, Portage, Pop. 11,455**
Maplewood Career Ctr SD
7075 State Route 88 44266 330-296-2892
Randy Griffith, supt. Fax 296-5680
www.mwood.cc
Maplewood Career Center Vo/Tech
7075 State Route 88 44266 330-296-2892
Craig Morgan, dir. Fax 296-5680

Ravenna CSD 2,500/PK-12
507 E Main St 44266 330-296-9679
Dennis Honkala, supt. Fax 297-4158
www.ravenna.portage.k12.oh.us
Brown MS 600/6-8
228 S Scranton St 44266 330-296-3849
Tara Reis, prin. Fax 297-4146
Ravenna HS 800/9-12
6589 N Chestnut St 44266 330-296-3844
Beth Coleman, prin. Fax 296-1855

Southeast Local SD 1,500/K-12
8245 Tallmadge Rd 44266 330-654-5841
Robert Dunn, supt. Fax 654-9110
www.sepirates.org
Southeast HS 600/9-12
8423 Tallmadge Rd 44266 330-654-1960
David Kennedy, prin. Fax 654-9110
Other Schools – See Diamond

---

Fortis College Post-Sec.
653 Enterprise Pkwy 44266 330-297-7319

**Rawson, Hancock, Pop. 564**
Cory-Rawson Local SD 400/PK-12
3930 County Road 26 45881 419-963-3415
Robert Hlasko, supt. Fax 963-4400
cory-rawson.k12.oh.us
Cory-Rawson HS 200/7-12
3930 County Road 26 45881 419-963-2611
Heath Huffman, prin. Fax 963-4400

**Rayland, Jefferson, Pop. 413**
Buckeye Local SD
Supt. — See Dillonvale
Buckeye HS 600/9-12
10692 State Route 150 43943 740-859-2196
Coy Sudvary, prin. Fax 859-2857
Buckeye JHS 300/7-8
10692 State Route 150 43943 740-859-2196
Jason Kovalski, prin. Fax 859-2857

**Reading, Hamilton, Pop. 10,188**
Reading Community CSD 1,600/K-12
1301 Bonnell St 45215 513-554-1800
Joel Anderson, supt. Fax 483-6754
www.readingschools.org
Reading Community HS 400/9-12
810 E Columbia Ave 45215 513-733-4422
Charles LaFata, prin. Fax 483-6766
Reading Community MS 400/6-8
230 Halker Ave 45215 513-842-5151
Ian Frank, prin. Fax 842-5146

---

Mt. Notre Dame HS 700/9-12
711 E Columbia Ave 45215 513-821-3044
Judy Gerwe, head sch Fax 821-6068

**Reedsville, Meigs**
Eastern Local SD 800/K-12
50008 State Route 681 45772 740-667-6079
Scot Gheen, supt. Fax 667-3978
www.easternlocal.com
Eastern HS 200/9-12
38900 State Route 7 45772 740-985-3329
Shawn Bush, prin. Fax 985-3778
Eastern MS 300/5-8
38850 State Route 7 45772 740-985-3304
William Francis, prin. Fax 985-3304

**Reynoldsburg, Franklin, Pop. 34,685**
Reynoldsburg CSD 3,900/PK-12
7244 E Main St 43068 614-501-1020
Tina Thomas-Manning, supt. Fax 501-1050
www.reyn.org/
Baldwin Road JHS 400/7-8
2300 Baldwin Pl 43068 614-367-1600
Michelle Watts, prin. Fax 367-1625
BELL Academy 300/9-12
6699 E Livingston Ave 43068 614-501-4000
Erica Dodson, prin.
ENCORE Academy 9-12
8579 Summit Rd 43068 614-501-2300
Jocelyn Cosgrave, prin.
eSTEM Academy 400/9-12
6699 E Livingston Ave 43068 614-501-4000
Scott Bennett, prin.
HS2 Academy 300/9-12
6699 E Livingston Ave 43068 614-501-4000
Dawn McCloud, prin. Fax 575-3098
Waggoner Road JHS 600/7-8
360 Waggoner Rd 43068 614-501-5700
Chris Brooks, prin. Fax 501-5700

**Richfield, Summit, Pop. 3,610**
Revere Local SD 2,700/K-12
3496 Everett Rd 44286 330-666-4155
Matthew Montgomery, supt. Fax 659-3127
www.revereschools.org
Other Schools – See Bath

**Richmond, Jefferson, Pop. 480**
Edison Local SD
Supt. — See Hammondsville
Edison HS 600/7-12
9890 State Route 152 43944 740-765-4313
Matthew Morrison, prin. Fax 765-4961

**Richmond Heights, Cuyahoga, Pop. 10,347**
Richmond Heights SD 800/PK-12
447 Richmond Rd 44143 216-692-0086
Renee Willis Ph.D., supt.
www.richmondheightsschools.org
Richmond Heights MSHS 400/7-12
447 Richmond Rd 44143 216-692-0094
Marnisha Brown, prin. Fax 692-8495

**Richwood, Union, Pop. 2,209**
North Union Local SD 1,500/PK-12
12920 State Route 739 43344 740-943-2509
Dr. Richard Baird, supt. Fax 943-2534
www.n-union.k12.oh.us
North Union HS 400/9-12
401 N Franklin St 43344 740-943-3012
Diana Martin, prin. Fax 943-2046
North Union MS 400/6-8
12555 Mulvane Rd 43344 740-943-2369
Matt Burggraf, prin. Fax 943-9279

**Rio Grande, Gallia, Pop. 808**
Gallia-Jackson-Vinton JVSD
PO Box 157 45674 740-245-5334
Fax 245-9465
bhcc.k12.oh.us/
Buckeye Hills Career Center Vo/Tech
PO Box 157 45674 740-245-5334
Fax 245-9465

---

University of Rio Grande Post-Sec.
PO Box 500 45674 740-245-5353

**Ripley, Brown, Pop. 1,713**
Ripley-Union-Lewis-Huntington Local SD 1,000/PK-12
PO Box 85 45167 937-392-4396
Dr. Linda Naylor, supt. Fax 392-7003
www.ripley.k12.oh.us
Ripley-Union-Lewis-Huntington HS 300/9-12
1317 S 2nd St 45167 937-392-4384
Susie Skinner, prin. Fax 392-7017
Other Schools – See Aberdeen

**Rittman, Wayne, Pop. 6,392**
Rittman EVD 1,000/K-12
100 Saurer St 44270 330-927-7401
James Ritchie, supt. Fax 927-7405
www.rittman.k12.oh.us/
Rittman HS 300/8-12
50 Saurer St 44270 330-927-7141
Nick Evans, prin. Fax 927-7145

**Rockford, Mercer, Pop. 1,102**
Parkway Local SD 1,100/PK-12
400 Buckeye St 45882 419-363-3045
Gregory Puthoff, supt. Fax 363-2595
www.parkwayschools.org/
Parkway HS 300/9-12
400 Buckeye St 45882 419-363-3045
Brian Fortkamp, prin. Fax 363-2596
Parkway MS 300/5-8
400 Buckeye St 45882 419-363-3045
Brian Woods, prin. Fax 363-2597

**Rocky River, Cuyahoga, Pop. 19,974**
Rocky River CSD 2,600/K-12
1101 Morewood Pkwy 44116 440-333-6000
Dr. Michael Shoaf, supt. Fax 356-6014
www.rrcs.org
Rocky River HS 900/9-12
20951 Detroit Rd 44116 440-356-6800
Debra Bernard, prin. Fax 331-2189
Rocky River MS 600/6-8
1631 Lakeview Ave 44116 440-356-6870
Megan Rose, prin. Fax 356-6881

---

Lutheran HS West 400/9-12
3850 Linden Rd 44116 440-333-1660
Dale Wolfgram, prin. Fax 333-1729
Magnificat HS 800/9-12
20770 Hilliard Blvd 44116 440-331-1572
Marilyn Arundel, dean Fax 331-7257

**Rootstown, Portage**
Rootstown Local SD 1,200/K-12
4140 State Route 44 44272 330-325-9911
Andrew Hawkins, supt. Fax 325-4105
rootstown.sparcc.org
Rootstown HS 300/9-12
4140 State Route 44 44272 330-325-7911
James Conley, prin. Fax 325-8506
Rootstown MS 300/6-8
4140 State Route 44 44272 330-325-9956
Robert Campbell, prin. Fax 325-8505

---

Northeastern Ohio Medical University Post-Sec.
PO Box 95 44272 800-686-2511

**Rossford, Wood, Pop. 6,225**
Rossford EVD 1,700/PK-12
601 Superior St 43460 419-666-2010
Daniel Creps, supt. Fax 661-2856
www.rossfordschools.org/
Rossford HS 500/9-12
701 Superior St 43460 419-666-5262
Tony Brashear, prin. Fax 661-2831
Rossford JHS 300/6-8
651 Superior St 43460 419-666-5254
Lester Pierson, prin. Fax 661-2890

**Russia, Shelby, Pop. 636**
Russia Local SD 500/K-12
100 School St 45363 937-526-3156
Steven Rose, supt. Fax 526-0045
www.russiaschool.org
Russia JSHS 200/7-12
100 School St 45363 937-295-3454
Karen Bensman, prin. Fax 526-9519

**Sabina, Clinton, Pop. 2,532**
East Clinton Local SD 1,400/PK-12
97 Astro Way 45169 937-584-2461
Eric Magee, supt. Fax 584-2817
www.eastclinton.org/
East Clinton HS 400/9-12
174 Larrick Rd 45169 937-584-2474
Matt Baker, prin. Fax 584-4842
East Clinton MS 300/6-8
174 Larrick Rd 45169 937-584-9267
Robbin Luck, prin. Fax 584-9558

**Saint Bernard, Hamilton, Pop. 4,269**
St. Bernard-Elmwood Place CSD 1,000/PK-12
105 Washington Ave 45217 513-482-7121
Dr. Mimi Webb, supt. Fax 641-0066
www.sbepschools.org
Saint Bernard-Elmwood Place JSHS 400/7-12
4615 Tower Ave 45217 513-482-7100
Alison Gates, prin. Fax 641-4878

**Saint Clairsville, Belmont, Pop. 5,119**
Belmont-Harrison Area JVSD
110 Fox Shannon Pl 43950 740-695-9130
Richard Schoene, supt. Fax 695-5340
bhccenters.com
Belmont Career Center Vo/Tech
110 Fox Shannon Pl 43950 740-695-9130
Frank Gregory, prin. Fax 695-5330
Other Schools – See Cadiz

St. Clairsville-Richland CSD 1,700/PK-12
108 Woodrow Ave 43950 740-695-1624
Dr. Walter Skaggs, supt. Fax 695-1627
www.stcschools.com
St. Clairsville HS 500/9-12
102 Woodrow Ave 43950 740-695-1584
Dr. Walter Skaggs, prin. Fax 695-2513
St. Clairsville MS 600/5-8
104 Woodrow Ave 43950 740-695-1591
Michael Mckeever, prin. Fax 695-2317

---

Belmont College Post-Sec.
120 Fox Shannon Pl 43950 740-695-9500
East Richland Christian S 100/PK-12
67888 Friends Church Rd 43950 740-695-2279
April Woods, admin. Fax 699-0562
Ohio University Post-Sec.
45425 National Rd W 43950 740-695-1720

**Saint Henry, Mercer, Pop. 2,423**
St. Henry Consolidated Local SD 1,000/K-12
391 E Columbus St 45883 419-678-4834
Julie Garke, supt. Fax 678-1724
sthenryschools.org
Saint Henry HS 300/9-12
391 E Columbus St 45883 419-678-4834
Eric Rosenbeck, prin. Fax 678-1724
Saint Henry MS 300/5-8
381 E Columbus St 45883 419-678-4834
Kyle Kunk, prin. Fax 678-1724

**Saint Martin, Brown, Pop. 128**

---

Chatfield College Post-Sec.
20918 State Route 251 45118 513-875-3344

**Saint Marys, Auglaize, Pop. 8,208**
St. Marys CSD 2,200/K-12
100 W Spring St 45885 419-394-4312
Shawn Brown, supt. Fax 394-5638
sm.k12.oh.us
St. Marys Memorial HS 800/9-12
2250 State Route 66 45885 419-394-4011
Bill Ruane, prin. Fax 394-1932
St. Marys MS 500/6-8
2250 State Route 66 45885 419-394-2112
Mary Miller, prin. Fax 394-1932

---

Grand Lake Christian S 100/PK-12
1001 Holly St 45885 419-300-9001
David Wilson, supt. Fax 300-9001

**Saint Paris, Champaign, Pop. 2,056**
Graham Local SD 2,100/PK-12
7790 US Highway 36 43072 937-663-4123
Norm Glismann, supt. Fax 663-4670
www.grahamlocalschools.org
Graham HS 600/9-12
7800 US Highway 36 43072 937-663-4127
Joe Hurst, prin. Fax 663-0396
Graham MS 500/6-8
9644 US Highway 36 43072 937-663-5339
Adam Kunkle, prin. Fax 663-4674

**Salem, Columbiana, Pop. 12,168**
Salem CSD 2,100/K-12
1226 E State St 44460 330-332-0316
Dr. Joseph Shivers, supt. Fax 332-8936
www.salemquakers.org
Salem HS 600/9-12
1200 E 6th St 44460 330-332-8905
Sean Kirkland, prin. Fax 332-8943
Salem JHS 300/7-8
1200 E 6th St 44460 330-332-8914
Sean Kirkland, prin. Fax 332-8923

---

Allegheny Wesleyan College Post-Sec.
2161 Woodsdale Rd 44460 330-337-6403
Kent State University-Salem Campus Post-Sec.
2491 State Route 45 S 44460 330-332-0361
Salem Wesleyan Academy 100/K-12
1095 Newgarden Ave 44460 330-332-4819
Dan Forrider, prin. Fax 332-4819

**Salineville, Columbiana, Pop. 1,294**
Southern Local SD 900/K-12
38095 State Route 39 43945 330-679-2343
John Wilson, supt. Fax 679-0193
www.southern.k12.oh.us
Southern Local JSHS 400/7-12
38095 State Route 39 43945 330-679-2305
Dallas Saunders, prin. Fax 679-3005

**Sandusky, Erie, Pop. 24,586**
Perkins Local SD 2,300/K-12
3714 Campbell St Ste B 44870 419-625-0484
Jodie Hausmann Ed.D., supt. Fax 621-2052
www.perkinsschools.org
Briar MS 600/6-8
3700 South Ave 44870 419-625-0132
Stephen Finn, prin. Fax 625-0523
Perkins HS 700/9-12
3714 Campbell St 44870 419-625-1252
Dean Stanfield, prin. Fax 621-2057

Sandusky CSD 2,800/PK-12
407 Decatur St 44870 419-626-6940
Eugene Sanders Ph.D., supt. Fax 621-2784
www.scs-k12.net
Sandusky Career Center Vo/Tech
2130 Hayes Ave 44870 419-984-1000
Nancy Zechman, dir. Fax 621-2893
Sandusky Digital Academy Alt
318 Columbus Ave 44870 419-627-3969
Todd Peugeot, dir. Fax 627-3996
Sandusky HS 900/9-12
2130 Hayes Ave 44870 419-984-1068
Theodore Caleris, prin. Fax 621-2751
Sandusky MS 7-8
2130 Hayes Ave 44870 419-984-1182
Linda Wohl, prin. Fax 621-2849

---

Firelands Regional Medical Center Post-Sec.
1912 Hayes Ave 44870 419-557-7110
Ohio Business College Post-Sec.
5202 Timber Commons Dr 44870 419-627-8345
Sandusky Central Catholic S 600/PK-12
410 W Jefferson St 44870 419-626-1892
Dennis Antonelli, prin. Fax 621-2252

**Sarahsville, Noble, Pop. 166**
Noble Local SD 900/PK-12
20977 Zep Rd E 43779 740-732-2084
Daniel Leffingwell, supt. Fax 732-7669
www.gozeps.org/
Shenandoah HS 300/9-12
49346 Seneca Lake Rd 43779 740-732-2361
Justin Denius, prin. Fax 732-6479

**Seaman, Adams, Pop. 934**
Adams County/Ohio Valley Local SD
Supt. — See West Union
North Adams HS 500/7-12
96 Green Devil Dr 45679 937-386-2528
Matthew Young, prin. Fax 386-2888

**Sebring, Mahoning, Pop. 4,362**
Sebring Local SD 600/K-12
510 N 14th St 44672 330-938-6165
Toni Viscounte, supt. Fax 938-4701
www.sebring.k12.oh.us/
McKinley JSHS 300/7-12
225 E Indiana Ave 44672 330-938-2963
Chris Corbi, prin. Fax 938-4702

**Senecaville, Guernsey, Pop. 454**
Mid-East Career & Technology Centers
Supt. — See Zanesville
Mid-East Career & Tech Center - Buffalo Vo/Tech
57090 Vocational Rd 43780 740-685-2516
Daniel Coffman, dir. Fax 685-2518

**Seven Hills, Cuyahoga, Pop. 11,709**

---

DeVry University Post-Sec.
4141 Rockside Rd Ste 110 44131 216-328-8754
Hondros College Post-Sec.
4100 Rockside Rd 44131 216-524-1143

**Seville, Medina, Pop. 2,268**
Cloverleaf Local SD
Supt. — See Lodi
Cloverleaf MS 700/6-8
7500 Buffham Rd 44273 330-721-3606
Brian Madigan, prin. Fax 721-3619

**Shadyside, Belmont, Pop. 3,765**
Shadyside Local SD 800/PK-12
3890 Lincoln Ave 43947 740-676-3121
John Haswell, supt. Fax 676-6616
www.shadyside.k12.oh.us
Shadyside JSHS 300/7-12
3890 Lincoln Ave 43947 740-676-3235
John Haswell, prin. Fax 676-6616

**Shaker Heights, Cuyahoga, Pop. 27,675**
Shaker Heights CSD 5,400/PK-12
15600 Parkland Dr 44120 216-295-1400
Gregory C. Hutchings Ed.D., supt. Fax 295-4340
www.shaker.org
Shaker Heights HS 1,700/9-12
15911 Aldersyde Dr 44120 216-295-4200
James Reed, prin. Fax 295-4277
Shaker Heights MS 800/7-8
20600 Shaker Blvd 44122 216-295-4100
David Glasner, prin. Fax 295-4129

---

Hathaway Brown S 800/PK-12
19600 N Park Blvd 44122 216-932-4214
William Christ, hdmstr. Fax 371-1501
Laurel S 700/PK-12
1 Lyman Cir 44122 216-464-1441
Ann V. Klotz, head sch Fax 464-8995

**Sharonville, Hamilton, Pop. 13,127**

---

Miami-Jacobs Career College Post-Sec.
2 Crowne Point Ct Ste 100 45241 513-693-4400

**Sheffield Lake, Lorain, Pop. 8,982**
Sheffield-Sheffield Lake CSD 1,800/PK-12
1824 Harris Rd 44054 440-949-6181
Michael Cook, supt. Fax 949-4204
www.sheffield.k12.oh.us
Other Schools – See Sheffield Vlg

**Sheffield Vlg, Lorain**
Sheffield-Sheffield Lake CSD
Supt. — See Sheffield Lake
Brookside HS 600/9-12
1662 Harris Rd 44054 440-949-4220
Angela Terella, prin. Fax 949-4204
Brookside MS 500/7-8
1662 Harris Rd 44054 440-949-4228
Gretchen Loper, prin. Fax 949-4204

---

Ohio Business College Post-Sec.
5095 Waterford Dr 44035 888-514-3126

**Shelby, Richland, Pop. 9,228**
Pioneer Career & Technology Center
27 Ryan Rd 44875 419-347-7926
Glenna Cannon, supt. Fax 347-4709
www.pctc.k12.oh.us/
Pioneer Career & Technology Center Vo/Tech
27 Ryan Rd 44875 419-347-7744
Fax 347-4977

Shelby CSD 1,600/K-12
PO Box 31 44875 419-342-3520
Tim Tarvin, supt. Fax 347-3586
www.shelbyk12.org
Shelby HS 500/9-12
1 Whippet Way 44875 419-342-5065
John Gies, prin. Fax 342-5095
Shelby MS 300/5-8
109 W Smiley Ave 44875 419-347-5451
Jeff Eichorn, prin. Fax 347-2095

**Sherrodsville, Carroll, Pop. 303**
Conotton Valley Union Local SD 400/PK-12
PO Box 187 44675 740-269-2000
Jerry Herman, supt. Fax 269-7901
www.conottonvalley.k12.oh.us
Other Schools – See Bowerston

**Sherwood, Defiance, Pop. 819**
Central Local SD 1,100/K-12
6289 US Highway 127 43556 419-658-2808
Vicki L. Brunn, supt. Fax 658-4011
www.centrallocal.org
Fairview HS 300/9-12
6289 US Highway 127 43556 419-658-2378
Phil Witker, prin. Fax 658-4011
Fairview MS 300/6-8
6289 US Highway 127 43556 419-658-2331
Suzanne Geis, prin. Fax 658-4010

**Sidney, Shelby, Pop. 20,551**
Fairlawn Local SD 600/PK-12
18800 Johnston Rd 45365 937-492-1974
Steve Mascho, supt. Fax 492-8613
www.fairlawn.k12.oh.us
Fairlawn MSHS 300/7-12
18800 Johnston Rd 45365 937-492-5930
Jo DeMotte, prin. Fax 492-5225

Sidney CSD 3,400/K-12
750 S 4th Ave 45365 937-497-2200
John Scheu, supt. Fax 497-2211
www2.sidney.k12.oh.us
Sidney Alternative S 50/Alt
315 W Russell Rd 45365 937-494-2003
Clayton Westerbeck, prin.
Sidney HS 1,000/9-12
1215 Campbell Rd 45365 937-497-2238
Jon Geuy, prin. Fax 497-2216
Sidney MS 800/5-8
980 Fair Rd 45365 937-497-2225
Diane Voress, prin. Fax 497-2204

---

Christian Academy S 100/K-12
2151 W Russell Rd 45365 937-492-7556
Mary Smith, supt. Fax 492-5399
Lehman HS 200/9-12
2400 Saint Marys Rd 45365 937-498-1161
Denise Stauffer, prin. Fax 492-9877

**Smithville, Wayne, Pop. 1,248**
Green Local SD 1,100/K-12
PO Box 438 44677 330-669-3921
Judith Robinson, supt. Fax 669-2121
www.green-local.k12.oh.us/
Green MS 400/5-8
200 Smithie Dr 44677 330-669-3165
Jason DeMassimo, prin. Fax 669-2069
Smithville HS 300/9-12
200 Smithie Dr 44677 330-669-3165
Nathan Gaubatz, prin. Fax 669-2999

Wayne County JVSD
518 W Prospect St 44677 330-669-7000
Dr. Kip Crain, supt. Fax 669-7001
www.wcscc.org
Wayne County Schools Career Center Vo/Tech
518 W Prospect St 44677 330-669-7000
Matt Brown, prin. Fax 669-7001

**Solon, Cuyahoga, Pop. 23,009**
Solon CSD 5,100/K-12
33800 Inwood Dr 44139 440-248-1600
Joseph Regano, supt. Fax 248-7665
www.solonschools.org
Solon HS 1,700/9-12
33600 Inwood Dr 44139 440-349-6230
Erin Short, prin. Fax 349-8041
Solon MS 800/7-8
6835 Som Center Rd 44139 440-349-3848
Scott Hatteberg, prin. Fax 349-8034

**South Amherst, Lorain, Pop. 1,662**
Firelands Local SD 1,800/K-12
112 N Lake St 44001 440-965-5821
Dr. Michael Von Gunten, supt. Fax 986-5990
www.firelandsschools.org/
South Amherst MS 400/6-8
152 W Main St 44001 440-986-7021
Cara Gomez, prin. Fax 986-7022
Other Schools – See Oberlin

**South Charleston, Clark, Pop. 1,672**
Southeastern Local SD 600/K-12
226 Clifton Rd 45368 888-627-6745
David Shea, supt. Fax 650-9129
www.sels.us
Southeastern HS 200/9-12
PO Box Z 45368 937-462-8308
P.J. Bertemes, prin. Fax 462-8394
Southeastern JHS 100/7-8
PO Box Z 45368 937-462-8308
P.J. Bertemes, prin. Fax 462-8394

**Southington, Trumbull**
Southington Local SD 600/PK-12
2482 State Route 534 44470 330-898-7480
Rocco Nero, supt. Fax 898-4828
www.southington.k12.oh.us/
Chalker HS 200/9-12
2482 State Route 534 44470 330-898-1781
Robert Kujala, prin. Fax 898-4828
Southington MS 200/5-8
2482 State Route 534 44470 330-898-1781
Robert Kujala, prin. Fax 898-4828

**South Point, Lawrence, Pop. 3,885**
South Point Local SD 1,800/K-12
302 High St 45680 740-377-4315
Mark Christian, supt. Fax 377-9735
www.southpoint.k12.oh.us
South Point HS 500/9-12
983 County Road 60 45680 740-377-4323
Benjamin Coleman, prin. Fax 377-4326
South Point MS 400/6-8
983 County Road 60 45680 740-377-4343
Mylissa Bentley, prin. Fax 377-3228

---

Tri-State Bible College Post-Sec.
PO Box 445 45680 740-377-2520

**South Vienna, Clark, Pop. 375**
Northeastern Local SD
Supt. — See Springfield
South Vienna MS 300/6-8
140 W Main St 45369 937-346-0880
Todd Justice, prin. Fax 568-4988

**South Webster, Scioto, Pop. 856**
Bloom-Vernon Local SD 900/K-12
PO Box 237 45682 740-778-2281
Marc Kreischer, supt. Fax 778-2526
www.bv.k12.oh.us/
South Webster JSHS 300/7-12
PO Box 100 45682 740-778-2320
Brett Roberts, prin. Fax 778-3227

**Spencerville, Allen, Pop. 2,168**
Spencerville Local SD 900/K-12
600 School St 45887 419-647-4111
Dennis Fuge, supt. Fax 647-6498
www.spencervillebearcats.com
Spencerville HS 200/9-12
2500 Wisher Dr 45887 419-647-4111
Scott Gephart, prin. Fax 647-5124
Spencerville MS 300/5-8
2500 Wisher Dr 45887 419-647-4112
Susan Wagner, prin. Fax 647-5124

**Springboro, Warren, Pop. 17,124**
Springboro Community CSD 4,500/K-12
1685 S Main St 45066 937-748-3960
Todd Petrey, supt. Fax 748-3956
www.springboro.org
Springboro HS 1,500/9-12
1675 S Main St 45066 937-748-3950
Dr. Kyle Martin, prin. Fax 748-3983
Springboro JHS 900/7-8
1605 S Main St 45066 937-748-3953
James Aker, prin. Fax 748-3964

---

Miami-Jacobs Career College Post-Sec.
875 W Central Ave 45066 937-746-1830

**Springfield, Clark, Pop. 58,259**
Clark-Shawnee Local SD 1,500/PK-12
3680 Selma Rd 45502 937-328-5378
Gregg Morris, supt. Fax 328-5379
www.cslocal.org
Shawnee HS 600/9-12
1675 E Possum Rd 45502 937-325-9296
Nathan Dockter, prin. Fax 328-5389

Greenon Local SD
Supt. — See Enon
Greenon JSHS 600/7-12
3950 S Tecumseh Rd 45502 937-340-6372
Rick Newsock, prin. Fax 340-6371

Northeastern Local SD 3,500/K-12
1414 Bowman Rd 45502 937-325-7615
John Kronour, supt. Fax 328-6592
www.nelsd.org/
Kenton Ridge HS 700/9-12
4444 Middle Urbana Rd 45503 937-390-1274
John Hill, prin. Fax 390-0013
Northeastern HS 500/9-12
1480 Bowman Rd 45502 937-328-6575
Allyson Thurman, prin. Fax 328-6581
Northridge MS 500/6-8
4445 Ridgewood Rd E 45503 937-399-2852
Gary Miller, prin. Fax 342-4631
Other Schools – See South Vienna

Northwestern Local SD 1,200/PK-12
5610 Troy Rd 45502 937-964-1318
Jesse Steiner, supt. Fax 964-6019
www.northwestern.k12.oh.us
Northwestern JSHS 500/7-12
5780 Troy Rd 45502 937-964-1324
Lori Swafford, prin. Fax 964-6006

Springfield CSD 7,400/PK-12
1500 W Jefferson St 45506 937-505-2800
Robert F. Hill Ed.D., supt. Fax 505-2978
www.spr.k12.oh.us
Hayward MS 400/7-8
1700 Clifton Ave 45505 937-505-4190
Susie Samuels, prin. Fax 323-9812
Keifer Alternative Center 300/Alt
601 Selma Rd 45505 937-505-4120
Gary Cross, prin. Fax 323-8785
Roosevelt MS 400/7-8
721 E Home Rd 45503 937-505-4370
Monte Brigham, prin. Fax 342-0280
Schaefer MS 300/7-8
147 S Fostoria Ave 45505 937-505-4390
Kimberly Watkins, prin. Fax 325-8974
Springfield HS 1,600/9-12
701 E Home Rd 45503 937-342-4320
Jonathan Kuehnle, prin. Fax 342-4110

Springfield-Clark Career Technology Ctr
1901 Selma Rd 45505 937-325-7368
Rick Smith, supt. Fax 325-7452
www.scctc.org
Springfield-Clark Career Technology Ctr Vo/Tech
1901 Selma Rd 45505 937-325-7368
Chris James, dir. Fax 325-7452

---

Carousel Beauty College Post-Sec.
1475 Upper Valley Pike #956 45504 937-323-0277
Catholic Central JSHS 400/7-12
1200 E High St 45505 937-325-9204
Dr. Karen Juliano, prin. Fax 328-7426
Clark State Community College Post-Sec.
PO Box 570 45501 937-325-0691
Emmanuel Christian Academy 500/PK-12
2177 Emmanuel Way 45502 937-390-3777
Dr. David Hook, supt. Fax 390-0966
Nightingale Montessori S 50/PK-12
1106 E High St 45505 937-324-0336
Maria Taylor, prin. Fax 398-0086
Wittenberg University Post-Sec.
PO Box 720 45501 937-327-6231

**Steubenville, Jefferson, Pop. 18,007**
Steubenville CSD 2,500/PK-12
PO Box 189 43952 740-283-3767
Melinda Young, supt. Fax 283-8930
scs.steubenville.k12.oh.us

Harding MS 700/5-8
2002 Sunset Blvd 43952 740-282-3481
Joseph Yanok, prin. Fax 283-8949
Steubenville HS 600/9-12
420 N 4th St 43952 740-282-9741
Ted Gorman, prin. Fax 283-8943

---

Bishop John King Mussio Central JHS 7-8
320 Westview Ave Ste 2 43952 740-346-0028
Theresa Danaher, prin. Fax 346-0070
Catholic Central HS 300/9-12
320 Westview Ave Ste 1 43952 740-264-5538
Richard Wilinski, prin. Fax 264-5443
Eastern Gateway Community College Post-Sec.
4000 Sunset Blvd 43952 740-264-5591
Franciscan University of Steubenville Post-Sec.
1235 University Blvd 43952 800-783-6220
Ohio Valley Hospital Post-Sec.
1 Ross Park Blvd 43952 740-283-7273
Trinity Medical Center East Post-Sec.
380 Summit Ave 43952 740-283-7213

**Stewart, Athens, Pop. 244**
Federal Hocking Local SD 1,000/PK-12
8461 State Route 144 45778 740-662-6691
Dr. George Wood, supt. Fax 662-5065
www.fedhock.com
Federal Hocking HS 200/9-12
8461 State Route 144 45778 740-662-6691
Cliff Bonner, prin. Fax 662-3805
Federal Hocking MS 200/7-8
8461 State Route 144 45778 740-662-6691
Cliff Bonner, prin. Fax 662-5065

**Stow, Summit, Pop. 34,347**
Stow-Munroe Falls CSD 5,400/PK-12
4350 Allen Rd 44224 330-689-5445
Thomas Bratten, supt. Fax 688-1629
www.smfschools.org
Stow-Munroe Falls HS 1,800/9-12
3227 Graham Rd 44224 330-689-5300
Jeffrey Hartmann, prin. Fax 678-3899
Other Schools – See Munroe Falls

---

National College Post-Sec.
3855 Fishcreek Rd 44224 330-676-1351

**Strasburg, Tuscarawas, Pop. 2,588**
Strasburg-Franklin Local SD 600/K-12
140 N Bodmer Ave 44680 330-878-5571
Cynthia Brown, supt. Fax 878-7900
www.strasburg.k12.oh.us/
Strasburg-Franklin HS 300/6-12
140 N Bodmer Ave 44680 330-878-5571
Brian Garrett, prin. Fax 878-7900

**Streetsboro, Portage, Pop. 15,768**
Streetsboro CSD 2,000/PK-12
9000 Kirby Ln 44241 330-626-4900
Aireane Curtis, dir. Fax 626-8102
www.streetsboroschools.com
Streetsboro HS 600/9-12
1900 Annalane Dr 44241 330-626-4902
James Hogue, prin. Fax 626-8103
Streetsboro MS 300/7-8
1951 Annalane Dr 44241 330-626-4905
Steve Hatch, prin. Fax 626-8104

**Strongsville, Cuyahoga, Pop. 44,134**
Strongsville CSD 6,500/PK-12
13200 Pearl Rd 44136 440-572-7000
Cameron Ryba, supt. Fax 572-7041
strongnet.org
Albion MS 500/7-8
11109 Webster Rd 44136 440-572-7070
Tom Kairis, prin. Fax 572-7079
Center MS 500/7-8
13200 Pearl Rd 44136 440-572-7090
Steve Deitrick, prin. Fax 572-7094
Strongsville HS 2,400/9-12
20025 Lunn Rd 44149 440-572-7100
Mark Smithberger, prin. Fax 572-7107

---

ITT Technical Institute Post-Sec.
14955 W Sprague Rd 44136 440-234-9091

**Struthers, Mahoning, Pop. 10,554**
Struthers CSD 1,900/K-12
99 Euclid Ave 44471 330-750-1061
Joseph Nohra, supt. Fax 750-5516
www.strutherscityschools.org
Struthers HS 600/9-12
111 Euclid Ave 44471 330-750-1062
Roger Day, prin. Fax 755-4525
Struthers MS 600/5-8
800 5th St 44471 330-750-1064
Peter Pirone, prin. Fax 755-4749

**Stryker, Williams, Pop. 1,320**
Stryker Local SD 400/K-12
400 S Defiance St 43557 419-682-6961
Nate Johnson, supt. Fax 682-2646
www.stryker.k12.oh.us
Stryker JSHS 200/7-12
400 S Defiance St 43557 419-682-4591
Denise Meyer, prin. Fax 682-3508

**Sugarcreek, Tuscarawas, Pop. 2,197**
Garaway Local SD 1,100/K-12
146 Dover Rd NW 44681 330-852-2421
Dr. James Millet, supt. Fax 852-2991
www.garaway.org
Garaway JSHS 300/7-12
146 Dover Rd NW 44681 330-852-4292
Brian Gibson, prin. Fax 852-4382

**Sugar Grove, Fairfield, Pop. 424**
Berne Union Local SD 600/PK-12
PO Box 187 43155 740-746-8341
Richard Spindler, supt. Fax 746-9824
www.buschools.com
Berne Union HS 300/7-12
PO Box 187 43155 740-746-9956
Jon Parker, prin. Fax 746-9824

**Sullivan, Ashland**
Black River Local SD 1,300/PK-12
257A County Road 40 44880 419-736-3300
Chris Clark, supt. Fax 736-3308
www.blackriver.k12.oh.us/
Black River HS 400/9-12
233 County Road 40 44880 419-736-3303
Martin Yoder, prin. Fax 736-3302
Black River MS 400/6-8
257 County Road 40 44880 419-736-3304
Tammy Starkey, prin. Fax 736-3309

**Sunbury, Delaware, Pop. 4,313**
Big Walnut Local SD 2,500/PK-12
105 Baughman St 43074 740-965-3010
Angela Pollock, supt. Fax 965-4688
www.bwls.net
Big Walnut HS 900/9-12
555 S Old 3C Rd 43074 740-965-3766
Jeffrey Jones, prin. Fax 965-1954
Big Walnut MS 500/6-8
777 Cheshire Rd 43074 740-965-3006
Penny Sturtevant, prin. Fax 965-6471

**Swanton, Fulton, Pop. 3,658**
Swanton Local SD 1,300/K-12
108 N Main St 43558 419-826-7085
Jeffrey Schlade, supt. Fax 825-1197
www.swanton.k12.oh.us
Swanton HS 400/9-12
601 N Main St 43558 419-826-3045
Steven Gfell, prin. Fax 826-1611
Swanton MS 300/6-8
206 Cherry St 43558 419-826-4016
Ted Haselman, prin. Fax 826-5176

**Sycamore, Wyandot, Pop. 857**
Mohawk Local SD 900/PK-12
605 State Highway 231 44882 419-927-2414
Kenneth Ratliff, supt. Fax 927-2393
www.mohawklocal.org
Mohawk JSHS 400/7-12
605 State Highway 231 44882 419-927-6222
Brett Graham, prin. Fax 927-6297

**Sylvania, Lucas, Pop. 18,670**
Sylvania CSD 7,500/K-12
4747 N Holland Sylvania Rd 43560 419-824-8500
Scott D. Nelson, supt. Fax 824-8503
www.sylvaniaschools.org
Arbor Hills JHS 600/6-8
5334 Whiteford Rd 43560 419-824-8640
Timothy Zieroff, prin. Fax 824-8659
McCord JHS 600/6-8
4304 N McCord Rd 43560 419-824-8650
Amanda Ogren, prin. Fax 824-8619
Northview HS 1,200/9-12
5403 Silica Dr 43560 419-824-8570
Steve Swaggerty, prin. Fax 824-8698
Southview HS 1,300/9-12
7225 Sylvania Ave 43560 419-824-8580
Dave McMurray, prin. Fax 824-8678
Timberstone JHS 600/6-8
9000 Sylvania Ave 43560 419-824-8680
Mike Bader, prin. Fax 824-8690

---

Lourdes University Post-Sec.
6832 Convent Blvd 43560 419-885-3211
Toledo Islamic Academy 200/PK-12
5225 Alexis Rd 43560 419-882-3339
Dr. Nabila Gomaa Ph.D., prin. Fax 882-3334

**Tallmadge, Summit, Pop. 17,273**
Tallmadge CSD 2,600/K-12
486 East Ave 44278 330-633-3291
Jeffrey Ferguson, supt. Fax 633-5331
www.tallmadgeschools.org
Tallmadge HS 900/9-12
140 N Munroe Rd 44278 330-633-5505
Rebecca Decapua, prin. Fax 475-0567
Tallmadge MS 600/6-8
484 East Ave 44278 330-633-4994
Robert Kearns, prin. Fax 630-5984

**The Plains, Athens, Pop. 2,987**
Athens CSD 2,500/PK-12
25 S Plains Rd 45780 740-797-4544
Dr. Thomas J. Gibbs, supt. Fax 797-2486
www.athenscsd.org
Athens HS 700/9-12
1 High School Rd 45780 740-797-4521
David Hanning, prin. Fax 797-1421
Other Schools – See Athens

**Thompson, Geauga**
Ledgemont Local SD 400/K-12
16200 Burrows Rd 44086 440-298-3341
Julie Ramos, supt. Fax 298-3342
www.ledgemontschools.org
Ledgemont JSHS 200/7-12
16200 Burrows Rd 44086 440-298-3343
Fax 298-1481

**Thornville, Perry, Pop. 982**
Northern Local SD 2,200/K-12
8700 Sheridan Dr 43076 740-743-1303
Thomas Perkins, supt. Fax 743-3301
nlsd.k12.oh.us
Sheridan HS 700/9-12
8725 Sheridan Dr 43076 740-743-1335
Chris King, prin. Fax 743-3311
Sheridan MS 500/6-8
8660 Sheridan Dr 43076 740-743-1315
Jay Hickman, prin. Fax 743-3319

**Tiffin, Seneca, Pop. 17,722**
Tiffin CSD 1,800/PK-12
244 S Monroe St 44883 419-447-2515
Vicki Wheatley Ed.D., supt. Fax 448-5202
www.tiffin.k12.oh.us
Columbian HS 800/9-12
300 S Monroe St 44883 419-447-6331
Douglas Hartenstein, prin. Fax 448-5252
Tiffin MS 700/6-8
103 Shepherd Dr 44883 419-447-3358
Robert Boes, prin. Fax 448-5250

Vanguard-Sentinel JVSD
Supt. — See Fremont
Sentinel Career Center Vo/Tech
793 E Township Road 201 44883 419-448-1212
Elissa Heal, prin. Fax 447-2544

---

Calvert JSHS 200/6-12
152 Madison St 44883 419-447-3844
Gerald Schoen, prin. Fax 447-2922
Heidelberg University Post-Sec.
310 E Market St 44883 419-448-2000
Tiffin Academy of Hair Design Post-Sec.
104 E Market St 44883 419-447-3117
Tiffin University Post-Sec.
155 Miami St 44883 800-968-6446

**Tipp City, Miami, Pop. 9,564**
Bethel Local SD 900/K-12
7490 State Route 201 45371 937-845-9414
Virginia Potter, supt. Fax 845-5007
www.bethel.k12.oh.us
Bethel HS 200/9-12
7490 State Route 201 45371 937-845-9487
John Zigler, prin. Fax 845-5007
Bethel MS 200/6-8
7490 State Route 201 45371 937-845-9430
Tim Zigler, prin. Fax 845-5007

Tipp City EVD 2,200/K-12
90 S Tippecanoe Dr 45371 937-667-8444
Dr. Gretta Kumpf, supt. Fax 667-6886
www.tippcityschools.com/
Tippecanoe HS 800/9-12
615 E Kessler Cowlesville 45371 937-667-8448
Belinda Banks, prin. Fax 667-0912
Tippecanoe MS 600/6-8
555 N Hyatt St 45371 937-667-8454
Greg Southers, prin. Fax 667-0874

**Toledo, Lucas, Pop. 278,478**
ESC of Lake Erie West 100/
2275 Collingwood Blvd 43620 419-245-4150
Sandra C. Frisch, supt. Fax 245-4186
www.esclakeeriewest.org
Alternate Learning Center Alt
3939 Wrenwood Rd 43623 419-473-3442
Brittani Paszko, prin. Fax 473-3445

Toledo CSD 22,900/PK-12
420 E Manhattan Blvd 43608 419-671-8200
Dr. Romules Durant, supt. Fax 671-8425
www.tps.org
Bowsher HS 1,300/9-12
2200 Arlington Ave 43614 419-671-2000
Teri Sherwood, prin. Fax 671-2060
Jones Leadership Academy 400/7-10
430 Nebraska Ave 43604 419-671-5400
Ward Barnett, prin. Fax 671-5460
Natural Science Technology Center Vo/Tech
5561 Elmer Dr 43615 419-537-1198
Fax 534-5819
Rogers HS 800/9-12
222 McTigue Dr 43615 419-671-1000
Kelly Welch, prin. Fax 671-1060
Scott HS 300/9-12
2400 Collingwood Blvd 43620 419-671-4000
Treva Jeffries, prin. Fax 671-4052
Start HS 1,300/9-12
2010 Tremainsville Rd 43613 419-671-3000
Edward Perozek, prin. Fax 671-3060
Toledo Early College HS 200/9-12
2225 Nebraska Ave 43607 419-530-3003
Dr. Robin Wheatley, prin. Fax 530-3040
Toledo Technology Academy Vo/Tech
3301 Upton Ave 43613 419-671-3900
Gary Thompson, prin. Fax 479-3192
Waite HS 1,000/9-12
301 Morrison Dr 43605 419-671-7000
Todd Deem, prin. Fax 671-7060
Woodward HS 700/9-12
701 E Central Ave 43608 419-671-6000
Jack Renz, prin. Fax 671-6050

Washington Local SD 6,700/PK-12
3505 W Lincolnshire Blvd 43606 419-473-8220
Patrick Hickey, supt. Fax 473-8200
www.wls4kids.org
Career & Tech Center Vo/Tech
5719 Clegg Dr 43613 419-473-8339
Debra Heban, dir. Fax 473-8309
Jefferson JHS 500/8-8
5530 Whitmer Dr 43613 419-473-8482
Scott Scharf, prin. Fax 473-8393
Whitmer HS 2,100/9-12
5601 Clegg Dr 43613 419-473-8490
Kristine Martin, prin. Fax 473-8461

---

Central Catholic HS 1,000/9-12
2550 Cherry St 43608 419-255-2280
Thomas Maj, pres. Fax 259-2848
Davis College Post-Sec.
4747 Monroe St 43623 419-473-2700

Emmanuel Christian S 400/K-12
4607 W Laskey Rd 43623 419-885-3558
Jeff Wilcox, supt. Fax 885-0139

Maumee Valley Country Day S 500/PK-12
1715 S Reynolds Rd 43614 419-381-1313
Gary Boehm, head sch Fax 381-8341

Mercy College of Ohio Post-Sec.
2221 Madison Ave 43604 419-251-1313

Notre Dame Academy 700/7-12
3535 W Sylvania Ave 43623 419-475-9359
Kimberly Grilliot, prin. Fax 725-1262

Owens Community College Post-Sec.
PO Box 10000 43699 567-661-7000

Riverside Hospital Post-Sec.
3404 W Sylvania Ave 43623 419-729-6059

St. Francis De Sales HS 600/9-12
2323 W Bancroft St 43607 419-531-1618
Eric Smola, prin. Fax 531-9740

St. John's Jesuit Academy 900/7-12
5901 Airport Hwy 43615 419-865-5743
Mike Savona, prin. Fax 861-5002

St. Ursula Academy 500/6-12
4025 Indian Rd 43606 419-531-1693
Nichole Flores, prin. Fax 534-5777

Toledo Christian S 600/PK-12
2303 Brookford Dr 43614 419-389-8700
Scott Gibson, supt. Fax 389-8703

University of Toledo Post-Sec.
2801 W Bancroft St 43606 419-530-4636

**Tontogany, Wood, Pop. 367**

Otsego Local SD 800/PK-12
PO Box 290 43565 419-823-4381
Adam Koch, supt. Fax 823-3035
www.otsegoknights.org

Otsego HS 400/9-12
PO Box 290 43565 419-823-4381
Kevin O'Shea, prin. Fax 823-1397

Otsego JHS 400/6-8
PO Box 290 43565 419-823-4381
Mike Wiley, prin. Fax 823-0944

**Toronto, Jefferson, Pop. 5,027**

Toronto CSD 900/PK-12
1307 Dennis Way 43964 740-537-2456
Frederick Burns, supt. Fax 537-1102
www.torontocityschools.k12.oh.us

Toronto HS 400/6-12
1305 Dennis Way 43964 740-537-2442
Maureen Taggart, prin. Fax 537-1102

**Trenton, Butler, Pop. 11,671**

Edgewood CSD 3,300/PK-12
3440 Busenbark Rd 45067 513-863-4692
Simon Fussnecker, supt. Fax 867-7421
www.edgewoodschools.com

Edgewood HS 1,000/9-12
3045 Busenbark Rd 45067 513-867-6300
Adrienne Sanders, prin. Fax 867-6341

Edgewood MS 900/6-8
5005 State Route 73 45067 513-867-7425
David Slamer, prin. Fax 867-7428

**Trotwood, Montgomery, Pop. 23,764**

Trotwood-Madison CSD 2,500/PK-12
3594 N Snyder Rd 45426 937-854-3050
Kevin Bell, supt. Fax 854-3057
www.trotwood.k12.oh.us/

Trotwood-Madison HS 800/9-12
4440 N Union Rd 45426 937-854-4908
David White, prin. Fax 854-0594

Trotwood-Madison MS 200/5-8
4420 N Union Rd 45426 937-854-0017
Phillitia Charlton, prin. Fax 854-8433

**Troy, Miami, Pop. 24,463**

Troy CSD 4,400/K-12
500 N Market St 45373 937-332-6700
Eric Herman, supt. Fax 332-6771
www.troy.k12.oh.us

Troy HS 1,300/9-12
151 Staunton Rd 45373 937-332-6710
William Overla, prin. Fax 332-6738

Troy JHS 700/7-8
556 Adams St 45373 937-332-6720
Dave Dilbone, prin. Fax 332-3812

---

Hobart Institute of Welding Technology Post-Sec.
400 Trade Sq E 45373 800-332-9448

Miami-Jacobs Career College Post-Sec.
865 W Market St 45373 937-332-8585

Troy Christian HS 300/7-12
700 S Dorset Rd 45373 937-339-5692
Dr. Gary Wilber, supt. Fax 335-6258

**Tuscarawas, Tuscarawas, Pop. 1,051**

Indian Valley Local SD
Supt. — See Gnadenhutten

Indian Valley MS 400/6-8
PO Box 356 44682 740-922-4226
Brent Carter, prin. Fax 922-2493

**Twinsburg, Summit, Pop. 18,443**

Twinsburg CSD 4,400/PK-12
11136 Ravenna Rd 44087 330-486-2000
Kathryn Powers, supt. Fax 425-7216
www.twinsburg.k12.oh.us

Chamberlin MS 700/7-8
10270 Ravenna Rd 44087 330-486-2281
James Ries, prin. Fax 963-8313

Twinsburg HS 1,400/9-12
10084 Ravenna Rd 44087 330-486-2400
Louise Teringo, prin. Fax 405-7406

---

The Ohio Academy Post-Sec.
10735 Ravenna Rd Ste 3 44087 330-282-3312

**Uhrichsville, Tuscarawas, Pop. 5,330**

Claymont CSD
Supt. — See Dennison

Claymont HS 600/9-12
4205 Indian Hill Rd SE 44683 740-922-3471
Scott Golec, prin. Fax 922-1031

Claymont JHS 400/7-8
215 E 6th St 44683 740-922-5241
Brian Watkins, prin. Fax 922-7330

**Union City, Darke, Pop. 1,628**

Mississinawa Valley Local SD 700/K-12
1469 State Road 47 E 45390 937-968-5656
James Atchley, supt. Fax 968-6731
www.mississinawa.k12.oh.us

Mississinawa Valley JSHS 300/7-12
10480 Staudt Rd 45390 937-968-4464
Jeffrey Winchester, prin. Fax 968-3434

**Uniontown, Stark, Pop. 3,274**

Green Local SD 4,100/PK-12
1755 Town Park Blvd 44685 330-896-7500
Jeffrey Miller, supt. Fax 896-7580
www.greenlocalschools.org

Green HS 1,300/9-12
1474 Boettler Rd 44685 330-896-7575
Cynthia Brown, prin. Fax 896-7550

Green MS 700/7-8
1711 Steese Rd 44685 330-896-7710
Jeff Wells, prin. Fax 896-7760

Lake Local SD 3,500/K-12
436 King Church Ave SW 44685 330-877-9383
Jeff Wendorf, supt. Fax 877-4754
www.lakelocal.org

Lake HS 1,200/9-12
1025 Lake Center St SW 44685 330-877-4282
Kevin Tobin, prin. Fax 877-0853

Other Schools – See Hartville

Portage Lakes JVSD
4401 Shriver Rd 44685 330-896-8200
Benjamin Moore, supt. Fax 896-8297
www.plcc.edu/

Portage Lakes Career Center Vo/Tech
4401 Shriver Rd 44685 330-896-8200
Michael Kaschak, prin. Fax 896-8297

**University Heights, Cuyahoga, Pop. 13,323**

Cleveland Hts - University Hts CSD 5,800/PK-12
2155 Miramar Blvd 44118 216-371-7171
Dr. Talisa Dixon, supt. Fax 397-3880
www.chuh.org

Heights HS 1,900/9-12
2181 Miramar Blvd 44118 216-371-7101
Zoraba Ross, admin. Fax 371-6506

Other Schools – See Cleveland Heights

**Upper Arlington, Franklin, Pop. 33,225**

Upper Arlington CSD 5,700/K-12
1950 N Mallway Dr 43221 614-487-5000
Paul Imhoff, supt. Fax 487-5012
www.uaschools.org

Hastings MS 700/6-8
1850 Hastings Ln 43220 614-487-5100
Robb Gonda, prin. Fax 487-5116

Jones MS 700/6-8
2100 Arlington Ave 43221 614-487-5080
Jason Fine, prin. Fax 487-5307

Upper Arlington HS 1,800/9-12
1650 Ridgeview Rd 43221 614-487-5200
Andrew Theado, prin. Fax 487-5238

**Upper Sandusky, Wyandot, Pop. 6,540**

Upper Sandusky EVD 1,700/K-12
800 N Sandusky Ave 43351 419-294-2307
Laurie Vent, supt. Fax 294-6891
www.uppersandusky.k12.oh.us

Union MS 600/4-8
390 W Walker St 43351 419-294-5721
James Wheeler, prin. Fax 294-2586

Upper Sandusky HS 500/9-12
800 N Sandusky Ave 43351 419-294-2308
James Clifford, prin. Fax 294-6889

**Urbana, Champaign, Pop. 11,459**

Urbana CSD 1,800/K-12
711 Wood St 43078 937-653-1402
Charles Thiel, supt. Fax 652-3845
www.urbana.k12.oh.us

Urbana HS 600/9-12
500 Washington Ave 43078 937-653-1412
Kristin Mays, prin. Fax 653-1487

Urbana JHS 300/6-8
500 Washington Ave 43078 937-653-1439
Joanne Petty, prin. Fax 658-1487

---

Urbana University Post-Sec.
579 College Way 43078 937-484-1400

**Utica, Licking, Pop. 2,106**

North Fork Local SD 1,700/K-12
PO Box 497 43080 740-892-3666
Scott Hartley, supt. Fax 892-2937
www.northfork.k12.oh.us

Utica HS 500/9-12
PO Box 677 43080 740-892-2855
Mark Bowman, prin. Fax 892-2090

Utica JHS 300/7-8
PO Box 647 43080 740-892-2691
Marcia Rutherford, prin. Fax 892-2203

**Van Buren, Hancock, Pop. 327**

Van Buren Local SD 1,000/PK-12
217 S Main St 45889 419-299-3578
Timothy Myers, supt. Fax 299-3668
www.vbschools.net

Van Buren HS 300/9-12
217 S Main St 45889 419-299-3384
Michael Brand, prin. Fax 299-3340

Van Buren MS 200/6-8
217 S Main St 45889 419-299-3385
Jason Clark, prin. Fax 299-3340

**Vandalia, Montgomery, Pop. 14,921**

Vandalia-Butler CSD 2,600/PK-12
306 S Dixie Dr 45377 937-415-6400
Bradley Neavin, supt. Fax 415-6429
www.vbcsd.com

Butler HS 1,000/9-12
600 S Dixie Dr 45377 937-415-6300
Chad Hill, prin. Fax 415-6457

Morton MS 400/6-8
8555 Peters Pike 45377 937-415-6600
Shannon White, prin. Fax 415-6648

**Vanlue, Hancock, Pop. 358**

Vanlue Local SD 200/K-12
PO Box 250 45890 419-387-7724
Traci Conley, supt. Fax 387-7722
vanlueschool.org

Vanlue JSHS 100/6-12
PO Box 250 45890 419-387-7724
Robyn Hoadley, prin. Fax 387-7722

**Van Wert, Van Wert, Pop. 10,671**

Lincolnview Local SD 900/K-12
15945 Middle Point Rd 45891 419-968-2226
Jeffrey Synder, supt. Fax 968-2227
www.lincolnview.k12.oh.us

Lincolnview JSHS 400/7-12
15945 Middle Point Rd 45891 419-968-2214
Brad Mendenhall, prin. Fax 968-2227

Lincolnview Marsh S 50/Alt
PO Box 150 45891 419-238-1695
Robbie Breese, prin. Fax 238-3986

Van Wert CSD 1,200/PK-12
205 W Crawford St 45891 419-238-0648
Kenneth Amstutz, supt. Fax 238-3974
www.vanwertcougars.net

Van Wert HS 500/9-12
10708 State Route 118 45891 419-238-3350
William Clifton, prin. Fax 238-0526

Van Wert MS 500/6-8
10694 State Route 118 45891 419-238-0727
Mark Bagley, prin. Fax 238-7166

Vantage JVSD
818 N Franklin St 45891 419-238-5411
Staci Kaufman, supt. Fax 238-4058
www.vantagecareercenter.com

Vantage Career Center Vo/Tech
818 N Franklin St 45891 419-238-5411
Ben Winans, dir. Fax 238-4058

**Vermilion, Erie, Pop. 10,413**

Vermilion Local SD 1,400/K-12
1250 Sanford St 44089 440-204-1700
Philip Pempin, supt. Fax 204-1771
vermilionschools.org

Vermilion HS 900/8-12
1250 Sanford St 44089 440-204-1701
Timothy Lamb, prin. Fax 204-1781

**Versailles, Darke, Pop. 2,673**

Versailles EVD 1,400/K-12
PO Box 313 45380 937-526-4773
Dr. Aaron Moran, supt. Fax 526-5745
www.versailles.k12.oh.us

Versailles HS 400/9-12
PO Box 313 45380 937-526-4427
Roger McEldowney, prin. Fax 526-4356

Versailles MS 400/5-8
PO Box 313 45380 937-526-4426
Jeanne Osterfeld, prin. Fax 526-3085

**Vienna, Trumbull, Pop. 1,067**

Mathews Local SD 700/K-12
4434 Warren Sharon Rd Ste B 44473 330-394-1800
Lew Lowery, supt. Fax 394-1930
www.mathews.k12.oh.us

Mathews JSHS 200/7-12
4429 Warren Sharon Rd 44473 330-394-1138
Robert Cameron, prin.

---

Pittsburgh Institute of Aeronautics Post-Sec.
1453 Youngstown Kingsville 44473 330-399-9992

**Vincent, Washington, Pop. 337**

Warren Local SD 2,300/K-12
220 Sweetapple Rd 45784 740-678-2366
Kyle Newton, supt. Fax 678-8275
www.warrenlocal.org

Warren HS 700/9-12
130 Warrior Dr 45784 740-678-2393
Benjamin Cunningham, prin. Fax 678-2783

**Wadsworth, Medina, Pop. 21,350**

Wadsworth CSD 4,800/PK-12
524 Broad St 44281 330-336-3571
Andrew Hill Ed.D., supt. Fax 335-1313
www.wadsworthschools.org

Wadsworth HS 1,600/9-12
625 Broad St 44281 330-335-1400
Steven Moore, prin. Fax 335-1376

Wadsworth MS 800/7-8
150 Silvercreek Rd 44281 330-335-1410
Eric Jackson, prin. Fax 336-3820

**Wapakoneta, Auglaize, Pop. 9,743**

Wapakoneta CSD 2,700/PK-12
1102 Gardenia Dr 45895 419-739-2900
Keith Horner, supt. Fax 739-2918
www.wapak.org/

Wapakoneta HS 800/8-12
1 Redskin Trl 45895 419-739-5200
Scott Minnig, prin. Fax 739-5305

**Warren, Trumbull, Pop. 40,148**
Champion Local SD 1,500/K-12
5759 Mahoning Ave NW 44483 330-847-2330
Pamela Hood, supt. Fax 847-2336
championlocal.org
Champion HS 500/9-12
5976 Mahoning Ave NW 44483 330-847-2305
John Grabowski, prin. Fax 847-2353
Champion MS 500/5-8
5435 Kuszmaul Ave NW 44483 330-847-2340
Heather Campbell, prin. Fax 847-2355

Howland Local SD 3,000/K-12
8200 South St SE 44484 330-856-8200
Kevin Spicher, supt. Fax 856-8214
www.howlandschools.com
Howland HS 1,000/9-12
200 Shaffer Dr NE 44484 330-856-8220
Sandra Williams, prin. Fax 856-7827
Howland MS 700/6-8
8100 South St SE 44484 330-856-8250
Stephen Kovach, prin. Fax 856-2157

Lordstown Local SD 500/K-12
1824 Salt Springs Rd W 44481 330-824-2534
Terry P. Armstrong, supt. Fax 824-2847
www.lordstown.k12.oh.us/
Lordstown JSHS 200/7-12
1824 Salt Springs Rd W 44481 330-824-2581
James Vivo, prin. Fax 824-2586

Trumbull Career & Technical Center
528 Educational Hwy NW 44483 330-847-0503
Jason Gray, supt. Fax 847-6817
www.tctchome.com
Trumbull Career & Technical Center Vo/Tech
528 Educational Hwy NW 44483 330-847-0503
Mary Flint, dir. Fax 847-0339

Warren CSD 5,300/PK-12
105 High St NE 44481 330-841-2321
Stephen Chiaro, supt. Fax 841-2434
www.warrenschools.k12.oh.us
Harding HS 1,500/9-12
860 Elm Rd NE 44483 330-841-2316
Dante Capers, prin. Fax 841-2289

Kennedy HS 300/7-12
2550 Central Parkway Ave SE 44484 330-369-1804
Joseph Kenneally, prin. Fax 369-1125
Kent State University-Trumbull Campus Post-Sec.
4314 Mahoning Ave NW 44483 330-847-0571
Trumbull Business College Post-Sec.
3200 Ridge Ave SE 44484 330-369-3200

**Warrensville Heights, Cuyahoga, Pop. 13,282**
Warrensville Heights CSD 1,700/PK-12
4500 Warrensville Center Rd 44128 216-865-4717
Donald J. Jolly, supt. Fax 921-5942
www.warrensville.k12.oh.us
Warrensville Heights HS 500/8-12
4270 Northfield Rd 44128 216-752-8585
Janet McDowell, prin. Fax 752-8116

ITT Technical Institute Post-Sec.
24865 Emery Rd 44128 216-896-6500

**Warsaw, Coshocton, Pop. 679**
River View Local SD 2,000/PK-12
26496 State Route 60 43844 740-824-3521
Dalton Summers, supt. Fax 824-3760
www.river-view.k12.oh.us
River View HS 600/9-12
26496 State Route 60 43844 740-824-3522
Chuck Rinkes, prin. Fax 824-4746
River View MS 300/7-8
26546 State Route 60 43844 740-824-3523
Jerry Olinger, prin. Fax 824-5241

**Washington Court House, Fayette, Pop. 13,899**
Miami Trace Local SD 2,400/K-12
3818 State Route 41 NW 43160 740-335-3010
David Lewis, supt. Fax 335-1959
miamitrace.k12.oh.us
Miami Trace HS 700/9-12
3722 State Route 41 NW 43160 740-333-4700
Robert Enochs, prin. Fax 636-2010
Miami Trace MS 500/6-8
3800 State Route 41 NW 43160 740-333-4900
Jeffrey Conroy, prin. Fax 333-4901

Washington Court House CSD 2,300/K-12
306 Highland Ave 43160 740-335-6620
Matthew McCorkle M.Ed., supt. Fax 335-1245
www.washingtonch.k12.oh.us
Washington HS 700/9-12
400 S Elm St 43160 740-636-4221
Tracy Rose, prin. Fax 636-4261
Washington MS 600/6-8
500 S Elm St 43160 740-335-0291
Eric Wayne, prin. Fax 333-3606

**Waterford, Washington, Pop. 445**
Wolf Creek Local SD 600/K-12
PO Box 67 45786 740-984-2373
Robert Caldwell M.A., supt. Fax 984-4420
www.wolfcreek.k12.oh.us
Waterford HS 200/9-12
PO Box 67 45786 740-984-2373
Suellen Coleman M.S., prin. Fax 984-4420

**Wauseon, Fulton, Pop. 7,227**
Wauseon EVD 1,800/K-12
126 S Fulton St 43567 419-335-6616
Larry Brown, supt. Fax 335-3978
www.wauseon.k12.oh.us
Wauseon HS 600/9-12
840 Parkview St 43567 419-335-5756
Keith Leatherman, prin. Fax 335-4228
Wauseon MS 400/6-8
940 E Oak St 43567 419-335-2701
Joe Friess, prin. Fax 335-0089

**Waverly, Pike, Pop. 5,086**
Waverly CSD 1,900/PK-12
1 Tiger Dr 45690 740-947-4770
Cheryl Francis, supt. Fax 947-4483
www.waverly.k12.oh.us
Waverly HS 500/9-12
1 Tiger Dr 45690 740-947-7701
Bill Hoover, prin. Fax 947-8877
Waverly JHS 400/6-8
3 Tiger Dr 45690 740-947-4527
Cynthia Houk, prin. Fax 947-8047

Pike Christian Academy 100/PK-12
400 Clough St 45690 740-947-5700
Rev. Dylan Rowland, prin. Fax 947-9500

**Waynesfield, Auglaize, Pop. 843**
Waynesfield-Goshen Local SD 600/K-12
500 N Westminster St 45896 419-568-9100
J. Chris Pfister, supt. Fax 568-8024
www.wgschools.org
Waynesfield-Goshen Local MSHS 300/6-12
500 N Westminster St 45896 419-568-9100
Rebecca Diglia, prin. Fax 568-6282

**Waynesville, Warren, Pop. 2,780**
Wayne Local SD 1,500/K-12
659 Dayton Rd 45068 513-897-6971
Patrick Dubbs, supt. Fax 897-9605
www.wayne-local.com
Waynesville HS 400/9-12
735 Dayton Rd 45068 513-897-2776
Randy Gebhardt, prin. Fax 897-2713
Waynesville MS 400/6-8
723 Dayton Rd 45068 513-897-4706
Randy Gebhardt, prin. Fax 897-2083

**Wellington, Lorain, Pop. 4,725**
Wellington EVD 1,300/PK-12
201 S Main St 44090 440-647-4286
Dennis Mock, supt. Fax 647-4806
www.wellington.k12.oh.us
Wellington HS 400/8-12
629 N Main St 44090 440-647-3734
Tina Drake, prin. Fax 647-7318

**Wellston, Jackson, Pop. 5,598**
Wellston CSD 1,500/PK-12
1 E Broadway St 45692 740-384-2152
Karen Boch, supt. Fax 384-3948
www.wcs.k12.oh.us
Wellston HS 400/9-12
200 Golden Rocket Dr 45692 740-384-2162
Megan Sowers, prin. Fax 384-9581
Wellston MS 400/6-8
227 Golden Rocket Dr 45692 740-384-2251
Tyler Swackhammer, prin. Fax 384-9801

**Wellsville, Columbiana, Pop. 3,433**
Wellsville Local SD 700/PK-12
929 Center St 43968 330-532-2643
Richard Bereschik, supt. Fax 532-6204
www.wellsville.k12.oh.us
Wellsville JSHS 200/7-12
1 Bengal Blvd 43968 330-532-1188
Linda Rolley, prin. Fax 532-9004

**West Alexandria, Preble, Pop. 1,321**
Twin Valley Community Local SD 800/K-12
100 Education Dr 45381 937-839-4688
Clinton Moore Ed.D., supt. Fax 839-4898
www.tvs.k12.oh.us
Twin Valley South HS 300/9-12
100 Education Dr 45381 937-839-4693
Scott Cottingim, prin. Fax 839-4898
Twin Valley South MS 200/7-8
100 Education Dr 45381 937-839-4165
Scott Cottingim, prin. Fax 839-4898

**West Carrollton, Montgomery, Pop. 12,886**
West Carrollton CSD 3,800/PK-12
430 E Pease Ave 45449 937-859-5121
Rusty Clifford Ph.D., supt. Fax 859-5250
www.westcarrolltonschools.com
West Carrollton HS 1,000/9-12
5833 Student St 45449 937-859-5121
Craig Myers, prin. Fax 435-2315
West Carrollton MS 900/6-8
424 E Main St 45449 937-859-5121
Doug Mescher, prin. Fax 859-2780

**West Chester, Butler**
Lakota Local SD
Supt. — See Liberty Twp
Hopewell JHS 600/7-8
8200 Cox Rd 45069 513-777-2258
Jeff Rouff, prin. Fax 777-1908
Lakota Ridge JHS 600/7-8
6199 Beckett Ridge Blvd 45069 513-777-0552
Andre Gendreau, prin. Fax 777-0919
Lakota West Freshman HS 600/9-9
5050 Tylersville Rd 45069 513-874-8390
Gary Card, prin. Fax 682-4230
Lakota West HS 1,900/10-12
8940 Union Centre Blvd 45069 513-874-5699
Gary Card, prin. Fax 682-4133

Hondros College Post-Sec.
7600 Tylers Place Blvd 45069 888-466-3767

**Westerville, Franklin, Pop. 35,380**
Westerville CSD 14,400/PK-12
936 Eastwind Dr 43081 614-797-5700
Dr. John R. Kellogg, supt. Fax 797-5701
www.wcsoh.org
Blendon MS 700/6-8
223 S Otterbein Ave 43081 614-797-6400
Kendall Harris, prin. Fax 797-6401
Genoa MS 1,000/6-8
5948 S Old 3C Hwy 43082 614-797-6500
Carrie Trusley, prin. Fax 797-6501
Heritage MS 900/6-8
390 N Spring Rd 43082 614-797-6600
Joseph Kacsandi, prin. Fax 797-6601
Walnut Springs MS 900/6-8
888 E Walnut St 43081 614-797-6700
Becca Yanni, prin. Fax 797-6701
Westerville Central HS 1,600/9-12
7118 Mount Royal Ave 43082 614-797-6800
Todd Spinner, prin. Fax 797-6801
Westerville-North HS 1,500/9-12
950 County Line Rd 43081 614-797-6200
Kurt Yancey, prin. Fax 797-6201
Westerville-South HS 1,500/9-12
303 S Otterbein Ave 43081 614-797-6000
Steven Andersson, prin. Fax 797-6001

Fortis College Post-Sec.
4151 Executive Pkwy Ste 120 43081 614-882-2551
Genoa Christian Academy 300/PK-12
7562 Lewis Center Rd 43082 740-965-5433
Craig Bartley, prin. Fax 965-8214
Hondros College Post-Sec.
4140 Executive Pkwy 43081 614-508-7277
Northside Christian S 200/K-12
2655 W Schrock Rd 43081 614-882-1493
John Taylor, prin.
Ohio State Cosmetology School Post-Sec.
5970 Westerville Rd 43081 614-890-3535
Otterbein University Post-Sec.
1 S Grove St 43081 614-890-3000
Worthington Christian MS 200/6-8
8225 Worthington Galena Rd 43081 614-431-8230
Tamara Evans, prin. Fax 431-8216

**West Jefferson, Madison, Pop. 4,287**
Jefferson Local SD 1,200/PK-12
906 W Main St 43162 614-879-7654
William Mullett, supt. Fax 879-5376
www.west-jefferson.k12.oh.us
West Jefferson HS 300/9-12
1 Roughrider Dr 43162 614-879-7681
David Metz, prin. Fax 879-5381
West Jefferson MS 300/6-8
2 Roughrider Dr 43162 614-879-8345
Deborah Omen, prin. Fax 879-5399

**West Lafayette, Coshocton, Pop. 2,307**
Ridgewood Local SD 1,300/PK-12
301 S Oak St 43845 740-545-6354
John Marks, supt. Fax 545-6336
www.ridgewood.k12.oh.us
Ridgewood HS 400/8-12
602 Johnson St 43845 740-545-6345
Todd Stoffer, prin. Fax 545-5311

**Westlake, Cuyahoga, Pop. 32,199**
Westlake CSD 4,000/PK-12
27200 Hilliard Blvd 44145 440-871-7300
Geoffrey Palmer, supt. Fax 871-6034
www.wlake.org
Burneson MS 600/7-8
2260 Dover Center Rd 44145 440-835-6340
Paul Wilson, prin. Fax 835-5987
Westlake HS 1,400/9-12
27830 Hilliard Blvd 44145 440-250-1002
Timothy Freeman, prin. Fax 835-5572

**West Liberty, Champaign, Pop. 1,773**
West Liberty-Salem Local SD 1,200/K-12
7208 US Highway 68 N 43357 937-465-1075
Kraig Hissong, supt. Fax 465-1095
www.wlstigers.org/
West Liberty-Salem MSHS 700/6-12
7208 US Highway 68 N 43357 937-465-1060
Greg Johnson, prin. Fax 465-1095

**West Milton, Miami, Pop. 4,568**
Milton-Union EVD 1,400/PK-12
7610 Milton Potsdam Rd 45383 937-884-7910
Dr. Virginia Rammel, supt. Fax 884-7911
www.milton-union.k12.oh.us
Milton-Union HS 400/9-12
7640 Milton Potsdam Rd 45383 937-884-7940
Scott Bloom, prin. Fax 884-7941
Milton-Union MS 300/5-8
7630 Milton Potsdam Rd 45383 937-884-7930
Katie Hartley, prin. Fax 884-7931

**West Portsmouth, Scioto, Pop. 3,091**
Washington-Nile Local SD 1,500/K-12
15332 US Highway 52 45663 740-858-1111
Jeff Stricklett, supt. Fax 858-1110
www.west.k12.oh.us
Portsmouth West HS 400/9-12
15332 US Highway 52 45663 740-858-1103
Anthony Bazler, prin. Fax 858-1110
Portsmouth West MS 500/5-8
15332 US Highway 52 Unit B 45663 740-858-6668
Christopher Jordan, prin. Fax 858-4101

**West Salem, Wayne, Pop. 1,452**
Northwestern Local SD 1,400/K-12
7571 N Elyria Rd 44287 419-846-3151
Jeffrey Layton, supt. Fax 846-3361
www.northwestern-wayne.k12.oh.us
Northwestern HS 400/9-12
7473 N Elyria Rd 44287 419-846-3833
Michael Burkholder, prin. Fax 846-3163
Northwestern MS 300/6-8
7569 N Elyria Rd 44287 419-846-3974
Joseph Brightbill, prin. Fax 846-3750

**West Union, Adams, Pop. 3,193**
Adams County/Ohio Valley Local SD 3,900/PK-12
141 Lloyd Rd 45693 937-544-5586
Richard Seas, supt. Fax 544-3720
www.ovsd.us
Ohio Valley Career & Technical Center Vo/Tech
175 Lloyd Rd 45693 937-544-2336
Jason Vesey, dir. Fax 544-5176
West Union HS 600/7-12
97 Dragon Lair Dr 45693 937-544-5553
Benjamin King, prin. Fax 544-5361
Other Schools – See Peebles, Seaman

Adams County Christian S 100/K-12
187 Willow Dr 45693 937-544-5502
Rev. Kenneth Jones, admin. Fax 544-5503

**West Unity, Williams, Pop. 1,653**
Millcreek-West Unity Local SD 600/K-12
1401 W Jackson St 43570 419-924-2365
Larry E Long, supt. Fax 924-2367
www.hilltop.k12.oh.us
Hilltop HS 300/7-12
1401 W Jackson St 43570 419-924-2365
Steven J. Riley, prin. Fax 924-2367

**Wheelersburg, Scioto, Pop. 6,353**
Wheelersburg Local SD 1,500/PK-12
PO Box 340 45694 740-574-8484
Mark Knapp, supt. Fax 574-6134
www.wheelersburg.net
Wheelersburg HS 400/9-12
800 Pirate Dr 45694 740-574-2527
Christopher Porter, prin. Fax 574-6178
Wheelersburg MS 600/4-8
800 Pirate Dr 45694 740-574-2515
David Rucker, prin. Fax 574-9201

**Whitehall, Franklin, Pop. 17,402**
Whitehall CSD 2,800/PK-12
625 S Yearling Rd 43213 614-417-5000
Brian Hamler, supt. Fax 417-5023
www.wcsrams.org
Rosemore MS 700/6-8
4800 Langley Ave 43213 614-417-5200
Rochelle Rankin, prin. Fax 417-5212
Whitehall-Yearling HS 700/9-12
675 S Yearling Rd 43213 614-417-5100
Carl Svagerko, prin. Fax 417-5133

**Whitehouse, Lucas, Pop. 4,098**
Anthony Wayne Local SD 4,300/K-12
PO Box 2487 43571 419-877-5377
Jim Fritz, supt. Fax 877-9352
www.anthonywayneschools.org
Wayne HS 1,300/9-12
5967 Finzel Rd 43571 419-877-0466
Jeri Hoellrich, prin. Fax 877-5028
Wayne JHS 700/7-8
6035 Finzel Rd 43571 419-877-5342
Kevin Pfefferle, prin. Fax 877-4908

**Wickliffe, Lake, Pop. 12,545**
Wickliffe CSD 1,500/PK-12
2221 Rockefeller Rd 44092 440-943-6900
Joseph Spiccia, supt. Fax 943-7738
www.wickliffeschools.org
Wickliffe HS 500/9-12
2255 Rockefeller Rd 44092 440-944-0800
Cynthia Anderson, prin. Fax 943-7738
Wickliffe MS 500/5-8
29240 Euclid Ave 44092 440-943-3220
William Basel, prin. Fax 943-7755

Rabbinical College of Telshe Post-Sec.
28400 Euclid Ave 44092 440-943-5300
St. Mary Seminary/Graduate Sch. Theology Post-Sec.
28700 Euclid Ave 44092 440-943-7600
Telshe HS 100/9-12
28400 Euclid Ave 44092 440-944-0299

**Wilberforce, Greene, Pop. 2,180**

Central State University Post-Sec.
PO Box 1004 45384 937-376-6011
Payne Theological Seminary Post-Sec.
PO Box 474 45384 937-376-2946
Wilberforce University Post-Sec.
PO Box 1001 45384 937-376-2911

**Willard, Huron, Pop. 6,140**
Willard CSD 1,100/PK-12
110 S Myrtle Ave 44890 419-935-1541
Jeffrey Ritz, supt. Fax 935-8491
www.willardschools.org/
Willard MSHS 500/PK-12
1 Flashes Ave 44890 419-935-0181
Chris Schaaf, prin. Fax 933-6701

**Williamsburg, Clermont, Pop. 2,468**
Williamsburg Local SD 1,000/PK-12
549 W Main St Ste A 45176 513-724-3077
Matthew Earley, supt. Fax 724-1504
www.burgschools.org
Williamsburg MSHS 500/6-12
500 S 5th St 45176 513-724-2211
Heather Powell, prin. Fax 724-6577

**Williamsport, Pickaway, Pop. 1,007**
Westfall Local SD 1,600/PK-12
19463 Pherson Pike 43164 740-986-3671
Cara Riddel, supt. Fax 986-8375
www.westfallschools.com
Westfall HS 500/9-12
19463 Pherson Pike 43164 740-986-2911
Billy Dennis, prin. Fax 986-8897
Westfall MS 400/6-8
19545 Pherson Pike 43164 740-986-2941
Jason Fife, prin. Fax 986-8882

**Willoughby, Lake, Pop. 21,949**
Willoughby-Eastlake CSD 8,100/K-12
37047 Ridge Rd 44094 440-946-5000
Stephen Thompson, supt. Fax 946-4671
www.weschools.org
South HS 1,400/9-12
5000 Shankland Rd 44094 440-975-3647
Patrick Ward, prin. Fax 975-3645
Willoughby-Eastlake Career Academy Vo/Tech
25 Public Sq 44094 440-946-7085
Susan Vargo Roseum, dir. Fax 975-3741
Willoughby MS 900/6-8
36901 Ridge Rd 44094 440-975-3600
Lawrence Keller, prin. Fax 975-3618
Other Schools – See Eastlake, Willowick

Andrews Osborne Academy 400/PK-12
38588 Mentor Ave 44094 440-942-3600
Larry Goodman Ph.D., head sch Fax 942-3660

**Willoughby Hills, Lake, Pop. 9,326**

Cornerstone Christian Academy 400/PK-12
2846 SOM Center Rd, 440-943-9260
Sandra Ortiz, coord. Fax 943-9262
National College Post-Sec.
27557 Chardon Rd 44092 440-944-0825

**Willowick, Lake, Pop. 14,003**
Willoughby-Eastlake CSD
Supt. — See Willoughby
Willowick MS 600/6-8
31500 Royalview Dr 44095 440-943-2950
Loretta Rodman, prin. Fax 943-9964

**Willow Wood, Lawrence**
Symmes Valley Local SD 800/K-12
14778 State Route 141 45696 740-643-2451
Jeff Saunders, supt. Fax 643-1219
www.sv.k12.oh.us
Symmes Valley HS 200/9-12
14778 State Route 141 45696 740-643-2371
Greg Bowman, prin. Fax 643-1606

**Wilmington, Clinton, Pop. 12,076**
Great Oaks Institute of Technology
Supt. — See Cincinnati
Laurel Oaks CDC Vo/Tech
300 Oak Dr 45177 937-382-1411
Mike Thomas, prin. Fax 383-2095

Wilmington CSD 3,100/K-12
341 S Nelson Ave 45177 937-382-1641
Ronald Sexton, supt. Fax 382-1645
www.wilmingtoncityschools.com
Borror MS 700/6-8
275 Thorne Ave 45177 937-382-7556
Jeffrey Sherby, prin. Fax 382-3295
Wilmington HS 800/9-12
300 Richardson Pl 45177 937-382-7716
Mindy McCarty-Stewart, prin. Fax 382-1139

Wilmington Christian Academy 50/K-12
642 Davids Dr 45177 937-383-1319
Tari Heath, admin. Fax 283-9541
Wilmington College Post-Sec.
1870 Quaker Way 45177 937-382-6661

**Winchester, Adams, Pop. 1,044**
Eastern Local SD 1,300/K-12
11479 US Highway 62 45697 937-378-3981
Michele Filon, supt. Fax 695-9046
www.eb.k12.oh.us
Eastern HS 300/9-12
11557 US Highway 62 45697 937-695-0959
Jennifer Grimes, prin. Fax 695-0303
Eastern MS 300/6-8
11479 US Highway 62 45697 937-695-1249
Rob Beucler, prin. Fax 695-1299

**Windham, Portage, Pop. 2,132**
Windham EVD 700/PK-12
9530 Bauer Ave 44288 330-326-2711
Gregory Isler, supt. Fax 326-2134
www.windham-schools.org
Windham HS 200/9-12
9530 Bauer Ave 44288 330-326-2711
Laura Amero, prin. Fax 326-2052
Windham JHS 200/6-8
9530 Bauer Ave 44288 330-326-2711
Laura Amero, prin. Fax 326-3713

**Wintersville, Jefferson, Pop. 3,879**
Indian Creek Local SD 1,700/PK-12
587 Bantam Ridge Rd 43953 740-264-3502
Dr. T.C. Chappelear Ed.D., supt. Fax 266-2915
www.indian-creek.k12.oh.us
Indian Creek HS 600/9-12
200 Park Dr 43953 740-264-1163
Albert Hartman, prin. Fax 266-2929
Other Schools – See Mingo Junction

Jefferson County Christian S 100/PK-12
125 Fernwood Rd 43953 740-275-4326
Diane Hutchison, prin. Fax 275-4296

**Woodsfield, Monroe, Pop. 2,354**
Switzerland of Ohio Local SD 2,400/PK-12
304 Mill St 43793 740-472-5801
John Hall, supt. Fax 472-5806
www.swissohio.k12.oh.us
Monroe Central HS 300/9-12
469 Lewisville Rd 43793 740-472-0414
Jerry Calder, prin. Fax 472-2055
Swiss Hills Career Center Vo/Tech
46601 State Route 78 43793 740-472-0722
Marc Ring, prin. Fax 472-0367
Other Schools – See Beallsville, Hannibal

**Woodville, Sandusky, Pop. 2,126**
Woodmore Local SD
Supt. — See Elmore
Woodmore MS 6-8
800 W Main St 43469 419-862-1070
Kevin Ball, prin. Fax 849-2132

**Wooster, Wayne, Pop. 25,513**
Triway Local SD 1,700/K-12
3205 Shreve Rd 44691 330-264-9491
David Rice, supt. Fax 262-3955
www.tccsa.net/dp/trwy
Triway HS 500/9-12
3205 Shreve Rd 44691 330-264-8685
Scott Wharton, prin. Fax 262-3955
Triway JHS 300/7-8
3145 Shreve Rd 44691 330-264-2114
Joshua Stutz, prin. Fax 264-6025

Wooster CSD 2,400/PK-12
144 N Market St 44691 330-988-1111
Dr. Michael Tefs, supt. Fax 262-3407
www.woostercityschools.org
Boys Village S 100/Alt
3011 Akron Rd 44691 330-262-3442
Anita Jorney-Gifford, prin. Fax 202-3890
Wooster HS 1,100/8-12
515 Oldman Rd 44691 330-988-1111
Tyler Keener, prin. Fax 345-3501

College of Wooster Post-Sec.
1189 Beall Ave 44691 330-263-2000
Ohio State University-A & T Institute Post-Sec.
1328 Dover Rd 44691 330-287-1331

**Worthington, Franklin, Pop. 13,300**
Worthington CSD 9,300/PK-12
200 E Wilson Bridge Rd 43085 614-450-6000
Trent Bowers Ph.D., supt. Fax 883-3010
www.worthington.k12.oh.us
Kilbourne MS 400/7-8
50 E Dublin Granville Rd 43085 614-450-4200
Pete Scully, prin. Fax 883-3510
Linworth Campus Alternative Program Alt
2075 W Dublin Granville Rd 43085 614-450-6900
Chris Hasebrook, dir. Fax 883-3710
Phoenix MS 200/Alt
2341 Snouffer Rd 43085 614-450-4100
Adham Schirg, prin. Fax 883-3610
Worthington HS 1,500/9-12
300 W Dublin Granville Rd 43085 614-450-6200
James Gaskill, prin. Fax 450-6390
Worthingway MS 400/7-8
6625 Guyer St 43085 614-450-4300
Nathan Kellenberger, prin. Fax 883-3660
Other Schools – See Columbus

Worthington Christian HS 300/9-12
6670 Worthington Galena Rd 43085 614-431-8210
Dr. Scott Inboden, prin. Fax 431-8213

**Wyoming, Hamilton, Pop. 8,224**
Wyoming CSD 1,900/K-12
420 Springfield Pike 45215 513-206-7000
Dr. Susan Lang, supt. Fax 672-3355
www.wyomingcityschools.org
Wyoming HS 600/9-12
106 Pendery Ave 45215 513-206-7050
Aaron Marshall, prin. Fax 206-7132
Wyoming MS 600/5-8
17 Wyoming Ave 45215 513-206-7170
Tiffany Brennan, prin. Fax 206-7245

**Xenia, Greene, Pop. 24,906**
Beavercreek CSD
Supt. — See Beavercreek
Coy MS 6-8
1786 Dayton Xenia Rd 45385 937-429-7577
Theresa Noe, prin. Fax 429-7686

Greene County JVSD 937-372-6941
2960 W Enon Rd 45385 Fax 372-8283
Daniel Schroer, supt.
www.greeneccc.com
Greene County Career Center Vo/Tech
2960 W Enon Rd 45385 937-426-6636
Matthew Lindley, dir. Fax 372-8283

Xenia Community SD 4,000/PK-12
819 Colorado Dr 45385 937-376-2961
Dennis Morrison, supt. Fax 372-4701
www.xenia.k12.oh.us
Warner MS 700/6-8
600 Buckskin Trl 45385 937-376-9488
Michael Earley, prin. Fax 374-4228
Xenia HS 1,200/9-12
303 Kinsey Rd 45385 937-372-6983
Ted Holop, prin. Fax 374-4390

Xenia Christian S 400/PK-12
1101 Wesley Ave 45385 937-352-1640
Dr. Dan Bragg, prin. Fax 352-1641

**Yellow Springs, Greene, Pop. 3,226**
Yellow Springs EVD 700/K-12
201 S Walnut St 45387 937-767-7381
Mario Basora, supt. Fax 767-6604
www.yellow-springs.k12.oh.us/
Yellow Springs HS / McKinney MS 300/7-12
420 E Enon Rd 45387 937-767-7224
Tim Krier, prin. Fax 767-6154

Antioch University Midwest Post-Sec.
900 Dayton St 45387 937-769-1800

**Youngstown, Mahoning, Pop. 65,039**

Austintown Local SD — 2,900/K-12
700 S Raccoon Rd 44515 — 330-797-3900
Vincent Colauca, supt. — Fax 792-8625
www.austintown.k12.oh.us

Austintown MS — 1,300/6-8
800 S Raccoon Rd 44515 — 330-797-3900
James Penk, prin. — Fax 792-9130

Fitch HS — 1,600/9-12
4560 Falcon Dr 44515 — 330-797-3900
Christopher Berni, prin. — Fax 797-3944

Boardman Local SD — 4,600/K-12
7410 Market St 44512 — 330-726-3404
Frank Lazzeri, supt. — Fax 726-3432
www.boardmanschools.org

Boardman HS — 1,500/9-12
7777 Glenwood Ave 44512 — 330-758-7511
Cindy Fernback, prin. — Fax 758-7515

Center MS — 700/5-8
7410 Market St 44512 — 330-726-3400
Randall Ebie, prin. — Fax 726-3431

Glenwood MS — 700/5-8
7635 Glenwood Ave 44512 — 330-726-3414
Bart Smith, prin. — Fax 758-8067

Liberty Local SD — 1,300/K-12
4115 Shady Rd 44505 — 330-759-0807
Stanley Watson, supt. — Fax 759-1209
sites.liberty.k12.oh.us

Guy MS — 400/5-8
4115 Shady Rd 44505 — 330-759-1733
Melissa Malone, prin. — Fax 759-4507

Liberty HS — 500/9-12
1 Leopard Way 44505 — 330-759-2301
Rocco Adduci, prin. — Fax 759-4506

Youngstown CSD — 3,900/PK-12
PO Box 550 44501 — 330-744-6900
Stephen Stohla Ph.D., supt. — Fax 743-1157
www.youngstown.k12.oh.us

Chaney VPA/STEM Campus — 400/6-12
731 S Hazelwood Ave 44509 — 330-744-8822
Joseph Krumpak, prin. — Fax 480-1909

East HS — 500/9-11
474 Bennington Ave 44505 — 330-744-4005
Tryvan Leech, prin. — Fax 742-6464

Programs of Promise at Wilson — Alt
2725 Gibson St 44502 — 330-744-7535
Tod Morris, prin. — Fax 788-1326

Rayen Early College MS — 200/6-8
731 S Hazelwood Ave 44509 — 330-744-7602
Deborah DiFrancesco, prin. — Fax 793-9675

Youngstown Early College HS — 200/9-12
Fedor Hall 644 Elm St 44555 — 330-744-7923
Monica Jones, dean — Fax 480-5875

---

Cardinal Mooney HS — 600/9-12
2545 Erie St 44507 — 330-788-5007
Mark Vollmer, prin. — Fax 788-4511

ITT Technical Institute — Post-Sec.
1030 N Meridian Rd 44509 — 330-270-1600

National College — Post-Sec.
3487 Belmont Ave 44505 — 330-759-0205

St. Elizabeth Hospital — Post-Sec.
PO Box 1790 44501 — 330-746-7211

Ursuline HS — 400/9-12
750 Wick Ave 44505 — 330-744-4563
Matt Sammartino, prin. — Fax 744-3358

Valley Christian S — 500/PK-12
4401 Southern Blvd 44512 — 330-788-8088
Michael Pecchia, pres. — Fax 788-2875

Western Reserve Care System — Post-Sec.
345 Oak Hill Ave 44502 — 330-747-0777

Youngstown State University — Post-Sec.
1 University Plz 44555 — 330-941-3000

**Zanesville, Muskingum, Pop. 24,279**

Maysville Local SD — 2,100/K-12
3715 Panther Dr 43701 — 740-453-0754
Monte Bainter, supt. — Fax 455-4081
maysvillesd.schoolwires.com/

Maysville HS — 600/9-12
3725 Panther Dr 43701 — 740-454-7999
Jason Bunting, prin. — Fax 452-9921

Maysville MS — 600/6-8
3725 Panther Dr 43701 — 740-454-7982
Erik Winland, prin. — Fax 452-9921

Mid-East Career & Technology Centers
400 Richards Rd 43701 — 740-454-0105
Richard Hall, supt. — Fax 454-0731
www.mideastctc.org

Mid-East Career & Tech Ctr - Zanesville — Vo/Tech
400 Richards Rd 43701 — 740-454-0101
Mike Hawley, dir. — Fax 454-0723

Adult Center for Education — Adult
400 Richards Rd 43701 — 740-455-3111
Tony Hartman, dir. — Fax 455-2043
Other Schools – See Senecaville

West Muskingum Local SD — 1,300/PK-12
4880 West Pike 43701 — 740-455-4052
Dr. William Harbron, supt. — Fax 455-4063
www.westm.k12.oh.us

West Muskingum HS — 400/9-12
150 Kimes Rd 43701 — 740-455-4050
Ray Peyton, prin. — Fax 452-7648

West Muskingum MS — 400/5-8
100 Kimes Rd 43701 — 740-455-4055
Greg Stickel, prin. — Fax 455-9717

Zanesville CSD — 3,100/PK-12
956 Moxahala Ave 43701 — 740-454-9751
Terry Martin, supt. — Fax 455-4325
www.zanesville.k12.oh.us

Zanesville HS — 900/9-12
1701 Blue Ave 43701 — 740-453-0335
Garry Young, prin. — Fax 455-4329

Zanesville MS — 500/7-8
1429 Blue Ave 43701 — 740-453-0711
Jason Taylor, prin. — Fax 454-7005

---

Bishop Fenwick MS — 100/4-8
1030 E Main St 43701 — 740-453-2637
Kelly Sagan, prin. — Fax 454-0653

Bishop Rosecrans HS — 200/9-12
1040 E Main St 43701 — 740-452-7504
Jennifer Mallett, prin. — Fax 455-5080

Ohio University — Post-Sec.
1425 Newark Rd 43701 — 740-453-0762

Valley Beauty School — Post-Sec.
627 Main St 43701 — 740-452-6821

Zane State College — Post-Sec.
1555 Newark Rd 43701 — 740-454-2501

**Zoarville, Tuscarawas**

Tuscarawas Valley Local SD — 1,500/PK-12
2637 Tusky Valley Rd NE 44656 — 330-859-2213
Mark Murphy, supt. — Fax 859-2706
www.tvtrojans.org/

Tuscarawas Valley HS — 400/9-12
2637 Tusky Valley Rd NE 44656 — 330-859-2421
Jason Phillips, prin. — Fax 859-8805

Tuscarawas Valley MS — 500/5-8
2633 Tusky Valley Rd NE 44656 — 330-859-2427
Scott Young, prin. — Fax 859-8845

# OKLAHOMA

## OKLAHOMA DEPARTMENT OF EDUCATION
**2500 N Lincoln Blvd Rm 112, Oklahoma City 73105-4503**
**Telephone 405-521-3301**
**Fax 405-521-6205**
**Website http://www.sde.state.ok.us**

Superintendent of Public Instruction Janet Barresi

## OKLAHOMA BOARD OF EDUCATION
**2500 N Lincoln Blvd Rm 112, Oklahoma City 73105-4596**

Chairperson Janet Baressi

## INTERLOCAL COOPERATIVES (IC)

Choctaw Nation IC
Ken Keeling, dir. 580-931-0691
PO Box 602, Durant 74702 Fax 931-0120
choctawinterlocal.org
Five Star IC
Nancy Anderson, dir. 918-225-5600
1405 E Moses St, Cushing 74023 Fax 225-3026
www.fsilc.k12.ok.us

Osage County IC
Jacque Canady, dir. 918-885-2667
207 E Main St, Hominy 74035 Fax 885-6742
www.ocic.k12.ok.us/
Seminole County IC 405-382-6121
, 630 Golf Rd, Seminole 74868 Fax 382-5254

Southeastern Oklahoma IC
Tracy Mussett, dir. 580-286-3344
103 NE Ave A, Idabel 74745 Fax 286-5598
Tri-County IC 580-673-2310
, PO Box 217, Fox 73435 Fax 673-2309

## PUBLIC, PRIVATE AND CATHOLIC SECONDARY SCHOOLS

**Achille, Bryan, Pop. 443**
Achille ISD 300/PK-12
PO Box 280 74720 580-283-3775
Rick Beene, supt. Fax 283-3787
achilleisd.org
Achille HS 100/9-12
PO Box 280 74720 580-283-3775
Dana Beene, prin. Fax 283-3524

**Ada, Pontotoc, Pop. 15,623**
Ada ISD 2,700/PK-12
324 W 20th St 74820 580-310-7200
Pat Harrison, supt. Fax 310-7206
www.adapss.com/
Ada JHS 500/7-9
223 W 18th St 74820 580-310-7260
Bryan Harwell, prin. Fax 310-7261
Ada SHS 500/10-12
1400 Stadium Dr 74820 580-310-7220
Jeff Maloy, prin. Fax 310-7221

Byng ISD 1,800/PK-12
500 S New Bethel Blvd 74820 580-436-3020
Todd Crabtree, supt. Fax 436-3052
www.byngschools.com
Byng JHS 300/7-9
500 S New Bethel Blvd 74820 580-310-6743
Kevin Wilson, prin. Fax 310-6741
Byng SHS 300/10-12
500 S New Bethel Blvd 74820 580-310-6732
Scott Lowrance, prin. Fax 310-6730

Latta ISD 700/PK-12
13925 County Road 1560 74820 580-332-2092
Cliff Johnson, supt. Fax 332-3116
www.latta.k12.ok.us/
Latta HS 200/9-12
13925 County Road 1560 74820 580-332-3300
Stan Cochran, prin.
Latta MS 100/5-8
13925 County Road 1560 74820 580-332-8180
Terry Painter, prin.

OK Dept. of Voc. & Tech. Education
Supt. — None
Pontotoc Technology Center Vo/Tech
601 W 33rd St 74820 580-310-2200
David Lassiter, supt. Fax 436-0236

Vanoss ISD 500/PK-12
4665 County Road 1555 74820 580-759-2251
Marjana Tharp, supt. Fax 759-3080
www.vanoss.k12.ok.us
Vanoss HS 200/9-12
4665 County Road 1555 74820 580-759-2503
Charles Hill, prin. Fax 759-3080
Vanoss MS 200/6-8
4665 County Road 1555 74820 580-759-2623
Charles Hill, prin. Fax 759-3080

East Central University Post-Sec.
1100 E 14th St 74820 580-332-8000
Valley View Regional Hospital Post-Sec.
430 N Monte Vista St 74820 580-332-2323

**Adair, Mayes, Pop. 736**
Adair ISD 1,000/PK-12
PO Box 197 74330 918-785-2424
Tom Linihan, supt. Fax 785-2491
adair.k12.ok.us/APS/
Adair HS 300/9-12
PO Box 197 74330 918-785-2424
Mark Lippe, prin. Fax 785-2491
Adair MS 200/6-8
PO Box 197 74330 918-785-2425
Brad Rogers, prin. Fax 785-2491

**Afton, Ottawa, Pop. 950**
Afton ISD 500/PK-12
PO Box 100 74331 918-257-4470
Randy Gardner, supt. Fax 257-4846
www.aftonschools.net/
Afton HS 100/9-12
PO Box 100 74331 918-257-8305
Owen Bowen, prin. Fax 257-5406

OK Dept. of Voc. & Tech. Education
Supt. — None
Northeast Tech Center Afton Campus Vo/Tech
PO Box 219 74331 918-257-8324
Paul Hocutt, dir. Fax 257-4342

**Agra, Lincoln, Pop. 313**
Agra ISD 400/PK-12
PO Box 279 74824 918-375-2261
Don Gray, supt. Fax 375-2263
www.agra.k12.ok.us/
Agra HS 100/9-12
PO Box 279 74824 918-375-2261
Tony Holt, prin. Fax 375-2260

**Alex, Grady, Pop. 528**
Alex ISD 200/PK-12
PO Box 188 73002 405-785-2605
Dr. Jason James, supt. Fax 785-2914
www.alex.k12.ok.us
Alex HS 100/9-12
PO Box 188 73002 405-785-2264
Doug Tolson, prin. Fax 785-9976

**Aline, Alfalfa, Pop. 202**
Aline-Cleo ISD 200/PK-12
PO Box 49 73716 580-463-2255
Barry Nault, supt. Fax 463-2256
www.alinecleo.k12.ok.us
Aline-Cleo Springs HS 50/9-12
PO Box 49 73716 580-463-2256
Kurt Myers, prin. Fax 463-2256

**Allen, Pontotoc, Pop. 878**
Allen ISD 400/PK-12
PO Box 430 74825 580-857-2417
Bob Gragg, supt. Fax 857-2636
www.allen.k12.ok.us
Allen HS 100/9-12
PO Box 430 74825 580-857-2416
Chad Ward, prin. Fax 857-2636

**Altus, Jackson, Pop. 19,118**
Altus ISD 3,900/PK-12
PO Box 558 73522 580-481-2100
Roger Hill, supt. Fax 481-2129
www.altusps.com
Altus JHS 500/7-8
PO Box 558 73522 580-481-2173
Roe Worbes, prin. Fax 481-2547
Altus SHS 1,000/9-12
PO Box 558 73522 580-481-2167
Mark Haught, prin. Fax 481-2545

Navajo ISD 300/PK-12
15695 S County Road 210 73521 580-482-7742
Vicki Nance, supt. Fax 482-7749
www.navajo.k12.ok.us
Navajo JSHS 100/7-12
15695 S County Road 210 73521 580-482-7742
Floyd Roach, prin. Fax 482-7749

OK Dept. of Voc. & Tech. Education
Supt. — None
Southwest Technology Center Vo/Tech
711 W Tamarack Rd 73521 580-477-2250
Dale Latham, supt. Fax 477-0138

Western Oklahoma State College Post-Sec.
2801 N Main St 73521 580-477-2000

**Alva, Woods, Pop. 4,829**
Alva ISD 800/PK-12
418 Flynn St 73717 580-327-4823
J. Stephen Parkhurst, supt. Fax 327-2965
www.alvaschools.com
Alva HS 200/9-12
501 14th St 73717 580-327-3682
Les Potter, prin. Fax 327-4240
Alva MS 200/6-8
800 Flynn St 73717 580-327-0608
Ron Sunderland, prin. Fax 327-4255

OK Dept. of Voc. & Tech. Education
Supt. — None
Northwest Technology Center Vo/Tech
1801 11th St 73717 580-327-0344
Daren Slater, dir. Fax 327-5467

Northwestern Oklahoma State University Post-Sec.
709 Oklahoma Blvd 73717 580-327-1700

**Amber, Grady, Pop. 416**
Amber-Pocasset ISD 500/PK-12
PO Box 38 73004 405-224-5768
Chad Hance, supt. Fax 224-5115
www.ampo.k12.ok.us/
Amber-Pocasset HS 100/10-12
PO Box 38 73004 405-224-4017
Jerime Parker, prin. Fax 224-5115
Amber-Pocasset JHS 100/7-9
PO Box 38 73004 405-224-4017
Jerime Parker, prin. Fax 224-5115

**Anadarko, Caddo, Pop. 6,230**
Anadarko ISD 2,000/PK-12
1400 S Mission St 73005 405-247-6605
Cindy Hackney, supt. Fax 247-6819
www.apswarriors.com
Anadarko HS 500/9-12
1400 Warrior Dr 73005 405-247-2486
Mike Sparks, prin. Fax 247-7066
Anadarko MS 400/6-8
900 W College St 73005 405-247-6671
Doug Hall, prin. Fax 247-3666

**Antlers, Pushmataha, Pop. 2,335**
Antlers ISD 1,000/K-12
219 NE A St 74523 580-298-5504
Cary Ammons, supt. Fax 298-4006
www.antlers.k12.ok.us
Antlers HS 300/9-12
219 NE A St 74523 580-298-2141
Bryan McNutt, prin. Fax 298-4019

Obuch MS 200/6-8
219 NE A St 74523 580-298-3308
William Neyman, prin. Fax 298-4012

OK Dept. of Voc. & Tech. Education
Supt. — None
Kiamichi Technology Center Vo/Tech
PO Box 70 74523 580-298-6354
Scott Garrett, dir. Fax 298-6412

**Apache, Caddo, Pop. 1,370**
Boone-Apache ISD 500/PK-12
PO Box 354 73006 580-588-3369
Don Schneberger, supt. Fax 588-3400
www.apache.k12.ok.us
Apache HS 100/9-12
PO Box 354 73006 580-588-3358
Todd Vail, prin. Fax 588-2079
Apache MS 100/6-8
PO Box 354 73006 580-588-2122
Steven Base, prin. Fax 588-3026

**Arapaho, Custer, Pop. 774**
Arapaho-Butler ISD 400/PK-12
PO Box 160 73620 580-323-3262
James Edelen, supt. Fax 323-5886
www.arapaho.k12.ok.us
Arapaho-Butler HS 100/9-12
PO Box 160 73620 580-323-3261
Ken Downs, prin. Fax 323-5886

**Ardmore, Carter, Pop. 22,734**
Ardmore ISD 3,100/PK-12
PO Box 1709 73402 580-223-2483
Sonny Bates, supt. Fax 226-2472
www.ardmoreschools.org
Ardmore HS 800/9-12
PO Box 1709 73402 580-226-7680
Jake Falvey, prin. Fax 221-3012
Ardmore MS 600/6-8
PO Box 1709 73402 580-223-2475
Cindy Huddleston, prin. Fax 221-3060

Dickson ISD 1,300/PK-12
4762 State Highway 199 73401 580-223-9557
Larry Case, supt. Fax 223-3624
www.dickson.k12.ok.us
Dickson HS 400/9-12
4762 State Highway 199 73401 580-226-0633
Rex Trent, prin. Fax 226-3974
Dickson MS 300/6-8
4762 State Highway 199 73401 580-223-2700
Matt Krimmer, prin. Fax 223-3972

Lone Grove ISD
Supt. — See Lone Grove
Lone Grove HS 400/9-12
6286 Meridian Rd 73401 580-657-3133
Chris Sudderth, prin. Fax 657-6624
Lone Grove MS 400/6-8
6362 Meridian Rd 73401 580-657-3132
Richie McKee, prin. Fax 657-2691

OK Dept. of Voc. & Tech. Education
Supt. — None
Southern Oklahoma Technology Center Vo/Tech
2610 Sam Noble Pkwy 73401 580-223-2070
Dr. David Powell, supt. Fax 223-2120

Plainview ISD 1,500/PK-12
1140 S Plainview Rd 73401 580-223-6319
Karl Stricker, supt. Fax 490-3190
www.plainview.k12.ok.us/
Plainview HS 400/9-12
1140 S Plainview Rd 73401 580-223-5877
Brian Nickel, prin. Fax 490-3191
Plainview MS 400/6-8
1140 S Plainview Rd 73401 580-223-6502
Tim Parham, prin. Fax 490-3192

---

Ardmore Adventist Academy 50/1-10
154 Beaver Academy Rd 73401 580-223-4948
Oklahoma State Horseshoeing School Post-Sec.
4802 Dogwood Rd 73401 580-223-0064

**Arkoma, LeFlore, Pop. 1,878**
Arkoma ISD 400/PK-12
PO Box 349 74901 918-875-3351
John Turner Ed.D., supt. Fax 875-3780
sites.google.com/site/arkomak12/
Arkoma JSHS 100/7-12
PO Box 349 74901 918-875-3353
Cyal Walden, prin. Fax 875-3780

**Arnett, Ellis, Pop. 514**
Arnett ISD 200/PK-12
PO Box 317 73832 580-885-7811
Danny Cochran, supt. Fax 885-7307
www.arnett.k12.ok.us/
Arnett HS 100/7-12
PO Box 317 73832 580-885-7285
Bob Dobrinski, prin. Fax 885-7922

**Asher, Pottawatomie, Pop. 357**
Asher ISD 200/PK-12
PO Box 168 74826 405-784-2332
Terry Grissom, supt. Fax 784-2306
www.asher.k12.ok.us
Asher HS 100/9-12
PO Box 168 74826 405-784-2331
Jeremy Frye, prin. Fax 784-2306

**Atoka, Atoka, Pop. 2,819**
Atoka ISD 900/PK-12
801 Greathouse Dr 74525 580-889-6611
Jay McAdams, supt. Fax 889-2513
atoka.org
Atoka HS 300/9-12
800 S Greathouse Dr 74525 580-889-3361
Jay McAdams, prin. Fax 889-6453

McCall MS 200/6-8
1003 W 11th St 74525 580-889-5640
Jay McAdams, prin. Fax 889-4064

OK Dept. of Voc. & Tech. Education
Supt. — None
Kiamichi Technology Center Vo/Tech
PO Box 240 74525 580-889-7321
Elaine Gee, dir. Fax 889-5642

Tushka ISD 500/PK-12
261 W Boggy Depot Rd 74525 580-889-7355
Bill Pingleton, supt. Fax 889-6144
www.tushka.k12.ok.us
Tushka HS 200/9-12
261 W Boggy Depot Rd 74525 580-889-7355
Matt Simpson, prin. Fax 889-6144

**Balko, Beaver**
Balko ISD, RR 1 Box 37 73931 200/PK-12
Larry Mills, supt. 580-646-3385
www.balko.k12.ok.us/
Balko HS, RR 1 Box 37 73931 50/9-12
Tammie Heathman, prin. 580-646-3385

**Barnsdall, Osage, Pop. 1,134**
Barnsdall ISD 400/PK-12
PO Box 629 74002 918-847-2271
Rick Loggins, supt. Fax 847-3029
www.barnsdallschools.org
Barnsdall HS, PO Box 629 74002 100/9-12
Sayra Bryant, prin. 918-847-2721
Barnsdall JHS, PO Box 629 74002 100/7-8
Sayra Bryant, prin. 918-847-2721

**Bartlesville, Washington, Pop. 33,922**
Bartlesville ISD 5,900/PK-12
PO Box 1357 74005 918-336-8600
Dr. Gary Quinn, supt. Fax 337-3643
www.bps-ok.org
Bartlesville Mid HS 900/9-10
5900 Baylor Dr 74006 918-333-4444
Jason Langham, prin. Fax 335-6311
Bartlesville SHS 800/11-12
1700 Hillcrest Dr 74003 918-336-3311
LaDonna Chancellor, prin. Fax 337-6226
Bruin Academy Alt
1700 Hillcrest Dr 74003 918-336-3311
Bill Wright, prin. Fax 337-6226
Central MS 600/6-8
408 E 9th St 74003 918-336-9302
Ryan Huff, prin. Fax 337-6270
Madison MS 600/6-8
500 S Madison Blvd 74006 918-333-3176
Joey Eidson, prin. Fax 335-6377

OK Dept. of Voc. & Tech. Education
Supt. — None
Tri-County Technology Center Vo/Tech
6101 Nowata Rd 74006 918-333-2422
Lindel Fields, supt. Fax 331-3274

---

Oklahoma Wesleyan University Post-Sec.
2201 Silver Lake Rd 74006 918-333-6151
Wesleyan Christian S 300/PK-12
1780 Silver Lake Rd 74006 918-333-8631
Rocky Clark, admin. Fax 333-8632

**Battiest, McCurtain**
Battiest ISD 300/PK-12
PO Box 199 74722 580-241-7810
Stace Ebert, supt. Fax 241-7847
www.battiest.k12.ok.us
Battiest HS 100/9-12
PO Box 199 74722 580-241-5550
Don Mullenix, prin. Fax 241-7847

**Beaver, Beaver, Pop. 1,494**
Beaver ISD 400/PK-12
PO Box 580 73932 580-625-3444
Scott Kinsey, supt. Fax 625-3690
www.beaver.k12.ok.us
Beaver HS 100/9-12
PO Box 580 73932 580-625-3444
Michael McVay, prin. Fax 625-3690

**Beggs, Okmulgee, Pop. 1,177**
Beggs ISD 1,000/PK-12
1201 W 9th St 74421 918-267-3628
Cindy Swearingen, supt. Fax 267-3635
www.beggs.k12.ok.us
Beggs HS 300/9-12
1201 W 9th St 74421 918-267-3625
Kristi Smith, prin. Fax 267-3624
Beggs MS 200/5-8
1201 W 9th St 74421 918-267-4916
Kenny Hurst, prin. Fax 267-4779

**Bennington, Bryan, Pop. 304**
Bennington ISD 300/PK-12
729 N Perry St 74723 580-847-2737
Pamela Reynolds, supt. Fax 847-2787
www.benningtonisd.org/
Bennington HS 100/9-12
729 N Perry St 74723 580-847-2310
Jon Shepard, prin. Fax 847-2787

**Bethany, Oklahoma, Pop. 18,252**
Bethany ISD 1,600/PK-12
6721 NW 42nd St 73008 405-789-3801
Dr. Kent Shellenberger, supt. Fax 499-4606
www.bethanyschools.com/
Bethany HS 500/9-12
6721 NW 42nd St 73008 405-789-6370
Dr. Don Wentroth, prin. Fax 499-4634
Bethany MS 400/6-8
6721 NW 42nd St 73008 405-787-3240
Matthew Flinton, prin. Fax 499-4606

Putnam City ISD
Supt. — See Oklahoma City
Western Oaks MS 700/6-8
7200 NW 23rd St 73008 405-789-4434
Meggan Wilson, prin. Fax 491-7616

---

Southern Nazarene University Post-Sec.
6729 NW 39th Expy 73008 405-789-6400
Southwestern Christian University Post-Sec.
PO Box 340 73008 405-789-7661

**Billings, Noble, Pop. 499**
Billings ISD 100/PK-12
PO Box 39 74630 580-725-3271
Rodney Vollmer, supt. Fax 725-3278
www.billings.k12.ok.us
Billings HS 50/9-12
PO Box 39 74630 580-725-3271
Rodney Vollmer, prin. Fax 725-3278

**Binger, Caddo, Pop. 635**
Binger-Oney ISD 300/PK-12
323 S Apache 73009 405-656-2304
Sharon Kniffin, supt. Fax 656-2267
www.binger-oney.k12.ok.us/
Binger-Oney HS 100/9-12
323 S Apache 73009 405-656-2304
Larry Milligan, prin. Fax 656-2267

**Bixby, Tulsa, Pop. 19,948**
Bixby ISD 4,800/PK-12
109 N Armstrong St 74008 918-366-2200
Dr. Kyle Wood, supt. Fax 366-4241
www.bixbyps.org
Bixby HS 1,300/10-12
109 N Armstrong St 74008 918-366-2234
Terry Adams, prin. Fax 366-2350
Bixby MS 800/7-8
109 N Armstrong St 74008 918-366-2201
Mike Lemon, prin. Fax 366-2337
9th Grade Center 9-9
109 N Armstrong St 74008 918-366-2200
Kate Creekmore, prin. Fax 366-4241

**Blackwell, Kay, Pop. 6,745**
Blackwell ISD 1,500/PK-12
201 E Blackwell Ave 74631 580-363-2570
Rick Riggs, supt. Fax 363-5513
www.blackwell.k12.ok.us
Blackwell HS 400/9-12
303 E Coolidge Ave 74631 580-363-3553
Jaylene Soulek, prin. Fax 363-2133
Blackwell MS 300/6-8
1041 S 1st St 74631 580-363-2100
Preston Kysar, prin. Fax 363-7010

**Blair, Jackson, Pop. 786**
Blair ISD 300/PK-12
PO Box 428 73526 580-563-2632
Jimmy Smith, supt. Fax 563-9166
www.blairschool.org
Blair HS 100/9-12
PO Box 428 73526 580-563-2486
Ronnie McKee, prin. Fax 563-9166

**Blanchard, McClain, Pop. 7,360**
Blanchard ISD 1,600/PK-12
211 N Tyler Ave 73010 405-485-3391
Dr. Jim Beckham, supt. Fax 485-2985
www.blanchard.k12.ok.us/
Blanchard HS 500/9-12
211 N Tyler Ave 73010 405-485-3392
Greg Jackson, prin. Fax 485-9549
Blanchard MS 300/6-8
211 N Tyler Ave 73010 405-485-3393
Larry McVay, prin. Fax 485-9103

Bridge Creek ISD 1,400/PK-12
2209 E Sooner Rd 73010 405-387-4880
David Morrow, supt. Fax 387-4882
www.bridgecreek.k12.ok.us/
Bridge Creek HS 400/9-12
2209 E Sooner Rd 73010 405-387-3981
K.B. Wedel, prin. Fax 387-2554
Bridge Creek MS 300/6-8
2209 E Sooner Rd 73010 405-387-9681
Kenneth Ward, prin. Fax 387-2552

**Bluejacket, Craig, Pop. 318**
Bluejacket ISD 200/PK-12
PO Box 29 74333 918-784-2365
Shellie Baker, supt. Fax 784-2130
www.bluejacket.k12.ok.us
Bluejacket HS 100/9-12
PO Box 29 74333 918-784-2133
Shellie Baker, prin. Fax 784-2130
Bluejacket MS, PO Box 29 74333 100/6-8
Tracy Mendez, prin. 918-784-2133

**Boise City, Cimarron, Pop. 1,253**
Boise City ISD 300/PK-12
PO Box 1116 73933 580-544-3110
Dr. Ira Harris, supt. Fax 544-2972
www.boisecity.k12.ok.us/
Boise City HS, PO Box 1115 73933 100/9-12
Cassie Graham, prin. 580-544-3111

**Bokchito, Bryan, Pop. 591**
Rock Creek ISD 400/PK-12
200 E Steakley St 74726 580-295-3137
Preston Burns, supt. Fax 295-3762
www.rockcreekisd.net
Rock Creek HS 100/9-12
200 E Steakley St 74726 580-295-3761
John Cartwright, prin. Fax 295-3854

**Bokoshe, LeFlore, Pop. 466**
Bokoshe ISD 200/PK-12
PO Box 158 74930 918-969-2341
Dennis Shoup, supt. Fax 969-2117
www.bokosheschools.org

Bokoshe HS 50/10-12
PO Box 158 74930 918-969-2341
John Speir, prin. Fax 969-2117
Bokoshe JHS 50/7-9
PO Box 158 74930 918-969-2341
John Speir, prin. Fax 969-2117

**Boswell, Choctaw, Pop. 659**
Boswell ISD 400/PK-12
PO Box 839 74727 580-566-2558
Keith Edge, supt. Fax 566-2265
www.boswellschools.org/
Boswell HS 100/9-12
PO Box 839 74727 580-566-2735
Rick Grimes, prin. Fax 566-2265
Boswell MS 50/7-8
PO Box 839 74727 580-566-2735
Rick Grimes, prin. Fax 566-2265

**Bowlegs, Seminole, Pop. 377**
Bowlegs ISD 300/PK-12
PO Box 88 74830 405-398-4172
Tommy Eaton, supt. Fax 398-4175
www.bowlegs.k12.ok.us
Bowlegs HS 100/9-12
PO Box 88 74830 405-398-4321
Sammye Davis, prin. Fax 398-4327

**Braggs, Muskogee, Pop. 242**
Braggs ISD 200/PK-12
PO Box 59 74423 918-487-5265
Michael Broyles, supt. Fax 487-7171
www.braggs.k12.ok.us
Braggs HS 100/9-12
PO Box 59 74423 918-487-5265
Shawndy Young, prin. Fax 487-7171

**Bristow, Creek, Pop. 3,811**
Bristow ISD 1,700/PK-12
420 N Main St 74010 918-367-5555
Curtis Shelton, supt. Fax 367-5848
www.bristow.k12.ok.us
Bristow HS 500/9-12
420 N Main St 74010 918-367-2241
Brandon Poteet, prin. Fax 367-5849
Bristow MS 400/6-8
420 N Main St 74010 918-367-3551
Brian Burden, prin. Fax 367-1362

**Broken Arrow, Tulsa, Pop. 94,005**
Broken Arrow ISD 13,200/PK-12
701 S Main St 74012 918-259-5700
Jarod Mendenhall Ed.D., supt. Fax 258-0399
www.baschools.org/
Broken Arrow Academy Alt
637 E College St 74012 918-259-4600
Jack Pugh, prin. Fax 258-7531
Broken Arrow Freshman Academy 500/9-9
301 W New Orleans St 74011 918-259-4330
Margaret Coates, prin. Fax 451-1964
Broken Arrow SHS 2,200/10-12
1901 E Albany St 74012 918-259-4310
Elizabeth Burns, prin. Fax 355-3676
Centennial MS 1,000/6-8
225 E Omaha St 74012 918-259-4340
Kenny Kinzer, prin. Fax 251-8347
Childers MS 600/6-8
301 E Tucson St 74011 918-259-4350
Stacy Replogle, prin. Fax 451-5465
Oliver MS 800/6-8
3100 W New Orleans St 74011 918-259-4590
Jill Whitaker, prin. Fax 250-8185
Oneta Ridge MS 6-8
6800 E Quincy Pl 74014 918-259-4360
Mickey Replogle, prin. Fax 251-8685
Sequoyah MS 500/6-8
2701 S Elm Pl 74012 918-259-4370
Beth Gilbert, prin. Fax 451-2167

OK Dept. of Voc. & Tech. Education
Supt. — None
Tulsa Tech Center Broken Arrow Campus Vo/Tech
4000 W Florence St 74011 918-828-3000
Brad Wayman, dir. Fax 828-3009

Union ISD
Supt. — See Tulsa
Union 9th Grade Center 1,100/9-9
7616 S Garnett Rd 74012 918-357-4324
John Federline, prin. Fax 357-7696
Union Eighth Grade Center 1,100/8-8
6501 S Garnett Rd 74012 918-357-4325
Marla Robinson, prin. Fax 357-7899

---

Broken Arrow Beauty College Post-Sec.
400 S Elm Pl 74012 918-251-9660
Immanuel Lutheran Christian Academy 100/K-12
400 N Aspen Ave 74012 918-251-5422
Katherine McGrew, hdmstr. Fax 251-8365
Summit Christian Academy 500/K-12
200 E Broadway St 74012 918-251-1997
Dan Giddens, supt. Fax 251-2831

**Broken Bow, McCurtain, Pop. 3,865**
Broken Bow ISD 1,700/PK-12
108 W 5th St 74728 580-584-3306
Carla Ellisor, supt. Fax 584-9482
www.bbisd.org
Broken Bow HS 600/9-12
108 W 5th St 74728 580-584-3365
Rod Davis, prin. Fax 584-2064
Rector Johnson MS 400/6-8
108 W 5th St 74728 580-584-9603
Belinda Highful, prin. Fax 584-2549

**Buffalo, Harper, Pop. 1,288**
Buffalo ISD 100/K-12
PO Box 130 73834 580-735-2448
Martin Adams, supt. Fax 735-2619
www.buffalo.k12.ok.us
Buffalo S 100/K-12
PO Box 130 73834 580-735-2448
Kenneth Horn, prin. Fax 735-2619

**Bunch, Adair**
Cave Springs ISD 100/PK-12
PO Box 200 74931 918-775-2364
Geary Brown, supt. Fax 776-2052
www.cavesprings.k12.ok.us
Cave Springs HS, PO Box 200 74931 100/9-12
Geary Brown, prin. 918-776-2050

**Burlington, Alfalfa, Pop. 145**
Burlington ISD 200/PK-12
PO Box 17 73722 580-431-2501
Glen Elliott, supt. Fax 431-2237
www.burlingtonschool.com/
Burlington HS 100/9-12
PO Box 17 73722 580-431-2222
Shane Feely, prin. Fax 431-2237

**Burneyville, Love**
Turner ISD 300/PK-12
PO Box 159 73430 580-276-1307
Jerry Garrett, supt. Fax 276-2006
www.turnerisd.org
Turner HS 100/9-12
PO Box 159 73430 580-276-3873
Burl Solie, prin. Fax 276-2493

**Burns Flat, Washita, Pop. 1,998**
Burns Flat-Dill City ISD 700/PK-12
PO Box 129 73624 580-562-4844
Ron Hughes, supt. Fax 562-4847
www.bfdc.k12.ok.us
Burns Flat-Dill City HS 100/9-12
PO Box 129 73624 580-562-4846
Cliff McCown, prin.

OK Dept. of Voc. & Tech. Education
Supt. — None
Western Technology Center Vo/Tech
PO Box 1469 73624 580-562-3181
Hoyt Lewis, supt. Fax 562-4476

**Cache, Comanche, Pop. 2,626**
Cache ISD 1,400/PK-12
102 E H Ave 73527 580-429-3266
Randy Batt, supt. Fax 429-3271
www.cacheps.org
Cache HS, 102 E H Ave 73527 500/9-12
Corey Holland, prin. 580-429-3214
Cache MS, 102 E H Ave 73527 300/7-8
Mitch Ange, prin. 580-429-8489

**Caddo, Bryan, Pop. 914**
Caddo ISD 500/PK-12
PO Box 128 74729 580-367-2208
Richard Thomas, supt. Fax 367-2837
www.caddoisd.org
Caddo HS 100/9-12
PO Box 128 74729 580-367-2208
J.T. Busby, prin. Fax 367-2837

**Calera, Bryan, Pop. 1,972**
Calera ISD 700/PK-12
PO Box 386 74730 580-434-5700
Gerald Parks, supt. Fax 434-5800
www.caleraisd.k12.ok.us
Calera HS 200/9-12
PO Box 386 74730 580-434-5158
Kevin Robinson, prin. Fax 434-7842

**Calumet, Canadian, Pop. 484**
Calumet ISD 300/PK-12
PO Box 10 73014 405-893-2222
Keith Weldon, supt. Fax 893-8019
www.chs.k12.ok.us
Calumet HS 100/9-12
PO Box 10 73014 405-893-2222
Chuck Hood, prin. Fax 893-8019
Calumet JHS 50/7-8
PO Box 10 73014 405-893-2222
Chuck Hood, prin. Fax 893-8019

**Calvin, Hughes, Pop. 277**
Calvin ISD 200/PK-12
PO Box 127 74531 405-645-2411
Chris Karch, supt. Fax 645-2384
www.calvin.k12.ok.us
Calvin HS 50/9-12
PO Box 127 74531 405-645-2411
Larry Marlow, prin. Fax 645-2384

**Cameron, LeFlore, Pop. 274**
Cameron ISD 300/PK-12
PO Box 190 74932 918-654-3225
Jim Caughern, supt. Fax 654-7387
www.cameron.k12.ok.us
Cameron HS 100/9-12
PO Box 190 74932 918-654-3224
Jose Obregon, prin. Fax 654-3826

**Canadian, Pittsburg, Pop. 206**
Canadian ISD 400/PK-12
PO Box 168 74425 918-339-7251
Rodney Karch, supt. Fax 339-2393
www.canadian.k12.ok.us
Canadian HS 100/9-12
PO Box 168 74425 918-339-2705
Bud Rattan, prin. Fax 339-2393

**Caney, Atoka, Pop. 176**
Caney ISD 300/PK-12
PO Box 60 74533 580-889-1996
Lori Boehme, supt. Fax 889-5033
www.caneyisd.org
Caney HS 100/9-12
PO Box 60 74533 580-889-6607
Matt Brister, prin. Fax 889-7922

**Canton, Blaine, Pop. 594**
Canton ISD 400/PK-12
PO Box 639 73724 580-886-3516
Carl Baker, supt. Fax 886-3501
www.canton.k12.ok.us
Canton HS 100/9-12
PO Box 639 73724 580-886-2256
Marcus Chapman, prin. Fax 886-2306

**Canute, Washita, Pop. 537**
Canute ISD 400/PK-12
PO Box 490 73626 580-472-3295
Larry Parrish, supt. Fax 472-3187
www.canutepublicschool.com
Canute HS 100/9-12
PO Box 490 73626 580-472-3295
Kevin Merz, prin. Fax 472-3187

**Carnegie, Caddo, Pop. 1,645**
Carnegie ISD 600/PK-12
330 W Wildcat Dr 73015 580-654-1470
Mark Batt, supt. Fax 654-1644
www.carnegie.k12.ok.us
Carnegie HS 100/9-12
330 W Wildcat Dr 73015 580-654-1266
Jerry Hulme, prin. Fax 654-2772
Carnegie MS 100/6-8
330 W Wildcat Dr 73015 580-654-1766
Jane Nix, prin. Fax 654-2281

**Carney, Lincoln, Pop. 589**
Carney ISD 200/PK-12
PO Box 240 74832 405-865-2344
Dewayne Osborn, supt. Fax 865-2345
www.carney.k12.ok.us/
Carney HS, PO Box 240 74832 100/9-12
Sandra Butler, prin. 405-865-2344

**Cashion, Logan, Pop. 779**
Cashion ISD 500/PK-12
101 N Euclid Ave 73016 405-433-2741
Sammy Jackson, supt. Fax 433-2646
www.cashionps.org
Cashion HS 100/9-12
101 N Euclid Ave 73016 405-433-2575
Ryan Schenk, prin. Fax 433-2646

**Catoosa, Rogers, Pop. 6,601**
Catoosa SD 2,200/PK-12
2000 S Cherokee St 74015 918-266-8603
Rick Kibbe, supt. Fax 266-8647
www.catoosaps.net/
Catoosa HS 700/9-12
2000 S Cherokee St 74015 918-266-8619
Darren Peaster, prin. Fax 266-1486
Wells MS 500/6-8
2000 S Cherokee St 74015 918-266-8623
Della Parrish, prin. Fax 266-1282

**Cement, Caddo, Pop. 491**
Cement ISD 200/PK-12
PO Box 60 73017 405-489-3216
Daniel Pittman, supt. Fax 489-3219
www.cement.k12.ok.us
Cement HS 100/9-12
PO Box 60 73017 405-489-3216
Steve Pelzer, prin. Fax 489-3219

**Chandler, Lincoln, Pop. 2,922**
Chandler ISD 1,100/PK-12
901 S CHS 74834 405-258-1450
Wayland Kimble, supt. Fax 258-2657
www.chandler.k12.ok.us
Chandler HS 300/9-12
901 S CHS 74834 405-258-1269
Randy Hedge, prin. Fax 258-0071
Chandler JHS 200/7-8
901 S CHS 74834 405-258-0183
Kent Barton, prin. Fax 258-1850

**Chattanooga, Comanche, Pop. 452**
Chattanooga ISD 300/PK-12
PO Box 129 73528 580-597-3347
Jerry Brown, supt. Fax 597-3344
www.chatty.k12.ok.us/
Chattanooga HS 100/9-12
PO Box 129 73528 580-597-3347
James Higdon, prin. Fax 597-3344

**Checotah, McIntosh, Pop. 3,060**
Checotah ISD 1,600/PK-12
PO Box 289 74426 918-473-5610
Janet Blocker, supt. Fax 473-1020
www.checotah.k12.ok.us/
Checotah HS 500/9-12
PO Box 289 74426 918-473-9100
Brian Terry, prin. Fax 473-7174
Checotah MS 400/6-8
PO Box 289 74426 918-473-2239
Jason Donathan, prin. Fax 473-2532

**Chelsea, Rogers, Pop. 1,729**
Chelsea ISD 700/PK-12
401 Redbud Ln 74016 918-789-2528
Rich McSpadden, supt. Fax 789-3271
www.chelseadragons.net
Chelsea HS, 401 Redbud Ln 74016 300/9-12
Howard Hill, prin. 918-789-2533
Chelsea MS, 401 Redbud Ln 74016 200/6-8
Debbie Hoskins, prin. 918-789-2521

**Cherokee, Alfalfa, Pop. 1,474**
Cherokee ISD 300/PK-12
PO Box 325 73728 580-596-3391
Donna Anderson, supt. Fax 596-2319
www.cherokee.k12.ok.us
Cherokee HS 100/9-12
PO Box 325 73728 580-596-3391
Jeremy Hickman, prin. Fax 596-2319

**Cheyenne, Roger Mills, Pop. 783**
Cheyenne ISD 300/PK-12
PO Box 650 73628 580-497-3371
Rick Garrison, supt. Fax 497-3373
www.cheyenne.k12.ok.us
Cheyenne HS 100/9-12
PO Box 650 73628 580-497-3371
Whitney Moore, prin. Fax 497-3373

**Chickasha, Grady, Pop. 15,287**
Chickasha ISD 1,900/PK-12
900 W Choctaw Ave 73018 405-222-6500
David Cash, supt. Fax 222-6590
www.chickasha.k12.ok.us/
Chickasha HS 700/9-12
900 W Choctaw Ave 73018 405-222-6550
Steven Couch, prin. Fax 222-6558
Chickasha MS 300/7-8
900 W Choctaw Ave 73018 405-222-6530
Dan Turner, prin. Fax 222-6594

OK Dept. of Voc. & Tech. Education
Supt. — None
Canadian Valley Technology Center Vo/Tech
1401 W Michigan Ave 73018 405-224-7220
Tracy Goyne, dir. Fax 222-3839

Academy of Cosmetology Post-Sec.
607 W Grand Ave 73018 405-222-2323
Caraway Christian S K-12
730 County Road 1330 73018 405-224-1998
University of Sciences & Arts of OK Post-Sec.
1727 W Alabama Ave 73018 405-224-3140

**Choctaw, Oklahoma, Pop. 10,497**
Choctaw-Nicoma Park ISD 5,200/PK-12
12880 NE 10th St 73020 405-769-4859
Dr. Jim McCharen, supt. Fax 769-9821
www.cnpschools.org
Choctaw HS 1,500/9-12
14300 NE 10th St 73020 405-390-8899
David Reid, prin. Fax 390-2275
Choctaw MS 600/6-8
14667 NE 3rd St 73020 405-390-2207
JeanAnn Gaona, prin. Fax 390-4439
Nicoma Park MS 500/6-8
1321 Hickman Ave 73020 405-769-3106
Brent Ingraham, prin. Fax 769-9355

OK Dept. of Voc. & Tech. Education
Supt. — None
Eastern Oklahoma County Technology Ctr Vo/Tech
4601 N Choctaw Rd 73020 405-390-9591
Dr. Terry Underwood, supt. Fax 390-9598

Life Christian Academy 200/PK-12
3200 N Choctaw Rd 73020 405-390-5081
Rodney Burchett, admin. Fax 390-5086

**Chouteau, Mayes, Pop. 1,930**
Chouteau-Mazie ISD 900/PK-12
PO Box 969 74337 918-476-8376
Kenny Mason, supt. Fax 476-8538
www.chouteauwildcats.com
Chouteau-Mazie HS 200/9-12
PO Box 969 74337 918-476-8337
Glen Bibelheimer, prin. Fax 476-8372
Chouteau-Mazie MS 200/6-8
PO Box 969 74337 918-476-8337
Michelle Middleton, prin. Fax 476-8306

**Claremore, Rogers, Pop. 17,084**
Claremore ISD 3,700/PK-12
102 W 10th St 74017 918-923-4200
Mike McClaren, supt. Fax 341-8447
www.claremore.k12.ok.us
Claremore HS 1,300/9-12
201 E Stuart Roosa Dr 74017 918-923-4211
Todd Steidley, prin. Fax 343-6331
Rogers JHS 900/6-8
1915 N Florence Ave 74017 918-923-4205
Lindsey Schnoebelen, prin. Fax 343-6332

Justus-Tiawah SD 600/PK-8
14902 E School Rd, 918-341-3626
David Garroutte, supt. Fax 341-4920
www.justustiawah.com
Justus-Tiawah JHS North Campus 100/7-8
14902 E School Rd, 918-341-1252
David Garroutte, prin. Fax 341-4920

OK Dept. of Voc. & Tech. Education
Supt. — None
Northeast Technology Center - Claremore Vo/Tech
1901 N Highway 88 74017 918-342-8066
Rick Reimer, supt. Fax 342-9066

Sequoyah ISD 1,200/PK-12
16441 S 4180 Rd 74017 918-341-5472
Terry Saul, supt. Fax 341-5764
www.sequoyaheagles.net
Sequoyah HS 200/11-12
16401 S 4180 Rd 74017 918-341-0642
Steve Johnson, prin. Fax 343-8105
Sequoyah MS 300/6-8
16403 S 4180 Rd 74017 918-343-5105
Barry Bulman, prin. Fax 343-8109
Sequoyah Mid HS 100/9-10
16405 S 4180 Rd 74017 918-341-5537
Josh Berg, prin. Fax 343-8102

Verdigris ISD 800/PK-12
26501 S 4110 Rd, 918-266-7227
Michael Payne, supt. Fax 266-3910
vps.k12.ok.us
Verdigris JSHS 400/7-12
26501 S 4110 Rd, 918-266-2336
Greg Kelley, prin. Fax 266-0546

Claremore Beauty College Post-Sec.
200 N Cherokee Ave 74017 918-341-4370
Claremore Christian S 100/PK-12
1055 W Blue Starr Dr 74017 918-341-1765
Ryan Mullins, prin. Fax 341-1011
Rogers State University Post-Sec.
1701 W Will Rogers Blvd 74017 918-343-7777

**Clayton, Pushmataha, Pop. 740**
Clayton ISD 300/PK-12
PO Box 190 74536 918-569-4492
Randall Erwin, supt. Fax 569-7757
www.clayton.k12.ok.us/
Clayton HS 100/9-12
PO Box 190 74536 918-569-4156
Keith Milligan, prin. Fax 569-4680

**Cleveland, Pawnee, Pop. 3,054**
Cleveland ISD 1,700/PK-12
600 N Gilbert Ave 74020 918-358-2210
Aaron Espolt, supt. Fax 358-3071
www.clevelandtigers.com/
Cleveland HS 500/9-12
323 N Gilbert Ave 74020 918-358-2210
Dr. Alan Baker, prin. Fax 358-2141
Cleveland MS 400/6-8
322 N Gilbert Ave 74020 918-358-2210
Noel Nation, prin. Fax 358-2534

**Clinton, Custer, Pop. 8,804**
Clinton ISD 2,200/PK-12
PO Box 729 73601 580-323-1800
Kevin Hime, supt. Fax 323-1804
www.clintonokschools.org/
Clinton HS 500/9-12
PO Box 729 73601 580-323-1230
Kenny Stringer, prin. Fax 323-1236
Clinton MS 300/7-8
PO Box 729 73601 580-323-4228
Mark Moring, prin. Fax 323-3896

**Coalgate, Coal, Pop. 1,800**
Coalgate SD 700/PK-12
2 W Cedar Ave 74538 580-927-2351
Jim Girten, supt. Fax 927-2694
www.coalgateschools.org
Byrd MS 100/7-8
2 W Cedar Ave 74538 580-927-3560
Phillip Wilkinson, prin. Fax 927-4031
Coalgate HS 300/9-12
2 W Cedar Ave 74538 580-927-2592
Kris Hall, prin. Fax 927-4020

**Colbert, Bryan, Pop. 1,037**
Colbert ISD 900/PK-12
PO Box 310 74733 580-296-2624
Jarvis Dobbs, supt. Fax 296-2219
www.colbert.k12.ok.us/
Colbert HS 200/9-12
PO Box 310 74733 580-296-2590
Gary Walton, prin. Fax 296-2219
Colbert MS 100/7-8
PO Box 310 74733 580-296-2590
Gary Walton, prin. Fax 296-2219

**Colcord, Delaware, Pop. 719**
Colcord ISD 600/PK-12
433 S Larmon 74338 918-326-4116
Bud Simmons, supt. Fax 326-4471
www.colcordschools.com
Colcord HS 200/9-12
433 S Larmon 74338 918-326-4107
Jerry Swank, prin. Fax 326-0035
Colcord MS 100/6-8
433 S Larmon 74338 918-326-4852
Sandy Shackelford, prin. Fax 326-4468

**Coleman, Johnston**
Coleman ISD 200/PK-12
PO Box 188 73432 580-937-4418
James Miller, supt. Fax 937-4866
www.colemanschools.org
Coleman HS 100/9-12
PO Box 188 73432 580-937-4418
Delane Jackson, prin. Fax 937-4866

**Collinsville, Tulsa, Pop. 5,212**
Collinsville ISD 2,600/PK-12
1092 W Maple St 74021 918-371-2386
Lance West, supt. Fax 371-4285
www.collinsville.k12.ok.us
Collinsville HS 700/9-12
2400 W Broadway St 74021 918-371-3382
Jon Coleman, prin. Fax 371-6904
Collinsville MS 600/7-8
1415 W Center St 74021 918-371-2541
Dale Harp, prin. Fax 371-1302

**Comanche, Stephens, Pop. 1,590**
Comanche ISD 1,000/K-12
1030 Ash Ave 73529 580-439-2900
Terry Davidson, supt. Fax 439-2907
www.cpsok.org
Comanche HS 300/9-12
1030 Ash Ave 73529 580-439-2933
Steven Dunham, prin. Fax 439-2950
Comanche MS 200/6-8
1030 Ash Ave 73529 580-439-2922
Brent Crow, prin. Fax 439-2979

**Commerce, Ottawa, Pop. 2,364**
Commerce ISD 900/PK-12
217 Commerce St 74339 918-675-4316
Jimmy R. Haynes, supt. Fax 675-4464
www.commercetigers.net
Commerce HS 200/9-12
420 Doug Furnas Blvd 74339 918-675-4343
Jim Buttram, prin. Fax 675-4682
Commerce MS 200/6-8
500 Commerce St 74339 918-675-4101
Jack Kelley, prin. Fax 675-5353

**Copan, Washington, Pop. 683**
Copan ISD 200/PK-12
PO Box 429 74022 918-532-4344
Rick Ruckman, supt. Fax 532-4649
www.copan.k12.ok.us/
Copan HS 100/9-12
PO Box 429 74022 918-532-4344
Chris Tanner, prin. Fax 532-4649

**Cordell, Washita, Pop. 2,865**
Cordell ISD 800/PK-12
PO Box 290 73632 580-832-3420
Brad Overton, supt. Fax 832-1090
www.cordell.k12.ok.us
Cordell JHS 200/7-9
PO Box 290 73632 580-832-3420
Larry Johnson, prin. Fax 832-1091
Cordell SHS 100/10-12
PO Box 290 73632 580-832-3420
Larry Johnson, prin. Fax 832-1091

**Corn, Washita, Pop. 497**

Corn Bible Academy 100/7-12
PO Box 38 73024 580-343-2262
Mark Thiessen, prin. Fax 343-2261

**Council Hill, Muskogee, Pop. 140**
Midway ISD 200/PK-12
PO Box 127 74428 918-474-3434
Bruce Douglas, supt. Fax 474-3636
www.midway.k12.ok.us
Midway HS 100/9-12
PO Box 127 74428 918-474-3434
Bruce Douglas, prin. Fax 474-3900

**Covington, Garfield, Pop. 512**
Covington-Douglas ISD 300/PK-12
400 E Main St 73730 580-864-7481
Darren Sharp, supt. Fax 864-7644
www.c-d.k12.ok.us
Covington-Douglas HS 100/9-12
400 E Main St 73730 580-864-7482
Brian Smith, prin. Fax 864-7644

**Coweta, Wagoner, Pop. 9,182**
Coweta ISD 3,300/PK-12
PO Box 550 74429 918-486-6506
Jeff Holmes, supt. Fax 486-4167
www.cowetaps.com/
Coweta Intermediate HS 300/9-9
PO Box 550 74429 918-486-6103
Leslie Frazier, prin.
Coweta JHS 500/7-8
PO Box 550 74429 918-486-2127
Scott Kempenich, prin. Fax 486-7307
Coweta SHS 700/10-12
PO Box 550 74429 918-486-4474
Gary Ellis, prin. Fax 486-1062

**Coyle, Logan, Pop. 317**
Coyle ISD 300/PK-12
PO Box 287 73027 405-466-2242
Josh Sumrall M.Ed., supt. Fax 466-2448
www.coyle.k12.ok.us
Coyle HS 100/9-12
PO Box 287 73027 405-466-2242
Patrick Smith, prin. Fax 466-2448

**Crescent, Logan, Pop. 1,340**
Crescent ISD 600/PK-12
PO Box 719 73028 405-969-3738
H.T. Gee, supt. Fax 969-2003
www.crescentok.com/
Crescent HS 200/9-12
PO Box 719 73028 405-969-2545
Bart Watkins, prin. Fax 969-2003
Crescent MS 100/6-8
PO Box 719 73028 405-969-2227
Mickey Hart, prin. Fax 969-2003

**Cromwell, Seminole, Pop. 270**
Butner ISD 200/PK-12
PO Box 157 74837 405-944-5530
Melissa Walden, supt. Fax 944-5746
Butner HS 100/9-12
PO Box 157 74837 405-944-5526
Melissa Walden, prin. Fax 944-5746

**Crowder, Pittsburg, Pop. 420**
Crowder ISD 500/PK-12
PO Box B 74430 918-334-3203
Robert Florenzano, supt. Fax 334-3295
www.crowder.k12.ok.us
Crowder HS, PO Box B 74430 200/9-12
Preston James, prin. 918-334-3204

**Cushing, Payne, Pop. 7,369**
Cushing ISD 1,800/PK-12
PO Box 1609 74023 918-225-3425
Koln Knight, supt. Fax 225-5256
cushing.k12.ok.us
Cushing HS 500/9-12
1700 E Walnut St 74023 918-225-6622
James Lauerman, prin. Fax 225-0933
Cushing MS 5-8
521 S Harmony Rd 74023 918-225-1311
Pat Elder, prin.

**Cyril, Caddo, Pop. 1,013**
Cyril ISD 300/PK-12
PO Box 449 73029 580-464-2272
Jamie Mitchell, supt. Fax 464-2445
www.cyrilschools.org
Cyril HS 100/7-12
PO Box 449 73029 580-464-2272
Tim Persinger, prin. Fax 464-2445

**Dale, Pottawatomie, Pop. 176**
Dale ISD 700/PK-12
300 Smith Ave 74851 405-964-5558
Charles Dickinson, supt. Fax 964-5559
www.dale.k12.ok.us
Dale HS 200/9-12
300 Smith Ave 74851 405-964-5555
Ky Wilkins, prin. Fax 964-5539
Dale MS, 300 Smith Ave 74851 200/6-8
Ky Wilkins, prin. 405-964-2799

**Davenport, Lincoln, Pop. 781**
Davenport ISD 400/PK-12
PO Box 849 74026 918-377-2277
Daniel Acord, supt. Fax 377-2553
www.davenport.k12.ok.us/
Davenport HS 100/9-12
PO Box 849 74026 918-377-2278
Daniel Acord, admin. Fax 377-4001

**Davidson, Tillman, Pop. 307**
Davidson ISD 100/PK-12
PO Box 338 73530 580-568-2423
Phillip Ratcliff, supt. Fax 568-2219
www.davidson.k12.ok.us/
Davidson HS 50/9-12
PO Box 338 73530 580-568-2261
Phillip Ratcliff, prin. Fax 568-2219

**Davis, Murray, Pop. 2,557**
Davis ISD 1,100/PK-12
400 E Atlanta Ave 73030 580-369-2386
Mike Martin, supt. Fax 369-3507
www.daviswolves.org
Davis HS 300/9-12
400 E Atlanta Ave 73030 580-369-5541
Rod Maynard, prin. Fax 369-3071
Davis MS 300/5-8
400 E Atlanta Ave 73030 580-369-5565
Jeff Jennings, prin. Fax 369-3289

**Del City, Oklahoma, Pop. 19,870**
Midwest City-Del City ISD
Supt. — See Midwest City
Del City SHS 1,300/9-12
1900 S Sunnylane Rd 73115 405-677-5777
Gina Hill, prin. Fax 671-8675
Del Crest MS 500/6-8
4731 Judy Dr 73115 405-671-8615
Scott Perry, prin. Fax 671-8618
Kerr MS 700/6-8
2300 Linda Ln 73115 405-671-8625
Rob Cherry, prin. Fax 671-8626

---

Christian Heritage Academy 600/PK-12
4400 SE 27th St 73115 405-672-1787
Josh Bullard, hdmstr. Fax 672-1839
Destiny Christian S 500/PK-12
3801 SE 29th St 73115 405-677-6000
Jim Howard, admin. Fax 677-6066

**Depew, Creek, Pop. 440**
Depew ISD 400/PK-12
PO Box 257 74028 918-324-5466
Leon Hiett, supt. Fax 324-5336
depew.k12.ok.us
Depew HS 100/9-12
PO Box 257 74028 918-324-5543
Tony Martin, prin. Fax 324-5336

**Dewar, Okmulgee, Pop. 790**
Dewar ISD 400/PK-12
PO Box 790 74431 918-652-9625
Todd Been, supt. Fax 652-3096
www.dewar.k12.ok.us/
Dewar HS 100/9-12
PO Box 790 74431 918-652-9625
Josh Kilhoffer, prin. Fax 652-3096
Dewar MS 100/6-8
PO Box 790 74431 918-652-9625
Josh Kilhoffer, prin. Fax 652-3096

**Dewey, Washington, Pop. 3,212**
Dewey ISD 1,200/PK-12
1 Bulldogger Rd 74029 918-534-2241
Dr. David Wilkins, supt. Fax 534-0149
www.deweyk12.org
Dewey HS, 1 Bulldogger Rd 74029 400/9-12
Brent Dugger, prin. 918-534-0933
Dewey MS, 1 Bulldogger Rd 74029 300/6-8
Brent Massey, prin. 918-534-0111

**Dibble, McClain, Pop. 838**
Dibble ISD 700/PK-12
PO Box 9 73031 405-344-6375
Chad Clanton, supt. Fax 344-6977
dibble.k12.ok.us
Dibble HS, PO Box 9 73031 200/9-12
Damon Garner, prin. 405-344-6380
Dibble MS 200/6-8
PO Box 9 73031 405-344-6380
Darlene Hayhurst, prin. Fax 344-7275

**Dover, Kingfisher, Pop. 461**
Dover ISD 200/PK-12
PO Box 195 73734 405-828-4206
Shannon Grimes, supt. Fax 828-7150
www.dover.k12.ok.us
Dover HS 100/9-12
PO Box 195 73734 405-828-4204
Shannon Grimes, prin. Fax 828-8019

**Drummond, Garfield, Pop. 444**
Drummond ISD 300/PK-12
PO Box 240 73735 580-493-2216
Mike Woods, supt. Fax 493-2273
www.drummond.k12.ok.us/
Drummond HS, PO Box 240 73735 100/9-12
Greg Kokojan, prin. 580-493-2271

**Drumright, Creek, Pop. 2,673**
Drumright ISD 600/PK-12
505 W 2nd St 74030 918-352-2492
Robbie Dorsey, supt. Fax 352-4430
www.drumright.k12.ok.us/
Cooper MS 100/6-8
510 S Skinner Ave 74030 918-352-2318
Kevin Bilyeu, prin. Fax 352-4033
Drumright HS 200/9-12
301 S Pennsylvania Ave 74030 918-352-2152
Judd Matthes, prin. Fax 352-9845

OK Dept. of Voc. & Tech. Education
Supt. — None
Central Tech Vo/Tech
3 Central Tech Cir 74030 918-352-2551
Fax 352-4117

Olive ISD 400/PK-12
9352 S 436th West Ave 74030 918-352-9567
Jimmy Reynolds, supt. Fax 352-4379
www.olive.k12.ok.us
Olive HS 100/9-12
9352 S 436th West Ave 74030 918-352-9568
Jeremy McKenny, dean Fax 352-4379

**Duke, Jackson, Pop. 417**
Duke ISD 200/PK-12
PO Box 160 73532 580-679-3014
Kevin Brown, supt. Fax 679-3017
www.dukeschools.com/
Duke HS, PO Box 160 73532 50/9-12
Heath Selcer, prin. 580-679-3311

**Duncan, Stephens, Pop. 22,474**
Duncan ISD 3,800/PK-12
PO Box 1548 73534 580-255-0686
Glenda Cobb, supt. Fax 252-2453
www.duncanps.org
Duncan HS 1,000/9-12
PO Box 1548 73534 580-255-0700
Justin Smith, prin. Fax 252-2445
Duncan MS 900/6-8
PO Box 1548 73534 580-470-8106
Dewey Ivey, prin. Fax 470-8743
Edge Academy Alt
PO Box 1548 73534 580-252-2403
Carol Phipps, prin. Fax 252-3515

Empire SD 400/PK-12
276803 E 1760 Rd 73533 580-252-5392
Vicki Davison, supt. Fax 252-4231
www.empireschools.org
Empire JSHS 100/7-12
276803 E 1760 Rd 73533 580-255-7515
Jodie Roberts, prin. Fax 255-2971

OK Dept. of Voc. & Tech. Education
Supt. — None
Red River Technology Center Vo/Tech
PO Box 1807 73534 580-255-2903
Dennis Loafman, supt. Fax 255-5652

---

Eve's College of Hairstyling Post-Sec.
PO Box 1545 73534 580-355-6620

**Durant, Bryan, Pop. 14,924**
Durant ISD 3,500/PK-12
1323 Waco St 74701 580-924-1276
Duane Merideth, supt. Fax 924-6019
www.durantisd.org
Durant HS 900/9-12
950 Gerlach Dr 74701 580-924-4424
Cheryl Conditt, prin. Fax 924-3642
Durant MS 500/7-8
802 W Walnut St 74701 580-924-1321
Kenny Chaffin, prin. Fax 924-8278

OK Dept. of Voc. & Tech. Education
Supt. — None
Kiamichi Technology Center Vo/Tech
810 Waldron Dr 74701 580-924-7081
Mike Goodwin, dir. Fax 924-2790

Silo ISD 800/PK-12
122 W Bourne St 74701 580-924-7000
Donna Anderson, supt. Fax 920-7988
www.siloisd.org
Silo HS 200/9-12
122 W Bourne St 74701 580-924-7000
Jeremy Atwood, prin. Fax 924-7045
Silo JHS 100/7-8
122 W Bourne St 74701 580-924-7000
Mike Lawless, prin. Fax 924-7045

---

Southeastern Oklahoma State University Post-Sec.
1405 N 4th Ave 74701 580-745-2000
Southern School of Beauty Post-Sec.
140 W Main St 74701 580-924-1049
Victory Life Academy 100/K-12
3412 W University Blvd 74701 580-920-0850
Sarah Morrison M.Ed., hdmstr. Fax 920-9923

**Eagletown, McCurtain, Pop. 515**
Eagletown ISD 100/PK-12
PO Box 38 74734 580-835-2242
Brian Armstrong, supt. Fax 835-7420
www.eagletownisd.org
Eagletown HS 100/9-12
PO Box 38 74734 580-835-2242
Brian Armstrong, prin. Fax 835-7420

**Earlsboro, Pottawatomie, Pop. 569**
Earlsboro ISD 200/PK-12
PO Box 10 74840 405-997-5616
Mark Maloy, supt. Fax 997-3181
www.earlsboro.k12.ok.us
Earlsboro HS 100/9-12
PO Box 10 74840 405-997-5252
Mark Maloy, prin. Fax 997-3181

**Edmond, Oklahoma, Pop. 78,271**
Deer Creek ISD 3,600/PK-12
20701 N MacArthur Blvd, 405-348-6100
Ranet Tippens, supt. Fax 348-3049
www.deercreekschools.org
Deer Creek Freshman Academy 300/9-9
6101 NW 206th St, 405-348-5720
Melissa Jordan, prin. Fax 359-3179
Deer Creek HS 800/10-12
6101 NW 206th St, 405-348-5720
Melissa Jordan, prin. Fax 359-3179
Deer Creek MS 700/7-8
2601 NW 234th St, 405-348-4830
Kristy VanDorn, prin. Fax 359-2292

Edmond ISD 21,900/PK-12
1001 W Danforth Rd 73003 405-340-2800
Dr. David Goin, supt. Fax 340-2835
www.edmondschools.net/
Boulevard Academy Alt
215 N Boulevard 73034 405-340-2865
Mark Andrus, dir. Fax 330-6057
Central MS 800/6-8
500 E 9th St 73034 405-340-2890
Dana Renner, prin. Fax 340-3961
Cheyenne MS 1,000/6-8
1271 W Covell Rd 73003 405-340-2940
Susie Schinnerer, prin. Fax 330-7397
Cimarron MS 800/6-8
3701 S Bryant Ave 73013 405-340-2935
Cordell Ehrich, prin. Fax 330-3398
Edmond Memorial HS 2,100/9-12
1000 E 15th St 73013 405-340-2850
Justin Coffelt, prin. Fax 340-2856
Edmond North HS 2,500/9-12
215 W Danforth Rd 73003 405-340-2875
Jason Pittenger, prin. Fax 330-7349
Edmond Santa Fe HS 2,000/9-12
1901 W 15th St 73013 405-340-2230
Jason Hayes, prin. Fax 340-2240
Sequoyah MS 1,200/6-8
1125 E Danforth Rd 73034 405-340-2900
Jason Galloway, prin. Fax 340-2909
Summit MS 1,000/6-8
1703 NW 150th St 73013 405-340-2920
Shana Perry, prin. Fax 340-2933

---

Mercy S Institute PK-12
14001 N Harvey 73013 405-748-5500
Oklahoma Christian Academy 300/PK-12
1101 E 9th St 73034 405-844-6478
Oklahoma Christian S 900/PK-12
PO Box 509 73083 405-341-2265
Dr. Al King, hdmstr. Fax 341-4710
University of Central Oklahoma Post-Sec.
100 N University Dr 73034 405-974-2000

**Eldorado, Jackson, Pop. 420**
Eldorado SD I025 100/PK-12
PO Box J 73537 580-633-2219
Dr. Harold Hayes, supt. Fax 633-2316
www.eldorado.k12.ok.us/
Eldorado HS 50/9-12
PO Box J 73537 580-633-2219
Chrystal Bryant, prin. Fax 633-2316

**Elgin, Comanche, Pop. 2,058**
Elgin ISD 2,000/PK-12
PO Box 369 73538 580-492-3663
Tom Crimmins, supt. Fax 492-4084
www.elginps.org
Elgin HS 600/9-12
PO Box 369 73538 580-492-3670
Curtis Lorah, prin. Fax 492-3697
Elgin MS 600/5-8
PO Box 369 73538 580-492-3655
Melissa Hitt, prin. Fax 492-3658

**Elk City, Beckham, Pop. 11,396**
Elk City ISD 2,300/PK-12
222 W Broadway Ave 73644 580-225-0175
Buddy Wood, supt. Fax 225-8644
www.elkcityschools.com
EC Alternative Education Alt
222 W Broadway Ave 73644 580-333-0555
Jeff Lewallen, dir.
Elk City HS 400/10-12
222 W Broadway Ave 73644 580-225-0105
Jeff Lewallen, prin. Fax 225-1359
Elk City JHS 300/8-9
222 W Broadway Ave 73644 580-225-0476
Tammy Russell, prin. Fax 225-0208
Adult Education Adult
222 W Broadway Ave 73644 580-225-4154
Sheryl Kimball, admin.

Merritt ISD 600/PK-12
19693 E 1130 Rd 73644 580-225-5460
Jeff Daugherty, supt. Fax 225-5469
www.merritt.k12.ok.us
Merritt HS 100/9-12
19693 E 1130 Rd 73644 580-225-5460
Don Bradshaw, prin. Fax 225-5469

**Elmore City, Garvin, Pop. 671**
Elmore City-Pernell ISD 400/PK-12
100 N Muse Ave 73433 580-788-2565
Donny Darrow, supt. Fax 788-4665
www.ecphs.k12.ok.us
Elmore City-Pernell HS 100/7-12
100 N Muse Ave 73433 580-788-2565
Jackie Sadler, prin. Fax 788-4665

**El Reno, Canadian, Pop. 16,130**
El Reno ISD 2,300/PK-12
PO Box 580 73036 405-262-1703
Craig McVay, supt. Fax 262-8620
www.elrenops.org

Dale JHS 200/7-8
PO Box 580 73036 405-262-3253
Kim Landers, prin. Fax 262-8650
El Reno HS 600/9-12
PO Box 580 73036 405-262-3254
Pat Liticker, prin. Fax 262-8629

OK Dept. of Voc. & Tech. Education
Supt. — None
Canadian Valley Technology Center Vo/Tech
6505 E US Highway 66 73036 405-262-2629
Gayla Lutts, dir.

---

Canadian Valley Area Voc-Tech School Post-Sec.
6505 E US Highway 66 73036 405-262-2629
Redlands Community College Post-Sec.
1300 S Country Club Rd 73036 405-262-2552

**Enid, Garfield, Pop. 46,752**
Chisholm ISD 900/PK-12
300 Colorado Ave 73701 580-237-5512
Roydon Tilley, supt. Fax 234-5334
www.chisholm.k12.ok.us
Chisholm HS 300/9-12
4018 W Carrier Rd 73703 580-233-2852
Shane Dent, prin. Fax 233-9325
Chisholm MS 200/6-8
4202 W Carrier Rd 73703 580-234-0234
Crystal Szymanski, prin. Fax 234-0343

Enid ISD 7,200/PK-12
500 S Independence St 73701 580-366-7000
Dr. Darrell Floyd, supt. Fax 366-8900
www.enidpublicschools.org
Emerson MS 400/6-8
700 W Elm Ave 73701 580-366-7250
Candice Wojciechowsky, prin. Fax 366-8903
Enid HS 1,800/9-12
611 W Wabash Ave 73701 580-366-8300
Jim Beierschmitt, prin. Fax 366-8905
Longfellow MS 400/6-8
900 E Broadway Ave 73701 580-366-8200
Scott Fitzgerald, prin. Fax 366-8912
Waller MS 600/6-8
2604 W Randolph Ave 73703 580-366-7900
Adam Beauchamp, prin. Fax 366-8917

OK Dept. of Voc. & Tech. Education
Supt. — None
Autry Technology Center Vo/Tech
1201 W Willow Rd 73703 580-242-2750
Brady McCullough, supt. Fax 233-8262

---

Enid Beauty College Post-Sec.
3905 S La Mesa Dr 73703 580-237-6677
Northern Oklahoma College Post-Sec.
PO Box 2300 73702 580-242-6300
Oklahoma Bible Academy 300/6-12
5913 W Chestnut Ave 73703 580-242-4104
Dallas Caldwell, hdmstr. Fax 242-4106
O T Autry Area Vocational Tech Center Post-Sec.
1201 W Willow Rd 73703 580-242-2750
St. Mary's Hospital Post-Sec.
305 S 5th St 73701 580-233-6100

**Erick, Beckham, Pop. 1,034**
Erick ISD 200/PK-12
PO Box 9 73645 580-526-3476
Jeff Kelly, supt. Fax 526-3308
www.erickps.k12.ok.us/
Erick HS 100/6-12
PO Box 9 73645 580-526-3351
Lantze Blevins, prin. Fax 526-3308

**Eufaula, McIntosh, Pop. 2,615**
Eufaula ISD 1,300/PK-12
215 N 6th St 74432 918-689-2152
Jeanette Smith, supt. Fax 689-1080
www.eufaula.k12.ok.us
Eufaula HS 400/9-12
1 Bell Anderson 74432 918-689-2556
Michael Tamez, prin. Fax 689-1099
Eufaula MS 300/6-8
1711 W J M Bailey Hwy 74432 918-689-2711
Chris Whelan, prin. Fax 689-2874

**Fairfax, Osage, Pop. 1,241**
Woodland SD 400/PK-12
100 N 6th St 74637 918-642-3297
Todd Kimrey, supt. Fax 642-5754
www.woodland.k12.ok.us/
Woodland HS 100/9-12
100 N 6th St 74637 918-642-3295
Rick Rogers, prin. Fax 642-5754
Other Schools – See Ralston

**Fairland, Ottawa, Pop. 935**
Fairland ISD 500/PK-12
202 W Washington Ave 74343 918-676-3811
Mark Alexander, supt. Fax 676-3594
www.fairlandowls.com
Fairland HS 200/9-12
202 W Washington Ave 74343 918-676-3246
Jerry Johnson, prin.
Fairland MS 6-8
202 W Washington Ave 74343 918-676-3246
Jerry Johnson, prin.

**Fairview, Major, Pop. 2,532**
Fairview ISD 600/PK-12
408 E Broadway 73737 580-227-2531
Rocky Burchfield, supt. Fax 227-2642
www.fairviewhigh.com
Chamberlain MS 100/6-8
1000 E Elm St 73737 580-227-2555
Cheryl Hasty, prin. Fax 227-2642
Fairview HS 200/9-12
316 N 8th Ave 73737 580-227-4446
Brian Hamar, prin. Fax 227-1004

OK Dept. of Voc. & Tech. Education
Supt. — None
Northwest Technology Center Vo/Tech
801 S Vo Tech Dr 73737 580-227-3708
Colt Shaw, dir. Fax 227-2651

**Fargo, Ellis, Pop. 359**
Fargo ISD 200/PK-12
PO Box 200 73840 580-698-2298
Terry Stevens, supt. Fax 698-8019
www.fargo.k12.ok.us
Fargo HS 100/9-12
PO Box 200 73840 580-698-2298
Sherri Tune, prin. Fax 698-8019

**Felt, Cimarron, Pop. 89**
Felt ISD 100/PK-12
PO Box 47 73937 580-426-2220
Lewetta Hefley, supt. Fax 426-2799
www.felt.k12.ok.us
Felt HS 50/9-12
PO Box 47 73937 580-426-2220
Christopher May, prin. Fax 426-2799

**Fletcher, Comanche, Pop. 1,123**
Fletcher ISD 400/PK-12
PO Box 489 73541 580-549-6027
Shane Gilbreath, supt. Fax 549-6016
www.fletcherschools.org/
Fletcher JSHS, PO Box 489 73541 100/7-12
Amanda Grimes, prin. 580-549-6015

**Forgan, Beaver, Pop. 539**
Forgan ISD 200/PK-12
PO Box 406 73938 580-487-3366
Travis Smalts, supt. Fax 487-3368
www.forgan.k12.ok.us
Forgan HS 50/9-12
PO Box 406 73938 580-487-3366
Todd Kerr, prin. Fax 487-3368

**Fort Cobb, Caddo, Pop. 599**
Fort Cobb-Broxton ISD 300/PK-12
PO Box 130 73038 405-643-2336
Kyle Lierle, supt. Fax 643-2547
www.fcbmustangs.com
Fort Cobb-Broxton HS 100/9-12
PO Box 130 73038 405-643-2820
Kyle Lierle, prin. Fax 643-3115
Fort Cobb-Broxton MS 100/6-8
PO Box 130 73038 405-643-2820
James Biddy, prin.

OK Dept. of Voc. & Tech. Education
Supt. — None
Caddo-Kiowa Technology Center Vo/Tech
PO Box 190 73038 405-643-5511
Dennis Ruttman, supt. Fax 643-3014

**Fort Gibson, Muskogee, Pop. 3,804**
Fort Gibson ISD 1,900/PK-12
500 Ross Ave 74434 918-478-2474
Derald Glover, supt. Fax 478-8533
www.ftgibson.k12.ok.us
Fort Gibson HS 600/9-12
500 Ross Ave 74434 918-478-2452
Gary Sparks, prin. Fax 478-6244
Fort Gibson MS 400/6-8
500 Ross Ave 74434 918-478-2471
Gregory Phares, prin. Fax 478-6412

**Fort Supply, Woodward, Pop. 320**
Fort Supply ISD 100/PK-12
PO Box 160 73841 580-766-2611
Melva Little, supt. Fax 766-8019
www.fortsupply.k12.ok.us/
Fort Supply HS 50/9-12
PO Box 160 73841 580-766-2611
Theron Graybill, prin. Fax 766-8019

**Fort Towson, Choctaw, Pop. 508**
Fort Towson ISD 400/PK-12
PO Box 39 74735 580-873-2712
Jason Price, supt. Fax 873-1053
www.forttowson.k12.ok.us/
Fort Towson JSHS 100/7-12
PO Box 39 74735 580-873-2325
Phil Hall, prin. Fax 873-2677

**Fox, Carter**
Fox ISD 300/PK-12
PO Box 248 73435 580-673-2081
Brent Phelps, supt. Fax 673-2389
www.foxps.k12.ok.us
Fox HS 100/9-12
PO Box 248 73435 580-673-2082
Jason Wright, prin. Fax 673-2389

**Foyil, Rogers, Pop. 287**
Foyil ISD 500/PK-12
PO Box 49 74031 918-341-1113
Rod Carter, supt. Fax 341-1223
Foyil HS 100/10-12
PO Box 49 74031 918-342-1782
Lance Williams, prin. Fax 341-1223
Foyil JHS 7-9
PO Box 49 74031 918-342-1782
Benny Ballard, prin. Fax 341-1223

**Frederick, Tillman, Pop. 3,832**
Frederick ISD 600/PK-12
817 N 15th St 73542 580-335-5516
Shannon Vanderburg, supt. Fax 335-2324
www.frederickbombers.net
Frederick HS 200/9-12
817 N 15th St 73542 580-335-5521
Randy Biggs, prin. Fax 335-2634
Frederick MS 200/6-8
817 N 15th St 73542 580-335-2014
Jeremy Newton, prin. Fax 335-2763

OK Dept. of Voc. & Tech. Education
Supt. — None
Great Plains Technology Center Vo/Tech
2001 E Gladstone Ave 73542 580-335-5525
Gary Tyler, admin. Fax 335-2209

**Freedom, Woods, Pop. 280**
Freedom ISD 100/PK-12
PO Box 5 73842 580-621-3271
Danny McCuiston, supt. Fax 621-3699
www.freedom.k12.ok.us
Freedom HS 50/9-12
PO Box 5 73842 580-621-3272
Brett Hill, prin. Fax 621-3699

**Gage, Ellis, Pop. 437**
Gage ISD 100/PK-12
PO Box 60 73843 580-923-7666
Greg Gregory, supt. Fax 923-7907
www.gage.k12.ok.us/
Gage HS 50/9-12
PO Box 60 73843 580-923-7909
Greg Gregory, admin. Fax 923-7907

**Gans, Sequoyah, Pop. 289**
Gans ISD 400/PK-12
PO Box 70 74936 918-775-2236
Larry Calloway, supt. Fax 775-5145
www.gans.k12.ok.us
Gans HS 100/9-12
PO Box 70 74936 918-775-2236
Shawn Gillespie, prin. Fax 775-5145

**Garber, Garfield, Pop. 806**
Garber ISD 300/PK-12
PO Box 539 73738 580-863-2220
Jim Lamer, supt. Fax 863-2259
www.garber.k12.ok.us/
Garber HS, PO Box 539 73738 100/9-12
Marc Hatton, prin. 580-863-2231

**Geary, Blaine, Pop. 1,213**
Geary ISD 400/PK-12
110 SW Embree Dr 73040 405-884-2411
Todd Glasgow, supt. Fax 884-2099
www.gearyschools.org
Bison Alternative Academy Alt
110 SW Embree Dr 73040 405-884-5605
Jim Shelton, dir.
Geary HS 100/9-12
110 SW Embree Dr 73040 405-884-2362
Jim Shelton, prin. Fax 884-5487
Geary MS 100/6-8
110 SW Embree Dr 73040 405-884-2362
Jim Shelton, prin. Fax 884-5487

**Geronimo, Comanche, Pop. 1,179**
Geronimo ISD 300/PK-12
800 W Main St 73543 580-355-3160
Bill Pascoe, supt. Fax 357-8307
www.geronimo.k12.ok.us
Geronimo HS 100/9-12
800 W Main St 73543 580-355-3160
Trae Koch, prin. Fax 357-8307
Geronimo MS 7-8
800 W Main St 73543 580-355-3160
Heath Selcer, prin. Fax 357-8307

**Glencoe, Payne, Pop. 577**
Glencoe ISD 300/PK-12
201 E Lone Chimney Rd 74032 580-669-2261
John Lazenby, supt. Fax 669-2961
www.glencoe.k12.ok.us
Glencoe HS 100/9-12
201 E Lone Chimney Rd 74032 580-669-2261
Chad Speer, prin. Fax 669-2961

**Glenpool, Tulsa, Pop. 9,951**
Glenpool ISD 2,400/PK-12
PO Box 1149 74033 918-322-9500
Jerry Olansen, supt. Fax 322-1529
www.glenpool.k12.ok.us
Glenpool HS 600/9-12
PO Box 1149 74033 918-322-9500
Kim Coody, prin. Fax 322-6410
Glenpool MS 500/6-8
PO Box 1149 74033 918-322-9500
Matt Fore, prin. Fax 322-6411

**Goodwell, Texas, Pop. 1,268**
Goodwell ISD 200/PK-12
PO Box 580 73939 580-349-2271
Freida Burgess, supt. Fax 349-2531
www.goodwell.k12.ok.us
Goodwell HS 100/9-12
PO Box 580 73939 580-349-2271
Jason Schreiner, prin. Fax 349-2531

Yarbrough ISD 100/PK-12
RR 1 Box 31 73939 580-545-3329
Jim Wiggin, supt. Fax 545-3392
www.yarbrough.k12.ok.us/
Yarbrough HS 50/9-12
RR 1 Box 31 73939 580-545-3328
Brent Meeks, prin. Fax 545-3392

---

Oklahoma Panhandle State University Post-Sec.
PO Box 430 73939 580-349-2611

**Gore, Sequoyah, Pop. 891**
Gore ISD 500/PK-12
1200 N Highway 10 74435 918-489-5587
Lucky McCrary, supt. Fax 489-5664
www.gorepublicschools.org
Gore HS 200/9-12
1200 N Highway 10 74435 918-489-5587
Beverly Robison, prin. Fax 489-5664
Gore MS 100/6-8
1200 N Highway 10 74435 918-487-5587
Beverly Robison, prin. Fax 489-5664

**Gracemont, Caddo, Pop. 298**
Gracemont ISD 200/PK-12
PO Box 5 73042 405-966-2236
Mike Jones, supt. Fax 966-2395
www.gracemont.k12.ok.us
Gracemont HS 50/9-12
PO Box 5 73042 405-966-2233
Mike Jones, prin. Fax 966-2395

**Grandfield, Tillman, Pop. 1,001**
Grandfield ISD 300/PK-12
PO Box 639 73546 580-479-5237
Eva Spaulding, supt. Fax 479-3381
www.grandfield.k12.ok.us/
Grandfield HS 100/9-12
PO Box 639 73546 580-479-3140
Matthew Fox, prin. Fax 479-5563

**Granite, Greer, Pop. 2,034**
Granite ISD 300/PK-12
PO Box 98 73547 580-535-2104
Rodney Calhoun, supt. Fax 535-2106
www.granite.k12.ok.us
Granite HS 100/9-12
PO Box 98 73547 580-535-2104
Listena Prickett, prin. Fax 535-2106

**Grove, Delaware, Pop. 6,167**
Grove ISD 2,500/PK-12
PO Box 450789 74345 918-786-3003
Sandy Coaly, supt. Fax 786-9365
www.ridgerunners.net
Grove HS 700/9-12
PO Box 450789 74345 918-786-2208
Renae Dozier, prin. Fax 787-5238
Grove MS 400/7-8
PO Box 450789 74345 918-786-2209
Pat Dodson, prin. Fax 786-6454

**Guthrie, Logan, Pop. 9,702**
Guthrie ISD 3,300/PK-12
802 E Vilas Ave 73044 405-282-8900
Dr. Mike Simpson, supt. Fax 282-5904
www.guthrie.k12.ok.us
Faver Alternative S Alt
1021 E Perkins Ave 73044 405-282-5941
Pat Hughes, dir. Fax 282-5931
Guthrie HS 900/9-12
200 N Crooks Dr 73044 405-282-5906
Chris LeGrande, prin. Fax 282-5909
Guthrie JHS 500/7-8
705 E Oklahoma Ave 73044 405-282-5936
Robbie Rainwater, prin. Fax 282-3598

**Guymon, Texas, Pop. 11,299**
Guymon ISD 2,800/PK-12
PO Box 1307 73942 580-338-4340
Doug Melton, supt. Fax 338-3812
www.guymontigers.com
Central JHS 400/7-8
PO Box 1307 73942 580-338-4360
Claudia Winters, prin. Fax 338-0212
Guymon HS 700/9-12
PO Box 1307 73942 580-338-4350
Randy Williams, prin. Fax 338-0994

**Haileyville, Pittsburg, Pop. 762**
Haileyville ISD 400/PK-12
PO Box 29 74546 918-297-2626
Roger Hemphill, supt. Fax 297-7136
www.haileyville.k12.ok.us
Haileyville HS 100/9-12
PO Box 29 74546 918-297-2627
Brandie Kirkes, prin. Fax 297-3215

**Hammon, Roger Mills, Pop. 547**
Hammon ISD 300/PK-12
PO Box 279 73650 580-473-2221
Robert Stafford, supt. Fax 473-2464
www.hammon.k12.ok.us/
Hammon HS 100/9-12
PO Box 279 73650 580-473-2737
Mike Higgins, prin. Fax 473-2464

**Hanna, McIntosh, Pop. 131**
Hanna ISD 300/PK-12
PO Box 10 74845 918-657-2523
Richard Boatright, supt. Fax 657-2424
www.hanna.k12.ok.us
Hanna HS 200/9-12
PO Box 10 74845 918-657-2527
David Dewalt, prin. Fax 657-2424

**Hardesty, Texas, Pop. 209**
Hardesty ISD 100/PK-12
PO Box 129 73944 580-888-4258
Greg Faris, supt. Fax 888-4560
www.hardesty.k12.ok.us
Hardesty HS 50/9-12
PO Box 129 73944 580-888-4258
Greg Faris, prin. Fax 888-4560

**Harrah, Oklahoma, Pop. 4,831**
Harrah ISD 2,200/PK-12
20670 Walker St 73045 405-454-6244
Paul Blessington, supt. Fax 454-0022
www.harrahschools.com
Harrah HS 500/9-12
20370 Elm St 73045 405-454-2416
Kenneth Riddle, prin. Fax 454-6842
Harrah MS 300/6-8
20665 Walker St 73045 405-347-2700
Dianna Hilburn, prin. Fax 454-6841

**Hartshorne, Pittsburg, Pop. 1,925**
Hartshorne ISD 800/PK-12
520 S 5th St 74547 918-297-2534
Mark Ichord, supt. Fax 297-2698
www.hartshorne.k12.ok.us
Hartshorne HS 200/10-12
520 S 5th St 74547 918-297-2536
Mike Reddick, prin. Fax 297-2025
Hartshorne JHS 200/7-9
520 S 5th St 74547 918-297-2433
Jason Lindley, prin. Fax 297-2698

**Haskell, Muskogee, Pop. 1,802**
Haskell ISD 900/PK-12
900 N Ohio Ave 74436 918-482-5221
Sharon Herrington, supt. Fax 482-3346
www.haskell.k12.ok.us
Beavers MS 200/6-8
900 N Ohio Ave 74436 918-482-5221
Erin Jones, prin. Fax 482-3346
Haskell HS 300/9-12
900 N Ohio Ave 74436 918-482-5223
Erin Jones, prin. Fax 482-3346

**Haworth, McCurtain, Pop. 273**
Haworth ISD 600/PK-12
300 N Maple St 74740 580-245-1406
Ted Brewer, supt. Fax 245-2265
www.haworth.k12.ok.us
Haworth HS 100/10-12
300 N Maple St 74740 580-245-1406
Johnny Crabtree, prin. Fax 245-4913
Haworth JHS 200/7-9
300 N Maple St 74740 580-245-1406
Brandy Wall, prin. Fax 245-4911

**Healdton, Carter, Pop. 2,670**
Healdton ISD 500/PK-12
PO Box 490 73438 580-229-0566
Terry D. Shaw, supt. Fax 229-1522
www.healdtonschools.org/
Healdton HS 100/9-12
PO Box 490 73438 580-229-0540
Justin Kana, prin. Fax 229-0557
Healdton MS 100/6-8
PO Box 490 73438 580-229-0303
Greg Munholland, prin. Fax 229-1475

**Heavener, LeFlore, Pop. 3,279**
Heavener ISD 1,100/PK-12
PO Box 698 74937 918-653-7223
Edward Wilson, supt. Fax 653-7843
www.heavenerschools.org
Heavener HS, PO Box 698 74937 300/9-12
Aaron Alexander, prin. 918-653-4307

**Helena, Alfalfa, Pop. 1,366**
Timberlake ISD 200/PK-12
PO Box 287 73741 580-852-3307
Brent Rousey, supt. Fax 852-8019
www.tlake.k12.ok.us
Timberlake HS 100/9-12
PO Box 287 73741 580-852-3281
Charlie Berg, prin. Fax 852-3280

**Hennessey, Kingfisher, Pop. 2,093**
Hennessey ISD 800/PK-12
604 E Oklahoma St 73742 405-853-4321
Joe McCulley, supt. Fax 853-4439
www.hps.k12.ok.us
Hennessey HS 200/9-12
707 E Oklahoma St 73742 405-853-4394
Brady Barnes, prin. Fax 853-4644
Hennessey MS 200/5-8
120 N Mitchell Rd 73742 405-853-4303
Stacy Schovanec, prin. Fax 853-4848

**Henryetta, Okmulgee, Pop. 5,595**
Henryetta ISD 1,300/PK-12
1801 W Troy Aikman Dr 74437 918-652-6523
Dwayne Noble, supt. Fax 652-6510
www.henryetta.k12.ok.us
Henryetta HS 300/9-12
1801 W Troy Aikman Dr 74437 918-652-6571
Scott Bein, prin. Fax 652-6572
Henryetta MS 300/6-8
1801 W Troy Aikman Dr 74437 918-652-6578
Brad Wion, prin. Fax 652-6506

Wilson ISD 300/PK-12
8867 Chestnut Rd 74437 918-652-3374
Andrea James, supt. Fax 652-8140
www.wpstigers.k12.ok.us
Wilson HS 100/9-12
8867 Chestnut Rd 74437 918-652-3384
Vernie Thomas, prin. Fax 650-9725

**Hinton, Caddo, Pop. 3,079**
Hinton ISD 700/PK-12
PO Box 1036 73047 405-542-3257
Richard Brownen, supt. Fax 542-3286
www.hintonschools.org
Hinton HS 200/9-12
PO Box 1036 73047 405-542-3235
Rennie Nickell, prin. Fax 542-3286
Hinton MS 100/6-8
PO Box 1036 73047 405-542-3235
Rennie Nickell, prin. Fax 542-3286

**Hobart, Kiowa, Pop. 3,599**
Hobart ISD 800/PK-12
PO Box 899 73651 580-726-5691
Cathy Hunt, supt. Fax 726-2855
www.hobart.k12.ok.us
Hobart HS, PO Box 899 73651 200/9-12
Mark Harmon, prin. 580-726-5611
Hobart MS, PO Box 899 73651 200/6-8
Kim Reed, prin. 580-726-5615

OK Dept. of Voc. & Tech. Education
Supt. — None
Western Technology Center Vo/Tech
PO Box 659 73651 580-726-8400
Jeff Ledford, dir. Fax 726-8470

**Holdenville, Hughes, Pop. 5,493**
Holdenville ISD 1,100/PK-12
210 Grimes Ave 74848 405-379-5483
Randy Davenport, supt. Fax 379-5874
www.holdenville.k12.ok.us
Holdenville HS 300/9-12
210 Grimes Ave 74848 405-379-3387
Travis Graham, prin. Fax 379-2012
Thomas MS 300/4-8
210 Grimes Ave 74848 405-379-6661
Mark Turner, prin. Fax 379-8118

Moss ISD 300/PK-12
8087 E 134 Rd 74848 405-379-2273
Gil Turpin, supt. Fax 379-2333
www.mossps.k12.ok.us/
Moss HS 100/9-12
8087 E 134 Rd 74848 405-379-7251
Bob Sifers, prin. Fax 379-2333

**Hollis, Harmon, Pop. 1,997**
Hollis ISD 500/PK-12
PO Box 193 73550 580-688-3450
Jennifer McQueen, supt. Fax 688-2532
www.hollis.k12.ok.us
Hollis HS, PO Box 193 73550 100/9-12
Marty Webb, prin. 580-688-2707
Hollis MS, PO Box 193 73550 100/6-8
Marty Webb, prin. 580-688-2707

**Hominy, Osage, Pop. 3,347**
Hominy ISD 500/PK-12
200 S Pettit Ave 74035 918-885-6511
Russell Hull, supt. Fax 885-2538
www.hominy.k12.ok.us
Hominy HS 200/9-12
200 S Pettit Ave 74035 918-885-2141
Doyle Edwards, prin. Fax 885-6369
Hominy MS 100/6-8
200 S Pettit Ave 74035 918-885-6253
Scott Harmon, prin. Fax 885-6369

**Hooker, Texas, Pop. 1,875**
Hooker ISD 600/PK-12
PO Box 247 73945 580-652-2162
Dan Faulkner, supt. Fax 652-3118
Hooker HS, PO Box 247 73945 100/9-12
Brian Stalder, prin. 580-652-2516

**Howe, LeFlore, Pop. 762**
Howe ISD 500/PK-12
PO Box 259 74940 918-658-3666
Scott Parks, supt. Fax 658-2233
www.howeschools.org
Howe HS 200/9-12
PO Box 259 74940 918-658-3368
Don McGee, prin. Fax 658-2233

**Hugo, Choctaw, Pop. 4,926**
Hugo ISD 1,200/PK-12
208 N 2nd St 74743 580-326-6483
Tod Harrison, supt. Fax 326-2480
www.hugoschools.com
Hugo HS 300/9-12
208 N 2nd St 74743 580-326-9648
Earl Dalke, prin. Fax 326-4811
Hugo MS 200/6-8
208 N 2nd St 74743 580-326-3365
Anna Pate, prin. Fax 326-7352

OK Dept. of Voc. & Tech. Education
Supt. — None
Kiamichi Technology Center Vo/Tech
PO Box 699 74743 580-326-6491
Scott Garrett, dir. Fax 326-5696

**Hulbert, Cherokee, Pop. 518**
Hulbert ISD 500/PK-12
PO Box 188 74441 918-772-2501
Dr. Marilyn Dewoody, supt. Fax 772-2766
www.hulbertriders.com
Hulbert JSHS 200/7-12
PO Box 188 74441 918-772-2501
Brad Ferguson, prin. Fax 772-1275

**Hydro, Caddo, Pop. 947**
Hydro-Eakly ISD 500/PK-12
407 E 7th St 73048 405-663-2774
Bill Derryberry, supt. Fax 663-2139
www.hydroeakly.k12.ok.us/
Hydro-Eakly HS 100/9-12
407 E 7th St 73048 405-663-2246
Jeremy Bussey, prin. Fax 663-2139
Hydro-Eakly MS 100/6-8
407 E 7th St 73048 405-663-2246
Jeremy Bussey, prin. Fax 663-2139

**Idabel, McCurtain, Pop. 6,641**
Idabel ISD 1,300/PK-12
200 NE Ave C 74745 580-286-7639
Doug Brown, supt. Fax 286-5585
www.idabelps.org
Idabel HS 400/9-12
901 E Lincoln Rd 74745 580-286-7693
Alan Bryant, prin. Fax 286-6755
Idabel MS 200/6-8
100 NE Ave D 74745 580-286-6558
Laura Bullock, prin. Fax 286-8272

OK Dept. of Voc. & Tech. Education
Supt. — None
Kiamichi Technology Center Vo/Tech
3205 NE Lincoln Rd 74745 580-286-7555
Johnnie Meredith, dir. Fax 286-3753

**Indiahoma, Comanche, Pop. 331**
Indiahoma ISD 200/PK-12
PO Box 8 73552 580-246-3448
Deanna Voegeli, supt. Fax 246-3372
www.indiahoma.k12.ok.us

| | |
|---|---|
| Indiahoma HS | 100/9-12 |
| PO Box 8 73552 | 580-246-3333 |
| Greg Ellis, prin. | Fax 246-3372 |

**Indianola, Pittsburg, Pop. 149**

| | |
|---|---|
| Indianola ISD | 200/PK-12 |
| PO Box 119 74442 | 918-823-4231 |
| Mark Baumann, supt. | Fax 823-4234 |
| www.indianola.k12.ok.us | |
| Indianola HS, PO Box 119 74442 | 100/9-12 |
| Gina Hernandez, prin. | 918-823-4231 |

**Inola, Rogers, Pop. 1,643**

| | |
|---|---|
| Inola ISD | 1,300/PK-12 |
| PO Box 1149 74036 | 918-543-2255 |
| Dr. Kent Holbrook, supt. | Fax 543-8754 |
| www.inola.k12.ok.us | |
| Inola HS | 400/9-12 |
| PO Box 789 74036 | 918-543-2404 |
| Paul Gruenberg, prin. | Fax 543-2345 |
| Inola MS | 400/5-8 |
| PO Box 819 74036 | 918-543-2434 |
| Jeff Unrau, prin. | Fax 543-6268 |

**Jay, Delaware, Pop. 2,212**

| | |
|---|---|
| Jay ISD | 1,800/PK-12 |
| PO Box 630 74346 | 918-253-4293 |
| Charles Thomas, supt. | Fax 253-8970 |
| www.jay.k12.ok.us | |
| Jay HS | 500/9-12 |
| PO Box 630 74346 | 918-253-4466 |
| James Bryant, prin. | Fax 253-6249 |
| Jay MS | 200/6-8 |
| PO Box 630 74346 | 918-253-8510 |
| Melissa McCullough, prin. | Fax 253-3342 |

**Jenks, Tulsa, Pop. 16,162**

| | |
|---|---|
| Jenks ISD | 10,700/PK-12 |
| 205 E B St 74037 | 918-299-4411 |
| Dr. Stacey Butterfield, supt. | Fax 299-9197 |
| www.jenksps.org | |
| Jenks Alternative Center | Alt |
| 205 E B St 74037 | 918-299-4411 |
| Amie Hardy, prin. | Fax 298-6640 |
| Jenks Freshman Academy | 900/9-9 |
| 205 E B St 74037 | 918-299-4411 |
| Judi Thorn, prin. | Fax 298-0807 |
| Jenks HS | 2,200/10-12 |
| 205 E B St 74037 | 918-299-4411 |
| Mike Means, prin. | Fax 298-0336 |
| Other Schools – See Tulsa | |

| | |
|---|---|
| Jenks Beauty College | Post-Sec. |
| 535 W Main St 74037 | 918-299-0901 |

**Jones, Oklahoma, Pop. 2,585**

| | |
|---|---|
| Jones ISD | 1,200/PK-12 |
| 412 SW 3rd St 73049 | 405-399-9215 |
| Dr. Carl Johnson, supt. | Fax 399-9212 |
| www.jones.k12.ok.us | |
| Jones HS | 300/9-12 |
| 304 Dr Lee Simmons 73049 | 405-399-9122 |
| Curtis Moses, prin. | Fax 399-9212 |
| Jones MS | 300/6-8 |
| 16011 E Wilshire Blvd 73049 | 405-399-9114 |
| Adam McPhail, prin. | Fax 399-6101 |

**Kansas, Delaware, Pop. 726**

| | |
|---|---|
| Kansas ISD | 1,000/PK-12 |
| PO Box 196 74347 | 918-868-2562 |
| Leann Barnwell, supt. | Fax 868-3103 |
| www.kansasps.com/ | |
| Kansas HS | 300/9-12 |
| PO Box 196 74347 | 918-868-3308 |
| Phil Isom, prin. | Fax 868-3103 |
| Kansas JHS | 200/6-8 |
| PO Box 196 74347 | 918-868-5308 |
| Bryon Arnold, prin. | Fax 868-5582 |

| | |
|---|---|
| OK Dept. of Voc. & Tech. Education | |
| Supt. — None | |
| Northeast Tech Center Kansas Campus | Vo/Tech |
| PO Box 30 74347 | 918-868-3535 |
| Greg Mitchell, supt. | Fax 868-3530 |

**Kaw City, Kay, Pop. 358**

| | |
|---|---|
| Shidler ISD | |
| Supt. — See Shidler | |
| Shidler MS | 100/5-8 |
| 904 Washunga Dr 74641 | 580-269-2911 |
| Janice Finton, prin. | Fax 269-2992 |

**Kellyville, Creek, Pop. 1,083**

| | |
|---|---|
| Kellyville ISD | 1,200/PK-12 |
| PO Box 99 74039 | 918-247-6133 |
| Joe Pierce, supt. | Fax 247-6120 |
| www.kellyvilleschools.org/ | |
| Kellyville HS, PO Box 99 74039 | 400/9-12 |
| Danny Wood, prin. | 918-247-6333 |
| Kellyville MS, PO Box 99 74039 | 200/7-8 |
| Danny Wood, prin. | 918-247-6134 |

**Keota, Haskell, Pop. 531**

| | |
|---|---|
| Keota ISD | 400/PK-12 |
| 110 NE 6th St 74941 | 918-966-3950 |
| Kelly Husted, supt. | Fax 966-3247 |
| www.keota.k12.ok.us | |
| Keota HS | 100/9-12 |
| 110 NE 6th St 74941 | 918-966-3950 |
| Richard Reed, prin. | Fax 966-3247 |

**Ketchum, Mayes, Pop. 396**

| | |
|---|---|
| Ketchum ISD | 600/PK-12 |
| PO Box 720 74349 | 918-782-5091 |
| Jerry Pete Hiseley, supt. | Fax 782-9018 |
| www.ketchumwarriors.com | |
| Ketchum HS | 200/9-12 |
| PO Box 720 74349 | 918-782-4481 |
| Joe Gramlich, prin. | Fax 782-4848 |
| Ketchum MS | 100/6-8 |
| PO Box 720 74349 | 918-782-3242 |
| Jennifer Turner, prin. | Fax 782-3016 |

**Keyes, Cimarron, Pop. 321**

| | |
|---|---|
| Keyes ISD | 100/PK-12 |
| PO Box 47 73947 | 580-546-7231 |
| Sherri Hitchings, supt. | Fax 546-7338 |
| www.keyes.k12.ok.us | |
| Keyes HS | 50/9-12 |
| PO Box 47 73947 | 580-546-7231 |
| Jim Washburn, prin. | Fax 546-7338 |

**Kiefer, Creek, Pop. 1,550**

| | |
|---|---|
| Kiefer ISD | 600/PK-12 |
| 4600 W 151st St S 74041 | 918-321-3421 |
| Mary Murrell, supt. | Fax 321-5216 |
| www.kiefer.k12.ok.us/ | |
| Kiefer HS | 100/9-12 |
| 4600 W 151st St S 74041 | 918-321-3533 |
| Sabrina Shaw, prin. | Fax 321-4443 |
| Rongey MS | 100/7-8 |
| 4600 W 151st St S 74041 | 918-321-3533 |
| Cory Campbell, prin. | Fax 321-4443 |

**Kingfisher, Kingfisher, Pop. 4,523**

| | |
|---|---|
| Kingfisher SD | 1,300/PK-12 |
| 602 W Chisholm Dr 73750 | 405-375-4194 |
| Jason Sternberger, supt. | Fax 375-5565 |
| www.kingfisher.k12.ok.us | |
| Kingfisher HS | 300/9-12 |
| 1500 S 13th St 73750 | 405-375-4191 |
| Todd Overstreet, prin. | Fax 375-4456 |
| Kingfisher MS | 400/5-8 |
| 601 S 13th St 73750 | 405-375-6607 |
| Keith Campbell, prin. | Fax 375-6410 |

**Kingston, Marshall, Pop. 1,514**

| | |
|---|---|
| Kingston ISD | 1,200/PK-12 |
| PO Box 370 73439 | 580-564-9033 |
| Ron Whipkey, supt. | Fax 564-9516 |
| www.kingston.k12.ok.us | |
| Kingston HS | 300/9-12 |
| PO Box 370 73439 | 580-564-2384 |
| Brenda Foster, prin. | Fax 564-0901 |
| Kingston MS | 300/6-8 |
| PO Box 370 73439 | 580-564-2996 |
| Brian Brister, prin. | Fax 564-0902 |

**Kinta, Haskell, Pop. 279**

| | |
|---|---|
| Kinta ISD | 200/PK-12 |
| PO Box 219 74552 | 918-768-3338 |
| Patricia Deville, supt. | Fax 768-3321 |
| www.kinta.k12.ok.us | |
| Kinta HS | 100/9-12 |
| PO Box 219 74552 | 918-768-3338 |
| Patricia Deville, prin. | Fax 768-3321 |

**Kiowa, Pittsburg, Pop. 681**

| | |
|---|---|
| Kiowa ISD | 300/PK-12 |
| PO Box 6 74553 | 918-432-5631 |
| Rick Pool, supt. | Fax 432-5683 |
| www.kiowa.k12.ok.us | |
| Kiowa HS | 100/9-12 |
| PO Box 6 74553 | 918-432-5631 |
| Ron Slawson, prin. | Fax 432-5683 |

**Konawa, Seminole, Pop. 1,168**

| | |
|---|---|
| Konawa ISD | 700/PK-12 |
| 701 W South St 74849 | 580-925-3244 |
| Andy Gower, supt. | Fax 925-2146 |
| www.konawa.k12.ok.us | |
| Konawa HS | 200/9-12 |
| 701 W South St 74849 | 580-925-3221 |
| Torrey Gaines, prin. | Fax 925-2146 |
| Konawa MS | 200/6-8 |
| 701 W South St 74849 | 580-925-3221 |
| Sean Walker, prin. | Fax 925-2146 |

**Kremlin, Garfield, Pop. 247**

| | |
|---|---|
| Kremlin-Hillsdale ISD | 300/PK-12 |
| PO Box 198 73753 | 580-874-2284 |
| Jim Patton, supt. | |
| www.kremlin.k12.ok.us/ | |
| Kremlin-Hillsdale HS | 100/6-12 |
| PO Box 198 73753 | 580-874-2281 |
| Jeremy Brashears B.S., prin. | |

**Lahoma, Garfield, Pop. 597**

| | |
|---|---|
| Cimarron ISD | 300/PK-12 |
| PO Box 8 73754 | 580-796-2204 |
| Steve Walker, supt. | Fax 796-2350 |
| www.cimarron.k12.ok.us | |
| Cimarron HS | 100/9-12 |
| PO Box 8 73754 | 580-796-2204 |
| Gene Novosad, prin. | Fax 796-2350 |

**Lamont, Grant, Pop. 412**

| | |
|---|---|
| Deer Creek-Lamont ISD | 200/PK-12 |
| PO Box 10 74643 | 580-388-4333 |
| James Lewis, supt. | Fax 388-4341 |
| www.dcla.k12.ok.us/ | |
| Deer Creek-Lamont HS | 100/9-12 |
| PO Box 10 74643 | 580-388-4333 |
| Kevin Engle, prin. | Fax 388-4341 |

**Langston, Logan, Pop. 1,691**

| | |
|---|---|
| Langston University | Post-Sec. |
| PO Box 1500 73050 | 405-466-2231 |

**Laverne, Harper, Pop. 1,316**

| | |
|---|---|
| Laverne ISD | 500/PK-12 |
| PO Box 40 73848 | 580-921-3362 |
| Ed Thomas, supt. | Fax 921-3636 |
| www.laverne.k12.ok.us | |
| Laverne HS | 100/9-12 |
| PO Box 40 73848 | 580-921-3361 |
| Kyndra Allen, prin. | Fax 921-3936 |

**Lawton, Comanche, Pop. 91,002**

| | |
|---|---|
| Lawton ISD | 15,600/PK-12 |
| PO Box 1009 73502 | 580-357-6900 |
| Dr. Tom Deighan, supt. | Fax 585-6319 |
| www.lawtonps.org | |
| Central MS | 700/6-8 |
| 1201 NW Fort Sill Blvd 73507 | 580-355-8544 |
| Dr. Regina DeLoach, prin. | Fax 585-6452 |
| Eisenhower HS | 1,400/9-12 |
| 5202 W Gore Blvd 73505 | 580-355-9144 |
| Rod Elam, prin. | Fax 585-6329 |
| Eisenhower MS | 1,000/6-8 |
| 5702 W Gore Blvd 73505 | 580-353-1040 |
| Beverly Mattingly, prin. | Fax 585-6436 |
| Gateway Success Center | Alt |
| 1701 NW Taft Ave 73507 | 580-353-4903 |
| Gary Barrett, prin. | Fax 585-6479 |
| Lawton HS | 1,800/9-12 |
| 601 NW Fort Sill Blvd 73507 | 580-355-5170 |
| Jerri Manning, prin. | Fax 585-6433 |
| MacArthur HS | 1,100/9-12 |
| 4402 E Gore Blvd 73501 | 580-355-5230 |
| Charlotte Oates, prin. | Fax 585-6434 |
| MacArthur MS | 800/6-8 |
| 510 NE 45th St 73507 | 580-353-5111 |
| Regina Lambert, prin. | Fax 585-6435 |
| Tomlinson MS | 800/6-8 |
| 702 NW Homestead Dr 73505 | 580-585-6416 |
| Eddie Williams, prin. | Fax 585-6451 |

| | |
|---|---|
| OK Dept. of Voc. & Tech. Education | |
| Supt. — None | |
| Great Plains Technology Center | Vo/Tech |
| 4500 SW Lee Blvd 73505 | 580-355-6371 |
| Dr. Tom Thomas, supt. | Fax 250-5677 |

| | |
|---|---|
| Cameron University | Post-Sec. |
| 2800 W Gore Blvd 73505 | 580-581-2200 |
| Comanche Co. Memorial Hospital | Post-Sec. |
| PO Box 129 73502 | 580-355-8620 |
| Comanche Nation College | Post-Sec. |
| 1608 SW 9th St 73501 | 580-591-0203 |
| Great Plains Area Voc. Tech. School | Post-Sec. |
| 4500 SW Lee Blvd 73505 | 580-355-6371 |
| Lawton Academy of Arts and Sciences | 100/PK-12 |
| 1911 NW 72nd 73505 | 580-536-1900 |
| Lawton Christian S | 500/PK-12 |
| 1 NW Crusader Dr 73505 | 580-536-6885 |
| Patti Rhea, supt. | Fax 536-5242 |
| Platt College | Post-Sec. |
| 112 SW 11th St 73501 | 580-355-4416 |

**Leedey, Dewey, Pop. 416**

| | |
|---|---|
| Leedey ISD | 200/PK-12 |
| 505 E 6th St 73654 | 580-488-3424 |
| Rusty Puffinbarger, supt. | Fax 488-3428 |
| www.leedey.k12.ok.us | |
| Leedey HS, 500 E 6th St 73654 | 100/9-12 |
| Darren Danielson, prin. | 580-488-3377 |

**LeFlore, LeFlore, Pop. 182**

| | |
|---|---|
| LeFlore ISD | 200/PK-12 |
| PO Box 147 74942 | 918-753-2345 |
| Lane Jackson, supt. | Fax 753-2604 |
| www.leflorepss.k12.ok.us | |
| LeFlore HS | 100/9-12 |
| PO Box 147 74942 | 918-753-2345 |
| Tracy Loyd, dean | Fax 753-2604 |

**Lexington, Cleveland, Pop. 2,050**

| | |
|---|---|
| Lexington ISD | 1,100/PK-12 |
| 420 NE 4th St 73051 | 405-527-7236 |
| Denny Prince, supt. | Fax 527-9517 |
| www.lexington.k12.ok.us/ | |
| Lexington HS | 200/9-12 |
| 801 E Broadway St 73051 | 405-527-3810 |
| David McLain, prin. | Fax 527-3814 |
| Lexington MS | 200/6-8 |
| 420 NE 4th St 73051 | 405-527-7236 |
| Jeff Hall, prin. | Fax 527-1415 |

**Lindsay, Garvin, Pop. 2,771**

| | |
|---|---|
| Lindsay ISD | 1,200/PK-12 |
| 800 W Creek St 73052 | 405-756-3131 |
| Dan Chapman, supt. | Fax 756-8819 |
| www.lindsay.k12.ok.us | |
| Lindsay HS | 300/9-12 |
| 800 W Creek St 73052 | 405-756-3132 |
| Chuck Karpe, prin. | Fax 756-8554 |
| Lindsay MS, 800 W Creek St 73052 | 300/6-8 |
| Tommy Ferguson, prin. | 405-756-3133 |

**Locust Grove, Mayes, Pop. 1,264**

| | |
|---|---|
| Locust Grove ISD | 1,500/PK-12 |
| PO Box 399 74352 | 918-479-5243 |
| Lori Helton, supt. | Fax 479-6468 |
| www.lg.k12.ok.us | |
| Locust Grove HS | 500/9-12 |
| PO Box 399 74352 | 918-479-5247 |
| Clint Hall, prin. | Fax 479-2743 |
| Locust Grove MS | 300/6-8 |
| PO Box 399 74352 | 918-479-5244 |
| Coy Graves, prin. | Fax 479-2930 |

**Lone Grove, Carter, Pop. 4,751**

| | |
|---|---|
| Lone Grove ISD | 1,600/PK-12 |
| PO Box 1330 73443 | 580-657-3131 |
| Meri Jayne Miller, supt. | Fax 657-4355 |
| www.lonegrove.k12.ok.us/ | |
| Other Schools – See Ardmore | |

**Lone Wolf, Kiowa, Pop. 435**

| | |
|---|---|
| Lone Wolf ISD | 100/PK-12 |
| PO Box 158 73655 | 580-846-9091 |
| James Sutherland, supt. | Fax 846-5266 |
| lonewolfschool.com | |
| Lone Wolf HS | 50/9-12 |
| PO Box 158 73655 | 580-846-9091 |
| James Sutherland, prin. | Fax 846-5266 |

**Lookeba, Caddo, Pop. 163**
Lookeba-Sickles ISD — 300/PK-12
10108 County Road 1150 73053 — 405-457-6623
Mike Davis, supt. — Fax 457-6382
www.lookeba.k12.ok.us
Lookeba-Sickles HS — 100/9-12
10108 County Road 1150 73053 — 405-457-6621
Shirley Gathers, prin. — Fax 457-6619

**Luther, Oklahoma, Pop. 1,168**
Luther ISD — 900/PK-12
PO Box 430 73054 — 405-277-3233
Dr. Sheldon Buxton, supt. — Fax 277-3498
www.lutherlions.org
Luther HS — 200/9-12
PO Box 430 73054 — 405-277-3263
Jan Scheffler, prin. — Fax 277-3630
Luther MS — 300/5-8
PO Box 430 73054 — 405-277-3264
Barry Gunn, prin. — Fax 277-3877

**McAlester, Pittsburg, Pop. 17,248**
McAlester ISD — 3,000/PK-12
PO Box 1027 74502 — 918-423-4771
Marsha Gore, supt. — Fax 423-8166
www.mcalester.k12.ok.us
McAlester HS — 900/9-12
PO Box 1027 74502 — 918-423-4776
Paula Meadows, prin. — Fax 423-8689
Puterbaugh MS — 400/7-8
PO Box 1027 74502 — 918-423-5445
Caroline Miller, prin. — Fax 423-7021

OK Dept. of Voc. & Tech. Education
Supt. — None
Kiamichi Technology Center — Vo/Tech
301 Kiamichi Dr 74501 — 918-426-0940
Angela Evans, dir. — Fax 426-1626

---

Lakewood Christian S — 200/PK-12
840 S George Nigh Expwy 74501 — 918-426-2000

**Mc Curtain, Haskell, Pop. 484**
McCurtain ISD — 200/PK-12
PO Box 189 74944 — 918-945-7237
Dart Drummonds, supt. — Fax 945-7064
www.mccurtain.k12.ok.us/
McCurtain HS — 100/9-12
PO Box 189 74944 — 918-945-7237
Perry Arnwine, prin. — Fax 945-7064

**Mc Loud, Pottawatomie, Pop. 3,818**
McLoud ISD — 1,800/PK-12
PO Box 240, — 405-964-3314
Doran Smith, supt. — Fax 964-2801
www.mcloudschools.us/
McLoud HS — 600/9-12
PO Box 60, — 405-964-3314
Leigh Todd, prin. — Fax 964-3498
McLoud JHS — 300/7-8
PO Box 730, — 405-964-3314
Angie Drew, prin. — Fax 964-7530

**Macomb, Pottawatomie, Pop. 32**
Macomb ISD — 400/PK-12
36591 Highway 59B 74852 — 405-598-3892
Matthew Riggs, supt. — Fax 598-8041
www.macomb.k12.ok.us
Macomb HS — 100/9-12
36591 Highway 59B 74852 — 405-598-5420
Scott Frazier, prin. — Fax 598-3295

**Madill, Marshall, Pop. 3,605**
Madill ISD — 1,800/PK-12
601 W McArthur St 73446 — 580-795-3303
Jon Tuck, supt. — Fax 795-3210
www.madillok.com
Madill HS — 500/9-12
700 S 5th Ave 73446 — 580-795-3339
Andy Gower, prin. — Fax 795-2657
Madill MS — 400/6-8
601 W McArthur St 73446 — 580-795-7373
Tena Houser, prin. — Fax 795-6930

**Mangum, Greer, Pop. 2,935**
Mangum ISD — 700/PK-12
400 N Pennsylvania Ave 73554 — 580-782-3371
Mike Southall, supt. — Fax 782-2313
www.mangum.k12.ok.us/
Mangum HS — 200/9-12
301 N Oklahoma Ave 73554 — 580-782-3343
Lori Cooksey, prin. — Fax 782-3265
Mangum JHS — 100/7-8
400 N Oklahoma Ave 73554 — 580-782-2702
Barbara Gahagan, prin. — Fax 782-5911

**Mannford, Creek, Pop. 2,901**
Mannford ISD — 1,500/PK-12
136 Evans Ave 74044 — 918-865-4062
Dr. Steve Waldvogel, supt. — Fax 865-3405
www.mannford.k12.ok.us
Mannford HS — 500/9-12
220 Evans Ave 74044 — 918-865-3841
Tim Wright, prin. — Fax 865-2813
Mannford MS — 300/6-8
100 Green Valley Rd 74044 — 918-865-4680
Steve Anderson, prin. — Fax 865-2862

**Marietta, Love, Pop. 2,521**
Marietta ISD — 1,000/PK-12
PO Box 289 73448 — 580-276-9444
Joe Neely, supt. — Fax 276-4037
www.mariettaisd.org/
Marietta HS — 300/9-12
PO Box 289 73448 — 580-276-3204
Rodd Davis, prin. — Fax 276-1208
Marietta MS — 200/6-8
PO Box 289 73448 — 580-276-3886
Brandi Naylor, prin. — Fax 276-1203

**Marlow, Stephens, Pop. 4,444**
Bray-Doyle ISD — 400/PK-12
1205 S Brooks Rd 73055 — 580-658-5076
David Eads, supt. — Fax 658-5888
www.braydoyle.k12.ok.us
Bray-Doyle HS — 100/9-12
1205 S Brooks Rd 73055 — 580-658-5071
James Vines, prin. — Fax 658-5888

Central High ISD — 400/PK-12
274801 Bronco Rd 73055 — 580-658-6858
Bennie Newton M.Ed., supt. — Fax 658-8006
www.central.k12.ok.us
Central JSHS — 100/7-12
274801 Bronco Rd 73055 — 580-658-2929
Mark Perry M.Ed., prin. — Fax 658-8010

Marlow ISD — 1,400/PK-12
PO Box 73 73055 — 580-658-2719
George Coffman, supt. — Fax 658-6455
www.marlow.k12.ok.us
Marlow HS — 400/9-12
PO Box 73 73055 — 580-658-1516
Bryan Brantley, prin. — Fax 658-2718
Marlow MS — 300/6-8
PO Box 73 73055 — 580-658-2619
Ross Ridge, prin. — Fax 658-1169

**Mason, Okfuskee**
Mason ISD — 300/PK-12
374006 E 1000 Rd 74859 — 918-623-0231
Jerry Bogle, supt. — Fax 623-0884
www.mason.k12.ok.us/
Mason HS — 100/9-12
374006 E 1000 Rd 74859 — 918-623-0107
Eddie Weaver, prin. — Fax 623-0147

**Maud, Pottawatomie, Pop. 993**
Maud ISD — 300/PK-12
PO Box 130 74854 — 405-374-2416
Jerry McCormick, supt. — Fax 374-2628
www.maud.k12.ok.us
Maud HS — 100/9-12
PO Box 130 74854 — 405-374-2425
Darrell Reid, prin. — Fax 374-2895

**Maysville, Garvin, Pop. 1,159**
Maysville ISD — 400/PK-12
600 1st St 73057 — 888-806-5220
Dr. Shelly Hildebrand-Beach, supt. — Fax 867-4864
maysville.k12.ok.us
Maysville HS — 100/9-12
600 1st St 73057 — 888-806-5330
Dr. Shelly Hildebrand-Beach, prin. — Fax 867-4864

**Medford, Grant, Pop. 970**
Medford ISD — 300/PK-12
301 N Main St 73759 — 580-395-2392
Mickey Geurkink, supt. — Fax 395-2391
www.medford.k12.ok.us/
Medford HS — 100/9-12
301 N Main St 73759 — 580-395-2392
Micheal Thompson, prin. — Fax 395-2391

**Meeker, Lincoln, Pop. 1,096**
Meeker ISD — 900/PK-12
214 E Carl Hubbell Blvd 74855 — 405-788-4540
Rita Palmer, supt. — Fax 279-2765
www.meeker.k12.ok.us/
Meeker HS — 300/9-12
214 E Carl Hubbell Blvd 74855 — 405-788-4540
Mike Hedge, prin. — Fax 279-2765
Meeker MS — 200/6-8
214 E Carl Hubbell Blvd 74855 — 405-788-4540
Virgil Fowler, dean — Fax 279-2765

**Miami, Ottawa, Pop. 12,277**
Miami ISD — 2,500/PK-12
26 N Main St 74354 — 918-542-8455
Loretta Robinson, supt. — Fax 542-1236
www.miami.k12.ok.us
Miami HS — 700/9-12
2000 E Central Ave 74354 — 918-542-4421
Lisa Munson, prin. — Fax 542-7421
Rogers MS — 600/6-8
504 Goodrich Blvd 74354 — 918-542-5588
Justin Chase, prin. — Fax 542-4400

---

Northeastern Oklahoma A&M College — Post-Sec.
200 I St NE 74354 — 918-542-8441

**Midwest City, Oklahoma, Pop. 51,213**
Midwest City-Del City ISD — 14,500/PK-12
7217 SE 15th St 73110 — 405-737-4461
Dr. Rick Cobb, supt. — Fax 739-1615
www.mid-del.net
Albert MS — 800/6-8
2515 S Post Rd 73130 — 405-739-1761
Cindy Anderson, prin. — Fax 739-1780
Albert SHS — 1,100/9-12
2009 S Post Rd 73130 — 405-739-1726
Kristin Goggans, prin. — Fax 739-1685
Career Academy — Alt
1730 Center Dr 73110 — 405-582-7099
Dr. Rodney Stearns, prin.
Jarman MS — 500/6-8
5 MacArthur Dr 73110 — 405-739-1771
LaShonda Broiles, prin. — Fax 739-1773
Midwest City SHS — 1,500/9-12
213 Elm St 73110 — 405-739-1741
Chris Reynolds, prin. — Fax 739-1675
Monroney MS — 600/6-8
7400 E Reno Ave 73110 — 405-739-1786
Mark Flies, prin. — Fax 739-1789
Other Schools – See Del City

OK Dept. of Voc. & Tech. Education
Supt. — None
Mid-Del Technology Center — Vo/Tech
1621 Maple Dr 73110 — 405-739-1707
Fax 739-1716

---

Rose State College — Post-Sec.
6420 SE 15th St 73110 — 405-733-7673

**Milburn, Johnston, Pop. 295**
Milburn ISD — 200/PK-12
PO Box 429 73450 — 580-443-5522
Joey McBride, supt. — Fax 443-5303
www.milburnps.org
Milburn HS — 100/9-12
PO Box 429 73450 — 580-443-5522
Joey McBride, prin. — Fax 443-5303

**Mill Creek, Johnston, Pop. 283**
Mill Creek ISD — 100/PK-12
602 S Chickasaw Ave 74856 — 580-384-5514
Lorinda Chancellor, supt. — Fax 384-3920
Mill Creek HS — 50/9-12
602 S Chickasaw Ave 74856 — 580-384-5514
Lorinda Chancellor, prin. — Fax 384-3920

**Minco, Grady, Pop. 1,580**
Minco ISD — 600/PK-12
PO Box 428 73059 — 405-352-4867
Kevin Sims, supt. — Fax 352-4006
www.minco.k12.ok.us
Minco HS — 200/9-12
PO Box 428 73059 — 405-352-4377
Clint Shirley, prin. — Fax 352-4006
Minco MS — 100/6-8
PO Box 428 73059 — 405-352-4377
Troy Wittrock, prin. — Fax 352-4006

**Moore, Cleveland, Pop. 51,925**
Moore ISD — 21,700/PK-12
1500 SE 4th St 73160 — 405-735-4200
Dr. Robert Romines, supt. — Fax 735-4392
www.mooreschools.com
Central JHS — 500/7-8
400 N Broadway St 73160 — 405-735-4560
Tammy Baker, prin. — Fax 895-7398
Highland East JHS — 700/7-8
1200 SE 4th St 73160 — 405-735-4580
Mark Archer, prin. — Fax 793-3198
Highland West JHS — 600/7-8
901 N Santa Fe Ave 73160 — 405-735-4600
Peggy Pate, prin. — Fax 793-3218
Moore HS — 2,200/9-12
300 N Eastern Ave 73160 — 405-735-4700
Mike Coyle, prin. — Fax 793-3140
Southmoore HS — 2,000/9-12
2901 S Santa Fe Ave 73160 — 405-735-4900
Roy Smith, prin. — Fax 735-4992
Vista Academy — Alt
224 SE 4th St 73160 — 405-735-4640
Dr. Sandra Ludwig, prin. — Fax 793-3062
Vista Academy HS — Alt
224 SE 4th St 73160 — 405-735-4640
Dr. Sandra Ludwig, prin. — Fax 793-3062
Vista MAST Academy — Alt
624 NW 5th St 73160 — 405-799-3379
Fax 799-0912
Other Schools – See Oklahoma City

---

Hillsdale Free Will Baptist College — Post-Sec.
PO Box 7208 73153 — 405-912-9000
Platt College — Post-Sec.
201 N Eastern Ave 73160 — 405-912-3260

**Mooreland, Woodward, Pop. 1,172**
Mooreland ISD — 500/PK-12
PO Box 75 73852 — 580-994-5388
Terry W. Kellner M.S., supt. — Fax 994-5900
www.mooreland.k12.ok.us
Mooreland HS — 100/9-12
PO Box 75 73852 — 580-994-5426
Ron Wilson, prin. — Fax 994-2344

**Morris, Okmulgee, Pop. 1,388**
Morris ISD — 1,000/PK-12
307 S 6th St 74445 — 918-733-9072
James Lyons, supt. — Fax 733-4205
www.morris.k12.ok.us/
Morris HS — 300/9-12
307 S 6th St 74445 — 918-733-9072
Andrew Ewton, prin. — Fax 733-4205
Morris MS — 200/6-8
307 S 6th St 74445 — 918-733-9072
Monte Womack, prin. — Fax 733-4205

**Morrison, Noble, Pop. 700**
Morrison ISD — 400/PK-12
PO Box 176 73061 — 580-724-3341
Jay Vernon, supt. — Fax 724-3004
www.morrisonps.com
Morrison HS, PO Box 176 73061 — 100/9-12
Shalon Reynolds, prin. — 580-724-3307

**Mounds, Creek, Pop. 1,107**
Liberty ISD — 600/PK-12
2727 E 201st St S 74047 — 918-366-8496
Donna Campo, supt. — Fax 366-8497
libertyoc.liberty.k12.ok.us
Liberty HS, 2727 E 201st St S 74047 — 200/9-12
Matthew Sweet, prin. — 918-366-8784

Mounds ISD — 500/PK-12
PO Box 189 74047 — 918-827-6100
Alfred Gaches, supt. — Fax 827-3704
www.moundsps.com
Mounds HS — 200/9-12
PO Box 189 74047 — 918-827-6100
Stephen Sturgeon, prin. — Fax 827-3705

**Mountain View, Kiowa, Pop. 770**
Mountain View-Gotebo ISD — 300/PK-12
RR 2 Box 88 73062 — 580-347-2211
Sam Belcher, supt. — Fax 347-2869
www.mvgschools.com

Mountain View-Gotebo HS 100/9-12
150 S 1st St 73062 580-347-2211
Sam Belcher, prin.

**Moyers, Pushmataha**
Moyers ISD 200/PK-12
PO Box 88 74557 580-298-5549
Donna Dudley, supt. Fax 298-2022
moyersisd.org
Moyers HS 100/9-12
PO Box 88 74557 580-298-5547
LaWanda Vaughn, prin. Fax 298-2022

**Muldrow, Sequoyah, Pop. 3,165**
Muldrow ISD 1,700/PK-12
PO Box 660 74948 918-427-7406
Ron Flanagan, supt. Fax 427-6088
www.muldrowps.org
Muldrow HS 500/9-12
PO Box 660 74948 918-427-3274
Steve Page, prin. Fax 427-1035
Muldrow MS 500/5-8
PO Box 660 74948 918-427-5421
Angela Williams, prin. Fax 427-1034

**Muskogee, Muskogee, Pop. 36,324**
Hilldale ISD 1,800/PK-12
500 E Smith Ferry Rd 74403 918-683-0273
Dr. Kaylin Coody, supt. Fax 683-8725
www.hilldale.k12.ok.us
Hilldale HS 500/9-12
300 E Smith Ferry Rd 74403 918-683-3253
Deborah Tennison, prin. Fax 683-0622
Hilldale MS 400/6-8
400 E Smith Ferry Rd 74403 918-683-0763
Darren Riddle, prin. Fax 683-0766

Muskogee ISD 6,200/PK-12
202 W Broadway St 74401 918-684-3700
Peggy Jones, supt. Fax 684-3827
www.mpsi20.org
Muskogee HS 1,600/9-12
3200 E Shawnee Rd 74403 918-684-3750
Dewayne Pemberton, prin. Fax 684-3751
Robertson JHS 700/7-8
402 N S St 74403 918-684-3775
Dr. Edwin Strickland, prin. Fax 684-3776
Rougher Alternative Academy Alt
600 Altamont St 74401 918-684-3705
Steve Barton, prin. Fax 684-3706

OK Dept. of Voc. & Tech. Education
Supt. — None
Indian Capital Technology Center Vo/Tech
2403 N 41st St E 74403 918-687-6383
Anthony Pivec, supt. Fax 687-6624

---

Bacone College Post-Sec.
2299 Old Bacone Rd 74403 918-683-4581
Muskogee General Hospital Post-Sec.
300 Rockefeller Dr 74401 918-682-5501
Parkview School OK School for the Blind Post-Sec.
3300 Gibson St 74403 918-682-6641
Virgil's Beauty College Post-Sec.
111 S 9th St 74401 918-682-9429

**Mustang, Canadian, Pop. 16,780**
Mustang ISD 7,900/PK-12
906 S Heights Dr 73064 405-376-2461
Dr. Sean McDaniel, supt. Fax 376-7333
www.mustangps.org
Mustang HS 1,800/9-12
906 S Heights Dr 73064 405-376-2404
Teresa Wilkerson, prin. Fax 376-7347
Mustang MS 700/7-8
906 S Heights Dr 73064 405-376-2448
Kathy Knowles, prin. Fax 376-7373
Mustang North MS 700/7-8
906 S Heights Dr 73064 405-324-2236
Christy Bradley, prin. Fax 324-2258

**Mutual, Woodward, Pop. 59**
Sharon-Mutual ISD 300/PK-12
210 S Maple St 73853 580-989-3210
Jeff Thompson, supt. Fax 989-3241
www.smps.k12.ok.us
Sharon-Mutual HS 100/9-12
210 S Maple St 73853 580-989-3231
Rustin Donaldson, prin. Fax 989-8019

**Newcastle, McClain, Pop. 7,304**
Newcastle ISD 1,400/PK-12
101 N Main St 73065 405-387-2890
Tony O'Brien, supt. Fax 387-3482
www.newcastle.k12.ok.us
Newcastle HS 500/9-12
101 N Main St 73065 405-387-4304
Rob Gilstrap, prin. Fax 387-3461
Newcastle MS 400/6-8
611 E Fox Ln 73065 405-387-3139
John Harris, prin. Fax 387-5563

**Newkirk, Kay, Pop. 2,182**
Newkirk ISD 800/PK-12
625 W South St 74647 580-362-2388
Steve Stanley, supt. Fax 362-3413
www.newkirk.k12.ok.us
Newkirk HS 300/9-12
221 S Main St 74647 580-362-6241
Dr. Maurisa Pruett, prin. Fax 362-6242
Newkirk MS 200/5-8
711 S Academy Ave 74647 580-362-2516
Jeff Wilson, prin. Fax 362-1150

**Ninnekah, Grady, Pop. 970**
Ninnekah ISD 500/PK-12
PO Box 275 73067 405-224-4092
Todd Bunch, supt. Fax 224-4096
www.ninnekah.ok.nph.schoolinsites.com/
Ninnekah HS 100/9-12
PO Box 275 73067 405-224-4299
David Pitts, prin. Fax 224-4665
Ninnekah JHS 100/7-8
PO Box 275 73067 405-224-4299
Glen Shoemake, prin. Fax 224-4665

**Noble, Cleveland, Pop. 6,155**
Noble ISD 2,900/PK-12
PO Box 499 73068 405-872-3452
Greg Kasbaum, supt. Fax 872-3271
www.nobleps.com
Inge MS 700/6-8
1201 N 8th St 73068 405-872-3495
Ronald Fulks, prin. Fax 872-8670
Noble HS 800/9-12
4601 E Etowah Rd 73068 405-872-3441
Steve Barrett, prin. Fax 872-9824

**Norman, Cleveland, Pop. 105,378**
Little Axe ISD 1,200/PK-12
2000 168th Ave NE 73026 405-329-7691
Tony Smith, supt. Fax 579-2929
littleaxeps.org/
Little Axe HS 300/9-12
2000 168th Ave NE 73026 405-329-1612
Barry Thomas, prin. Fax 329-2914
Little Axe MS 300/6-8
2000 168th Ave NE 73026 405-329-2156
Dalton Griffin, prin. Fax 579-2937

Norman ISD 14,500/PK-12
131 S Flood Ave 73069 405-364-1339
Dr. Joseph Siano, supt. Fax 366-5851
www.norman.k12.ok.us
Alcott MS 600/6-8
1919 W Boyd St 73069 405-366-5845
Dr. Dana Morris, prin. Fax 447-6572
Dimensions Academy Alt
1101 E Main St 73071 405-579-1880
Paul Tryggestad, prin. Fax 579-1881
Irving MS 800/6-8
125 Vicksburg Ave 73071 405-366-5941
Alice Graddy, prin. Fax 366-5944
Longfellow MS 600/6-8
215 N Ponca Ave 73071 405-366-5948
Shelly Ellis, prin. Fax 366-5952
Norman HS 1,800/9-12
911 W Main St 73069 405-366-5812
Dr. Scott Beck, prin. Fax 366-5945
Norman North HS 2,100/9-12
1809 Stubbeman Ave 73069 405-366-5954
Dr. Peter Liesenfeld, prin. Fax 573-3590
Whittier MS 1,100/6-8
2000 W Brooks St 73069 405-366-5956
Gayla Mears, prin. Fax 447-6562

OK Dept. of Voc. & Tech. Education
Supt. — None
Moore Norman Technology Center Vo/Tech
PO Box 4701 73070 405-364-5763
Dr. Jane Bowen, supt. Fax 217-8277

---

Community Christian S 700/PK-12
3002 Broce Dr 73072 405-329-2500
Hollywood Cosmetology Center Post-Sec.
1708 W Lindsey St 73069 405-364-3375
University of Oklahoma Post-Sec.
660 Parrington Oval 73019 405-325-0311

**Nowata, Nowata, Pop. 3,335**
Nowata ISD 1,000/PK-12
707 W Osage Ave 74048 918-273-3425
Leon Ashlock, supt. Fax 273-2105
www.npsok.org
Nowata HS 300/9-12
707 W Osage Ave 74048 918-273-2221
Bron Williams, prin. Fax 273-2105
Nowata MS 200/6-8
707 W Osage Ave 74048 918-273-1346
Shawn Imhoff, prin. Fax 273-2105

**Oaks, Delaware, Pop. 277**
Oaks-Mission ISD 300/PK-12
PO Box 160 74359 918-868-2183
Dr. John Sheridan, supt. Fax 868-2707
Oaks-Mission HS 100/9-12
PO Box 160 74359 918-868-2499
John Sheridan, prin. Fax 868-5012

**Oilton, Creek, Pop. 965**
Oilton ISD 300/PK-12
PO Box 130 74052 918-862-3954
Matt Posey, supt. Fax 862-3955
www.oilton.k12.ok.us
Oilton HS 100/9-12
PO Box 130 74052 918-862-3272
Tim Kruse, prin. Fax 862-3763

**Okarche, Kingfisher, Pop. 1,196**
Okarche ISD 300/PK-12
PO Box 276 73762 405-263-7300
Robert Friesen, supt. Fax 263-7515
www.okarche.k12.ok.us
Okarche HS 100/10-12
PO Box 276 73762 405-263-7212
Robert Friesen, prin. Fax 263-7515
Okarche JHS 100/7-9
PO Box 276 73762 405-263-7212
Robert Friesen, prin. Fax 263-7515

**Okay, Wagoner, Pop. 586**
Okay ISD 500/PK-12
PO Box 830 74446 918-682-2548
Charles McMahan, supt. Fax 683-8331
www.okayps.org
Okay HS 100/9-12
PO Box 830 74446 918-682-0371
Mark Hayes, prin. Fax 682-7653

**Okeene, Blaine, Pop. 1,187**
Okeene ISD 300/PK-12
PO Box 409 73763 580-822-3268
Ron Pittman, supt. Fax 822-4123
www.okeene.k12.ok.us
Okeene JSHS 100/7-12
PO Box 409 73763 580-822-3219
Jeremy Osmus, prin. Fax 822-4123

**Okemah, Okfuskee, Pop. 3,000**
Okemah ISD 800/PK-12
107 W Date St 74859 918-623-1874
Tony Dean, supt. Fax 623-1203
www.okemahk12.com
Okemah HS 300/9-12
704 E Date St 74859 918-623-1874
Ronald Vick, prin. Fax 623-1884
Okemah MS 200/4-8
107 W Date St 74859 918-623-1874
Sandra Lambert, prin. Fax 623-9151

**Oklahoma City, Oklahoma, Pop. 555,623**
Crooked Oak ISD 1,100/PK-12
1450 S Eastern Ave 73129 405-677-5252
Brad Richards, supt. Fax 670-8070
www.crookedoak.org
Crooked Oak HS 300/9-12
1450 S Eastern Ave 73129 405-677-3452
Barbara Jaramillo, prin. Fax 670-8072
Crooked Oak MS 300/6-8
1450 S Eastern Ave 73129 405-677-5133
Dennis McCray, prin. Fax 670-2256

Millwood ISD 1,100/PK-12
6724 N Martin Luther King 73111 405-478-1336
Cecilia Robinson, supt. Fax 478-4698
millwood.k12.ok.us
Millwood Arts Academy 6-8
6700 N Martin Luther King 73111 405-478-0630
Candice Greene, prin. Fax 478-7134
Millwood HS 300/9-12
6718 N Martin Luther King 73111 405-475-1015
Eldridge Moore, prin. Fax 478-4194

Moore ISD
Supt. — See Moore
Brink JHS 900/7-8
11420 S Western Ave 73170 405-735-4540
David Peak, prin. Fax 692-5634
Moore West JHS 700/7-8
9400 S Pennsylvania Ave 73159 405-735-4620
Danny Reed, prin. Fax 692-5660
Westmoore HS 2,000/9-12
12613 S Western Ave 73170 405-735-4800
Mark Hunt, prin. Fax 692-5711

OK Dept. of Voc. & Tech. Education
Supt. — None
Metro Tech-Aviation Career Center Vo/Tech
5600 S MacArthur Blvd 73179 405-424-8324
Dr. Elaine Stith, supt.
Metro Tech Downtown Vo/Tech
100 N Broadway 73102 405-424-8324
Metro Tech South Bryant Campus Vo/Tech
4901 S Bryant Ave 73129 405-424-8324
Dr. Elaine Stith, supt. Fax 670-6895
Metro Tech-Springlake Campus Vo/Tech
1900 Springlake Dr 73111 405-424-8324
Dr. Elaine Stith, supt. Fax 424-8589
Tuttle-Portland Campus Vo/Tech
3500 NW 150th St 73134 405-717-7799
Dr. Tom Friedemann, supt. Fax 755-0028
Tuttle-Reno Campus Vo/Tech
7301 W Reno Ave 73127 405-717-4646
Dr. Tom Friedemann, supt.
Tuttle-Rockwell Campus Vo/Tech
12777 N Rockwell Ave 73142 405-717-7799
Dr. Tom Friedemann, supt. Fax 717-4112

Oklahoma City ISD 38,300/PK-12
900 N Klein Ave 73106 405-587-0000
Rob Neu, supt. Fax 587-0443
www.okcps.org
Belle Isle Enterprise MS 500/6-8
5904 N Villa Ave 73112 405-587-6600
Lynn Kellert, prin. Fax 587-6605
Capitol Hill HS 1,000/9-12
500 SW Grand Blvd 73109 405-587-9000
Alex Souza, prin. Fax 587-9005
Classen S of Advanced Studies 500/6-12
1901 N Ellison Ave 73106 405-587-5400
Dr. Ashley Davis, prin. Fax 587-5405
Douglass MSHS 500/7-12
900 N Martin Luther King Av 73117 405-587-4200
Dr. Barbara Davis, prin. Fax 587-4205
Emerson HS 400/Alt
715 N Walker Ave 73102 405-232-5273
Sheryl Kishore, prin. Fax 231-2014
Grant HS 1,500/9-12
5016 S Pennsylvania Ave 73119 405-587-2200
Barbara Jaramillo, prin. Fax 587-2205
Jefferson MS 1,000/6-8
6800 S Blackwelder Ave 73159 405-587-1300
Greg Frederick, prin. Fax 587-1305
Marshall MSHS 400/6-12
12201 N Portland Ave 73120 405-587-7200
Aspasia Carlson, prin. Fax 587-7205
Northeast Academy for Health Sci./Eng. 200/6-12
3100 N Kelley Ave 73111 405-587-3300
Scot McAdoo, prin. Fax 587-3305
Northwest Classen HS 1,000/9-12
2801 NW 27th St 73107 405-587-6300
Brad Herzer, prin. Fax 587-6305
Oklahoma Centennial MSHS 400/6-12
1301 NE 101st St 73131 405-587-5200
Charmaine Johnson, prin. Fax 587-5205
Roosevelt MS 1,000/6-8
3233 SW 44th St 73119 405-587-8300
Julie Roach, prin. Fax 587-8305

Southeast HS 700/9-12
5401 S Shields Blvd 73129 405-587-9600
Pat Borelli, prin. Fax 587-9605
Taft MS 800/6-8
2901 NW 23rd St 73107 405-946-1431
Eric Schellenger, prin. Fax 945-1126
Webster MS 700/6-8
6708 S Santa Fe Ave 73139 405-632-6653
Mylissa Hall, prin. Fax 636-5096
Other Schools – See Spencer

Oklahoma School of Science & Math 11-12
1141 N Lincoln Blvd 73104 405-521-6436
Dr. Frank Wang, pres. Fax 522-4586
www.ossm.edu/
Oklahoma S of Science & Math 11-12
1141 N Lincoln Blvd 73104 405-521-6436
Dr. Frank Wang, pres. Fax 522-4586

Putnam City ISD 18,500/PK-12
5401 NW 40th St 73122 405-495-5200
Dr. Fred Rhodes, supt. Fax 495-8648
www.putnamcityschools.org
Cooper MS 700/6-8
8001 River Bend Blvd 73132 405-720-9887
Mark Lebsack, prin. Fax 728-5632
Hefner MS 1,100/6-8
8400 N MacArthur Blvd 73132 405-721-2411
Toye Mitchell, prin. Fax 728-5645
Mayfield MS 700/6-8
1600 N Purdue Ave 73127 405-947-8693
Tracy Sowinski, prin. Fax 948-9000
Putnam City North HS 2,000/9-12
11800 N Rockwell Ave 73162 405-722-4220
Dr. Brian Chastain, prin. Fax 721-4946
Putnam City West HS 1,600/9-12
8500 NW 23rd St 73127 405-787-1140
Buster Meeks, prin. Fax 491-7602
Other Schools – See Bethany, Warr Acres

Western Heights ISD 4,200/PK-12
8401 SW 44th St 73179 405-350-3410
Joe Kitchens, supt. Fax 745-6322
www.westernheights.k12.ok.us
Western Heights 9th Grade Center 600/9-9
8201 SW 44th St 73179 405-350-3415
Alan Dale, prin. Fax 261-0280
Western Heights Academy Alt
8435 SW 44th St 73179 405-350-3485
Khristi Mize, prin. Fax 745-6364
Western Heights HS 600/10-12
8201 SW 44th St 73179 405-350-3435
John Erickson, prin. Fax 745-6315
Western Heights MS 600/7-8
8435 SW 44th St 73179 405-350-3455
Carolyn Erickson, prin. Fax 745-6341

---

Academy of Classical Christian Studies 500/PK-12
1120 E Hefner Rd 73131 405-478-2077
Bishop McGuinness HS 700/9-12
801 NW 50th St 73118 405-842-6638
David Morton, prin. Fax 858-9550
Brookline College Post-Sec.
9801 Broadway Ext 73114 405-842-9400
Brown Mackie College Post-Sec.
7101 NW Expressway Ste 800 73132 405-621-8000
Casady S 900/PK-12
9500 N Pennsylvania Ave 73120 405-749-3100
Nathan Sheldon, head sch Fax 749-3214
CC's Cosmetology College Post-Sec.
4439 NW 50th St 73112 405-943-2300
Central State Beauty Academy Post-Sec.
8494 NW Expressway 73162 405-722-4499
Crossings Christian S 700/PK-12
14400 N Portland Ave 73134 405-842-8495
Paul S. MacDonald, hdmstr. Fax 767-1520
DeVry University Post-Sec.
4013 NW Expressway Ste 100 73116 405-767-9516
Heritage College Post-Sec.
7100 S I 35 Service Rd 7118 73149 405-631-3399
Heritage Hall S 900/PK-12
1800 NW 122nd St 73120 405-749-3001
Guy Bramble, hdmstr. Fax 751-7372
ITT Technical Institute Post-Sec.
1900 NW Expressway Ste 305R 73118
405-810-4100
Metro Area Vocational Technical School Post-Sec.
1900 Springlake Dr 73111 405-424-8324
Mid-America Christian University Post-Sec.
3500 SW 119th St 73170 405-691-3800
Oklahoma Christian University Post-Sec.
PO Box 11000 73136 405-425-5000
Oklahoma City Community College Post-Sec.
7777 S May Ave 73159 405-682-1611
Oklahoma City University Post-Sec.
2501 N Blackwelder Ave 73106 405-208-5000
Oklahoma State University-Oklahoma City Post-Sec.
900 N Portland Ave 73107 405-947-4421
Parkview Adventist Academy 100/PK-12
4201 N Martin Luther King 73111 405-427-6525
Platt College Post-Sec.
309 S Ann Arbor Ave 73128 405-946-7799
Platt College Post-Sec.
2727 W Memorial Rd 73134 405-749-2433
Tuttle Vocational Technical Center Post-Sec.
12777 N Rockwell Ave 73142 405-722-7799
University Hospital of Oklahoma City Post-Sec.
PO Box 26307 73126 405-271-4000
University of Oklahoma Health Sciences Post-Sec.
1100 N Lindsay Ave 73104 405-271-4000
Wright Career College Post-Sec.
2219 W I 240 Service Rd 73159 405-681-2300

**Okmulgee, Okmulgee, Pop. 11,317**
OK Dept. of Voc. & Tech. Education
Supt. — None
Green Country Technology Center Vo/Tech
PO Box 1217 74447 918-758-0840
Larry Killebrew, supt. Fax 758-0422

Okmulgee ISD 1,600/PK-12
PO Box 1346 74447 918-758-2000
Tod Williams, supt. Fax 758-2088
www.okmulgeeps.com
Alternative Education 50/Alt
1421 Martin Luther King Dr 74447 918-758-2050
Cathryn Umsted, dir. Fax 758-2095
Okmulgee HS 400/9-12
415 W 3rd St 74447 918-758-2075
Jeremy Ramsey, prin. Fax 758-2096
Okmulgee MS 300/6-8
1421 Martin Luther King Dr 74447 918-758-2050
Bradley Ferguson, prin. Fax 758-2095

---

College of Muscogee Nation Post-Sec.
PO Box 917 74447 918-549-2800
Oklahoma State Univ Institute of Tech Post-Sec.
1801 E 4th St 74447 800-722-4471

**Oktaha, Muskogee, Pop. 343**
Oktaha ISD 700/PK-12
PO Box 9 74450 918-687-7556
Jerry Needham M.Ed., supt. Fax 687-0074
www.oktahaschool.com/
Oktaha HS 200/9-12
PO Box 9 74450 918-687-3672
Chris Burt M.Ed., prin. Fax 687-8551

**Olustee, Jackson, Pop. 583**
Olustee ISD 200/PK-12
PO Box 70 73560 580-648-2243
Gaylene Freeman, supt. Fax 648-2501
www.olustee.k12.ok.us
Olustee HS 100/9-12
PO Box 70 73560 580-648-2243
Brent Drury, prin. Fax 648-2501

**Omega, Kingfisher**
Lomega ISD 200/PK-12
18319 N 2700 Rd 73764 405-729-4215
Karen Castonguay, supt. Fax 729-4666
www.lomega.k12.ok.us
Lomega HS 50/9-12
18319 N 2700 Rd 73764 405-729-4281
Karen Castonguay, prin. Fax 729-4666

OK Dept. of Voc. & Tech. Education
Supt. — None
Chisholm Trail Technology Center Vo/Tech
283 State Highway 33 73764 405-729-8324
Max Thomas, supt. Fax 729-8335

**Oologah, Rogers, Pop. 1,080**
Oologah-Talala ISD 1,800/PK-12
PO Box 189 74053 918-443-6000
Max Tanner, supt. Fax 443-9088
www.oologah.k12.ok.us
Oologah HS 600/9-12
PO Box 189 74053 918-443-6211
Melissa Overcash, prin. Fax 443-2418
Oologah MS 400/6-8
PO Box 189 74053 918-443-6161
Kelli Dixon, prin. Fax 443-2875

**Orlando, Logan, Pop. 142**
Mulhall-Orlando ISD 200/PK-12
100 E Main 73073 405-649-2000
Michael Parsons, supt. Fax 649-2020
www.mulhall-orlando.k12.ok.us
Mulhall-Orlando HS 100/9-12
100 E Main 73073 580-455-2211
Joline Oldenburg, prin. Fax 455-8019

**Owasso, Tulsa, Pop. 27,251**
OK Dept. of Voc. & Tech. Education
Supt. — None
Tulsa Tech Center Owasso Campus Vo/Tech
10800 N 140th East Ave 74055 918-828-1400
Kent Inouye, dir. Fax 376-4107

Owasso ISD 9,000/PK-12
1501 N Ash St 74055 918-272-5367
Dr. Clark Ogilvie, supt. Fax 272-8111
www.owassops.org
Owasso Eighth Grade Center 700/8-8
13901 E 86th St N 74055 918-272-6274
Deirdre Hodge, prin. Fax 272-5562
Owasso HS 1,300/11-12
12901 E 86th St N 74055 918-272-5334
Matt Roberts, prin. Fax 272-8108
Owasso Mid HS 1,400/9-10
8800 N 129th East Ave 74055 918-274-3000
Don Huggins, prin. Fax 274-3006
Owasso Ram Academy Alt
202 E Broadway St 74055 918-272-8040
Johanna Woodard, coord. Fax 272-0712

---

Rejoice Christian S 300/PK-12
12200 E 86th St N 74055 918-516-0050
Dr. Craig Shaw, supt. Fax 516-0299

**Paden, Okfuskee, Pop. 430**
Paden ISD 200/PK-12
PO Box 370 74860 405-932-5053
Lee Northcutt, supt. Fax 932-4132
www.paden.k12.ok.us
Paden HS, PO Box 370 74860 100/9-12
Chris Howk, prin. 405-932-4465

**Panama, LeFlore, Pop. 1,335**
Panama ISD 500/PK-12
PO Box 1680 74951 918-963-2215
Grant Ralls, supt. Fax 963-4860
www.panama.k12.ok.us
Panama HS 200/9-12
PO Box 1680 74951 918-963-2215
Richard Haynes, prin. Fax 963-2638
Panama MS 100/6-8
PO Box 1680 74951 918-963-4479
James Hoffman, dean Fax 963-4493

**Panola, Latimer**
Panola ISD 200/PK-12
PO Box 6 74559 918-465-3298
Brad Corcoran, supt. Fax 465-3656
panolabearcats.org
Panola HS 100/9-12
PO Box 6 74559 918-465-3813
Linda Albright, prin. Fax 465-2996

**Paoli, Garvin, Pop. 587**
Paoli ISD 200/PK-12
PO Box 278 73074 405-484-7336
David Morris, supt. Fax 484-7268
www.paoli.k12.ok.us/
Paoli HS 100/9-12
PO Box 278 73074 405-484-7336
David Morris, prin. Fax 484-7268

**Park Hill, Cherokee, Pop. 3,515**
Keys ISD 900/PK-12
26622 S 520 Rd 74451 918-458-1835
Vol Woods, supt. Fax 456-1656
www.keys.k12.ok.us
Keys HS 400/9-12
26622 S 520 Rd 74451 918-458-1835
Steven Goss, prin. Fax 456-7502

**Pauls Valley, Garvin, Pop. 5,834**
Pauls Valley ISD 1,300/PK-12
PO Box 780 73075 405-238-6453
Darsha Huckabaa, supt. Fax 238-9178
www.paulsvalleyschools.com/
Pauls Valley HS 300/10-12
PO Box 780 73075 405-238-6497
Chris Caldwell, prin. Fax 238-1236
Pauls Valley JHS 300/7-9
PO Box 780 73075 405-238-1239
Martha Graham, prin. Fax 238-1410

**Pawhuska, Osage, Pop. 3,306**
Pawhuska ISD 900/PK-12
1801 McKenzie Rd 74056 918-287-1281
Dr. Landon Berry, supt. Fax 287-4461
www.pawhuskadistrict.org/
Pawhuska HS 300/8-12
621 E 15th St 74056 918-287-1266
Joe Sindelar, prin. Fax 287-1236

**Pawnee, Pawnee, Pop. 2,051**
Pawnee ISD 700/PK-12
615 Denver St 74058 918-762-3676
Ned Williams, supt. Fax 762-2704
www.pawnee.k12.ok.us
Pawnee HS 200/9-12
615 Denver St 74058 918-762-3676
Bobby Miller, prin. Fax 762-2704
Pawnee MS 100/6-8
605 Denver St 74058 918-762-3055
Stacy Womack, prin. Fax 762-3585

**Perkins, Payne, Pop. 2,678**
Perkins-Tryon ISD 1,200/PK-12
PO Box 549 74059 405-547-5703
James Ramsey, supt. Fax 547-2020
www.p-t.k12.ok.us
Perkins-Tryon HS 300/9-12
PO Box 549 74059 405-547-5724
Joe McElroy, prin. Fax 547-5760
Perkins-Tryon JHS 200/6-8
PO Box 549 74059 405-547-5715
Jerry Burnett, prin. Fax 547-5761

**Perry, Noble, Pop. 4,921**
Perry ISD 1,200/PK-12
900 Fir St 73077 580-336-4511
Scott Chenoweth, supt. Fax 336-5185
www.perry.k12.ok.us/
Perry HS 300/9-12
900 Fir St 73077 580-336-4415
Les Justus, prin. Fax 336-3163
Perry JHS 200/7-8
901 Elm St 73077 580-336-2265
Bryan Hall, prin. Fax 336-4211

**Piedmont, Canadian, Pop. 5,527**
Piedmont ISD 2,400/PK-12
713 Piedmont Rd N 73078 405-373-2311
James White, supt. Fax 373-0912
www.piedmontschools.org
Piedmont HS 700/9-12
1055 Edmond Rd NW 73078 405-373-5011
Layne Jones, prin. Fax 373-3055
Piedmont MS 400/7-8
823 2nd St NW 73078 405-373-1315
Trinity Johnson, prin. Fax 373-5006

**Pittsburg, Pittsburg, Pop. 206**
Pittsburg ISD 200/PK-12
PO Box 200 74560 918-432-5062
Chad Graham, supt. Fax 432-5312
www.pittsburg.k12.ok.us
Pittsburg HS, PO Box 200 74560 50/9-12
Chad Graham, prin. 918-432-5513

**Pocola, LeFlore, Pop. 3,869**
Pocola ISD 800/PK-12
600 E Pryor Ave 74902 918-436-2424
Monty Guthrie, supt. Fax 436-2437
www.pocola.k12.ok.us
Pocola HS 200/9-12
603 E Pryor Ave 74902 918-436-2042
Randy Ragland, prin. Fax 436-2920

Pocola MS 200/6-8
603 E Pryor Ave 74902 918-436-2091
Mark McKenzie, prin. Fax 436-9880

**Ponca City, Kay, Pop. 24,217**
OK Dept. of Voc. & Tech. Education
Supt. — None
Pioneer Technology Center Vo/Tech
2101 N Ash St 74601 580-762-8336
Bruce DeMuth, supt. Fax 762-3107

Ponca City ISD 5,200/PK-12
111 W Grand Ave 74601 580-767-8000
Dr. David Pennington, supt. Fax 767-8007
www.pcps.us
East MS 400/8-8
612 E Grand Ave 74601 580-767-8010
Barbara Davis, prin. Fax 762-5301
Ponca City HS 1,600/9-12
927 N 5th St 74601 580-767-9500
Thad Dilbeck, prin. Fax 767-9515

---

Ponca City Beauty College Post-Sec.
122 N 1st St 74601 888-557-6709

**Pond Creek, Grant, Pop. 839**
Pond Creek-Hunter ISD 200/PK-12
200 E Broadway St 73766 580-532-4242
Joel Quinn, supt. Fax 532-4965
www.pondcreek-hunter.k12.ok.us
Pond Creek-Hunter HS 100/9-12
200 E Broadway St 73766 580-532-4241
Kelly Childress, prin. Fax 532-4965
Pond Creek-Hunter MS 5-8
200 E Broadway St 73766 580-532-4262
Jamie Ronck, prin. Fax 532-4965

**Porter, Wagoner, Pop. 534**
Porter Consolidated ISD 600/PK-12
PO Box 120 74454 918-483-2401
Mark Fenton, supt. Fax 483-2310
www.porter.k12.ok.us
Porter Consolidated HS 200/9-12
PO Box 120 74454 918-483-7011
Larry Shackelford, prin. Fax 483-2310

**Porum, Muskogee, Pop. 622**
Porum ISD 500/PK-12
PO Box 189 74455 918-484-5121
Curtis Curry, supt. Fax 484-2310
www.porum.k12.ok.us/
Porum HS 100/9-12
PO Box 189 74455 918-484-5122
Brent Pearce, prin. Fax 484-5121

**Poteau, LeFlore, Pop. 8,045**
OK Dept. of Voc. & Tech. Education
Supt. — None
Kiamichi Technology Center Vo/Tech
PO Box 825 74953 918-647-4525
Doug Hall, dir. Fax 647-4527

Poteau ISD 2,400/PK-12
100 Mockingbird Ln 74953 918-647-7700
Dr. Don Sjoberg, supt. Fax 647-9357
www.poteau.k12.ok.us
Kidd MS 500/6-8
100 Mockingbird Ln 74953 918-647-7741
Joe Ballard, prin. Fax 647-4286
Poteau HS 600/9-12
100 Mockingbird Ln 74953 918-647-7716
Cory Wood, prin. Fax 647-4383

---

Carl Albert State College Post-Sec.
1507 S McKenna St 74953 918-647-1200

**Prague, Lincoln, Pop. 2,232**
Prague ISD 1,000/K-12
3504 NBU 74864 405-567-4455
Justin Lockwood, supt. Fax 567-3095
www.prague.k12.ok.us
Prague HS 300/9-12
3504 NBU 74864 405-567-2281
Fax 567-4982
Prague MS 200/6-8
3504 NBU 74864 405-567-2281
Benny Burnett, prin. Fax 567-3095

**Preston, Okmulgee**
Preston ISD 600/PK-12
PO Box 40 74456 918-756-3388
Mark Hudson, supt. Fax 756-2122
www.preston.k12.ok.us/
Preston HS 200/9-12
PO Box 40 74456 918-756-8636
Pam Snowden, prin. Fax 756-2122

**Prue, Osage, Pop. 443**
Prue ISD 300/PK-12
PO Box 130 74060 918-242-3351
Tom Scully, supt. Fax 242-3392
www.prue.k12.ok.us/
Prue HS 100/9-12
PO Box 130 74060 918-242-3384
Tom Scully, prin. Fax 242-3888

**Pryor, Mayes, Pop. 8,842**
OK Dept. of Voc. & Tech. Education
Supt. — None
Northeast Tech Center Pryor Campus Vo/Tech
PO Box 825 74362 918-825-5555
Debby Peaster, dir. Fax 825-6281

Pryor ISD 2,700/PK-12
PO Box 548 74362 918-825-1255
Don Raleigh, supt. Fax 825-3938
sites.google.com/a/pryorschools.org/pryorschools-org
Pryor HS 600/10-12
PO Box 548 74362 918-825-2340
Brad Bates, prin. Fax 825-3914
Pryor JHS 600/7-9
PO Box 548 74362 918-825-2371
Terry Gwartney, prin. Fax 825-3950

---

Bradford Christian S 50/K-12
2320 NE 1st St 74361 918-825-7038
Amanda Rutherford, admin. Fax 825-7037
Pryor Beauty College Post-Sec.
330 W Graham Ave 74361 918-825-2795

**Purcell, McClain, Pop. 5,558**
Purcell ISD 1,300/PK-12
919 1/2 N 9th Ave 73080 405-527-2146
Dr. Kathy Draper, supt. Fax 527-6366
www.purcellps.org/
Purcell HS 400/9-12
2020 N Green Ave 73080 405-527-4400
Bret Petty, prin. Fax 527-4410
Purcell JHS 200/6-8
201 Lester Ln 73080 405-527-6591
Byron Mooney, prin. Fax 527-6593

**Quapaw, Ottawa, Pop. 859**
Quapaw ISD 700/PK-12
305 W 1st St 74363 918-674-2501
Dr. Randy D. Darr Ed.D., supt. Fax 674-2721
www.quapaw.k12.ok.us
Quapaw HS 200/9-12
305 W 1st St 74363 918-674-2474
Terry Tyree, prin. Fax 674-2721
Quapaw MS 100/6-8
305 W 1st St 74363 918-674-2496
Tamara Bacon, prin. Fax 674-2721

**Quinton, Pittsburg, Pop. 953**
Quinton ISD 600/PK-12
PO Box 670 74561 918-469-3100
Don Cox, supt. Fax 469-3308
www.quintonschools.com/pages/Quinton_Independent_SD
Quinton HS 200/9-12
PO Box 670 74561 918-469-3309
Dane Lemons, prin. Fax 469-2310

**Ralston, Pawnee, Pop. 314**
Woodland SD
Supt. — See Fairfax
Woodland MS 100/5-8
6th & McKinley 74650 918-738-4286
Shelly Doshier, prin. Fax 738-4287

**Ramona, Washington, Pop. 498**
Caney Valley ISD 800/PK-12
PO Box 410 74061 918-536-2500
Rick Peters, supt. Fax 536-2600
www.caneyvalleyschool.org/
Caney Valley HS 200/9-12
PO Box 410 74061 918-536-3425
Debra Keil, prin. Fax 536-7105
Caney Valley MS 200/6-8
PO Box 410 74061 918-536-2705
Travis Lashbrook, prin. Fax 536-7105

**Randlett, Cotton, Pop. 435**
Big Pasture ISD 200/PK-12
PO Box 167 73562 580-281-3831
Nat Lunn, supt. Fax 281-3299
www.bigpasture.org
Big Pasture HS 100/9-12
PO Box 167 73562 580-281-3276
Nat Lunn, prin. Fax 281-3299

**Rattan, Pushmataha, Pop. 299**
Rattan ISD 500/PK-12
PO Box 44 74562 580-587-2546
Shari Pillow, supt. Fax 587-4000
www.rattan.k12.ok.us
Rattan JHS 100/7-8
PO Box 44 74562 580-587-2715
Neil Birchfield, prin. Fax 587-2476
Rattan SHS 100/9-12
PO Box 44 74562 580-587-2715
Neil Birchfield, prin. Fax 587-2476

**Red Oak, Latimer, Pop. 508**
Red Oak ISD 200/PK-12
PO Box 310 74563 918-754-2426
Bryan Deatherage, supt. Fax 754-2898
redoak.k12.ok.us
Red Oak HS 100/9-12
PO Box 310 74563 918-754-2283
Bryan Deatherage, prin. Fax 754-2898

**Red Rock, Noble, Pop. 265**
Frontier ISD 300/PK-12
PO Box 130 74651 580-723-4361
Tracy Kincannon, supt. Fax 723-4516
www.frontierok.com
Frontier HS 100/9-12
PO Box 130 74651 580-723-4360
Doug Sinor, prin. Fax 723-4516

**Reydon, Roger Mills, Pop. 205**
Reydon ISD 200/PK-12
PO Box 10 73660 580-655-4375
Phil Drouhard, supt. Fax 655-4622
www.reydon.k12.ok.us
Reydon HS, PO Box 10 73660 50/9-12
Ryan Baker, prin. 580-655-4375

**Ringling, Jefferson, Pop. 968**
Ringling ISD 500/PK-12
PO Box 1010 73456 580-662-2385
Rick Hatfield, supt. Fax 662-2683
www.ringlingps.org
Ringling HS 100/10-12
PO Box 1010 73456 580-662-2386
Tracy Gandy, prin. Fax 662-3323
Ringling JHS 100/7-9
PO Box 1010 73456 580-662-2386
Tracy Gandy, prin. Fax 662-3323

**Ringwood, Major, Pop. 490**
Ringwood ISD 400/PK-12
101 W 5th St 73768 580-883-2201
Wade Detrick, supt. Fax 883-2220
www.ringwood.k12.ok.us
Ringwood HS 100/9-12
101 W 5th St 73768 580-883-2201
Pete Maples, prin. Fax 883-2220

**Ripley, Payne, Pop. 385**
Ripley ISD 500/PK-12
PO Box 97 74062 918-372-4567
Dr. Kenny Beams, supt. Fax 372-4608
www.ripley.k12.ok.us/
Ripley HS 200/9-12
PO Box 97 74062 918-372-4245
Joshua Calavan, prin. Fax 372-4608

**Roff, Pontotoc, Pop. 687**
Roff ISD 300/PK-12
PO Box 157 74865 580-456-7663
Scott Morgan, supt. Fax 456-7245
www.roff.k12.ok.us
Roff HS 100/9-12
PO Box 157 74865 580-456-7252
Ead Simon, prin. Fax 456-7499

**Roland, Sequoyah, Pop. 2,907**
Roland ISD 1,200/PK-12
300 Ranger Blvd 74954 918-427-4601
Paul Wood, supt. Fax 427-1785
www.rolandschools.org
Roland HS 300/10-12
300 Ranger Blvd 74954 918-427-7419
Steven Barrick, prin. Fax 427-6993
Roland JHS 300/7-9
300 Ranger Blvd 74954 918-427-4631
John Speir, prin. Fax 427-0093

**Rush Springs, Grady, Pop. 1,191**
Rush Springs ISD 600/PK-12
PO Box 308 73082 580-476-3929
Mike Zurline, supt. Fax 476-2018
www.rushsprings.k12.ok.us
Rush Springs HS 200/9-12
PO Box 308 73082 580-476-3596
Shawn Haskins, prin. Fax 476-2018
Rush Springs MS 100/6-8
PO Box 308 73082 580-476-3447
Billy Langford, prin. Fax 476-2148

**Ryan, Jefferson, Pop. 785**
Ryan ISD 200/PK-12
1201 Washington St 73565 580-757-2308
Larry Ninman, supt. Fax 757-2609
Ryan HS, 1201 Washington St 73565 100/9-12
Pete Maples, prin. 580-757-2296

**Salina, Mayes, Pop. 1,257**
Salina ISD 900/PK-12
PO Box 98 74365 918-434-5091
Tony Thomas, supt. Fax 434-5346
www.salina.k12.ok.us
Salina HS 300/9-12
PO Box 98 74365 918-434-5347
Kyle Fowler, prin. Fax 434-5537
Salina MS 200/6-8
PO Box 98 74365 918-434-5311
Debbie Cox, prin. Fax 434-5173

**Sallisaw, Sequoyah, Pop. 7,974**
Central ISD 500/PK-12
108089 S 4670 Rd 74955 918-775-5525
Larry Henson, supt. Fax 775-8557
www.centralps.k12.ok.us
Central HS 200/9-12
108089 S 4670 Rd 74955 918-775-5525
Brooks Cawhorn, prin. Fax 775-8557

OK Dept. of Voc. & Tech. Education
Supt. — None
Indian Capital Technology Center Vo/Tech
401 E Houser Blvd 74955 918-775-9119
Dr. Curtis Shumaker, dir. Fax 775-7305

Sallisaw ISD 2,100/PK-12
701 S J T Stites St 74955 918-775-5544
Scott Farmer, supt. Fax 775-1257
sallisawps.org
Sallisaw HS 600/9-12
2301 W Ruth Ave 74955 918-775-7761
Ernie Martens, prin. Fax 775-1275
Spear MS 400/6-8
211 S Main St 74955 918-775-6561
Greg Cast, prin. Fax 775-1276

**Sand Springs, Tulsa, Pop. 17,953**
OK Dept. of Voc. & Tech. Education
Supt. — None
Tulsa Tech Center Sand Springs Campus Vo/Tech
924 E Charles Page Blvd 74063 918-828-1300
Derek Beller, dir. Fax 828-1309

Sand Springs ISD 5,200/PK-12
11 W Broadway St 74063 918-246-1400
Lloyd Snow, supt. Fax 246-1401
www.sandites.org/
Boyd MS 1,200/6-8
305 W 35th St 74063 918-246-1535
Nancy Ogle, prin. Fax 246-1544
Central 9th Grade Center 400/9-9
14 W 4th St 74063 918-246-1440
Ernie Kothe, prin. Fax 246-1446
Page Academy 100/Alt
104 W 4th St 74063 918-246-1564
Janice Marr, admin. Fax 246-1565
Page HS 1,200/10-12
500 N Adams Rd 74063 918-246-1470
Stan Trout, prin. Fax 246-1480

Moriah Christian Academy 100/PK-12
680 E 41st St 74063 918-241-8410
Kim Ervin, admin. Fax 246-1109
Sand Springs Beauty College Post-Sec.
28 E 2nd St 74063 918-245-6627

**Sapulpa, Creek, Pop. 19,322**
OK Dept. of Voc. & Tech. Education
Supt. — None
Central Tech Vo/Tech
1720 S Main St 74066 918-224-9300
Fax 224-3190

Sapulpa ISD 3,300/PK-12
511 E Lee Ave 74066 918-224-3400
Kevin Burr, supt. Fax 227-8347
www.sapulpaps.org
Bartlett Academy Alt
603 S Park St 74066 918-224-7958
Dr. Corey Barton, prin. Fax 224-0049
Sapulpa JHS 700/8-9
7 S Mission St 74066 918-224-6710
Johnny Bilby, prin. Fax 227-0473
Sapulpa SHS 1,000/10-12
3 S Mission St 74066 918-224-6560
Johnny Bilby, prin. Fax 224-0174

Eagle Point Christian Academy 100/PK-12
602 S Mounds St 74066 918-227-2441
Jim Pryor, admin. Fax 248-3117

**Sasakwa, Seminole, Pop. 141**
Sasakwa ISD 200/PK-12
PO Box 323 74867 405-941-3250
Kyle Wilson, supt. Fax 941-3561
www.sasakwaschools.org
Sasakwa HS 100/9-12
PO Box 323 74867 405-941-3250
Brent Griffin, prin. Fax 941-3561

**Savanna, Pittsburg, Pop. 629**
Savanna ISD 400/PK-12
PO Box 266 74565 918-548-3777
Gary Reeder, supt. Fax 548-3836
www.savanna.k12.ok.us/
Savanna HS 200/9-12
PO Box 266 74565 918-548-3777
Brad Kellogg, prin. Fax 548-3836

**Sayre, Beckham, Pop. 4,304**
OK Dept. of Voc. & Tech. Education
Supt. — None
Western Technology Center Vo/Tech
2002 NE Highway 66 73662 580-928-2097
Hal Holt, dir. Fax 928-9827

Sayre ISD 700/PK-12
716 NE Highway 66 73662 580-928-5531
Todd Winn, supt. Fax 928-5538
www.sayre.k12.ok.us
Sayre HS 200/9-12
716 NE Highway 66 73662 580-928-5576
Danny Crabb, prin. Fax 928-3045
Sayre MS 200/6-8
716 NE Highway 66 73662 580-928-5578
Danny Clifton, prin. Fax 928-3045

Southwestern Oklahoma State University Post-Sec.
409 E Mississippi Ave 73662 580-928-5533

**Schulter, Okmulgee, Pop. 449**
Schulter ISD 200/PK-12
PO Box 203 74460 918-652-8219
Allen Callahan, supt. Fax 652-8474
www.schulter.k12.ok.us/
Schulter HS 50/9-12
PO Box 203 74460 918-652-8200
Allen Callahan, prin. Fax 652-8474

**Seiling, Dewey, Pop. 824**
Seiling ISD 300/PK-12
PO Box 780 73663 580-922-7383
Randy Seifried, supt. Fax 922-8019
www.seiling.k12.ok.us
Seiling JSHS 100/7-12
PO Box 780 73663 580-922-7382
Gary Baker, prin. Fax 922-8019

**Seminole, Seminole, Pop. 6,934**
Seminole ISD 1,600/PK-12
PO Box 1031 74818 405-382-5085
Bill Weldon, supt. Fax 382-8281
seminole1.schooldesk.net/
Seminole HS 500/9-12
PO Box 1031 74818 405-382-1415
Steven Osborn, prin. Fax 382-1062
Seminole MS 300/7-8
PO Box 1031 74818 405-382-5065
David Dean, prin. Fax 382-8653

Strother ISD 400/PK-12
36085 EW 1140 74868 405-382-4014
Chad Broughton, supt. Fax 382-3339
www.strother.k12.ok.us/
Strother HS 100/9-12
36085 EW 1140 74868 405-382-4014
Scott Douthit, prin. Fax 382-3339

Varnum ISD 300/PK-12
11929 NS 3550 74868 405-382-1448
David Brewer, supt. Fax 382-8618
www.varnum.k12.ok.us
Varnum HS 100/9-12
11929 NS 3550 74868 405-382-1408
Kevin Romine, prin. Fax 382-8618

Seminole State College Post-Sec.
PO Box 351 74818 405-382-9950

**Sentinel, Washita, Pop. 867**
Sentinel ISD 300/PK-12
PO Box 640 73664 580-393-2101
Jason Goostree, supt. Fax 393-4334
www.sentinel.k12.ok.us/
Thomas HS 100/9-12
PO Box 640 73664 580-393-2112
Benny Barnett, prin. Fax 393-4334

**Shattuck, Ellis, Pop. 1,338**
Shattuck ISD 400/PK-12
PO Box 159 73858 580-938-2586
Randy Holley, supt. Fax 938-8019
www.shattuck.k12.ok.us/
Shattuck HS 100/9-12
PO Box 159 73858 580-938-2586
Terry Conder, prin. Fax 938-8019

**Shawnee, Pottawatomie, Pop. 28,106**
Bethel ISD 1,300/PK-12
36000 Clearpond Rd 74801 405-273-0385
Jerry M. Johnson M.Ed., supt. Fax 273-5056
bethel.k12.ok.us
Bethel HS 400/9-12
36000 Clearpond Rd 74801 405-273-3633
J. Stewart, prin. Fax 878-5571
Bethel MS 300/6-8
36000 Clearpond Rd 74801 405-273-5944
Tina Moon M.Ed., prin. Fax 273-6025

OK Dept. of Voc. & Tech. Education
Supt. — None
Cooper Technology Center Vo/Tech
1 John C Bruton Blvd 74804 405-273-7493
Marty Lewis, supt. Fax 273-4704

Shawnee ISD 4,100/PK-12
326 N Union Ave 74801 405-273-0653
Marc Moore, supt. Fax 273-6818
www.shawnee.k12.ok.us
Shawnee HS 1,200/9-12
1001 N Kennedy Ave 74801 405-275-3084
Angela Avila, prin. Fax 275-9501
Shawnee MS 800/6-8
4300 N Union Ave 74804 405-273-0403
Colby Cagle, prin. Fax 275-9651
Thorpe Academy Alt
1111 N Kennedy Ave 74801 405-273-3525
Debra Watson, dir. Fax 878-1046

Family of Faith Christian S 100/K-12
PO Box 1442 74802 405-273-5331
Christopher Belyeu, admin. Fax 273-8535
Family of Faith College Post-Sec.
PO Box 1805 74802 405-273-5331
Liberty Academy 300/PK-12
PO Box 1176 74802 405-273-3022
Susan Harmon, supt. Fax 273-3029
Oklahoma Baptist University Post-Sec.
500 W University St 74804 405-275-2850
St. Gregory's University Post-Sec.
1900 W MacArthur St 74804 888-784-7347
Shawnee Beauty College Post-Sec.
410 E Main St 74801 405-275-3182

**Shidler, Osage, Pop. 394**
Shidler ISD 300/PK-12
PO Box 85 74652 918-793-2021
John Herzig, supt. Fax 793-2061
www.shidlerpublicschools.org
Shidler HS 100/9-12
PO Box 85 74652 918-793-2461
Cory Smith, prin. Fax 793-2062
Other Schools – See Kaw City

**Skiatook, Tulsa, Pop. 6,871**
Skiatook ISD 2,600/PK-12
355 S Osage St 74070 918-396-1792
Rick Thomas, supt. Fax 396-1799
www.skiatookschools.org
Newman MS 600/6-8
355 S Osage St 74070 918-396-2307
Steve Cantrell, prin. Fax 396-1799
Skiatook HS 800/9-12
355 S Osage St 74070 918-396-1790
William Parker, prin. Fax 396-1799

**Smithville, McCurtain, Pop. 106**
Smithville ISD 300/PK-12
PO Box 8 74957 580-244-3333
Delbert McBroom, supt. Fax 244-3101
www.smithville.k12.ok.us
Smithville HS 100/9-12
PO Box 8 74957 580-244-3281
Delbert McBroom, prin. Fax 244-7277
Smithville MS 100/6-8
PO Box 8 74957 580-244-7212
Stacy Nichols, prin. Fax 244-3651

**Snyder, Kiowa, Pop. 1,354**
Snyder ISD 500/PK-12
PO Box 368 73566 580-569-2773
Robert Trammell, supt. Fax 569-4205
www.snyder.k12.ok.us
Snyder HS 200/9-12
PO Box 368 73566 580-569-2730
Ken McKee, prin. Fax 569-4033
Snyder MS 200/4-8
PO Box 368 73566 580-569-2691
Carol McPhail, prin. Fax 569-4657

**Soper, Choctaw, Pop. 237**
Soper ISD 400/PK-12
PO Box 149 74759 580-345-2757
Scotty Van Worth, supt. Fax 345-2222
soperisd.com
Soper HS 100/9-12
PO Box 149 74759 580-345-2212
James Eberts M.A., prin. Fax 345-2896

**South Coffeyville, Nowata, Pop. 715**
Oklahoma Union ISD 700/PK-12
RR 1 Box 377-7 74072 918-255-6550
Kevin Stacy, supt. Fax 255-6817
www.okunion.k12.ok.us/
Oklahoma Union HS 200/9-12
RR 1 Box 377-7 74072 918-255-6550
David Lovelace, prin. Fax 255-6817
Oklahoma Union MS 200/6-8
RR 1 Box 377-7 74072 918-255-6550
Dale Wicks, prin. Fax 255-6817

South Coffeyville ISD 300/PK-12
PO Box 190 74072 918-255-6202
Clemo Haddox, supt. Fax 255-6230
www.scps.k12.ok.us
South Coffeyville HS 100/9-12
PO Box 190 74072 918-255-6087
Steve Johns, prin. Fax 255-6115

**Spencer, Oklahoma, Pop. 3,660**
Oklahoma City ISD
Supt. — See Oklahoma City
Rogers MS 400/6-8
4000 Spencer Rd 73084 405-771-3205
Jahree Herzer, prin. Fax 771-2114
Star Spencer HS 400/9-12
3001 Spencer Rd 73084 405-587-8800
Chris Gardner, prin. Fax 587-8805

**Sperry, Tulsa, Pop. 1,118**
Sperry ISD 1,400/PK-12
400 W Main St 74073 918-288-6258
Brian Beagles Ed.D., supt. Fax 288-7067
www.sperry.k12.ok.us
Sperry HS 300/9-12
400 W Main St 74073 918-288-7213
Mike Haney, prin. Fax 288-7230
Sperry MS 300/6-8
400 W Main St 74073 918-288-7213
Mike Juby, prin. Fax 288-7231

Oklahoma Farriers College Post-Sec.
PO Box 788 74073 918-288-7221

**Spiro, LeFlore, Pop. 2,077**
OK Dept. of Voc. & Tech. Education
Supt. — None
Kiamichi Technology Center Vo/Tech
610 SW 3rd St 74959 918-962-3722
Doug Hall, dir. Fax 962-4627

Spiro ISD 1,200/K-12
600 W Broadway St 74959 918-962-2463
Don Atkinson, supt. Fax 962-2757
www.spiro.k12.ok.us
Spiro HS, 600 W Broadway St 74959 300/9-12
Larry Greenwood, prin. 918-962-2493
Spiro MS, 600 W Broadway St 74959 200/6-8
Nick Carter, prin. 918-962-2488

**Springer, Carter, Pop. 636**
Springer ISD 200/PK-12
PO Box 249 73458 580-653-2656
Cynthia Hunter, supt. Fax 653-2666
www.springerschools.com
Springer HS, PO Box 249 73458 100/9-12
Russell Noland, prin. 580-653-2471

**Sterling, Comanche, Pop. 758**
Sterling ISD 400/PK-12
PO Box 158 73567 580-365-4307
Julie Poteete, supt. Fax 365-4705
www.sterling.k12.ok.us/
Sterling HS 100/9-12
PO Box 158 73567 580-365-4303
Marty Curry, prin. Fax 365-4705

**Stigler, Haskell, Pop. 2,525**
OK Dept. of Voc. & Tech. Education
Supt. — None
Kiamichi Technology Center Vo/Tech
1410 Old Military Rd 74462 918-967-2801
April Murray, dir. Fax 967-2804

Stigler ISD 1,200/PK-12
309 NW E St 74462 918-967-2805
Clayton Edwards, supt. Fax 967-4550
www.stigler.k12.ok.us
Stigler HS 400/9-12
309 NW E St 74462 918-967-8834
David Morgan, prin. Fax 967-8974
Stigler MS 300/5-8
309 NW E St 74462 918-967-2521
Tony Gilmore, prin. Fax 967-5125

**Stillwater, Payne, Pop. 43,498**
OK Dept. of Voc. & Tech. Education
Supt. — None
Meridian Technology Center Vo/Tech
1312 S Sangre Rd 74074 405-377-3333
Dr. Douglas Major, supt. Fax 372-3466
Other Schools – See Ada OK, Afton OK, Altus OK, Alva OK, Antlers OK, Ardmore OK, Atoka OK, Bartlesville OK, Broken Arrow OK, Burns Flat OK, Chickasha OK, Choctaw OK, Claremore OK, Drumright OK, Duncan OK, Durant OK, El Reno OK, Enid OK, Fairview OK, Fort Cobb OK, Frederick OK, Hobart OK, Hugo OK, Idabel OK, Kansas OK, Lawton OK, McAlester OK, Midwest City OK, Muskogee OK, Norman OK, Oklahoma City OK, Okmulgee OK, Omega OK, Owasso OK, Ponca City OK, Poteau OK, Pryor OK, Sallisaw OK, Sand Springs OK, Sapulpa OK, Sayre OK, Shawnee OK, Spiro OK, Stigler OK, Stilwell OK, Tahlequah OK, Talihina OK, Tulsa OK, Wayne OK, Weatherford OK, Wetumka OK, Wilburton OK, Woodward OK, Yukon OK

Stillwater ISD 5,900/PK-12
314 S Lewis St 74074 405-533-6300
Dr. Ann Caine, supt. Fax 743-6311
www.stillwaterschools.com
Lincoln Alternative Academy Alt
215 E 12th Ave 74074 405-533-6331
Trent Swanson, prin. Fax 377-7725
Stillwater HS 1,100/10-12
1224 N Husband St 74075 405-533-6450
Uwe Gordon, prin. Fax 743-6488
Stillwater JHS 700/8-9
1900 N Skyline St 74075 405-533-6420
John Fields, prin. Fax 743-6444

Meridian Technology Center Post-Sec.
1312 S Sangre Rd 74074 405-377-3333
Northern Oklahoma College Post-Sec.
PO Box 1869 74076 405-744-2246
Oklahoma State University 74078 Post-Sec.
405-744-5000
Stillwater Beauty Academy Post-Sec.
1684 Cimarron Plz 74075 405-377-4100

**Stilwell, Adair, Pop. 3,604**
OK Dept. of Voc. & Tech. Education
Supt. — None
Indian Capital Technology Center Vo/Tech
RR 6 Box 3320 74960 918-696-3111
Dan Collins, dir. Fax 696-3031

Stilwell ISD 1,300/PK-12
1801 W Locust St 74960 918-696-7001
Geri Gilstrap, supt. Fax 696-2193
www.stilwellk12.org
Stilwell HS 600/9-12
1801 W Locust St 74960 918-696-7276
Ramona Ketcher, prin. Fax 696-4695
Stilwell MS 300/5-8
12 N 7th St 74960 918-696-2685
Dale Girdner, prin. Fax 696-7761

**Stonewall, Pontotoc, Pop. 416**
Stonewall ISD 400/PK-12
600 Highschool 74871 580-265-4241
Kevin Flowers, supt. Fax 265-4536
www.stonewall.k12.ok.us
McLish MS 100/5-8
600 Highschool 74871 580-777-2240
Jack Wofford, prin. Fax 777-2222
Stonewall HS 100/9-12
600 Highschool 74871 580-265-4242
Tamara Newberry, prin. Fax 265-4231

**Stratford, Garvin, Pop. 1,461**
Stratford ISD 600/PK-12
PO Box 589 74872 580-759-3615
Michael Blackburn, supt. Fax 759-2669
www.stratford.k12.ok.us
Stratford HS 200/9-12
PO Box 589 74872 580-759-2381
Paul Savage, prin. Fax 759-8913
Stratford MS 200/6-8
PO Box 589 74872 580-759-3615
Tracy Felan, prin. Fax 759-2513

**Stringtown, Atoka, Pop. 364**
Stringtown ISD 200/PK-12
PO Box 130 74569 580-346-7423
Tony Potts, supt. Fax 346-7726
Stringtown HS 100/9-12
PO Box 130 74569 580-346-7423
Tony Potts, prin. Fax 346-7726

**Stroud, Lincoln, Pop. 2,575**
Stroud ISD 900/PK-12
212 W 7th St 74079 918-968-2541
Joe Van Tuyl, supt. Fax 968-2582
www.stroud.k12.ok.us
Stroud HS 200/9-12
212 W 7th St 74079 918-968-2542
Scott Baade, prin. Fax 968-3656
Stroud MS 200/6-8
212 W 7th St 74079 918-968-2200
Betty Wages, prin. Fax 968-2391

**Stuart, Hughes, Pop. 165**
Stuart ISD 300/PK-12
8837 4th St 74570 918-546-2476
Bill San Millan, supt. Fax 546-2329
www.stuart.k12.ok.us/
Stuart HS 100/9-12
8837 4th St 74570 918-546-2474
Tracy Blasengame, prin. Fax 546-2329

**Sulphur, Murray, Pop. 4,613**
Sulphur ISD 1,500/PK-12
1021 W 9th St 73086 580-622-2061
Gary Jones, supt. Fax 622-6789
www.sis.sulphurk12.org
Sulphur HS 400/9-12
1021 W 9th St 73086 580-622-3174
Clete Cole, prin. Fax 622-5735
Sulphur JHS 400/6-8
1021 W 9th St 73086 580-622-4010
Dub Grisham, prin. Fax 622-3900

Oklahoma School for the Deaf Post-Sec.
1100 E Oklahoma Ave 73086 580-622-4900

**Sweetwater, Roger Mills, Pop. 86**
Sweetwater ISD 100/PK-12
11107 N Highway 30 73666 580-534-2272
Casey Reed, supt. Fax 534-2273
www.sweetwater.k12.ok.us/
Sweetwater HS 50/9-12
11107 N Highway 30 73666 580-534-2272
Casey Reed, prin. Fax 534-2273

**Tahlequah, Cherokee, Pop. 14,483**
OK Dept. of Voc. & Tech. Education
Supt. — None
Indian Capital Technology Center Vo/Tech
240 Vo Tech Dr 74464 918-456-2594
Robin Roberts, dir. Fax 456-0140

Tahlequah SD 3,200/PK-12
PO Box 517 74465 918-458-4100
Lisa Presley, supt. Fax 458-4103
www.tahlequahschools.org
Tahlequah HS 1,200/9-12
591 Pendleton St 74464 918-458-4150
Cory Slagle, prin. Fax 458-4152
Tahlequah MS 900/6-8
871 Pendleton St 74464 918-458-4140
Jaycie Smith, prin. Fax 458-4142

Academy of Salon and Spa Post-Sec.
3040 S Muskogee Ave Ste 105 74464 918-506-4071
Beauty Technical College Post-Sec.
PO Box 1506 74465 918-456-6360
Northeastern State University Post-Sec.
600 N Grand Ave 74464 918-456-5511

**Talihina, Latimer, Pop. 1,013**
Buffalo Valley ISD 200/PK-12
4384 SE Highway 63 74571 918-522-4426
Justin Kennedy, supt. Fax 522-4287
www.buffalovalley.k12.ok.us
Buffalo Valley HS 100/9-12
4384 SE Highway 63 74571 918-522-4803
Diana Hames, prin. Fax 522-4287

OK Dept. of Voc. & Tech. Education
Supt. — None
Kiamichi Technology Center Vo/Tech
13739 SE 202nd Rd 74571 918-567-2264
Larry Brooks, dir. Fax 567-3359

Talihina ISD 600/PK-12
PO Box 38 74571 918-567-2259
Jason Lockhart, supt. Fax 567-3507
www.talihina.k12.ok.us/
Talihina HS 100/9-12
PO Box 38 74571 918-567-2266
Maria Carden, prin. Fax 567-3507
Talihina JHS, PO Box 38 74571 100/7-8
Maria Carden, prin. 918-567-2266

**Taloga, Dewey, Pop. 290**
Taloga ISD 100/PK-12
PO Box 158 73667 580-328-5577
Darci Brown, supt. Fax 328-5237
www.taloga.k12.ok.us
Taloga HS 50/9-12
PO Box 158 73667 580-328-5586
Lora Burch, prin. Fax 328-5237

**Tecumseh, Pottawatomie, Pop. 6,036**
Tecumseh ISD 2,100/PK-12
1301 E Highland St 74873 405-598-3739
Tom Wilsie, supt. Fax 598-2861
www.tecumseh.k12.ok.us
Tecumseh HS 600/9-12
901 N 13th St 74873 405-598-2113
Danny Sterling, prin. Fax 598-2432
Tecumseh MS 500/6-8
315 W Park St 74873 405-598-3744
Robert Kinsey, prin. Fax 598-1948

**Temple, Cotton, Pop. 952**
Temple ISD 200/PK-12
PO Box 400 73568 580-342-6230
Kolby Johnson, supt. Fax 342-6463
www.temple.k12.ok.us/
Temple HS 100/9-12
PO Box 400 73568 580-342-6221
Kolby Johnson, prin. Fax 342-6463

**Texhoma, Texas, Pop. 917**
Texhoma ISD 200/5-12
PO Box 648 73949 580-423-7371
Tom Schroeder, supt. Fax 423-7096
www.texhoma61.net
Texhoma ES 100/5-8
PO Box 648 73949 580-423-7371
Kayla Yates, prin. Fax 423-7141
Texhoma HS 100/9-12
PO Box 648 73949 580-423-7371
Kayla Yates, prin. Fax 423-7096

**Thackerville, Love, Pop. 429**
Thackerville ISD 300/PK-12
PO Box 377 73459 580-276-2630
Greg Raper, supt. Fax 276-2638
www.thackervilleschools.org
Thackerville HS 100/9-12
PO Box 377 73459 580-276-3610
Carrie Tucker, prin. Fax 276-8314

**Thomas, Custer, Pop. 1,152**
Thomas-Fay-Custer Unified ISD 400/PK-12
PO Box 190 73669 580-661-3522
Rob Royalty, supt. Fax 661-3589
thomas.k12.ok.us/
Thomas-Fay-Custer HS 100/10-12
PO Box 190 73669 580-661-3522
Ray Oakes, prin. Fax 661-3589
Thomas-Fay-Custer JHS 7-9
PO Box 190 73669 580-661-3522
Ray Oakes, prin. Fax 661-3589

**Tipton, Tillman, Pop. 830**
Tipton ISD 200/K-12
PO Box 340 73570 580-667-5268
Shane Boothe, supt. Fax 667-5267
www.tiptontigers.net
Tipton HS 100/9-12
PO Box 340 73570 580-667-5268
Steve Glenn, prin. Fax 667-5478

**Tishomingo, Johnston, Pop. 2,754**
Tishomingo ISD 900/PK-12
1300 E Main St 73460 580-371-9190
Kevin Duncan, supt. Fax 371-3765
www.tishomingo.k12.ok.us/
Tishomingo HS, 1300 E Main St 73460 300/9-12
Jon Holmes, prin. 580-371-2322
Tishomingo MS, 1300 E Main St 73460 200/5-8
Charles Hook, prin. 580-371-3602

Murray State College Post-Sec.
1 Murray Campus St 73460 580-371-2371

**Tonkawa, Kay, Pop. 3,131**
Tonkawa ISD 600/PK-12
500 E North Ave 74653 580-628-3597
Lori Simpson, supt. Fax 628-5132
www.tonkawa.k12.ok.us/
Tonkawa JSHS 200/6-12
500 E North Ave 74653 580-628-2566
Kyle Simpson, prin. Fax 628-3646

Northern Oklahoma College Post-Sec.
PO Box 310 74653 580-628-6200

**Tulsa, Tulsa, Pop. 371,916**
Berryhill ISD 1,200/PK-12
3128 S 63rd West Ave 74107 918-446-1966
Mike Campbell, supt. Fax 446-6370
www.berryhillschools.org/
Berryhill HS 400/9-12
3128 S 63rd West Ave 74107 918-445-6035
Donnie Bridgeman, prin. Fax 445-6015
Berryhill MS 200/7-8
3128 S 63rd West Ave 74107 918-445-6039
Ronna Taylor, prin. Fax 445-6018

Jenks ISD
Supt. — See Jenks
Jenks MS 1,600/7-8
3019 E 101st St 74137 918-299-4411
Dr. Nick Brown, prin. Fax 298-0652

OK Dept. of Voc. & Tech. Education
Supt. — None
Tulsa Tech Center Lemley Vo/Tech
PO Box 477200 74147 918-828-1000
Randy Dean, dir. Fax 828-1009
Tulsa Tech Center Peoria Vo/Tech
PO Box 477200 74147 918-828-2000
Randy Craven, dir. Fax 828-2009
Tulsa Tech Center Riverside Campus Vo/Tech
PO Box 477200 74147 918-828-4000
Brad Hanselman, dir. Fax 828-4119

Tulsa ISD 36,100/PK-12
PO Box 470208 74147 918-746-6800
Dr. Deborah Gist, supt. Fax 746-6850
www.tulsaschools.org
Carver MS 600/6-8
624 E Oklahoma Pl 74106 918-925-1420
Melissa Woolridge, prin. Fax 925-1450
Central JSHS Fine & Performing Arts 600/7-12
3101 W Edison St 74127 918-833-8400
Dr. Ebony Johnson, prin. Fax 833-8417
Clinton MS 300/6-8
2224 W 41st St 74107 918-746-8640
Dixie Speer, prin. Fax 746-8691
East Central HS 1,100/9-12
12150 E 11th St 74128 918-746-9700
Mike Crase, prin. Fax 746-9760
East Central JHS 700/6-8
12121 E 21st St 74129 918-746-9500
Joshua Regnier, prin. Fax 746-9519
Edison Preparatory MSHS 1,300/6-12
2906 E 41st St 74105 918-746-8500
Derrick Schmidt, prin. Fax 746-8511
Hale HS 1,300/9-12
6960 E 21st St 74129 918-925-1200
Caleb Starr, prin. Fax 925-1262
Hale JHS 800/6-8
2177 S 67th East Ave 74129 918-746-9260
Jody Parsons, prin. Fax 746-9291
McLain JSHS for Science & Technology 500/8-12
4929 N Peoria Ave 74126 918-833-8500
Enna Dancy, prin. Fax 833-8559
Memorial HS 1,200/9-12
5840 S Hudson Ave 74135 918-833-9600
Darin Schmidt, prin. Fax 833-9659
Memorial JHS 500/6-8
7502 E 57th St 74145 918-833-9520
Ginger Bunnell, prin. Fax 833-9551
Monroe Demonstration Academy 50/6-8
2010 E 48th St N 74130 918-833-8900
Kiana Smith, prin. Fax 833-8918
Phoenix Rising S Alt
1205 W Newton St 74127 918-833-8376
Diane Dross, dir.
Rogers JSHS 200/7-12
3909 E 5th Pl 74112 918-833-9000
Nicolette Dennis, prin. Fax 833-9065
Street S Alt
1135 S Yale Ave 74112 918-833-9800
Lori McGinnis Ed.D., dir. Fax 833-9858
Thoreau Demonstration Academy 600/6-8
7370 E 71st St 74133 918-833-9700
Thomas Padalino, prin. Fax 833-9720
TRAICE MSHS Academy 600/Alt
2740 E 41st St N 74110 918-925-1360
Elizabeth Martin, prin.
Tulsa Met JSHS 100/Alt
6201 E Virgin St 74115 918-746-9300
Michelle Butler, prin. Fax 833-9875
Washington HS 1,300/9-12
1514 E Zion St 74106 918-925-1000
Nanette Coleman, prin. Fax 928-1001

Webster HS 600/9-12
1919 W 40th St 74107 918-746-8000
Shelly Holman, prin. Fax 746-8056

Union ISD 13,900/PK-12
8506 E 61st St 74133 918-357-4321
Dr. Kirt Hartzler, supt. Fax 357-6019
www.unionps.org
Union Alternative S Alt
5656 S 129th East Ave 74134 918-357-4327
Chris Ducker, prin. Fax 357-7094
Union SHS 2,200/10-12
6636 S Mingo Rd 74133 918-357-4323
Tony Tempest, prin. Fax 357-7210
Other Schools – See Broken Arrow

---

Bishop Kelley HS 800/9-12
3905 S Hudson Ave 74135 918-627-3390
Fr. Brian O'Brien, pres. Fax 664-2134
Brown Mackie College Post-Sec.
4608 S Garnett Rd Ste 110 74146 918-628-3700
Career Point College Post-Sec.
3138 S Garnett Rd 74146 918-627-8074
Cascia Hall Preparatory S 600/6-12
2520 S Yorktown Ave 74114 918-746-2600
Roger Carter, hdmstr. Fax 746-2636
CC's Cosmetology College Post-Sec.
11630 E 21st St 74129 918-234-9444
Clary Sage College Post-Sec.
3131 S Sheridan Rd 74145 918-298-8200
Community Care College Post-Sec.
4242 S Sheridan Rd 74145 918-610-0027
Holland Hall 1,000/PK-12
5666 E 81st St 74137 918-481-1111
J.P. Culley, head sch Fax 481-1145
ITT Technical Institute Post-Sec.
4500 S 129th East Ave # 152 74134 918-615-3900
Lincoln Christian S 800/PK-12
1003 N 129th East Ave 74116 918-234-8863
Trandy Birch, prin. Fax 234-8864
Metro Christian Academy 1,000/PK-12
6363 S Trenton Ave 74136 918-745-9868
Roger Gerstenberger, hdmstr. Fax 747-8724
Mingo Valley Christian S 300/PK-12
8720 E 61st St 74133 918-294-0404
Dr. Boyd Chitwood, supt. Fax 294-0555
Oklahoma State University Post-Sec.
700 N Greenwood Ave 74106 918-594-8000
Oklahoma Technical College Post-Sec.
4444 S Sheridan Rd 74145 918-895-7500
Oral Roberts University Post-Sec.
7777 S Lewis Ave 74171 918-495-6161
OSU Center for Health Sciences Post-Sec.
1111 W 17th St 74107 918-582-1972
Peace Academy PK-12
4620 S Irvington Ave 74135 918-627-1040
Phillips Theological Seminary Post-Sec.
901 N Mingo Rd 74116 918-610-8303
Platt College Post-Sec.
3801 S Sheridan Rd 74145 918-663-9000
St. Francis Hospital Post-Sec.
6161 S Yale Ave 74136 918-494-1370
San Miguel MS 100/6-8
2444 E Admiral Blvd 74110 918-728-7337
John Dowdell, prin. Fax 660-2040
Spartan Coll of Aeronautics & Technology Post-Sec.
8820 E Pine St 74115 800-331-1204
Technical Institute of Cosmetology Arts Post-Sec.
822 E 6th St 74120 918-660-8828
Tulsa Adventist Academy 100/PK-10
900 S New Haven Ave 74112 918-834-1107
Tulsa Community College Post-Sec.
3727 E Apache St 74115 918-595-7000
Tulsa Community College Metro Campus Post-Sec.
909 S Boston Ave 74119 918-595-7000
Tulsa Community College Southeast Campus Post-Sec.
10300 E 81st St 74133 918-595-7000
Tulsa Community College West Campus Post-Sec.
7505 W 41st St 74107 918-595-7000
Tulsa Welding School Post-Sec.
2545 E 11th St 74104 918-587-6789
University of Oklahoma Tulsa Post-Sec.
4502 E 41st St 74135 918-660-3000
University of Tulsa Post-Sec.
800 Tucker Dr 74104 918-631-2000
Vatterott College Post-Sec.
4343 S 118th East Ave Ste A 74146 918-835-8288
Victory Christian S 1,100/PK-12
7700 S Lewis Ave 74136 918-491-7720
Dr. Dennis Demuth, supt. Fax 491-7727
Virginia College Post-Sec.
5124 S Peoria Ave 74105 918-960-5400
Wichita Technical Institute - Tulsa Post-Sec.
8421 E 61st St Ste U 74133 888-859-4564
Wright Career College Post-Sec.
4908 S Sheridan Rd 74145 918-628-7700
Wright Christian Academy 200/PK-12
11391 E Admiral Pl 74116 918-438-0922
Jeffrey L. Brown, supt. Fax 438-0700

**Tupelo, Coal, Pop. 308**
Tupelo ISD 300/PK-12
PO Box 239 74572 580-845-2460
Jerry Romines, supt. Fax 845-2565
www.tupelo.k12.ok.us
Tupelo HS 100/9-12
PO Box 239 74572 580-845-2381
Jeff Hiatt, prin. Fax 845-2565

**Turpin, Beaver, Pop. 457**
Turpin ISD 300/PK-12
PO Box 187 73950 580-778-3333
Bret Rider, supt. Fax 778-3179
www.turpinps.org
Turpin HS 100/7-12
PO Box 187 73950 580-778-3333
Gary Wallace, prin. Fax 778-3179

**Tuttle, Grady, Pop. 5,837**
Tuttle ISD 1,800/PK-12
PO Box 780 73089 405-381-2605
Bobby Waitman, supt. Fax 381-4008
www.tuttleschools.info/
Tuttle HS 500/9-12
PO Box 780 73089 405-381-2396
Pat Ragsdale, prin. Fax 381-4637
Tuttle MS 400/6-8
PO Box 780 73089 405-381-2062
Scott Moore, prin. Fax 381-4630

**Tyrone, Texas, Pop. 753**
Tyrone ISD 300/PK-12
PO Box 168 73951 580-854-6298
Josh Bell, supt. Fax 854-6474
www.tyrone.k12.ok.us/
Tyrone HS 100/9-12
PO Box 168 73951 580-854-6298
Donovan Smith, prin. Fax 854-6474

**Union City, Canadian, Pop. 1,578**
Union City ISD 300/PK-12
PO Box 279 73090 405-483-3531
Todd Carel, supt. Fax 483-5599
www.unioncity.k12.ok.us/
Union City HS 100/9-12
PO Box 279 73090 405-483-3531
Todd Carel, admin. Fax 483-5599

**Valliant, McCurtain, Pop. 701**
Valliant ISD 1,000/PK-12
604 E Lucas St 74764 580-933-7232
Craig Wall, supt. Fax 933-7289
www.vpsd.org
Valliant HS 300/9-12
604 E Lucas St 74764 580-933-7292
Cale Haley, prin. Fax 933-7278
Valliant MS 200/6-8
604 E Lucas St 74764 580-933-4253
Dennis Robberson, prin. Fax 933-4254

**Velma, Stephens, Pop. 608**
Velma-Alma ISD 300/PK-12
PO Box 8 73491 580-444-3355
Raymond Rice, supt. Fax 444-2554
www.velma-alma.k12.ok.us
Velma-Alma HS 100/6-12
PO Box 8 73491 580-444-3356
Mike Thompson, prin. Fax 444-2554

**Verden, Grady, Pop. 510**
Verden ISD 300/PK-12
PO Box 99 73092 405-453-7247
David Davidson, supt. Fax 453-7246
www.verdenschools.org
Verden HS 100/7-12
PO Box 99 73092 405-453-7836
David Davidson, prin. Fax 453-7246

**Vian, Sequoyah, Pop. 1,346**
Vian ISD 1,000/PK-12
PO Box 434 74962 918-773-5798
Victor Salcedo, supt. Fax 773-3051
www.vian.k12.ok.us
Vian HS 300/9-12
PO Box 434 74962 918-773-5475
Richard Moseley, prin. Fax 773-3051
Vian MS 200/6-8
PO Box 434 74962 918-773-8631
Steve Barton, prin. Fax 773-3051

**Vici, Dewey, Pop. 673**
Vici ISD 300/PK-12
PO Box 60 73859 580-995-4744
Coby Nelson, supt. Fax 995-3101
www.vicischools.k12.ok.us
Vici HS 100/9-12
PO Box 60 73859 580-995-4251
Sheldon Halderman, prin. Fax 995-3101

**Vinita, Craig, Pop. 5,215**
Vinita ISD 1,600/PK-12
114 S Scraper St 74301 918-256-6778
Kelly Grimmett, supt. Fax 256-5617
www.vinitahornets.com
Vinita HS 500/9-12
801 N Adair St 74301 918-256-6777
Michelle Gibson, prin. Fax 256-5300
Vinita MS 300/6-8
226 N Miller St 74301 918-256-2402
Duwayne King, prin. Fax 256-5401

---

Ketchum Adventist Academy 50/PK-10
35369 S Highway 82 74301 918-782-2986

**Wagoner, Wagoner, Pop. 7,460**
Wagoner ISD 2,500/PK-12
PO Box 508 74477 918-485-4046
Monte Thompson, supt. Fax 485-8710
www.wagonerps.org
Lincoln Academy 200/Alt
902 Martin Luther King Blvd 74467 918-485-7615
Robert Schaefer, prin.
Wagoner HS 700/9-12
300 Bulldog Cir 74467 918-485-5553
Nick Humphries, admin. Fax 485-8886
Wagoner MS 500/6-8
500 Bulldog Cir 74467 918-485-9541
Jeremy Holmes, prin. Fax 485-4149

**Walters, Cotton, Pop. 2,379**
Walters ISD 700/PK-12
418 S Broadway St 73572 580-875-2568
Jimmie Dedmon, supt. Fax 875-2831
blued.org
Walters HS 200/9-12
418 S Broadway St 73572 580-875-3257
Laura Booher, prin. Fax 875-6097
Walters MS 100/6-8
418 S Broadway St 73572 580-875-3214
Laurie Graham, prin. Fax 875-3401

**Wanette, Pottawatomie, Pop. 331**
Wanette ISD 200/PK-12
PO Box 161 74878 405-383-2656
Crystal Shaw, supt. Fax 383-2449
www.wanette.k12.ok.us/
Wanette HS 100/9-12
PO Box 161 74878 405-383-2254
Silvia McNeely, prin. Fax 383-2180

**Wapanucka, Johnston, Pop. 399**
Wapanucka ISD 200/PK-12
PO Box 188 73461 580-937-4466
Stanley Williams, supt. Fax 937-4801
www.wpss.k12.ok.us
Wapanucka HS, PO Box 188 73461 100/9-12
Max Rowland, prin. 580-937-4288

**Warner, Muskogee, Pop. 1,489**
Warner ISD 700/PK-12
1012 5th Ave 74469 918-463-5171
David Vinson, supt. Fax 463-2542
www.warner.k12.ok.us
Warner HS 200/9-12
1012 5th Ave 74469 918-463-5172
Jeremy Jackson, prin. Fax 463-2378

---

Connors State College Post-Sec.
700 College Rd 74469 918-463-2931

**Warr Acres, Oklahoma, Pop. 9,574**
Putnam City ISD
Supt. — See Oklahoma City
Capps MS 900/6-8
4020 N Grove Ave 73122 405-787-3660
Keely Frayser, prin. Fax 491-7536
Putnam City Academy Alt
5604 NW 41st St Ste 300 73122 405-495-8838
Shelly Roper, prin. Fax 491-7529
Putnam City HS 1,800/9-12
5300 NW 50th St 73122 405-789-4350
Clay Vinyard, prin. Fax 789-1662

---

Vatterott College - Oklahoma City Post-Sec.
5537 NW Expressway 73132 405-234-3600

**Washington, McClain, Pop. 585**
Washington ISD 900/PK-12
PO Box 98 73093 405-288-6190
A.J. Brewer, supt. Fax 288-6214
www.washington.k12.ok.us/
Washington HS 300/9-12
PO Box 98 73093 405-288-2354
David Crabbe, prin. Fax 288-6214
Washington MS 200/6-8
PO Box 98 73093 405-288-2428
Stuart McPherson, prin. Fax 288-6214

**Watonga, Blaine, Pop. 4,947**
Watonga ISD 700/PK-12
1020 N Noble Ave 73772 580-623-7364
Bill Seitter, supt. Fax 623-7370
www.watonga.k12.ok.us
Watonga HS 200/9-12
PO Box 310 73772 580-623-7362
David Lorenz, prin. Fax 623-8019
Watonga MS 200/6-8
PO Box 310 73772 580-623-7361
Robin Roof, prin. Fax 623-7371

**Watts, Adair, Pop. 292**
Watts ISD 400/PK-12
RR 2 Box 1 74964 918-422-5311
Lisa Weaver, supt. Fax 422-5556
www.wattsschool.com
Watts HS 100/9-12
RR 2 Box 1 74964 918-422-5132
Martin Bradford, prin. Fax 422-5556

**Waukomis, Garfield, Pop. 1,254**
Pioneer-Pleasant Vale ISD 600/PK-12
6520 E Wood Rd 73773 580-758-3282
Brent Koontz, supt. Fax 758-3504
www.ppv.k12.ok.us/
Pioneer-Pleasant Vale HS 100/9-12
6520 E Wood Rd 73773 580-758-3282
Tom Betchan, prin. Fax 758-1541
Pioneer-Pleasant Vale JHS 100/7-8
6520 E Wood Rd 73773 580-758-3282
Tom Betchan, prin. Fax 758-1541

Waukomis ISD 300/PK-12
PO Box 729 73773 580-758-3247
Shawn Tennyson, supt. Fax 758-3834
www.waukomis.k12.ok.us
Waukomis HS 100/6-12
PO Box 729 73773 580-758-3245
Matt Cue, prin. Fax 758-3256

**Waurika, Jefferson, Pop. 1,993**
Waurika ISD 300/PK-12
600 E Florida Ave 73573 580-228-3373
Roxie Terry M.Ed., supt. Fax 228-3428
www.waurikaschools.org
Waurika MSHS 100/6-12
600 E Florida Ave 73573 580-228-2341
Dale Spradlin, prin. Fax 228-3428

**Wayne, McClain, Pop. 635**
OK Dept. of Voc. & Tech. Education
Supt. — None
Mid-America Technology Center Vo/Tech
PO Box H 73095 405-449-3391
Dusty Ricks, supt. Fax 449-7321

Wayne ISD 500/PK-12
212 S Seifried St 73095 405-449-3646
David Powell, supt. Fax 449-7095
www.wayne.k12.ok.us
Wayne HS 200/9-12
212 S Seifried St 73095 405-449-3317
Toby Ringwald, prin. Fax 449-7095
Wayne MS 100/6-8
212 S Seifried St 73095 405-449-7047
Brandon Sharp, prin. Fax 449-7095

**Waynoka, Woods, Pop. 895**
Waynoka ISD 300/PK-12
2134 Lincoln St 73860 580-824-4341
Loren Tackett, supt. Fax 824-0656
www.waynoka.k12.ok.us/
Waynoka HS 100/9-12
2134 Lincoln St 73860 580-824-4341
Michael Meriwether, prin. Fax 824-0656

**Weatherford, Custer, Pop. 10,475**
OK Dept. of Voc. & Tech. Education
Supt. — None
Western Technology Center Vo/Tech
2605 E Main St 73096 580-774-0224
Audie Corning, dir. Fax 774-0274

Weatherford ISD 1,900/PK-12
516 N Broadway St 73096 580-772-3327
Matt Holder, supt. Fax 774-0821
www.wpsok.org
Weatherford HS 500/9-12
1500 N Washington St 73096 580-772-3385
Mark Shadid, prin. Fax 774-1939
Weatherford MS 400/6-8
509 N Custer St 73096 580-772-2270
Steven Callen, prin. Fax 774-1981

---

Southwestern Oklahoma State University Post-Sec.
100 Campus Dr 73096 580-772-6611

**Webbers Falls, Muskogee, Pop. 572**
Webbers Falls ISD 300/PK-12
PO Box 300 74470 918-464-2580
Dixie Swearingen Ph.D., supt. Fax 464-2313
www.webbersfalls.k12.ok.us
Webbers Falls HS 100/9-12
PO Box 300 74470 918-464-2334
Jim McCabe, prin. Fax 464-2313

**Welch, Craig, Pop. 576**
Welch ISD 400/PK-12
PO Box 189 74369 918-788-3129
Dr. Clark McKeon, supt. Fax 788-3734
welchwildcats.net
Welch HS 100/9-12
PO Box 189 74369 918-788-3129
Dr. Clark McKeon, prin. Fax 788-3734
Welch MS 50/7-8
PO Box 189 74369 918-788-3129
Kim Hall, prin. Fax 788-3734

**Weleetka, Okfuskee, Pop. 906**
Graham-Dustin SD 200/PK-12
116118 Highway 84 74880 918-652-8935
Dusty Chancey, supt. Fax 652-2422
www.graham-dustin.k12.ok.us
Graham HS 100/9-12
116118 Highway 84 74880 918-652-8935
Linda Riddle, prin. Fax 652-2422
Graham MS 50/5-8
116118 Highway 84 74880 918-652-8935
Linda Riddle, prin. Fax 652-2422

Weleetka ISD 500/PK-12
PO Box 278 74880 405-786-2203
Chris Carter, supt. Fax 786-2625
www.weleetka.k12.ok.us
Weleetka HS 100/10-12
PO Box 278 74880 405-786-2203
Rusty Johnson, prin. Fax 786-2625
Weleetka JHS 100/7-9
PO Box 278 74880 405-786-2204
Rusty Johnson, prin. Fax 786-2625

**Wellston, Lincoln, Pop. 751**
Wellston ISD 700/PK-12
PO Box 60 74881 405-356-2534
Dwayne Danker, supt. Fax 356-2838
www.wellstonschools.org
Wellston HS 200/9-12
PO Box 60 74881 405-356-2533
Tracy Fredman, prin. Fax 356-2838
Wellston MS 100/6-8
PO Box 60 74881 405-356-2533
Tracy Fredman, prin. Fax 356-2838

**Westville, Adair, Pop. 1,479**
Westville ISD 1,100/PK-12
PO Box 410 74965 918-723-3181
Terry Heustis, supt. Fax 723-3042
www.westville.k12.ok.us
Westville HS 300/10-12
PO Box 410 74965 918-723-5644
Renae Price, prin. Fax 723-3042
Westville JHS 200/7-9
PO Box 410 74965 918-723-3432
Shelly Cooper, prin. Fax 723-3042

**Wetumka, Hughes, Pop. 1,171**
OK Dept. of Voc. & Tech. Education
Supt. — None
Watkins Technology Center Vo/Tech
7892 Highway 9 74883 405-452-5500
Wade Walling, supt. Fax 452-3561

Wetumka ISD 500/PK-12
416 S Tiger St 74883 405-452-5150
Donna McGee, supt. Fax 452-3052
www.wetumka.k12.ok.us/
Wetumka HS 100/9-12
416 S Tiger St 74883 405-452-3291
Dusty Sifers, prin. Fax 452-5836

**Wewoka, Seminole, Pop. 3,192**
New Lima ISD 300/PK-12
116 Gross St 74884 405-257-5771
Gil Turpin, supt. Fax 257-3127
www.newlima.k12.ok.us
New Lima HS 100/9-12
116 Gross St 74884 405-257-5771
Rhonda Barkhimer, prin. Fax 257-2587

Wewoka ISD 600/PK-12
PO Box 870 74884 405-257-5475
Sam McElvany, supt. Fax 257-2303
www.wps.k12.ok.us/
Wewoka HS 200/9-12
PO Box 870 74884 405-257-5473
Steven Edwards, prin. Fax 257-2303
Wewoka MS 100/7-8
PO Box 870 74884 405-257-2347
Darrell Brown, prin. Fax 257-2303

**Whitesboro, LeFlore, Pop. 244**
Whitesboro ISD 200/PK-12
PO Box 150 74577 918-567-2556
Katie Blagg, supt. Fax 567-2842
www.whitesborops.k12.ok.us/
Whitesboro HS, PO Box 150 74577 100/9-12
Katie Blagg, prin. 918-567-2624

**Wilburton, Latimer, Pop. 2,654**
OK Dept. of Voc. & Tech. Education
Supt. — None
Kiamichi Technology Center Vo/Tech
PO Box 548 74578 918-465-2323
Shelley Free, supt. Fax 465-3666

Wilburton ISD 1,000/PK-12
1201 W Blair Ave 74578 918-465-2100
Dr. Trice Butler, supt. Fax 465-3086
wilburtondiggers.org
Wilburton HS 300/9-12
1201 W Blair Ave 74578 918-465-3125
Gary Lay, prin. Fax 465-1141
Wilburton MS 200/6-8
1201 W Blair Ave 74578 918-465-2281
Kyle Vanderburg, prin. Fax 465-3094

---

Eastern Oklahoma State College Post-Sec.
1301 W Main St 74578 918-465-2361

**Wilson, Carter, Pop. 1,643**
Wilson ISD 500/PK-12
1860 Hewitt Rd 73463 580-668-2306
Eric Smith, supt. Fax 668-2170
www.wilson.k12.ok.us
Wilson HS 200/9-12
1860 Hewitt Rd 73463 580-668-2317
Gary Labeth, prin. Fax 668-2412

**Wister, LeFlore, Pop. 1,038**
Wister ISD 600/PK-12
201 Logan St 74966 918-655-7381
Jerry Carpenter, supt. Fax 655-7402
www.wister.k12.ok.us
Wister HS 200/9-12
201 Logan St 74966 918-655-7276
Albert Cole, prin. Fax 655-7402

**Woodward, Woodward, Pop. 11,818**
OK Dept. of Voc. & Tech. Education
Supt. — None
High Plains Technology Center Vo/Tech
3921 34th St 73801 580-256-6618
Dwight Hughes, supt. Fax 571-6190

Woodward ISD 2,800/PK-12
PO Box 668 73802 580-256-6063
Kyle Reynolds, supt. Fax 256-4391
www.woodwardps.net
Woodward HS 600/9-12
PO Box 668 73802 580-256-5329
Brad Logan, prin. Fax 256-8716
Woodward MS 600/6-8
PO Box 668 73802 580-256-7901
Sarah Hall, prin. Fax 256-8014

---

Woodward Beauty College Post-Sec.
502 Texas St 73801 580-256-7520

**Wright City, McCurtain, Pop. 687**
Wright City ISD 400/PK-12
PO Box 329 74766 580-981-2824
David Hawkins, supt. Fax 981-2115
www.wcisd.org/
Wright City HS 100/9-12
PO Box 329 74766 580-981-2558
Mike Converse, prin. Fax 981-2329
Wright City JHS 100/7-8
PO Box 329 74766 580-981-2558
Mike Converse, prin. Fax 981-2329

**Wyandotte, Ottawa, Pop. 310**
Wyandotte ISD 800/PK-12
PO Box 360 74370 918-678-2255
Troy Gray M.A., supt. Fax 678-2304
www.wyandotte.k12.ok.us
Wyandotte HS 200/9-12
PO Box 360 74370 918-678-2222
Steve Buckingham, prin. Fax 678-3906
Wyandotte MS 200/6-8
PO Box 360 74370 918-678-2222
Stacy Sloan, prin. Fax 678-3906

**Wynnewood, Garvin, Pop. 2,125**
Wynnewood ISD 700/PK-12
702 E Robert S Kerr Blvd 73098 405-665-2004
Raymond Cole, supt. Fax 665-5425
www.wynnewood.k12.ok.us/
Wynnewood HS 200/9-12
702 E Robert S Kerr Blvd 73098 405-665-2045
Steve Musgrove, prin.
Wynnewood MS 200/5-8
702 E Robert S Kerr Blvd 73098 405-665-4105
Kevin Lynch, prin.

**Wynona, Osage, Pop. 396**
Wynona ISD 300/PK-12
PO Box 700 74084 918-846-2467
Shelly Shulanberger, supt. Fax 846-2883
www.wynona.k12.ok.us
Wynona HS 200/9-12
PO Box 700 74084 918-846-2467
Dixie Hurd, prin. Fax 846-2883

**Yale, Payne, Pop. 1,132**
Yale ISD 500/PK-12
315 E Chicago Ave 74085 918-387-2118
Dale Bledsoe, supt. Fax 387-4243
www.yale.k12.ok.us
Yale HS 100/9-12
315 E Chicago Ave 74085 918-387-2118
Rocky Kennedy, prin. Fax 387-4243
Yale JHS 100/7-8
315 E Chicago Ave 74085 918-387-2118
Rocky Kennedy, prin. Fax 387-4243

**Yukon, Canadian, Pop. 21,966**
OK Dept. of Voc. & Tech. Education
Supt. — None
Canadian Valley Technology Center Vo/Tech
1000 Garth Brooks Blvd 73099 405-262-2629
Gayla Lutts, prin.
Canadian Valley Technology Center Vo/Tech
1701 S Czech Hall Rd 73099 405-345-3333
Greg Taylor, dir.

Yukon ISD 8,500/PK-12
600 Maple St 73099 405-354-2587
Dr. Jason Simeroth, supt. Fax 354-4208
www.yukonps.com
Yukon HS 2,200/9-12
1777 S Yukon Pkwy 73099 405-354-6692
Melissa Barlow, prin. Fax 354-8411
Yukon MS 1,700/6-8
801 Garth Brooks Blvd 73099 405-354-5274
Cecil Bowles, prin. Fax 354-6640

---

Southwest Covenant S 300/PK-12
2300 S Yukon Pkwy 73099 405-354-0772
Steve Lessman, hdmstr. Fax 350-2670
Yukon Beauty College Post-Sec.
221 W Main St 73099 405-354-3172

# OREGON

## OREGON DEPARTMENT OF EDUCATION
**255 Capitol St NE, Salem 97310-0406**
**Telephone 503-947-5600**
**Fax 503-378-5156**
**Website http://www.ode.state.or.us**

Superintendent of Public Instruction Vacant

## OREGON BOARD OF EDUCATION
**255 Capitol St NE, Salem 97310-0406**

Chairperson Artemio Paz

## EDUCATION SERVICE DISTRICTS (ESD)

Clackamas ESD
Milt Dennison, supt. 503-675-4000
13455 SE 97th Ave Fax 675-4200
Clackamas 97015
www.clackesd.k12.or.us

Columbia Gorge ESD
Gary Peterson, supt. 541-298-5155
400 E Scenic Dr Ste 207 Fax 296-2965
The Dalles 97058
www.cgesd.k12.or.us

Douglas ESD
Michael Lasher, supt. 541-440-4777
1871 NE Stephens St Fax 440-4771
Roseburg 97470
www.douglasesd.k12.or.us

Grant ESD
Robert Waltenburg, supt. 541-575-1349
835 S Canyon Blvd Ste A Fax 575-3601
John Day 97845
www.grantesd.k12.or.us

Harney ESD
Charles Beck, supt. 541-573-2426
779 W Fillmore St, Burns 97720 Fax 573-1002
www.harneyesd.k12.or.us

High Desert ESD
John Rexford, supt. 541-693-5614
2804 SW 6th St, Redmond 97756 Fax 693-5601
www.hdesd.org

InterMountain ESD
Mark Mulvihill Ed.D., supt. 541-276-6616
2001 SW Nye Ave Fax 276-4252
Pendleton 97801
www.imesd.k12.or.us

Jefferson ESD
Richard Molitor, supt. 541-475-2804
295 SE Buff St, Madras 97741 Fax 475-2827
www.jcesd.k12.or.us

Lake ESD
Bob Nash, supt. 541-947-3371
357 N L St, Lakeview 97630 Fax 947-3373
www.lakeesd.k12.or.us

Lane ESD
Larry Sullivan, supt. 541-461-8200
1200 Highway 99 N, Eugene 97402 Fax 461-8298
www.lesd.k12.or.us

Linn-Benton-Lincoln ESD
Mary McKay, supt. 541-812-2600
905 4th Ave SE, Albany 97321 Fax 926-6047
www.lblesd.k12.or.us

Malheur ESD
Stephen Phillips, supt. 541-473-3138
363 A St W, Vale 97918 Fax 473-3915
www.malesd.k12.or.us

Multnomah ESD
Jim Rose, supt. 503-255-1841
PO Box 301039, Portland 97294 Fax 257-1519
www.mesd.k12.or.us

North Central ESD
Robert Waltenberg, supt. 541-384-2732
PO Box 637, Condon 97823 Fax 384-2752
www.ncesd.k12.or.us

Northwest Regional ESD
Rob Saxton, supt. 503-614-1428
5825 NE Ray Cir, Hillsboro 97124 Fax 614-1440
www.nwresd.k12.or.us

Region 18 ESD
Karen Patton, supt. 541-426-7600
107 SW 1st St Ste 105 Fax 426-3732
Enterprise 97828
www.r18esd.org

South Coast ESD
Tenneal Wetherell, supt. 541-269-1611
1350 Teakwood Ave Fax 266-4040
Coos Bay 97420
www.scesd.k12.or.us

Southern Oregon ESD
Scott Beveridge, supt. 541-776-8590
101 N Grape St, Medford 97501 Fax 779-2018
www.soesd.k12.or.us

Willamette ESD
Dave Novotney, supt. 503-588-5330
2611 Pringle Rd SE, Salem 97302 Fax 363-5787
www.wesd.org

## PUBLIC, PRIVATE AND CATHOLIC SECONDARY SCHOOLS

**Adel, Lake**
Adel SD 21
Supt. — See Lakeview
Adel ES, PO Box 117 97620 50/4-8
Bob Nash, prin. 541-947-3371

**Adrian, Malheur, Pop. 173**
Adrian SD 61 300/K-12
PO Box 108 97901 541-372-2335
Gene Mills, supt. Fax 372-5380
www.adriansd.com
Adrian HS 100/9-12
PO Box 108 97901 541-372-2335
Kevin Purnell, prin. Fax 372-5380

**Albany, Linn, Pop. 48,696**
Greater Albany SD 8J 9,100/K-12
718 7th Ave SW 97321 541-967-4501
Jim Golden, supt. Fax 967-4587
albany.k12.or.us
Albany Options S 100/Alt
701 19th Ave SE, 541-967-4563
John Hunter, prin. Fax 924-3780
Calapooia MS 600/6-8
830 24th Ave SE, 541-967-4555
Pat Weidmann, prin. Fax 924-3702
Memorial MS 600/6-8
1050 Queen Ave SW 97321 541-967-4537
Ken Gilbert, prin. Fax 924-3703
North Albany MS 500/6-8
1205 NW North Albany Rd 97321 541-967-4541
Jon Dilbone, prin. Fax 924-3704
South Albany HS 1,300/9-12
3705 Columbus St SE, 541-967-4522
Brent Belveal, prin. Fax 924-3700
Timber Ridge S 700/3-8
373 Timber Ridge St NE, 541-704-1095
Jodi Dedera, prin. Fax 704-1099
West Albany HS 1,400/9-12
1130 Queen Ave SW 97321 541-967-4545
Susie Orsborn, prin. Fax 924-3701

---

Linn-Benton Community College Post-Sec.
6500 Pacific Blvd SW 97321 541-917-4999

**Aloha, Washington, Pop. 47,267**

---

Life Christian S 200/PK-12
5585 SW 209th Ave, 503-259-1329
Angie Taylor, prin. Fax 649-5484

**Alsea, Benton, Pop. 157**
Alsea SD 7J 100/K-12
PO Box B 97324 541-487-4305
Marc Thielman, supt. Fax 487-4089
www.alsea.k12.or.us
Alsea HS 100/7-12
PO Box B 97324 541-487-4305
Marc Thielman, prin. Fax 487-4089

**Amity, Yamhill, Pop. 1,569**
Amity SD 4J 800/K-12
807 S Trade St 97101 503-835-2171
Jeff Clark, supt. Fax 835-5050
www.amity.k12.or.us
Amity HS 300/9-12
807 S Trade St 97101 503-835-2181
Chris Daniels, prin. Fax 835-6113
Amity MS 200/6-8
807 S Trade St 97101 503-835-0518
Dave Lund, prin. Fax 835-0418

Perrydale SD 21 300/PK-12
7445 Perrydale Rd 97101 503-835-3184
Eric Milburn, supt. Fax 835-0631
www.perrydale.k12.or.us
Perrydale JSHS 200/6-12
7445 Perrydale Rd 97101 503-835-3184
Eric Milburn, prin. Fax 835-0631

**Ashland, Jackson, Pop. 19,339**
Ashland SD 5 2,600/K-12
885 Siskiyou Blvd 97520 541-482-2811
Jay Hummel, supt. Fax 482-2185
www.ashland.k12.or.us
Ashland HS 1,000/9-12
201 S Mountain Ave 97520 541-482-8771
Erika Bare, prin. Fax 482-2172
Ashland MS 500/6-8
100 Walker Ave 97520 541-482-1611
Steve Retzlaff, prin. Fax 482-8112

---

Southern Oregon University Post-Sec.
1250 Siskiyou Blvd 97520 541-552-7672

**Astoria, Clatsop, Pop. 9,193**
Astoria SD 1 1,900/K-12
785 Alameda Ave 97103 503-325-6441
Craig Hoppes, supt. Fax 325-6524
www.astoria.k12.or.us
Astoria HS 600/9-12
1001 W Marine Dr 97103 503-325-3911
Lynn Jackson, prin. Fax 325-2891
Astoria MS 500/6-8
1100 Klaskanine Ave 97103 503-325-4331
Linda Berger, prin. Fax 325-3040

Knappa SD 4 500/K-12
41535 Old Highway 30 97103 503-458-5993
Terrence Smyth, supt. Fax 458-6979
www.knappa.k12.or.us
Knappa HS 100/9-12
41535 Old Highway 30 97103 503-458-6166
Terrence Smyth, prin. Fax 458-5466

---

Clatsop Community College Post-Sec.
1651 Lexington Ave 97103 503-325-0910

**Athena, Umatilla, Pop. 1,106**
Athena-Weston SD 29RJ 500/K-12
375 S 5th St 97813 541-566-3551
James Reager, supt. Fax 566-9454
www.athwest.k12.or.us
Weston-McEwen HS 200/9-12
540 E Main St 97813 541-566-3555
Rollie Marshall, prin. Fax 566-2751
Other Schools – See Weston

**Aumsville, Marion, Pop. 3,437**
Cascade SD 5
Supt. — See Turner
West Stayton Alternative S Alt
11463 W Stayton Rd SE 97325 503-749-8020
Matt Thatcher, prin. Fax 749-8029

**Aurora, Marion, Pop. 900**
North Marion SD 15 1,900/PK-12
20256 Grim Rd NE 97002 503-678-7100
Boyd Keyser, supt. Fax 678-1473
www.nmarion.k12.or.us
North Marion HS 600/9-12
20167 Grim Rd NE 97002 503-678-7123
De Ann Jenness, prin. Fax 678-7186
North Marion MS 500/6-8
20246 Grim Rd NE 97002 503-678-7118
David Sheldon, prin. Fax 678-7185

**Baker City, Baker, Pop. 9,619**
Baker SD 5J 1,700/K-12
2090 4th St 97814 541-524-2260
Mark Witty, supt. Fax 524-2564
www.baker.k12.or.us
Baker HS 500/9-12
2500 E St 97814 541-524-2600
Ben Merrill, prin. Fax 524-2699
Baker MS 300/7-8
2320 Washington Ave 97814 541-524-2500
Chris Carmiencke, prin. Fax 524-2563
EAGLE CAP Innovative HS Alt
2725 7th St 97814 541-524-2285
Jerry Peacock, prin. Fax 359-2564

**Bandon, Coos, Pop. 2,978**
Bandon SD 54 700/K-12
455 9th St SW 97411 541-347-4411
Doug Ardiana, supt. Fax 347-3974
www.bandon.k12.or.us
Bandon HS 200/9-12
550 9th St SW 97411 541-347-4413
Sabrina Belletti, prin. Fax 347-3714
Harbor Lights MS 200/5-8
390 9th St SW 97411 541-347-4415
Michelle Inskeep, prin. Fax 347-1280

---

Bandon Pacific Christian S 50/PK-12
PO Box 949 97411 541-290-7322
Fax 347-3922

**Banks, Washington, Pop. 1,714**
Banks SD 13 1,100/K-12
12950 NW Main St 97106 503-324-8591
Jeff Leo, supt. Fax 324-6969
www.banks.k12.or.us
Banks HS 400/9-12
13050 NW Main St 97106 503-324-2281
Mark Everett, prin. Fax 324-8221
Banks MS 200/6-8
12850 NW Main St 97106 503-324-3111
Shelley Mitchell, prin. Fax 324-7441

**Beaverton, Washington, Pop. 86,161**
Beaverton SD 48J 38,600/K-12
16550 SW Merlo Rd, 503-356-4500
Jeff Rose, supt.
www.beaverton.k12.or.us
Aloha HS 2,100/9-12
18550 SW Kinnaman Rd 97078 503-356-2760
Ken Yarnell, prin. Fax 356-2765
Arts & Communication Magnet Academy 400/6-12
11375 SW Center St 97005 503-672-3700
Michael Johnson, prin. Fax 672-3706
Beaverton HS 1,700/9-12
13000 SW 2nd St 97005 503-259-5000
Anne Erwin, prin. Fax 259-4990
Bridges Academy Alt
18640 NW Walker Rd 97006 503-591-4131
Ashley Marston, prin. Fax 591-4132
Carson Environmental MS 200/6-8
1600 NW 173rd Ave 97006 503-533-1890
Shirley Brock, prin. Fax 533-1898
Conestoga MS 900/6-8
12250 SW Conestoga Dr 97008 503-524-1345
Zan Hess, prin. Fax 524-1349
Five Oaks MS 1,100/6-8
1600 NW 173rd Ave 97006 503-533-1890
Shirley Brock, prin. Fax 533-1898
Health & Science HS 700/6-12
18640 NW Walker Rd 97006 503-533-1853
Brian Sica, prin. Fax 533-1856
Highland Park MS 800/6-8
7000 SW Wilson Ave 97008 503-672-3640
David Nieslanik, prin. Fax 672-3644
International S of Beaverton 700/6-12
17770 SW Blanton St 97078 503-259-3800
Jill O'Neill, prin. Fax 259-3803
Meadow Park MS 800/6-8
14100 SW Downing St 97006 503-672-3660
Jared Freeman, prin. Fax 672-3664
Merlo Station Community HS 200/Alt
1841 SW Merlo Dr, 503-259-5575
MaryJean Katz, prin. Fax 259-4220
Mountain View MS 900/6-8
17500 SW Farmington Rd 97007 503-259-3890
Matt Pedersen, prin. Fax 259-3894
School of Science & Technology 200/9-12
1841 SW Merlo Dr, 503-259-5575
MaryJean Katz, prin. Fax 259-4220
Southridge HS 1,900/9-12
9625 SW 125th Ave 97008 503-259-5400
Todd Corsetti, prin. Fax 259-5425
Whitford MS 800/6-8
7935 SW Scholls Ferry Rd 97008 503-672-3680
Aaron Persons, prin. Fax 672-3684
Merlo Station Night S Adult
1841 SW Merlo Dr, 503-259-5575
MaryJean Katz, prin. Fax 259-4220
Other Schools – See Portland

---

Anthem College Post-Sec.
4145 SW Watson Ave Ste 300 97005 503-646-6000
Valley Catholic HS 300/9-12
4275 SW 148th Ave 97078 503-644-3745
Ross Thomas, prin. Fax 646-4054

**Bend, Deschutes, Pop. 74,904**
Bend-LaPine Administrative SD 1 15,900/K-12
520 NW Wall St 97701 541-355-1000
Shay Mikalson, supt. Fax 383-6003
www.bend.k12.or.us
Bend HS 1,600/9-12
230 NE 6th St 97701 541-355-3700
Christopher Reese, prin. Fax 383-6465
Cascade MS 900/6-8
19619 Mountaineer Way 97702 541-355-7000
Stephanie Bennett, prin. Fax 383-6499
High Desert MS 800/6-8
61000 Diamondback Ln 97702 541-355-7200
Brian Moran-Crook, prin. Fax 383-6499
Marshall HS 200/Alt
1291 NE 5th St 97701 541-355-3500
Julie Linhares, prin. Fax 383-6584
Mountain View HS 1,400/9-12
2755 NE 27th St 97701 541-355-4400
Kathryn Legace, prin. Fax 383-6469
Pilot Butte MS 600/6-8
1501 NE Neff Rd 97701 541-355-7400
Michael Hecker, prin. Fax 383-6286
Sky View MS 800/6-8
63555 18th St 97701 541-355-7600
Scott Olszewski, prin. Fax 322-5217
Summit HS 1,400/9-12
2855 NW Clearwater Dr 97701 541-355-4000
Alice Dewittie, prin. Fax 322-3310
Other Schools – See La Pine

---

Cascades Academy 200/PK-12
19860 Tumalo Reservoir Rd, 541-382-0699
Julie Amberg, head sch Fax 382-0225
Central Oregon Community College Post-Sec.
2600 NW College Way 97701 541-383-7700
Phagans' Central Oregon Beauty College Post-Sec.
1310 NE Cushing Dr 97701 541-382-6171
Trinity Lutheran S 300/PK-12
2550 NE Butler Market Rd 97701 541-382-1850
Hanne Krause, prin. Fax 382-1850

**Boardman, Morrow, Pop. 3,160**
Morrow SD 1
Supt. — See Heppner
Riverside JSHS 400/7-12
210 NE Boardman Ave 97818 541-481-2525
Marie Shimer, prin. Fax 481-2047

**Bonanza, Klamath, Pop. 407**
Klamath County SD
Supt. — See Klamath Falls
Bonanza S 200/K-12
PO Box 128 97623 541-545-6581
Art Ochoa, prin. Fax 545-1719

**Boring, Clackamas**
Oregon Trail SD 46
Supt. — See Sandy
Boring MS 400/6-8
27801 SE Dee St 97009 503-668-9393
Tim Werner, prin. Fax 668-5291

**Brookings, Curry, Pop. 6,146**
Brookings-Harbor SD 17C 1,600/K-12
629 Easy St 97415 541-469-7443
Sean Gallagher, supt. Fax 463-6599
www.brookings.k12.or.us
Azalea MS 400/6-8
629 Easy St 97415 541-469-7427
Nicole Medrano, prin. Fax 469-7080
Brookings-Harbor HS 600/9-12
629 Easy St 97415 541-469-2108
Lisa Dion, prin. Fax 469-0176

---

Brookings Harbor Christian S 100/PK-10
PO Box 5809 97415 541-469-6478
Kari Schultz, dir. Fax 412-7242

**Brooks, Marion, Pop. 395**

---

Willamette Valley Christian S 100/PK-12
9075 Pueblo Ave NE 97305 503-393-5236
Debbie Tipton, prin. Fax 485-8203

**Burns, Harney, Pop. 2,728**
Harney County SD 3 800/K-12
550 N Court Ave 97720 541-573-6811
Dr. Marilyn McBride, supt. Fax 573-7557
www.burnsschools.k12.or.us
Burns Alternative S 50/Alt
550 N Court Ave 97720 541-573-8198
Ronald Wassom, prin. Fax 573-7557
Burns HS 200/9-12
1100 Oregon Ave 97720 541-573-2044
Brandon Yant, prin. Fax 573-5456
Other Schools – See Hines

**Canby, Clackamas, Pop. 15,520**
Canby SD 86 4,400/K-12
1130 S Ivy St 97013 503-266-7861
Samuel Goodall, supt. Fax 266-0022
www.canby.k12.or.us
Baker Prairie MS 600/7-8
1859 SE Township Rd 97013 503-263-7170
Jennifer Turner, prin. Fax 263-7189
Canby HS 1,500/9-12
721 SW 4th Ave 97013 503-263-7200
Greg Dinse, prin. Fax 263-7211

**Canyon City, Grant, Pop. 694**
Grant SD 3 600/K-12
401 N Canyon City Blvd 97820 541-575-1280
Curt Shelley, supt. Fax 575-3614
www.grantesd.k12.or.us
Other Schools – See John Day

**Canyonville, Douglas, Pop. 1,804**

---

Canyonville Christian Academy 100/9-12
PO Box 1100 97417 541-839-4401
Cathy Lovato, head sch Fax 839-6228

**Cave Junction, Josephine, Pop. 1,818**
Three Rivers SD
Supt. — See Grants Pass
Byrne MS 300/6-8
101 S Junction Ave 97523 541-592-2163
Scott Polen, prin. Fax 592-4851
Illinois Valley HS 400/9-12
625 E River St 97523 541-592-2116
Jamie Ongman, prin. Fax 592-4853

**Central Point, Jackson, Pop. 16,683**
Central Point SD 6 4,400/K-12
300 Ash St 97502 541-494-6200
Samantha Steele, supt. Fax 664-1637
www.district6.org
Crater Acad of Health & Public Service 500/9-12
655 N 3rd St 97502 541-494-6300
Julie Howland, prin. Fax 664-7589
Crater Renaissance Academy 500/9-12
655 N 3rd St 97502 541-494-6300
Bob King, prin. Fax 664-7589
Crater S of Business Innovation Science 500/9-12
655 N 3rd St 97502 541-494-6300
Tiffany Slaughter, prin. Fax 664-7589
Scenic MS 800/6-8
1955 Scenic Ave 97502 541-494-6400
Brad Eaton, prin. Fax 664-8534
Other Schools – See Gold Hill

**Chiloquin, Klamath, Pop. 678**
Klamath County SD
Supt. — See Klamath Falls
Chiloquin JSHS 200/7-12
PO Box 397 97624 541-783-2321
Denise Brumels, prin. Fax 783-2792

**Christmas Valley, Lake**

---

Solid Rock Christian S 50/K-12
PO Box 745 97641 541-576-2895
Dr. Megan Eide, prin. Fax 576-3554

**Clackamas, Clackamas, Pop. 2,578**
North Clackamas SD 12
Supt. — See Milwaukie
Clackamas HS 2,300/9-12
14486 SE 122nd Ave 97015 503-353-5800
Christine Garcia, prin. Fax 353-5815
Rock Creek MS 900/6-8
14897 SE Parklane Dr 97015 503-353-5680
John Brooks, prin. Fax 353-5695

---

Northwest College of Hair Design Post-Sec.
8307 SE Monterey Ave 97086 503-659-2834
Pioneer Pacific College Post-Sec.
8800 SE Sunnyside Rd 97015 503-654-8000
Spring Mountain Christian Academy PK-12
12152 SE Mather Rd 97015 503-454-0319
Hanna Grishkevich M.Ed., prin. Fax 286-0473

**Clatskanie, Columbia, Pop. 1,681**
Clatskanie SD 6J 800/K-12
PO Box 678 97016 503-728-0587
Dr. Lloyd Hartley, supt. Fax 728-0608
www.csd.k12.or.us
Clatskanie MSHS 400/7-12
PO Box 68 97016 503-728-2146
Amy McNeil, prin. Fax 728-4632

**Cloverdale, Tillamook, Pop. 245**
Nestucca Valley SD 101 500/K-12
PO Box 99 97112 503-392-4892
David Phelps, supt. Fax 392-9061
www.nestucca.k12.or.us
Nestucca JSHS 300/7-12
PO Box 38 97112 503-392-3194
David Phelps, prin. Fax 392-3724

**Colton, Clackamas**
Colton SD 53 600/K-12
30429 S Grays Hill Rd 97017 503-824-3535
Jay Kosik, supt. Fax 824-3530
www.colton.k12.or.us
Colton HS 200/9-12
30205 S Wall St 97017 503-824-2311
Tom Crane, prin. Fax 824-2312
Colton MS 200/6-8
21580 S Schieffer Rd 97017 503-824-2319
Susan Inman, prin. Fax 824-2309

**Condon, Gilliam, Pop. 677**
Condon SD 25J 100/K-12
210 E Bayard St 97823 541-384-2441
Robert Waltenburg, supt. Fax 384-2504
www.condon.k12.or.us
Condon HS 100/9-12
210 E Bayard St 97823 541-384-2441
Michelle Geer, prin. Fax 384-2504

**Coos Bay, Coos, Pop. 15,210**
Coos Bay SD 9 2,900/K-12
1255 Hemlock Ave 97420 541-267-3104
Dawn Granger, supt. Fax 269-5366
www.cbd9.net
Destinations S 100/Alt
1255 Hemlock Ave 97420 541-267-1485
Shelly McKnight, prin. Fax 266-7314
Harding Learning Center Alt
1255 Hemlock Ave 97420 541-267-1485
Shelly McKnight, prin. Fax 266-7314
Marshfield HS 1,100/8-12
1255 Hemlock Ave 97420 541-267-1405
Travis Howard, prin. Fax 269-0161

---

Southwestern Oregon Community College Post-Sec.
1988 Newmark Ave 97420 541-888-2525

**Coquille, Coos, Pop. 3,760**
Coquille SD 8 700/PK-12
1366 N Gould St 97423 541-396-2181
Tim Sweeney, supt. Fax 396-5015
www.coquille.k12.or.us
Coquille JSHS 300/7-12
499 W Central Blvd 97423 541-396-2163
Jeff Philley, prin. Fax 396-4635
Winter Lakes S 100/Alt
180 N Baxter 97423 541-824-0115
Tony Jones, prin. Fax 824-0116

**Corbett, Multnomah**
Corbett SD 39 | 1,200/K-12
35800 E Historic Colmb Riv 97019 | 503-261-4211
Dr. Randy Trani, supt. | Fax 695-3641
corbett.k12.or.us
Corbett HS | 200/9-12
35800 E Historic Colmb Riv 97019 | 503-261-4226
Dr. Phillip Pearson, prin. | Fax 695-3641
Corbett MS | 200/6-8
35800 E Historic Colmb Riv 97019 | 503-261-4226
Randy Trani, prin. | Fax 695-3641

**Corvallis, Benton, Pop. 52,340**
Corvallis SD 509J | 6,400/K-12
PO Box 3509J 97339 | 541-757-5811
Dr. Erin Prince, supt. | Fax 757-5703
www.corvallis.k12.or.us
Cheldelin MS | 500/6-8
987 NE Conifer Blvd 97330 | 541-757-5971
Jeff Brew, prin. | Fax 757-4596
Corvallis HS | 1,200/9-12
1400 NW Buchanan Ave 97330 | 541-757-5871
Matt Boring, prin. | Fax 757-5875
Crescent Valley HS | 1,000/9-12
4444 NW Highland Dr 97330 | 541-757-5801
Cherie Stroud, prin. | Fax 757-4522
Pauling MS | 700/6-8
1111 NW Cleveland Ave 97330 | 541-757-5961
Alicia Ward-Satey, prin. | Fax 757-4598

Oregon State University 97333 | Post-Sec.
541-737-1000
Phagans' Beauty College | Post-Sec.
1565 SW 53rd St 97333 | 541-753-6466
Santiam Christian S | 700/PK-12
7220 NE Arnold Ave 97330 | 541-745-5524
Lance Villers, supt. | Fax 745-6338

**Cottage Grove, Lane, Pop. 9,371**
South Lane SD 45J3 | 2,600/K-12
PO Box 218 97424 | 541-942-3381
Krista Parent, supt. | Fax 942-8098
www.slane.k12.or.us
Cottage Grove HS | 800/9-12
1375 S River Rd 97424 | 541-942-3391
Iton Udosenata, prin. | Fax 942-7492
Kennedy Alternative HS | 100/Alt
PO Box 218 97424 | 541-942-1962
Mike Ingman, prin. | Fax 942-3672
Lincoln MS | 600/6-8
1565 S 4th St 97424 | 541-942-3316
Jeremy Smith, prin. | Fax 942-9801

**Crane, Harney, Pop. 128**
Harney County UNHSD 1J | 100/9-12
PO Box 828 97732 | 541-493-2641
Matthew Hawley, supt. | Fax 493-2051
cranehighschool.org
Crane Union HS | 100/9-12
PO Box 828 97732 | 541-493-2641
Matthew Hawley, prin. | Fax 493-2051

**Creswell, Lane, Pop. 4,867**
Creswell SD 40 | 1,300/K-12
998 A St 97426 | 541-895-6000
Todd Hamilton, supt. | Fax 895-6019
www.creswell.k12.or.us
Creswell HS | 400/9-12
33390 Nieblock Ln 97426 | 541-895-6020
Andy Bracco, prin. | Fax 895-6089
Creswell MS | 300/6-8
655 W Oregon Ave 97426 | 541-895-6090
Shirley Burrus, prin. | Fax 895-6139

Creswell Christian S | 50/PK-12
PO Box 217 97426 | 541-895-4622
Rebecca Lake, admin. | Fax 895-4622

**Culver, Jefferson, Pop. 1,338**
Culver SD 4 | 600/K-12
PO Box 259 97734 | 541-546-2541
Stefanie Garber, supt. | Fax 546-7517
www.culver.k12.or.us/
Culver HS | 200/9-12
PO Box 259 97734 | 541-546-2251
Tim Fields, prin. | Fax 546-2201
Culver MS | 200/6-8
PO Box 259 97734 | 541-546-3090
Brad Kudlac, prin. | Fax 546-2137

**Dallas, Polk, Pop. 14,264**
Dallas SD 2 | 3,100/K-12
111 SW Ash St 97338 | 503-623-5594
Michelle Johnstone, supt. | Fax 623-5597
www.dallas.k12.or.us
Dallas HS | 1,000/9-12
1250 SE Holman Ave 97338 | 503-623-8336
Steve Spencer, prin. | Fax 623-4669
LaCreole MS | 700/6-8
701 SE Lacreole Dr 97338 | 503-623-6662
Jamie Richardson, prin. | Fax 623-8477

**Damascus, Clackamas, Pop. 10,286**
Gresham-Barlow SD 10J
Supt. — See Gresham
Damascus MS | 200/6-8
14151 SE 242nd Ave, | 503-658-3171
Lori Walter, prin. | Fax 658-6275

Damascus Christian S | 200/K-12
14251 SE Rust Way, | 503-658-4100
Zach Davidson, prin. | Fax 658-5827

**Days Creek, Douglas, Pop. 264**

Milo Adventist Academy | 100/9-12
PO Box 278 97429 | 541-825-3200

**Dayton, Yamhill, Pop. 2,476**
Dayton SD 8 | 1,000/K-12
PO Box 219 97114 | 503-864-2215
Janelle Beers, supt. | Fax 864-3927
daytonk12.org
Dayton HS | 300/9-12
801 Ferry St 97114 | 503-864-2273
Jami Fluke, prin. | Fax 864-2932
Dayton JHS | 200/6-8
801 Ferry St 97114 | 503-864-2246
Jami Fluke, prin. | Fax 864-3697

**Dayville, Grant, Pop. 148**
Dayville SD 16J | 100/PK-12
PO Box C 97825 | 541-987-2412
Kathryn Hedrick, supt. | Fax 987-2155
www.grantesd.k12.or.us/dayville
Dayville S | 100/PK-12
PO Box C 97825 | 541-987-2412
Denise Folston, prin. | Fax 987-2155

**Dillard, Douglas**
Winston-Dillard SD 116
Supt. — See Winston
Dillard Alternative HS | 50/Alt
165 Dyke Rd 97432 | 541-679-3023
Jon Martz, prin. | Fax 784-2620

**Drain, Douglas, Pop. 1,120**
North Douglas SD 22 | 300/K-12
PO Box 428 97435 | 541-836-2223
John Lahley, supt. | Fax 836-7558
www.northdouglas.k12.or.us
North Douglas HS | 100/9-12
PO Box 488 97435 | 541-836-2222
Scott Yakovich, prin. | Fax 836-2387

**Dufur, Wasco, Pop. 590**
Dufur SD 29 | 300/K-12
802 NE 5th St 97021 | 541-467-2509
Jack Henderson, supt. | Fax 467-2589
www.dufur.k12.or.us
Dufur S | 300/K-12
802 NE 5th St 97021 | 541-467-2509
Leo Baptiste, prin. | Fax 467-2589

**Eagle Point, Jackson, Pop. 8,245**
Jackson County SD 9 | 4,000/K-12
PO Box 548 97524 | 541-830-6551
Cynda Rickert, supt. | Fax 830-6550
www.eaglepnt.k12.or.us
Eagle Point HS | 1,200/9-12
PO Box 198 97524 | 541-830-1300
Tom McGuire, prin. | Fax 830-6682
Eagle Point MS | 500/6-8
PO Box 218 97524 | 541-830-1250
Joni Parsons, prin. | Fax 830-6086
Other Schools – See White City

**Echo, Umatilla, Pop. 686**
Echo SD 5 | 300/PK-12
600 E Gerone St 97826 | 541-376-8436
Raymon Smith, supt. | Fax 376-8473
www.echo.k12.or.us
Echo S | 300/PK-12
600 E Gerone St 97826 | 541-376-8436
Raymon Smith, prin. | Fax 376-8473

**Elgin, Union, Pop. 1,678**
Elgin SD 23 | 400/PK-12
PO Box 68 97827 | 541-437-1211
Dianne Greif, supt. | Fax 437-1231
www.elgin.k12.or.us
Elgin HS | 100/9-12
PO Box 68 97827 | 541-437-2021
Thomas Grimes, prin. | Fax 437-1705

**Elmira, Lane**
Fern Ridge SD 28J | 1,400/K-12
88834 Territorial Rd 97437 | 541-935-2253
Sally J. Storm Ph.D., supt. | Fax 935-8222
www.fernridge.k12.or.us
Elmira HS | 500/9-12
24936 Fir Grove Ln 97437 | 541-935-8200
Gary Carpenter, prin. | Fax 935-8205
Fern Ridge MS | 300/6-8
88831 Territorial Rd 97437 | 541-935-8230
Peter Barsotti, prin. | Fax 935-8234

**Enterprise, Wallowa, Pop. 1,904**
Enterprise SD 21 | 400/K-12
201 SE 4th St 97828 | 541-426-3193
Brad Royse, supt. | Fax 426-3504
www.enterprise.k12.or.us/
Enterprise HS | 200/7-12
201 SE 4th St 97828 | 541-426-3193
Blake Carlsen, prin. | Fax 426-3504

Enterprise SDA S | 50/K-10
PO Box N 97828 | 541-426-8339

**Estacada, Clackamas, Pop. 2,646**
Estacada SD 108 | 2,100/K-12
255 NE 6th Ave 97023 | 503-630-6871
Marla Stephenson, supt. | Fax 630-8513
www.estacada.k12.or.us
Estacada HS | 700/9-12
355 NE 6th Ave 97023 | 503-630-8515
Ryan Carpenter, prin. | Fax 630-8699
Estacada MS | 300/6-8
500 NE Main St 97023 | 503-630-8516
Kristin Turnquist, prin. | Fax 630-8693

**Eugene, Lane, Pop. 149,658**
Bethel SD 52 | 5,700/K-12
4640 Barger Dr 97402 | 541-689-3280
Colt Gill, supt. | Fax 689-0719
www.bethel.k12.or.us
Cascade MS | 400/6-8
1525 Echo Hollow Rd 97402 | 541-689-0641
Natalie Oliver, prin. | Fax 689-9622
Kalapuya HS | 100/Alt
1200 N Terry St 97402 | 541-607-9853
Stefan Aumack, prin. | Fax 607-9857
Shasta MS | 500/6-8
4656 Barger Dr 97402 | 541-688-9611
Brady Cottle, prin. | Fax 689-9382
Willamette HS | 1,500/9-12
1801 Echo Hollow Rd 97402 | 541-689-0731
Mindy LeRoux, prin. | Fax 689-7119

Crow-Applegate-Lorane SD 66 | 300/K-12
85955 Territorial Hwy 97402 | 541-935-2100
Aaron Brown, supt. | Fax 935-6107
www.cal.k12.or.us
Crow MSHS | 100/7-12
25863 Crow Rd 97402 | 541-935-2227
Carla DeShaw, prin. | Fax 935-6829

Eugene SD 4J | 16,400/K-12
200 N Monroe St 97402 | 541-790-7700
Dr. Gustavo Balderas, supt. | Fax 790-7711
www.4j.lane.edu
Arts and Technology Academy at Jefferson | 400/6-8
1650 W 22nd Ave 97405 | 541-790-5700
Jeff Johnson, prin. | Fax 790-5705
Churchill HS | 1,000/9-12
1850 Bailey Hill Rd 97405 | 541-790-5100
B.J. Blake, prin. | Fax 790-5110
Eugene College and Career Options | Alt
4000 E 30th Ave 97405 | 541-463-3930
Brad New, prin. | Fax 463-3937
French Immersion MS | 6-8
680 E 24th Ave 97405 | 541-790-8500
Chris Mitchell, prin. | Fax 790-8505
International HS Churchill Campus | 9-12
1850 Bailey Hill Rd 97405 | 541-790-5225
Jessica Schabtach, prin. | Fax 790-5110
International HS Sheldon Campus | 9-12
2455 Willakenzie Rd 97401 | 541-790-6636
Jessica Schabtach, prin. | Fax 790-6605
International HS South Eugene Campus | 9-12
400 E 19th Ave 97401 | 541-790-8030
Jessica Schabtach, prin. | Fax 790-8005
Kelly MS | 400/6-8
850 Howard Ave 97404 | 541-790-4740
Wes Flinn, prin. | Fax 790-4746
Kennedy MS | 500/6-8
2200 Bailey Hill Rd 97405 | 541-790-5500
Charlie Smith, prin. | Fax 790-5505
Madison MS | 500/6-8
875 Wilkes Dr 97404 | 541-790-4300
Scott Marsh, prin. | Fax 790-4320
Monroe MS | 500/6-8
2800 Bailey Ln 97401 | 541-790-6300
Mike Johnson, prin. | Fax 790-6305
North Eugene HS | 1,100/9-12
200 Silver Ln 97404 | 541-790-4500
Casandra Kamens, prin. | Fax 790-4440
Roosevelt MS | 500/6-8
680 E 24th Ave 97405 | 541-790-8500
Chris Mitchell, prin. | Fax 790-8505
Sheldon HS | 1,500/9-12
2455 Willakenzie Rd 97401 | 541-790-6600
Bob Bolden, prin. | Fax 790-6605
South Eugene HS | 1,400/9-12
400 E 19th Ave 97401 | 541-790-8000
Stephanie Cannon, prin. | Fax 790-8005
Spanish Immersion MS | 6-8
2800 Bailey Ln 97401 | 541-790-6300
Mike Johnson, prin. | Fax 790-6305
Spencer Butte MS | 400/6-8
500 E 43rd Ave 97405 | 541-790-8300
Greg Borgerding, prin. | Fax 790-8305
Young MS | 600/6-8
2555 Gilham Rd 97408 | 541-790-6400
Kim Watry, prin. | Fax 790-6456
Yujin Gakuen Japanese MS | 6-8
850 Howard Ave 97404 | 541-790-4740
Wes Flinn, prin. | Fax 790-4746

Gutenberg College | Post-Sec.
1883 University St 97403 | 541-683-5141
Lane Community College | Post-Sec.
4000 E 30th Ave 97405 | 541-463-3000
Lifegate Christian S | 50/6-12
1052 Fairfield Ave 97402 | 541-689-5847
Dr. Mike McCoy, prin. | Fax 689-6028
Marist HS | 500/9-12
1900 Kingsley Rd 97401 | 541-686-2234
Stacey Baker, prin. | Fax 342-6451
New Hope Christian College | Post-Sec.
2155 Bailey Hill Rd 97405 | 541-485-1780
Northwest Christian University | Post-Sec.
828 E 11th Ave 97401 | 541-343-1641
Oak Hill S | 100/K-12
86397 Eldon Schafer Dr 97405 | 541-744-0954
Robert Sarkisian, head sch | Fax 741-6968
University of Oregon | Post-Sec.
1217 University of Oregon 97403 | 541-346-1000
Wellsprings Friends S | 100/9-12
3590 W 18th Ave 97402 | 541-686-1223
Dennis Hoerner Ph.D., head sch | Fax 687-1493

**Fairview, Multnomah, Pop. 8,478**
Reynolds SD 7 | 11,100/K-12
1204 NE 201st Ave 97024 | 503-661-7200
Linda Florence, supt. | Fax 667-6932
www.reynolds.k12.or.us
Reynolds MS | 900/6-8
1200 NE 201st Ave 97024 | 503-665-8166
Stacy Talus, prin. | Fax 667-6751
Reynolds Learning Academy | Adult
20234 NE Halsey St 97024 | 503-667-4673
Erin Ferguson, prin. | Fax 667-0530
Other Schools – See Portland, Troutdale

**Falls City, Polk, Pop. 925**
Falls City SD 57 100/K-12
111 N Main St 97344 503-787-3521
Jack Thompson, supt. Fax 787-5805
www.fallscityschools.org/
Falls City HS 50/9-12
111 N Main St 97344 503-787-3521
Jack Thompson, prin. Fax 787-1507

**Finn Rock, Lane**
McKenzie SD 68 200/K-12
51187 Blue River Dr, Vida OR 97488 541-822-3338
Jim Thomas, supt. Fax 822-8014
www.mckenzie.k12.or.us
McKenzie HS 100/9-12
51187 Blue River Dr, Vida OR 97488 541-822-3313
Lane Tompkins, prin. Fax 822-8014

**Florence, Lane, Pop. 8,201**
Siuslaw SD 97J 1,400/K-12
2111 Oak St 97439 541-997-2651
Ethel Angal, supt. Fax 997-6748
www.siuslaw.k12.or.us
Siuslaw HS 500/9-12
2975 Oak St 97439 541-997-3448
Kerri Tatum, prin. Fax 997-4160
Siuslaw MS 300/6-8
2525 Oak St 97439 541-997-8241
Andrew Grzeskowiak, prin. Fax 997-4161

**Forest Grove, Washington, Pop. 20,448**
Forest Grove SD 15 6,000/K-12
1728 Main St 97116 503-357-6171
Dr. Yvonne Curtis, supt. Fax 359-2520
www.fgsd.k12.or.us
Armstrong MS 900/7-8
1777 Mountain View Ln 97116 503-359-2465
Brandon Hundley, prin. Fax 359-2560
Forest Grove HS 1,900/9-12
1401 Nichols Ln 97116 503-359-2432
Karen O'Neill, prin. Fax 359-2521

---

Pacific University Post-Sec.
2043 College Way 97116 800-677-6712

**Gaston, Washington, Pop. 631**
Gaston SD 511J 500/K-12
PO Box 68 97119 503-985-0210
Susy McKenzie, supt. Fax 985-3366
www.gaston.k12.or.us
Gaston JSHS 200/7-12
PO Box 68 97119 503-985-7516
Christine Collins, prin. Fax 985-3279

**Gervais, Marion, Pop. 2,415**
Gervais SD 1 600/PK-12
PO Box 100 97026 503-792-3803
Matt Henry, supt. Fax 792-3809
www.gervais.k12.or.us
Brown Academy Alt
PO Box 100 97026 503-792-3830
Kim Kellison, prin. Fax 792-3809
Gervais HS 300/9-12
PO Box 195 97026 503-792-3656
Mike Solem, prin. Fax 792-3770
Gervais MS 300/6-8
PO Box 176 97026 503-792-3626
Ann O'Connell, prin. Fax 792-3770

**Gilchrist, Klamath**
Klamath County SD
Supt. — See Klamath Falls
Gilchrist S 100/K-12
PO Box 668 97737 541-433-2295
Scott Reed, prin. Fax 433-2688

**Gladstone, Clackamas, Pop. 11,109**
Gladstone SD 115 2,000/PK-12
17789 Webster Rd 97027 503-655-2777
Bob Stewart, supt. Fax 655-5201
www.gladstone.k12.or.us
Gladstone HS 700/9-12
18800 Portland Ave 97027 503-655-2544
Natalie Osburn, prin. Fax 655-0320
Kraxberger MS 500/6-8
17777 Webster Rd 97027 503-655-3636
Becky Lukens, prin. Fax 650-2596

---

Grace Christian S 100/PK-12
6460 Glen Echo Ave 97027 503-655-3074

**Glide, Douglas, Pop. 1,756**
Glide SD 12 700/K-12
301 Glide Loop Dr 97443 541-496-3521
Mike Narkiewicz, supt. Fax 496-4300
www.glide.k12.or.us
Glide HS 200/9-12
18990 N Umpqua Hwy 97443 541-496-3554
Kristina Haug, prin. Fax 496-4304
Glide MS 100/7-8
18990 N Umpqua Hwy 97443 541-496-3516
Kristina Haug, prin. Fax 496-4302

**Gold Beach, Curry, Pop. 2,158**
Central Curry SD 1 500/K-12
29516 Ellensburg Ave 97444 541-247-2003
Roy Durfee, supt. Fax 247-9717
www.ccsd.k12.or.us
Gold Beach HS 200/9-12
29516 Ellensburg Ave 97444 541-247-6647
Roy Durfee, prin. Fax 247-4557

**Gold Hill, Jackson, Pop. 1,181**
Central Point SD 6
Supt. — See Central Point
Hanby MS 200/6-8
806 6th Ave 97525 541-494-6800
Scott Dippel, prin. Fax 855-1120

**Grants Pass, Josephine, Pop. 33,499**
Grants Pass SD 7 5,800/K-12
725 NE Dean Dr 97526 541-474-5700
John Higgins, supt. Fax 474-5705
www.grantspass.k12.or.us
Grants Pass HS 1,900/9-12
830 NE 9th St 97526 541-474-5710
Ryan Thompson, prin. Fax 474-5717
Grants Pass HS - Gladiola Campus Alt
1137 SE Gladiola Dr 97526 541-474-5790
Kelly Marval, admin. Fax 474-0098
North MS 700/6-8
1725 NW Highland Ave 97526 541-474-5740
Doug Ely, prin. Fax 474-5739
South MS 600/6-8
350 W Harbeck Rd 97527 541-474-5750
Jeff Weiss, prin. Fax 474-9742

Three Rivers SD 4,600/K-12
8550 New Hope Rd 97527 541-862-3111
David Holmes, supt. Fax 862-3119
www.threerivers.k12.or.us
Fleming MS 400/6-8
6001 Monument Dr 97526 541-476-8284
Sidney Hobgood, prin. Fax 471-2458
Hidden Valley HS 700/9-12
651 Murphy Creek Rd 97527 541-862-2124
Daye Stone, prin. Fax 862-2872
Lincoln Savage MS 400/6-8
8551 New Hope Rd 97527 541-862-2171
Mark Higgins, prin. Fax 862-2713
North Valley HS 600/9-12
6741 Monument Dr 97526 541-479-3388
Dennis Misner, prin. Fax 471-2462
Other Schools – See Cave Junction, Merlin

---

Brighton Academy 100/PK-12
1121 NE 7th St 97526 541-474-6865
New Hope Christian S 200/PK-12
5961 New Hope Rd 97527 541-476-4588
Ernest Stone, admin. Fax 474-7626
Phagans' Grants Pass College of Beauty Post-Sec.
304 NE Agness Ave Ste F 97526 541-479-6678
Rogue Community College Post-Sec.
3345 Redwood Hwy 97527 541-956-7500
Vineyard Christian S 100/PK-12
275 Potts Way 97526 541-479-9649
Doug Thomas, prin. Fax 479-3506

**Grass Valley, Sherman, Pop. 160**
Sherman County SD 200/K-12
PO Box 68 97029 541-565-3500
Wes Owens, supt. Fax 565-3319
shermancountyschooldistrict.weebly.com
Other Schools – See Moro

**Gresham, Multnomah, Pop. 101,317**
Centennial SD 28J
Supt. — See Portland
Centennial HS 1,800/9-12
3505 SE 182nd Ave 97030 503-762-6180
Mairi Scott-Aguirre, prin. Fax 661-5296

Gresham-Barlow SD 10J 11,800/PK-12
1331 NW Eastman Pkwy 97030 503-261-4550
Jim Schlachter, supt. Fax 261-4552
www.gresham.k12.or.us
Barlow HS 1,800/9-12
5105 SE 302nd Ave 97080 503-258-4850
Bruce Schmidt, prin. Fax 258-4840
Clear Creek MS 700/6-8
219 NE 219th Ave 97030 503-492-6700
David Atherton, prin. Fax 492-6707
Gresham HS 1,800/9-12
1200 N Main Ave 97030 503-674-5500
John Koch, prin. Fax 674-5549
McCarty MS 700/6-8
1400 SE 5th St 97080 503-665-0148
John George, prin. Fax 669-1892
Russell MS 800/6-8
3625 SE Powell Valley Rd 97080 503-667-6900
Rolland Hayden, prin. Fax 492-6708
Springwater Trail HS 200/9-12
1440 SE Fleming Ave 97080 503-261-4600
Ryan Blaszak, prin. Fax 261-4630
West Orient MS 400/6-8
29805 SE Orient Dr 97080 503-663-3323
Elise Cantanese, prin. Fax 663-2504
Other Schools – See Damascus

Multnomah ESD
Supt. — See Portland
Alpha HS 100/Alt
876 NE 8th St 97030 503-262-4050
Peter Kane, prin. Fax 262-4065

---

Mt. Hood Community College Post-Sec.
26000 SE Stark St 97030 503-491-6422
Phonics Phactory 300/PK-10
PO Box 2128 97030 503-661-5632
Rev. Brian Mayer, admin. Fax 907-5827

**Halsey, Linn, Pop. 874**
Central Linn SD 552 700/K-12
PO Box 200 97348 541-369-2813
Brian Gardner, supt. Fax 369-3439
www.centrallinn.k12.or.us
Central Linn HS 300/7-12
32433 Highway 228 97348 541-369-2811
Jon Zwemke, prin. Fax 369-3455

**Happy Valley, Clackamas, Pop. 13,434**
North Clackamas SD 12
Supt. — See Milwaukie
Happy Valley MS 1,000/6-8
13865 SE King Rd Ste B, 503-353-1920
Emily Behunin, prin. Fax 353-1935

---

Phagans' School of Hair Design Post-Sec.
11860 SE 82nd Ave # K-217, 503-652-2668

**Harrisburg, Linn, Pop. 3,472**
Harrisburg SD 7 900/K-12
PO Box 208 97446 541-995-6626
Bryan Starr, supt. Fax 995-3453
www.harrisburg.k12.or.us
Harrisburg HS 300/9-12
PO Box 209 97446 541-995-6626
Steve Atkinson, prin. Fax 995-6697
Harrisburg MS 200/6-8
PO Box 317 97446 541-995-6551
Darci Stuller, prin. Fax 995-5120

---

Harris S 100/PK-12
PO Box 347 97446 541-995-6444

**Helix, Umatilla, Pop. 175**
Helix SD 1 200/K-12
PO Box 398 97835 541-457-2175
Darrick Cope, supt. Fax 457-2481
www.helix.k12.or.us
Helix S 200/K-12
PO Box 398 97835 541-457-2175
Darrick Cope, prin. Fax 457-2481

**Heppner, Morrow, Pop. 1,251**
Morrow SD 1 2,200/K-12
PO Box 100 97836 541-676-9128
Dirk Dirksen, supt. Fax 676-5742
www.morrow.k12.or.us
Heppner JSHS 200/7-12
PO Box 67 97836 541-676-9138
Matt Combe, prin. Fax 676-5836
Other Schools – See Boardman, Irrigon

**Hermiston, Umatilla, Pop. 16,457**
Hermiston SD 8 5,100/K-12
305 SW 11th St 97838 541-667-6000
Dr. Fred Maiocco, supt. Fax 667-6050
www.hermiston.k12.or.us
Hermiston HS 1,400/9-12
600 S 1st St 97838 541-667-6100
Tom Spoo, prin. Fax 667-6150
Innovative Learning Center 50/Alt
581 S 1st St 97838 541-667-6100
Tom Spoo, prin. Fax 667-6153
Larive MS 600/6-8
1497 SW 9th St 97838 541-667-6200
Stacie Roberts, prin. Fax 667-6250
Sandstone MS 500/6-8
400 NE 10th St 97838 541-667-6300
Larry Usher, prin. Fax 667-6350

**Hillsboro, Washington, Pop. 88,100**
Hillsboro SD 1J 20,700/K-12
3083 NE 49th Pl 97124 503-844-1500
Mike Scott, supt. Fax 844-1540
www.hsd.k12.or.us
Brown MS 800/7-8
1505 SW Cornelius Pass Rd 97123 503-844-1070
Koreen Barreras-Brown, prin. Fax 844-1071
Century HS 1,700/9-12
2000 SE Century Blvd 97123 503-844-1800
Martha Guise, prin. Fax 844-1825
Evergreen MS 800/7-8
29850 NW Evergreen Rd 97124 503-844-1400
Rian Petrick, prin. Fax 844-1402
Glencoe HS 1,600/9-12
2700 NW Glencoe Rd 97124 503-844-1900
Claudia Ruf, prin. Fax 844-1949
Hillsboro HS 1,500/9-12
3285 SE Rood Bridge Rd 97123 503-844-1980
Arturo Lomeli, prin. Fax 844-1999
Liberty HS 1,400/9-12
21945 NW Wagon Way 97124 503-844-1250
Greg Timmons, prin. Fax 844-1299
Miller Education Center 50/Alt
440 SE Oak St 97123 503-844-1680
Gregg O'Mara, prin. Fax 844-1684
Miller Education Center 100/Alt
215 SE 6th Ave 97123 503-844-1000
Gregg O'Mara, prin. Fax 844-1019
Poynter MS 700/7-8
1535 NE Grant St 97124 503-844-1580
Jon Pede, prin. Fax 844-1583
South Meadows MS 800/7-8
4690 SE Davis Rd 97123 503-844-1220
Rebecca Smith, prin. Fax 844-1221

---

Airman Proficiency Center Post-Sec.
3565 NE Cornell Rd 97124 503-648-2831
Faith Bible Christian HS 100/9-12
2299 SE 45th Ave 97123 503-681-8254
Kevin Rex, supt. Fax 681-9274

**Hines, Harney, Pop. 1,525**
Harney County SD 3
Supt. — See Burns
Hines MS 200/6-8
PO Box 38 97738 541-573-6436
Jerry Mayes, prin. Fax 573-7255

**Hood River, Hood River, Pop. 7,008**
Hood River County SD 4,000/K-12
1011 Eugene St 97031 541-386-2511
Dan Goldman, supt. Fax 387-5099
www.hoodriver.k12.or.us
Hood River MS 500/6-8
1602 May St 97031 541-386-2114
Brent Emmons, prin. Fax 387-5070
Hood River Valley HS 1,200/9-12
1220 Indian Creek Rd 97031 541-386-4500
Rich Polkinghorn, prin. Fax 386-2400
Wy'East MS 400/6-8
3000 Wyeast Rd 97031 541-354-1548
Sarah Braman-Smith, prin. Fax 354-5120

---

Horizon Christian S 200/PK-12
700 Pacific Ave 97031 541-387-3200
Ken Block, supt. Fax 387-3651

Mid-Columbia Adventist Academy 50/K-10
1100 22nd St 97031 541-386-3187

**Huntington, Baker, Pop. 429**
Huntington SD 16J 100/K-12
520 3rd St E 97907 541-869-2204
Scott Bullock, supt. Fax 869-2444
www.huntington.k12.or.us/
Huntington S 100/K-12
520 3rd St E 97907 541-869-2204
Scott Bullock, admin. Fax 869-2444

**Independence, Polk, Pop. 8,352**
Central SD 13J 2,700/K-12
750 S 5th St 97351 503-838-0030
Buzz Brazeau, supt. Fax 838-0033
www.central.k12.or.us
Central HS 900/9-12
1530 Monmouth St 97351 503-838-0480
Greg Mitchell, prin. Fax 838-0483
Talmadge MS 700/6-8
51 S 16th St 97351 503-606-2252
Perry LaBounty, prin. Fax 606-2436

**Irrigon, Morrow, Pop. 1,788**
Morrow SD 1
Supt. — See Heppner
Irrigon JSHS 300/7-12
315 E Wyoming Ave 97844 541-922-5551
Ryan Keefauver, prin. Fax 922-5558
Morrow Education Center 100/Alt
240 W Columbia Ln 97844 541-922-4004
Craig Bensen, dir. Fax 922-4122

**Jasper, Lane**

---

Laurelwood Academy 50/9-12
PO Box 2072 97438 541-726-8340

**Jefferson, Marion, Pop. 3,013**
Jefferson SD 14J 900/K-12
1328 N 2nd St 97352 541-327-3337
Kent Klewitz, supt. Fax 327-2960
www.jefferson.k12.or.us
Jefferson HS 300/9-12
2200 Talbot Rd SE 97352 541-327-3337
Cathy Emmert, prin. Fax 327-1867
Jefferson MS 200/6-8
1344 N 2nd St 97352 541-327-3337
Tracy Keuler, prin. Fax 327-7762

**John Day, Grant, Pop. 1,713**
Grant SD 3
Supt. — See Canyon City
Grant Union JSHS 300/7-12
911 S Canyon Blvd 97845 541-575-1799
Ryan Gerry, prin. Fax 575-2754

**Jordan Valley, Malheur, Pop. 179**
Jordan Valley SD 3 100/K-12
PO Box 99 97910 541-586-2213
Rusty Bengoa, supt. Fax 586-2568
www.jordanvalley.k12.or.us
Jordan Valley HS 50/7-12
PO Box 99 97910 541-586-2213
Rusty Bengoa, supt. Fax 586-2568

**Junction City, Lane, Pop. 5,249**
Junction City SD 69 1,700/K-12
325 Maple St 97448 541-998-6311
Dr. Kathleen Rodden-Nord, supt. Fax 998-3926
www.junctioncity.k12.or.us
Junction City HS 500/9-12
1135 W 6th Ave 97448 541-998-2343
Malcolm McRae, prin. Fax 998-6303
Oaklea MS 500/5-8
1515 Rose St 97448 541-998-3381
Brian Young, prin. Fax 998-3383

**Keizer, Marion, Pop. 35,273**
Salem-Keizer SD 24J
Supt. — See Salem
Claggett Creek MS 900/6-8
1810 Alder Dr NE 97303 503-399-3701
Rob Schoepper, prin. Fax 399-3708
McNary HS 2,000/9-12
595 Chemawa Rd N 97303 503-399-3233
Erik Jespersen, prin. Fax 391-4025
Whiteaker MS 800/6-8
1605 Lockhaven Dr NE 97303 503-399-3224
Julia DeWitt, prin. Fax 375-7872

**Klamath Falls, Klamath, Pop. 20,019**
Klamath County SD 5,900/K-12
10501 Washburn Way 97603 541-883-5000
Greg Thede, supt. Fax 883-6677
www.kcsd.k12.or.us
Brixner JHS 400/7-8
4727 Homedale Rd 97603 541-883-5025
Leslie Garrett, prin. Fax 883-5019
Falcon Heights Academy 100/Alt
5825 Climax Ave 97603 541-883-6699
Laura Blair, prin. Fax 273-8763
Henley HS 700/9-12
8245 Highway 39 97603 541-883-5040
Jack Lee, prin. Fax 883-6663
Henley MS 400/7-8
7925 Highway 39 97603 541-883-5050
Kristine Creed, prin. Fax 883-5012
Mazama HS 800/9-12
3009 Summers Ln 97603 541-883-5024
Steve Morosin, prin. Fax 883-5044
Other Schools – See Bonanza, Chiloquin, Gilchrist, Merrill

Klamath Falls CSD 2,700/K-12
1336 Avalon St 97603 541-883-4700
Dr. Paul Hillyer, supt. Fax 850-2766
www.kfalls.k12.or.us
Klamath Union HS 700/9-12
1300 Monclaire St 97601 541-883-4710
Charlene Herron, prin. Fax 885-4276

Link River HS 100/Alt
2858 Eberlein Ave 97603 541-850-7653
Scott Mason, admin.
Ponderosa JHS 500/6-8
2554 Main St 97601 541-883-4740
Daymond Monteith, prin. Fax 885-4286

---

College of Cosmetology Post-Sec.
357 E Main St 97601 541-882-6644
Hosanna Christian S 300/PK-12
5000 Hosanna Way 97603 541-882-7732
Barney Simonsen, admin. Fax 882-6940
Klamath Community College Post-Sec.
7390 S 6th St 97603 541-882-3521
Oregon Institute of Technology Post-Sec.
3201 Campus Dr 97601 541-885-1000
Triad S 200/PK-12
2450 Summers Ln 97603 541-885-7940

**La Grande, Union, Pop. 12,606**
La Grande SD 1 2,100/K-12
1305 N Willow St 97850 541-663-3202
Larry Glaze, supt. Fax 663-3223
www.lagrandesd.org
La Grande HS 600/9-12
708 K Ave 97850 541-663-3301
Brett Baxter, prin. Fax 663-3313
La Grande MS 500/6-8
1108 4th St 97850 541-663-3421
Kyle McKinney, prin. Fax 663-3422

---

Eastern Oregon University Post-Sec.
1 University Blvd 97850 541-962-3672

**Lake Oswego, Clackamas, Pop. 35,589**
Lake Oswego SD 7J 5,500/K-12
PO Box 70 97034 503-534-2000
Dr. Heather Beck, supt. Fax 534-2030
www.loswego.k12.or.us
Lake Oswego HS 1,200/9-12
PO Box 310 97034 503-534-2313
Cindy Schubert, prin. Fax 534-2327
Lake Oswego JHS 600/6-8
2500 Country Club Rd 97034 503-534-2335
Robert Caplinger, prin. Fax 534-2341
Lakeridge HS 1,100/9-12
PO Box 739 97034 503-534-2319
Jennifer Schiele, prin. Fax 534-2392
Lakeridge JHS 500/6-8
4700 Jean Rd 97035 503-534-2343
Kurt Schultz, prin. Fax 534-2276

**Lakeview, Lake, Pop. 2,216**
Adel SD 21 50/4-8
357 N L St 97630 541-947-5418
Bob Nash, admin. Fax 947-3373
www.lakeesd.k12.or.us
Other Schools – See Adel

Lake County SD 7 600/K-12
1341 S 1st St 97630 541-947-3347
Will Cahill, supt. Fax 947-3386
www.lakeview.k12.or.us
Daly MS 100/7-8
220 S H St 97630 541-947-2257
Steve Prock, prin. Fax 947-3506
Lakeview HS 200/9-12
906 S 3rd St 97630 541-947-2287
Steve Prock, prin. Fax 947-3601

**La Pine, Deschutes, Pop. 1,617**
Bend-LaPine Administrative SD 1
Supt. — See Bend
La Pine HS 500/9-12
51633 Coach Rd 97739 541-355-8400
Matt Montgomery, prin. Fax 322-5352
La Pine MS 300/6-8
16360 1st St 97739 541-355-8200
Robi Phinney, prin. Fax 355-8210

**Lebanon, Linn, Pop. 15,042**
Lebanon Community SD 9 4,200/K-12
485 S 5th St 97355 541-451-8511
Rob Hess, supt. Fax 259-6857
www.lebanon.k12.or.us
Lebanon HS 1,200/9-12
1700 S 5th St 97355 541-451-8555
Brad Shreve, prin. Fax 451-8550
Seven Oak MS 600/6-8
550 Cascade Dr 97355 541-451-8416
Wayne Raposa, prin. Fax 451-8431

---

East Linn Christian Academy 300/PK-12
36883 Victory Dr 97355 541-259-2324
Janelle Detweiler M.Ed., supt. Fax 451-3800

**Lincoln City, Lincoln, Pop. 7,723**
Lincoln County SD
Supt. — See Newport
Taft HS 700/7-12
3780 SE Spy Glass Ridge Dr 97367 541-996-2115
Majalise Tolan, prin. Fax 996-4335

---

Lincoln City Seventh-day Adventist S 100/1-12
2126 NE Surf Ave 97367 541-994-5181
Joan Oksenholt, prin. Fax 994-5181

**Long Creek, Grant, Pop. 191**
Long Creek SD 17 50/PK-12
PO Box 429 97856 541-421-3896
Bill Delong, supt. Fax 421-3012
www.longcreekschool.com
Long Creek S 50/PK-12
PO Box 429 97856 541-421-3896
Bill Delong, prin. Fax 421-3012

**Lowell, Lane, Pop. 983**
Lowell SD 71 300/K-12
65 S Pioneer St 97452 541-937-8405
Dr. Walt Hanline, supt. Fax 937-2112
www.lowell.k12.or.us

Lowell JSHS 100/7-12
65 S Pioneer St 97452 541-937-2124
Kay Graham, prin. Fax 937-2112

**Mc Minnville, Yamhill, Pop. 31,337**
McMinnville SD 40 6,500/K-12
1500 NE Baker St 97128 503-565-4000
Maryalice Russell, supt. Fax 565-4043
www.msd.k12.or.us
Duniway MS 800/6-8
575 NW Michelbook Ln 97128 503-565-4400
Cathy Carnahan, prin. Fax 565-4414
McMinnville HS 2,000/9-12
615 NE 15th St 97128 503-565-4200
Kris Olsen, prin. Fax 565-4244
Patton MS 800/6-8
1175 NE 19th St 97128 503-565-4500
Brian Crain, prin. Fax 565-4515

---

Linfield College Post-Sec.
900 SE Baker St 97128 503-883-2200

**Madras, Jefferson, Pop. 5,846**
Jefferson County SD 509J 2,800/K-12
445 SE Buff St 97741 541-475-6192
Dr. Rick Molitor, supt. Fax 475-6856
www.jcsd.k12.or.us
Jefferson County MS 600/6-8
1180 SE Kemper Way 97741 541-475-7253
Simon White, prin. Fax 475-4825
Madras HS 800/9-12
390 SE 10th St 97741 541-475-7265
Marl Neffendorf, prin. Fax 475-7744

**Mapleton, Lane**
Mapleton SD 32 200/K-12
10868 E Mapleton Rd 97453 541-268-4312
Jodi O'Mara, supt. Fax 268-4632
www.mapleton.k12.or.us
Mapleton MSHS 100/7-12
10868 E Mapleton Rd 97453 541-268-4322
Brenda Moyer, prin. Fax 268-4632

**Marcola, Lane**
Marcola SD 79J 200/K-12
PO Box 820 97454 541-933-2512
Bill Watkins, supt. Fax 933-2338
www.marcola.k12.or.us
Mohawk HS 100/7-12
38300 Wendling Rd 97454 541-933-2512
Bill Watkins, prin. Fax 933-2338

**Marylhurst, Clackamas**

---

Marylhurst University Post-Sec.
PO Box 261 97036 503-636-8141

**Maupin, Wasco, Pop. 405**
South Wasco County SD 1 200/K-12
PO Box 346 97037 541-395-2645
Ryan Wraught, supt. Fax 395-2679
www.swasco.net
South Wasco County HS 100/7-12
PO Box 347 97037 541-395-2225
Lynn Cowdrey, prin. Fax 395-2223

**Medford, Jackson, Pop. 72,448**
Medford SD 549C 11,900/K-12
815 S Oakdale Ave 97501 541-842-3636
Brian Shumate, supt. Fax 842-1087
www.medford.k12.or.us
Central Medford HS 200/Alt
815 S Oakdale Ave 97501 541-842-3669
Amy Herbst, prin. Fax 842-2183
Hedrick MS 900/7-8
1501 E Jackson St 97504 541-842-3700
Beth Anderson, prin. Fax 842-1548
McLoughlin MS 800/7-8
320 W 2nd St 97501 541-842-3720
Linda White, prin. Fax 842-1652
North Medford HS 1,700/9-12
1900 N Keene Way Dr 97504 541-842-3670
Dan Smith, prin. Fax 842-5206
South Medford HS 1,800/9-12
1551 Cunningham Ave 97501 541-842-3680
Damian Crowson, prin. Fax 842-1513

---

Abdill Career College Post-Sec.
843 E Main St Ste 203 97504 541-779-8384
Cascade Christian HS 400/9-12
855 Chevy Way 97504 541-772-0606
Dr. Phil Long, prin. Fax 608-1369
Phagans' Medford Beauty School Post-Sec.
2320 Poplar Dr 97504 541-772-6155
Rogue Valley Adventist Academy 100/K-12
3675 S Stage Rd 97501 541-773-2988
Fax 779-7575
St. Mary's HS 400/6-12
816 Black Oak Dr 97504 541-773-7877
Frank Phillips, pres. Fax 772-8973

**Merlin, Josephine, Pop. 1,565**
Three Rivers SD
Supt. — See Grants Pass
Merlin Alternative Center Alt
345 Merlin Rd 97532 541-476-2524
Mike Herzog, admin. Fax 476-6899

**Merrill, Klamath, Pop. 817**
Klamath County SD
Supt. — See Klamath Falls
Lost River JSHS 200/7-12
23330 Highway 50 97633 541-798-5666
Steve Johnson, prin. Fax 798-5072

**Mill City, Linn, Pop. 1,789**
Santiam Canyon SD 129J 300/K-12
PO Box 197 97360 503-897-2321
Todd Miller, supt.
www.santiam.k12.or.us

Santiam JSHS 200/7-12
PO Box 199 97360 503-897-2311
David Plotts, prin. Fax 897-3154

**Milton Freewater, Umatilla, Pop. 6,982**
Milton-Freewater USD 7 2,000/K-12
1020 S Mill St 97862 541-938-3551
Dr. Robert Clark, supt. Fax 938-6704
www.miltfree.k12.or.us
Central MS 400/6-8
306 SW 2nd Ave 97862 541-938-5504
Tim Sprenger, prin. Fax 938-6615
McLoughlin HS 500/9-12
120 S Main St 97862 541-938-5591
Mindi Vaughan, prin. Fax 938-5593

**Milwaukie, Clackamas, Pop. 19,622**
North Clackamas SD 12 17,100/K-12
4444 SE Lake Rd 97222 503-353-6000
Matt Utterback, supt. Fax 353-6007
www.nclack.k12.or.us
Alder Creek MS 1,000/6-8
13801 SE Webster Rd 97267 503-353-5700
Alyson Brant, prin. Fax 353-5715
Milwaukie HS 1,100/9-12
11300 SE 23rd Ave 97222 503-353-5830
Mark Pinder, prin. Fax 353-5845
New Urban HS 200/Alt
1901 SE Oak Grove Blvd 97267 503-353-5925
Noah Hurd, prin. Fax 353-5928
Putnam HS 1,300/9-12
4950 SE Roethe Rd 97267 503-353-5860
Kathleen Walsh, prin. Fax 353-5875
Rowe MS 1,000/6-8
3606 SE Lake Rd 97222 503-353-5725
Greg Harris, prin. Fax 353-5740
Sabin-Schellenberg Professional-Tech Ctr Vo/Tech
14211 SE Johnson Rd 97267 503-353-5900
Karen Phillips, prin. Fax 353-5915
Other Schools – See Clackamas, Happy Valley

---

LaSalle College Prep HS 600/9-12
11999 SE Fuller Rd 97222 503-659-4155
Andrew Kuffner, prin. Fax 659-2535
National Coll of Technical Instruction Post-Sec.
9800 SE McBrod Ave 97222 971-236-9231
Portland Waldorf S 300/PK-12
2300 SE Harrison St 97222 503-654-2200
Wendy Rea, dir. Fax 652-5162

**Mitchell, Wheeler, Pop. 123**
Mitchell SD 55 100/K-12
PO Box 247 97750 541-462-3311
Tim Wilson, supt. Fax 462-3849
www.mitchell.k12.or.us
Mitchell S 100/K-12
PO Box 247 97750 541-462-3311
Tim Wilson, prin. Fax 462-3849

**Molalla, Clackamas, Pop. 7,927**
Molalla River SD 35 2,800/K-12
PO Box 188 97038 503-829-2359
Tony Mann, supt. Fax 829-5540
www.molallariv.k12.or.us
Molalla HS 800/9-12
PO Box 309 97038 503-829-2355
Randy Dalton, prin. Fax 829-5680
Molalla River MS 600/6-8
PO Box 225 97038 503-829-6133
Mike Nelson, prin. Fax 829-5680

---

Country Christian S 200/K-12
16975 S Highway 211 97038 503-829-5503

**Monmouth, Polk, Pop. 9,171**

---

Mid Valley Christian Academy 100/PK-12
1483 N 16th St 97361 503-838-2818
Gaye Stewart, admin.
Western Oregon University Post-Sec.
345 Monmouth Ave N 97361 503-838-8000

**Monroe, Benton, Pop. 601**
Monroe SD 1J 500/K-12
365 N 5th St 97456 541-847-6292
Fax 847-6290
www.monroe.k12.or.us
Monroe HS 100/9-12
365 N 5th St 97456 541-847-5161
Bill Crowson, prin. Fax 847-6161

**Monument, Grant, Pop. 127**
Monument SD 8 50/K-12
PO Box 127 97864 541-934-2646
Earl Pettit, supt. Fax 934-2005
www.grantesd.k12.or.us/Monument/
Monument S 50/K-12
PO Box 127 97864 541-934-2646
Earl Pettit, prin. Fax 934-2005

**Moro, Sherman, Pop. 321**
Sherman County SD
Supt. — See Grass Valley
Sherman JSHS 100/7-12
65912 High School Loop 97039 541-565-3500
Bill Blevins, prin. Fax 565-3319

**Mount Angel, Marion, Pop. 3,231**
Mt. Angel SD 91 700/K-12
PO Box 1129 97362 503-845-2345
Troy Stoops, supt. Fax 845-2789
www.mtangel.k12.or.us
Kennedy HS 200/9-12
890 E Marquam St 97362 503-845-6128
Sean Aker, prin. Fax 845-9586
Mount Angel MS 200/6-8
460 E Marquam St 97362 503-845-6137
Jennifer McCallum, prin. Fax 845-2856

**Myrtle Creek, Douglas, Pop. 3,296**
South Umpqua SD 19 1,400/K-12
558 Chadwick Ln 97457 541-863-3115
Jim Howard, supt. Fax 863-5212
www.susd.k12.or.us
Coffenberry MS 300/6-8
591 Rice St 97457 541-863-3104
Douglas Park, prin. Fax 863-5187
South Umpqua HS 400/9-12
501 Chadwick Ln 97457 541-863-3118
Kristi McGree, prin. Fax 863-5486

**Myrtle Point, Coos, Pop. 2,411**
Myrtle Point SD 41 600/K-12
413 C St 97458 541-572-1220
Bruce Shull, supt. Fax 572-5401
www.mpsd.k12.or.us
Myrtle Point JSHS 300/7-12
717 4th St 97458 541-572-1270
Ken Smith, prin. Fax 572-5221

**Newberg, Yamhill, Pop. 21,511**
Newberg SD 29J 5,100/K-12
714 E 6th St 97132 503-554-5000
Dr. Kym LeBlanc-Esparza, supt. Fax 538-4374
www.newberg.k12.or.us
Catalyst S Alt
1421 Deborah Rd 97132 503-554-4492
Bill Rogers, prin. Fax 554-4521
Chehalem Valley MS 600/6-8
403 W Foothills Dr 97132 503-554-4600
Karen Pugsley, prin. Fax 537-3239
Mountain View MS 600/6-8
2015 N Emery Dr 97132 503-554-4500
Michele Paton, prin. Fax 537-3337
Newberg HS 1,600/9-12
2400 Douglas Ave 97132 503-554-4525
Dave Parker, prin. Fax 554-4440

---

Country Faith Christian Academy 50/3-12
26155 NE Bell Rd 97132
Jolaine Davis, prin.
George Fox University Post-Sec.
414 N Meridian St 97132 503-538-8383
Lewis Academy 200/PK-12
PO Box 3250 97132 503-538-0114
Michael Wenger, prin. Fax 538-4113

**Newport, Lincoln, Pop. 9,688**
Lincoln County SD 4,900/K-12
PO Box 1110 97365 541-265-9211
Steve Boynton, supt. Fax 265-0511
www.lincoln.k12.or.us
Newport HS 600/9-12
322 NE Eads St 97365 541-265-9281
Jon Zagel, prin. Fax 574-2228
Newport MS 300/6-8
825 NE 7th St 97365 541-265-6601
Aaron Belloni, prin. Fax 265-6493
Newport Prep Academy 200/7-8
322 NE Eads St 97365 541-265-9281
Jon Zagel, prin. Fax 574-2228
Newton Magnet S 100/6-8
825 NE 7th St 97365 541-265-6601
Tiana Tucker, prin. Fax 265-6493
Other Schools – See Lincoln City, Toledo, Waldport

---

Phagans' Newport Academy of Cosmetology Post-Sec.
158 E Olive St 97365 541-265-3083

**North Bend, Coos, Pop. 9,275**
North Bend SD 13 3,600/K-12
1913 Meade St 97459 541-756-2521
Bill Yester, supt. Fax 756-1313
www.nbend.k12.or.us
North Bend HS 400/9-12
2323 Pacific St 97459 541-756-8328
Bill Lucero, prin. Fax 756-6945
North Bend MS 400/6-8
1500 16th St 97459 541-756-8341
Marci Stadiem, prin. Fax 756-6460

---

Kingsview Christian S 100/PK-12
1850 Clark St 97459 541-756-1411
Dr. Michael Myers, admin. Fax 756-0105

**Nyssa, Malheur, Pop. 3,244**
Nyssa SD 26 1,100/K-12
804 Adrian Blvd 97913 541-372-2275
Janine Weeks, supt. Fax 372-2204
www.nyssa.k12.or.us
Nyssa HS 300/9-12
824 Adrian Blvd 97913 541-372-2287
Shawn Jensen, prin. Fax 372-5634
Nyssa MS 300/6-8
101 S 11th St 97913 541-372-3891
Luke Cleaver, prin. Fax 372-3260

**Oakland, Douglas, Pop. 890**
Oakland SD 1 500/K-12
PO Box 390 97462 541-459-4341
Nanette Hagen, supt. Fax 459-4120
www.oakland.k12.or.us
Lincoln MS 200/5-8
PO Box 420 97462 541-459-3407
Diana Sweeden, prin. Fax 459-9167
Oakland HS 200/9-12
PO Box 479 97462 541-459-2597
Jeff Clark, prin. Fax 459-4765

**Oakridge, Lane, Pop. 3,091**
Oakridge SD 76 600/K-12
76499 Rose St 97463 541-782-2813
Dr. Donald Kordosky, supt. Fax 782-2982
www.oakridge.k12.or.us
Oakridge HS 200/9-12
47997 W 1st St 97463 541-782-2231
Tamara Skordahl, prin. Fax 782-4692
Oakridge JHS 100/7-8
76486 Rose St 97463 541-782-2731
Tamara Skordahl, prin. Fax 782-4647

**Ontario, Malheur, Pop. 11,152**
Ontario SD 8C 2,300/K-12
195 SW 3rd Ave 97914 541-889-5374
Nicole Albisu, supt. Fax 889-8553
www.ontario.k12.or.us
Ontario HS 700/9-12
1115 W Idaho Ave 97914 541-889-5309
Andy Kovach, prin. Fax 889-8117
Ontario MS 400/7-8
573 SW 2nd Ave 97914 541-889-5377
Lisa Estrada, prin. Fax 881-0060

---

Treasure Valley Christian S 100/PK-12
386 N Verde Dr 97914 541-889-4662
Fran Renk, prin. Fax 889-9199
Treasure Valley Community College Post-Sec.
650 College Blvd 97914 541-881-8822

**Oregon City, Clackamas, Pop. 30,976**
Oregon City SD 62 6,600/K-12
PO Box 2110 97045 503-785-8000
Larry Didway, supt. Fax 657-2492
www.orecity.k12.or.us
Gardiner MS 600/6-8
180 Ethel St 97045 503-785-8200
Kelly Schmidt, prin. Fax 650-5482
Ogden MS 600/6-8
14133 Donovan Rd 97045 503-785-8300
Peter Danner, prin. Fax 657-2508
Oregon City HS 2,200/9-12
19761 Beavercreek Rd 97045 503-785-8900
Tom Lovell, prin. Fax 785-8578

---

Clackamas Community College Post-Sec.
19600 Molalla Ave 97045 503-594-6000
North Clackamas Christian S 200/PK-12
19575 Sebastian Way 97045 503-655-5961
Tim Tutty, admin. Fax 655-4875

**Pendleton, Umatilla, Pop. 16,180**
Pendleton SD 16 3,200/PK-12
1100 Southgate Ste 8 97801 541-276-6711
Jon Peterson, supt. Fax 278-3208
www.pendleton.k12.or.us
Hawthorne Alternative JSHS Alt
1207 SW Frazer Ave 97801 541-966-3378
Curt Thompson, prin. Fax 966-3291
Pendleton HS 900/9-12
1800 NW Carden Ave 97801 541-966-3804
Dan Greenough, prin. Fax 966-3813
Sunridge MS 800/6-8
700 SW Runnion Ave 97801 541-276-4560
David Williams, prin. Fax 276-4724

---

Blue Mountain Community College Post-Sec.
PO Box 100 97801 541-276-1260
Harris Junior Academy 100/PK-10
3121 SW Hailey Ave 97801 541-276-0615

**Philomath, Benton, Pop. 4,445**
Philomath SD 17J 1,500/K-12
535 S 19th St 97370 541-929-3169
Melissa Goff, supt. Fax 929-3991
www.philomath.k12.or.us
Philomath HS 500/9-12
2054 Applegate St 97370 541-929-3211
Ken Ball, prin. Fax 929-3244
Philomath MS 300/6-8
2021 Chapel Dr 97370 541-929-3167
Steve Bell, prin. Fax 929-3180

**Phoenix, Jackson, Pop. 4,376**
Phoenix-Talent SD 4 2,600/K-12
PO Box 698 97535 541-535-1517
Teresa Sayre, supt. Fax 535-3928
www.phoenix.k12.or.us
Phoenix HS 800/9-12
PO Box 697 97535 541-535-1526
Jani Hale, prin. Fax 535-7511
Other Schools – See Talent

**Pilot Rock, Umatilla, Pop. 1,457**
Pilot Rock SD 2 400/K-12
PO Box BB 97868 541-443-8291
Steve Staniak, supt. Fax 443-8000
www.pilotrock.k12.or.us
Pilot Rock JSHS 200/7-12
PO Box BB 97868 541-443-2671
Anna Tester, prin. Fax 443-2120

**Pleasant Hill, Lane**
Pleasant Hill SD 1 800/K-12
36386 Highway 58 97455 541-746-9646
Tony Scurto, supt. Fax 746-2537
www.pleasanthill.k12.or.us
Pleasant Hill HS 400/7-12
36386 Highway 58 97455 541-747-4541
Randy Fisher, prin. Fax 744-3351

---

Emerald Christian Academy 100/K-12
35582 Zephyr Way 97455 541-746-1708

**Portland, Multnomah, Pop. 557,791**
Beaverton SD 48J
Supt. — See Beaverton
Cedar Park MS 900/6-8
11100 SW Park Way 97225 503-672-3620
Ken Struckmeier, prin. Fax 672-3626
Early College HS 11-12
17705 NW Springville Rd 97229 971-722-7473
Drew Cronk, admin. Fax 722-7553
Stoller MS 1,200/6-8
14141 NW Laidlaw Rd 97229 503-356-2680
Florence Richey, prin. Fax 356-2685

Sunset HS 2,000/9-12
13840 NW Cornell Rd 97229 503-259-5050
John Huelskamp, prin. Fax 259-5066
Westview HS 2,500/9-12
4200 NW 185th Ave 97229 503-259-5218
Jon Franco, prin. Fax 259-5230

Centennial SD 28J 6,200/K-12
18135 SE Brooklyn St 97236 503-760-7990
Sam Breyer, supt. Fax 762-3689
www.centennial.k12.or.us
Centennial MS 1,000/7-8
17650 SE Brooklyn St 97236 503-762-3206
Rise' Hawley, prin. Fax 762-3236
Centennial Park S 100/Alt
17630 SE Main St 97233 503-762-3202
Ajai Huja, prin. Fax 760-1651
Other Schools – See Gresham

David Douglas SD 40 10,800/PK-12
11300 NE Halsey St 97220 503-252-2900
Don Grotting, supt. Fax 261-8208
www.ddouglas.k12.or.us
Douglas HS 3,200/9-12
1001 SE 135th Ave 97233 503-261-8300
John Bier, prin. Fax 261-8399
Fir Ridge Campus 200/Alt
11215 SE Market St 97216 503-256-6530
Joy O'Renick, prin. Fax 261-8433
Light MS 800/6-8
10800 SE Washington St 97216 503-256-6511
Doug Pease, prin. Fax 261-8423
Ott MS 700/6-8
12500 SE Ramona St 97236 503-256-6510
James Johnston, prin. Fax 261-8403
Russell MS 800/6-8
3955 SE 112th Ave 97266 503-256-6519
Andy Long, prin. Fax 761-7246

Multnomah ESD 300/
PO Box 301039 97294 503-255-1841
Jim Rose, supt. Fax 257-1519
www.mesd.k12.or.us
Helensview HS 200/Alt
8678 NE Sumner St 97220 503-262-4150
Kris Persson, prin. Fax 255-1767
Other Schools – See Gresham

Parkrose SD 3 3,400/K-12
10636 NE Prescott St 97220 503-408-2100
Dr. Karen Fischer Gray, supt. Fax 408-2140
www.parkrose.k12.or.us
Parkrose HS 1,000/9-12
12003 NE Shaver St 97220 503-408-2600
Molly Ouche, prin. Fax 408-2739
Parkrose MS 800/6-8
11800 NE Shaver St 97220 503-408-2700
Annette Sweeney, prin. Fax 408-2998

Portland SD 1J 42,700/PK-12
PO Box 3107 97208 503-916-2000
Carole Smith, supt. Fax 916-3107
www.pps.k12.or.us
Alliance HS 200/9-12
4039 NE Alberta Ct 97211 503-916-5747
Lorna Fast Buffalo Horse, prin. Fax 916-2680
Alliance HS @ Benson 11-12
546 NE 12th Ave 97232 503-916-6486
Lorna Fast Buffalo Horse, prin. Fax 916-2696
Beaumont MS 500/6-8
4043 NE Fremont St 97212 503-916-5610
Macarre Traynham, prin. Fax 916-2609
Benson Polytechnic HS Vo/Tech
546 NE 12th Ave 97232 503-916-5100
Curtis Wilson, prin. Fax 916-2690
Cleveland HS 1,500/9-12
3400 SE 26th Ave 97202 503-916-5120
Tammy O'Neill, prin. Fax 916-2692
Da Vinci Arts MS 500/6-8
2508 NE Everett St 97232 503-916-5356
Fred Locke, prin. Fax 916-2721
Franklin HS 1,500/9-12
3905 SE 91st Ave 97266 503-916-5140
Juanita Valder, prin. Fax 916-2694
George MS 400/6-8
10000 N Burr Ave 97203 503-916-6262
Lavert Robertson, prin. Fax 916-2627
Grant HS 1,600/9-12
2245 NE 36th Ave 97212 503-916-5160
Carol Campbell, prin. Fax 916-2695
Gray MS 400/6-8
5505 SW 23rd Ave, 503-916-5676
Beth Madison, prin. Fax 916-2629
Hosford International MS 500/6-8
2303 SE 28th Pl 97214 503-916-5640
Kristyn Westphal, prin. Fax 916-2637
Jackson MS 500/6-8
10625 SW 35th Ave 97219 503-916-5680
Kevin Crotchett, prin. Fax 916-2640
Jefferson HS 600/9-12
5210 N Kerby Ave 97217 503-916-5180
Margaret Calvert, prin. Fax 916-2698
Lane MS 400/6-8
7200 SE 60th Ave 97206 503-916-6355
Brenda Fox, prin. Fax 916-2648
Lincoln HS 1,500/9-12
1600 SW Salmon St 97205 503-916-5200
Peyton Chapman, prin. Fax 916-2700
Madison HS 1,200/9-12
2735 NE 82nd Ave 97220 503-916-5220
Petra Callin, prin. Fax 916-2702
Metropolitan Learning Center S 400/Alt
2033 NW Glisan St 97209 503-916-5737
Pamela Joyner, prin. Fax 916-2658
Mt. Tabor MS 600/6-8
5800 SE Ash St 97215 503-916-5646
Robi Osborne, prin. Fax 916-2659
Ockley Green S 300/4-8
6031 N Montana Ave 97217 503-916-5660
Molly Chun, prin. Fax 916-2661

PISA @ Benson 9-12
546 NE 12th Ave 97232 503-916-5252
Tonjya Mjelde, prin.
Roosevelt HS 300/9-12
6941 N Central St 97203 503-916-5260
Filip Hristic, prin. Fax 916-2704
Sellwood MS 500/6-8
8300 SE 15th Ave 97202 503-916-5656
Brian Anderson, prin. Fax 916-2672
West Sylvan MS 600/6-8
8111 SW West Slope Dr 97225 503-916-5690
John Ferraro, prin. Fax 916-2681
Wilson HS 1,400/9-12
1151 SW Vermont St 97219 503-916-5280
Brian Chatard, prin. Fax 916-2705
Portland Evening Scholars Adult
546 NE 12th Ave 97232 503-916-5100
Ginger Taylor, admin.

Reynolds SD 7
Supt. — See Fairview
Lee MS 800/6-8
1121 NE 172nd Ave 97230 503-255-5686
Dan Kimbrow, prin. Fax 252-0522

Riverdale SD 51J 600/K-12
11733 SW Breyman Ave 97219 503-262-4840
Terry Brandon, supt. Fax 262-4841
www.riverdaleschool.com
Riverdale HS 300/9-12
9727 SW Terwilliger Blvd 97219 503-262-4844
Paula Robinson, prin. Fax 262-4845

---

American College of Healthcare Sciences Post-Sec.
5940 SW Hood Ave, 800-487-8839
Art Institute of Portland Post-Sec.
1122 NW Davis St 97209 503-228-6528
Beau Monde College Acad of Cosmetology Post-Sec.
525 SW 12th Ave 97205 503-252-7444
Beau Monde College of Hair Design Post-Sec.
1221 SW 12th Ave 97205 503-226-7355
Birthingway College of Midwifery Post-Sec.
12113 SE Foster Rd 97266 503-760-3131
Catlin Gabel S 700/PK-12
8825 SW Barnes Rd 97225 503-297-1894
Timothy Bazemore, head sch Fax 297-0139
Central Catholic HS 800/9-12
2401 SE Stark St 97214 503-235-3138
John Garrow, prin. Fax 233-0073
City Christian S 400/PK-12
9200 NE Fremont St 97220 503-252-5207
Columbia Christian S 200/PK-12
413 NE 91st Ave 97220 503-252-8577
Ami Vensel, prin. Fax 252-2108
Concorde Career Institute Post-Sec.
1425 NE Irving St Ste 300 97232 503-281-4181
Concordia University Post-Sec.
2811 NE Holman St 97211 503-288-9371
De La Salle North HS 300/9-12
7528 N Fenwick Ave 97217 503-285-9385
Matt Powell, prin. Fax 285-9546
DeVry University Post-Sec.
9755 SW Barnes Rd Ste 150 97225 503-296-7468
Edison HS 100/9-12
9020 SW Bvrtn Hillsdale Hwy 97225 503-297-2336
Everest College Post-Sec.
425 SW Washington St 97204 503-222-3225
Heald College Post-Sec.
6035 NE 78th Ct 97218 503-229-0492
ITT Technical Institute Post-Sec.
9500 NE Cascades Pkwy 97220 503-255-6500
Jesuit HS 1,200/9-12
9000 SW Beaverton Hillsdale 97225 503-292-2663
Paul Hogan, prin. Fax 291-5464
Le Cordon Bleu College of Culinary Arts Post-Sec.
600 SW 10th Ave Ste 500 97205 503-223-2245
Lewis and Clark College Post-Sec.
0615 SW Palatine Hill Rd 97219 503-768-7000
Linfield College Post-Sec.
2255 NW Northrup St 97210 503-413-8481
Multnomah University Post-Sec.
8435 NE Glisan St 97220 503-255-0332
National College of Natural Medicine Post-Sec.
049 SW Porter St 97201 503-552-1555
Oregon College of Art and Craft Post-Sec.
8245 SW Barnes Rd 97225 503-297-5544
Oregon College of Oriental Medicine Post-Sec.
75 NW Couch St 97209 503-253-3443
Oregon Culinary Institute Post-Sec.
1701 SW Jefferson St 97201 503-961-6200
Oregon Episcopal S 800/PK-12
6300 SW Nicol Rd 97223 503-246-7771
Mo Copeland, head sch Fax 293-1105
Oregon Health & Science University Post-Sec.
3181 SW Sam Jackson Park Rd, 503-494-8311
Pacific Crest Community S 100/6-12
116 NE 29th Ave 97232 503-234-2826
Pacific Northwest College of Art Post-Sec.
1241 NW Johnson St 97209 503-226-4391
Phagans' School of Hair Design Post-Sec.
1542 NE Weidler St 97232 503-239-0838
Portland Adventist Academy 200/9-12
1500 SE 96th Ave 97216 503-255-8372
Portland Christian JSHS 300/6-12
12425 NE San Rafael St 97230 503-256-3960
Jim Hill M.Ed., prin. Fax 256-2773
Portland Community College Post-Sec.
PO Box 19000 97280 971-722-6111
Portland State University Post-Sec.
PO Box 751 97207 503-725-3000
Reed College Post-Sec.
3203 SE Woodstock Blvd 97202 503-771-1112
St. Andrew Nativity S 100/6-8
4925 NE 9th Ave 97211 503-335-9600
Michael Chambers, prin. Fax 335-9494
St. Mary's Academy 600/9-12
1615 SW 5th Ave 97201 503-228-8306
Kelli Clark, prin. Fax 223-0995

St. Vincent Hospital & Medical Center Post-Sec.
9205 SW Barnes Rd 97225 503-216-3031
Sumner College Post-Sec.
8909 SW Barbur Blvd 97219 503-223-5100
University of Portland Post-Sec.
5000 N Willamette Blvd 97203 503-943-8000
University of Western States Post-Sec.
2900 NE 132nd Ave 97230 503-256-3180
Veterans Administration Medical Center Post-Sec.
PO Box 1034 97207 503-220-8262
Walla Walla University School of Nursing Post-Sec.
10345 SE Market St 97216 503-251-6115
Warner Pacific College Post-Sec.
2219 SE 68th Ave 97215 503-517-1000
Western Seminary Post-Sec.
5511 SE Hawthorne Blvd 97215 503-517-1800

**Port Orford, Curry, Pop. 1,095**
Port Orford-Langlois SD 2CJ 300/K-12
PO Box 8 97465 541-366-2111
Christine Nichols, supt. Fax 332-0190
www.2cj.com
Other Schools – See Sixes

**Powers, Coos, Pop. 625**
Powers SD 31 100/K-12
PO Box 479 97466 541-439-2291
Matt Shorb, supt. Fax 439-2875
www.powers.k12.or.us
Powers HS 100/7-12
PO Box 479 97466 541-439-2291
Matt Shorb, prin. Fax 439-2875

**Prairie City, Grant, Pop. 882**
Prairie City SD 4 100/K-12
PO Box 345 97869 541-820-3314
Julie Gurczynski, supt. Fax 820-4352
www.grantesd.k12.or.us/Prairie-City/
Prairie City S 100/K-12
PO Box 345 97869 541-820-3314
Julie Gurczynski, prin. Fax 820-4352

**Prineville, Crook, Pop. 9,076**
Crook County SD 2,700/K-12
471 NE Ochoco Plaza Dr 97754 541-447-5664
Dr. Duane Yecha, supt. Fax 447-3645
www.crookcounty.k12.or.us
Crook County HS 800/9-12
1100 SE Lynn Blvd 97754 541-416-6900
Michelle Jonas, prin. Fax 416-6907
Crook County MS 700/6-8
100 NE Knowledge St 97754 541-447-6283
Kurt Sloper, prin. Fax 447-3293
Pioneer Alternative HS Alt
297 NE Holly St 97754 541-447-1268
Michelle Jonas, prin. Fax 447-1862

**Rainier, Columbia, Pop. 1,842**
Rainier SD 13 1,100/K-12
28168 Old Rainier Rd 97048 503-556-3777
R. Michael Carter, supt. Fax 556-3778
www.rainier.k12.or.us
Rainier JSHS 500/7-12
28170 Old Rainier Rd 97048 503-556-4215
Graden Blue, prin. Fax 556-1120

**Redmond, Deschutes, Pop. 25,592**
Redmond SD 2J 7,000/K-12
145 SE Salmon Ave 97756 541-923-5437
Mike McIntosh, supt. Fax 923-5142
www.redmondschools.org
Brown Education Center 100/Alt
850 SW Antler Ave 97756 541-923-4868
Mark Keel, admin. Fax 923-4867
Gregory MS 700/6-8
1220 NW Upas Ave 97756 541-526-6440
Tracie Renwick, prin. Fax 526-6441
Obsidian MS 700/6-8
1335 SW Obsidian Ave 97756 541-923-4900
Tami Nakamura, prin. Fax 923-6509
Redmond HS 1,800/9-12
675 SW Rimrock Way 97756 541-923-4800
Tony Pupo, prin. Fax 548-0809
Ridgeview HS 9-12
4555 SW Elkhorn Ave 97756 541-504-3600
Lee Loving, prin. Fax 548-0809

---

Central Christian S 300/PK-12
2731 SW Airport Way 97756 541-548-7803
Elisa Carlson, head sch Fax 548-2801

**Riddle, Douglas, Pop. 1,134**
Riddle SD 70 400/K-12
PO Box 45 97469 541-874-3131
Dave Gianotti, supt. Fax 874-2345
www.riddle.k12.or.us
Riddle JSHS, PO Box 45 97469 200/7-12
William Starkweather, prin. 541-874-2251

**Rockaway, Tillamook, Pop. 1,282**
Neah-Kah-Nie SD 56 700/K-12
PO Box 28 97136 503-355-2222
Paul Erlebach, supt. Fax 355-3434
www.nknsd.org
Neah-Kah-Nie HS 200/9-12
24705 Highway 101 N 97136 503-355-2272
Heidi Buckmaster, prin. Fax 355-8200
Neah-Kah-Nie MS 200/6-8
25111 Highway 101 N 97136 503-355-2990
Leo Lawyer, prin. Fax 355-8514

**Rogue River, Jackson, Pop. 2,091**
Rogue River SD 35 800/K-12
PO Box 1045 97537 541-582-3235
Paul Young, supt. Fax 582-1600
www.rogueriver.k12.or.us
Rogue River JSHS 400/7-12
PO Box 1045 97537 541-582-3297
Paul Cataldo, prin. Fax 582-6005

**Roseburg, Douglas, Pop. 20,494**
Douglas County SD 4 6,200/K-12
1419 NW Valley View Dr, 541-440-4015
Gerry Washburn, supt. Fax 440-4003
www.roseburg.k12.or.us
Fremont MS 700/6-8
850 W Keady Ct, 541-440-4055
Ben Bentea, prin. Fax 440-4060
Lane MS 700/6-8
2153 NE Vine St 97470 541-440-4104
Bill Bartlett, prin. Fax 440-4100
Roseburg HS 1,800/9-12
400 W Harvard Ave 97470 541-440-4142
Jill Weber, prin. Fax 440-8296

---

Geneva Academy 100/K-12
PO Box 1154 97470 541-637-7500
Brian Turner, hdmstr.
Roseburg Beauty College Post-Sec.
700 SE Stephens St 97470 541-673-5533
Umpqua Community College Post-Sec.
PO Box 967 97470 541-440-4600
Umpqua Valley Christian S 100/7-12
18585 Dixonville Rd 97470 541-679-4964
Adam Armstrong, head sch

**Saint Benedict, Marion, Pop. 55**

---

Mt. Angel Seminary Post-Sec.
1 Abbey Dr 97373 503-845-3951

**Saint Helens, Columbia, Pop. 12,364**
Saint Helens SD 502 3,100/K-12
474 N 16th St 97051 503-397-3085
Scot Stockwell, supt. Fax 397-1907
www.sthelens.k12.or.us
Columbia County Education Campus 100/Alt
474 N 16th St 97051 503-366-3207
Colleen Grogan, dir. Fax 397-2723
Saint Helens HS 1,100/9-12
2375 Gable Rd 97051 503-397-1900
B.G. Aguirre, prin. Fax 397-1828
Saint Helens MS 500/7-8
354 N 15th St 97051 503-366-7300
Carol Dowsett, prin. Fax 366-7306

**Saint Paul, Marion, Pop. 420**
St. Paul SD 45 300/PK-12
20449 Main St NE 97137 503-633-2541
Joseph Wehrli, supt. Fax 633-2540
www.stpaul.k12.or.us
Saint Paul JSHS 100/7-12
20449 Main St NE 97137 503-633-2541
Tony Smith, prin. Fax 633-2540

**Salem, Marion, Pop. 148,676**
Salem-Keizer SD 24J 38,200/PK-12
PO Box 12024 97309 503-399-3000
Christy Perry, supt. Fax 399-5579
www.salkeiz.k12.or.us
Crossler MS 800/6-8
1155 Davis Rd S 97306 503-399-3444
Kristine Walton, prin. Fax 391-4005
Early College HS 200/Alt
4071 Winema Pl NE Ste 50 97305 503-365-4800
Jay Weeks, prin. Fax 365-4703
Houck MS 1,000/6-8
1155 Connecticut St SE, 503-399-3446
Mark Thompson, prin. Fax 391-4167
Judson MS 1,000/6-8
4512 Jones Rd SE 97302 503-399-3201
Alicia Kruska, prin. Fax 391-4041
Leslie MS 800/6-8
3850 Pringle Rd SE 97302 503-399-3206
Denny McCarthy, prin. Fax 399-3479
McKay HS 1,800/9-12
2440 Lancaster Dr NE 97305 503-399-3080
Sara LeRoy, prin. Fax 375-7807
North Salem HS 1,900/9-12
765 14th St NE 97301 503-399-3241
Cynthia Richardson, prin. Fax 375-7808
Parrish MS 700/6-8
802 Capitol St NE 97301 503-399-3210
Steve Nelson, prin. Fax 391-4004
Roberts HS 500/Alt
3620 State St 97301 503-399-5550
Jay Weeks, prin. Fax 391-4075
South Salem HS 2,000/9-12
1910 Church St SE 97302 503-399-3252
Lara Tiffin, prin. Fax 375-7805
Sprague HS 1,800/9-12
2373 Kuebler Rd S 97302 503-399-3261
Craig Swanson, prin. Fax 391-4046
Stephens MS 1,000/6-8
4962 Hayesville Dr NE 97305 503-399-3442
Jennie Madland, prin. Fax 391-4079
Straub MS 700/6-8
1920 Wilmington Ave NW 97304 503-399-2030
Laura Perez, prin. Fax 399-2032
Waldo MS 800/6-8
2805 Lansing Ave NE 97301 503-399-3215
Tricia Nelson, prin. Fax 391-4070
Walker MS 500/6-8
1075 8th St NW 97304 503-399-3220
Bridget Weldon, prin. Fax 399-5540
West Salem HS 1,700/9-12
1776 Titan Dr NW 97304 503-399-5533
Ken Phillips, prin. Fax 584-5004
Other Schools – See Keizer

---

Academy of Hair Design Post-Sec.
305 Court St NE 97301 503-585-8122
Blanchet S 400/6-12
4373 Market St NE 97301 503-391-2639
Brian Heinze, prin. Fax 399-1259
Chemeketa Community College Post-Sec.
PO Box 14007 97309 503-399-5000
College of Hair Design Careers Post-Sec.
1684 Clay St NE 97301 503-588-5888
Corban University Post-Sec.
5000 Deer Park Dr SE, 503-581-8600
Institute of Technology Post-Sec.
4700 Silverton Rd NE 97305 877-887-8007
ITT Technical Institute Post-Sec.
4825 Commercial St SE 97302 503-576-2300
Livingstone Adventist Academy 200/PK-12
5771 Fruitland Rd NE, 503-363-9408
Joel Reyes, prin. Fax 363-5721
Oregon State School for the Deaf Post-Sec.
999 Locust St NE 97301
Phagans' School of Beauty Post-Sec.
622 Lancaster Dr NE 97301 503-363-6800
Salem Academy 700/PK-12
942 Lancaster Dr NE 97301 503-378-1219
Jeff Williamson, supt. Fax 375-3522
Western Mennonite S 200/6-12
9045 Wallace Rd NW 97304 503-363-2000
Paul Schultz, head sch Fax 370-9455
Willamette University Post-Sec.
900 State St 97301 503-370-6300

**Sandy, Clackamas, Pop. 9,279**
Oregon Trail SD 46 3,900/K-12
PO Box 547 97055 503-668-5541
Aaron Bayer, supt. Fax 668-7906
www.oregontrailschools.com
Cedar Ridge MS 400/6-8
17225 Smith Ave 97055 503-668-8067
Nicole Johnston, prin. Fax 668-3977
Sandy HS 1,300/9-12
37400 Bell St 97055 503-668-8011
Kim Ball, prin. Fax 668-7646
Other Schools – See Boring

**Scappoose, Columbia, Pop. 6,380**
Scappoose SD 1J 2,300/K-12
33589 High School Way 97056 971-200-8000
Stephen Jupe, supt. Fax 543-7011
www.scappoose.k12.or.us
Scappoose HS 700/9-12
33700 High School Way 97056 971-200-8005
Jim Jones, prin. Fax 200-8000
Scappoose MS 400/7-8
52265 Columbia River Hwy 97056 503-543-7163
Ron Alley, prin. Fax 543-7917

**Scio, Linn, Pop. 809**
Scio SD 95 3,600/K-12
38875 NW 1st Ave 97374 503-394-3261
Gary Tempel, supt. Fax 394-3920
www.scio.k12.or.us
Scio HS 200/9-12
38875 NW 1st Ave 97374 503-394-3276
Patrick Dutcher, prin. Fax 394-3236
Scio MS 200/6-8
38875 NW 1st Ave 97374 503-394-3271
Greg Nolan, prin. Fax 394-4042

**Seaside, Clatsop, Pop. 6,285**
Jewell SD 8 100/PK-12
83874 Highway 103 97138 503-755-2451
Alice Hunsaker, supt. Fax 755-0616
www.jewell.k12.or.us
Jewell S 100/PK-12
83874 Highway 103 97138 503-755-2451
Mike Scott, prin. Fax 755-0616

Seaside SD 10 1,400/K-12
1801 S Franklin St 97138 503-738-5591
Doug Dougherty, supt. Fax 738-3471
www.seaside.k12.or.us
Broadway MS 300/6-8
1120 Broadway St 97138 503-738-5560
John McAndrews, prin. Fax 738-3900
Seaside HS 500/9-12
1901 N Holladay Dr 97138 503-738-5586
Sheila Roley, prin. Fax 738-5589

**Sheridan, Yamhill, Pop. 5,880**
Sheridan SD 48J 1,000/K-12
435 S Bridge St 97378 971-261-6959
Steven Sugg, supt. Fax 843-3505
www.sheridan.k12.or.us
Sheridan HS 9-12
433 S Bridge St 97378 971-261-6970
Dean Rech, admin. Fax 843-3466
Sheridan Spartan Academy 200/Alt
433 S Bridge St 97378 971-261-6970
Dean Rech, prin. Fax 843-3466

---

Delphian S 200/PK-12
20950 SW Rock Creek Rd 97378 503-843-3521

**Sherwood, Washington, Pop. 17,504**
Sherwood SD 88J 5,000/PK-12
23295 SW Main St 97140 503-825-5000
Heather Cordie, supt. Fax 825-5001
www.sherwood.k12.or.us
Laurel Ridge MS 500/6-8
21416 SW Copper Ter 97140 503-825-5800
Penny Salm, prin. Fax 825-5801
Sherwood HS 1,500/9-12
16956 SW Meinecke Rd 97140 503-825-5500
Ken Bell, prin. Fax 825-5501
Sherwood MS 600/6-8
21970 SW Sherwood Blvd 97140 503-825-5400
Marianne Funderhide, prin. Fax 825-5401

**Silver Lake, Lake, Pop. 147**
North Lake SD 14 200/K-12
57566 Fort Rock Rd 97638 541-576-2121
Dave Kerr, supt. Fax 576-2705
www.nlake.k12.or.us/
North Lake S 200/K-12
57566 Fort Rock Rd 97638 541-576-2121
Dave Kerr, admin. Fax 576-2705

**Silverton, Marion, Pop. 9,064**
Silver Falls SD 4J 3,700/K-12
802 Schlador St 97381 503-873-5303
Andy Bellando, supt. Fax 873-2936
silverfallsschools.org
Silverton HS 1,200/9-12
1456 Pine St 97381 503-873-6331
Mark Hannan, prin. Fax 873-8606
Twain MS 300/7-8
425 N Church St 97381 503-873-5317
Nancy Griffith, prin. Fax 873-7108

**Sisters, Deschutes, Pop. 2,007**
Sisters SD 6 1,200/K-12
525 E Cascade Ave 97759 541-549-8521
Curtiss Scholl, supt. Fax 549-8951
www.sisters.k12.or.us
Sisters HS 500/9-12
1700 W McKinney Butte Rd 97759 541-549-4045
Joe Hosang, prin. Fax 549-4051
Sisters MS 400/5-8
15200 McKenzie Hwy 97759 541-549-2099
Marshall Jackson, prin. Fax 549-2098

**Sixes, Curry**
Port Orford-Langlois SD 2CJ
Supt. — See Port Orford
Pacific HS 100/9-12
45525 Highway 101 97476 541-348-2293
Krista Nieraeth, prin. Fax 348-2389

**Spray, Wheeler, Pop. 157**
Spray SD 1 50/K-12
PO Box 230 97874 541-468-2226
Phil Starkey, supt. Fax 468-2630
www.spray.k12.or.us
Spray S 50/K-12
PO Box 230 97874 541-468-2226
Phil Starkey, prin. Fax 468-2630

**Springfield, Lane, Pop. 57,056**
Springfield SD 19 10,100/K-12
525 Mill St 97477 541-747-3331
Susan Rieke-Smith Ed.D., supt. Fax 726-3312
www.springfield.k12.or.us
Briggs MS 600/6-8
2355 Yolanda Ave 97477 541-744-6350
Jeff Mather, prin. Fax 744-6354
Gateways HS 100/9-12
665 Main St 97477 541-744-8862
Paul Weill, prin. Fax 744-8863
Hamlin MS 600/6-8
326 Centennial Blvd 97477 541-744-6356
Kevin Wright, prin. Fax 744-6360
Springfield HS 1,400/9-12
875 7th St 97477 541-744-4700
Jose de Silva, prin. Fax 744-4875
Stewart MS 600/6-8
900 S 32nd St 97478 541-988-2520
Jeff Fuller, prin. Fax 988-2530
Thurston HS 1,500/9-12
333 58th St 97478 541-744-5000
Chad Towe, prin. Fax 744-5029
Thurston MS 600/6-8
6300 Thurston Rd 97478 541-744-6368
Brandi Starck, prin. Fax 744-6372

---

Pioneer Pacific College Post-Sec.
3800 Sports Way 97477 541-684-4644
Springfield College of Beauty Post-Sec.
307 Q St 97477 541-746-4473

**Stanfield, Umatilla, Pop. 1,997**
Stanfield SD 61 500/K-12
1120 N Main St 97875 541-449-8766
Shelley Liscom, supt. Fax 449-8768
www.stanfield.k12.or.us
Stanfield Secondary S 300/7-12
1120 N Main St 97875 541-449-3851
Bryan Johnson, prin. Fax 449-8751

**Stayton, Marion, Pop. 7,435**
North Santiam SD 29J 2,400/K-12
1155 N 3rd Ave 97383 503-769-6924
Andrew Gardner, supt. Fax 769-3578
www.nsantiam.k12.or.us
Stayton HS 800/9-12
757 W Locust St 97383 503-769-2171
Alan Kirby, prin. Fax 769-6050
Stayton Intermediate / MS 600/4-8
1021 Shaff Rd 97383 503-769-2198
Michael Proctor, prin. Fax 769-9524

---

Regis HS 200/9-12
550 W Regis St 97383 503-769-2159
Scott Coulter, prin. Fax 769-1706

**Sutherlin, Douglas, Pop. 7,596**
Sutherlin SD 130 1,400/K-12
531 E Central Ave 97479 541-459-2228
Steve Perkins, supt. Fax 459-2484
www.sutherlin.k12.or.us
Sutherlin HS 500/9-12
500 E Fourth Ave 97479 541-459-9551
Justin Huntley, prin. Fax 459-4887
Sutherlin MS 200/7-8
649 E Fourth Ave 97479 541-459-2668
Terry Prestianni, prin. Fax 459-2047

**Sweet Home, Linn, Pop. 8,693**
Sweet Home SD 55 2,300/K-12
1920 Long St 97386 541-367-7126
Keith Winslow, supt. Fax 367-7105
www.sweethome.k12.or.us
Sweet Home HS 700/9-12
1641 Long St 97386 541-367-7142
Ralph Brown, prin. Fax 367-7196
Sweet Home JHS 400/7-8
880 22nd Ave 97386 541-367-7187
Colleen Henry, prin. Fax 367-7107

**Talent, Jackson, Pop. 5,873**
Phoenix-Talent SD 4
Supt. — See Phoenix
Talent MS 600/6-8
PO Box 359 97540 541-535-1552
Aaron Santi, prin. Fax 535-7532

**The Dalles, Wasco, Pop. 13,258**
North Wasco County SD 21 3,000/K-12
3632 W 10th St 97058 541-506-3420
Candy Armstrong, supt. Fax 298-6018
www.nwasco.k12.or.us
The Dalles HS 900/9-12
220 E 10th St 97058 541-506-3400
Nick Nelson, prin. Fax 298-4964
The Dalles MS 600/6-8
1100 E 12th St 97058 541-506-3380
Fax 298-1942
Wahtonka Community S Alt
3601 W 10th St 97058 541-506-3410
Brian Goodwin, admin.

---

Columbia Gorge Community College Post-Sec.
400 E Scenic Dr 97058 541-506-6000

**Tigard, Washington, Pop. 46,005**
Tigard-Tualatin SD 23J 12,600/K-12
6960 SW Sandburg St 97223 503-431-4000
Ernest Brown, supt. Fax 431-4047
www.ttsdschools.org
Durham Center 100/Alt
8040 SW Durham Rd 97224 503-431-4580
Andy McFarlane, dir. Fax 431-4590
Fowler MS 800/6-8
10865 SW Walnut St 97223 503-431-5000
Dan Busch, prin. Fax 431-5010
Tigard HS 2,000/9-12
9000 SW Durham Rd 97224 503-431-5400
Andy Van Fleet, prin. Fax 431-5410
Twality MS 1,000/6-8
14650 SW 97th Ave 97224 503-431-5200
Carol Kinch, prin. Fax 431-5210
Other Schools – See Tualatin

---

Everest Institute Post-Sec.
9600 SW Oak St Fl 4 97223 503-892-8100
Phagans' Tigard Beauty School Post-Sec.
8820 SW Center St 97223 503-639-6107
Westside Christian HS 200/9-12
8200 SW Pfaffle St 97223 503-697-4711
Dr. Debi Miller, head sch Fax 697-4605

**Tillamook, Tillamook, Pop. 4,782**
Tillamook SD 9 2,000/K-12
2510 1st St 97141 503-842-4414
Randy Schild, supt. Fax 842-6854
www.tillamook.k12.or.us
Tillamook HS 700/9-12
2605 12th St 97141 503-842-2566
Greg English, prin. Fax 842-1340
Tillamook JHS 300/7-8
3906 Alder Ln 97141 503-842-7531
J.P. Richards, prin. Fax 842-1349
Tillamook Options Program Alt
2510 1st St 97141 503-842-7538
Rachel Sip, prin. Fax 842-1378
Trask River HS 50/Alt
6700 Officers Row 97141 503-842-2565
Jerry Dorland, prin. Fax 842-4918

---

Tillamook Adventist S 100/PK-10
4300 12th St 97141 503-842-6533
Fax 842-6236
Tillamook Bay Community College Post-Sec.
4301 3rd St 97141 503-842-8222

**Toledo, Lincoln, Pop. 3,349**
Lincoln County SD
Supt. — See Newport
Toledo JSHS 300/7-12
1800 NE Sturdevant Rd 97391 541-336-5104
Clint Raever, prin. Fax 336-2970

---

Mid Coast Christian S 50/K-12
1811 NE Arcadia Dr Ste C 97391 541-336-2234
Greg Wood, prin. Fax 336-2702

**Troutdale, Multnomah, Pop. 15,404**
Reynolds SD 7
Supt. — See Fairview
Morey MS 700/6-8
2801 SW Lucas Ave 97060 503-491-1935
Tanya Pruett, prin. Fax 491-0245
Reynolds HS 2,700/9-12
1698 SW Cherry Park Rd 97060 503-667-3186
Wade Bakley, prin. Fax 669-0776

**Tualatin, Washington, Pop. 25,026**
Tigard-Tualatin SD 23J
Supt. — See Tigard
Hazelbrook MS 1,000/6-8
11300 SW Hazelbrook Rd 97062 503-431-5100
Eric Nesse, prin. Fax 431-5110
Tualatin HS 1,900/9-12
22300 SW Boones Ferry Rd 97062 503-431-5600
Darin Barnard, prin. Fax 431-5610

West Linn-Wilsonville SD 3J 8,400/PK-12
22210 SW Stafford Rd 97062 503-673-7000
Dr. William Rhoades, supt. Fax 673-7001
www.wlwv.k12.or.us
Athey Creek MS 600/6-8
2900 SW Borland Rd 97062 503-673-7400
Joel Sebastian, prin. Fax 638-8302
Other Schools – See West Linn, Wilsonville

---

Horizon Christian HS 100/9-12
PO Box 2690 97062 503-612-6521
Bill Smethurst, dir.
Northwest College of Hair Design Post-Sec.
8345 SW Nyberg St 97062 503-218-2265

**Turner, Marion, Pop. 1,825**
Cascade SD 5 2,200/K-12
10226 Marion Rd SE 97392 503-749-8010
Darin Drill, supt. Fax 749-8019
www.cascade.k12.or.us
Cascade HS 700/9-12
10226 Marion Rd SE 97392 503-749-8020
Matt Thatcher, prin. Fax 749-8029
Cascade JHS 500/6-8
10226 Marion Rd SE 97392 503-749-8030
Peter Rasmussen, prin. Fax 749-8039
Other Schools – See Aumsville

---

Crosshill Christian S 200/PK-12
2707 Maranatha Ct SE 97392 503-391-9082
Adam Kronberger, supt. Fax 378-0507

**Ukiah, Umatilla, Pop. 181**
Ukiah SD 80R 50/K-12
PO Box 218 97880 541-427-3731
Dan Korber, supt. Fax 427-3730
www.ukiah.k12.or.us
Ukiah S 50/K-12
PO Box 218 97880 541-427-3731
Dan Korber, supt. Fax 427-3730

**Umatilla, Umatilla, Pop. 6,845**
Umatilla SD 6R 1,400/K-12
1001 6th St 97882 541-922-6500
Heidi Sipe, supt. Fax 922-6507
www.umatilla.k12.or.us
Brownell MS 300/6-8
1300 7th St 97882 541-922-6625
Liz Durant, prin. Fax 922-6507
Umatilla HS 400/9-12
1400 7th St 97882 541-922-6525
Beth Burton, prin. Fax 922-6599

**Union, Union, Pop. 2,065**
Union SD 5 400/K-12
PO Box K 97883 541-562-5166
Carter Wells, supt. Fax 562-8116
www.union.k12.or.us
Union JSHS 200/7-12
PO Box 908 97883 541-562-5166
Carter Wells, prin. Fax 562-8116

**Vale, Malheur, Pop. 1,833**
Vale SD 84 900/K-12
403 E St W 97918 541-473-0201
Scott Linenberger, supt. Fax 473-3294
www.vale.k12.or.us
Vale HS 300/9-12
505 Viking Dr 97918 541-473-0290
Mary Jo Sharp, prin. Fax 473-2364
Vale MS 100/7-8
403 E St W 97918 541-473-0241
Jeri Schaffeld, prin. Fax 473-3293

**Vernonia, Columbia, Pop. 2,091**
Vernonia SD 47J 600/K-12
1201 Texas Ave 97064 503-429-5891
Aaron Miller, supt. Fax 429-7742
www.vernonia.k12.or.us/
Vernonia HS 200/9-12
1000 Missouri Ave 97064 503-429-1333
Nate Underwood, prin. Fax 429-0588
Vernonia MS 100/6-8
1000 Missouri Ave 97064 503-429-1333
Nate Underwood, prin. Fax 429-0588

**Waldport, Lincoln, Pop. 1,936**
Lincoln County SD
Supt. — See Newport
Waldport HS 200/9-12
PO Box 370 97394 541-563-3243
Diana MacKenzie, prin. Fax 563-4145

**Wallowa, Wallowa, Pop. 785**
Wallowa SD 12 200/K-12
PO Box 425 97885 541-886-2061
Bret Uptmor, supt. Fax 886-7355
www.wallowa.k12.or.us/
Wallowa JSHS 100/7-12
PO Box 425 97885 541-886-2951
Rebecca Nordtvedt, prin. Fax 886-7355

**Warrenton, Clatsop, Pop. 4,827**
Warrenton-Hammond SD 30 800/K-12
820 SW Cedar Ave 97146 503-861-2281
Mark Jeffery, supt. Fax 861-2911
www.warrentonschools.com
Warrenton HS 200/9-12
1700 S Main Ave 97146 503-861-3317
Rod Heyen, prin. Fax 861-2997

**West Linn, Clackamas, Pop. 24,356**
West Linn-Wilsonville SD 3J
Supt. — See Tualatin
Rosemont Ridge MS 700/6-8
20001 Salamo Rd 97068 503-673-7550
Debi Briggs-Crispin, prin. Fax 657-8720
West Linn HS 1,500/9-12
5464 W A St 97068 503-673-7800
Kevin Mills, prin. Fax 657-8710

**Weston, Umatilla, Pop. 646**
Athena-Weston SD 29RJ
Supt. — See Athena
Weston MS 200/4-8
PO Box 188 97886 541-566-3548
Ann Vescio, prin. Fax 566-2326

**White City, Jackson, Pop. 7,814**
Jackson County SD 9
Supt. — See Eagle Point
White Mountain MS 400/6-8
550 Wilson Way 97503 541-830-6315
Karina Rizo, prin. Fax 830-6751

**Willamina, Yamhill, Pop. 1,910**
Willamina SD 30J 800/K-12
PO Box 1000 97396 503-876-4525
Carrie Zimbrick, supt. Fax 876-3610
www.willamina.k12.or.us
Willamina HS 200/9-12
PO Box 1000 97396 503-876-2545
Tim France, prin. Fax 876-2511
Willamina MS 100/7-8
PO Box 1000 97396 503-876-2545
Tim France, prin. Fax 876-2511

**Wilsonville, Clackamas, Pop. 18,997**
West Linn-Wilsonville SD 3J
Supt. — See Tualatin
Arts and Technology HS PK-PK, 9-
29796 SW Town Center Loop E 97070 503-673-7375
Saskia Dresler, prin. Fax 570-8720
Wilsonville HS 1,100/9-12
6800 SW Wilsonville Rd 97070 503-673-7600
Dan Schumaker, prin. Fax 682-0917
Wood MS 700/6-8
11055 SW Wilsonville Rd 97070 503-673-7500
Jim Severson, prin. Fax 682-9109

---

Pioneer Pacific College Post-Sec.
27501 SW Parkway Ave 97070 503-682-3903

**Winston, Douglas, Pop. 5,205**
Winston-Dillard SD 116 1,400/K-12
620 NW Elwood St 97496 541-679-3000
Kevin Miller, supt. Fax 679-4819
www.wdsd.org
Douglas HS 500/9-12
1381 NW Douglas Blvd 97496 541-679-3001
Jon Martz, prin. Fax 679-7284
Winston MS 200/7-8
330 SE Thompson Ave 97496 541-679-3002
David Welker, prin. Fax 679-3026
Other Schools – See Dillard

**Woodburn, Marion, Pop. 23,765**
Woodburn SD 103 5,500/PK-12
965 N Boones Ferry Rd 97071 503-981-9555
Charles Ransom, supt. Fax 981-8018
www.woodburnsd.org
Academy of International Studies 300/9-12
1785 N Front St 97071 503-980-6100
Victor Vergara, prin. Fax 981-2629
French Prairie MS 600/6-8
1025 N Boones Ferry Rd 97071 971-983-3550
Ricardo Marquez, prin. Fax 981-2724
Valor MS 600/6-8
450 Parr Rd 97071 503-981-2750
Danny Nanez, prin. Fax 981-2790
Wellness Business and Sports S 300/9-12
1785 N Front St 97071 503-980-6150
Eric Swenson, prin. Fax 981-2621
Woodburn Acad Art Science & Technology 300/9-12
1785 N Front St 97071 503-980-6200
Geri Federico, prin. Fax 980-6209
Woodburn Arts and Communication Academy 400/9-12
1785 N Front St 97071 503-980-6250
Greg Baisch, prin. Fax 980-6255
Woodburn Success HS 200/Alt
610 Young St 97071 503-980-6185
Jennifer Dixon, prin. Fax 982-8372

**Yamhill, Yamhill, Pop. 999**
Yamhill-Carlton SD 1 1,200/K-12
120 N Larch 97148 503-852-6980
Charan Cline, supt. Fax 662-4931
www.ycsd.k12.or.us
Yamhill-Carlton HS 400/9-12
275 N Maple St 97148 503-852-7600
Greg Neuman, prin. Fax 662-3220
Yamhill-Carlton IS 400/5-8
310 E Main St 97148 503-852-7680
Michael Fisher, prin. Fax 662-4079

**Yoncalla, Douglas, Pop. 1,008**
Yoncalla SD 32 300/K-12
PO Box 568 97499 541-849-2782
Jan Zarate, supt. Fax 849-2190
www.yoncalla.k12.or.us
Yoncalla HS 100/7-12
PO Box 568 97499 541-849-2175
Brian Berry, prin. Fax 849-2669

# PENNSYLVANIA

## PENNSYLVANIA DEPARTMENT OF EDUCATION
**333 Market St Fl 9, Harrisburg 17101-2215**
**Telephone 717-783-6788**
**Fax 717-787-7222**
**Website http://www.education.state.pa.us**

Secretary of Education Carolyn Dumaresq

## PENNSYLVANIA BOARD OF EDUCATION
**333 Market St Fl 10, Harrisburg 17101-2215**

Chairperson James Barker

### INTERMEDIATE UNITS (IU)

Allegheny IU 3
Dr. Linda Hippert, dir. 412-394-5700
475 E Waterfront Dr Fax 394-5706
Homestead 15120
www.aiu3.net/

Appalachia IU 8
Dr. Thomas Butler, dir. 814-940-0223
4500 6th Ave, Altoona 16602 Fax 949-0984
www.iu08.org/

ARIN IU 28
James Wagner, dir. 724-463-5300
2895 W Pike Rd, Indiana 15701 Fax 463-5315
www.iu28.org

Beaver Valley IU 27
Eric Rosendale, dir. 724-774-7800
147 Poplar Ave, Monaca 15061 Fax 774-4751
www.bviu.org/

Berks County IU 14
Dr. Jill Hackman, dir. 610-987-2248
PO Box 16050, Reading 19612 Fax 987-8400
www.berksiu.org

BLaST IU 17
William Martens, dir. 570-323-8561
PO Box 3609, Williamsport 17701 Fax 323-1738
www.iu17.org

Bucks County IU 22
Dr. Mark Hoffman, dir. 800-770-4822
705 N Shady Retreat Rd Fax 340-1964
Doylestown 18901
www.bucksiu.org

Capital Area IU 15
Cindy Mortzfeldt, dir. 717-732-8400
55 Miller St, Enola 17025 Fax 732-8421
www.caiu.org

Carbon-Lehigh IU 21
Elaine Eib Ed.D., dir. 610-769-4111
4210 Independence Dr Fax 769-1290
Schnecksville 18078
www.cliu.org

Central IU 10
Dr. Hugh Dwyer, dir. 814-342-0884
345 Link Rd, West Decatur 16878 Fax 342-5137
www.ciu10.com

Central Susquehanna IU 16
Dr. Kevin Singer, dir. 570-523-1155
90 Lawton Ln, Milton 17847 Fax 524-7104
www.csiu.org/

Chester County IU 24
Joseph Lubitsky, dir. 484-237-5000
455 Boot Rd, Downingtown 19335 Fax 237-5154
www.cciu.org/

IU 1
Charles Mahoney, dir. 724-938-3241
1 Intermediate Unit Dr Fax 938-6665
Coal Center 15423
www.iu1.k12.pa.us/

Colonial IU 20
Dr. Charlene Brennan, dir. 610-252-5550
6 Danforth Rd, Easton 18045 Fax 252-5740
www.ciu20.org

Delaware County IU 25
Maria Edelberg Ed.D., dir. 610-938-9000
200 Yale Ave, Morton 19070 Fax 938-9887
www.dciu.org/

Lancaster-Lebanon IU 13
Dr. Brian Barnhart, dir. 717-606-1600
1020 New Holland Ave
Lancaster 17601
www.iu13.org

Lincoln IU 12
Dr. LeeAnn Zeroth, dir. 717-624-4616
PO Box 70, New Oxford 17350 Fax 624-6519
www.iu12.org

Luzerne IU 18
Dr. Anthony Grieco, dir. 570-287-9681
368 Tioga Ave, Kingston 18704 Fax 287-5721
www.liu18.org/

Midwestern IU 4
Dr. Wayde Killmeyer, dir. 724-458-6700
453 Maple St, Grove City 16127 Fax 458-5083
www.miu4.k12.pa.us/

Montgomery County IU 23
Dr. John George, dir. 610-539-8550
1605 W Main St Ste B Fax 539-5973
Norristown 19403
www.mciu.org

Northeastern Educational IU 19
Bob McTiernan, dir. 570-876-9200
1200 Line St, Archbald 18403 Fax 876-8660
www.iu19.org

Northwest Tri-County IU 5
Dr. Frederick Johnson, dir. 814-734-5610
252 Waterford St, Edinboro 16412 Fax 734-5806
www.iu5.org/

Philadelphia IU 26
Dr. William Hite, dir. 215-400-4000
440 N Broad St, Philadelphia 19130
www.phila.k12.pa.us/

Pittsburgh/Mt. Oliver IU 2
Dr. Linda Lane, dir. 412-224-4580
1305 Muriel St, Pittsburgh 15203 Fax 224-4583
www.pmoiu2.k12.pa.us/

Riverview IU 6
Jeff Brown, dir. 814-226-7103
270 Mayfield Rd, Clarion 16214 Fax 226-4850
www.riu6.org/

Schuylkill IU 29
Dr. Diane Niederriter, dir. 570-544-9131
PO Box 130, Mar Lin 17951 Fax 544-6412
www.iu29.org/

Seneca Highlands IU 9
Don Wismar, dir. 814-887-5512
PO Box 1566, Smethport 16749 Fax 887-2157
www.iu9.org

Tuscarora IU 11
Dr. Kendra Trail, dir. 717-899-7143
2527 US Highway 522 S
Mc Veytown 17051
www.tiu11.org

Westmoreland IU 7
Dr. Jason Conway, dir. 724-836-2460
102 Equity Dr, Greensburg 15601 Fax 836-1747
wiu.k12.pa.us/

### PUBLIC, PRIVATE AND CATHOLIC SECONDARY SCHOOLS

**Abington, Montgomery, Pop. 56,600**

Abington SD 7,300/K-12
970 Highland Ave 19001 215-884-4700
Amy Sichel Ph.D., supt. Fax 881-2545
www.abington.k12.pa.us

Abington JHS 1,700/7-9
2056 Susquehanna Rd 19001 215-884-4700
Dr. Mark Pellico, prin. Fax 885-0293

Abington SHS 1,800/10-12
900 Highland Ave 19001 215-884-4700
Angelo Berrios, prin. Fax 886-1871

---

Abington Memorial Hospital Post-Sec.
1200 Old York Rd 19001 215-576-2000

Penn State Abington Post-Sec.
1600 Woodland Rd 19001 215-881-7300

**Albion, Erie, Pop. 1,497**

Northwestern SD 1,600/K-12
100 Harthan Way 16401 814-756-9400
Dr. Karen Downie, supt. Fax 756-9414
www.nwsd.org

Northwestern HS 600/9-12
200 Harthan Way 16401 814-756-9400
Daniel Shreve, prin. Fax 756-9411

Northwestern MS 400/6-8
150 Harthan Way 16401 814-756-9400
Greg Lehman, prin. Fax 756-9415

**Alexandria, Huntingdon, Pop. 344**

Juniata Valley SD 800/K-12
PO Box 318 16611 814-669-9150
David Christopher, supt. Fax 669-4492
www.jvsd.org

Juniata Valley JSHS 400/7-12
PO Box 318 16611 814-669-4401
Michael Estep, prin. Fax 669-4421

**Aliquippa, Beaver, Pop. 9,176**

Aliquippa SD 1,200/K-12
800 21st St 15001 724-857-7500
David Wytiaz, supt. Fax 857-3404
www.quipsd.org

Aliquippa JSHS 500/7-12
800 21st St 15001 724-857-7500
Alvin Gipson, prin. Fax 857-7560

Hopewell Area SD 2,300/K-12
2354 Brodhead Rd 15001 724-375-6691
Dr. Charles Reina, supt. Fax 375-0942
www.hopewell.k12.pa.us

Hopewell HS 800/9-12
1215 Longvue Ave 15001 724-378-8565
Michael Allison, prin. Fax 378-4952

Hopewell JHS 700/5-8
2354 Brodhead Rd 15001 724-375-6691
Edward Katkich, prin. Fax 378-2594

**Allentown, Lehigh, Pop. 115,413**

Allentown CSD 16,600/PK-12
PO Box 328 18105 484-765-4000
Dr. C. Russ Mayo, supt. Fax 765-4239
www.allentownsd.org/

Allen HS 2,800/9-12
126 N 17th St 18104 484-765-5000
Luke Shafnisky, prin. Fax 765-5010

Building 21 HS, 265 Lehigh St 18102 9-9
Janice Mathesz, prin. 484-765-4400

Dieruff HS 1,800/9-12
815 N Irving St 18109 484-765-5500
Susan Bocian, prin. Fax 765-5512

Harrison-Morton MS 900/6-8
137 N 2nd St 18101 484-765-5700
Daria Custer, prin. Fax 765-5715

Raub MS 900/6-8
102 S Saint Cloud St 18104 484-765-5300
Susan Elliott, prin. Fax 765-5310

South Mountain MS 1,100/6-8
709 W Emaus Ave 18103 484-765-4300
Frank Derrick, prin. Fax 765-4310

Trexler MS 1,000/6-8
851 N 15th St 18102 484-765-4600
Steve Serensits, prin. Fax 765-4610

Parkland SD 9,300/K-12
1210 Springhouse Rd 18104 610-351-5503
Richard Sniscak, supt. Fax 351-5509
www.parklandsd.org

Parkland HS 3,100/9-12
2700 N Cedar Crest Blvd 18104 610-351-5600
James Moniz, prin. Fax 351-5656

Springhouse MS 1,100/6-8
1200 Springhouse Rd 18104 610-351-5700
Michelle Minotti, prin. Fax 351-5748

Other Schools – See Orefield

Salisbury Township SD 1,600/K-12
1140 Salisbury Rd 18103 610-797-2062
Dr. Randy Ziegenfuss, supt. Fax 791-9983
www.stsd.org

Salisbury HS 600/9-12
500 E Montgomery St 18103 610-797-4107
Heather Morningstar, prin. Fax 797-1972

Salisbury MS 400/6-8
3301 Devonshire Rd 18103 610-791-0830
Ken Parliman, prin. Fax 797-9648

---

Allentown Central Catholic HS 800/9-12
301 N 4th St 18102 610-437-4601
Blair Tiger, prin. Fax 437-6760
Allentown School of Cosmetology Post-Sec.
1921 Union Blvd 18109 610-437-4626
Blackstone Career Institute Post-Sec.
PO Box 3717 18106 610-871-0031
Cedar Crest College Post-Sec.
100 College Dr 18104 610-437-4471
Lehigh Valley Christian HS 100/9-12
3436 Winchester Rd 18104 610-403-1000
Brendan O'Brien, head sch
Lehigh Valley Hospital & Health Network Post-Sec.
PO Box 7017 18105 610-402-2556
Lincoln Technical Institute Post-Sec.
5151 W Tilghman St 18104 610-398-5300
McCann School of Business & Technology Post-Sec.
2200 N Irving St 18109 484-223-4600
Muhlenberg College Post-Sec.
2400 Chew St 18104 484-664-3100
Sacred Heart Hospital Post-Sec.
421 Chew St 18102 610-776-4745
Welder Training & Testing Institute Post-Sec.
729 E Highland St 18109 610-437-9720

**Allison Park, Allegheny, Pop. 21,377**
Area Vocational Technical School
Supt. — None
Beattie Career Center Vo/Tech
9600 Babcock Blvd 15101 412-366-2800
Eric Heasley, prin. Fax 366-9600

Hampton Township SD 3,100/K-12
4591 School Dr 15101 412-486-6000
Dr. John Hoover, supt.
www.ht-sd.org/
Hampton HS 1,100/9-12
2929 McCully Rd 15101 412-492-6376
Dr. Marguerite Imbarlina, prin. Fax 486-7050
Hampton MS 700/6-8
4589 School Dr 15101 412-492-6356
Dr. Eric Stennett, prin. Fax 487-7544

**Altoona, Blair, Pop. 45,425**
Altoona Area SD 7,300/K-12
1415 6th Ave 16602 814-946-8211
John Kopicki, supt. Fax 946-8226
www.aasdcat.com/aasd/
Altoona Area JHS 1,800/7-9
1400 7th Ave 16602 814-381-7500
Lori Mangan, prin. Fax 381-7501
Altoona Area SHS 1,700/10-12
1415 6th Ave 16602 814-946-8273
Patricia Burlingame, prin. Fax 946-8272
Kimmel Alternative S 100/Alt
900 S Jaggard St 16602 814-946-8246
Paul Hasson, prin. Fax 946-8402

Area Vocational Technical School
Supt. — None
Greater Altoona CTC Vo/Tech
1500 4th Ave 16602 814-946-8450
Dr. Donna Miller, prin. Fax 946-8351

---

Altoona Beauty School Post-Sec.
1528 Valley View Blvd 16602 814-942-3141
Altoona Central Catholic MS 300/5-8
1400 4th Ave 16602 814-944-1250
Sherry Buck, prin. Fax 944-1452
Altoona Hospital Post-Sec.
620 Howard Ave 16601 814-946-2223
Bishop Guilfoyle Catholic HS 300/9-12
2400 Pleasant Valley Blvd 16602 814-944-4014
Joan Donnelly, prin. Fax 944-8695
Great Commission S 200/PK-12
1100 6th Ave 16602 814-942-9710
Kimberly Salyards, supt. Fax 942-7147
Penn State Altoona Post-Sec.
3000 Ivyside Park 16601 814-949-5000
Pruonto's Hair Design Institute Post-Sec.
705 12th St 16602 814-944-4494
South Hills School of Business & Tech. Post-Sec.
541 58th St 16602 814-944-6134
YTI Career Institute Post-Sec.
2900 Fairway Dr 16602 814-944-5643

**Alverton, Westmoreland**
Southmoreland SD
Supt. — See Scottdale
Southmoreland HS 700/9-12
PO Box A 15612 724-887-2010
Dan Krofcheck, prin. Fax 887-2980

**Ambler, Montgomery, Pop. 6,216**
Wissahickon SD 4,300/K-12
601 Knight Rd 19002 215-619-8000
Dr. James Crisfield, supt. Fax 619-8002
wsdweb.org
Wissahickon HS 1,500/9-12
521 Houston Rd 19002 215-619-8112
Dr. Lynne Blair, prin. Fax 619-8113
Wissahickon MS 1,000/6-8
500 Houston Rd 19002 215-619-8110
Elizabeth Bauer, prin. Fax 619-8111

---

Ambler Beauty Academy Post-Sec.
50 E Butler Ave 19002 215-643-5994

**Ambridge, Beaver, Pop. 6,737**
Ambridge Area SD 2,700/K-12
901 Duss Ave 15003 724-266-2833
Dr. Cynthia Zurchin, supt. Fax 266-3981
www.ambridge.k12.pa.us
Ambridge Area HS 800/9-12
909 Duss Ave 15003 724-266-2833
Janice Zupsic, prin. Fax 266-5056
Other Schools – See Freedom

---

Trinity School for Ministry Post-Sec.
311 11th St 15003 724-266-3838

**Annville, Lebanon, Pop. 4,714**
Annville-Cleona SD 1,200/K-12
520 S White Oak St 17003 717-867-7600
Dr. Steven E. Houser, supt. Fax 867-7610
www.acschools.org
Annville-Cleona JSHS 500/7-12
500 S White Oak St 17003 717-867-7700
David Wright, prin. Fax 867-7712

---

Lebanon Valley College Post-Sec.
101 N College Ave 17003 717-867-6100

**Apollo, Armstrong, Pop. 1,610**
Apollo-Ridge SD 1,300/K-12
1825 State Route 56 15613 724-478-6000
Dr. Matthew E. Curci, supt. Fax 478-1149
www.apolloridge.com/
Other Schools – See Spring Church

**Archbald, Lackawanna, Pop. 6,931**
Valley View SD 2,500/K-12
1 Columbus Dr 18403 570-876-5080
Donald Kanavy, supt. Fax 876-6365
www.valleyviewsd.org/
Valley View HS 800/9-12
1 Columbus Dr 18403 570-876-4110
Peter Chapla, prin. Fax 803-0217
Valley View MS 600/6-8
1 Columbus Dr 18403 570-876-6461
Craig Sweeney, prin. Fax 803-0276

**Ardmore, Montgomery, Pop. 12,170**
Lower Merion SD 7,300/K-12
301 E Montgomery Ave 19003 610-645-1800
Robert Copeland, supt. Fax 645-9772
www.lmsd.org
Lower Merion HS 1,300/9-12
315 E Montgomery Ave 19003 610-645-1810
Sean Hughes, prin. Fax 645-9657
Other Schools – See Bala Cynwyd, Narberth, Rosemont

**Armagh, Indiana, Pop. 121**
United SD 1,200/PK-12
10780 Route 56 Hwy E 15920 814-446-5615
Dr. Barbara Parkins, supt. Fax 446-6615
www.unitedsd.net/
United JSHS 500/7-12
10780 Route 56 Hwy E 15920 814-446-5615
Michael Worthington, prin. Fax 446-6615

**Ashland, Schuylkill, Pop. 2,790**
North Schuylkill SD 1,900/K-12
15 Academy Ln 17921 570-874-0466
Dr. Robert Ackell, supt. Fax 874-3334
www.northschuylkill.net
North Schuylkill JSHS 900/7-12
15 Academy Ln 17921 570-874-0495
Ken Roseberry, prin. Fax 874-1531

**Aston, Delaware**
Area Vocational Technical School
Supt. — None
Delaware County Technical HS Aston Vo/Tech
100 Crozerville Rd 19014 610-459-3050
Christopher Moritzen, prin.

Chichester SD 3,400/K-12
401 Cherry Tree Rd 19014 610-485-6881
Dr. Kathleen Sherman, supt. Fax 485-3086
www.chichestersd.org
Other Schools – See Boothwyn

Penn-Delco SD 3,400/K-12
2821 Concord Rd 19014 610-497-6300
Dr. George Steinhoff, supt. Fax 497-1798
www.pdsd.org
Northley MS 800/6-8
2801 Concord Rd 19014 610-497-6300
Lanny Blair, prin. Fax 497-5737
Sun Valley HS 1,100/9-12
2881 Pancoast Ave 19014 610-497-6300
Pete Donaghy, prin. Fax 497-2863

---

Neumann University Post-Sec.
1 Neumann Dr 19014 610-459-0905

**Atglen, Chester, Pop. 1,387**
Octorara Area SD 2,600/K-12
228 Highland Rd Ste 1 19310 610-593-8238
Dr. Thomas Newcome, supt. Fax 593-6425
www.octorara.k12.pa.us
Octorara Area HS 900/9-12
226 Highland Rd 19310 610-593-8238
Scott Rohrer, prin. Fax 593-4945
Octorara Area JHS 400/7-8
228 Highland Rd 19310 610-593-8238
Dr. Scott Rohrer, prin. Fax 593-5185

**Athens, Bradford, Pop. 3,332**
Athens Area SD 1,700/K-12
401 W Frederick St 18810 570-888-7766
Craig Stage, supt. Fax 882-6250
www.athensasd.org
Athens Area HS 500/9-12
401 W Frederick St 18810 570-888-7766
William Clark, prin. Fax 888-4038
Rowe MS 200/6-8
116 W Pine St Ste 1 18810 570-888-7766
Donald Jones, prin. Fax 888-9536

**Austin, Potter, Pop. 562**
Austin Area SD 200/PK-12
138 Costello Ave 16720 814-647-8603
Jerome Sasala, supt. Fax 647-8869
www.austinsd.net
Austin Area HS 100/7-12
138 Costello Ave 16720 814-647-8603
Jerome Sasala, prin. Fax 647-8869

**Avella, Washington, Pop. 795**
Avella Area SD 600/K-12
1000 Avella Rd 15312 724-356-2218
Cyril Walther, supt. Fax 356-2207
www.avella.k12.pa.us
Avella Area JSHS 300/7-12
1000 Avella Rd 15312 724-356-2216
Sheryl Wright-Brown, prin. Fax 356-7905

**Avis, Clinton, Pop. 1,476**

---

Walnut Street Christian S 200/PK-12
PO Box 616 17721 570-753-3400

**Baden, Beaver, Pop. 4,097**

---

Quigley HS 100/9-12
200 Quigley Dr 15005 724-869-2188
Rita McCormick, prin. Fax 869-3091

**Bala Cynwyd, Montgomery, Pop. 8,000**
Lower Merion SD
Supt. — See Ardmore
Bala Cynwyd MS 900/6-8
510 Bryn Mawr Ave 19004 610-645-1480
Jason Potten, prin. Fax 664-2798

---

Kosloff Torah Academy HS 100/9-12
50 Montgomery Ave 19004 610-660-5010
Barry Lichtenstein, prin. Fax 667-5005

**Bangor, Northampton, Pop. 5,192**
Bangor Area SD 3,200/K-12
123 Five Points Richmond Rd 18013 610-588-2163
Dr. Frank J. DeFelice, supt. Fax 599-7040
www.bangor.k12.pa.us
Bangor Area HS 1,100/9-12
187 Five Points Richmond Rd 18013 610-599-7011
Tami Gary, prin. Fax 599-7043
Bangor Area MS 500/7-8
401 Five Points Richmond Rd 18013 610-599-7012
Allison Tucker, prin. Fax 599-7045

**Bartonsville, Monroe**
Area Vocational Technical School
Supt. — None
Monroe Career & Tech Institute Vo/Tech
194 Laurel Lake Rd 18321 570-629-2001
Adam Lazarchak, dir. Fax 629-9698

**Beaver, Beaver, Pop. 4,471**
Beaver Area SD 2,000/K-12
1300 5th St 15009 724-774-4021
Dr. John Hansen, supt. Fax 774-8770
www.basd.k12.pa.us/
Beaver Area HS 600/9-12
Gypsy Glenn Rd 15009 724-774-0251
Steve Wellendorf, prin. Fax 774-3926
Beaver Area MS 300/7-8
Gypsy Glen Rd 15009 724-774-0253
Jeff Beltz, prin. Fax 774-3926

---

Medical Center of Beaver County Post-Sec.
1000 Dutch Ridge Rd 15009 724-728-7000

**Beaver Falls, Beaver, Pop. 8,590**
Big Beaver Falls Area SD 1,700/K-12
1503 8th Ave 15010 724-843-3470
Dr. Donna Nugent, supt. Fax 843-2360
www.tigerweb.org
Beaver Falls Area HS 500/9-12
1701 8th Ave 15010 724-843-7470
Mary Beth Leeman, prin. Fax 843-0892
Beaver Falls MS 300/6-8
1601 8th Ave 15010 724-846-5470
Thomas House, prin. Fax 846-2579

Blackhawk SD 2,200/K-12
500 Blackhawk Rd 15010 724-846-6600
Dr. Melanie Kerber, supt. Fax 846-2021
www.bsd.k12.pa.us
Blackhawk HS 800/9-12
500 Blackhawk Rd 15010 724-846-9600
Scott Nelson, prin. Fax 891-7113
Highland MS 400/6-8
402 Shenango Rd 15010 724-843-1700
Amy Anderson, prin. Fax 843-0934

---

Beaver County Christian HS 9-12
510 37th St 15010 724-843-3002
Doug Carson, prin. Fax 843-5224
Beaver Falls Beauty Academy Post-Sec.
720 13th St 15010 724-843-7700
Geneva College Post-Sec.
3200 College Ave 15010 724-846-5100

**Bedford, Bedford, Pop. 2,806**
Bedford Area SD 1,800/K-12
330 E John St 15522 814-623-4290
Dr. Allen Sell, supt. Fax 623-4299
www.bedford.k12.pa.us
Bedford HS 600/9-12
330 E John St 15522 814-623-4250
Kyle Kane, prin. Fax 623-4265
Bedford MS 500/6-8
440 E Watson St 15522 814-623-4200
Kevin Windows, prin. Fax 623-4214

**Bellefonte, Centre, Pop. 6,107**
Bellefonte Area SD 2,900/K-12
318 N Allegheny St 16823 814-355-4814
Dr. Cheryl Potteiger, supt. Fax 353-5342
www.basd.net
Bellefonte Area HS 900/9-12
830 E Bishop St 16823 814-355-4833
Jennifer Brown, prin. Fax 353-5320
Bellefonte Area MS 600/6-8
100 N School St 16823 814-355-5466
Sommer Garman, prin. Fax 353-5350

**Belle Vernon, Fayette, Pop. 1,081**
Belle Vernon Area SD 2,200/K-12
270 Crest Ave 15012 724-808-2500
Dr. John Wilkinson, supt. Fax 929-5598
www.bellevernonarea.net/bvasd/site/default.asp
Belle Vernon Area HS 900/9-12
425 Crest Ave 15012 724-808-2500
Jason Boone, prin.
Belle Vernon Area MS 200/7-8
500 Perry Ave 15012 724-808-2500
Greg Zborovancik, prin.

**Belleville, Mifflin, Pop. 1,819**

Belleville Mennonite S 200/PK-12
4105 Front Mountain Rd 17004 717-935-2184
Starla Fogleman, supt. Fax 935-5641

**Bellwood, Blair, Pop. 1,814**
Bellwood-Antis SD 1,300/K-12
300 Martin St 16617 814-742-2271
Dr. Thomas McInroy, supt. Fax 742-9049
moss.blwd.k12.pa.us
Bellwood-Antis HS 400/9-12
400 Martin St 16617 814-742-2274
Richard Schreier, prin. Fax 742-9817
Bellwood-Antis MS 400/5-8
400 Martin St 16617 814-742-2273
Donald Wagner, prin. Fax 742-9817

**Bensalem, Bucks, Pop. 59,700**
Bensalem Township SD 6,300/K-12
3000 Donallen Dr 19020 215-750-2800
Dr. Samuel Lee, supt. Fax 359-0181
www.bensalemsd.org/
Bensalem HS 1,900/9-12
4319 Hulmeville Rd 19020 215-750-2800
William Ferrara, prin. Fax 244-2970
Shafer MS 600/7-8
3333 Hulmeville Rd 19020 215-750-2800
William Incollingo, prin. Fax 244-2964
Snyder MS 400/7-8
3330 Hulmeville Rd 19020 215-750-2800
Dr. Thomas Evert, prin. Fax 244-2851

Everest Institute Post-Sec.
3050 Tillman Dr 19020 267-223-2900
Holy Ghost Prep S 500/9-12
2429 Bristol Pike 19020 215-639-2102
Jeff Danilak, prin. Fax 639-4225

**Bentleyville, Washington, Pop. 2,539**
Bentworth SD 1,200/K-12
150 Bearcat Dr 15314 724-239-2861
Scott Martin, supt. Fax 239-2865
bentworth.org
Bentworth HS 400/9-12
75 Bearcat Dr 15314 724-239-5911
Keith Konyk, prin. Fax 239-4010
Bentworth MS 400/5-8
563 Lincoln Ave 15314 724-239-4431
David Schreiber, prin. Fax 239-5889

**Benton, Columbia, Pop. 821**
Benton Area SD 700/K-12
600 Green Acres Rd 17814 570-925-6651
Coleen Genovese, supt. Fax 925-6973
www.bentonsd.k12.pa.us/
Benton Area MSHS 300/7-12
400 Park St 17814 570-925-2651
Coleen Genovese, prin. Fax 925-0956

**Berlin, Somerset, Pop. 2,084**
Berlin Brothersvalley SD 900/K-12
1025 Main St 15530 814-267-4621
Dwayne Northcraft, supt. Fax 267-6060
www.bbsd.com/
Berlin Brothersvalley HS 300/9-12
1025 Main St 15530 814-267-4622
Brian Thompson, prin. Fax 267-6060
Berlin Brothersvalley MS 300/5-8
1025 Main St 15530 814-267-6931
Martin Mudry, prin. Fax 267-6060

**Bernville, Berks, Pop. 942**
Tulpehocken Area SD
Supt. — See Bethel
Tulpehocken Area JSHS 800/7-12
430 New Schaefferstown Rd 19506 610-488-6286
Andrew Netznik, prin. Fax 488-7976

**Berwick, Columbia, Pop. 10,321**
Berwick Area SD 3,100/K-12
500 Line St 18603 570-759-6400
Wayne Brookhart, supt. Fax 759-6439
www.berwicksd.org
Berwick Area HS 900/9-12
1100 Fowler Ave 18603 570-759-6400
Robert Croop, prin. Fax 759-6466
Berwick Area MS 700/6-8
1100 Evergreen Dr 18603 570-759-6400
Christopher Rivera, prin. Fax 759-7978

**Berwyn, Chester, Pop. 3,583**
Tredyffrin-Easttown SD
Supt. — See Wayne
Conestoga HS 2,100/9-12
200 Irish Rd 19312 610-240-1000
Dr. Amy Meisinger, prin. Fax 240-1055
Tredyffrin-Easttown MS 1,000/5-8
801 Conestoga Rd 19312 610-240-1200
Mark Cataldi, prin. Fax 240-1225

**Bessemer, Lawrence, Pop. 1,097**
Mohawk Area SD 1,500/K-12
PO Box 25 16112 724-667-7723
Michael Leitera, supt. Fax 667-0602
www.mohawk.k12.pa.us
Mohawk JSHS 700/7-12
PO Box 25 16112 724-667-7782
Raymond Omer, prin. Fax 667-0602

**Bethel, Berks, Pop. 495**
Tulpehocken Area SD 1,500/K-12
27 Rehrersburg Rd 19507 717-933-4611
Dr. Robert Schultz, supt. Fax 933-9724
www.tulpehocken.org
Other Schools – See Bernville

Bethel Dunkard Brethren Church S 1,300/K-12
5450 Four Point Rd 19507 717-933-5510

**Bethel Park, Allegheny, Pop. 32,035**
Bethel Park SD 4,600/K-12
301 Church Rd 15102 412-854-8402
Nancy Aloi Rose, supt. Fax 854-8430
www.bpsd.org
Bethel Park HS 1,700/9-12
309 Church Rd 15102 412-854-8581
Zeb Jansante, prin. Fax 854-8552
Independence MS 700/7-8
2807 Bethel Church Rd 15102 412-854-8677
David Muench, prin. Fax 854-8732

Hillcrest Christian Academy 300/PK-12
2500 Bethel Church Rd 15102 412-854-4040
Dr. Kenneth Barbour Ph.D., prin. Fax 854-4051

**Bethlehem, Northampton, Pop. 73,573**
Area Vocational Technical School
Supt. — None
Bethlehem AVTS Vo/Tech
3300 Chester Ave 18020 610-866-8013
Brian Williams, dir. Fax 866-6124

Bethlehem Area SD 14,300/K-12
1516 Sycamore St 18017 610-861-0500
Dr. Joseph J. Roy, supt. Fax 807-5599
www.beth.k12.pa.us
Broughal MS 600/6-8
114 W Morton St 18015 610-866-5041
Dr. Detrick McGriff, prin. Fax 807-5909
East Hills MS 1,100/6-8
2005 Chester Rd 18017 610-867-0541
David Horvath, prin. Fax 807-5941
Freedom HS 1,900/9-12
3149 Chester Ave 18020 610-867-5843
Michael LaPorta, prin. Fax 867-7360
Liberty HS 2,800/9-12
1115 Linden St 18018 610-691-7200
Harrison Bailey, prin. Fax 691-0741
Nitschmann MS 900/6-8
909 W Union Blvd 18018 610-866-5781
Peter Mayes, prin. Fax 866-1435
Northeast MS 800/6-8
1170 Fernwood St 18018 610-868-8581
Joseph Rahs, prin. Fax 807-5997

Bethlehem Catholic HS 800/9-12
2133 Madison Ave 18017 610-866-0791
John Petruzzelli M.Ed., prin. Fax 866-4429
International Inst Restorative Practices Post-Sec.
PO Box 229 18016 610-807-9221
Lehigh University Post-Sec.
27 Memorial Dr W 18015 610-758-3000
Moravian Academy MS 200/6-8
11 W Market St 18018 610-866-6677
George N. King, hdmstr. Fax 866-6337
Moravian Academy - Upper S 300/9-12
4313 Green Pond Rd 18020 610-691-1600
George King, hdmstr. Fax 691-3354
Moravian College Post-Sec.
1200 Main St 18018 610-861-1300
Moravian Theological Seminary Post-Sec.
60 W Locust St 18018 610-861-1516
Northampton Community College Post-Sec.
3835 Green Pond Rd 18020 610-861-5300
St. Luke's Hospital Post-Sec.
801 Ostrum St 18015 610-954-3400
Triangle Tech Post-Sec.
3184 Airport Rd 18017 610-266-2910

**Biglerville, Adams, Pop. 1,195**
Upper Adams SD 1,700/K-12
PO Box 847 17307 717-677-7191
Fax 677-9807
upperadams.org
Biglerville HS 500/9-12
161 N Main St 17307 717-677-7191
Richard Sterner, prin. Fax 677-0142
Upper Adams MS 300/7-8
161 N Main St 17307 717-677-7191
David Zinn, prin. Fax 677-0219

**Birdsboro, Berks, Pop. 5,083**
Daniel Boone Area SD
Supt. — See Douglassville
Boone Area HS 1,200/9-12
PO Box 450 19508 610-582-6100
Preston McKnight, prin. Fax 582-5400

Berks Christian S 100/PK-12
926 Philadelphia Ter 19508 610-582-1000
Philip Warner, admin. Fax 404-0126

**Blairsville, Indiana, Pop. 3,366**
Blairsville-Saltsburg SD 1,800/PK-12
102 School Ln 15717 724-459-5500
Tammy Whitfield Ed.D., supt. Fax 459-9209
www.b-ssd.org
Blairsville HS 400/9-12
100 School Ln 15717 724-459-8882
Allan Berkhimer, prin. Fax 459-3392
Blairsville MS 200/6-8
104 School Ln 15717 724-459-8880
Allan Berkhimer, prin. Fax 459-0213
Other Schools – See Saltsburg

WyoTech - Blairsville Post-Sec.
500 Innovation Dr 15717 724-459-9500

**Bloomsburg, Columbia, Pop. 14,675**
Area Vocational Technical School
Supt. — None
Columbia-Montour AVTS Vo/Tech
5050 Sweppenheiser Dr 17815 570-784-8040
Dave Bacher, dir. Fax 784-3565

Bloomsburg Area SD 1,600/K-12
728 E 5th St 17815 570-784-5000
Dr. Cosmas Curry, supt. Fax 387-8832
bloomsburgasd.schoolwires.com
Bloomsburg Area HS 400/9-12
1200 Railroad St 17815 570-784-6100
Daniel Bonomo M.Ed., prin. Fax 387-3492
Bloomsburg Area MS 400/6-8
1100 Railroad St 17815 570-784-9100
Marc Freeman, prin. Fax 387-3491

Central Columbia SD 1,900/K-12
4777 Old Berwick Rd 17815 570-784-2850
Harry Mathias, supt. Fax 387-0192
www.ccsd.cc
Central Columbia HS 600/9-12
4777 Old Berwick Rd 17815 570-784-2850
Jeffrey Groshek, prin. Fax 784-0863
Central Columbia MS 600/5-8
4777 Old Berwick Rd 17815 570-784-2850
Chad Heintzelman, prin. Fax 784-4935

Bloomsburg University of Pennsylvania Post-Sec.
400 E 2nd St 17815 570-389-4000
Columbia County Christian S 200/PK-12
123 Schoolhouse Rd 17815 570-784-2977
Daniel Thompson, prin. Fax 784-1755

**Blossburg, Tioga, Pop. 1,532**
Southern Tioga SD 2,000/K-12
241 Main St 16912 570-638-2183
Sam Rotella, supt. Fax 638-3512
www.southerntioga.org
Other Schools – See Liberty, Mansfield

**Blue Bell, Montgomery, Pop. 6,001**

Montgomery County Community College Post-Sec.
340 Dekalb Pike 19422 215-641-6300
Reformed Episcopal Seminary Post-Sec.
826 2nd Ave 19422 610-292-9852

**Boalsburg, Centre, Pop. 3,655**

St. Joseph's Catholic Academy 9-12
901 Boalsburg Pike 16827 814-808-6118
Christopher Chirieleison, prin. Fax 808-6170

**Boiling Springs, Cumberland, Pop. 3,185**
South Middleton SD 2,100/K-12
4 Forge Rd 17007 717-258-6484
Dr. Alan Moyer, supt. Fax 258-1214
www.smsd.us
Boiling Springs HS 700/9-12
4 Forge Rd 17007 717-258-6484
Joel Hain, prin. Fax 258-5014
Yellow Breeches MS 500/6-8
4 Forge Rd 17007 717-258-6484
Dr. Jesse White, prin. Fax 258-0301

**Boothwyn, Delaware, Pop. 4,830**
Chichester SD
Supt. — See Aston
Chichester HS 1,100/9-12
3333 Chichester Ave 19061 610-485-6881
Michael Stankavage, prin. Fax 485-6510
Chichester MS 1,000/5-8
925 Meetinghouse Rd 19061 610-485-6881
Ken Salamone, prin. Fax 494-3064

**Boswell, Somerset, Pop. 1,262**
North Star SD 1,100/PK-12
1200 Morris Ave 15531 814-629-5631
Dr. B. Christopher Cooper, supt. Fax 629-6181
www.nscougars.com
North Star HS 400/9-12
400 Ohio St 15531 814-629-6651
Thaddeus Kiesnowski, prin. Fax 629-9346
Other Schools – See Stoystown

**Boyertown, Berks, Pop. 4,017**
Boyertown Area SD 7,100/K-12
911 Montgomery Ave 19512 610-367-6031
Dr. Richard Faidley, supt. Fax 369-7620
www.boyertownasd.org
Boyertown Area JHS West 800/7-9
380 S Madison St 19512 610-369-7471
Gregory Galtere, prin. Fax 369-7476
Boyertown Area SHS 1,700/10-12
120 N Monroe St 19512 610-369-7435
Brett Cooper, prin. Fax 369-7359
Other Schools – See Gilbertsville

**Bradford, McKean, Pop. 8,658**
Bradford Area SD 2,600/PK-12
PO Box 375 16701 814-362-3841
Katharine Pude, supt. Fax 362-2552
www.bradfordareaschools.org
Bradford Area HS 800/9-12
81 Interstate Pkwy 16701 814-362-3845
David Ray, prin. Fax 362-1765
Fretz MS 600/6-8
140 Lorana Ave 16701 814-362-3500
Tina Slaven, prin. Fax 362-1812

Bradford Regional Medical Center Post-Sec.
116 Interstate Pkwy 16701 814-362-8292
University of Pittsburgh at Bradford Post-Sec.
300 Campus Dr 16701 814-362-7500

**Bridgeville, Allegheny, Pop. 5,046**
Chartiers Valley SD
Supt. — See Pittsburgh

Chartiers Valley HS 1,100/9-12
50 Thoms Run Rd 15017 412-429-2241
Valerie Keys, prin. Fax 276-5808
Chartiers Valley MS 800/6-8
50 Thoms Run Rd 15017 412-429-2223
Adrienne Floro, prin. Fax 429-2226

**Bristol, Bucks, Pop. 9,494**
Bristol Borough SD 1,000/PK-12
1776 Farragut Ave 19007 215-781-1000
Dr. Thomas Shaffer, supt. Fax 781-1012
www.bbsd.org
Bristol HS, 1801 Wilson Ave 19007 300/9-12
Dr. Thomas Shaffer, prin. 215-781-1000

Bristol Township SD
Supt. — See Levittown
Roosevelt MS 500/7-8
1001 New Rodgers Rd 19007 215-788-0436
Kevin Boles, prin. Fax 788-2629

---

Pennco Tech Post-Sec.
3815 Otter St 19007 215-785-0111

**Brockway, Jefferson, Pop. 2,057**
Brockway Area SD 1,000/K-12
40 North St 15824 814-265-8411
Daniel Hawkins, supt. Fax 265-8498
www.brockway.k12.pa.us/
Brockway Area JSHS 500/7-12
100 Alexander St 15824 814-265-8414
Mark Dippold, prin. Fax 265-8413

**Brodheadsville, Monroe, Pop. 1,776**
Pleasant Valley SD 4,100/K-12
2233 Route 115 Ste 100 18322 570-402-1000
Carole Geary, supt. Fax 992-7275
www.pvbears.org
Pleasant Valley HS 1,600/9-12
1671 Route 209 18322 570-402-1000
John Gress, prin. Fax 992-7733
Pleasant Valley MS 500/7-8
2233 Route 115 18322 570-402-1000
Rocco Seiler, prin. Fax 992-6968

**Brookhaven, Delaware, Pop. 7,890**
Chester-Upland SD
Supt. — See Chester
Toby Farms IS 300/4-8
201 Bridgewater Rd 19015 610-447-3815
R. Victoria Pressley, prin. Fax 499-3814

---

Christian Academy 400/K-12
4301 Chandler Dr 19015 610-872-7600
Dr. Timothy Sierer, hdmstr. Fax 876-2173

**Brookville, Jefferson, Pop. 3,884**
Brookville Area SD 1,600/K-12
PO Box 479 15825 814-849-1100
Dr. Robin Fillman, supt. Fax 849-6842
www.basd.us
Brookville Area JSHS 700/7-12
PO Box 479 15825 814-849-1106
Robert Rocco, prin. Fax 849-1117

**Broomall, Delaware, Pop. 10,688**
Area Vocational Technical School
Supt. — None
Delaware County Technical HS - Marple Vo/Tech
85 N Malin Rd 19008 610-423-7000
Dr. Philip Lachimia, dir.

Marple Newtown SD
Supt. — See Newtown Square
Paxon Hollow MS 900/6-8
815 Paxon Hollow Rd 19008 610-359-4320
Stephen Subers Ed.D., prin. Fax 353-4061

---

Kaplan Career Institute Post-Sec.
1991 Sproul Rd Ste 42 19008 610-353-7630

**Brownstown, Lancaster, Pop. 741**
Area Vocational Technical School
Supt. — None
Lancaster County CTC-Brownstown Vo/Tech
PO Box 519 17508 717-859-5100
Margaret Roth, prin. Fax 859-4529

**Brownsville, Fayette, Pop. 2,220**
Brownsville Area SD 1,300/K-12
5 Falcon Dr 15417 724-785-2021
Dr. Philip Savini, supt. Fax 785-6988
www.basd.org
Brownsville Area HS 400/9-12
1 Falcon Dr 15417 724-785-8200
Jason Kushak, prin. Fax 785-8930
Brownsville MS 300/7-8
3 Falcon Dr 15417 724-785-2155
Vincent Nesser, prin. Fax 785-2502

**Bryn Athyn, Montgomery, Pop. 1,347**

---

Academy of the New Church-Boys S 100/9-12
PO Box 707 19009 267-502-2500
Jeremy Irwin, prin. Fax 502-2617
Academy of the New Church Girls S 100/9-12
PO Box 707 19009 267-502-2556
Susan Odhner, prin. Fax 502-2617
Bryn Athyn College Post-Sec.
PO Box 462 19009 267-502-6000

**Bryn Mawr, Montgomery, Pop. 3,647**

---

American College Post-Sec.
270 S Bryn Mawr Ave 19010 610-526-1000
Baldwin S 600/PK-12
701 Montgomery Ave 19010 610-525-2700
Sally Powell, hdmstr. Fax 525-7534
Barrack Hebrew Academy 300/6-12
272 S Bryn Mawr Ave 19010 610-922-2300
Sharon Levin, head sch Fax 922-2301

Bryn Mawr College Post-Sec.
101 N Merion Ave 19010 610-526-5000
Country Day S of the Sacred Heart 300/PK-12
480 S Bryn Mawr Ave 19010 610-527-3915
Sr. Anita MacDonald Ph.D., hdmstr. Fax 527-0942
Harcum College Post-Sec.
750 Montgomery Ave 19010 610-525-4100
Shipley S 800/PK-12
814 Yarrow St 19010 610-525-4300
Dr. Steven Piltch, hdmstr. Fax 525-5082

**Burgettstown, Washington, Pop. 1,365**
Burgettstown Area SD 1,300/K-12
100 Bavington Rd 15021 724-947-8136
Dr. James Walsh, supt. Fax 947-8143
www.burgettstown.k12.pa.us
Burgettstown MSHS 800/6-12
104 Bavington Rd 15021 724-947-8100
Brian Fadden, prin. Fax 947-3325

---

Tri State Christian Academy 100/PK-12
750 Steubenville Pike 15021 724-947-8722
Jarrett Gum, prin. Fax 947-0821

**Butler, Butler, Pop. 13,451**
Area Vocational Technical School
Supt. — None
Butler County AVTS Vo/Tech
210 Campus Ln 16001 724-282-0735
Regina Hiler, prin. Fax 282-7448

Butler Area SD 7,500/K-12
110 Campus Ln 16001 724-287-8721
Dr. Dale Lumley, supt. Fax 287-1802
www.basdk12.org
Butler Area Intermediate HS 1,200/7-9
551 Fairground Hill Rd 16001 724-287-8721
John Wyllie, prin. Fax 287-5457
Butler Area SHS 1,200/10-12
120 Campus Ln 16001 724-287-8721
Jeffery Schnur, prin. Fax 287-1596

---

Butler Beauty School Post-Sec.
233 S Main St 16001 724-287-0708
Butler County Community College Post-Sec.
107 College Dr 16002 724-287-8711
First Baptist Christian S 100/PK-12
221 New Castle St 16001 724-287-1188

**Cairnbrook, Somerset, Pop. 520**
Shade-Central CSD 600/K-12
203 McGreagor Ave 15924 814-754-4648
John Krupper, supt. Fax 754-5848
www.shade.k12.pa.us
Shade JSHS 300/7-12
203 McGreagor Ave 15924 814-754-4648
Sean Wechtenhiser, prin.

**California, Washington, Pop. 6,712**

---

California University of Pennsylvania Post-Sec.
250 University Ave 15419 724-938-4000

**Cambridge Springs, Crawford, Pop. 2,577**
PENNCREST SD
Supt. — See Saegertown
Cambridge Springs JSHS 600/7-12
641 Venango Ave 16403 814-398-4631
David Nuhfer, prin. Fax 398-8343

**Camp Hill, Cumberland, Pop. 7,766**
Camp Hill SD 1,300/K-12
2627 Chestnut St 17011 717-901-2401
Dr. David Reeder, supt. Fax 901-2421
www.camphillsd.k12.pa.us
Camp Hill HS 400/9-12
100 S 24th St 17011 717-901-2500
Mark Ziegler, prin. Fax 901-2614
Camp Hill MS 300/6-8
2401 Chestnut St 17011 717-901-2450
Leslee DeLong, prin. Fax 901-2573

West Shore SD
Supt. — See Lewisberry
Allen MS 400/6-8
4225 Gettysburg Rd 17011 717-901-9552
Tara Lingle, prin. Fax 901-8201
Cedar Cliff HS 1,300/9-12
1301 Carlisle Rd 17011 717-737-8654
Kevin Fillgrove, prin. Fax 737-0874

---

Holy Spirit Hospital Post-Sec.
505 N 21st St 17011 717-763-2106
Trinity HS 600/9-12
3601 Simpson Ferry Rd 17011 717-761-1116
Joseph Gressock, prin. Fax 761-7309

**Canonsburg, Washington, Pop. 8,707**
Area Vocational Technical School
Supt. — None
Western Area CTC Vo/Tech
688 Western Ave 15317 724-746-2890
Dr. Dennis McCarthy, prin. Fax 746-0817

Canon-McMillan SD 5,000/K-12
1 N Jefferson Ave 15317 724-746-2940
Michael Daniels, supt. Fax 746-9184
www.cmsd.k12.pa.us
Canon-McMillan HS 1,500/9-12
314 Elm Street Ext 15317 724-745-1400
Dave Helinski, prin. Fax 745-2258
Canonsburg MS 800/7-8
25 E College St 15317 724-745-9030
Greg Taranto, prin. Fax 873-5230

**Canton, Bradford, Pop. 1,948**
Canton Area SD 1,000/K-12
509 E Main St 17724 570-673-3191
Mathew Gordon, supt. Fax 673-3680
www.canton.k12.pa.us

Canton JSHS 400/7-12
509 E Main St 17724 570-673-5134
Craig Coleman, prin. Fax 673-5566

**Carbondale, Lackawanna, Pop. 8,778**
Carbondale Area SD 1,600/PK-12
101 Brooklyn St 18407 570-282-2507
Joseph M. Gorham, supt. Fax 282-6988
gateway.ca.k12.pa.us
Carbondale Area JSHS 600/7-12
101 Brooklyn St 18407 570-282-4500
Joseph Farrell, prin. Fax 282-3394

**Carlisle, Cumberland, Pop. 18,109**
Carlisle Area SD 4,900/K-12
623 W Penn St 17013 717-240-6800
Dr. John W. Friend, supt. Fax 240-6898
www.carlisleschools.org
Carlisle HS 1,500/9-12
623 W Penn St 17013 717-240-6800
Jay Rauscher, prin. Fax 240-7145
Lamberton MS 600/6-8
623 W Penn St 17013 717-240-6800
Keith Colestock, prin. Fax 240-2066
Wilson MS 600/6-8
623 W Penn St 17013 717-240-6800
Colleen Friend, prin. Fax 240-2050

---

Carlisle Christian Academy 100/K-12
1412 Holly Pike, 717-249-3692
Christine Tiday, prin. Fax 240-0644
Dickinson College Post-Sec.
PO Box 1773 17013 717-243-5121
McCann School of Business & Technology Post-Sec.
346 York Rd 17013 714-218-3400

**Carmichaels, Greene, Pop. 473**
Carmichaels Area SD 1,100/K-12
300 W Greene St 15320 724-966-5045
John Menhart, supt. Fax 966-8793
www.carmarea.org/Carm_Web/MainIndex.htm
Carmichaels Area JSHS 500/7-12
300 W Greene St 15320 724-966-5045
Lisa Zdravecky, prin. Fax 966-5556

**Carnegie, Allegheny, Pop. 7,765**
Carlynton SD 1,400/K-12
435 Kings Hwy 15106 412-429-8400
Gary D. Peiffer, supt. Fax 429-2502
www.carlynton.k12.pa.us
Carlynton JSHS 700/7-12
435 Kings Hwy 15106 412-429-2500
Fax 429-2508

**Catasauqua, Lehigh, Pop. 6,277**
Catasauqua Area SD 1,500/K-12
201 N 14th St 18032 610-264-5571
Robert Spengler, supt. Fax 264-5618
www.cattysd.org
Catasauqua MS 500/5-8
850 Pine St 18032 610-264-4341
Melissa Inselmann, prin. Fax 264-5458
Other Schools – See Northampton

**Catawissa, Columbia, Pop. 1,525**
Southern Columbia Area SD 1,400/K-12
800 Southern Dr 17820 570-356-2331
Paul Caputo, supt. Fax 356-2892
www.scasd.us
Southern Columbia Area HS 400/9-12
812 Southern Dr 17820 570-356-3450
James Becker, prin. Fax 356-2835
Southern Columbia Area MS 500/5-8
810 Southern Dr 17820 570-356-3400
Angela Farronato, prin. Fax 356-2835

**Center Valley, Lehigh**
Southern Lehigh SD 3,100/K-12
5775 Main St 18034 610-282-3121
Dr. Leah M. Christman, supt. Fax 282-0193
www.slsd.org
Southern Lehigh HS 1,000/9-12
5800 Main St Unit 1 18034 610-282-1421
Christine Siegfried, prin. Fax 282-2965
Southern Lehigh MS 500/7-8
3715 Preston Ln 18034 610-282-3700
Dr. Edward Donahue, prin. Fax 282-2963

---

Achieve Test Prep Post-Sec.
3477 Corporate Pkwy 18034 610-628-0912
DeSales University Post-Sec.
2755 Station Ave 18034 610-282-1100
Penn State Lehigh Valley Post-Sec.
2809 Saucon Valley Rd 18034 610-285-5000

**Chalfont, Bucks, Pop. 3,976**
Central Bucks SD
Supt. — See Doylestown
Unami MS 900/7-9
160 Moyer Rd 18914 267-893-3400
Christina Lang, prin. Fax 893-5820

**Chambersburg, Franklin, Pop. 19,639**
Area Vocational Technical School
Supt. — None
Franklin County CTC Vo/Tech
2463 Loop Rd, 717-263-9033
James Duffey, dir. Fax 263-6568

Chambersburg Area SD 8,200/K-12
435 Stanley Ave 17201 717-263-9281
Dr. Joseph Padasak, supt. Fax 261-3321
casdonline.org
Career Magnet S 9-12
2459 Loop Rd, 717-261-5656
Mark Long, admin. Fax 261-5658
Chambersburg Area MS North 1,000/6-8
1957 Scotland Ave 17201 717-261-3366
Kurt Widmann, prin. Fax 261-3379
Chambersburg Area MS South 1,000/6-8
1151 E McKinley St 17201 717-261-3385
Melissa Cashdollar, prin. Fax 261-3401

Chambersburg Area SHS — 2,400/9-12
511 S 6th St 17201 — 717-261-3322
Burdette Chapel, prin. — Fax 263-6532

Cumberland Valley Christian S — 400/PK-12
600 Miller St 17201 — 717-264-3266
Dr. Wilford Rathel, admin. — Fax 264-0416
Shalom Christian Academy — 400/PK-12
126 Social Island Rd, — 717-375-2223
Angie Petersheim, admin. — Fax 375-2224
Wilson College — Post-Sec.
1015 Philadelphia Ave 17201 — 717-264-4141

**Charleroi, Washington, Pop. 4,003**
Area Vocational Technical School
Supt. — None
Mon Valley CTC — Vo/Tech
5 Guttman Blvd 15022 — 724-489-9581
Neil Henehan, dir. — Fax 489-0711

Charleroi Area SD — 1,600/K-12
125 Fecsen Dr 15022 — 724-483-3509
Edward Zelich, supt. — Fax 483-3776
www.charleroisd.org
Charleroi Area HS — 500/9-12
100 Fecsen Dr 15022 — 724-483-3573
Dr. Patricia Mason, prin. — Fax 483-2294
Charleroi Area MS — 400/6-8
100 Fecsen Dr 15022 — 724-483-3600
Adam Brewer, prin. — Fax 489-9128

**Chester, Delaware, Pop. 33,256**
Chester-Upland SD — 1,800/PK-12
232 W 9th St 19013 — 610-447-3600
Gregory Shannon M.Ed., supt. — Fax 447-3616
www.chesteruplandsd.org/
Chester HS — 800/9-12
232 W 9th St 19013 — 610-447-3700
Constance McAlister, prin. — Fax 447-3682
STEM at Showalter — 7-12
1100 W 10th St 19013 — 610-477-3650
Anthony Womack, prin.
Other Schools – See Brookhaven

Widener University — Post-Sec.
1 University Pl 19013 — 610-499-4000

**Cheswick, Allegheny, Pop. 1,738**
Allegheny Valley SD — 1,000/K-12
300 Pearl Ave 15024 — 724-274-5300
Patrick Graczyk Ed.D., supt. — Fax 274-8040
www.avsd.k12.pa.us
Other Schools – See Springdale

Deer Lakes SD — 2,000/K-12
19 E Union Rd 15024 — 724-265-5300
Dr. Janell Logue-Belden, supt. — Fax 265-5025
www.deerlakes.net
Deer Lakes HS — 600/9-12
163 E Union Rd 15024 — 724-265-5320
David Palmer, prin. — Fax 265-3970
Deer Lakes MS — 500/6-8
17 E Union Rd 15024 — 724-265-5310
David Campos, prin. — Fax 265-3711

Cheswick Christian Academy — 200/K-12
1407 Pittsburgh St 15024 — 724-274-4846

**Cheyney, Delaware**

Cheyney University of Pennsylvania — Post-Sec.
PO Box 200 19319 — 610-399-2275

**Clairton, Allegheny, Pop. 6,590**
Clairton CSD — 700/PK-12
501 Waddell Ave 15025 — 412-233-9200
Dr. Ginny Hunt, supt. — Fax 233-4755
www.ccsdbears.org
Clairton MSHS — 300/6-12
501 Waddell Ave 15025 — 412-233-9200
Thomas McCloskey, prin. — Fax 233-3243

**Clarion, Clarion, Pop. 5,178**
Clarion Area SD — 800/K-12
221 Liberty St 16214 — 814-226-6110
Dr. Michael Stahlman, supt. — Fax 226-9292
www.clarion-schools.com
Clarion Area JSHS — 400/7-12
219 Liberty St 16214 — 814-226-8112
John Kimmel, prin. — Fax 226-9004

Clarion University of Pennsylvania — Post-Sec.
840 Wood St 16214 — 814-393-2000

**Clarks Green, Lackawanna, Pop. 1,470**

Abington Christian Academy — 100/PK-10
204 S Abington Rd 18411 — 570-586-5270
Janet Wells M.Ed., admin. — Fax 587-4648

**Clarks Summit, Lackawanna, Pop. 5,073**
Abington Heights SD — 3,400/K-12
200 E Grove St 18411 — 570-586-2511
Michael Mahon, supt. — Fax 586-1756
www.ahsd.org
Abington Heights HS — 1,100/9-12
222 Noble Rd 18411 — 570-585-5300
Dr. Pamela Murray, prin. — Fax 586-7093
Abington Heights MS — 1,100/5-8
1555 Newton Ransom Blvd 18411 — 570-586-1281
Dr. Michael Elia, prin. — Fax 586-6361

Baptist Bible College and Seminary — Post-Sec.
538 Venard Rd 18411 — 570-586-2400

**Claysburg, Blair, Pop. 1,606**
Claysburg-Kimmel SD — 900/K-12
531 Bedford St 16625 — 814-239-5141
Royce Boyd, supt. — Fax 239-5896
www.cksdbulldogs.com
Claysburg-Kimmel JSHS — 400/7-12
531 Bedford St 16625 — 814-239-5141
Michael O'Dellick, prin. — Fax 239-8949

**Claysville, Washington, Pop. 815**
McGuffey SD — 1,900/K-12
90 McGuffey Dr 15323 — 724-948-3731
Dr. Erica Kolat, supt. — Fax 948-3769
www.mcguffey.k12.pa.us
McGuffey HS — 600/9-12
86 McGuffey Dr 15323 — 724-948-3328
Mark Bonus, prin. — Fax 948-3344
McGuffey MS — 500/6-8
86 McGuffey Dr 15323 — 724-948-3323
Michael Wilson, prin. — Fax 948-2413

**Clearfield, Clearfield, Pop. 6,141**
Area Vocational Technical School
Supt. — None
Clearfield County CTC — Vo/Tech
1620 River Rd 16830 — 814-765-5308
Elizabeth Frankhouser, dir. — Fax 765-5474

Clearfield Area SD — 2,300/K-12
PO Box 710 16830 — 814-765-5511
Terry Struble, supt. — Fax 765-5515
www.clearfield.org
Clearfield Area JSHS — 800/7-12
PO Box 910 16830 — 814-765-2401
Tim Janocko, prin. — Fax 765-2405

Clearfield Alliance Christian S — 200/K-12
56 Alliance Rd 16830 — 814-765-0216
Clearfield Beauty Academy — Post-Sec.
22 N 3rd St 16830 — 814-765-2022
Clearfield Hospital — Post-Sec.
PO Box 992 16830 — 814-768-2496
Lock Haven University-Clearfield Campus — Post-Sec.
201 University Dr 16830 — 814-768-3405

**Clymer, Indiana, Pop. 1,351**
Penns Manor Area SD — 900/PK-12
6003 Route 553 Hwy 15728 — 724-254-2666
Daren Johnston, supt. — Fax 254-3418
www.pennsmanor.org
Penns Manor Area JSHS — 400/6-12
6003 Route 553 Hwy 15728 — 724-254-2666
Michelle Dolges, prin. — Fax 254-3417

**Coal Center, Washington, Pop. 134**
California Area SD — 800/K-12
11 Trojan Way Ste 100 15423 — 724-785-5800
Brian R. Jackson, supt. — Fax 785-4866
www.calsd.org/
California Area HS — 300/9-12
11 Trojan Way 15423 — 724-785-5800
Leigh Ann Folmar, prin. — Fax 785-8860
California Area MS — 100/5-8
40 Trojan Way 15423 — 724-785-5800
Raymond Huffman, prin. — Fax 785-5458

**Coal Township, Northumberland, Pop. 9,922**
Area Vocational Technical School
Supt. — None
Northumberland County AVTS — Vo/Tech
1700 W Montgomery St 17866 — 570-644-0304
James Monaghan, admin.

Shamokin Area SD — 2,600/PK-12
2000 W State St 17866 — 570-648-5752
James Zack, supt. — Fax 648-2592
www.indians.k12.pa.us/
Shamokin Area JSHS — 1,300/7-12
2000 W State St 17866 — 570-648-5731
Chris Venna, prin.

Our Lady of Lourdes Regional S — 300/PK-12
2001 Clinton Ave 17866 — 570-644-0375
Martin McCarthy, admin. — Fax 644-7655

**Coatesville, Chester, Pop. 12,560**
Coatesville Area SD
Supt. — See Thorndale
Coatesville Area 9-10 Center — 1,200/9-10
1425 E Lincoln Hwy 19320 — 610-383-3735
Brian Chenger, prin. — Fax 383-3723
Coatesville Area SHS — 1,000/11-12
1445 E Lincoln Hwy 19320 — 610-383-3730
Robert Fisher, prin. — Fax 383-3725
North Brandywine MS — 500/6-8
256 Reeceville Rd 19320 — 610-383-3745
Chamise Taylor, prin. — Fax 383-3749
Scott MS — 400/6-8
800 Olive St 19320 — 610-383-6946
Dr. Denise Ray, prin. — Fax 383-7110
South Brandywine MS — 600/6-8
600 Doe Run Rd 19320 — 610-383-3750
Michelle Snyder, prin. — Fax 383-3754

Brandywine Hospital — Post-Sec.
201 Reeceville Rd 19320 — 610-383-9000

**Cochranton, Crawford, Pop. 1,126**
Crawford Central SD
Supt. — See Meadville
Cochranton JSHS — 400/7-12
PO Box 127 16314 — 814-425-7421
Donald Wigton, prin. — Fax 425-2071

**Collegeville, Montgomery, Pop. 4,996**
Perkiomen Valley SD — 5,800/K-12
3 Iron Bridge Dr 19426 — 610-489-8506
Dr. Clifford Rogers, supt. — Fax 489-2974
www.pvsd.org
Perkiomen Valley East MS — 800/6-8
100 Kagey Rd 19426 — 610-409-8580
Dr. Seamus Clune, prin. — Fax 489-4815
Perkiomen Valley HS — 1,800/9-12
509 Gravel Pike 19426 — 610-489-1230
Cyndi Lewis, prin. — Fax 489-1921
Other Schools – See Zieglerville

Ursinus College — Post-Sec.
PO Box 1000 19426 — 610-409-3000
Valley Forge Baptist Academy — 200/K-12
616 S Trappe Rd 19426 — 610-792-1884

**Columbia, Lancaster, Pop. 10,150**
Columbia Borough SD — 1,300/K-12
200 N 5th St 17512 — 717-684-2283
Dr. Carol Powell, supt. — Fax 681-2220
www.columbia.k12.pa.us
Columbia HS — 500/9-12
901 Ironville Pike 17512 — 717-684-7500
Maura Meiser, prin. — Fax 681-2219
Columbia MS Hill Campus — 7-8
901 Ironville Pike 17512 — 717-684-7500
Jodie Parkinson, prin.

**Commodore, Indiana, Pop. 325**
Purchase Line SD — 900/K-12
16559 Route 286 Hwy E 15729 — 724-254-4312
Joseph Bradley, supt. — Fax 254-1621
www.plsd.k12.pa.us/
Purchase Line JSHS — 500/7-12
16559 Route 286 Hwy E 15729 — 724-254-4312
James Price, prin. — Fax 254-2306

**Confluence, Somerset, Pop. 758**
Turkeyfoot Valley Area SD — 400/K-12
172 Turkeyfoot Rd 15424 — 814-395-3621
Jeffrey Malaspino, supt. — Fax 395-3366
www.turkeyfoot.k12.pa.us
Turkeyfoot Valley Area JSHS — 200/7-12
172 Turkeyfoot Rd 15424 — 814-395-3622
Richard Berkley, prin. — Fax 395-3366

**Conneaut Lake, Crawford, Pop. 646**
Conneaut SD
Supt. — See Linesville
Conneaut Lake MS — 100/5-8
10331 US Highway 6 16316 — 814-382-5315
Joel Wentling, prin. — Fax 382-0165

**Conneautville, Crawford, Pop. 765**
Conneaut SD
Supt. — See Linesville
Conneaut Valley MS — 100/5-8
22154 State Highway 18 16406 — 814-587-2091
Kevin Burns, prin. — Fax 587-2094

**Connellsville, Fayette, Pop. 7,510**
Area Vocational Technical School
Supt. — None
Connellsville Area CTC — Vo/Tech
720 Locust St 15425 — 724-626-0236
Kevin O'Donnell, dir.

Connellsville Area SD — 4,000/K-12
732 Rockridge Rd 15425 — 724-628-3300
Dr. Daniel Lujetic, supt. — Fax 628-9002
www.casdfalcons.org
Connellsville Area HS — 900/9-12
201 Falcon Dr 15425 — 724-628-1350
Nicholas Bosnic, prin. — Fax 628-0280
Connellsville JHS — 400/7-8
710 Locust St 15425 — 724-628-8910
Richard Evans, prin. — Fax 628-9293

Geibel Catholic JSHS — 200/7-12
611 E Crawford Ave 15425 — 724-628-5600
Donald Favero, prin. — Fax 626-5700

**Coraopolis, Allegheny, Pop. 5,475**
Cornell SD — 700/K-12
1099 Maple Street Ext 15108 — 412-264-5010
Aaron Thomas, supt. — Fax 264-1445
www.cornell.k12.pa.us
Cornell JSHS — 300/7-12
1099 Maple Street Ext 15108 — 412-264-5010
Doug Szokoly, prin. — Fax 264-1445

Montour SD
Supt. — See Mc Kees Rocks
Williams MS — 900/5-8
Porters Hollow Rd 15108 — 412-771-8802
Dominic Salpeck, prin. — Fax 771-3772

Our Lady of Sacred Heart HS — 400/9-12
1504 Woodcrest Ave 15108 — 412-264-5140
Tim Plocinik, prin. — Fax 264-4143

**Corry, Erie, Pop. 6,515**
Corry Area SD — 1,400/PK-12
540 E Pleasant St 16407 — 814-664-4677
Fax 664-9645
www.corrysd.net
Career & Technical Center — Vo/Tech
534 E Pleasant St 16407 — 814-664-4677
Susan Barra, dir. — Fax 663-0722
Corry Area HS — 800/9-12
534 E Pleasant St 16407 — 814-665-8297
Kelly Cragg, prin. — Fax 664-3650
Corry Area MS — 400/6-8
534 E Pleasant St 16407 — 814-665-8297
Gail Swank, prin. — Fax 664-3650

**Coudersport, Potter, Pop. 2,519**
Coudersport Area SD — 800/K-12
698 Dwight St 16915 — 814-274-9480
Alanna Huck, supt. — Fax 274-7551
www.coudyschools.net
Coudersport Area JSHS — 400/7-12
698 Dwight St 16915 — 814-274-8500
Steve Mongillo, prin. — Fax 274-8053

**Cranberry Township, Butler**

Cardinal Wuerl North Catholic HS — 200/9-12
1617 Route 228 16066 — 412-321-4823
Dr. Ann Gaudino, prin. — Fax 776-2287

**Cresson, Cambria, Pop. 1,702**
Penn Cambria SD 1,700/PK-12
201 6th St 16630 814-886-8121
William Marshall, supt. Fax 886-4809
www.pcam.org
Penn Cambria HS 500/9-12
401 Linden Ave 16630 814-886-8188
William Marshall, prin. Fax 884-3977
Other Schools – See Gallitzin

---

Mount Aloysius College Post-Sec.
7373 Admiral Peary Hwy 16630 814-886-4131

**Curwensville, Clearfield, Pop. 2,529**
Curwensville Area SD 1,100/K-12
650 Beech St 16833 814-236-1101
Ronald Matchock, supt. Fax 236-1103
www.curwensville.org
Curwensville Area JSHS 600/7-12
650 Beech St 16833 814-236-1100
William Hayward, prin. Fax 236-2392

**Dallas, Luzerne, Pop. 2,782**
Dallas SD 2,800/K-12
PO Box 2000 18612 570-674-7221
Dr. Thomas Duffy, supt. Fax 674-7295
www.dallassd.com/
Dallas HS 900/9-12
PO Box 2000 18612 570-674-7230
Jeffrey Shaffer, prin. Fax 674-6843
Dallas MS 700/6-8
PO Box 2000 18612 570-674-7245
Dr. Thomas Duffy, prin. Fax 674-7219

Lake-Lehman SD 2,000/K-12
1237 Market St 18612 570-675-2165
James McGovern, supt. Fax 675-7657
www.lake-lehman.k12.pa.us/
Other Schools – See Lehman

---

Misericordia University Post-Sec.
301 Lake St 18612 570-674-6400

**Dallastown, York, Pop. 3,985**
Dallastown Area SD 5,900/K-12
700 New School Ln 17313 717-244-4021
Dr. Ronald Dyer, supt. Fax 894-0583
www.dallastown.net
Dallastown Area HS 1,900/9-12
700 New School Ln 17313 717-244-4021
Dr. Kevin Duckworth, prin. Fax 223-7505
Dallastown Area MS 1,000/7-8
700 New School Ln 17313 717-244-4021
Chad Bumsted, prin. Fax 233-9796

**Danville, Montour, Pop. 4,646**
Danville Area SD 2,000/K-12
600 Walnut St 17821 570-271-3268
Cheryl Latorre, supt. Fax 275-7712
www.danville.k12.pa.us
Danville Area HS 700/9-12
600 Walnut St 17821 570-271-3268
Lee Gump, prin. Fax 275-5463
Danville Area MS 500/6-8
120 Northumberland St 17821 570-271-3268
Charles Smargiassi, prin. Fax 284-4943

---

Geisinger Medical Center Post-Sec.
100 N Academy Ave 17822 570-271-5200

**Darby, Delaware, Pop. 10,364**
William Penn SD
Supt. — See Lansdowne
Penn Wood MS 800/7-8
121 Summit St 19023 610-586-1804
Brian Wilson, prin. Fax 586-7372

**Davidsville, Somerset, Pop. 1,129**
Conemaugh Township Area SD 1,000/K-12
PO Box 407 15928 814-479-7575
Thomas Kakabar, supt. Fax 479-2620
www.ctasd.org
Conemaugh Township Area MSHS 500/6-12
PO Box 407 15928 814-479-4014
James Foster, prin. Fax 479-2038

**Denver, Lancaster, Pop. 3,812**
Cocalico SD 3,200/PK-12
PO Box 800 17517 717-336-1413
Dr. Bruce Sensenig, supt. Fax 336-1415
www.cocalico.org/
Cocalico HS 1,000/9-12
PO Box 800 17517 717-336-1423
Christopher Irvine, prin. Fax 336-1418
Cocalico MS 800/6-8
PO Box 800 17517 717-336-1471
Dr. Stephen Melnyk, prin. Fax 336-1482

---

Gehmans Mennonite S 100/K-12
650 Gehman School Rd 17517 717-484-4222

**Derry, Westmoreland, Pop. 2,670**
Derry Area SD 2,200/K-12
982 N Chestnut Street Ext 15627 724-694-1401
Cheryl Walters, supt. Fax 694-1429
derryasd.schoolwires.com/Page/1
Derry Area HS 700/9-12
988 N Chestnut Street Ext 15627 724-694-2780
Dr. Kathy Perry, prin. Fax 694-1482
Derry Area MS 500/6-8
994 N Chestnut Street Ext 15627 724-694-8231
Lisa Dubich, prin. Fax 694-0288

**Devon, Chester, Pop. 1,486**

---

Devon Preparatory S 300/6-12
363 N Valley Forge Rd 19333 610-688-7337
James Shea, hdmstr. Fax 688-2409

**Dickson City, Lackawanna, Pop. 5,996**

---

McCann School of Business & Technology Post-Sec.
2227 Scranton Carbondale 18519 570-969-4330

**Dillsburg, York, Pop. 2,514**
Northern York County SD 3,200/K-12
149 S Baltimore St 17019 717-432-8691
Dr. Eric Eshbach, supt. Fax 432-1421
www.northernpolarbears.com
Northern HS 1,000/9-12
653 S Baltimore St 17019 717-432-8691
Matthew LaBuda, prin. Fax 432-0375
Northern MS 700/6-8
655 S Baltimore St 17019 717-432-8691
Sylvia Murray, prin. Fax 432-5889

**Dimock, Susquehanna**
Elk Lake SD 1,200/K-12
PO Box 100 18816 570-278-1106
Dr. Kenneth Cuomo, supt. Fax 278-4838
www.elklakeschool.org
Elk Lake JSHS 500/7-12
PO Box 100 18816 570-278-1106
Brian Mallery, prin. Fax 278-4838

**Dingmans Ferry, Pike**
Delaware Valley SD
Supt. — See Milford
Dingman-Delaware MS 700/6-8
1365 Route 739 18328 570-296-3140
James Mitchell, prin. Fax 296-3170

East Stroudsburg Area SD
Supt. — See East Stroudsburg
East Stroudsburg HS North 1,300/9-12
279 Timberwolf Dr 18328 570-588-4420
Stephen Zall, prin. Fax 588-4421
Lehman IS 800/6-8
257 Timberwolf Dr 18328 570-588-4410
Robert Dilliplane, prin. Fax 588-4411

**Donegal, Westmoreland, Pop. 120**

---

Champion Christian S 100/PK-PK, 5-
1076 Kings Way 15628 724-593-9200
Dr. D. Merle Skinner, dir. Fax 593-9210

**Douglassville, Berks, Pop. 444**
Daniel Boone Area SD 3,400/K-12
2144 Weavertown Rd 19518 610-582-6140
Dr. Robert Hurley, supt. Fax 689-6215
www.dboone.org
Boone Area MS 1,000/6-8
1845 Weavertown Rd 19518 610-689-6300
Jenny Rexrode, prin. Fax 689-6306
Other Schools – See Birdsboro

**Dover, York, Pop. 1,967**
Dover Area SD 3,600/K-12
101 Edgeway Rd 17315 717-292-3671
Ken Cherry, supt. Fax 292-9659
www.doversd.org/
Dover Area HS 1,000/9-12
46 W Canal St 17315 717-292-8066
William Rickard, prin. Fax 292-7303
Dover Area IS 500/7-8
4500 Intermediate Ave 17315 717-292-8067
Dr. Philip Livelsberger, prin. Fax 292-9849

**Downingtown, Chester, Pop. 7,678**
Area Vocational Technical School
Supt. — None
Technical College HS - Brandywine Campus Vo/Tech
443 Boot Rd 19335 484-593-5100
Seth Schram, prin.

Downingtown Area SD 11,400/K-12
540 Trestle Pl 19335 610-269-8460
Lawrence Mussoline Ph.D., supt. Fax 873-1404
www.dasd.org
Downingtown HS - West Campus 1,500/9-12
445 Manor Ave 19335 610-269-4400
Kurt Barker, prin. Fax 269-1801
Downingtown MS 1,300/7-8
115 Rock Raymond Rd 19335 610-518-0685
Nick Indeglio, prin. Fax 518-0685
Downingtown STEM Academy 400/9-12
335 Manor Ave 19335 610-269-8460
Arthur Campbell, prin.
Other Schools – See Exton

---

Bishop Shanahan HS 1,200/9-12
220 Woodbine Rd 19335 610-518-1300
Sr. Maureen McDermott, prin. Fax 343-6220

**Doylestown, Bucks, Pop. 8,255**
Central Bucks SD 20,100/K-12
20 Weldon Dr 18901 267-893-2000
Dr. David Weitzel, supt. Fax 893-5800
www.cbsd.org
Central Bucks SHS - East 1,600/10-12
2804 Holicong Rd, 267-893-2300
Abram Lucabaugh, prin. Fax 794-5446
Central Bucks SHS - West 1,500/10-12
375 W Court St 18901 267-893-2500
Jason Bucher, prin. Fax 348-9832
Holicong MS 1,200/7-9
2900 Holicong Rd, 267-893-2700
Kevin Shillingford, prin. Fax 893-5816
Lenape MS 900/7-9
313 W State St 18901 267-893-2800
Timothy Donovan, prin. Fax 345-4699
Tohickon MS 1,100/7-9
5051 Old Easton Rd, 267-893-3300
Kevin Marton, prin. Fax 893-5819
Other Schools – See Chalfont, Warrington

---

Delaware Valley College Post-Sec.
700 E Butler Ave 18901 215-345-1500

**Dresher, Montgomery**
Upper Dublin SD
Supt. — See Maple Glen
Sandy Run MS 1,000/6-8
520 Twining Rd 19025 215-576-3280
Dr. Jill Clark, prin. Fax 572-3886

**Drexel Hill, Delaware, Pop. 27,609**
Upper Darby SD 12,100/K-12
4611 Bond Ave 19026 610-789-7200
Dr. Richard Dunlap, supt. Fax 789-8671
www.upperdarbysd.org
Drexel Hill MS, 3001 State Rd 19026 1,300/6-8
Frank Salerno, prin. 610-853-4580
Upper Darby HS 3,700/9-12
601 N Lansdowne Ave 19026 610-622-7000
Edward Roth, prin. Fax 622-7844
Other Schools – See Upper Darby

---

Bonner/Prendergast HS 1,300/9-12
403 N Lansdowne Ave 19026 610-259-0280
Dr. Tracey Rush, prin. Fax 259-1630

**Du Bois, Clearfield, Pop. 7,711**
Du Bois Area SD 3,900/K-12
500 Liberty Blvd 15801 814-371-2700
J. Mark Heckman, supt. Fax 371-2544
www.dasd.k12.pa.us
Du Bois Area HS 1,200/9-12
425 Orient Ave 15801 814-371-8111
Jeffrey Vizza, prin. Fax 371-3928
Du Bois Area MS 1,000/6-8
404 Liberty Blvd 15801 814-375-8770
Wendy Benton, prin. Fax 375-8775

---

Du Bois Area Catholic HS 200/9-12
PO Box 567 15801 814-371-3060
Dawn Bressler, prin. Fax 371-3215
Du Bois Area Catholic MS 100/6-8
PO Box 567 15801 814-371-3060
Dawn Bressler, prin. Fax 371-3215
DuBois Business College Post-Sec.
1 Beaver Dr 15801 814-371-6920
DuBois Christian S 100/PK-12
197 Eastern Ave 15801 814-371-7395
Dan Kennard B.A., prin. Fax 371-7399
Penn State Du Bois Post-Sec.
1 College Place 15801 814-375-4700
PA Academy of Cosmetic Arts & Sciences Post-Sec.
19 N Brady St 15801 814-371-4151
Triangle Tech Post-Sec.
PO Box 551 15801 814-371-2090

**Duke Center, McKean**
Otto-Eldred SD 700/PK-12
143 Sweitzer Dr 16729 814-817-1380
Matthew D. Splain, supt. Fax 966-3911
www.ottoeldred.org
Otto-Eldred JSHS 300/7-12
143 Sweitzer Dr 16729 814-817-1380
Harley D. Ramsey, prin. Fax 966-3911

**Duncannon, Perry, Pop. 1,503**
Susquenita SD 1,800/K-12
1725 Schoolhouse Rd 17020 717-957-6000
Kent R. Smith, supt. Fax 957-2463
www.susq.k12.pa.us/
Susquenita HS 600/9-12
309 Schoolhouse Rd 17020 717-957-6000
Craig Funk, prin. Fax 957-1792
Susquenita MS 600/5-8
200 Susquenita Dr 17020 717-957-6000
William Quigley, prin. Fax 957-6022

**Dunmore, Lackawanna, Pop. 13,930**
Dunmore SD 1,600/K-12
300 W Warren St 18512 570-343-2110
Richard McDonald, supt. Fax 343-1458
www.dunmoreschooldistrict.net/
Dunmore HS 500/9-12
300 W Warren St 18512 570-346-2043
Matthew Quinn, prin. Fax 343-5923
Dunmore MS 300/7-8
300 W Warren St 18512 570-207-9590
Matthew Quinn, prin. Fax 346-5923

---

Holy Cross HS 500/9-12
501 E Drinker St 18512 570-346-7541
Ben Tolerico, prin. Fax 348-1070
ITT Technical Institute Post-Sec.
1000 Meade St 18512 570-330-0600
Penn State Worthington Scranton Post-Sec.
120 Ridgeview Dr 18512 570-963-2500

**Eagleville, Montgomery, Pop. 4,719**
Methacton SD 4,500/K-12
1001 Kriebel Mill Rd 19403 610-489-5000
Dr. David Zerbe, supt. Fax 489-5019
www.methacton.org
Arcola IS 800/7-8
4001 Eagleville Rd Ste A 19403 610-489-5000
Lucretia Page, prin. Fax 831-5317
Methacton HS 1,800/9-12
1005 Kriebel Mill Rd 19403 610-489-5000
Judith Landis, prin. Fax 489-8165

**East Greenville, Montgomery, Pop. 2,902**
Upper Perkiomen SD
Supt. — See Pennsburg
Upper Perkiomen MS 700/6-8
510 Jefferson St 18041 215-679-6288
Duane Wickard, prin. Fax 679-3091

**Easton, Northampton, Pop. 25,861**
Area Vocational Technical School
Supt. — None
Career Institute of Technology Vo/Tech
5335 Kesslersville Rd 18040 610-258-2857
Dr. Ronald Roth, dir.

Easton Area SD 9,000/K-12
1801 Bushkill Dr 18040 610-250-2400
John Reinhart, supt. Fax 923-8954
www.eastonsd.org
Easton Area Academy Alt
2035 Edgewood Ave 18045 610-829-5700
Kyle Geiger, dean Fax 829-5708
Easton Area HS 2,700/9-12
2601 William Penn Hwy 18045 610-250-2481
Michael Koch, prin. Fax 250-2483
Easton Area MS 7/8 1,400/7-8
1010 Echo Trl 18040 610-250-2460
Dr. Charlene Symia, prin. Fax 250-2613

Wilson Area SD 2,200/K-12
2040 Washington Blvd 18042 484-373-6000
Douglas Wagner, supt. Fax 258-6421
www.wilsonareasd.org
Wilson Area HS 700/9-12
424 Warrior Ln 18042 484-373-6030
John Martuscelli, prin. Fax 258-8831
Wilson Area IS 700/5-8
2400 Firmstone St 18042 484-373-6110
Anthony Tarsi, prin. Fax 258-4014

---

Bethlehem Christian S Calvary Campus 100/5-8
5300 Green Pond Rd 18045 610-365-8176
Carol Aversa, prin. Fax 365-8407
Lafayette College Post-Sec.
730 High St 18042 610-330-5000
Notre Dame HS 600/9-12
3417 Church Rd 18045 610-868-1431
Mario Lucrezi, prin. Fax 868-6710
Rock Christian Academy 50/PK-12
PO Box 636 18044 610-253-8161
Rev. Arlene Santos, admin. Fax 250-8794

**East Stroudsburg, Monroe, Pop. 9,606**
East Stroudsburg Area SD 7,600/K-12
50 Vine St 18301 570-424-8500
Sharon Laverdure, supt. Fax 424-5646
www.esasd.net
East Stroudsburg HS South 1,500/9-12
279 N Courtland St 18301 570-424-8471
Michael Catrillo, prin. Fax 420-8338
Lambert IS 1,000/6-8
2000 Milford Rd 18301 570-424-8430
Heather Piperato, prin. Fax 476-0464
Other Schools – See Dingmans Ferry

---

East Stroudsburg University of PA Post-Sec.
200 Prospect St 18301 570-422-3211
Notre Dame HS 200/6-12
60 Spangenburg Ave 18301 570-421-0466
Jeffrey Lyons, prin. Fax 476-0629

**Ebensburg, Cambria, Pop. 3,337**
Area Vocational Technical School
Supt. — None
Admiral Peary AVTS Vo/Tech
948 Ben Franklin Hwy 15931 814-472-6490
Ken Jubas, dir. Fax 472-6494

Central Cambria SD 1,800/K-12
208 Schoolhouse Rd 15931 814-472-8870
Vincent DiLeo Ed.D., supt. Fax 472-9695
www.cchs.k12.pa.us/
Central Cambria HS 600/9-12
204 Schoolhouse Rd 15931 814-472-8860
Kimberly McDermott, prin. Fax 472-8886
Central Cambria MS 400/6-8
206 Schoolhouse Rd 15931 814-472-6505
Christopher Santini, prin. Fax 472-4187

---

Bishop Carroll Catholic HS 200/9-12
728 Ben Franklin Hwy 15931 814-472-7500
Lorie Ratchford, prin. Fax 472-8020
Pennsylvania Institute of Taxidermy Post-Sec.
118 Industrial Park Rd 15931 814-472-4510

**Edinboro, Erie, Pop. 6,330**
General McLane SD 2,200/K-12
11771 Edinboro Rd 16412 814-273-1033
Richard Scaletta, supt. Fax 273-1030
www.generalmclane.org
McLane HS 700/9-12
11761 Edinboro Rd 16412 814-273-1033
Daniel Mennow, prin. Fax 273-1035
Parker MS 700/5-8
11781 Edinboro Rd 16412 814-273-1033
John Hansen, prin. Fax 273-1038

---

Edinboro University of Pennsylvania Post-Sec.
219 Meadville St 16444 814-732-2000

**Elizabeth, Allegheny, Pop. 1,455**
Elizabeth Forward SD 2,400/K-12
401 Rock Run Rd 15037 412-896-2312
Dr. Bart Rocco, supt. Fax 751-9483
www.efsd.net
Elizabeth Forward HS 900/9-12
1000 Weigles Hill Rd 15037 412-896-2349
Michael Routh, prin. Fax 384-2030
Elizabeth Forward MS 600/6-8
401 Rock Run Rd 15037 412-896-2335
Trisha Martell, prin. Fax 751-6669

**Elizabethtown, Lancaster, Pop. 11,397**
Elizabethtown Area SD 3,000/K-12
600 E High St 17022 717-367-1521
Dr. Michele Balliet, supt. Fax 367-1920
www.etownschools.org
Elizabethtown Area HS 1,300/9-12
600 E High St 17022 717-367-1533
Daniel Serfass, prin. Fax 367-4149
Elizabethtown Area MS 600/7-8
600 E High St 17022 717-361-7525
Dr. Nathan Frank, prin. Fax 361-2597

---

Elizabethtown College Post-Sec.
1 Alpha Dr 17022 717-361-1000
Mt. Calvary Christian S 300/PK-12
629 Holly St 17022 717-367-1649
Dr. Daniel Sheard, hdmstr. Fax 367-5672

**Elizabethville, Dauphin, Pop. 1,493**
Upper Dauphin Area SD
Supt. — See Lykens
Upper Dauphin Area HS 400/9-12
220 N Church St 17023 717-362-8181
Dermot Garrett, prin. Fax 362-8088

**Elkins Park, Montgomery, Pop. 4,700**
Cheltenham Township SD 4,500/K-12
2000 Ashbourne Rd 19027 215-886-9500
Dr. Wagner Marseille, supt. Fax 884-3029
www.cheltenham.org
Other Schools – See Philadelphia, Wyncote

---

Medical College Hospitals Post-Sec.
60 Township Line Rd 19027 215-663-6150
Salus University Post-Sec.
8360 Old York Rd 19027 215-780-1400

**Elkland, Tioga, Pop. 1,798**
Northern Tioga SD 2,100/K-12
110 Ellison Rd 16920 814-258-5642
Dr. Diane Barnes, supt. Fax 258-7083
www.ntiogasd.org
Other Schools – See Tioga, Westfield

**Elliottsburg, Perry**
West Perry SD 2,600/PK-12
2606 Shermans Valley Rd 17024 717-789-3934
Dr. Michael O'Brien, supt. Fax 789-4997
www.westperry.org
West Perry HS 800/9-12
2608 Shermans Valley Rd 17024 717-789-3931
Christopher Rahn, prin. Fax 789-2110
West Perry MS 600/6-8
2620 Shermans Valley Rd 17024 717-789-3012
Renee LeDonne, prin. Fax 789-3393

**Ellwood City, Lawrence, Pop. 7,833**
Ellwood City Area SD 1,200/K-12
501 Crescent Ave 16117 724-752-1591
Joseph Mancini, supt. Fax 752-8556
www.ellwood.k12.pa.us
Lincoln JSHS 900/7-12
501 Crescent Ave 16117 724-752-1591
Kirk Lape, prin. Fax 752-8556

Riverside Beaver County SD 1,200/PK-12
318 Country Club Dr 16117 724-758-7512
Dr. David Anney, supt. Fax 758-2070
www.riverside.k12.pa.us
Riverside HS 600/9-12
300 Country Club Dr 16117 724-758-7512
Michael Brooks, prin. Fax 758-7519
Riverside MS 300/6-8
302 Country Club Dr 16117 724-758-7512
Alicia Dwyer, prin. Fax 758-0919

**Elverson, Chester, Pop. 1,218**
Twin Valley SD 3,400/K-12
4851 N Twin Valley Rd 19520 610-286-8611
Dr. Robert Pleis, supt. Fax 286-8608
www.tvsd.org
Twin Valley HS 1,000/9-12
4897 N Twin Valley Rd 19520 610-286-8600
William Clements, prin. Fax 286-8604
Twin Valley MS 1,100/5-8
770 Clymer Hill Rd 19520 610-286-8660
Dr. Gerald Catagnus, prin. Fax 286-8662

**Emmaus, Lehigh, Pop. 11,070**
East Penn SD 7,400/K-12
800 Pine St 18049 610-966-8300
Michael Schilder Ed.D., supt. Fax 966-8339
new.eastpennsd.org
Emmaus HS 2,500/9-12
500 N Macungie St 18049 610-966-1651
David Piperato, prin.
Other Schools – See Macungie

**Emporium, Cameron, Pop. 2,061**
Cameron County SD 700/K-12
601 Woodland Ave 15834 814-486-4000
Christine Holjencin, supt. Fax 486-4006
www.camcosd.org/
Cameron County JSHS 300/7-12
601 Woodland Ave 15834 814-486-4000
Amy Schwab, prin. Fax 486-4003

**Enola, Cumberland, Pop. 5,946**
East Pennsboro Area SD 2,700/K-12
890 Valley St 17025 717-732-3601
Dr. Jay Burkhart, supt. Fax 732-8927
www.epasd.k12.pa.us
East Pennsboro Area HS 800/9-12
425 W Shady Ln 17025 717-732-0723
Craig Robbins, prin. Fax 732-8932
East Pennsboro Area MS 900/5-8
529 N Enola Dr 17025 717-732-0771
Michael Sim, prin. Fax 732-8948

**Ephrata, Lancaster, Pop. 13,209**
Ephrata Area SD 4,100/K-12
803 Oak Blvd 17522 717-721-1400
Dr. Brian Troop, supt. Fax 721-1514
www.easdpa.org
Ephrata HS 1,300/9-12
803 Oak Blvd 17522 717-721-1478
Scott Galen, prin. Fax 721-1129
Ephrata MS 600/7-8
957 Hammon Ave 17522 717-721-1468
Kevin Deemer, prin. Fax 721-1469

---

Ephrata Mennonite S 200/K-10
598 Stevens Rd 17522 717-738-4266
Pleasant Valley Mennonite S 100/K-12
144 Pleasant Valley Rd 17522 717-738-1833
Larry Weaver, prin. Fax 738-3941

**Erdenheim, Montgomery**
Springfield Township SD
Supt. — See Oreland
Springfield Township HS 600/9-12
1801 Paper Mill Rd 19038 215-233-6030
Dr. Charles Rittenhouse, prin. Fax 233-0691

---

Antonelli Institute Post-Sec.
300 Montgomery Ave 19038 215-836-2222
Philadelphia-Montgomery Christian Acad 300/K-12
35 Hillcrest Rd 19038 215-233-0782
Donald Beebe, hdmstr. Fax 233-0829

**Erie, Erie, Pop. 98,321**
Area Vocational Technical School
Supt. — None
Erie County Technical S Vo/Tech
8500 Oliver Rd 16509 814-464-8600
Joseph Tarasovich, prin. Fax 464-8625

Erie CSD 10,400/PK-12
148 W 21st St 16502 814-874-6000
Dr. Jay Badams, supt. Fax 874-6010
eriesd.org
Central Career and Technical S Vo/Tech
3325 Cherry St 16508 814-874-6200
Pamela Mackowski, prin. Fax 874-6207
East HS 1,000/9-12
1001 Atkins St 16503 814-874-6400
Jill Crable, prin. Fax 874-6407
Northwest Pennsylvania Collegiate Acad 900/9-12
2825 State St 16508 814-874-6300
James Vieira, dean Fax 874-6307
Roosevelt MS 300/6-8
3325 Cherry St 16508 814-874-6800
Teresa Szumigala, prin. Fax 874-6807
Vincent HS 800/9-12
1330 W 8th St 16502 814-874-6500
Scherry Prater, prin. Fax 874-6507
Wilson MS 600/6-8
718 E 28th St 16504 814-874-6600
Donald Orlando, prin. Fax 874-6607

Iroquois SD, 800 Tyndall Ave 16511 1,200/K-12
Shane S. Murray, supt. 814-899-7643
www.iroquoissd.org
Iroquois JSHS 500/7-12
4301 Main St 16511 814-899-7643
Fax 898-4105

Millcreek Township SD 6,800/PK-12
3740 W 26th St 16506 814-835-5300
William Hall, supt. Fax 835-5307
www.mtsd.org
McDowell Intermediate HS 1,200/9-10
3320 Caughey Rd 16506 814-835-5487
Dr. Timothy Stoops, prin. Fax 835-5417
McDowell SHS 1,200/11-12
3580 W 38th St 16506 814-835-5403
Timothy Rankin, prin. Fax 836-6810
Millcreek Learning Center 100/Alt
3814 Asbury Rd 16506 814-836-6888
James Smith, coord. Fax 836-6871
Westlake MS 600/PK-PK, 6-
4330 W Lake Rd 16505 814-835-5750
Marty Kaverman, prin. Fax 835-5770
Wilson MS 600/6-8
901 W 54th St 16509 814-835-5500
Terry Costello, prin. Fax 835-5542
Other Schools – See Fairview

Wattsburg Area SD 1,500/K-12
10782 Wattsburg Rd 16509 814-824-3400
Kenneth Berlin, supt. Fax 824-5200
www.wattsburg.org/
Seneca HS 500/9-12
10770 Wattsburg Rd 16509 814-824-3400
Keith Miller, prin. Fax 825-2262
Wattsburg Area MS 500/5-8
10774 Wattsburg Rd 16509 814-824-3400
Christopher Paris, prin. Fax 825-6337

---

Bethel Christian S of Erie 100/PK-12
1781 W 38th St 16508 814-868-2365
Garry Shultz, admin. Fax 864-7674
Cathedral Preparatory HS 500/9-12
225 W 9th St 16501 814-453-7737
Trevor Murnock, prin. Fax 453-6180
Erie Business Center Post-Sec.
246 W 9th St 16501 814-456-7504
Erie First Christian Academy 200/PK-12
8150 Oliver Rd 16509 814-866-6979
John Richardson, supt. Fax 866-5829
Erie Institute of Technology Post-Sec.
940 Millcreek Mall 16565 814-868-9900
Gannon University Post-Sec.
109 University Sq 16541 814-871-7000
Great Lakes Institute of Technology Post-Sec.
5100 Peach St 16509 814-864-6666
Lake Erie College\Osteopathic Medicine Post-Sec.
1858 W Grandview Blvd 16509 814-866-6641
Mercyhurst Prep S 600/9-12
538 E Grandview Blvd 16504 814-824-2210
Deborah Laughlin, prin. Fax 824-3638
Mercyhurst University Post-Sec.
501 E 38th St 16546 814-824-2000
Northwest Regional Technology Institute Post-Sec.
3104 State St 16508 814-455-4446
Penn State Erie The Behrend College Post-Sec.
4701 College Dr 16563 814-898-6000
Toni & Guy Hairdressing Academy Post-Sec.
930 Peach St 16501 800-775-4187
Triangle Tech Post-Sec.
2000 Liberty St 16502 814-453-6016
Tri-State Business Institute Post-Sec.
5757 W 26th St 16506 814-838-7673

Villa Maria Academy 300/9-12
2403 W 8th St 16505 814-838-2061
Sr. Mary Drexler, prin. Fax 836-0881

**Essington, Delaware**

---

All-State Career School Post-Sec.
50 W Powhattan Ave 19029 610-362-1124

**Everett, Bedford, Pop. 1,810**
Area Vocational Technical School
Supt. — None
Bedford County Technical Center Vo/Tech
195 Pennknoll Rd 15537 814-623-2760
David DiPasquale, prin. Fax 623-7234

Everett Area SD 1,200/K-12
427 E South St 15537 814-652-9114
Dr. Danny Webb, supt. Fax 652-6191
www.everett.k12.pa.us
Everett Area HS 400/9-12
1 Renaissance Cir 15537 814-652-9114
Christina Ramsey, prin. Fax 652-0107
Everett Area MS 200/6-8
1 Renaissance Cir 15537 814-652-9114
Laurie Criswell, prin. Fax 652-0107

---

Foundations Christian Academy 50/PK-12
377 Upper Snake Spring Rd 15537 814-623-2840
Amy Will M.A., admin. Fax 623-4864

**Exeter, Luzerne, Pop. 5,622**
Wyoming Area SD 2,500/K-12
20 Memorial St 18643 570-655-2836
Janet Serino, supt. Fax 883-1280
www.wyomingarea.org
Wyoming Area JSHS 1,200/7-12
20 Memorial St 18643 570-655-2836
Vito Quaglia, prin. Fax 883-1280

**Exton, Chester, Pop. 4,742**
Downingtown Area SD
Supt. — See Downingtown
Downingtown HS - East Campus 1,700/9-12
50 Devon Dr 19341 610-363-6400
Paul Hurley, prin. Fax 903-1047
Lionville MS 1,600/7-8
550 W Uwchlan Ave 19341 610-524-6300
Jonathan Ross, prin. Fax 524-0152

---

Automotive Training Center Post-Sec.
114 Pickering Way 19341 610-363-6716
Church Farm S 200/7-12
1001 E Lincoln Hwy 19341 610-363-7500
Rev. Edmund Sherrill, hdmstr. Fax 363-5367
Universal Technical Institute Post-Sec.
750 Pennsylvania Dr 19341 877-884-3986

**Factoryville, Wyoming, Pop. 1,146**
Lackawanna Trail SD 1,100/K-12
PO Box 85 18419 570-945-5184
Matthew Rakauskas, supt. Fax 945-3154
www.ltsd.org
Lackawanna Trail JSHS 500/7-12
PO Box 85 18419 570-945-5181
Dr. Mark Murphy Ph.D., prin. Fax 945-3832

**Fairfield, Adams, Pop. 504**
Fairfield Area SD 1,200/K-12
4840 Fairfield Rd 17320 717-642-8228
Karen Kugler, supt. Fax 642-2036
www.fairfieldpaschools.org/
Fairfield Area HS 400/9-12
4840 Fairfield Rd 17320 717-642-2004
Brian McDowell, prin. Fax 642-2029
Fairfield Area MS 400/5-8
4840 Fairfield Rd 17320 717-642-2005
Patricia Weber, prin. Fax 642-2030

**Fairless Hills, Bucks, Pop. 8,316**
Area Vocational Technical School
Supt. — None
Bucks County Technical HS Vo/Tech
610 Wistar Rd 19030 215-949-1700
Dr. Leon Poeske, dir.

Bristol Township SD
Supt. — See Levittown
Armstrong MS 500/7-8
475 Wistar Rd 19030 215-945-4940
Edward Dayton, prin. Fax 945-1664

Pennsbury SD
Supt. — See Fallsington
Pennsbury HS East 3,200/9-12
705 Hood Blvd 19030 215-949-6700
Shawn Neely, prin. Fax 949-3896
Pennsbury HS West 9-12
608 S Olds Blvd 19030 215-949-6780
Lisa Becker, prin. Fax 949-6857

---

Conwell-Egan HS 600/9-12
611 Wistar Rd 19030 215-945-6200
Dr. Marion Mann, prin. Fax 945-6206

**Fairview, Erie, Pop. 2,337**
Fairview SD 1,600/K-12
7460 McCray Rd 16415 814-474-2600
Erik Kincade, supt. Fax 474-5497
www.fairviewschools.org/
Fairview HS 600/9-12
7460 McCray Rd 16415 814-474-2600
David Park, prin. Fax 474-1367
Fairview MS 500/5-8
4967 Avonia Rd 16415 814-474-2600
Steve Ferringer, prin. Fax 474-1640

Millcreek Township SD
Supt. — See Erie
Walnut Creek MS 600/PK-PK, 6-
5901 Sterrettania Rd 16415 814-835-5700
Marcie Morgan, prin. Fax 835-5720

**Fallsington, Bucks**
Pennsbury SD 10,600/K-12
134 Yardley Ave 19054 215-428-4100
Dr. Kevin McHugh, supt. Fax 295-8912
www.pennsbury.k12.pa.us
Other Schools – See Fairless Hills, Yardley

**Farrell, Mercer, Pop. 4,855**
Farrell Area SD 900/PK-12
1600 Roemer Blvd 16121 724-346-6585
Rev. Lora Adams-King, supt. Fax 346-0223
www.farrellareaschools.com
Farrell Area MSHS 400/7-12
1700 Roemer Blvd 16121 724-346-6585
Matthew Fowler, prin. Fax 346-2381

**Fawn Grove, York, Pop. 449**
South Eastern SD 2,900/PK-12
377 Main St 17321 717-382-4843
Dr. Rona Kaufmann, supt. Fax 382-4769
www.sesdweb.net/
Kennard-Dale HS 900/9-12
393 Main St 17321 717-382-4871
Heather Venne, prin. Fax 382-4869
South Eastern MS 400/7-8
375 Main St 17321 717-382-4851
Jon Horton, prin. Fax 382-9033

**Feasterville, Bucks, Pop. 3,026**
Neshaminy SD
Supt. — See Langhorne
Poquessing MS 500/6-8
300 Heights Ln 19053 215-809-6210
Joann Holland, prin.

---

Bucks County School of Beauty Culture Post-Sec.
1761 Bustleton Pike 19053 215-322-0666

**Finleyville, Washington, Pop. 453**
Ringgold SD
Supt. — See New Eagle
Ringgold MS 700/6-8
6023 State Route 88 15332 724-348-7154
Mark Alberta, prin. Fax 348-8839

**Fishertown, Bedford**
Chestnut Ridge SD 1,600/K-12
3281 Valley Rd 15539 814-839-4195
Mark Kudlawiec, supt. Fax 839-2088
www.crsd.k12.pa.us/
Other Schools – See New Paris

**Fleetwood, Berks, Pop. 4,046**
Fleetwood Area SD 2,700/K-12
801 N Richmond St 19522 610-944-9598
Dr. Paul Eaken, supt. Fax 944-9408
www.fleetwoodasd.k12.pa.us
Fleetwood Area HS 800/9-12
803 N Richmond St 19522 610-944-7656
Stephen Herman, prin. Fax 944-6952
Fleetwood Area MS 800/5-8
407 N Richmond St 19522 610-944-7634
Gangi Cucciuffo, prin. Fax 944-5307

**Flinton, Cambria**
Glendale SD 800/K-12
1466 Beaver Valley Rd 16640 814-687-3402
Edward DiSabato, supt. Fax 687-3341
www.gsd1.org
Glendale JSHS 400/7-12
1466 Beaver Valley Rd 16640 814-687-4261
Richard Stackhouse, prin. Fax 687-4718

**Flourtown, Montgomery, Pop. 4,474**

---

Mount St. Joseph Academy 600/9-12
120 W Wissahickon Ave 19031 215-233-3177
Dr. Judith Caviston, prin. Fax 233-4734

**Folcroft, Delaware, Pop. 6,473**
Area Vocational Technical School
Supt. — None
Delaware County Technical HS - Folcroft Vo/Tech
701 Henderson Blvd 19032 610-583-7620
Ryan Coughlin, prin. Fax 583-6537

Southeast Delco SD 4,000/K-12
1560 Delmar Dr 19032 610-522-4300
Dr. Stephen D. Butz, supt. Fax 461-4874
www.sedelco.org
Other Schools – See Sharon Hill

**Folsom, Delaware, Pop. 8,224**
Ridley SD 5,700/K-12
901 Morton Ave 19033 610-534-1900
Lee Ann Wentzel, supt. Fax 534-2335
www.ridleysd.org/
Ridley HS 2,100/9-12
901 Morton Ave 19033 610-237-8034
Dr. Kenneth Acker, prin. Fax 237-9641
Other Schools – See Ridley Park

**Ford City, Armstrong, Pop. 2,961**
Area Vocational Technical School
Supt. — None
Lenape Tech Vo/Tech
2215 Chaplin Ave 16226 724-763-7116
Dawn Kocher-Taylor, dir.

**Forest City, Susquehanna, Pop. 1,887**
Forest City Regional SD 800/PK-12
100 Susquehanna St 18421 570-785-2400
Dr. Jessica Aquilina, supt. Fax 785-9557
www.fcrsd.org
Forest City Regional JSHS 400/7-12
100 Susquehanna St 18421 570-785-2400
Peter Jordan, prin. Fax 785-3785

**Fort Washington, Montgomery, Pop. 5,372**
Upper Dublin SD
Supt. — See Maple Glen
Upper Dublin HS 1,500/9-12
800 Loch Alsh Ave 19034 215-643-8900
Robert Schultz M.Ed., prin. Fax 643-8898

---

DeVry University Post-Sec.
1140 Virginia Dr 19034 215-591-5700
Germantown Academy 1,100/PK-12
340 Morris Rd 19034 215-646-3300
James Connor, hdmstr. Fax 646-1216

**Forty Fort, Luzerne, Pop. 4,182**

---

Fortis Institute Post-Sec.
166 Slocum St 18704 570-288-8400

**Foxburg, Clarion, Pop. 183**
Allegheny-Clarion Valley SD 800/K-12
PO Box 100 16036 724-659-5820
David McDeavitt, supt. Fax 659-2963
www.acvsd.org/
Allegheny-Clarion Valley JSHS 400/7-12
PO Box 345 16036 724-659-4661
William Jordan, prin. Fax 659-4774

**Frackville, Schuylkill, Pop. 3,786**
Area Vocational Technical School
Supt. — None
Schuylkill Technology Center - North Vo/Tech
101 Technology Dr 17931 570-874-1034
Jeff Sweda, admin. Fax 874-4028

**Franklin, Venango, Pop. 6,385**
Franklin Area SD 1,800/K-12
702 Liberty St 16323 814-432-8917
Dr. Pamela Dye, supt. Fax 437-5754
www.fasd.k12.pa.us/
Franklin Area HS 600/9-12
246 Pone Ln 16323 814-432-2121
Gary Canfora, prin. Fax 432-5031
Franklin Area MS 300/7-8
246 Pone Ln 16323 814-432-2224
Christine Cohlhepp, prin. Fax 437-1491

Valley Grove SD 1,000/K-12
429 Wiley Ave 16323 814-432-4919
Jeffrey Clark, supt. Fax 437-1243
www.vgsd.org/
Rocky Grove JSHS 400/7-12
403 Rocky Grove Ave 16323 814-437-3759
Matthew LaVerde, prin. Fax 437-1062

**Fredericksburg, Lebanon, Pop. 1,345**
Northern Lebanon SD
Supt. — See Jonestown
Northern Lebanon HS 800/9-12
PO Box 100 17026 717-865-2117
Joshua Kuehner, prin. Fax 865-7818
Northern Lebanon MS 400/6-8
PO Box 100 17026 717-865-2117
Bradly Reist, prin. Fax 865-5835

**Fredericktown, Washington, Pop. 397**
Bethlehem-Center SD 1,300/K-12
194 Crawford Rd 15333 724-267-4910
Linda Marcolini, supt. Fax 267-4904
www.bc.k12.pa.us
Bethlehem-Center HS 400/9-12
179 Crawford Rd 15333 724-267-4944
Aaron Cornell, prin. Fax 267-4907
Bethlehem-Center MS 300/6-8
136 Crawford Rd 15333 724-267-4935
Amanda Kinneer, prin. Fax 267-4937

**Freedom, Beaver, Pop. 1,529**
Ambridge Area SD
Supt. — See Ambridge
Ambridge Area JHS 400/7-8
401 1st St 15042 724-266-2833
Shawn Cooke, prin. Fax 869-5321

Freedom Area SD 1,300/K-12
1702 School St 15042 724-775-5464
Dr. Jeffrey Fuller, supt. Fax 775-7434
www.freedomareaschools.org
Freedom Area HS 500/9-12
1190 Bulldog Dr 15042 724-775-7400
William Deal, prin. Fax 775-7753
Freedom Area MS 200/5-8
1702 School St 15042 724-775-7641
Frank Hernandez, prin. Fax 775-7748

**Freeland, Luzerne, Pop. 3,500**

---

MMI Prep S 200/6-12
154 Centre St 18224 570-636-1108
Thomas G. Hood, head sch Fax 636-0742

**Freeport, Armstrong, Pop. 1,775**
Freeport Area SD
Supt. — See Sarver
Freeport Area MS 300/6-8
325 4th St 16229 724-295-9020
Donald Dell, prin. Fax 295-4630

**Friedens, Somerset, Pop. 1,520**
Shanksville-Stonycreek SD 300/PK-12
1325 Corner Stone Rd 15541 814-267-6499
Samuel Romesberg, supt. Fax 267-4372
www.sssd.com
Other Schools – See Shanksville

**Galeton, Potter, Pop. 1,134**
Galeton Area SD 400/PK-12
27 Bridge St 16922 814-435-6571
Dr. Brenda Freeman, supt. Fax 435-6981
gasd.net
Galeton Area S 400/PK-12
27 Bridge St 16922 814-435-6571
Dr. Brenda Freeman, supt. Fax 435-6981

**Gallitzin, Cambria, Pop. 1,656**
Penn Cambria SD
Supt. — See Cresson
Penn Cambria MS 500/5-8
401 Division St 16641 814-886-4181
Jeff Baird, prin. Fax 886-9308

**Geigertown, Berks**

High Point Baptist Academy 200/K-12
PO Box 188 19523 610-286-5942
Brad Feldmeier, admin. Fax 286-7525

**Gettysburg, Adams, Pop. 7,466**
Gettysburg Area SD 2,900/K-12
900 Biglerville Rd 17325 717-334-6254
Dr. Larry Redding, supt. Fax 334-5220
www.gettysburg.k12.pa.us
Gettysburg Area HS 1,100/9-12
1130 Old Harrisburg Rd 17325 717-334-6254
Mark Blanchard, prin. Fax 337-4439
Gettysburg Area MS 700/6-8
37 Lefever St 17325 717-334-6254
Elwood Strait, prin. Fax 334-6999

Adams County Christian Academy 100/PK-12
1865 Biglerville Rd 17325 717-334-9177
Rhonda Fertich, prin. Fax 334-7691
Freedom Christian S 100/PK-12
3185 York Rd 17325 717-624-3884
Karen Trout, prin. Fax 624-1562
Gettysburg College Post-Sec.
300 N Washington St 17325 717-337-6300
Lutheran Theological Seminary Post-Sec.
61 Seminary Rdg 17325 717-334-6286

**Gibsonia, Allegheny, Pop. 2,710**
Pine-Richland SD 4,600/K-12
702 Warrendale Rd 15044 724-625-7773
Dr. Brian Miller, supt. Fax 625-1490
www.pinerichland.org
Pine-Richland HS 1,500/9-12
700 Warrendale Rd 15044 724-625-4444
Nancy Bowman, prin. Fax 625-4640
Pine-Richland MS 700/7-8
100 Logan Rd 15044 724-625-3111
Dr. David Kristofic, prin. Fax 625-3144

Aquinas Academy 300/K-12
2308 W Hardies Rd 15044 724-444-0722
Leslie Mitros, hdmstr. Fax 444-0750

**Gilbertsville, Montgomery, Pop. 4,774**
Boyertown Area SD
Supt. — See Boyertown
Boyertown Area JHS East 800/7-9
2020 Big Rd 19525 610-754-9550
Andrew Ruppert, prin. Fax 754-9567

**Girard, Erie, Pop. 3,073**
Girard SD 1,900/PK-12
1203 Lake St 16417 814-774-5666
Dr. James Tracy, supt. Fax 774-4220
www.girardsd.org
Girard HS 600/9-12
1135 Lake St 16417 814-774-5607
Gregg McClelland, prin. Fax 774-2239
Rice Avenue MS 600/5-8
1100 Rice Ave 16417 814-774-5604
David Koma, prin. Fax 774-5259

**Glen Mills, Delaware**
Garnet Valley SD, 80 Station Rd 19342 4,800/K-12
Dr. Marc Bertrando, supt. 610-579-7300
www.garnetvalleyschools.com/
Garnet Valley HS 1,500/9-12
552 Smithbridge Rd 19342 610-579-7745
Dr. Janet Girolami, prin.
Garnet Valley MS 1,200/6-8
601 Smithbridge Rd 19342 610-579-5100
Dr. Kenneth Acker, prin.

**Glen Rock, York, Pop. 1,997**
Southern York County SD 3,200/K-12
PO Box 128 17327 717-235-4811
Dr. Sandra Lemmon, supt. Fax 235-0863
www.syc.k12.pa.us
Southern MS 500/7-8
PO Box 128 17327 717-235-4811
Dr. Len Reppert, prin. Fax 227-9681
Susquehannock HS 1,000/9-12
PO Box 128 17327 717-235-4811
Dr. Robert Bryson, prin. Fax 227-1951

**Glenshaw, Allegheny, Pop. 8,914**
Shaler Area SD 4,800/K-12
1800 Mount Royal Blvd 15116 412-492-1200
Dr. Victor Morrone, supt. Fax 492-1293
www.sasd.k12.pa.us
Shaler Area MS 700/7-8
1810 Mount Royal Blvd 15116 412-492-1200
Martin Martynuska, prin. Fax 492-1237
Other Schools – See Pittsburgh

**Glenside, Montgomery, Pop. 8,249**

Arcadia University Post-Sec.
450 S Easton Rd 19038 215-572-2900
LaSalle College HS 1,100/9-12
8605 Cheltenham Ave 19038 215-233-2911
Michael O'Toole, prin. Fax 233-1418
Princeton Information Technology Center Post-Sec.
140 S Easton Rd 19038 215-576-5650
Won Institute of Graduate Studies Post-Sec.
137 S Easton Rd 19038 215-884-8942

**Greencastle, Franklin, Pop. 3,946**
Greencastle-Antrim SD 3,000/K-12
500 Leitersburg St 17225 717-597-3226
Dr. C. Gregory Hoover Ed.D., supt. Fax 597-2180
www.gcasd.org
Greencastle-Antrim HS 900/9-12
300 S Ridge Ave 17225 717-597-3226
Edward Rife, prin. Fax 597-2912
Greencastle-Antrim MS 700/6-8
370 S Ridge Ave 17225 717-597-3226
Mark Herman, prin. Fax 597-6468

Shady Grove Mennonite S 200/1-10
1442 Buchanan Trl E 17225 717-597-0843

**Greensboro, Greene, Pop. 254**
Southeastern Greene SD 600/K-12
1000 Mapletown Rd 15338 724-943-3630
Rich Pekar, supt. Fax 943-3052
www.segsd.org
Mapletown JSHS 300/7-12
1000 Mapletown Rd 15338 724-943-3401
Bart Donley, prin. Fax 943-4769

**Greensburg, Westmoreland, Pop. 14,523**
Greensburg Salem SD 2,900/K-12
1 Academy Hill Pl 15601 724-832-2901
Dr. Eileen Amato, supt. Fax 832-2968
www.greensburgsalem.org
Greensburg Salem HS 900/9-12
65 Mennel Dr 15601 724-832-2960
David Zilli, prin. Fax 832-2922
Greensburg Salem MS 600/6-8
301 N Main St 15601 724-832-2930
Adam Jones, prin. Fax 832-2937

Hempfield Area SD 5,800/K-12
4347 State Route 136 15601 724-834-2590
Dr. Barbara J. Marin, supt. Fax 850-2298
www.hasdpa.net
Harrold MS 400/6-8
1368 Middletown Rd 15601 724-850-2301
Jason Lochner, prin. Fax 850-2302
Hempfield Area HS 1,900/9-12
4345 State Route 136 15601 724-834-9000
Kathy Charlton, prin. Fax 850-2090
Wendover MS 500/6-8
425 Wendover Jr High Rd 15601 724-838-4070
Deanna Mikesic, prin. Fax 838-4071
Other Schools – See Irwin

Education and Technology Institute Post-Sec.
219 Donohoe Rd 15601 724-836-2395
Greensburg Central Catholic JSHS 500/7-12
911 Armory Dr 15601 724-834-0310
Donald Teti, prin. Fax 834-2472
Seton Hill University Post-Sec.
Seton Hill Dr 15601 724-834-2200
Triangle Tech Post-Sec.
222 E Pittsburgh St # A 15601 724-832-1050
University of Pittsburgh Post-Sec.
150 Finoli Dr 15601 724-837-7040
Westmoreland Christian Academy 100/PK-12
538 Rugh St 15601 724-853-8308
Jordan Tomson, prin. Fax 836-7472

**Greenville, Mercer, Pop. 5,850**
Greenville Area SD 1,400/K-12
9 Donation Rd 16125 724-588-2500
Mark Ferrara, supt. Fax 588-5024
www.greenville.k12.pa.us
Greenville JSHS 700/7-12
9 Donation Rd 16125 724-588-2500
Brian Tokar, prin. Fax 588-4397

Reynolds SD 1,200/PK-12
531 Reynolds Rd 16125 724-646-5501
Joseph Neuch, supt. Fax 646-5505
www.reynolds.k12.pa.us
Reynolds JSHS 600/7-12
531 Reynolds Rd 16125 724-646-5701
Scott Shearer, prin. Fax 646-5705

Living Word Christian S 100/1-12
12 N Diamond St 16125 724-588-2140
Jan Chapin, admin. Fax 588-8742
Thiel College Post-Sec.
75 College Ave 16125 724-589-2000

**Grove City, Mercer, Pop. 8,236**
Grove City Area SD 2,000/K-12
511 Highland Ave 16127 724-458-6733
Dr. Lawrence Connelly, supt. Fax 458-5868
www.grovecity.k12.pa.us
Grove City Area HS 700/9-12
511 Highland Ave 16127 724-458-5456
Dr. RaeLin Howard, prin. Fax 450-0678
Grove City Area MS 500/6-8
100 Middle School Dr 16127 724-458-8040
Larry Connelly, prin. Fax 450-0780

Grove City College Post-Sec.
100 Campus Dr 16127 724-458-2000

**Guys Mills, Crawford, Pop. 121**
PENNCREST SD
Supt. — See Saegertown
Maplewood JSHS 600/7-12
30383 Guys Mills Rd 16327 814-789-3666
Kenneth Wolfarth, prin. Fax 789-2409

Faith Builders Christian S 100/1-12
28527 Guys Mills Rd 16327 814-789-2303
Gerald Miller, admin. Fax 789-3396

**Gwynedd Valley, Montgomery**

Gwynedd-Mercy Academy 400/9-12
PO Box 902 19437 215-646-8815
Sr. Patricia Flynn, prin. Fax 646-4361
Gwynedd-Mercy University Post-Sec.
PO Box 901 19437 215-646-7300

**Hadley, Mercer**
Commodore Perry SD 500/K-12
3002 Perry Hwy 16130 724-253-3255
Kim Zippie, supt. Fax 253-3467
www.cppanthers.org/CPWeb.htm
Perry JSHS 300/7-12
3002 Perry Hwy 16130 724-253-2232
Doug Mays, prin. Fax 253-3467

**Halifax, Dauphin, Pop. 814**
Halifax Area SD 1,100/PK-12
3940 Peters Mountain Rd 17032 717-896-3416
Dr. Michele Orner, supt. Fax 896-3976
www.hasd.us
Halifax Area HS 400/9-12
3940 Peters Mountain Rd 17032 717-896-3416
David Hatfield, prin. Fax 896-3976
Halifax Area MS 300/6-8
3940 Peters Mountain Rd 17032 717-896-3416
Rick Ansel, prin. Fax 896-3976

**Hamburg, Berks, Pop. 4,259**
Hamburg Area SD 2,100/K-12
Windsor St 19526 610-562-2241
Dr. Richard Mextorf, supt. Fax 562-2634
www.hasdhawks.org
Hamburg Area HS 800/9-12
701 Windsor St 19526 610-562-3861
Christopher Spohn, prin. Fax 561-3394
Hamburg Area MS 600/5-8
Windsor St 19526 610-562-3990
Geno McGorry, prin. Fax 562-1425

Blue Mountain Academy 200/9-12
2363 Mountain Rd 19526 484-662-7000

**Hanover, York, Pop. 15,077**
Hanover Public SD 1,600/K-12
403 Moul Ave 17331 717-637-9000
Dr. John Scola, supt. Fax 630-4617
www.hanoverpublic.org
Hanover HS 500/9-12
401 Moul Ave 17331 717-637-9000
Catherine Houck, prin. Fax 630-4634
Hanover MS 500/5-8
300 Keagy Ave 17331 717-637-9000
Mark Hershner, prin. Fax 630-4632

South Western SD 4,100/K-12
225 Bowman Rd 17331 717-632-2500
Dr. Barbara Rupp, supt. Fax 632-7993
www.swsd.k12.pa.us/
Markle IS 900/6-8
225 Bowman Rd Ste 1 17331 717-633-4840
Dr. Daniel Hartman, prin. Fax 633-7073
South Western HS 1,300/9-12
200 Bowman Rd 17331 717-633-4807
Dr. Judy Berryman, prin. Fax 633-4819

Empire Beauty School Post-Sec.
1000 Carlisle St 17331 717-633-6201
St. Joseph MS 100/6-8
5125 Grandview Rd 17331 717-632-0118
Susan Mummert, prin. Fax 632-0030

**Hanover Twp, Lehigh**
Hanover Area SD 1,900/K-12
1600 Sans Souci Pkwy 18706 570-831-2300
Andrew Kuhl, supt. Fax 831-2322
www.hanoverarea.org
Hanover Area JSHS 900/7-12
1600 Sans Souci Pkwy 18706 570-831-2300
Daniel Malloy, prin. Fax 831-2316

**Harborcreek, Erie**
Harbor Creek SD 2,000/K-12
6375 Buffalo Rd 16421 814-897-2100
Kelly Hess, supt. Fax 897-2142
www.hcsd.iu5.org
Harbor Creek HS 700/9-12
6375 Buffalo Rd 16421 814-897-2100
Pamela Chodubski, prin. Fax 897-2136
Harbor Creek JHS 300/7-8
6375 Buffalo Rd 16421 814-897-2100
Andrew Krahe, prin. Fax 897-2121

**Harleysville, Montgomery, Pop. 9,178**
Souderton Area SD
Supt. — See Souderton
Indian Valley MS 800/6-8
130 Maple Ave 19438 215-256-8896
Dr. Dale Burkhard, prin. Fax 256-1288

**Harmony, Butler, Pop. 882**
Seneca Valley SD 7,300/K-12
124 Seneca School Rd 16037 724-452-6040
Dr. Tracy Vitale, supt. Fax 452-6105
www.svsd.net/
Seneca Valley Intermediate HS 1,200/9-10
126 Seneca School Rd 16037 724-452-6040
Matthew Delp, prin. Fax 452-3718
Seneca Valley MS 1,200/7-8
122 Seneca School Rd 16037 724-452-6040
Robert Ceh, prin. Fax 452-0331
Seneca Valley SHS 1,100/11-12
128 Seneca School Rd 16037 724-452-6040
Mark Korcinsky, prin. Fax 452-8357

**Harrisburg, Dauphin, Pop. 47,794**
Area Vocational Technical School
Supt. — None
Dauphin County Technical S Vo/Tech
6001 Locust Ln 17109 717-652-3170
Dr. Peggy Grimm, prin. Fax 652-9326

Other Schools – See Allison Park PA, Altoona PA, Aston PA, Bartonsville PA, Bethlehem PA, Bloomsburg PA, Broomall PA, Brownstown PA, Butler PA, Canonsburg PA, Chambersburg PA, Charleroi PA, Clearfield PA, Coal Township PA, Connellsville PA, Downingtown PA, Easton PA, Ebensburg PA, Erie PA, Everett PA, Fairless Hills PA, Folcroft PA, Ford City PA, Frackville PA, Hazle Township PA, Hughesville PA, Indiana PA, Jamison PA, Jefferson Hills PA, Jim Thorpe PA, Johnstown PA, Kingston PA, Lansdale PA, Latrobe PA, Lebanon PA, Leesport PA, Lewistown PA, Limerick PA, Mc Connellsburg PA, Mc Keesport PA, Mar Lin PA, Meadville PA, Mechanicsburg PA, Mercer PA, Mill Creek PA, Mill Hall PA, Monaca PA, Monroeville PA, Mount Joy PA, New Berlin PA, New Castle PA, New Kensington PA, New Stanton PA, Oakdale PA, Oil City PA, Oley PA, Perkasie PA, Philadelphia PA, Phoenixville PA, Pleasant Gap PA, Plymouth Meeting PA, Port Allegany PA, Pottsville PA, Reading PA, Reynoldsville PA, Schnecksville PA, Scranton PA, Shippenville PA, Somerset PA, Springville PA, Towanda PA, Uniontown PA, Warren PA, Waynesburg PA, West Grove PA, Wilkes Barre PA, Willow Grove PA, Willow Street PA, York PA

Central Dauphin SD 10,600/K-12
600 Rutherford Rd 17109 717-545-4703
Dr. Carol Johnson, supt. Fax 657-4999
www.cdschools.org
Central Dauphin East HS 1,300/9-12
626 Rutherford Rd 17109 717-541-1662
Dr. Jesse Rawls, prin. Fax 545-7139
Central Dauphin East MS 600/6-8
628 Rutherford Rd 17109 717-545-4703
Christine Miller, prin. Fax 657-4987
Central Dauphin HS 1,800/9-12
437 Piketown Rd 17112 717-703-5360
Ken Miller, prin. Fax 703-5730
Central Dauphin MS 700/6-8
4600 Locust Ln 17109 717-540-4606
Jeffrey Matzner, prin. Fax 214-5055
Linglestown MS 700/6-8
1200 N Mountain Rd 17112 717-657-3060
Mickey Termin, prin. Fax 657-0537
Other Schools – See Steelton

Harrisburg City SD 5,100/K-12
1601 State St 17103 717-703-4000
Dr. Sybil Knight-Burney, supt. Fax 703-4115
www.hbgsd.k12.pa.us
Camp Curtin Academy 400/5-8
2900 N 6th St 17110 717-703-4200
Portia Slaughter, prin. Fax 703-4225
Harrisburg HS 1,300/9-12
2451 Market St 17103 717-703-4300
Eugene Spells, prin. Fax 703-4333
Marshall Math Science Academy 200/5-8
301 Hale Ave 17104 717-703-1400
Marisol Craig, prin. Fax 703-1420
Rowland Academy 600/5-8
1842 Derry St 17104 717-703-4500
Roma Benjamin, prin. Fax 703-4520
Sci-Tech HS 400/9-12
215 Market St 17101 717-703-1900
Sieta Achampong, dir. Fax 703-1915

Susquehanna Township SD 2,900/K-12
2579 Interstate Dr 17110 717-657-5100
Dr. Tod F. Kline Ed.D., supt. Fax 724-1851
www.hannasd.org
Susquehanna Township HS 1,000/9-12
3500 Elmerton Ave 17109 717-657-5117
Keith Still, prin. Fax 657-2919
Susquehanna Township MS 700/6-8
801 Wood St 17109 717-657-5125
Kenneth R. Edwards, prin. Fax 657-2919

---

Bishop McDevitt HS 700/9-12
1 Crusader Way 17111 717-236-7973
Sr. Mary Anne Bednar, prin. Fax 234-1270
Covenant Christian Academy 200/PK-12
1982 Locust Ln 17109 717-540-9885
Empire Beauty School Post-Sec.
3941 Jonestown Rd 17109 717-652-8500
Harrisburg Area Community College Post-Sec.
1 Hacc Dr 17110 717-780-2300
Harrisburg Christian S 300/K-12
2000 Blue Mountain Pkwy 17112 717-545-3728
Phillip Puleo, hdmstr. Fax 545-9370
Harrisburg University of Science & Tech Post-Sec.
326 Market St 17101 717-901-5100
ITT Technical Institute Post-Sec.
449 Eisenhower Blvd Ste 100 17111 717-565-1700
Kaplan Career Institute Post-Sec.
5650 Derry St 17111 717-564-4112
Keystone Technical Institute Post-Sec.
2301 Academy Dr 17112 717-545-4747
Widener University School of Law Post-Sec.
PO Box 69380 17106 717-541-3900

**Harrison City, Westmoreland, Pop. 134**
Penn-Trafford SD 4,200/K-12
PO Box 530 15636 724-744-4496
Dr. Matthew Harris, supt. Fax 744-4016
www.penntrafford.org
Penn-Trafford HS 1,500/9-12
3381 Route 130 15636 724-744-4471
Tony Aquilio, prin. Fax 744-1214
Other Schools – See Jeannette, Trafford

**Hatboro, Montgomery, Pop. 7,268**
Upper Moreland Township SD
Supt. — See Willow Grove
Upper Moreland MS 700/6-8
4000 Orangemans Rd 19040 215-674-4185
Charles Hafele, prin. Fax 956-1906

**Hatfield, Montgomery, Pop. 3,211**
North Penn SD
Supt. — See Lansdale
Northbridge S Alt
2374 N Penn Rd 19440 215-412-4009
Kyle Hassler, prin. Fax 853-1627
Pennfield MS 800/7-9
726 Forty Foot Rd 19440 215-368-9600
Dr. Barbara Galloway, prin. Fax 368-9791

---

Biblical Theological Seminary Post-Sec.
200 N Main St 19440 800-235-4021

**Haverford, Montgomery, Pop. 6,000**

---

Haverford College Post-Sec.
370 Lancaster Ave 19041 610-896-1000
Haverford S 1,000/PK-12
450 Lancaster Ave 19041 610-642-3020
Dr. John Nagl, hdmstr. Fax 649-4898

**Havertown, Delaware, Pop. 30,000**
Haverford Township SD 5,600/K-12
50 E Eagle Rd 19083 610-853-5900
Dr. Maureen Reusche, supt. Fax 853-5942
www.haverford.k12.pa.us
Haverford HS 1,800/9-12
200 Mill Rd 19083 610-853-5900
Jeffrey Nesbitt Ed.D., prin. Fax 853-5952
Haverford MS 1,300/6-8
1701 Darby Rd 19083 610-853-5900
Daniel Horan, prin. Fax 853-5937

**Hawley, Pike, Pop. 1,191**
Wallenpaupack Area SD 3,500/K-12
2552 Route 6 18428 570-226-4557
Michael Silsby, supt. Fax 226-0638
www.wallenpaupack.org/
Hawley Center 100/Alt
500 Academy St 18428 570-226-4557
Fax 251-3010
Wallenpaupack Area HS 1,300/9-12
2552 Route 6 18428 570-226-4557
Jay Starnes, prin. Fax 251-3153
Wallenpaupack Area MS 900/6-8
139 Atlantic Ave 18428 570-226-4557
Keith Gunuskey, prin. Fax 251-3165

**Hazleton, Luzerne, Pop. 25,114**
Hazleton Area SD
Supt. — See Hazle Township
Hazleton S 1,100/3-8
700 N Wyoming St 18201 570-459-3221
Maureen DeRose, prin. Fax 501-8433

---

Academy of Hair Design Post-Sec.
1057 N Church St # A 18202 570-784-1020
Immanuel Christian S 100/K-12
725 N Locust St 18201 570-459-1111
Kelly Knowlden, head sch Fax 459-6920
McCann School of Business & Technology Post-Sec.
370 Maplewood Dr 18202 570-454-6172
Penn State Hazleton Post-Sec.
76 University Dr 18202 570-450-3000

**Hazle Township, Luzerne**
Area Vocational Technical School
Supt. — None
Hazleton Area Career Center Vo/Tech
1451 W 23rd St, 570-459-3221
Lori Herman, prin. Fax 459-3181

Hazleton Area SD 10,200/PK-12
1515 W 23rd St 18202 570-459-3111
Dr. Craig Butler, supt. Fax 459-3118
www.hasdk12.org
Hazleton Area HS 2,400/9-12
1601 W 23rd St, 570-459-3221
Rocco Petrone, prin. Fax 459-3242
Other Schools – See Hazleton

**Hegins, Schuylkill, Pop. 805**
Tri-Valley SD
Supt. — See Valley View
Tri-Valley JSHS 400/7-12
155 E Main St 17938 570-682-3125
Charles Hall, prin. Fax 682-9873

**Hellertown, Northampton, Pop. 5,840**
Saucon Valley SD 2,300/K-12
2097 Polk Valley Rd 18055 610-838-7026
Monica McHale-Small, supt. Fax 838-6419
www.svpanthers.org
Saucon Valley HS 800/9-12
2100 Polk Valley Rd 18055 610-838-7001
Eric Kahler, prin. Fax 838-2365
Saucon Valley MS 600/6-8
2095 Polk Valley Rd 18055 610-838-7071
Pamela Bernardo, prin. Fax 838-7473

**Herminie, Westmoreland, Pop. 785**
Yough SD 2,200/K-12
915 Lowber Rd 15637 724-446-7272
Dr. Janet Sardon, supt. Fax 446-5017
www.youghsd.net
Yough HS 700/9-12
919 Lowber Rd 15637 724-446-5520
Earl Thompson, prin. Fax 446-6008
Other Schools – See Ruffs Dale

**Hermitage, Mercer, Pop. 16,014**
Hermitage SD 1,900/K-12
411 N Hermitage Rd 16148 724-981-8750
Dr. Daniel Bell, supt. Fax 981-5080
www.hermitage.k12.pa.us
Hickory HS 700/8-12
640 N Hermitage Rd 16148 724-981-8750
Chris Gill, prin. Fax 347-4558

---

Kennedy Catholic HS 300/9-12
2120 Shenango Valley Fwy 16148 724-346-5531
Heidi Patterson, prin. Fax 346-3011
Kennedy Catholic MS 100/6-8
2120 Shenango Valley Fwy 16148 724-346-5531
Victoria Wagner, prin. Fax 346-3011

**Herndon, Northumberland, Pop. 322**
Line Mountain SD 800/K-12
185 Line Mountain Rd 17830 570-758-2640
David Campbell, supt. Fax 758-2842
www.linemountain.com
Line Mountain HS 600/9-12
187 Line Mountain Rd 17830 570-758-2011
Jeffrey Roadcap, prin. Fax 758-1514
Line Mountain MS 5-8
187 Line Mountain Rd 17830 570-758-2011
Jeffrey Roadcap, prin.

**Hershey, Dauphin, Pop. 13,934**
Derry Township SD 3,600/K-12
PO Box 898 17033 717-534-2501
Joseph McFarland, supt. Fax 533-4357
www.hershey.k12.pa.us
Hershey HS 1,100/9-12
PO Box 898 17033 717-531-2244
Dale Reimann Ed.D., prin. Fax 534-2684
Hershey MS 900/6-8
PO Box 898 17033 717-531-2222
Erick Valentin, prin. Fax 531-2245

---

Hershey S 1,800/PK-12
PO Box 830 17033 717-520-2000
Freda Martine, prin. Fax 520-2002
M. Hershey Medical Center Coll of Med. Post-Sec.
500 University Dr 17033 717-531-8521

**Hilltown, Bucks**

---

St. Agnes-Sacred Heart MS 100/4-8
PO Box 31 18927 215-822-9174
Margaret Graham, prin. Fax 822-7942

**Holland, Bucks, Pop. 5,300**
Council Rock SD
Supt. — See Newtown
Council Rock HS South 2,000/9-12
2002 Rock Way 18966 215-944-1100
Al Funk, prin. Fax 944-1145
Holland MS 600/7-8
400 E Holland Rd 18966 215-944-2700
Daniel Greenland, prin. Fax 944-2789

---

Villa Joseph Marie HS 400/9-12
1180 Holland Rd 18966 215-357-8810
Lauren Carr, prin. Fax 357-2477

**Hollidaysburg, Blair, Pop. 5,745**
Hollidaysburg Area SD 3,200/K-12
405 Clark St 16648 814-696-4454
Dr. Robert Gildea, supt. Fax 695-2315
www.tigerwires.com
Hollidaysburg Area JHS 800/7-9
1000 Hewit St 16648 814-695-4426
Edward Barton, prin. Fax 696-2959
Hollidaysburg Area SHS 800/10-12
1500 N Montgomery St 16648 814-695-4416
Dr. Maureen Letcher, prin. Fax 696-2958

**Hollsopple, Somerset**

---

Johnstown Christian S 200/PK-12
125 Christian School Rd 15935 814-288-2588
Dr. Kathy Keafer, admin. Fax 288-1447

**Homer City, Indiana, Pop. 1,691**
Homer-Center SD 900/K-12
65 Wildcat Ln 15748 724-479-8080
Dr. Charles Koren, supt. Fax 479-3967
homercenter.org/
Homer-Center JSHS 400/7-12
70 Wildcat Ln 15748 724-479-8026
Jody Rainey, prin. Fax 479-4236

**Honesdale, Wayne, Pop. 4,431**
Wayne Highlands SD 2,900/K-12
474 Grove St 18431 570-253-4661
Gregory Frigoletto, supt. Fax 253-9409
www.waynehighlands.org
Honesdale HS 1,000/9-12
459 Terrace St 18431 570-253-2046
Diane Scarfalloto, prin. Fax 253-1502
Wayne Highlands MS 500/6-8
482 Grove St 18431 570-253-5900
Chris Pietraszewski, prin. Fax 253-5259

**Hookstown, Beaver, Pop. 144**
South Side Area SD 1,100/PK-12
4949 Route 151 15050 724-573-9581
Tamara Adams, supt. Fax 573-0414
www.sssd.k12.pa.us
South Side HS 400/9-12
4949 Route 151 15050 724-573-9581
Anthony Paull, prin. Fax 573-0449
South Side MS 300/6-8
4949 Route 151 15050 724-573-9581
Samuel Adams, prin. Fax 573-0449

**Horsham, Montgomery, Pop. 14,608**
Hatboro-Horsham SD 4,800/K-12
229 Meetinghouse Rd 19044 215-420-5000
Dr. Curtis Griffin, supt. Fax 420-5262
www.hatboro-horsham.org
Hatboro-Horsham HS 1,700/9-12
899 Horsham Rd 19044 215-420-5500
Dennis Williams, prin. Fax 420-5613
Keith Valley MS 1,200/6-8
227 Meetinghouse Rd 19044 215-420-5050
Jonathan Kircher, prin. Fax 420-5291

**Houston, Washington, Pop. 1,253**
Chartiers-Houston SD 1,200/K-12
2020 W Pike St 15342 724-746-1400
John George, supt. Fax 746-3971
www.chbucs.k12.pa.us/
Chartiers-Houston JSHS 500/7-12
2050 W Pike St 15342 724-745-3350
Philip Mary, prin. Fax 745-3495

**Houtzdale, Clearfield, Pop. 791**
Moshannon Valley SD 900/K-12
4934 Green Acre Rd 16651 814-378-7609
John Zesiger, supt. Fax 378-7100
www.movalley.org
Moshannon Valley JSHS 400/7-12
4934 Green Acre Rd 16651 814-378-7616
Fax 378-5205

**Hughesville, Lycoming, Pop. 2,101**
Area Vocational Technical School
Supt. — None
Lycoming CTC Vo/Tech
293 Cemetery St 17737 570-584-2300
Eric Butler, prin.

East Lycoming SD 1,600/PK-12
349 Cemetery St 17737 570-584-2131
Michael Pawlik, supt. Fax 584-5701
www.eastlycoming.net
Hughesville JSHS 800/7-12
349 Cemetery St 17737 570-584-5111
Ron Lorson, prin. Fax 584-5378

**Hummelstown, Dauphin, Pop. 4,481**
Lower Dauphin SD 3,800/K-12
291 E Main St 17036 717-566-5300
Dr. Sherri L. Smith, supt. Fax 566-3670
www.ldsd.org
Lower Dauphin HS 1,200/9-12
201 S Hanover St 17036 717-566-5330
Todd Neuhard, prin. Fax 566-3970
Lower Dauphin MS 900/6-8
251 Quarry Rd 17036 717-566-5310
Daniel Berra, prin. Fax 566-5383
Price S, 101 E High St 17036 Alt
Dr. David Wuestner, prin. 717-566-5326

---

Hershey Christian S 300/K-12
1525 Sand Hill Rd 17036 717-533-4900
Miles Yoder, admin. Fax 835-0256

**Hunker, Westmoreland, Pop. 283**

---

Armbrust Christian Academy 100/PK-12
7786 State Route 819 15639 724-925-3830
Susan Stoner, head sch Fax 925-2523

**Huntingdon, Huntingdon, Pop. 6,994**
Huntingdon Area SD 2,100/K-12
2400 Cassady Ave Ste 2 16652 814-643-4140
Fred Foster, supt. Fax 643-6244
www.hasd.tiu.k12.pa.us/
Huntingdon Area HS 700/9-12
2400 Cassady Ave 16652 814-643-1080
Deborah Luffy, prin. Fax 643-3800
Huntingdon Area MS 500/6-8
2500 Cassady Ave 16652 814-643-2900
Deborah Luffy, prin. Fax 643-6513

---

DuBois Business College Post-Sec.
1001 Moore St 16652 814-641-0440
Juniata College Post-Sec.
1700 Moore St 16652 814-641-3000

**Huntingdon Valley, Montgomery, Pop. 10,000**
Lower Moreland Township SD 2,100/K-12
2551 Murray Ave 19006 215-938-0270
Dr. Marykay Feeley, supt. Fax 947-6933
www.lmtsd.org
Lower Moreland HS 700/9-12
555 Red Lion Rd 19006 215-938-0220
Bill Miles, prin. Fax 947-0333
Murray Avenue MS 500/6-8
2551 Murray Ave 19006 215-938-0230
Jennifer Dilks, prin. Fax 947-3697

---

Huntingdon Valley Christian Academy 100/PK-10
1845 Byberry Rd 19006 215-947-6595

**Immaculata, Chester**

---

Immaculata University Post-Sec.
1145 King Rd 19345 610-647-4400

**Imperial, Allegheny, Pop. 2,507**
West Allegheny SD 3,300/K-12
PO Box 55 15126 724-695-3422
Dr. Jerri Lynn Lippert, supt. Fax 695-3788
www.westasd.org
West Allegheny HS 1,000/9-12
205 W Allegheny Rd 15126 724-695-5245
Daniel Smith, prin. Fax 695-8690
West Allegheny MS 800/6-8
207 W Allegheny Rd 15126 724-695-8979
Rick Smith, prin. Fax 695-8211

**Indiana, Indiana, Pop. 13,787**
Area Vocational Technical School
Supt. — None
Indiana County Technology Center Vo/Tech
441 Hamill Rd 15701 724-349-6700
Carol Fry, dir.

Indiana Area SD 2,700/PK-12
501 E Pike Rd 15701 724-463-8713
Dale Kirsch, supt. Fax 463-0868
www.iasd.cc
Indiana Area JHS 600/6-8
245 N 5th St 15701 724-463-8568
Michael Minnick, prin. Fax 463-2133
Indiana Area SHS 800/9-12
450 N 5th St 15701 724-463-8562
Wade McElheny, prin. Fax 463-9709

---

Cambria-Rowe Business College Post-Sec.
422 S 13th St 15701 724-463-0222
Indiana University of Pennsylvania Post-Sec.
1011 South Dr 15705 724-357-2100

Seeds of Faith Christian Academy 100/PK-12
640 Church St 15701 724-463-7719
Erica Parks, admin. Fax 463-8097

**Industry, Beaver, Pop. 1,815**
Western Beaver County SD
Supt. — See Midland
Western Beaver County JSHS 400/6-12
216 Engle Rd 15052 724-643-8500
David Brandon, prin. Fax 643-8504

**Irwin, Westmoreland, Pop. 3,935**
Hempfield Area SD
Supt. — See Greensburg
West Hempfield MS 500/6-8
156 Northumberland Dr 15642 724-850-2140
Aaron Steinly, prin. Fax 850-2141

**Jamestown, Mercer, Pop. 614**
Jamestown Area SD 600/K-12
PO Box 217 16134 724-932-5557
Tracy Reiser, supt. Fax 932-5632
www.jamestown.k12.pa.us
Jamestown Area JSHS 300/7-12
PO Box 217 16134 724-932-3186
Brian Keyser, prin.

**Jamison, Bucks**
Area Vocational Technical School
Supt. — None
Middle Bucks Institute of Tech Vo/Tech
2740 York Rd 18929 215-343-2480
Kathryn Strouse, hdmstr. Fax 343-8626

**Jeannette, Westmoreland, Pop. 9,284**
Jeannette CSD 1,200/K-12
800 Florida Ave 15644 724-523-5497
Matthew Hutcheson, supt. Fax 523-3289
www.jeannette.k12.pa.us/
Jeannette HS 400/9-12
800 Florida Ave 15644 724-523-5591
Patricia Rozycki, prin. Fax 523-2313

Penn-Trafford SD
Supt. — See Harrison City
Penn MS 600/6-8
11 Penn Middle Way 15644 724-744-4431
James Simpson, prin. Fax 744-1215

**Jefferson, Greene, Pop. 979**
Jefferson-Morgan SD 800/PK-12
PO Box 158 15344 724-883-2310
Donna Furnier, supt. Fax 883-4942
www.jmsd.org/
Jefferson-Morgan MSHS 400/7-12
PO Box 158 15344 724-883-2310
Joseph Orr, prin. Fax 883-3786

**Jefferson Hills, Allegheny, Pop. 9,642**
Area Vocational Technical School
Supt. — None
Steel Center for Career and Technical Ed Vo/Tech
565 N Lewis Run Rd 15025 412-469-3200
Kevin Rice, prin. Fax 469-2196

West Jefferson Hills SD 2,800/K-12
835 Old Clairton Rd 15025 412-655-8450
Dr. Michael A. Panza, supt. Fax 655-9544
www.wjhsd.net
Jefferson HS 900/9-12
310 Old Clairton Rd 15025 412-655-8610
Christopher Sefcheck, prin. Fax 655-8618
Other Schools – See Pittsburgh

**Jenkintown, Montgomery, Pop. 4,346**
Jenkintown SD 600/K-12
325 Highland Ave 19046 215-885-3722
Dr. Timothy Wade, supt. Fax 885-2090
www.jenkintown.org/
Jenkintown JSHS 300/7-12
325 Highland Ave 19046 215-884-1801
Thomas Roller, prin. Fax 885-2090

---

Abington Friends S 700/PK-12
575 Washington Ln 19046 215-886-4350
Richard Nourie, hdmstr. Fax 886-9143
Manor College Post-Sec.
700 Fox Chase Rd 19046 215-885-2360
St. Basil Academy 300/9-12
711 Fox Chase Rd 19046 215-885-3771
Gwenda Coto, prin. Fax 885-4025

**Jersey Shore, Lycoming, Pop. 4,319**
Jersey Shore Area SD 2,400/K-12
175 A and P Dr 17740 570-398-1561
Dr. Dorothy Chappel, supt. Fax 398-5089
www.jsasd.k12.pa.us
Jersey Shore Area HS 900/9-12
701 Cemetery St 17740 570-398-7170
Reed Mellinger, prin. Fax 398-5612
Jersey Shore Area MS 600/6-8
601 Thompson St 17740 570-398-7400
Laura Milarch, prin. Fax 398-5618

**Jessup, Lackawanna, Pop. 4,627**

---

LaSalle Academy 200/4-8
309 1st Ave 18434 570-489-2010
Ellen Murphy, prin. Fax 489-3887

**Jim Thorpe, Carbon, Pop. 4,724**
Area Vocational Technical School
Supt. — None
Carbon Career & Technical Institute Vo/Tech
150 W 13th St 18229 570-325-3682
David Reinbold, prin.

Jim Thorpe Area SD 2,100/K-12
410 Center Ave 18229 570-325-3691
Brian Gasper, supt. Fax 325-3699
www.jimthorpesd.org/
Jim Thorpe Area HS 600/9-12
1 Olympian Way 18229 570-325-3663
Thomas Lesisko, prin. Fax 325-8973

**Johnsonburg, Elk, Pop. 2,464**
Johnsonburg Area SD 600/PK-12
315 High School Rd 15845 814-965-2536
Dennis Crotzer, supt. Fax 965-5809
www.johnsonburgareaschooldistrict.net
Johnsonburg Area JSHS 300/7-12
315 High School Rd 15845 814-965-2556
Brock Benson, prin. Fax 965-5809

**Johnstown, Cambria, Pop. 20,140**
Area Vocational Technical School
Supt. — None
Greater Johnstown Career and Tech Center Vo/Tech
445 Schoolhouse Rd 15904 814-266-6073
John Augustine, prin. Fax 269-4394

Conemaugh Valley SD 900/PK-12
1340 William Penn Ave 15906 814-535-5005
David Lehman, supt. Fax 536-8902
www.cvk12.org/
Conemaugh Valley JSHS 400/7-12
1342 William Penn Ave 15906 814-535-5523
Shane Hazenstab, prin. Fax 536-4025

Ferndale Area SD 800/K-12
100 Dartmouth Ave 15905 814-535-1507
Carole Kakabar, supt. Fax 535-8527
www.fasdk12.org
Ferndale Area JSHS 300/7-12
600 Harlan Ave 15905 814-288-5757
Matthew Thomas, prin. Fax 288-5224

Greater Johnstown SD 3,100/PK-12
1091 Broad St 15906 814-533-5651
Dr. James Cekada, supt. Fax 533-5655
www.gjsd.net
Greater Johnstown HS 900/9-12
222 Central Ave 15902 814-533-5601
Michael Dadey, prin. Fax 533-5698
Greater Johnstown MS 600/6-8
280 Decker Ave 15906 814-533-5570
Douglas Henry, prin. Fax 533-5564

Richland SD 1,600/K-12
319 Schoolhouse Rd 15904 814-266-6063
Arnold Nadonley, supt. Fax 266-7349
www.richlandsd.com/
Richland HS 800/7-12
1 Academic Ave 15904 814-266-6081
Brandon Bailey, prin. Fax 269-9506

Westmont Hilltop SD 1,700/K-12
827 Diamond Blvd 15905 814-255-6751
Donald Irwin, supt. Fax 255-7735
www.whsd.org
Westmont Hilltop HS 600/9-12
200 Fair Oaks Dr 15905 814-255-8726
Thomas Mitchell, prin. Fax 255-2704
Westmont Hilltop MS 500/5-8
827 Diamond Blvd 15905 814-255-8704
Steve McGee, prin. Fax 255-8783

---

Bishop McCort Catholic HS 400/9-12
25 Osborne St 15905 814-536-8991
Thomas Fleming, prin. Fax 535-4118
Cambria County Christian S 100/PK-12
561 Pike Rd 15909 814-749-7406
Fax 749-7028
Cambria-Rowe Business College Post-Sec.
221 Central Ave 15902 814-536-5168
Commonwealth Technical Institute Post-Sec.
727 Goucher St 15905 814-255-8200
Conemaugh Valley Memorial Hospital Post-Sec.
1086 Franklin St 15905 814-534-9118
Greater Johnstown Area Voc Tech School Post-Sec.
445 Schoolhouse Rd 15904 814-266-6073
PA Academy of Cosmetic Arts & Sciences Post-Sec.
2445 Bedford St 15904 814-269-3444
Pennsylvania Highlands Community College Post-Sec.
101 Community College Way 15904 814-262-6400
University of Pittsburgh at Johnstown Post-Sec.
450 Schoolhouse Rd 15904 814-269-7000

**Jonestown, Lebanon, Pop. 1,873**
Northern Lebanon SD 2,400/K-12
40 Fisher Ave 17038 717-865-2117
Dr. Don Bell, supt. Fax 865-0606
www.norleb.k12.pa.us
Other Schools – See Fredericksburg

---

Blue Mountain Christian S 50/PK-12
14 Silvertown Rd 17038 717-865-9650
Greg Firestone, admin. Fax 865-4732

**Kane, McKean, Pop. 3,695**
Kane Area SD 1,200/K-12
400 W Hemlock Ave 16735 814-837-9570
Robert Gaetano, supt. Fax 837-7450
www.kasd.net
Kane Area HS 400/9-12
6965 Route 321 16735 814-837-6821
James Fryzlewicz, prin. Fax 837-6158
Kane Area MS 300/6-8
400 W Hemlock Ave 16735 814-837-6030
Todd Stanko, prin. Fax 837-9133

**Karns City, Butler, Pop. 209**
Karns City Area SD 1,500/K-12
1446 Kittanning Pike 16041 724-756-2030
Eric Ritzert, supt. Fax 756-2121
www.karnscity.k12.pa.us
Karns City JSHS 800/7-12
1446 Kittanning Pike 16041 724-756-2030
Ed Conto, prin. Fax 756-2121

**Kennett Square, Chester, Pop. 6,014**
Kennett Consolidated SD 3,900/K-12
300 E South St 19348 610-444-6600
Dr. Barry Tomasetti, supt. Fax 444-6614
kcsd.org

Kennett HS 1,300/9-12
100 E South St 19348 610-444-6620
Jeremy Hritz, prin. Fax 444-7013
Other Schools – See Landenberg

Unionville-Chadds Ford SD 4,100/K-12
740 Unionville Rd 19348 610-347-0970
Dr. John Sanville, supt. Fax 347-0976
www.ucfsd.org
Patton MS 1,000/6-8
760 Unionville Rd 19348 610-347-2000
Timothy V. Hoffman, prin. Fax 347-0421
Unionville HS 1,400/9-12
750 Unionville Rd 19348 610-347-1600
James Conley, prin. Fax 347-1890

**Kimberton, Chester**

---

Kimberton Waldorf S 300/PK-12
PO Box 350 19442 610-933-3635
Kevin Hughes, dean Fax 935-6985

**King of Prussia, Montgomery, Pop. 19,511**
Upper Merion Area SD 3,900/K-12
435 Crossfield Rd 19406 610-205-6401
Dr. John Toleno, supt. Fax 205-6433
www.umasd.org
Upper Merion HS 1,100/9-12
440 Crossfield Rd 19406 610-205-3801
Jonathan Bauer, prin. Fax 205-3993
Upper Merion MS 1,200/5-8
450 Keebler Rd 19406 610-205-8801
Dr. Karen Geller, prin. Fax 205-8999

---

Achieve Test Prep Post-Sec.
1150 1st Ave 19406 267-687-0333
Cortiva Institute - King of Prussia Post-Sec.
211 S Gulph Rd 19406 484-690-1400
DeVry University Post-Sec.
150 Allendale Rd Ste 3250 19406 610-205-3130
Palmer Theological Seminary Post-Sec.
588 N Gulph Rd 19406 610-896-5000

**Kingsley, Susquehanna**
Mountain View SD 1,100/K-12
11748 State Route 106 18826 570-434-2180
Karen Voigt, supt. Fax 434-2404
www.mvsd.net
Mountain View JSHS 600/7-12
11748 State Route 106 18826 570-434-2501
Robert Presley, prin. Fax 434-9582

**Kingston, Luzerne, Pop. 12,983**
Area Vocational Technical School
Supt. — None
West Side CTC, 75 Evans St 18704 Vo/Tech
Dr. Thomas Viviano, dir. 570-288-8493

Wyoming Valley West SD 4,300/K-12
450 N Maple Ave 18704 570-288-6551
Charles R. Suppon, supt. Fax 714-6948
www.wvwsd.org/
Wyoming Valley West MS 1,200/6-8
201 Chester St 18704 570-287-2131
Deborah Troy, prin. Fax 287-6343
Other Schools – See Plymouth

---

Wyoming Seminary Upper S 400/9-12
201 N Sprague Ave 18704 570-270-2100
Kevin Rea, pres. Fax 270-2199

**Kintnersville, Bucks**
Palisades SD 1,800/K-12
39 Thomas Free Dr 18930 610-847-5131
Dr. Bridget O'Connell, supt. Fax 847-8116
www.palisadessd.org
Palisades HS 700/9-12
35 Church Hill Rd 18930 610-847-5131
Richard Heffernan, prin. Fax 847-2562
Palisades MS 400/6-8
4710 Durham Rd 18930 610-847-5131
Zachary Fuller, prin. Fax 847-2691

**Kinzers, Lancaster**
Pequea Valley SD 1,700/K-12
PO Box 130 17535 717-768-5530
Erik Orndorff, supt. Fax 768-7176
www.pequeavalley.org
Pequea Valley HS 600/9-12
PO Box 287 17535 717-768-5500
Arlen Mummau, prin. Fax 768-5523
Pequea Valley IS 400/7-8
PO Box 257 17535 717-768-5535
Sharon Ray, prin. Fax 768-5656

**Kittanning, Armstrong, Pop. 3,989**
Armstrong SD 5,000/K-12
181 Heritage Park Dr Ste 2 16201 724-548-7200
Chris DeVivo, supt. Fax 548-7201
www.asd.k12.pa.us
Armstrong JSHS 7-12
300 Buffington Dr 16201 724-548-7600
James Rummel, prin.
Other Schools – See Rural Valley

---

Armstrong County Memorial Hospital Post-Sec.
1 Nolte Dr 16201 724-543-8404
Grace Christian S 100/PK-12
215 Arthur St 16201 724-543-4019
Sandy Hankinson, prin. Fax 545-6738
Kittanning Beauty School Post-Sec.
120 Market St 16201 800-833-4247

**Knox, Clarion, Pop. 1,139**
Keystone SD 1,100/K-12
451 Huston Ave 16232 814-797-5921
Shawn Algoe, supt. Fax 797-2382
www.keyknox.com
Keystone JSHS 500/7-12
700 Beatty Ave 16232 814-797-1261
Brad Wagner, prin. Fax 797-2868

**Kutztown, Berks, Pop. 4,969**
Kutztown Area SD 1,400/K-12
251 Long Lane Rd 19530 610-683-7361
Katherine Metrick, supt. Fax 683-7230
www.kasd.org
Kutztown Area HS 500/9-12
50 Trexler Ave 19530 610-683-7346
Fax 894-4801
Kutztown Area MS 300/6-8
10 Deisher Ln 19530 610-683-3575
James Brown, prin. Fax 683-5460

---

Kutztown University of Pennsylvania Post-Sec.
15200 Kutztown Rd 19530 610-683-4000

**Lake Ariel, Wayne**
Western Wayne SD 1,600/PK-12
1970 Easton Tpke Bldg C 18436 800-321-9973
Joseph Adams, supt. Fax 341-1221
www.westernwayne.org
Western Wayne HS 700/9-12
1970 Easton Tpke Bldg A 18436 800-321-9973
Paul Blaum, prin.
Western Wayne MS 500/6-8
1970 Easton Tpke Bldg B 18436 800-321-9973
Kristin Donohue, prin.

---

Canaan Christian Academy 200/PK-12
30 Hemlock Rd 18436 570-937-4848

**Lancaster, Lancaster, Pop. 57,600**
Conestoga Valley SD 4,200/K-12
2110 Horseshoe Rd 17601 717-397-2421
Dr. Gerald Huesken, supt. Fax 397-0442
www.conestogavalley.org
Conestoga Valley HS 1,400/9-12
2110 Horseshoe Rd 17601 717-397-5231
Michael Thornton, prin. Fax 397-8841
Conestoga Valley MS 700/7-8
500 Mount Sidney Rd 17602 717-397-1294
Baron Jones, prin. Fax 397-4404

Hempfield SD
Supt. — See Landisville
Centerville MS 600/7-8
865 Centerville Rd 17601 717-898-5580
James Dague, prin. Fax 618-0999

Lampeter-Strasburg SD 2,800/K-12
1600 Book Rd 17602 717-464-3311
Dr. Kevin Peart Ed.D., supt. Fax 464-4699
www.l-spioneers.org
Lampeter-Strasburg HS 1,000/9-12
1600 Book Rd 17602 717-464-3311
Eric Spencer, prin. Fax 509-0485
Meylin MS 700/6-8
1600 Book Rd 17602 717-464-3311
Jamie Raum, prin. Fax 509-0289

Lancaster SD 10,400/K-12
251 S Prince St 17603 717-299-2700
Dr. Stephen Iovino, supt. Fax 339-6844
www.lancaster.k12.pa.us
Hand MS 500/6-8
431 S Ann St 17602 717-291-6161
Mark Simms, prin. Fax 391-8600
Lincoln MS 600/6-8
1001 Lehigh Ave 17602 717-291-6187
Josh Keene, prin. Fax 399-6408
McCaskey East HS 9-12
1051 Lehigh Ave 17602 717-291-6172
Bill Jimenez, prin. Fax 391-8601
McCaskey HS 2,700/9-12
445 N Reservoir St 17602 717-291-6211
Bill Jimenez, prin. Fax 390-2567
Phoenix Academy 300/Alt
630 Rockland St 17602 717-735-7860
Aura Beck, prin. Fax 399-3427
Reynolds MS 500/6-8
605 W Walnut St 17603 717-291-6257
Stephen Sohonyay, prin. Fax 396-6823
Wheatland MS 600/6-8
919 Hamilton Park Dr 17603 717-291-6285
Donald Trost, prin. Fax 399-6411

Manheim Township SD 5,400/K-12
PO Box 5134 17606 717-569-8231
John Nodecker, supt. Fax 569-3729
www.mtwp.net
Manheim Township HS 1,800/9-12
PO Box 5134 17606 717-560-3097
Deborah Mitchell, prin. Fax 569-2806
Manheim Township MS 1,000/7-8
PO Box 5134 17606 717-560-3111
Karen Evans, prin. Fax 569-1670

Penn Manor SD 5,100/K-12
2950 Charlestown Rd 17603 717-872-9500
Dr. Michael Leichliter, supt. Fax 872-9505
www.pennmanor.net
Manor MS 500/7-8
2950 Charlestown Rd 17603 717-872-9510
Dr. Dana Edwards, prin. Fax 872-9505
Other Schools – See Millersville, Pequea

---

Consolidated School of Business Post-Sec.
2124 Ambassador Cir 17603 717-394-6211
Empire Beauty School Post-Sec.
1801 Columbia Ave 17603 717-394-8561
Franklin & Marshall College Post-Sec.
PO Box 3003 17604 717-291-3911
Lancaster Bible College Post-Sec.
901 Eden Rd 17601 717-569-7071
Lancaster Country Day S 600/PK-12
725 Hamilton Rd 17603 717-392-2916
Stephen Lisk, head sch Fax 392-0425
Lancaster Co. Christian S - Leola Campus 300/PK-12
2390 New Holland Pike 17601 717-556-0711
Becky Sprenkle, prin. Fax 656-4868
Lancaster General College of Nursing Post-Sec.
410 N Lime St 17602 800-622-5443
Lancaster HS 800/9-12
650 Juliette Ave 17601 717-509-0315
Terry Klugh, prin. Fax 509-0312
Lancaster Mennonite HS 800/6-12
2176 Lincoln Hwy E 17602 717-299-0436
J. Richard Thomas, supt. Fax 299-0823
Lancaster School of Cosmetology Post-Sec.
50 Ranck Ave 17602 717-299-0200
Lancaster Theological Seminary Post-Sec.
555 W James St 17603 717-393-0654
Pennsylvania College of Art and Design Post-Sec.
PO Box 59 17608 717-396-7833
Thaddeus Stevens College of Technology Post-Sec.
750 E King St 17602 717-299-7730
YTI Career Institute Post-Sec.
3050 Hempland Rd 17601 717-295-1100

**Landenberg, Chester**
Kennett Consolidated SD
Supt. — See Kennett Square
Kennett MS, 195 Sunny Dell Rd 19350 1,000/6-8
Lorenzo DeAngelis, prin. 610-268-5800

**Landisville, Lancaster, Pop. 1,881**
Hempfield SD 6,900/K-12
200 Church St 17538 717-898-5564
Dr. Brenda Becker, supt. Fax 898-5628
www.hempfieldsd.org
Hempfield HS 2,200/9-12
200 Stanley Ave 17538 717-898-5510
Dr. Wilbur Stout, prin. Fax 618-1210
Landisville Education Center Alt
220 Church St 17538 717-406-3400
Brendan Cregan, prin. Fax 618-1992
Landisville MS 500/7-8
340 Mumma Dr 17538 717-898-5607
Douglas Dandridge, prin. Fax 618-0871
Other Schools – See Lancaster

**Langhorne, Bucks, Pop. 1,596**
Neshaminy SD 8,500/K-12
2001 Old Lincoln Hwy 19047 215-809-6500
Dr. David Baugh Ed.D., supt. Fax 809-6502
www.neshaminy.k12.pa.us
Maple Point MS 1,000/6-8
2250 Langhorne Yardley Rd 19047 215-809-6230
Matthew Sokol, prin.
Neshaminy HS 2,700/9-12
2001 Old Lincoln Hwy 19047 215-809-6102
Dr. Rob McGee, prin.
Other Schools – See Feasterville, Levittown

---

Cairn University Post-Sec.
200 Manor Ave 19047 215-752-5800
Woods Services Post-Sec.
PO Box 36 19047 800-782-3646

**Lansdale, Montgomery, Pop. 15,885**
Area Vocational Technical School
Supt. — None
North Montco Tech Career Center Vo/Tech
1265 Sumneytown Pike 19446 215-368-1177
Michael Lucas, dir.

North Penn SD 12,600/K-12
401 E Hancock St 19446 215-368-0400
Dr. Curtis Dietrich, supt. Fax 368-3161
www.npenn.org
North Penn HS 3,100/10-12
1340 S Valley Forge Rd 19446 215-368-9800
Burton Hynes, prin. Fax 855-0632
Penndale MS 1,400/7-9
400 Penn St 19446 215-368-2700
Dr. Sean O'Sullivan, prin. Fax 368-6817
Other Schools – See Hatfield, North Wales

---

Calvary Baptist S 400/PK-12
1380 S Valley Forge Rd 19446 215-368-1100
Calvary Baptist Theological Seminary Post-Sec.
1380 S Valley Forge Rd 19446 215-368-7538
Dock Mennonite HS 400/9-12
1000 Forty Foot Rd 19446 215-362-2675
Dr. Conrad J. Swartzentruber, supt. Fax 362-2943
Lansdale Catholic HS 800/9-12
700 Lansdale Ave 19446 215-362-6160
Rita McGovern, prin. Fax 362-5746
Lansdale School of Cosmetology Post-Sec.
215 W Main St 19446 215-362-2322

**Lansdowne, Delaware, Pop. 10,265**
William Penn SD 5,200/K-12
100 Green Ave 19050 610-284-8000
Joseph Bruni, supt. Fax 284-8054
www.williampennsd.org
Penn Wood HS Green Ave Campus 700/11-12
100 Green Ave 19050 610-284-8080
Dr. D. Brandon Cooley, prin. Fax 284-2141
Other Schools – See Darby, Yeadon

**Lansford, Carbon, Pop. 3,876**
Panther Valley SD 1,700/K-12
1 Panther Way 18232 570-645-4248
Dennis Kergick, supt. Fax 645-6232
www.panthervalley.org/
Panther Valley JSHS 400/7-12
912 Coal Region Way 18232 570-645-2171
Joseph Gunnels, prin. Fax 645-2507

**La Plume, Lackawanna**

---

Keystone College Post-Sec.
PO Box 50 18440 570-945-8000

**Laporte, Sullivan, Pop. 316**
Sullivan County SD 500/K-12
PO Box 240 18626 570-946-8200
Patricia A. Cross, supt. Fax 946-8210
www.sulcosd.k12.pa.us
Sullivan County JSHS 300/7-12
PO Box 98 18626 570-946-7001
Edward J. Pietroski, prin. Fax 946-5070

**Latrobe, Westmoreland, Pop. 8,261**
Area Vocational Technical School
Supt. — None
Eastern Westmoreland CTC Vo/Tech
4904 State Route 982 15650 724-539-9788
Marie Bowers, dir. Fax 539-1907

Greater Latrobe SD 4,200/K-12
1816 Lincoln Ave 15650 724-539-4200
Judith Swigart, supt. Fax 539-4202
www.glsd.us
Greater Latrobe JHS 1,000/7-9
130 High School Rd 15650 724-539-4265
Chad Krehlik, prin. Fax 539-4223
Greater Latrobe SHS 1,000/10-12
131 High School Rd 15650 724-539-4225
Steven LoCascio, prin. Fax 539-4295

---

Latrobe Area Hospital Post-Sec.
101 W 2nd Ave 15650 724-537-1001
St. Vincent College Post-Sec.
300 Fraser Purchase Rd 15650 724-532-6600
St. Vincent Seminary Post-Sec.
300 Fraser Purchase Rd 15650 724-805-2592

**Laureldale, Berks, Pop. 3,857**
Muhlenberg SD 3,500/K-12
801 E Bellevue Ave 19605 610-921-8000
Dr. Joseph Macharola, supt. Fax 921-8076
www.muhlsdk12.org
Muhlenberg HS 900/10-12
400 Sharp Ave 19605 610-921-8078
Michael Mish, prin. Fax 921-7925
Muhlenberg MS 900/7-9
801 E Bellevue Ave 19605 610-921-8034
Kevin Vanino, prin. Fax 921-8038

**Lebanon, Lebanon, Pop. 25,113**
Area Vocational Technical School
Supt. — None
Lebanon County CTC Vo/Tech
833 Metro Dr 17042 717-273-8551
George Custer, dir. Fax 273-0534

Cornwall-Lebanon SD 4,700/K-12
105 E Evergreen Rd 17042 717-272-2031
Dr. Philip Domencic, supt. Fax 274-2786
www.clsd.k12.pa.us
Cedar Crest HS 1,600/9-12
115 E Evergreen Rd 17042 717-272-2033
Nicole Malinoski, prin. Fax 389-1823
Cedar Crest MS 1,100/6-8
101 E Evergreen Rd 17042 717-272-2032
Dean Bozman, prin. Fax 389-1856

Lebanon SD 4,600/PK-12
1000 S 8th St 17042 717-273-9391
Dr. Marianne Bartley, supt. Fax 270-6778
www.lebanon.k12.pa.us
Lebanon HS 1,200/9-12
1000 S 8th St 17042 717-273-9391
William Giovino, prin. Fax 270-6778
Lebanon MS 900/6-8
350 N 8th St 17046 717-273-9391
Dawn Connelly, prin. Fax 270-6859

---

Empire Beauty School Post-Sec.
1776 Quentin Rd 17042 717-272-3323
Lebanon Catholic S 300/PK-12
1400 Chestnut St 17042 717-273-3731
Rose Kury, prin. Fax 274-5167
Lebanon County Career School Post-Sec.
18 E Weidman St 17046 717-274-8804
New Covenant Christian S 200/PK-12
452 Ebenezer Rd 17046 717-274-2423
James Hubbard, prin. Fax 274-9830

**Leechburg, Armstrong, Pop. 2,128**
Kiski Area SD 3,500/K-12
250 Hyde Park Rd 15656 724-845-2022
Dr. Timothy Scott, supt. Fax 842-0444
www.kiskiarea.com
Kiski Area HS 1,300/9-12
250 Hyde Park Rd 15656 724-845-8181
Chad Roland, prin. Fax 842-0403
Kiski Area IS 700/7-8
260 Hyde Park Rd 15656 724-845-2219
Jason Lohr, prin. Fax 845-3208

Leechburg Area SD 800/K-12
210 Penn Ave 15656 724-842-9681
Ian Magness M.Ed., supt. Fax 845-2241
www.leechburg.k12.pa.us
Leechburg Area HS 200/9-12
215 1st St 15656 724-842-0571
Matthew Kruluts B.S., prin. Fax 845-4761
Leechburg Area JHS 200/7-8
215 1st St 15656 724-842-0571
Matthew Kruluts B.S., prin. Fax 845-4761

**Leesport, Berks, Pop. 1,904**
Area Vocational Technical School
Supt. — None
Berks CTC - West Vo/Tech
1057 County Road 19533 610-374-4073
Christian Hansen, prin. Fax 987-6106

Schuylkill Valley SD 1,900/K-12
929 Lakeshore Dr 19533 610-916-0957
Dr. Warren Mata, supt. Fax 926-3960
www.schuylkillvalley.org/
Schuylkill Valley HS 600/9-12
929 Lakeshore Dr 19533 610-926-1706
Patrick Sasse, prin. Fax 926-8341
Schuylkill Valley MS 600/5-8
114 Ontelaunee Dr 19533 610-926-7111
Michael Mitchell, prin. Fax 926-3321

**Leetsdale, Allegheny, Pop. 1,172**
Quaker Valley SD 1,900/K-12
100 Leetsdale Industrial Dr 15056 412-749-3600
Dr. Heidi Ondek, supt. Fax 749-3601
www.qvsd.org
Quaker Valley HS 700/9-12
625 Beaver St 15056 412-749-6020
Deborah Riccobelli, prin. Fax 749-1226
Other Schools – See Sewickley

**Lehighton, Carbon, Pop. 5,438**
Lehighton Area SD 2,300/K-12
1000 Union St 18235 610-377-4490
Jonathan J. Cleaver, supt. Fax 577-0035
www.lehighton.org/
Lehighton Area HS 700/9-12
1 Indian Ln 18235 610-377-6180
Craig Reichl, prin. Fax 377-1852
Lehighton Area MS 700/5-8
301 Beaver Run Rd 18235 610-377-6535
Mark McGalla Ph.D., prin. Fax 377-6503

**Lehman, Luzerne**
Lake-Lehman SD
Supt. — See Dallas
Lake-Lehman JSHS 1,000/7-12
PO Box 38 18627 570-675-7458
Douglas Klopp, prin. Fax 675-2951

---

Penn State Wilkes-Barre Post-Sec.
PO Box PSU 18627 570-675-2171

**Lemont Furnace, Fayette, Pop. 807**

---

Penn State Fayette Eberly Campus Post-Sec.
2201 University Dr 15456 724-430-4100

**Leola, Lancaster, Pop. 7,126**

---

Veritas Academy 200/PK-12
26 Hillcrest Ave 17540 717-556-0690

**Lester, Delaware**

---

All-State Career School Post-Sec.
501 Seminole St 19029 610-521-1818

**Levittown, Bucks, Pop. 52,008**
Bristol Township SD 6,200/K-12
6401 Mill Creek Rd 19057 215-943-3200
Dr. Melanie Gehrens, supt. Fax 949-2210
www.btsd.us/
Truman HS 1,600/9-12
3001 Green Ln 19057 215-547-3000
James Moore, prin. Fax 547-4802
Other Schools – See Bristol, Fairless Hills

Neshaminy SD
Supt. — See Langhorne
Sandburg MS 600/6-8
30 Harmony Rd 19056 215-809-6220
Dawn Kelly, prin. Fax 809-6701

---

ITT Technical Institute Post-Sec.
311 Veterans Hwy Ste 100E 19056 215-702-3600
Levittown Beauty Academy Post-Sec.
8919 New Falls Rd 19054 215-943-0298

**Lewisberry, York, Pop. 357**
West Shore SD 7,300/K-12
507 Fishing Creek Rd 17339 717-938-9577
Dr. Todd Stoltz, supt. Fax 938-2779
www.wssd.k12.pa.us
Crossroads MS 600/6-8
535 Fishing Creek Rd 17339 717-932-1295
Melissa Resek, prin. Fax 938-3599
Red Land HS 1,200/9-12
560 Fishing Creek Rd 17339 717-938-6561
Holly Sayre, prin. Fax 938-0886
Other Schools – See Camp Hill, New Cumberland

**Lewisburg, Union, Pop. 5,667**
Lewisburg Area SD 1,900/K-12
1951 Washington Ave 17837 570-523-3220
Dr. Mark DiRocco, supt. Fax 522-3278
www.dragon.k12.pa.us
Eichhorn MS 400/6-8
2057 Washington Ave 17837 570-523-3220
George Drogin, prin. Fax 522-3331
Lewisburg Area HS 600/9-12
815 Market St 17837 570-523-3220
David Himes, prin. Fax 524-9484

---

Bucknell University Post-Sec.
1 Dent Dr 17837 570-577-2000

**Lewistown, Mifflin, Pop. 8,199**
Area Vocational Technical School
Supt. — None
Academy Vo/Tech
700 Pitt St 17044 717-248-3933
Daniel Potutschnig, dir. Fax 248-5148

Mifflin County SD 3,000/K-12
201 8th St 17044 717-248-0148
James Estep, supt. Fax 248-5345
www.mcsdk12.org
Mifflin County HS 500/10-12
501 6th St 17044 717-242-0240
Mark Crosson, prin. Fax 447-2600
Mifflin County JHS 900/8-9
700 Cedar St 17044 717-248-5441
Mike Zinobile, prin. Fax 242-5806

---

Mifflin-Juniata Career & Technology Ctr Post-Sec.
700 Pitt St 17044 717-248-3933

**Liberty, Tioga, Pop. 247**
Southern Tioga SD
Supt. — See Blossburg

North Penn - Liberty JSHS 200/7-12
8675 Route 414 16930 570-324-2071
Joseph Eglesia, prin. Fax 324-2313

**Ligonier, Westmoreland, Pop. 1,565**
Ligonier Valley SD 1,700/K-12
339 W Main St 15658 724-238-5696
Dr. Christine Oldham Ed.D., supt. Fax 238-7877
lvsd.k12.pa.us
Ligonier Valley HS 600/9-12
40 Springer Rd 15658 724-238-9531
Timothy Kantor, prin. Fax 238-2675
Ligonier Valley MS 400/6-8
536 Bell Street Ext 15658 724-238-6412
David Steimer, prin. Fax 238-2358

**Limerick, Montgomery**
Area Vocational Technical School
Supt. — None
Western Montgomery Career/Technology Ctr Vo/Tech
77 Gratersford Rd 19468 610-489-7272
Christopher Moritzen, dir.

**Lincoln University, Chester, Pop. 1,678**

---

Lincoln University Post-Sec.
PO Box 179 19352 484-365-8000

**Linesville, Crawford, Pop. 1,024**
Conneaut SD 1,100/K-12
219 W School Dr 16424 814-683-5900
Jarrin Sperry, supt. Fax 683-4127
www.conneautsd.org
Conneaut Area SHS 300/9-12
302 W School Dr 16424 814-683-5551
David Maskrey, prin. Fax 683-5221
Other Schools – See Conneaut Lake, Conneautville

**Lititz, Lancaster, Pop. 9,235**
Warwick SD 4,400/K-12
301 W Orange St 17543 717-626-3734
Dr. April Hershey, supt. Fax 626-3850
www.warwicksd.org/
Warwick HS 1,500/9-12
301 W Orange St 17543 717-626-3700
Ryan Axe, prin. Fax 626-6199
Warwick MS 700/7-8
401 Maple St 17543 717-626-3701
Dr. Michael Smith, prin. Fax 627-6089

---

Linden Hall 200/5-12
212 E Main St 17543 717-626-8512
Dr. Jay White, head sch Fax 627-1384
Lititz Christian S 200/PK-12
501 W Lincoln Ave 17543 717-626-9518
Rick Bernhardt, admin. Fax 626-9028
New Haven Mennonite S 100/1-12
225 Crest Rd 17543 717-626-1603

**Littlestown, Adams, Pop. 4,373**
Littlestown Area SD 2,000/K-12
162 Newark St 17340 717-359-4146
Christopher Bigger, supt. Fax 359-9617
www.lasd.k12.pa.us
Littlestown HS 700/9-12
200 E Myrtle St 17340 717-359-4146
Dr. Matthew Meakin, prin. Fax 359-9461
Maple Avenue MS 500/6-8
75 Maple Ave 17340 717-359-4146
Eric Naylor, prin. Fax 359-9617

**Lock Haven, Clinton, Pop. 9,648**

---

Lock Haven University Post-Sec.
401 N Fairview St 17745 570-484-2011

**Loretto, Cambria, Pop. 1,282**

---

St. Francis University Post-Sec.
PO Box 600 15940 814-472-3000

**Lower Burrell, Westmoreland, Pop. 11,648**
Burrell SD 1,900/K-12
1021 Puckety Church Rd 15068 724-334-1406
Shannon Wagner, supt. Fax 334-1429
www.burrell.k12.pa.us
Burrell HS 600/9-12
1021 Puckety Church Rd 15068 724-334-1403
Dr. John Boylan, prin. Fax 334-1420
Huston MS 400/6-8
1020 Puckety Church Rd 15068 724-334-1443
Brian Ferra, prin. Fax 334-1434

---

Newport Business Institute Post-Sec.
945 Greensburg Rd 15068 724-339-7542

**Loysburg, Bedford**
Northern Bedford County SD 1,100/PK-12
152 NBC Dr 16659 814-766-2221
Todd B. Beatty, supt. Fax 766-3772
www.nbcsd.org/
Northern Bedford County HS 300/9-12
152 NBC Dr 16659 814-766-2221
David Burkett, prin. Fax 766-3772
Northern Bedford County MS 200/6-8
152 NBC Dr 16659 814-766-2221
Wayne Sherlock, prin. Fax 766-3772

**Lykens, Dauphin, Pop. 1,762**
Upper Dauphin Area SD 1,200/K-12
5668 State Route 209 17048 717-362-8134
Evan Williams, supt. Fax 362-3050
www.udasd.org/
Upper Dauphin Area MS 400/5-8
5668 State Route 209 17048 717-362-8177
Jared Shade, prin. Fax 362-6567
Other Schools – See Elizabethville

**Mc Alisterville, Juniata, Pop. 971**
Juniata County SD
Supt. — See Mifflintown

East Juniata JSHS 500/7-12
32944 Route 35 N 17049 717-463-2111
Benjamin Fausey, prin. Fax 463-3268

Juniata Mennonite S 200/K-12
289 Leonard Hill Rd 17049 717-463-2898
Tom Getz, admin. Fax 463-0134

**Mc Clellandtown, Fayette**
Albert Gallatin Area SD
Supt. — See Uniontown
Gallatin North MS 500/6-8
113 College Ave 15458 724-737-5423
Randy Wilson, prin. Fax 737-5312

**Mc Connellsburg, Fulton, Pop. 1,183**
Area Vocational Technical School
Supt. — None
Fulton County AVTS Vo/Tech
145 E Cherry St 17233 717-485-5813
Tony Payne, dir.

Central Fulton SD 1,000/PK-12
151 E Cherry St 17233 717-485-3183
Dixie Paruch, supt. Fax 485-5984
www.cfsd.info
Mc Connellsburg HS 200/9-12
151 E Cherry St 17233 717-485-3195
Erich May, prin. Fax 485-0175
Mc Connellsburg MS 200/6-8
151 E Cherry St 17233 717-485-3195
Erich May, prin. Fax 485-0175

**Mc Donald, Washington, Pop. 2,125**
Fort Cherry SD 1,100/K-12
110 Fort Cherry Rd 15057 724-796-1551
Dr. Jill Jacoby, supt. Fax 796-0065
www.fortcherry.org
Fort Cherry HS 500/9-12
110 Fort Cherry Rd 15057 724-796-1551
Robert N. Motte, prin. Fax 356-2769
Fort Cherry JHS 100/7-8
110 Fort Cherry Rd 15057 724-796-1551
Daniel Mayer, prin. Fax 356-2769

South Fayette Township SD 2,600/K-12
3680 Old Oakdale Rd 15057 412-221-4542
Dr. Bille Rondinelli, supt. Fax 693-2883
www.southfayette.org
South Fayette Township HS 700/9-12
3640 Old Oakdale Rd 15057 412-221-4542
Scott Milburn, prin. Fax 693-9843
South Fayette Township MS 600/6-8
3700 Old Oakdale Rd 15057 412-221-4542
David Deramo, prin. Fax 693-0860

**Mc Keesport, Allegheny, Pop. 18,886**
Area Vocational Technical School
Supt. — None
McKeesport Area Tech Center Vo/Tech
1960 Eden Park Blvd, 412-664-3664
Dr. Rula Skezas, dir. Fax 664-3784

McKeesport Area SD 3,000/K-12
3590 Oneil Blvd, 412-664-3610
Dr. Rula Skezas, supt. Fax 664-3638
www.mckasd.net
Founders Hall MS 600/7-8
3600 Oneil Blvd, 412-664-3690
Paul Sebelia, prin. Fax 664-3768
McKeesport Area HS 1,200/9-12
1960 Eden Park Blvd, 412-664-3650
Thomas Bauman, prin. Fax 664-3787

South Allegheny SD 1,600/PK-12
2743 Washington Blvd, 412-675-3070
Wayne Gdovic, supt. Fax 672-2836
www.southallegheny.org
South Allegheny MSHS 500/7-12
2743 Washington Blvd, 412-675-3070
Hal Minford, prin. Fax 673-4903

Penn State Greater Allegheny Post-Sec.
4000 University Dr 15131 412-675-9000
Serra Catholic HS 400/9-12
200 Hershey Dr, 412-751-2020
Timothy Chirdon, prin. Fax 751-3488

**Mc Kees Rocks, Allegheny, Pop. 5,853**
Montour SD 2,300/K-12
225 Clever Rd 15136 412-490-6500
Michael Ghilani, supt. Fax 788-1196
www.montourschools.com
Montour HS 1,000/9-12
223 Clever Rd 15136 412-490-6500
Todd Price, prin. Fax 494-9747
Other Schools – See Coraopolis

Sto-Rox SD 1,400/K-12
600 Russellwood Ave 15136 412-771-3213
Terry DeCarbo, supt. Fax 771-5205
www.srsd.k12.pa.us
Sto-Rox HS 400/9-12
1105 Valley St 15136 412-771-3213
Tim Beck, prin. Fax 771-8395
Sto-Rox MS 300/6-8
298 Ewing Rd 15136 412-331-2170
Maurice Wigley, prin. Fax 771-3848

Ohio Valley General Hospital Post-Sec.
25 Heckel Rd 15136 412-777-6207
Robinson Township Christian S 100/PK-12
77 Phillips Ln 15136 412-787-5919
Arthur Broadwick, prin. Fax 787-1558

**Mc Murray, Washington, Pop. 4,622**
Peters Township SD 4,400/K-12
631 E McMurray Rd 15317 724-941-6251
Dr. Jeannine French, supt. Fax 941-6565
www.ptsd.k12.pa.us
Peters Township HS 1,500/9-12
264 E McMurray Rd 15317 724-941-6250
Lori Pavlik, prin. Fax 942-0915
Peters Township MS 700/7-8
625 E McMurray Rd 15317 724-941-2688
Adam Sikorski, prin. Fax 941-1426

**Mc Sherrystown, Adams, Pop. 3,006**

Delone Catholic HS 500/9-12
140 S Oxford Ave 17344 717-637-5969
Dr. Maureen Thiec, prin. Fax 637-0442

**Macungie, Lehigh, Pop. 3,024**
East Penn SD
Supt. — See Emmaus
Eyer MS, 5616 Buckeye Rd 18062 900/6-8
Michael Kelly, prin. 610-965-1600
Lower Macungie MS 1,100/6-8
6299 Lower Macungie Rd 18062 610-395-8593
Suzanne Vincent, prin. Fax 398-4385

Salem Christian S 200/PK-12
8031 Salem Bible Church Rd 18062 610-966-5823
Mark Stanton, head sch Fax 965-8368

**Mahanoy City, Schuylkill, Pop. 4,109**
Mahanoy Area SD 1,000/K-12
1 Golden Bear Dr 17948 570-773-3443
Dr. Joie Green, supt. Fax 773-2913
www.mabears.net
Mahanoy Area HS 300/9-12
1 Golden Bear Dr 17948 570-773-3443
Thomas Smith, prin. Fax 773-4020
Mahanoy Area MS 300/5-8
1 Golden Bear Dr 17948 570-773-3443
Michael Heater, prin. Fax 773-4034

**Malvern, Chester, Pop. 2,955**
Great Valley SD 4,000/K-12
47 Church Rd 19355 610-889-2100
Dr. Regina Palubinsky, supt. Fax 889-2120
www.gvsd.org
Great Valley HS 1,300/9-12
225 Phoenixville Pike 19355 610-889-1900
Michael Flick, prin. Fax 695-8901
Great Valley MS 1,000/6-8
255 Phoenixville Pike 19355 610-644-6440
Dr. Edward Souders, prin. Fax 889-1166

Malvern Prep S 600/6-12
418 S Warren Ave 19355 484-595-1100
Christian Talbot, head sch Fax 595-1124
Penn State Great Valley Grad Prof Stds Post-Sec.
30 E Swedesford Rd 19355 610-648-3200
Phelps S 100/6-12
583 Sugartown Rd 19355 610-644-1754
Daniel Knopp, head sch Fax 644-6679
Villa Maria Academy 400/9-12
370 Old Lincoln Hwy 19355 610-644-2551
Sr. Regina Ryan, prin. Fax 644-2866

**Manchester, York, Pop. 2,703**
Northeastern York SD 3,800/K-12
41 Harding St 17345 717-266-3667
Dr. Shawn Minnich, supt. Fax 266-5792
www.nesd.k12.pa.us
Northeastern HS 1,000/9-12
300 High St 17345 717-266-3644
Mathew Gay, prin. Fax 266-0616
Other Schools – See Mount Wolf

**Manheim, Lancaster, Pop. 4,777**
Manheim Central SD 2,400/K-12
71 N Hazel St 17545 717-664-8540
Dr. Norman Hatten, supt. Fax 664-8539
www.manheimcentral.org
Manheim Central HS 900/9-12
400 Adele Ave 17545 717-664-8400
Jeffrey Hughes, prin. Fax 664-8420
Manheim Central MS 500/7-8
261 White Oak Rd 17545 717-664-1700
Scott Richardson, prin. Fax 664-1859

**Mansfield, Tioga, Pop. 3,545**
Southern Tioga SD
Supt. — See Blossburg
North Penn - Mansfield JSHS 400/7-12
73 W Wellsboro St 16933 570-662-2674
Bill David, prin. Fax 662-2808

Mansfield University of Pennsylvania Post-Sec.
71 S Academy St 16933 570-662-4000
New Covenant Academy 200/PK-12
310 Extension St 16933 570-662-2996
Brian Barden, hdmstr. Fax 662-0272

**Maple Glen, Montgomery, Pop. 6,682**
Upper Dublin SD 4,200/K-12
1580 Fort Washington Ave 19002 215-643-8800
Dr. Deborah Wheeler, supt. Fax 643-8808
www.udsd.org
Other Schools – See Dresher, Fort Washington

**Marienville, Forest, Pop. 3,126**
Forest Area SD
Supt. — See Tionesta
East Forest JSHS 100/7-12
120 W Birch St 16239 814-927-6688
Debra Arner, prin. Fax 927-8452

**Marion Center, Indiana, Pop. 450**
Marion Center Area SD 1,400/PK-12
PO Box 156 15759 724-397-5551
Frank Garritano Ed.D., supt. Fax 397-9144
www.mcasd.net/
Marion Center Area JSHS 700/7-12
PO Box 209 15759 724-397-5551
Matt Jioio, prin. Fax 397-9162

**Markleysburg, Fayette, Pop. 283**
Uniontown Area SD
Supt. — See Uniontown
McMullen MS 200/6-8
4773 National Pike 15459 724-329-8811
Tracy Holesapple, prin. Fax 329-4696

**Mar Lin, Schuylkill, Pop. 649**
Area Vocational Technical School
Supt. — None
Schuylkill Technology Center - South Vo/Tech
PO Box 110 17951 570-544-4748
Stacey Minahan, admin. Fax 544-3895

**Mars, Butler, Pop. 1,685**
Mars Area SD 3,200/K-12
545 Route 228 16046 724-625-1518
Dr. Wesley Shipley, supt. Fax 625-1060
www.marsk12.org
Mars Area HS 1,000/9-12
520 Route 228 16046 724-625-1581
Todd Kolson, prin. Fax 625-4541
Mars Area MS 500/7-8
1775 Three Degree Rd 16046 724-625-3145
Dale Sleva, prin. Fax 625-2147

**Martinsburg, Blair, Pop. 1,949**
Spring Cove SD
Supt. — See Roaring Spring
Central HS 600/9-12
718 Central High Rd 16662 814-793-2111
David Crumrine, prin. Fax 793-4942

**Meadville, Crawford, Pop. 13,058**
Area Vocational Technical School
Supt. — None
Crawford County CTC Vo/Tech
860 Thurston Rd 16335 814-724-6024
Kevin Sprong, dir. Fax 337-0602

Crawford Central SD 3,900/K-12
11280 Mercer Pike 16335 814-724-3960
Thomas Washington, supt. Fax 333-8731
www.craw.org
Meadville Area HS 900/9-12
930 North St 16335 814-336-1121
John Higgins, prin. Fax 337-1486
Meadville Area MS 400/7-8
974 North St 16335 814-333-1188
Scott Lynch, prin. Fax 333-2799
Other Schools – See Cochranton

Allegheny College Post-Sec.
520 N Main St 16335 814-332-3100
Calvary Baptist Christian Academy 200/PK-12
543 Randolph St 16335 814-724-6606
Daryl Van Norman, admin. Fax 337-4357
Laurel Technical Institute Post-Sec.
847 N Main St Ste 204 16335 814-724-0700
Precision Manufacturing Institute Post-Sec.
764 Bessemer St 16335 814-333-2415

**Mechanicsburg, Cumberland, Pop. 8,802**
Area Vocational Technical School
Supt. — None
Cumberland-Perry AVTS Vo/Tech
110 Old Willow Mill Rd 17050 717-697-0354
Justin Bruhn, dir. Fax 697-0592

Cumberland Valley SD 7,800/K-12
6746 Carlisle Pike 17050 717-697-8261
Frederick Withum, supt. Fax 506-3302
www.cvschools.org
Cumberland Valley HS 2,500/9-12
6746 Carlisle Pike 17050 717-766-0217
Judy Baumgardner, prin. Fax 506-3777
Eagle View MS 900/6-8
6746 Carlisle Pike 17050 717-766-0217
John Gallagher, prin. Fax 506-3806
Good Hope MS 1,000/6-8
451 Skyport Rd 17050 717-761-1865
Jeff Hosenfeld, prin. Fax 761-5910

Mechanicsburg Area SD 3,700/K-12
100 E Elmwood Ave 17055 717-691-4500
Mark K. Leidy Ed.D., supt. Fax 691-3438
www.mbgsd.org
Mechanicsburg Area HS 1,200/9-12
500 S Broad St 17055 717-691-4530
David R. Harris, prin. Fax 691-7632
Mechanicsburg MS 900/6-8
1750 S Market St 17055 717-691-4560
Joel A. Yohn, prin. Fax 791-7977

Faith Tabernacle S 200/1-12
1410 Good Hope Rd 17050 717-975-0641
Messiah College Post-Sec.
1 College Ave 17055 717-766-2511

**Media, Delaware, Pop. 5,231**
Rose Tree Media SD 3,800/K-12
308 N Olive St 19063 610-627-6000
James Wigo, supt. Fax 891-0959
www.rtmsd.org
Penncrest HS 1,300/9-12
134 Barren Rd 19063 610-627-6200
Richard Gregg, prin. Fax 891-0898
Springton Lake MS 800/6-8
1900 N Providence Rd 19063 610-627-6500
Dr. Robert Salladino, prin. Fax 566-8665

Delaware County Community College Post-Sec.
901 Media Line Rd 19063 610-359-5000
Penn State Brandywine Post-Sec.
25 Yearsley Mill Rd 19063 610-892-1200
Pennsylvania Institute of Technology Post-Sec.
800 Manchester Ave 19063 610-892-1500
Williamson Free School of Mech. Trades Post-Sec.
106 S New Middletown Rd 19063 610-566-1776

**Melrose Park, Montgomery, Pop. 6,500**

---

Gratz College — Post-Sec.
7605 Old York Rd 19027 — 215-635-7300

**Mercer, Mercer, Pop. 1,978**
Area Vocational Technical School
Supt. — None
Mercer County Career Center — Vo/Tech
776 Greenville Rd 16137 — 724-662-3000
Rachel Martin, dir. — Fax 662-1025

Mercer Area SD — 1,300/K-12
545 W Butler St 16137 — 724-662-5100
Dr. William Gathers, supt. — Fax 662-5109
www.mercer.k12.pa.us
Mercer Area HS — 500/9-12
545 W Butler St 16137 — 724-662-5104
Michael Piddington, prin. — Fax 662-2993
Mercer Area MS — 200/7-8
545 W Butler St 16137 — 724-662-5104
Michael Piddington, prin. — Fax 662-2993

---

Creative Learning Christian S — 50/PK-12
550 Grant St 16137 — 724-269-7400
Jillian Morgan, prin.

**Mercersburg, Franklin, Pop. 1,540**
Tuscarora SD — 2,600/K-12
100 W Seminary St 17236 — 717-328-3127
Dr. Charles A. Prijatelj Ed.D., supt. — Fax 328-9316
www.tus.k12.pa.us
Buchanan HS — 800/9-12
4773 Fort Loudon Rd 17236 — 717-328-2146
Rodney Benedick, prin. — Fax 328-5428
Buchanan MS — 600/6-8
5191 Fort Loudon Rd 17236 — 717-328-5221
James Carbaugh, prin. — Fax 328-9081

---

Mercersburg Academy — 400/9-12
300 E Seminary St 17236 — 717-328-6173
Douglas Hale, head sch — Fax 328-6319

**Merion Station, Montgomery, Pop. 700**

---

Merion Mercy Academy — 500/9-12
511 Montgomery Ave 19066 — 610-664-6655
Sr. Barbara Buckley, prin. — Fax 664-6322

**Mertztown, Berks, Pop. 656**
Brandywine Heights Area SD
Supt. — See Topton
Brandywine Heights Area HS — 600/9-12
103 Old Topton Rd 19539 — 610-682-5102
Josh Ziatyk, prin. — Fax 682-5139

**Meyersdale, Somerset, Pop. 2,169**
Meyersdale Area SD — 900/K-12
309 Industrial Park Rd 15552 — 814-634-5123
Dr. Tracey Karlie, supt. — Fax 634-0832
www.masd.net
Meyersdale Area HS — 300/9-12
1349 Shaw Mines Rd 15552 — 814-634-5123
John Wiltrout, prin. — Fax 634-0832
Meyersdale Area MS — 200/6-8
1353 Shaw Mines Rd 15552 — 814-634-5123
Wayne Miller, dean — Fax 634-0832

**Middleburg, Snyder, Pop. 1,296**
Midd-West SD — 1,500/K-12
568 E Main St 17842 — 570-837-0046
Richard J. Musselman, supt. — Fax 837-3018
www.mwsd.cc
Midd-West HS — 600/8-12
540 E Main St 17842 — 570-837-0046
Cynthia L. Hutchinson, prin. — Fax 837-5267

**Middletown, Dauphin, Pop. 8,620**
Middletown Area SD — 2,300/K-12
55 W Water St 17057 — 717-948-3300
Lori Suski Ed.D., supt. — Fax 948-3329
www.raiderweb.org
Middletown Area HS — 700/9-12
1155 N Union St 17057 — 717-948-3333
Michael Carnes, prin. — Fax 948-3359
Middletown Area MS — 600/6-8
215 Oberlin Rd 17057 — 717-930-0739
Kevin Cook, prin. — Fax 944-0951

---

Penn State Harrisburg — Post-Sec.
777 W Harrisburg Pike 17057 — 717-948-6250

**Midland, Beaver, Pop. 2,534**
Western Beaver County SD — 700/PK-12
343 Ridgemont Dr 15059 — 724-643-9310
Dr. Robert Postupac, supt. — Fax 643-8048
www.westernbeaver.org
Other Schools – See Industry

**Mifflinburg, Union, Pop. 3,516**
Mifflinburg Area SD — 2,100/K-12
178 Maple St 17844 — 570-966-8200
Daniel Lichtel, supt. — Fax 966-8210
www.mifflinburg.org
Mifflinburg Area HS — 600/9-12
75 Market St 17844 — 570-966-8230
Michelle Shearer, prin. — Fax 966-8260
Mifflinburg Area MS — 500/6-8
100 Mabel St 17844 — 570-966-8290
Daryl Hunsberger, prin. — Fax 966-8304

**Mifflintown, Juniata, Pop. 920**
Juniata County SD — 3,000/K-12
75 S 7th St 17059 — 717-436-2111
Keith Yarger, supt. — Fax 436-2777
www.jcsdk12.org
Juniata HS — 600/9-12
3931 William Penn Hwy 17059 — 717-436-2193
Edward Apple, prin. — Fax 436-2858
Tuscarora JHS — 400/6-8
3873 William Penn Hwy 17059 — 717-436-2165
Aaron Bennett, prin. — Fax 436-5999

Other Schools – See Mc Alisterville

**Milford, Pike, Pop. 1,003**
Delaware Valley SD — 4,000/K-12
236 Route 6 and 209 18337 — 570-296-1800
John Bell, supt. — Fax 296-3172
www.dvsd.org
Delaware Valley HS 9-10 — 9-10
256 Route 6 and 209 18337 — 570-409-2001
Brian Blaum, prin. — Fax 409-2002
Delaware Valley HS 11-12 — 900/11-12
252 Route 6 and 209 18337 — 570-296-1850
Brian Blaum, prin. — Fax 296-3160
Delaware Valley MS — 400/6-8
258 Route 6 and 209 18337 — 570-296-1830
Peter Ioppolo, prin. — Fax 296-3162
Other Schools – See Dingmans Ferry

**Mill Creek, Huntingdon, Pop. 326**
Area Vocational Technical School
Supt. — None
Huntingdon County CTC — Vo/Tech
PO Box E 17060 — 814-643-0951
Mary Lou Lebo, prin.

**Millersburg, Dauphin, Pop. 2,536**
Millersburg Area SD — 800/K-12
799 Center St 17061 — 717-692-2108
Thomas Haupt, supt. — Fax 692-2895
www.mlbgsd.k12.pa.us/
Millersburg Area HS — 300/9-12
799 Center St 17061 — 717-692-2108
David Shover, prin. — Fax 692-2895
Millersburg Area MS — 200/6-8
799 Center St 17061 — 717-692-2108
Jennifer Wicht, prin. — Fax 692-2895

---

Northern Dauphin Christian S — 100/PK-12
1072 State Route 25 17061 — 717-692-1940
JoAnn Kieffer, admin.

**Millerstown, Perry, Pop. 664**
Greenwood SD — 700/K-12
405 E Sunbury St 17062 — 717-589-3117
Dr. Nicholas Guarente, supt. — Fax 589-1017
www.greenwoodsd.org
Greenwood HS — 200/9-12
405 E Sunbury St 17062 — 717-589-3116
Michele Dubaich, prin. — Fax 589-1016
Greenwood MS — 100/6-8
405 E Sunbury St 17062 — 717-589-3116
Michele Dubaich, prin. — Fax 589-1016

**Millersville, Lancaster, Pop. 8,074**
Penn Manor SD
Supt. — See Lancaster
Penn Manor HS — 1,600/9-12
PO Box 1001 17551 — 717-872-9520
Dr. Philip Gale, prin. — Fax 872-0934

---

Millersville University of Pennsylvania — Post-Sec.
PO Box 1002 17551 — 717-872-3024

**Mill Hall, Clinton, Pop. 1,602**
Area Vocational Technical School
Supt. — None
Keystone Central CTC — Vo/Tech
64 Keystone Central Dr 17751 — 570-748-6584
Scott Owens, prin. — Fax 748-5467

Keystone Central SD — 4,200/K-12
86 Administration Dr 17751 — 570-893-4900
Kelly Hastings, supt. — Fax 893-4923
www.kcsd.k12.pa.us
Central Mountain HS — 1,300/9-12
64 Keystone Central Dr 17751 — 570-893-4646
Dr. Steve Turchetta, prin. — Fax 893-4946
Central Mountain MS — 1,000/6-8
200 Ben Ave 17751 — 570-726-3141
Justin Evey, prin. — Fax 726-7227
Other Schools – See Renovo

**Millville, Columbia, Pop. 940**
Millville Area SD — 700/K-12
PO Box 260 17846 — 570-458-5538
Cynthia Jenkins, supt. — Fax 458-5584
www.millville.k12.pa.us
Millville Area JSHS — 300/7-12
PO Box 260 17846 — 570-458-5538
Eric Stair, prin. — Fax 458-5583

**Milton, Northumberland, Pop. 6,900**
Milton Area SD — 2,200/K-12
700 Mahoning St 17847 — 570-742-7614
Cathy Keegan, supt. — Fax 742-4523
www.miltonsd.org/
Milton Area HS — 700/9-12
700 Mahoning St 17847 — 570-742-7611
Bryan Noaker, prin. — Fax 742-4928
Milton Area MS — 500/6-8
700 Mahoning St 17847 — 570-742-7685
Gregory Scoggins, prin. — Fax 742-4857

---

Meadowbrook Christian S — 300/PK-12
363 Stamm Rd 17847 — 570-742-2638
Rodney Baughman M.Ed., admin. — Fax 742-4710

**Minersville, Schuylkill, Pop. 4,345**
Minersville Area SD — 1,200/PK-12
PO Box 787 17954 — 570-544-1400
Carl McBreen, supt. — Fax 544-6162
www.battlinminers.com
Minersville Area JSHS — 500/7-12
PO Box 787 17954 — 570-544-1400
James Grabusky, prin. — Fax 544-5866

**Mohrsville, Berks, Pop. 375**

---

King's Academy — 200/PK-12
1562 Main St 19541 — 610-926-9639
Michelle Goodman, head sch — Fax 926-8089

**Monaca, Beaver, Pop. 5,641**
Area Vocational Technical School
Supt. — None
Beaver County CTC — Vo/Tech
145 Poplar Dr 15061 — 724-728-5800
Robert Edwards, dir. — Fax 775-2299

Central Valley SD — 2,400/K-12
160 Baker Road Ext 15061 — 724-775-5600
Nicholas Perry, supt. — Fax 775-4302
www.centralvalleysd.org
Central Valley HS — 800/9-12
160 Baker Road Ext 15061 — 724-775-5600
Anthony Mendicino, prin. — Fax 775-6560
Central Valley MS — 600/6-8
1500 Allen Ave 15061 — 724-775-5600
Michael McCullough, prin. — Fax 775-4302

---

Community College of Beaver County — Post-Sec.
1 Campus Dr 15061 — 724-480-2222
Penn State Beaver — Post-Sec.
100 University Dr 15061 — 724-773-3800

**Monessen, Westmoreland, Pop. 7,447**
Monessen CSD — 900/K-12
1275 Rostraver St 15062 — 724-684-3600
Dr. Leanne Spazak, supt. — Fax 684-6782
monessenschooldistrict.com
Monessen HS — 300/9-12
1245 State Rd 15062 — 724-684-7100
Eric Manko, prin. — Fax 684-7925
Monessen MS — 200/6-8
1245 State Rd 15062 — 724-684-6282
Eric Manko, prin. — Fax 684-7931

---

Douglas Education Center — Post-Sec.
130 7th St 15062 — 724-684-3684

**Monongahela, Washington, Pop. 4,226**
Ringgold SD
Supt. — See New Eagle
Ringgold HS — 1,000/9-12
1 Ram Dr 15063 — 724-258-2200
Jason Minniti, prin. — Fax 258-7360

**Monroeville, Allegheny, Pop. 28,591**
Area Vocational Technical School
Supt. — None
Forbes Road CTC — Vo/Tech
607 Beatty Rd 15146 — 412-373-8100
Edward McMullen, dir. — Fax 373-8106

Gateway SD — 3,800/K-12
9000 Gateway Campus Blvd 15146 — 412-372-5300
Dr. Nina Zetty, supt. — Fax 373-5731
www.gatewayk12.org
Gateway HS — 1,400/9-12
3000 Gateway Campus Blvd 15146 — 412-373-5744
Peter Murphy, prin. — Fax 373-5872
Gateway MS — 600/7-8
4450 Old William Penn Hwy 15146 — 412-373-5780
Rocco Telli, prin. — Fax 373-5794

---

Career Training Academy — Post-Sec.
4314 Old William Penn # 103 15146 — 412-372-3900
Community College of Allegheny County — Post-Sec.
595 Beatty Rd 15146 — 724-327-1327
Empire Beauty School — Post-Sec.
320 Mall Blvd 15146 — 412-373-7727

**Mont Alto, Franklin, Pop. 1,684**

---

Penn State Mont Alto — Post-Sec.
1 Campus Dr 17237 — 717-749-6000

**Montgomery, Lycoming, Pop. 1,554**
Montgomery Area SD — 900/K-12
120 Penn St 17752 — 570-547-1608
Daphne Bowers, supt. — Fax 547-6271
www.montasd.org
Montgomery JSHS — 300/7-12
120 Penn St 17752 — 570-547-1608
Michael Prowant, prin. — Fax 547-6755

**Montoursville, Lycoming, Pop. 4,566**
Montoursville Area SD — 1,900/K-12
50 N Arch St 17754 — 570-368-2491
Dr. Timothy Bowers, supt. — Fax 368-3501
www.montoursville.k12.pa.us/
McCall MS — 600/5-8
600 Willow St 17754 — 570-368-2441
Jeffrey Moore, prin. — Fax 368-3521
Montoursville Area HS — 600/9-12
100 N Arch St 17754 — 570-368-2611
Daniel Taormina, prin. — Fax 368-2768

**Montrose, Susquehanna, Pop. 1,608**
Montrose Area SD — 1,500/K-12
273 Meteor Way 18801 — 570-278-6221
Carol Boyce, supt. — Fax 278-4798
www.masd.info
Montrose JSHS — 800/7-12
75 Meteor Way 18801 — 570-278-3731
William King, prin. — Fax 278-9143

**Moon Township, Allegheny, Pop. 10,187**
Moon Area SD — 3,700/K-12
8353 University Blvd 15108 — 412-264-9440
Curt Baker, supt. — Fax 264-3268
www.moonarea.net
Moon Area HS — 1,100/9-12
8353 University Blvd 15108 — 412-264-9440
Barry Balaski, prin. — Fax 264-1271
Moon Area MS — 900/5-8
904 Beaver Grade Rd 15108 — 412-264-9440
Melissa Heasley, prin. — Fax 264-3013

---

Robert Morris University — Post-Sec.
6001 University Blvd 15108 — 412-397-3000

**Moosic, Lackawanna, Pop. 5,672**

Empire Beauty School — Post-Sec.
3370 Birney Ave 18507 — 570-823-5987

**Morgantown, Lancaster, Pop. 817**

Conestoga Christian S — 200/PK-12
2760 Main St 19543 — 610-286-0353
Kenneth Parris, admin. — Fax 286-0350

**Morrisdale, Clearfield, Pop. 747**
West Branch Area SD — 1,100/K-12
516 Allport Cutoff 16858 — 814-345-5615
Michelle Dutrow, supt. — Fax 345-5220
www.westbranch.org
West Branch Area JSHS — 600/7-12
444 Allport Cutoff 16858 — 814-345-5615
Joseph Holenchik, prin. — Fax 345-6116

**Morrisville, Bucks, Pop. 8,532**
Morrisville Borough SD — 800/K-12
550 W Palmer St 19067 — 215-736-2681
Michael Kopakowski, supt. — Fax 736-2413
mv.org
Morrisville HS — 200/9-12
550 W Palmer St 19067 — 215-736-5260
Michael Kopakowski, supt. — Fax 736-3958
Morrisville IS, 550 W Palmer St 19067 — 400/3-8
Michael Kopakowski, supt. — 215-736-5270

**Moscow, Lackawanna, Pop. 2,016**
North Pocono SD — 3,100/K-12
701 Church St 18444 — 570-842-7659
Bryan McGraw, supt. — Fax 842-0886
www.npsd.org/
North Pocono HS — 1,000/9-12
97 Bochicchio Blvd 18444 — 570-842-7606
Ronald Collins, prin. — Fax 842-2163
North Pocono MS — 700/6-8
701 Church St 18444 — 570-842-4588
Edward Bugno, prin. — Fax 842-1783

**Mountain Top, Luzerne, Pop. 10,876**
Crestwood SD — 3,000/K-12
281 S Mountain Blvd 18707 — 570-474-6782
Dave McLaughlin-Smith, supt. — Fax 474-2254
www.csdcomets.org/
Crestwood HS — 1,000/9-12
281 S Mountain Blvd 18707 — 570-474-6782
Christopher Gegaris, prin. — Fax 474-1175
Crestwood MS — 500/7-8
281 S Mountain Blvd 18707 — 570-474-6782
Bonnie Gregory, prin. — Fax 474-2254

**Mount Braddock, Fayette**

Pennsylvania Institute of Health & Tech — Post-Sec.
PO Box 278 15465 — 724-437-4600

**Mount Carmel, Northumberland, Pop. 5,840**
Mt. Carmel Area SD — 1,300/PK-12
600 W 5th St 17851 — 570-339-1500
Bernard Stellar, supt. — Fax 339-0487
www.mca.k12.pa.us
Mt. Carmel Area JSHS — 500/7-12
600 W 5th St 17851 — 570-339-1500
Lisa Varano, prin. — Fax 339-0487

**Mount Joy, Lancaster, Pop. 7,283**
Area Vocational Technical School
Supt. — None
Lancaster County CTC-Mt. Joy — Vo/Tech
PO Box 537 17552 — 717-653-3000
David Smith, prin. — Fax 653-0901

Donegal SD — 2,000/K-12
1051 Koser Rd 17552 — 717-653-1447
Susan Ursprung Ed.D., supt. — Fax 492-1350
www.donegal.k12.pa.us
Donegal HS — 800/9-12
1025 Koser Rd 17552 — 717-653-1871
John Felix, prin. — Fax 492-1241
Donegal JHS — 500/7-8
915 Anderson Ferry Rd 17552 — 717-928-2900
Judy Haugh, prin. — Fax 928-2911

**Mount Pleasant, Westmoreland, Pop. 4,419**
Mt. Pleasant Area SD — 1,800/K-12
271 State St 15666 — 724-547-4100
Dr. Timothy Gabauer, supt. — Fax 547-0629
www.mpasd.net
Mount Pleasant Area HS — 700/9-12
265 State St 15666 — 724-547-4100
John Campbell, prin. — Fax 547-0526
Mount Pleasant Area JHS — 300/7-8
265 State St 15666 — 724-547-4100
Robert Gumbita, admin. — Fax 547-0526

**Mount Union, Huntingdon, Pop. 2,343**
Mt. Union Area SD — 1,500/K-12
603 N Industrial Dr 17066 — 814-542-8631
Dr. Brett Gilliland, supt. — Fax 542-8633
www.muasd.org/
Mount Union Area HS — 500/9-12
706 N Shaver St 17066 — 814-542-2518
Curt Whitsel, prin. — Fax 542-5451
Mount Union JHS — 200/7-8
706 N Shaver St 17066 — 814-542-9311
Amy Smith, prin.

**Mountville, Lancaster, Pop. 2,760**

Dayspring Christian Academy — 200/PK-12
120 College Ave 17554 — 717-285-2000
Dr. Michael Myers, hdmstr.

**Mount Wolf, York, Pop. 1,367**
Northeastern York SD
Supt. — See Manchester
Northeastern MS — 600/7-8
4855 Board Rd 17347 — 717-266-3676
Michael Alessandroni, prin. — Fax 266-9735

**Muncy, Lycoming, Pop. 2,457**
Muncy SD — 1,000/K-12
206 Sherman St 17756 — 570-546-3125
Craig Skaluba, supt. — Fax 546-6676
www.muncysd.org
Muncy JSHS — 500/7-12
200 W Penn St 17756 — 570-546-3127
Timothy Welliver, prin. — Fax 546-7688

**Munhall, Allegheny, Pop. 11,221**
Steel Valley SD — 1,800/K-12
220 E Oliver Rd 15120 — 412-464-3600
Edward Wehrer, supt. — Fax 464-3626
steelvalleysd.org
Steel Valley HS — 600/9-12
3113 Main St 15120 — 412-464-3600
Lisa Duval, prin. — Fax 464-3609
Steel Valley MS — 400/6-8
3114 Main St 15120 — 412-464-3600
Bryan Macuga, admin. — Fax 326-0315

**Murrysville, Westmoreland, Pop. 19,098**
Franklin Regional SD — 3,700/K-12
3210 School Rd 15668 — 724-327-5456
Dr. Gennaro R. Piraino Ed.D., supt. — Fax 327-6149
www.franklinregional.k12.pa.us
Franklin Regional HS — 1,200/9-12
3200 School Rd 15668 — 724-327-5456
Ron Suvak, prin. — Fax 327-2782
Franklin Regional MS — 900/6-8
4660 Old William Penn Hwy 15668 — 724-327-5456
Andy Leviski, prin. — Fax 733-0949

**Myerstown, Lebanon, Pop. 3,030**
Eastern Lebanon County SD — 2,500/K-12
180 Elco Dr 17067 — 717-866-7117
Dr. David Zuilkoski, supt. — Fax 866-7084
www.elcosd.org/
Eastern Lebanon County HS — 700/9-12
180 Elco Dr 17067 — 717-866-7447
Jennifer Haas, prin. — Fax 866-7287
Eastern Lebanon County MS — 600/6-8
60 Evergreen Dr 17067 — 717-866-6591
Michael Gerhart, prin. — Fax 866-5837

Evangelical Theological Seminary — Post-Sec.
121 S College St 17067 — 717-866-5775
Lebanon Valley Christian S — 100/1-12
7821 Lancaster Ave 17067 — 717-933-5171
Myerstown Mennonite S — 100/1-12
739 E Lincoln Ave 17067 — 717-866-5667

**Nanticoke, Luzerne, Pop. 10,349**
Greater Nanticoke Area SD — 2,200/K-12
427 Kosciuszko St 18634 — 570-735-1270
Dr. Ronald Grevera, supt. — Fax 735-1350
www.gnasd.com
Greater Nanticoke Area HS — 800/8-12
425 Kosciuszko St 18634 — 570-735-7781
Joseph Long, prin. — Fax 733-1002

Luzerne County Community College — Post-Sec.
1333 S Prospect St 18634 — 570-740-0200

**Nanty Glo, Cambria, Pop. 2,702**
Blacklick Valley SD — 700/PK-12
555 Birch St 15943 — 814-749-9211
Dr. John Mastillo, supt. — Fax 749-8627
www.bvsd.k12.pa.us
Blacklick Valley JSHS — 300/7-12
555 Birch St 15943 — 814-749-9211
Dr. Laura Fisanick, prin. — Fax 749-8627

**Narberth, Montgomery, Pop. 4,161**
Lower Merion SD
Supt. — See Ardmore
Welsh Valley MS — 900/6-8
325 Tower Ln 19072 — 610-658-3920
Chris Hall, prin. — Fax 667-4749

**Natrona Heights, Allegheny, Pop. 11,400**
Highlands SD — 2,600/K-12
PO Box 288 15065 — 724-226-2400
Dr. Michael Bjalobok, supt. — Fax 226-8437
www.goldenrams.com
Highlands HS — 800/9-12
1500 Pacific Ave 15065 — 724-226-1000
Catherine Russo, prin. — Fax 226-9611
Highlands MS — 600/6-8
1350 Broadview Blvd 15065 — 724-226-0600
Charles Mort, prin. — Fax 226-3287

Allegheny Valley Hospital — Post-Sec.
1301 Carlisle St 15065 — 724-226-7000
St. Joseph HS — 200/9-12
800 Montana Ave 15065 — 724-224-5552
Beverly Kaniecki, prin. — Fax 224-3205

**Nazareth, Northampton, Pop. 5,699**
Nazareth Area SD — 4,600/K-12
1 Education Plz 18064 — 610-759-1170
Dr. Dennis L. Riker, supt. — Fax 759-9637
www.nazarethasd.k12.pa.us
Nazareth Area HS — 1,500/9-12
501 E Center St 18064 — 610-759-1730
Alan Davis, prin. — Fax 746-2599
Nazareth Area MS — 800/7-8
94 Friedensthal Ave 18064 — 610-759-3350
Robert Kern, prin. — Fax 759-3725

**Needmore, Fulton, Pop. 168**

Fulton County Community Christian S — 50/PK-12
PO Box 235 17238 — 717-573-4400
Dr. Louise Hine, admin. — Fax 573-2731

**New Berlin, Union, Pop. 870**
Area Vocational Technical School
Supt. — None
SUN Area Technology Institute — Vo/Tech
815 Market St 17855 — 570-966-1031
Jennifer Hain, dir. — Fax 966-9492

**New Bethlehem, Clarion, Pop. 986**
Redbank Valley SD — 800/K-12
920 Broad St 16242 — 814-275-2426
Michael Drzewiecki, supt. — Fax 275-2428
www.redbankvalley.net/
Redbank Valley JSHS — 600/7-12
910 Broad St 16242 — 814-275-2424
Amy Rupp, prin. — Fax 275-2428

**New Bloomfield, Perry, Pop. 1,237**

Carson Long Military Academy — 100/6-12
200 N Carlisle St 17068 — 717-582-2121
David Pearson, pres. — Fax 582-8763

**New Brighton, Beaver, Pop. 5,744**
New Brighton Area SD — 1,600/K-12
3225 43rd St 15066 — 724-843-1795
Dr. Joseph Guarino, supt. — Fax 843-6144
www.nbasd.org
New Brighton Area HS — 500/9-12
3202 43rd St 15066 — 724-846-1050
Ryan Yates, prin. — Fax 846-2204
New Brighton Area MS — 400/6-8
901 Penn Ave 15066 — 724-846-8100
Julian Underwood, prin. — Fax 846-2337

**New Castle, Lawrence, Pop. 22,422**
Area Vocational Technical School
Supt. — None
Lawrence County CTC — Vo/Tech
750 Phelps Way 16101 — 724-658-3583
Regina Hiler, prin. — Fax 658-8530

Laurel SD — 1,300/K-12
2497 Harlansburg Rd 16101 — 724-658-8940
Sandra Hennon Ph.D., supt. — Fax 658-2992
www.laurel.k12.pa.us
Laurel JSHS — 700/7-12
2497 Harlansburg Rd 16101 — 724-658-9056
Mark Frengel M.D., prin. — Fax 658-2992

Neshannock Township SD — 1,300/K-12
3834 Mitchell Rd 16105 — 724-654-4793
Dr. Terence Meehan, supt. — Fax 658-1828
www.neshannock.k12.pa.us
Neshannock HS — 400/9-12
3834 Mitchell Rd 16105
Luca Passarelli, prin.
Neshannock JHS — 600/7-8
3834 Mitchell Rd 16105 — 724-658-5513
Dr. Tracy McCalla, prin. — Fax 657-8169

New Castle Area SD — 2,500/PK-12
420 Fern St 16101 — 724-656-4756
John Sarandrea, supt. — Fax 656-4767
www.ncasd.com
New Castle HS — 1,300/9-12
300 E Lincoln Ave 16101 — 724-656-4700
Richard Litrenta, prin. — Fax 658-3916
New Castle JHS — 7-8
310 E Lincoln Ave 16101 — 724-656-4700
Carol Morrell, prin. — Fax 658-6276

Shenango Area SD — 1,200/K-12
2501 Old Pittsburgh Rd 16101 — 724-658-7287
Dr. Michael Schreck, supt. — Fax 658-5370
www.shenango.k12.pa.us
Shenango HS — 600/7-12
2550 Ellwood Rd 16101 — 724-658-5537
Dr. Joseph McCormick, prin. — Fax 658-7584

Union Area SD — 600/K-12
2106 Camden Ave 16101 — 724-658-4775
Michael Ross, supt. — Fax 658-5151
www.union.k12.pa.us/
Union Area MSHS — 200/5-12
2106 Camden Ave 16101 — 724-658-4501
Robin Nogay, prin. — Fax 658-8617

Erie Business Center South — Post-Sec.
170 Cascade Galleria 16101 — 724-658-9066
Jameson Memorial Hosp School of Nursing — Post-Sec.
1211 Wilmington Ave 16105 — 724-656-4240
New Castle School of Beauty Culture — Post-Sec.
314 E Washington St 16101 — 724-654-6611
New Castle School of Trades — Post-Sec.
4117 Pulaski Rd 16101 — 800-837-8299

**New Cumberland, Cumberland, Pop. 7,166**
West Shore SD
Supt. — See Lewisberry
New Cumberland MS — 400/6-8
331 8th St 17070 — 717-774-0162
Fax 901-9474

**New Eagle, Washington, Pop. 2,165**
Ringgold SD — 2,900/K-12
400 Main St 15067 — 724-258-9329
Dr. Karen Polkabla, supt. — Fax 258-5363
www.ringgold.org
Other Schools – See Finleyville, Monongahela

**New Holland, Lancaster, Pop. 5,286**
Eastern Lancaster County SD — 3,100/K-12
PO Box 609 17557 — 717-354-1500
Dr. Robert Hollister, supt. — Fax 354-1512
www.elanco.org
Garden Spot HS — 1,000/9-12
PO Box 609 17557 — 717-354-1550
Matthew Sanger, prin. — Fax 354-1128
Garden Spot MS — 500/7-8
PO Box 609 17557 — 717-354-1560
Jeffrey Starr, prin. — Fax 354-1129

**New Hope, Bucks, Pop. 2,495**
New Hope-Solebury SD — 1,600/K-12
180 W Bridge St 18938 — 215-862-2552
Dr. Raymond Boccuti, supt. — Fax 744-6012
www.nhsd.org
New Hope-Solebury HS — 500/9-12
182 W Bridge St 18938 — 215-862-2028
Charles Malone, prin. — Fax 862-3198

New Hope-Solebury MS 400/6-8
184 W Bridge St 18938 215-862-0608
Dr. Christina Cortellessa, prin. Fax 862-2862

---

Solebury S 200/7-12
6832 Phillips Mill Rd 18938 215-862-5261
Tom Wilschutz, head sch Fax 862-3366

**New Kensington, Westmoreland, Pop. 12,575**
Area Vocational Technical School
Supt. — None
Northern Westmoreland CTC Vo/Tech
705 Stevenson Blvd 15068 724-335-9389
Kurt Kiefer, dir. Fax 337-9010

New Kensington-Arnold SD 2,100/PK-12
707 Stevenson Blvd 15068 724-335-4401
Dr. John Pallone J.D., supt. Fax 994-1213
nkasd.com
Valley JSHS 600/7-12
703 Stevenson Blvd 15068 724-337-4536
Jon Banko, prin. Fax 337-8054

---

Career Training Academy Post-Sec.
950 5th Ave 15068 724-337-1000
Citizens General Hospital Post-Sec.
651 4th Ave 15068 724-337-5090
Mary Queen of Apostles S 100/4-8
1129 Leishman Ave 15068 724-339-4411
Catherine Collett, prin. Fax 337-6457
Penn State New Kensington Post-Sec.
3550 7th Street Rd 15068 724-334-5466

**New Milford, Susquehanna, Pop. 860**
Blue Ridge SD 1,100/PK-12
5058 School Rd 18834 570-465-3141
Matthew Button, supt. Fax 465-3148
www.brsd.org
Blue Ridge HS 300/9-12
5058 School Rd 18834 570-465-3144
Matthew Nebzydoski, prin. Fax 465-3148
Blue Ridge MS 200/6-8
5058 School Rd 18834 570-465-3177
Matthew Nebzydoski, prin. Fax 465-3148

**New Oxford, Adams, Pop. 1,767**
Conewago Valley SD 4,000/K-12
130 Berlin Rd 17350 717-624-2157
Dr. Russell Greenholt, supt. Fax 624-5020
www.conewago.k12.pa.us
New Oxford HS 1,300/9-12
130 Berlin Rd 17350 717-624-2157
Kevin Thomas, prin. Fax 624-5021
New Oxford MS 600/7-8
130 Berlin Rd 17350 717-624-2157
Dr. Gretchen Gates, prin. Fax 624-6560

**New Paris, Bedford, Pop. 183**
Chestnut Ridge SD
Supt. — See Fishertown
Chestnut Ridge HS 500/8-12
2588 Quaker Valley Rd 15554 814-839-4195
Max Shoemaker, prin. Fax 839-0018

**Newport, Perry, Pop. 1,551**
Newport SD 1,100/K-12
PO Box 9 17074 717-567-3806
Ryan Neuhard, supt. Fax 567-6468
www.newportsd.org
Newport HS 400/9-12
PO Box 9 17074 717-567-3806
Scott McGrady, prin. Fax 567-2619
Newport MS 200/6-8
PO Box 9 17074 717-567-3806
Bryan Rehmeyer, prin. Fax 567-2619

**New Stanton, Westmoreland, Pop. 2,152**
Area Vocational Technical School
Supt. — None
Central Westmoreland CTC Vo/Tech
240 Arona Rd 15672 724-925-3532
Brad Elwood, dir. Fax 925-1423

**Newtown, Bucks, Pop. 2,215**
Council Rock SD 11,600/K-12
30 N Chancellor St 18940 215-944-1000
Dr. Robert Fraser, supt. Fax 944-1031
www.crsd.org
Council Rock HS North 2,000/9-12
62 Swamp Rd 18940 215-944-1300
Susan McCarthy, prin. Fax 944-1387
Newtown MS 900/7-8
116 Richboro Newtown Rd 18940 215-944-2600
Timothy Long, prin. Fax 944-2698
Other Schools – See Holland, Richboro

---

Bucks County Community College Post-Sec.
275 Swamp Rd 18940 215-968-8000
George S 500/9-12
PO Box 4460 18940 215-579-6547
Nancy Starmer, head sch Fax 579-6549

**Newtown Square, Delaware, Pop. 11,300**
Marple Newtown SD 3,300/K-12
40 Media Line Rd 19073 610-359-4256
Dr. Carol Cary, supt. Fax 723-3340
www.mnsd.net
Marple Newtown HS 1,100/9-12
120 Media Line Rd 19073 610-359-4218
Greg Puckett, prin. Fax 356-2194
Other Schools – See Broomall

---

Delaware County Christian HS 500/6-12
462 Malin Rd 19073 610-353-6522
Dr. Timothy Wiens, head sch Fax 356-9684
Episcopal Academy 1,200/PK-12
1785 Bishop White Dr 19073 484-424-1400
Dr. Thomas Locke, hdmstr. Fax 424-1600

**New Tripoli, Lehigh, Pop. 887**
Northwestern Lehigh SD 2,300/K-12
6493 Route 309 18066 610-298-8661
Mary Anne Wright Ph.D., supt. Fax 298-8002
www.nwlehighsd.org
Northwestern Lehigh HS 700/9-12
6493 Route 309 18066 610-298-8661
Aileen Yadush, prin. Fax 298-4645
Northwestern Lehigh MS 600/6-8
6636 Northwest Rd 18066 610-298-8661
William Dovico, prin. Fax 298-8178

**Newville, Cumberland, Pop. 1,313**
Big Spring SD 2,800/K-12
45 Mount Rock Rd 17241 717-776-2000
Richard Fry, supt. Fax 776-4428
www.bigspring.k12.pa.us
Big Spring HS 900/9-12
100 Mount Rock Rd 17241 717-776-2000
William August, prin. Fax 776-2433
Big Spring MS 700/6-8
47 Mount Rock Rd 17241 717-776-2000
Dr. Linda Wilson, prin. Fax 776-2468

**New Wilmington, Lawrence, Pop. 2,444**
Wilmington Area SD 1,300/K-12
300 Wood St 16142 724-656-8866
Dr. Michelle Miller, supt. Fax 946-8982
www.wilmington.k12.pa.us/
Wilmington Area HS 500/9-12
350 Wood St 16142 724-656-8866
Benjamin Fenwick, prin.
Wilmington Area MS 400/5-8
400 Wood St 16142 724-656-8866
George Endrizzi, prin.

---

Westminster College Post-Sec.
319 S Market St 16172 724-946-7100

**Norristown, Montgomery, Pop. 33,250**
Norristown Area SD 7,000/PK-12
401 N Whitehall Rd 19403 610-630-5000
Janet Samuels Ph.D., supt. Fax 630-5013
www.nasd.k12.pa.us
East Norriton MS 900/5-8
330 Roland Dr 19401 610-275-6520
Dr. Christina Spink, prin. Fax 272-0531
Eisenhower MS 500/5-8
1601 Markley St 19401 610-277-8720
Christina Taylor, prin. Fax 270-2901
Norristown Area HS 1,800/9-12
1900 Eagle Dr 19403 610-630-5090
Jeffrey Smith, prin. Fax 630-5115
Roosevelt Alternative S 100/Alt
1161 Markley St 19401 610-275-9720
Dr. Carla Queenan, prin. Fax 272-0552
Stewart MS 500/5-8
1315 W Marshall St 19401 610-275-6870
Martina Walls, prin. Fax 272-0560

---

Star Career Academy Post-Sec.
2501 Monroe Blvd 19403 610-783-7827
The Pathway School Post-Sec.
162 Egypt Rd 19403 610-277-0660

**Northampton, Northampton, Pop. 9,830**
Catasauqua Area SD
Supt. — See Catasauqua
Catasauqua HS 500/9-12
2500 W Bullshead Rd 18067 610-697-0111
David Ascani, prin. Fax 697-0116

Northampton Area SD 5,500/K-12
2014 Laubach Ave 18067 610-262-7811
Joseph Kovalchik, supt. Fax 262-1150
www.nasdschools.org/
Northampton Area HS 1,700/9-12
1619 Laubach Ave 18067 610-262-7812
Stephen Seier, prin. Fax 262-3024
Northampton Area MS 800/6-8
1617 Laubach Ave 18067 610-262-7817
Patrice Turner, prin. Fax 262-6583

**North Braddock, Allegheny, Pop. 4,701**
Woodland Hills SD 3,800/K-12
531 Jones Ave, 412-731-1300
Alan Johnson, supt. Fax 731-1562
www.whsd.net
Other Schools – See Pittsburgh

**North East, Erie, Pop. 4,255**
North East SD 1,700/K-12
50 E Division St 16428 814-725-8671
Dr. Frank McClard, supt. Fax 725-9380
www.nesd1.org/
North East HS 500/9-12
1901 Freeport Rd 16428 814-725-8671
Regan Tanner, prin. Fax 725-3357
North East MS 400/6-8
1903 Freeport Rd 16428 814-725-8671
Gregory Beardsley, prin. Fax 725-1086

**Northern Cambria, Cambria, Pop. 4,022**
Northern Cambria SD 1,200/K-12
601 Joseph St 15714 814-948-5481
Joseph Kimmel, supt. Fax 948-6058
www.ncsd.k12.pa.us
Northern Cambria HS 400/9-12
813 35th St 15714 814-948-6800
Rebecca Pupo, prin. Fax 948-9810
Northern Cambria MS 300/6-8
601 Joseph St 15714 814-948-5880
Marilyn Wargo, prin. Fax 948-5561

**North Huntingdon, Westmoreland, Pop. 28,158**
Norwin SD 5,200/K-12
281 McMahon Dr 15642 724-861-3000
Dr. William Kerr, supt. Fax 863-9467
www.norwinsd.org
Norwin HS 1,600/9-12
251 McMahon Dr 15642 724-861-3005
Timothy Kotch, prin. Fax 861-0581
Norwin MS 800/7-8
10870 Mockingbird Dr 15642 724-863-5707
Robert Suman, prin. Fax 863-5408

**Northumberland, Northumberland, Pop. 3,769**

---

Northumberland Christian S 200/K-12
351 5th St 17857 570-473-9786
Sunbury Christian Academy 200/PK-12
135 Spruce Hollow Rd 17857 570-473-7592
Richard Hennett, admin. Fax 473-7531

**North Versailles, Allegheny, Pop. 12,302**
East Allegheny SD 1,800/PK-12
1150 Jacks Run Rd 15137 412-824-8012
Donald MacFann, supt. Fax 824-1062
www.eawildcats.net
East Allegheny JSHS 600/7-12
1150 Jacks Run Rd 15137 412-824-9700
Betsy D'Emidio, prin. Fax 825-4570

**North Wales, Montgomery, Pop. 3,136**
North Penn SD
Supt. — See Lansdale
Pennbrook MS 800/7-9
1201 N Wales Rd 19454 215-699-9287
Jim Galante, prin. Fax 699-0151

---

Lansdale School of Business Post-Sec.
290 Wissahickon Ave 19454 215-699-5700

**Oakdale, Allegheny, Pop. 1,442**
Area Vocational Technical School
Supt. — None
Parkway West CTC Vo/Tech
7101 Steubenville Pike 15071 412-923-1772
Dr. Darby Copeland, dir. Fax 787-7257

---

Pittsburgh Technical Institute Post-Sec.
1111 McKee Rd 15071 800-784-9675

**Oakmont, Allegheny, Pop. 6,258**
Riverview SD 1,000/K-12
701 10th St 15139 412-828-1800
Margaret DiNinno, supt. Fax 828-9346
www.rsd.k12.pa.us
Riverview HS 500/7-12
100 Hulton Rd 15139 412-828-1800
Jay Moser, prin. Fax 828-6296

**Oil City, Venango, Pop. 10,397**
Area Vocational Technical School
Supt. — None
Venango Technology Center Vo/Tech
1 Vo Tech Dr 16301 814-677-3097
Mario Fontanazza, dir. Fax 676-0075

Oil City Area SD 2,100/K-12
825 Grandview Rd 16301 814-676-1867
Patrick Gavin, supt. Fax 676-2211
www.ocasd.org
Oil City Area MS 700/5-8
8 Lynch Blvd 16301 814-676-5702
Joy Zuck, prin. Fax 676-2306
Oil City HS 700/9-12
10 Lynch Blvd 16301 814-676-2771
Scott Stahl, prin. Fax 677-7256

---

DuBois Business College Post-Sec.
701 E 3rd St 16301 814-677-1322
Venango Catholic HS 100/9-12
1505 W 1st St 16301 814-677-3098
Rev. T. Shane Mathew, hdmstr. Fax 676-4453
Venango College of Clarion University Post-Sec.
1801 W 1st St 16301 814-676-6591

**Old Forge, Lackawanna, Pop. 8,255**
Old Forge SD 900/K-12
300 Marion St 18518 570-457-6721
John Rushefski, supt. Fax 457-8389
www.ofsd.cc
Old Forge JSHS 400/7-12
300 Marion St 18518 570-457-6721
Christopher Thomas, prin. Fax 414-0997

**Oley, Berks, Pop. 1,277**
Area Vocational Technical School
Supt. — None
Berks CTC - East Vo/Tech
3307 Friedensburg Rd 19547 610-987-6201
Ronald Wilson, prin. Fax 987-6106

Oley Valley SD 1,800/K-12
17 Jefferson St 19547 610-987-4100
Tracy Shank Ed.D., supt. Fax 987-4138
www.oleyvalleysd.org
Oley Valley HS 600/9-12
17 Jefferson St 19547 610-987-4100
Michael Stauffer, prin. Fax 987-4138
Oley Valley MS 400/6-8
3247 Friedensburg Rd 19547 610-987-4100
Dan Marks, prin. Fax 987-4240

**Orefield, Lehigh**
Parkland SD
Supt. — See Allentown
Orefield MS 1,100/6-8
2675 PA Route 309 18069 610-351-5750
Todd Gombos, prin. Fax 351-5799

**Oreland, Montgomery, Pop. 5,575**
Springfield Township SD 2,200/K-12
1901 Paper Mill Rd 19075 215-233-6000
Dr. Nancy Hacker, supt. Fax 233-5815
www.sdst.org
Springfield Township MS 500/6-8
1901 Paper Mill Rd 19075 215-233-6070
Lauren Patterson, prin. Fax 233-6091
Other Schools – See Erdenheim

**Orwigsburg, Schuylkill, Pop. 3,077**
Blue Mountain SD 2,900/K-12
PO Box 188 17961 570-366-0515
Dr. Robert Urzillo, supt. Fax 366-0838
www.bmsd.org
Blue Mountain MS 700/6-8
PO Box 279 17961 570-366-0546
James McGonigle, prin. Fax 366-2513
Other Schools – See Schuylkill Haven

**Oxford, Chester, Pop. 4,949**
Oxford Area SD 3,800/K-12
125 Bell Tower Ln 19363 610-932-6600
David Woods, supt. Fax 932-6614
www.oxford.k12.pa.us
Oxford Area HS 1,200/9-12
705 Waterway Rd 19363 610-932-6640
Christopher Dormer, prin. Fax 932-6649
Penn's Grove S 600/7-8
301 S 5th St 19363 610-932-6615
James Canaday, prin. Fax 932-6619

**Palmerton, Carbon, Pop. 5,366**
Palmerton Area SD 1,800/K-12
680 4th St 18071 610-826-7101
Scot Engler, supt. Fax 826-4958
www.palmerton.org/
Palmerton Area HS 600/9-12
3525 Fireline Rd 18071 610-826-3155
Paula Husar, prin. Fax 826-4929
Palmerton Area JHS 300/7-8
3529 Fireline Rd 18071 610-826-2492
Richard DeSocio, prin. Fax 826-2366

**Palmyra, Lebanon, Pop. 7,238**
Palmyra Area SD 2,900/K-12
1125 Park Dr 17078 717-838-3144
Lisa Brown, supt. Fax 838-5105
www.pasd.us
Palmyra Area HS 900/9-12
1125 Park Dr 17078 717-838-1331
Dr. Benjamin Ruby, prin. Fax 838-7915
Palmyra Area MS 800/6-8
50 W Cherry St 17078 717-838-1331
Walter Popejoy, prin. Fax 838-4402

**Paoli, Chester, Pop. 5,479**

---

Royer-Greaves School for Blind Post-Sec.
118 S Valley Rd 19301

**Patton, Cambria, Pop. 1,764**
Cambria Heights SD 1,500/PK-12
PO Box 66 16668 814-674-6072
Michael Strasser, supt. Fax 674-5411
www.chsd1.org/
Cambria Heights HS 500/9-12
PO Box 6 16668 814-674-3601
Kenneth Kerchenske, prin. Fax 674-5605
Cambria Heights MS 300/6-8
PO Box 216 16668 814-674-6290
David Caldwell, prin. Fax 674-5054

**Pen Argyl, Northampton, Pop. 3,551**
Pen Argyl Area SD 1,800/K-12
1620 Teels Rd 18072 610-863-3191
William Haberl Ed.D., supt. Fax 863-7040
www.edline.net/pages/Pen_Argyl_ASD
Pen Argyl Area HS 600/9-12
501 W Laurel Ave 18072 610-863-1293
David Domchek, prin. Fax 863-7660
Wind Gap MS 700/4-8
1620 Teels Rd 18072 610-863-9093
Dr. Terry Barry, prin. Fax 863-3817

**Pennsburg, Montgomery, Pop. 3,798**
Upper Perkiomen SD 3,200/K-12
2229 E Buck Rd 18073 215-679-7961
Dr. Alexis McGloin, supt. Fax 679-6214
www.upsd.org
Upper Perkiomen HS 1,000/9-12
2 Walt Rd 18073 215-679-5935
Dr. William Shirk, prin. Fax 679-0911
Other Schools – See East Greenville

---

Perkiomen S 300/6-12
200 Seminary St 18073 215-679-9511
Mark Devey, hdmstr. Fax 679-5202

**Penns Creek, Snyder, Pop. 711**

---

Penn View Christian Academy 100/PK-12
PO Box 970 17862 570-837-1855
Rev. Brent Lenhart, prin. Fax 837-1865

**Pequea, Lancaster**
Penn Manor SD
Supt. — See Lancaster
Marticville MS 300/7-8
356 Frogtown Rd 17565 717-284-4135
Christine Santaniello, prin. Fax 284-5954

**Perkasie, Bucks, Pop. 8,390**
Area Vocational Technical School
Supt. — None
Upper Bucks County AVTS Vo/Tech
3115 Ridge Rd 18944 215-795-2911
Bernard Wagenseller, dir. Fax 795-0530

Pennridge SD 7,400/K-12
1200 N 5th St 18944 215-257-5011
Dr. Jacqueline Rattigan, supt. Fax 453-8699
www.pennridge.org
Pennridge Central MS 600/6-8
144 N Walnut St 18944 215-258-0939
Christian Temchatin, prin. Fax 258-0938
Pennridge HS 2,300/9-12
1228 N 5th St 18944 215-453-6944
Gina DeBona, prin. Fax 257-4986
Pennridge North MS 700/6-8
1500 N 5th St 18944 215-453-6932
Dr. Matthew Cole, prin. Fax 453-7867
Pennridge South MS 500/6-8
610 S 5th St 18944 215-257-0467
Dr. Felicia McAllister, prin. Fax 257-3094

**Perryopolis, Fayette, Pop. 1,762**
Frazier SD 1,200/PK-12
142 Constitution St 15473 724-736-4427
William Henderson, supt. Fax 736-0688
www.frazierschooldistrict.org/pages/frazier_sd
Frazier HS 400/9-12
142 Constitution St 15473 724-736-4426
Jason Pappas, prin. Fax 736-0688
Frazier MS 300/6-8
142 Constitution St 15473 724-736-4428
Michael Turek, prin. Fax 736-0688

**Philadelphia, Philadelphia, Pop. 1,493,502**
Area Vocational Technical School
Supt. — None
Dobbins AVTS Vo/Tech
2150 W Lehigh Ave 19132 215-227-4421
Dr. Toni Damon, prin. Fax 227-4944
Edison HS Vo/Tech
151 W Luzerne St 19140 215-324-9599
Awilda Ortiz, prin. Fax 329-5824
Kensington Culinary Arts S Vo/Tech
2463 Emerald St 19125 215-291-5185
James Williams, prin. Fax 291-6320
Mastbaum AVTS Vo/Tech
3116 Frankford Ave 19134 215-291-4703
Dr. Warren Bowman, prin. Fax 291-5657
Randolph AVTS Vo/Tech
3101 Henry Ave 19129 215-227-4407
Darryl Overton, prin. Fax 227-8655
Saul Agricultural S Vo/Tech
7100 Henry Ave 19128 215-487-4467
Tamera Conaway, prin. Fax 487-4844
School for Exceptional Adults AVTS Vo/Tech
1400 W Olney Ave 19141 215-299-3699
Swenson Arts & Technology HS Vo/Tech
2750 Red Lion Rd 19114 215-961-2009
Colette Langston, prin. Fax 961-2081

Cheltenham Township SD
Supt. — See Elkins Park
Cedarbrook MS 700/7-8
1331 Ivy Hill Rd 19150 215-881-6423
Russell Bender, prin. Fax 576-5610

Philadelphia CSD 165,700/PK-12
440 N Broad St 19130 215-400-4000
William Hite Ed.D., supt.
www.philasd.org/
Academy at Palumbo 600/9-12
1100 Catharine St 19147 215-351-7618
Kiana Thompson, prin. Fax 351-7685
Alternative Ed Regional Ctr at 440 Alt
440 N Broad St 19130 215-400-4230
Arts Academy at Benjamin Rush 500/9-12
11081 Knights Rd 19154 215-281-2603
Lori DeFields, prin. Fax 281-2674
Baldi MS 1,200/6-8
8801 Verree Rd 19115 215-961-2003
Luke Hostetter, prin. Fax 961-2116
Bartram HS 1,000/9-12
2401 S 67th St 19142 215-492-6450
Abdul-Mubdi Muhammad, prin. Fax 492-6117
Beeber MS 300/7-8
5925 Malvern Ave 19131 215-581-5513
Khary Moody, prin. Fax 581-5694
Bodine HS for International Affairs 600/9-12
1101 N 4th St 19123 215-351-7332
Karen Thomas, prin. Fax 351-7370
Building 21, 2000 N 7th St 19122 9-9
Tara Ranzy, prin. 215-684-2030
Carver HS for Engineering & Science 700/9-12
1600 W Norris St 19121 215-684-5079
Ted Domers, prin. Fax 684-5151
Central HS 2,400/9-12
1700 W Olney Ave 19141 215-276-5262
Tim McKenna, prin. Fax 276-4721
Clemente MS 600/6-8
122 W Erie Ave 19140 215-291-5400
Edward Penn, prin. Fax 291-5421
Constitution HS 400/9-12
18 S 7th St 19106 215-351-7310
Dr. Tom Davidson, prin. Fax 351-7694
Conwell MS 700/5-8
1849 E Clearfield St 19134 215-291-4722
Erica Green, prin. Fax 291-5019
Creative & Performing Arts HS 700/9-12
901 S Broad St 19147 215-952-2462
Joanne Beaver, prin. Fax 952-6472
Fels HS 1,300/9-12
5500 Langdon St 19124 215-537-2516
Shawn McGuigan, prin. Fax 537-2556
Feltonville Arts & Sciences MS 700/6-8
210 E Courtland St 19120 215-456-5603
John Piniat, prin. Fax 456-5614
Frankford HS 1,600/9-12
5000 Oxford Ave 19124 215-537-2519
Michael Calderone, prin. Fax 537-2598
Franklin HS 600/9-12
550 N Broad St 19130 215-299-4662
Greg Haley, prin. Fax 299-7285
Franklin Learning Center 700/Alt
616 N 15th St 19130 215-684-5916
Joyce Hoog, prin. Fax 684-8969
Furness HS 600/9-12
1900 S 3rd St 19148 215-952-6226
Daniel Peou, prin. Fax 952-8635
Girard Academic Music Program 500/5-12
2136 W Ritner St 19145 215-952-8589
Carol Domb, prin. Fax 952-6544
Harding MS 700/6-8
2000 Wakeling St 19124 215-537-2528
Mary Sanchez, prin. Fax 537-2850
High School of the Future 400/9-12
4021 Parkside Ave 19104 215-823-5502
Richard Sherin, prin. Fax 823-5504
Hill-Freedman World Academy 200/6-12
6200 Crittenden St 19138 215-276-5260
Anthony Majewski, prin. Fax 276-5873
Kensington Business & Finance HS 400/9-12
2501 Coral St 19125 215-291-5168
Renato Lajara, prin. Fax 291-5708
Kensington CAPA HS 400/9-12
1901 N Front St 19122 215-291-5010
Lisette Agosto-Clintron, prin. Fax 291-6334
Kensington Health Sciences S Vo/Tech
2463 Emerald St 19125 215-291-5185
James Williams, prin. Fax 291-6320
Kensington Urban Education 200/Alt
2051 E Cumberland St 19125 215-291-5420
Renato Lajara, prin. Fax 291-5427
King HS 800/9-12
6100 Stenton Ave 19138 215-276-5253
William Wade, prin. Fax 276-5844
LaBrum MS 200/6-8
10800 Hawley Rd 19154 215-281-2607
William Griffin, prin. Fax 281-5800
Lankenau HS 300/9-12
201 Spring Ln 19128 215-487-4465
Karen Dean, prin. Fax 487-4879
Leeds MS 300/7-8
1100 E Mount Pleasant Ave 19150 215-248-6602
Kala Johnstone, prin. Fax 248-6623
Linc 9-10
122 W Erie Ave 19122 215-291-5432
Bridget Bujak, prin. Fax 291-5449
Lincoln HS 1,800/9-12
3201 Ryan Ave 19136 215-335-5653
Jack Nelson, prin. Fax 335-5997
Masterman MSHS 1,200/5-12
1699 Spring Garden St 19130 215-299-4661
Jessica Brown, prin. Fax 299-3425
Meehan MS 600/7-8
3001 Ryan Ave 19152 215-335-5654
Mary Jackson, prin. Fax 335-5992
Middle Years Alternative-MYA 300/Alt
4725 Fairmount Ave 19139 215-581-5633
Shakae Dupre, prin. Fax 581-5668
Motivation HS 200/9-12
5900 Baltimore Ave 19143 215-471-2906
Rennu Teli, prin. Fax 492-6924
Northeast HS 3,100/9-12
1601 Cottman Ave 19111 215-728-5018
Sharon McCLoskey, prin. Fax 728-5004
Overbrook HS 1,400/9-12
5898 Lancaster Ave 19131 215-581-5507
Yvette Jackson, prin. Fax 581-3406
Parkway Center City HS 400/9-12
540 N 13th St 19123 215-351-7095
Karren Dunkley, prin. Fax 351-7097
Parkway Northwest HS 300/9-12
1100 E Mount Pleasant Ave 19150 215-248-6220
Gina Steiner, prin. Fax 248-6015
Parkway West HS 300/9-12
4725 Fairmount Ave 19139 215-581-5510
Dr. Kathleen McCladdie, prin. Fax 581-5600
Penn Treaty MSHS 300/6-12
600 E Thompson St 19125 215-291-4715
Sam Howell, prin. Fax 291-5172
Philadelphia HS for Girls 1,000/9-12
1400 W Olney Ave 19141 215-276-5258
Parthenia Moore, prin. Fax 276-5738
Philadelphia Military Academy 200/9-12
2118 N 13th St 19122 215-684-5091
Patricia Randzo, prin. Fax 684-5507
Robeson HS for Human Services 300/9-12
4125 Ludlow St 19104 215-823-8207
Richard Gordon, prin. Fax 823-8252
Roxborough HS 500/9-12
6498 Ridge Ave 19128 215-487-4464
Dana Jenkins, prin. Fax 487-4843
Sayre HS 600/9-12
5800 Walnut St 19139 215-471-2904
Jamie Eberle, prin. Fax 471-3486
Science Leadership Academy 500/9-12
55 N 22nd St 19103 215-979-5620
Christopher Lehmann, prin. Fax 567-2809
Science Leadership Academy @ Beeber 9-10
5925 Malvern Ave 19131 215-581-2715
Christopher Johnson, prin. Fax 581-2109
South Philadelphia HS 900/9-12
2101 S Broad St 19148 215-952-6220
Otis Hackney, prin. Fax 551-2275
Strawberry Mansion HS 400/9-12
3133 Ridge Ave 19121 215-684-5089
Linda Cliatt-Wayman, prin. Fax 684-5380
The U School: Innovative Lab 9-10
2000 N 7th St 19122 215-684-3266
Neil Geyette, prin. Fax 684-2476
Tilden MS 300/6-8
6601 Elmwood Ave 19142 215-492-6454
Brian Johnson, prin. Fax 492-6128
Wagner MS 500/6-8
1701 W Chelten Ave 19126 215-276-5252
Maya Johnstone, prin. Fax 276-5849
Washington HS 1,900/9-12
10175 Bustleton Ave 19116 215-961-2001
Gene Jones, prin. Fax 961-2545
Washington Jr. MS 700/5-8
201 E Olney Ave 19120 215-456-0422
Jovan Moore, prin. Fax 456-2181
West Philadelphia HS 800/9-12
4901 Chestnut St 19139 215-471-2902
Mary Dean, prin. Fax 471-6402
Wilson MS 1,200/6-8
1800 Cottman Ave 19111 215-728-5015
Stefanie Ressler, prin. Fax 728-5051
Workshop HS Alt
221 S Hanson St 19139 215-471-2960
Simon Hauger, prin. Fax 471-2948

---

Achieve Test Prep Post-Sec.
1015 Chestnut St Ste 515 19107 610-400-1641
Al-Aqsa Islamic Academy 300/PK-12
1501 Germantown Ave 19122 215-765-6660

Albert Einstein Medical Center — Post-Sec.
5501 Old York Rd 19141 — 215-456-7010
American Beauty Academy — Post-Sec.
6912 Frankford Ave 19135 — 215-331-1515
ARAMARK Healthcare Support Services — Post-Sec.
1101 Market St Fl 12 19107 — 610-687-8600
Archbishop Ryan HS — 1,600/9-12
11201 Academy Rd 19154 — 215-637-1800
James Meredith, prin. — Fax 637-8833
Aria Health School of Nursing — Post-Sec.
4918 Penn St 19124 — 215-831-6740
Aviation Institute of Maintenance — Post-Sec.
3001 Grant Ave 19114 — 215-676-7700
Calvary Christian Academy — 1,000/PK-12
13500 Philmont Ave 19116 — 215-969-1579
Chestnut Hill College — Post-Sec.
9601 Germantown Ave 19118 — 215-248-7001
City S, 860 N 24th St 19130 — 200/K-12
Jake Becker, head sch — 215-765-5363
Community College of Philadelphia — Post-Sec.
1700 Spring Garden St 19130 — 215-751-8000
Crefeld S — 100/7-12
8836 Crefeld St 19118 — 215-242-5545
George Zeleznik, head sch — Fax 242-8869
Curtis Institute of Music — Post-Sec.
1726 Locust St 19103 — 215-893-5252
DeVry University — Post-Sec.
1800 JFK Blvd Ste 200 19103 — 215-568-2911
Drexel University — Post-Sec.
3141 Chestnut St 19104 — 215-895-2000
Empire Beauty School — Post-Sec.
4026 Woodhaven Rd 19154 — 215-637-3700
Empire Beauty School — Post-Sec.
1522 Chestnut St 19102 — 215-568-3980
Faith Tabernacle S — 200/1-12
PO Box 46245 19160 — 215-221-0909
Father Judge HS — 1,100/9-12
3301 Solly Ave 19136 — 215-338-9494
Rev. James Dalton, prin. — Fax 338-0250
Finshing Trades Institute — Post-Sec.
2190 Hornig Rd 19116 — 215-501-0130
First Century Gospel S — 200/1-10
6807 Rising Sun Ave 19111 — 215-742-6615
Friends Select S — 600/PK-12
1651 Benjamin Franklin Pkwy 19103 — 215-561-5900
Rose Hagan, hdmstr. — Fax 864-2979
Germantown Friends S — 900/K-12
31 W Coulter St 19144 — 215-951-2300
Dana Weeks, head sch — Fax 951-2312
Girard College — 500/1-12
2101 S College Ave 19121 — 215-787-2600
Clarence Armbrister, pres. — Fax 787-2725
Hallahan HS — 600/9-12
311 N 19th St 19103 — 215-563-8930
Michelle Beachy, prin. — Fax 563-3809
Holy Family University — Post-Sec.
9801 Frankford Ave 19114 — 215-637-7700
Hope Church S — 200/PK-12
6707 Old York Rd 19126 — 215-927-7770
Dr. Raahsahn Bowden, supt. — Fax 927-8070
Hussian School of Art — Post-Sec.
111 S Indpndnce Mall E #300 19106 — 215-574-9600
International Christian HS — 100/9-12
413 E Tabor Rd 19120 — 267-900-2000
Ben Brittin, admin. — Fax 455-7198
ITT Technical Institute — Post-Sec.
105 S 7th St Ste 100 19106 — 215-413-4300
Jean Madeline Educ. Ctr. for Cosmetology — Post-Sec.
315A Bainbridge St 19147 — 215-238-9998
JNA Institute of Culinary Arts — Post-Sec.
1212 S Broad St 19146 — 215-468-8800
Kaplan Career Institute — Post-Sec.
3010 Market St 19104 — 215-594-4000
Kaplan Career Institute — Post-Sec.
177 Franklin Mills Blvd 19154 — 215-612-6600
La Salle Academy — 100/3-8
1434 N 2nd St 19122 — 215-739-5804
Teresa Diamond, prin. — Fax 739-1664
La Salle University — Post-Sec.
1900 W Olney Ave 19141 — 215-951-1000
Lincoln Technical Institute — Post-Sec.
9191 Torresdale Ave 19136 — 215-335-0800
Lincoln Technical Institute — Post-Sec.
3600 Market St 19104 — 215-382-1553
Lincoln Technical Institute — Post-Sec.
2180 Hornig Rd 19116 — 215-969-0869
Little Flower HS — 700/9-12
1000 W Lycoming St 19140 — 215-455-6900
Sr. Kathleen Klarich, prin. — Fax 329-0478
L.T. International Beauty School — Post-Sec.
830 N Broad St 19130 — 215-922-4478
Lutheran Theological Seminary — Post-Sec.
7301 Germantown Ave 19119 — 215-248-4616
Mercy Vocational HS — Vo/Tech
2900 W Hunting Park Ave 19129 — 215-226-1225
Sr. Rosemary Herron, pres. — Fax 228-6337
Methodist Hospital — Post-Sec.
2301 S Broad St 19148 — 215-952-9402
Metropolitan Career Center — Post-Sec.
100 S Broad St Ste 830 19110 — 215-568-9215
Moore College of Art and Design — Post-Sec.
20th St and The Parkway 19103 — 215-965-4000
Nazareth Academy HS — 400/9-12
4001 Grant Ave 19114 — 215-637-7676
Sr. Mary Joan Jacobs, prin. — Fax 637-8523
Nazareth Hospital — Post-Sec.
2601 Holme Ave 19152 — 215-335-6000
Northeastern Hospital School of Nursing — Post-Sec.
2301 E Allegheny Ave 19134 — 215-291-3145
Northeast Prep S — 100/7-12
1309 Cottman Ave 19111 — 215-342-5500
Orleans Technical Institute — Post-Sec.
2770 Red Lion Rd 19114 — 215-728-4700
Our Mother of Sorrows S — 100/4-8
1008 N 48th St 19131 — 215-473-5828
Sr. Patricia Bonner, prin. — Fax 473-3096
Overbrook School for the Blind — Post-Sec.
6333 Malvern Ave 19151 — 215-877-0313
Peirce College — Post-Sec.
1420 Pine St 19102 — 215-545-6400

Penn Charter S — 1,000/PK-12
3000 W School House Ln 19144 — 215-844-3460
Dr. Darryl J. Ford, head sch — Fax 843-3939
Pennsylvania Academy of the Fine Arts — Post-Sec.
128 N Broad St 19102 — 215-972-7600
Pennsylvania Hospital — Post-Sec.
800 Spruce St 19107 — 215-829-3312
Pennsylvania School for the Deaf — Post-Sec.
100 W School House Ln 19144
Philadelphia Coll. Osteopathic Medicine — Post-Sec.
4170 City Ave 19131 — 215-871-6100
Philadelphia University — Post-Sec.
4201 Henry Ave 19144 — 215-951-2700
Restaurant School at Walnut Hill College — Post-Sec.
4207 Walnut St 19104 — 215-222-4200
Roman Catholic HS — 1,100/9-12
301 N Broad St 19107 — 215-627-1270
Robert O'Neill, prin. — Fax 627-4979
Roxborough Memorial Hospital — Post-Sec.
5800 Ridge Ave 19128 — 215-487-4459
St. Hubert HS — 700/9-12
7320 Torresdale Ave 19136 — 215-624-6840
Dr. Joanne Walls, prin. — Fax 624-5940
St. James S — 5-8
3217 W Clearfield St 19132 — 215-226-1276
David Kasievich, head sch
St. Joseph's Prep S — 1,000/9-12
1733 W Girard Ave 19130 — 215-978-1950
Fr. George Bur, pres. — Fax 765-1710
St. Joseph's University — Post-Sec.
5600 City Ave 19131 — 610-660-1000
St. Monica S - Senior Campus — 200/4-8
2500 S 16th St 19145 — 215-467-5338
Barbara Inforzato, prin. — Fax 467-4599
Settlement Music School — Post-Sec.
416 Queen St 19147 — 215-336-0400
Springside Chestnut Hill Academy — 500/PK-12
500 W Willow Grove Ave 19118 — 215-247-4700
Dr. Mark Segar, pres. — Fax 247-8516
SS. John Neumann/Maria Goretti HS — 700/9-12
1736 S 10th St 19148 — 215-465-8437
Kevin Dugan, prin. — Fax 462-2410
Star Career Academy — Post-Sec.
2371 Welsh Rd 19114 — 215-969-5877
Talmudical Yeshiva of Philadelphia — Post-Sec.
6063 Drexel Rd 19131 — 215-473-1212
Talmudical Yeshiva of Philadelphia — 100/9-12
6063 Drexel Rd 19131 — 215-477-1000
Rabbi Pinchas Lando, admin. — Fax 477-5065
Temple University — Post-Sec.
1801 N Broad St 19122 — 215-204-7000
The Art Institute of Philadelphia — Post-Sec.
1622 Chestnut St 19103 — 215-567-7080
Thomas Jefferson University — Post-Sec.
1020 Walnut St 19107 — 215-955-6000
University of Pennsylvania — Post-Sec.
3451 Walnut St 19104 — 215-898-5000
University of the Arts — Post-Sec.
320 S Broad St 19102 — 215-717-6000
University of the Sciences Philadelphia — Post-Sec.
600 S 43rd St 19104 — 215-596-8800
Westminster Theological Seminary — Post-Sec.
PO Box 27009 19118 — 215-887-5511
West Philadephia Catholic HS — 400/9-12
4501 Chestnut St 19139 — 215-386-2244
Sr. Mary Bur, prin. — Fax 222-1651

**Philipsburg, Centre, Pop. 2,742**
Philipsburg-Osceola Area SD — 1,400/K-12
200 Short St 16866 — 814-342-1050
Dr. Gregg Paladina, supt. — Fax 342-7208
www.pomounties.org
Philipsburg-Osceola Area HS — 600/9-12
502 Philips St 16866 — 814-342-1521
Justin Hazelton, prin. — Fax 342-7521
Philipsburg-Osceola Area MS — 100/5-8
200 Short St 16866 — 814-342-4906
Susan Pritchard-Harris, prin. — Fax 342-7532

**Phoenixville, Chester, Pop. 15,988**
Area Vocational Technical School
Supt. — None
Technical College HS - Pickering Campus — Vo/Tech
1580 Charlestown Rd 19460 — 610-933-8877
Frank McKnight, prin. — Fax 983-0680

Phoenixville Area SD — 3,300/K-12
386 City Line Ave 19460 — 484-927-5000
Dr. Alan Fegley, supt. — Fax 983-3729
www.pasd.com
Phoenixville Area HS — 900/9-12
1200 Gay St 19460 — 484-927-5100
Dr. Craig Parkinson, prin. — Fax 933-6009
Phoenixville Area MS — 800/6-8
1000 Purple Pride Pkwy 19460 — 484-927-5200
Dr. Frank Garritano, prin. — Fax 933-6121

---

Valley Forge Christian College — Post-Sec.
1401 Charlestown Rd 19460 — 610-935-0450

**Pine Forge, Berks**

---

Pine Forge Academy — 200/9-12
PO Box 338 19548 — 610-326-5800
Nicole Falconer, prin. — Fax 326-4260

**Pine Grove, Schuylkill, Pop. 2,160**
Pine Grove Area SD — 1,600/K-12
103 School St 17963 — 570-345-2731
Dr. Kendy Hinkel, supt. — Fax 345-2790
www.pgasd.com
Pine Grove Area HS — 500/9-12
101 School St 17963 — 570-345-2731
Michael Janicelli, prin. — Fax 345-2793
Pine Grove Area MS — 500/5-8
105 School St 17963 — 570-345-2731
Cassidy Shults, prin. — Fax 345-2791

**Pittsburgh, Allegheny, Pop. 297,895**
Avonworth SD — 1,500/K-12
258 Josephs Ln 15237 — 412-369-8738
Dr. Thomas W. Ralston, supt. — Fax 369-8746
www.avonworth.k12.pa.us
Avonworth HS — 400/9-12
304 Josephs Ln 15237 — 412-366-6360
Dr. Kenneth Lockette, prin. — Fax 366-7603
Avonworth MS — 300/6-8
256 Josephs Ln 15237 — 412-366-9650
Michael Hall, prin. — Fax 358-9621

Baldwin-Whitehall SD — 4,200/K-12
4900 Curry Rd 15236 — 412-884-6300
Dr. Randal A. Lutz, supt. — Fax 885-7802
www.bwschools.net/
Baldwin HS — 1,500/9-12
4653 Clairton Blvd 15236 — 412-885-7500
Walter Graves, prin. — Fax 885-6652
Harrison MS — 900/6-8
129 Windvale Dr 15236 — 412-885-7530
Michael Wetmiller, prin. — Fax 885-6766

Brentwood Borough SD — 1,300/K-12
3601 Brownsville Rd 15227 — 412-881-2227
Dr. Amy Burch, supt. — Fax 881-1640
www.brentwoodpgh.k12.pa.us
Brentwood HS — 400/9-12
3601 Brownsville Rd 15227 — 412-881-4940
Jason Olexa, prin. — Fax 881-4170
Brentwood MS — 300/6-8
3601 Brownsville Rd 15227 — 412-881-4940
David Radcliffe Ph.D., prin. — Fax 881-4170

Chartiers Valley SD — 3,400/K-12
2030 Swallow Hill Rd 15220 — 412-429-2201
Dr. Brian White, supt. — Fax 429-2237
Other Schools – See Bridgeville

Fox Chapel Area SD — 4,300/K-12
611 Field Club Rd 15238 — 412-963-9600
Dr. Gene Freeman, supt. — Fax 967-0697
www.fcasd.edu
Dorseyville MS — 1,000/6-8
3732 Saxonburg Blvd 15238 — 412-767-5343
Jonathan Nauhaus, prin. — Fax 967-2531
Fox Chapel Area HS — 1,400/9-12
611 Field Club Rd 15238 — 412-967-2430
Michael Hower, prin. — Fax 967-0697

Keystone Oaks SD — 2,100/K-12
1000 Kelton Ave 15216 — 412-571-6000
Dr. William Stropkaj, supt. — Fax 571-6006
www.kosd.org
Keystone Oaks HS — 700/9-12
1000 Kelton Ave 15216 — 412-571-6040
Scott Hagy, prin. — Fax 571-6043
Keystone Oaks MS — 500/6-8
1002 Kelton Ave 15216 — 412-571-6146
Jeffrey Kattan, prin. — Fax 571-6092

Mt. Lebanon SD — 5,300/K-12
7 Horsman Dr 15228 — 412-344-2077
Dr. Timothy Steinhauer, supt. — Fax 344-2047
www.mtlsd.org
Jefferson MS — 600/6-8
21 Moffett St 15243 — 412-344-2123
Kelly Szesterniak, prin. — Fax 344-1252
Mellon MS — 600/6-8
11 Castle Shannon Blvd 15228 — 412-344-2122
Christopher Wolfson, prin. — Fax 344-0590
Mt. Lebanon HS — 1,800/9-12
155 Cochran Rd 15228 — 412-344-2003
Brian McFeeley, prin. — Fax 344-2021

North Allegheny SD — 8,200/K-12
200 Hillvue Ln 15237 — 412-366-2100
Dr. Raymond D. Gualtieri Ed.D., admin. — Fax 369-5513
www.northallegheny.org
Carson MS — 700/6-8
300 Hillvue Ln 15237 — 412-369-5520
Katherine Jenkins, prin. — Fax 630-5819
Ingomar MS — 600/6-8
1521 Ingomar Heights Rd 15237 — 412-358-1470
Heidi Stark, prin. — Fax 366-4487
North Allegheny Intermediate HS — 1,400/9-10
350 Cumberland Rd 15237 — 412-369-5530
Dr. Brendan Hyland, prin. — Fax 369-4825
Other Schools – See Wexford

North Hills SD — 3,600/K-12
135 6th Ave 15229 — 412-318-1000
Dr. Patrick Mannarino, supt. — Fax 318-1084
www.nhsd.net
North Hills HS — 1,100/9-12
53 Rochester Rd 15229 — 412-318-1400
Beth Williams, prin. — Fax 318-1403
North Hills MS — 700/7-8
55 Rochester Rd 15229 — 412-318-1450
Dave Lieberman, prin. — Fax 318-1453

Northgate SD — 1,200/K-12
591 Union Ave 15202 — 412-732-3300
Dr. Joseph Pasquerilla, supt. — Fax 734-8008
www.northgate.k12.pa.us
Northgate MSHS — 500/7-12
589 Union Ave 15202 — 412-732-3300
Bryan Kyle, prin. — Fax 734-8086

Penn Hills SD — 4,000/PK-12
260 Aster St 15235 — 412-793-7000
Dr. Nancy Hines, supt. — Fax 793-7825
www.phsd.k12.pa.us
Linton MS — 1,300/5-8
250 Aster St 15235 — 412-793-7000
Katie Friend, prin. — Fax 795-6087
Penn Hills HS — 1,400/9-12
309 Collins Dr 15235 — 412-793-7000
Eric Kostic, prin. — Fax 712-1047

Pittsburgh SD 22,700/PK-12
341 S Bellefield Ave 15213 412-622-3500
Dr. Linda Lane, supt. Fax 622-7920
www.pps.k12.pa.us
Pittsburgh Allderdice HS 1,400/9-12
2409 Shady Ave 15217 412-422-4800
Melissa Friez, prin. Fax 422-4803
Pittsburgh Allegheny 6-8 400/6-8
810 Arch St 15212 412-323-4115
Toni Kendrick, prin. Fax 323-4114
Pittsburgh Arlington 3-8 200/3-8
2500 Jonquil St 15210 412-488-3641
Kevin McGuire, prin. Fax 488-3760
Pittsburgh Arsenal 6-8 200/6-8
220 40th St 15201 412-622-5740
Patti Camper, prin. Fax 622-5743
Pittsburgh Brashear HS 1,200/9-12
590 Crane Ave 15216 412-571-7300
Kimberly Safran, prin. Fax 571-7305
Pittsburgh CAPA 6-12 900/6-12
111 9th St 15222 412-338-6100
Melissa Pearlman, prin. Fax 338-6143
Pittsburgh Carrick HS 800/9-12
125 Parkfield St 15210 412-885-7700
Dennis Chakey, prin. Fax 885-7708
Pittsburgh Classical 6-8 300/6-8
1463 Chartiers Ave 15220 412-928-3110
Valerie Merlo, prin. Fax 928-3106
Pittsburgh Milliones 6-12 700/6-12
3117 Centre Ave 15219 412-622-5900
Derrick Hardy, prin. Fax 622-5925
Pittsburgh Morrow 5-8 5-8
3530 Fleming Ave 15212 412-529-6600
Alivia Clark, prin. Fax 734-6606
Pittsburgh Obama 6-12 900/6-12
515 N Highland Ave 15206 412-622-5980
Dr. Wayne Walters, prin. Fax 622-5983
Pittsburgh Perry HS 700/9-12
3875 Perrysville Ave 15214 412-323-3400
Nina Sacco, prin. Fax 323-3404
Pittsburgh Schiller 6-8 200/6-8
1018 Peralta St 15212 412-323-4190
Paula Heinzman, prin. Fax 323-4192
Pittsburgh Science\Technology Acad 6-12 400/6-12
107 Thackeray St 15213 412-325-7620
Shawn McNeil, prin. Fax 622-5991
Pittsburgh South Brook 6-8 500/6-8
779 Dunster St 15226 412-572-8170
Jennifer McNamara, prin. Fax 572-8177
Pittsburgh South Hills 6-8 500/6-8
595 Crane Ave 15216 412-572-8130
Jacqueline Hale, prin. Fax 572-8148
Pittsburgh Sterrett 6-8 400/6-8
7100 Reynolds St 15208 412-247-7870
Dr. MiChele Holly, prin. Fax 247-7877
Pittsburgh Student Achievement Center 200/Alt
925 Brushton Ave 15208 412-529-7860
Dalhart Dobbs, prin. Fax 529-7926
Pittsburgh Westinghouse Academy 6-12 300/6-12
1101 N Murtland St 15208 412-665-3940
Alexander Herring, prin. Fax 665-4977

Plum Borough SD 4,000/K-12
900 Elicker Rd 15239 412-795-0100
Dr. Timothy Glasspool, supt. Fax 795-9115
www.pbsd.k12.pa.us
O'Block JHS 700/7-8
440 Presque Isle Dr 15239 724-733-2400
Joseph Fishell, prin. Fax 798-6347
Plum HS 1,400/9-12
900 Elicker Rd 15239 412-795-4880
Ryan Kociela, prin. Fax 795-6823

Shaler Area SD
Supt. — See Glenshaw
Shaler Area HS 1,600/9-12
381 Wible Run Rd 15209 412-492-1200
Timothy Royall, prin. Fax 684-1076

Upper St. Clair SD
Supt. — See Upper Saint Clair
Ft. Couch MS 700/7-8
515 Fort Couch Rd 15241 412-833-1600
Joseph DeMar, prin. Fax 854-3095
Upper Saint Clair HS 1,400/9-12
1825 Mclaughlin Run Rd 15241 412-833-1600
Dr. Michael Ghilani, prin. Fax 833-4889

West Jefferson Hills SD
Supt. — See Jefferson Hills
Pleasant Hills MS 700/6-8
404 Old Clairton Rd 15236 412-655-8680
Daniel Como, prin. Fax 655-5691

Woodland Hills SD
Supt. — See North Braddock
Woodland Hills JSHS 1,300/8-12
2550 Greensburg Pike 15221 412-244-1100
Kevin Murray, prin. Fax 242-2344

---

Academy of Court Reporting & Technology Post-Sec.
717 Liberty Ave Fl 13 15222 216-834-1400
Bidwell Training Center Post-Sec.
1815 Metropolitan St 15233 412-323-4000
Bishop Canevin Catholic HS 400/9-12
2700 Morange Rd 15205 412-922-7400
Karen Walker, prin. Fax 922-7403
Bradford School Post-Sec.
125 W Station Square # 129 15219 412-391-6710
Byzantine Catholic Seminary Post-Sec.
3605 Perrysville Ave 15214 412-321-8383
Career Training Academy Post-Sec.
1500 Shoppes Northway Mall 15237 412-367-4000
Carlow University Post-Sec.
3333 5th Ave 15213 412-578-6000
Carnegie Mellon University Post-Sec.
5000 Forbes Ave 15213 412-268-2000
Center for Emergency Medicine/Western PA Post-Sec.
230 McKee Pl # 500 15213 412-647-4665
Central Catholic HS 800/9-12
4720 5th Ave 15213 412-208-3400
Br. Robert Schaefer, prin. Fax 208-0555
Chatham University Post-Sec.
Woodland Rd 15232 412-365-1100
Community College of Allegheny County Post-Sec.
808 Ridge Ave 15212 412-237-2525
Community College of Allegheny County Post-Sec.
8701 Perry Hwy 15237 412-366-7000
Dean Institute of Technology Post-Sec.
1501 W Liberty Ave 15226 412-531-4433
DeVry University Post-Sec.
210 6th Ave Ste 200 15222 412-642-9072
Duquesne University Post-Sec.
600 Forbes Ave 15282 412-396-6000
Ellis S 500/PK-12
6425 5th Ave 15206 412-661-5992
Robin Newham M.Ed., head sch Fax 661-3979
Empire Beauty School Post-Sec.
1000 McKnight Park Dr #1006 15237 800-575-5983
Everest Institute Post-Sec.
100 Forbes Ave # 1200 15222 412-261-4520
Hillel Academy of Pittsburgh 200/K-12
5685 Beacon St 15217 412-521-8131
Home for Crippled Children Post-Sec.
1426 Denniston St 15217
Imani Christian Academy 200/K-12
2150 E Hills Dr 15221 412-731-7982
ITT Technical Institute Post-Sec.
5460 Campbells Run Rd 15205 412-446-2900
Kaplan Career Institute Post-Sec.
933 Penn Ave 15222 412-338-4770
La Roche College Post-Sec.
9000 Babcock Blvd 15237 412-367-9300
Mercy Hospital School of Nursing Post-Sec.
1401 Blvd of the Allies 15219 412-232-7940
Neighborhood Academy 100/8-12
709 N Aiken Ave 15206 412-362-2001
Rev. Thomas Johnson, head sch Fax 362-2004
North Hills Beauty Academy Post-Sec.
813 W View Park Dr 15229 412-931-8563
Oakland Catholic HS 600/9-12
144 N Craig St 15213 412-682-6633
Sharyn Zalno, prin. Fax 682-2496
Pennsylvania Gunsmith School Post-Sec.
812 Ohio River Blvd 15202 412-766-1812
Pittsburgh Institute of Aeronautics Post-Sec.
PO Box 10897 15236 412-346-2100
Pittsburgh Institute of Mortuary Science Post-Sec.
5808 Baum Blvd 15206 412-362-8500
Pittsburgh Theological Seminary Post-Sec.
616 N Highland Ave 15206 412-362-5610
Point Park University Post-Sec.
201 Wood St 15222 412-391-4100
Point Park Univ.-St. Francis Med. Ctr. Post-Sec.
201 Wood St 15222 412-392-3879
Pressley Ridge School Post-Sec.
530 Marshall Ave 15214 412-442-4468
Reformed Presbyterian Theological Sem. Post-Sec.
7418 Penn Ave 15208 412-731-6000
Rosedale Technical Institute Post-Sec.
215 Beecham Dr Ste 2 15205 412-521-6200
St. Margaret Schools of Nursing Post-Sec.
221 7th St Ste 100 15238 412-784-4980
Seton-LaSalle HS 500/9-12
1000 McNeilly Rd 15226 412-561-3583
Lauren Martin, prin. Fax 561-9097
Shady Side Academy MS 200/6-8
500 Squaw Run Rd E 15238 412-968-3100
Amy Nixon, head sch Fax 968-3008
Shady Side Academy Senior S 500/9-12
423 Fox Chapel Rd 15238 412-968-3000
Katharine Vavpetic, head sch Fax 968-3002
Shadyside Hospital Post-Sec.
5230 Centre Ave 15232 412-622-2010
South Hills Beauty Academy Post-Sec.
3269 W Liberty Ave 15216 412-561-3381
The Art Institute of Pittsburgh Post-Sec.
420 Blvd of the Allies 15219 412-263-6600
Triangle Tech Post-Sec.
1940 Perrysville Ave 15214 412-359-1000
Trinity Christian S 300/K-12
299 Ridge Ave 15221 412-242-8886
Kennedy Henriquez, head sch Fax 242-8859
University Health Center Post-Sec.
300 Halket St 15213 412-641-4664
University of Pittsburgh Post-Sec.
4200 5th Ave 15213 412-624-4141
UPMC School of Medical Imaging Post-Sec.
3434 Forbes Ave 15213 412-647-3528
Vet Tech Institute Post-Sec.
125 7th St 15222 412-391-7021
Vincentian Academy 200/9-12
8100 McKnight Rd 15237 412-364-1616
Edward Bernot, prin. Fax 367-5722
Western Pennsylvania Hospital Post-Sec.
4900 Friendship Ave 15224 412-578-5538
Western Pennsylvania School for Blind Post-Sec.
Bayard at Bellefield 15213
Western Pennsylvania School for the Deaf Post-Sec.
300 E Swissvale Ave 15218 412-371-7000
Winchester Thurston S 700/PK-12
555 Morewood Ave 15213 412-578-7500
Gary Niels, hdmstr. Fax 578-7504
Yeshiva S of Pittsburgh 100/PK-12
2100 Wightman St 15217 412-422-7300
Rabbi Yisroel Rosenfeld, dean Fax 422-5930

**Pittston, Luzerne, Pop. 7,622**
Pittston Area SD 2,600/K-12
5 Stout St 18640 570-654-2415
Dr. Michael Garzella, supt. Fax 654-5548
www.pittstonarea.com
Pittston Area HS 1,100/9-12
5 Stout St 18640 570-654-3541
John Haas, prin. Fax 602-0823
Pittston Area MS 700/5-8
120 New St 18640 570-655-2927
Patrick Bilbow, prin. Fax 654-0862

**Plains, Luzerne, Pop. 4,288**
Wilkes-Barre Area SD
Supt. — See Wilkes Barre
Solomon/Plains JHS 500/7-8
43 Abbott St 18705 570-826-7224
John Woloski, prin. Fax 820-3715

**Pleasant Gap, Centre, Pop. 2,844**
Area Vocational Technical School
Supt. — None
Central PA Institute of Science & Tech Vo/Tech
540 N Harrison Rd 16823 814-359-2793
Dr. Richard Makin, dir. Fax 359-2599

**Plumsteadville, Bucks, Pop. 2,600**

---

Plumstead Christian S - Middle Upper Cps 200/6-12
PO Box 216 18949 215-766-8073
Patrick Fitzpatrick, hdmstr. Fax 766-2033

**Plymouth, Luzerne, Pop. 5,852**
Wyoming Valley West SD
Supt. — See Kingston
Wyoming Valley West HS 1,300/9-12
150 Wadham St 18651 570-779-5361
David Novrocki, prin. Fax 779-9510

**Plymouth Meeting, Montgomery, Pop. 6,092**
Area Vocational Technical School
Supt. — None
Central Montco Technical HS Vo/Tech
821 Plymouth Rd 19462 610-277-2301
Walter Slauch, dir.

Colonial SD 4,700/K-12
230 Flourtown Rd 19462 610-834-1670
Dr. Mary Ellen Gorodetzer, supt. Fax 834-7535
www.colonialsd.org
Colonial MS 1,100/6-8
716 Belvoir Rd 19462 610-275-5100
Robert Fahler, prin. Fax 278-2447
Plymouth-Whitemarsh HS 1,600/9-12
201 E Germantown Pike 19462 610-825-1500
Jason Bacani, prin. Fax 832-0766

---

ITT Technical Institute Post-Sec.
220 W Germantown Pike # 100 19462 610-832-3400

**Pocono Summit, Monroe**
Pocono Mountain SD
Supt. — See Swiftwater
Pocono Mountain West HS 1,500/9-12
181 Panther Ln 18346 570-839-7121
Mark Wade, prin. Fax 839-5968
Pocono Mountain West JHS 500/7-8
180 Panther Ln 18346 570-839-7121
Dr. Eric Vogt, prin. Fax 839-7397

**Point Marion, Fayette, Pop. 1,152**
Albert Gallatin Area SD
Supt. — See Uniontown
Gallatin South MS 400/6-8
224 New Geneva Rd 15474 724-725-5241
Joetta Britvich, prin. Fax 725-5424

**Portage, Cambria, Pop. 2,610**
Portage Area SD 900/PK-12
84 Mountain Ave 15946 814-736-9636
Eric Zelanko, supt. Fax 736-9634
www.portageareasd.org
Portage Area JSHS 400/7-12
85 Mountain Ave 15946 814-736-9636
Ralph Cecere, prin. Fax 736-9597

**Port Allegany, McKean, Pop. 2,134**
Area Vocational Technical School
Supt. — None
Seneca Highlands Career & Technical Ctr Vo/Tech
PO Box 219 16743 814-642-2573
James Young, dir.

Port Allegany SD 900/K-12
20 Oak St 16743 814-642-2596
Gary Buchsen, supt. Fax 642-9574
www.pahs.net
Port Allegany JSHS 500/7-12
20 Oak St 16743 814-642-2544
Marc Budd, prin. Fax 642-5082

**Portersville, Butler, Pop. 235**

---

Portersville Christian S 200/PK-12
343 E Portersville Rd 16051 724-368-8787
Lee Saunders, head sch Fax 368-3100

**Pottstown, Montgomery, Pop. 21,544**
Owen J. Roberts SD 5,000/K-12
901 Ridge Rd 19465 610-469-5100
Dr. Michael Christian, supt. Fax 469-0403
www.ojrsd.com
Roberts HS 1,500/9-12
981 Ridge Rd 19465 610-469-5101
Dr. Richard Marchini, prin. Fax 469-5898
Roberts MS 800/7-8
881 Ridge Rd 19465 610-469-5102
Sean Burns, prin. Fax 469-5832

Pottsgrove SD 3,300/K-12
1301 Kauffman Rd 19464 610-327-2277
Dr. Shellie Feola, supt. Fax 327-2530
www.pgsd.org
Pottsgrove HS 1,100/9-12
1345 Kauffman Rd 19464 610-326-5105
Dr. William Ziegler, prin. Fax 970-6191
Pottsgrove MS 800/6-8
1351 N Hanover St 19464 610-326-8243
Dr. David Ramage, prin. Fax 718-0581

Pottstown SD 2,700/PK-12
230 Beech St 19464 610-323-8200
Dr. Jeffrey Sparagana, supt. Fax 326-6540
www.pottstownschools.com
Pottstown HS 800/9-12
750 N Washington St 19464 610-970-6700
Danielle McCoy, prin. Fax 970-1363
Pottstown MS 600/6-8
600 N Franklin St 19464 610-970-6665
David Todd, prin. Fax 970-8738

Antonelli Medical & Professional Inst Post-Sec.
1700 Industrial Hwy 19464 610-323-7270
Coventry Christian S 300/PK-12
699 N Pleasantview Rd 19464 610-326-3320
Paul Q. Fisher M.Ed., hdmstr. Fax 326-0085
Empire Beauty School Post-Sec.
141 E High St 19464 610-327-1313
Hill S 500/9-12
717 E High St 19464 610-326-1000
Zachary Lehman, hdmstr. Fax 705-1753
West-Mont Christian Academy 300/K-12
873 S Hanover St 19465 610-326-7690
Dr. James Smock, admin. Fax 326-7126

**Pottsville, Schuylkill, Pop. 14,045**
Area Vocational Technical School
Supt. — None
Schuylkill Technology Center - Airport Vo/Tech
240 Airport Rd 17901 570-544-4904
Dr. Diane Niederriter, dir.

Pottsville Area SD 2,900/K-12
1501 Laurel Blvd 17901 570-621-2900
Dr. Jeffrey Zweibel, supt. Fax 621-2025
www.pottsville.k12.pa.us/
Lengel MS 800/5-8
1541 Laurel Blvd 17901 570-621-2924
Michael Maley, prin. Fax 621-2999
Pottsville Area HS 1,100/9-12
1600 Elk Ave 17901 570-621-2962
Tiffany Reedy, prin. Fax 621-2036

McCann School of Business & Technology Post-Sec.
2650 Woodglen Rd 17901 570-622-7622
Nativity BVM HS 200/9-12
1 Lawtons Hl 17901 570-622-8110
Lynn Sabol, prin. Fax 622-0454
Schuylkill Health School of Nursing Post-Sec.
420 S Jackson St 17901 570-621-5027

**Prospect Park, Delaware, Pop. 6,344**
Interboro SD 3,600/K-12
900 Washington Ave 19076 610-461-6700
Bernadette Reiley, supt. Fax 583-1678
www.interborosd.org
Interboro HS 1,200/9-12
500 16th Ave 19076 610-237-6410
Ryan Johnston, prin. Fax 237-8103

**Punxsutawney, Jefferson, Pop. 5,912**
Punxsutawney Area SD 2,200/K-12
475 Beyer Ave 15767 814-938-5151
Dr. Keith Wolfe, supt. Fax 938-6677
www.punxsy.k12.pa.us/
Punxsutawney Area HS 900/8-12
500 N Findley St 15767 814-938-5151
David London, prin. Fax 938-5101

Punxsutawney Christian S 200/PK-12
216 N Jefferson St 15767 814-938-2295
Lori Galbraith, admin. Fax 938-2251

**Quakertown, Bucks, Pop. 8,835**
Quakertown Community SD 5,200/K-12
100 Commerce Dr 18951 215-529-2000
William Harner Ph.D., supt. Fax 529-2042
www.qcsd.org
Freshman Center 400/9-9
349 S 9th St 18951 267-371-1200
Erin Oleksa, prin. Fax 371-1201
Milford MS 400/6-8
2255 Allentown Rd 18951 215-529-2210
Dr. Deb Lock, prin. Fax 529-2211
Quakertown Community HS 1,200/10-12
600 Park Ave 18951 215-529-2060
David Finnerty, prin. Fax 529-2061
Strayer MS 800/6-8
1200 Ronald Reagan Dr 18951 215-529-2290
Derek Peiffer, prin. Fax 529-2291

Quakertown Christian S 200/PK-12
50 E Paletown Rd 18951 215-536-6970
Dr. Mark Slider, head sch Fax 536-2115

**Quarryville, Lancaster, Pop. 2,535**
Solanco SD 3,700/K-12
121 S Hess St 17566 717-786-8401
Dr. Brian A. Bliss, supt. Fax 786-8245
www.solanco.k12.pa.us
Smith MS 500/6-8
645 Kirkwood Pike 17566 717-786-2244
Paul Gladfelter, prin. Fax 786-8796
Solanco HS 1,100/9-12
585 Solanco Rd 17566 717-786-2151
Brian Gallagher, prin. Fax 786-1808
Swift MS 400/6-8
1866 Robert Fulton Hwy 17566 717-548-2187
Paul Gladfelter, prin. Fax 548-3350

**Radnor, Delaware, Pop. 31,300**
Radnor Township SD
Supt. — See Wayne
Radnor HS 1,200/9-12
130 King of Prussia Rd 19087 610-293-0855
Daniel Bechtold, prin. Fax 989-9146

Archbishop Carroll HS 1,000/9-12
211 Matsonford Rd 19087 610-688-7610
Joseph Denelsbeck, prin. Fax 688-8326

Cabrini College Post-Sec.
610 King of Prussia Rd 19087 610-902-8100

**Reading, Berks, Pop. 86,403**
Antietam SD 1,000/K-12
100 Antietam Rd 19606 610-779-0554
Dr. Melissa G. Brewer, supt. Fax 779-4424
www.antietamsd.org
Antietam MSHS 500/7-12
100 Antietam Rd 19606 610-779-3545
Dr. Felice Stern, prin. Fax 779-0378

Area Vocational Technical School
Supt. — None
Reading-Muhlenberg CTC Vo/Tech
2615 Warren Rd 19604 610-921-7300
Gerald Witmer, admin. Fax 921-7367

Exeter Township SD 3,800/K-12
200 Elm St 19606 610-779-0700
Dr. Beverly Martin, supt. Fax 779-7104
www.exeter.k12.pa.us
Exeter Township HS 1,400/9-12
201 E 37th St 19606 610-779-3060
William Cain, prin. Fax 370-0518
Exeter Township JHS 700/7-8
151 E 39th St 19606 610-779-3320
Eric Flamm, prin. Fax 370-0678

Reading SD 12,800/PK-12
800 Washington St 19601 610-371-5611
Dr. Khalid Mumin, supt. Fax 371-5971
www.readingsd.org
Reading HS 2,600/10-12
801 N 13th St 19604 610-371-5710
Eric Turman, prin. Fax 371-8723
Reading Intermediate HS 8-9
215 N 12th St 19604 484-258-7365
Alex Brown, prin. Fax 258-7333

Albright College Post-Sec.
PO Box 15234 19612 610-921-2381
Alvernia University Post-Sec.
400 Saint Bernardine St 19607 610-796-8200
Berks Catholic HS 500/9-12
955 E Wyomissing Blvd 19611 610-374-8361
Tony Balistiere, prin. Fax 374-4309
Empire Beauty School Post-Sec.
2302 N 5th Street Hwy 19605 610-372-2777
Fairview Christian S 200/K-12
410 S 14th St 19602 610-372-8826
Pace Institute Post-Sec.
606 Court St 19601 610-375-1212
Penn State Berks Post-Sec.
PO Box 7009 19610 610-396-6000
Reading Area Community College Post-Sec.
PO Box 1706 19603 610-372-4721
Reading Hospital & Medical Center Post-Sec.
PO Box 16052 19612 610-378-6664
Reading Junior Academy 100/PK-10
309 N Kenhorst Blvd 19607 610-777-8424
St. Joseph's Hospital Post-Sec.
PO Box 316 19603 610-378-2000

**Red Lion, York, Pop. 6,289**
Red Lion Area SD 5,600/K-12
696 Delta Rd 17356 717-244-4518
Dr. Scott Deisley, supt. Fax 244-2196
www.rlasd.net
Red Lion Area JHS 900/7-8
200 Country Club Rd 17356 717-244-1448
Shane Mack, prin. Fax 244-6160
Red Lion Area SHS 1,700/9-12
200 Horace Mann Ave 17356 717-246-1611
Mark Shue, prin. Fax 246-9181

Red Lion Christian S 200/PK-12
105 Springvale Rd 17356 717-244-3905

**Renovo, Clinton, Pop. 1,205**
Keystone Central SD
Supt. — See Mill Hall
Bucktail Area JSHS 200/7-12
1300 Bucktail Ave 17764 570-923-1166
Betsy Dickey, prin. Fax 923-2233

**Reynoldsville, Jefferson, Pop. 2,735**
Area Vocational Technical School
Supt. — None
Jefferson County-Dubois AVTS Vo/Tech
576 Vo Tech Rd 15851 814-653-8265
Barry Fillman, dir. Fax 653-8425

**Richboro, Bucks, Pop. 6,518**
Council Rock SD
Supt. — See Newtown
Richboro MS 500/7-8
98 Upper Holland Rd 18954 215-944-2500
Richard Hollahan, prin. Fax 944-2598

**Ridgway, Elk, Pop. 4,043**
Ridgway Area SD 1,000/K-12
PO Box 447 15853 814-773-3146
Robert Rocco, supt. Fax 776-4299
www.ridgwayareaschooldistrict.com
Ridgway Area HS 300/9-12
PO Box 447 15853 814-773-3164
Brice Benson, prin. Fax 776-4247
Ridgway Area MS 200/6-8
PO Box 447 15853 814-773-3156
Brice Benson, prin. Fax 776-4239

**Ridley Park, Delaware, Pop. 6,923**
Ridley SD
Supt. — See Folsom
Ridley MS 1,300/6-8
400 Free St 19078 610-237-8034
Adam Staples, prin. Fax 237-8032

**Rimersburg, Clarion, Pop. 942**
Union SD 600/K-12
354 Baker St Ste 2 16248 814-473-6311
Jean McCleary, supt. Fax 473-8201
www.unionsd.net/
Union JSHS 300/7-12
354 Baker St Ste 1 16248 814-473-3121
Mark Schlosser, prin. Fax 473-8201

**Roaring Spring, Blair, Pop. 2,566**
Spring Cove SD 1,800/K-12
1100 E Main St 16673 814-224-5124
Robert Vadella, supt. Fax 224-5516
scsd.schoolwires.net
Spring Cove MS 400/6-8
185 Spring Cove Dr 16673 814-224-2106
Candace Claar, prin. Fax 224-2842
Other Schools – See Martinsburg

**Robesonia, Berks, Pop. 2,034**
Conrad Weiser Area SD 2,800/K-12
44 Big Spring Rd 19551 610-693-8545
Dr. Randall Grove, supt. Fax 693-8586
www.conradweiser.org
Weiser HS 1,000/9-12
44 Big Spring Rd 19551 610-693-8528
Robert G. Galtere, prin. Fax 693-8511
Weiser MS 900/5-8
347 E Penn Ave 19551 610-693-8514
R. Kenneth Buck, prin. Fax 693-8543

**Rochester, Beaver, Pop. 3,481**
Rochester Area SD 700/K-12
540 Reno St 15074 724-775-7500
Dr. Jane W. Bovalino Ed.D., supt. Fax 775-4077
www.rasd.org
Rochester Area HS 300/9-12
540 Reno St 15074 724-775-7500
Michael Damon, prin. Fax 775-9268
Rochester Area MS 6-8
540 Reno St 15074 724-775-7500
Michael Damon, prin. Fax 775-9268

**Rockwood, Somerset, Pop. 885**
Rockwood Area SD 800/K-12
439 Somerset Ave 15557 814-926-4688
Mark Bower, supt. Fax 926-2880
www.rockwoodschools.org
Rockwood Area JSHS 400/7-12
437 Somerset Ave 15557 814-926-4631
Mark Bower, prin. Fax 926-2631

**Rome, Bradford, Pop. 437**
Northeast Bradford SD 800/K-12
526 Panther Ln 18837 570-744-2521
Heather McPherson, supt. Fax 744-2933
www.neb.k12.pa.us
Northeast Bradford JSHS 400/7-12
526 Panther Ln 18837 570-744-2521
Gary Martell, prin. Fax 744-1445

North Rome Christian S 200/K-12
3376 N Rome Rd 18837 570-247-2800
Lee Ann Carmichael, admin. Fax 247-7288

**Rosemont, Montgomery**
Lower Merion SD
Supt. — See Ardmore
Harriton HS 1,100/9-12
600 N Ithan Ave 19010 610-658-3950
Scott Eveslage, prin. Fax 525-6771

Hill Top Preparatory S 100/5-12
737 S Ithan Ave 19010 610-527-3230
Tom Needham, head sch Fax 527-7683
Irwin S 700/PK-12
275 S Ithan Ave 19010 610-525-8400
Dr. Wendy Hill, head sch Fax 525-8908
Rosemont College Post-Sec.
1400 Montgomery Ave 19010 610-527-0200

**Roseto, Northampton, Pop. 1,552**

Faith Christian S 200/K-12
122 Dante St 18013 610-588-3414
Philip Norris, prin. Fax 588-8103

**Royersford, Montgomery, Pop. 4,653**
Spring-Ford Area SD 7,800/K-12
857 S Lewis Rd 19468 610-705-6000
Dr. David Goodin, supt. Fax 705-6245
www.spring-ford.net
Spring-Ford 9th Grade Center 600/9-9
400 S Lewis Rd 19468 610-705-6011
Dr. Theresa Weidenbaugh, prin. Fax 705-6233
Spring-Ford HS 1,700/10-12
350 S Lewis Rd 19468 610-705-6001
Dr. Patrick Nugent, prin. Fax 705-6258
Spring-Ford MS 8th Grade Center 600/8-8
700 Washington St 19468 610-705-6002
Michael Siggins, prin. Fax 705-6255

Pope John Paul II HS 800/9-12
181 Rittenhouse Rd 19468 484-975-6500
Sr. Janet Purcell, prin. Fax 792-3082

**Ruffs Dale, Westmoreland**
Yough SD
Supt. — See Herminie
Yough MS 700/5-8
171 State Route 31 15679 724-872-5164
Kevin Smetak, prin. Fax 872-5319

**Rural Valley, Armstrong, Pop. 873**
Armstrong SD
Supt. — See Kittanning
West Shamokin JSHS 500/7-12
178 Wolf Dr 16249 724-783-7040
Dr. Stephen Shutters, prin. Fax 783-6747

**Russell, Warren, Pop. 1,393**
Warren County SD 4,300/K-12
6820 Market Street Ext 16345 814-723-6900
Dr. William Clark, supt.
www.wcsdpa.org
Eisenhower MSHS 500/6-12
3700 Route 957 16345 814-757-8878
Kelly Martin, prin. Fax 757-8516
Other Schools – See Sheffield, Warren, Youngsville

**Saegertown, Crawford, Pop. 988**
PENNCREST SD 3,400/K-12
PO Box 808 16433 814-763-2323
Michael J. Healey, supt. Fax 763-5129
www.penncrest.org
Saegertown JSHS 600/7-12
18079 Mook Rd 16433 814-763-2615
Douglas Wilson, prin. Fax 763-6702
Other Schools – See Cambridge Springs, Guys Mills

**Saint Davids, Delaware**

Eastern University Post-Sec.
1300 Eagle Rd 19087 610-341-5800

**Saint Marys, Elk, Pop. 12,994**
Saint Marys Area SD 2,200/K-12
977 S Saint Marys St 15857 814-834-7831
Dr. Brian Toth, supt. Fax 781-2190
smasd.org
Saint Marys Area HS 700/9-12
977 S Saint Marys St 15857 814-834-7831
Joseph Collins, prin. Fax 781-2190
Saint Marys Area MS 600/6-8
979 S Saint Marys St 15857 814-834-7831
James Wortman, prin. Fax 781-2191

Elk County Catholic HS 300/9-12
600 Maurus St 15857 814-834-7800
Sandra Florig, prin. Fax 781-3441
St. Marys Catholic MS 100/6-8
600 Maurus St 15857 814-834-7800
John Schneider, prin. Fax 781-3441

**Salisbury, Somerset, Pop. 724**
Salisbury-Elk Lick SD 300/PK-12
PO Box 68 15558 814-662-2733
Joseph Renzi, supt. Fax 662-2544
selsd.com
Salisbury-Elk Lick JSHS 100/7-12
PO Box 68 15558 814-662-2741
Kenneth Fusina, prin. Fax 662-2091

**Saltsburg, Indiana, Pop. 862**
Blairsville-Saltsburg SD
Supt. — See Blairsville
Saltsburg MSHS 400/6-12
84 Trojan Ln 15681 724-639-3547
Tracy Richards, prin. Fax 639-0071

Kiski S 200/9-12
1888 Brett Ln 15681 724-639-3586
Christopher Brueningsen, hdmstr. Fax 639-8596

**Sarver, Butler**
Freeport Area SD 2,000/K-12
621 S Pike Rd 16055 724-295-5141
Chris DeVivo, supt. Fax 295-3001
www.freeport.k12.pa.us
Freeport Area HS 600/9-12
625 S Pike Rd 16055 724-295-5143
Michael Kleckner, prin. Fax 295-2390
Other Schools – See Freeport

Evangel Heights Christian Academy 300/PK-12
120 Beale Rd 16055 724-295-9199
Rev. Jeffrey Bogaczyk, dir. Fax 295-9009

**Saxonburg, Butler, Pop. 1,517**
South Butler County SD 2,600/K-12
328 Knoch Rd 16056 724-352-1700
David Zupsic, supt. Fax 352-3622
southbutler.org
Knoch HS 1,000/9-12
345 Knoch Rd 16056 724-352-1700
Todd Trofimuk, prin. Fax 352-0160
Knoch MS 600/6-8
754 Dinnerbell Rd 16056 724-352-1700
Frank Moxie, prin. Fax 352-0170

**Saxton, Bedford, Pop. 730**
Tussey Mountain SD 900/PK-12
199 Front St 16678 814-635-3670
Mark Bollman, supt. Fax 635-3928
www.tmsd.net
Tussey Mountain HS 400/7-12
199 Front St 16678 814-635-2975
Melinda Damiano, prin.
Tussey Mountain JHS 200/7-8
199 Front St 16678 814-635-2975
Zachary Treece, prin. Fax 635-3713

**Sayre, Bradford, Pop. 5,530**
Sayre Area SD 1,100/PK-12
333 W Lockhart St 18840 570-888-7615
Dr. Sherry Griggs Ph.D., supt. Fax 888-8248
www.sayresd.org
Sayre Area JSHS 500/7-12
331 W Lockhart St 18840 570-888-6622
Dayton Handrick, prin. Fax 882-9385

Robert Packer Hospital Post-Sec.
1 Guthrie Sq 18840 570-888-6666

**Schnecksville, Lehigh, Pop. 2,900**
Area Vocational Technical School
Supt. — None
Lehigh Career & Technical Institute Vo/Tech
4500 Education Park Dr 18078 610-799-1323

Lehigh Carbon Community College Post-Sec.
4525 Education Park Dr 18078 610-799-2121

**Schuylkill Haven, Schuylkill, Pop. 5,373**
Blue Mountain SD
Supt. — See Orwigsburg
Blue Mountain HS 1,000/9-12
1076 W Market St 17972 570-366-0511
Kevin Berger, prin. Fax 366-1965

Schuylkill Haven Area SD 1,300/K-12
501 E Main St 17972 570-385-6705
Lorraine Felker, supt. Fax 385-6736
www.haven.k12.pa.us/
Schuylkill Haven Area HS 500/8-12
501 E Main St 17972 570-385-6717
Sarah Yoder, prin. Fax 385-6745

Penn State Schuylkill Post-Sec.
200 University Dr 17972 570-385-6000

**Scottdale, Westmoreland, Pop. 4,332**
Southmoreland SD 2,000/K-12
200 Scottie Way 15683 724-887-2005
Dr. John Molnar, supt. Fax 887-2055
www.southmoreland.net
Southmoreland MS 500/6-8
200 Scottie Way 15683 724-887-2029
Vince Mascia, prin. Fax 887-2032
Other Schools – See Alverton

**Scott Township, Allegheny, Pop. 17,118**
Lakeland SD 1,600/K-12
1355 Lakeland Dr, 570-254-9485
R. Scott Jeffery, supt. Fax 254-9224
www.lakelandsd.org
Lakeland JSHS 800/7-12
1355 Lakeland Dr, 570-254-9485
Thomas Kameroski, prin. Fax 254-6730

**Scranton, Lackawanna, Pop. 74,482**
Area Vocational Technical School
Supt. — None
CTC of Lackawanna County Vo/Tech
3201 Rockwell Ave 18508 570-346-8471
Thomas Baileys, dir. Fax 342-4251

Scranton SD 8,600/PK-12
425 N Washington Ave 18503 570-348-3400
Dr. Alexis Kirijan, admin. Fax 348-3563
www.scrsd.org/
Northeast IS, 721 Adams Ave 18510 800/6-8
Robert Butka, prin. 570-348-3651
Scranton HS 1,800/9-12
63 Munchak Way 18508 570-348-3481
John Coyle, prin. Fax 348-3561
South Scranton IS 500/6-8
355 Maple St 18505 570-348-3631
Melissa McTiernan, prin.
West Scranton HS 1,000/9-12
1201 Luzerne St 18504 570-348-3616
Robert Gentilezza, prin. Fax 348-3594
West Scranton IS 700/6-8
1401 Fellows St 18504 570-348-3475
Paul Dougherty, prin.

Bais Yaakov of Scranton 50/9-12
1025 Vine St 18510 570-347-5003
Bnos Yisroel of Scranton 100/9-12
620 Monroe Ave 18510 570-558-1370
Fortis Institute Post-Sec.
517 Ash St 18509 570-558-1818
Gregory the Great Academy 100/9-12
621 N Bromley Ave 18504 571-295-6244
Johnson College Post-Sec.
3427 N Main Ave 18508 570-342-6404
Lackawanna College Post-Sec.
501 Vine St 18509 570-961-7810
Marywood University Post-Sec.
2300 Adams Ave 18509 570-348-6211
Penn Foster Career School Post-Sec.
925 Oak St 18515 570-342-7701
St. Clare/St. Paul S-Main Campus 300/3-8
1527 Penn Ave 18509 570-343-7880
Douglas Workman, prin. Fax 343-0069
Scranton Prep S 800/9-12
1000 Wyoming Ave 18509 570-941-7737
Matthew Bernard, prin. Fax 941-6118
Scranton State School for the Deaf Post-Sec.
1800 N Washington Ave 18509
The Commonwealth Medical College Post-Sec.
525 Pine St 18509 570-504-7000
University of Scranton Post-Sec.
800 Linden St 18510 570-941-7400
Yeshiva Beth Moshe Post-Sec.
930 Hickory St 18505 570-346-1747
Yeshiva Beth Moshe 100/9-12
930 Hickory St 18505 570-346-1747

**Selinsgrove, Snyder, Pop. 5,582**
Selinsgrove Area SD 2,500/K-12
401 18th St 17870 570-374-1144
Chad Cohrs, supt. Fax 372-2222
www.seal-pa.org/
Selinsgrove Area HS 900/9-12
500 N Broad St 17870 570-372-2230
Dr. Lorinda Krause, prin. Fax 372-2240
Selinsgrove Area MS 400/6-8
401 18th St 17870 570-372-2250
John Bohle, prin. Fax 372-2251

Susquehanna University Post-Sec.
514 University Ave 17870 570-374-0101

**Sellersville, Bucks, Pop. 4,161**

Faith Christian Academy 300/K-12
700 N Main St 18960 215-257-4577
Ryan Clymer, hdmstr. Fax 534-0842

Upper Bucks Christian S 300/PK-12
754 E Rockhill Rd 18960 215-536-9200

**Seneca, Venango, Pop. 1,053**
Cranberry Area SD 1,200/K-12
3 Education Dr 16346 814-676-5628
William Vonada, supt. Fax 677-5728
www.edline.net/pages/cranberry_area_school_district
Cranberry Area JSHS 500/7-12
1 Education Dr 16346 814-676-8504
Richard Smith, prin. Fax 676-5156

Christian Life Academy 100/PK-12
3973 State Route 257 Ste 1 16346 814-676-9360
Lanny Williams, admin. Fax 676-2908
Northwest Medical Center Post-Sec.
100 Fairfield Dr 16346 814-677-1711

**Sewickley, Allegheny, Pop. 3,749**
Quaker Valley SD
Supt. — See Leetsdale
Quaker Valley MS 400/6-8
618 Harbaugh St 15143 412-749-5079
Fax 749-9844

Eden Christian Academy - Mt. Nebo Campus 200/7-12
318 Nicholson Rd 15143 412-741-2825
Todd Aiken, prin. Fax 324-1101
Sewickley Academy 700/PK-12
315 Academy Ave 15143 412-741-2230
Kolia John O'Connor, head sch Fax 741-9234
Sewickley Valley Hospital Post-Sec.
700 Blackburn Rd 15143 412-741-6600
The Education Center at Watson Inst. Post-Sec.
301 Campmeeting Rd 15143 412-741-1800

**Shamokin Dam, Snyder, Pop. 1,672**

Empire Beauty School Post-Sec.
PO Box 397 17876 570-743-1410

**Shanksville, Somerset, Pop. 229**
Shanksville-Stonycreek SD
Supt. — See Friedens
Shanksville-Stonycreek MSHS 100/6-12
PO Box 128 15560 814-267-4649
Reno Barkman, prin. Fax 267-4372

**Sharon, Mercer, Pop. 13,523**
Sharon CSD 2,100/K-12
215 Forker Blvd 16146 724-983-4000
Michael Calla, supt. Fax 981-0844
sharoncitysd.schoolwires.com
Sharon HS 600/9-12
1129 E State St 16146 724-983-4030
Mike Fitzgerald, prin. Fax 981-0840
Sharon MS 300/7-8
1129 E State St 16146 724-983-4032
Terry Karsonovich, prin. Fax 983-4050

Laurel Technical Institute Post-Sec.
200 Sterling Ave 16146 724-983-0700
Penn State Shenango Post-Sec.
147 Shenango Ave 16146 724-983-2803
Sharon Regional Health System Post-Sec.
740 E State St 16146 724-983-5603

**Sharon Hill, Delaware, Pop. 5,504**
Southeast Delco SD
Supt. — See Folcroft
Academy Park HS 1,100/9-12
300 Calcon Hook Rd 19079 610-522-4330
Nathaniel Robinson, prin. Fax 522-4335

Venus Beauty Academy Post-Sec.
1033 Chester Pike 19079 610-586-2500

**Sharpsville, Mercer, Pop. 4,343**
Sharpsville Area SD 1,300/K-12
701 Pierce Ave 16150 724-962-7874
Dr. Brad Ferko, supt. Fax 962-7873
www.sharpsville.k12.pa.us/
Sharpsville Area HS 400/9-12
301 Blue Devil Way 16150 724-962-7861
Tim Dadich, prin. Fax 962-7730
Sharpsville Area MS 300/6-8
303 Blue Devil Way 16150 724-962-7863
Heidi AbiNader, prin. Fax 962-7891

**Sheffield, Warren, Pop. 1,128**
Warren County SD
Supt. — See Russell
Sheffield Area MSHS 300/6-12
6760 Route 6 16347 814-968-3720
Kimberly Yourchisin, prin. Fax 968-4233

**Shenandoah, Schuylkill, Pop. 5,009**
Shenandoah Valley SD 1,200/PK-12
805 W Centre St 17976 570-462-1936
Dr. Stanley Rakowsky, supt. Fax 462-4611
www.svbluedevils.org
Shenandoah Valley JSHS 500/7-12
805 W Centre St 17976 570-462-1957
Phillip Andras, prin. Fax 462-2982

**Shickshinny, Luzerne, Pop. 832**
Northwest Area SD 1,200/K-12
243 Thorne Hill Rd 18655 570-542-4126
James McGovern, supt. Fax 542-0187
www.northwest.k12.pa.us/
Northwest Area MSHS 500/7-12
243 Thorne Hill Rd 18655 570-542-4126
Ryan Miner, prin. Fax 542-7538

**Shillington, Berks, Pop. 5,201**
Governor Mifflin SD 4,200/K-12
10 S Waverly St 19607 610-775-1461
Dr. Steven Gerhard, supt. Fax 775-6586
www.governormifflinsd.org
Mifflin HS 1,300/9-12
10 S Waverly St 19607 610-775-5089
John Althouse, prin. Fax 796-7471

Mifflin MS 600/7-8
10 S Waverly St 19607 610-775-1465
Kevin Hohl, prin. Fax 685-3760

**Shinglehouse, Potter, Pop. 1,122**
Oswayo Valley SD 400/PK-12
277 S Oswayo St 16748 814-260-1700
Dr. Michele Hartzell, supt. Fax 697-7439
www.oswayovalley.com
Oswayo Valley MSHS 200/6-12
318 S Oswayo St 16748 814-260-1701
Dr. Michele Hartzell, admin. Fax 697-6375

**Shippensburg, Cumberland, Pop. 5,366**
Shippensburg Area SD 3,400/K-12
317 N Morris St 17257 717-530-2700
Beth Bender, supt. Fax 530-2724
www.ship.k12.pa.us
Shippensburg Area HS 1,100/9-12
201 Eberly Dr 17257 717-530-2730
Bruce Levy, prin. Fax 530-2835
Shippensburg Area MS 800/6-8
101 Park Pl W 17257 717-530-2750
David Rice, prin. Fax 530-2757

---

Shippensburg University Post-Sec.
1871 Old Main Dr 17257 717-477-7447

**Shippenville, Clarion, Pop. 476**
Area Vocational Technical School
Supt. — None
Clarion County Career Center Vo/Tech
447 Career Ln 16254 814-226-4391
Mike Stahlman, dir. Fax 226-7350

**Shiremanstown, Cumberland, Pop. 1,540**

---

West Shore Christian Academy 400/PK-12
201 W Main St 17011 717-737-3550
Daniel Steinfield, head sch Fax 761-3977

**Sidman, Cambria, Pop. 430**
Forest Hills SD 2,000/PK-12
PO Box 158 15955 814-487-7613
Edwin Bowser, supt. Fax 487-7775
www.fhrangers.org
Forest Hills HS 500/10-12
PO Box 325 15955 814-487-7613
Curt Vasas, prin. Fax 487-2371
Forest Hills MS 500/7-9
1427 Frankstown Rd 15955 814-487-7613
Fax 495-7367

**Sinking Spring, Berks, Pop. 3,938**
Wilson SD
Supt. — See West Lawn
Wilson Southern MS 400/6-8
3100 Iroquois Ave 19608 610-670-0180
Dr. Stephen Burnham, prin. Fax 334-6445
Wilson West MS 500/6-8
450 Faust Rd 19608 610-670-0180
Kyle Wetherhold, prin. Fax 334-6440

**Slatington, Lehigh, Pop. 4,171**
Northern Lehigh SD 1,800/K-12
1201 Shadow Oaks Ln 18080 610-767-9800
Michael Michaels, supt. Fax 767-9809
www.nlsd.org
Northern Lehigh HS 600/9-12
1 Bulldog Ln 18080 610-767-9832
Robert Vlasaty, prin. Fax 767-9848
Northern Lehigh MS 300/7-8
600 Diamond St 18080 610-767-9812
Jill Chamberlain, prin. Fax 767-9850

**Slippery Rock, Butler, Pop. 3,557**
Slippery Rock Area SD 2,100/K-12
201 Kiester Rd 16057 724-794-2960
Dr. Alfonso Angelucci, supt. Fax 794-2001
www.slipperyrock.k12.pa.us
Slippery Rock Area HS 700/9-12
201 Kiester Rd 16057 724-794-2960
Cory Hake, prin. Fax 794-1952
Slippery Rock Area MS 500/6-8
201 Kiester Rd 16057 724-794-2960
Jacob Jefferis, prin. Fax 794-6265

---

Slippery Rock University Post-Sec.
1 Morrow Way 16057 724-738-9000

**Smethport, McKean, Pop. 1,646**
Smethport Area SD 900/PK-12
414 S Mechanic St 16749 814-887-5543
Dr. Charles Leasure, supt. Fax 887-5544
www.smethportschools.com/
Smethport Area JSHS 400/7-12
412 S Mechanic St 16749 814-887-5545
Robert Miller, prin. Fax 887-5546

**Somerset, Somerset, Pop. 6,210**
Area Vocational Technical School
Supt. — None
Somerset County Technology Center Vo/Tech
281 Technology Dr 15501 814-443-3651
Karen Remick, dir. Fax 445-6716

Somerset Area SD 2,300/PK-12
645 S Columbia Ave Ste 110 15501 814-443-2831
Krista Mathias, supt. Fax 443-1964
sasd.us
Somerset Area HS 700/9-12
645 S Columbia Ave Ste 130 15501 814-443-2831
Scott Shirley, prin. Fax 444-3202
Somerset Area MS 600/6-8
645 S Columbia Ave Ste 120 15501 814-443-2831
Lisa James, prin. Fax 444-3301

---

Somerset Christian S 100/PK-12
708 Stoystown Rd Ste 2 15501 814-443-1960
Susie Harshbarger, prin. Fax 443-9830
Somerset Community Hospital Post-Sec.
225 S Center Ave 15501 814-443-5221

**Souderton, Montgomery, Pop. 6,521**
Souderton Area SD 6,300/K-12
760 Lower Rd 18964 215-723-6061
Frank Gallagher, supt. Fax 723-8897
www.soudertonsd.org
Indian Crest MS 800/6-8
139 Harleysville Pike 18964 215-723-9193
Jeff Pammer, prin. Fax 723-8897
Souderton Area HS 2,200/9-12
625 Lower Rd 18964 215-723-2808
Dr. Sam Varano, prin. Fax 723-6352
Other Schools – See Harleysville

**South Abington, Lackawanna**

---

Summit Christian Academy 100/PK-12
660 Griffin Pond Rd, 570-587-1545
John Antolick, admin. Fax 309-0038

**Southampton, Bucks, Pop. 11,500**
Centennial SD
Supt. — See Warminster
Klinger MS 700/6-8
1415 2nd Street Pike 18966 215-364-5950
Travis Bloom, prin. Fax 364-5955

**South Canaan, Wayne**

---

St. Tikhon's Orthodox Theological Sem. Post-Sec.
PO Box 130 18459 570-561-1818

**South Park, Allegheny**
South Park SD 2,100/K-12
2005 Eagle Ridge Dr 15129 412-655-3111
Jeanine Gregory, supt. Fax 655-2952
www.sparksd.org
South Park HS 700/9-12
2005 Eagle Ridge Dr 15129 412-655-4900
David Palmer, prin. Fax 655-1463
South Park MS 600/6-8
2500 Stewart Rd 15129 412-831-7200
Kevin Monaghan, prin. Fax 831-7204

---

Cornerstone Christian Prep Academy 100/7-12
3701 Brownsville Rd 15129 412-835-1100
Cindi R. McCall, dir. Fax 835-1106

**South Williamsport, Lycoming, Pop. 6,306**
South Williamsport Area SD 1,300/K-12
515 W Central Ave 17702 570-327-1581
Dr. Mark Stamm, supt. Fax 326-0641
www.mounties.k12.pa.us
South Williamsport Area JSHS 600/7-12
700 Percy St 17702 570-326-2684
Jesse Smith, prin. Fax 326-2687

**Spring Church, Armstrong**
Apollo-Ridge SD
Supt. — See Apollo
Apollo-Ridge HS 400/9-12
1825 State Route 56 15686 724-478-6000
Clint Weimer, prin. Fax 478-9775
Apollo-Ridge MS 300/6-8
1829 State Route 56 15686 724-478-6000
Travis Barta, prin. Fax 478-3730

**Springdale, Allegheny, Pop. 3,373**
Allegheny Valley SD
Supt. — See Cheswick
Springdale JSHS 500/7-12
501 Butler Rd 15144 724-274-8100
Michele Welter, prin. Fax 274-2106

**Springfield, Delaware, Pop. 24,160**
Springfield SD 3,200/K-12
111 W Leamy Ave 19064 610-938-6000
Dr. Anthony Barber, supt. Fax 938-6005
www.ssdcougars.org
Richardson MS 800/6-8
20 W Woodland Ave 19064 610-938-6300
Daniel Tracy, prin. Fax 938-6305
Springfield HS 1,200/9-12
49 W Leamy Ave 19064 610-938-6100
Joseph Hepp, prin. Fax 938-6105

---

Anthem Institute Post-Sec.
400 S State Rd 19064 877-600-8860
Cardinal O'Hara HS 1,400/9-12
1701 S Sproul Rd 19064 610-544-3800
Thomas Fertal, pres. Fax 544-1189

**Spring Grove, York, Pop. 2,145**
Spring Grove Area SD 3,800/K-12
100 E College Ave 17362 717-225-4731
Dr. Robert Lombardo, supt. Fax 225-6028
www.sgasd.org
Spring Grove Area HS 1,100/9-12
1490 Roth Church Rd 17362 717-225-4731
Dr. Rosemary Cugliari, prin. Fax 225-0736
Spring Grove Area MS 600/7-8
244 Old Hanover Rd 17362 717-225-4731
Dr. Steve Guadagnino, prin. Fax 225-0146

**Spring Mills, Centre, Pop. 267**
Penns Valley Area SD 1,500/K-12
4528 Penns Valley Rd 16875 814-422-2000
Brian Griffith, supt. Fax 422-8020
www.pennsvalley.org
Penns Valley Area JSHS 700/7-12
4545 Penns Valley Rd 16875 814-422-8854
Dustin Dalton, prin. Fax 422-8280

**Springville, Susquehanna**
Area Vocational Technical School
Supt. — None
Susquehanna County Career & Tech. Center Vo/Tech
2380 Elk Lake School Rd 18844 570-278-9229
Dr. Alice Davis, dir. Fax 278-3913

**State College, Centre, Pop. 41,187**
State College Area SD 6,800/K-12
131 W Nittany Ave 16801 814-231-1011
Dr. Robert O'Donnell, supt. Fax 231-4130
www.scasd.org
Mount Nittany MS 700/6-8
656 Brandywine Dr 16801 814-272-4050
Brian Ishler, prin. Fax 272-4055
Park Forest MS 800/6-8
2180 School Dr 16803 814-237-5301
Dr. Karen Wiser, prin. Fax 272-0196
State College Area HS 2,400/9-12
653 Westerly Pkwy 16801 814-231-1111
Curtis Johnson, prin. Fax 231-5024

---

Empire Beauty School Post-Sec.
206 W Hamilton Ave 16801 814-238-1961
Grace Prep HS 100/9-12
848 Science Park Rd 16803 814-867-1177
Jane Auhl, prin. Fax 240-3977
South Hills School of Business & Tech. Post-Sec.
480 Waupelani Dr 16801 814-234-7755

**Steelton, Dauphin, Pop. 5,688**
Central Dauphin SD
Supt. — See Harrisburg
Swatara MS 500/6-8
1101 Highland St 17113 717-939-9363
Kelly Fowlkes, prin. Fax 939-2156

Steelton-Highspire SD 1,300/K-12
250 Reynders St 17113 717-704-3800
Dr. Ellen Castagneto, supt. Fax 704-3808
www.shsd.k12.pa.us
Steelton-Highspire JSHS 500/7-12
250 Reynders St 17113 717-704-3800
Willie Slade, prin. Fax 704-3808

**Stoneboro, Mercer, Pop. 1,041**
Lakeview SD 1,200/K-12
2482 Mercer St 16153 724-376-7911
Douglas J. Mays, supt. Fax 376-7910
www.lakeview.k12.pa.us
Lakeview HS 400/9-12
2482 Mercer St 16153 724-376-7911
Fax 376-7910
Lakeview MS 400/5-8
2482 Mercer St 16153 724-376-7911
David Blakley, prin. Fax 376-7910

**Stoystown, Somerset, Pop. 354**
North Star SD
Supt. — See Boswell
North Star MS 300/5-8
3598 Whistler Rd 15563 814-893-5616
Cheryl Slade, prin. Fax 893-5922

**Strafford, Chester, Pop. 4,500**

---

Woodlynde S 200/K-12
445 Upper Gulph Rd 19087 610-687-9660
Dr. Christopher Fulco Ed.D., head sch Fax 687-4752

**Strattanville, Clarion, Pop. 547**
Clarion-Limestone Area SD 900/K-12
4091 C L School Rd 16258 814-764-5111
Michael Stimac, supt. Fax 764-5729
www.clasd.net/
Clarion-Limestone JSHS 500/7-12
4091 C L School Rd 16258 814-764-5111
Doug Rodgers, prin. Fax 764-5274

**Stroudsburg, Monroe, Pop. 5,412**
Stroudsburg Area SD 5,500/K-12
123 Linden St 18360 570-421-1990
Dr. Charles Amuso, supt. Fax 424-5986
www.sburg.org
Stroudsburg HS 1,400/10-12
1100 W Main St 18360 570-421-1991
Jeff Sodl, prin. Fax 424-1383
Stroudsburg JHS 900/8-9
1901 Chipperfield Dr 18360 570-424-4848
Ryan Cron, prin. Fax 424-4839

---

Stroudsburg School of Cosmetology Post-Sec.
100 N 8th St 18360 570-421-3387

**Summerdale, Cumberland**

---

Central Penn College Post-Sec.
PO Box 309 17093 800-759-2727

**Sunbury, Northumberland, Pop. 9,716**
Shikellamy SD 2,700/K-12
200 Island Blvd 17801 570-286-3720
Ned Sodrick, supt. Fax 286-3776
www.shikbraves.org
Shikellamy HS 900/9-12
600 Walnut St 17801 570-286-3700
Michael Egan, prin. Fax 286-3775
Shikellamy MS 400/7-8
520 Walnut St 17801 570-286-3736
Dr. Mary Murphy-Kahn, prin. Fax 286-3780

---

McCann School of Business & Technology Post-Sec.
1147 N 4th St 17801 570-286-3058
Triangle Tech Post-Sec.
191 Performance Rd 17801 570-988-0700

**Susquehanna, Susquehanna, Pop. 1,631**
Susquehanna Community SD 900/K-12
3192 Turnpike St 18847 570-853-4921
Bronson Stone, supt. Fax 853-3768
www.scschools.org/
Susquehanna Community JSHS 400/7-12
3192 Turnpike St 18847 570-853-4921
Carmella Bullick, prin. Fax 853-3918

**Swarthmore, Delaware, Pop. 5,977**

Swarthmore College Post-Sec.
500 College Ave 19081 610-328-8000

**Swiftwater, Monroe**
Pocono Mountain SD 7,800/K-12
PO Box 200 18370 570-839-7121
Dr. Elizabeth Robison, supt. Fax 895-4768
www.pmsd.org
Pocono Mountain East HS 1,200/9-12
PO Box 200 18370 570-839-7121
Todd Burns, prin. Fax 839-5934
Pocono Mountain East JHS 400/7-8
PO Box 200 18370 570-839-7121
Dr. Kathy Fanelli, prin. Fax 839-3242
Swiftwater IS 400/7-8
PO Box 200 18370 570-839-7121
Kristine Kunsman, prin. Fax 839-7820
Other Schools – See Pocono Summit

**Tamaqua, Schuylkill, Pop. 7,032**
Tamaqua Area SD 2,100/K-12
138 W Broad St 18252 570-668-2570
Carol Makuta, supt. Fax 668-6850
www.tamaqua.k12.pa.us
Rush Academy 300/Alt
50 Meadow Ave 18252 570-668-6932
Tammy Recker, dir. Fax 668-6858
Tamaqua Area HS 700/9-12
500 Penn St 18252 570-668-1901
Stephen Toth, prin. Fax 668-2970
Tamaqua Area MS 500/6-8
502 Penn St 18252 570-668-1210
Christopher Czapla, prin. Fax 668-5027

Marian HS 300/9-12
166 Marian Ave 18252 570-467-3335
Sr. Bernard Agnes Smith, prin. Fax 467-0186

**Tarentum, Allegheny, Pop. 4,449**

ITT Technical Institute Post-Sec.
100 Pittsburgh Mills Cir 15084 724-274-1400

**Taylor, Lackawanna, Pop. 6,195**
Riverside SD 1,500/K-12
300 Davis St 18517 570-562-2121
Paul Brennan, supt. Fax 562-3205
www.riversidesd.com
Riverside JSHS 700/7-12
310 Davis St 18517 570-562-2121
Joseph Moceyunas, prin. Fax 562-7551

**Thorndale, Chester, Pop. 3,357**
Coatesville Area SD 7,000/K-12
3030 C G Zinn Rd 19372 610-466-2400
Dr. Cathy Taschner, supt. Fax 383-1426
casd.schoolwires.net
Other Schools – See Coatesville

**Three Springs, Huntingdon, Pop. 439**
Southern Huntingdon County SD 1,200/K-12
10339 Pogue Rd 17264 814-447-5529
Stacey Miller, supt. Fax 447-3967
shcsd.org
Southern Huntingdon County MSHS 700/6-12
10339 Pogue Rd 17264 814-447-5529
Michael Adamek, prin. Fax 447-3750

**Throop, Lackawanna, Pop. 4,041**
Mid Valley SD 1,600/K-12
52 Underwood Rd 18512 570-307-1108
Patrick Sheehan, supt. Fax 307-1107
www.mvsd.us
Mid Valley HS 500/7-12
52 Underwood Rd 18512 570-307-2180
Chad Vinansky, prin. Fax 307-1912

**Tioga, Tioga, Pop. 659**
Northern Tioga SD
Supt. — See Elkland
Williamson JSHS 600/7-12
33 Jct Cross Rd 16946 570-827-2191
Kris Kaufman, prin. Fax 827-3557

**Tionesta, Forest, Pop. 478**
Forest Area SD 500/PK-12
22318 Route 62 Unit 16 16353 814-755-4491
Amanda Hetrick, supt. Fax 755-2426
www.forestareaschools.org/
West Forest JSHS 100/7-12
22318 Route 62 Unit 15 16353 814-755-3611
Elisha Pospisil, prin. Fax 755-2427
Other Schools – See Marienville

North Clarion County SD 600/PK-12
10439 Route 36 16353 814-744-8536
Steven Young, supt. Fax 744-9378
www.northclarion.org
North Clarion County JSHS 300/7-12
10439 Route 36 16353 814-744-8544
Ryan Cornecki, prin. Fax 744-8762

**Titusville, Crawford, Pop. 5,544**
Titusville Area SD 2,100/PK-12
221 N Washington St 16354 814-827-2715
Karen Jez, supt. Fax 827-7761
www.gorockets.org/
Titusville HS 600/9-12
302 E Walnut St 16354 814-827-2715
Philip Knapp, prin. Fax 827-0551
Titusville MS 500/6-8
415 Water St 16354 814-827-2715
Douglas Gifford, prin. Fax 827-0552

University of Pittsburgh at Titusville Post-Sec.
504 E Main St # 287 16354 814-827-4400

**Topton, Berks, Pop. 2,055**
Brandywine Heights Area SD 1,500/K-12
200 W Weis St 19562 610-682-5100
Andrew Potteiger, supt. Fax 682-5136
www.bhasd.org
Brandywine Heights Area MS 400/6-8
200 W Weis St 19562 610-682-5131
Robert Farina, prin. Fax 682-5105
Other Schools – See Mertztown

**Towanda, Bradford, Pop. 2,864**
Area Vocational Technical School
Supt. — None
Northern Tier Career Center Vo/Tech
120 Career Center Ln 18848 570-265-8111
Elizabeth Frankhouser, dir. Fax 265-3002

Towanda Area SD 1,600/K-12
410 State St 18848 570-265-9154
Steve Gobble, supt. Fax 265-4881
www.tsd.k12.pa.us
Towanda Area JSHS 800/7-12
1 High School Dr 18848 570-265-2101
Dennis Peachey, prin. Fax 268-2069

**Tower City, Schuylkill, Pop. 1,337**
Williams Valley SD 1,000/K-12
10330 Route 209 Rd 17980 717-647-2167
Dr. Donald Burkhardt, supt. Fax 647-2055
www.wvschools.net
Williams Valley JSHS 500/7-12
10330 Route 209 Rd 17980 717-647-2167
Tracey Weller, prin. Fax 647-2055

**Trafford, Westmoreland, Pop. 3,138**
Penn-Trafford SD
Supt. — See Harrison City
Trafford MS 400/6-8
100 Brinton Ave 15085 412-372-6600
Roger Sullivan, prin. Fax 372-1554

**Trevose, Bucks, Pop. 3,515**

Strayer University Post-Sec.
3600 Horizon Blvd Ste 100 19053 215-354-2700

**Troy, Bradford, Pop. 1,340**
Troy Area SD 1,300/K-12
68 Fenner Ave 16947 570-297-2750
Charles Young, supt. Fax 297-1600
www.troyareasd.org/
Troy Area JSHS 700/7-12
150 High St 16947 570-297-2176
Susan Shipman, prin. Fax 297-2058

Martha Lloyd School Post-Sec.
66 Lloyd Ln 16947 570-297-2185

**Tunkhannock, Wyoming, Pop. 1,809**
Tunkhannock Area SD 2,700/K-12
41 Philadelphia Ave 18657 570-836-3111
Michael Healey, supt. Fax 836-2942
www.tasd.net/
Tunkhannock HS 900/9-12
135 Tiger Dr 18657 570-836-8223
Gregory Ellsworth, prin. Fax 836-4719
Tunkhannock MS 900/5-8
200 Franklin Ave 18657 570-836-8235
James Timmons, prin. Fax 836-5796

**Turbotville, Northumberland, Pop. 705**
Warrior Run SD 1,700/K-12
4800 Susquehanna Trl 17772 570-649-5138
Dr. John Kurelja, supt. Fax 649-5475
www.wrsd.org
Warrior Run HS 600/9-12
4800 Susquehanna Trl 17772 570-649-5166
Patricia Cross, prin. Fax 649-5591
Warrior Run MS 500/5-8
4800 Susquehanna Trl 17772 570-649-5135
Susan Mabus, prin. Fax 649-6173

**Tyrone, Blair, Pop. 5,415**
Tyrone Area SD 1,900/PK-12
701 Clay Ave 16686 814-684-0710
Cathy Harlow, supt. Fax 684-8408
www.tyrone.k12.pa.us
Tyrone Area HS 600/9-12
1001 Clay Ave 16686 814-684-4240
Thomas Yoder, prin. Fax 684-4245
Tyrone Area MS 500/5-8
1001 Clay Ave 16686 814-684-4240
Kristen N. Pinter, prin. Fax 682-1013

Grier S 300/7-12
PO Box 308 16686 814-684-3000
Gina Borst, head sch Fax 684-2177

**Ulysses, Potter, Pop. 619**
Northern Potter SD 600/PK-12
745 Northern Potter Rd 16948 814-848-7506
Scott Graham, supt. Fax 848-7431
www.northernpottersd.org
Northern Potter JSHS 300/7-12
763 Northern Potter Rd 16948 814-848-7534
Fax 848-9671

**Union City, Erie, Pop. 3,286**
Union City Area SD 1,200/PK-12
107 Concord St 16438 814-438-3804
Dr. Sandra Myers, supt. Fax 438-2030
www.ucasd.org
Union City HS 300/9-12
105 Concord St 16438 814-438-7673
Melissa Tomcho, prin. Fax 438-8079
Union City MS 300/6-8
105 Concord St 16438 814-438-7673
Melissa Tomcho, prin. Fax 438-8079

**Uniontown, Fayette, Pop. 10,023**
Albert Gallatin Area SD 3,600/K-12
2625 Morgantown Rd 15401 724-564-7190
Carl Bezjak, supt. Fax 564-7195
www.agasd.org
Gallatin Area HS 1,100/9-12
1119 Township Dr 15401 724-564-2024
Jason Hutchinson, prin. Fax 564-4525
Other Schools – See Mc Clellandtown, Point Marion

Area Vocational Technical School
Supt. — None
Fayette County Career & Technical Inst Vo/Tech
175 Georges Fairchance Rd 15401 724-437-2721
Dr. Edward Jeffreys, prin.

Laurel Highlands SD 3,300/K-12
304 Bailey Ave 15401 724-437-2821
Jesse Wallace, supt. Fax 437-8929
www.lhsd.org
Laurel Highlands HS 1,100/9-12
300 Bailey Ave 15401 724-437-4741
John Diamond, prin. Fax 437-5653
Laurel Highlands MS 700/6-8
18 Hookton Ave 15401 724-437-2865
Mike Rozgony, prin. Fax 437-8518

Uniontown Area SD 2,900/K-12
205 Wilson Ave 15401 724-438-4501
Dr. Charles D. Machesky, supt. Fax 437-7007
uasdraiders.org
Lafayette MS 100/6-8
303 Connellsville St 15401 724-438-3581
Joseph Galie, prin. Fax 439-5023
Uniontown Area HS 900/9-12
146 E Fayette St 15401 724-439-5000
Robert Manges, prin. Fax 439-5004
Other Schools – See Markleysburg

Chestnut Ridge Christian Academy 100/PK-12
115 Downer Ave 15401 724-439-1090
Patricia D. Cowsert, prin. Fax 439-4540
Laurel Business Institute Post-Sec.
PO Box 877 15401 724-439-4900

**University Park, See State College**

Penn State The Dickinson School of Law Post-Sec.
Lewis Katz Building 16802 814-865-8900
Penn State University Post-Sec.
201 Old Main 16802 814-865-4700

**Upper Darby, See Darby**
Upper Darby SD
Supt. — See Drexel Hill
Beverly Hills MS 1,500/6-8
1400 Garrett Rd 19082 610-626-9317
Kelley Simone, prin.

Harris School of Business Post-Sec.
20 S 69th St 19082 484-463-3800
Prism Career Institute Post-Sec.
6800 Market St 19082 610-789-6700

**Upper Saint Clair, Allegheny, Pop. 19,692**
Upper St. Clair SD 4,100/K-12
1820 McLaughlin Run Rd 15241 412-833-1600
Dr. Patrick O'Toole, supt. Fax 833-5535
www.uscsd.k12.pa.us
Other Schools – See Pittsburgh

**Valley View, Schuylkill, Pop. 1,675**
Tri-Valley SD 800/K-12
110 W Main St 17983 570-682-9013
Dr. Mark Snyder, supt. Fax 682-9544
www.tri-valley.k12.pa.us
Other Schools – See Hegins

**Verona, Allegheny, Pop. 2,433**

Redeemer Lutheran S 200/PK-12
700 Idaho Ave 15147 412-828-9323
Gail Holzer, prin. Fax 828-1860

**Villanova, Delaware**

Academy of Notre Dame De Namur 500/6-12
560 Sproul Rd 19085 610-687-0650
Jacqueline Coccia, prin. Fax 687-1912
Devereux Foundation in Pennsylvania Post-Sec.
444 Devereux Dr 19085 610-542-3030
Villanova University Post-Sec.
800 E Lancaster Ave 19085 610-519-4500

**Wallingford, Delaware**
Wallingford-Swarthmore SD 3,400/K-12
200 S Providence Rd 19086 610-892-3470
Dr. Rich Noonan, supt. Fax 892-3493
www.wssd.org
Strath Haven HS 1,200/9-12
205 S Providence Rd 19086 610-892-3470
Dr. Mary Jo Yannacone, prin. Fax 892-3494
Strath Haven MS 800/6-8
200 S Providence Rd 19086 610-892-3470
George King, prin. Fax 892-3492

**Warfordsburg, Fulton**
Southern Fulton SD 800/K-12
3072 Great Cove Rd Ste 100 17267 717-294-2203
Hervey P. Hann, supt. Fax 294-2207
sfsd.k12.pa.us
Southern Fulton JSHS 400/7-12
13083 Buck Valley Rd 17267 717-294-3251
Meredith Hendershot, prin. Fax 294-6248

**Warminster, Bucks, Pop. 32,400**
Centennial SD 5,200/K-12
433 Centennial Rd 18974 215-441-6000
Dr. Jennifer Polinchock, admin. Fax 441-5105
www.centennialsd.org

Log College MS 600/6-8
730 Norristown Rd 18974 215-441-6075
Fax 441-6073
Tennent HS 1,900/9-12
333 Centennial Rd 18974 215-441-6181
Dr. Dennis Best, prin. Fax 441-6175
Other Schools – See Southampton

---

Archbishop Wood HS 1,000/9-12
655 York Rd 18974 215-672-5050
Mary Harkins, prin. Fax 672-9572
Automotive Training Center Post-Sec.
900 Johnsville Blvd 18974 888-233-0476
Empire Beauty School Post-Sec.
435 York Rd 18974 215-443-8446

**Warren, Warren, Pop. 9,619**
Area Vocational Technical School
Supt. — None
Warren County Career Center Vo/Tech
347 E 5th Ave 16365 814-726-1260
James Evers, prin. Fax 726-9673

Warren County SD
Supt. — See Russell
Beaty-Warren MS 600/6-8
2 E 3rd Ave 16365 814-723-5200
Ann Ryan, prin. Fax 723-9503
Warren Area HS 700/9-12
345 E 5th Ave 16365 814-723-3370
Jeffrey Flickner, prin. Fax 726-3126

**Warrington, Bucks, Pop. 7,000**
Central Bucks SD
Supt. — See Doylestown
Central Bucks SHS - South 1,900/10-12
1100 Folly Rd 18976 267-893-3000
Scott Davidheiser, prin. Fax 893-5824
Tamanend MS 900/7-9
1492 Stuckert Rd 18976 267-893-2900
Cheryl Leatherbarrow, prin. Fax 893-5818

**Washington, Washington, Pop. 13,036**
Trinity Area SD 3,300/K-12
231 Park Ave 15301 724-223-2000
Michael Lucas, supt. Fax 228-2640
www.trinitypride.org
Trinity HS 1,100/9-12
231 Park Ave 15301 724-225-5380
Thomas Samosky, prin. Fax 228-9057
Trinity MS 800/6-8
50 Scenic Dr 15301 724-228-2112
Peter Keruskin, prin. Fax 228-1196

Washington SD 1,500/K-12
311 Allison Ave 15301 724-223-5112
Dr. Roberta DiLorenzo, supt. Fax 223-5024
www.washington.k12.pa.us
Washington HS 400/9-12
201 Allison Ave 15301 724-223-5080
Paul Kostelnik, prin. Fax 223-5046
Washington JHS 200/7-8
201 Allison Ave 15301 724-223-5060
Chet Henderson, prin. Fax 223-5123

---

Faith Christian S 200/PK-12
524 E Beau St 15301 724-222-5440
Lucy Hall, prin. Fax 222-5442
First Love Christian Academy 50/PK-PK, 9-
150 Sunset Blvd 15301 724-228-3547
Kathleen Miller, supt. Fax 228-3547
Penn Commercial Business/Technical Sch. Post-Sec.
242 Oak Spring Rd 15301 724-222-5330
Washington & Jefferson College Post-Sec.
60 S Lincoln St 15301 724-222-4400
Washington Hospital Post-Sec.
155 Wilson Ave 15301 724-223-3167

**Waterfall, Fulton**
Forbes Road SD 500/K-12
159 Red Bird Dr 16689 814-685-3866
James Foster, supt. Fax 685-3159
www.frsd.k12.pa.us
Forbes Road JSHS 200/7-12
159 Red Bird Dr 16689 814-685-3866
Maria Scott, prin. Fax 685-3159

**Waterford, Erie, Pop. 1,509**
Fort LeBoeuf SD 2,100/K-12
PO Box 810 16441 814-796-2638
Debra Spaulding, supt. Fax 796-6459
www.fortleboeuf.net/
Fort LeBoeuf HS 700/9-12
931 N High St 16441 814-796-2616
Martin Rimpa, prin. Fax 796-2141
Fort LeBoeuf MS 500/6-8
PO Box 516 16441 814-796-2681
Brent Holt, prin. Fax 796-4712

**Wayne, Delaware**
Radnor Township SD 3,600/K-12
135 S Wayne Ave 19087 610-688-8100
Dr. Michael Kelly, supt. Fax 687-3318
www.rtsd.org/
Radnor MS 900/6-8
150 Louella Ave 19087 610-386-6300
Esther Purnell, prin. Fax 688-2491
Other Schools – See Radnor

Tredyffrin-Easttown SD 6,500/K-12
940 W Valley Rd Ste 1700 19087 610-240-1900
Dr. Richard Gusick, supt. Fax 240-1965
www.tesd.net/
Valley Forge MS 1,000/5-8
105 W Walker Rd 19087 610-240-1300
Matthew Gibson, prin. Fax 240-1325
Other Schools – See Berwyn

---

Valley Forge Military Academy 300/7-12
1001 Eagle Rd 19087 610-989-1200
Jeffrey Brown Ed.D., hdmstr. Fax 989-1545
Valley Forge Military Academy & College Post-Sec.
1001 Eagle Rd 19087 610-989-1200

**Waynesboro, Franklin, Pop. 10,360**
Waynesboro Area SD 4,300/K-12
210 Clayton Ave 17268 717-762-1191
Sherran Diller, supt. Fax 762-0028
www.wasd.k12.pa.us
Waynesboro Area HS 1,300/9-12
550 E 2nd St 17268 717-762-1191
Steve Pappas, prin. Fax 762-3787
Waynesboro Area MS 700/7-8
702 E 2nd St 17268 717-762-1191
Aaron Taylor, prin. Fax 762-6566

**Waynesburg, Greene, Pop. 4,116**
Area Vocational Technical School
Supt. — None
Greene County CTC Vo/Tech
60 Zimmerman Dr 15370 724-627-3106
Karen Pflugh, dir.

Central Greene SD 2,000/K-12
PO Box 472 15370 724-627-8151
Brian Uplinger, supt. Fax 627-9591
www.cgsd.org
Bell MS 400/6-8
126 E Lincoln St 15370 724-852-2722
John Lipscomb, prin. Fax 627-0637
Waynesburg Central HS 600/9-12
30 Zimmerman Dr 15370 724-852-1050
Dave Mason, prin. Fax 852-2109

West Greene SD 500/K-12
1367 Hargus Creek Rd 15370 724-499-5183
Thelma Szarell, supt. Fax 499-5623
www.wgsd.org
West Greene MSHS 200/7-12
1352 Hargus Creek Rd 15370 724-499-5051
Scott Sakai, prin. Fax 499-5492

---

Waynesburg University Post-Sec.
51 W College St 15370 724-627-8191

**Weatherly, Carbon, Pop. 2,496**
Weatherly Area SD 700/K-12
602 6th St 18255 570-427-8681
Thomas McLaughlin, supt. Fax 427-8918
www.weatherlysd.org
Weatherly Area HS 200/9-12
601 6th St 18255 570-427-8521
Stuart Tripler, prin. Fax 427-4642
Weatherly Area MS 200/6-8
602 6th St 18255 570-427-8689
Sandra Slavick, prin. Fax 427-8918

**Wellsboro, Tioga, Pop. 3,220**
Wellsboro Area SD 1,500/K-12
227 Nichols St 16901 570-724-4424
Christopher Morral, supt. Fax 724-5103
www.wellsborosd.org
Butler MS 500/5-8
9 Nichols St 16901 570-724-2306
Michael Pietropola, prin. Fax 724-4143
Wellsboro Area HS 500/9-12
225 Nichols St 16901 570-724-3547
David Krick, prin. Fax 724-3027

**West Chester, Chester, Pop. 18,141**
West Chester Area SD 11,800/K-12
829 Paoli Pike 19380 484-266-1000
Dr. James R. Scanlon, supt. Fax 266-1175
www.wcasd.net
Fugett MS 1,000/6-8
500 Ellis Ln 19380 484-266-2900
Le Roy G. Whitehead, prin. Fax 266-2999
Peirce MS 900/6-8
1314 Burke Rd 19380 484-266-2500
Geoffrey Mills, prin. Fax 266-2599
Stetson MS 900/6-8
1060 Wilmington Pike 19382 484-266-2700
Dr. Charles A. Cognato, prin. Fax 266-2799
West Chester Bayard Rustin HS 1,300/9-12
1100 Shiloh Rd 19382 484-266-4300
Michael Marano, prin. Fax 266-4399
West Chester East HS 1,400/9-12
450 Ellis Ln 19380 484-266-3800
Kevin Fagan, prin. Fax 266-3899
West Chester Henderson HS 1,300/9-12
400 Montgomery Ave 19380 484-266-3300
Dr. Jason P. Sherlock, prin. Fax 266-3399

---

Devereux Kanner Center Post-Sec.
390 E Boot Rd 19380 866-532-2212
West Chester Christian S 100/K-12
1237 Paoli Pike 19380 610-692-3700
West Chester University of Pennsylvania Post-Sec.
S High St 19383 610-436-1000
Westtown S 700/PK-12
975 Westtown Rd 19382 610-399-0123
John Baird, hdmstr. Fax 399-3760

**Westfield, Tioga, Pop. 1,060**
Northern Tioga SD
Supt. — See Elkland
Cowanesque Valley JSHS 400/7-12
51 N Fork Rd 16950 814-367-2233
Matthew Sottolano, prin. Fax 367-5874

**West Grove, Chester, Pop. 2,811**
Area Vocational Technical School
Supt. — None
Technical College HS - Pennocks Bridge Vo/Tech
280 Pennocks Bridge Rd 19390 610-345-1800
Michael Katch, prin. Fax 345-1803

Avon Grove SD 5,300/K-12
375 S Jennersville Rd 19390 610-869-2441
Dr. Michael Marchese, supt. Fax 869-8651
www.avongrove.org/
Avon Grove HS 1,800/9-12
257 State Rd 19390 610-869-2446
Thomas Alexander, prin. Fax 869-4511
Engle MS 900/7-8
107 Schoolhouse Rd 19390 610-869-3022
Michael Berardi, prin. Fax 869-0827

**West Lawn, Berks, Pop. 1,678**
Wilson SD 4,600/K-12
2601 Grandview Blvd 19609 610-670-0180
Dr. Rudy Ruth, supt. Fax 334-6430
www.wilsonsd.org
Wilson HS 1,400/9-12
2601 Grandview Blvd 19609 610-670-0180
Dr. George Fiore, prin. Fax 670-9101
Other Schools – See Sinking Spring

**West Middlesex, Mercer, Pop. 850**
West Middlesex Area SD 900/K-12
3591 Sharon Rd 16159 724-634-3030
Dr. David Foley, supt. Fax 528-0380
www.wmasd.k12.pa.us
West Middlesex JSHS 400/7-12
3591 Sharon Rd 16159 724-634-3030
Kevin Briggs, prin. Fax 528-0380

**West Mifflin, Allegheny, Pop. 19,950**
West Mifflin Area SD 2,500/PK-12
1020 Lebanon Rd # 250 15122 412-466-9131
Dr. Daniel Castagna, supt. Fax 466-9260
www.wmasd.org
West Mifflin Area HS 1,100/9-12
91 Commonwealth Ave 15122 412-466-9131
Phillip Woods, prin. Fax 466-4595
West Mifflin Area MS 700/4-8
81 Commonwealth Ave 15122 412-466-9131
Brian Plichta, prin. Fax 466-0836

---

All-State Career School Post-Sec.
1200 Lebanon Rd 15122 412-823-1818
Community College of Allegheny County Post-Sec.
1750 Clairton Rd 15122 412-469-1100
Empire Beauty School Post-Sec.
2393 Mountain View Dr 15122 800-575-5983
Wilson Christian Academy 200/PK-12
1900 Clairton Rd 15122 412-466-1919
Laura Erb M.Ed., head sch Fax 466-0303

**Westover, Clearfield, Pop. 390**
Harmony Area SD 400/PK-12
5239 Ridge Rd 16692 814-845-7918
Dr. Jill M. Dillon, supt. Fax 845-2305
www.harmonyowls.com/
Harmony Area JSHS 100/7-12
5239 Ridge Rd 16692 814-845-7918
Terry Young, prin. Fax 845-2305

**West Sunbury, Butler, Pop. 190**
Moniteau SD 1,500/K-12
1810 W Sunbury Rd 16061 724-637-2117
George S. Svolos, supt. Fax 637-3862
www.moniteau.k12.pa.us
Moniteau JSHS 700/7-12
1810 W Sunbury Rd 16061 724-637-2091
Lance Fox, prin. Fax 637-3878

**Wexford, Allegheny**
North Allegheny SD
Supt. — See Pittsburgh
Marshall MS 600/6-8
5145 Wexford Run Rd 15090 724-934-6060
Daniel Swoger, prin. Fax 935-2474
North Allegheny SHS 1,300/11-12
10375 Perry Hwy 15090 724-934-7200
John Kreider, prin. Fax 935-5846

**Whitehall, Lehigh, Pop. 13,797**
Whitehall-Coplay SD 4,200/K-12
2940 MacArthur Rd 18052 610-439-1431
John Corby, supt. Fax 435-0124
www.whitehallcoplay.org/districtsite/
Whitehall-Coplay MS 1,000/6-8
2930 Zephyr Blvd 18052 610-439-1439
Peter Bugbee, prin. Fax 740-9308
Whitehall HS 1,400/9-12
3800 Mechanicsville Rd 18052 610-437-5081
Christopher Schiffert, prin. Fax 820-7520

---

Empire Beauty School Post-Sec.
1634 MacArthur Rd 18052 610-776-8908
Intl Academy of Medical Reflexology Post-Sec.
1000 4th St 18052 267-424-4549

**Wilkes Barre, Luzerne, Pop. 40,594**
Area Vocational Technical School
Supt. — None
Wilkes-Barre Area CTC Vo/Tech
PO Box 1699 18705 570-822-4131
Peter Halesey, dir. Fax 823-4304

Wilkes-Barre Area SD 7,000/K-12
730 S Main St 18702 570-826-7131
Dr. Bernard Prevuznak, supt. Fax 829-5031
www.wbasd.k12.pa.us
Coughlin HS 1,000/9-12
80 N Washington St 18701 570-826-7201
Patrick Patte, prin. Fax 826-7252
G.A.R. Memorial JSHS 900/7-12
250 S Grant St 18702 570-826-7165
Colleen Robatin, prin. Fax 826-7164
Meyers JSHS 900/7-12
341 Carey Ave 18702 570-826-7145
Michael Elias, prin. Fax 820-3770
Other Schools – See Plains

---

Academy of Creative Hair Design Post-Sec.
125 N Wilkes Barre Blvd 18702 570-825-8363

CDE Career Institute — Post-Sec.
100 N Wilkes Barre Ste 100 18702 — 570-823-3891
Holy Redeemer HS — 600/9-12
159 S Pennsylvania Ave 18701 — 570-829-2424
Anita Sirak, prin. — Fax 829-4412
King's College — Post-Sec.
133 N River St 18711 — 570-208-5900
McCann School of Business & Technology — Post-Sec.
264 Highland Park Blvd 18702 — 570-235-2200
Rock Solid Academy — 50/PK-12
106 S Lehigh St 18708 — 570-696-5466
Lauren Dennis, head sch — Fax 696-2413
Wilkes Barre General Hospital — Post-Sec.
575 N River St 18764 — 570-829-8111
Wilkes University — Post-Sec.
84 W South St 18766 — 570-408-5000

**Wilkinsburg, Allegheny, Pop. 15,450**
Wilkinsburg Borough SD — 900/PK-12
718 Wallace Ave 15221 — 412-371-9667
Dr. Joseph Petrella, supt. — Fax 371-4058
www.wilkinsburgschools.org
Wilkinsburg MSHS — 200/7-12
747 Wallace Ave 15221 — 412-371-9500
Stephen Puskar, prin. — Fax 871-2257

**Williamsburg, Blair, Pop. 1,244**
Williamsburg Community SD — 500/K-12
515 W 3rd St 16693 — 814-832-2125
Lisa Murgas M.Ed., supt. — Fax 832-3657
www.williamsburg.k12.pa.us/
Williamsburg Community JSHS — 200/7-12
515 W 3rd St 16693 — 814-832-2125
Travis Lee M.Ed., prin. — Fax 832-0115

**Williamsport, Lycoming, Pop. 28,270**
Loyalsock Township SD — 1,500/K-12
1605 Four Mile Dr 17701 — 570-326-6508
Gerald McLaughlin, supt. — Fax 326-0770
www.loyalsocklancers.org
Loyalsock Township HS — 500/9-12
1801 Loyalsock Dr 17701 — 570-326-3581
Dr. Matthew Reitz, prin. — Fax 322-3952
Loyalsock Township MS — 300/6-8
2101 Loyalsock Dr 17701 — 570-323-9439
Charles Greevy, prin. — Fax 323-5303

Williamsport Area SD — 3,600/K-12
2780 W 4th St 17701 — 570-327-5500
Don Adams, supt. — Fax 327-8122
www.wasd.org
Williamsport Area HS — 1,700/9-12
2990 W 4th St 17701 — 570-323-8411
Brandon Pardoe, prin. — Fax 322-4150
Williamsport Area MS — 7-8
2800 W 4th St 17701 — 570-323-6177
Reginald Fatherly, prin. — Fax 326-6851

---

Divine Providence Hospital — Post-Sec.
1100 Grampian Blvd 17701 — 570-326-8101
Empire Beauty School — Post-Sec.
1808 E 3rd St 17701 — 570-322-8243
Lycoming College — Post-Sec.
700 College Pl 17701 — 570-321-4000
Newport Business Institute — Post-Sec.
941 W 3rd St 17701 — 570-326-2869
Pennsylvania College of Technology — Post-Sec.
1 College Ave 17701 — 570-326-3761
St. John Neumann Regional Academy — 200/7-12
901 Penn St 17701 — 570-323-9953
Denise Tobin, prin. — Fax 321-7146
Williamsport Hospital — Post-Sec.
777 Rural Ave 17701 — 570-326-8101

**Willow Grove, Montgomery, Pop. 15,410**
Area Vocational Technical School
Supt. — None
Eastern Center for Arts & Technology — Vo/Tech
3075 Terwood Rd 19090 — 215-784-4800
Thomas Allen, dir. — Fax 784-4801

Upper Moreland Township SD — 3,000/K-12
2900 Terwood Rd 19090 — 215-830-1511
Robert Milrod Ph.D., supt. — Fax 659-3421
www.umtsd.org/
Upper Moreland HS — 1,000/9-12
3000 Terwood Rd 19090 — 215-830-1500
Joseph Carracappa, prin. — Fax 830-1581
Other Schools – See Hatboro

**Willow Hill, Franklin**
Fannett-Metal SD — 400/K-12
PO Box 91 17271 — 717-349-7172
Fax 349-2748
fmsd.schoolwires.net
Fannett-Metal MSHS — 200/6-12
PO Box 91 17271 — 717-349-2363
Adam Whitsel, prin. — Fax 349-2173

**Willow Street, Lancaster, Pop. 7,536**
Area Vocational Technical School
Supt. — None
Lancaster County CTC-Willow Street — Vo/Tech
PO Box 527 17584 — 717-464-7050
James Catino, dir. — Fax 464-9518

---

Lancaster County Career & Technology Ctr — Post-Sec.
1730 Hans Herr Dr 17584 — 717-464-7050

**Windber, Somerset, Pop. 4,117**
Windber Area SD — 1,200/PK-12
2301 Graham Ave 15963 — 814-467-5551
Rick Huffman, supt. — Fax 467-4208
www.windberschools.org
Windber Area HS — 400/9-12
2301 Graham Ave 15963 — 814-467-4567
Ric Lucas, prin. — Fax 467-0677
Windber Area MS — 300/6-8
2301 Graham Ave 15963 — 814-467-4620
Ric Lucas, prin. — Fax 467-6218

**Wingate, Centre**
Bald Eagle Area SD — 1,800/K-12
751 S Eagle Valley Rd 16823 — 814-355-4860
Jeffrey Miles, supt. — Fax 355-1028
www.beasd.org
Bald Eagle Area MSHS — 1,000/6-12
751 S Eagle Valley Rd 16823 — 814-355-4868
John Tobias, prin. — Fax 355-2146

**Wormleysburg, Cumberland, Pop. 3,002**

---

Harrisburg Academy — 400/PK-12
10 Erford Rd 17043 — 717-763-7811
Dr. James Newman, head sch — Fax 975-0894

**Wrightsville, York, Pop. 2,269**
Eastern York SD — 2,600/K-12
PO Box 150 17368 — 717-252-1555
Dr. Darla Pianowski, supt. — Fax 478-6000
www.eyork.k12.pa.us/
Eastern York HS — 700/9-12
PO Box 2002 17368 — 717-252-1551
Dr. Timothy Mitzel, prin. — Fax 252-4808
Eastern York MS — 600/6-8
PO Box 2003 17368 — 717-252-3400
Dr. Paula Westerman, prin. — Fax 252-4891

**Wyalusing, Bradford, Pop. 591**
Wyalusing Area SD — 1,000/K-12
PO Box 157 18853 — 570-746-1600
Dr. Chester Mummau, supt. — Fax 746-0281
www.wyalusingrams.com/
Wyalusing Valley JSHS — 600/7-12
11364 Wyalusing New Albany 18853 — 570-746-1218
Gary Otis, prin. — Fax 746-2053

**Wyncote, Montgomery, Pop. 2,980**
Cheltenham Township SD
Supt. — See Elkins Park
Cheltenham HS — 1,500/9-12
500 Rices Mill Rd 19095 — 215-517-3700
Iris Parker, prin. — Fax 517-3771

---

Bishop McDevitt HS — 700/9-12
125 Royal Ave 19095 — 215-887-5575
Mary Kirby, prin. — Fax 887-1371
Reconstructionist Rabbinical College — Post-Sec.
1299 Church Rd 19095 — 215-576-0800

**Wynnewood, Montgomery, Pop. 7,800**

---

Friends' Central S - Upper Campus — 600/6-12
1101 City Ave 19096 — 610-649-7440
Craig Sellers, hdmstr. — Fax 649-5669
Lankenau Hospital — Post-Sec.
100 E Lancaster Ave 19096 — 610-526-3019
St. Charles Borromeo Seminary — Post-Sec.
100 E Wynnewood Rd 19096 — 610-667-3394

**Wyomissing, Berks, Pop. 10,332**
Wyomissing Area SD — 1,800/K-12
630 Evans Ave 19610 — 610-374-0739
Julia Vicente, supt. — Fax 374-0948
www.wyoarea.org/
Wyomissing Area JSHS — 900/7-12
630 Evans Ave 19610 — 610-374-0739
Dr. Corey Jones, prin. — Fax 374-6012

---

Berks Technical Institute — Post-Sec.
2205 Ridgewood Rd 19610 — 610-372-1722

**Yardley, Bucks, Pop. 2,392**
Pennsbury SD
Supt. — See Fallsington
Boehm MS — 800/6-8
866 Big Oak Rd 19067 — 215-428-4220
Theresa Ricci, prin. — Fax 428-9605
Penn MS — 1,000/6-8
1524 Derbyshire Rd 19067 — 215-428-4280
Christopher Becker, prin. — Fax 428-1549
Pennwood MS — 1,000/6-8
1523 Makefield Rd 19067 — 215-428-4237
Elizabeth Aldridge, prin. — Fax 428-4265

**Yeadon, Delaware, Pop. 11,214**
William Penn SD
Supt. — See Lansdowne
Penn Wood HS Cypress Street Campus — 800/9-10
600 Cypress St 19050 — 610-626-3223
Dr. D. Brandon Cooley, prin. — Fax 284-8061

**York, York, Pop. 41,931**
Area Vocational Technical School
Supt. — None
York County School of Technology — Vo/Tech
2179 S Queen St 17402 — 717-741-0820
Dr. David Thomas, dir. — Fax 741-0694

Central York SD — 5,600/K-12
775 Marion Rd 17406 — 717-846-6789
Dr. Michael Snell, supt. — Fax 840-0451
www.cysd.k12.pa.us
Central York HS — 1,700/9-12
601 Mundis Mill Rd 17406 — 717-846-6789
Ryan Caufman, prin. — Fax 848-4684
Central York MS — 800/7-8
1950 N Hills Rd 17406 — 717-846-6789
Edmund McManama, prin.

West York Area SD — 3,100/K-12
2605 W Market St 17404 — 717-792-2796
Dr. Emilie Lonardi, supt. — Fax 792-5114
www.wyasd.k12.pa.us
West York Area HS — 900/9-12
1800 Bannister St 17404 — 717-845-6634
Janet May, prin. — Fax 846-9691
West York Area MS — 800/6-8
1700 Bannister St 17404 — 717-845-1671
Brad Sterner, prin. — Fax 845-9083

York CSD — 3,700/K-12
PO Box 1927 17405 — 717-845-3571
Dr. Eric Holmes, supt. — Fax 849-1394
www.ycs.k12.pa.us
Penn HS — 1,000/9-12
101 W College Ave 17401 — 717-849-1218
Brandon Carter, prin. — Fax 848-1143

York Suburban SD — 2,900/K-12
1800 Hollywood Dr 17403 — 717-885-1210
Dr. Michele Merkle, supt. — Fax 885-1211
www.yssd.org/
York Suburban HS — 900/9-12
1800 Hollywood Dr 17403 — 717-885-1270
Dr. Brian Ellis, prin. — Fax 885-1271
York Suburban MS — 700/6-8
455 Sundale Dr 17402 — 717-885-1260
Dr. Scott Krauser, prin. — Fax 885-1261

---

Art Institute of York - Pennsylvania — Post-Sec.
1409 Williams Rd 17402 — 717-755-2300
Baltimore School of Massage-York Campus — Post-Sec.
170 Red Rock Rd 17406 — 717-268-1881
Bible Baptist Christian Academy — 100/PK-12
4190 N Susquehanna Trl 17404 — 717-266-2544
Christian S of York — 400/PK-12
907 Greenbriar Rd 17404 — 717-767-6842
Kevin Hofer, hdmstr. — Fax 767-4904
Consolidated School of Business — Post-Sec.
1605 Clugston Rd 17404 — 717-764-9550
Empire Beauty School — Post-Sec.
2592 Eastern Blvd 17402 — 717-600-8111
Motorcycle Technology Center — Post-Sec.
52 Grumbacher Rd 17406 — 717-767-4300
Penn State York — Post-Sec.
1031 Edgecomb Ave 17403 — 717-771-4000
York Catholic HS — 600/7-12
601 E Springettsbury Ave 17403 — 717-846-8871
Katie Seufert, prin. — Fax 843-4588
York College of Pennsylvania — Post-Sec.
441 Country Club Rd 17403 — 717-846-7788
York Country Day S — 200/PK-12
1071 Regents Glen Blvd 17403 — 717-815-6700
Dr. Christine Heine, head sch — Fax 815-6769
York Hospital — Post-Sec.
1001 S George St 17403 — 717-851-2942
Yorktowne Business Institute — Post-Sec.
W 7th Ave 17404 — 717-846-5000
YTI Career Institute — Post-Sec.
1405 Williams Rd 17402 — 717-757-1100

**York Springs, Adams, Pop. 827**
Bermudian Springs SD — 2,000/K-12
7335 Carlisle Pike 17372 — 717-528-4113
Dr. Shane Hotchkiss, supt. — Fax 528-7981
www.bermudian.org
Bermudian Springs HS — 600/9-12
7335 Carlisle Pike 17372 — 717-528-5127
Jon DeFoe, prin. — Fax 528-4149
Bermudian Springs MS — 600/5-8
7335 Carlisle Pike 17372 — 717-528-5137
Wade Hunt, prin. — Fax 528-0034

**Youngsville, Warren, Pop. 1,716**
Warren County SD
Supt. — See Russell
Youngsville HS — 300/8-12
227 College St 16371 — 814-563-7573
Amy Beers, prin. — Fax 563-4459

---

Warren County Christian S — 100/K-12
165 Mead Run Rd 16371 — 814-563-4457
Richard Kolcharno, prin. — Fax 563-7647

**Youngwood, Westmoreland, Pop. 3,014**

---

Westmoreland County Community College — Post-Sec.
145 Pavilion Ln 15697 — 724-925-4000

**Zieglerville, Montgomery**
Perkiomen Valley SD
Supt. — See Collegeville
Perkiomen Valley West MS — 600/6-8
220 Big Rd 19492 — 484-977-7210
Kim Boyd, prin. — Fax 977-7212

# RHODE ISLAND

## RHODE ISLAND DEPARTMENT OF EDUCATION
**255 Westminster St, Providence 02903-3400**
**Telephone 401-222-4600**
**Fax 401-277-6178**
**Website http://www.ride.ri.gov**

Commissioner of Education Deborah Gist

## RHODE ISLAND BOARD OF REGENTS
**255 Westminster St, Providence 02903-3414**

Chairperson George Caruolo

## PUBLIC, PRIVATE AND CATHOLIC SECONDARY SCHOOLS

**Barrington, Bristol, Pop. 15,849**
Barrington SD 3,400/PK-12
PO Box 95 02806 401-245-5000
Michael Messore, supt. Fax 245-5003
barringtonschools.org
Barrington HS 1,100/9-12
220 Lincoln Ave 02806 401-247-3150
Joseph Hurley, prin. Fax 245-6170
Barrington MS 800/6-8
261 Middle Hwy 02806 401-247-3160
Dr. Andrew Anderson, prin. Fax 247-3164

---

Barrington Christian Academy 200/K-12
9 Old County Rd 02806 401-246-0113
Elsie R. Wright, head sch Fax 246-2540
St. Andrew's S 200/6-12
63 Federal Rd 02806 401-246-1230
David Tinagero, hdmstr. Fax 246-0510

**Block Island, Washington**
New Shoreham SD 100/K-12
PO Box 1890 02807 401-466-7732
Dr. Judith Lundsten, supt. Fax 466-3249
blockislandschool.net/
Block Island S 100/K-12
PO Box 1890 02807 401-466-5600
Kristine Monje, prin. Fax 466-5610

**Bristol, Bristol, Pop. 21,625**
Bristol Warren Regional SD 3,500/PK-12
151 State St 02809 401-253-4000
Mario Andrade Ed.D., supt. Fax 253-1740
www.bw.k12.ri.us
Mt. Hope HS 1,100/9-12
199 Chestnut St 02809 401-254-5980
Don Rebello, prin. Fax 254-5925
Other Schools – See Warren

---

Roger Williams University Post-Sec.
1 Old Ferry Rd 02809 401-253-1040

**Central Falls, Providence, Pop. 18,222**
Central Falls SD 2,500/PK-12
949 Dexter St 02863 401-727-7700
Frances Gallo, supt. Fax 727-7722
www.cfschools.net/
Calcutt MS 400/5-8
112 Washington St 02863 401-727-7726
Heather Dos Santos, prin. Fax 724-0870
Central Falls HS 800/9-12
24 Summer St 02863 401-727-7710
Joshua Laplante, prin. Fax 727-6157

**Coventry, Kent, Pop. 31,083**
Coventry SD 5,100/PK-12
1675 Flat River Rd 02816 401-822-9400
Michael Almeida, supt. Fax 822-9464
www.coventryschools.net
Career & Technical Center Vo/Tech
40 Reservoir Rd 02816 401-822-9499
Lori Ferguson, dir. Fax 822-9492
Coventry HS 1,700/9-12
40 Reservoir Rd 02816 401-822-9499
Michael Hobin, prin. Fax 822-9492
Feinstein MS of Coventry 1,200/6-8
15 Foster Dr 02816 401-822-9426
Dr. Arthur Lisi, prin. Fax 822-9469

**Cranston, Providence, Pop. 78,728**
Cranston SD 10,600/PK-12
845 Park Ave 02910 401-270-8000
Jeannine Nota-Masse, supt. Fax 270-8703
www.cpsed.net
Bain MS 400/7-8
135 Gansett Ave 02910 401-270-8010
Jenny Chan-Remka, prin. Fax 270-8567
Cranston Area Career & Technical Center Vo/Tech
100 Metropolitan Ave 02920 401-270-8070
Gerry Auth, prin. Fax 270-8611
Cranston HS East 1,600/9-12
899 Park Ave 02910 401-270-8126
Sean Kelly, prin. Fax 270-8509
Cranston HS West 1,600/9-12
80 Metropolitan Ave 02920 401-270-8049
Thomas Barbieri, prin. Fax 270-8526

Park View MS 400/7-8
25 Park View Blvd 02910 401-270-8090
Michael Crudale, prin. Fax 270-8527
Western Hills MS 700/7-8
400 Phenix Ave 02920 401-270-8030
Anthony Corrente, prin. Fax 270-8635

**Cumberland, Providence**
Cumberland SD 4,700/PK-12
2602 Mendon Rd 02864 401-658-1600
Dr. Philip Thornton Ed.D., supt. Fax 658-4620
www.cumberlandschools.org/
Cumberland HS 1,500/9-12
2600 Mendon Rd 02864 401-658-2600
Alan Tenreiro, prin. Fax 658-3124
McCourt MS 500/6-8
45 Highland Ave 02864 401-725-2092
Jason Masterson Ed.D., prin. Fax 723-1188
North Cumberland MS 600/6-8
400 Nate Whipple Hwy 02864 401-333-6306
Bethany Coughlin, prin. Fax 333-1926

**East Greenwich, Kent, Pop. 11,865**
East Greenwich SD 2,200/PK-12
111 Peirce St 02818 401-398-1201
Victor Mercurio, supt. Fax 886-3203
www.egsd.net
Cole MS 600/6-8
100 Cedar Ave 02818 401-886-3248
Alexis Meyer, prin. Fax 886-3283
East Greenwich HS 800/9-12
300 Avenger Dr 02818 401-886-3292
Michael Podraza, prin. Fax 885-1336

---

New England Institute of Technology Post-Sec.
One New England Tech Blvd 02818 401-467-7744
Rocky Hill S 300/PK-12
530 Ives Rd 02818 401-884-9070
Peter Branch, head sch Fax 885-4985

**East Providence, Providence, Pop. 44,064**
East Providence SD 5,400/PK-12
145 Taunton Ave 02914 401-435-7500
Kim Mercer, supt. Fax 435-7507
www.epschoolsri.com/
East Providence Career & Technical Ctr Vo/Tech
1998 Pawtucket Ave 02914 401-435-7815
Karen Mellen, dir. Fax 435-7854
East Providence HS 1,700/9-12
2000 Pawtucket Ave 02914 401-435-7806
Shani Wallace, prin. Fax 435-7864
Martin MS 600/6-8
111 Brown St 02914 401-435-7819
Dr. Sandra Forand, prin. Fax 435-7851
Other Schools – See Riverside

---

Providence Country Day S 200/6-12
660 Waterman Ave 02914 401-438-5170
Vince Watchorn, head sch Fax 435-4514
St. Mary Academy-Bay View 700/PK-12
3070 Pawtucket Ave 02915 401-434-0113
Colleen Gribbin, prin. Fax 438-5936

**Greenville, Providence, Pop. 8,588**

---

Mater Ecclesiae College Post-Sec.
60 Austin Ave 02828 401-949-2820
Overbrook Academy 100/6-9
60 Austin Ave 02828 401-349-3444

**Harrisville, Providence, Pop. 1,581**
Burrillville SD 2,400/PK-12
2300 Broncos Hwy 02830 401-568-1301
Dr. Frank Pallotta, supt. Fax 568-4111
www.bsd-ri.net/
Burrillville HS 700/9-12
425 East Ave 02830 401-568-1310
Michael Whaley, prin. Fax 568-1363
Burrillville MS 500/6-8
2220 Broncos Hwy 02830 401-568-1320
Dennis Kafalas, prin. Fax 568-1317

**Jamestown, Newport, Pop. 4,999**
Jamestown SD 500/PK-8
76 Melrose Ave 02835 401-423-7020
Dr. Carol Ann Blanchette, supt. Fax 423-7022
www.jamestownschools.org
Lawn Avenue S 200/5-8
55 Lawn Ave 02835 401-423-7010
Nathaniel Edmonds, prin. Fax 423-7012

**Johnston, Providence, Pop. 26,542**
Johnston SD 3,000/PK-12
10 Memorial Ave 02919 401-233-1900
Dr. Bernard DiLullo, supt. Fax 233-1907
www.johnstonschools.org
Ferri MS 700/6-8
10 Memorial Ave 02919 401-233-1930
Dennis Morrell, prin. Fax 233-1943
Johnston SHS 900/9-12
345 Cherry Hill Rd 02919 401-233-1920
Zachary Farrell, prin. Fax 233-0031

**Kingston, Washington, Pop. 6,817**

---

University of Rhode Island 02881 Post-Sec.
401-874-1000

**Lincoln, Providence, Pop. 18,045**
Lincoln SD 3,300/PK-12
1624 Lonsdale Ave 02865 401-721-3300
Georgia Fortunato, supt. Fax 728-5482
www.lincolnps.org/
Lincoln HS 1,000/9-12
135 Old River Rd 02865 401-334-7500
Kevin McNamara, prin. Fax 334-8753
Lincoln MS 800/6-8
152 Jenckes Hill Rd 02865 401-721-3400
Heidi Godowski, prin. Fax 721-3428

Rhode Island Technical Schools
Supt. — None
Davies Career-Technical HS Vo/Tech
50 Jenckes Hill Rd 02865 401-728-1500
Victoria Garrick, prin. Fax 728-8910

---

Lincoln Technical Institute Post-Sec.
622 George Washington Hwy 02865 401-334-2430

**Middletown, Newport, Pop. 3,400**
Middletown SD 2,200/PK-12
26 Oliphant Ln 02842 401-849-2122
Rosemarie Kraeger, supt. Fax 849-0202
www.mpsri.net/
Gaudet MS 700/4-8
1113 Aquidneck Ave 02842 401-846-6395
Beth Hayes, prin. Fax 847-7580
Middletown HS 700/9-12
130 Valley Rd 02842 401-846-7250
Gail Abromitis, prin. Fax 849-7170

---

St. George's S 400/9-12
372 Purgatory Rd 02842 401-847-7565
Eric Peterson, head sch Fax 842-6677

**Narragansett, Washington, Pop. 3,721**
Narragansett SD 1,400/PK-12
25 5th Ave 02882 401-792-9450
Katherine Sipala, supt. Fax 792-9439
www.narragansett.k12.ri.us/
Narragansett HS 500/9-12
245 S Pier Rd 02882 401-792-9400
Daniel Warner, prin. Fax 792-9410
Narragansett Pier MS 400/5-8
235 S Pier Rd 02882 401-792-9430
Marianne Kirby, prin. Fax 792-9436

**Newport, Newport, Pop. 23,495**
Newport SD 1,200/PK-12
15 Wickham Rd 02840 401-847-2100
Colleen Jermain Ed.D., supt. Fax 849-0170
www.npsri.net
Newport Area Career & Technical Center Vo/Tech
15 Wickham Rd 02840 401-849-3608
James Nelson, dir. Fax 849-4670

Rogers HS 600/9-12
15 Wickham Rd 02840 401-847-6235
Jeff Goss, prin. Fax 849-3295
Thompson MS 600/5-8
55 Broadway 02840 401-847-1493
Jaime Crowley, prin. Fax 849-3426

Rhode Island Technical Schools
Supt. — None
MET East Bay Campus Vo/Tech
1 York St 02840 401-849-7711
Brandee Lapisky, prin. Fax 846-5703

---

International Yacht Restoration School Post-Sec.
449 Thames St 02840 401-848-5777
Salve Regina University Post-Sec.
100 Ochre Point Ave 02840 401-847-6650

**North Kingstown, Washington, Pop. 2,800**
North Kingstown SD 4,300/PK-12
100 Fairway Dr 02852 401-268-6200
Philip Auger, supt. Fax 268-6405
www.nksd.net
Davisville MS 500/6-8
200 School St 02852 401-541-6300
Ruthanne Logan, prin. Fax 541-6310
North Kingstown HS 1,600/9-12
150 Fairway Dr 02852 401-268-6236
Thomas Kenworthy, prin. Fax 268-6210
Wickford MS 400/6-8
250 Tower Hill Rd 02852 401-268-6470
Terry Merkel, prin. Fax 268-6480

**North Providence, Providence, Pop. 32,500**
North Providence SD 3,300/PK-12
2240 Mineral Spring Ave 02911 401-233-1100
Melinda A. Smith M.Ed., supt. Fax 233-1106
www.northprovschools.org
Birchwood MS 400/6-8
10 Birchwood Dr 02904 401-233-1120
Steven Clarke, prin. Fax 353-6903
North Providence HS 1,000/9-12
1828 Mineral Spring Ave 02904 401-233-1150
Joseph Goho, prin. Fax 233-1166
Ricci MS 300/6-8
51 Intervale Ave 02911 401-233-1170
Lucille Delasanta, prin. Fax 232-5421

---

St. Joseph's Hospital Post-Sec.
200 High Service Ave 02904 401-456-3050

**North Scituate, Providence**
Foster-Glocester Regional SD 800/9-12
91 Anan Wade Rd 02857 401-710-7500
Michael Barnes Ph.D., supt.
www.fg.k12.ri.us/
Ponaganset HS 800/9-12
137 Anan Wade Rd 02857 401-710-7500
Renee Palazzo, prin. Fax 647-5743

Scituate SD 1,500/PK-12
PO Box 188 02857 401-647-4100
Dr. Paul Lescault, supt. Fax 647-4102
www.scituateri.net
Scituate HS 500/9-12
94 Trimtown Rd 02857 401-647-4120
Dr. Michael Sollitto, prin. Fax 647-4126
Scituate MS 400/6-8
94 Trimtown Rd 02857 401-647-4123
Michael Zajac, prin. Fax 647-4104

**North Smithfield, Providence, Pop. 10,497**
North Smithfield SD
Supt. — See Slatersville
North Smithfield HS 500/9-12
412 Greenville Rd 02896 401-766-2500
Robert Mezzanotte, prin. Fax 765-8629
North Smithfield MS 400/6-8
1850 Providence Pike 02896 401-597-6100
John Lahar, prin. Fax 597-6121

**Pawtucket, Providence, Pop. 64,391**
Pawtucket SD 8,700/PK-12
PO Box 388 02862 401-729-6300
Patti DiCenso, supt. Fax 727-1641
www.psdri.net
Alternative Learning Program Alt
286 Main St 02860 401-721-2127
Dr. Linda Gifford, prin. Fax 729-2126
Goff JHS 500/7-8
974 Newport Ave 02861 401-729-6500
Lisa Benedetti Ramzi, prin. Fax 721-2105
Jenks JHS 300/7-8
350 Division St 02860 401-729-6520
Elizabeth Fasteson, prin. Fax 729-6523
Shea HS 900/9-12
485 East Ave 02860 401-729-6445
Donald Miller, prin. Fax 729-6454
Slater JHS 500/7-8
281 Mineral Spring Ave 02860 401-729-6480
Dr. Jacqueline Ash, prin. Fax 729-6490
Tolman HS 1,200/9-12
150 Exchange St 02860 401-729-6400
Christopher Savastano, prin. Fax 729-6407
Walsh S of the Arts 100/9-12
350 Division St 02860 401-721-2148
Elizabeth Fasteson, prin. Fax 721-2147

---

New England Tractor Trailer Training Post-Sec.
600 Mshssuck Valley Ind Hwy 02860 401-725-1220
Newport School of Hairdressing Post-Sec.
226 Main St 02860 401-725-6882
St. Raphael Academy 400/9-12
123 Walcott St 02860 401-723-8100
Daniel Richard, prin. Fax 723-8740
Sawyer School Post-Sec.
101 Main St 02860 401-272-8400

**Portsmouth, Newport, Pop. 3,600**
Portsmouth SD 2,700/PK-12
29 Middle Rd 02871 401-683-1039
Ana C. Riley, supt. Fax 683-5204
portsmouthschoolsri.net
Portsmouth HS 1,000/9-12
120 Education Ln 02871 401-683-2124
Robert Littlefield, prin. Fax 683-1096
Portsmouth MS 1,000/4-8
125 Jepson Ln 02871 401-849-3700
Joseph Amaral, prin. Fax 841-8420

---

Portsmouth Abbey S 400/9-12
285 Corys Ln 02871 401-683-2000
Daniel McDonough, hdmstr. Fax 683-5888

**Providence, Providence, Pop. 170,517**
Providence SD 22,600/PK-12
797 Westminster St 02903 401-456-9211
Susan Lusi, supt. Fax 456-9252
www.providenceschools.org
Alvarez HS 500/9-12
375 Adelaide Ave 02907 401-456-0676
Janice Hawkins, prin. Fax 456-0679
Bishop MS 700/6-8
101 Sessions St 02906 401-456-9344
Kimberly Luca, prin. Fax 456-9110
Central HS 1,100/9-12
70 Fricker St 02903 401-456-9111
Julia Carlson, prin. Fax 456-9113
Classical HS 1,100/9-12
770 Westminster St 02903 401-456-9145
Scott Barr, prin. Fax 456-9155
Cooley Health & Science Technology HS 700/9-12
182 Thurbers Ave 02905 401-456-1781
Michaela Keegan, prin. Fax 456-1782
DelSesto MS 900/6-8
152 Springfield St 02909 401-278-0557
Arzinia Gill, prin. Fax 278-0564
E-Cubed Academy 400/9-12
812 Branch Ave 02904 401-456-0694
Regina Winkfield, prin. Fax 456-0696
Greene MS 900/6-8
721 Chalkstone Ave 02908 401-456-9347
Dr. Nicole Mathis, prin. Fax 453-8630
Hope HS 600/9-12
324 Hope St 02906 401-456-9161
John Hunt, prin. Fax 456-1747
Hopkins MS 500/6-8
480 Charles St 02904 401-456-9203
Gloria Jackson, prin. Fax 456-9226
Mt. Pleasant HS 1,000/9-12
434 Mount Pleasant Ave 02908 401-456-9181
Christopher Coleman, prin. Fax 453-8655
Providence Career And Technical Academy Vo/Tech
41 Fricker St 02903 401-456-9136
Ramon Torres, dir. Fax 456-9172
Stuart MS 700/6-8
188 Princeton Ave 02907 401-456-9340
Edward Halpin, prin. Fax 453-8659
West Broadway MS 6-8
29 Bainbridge Ave 02909 401-456-1733
William Black, prin. Fax 278-0527
Williams MS 800/6-8
278 Thurbers Ave 02905 401-456-9355
Jennifer Vorro, prin. Fax 453-8631

Rhode Island Technical Schools
Supt. — None
MET Equality S Vo/Tech
325 Public St 02905 401-752-2610
Steven Bartholomew, prin. Fax 752-2612
MET Justice Campus Vo/Tech
325 Public St 02905 401-752-2630
Janet Vilanueva-Williams, prin. Fax 752-2612
MET Liberty S Vo/Tech
325 Public St 02905 401-752-2680
Arthur Baraf, prin. Fax 752-2612
MET Peace Street Campus Vo/Tech
362 Dexter St 02907 401-752-3400
Chantel Wylie, prin. Fax 752-3425
MET Unity S Vo/Tech
325 Public St 02905 401-752-2650
Alin Bennett, prin. Fax 752-2612
Other Schools – See Lincoln RI, Newport RI

---

Brown S 800/PK-12
250 Lloyd Ave 02906 401-831-7350
Matt Glendinning, hdmstr. Fax 455-0084
Brown University Post-Sec.
1 Prospect St 02912 401-863-1000
Community Preparatory S 100/3-8
126 Somerset St 02907 401-521-9696
Dan Corley, head sch Fax 521-9715
Empire Beauty School Post-Sec.
151 Broadway 02903 401-272-4300
Johnson & Wales University Post-Sec.
8 Abbott Park Pl 02903 401-598-1000
LaSalle Academy 1,500/7-12
612 Academy Ave 02908 401-351-7750
Donald Kavanagh, prin. Fax 444-1782
Lincoln S 400/PK-12
301 Butler Ave 02906 401-331-9696
Suzanne Fogarty, head sch Fax 751-6670
Providence College Post-Sec.
1 Cunningham Sq 02918 401-865-1000
Providence Hebrew Day S 200/PK-12
450 Elmgrove Ave 02906 401-331-5327
Rabbi Peretz Scheinerman, dean Fax 331-0030
Rhode Island College Post-Sec.
600 Mount Pleasant Ave 02908 401-456-8000
Rhode Island Hospital Post-Sec.
593 Eddy St 02903 401-444-5123
Rhode Island School of Design Post-Sec.
2 College St 02903 401-454-6100

St. Patrick Academy 100/8-10
244 Smith St 02908 401-421-9300
Bruce Daigle, prin. Fax 421-0810
Sawyer School Post-Sec.
550 Hartford Ave 02909 401-272-3280
School One 100/9-12
220 University Ave 02906 401-331-2497
Jennifer Borman, head sch Fax 421-8869
Wheeler S 800/PK-12
216 Hope St 02906 401-421-8100
Dr. Dan Miller, head sch Fax 751-7674
Women & Infants Hospital Post-Sec.
101 Dudley St 02905 401-274-1100

**Riverside, See East Providence**
East Providence SD
Supt. — See East Providence
Riverside MS 600/6-8
179 Forbes St 02915 401-433-6230
Cheri Guerra, prin. Fax 433-6261

**Slatersville, Providence**
North Smithfield SD 1,600/PK-12
PO Box 72 02876 401-769-5492
Stephen Lindberg, supt. Fax 769-5493
www.northsmithfieldschools.com/
Other Schools – See North Smithfield

**Smithfield, Providence, Pop. 19,163**
Smithfield SD 2,400/PK-12
49 Farnum Pike 02917 401-231-6606
Robert O'Brien, supt. Fax 232-0870
www.smithfield-ps.org
Gallagher MS 600/6-8
10 Indian Run Trl 02917 401-949-2056
Laurie Beauvais, prin. Fax 949-5697
Smithfield HS 800/9-12
90 Pleasant View Ave 02917 401-949-2050
Daniel Kelley, prin. Fax 949-2052

---

Bryant University Post-Sec.
1150 Douglas Pike 02917 401-232-6000
Masters Regional Academy 200/7-12
915 Douglas Pike 02917 401-232-7061
Dr. Michael Dube Ed.D., prin. Fax 233-9267

**Tiverton, Newport, Pop. 7,434**
Tiverton SD 1,900/PK-12
100 N Brayton Rd 02878 401-624-8476
William Rearick, supt. Fax 624-4086
www.tivertonschools.org
Tiverton HS 600/9-12
100 N Brayton Rd 02878 401-624-8494
Steven Fezette, prin. Fax 624-8495
Tiverton MS 600/5-8
10 Quintal Dr 02878 401-624-6668
Laurie Dias-Mitchell, prin. Fax 624-6669

**Wakefield, Washington, Pop. 8,226**
South Kingstown SD 3,700/PK-12
307 Curtis Corner Rd 02879 401-360-1300
Dr. Kristen Stringfellow Ed.D., supt. Fax 360-1330
www.skschools.net/
Curtis Corner MS 600/7-8
301 Curtis Corner Rd 02879 401-360-1333
Patricia Aull, prin. Fax 360-1334
South Kingstown HS 1,100/9-12
215 Columbia St 02879 401-360-1000
Robert McCarthy, prin. Fax 360-1464

---

Prout S 600/9-12
4640 Tower Hill Rd 02879 401-789-9262
David Carradini, prin. Fax 782-2262

**Warren, Bristol, Pop. 11,385**
Bristol Warren Regional SD
Supt. — See Bristol
Kickemuit MS 800/6-8
525 Child St 02885 401-245-2010
Beth Hayes, prin. Fax 254-5960

**Warwick, Kent, Pop. 81,173**
Warwick SD 9,900/PK-12
34 Warwick Lake Ave 02889 401-734-3000
Dr. Richard D'Agostino, supt. Fax 734-3105
www.warwickschools.org
Aldrich JHS 500/7-8
789 Post Rd 02888 401-734-3500
John Livsey, prin. Fax 734-3508
Gorton JHS 500/7-8
69 Draper Ave 02889 401-734-3350
Jeffrey Taylor, prin. Fax 734-3359
Pilgrim HS 1,100/9-12
111 Pilgrim Pkwy 02888 401-734-3250
Marie Cote, prin. Fax 734-3264
Toll Gate HS 1,000/9-12
575 Centerville Rd Ste 1 02886 401-734-3300
Stephen Chrabaszcz, prin. Fax 734-3314
Warwick Area Career & Technical Center Vo/Tech
575 Centerville Rd 02886 401-734-3150
William McCaffrey, dir. Fax 734-3160
Warwick Veterans Memorial HS 1,000/9-12
2401 W Shore Rd 02889 401-734-3200
Gerry Habershaw, prin. Fax 734-3214
Winman JHS 500/7-8
575 Centerville Rd 02886 401-734-3375
Joanne Pelletier, prin. Fax 734-3385

---

Bishop Hendricken HS 900/9-12
2615 Warwick Ave 02889 401-739-3450
Joseph Brennan, prin. Fax 732-8261
Community College of Rhode Island Post-Sec.
400 East Ave 02886 401-825-1000
Warwick Academy of Beauty Culture Post-Sec.
1276 Bald Hill Rd Unit 100 02886 401-737-4946

**Westerly, Washington, Pop. 17,600**
Westerly SD — 3,000/PK-12
23 Highland Ave 02891 — 401-315-1500
Roy Seitsinger Ph.D., supt. — Fax 348-2707
www.westerly.k12.ri.us
Westerly HS — 1,000/9-12
23 Ward Ave 02891 — 401-596-2109
Todd Grimes, prin. — Fax 315-1586
Westerly MS — 900/5-8
10 Sandy Hill Rd 02891 — 401-348-2750
Paula Fusco, prin. — Fax 348-2752

**West Greenwich, Kent, Pop. 3,492**
Exeter-West Greenwich Regional SD — 1,800/PK-12
940 Nooseneck Hill Rd 02817 — 401-397-5125
James Erinakes M.Ed., supt. — Fax 397-2407
www.ewg.k12.ri.us
Exeter-West Greenwich Regional HS — 600/9-12
930 Nooseneck Hill Rd 02817 — 401-397-6893
Susan Chandler, prin. — Fax 392-0134
Exeter-West Greenwich Regional JHS — 300/7-8
930 Nooseneck Hill Rd 02817 — 401-397-6897
Mary Slattery, prin. — Fax 392-0109

**West Warwick, Kent, Pop. 29,600**
West Warwick SD — 3,400/PK-12
10 Harris Ave 02893 — 401-821-1180
Karen A. Tarasevich, supt. — Fax 822-8463
www.westwarwickpublicschools.com/
Deering MS — 1,000/5-8
2 Webster Knight Dr 02893 — 401-822-8445
Jeffrey Guiot, prin. — Fax 822-8474
West Warwick HS — 1,000/9-12
Webster Knight Dr 02893 — 401-821-6596
Phillip Solomon, prin. — Fax 822-8473

**Wood River Junction, Washington**
Chariho Regional SD — 3,500/PK-12
455A Switch Rd 02894 — 401-364-7575
Barry Ricci, supt. — Fax 415-6076
www.chariho.k12.ri.us/
Chariho Area Career & Technical Center — Vo/Tech
459 Switch Rd 02894 — 401-364-6869
Marilyn Massey, dir. — Fax 364-1191
Chariho Regional HS — 1,200/9-12
453 Switch Rd 02894 — 401-364-7778
Laurie Weber, prin. — Fax 415-0436
Chariho Regional MS — 1,000/5-8
455b Switch Rd 02894 — 401-364-0651
Gregory Zenion, prin. — Fax 223-4925
RYSE — 50/Alt
459 Switch Rd 02894 — 401-364-1160
Carolyn Garlick, dir. — Fax 223-9651

**Woonsocket, Providence, Pop. 39,726**
Woonsocket SD — 4,000/PK-12
108 High St 02895 — 401-767-4600
Patrick McGee, supt. — Fax 767-4607
www.woonsocketschools.com/
Woonsocket Area Career & Tech. Center — Vo/Tech
400 Aylsworth Ave 02895 — 401-767-4662
William Webb, dir. — Fax 767-4665
Woonsocket HS — 1,700/9-12
777 Cass Ave 02895 — 401-767-4700
Carnell Henderson, prin. — Fax 767-4748
Woonsocket MS at Hamlet — 6-8
60 Florence Dr 02895 — 401-235-6110
Steve Boss, prin.
Woonsocket MS at Villa Nova — 6-8
240 Florence Dr 02895 — 401-235-6125
Steve Boss, prin.

---

Good Shepherd Regional S — 200/3-8
1210 Mendon Rd 02895 — 401-767-5906
Lawrence Poitras, prin. — Fax 767-5905
Mt. St. Charles Academy — 900/7-12
800 Logee St 02895 — 401-769-0310
Edwin Burke, prin. — Fax 762-2327

# SOUTH CAROLINA

## SOUTH CAROLINA DEPARTMENT OF EDUCATION
**1429 Senate St Ste 100, Columbia 29201-3799**
**Telephone 803-734-8500**
**Fax 803-734-3389**
**Website ed.sc.gov/**

Superintendent of Education Mick Zais

## SOUTH CAROLINA BOARD OF EDUCATION
**1429 Senate St Ste 100, Columbia 29201-3730**

Chairperson Dennis Thompson

## PUBLIC, PRIVATE AND CATHOLIC SECONDARY SCHOOLS

**Abbeville, Abbeville, Pop. 5,157**
Abbeville County SD — 3,100/PK-12
400 Greenville St 29620 — 864-366-5427
Dr. Jonathan Phipps, supt. — Fax 366-8531
www.acsdsc.org
Abbeville County Career Center — Vo/Tech
100 Old Calhoun Falls Rd 29620 — 864-366-9069
Dorinda Bell-Dunlap, dir. — Fax 366-4774
Abbeville HS — 500/9-12
701 Washington St 29620 — 864-366-5916
Charles Costner, prin. — Fax 366-4939
Wright MS — 400/6-8
111 Highway 71 29620 — 864-366-5998
Skip Hopkins, prin. — Fax 366-4282
Other Schools – See Due West

**Aiken, Aiken, Pop. 29,094**
Aiken County SD — 23,800/PK-12
1000 Brookhaven Dr 29803 — 803-641-2428
Sean Alford Ph.D., supt. — Fax 642-8903
www.aiken.k12.sc.us
Aiken HS — 1,400/9-12
449 Rutland Dr NW 29801 — 803-641-2500
Garen Cofer, prin. — Fax 641-2501
Aiken MS — 600/6-8
101 Gator Ln 29801 — 803-641-2570
John Bradley, prin. — Fax 641-2578
Kennedy MS — 900/6-8
274 E Pine Log Rd 29803 — 803-641-2470
Teresa Mitchem, prin. — Fax 641-2405
Pinecrest Center — Alt
1050 Pinecrest Ave 29801 — 803-641-2680
Ben Osborne, prin. — Fax 641-2681
Schofield MS — 700/6-8
224 Kershaw St NE 29801 — 803-641-2770
Dr. Lloydette Young, prin. — Fax 641-2529
Silver Bluff HS — 700/9-12
64 Desoto Dr 29803 — 803-652-8100
Collette Johnson, prin. — Fax 652-8104
South Aiken HS — 1,500/9-12
232 E Pine Log Rd 29803 — 803-641-2600
Jill Jett, prin. — Fax 641-2607
Aiken County Adult Education — Adult
1000 Brookhaven Dr 29803 — 803-641-2476
Pat Keating, dir. — Fax 641-2492
Other Schools – See Graniteville, Jackson, Monetta, New Ellenton, North Augusta, Wagener, Warrenville

---

Aiken School of Cosmetology — Post-Sec.
225 Richland Ave E 29801 — 803-644-7133
Aiken Technical College — Post-Sec.
PO Box 696 29802 — 803-593-9231
Lacy Cosmetology School — Post-Sec.
3084 Whiskey Rd 29803 — 803-648-6181
South Aiken Baptist Christian S — 400/PK-12
980 Dougherty Rd 29803 — 803-648-7871
University of South Carolina — Post-Sec.
471 University Pkwy 29801 — 803-648-6851

**Allendale, Allendale, Pop. 3,449**

---

University of South Carolina — Post-Sec.
PO Box 617 29810 — 803-584-3446

**Anderson, Anderson, Pop. 26,180**
Anderson SD 3
Supt. — See Iva
Anderson County Alternative S — Alt
805 E Whitner St 29624 — 864-260-4888
Randolph Dillingham, dir. — Fax 260-4004

Anderson SD 4
Supt. — See Pendleton
Pendleton HS — 800/9-12
7324 Highway 187 29625 — 864-403-2100
Brian Couch, prin. — Fax 646-8066

Anderson SD 5 — 11,700/PK-12
PO Box 439 29622 — 864-260-5000
Thomas Wilson, supt. — Fax 260-5074
www.anderson5.net
Anderson College & Career Acad — 700/6-8
2302 Dobbins Bridge Rd 29626 — 864-716-3890
Leonard Galloway, prin. — Fax 716-4070
Anderson V Career Campus — Vo/Tech
1225 S McDuffie St 29624 — 864-260-5160
Cecil Bonner, prin. — Fax 260-5685
Glenview MS of Choice — 6-8
2725 Old Williamston Rd 29621 — 864-716-4060
Walter Mayfield, prin. — Fax 716-3883
Hanna HS IB World S — 1,700/9-12
2600 N Highway 81 29621 — 864-260-5110
Shawn Tobin, prin. — Fax 260-5213
Lakeside MS of Inquiry & Innovation — 700/6-8
315 Pearman Dairy Rd 29625 — 864-260-5135
Tiffany Osborne, prin. — Fax 260-5885
McCants MS IB World S — 800/6-8
2123 Marchbanks Ave 29621 — 864-260-5145
Leigh Burton, prin. — Fax 260-5846
Southwood Academy of the Arts — 100/6-8
1110 Southwood St 29624 — 864-260-5205
Jamie Smith, prin. — Fax 964-2607
Westside HS Early College Academy — 1,700/9-12
806 Pearman Dairy Rd 29625 — 864-260-5230
Kory Roberts, prin. — Fax 260-5007

---

Anderson Christian S — 200/PK-12
3902 Liberty Hwy 29621 — 864-224-7309
Anderson Memorial Hospital — Post-Sec.
800 N Fant St 29621 — 864-261-1109
Anderson University — Post-Sec.
316 Boulevard 29621 — 864-231-2000
Forrest College — Post-Sec.
601 E River St 29624 — 864-225-7653
Montessori S of Anderson — 200/PK-12
280 Sam McGee Rd 29621 — 864-226-5344
Dr. Craig Drennon Ph.D., admin. — Fax 231-6562

**Andrews, Georgetown, Pop. 2,842**
Georgetown County SD
Supt. — See Georgetown
Andrews HS — 600/9-12
12890 County Line Rd 29510 — 843-264-3414
Dr. Michelle Greene, prin. — Fax 264-3326
Rosemary MS — 500/6-8
12804 County Line Rd 29510 — 843-264-9780
LaTanya Goodson, prin. — Fax 264-9787

**Aynor, Horry, Pop. 554**
Horry County SD
Supt. — See Conway
Aynor HS — 700/9-12
201 Jordanville Rd 29511 — 843-488-7100
Michael McCracken, prin. — Fax 488-7101

**Bamberg, Bamberg, Pop. 3,560**
Bamberg SD 1 — 900/PK-12
3830 Faust St 29003 — 803-245-3053
Phyllis Schwarting, supt. — Fax 245-3056
www.bamberg1.com
Bamberg-Ehrhardt HS — 400/9-12
267 Red Raider Dr 29003 — 803-245-3030
Randall Maxwell, prin. — Fax 245-6502
Bamberg-Ehrhardt MS — 200/7-8
897 North St 29003 — 803-245-3058
Dr. Sandra Glover Ed.D., prin. — Fax 245-6501

**Barnwell, Barnwell, Pop. 4,670**
Barnwell SD 45 — 2,400/PK-12
770 Hagood Ave 29812 — 803-541-1300
J.H. Grissom, supt. — Fax 541-1348
www.barnwell45.org
Barnwell HS — 700/9-12
474 Jackson St 29812 — 803-541-1390
Jon Burdge, prin. — Fax 541-0726
Guinyard-Butler MS — 400/7-8
779 Allen St 29812 — 803-541-1370
Craig Hart, prin. — Fax 541-1306

**Batesburg, Lexington, Pop. 5,296**
Lexington County SD 3 — 2,000/PK-12
338 W Columbia Ave 29006 — 803-532-4423
Dr. Chester Floyd, supt. — Fax 532-8000
www.lex3.k12.sc.us
Batesburg-Leesville HS — 500/9-12
600 Summerland Ave 29006 — 803-532-9251
Pat Padgett, prin. — Fax 532-3232
Batesburg-Leesville MS — 500/6-8
425 Shealy Rd 29006 — 803-532-3831
Randall Price, prin. — Fax 532-8021

---

King Academy — 200/K-12
1046 Sardis Rd 29006 — 803-532-6682

**Beaufort, Beaufort, Pop. 12,089**
Beaufort County SD — 19,500/PK-12
PO Box 309 29901 — 843-322-2300
Jeffrey Moss, supt. — Fax 322-2330
www.beaufort.k12.sc.us
Battery Creek HS — 800/9-12
1 Blue Dolphin Dr 29906 — 843-322-5500
Edmond Burnes, prin. — Fax 322-5608
Beaufort HS — 1,500/9-12
84 Sea Island Pkwy, — 843-322-2000
Corey Murphy, prin. — Fax 322-2158
Beaufort MS — 600/6-8
2501 Mossy Oaks Rd 29902 — 843-322-5700
Carole Ingram, prin. — Fax 322-5723
Ladys Island MS — 800/6-8
30 Cougar Dr, — 843-322-3100
Mona Lise Dickson, prin. — Fax 322-3179
Adult Education S — Adult
2900 Mink Point Blvd 29902 — 843-322-2300
Dr. Juanita Murrell, prin. — Fax 322-2371
Other Schools – See Bluffton, Hilton Head Island, Seabrook

---

Beaufort Academy — 300/PK-12
240 Sams Point Rd, — 843-524-3393
Stephen Schools, head sch — Fax 524-1171
Beaufort Christian S — 100/PK-12
378 Parris Island Gtwy 29906 — 843-525-0635
Rev. Douglas Wadsworth, admin. — Fax 525-0635
Technical College of the Lowcountry — Post-Sec.
921 Ribaut Rd 29902 — 843-525-8211

**Belton, Anderson, Pop. 4,063**
Anderson SD 2
Supt. — See Honea Path
Belton MS — 500/6-8
102 Cherokee Rd 29627 — 864-338-6595
Josh Burton, prin. — Fax 338-3301

**Bennettsville, Marlboro, Pop. 8,964**
Marlboro County SD — 4,000/PK-12
PO Box 947 29512 — 843-479-4016
Dr. Helena Tillar, supt. — Fax 479-5944
www.marlboro.k12.sc.us
Marlboro County HS — 1,200/9-12
951 Fayetteville Avenue Ext 29512 — 843-479-5900
Kelvin Lemon, prin. — Fax 479-5916
Other Schools – See Clio

**Bishopville, Lee, Pop. 3,442**
Lee County SD — 2,300/PK-12
PO Box 507 29010 — 803-484-5327
Dr. Wanda Andrews, supt. — Fax 484-9107
www.leeschoolsk12.org
Lee Central HS — 600/9-12
1800 Wisacky Hwy 29010 — 803-428-4010
Dr. James White, prin. — Fax 428-4062
Lee Central MS — 600/6-8
41 Charlenes Ln 29010 — 803-428-2100
Tonya Addison, prin. — Fax 428-2174
Lee County Academic Learning Center — 100/Alt
123 E College St 29010 — 803-483-0111
Bernard McDaniel, dir. — Fax 483-0113
Lee County Career & Technology Center — Vo/Tech
521 Park St 29010 — 803-484-5327
Betty Lowery, coord. — Fax 484-4171

---

Lee Academy — 400/K-12
630 Cousar St 29010 — 803-484-5532

**Blacksburg, Cherokee, Pop. 1,800**
Cherokee County SD
Supt. — See Gaffney
Blacksburg HS — 600/9-12
201 W Ramseur Dr 29702 — 864-839-6371
Craig Bramlett, prin. — Fax 839-2960
Blacksburg MS — 400/6-8
101 London St 29702 — 864-839-6476
Virgil Hampton, prin. — Fax 839-2390

**Blackville, Barnwell, Pop. 2,378**
Area Vocational Schools
Supt. — None
Barnwell County Career Center Vo/Tech
5214 Reynolds Rd 29817 803-259-5512
H. Samuel McKay, dir. Fax 541-4701

Barnwell SD 19 800/PK-12
297 Pascallas St 29817 803-284-5605
Teresa Pope Ph.D., supt. Fax 284-4417
www.barnwell19.k12.sc.us
Blackville-Hilda HS 200/9-12
PO Box 245 29817 803-284-5700
Sterling Harris, prin. Fax 284-3766
Blackville-Hilda JHS 100/7-8
PO Box 245 29817 803-284-5900
Sterling Harris, prin. Fax 284-0961

---

Barnwell Christian S 100/1-12
5675 SC Highway 70 29817 803-259-2100
Patrick Heatwole, admin. Fax 259-2100
Davis Academy 200/K-12
5061 Hilda Rd 29817 803-284-2476
Eve Hogarth, head sch Fax 284-5544

**Bluffton, Beaufort, Pop. 12,248**
Beaufort County SD
Supt. — See Beaufort
Bluffton HS 1,000/10-12
12 H E McCracken Cir 29910 843-706-8800
Mark Dievendorf, prin. Fax 706-8819
McCracken MS 900/8-9
250 HE McCracken Cir 29910 843-706-8700
Todd Bornscheuer, prin. Fax 706-8778

---

Professional Golfers Career College Post-Sec.
4454 Bluffton Park Cres 200 29910 843-757-9611
University of South Carolina Post-Sec.
1 University Blvd, 843-208-8000

**Blythewood, Richland, Pop. 2,008**
Richland SD 2
Supt. — See Columbia
Blythewood Academy Alt
501 Main St 29016 803-691-6890
Dr. Perry Mills, prin. Fax 691-4396
Blythewood HS 2,200/9-12
10901 Wilson Blvd 29016 803-691-4090
Dr. Brenda Hafner, prin. Fax 691-4097
Blythewood MS 600/6-8
2351 Longtown Rd E 29016 803-691-6850
Karis Mazyck, prin. Fax 691-6860
Kelly Mill MS 900/6-8
1141 Kelly Mill Rd 29016 803-691-7210
Mark Sims, prin. Fax 691-7212
Muller Road MS 700/6-8
1031 Muller Rd 29016 803-691-6851
Ssean Bishton, prin. Fax 738-7531
Westwood HS 1,300/9-12
180 Turkey Farm Rd 29016 803-691-4049
Dr. Cheryl Guy, prin. Fax 738-7520

**Boiling Springs, Spartanburg, Pop. 8,098**
Spartanburg SD 2
Supt. — See Chesnee
Boiling Springs HS 9th Grade Campus 600/9-9
3655 Boiling Springs Rd 29316 864-578-2610
Eddie Cole, prin. Fax 578-2620
Boiling Springs HS 1,700/10-12
2251 Old Furnace Rd 29316 864-578-8465
Chuck Gordon, prin. Fax 578-6825

**Branchville, Orangeburg, Pop. 1,014**
Orangeburg County Consolidated SD 4
Supt. — See Cope
Branchville HS 300/7-12
PO Box 188 29432 803-274-8875
David Hess, prin. Fax 274-8645

**Camden, Kershaw, Pop. 6,772**
Kershaw County SD 10,300/PK-12
2029 W Dekalb St 29020 803-432-8416
Dr. Frank Morgan, supt. Fax 425-8918
www.kcsdschools.com
Applied Technical Education Campus Vo/Tech
874 Vocational Ln 29020 803-425-8982
Gordon Morris, dir. Fax 425-8983
Camden HS 900/9-12
1022 Ehrenclou Dr 29020 803-425-8930
Dan Matthews, prin. Fax 424-2861
Camden MS 800/6-8
902 McRae Rd 29020 803-425-8975
Byron Johnson, prin. Fax 425-7867
Continuous Learning Center Alt
1109 Campbell St 29020 803-425-7712
Tommy Gladden, dir. Fax 425-7713
Kershaw County Adult Education Adult
874 Vocational Ln 29020 803-425-8980
Weyland Burns, dir. Fax 425-8988
Other Schools – See Elgin, Kershaw, Lugoff

---

Camden Military Academy 300/7-12
520 Highway 1 N 29020 800-948-6291
Fax 425-1020

**Campobello, Spartanburg, Pop. 498**
Spartanburg SD 1 5,100/PK-12
PO Box 218 29322 864-472-2846
Dr. Ron Garner, supt. Fax 472-4118
www.spart1.org/do/
Landrum HS 600/9-12
18818 Asheville Hwy 29322 864-457-2606
Jason McCraw, prin. Fax 468-4004
Other Schools – See Inman, Landrum

**Cayce, Lexington, Pop. 12,278**
Lexington County SD 2
Supt. — See West Columbia
Brookland-Cayce HS 1,100/9-12
1300 State St 29033 803-791-5000
Gregg Morton, prin. Fax 739-4970

Busbee Creative Arts Academy 300/6-8
501 Bulldog Blvd 29033 803-739-4070
C.R. Hall, prin. Fax 739-4133

**Central, Pickens, Pop. 5,067**
Pickens County SD
Supt. — See Easley
Daniel HS 1,000/9-12
140 Blue and Gold Blvd 29630 864-397-2900
Josh Young, prin. Fax 654-9608
Edwards MS 800/6-8
1157 Madden Bridge Rd 29630 864-397-4200
Jeff Duncan, prin. Fax 624-4426

---

Southern Wesleyan University Post-Sec.
PO Box 1020 29630 864-644-5000

**Chapin, Lexington, Pop. 1,420**
SD Five of Lexington & Richland Counties
Supt. — See Irmo
Academy for Success Alt
11629 Broad River Rd 29036 803-575-5300
Donald Hardie, prin. Fax 575-5320
Center for Advanced Technical Studies 9-12
916 Mount Vernon Church Rd 29036
Dr. Bob Couch, dir. 803-476-8000
Chapin HS 1,300/9-12
300 Columbia Ave 29036 803-575-5400
Dr. Akil Ross, prin. Fax 575-5420
Chapin MS 1,100/6-8
1130 Old Lexington Hwy 29036 803-575-5700
Anna Miller, prin. Fax 575-5721
Spring Hill HS 9-12
11629 Broad River Rd 29036 803-476-8700
Dr. Michael Lofton, prin. Fax 476-8720

**Charleston, Charleston, Pop. 118,351**
Charleston County SD 44,400/PK-12
75 Calhoun St Fl 2 29401 843-937-6300
Michael Bobby, supt. Fax 937-6307
www.charleston.k12.sc.us
Academic Magnet HS 600/9-12
5109 W Enterprise St Ste A 29405 843-746-1300
Judith Peterson, prin. Fax 746-1310
Burke MSHS 600/7-12
244 President St 29403 843-579-4815
Maurice Cannon, prin. Fax 722-3651
Clark Corporate Academy 100/Alt
1929 N Grimball Rd 29412 843-762-2774
Dr. Andrew Halevi, dir. Fax 762-6218
Ft. Johnson MS 500/6-8
1825 Camp Rd 29412 843-762-2740
David Parler, prin. Fax 762-6212
James Island MS 400/6-8
1484 Camp Rd 29412 843-762-2784
Murton Hudson, prin. Fax 762-6209
West Ashley HS 1,900/9-12
4060 Wildcat Blvd 29414 843-573-1201
William Runyon, prin. Fax 573-1223
West Ashley MS 300/6-8
1776 William Kennerty Dr 29407 843-763-1546
LaCarma Brown-McMillan, prin. Fax 852-6557
Williams MS 600/6-8
640 Butte St 29414 843-763-1529
Kevin Smith, prin. Fax 763-5955
Other Schools – See Hollywood, Johns Island, Mc Clellanville, Mount Pleasant, North Charleston

---

Academy of Cosmetology Post-Sec.
5117 Dorchester Rd 29418 843-552-3241
Ashley Hall 700/PK-12
172 Rutledge Ave 29403 843-722-4088
Jill Muti, head sch Fax 720-2868
Bishop England HS 800/9-12
363 Seven Farms Dr 29492 843-849-9599
Patrick Finneran, prin. Fax 849-9221
Charleston Cosmetology Institute Post-Sec.
8484 Dorchester Rd 29420 843-552-3670
Charleston School of Law Post-Sec.
PO Box 535 29402 843-329-1000
Charleston Southern University Post-Sec.
9200 University Blvd 29406 843-863-7000
College of Charleston Post-Sec.
66 George St 29424 843-805-5507
First Baptist S of Charleston 500/PK-12
48 Meeting St 29401 843-722-6646
Thomas Mullins, head sch Fax 720-2521
James Island Christian S 200/PK-12
15 Crosscreek Dr 29412 843-795-1762
Jeremy Schwartz, admin. Fax 762-1619
Medical University of South Carolina Post-Sec.
171 Ashley Ave 29425 843-792-2300
Porter-Gaud S 900/1-12
300 Albemarle Rd 29407 843-556-3620
D. DuBose Egleston B.S., head sch Fax 556-7404
The Art Institute of Charleston Post-Sec.
24 N Market St 29401 866-211-0107
The Citadel Post-Sec.
171 Moultrie St 29409 843-225-3294
Trident Technical College Post-Sec.
PO Box 118067 29423 843-574-6111

**Cheraw, Chesterfield, Pop. 5,741**
Chesterfield County SD
Supt. — See Chesterfield
Cheraw HS 800/9-12
649 Chesterfield Hwy 29520 843-921-1000
Jason Bryant, prin. Fax 921-1006
Long MS 600/6-8
1010 W Greene St 29520 843-921-1010
Matthew Brantley, prin. Fax 921-1017

---

Northeastern Technical College Post-Sec.
1201 Chesterfield Hwy 29520 843-921-6900

**Chesnee, Spartanburg, Pop. 845**
Spartanburg SD 2 8,900/K-12
3231 Old Furnace Rd 29323 864-578-0128
Scott Mercer, supt. Fax 578-8924
www.spartanburg2.k12.sc.us
Chesnee HS 600/9-12
795 S Alabama Ave 29323 864-461-7318
Thomas Ezell, prin. Fax 461-4137
Chesnee MS 500/6-8
805 S Alabama Ave 29323 864-461-3900
Rob Hayes, prin. Fax 461-3950
Rainbow Lake MS 700/6-8
1951 Riveroak Rd 29323 864-253-5700
Greg Lovelace, prin. Fax 253-5701
Other Schools – See Boiling Springs, Inman

**Chester, Chester, Pop. 5,520**
Chester County SD 5,200/PK-12
509 District Office Dr 29706 803-385-6122
Agnes Slayman Ph.D., supt. Fax 581-6965
www.chester.k12.sc.us/
Chester County Career Center Vo/Tech
1324 J A Cochran Byp 29706 803-377-1991
Lee Green Ed.D., dir. Fax 581-0912
Chester HS 900/9-12
1330 J A Cochran Byp 29706 803-377-3161
Martin Tiller, prin. Fax 581-2363
Chester MS 600/6-8
1014 McCandless Rd 29706 803-377-8192
Cedrick Tidwell, prin. Fax 581-1875
Other Schools – See Great Falls, Richburg

**Chesterfield, Chesterfield, Pop. 1,462**
Chesterfield County SD 7,600/PK-12
401 West Blvd 29709 843-623-2175
Dr. Harrison Goodwin, supt. Fax 623-3434
www.chesterfieldschools.org
Chesterfield HS 600/9-12
401 N Page St 29709 843-623-2161
Scott Radkin, prin. Fax 623-2050
Chesterfield-Ruby MS 400/6-8
14445 Highway 9 29709 843-623-9401
Neil Adams, prin. Fax 623-9429
Palmetto Learning Center Alt
116 Edwards Rd 29709 843-623-5101
Thomas Brewer, coord. Fax 623-5105
Other Schools – See Cheraw, Jefferson, Mc Bee, Pageland

**Clemson, Pickens, Pop. 13,699**

---

Clemson University Post-Sec.
105 Sikes Hall 29634 864-656-3311

**Clinton, Laurens, Pop. 8,368**
Laurens County SD 56 3,000/PK-12
211 N Broad St Ste B 29325 864-833-0800
Dr. David O'Shields, supt. Fax 833-0804
www.laurens56.k12.sc.us
Clinton HS 800/9-12
18132 Highway 72 E 29325 864-833-0817
Maureen Tiller, prin. Fax 833-0825
Clinton MS 700/6-8
800 N Adair St 29325 864-833-0807
Brenda Romines, prin. Fax 833-0810

---

Presbyterian College Post-Sec.
503 S Broad St 29325 864-833-2820

**Clio, Marlboro, Pop. 720**
Marlboro County SD
Supt. — See Bennettsville
Marlboro School of Discovery 100/Alt
PO Box 517 29525 843-586-8376
William Jorgensen, prin. Fax 586-9078

**Clover, York, Pop. 5,008**
Clover SD 2 6,600/PK-12
604 Bethel St 29710 803-810-8005
Dr. Marc Sosne, supt. Fax 222-8010
www.clover2.k12.sc.us
Blue Eagle Academy Alt
300 Clinton Ave 29710 803-810-8420
Hezekiah Massey, dir. Fax 222-8042
Clover HS 1,900/9-12
1625 Highway 55 E 29710 803-810-8200
Rodney Ruth, prin. Fax 222-8021
Clover MS 700/6-8
1555 Highway 55 E 29710 803-810-8300
Calub Courtwright, prin. Fax 222-8034
Oakridge MS 900/6-8
5650 Highway 557 29710 803-631-8000
William Largen, prin. Fax 631-8102

**Columbia, Richland, Pop. 126,841**
Richland SD 1 23,800/PK-12
1616 Richland St 29201 803-231-7000
Dr. Cynthia Cash-Greene, supt. Fax 231-7502
www.richlandone.org/
Alcorn MS 400/6-8
5125 Fairfield Rd 29203 803-735-3439
Dr. Baron Davis, prin. Fax 735-3487
Columbia HS 700/9-12
1701 Westchester Dr 29210 803-731-8950
Shenequa Coles, prin. Fax 731-8953
Crayton MS 1,000/6-8
5000 Clemson Ave 29206 803-738-7224
Susan Childs, prin. Fax 738-7901
Dreher HS 1,200/9-12
3319 Millwood Ave 29205 803-253-7000
Jeanne Stiglbauer, prin. Fax 253-7007
Eau Claire HS 700/9-12
4800 Monticello Rd 29203 803-735-7600
June Page, prin. Fax 735-7629
Flora HS 1,200/9-12
1 Falcon Dr 29204 803-738-7300
Richard McClure, prin. Fax 738-7307
Gibbes MS 300/6-8
500 Summerlea Dr 29203 803-343-2942
Sarah Smith, prin. Fax 733-3040
Hand MS 900/6-8
2600 Wheat St 29205 803-343-2947
Marisa Vickers, prin. Fax 733-6173
Heyward Career & Technology Center Vo/Tech
3560 Lynhaven Dr 29204 803-735-3343
Sherry Rivers, prin. Fax 691-4253

Johnson HS 400/9-12
2219 Barhamville Rd 29204 803-253-7092
Nathan White, prin. Fax 253-5713
Keenan HS 700/9-12
361 Pisgah Church Rd 29203 803-714-2500
Alvin Pressley, prin. Fax 714-2593
Olympia Learning Center Alt
621 Bluff Rd 29201 803-400-1650
Ericka Hursey, prin. Fax 400-1700
Perry MS 300/6-8
2600 Barhamville Rd 29204 803-256-6347
Robert Smalls, prin. Fax 255-2262
St. Andrews MS 700/6-8
1231 Bluefield Dr 29210 803-731-8910
Ken Richardson, prin. Fax 731-8913
Sanders MS, 3455 Pine Belt Rd 29204 400/6-8
Andrenna Smith, prin. 803-738-7575
Adult & Community Education Adult
2612 Covenant Rd 29204 803-343-2935
Marva Coates, dir. Fax 212-1453
Other Schools – See Hopkins

Richland SD 2 24,300/PK-12
6831 Brookfield Rd 29206 803-787-1910
Debra Hamm Ph.D., supt. Fax 738-3334
www.richland2.org
Dent MS 1,300/6-8
2721 Decker Blvd 29206 803-699-2750
Dr. David Basile, prin. Fax 699-2754
Longleaf MS 600/6-8
1160 Longreen Pkwy 29229 803-691-4870
Angela Thom, prin. Fax 691-4043
Richland Northeast HS 1,400/9-12
7500 Brookfield Rd 29223 803-699-2800
Dr. Sabrina Suber, prin. Fax 699-3679
Ridge View HS 2,000/9-12
4801 Hard Scrabble Rd 29229 803-699-2999
Dr. Brenda Mack-Foxworth, prin. Fax 699-2888
Spring Valley HS 2,100/9-12
120 Sparkleberry Ln 29229 803-699-3500
Jeff Temoney, prin. Fax 699-3541
Summit Parkway MS 900/6-8
200 Summit Pkwy 29229 803-699-3580
Andrew Barbone, prin. Fax 699-3682
Wright MS 1,000/6-8
2740 Alpine Rd 29223 803-736-8740
Mary Paige Wylie, prin. Fax 736-8798
Rogers Adult Continuing Center Adult
750 Old Clemson Rd 29229 803-736-8787
Bobby Cunningham, prin. Fax 736-8785
Other Schools – See Blythewood

SD Five of Lexington & Richland Counties
Supt. — See Irmo
Irmo HS 1,800/9-12
6671 Saint Andrews Rd 29212 803-476-3000
David Riegel, prin. Fax 476-3020
Irmo MS 900/6-8
6051 Wescott Rd 29212 803-476-3600
Robert Jackson, prin. Fax 476-3620

---

Allen University Post-Sec.
1530 Harden St 29204 803-376-5700
Baptist Medical Center Post-Sec.
1519 Marion St 29201 803-771-5042
Benedict College Post-Sec.
1600 Harden St 29204 803-253-5000
Cardinal Newman HS 400/7-12
4701 Forest Dr 29206 803-782-2814
Jacquie Kasprowski, prin. Fax 782-9314
Centura College Post-Sec.
7500 Two Notch Rd 29223 803-754-7544
Columbia Biblical Seminary Post-Sec.
7435 Monticello Rd 29203 800-777-2227
Columbia College Post-Sec.
1301 Columbia College Dr 29203 800-277-1301
Columbia International University Post-Sec.
7435 Monticello Rd 29203 803-754-4100
Covenant Classical Christian S 100/K-12
3120 Covenant Rd 29204 803-787-0225
Kevin Bolen, admin. Fax 782-7309
ECPI University Post-Sec.
250 Berryhill Rd Ste 300 29210 803-772-3333
Fortis College Post-Sec.
246 Stoneridge Dr Ste 101 29210 803-678-4800
Hammond S 900/PK-12
854 Galway Ln 29209 803-776-0295
Christopher Angel, prin. Fax 776-0122
Heathwood Hall Episcopal S 500/PK-12
3000 S Beltline Blvd 29201 803-765-2309
Chris Hinchey, head sch Fax 748-4755
ITT Technical Institute Post-Sec.
1628 Browning Rd Ste 180 29210 803-216-6000
Kenneth Shuler's School of Cosmetology Post-Sec.
449 Saint Andrews Rd 29210 803-772-6042
Lippen S 500/PK-12
7401 Monticello Rd 29230 803-807-4100
Chip Jones, hdmstr. Fax 744-1387
Lutheran Theological Southern Seminary Post-Sec.
4201 N Main St 29203 803-786-5150
Midlands Technical College Post-Sec.
PO Box 2408 29202 803-738-8324
National Ctr for Credibility Assessment Post-Sec.
7540 Pickens Ave 29207 803-751-9100
Remington College Columbia Post-Sec.
607 Bush River Rd 29210 803-214-9000
Southeastern Institute Post-Sec.
1420 Colonial Life Blvd #80 29210 803-798-8800
South University Post-Sec.
9 Science Ct 29203 803-799-9082
Strayer University Post-Sec.
200 Center Point Cir # 300 29210 803-750-2500
University of South Carolina 29208 Post-Sec.
803-777-7700
Virginia College Post-Sec.
7201 Two Notch Rd 29223 803-509-7100
W.L. Bonner College Post-Sec.
4430 Argent Ct 29203 803-754-3950

**Conway, Horry, Pop. 16,872**
Horry County SD 39,100/PK-12
PO Box 260005 29528 843-488-6700
Dr. Rick Maxey, supt. Fax 488-6722
www.horrycountyschools.net
Academy for Technology and Academics Vo/Tech
5639 Highway 701 N 29526 843-488-6600
David Stoudenmire, prin. Fax 488-6601
Black Water MS 700/6-8
900 E Cox Ferry Rd 29526 843-903-8440
Candace Lane, prin. Fax 903-8441
Conway HS 1,500/9-12
2301 Church St 29526 843-488-0662
Velna Allen, prin. Fax 488-0686
Conway MS 700/6-8
1104 Elm St 29526 843-488-6040
Lee James, prin. Fax 488-0611
Early College HS 300/9-12
2050 E Highway 501 29526 843-349-7102
Kandi Fleming-Jones, dir. Fax 349-7895
Horry County Education Center Alt
2694 Highway 905 29526 843-488-7500
Maurice Murphy, prin. Fax 488-7501
Scholars Academy 9-12
215 University Hall 29526 843-349-4117
Norman McQueen, prin. Fax 349-6144
Whittemore Park MS 600/6-8
1808 Rhue St 29527 843-488-0669
Judy Beard, prin. Fax 488-0669
Other Schools – See Aynor, Galivants Ferry, Green Sea, Little River, Loris, Murrells Inlet, Myrtle Beach

---

Coastal Carolina University Post-Sec.
PO Box 261954 29528 843-347-3161
Conway Christian S 200/PK-12
PO Box 1245 29528 843-365-2005
Horry-Georgetown Technical College Post-Sec.
PO Box 261966 29528 843-347-3186
Miller-Motte Technical College Post-Sec.
2451 E Highway 501 29526 843-591-1100

**Cope, Orangeburg, Pop. 75**
Orangeburg County Consolidated SD 4 3,900/PK-12
PO Box 68 29038 803-534-8081
Brenda Turner, supt. Fax 531-5614
www.orangeburg4.com
Cope Area Career Center Vo/Tech
PO Box 128 29038 803-534-7661
Sandra Jameson, prin. Fax 535-4301
STAR Center for Learning 100/Alt
6064 Slab Landing Rd 29038 803-533-1783
Belinda Johnson, prin. Fax 533-1785
Other Schools – See Branchville, Cordova, Neeses

**Cordova, Orangeburg, Pop. 167**
Orangeburg County Consolidated SD 4
Supt. — See Cope
Carver-Edisto MS 600/6-8
PO Box 65 29039 803-534-3554
Jeannie Monson, prin. Fax 535-0937
Edisto HS 700/9-12
PO Box 101 29039 803-536-1553
David Damm, prin. Fax 531-5615

**Cowpens, Spartanburg, Pop. 2,133**
Spartanburg SD 3
Supt. — See Glendale
Cowpens MS 500/6-8
150 Foster St 29330 864-279-6400
Cynthia James, prin. Fax 279-6410

**Cross, Berkeley**
Berkeley County SD
Supt. — See Moncks Corner
Cross HS 300/7-12
1293 Old Highway 6 29436 843-899-8900
Adrian Busch, prin. Fax 899-8910

**Dalzell, Sumter, Pop. 2,975**
Sumter SD
Supt. — See Sumter
Hillcrest MS 500/6-8
4355 Peach Orchard Rd 29040 803-499-3341
Tarsha Staggers, prin. Fax 499-3353

**Darlington, Darlington, Pop. 6,253**
Darlington County SD 10,400/PK-12
PO Box 1117 29540 843-398-5100
Dr. Eddie Ingram, supt. Fax 398-5198
www.darlington.k12.sc.us
Darlington Co. Institute of Technology Vo/Tech
160 Pinedale Dr 29532 843-398-4796
Bert Guerry, dir. Fax 395-1044
Darlington County Intervention S Alt
100 Magnolia St 29532 843-393-5617
Zenobia Edwards, dir. Fax 398-2640
Darlington HS 1,100/9-12
525 Spring St 29532 843-398-5140
Dr. Gregory Harrison, prin. Fax 398-2739
Darlington MS 1,100/6-8
150 Pinedale Dr 29532 843-398-5088
Eddie Shuler, prin. Fax 398-3390
Mayo HS for Math Science & Technology 400/9-12
405 Chestnut St 29532 843-398-5050
Arlene Wallace, prin. Fax 398-2647
Other Schools – See Hartsville, Lamar

---

Trinity-Byrnes Collegiate S 100/6-12
5001 Hoffmeyer Rd 29532 843-395-9124
Ed Hoffman, hdmstr. Fax 395-6495

**Denmark, Bamberg, Pop. 3,519**
Bamberg SD 2 800/PK-12
62 Holly Ave 29042 803-793-3346
Dr. Thelma Sojourner, supt. Fax 793-2006
www.denmarkolarschooldistrict2.org
Denmark-Olar HS 200/9-12
197 Viking Cir 29042 803-793-3307
Mickey Pringle, prin. Fax 793-2004
Denmark-Olar MS 200/6-8
45 Green St 29042 803-793-3383
Daryl Brockington, prin. Fax 793-2038

---

Denmark Technical College Post-Sec.
PO Box 327 29042 803-793-5176
Voorhees College Post-Sec.
PO Box 678 29042 803-780-1234

**Dillon, Dillon, Pop. 6,694**
Area Vocational Schools
Supt. — None
Dillon County Technology Center Vo/Tech
PO Box 1130 29536 843-774-5143
Jerry Strickland, prin. Fax 774-7711

Dillon SD Four 3,900/PK-12
1738 Highway 301 N 29536 843-774-1200
D. Ray Rogers, supt. Fax 774-1203
www.dillon.k12.sc.us
Dillon HS 900/9-12
1730 Highway 301 N 29536 843-774-1230
Dr. Shawn Johnson, prin. Fax 774-1234
Dillon MS 500/6-8
1803 Joan Dr 29536 843-774-1212
Rodney Cook, prin. Fax 841-3616
Other Schools – See Lake View

---

Dillon Christian S 300/K-12
PO Box 151 29536 843-841-1000

**Dorchester, Dorchester**
Area Vocational Schools
Supt. — None
Dorchester Co. Career & Technology Ctr Vo/Tech
507 Schoolhouse Rd 29437 843-563-2361
James Villeponteaux, prin. Fax 563-9038
Other Schools – See Blackville SC, Dillon SC, Manning SC, Ridgeland SC, Williamston SC

Dorchester SD 4
Supt. — See Saint George
Harleyville-Ridgeville MS 200/6-8
1650 E Main St 29437 843-462-2470
LaShawna Rivers, admin. Fax 462-2479
Woodland HS 600/9-12
4128 Highway 78 29437 843-563-5956
Bernard Utsey, prin. Fax 563-5997

**Due West, Abbeville, Pop. 1,226**
Abbeville County SD
Supt. — See Abbeville
Dixie HS 400/8-12
1 Haynes St 29639 864-379-2186
Lori Brownlee-Brewton, prin. Fax 379-8187

---

Erskine College Post-Sec.
PO Box 338 29639 864-379-2131

**Duncan, Spartanburg, Pop. 3,086**
Spartanburg SD 5 7,300/K-12
PO Box 307 29334 864-949-2350
Dr. Scott Turner, supt. Fax 439-0051
www.spart5.net
Byrnes Freshman Academy 600/9-9
PO Box 277 29334 864-949-2320
Pat Monteith, prin. Fax 949-2328
Byrnes HS 1,600/10-12
PO Box 187 29334 864-949-2355
Dr. Jeff Rogers, prin. Fax 949-2362
Florence Chapel MS 600/7-8
290 Shoals Rd 29334 864-949-2310
Tammy White, prin. Fax 949-2315
Other Schools – See Lyman

**Easley, Pickens, Pop. 19,670**
Pickens County SD 15,600/K-12
1348 Griffin Mill Rd 29640 864-397-1000
Dr. Danny Merck, supt. Fax 855-8159
www.pickens.k12.sc.us
Dacusville MS 400/6-8
899 Thomas Mill Rd 29640 864-397-3525
Wanda Tharpe, prin. Fax 850-2094
Easley HS 1,600/9-12
154 Green Wave Blvd 29642 864-397-3100
Gary Culler, prin. Fax 855-8194
Gettys MS 1,400/6-8
510 S Pendleton St 29640 864-397-3900
Michael Cory, prin. Fax 855-1268
Adult Learning Center Adult
106 Glazner St 29640 864-397-3825
Dr. Mary Gaston, dir. Fax 850-8116
Other Schools – See Central, Liberty, Pickens

**Ehrhardt, Bamberg, Pop. 541**

---

Jackson Academy 100/K-12
7054 Broxton Bridge 29081 803-245-4810

**Elgin, Kershaw, Pop. 1,286**
Kershaw County SD
Supt. — See Camden
Stover MS 600/6-8
1649 Smyrna Rd 29045 803-438-7414
Mike Garity, prin. Fax 438-7014

**Estill, Hampton, Pop. 2,023**
Hampton SD 2 1,000/PK-12
PO Box 1028 29918 803-625-5000
Dr. Beverly Gurley, supt. Fax 625-2573
www.hampton2.k12.sc.us
Estill HS 300/9-12
PO Box 757 29918 803-625-5100
Kamar Lee, prin. Fax 625-4695
Estill MS 300/6-8
PO Box 817 29918 803-625-5200
Synetria Hawkins, prin. Fax 625-3588

---

Henry Academy 300/PK-12
8766 Savannah Hwy 29918 803-625-2440
Dr. Walter Banks, admin. Fax 625-3110

**Fairfax, Allendale, Pop. 2,023**
Allendale County SD 1,400/PK-12
3249 Allendale Fairfax Hwy 29827 803-584-4603
Walter Tobin, supt. Fax 584-5303
www.acs.k12.sc.us
Allendale-Fairfax MSHS 400/7-12
3581 Allendale Fairfax Hwy 29827 803-584-2311
Robert Hemby, prin. Fax 584-1787

**Florence, Florence, Pop. 36,588**
Florence County SD One 17,800/PK-12
319 S Dargan St 29506 843-673-1106
Randy Bridges, supt. Fax 292-1003
www.fsd1.org
Alfred Rush Academy Alt
1201 E Ashby Rd 29506 843-664-8911
Dr. Gerard Edwards, prin.
Beck Learning Center 7-12
1001 W Sumter St 29501 843-679-6768
Dr. Floyd Creech, dir.
Florence Career Ctr Vo/Tech
126 E Howe Springs Rd 29505 843-664-8465
Alphonso Bradley, dir. Fax 413-4688
Sneed MS 900/7-8
1102 S Ebenezer Rd 29501 843-673-1199
Hayley Cagle, prin. Fax 679-6890
South Florence HS 1,600/9-12
3200 S Irby St 29505 843-664-8190
Carol Hill, prin. Fax 664-8184
Southside MS 800/7-8
200 E Howe Springs Rd 29505 843-664-8467
Craig Washington, prin. Fax 673-5766
West Florence HS 1,700/9-12
221 N Beltline Dr 29501 843-664-8472
Pamela Quick, prin. Fax 664-8475
Williams MS 600/7-8
1119 N Irby St 29501 843-664-8162
Leon McCray, prin. Fax 664-8178
Wilson HS 1,200/9-12
1411 E Old Marion Hwy 29506 843-664-8440
Dr. Eric Robinson, prin. Fax 664-8176
Poynor Adult and Community Education Ctr Adult
301 S Dargan St 29506 843-664-8152
Til Morisey, dir. Fax 664-8155

---

Florence Christian S 700/PK-12
2308 S Irby St 29505 843-662-0454
Florence-Darlington Technical College Post-Sec.
PO Box 100548 29502 843-661-8324
Francis Marion University Post-Sec.
PO Box 100547 29502 843-661-1362
King's Academy 300/PK-12
1015 S Ebenezer Rd 29501 843-661-7464
Mike Hiltibidal, head sch Fax 661-7647
Maranatha Christian S 300/PK-12
2624 W Palmetto St 29501 843-665-6395
McLeod Regional Medical Center Post-Sec.
555 E Cheves St 29506 843-667-2297
Virgina College Post-Sec.
2400 David H McLeod Blvd 29501 843-407-2200

**Fort Mill, York, Pop. 10,605**
Fort Mill SD 10,200/K-12
2233 Deerfield Dr 29715 803-548-2527
James Epps Ph.D., supt. Fax 547-4696
www.fortmillschools.org
Fort Mill HS 1,600/9-12
215 Highway 21 Byp 29715 803-548-1900
Dee Christopher, prin. Fax 548-1911
Fort Mill MS 600/6-8
200 Springfield Pkwy 29715 803-547-5553
Greg Norton, prin. Fax 548-2911
Nation Ford HS 1,500/9-12
1400 A O Jones Blvd 29715 803-835-0000
Jason Johns, prin. Fax 835-0010
Springfield MS 700/6-8
1711 Springfield Pkwy 29715 803-548-8199
Keith Griffin, prin. Fax 547-1013
Other Schools – See Tega Cay

**Gaffney, Cherokee, Pop. 12,231**
Cherokee County SD 9,100/PK-12
PO Box 460 29342 864-206-2201
Dr. Quincie Moore, supt. Fax 902-3541
www.cherokee1.k12.sc.us
Cherokee Technology Center Vo/Tech
3206 Cherokee Ave 29340 864-489-3191
Amanda Painter, prin. Fax 487-1287
Copeland Community Learning Center Alt
243 Allison Dr 29341 864-206-6992
LaTunya Means, prin. Fax 487-1238
Ewing MS 400/6-8
171 E Junior High Rd 29340 864-489-3176
Dr. Denise Wooten, prin. Fax 489-8534
Gaffney HS 2,100/9-12
149 Twin Lake Rd 29341 864-902-3600
Dr. RaaShad Fitzpatrick, prin. Fax 902-3628
Gaffney MS 700/6-8
805 E Frederick St 29340 864-902-3630
Dr. Shirley Sealy, prin. Fax 902-3637
Granard MS 600/6-8
815 W Rutledge Ave 29341 864-206-2302
Dr. Mark Bunch, prin. Fax 488-1553
Adult & Community Education Adult
243 Allison Dr 29341 864-487-7152
Lisa Hannon, prin. Fax 487-1260
Other Schools – See Blacksburg

---

Limestone College Post-Sec.
1115 College Dr 29340 864-489-7151

**Galivants Ferry, Horry**
Horry County SD
Supt. — See Conway
Aynor MS 700/6-8
400 Frye Rd 29544 843-358-6000
Robbie Watkins, prin. Fax 358-5065

**Gaston, Lexington, Pop. 1,599**
Lexington County SD 4
Supt. — See Swansea
Sandhills MS 400/7-8
582 Meadowfield Rd 29053 803-490-7005
Justin Nutter, prin. Fax 926-1910

**Georgetown, Georgetown, Pop. 9,055**
Georgetown County SD 9,700/PK-12
2018 Church St 29440 843-436-7000
Dr. Randy Dozier, supt. Fax 436-7171
www.gcsd.k12.sc.us
Georgetown HS 1,000/9-12
2500 Anthuan Maybank St 29440 843-546-8516
Craig Evans, prin. Fax 546-8521
Georgetown MS 900/6-8
2400 Anthuan Maybank St 29440 843-527-4495
Rosemary Gray, prin. Fax 527-2290
Howard Adult Center & Optional S Adult
500 S Kaminski St 29440 843-546-0219
James Ferdon, dir.
Other Schools – See Andrews, Hemingway, Pawleys Island

**Gilbert, Lexington, Pop. 564**
Lexington County SD 1
Supt. — See Lexington
Gilbert HS 900/9-12
840 Main St 29054 803-821-1900
Ann O'Cain, prin. Fax 821-1903
Gilbert MS 700/6-8
120 Rikard Cir 29054 803-821-1700
Benji Ricard, prin. Fax 821-1703

**Glendale, Spartanburg, Pop. 305**
Spartanburg SD 3 3,000/PK-12
PO Box 267 29346 864-279-6000
Kenny Blackwood, supt. Fax 279-6010
www.spartanburg3.org/
Other Schools – See Cowpens, Pacolet, Spartanburg

**Goose Creek, Berkeley, Pop. 34,642**
Berkeley County SD
Supt. — See Moncks Corner
Goose Creek HS 1,700/9-12
1137 Red Bank Rd 29445 843-553-5300
Jimmy Huskey, prin. Fax 820-4064
Marrington MS of the Arts 400/6-8
109 Gearing St 29445 843-572-0313
Dr. Jim Spencer, prin. Fax 820-4063
Sedgefield MS 900/6-8
131 Charles B Gibson Blvd 29445 843-797-2620
Shameka Washington, prin. Fax 820-5401
Stratford HS 1,800/9-12
951 Crowfield Blvd 29445 843-820-4000
Heather Taylor, prin. Fax 820-4042
Westview MS 900/6-8
101 Westview Dr 29445 843-572-1700
Sharon Perry M.Ed., prin. Fax 820-3728

**Graniteville, Aiken, Pop. 2,553**
Aiken County SD
Supt. — See Aiken
Byrd Learning Center Alt
1 Willis Cir 29829 803-663-4920
Ben Osborne, prin. Fax 663-4921
Leavelle-McCampbell MS 500/6-8
82 Canal St 29829 803-663-4300
Johnny Spears, prin. Fax 663-4302
Midland Valley HS 1,200/9-12
227 Mustang Dr 29829 803-593-7100
Carl White, prin. Fax 593-7106

**Great Falls, Chester, Pop. 1,942**
Chester County SD
Supt. — See Chester
Great Falls HS 300/9-12
411 Sunset Ave 29055 803-482-2210
Brenda Fort, prin. Fax 482-4896
Great Falls MS 200/6-8
409 Sunset Ave 29055 803-482-2220
Brenda Fort, prin. Fax 482-6025

**Greeleyville, Williamsburg, Pop. 428**
Williamsburg County SD
Supt. — See Kingstree
Murray HS 300/9-12
PO Box 188 29056 843-426-2121
Dr. Janice Gamble, prin. Fax 426-2151
Murray MS 7-8
PO Box 188 29056 843-426-2121
Dr. Janice Gamble, prin. Fax 426-2151

**Green Sea, Horry**
Horry County SD
Supt. — See Conway
Green Sea-Floyds JSHS 600/6-12
4990 Tulip Grove Rd 29545 843-392-3131
Andrea Pridgen, prin. Fax 392-9805

**Greenville, Greenville, Pop. 57,469**
Anderson SD 1
Supt. — See Williamston
Powdersville HS 300/9-12
145 Hood Rd 29611 864-312-5641
Dr. Robby Roach, prin. Fax 312-5640
Powdersville MS 600/6-8
135 Hood Rd 29611 864-269-1821
Todd Binnicker, prin. Fax 269-0795

Greenville County SD 73,400/PK-12
PO Box 2848 29602 864-355-3100
W. Burke Royster, supt. Fax 241-4195
www.greenville.k12.sc.us/
Beck Academy 1,100/6-8
901 Woodruff Rd 29607 864-355-1400
Jennifer Meisten, prin. Fax 355-1490
Berea HS 1,100/9-12
201 Burdine Dr 29617 864-355-1600
Mike Noel, prin. Fax 355-1625
Berea MS 700/6-8
151 Berea Middle School Rd 29617 864-355-1700
Robin Mill, prin. Fax 355-1777
Carolina Academy 700/9-12
2725 Anderson Rd 29611 864-355-2300
Michael Delaney, prin. Fax 355-2375
Donaldson Career Center Vo/Tech
100 Vocational Dr 29605 864-355-4650
Cassina Allen, prin. Fax 355-4683
Enoree Career Center Vo/Tech
108 Scalybark Rd 29617 864-355-7400
Mike Parris, prin. Fax 355-7407
Fine Arts Center 400/11-12
102 Pine Knoll Dr 29609 864-355-2550
Dr. Roy Fluhrer, prin. Fax 355-2579
Golden Strip Career Ctr Vo/Tech
1120 E Butler Rd 29607 864-355-1050
J.F. Lucas, prin. Fax 355-1058
Greenville High Academy 1,400/9-12
1 Vardry St 29601 864-355-5500
Jason Warren, prin. Fax 355-5492
Greenville Middle Academy 800/6-8
339 Lowndes Ave 29607 864-355-5600
Dr. Robert Palmer, prin. Fax 355-5682
Hampton HS 1,600/9-12
100 Pine Knoll Dr 29609 864-355-0100
Eric Williamks, prin. Fax 355-0194
High School Alternative Program 100/Alt
206 Wilkins St 29605 864-355-5180
Stuart Holcombe, admin. Fax 355-5185
Hughes Academy 900/6-8
122 Deoyley Ave 29605 864-355-6200
Andrew Hooker, prin. Fax 355-6275
Lakeview MS 500/6-8
3801 Old Buncombe Rd 29617 864-355-6400
LaTonya Copeland, prin. Fax 355-6416
League Academy 800/6-8
125 Twin Lake Rd 29609 864-355-8100
Mary Leslie Anderson, prin. Fax 355-8160
Mann Academy 1,700/9-12
160 Fairforest Way 29607 864-355-6300
Charles Mayfield, prin. Fax 355-6329
Sevier MS 600/6-8
1000 Piedmont Park Rd 29609 864-355-8200
Karen Kapp, prin. Fax 355-8255
Southside HS 900/9-12
6630 Frontage Rd 29605 864-355-8700
Carlos Brooks, prin. Fax 355-8798
Star Academy - Donaldson Alt
100 Vocational Dr 29605 864-355-4669
Cassina Allen, admin. Fax 355-4683
Star Academy - Enoree Vo/Tech
108 Scalybark Rd 29617 864-355-7401
Shakeria McCullough, dir. Fax 355-7404
Tanglewood MS 600/6-8
44 Merriwoods Dr 29611 864-355-4500
William Price, prin. Fax 355-4512
Adult Education/Lifelong Learning Adult
206 Wilkins St 29605 864-355-6088
Dr. Chuck Welch, prin. Fax 355-6077
Other Schools – See Greer, Mauldin, Piedmont, Simpsonville, Taylors, Travelers Rest

State Supported Schools
Supt. — None
Governors S of Arts & Humanities 200/9-12
15 University St 29601 864-282-3777
Julie Allen, prin. Fax 241-1235

---

Academy of Hair Technology Post-Sec.
3715 E North St Ste F 29615 864-322-0300
Bob Jones University Post-Sec.
1700 Wade Hampton Blvd 29614 864-242-5100
Brown Mackie College Post-Sec.
75 Beattie Pl Ste 100 29601 864-239-5300
Christ Church Episcopal S 1,000/K-12
245 Cavalier Dr 29607 864-299-1522
Dr. Leonard Kupersmith, hdmstr. Fax 299-8861
ECPI University Post-Sec.
1001 Keys Dr # 100 29615 864-288-2828
Furman University Post-Sec.
3300 Poinsett Hwy 29613 864-294-2000
Greenville Technical College Post-Sec.
PO Box 5616 29606 864-250-8000
Hampton Park Christian S 500/PK-12
875 State Park Rd 29609 864-233-0556
Dr. Kevin Priest, admin. Fax 235-5621
ITT Technical Institute Post-Sec.
6 Independence Pt 29615 864-288-0777
Jones Academy 1,300/PK-12
1700 Wade Hampton Blvd 29614 864-770-1395
Dr. Dan Nelson, admin. Fax 271-7278
St. Joseph's HS 400/9-12
100 Saint Josephs Dr 29607 864-234-9009
Keith Kiser, hdmstr. Fax 234-5516
Shannon Forest Christian S 400/PK-12
829 Garlington Rd 29615 864-678-5107
Lori Horton, admin. Fax 281-9372
Strayer University Post-Sec.
555 N Pleasantburg Dr # 300 29607 864-250-7000
University of SC School of Medicine Post-Sec.
607 Grove Rd 29605 864-455-7992
Virginia College Post-Sec.
78 Global Dr Ste 200 29607 864-679-4900

**Greenwood, Greenwood, Pop. 22,959**
Greenwood SD 50 8,700/PK-12
PO Box 248 29648 864-941-5400
Dr. Darrell Johnson, supt. Fax 941-5427
www.gwd50.org
Brewer MS 700/6-8
1000 Emerald Rd 29646 864-941-5500
Corey Collington, prin. Fax 941-5527
Emerald HS 900/9-12
150 Bypass 225 29646 864-941-5730
Brad Nickles, prin. Fax 941-3487
Genesis Education Center Alt
400 Glenwood St 29649 864-941-5460
Damian Coleman, prin.
Greenwood HS 1,600/9-12
1816 Cokesbury Rd 29649 864-941-5600
Chad Evans, prin. Fax 941-5498

Northside MS 800/6-8
431 Deadfall Rd W 29649 864-941-5780
Cyndi Storer, prin. Fax 941-3434
Russell Career Center Vo/Tech
601 Northside Dr E 29649 864-941-5750
Bonnie Corbitt, prin. Fax 941-5375
Westview MS 700/6-8
1410 W Alexander Rd 29646 864-229-4301
Dr. Steve Glenn, prin. Fax 229-4827

---

Charzanne Beauty College Post-Sec.
1549 Highway 72 E 29649 864-223-7321
Greenwood Christian S 300/PK-12
2026 Woodlawn Rd 29649 864-229-2427
Dr. Chris Johns, hdmstr. Fax 852-5278
Lander University Post-Sec.
320 Stanley Ave 29649 864-388-8000
Palmetto Christian Academy of Greenwood 100/PK-12
308 Deadfall Rd W 29649 864-223-0391
Joan Gore, prin. Fax 396-5316
Piedmont Technical College Post-Sec.
PO Box 1467 29648 864-941-8324

**Greer, Greenville, Pop. 25,060**
Greenville County SD
Supt. — See Greenville
Blue Ridge HS 1,100/8-12
2151 Fews Chapel Rd 29651 864-355-1800
Reena Watson, prin. Fax 355-1821
Blue Ridge MS 1,000/6-8
2423 E Tyger Bridge Rd 29651 864-355-1900
Rebecca Greene, prin. Fax 355-1966
Bonds Resource Center Vo/Tech
505 N Main St 29650 864-355-8080
Wayne Rhodes, prin. Fax 355-8264
Greer HS 1,100/9-12
3000 E Gap Creek Rd 29651 864-355-5700
Marion Waters, prin. Fax 355-5725
Greer MS 900/6-8
3032 E Gap Creek Rd 29651 864-355-5800
Michael Ruthsatz, prin. Fax 355-5880
Riverside HS 1,500/9-12
794 Hammett Bridge Rd 29650 864-355-7800
Andy Crowley, prin. Fax 355-7898
Riverside MS 1,000/6-8
615 Hammett Bridge Rd 29650 864-355-7900
Kate Malone, prin. Fax 355-7918

**Hanahan, Berkeley, Pop. 17,513**
Berkeley County SD
Supt. — See Moncks Corner
Hanahan HS 1,000/9-12
6015 Murray Dr 29410 843-820-3710
Ric Raycroft, prin. Fax 820-3716
Hanahan MS 700/5-8
5815 Murray Dr 29410 843-820-3800
Robin Rogers, prin. Fax 820-3804
Fishburne Educational Center Adult
6215 Murray Dr 29410 843-820-3742
Dr. Paulette Walker, coord. Fax 820-3826

**Hardeeville, Jasper, Pop. 2,902**
Jasper County SD
Supt. — See Ridgeland
Hardeeville-Ridgeland MS 300/6-8
150 Hurricane Alley 29927 843-784-8600
Eric Jeffcoat, prin. Fax 784-8609

**Harleyville, Dorchester, Pop. 670**
Dorchester SD 4
Supt. — See Saint George
Odyssey Educational Center Alt
145 Hill St 29448 843-462-2270
Catherine Yates, prin. Fax 462-2275

**Hartsville, Darlington, Pop. 7,682**
Darlington County SD
Supt. — See Darlington
Hartsville HS 1,300/9-12
701 Lewellyn Ave 29550 843-383-3130
Dr. Charlie Burry, prin. Fax 857-3715
Hartsville MS 1,100/6-8
1427 14th St 29550 843-383-3121
Meredith Taylor, prin. Fax 857-4510

State Supported Schools
Supt. — None
Governers S of Science/Math 50/11-12
401 Railroad Ave 29550 843-383-3900
Dr. Murray Brockman, pres. Fax 383-3903

---

Coker College Post-Sec.
300 E College Ave 29550 843-383-8000
Emmanuel Christian S 400/PK-12
1001 N Marquis Hwy 29550 843-332-0164

**Hemingway, Williamsburg, Pop. 449**
Georgetown County SD
Supt. — See Georgetown
Carvers Bay HS 400/9-12
13002 Choppee Rd 29554 843-545-5837
Rich Neal, prin. Fax 558-6927
Carvers Bay MS 300/6-8
13000 Choppee Rd 29554 843-545-0918
Cometeia Pyatt, prin. Fax 558-6937

Williamsburg County SD
Supt. — See Kingstree
Hemingway Career and Technology Center Vo/Tech
1593 Hemingway Hwy 29554 843-558-5813
Torrance Wilson, admin. Fax 558-5991
Hemingway HS 400/9-12
PO Box 1509 29554 843-558-9413
Levi Keith, prin. Fax 558-9335
Hemingway M.B. Lee MS 6-8
PO Box 1509 29554 843-558-2721
Erica Barcus, prin. Fax 558-0792

**Hilton Head Island, Beaufort, Pop. 36,811**
Beaufort County SD
Supt. — See Beaufort
Hilton Head Island HS 1,200/9-12
70 Wilborn Rd 29926 843-689-4800
Elizabeth O'Nan, prin. Fax 689-4947
Hilton Head Island MS 900/6-8
55 Wilborn Rd 29926 843-689-4500
Gregory Stickel, prin. Fax 689-4600

---

Heritage Academy 100/6-12
11 New Orleans Rd 29928 866-925-5528
Hilton Head Christian Academy 400/PK-12
55 Gardner Dr 29926 843-681-2878
Hilton Head Preparatory S 400/PK-12
8 Foxgrape Rd 29928 843-671-2286
Jon Hopman, hdmstr. Fax 671-7624

**Holly Hill, Orangeburg, Pop. 1,261**
Orangeburg County Consolidated SD 3 3,100/PK-12
PO Box 98 29059 803-496-3288
Dr. Jesulon Gibbs-Brown, supt. Fax 496-5850
www.obg3.k12.sc.us
Holly Hill-Roberts MS 400/6-8
PO Box 879 29059 803-496-3818
Rodney Zimmerman, prin. Fax 496-7584
Other Schools – See Santee

---

Holly Hill Academy 300/K-12
PO Box 757 29059 803-496-3243

**Hollywood, Charleston, Pop. 4,680**
Charleston County SD
Supt. — See Charleston
Baptist Hill HS 400/7-12
5117 Baptist Hill Rd 29449 843-889-2276
Kala Goodwine, prin. Fax 889-2101

**Honea Path, Anderson, Pop. 3,518**
Anderson SD 2 3,600/PK-12
10990 Belton Honea Path Hwy 29654 864-369-7364
Dr. Richard Rosenberger, supt. Fax 369-4006
www.anderson2.k12.sc.us
Belton-Honea Path HS 1,100/9-12
11000 Belton Honea Path Hwy 29654 864-369-7382
Lester McCall, prin. Fax 369-4011
Honea Path MS 400/6-8
107 Brock Ave 29654 864-369-7641
Dr. John Snead, prin. Fax 369-4034
Other Schools – See Belton

**Hopkins, Richland, Pop. 2,838**
Richland SD 1
Supt. — See Columbia
Hopkins MS 500/6-8
1601 Clarkson Rd 29061 803-695-3331
Goler Collins, prin. Fax 695-3320
Lower Richland HS 1,200/9-12
2615 Lower Richland Blvd 29061 803-695-3000
Kelvin Wymbs, prin. Fax 695-3062
Southeast MS 500/6-8
731 Horrell Hill Rd 29061 803-695-5700
Stacey Whitaker, prin. Fax 695-5703

**Indian Land, Lancaster**
Lancaster County SD
Supt. — See Lancaster
Indian Land HS 700/9-12
8063 River Rd, 803-547-7571
David Shamble, prin. Fax 547-7366
Indian Land MS 600/6-8
8361 Charlotte Hwy, 803-578-2500
Chris Thorpe, prin. Fax 578-2549

**Inman, Spartanburg, Pop. 2,273**
Spartanburg SD 1
Supt. — See Campobello
Chapman HS 900/9-12
PO Box 389 29349 864-472-2836
Ty Dawkins, prin. Fax 472-0914
Mabry MS 400/7-8
35 Oakland Ave 29349 864-472-8402
Marsha Clark, prin. Fax 472-7438
Swofford Career Center Vo/Tech
5620 Highway 11 29349 864-592-2790
Scott Simpkins, dir. Fax 592-1469

Spartanburg SD 2
Supt. — See Chesnee
Boiling Springs MS 1,000/6-8
4801 Highway 9 29349 864-578-5954
Penny Atkinson, prin. Fax 599-5489

**Irmo, Richland, Pop. 10,848**
SD Five of Lexington & Richland Counties 16,500/PK-12
1020 Dutch Fork Rd 29063 803-476-8000
Dr. Stephen Hefner, supt. Fax 476-8217
www.lexrich5.org/
Dutch Fork HS 2,100/9-12
1400 Old Tamah Rd 29063 803-476-3300
Dr. Greg Owings, prin. Fax 476-3320
Dutch Fork MS 1,100/7-8
1528 Old Tamah Rd 29063 803-476-4800
Dr. Gerald Gary, prin. Fax 476-4820
Other Schools – See Chapin, Columbia

**Iva, Anderson, Pop. 1,209**
Anderson SD 3 2,600/PK-12
PO Box 118 29655 864-348-6196
Dr. Mason Gary, supt. Fax 348-6198
www.anderson3.k12.sc.us
Crescent HS 700/9-12
9104 Highway 81 S 29655 864-352-6175
Devon Smith, prin. Fax 352-2308
Other Schools – See Anderson, Starr

**Jackson, Aiken, Pop. 1,680**
Aiken County SD
Supt. — See Aiken
Jackson MS 300/6-8
18731 Atomic Rd 29831 803-279-3525
Jason Holt, prin. Fax 471-2202

**Jefferson, Chesterfield, Pop. 722**
Chesterfield County SD
Supt. — See Chesterfield
New Heights MS 500/6-8
5738 Highway 151 29718 843-658-6830
Dr. Diana Smith, prin. Fax 658-6812

**Johns Island, Charleston**
Charleston County SD
Supt. — See Charleston
Haut Gap MS 400/5-8
1861 Bohicket Rd 29455 843-559-6418
Travis Benintendo, prin. Fax 559-6439
St. Johns HS 300/9-12
1518 Main Rd 29455 843-559-6400
Andre Dukes, prin. Fax 559-6409

---

Charleston Collegiate S 200/PK-12
2024 Academy Rd 29455 843-559-5506
Hacker Burr, head sch Fax 559-6172

**Johnsonville, Florence, Pop. 1,455**
Florence County SD Five 1,500/PK-12
PO Box 98 29555 843-386-2358
Robert Smiley, supt. Fax 386-3139
www.flo5.k12.sc.us
Johnsonville HS 400/9-12
237 S Georgetown Hwy 29555 843-386-2707
Sam Tuten, prin. Fax 386-9058
Johnsonville MS 500/5-8
PO Box 67 29555 843-386-2066
Randy Willis, prin. Fax 386-3786

**Johnston, Edgefield, Pop. 2,346**
Edgefield County SD 3,900/PK-12
3 Par Dr 29832 803-275-4601
Greg Anderson, supt. Fax 275-4426
www.edgefield.k12.sc.us
JET MS 500/6-8
1095 Columbia Rd 29832 803-275-1997
Stephen Hampton, prin. Fax 275-1783
Thurmond Career Center Vo/Tech
17 Par Dr 29832 803-275-1767
Arthur Northrop, dir. Fax 275-1766
Thurmond HS 800/9-12
1131 Columbia Rd 29832 803-275-1768
Dr. Robert Ross, prin. Fax 275-1764
Other Schools – See North Augusta

---

Wardlaw Academy 200/PK-12
1296 Columbia Rd 29832 803-275-4794

**Kershaw, Lancaster, Pop. 1,779**
Kershaw County SD
Supt. — See Camden
North Central HS 500/9-12
3000 Lockhart Rd 29067 803-432-9858
David Branham, prin. Fax 425-8992
North Central MS 400/6-8
805 Keys Ln 29067 803-424-2740
Burch Richardson Ed.D., prin. Fax 424-2742

Lancaster County SD
Supt. — See Lancaster
Jackson HS 600/9-12
6925 Kershaw Camden Hwy 29067 803-475-2381
Alex Dabney, prin. Fax 475-7317
Jackson MS 500/6-8
6865 Kershaw Camden Hwy 29067 803-475-6021
Daryl Hinson, prin. Fax 475-8256

**Kingstree, Williamsburg, Pop. 3,310**
Williamsburg County SD 3,900/PK-12
PO Box 1067 29556 843-355-5571
Dr. Yvonne Jefferson-Barnes, supt. Fax 355-3213
wcsd.k12.sc.us/
Kingstree HS 700/9-12
616 Martin Luther King Ave 29556 843-355-6525
Alex Gordon, prin. Fax 355-7019
Kingstree Middle Magnet S of the Arts 500/6-8
710 3rd Ave 29556 843-355-1506
Roberta Cumbee, prin. Fax 355-9207
Other Schools – See Greeleyville, Hemingway

---

Williamsburg Academy 400/K-12
1000 Sandy Bay Rd 29556 843-355-9400
Williamsburg Technical College Post-Sec.
601 Martin Luther King Ave 29556 843-355-4110

**Ladson, Berkeley, Pop. 13,352**
Berkeley County SD
Supt. — See Moncks Corner
College Park MS 800/6-8
713 College Park Rd 29456 843-553-8300
Ingrid Dukes M.Ed., prin. Fax 820-4026
Sangaree MS 800/6-8
1050 Discovery Dr 29456 843-821-4028
Margaret Day, prin. Fax 871-8974

Dorchester SD 2
Supt. — See Summerville
Oakbrook MS 900/6-8
286 Old Fort Dr 29456 843-873-9750
Brion Rutherford, prin. Fax 821-3931

**Lake City, Florence, Pop. 6,625**
Florence County SD Three 3,400/PK-12
PO Box 1389 29560 843-374-8652
Laura Hickson, supt. Fax 374-2946
fsd3.org
Lake City HS 800/9-12
PO Box 1569 29560 843-374-3321
Ned Blake, prin. Fax 374-3138
McNair JHS 500/7-8
PO Box 1209 29560 843-374-8651
Margie Myers, prin. Fax 374-8504

---

Carolina Academy 200/PK-12
351 N Country Club Rd 29560 843-374-5485

**Lake View, Dillon, Pop. 805**
Dillon SD Four
Supt. — See Dillon
Lake View JSHS 300/6-12
PO Box 624 29563 843-759-3009
Edison Arnette, prin. Fax 759-3015

**Lamar, Darlington, Pop. 980**
Darlington County SD
Supt. — See Darlington
Lamar HS 300/9-12
216 N Darlington Ave 29069 843-326-5543
Kathy Gainey, prin. Fax 326-7507
Spaulding MS 300/6-8
400 Cartersville Hwy 29069 843-326-7625
Derrick Glover, prin. Fax 326-7656

**Lancaster, Lancaster, Pop. 8,450**
Lancaster County SD 11,700/PK-12
300 S Catawba St 29720 803-286-6972
Dr. Gene Moore, supt. Fax 416-8860
www.lancastercsd.com
Buford HS 600/9-12
4290 Tabernacle Rd 29720 803-286-7068
Rodney Miller, prin. Fax 286-8147
Buford MS 500/6-8
1890 N Rocky River Rd 29720 803-285-8473
Sheri Wells, prin. Fax 283-2023
Lancaster High Career Center Vo/Tech
625 Normandy Rd 29720 803-285-7404
Dr. Joe Keenan, prin. Fax 285-2720
Lancaster HS 1,500/9-12
617 Normandy Rd 29720 803-283-2001
Dr. Joseph Keenan, prin. Fax 286-6962
Rucker MS 500/6-8
422 Old Dixie Rd 29720 803-416-8555
Phillip Mickles, prin. Fax 285-1534
South MS 600/6-8
1551 Billings Dr 29720 803-283-8416
Joyce Crimminger, prin. Fax 283-8417
Adult Education Adult
610 E Meeting St 29720 803-285-7660
Dr. Kim Linton, dir. Fax 285-9281
Other Schools – See Indian Land, Kershaw

---

University of South Carolina Post-Sec.
PO Box 889 29721 803-313-7000

**Landrum, Spartanburg, Pop. 2,337**
Spartanburg SD 1
Supt. — See Campobello
Landrum MS 300/6-8
104 Redland Rd 29356 864-457-2629
Tucker Hamrick, prin. Fax 457-5372

**Latta, Dillon, Pop. 1,366**
Latta SD 1,600/PK-12
205 King St 29565 843-752-7101
Dr. John Kirby, supt. Fax 752-2081
www.dillon3.k12.sc.us
Latta HS 400/9-12
618 N Richardson St 29565 843-752-5751
George Liebenrood, prin. Fax 752-2707
Latta MS 400/5-8
612 N Richardson St 29565 843-752-7117
Debra Morris, prin. Fax 752-2722

**Laurens, Laurens, Pop. 9,035**
Laurens SD 55 5,900/PK-12
1029 W Main St 29360 864-984-3568
Dr. Billy Strickland, supt. Fax 984-8100
www.laurens55.k12.sc.us/
Laurens District 55 HS 1,500/9-12
5058 Highway 76 W 29360 864-682-3151
Sonya Bryant, prin. Fax 682-7426
Laurens MS 500/6-8
1035 W Main St 29360 864-984-2400
Dr. Rhett Harris, prin. Fax 984-6013
Sanders MS 400/6-8
609 Green St 29360 864-984-0354
Lacresha Byrd, prin. Fax 984-2452

---

Laurens Academy 200/PK-12
PO Box 425 29360 864-682-2324

**Lexington, Lexington, Pop. 17,606**
Lexington County SD 1 21,300/K-12
PO Box 1869 29071 803-821-1000
Karen Woodward Ed.D., supt. Fax 821-1010
www.lexington1.net
Carolina Springs MS 800/6-8
6180 Platt Springs Rd 29073 803-821-4900
Alan Zwart, prin. Fax 821-4903
Focus Program Alternative Learning Ctr Alt
420 Hendrix St 29072 803-821-1300
John Robert Jackson, coord. Fax 821-1303
Lexington HS 3,100/9-12
2463 Augusta Hwy 29072 803-821-3400
Melissa Rawl, prin. Fax 821-3403
Lexington MS 1,400/6-8
702 N Lake Dr 29072 803-821-3700
Ryan Pool, prin. Fax 821-3703
Lexington Technology Center Vo/Tech
2421 Augusta Hwy 29072 803-821-3000
Bryan Hearn, dir. Fax 821-3003
Meadow Glen MS 6-8
440 Ginny Ln 29072 803-821-0600
Bill Coon, prin. Fax 821-0603
Pleasant Hill MS 1,100/6-8
660 Rawl Rd 29072 803-821-2700
Thomas Rivers, prin. Fax 821-2703
River Bluff HS 9-12
320 Corley Mill Rd 29072 803-821-0702
Luke Clamp, prin. Fax 821-1156
White Knoll HS 1,900/9-12
5643 Platt Springs Rd 29073 803-821-5200
Ryan Player, prin. Fax 821-5203
Other Schools – See Gilbert, Pelion, West Columbia

---

Northside Christian Academy PK-12
4347 Sunset Blvd 29072 803-520-5656
Rev. Scott Crede, head sch Fax 520-5661

**Liberty, Pickens, Pop. 3,217**
● Pickens County SD
Supt. — See Easley
Liberty HS 700/9-12
124 Red Devil Dr 29657 864-397-2600
Josh Oxendine, prin. Fax 843-5828
Liberty MS 500/6-8
125 Falcon Ln 29657 864-397-3400
Dr. Tim Mullis, prin. Fax 843-5857
Pickens County Career & Technology Ctr Vo/Tech
990 Chastain Rd 29657 864-397-4500
Ken Hitchcock, dir. Fax 843-9064

**Little River, Horry, Pop. 8,858**
Horry County SD
Supt. — See Conway
North Myrtle Beach HS 1,200/9-12
3750 Sea Mountain Hwy 29566 843-399-6171
Trevor Strawderman, prin. Fax 399-6509
North Myrtle Beach MS 1,000/6-8
11240 Highway 90 29566 843-399-6136
Mark Porter, prin. Fax 399-2233

**Longs, Horry**

---

North Myrtle Beach Christian S 100/PK-12
9535 Highway 90 29568 843-399-7181

**Loris, Horry, Pop. 2,350**
Horry County SD
Supt. — See Conway
Loris HS 800/9-12
301 Loris Lions Rd 29569 843-390-6800
Dirk Gurley, prin. Fax 390-6801
Loris MS 700/6-8
5209 Highway 66 29569 843-756-2181
Ann Hall, prin. Fax 756-0522

**Lugoff, Kershaw, Pop. 7,335**
Kershaw County SD
Supt. — See Camden
Lugoff-Elgin HS 1,600/9-12
1284 Highway 1 S 29078 803-438-3481
Worth Thomasson, prin. Fax 438-8005
Lugoff-Elgin MS 700/6-8
1244 Highway 1 S 29078 803-438-3591
Karen Bullard, prin. Fax 438-8027

**Lyman, Spartanburg, Pop. 3,187**
Spartanburg SD 5
Supt. — See Duncan
Hill MS 600/7-8
PO Box 1329 29365 864-949-2370
Terry Glasgow, prin. Fax 949-2369

**Mc Bee, Chesterfield, Pop. 855**
Chesterfield County SD
Supt. — See Chesterfield
Mc Bee HS 500/7-12
PO Box 218 29101 843-335-8251
Dennis McDaniel, prin. Fax 335-6515

**Mc Clellanville, Charleston, Pop. 499**
Charleston County SD
Supt. — See Charleston
Lincoln MSHS 100/7-12
714 Lincoln Rd 29458 843-577-0970
Dr. Yvonne Commodore, prin. Fax 887-3116

**Mc Cormick, McCormick, Pop. 2,752**
McCormick County SD 800/PK-12
821 N Mine St 29835 864-852-2435
Dr. William Wright, supt. Fax 852-2883
www.mccormick.k12.sc.us
McCormick HS 300/9-12
6981 SC Highway 28 S 29835 864-443-0040
Steve English, prin. Fax 443-0049
McCormick MS 200/6-8
6979 SC Highway 28 S 29835 864-443-2243
Rodney Robinson, prin. Fax 443-3298

**Manning, Clarendon, Pop. 4,077**
Area Vocational Schools
Supt. — None
Dubose Career Center Vo/Tech
3351 Sumter Hwy 29102 803-473-2531
Susan Anderson, prin. Fax 473-4320

Clarendon SD 2 3,100/PK-12
PO Box 1252 29102 803-435-4435
John Tindal, supt. Fax 435-8172
www.clarendon2.k12.sc.us
Manning HS 800/9-12
2155 Paxville Hwy 29102 803-435-4417
Neshunda Walters, prin. Fax 435-4404
Manning JHS 400/7-8
1101 W L Hamilton Rd 29102 803-435-8195
Terrie Ard, prin. Fax 435-6848

---

Laurence Manning Academy 1,000/K-12
PO Box 278 29102 803-435-2114

**Marion, Marion, Pop. 6,862**
Marion County SD 5,300/PK-12
719 N Main St 29571 843-423-1811
Dr. Dan Strickland, supt. Fax 423-8328
www.marion.k12.sc.us
Creek Bridge HS 400/6-12
6641 S Highway 41 29571 843-362-3500
Darryl Woodberry, prin. Fax 362-3506
Johnakin MS 600/6-8
601 Gurley St 29571 843-423-8360
Rebecca Ford, prin. Fax 423-8383
Marion HS 800/9-12
1205 S Main St 29571 843-423-2571
Nathaniel Nelson, prin. Fax 423-8330
Other Schools – See Mullins

**Mauldin, Greenville, Pop. 22,445**
Greenville County SD
Supt. — See Greenville
Mauldin HS 2,100/9-12
701 E Butler Rd 29662 864-355-6500
Scott Rhymer, prin. Fax 355-6657

**Moncks Corner, Berkeley, Pop. 7,746**
Berkeley County SD 28,700/PK-12
PO Box 608 29461 843-899-8600
Michael Turner, supt. Fax 899-8791
www.berkeley.k12.sc.us
Berkeley Alternative S Alt
106 S Live Oak Dr 29461 843-899-8830
Don Brown, prin. Fax 899-8817
Berkeley County Middle College HS 100/11-12
1001 S Live Oak Dr 29461 843-899-8111
Claire Freeman, prin. Fax 899-8113
Berkeley HS 1,300/9-12
406 W Main St 29461 843-899-8800
Steven Steele, prin. Fax 899-8810
Berkeley MS 1,200/6-8
320 N Live Oak Dr 29461 843-899-8840
Mike Wilkerson, prin. Fax 899-8846
Macedonia MS 400/6-8
200 Macedonia Foxes Cir 29461 843-899-8940
Don Walton, prin. Fax 899-8929
Berkeley Educational Center Adult
113 E Main St 29461 843-899-8635
Dr. Lillie Caldwell, dir. Fax 899-8764
Other Schools – See Cross, Goose Creek, Hanahan, Ladson, Saint Stephen, Summerville

---

St. John's Christian Academy 300/PK-12
204 W Main St 29461 843-761-8539
Dr. Eric Denton, hdmstr. Fax 899-5514

**Monetta, Aiken, Pop. 227**
Aiken County SD
Supt. — See Aiken
Ridge Spring-Monetta MSHS 200/6-12
10 J P Kneece Dr 29105 803-685-2100
Kyle Blankenship, prin. Fax 685-2108

**Moore, Spartanburg**
Spartanburg County SD 6
Supt. — See Roebuck
Anderson Applied Technology Center Vo/Tech
PO Box 248 29369 864-576-5020
Sherri Yarborough, prin. Fax 576-8642
Dawkins MS 800/6-8
1300 E Blackstock Rd 29369 864-576-8088
Jay Seegars, prin. Fax 595-2418

**Mount Pleasant, Charleston, Pop. 67,140**
Charleston County SD
Supt. — See Charleston
Cario MS 1,400/6-8
3500 Thomas Cario Blvd 29466 843-856-4595
Sharon Randall, prin. Fax 856-4599
Laing MS of Science & Technology 600/6-8
2705 Bulrush Basket Ln 29466 843-849-2809
James Whitehair, prin. Fax 849-2895
Moultrie MS 900/6-8
645 Coleman Blvd 29464 843-849-2819
Anna Dassing, prin. Fax 849-2899
Wando HS 3,500/9-12
1000 Warrior Way 29466 843-849-2830
Lucy Beckham, prin. Fax 849-2890

---

Coastal Christian Preparatory S 300/PK-12
681 McCants Dr 29464 843-884-3663
Dr. David Piccolo, head sch Fax 884-9608
Palmetto Christian Academy 600/PK-12
361 Egypt Rd 29464 843-881-9967
Mike Lindsey, hdmstr. Fax 881-4662

**Mullins, Marion, Pop. 4,600**
Marion County SD
Supt. — See Marion
Academy of Careers and Technology Vo/Tech
2697 E Highway 76 29574 843-423-1941
Paul Crandall, dir. Fax 423-1943
Mullins HS 500/9-12
747 Millers Rd 29574 843-464-3710
Michael Stone, prin. Fax 464-3717
Palmetto MS 400/6-8
305 ONeal St 29574 843-464-3730
Rechel Anderson, prin. Fax 464-3736

---

Pee Dee Academy 400/PK-12
PO Box 449 29574 843-423-1771

**Murrells Inlet, Horry, Pop. 7,501**
Horry County SD
Supt. — See Conway
St. James HS 1,300/9-12
10800 Highway 707 29576 843-650-5600
Vann Pennell, prin. Fax 650-1004

**Myrtle Beach, Horry, Pop. 26,336**
Horry County SD
Supt. — See Conway
Academy for Arts Science & Technology Vo/Tech
895 International Dr 29579 843-903-8460
Robin Jones, prin. Fax 903-8461
Carolina Forest HS 2,000/9-12
700 Gardner Lacy Rd 29579 843-236-7997
Gaye Driggers, prin. Fax 236-7504
Forestbrook MS 1,000/6-8
4430 Gator Ln 29588 843-236-7300
April Scott, prin. Fax 236-8065
Myrtle Beach HS 1,200/9-12
3302 Robert M Grissom Pkwy 29577 843-448-7149
John Washburn, prin. Fax 445-2036
Myrtle Beach MS 900/6-8
950 Seahawk Way 29577 843-448-3932
Dr. Janice Christy, prin. Fax 448-1182

Ocean Bay MS 1,100/6-8
905 International Dr 29579 843-903-8420
Connie Huddle, prin. Fax 903-8421
St. James MS 1,100/6-8
9775 Saint James Rd 29588 843-650-5543
Dr. Dwight Boykin, prin. Fax 650-5610
Socastee HS 1,500/9-12
4900 Socastee Blvd 29588 843-293-2513
Dr. Paul Browning, prin. Fax 293-3393

Calvary Christian S 200/PK-12
4511 Dick Pond Rd 29588 843-650-2829
Mark Roland, prin. Fax 215-4125
Christian Academy of Myrtle Beach 300/K-12
291 Ronald McNair Blvd 29579 843-236-6222
Nancy Henry, head sch Fax 236-2262
Golf Academy of America Post-Sec.
3268 Waccamaw Blvd 29579 800-342-7342
ITT Technical Institute Post-Sec.
9654 N Kings Hwy Ste 101 29572 843-497-7820
Pittsburgh Institute of Aeronautics Post-Sec.
1038 Shine Ave 29577 800-444-1440
Risen Christ Lutheran S 100/PK-12
10595 Highway 17 N 29572 843-272-8163
Sean E. O'Connor, prin. Fax 272-4039
Strand College of Hair Design Post-Sec.
423 79th Ave N 29572 843-449-1017

**Neeses, Orangeburg, Pop. 371**
Orangeburg County Consolidated SD 4
Supt. — See Cope
Hunter-Kinard-Tyler HS 300/7-12
7066 Norway Rd 29107 803-263-4832
Ernest Holiday, prin. Fax 263-4467

**Newberry, Newberry, Pop. 10,123**
Newberry County SD 5,500/PK-12
PO Box 718 29108 803-321-2600
Bennie Bennett, supt. Fax 321-2604
www.newberry.k12.sc.us/
Newberry County Career Ctr Vo/Tech
3413 Main St 29108 803-321-2674
Buddy Livingston, prin. Fax 321-2676
Newberry HS 800/9-12
3113 Main St 29108 803-321-2621
Katrina Singletary, prin. Fax 321-2633
Newberry MS 700/6-8
125 ONeal St 29108 803-321-2640
Kimberly Hamilton, prin. Fax 321-2647
Other Schools – See Prosperity, Whitmire

Newberry Academy 200/PK-12
2055 Smith Rd 29108 803-276-2760
Newberry College Post-Sec.
2100 College St 29108 800-845-4955

**New Ellenton, Aiken, Pop. 1,998**
Aiken County SD
Supt. — See Aiken
New Ellenton MS 200/6-8
814 Main St S 29809 803-652-8200
Shunte Dugar, prin. Fax 652-8203

**Ninety Six, Greenwood, Pop. 1,979**
Greenwood SD 52 1,700/PK-12
605 Johnston Rd 29666 864-543-3100
Dr. Mark Petersen, supt. Fax 543-3704
www.greenwood52.org
Edgewood MS 400/6-8
644 S Cambridge St 29666 864-543-3511
Scott Parker, prin. Fax 543-4994
Ninety Six HS 500/9-12
640 S Cambridge St 29666 864-543-2911
Rex Ward, prin. Fax 543-3132

**North, Orangeburg, Pop. 730**
Orangeburg Consolidated SD 5
Supt. — See Orangeburg
North MSHS 300/6-12
692 Cromer Ave 29112 803-247-2541
Charles Gregory, prin. Fax 247-5090

**North Augusta, Aiken, Pop. 20,954**
Aiken County SD
Supt. — See Aiken
Knox MS 600/6-8
1804 Wells Rd 29841 803-442-6300
Kyle Smith, prin. Fax 442-6302
North Augusta HS 1,500/9-12
2000 Knobcone Ave 29841 803-442-6100
John Murphy, prin. Fax 442-6127
North Augusta MS 600/6-8
725 Old Edgefield Rd 29841 803-442-6200
Phyllis Gamble, prin. Fax 442-6202

Edgefield County SD
Supt. — See Johnston
Merriwether MS 400/6-8
430 Murrah Rd 29860 803-279-2511
Kevin Butler, prin. Fax 279-1710

Kenneth Shuler's School of Cosmetology Post-Sec.
736 Martintown Rd 29841 803-278-1200
Victory Christian S 100/K-12
620 W Martintown Rd 29841 803-278-0125
Dr. Ed Martin, prin. Fax 278-7310

**North Charleston, Charleston, Pop. 95,273**
Charleston County SD
Supt. — See Charleston
ARMS Academy at Morningside 6-8
1999 Singley St 29405 843-745-2030
Dr. Joseph Williams, prin. Fax 745-2029
Charleston County S of the Arts 1,100/6-12
5109 W Enterprise St 29405 843-529-4990
Dr. Shannon Cook, prin. Fax 529-4991
EXCEL Academy at Morningside 600/6-8
1999 Singley St 29405 843-745-2000
Dr. Joseph Williams, prin. Fax 745-7191
Garrett Academy of Technology Vo/Tech
2731 Gordon St 29405 843-745-7126
Charity Summers, prin. Fax 529-3914
Jenkins Creative Learning Center 200/Alt
2670 Bonds Ave 29405 843-747-6609
Jennifer Coker, prin. Fax 746-7438
Liberty Hill Academy 100/Alt
5025 W Enterprise St 29405 843-566-8892
Sarah Jamme, prin. Fax 566-8897
Military Magnet Academy 500/6-12
2950 Carner Ave 29405 843-745-7102
Anderson Townsend, prin. Fax 566-7791
North Charleston HS 500/9-12
1087 E Montague Ave 29405 843-745-7140
Robert Grimm, prin. Fax 566-1954
Northwoods MS 800/6-8
7763 Northside Dr 29420 843-764-2212
Toshawnka Mahone, prin. Fax 569-5466
Stall HS 1,000/9-12
3625 Ashley Phosphate Rd 29418 843-764-2200
Kim Wilson, prin. Fax 764-2240
Zucker Science MS 500/6-8
6401 Dorchester Rd 29418 843-767-8383
Jacob Perlmutter, prin. Fax 207-3073

Dorchester SD 2
Supt. — See Summerville
Fort Dorchester HS 2,100/9-12
8500 Patriot Blvd 29420 843-760-4450
Bert Postell, prin. Fax 760-4852
River Oaks MS 1,000/6-8
8642 River Oaks Dr 29420 843-695-2470
Scott Matthews, prin. Fax 695-2475

Cathedral Academy 300/K-12
PO Box 41129, 843-760-1192
Chris Bateman, head sch Fax 760-1197
Centura College Post-Sec.
8088 Rivers Ave 29406 843-569-0889
ECPI University Post-Sec.
7410 Northside Dr Ste G101 29420 843-414-0350
ITT Technical Institute Post-Sec.
2431 W Aviation Ave 29406 843-745-5700
Miller-Motte Technical College Post-Sec.
8085 Rivers Ave Ste E 29406 843-574-0101
Northside Christian S 400/PK-12
7800 Northside Dr 29420 843-797-2693
Northwood Academy 400/6-12
2263 Otranto Rd 29406 843-764-2284
Dr. Darlene Anderson, prin. Fax 764-3713
Southeastern Institute Post-Sec.
4600 Goer Dr Ste 105 29406 843-747-1279
Virginia College Post-Sec.
6185 Rivers Ave 29406 843-614-4300

**Orangeburg, Orangeburg, Pop. 13,823**
Orangeburg Consolidated SD 5 6,500/PK-12
578 Ellis Ave 29115 803-534-5454
Cynthia Wilson, supt. Fax 533-7953
www.ocsd5schools.org
Clark MS 800/6-8
919 Bennett St 29115 803-531-2200
Dr. Lana Williams, prin. Fax 533-6503
Howard MS 400/6-8
1255 Belleville Rd 29115 803-534-5470
Eric Brown, prin. Fax 535-1606
Orangeburg-Wilkinson HS 1,400/9-12
601 Bruin Pkwy 29118 803-534-6180
David Norman, prin. Fax 533-6310
Technology Center Vo/Tech
3720 Magnolia St 29118 803-536-4473
Dr. Cleve Pilot, prin. Fax 533-6365
Other Schools – See North, Rowesville

Claflin University Post-Sec.
400 Magnolia St 29115 803-535-5000
Orangeburg-Calhoun Technical College Post-Sec.
3250 Saint Matthews Rd 29118 803-536-0311
Orangeburg Preparatory S 800/PK-12
2651 North Rd 29118 803-534-7970
Dr. Brian Newsome, supt. Fax 535-2190
South Carolina State University Post-Sec.
300 College Ave 29115 803-536-7000
Southern Methodist College Post-Sec.
541 Broughton St 29115 803-534-7826

**Pacolet, Spartanburg, Pop. 2,212**
Spartanburg SD 3
Supt. — See Glendale
Middle School of Pacolet 200/6-8
850 Sunny Acres Rd 29372 864-279-6600
Max Deaton, prin. Fax 279-6610

**Pageland, Chesterfield, Pop. 2,713**
Chesterfield County SD
Supt. — See Chesterfield
Central HS 700/9-12
200 Zion Church Rd 29728 843-672-6115
Dr. Juddson Starling, prin. Fax 672-2694

South Pointe Christian S 200/PK-12
PO Box 188 29728 843-672-2760
Larry Stinson, prin. Fax 672-3913

**Pamplico, Florence, Pop. 1,212**
Florence County SD 2 1,200/PK-12
2121 S Pamplico Hwy 29583 843-493-2502
Robert Sullivan, supt. Fax 493-1912
www.flo2.k12.sc.us/
Hannah-Pamplico HS 300/9-12
2055 S Pamplico Hwy 29583 843-493-5781
Timothy Gibbs, prin. Fax 493-5424

**Pawleys Island, Georgetown, Pop. 101**
Georgetown County SD
Supt. — See Georgetown
Waccamaw HS 800/9-12
2412 Kings River Rd 29585 843-237-9899
Dr. David Hammel, prin. Fax 237-9883
Waccamaw MS 400/7-8
247 Wildcat Way 29585 843-237-0106
Jamie Curry, prin. Fax 237-0237

Lowcountry Preparatory S 100/K-12
300 Blue Stem Dr 29585 843-237-4147
Scott Gibson, head sch Fax 237-4147
Pawleys Island Christian Academy 100/PK-12
10304 Ocean Hwy 29585 843-237-9293

**Pelion, Lexington, Pop. 671**
Lexington County SD 1
Supt. — See Lexington
Pelion HS 700/9-12
600 Lydia Dr 29123 803-821-2200
Clark Cooper, prin. Fax 821-2203
Pelion MS 600/6-8
758 Magnolia St 29123 803-821-2300
Jeffrey Matthews, prin. Fax 821-2303

**Pendleton, Anderson, Pop. 2,884**
Anderson SD 4 2,800/K-12
PO Box 545 29670 864-403-2000
Dr. Joanne Avery Ph.D., supt. Fax 403-2029
www.anderson4.org
Riverside MS 400/7-8
458 Riverside St 29670 864-403-2200
Dr. Kevin Black, prin. Fax 646-8025
Other Schools – See Anderson

Tri-County Technical College Post-Sec.
PO Box 587 29670 864-646-8361

**Pickens, Pickens, Pop. 3,062**
Pickens County SD
Supt. — See Easley
Pickens HS 1,400/9-12
150 Blue Flame Dr 29671 864-397-3600
Marion Lawson, prin. Fax 898-5611
Pickens MS 800/6-8
140 Torch Dr 29671 864-397-4100
Reggia Stapleton, prin. Fax 878-9224

Lakeview Christian S 200/PK-12
107 Mauldin Lake Rd 29671 864-878-6959
Rev. Mike Belcher, admin. Fax 878-6927

**Piedmont, Greenville, Pop. 5,025**
Anderson SD 1
Supt. — See Williamston
Wren HS 1,500/9-12
905 Wren School Rd 29673 864-850-5900
Nichole Boseman, prin. Fax 850-5929
Wren MS 900/6-8
1010 Wren School Rd 29673 864-850-5930
Robin Fulbright, prin. Fax 850-5941

Greenville County SD
Supt. — See Greenville
Woodmont HS 1,600/9-12
2831 W Georgia Rd 29673 864-355-8600
Darryl Imperati, prin. Fax 355-8695
Woodmont MS 700/6-8
325 N Flat Rock Rd 29673 864-355-8500
Greg Scott, prin. Fax 355-8587

**Prosperity, Newberry, Pop. 1,173**
Newberry County SD
Supt. — See Newberry
Mid-Carolina HS 700/9-12
377 Cy Schumpert Rd 29127 803-364-2134
Ray Cooper, prin. Fax 364-4395
Mid-Carolina MS 600/6-8
6794 US Highway 76 29127 803-364-3634
Deedee Westwood, prin. Fax 364-4877

**Rembert, Sumter, Pop. 296**

Sumter Academy 400/PK-12
5265 Camden Hwy 29128 803-499-3378

**Richburg, Chester, Pop. 273**
Chester County SD
Supt. — See Chester
Lewisville HS 400/9-12
3971 Lewisville High School 29729 803-789-5131
James Knox, prin. Fax 789-3188
Lewisville MS 300/6-8
PO Box 280 29729 803-789-5858
H.L. Erwin, prin. Fax 789-6159

**Ridgeland, Jasper, Pop. 4,009**
Area Vocational Schools
Supt. — None
Beaufort-Jasper Acad Career Excellence Vo/Tech
80 Lowcountry Dr 29936 843-987-8107
Dr. Dandi Daniels, dir. Fax 987-1343

Jasper County SD 2,600/PK-12
10942 N Jacob Smart Blvd 29936 843-717-1100
Dr. Vashti Washington, supt. Fax 717-1199
www.jcsd.net
Ridgeland-Hardeeville HS 500/9-12
250 Jaguar Trl 29936 843-489-8844
Karen Parker, prin. Fax 717-1409
Other Schools – See Hardeeville

Heyward Academy 300/PK-12
1727 Malphrus Rd 29936 843-726-3673
Marilyn Davis, head sch Fax 726-5773
John Paul II Catholic S 7-10
4211 N Okatie Hwy 29936 843-645-3838
Walter Dupre, prin. Fax 645-3839

**Ridgeville, Dorchester, Pop. 1,972**
Dorchester SD 2
Supt. — See Summerville
Givhans Community S Adult
273 Highway 61 29472 843-832-5559
Joyce Dearing, prin. Fax 821-3944

**Rock Hill, York, Pop. 64,898**
Rock Hill SD 3 17,200/PK-12
PO Box 10072 29731 803-981-1000
Dr. Kelly U. Pew, supt. Fax 981-1094
www.rock-hill.k12.sc.us
Castle Heights MS 800/6-8
2382 Fire Tower Rd 29730 803-981-1400
Kelly Kane, prin. Fax 981-1430
Dutchman Creek MS 900/6-8
4757 Mount Gallant Rd 29732 803-985-1700
Norris Williams, prin. Fax 985-1740
Northwestern HS 1,700/9-12
2503 W Main St 29732 803-981-1200
James Blake, prin. Fax 981-1250
Phoenix Academy Alt
1234 Flint Street Ext 29730 803-981-1975
Dr. Walter Wolff, dir. Fax 981-1396
Rawlinson Road MS 700/6-8
2631 W Main St 29732 803-981-1500
Dr. Jean Dickson, prin. Fax 981-1532
Rebound Alternative S Alt
1234 Flint Street Ext 29730 803-981-1087
Hank Hammond, dir. Fax 981-1259
Renaissance Academy Alt
1234 Flint Street Ext 29730 803-985-3737
Fax 981-1396
Rock Hill Applied Technology Center Vo/Tech
2399 W Main St 29732 803-981-1100
Don Gillman, dir. Fax 981-1125
Rock Hill HS 1,900/9-12
320 W Springdale Rd 29730 803-981-1300
Ozzie Ahl, prin. Fax 981-1343
Saluda Trail MS 800/6-8
2300 Saluda Rd 29730 803-981-1800
Brenda Campbell, prin. Fax 981-1888
South Pointe HS 1,400/9-12
801 Neely Rd 29730 803-980-2100
Dr. Al Leonard, prin. Fax 980-2105
Sullivan MS 800/6-8
1825 Eden Ter 29730 803-981-1450
Shane Goodwin, prin. Fax 981-1456
Adult & Community Education Adult
1234 Flint Street Ext 29730 803-981-1375
Sandy Andrews, dir. Fax 981-1397

Clinton College Post-Sec.
1029 Crawford Rd 29730 803-327-7402
Westminster Catawba Christian S 500/PK-12
2650 India Hook Rd 29732 803-366-4119
Scott Dillon, head sch Fax 328-5465
Winthrop University Post-Sec.
701 W Oakland Ave 29733 803-323-2211
York Technical College Post-Sec.
452 Anderson Rd S 29730 803-327-8000

**Roebuck, Spartanburg, Pop. 2,173**
Spartanburg County SD 6 11,500/PK-12
1390 Cavalier Way 29376 864-576-4212
Dr. Darryl Owings, supt. Fax 574-6265
www.spart6.org
Dorman HS 2,400/10-12
1050 Cavalier Way 29376 864-582-4347
Ken Kiser, prin. Fax 587-8738
Dorman HS - Freshman Campus 800/9-9
1225 Cavalier Way 29376 864-582-3479
Mark Smith, prin. Fax 342-8997
Gable MS 800/6-8
198 Otts Shoals Rd 29376 864-576-3500
Matt Talley, prin. Fax 595-2428
Other Schools – See Moore, Spartanburg

**Rowesville, Orangeburg, Pop. 302**
Orangeburg Consolidated SD 5
Supt. — See Orangeburg
Bethune-Bowman MSHS 400/6-12
4857 Charleston Hwy 29133 803-516-6011
Marvin Foster, prin. Fax 516-6013

**Saint George, Dorchester, Pop. 2,077**
Dorchester SD 4 2,400/PK-12
500 Ridge St 29477 843-563-4535
Dr. Morris Ravenell, supt. Fax 563-9269
www.dorchester4.k12.sc.us
Saint George MS 300/6-8
600 Minus St 29477 843-563-3171
Jeffery Thompson, prin. Fax 563-5936
Other Schools – See Dorchester, Harleyville

Dorchester Academy 300/PK-12
234 Academy Rd 29477 843-563-9511

**Saint Matthews, Calhoun, Pop. 2,002**
Calhoun County SD 1,700/PK-12
PO Box 215 29135 803-655-7310
Dr. Steve Wilson, supt. Fax 655-7393
www.ccpsonline.net/
Calhoun County HS 400/9-12
150 Saints Ave 29135 803-874-3071
Cynthia Johnson, prin. Fax 655-5948

Calhoun Academy 400/PK-12
PO Box 526 29135 803-874-2734

**Saint Stephen, Berkeley, Pop. 1,670**
Berkeley County SD
Supt. — See Moncks Corner
Saint Stephen MS 200/6-8
225 Carolina Dr 29479 843-567-3128
Brenda Fleming, prin. Fax 567-8162
Timberland HS 800/9-12
1418 Gravel Hill Rd 29479 843-567-8110
Kerry Daugherty, prin. Fax 567-8116

**Salem, Oconee, Pop. 134**
Oconee County SD
Supt. — See Walhalla
Tamassee-Salem MSHS 300/6-12
4 Eagle Ln 29676 864-886-4545
Steve Moore, prin. Fax 886-4541

**Saluda, Saluda, Pop. 3,519**
Saluda SD 2,200/PK-12
404 N Wise Rd 29138 864-445-8441
David M. Mathis Ed.D., supt. Fax 445-9598
www.saludaschools.org
Saluda HS 600/9-12
160 Ivory Key Rd 29138 864-445-3011
Dr. Sarah Longshore, prin. Fax 445-3542
Saluda MS 500/6-8
140 Ivory Key Rd 29138 864-445-3767
Shawnda Brunson, prin. Fax 445-3980

**Santee, Orangeburg, Pop. 941**
Orangeburg County Consolidated SD 3
Supt. — See Holly Hill
Lake Marion HS 800/9-12
PO Box 650 29142 803-854-9213
Rose Pelzer, prin. Fax 854-5202

**Seabrook, Beaufort**
Beaufort County SD
Supt. — See Beaufort
Whale Branch Early College HS 500/9-12
169 Detour Rd 29940 843-466-2700
Priscilla Drake, prin. Fax 846-6827
Whale Branch MS 400/5-8
2009 Trask Pkwy 29940 843-466-3000
Matthew Hunt, prin. Fax 466-3087

**Seneca, Oconee, Pop. 7,931**
Oconee County SD
Supt. — See Walhalla
Hamilton Career Center Vo/Tech
100 Vocational Dr 29672 864-886-4425
Michael Pearson, prin. Fax 886-4426
Seneca HS 1,000/9-12
100 Bobcat Rdg 29678 864-886-4460
Cliff Roberts, prin. Fax 886-4457
Seneca MS 700/6-8
810 W South 4th St 29678 864-886-4455
Al LeRoy, prin. Fax 886-4452

Oconee Christian Academy 200/PK-12
150 His Way Cir 29672 864-882-6925
Harold Dean Bare, head sch Fax 882-7217

**Simpsonville, Greenville, Pop. 17,848**
Greenville County SD
Supt. — See Greenville
Bryson MS 1,100/6-8
3657 S Industrial Dr 29681 864-355-2100
Dr. Adrienne Davenport, prin. Fax 355-2194
Chandler MS 700/6-8
4231 Fork Shoals Rd 29680 864-452-0300
Rita Mantooth, prin. Fax 452-0365
Hillcrest HS 2,100/9-12
3665 S Industrial Dr 29681 864-355-3500
G. Bryan Skipper, prin. Fax 355-3382
Hillcrest MS 1,000/6-8
510 Garrison Rd 29681 864-355-6100
Kelli Farmer, prin. Fax 355-6120
Mauldin MS 1,200/6-8
1190 Holland Rd 29681 864-355-6770
Rosia Gardner, prin. Fax 355-6988

Greenville Classical Academy 100/K-12
2519 Woodruff Rd 29681 864-329-9884
Eric Woernle, prin.
Southside Christian S 1,100/PK-12
2211 Woodruff Rd 29681 864-234-7595
Dr. Stephen Reel, supt. Fax 234-7048

**Spartanburg, Spartanburg, Pop. 36,415**
Spartanburg County SD 6
Supt. — See Roebuck
Fairforest MS 800/6-8
4120 N Blackstock Rd 29301 864-576-1270
Dean Ledford, prin. Fax 576-2600

Spartanburg SD 3
Supt. — See Glendale
Broome HS 900/9-12
381 Cherry Hill Rd 29307 864-279-6700
Rodney Graves, prin. Fax 279-6710

Spartanburg SD 7 7,300/PK-12
PO Box 970 29304 864-594-4400
Dr. Russell W. Booker, supt. Fax 594-4406
www.spart7.org
Carver MS 500/6-8
467 S Church St 29306 864-594-4435
Nicole Thompson, prin. Fax 594-6144
McCracken MS 700/6-8
300 Webber Rd 29307 864-594-4457
Margaret Peach, prin. Fax 596-8418
Morgan Technology Center Vo/Tech
201 Zion Hill Rd 29307 864-579-2810
Bill Price, prin. Fax 579-7392
Spartanburg County Alternative S Alt
364 Successful Way 29303 864-594-4482
Paul Hughes, prin. Fax 594-6154
Spartanburg HS Freshman Academy 500/9-9
50 Emory Rd 29307 864-594-4513
Jada Kidd, prin. Fax 594-4518
Spartanburg SHS 1,400/10-12
500 Dupre Dr 29307 864-594-4410
Jeff Stevens, prin. Fax 594-6142

Converse College Post-Sec.
580 E Main St 29302 864-596-9000
Oakbrook Preparatory S 400/K-12
190 Lincoln School Rd 29301 864-587-2060
Sherman College of Chiropractic Post-Sec.
PO Box 1452 29304 864-578-8770
South Carolina School for Deaf and Blind Post-Sec.
355 Cedar Springs Rd 29302 864-577-7557
Spartanburg Christian Academy 500/PK-12
8740 Asheville Hwy 29316 864-578-4238
Robert McDonald, hdmstr. Fax 542-1846
Spartanburg Community College Post-Sec.
PO Box 4386 29305 864-592-4800
Spartanburg Day S 400/PK-12
1701 Skylyn Dr 29307 864-582-7539
Rachel Deems, head sch Fax 582-7530
Spartanburg Methodist College Post-Sec.
1000 Powell Mill Rd 29301 864-587-4000
University of South Carolina Post-Sec.
800 University Way 29303 864-503-5000
Virginia College Post-Sec.
8150 Warren H Abernathy Hwy 29301 864-504-3200
Westgate Christian S 200/PK-12
1990 Old Reidville Rd 29301 864-576-4953
Rev. Tony Seiber, admin. Fax 576-7581
Wofford College Post-Sec.
429 N Church St 29303 864-597-4000

**Starr, Anderson, Pop. 170**
Anderson SD 3
Supt. — See Iva
Starr-Iva MS 600/6-8
1034 Rainey Rd 29684 864-352-6146
Barry Jacks, prin. Fax 352-2095

**Summerton, Clarendon, Pop. 994**
Clarendon SD 1 900/PK-12
PO Box 38 29148 803-485-2325
Dr. Rose Wilder, supt. Fax 485-2822
www.clarendon1.k12.sc.us
Scott's Branch HS 200/9-12
9253 Alex Harvin Hwy 29148 803-478-7818
Dr. Gwendolyn Harris, prin. Fax 478-7659
Scott's Branch MS 100/7-8
1154 4th St 29148 803-485-2043
Dr. Gwendolyn Harris, prin. Fax 485-7012

Clarendon Hall S 200/PK-12
PO Box 609 29148 803-485-3550
Phillip Rizzo, hdmstr. Fax 485-3205

**Summerville, Dorchester, Pop. 42,232**
Berkeley County SD
Supt. — See Moncks Corner
Cane Bay HS 1,400/9-12
1624 State Rd 29483 843-899-8786
Dr. Lee Westberry, prin. Fax 899-8789
Cane Bay MS 5-8
1175 Cane Bay Blvd 29483 843-899-1857
Carol Beckmann-Bartlett, prin. Fax 899-1861

Dorchester SD 2 21,400/K-12
102 Greenwave Blvd 29483 843-873-2901
Joseph Pye, supt. Fax 821-3959
www.dorchester2.k12.sc.us
Alston MS 900/6-8
500 Bryan St 29483 843-873-3890
Thad Schmenk, prin. Fax 821-3978
Ashley Ridge HS 1,900/9-12
9800 Delemar Hwy 29485 843-695-4900
Karen Radcliffe, prin. Fax 695-4905
DuBose MS 1,000/6-8
1005 DuBose School Rd 29483 843-875-7012
Mona Caudle, prin. Fax 821-3995
Gregg MS 1,000/6-8
500 Greenwave Blvd 29483 843-871-3150
Lori Estep, prin. Fax 821-3992
Rollings MS of the Arts 700/6-8
815 S Main St 29483 843-873-3610
Dr. Kathy Sobolewski, prin. Fax 821-3985
Summerville HS 2,800/9-12
1101 Boone Hill Rd 29483 843-873-6460
Kenny Farrell, prin. Fax 821-3989
Other Schools – See Ladson, North Charleston, Ridgeville

Faith Christian S 300/PK-12
337 Farmington Rd 29483 843-873-8464
John Davis M.Ed., head sch Fax 923-6806
Pinewood Preparatory S 800/PK-12
1114 Orangeburg Rd 29483 843-873-1643
Stephen Mandell, hdmstr. Fax 821-4257

**Sumter, Sumter, Pop. 39,747**
Sumter SD 17,100/PK-12
1345 Wilson Hall Rd 29150 803-469-6900
J. Frank Baker, supt. Fax 469-3769
district.sumterschools.net
Alice Drive MS 800/6-8
40 Miller Rd 29150 803-775-0821
Jeannie Pressley, prin. Fax 778-2929
Bates MS 800/6-8
715 Estate St 29150 803-775-0711
Dr. Ayesha Hunter, prin. Fax 775-0715
Brewington Academy Alt
4300 E Brewington Rd 29153 803-495-8069
Robert Barth, prin. Fax 495-8068
Chestnut Oaks MS 500/6-8
1200 Oswego Hwy 29153 803-775-7272
Lashawnte Sarvis, prin. Fax 775-7601
Crestwood HS 1,200/9-12
2000 Oswego Hwy 29153 803-469-6200
Dr. Shirley Gamble, prin. Fax 469-7678
Ebenezer MS 400/6-8
3440 Ebenezer Rd 29153 803-469-8571
Marlene DeWit, prin. Fax 469-8575
Furman MS 900/6-8
3400 Bethel Church Rd 29154 803-481-8519
Maria Newton Ta'Bon, prin. Fax 481-8923
Lakewood HS 1,100/9-12
350 Old Manning Rd 29150 803-506-2700
John Michalik, prin. Fax 506-2712
Mayewood MS 200/6-8
4300 E Brewington Rd 29153 803-495-8014
John Koumas, prin. Fax 495-8016
Sumter Career and Technology Center Vo/Tech
2612 McCrays Mill Rd 29154 803-481-8575
Shirrie Miller, dir. Fax 481-4232
Sumter HS 2,300/9-12
2580 McCrays Mill Rd 29154 803-481-4480
Dana Fall, prin. Fax 481-4021

Sumter Adult Ed Center — Adult
905 N Main St 29150 — 803-778-6432
Sharon Teigue, dir. — Fax 775-4665
Other Schools – See Dalzell

---

Central Carolina Technical College — Post-Sec.
506 N Guignard Dr 29150 — 803-778-1961
Morris College — Post-Sec.
100 W College St 29150 — 803-934-3200
St. Francis Xavier HS — 50/9-12
15 School St 29150 — 803-773-0210
Raymond Reinsant, prin. — Fax 775-0119
Sumter Beauty College — Post-Sec.
921 Carolina Ave 29150 — 803-773-7311
Sumter Christian S — 200/PK-12
420 S Pike W 29150 — 803-773-1902
University of South Carolina — Post-Sec.
200 Miller Rd 29150 — 803-775-8727
Wilson Hall — 800/PK-12
520 Wilson Hall Rd 29150 — 803-469-3475
Fred Moulton, hdmstr. — Fax 469-3477

**Swansea, Lexington, Pop. 808**
Lexington County SD 4 — 2,800/PK-12
607 E 5th St 29160 — 803-490-7000
Dr. Linda Lavender, supt. — Fax 568-1020
www.lexington4.net
Swansea HS Freshman Academy — 50/9-9
1195 I W Hutto Rd 29160 — 803-490-7006
Craig Baker, prin. — Fax 568-1052
Swansea SHS — 600/10-12
500 E 1st St 29160 — 803-490-7007
Bryan Evans, prin. — Fax 568-1117
Other Schools – See Gaston

**Taylors, Greenville, Pop. 21,240**
Greenville County SD
Supt. — See Greenville
Eastside HS — 1,300/9-12
1300 Brushy Creek Rd 29687 — 864-355-2800
Mike Thorne, prin. — Fax 355-2992
Northwood MS — 900/6-8
710 Ikes Rd 29687 — 864-355-7000
Treva Lee, prin. — Fax 355-7077

**Tega Cay, York, Pop. 7,516**
Fort Mill SD
Supt. — See Fort Mill
Gold Hill MS — 800/6-8
1025 Dave Gibson Blvd 29708 — 803-548-8300
Matthew Wallace, prin. — Fax 548-8322

**Tigerville, Greenville, Pop. 1,267**

---

North Greenville University — Post-Sec.
PO Box 1892 29688 — 864-977-7000

**Timmonsville, Florence, Pop. 2,312**
Florence County SD Four — 700/PK-12
304 Kemper St 29161 — 843-346-3956
Dr. Andre Boyd Ph.D., supt. — Fax 346-5159
www.florence4.k12.sc.us
Johnson MS — 100/6-8
304 Kemper St 29161 — 843-346-4586
Langston Brown, prin. — Fax 346-5416
Timmonsville HS — 300/9-12
304 Kemper St 29161 — 843-346-4586
Langston Brown, prin. — Fax 346-5416
Timmonsville Adult Education Center — Adult
304 Kemper St 29161 — 843-420-5261
Gloria Q. Bracey, coord. — Fax 346-5159

**Travelers Rest, Greenville, Pop. 4,504**
Greenville County SD
Supt. — See Greenville
Northwest MS — 800/6-8
1606 Geer Hwy 29690 — 864-355-6900
David McDonald, prin. — Fax 355-6920
Travelers Rest HS — 1,200/9-12
301 N Main St 29690 — 864-355-0000
Louis Lavely, prin. — Fax 355-0088

**Turbeville, Clarendon, Pop. 765**
Clarendon SD 3 — 1,200/PK-12
PO Box 270 29162 — 843-659-2188
Connie Dennis Ph.D., supt. — Fax 659-3204
www.clarendon3.org/
East Clarendon MSHS — 600/6-12
PO Box 67 29162 — 843-659-2185
Jason Cook, prin. — Fax 659-2192

**Union, Union, Pop. 8,281**
Union County SD — 4,200/K-12
PO Box 907 29379 — 864-429-1740
Dr. Kristi Woodall, supt. — Fax 429-1745
www.union.k12.sc.us
Sims MS — 800/6-8
2200 Whitmire Hwy 29379 — 864-429-1755
Mickey Connolly, prin. — Fax 429-2811
Union County HS — 1,200/9-12
1163 Lakeside Dr 29379 — 864-429-1750
Floyd Lyles, prin. — Fax 429-5401
Adult Education / Lifelong Learning — Adult
517 E Main St 29379 — 864-429-1770
Cindy Langley, dir. — Fax 429-1771

---

University of South Carolina — Post-Sec.
PO Box 729 29379 — 864-429-8728

**Varnville, Hampton, Pop. 2,133**
Hampton SD 1 — 2,500/PK-12
372 Pine St E 29944 — 803-943-4576
Doug McTeer, supt. — Fax 943-5943
www.hampton1.org
Hampton HS — 700/9-12
115 Airport Rd 29944 — 803-943-3568
Barry Rosenburg, prin. — Fax 943-5036
North District MS — 400/7-8
PO Box 368 29944 — 803-943-3507
Patricia Brantley, prin. — Fax 943-4074

**Wagener, Aiken, Pop. 778**
Aiken County SD
Supt. — See Aiken
Corbett MS — 200/6-8
10 Corbett Cir 29164 — 803-564-1050
Dr. Laura Bacon, prin. — Fax 564-1058
Wagener-Salley HS — 300/9-12
272 Main St S 29164 — 803-564-1100
Ute Aadland, prin. — Fax 564-1109

**Walhalla, Oconee, Pop. 4,200**
Oconee County SD — 11,400/PK-12
414 S Pine St 29691 — 864-886-4400
Dr. Michael Thorsland, supt. — Fax 886-4408
www.oconee.k12.sc.us
Oconee Academy — Alt
177 Razorback Ln 29691 — 864-886-4431
Tracey Long, coord. — Fax 886-4432
Walhalla HS — 1,000/9-12
4701 N Highway 11 29691 — 864-886-4490
Steve Garrett, prin. — Fax 886-4488
Walhalla MS — 700/6-8
151 Razorback Ln 29691 — 864-886-4485
Scott Dixon, prin. — Fax 886-4483
Other Schools – See Salem, Seneca, Westminster

**Walterboro, Colleton, Pop. 5,325**
Colleton County SD — 5,100/PK-12
213 N Jefferies Blvd 29488 — 843-782-4510
Franklin Foster, supt. — Fax 549-2606
colletonsd.org
Colleton County HS — 1,700/9-12
150 Cougar Nation Dr 29488 — 843-782-0031
Cliff Warren, prin. — Fax 782-0042
Colleton MS — 1,400/6-8
1379 Tuskegee Airmen Dr 29488 — 843-782-0040
Senaca Baines, prin. — Fax 782-0041
Thunderbolt Career & Technology Center — Vo/Tech
1069 Thunderbolt Dr 29488 — 843-782-4514
Mr William Hayden, dir. — Fax 538-3009
Adult Education — Adult
609 Colleton Loop 29488 — 843-782-0018
Lynn Jones, dir. — Fax 549-6285

---

Colleton Prep Academy — 200/PK-12
PO Box 1426 29488 — 843-538-8959
Jill Burttram, head sch — Fax 538-8260
Cosmetic Arts Institute — Post-Sec.
1789 Hampton St 29488 — 843-549-8587

**Ware Shoals, Greenwood, Pop. 2,149**
Greenwood SD 51 — 1,000/PK-12
56 S Greenwood Ave 29692 — 864-456-7496
Dr. Fay Sprouse, supt.
www.gwd51.org
Ware Shoals HS — 500/9-12
56 S Greenwood Ave 29692 — 864-456-7923
Paul Anderson, prin. — Fax 456-2370
Ware Shoals MS — 200/5-8
45 W Main St 29692 — 864-456-2711
Nancy Brown, prin. — Fax 456-2153

**Warrenville, Aiken, Pop. 1,205**
Aiken County SD
Supt. — See Aiken
Aiken County Career & Technical Center — Vo/Tech
2455 Jefferson Davis Hwy 29851 — 803-593-7300
William Hudson, dir. — Fax 593-7115
Langley-Bath-Clearwater MS — 500/6-8
29 Lions Trl 29851 — 803-593-7260
Brenda DeLoache, prin. — Fax 593-7119

**West Columbia, Lexington, Pop. 14,742**
Lexington County SD 1
Supt. — See Lexington
White Knoll MS — 800/6-8
116 White Knoll Way 29170 — 803-821-4300
Guy Smith, prin. — Fax 821-4303

Lexington County SD 2 — 8,700/PK-12
715 9th St 29169 — 803-796-4708
Dr. William B. James Ph.D., supt. — Fax 739-4063
www.lex2.org/
Airport HS — 1,300/9-12
1315 Boston Ave 29170 — 803-822-5600
Dr. Dixon Brooks, prin. — Fax 822-5665
Fulmer MS — 600/6-8
1614 Walterboro St 29170 — 803-822-5660
Megan Carrero, prin. — Fax 822-5664
Northside MS — 600/6-8
157 Cougar Dr 29169 — 803-739-4190
Lisa Davis, prin. — Fax 739-3188
Pair Education Center — Alt
2325 Platt Springs Rd 29169 — 803-739-4085
Leonard Frierson, prin. — Fax 739-3195
Pine Ridge MS — 500/6-8
735 Pine Ridge Dr 29172 — 803-755-7400
Brad Coleman, prin. — Fax 755-7449
Other Schools – See Cayce

State Supported Schools
Supt. — None
Gray Opportunity S — 9-12
3300 W Campus Rd 29170 — 803-896-6480
Pat Smith, dir. — Fax 896-6463

**Westminster, Oconee, Pop. 2,380**
Oconee County SD
Supt. — See Walhalla
West-Oak HS — 1,000/9-12
130 Warrior Ln 29693 — 864-886-4530
Kurt Kreuzberger, prin. — Fax 886-4527
West Oak MS — 800/6-8
501 Westminster Hwy 29693 — 864-886-4525
Jami Verderosa, prin. — Fax 886-4524

---

Foothills Christian S — 100/K-12
126 Robin Rd 29693 — 864-647-1220
Joe Mullet, prin.

**Whitmire, Newberry, Pop. 1,424**
Newberry County SD
Supt. — See Newberry
Whitmire Community S — 200/K-12
2597 Hwy 66 29178 — 803-694-2320
Joey Haney, prin. — Fax 694-3835

**Williamston, Anderson, Pop. 3,887**
Anderson SD 1 — 9,000/PK-12
PO Box 99 29697 — 864-847-7344
David Havird, supt. — Fax 847-3543
www.anderson1.k12.sc.us
Palmetto HS — 900/9-12
804 N Hamilton St 29697 — 864-847-7311
Robert Roach, prin. — Fax 847-3532
Palmetto MS — 900/6-8
803 N Hamilton St 29697 — 864-847-4333
Barry Knight, prin. — Fax 847-3529
Other Schools – See Greenville, Piedmont

Area Vocational Schools
Supt. — None
Career & Technology Center — Vo/Tech
702 Belton Hwy 29697 — 864-847-4121
Dr. Hollie Harrell, dir. — Fax 847-3539

**Williston, Barnwell, Pop. 3,095**
Williston SD 29 — 1,000/PK-12
12255 Main St 29853 — 803-266-7878
Dr. Missoura G. Ashe, supt. — Fax 266-3879
www.williston.k12.sc.us
Williston-Elko HS — 300/9-12
12233 Main St 29853 — 803-266-3110
Joel Mitchell, prin. — Fax 266-5489
Williston-Elko MS — 200/6-8
12333 Main St 29853 — 803-266-3430
Greg Sweet, prin. — Fax 266-7623

**Winnsboro, Fairfield, Pop. 3,508**
Fairfield County SD — 3,300/PK-12
PO Box 622 29180 — 803-635-4607
Dr. J.R. Green, supt. — Fax 635-6578
www.fairfield.k12.sc.us/
Fairfield Career & Technology Center — Vo/Tech
1451 US Highway 321 N 29180 — 803-635-5506
Christopher Dinkins, prin. — Fax 635-9958
Fairfield Central HS — 800/9-12
836 US Highway 321 Byp S 29180 — 803-635-1441
Tracie Swilley, prin. — Fax 635-3997
Fairfield MS — 400/7-8
728 US Highway 321 Byp S 29180 — 803-635-4270
Robin Hardy, prin. — Fax 635-9108
Gordon Odyssey Academy — 200/Alt
560 Fairfield St 29180 — 803-635-4859
LaNisha Tindal Ed.D., dir. — Fax 635-5835

---

Winn Academy — 300/K-12
PO Box 390 29180 — 803-635-5494
Dr. Henry G. Selby, head sch — Fax 635-4310

**Woodruff, Spartanburg, Pop. 3,990**
Spartanburg SD 4 — 2,900/PK-12
118 McEdco Rd 29388 — 864-476-3186
Dr. W. Rallie Liston, supt. — Fax 476-8616
www.spartanburg4.org
Woodruff HS — 800/9-12
710 Cross Anchor Rd 29388 — 864-476-7045
Dr. Aaron Fulmer, prin. — Fax 476-7224
Woodruff MS — 700/6-8
205 SJ Workman Hwy 29388 — 864-476-3150
Denise Brown, prin. — Fax 476-6036

**York, York, Pop. 7,594**
York SD 1 — 5,200/PK-12
PO Box 770 29745 — 803-684-9916
Dr. Vernon Prosser, supt. — Fax 684-1903
www.york.k12.sc.us
Johnson Technology Center — Vo/Tech
275 E Alexander Love Hwy 29745 — 803-684-1910
Ron Roveri, prin. — Fax 684-1913
York Comprehensive HS — 1,400/9-12
275 E Alexander Love Hwy 29745 — 803-684-2336
Chris Black, prin. — Fax 684-1932
York MS — 800/7-8
1010 Devinney Rd 29745 — 803-684-5008
Richard Ball, prin. — Fax 684-1916
York One Academy — Alt
37 Pinckney St 29745 — 803-684-2381
Shelton Clinton, prin. — Fax 684-1932

# SOUTH DAKOTA

## SOUTH DAKOTA DEPARTMENT OF EDUCATION
**800 Governors Dr, Pierre 57501-2235**
**Telephone 605-773-3134**
**Fax 605-773-6139**
**Website doe.sd.gov/**

Secretary of Education Dr. Melody Schopp

## SOUTH DAKOTA BOARD OF EDUCATION
**700 Governors Dr, Pierre 57501-2291**

President Donald Kirkegaard

## PUBLIC, PRIVATE AND CATHOLIC SECONDARY SCHOOLS

**Aberdeen, Brown, Pop. 25,591**
Aberdeen SD 6-1 3,900/K-12
1224 S 3rd St 57401 605-725-7100
Dr. Becky Guffin, supt. Fax 725-7199
www.aberdeen.k12.sd.us
Central HS 1,200/9-12
2200 S Roosevelt St 57401 605-725-8100
Jason Uttermark, prin. Fax 725-8199
Holgate MS 400/6-8
2200 N Dakota St 57401 605-725-7700
Dr. Greg Aas, prin. Fax 725-7799
Simmons MS 500/6-8
1300 S 3rd St 57401 605-725-7900
Kelly Northrup, prin. Fax 725-7999

Aberdeen Christian S 100/PK-12
1500 N Highway 281 57401 605-225-2053
Eric Kline, head sch Fax 226-2106
Northern State University Post-Sec.
1200 S Jay St 57401 605-626-3011
Presentation College Post-Sec.
1500 N Main St 57401 800-437-6060
Roncalli HS 300/7-12
1400 N Dakota St 57401 605-226-2100
Ed Mitzel, prin. Fax 226-0616
St. Luke's Midland Regional Medical Ctr. Post-Sec.
305 S State St 57401 605-622-5230
South Dakota School Visually Handicapped Post-Sec.
423 17th Ave SE 57401 605-626-2580

**Alcester, Union, Pop. 801**
Alcester-Hudson SD 61-1 300/PK-12
PO Box 198 57001 605-934-1890
Tim Rhead, supt. Fax 934-1936
www.alcester-hudson.k12.sd.us
Alcester-Hudson HS 100/9-12
PO Box 198 57001 605-934-1890
LeeAnn Haisch, prin. Fax 934-1936
Alcester-Hudson JHS 50/7-8
PO Box 198 57001 605-934-1890
LeeAnn Haisch, prin. Fax 934-1936

**Alexandria, Hanson, Pop. 613**
Hanson SD 30-1 400/PK-12
PO Box 490 57311 605-239-4387
James Bridge, supt. Fax 239-4293
www.hanson.k12.sd.us/
Hanson HS 100/9-12
PO Box 490 57311 605-239-4387
Ray Slaba, prin. Fax 239-4293
Hanson MS 100/6-8
PO Box 490 57311 605-239-4387
Ray Slaba, prin. Fax 239-4293
Other Schools – See Mitchell

**Arlington, Kingsbury, Pop. 909**
Arlington SD 38-1 300/PK-12
PO Box 359 57212 605-983-5597
Chris Lund, supt. Fax 983-2820
www.arlington.k12.sd.us
Arlington HS 100/9-12
PO Box 359 57212 605-983-5598
Rhonda Gross, prin. Fax 983-4652
Arlington JHS 100/7-8
PO Box 359 57212 605-983-5598
Rhonda Gross, prin. Fax 983-4652

Oldham-Ramona SD 39-5
Supt. — See Ramona
Spring Lake Colony HS 9-12
21727 452nd Ave 57212 605-482-8244
Tom Ludens, prin. Fax 482-8282

**Armour, Douglas, Pop. 693**
Armour SD 21-1 200/K-12
PO Box 640 57313 605-724-2153
Burnell Glanzer, supt. Fax 724-2977
www.armour.k12.sd.us/
Armour HS 100/9-12
PO Box 640 57313 605-724-2153
Brad Preheim, prin. Fax 724-2799
Armour MS 100/6-8
PO Box 640 57313 605-724-2698
Burnell Glanzer, prin. Fax 724-2799

**Avon, Bon Homme, Pop. 586**
Avon SD 4-1 300/PK-12
PO Box 407 57315 605-286-3291
Tom Culver, supt. Fax 286-3712
www.avon.k12.sd.us/
Avon HS 100/9-12
PO Box 407 57315 605-286-3291
Matt Yost, prin. Fax 286-3510
Avon JHS 50/7-8
PO Box 407 57315 605-286-3291
Matt Yost, prin. Fax 286-3510

**Baltic, Minnehaha, Pop. 1,070**
Baltic SD 49-1 400/PK-12
PO Box 309 57003 605-529-5464
Robert Sittig, supt. Fax 529-5443
www.baltic.k12.sd.us/
Baltic HS 100/9-12
PO Box 309 57003 605-529-5461
James Aisenbrey, prin. Fax 529-5467
Baltic MS 100/6-8
PO Box 309 57003 605-529-5461
James Aisenbrey, prin. Fax 529-5467

**Batesland, Shannon, Pop. 108**
Oglala Lakota County SD 65-1 1,600/PK-8
PO Box 109 57716 605-288-1921
Dr. Julie Ertz, supt. Fax 288-1814
www.shannon.ws
Other Schools – See Pine Ridge, Porcupine

**Belle Fourche, Butte, Pop. 5,472**
Belle Fourche SD 9-1 1,400/K-12
2305 13th Ave 57717 605-723-3355
Dr. Steve Willard, supt. Fax 723-3366
www.bellefourche.k12.sd.us
Belle Fourche Education Connection 100/Alt
2305 13th Ave 57717 605-723-0955
Mathew Raba, prin. Fax 723-0941
Belle Fourche HS 400/9-12
2305 13th Ave 57717 605-723-3350
Mathew Raba, prin. Fax 723-3357
Belle Fourche MS 400/5-8
2305 13th Ave 57717 605-723-3367
Kevin Smidt, prin. Fax 723-3374

**Beresford, Union, Pop. 1,991**
Beresford SD 61-2 600/PK-12
301 W Maple St 57004 605-763-4293
Brian Field, supt. Fax 763-5305
www.beresford.k12.sd.us/
Beresford HS 200/9-12
301 W Maple St 57004 605-763-2145
Dustin Degen, prin. Fax 763-5305
Beresford MS 100/6-8
205 W Maple St 57004 605-763-2139
Dustin Degen, prin. Fax 763-5305

**Big Stone City, Grant, Pop. 465**
Big Stone CSD 25-1 100/PK-8
655 Walnut St 57216 605-862-8108
Roger DeGroot, supt. Fax 862-8640
bigstonecitylions.weebly.com
Big Stone City JHS 50/6-8
655 Walnut St 57216 605-862-8108
Roger DeGroot, prin. Fax 862-8640

**Bison, Perkins, Pop. 326**
Bison SD 52-1 100/K-12
PO Box 9 57620 605-244-5961
Marilyn Azevedo, supt. Fax 244-5276
www.bison.k12.sd.us/
Bison HS 100/9-12
PO Box 9 57620 605-244-5271
Marilyn Azevedo, supt. Fax 244-5276
Bison JHS 50/7-8
PO Box 9 57620 605-244-5271
Marilyn Azevedo, supt. Fax 244-5276

**Bonesteel, Gregory, Pop. 272**
South Central SD 26-5 100/PK-12
401 Birdsell St 57317 605-654-2314
Dr. Cheryl Thaler, supt.
www.southcentral.k12.sd.us/
South Central HS 50/9-12
401 Birdsell St 57317 605-654-2314
Dr. Cheryl Thaler, supt.
South Central MS 50/6-8
401 Birdsell St 57317 605-654-2314
Dr. Cheryl Thaler, supt.

**Bowdle, Edmunds, Pop. 501**
Bowdle SD 22-1 100/K-12
PO Box 563 57428 605-285-6272
Ryan Orrock, supt. Fax 285-6830
www.bowdle.k12.sd.us
Bowdle HS 50/9-12
PO Box 563 57428 605-285-6590
Ryan Orrock, prin. Fax 285-6830
Bowdle JHS 50/7-8
PO Box 563 57428 605-285-6590
Ryan Orrock, prin. Fax 285-6830

**Box Elder, Pennington, Pop. 7,381**
Douglas SD 51-1 2,600/PK-12
400 Patriot Dr 57719 605-923-0000
Alan Kerr, supt. Fax 923-0018
www.dsdk12.net
Douglas HS 700/9-12
420 Patriot Dr 57719 605-923-0030
Bud Gusso, prin. Fax 923-0031
Douglas MS 600/6-8
401 Tower Rd 57719 605-923-0050
Dan Baldwin, prin. Fax 923-0051

**Brandon, Minnehaha, Pop. 8,690**
Brandon Valley SD 49-2 3,400/PK-12
300 S Splitrock Blvd 57005 605-582-2049
David Pappone, supt. Fax 582-7456
brandonvalley.k12.sd.us
Brandon Valley HS 1,000/9-12
301 S Splitrock Blvd 57005 605-582-3211
Dr. Gregg Talcott, prin. Fax 582-2652
Brandon Valley MS 800/6-8
700 E Holly Blvd 57005 605-582-3214
Brad Thorson, prin. Fax 582-7206

**Bridgewater, McCook, Pop. 491**
Bridgewater-Emery SD 30-3 200/PK-12
PO Box 350 57319 605-729-2541
Jason Bailey, supt. Fax 449-4270
www.bridgewater-emery.k12.sd.us/
Bridgewater-Emery MS 100/6-8
PO Box 350 57319 605-449-4271
Christena Schultz, prin. Fax 449-4270
Other Schools – See Emery

**Britton, Marshall, Pop. 1,232**
Britton-Hecla SD 45-4 500/PK-12
PO Box 190 57430 605-448-2234
Kevin Coles, supt. Fax 448-5994
www.britton.k12.sd.us/
Britton-Hecla HS 200/9-12
PO Box 190 57430 605-448-2234
Carrie James, prin. Fax 448-5994
Britton-Hecla JHS 100/7-8
PO Box 190 57430 605-448-2234
Carrie James, prin. Fax 448-5994

**Brookings, Brookings, Pop. 21,716**
Brookings SD 5-1 2,900/K-12
2130 8th St S 57006 605-696-4700
Dr. Roger DeGroot, supt. Fax 696-4704
www.brookings.k12.sd.us/
Brookings HS 800/9-12
530 Elm Ave 57006 605-696-4100
Paul vonFischer, prin. Fax 696-4128
Mickelson MS 600/6-8
1801 12th St S 57006 605-696-4500
Tim Steffensen, prin. Fax 696-4506

South Dakota State University 57007 Post-Sec.
605-688-4151

**Buffalo, Harding, Pop. 328**
Harding County SD 31-1 200/K-12
PO Box 367 57720 605-375-3241
Ruth Krogh, supt. Fax 375-3246
www.hardingcounty.k12.sd.us/
Harding County HS 100/9-12
PO Box 367 57720 605-375-3241
Josh Page, prin. Fax 375-3246
Harding County MS 50/6-8
PO Box 367 57720 605-375-3241
Josh Page, prin. Fax 375-3246

**Burke, Gregory, Pop. 594**
Burke SD 26-2 200/PK-12
PO Box 382 57523 605-775-2644
Erik Person, supt. Fax 775-2468
www.burke.k12.sd.us
Burke HS 100/9-12
PO Box 382 57523 605-775-2645
Mark Otten, prin. Fax 775-2468
Burke MS 50/7-8
PO Box 382 57523 605-775-2645
Mark Otten, prin. Fax 775-2468

**Canistota, McCook, Pop. 646**
Canistota SD 43-1 200/K-12
PO Box 8 57012 605-296-3458
Larry Nebelsick, supt. Fax 296-3158
www.canistota.k12.sd.us
Canistota HS 100/9-12
PO Box 8 57012 605-296-3458
Lenny Schroeder, prin. Fax 296-3158
Canistota MS 50/6-8
PO Box 8 57012 605-296-3458
Lenny Schroeder, prin. Fax 296-3158

**Canton, Lincoln, Pop. 3,010**
Canton SD 41-1 800/PK-12
800 N Main St 57013 605-764-2706
Terry Gerber, supt. Fax 764-2700
www.canton.k12.sd.us
Canton HS 200/9-12
800 N Main St 57013 605-764-2706
Russell Townsend, prin. Fax 764-2700
Canton MS 200/6-8
800 N Main St 57013 605-764-2706
Russell Townsend, prin. Fax 764-2700

**Carpenter, Clark**
Willow Lake SD 12-3
Supt. — See Willow Lake
Shamrock Colony Alternative HS 50/Alt
19087 413th Ave 57322 605-625-5945
Hector Serna, prin. Fax 625-3103

**Castlewood, Hamlin, Pop. 623**
Castlewood SD 28-1 300/PK-12
310 E Harry St 57223 605-793-2497
Keith Fodness, supt. Fax 793-2679
www.castlewood.k12.sd.us/
Castlewood HS 100/9-12
310 E Harry St 57223 605-793-2497
Keith Fodness, prin. Fax 793-2679
Castlewood JHS 50/7-8
310 E Harry St 57223 605-793-2497
Keith Fodness, prin. Fax 793-2679

**Centerville, Turner, Pop. 877**
Centerville SD 60-1 200/PK-12
PO Box 100 57014 605-563-2291
Chad Conaway, supt. Fax 563-2615
www.centerville.k12.sd.us
Centerville HS 100/9-12
PO Box 100 57014 605-563-2291
Chad Conaway, prin. Fax 563-2615
Centerville JHS 50/5-8
PO Box 100 57014 605-563-2291
Chad Conaway, prin. Fax 563-2615

**Chamberlain, Brule, Pop. 2,326**
Chamberlain SD 7-1 900/PK-12
PO Box 119 57325 605-234-4477
Debra Johnson, supt. Fax 234-4479
www.chamberlain.k12.sd.us
Chamberlain HS 300/9-12
PO Box 119 57325 605-234-4467
Karen Fox, prin. Fax 234-4479
Chamberlain JHS 100/7-8
PO Box 119 57325 605-234-4467
Karen Fox, prin. Fax 234-4479

**Chester, Lake, Pop. 257**
Chester Area SD 39-1 600/PK-12
PO Box 159 57016 605-489-2411
Heath Larson, supt. Fax 489-2413
www.chester.k12.sd.us
Chester HS 100/9-12
PO Box 159 57016 605-489-2411
Julie Eppard, prin. Fax 489-2413
Chester MS 100/6-8
PO Box 159 57016 605-489-2411
Julie Eppard, prin. Fax 489-2413
High Plains Alternative S 50/Alt
PO Box 159 57016 605-489-2411
Heath Larson, prin. Fax 489-2413

**Clark, Clark, Pop. 1,130**
Clark SD 12-2 400/PK-12
220 N Clinton St 57225 605-532-3603
Luanne Warren, supt. Fax 532-3600
clark.k12.sd.us/
Clark HS 100/9-12
220 N Clinton St 57225 605-532-3605
Jerry Hartley, prin. Fax 532-3600
Clark MS 100/5-8
220 N Clinton St 57225 605-532-3603
Jerry Hartley, prin. Fax 532-3600

**Clear Lake, Deuel, Pop. 1,256**
Deuel SD 19-4 500/PK-12
PO Box 770 57226 605-874-2161
Dean Christensen, supt. Fax 874-8585
www.deuel.k12.sd.us/
Clear Lake MS 100/6-8
PO Box 770 57226 605-874-2162
Eric Bass, prin. Fax 874-8585
Deuel HS 100/9-12
PO Box 770 57226 605-874-2163
Eric Bass, prin. Fax 874-8585

**Colman, Moody, Pop. 586**
Colman-Egan SD 50-5 300/K-12
200 S Loban Ave 57017 605-534-3534
Tracey Olson, supt. Fax 534-3670
www.colman-egan.k12.sd.us
Colman-Egan HS 100/9-12
200 S Loban Ave 57017 605-534-3534
Scott Hemmer, prin. Fax 534-3670
Colman-Egan JHS 50/7-8
200 S Loban Ave 57017 605-534-3534
Scott Hemmer, prin. Fax 534-3670

**Colome, Tripp, Pop. 291**
Colome SD 59-3 200/PK-12
PO Box 367 57528 605-842-1624
Alan Armstrong, supt. Fax 842-0783
www.colome.k12.sd.us/
Colome HS 100/9-12
PO Box 367 57528 605-842-1624
Alan Armstrong, prin. Fax 842-0783
Colome JHS 50/7-8
PO Box 367 57528 605-842-1624
Alan Armstrong, prin. Fax 842-0783

**Colton, Minnehaha, Pop. 682**
Tri-Valley SD 49-6 800/PK-12
46450 252nd St 57018 605-446-3538
Mike Lodmel, supt. Fax 446-3520
www.tri-valley.k12.sd.us/
Tri-Valley HS 300/9-12
46450 252nd St 57018 605-446-3538
Tim Pflanz, prin. Fax 446-3520
Tri-Valley JHS 100/7-8
46450 252nd St 57018 605-446-3538
Tim Pflanz, prin. Fax 446-3520

**Corsica, Douglas, Pop. 584**
Corsica SD 21-2 200/PK-12
120 S Napoleon Ave 57328 605-946-5475
Vern DeGeest, supt. Fax 946-5607
www.corsica.k12.sd.us
Corsica HS 100/9-12
120 S Napoleon Ave 57328 605-946-5475
Scott Muckey, prin. Fax 946-5607
Corsica MS 50/6-8
120 S Napoleon Ave 57328 605-946-5475
Vern DeGeest, prin. Fax 946-5607

---

Dakota Christian S 100/PK-12
37614 SD Highway 44 57328 605-243-2211
Donald Mitchell, admin. Fax 243-2379

**Custer, Custer, Pop. 2,043**
Custer SD 16-1 700/PK-12
527 Montgomery St 57730 605-673-3154
Mark Naugle, supt. Fax 673-5607
www.csd.k12.sd.us
Custer JSHS 300/7-12
1645 Wild Cat Ln 57730 605-673-4473
Derek Barrios, prin. Fax 673-4710

**Dell Rapids, Minnehaha, Pop. 3,605**
Dell Rapids SD 49-3 900/K-12
1216 N Garfield Ave 57022 605-428-5473
Summer Schultz, supt. Fax 428-5609
dr-k12.org
Dell Rapids HS 300/9-12
1216 N Garfield Ave 57022 605-428-5473
Kimberly Kludt, prin. Fax 428-5609
Dell Rapids MS 300/5-8
1216 N Garfield Ave 57022 605-428-5473
Fran Ruesink, prin. Fax 428-5609

---

St. Mary HS 100/7-12
812 N State Ave 57022 605-428-5591
Casey Michel, prin. Fax 428-5377

**De Smet, Kingsbury, Pop. 1,084**
De Smet SD 38-2 300/K-12
PO Box 157 57231 605-854-3423
Jim Altenburg, admin. Fax 854-9138
www.desmet.k12.sd.us
De Smet HS 100/9-12
PO Box 157 57231 605-854-3423
Jim Altenburg, prin. Fax 854-9138
De Smet MS 100/6-8
PO Box 157 57231 605-854-3423
Jim Altenburg, prin. Fax 854-9138

**Dewey, Custer**
Elk Mountain SD 16-2 50/K-12
10222 Valley Rd 57735 605-749-2258
Susan Ostenson M.Ed., admin. Fax 749-2258
Elk Mountain S 50/K-12
10222 Valley Rd 57735 605-749-2258
Susan Ostenson M.Ed., admin. Fax 749-2258

**Doland, Spink, Pop. 180**
Doland SD 56-2 100/K-12
PO Box 385 57436 605-635-6302
Jim Hulscher, supt. Fax 635-6504
www.doland.k12.sd.us/
Doland HS 50/9-12
PO Box 385 57436 605-635-6241
Jim Hulscher, prin. Fax 635-6504
Doland JHS 50/7-8
PO Box 385 57436 605-635-6241
Jim Hulscher, prin. Fax 635-6504

**Dupree, Ziebach, Pop. 511**
Dupree SD 64-2 300/PK-12
PO Box 10 57623 605-365-5140
Brian Shanks, supt. Fax 365-5514
www.dupree.k12.sd.us
Dupree HS 100/9-12
PO Box 10 57623 605-365-5140
Pandi Pittman, prin. Fax 365-5514
Dupree JHS 50/7-8
PO Box 10 57623 605-365-5140
Pandi Pittman, prin. Fax 365-5514

**Eagle Butte, Dewey, Pop. 1,279**
Eagle Butte SD 20-1 300/K-12
PO Box 260 57625 605-964-4911
Carol Veit, supt. Fax 964-4912
www.c-eb.com/
Eagle Butte HS 50/9-12
PO Box 672 57625 605-964-8744
Dora Gwin, prin. Fax 964-8700
Eagle Butte JHS 50/7-8
PO Box 672 57625 605-964-7841
Dr. Kathie Bowker, prin. Fax 964-1224
E.A.G.L.E. Center 50/Alt
PO Box 672 57625 605-964-8773
Dr. Vicki Birkeland, prin. Fax 964-1218

**Edgemont, Fall River, Pop. 746**
Edgemont SD 23-1 200/K-12
PO Box 29 57735 605-662-7294
Dave Cortney, supt. Fax 662-7721
edgemont.k12.sd.us
Edgemont HS 50/9-12
PO Box 29 57735 605-662-7254
Dave Cortney, admin. Fax 662-7721

**Elk Point, Union, Pop. 1,939**
Elk Point-Jefferson SD 61-7 600/PK-12
PO Box 578 57025 605-356-5950
Sheri Hardman, supt. Fax 356-5953
www.epj.k12.sd.us
Elk Point-Jefferson HS 200/9-12
PO Box 578 57025 605-356-5900
Travis Aslesen, prin. Fax 356-5999
Elk Point-Jefferson MS 100/6-8
PO Box 578 57025 605-356-5900
Travis Aslesen, prin. Fax 356-5999

**Elkton, Brookings, Pop. 721**
Elkton SD 5-3 300/PK-12
PO Box 190 57026 605-542-2541
Brian Jandahl, supt. Fax 542-4441
elkton.k12.sd.us
Elkton HS 100/9-12
PO Box 190 57026 605-542-2541
Kelly Neill, prin. Fax 542-4441
Elkton JHS 50/7-8
PO Box 190 57026 605-542-2541
Kelly Neill, prin. Fax 542-4441

**Ellsworth AFB, Meade, Pop. 7,017**

---

National American University Post-Sec.
1000 Ellsworth St Ste 2400B 57706 605-718-6550

**Emery, Hanson, Pop. 443**
Bridgewater-Emery SD 30-3
Supt. — See Bridgewater
Bridgewater-Emery HS 100/9-12
130 N 6th St 57332 605-449-4271
Christena Schultz, prin. Fax 449-4270

**Estelline, Hamlin, Pop. 763**
Estelline SD 28-2 200/K-12
PO Box 306 57234 605-873-2201
Patrick Kraning, supt. Fax 873-2102
www.estelline.k12.sd.us
Estelline HS 100/7-12
PO Box 306 57234 605-873-2201
Patrick Kraning, prin. Fax 873-2102
Estelline JHS 7-8
PO Box 306 57234 605-873-2203
Justin Pitts, prin. Fax 873-2102

**Ethan, Davison, Pop. 328**
Ethan SD 17-1 200/PK-12
PO Box 169 57334 605-227-4211
Terry Eckstaine, supt. Fax 227-4236
www.ethan.k12.sd.us/
Ethan HS 100/9-12
PO Box 169 57334 605-227-4211
Tim Hawkins, prin. Fax 227-4236
Ethan JHS 50/7-8
PO Box 169 57334 605-227-4211
Tim Hawkins, prin. Fax 227-4236

**Eureka, McPherson, Pop. 856**
Eureka SD 44-1 100/PK-12
PO Box 10 57437 605-284-2875
Bo Beck, supt. Fax 284-2810
www.eureka.k12.sd.us/
Eureka HS 100/9-12
PO Box 10 57437 605-284-2521
Bo Beck, prin. Fax 284-2810
Eureka MS 50/6-8
PO Box 10 57437 605-284-2521
Bo Beck, prin. Fax 284-2810

**Faith, Meade, Pop. 405**
Faith SD 46-2 200/PK-12
PO Box 619 57626 605-967-2152
Kelly Daughters, supt. Fax 967-2153
www.faith.k12.sd.us/
Faith HS 100/9-12
PO Box 619 57626 605-967-2152
Kelly Daughters, supt. Fax 967-2153
Faith JHS 50/7-8
PO Box 619 57626 605-967-2152
Don Kraemer, supt. Fax 967-2153

**Faulkton, Faulk, Pop. 724**
Faulkton Area SD 24-4 300/K-12
PO Box 308 57438 605-598-6266
Joel Price, supt. Fax 598-6666
www.faulkton.k12.sd.us
Faulkton HS 100/9-12
PO Box 308 57438 605-598-6266
Craig Cassens, prin. Fax 598-6666
Faulkton JHS 50/7-8
PO Box 308 57438 605-598-6266
Craig Cassens, prin. Fax 598-6666

**Flandreau, Moody, Pop. 2,264**
Flandreau SD 50-3 600/K-12
600 W Community Dr 57028 605-997-3263
Rick Weber, supt. Fax 997-2457
www.flandreau.k12.sd.us
Flandreau HS 200/9-12
600 W Community Dr 57028 605-997-2455
Ross Rollinger, prin. Fax 997-2457
Flandreau MS 100/6-8
700 W Community Dr 57028 605-997-2705
Brian Relf, prin. Fax 997-2457

**Florence, Codington, Pop. 370**
Florence SD 14-1 200/PK-12
PO Box 66 57235 605-758-2412
Gary Leighton, supt. Fax 758-2433
www.florence.k12.sd.us/
Florence HS 100/9-12
PO Box 66 57235 605-758-2412
Gary Leighton, prin. Fax 758-2433
Florence JHS 50/7-8
PO Box 66 57235 605-758-2412
Gary Leighton, prin. Fax 758-2433

**Forestburg, Sanborn, Pop. 70**
Sanborn Central SD 55-5 200/PK-12
40405 SD Highway 34 57314 605-495-4183
Linda Whitney, supt. Fax 495-4185
www.sanborncentral.com/
Sanborn Central HS 100/9-12
40405 SD Highway 34 57314 605-495-4183
Linda Whitney, prin. Fax 495-4185
Sanborn Central MS 50/6-8
40405 SD Highway 34 57314 605-495-4183
Connie Vermeulen, prin. Fax 495-4185

**Fort Pierre, Stanley, Pop. 2,009**
Stanley County SD 57-1 300/K-12
PO Box 370 57532 605-223-7741
Dan Martin, supt. Fax 223-7750
www.stanleycounty.k12.sd.us
Stanley County MSHS 100/6-12
PO Box 370 57532 605-223-7743
Thomas O'Boyle M.S., prin. Fax 223-7751

**Frederick, Brown, Pop. 197**
Frederick Area SD 6-2 200/PK-12
PO Box 486 57441 605-329-2145
Beverly Myer, supt. Fax 329-2722
www.frederickarea.k12.sd.us/
Frederick HS 100/9-12
PO Box 486 57441 605-329-2145
Justin Downes, prin. Fax 329-2722
Frederick JHS 50/7-8
PO Box 486 57441 605-329-2145
Justin Downes, prin. Fax 329-2722

**Freeman, Hutchinson, Pop. 1,290**
Freeman SD 33-1 300/PK-12
PO Box 220 57029 605-925-4214
Don Hotchkiss, supt. Fax 925-4814
www.freeman.k12.sd.us
Freeman HS 100/9-12
PO Box 220 57029 605-925-4214
Tim Hansen, prin. Fax 925-4814
Freeman JHS 50/7-8
PO Box 220 57029 605-925-4214
Tim Hansen, prin. Fax 925-4814

---

Freeman Academy 100/1-12
PO Box 1000 57029 605-925-4237
Katie Minster, prin. Fax 925-4271

**Garretson, Minnehaha, Pop. 1,155**
Garretson SD 49-4 600/PK-12
PO Box C 57030 605-594-3451
Guy Johnson, supt. Fax 594-3443
www.garretson.k12.sd.us/
Garretson HS 200/9-12
PO Box C 57030 605-594-3452
Chris Long, prin. Fax 594-3443
Garretson MS 100/6-8
PO Box C 57030 605-594-3452
Chris Long, prin. Fax 594-3443

**Gayville, Yankton, Pop. 403**
Gayville-Volin SD 63-1 200/K-12
PO Box 158 57031 605-267-4476
Jason Selchert, supt. Fax 267-4294
www.gayvillevolin.k12.sd.us/
Gayville-Volin HS 100/9-12
PO Box 158 57031 605-267-4476
Tom Rice, prin. Fax 267-4294
Gayville-Volin MS 50/7-8
PO Box 158 57031 605-267-4476
Tom Rice, prin. Fax 267-4294

**Gettysburg, Potter, Pop. 1,150**
Gettysburg SD 53-1 200/K-12
100 E King Ave 57442 605-765-2436
Tim Hagedorn, supt. Fax 765-2249
www.gettysburg.k12.sd.us/
Gettysburg HS 100/9-12
100 E King Ave 57442 605-765-2436
Wendy Smith, prin. Fax 765-2249
Gettysburg JHS 50/7-8
100 E King Ave 57442 605-765-2436
Wendy Smith, prin. Fax 765-2249

**Gregory, Gregory, Pop. 1,270**
Gregory SD 26-4 400/K-12
PO Box 438 57533 605-835-9651
Sara Klein, supt. Fax 835-8146
www.gregory.k12.sd.us/
Gregory HS 100/9-12
PO Box 438 57533 605-835-9672
Jeff Determan, prin. Fax 835-8146
Gregory JHS 100/7-8
PO Box 438 57533 605-835-8771
Jeff Determan, prin. Fax 835-8744

**Groton, Brown, Pop. 1,444**
Groton Area SD 6-6 600/PK-12
PO Box 410 57445 605-397-2351
Joe Schwan, supt. Fax 397-8453
www.grotonarea.com/
Groton HS 200/9-12
PO Box 410 57445 605-397-8381
Anna Schwan, prin. Fax 397-8453
Groton MS 100/6-8
PO Box 410 57445 605-397-8381
Anna Schwan, prin. Fax 397-8453

**Harrisburg, Lincoln, Pop. 4,018**
Harrisburg SD 41-2 2,400/PK-12
PO Box 187 57032 605-743-2567
James Holbeck, supt. Fax 743-2569
www.harrisburg.k12.sd.us
Harrisburg HS 500/9-12
PO Box 339 57032 605-743-2567
Kevin Lein, prin. Fax 743-9040
Harrisburg South MS 500/6-8
PO Box 309 57032 605-743-2567
Darren Ellwein, prin. Fax 743-5630
Other Schools – See Sioux Falls

**Hartford, Minnehaha, Pop. 2,498**
West Central SD 49-7 1,300/PK-12
PO Box 730 57033 605-528-3217
Dr. Jeff Danielsen, supt. Fax 528-3219
www.westcentral.k12.sd.us/
West Central HS 400/9-12
PO Box 730 57033 605-528-6236
Melinda Jensen, prin. Fax 528-6217
West Central MS 300/6-8
PO Box 730 57033 605-528-3799
Mark Rockafellow, prin. Fax 528-3702

**Hayti, Hamlin, Pop. 381**
Hamlin SD 28-3 700/PK-12
44577 188th St 57241 605-783-3631
Joel Jorgenson, supt. Fax 783-3632
www.hamlin.k12.sd.us/
Hamlin HS 200/9-12
44577 188th St 57241 605-783-3644
Jeff Sheehan, prin. Fax 783-3360
Hamlin MS 100/6-8
44577 188th St 57241 605-783-3644
Jeff Sheehan, prin. Fax 783-3632

**Henry, Codington, Pop. 264**
Henry SD 14-2 200/K-12
PO Box 8 57243 605-532-5364
Steve Zirbel, supt. Fax 532-3795
www.henry.k12.sd.us/
Henry HS 100/9-12
PO Box 8 57243 605-532-5364
Philip Schonebaum, prin. Fax 532-3795
Henry MS 50/5-8
PO Box 8 57243 605-532-5364
Philip Schonebaum, prin. Fax 532-3795

**Herreid, Campbell, Pop. 436**
Herreid SD 10-1 100/K-12
PO Box 276 57632 605-437-2263
Jeff Kosters, supt. Fax 437-2264
herreid.k12.sd.us
Herreid HS 50/9-12
PO Box 276 57632 605-437-2263
Jeff Kosters, supt. Fax 437-2264
Herreid MS 50/6-8
PO Box 276 57632 605-437-2263
Jeff Kosters, supt. Fax 437-2264

**Highmore, Hyde, Pop. 788**
Highmore-Harrold SD 34-2 300/PK-12
PO Box 416 57345 605-852-2275
Chip Sundberg, supt. Fax 852-2295
www.highmore.k12.sd.us
Highmore HS 100/9-12
PO Box 416 57345 605-852-2275
Quinton Cermak M.Ed., prin. Fax 852-2295
Highmore JHS 50/7-8
PO Box 416 57345 605-852-2275
Quinton Cermak M.Ed., prin. Fax 852-2295

**Hill City, Pennington, Pop. 926**
Hill City SD 51-2 500/PK-12
PO Box 659 57745 605-574-3030
Mike Hanson, supt. Fax 574-3031
hillcity.sd.schoolwebpages.com
Hill City HS 100/9-12
PO Box 659 57745 605-574-3000
Todd Satter, prin. Fax 574-3040
Hill City MS 100/6-8
PO Box 659 57745 605-574-3032
Blake Gardner, prin. Fax 574-3044

**Hot Springs, Fall River, Pop. 3,587**
Hot Springs SD 23-2 900/PK-12
1609 University Ave 57747 605-745-4145
Danielle Root, supt. Fax 745-4178
www.hssd.k12.sd.us
Hot Springs HS 300/9-12
1609 University Ave 57747 605-745-4147
Mary Weiss, prin. Fax 745-4166
Hot Springs MS 200/6-8
1609 University Ave 57747 605-745-4146
Liz Baker, prin. Fax 745-6389

**Hoven, Potter, Pop. 401**
Hoven SD 53-2 100/PK-12
PO Box 128 57450 605-948-2252
Dr. Pat Jones, supt. Fax 948-2477
www.hoven.k12.sd.us/
Hoven HS 50/9-12
PO Box 128 57450 605-948-2252
Dr. Pat Jones, prin. Fax 948-2477
Hoven JHS 50/7-8
PO Box 128 57450 605-948-2252
Dr. Pat Jones, prin. Fax 948-2477

**Howard, Miner, Pop. 846**
Howard SD 48-3 400/PK-12
500 N Section Line St 57349 605-772-5515
Mike Cullen, supt. Fax 772-5516
www.howard.k12.sd.us/
Howard HS 100/9-12
500 N Section Line St 57349 605-772-5515
Mike Cullen, prin. Fax 772-5516
Howard JHS 50/7-8
500 N Section Line St 57349 605-772-5515
Mike Cullen, prin. Fax 772-5516

**Hurley, Turner, Pop. 413**
Viborg-Hurley SD 60-6
Supt. — See Viborg
Viborg-Hurley MS 50/5-8
PO Box 278 57036 605-238-5221
Amy Brandriet, prin. Fax 238-5223

**Huron, Beadle, Pop. 12,413**
Huron SD 2-2 1,800/K-12
PO Box 949 57350 605-353-6990
Terry Nebelsick Ed.D., supt. Fax 353-6994
www.huron.k12.sd.us
Huron HS 700/9-12
PO Box 949 57350 605-353-7800
Demetria Moon, prin. Fax 353-7807
Huron MS 600/6-8
PO Box 949 57350 605-353-6900
Michael Taplett, prin. Fax 353-6913

---

James Valley Christian S 200/PK-12
1550 Dakota Ave N 57350 605-352-7737
Brian Held, admin. Fax 352-9893

**Ipswich, Edmunds, Pop. 945**
Ipswich SD 22-6 400/PK-12
PO Box 306 57451 605-426-6571
Trent Osborne, supt. Fax 426-6029
www.ipswich.k12.sd.us
Ipswich HS 100/9-12
PO Box 306 57451 605-426-6571
Trent Osborne, prin. Fax 426-6029
Ipswich MS 100/6-8
PO Box 306 57451 605-426-6571
Mathew Pollock, prin. Fax 426-6029

**Irene, Yankton, Pop. 419**
Irene-Wakonda SD 13-3 300/PK-12
PO Box 5 57037 605-263-3311
David Hutchison, supt. Fax 263-3316
www.irene-wakonda.k12.sd.us/
Irene-Wakonda JSHS 100/7-12
PO Box 5 57037 605-263-3313
Bruce Bailey, prin. Fax 263-3316

**Iroquois, Kingsbury, Pop. 263**
Iroquois SD 2-3 200/PK-12
PO Box 98 57353 605-546-2210
Mike Ruth, supt. Fax 546-8540
www.iroquois.k12.sd.us/
Iroquois HS 50/9-12
PO Box 98 57353 605-546-2426
Rick Soma, prin. Fax 546-8540
Iroquois MS 50/6-8
PO Box 98 57353 605-546-2426
Rick Soma, prin. Fax 546-8540

**Kadoka, Jackson, Pop. 622**
Kadoka Area SD 35-2 400/PK-12
PO Box 99 57543 605-837-2175
Jamie Hermann, supt. Fax 837-2176
kadoka.k12.sd.us/
Kadoka HS 100/9-12
PO Box 99 57543 605-837-2172
George Seiler, prin. Fax 837-2176

**Kennebec, Lyman, Pop. 232**
Lyman SD 42-1
Supt. — See Presho
Lyman MS 100/6-8
PO Box 188 57544 605-869-2213
Rene Lillebo, prin. Fax 869-2283

**Kimball, Brule, Pop. 698**
Kimball SD 7-2 200/PK-12
PO Box 479 57355 605-778-6232
Jeff Rieckman, supt. Fax 778-6393
www.kimball.k12.sd.us
Grass Ranch HS 50/9-12
PO Box 479 57355 605-778-6231
Erik Sommervold, prin. Fax 778-6393
Kimball HS 100/9-12
PO Box 479 57355 605-778-6232
Erik Sommervold, prin. Fax 778-6393
Kimball MS 50/5-8
PO Box 479 57355 605-778-6231
Erik Sommervold, prin. Fax 778-6393

**Kyle, Shannon, Pop. 840**

---

Oglala Lakota College Post-Sec.
PO Box 490 57752 605-455-6000

**Lake Andes, Charles Mix, Pop. 832**
Andes Central SD 11-1 400/PK-12
PO Box 40 57356 605-487-7671
Debera Lucas, supt. Fax 487-7051
www.andescentral.k12.sd.us/
Andes Central HS 100/9-12
PO Box 40 57356 605-487-7671
Rocky Brinkman, prin. Fax 487-7051
Andes Central JHS 50/7-8
PO Box 40 57356 605-487-7671
Rocky Brinkman, prin. Fax 487-7051

**Lake Preston, Kingsbury, Pop. 595**
Lake Preston SD 38-3 200/K-12
300 1st St NE 57249 605-847-4455
Tim Casper, supt. Fax 847-4311
www.lakepreston.k12.sd.us
Lake Preston HS 100/9-12
300 1st St NE 57249 605-847-4455
Tim Casper, prin. Fax 847-4311
Lake Preston JHS 50/7-8
300 1st St NE 57249 605-847-4455
Tim Casper, prin. Fax 847-4311

**Langford, Marshall, Pop. 312**
Langford SD 45-5 200/PK-12
PO Box 127 57454 605-493-6454
Monte Nipp, supt. Fax 493-6447
www.langford.k12.sd.us/
Langford HS 100/9-12
PO Box 127 57454 605-493-6454
Toni Brown, prin. Fax 493-6447
Langford MS 50/6-8
PO Box 127 57454 605-493-6454
Toni Brown, prin. Fax 493-6447

**Lead, Lawrence, Pop. 3,058**
Lead-Deadwood SD 40-1 — 900/PK-12
320 S Main St 57754 — 605-717-3890
Dr. Dan Leikvold, supt. — Fax 717-2813
www.lead-deadwood.k12.sd.us/
Lead-Deadwood HS — 300/9-12
320 S Main St 57754 — 605-717-3899
Tony Biesiot, prin. — Fax 717-2815
Lead-Deadwood MS — 200/6-8
234 S Main St 57754 — 605-717-3898
Jay Beagle, prin. — Fax 717-2821
Other Schools – See Nemo

**Lemmon, Perkins, Pop. 1,211**
Lemmon SD 52-4 — 300/PK-12
209 3rd St W 57638 — 605-374-3762
Rick Herbel, supt. — Fax 374-3562
www.lemmon.k12.sd.us
Lemmon HS — 100/9-12
209 3rd St W 57638 — 605-374-3762
Rick Herbel, prin. — Fax 374-3562
Lemmon JHS — 50/7-8
209 3rd St W 57638 — 605-374-3784
Rick Herbel, prin. — Fax 374-3562

**Lennox, Lincoln, Pop. 2,100**
Lennox SD 41-4 — 1,000/PK-12
PO Box 38 57039 — 605-647-2203
Kirk Easton, supt. — Fax 647-2201
www.lennox.k12.sd.us
Lennox HS — 300/9-12
PO Box 38 57039 — 605-647-2203
Tim Raabe, prin. — Fax 647-6045
Lennox MS — 200/6-8
PO Box 38 57039 — 605-647-2203
Chad Allison, prin. — Fax 647-2502

**Leola, McPherson, Pop. 451**
Leola SD 44-2 — 200/K-12
PO Box 350 57456 — 605-439-3477
Brian Heupel, supt. — Fax 439-3206
www.leola.k12.sd.us/
Leola HS — 50/9-12
PO Box 350 57456 — 605-439-3477
Beverly Myer, prin. — Fax 439-3206
Leola JHS — 50/6-8
PO Box 350 57456 — 605-439-3477
Beverly Myer, prin. — Fax 439-3206

**Mc Intosh, Corson, Pop. 167**
Mc Intosh SD 15-1 — 200/PK-12
PO Box 80 57641 — 605-273-4298
Rob Davis, supt. — Fax 273-4531
www.mcintosh.k12.sd.us/
Mc Intosh HS — 50/9-12
PO Box 80 57641 — 605-273-4298
Rob Davis, prin. — Fax 273-4531
Mc Intosh JHS — 50/7-8
PO Box 80 57641 — 605-273-4298
Rob Davis, prin. — Fax 273-4531

**Mc Laughlin, Corson, Pop. 634**
Mc Laughlin SD 15-2 — 400/PK-12
PO Box 880 57642 — 605-823-4484
Scott Lepke, supt. — Fax 823-4886
www.mclaughlin.k12.sd.us
McLaughlin HS — 100/9-12
PO Box 880 57642 — 605-823-4484
Fax 823-4481
McLaughlin MS — 100/6-8
PO Box 880 57642 — 605-823-4484
Fax 823-4481

**Madison, Lake, Pop. 6,389**
Madison Central SD 39-2 — 1,100/K-12
800 NE 9th St 57042 — 605-256-7700
Vincent Schaefer, supt. — Fax 256-7711
www.madison.k12.sd.us
Madison HS — 300/9-12
800 NE 9th St 57042 — 605-256-7706
Adam Shaw, prin. — Fax 256-7711
Madison MS — 300/6-8
830 NE 9th St 57042 — 605-256-7717
Cotton Koch, prin. — Fax 256-7728

---

Dakota State University — Post-Sec.
820 N Washington Ave 57042 — 605-256-5111

**Marion, Turner, Pop. 780**
Marion SD 60-3 — 200/PK-12
PO Box 207 57043 — 605-648-3615
E. David Colberg, supt. — Fax 648-3652
marion.k12.sd.us
Marion HS — 100/9-12
PO Box 207 57043 — 605-648-3615
Michelle Larson, prin. — Fax 648-3617
Marion MS — 50/6-8
PO Box 207 57043 — 605-648-3615
Michelle Larson, prin. — Fax 648-3617

**Martin, Bennett, Pop. 986**
Bennett County SD 3-1 — 500/PK-12
PO Box 580 57551 — 605-685-6697
Stacy Halverson, supt. — Fax 685-6694
www.bennettco.k12.sd.us/
Bennett County HS — 200/9-12
PO Box 580 57551 — 605-685-6330
Nicholas Redden, prin. — Fax 685-6935
Bennett County JHS — 100/7-8
PO Box 580 57551 — 605-685-6343
Belinda Ready, prin. — Fax 685-6935

**Mellette, Spink, Pop. 205**
Northwestern Area SD 56-7 — 300/PK-12
221 3rd St 57461 — 605-887-3467
Ryan Bruns, supt. — Fax 887-3101
www.northwestern.k12.sd.us
Northwestern HS — 100/9-12
221 3rd St 57461 — 605-887-3467
Richard Osborn, prin. — Fax 887-3101
Northwestern MS — 100/6-8
221 3rd St 57461 — 605-887-3467
Richard Osborn, prin. — Fax 887-3101

**Menno, Hutchinson, Pop. 603**
Menno SD 33-2 — 300/PK-12
PO Box 346 57045 — 605-387-5161
Dr. Chris Christensen, supt. — Fax 387-5171
www.menno.k12.sd.us/
Menno HS — 100/9-12
PO Box 346 57045 — 605-387-5161
Dr. Chris Christensen, prin. — Fax 387-5171
Menno MS — 50/6-8
PO Box 346 57045 — 605-387-5161
Dr. Charlene Crosswait, prin. — Fax 387-5171

**Milbank, Grant, Pop. 3,335**
Milbank SD 25-4 — 900/K-12
1001 E Park Ave 57252 — 605-432-5579
Tim Graf, supt. — Fax 432-4137
www.milbankschooldistrict.com
Milbank HS — 300/9-12
1001 E Park Ave 57252 — 605-432-5546
Dan Snaza, prin. — Fax 432-5514
Milbank MS — 200/6-8
1001 E Park Ave 57252 — 605-432-5519
Kristopher Evje, dean — Fax 432-4137

**Miller, Hand, Pop. 1,475**
Miller SD 29-4 — 400/PK-12
PO Box 257 57362 — 605-853-2614
Dan Trefz, supt. — Fax 853-3041
www.miller.k12.sd.us/
Miller HS — 100/9-12
PO Box 257 57362 — 605-853-2455
Steve Schumacher, prin. — Fax 853-3041
Miller JHS — 100/7-8
PO Box 257 57362 — 605-853-2455
Steve Schumacher, prin. — Fax 853-3041

---

Sunshine Bible Academy — 100/K-12
400 Sunshine Dr 57362 — 605-853-3071
Jason Watson, supt. — Fax 853-3072

**Mission, Todd, Pop. 1,157**
Todd County SD 66-1 — 1,900/K-12
PO Box 87 57555 — 605-856-3501
Dr. Karen Whitney, supt. — Fax 856-2449
www.tcsdk12.org/
Todd County HS — 500/9-12
PO Box 726 57555 — 605-856-3503
Cheryl Whirlwind Soldier, prin. — Fax 856-4723
Todd County MS — 400/6-8
PO Box 248 57555 — 605-856-3504
Linda Bordeaux, prin. — Fax 856-2032

---

Sinte Gleska University — Post-Sec.
PO Box 105 57555 — 605-856-5880

**Mitchell, Davison, Pop. 15,009**
Hanson SD 30-1
Supt. — See Alexandria
Hanson Colony Alternative HS — Alt
41659 256th St 57301 — 605-239-4387
Ray Slaba, prin. — Fax 239-4293

Mitchell SD 17-2 — 2,600/K-12
821 N Capital St 57301 — 605-995-3010
Dr. Joseph Graves, supt. — Fax 995-3089
www.mitchell.k12.sd.us
Mitchell Career & Technical Educ Academy — 9-12
821 N Capital St 57301 — 605-995-7533
Denise Hoffman, dir. — Fax 995-3099
Mitchell HS — 800/9-12
920 N Capital St 57301 — 605-995-3034
Joe Childs, prin. — Fax 995-3047
Mitchell MS — 500/6-8
800 W 10th Ave 57301 — 605-995-3051
Justin Zajic, prin. — Fax 995-3037
Mitchell Technical Institute — Vo/Tech
1800 E Spruce St 57301 — 800-684-1969
Greg Von Wald, pres. — Fax 995-3083
Second Chance HS — 100/Alt
821 N Capital St 57301 — 605-995-7509
Shane Thill, dir. — Fax 995-8099

---

Dakota Wesleyan University — Post-Sec.
1200 W University Ave 57301 — 605-995-2600
Mitchell Christian S — 200/PK-12
805 W 18th Ave 57301 — 605-996-8861
Dr. Gary Cookson, admin. — Fax 996-3642
Mitchell Technical Institute — Post-Sec.
1800 E Spruce St 57301 — 800-684-1969
Queen of Peace Hospital — Post-Sec.
5th & Foster 57301 — 605-995-2250

**Mobridge, Walworth, Pop. 3,357**
Mobridge-Pollock SD 62-6 — 700/PK-12
1107 1st Ave E 57601 — 605-845-9200
Tim Frederick, supt. — Fax 845-3455
www.mobridge-pollock.k12.sd.us/
Mobridge-Pollock HS — 200/9-12
1107 1st Ave E 57601 — 605-845-9200
Joe Lenz, prin. — Fax 845-3455
Mobridge-Pollock MS — 200/6-8
1107 1st Ave E 57601 — 605-845-9200
Joe Lenz, prin. — Fax 845-3455

**Montrose, McCook, Pop. 466**
Montrose SD 43-2 — 200/K-12
309 S Church Ave 57048 — 605-363-5025
Lonny Johnson, supt. — Fax 363-3513
www.montroseschool.k12.sd.us
Montrose HS — 50/9-12
309 S Church Ave 57048 — 605-363-5025
Lonny Johnson, prin. — Fax 363-3513
Montrose JHS — 50/6-8
309 S Church Ave 57048 — 605-363-5025
Sam Jacobs, prin. — Fax 363-3513

**Mount Vernon, Davison, Pop. 457**
Mount Vernon SD 17-3 — 300/PK-12
PO Box 46 57363 — 605-236-5237
Patrick Mikkonen, supt. — Fax 236-5604
www.mtvernon.k12.sd.us
Mount Vernon HS — 100/9-12
PO Box 46 57363 — 605-236-5237
Patrick Mikkonen, prin. — Fax 236-5604
Mount Vernon MS — 100/6-8
PO Box 46 57363 — 605-236-5237
Margaret Freidel, prin. — Fax 236-5604

**Murdo, Jones, Pop. 476**
Jones County SD 37-3 — 100/PK-12
PO Box 109 57559 — 605-669-2297
Lorrie Esmay, supt. — Fax 669-3248
jonesco.k12.sd.us
Jones County HS — 100/9-12
PO Box 109 57559 — 605-669-2258
JayTee Sealey, prin. — Fax 669-2904
Jones County MS — 50/7-8
PO Box 109 57559 — 605-669-2258
JayTee Sealey, prin. — Fax 669-2904

**Nemo, Lawrence**
Lead-Deadwood SD 40-1
Supt. — See Lead
Career & Technical Education Campus — Vo/Tech
PO Box 110 57759 — 605-578-2371
Bonnie Fuller, dir. — Fax 578-1157

**Newell, Butte, Pop. 575**
Newell SD 9-2 — 300/PK-12
PO Box 99 57760 — 605-456-2393
Joel Hovland, supt. — Fax 456-2395
www.newell.k12.sd.us
Newell HS — 100/9-12
PO Box 99 57760 — 605-456-2393
Joel Hovland, prin. — Fax 456-2395
Newell MS — 100/6-8
PO Box 99 57760 — 605-456-0102
Barb Paulson, prin. — Fax 456-2395

**New Underwood, Pennington, Pop. 640**
New Underwood SD 51-3 — 300/K-12
PO Box 128 57761 — 605-754-6485
George Seiler, supt. — Fax 754-6492
newunderwood.k12.sd.us
New Underwood HS — 100/9-12
PO Box 128 57761 — 605-754-6485
Peggy Petersen, prin. — Fax 754-6492
New Underwood JHS — 50/7-8
PO Box 128 57761 — 605-754-6485
Peggy Petersen, prin. — Fax 754-6492

**North Sioux City, Union, Pop. 2,476**
Dakota Valley SD 61-8 — 900/K-12
1150 Northshore Dr 57049 — 605-422-3800
Al Leber, supt. — Fax 422-3807
www.dakotavalley.k12.sd.us/
Dakota Valley HS — 300/9-12
1150 Northshore Dr 57049 — 605-422-3820
Dr. Jerry Rasmussen, prin. — Fax 422-3827
Dakota Valley MS — 200/5-8
1150 Northshore Dr 57049 — 605-422-3830
Harlan Halverson, prin. — Fax 422-3837

**Oelrichs, Fall River, Pop. 123**
Oelrichs SD 23-3 — 100/K-12
PO Box 65 57763 — 605-535-2631
LuAnn Werdel, supt. — Fax 535-2046
www.oelrichs.k12.sd.us/
Oelrichs HS — 100/9-12
PO Box 65 57763 — 605-535-2631
Fax 535-2046
Oelrichs JHS — 50/7-8
PO Box 65 57763 — 605-535-2631
Fax 535-2046

**Onida, Sully, Pop. 643**
Agar-Blunt-Onida SD 58-3 — 300/K-12
PO Box 205 57564 — 605-258-2618
Kevin Pickner, supt. — Fax 258-2361
www.abo.k12.sd.us
Sully Buttes HS — 100/9-12
PO Box 205 57564 — 605-258-2618
Jeremy Chicoine, prin. — Fax 258-2361
Sully Buttes JHS — 50/7-8
PO Box 205 57564 — 605-258-2618
Jeremy Chicoine, prin. — Fax 258-2361

**Parker, Turner, Pop. 1,005**
Parker SD 60-4 — 300/K-12
PO Box 517 57053 — 605-297-3456
Dr. Donavan DeBoer, supt. — Fax 297-4381
parker.k12.sd.us
Parker HS — 100/9-12
PO Box 517 57053 — 605-297-3456
Bill Leberman, prin. — Fax 297-4381
Parker JHS — 50/7-8
PO Box 517 57053 — 605-297-3456
Bill Leberman, prin. — Fax 297-4381

**Parkston, Hutchinson, Pop. 1,496**
Parkston SD 33-3 — 600/PK-12
102C S Chapman Dr 57366 — 605-928-3368
Shayne McIntosh, supt. — Fax 928-7284
www.parkston.k12.sd.us
Parkston HS — 200/9-12
102A S Chapman Dr 57366 — 605-928-3368
Joseph Kollmann, prin. — Fax 928-4032
Parkston JHS — 100/7-8
102A S Chapman Dr 57366 — 605-928-3368
Joseph Kollmann, prin. — Fax 928-4032

**Philip, Haakon, Pop. 760**
Haakon SD 27-1 — 300/PK-12
PO Box 730 57567 — 605-859-2679
Keven Morehart, supt. — Fax 859-3005
www.philip.k12.sd.us
Philip HS — 100/9-12
PO Box 730 57567 — 605-859-2680
Mandie Menzel, prin. — Fax 859-3550
Philip MS — 50/7-8
PO Box 730 57567 — 605-859-2680
Mandie Menzel, prin. — Fax 859-3550

**Pierre, Hughes, Pop. 13,369**
Pierre SD 32-2 2,500/PK-12
211 S Poplar Ave 57501 605-773-7300
Dr. Kelly Glodt, supt. Fax 773-7304
www.pierre.k12.sd.us
Morse MS 600/6-8
309 E Capitol Ave 57501 605-773-7330
Dr. Kyley Cumbow, prin. Fax 773-7338
Riggs HS 800/9-12
1010 E Broadway Ave 57501 605-773-7350
Kevin Mutchelknaus, prin. Fax 773-7360

**Pine Ridge, Shannon, Pop. 3,284**
Oglala Lakota County SD 65-1
Supt. — See Batesland
Wolf Creek Upper ES 200/5-8
PO Box 469 57770 605-867-5174
Darrell Eagle Bull, prin. Fax 867-5067

---

Red Cloud Indian S 200/PK-12
100 Mission Dr 57770 605-867-5888
Bob Brave Heart, supt. Fax 867-2528

**Plankinton, Aurora, Pop. 706**
Plankinton SD 1-1 300/PK-12
PO Box 190 57368 605-942-7743
Steve Randall, supt. Fax 942-7453
www.plankinton.k12.sd.us
Plankinton HS 100/9-12
PO Box 190 57368 605-942-7743
Steve Randall, admin. Fax 942-7453
Plankinton JHS 50/7-8
PO Box 190 57368 605-942-7743
Steve Randall, admin. Fax 942-7453

**Platte, Charles Mix, Pop. 1,219**
Platte-Geddes SD 11-5 400/PK-12
PO Box 140 57369 605-337-3391
Joel Bailey, supt. Fax 337-2549
www.platte-geddes.k12.sd.us/
Platte HS 100/9-12
PO Box 140 57369 605-337-3391
Steve Randall, prin. Fax 337-2549
Platte JHS 50/7-8
PO Box 140 57369 605-337-3391
Steve Randall, prin. Fax 337-2549

**Porcupine, Shannon, Pop. 1,058**
Oglala Lakota County SD 65-1
Supt. — See Batesland
Rockyford Upper ES 200/5-8
HC 49 Box 175 57772 605-455-6300
Monica Whirlwind Horse, prin. Fax 455-2091

**Presho, Lyman, Pop. 489**
Lyman SD 42-1 400/PK-12
PO Box 1000 57568 605-895-2579
Lynn Vlasman, supt. Fax 895-2216
www.lyman.k12.sd.us/
Lyman HS 100/9-12
PO Box 1000 57568 605-895-2579
Jon Boer, prin. Fax 895-2216
Other Schools – See Kennebec

**Ramona, Lake, Pop. 174**
Oldham-Ramona SD 39-5 100/PK-12
PO Box 8 57054 605-482-8244
Tom Ludens, supt. Fax 482-8282
www.oldhamramona.k12.sd.us
Oldham-Ramona HS 50/9-12
PO Box 8 57054 605-482-8244
Tom Ludens, prin. Fax 482-8282
Oldham-Ramona JHS 50/7-8
PO Box 8 57054 605-482-8244
Tom Ludens, prin. Fax 482-8282
Other Schools – See Arlington

**Rapid City, Pennington, Pop. 65,557**
Rapid City Area SD 51-4 13,200/PK-12
300 6th St 57701 605-394-4031
Dr. Timothy Mitchell, supt. Fax 394-2514
www.rcas.org
Central HS 2,000/9-12
433 N Mount Rushmore Rd 57701 605-394-4023
Mike Talley, prin. Fax 355-3041
East MS 700/6-8
4860 Homestead St 57703 605-394-4092
Scott Phares, prin. Fax 394-6935
North MS 500/6-8
1501 N Maple Ave 57701 605-394-4042
Danny Janklow, prin. Fax 394-6120
Rapid City HS 500/Alt
601 Columbus St 57701 605-394-4048
Deb Steele, prin. Fax 394-6941
South MS 700/6-8
2 Indiana St 57701 605-394-4024
Larry Stevens, prin. Fax 394-5834
Southwest MS 500/6-8
4501 Park Dr 57702 605-394-6792
Jackie Talley, prin. Fax 355-3095
Stevens HS 1,600/9-12
4215 Raider Rd 57702 605-394-4051
John Julius, prin. Fax 394-1820
West MS 600/6-8
1003 Soo San Dr 57702 605-394-4033
Doug Foley, prin. Fax 394-1889

---

Black Hills Beauty College Post-Sec.
623 Saint Joseph St 57701 605-342-0697
Black Hills Lutheran S 50/6-12
PO Box 3034 57709 605-721-0760
Lacey Hoogland, admin.
National American University Post-Sec.
5301 S Highway 16 57701 605-394-4800
Rapid City Christian HS 100/6-12
23757 Arena Dr 57702 605-341-3377
Julie Hewitt, admin. Fax 341-2248
Rapid City Regional Hospital Post-Sec.
353 Fairmont Blvd 57701 605-341-8100
St. Thomas More HS 300/9-12
300 Fairmont Blvd 57701 605-343-8484
Wayne Sullivan, prin. Fax 343-1315
St. Thomas More MS 200/6-8
424 Fairmont Blvd 57701 605-348-1477
Keiz Shultz, prin. Fax 342-4367
South Dakota School Mines and Technology Post-Sec.
501 E Saint Joseph St 57701 605-394-2511
Western Dakota Technical Institute Post-Sec.
800 Mickelson Dr 57703 605-394-4034

**Redfield, Spink, Pop. 2,312**
Redfield SD 56-4 600/PK-12
PO Box 560 57469 605-472-4520
Shad Storley, supt. Fax 472-4525
www.redfield.k12.sd.us
Mickelson Alternative Program 50/Alt
PO Box 560 57469 605-472-4520
Brenda Stover, prin. Fax 472-4525
Redfield HS 200/9-12
PO Box 560 57469 605-472-4520
Rob Lewis, prin. Fax 472-4525
Redfield JHS 100/7-8
PO Box 560 57469 605-472-4520
Rob Lewis, prin. Fax 472-4525

**Revillo, Grant, Pop. 117**
Grant-Deuel SD 25-3 100/PK-12
16370 482nd Ave 57259 605-623-4241
Allen W. Stewart M.Ed., supt. Fax 623-4215
www.grant-deuel.k12.sd.us/
Grant-Deuel HS 100/9-12
16370 482nd Ave 57259 605-623-4241
Allen W. Stewart M.Ed., supt. Fax 623-4215
Grant-Deuel JHS 50/6-8
16370 482nd Ave 57259 605-623-4241
Allen W. Stewart M.Ed., supt. Fax 623-4215

**Roscoe, Edmunds, Pop. 323**
Edmunds Central SD 22-5 100/PK-12
PO Box 317 57471 605-287-4251
Shawn Yates, supt. Fax 287-4813
www.echs.k12.sd.us/
Edmunds Central HS 50/9-12
PO Box 317 57471 605-287-4251
Shawn Yates, prin. Fax 287-4813
Edmunds Central MS 50/6-8
PO Box 317 57471 605-287-4251
Shawn Yates, prin. Fax 287-4813

**Rosholt, Roberts, Pop. 406**
Rosholt SD 54-4 200/PK-12
PO Box 106 57260 605-537-4283
Teresa Appel, supt. Fax 537-4285
www.rosholt.k12.sd.us/
Rosholt HS 100/9-12
PO Box 106 57260 605-537-4278
Teresa Appel, prin. Fax 537-4285
Rosholt JHS 50/7-8
PO Box 106 57260 605-537-4278
Teresa Appel, prin. Fax 537-4285

**Rutland, Lake**
Rutland SD 39-4 100/PK-12
102 School St 57057 605-586-4352
Dr. Carl Fahrenwald, supt. Fax 586-4343
www.rutland.k12.sd.us
Rutland HS 50/9-12
102 School St 57057 605-586-4352
Carl Fahrenwald, supt. Fax 586-4343
Rutland JHS 50/7-8
102 School St 57057 605-586-4352
Kathleen Trower, lead tchr. Fax 586-4343

**Salem, McCook, Pop. 1,343**
McCook Central SD 43-7 400/PK-12
PO Box 310 57058 605-425-2264
Dr. Dan Swartos, supt. Fax 425-2079
www.mccookcentral.k12.sd.us/
McCook Central HS 100/9-12
PO Box 310 57058 605-425-2264
Brad Seamer, prin. Fax 425-2079
McCook Central MS 100/5-8
PO Box 310 57058 605-425-2264
Brad Seamer, prin. Fax 425-2079

**Scotland, Bon Homme, Pop. 830**
Scotland SD 4-3 300/PK-12
711 4th St 57059 605-583-2237
Damon Alvey, supt. Fax 583-2239
www.scotland.k12.sd.us
Scotland HS 100/9-12
711 4th St 57059 605-583-2237
Chris McGregor, prin. Fax 583-2239
Scotland MS 100/6-8
711 4th St 57059 605-583-2237
Chris McGregor, prin. Fax 583-2239

**Selby, Walworth, Pop. 634**
Selby Area SD 62-5 200/PK-12
PO Box 324 57472 605-649-7818
Darrel McFarland, supt. Fax 649-7282
www.selby.k12.sd.us/
Selby Area HS 50/9-12
PO Box 324 57472 605-649-7818
Yvette Houck, prin. Fax 649-7282
Selby Area JHS 50/7-8
PO Box 324 57472 605-649-7818
Yvette Houck, prin. Fax 649-7282

**Sioux Falls, Minnehaha, Pop. 150,371**
Harrisburg SD 41-2
Supt. — See Harrisburg
Harrisburg North MS 6-8
2201 W 95th St 57108 605-743-2567
Tim Koehler, prin. Fax 275-9140

Sioux Falls SD 49-5 22,200/PK-12
201 E 38th St 57105 605-367-7900
Dr. Brian Maher, supt. Fax 367-4637
www.sf.k12.sd.us
Axtell Park S 400/Alt
201 N West Ave 57104 605-367-7647
Erika Paladino-Hazlett, admin. Fax 367-8326
Career and Technical Education Academy Vo/Tech
4700 W Career Cir 57107 605-367-5504
Jim Kayl, prin. Fax 367-5508
Edison MS 800/6-8
2101 S West Ave 57105 605-367-7643
Steve Griffith, prin. Fax 367-8457
Henry MS 1,100/6-8
2200 S 5th Ave 57105 605-367-7639
Darryl Walker, prin. Fax 367-7693
Lincoln HS 2,000/9-12
2900 S Cliff Ave 57105 605-367-7990
Val Fox, prin. Fax 367-8492
McGovern MS 700/6-8
6221 W Maple St 57107 605-367-4440
LaVonna Emanuel, prin. Fax 367-4434
Memorial MS 1,000/6-8
1401 S Sertoma Ave 57106 605-362-2785
Carrie Aaron, prin. Fax 362-2790
Roosevelt HS 2,000/9-12
6600 W 41st St 57106 605-362-2860
Tim Hazlett, prin. Fax 362-2883
MS Immersion Center 50/Alt
6221 W Maple St 57107 605-367-4440
LaVonna Emanuel, prin. Fax 367-4434
Sioux Falls New Technology HS 200/9-12
2205 N Career Ave 57107 605-367-5850
Dolly Ellwein, prin. Fax 367-5852
Washington HS 2,100/9-12
501 N Sycamore Ave 57110 605-367-7970
James Nold, prin. Fax 367-8494
Whittier MS 900/6-8
930 E 6th St 57103 605-367-7620
Twaine Fink, prin. Fax 367-8357

---

Augustana College Post-Sec.
2001 S Summit Ave 57197 605-274-0770
Globe University Post-Sec.
5101 S Broadband Ln 57108 605-977-0705
Kilian Community College Post-Sec.
300 E 6th St 57103 605-221-3100
Lutheran HS of Sioux Falls 50/9-12
5000 S Western Ave 57108 605-275-2024
Derek Bult, prin. Fax 275-2034
McKennan Hospital Post-Sec.
800 E 21st St 57105 605-339-8113
National American University Post-Sec.
5801 S Corporate Pl 57108 605-336-4600
O'Gorman HS 700/9-12
3201 S Kiwanis Ave 57105 605-336-3644
Kyle Groos, prin. Fax 336-9272
O'Gorman JHS 400/7-8
3100 W 41st St 57105 605-988-0546
Wade Charron, prin. Fax 336-9839
Sioux Falls Christian S 400/PK-12
6120 S Charger Cir 57108 605-334-1422
Jay Woudstra, supt. Fax 334-6928
Sioux Falls Seminary Post-Sec.
2100 S Summit Ave 57105 605-336-6588
Sioux Valley Hospital Post-Sec.
PO Box 5039 57117 605-333-6424
South Dakota School for the Deaf Post-Sec.
2001 E 8th St 57103 605-367-5200
Southeast Technical Institute Post-Sec.
2320 N Career Ave 57107 605-367-7624
Stewart School Post-Sec.
604 N West Ave 57104 605-336-2775
University of Sioux Falls Post-Sec.
1101 W 22nd St 57105 605-331-5000

**Sisseton, Roberts, Pop. 2,369**
Sisseton SD 54-2 1,000/K-12
516 8th Ave W 57262 605-698-7613
Dr. Stephen Schulte, supt. Fax 698-3032
www.sisseton.k12.sd.us/
Sisseton HS 300/9-12
516 8th Ave W 57262 605-698-7613
Jim Frederick, prin. Fax 698-7353
Sisseton MS 200/6-8
516 8th Ave W 57262 605-698-7613
Tammy Meyer, prin. Fax 698-7487

---

Sisseton-Wahpeton College Post-Sec.
PO Box 689 57262 605-698-3966

**Spearfish, Lawrence, Pop. 10,283**
Spearfish SD 40-2 2,000/PK-12
525 E Illinois St 57783 605-717-1201
Dave Peters, supt. Fax 717-1200
www.spearfish.k12.sd.us
Spearfish HS 600/9-12
525 E Illinois St 57783 605-717-1212
Steve Morford, prin. Fax 717-1211
Spearfish MS 400/6-8
525 E Illinois St 57783 605-717-1215
Don Lyon, prin. Fax 717-1252

---

Black Hills State University Post-Sec.
1200 University St 57799 605-642-6011

**Stickney, Aurora, Pop. 284**
Stickney SD 1-2 100/PK-12
PO Box 67 57375 605-732-4221
Robert Krietlow, supt. Fax 732-4281
www.stickney.k12.sd.us/
Stickney HS 50/9-12
PO Box 67 57375 605-732-4221
Robert Krietlow, prin. Fax 732-4281
Stickney JHS 50/7-8
PO Box 67 57375 605-732-4221
Robert Krietlow, prin. Fax 732-4281

**Sturgis, Meade, Pop. 6,462**
Meade SD 46-1 2,500/K-12
1230 Douglas St 57785 605-347-2523
Don Kirkegaard, supt. Fax 347-0005
meade.k12.sd.us
Sturgis Brown HS 700/9-12
12930 SD Highway 34 57785 605-347-2686
Jeff Simmons, prin. Fax 347-0225
Sturgis Williams MS 500/6-8
1425 Cedar St 57785 605-347-5232
Lonny Harter, prin. Fax 720-0190
Other Schools – See Union Center

**Summit, Roberts, Pop. 270**
Summit SD 54-6 200/PK-12
PO Box 791 57266 605-398-6211
Kurt Jensen, supt. Fax 398-6311
www.summit.k12.sd.us
Summit HS 50/9-12
PO Box 791 57266 605-398-6211
Kurt Jensen, prin. Fax 398-6311

**Tabor, Bon Homme, Pop. 415**
Bon Homme SD 4-2
Supt. — See Tyndall
Hutterische Colony Alternative HS Alt
31232 Colony Rd 57063 605-589-3387
Cory Lambley, prin. Fax 589-3468

**Tea, Lincoln, Pop. 3,745**
Tea Area SD 41-5 1,500/K-12
PO Box 488 57064 605-498-2700
Jennifer Lowery, supt. Fax 498-2702
www.teaschools.k12.sd.us/
Tea Area HS 300/9-12
PO Box 488 57064 605-498-2700
Collin Knudson, prin. Fax 498-0280
Tea Area MS 300/6-8
PO Box 488 57064 605-498-2700
Chris Fechner, prin. Fax 498-0280

**Timber Lake, Dewey, Pop. 419**
Timber Lake SD 20-3 300/K-12
PO Box 1000 57656 605-865-3654
Jarod Larson, supt. Fax 865-3294
www.tls.new.rschooltoday.com
Timber Lake HS 100/9-12
PO Box 1000 57656 605-865-3654
Julie Marshall, prin. Fax 865-3294
Timber Lake MS 100/6-8
PO Box 1000 57656 605-865-3654
Julie Marshall, prin. Fax 865-3294

**Tripp, Hutchinson, Pop. 645**
Tripp-Delmont SD 33-5 200/PK-12
PO Box 430 57376 605-935-6766
Gail Swenson, supt. Fax 935-6507
www.tridel.k12.sd.us/
Tripp-Delmont HS 50/9-12
PO Box 430 57376 605-935-6766
Gail Swenson, prin. Fax 935-6507

**Tulare, Spink, Pop. 205**
Hitchcock-Tulare SD 56-6 200/PK-12
PO Box 108 57476 605-266-2151
Jeff Clark, supt. Fax 266-2160
www.hitchcock-tulare.k12.sd.us/
Hitchcock-Tulare HS 100/9-12
PO Box 108 57476 605-596-4171
Bill Barrie, prin. Fax 596-4150
Hitchcock-Tulare JHS 50/7-8
PO Box 108 57476 605-596-4171
Bill Barrie, prin. Fax 596-4150

**Tyndall, Bon Homme, Pop. 1,060**
Bon Homme SD 4-2 600/PK-12
PO Box 28 57066 605-589-3388
Dr. Mike Elsberry, supt. Fax 589-3468
www.bonhomme.k12.sd.us/
Bon Homme HS 200/9-12
PO Box 28 57066 605-589-3387
Cory Lambley, prin. Fax 589-3468
Bon Homme MS 100/6-8
PO Box 28 57066 605-589-3387
cory lambley, prin. Fax 589-3468
Other Schools – See Tabor

**Union Center, Meade**
Meade SD 46-1
Supt. — See Sturgis
Union Center S 50/6-8
1700 SD Highway 34 57787 605-269-2264
Bev Rosenboom, prin. Fax 269-2099

**Vermillion, Clay, Pop. 10,331**
Vermillion SD 13-1 1,200/PK-12
17 Prospect St 57069 605-677-7000
Dr. Mark Froke, supt. Fax 677-7002
www.vermillion.k12.sd.us
Vermillion Area Alternative Education Alt
840 E Cherry St 57069 605-677-7000
Terri Trumm, dir.
Vermillion HS 400/9-12
1001 E Main St 57069 605-677-7035
Curt Cameron, prin. Fax 677-7042
Vermillion MS 300/6-8
422 Princeton St 57069 605-677-7025
Pat Anderson, prin. Fax 677-7028

---

University of South Dakota Post-Sec.
414 E Clark St 57069 605-677-5011

**Viborg, Turner, Pop. 777**
Viborg-Hurley SD 60-6 200/PK-12
PO Box 397 57070 605-766-5418
Rob Sylliaasen, supt. Fax 766-5635
www.viborg-hurley.k12.sd.us
Viborg-Hurley HS 100/9-12
PO Box 397 57070 605-766-5418
Brett Mellem, prin. Fax 766-5635
Other Schools – See Hurley

**Volga, Brookings, Pop. 1,762**
Sioux Valley SD 5-5 600/PK-12
PO Box 278 57071 605-627-5657
Thomas Oster, supt. Fax 627-5291
www.svs.k12.sd.us/
Sioux Valley HS 200/9-12
PO Box 278 57071 605-627-5657
Belinda Miller, prin. Fax 627-5291
Sioux Valley MS 100/6-8
PO Box 278 57071 605-627-5657
Belinda Miller, prin. Fax 627-5291

**Wagner, Charles Mix, Pop. 1,520**
Wagner Community SD 11-4 900/PK-12
101 Walnut Ave SW 57380 605-384-3677
Linda Foos, supt. Fax 384-3678
www.wagner.k12.sd.us/
Wagner HS 200/9-12
101 Walnut Ave SW 57380 605-384-5426
Neil Goter, prin. Fax 384-3200
Wagner MS 200/5-8
101 Walnut Ave SW 57380 605-384-3913
Steve Petry, prin. Fax 384-3678

**Wakpala, Corson**
Smee SD 15-3 200/PK-12
PO Box B 57658 605-845-3040
Greg East, supt. Fax 845-7244
www.smee.k12.sd.us
Wakpala HS 100/9-12
PO Box B 57658 605-845-3040
Curtis Huffman, prin. Fax 845-7244
Wakpala MS 50/6-8
PO Box B 57658 605-845-3040
Curtis Huffman, prin. Fax 845-7244

**Wall, Pennington, Pop. 739**
Wall SD 51-5 200/K-12
PO Box 414 57790 605-279-2156
Cooper Garnos, supt. Fax 279-2613
www.wall.k12.sd.us
Wall HS 100/9-12
PO Box 414 57790 605-279-2156
Cooper Garnos, prin. Fax 279-2613
Wall MS 50/7-8
PO Box 414 57790 605-279-2156
Cooper Garnos, prin. Fax 279-2613

**Warner, Brown, Pop. 453**
Warner SD 6-5 300/K-12
PO Box 20 57479 605-225-6397
Michael Kroll, supt. Fax 225-0007
www.warner.k12.sd.us/
Warner HS 100/9-12
PO Box 20 57479 605-225-6194
Lori Enright, prin. Fax 225-0007
Warner MS 100/6-8
PO Box 20 57479 605-225-6194
Lori Enright, prin. Fax 225-0007

**Watertown, Codington, Pop. 21,216**
Northeast Technical HSD
1311 3rd Ave NE 57201 605-882-6380
Bert Falak, dir. Fax 882-6381
northeasttechnicalhighschool.k12.sd.us
Northeast Technical HS Vo/Tech
1311 3rd Ave NE 57201 605-882-6380
Bert Falak, dir. Fax 882-6381

Watertown SD 14-4 3,800/PK-12
PO Box 730 57201 605-882-6312
Dr. Lesli Jutting, supt. Fax 882-6327
www.watertown.k12.sd.us/
Watertown HS 1,100/9-12
200 9th St NE 57201 605-882-6316
Dr. Michael Butts, prin. Fax 882-6327
Watertown MS 600/7-8
1700 11th St NE 57201 605-882-6370
Dr. Todd Brist, prin. Fax 886-6372

---

Great Plains Lutheran HS 100/9-12
1200 Luther Ln NE 57201 605-886-0672
Rev. David Maertz, pres. Fax 882-9089
Lake Area Technical Institute Post-Sec.
PO Box 730 57201 605-882-5284

**Waubay, Day, Pop. 561**
Waubay SD 18-3 200/PK-12
202 W School Rd 57273 605-947-4529
Dean Jones M.A., supt. Fax 947-4243
www.waubay.k12.sd.us/
Waubay HS 100/9-12
202 W School Rd 57273 605-947-4529
Dean Jones M.A., prin. Fax 947-4243
Waubay MS 50/6-8
202 W School Rd 57273 605-947-4529
Dean Jones M.A., prin. Fax 947-4243

**Waverly, Codington, Pop. 37**
Waverly SD 14-5 200/PK-12
319 Mary Pl, 605-886-9174
John Bjorkman, supt. Fax 886-6630
www.waverly.k12.sd.us
Waverly/South Shore HS 100/9-12
319 Mary Pl, 605-886-9174
John Bjorkman, prin. Fax 886-6630
Waverly/South Shore MS 100/6-8
319 Mary Pl, 605-886-9174
John Bjorkman, prin. Fax 886-6630

**Webster, Day, Pop. 1,853**
Webster Area SD 18-4 500/PK-12
102 E 9th Ave 57274 605-345-3548
Dr. James Block, supt. Fax 345-4421
www.webster.k12.sd.us/
Webster Area HS 200/9-12
102 E 9th Ave 57274 605-345-4653
James Block, prin. Fax 345-4421
Webster Area MS 100/6-8
102 E 9th Ave 57274 605-345-4651
Craig Case, prin. Fax 345-4421

**Wessington Springs, Jerauld, Pop. 954**
Wessington Springs SD 36-2 300/PK-12
PO Box 449 57382 605-539-9391
Lance Witte, supt. Fax 539-1029
www.wessingtonsprings.k12.sd.us
Spring Valley HS 50/9-12
PO Box 449 57382 605-539-9687
Jason Kolousek, prin. Fax 539-1029
Wessington Springs HS 100/9-12
PO Box 449 57382 605-539-9391
Jason Kolousek, prin. Fax 539-1029
Wessington Springs JHS 50/7-8
PO Box 449 57382 605-539-9311
Jason Kolousek, prin. Fax 539-1029

**White, Brookings, Pop. 482**
Deubrook Area SD 5-6 300/K-12
PO Box 346 57276 605-629-1100
Kevin Keenaghan, supt. Fax 629-3701
www.deubrook.com
Deubrook JSHS 100/7-12
PO Box 346 57276 605-629-1114
Paul Nepodal, prin. Fax 629-3701

**White Lake, Aurora, Pop. 368**
White Lake SD 1-3 100/PK-12
PO Box 246 57383 605-249-2251
Robert Schroeder, supt. Fax 249-2725
www.whitelake.k12.sd.us/
White Lake HS 50/9-12
PO Box 246 57383 605-249-2251
Robert Schroeder, prin. Fax 249-2725
White Lake JHS 50/7-8
PO Box 246 57383 605-249-2251
Robert Schroeder, prin. Fax 249-2725

**White River, Mellette, Pop. 529**
White River SD 47-1 400/PK-12
PO Box 273 57579 605-259-3311
Thomas Cameron, supt. Fax 259-3133
www.whiteriver.k12.sd.us/
White River HS 100/9-12
PO Box 273 57579 605-259-3135
David Colberg, prin. Fax 259-3133
White River MS 100/6-8
PO Box 273 57579 605-259-3135
Kendra Becker, prin. Fax 259-3133

**Willow Lake, Clark, Pop. 262**
Willow Lake SD 12-3 200/PK-12
PO Box 170 57278 605-625-5945
Scott Klaudt, supt. Fax 625-3103
www.willowlake.k12.sd.us
Willow Lake HS 50/9-12
PO Box 170 57278 605-625-5945
Hector Serna, prin. Fax 625-3103
Willow Lake MS 50/6-8
PO Box 170 57278 605-625-5945
Hector Serna, prin. Fax 625-3103
Other Schools – See Carpenter

**Wilmot, Roberts, Pop. 481**
Wilmot SD 54-7 200/PK-12
PO Box 100 57279 605-938-4647
Larry Hulscher, supt. Fax 938-4185
www.wilmot.k12.sd.us
Wilmot HS 100/9-12
PO Box 100 57279 605-938-4647
Larry Hulscher, prin. Fax 938-4185
Wilmot MS 50/6-8
PO Box 100 57279 605-938-4647
Mike Schmidt, prin. Fax 938-4185

**Winner, Tripp, Pop. 2,819**
Winner SD 59-2 500/K-12
PO Box 231 57580 605-842-8101
Bruce Carrier, supt. Fax 842-8120
www.winner.k12.sd.us
Winner MSHS 200/6-12
PO Box 231 57580 605-842-8125
Gerald Witte, prin. Fax 842-8121

**Wolsey, Beadle, Pop. 376**
Wolsey-Wessington SD 2-6 300/K-12
375 Ash St SE 57384 605-883-4221
James Cutshaw, supt. Fax 883-4720
www.wolsey-wessington.k12.sd.us
Wolsey-Wessington HS 100/9-12
375 Ash St SE 57384 605-883-4221
James Cutshaw, prin. Fax 883-4720
Wolsey-Wessington MS 100/6-8
375 Ash St SE 57384 605-883-4221
Carol Rowen, prin. Fax 883-4720

**Woonsocket, Sanborn, Pop. 652**
Woonsocket SD 55-4 200/PK-12
PO Box 428 57385 605-796-4431
Dr. Rodrick Weber, supt. Fax 796-4352
www.woonsocket.k12.sd.us/
Woonsocket HS 50/9-12
PO Box 428 57385 605-796-4431
Dr. Rodrick Weber, prin. Fax 796-4352

**Yankton, Yankton, Pop. 14,259**
Yankton SD 63-3 2,700/PK-12
PO Box 738 57078 605-665-3998
Dr. Wayne Kindle, supt. Fax 665-1422
www.ysd.k12.sd.us
Alternative Learning Center Alt
PO Box 738 57078 605-665-2073
Dr. Jennifer Johnke, prin. Fax 655-5948
Yankton HS 900/9-12
PO Box 738 57078 605-665-2073
Dr. Jennifer Johnke, prin. Fax 655-5948
Yankton MS 600/6-8
PO Box 738 57078 605-665-2419
Todd Dvoracek, prin. Fax 665-6239

---

Mt. Marty College Post-Sec.
1105 W 8th St 57078 605-668-1545
Sacred Heart Hospital Post-Sec.
501 Summit St 57078 605-655-9371
Sacred Heart MS 5-8
504 Capitol St 57078 605-665-1808
Dr. Tim Mulhair, prin. Fax 260-9787

# TENNESSEE

## TENNESSEE DEPARTMENT OF EDUCATION
**710 James Robertson Pkwy, Nashville 37243-1219**
**Telephone 615-741-2731**
**Fax 615-532-4791**
**Website http://www.state.tn.us/education**

Commissioner of Education Kevin Huffman

## TENNESSEE BOARD OF EDUCATION
**710 James Robertson Pkwy, Nashville 37243-1219**

Executive Director Dr. Gary Nixon

## PUBLIC, PRIVATE AND CATHOLIC SECONDARY SCHOOLS

**Adamsville, McNairy, Pop. 2,170**
McNairy County SD
Supt. — See Selmer
Adamsville JSHS 700/7-12
PO Box 407 38310 731-632-3273
Greg Martin, prin. Fax 632-3080

**Afton, Greene**
Greene County SD
Supt. — See Greeneville
Chuckey-Doak HS 700/9-12
365 Ripley Island Rd 37616 423-798-2636
Mike Garland, prin. Fax 639-5761
Chuckey Doak MS 400/6-8
120 Chuckey Doak Rd 37616 423-787-2038
Tim Shelton, prin. Fax 787-2096

**Alamo, Crockett, Pop. 2,420**
Crockett County SD 1,900/PK-12
102 N Cavalier Dr 38001 731-696-2604
Robert Mullins, supt. Fax 696-4734
www.ccschools.net
Crockett County HS 800/9-12
402 Highway 88 38001 731-696-4525
Jared Foust, prin. Fax 696-3124
Crockett County MS 600/6-8
497 N Cavalier Dr 38001 731-696-5583
Bobby McLaughlin, prin. Fax 696-2034

**Alcoa, Blount, Pop. 8,239**
Alcoa CSD 1,800/PK-12
524 Faraday St 37701 865-984-0531
Dr. Brian Bell, supt. Fax 984-5832
www.alcoaschools.net/
Alcoa HS 500/9-12
1205 Lodge St 37701 865-982-4631
Becky Stone, prin. Fax 380-2240
Alcoa MS 500/6-8
532 Faraday St 37701 865-982-5211
Dr. Scott Porter, prin. Fax 380-2533

**Algood, Putnam, Pop. 3,428**
Putnam County SD
Supt. — See Cookeville
Algood MS 800/PK-PK, 5-
540 Dry Valley Rd, Cookeville TN 38506
931-537-6141
Tim Martin, prin. Fax 537-3700

**Allardt, Fentress, Pop. 632**
Fentress County SD
Supt. — See Jamestown
Fentress County Adult HS Adult
220 Portland Ave 38504 931-752-8316
David Garrett, lead tchr. Fax 879-7428

**Altamont, Grundy, Pop. 1,042**
Grundy County SD 2,300/PK-12
PO Box 97 37301 931-692-3467
Dr. William Childers Ed.D., dir. Fax 692-2188
www.grundycoschools.com
Other Schools – See Coalmont

**Antioch, Davidson**
Metropolitan Nashville SD
Supt. — See Nashville
Antioch HS 1,900/9-12
1900 Hobson Pike 37013 615-641-5400
Dr. Adrienne Battle-Koger, prin. Fax 641-5422
Antioch MS 500/5-8
5050 Blue Hole Rd 37013 615-333-5642
Celia Conley, prin. Fax 333-5053
Apollo MS 500/5-8
631 Richards Rd 37013 615-333-5025
Shawn Lawrence, prin. Fax 333-5029
Cane Ridge HS 1,500/9-12
12848 Old Hickory Blvd 37013 615-687-4000
Michel Sanchez-Wall, prin. Fax 641-5007
Kennedy MS 900/5-8
2087 Hobson Pike 37013 615-501-7900
Dr. Sam Braden, prin.
Marshall MS, 5832 Pettus Rd 37013 900/5-8
Roderick Webb, prin. 615-941-7515
Academy at Hickory Hollow Adult
5248 Hickory Hollow Pkwy 37013 615-687-4028
Billy Fellman, prin.

---

Ezell-Harding Christian S 600/PK-12
574 Bell Rd 37013 615-367-0532
Ronnie Rummage, pres. Fax 399-8747
Jon Nave University of Cosmetology Post-Sec.
5510 Crossings Cir 37013 - -
Lighthouse Christian S 600/PK-12
5100 Blue Hole Rd 37013 615-331-6286
Brian Sweatt, hdmstr. Fax 331-2491

**Arlington, Shelby, Pop. 11,290**
Arlington Community SD K-12
5475 Airline Rd 38002 901-389-2497
Tamara Mason, supt. Fax 389-2498
www.acsk-12.org
Arlington HS 2,400/9-12
5475 Airline Rd 38002 901-867-1541
Chris Duncan, prin. Fax 867-1546
Arlington MS 1,100/6-8
5470 Lamb Rd 38002 901-867-6015
Dr. Allison Clark, prin. Fax 867-7080

Bartlett CSD
Supt. — See Bartlett
Bartlett Ninth Grade Academy 9-9
4734 Shadowlawn Rd 38002 901-373-2654
John McDonald, prin. Fax 373-1363

Shelby County SD
Supt. — See Memphis
Bolton HS 1,900/9-12
7323 Brunswick Rd 38002 901-873-8150
Chad Stevens, prin. Fax 829-2435

---

Macon Road Baptist S - East 400/K-12
11017 Highway 64 38002 901-867-8161

**Ashland City, Cheatham, Pop. 4,449**
Cheatham County SD 6,800/PK-12
102 Elizabeth St 37015 615-792-5664
Dr. Stan Curtis, dir. Fax 792-2551
www.cheathamcountyschools.net
Cheatham County Central HS 700/9-12
1 Cub Cir 37015 615-792-5641
Fax 792-2090
Cheatham MS 700/5-8
700 Scoutview Rd 37015 615-792-2334
Linda Owen, prin. Fax 792-2337
Cheatham County Adult HS Adult
102 Elizabeth St 37015 615-792-9287
Jo Jones, prin.
Other Schools – See Kingston Springs, Pleasant View

**Athens, McMinn, Pop. 13,106**
Athens CSD 1,600/PK-8
943 Crestway Dr 37303 423-745-2863
Robert Greene, dir. Fax 745-9041
www.athenscityschools.net
Athens City MS 500/6-8
200 Keith Ln 37303 423-745-1177
Michael Simmons, prin. Fax 745-9679

McMinn County SD 6,200/PK-12
3 S Hill St 37303 423-745-1612
Mickey Blevins Ed.D., supt. Fax 744-1641
www.mcminn.k12.tn.us
McMinn County Career Technical Center Vo/Tech
3 S Hill St 37303 423-745-1612
Mickey Blevins, prin. Fax 744-1641
McMinn County HS 1,500/9-12
2215 Congress Pkwy S 37303 423-745-4142
John Burroughs, prin. Fax 745-0584
Other Schools – See Englewood

---

Christ's Legacy Academy 100/K-12
964 County Road 180 37303 423-649-0040
Dr. Shane Arnold Ph.D., head sch
Fairview Christian Academy 100/PK-12
261 County Road 439 37303 423-745-6781
Greg Ranck, admin.
Liberty Christian S 100/K-12
PO Box 1555 37371 423-745-9248
Tennessee Technology Center at Athens Post-Sec.
PO Box 848 37371 423-744-2814

Tennessee Wesleyan College Post-Sec.
204 E College St 37303 423-745-7504

**Atwood, Carroll, Pop. 925**
West Carroll Special SD 1,000/PK-12
1415 State Route 77 38220 731-662-4200
Eric Williams, dir. Fax 662-4250
www.wcssd.org
West Carroll JSHS 500/7-12
760 State Route 77 38220 731-662-7116
Lex Suite, prin. Fax 662-4198

**Bartlett, Shelby, Pop. 53,815**
Bartlett CSD K-12
5650 Woodlawn St 38134 901-202-0855
David Stephens, supt. Fax 202-0854
www.bartlettschools.org
Appling MS 700/6-8
3700 Appling Rd 38133 901-373-1410
Dr. Keshia Newborn, prin. Fax 373-1360
Bartlett HS 1,700/10-12
5688 Woodlawn St 38134 901-373-2620
Tim Jones, prin. Fax 373-2624
Bon Lin MS 600/6-8
3862 N Germantown Rd 38133 901-347-1520
Cody Duncan, prin. Fax 347-1491
Elmore Park MS 600/6-8
6330 Althorne Rd 38134 901-373-2642
Ethan Randle, prin. Fax 373-1361
Other Schools – See Arlington

Shelby County SD
Supt. — See Memphis
Renaissance Academy Lakeside Alt
2911 Brunswick Rd 38133 901-377-4700
Tyria Butler, admin.

---

National College of Business & Tech Post-Sec.
5760 Stage Rd 38134 901-213-1681

**Baxter, Putnam, Pop. 1,354**
Putnam County SD
Supt. — See Cookeville
Upperman HS 700/PK-PK, 9-
6950 Nashville Hwy 38544 931-858-3112
Penny Nash, prin. Fax 858-4641
Upperman MS 5-8
6750 Nashville Hwy 38544 931-858-6601
Billy Stepp, admin. Fax 858-6637

**Bell Buckle, Bedford, Pop. 495**

---

Webb S 300/6-12
PO Box 488 37020 931-389-6003
Raymond Broadhead, head sch Fax 389-6657

**Benton, Polk, Pop. 1,374**
Polk County SD 2,700/PK-12
PO Box 665 37307 423-299-0471
James Jones, supt. Fax 338-2691
www.polk-schools.com
Chilhowee MS 400/6-8
PO Box 977 37307 423-338-3102
Connie Dunn, prin. Fax 338-3158
Polk County HS 600/9-12
PO Box 188 37307 423-299-0078
Jason Bell, prin. Fax 338-4521
Other Schools – See Copperhill

**Big Sandy, Benton, Pop. 553**
Benton County SD
Supt. — See Camden
Big Sandy S 300/K-12
13305 Highway 69A 38221 731-593-3221
Marty Caruthers, prin. Fax 593-3245

**Blountville, Sullivan, Pop. 3,052**
Sullivan County SD 10,000/PK-12
PO Box 306 37617 423-354-1000
Evelyn Rafalowski, supt. Fax 354-1004
www.sullivank12.net
Blountville MS 400/6-8
1651 Blountville Blvd 37617 423-354-1600
Michael Wilson, prin. Fax 354-1606

Holston MS 400/6-8
2348 Highway 75 37617 423-354-1500
Bill Miller, prin. Fax 354-1505
Sullivan Central HS 1,000/9-12
131 Shipley Ferry Rd 37617 423-354-1200
Mark Foster, prin. Fax 354-1206
Other Schools – See Bluff City, Bristol, Kingsport

---

Northeast State Community College Post-Sec.
PO Box 246 37617 423-323-3191
Tri-Cities Christian S 400/PK-12
1500 Highway 75 37617 423-323-7128

**Bluff City, Sullivan, Pop. 1,717**
Sullivan County SD
Supt. — See Blountville
Bluff City MS 400/6-8
337 Carter St 37618 423-354-1801
Greg Stallcup, prin. Fax 354-1818
Sullivan East HS 900/9-12
4180 Weaver Pike 37618 423-354-1900
Angie Buckles, prin. Fax 354-1906

**Bolivar, Hardeman, Pop. 5,360**
Hardeman County SD 4,200/PK-12
10815 Old Highway 64 38008 731-658-2510
Warner Ross, dir. Fax 658-2061
www.hardemancountyschools.org
Bolivar MS 400/6-8
915 Pruitt St 38008 731-658-3656
Mary Ann Polk, prin. Fax 658-6625
Central HS 800/9-12
313 Harris St 38008 731-658-3151
Fred Kessler, prin. Fax 658-6697
Other Schools – See Middleton

**Bradford, Gibson, Pop. 1,036**
Bradford Special SD 600/PK-12
PO Box 220 38316 731-742-3180
Dan Black, supt. Fax 742-3994
www.bradfordssd.schoolinsites.com
Bradford JSHS 200/7-12
136 Highway 45 S 38316 731-742-3729
Shane Paschall, prin. Fax 742-3088

**Brentwood, Williamson, Pop. 36,506**
Williamson County SD
Supt. — See Franklin
Brentwood HS 1,600/9-12
5304 Murray Ln 37027 615-472-4220
Kevin Keidel, prin. Fax 472-4241
Brentwood MS 1,200/6-8
5324 Murray Ln 37027 615-472-4250
Dr. Brandon Barkley, prin. Fax 472-4263
Ravenwood HS 1,900/9-12
1724 Wilson Pike 37027 615-472-4800
Dr. Pam Vaden, prin. Fax 472-4821
Sunset MS 800/6-8
200 Sunset Trl 37027 615-472-5040
Dr. Tim Brown, prin. Fax 472-5050
Woodland MS 800/6-8
1500 Volunteer Pkwy 37027 615-472-4930
Priscilla Fizer, prin. Fax 472-4941

---

Brentwood Academy 800/6-12
219 Granny White Pike 37027 615-373-0611
Curt Masters, hdmstr. Fax 377-3709
Currey Ingram Academy 300/K-12
6544 Murray Ln 37027 615-507-3242
Jeffrey Mitchell, head sch Fax 507-3170

**Brighton, Tipton, Pop. 2,690**
Tipton County SD
Supt. — See Covington
Brighton HS 1,500/9-12
8045 Highway 51 S 38011 901-837-5800
Christie Huffman, prin. Fax 837-5829
Brighton MS 1,100/6-8
7785 Highway 51 S 38011 901-837-5600
Sabrina Sneed-Mathews, prin. Fax 837-5625

**Bristol, Sullivan, Pop. 26,322**
Bristol CSD 4,000/PK-12
615 Martin Luther King Blvd 37620 423-652-9451
Dr. Gary Lilly, dir. Fax 652-9238
www.btcs.org
Tennessee HS 1,200/9-12
1112 Edgemont Ave 37620 423-652-9494
Mary Rouse, prin. Fax 652-9327
Vance MS 600/7-8
815 Edgemont Ave 37620 423-652-9449
Dr. Amy Scott, prin. Fax 652-9297

Sullivan County SD
Supt. — See Blountville
Holston Valley MS 200/6-8
1717 Bristol Caverns Hwy 37620 423-354-1880
Jess Lockhart, prin. Fax 354-1891

---

King University Post-Sec.
1350 King College Rd 37620 423-968-1187
National College of Business & Tech Post-Sec.
1328 Highway 11 W 37620 423-878-4440

**Brownsville, Haywood, Pop. 10,196**
Haywood County SD 2,700/PK-12
900 E Main St 38012 731-772-9613
Teresa Russell, dir. Fax 772-3275
www.haywoodschools.com
Haywood HS 1,000/9-12
1175 E College St 38012 731-772-1845
Dr. Jerry Pyron, prin. Fax 772-6079
Haywood JHS 500/6-8
1201 Haralson St 38012 731-772-3265
Yvette Blue, prin. Fax 772-3352

**Bruceton, Carroll, Pop. 1,455**
Hollow Rock-Bruceton Special SD 700/PK-12
29590 Broad St 38317 731-418-4180
David Duncan, supt. Fax 418-4188
www.hrbedu.org
Central HS, 29590 Broad St 38317 200/9-12
Tim Gilmer, prin. 731-418-4189
Central MS 200/6-8
29590 Broad St 38317 731-418-4167
Joe Norval, prin. Fax 418-4188

**Buchanan, Henry**
Henry County SD
Supt. — See Paris
Lakewood MS 300/6-8
6745 Highway 79 N Ste B 38222 731-644-1600
Mike Bell, prin. Fax 644-0680

**Byrdstown, Pickett, Pop. 803**
Pickett County SD 800/PK-12
141 Skyline Dr 38549 931-864-3123
Diane Elder, supt. Fax 864-7185
pickett.k12tn.net/
Pickett County HS 200/9-12
130 Skyline Dr 38549 931-864-3422
Jane Winningham, prin. Fax 864-6297

**Camden, Benton, Pop. 3,542**
Benton County SD 2,300/PK-12
197 Briarwood St 38320 731-584-6111
Mark Florence, supt. Fax 584-8142
www.bcos.org
Benton County Career/Technical Center Vo/Tech
155 Schools Dr 38320 731-584-4492
Dr. Randy Shannon, prin. Fax 584-1864
Camden Central HS 600/9-12
115 Schools Dr 38320 731-584-7254
Shawn McDowell, prin. Fax 584-2799
Camden JHS 400/6-8
75 Schools Dr 38320 731-584-4518
Michelle Leonard, prin. Fax 584-5958
Other Schools – See Big Sandy

**Carthage, Smith, Pop. 2,267**
Smith County SD 3,300/PK-12
126 Smith Co Middle Schl Ln 37030 615-735-9625
Barry Smith, dir. Fax 735-8271
boe.smithcounty.com/
Smith County HS 600/9-12
312 Fite Ave E 37030 615-735-9219
Jeanie Hix, prin. Fax 735-9049
Smith County MS 400/5-8
134 Smith Co Mid School Ln 37030 615-735-8277
Mike Lytle, prin. Fax 735-8255
Other Schools – See Gordonsville

**Cedar Hill, Robertson, Pop. 308**
Robertson County SD
Supt. — See Springfield
Byrns HS 500/6-12
7025 Highway 41 N 37032 615-696-2251
Doug Haskins, prin. Fax 696-0526

**Celina, Clay, Pop. 1,478**
Clay County SD 1,000/PK-12
PO Box 469 38551 931-243-3310
Jerry Strong, dir. Fax 243-3706
www.clayedu.com
Clay County HS 300/9-12
860 Clay County Hwy 38551 931-243-2340
Melissa White, prin. Fax 243-2376

**Centerville, Hickman, Pop. 3,602**
Hickman County SD 3,800/PK-12
115 Murphree Ave 37033 931-729-3391
Dr. Jerry Nash, dir. Fax 729-3834
www.hickmank12.org
Hickman County HS 600/9-12
1645 Bulldog Blvd 37033 931-729-2616
Philip Jacobs, prin. Fax 729-2925
Hickman County MS 400/6-8
1639 Bulldog Blvd 37033 931-729-4234
Jeremy Qualls, prin. Fax 729-5688
Other Schools – See Lyles

**Chapel Hill, Marshall, Pop. 1,427**
Marshall County SD
Supt. — See Lewisburg
Forrest MSHS 900/7-12
310 N Horton Pkwy 37034 931-246-4733
Davy McClaran, prin. Fax 246-4732

**Charleston, Bradley, Pop. 646**

---

Candies Creek Academy 100/K-12
294 Old Eureka Rd 37310 423-790-5660

**Charlotte, Dickson, Pop. 1,221**
Dickson County SD
Supt. — See Dickson
Charlotte MS 400/6-8
250 Humphries St 37036 615-740-6060
Ray Lecomte, prin. Fax 789-7033
Creek Wood HS 900/9-12
3499 Highway 47 N 37036 615-740-6000
Dr. Andrew Williams, prin. Fax 441-2868
New Directions Academy 100/Alt
4000 Highway 48 N 37036 615-740-6070
Karen Willey, prin. Fax 789-7032

**Chattanooga, Hamilton, Pop. 164,861**
Hamilton County SD 42,500/PK-12
3074 Hickory Valley Rd 37421 423-209-8400
Rick Smith, supt. Fax 209-8601
www.hcde.org
Brainerd HS 600/9-12
1020 N Moore Rd 37411 423-855-2615
Uras Agee, prin. Fax 855-2651
Chattanooga HS Center for Creative Arts 600/6-12
1301 Dallas Rd 37405 423-209-5929
Deborah Smith, prin. Fax 209-5930
Dalewood MS 300/6-8
1300 Shallowford Rd 37411 423-493-0323
Christian Earl, prin. Fax 493-0327
East Lake Academy of Fine Arts 400/6-8
2700 E 34th St 37407 423-493-0334
Lakesha Carson, prin. Fax 493-0343
East Ridge HS 800/9-12
4320 Bennett Rd 37412 423-867-6200
Tamera Helton, prin. Fax 867-6220
East Ridge MS 700/6-8
4400 Bennett Rd 37412 423-867-6214
Steven Robinson, prin. Fax 867-6226
Howard HS Vo/Tech
2500 S Market St 37408 423-209-5868
Zac Brown, prin. Fax 209-5869
Lookout Valley MSHS 400/6-12
350 Lookout High St 37419 423-825-7352
Derrick Rushworth, prin. Fax 821-7951
Middle College HS at Chattanooga State 100/10-12
4501 Amnicola Hwy 37406 423-697-4492
Dr. Sonja Rich, coord. Fax 697-2676
Normal Park Museum Magnet S 800/6-8
1219 W Mississippi Ave 37405 423-209-5900
Susan Kennedy, prin. Fax 209-5901
Orchard Knob MS 400/6-8
500 N Highland Park Ave 37404 423-493-7793
Crystal Sorrells, prin. Fax 493-7795
Red Bank HS 800/9-12
640 Morrison Springs Rd 37415 423-874-1900
Dr. Justin Robertson, prin. Fax 874-1924
Red Bank MS 600/6-8
3701 Tom Weathers Dr 37415 423-874-1908
John Pierce, prin. Fax 874-1938
STEM S Chattanooga 9-12
4501 Amnicola Hwy 37406 423-531-6270
Dr. Tony Donen, prin. Fax 531-6268
Tyner Academy 500/9-12
6836 Tyner Rd 37421 423-855-2635
Carol Goss, prin. Fax 855-9417
Tyner Middle Academy 500/6-8
6837 Tyner Rd 37421 423-855-2648
Mark Smith, prin. Fax 855-2699
Washington Alternative Learning Center 50/Alt
7821 Hancock Rd 37416 423-893-3520
Dr. Rodney Knox, prin. Fax 893-3521
Other Schools – See Harrison, Hixson, Ooltewah, Sale Creek, Signal Mountain, Soddy Daisy

---

Baylor S 1,100/6-12
171 Baylor School Rd 37405 423-267-8505
Scott Wilson, hdmstr. Fax 265-4276
Boyd-Buchanan S 900/PK-12
4650 Buccaneer Trl 37411 423-622-6177
Calvary Christian S 200/PK-12
4601 North Ter 37411 423-622-2181
Les Wallace, admin.
Chattanooga Christian S 1,100/K-12
3354 Charger Dr 37409 423-265-6411
Chad Dirkse, pres. Fax 756-4044
Chattanooga College Post-Sec.
248 Northgate Mall Dr 37415 423-624-0078
Chattanooga State Community College Post-Sec.
4501 Amnicola Hwy 37406 423-697-4400
Girls Preparatory S 600/6-12
PO Box 4736 37405 423-634-7600
Dr. Autumn Graves, head sch Fax 634-7643
Grace Baptist Academy 600/PK-12
7815 Shallowford Rd 37421 423-892-8224
Matt Pollock, hdmstr. Fax 892-1194
Hamilton Heights Christian Academy 100/9-12
2201 Hickory Valley Rd 37421 423-894-0597
Rev. Duke Stone, admin. Fax 894-4259
ITT Technical Institute Post-Sec.
5600 Brainerd Rd Ste G1 37411 423-510-6800
McCallie S 900/6-12
500 Dodds Ave 37404 423-624-8300
Lee Burns, hdmstr. Fax 493-5690
Miller-Motte Technical College Post-Sec.
6020 Shallowford Rd Ste 100 37421 423-510-9675
Notre Dame HS 400/9-12
2701 Vermont Ave 37404 423-624-4618
George Valadie, pres. Fax 624-4621
Silverdale Baptist Academy 1,000/PK-12
7236 Bonny Oaks Dr 37421 423-892-2319
Rebecca Hansard, hdmstr. Fax 648-7600
Tennessee Temple University Post-Sec.
1815 Union Ave 37404 800-553-4050
University of Tennessee Post-Sec.
615 McCallie Ave 37403 423-425-4111
Virginia College Post-Sec.
721 Eastgate Loop 37411 423-893-2000

**Christiana, Rutherford**
Rutherford County SD
Supt. — See Murfreesboro
Christiana MS 800/6-8
4675 Shelbyville Pike 37037 615-904-3885
Bob Horne, prin. Fax 904-3886

**Church Hill, Hawkins, Pop. 6,688**
Hawkins County SD
Supt. — See Rogersville
Church Hill MS 500/7-8
211 Oak St 37642 423-357-3051
Scott Jones, prin. Fax 357-9873
Volunteer HS 1,200/9-12
1050 Volunteer St 37642 423-357-3641
Bobby Wines, prin. Fax 357-6694

**Clarkrange, Fentress, Pop. 575**
Fentress County SD
Supt. — See Jamestown
Clarkrange HS 300/9-12
5801 S York Hwy 38553 931-863-3143
Marty Walker, prin. Fax 863-3981

**Clarksville, Montgomery, Pop. 126,966**
Clarksville-Montgomery County SD 30,200/PK-12
621 Gracey Ave 37040 931-648-5600
Dr. B.J. Worthington, supt. Fax 648-5612
www.cmcss.net
Alternative S Alt
430 Greenwood Ave 37040 931-542-5057
Kim Sigears, prin. Fax 503-3411
Clarksville HS 1,400/9-12
151 Richview Rd 37043 931-648-5690
Jean Luna, prin. Fax 648-5624
Kenwood HS 1,000/9-12
251 E Pine Mountain Rd 37042 931-905-7900
Hal Bedell, prin. Fax 905-7906
Kenwood MS 900/6-8
241 E Pine Mountain Rd 37042 931-553-2080
Evelyn Martinez, prin. Fax 552-3080
Middle College HS at APSU 100/9-12
PO Box 4654 37044 931-221-1350
Melissa Champion-Emerson, prin. Fax 221-1360
New Providence MS 1,000/6-8
146 Cunningham Ln 37042 931-648-5655
Laura Barnett, prin. Fax 503-3409
Northeast HS 900/9-12
3701 Trenton Rd 37040 931-648-5640
Garry Chadwell, prin. Fax 647-6025
Northeast MS 900/6-8
3703 Trenton Rd 37040 931-648-5665
Tracy Hollinger, prin. Fax 503-3410
Northwest HS 1,200/9-12
800 Lafayette Rd 37042 931-648-5675
Dr. Theresa Muckleroy, prin. Fax 648-0094
Richview MS 1,100/6-8
2350 Memorial Drive Ext 37043 931-648-5620
Lisa Clark, prin. Fax 551-8111
Rossview HS 1,500/9-12
1237 Rossview Rd 37043 931-553-2070
Frank Myers, prin. Fax 503-3419
Rossview MS 1,200/6-8
2265 Cardinal Ln 37043 931-920-6150
Christina Harris, prin. Fax 920-6147
STEM Academy 9-12
251 E Pine Mountain Rd 37042 931-905-7900
Christi Fordham, prin. Fax 905-7906
West Creek HS 1,200/9-12
1210 W Creek Coyote Trl 37042 931-503-1788
Christopher Neidigh, prin. Fax 503-1802
West Creek MS 1,100/6-8
1200 W Creek Coyote Trl 37042 931-503-3288
Bryan Feldman, prin. Fax 503-3296
Other Schools – See Cunningham

---

Austin Peay State University Post-Sec.
601 College St 37044 931-221-7011
Clarksville Academy 600/PK-12
710 N 2nd St 37040 931-647-6311
Clarksville Christian S 100/PK-12
505 Highway 76 37043 931-647-8180
Amanda Binkley, prin. Fax 741-0953
Draughons Junior College Post-Sec.
2691 Trenton Rd 37040 931-552-7600
Miller-Motte Technical College Post-Sec.
1820 Business Park Dr 37040 931-553-0071
North Central Institute Post-Sec.
168 Jack Miller Blvd 37042 931-431-9700
Queen City College Post-Sec.
1594 Fort Campbell Blvd 37042 931-645-2361

**Cleveland, Bradley, Pop. 40,418**
Bradley County SD 10,100/PK-12
800 S Lee Hwy 37311 423-476-0620
Dr. Linda Cash, dir. Fax 476-0485
www.bradleyschools.org
Bradley Central HS 1,600/9-12
1000 S Lee Hwy 37311 423-476-0650
Todd Shoemaker, prin. Fax 476-0613
Goal Academy 50/Alt
209 Sunset Dr NW 37312 423-476-0699
Kyle Page, prin. Fax 478-8829
Lake Forest MS 1,100/6-8
610 Kile Lake Rd SE 37323 423-478-8821
Ritchie Stevenson, prin. Fax 478-8832
Ocoee MS 1,300/6-8
2250 N Ocoee St 37311 423-476-0630
Ron Spangler, prin. Fax 476-0588
Walker Valley HS 1,500/9-12
750 Lauderdale Mem Hwy NW 37312 423-336-1383
Nat Akiona, prin. Fax 336-1578
REACH Adult HS Adult
1450 Strawberry Ln NE 37311 423-473-8473
Rachel Wilson, prin. Fax 473-8483

Cleveland CSD 5,100/K-12
4300 Mouse Creek Rd NW 37312 423-472-9571
Dr. Martin Ringstaff, dir. Fax 472-3390
www.clevelandschools.org
Cleveland HS 1,300/9-12
850 Raider Dr NW 37312 423-478-1113
Autumn O'Bryan, prin. Fax 559-1560
Cleveland MS 1,200/6-8
3635 Georgetown Rd NW 37312 423-479-9641
Michael Collier, prin. Fax 479-9553
Teen Learning Center Alt
350 Central Ave NW 37311 423-339-0902
Barbra Ector, prin. Fax 559-9477

---

Cleveland Christian S 100/K-12
695 S Ocoee St 37311 423-476-2642
Cleveland State Community College Post-Sec.
PO Box 3570 37320 423-472-7141
Franklin Academy Post-Sec.
1605 Professional Park Dr N 37312 423-476-3742
Lee University Post-Sec.
1120 N Ocoee St 37311 800-533-9930
Pentecostal Theological Seminary Post-Sec.
900 Walker St NE 37311 423-478-1131

Tennessee Christian Preparatory S 200/PK-12
4995 N Lee Hwy 37312 423-559-8939
Dr. Bill Balzano, pres. Fax 476-4974

**Clifton, Wayne, Pop. 2,664**
Wayne County SD
Supt. — See Waynesboro
Hughes S 300/PK-12
PO Box A 38425 931-676-3325
Tracy Love, prin. Fax 676-3903

**Clinton, Anderson, Pop. 9,667**
Anderson County SD 7,900/PK-12
101 S Main St 37716 865-463-2800
Larry Foster, supt. Fax 457-9157
www2.acs.ac
Anderson County Career & Technical Ctr Vo/Tech
140 Maverick Cir 37716 865-457-4205
Kelly Myers, prin. Fax 457-1715
Anderson County HS 1,000/9-12
130 Maverick Cir 37716 865-457-4716
Andrea Russell, prin. Fax 457-3398
Clinch River Community S 100/Alt
160 Maverick Cir 37716 865-457-7462
Darren Leach, prin. Fax 457-6546
Clinton HS 1,200/9-12
425 Dragon Dr 37716 865-457-2611
Eric Snider, prin. Fax 457-8805
Clinton MS 700/6-8
110 N Hicks St 37716 865-457-3451
Chris Goodwyne, prin. Fax 457-9486
Other Schools – See Lake City, Norris, Oliver Springs

**Coalfield, Morgan, Pop. 2,425**
Morgan County SD
Supt. — See Wartburg
Coalfield S 500/K-12
PO Box 98 37719 865-435-7332
Matthew Murphy, prin. Fax 435-2646

**Coalmont, Grundy, Pop. 825**
Grundy County SD
Supt. — See Altamont
Grundy County HS 700/9-12
24970 SR 108 37313 931-692-5400
Jamie Ruehling, prin. Fax 692-5403

**Collegedale, Hamilton, Pop. 8,113**

---

Collegedale Academy 400/9-12
PO Box 628 37315 423-396-2124
Collegedale Adventist MS 50/6-8
4856 College Dr E 37315 423-396-3020
Southern Adventist University Post-Sec.
PO Box 370 37315 423-236-2000

**Collierville, Shelby, Pop. 43,413**
Collierville SD, 146 College St 38017 K-12
John Aitken, supt. 901-861-7000
www.colliervilleschools.org
Collierville HS 1,900/9-12
1101 New Byhalia Rd 38017 901-853-3310
Chip Blanchard, prin. Fax 853-3313
Collierville MS 900/6-8
580 Quinn Rd 38017 901-853-3320
Roger Jones, prin. Fax 853-3327
Schilling Farms MS 1,000/6-8
935 Colbert St S 38017 901-854-2345
Jeff Jones, prin. Fax 854-8200

---

St. George's Independent S Collierville 700/6-12
1880 Wolf River Blvd 38017 901-457-2000
J. Ross Peters, head sch Fax 457-2121

**Collinwood, Wayne, Pop. 979**
Wayne County SD
Supt. — See Waynesboro
Collinwood HS 300/9-12
401 N Trojan Blvd 38450 931-724-4316
Benita Smith, prin. Fax 724-4488
Collinwood MS 300/5-8
300 4th Ave N 38450 931-724-9510
Walter Butler, prin. Fax 924-2519

**Columbia, Maury, Pop. 33,976**
Maury County SD 11,900/PK-12
501 W 8th St 38401 931-388-8403
Dr. Chris Marczak, dir. Fax 840-4410
www.mauryk12.org
Columbia Central HS 1,300/9-12
921 Lion Pkwy 38401 931-381-2222
Roger White, prin. Fax 381-6434
Cox MS 600/5-8
633 Bear Creek Pike 38401 931-840-3902
Tim Webb, prin. Fax 840-3903
Porter S Alt
1101 Bridge St 38401 931-381-1474
Robert Busch, admin. Fax 840-4432
Spring Hill HS 900/9-12
1 Raider Ln 38401 931-486-2207
Dr. Christine Potts, prin. Fax 486-3113
Whitthorne MS 1,100/5-8
915 Lion Pkwy 38401 931-388-2558
Linda Lester, prin. Fax 380-4684
Other Schools – See Culleoka, Hampshire, Mount Pleasant, Santa Fe, Spring Hill

---

Agathos Classical S 100/PK-12
1201 Mapleash Ave 38401 931-388-0556
Ted Trainor, hdmstr. Fax 388-0538
Columbia Academy 600/PK-12
1101 W 7th St 38401 931-388-5363
Columbia State Community College Post-Sec.
1665 Hampshire Pike 38401 931-540-2722
Zion Christian Academy 500/PK-12
6901 Old Zion Rd 38401 931-388-5731
Don Wahlman, hdmstr. Fax 388-5842

**Cookeville, Putnam, Pop. 29,908**
Putnam County SD 10,800/PK-12
1400 E Spring St 38506 931-526-9777
Jerry S. Boyd, dir. Fax 528-6942
www.pcsstn.com
Cookeville HS 2,200/PK-PK, 9-
1 Cavalier Dr 38501 931-520-2287
Edward L. Ward, prin. Fax 520-2268
Prescott South MS 800/5-8
1859 S Jefferson Ave 38506 931-528-3647
Trey Upchurch, prin. Fax 520-2019
Trace MS 700/5-8
230 Raider Dr 38501 931-520-2200
Michael Miehls, prin. Fax 520-2204
White Plains Academy 100/Alt
288 E Main St 38506 931-537-3862
Joe Matheney, prin. Fax 537-3062
Adult Learning Center Adult
288 E Main St 38506 931-528-8685
Robyn Nabors, prin. Fax 537-2516
Other Schools – See Algood, Baxter, Monterey

---

Fortis Institute Post-Sec.
1025 Highway 111 38501 931-526-3660
Genesis Career College Post-Sec.
880 E 10th St Ste A 38501 931-526-8735
Mister Wayne's Sch of Unisex Hair Design Post-Sec.
170 S Willow Ave 38501 931-526-1478
Tennessee Technological University Post-Sec.
1 William L Jones Dr 38505 931-372-3101

**Copperhill, Polk, Pop. 348**
Polk County SD
Supt. — See Benton
Copper Basin HS 300/7-12
300 Cougar Dr 37317 423-496-3291
Jared Bigham, prin. Fax 496-5308

**Cordova, Shelby**
Shelby County SD
Supt. — See Memphis
Cordova HS 1,800/9-12
1800 Berryhill Rd 38016 901-416-4540
Kymberli Chandler, prin. Fax 416-4545
Cordova MS 900/6-8
900 N Sanga Rd 38018 901-416-2189
Stephanie Beach, prin. Fax 416-2191
Dexter MS 500/5-8
6998 Raleigh LaGrange Rd 38018 901-373-3134
Dr. Phyllis Jones, prin. Fax 373-3378
Mt. Pisgah MS 600/6-8
1444 Pisgah Rd 38016 901-756-2386
LaVonda Jones, prin. Fax 756-2306

---

Evangelical Christian S - Macon Campus 700/6-12
PO Box 1030 38088 901-754-7217
Barrett Luketic, prin. Fax 754-8123
First Assembly Christian S 800/PK-12
8650 Walnut Grove Rd 38018 901-458-5543
ITT Technical Institute Post-Sec.
7260 Goodlett Farms Pkwy 38016 901-381-0200
L'Ecole Culinaire Post-Sec.
1245 N Germantown Pkwy 38016 901-754-7115
Mid-America Baptist Theological Seminary Post-Sec.
2095 Appling Rd 38016 901-751-8453
St. Benedict HS 800/9-12
8250 Varnavas Dr 38016 901-260-2840
Sondra Morris, prin. Fax 260-2850

**Cornersville, Marshall, Pop. 1,184**
Marshall County SD
Supt. — See Lewisburg
Cornersville JSHS 400/7-12
323 S Main St 37047 931-246-4170
Brent Adcox, prin. Fax 246-4153

**Corryton, Knox, Pop. 100**
Knox County SD
Supt. — See Knoxville
Gibbs HS 1,000/9-12
7628 Tazewell Pike 37721 865-689-9130
Tom Brown, prin. Fax 689-9128

**Cosby, Cocke**
Cocke County SD
Supt. — See Newport
Cosby HS 400/9-12
3320 Cosby Hwy 37722 423-487-5602
Patrick O'Neil, prin. Fax 487-5502

**Covington, Tipton, Pop. 8,910**
Tipton County SD 11,800/PK-12
1580 Highway 51 S 38019 901-476-7148
Dr. William Bibb, dir. Fax 476-4870
www.tipton-county.com
Covington HS 800/9-12
803 S College St 38019 901-475-5850
Marcus Heaston, prin. Fax 476-5778
Crestview MS 600/6-8
201 Mark Walker Dr 38019 901-475-5900
Steve Maclin, prin. Fax 475-2607
Tipton Co. Alternative Learning Center 100/Alt
800 Bert Johnston Ave 38019 901-837-5755
Steve Zurhellen, prin. Fax 476-4612
Other Schools – See Brighton, Munford

---

Tennessee Technology Center at Covington Post-Sec.
1600 Highway 51 S 38019 901-475-2526

**Cowan, Franklin, Pop. 1,690**
Franklin County SD
Supt. — See Winchester
South MS 400/6-8
601 Cumberland St W 37318 931-967-7355
Derrick Crutchfield, prin. Fax 967-1413

**Cross Plains, Robertson, Pop. 1,691**
Robertson County SD
Supt. — See Springfield

East Robertson HS 800/6-12
158 Kilgore Trce 37049 615-654-2191
Mary Cook, prin. Fax 654-4563

**Crossville, Cumberland, Pop. 10,670**
Cumberland County SD 7,500/PK-12
368 Fourth St 38555 931-484-6135
Donald Andrews, supt. Fax 484-6491
ccschools.k12tn.net/
Cumberland County HS 1,100/9-12
660 Stanley St 38555 931-484-6194
Janet Graham, prin. Fax 456-6872
Stone Memorial HS 1,100/9-12
2800 Cook Rd 38571 931-484-5767
Scott Maddox, prin. Fax 484-4801

Christian Academy of the Cumberlands 100/PK-12
325 Braun St 38555 931-707-9540
Douglas Reid, prin. Fax 707-9545
Tennessee Technology Center Crossville Post-Sec.
910 Miller Ave 38555 931-484-7502

**Crump, Hardin, Pop. 1,405**

Tennessee Technology Center at Crump Post-Sec.
PO Box 89 38327 731-632-3393

**Culleoka, Maury**
Maury County SD
Supt. — See Columbia
Culleoka S 1,000/K-12
1921 Warrior Way 38451 931-987-2511
Penny Love, prin. Fax 987-2594

Hopewell Church Covenant Family S 50/1-12
3886 Hopewell Rd 38451 931-505-1624
Charles Mangum, admin. Fax 406-4971

**Cumberland Gap, Claiborne, Pop. 477**
Claiborne County SD
Supt. — See Tazewell
Cumberland Gap HS 600/9-12
661 Old Jacksboro Pike 37724 423-869-9964
Linda Keck, prin. Fax 869-4352

**Cunningham, Montgomery**
Clarksville-Montgomery County SD
Supt. — See Clarksville
Montgomery Central HS 900/9-12
3955 Highway 48 37052 931-387-3201
Christy Houston, prin. Fax 387-4578
Montgomery Central MS 800/6-8
3941 Highway 48 37052 931-387-2575
Dee-Etta Whitlock, prin. Fax 387-3391

**Dandridge, Jefferson, Pop. 2,785**
Jefferson County SD 8,200/PK-12
PO Box 190 37725 865-397-3194
Dr. Charles Edmonds, dir. Fax 397-3301
jc-schools.net/
Jefferson County HS 2,200/9-12
115 W Dumplin Valley Rd 37725 865-397-3182
Dr. Scott Walker, prin. Fax 397-4121
Maury MS 600/6-8
965 Maury Cir 37725 865-397-3424
Michelle Walker, prin. Fax 397-4253
Other Schools – See Jefferson City

**Dayton, Rhea, Pop. 7,052**
Rhea County SD 4,400/PK-12
305 California Ave 37321 423-775-7812
Jerry Levengood, dir. Fax 775-7831
www.rheacounty.org
Other Schools – See Evensville, Spring City

Bryan College Post-Sec.
PO Box 7000 37321 423-775-2041
Laurelbrook Academy 100/9-12
114 Campus Dr 37321 423-775-3339
Oxford Graduate School Post-Sec.
500 Oxford Dr 37321 423-775-6596

**Decatur, Meigs, Pop. 1,593**
Meigs County SD 1,800/PK-12
345 N Main St 37322 423-334-5793
Donald Roberts, supt. Fax 334-1462
www.meigscounty.net
Meigs County HS 500/9-12
PO Box 1182 37322 423-334-5797
Clint Baker, prin. Fax 334-5732
Meigs MS 400/6-8
564 N Main St 37322 423-334-9187
Ronald Woods, prin. Fax 334-1353

**Decaturville, Decatur, Pop. 853**
Decatur County SD 1,600/PK-12
PO Box 369 38329 731-852-2391
Branson Townsend, supt. Fax 852-2960
www.decaturcountyschools.org
Riverside HS 500/9-12
4250 Highway 641 S 38329 731-852-3941
Hugh Smith, prin. Fax 852-3955
Other Schools – See Parsons

**Denmark, Madison**
Jackson-Madison County SD
Supt. — See Jackson
West MS 500/6-8
317 Denmark Rd 38391 731-988-3810
John Burks, prin. Fax 988-3814

**Dickson, Dickson, Pop. 14,179**
Dickson County SD 8,500/PK-12
817 N Charlotte St 37055 615-446-7571
Dr. Danny Weeks, dir. Fax 441-1375
www.dicksoncountyschools.org
Dickson County HS 1,500/9-12
509 Henslee Dr 37055 615-446-9003
Joey Holley, prin. Fax 441-4135
Dickson MS 1,200/6-8
401 E College St 37055 615-446-2273
Dr. Robbie Faulkner, prin. Fax 441-4139
Other Schools – See Charlotte, White Bluff

Tennessee Technology Center at Dickson Post-Sec.
740 Highway 46 S 37055 615-441-6220

**Dover, Stewart, Pop. 1,392**
Stewart County SD 2,200/PK-12
PO Box 433 37058 931-232-5176
Leta Joiner, dir. Fax 232-5390
stewartcountyschools.net
Stewart County HS 700/9-12
120 Robertson Hill Rd 37058 931-232-5179
Michael Craig, prin. Fax 232-3119
Stewart County MS 500/6-8
PO Box 1001 37058 931-232-9112
Steve Nolen, prin. Fax 232-4608

**Dresden, Weakley, Pop. 2,945**
Weakley County SD 4,700/PK-12
8319 Highway 22 Ste A 38225 731-364-2247
Randy Frazier, supt. Fax 364-2662
www.weakleycountyschools.com
Dresden HS 400/9-12
7150 Highway 22 38225 731-364-2949
Charles West, prin. Fax 364-5328
Dresden MS 400/5-8
759 Linden St Ste A 38225 731-364-2407
David Lewellen, prin. Fax 364-5840
Weakley County Adult Learning Center Adult
8250 Highway 22 38225 731-364-5481
Shirley Callis, prin. Fax 364-3580
Other Schools – See Gleason, Greenfield, Martin

**Dunlap, Sequatchie, Pop. 4,760**
Bledsoe County SD
Supt. — See Pikeville
Bledsoe County Vocational Center Vo/Tech
26297 US 127 37327 423-554-3293
Steve Reel, dir. Fax 554-3142

Sequatchie County SD 2,300/PK-12
PO Box 488 37327 423-949-3617
Michael L. Swafford, dir. Fax 949-5257
sequatchieschools.net
Sequatchie County HS 700/9-12
PO Box 759 37327 423-949-2154
Tommy Layne, prin. Fax 949-4696
Sequatchie County MS 700/5-8
PO Box 789 37327 423-949-4149
Devona Smith, prin. Fax 949-4140

Sequatchie Valley Preparatory Academy 50/K-12
1050 Ray Hixson Rd 37327 423-554-4677
Robert Young, admin. Fax 554-4398

**Dyer, Gibson, Pop. 2,288**
Gibson County Special SD 3,700/PK-12
PO Box 60 38330 731-692-3803
Eddie Pruett, dir. Fax 692-4375
www.gcssd.org
Gibson County HS 500/9-12
PO Box 190 38330 731-692-3616
Jim Hughes, prin. Fax 692-2123
Other Schools – See Medina

**Dyersburg, Dyer, Pop. 16,802**
Dyer County SD 3,800/PK-12
159 Everett Ave 38024 731-285-6712
Dr. Dwight Hedge, dir. Fax 286-6721
www.dyercs.net
Three Oaks MS 500/6-8
3200 Upper Finley Rd 38024 731-285-3100
Laura Brimm, prin. Fax 285-3360
Other Schools – See Newbern

Dyersburg CSD 3,000/PK-12
509 Lake Rd 38024 731-286-3600
Neel Durbin, dir. Fax 286-2754
www.dyersburgcityschools.org/
Dyersburg HS 900/9-12
125 US Highway 51 Byp W 38024 731-286-3630
Kim Worley, prin. Fax 286-2209
Dyersburg MS 700/6-8
400 Frank Maynard Dr 38024 731-286-3625
Cal Johnson, prin. Fax 286-3624

Dyersburg State Community College Post-Sec.
1510 Lake Rd 38024 731-286-3200
Emmanuel Christian S 50/PK-12
92 Kendall Ln 38024 731-377-3386
Thomas Kendall, supt. Fax 445-4816

**Eads, Shelby**

Briarcrest Christian S 300/PK-12
76 S Houston Levee Rd 38028 901-765-4600
Steve Simpson, hdmstr. Fax 765-4667

**Eagleville, Rutherford, Pop. 600**
Rutherford County SD
Supt. — See Murfreesboro
Eagleville S 800/PK-12
500 Old Highway 99 37060 615-904-6710
Bill Tollett, prin. Fax 274-6859

**Elizabethton, Carter, Pop. 13,969**
Carter County SD 5,500/PK-12
305 Academy St 37643 423-547-4000
Dr. Kevin Ward Ed.D., dir. Fax 542-7560
carter.k12.tn.us
Happy Valley HS 500/9-12
121 Warpath Ln 37643 423-547-4094
Terry Hubbard, prin. Fax 547-4083
Happy Valley MS 500/5-8
163 Warpath Ln 37643 423-547-4070
Jonathan Minton, prin. Fax 547-8352
Siam Learning Center 50/Alt
2453 Siam Rd 37643 423-547-4050
C.B. Hardin, prin. Fax 547-4061
Unaka HS 300/9-12
119 Robinson Ln 37643 423-474-4100
Betsy Oliver, prin. Fax 474-4108
Other Schools – See Hampton, Roan Mountain

Elizabethton CSD 2,400/PK-12
804 S Watauga Ave 37643 423-547-8000
Dr. Corey R. Gardenhour, supt. Fax 547-8929
www.ecschools.net
Dugger JHS 600/6-8
306 W E St 37643 423-547-8025
Randy Little, prin. Fax 547-8021
Elizabethton HS 800/9-12
907 Jason Witten Way 37643 423-547-8015
David Wright, prin. Fax 547-8016

Tennessee Technology Center Elizabethton Post-Sec.
426 Highway 91 37643 423-543-0070

**Englewood, McMinn, Pop. 1,491**
McMinn County SD
Supt. — See Athens
Central HS 800/9-12
145 County Road 461 37329 423-263-5541
Roger Freeman, prin. Fax 263-0399

**Erin, Houston, Pop. 1,288**
Houston County SD 1,400/PK-12
PO Box 209 37061 931-289-4148
Cathy Harvey, dir. Fax 289-5543
www.houston.k12.tn.us
Houston County HS 400/9-12
2500 Highway 149 37061 931-289-4447
Linda Jolly, prin. Fax 289-4924
Houston County MS 300/6-8
3460 W Main St 37061 931-289-5591
Anita Gray, prin. Fax 289-5599
Houston County Adult S Adult
2500 Highway 149 37061 931-289-5525
Linda McDonough, prin.

**Erwin, Unicoi, Pop. 6,036**
Unicoi County SD 2,600/PK-12
100 Nolichucky Ave 37650 423-743-1600
Denise Brown, dir. Fax 743-1615
www.unicoischools.com/
Unicoi County Career & Technical S Vo/Tech
100 Okolona Dr 37650 423-743-1639
Fax 743-1671
Unicoi County HS 700/9-12
700 S Mohawk Dr 37650 423-743-1632
Becky Love, prin. Fax 743-1636
Unicoi County MS 600/6-8
599 S Mohawk Dr 37650 423-735-0236
John English, prin. Fax 735-0728

**Evensville, Rhea**
Rhea County SD
Supt. — See Dayton
Rhea County HS 1,400/9-12
885 Eagle Ln 37332 423-775-7821
Jesse Messimer, prin. Fax 775-7889
Rhea County MS 700/6-8
405 Pierce Rd 37332 423-775-7821
Doug Keylon, prin. Fax 775-7823

**Fairview, Williamson, Pop. 7,635**
Williamson County SD
Supt. — See Franklin
Fairview HS 600/9-12
2595 Fairview Blvd 37062 615-472-4400
Dr. Juli Oyer, prin. Fax 472-4421
Fairview MS 600/6-8
7200 Cumberland Dr 37062 615-472-4430
Gary Shrader, prin. Fax 472-4441

**Fayetteville, Lincoln, Pop. 6,705**
Fayetteville CSD 1,100/PK-12
110 Elk Ave S Ste 200 37334 931-433-5542
Dr. Janine M. Wilson, supt. Fax 433-7499
www.fcsboe.org
Fayetteville HS 100/9-12
1800 Wilson Pkwy Ste A 37334 931-433-3158
Eric Jones, prin. Fax 433-4611
Fayetteville MS 300/5-8
1800 Wilson Pkwy Ste A 37334 931-438-2533
John D. Wilson, prin. Fax 438-2539

Lincoln County SD 4,100/PK-12
206 Davidson St E 37334 931-433-3565
Wanda Shelton Ed.D., dir. Fax 433-7397
www.lcdoe.org
Lincoln County HS 1,100/10-12
1233 Huntsville Hwy 37334 931-433-6505
Sarah Wallace, prin. Fax 438-1490
Ninth Grade Academy 300/9-9
900 Main Ave S 37334 931-433-6156
Spring Brindley, prin. Fax 438-2465

Fayetteville College of Cosmetology Post-Sec.
201 College St W 37334 931-433-1305
Riverside Christian Academy 400/PK-12
PO Box 617 37334 931-438-4722
James Bryant, head sch Fax 438-4727

**Franklin, Williamson, Pop. 61,495**
Franklin Special SD 3,900/PK-8
507 New Highway 96 W 37064 615-794-6624
Dr. David Snowden Ph.D., supt. Fax 790-4716
www.fssd.org
Freedom MS 600/7-8
750 New Highway 96 W 37064 615-794-0987
Kristi Jefferson Ed.D., prin. Fax 790-4742
Poplar Grove MS 400/5-8
2959 Del Rio Pike 37069 615-790-4721
Tracie Clark, prin. Fax 790-4730

Williamson County SD 31,100/PK-12
1320 W Main St Ste 202 37064 615-472-4000
Dr. Michael Looney, supt. Fax 472-4190
www.wcs.edu
Centennial HS 1,600/9-12
5050 Mallory Ln 37067 615-472-4270
Dr. Leigh Webb, prin. Fax 472-4291
Franklin HS 1,800/9-12
810 Hillsboro Rd 37064 615-472-4450
Willie Dickerson, prin. Fax 472-4478
Grassland MS 1,000/6-8
2390 Hillsboro Rd 37069 615-472-4500
Dr. Lily Leffler, prin. Fax 472-4511
Page HS 800/9-12
6281 Arno Rd 37064 615-472-4730
Shane Pantall, prin. Fax 472-4751
Page MS 800/6-8
6262 Arno Rd 37064 615-472-4760
Dr. Eric Lifsey, prin. Fax 472-4771
Renaissance HS 100/9-12
108 Everbright St 37064 615-472-4670
Dr. Brian Bass, prin. Fax 472-4675
Other Schools – See Brentwood, Fairview, Nolensville, Spring Hill, Thompsons Station

---

Battle Ground Academy 900/K-12
336 Ernest Rice Ln 37069 615-794-3501
William F. Kesler, head sch Fax 567-8360
Classical Academy of Franklin 200/PK-12
810 Del Rio Pike 37064 615-790-8556
Eric Van Gorden, admin. Fax 790-8617
Comenius S K-12
PO Box 1601 37065 615-528-3778
Jenna L. Coghlan, dir. Fax 528-9432
Franklin Christian Academy 100/5-12
PO Box 157 37065 615-599-9229
Hugh Harris, hdmstr. Fax 599-9441
Franklin Classical S 100/K-12
PO Box 1601 37065 615-528-3777
Jeff Dokkestul, prin. Fax 528-9432
Grace Christian Academy 200/PK-12
3279 Southall Rd 37064 615-591-3017
Robbie Mason, hdmstr. Fax 591-5576
O'More College of Design Post-Sec.
423 S Margin St 37064 615-794-4254
Williamson Christian College Post-Sec.
274 Mallory Station Rd 37067 615-771-7821

**Friendsville, Blount, Pop. 902**
Blount County SD
Supt. — See Maryville
Union Grove MS 800/6-8
334 S Old Grey Ridge Rd 37737 865-980-1320
Alicia Lail, prin. Fax 980-1323

**Gainesboro, Jackson, Pop. 959**
Jackson County SD 1,600/PK-12
711 School Dr 38562 931-268-0268
Joe Barlow, supt. Fax 268-3647
volweb.utk.edu/school/jackson/
Jackson County HS 500/9-12
190 Blue Devil Ln 38562 931-268-9771
Charles Breidert, prin. Fax 268-9433
Jackson County MS 500/PK-PK, 4-
170 Blue Devil Ln 38562 931-268-9779
Gail Myers, prin. Fax 268-9413

**Gallatin, Sumner, Pop. 29,705**
Sumner County SD 27,900/PK-12
695 E Main St 37066 615-451-5200
Dr. Del Phillips, dir. Fax 451-5216
www.sumnerschools.org
Fisher Alternative S 100/Alt
455 N Boyers Ave 37066 615-451-6558
Bob Gideon, prin. Fax 451-5290
Gallatin HS 1,400/9-12
700 Dan P Herron Dr 37066 615-452-2621
Dr. Ron Becker, prin. Fax 451-5426
Rucker-Stewart MS 700/6-8
350 Hancock St 37066 615-452-1734
Bryan Adams, prin. Fax 451-5297
Shafer MS 700/6-8
240 Albert Gallatin Ave 37066 615-452-9100
David Hallman, prin. Fax 451-6545
Station Camp HS 1,400/9-12
1040 Bison Trl 37066 615-451-6551
Art Crook, prin. Fax 451-6556
Station Camp MS 600/6-8
281 Big Station Camp Blvd 37066 615-206-0116
Mike Brown, prin. Fax 206-0165
Sumner County Middle College HS 9-12
1480 Nashville Pike 37066 615-230-3470
Brad Schreiner, prin.
Wilson HS, 685 E Main St 37066 9-12
Jennifer Holdren, prin. 615-230-6948
Other Schools – See Hendersonville, Portland, Westmoreland, White House

---

Volunteer State Community College Post-Sec.
1480 Nashville Pike 37066 615-452-8600

**Gatlinburg, Sevier, Pop. 3,902**
Sevier County SD
Supt. — See Sevierville
Gatlinburg-Pittman HS 600/9-12
150 Proffitt Rd 37738 865-436-5637
Tony Ogle, prin. Fax 436-2567

**Germantown, Shelby, Pop. 38,412**
Germantown Municipal SD K-12
6685 Poplar Ave Ste 202 38138 901-752-7900
Jason Manuel, supt. Fax 757-6479
www.gmsdk12.org
Houston HS 1,700/9-12
9755 Wolf River Blvd 38139 901-756-2370
Kyle Cherry, prin. Fax 756-2377
Houston MS 900/6-8
9400 Wolf River Blvd 38139 901-756-2366
Liz Dias, prin. Fax 756-2346

Shelby County SD
Supt. — See Memphis
Germantown HS 2,100/9-12
7653 Poplar Pike 38138 901-756-2350
Barbara Harmon, prin. Fax 756-2356
Germantown MS 700/6-8
7925 CD Smith Rd 38138 901-756-2338
Amie Marsh, prin. Fax 759-4521

**Gleason, Weakley, Pop. 1,427**
Weakley County SD
Supt. — See Dresden
Gleason S 600/PK-12
9299 State Championship Dr 38229 731-648-5351
Trish Price, prin. Fax 648-9199

**Gordonsville, Smith, Pop. 1,200**
Smith County SD
Supt. — See Carthage
Gordonsville HS 500/7-12
110 Main St E 38563 615-683-8245
Ronnie Scudder, prin. Fax 683-5193

**Gray, Washington, Pop. 1,206**
Washington County SD
Supt. — See Jonesborough
Boone HS 1,400/9-12
1440 Suncrest Dr 37615 423-477-1600
Roger Jackson, prin. Fax 477-1625

**Greenback, Loudon, Pop. 1,059**
Loudon County SD
Supt. — See Loudon
Greenback S 600/PK-12
6945 Morganton Rd 37742 865-856-3028
Mike Casteel, prin. Fax 856-8379

**Greenbrier, Robertson, Pop. 6,354**
Robertson County SD
Supt. — See Springfield
Greenbrier HS 800/9-12
126 Cuniff Dr 37073 615-643-4526
Dr. Katie Osborne, prin. Fax 643-8873
Greenbrier MS 600/6-8
2450 Highway 41 S 37073 615-643-7823
Kathy Carroll, prin. Fax 643-4580

---

Dayspring Academy 100/PK-12
2838 Heights Circle Dr 37073 615-672-9650

**Greeneville, Greene, Pop. 14,821**
Greene County SD 7,400/PK-12
910 W Summer St 37743 423-639-4194
David McLain, dir. Fax 639-1615
www.greenek12.org
North Greene HS 400/9-12
4675 Old Baileyton Rd 37745 423-234-1752
David McLain, prin. Fax 234-3103
South Greene HS 500/9-12
7469 Asheville Hwy 37743 423-639-3790
Dr. Cindy Bowman, prin. Fax 636-3791
Other Schools – See Afton, Mosheim

Greeneville CSD 2,800/PK-12
PO Box 1420 37744 423-787-8000
Dr. Linda Stroud, dir. Fax 638-2540
www.gcschools.net
Greeneville HS 800/9-12
210 Tusculum Blvd 37745 423-787-8030
Dr. Linda Stroud, prin. Fax 787-8028
Greeneville MS 600/6-8
433 E Vann Rd 37743 423-639-7841
Heather Boegemann, prin. Fax 639-4112
Greeneville/Greene Co. Ctr for Technology Vo/Tech
1121 Hal Henard Rd 37743 423-639-0171
Jerry Ayers, prin. Fax 639-0176

---

Greeneville Adventist Academy 100/K-12
305 Takoma Ave 37743 423-639-2011
Randy Nomura, prin. Fax 639-5002
Tusculum College Post-Sec.
60 Shiloh Rd 37745 423-636-7300

**Greenfield, Weakley, Pop. 2,162**
Weakley County SD
Supt. — See Dresden
Greenfield S 600/PK-12
319 W Main St 38230 731-235-3424
Mike Riggs, prin. Fax 235-3480

**Gruetli Laager, Grundy, Pop. 1,795**

---

Faith Missionary Academy 100/K-12
495 Red Barn Rd 37339 931-779-3338

**Halls, Lauderdale, Pop. 2,218**
Lauderdale County SD
Supt. — See Ripley
Halls HS 400/9-12
800 W Tigrett St 38040 731-836-9642
Andy Pugh, prin. Fax 836-1072
Halls JHS 200/7-8
800 W Tigrett St 38040 731-836-5579
Michael Blackwood, prin. Fax 836-5555

**Hampshire, Maury**
Maury County SD
Supt. — See Columbia
Hampshire S 400/K-12
4235 Old State Rd 38461 931-285-2300
Sonya Booker Cathey, prin. Fax 285-2612

**Hampton, Carter**
Carter County SD
Supt. — See Elizabethton
Hampton HS 400/9-12
766 First Ave 37658 423-725-5200
Jeff Bradley, prin. Fax 725-5204

**Harriman, Roane, Pop. 6,223**
Roane County SD
Supt. — See Kingston
Harriman HS 300/9-12
920 N Roane St 37748 865-882-1821
Scott Calahan, prin. Fax 882-6479
Harriman MS 300/6-8
1025 Cumberland St 37748 865-882-1727
Leslie Smith, prin. Fax 882-6285
Midtown Educational Center 100/Alt
3096 Roane State Hwy 37748 865-882-0242
Chris Johnson, prin. Fax 882-7734

---

Roane State Community College Post-Sec.
276 Patton Ln 37748 865-354-3000
Tennessee Technology Center at Harriman Post-Sec.
PO Box 1109 37748 865-882-6703

**Harrison, Hamilton, Pop. 7,602**
Hamilton County SD
Supt. — See Chattanooga
Brown MS 500/6-8
5716 Highway 58 37341 423-344-1439
Jane Reynolds, prin. Fax 344-1471
Central HS 1,000/9-12
5728 Highway 58 37341 423-344-1447
Ronald King, prin. Fax 344-1470

**Harrogate, Claiborne, Pop. 4,333**
Claiborne County SD
Supt. — See Tazewell
Livesay MS 300/5-8
PO Box 460 37752 423-869-4663
Karyn Clark, prin. Fax 869-8389

---

Lincoln Memorial University Post-Sec.
6965 Cumberland Gap Pkwy 37752 423-869-3611
White Academy 100/5-12
6965 Cumberland Gap Pkwy 37752 423-869-6234

**Hartsville, Trousdale, Pop. 2,373**
Trousdale County SD 1,200/K-12
103 Lock Six Rd 37074 615-374-2193
Clint Satterfield, dir. Fax 374-1108
www.tcschools.org
Satterfield MS 300/6-8
210 Damascus St 37074 615-374-2748
Amanda Gregory, prin. Fax 374-2602
Trousdale County HS 400/9-12
262 McMurry Blvd W 37074 615-374-2201
Teresa Dickerson, prin. Fax 374-1120

---

Tennessee Technology Center Hartsville Post-Sec.
716 McMurry Blvd E 37074 615-374-2147

**Henderson, Chester, Pop. 6,177**
Chester County SD 2,800/PK-12
PO Box 327 38340 731-989-5134
Troy Kilzer, supt. Fax 989-4755
www.chestercountyschools.org
Chester County HS 800/9-12
552 E Main St 38340 731-989-8125
Dr. Ricky Catlett, prin. Fax 989-8131
Chester County JHS 700/6-8
930 E Main St 38340 731-989-8135
Kris Todd, prin. Fax 989-8137

---

Freed-Hardeman University Post-Sec.
158 E Main St 38340 731-989-6000

**Hendersonville, Sumner, Pop. 50,488**
Sumner County SD
Supt. — See Gallatin
Beech HS 1,300/9-12
3126 Long Hollow Pike 37075 615-824-6200
Kenny Powell, prin. Fax 264-6553
Ellis MS 600/6-8
100 Indian Lake Rd 37075 615-264-6093
Darren Frank, prin. Fax 264-5800
Hawkins MS 500/6-8
487A Walton Ferry Rd 37075 615-824-3456
Mitch Flood, prin. Fax 264-6003
Hendersonville HS 1,500/9-12
123 Cherokee Rd 37075 615-824-6162
Bob Cotter, prin. Fax 264-6027
Hunter MS 700/6-8
2101 New Hope Rd 37075 615-822-4720
Ahmed White, prin. Fax 264-6036
Hyde Magnet S 700/K-12
128 Township Dr 37075 615-264-6543
Todd Stinson, prin. Fax 264-6546
Knox Doss MS 500/6-8
1338 Drakes Creek Rd 37075 615-824-8383
Kenny Powell, prin. Fax 824-8448

---

Hendersonville Christian Academy 300/PK-12
355 Old Shackle Island Rd 37075 615-824-1550
Pope John Paul II HS 600/9-12
117 Caldwell Dr 37075 615-822-2375
Faustin Weber, hdmstr. Fax 822-6226

**Hermitage, See Nashville**
Metropolitan Nashville SD
Supt. — See Nashville
DuPont-Tyler MS 600/5-8
431 Tyler Dr 37076 615-885-8827
Dr. Damon Cathey, prin. Fax 847-7322

**Hixson, See Chattanooga**
Hamilton County SD
Supt. — See Chattanooga
Hixson HS 800/9-12
5705 Middle Valley Rd 37343 423-847-4800
Lee Sims, prin. Fax 847-4801

Hixson MS 600/6-8
5681 Old Hixson Pike 37343 423-847-4810
Leangela Rogers, prin. Fax 847-4811
Loftis MS 700/6-8
8611 Columbus Rd 37343 423-843-4749
Brentley Eller, prin. Fax 843-4758

---

Berean Academy 300/PK-12
441 Berean Ln 37343 423-877-1288

**Hohenwald, Lewis, Pop. 3,706**
Lewis County SD 2,000/PK-12
206 S Court St 38462 931-796-3264
Benny Pace, supt. Fax 796-5127
www.lewis.k12.tn.us
Lewis County HS 600/9-12
818 W Main St 38462 931-796-4085
Clayton Callicott, prin. Fax 796-1172
Lewis County MS 400/6-8
207 S Court St 38462 931-796-4586
Steve Edwards, prin. Fax 796-7601

---

Tennessee Technology Center at Hohenwald Post-Sec.
813 W Main St 38462 931-796-5351

**Humboldt, Gibson, Pop. 8,376**
Humboldt CSD 1,300/PK-12
2602 Viking Dr 38343 731-784-2652
Dr. Versie Hamlett, supt. Fax 784-2480
www.humboldtschools.com
Humboldt HS 400/7-12
2600 Viking Dr 38343 731-784-2781
James Walker, prin. Fax 784-8536

**Huntingdon, Carroll, Pop. 3,896**
Carroll County SD
PO Box 799 38344 731-986-4482
Johnny McAdams, supt. Fax 986-0198
www.carrollschools.com
Carroll County Technical Center Vo/Tech
1235 Buena Vista Rd 38344 731-986-8908
Dennis Stokes, prin. Fax 986-3200

Huntingdon Special SD 1,300/PK-12
585 High St 38344 731-986-2222
Pat Dillahunty, supt. Fax 986-4365
www.huntingdonschools.net
Huntingdon HS 400/9-12
475 Mustang Dr 38344 731-986-8223
Dr. Jonathan Kee, prin. Fax 986-4031
Huntingdon MS 500/4-8
199 Browning Ave 38344 731-986-4544
Scott Carter, prin. Fax 986-8689

South Carroll County Special SD 400/PK-12
145 Clarksburg Rd 38344 731-986-4534
Dr. Tony Tucker, supt. Fax 986-4562
www.rocketsonline.org
Clarksburg S 400/PK-12
145 Clarksburg Rd 38344 731-986-3165
Angela Bartholomew, prin. Fax 986-4562

**Huntland, Franklin, Pop. 866**
Franklin County SD
Supt. — See Winchester
Huntland S 700/PK-12
400 Gore St 37345 931-469-7506
Ken Bishop, prin. Fax 469-0590

**Huntsville, Scott, Pop. 1,235**
Scott County SD 3,100/PK-12
PO Box 37 37756 423-663-2159
Bill Hall, supt. Fax 663-9682
www.scottcounty.net
Huntsville MS 300/5-8
3101 Baker Hwy 37756 423-663-2192
Donna Goodman, prin. Fax 663-2967
Scott HS 800/9-12
400 Scott High Dr 37756 423-663-2801
Melissa Rector, prin. Fax 663-2368

---

Tennessee Technology Center Oneida/Hunts Post-Sec.
355 Scott High Dr 37756 423-663-4900

**Jacksboro, Campbell, Pop. 2,000**
Campbell County SD 6,000/PK-12
172 Valley St 37757 423-562-8377
Larry Nidiffer, dir. Fax 566-7562
www.campbell.k12.tn.us
Campbell County Comprehensive HS 1,300/9-12
150 Cougar Ln 37757 423-562-8308
Jamie Wheeler, prin. Fax 566-2019
Jacksboro MS 500/6-8
150 Eagle Cir 37757 423-562-3773
Steve Rutherford, prin. Fax 562-8994
Other Schools – See Jellico, La Follette

---

Tennessee Technology Center at Jacksboro Post-Sec.
PO Box 419 37757 423-566-9629

**Jackson, Madison, Pop. 64,311**
Jackson-Madison County SD 13,300/PK-12
310 N Parkway 38305 731-664-2592
Verna Ruffin, supt. Fax 664-2502
www.jmcss.org
Jackson Central-Merry HS 600/9-12
332 Lane Ave 38301 731-424-2200
Dr. Michael Booker, prin. Fax 423-6158
Liberty Technology Magnet HS Vo/Tech
3470 Ridgecrest Road Ext 38305 731-423-9086
Dr. June Murry, prin. Fax 424-3445
Madison Academic Magnet S 500/9-12
179 Allen Ave 38301 731-427-3501
Janice Epperson, prin. Fax 427-3587
Northeast MS 600/6-8
2665 Christmasville Rd 38305 731-422-6687
Clennon Saulsberry, prin. Fax 423-1805
North Parkway MS 600/6-8
1341 N Parkway 38305 731-427-3384
Tracey Vowell, prin. Fax 427-2591
North Side HS 1,100/9-12
3066 N Highland Ave 38305 731-668-3171
Ricky Catlett, prin. Fax 661-9756
Parkview Learning Center 100/Alt
905 E Chester St 38301 731-427-2841
Jason Newman, prin. Fax 427-2529
Rose Hill MS 500/6-8
2233 Beech Bluff Rd 38301 731-423-6170
Ned Lewis, prin. Fax 423-6171
South Side HS 800/9-12
84 Harts Bridge Rd 38301 731-422-9923
Anita Tucker, prin. Fax 423-3411
Tigrett MS 500/6-8
716 Westwood Ave 38301 731-988-3840
Tenganyike Cook, prin. Fax 988-3838
Other Schools – See Denmark

---

Augustine S 100/PK-12
1171 Old Humboldt Rd 38305 731-660-6822
Donna Nelson, admin. Fax 660-6833
Jackson Christian S 800/PK-12
832 Country Club Ln 38305 731-668-8055
Jackson Preparatory S 200/PK-12
130 Old Denmark Rd 38301 731-554-9647
Jackson State Community College Post-Sec.
2046 N Parkway 38301 731-424-3520
Lane College Post-Sec.
545 Lane Ave 38301 731-426-7500
Sacred Heart of Jesus & Mary HS 9-12
185 Greenfield Dr 38305 731-660-4774
Ann Keyl, prin. Fax 984-7200
Tennessee Technology Center at Jackson Post-Sec.
2468 Technology Center Dr 38301 731-424-0691
Trinity Christian Academy 700/PK-12
10 Windy City Rd 38305 731-668-8500
Jon Holley, head sch Fax 668-3232
Union University Post-Sec.
1050 Union University Dr 38305 731-668-1818
University S of Jackson 1,100/PK-12
232 McClellan Rd 38305 731-664-0812
Stuart Hirstein, hdmstr. Fax 664-5046
West Tennessee Business College Post-Sec.
1186 Highway 45 Byp 38301 800-737-9822

**Jamestown, Fentress, Pop. 1,935**
Fentress County SD 2,500/PK-12
1011 Old Highway 127 S 38556 931-879-9218
Mike Jones, dir. Fax 879-4050
www.fentress.k12tn.net
Other Schools – See Allardt, Clarkrange

**Jasper, Marion, Pop. 3,248**
Marion County SD 4,300/PK-12
204 Betsy Pack Dr 37347 423-942-3434
Mark Griffith, supt. Fax 942-4210
www.marionschools.org/
Central Prep Academy Alt
230 Ridley Dr 37347 423-805-9861
Jennifer Rector, prin. Fax 805-9861
Jasper MS 500/5-8
601 Elm Ave 37347 423-942-6251
Ramona McEntyre, prin. Fax 942-0141
Marion County HS 500/9-12
160 Ridley Ave 37347 423-942-5120
Larry Ziegler, prin. Fax 942-5544
Other Schools – See South Pittsburg, Whitwell

**Jefferson City, Jefferson, Pop. 7,885**
Jefferson County SD
Supt. — See Dandridge
Jefferson MS 600/6-8
361 W Broadway Blvd 37760 865-475-6133
Joel Sanford, prin. Fax 471-6878

---

Carson-Newman University Post-Sec.
1646 Russell Ave 37760 865-471-2000

**Jellico, Campbell, Pop. 2,326**
Campbell County SD
Supt. — See Jacksboro
Jellico HS 400/9-12
141 High School Ln 37762 423-784-9455
Dr. Donna Singley, prin. Fax 784-9456

**Joelton, See Nashville**
Metropolitan Nashville SD
Supt. — See Nashville
Joelton MS 300/5-8
3500 Old Clarksville Pike 37080 615-876-5100
Peggy Brodien, prin.

**Johnson City, Washington, Pop. 61,881**
Johnson City SD 5,900/PK-12
PO Box 1517 37605 423-434-5200
Dr. Richard Bales, supt. Fax 218-4968
www.jcschools.org
Liberty Bell MS 7-8
806 Morningside Dr 37604 423-232-2192
Tammy Pearce, prin.
Science Hill Career Technical Center Vo/Tech
251 Cotty Jones Dr 37604 423-232-2200
Dr. Julia Decker, dir. Fax 461-1695
Science Hill HS 2,200/9-12
1509 John Exum Pkwy 37604 423-232-2190
Melanie Riden-Bacon, prin. Fax 434-5570

Washington County SD
Supt. — See Jonesborough
Asbury Optional HS Alt
2002 Indian Ridge Rd 37604 423-434-4900
Kari Arnold, prin. Fax 434-4902
Boones Creek MS 400/5-8
4352 N Roan St 37615 423-283-3520
Mike Edmonds, prin. Fax 283-3524

---

East Tennessee State University Post-Sec.
807 University Pkwy 37614 423-439-1000
Emmanuel School of Religion Post-Sec.
1 Walker Dr 37601 423-926-1186
ITT Technical Institute Post-Sec.
4721 Lake Park Dr Ste 100 37615 423-952-4400
Providence Academy 500/K-12
2788 Carroll Creek Rd 37615 423-854-9819
Jerry Williams, admin. Fax 854-8958

**Jonesborough, Washington, Pop. 4,977**
Washington County SD 9,100/PK-12
405 W College St 37659 423-753-1100
Ronald Dykes, dir. Fax 753-1114
www.wcde.org
Crockett HS 1,200/9-12
684 Old State Route 34 37659 423-753-1150
Andy Hare, prin. Fax 753-1167
Jonesborough MS 400/5-8
308 Forrest Dr 37659 423-753-1190
Terry Crowe, prin. Fax 753-1570
Other Schools – See Gray, Johnson City

**Kingsport, Sullivan, Pop. 47,353**
Kingsport CSD 6,900/PK-12
400 Clinchfield St Ste 200 37660 423-378-2100
Dr. Lyle Ailshie, supt. Fax 378-2120
www.k12k.com/
D-B EXCEL at Cora Cox Academy Alt
520 Myrtle St 37660 423-378-2185
Shanna Hensley, prin. Fax 378-2187
Dobyns-Bennett HS 1,900/9-12
1800 Legion Dr 37664 423-378-8400
Dr. Chris Hampton, prin. Fax 378-8535
Robinson MS 900/6-8
1517 Jessee St 37664 423-378-2200
Brian Partin, prin. Fax 378-2220
Sevier MS 800/6-8
1200 Wateree St 37660 423-378-2450
Holly Flora, prin. Fax 378-2430

Sullivan County SD
Supt. — See Blountville
Colonial Heights MS 500/6-8
415 Lebanon Rd 37663 423-354-1360
Bill Dunham, prin. Fax 354-1365
Sullivan North HS 600/9-12
2533 N John B Dennis Hwy 37660 423-354-1400
Brent Palmer, prin. Fax 354-1406
Sullivan North MS 6-8
2533 N John B Dennis Hwy 37660 423-354-1750
Wayne King, admin. Fax 354-1459
Sullivan South HS 1,000/9-12
1236 Moreland Dr 37664 423-354-1300
Greg Harvey, prin. Fax 354-1306

---

Appalachian Christian S 50/K-12
1044 New Beason Well Rd 37660 423-288-3352
Newl Dotson, dir. Fax 288-3354
Cedar View Christian School 200/PK-12
PO Box 143 37662 423-245-6341

**Kingston, Roane, Pop. 5,854**
Roane County SD 7,100/PK-12
105 Bluff Rd 37763 865-376-5592
Gary Aytes, dir. Fax 376-1284
www.roaneschools.com
Cherokee MS 600/6-8
200 Paint Rock Ferry Rd 37763 865-376-9281
Elizabeth Rose, prin. Fax 376-8525
Midway HS 300/9-12
530 Loudon Hwy 37763 865-376-5645
Scott Mason, prin. Fax 376-8516
Roane County HS 700/9-12
540 W Cumberland St 37763 865-376-6534
Lance Duff, prin. Fax 376-8530
Other Schools – See Harriman, Oliver Springs, Rockwood, Ten Mile

**Kingston Springs, Cheatham, Pop. 2,732**
Cheatham County SD
Supt. — See Ashland City
Harpeth HS 600/9-12
170 E Kingston Springs Rd 37082 615-952-2811
Dr. Ryan Longnecker, prin. Fax 952-5013
Harpeth MS 600/5-8
170 Harpeth View Trl 37082 615-952-2293
Lucas Winstead, prin. Fax 952-4527

**Knoxville, Knox, Pop. 174,475**
Knox County SD 57,000/PK-12
PO Box 2188 37901 865-594-1800
Dr. James McIntyre, supt. Fax 594-1627
knoxschools.org
Austin-East HS 600/9-12
2800 Martin Luther King Jr 37914 865-594-3792
Benny Perry, prin. Fax 594-1165
Bearden HS 1,900/9-12
8352 Kingston Pike 37919 865-539-7800
Dr. John Bartlett, prin. Fax 539-7805
Bearden MS 1,100/6-8
1000 Francis Rd 37909 865-539-7839
Sonya Winstead, prin. Fax 539-7851
Byington-Solway Technology Center Vo/Tech
2700 Byington Solway Rd 37931 865-693-3511
David Bell, admin. Fax 694-7094
Career Technical Education Vo/Tech
535 Chickamauga Ave 37917 865-689-1454
Don Lawson, dir. Fax 689-1456
Cedar Bluff MS 600/6-8
707 N Cedar Bluff Rd 37923 865-539-7891
Christine Oehler, prin. Fax 539-7792
Central HS 1,100/9-12
5321 Jacksboro Pike 37918 865-689-1400
Jody Goins, prin. Fax 689-1403
Farragut HS 1,700/9-12
11237 Kingston Pike, 865-966-9775
Mike Reynolds, prin. Fax 671-7120

Farragut MS 1,300/6-8
200 W End Ave, 865-966-9756
Danny Trent, prin. Fax 671-7048
Fulton HS 900/9-12
2509 N Broadway St 37917 865-594-1240
Rob Speas, prin. Fax 594-1228
Gresham MS 800/6-8
500 Gresham Rd 37918 865-689-1430
Donna Parker, prin. Fax 689-7437
Halls HS 1,300/9-12
4321 E Emory Rd 37938 865-922-7757
Mark Duff, prin. Fax 925-7700
Halls MS 1,100/6-8
4317 E Emory Rd 37938 865-922-7494
Tim Wiegenstein, prin. Fax 925-7439
Hardin Valley Academy 1,900/9-12
11345 Hardin Valley Rd 37932 865-690-9690
Sallee Reynolds, prin. Fax 690-9260
Holston MS 900/6-8
600 N Chilhowee Dr 37924 865-594-1300
Ashley Jessie, prin. Fax 594-4429
Karns HS 1,300/9-12
2710 Byington Solway Rd 37931 865-539-8670
Kim Towe, prin. Fax 539-8679
Karns MS 1,300/6-8
2925 Gray Hendrix Rd 37931 865-539-7732
Brad Corum, prin. Fax 539-7745
Kelley Volunteer Academy Alt
3001 Knoxville Center Dr 37924 865-525-0069
Alan Hill, prin. Fax 525-2666
L & N STEM Academy 50/10-12
401 Henley St 37902 865-329-8440
Becky Ashe, prin. Fax 329-8457
North Knox Vocational Center Vo/Tech
7411 Ledgerwood Rd 37938 865-922-7576
Fax 925-7551
Northwest MS 700/6-8
5301 Pleasant Ridge Rd 37912 865-594-1345
Dr. Karen Loy, prin. Fax 594-1339
South-Doyle HS 1,100/9-12
2020 Tipton Station Rd 37920 865-577-4475
Tim Berry, prin. Fax 577-4540
South-Doyle MS 1,100/6-8
3900 Decatur Dr 37920 865-579-2133
Beth Blevins, prin. Fax 579-2128
Vine MS 300/6-8
1807 Martin Luther King Jr 37915 865-594-4461
Cindy White, prin. Fax 594-1702
West HS 1,200/9-12
3300 Sutherland Ave 37919 865-594-4477
Katherine Banner, prin. Fax 594-4486
West Valley MS 1,200/6-8
9118 George Williams Rd 37922 865-539-5145
Renee Kelly, prin. Fax 539-5155
Whittle Springs MS 500/6-8
2700 White Oak Ln 37917 865-594-4474
Nadriene Jackson, prin. Fax 594-1132
Yoakley S 100/Alt
4415 Washington Pike 37917 865-594-3790
Tom Watson, prin. Fax 594-3770
Knox County Adult HS Adult
3001 Knoxville Center Dr 37924 865-594-8718
Nancy Seely, prin.
Other Schools – See Corryton, Powell, Strawberry Plains

---

Apostolic Christian S 100/K-12
5020 Pleasant Ridge Rd 37912 865-523-5262
Berean Christian S 400/PK-12
2329 Prosser Rd 37914 865-521-6054
George Waller, hdmstr. Fax 522-5063
Christian Academy of Knoxville 1,200/PK-12
529 Academy Way 37923 865-690-4721
Robert Neu, head sch Fax 690-4752
Concord Christian S 400/K-12
11704 Kingston Pike, 865-966-8858
Ruston Pierce, hdmstr. Fax 288-1617
Fort Sanders School of Nursing Post-Sec.
9821 Cogdill Rd Ste 2 37932
Fountainhead College of Technology Post-Sec.
10208 Technology Dr 37932 865-688-9422
Grace Christian Academy 900/K-12
5914 Beaver Ridge Rd 37931 865-691-3427
Rob Hammond, head sch Fax 342-3827
Huntington College of Health Sciences Post-Sec.
117 Legacy View Way 37918 865-524-8079
ITT Technical Institute Post-Sec.
9123 Executive Park Dr 37923 865-342-2300
Johnson University Post-Sec.
7900 Johnson Dr 37998 865-573-4517
Knoxville Catholic HS 700/9-12
9245 Fox Lonas Rd 37923 865-560-0313
Dickie Sompayrac Ed.D., prin. Fax 560-0314
Knoxville Christian S 200/PK-12
11549 Snyder Rd 37932 865-966-7060
Jarra Snyder, prin. Fax 671-2148
National College of Business & Tech Post-Sec.
8415 Kingston Pike 37919 865-539-2011
Paideia Academy 100/PK-12
10825 Yarnell Rd 37932 865-670-0440
Kent Capps, prin. Fax 474-1476
Pellissippi State Community College Post-Sec.
PO Box 22990 37933 865-694-6400
Reuben Allen College Post-Sec.
120 Center Park Dr 37922 865-966-0400
River's Edge Christian Academy 200/PK-12
PO Box 31733 37930 865-693-6779
Brian Beemer, admin. Fax 317-2443
South College Post-Sec.
3904 Lonas Dr 37909 865-251-1800
Tennessee School for the Deaf Post-Sec.
2725 Island Home Blvd 37920 865-594-6022
Tennessee School of Beauty Post-Sec.
4704 Western Ave 37921 865-588-7878
Tennessee Technology Center at Knoxville Post-Sec.
1100 Liberty St 37919 865-546-5567
University of Tennessee Knoxville Post-Sec.
320 Student Services Bldg 37996 865-974-1000
University of Tennessee Medical Center Post-Sec.
1924 Alcoa Hwy 37920 865-546-5567
Virginia College Post-Sec.
5003 N Broadway St 37918 865-745-4500
Webb S of Knoxville 1,100/K-12
9800 Webb School Ln 37923 865-693-0011
Michael McBrien, pres. Fax 691-8057

**Kodak, Sevier**
Sevier County SD
Supt. — See Sevierville
Northview Junior Academy 200/7-9
2719 Northview Academy Ln 37764 865-933-5880
Greg Clark, prin. Fax 933-4018
Northview Senior Academy 10-11
2719 Northview Academy Ln 37764 865-933-5880
Kevin DeBow, admin. Fax 933-4018

**Lafayette, Macon, Pop. 4,440**
Macon County SD 3,700/PK-12
501 College St 37083 615-666-2125
Tony Boles, dir. Fax 666-7878
www.maconcountyschools.com/
Macon County HS 900/9-12
2550 Days Rd 37083 615-666-4320
B.J. West, prin. Fax 666-4757
Macon County JHS 700/6-8
1003 Highway 52 Byp E 37083 615-666-7545
Tracy Strong, prin. Fax 666-9264
Other Schools – See Red Boiling Springs

---

Lighthouse Academy 300/PK-12
5576 Highway 52 W 37083 615-666-7151

**La Follette, Campbell, Pop. 7,339**
Campbell County SD
Supt. — See Jacksboro
La Follette MS 500/6-8
1309 E Central Ave 37766 423-562-8448
Robbie Heatherly, prin. Fax 562-2107
Campbell County Adult HS Adult
318 W Beech St 37766 423-566-5436
Dr. Jamie Wheeler, prin. Fax 562-5219

**Lake City, Anderson, Pop. 1,756**
Anderson County SD
Supt. — See Clinton
Lake City MS 300/6-8
1132 S Main St 37769 865-426-2609
Kelvin McCullom, prin. Fax 426-9319

**La Vergne, Rutherford, Pop. 31,758**
Rutherford County SD
Supt. — See Murfreesboro
La Vergne HS 2,100/9-12
250 Wolverine Trl 37086 615-904-3870
Dirk Ash, prin. Fax 904-3871
La Vergne MS 1,000/6-8
382 Stones River Rd 37086 615-904-3877
Cary Holman, prin. Fax 904-3878

**Lawrenceburg, Lawrence, Pop. 10,194**
Lawrence County SD 6,800/PK-12
700 Mahr Ave 38464 931-762-3581
Dr. Bill Heath, supt. Fax 762-7299
www.lcss.us
Coffman MS 400/7-8
111 Lafayette Ave 38464 931-762-6395
Sarah Cope, prin. Fax 762-7176
Lawrence County HS 1,100/9-12
1800 Springer Rd 38464 931-762-9412
Michael Adkins, prin. Fax 766-0761
LCSS Career-Technical Education Vo/Tech
700 Mahr Ave 38464 931-762-2273
Jay Ridgway, prin.
Barnett Education Center Adult
610 Mahr Ave 38464 931-762-5251
Other Schools – See Loretto, Summertown

**Lebanon, Wilson, Pop. 25,677**
Lebanon Special SD 3,300/PK-8
701 Coles Ferry Pike 37087 615-449-6060
Scott Benson, dir. Fax 449-5673
www.lssd.org
Baird MS 500/6-8
131 WJB Pride Ln 37087 615-444-2190
Pam Sampson, prin. Fax 453-2690
Winfree Bryant MS 500/6-8
1213 Leeville Pike 37090 615-449-4560
Becky Kegley, prin. Fax 449-4590

Wilson County SD 15,900/PK-12
351 Stumpy Ln 37090 615-444-3282
Dr. Donna Wright, dir. Fax 449-3858
www.wcschools.com
Lebanon HS 1,600/9-12
500 Blue Devil Blvd 37087 615-444-9610
Myra Sloan, prin. Fax 443-1373
MAP Academy Alt
205 Stumpy Ln 37090 615-453-3400
Rick Miller, prin. Fax 453-3401
Wilson Central HS 1,700/9-12
419 Wildcat Way 37090 615-453-4600
Pat Suddarth, prin. Fax 453-4610
Adult Basic Education Adult
351 Stumpy Ln 37090 615-443-8731
Betty Byrd, dir. Fax 453-2529
Wilson County Adult HS Adult
207 J Branham Dr 37087 615-443-7199
Mary Ashby, prin. Fax 443-2690
Other Schools – See Mount Juliet, Watertown

---

Cumberland University Post-Sec.
1 Cumberland Sq 37087 615-444-2562
Friendship Christian S 500/PK-12
5400 Coles Ferry Pike 37087 615-449-1573
Jon Shoulders, pres. Fax 449-2769

**Lenoir City, Loudon, Pop. 8,520**
Lenoir CSD 2,400/PK-12
2145 Harrison Ave 37771 865-986-8058
Dr. Jeanne Barker, dir. Fax 988-6732
www.lenoircityschools.com/
Lenoir City HS 1,300/9-12
1485 Old Highway 95 37771 865-986-2072
Chip Orr, prin. Fax 988-2054
Lenoir City Intermediate MS 600/4-8
2141 Harrison Ave 37771 865-986-2038
Brandee Hoglund, prin. Fax 988-1964

Loudon County SD
Supt. — See Loudon
North MS 800/5-8
421 Hickory Creek Rd 37771 865-986-9944
Mattthew Tinker, prin. Fax 988-9089

---

Crossroads Christian Academy 100/PK-12
1963 Martel Rd 37772 865-986-9823

**Lewisburg, Marshall, Pop. 10,852**
Marshall County SD 4,200/PK-12
700 Jones Cir 37091 931-359-1581
Jackie Abernathy, dir. Fax 270-8816
www.k12marshall.net
Lewisburg MS 400/7-8
500 Tiger Blvd 37091 931-359-1265
Randy Hubbell, prin. Fax 359-4030
Marshall County HS 800/9-12
597 W Ellington Pkwy 37091 931-359-1549
John Bush, prin. Fax 359-4784
Spot Lowe Vocational S Vo/Tech
1771 Jason Maxwell Blvd 37091 931-359-4911
Lyn Stacey, dir. Fax 359-3041
Other Schools – See Chapel Hill, Cornersville

**Lexington, Henderson, Pop. 7,427**
Henderson County SD 3,900/PK-12
35 E Wilson St 38351 731-968-3661
Steve Wilkinson, dir. Fax 968-9457
hcschoolstn.org
Lexington HS 900/9-12
284 White St 38351 731-968-2961
Steve Lindsey, prin. Fax 968-9399
Other Schools – See Reagan

Lexington CSD 1,100/PK-8
99 Monroe Ave 38351 731-967-5591
Susan Bunch, dir. Fax 967-0794
www.caywood.org
Lexington MS 300/6-8
112 Airways Dr 38351 731-968-8457
Beth Deere, prin. Fax 967-7130

**Linden, Perry, Pop. 889**
Perry County SD 1,200/PK-12
857 Squirrel Hollow Dr 37096 931-589-2102
Eric Lomax, dir. Fax 589-5110
www.perrycountyschools.us
Linden MS 200/5-8
130 College Ave 37096 931-589-5000
Brent Cunningham, prin. Fax 589-3685
Perry County HS 400/9-12
1056 Squirrel Hollow Dr 37096 931-589-2831
Mike Rhodes, prin. Fax 589-5063

**Livingston, Overton, Pop. 4,018**
Overton County SD 3,400/K-12
302 Zachary St 38570 931-823-1287
Pamela Smith-Gordon, dir. Fax 823-4673
www.overtoncountyschools.net
Livingston Academy HS 1,000/9-12
120 Melvin Johnson Dr 38570 931-823-5911
Leslie Riddle, prin. Fax 823-8626
Livingston MS 400/5-8
216 Bilbrey St 38570 931-823-5917
Doug Smith, prin. Fax 823-7549
Reach Academy 50/Alt
312 W Broad St 38570 931-823-9388
cindy prater, prin. Fax 823-4673
Overton Adult HS Adult
112 Bussell St 38570 931-823-7761
Marsha Wyatt, admin. Fax 823-8852

---

Tennessee Technology Center Livingston Post-Sec.
740 HI Tech Dr 38570 931-823-5525

**Loretto, Lawrence, Pop. 1,696**
Lawrence County SD
Supt. — See Lawrenceburg
Loretto HS 500/9-12
525 2nd Ave S 38469 931-853-4324
Dr. Jennifer Littleton, prin. Fax 853-4340

**Loudon, Loudon, Pop. 5,315**
Loudon County SD 5,000/PK-12
100 River Rd 37774 865-458-5411
Jason Vance, dir. Fax 458-6138
www.loudoncounty.org/
Ft. Loudoun MS 400/6-8
1083 Mulberry St 37774 865-458-2026
Christie Amburn, prin. Fax 458-6611
Loudon HS 700/9-12
1039 Mulberry St 37774 865-458-4326
Cheri Parrish, prin. Fax 458-0717
Other Schools – See Greenback, Lenoir City

**Lyles, Hickman, Pop. 722**
Hickman County SD
Supt. — See Centerville
East Hickman HS 600/9-12
7700 Highway 7 37098 931-670-1366
Bruce Jackson, prin. Fax 670-1039
East Hickman MS 500/6-8
9414 E Eagle Dr 37098 931-670-4237
Julia Thomasson, prin. Fax 670-4239

**Lynchburg, Moore, Pop. 5,241**
Moore County SD 1,000/K-12
PO Box 219 37352 931-759-7303
Chad Moorehead, supt. Fax 759-6386
www.moorecountyschools.net
Moore County JSHS 500/7-12
1502 Lynchburg Hwy 37352 931-759-4231
Brantley Smith, prin. Fax 759-6390

---

Motlow State Community College Post-Sec.
PO Box 8500 37352 931-393-1500

**Lynnville, Giles, Pop. 286**
Giles County SD
Supt. — See Pulaski
Richland MSHS 700/5-12
10610 Columbia Hwy 38472 931-527-3577
Micah Landers, prin. Fax 527-3720

**Mc Ewen, Humphreys, Pop. 1,735**
Humphreys County SD
Supt. — See Waverly
Mc Ewen HS 300/9-12
335 Melrose St 37101 931-582-6950
Jerry Honea, prin. Fax 582-6952
McEwen JHS 200/6-8
365 Melrose St 37101 931-582-8417
T. Coleman, prin. Fax 582-8418

**Mc Kenzie, Carroll, Pop. 5,208**
Mc Kenzie Special SD 1,400/PK-12
114 Bell Ave 38201 731-352-2246
Lynn Watkins, dir. Fax 352-7550
www.mckenzieschools.org
Mc Kenzie HS 400/9-12
23292 Highway 22 38201 731-352-2133
Tim Watkins, prin. Fax 352-1424
Mc Kenzie MS 500/5-8
80 Woodrow Ave 38201 731-352-2792
David Duncan, prin. Fax 352-4709

---

Bethel University Post-Sec.
325 Cherry Ave 38201 731-352-4000
Tennessee Technology Center at Mc Kenzie Post-Sec.
16940 Highland Dr 38201 731-352-5364

**Mc Minnville, Warren, Pop. 13,384**
Warren County SD 6,700/PK-12
2548 Morrison St 37110 931-668-4022
John R. Cox, dir. Fax 815-2685
www.warrenschools.com
Warren Academy 50/Alt
421 N Spring St 37110 931-473-8723
Frank Fisher, prin. Fax 473-6094
Warren County HS 1,900/9-12
199 Pioneer Ln 37110 931-668-5858
Jimmy Walker, prin. Fax 668-5801
Warren County MS 900/6-8
200 Caldwell St 37110 931-473-6557
Gerald Tidwell, prin. Fax 473-2432

---

Boyd Christian S 100/PK-12
806 Morrison St 37110 931-473-9631
Covenant Academy 100/PK-12
1079 Country Club Dr 37110 931-668-6185
Tennessee Technology Center Mc Minnville Post-Sec.
241 Vo Tech Dr 37110 931-473-5587

**Madison, See Nashville**
Metropolitan Nashville SD
Supt. — See Nashville
Madison MS 800/5-8
300 W Old Hickory Blvd 37115 615-684-4018
Kelli Lorton, prin. Fax 612-3664
Neelys Bend MS 600/5-8
1251 Neelys Bend Rd 37115 615-860-1477
Michelle Brock Demps, prin. Fax 612-3669

---

Goodpasture Christian S 900/PK-12
619 W Due West Ave 37115 615-868-2600
Madison Academy 100/9-12
100 Academy Rd 37115 615-865-4055
Middle Tennessee School of Anesthesia Post-Sec.
PO Box 417 37116 615-732-7662
Miller-Motte Technical College Post-Sec.
1515 Gallatin Pike N 37115 615-859-8090
Nashville College of Medical Careers Post-Sec.
1556 Crestview Dr 37115 615-868-2963
National College of Business & Tech Post-Sec.
900 Madison Sq 37115 615-612-3015
Nossi College of Art Post-Sec.
590 Cheron Rd 37115 615-514-2787
Volunteer Beauty Academy Post-Sec.
1793 Gallatin Pike N 37115 615-860-4200

**Madisonville, Monroe, Pop. 4,500**
Monroe County SD 5,500/PK-12
205 Oak Grove Rd 37354 423-442-2373
Tim Blankenship, dir. Fax 442-1389
www.monroe.k12.tn.us/
Madisonville MS 500/6-8
175 Oak Grove Rd 37354 423-442-4137
Sheryl Debity, prin. Fax 442-9338
Sequoyah HS 1,000/9-12
3128 Highway 411 37354 423-442-9230
Debi Tipton, prin. Fax 442-5520
Other Schools – See Sweetwater, Tellico Plains, Vonore

---

Hiwassee College Post-Sec.
225 Hiwassee College Dr 37354 423-442-2001

**Manchester, Coffee, Pop. 9,924**
Coffee County SD 4,600/PK-12
1343 McArthur St 37355 931-723-5150
Dr. LaDonna McFall, dir. Fax 723-5153
www.coffeecountyschools.com/
Coffee County Central HS 1,600/10-12
100 Red Raider Dr 37355 931-723-5159
Joey Vaughn, prin. Fax 723-5161
Coffee County Koss Center 50/Alt
1756 McMinnville Hwy 37355 931-723-5189
Major Shelton, prin. Fax 723-5172
Coffee County MS 1,000/6-8
3063 Woodbury Hwy 37355 931-723-5177
Kimberly Aaron, prin. Fax 723-5180
Coffee County Raider Academy 9-9
865 McMinnville Hwy 37355 931-723-3309
Angela Gribble, prin. Fax 723-8273

Manchester CSD 1,200/PK-8
215 E Fort St 37355 931-728-2316
Sandra Morris, supt. Fax 728-7075
www.manchestercitysch.org
Westwood MS 300/6-8
505 E Taylor St 37355 931-728-2071
Chad Fletcher, prin. Fax 728-0962

**Martin, Weakley, Pop. 11,280**
Weakley County SD
Supt. — See Dresden
Martin MS 500/6-8
700 Fowler Rd 38237 731-587-2346
Nate Holmes, prin. Fax 588-0529
Westview HS 600/9-12
8161 Highway 45 S 38237 731-587-4202
Jeromy Davidson, prin. Fax 588-0806

---

University of Tennessee Post-Sec.
554 University Ct 38237 731-881-7000

**Maryville, Blount, Pop. 26,990**
Blount County SD 11,200/PK-12
831 Grandview Dr 37803 865-984-1212
Rob Britt, dir. Fax 980-1002
www.blountk12.org
Blount 9th Grade Academy 500/9-9
1126 William Blount Dr 37801 865-984-5500
Chris Merrit, prin. Fax 980-1183
Blount HS 1,300/10-12
219 County Farm Rd 37801 865-984-5500
Rob Clark, prin. Fax 977-0153
Carpenters MS 700/6-8
920 Huffstetler Rd 37803 865-980-1414
Jon Young, prin. Fax 980-1404
Eagleton MS 400/6-8
2610 Cinema Dr 37804 865-982-3211
Tony Schultz, prin. Fax 982-4203
Everett Learning Opportunity Center 100/Alt
1500 Jett Rd 37804 865-984-9420
Danny Galyon, prin. Fax 984-7189
Heritage HS 1,600/9-12
3741 E Lamar Alexander Pkwy 37804 865-984-8110
Jake Jones, prin. Fax 984-0147
Heritage MS 900/6-8
3737 E Lamar Alexander Pkwy 37804 865-980-1300
Dr. Steve Moser, prin. Fax 980-1281
Other Schools – See Friendsville

Maryville CSD 3,600/PK-12
833 Lawrence Ave 37803 865-982-7121
Dr. Mike Winstead, supt. Fax 977-5055
www.maryville-schools.org
Maryville HS 1,100/10-12
825 Lawrence Ave 37803 865-982-1132
Greg Roach, prin. Fax 983-1440
Maryville JHS 400/8-9
805 Montvale Station Rd 37803 865-983-2070
Lisa McGinley, prin. Fax 977-9413

---

Apostolic Christian Academy 100/PK-12
1723 William Blount Dr 37801 865-984-0046
Cherie Johnson, prin. Fax 982-0046
Clayton-Bradley STEM Academy 100/PK-10
425 Alcoa Tr 37804 865-494-1222
Maryville Christian S 400/PK-12
2525 Morganton Rd 37801 865-681-3205
Dr. Glenn Slater, admin. Fax 681-4086
Maryville College Post-Sec.
502 E Lamar Alexander Pkwy 37804 865-981-8000

**Maynardville, Union, Pop. 2,385**
Union County SD 3,000/PK-12
PO Box 10 37807 865-992-5466
Dr. James Carter, dir. Fax 992-0126
www.ucps.org/
Maynard MS 700/6-8
PO Box 669 37807 865-992-1030
Greg Clay, prin. Fax 992-1060
Union County Alternative Learning Center Alt
PO Box 609 37807 865-992-7747
Chris Price, prin. Fax 992-9076
Union County HS 800/9-12
150 Main St 37807 865-992-5232
Linda Harrell, prin. Fax 992-5724

**Medina, Gibson, Pop. 3,452**
Gibson County Special SD
Supt. — See Dyer
Medina MS 900/3-8
PO Box 369 38355 731-783-1962
Steve Maloan, prin. Fax 783-1964
South Gibson County HS 600/9-12
PO Box 249 38355 731-783-0999
Phil Rogers, prin. Fax 783-0011

**Memphis, Shelby, Pop. 639,057**
Achievement SD 3,400/PK-12
477 S Main St Fl 4 38103 901-260-9649
Chris Barbic, supt.
www.achievementschooldistrict.org/
Pathways in Education - Memphis Frayser Alt
3156 Thomas St 38127 901-308-8471
Jennifer Isom, prin.
Westside Achievement MS 500/6-8
3389 Dawn Dr 38127 901-416-3700
Michael Brown, prin. Fax 416-3701

Shelby County SD 144,300/PK-12
160 S Hollywood St 38112 901-321-2500
Dorsey Hopson, supt. Fax 321-2501
www.scsk12.org/
Airways MS 300/6-8
2601 Ketchum Rd 38114 901-416-5006
Dr. LeCharle Harris, prin. Fax 416-5009
American Way MS 800/6-8
3805 American Way 38118 901-416-1250
Lisa Maclin-Love, prin. Fax 416-1251
Bellevue MS 500/6-8
575 S Bellevue Blvd 38104 901-416-4488
Kevin Malone, prin. Fax 416-4490
Bond MS 1,100/6-8
2737 Kate Bond Rd 38133 901-416-0640
Angela Brown, prin. Fax 416-7962
Carver HS 500/9-12
1591 Pennsylvania St 38109 901-416-7594
Alvin Harris, prin. Fax 416-2235
Central HS 1,800/9-12
306 S Bellevue Blvd 38104 901-416-4500
Gregory McCullough, prin. Fax 416-4506
Chickasaw MS 400/6-8
4060 Westmont Rd 38109 901-416-8134
Veda Turner, prin. Fax 416-8139
Colonial MS 1,200/6-8
1370 Colonial Rd 38117 901-416-8980
Marty Pettigrew, prin. Fax 416-8996
Craigmont HS 1,100/9-12
3333 Covington Pike 38128 901-416-4312
Sherilyn Brown, prin. Fax 416-7675
Craigmont MS 800/6-8
3455 Covington Pike 38128 901-416-7780
LaTrenda Hicks, prin. Fax 416-1454
Douglass HS 700/9-12
3200 Mount Olive Rd 38108 901-416-0990
Janet Thompson, prin. Fax 416-9887
East HS 900/9-12
3206 Poplar Ave 38111 901-416-6160
Eric Harris, prin. Fax 416-6161
Frayser Success Academy Alt
1530 Dellwood Ave 38127 901-416-2820
Robert Washington, prin. Fax 416-2831
Geeter MS 400/6-8
4649 Horn Lake Rd 38109 901-416-8157
Lori Oduyoye, prin. Fax 416-8160
Georgian Hills MS 300/6-8
3925 Denver St 38127 901-416-3740
Deartis Barber, prin. Fax 416-6500
Grandview Heights MS 400/6-8
2342 Clifton Ave 38127 901-416-3940
Christine Vandiver-Tate, prin. Fax 416-3923
Hamilton HS 900/9-12
1363 E Person Ave 38106 901-416-7838
Curtis Weathers, prin. Fax 416-7829
Hamilton MS 400/6-8
1478 Wilson St 38106 901-416-7832
Kelly Henderson, prin. Fax 416-3314
Hamilton Success Academy Alt
1478 Wilson St 38106 901-416-7949
Dr. James Suggs, prin. Fax 416-7948
Havenview MS 900/6-8
1481 Hester Rd 38116 901-416-3092
Michael Bates, prin. Fax 416-3093
Hickory Ridge MS 900/6-8
3920 Ridgeway Rd 38115 901-416-9337
Cedric Smith, prin. Fax 416-9210
Highland Oaks MS 900/6-8
5600 Meadowbriar Trl 38125 901-432-4114
Monica Bates, prin. Fax 432-4122
Hillcrest HS 700/9-12
4184 Graceland Dr 38116 901-416-3104
Eric Moore, prin. Fax 416-9432
Kingsbury Career Technology Center Vo/Tech
1328 N Graham St 38122 901-416-6000
Timothy Batts, prin. Fax 416-6003
Kingsbury HS 1,100/9-12
1270 N Graham St 38122 901-416-6060
Terry Ross, prin. Fax 416-6061
Kingsbury MS 400/6-8
1276 N Graham St 38122 901-416-6040
Melvin Harris, prin. Fax 416-6058
Kirby HS 1,500/9-12
4080 Kirby Pkwy 38115 901-416-1960
Daniel Jack, prin. Fax 416-1968
Kirby MS 800/6-8
6670 E Raines Rd 38115 901-416-1980
Pamela Yancy-Taylor, prin. Fax 416-0974
Lester MS 400/7-8
320 Carpenter St 38112 901-416-5969
Elaine Stewart-Price, prin. Fax 416-5971
Manassas HS 600/9-12
1111 N Manassas St 38107 901-416-3244
James Griffin, prin. Fax 416-3248
Melrose HS 1,000/9-12
2870 Deadrick Ave 38114 901-416-5974
Mark Neal, prin. Fax 416-5984
Memphis Health Careers Academy 100/Alt
80 W Olive Ave 38106 901-416-1950
Brenda Diaz Williams, prin. Fax 416-1951
Messick Career & Technology Center Vo/Tech
703 S Greer St 38111 901-416-4840
Rochelle Griffin, prin. Fax 416-4842
Middle College SHS 200/10-12
750 E Parkway S 38104 901-416-4550
Docia Generette, prin. Fax 416-4555
Mitchell HS 600/9-12
658 W Mitchell Rd 38109 901-416-8174
Kelvin Meeks, prin. Fax 416-8176
Northeast Prep Academy 300/Alt
968 N Mendenhall Rd 38122 901-416-2132
Kenneth Dickerson, prin. Fax 416-2157

Northside HS 400/9-12
1212 Vollintine Ave 38107 901-416-4582
Vincent Thompson, prin. Fax 416-9813
Northwest Prep Academy 500/Alt
1266 Poplar Ave 38104 901-416-4400
Roger Jones, prin. Fax 416-4683
Oakhaven HS 500/9-12
3125 Ladbrook Rd 38118 901-416-2300
Melanie Black, prin. Fax 416-2301
Oakhaven MS 200/6-8
3125 Ladbrook Rd 38118 901-416-2380
Shari Jones, prin. Fax 416-9780
Overton HS 1,300/9-12
1770 Lanier Ln 38117 901-416-2136
Brett Lawson, prin. Fax 416-2135
Price Middle College HS 200/9-12
807 Walker Ave 38126 901-435-1765
Sandra Barnes, prin. Fax 435-1779
Raleigh-Egypt HS 1,000/9-12
3970 Voltaire Ave 38128 901-416-4108
James Griffin, prin. Fax 416-4143
Raleigh-Egypt MS 700/6-8
4215 Alice Ann Dr 38128 901-416-4141
Rommie Mackin, prin. Fax 416-4110
Reconation Academy Alt
868 N Manassas St 38107 901-577-2500
Michael Smith, prin. Fax 578-3435
Ridgeway HS 1,200/9-12
2009 Ridgeway Rd 38119 901-416-8820
Dr. Jonathan Stencel, prin. Fax 416-2199
Ridgeway MS 800/6-8
6333 Quince Rd 38119 901-416-1588
Corey Williams, prin. Fax 416-1477
Riverview MS 300/6-8
241 Majuba Ave 38109 901-416-7340
Dr. Rosalind Martin, prin. Fax 416-7343
Sheffield Career & Tech Center Vo/Tech
4350 Chuck Ave 38118 901-416-2340
Charles Grove, prin. Fax 416-2394
Sheffield HS 1,000/9-12
4315 Sheffield Ave 38118 901-416-2370
Anthony Frigo, prin. Fax 416-2407
Sherwood MS 600/6-8
3480 Rhodes Ave 38111 901-416-4870
Corey Kelly, prin. Fax 416-4881
Smith STEAM Academy 300/6-8
750 E Parkway S 38104 901-416-4536
Lischa Brooks, prin. Fax 416-4539
Southeast Success Academy Alt
5396 Mendenhall Park Pl 38115 901-416-1436
Shawnh Curry, admin. Fax 416-1422
South Side MS 300/6-8
1880 Prospect St 38106 901-416-7420
Kobie Sweeten, prin. Fax 416-7381
Southwest Career & Technology Center Vo/Tech
3746 Horn Lake Rd 38109 901-416-8186
Leroy McClain, prin. Fax 416-8188
Southwest Prep Academy 200/Alt
1237 College St 38106 901-416-7884
Tyria Butler, prin. Fax 416-7886
Southwind HS 1,700/9-12
7900 E Shelby Dr 38125 901-752-2881
Terrence Brown, prin. Fax 752-2898
Treadwell MS 400/6-8
920 N Highland St 38122 901-416-6100
Tonya McBride, prin. Fax 416-6133
Trezevant Career & Tech Center Vo/Tech
3224 Range Line Rd 38127 901-416-3800
Eleanor Thomas, prin. Fax 416-3839
Trezevant HS 700/9-12
3350 N Trezevant St 38127 901-416-3760
Dr. Joe Canada, prin. Fax 416-3761
Walker MS 600/6-8
1900 E Raines Rd 38116 901-416-1030
Terrence Brittenum, prin. Fax 416-1075
Washington HS 500/6-12
715 S Lauderdale St 38126 901-416-7240
Alisha Kiner, prin. Fax 416-7228
Westhaven Success Academy Alt
4585 Hodge Rd 38109 901-416-7122
Valerie Matthews, prin. Fax 416-7121
Westwood HS 600/9-12
4480 Westmont Rd 38109 901-416-8000
Isaac White, prin. Fax 416-8027
Whitehaven HS 2,100/9-12
4851 Elvis Presley Blvd 38116 901-416-3000
Dr. Vincent Hunter, prin. Fax 416-3058
White Station HS 2,300/9-12
514 S Perkins Rd 38117 901-416-8880
David Mansfield, prin. Fax 416-8910
White Station MS 900/6-8
5465 Mason Rd 38120 901-416-2184
Shawn Page, prin. Fax 416-2187
Wooddale HS 1,500/9-12
5151 Scottsdale Ave 38118 901-416-2440
Michael Kyle, prin. Fax 416-2476
Wooddale MS 900/6-8
3467 Castleman St 38118 901-416-2420
Julia Callaway, prin. Fax 416-2426
Other Schools – See Arlington, Bartlett, Cordova, Germantown, Millington

---

All Saints Bible College Post-Sec.
930 Mason St 38126 901-322-0120
Anthem College Post-Sec.
5865 Shelby Oaks Cir #100 38134 901-432-3800
Baptist College of Health Sciences Post-Sec.
1003 Monroe Ave 38104 901-575-2247
Baptist Memorial Hospital Post-Sec.
350 N Humphreys Blvd #EagB2 38103
901-227-5121
Central Baptist S 200/PK-12
5470 Raleigh LaGrange Rd 38134 901-386-8161
Christian Brothers HS 800/9-12
5900 Walnut Grove Rd 38120 901-261-4900
Chris Fay, prin. Fax 261-4909
Christian Brothers University Post-Sec.
650 E Parkway S 38104 901-321-3000
Collegiate S of Memphis 300/9-12
3353 Faxon Ave 38122 901-591-8200
Concorde Career College Post-Sec.
5100 Poplar Ave Ste 132 38137 901-761-9494
Creative Life Preparatory S 50/PK-12
1222 Riverside Blvd 38106 901-775-0304
Dr. Carolyn Bibbs, pres. Fax 946-5433
DeVry University Post-Sec.
6401 Poplar Ave Ste 600 38119 901-537-2560
Gateway Christian S 1,300/1-12
4070 Macon Rd 38122 901-458-4276
Donna Bumgardner, prin. Fax 323-0914
Harding Academy of Memphis 500/7-12
1100 Cherry Rd 38117 901-767-4949
Harding School of Theology Post-Sec.
1000 Cherry Rd 38117 901-761-1350
Hutchison S 900/PK-12
1740 Ridgeway Rd 38119 901-761-2220
Dr. Annette Smith Ed.D., head sch Fax 432-6655
Immaculate Conception Cathedral S 200/PK-12
1695 Central Ave 38104 901-725-2705
Robin Perry, head sch Fax 725-2701
Lausanne Collegiate S 800/PK-12
1381 W Massey Rd 38120 901-474-1000
Le Moyne-Owen College Post-Sec.
807 Walker Ave 38126 901-435-1000
Margolin Hebrew Academy 200/PK-12
390 S White Station Rd 38117 901-682-2400
Memphis Catholic MSHS 200/7-12
61 N McLean Blvd 38104 901-276-1221
Kevin Kimberly, prin. Fax 725-1447
Memphis College of Art Post-Sec.
1930 Poplar Ave 38104 901-272-5100
Memphis Junior Academy 100/PK-10
50 N Mendenhall Rd 38117 901-683-1061
Memphis Theological Seminary Post-Sec.
168 E Parkway S 38104 901-458-8232
Memphis University S 700/7-12
6191 Park Ave 38119 901-260-1300
Ellis Haguewood, hdmstr. Fax 260-1301
Methodist Hospital Post-Sec.
1265 Union Ave 38104 901-726-8274
Mid-South Christian College Post-Sec.
3097 Knight Rd 38118 901-375-4400
National College of Business & Tech Post-Sec.
2576 Thousand Oaks Blvd 38118 901-363-9046
New Wave Hair Academy Post-Sec.
3250 Coleman Rd 38128 901-323-6100
New Wave Hair Academy Post-Sec.
804 S Highland St 38111 901-320-9283
Plaza Beauty School Post-Sec.
4682 Spottswood Ave 38117 901-761-4445
Pleasant View S 200/PK-12
1888 Bartlett Rd 38134 901-380-0122
Mohammed Malley, prin. Fax 380-1527
Remington College Post-Sec.
2710 Nonconnah Blvd # 160 38132 901-345-1000
Rhodes College Post-Sec.
2000 N Parkway 38112 901-843-3000
St. Agnes Academy/St. Dominic S 400/PK-12
4830 Walnut Grove Rd 38117 901-767-1356
Barbara Daush, pres. Fax 435-5866
St. Mary's Episcopal S 800/PK-12
60 Perkins Ext 38117 901-537-1472
Albert L. Throckmorton, hdmstr. Fax 682-0119
Southern College of Optometry Post-Sec.
1245 Madison Ave 38104 901-722-3200
Southern Institute of Cosmetology Post-Sec.
4030 Muirfield Dr 38125 - -
Southern Institute of Cosmetology Post-Sec.
3099 S Perkins Rd 38118 901-363-3553
Southwest Tennessee Community College Post-Sec.
PO Box 780 38101 901-333-5000
Strayer University Post-Sec.
2620 Thousand Oaks Ste 1100 38118 901-369-0835
Strayer University Post-Sec.
7275 Appling Farms Pkwy 38133 901-251-7100
Tennessee Academy of Cosmetology Post-Sec.
7041 Stage Rd Ste 101 38133 901-382-9085
Tennessee Academy of Cosmetology Post-Sec.
7020 E Shelby Dr Ste 104 38125 901-757-4166
Tennessee Technology Center at Memphis Post-Sec.
550 Alabama Ave 38105 901-543-6100
The Beauty Institute Post-Sec.
568 Colonial Rd 38117 901-761-1888
University of Memphis 38152 Post-Sec.
901-678-2000
Univ. of Tennessee Health Science Center Post-Sec.
800 Madison Ave 38163 901-448-5500
Vatterott Career College Post-Sec.
6991 Appling Farms Pkwy 38133 901-372-2399
Vatterott College Post-Sec.
2655 Dividend Dr 38132 901-761-5730
Victory University Post-Sec.
255 N Highland St 38111 800-960-9777
Visible Music College Post-Sec.
200 Madison Ave 38103 901-381-3939
Westminster Academy 300/PK-12
2500 Ridgeway Rd 38119 901-380-9192
William Moore College of Technology Post-Sec.
1200 Poplar Ave 38104 901-726-1977
Word of Faith Christian Academy 100/PK-12
3528 Sharpe Ave 38111 901-744-4061

**Middleton, Hardeman, Pop. 695**
Hardeman County SD
Supt. — See Bolivar
Middleton HS 600/7-12
138 Florida Ave 38052 731-376-8391
Darlene Cardwell, prin. Fax 376-8157

**Milan, Gibson, Pop. 7,701**
Milan Special SD 2,200/PK-12
1165 S Main St 38358 731-686-0844
Mary Reel Ed.D., dir. Fax 686-8781
www.milanssd.org
Milan HS 600/9-12
7060 E Van Hook St 38358 731-686-0841
Kris Todd, prin. Fax 686-9829
Milan MS 700/5-8
4040 Middle Rd 38358 731-686-7232
Sam Rhodes, prin. Fax 723-8872

---

Arnold's Beauty School Post-Sec.
1179 S 2nd St 38358 731-686-7351

**Milligan College, Carter**

---

Milligan College Post-Sec.
PO Box 500 37682 423-461-8700

**Millington, Shelby, Pop. 9,878**
Millington Municipal SD K-12
5020 2nd Ave 38053 901-873-5680
Dr. David Roper, supt. Fax 873-5699
www.millingtonschools.org
Millington Central HS 1,300/9-12
8050 West St 38053 901-873-8100
Mark Neal, prin. Fax 873-8105
Millington MS 500/6-8
4964 Cuba Millington Rd 38053 901-873-8130
Amie Mansh, prin. Fax 873-8136

Shelby County SD
Supt. — See Memphis
Renaissance Academy North Alt
4885 Bill Knight Rd 38053 901-873-8146
David Matykiewicz, prin.
Woodstock MSHS 500/6-12
5885 Woodstock Cuba Rd 38053 901-353-8590
Eric Linsy, prin. Fax 353-8599

---

Faith Heritage Christian Academy 100/PK-12
PO Box 157 38053 901-872-0828
M.O. Eckel M.D., hdmstr. Fax 872-0803
Lighthouse Christian Academy 200/PK-12
3660 Shelby Rd 38053 901-873-3353
Kim Kellum, admin. Fax 873-3394
Tipton-Rosemark Academy 600/PK-12
8696 Rosemark Rd 38053 901-829-6500
John Scott, head sch Fax 829-4477

**Monterey, Putnam, Pop. 2,832**
Putnam County SD
Supt. — See Cookeville
Monterey HS 300/PK-PK, 9-
112 N Elm St 38574 931-839-2970
Sonja Farley, prin. Fax 839-6070

**Morristown, Hamblen, Pop. 28,494**
Hamblen County SD 10,100/K-12
210 E Morris Blvd 37813 423-586-7700
Dale Lynch, supt. Fax 586-7747
www.hcboe.net
Lincoln Heights MS 500/6-8
219 Lincoln Ave 37813 423-581-3200
Joe Ely, prin. Fax 585-3763
Meadowview MS 500/6-8
1623 Meadowview Ln 37814 423-581-6360
Dominique Salaciak, prin. Fax 585-3771
Miller Boyd Alternative S 50/Alt
376 Snyder Rd 37813 423-585-3785
Calvin Decker, prin. Fax 585-3786
Morristown-Hamblen HS East 1,400/9-12
1 Hurricane Ln 37813 423-586-2543
Gary Johnson, prin. Fax 585-3779
Morristown-Hamblen HS West 1,400/9-12
1 Trojan Trl 37813 423-581-1600
Jeff Moorhouse, prin. Fax 585-3791
West View MS 700/6-8
1 Indian Path 37813 423-581-2407
Rebekah Patrick, prin. Fax 585-3807
Other Schools – See Whitesburg

---

Cornerstone Academy 200/PK-12
260 Jacobs Rd 37813 423-307-1189
Ben Holland, hdmstr.
Tennessee Technology Center Morristown Post-Sec.
821 W Louise Ave 37813 423-586-5771
Walters State Community College Post-Sec.
500 S Davy Crockett Pkwy 37813 423-585-2600

**Mosheim, Greene, Pop. 2,337**
Greene County SD
Supt. — See Greeneville
West Greene HS 700/9-12
275 W Greene Dr 37818 423-422-4061
Steven Tunnell, prin. Fax 638-3180

**Mountain City, Johnson, Pop. 2,508**
Johnson County SD 2,300/PK-12
211 N Church St 37683 423-727-2640
Dr. Mischelle Simcox, dir. Fax 727-2663
www.jocoed.k12tn.net
Johnson County HS 700/9-12
510 Fairground Ln 37683 423-727-2620
Lisa Arnold, prin. Fax 727-2677
Johnson County MS 400/7-8
500 Fairground Ln 37683 423-727-2600
Edna Miller, prin. Fax 727-2608
Johnson County Vocational S Vo/Tech
520 Fairground Ln 37683 423-727-1860
Herbie Adams, prin. Fax 727-2693

**Mount Juliet, Wilson, Pop. 23,208**
Wilson County SD
Supt. — See Lebanon
Mount Juliet HS 1,900/9-12
1800 Curd Rd 37122 615-758-5606
Mel Brown, prin. Fax 758-5645
Mount Juliet MS 1,400/6-8
3565 N Mount Juliet Rd 37122 615-754-6688
Tim Bell, prin. Fax 754-7566

West Wilson MS 1,000/6-8
935 N Mount Juliet Rd 37122 615-758-5152
Wendell Marlowe, prin. Fax 758-5283

---

Heritage Christian Academy - Mt. Juliet 300/K-12
PO Box 1135 37121 615-604-0564
Katrina Hagerty, prin.
Mt. Juliet Christian Academy 500/PK-12
735 N Mount Juliet Rd 37122 615-758-2427
Dr. Mike Lee, head sch Fax 758-3662

**Mount Pleasant, Maury, Pop. 4,471**
Maury County SD
Supt. — See Columbia
Mount Pleasant HS 400/9-12
600 Greenwood St 38474 931-379-5583
Dr. John Gunn, prin. Fax 379-2093
Mt. Pleasant MS of Visual/Performing Art 500/5-8
410 Gray Ln 38474 931-379-1100
Kevin Eady, prin. Fax 379-1108

**Munford, Tipton, Pop. 5,823**
Tipton County SD
Supt. — See Covington
Munford HS 1,300/9-12
1080 McLaughlin Dr 38058 901-837-5701
Courtney Fee, prin. Fax 837-5729
Munford MS 1,100/6-8
100 Education Ave 38058 901-837-1700
Vicki Shipley, prin. Fax 837-5749

**Murfreesboro, Rutherford, Pop. 106,177**
Rutherford County SD 39,500/PK-12
2240 Southpark Dr 37128 615-893-5812
Don Odom, dir. Fax 898-7940
www.rcs.k12.tn.us
Blackman HS 2,300/9-12
3956 Blaze Dr 37128 615-904-3850
Gail Vick, prin. Fax 904-3851
Blackman MS 1,000/6-8
3945 Blaze Dr 37128 615-904-3860
Will Shelton, prin. Fax 904-3861
Central Magnet S 900/6-12
701 E Main St 37130 615-904-6789
Dr. John Ash, prin. Fax 904-6788
Holloway HS 100/9-12
619 S Highland Ave 37130 615-890-6004
Sumatra Drayton, prin. Fax 904-7508
McKee Alternative S 100/Alt
2623 Halls Hill Pike 37130 615-890-2282
Mary Jo Yeager, prin. Fax 898-7726
Oakland HS 1,800/9-12
2225 Patriot Dr 37130 615-904-3780
Bill Spurlock, prin. Fax 904-3781
Oakland MS 1,000/6-8
853 Dejarnette Ln 37130 615-904-6760
Kim Edwards, prin. Fax 904-6761
Riverdale HS 2,000/9-12
802 Warrior Dr 37128 615-890-6450
Tom Nolan, prin. Fax 890-9790
Siegel HS 1,900/9-12
3300 Siegel Rd 37129 615-904-3800
Jason Bridgeman, prin. Fax 904-3801
Siegel MS 1,000/6-8
355 W Thompson Ln 37129 615-904-3830
Tom Delbridge, prin. Fax 904-3831
Whitworth-Buchanan MS 700/6-8
5555 Manchester Pike 37127 615-904-6765
Avy Seymore, prin. Fax 904-6766
Other Schools – See Christiana, Eagleville, La Vergne, Rockvale, Smyrna

---

Daymar Institute Post-Sec.
415 Golden Bear Ct 37128 615-217-9347
Franklin Road Christian S 300/PK-12
3124 Franklin Rd 37128 615-890-0894
Kenton Kramer, admin. Fax 893-2837
Middle Tennessee Christian S 700/PK-12
100 E MTCS Rd 37129 615-893-0601
Dr. Phil Ellenburg, pres. Fax 895-8815
Middle Tennessee State University Post-Sec.
1301 E Main St 37132 615-898-2300
Providence Christian Academy 300/PK-12
410 Dejarnette Ln 37130 615-904-0902
Dr. Bill Mott, hdmstr. Fax 904-0859
Rice Christian Academy 100/K-12
627 Bill Rice Ranch Rd 37128 615-893-2767
Tennessee Technology Center Murfreesboro Post-Sec.
1303 Old Fort Pkwy 37129 615-898-8010

**Nashville, Davidson, Pop. 588,359**
Metropolitan Nashville SD 77,500/PK-12
2601 Bransford Ave 37204 615-259-4636
Chris Henson, dir. Fax 214-8897
www.mnps.org
Allen MS 500/5-8
500 Spence Ln 37210 615-291-6385
Kisha Stinson-Cox, prin. Fax 291-6066
Bailey MS 500/5-8
2000 Greenwood Ave 37206 615-262-6670
Charlie Mc Reynolds, prin. Fax 262-6979
Bass Learning Center Alt
5200 Delaware Ave 37209 615-298-3278
Henry Johnson, prin.
Baxter MS 500/5-8
350 Hart Ln 37207 615-262-6710
Miriam Harrington, prin. Fax 262-6743
Bellevue MS 700/5-8
655 Colice Jeanne Rd 37221 615-662-3000
Mark Pittman, prin. Fax 662-5728
Cohn S 100/Alt
4805 Park Ave 37209 615-298-6617
Debbie Booker, prin. Fax 298-8052
Creswell MS of the Arts 500/5-8
3500 John Mallette Dr 37218 615-291-6515
Dr. Ted Murcray, prin. Fax 291-5326
Croft Design Center MS 800/5-8
482 Elysian Fields Rd 37211 615-332-0217
Dr. Barbara Springer, prin. Fax 333-5650
Donelson MS 700/5-8
110 Stewarts Ferry Pike 37214 615-884-4080
Jennifer Rheinecker, prin. Fax 885-8970
Early Museum Magnet MS 400/5-8
1000 Cass St 37208 615-291-6369
Rise Pope, prin. Fax 298-8497
East Nashville Magnet S 1,200/5-12
110 Gallatin Ave 37206 615-262-6947
Steve Ball, prin. Fax 262-3972
Glencliff Comprehensive HS 1,300/9-12
160 Antioch Pike 37211 615-333-5070
Clint Wilson, prin. Fax 333-5003
Goodlettsville MS 500/5-8
1460 McGavock Pike 37216 615-227-1042
Katrina Frazier, prin. Fax 859-8965
Gra-Mar MS 400/5-8
575 Joyce Ln 37216 615-262-6685
Sonya Brooks, prin. Fax 262-6901
Haynes Health/Medical Science Design Ctr 300/5-8
510 W Trinity Ln 37207 615-262-6688
Dr. Canidra Henderson, prin. Fax 298-8084
Head MS 600/5-8
1830 Jo Johnston Ave 37203 615-329-8160
Dr. Tonja Williams, prin. Fax 321-8389
Hill MS 600/5-8
150 Davidson Rd 37205 615-353-2020
Connie Gwinn, prin. Fax 884-4028
Hillsboro Comprehensive HS 1,100/9-12
3812 Hillsboro Pike 37215 615-298-8400
Dr. Andrew Shuler Pelham, prin. Fax 353-1159
Hillwood Comprehensive HS 1,200/9-12
400 Davidson Rd 37205 615-353-2025
Dr. Steve Chauncy, prin. Fax 298-8402
Hume-Fogg Magnet HS 900/9-12
700 Broadway 37203 615-291-6300
Dr. Kellie Hargis, prin. Fax 291-6065
Hunters Lane Comprehensive HS 1,800/9-12
1150 Hunters Ln 37207 615-860-1401
Dr. Susan Kessler, prin. Fax 291-6304
Johnson Alternative Learning Center Alt
1200 2nd Ave S 37210 615-749-3067
Dr. Sharon Braden, prin. Fax 749-3076
King Magnet JSHS 1,200/7-12
613 17th Ave N 37203 615-329-8400
Dr. Angela Carr, prin. Fax 501-7907
Litton MS 300/5-8
4601 Hedgewood Dr 37216 615-262-6700
Chara Rand, prin. Fax 262-6995
Maplewood Comprehensive HS 1,000/9-12
401 Walton Ln 37216 615-262-6770
Dr. Ron Woodard, prin. Fax 262-6772
McGavock Comprehensive HS 2,300/9-12
3150 Mcgavock Pike 37214 615-885-8850
Robbin Wall, prin. Fax 885-8900
McKissack MS 300/5-8
915 38th Ave N 37209 615-329-8170
Darren Kennedy, prin. Fax 329-8183
McMurray MS 800/5-8
520 McMurray Dr 37211 615-333-5126
T'Shaka Coverson, prin. Fax 333-5125
Meigs Magnet MS 700/5-8
713 Ramsey St 37206 615-271-3222
Dr. Scott Underwood, prin. Fax 271-3223
Middle College HS 100/10-12
120 White Bridge Pike 37209 615-353-3742
Roderick Manuel, prin.
Moore MS 600/5-8
4425 Granny White Pike 37204 615-298-8095
Dr. Gary Hughes, prin. Fax 298-8452
Nashville Big Picture HS 200/9-12
160 Rural Ave 37209 615-353-2081
Chaerea Denning-Snorten, prin.
Nashville S of the Arts 700/9-12
1250 Foster Ave 37210 615-291-6600
Dr. Gregory Stewart, prin. Fax 271-1767
Oliver MS 800/5-8
6211 Nolensville Pike 37211 615-332-3011
Jeanna Collins, prin. Fax 332-3019
Overton Comprehensive HS 1,900/9-12
4820 Franklin Pike 37220 615-333-5135
Dr. Jill Pittman, prin. Fax 333-5141
Pearl-Cohn Entertainment Industry HS 900/9-12
904 26th Ave N 37208 615-329-8150
Sonia Stewart, prin. Fax 329-8192
Rose Park Math/Science MS 500/5-8
1025 9th Ave S 37203 615-291-6405
Robert Blankenship, prin. Fax 262-6717
Stratford STEM HS 700/9-12
1800 Stratford Ave 37216 615-242-6730
Michael Steele, prin. Fax 885-8929
Two Rivers MS 700/5-8
2991 Mcgavock Pike 37214 615-885-8931
Dr. Shelly Dunaway, prin. Fax 333-5641
West End MS, 3529 W End Ave 37205 400/5-8
Dr. Craig Hammond, prin. 615-298-8425
Wright MS 900/5-8
180 McCall St 37211 615-333-5189
Dr. Erin Anderson, prin. Fax 333-5635
Academy at Old Cockrill HS Adult
610 49th Ave N 37209 615-298-2294
Carl Carter, prin.
Academy at Opry Mills HS Adult
437 Opry Mills Dr 37214 615-810-8306
Carmon Brown, prin.
Other Schools – See Antioch, Hermitage, Joelton, Madison, Old Hickory, Whites Creek

---

American Baptist College Post-Sec.
1800 Baptist World Ctr Dr 37207 615-256-1463
Anthem Career College Post-Sec.
560 Royal Pkwy 37214 615-232-3700
Aquinas College Post-Sec.
4210 Harding Pike 37205 615-297-7545
Argosy University / Nashville Post-Sec.
100 Centerview Dr Ste 225 37214 615-525-2800
Art Institute of Tennessee - Nashville Post-Sec.
100 Centerview Dr Ste 250 37214 866-747-5770
Belmont University Post-Sec.
1900 Belmont Blvd 37212 615-460-6000
Christ Presbyterian Academy 1,000/PK-12
2323A Old Hickory Blvd 37215 615-373-9550
Nathaniel Morrow, hdmstr. Fax 370-0884
Davidson Academy 700/PK-12
1414 Old Hickory Blvd 37207 615-860-5300
Tim Johnson M.Ed., hdmstr. Fax 868-7918
Daymar Institute Post-Sec.
340 Plus Park Blvd 37217 615-361-7555
DeVry University Post-Sec.
3343 Perimeter Hill Dr #200 37211 615-445-3456
Diamond Council of America Post-Sec.
3212 W End Ave Ste 202 37203 615-385-5301
Donelson Christian Academy 800/PK-12
300 Danyacrest Dr 37214 615-883-2926
Ensworth S 1,100/K-12
211 Ensworth Ave 37205 615-383-0661
David Braemer, head sch Fax 269-4840
Father Ryan HS 900/9-12
700 Norwood Dr 37204 615-383-4200
Paul Davis, prin. Fax 383-9056
Fisk University Post-Sec.
1000 17th Ave N 37208 615-329-8500
Franklin Road Academy 800/PK-12
4700 Franklin Pike 37220 615-832-8845
Sean Casey, head sch Fax 834-4137
Harpeth Hall S 700/5-12
3801 Hobbs Rd 37215 615-297-9543
Stephanie Balmer, head sch Fax 297-0480
ITT Technical Institute Post-Sec.
2845 Elm Hill Pike 37214 615-889-8700
John A. Gupton College Post-Sec.
1616 Church St 37203 615-327-3927
Kaplan Career Institute Post-Sec.
750 Envious Ln 37217 615-279-8300
Lincoln College of Technology Post-Sec.
1524 Gallatin Ave 37206 615-226-3990
Lipscomb Academy 1,300/PK-12
3901 Granny White Pike 37204 615-966-1600
Greg Glenn, head sch Fax 966-7633
Lipscomb University Post-Sec.
1 University Park Dr 37204 800-333-4358
Meharry Medical College Post-Sec.
1005 Dr DB Todd Jr Blvd 37208 615-327-6111
Montgomery Bell Academy 700/7-12
4001 Harding Pike 37205 615-298-5514
Bradford Gioia, hdmstr. Fax 297-0271
Nashville Christian S 600/PK-12
7555 Sawyer Brown Rd 37221 615-356-5600
Nashville State Community College Post-Sec.
120 White Bridge Pike 37209 615-353-3333
National College of Business & Tech. Post-Sec.
1638 Bell Rd 37211 615-333-3344
Remington College Post-Sec.
441 Donelson Pike Ste 150 37214 615-889-5520
SAE Institute Nashville Post-Sec.
7 Music Cir N 37203 615-244-5848
St. Cecilia Academy 300/9-12
4210 Harding Pike Ste 2 37205 615-298-4525
Sr. Anne Catherine, prin. Fax 783-0561
St. Thomas Hospital Post-Sec.
PO Box 380 37202 615-222-2111
Seminary Ext. Independent Study Inst. Post-Sec.
901 Commerce St Ste 500 37203 800-229-4612
Strayer University Post-Sec.
1809 Dabbs Ave 37210 615-871-2260
Tennessee School for the Blind Post-Sec.
115 Stewarts Ferry Pike 37214 615-231-7300
Tennessee State University Post-Sec.
3500 John A Merritt Blvd 37209 615-963-5000
Tennessee Technology Center at Nashville Post-Sec.
100 White Bridge Pike 37209 615-425-5500
Trevecca Nazarene University Post-Sec.
333 Murfreesboro Pike 37210 615-248-1200
University S of Nashville 1,000/K-12
2000 Edgehill Ave 37212 615-321-8000
Vincent Durnan, dir. Fax 321-0889
Vanderbilt University Post-Sec.
2301 Vanderbilt Pl 37235 615-322-7311
Watkins College of Art Design and Film Post-Sec.
2298 Rosa L Parks Blvd 37228 615-383-4848
Welch College Post-Sec.
3606 W End Ave 37205 615-844-5000

**Newbern, Dyer, Pop. 3,269**
Dyer County SD
Supt. — See Dyersburg
Dyer County HS 1,100/9-12
1000 W Main St 38059 731-627-2229
Peggy Dodds, prin. Fax 627-2152
Northview MS 400/6-8
820 Williams St 38059 731-627-3713
Anthony Jones, prin. Fax 627-4823

---

Tennessee Technology Center at Newbern Post-Sec.
340 Washington St 38059 731-627-2511

**Newport, Cocke, Pop. 6,817**
Cocke County SD 4,900/PK-12
305 Hedrick Dr 37821 423-623-7821
Manney Moore, dir. Fax 625-3947
www.cocke.k12.tn.us
Cocke County Alternative S Alt
345 Hedrick Dr 37821 423-625-9768
Bryan Douglas, prin. Fax 625-1807
Cocke County HS 1,300/9-12
216 Hedrick Dr 37821 423-623-8718
Dr. Marvin Stewart, prin. Fax 623-1213
Hooper Career & Technical Center Vo/Tech
210 Hedrick Dr 37821 423-623-6072
Gail Burchette, prin. Fax 623-6070

Cocke County Adult School — Adult
345 Hedrick Dr 37821 — 423-625-3427
Bryan Douglas, prin. — Fax 625-3421
Other Schools – See Cosby

**New Tazewell, Claiborne, Pop. 2,986**
Claiborne County SD
Supt. — See Tazewell
Claiborne HS — 800/9-12
815 Davis Dr 37825 — 423-626-3532
Jody Goins, prin. — Fax 626-3555

**Nolensville, Williamson, Pop. 5,749**
Williamson County SD
Supt. — See Franklin
Mill Creek MS, 200 York Trl 37135 — 6-8
Kari Miller, admin. — 615-472-5250
Nolensville HS — 9-10
1600 Summerlyn Dr 37135 — 615-472-5200
Bill Harlin, admin.

**Norris, Anderson, Pop. 1,472**
Anderson County SD
Supt. — See Clinton
Norris MS — 500/6-8
PO Box 980 37828 — 865-494-7171
Jeff Harshbarger, prin. — Fax 494-6693

**Oakdale, Morgan, Pop. 205**
Morgan County SD
Supt. — See Wartburg
Oakdale S — 600/K-12
225 Clifty Creek Rd 37829 — 423-369-3885
Rory Foster, prin. — Fax 369-2821

**Oakland, Fayette, Pop. 6,569**
Fayette County SD
Supt. — See Somerville
West JHS — 400/6-8
13100 Highway 194 38060 — 901-465-9213
Stephanie Neal, prin. — Fax 465-1599

**Oak Ridge, Anderson, Pop. 28,500**
Oak Ridge CSD — 4,700/PK-12
PO Box 6588 37831 — 865-425-9001
Dr. Bruce Borchers, supt. — Fax 425-9070
www.ortn.edu
Jefferson MS — 700/5-8
200 Fairbanks Rd 37830 — 865-425-9301
Phil Cox, prin. — Fax 425-9339
Oak Ridge HS — 1,400/9-12
1450 Oak Ridge Tpke 37830 — 865-425-9601
David Bryant, prin. — Fax 425-9678
Robertsville MS — 700/5-8
245 Robertsville Rd 37830 — 865-425-9201
Bruce Lay, prin. — Fax 425-9236

**Old Hickory, See Nashville**
Metropolitan Nashville SD
Supt. — See Nashville
DuPont-Hadley MS — 700/5-8
1901 Old Hickory Blvd 37138 — 615-847-7300
Dr. Kevin Armstrong, prin. — Fax 847-7311

---

Academy for G.O.D. — K-12
401 Center St 37138 — 615-722-7107
Betsy Johnson, prin. — Fax 246-2719

**Oliver Springs, Morgan, Pop. 3,166**
Anderson County SD
Supt. — See Clinton
Norwood MS — 200/6-8
803 E Tri County Blvd 37840 — 865-435-7749
Rae Ann Owens, prin. — Fax 435-5426

Roane County SD
Supt. — See Kingston
Oliver Springs HS — 400/9-12
419 Kingston Ave 37840 — 865-435-7216
Justin Nivens, prin. — Fax 435-6774
Oliver Springs MS — 300/6-8
317 Roane St 37840 — 865-435-0011
Nancy Wilson, prin. — Fax 435-1621

---

Faith Christian Academy — 50/PK-12
864 Poplar Creek Rd 37840 — 828-435-0670
Dr. Paul Cates, prin. — Fax 435-0670

**Oneida, Scott, Pop. 3,699**
Oneida Special SD — 1,300/PK-12
PO Box 4819 37841 — 423-569-8912
Ann Sexton, dir. — Fax 569-2201
www.oneidaschools.org/
Oneida HS — 400/9-12
372 N Main St 37841 — 423-569-8818
Kevin Byrd, prin. — Fax 569-1681
Oneida MS — 300/6-8
376 N Main St 37841 — 423-569-2468
Kevin Byrd, prin. — Fax 569-5977

**Ooltewah, Hamilton, Pop. 676**
Hamilton County SD
Supt. — See Chattanooga
East Hamilton MSHS — 2,000/6-12
2015 Ooltewah Ringgold Rd 37363 — 423-893-3535
Gail Chuy, prin. — Fax 893-3536
Hamilton County HS — 200/Alt
9050 Career Ln 37363 — 423-344-1433
Gary Kuehn, prin. — Fax 344-1434
Hunter MS — 600/6-8
6810 Teal Ln 37363 — 423-344-1474
Robert Alford, prin. — Fax 344-1485
Ooltewah HS — 1,400/9-12
6123 Mountain View Rd 37363 — 423-238-5221
Mark Bean, prin. — Fax 238-5871
Ooltewah MS — 800/6-8
5100 Ooltewah Ringgold Rd 37363 — 423-238-5732
Chrissy Easterly, prin. — Fax 238-5735

**Paris, Henry, Pop. 9,926**
Henry County SD — 3,200/PK-12
217 Grove Blvd 38242 — 731-642-9733
Sam Miles, dir. — Fax 642-8073
www.henryk12.net/
Grove S — 300/9-9
215 Grove Blvd 38242 — 731-642-4586
Samuel Tharpe, prin. — Fax 642-4577
Henry County HS — 1,100/10-12
315 S Wilson St 38242 — 731-642-5232
Lennies McFerren, prin. — Fax 642-5240
Other Schools – See Buchanan

Paris Special SD — 1,700/PK-8
1219 Highway 641 S 38242 — 731-642-9322
Mike Brown, supt. — Fax 642-9327
www.parisssd.org/
Inman MS — 500/6-8
400 Harrison St 38242 — 731-642-8131
Jason Scarbrough, prin. — Fax 642-8209

---

Tennessee Technology Center at Paris — Post-Sec.
312 S Wilson St 38242 — 731-644-7365

**Parsons, Decatur, Pop. 2,355**
Decatur County SD
Supt. — See Decaturville
Decatur County MS — 500/5-8
2740 Highway 641 S 38363 — 731-847-6510
Chris Villaflor, prin. — Fax 847-6572

**Pigeon Forge, Sevier, Pop. 5,787**
Sevier County SD
Supt. — See Sevierville
Pigeon Forge HS — 700/9-12
414 Tiger Dr 37863 — 865-774-5790
Ben Clabo, prin. — Fax 774-5798
Pigeon Forge MS — 500/5-8
300 Wears Valley Rd 37863 — 865-453-2401
Scott Hensley, prin. — Fax 453-0799

**Pikeville, Bledsoe, Pop. 1,590**
Bledsoe County SD — 2,000/PK-12
PO Box 369 37367 — 423-447-2914
Jennifer Terry, dir. — Fax 447-7135
bledsoecounty.schoolinsites.com/
Bledsoe County HS — 600/9-12
877 Main St 37367 — 423-447-6851
Linda Pickett, prin. — Fax 447-6286
Bledsoe County MS — 400/6-8
PO Box 147 37367 — 423-447-3212
Melissa Reel, prin. — Fax 447-3085
Other Schools – See Dunlap

**Pleasant View, Cheatham, Pop. 4,108**
Cheatham County SD
Supt. — See Ashland City
Sycamore HS — 800/9-12
1021 Old Clarksville Pike 37146 — 615-746-5013
Jennifer Anderson, prin. — Fax 746-3653
Sycamore MS — 800/5-8
1025 Old Clarksville Pike 37146 — 615-746-8852
Lisa Young, prin. — Fax 746-5770

---

Pleasant View Christian S — 300/PK-12
160 Hicks Edgen Rd 37146 — 615-746-8555
Dr. Seldon Buck, admin. — Fax 746-2646

**Portland, Sumner, Pop. 11,308**
Sumner County SD
Supt. — See Gallatin
Portland East MS — 400/6-8
604 S Broadway St 37148 — 615-325-4146
Jackson Howell, prin. — Fax 325-5320
Portland HS — 1,100/9-12
600 College St 37148 — 615-325-9201
David Woods, prin. — Fax 325-5302
Portland West MS — 500/6-8
110 Nolan Private Dr 37148 — 615-325-8066
Cam MacLean, prin. — Fax 325-4073

---

Highland Academy — 100/9-12
211 Highland Circle Dr 37148 — 615-325-2036

**Powell, Knox, Pop. 7,534**
Knox County SD
Supt. — See Knoxville
Powell HS — 1,400/9-12
2136 W Emory Rd 37849 — 865-938-2171
Nathan Langlois, prin. — Fax 947-2805
Powell MS — 1,100/6-8
3329 W Emory Rd 37849 — 865-938-9008
Gary Critselous, prin. — Fax 947-4357

---

First Baptist Academy — 200/K-12
7706 Ewing Rd 37849 — 865-947-8503
Matt Mercer, hdmstr. — Fax 961-6525
Temple Baptist Academy — 200/PK-12
PO Box 159 37849 — 865-938-8180
David Whitaker, prin. — Fax 938-8147
The Crown College of the Bible — Post-Sec.
2307 W Beaver Creek Dr 37849 — 865-938-8186

**Pulaski, Giles, Pop. 7,654**
Giles County SD — 4,100/PK-12
270 Richland Dr 38478 — 931-363-4558
J.B. Smith, dir. — Fax 363-8975
www.giles-lea.giles.k12.tn.us
Bridgeforth MS — 400/6-8
1051 Bridgeforth Cir 38478 — 931-363-7526
Cathie White, prin. — Fax 424-7021
Giles County HS — 800/9-12
200 Sheila Frost Dr 38478 — 931-363-6532
Mark Cardin, prin. — Fax 424-7010
Other Schools – See Lynnville

---

Martin Methodist College — Post-Sec.
433 W Madison St 38478 — 931-363-9800

Tennessee Technology Center at Pulaski — Post-Sec.
PO Box 614 38478 — 931-424-4014

**Reagan, Henderson**
Henderson County SD
Supt. — See Lexington
Scotts Hill HS — 500/9-12
7871 Highway 100 38368 — 731-602-6112
Beverly Ivy, prin. — Fax 602-6118

**Red Boiling Springs, Macon, Pop. 1,106**
Macon County SD
Supt. — See Lafayette
Red Boiling Springs JSHS — 300/6-12
415 Hillcrest Dr 37150 — 615-699-3125
Don Jones, prin. — Fax 699-3371

**Ripley, Lauderdale, Pop. 8,322**
Lauderdale County SD — 4,700/PK-12
PO Box 350 38063 — 731-635-2941
Joey Hassell, supt. — Fax 635-7985
www.lced.net
Lauderdale MS — 700/6-8
309 Charles Griggs St 38063 — 731-635-1391
Latonya Jackson, prin. — Fax 635-0028
Ripley HS — 900/9-12
254 S Jefferson St 38063 — 731-635-2642
Joe Bridges, prin. — Fax 635-7151
Other Schools – See Halls

---

Tennessee Technology Center at Ripley — Post-Sec.
127 Industrial Dr 38063 — 731-635-3368

**Roan Mountain, Carter, Pop. 1,355**
Carter County SD
Supt. — See Elizabethton
Cloudland JSHS — 300/7-12
476 Cloudland Dr 37687 — 423-772-5300
Randy Birchfield, prin. — Fax 772-5309

**Rockvale, Rutherford**
Rutherford County SD
Supt. — See Murfreesboro
Rockvale MS — 800/6-8
6543 Highway 99 37153 — 615-904-6745
Fred Barlow, prin. — Fax 904-6746

**Rockwood, Roane, Pop. 5,395**
Roane County SD
Supt. — See Kingston
Rockwood HS — 400/9-12
512 W Rockwood St 37854 — 865-354-0882
Alan Reed, prin. — Fax 354-5170
Rockwood MS — 400/6-8
434 W Rockwood St 37854 — 865-354-0931
Amanda Evans, prin. — Fax 354-5160

**Rogersville, Hawkins, Pop. 4,364**
Hawkins County SD — 7,600/PK-12
200 N Depot St 37857 — 423-272-7629
Steve Starnes, dir. — Fax 272-2207
www.hck12.net
Cherokee HS — 1,100/9-12
2927 Highway 66 S 37857 — 423-272-6507
Thomas Floyd, prin. — Fax 272-3556
Rogersville MS — 500/6-8
958 E Mckinney Ave 37857 — 423-272-7603
Jim Ailshie, prin. — Fax 272-0185
Other Schools – See Church Hill, Sneedville, Surgoinsville

**Rossville, Fayette, Pop. 656**

---

Rossville Christian Academy — 300/K-12
PO Box 369 38066 — 901-853-0200

**Rutledge, Grainger, Pop. 1,113**
Grainger County SD — 3,600/PK-12
PO Box 38 37861 — 865-828-3611
Edwin Jarnagin, dir. — Fax 828-4357
www.grainger.k12.tn.us/
Grainger Academy — 50/Alt
232 Pioneer Dr 37861 — 865-828-6330
Kip Combs, prin. — Fax 828-3364
Grainger HS — 900/9-12
2201 Highway 11W S 37861 — 865-828-5291
Mark Briscoe, prin. — Fax 828-4828
Rutledge MS — 500/7-8
140 Pioneer Dr 37861 — 865-828-3366
Lynn Jones, prin. — Fax 828-3364
Grainger County Adult S — Adult
PO Box 38 37861 — 865-828-3611
Dr. James Atkins, prin. — Fax 828-4357
Other Schools – See Washburn

**Sale Creek, Hamilton, Pop. 2,811**
Hamilton County SD
Supt. — See Chattanooga
Sale Creek MSHS — 500/6-12
211 Patterson Rd 37373 — 423-332-8819
Tobin Davidson, prin. — Fax 332-8847

**Santa Fe, Maury**
Maury County SD
Supt. — See Columbia
Santa Fe S — 700/PK-12
2629 Santa Fe Pike 38482 — 931-682-2172
Leigh Ann Willey, prin. — Fax 682-2606

**Savannah, Hardin, Pop. 6,820**
Hardin County SD — 3,700/PK-12
155 Guinn St 38372 — 731-925-3943
Michael Davis, dir. — Fax 925-7313
www.hardincountyschools.net
Hardin County HS — 1,100/9-12
1170 Pickwick St 38372 — 731-925-3976
William McAdams, prin. — Fax 925-7407
Hardin County MS — 700/6-8
299 Lacefield Dr 38372 — 731-925-9037
Steve Haffly, prin. — Fax 925-0253

**Selmer, McNairy, Pop. 4,308**
McNairy County SD 4,300/K-12
170 W Court Ave 38375 731-645-3267
John Prince, supt. Fax 645-8085
www.mcnairy.org
McNairy Central HS 800/9-12
493 High School Rd 38375 731-645-3226
Cecil Stroup, prin. Fax 645-8014
Selmer MS 400/5-8
635 E Poplar Ave 38375 731-645-7977
Dr. Brenda Armstrong, prin. Fax 645-6377
Other Schools – See Adamsville

Styles and Profiles Beauty College Post-Sec.
119 S 2nd St 38375 731-645-9728

**Sevierville, Sevier, Pop. 14,595**
Sevier County SD 14,400/PK-12
226 Cedar St 37862 865-453-4671
Dr. Jack Parton, supt. Fax 522-1497
www.sevier.org
Alternative Learning Center 50/Alt
2540 Boyds Creek Hwy 37876 865-453-8338
Jason Kerley, prin. Fax 453-7875
Hardin Academy 100/9-12
2540 Boyds Creek Hwy 37876 865-453-8338
Jason Kerley, prin.
Sevier County HS 1,800/9-12
1200 Dolly Parton Pkwy 37862 865-453-5525
Toby Ward, prin. Fax 428-5867
Sevierville MS 600/6-8
520 High St 37862 865-453-0311
Donna Rolen, prin. Fax 428-2316
Whites Adult HS Adult
226 Cedar St 37862 865-429-1492
Curtis Clabo, prin. Fax 774-4564
Other Schools – See Gatlinburg, Kodak, Pigeon Forge, Seymour

Christian Academy of the Smokies 100/PK-12
1625 Old Newport Hwy 37862 865-774-0012
Smokey Mountain Trucking Institute Post-Sec.
3173 Newport Hwy 37876 800-495-4056

**Sewanee, Franklin, Pop. 2,295**

St. Andrew's-Sewanee S 300/6-12
290 Quintard Rd 37375 931-598-5651
Judith Chamberlain, head sch Fax 914-1224
Sewanee The University of the South Post-Sec.
735 University Ave 37383 931-598-1000

**Seymour, Sevier, Pop. 10,811**
Sevier County SD
Supt. — See Sevierville
Seymour HS 1,300/9-12
732 Boyds Creek Hwy 37865 865-577-7040
Kristy Wallen, prin. Fax 579-1492
Seymour MS 700/6-8
737 Boyds Creek Hwy 37865 865-579-0730
David Loy, prin. Fax 579-0905

King's Academy 500/PK-12
202 Smothers Rd 37865 865-573-8321
Dr. Walter Grubb, hdmstr. Fax 573-8323
Seymour Community Christian S 100/PK-12
PO Box 849 37865 865-577-5500

**Shelbyville, Bedford, Pop. 19,855**
Bedford County SD 8,000/PK-12
500 Madison St 37160 931-684-3284
Don Embry, supt. Fax 684-1133
www.bedfordk12tn.com/
Harris MS 800/6-8
570 Eagle Blvd 37160 931-684-5195
James Sullivan, prin. Fax 685-9455
Shelbyville Central HS 1,200/9-12
401 Eagle Blvd 37160 931-684-5672
Whit Taylor, prin. Fax 684-9359
Other Schools – See Unionville, Wartrace

Tennessee Technology Center Shelbyville Post-Sec.
1405 Madison St 37160 931-685-5013
Victory Baptist Academy 100/K-12
2200 N Main Street 37160 931-684-8115

**Signal Mountain, Hamilton, Pop. 7,474**
Hamilton County SD
Supt. — See Chattanooga
Signal Mountain MSHS 1,300/6-12
2650 Sam Powell Trl 37377 423-886-0880
Robin Copp, prin. Fax 886-0881

**Smithville, DeKalb, Pop. 4,481**
DeKalb County SD 3,000/PK-12
110 S Public Sq 37166 615-597-4084
Mark Willoughby, supt. Fax 597-6326
www.dekalbschools.net
DeKalb County HS 800/9-12
1130 W Broad St 37166 615-597-4094
Patrick Cripps, prin. Fax 597-8104
DeKalb MS 500/6-8
1132 W Broad St 37166 615-597-7987
Randy Jennings, prin. Fax 597-2640

**Smyrna, Rutherford, Pop. 39,070**
Rutherford County SD
Supt. — See Murfreesboro
Rock Springs MS 1,000/6-8
3301 Rock Springs Rd 37167 615-904-3825
Chris Treadway, prin. Fax 904-3826
Smyrna HS 2,000/9-12
100 Bulldog Dr 37167 615-904-3865
Rick Powell, prin. Fax 904-3866
Smyrna MS 1,000/6-8
712 Hazelwood Dr 37167 615-904-3845
Jeannie Fitzpatrick, prin. Fax 904-3846
Smyrna West Alternative S 100/Alt
12619 Old Nashville Hwy 37167 615-904-3856
Kay Davenport, prin. Fax 904-3857
Stewart's Creek HS 9-12
301 Red Hawk Blvd 37167 615-904-6771
Dr. Clark Harrell, prin. Fax 904-6772
Stewarts Creek MS 900/6-8
400 Red Hawk Blvd 37167 615-904-6700
Larry Creasy, prin. Fax 904-6701

Lancaster Christian Academy 500/PK-12
150 Soccer Way 37167 615-223-0451

**Sneedville, Hancock, Pop. 1,364**
Hancock County SD 1,000/K-12
PO Box 629 37869 423-733-2591
Mike Antrican, dir. Fax 733-8757
www.hancockcountyschools.com/
Hancock County MSHS 500/6-12
2700 Main St 37869 423-733-4611
Dr. Michael Belcher, prin. Fax 733-1427

Hawkins County SD
Supt. — See Rogersville
Clinch S 100/K-12
1540 Clinch Valley Rd 37869 423-272-3202
George Barton, prin. Fax 272-3207

**Soddy Daisy, Hamilton, Pop. 12,577**
Hamilton County SD
Supt. — See Chattanooga
Sequoya HS Vo/Tech
9517 W Ridge Trail Rd 37379 423-843-4707
Todd Jackson, prin. Fax 843-4719
Soddy Daisy HS 1,400/9-12
618 Sequoyah Access Rd 37379 423-332-8828
Daniel Gilbert, prin. Fax 332-8831
Soddy Daisy MS 600/6-8
200 Turner Rd 37379 423-332-8800
Blake Freeman, prin. Fax 332-8810

**Somerville, Fayette, Pop. 3,069**
Fayette County SD 3,800/PK-12
PO Box 9 38068 901-465-5260
Dr. Lonnie Harris, supt. Fax 466-0078
www.fcsk12.net
East JHS 400/6-8
400 Leach Dr 38068 901-465-3151
Kathy Redditt, prin. Fax 465-5084
Fayette-Ware HS 900/9-12
13520 Highway 59 38068 901-465-9838
Diane Watkins, prin. Fax 465-1377
Other Schools – See Oakland

Fayette Academy 700/PK-12
PO Box 130 38068 901-465-3241
Ron Canada, hdmstr. Fax 465-2141

**South Fulton, Obion, Pop. 2,320**
Obion County SD
Supt. — See Union City
South Fulton MSHS 500/6-12
1302 John C Jones Pkwy 38257 731-479-1441
Keith Frazier, prin. Fax 479-0586

**South Pittsburg, Marion, Pop. 2,934**
Marion County SD
Supt. — See Jasper
South Pittsburg JSHS 400/7-12
717 Elm Ave 37380 423-837-7561
Danny Wilson, prin. Fax 837-4532

Richard CSD 400/PK-12
1620 Hamilton Ave 37380 423-837-7282
Cindy Blevins, dir. Fax 837-0641
www.richardhardy.org
Hardy Memorial S 400/PK-12
1620 Hamilton Ave 37380 423-837-7282
Beth Webb, prin. Fax 837-0641

**Sparta, White, Pop. 4,841**
White County SD 4,100/PK-12
136 Baker St 38583 931-836-2229
Sandra Crouch, dir. Fax 836-8128
www.whitecoschools.net
White County HS 1,200/9-12
267 Allen Dr 38583 931-836-3214
Grant Swallows, prin. Fax 836-6295
White County MS 1,000/6-8
300 Turn Table Rd 38583 931-738-9238
Craig Lynn, prin. Fax 738-9271

**Spencer, Van Buren, Pop. 1,580**
Van Buren County SD 800/PK-12
PO Box 98 38585 931-946-2242
Cheryl Cole, dir. Fax 946-2858
Van Buren County JSHS 400/6-12
337 Sparta St 38585 931-946-2442
Jamie Simmons, prin. Fax 946-2265

**Spring City, Rhea, Pop. 1,936**
Rhea County SD
Supt. — See Dayton
Spring City MS 300/6-8
751 Wassom Memorial Hwy 37381 423-365-9105
Buddy Jackson, prin. Fax 365-9102

**Springfield, Robertson, Pop. 16,188**
Robertson County SD 11,200/PK-12
PO Box 130 37172 615-384-5588
Mike Davis, dir. Fax 384-9749
www.rcstn.net/
Coopertown MS 600/4-8
3820 Highway 49 W 37172 615-382-4166
Lewis Walling, prin. Fax 382-4171
Robertson County Alternative Program Alt
800 M S Couts Blvd 37172 615-382-2328
Nancy Williams, prin. Fax 382-2328
Springfield HS 1,100/9-12
5240 Highway 76 E 37172 615-384-3516
Teresa Leavitt, prin. Fax 384-5484
Springfield MS 600/6-8
715 5th Ave W 37172 615-384-4821
Dr. Grant Bell, prin. Fax 382-7890
Other Schools – See Cedar Hill, Cross Plains, Greenbrier, White House

South Haven Christian S 400/PK-12
112 Academy Dr 37172 615-384-5073

**Spring Hill, Maury, Pop. 28,520**
Maury County SD
Supt. — See Columbia
Spring Hill MS 700/5-8
3501 Cleburne Rd 37174 931-451-1531
Shanda Sparrow, prin. Fax 486-3954
Northfield Academy Adult
500 Northfield Ln 37174 931-486-1134
Dianne Kirk, coord. Fax 840-4410

Williamson County SD
Supt. — See Franklin
Spring Station MS 1,000/6-8
1000 Spring Station Dr 37174 615-472-5080
Paula Pulliam, prin. Fax 472-5091
Summit HS 500/9-12
2830 Twin Lakes Dr 37174 615-472-5100
Sarah Lamb, prin. Fax 472-5121

**Strawberry Plains, Jefferson**
Knox County SD
Supt. — See Knoxville
Carter HS 900/9-12
210 N Carter School Rd 37871 865-933-3434
Ryan Siebe, prin. Fax 932-8180
Carter MS 800/6-8
204 N Carter School Rd 37871 865-933-3426
Michael Derrick, prin. Fax 932-8170

Blue Springs Christian Academy 50/PK-12
3265 Blue Springs Rd 37871 865-932-7603
June Ingram, prin.

**Summertown, Lawrence, Pop. 852**
Lawrence County SD
Supt. — See Lawrenceburg
Summertown JSHS 500/7-12
411 W College St 38483 931-964-3539
Brent Long, prin. Fax 964-3302

**Sunbright, Morgan, Pop. 550**
Morgan County SD
Supt. — See Wartburg
Sunbright S 600/K-12
PO Box 129 37872 423-628-2244
Ron Treadway, prin. Fax 628-2120

**Surgoinsville, Hawkins, Pop. 1,786**
Hawkins County SD
Supt. — See Rogersville
Surgoinsville MS 300/5-8
1044 Main St 37873 423-345-2252
Dr. Scott Trent, prin. Fax 345-3598

**Sweetwater, Monroe, Pop. 5,664**
Monroe County SD
Supt. — See Madisonville
Sweetwater HS 600/9-12
414 S High St 37874 423-337-7881
Eric Weaver, prin. Fax 337-0685

Sweetwater CSD 1,500/PK-8
PO Box 231 37874 423-337-7051
Rodney Boruff, supt. Fax 337-6773
www.compurdy.com/scs2/
Sweetwater JHS 300/7-8
1013 Cannon Ave 37874 423-337-7336
Jaime Downs, prin. Fax 337-7360

Cross Creek Christian S 100/PK-12
501 E North St 37874 423-337-9330
Sabra McDonald, admin. Fax 337-9335

**Tazewell, Claiborne, Pop. 2,172**
Claiborne County SD 4,800/PK-12
PO Box 179 37879 423-626-3543
Connie Holdway, dir. Fax 626-5945
www.claibornecountyschools.com
Soldiers Memorial MS 500/5-8
1510 Legion St 37879 423-626-3531
Lisa Jessie, prin. Fax 626-2151
Claiborne Adult HS Adult
PO Box 600 37879 423-626-8222
Starla Ray, prin. Fax 626-5945
Other Schools – See Cumberland Gap, Harrogate, New Tazewell

**Tellico Plains, Monroe, Pop. 866**
Monroe County SD
Supt. — See Madisonville
Tellico Plains HS 400/9-12
9180 Highway 68 37385 423-253-2530
Russell Harris, prin. Fax 253-2541
Tellico Plains JHS 300/5-8
120 Old High School Rd 37385 423-253-2250
Ruthie Hunt, prin. Fax 253-7824

**Ten Mile, Roane**
Roane County SD
Supt. — See Kingston
Midway MS 200/6-8
104 Dogtown Rd 37880 865-717-5464
Amy Cawood, prin. Fax 376-0948

**Thompsons Station, Williamson, Pop. 2,172**
Williamson County SD
Supt. — See Franklin

Heritage MS 700/6-8
4803 Columbia Pike 37179 615-472-4540
Dr. Dana Finch, prin. Fax 472-4553
Independence HS 1,500/9-12
1776 Declaration Way 37179 615-472-4600
Dr. Todd Campbell, prin. Fax 472-4621

**Tiptonville, Lake, Pop. 4,409**
Lake County SD 1,000/PK-12
PO Box 397 38079 731-253-6601
Sherry Darnell, supt. Fax 253-7111
lake.k12.tn.us
Lake County HS 200/9-12
300 Cochran St 38079 731-253-7733
Kim Decker, prin. Fax 253-7766

**Trenton, Gibson, Pop. 4,197**
Trenton Special SD 1,400/PK-12
201 W 10th St 38382 731-855-1191
Sandra Harper, supt. Fax 855-1414
www.trentonssd.org
Peabody HS 400/9-12
2069 US Highway 45 Byp N 38382 731-855-2601
Tim Haney, prin. Fax 855-1217
Trenton Rosenwald MS 400/5-8
2065 US Highway 45 Byp S 38382 731-855-2422
Paul Pillow, prin. Fax 855-1826

**Troy, Obion, Pop. 1,363**
Obion County SD
Supt. — See Union City
Career Technology Center Vo/Tech
528 N US Highway 51 38260 731-536-4688
George Leake, prin. Fax 536-0469
Obion County Central HS 900/9-12
528 N US Highway 51 38260 731-536-4688
Linda Crigger, prin. Fax 536-0469

**Tullahoma, Coffee, Pop. 18,247**
Tullahoma CSD 3,400/PK-12
510 S Jackson St 37388 931-454-2600
Dr. Dan Lawson, dir. Fax 454-2642
www.tcsedu.net
East MS 400/6-8
908 Country Club Dr 37388 931-454-2632
Charles Lawson, prin. Fax 454-2660
Tullahoma HS 1,100/9-12
927 N Jackson St 37388 931-454-2620
Kathy Rose, prin. Fax 454-2662
West MS 400/6-8
90 Hermitage Dr 37388 931-454-2605
Dr. Mickey Shuran, prin. Fax 454-2661

**Union City, Obion, Pop. 10,735**
Obion County SD 4,000/PK-12
1700 N 5th St 38261 731-885-9743
Russell J. Davis, dir. Fax 885-4902
www.ocboe.com
Other Schools – See South Fulton, Troy

Union CSD 1,500/PK-12
PO Box 749 38281 731-885-3922
Gary Houston, dir. Fax 885-6033
www.tornadotouch.net
Union City HS 300/9-12
1305 High School Dr 38261 731-885-2373
Wesley Kennedy, prin. Fax 885-5011
Union City MS 300/6-8
1111 High School Dr 38261 731-885-2901
Michael Paul Miller, prin. Fax 885-3677

**Unionville, Bedford, Pop. 1,363**
Bedford County SD
Supt. — See Shelbyville
Community HS 500/9-12
100 Community Xing 37180 931-685-1418
Robert Ralston, prin. Fax 294-2107
Community MS 400/6-8
3470 Highway 41A N 37180 931-685-1426
Tony Garrette, prin. Fax 294-5126

**Vonore, Monroe, Pop. 1,458**
Monroe County SD
Supt. — See Madisonville
Vonore MS 300/5-8
414 Hall St 37885 423-884-2730
Matt Conley, prin. Fax 884-2731

**Wartburg, Morgan, Pop. 898**
Morgan County SD 3,200/K-12
136 Flat Fork Rd 37887 423-346-6214
Dr. Ronald Wilson, supt. Fax 346-6043
mcsed.net/
Central HS 400/9-12
1119 Knoxville Hwy 37887 423-346-6616
Carol Staten, prin. Fax 346-5665
Central MS 300/6-8
146 Liberty Rd 37887 423-346-2800
Dr. Lisa Bunch, prin. Fax 346-2805
Morgan County Career & Technical Center Vo/Tech
132 Flat Fork Rd 37887 423-346-6285
Dr. Joseph Miller, prin. Fax 346-5857
Other Schools – See Coalfield, Oakdale, Sunbright

**Wartrace, Bedford, Pop. 637**
Bedford County SD
Supt. — See Shelbyville
Cascade HS 500/9-12
1165 Bell Buckle Wartrace 37183 931-389-9389
Tim Harwell, prin. Fax 389-6223
Cascade MS 400/6-8
1165 Bell Buckle Wartrace 37183 931-389-9389
David Parker, prin. Fax 389-6223

**Washburn, Grainger**
Grainger County SD
Supt. — See Rutledge
Washburn S 600/PK-12
7925 Highway 131 37888 865-497-2557
Ginny McElhaney, prin. Fax 497-2934

**Watertown, Wilson, Pop. 1,450**
Wilson County SD
Supt. — See Lebanon
Watertown HS 800/9-12
9360 Sparta Pike 37184 615-237-3434
Jeff Luttrell, prin. Fax 237-3030
Watertown MS 6-8
515 W Main St 37184 615-237-4000
Michael Pigg, prin. Fax 237-3643

**Waverly, Humphreys, Pop. 4,056**
Humphreys County SD 3,100/PK-12
2443 Highway 70 E 37185 931-296-2568
James Long, supt. Fax 296-6501
www.hcss.org
Humphreys County Vocational Center Vo/Tech
1327 Highway 70 W 37185 931-296-7867
Lori Dell, dir. Fax 296-7252
Waverly Central HS 600/9-12
1325 Highway 70 W 37185 931-296-3911
Robert Martin, prin. Fax 296-2575
Waverly JHS 600/4-8
520 E Main St 37185 931-296-4514
Andy Daniels, prin. Fax 296-6507
Other Schools – See Mc Ewen

**Waynesboro, Wayne, Pop. 2,423**
Wayne County SD 2,500/PK-12
PO Box 658 38485 931-722-3548
Gailand Grinder, supt. Fax 722-7579
www.waynetn.net/
Wayne County HS 300/9-12
707 S Main St 38485 931-722-3238
David Byrd, prin. Fax 722-7641
Wayne County Technology Center Vo/Tech
703 S Main St 38485 931-722-5495
Beverly Hall, prin. Fax 722-5496
Waynesboro MS 300/5-8
PO Box 657 38485 931-722-5545
Talitha Willard, prin. Fax 722-3953
Other Schools – See Clifton, Collinwood

**Westmoreland, Sumner, Pop. 2,182**
Sumner County SD
Supt. — See Gallatin
Westmoreland HS 500/9-12
4300 Hawkins Dr 37186 615-644-2280
Rick Duffer, prin. Fax 644-3395
Westmoreland MS 400/6-8
4128 Hawkins Dr 37186 615-644-3003
Danny Robinson, prin. Fax 644-5584

**White Bluff, Dickson, Pop. 3,171**
Dickson County SD
Supt. — See Dickson
James MS 200/6-8
3030 Trace Creek Rd 37187 615-740-5770
Jan Ford, prin. Fax 797-6401

**White House, Sumner, Pop. 10,123**
Robertson County SD
Supt. — See Springfield
White House-Heritage HS 800/7-12
7744 Highway 76 E 37188 615-672-0311
Mary Jo Holmes, prin. Fax 672-7178

Sumner County SD
Supt. — See Gallatin
White House HS 900/9-12
508 Tyree Springs Rd 37188 615-672-3761
Scott Langford, prin. Fax 672-6404
White House MS 700/6-8
2020 Highway 31 W 37188 615-672-4379
Jerry Apple, prin. Fax 672-6409

---

Christian Community Schools 300/PK-12
506 Hester Dr 37188 615-672-6949
Steve Gillespie, dir. Fax 616-1330

**Whitesburg, Hamblen**
Hamblen County SD
Supt. — See Morristown
East Ridge MS 600/6-8
6595 Saint Clair Rd 37891 423-581-3041
James Templin, prin. Fax 585-3765

**Whites Creek, See Nashville**
Metropolitan Nashville SD
Supt. — See Nashville
Whites Creek Comprehensive HS 1,000/9-12
7277 Old Hickory Blvd 37189 615-876-5132
Dr. James Bailey, prin. Fax 321-8720

---

Edwards Classical Academy 100/K-10
4479 Jackson Rd 37189 615-876-7291

**Whiteville, Hardeman, Pop. 4,622**

---

Tennessee Technology Center Whiteville Post-Sec.
1685 US Highway 64 38075 731-254-8521

**Whitwell, Marion, Pop. 1,684**
Marion County SD
Supt. — See Jasper
Whitwell HS 400/9-12
200 Tiger Trl 37397 423-658-5141
Teena Casseday, prin. Fax 658-0313
Whitwell MS 400/5-8
1 Butterfly Ln 37397 423-658-5635
Kim Headrick, prin. Fax 658-6949

**Winchester, Franklin, Pop. 8,370**
Franklin County SD 6,000/PK-12
215 S College St 37398 931-967-0626
Dr. Amie W. Lonas, supt. Fax 967-7832
www.fcstn.net
Franklin County HS 1,400/9-12
833 Bypass Rd 37398 931-967-2821
Greg Mantooth, prin. Fax 967-6945
North MS 700/6-8
2990 Decherd Blvd 37398 931-967-5323
Stanley Bean, prin. Fax 967-1413
Other Schools – See Cowan, Huntland

**Woodbury, Cannon, Pop. 2,647**
Cannon County SD 2,500/PK-12
301 W Main St Ste 100 37190 615-563-5752
Barbara Parker, supt. Fax 563-2716
www.ccstn.com/
Cannon County HS 700/9-12
1 Lion Dr 37190 615-563-2144
Mike Jones, prin. Fax 563-8068

# TEXAS

## TEXAS EDUCATION AGENCY
**1701 Congress Ave, Austin 78701-1494**
**Telephone 512-463-9734**
**Fax 512-463-9838**
**Website http://www.tea.state.tx.us**

Commissioner of Education Michael Williams

## TEXAS BOARD OF EDUCATION
**1701 Congress Ave, Austin 78701-1402**

Chairperson Barbara Cargill

## REGIONAL EDUCATION SERVICE CENTERS (RESC)

Region 1 ESC
Dr. Cornelia Gonzalez, dir. 956-984-6000
1900 W Schunior St, Edinburg Fax 984-7655
www.esc1.net

Region 2 ESC
Dr. Rick Alvarado Ph.D., dir. 361-561-8400
209 N Water St Fax 883-3442
Corpus Christi 78401
www.esc2.net

Region 3 ESC
Dr. Patricia Shafer, dir. 361-573-0731
1905 Leary Ln, Victoria 77901 Fax 576-4804
www.esc3.net/

Region 4 ESC
Dr. Pam Wells, dir. 713-462-7708
7145 W Tidwell Rd, Houston 77092 Fax 744-6514
www.esc4.net/

Region 5 ESC
Dr. Danny Lovett, dir. 409-951-1700
350 Pine St Ste 500 Fax 951-1800
Beaumont 77701
www.esc5.net

Region 6 ESC
Michael Holland, dir. 936-435-8400
3332 Montgomery Rd Fax 435-8484
Huntsville 77340
www.esc6.net

Region 7 ESC
Elizabeth Abernethy, dir. 903-988-6700
1909 N Longview St, Kilgore 75662 Fax 988-6708
www.esc7.net/

Region 8 ESC
Dr. David Fitts, dir. 903-572-8551
4845 US Highway 271 N Fax 575-2611
Pittsburg 75686
www.reg8.net/

Region 9 ESC
Wes Pierce, dir. 940-322-6928
301 Loop 11, Wichita Falls 76306 Fax 767-3836
www.esc9.net

Region 10 ESC
Dr. Gordon Taylor, dir. 972-348-1700
400 E Spring Valley Rd Fax 231-3642
Richardson 75081
www.region10.org/

Region 11 ESC
Dr. Clyde Steelman, dir. 817-740-3600
1451 S Cherry Ln Fax 740-7600
Fort Worth 76108
www.esc11.net

Region 12 ESC
Dr. Jerry Maze, dir. 254-297-1212
PO Box 23409, Waco 76702 Fax 666-0823
www.esc12.net

Region 13 ESC
Rich Elsasser, dir. 512-919-5313
5701 Springdale Rd, Austin 78723 Fax 919-5374
www5.esc13.net/

Region 14 ESC
Ronnie Kincaid, dir. 325-675-8600
1850 State Highway 351 Fax 675-8659
Abilene 79601
www.esc14.net/

Region 15 ESC
Scot Goen, dir. 325-658-6571
PO Box 5199, San Angelo 76902 Fax 655-4823
www.netxv.net/

Region 16 ESC
Ray Cogburn, dir. 806-677-5000
5800 Bell St, Amarillo 79109 Fax 677-5001
www.esc16.net

Region 17 ESC
Dr. Kyle Wargo, dir. 806-792-4000
1111 W Loop 289, Lubbock 79416 Fax 792-1523
www.esc17.net/

Region 18 ESC
John Thomas, dir. 432-563-2380
PO Box 60580, Midland 79711 Fax 567-3290
www.esc18.net

Region 19 ESC
Dr. Armando Aguirre, dir. 915-780-1919
PO Box 971127, El Paso 79997 Fax 780-6537
www.esc19.net/

Region 20 ESC
Dr. Ronald Beard, dir. 210-370-5200
1314 Hines, San Antonio 78208 Fax 370-5750
www.esc20.net

## PUBLIC, PRIVATE AND CATHOLIC SECONDARY SCHOOLS

**Abbott, Hill, Pop. 355**
Abbott ISD 300/PK-12
PO Box 226 76621 254-582-3011
Richard Edison, supt. Fax 582-5430
www.abbottisd.org
Abbott S 300/PK-12
PO Box 226 76621 254-582-3011
Eric Pustejovsky, prin. Fax 582-5430

**Abernathy, Hale, Pop. 2,787**
Abernathy ISD 800/PK-12
505 7th St 79311 806-298-4940
Glen Teal Ed.D., supt. Fax 298-2400
www.abernathyisd.com
Abernathy HS 200/9-12
505 7th St 79311 806-298-4902
Gary Pugh, prin. Fax 298-4653
Abernathy JHS 200/6-8
505 7th St 79311 806-298-4921
Kelly Priest, prin. Fax 298-4775

**Abilene, Taylor, Pop. 114,633**
Abilene ISD 16,100/PK-12
PO Box 981 79604 325-677-1444
Dr. David Young, supt. Fax 794-1325
www.abileneisd.org
Abilene HS 1,900/9-12
2800 N 6th St 79603 325-677-1731
Royce Curtis, prin. Fax 794-1387
Academy for Tech/Eng/Math/Science 300/9-12
650 US Highway 80 E 79601 325-794-4140
Ketta Garduno, dir. Fax 794-1341
Clack MS 800/6-8
1610 Corsicana Ave 79605 325-692-1961
Rodney Brown, prin. Fax 794-1371
Cooper HS 1,900/9-12
3639 Sayles Blvd 79605 325-691-1000
Karen Munoz, prin. Fax 794-1375
Craig MS 900/6-8
702 S Judge Ely Blvd 79602 325-794-4100
Daniel Dukes, prin. Fax 794-1385
Holland Medical HS 9-12
2442 Cedar St 79601 325-794-4120
Michael Trook, prin. Fax 794-1377
Jefferson Opportunity Center 50/Alt
1741 S 14th St 79602 325-794-4150
Jane Allred-May, admin. Fax 794-1367
Madison MS 900/6-8
3145 Barrow St 79605 325-692-5661
Cyndi Smith, prin. Fax 794-1313
Mann MS 800/6-8
2545 Mimosa Dr 79603 325-672-8493
Kathy Walker, prin. Fax 794-1374
Woodson Center for Excellence 200/Alt
342 Cockerell Dr 79601 325-671-4736
Jaime Tindall, prin. Fax 794-1377
Adult Learning Center Adult
1929 S 11th St 79602 325-671-4419
Mignon Lawson, dir. Fax 794-1327

Wylie ISD 2,900/PK-12
6251 Buffalo Gap Rd 79606 325-692-4353
Joey Light, supt. Fax 695-3438
www.wyliebulldogs.org
Wylie HS 900/9-12
4502 Antilley Rd 79606 325-690-1181
Tommy Vaughn, prin. Fax 690-0320
Wylie JHS 800/6-8
4010 Beltway S 79606 325-695-1910
Rob Goodenough, prin. Fax 692-5786

---

Abilene Christian S 300/PK-12
2550 N Judge Ely Blvd 79601 325-672-9200
Abilene Christian University Post-Sec.
ACU Box 29000 79699 325-674-2000
American Commercial College Post-Sec.
402 Butternut St 79602 325-672-8495
Hardin-Simmons University Post-Sec.
2200 Hickory St 79698 325-670-1000
Hendrick Medical Center Post-Sec.
1900 Pine St 79601 325-670-2201
McMurry University Post-Sec.
1 McMurry Sta 79697 325-793-3800
Texas College of Cosmetology Post-Sec.
117 Sayles Blvd 79605 325-677-0532

**Ackerly, Dawson, Pop. 220**
Sands Consolidated ISD 200/PK-12
PO Box 218 79713 432-353-4888
Wayne Henderson, supt. Fax 353-4650
sands.esc17.net
Sands S 200/PK-12
PO Box 218 79713 432-353-4888
Lenny Morrow, prin. Fax 353-4650

**Addison, Dallas, Pop. 12,782**

---

Greenhill S 1,300/PK-12
4141 Spring Valley Rd 75001 972-628-5400
Scott Griggs, head sch Fax 404-8217
Trinity Christian Academy 1,500/PK-12
17001 Addison Rd 75001 972-931-8325
David Delph, hdmstr. Fax 931-8923

**Adrian, Oldham, Pop. 165**
Adrian ISD 100/PK-12
PO Box 189 79001 806-538-6203
Mike Winter, supt. Fax 538-6291
www.adrianisd.net
Adrian S 100/PK-12
PO Box 189 79001 806-538-6203
Maritssa Flores, prin. Fax 538-6291

**Afton, Dickens**
Patton Springs ISD 100/PK-12
PO Box 32 79220 806-689-2220
Larry McClenny, supt. Fax 689-2253
pattonsprings.net
Patton Springs S 100/PK-12
PO Box 32 79220 806-689-2220
Bryan White, prin. Fax 689-2253

**Agua Dulce, Nueces, Pop. 795**
Agua Dulce ISD 400/PK-12
PO Box 250 78330 361-998-2542
Dr. Russ Perry, supt. Fax 998-2816
www.adisd.net
Agua Dulce JSHS 200/6-12
PO Box 250 78330 361-998-2214
Guadalupe Martinez, prin. Fax 998-2994

**Alamo, Hidalgo, Pop. 18,315**
Pharr-San Juan-Alamo ISD
Supt. — See Pharr
Alamo MS 800/6-8
1819 W US Highway 83 78516 956-354-2550
Adrian Karr, prin. Fax 354-3188
Murphy MS 700/6-8
924 Sioux Rd 78516 956-354-2530
Lizette Longoria, prin. Fax 354-3224
Pharr-San Juan-Alamo Memorial HS 2,000/9-12
800 S Alamo Rd 78516 956-354-2420
Juan Garza, prin. Fax 354-3124

Valley Christian Heritage S 100/PK-12
932 N Alamo Rd 78516 956-787-9743

**Alba, Wood, Pop. 497**
Alba-Golden ISD 900/PK-12
1373 County Road 2377 75410 903-768-2472
Dwayne Ellis, supt. Fax 768-2593
www.agisd.com
Alba-Golden JSHS 500/6-12
1373 County Road 2377 75410 903-768-2472
Michael Mize, prin. Fax 768-2303

**Albany, Shackelford, Pop. 1,992**
Albany ISD 500/PK-12
PO Box 2050 76430 325-762-2823
Shane Fields, supt. Fax 762-3876
www.albanyisd.net
Albany JSHS 200/7-12
PO Box 2050 76430 325-762-3974
Kevin Hill, prin. Fax 762-3850

**Aledo, Parker, Pop. 2,690**
Aledo ISD 4,600/PK-12
1008 Bailey Ranch Rd 76008 817-441-8327
Dr. Derek Citty, supt. Fax 441-5144
aledo.schoolfusion.us
Aledo HS 1,100/10-12
1000 Bailey Ranch Rd 76008 817-441-8711
Dan Peterson, prin. Fax 441-5136
Aledo Learning Center 50/Alt
1016 Bailey Ranch Rd 76008 817-441-5176
Ron Miller, prin. Fax 441-9488
Aledo MS 700/7-8
416 S FM 1187 76008 817-441-5198
Cheryl Jones, prin. Fax 441-5133
Daniel 9th Grade Campus 400/9-9
990 Bailey Ranch Rd 76008 817-441-4504
Angela Tims, prin. Fax 441-2146

**Alice, Jim Wells, Pop. 19,053**
Alice ISD 5,400/PK-12
2 Coyote Trl 78332 361-664-0981
Dr. Grace Everett, supt. Fax 660-2113
www.aliceisd.net
Adams MS 800/7-8
901 E 3rd St 78332 361-660-2055
Dr. Ruben Pena, prin. Fax 660-2094
Alice HS 1,400/9-12
1 Coyote Trl 78332 361-664-0126
Debra Garcia, prin. Fax 660-2128

Alice Christian S 50/PK-12
1200 N Stadium Rd 78332 361-668-6636
Jaye Lynn Watson, prin. Fax 668-0840

**Allen, Collin, Pop. 82,168**
Allen ISD 19,400/PK-12
PO Box 13 75013 972-727-0511
Dr. Lance Hindt, supt. Fax 727-0500
www.allenisd.org
Allen SHS 4,000/10-12
300 Rivercrest Blvd 75002 972-727-0400
Steve Payne, prin. Fax 727-0515
Curtis MS 1,000/7-8
1530 Rivercrest Blvd 75002 972-727-0340
Sonya Pitcock, prin. Fax 727-0345
Dillard Special Achievement Center Alt
610 E Bethany Dr 75002 972-727-7163
Eric Pacheco, dir. Fax 727-7162
Ereckson MS 1,100/7-8
450 Tatum Dr 75013 972-747-3308
Leslie Norris, prin. Fax 747-3311
Ford MS 1,000/7-8
630 Park Place Dr 75002 972-727-0590
Susan Horowitz, prin. Fax 727-0596
Lowery Freshman Center 1,400/9-9
601 E Main St 75002 972-396-6975
Jill Stafford, prin. Fax 396-6981

Lovejoy ISD 2,900/K-12
259 Country Club Rd 75002 469-742-8000
Ted Moore, supt. Fax 742-8001
www.lovejoyisd.net/
Other Schools – See Lucas

**Alpine, Brewster, Pop. 5,819**
Alpine ISD 1,100/PK-12
704 W Sul Ross Ave 79830 432-837-7700
Becky Watley, supt. Fax 837-7740
www.alpine.esc18.net
Alpine HS 300/9-12
300 E Hendryx Ave 79830 432-837-7710
Panchi Scown, prin. Fax 837-9813
Alpine MS 300/5-8
801 Middle School Dr 79830 432-837-7720
Justin Gonzales, prin. Fax 837-9814

Sul Ross State University Post-Sec.
PO Box C114 79832 432-837-8032

**Altair, Colorado**
Rice Consolidated ISD 1,300/PK-12
PO Box 338 77412 979-234-3531
Bill Hefner, supt. Fax 234-3409
www.ricecisd.org
Rice HS 300/9-12
PO Box 338 77412 979-234-3531
Eric Grogan, prin. Fax 234-5901
Rice JHS 200/6-8
PO Box 338 77412 979-234-3531
John Post, prin. Fax 234-3191

**Alto, Cherokee, Pop. 1,204**
Alto ISD 700/PK-12
244 County Road 2429 75925 936-858-7101
Kerry Birdwell, supt. Fax 858-2101
www.alto.esc7.net/
Alto HS 200/9-12
248 County Road 2429 75925 936-858-7110
Scott Walters, prin. Fax 858-4387
Alto MS 200/5-8
240 County Road 2429 75925 936-858-7140
Kelly West, prin. Fax 858-4579

**Alton, Hidalgo, Pop. 12,339**
La Joya ISD
Supt. — See La Joya
Trevino MS 900/6-8
301 S Inspiration Blvd, 956-581-3050
Jose T. Garcia, prin. Fax 581-3099

Mission Consolidated ISD
Supt. — See Mission
Alton Memorial JHS 800/6-8
521 S Los Ebanos Blvd, 956-323-5000
Sylvia Garcia, prin. Fax 323-5045

**Alvarado, Johnson, Pop. 3,699**
Alvarado ISD 3,300/PK-12
PO Box 387 76009 817-783-6800
Dr. Kenneth Estes, supt. Fax 783-3844
www.alvaradoisd.net/
Alvarado HS 1,000/9-12
PO Box 387 76009 817-783-6940
Chris Magee, prin. Fax 783-6944
Alvarado JHS 500/7-8
PO Box 387 76009 817-783-6840
Melodye Brooks, prin. Fax 783-6844

**Alvin, Brazoria, Pop. 23,976**
Alvin ISD 17,600/PK-12
301 E House St 77511 281-388-1130
Dr. Buck Gilcrease, supt. Fax 388-2719
www.alvinisd.net
Alvin HS 2,400/9-12
802 S Johnson St 77511 281-245-3000
Dr. Johnny Briseno, prin. Fax 331-3053
Alvin JHS 700/6-8
2300 W South St 77511 281-245-2770
Trent Thrasher, prin. Fax 331-5926
ASSETS Learning Center 200/Alt
605 W House St 77511 281-331-1690
Traci Hummel, dir. Fax 331-1667
Fairview JHS 900/6-8
2600 County Road 190 77511 281-245-3100
Bobby Martinez, prin. Fax 245-3213
Harby JHS 700/6-8
1500 Heights Rd 77511 281-585-6626
Lisa Burns, prin. Fax 388-2247
Other Schools – See Manvel, Pearland

Alvin Community College Post-Sec.
3110 Mustang Rd 77511 281-756-3500
Living Stones Christian S 200/PK-12
1407 Victory Ln 77511 281-331-0086
Jessica Sanders, admin. Fax 331-6747

**Alvord, Wise, Pop. 1,324**
Alvord ISD 700/PK-12
PO Box 70 76225 940-427-5975
Dr. Randy Brown, supt. Fax 427-2313
www.alvordisd.net
Alvord HS 200/9-12
PO Box 70 76225 940-427-9643
Dr. Rhett King, prin. Fax 427-9648
Alvord MS 200/6-8
PO Box 70 76225 940-427-5511
Janis Branum, prin. Fax 427-2461

**Amarillo, Potter, Pop. 187,598**
Amarillo ISD 32,700/PK-12
7200 W Interstate 40 79106 806-326-1000
Dr. Dana West, supt. Fax 354-4378
www.amaisd.org
Amarillo Area Ctr for Advanced Learning 50/Alt
1100 N Forest St 79106 806-326-2800
Jay Barrett, prin. Fax 371-6100
Amarillo HS 2,100/9-12
4225 Danbury Dr 79109 806-326-2000
Mark Webster, prin. Fax 354-5092
Austin MS 800/6-8
1808 Wimberly Rd 79109 806-326-3000
Alan Nickson, prin. Fax 356-4802
Bonham MS 800/6-8
5600 SW 49th Ave 79109 806-326-3100
David Vincent, prin. Fax 356-4865
Bowie MS 1,000/7-8
2901 Tee Anchor Blvd 79104 806-326-3200
John Smith, prin. Fax 371-6016
Caprock HS 1,900/9-12
3001 E 34th Ave 79103 806-326-2200
David Bishop, prin. Fax 371-6042
Crockett MS 800/6-8
4720 Floyd Ave 79106 806-326-3300
Lisa Loan, prin. Fax 356-4873
de Zavala MS 400/5-8
2801 N Coulter St 79124 806-326-3400
Angie Noel, prin. Fax 354-4286
Fannin MS 600/6-8
4627 S Rusk St 79110 806-326-3500
Nathan Culwell, prin. Fax 354-4588
Houston MS 800/6-8
815 S Independence St 79106 806-326-3600
Renee Mott, prin. Fax 371-5577
Mann MS 400/7-8
610 N Buchanan St 79107 806-326-3700
Tammie Villarreal, prin. Fax 371-5617
North Heights Alternative S 300/Alt
607 N Hughes St 79107 806-326-2850
Mark Leach, prin. Fax 371-5715
Palo Duro HS 1,900/9-12
1400 N Grant St 79107 806-326-2400
Amy Dorris, prin. Fax 381-7166
Tascosa HS 2,300/9-12
3921 Westlawn St 79102 806-326-2600
Dr. Lynn Pulliam, prin. Fax 356-4805
Travis MS 900/7-8
2815 Martin Rd 79107 806-326-3800
David Manchee, prin. Fax 381-7207

Canyon ISD
Supt. — See Canyon
Midway Alternative HS 50/Alt
13501 Bell St 79118 806-677-2455
Shawn Neeley, prin. Fax 677-2459
Randall HS 1,400/9-12
5800 Attebury Dr 79118 806-677-2333
Steve Williams, prin. Fax 677-2329
Westover Park JHS 800/7-8
7200 Pinnacle Dr 79119 806-677-2420
Doug Voran, prin. Fax 677-2439
Youth Center S 100/Alt
9300 S Georgia St 79118 806-677-2450
Shawn Neeley, prin. Fax 468-5714

Highland Park ISD 900/PK-12
PO Box 30430 79120 806-335-2823
Buddy Freeman, supt. Fax 335-3547
www.hpisd.net
Highland Park HS 200/9-12
PO Box 30430 79120 806-335-2821
Shawn Read, prin. Fax 335-3215
Highland Park MS 200/6-8
PO Box 30430 79120 806-335-2821
Neila Malcom, prin. Fax 335-3215

River Road ISD 1,500/PK-12
9500 N US Highway 287 79108 806-381-7800
Randy Owen, supt. Fax 381-1357
www.rrisd.net
River Road HS 400/9-12
101 W Mobley St 79108 806-383-8867
Mike Cheverier, prin. Fax 381-7818
River Road MS 300/7-8
9500 N US Highway 287 79108 806-383-8721
Penny Rosson, prin. Fax 381-7815

Amarillo College Post-Sec.
PO Box 447 79178 806-371-5000
Exposito School of Hair Design Post-Sec.
3710 Mockingbird Ln 79109 806-355-9111
Holy Cross Catholic Academy 100/6-12
4110 S Bonham St 79110 806-355-9637
Fr. Robert Busch, head sch Fax 353-9520
Milan Institute Post-Sec.
7001 W Interstate 40 79106 806-353-3500
Milan Institute of Cosmetology Post-Sec.
2400 SE 27th Ave 79103 806-371-7600
San Jacinto Christian Academy 400/PK-12
PO Box 3428 79116 806-372-2285
Randy Down, supt. Fax 376-6712
Vista College Post-Sec.
3440 Bell St Unit 100 79109 866-442-4197

**Amherst, Lamb, Pop. 712**
Amherst ISD 100/PK-12
PO Box 248 79312 806-246-3221
Joel Rodgers, supt. Fax 246-3494
www.amherstisd.com/
Amherst S 100/PK-12
PO Box 248 79312 806-246-3221
Mike Ritchie, prin. Fax 246-3649

**Anahuac, Chambers, Pop. 2,205**
Anahuac ISD 1,200/PK-12
PO Box 369 77514 409-267-3600
James Hopper, supt. Fax 267-3855
www.anahuacisd.net
Anahuac HS 300/9-12
PO Box 1560 77514 409-267-2010
Eric Humphrey, prin. Fax 267-5192
Anahuac MS 300/6-8
PO Box 849 77514 409-267-2040
Tammy Duhon, prin. Fax 267-2046

**Anderson, Grimes, Pop. 220**
Anderson - Shiro Consolidated ISD 700/PK-12
458 FM 149 Rd W 77830 936-873-4500
Sara Goolsby, supt. Fax 873-4515
www.ascisd.net
Anderson - Shiro JSHS 400/6-12
458 FM 149 Rd W 77830 936-873-4550
Diana Branch, prin. Fax 873-4575

**Andrews, Andrews, Pop. 10,989**
Andrews ISD 3,400/PK-12
405 NW 3rd St 79714 432-523-3640
Bobby Azam, supt. Fax 523-3343
www.andrews.esc18.net
Andrews Education Center 50/Alt
405 NW 3rd St 79714 432-523-3640
Charlie Falcon, prin. Fax 524-1989
Andrews HS 900/9-12
405 NW 3rd St 79714 432-523-3640
Kyle Clark, prin. Fax 523-6807
Andrews MS 700/6-8
405 NW 3rd St 79714 432-523-3640
Chris Dulin, prin. Fax 524-1904

**Angleton, Brazoria, Pop. 18,559**
Angleton ISD 6,400/PK-12
1900 N Downing Rd 77515 979-864-8000
Patricia Montgomery Ed.D., supt. Fax 864-8070
www.angletonisd.net/
Angleton HS 1,800/9-12
1 Campus Dr 77515 979-864-8001
Jerry Crowell, prin. Fax 864-8090
Angleton JHS 1,400/6-8
1201 W Henderson Rd 77515 979-849-8206
Doreen Martinez, prin. Fax 864-8675

Angleton Christian S 100/PK-12
3133 N Valderas St 77515 979-864-3842

**Anna, Collin, Pop. 8,055**
Anna ISD 2,000/PK-12
501 S Sherley Ave 75409 972-924-1000
Pete Slaughter, supt. Fax 924-1001
www.annaisd.org

Anna HS 600/9-12
501 S Sherley Ave 75409 972-924-1100
Jennifer Kelley, prin. Fax 924-1101
Anna MS 500/6-8
501 S Sherley Ave 75409 972-924-1200
Thance Springer, prin. Fax 924-1201

**Anson, Jones, Pop. 2,396**
Anson ISD 700/PK-12
1431 Commercial Ave 79501 325-823-3671
Jay Baccus, supt. Fax 823-4444
www.ansontigers.com
Anson HS 200/9-12
1509 Commercial Ave 79501 325-823-2404
Troy Hinds, prin. Fax 823-2514
Anson MS 100/6-8
1120 Avenue M 79501 325-823-2771
David Hagler, prin. Fax 823-3667

**Anthony, El Paso, Pop. 4,964**
Anthony ISD 800/PK-12
840 6th St 79821 915-886-6500
Dr. Steven Saldivar, supt. Fax 886-2420
www.anthonyisd.net
Anthony HS 200/9-12
825 Wildcat Dr 79821 915-886-6550
Oscar Troncoso, prin. Fax 886-3875
Anthony MS 200/6-8
813 6th St 79821 915-886-6530
Oscar Troncoso, prin. Fax 886-3875

**Anton, Hockley, Pop. 1,117**
Anton ISD 100/PK-12
PO Box 309 79313 806-997-2301
Jim Knight, supt. Fax 997-2062
www.antonisd.org
Anton S 100/PK-12
PO Box 309 79313 806-997-5211
Dwight Rice, prin. Fax 997-2196

**Apple Springs, Trinity**
Apple Springs ISD 200/PK-12
PO Box 125 75926 936-831-3344
Cody Moree, supt. Fax 831-2824
www.asisd.com/
Apple Springs JSHS 100/7-12
PO Box 125 75926 936-831-2241
Kevin Plotts, prin. Fax 831-2824

**Aquilla, Hill, Pop. 108**
Aquilla ISD 300/PK-12
404 N Richards 76622 254-694-3770
David Edison, supt. Fax 694-6237
www.aquillaisd.net
Aquilla S 300/PK-12
404 N Richards 76622 254-694-3770
Andrew Christian, prin. Fax 694-6237

**Aransas Pass, San Patricio, Pop. 8,090**
Aransas Pass ISD 1,600/PK-12
2300 McMullen Ln Ste 600 78336 361-758-3466
Mark Kemp, supt. Fax 758-2962
www.apisd.org
Aransas Pass HS 400/9-12
450 S Avenue A 78336 361-758-3248
Wayne Bennett, prin. Fax 758-3251
Blunt MS 300/6-8
2103 Demory Ln 78336 361-758-2711
Martha Rose, prin. Fax 758-4690

**Archer City, Archer, Pop. 1,806**
Archer City ISD 500/PK-12
PO Box 926 76351 940-574-4536
C.D. Knobloch, supt. Fax 574-4051
www.archercityisd.net
Archer City JSHS 200/7-12
PO Box 926 76351 940-574-4713
Vance Morris, prin. Fax 574-4051

**Argyle, Denton, Pop. 3,241**
Argyle ISD 1,700/PK-12
800 Eagle Dr 76226 940-464-7241
Dr. Telena Wright, supt. Fax 464-7297
www.argyleisd.com
Argyle HS 700/9-12
800 Eagle Dr 76226 940-262-7777
James Hill, prin. Fax 262-7783
Argyle MS 300/7-8
800 Eagle Dr 76226 940-246-2126
Scott Gibson, prin. Fax 246-2128

Denton ISD
Supt. — See Denton
Harpool MS 1,000/6-8
9601 Stacee Ln 76226 940-369-1700
Jeff Smith, prin. Fax 241-1342

---

Liberty Christian S 1,300/PK-12
1301 S US Highway 377 76226 940-294-2000
Dr. Rodney Haire, pres. Fax 294-2045

**Arlington, Tarrant, Pop. 357,280**
Arlington ISD 63,900/PK-12
1203 W Pioneer Pkwy 76013 682-867-4611
Dr. Marcelo Cavazos, supt. Fax 459-7299
www.aisd.net
Arlington Collegiate HS at TCC-SE 9-12
2224 Southeast Pkwy 76018 817-515-3550
Dr. Ben Bholan, prin. Fax 515-3540
Arlington HS 2,900/9-12
818 W Park Row Dr 76013 682-867-8100
Shahveer Dhalla, prin. Fax 801-6105
Bailey JHS 800/7-8
2411 Winewood Ln 76013 682-867-0700
Tiffany Benavides, prin. Fax 801-0705
Barnett JHS 1,100/7-8
2101 E Sublett Rd 76018 682-867-5000
Stephanie Hawthorne, prin. Fax 419-5005
Boles JHS 800/7-8
3900 SW Green Oaks Blvd 76017 682-867-8000
Jeff Provence, prin. Fax 561-8005
Bowie HS 3,000/9-12
2101 Highbank Dr 76018 682-867-4400
Bill Manley, prin. Fax 472-4444
Carter JHS 900/7-8
701 Tharp St 76010 682-867-1700
Reny Lizardo, prin. Fax 801-1705
Gunn JHS 500/7-8
3000 S Fielder Rd 76015 682-867-5400
Juan Villarreal, prin. Fax 419-5405
Houston HS 3,100/9-12
2000 Sam Houston Dr 76014 682-867-8200
Fernando Benavides, prin. Fax 801-4505
Lamar HS 2,900/9-12
1400 W Lamar Blvd 76012 682-867-8300
Andrew Hagman, prin. Fax 801-6255
Martin HS 3,300/9-12
4501 W Pleasant Ridge Rd 76016 682-867-8600
Marlene Roddy, prin. Fax 561-8705
Newcomer Center 200/Alt
600 SE Green Oaks Blvd 76018 682-867-7100
Christy Strybosch, prin. Fax 419-1221
Nichols JHS 900/7-8
2201 Ascension Blvd 76006 682-867-2600
Julie Harcrow, prin. Fax 801-2605
Ousley JHS 600/7-8
950 Southeast Pkwy 76018 682-867-5700
Lora Thurston, prin. Fax 419-5705
Seguin HS 1,700/9-12
7001 Silo Rd 76002 682-867-6700
Sam Nix, prin. Fax 375-6705
Shackelford JHS 800/7-8
2000 N Fielder Rd 76012 682-867-3600
Jerod Zahn, prin. Fax 801-3605
Turning Point Alternative HS 100/Alt
5618 W Arkansas Ln 76016 682-867-3000
Ray Borden, prin. Fax 492-3005
Turning Point Alternative JHS 50/Alt
2209 N Davis Dr 76012 682-867-3050
Linda Williams, prin. Fax 459-7331
Venture Alternative HS 300/Alt
4900 W Arkansas Ln 76016 682-867-6400
Beverley McReynolds, prin. Fax 492-6405
Workman JHS 600/7-8
701 E Arbrook Blvd 76014 682-867-1200
Inelda Acosta, prin. Fax 419-1205
Young JHS 800/7-8
3200 Woodside Dr 76016 682-867-3400
Kelly Hastings, prin. Fax 492-3405

Mansfield ISD
Supt. — See Mansfield
Coble MS 600/7-8
1200 Ballweg Rd 76002 682-314-4900
Winston Gipson, prin. Fax 453-7331
Howard MS 900/7-8
7501 Calendar Rd 76001 682-314-1050
Dr. Maria Gamell, prin. Fax 561-3840
Summit HS 2,100/9-12
1071 Turner Warnell Rd 76001 682-314-0800
Dr. Charlotte Ford, prin. Fax 473-5732
Timberview HS 2,600/9-12
7700 S Watson Rd 76002 682-314-1300
Derrell Douglas, prin. Fax 472-2978

---

Arlington Baptist College Post-Sec.
3001 W Division St 76012 817-461-8741
Arlington Medical Institute Post-Sec.
1001 NE Green Oaks Ste 190 76006 817-265-0706
B.H. Carroll Theological Institute Post-Sec.
301 S Center St Ste 100 76010 817-274-4284
Burton Adventist Academy 300/PK-12
4611 Kelly Elliott Rd 76017 817-572-0081
Concorde Career Institute Post-Sec.
600 E Lamar Blvd Ste 200 76011 817-261-1594
Everest College Post-Sec.
300 Six Flags Dr Ste 100 76011 817-652-7790
Grace Preparatory Academy 400/K-12
PO Box 170958 76003 817-557-3399
High Point Preparatory Academy 200/K-12
2500 E Arbrook Blvd 76014 817-394-3130
Shawn King, prin. Fax 394-3101
ITT Technical Institute Post-Sec.
551 Ryan Plaza Dr 76011 817-794-5100
Northstar S 100/7-12
4620 Park Springs Blvd 76017 817-478-5852
Oakridge S 900/PK-12
5900 W Pioneer Pkwy 76013 817-451-4994
Jon Kellam, hdmstr. Fax 457-6681
Ogle School of Hair Design Post-Sec.
2200 W Park Row Dr Ste 106 76013 888-820-4224
Pantego Christian Academy 800/PK-12
2201 W Park Row Dr 76013 817-460-3315
Dr. Jeffrey Potts Ed.D., hdmstr. Fax 459-4687
St. Paul's Preparatory Academy 200/PK-12
6900 US 287 Hwy 76001 817-561-3500
Gayla Rockwell, prin. Fax 561-3408
Tarrant County College Post-Sec.
2100 Southeast Pkwy 76018 817-515-8223
University of Texas Post-Sec.
701 S Nedderman Dr 76019 817-272-2011

**Arp, Smith, Pop. 957**
Arp ISD 900/PK-12
PO Box 70 75750 903-859-8482
Dwight Thomas, supt. Fax 859-2621
home.arpisd.org
Arp HS 300/9-12
PO Box 70 75750 903-859-4917
Shannon Arrington, prin. Fax 859-1541
Arp JHS 200/6-8
PO Box 70 75750 903-859-4936
Dwight Thomas, prin. Fax 859-3980

**Aspermont, Stonewall, Pop. 909**
Aspermont ISD 200/PK-12
PO Box 549 79502 940-989-3355
Gary Harrell, supt. Fax 989-3353
www.aspermontisd.com
Aspermont JSHS 100/6-12
PO Box 549 79502 940-989-2707
Zach Morris, prin. Fax 989-3486

**Atascosa, Bexar**
Southwest ISD
Supt. — See San Antonio
McNair MS 1,000/6-8
11553 Old Pearsall Rd 78002 210-622-4480
Joseph Guidry, prin. Fax 622-4481

**Athens, Henderson, Pop. 12,562**
Athens ISD 3,400/PK-12
104 Hawn St 75751 903-677-6900
Blake Stiles, supt. Fax 677-6908
www.athensisd.net
Athens HS 900/9-12
708 E College St 75751 903-677-6920
Jami Ivey, prin. Fax 677-6925
Athens MS 800/6-8
6800 State Highway 19 S 75751 903-677-3030
Ginger Morrison, prin. Fax 677-2111
Bridges Center 50/Alt
104 Hawn St 75751 903-677-6900
Vicki Weatherford, coord. Fax 677-6908

---

Trinity Valley Community College Post-Sec.
100 Cardinal St 75751 903-677-8822

**Atlanta, Cass, Pop. 5,585**
Atlanta ISD 1,500/PK-12
106 W Main St 75551 903-796-4194
Sidney Harrist, supt. Fax 799-1004
www.atlisd.net
Atlanta HS 500/9-12
705 Rabbit Blvd 75551 903-796-4411
Nancy Rinehart, prin. Fax 799-1033
Atlanta MS 400/5-8
600 High School Ln 75551 903-796-7928
Jay Wylie, prin. Fax 799-1021

**Aubrey, Denton, Pop. 2,543**
Aubrey ISD 1,900/PK-12
415 Tisdell Ln 76227 940-668-0060
Debby Sanders, supt. Fax 365-2627
www.aubreyisd.net/
Aubrey HS 500/9-12
510 Spring Hill Rd 76227 940-668-3900
Dr. Shannon Saylor, prin. Fax 668-3903
Aubrey MS 500/5-8
815 W Sherman Dr 76227 940-668-0200
Karen Wright, prin. Fax 365-3135

Denton ISD
Supt. — See Denton
Navo MS 800/6-8
1701 Navo Rd 76227 972-347-7500
Dr. Mario Layne, prin. Fax 346-2562

**Austin, Travis, Pop. 774,864**
Austin ISD 85,500/PK-12
1111 W 6th St 78703 512-414-1700
Dr. Paul Cruz, supt. Fax 414-1707
www.austinisd.org
Akins HS 2,700/9-12
10701 S 1st St 78748 512-841-9900
Brandi Hosack, prin. Fax 841-9903
Alternative Learning Center 200/Alt
901 Neal St 78702 512-414-2554
Dennis Harms, prin. Fax 476-2809
Anderson HS 2,000/9-12
8403 Mesa Dr 78759 512-414-2538
Donna Houser, prin. Fax 338-1293
Austin HS 2,200/9-12
1715 W Cesar Chavez St 78703 512-414-2505
Amy Taylor, prin. Fax 414-7373
Bailey MS 1,000/6-8
4020 Lost Oasis Holw 78739 512-414-4990
John Rocha, prin. Fax 292-0898
Bedichek MS 1,000/6-8
6800 Bill Hughes Rd 78745 512-414-3265
Dan Diehl, prin. Fax 444-4382
Bowie HS 2,900/9-12
4103 W Slaughter Ln 78749 512-414-5247
Stephen Kane, prin. Fax 292-0527
Burnet MS 1,000/6-8
8401 Hathaway Dr 78757 512-414-3225
David Dean, prin. Fax 452-0695
Covington MS 700/6-8
3700 Convict Hill Rd 78749 512-414-3276
Shannon Sellstrom, prin. Fax 892-4547
Crockett HS 1,500/9-12
5601 Manchaca Rd 78745 512-414-2532
Craig Shapiro, prin. Fax 447-0489
Dobie MS 700/6-8
1200 E Rundberg Ln 78753 512-414-3270
Maggie Araujo, prin. Fax 836-8411
Eastside Memorial HS 600/9-12
1012 Arthur Stiles Rd 78721 512-414-5810
Bryan Miller, prin. Fax 841-5935
Fulmore MS 1,000/6-8
201 E Mary St 78704 512-414-3207
Lisa Bush, prin. Fax 441-3129
Garcia Young Men's Leadership Academy 400/6-8
7414 Johnny Morris Rd 78724 512-841-9400
Sterlin McGruder, prin. Fax 841-9401
Garza Independence HS 300/11-12
1600 Chicon St 78702 512-414-8600
Dr. Linda Webb, prin. Fax 414-8610
Gorzycki MS 1,100/6-8
7412 W Slaughter Ln 78749 512-841-8600
Cathryn Mitchell, prin. Fax 841-8601
Henry MS 1,000/6-8
2610 W 10th St 78703 512-414-3229
Peter Price, prin. Fax 477-7428
International HS 100/9-10
1012 Arthur Stiles Rd 78721 512-414-6817
Susan Galvan, prin. Fax 841-5621
Johnson Early College HS 900/9-12
7309 Lazy Creek Dr 78724 512-414-2543
Sheila Henry, prin. Fax 929-3955

Kealing MS — 1,200/6-8
1607 Pennsylvania Ave 78702 — 512-414-3214
Kenisha Coburn, prin. — Fax 478-9133
Lamar MS — 600/6-8
6201 Wynona Ave 78757 — 512-414-3217
George Llewellyn, prin. — Fax 467-6862
Lanier Health Sciences Inst of Austin — 200/9-12
1201 Payton Gin Rd 78758 — 512-414-2514
Fax 832-1203
Lanier HS — 1,600/9-12
1201 Payton Gin Rd 78758 — 512-414-2514
Ryan Hopkins, prin. — Fax 832-1203
Liberal Arts & Science Academy — 900/9-12
7309 Lazy Creek Dr 78724 — 512-414-5272
Stacia Crescenzi, dir. — Fax 414-6050
Martin MS — 600/6-8
1601 Haskell St 78702 — 512-414-3243
Rey Garcia, prin. — Fax 320-0125
McCallum HS — 1,700/9-12
5600 Sunshine Dr 78756 — 512-414-2519
Michael Garrison, prin. — Fax 453-2599
Mendez MS — 1,000/6-8
5106 Village Square Dr 78744 — 512-414-3284
Ron Gonzales, prin. — Fax 442-5738
Murchison MS — 1,400/6-8
3700 N Hills Dr 78731 — 512-414-3254
Sammilu Harrison, prin. — Fax 343-1710
Paredes MS — 1,000/6-8
10100 S Mary Moore Searight 78748 — 512-841-6800
Valeria Torres-Solis, prin. — Fax 841-7036
Reagan HS — 1,000/9-12
7104 Berkman Dr 78752 — 512-414-2523
Anabel Garza, prin. — Fax 452-7089
Richards S for Young Women Leaders — 600/6-12
2206 Prather Ln 78704 — 512-414-3236
Jeanne Goka, prin. — Fax 441-5208
Small MS — 900/6-8
4801 Monterey Oaks Blvd 78749 — 512-841-6700
Sheri Lepine, prin. — Fax 841-6703
Travis HS — 1,500/9-12
1211 E Oltorf St 78704 — 512-414-2527
Ty Davidson, prin. — Fax 707-0050
Webb MS — 700/6-8
601 E Saint Johns Ave 78752 — 512-414-3258
Raul Sanchez, prin. — Fax 452-9683

Del Valle ISD
Supt. — See Del Valle
Dailey MS — 800/6-8
14000 Westall 78725 — 512-386-3600
Mario Palacios, prin. — Fax 386-3630
Ojeda MS — 900/6-8
4900 McKinney Falls Pkwy 78744 — 512-386-3500
Sarah Reuwsaat, prin. — Fax 386-3505

Eanes ISD — 7,800/PK-12
601 Camp Craft Rd 78746 — 512-732-9001
Dr. Tom Leonard, supt. — Fax 732-9005
www.eanesisd.net
Hill Country MS — 900/6-8
1300 Walsh Tarlton Ln 78746 — 512-732-9220
Kathleen Sullivan, prin. — Fax 732-9229
Westlake HS — 2,600/9-12
4100 Westbank Dr 78746 — 512-732-9280
Dr. John Carter, prin. — Fax 732-9289
West Ridge MS — 900/6-8
9201 Scenic Bluff Dr 78733 — 512-732-9240
Steve Ramsey, prin. — Fax 732-9249
Other Schools – See West Lake Hills

Lake Travis ISD — 7,400/PK-12
3322 Ranch Road 620 S 78738 — 512-533-6000
Brad Lancaster, supt. — Fax 533-6001
www.ltisdschools.org/
Hudson Bend MS — 900/6-8
15600 Lariat Trl 78734 — 512-533-6400
Mark Robinson, prin. — Fax 533-6401
Lake Travis HS — 2,200/9-12
3324 Ranch Road 620 S 78738 — 512-533-6100
Kim Brents, prin. — Fax 533-6102
Other Schools – See Spicewood

Leander ISD
Supt. — See Leander
Canyon Ridge MS — 1,000/6-8
12601 Country Trl 78732 — 512-570-3500
Susan Sullivan, prin. — Fax 570-3505
Four Points MS — 600/6-8
9700 McNeil Dr 78750 — 512-570-3700
Dr. Joe Ciccarelli, prin. — Fax 570-3705
Vandegrift HS — 1,500/9-12
9500 McNeil Dr 78750 — 512-570-2300
Charlie Little, prin. — Fax 570-2305

Manor ISD
Supt. — See Manor
Decker MS — 700/6-8
8104 Decker Ln 78724 — 512-278-4630
Jon Bailey, prin. — Fax 278-4654

Pflugerville ISD
Supt. — See Pflugerville
Connally HS — 2,000/9-12
13212 N Lamar Blvd 78753 — 512-594-0800
Kermit Ward, prin. — Fax 594-0805
Dessau MS — 1,000/6-8
12900 Dessau Rd 78754 — 512-594-2600
Jeremy LeJeune, prin. — Fax 594-2605
Westview MS — 900/6-8
1805 Scofield Ln 78727 — 512-594-2200
Amanda Johnson, prin. — Fax 594-2205

Round Rock ISD
Supt. — See Round Rock
Canyon Vista MS — 1,300/6-8
8455 Spicewood Springs Rd 78759 — 512-464-8100
Nicole Hagerty, prin. — Fax 464-8210
Cedar Valley MS — 1,200/6-8
8139 Racine Trl 78717 — 512-428-2300
Matt Groff, prin. — Fax 428-2420
Deerpark MS — 1,000/6-8
8849 Anderson Mill Rd 78729 — 512-464-6600
Sonya Hayes, prin. — Fax 464-6740
Grisham MS — 700/6-8
10805 School House Ln 78750 — 512-428-2650
Kim Winters, prin. — Fax 428-2790
McNeil HS — 2,400/9-12
5720 McNeil Dr 78729 — 512-464-6300
Courtney Acosta, prin. — Fax 464-6550
Westwood HS — 2,500/9-12
12400 Mellow Meadow Dr 78750 — 512-464-4000
Laurelyn Arterbury, prin. — Fax 464-4020

---

ACE Academy — 200/PK-12
3901 Shoal Creek Blvd 78756 — 512-206-4070
AESA Prep Academy — 100/2-12
14101 Canonade 78737 — 512-560-5584
A New Beginning School of Massage — Post-Sec.
2525 Wallingwood Dr # 1501 78746 — 512-306-0975
AOMA Graduate School of Integrative Med — Post-Sec.
4701 W Gate Blvd 78745 — 512-454-1188
Austin Community College — Post-Sec.
5930 Middle Fiskville Rd 78752 — 512-223-7000
Austin Graduate School of Theology — Post-Sec.
7640 Guadalupe St 78752 — 512-476-2772
Austin Montessori S - Gaines Creek Cmps — 50/7-9
5006 Sunset Trl 78745 — 512-892-0826
Austin Peace Academy — 200/PK-12
5110 Manor Rd 78723 — 512-926-1737
Diana Abdi, prin. — Fax 926-9688
Austin Presbyterian Theological Seminary — Post-Sec.
100 E 27th St 78705 — 512-404-4800
Austin Tennis Academy — 50/6-12
6800 Spanish Oaks Club Blvd 78738 — 512-276-2271
Austin Waldorf S — 400/K-12
8700 S View Rd 78737 — 512-288-5942
Baldwin Beauty School - North — Post-Sec.
8440 Burnet Rd 78757 — 512-458-4127
Baldwin Beauty School - South — Post-Sec.
3005 S Lamar Blvd Ste 103 78704 — 512-441-6898
Brentwood Christian S — 700/PK-12
11908 N Lamar Blvd 78753 — 512-835-5983
Jay Burcham, pres. — Fax 835-2184
Capitol City Careers — Post-Sec.
5424 W Highway 290 Ste 200 78735 — 512-892-2640
Capitol City Trade and Technical School — Post-Sec.
205 E Riverside Dr 78704 — 512-444-3257
Concordia University Texas — Post-Sec.
11400 Concordia Univ Dr 78726 — 512-313-3000
DeVry University — Post-Sec.
11044 Research Blvd # B100 78759 — 512-231-2500
Escoffier School of Culinary Arts — Post-Sec.
6020 Dillard Cir Ste B 78752 — 512-451-5743
Everest Institute — Post-Sec.
9100 E Highway 290 # 100 78724 — 512-928-1933
Hill Country Christian S of Austin — 500/PK-12
12124 Ranch Road 620 N 78750 — 512-331-7036
Bill McGee, hdmstr. — Fax 257-4190
Huntington-Surrey S — 50/8-12
5206 Balcones Dr 78731 — 512-478-4743
Dr. Light German, prin. — Fax 457-0235
Huston-Tillotson University — Post-Sec.
900 Chicon St 78702 — 512-505-3000
Hyde Park HS - Quarries Campus — 200/9-12
PO Box 4486 78765 — 512-465-8333
Dr. Chris Coy, prin. — Fax 827-2020
ITT Technical Institute — Post-Sec.
6330 E Highway 290 Ste 150 78723 — 512-467-6800
Khabele S — 200/PK-12
801 Rio Grande St 78701 — 512-480-8142
Kirby Hall S — 200/PK-12
306 W 29th St 78705 — 512-474-1770
Kussad Institute of Court Reporting — Post-Sec.
2800 S Interstate 35 # 110 78704 — 512-443-7286
Le Cordon Bleu College of Culinary Arts — Post-Sec.
3110 Esperanza Xing Ste 100 78758 — 512-837-2665
Mediatech Institute — Post-Sec.
4719 S Congress Ave 78745 — 512-447-2002
Rawson Saunders School — 100/1-10
2614 A Exposition Blvd 78703 — 512-476-8382
Laura Steinbach M.Ed., head sch — Fax 476-1132
Regents S of Austin — 900/K-12
3230 Travis Country Cir 78735 — 512-899-8095
Rod Gilbert, hdmstr. — Fax 899-8623
Renaissance Academy — 200/PK-12
14401 Owen-Tech Blvd 78728 — 512-252-2277
St. Andrew's Episcopal S — 300/9-12
5901 Southwest Pkwy 78735 — 512-299-9700
Sean Murphy, head sch — Fax 299-9660
St. Domic Savio Catholic HS — 300/9-12
9300 Neenah Ave 78717 — 512-388-8846
Morgan Daniels, prin. — Fax 388-1335
St. Edward's University — Post-Sec.
3001 S Congress Ave 78704 — 512-448-8400
St. Michael's Catholic Academy — 400/9-12
3000 Barton Creek Blvd 78735 — 512-328-2323
Dr. Dan Dolan, head sch — Fax 328-2327
St. Stephen's Episcopal S — 700/6-12
6500 Saint Stephens Dr 78746 — 512-327-1213
Robert Kirkpatrick, head sch — Fax 327-6771
San Juan Diego Catholic HS — 100/8-12
800 Herndon Ln 78704 — 512-804-1935
Pamela Jupe, prin. — Fax 804-1937
Seminary of the Southwest — Post-Sec.
PO Box 2247 78768 — 512-472-4133
Southern Careers Institute — Post-Sec.
2301 S Congress Ave Ste 27 78704 — 512-448-4795
Texas Health and Science University — Post-Sec.
4005 Manchaca Rd 78704 — 512-444-8082
The College of Health Care Professions — Post-Sec.
6505 Airport Blvd Ste 102 78752 — 512-892-2835
University of Texas at Austin — Post-Sec.
1 University Sta 78712 — 512-471-3434
Veritas Academy — 500/PK-12
PO Box 90517 78709 — 512-891-1673
Virginia College Austin — Post-Sec.
6301 E Highway 290 78723 — 512-371-3500

**Avalon, Ellis**
Avalon ISD — 300/PK-12
PO Box 455 76623 — 972-627-3251
Dr. David Del Bosque, supt. — Fax 627-3220
www.avalonisd.net
Avalon S — 300/PK-12
PO Box 455 76623 — 972-627-3251
Khristopher Marshall, prin. — Fax 627-3220

**Avery, Red River, Pop. 482**
Avery ISD — 400/PK-12
150 San Antonio St 75554 — 903-684-3460
Kelly Burns, supt. — Fax 684-3294
www.averyisd.net/
Avery HS — 100/9-12
150 San Antonio St 75554 — 903-684-3431
Daniel Pritchett, prin. — Fax 684-3294
Avery MS — 100/5-8
150 San Antonio St 75554 — 903-684-3079
Rhonda Christophersen, prin. — Fax 684-3294

**Avinger, Cass, Pop. 437**
Avinger ISD — 100/PK-12
245 Conner 75630 — 903-562-1355
Jacquelyn Smith, supt. — Fax 562-1271
www.avingerisd.net/
Avinger S — 100/PK-12
245 Conner 75630 — 903-562-1355
Dr. Tom Phy, prin. — Fax 562-1271

**Avoca, Jones**
Lueders-Avoca ISD
Supt. — See Lueders
Lueders-Avoca HS — 50/9-12
8762 County Road 604 79503 — 325-773-2785
Bob Spikes, supt. — Fax 773-3072

**Axtell, McLennan**
Axtell ISD — 700/PK-12
308 Ottawa 76624 — 254-863-5301
Dr. J.R. Proctor, supt. — Fax 863-5651
www.axtellisd.net
Axtell HS — 200/9-12
308 Ottawa 76624 — 254-863-5301
Dale Monsey, prin. — Fax 863-5651
Axtell MS — 200/6-8
308 Ottawa 76624 — 254-863-5301
Dale Monsey, prin. — Fax 863-5651

**Azle, Tarrant, Pop. 10,777**
Azle ISD — 5,900/PK-12
300 Roe St 76020 — 817-444-3235
Ray Lea, supt. — Fax 444-6866
www.azleisd.net
Azle HS — 1,800/9-12
1200 Boyd Rd 76020 — 817-444-5555
Sam Robinson, prin. — Fax 444-8884
Azle JHS — 500/7-8
201 School St 76020 — 817-444-2564
Brian Roberts, prin. — Fax 270-0880
Forte JHS — 400/7-8
479 Sandy Beach Rd 76020 — 817-270-1133
Dianne Boone, prin. — Fax 270-1157

---

Azle Christian S — 100/PK-12
1801 S Stewart St 76020 — 817-444-9964
Shery Rushing, admin. — Fax 444-9914

**Baird, Callahan, Pop. 1,483**
Baird ISD — 300/PK-12
PO Box 1147 79504 — 325-854-1400
Jarod Bellar, supt. — Fax 854-2058
www.bairdisd.net
Baird HS — 100/9-12
PO Box 1147 79504 — 325-854-1400
Perry Simmons, prin. — Fax 854-2808
Baird JHS — 100/6-8
PO Box 1147 79504 — 325-854-1400
Cynthia Bessent, prin. — Fax 854-2808

**Balch Springs, Dallas, Pop. 23,383**
Dallas ISD
Supt. — See Dallas
Balch Springs MS — 6-8
710 Cheyenne Rd 75180 — 972-892-5800
Clarita Rivera, prin.

**Ballinger, Runnels, Pop. 3,731**
Ballinger ISD — 1,000/PK-12
PO Box 231 76821 — 325-365-3588
Jeff Butts, admin. — Fax 365-5920
www.ballingerisd.net
Ballinger HS — 300/9-12
PO Box 231 76821 — 325-365-3547
Alan Gillespie, prin. — Fax 365-5422
Ballinger JHS — 200/6-8
PO Box 231 76821 — 325-365-3537
Stacy Tucker, prin. — Fax 365-5420

**Balmorhea, Reeves, Pop. 479**
Balmorhea ISD — 100/PK-12
PO Box 368 79718 — 432-375-2223
Manuel Espino, supt. — Fax 375-2511
www.bisdbears.esc18.net
Balmorhea S — 100/PK-12
PO Box 368 79718 — 432-375-2223
Teri Barragan, prin. — Fax 375-2511

**Bandera, Bandera, Pop. 852**
Bandera ISD — 2,400/PK-12
PO Box 727 78003 — 830-796-3313
Regina Howell, supt. — Fax 796-6238
www.banderaisd.net
Bandera HS — 800/9-12
PO Box 727 78003 — 830-796-6254
Sergio Menchaca, prin. — Fax 796-6251
Bandera MS — 600/6-8
PO Box 727 78003 — 830-796-6270
Donald Tosh, prin. — Fax 796-6277

**Bangs, Brown, Pop. 1,570**
Bangs ISD 1,000/PK-12
PO Box 969 76823 325-752-6612
Bill Foster, supt. Fax 752-6253
www.bangsisd.net
Bangs HS 300/9-12
PO Box 969 76823 325-752-6822
Tony Truelove, prin. Fax 752-7028
Bangs MS 300/5-8
PO Box 969 76823 325-752-6088
Tony Truelove, prin. Fax 752-6253

**Banquete, Nueces, Pop. 721**
Banquete ISD 800/PK-12
PO Box 369 78339 361-387-2551
Dr. Max Thompson, supt. Fax 387-7188
www.banqueteisd.esc2.net/
Banquete HS 200/9-12
PO Box 369 78339 361-387-8588
Nancy Mooney, prin. Fax 767-6504
Banquete JHS 200/6-8
PO Box 369 78339 361-387-6504
Ramiro Pena, prin. Fax 387-7051

**Barksdale, Edwards**
Nueces Canyon Consolidated ISD 300/K-12
PO Box 118 78828 830-234-3514
Kristi Powers, supt. Fax 234-3435
www.nccisd.net/
Nueces Canyon JSHS 200/7-12
PO Box 118 78828 830-234-3524
Luci Harmon, prin. Fax 234-4129

**Bartlett, Bell, Pop. 1,605**
Bartlett ISD 400/PK-12
PO Box 170 76511 254-527-4247
Brett Springston M.Ed., supt. Fax 527-3340
www.bartlett.txed.net
Bartlett S 400/PK-12
PO Box 170 76511 254-527-4247
Jay Harris M.Ed., prin. Fax 527-3340

**Bastrop, Bastrop, Pop. 7,084**
Bastrop ISD 9,100/PK-12
906 Farm St 78602 512-772-7100
Steve Murray, supt. Fax 321-7469
www.bisdtx.org/
Bastrop HS 1,500/9-12
1614 Chambers St 78602 512-772-7200
Dr. Jason Hewitt, prin. Fax 321-7502
Bastrop MS 700/7-8
725 Old Austin Hwy 78602 512-772-7400
Dr. Christopher Julian, prin. Fax 321-1557
Colorado River Collegiate Academy 9-12
1602 Hill St 78602 512-772-7230
Martin Conrardy, prin.
Gateway Alternative S 50/Alt
1019 Lovers Ln 78602 512-772-7820
Patricia Alford, prin. Fax 332-0498
Genesis HS 100/Alt
1602 Hill St 78602 512-772-7230
Martin Conrardy, prin. Fax 321-3212
Other Schools – See Cedar Creek

**Bay City, Matagorda, Pop. 17,441**
Bay City ISD 3,800/PK-12
PO Box 2510 77404 979-245-5766
Keith Brown, supt. Fax 245-3175
www.bcblackcats.net
Bay City HS 1,100/9-12
400 7th St 77414 979-245-5771
Chris Townsend, prin. Fax 245-1220
Bay City JHS 800/6-8
1507 Sycamore Ave 77414 979-245-6345
Glenn Ging, prin. Fax 245-1419

**Baytown, Harris, Pop. 70,920**
Barbers Hill ISD
Supt. — See Mont Belvieu
Barbers Hill MS South 6-8
9600 Eagle Dr, 281-576-2221
Dennis Wagner, prin. Fax 576-3350

Goose Creek Consolidated ISD 21,100/PK-12
PO Box 30 77522 281-420-4800
Randal O'Brien, supt. Fax 420-4815
www.gccisd.net
Baytown JHS 800/6-8
7707 Bayway Dr 77520 281-420-4560
Matthew Bolinger, prin. Fax 420-4908
Cedar Bayou JHS 1,000/6-8
2610 Elvinta St 77520 281-420-4570
Bruce Davis, prin. Fax 420-4569
Gentry JHS 1,000/6-8
1919 E Archer Rd 77521 281-420-4590
Murrell Stewart, prin. Fax 420-4909
Goose Creek Memorial HS 1,700/9-12
6001 E Wallisville Rd 77521 281-421-4400
Susan Jackson, prin. Fax 421-4444
Hyland Center 200/Alt
1906 Decker Dr 77520 281-420-4555
Michelle Verdun, prin. Fax 420-4558
Impact Early College HS 200/9-12
200 Lee Dr 77520 281-420-4802
Laura Reyes, prin. Fax 556-5781
Lee HS 1,600/9-12
1809 Market St 77520 281-420-4535
Greg Lynd, prin. Fax 420-4548
Mann JHS 900/6-8
310 S Highway 146 77520 281-420-4585
Erica Navejar, prin. Fax 420-4664
Sterling HS 2,300/9-12
300 W Baker Rd 77521 281-420-4500
Kevin Foxworth, prin. Fax 420-4974
Stuart Career Center Vo/Tech
300 YMCA Dr 77521 281-420-4550
Renea Dillon, dir. Fax 420-4553
Other Schools – See Highlands

Baytown Christian Academy 200/PK-12
5555 N Main St 77521 281-421-4150
Al Richard, hdmstr. Fax 421-4038
Lee College Post-Sec.
PO Box 818 77522 281-427-5611

**Beaumont, Jefferson, Pop. 116,638**
Beaumont ISD 18,100/PK-12
3395 Harrison Ave 77706 409-617-5000
Dr. John Frossard, supt. Fax 617-5184
www.bmtisd.com
Brown Center 100/Alt
3410 Austin St 77706 409-617-5720
Jackie Cotton, prin. Fax 617-5738
Central HS 1,800/9-12
88 Jaguar Dr 77702 409-617-5300
Ronald Jackson, prin. Fax 617-5396
King MS 400/6-8
1400 Avenue A 77701 409-617-5850
Dana Lewis, prin. Fax 617-5873
Marshall MS 800/6-8
6455 Gladys Ave 77706 409-617-5900
Shannon Allen, prin. Fax 617-5924
Odom Academy 900/6-8
2550 W Virginia St 77705 409-617-5925
Tillie Hickman, prin. Fax 617-5949
Ozen HS 1,200/9-12
3443 Fannett Rd 77705 409-617-5400
Odis Norris, prin. Fax 617-5496
Pathways Learning Center 100/Alt
3410 Austin St 77706 409-617-5700
Jackie Cotton, prin. Fax 617-5718
Smith MS 500/6-8
4415 Concord Rd 77703 409-617-5825
Dr. Tyrus Doctor, prin. Fax 617-5848
South Park MS 400/6-8
4500 Highland Ave 77705 409-617-5875
Sharon Hendrix, prin. Fax 617-5899
Taylor Career Center Vo/Tech
2330 North St 77702 409-617-5740
Michael Shelton, prin. Fax 617-5759
Vincent MS 800/6-8
350 Eldridge Dr 77707 409-617-5950
Dr. Brian Abel, prin. Fax 617-5974
West Brook HS 2,300/9-12
8750 Phelan Blvd 77706 409-617-5500
Kristi Fuselier, prin. Fax 617-5582

Hamshire-Fannett ISD
Supt. — See Hamshire
Hamshire-Fannett MS 300/7-8
11375 Dugat Rd 77705 409-794-2361
Shawn Clubb, prin. Fax 794-3042

Baptist Hospital of Southeast Texas Post-Sec.
3030 Fannin St Ste A 77701 409-212-5724
Kaplan College Post-Sec.
6115 Eastex Fwy 77706 409-347-5900
Lamar Institute of Technology Post-Sec.
PO Box 10043 77710 409-880-8321
Lamar University Post-Sec.
PO Box 10009 77710 409-880-7011
Legacy Christian Academy 300/PK-12
8200 Highway 105 77713 409-924-0500
Jon Cregor, dir. Fax 924-0953
Monsignor Kelly Catholic HS 400/9-12
5950 Kelly Dr 77707 409-866-2351
Roger Bemis, prin. Fax 866-0917
St. Elizabeth Hospital Post-Sec.
2830 Calder St 77702 409-892-7171
Vista College Post-Sec.
3871 Stagg Dr Ste 194 77701 409-291-4900

**Beckville, Panola, Pop. 830**
Beckville ISD 700/PK-12
PO Box 37 75631 903-678-3311
Devin Tate, supt. Fax 678-2157
www.beckvilleisd.net/
Beckville HS 200/9-12
PO Box 37 75631 903-678-3591
Phillip Works, prin. Fax 678-3645
Beckville JHS 100/6-8
PO Box 37 75631 903-678-3851
Loretta Blair, prin. Fax 678-3827

**Bedford, Tarrant, Pop. 45,838**
Hurst-Euless-Bedford ISD 21,500/PK-12
1849 Central Dr Ste A 76022 817-283-4461
Steven Chapman, supt. Fax 354-3311
www.hebisd.edu
Bedford JHS 800/7-9
325 Carolyn Dr 76021 817-788-3101
Michael Martinak, prin. Fax 788-3105
Harwood JHS 1,000/7-9
3000 Martin Dr 76021 817-354-3360
Leslie Guajardo, prin. Fax 354-3369
Technical Education Center Vo/Tech
1849 Central Dr 76022 817-354-3542
Lisa Karr, prin. Fax 354-3546
Other Schools – See Euless, Hurst

Brown Mackie College - Dallas/Ft. Worth Post-Sec.
2200 Highway 121 Ste 250 76021 817-799-0500

**Beeville, Bee, Pop. 12,739**
Beeville ISD 2,400/PK-12
201 N Saint Marys St 78102 361-358-7111
Erasmo Rodriguez, supt. Fax 362-6046
www.beevilleisd.net
Jones HS 1,000/9-12
1902 N Adams St 78102 361-362-6000
DeeDee Bernal, prin. Fax 362-6016
Moreno MS 600/7-8
301 N Minnesota St 78102 361-358-6262
Joni Barber, prin. Fax 362-6092

Coastal Bend College Post-Sec.
3800 Charco Rd 78102 361-358-2838

**Bellaire, Harris, Pop. 16,508**
Houston ISD
Supt. — See Houston
Bellaire HS 3,500/9-12
5100 Maple St 77401 713-295-3704
Michael McDonough, prin. Fax 295-3763
Pin Oak MS 1,200/6-8
4601 Glenmont St 77401 713-295-6500
Rita Graves, prin. Fax 295-6511

Episcopal HS 700/9-12
4650 Bissonnet St 77401 713-512-3400
Ned Smith, hdmstr. Fax 512-3603
Post Oak S 400/PK-12
4600 Bissonnet St 77401 713-661-6688
John Long, head sch Fax 661-4959

**Bellevue, Clay, Pop. 360**
Bellevue ISD 200/K-12
PO Box 38 76228 940-928-2104
Dean Gilstrap, supt. Fax 928-2583
www.bellevueisd.org/
Bellevue S 200/K-12
PO Box 38 76228 940-928-2104
Michael Qualls, prin. Fax 928-2583

**Bells, Grayson, Pop. 1,356**
Bells ISD 800/PK-12
1550 Ole Ambrose Rd 75414 903-965-7721
Joe Moore, supt. Fax 965-7036
bellsisd.net/
Bells HS 200/9-12
1500 Ole Ambrose Rd 75414 903-965-7315
Josh Weger, prin. Fax 965-5205
Prichard JHS 200/6-8
1510 Ole Ambrose Rd 75414 903-965-4835
Will Steger, prin. Fax 965-7428

**Bellville, Austin, Pop. 4,068**
Bellville ISD 2,100/PK-12
518 S Mathews St 77418 979-865-3133
Mike Coker, supt. Fax 865-8591
www.bellvilleisd.org
Bellville HS 700/9-12
518 S Mathews St 77418 979-865-3681
Dr. Michael Coopersmith, prin. Fax 865-7080
Bellville JHS 500/6-8
518 S Mathews St 77418 979-865-5966
Natalie Jones, prin. Fax 865-7060
Spicer Alternative Education Center Alt
518 S Mathews St 77418 979-865-7095
Sean McEnerney, coord. Fax 865-7094

Faith Academy 200/PK-12
12177 Highway 36 77418 979-865-1811
Fax 865-2454

**Belton, Bell, Pop. 17,870**
Belton ISD 8,700/PK-12
PO Box 269 76513 254-215-2000
Dr. Susan Kincannon, supt. Fax 215-2001
www.bisd.net
Belton HS 2,400/9-12
600 Lake Rd 76513 254-215-2200
Chris DuBois, prin. Fax 215-2201
Belton New Tech HS @ Waskow 100/9-12
320 N Blair St 76513 254-215-2500
Jill Ross, prin. Fax 215-2501
South Belton MS 6-8
805 Sage Brush 76513 254-215-3000
Keonna White, prin. Fax 215-3001
Other Schools – See Temple

University of Mary Hardin-Baylor Post-Sec.
900 College St 76513 254-295-8642

**Benavides, Duval, Pop. 1,353**
Benavides ISD 400/PK-12
PO Box P 78341 361-256-3003
Adell Cueva, supt. Fax 256-3002
www.benavidesisd.net
Benavides HS 200/7-12
PO Box P 78341 361-256-3040
Marco Ramirez, prin. Fax 256-3043

**Ben Bolt, Jim Wells**
Ben Bolt-Palito Blanco ISD 600/PK-12
PO Box 547 78342 361-664-9904
Dr. Timothy Little, supt. Fax 668-0446
www.bbpbschools.net
Ben Bolt MS 300/4-8
PO Box 547 78342 361-664-9568
Fernando Galvan, prin. Fax 664-5235
Ben Bolt-Palito Blanco HS 200/9-12
PO Box 547 78342 361-664-9822
Terry Young, prin. Fax 664-5481

**Benbrook, Tarrant, Pop. 20,889**
Fort Worth ISD
Supt. — See Fort Worth
Benbrook MS 600/6-8
201 Overcrest Dr 76126 817-815-7100
Richard Penland, prin. Fax 815-7150
Leonard MS 800/6-8
8900 Chapin Rd 76116 817-815-6200
Cathy Williams-Ridley, prin. Fax 815-6250
Western Hills HS 1,400/9-12
3600 Boston Ave 76116 817-815-6000
James Wellman, prin. Fax 815-6050

**Benjamin, Knox, Pop. 256**
Benjamin ISD 100/K-12
PO Box 166 79505 940-459-2231
Olivia Gloria, supt. Fax 459-2007
www.benjaminisd.net/
Benjamin S 100/K-12
PO Box 166 79505 940-459-2231
Olivia Gloria, prin. Fax 459-2007

**Ben Wheeler, Van Zandt**
Martins Mill ISD 500/PK-12
301 FM 1861 75754 903-479-3872
James Oliver, supt. Fax 479-3711
www.martinsmillisd.net
Martins Mill HS 200/7-12
301 FM 1861 75754 903-479-3234
Cory Hines, prin. Fax 479-3486

**Big Lake, Reagan, Pop. 2,917**
Reagan County ISD 800/PK-12
1111 E 12th St 76932 325-884-3705
Steve Long, supt. Fax 884-3021
www.rcisd.net
Reagan County HS 200/9-12
1111 E 12th St 76932 325-884-3714
Kara Garlitz, prin. Fax 884-5759
Reagan County MS 200/6-8
500 N Pennsylvania Ave 76932 325-884-3728
David Kohutek, prin. Fax 884-2327

**Big Sandy, Upshur, Pop. 1,325**
Big Sandy ISD 700/PK-12
PO Box 598 75755 903-636-5287
Scott Beene, supt. Fax 636-5111
www.bigsandyisd.org
Big Sandy HS 200/9-12
PO Box 598 75755 903-636-5287
Kim Stradley, prin. Fax 636-5111
Big Sandy JHS 200/6-8
PO Box 598 75755 903-636-5287
Lance Morrow, prin. Fax 636-5111

Harmony ISD 1,100/PK-12
9788 State Highway 154 W 75755 903-725-5492
Dennis Glenn, supt. Fax 725-6737
www.harmonyisd.net
Harmony HS 400/9-12
9788 State Highway 154 W 75755 903-725-5495
Michael Alphin, prin. Fax 725-7079
Harmony JHS 200/6-8
9788 State Highway 154 W 75755 903-725-5485
Pamela Beall, prin. Fax 725-7270

**Big Spring, Howard, Pop. 26,933**
Big Spring ISD 3,200/PK-12
708 E 11th Pl 79720 432-264-3600
Chris Wigington, supt. Fax 264-3646
www.bsisd.esc18.net
Big Spring HS 1,000/9-12
708 E 11th Pl 79720 432-264-3641
Mike Ritchey, prin. Fax 264-4113
Big Spring JHS 500/7-8
708 E 11th Pl 79720 432-264-4135
Rebecca Otto, prin. Fax 264-4196
D.A.E.P. Alt
708 E 11th Pl 79720 432-264-3641
Bert Otto, prin. Fax 264-4113

---

Howard College Post-Sec.
1001 N Birdwell Ln 79720 432-264-5000
Scenic Mountain Medical Center Post-Sec.
1601 W 11th Pl 79720 432-263-1211

**Bishop, Nueces, Pop. 3,126**
Bishop Consolidated ISD 1,300/PK-12
719 E 6th St 78343 361-584-3591
Christina Gutierrez, supt. Fax 584-3147
www.bishopcisd.net
Bishop HS 400/9-12
100 Badger Ln 78343 361-584-2547
Ray Garza, prin. Fax 584-2549
Luehrs JHS 200/7-8
717 E 6th St 78343 361-584-3576
Kenna Moody, prin. Fax 584-3577

**Blackwell, Nolan, Pop. 309**
Blackwell Consolidated ISD 200/PK-12
PO Box 505 79506 325-282-2311
Abe Gott, supt. Fax 282-2027
www.blackwellhornets.org
Blackwell S 200/PK-12
PO Box 505 79506 325-282-2311
Bryan Shipman, prin. Fax 282-2027

**Blanco, Blanco, Pop. 1,722**
Blanco ISD 1,000/PK-12
814 11th St 78606 830-833-4414
Dr. Buck Ford, supt. Fax 833-2019
www.blancoisd.com
Blanco HS 300/9-12
814 11th St 78606 830-833-4337
Casey Hollomon, prin. Fax 833-5028
Blanco MS 200/6-8
814 11th St 78606 830-833-5570
Keitha St. Clair, prin. Fax 833-2507

**Blanket, Brown, Pop. 382**
Blanket ISD 200/K-12
901 Avenue H 76432 325-748-5311
Vick Orlando, supt. Fax 748-3391
www.blanketisd.net
Blanket HS 100/9-12
901 Avenue H 76432 325-748-5311
Kay Ribble, prin. Fax 748-2110

**Bloomburg, Cass, Pop. 398**
Bloomburg ISD 300/PK-12
307 W Cypress St 75556 903-728-5216
Brian Stroman, supt. Fax 728-5399
www.bloomburgisd.net
Bloomburg HS 100/6-12
307 W Cypress St 75556 903-728-5216
Clinton Coyne, prin. Fax 728-5399

**Blooming Grove, Navarro, Pop. 812**
Blooming Grove ISD 800/PK-12
PO Box 258 76626 903-695-2541
Marshall Harrison, supt. Fax 695-2594
www.bgisd.org
Blooming Grove HS 300/9-12
PO Box 258 76626 903-695-2541
Karen Lane, prin. Fax 695-2594
Blooming Grove JHS 200/6-8
PO Box 258 76626 903-695-4201
Doyle Bell, prin. Fax 695-4601

**Bloomington, Victoria, Pop. 2,445**
Bloomington ISD
Supt. — See Victoria
Bloomington HS 200/9-12
PO Box 158 77951 361-897-1551
James Pieper, prin. Fax 897-1888
Bloomington MS 200/6-8
PO Box 158 77951 361-897-2260
Abbie Barnett, prin. Fax 897-3822

**Blue Ridge, Collin, Pop. 807**
Blue Ridge ISD 700/PK-12
318 School St 75424 972-752-5554
Todd Lintzen, supt. Fax 752-9084
brisd.net
Blue Ridge HS 200/9-12
11020 County Road 504 75424 972-752-5554
Justin Minzenmayer, prin. Fax 752-5361
Blue Ridge MS 100/6-8
710 Tiger Pride Cir 75424 972-752-5554
Justin Minzenmayer, prin. Fax 752-5363

**Blum, Hill, Pop. 439**
Blum ISD 400/PK-12
PO Box 520 76627 254-874-5231
Elsa Scott, supt. Fax 874-5233
www.blumisd.net
Blum JSHS 200/6-12
PO Box 520 76627 254-874-5231
Jeff Sanders, prin. Fax 874-5233

**Boerne, Kendall, Pop. 10,349**
Boerne ISD 6,800/PK-12
123 Johns Rd 78006 830-357-2000
David Stelmazewski, supt. Fax 357-2009
www.boerne-isd.net
Boerne Academy Alt
210 Live Oak St 78006 830-357-2925
Cory Bell, admin. Fax 357-2919
Boerne HS 1,000/9-12
1 Greyhound Ln 78006 830-357-2200
Natalie Farber, prin. Fax 357-2299
Boerne MS - North 500/6-8
240 Johns Rd 78006 830-357-3100
Tommy Hungate, prin. Fax 357-3199
Boerne MS - South 600/6-8
10 Cascade Caverns Rd 78015 830-357-3300
Georgia Franks, prin. Fax 357-3399
Boerne-Samuel V. Champion HS 1,300/9-12
201 Charger Blvd 78006 830-357-2600
Dr. Jodi Spoor, prin. Fax 357-2699

---

Blessed Hope Academy 100/9-12
PO Box 1453 78006 210-697-9191
Alice Ashcraft, dir. Fax 690-9299
Geneva S 500/K-12
113 Cascade Caverns Rd 78015 830-775-6101

**Bogata, Red River, Pop. 1,141**
Rivercrest ISD 700/PK-12
4100 US Highway 271 S 75417 903-632-5205
Stanley Jessee, supt. Fax 632-4691
www.rivercrestisd.net
Rivercrest HS 200/9-12
4126 US Highway 271 S 75417 903-632-5204
Ronny Alsup, prin. Fax 632-5231
Rivercrest JHS 200/6-8
4100 US Highway 271 S 75417 903-632-0878
Lee Wilson, prin. Fax 632-4691

**Boling, Wharton, Pop. 1,118**
Boling ISD 1,000/PK-12
PO Box 160 77420 979-657-2770
Wade Stidevent, supt. Fax 657-3265
www.bolingisd.net
Boling HS 300/9-12
PO Box 119 77420 979-657-2816
Keith Jedlicka, prin. Fax 657-2026
Iago JHS 300/6-8
PO Box 89 77420 979-657-2826
Brett Pohler, prin. Fax 657-2828

**Bonham, Fannin, Pop. 9,979**
Bonham ISD 1,800/PK-12
1005 Chestnut St 75418 903-583-5526
Dr. Marvin Beaty, supt. Fax 583-8463
www.bonhamisd.org/
Bonham HS 500/9-12
1002 War Path St 75418 903-583-5567
David Ketcher, prin. Fax 583-5560
Rather JHS 300/7-8
1201 N Main St 75418 903-583-7474
Ryan Prock, prin. Fax 583-3713

**Booker, Lipscomb, Pop. 1,488**
Booker ISD 400/PK-12
PO Box 288 79005 806-658-4501
Terri Zink, supt. Fax 658-4503
www.bookerisd.net/
Booker JSHS 200/6-12
PO Box 288 79005 806-658-4521
Kelly Lampe, prin. Fax 658-4503

**Borger, Hutchinson, Pop. 13,012**
Borger ISD 2,800/PK-12
200 E 9th St 79007 806-273-1000
Chance Welch, supt. Fax 273-1066
www.borgerisd.net
Borger HS 800/9-12
600 W 1st St 79007 806-273-1029
Matt Ammerman, prin. Fax 273-1036
Borger MS 600/6-8
1321 S Florida St 79007 806-273-1037
Michael Cano, prin. Fax 273-1069

---

Frank Phillips College Post-Sec.
PO Box 5118 79008 806-457-4200

**Bovina, Parmer, Pop. 1,863**
Bovina ISD 500/PK-12
PO Box 70 79009 806-251-1336
Denise Anderson, supt. Fax 251-1578
www.bovinaisd.org
Bovina HS 100/9-12
PO Box 70 79009 806-251-1317
Steve Arias, prin. Fax 251-1002
Bovina MS 100/6-8
PO Box 70 79009 806-251-1336
Mark Barnes, prin. Fax 251-1578

**Bowie, Montague, Pop. 5,161**
Bowie ISD 1,600/PK-12
PO Box 1168 76230 940-872-1151
Steven Monkres, supt. Fax 872-5979
www.bowieisd.net/
Bowie HS 400/9-12
341 US Highway 287 N Access 76230940-872-1154
Kelly Shackelford, prin. Fax 872-1299
Bowie JHS 400/6-8
501 E Tarrant St 76230 940-872-1152
Amy Murphey, prin. Fax 872-8921

Gold-Burg ISD 100/PK-12
468 Prater Rd 76230 940-872-3562
Roger Ellis, supt. Fax 872-5933
www.goldburgisd.net
Gold-Burg S 100/PK-12
468 Prater Rd 76230 940-872-3562
Aaron Tefertiller, prin. Fax 872-5933

**Boyd, Wise, Pop. 1,184**
Boyd ISD 1,100/PK-12
PO Box 92308 76023 940-433-2327
Ted West, supt. Fax 433-9569
www.boydisd.net
Boyd HS 400/9-12
PO Box 92308 76023 940-433-2327
Scott Nedrow, prin. Fax 433-9593
Boyd MS 200/7-8
PO Box 92308 76023 940-433-2327
James McDonald, prin. Fax 433-9568

**Boys Ranch, Oldham, Pop. 281**
Boys Ranch ISD 300/K-12
PO Box 219 79010 806-534-2221
Dr. Vita Sotelo, supt. Fax 534-2384
www.boysranchisd.org/
Blakemore MS 100/6-8
PO Box 219 79010 806-534-2361
Kenneth Brown, prin. Fax 534-0041
Boys Ranch HS 200/9-12
PO Box 219 79010 806-534-0032
Mark Kellogg, prin. Fax 534-0033
STARR Academy 50/Alt
PO Box 219 79010 806-533-1413
Shelly Allen, prin. Fax 533-2220

**Brackettville, Kinney, Pop. 1,675**
Brackett ISD 600/PK-12
PO Box 586 78832 830-563-2491
Kevin Newsom, supt. Fax 563-9264
www.brackettisd.net/
Brackett HS 200/9-12
PO Box 586 78832 830-563-2480
Daron Worrell, prin. Fax 563-3213
Brackett JHS 100/6-8
PO Box 586 78832 830-563-2480
Christy Price, prin. Fax 563-9559

**Brady, McCulloch, Pop. 5,490**
Brady ISD 1,200/PK-12
1003 W 11th St 76825 325-597-2301
Johnny Clawson, supt. Fax 597-3984
www.bradyisd.org
Brady HS 300/9-12
1003 W 11th St 76825 325-597-2491
Eric Bierman, prin. Fax 597-2147
Brady MS 300/6-8
1003 W 11th St 76825 325-597-8110
Shona Moore, prin. Fax 597-4166

**Brazoria, Brazoria, Pop. 2,978**
Columbia-Brazoria ISD
Supt. — See West Columbia
West Brazos JHS 500/7-8
111 Roustabout Dr 77422 979-799-1730
Robert McReynolds, prin. Fax 798-8000

**Breckenridge, Stephens, Pop. 5,738**
Breckenridge ISD 1,500/PK-12
PO Box 1738 76424 254-522-9600
Timothy Seymore, supt. Fax 522-9600
www.breckenridgeisd.org
Breckenridge HS 400/9-12
500 W Lindsey St 76424 254-212-4730
Bryan Dieterich, prin. Fax 212-4730
Breckenridge JHS 200/7-8
502 W Lindsey St 76424 254-212-4311
Jessica Stapp, prin. Fax 212-4311

**Bremond, Robertson, Pop. 926**
Bremond ISD 400/PK-12
601 W Collins St 76629 254-746-7145
Daryl Stuard, supt. Fax 746-7726
www.bremondisd.net
Bremond HS 100/9-12
601 W Collins St 76629 254-746-7145
Harold Schroeder, prin. Fax 746-7726
Bremond MS 100/6-8
601 W Collins St 76629 254-746-7145
John Burnett, prin. Fax 746-7726

**Brenham, Washington, Pop. 15,543**
Brenham ISD 4,900/PK-12
PO Box 1147 77834 979-277-3700
Walter Jackson Ed.D., supt. Fax 277-3701
www.brenhamisd.net

Brenham HS 1,400/9-12
525 A H Ehrig Dr 77833 979-277-3800
Steve Skrla, prin. Fax 277-3801
Brenham JHS 700/7-8
1200 Carlee Dr 77833 979-277-3830
Bryan Bryant, prin. Fax 277-3831
PRIDE Academy 50/Alt
1301 S Market St 77833 979-277-3890
Michael Watts, prin. Fax 277-3891

---

Blinn College Post-Sec.
902 College Ave 77833 979-830-4000
Brenham Christian Academy 100/PK-12
2111 S Blue Bell Rd 77833 979-830-8480
Dr. Charles Loyd, head sch Fax 830-1687

**Bridge City, Orange, Pop. 7,734**
Bridge City ISD 2,200/PK-12
1031 W Round Bunch Rd 77611 409-735-1500
Mike King, supt. Fax 735-1512
www.bridgecityisd.net/
Bridge City HS 800/9-12
2690 Texas Ave 77611 409-735-1501
Elisha Bell, prin. Fax 735-1519
Bridge City MS 600/6-8
300 Bower Dr 77611 409-735-1513
Lydia Gonzales, prin. Fax 735-1517

**Bridgeport, Wise, Pop. 5,936**
Bridgeport ISD 2,300/PK-12
2107 15th St 76426 940-683-5124
Eddie Bland, supt. Fax 683-4268
www.bridgeportisd.net
Alternative Learning Center Alt
1101 17th St 76426 940-683-1830
Jennifer Miller, prin. Fax 683-3582
Bridgeport HS 600/9-12
1 Maroon Dr 76426 940-683-4064
Jaime Sturdivant, prin. Fax 683-4014
Bridgeport MS 600/6-8
702 17th St 76426 940-683-2273
Travis Whisenant, prin. Fax 683-5812

**Briscoe, Wheeler**
Fort Elliott Consolidated ISD 100/PK-12
PO Box 138 79011 806-375-2454
Brad Slatton, supt. Fax 375-2327
www.fecisd.net
Ft. Elliott JSHS 100/6-12
PO Box 138 79011 806-375-2454
Benny Barnett, prin. Fax 375-2327

**Broaddus, San Augustine, Pop. 202**
Broaddus ISD 500/PK-12
PO Box 58 75929 936-872-3041
Shane McGown, supt. Fax 872-3699
www.broaddusisd.net
Broaddus JSHS 200/6-12
PO Box 58 75929 936-872-3610
Brad Hranicky, prin. Fax 872-9020

**Brock, Parker**
Brock ISD 900/K-12
410 Eagle Spirit Ln 76087 817-594-7642
Scott Drillette, supt. Fax 599-3246
www.brockisd.net
Brock HS 300/9-12
400 Eagle Spirit Ln 76087 817-596-7425
Rick Howell, prin. Fax 594-2509
Brock MS 200/6-8
300 Grindstone Rd 76087 817-594-3195
Ingia Saxton, prin. Fax 594-3191

**Bronte, Coke, Pop. 986**
Bronte ISD 300/PK-12
PO Box 670 76933 325-473-2511
Tim Siler, supt. Fax 473-2313
www.bronteisd.net
Bronte JSHS 100/7-12
PO Box 670 76933 325-473-2521
Terry Marrs, prin. Fax 473-2022

**Brookeland, Sabine**
Brookeland ISD 400/PK-12
187 Wildcat Walk 75931 409-698-2677
Kevin McCugh, supt. Fax 698-2533
www.brookelandisd.net
Brookeland JSHS 200/6-12
187 Wildcat Walk 75931 409-698-2413
Charlotte Odom, prin. Fax 698-2891

**Brookesmith, Brown**
Brookesmith ISD 200/PK-12
PO Box 706 76827 325-643-3023
Guy Birdwell, supt. Fax 643-3378
www.brookesmithisd.net/
Brookesmith S 200/PK-12
PO Box 706 76827 325-643-3023
Guy Birdwell, supt. Fax 643-3378

**Brookshire, Waller, Pop. 4,653**
Royal ISD
Supt. — See Pattison
Royal HS 500/9-12
34499 Royal Rd 77423 281-934-2215
Dr. Ostrova McGary, prin. Fax 934-2866
Royal JHS 400/6-8
2520 Durkin Rd 77423 281-934-2241
Justin Johnston, prin. Fax 934-2329

**Brownfield, Terry, Pop. 9,594**
Brownfield ISD 1,600/PK-12
601 E Tahoka Rd 79316 806-637-2591
Tanya Monroe, supt. Fax 637-9208
www.brownfieldisd.net
Brownfield Education Center Alt
321 School Dr 79316 905-555-3533
Chris Edwards, prin. Fax 555-7836
Brownfield HS 400/9-12
701 Cub Dr 79316 806-637-4523
Paul Coronado, prin. Fax 637-3801
Brownfield MS 400/6-8
1001 E Broadway St 79316 806-637-7521
Aaron Waldrip, prin. Fax 637-2919

**Brownsboro, Henderson, Pop. 1,031**
Brownsboro ISD 2,900/PK-12
PO Box 465 75756 903-852-3701
Dr. Christopher Moran, supt. Fax 852-3957
www.gobearsgo.net
Brownsboro HS 900/9-12
PO Box 465 75756 903-852-2321
Brandon Jones, prin. Fax 852-5195
Brownsboro JHS 500/7-8
PO Box 465 75756 903-852-6931
Bradley Robertson, prin. Fax 852-5238

**Brownsville, Cameron, Pop. 174,679**
Brownsville ISD 47,900/PK-12
1900 Price Rd 78521 956-548-8000
Dr. Esperanza Zendejas, supt. Fax 548-8010
www.bisd.us
Besteiro MS 900/6-8
6280 Southmost Rd 78521 956-544-3900
Kathleen Jimenez, prin. Fax 544-3946
Brownsville Academic Center Alt
3308 Robindale Rd 78526 956-504-6305
Felipe Reyes, prin. Fax 831-8267
Brownsville Early College HS 300/9-12
343 Ringgold Rd 78520 956-698-1476
Acacia Ameel, prin. Fax 548-8842
Brownsville Learning Academy Alt
4350 Morrison Rd 78526 956-982-2860
Dawn Hall, prin. Fax 982-3028
Cummings MS 700/6-8
1800 Cummings Pl 78520 956-548-8630
Teresa Nunez, prin. Fax 548-8218
Faulk MS 800/6-8
2000 Roosevelt St 78521 956-548-8500
Benita Villarreal, prin. Fax 548-8507
Garcia MS 1,200/6-8
5701 FM 802 78526 956-832-6300
Noe Garcia, prin. Fax 832-6304
Hanna HS 3,000/9-12
2615 E Price Rd 78521 956-548-7600
Bertha Presas, prin. Fax 548-7603
Lopez HS 2,300/9-12
3205 S Dakota Ave 78521 956-982-7400
Dahlia Aguilar, prin. Fax 982-7499
Lucio MS 1,100/6-8
300 N Vermillion Ave 78521 956-831-4550
Jennifer Gonzales, prin. Fax 838-2298
Manzano MS 700/6-8
2580 W Alton Gloor Blvd 78520 956-548-9800
Marisol Trevino, prin. Fax 548-6772
Oliveira MS 1,200/6-8
444 Land O Lakes Dr 78521 956-548-8530
Cynthia Castro, prin. Fax 544-3968
Pace HS 1,800/9-12
314 W Los Ebanos Blvd 78520 956-548-7700
Rose Longoria, prin. Fax 548-7710
Perkins MS 900/6-8
4750 Austin Rd 78521 956-831-8770
Beatriz Hernandez, prin. Fax 831-8789
Porter HS 2,000/9-12
3500 International Blvd 78521 956-548-7800
Hector Hernandez, prin. Fax 982-2892
Rivera HS 2,200/9-12
6955 FM 802 78526 956-831-8700
Aimee Garza-Limon, prin. Fax 831-8705
Stell MS 1,100/6-8
1105 E Los Ebanos Blvd 78520 956-548-8560
Liz Valdez, prin. Fax 546-2579
Stillman MS 1,000/6-8
2977 W Tandy Rd 78520 956-698-1000
Eduardo Martinez, prin. Fax 350-3231
Vela MS 1,200/6-8
4905 Paredes Line Rd 78526 956-548-7770
Rosie Ara, prin. Fax 548-7780
Veterans Memorial HS 9-12
4550 US Highway 281 78520 956-574-5600
Mary Solis, prin. Fax 452-1341

---

First Baptist S 300/PK-12
1600 Boca Chica Blvd 78520 956-542-4854
Terry Roberts, supt. Fax 542-6188
Guadalupe Regional MS 100/6-8
1214 Lincoln St 78521 956-504-5568
Maria Alvarado, prin. Fax 504-9393
Kaplan College Post-Sec.
1900 N Expressway 78521 956-547-8200
St. Joseph Academy 700/7-12
101 Saint Joseph Dr 78520 956-542-3581
Lori Trott, prin. Fax 542-4748
University of Texas at Brownsville Post-Sec.
1 W University Blvd 78520 956-882-8200
Valley Christian HS 100/9-12
PO Box 4220 78523 956-542-5222
Gail Hanson, prin. Fax 544-0038

**Brownwood, Brown, Pop. 19,003**
Brownwood ISD 3,500/PK-12
PO Box 730 76804 325-643-5644
Liesa Land, supt. Fax 643-5640
www.brownwoodisd.org
Brownwood HS 900/9-12
2100 Slayden St 76801 325-646-9549
Mitchell Moore, prin. Fax 643-1965
Brownwood MS 500/7-8
1600 Calvert Rd 76801 325-646-9545
Bryan Allen, prin. Fax 646-3785

---

Howard Payne University Post-Sec.
1000 Fisk Ave 76801 325-646-2502
Victory Life Academy 100/PK-12
PO Box 940 76804 325-641-2223
Cathy Roberts, supt. Fax 643-9772

**Bruni, Webb, Pop. 377**
Webb Consolidated ISD 400/PK-12
PO Box 206 78344 361-747-5415
Dr. Severita Sanchez, supt. Fax 747-5202
webbcisd.org
Bruni HS 100/9-12
PO Box 206 78344 361-747-5415
Juan Maldonado, prin. Fax 747-5301
Bruni MS 100/6-8
PO Box 206 78344 361-747-5415
Sandra Castillo, prin. Fax 747-5298

**Bryan, Brazos, Pop. 75,248**
Bryan ISD 15,100/PK-12
101 N Texas Ave 77803 979-209-1000
Dr. Thomas Wallis, supt. Fax 209-1004
www.bryanisd.org
Austin MS 900/6-8
801 S Ennis St 77803 979-209-6700
Brandon Jayroe, prin. Fax 209-6741
Bryan Collegiate HS 300/9-12
1901 E Villa Maria Rd 77802 979-209-2790
Christina Richardson, prin. Fax 209-2704
Bryan HS 2,300/9-12
3450 Campus Dr 77802 979-209-2400
Lane Buban, prin. Fax 209-2402
Davila MS 600/6-8
2751 N Earl Rudder Fwy 77803 979-209-7150
Shannon McGehee, prin. Fax 209-7151
Harris S, 1305 Memorial Dr 77802 100/Alt
Leroy Morales, prin. 979-209-2812
Long MS 1,000/6-8
1106 N Harvey Mitchell Pkwy 77803 979-209-6500
Lindsay Harris, prin. Fax 209-6566
Rayburn MS 800/6-8
1048 N Earl Rudder Fwy 77802 979-209-6600
Walter Hunt, prin. Fax 209-6611
Rudder HS 1,300/9-12
3251 Austins Colony Pkwy 77808 979-209-7900
Bennie Mayes, prin. Fax 209-7901
Adult Learning Center Adult
1700 Palasota Dr 77803 979-703-7740

---

Allen Academy 300/PK-12
3201 Boonville Rd 77802 979-776-0731
Dr. Matthew Rush, head sch Fax 774-7769
Brazos Christian S 400/PK-12
3000 W Villa Maria Rd 77807 979-823-1000
Dr. Jeff McMaster, hdmstr. Fax 823-1774
Charlie & Sue's School of Hair Design Post-Sec.
1711 Briarcrest Dr 77802 979-776-4375
St. Joseph Catholic HS 200/6-12
600 S Coulter Dr 77803 979-822-6641
Blake Evans, prin. Fax 779-2810
St. Michael's Episcopal S 100/PK-12
2500 S College Ave 77801 979-822-2715
Still Creek Christian Academy 100/K-12
6055 Hearne Rd 77808 979-589-1816
Texas A&M University Health Science Ctr Post-Sec.
8441 State Highway 47 #3100 77807 979-436-9100

**Bryson, Jack, Pop. 518**
Bryson ISD 200/PK-12
300 N McCloud St 76427 940-392-3281
David Stout, supt. Fax 392-2086
www.brysonisd.net
Bryson S 200/PK-12
300 N McCloud St 76427 940-392-3281
Eric Wilson, prin. Fax 392-2086

**Buckholts, Milam, Pop. 513**
Buckholts ISD 200/PK-12
PO Box 248 76518 254-593-2744
Dr. Dirk D. Dykstra, supt. Fax 593-2270
www.buckholtsisd.net
Buckholts S 200/PK-12
PO Box 248 76518 254-593-2744
Myron Spencer, prin. Fax 593-2270

**Buda, Hays, Pop. 7,167**
Hays Consolidated ISD
Supt. — See Kyle
Barton MS 900/6-8
4950 Jack C Hays Trl 78610 512-268-1472
Teri Eubank, prin. Fax 268-1610
Dahlstrom MS 800/6-8
3600 FM 967 78610 512-268-8441
Rod Trevino, prin. Fax 295-5346
Hays HS 2,000/9-12
4800 Jack C Hays Trl 78610 512-268-2911
David Pierce, prin. Fax 268-1394
Impact Center 100/Alt
4125 FM 967 78610 512-268-8473
Sylvia Villejo, prin. Fax 295-5006
Live Oak Academy 100/Alt
4820 Jack C Hays Trl 78610 512-268-8462
Dr. Michael Watson, prin. Fax 268-4142

**Buffalo, Leon, Pop. 1,845**
Buffalo ISD 900/PK-12
708 Cedar Creek Rd 75831 903-322-3765
Lacy Freeman, supt. Fax 322-3091
www.buffaloisd.net
Buffalo HS 300/9-12
1724 N Buffalo Ave 75831 903-322-4243
Tracy Gleghorn, prin. Fax 322-5806
Buffalo JHS 300/3-8
335 Bison Trl 75831 903-322-4340
Greg Kennedy, prin. Fax 322-4803

**Bullard, Smith, Pop. 2,447**
Bullard ISD 2,100/PK-12
PO Box 250 75757 903-894-6639
Todd Schneider, supt. Fax 894-9291
www.bullardisd.net
Bullard HS 600/9-12
PO Box 250 75757 903-894-3272
Scott Franks, prin. Fax 894-3051
Bullard MS 400/7-8
PO Box 250 75757 903-894-6533
Cheryl Hendrix, prin. Fax 894-7592

Brook Hill S 500/PK-12
1051 N Houston St 75757 903-894-5000
Rod Fletcher, head sch Fax 894-6332

**Bulverde, Comal, Pop. 4,570**

Bracken Christian S 300/PK-12
670 Old Boerne Rd 78163 830-438-3211
Jason Detty M.Ed., admin. Fax 980-2327
Gloria Deo Academy 100/PK-12
1100 Bulverde Rd Ste 100 78163 830-980-8511

**Buna, Jasper, Pop. 2,103**
Buna ISD 1,600/PK-12
PO Box 1087 77612 409-994-5101
Dr. Steve Hyden, supt. Fax 994-4808
www.bunaisd.net
Buna HS 500/9-12
PO Box 1087 77612 409-994-4811
Roy Farias, prin. Fax 994-4818
Buna JHS 300/6-8
PO Box 1087 77612 409-994-4860
Amber Flowers, prin. Fax 994-4808

**Burkburnett, Wichita, Pop. 10,638**
Burkburnett ISD 3,300/PK-12
416 Glendale St 76354 940-569-3326
Fax 569-4776
www.burkburnettisd.org
Burkburnett HS 800/9-12
109 W Kramer Rd 76354 940-569-1411
Brad Owen, prin. Fax 569-1512
Burkburnett MS 700/6-8
108 S Avenue D 76354 940-569-3381
Scott Slater, prin. Fax 569-7116
Gateway Alternative Education Center 50/Alt
200 E 3rd St 76354 940-569-0850
Del Hardaway, admin. Fax 569-3030

**Burke, Angelina, Pop. 734**

Crimson Christian Academy 50/K-12
7020 S Highway 59, 936-639-1222

**Burkeville, Newton**
Burkeville ISD 300/PK-12
PO Box 218 75932 409-565-2201
Dr. Brant Graham, supt. Fax 565-2012
www.burkevilleisd.org
Burkeville JSHS 100/7-12
PO Box 218 75932 409-565-2201
Dr. Keri Launius, prin. Fax 565-2461

**Burleson, Johnson, Pop. 36,116**
Burleson ISD 10,200/PK-12
1160 SW Wilshire Blvd 76028 817-245-1000
Dr. Bret Jimerson, supt. Fax 447-5737
www.burlesonisd.net
Burleson HS 1,600/9-12
100 Elk Dr 76028 817-245-0000
Wayne Leek, prin. Fax 447-5796
Centennial HS 1,200/9-12
201 S Hurst Rd 76028 817-245-0250
Jimmy Neal, prin. Fax 447-2152
Crossroads HS 100/Alt
505 Pleasant Manor Ave 76028 817-245-0500
Mekasha Brown, prin. Fax 447-5889
Hughes MS 1,100/6-8
316 SW Thomas St 76028 817-245-0600
Mekasha Brown, prin. Fax 447-5748
Kerr MS 1,200/6-8
517 SW Johnson Ave 76028 817-245-0750
Dr. Miller Beaird, prin. Fax 447-5742
STEAM MS, 201 S Hurst Rd 76028 600/6-8
Brandon Johnson, prin. 817-245-1000

**Burnet, Burnet, Pop. 5,927**
Burnet Consolidated ISD 3,000/PK-12
208 E Brier Ln 78611 512-756-2124
Keith McBurnett, supt. Fax 756-7498
www.burnetcisd.net
Burnet HS 900/9-12
1000 The Green Mile Rd 78611 512-756-6193
Mark Kincaid, prin. Fax 756-4553
Burnet MS 700/6-8
1401 N Main St 78611 512-756-6182
Steve Grant, prin. Fax 756-7955
Quest HS 50/Alt
303 N Pierce St 78611 512-756-6747
Douglas Marvin Ed.D., prin. Fax 756-6289

**Burton, Washington, Pop. 298**
Burton ISD 400/PK-12
PO Box 37 77835 979-289-3131
Dr. Edna Kennedy, supt. Fax 289-3076
www.burtonisd.net
Burton JSHS 200/7-12
PO Box 499 77835 979-289-3830
Karen Steenken, prin. Fax 289-4609

**Bushland, Potter**
Bushland ISD 1,400/PK-12
PO Box 60 79012 806-359-6683
Don Wood, supt. Fax 359-6769
www.bushlandisd.org
Bushland HS 400/9-12
PO Box 60 79012 806-359-6683
Rick Davis, prin. Fax 322-1180
Bushland MS 400/5-8
PO Box 60 79012 806-359-5418
Jack Turner, prin. Fax 355-2841

**Bynum, Hill, Pop. 197**
Bynum ISD 300/PK-12
PO Box 68 76631 254-623-4251
Larry Mynarcik, supt. Fax 623-4290
www.bynumisd.net/
Bynum S 300/PK-12
PO Box 68 76631 254-623-4251
Lyndsey Pederson, prin. Fax 623-4290

**Caddo Mills, Hunt, Pop. 1,323**
Caddo Mills ISD 1,600/PK-12
PO Box 160 75135 903-527-6056
Vicki Payne, supt. Fax 527-4883
www.caddomillsisd.org/caddomillsisd/site/default.asp
Caddo Mills HS 400/9-12
PO Box 160 75135 903-527-3164
Jana Everett, prin. Fax 527-4772
Caddo Mills MS 400/6-8
PO Box 160 75135 903-527-3161
Anne Payne, prin. Fax 527-2379

**Caldwell, Burleson, Pop. 4,063**
Caldwell ISD 1,900/PK-12
203 N Gray St 77836 979-567-2400
Dr. Tim Cuff, supt. Fax 567-9876
caldwellisd.net
Caldwell HS 500/9-12
203 N Gray St 77836 979-567-2401
Vicki Ochs, prin. Fax 567-6735
Caldwell MS 400/6-8
203 N Gray St 77836 979-567-2402
Kim McManus, prin. Fax 567-7433

**Callisburg, Cooke, Pop. 352**
Callisburg ISD 1,100/PK-12
148 Dozier St, 940-665-0540
Steve Clugston, supt. Fax 668-2706
www.cisdtx.net
Callisburg HS 300/9-12
148 Dozier St, 940-665-0961
Tommy Cummings, prin. Fax 665-2849
Callisburg MS 300/6-8
148 Dozier St, 940-665-0961
Bronwyn Werts, prin. Fax 665-2849

**Calvert, Robertson, Pop. 1,179**
Calvert ISD 200/PK-12
PO Box 7 77837 979-364-2824
Maxie Morgan, supt. Fax 364-2468
www.calvertisd.com/
Calvert S 200/PK-12
PO Box 7 77837 979-364-2824
Tom Kelly, prin. Fax 364-2468

**Cameron, Milam, Pop. 5,512**
Cameron ISD 1,600/PK-12
PO Box 712 76520 254-697-3512
Allan Sapp, supt. Fax 697-2448
www.cameronisd.net
Cameron JHS 300/6-8
PO Box 712 76520 254-697-2131
Wendy Mahan, prin. Fax 605-0379
Yoe HS 400/9-12
PO Box 712 76520 254-697-3902
Kenneth Driska, prin. Fax 605-0413

**Campbell, Hunt, Pop. 622**
Campbell ISD 300/PK-12
480 N Patterson St 75422 903-862-3259
Mark Keahey, supt. Fax 862-2222
www.campbellisd.org
Campbell JSHS 100/6-12
480 N Patterson St 75422 903-862-3257
James Daugherty, admin. Fax 862-3547

**Canadian, Hemphill, Pop. 2,631**
Canadian ISD 900/PK-12
800 Hillside Ave 79014 806-323-5393
Kyle Lynch, supt. Fax 323-8143
www.canadianisd.net
Canadian HS 200/9-12
800 Hillside Ave 79014 806-323-5373
Rick Berry, prin. Fax 323-9345
Canadian MS 200/6-8
800 Hillside Ave 79014 806-323-5351
Bruce Bryant, prin. Fax 323-8791

**Canton, Van Zandt, Pop. 3,519**
Canton ISD 2,000/PK-12
1045 S Buffalo St 75103 903-567-4179
Jay Tullos, supt. Fax 567-2370
www.cantonisd.net
Canton HS 600/9-12
1110 W Highway 243 75103 903-567-6561
Jarrod Bitter, prin. Fax 567-6562
Canton JHS 500/6-8
1115 S Buffalo St 75103 903-567-4329
Amy Autry, prin. Fax 567-1298

**Canutillo, El Paso, Pop. 6,297**
Canutillo ISD
Supt. — See El Paso
Alderete MS 600/6-8
PO Box 100 79835 915-877-6600
Geoffrey Kimble, prin. Fax 877-6607
Canutillo MS 700/6-8
PO Box 100 79835 915-877-7900
Mark Paz, prin. Fax 877-7907

**Canyon, Randall, Pop. 13,164**
Canyon ISD 9,000/PK-12
PO Box 899 79015 806-677-2600
Darryl Flusche, supt. Fax 677-2659
www.canyonisd.net
Canyon HS 1,200/9-12
1701 23rd St 79015 806-677-2740
Tim Gilliland, prin. Fax 677-2779
Canyon JHS 600/7-8
910 9th Ave 79015 806-677-2700
Kirk Kear, prin. Fax 677-2739
Other Schools – See Amarillo

West Texas A&M University Post-Sec.
2501 4th Ave 79016 806-651-0000

**Carmine, Fayette, Pop. 250**
Round Top - Carmine ISD 300/PK-12
PO Box 385 78932 979-249-3200
Adren Pilger, supt. Fax 249-4084
www.rtcisd.net
Round Top - Carmine HS 100/7-12
PO Box 385 78932 979-278-3252
Brandon Schovajsa, prin. Fax 278-3063

**Carrizo Springs, Dimmit, Pop. 5,350**
Carrizo Springs Consolidated ISD 2,400/PK-12
300 N 7th St 78834 830-876-2473
Dr. Jesse Salazar, supt. Fax 876-9700
www.cscisd.net
Carrizo Springs HS 600/9-12
300 N 7th St 78834 830-876-5237
Michelle Gonzalez, prin. Fax 876-3052
Carrizo Springs JHS 500/7-8
300 N 7th St 78834 830-876-2496
Maria Villarreal, prin. Fax 876-3655

**Carrollton, Denton, Pop. 116,719**
Carrollton-Farmers Branch ISD 25,800/PK-12
PO Box 115186 75011 972-968-6100
Dr. Bobby Burns, supt. Fax 968-6210
www.cfbisd.edu
Blalack MS 1,000/6-8
1706 E Peters Colony Rd 75007 972-968-3500
Dr. Lance Hamlin, prin. Fax 968-3510
Creekview HS 2,000/9-12
3201 Old Denton Rd 75007 972-968-4800
Joe LaPuma, prin. Fax 968-4810
Grimes Education Center 200/Alt
1745 Hutton Dr 75006 972-968-5600
Bob Tipton, prin. Fax 968-5610
Perry MS 900/6-8
1709 E Belt Line Rd 75006 972-968-4400
Asheley Brown, prin. Fax 968-4410
Polk MS 1,100/6-8
2001 Kelly Blvd 75006 972-968-4600
Melanie Magee, prin. Fax 968-4610
Salazar S 100/Alt
2416 Keller Springs Rd 75006 972-968-5600
Melissa Wesley, prin. Fax 968-5610
Smith HS 2,100/9-12
2335 N Josey Ln 75006 972-968-5200
Joe Pouncey, prin. Fax 968-5210
Turner HS 2,100/9-12
1600 S Josey Ln Bldg 1 75006 972-968-5400
Brooke Puricelli, prin. Fax 968-5410
Other Schools – See Dallas, Farmers Branch, Irving

Lewisville ISD
Supt. — See Flower Mound
Arbor Creek MS 900/6-8
2109 Arbor Creek Dr 75010 469-713-5971
Joanie Finch, prin. Fax 350-9163
Creek Valley MS 700/6-8
4109 Creek Valley Blvd 75010 469-713-5184
Nicole Jund, prin. Fax 350-9172
Hebron HS 2,200/10-12
4207 Plano Pkwy 75010 469-713-5183
Scot Finch, prin. Fax 350-9255
Hebron Ninth Grade Center 50/9-9
4211 Plano Pkwy 75010 469-713-5996
Mark Dalton, prin. Fax 626-1630

Carrollton Christian Academy 300/K-12
2205 E Hebron Pkwy 75010 972-242-6688
Rev. David Culpepper, head sch Fax 245-0321
Prince of Peace Christian S 900/PK-12
4004 Midway Rd 75007 972-447-0532
Chris Hahn, hdmstr. Fax 267-4202
Toni & Guy Hairdressing Academy Post-Sec.
2810 E Trinity Mills Rd 75006 972-416-8396

**Carthage, Panola, Pop. 6,679**
Carthage ISD 2,900/PK-12
1 Bulldog Dr 75633 903-693-3806
J. Glenn Hambrick, supt. Fax 693-3650
www.carthageisd.org
Carthage HS 700/9-12
1 Bulldog Dr 75633 903-693-2552
Otis Amy, prin. Fax 693-9752
Carthage JHS 400/7-8
1 Bulldog Dr 75633 903-693-2751
Mike Baysinger, prin. Fax 693-9582

Panola College Post-Sec.
1109 W Panola St 75633 903-693-2000

**Castroville, Medina, Pop. 2,662**
Medina Valley ISD 3,500/PK-12
8449 FM 471 S 78009 830-931-2243
Joe Lee, supt. Fax 931-4050
www.mvisd.com
Medina Valley HS 1,000/9-12
8365 FM 471 S 78009 830-931-2243
Toby Tyler, prin. Fax 931-0371
Medina Valley MS 800/6-8
8395 FM 471 S 78009 830-931-2243
Justin Russell, prin. Fax 931-3258

**Cayuga, Anderson**
Cayuga ISD 600/PK-12
PO Box 427 75832 903-928-2102
Dr. Rick Webb, supt. Fax 928-2646
www.cayugaisd.com
Cayuga HS 200/9-12
PO Box 427 75832 903-928-2294
Russell Holden, prin. Fax 928-2646
Cayuga MS 200/6-8
PO Box 427 75832 903-928-2699
Sherri McInnis, prin. Fax 928-2646

**Cedar Creek, Bastrop**
Bastrop ISD
Supt. — See Bastrop
Cedar Creek HS 900/9-12
793 Union Chapel Rd 78612 512-772-7300
Bridgette Cornelius, prin. Fax 772-7930
Cedar Creek MS 800/7-8
125 Voss Pkwy 78612 512-772-7425
Robert Hensarling, prin. Fax 332-2631

**Cedar Hill, Dallas, Pop. 44,182**
Cedar Hill ISD 8,100/PK-12
285 Uptown Blvd Ste 300 75104 972-291-1581
Orlando Riddick, supt. Fax 291-5231
www.chisd.net
Cedar Hill Collegiate Academy MS 6-8
1533 High Pointe Ln 75104 469-272-2021
Jackie Fagan, prin.
Cedar Hill SHS 1,600/10-12
1 Longhorn Blvd 75104 469-272-2000
Tammy Mariani, prin. Fax 293-7125
Coleman MS 400/6-8
1208 E Pleasant Run Rd 75104 972-293-4505
Jason Miller, prin. Fax 272-9445
Ninth Grade Center 600/9-9
1515 W Belt Line Rd 75104 469-272-2050
Dr. Denise Roache-Davis, prin. Fax 272-3443
Permenter MS 800/6-8
431 W Parkerville Rd 75104 972-291-5270
Dr. Shauntee Mayfield, prin. Fax 291-5296

Northwood University Post-Sec.
1114 W FM 1382 75104 800-622-9000
Trinity Christian S 600/PK-12
1231 E Pleasant Run Rd 75104 972-291-2505
Mark Hennesy, supt. Fax 291-4739

**Cedar Park, Williamson, Pop. 47,764**
Leander ISD
Supt. — See Leander
Cedar Park HS 1,800/9-12
2150 Cypress Creek Rd 78613 512-570-1200
John Sloan, prin. Fax 570-1205
Cedar Park MS 1,300/6-8
2100 Sun Chase Blvd 78613 512-570-3100
Sandra Stewart, prin. Fax 570-3105
Henry MS 1,500/6-8
100 N Vista Ridge Pkwy 78613 512-570-3400
Dr. David Ellis, prin. Fax 570-3405
Running Brushy MS 1,200/6-8
2303 N Lakeline Blvd 78613 512-570-3300
Karin Johnson, prin. Fax 570-3305
Vista Ridge HS 1,800/9-12
200 S Vista Ridge Pkwy 78613 512-570-1800
Paul Johnson, prin. Fax 570-1805

Summit Christian Academy of Cedar Park 300/PK-12
2121 Cypress Creek Rd 78613 512-250-1369
Shannon Dare, hdmstr. Fax 257-1851

**Celeste, Hunt, Pop. 800**
Celeste ISD 500/PK-12
PO Box 67 75423 903-568-4825
Brad Connelly, supt. Fax 568-4495
www.celesteisd.org/
Celeste HS 200/9-12
PO Box 67 75423 903-568-4721
James Branam, prin. Fax 568-4115
Celeste JHS 100/6-8
PO Box 67 75423 903-568-4721
Staci Beadles, prin. Fax 568-4277

**Celina, Collin, Pop. 5,948**
Celina ISD 2,000/PK-12
205 S Colorado St 75009 469-742-9100
Donny O'Dell M.Ed., supt. Fax 382-3607
www.celinaisd.com/
Celina HS 600/9-12
3455 N Preston Rd 75009 469-742-9102
Bill Hemby M.Ed., prin. Fax 382-4830
Celina JHS 500/7-8
710 E Pecan St 75009 469-742-9101
John Mathews M.Ed., prin. Fax 382-4258

**Center, Shelby, Pop. 5,149**
Center ISD 2,700/PK-12
PO Box 1689 75935 936-598-5642
James Hockenberry, supt. Fax 598-1515
www.centerisd.org/
Center HS 600/9-12
658 Rough Rider Dr 75935 936-598-6173
Matthew Gregory, prin. Fax 598-1557
Center MS 500/6-8
302 Kennedy St 75935 936-598-5619
Jake Henson, prin. Fax 598-1534

**Center Point, Kerr**
Center Point ISD 600/PK-12
PO Box 377 78010 830-634-2171
Cody Newcomb, supt. Fax 634-2254
www.cpisd.net
Center Point HS 200/9-12
PO Box 377 78010 830-634-2244
Keith Mills, prin. Fax 634-7430
Center Point MS 100/6-8
PO Box 377 78010 830-634-2533
Keith Mills, prin. Fax 634-7825

**Centerville, Leon, Pop. 862**
Centerville ISD 700/PK-12
813 S Commerce St 75833 903-536-7812
Jason Jeitz, supt. Fax 536-7148
www.centerville.k12.tx.us
Centerville JSHS 300/7-12
813 S Commerce St 75833 903-536-2935
Dan Parker, prin. Fax 536-3133

**Channelview, Harris, Pop. 37,941**
Channelview ISD 8,400/PK-12
828 Sheldon Rd 77530 281-452-8002
Greg Ollis, supt. Fax 452-8001
www.cvisd.org
Channelview HS 1,600/10-12
1100 Sheldon Rd 77530 281-452-1450
Cindi Ollis, prin. Fax 457-7346
Endeavor S 100/Alt
915 Sheldon Rd 77530 281-457-0086
Mark Sims, prin. Fax 860-3801
Johnson JHS 1,300/6-8
15500 Proctor St 77530 281-452-8030
Jules Pichon, prin. Fax 452-1022
Kolarik 9th Grade Center 800/9-9
1120 Sheldon Rd 77530 713-378-3400
Cindi Ollis, prin. Fax 378-3498
Other Schools – See Houston

**Channing, Hartley, Pop. 363**
Channing ISD 200/PK-12
PO Box A 79018 806-235-3719
Robert McLain, supt. Fax 235-2609
www.channingisd.net/
Channing S 200/PK-12
PO Box A 79018 806-235-3719
Forrest Herbert, prin. Fax 235-2609

**Charlotte, Atascosa, Pop. 1,708**
Charlotte ISD 500/PK-12
PO Box 489 78011 830-277-1431
Mario Sotelo, supt. Fax 277-1551
www.charlotteisd.net
Charlotte HS 100/9-12
PO Box 489 78011 830-277-1432
Denise Cruz, prin. Fax 277-1605
Charlotte MS 200/5-8
PO Box 489 78011 830-277-1646
Roger Solis, prin. Fax 277-1654

**Cherokee, San Saba**
Cherokee ISD 100/K-12
PO Box 100 76832 325-622-4298
Chris Perry, supt. Fax 622-4430
www.cherokeeisd.net
Cherokee S 100/K-12
PO Box 100 76832 325-622-4298
Randy Gartman, prin. Fax 622-4430

**Chester, Tyler, Pop. 312**
Chester ISD 200/PK-12
273 Yellow Jacket Dr 75936 936-969-2371
Wayne Ivey, supt. Fax 969-2080
www.chesterisd.com
Chester JSHS 100/6-12
273 Yellow Jacket Dr 75936 936-969-2353
Wayne Ivey, supt. Fax 969-2080

**Chico, Wise, Pop. 994**
Chico ISD 600/PK-12
PO Box 95 76431 940-644-2228
Mike Jones, supt. Fax 644-5642
www.chico.k12.tx.us
Chico HS 200/9-12
PO Box 95 76431 940-644-5783
Randy Cobb, prin. Fax 644-5876
Chico MS 100/6-8
PO Box 95 76431 940-644-5550
Randy Brawner, prin. Fax 644-5642

**Childress, Childress, Pop. 6,037**
Childress ISD 1,100/PK-12
PO Box 179 79201 940-937-2501
Rick Teran, supt. Fax 937-2938
www.childressisd.net/
Childress HS 300/9-12
800 Avenue J NW 79201 940-937-6131
Joe Waldron, prin. Fax 937-2039
Childress JHS 200/6-8
700 Commerce St 79201 940-937-3641
Marsha Meacham, prin. Fax 937-8427

**Chillicothe, Hardeman, Pop. 698**
Chillicothe ISD 200/PK-12
PO Box 418 79225 940-852-5391
Todd Wilson, supt. Fax 852-5269
cisd-tx.net
Chillicothe JSHS 100/7-12
PO Box 550 79225 940-852-5391
Tony Martinez, prin. Fax 852-5465

**Chilton, Falls, Pop. 896**
Chilton ISD 500/PK-12
PO Box 488 76632 254-546-1200
Benny Bobo, supt. Fax 546-1201
www.chiltonisd.org
Chilton JSHS 300/6-12
PO Box 488 76632 254-546-1200
Brandon Hubbard, prin. Fax 546-1201

**China Spring, McLennan, Pop. 1,276**
China Spring ISD
Supt. — See Waco
China Spring HS 700/9-12
7301 N River Xing 76633 254-836-1771
Kevin Pitts, prin. Fax 836-1418
China Spring MS 400/7-8
7201 N River Xing 76633 254-836-4611
Mike Kelly, prin. Fax 836-4777

**Chireno, Nacogdoches, Pop. 378**
Chireno ISD 300/PK-12
PO Box 85 75937 936-362-2132
Tim Norman, supt. Fax 362-2490
www.chirenoisd.org/
Chireno JSHS 100/7-12
PO Box 85 75937 936-362-2132
Brian King, prin. Fax 362-9331

**Christoval, Tom Green, Pop. 503**
Christoval ISD 400/K-12
PO Box 162 76935 325-896-2520
Dr. David Walker, supt. Fax 896-7405
www.christovalisd.org
Christoval JSHS 300/6-12
PO Box 162 76935 325-896-2355
John Choate, prin. Fax 896-2671

**Cibolo, Guadalupe, Pop. 14,799**
Schertz-Cibolo-Universal City ISD
Supt. — See Schertz
Dobie JHS 1,100/7-8
395 W Borgfeld Rd 78108 210-619-4100
Vernon Simmons, prin. Fax 619-4142
Steele HS 100/9-12
1300 FM 1103 78108 210-619-4000
Jana Cervantes, prin. Fax 619-4057

**Cisco, Eastland, Pop. 3,863**
Cisco ISD 900/PK-12
PO Box 1645 76437 254-442-3056
Kelly West, supt. Fax 442-1412
www.ciscoisd.net/
Cisco HS 200/9-12
PO Box 1645 76437 254-442-3051
Craig Kent, prin. Fax 442-2516
Cisco JHS 200/6-8
PO Box 1645 76437 254-442-3004
Mark Lewis, prin. Fax 442-1832
Cisco Learning Center 50/Alt
PO Box 1645 76437 254-442-4852
Julie Patterson, prin. Fax 442-1917

Cisco College Post-Sec.
101 College Hts 76437 254-442-5000

**Clarendon, Donley, Pop. 1,994**
Clarendon ISD 500/PK-12
PO Box 610 79226 806-874-2062
Michael Norrell, supt. Fax 874-2579
www.clarendonisd.net
Clarendon HS 200/9-12
PO Box 610 79226 806-874-2181
Larry Jeffers, prin. Fax 874-3428
Clarendon JHS 100/6-8
PO Box 610 79226 806-874-3232
John Taylor, prin. Fax 874-9748

Clarendon College Post-Sec.
PO Box 968 79226 806-874-3571

**Clarksville, Red River, Pop. 3,231**
Clarksville ISD 700/PK-12
1500 W Main St 75426 903-427-3891
Pam Bryant, supt. Fax 427-5071
www.clarksvilleisd.net
Clarksville MSHS 200/6-12
1500 W Main St 75426 903-427-3891
James Johnson, prin. Fax 427-5116

**Claude, Armstrong, Pop. 1,174**
Claude ISD 400/PK-12
PO Box 209 79019 806-226-7331
Jeff Byrd, supt. Fax 226-2244
www.claudeisd.net/
Claude JSHS 200/6-12
PO Box 209 79019 806-226-2191
Derek Davis, prin. Fax 226-2244

**Cleburne, Johnson, Pop. 28,861**
Cleburne ISD 6,700/PK-12
505 N Ridgeway Dr Ste 100 76033 817-202-1100
Dr. Kyle Heath, supt. Fax 202-1460
www.cleburne.k12.tx.us/
Cleburne HS 1,700/9-12
1501 Harlin Dr 76033 817-202-1200
Dr. Chris Jackson, prin. Fax 202-1470
Smith MS 800/6-8
1710 Country Club Rd 76033 817-202-1500
William Allen, prin. Fax 202-1475
TEAM 100/Alt
1005 S Anglin St 76031 817-202-2160
Georganne Storm, prin. Fax 202-1489
Wheat MS 700/6-8
810 N Colonial Dr 76033 817-202-1300
Suzanne Keesee, prin. Fax 202-1479

Cleburne Christian Academy 100/K-12
PO Box 2017 76033 817-641-2857
Eddie Baca M.Ed., admin. Fax 641-0220

**Cleveland, Liberty, Pop. 7,571**
Cleveland ISD 2,800/PK-12
316 E Dallas St 77327 281-592-8717
Dr. Darrell Myers, supt. Fax 592-8283
www.clevelandisd.org
Cleveland HS 900/9-12
1600 E Houston St 77327 281-592-8752
Stephen McCanless, prin. Fax 592-7485
Cleveland MS 500/7-8
2000 E Houston St 77327 281-593-1148
Glenn Barnes, prin. Fax 593-3400
Disciplinary Alternative Education Prgrm Alt
200 Charles St 77327 281-432-0478
Victor Fulton, prin. Fax 432-0538
Douglass Learning Academy 100/Alt
900 Sam Wiley Dr 77327 281-592-7595
Sandy Williamson, prin. Fax 432-2754

Tarkington ISD 1,900/PK-12
2770 FM 163 Rd 77327 281-592-8781
Kevin Weldon, supt. Fax 592-3969
www.tarkingtonisd.net/
Tarkington HS 600/9-12
2770 FM 163 Rd 77327 281-592-7739
Daniel Barton, prin. Fax 592-0693
Tarkington MS 500/6-8
2770 FM 163 Rd 77327 281-592-7737
David Opp, prin. Fax 592-5241

**Clifton, Bosque, Pop. 3,399**
Clifton ISD 1,100/PK-12
1102 Key St 76634 254-675-2827
Rhoda White, supt. Fax 675-4351
www.cliftonisd.org
Clifton HS 300/9-12
1101 N Avenue Q 76634 254-675-1845
Becky Burnett, prin. Fax 675-8002
Clifton MS 300/6-8
1102 Key St 76634 254-675-1855
Andy Ball, prin. Fax 675-2005

**Clint, El Paso, Pop. 926**
Clint ISD
Supt. — See El Paso
Clint HS 600/9-12
13890 Alameda Ave 79836 915-926-8300
Daniel Gurany, prin. Fax 851-5375

Clint ISD Early College Academy 100/9-12
13100 Alameda Ave 79836 915-926-8100
Edmond Martinez, prin. Fax 851-3459
Clint JHS 500/6-8
12625 Alameda Ave 79836 915-926-8000
Josephine A. Guzman, prin. Fax 851-3895

**Clute, Brazoria, Pop. 11,087**
Brazosport ISD 12,400/PK-12
301 W Brazoswood Dr 77531 979-730-7000
Danny Massey, supt. Fax 266-2409
www.brazosportisd.net
Brazoswood HS 2,400/9-12
302 W Brazoswood Dr 77531 979-730-7300
Tracie Phillips, prin. Fax 266-2447
Clute IS 900/5-8
421 E Main St 77531 979-730-7230
Chris Loftin, prin. Fax 730-7363
Lighthouse Learning Center 50/Alt
1035 Dixie Dr 77531 979-730-7340
Robert Rasberry, prin. Fax 730-7369
Other Schools – See Freeport, Lake Jackson

**Clyde, Callahan, Pop. 3,655**
Clyde Consolidated ISD 1,500/PK-12
PO Box 479 79510 325-893-4222
Keith Scharnhorst, supt. Fax 893-4024
www.clyde.esc14.net
Clyde HS 400/9-12
500 N Hays Rd 79510 325-893-2161
Gregg Wilson, prin. Fax 893-2993
Clyde JHS 300/6-8
211 S 3rd St W 79510 325-893-5788
Kenneth Berry, prin. Fax 893-5319

Eula ISD 300/PK-12
6040 FM 603 79510 325-529-3186
Tim Kelley, supt. Fax 529-4461
www.eulaisd.us
Eula JSHS 100/7-12
6040 FM 603 79510 325-529-3605
Candilyn Smith, prin. Fax 529-5534

**Coahoma, Howard, Pop. 815**
Coahoma ISD 700/PK-12
600 N Main St 79511 432-394-5000
Dr. Amy Jacobs, supt. Fax 394-4302
www.coahomaisd.com/
Coahoma HS 200/9-12
606 N Main St 79511 432-394-5000
Charlotte Stovall, prin. Fax 394-4301
Coahoma JHS 100/6-8
501 High School Dr 79511 432-394-5000
Carrie Conley, prin. Fax 394-4419

**Coldspring, San Jacinto, Pop. 837**
Coldspring-Oakhurst Consolidated ISD 1,700/PK-12
PO Box 39 77331 936-653-1115
Jerry Gibson, supt. Fax 653-2197
www.cocisd.org
Coldspring-Oakhurst HS 500/9-12
PO Box 39 77331 936-653-1140
Donna Thompson, prin. Fax 653-3687
Lincoln JHS 400/6-8
PO Box 39 77331 936-653-1166
Christopher Oldham, prin. Fax 653-3688

**Coleman, Coleman, Pop. 4,660**
Coleman ISD 900/PK-12
PO Box 900 76834 325-625-3575
Royce Young, supt. Fax 625-4751
www.colemanisd.org
Coleman HS 200/9-12
201 15th St 76834 325-625-2156
Diana Dobbins, prin. Fax 625-4557
Coleman JHS 200/5-8
301 15th St 76834 325-625-3593
Amy Flippin, prin. Fax 625-3358

**College Station, Brazos, Pop. 92,151**
College Station ISD 10,300/PK-12
1812 Welsh Ave 77840 979-764-5400
Dr. Clark Ealy Ph.D., supt. Fax 764-5535
www.csisd.org
A & M Consolidated HS 2,800/9-12
1801 Harvey Mitchell Pkwy S 77840 979-764-5500
Gwen Elder, prin. Fax 693-0212
A & M Consolidated MS 800/7-8
105 Holik St 77840 979-764-5575
Jeff Mann, prin. Fax 764-5577
Alternative Education Programs 100/Alt
105 Timber St 77840 979-764-5540
Margie Martinez, prin. Fax 764-5564
College Station HS 1,600/9-12
4002 Victoria Ave 77845 979-694-5800
Mike Martindale, prin. Fax 394-5865
College Station MS 800/7-8
900 Rock Prairie Rd 77845 979-764-5545
Oliver Hadnot, prin. Fax 764-5557

---

Brazos Valley Cornerstone Christian Acad 100/K-12
2475 Earl Rudder Fwy S 77845 979-694-8200
Texas A&M University 77843 Post-Sec.
979-845-3211

**Colleyville, Tarrant, Pop. 22,415**
Grapevine-Colleyville ISD
Supt. — See Grapevine
BRIDGES S 100/Alt
5800 Colleyville Blvd 76034 817-251-5474
Dr. Lynda Burr, prin. Fax 581-4893
Colleyville Heritage HS 2,300/9-12
5401 Heritage Ave 76034 817-305-4700
Conrad Streeter, prin. Fax 358-4765
Colleyville MS 700/6-8
1100 Bogart Dr 76034 817-305-4900
Ryan Martin, prin. Fax 498-9764
Heritage MS 900/6-8
5300 Heritage Ave 76034 817-305-4790
Scott Saettel, prin. Fax 267-9929

Vista Alternative Learning Center Alt
5800 Colleyville Blvd 76034 817-251-5466
Roger Alzamora, prin. Fax 251-5466

---

Covenant Christian Academy 600/PK-12
901 Cheek Sparger Rd 76034 817-281-4333
Keith Castello, hdmstr. Fax 334-0367

**Collinsville, Grayson, Pop. 1,601**
Collinsville ISD 600/PK-12
PO Box 49 76233 903-429-6272
Dwain Milam, supt. Fax 429-6665
www.collinsvilleisd.org
Collinsville JSHS 300/7-12
PO Box 49 76233 903-429-6164
Mark Dykes, prin. Fax 429-6493

**Colmesneil, Tyler, Pop. 588**
Colmesneil ISD 400/PK-12
PO Box 37 75938 409-837-5757
Angela Matterson, supt. Fax 837-9107
www.colmesneilisd.net
Colmesneil JSHS 200/7-12
PO Box 37 75938 409-837-2225
Walter McAlpin, prin. Fax 837-9107

**Colorado City, Mitchell, Pop. 4,115**
Colorado ISD 1,100/PK-12
PO Box 1268 79512 325-728-3721
Reggy Spencer, supt. Fax 728-8471
www.ccity.esc14.net
Colorado HS 300/9-12
1500 Lone Wolf Blvd 79512 325-728-3424
Mark Merrell, prin. Fax 728-1083
Colorado MS 200/6-8
312 E 12th St 79512 325-728-2673
Robby Russell, prin. Fax 728-1051

**Columbus, Colorado, Pop. 3,623**
Columbus ISD 1,600/PK-12
105 Cardinal Ln 78934 979-732-5704
Ester Chandler, supt. Fax 732-5960
www.columbusisd.org/
Columbus Alternative S Alt
1421 Austin 78934 979-732-2963
Michael Koehl, prin. Fax 732-8862
Columbus HS 500/9-12
103 Cardinal Ln 78934 979-732-5746
Robert Russell, prin. Fax 732-8862
Columbus JHS 300/6-8
702 Rampart St 78934 979-732-2891
Gary leopold, prin. Fax 732-9081

**Comanche, Comanche, Pop. 4,301**
Comanche ISD 1,200/PK-12
1414 N Austin St 76442 325-356-2727
Rick Howard, supt. Fax 356-2312
www.comancheisd.net
Comanche HS 300/9-12
1600 N Austin St 76442 325-356-2581
Chad Gee, prin. Fax 356-2658
Jeffries JHS 200/6-8
1 Valley Forge Dr 76442 325-356-5220
Joseph Simmons, prin. Fax 356-1949

**Comfort, Kendall, Pop. 2,348**
Comfort ISD 1,100/PK-12
PO Box 398 78013 830-995-6400
Leslie Vann, supt. Fax 995-2236
www.comfort.txed.net
Comfort HS 300/9-12
PO Box 280 78013 830-995-6430
Katherine Kuenstler, prin. Fax 995-2261
Comfort MS 200/6-8
PO Box 187 78013 830-995-6420
Christopher Yeschke, prin. Fax 995-2248

**Commerce, Hunt, Pop. 7,851**
Commerce ISD 1,600/PK-12
3315 Washington St 75428 903-886-3755
Blake Cooper, supt. Fax 886-6025
www.commerceisd.org
Commerce HS 400/9-12
3315 Washington St 75428 903-886-3756
Steve Drummond, prin. Fax 886-6209
Commerce MS 400/6-8
3315 Washington St 75428 903-886-3795
Patrick Just, prin. Fax 886-6102

---

Texas A&M University Commerce Post-Sec.
PO Box 3011 75429 903-886-5102

**Como, Hopkins, Pop. 696**
Como-Pickton Consolidated ISD 800/PK-12
PO Box 18 75431 903-488-3671
Dr. Kay Handlin, supt. Fax 488-3133
www.cpcisd.net
Como-Pickton S 200/PK-12
PO Box 18 75431 903-488-3671
Dustin Carr, prin. Fax 488-3133

**Comstock, Val Verde**
Comstock ISD 200/K-12
PO Box 905 78837 432-292-4444
Orlie Wolfenbarger, supt. Fax 292-4436
www.comstockisd.net/
Comstock S 200/K-12
PO Box 905 78837 432-292-4444
Darlene Stevens, prin. Fax 292-4436

**Conroe, Montgomery, Pop. 55,526**
Conroe ISD 52,300/PK-12
3205 W Davis St 77304 936-709-7751
Dr. Don Stockton, supt. Fax 709-9701
www.conroeisd.net
Academy for Science & Health Professions 9-12
3200 W Davis St 77304 936-709-5731
Dr. Mike Papadimitriou, hdmstr. Fax 709-5842
Caney Creek HS 1,800/9-12
13470 FM 1485 Rd 77306 936-709-2000
Trish McClure, prin. Fax 709-2099
Conroe HS 9th Grade Campus 900/9-9
400 Sgt Ed Holcomb Blvd N 77304 936-709-4000
Bryan Gorka, prin. Fax 709-4099
Conroe SHS 2,200/10-12
3200 W Davis St 77304 936-709-5700
Dr. Mark Weatherly, prin. Fax 709-5655
Hauke Academic Alternative HS 200/Alt
701 N 3rd St 77301 936-709-3420
Paula Nicolini, prin. Fax 709-3499
Irons JHS 7-8
16780 Needham Rd 77385 936-709-8500
Jeff Fuller, prin. Fax 709-8599
Moorehead JHS 1,000/7-8
13475 FM 1485 Rd 77306 936-709-2400
Dr. Jeff Stichler, prin. Fax 709-2499
Oak Ridge 9th Grade Campus 900/9-9
27310 Oak Ridge School Rd 77385 281-465-5000
Julie Miller, prin. Fax 465-5099
Oak Ridge SHS 2,200/10-12
27330 Oak Ridge School Rd 77385 832-592-5300
Tommy Johnson, prin. Fax 592-5544
Peet JHS 1,100/7-8
1895 Longmire Rd 77304 936-709-3700
Tasha Smith, prin. Fax 709-3828
Washington JHS 600/7-8
507 Dr Martin Luther King 77301 936-709-7400
Hartwell Brown, prin. Fax 709-7492
Other Schools – See Spring, The Woodlands

---

Adventist Christian Academy of Texas 100/PK-12
3601 S Loop 336 E 77301 936-756-5078
Calvary Baptist S 200/PK-12
3401 N Frazier St 77303 936-756-0743
Rev. Mark Parker, admin. Fax 756-0764
Covenant Christian S 300/PK-12
4503 Interstate 45 N 77304 936-890-8080
Dr. Glenn Slater, head sch Fax 890-5343
Lifestyle Christian S 100/K-12
3993 Interstate 45 N 77304 936-756-9383
Robert Meade, prin. Fax 760-3003
Lone Star College - Montgomery Post-Sec.
3200 College Park Dr 77384 936-273-7000
PCAL Christian S 100/PK-12
9268 Highway 242 77385 936-273-6464
Karen Parish, admin. Fax 273-4082

**Converse, Bexar, Pop. 17,584**
Judson ISD
Supt. — See Live Oak
Judson Alternative S 50/Alt
102 School St 78109 210-619-0330
Marsha Bellinger, prin. Fax 658-2206
Judson HS 3,500/9-12
9142 FM 78 78109 210-945-1100
Jesus Hernandez, prin. Fax 659-4359
Judson MS 900/6-8
9695 Schaefer Rd 78109 210-357-0801
Ted Haynes, prin. Fax 659-8769
Judson STEM Academy 100/6-8
9695 Schaefer Rd 78109 210-945-1159
Dawn Worley, dir.
Thompson Learning Center 50/Alt
PO Box 369 78109 210-945-5053
Joe Gonzalez, prin. Fax 945-7525

**Coolidge, Limestone, Pop. 937**
Coolidge ISD 300/PK-12
PO Box 70 76635 254-786-2206
Dr. Robert Lowry, supt. Fax 786-4835
www.coolidge.k12.tx.us/
Coolidge HS 100/6-12
PO Box 70 76635 254-786-4822
Oscar Muniz, prin. Fax 786-4835

**Cooper, Delta, Pop. 1,923**
Cooper ISD 800/PK-12
PO Box 478 75432 903-395-2111
Denicia Hohenberger, supt. Fax 395-2117
www.cooperisd.net/
Cooper HS 200/9-12
PO Box 429 75432 903-395-2111
Chris Kiser, prin. Fax 395-2382
Cooper JHS 200/6-8
PO Box 429 75432 903-395-2111
Richard Roan, prin. Fax 395-2382

**Coppell, Dallas, Pop. 37,827**
Coppell ISD 10,700/PK-12
200 S Denton Tap Rd 75019 214-496-6000
Dr. Mike Waldrip, supt. Fax 496-6036
www.coppellisd.com
Coppell HS 2,800/9-12
185 W Parkway Blvd 75019 214-496-6100
Mike Jasso, prin. Fax 496-6166
Coppell MS East 800/6-8
400 Mockingbird Ln 75019 214-496-6600
Laura Springer, prin. Fax 496-6603
Coppell MS North 900/6-8
120 Natches Trce 75019 214-496-7100
Amanda Ziaer, prin. Fax 496-7103
Coppell MS West 900/6-8
1301 Wrangler Cir 75019 214-496-8600
Emily Froese, prin. Fax 496-8606
New Tech HS @ Coppell 500/9-12
113 Samuel Blvd 75019 214-496-5900
Dr. Leanne Shivers, prin. Fax 496-5906

**Copperas Cove, Coryell, Pop. 30,055**
Copperas Cove ISD 7,500/PK-12
703 W Avenue D 76522 254-547-1227
Dr. Joe Burns, supt. Fax 547-7060
www.ccisd.com
Avenue E Alternative Learning Center 100/Alt
306 E Avenue E 76522 254-547-9164
Miguel Timarky, prin. Fax 547-4039
Copperas Cove HS 2,100/9-12
400 S 25th St 76522 254-547-2534
Earl Parcell, prin. Fax 547-9870
Copperas Cove JHS 800/6-8
702 Sunny Ave 76522 254-547-6959
Randy Troub, prin. Fax 518-2620

Lee JHS 800/6-8
1205 Courtney Ln 76522 254-542-7877
Kayleen Love, prin. Fax 542-8103

**Corinth, Denton, Pop. 19,502**
Denton ISD
Supt. — See Denton
Crownover MS 1,000/6-8
1901 Creekside Dr 76210 940-369-4700
Jason Rainey, prin. Fax 321-0502

Lake Dallas ISD
Supt. — See Lake Dallas
Lake Dallas HS 1,200/9-12
3016 Parkridge Dr 76210 940-497-4031
Kristi Strickland, prin. Fax 497-1524

**Corpus Christi, Nueces, Pop. 301,876**
Calallen ISD 4,000/PK-12
4205 Wildcat Dr 78410 361-242-5600
Dr. Arturo Almendarez, supt. Fax 242-5620
www.calallen.org
Calallen HS 1,200/9-12
4001 Wildcat Dr 78410 361-242-5626
Yvonne Marquez-Neth, prin. Fax 242-5632
Calallen MS 900/6-8
4602 Cornett Dr 78410 361-242-5672
Marcos Flores, prin. Fax 242-0628

Corpus Christi ISD 36,700/PK-12
PO Box 110 78403 361-695-7200
Dr. Roland Hernandez, supt. Fax 886-9109
echalkweb.ccisd.us
Adkins MS 6-8
2402 Ennis Joslin Rd 78414 361-878-3800
Norma Cullum, prin. Fax 878-3828
Baker MS 1,000/6-8
3445 Pecan St 78411 361-878-4600
John Dobbins, prin. Fax 878-1834
Branch Acad for Career & Tech Education 9-12
3902 Morgan Ave 78405 361-878-4780
Browne MS 800/6-8
4301 Schanen Blvd 78413 361-878-4270
John Trevino, prin. Fax 878-1836
Carroll HS 2,200/9-12
5301 Weber Rd 78411 361-878-5140
Kelly Manlove, prin. Fax 878-2403
Coles HS & Education Ctr 300/Alt
924 Winnebago St 78401 361-844-0432
Monica Bayarena, prin. Fax 844-0436
Cullen Place MS 500/6-8
5225 Greely Dr 78412 361-878-2960
George Lerma, prin. Fax 994-3624
Cunningham MS 600/6-8
4321 Prescott St 78416 361-878-4630
Sandy Salinas-Deleon, prin. Fax 878-1838
Driscoll MS 800/6-8
3501 Kenwood Dr 78408 361-878-4660
Bruce Wilson, prin. Fax 886-9890
Grant MS 1,000/6-8
4350 Aaron Dr 78413 361-878-3740
Carla Rosa-Villarreal, prin. Fax 878-1871
Haas MS 600/6-8
6630 McArdle Rd 78412 361-878-4240
Dr. Lynda DeLeon, prin. Fax 994-3626
Hamlin MS 700/6-8
3900 Hamlin Dr 78411 361-878-4210
Tommy Whitehead, prin. Fax 878-1839
Kaffie MS 1,000/6-8
5922 Brockhampton St 78414 361-878-3700
Patti Heiland, prin. Fax 994-3604
King HS 2,400/9-12
5225 Gollihar Rd 78412 361-906-3400
Elizabeth Perez, prin. Fax 994-6918
Martin Special Emphasis S 600/6-8
3502 Greenwood Dr 78416 361-878-4690
Javier Granados, prin. Fax 878-2455
Miller HS 1,000/9-12
1 Battlin Buc Blvd 78408 361-878-5100
Stella Torres, prin. Fax 883-1928
Moody HS 1,800/9-12
1818 Trojan Dr 78416 361-878-7340
Dr. Sandra Clement, prin. Fax 857-8253
Ray HS 1,900/9-12
1002 Texan Trl 78411 361-878-7300
Cissy Perez, prin. Fax 852-6528
South Park MS 500/6-8
3001 McArdle Rd 78415 361-878-4720
Anna Marie Fuentes, prin. Fax 878-1844
Student Support Center 200/Alt
4401 Greenwood Dr 78416 361-878-2840
Douglas Cross, prin. Fax 878-1437
Veterans Memorial HS 9-12
3750 Cimarron 78414 361-878-7900
Kim James, prin. Fax 878-7910

Flour Bluff ISD 5,600/PK-12
2505 Waldron Rd 78418 361-694-9000
Joe Kelley, supt. Fax 694-9800
www.flourbluffschools.net
Flour Bluff HS 1,800/9-12
2505 Waldron Rd 78418 361-694-9100
James Crenshaw, prin. Fax 694-9802
Flour Bluff JHS 900/7-8
2505 Waldron Rd 78418 361-694-9300
Cindy Holder, prin. Fax 694-9803

London ISD 500/PK-12
1306 FM 43 78415 361-855-0092
David Freeman, supt. Fax 855-0198
www.londonisd.net
London HS 500/6-12
1306 FM 43 78415 361-855-0092
Rebecca Hitchcock, prin. Fax 855-0198

Tuloso-Midway ISD 3,500/PK-12
PO Box 10900 78460 361-903-6400
Dr. Sue Nelson, supt. Fax 241-5836
www.tmisd.us
Tuloso-Midway HS 1,100/9-12
PO Box 10900 78460 361-903-6700
Ann Bartosh, prin. Fax 241-4258
Tuloso-Midway MS 800/6-8
PO Box 10900 78460 361-903-6600
Adriana Tagle, prin. Fax 242-9829

West Oso ISD 1,900/PK-12
5050 Rockford Dr 78416 361-806-5900
Elizabeth Saenz, supt. Fax 225-8308
www.westosoisd.net
West Oso HS 600/9-12
754 Flato Rd 78405 361-806-5960
Harrison Jones, prin. Fax 299-3111
West Oso JHS 500/6-8
5202 Bear Ln 78405 361-806-5950
Terry Avery, prin. Fax 299-3111

---

Annapolis Christian Academy 200/PK-12
3875 S Staples St 78411 361-991-6004
Peter Hansen, hdmstr. Fax 232-5629
Arlington Heights Christian S 100/PK-12
9550 Leopard St 78410 361-241-0090
Leanne Isom, admin. Fax 242-9284
Bishop Garriga MS 200/6-8
3114 Saratoga Blvd 78415 361-851-0853
Rene Gonzalez, prin. Fax 853-5145
Coggin Memorial S 50/PK-10
6645 Downing St 78414 361-991-6968
Del Mar College Post-Sec.
101 Baldwin Blvd 78404 361-698-1200
Incarnate Word Academy 200/6-8
2917 Austin St 78404 361-883-0857
Adolfo Garza, prin. Fax 882-9193
Incarnate Word Academy 300/9-12
2910 S Alameda St 78404 361-883-0857
Jose Torres, prin. Fax 881-8742
Institute of Cosmetic Arts and Science Post-Sec.
1105 Airline Rd 78412 361-991-8868
Kaplan College Post-Sec.
1620 S Padre Island Dr #600 78416 361-852-2900
St. John Paul II HS 400/9-12
3036 Saratoga Blvd 78415 361-855-5744
Perry LeGrange M.Ed., prin. Fax 855-1343
Southern Careers Institute Post-Sec.
2422 Airline Rd 78414 361-857-5700
South Texas Barber College Post-Sec.
3917 Ayers St 78415 361-855-0262
Texas A&M University Corpus Christi Post-Sec.
6300 Ocean Dr 78412 361-825-5700
Yorktown Christian Academy 200/PK-12
5025 Yorktown Blvd Ste A 78413 361-985-9960
John Gilbert, admin. Fax 985-9821

**Corrigan, Polk, Pop. 1,578**
Corrigan-Camden ISD 1,000/PK-12
504 S Home St 75939 936-398-4040
Sherry Hughes, supt. Fax 398-4616
www.ccisdtx.com
Corrigan-Camden HS 300/9-12
504 S Home St 75939 936-398-2341
Kyle Spivey, prin. Fax 398-4928
Corrigan-Camden JHS 200/6-8
504 S Home St 75939 936-398-2341
Robert Elliott, prin. Fax 398-4928

**Corsicana, Navarro, Pop. 23,195**
Corsicana ISD 5,800/PK-12
2200 W 4th Ave 75110 903-874-7441
Dr. Diane Frost, supt. Fax 872-2100
www.cisd.org
Collins MS 800/7-8
1500 Dobbins Rd 75110 903-872-3979
Darla Nolen, prin. Fax 874-1423
Corsicana HS 1,500/9-12
3701 W State Highway 22 75110 903-874-8211
Eldon Franco, prin. Fax 874-7403

Mildred ISD 700/K-12
5475 S US Highway 287 75109 903-872-6505
Becky Burns, supt. Fax 872-1341
www.mildredisd.org/
Mildred JSHS 400/6-12
5475 S US Highway 287 75109 903-872-0392
Aaron Tidwell, prin. Fax 641-0356

---

Navarro College Post-Sec.
3200 W 7th Ave 75110 903-874-6501

**Cotton Center, Hale**
Cotton Center ISD 100/PK-12
PO Box 350 79021 806-879-2160
Rocky J. Stone M.Ed., supt. Fax 879-2175
www.cottoncenterisd.org
Cotton Center S 100/PK-12
PO Box 350 79021 806-879-2176
Clay Williams, prin. Fax 879-2175

**Cotulla, LaSalle, Pop. 3,594**
Cotulla ISD 1,200/PK-12
310 N Main St 78014 830-879-3073
Dr. Jack Seals, supt. Fax 879-3609
www.cotullaisd.org
Cotulla HS 300/9-12
310 N Main St 78014 830-879-2374
Joe Reyes, prin. Fax 879-4302
Newman MS 300/6-8
310 N Main St 78014 830-879-2224
Dr. Brenda Jirasek, prin. Fax 879-4357

**Covington, Hill, Pop. 269**
Covington ISD 300/PK-12
501 N Main 76636 254-854-2215
Diane Innis, supt. Fax 854-2272
www.covingtonisd.org/
Covington S 300/PK-12
501 N Main 76636 254-854-2215
Sherry Abbott, prin. Fax 854-2272

**Crandall, Kaufman, Pop. 2,834**
Crandall ISD 2,700/PK-12
PO Box 128 75114 972-427-6000
Dr. Robert Jolly, supt. Fax 427-6036
www.crandall-isd.net
Crandall Alternative Center 50/Alt
PO Box 400 75114 972-472-6100
Emily Christensen, prin.
Crandall HS 800/9-12
PO Box 520 75114 972-427-8030
David Williams, prin. Fax 427-8234
Crandall MS 500/6-8
PO Box 490 75114 972-427-6080
Amy Teague, prin. Fax 427-8031

**Crane, Crane, Pop. 3,329**
Crane ISD 1,000/PK-12
511 W 8th St 79731 432-558-1022
Jim Rumage, supt. Fax 558-1025
www.craneisd.com/css/home.htm
Crane HS 300/9-12
511 W 8th St 79731 432-558-1030
Tony Priest, prin. Fax 558-1056
Crane MS 200/6-8
511 W 8th St 79731 432-558-1040
Lori Schulze, prin. Fax 558-1046

**Cranfills Gap, Bosque, Pop. 280**
Cranfills Gap ISD 100/PK-12
PO Box 67 76637 254-597-2505
Vincent Gilbert, supt. Fax 597-0001
www.cranfillsgapisd.net
Cranfills Gap S 100/PK-12
PO Box 67 76637 254-597-2505
Monti Parchman, prin. Fax 597-0001

**Crawford, McLennan, Pop. 703**
Crawford ISD 600/K-12
200 Pirate Dr 76638 254-486-2381
Kenneth Hall, supt. Fax 486-2198
www.crawford-isd.net
Crawford HS 300/7-12
200 Pirate Dr 76638 254-486-2381
Don Harris, prin. Fax 486-2198

**Crockett, Houston, Pop. 6,873**
Crockett ISD 1,300/PK-12
1400 W Austin St 75835 936-544-2125
Terry Myers, supt. Fax 544-5727
www.crockettisd.net
Crockett Alternative Campus 50/Alt
1400 W Austin St 75835 936-546-5972
Mecheal Abbs, prin. Fax 546-0721
Crockett HS 300/9-12
1400 W Austin St 75835 936-544-2193
Deborah Revels, prin. Fax 546-0104
Crockett JHS 300/6-8
1400 W Austin St 75835 936-544-2125
Judy Leediker, prin. Fax 544-4164

**Crosby, Harris, Pop. 2,268**
Crosby ISD 4,900/PK-12
PO Box 2009 77532 281-328-9200
Keith Moore Ed.D., supt. Fax 328-9208
www.crosbyisd.org
Crosby HS 1,400/9-12
PO Box 2009 77532 281-328-9237
Greg Bower, prin. Fax 328-9219
Crosby MS 800/7-8
PO Box 2009 77532 281-328-9264
Robert Hicks, prin. Fax 328-9356

**Crosbyton, Crosby, Pop. 1,731**
Crosbyton Consolidated ISD 400/PK-12
204 S Harrison St 79322 806-675-7331
Shawn Mason, supt. Fax 675-2409
www.crosbyton.k12.tx.us
Crosbyton Secondary S 100/6-12
204 S Harrison St 79322 806-675-7331
Royce Roark, prin. Fax 675-1049

**Cross Plains, Callahan, Pop. 974**
Cross Plains ISD 400/PK-12
700 N Main St 76443 254-725-6121
Phil Mitchell, supt. Fax 725-6559
www.crossplains.esc14.net/
Cross Plains JSHS 200/7-12
700 N Main St 76443 254-725-6121
Brad Jones, prin. Fax 725-6559

**Crowell, Foard, Pop. 945**
Crowell ISD 200/PK-12
PO Box 239 79227 940-684-1403
Steven Pyburn, supt. Fax 684-1616
www.crowellisd.net/
Crowell JSHS 100/7-12
PO Box 239 79227 940-684-1331
Steven Pyburn, admin. Fax 684-1616

**Crowley, Tarrant, Pop. 12,575**
Crowley ISD 15,000/PK-12
PO Box 688 76036 817-297-5800
Dr. Dan Powell, supt. Fax 297-5805
www.crowleyisdtx.org/
Crowley 9th Grade Campus 500/9-9
1016 FM 1187 W 76036 817-297-5845
Christopher White, prin. Fax 297-5847
Crowley HS 1,300/10-12
1005 W Main St 76036 817-297-5810
Lyndsae Benton, prin. Fax 297-5854
Crowley Learning Center Alt
PO Box 688 76036 817-297-6992
Jose Lara, prin. Fax 297-4087
Johnson Career & Tech Center Vo/Tech
1033 McCart Ave 76036 817-297-3018
Kady Donaghey, dir. Fax 297-1839
Stevens MS 900/7-8
940 N Crowley Rd 76036 817-297-5840
Jim Phillips, prin. Fax 297-5850

Summer Creek MS 800/7-8
10236 Summercreek Dr 76036 817-297-5090
Pam Berry, prin. Fax 297-5094
Other Schools – See Fort Worth

---

Nazarene Christian Academy 400/K-12
2001 E Main St 76036 817-297-7003
Kathie Starks, prin. Fax 297-1509

**Crystal City, Zavala, Pop. 7,131**
Crystal City ISD 2,100/PK-12
805 E Crockett St 78839 830-374-2367
Imelda Allen, supt. Fax 374-8004
www.crystalcityisd.org
Alternative S, 805 E Crockett St 78839 Alt
Laura Barajas, admin. 830-374-9840
Crystal City HS 500/9-12
805 E Crockett St 78839 830-374-2341
Russell Baldwin, prin. Fax 374-8012
Fly JHS 300/7-8
805 E Crockett St 78839 830-374-2371
Gabriel Garcia, prin. Fax 374-8060

**Cuero, DeWitt, Pop. 6,679**
Cuero ISD 2,000/PK-12
960 E Broadway 77954 361-275-1900
Jim Haley, supt. Fax 275-2981
www.cueroisd.org
Cuero HS 600/9-12
920 E Broadway St 77954 361-275-1900
Dr. Kristi Lee, prin. Fax 275-2430
Cuero JHS 300/6-8
608 Jr High Dr 77954 361-275-1900
Gregory Crockett, prin. Fax 275-6912

**Cumby, Hopkins, Pop. 769**
Cumby ISD 400/PK-12
303 Sayle St 75433 903-994-2260
Shelly Slaughter, supt. Fax 994-2399
www.cumbyisd.net
Cumby HS 200/7-12
303 Sayle St 75433 903-994-2260
Hector Madrigal, prin. Fax 994-2510

Miller Grove ISD 300/PK-12
7819 Farm Road 275 S 75433 903-459-3288
Steve Johnson, supt. Fax 459-3744
www.mgisd.net
Miller Grove S 100/PK-12
7819 Farm Road 275 S 75433 903-459-3288
Gary Billingsley, prin. Fax 459-3744

**Cushing, Nacogdoches, Pop. 594**
Cushing ISD 500/PK-12
PO Box 337 75760 936-326-4890
Michael Davis, supt. Fax 326-4115
www.cushingisd.org
Cushing MSHS 300/6-12
PO Box 337 75760 936-326-4890
Andy Gresham, prin. Fax 326-4131

**Cypress, Harris**
Cypress-Fairbanks ISD
Supt. — See Houston
Anthony MS 6-8
10215 Greenhouse Rd 77433 281-373-5660
Sherma Duck, prin. Fax 373-5661
Arnold MS 1,600/6-8
11111 Telge Rd 77429 281-897-4700
Vicki Snokhous, prin. Fax 807-8610
Carlton Vocational Center Vo/Tech
13550 Woods Spillane Blvd 77429 281-213-1950
Rhonda Turns, dir. Fax 213-1951
Cy-Fair HS 3,400/9-12
22602 Hempstead Hwy 77429 281-897-4600
Mike Smith, prin. Fax 517-6530
Cypress Ranch HS 2,600/9-12
10700 Fry Rd 77433 281-373-2300
Robert Hull, prin. Fax 213-1979
Cypress Springs HS 2,500/9-12
7909 Fry Rd 77433 281-345-3000
Dr. Cheryl Henry, prin. Fax 345-3010
Cypress Woods HS 2,800/9-12
13550 Woods Spillane Blvd 77429 281-213-1800
Gary Kinninger, prin. Fax 213-1827
Goodson MS 1,100/6-8
17333 Huffmeister Rd 77429 281-373-2350
Sheri McCaig, prin. Fax 373-2355
Hamilton MS 1,600/6-8
12330 Kluge Rd 77429 281-320-7000
Kim Sempe, prin. Fax 320-7021
Hopper MS 1,400/6-8
7811 Fry Rd 77433 281-463-5353
Wendi Whitthaus, prin. Fax 463-5354
Salyards MS 1,400/6-8
21757 Fairfield Place Dr 77433 281-373-2400
Liz Wood, prin. Fax 373-2425
Smith MS 1,600/6-8
10300 Warner Smith Blvd 77433 281-213-1010
Susan Higgins, prin. Fax 213-1020
Spillane MS 1,100/6-8
13403 Woods Spillane Blvd 77429 281-213-1645
Michael Maness, prin. Fax 213-1799

---

Connection S of Houston 100/K-12
15815 House Hahl Rd 77433 832-544-6031
Kathleen Wrobleske, dir. Fax 286-3088
Covenant Academy 200/K-12
11711 Telge Rd 77429 281-373-2233
Leslie Collins, head sch Fax 588-8227
Lone Star College Cyfair Post-Sec.
9191 Barker Cypress Rd 77433 281-290-3200
Oaks Adventist Christian S 100/PK-12
11735 Grant Rd 77429 713-896-0071

**Daingerfield, Morris, Pop. 2,512**
Daingerfield-Lone Star ISD 1,200/PK-12
200 Tiger Dr 75638 903-645-2239
Sandra Quarles, supt. Fax 645-2137
www.dlsisd.org
Daingerfield HS 400/9-12
202 Tiger Dr 75638 903-645-3968
Ryan Carroll, prin. Fax 645-7662
Daingerfield JHS 200/6-8
200 Texas St 75638 903-645-2261
Linda Rhymes, prin. Fax 645-4010

**Daisetta, Liberty, Pop. 957**
Hull-Daisetta ISD 500/PK-12
PO Box 477 77533 936-536-6321
Mary Huckabay, supt. Fax 536-6251
www.hdisd.net/
Hull-Daisetta HS 200/9-12
PO Box 477 77533 936-536-6321
Quinn Godwin, prin. Fax 536-3839
Hull-Daisetta JHS 100/7-8
PO Box 477 77533 936-536-6321
Quinn Godwin, prin. Fax 536-3839

**Dalhart, Dallam, Pop. 7,836**
Dalhart ISD 1,800/PK-12
701 E 10th St 79022 806-244-7810
John Massey, supt. Fax 244-7822
www.dalhartisd.org
Dalhart HS 500/9-12
701 E 10th St 79022 806-244-7300
Kevin Douglas, prin. Fax 244-7307
Dalhart JHS 400/6-8
701 E 10th St 79022 806-244-7825
Shannon Marshall, prin. Fax 244-7835
XIT Secondary S 50/Alt
701 E 10th St 79022 806-244-7340
Derek Hollingsworth, prin. Fax 244-7345

**Dallardsville, Polk**
Big Sandy ISD 500/PK-12
PO Box 188 77332 936-563-1000
Gary Gazaway, supt. Fax 563-1010
www.bigsandyisd.net
Other Schools – See Livingston

**Dallas, Dallas, Pop. 1,183,449**
Carrollton-Farmers Branch ISD
Supt. — See Carrollton
Long MS 800/6-8
2525 Frankford Rd 75287 972-968-4100
Joe Copeland, prin. Fax 968-4110

Dallas ISD 151,100/PK-12
3700 Ross Ave 75204 972-925-3700
Michael Hinojosa Ed.D., supt. Fax 925-3201
www.dallasisd.org
Adams HS 1,900/9-12
2101 Millmar Dr 75228 972-502-4900
Richard Kastl, prin. Fax 502-4901
Adamson HS 1,400/9-12
309 E 9th St 75203 972-749-1400
Janie Ortega, prin. Fax 749-1401
Angelou HS 50/Alt
4528 Rusk Ave 75204 972-749-2200
Lynn Smith, prin. Fax 749-2264
Atwell Law Academy 800/6-8
1303 Reynoldston Ln 75232 972-794-6400
Selena Deboskie, prin. Fax 794-6401
Browne MS 800/7-8
3333 Sprague Dr 75233 972-502-2500
Jonathan Smith, prin. Fax 502-2501
Carter HS 1,000/9-12
1819 W Wheatland Rd 75232 214-932-5700
Fred Davis, prin. Fax 932-5701
Cary MS 600/6-8
3978 Killion Dr 75229 972-502-7600
Ben Dickerson, prin. Fax 502-7601
Collins-Sorrells S of Educ & Social Srvc 300/9-12
1201 E 8th St 75203 972-925-5940
Shelia Brown, prin. Fax 925-5901
Comstock MS 1,200/7-8
7044 Hodde St 75217 972-794-1300
Willie Johnson, prin. Fax 794-1301
Conrad HS 1,400/9-12
7502 Fair Oaks Ave 75231 972-502-2300
Anthony Mays, prin. Fax 502-2301
Dade Learning Center 400/6-8
2727 Grand Ave 75215 972-749-3800
Tracie Washington, prin. Fax 749-3801
Dallas Environmental Science Academy 200/6-8
3635 Greenleaf St 75212 972-794-3950
Diana Vega, prin. Fax 794-3951
Edison MS 800/6-8
2940 Singleton Blvd 75212 972-794-4100
Luis Valdez, prin. Fax 794-4101
Florence MS 900/6-8
1625 N Masters Dr 75217 972-749-6000
Dawn Walker, prin. Fax 749-6001
Franklin MS 900/6-8
6920 Meadow Rd 75230 972-502-7100
Joseph Sotelo, prin. Fax 502-7101
Garcia MS, 700 E 8th St 75203 1,000/6-8
Gary Auld, prin. 972-502-5500
Garza Early College HS 400/9-12
4849 W Illinois Ave Rm W53A 75211 214-860-3680
Janice Lombardi, prin. Fax 860-3639
Gaston MS 1,200/6-8
9565 Mercer Dr 75228 972-502-5400
Sharon Stauss, prin. Fax 502-5401
Gilliam Collegiate Academy 300/9-12
1700 E Camp Wisdom Rd 75241 214-925-1400
Tamara Francis, prin. Fax 925-1401
Greiner Exploratory Arts Academy 1,800/6-8
501 S Edgefield Ave 75208 972-925-7100
Yvonne Rojas, prin. Fax 925-7101
Hillcrest HS 1,200/9-12
9924 Hillcrest Rd 75230 972-502-6800
Leeann Bartee, prin. Fax 502-6801
Hill MS 900/6-8
505 Easton Rd 75218 972-502-5700
Candice Ruiz, prin. Fax 502-5701
Holmes Classical Academy 900/6-8
2001 E Kiest Blvd 75216 972-925-8500
Sharron Jackson, prin. Fax 925-8501
Holmes MS 6-8
2939 Saint Rita Dr 75233 214-932-7800
Barbara Moham, prin. Fax 932-7801
Hood MS 1,400/6-8
7625 Hume Dr 75227 972-749-4100
Latonya Lockhart, prin. Fax 749-4101
Innovation Design Entrepreneurship Acad 9-12
4800 Ross Ave 75204 972-794-6800
Sarah Ritsema, prin.
Jefferson HS 1,400/9-12
4001 Walnut Hill Ln 75229 972-502-7300
Sandi Massey, prin. Fax 502-7301
Kennedy-Curry MS 700/6-8
6605 Sebring Dr 75241 972-925-1600
Dennis Taylor, prin.
Kimball HS 1,300/9-12
3606 S Westmoreland Rd 75233 972-502-2100
Earl Jones, prin. Fax 502-2101
Lang MS, 1678 Chenault St 75228 1,300/6-8
Johanna Weaver, prin. 972-925-2400
Lassiter Early College HS 200/9-12
701 Elm St 75202 214-860-2356
Michael St. Ama, prin. Fax 860-2359
Learning Alt Ctr for Empowering Youth 100/Alt
4949 Village Fair Dr 75224 972-925-7060
Gail Dupree, prin. Fax 925-7061
Lincoln Humanities/Communications HS 700/9-12
2826 Hatcher St 75215 972-925-7600
Chanel Howard-Veazy, prin. Fax 925-7601
Longfellow Career Academy 400/6-8
5314 Boaz St 75209 972-749-5400
Cheryl Breedlove-Wright, prin. Fax 749-5401
Long MS 1,200/6-8
6116 Reiger Ave 75214 972-502-4700
Chandra Hooper-Barnett, prin. Fax 502-4701
Madison HS 500/9-12
3000 Mrtn Lthr King Jr Blvd 75215 972-925-2800
Gayle Smith, prin. Fax 925-2801
Manns Education Center 200/Alt
3313 S Beckley Ave 75224 972-932-7300
Letice Portley, prin.
Marsh MS 1,200/6-8
3838 Crown Shore Dr 75244 972-502-6600
Nicky Niewinski, prin. Fax 502-6601
Medrano MS 800/6-8
9815 Brockbank Dr 75220 972-925-1300
Theresa Sigurdson, prin. Fax 925-1301
Molina HS 2,000/9-12
2355 Duncanville Rd 75211 972-502-1000
Jeffrey Saldivar, prin. Fax 502-1001
Multiple Careers Magnet HS Vo/Tech
4528 Rusk Ave 75204 972-925-2200
Lynn Smith, prin. Fax 925-2201
North Dallas HS 1,300/9-12
3120 N Haskell Ave 75204 972-925-1500
Blanca Rodriguez, prin. Fax 925-1501
Obama Male Leadership Academy 200/6-8
4730 S Lancaster Rd 75216 972-749-2100
Nakia Douglas, prin.
Patton Academic Center 600/Alt
3313 S Beckley Ave 75224 214-932-5160
Leslie Swann, prin. Fax 932-5149
Pinkston HS 1,000/9-12
2200 Dennison St 75212 972-502-2700
Dwain Simmons, prin. Fax 502-2701
Quintanilla MS 800/7-8
2700 Remond Dr 75211 972-502-3200
Angela West, prin. Fax 502-3201
Rangel Young Women's Leadership S 200/6-12
1718 Robert B Cullum Blvd 75210 972-749-5200
Lisa Curry, prin. Fax 749-5201
Richards MS 6-8
3831 Prairie Creek Rd 75227 972-892-5400
Francine Taylor, prin.
Roosevelt HS 600/9-12
525 Bonnie View Rd 75203 972-925-6800
Brian DeVeaux, prin. Fax 925-6801
Rusk MS 700/6-8
2929 Inwood Rd 75235 972-925-2000
Mariela Magro Malo, prin. Fax 925-2001
Samuell HS 1,900/9-12
8928 Palisade Dr 75217 972-892-5100
Juan Vega, prin. Fax 892-5101
Sanders Magnet Center for Law 400/9-12
1201 E 8th St Ste 203 75203 972-925-5950
Michael Dang, prin. Fax 925-6010
School Community Guidance Center 200/Alt
4949 Village Fair Dr 75224 972-925-7020
Gail Dupree, prin. Fax 925-7021
School for the Talented & Gifted 200/9-12
1201 E 8th St Ste 216 75203 972-925-5970
Ben Mackey, prin. Fax 925-6018
School of Business & Management 500/9-12
1201 E 8th St Ste 241 75203 972-925-5920
Michelle Broughton, prin. Fax 925-5901
School of Health Professions 500/9-12
1201 E 8th St Ste 281 75203 972-925-5930
LaSandra Sanders, prin. Fax 925-6007
School of Science & Engineering HS 400/9-12
1201 E 8th St 75203 972-925-5960
Tiffany Huitt, prin. Fax 925-6016
Seagoville HS 1,000/9-12
15920 Seagoville Rd 75253 972-892-5900
Michael Jones, prin. Fax 892-5901
Seagoville MS 1,000/6-8
950 N Woody Rd 75253 972-892-7100
Deidrea Stevens, prin. Fax 892-7101
Skyline HS 4,300/9-12
7777 Forney Rd 75227 972-502-3400
Marlon Brooks, prin. Fax 502-3401
Smith New Tech HS 800/9-12
3030 Stag Rd 75241 214-932-7600
Lisa DeVeaux, prin. Fax 932-7601
South Oak Cliff HS 1,300/9-12
3601 S Marsalis Ave 75216 214-932-7000
Shon Joseph, prin. Fax 932-7001
Spence Talented/Gifted Academy 1,100/6-8
4001 Capitol Ave 75204 972-925-2300
Deardra Hayes-Whigham, prin. Fax 925-2301

Spruce HS 1,400/9-12
9733 Old Seagoville Rd 75217 972-892-5500
Danielle Petters, prin. Fax 892-5501
STEAM MS at Hulcy 6-8
9339 S Polk St 75232 214-932-7400
Jonica Crowder-Lockwood, prin.
Stockard MS 900/7-8
2300 S Ravinia Dr 75211 972-794-5700
Adam Varrassi, prin. Fax 794-5701
Storey MS 600/6-8
3000 Maryland Ave 75216 972-925-8700
JoAnn Jackson, prin. Fax 925-8701
Sunset HS 2,200/9-12
2120 W Jefferson Blvd 75208 972-502-1500
Luz Martinez, prin. Fax 502-1501
Tasby MS 800/6-8
7001 Fair Oaks Ave 75231 972-502-1900
Audrey de la Cruz, prin. Fax 502-1901
Travis Academy 100/4-8
3001 McKinney Ave 75204 972-794-7500
Mari Smith, prin. Fax 794-7501
Walker MS 800/6-8
12532 Nuestra Dr 75230 972-502-6100
Dr. Laura Stout, prin. Fax 502-6101
Washington Performing & Visual Arts HS 900/9-12
2501 Flora St 75201 972-925-1200
Scott Rudes, prin. Fax 925-1201
White HS 2,400/9-12
4505 Ridgeside Dr 75244 972-502-6200
Michelle Thompson, prin. Fax 502-6201
Wilmer-Hutchins HS 800/9-12
5520 Langdon Rd 75241 972-925-2900
Tamika Prentiss Barnett, prin.
Wilson HS 1,600/9-12
100 S Glasgow Dr 75214 972-502-4400
Russell Richardson, prin. Fax 502-4401
Zumwalt MS 500/6-8
2445 E Ledbetter Dr 75216 972-749-3600
Troy Tyson, prin. Fax 749-3601
Evening Academy Adult
7777 Forney Rd 75227 972-502-3458
Fax 502-3633

Other Schools – See Balch Springs

Duncanville ISD
Supt. — See Duncanville
Kennemer MS 800/7-8
7101 W Wheatland Rd 75249 972-708-3600
Brandee King, prin. Fax 708-3636

Highland Park ISD 6,800/PK-12
7015 Westchester Dr 75205 214-780-3000
Dr. Tom Trigg, supt. Fax 780-3099
www.hpisd.org
Highland Park Alternative Education Ctr Alt
4220 Emerson Ave 75205 214-780-3700
Walter Kelly, prin. Fax 780-3799
Highland Park HS 2,000/9-12
4220 Emerson Ave 75205 214-780-3700
Walter Kelly, prin. Fax 780-3799
Highland Park MS 1,000/7-8
3555 Granada Ave 75205 214-780-3600
Dr. Laurie Hitzelberger, prin. Fax 780-3699

Plano ISD
Supt. — See Plano
Frankford MS 1,100/6-8
7706 Osage Plaza Pkwy 75252 469-752-5200
Shurandia Holden, prin. Fax 752-5201

Richardson ISD
Supt. — See Richardson
Forest Meadow JHS 700/7-8
9373 Whitehurst Dr 75243 469-593-1500
Kerri Jones, prin. Fax 593-1461
Lake Highlands Freshman Center 700/9-9
10200 White Rock Trl 75238 469-593-1300
Bill Gallo, prin. Fax 593-1327
Lake Highlands HS 1,600/10-12
9449 Church Rd 75238 469-593-1000
Frank Miller, prin. Fax 593-1030
Lake Highlands JHS 700/7-8
10301 Walnut Hill Ln 75238 469-593-1600
Veronica Escalante, prin. Fax 593-1606
Liberty JHS 600/7-9
10330 Lawler Rd 75243 469-593-7888
Doug Planey, prin. Fax 593-7764
Parkhill JHS 600/7-9
16500 Shadybank Dr 75248 469-593-5600
Farrah Smock, prin. Fax 593-5500
Westwood Magnet JHS 700/7-9
7630 Arapaho Rd 75248 469-593-3600
Troy Gray, prin. Fax 593-3508

---

Argosy University/Dallas Post-Sec.
5001 Lyndon B Johnson # 176 75244 214-890-9900
Art Institute of Dallas Post-Sec.
8080 Park Ln Ste 100 75231 214-692-8080
Bending Oaks HS 50/8-12
11884 Greenville Ave # 120 75243 972-669-0000
Bishop Dunne Catholic S 600/6-12
3900 Rugged Dr 75224 214-339-6561
Kate Dailey, pres. Fax 339-1438
Bishop Lynch HS 1,100/9-12
9750 Ferguson Rd 75228 214-324-3607
Chris Rebuck, pres. Fax 324-3600
Cambridge S of Dallas 100/6-12
3877 Walnut Hill Ln 75229 214-357-2995
Paul Wolfe, hdmstr. Fax 357-0880
Choices Leadership Academy 50/5-8
18106 Marsh Ln 75287 972-662-0665
Concorde Career College Post-Sec.
12606 Greenville Ave # 130 75243 469-221-3400
Cornerstone Crossroads Academy 50/10-12
PO Box 151062 75315 214-426-3282
Dr. Kristi Lichtenberg, prin. Fax 741-0066
Court Reporting Institute of Dallas Post-Sec.
1341 W Mockingbird Ln #200E 75247 214-350-9722
Covenant S 500/K-12
7300 Valley View Ln 75240 214-358-5818
Dr. Robert Woods, head sch Fax 358-5809
Cristo Rey Dallas Prep 9-9
1064 N Saint Augustine Dr 75217 214-888-5057
Kelby Woodard, admin.
Criswell College Post-Sec.
4010 Gaston Ave 75246 214-821-5433
Dallas Academy 200/1-12
950 Tiffany Way 75218 214-324-1481
Dallas Baptist University Post-Sec.
3000 Mountain Creek Pkwy 75211 214-333-7100
Dallas Barber and Stylist College Post-Sec.
9357 Forest Ln 75243 214-575-2168
Dallas Christian Academy 100/PK-12
4025 N Central Expy 75204 214-528-6327
Dallas Christian College Post-Sec.
2700 Christian Pkwy 75234 972-241-3371
Dallas Institute of Funeral Service Post-Sec.
3909 S Buckner Blvd 75227 214-388-5466
Dallas Lutheran HS 200/7-12
8494 Stults Rd 75243 214-349-8912
David Bangert, dir. Fax 340-3095
Dallas Nursing Institute Post-Sec.
12170 Abrams Rd Ste 200 75243 888-201-8806
Dallas Theological Seminary Post-Sec.
3909 Swiss Ave 75204 214-887-5504
El Centro College Post-Sec.
801 Main St 75202 214-860-2000
Episcopal S of Dallas 700/5-12
4100 Merrell Rd 75229 214-358-4368
Meredyth Cole, head sch Fax 357-1232
Everest College Post-Sec.
6080 N Central Expy 75206 214-234-4850
First Baptist Academy 300/PK-12
1606 Patterson St 75201 214-969-7861
Jason Lovvorn, hdmstr. Fax 969-7797
Golf Academy of America Post-Sec.
1861 Valley View Ln Ste 100 75234 972-763-8100
Graduate Institute of Applied Linguistic Post-Sec.
7500 W Camp Wisdom Rd 75236 972-708-7340
Hockaday S 1,100/PK-12
11600 Welch Rd 75229 214-363-6311
Elizabeth Lee, head sch Fax 360-6563
Jesuit College Preparatory S 1,100/9-12
12345 Inwood Rd 75244 972-387-8700
Mike Earsing, pres. Fax 661-9349
Kaplan College Post-Sec.
12005 Ford Rd Ste 100 75234 972-385-1446
KD Studio - Actors Conservatory Post-Sec.
2600 N Stemmons Fwy Ste 117 75207 214-638-0484
Lakehill Prep S 400/K-12
2720 Hillside Dr 75214 214-826-2931
Roger Perry, hdmstr. Fax 826-4623
Lawyer's Assistant School of Dallas Post-Sec.
8150 N Central Expy # M2240 75206 214-777-6433
Le Cordon Bleu Inst of Culinary Arts Post-Sec.
11830 Webb Chapel Rd # 1200 75234
214-647-8500
Lighthouse College Post-Sec.
9400 N Central Expy Ste 200 75231 214-368-3680
Mediatech Institute Post-Sec.
13370 Branch View Ln # 135 75234 866-498-1122
Mesorah HS for Girls 50/9-12
12712 Park Central Dr #B190 75251 214-420-1990
MJ's Beauty Academy Post-Sec.
3939 S Polk St Ste 505 75224 214-374-7500
Mountain View College Post-Sec.
4849 W Illinois Ave 75211 214-860-8680
Neilson Beauty College Post-Sec.
416 W Jefferson Blvd 75208 214-941-8756
Ogle School of Hair Design Post-Sec.
6333 E Mockingbird Ln #201 75214 214-821-0819
Parish Episcopal S 1,100/PK-12
4101 Sigma Rd 75244 972-239-8011
David Monaco, head sch Fax 991-1237
Parker University Post-Sec.
2540 Walnut Hill Ln 75229 972-438-6932
Paul Quinn College Post-Sec.
3837 Simpson Stuart Rd 75241 214-376-1000
PCI Health Training Center Post-Sec.
8101 John W Carpenter Fwy 75247 214-380-4322
Presbyterian Hospital Post-Sec.
8200 Walnut Hill Ln 75231 214-345-7558
Redeemer Seminary Post-Sec.
6060 N Central Expy Ste 700 75206 214-528-8600
Richland College Post-Sec.
12800 Abrams Rd 75243 972-238-6100
St. Marks S of Texas 900/1-12
10600 Preston Rd 75230 214-346-8000
David Dini, hdmstr. Fax 346-8002
Sanford-Brown College Post-Sec.
1250 W Mockingbird Ln # 150 75247 214-459-8490
Southern Methodist University Post-Sec.
PO Box 750100 75275 214-768-2000
Sterling Health Center Post-Sec.
17084 Dallas Pkwy 75248 972-991-9293
Texas A&M Univ.-Baylor Coll. Dentistry Post-Sec.
3302 Gaston Ave 75246 214-828-8100
Texas Barber Colleges & Hairstyling Sch Post-Sec.
5148 S Lancaster Rd 75241 214-943-7255
Texas Torah Institute 50/9-12
6506 Frankford Rd 75252 214-250-4888
Sarah Broderick, admin. Fax 250-4889
Texas Women's Univ Pickens Inst Health Post-Sec.
5500 Southwestern Medical 75235 214-689-6500
Tint School of Makeup & Cosmetology Post-Sec.
10909 Webb Chapel Rd # 129 75229 214-956-0088
Tyler Street Christian Academy 200/PK-12
915 W 9th St 75208 214-941-9717
Dr. Karen Egger, supt. Fax 941-0324
University of North Texas at Dallas Post-Sec.
7300 University Hills Blvd 75241 972-780-3600
University of Texas S.W. Medical Center Post-Sec.
5323 Harry Hines Blvd 75390 214-648-3111
Ursuline Academy 800/9-12
4900 Walnut Hill Ln 75229 469-232-1800
Gretchen Kane, pres. Fax 232-1836
Velma B's Beauty Academy Post-Sec.
1511 S Ewing Ave 75216 214-942-1541
Wade College Dallas Market Center Post-Sec.
1950 N Stemmons Ste 4080 75207 800-624-4850
West Coast University Post-Sec.
8435 N Stemmons Fwy 75247 214-453-4533
Westwood S 300/PK-12
14340 Proton Rd 75244 972-239-8598
Winston S 200/K-12
5707 Royal Ln 75229 214-691-6950
Rebbie Evans, head sch Fax 691-1509
Yavneh Academy of Dallas 100/9-12
12324 Merit Dr 75251 214-295-3500
Dr. David Portnoy, head sch Fax 295-3505

**Damon, Brazoria, Pop. 543**
Damon ISD 200/PK-10
PO Box 429 77430 979-742-3457
Dr. Donald Rhodes, supt. Fax 742-3275
www.damonisd.net/
Damon S 200/PK-10
PO Box 429 77430 979-742-3457
Dr. Donald Rhodes, supt. Fax 742-3275

**Danbury, Brazoria, Pop. 1,690**
Danbury ISD 700/PK-12
PO Box 378 77534 979-922-1218
Greg Anderson, supt. Fax 922-8246
www.danburyisd.org/
Danbury HS 200/9-12
PO Box 377 77534 979-922-1226
Jon Hill, prin. Fax 922-1051
Danbury MS 100/7-8
PO Box 586 77534 979-922-1226
Jon Hill, prin. Fax 922-1051

**Darrouzett, Lipscomb, Pop. 347**
Darrouzett ISD 100/PK-12
PO Box 98 79024 806-624-2221
Brian Patterson, supt. Fax 624-4361
www.darrouzettisd.net
Darrouzett S 100/PK-12
PO Box 98 79024 806-624-2221
Troy Humphrey, prin. Fax 624-4361

**Dawson, Navarro, Pop. 793**
Dawson ISD 500/PK-12
199 N School Ave 76639 254-578-1031
Stacy Henderson, supt. Fax 578-1721
www.dawsonisd.net/
Dawson HS 200/7-12
199 N School Ave 76639 254-578-1031
Robert Bray, prin. Fax 578-1721

**Dayton, Liberty, Pop. 7,114**
Dayton ISD 4,900/PK-12
PO Box 248 77535 936-258-2667
Dr. Jessica Johnson, supt. Fax 258-5616
www.daytonisd.net/
Dayton HS 1,400/9-12
PO Box 248 77535 936-258-2510
Travis Young, prin. Fax 257-4047
Wilson JHS 800/7-8
PO Box 248 77535 936-258-2309
Rita Gilmore, prin. Fax 257-4109

**Decatur, Wise, Pop. 6,000**
Decatur ISD 3,100/PK-12
307 S Cates St 76234 940-393-7100
Rod Townsend, supt. Fax 627-3141
www.decaturisd.us/
Decatur HS 900/9-12
750 E Eagle Smt 76234 940-393-7200
Jeff Russell, prin. Fax 627-3669
McCarroll MS 700/6-8
1201 W Thompson St 76234 940-393-7300
Dewayne Tamplen, prin. Fax 627-2497

**Deer Park, Harris, Pop. 31,669**
Deer Park ISD 15,100/PK-12
2800 Texas Ave 77536 832-668-7000
Victor White, supt. Fax 930-4638
www.dpisd.org
Bonnette JHS 800/6-8
5010 W Pasadena Blvd 77536 832-668-7700
Paul Moore, prin. Fax 930-4756
Deer Park HS - North Campus 3,800/9-9
402 Ivy Ave 77536 832-668-7300
Ernie Salazar, prin. Fax 930-4840
Deer Park HS - South Campus 2,800/10-12
710 W San Augustine St 77536 832-668-7200
Steve Corry, prin. Fax 930-4894
Deer Park JHS 800/6-8
410 E 9th St 77536 832-668-7500
Dr. Tiffany Regan, prin. Fax 930-4726
Wolters Accelerated HS Alt
204 Ivy Ave 77536 832-668-7400
Clyde Skarke, prin. Fax 930-0525
Other Schools – See Pasadena

**De Kalb, Bowie, Pop. 1,672**
De Kalb ISD 800/PK-12
101 Maple St 75559 903-667-2566
Dr. John Booth, supt. Fax 667-3791
www.dekalbisd.net
De Kalb HS 200/9-12
152 Maple St 75559 903-667-2422
Neilan Hensley, prin. Fax 667-4086
De Kalb MS 200/5-8
929 W Grizzley St 75559 903-667-2834
Clayton Little, prin. Fax 667-5509

**De Leon, Comanche, Pop. 2,226**
De Leon ISD 700/PK-12
425 S Texas St 76444 254-893-8210
Dr. Dana Marable Ph.D., supt. Fax 893-8214
www.deleonisd.net
De Leon HS 200/9-12
425 S Texas St 76444 254-893-8240
Liesa Nowlin, prin. Fax 893-4985

Perkins MS 200/6-8
425 S Texas St 76444 254-893-8230
Liesa Nowlin, prin. Fax 893-8234

**Dell City, Hudspeth, Pop. 357**
Dell City ISD 100/K-12
PO Box 37 79837 915-964-2663
Fabian Gomez, supt. Fax 964-2473
dellcity.schoolwires.com
Dell City S 100/K-12
PO Box 37 79837 915-964-2663
Patricia Duran, admin. Fax 964-2473

**Del Rio, Val Verde, Pop. 35,427**
San Felipe-Del Rio Consolidated ISD 10,300/PK-12
PO Box 428002 78842 830-778-4000
Carlos Rios Ed.D., supt. Fax 774-9892
www.sfdr-cisd.org
Del Rio Freshman S 800/9-9
PO Box 428002 78842 830-778-4400
Tomas Cabello, prin. Fax 774-9873
Del Rio HS 1,900/10-12
PO Box 428002 78842 830-778-4329
Dr. Celia Zuniga-Barrera, prin. Fax 774-9320
Del Rio MS 1,500/7-8
PO Box 428002 78842 830-778-4530
Jorge Limon, prin. Fax 778-4912

**Del Valle, Travis**
Del Valle ISD 10,400/PK-12
5301 Ross Rd 78617 512-386-3000
Kelly Crook Ph.D., supt. Fax 386-3015
delvalle.tx.schoolwebpages.com/
Del Valle HS 2,500/9-12
5201 Ross Rd 78617 512-386-3200
David Williams, prin. Fax 386-3205
Del Valle MS 800/6-8
5500 Ross Rd 78617 512-386-3400
James Cruz, prin. Fax 386-3440
Del Valle Opportunity Center 300/Alt
5301 Ross Rd Ste B 78617 512-386-3300
Ray Macias, prin. Fax 386-3316
Other Schools – See Austin

**Denison, Grayson, Pop. 22,067**
Denison ISD 4,200/PK-12
1201 S Rusk Ave 75020 903-462-7000
Dr. Henry Scott, supt. Fax 462-7002
www.denisonisd.net
Denison HS 1,200/9-12
4200 N State Highway 91 75020 903-462-7125
Dr. Cavin Boettger, prin. Fax 462-7217
Pathways HS 50/Alt
318 W Morgan St 75020 903-462-7150
Lance SanMillan, prin. Fax 462-7220
Scott MS 7-8
1901 S Mirick Ave 75020 903-462-7180
John Parker, prin. Fax 462-7342

Sherman ISD
Supt. — See Sherman
Perrin Learning Center 100/Alt
81 Vandenburg Dr 75020 903-891-6680
Art Urquidi, prin. Fax 786-4766

---

Grayson College Post-Sec.
6101 FM 691 75020 903-465-6030

**Denton, Denton, Pop. 110,797**
Denton ISD 23,900/PK-12
1307 N Locust St 76201 940-369-0000
Dr. Jamie Wilson, supt. Fax 369-4982
www.dentonisd.org
Calhoun MS 900/6-8
709 W Congress St 76201 940-369-2400
Paul Martinez, prin. Fax 369-4939
Davis S 100/Alt
1125 Davis St 76209 940-369-4050
Jeff Tinch, prin. Fax 369-4966
Denton HS 1,800/9-12
1007 Fulton St 76201 940-369-2000
Dan Ford, prin. Fax 369-4953
Guyer HS 2,100/9-12
7501 Teasley Ln 76210 940-369-1000
Shaun Perry, prin. Fax 369-4965
LaGrone Advanced Technology Complex Vo/Tech
1504 Long Rd 76207 940-369-4850
Marcus Bourland, prin. Fax 380-0243
McMath MS 800/6-8
1900 Jason Dr 76205 940-369-3300
Dr. Debra Nobles, prin. Fax 369-4946
Moore HS 100/Alt
815 Cross Timber St 76205 940-369-4000
Beth Kelly, prin. Fax 369-4957
Ryan HS 2,100/9-12
5101 E McKinney St 76208 940-369-3000
Vernon Reeves, prin. Fax 369-4960
Strickland MS 900/6-8
324 E Windsor Dr 76209 940-369-4200
Kathleen Carmona, prin. Fax 369-4950
Other Schools – See Argyle, Aubrey, Corinth, Shady Shores

---

Denton Calvary Academy 200/K-12
PO Box 2414 76202 940-320-1944
Selwyn College Preparatory S 200/PK-12
3333 W University Dr 76207 940-382-6771
Karen Morris M.Ed., head sch Fax 383-0704
Texas Woman's University Post-Sec.
PO Box 425589 76204 940-898-2000
University of North Texas Post-Sec.
1155 Union Cir # 311277 76203 940-565-2000

**Denver City, Yoakum, Pop. 4,445**
Denver City ISD 1,600/PK-12
501 Mustang Dr 79323 806-592-5900
Gary Davis, supt. Fax 592-5909
www.dcisd.org
Denver City HS 400/9-12
601 Mustang Dr 79323 806-592-5950
Bruce Patterson, prin. Fax 592-5959

Gravitt JHS 400/6-8
419 Mustang Dr 79323 806-592-5940
Billy Moore, prin. Fax 592-5949

**DeSoto, Dallas, Pop. 48,350**
De Soto ISD 9,000/PK-12
200 E Belt Line Rd 75115 972-223-6666
Dr. David Harris, supt. Fax 274-8209
www.desotoisd.org
DeSoto Alternative Education Center 50/Alt
200 E Belt Line Rd 75115 972-223-6666
Homer Webb, admin. Fax 274-8011
De Soto East MS 600/6-8
601 E Belt Line Rd 75115 972-223-0690
Donna Blackburn, prin. Fax 274-8156
De Soto HS 2,000/9-12
600 Eagle Dr 75115 972-230-0726
Dr. Thurston Lamb, prin. Fax 274-8115
De Soto West MS 700/6-8
800 N Westmoreland Rd 75115 972-230-1820
Reginald Lewis, prin. Fax 274-8183
WINGS Drop Out Recovery Alt
200 E Belt Line Rd 75115 972-274-8219
Homer Webb, prin. Fax 274-8246
Other Schools – See Glenn Heights

---

Canterbury Episcopal S 300/PK-12
1708 N Westmoreland Rd 75115 972-572-7200
Sandy Doerge, admin. Fax 572-7400
ITT Technical Institute Post-Sec.
921 W Belt Line Rd Ste 181 75115 972-274-8600
PC Center Post-Sec.
1229 E Pleasant Run Rd 75115 972-224-9800

**Detroit, Red River, Pop. 712**
Detroit ISD 500/PK-12
110 E Garner St 75436 903-674-6131
Brian Howie, supt. Fax 674-2478
www.detroiteagles.net
Detroit HS 100/9-12
110 E Garner St 75436 903-674-2646
Jonathan Lloyd, prin. Fax 674-2206
Detroit JHS 100/6-8
110 E Garner St 75436 903-674-2646
Jonathan Lloyd, prin. Fax 674-2206

**Devers, Liberty, Pop. 439**
Devers ISD 200/PK-8
PO Box 488 77538 936-549-7135
Elizabeth A. Harris, supt. Fax 549-7595
www.deversisd.net
Devers JHS 50/6-8
PO Box 488 77538 936-549-7591
Elizabeth A. Harris, admin. Fax 549-7595

**Devine, Medina, Pop. 4,321**
Devine ISD 1,900/PK-12
605 W Hondo Ave 78016 830-851-0795
Linda McAnelly, supt. Fax 663-6706
www.devineisd.org
Devine HS 600/9-12
1225 W Hondo Ave 78016 830-851-0895
Derrick Byrd, prin. Fax 663-6792
Devine MS 400/6-8
400 Cardinal Dr 78016 830-851-0695
Michael Murphy, prin. Fax 663-6769

**Deweyville, Newton, Pop. 997**
Deweyville ISD 600/PK-12
PO Box 408 77614 409-746-2731
Kevin Clark, supt. Fax 746-3360
www.deweyvilleisd.com
Other Schools – See Orange

**D Hanis, Medina, Pop. 845**
D'Hanis ISD 300/PK-12
PO Box 307 78850 830-363-7216
Scott Higgins, supt. Fax 363-7390
www.dhanisisd.net/
D'Hanis MSHS 300/PK-12
PO Box 307 78850 830-363-7217
Kurt Schumacher, prin. Fax 363-7390

**Diana, Upshur**
New Diana ISD 1,000/PK-12
1373 US Highway 259 S 75640 903-663-8000
Carl Key, supt. Fax 241-7393
www.ndisd.org
New Diana HS 300/9-12
11826 State Highway 154 E 75640 903-663-8001
Jenifer Politi, prin. Fax 663-2200
New Diana MS 200/6-8
11854 State Highway 154 E 75640 903-663-8002
Greg Pope, prin. Fax 663-1812

**Diboll, Angelina, Pop. 4,716**
Diboll ISD 1,700/PK-12
PO Box 550 75941 936-829-4718
Gary Martel, supt. Fax 829-5558
www.dibollisd.com
Diboll HS 500/9-12
1000 Lumberjack Dr 75941 936-829-5626
John Clements, prin. Fax 829-5708
Diboll JHS 300/7-8
403 Dennis St 75941 936-829-5225
Mark Kettering, prin. Fax 829-5848

**Dickinson, Galveston, Pop. 18,370**
Dickinson ISD 8,400/PK-12
PO Box Z 77539 281-229-6000
Vicki Mims, supt. Fax 229-6023
www.dickinsonisd.org
Dickinson Continuation Center Alt
2805 Oak Park Dr 77539 281-229-6350
Wendy Chide, prin. Fax 229-6351
Dickinson HS 2,300/9-12
3800 Baker Dr 77539 281-229-6400
Dr. Billye Smith, prin. Fax 229-6401
McAdams JHS 1,300/7-8
11415 Hughes Rd 77539 281-229-7100
Rachelle Joseph, prin. Fax 229-7101

---

Pine Drive Christian S 200/PK-12
705 FM 517 Rd E 77539 281-534-4881
Frances Templeton, dir. Fax 534-4318

**Dilley, Frio, Pop. 3,879**
Dilley ISD 1,000/PK-12
245 W FM 117 78017 830-965-1912
Clint McLain, supt. Fax 965-4069
dilleyisd.net
Dilley HS 200/9-12
245 W FM 117 78017 830-965-1814
Jadie Matthew, prin. Fax 965-1276
Harper MS 200/6-8
245 W FM 117 78017 830-965-2195
Jennifer Torres, prin. Fax 965-2171

**Dime Box, Lee**
Dime Box ISD 200/PK-12
PO Box 157 77853 979-884-2324
David Rains, supt. Fax 884-0106
www.dimeboxisd.net
Dime Box S 200/PK-12
PO Box 157 77853 979-884-3366
James Lynn Ponder, prin. Fax 884-0106

**Dimmitt, Castro, Pop. 4,377**
Dimmitt ISD 1,200/PK-12
608 W Halsell St 79027 806-647-3101
Bryan Davis, supt. Fax 647-5433
www.dimmittisd.net
Dimmitt HS 300/9-12
1405 Western Cir 79027 806-647-3105
David Cox, prin. Fax 647-5795
Dimmitt MS 300/5-8
1505 Western Cir 79027 806-647-3108
Jill Millican, prin. Fax 647-2996

**Dodd City, Fannin, Pop. 356**
Dodd City ISD 300/PK-12
602 N Main St 75438 903-583-7585
Craig Reed, supt. Fax 583-9545
www.doddcityisd.org
Dodd City S 300/PK-12
602 N Main St 75438 903-583-7585
Lesia Bridges, prin. Fax 583-9545

**Donna, Hidalgo, Pop. 15,775**
Donna ISD 15,000/PK-12
116 N 10th St 78537 956-464-1600
Fernando Castillo, supt. Fax 464-1752
www.donnaisd.net
Donna HS 2,300/9-12
116 N 10th St 78537 956-464-1700
Nancy Castillo, prin. Fax 464-1629
Donna North HS, 116 N 10th St 78537 9-12
Bernadett Caceras, prin. 956-464-4190
Excel Academy, 116 N 10th St 78537 Alt
Emmy De La Garza, prin. 956-464-1771
Sauceda MS 1,000/6-8
116 N 10th St 78537 956-464-1360
Adela Troncoso, prin. Fax 464-1349
Solis MS 1,000/6-8
116 N 10th St 78537 956-464-1650
Mary Lou Rodriguez, prin. Fax 464-1649
3D Academy 100/Alt
116 N 10th St 78537 956-464-1771
Lydia Lugo, prin. Fax 464-2375
Todd MS 1,000/6-8
116 N 10th St 78537 956-464-1800
Labrado DeHoyos, prin. Fax 464-1824
Veterans MS 1,200/6-8
116 N 10th St 78537 956-464-1350
Claudia Guerrero, prin. Fax 464-1356

**Douglass, Nacogdoches**
Douglass ISD 400/K-12
PO Box 38 75943 936-569-9804
Walter Peddy, supt. Fax 569-9446
www.douglassisd.com
Douglass S 400/K-12
PO Box 38 75943 936-569-9804
Jeffrey Roquemore, prin. Fax 569-9446

**Dripping Springs, Hays, Pop. 1,763**
Dripping Springs ISD 4,600/PK-12
PO Box 479 78620 512-858-3002
Bruce Gearing Ed.D., supt. Fax 858-3099
www.dsisd.txed.net
Dripping Springs HS 1,300/9-12
PO Box 479 78620 512-858-3100
Joe Burns, prin. Fax 858-3199
Dripping Springs MS 1,100/6-8
PO Box 479 78620 512-858-3400
Blake Hays, prin. Fax 858-3499

---

Dripping Springs Christian Academy 50/K-12
800 W Hwy 290 Bldg C # 290 78620 512-858-9738

**Dublin, Erath, Pop. 3,617**
Dublin ISD 1,100/PK-12
PO Box 169 76446 254-445-3341
Rodney Schneider, supt. Fax 445-3345
www.dublinisd.us
Dublin HS 300/7-12
PO Box 169 76446 254-445-0362
Keith Owen, prin. Fax 445-1706

**Dumas, Moore, Pop. 14,542**
Dumas ISD 4,500/PK-12
PO Box 615 79029 806-935-6461
Monty Hysinger, supt. Fax 935-6275
www.dumas-k12.net
Dumas HS 1,100/9-12
PO Box 695 79029 806-935-4151
Brett Beesley, prin. Fax 934-1433
Dumas JHS 700/7-8
PO Box 697 79029 806-935-4155
Kurt Baxter, prin. Fax 934-1434

**Duncanville, Dallas, Pop. 38,022**
Duncanville ISD 13,100/PK-12
710 S Cedar Ridge Dr 75137 972-708-2000
Dr. Deborah Cron, supt. Fax 708-2020
www.duncanvilleisd.org
Byrd MS 800/7-8
1040 W Wheatland Rd 75116 972-708-3400
Michael McDonald, prin. Fax 708-3434
Duncanville HS 3,900/9-12
900 W Camp Wisdom Rd 75116 972-708-3700
Dr. Andre Smith, prin. Fax 708-3737
PACE HS 100/Alt
502 E Freeman St 75116 972-708-2470
Keith Butcher, prin. Fax 708-2474
Reed MS 600/7-8
530 E Freeman St 75116 972-708-3500
Dr. Ryan McCoy, prin. Fax 708-3535
Summit Learning Center Alt
900 S Cedar Ridge Dr #300A 75137 972-708-2570
Dwight Weaver, prin. Fax 708-2585
Other Schools – See Dallas

State Beauty Academy Post-Sec.
663 Oriole Blvd 75116 972-298-0100

**Eagle Pass, Maverick, Pop. 26,203**
Eagle Pass ISD 14,900/PK-12
1420 Eidson Rd 78852 830-773-5181
Gilberto Gonzalez, supt. Fax 773-7252
www.eaglepassisd.net
Eagle Pass HS 2,200/9-12
2020 2nd St 78852 830-773-2381
Valeriano Moreno, prin. Fax 758-1795
Eagle Pass JHS 1,200/7-8
1750 N Bibb Ave 78852 830-758-7037
Mario Escobar, prin. Fax 757-1278
Memorial JHS 1,000/7-8
1800 Lewis St 78852 830-758-7053
Maria Sumpter, prin. Fax 773-8900
Winn HS 2,000/9-12
265 Foster Maldonado Blvd 78852 830-757-0828
Jesus Diaz-Wever, prin. Fax 757-3268

Southwest School Post-Sec.
272 Commercial St 78852 830-773-1373

**Early, Brown, Pop. 2,720**
Early ISD 1,200/PK-12
PO Box 3315, Brownwood TX 76803 325-646-7934
Wes Beck, supt. Fax 646-9238
www.earlyisd.net
Early HS 300/9-12
PO Box 3315, Brownwood TX 76803 325-643-4593
Jennifer Kent, prin. Fax 646-4061
Early MS 300/6-8
PO Box 3315, Brownwood TX 76803 325-643-5665
Robert Weyman, prin. Fax 646-9972

**Earth, Lamb, Pop. 1,057**
Springlake-Earth ISD 400/PK-12
PO Box 130 79031 806-257-3310
Denver Crum, supt. Fax 257-3927
www.springlake-earth.org
Springlake-Earth HS 100/8-12
PO Box 130 79031 806-257-3819
Cindy Furr, prin. Fax 257-3370

**East Bernard, Wharton, Pop. 2,255**
East Bernard ISD 900/PK-12
723 College St 77435 979-335-7519
Courtney Hudgins, supt. Fax 335-6561
www.ebisd.org
East Bernard HS 300/9-12
723 College St 77435 979-335-7519
Jay Janczak, prin. Fax 335-6085
East Bernard JHS 300/5-8
723 College St 77435 979-335-7519
Emmett Tugwell M.Ed., prin. Fax 335-6415

**Eastland, Eastland, Pop. 3,922**
Eastland ISD 1,100/PK-12
PO Box 31 76448 254-631-5120
Jason Cochran, supt. Fax 631-5126
www.eastlandisd.net/
Eastland HS 300/9-12
PO Box 31 76448 254-631-5000
Steven Valkenaar, prin. Fax 631-5025
Eastland MS 200/6-8
PO Box 31 76448 254-631-5040
Jason Henry, prin. Fax 631-5049

**Ector, Fannin, Pop. 677**
Ector ISD 200/PK-12
PO Box 128 75439 903-961-2355
Gary Bohannon, supt. Fax 961-2110
www.ectorisd.net
Ector HS 100/7-12
PO Box 128 75439 903-961-2076
Brad Evans, prin. Fax 961-2356

**Edcouch, Hidalgo, Pop. 3,161**
Edcouch-Elsa ISD 5,200/PK-12
PO Box 127 78538 956-262-6000
Dr. Richard Rivera, supt. Fax 262-6032
www.eeisd.org
Other Schools – See Elsa

**Eddy, McLennan, Pop. 1,113**
Bruceville-Eddy ISD 800/PK-12
1 Eagle Dr 76524 254-859-5832
Richard Kilgore, supt. Fax 859-4023
www.beisd.net
Bruceville-Eddy HS 300/9-12
1 Eagle Dr 76524 254-859-5848
Grady Fulbright, prin. Fax 859-5001
Bruceville-Eddy MS 100/7-8
1 Eagle Dr 76524 254-859-5525
Mike Hawkins, prin. Fax 859-3207
Other Schools – See Waco

**Eden, Concho, Pop. 2,753**
Eden Consolidated ISD 200/K-12
PO Box 988 76837 325-869-4121
Kent Coker, supt. Fax 869-5210
www.edencisd.net
Eden JSHS 100/6-12
PO Box 988 76837 325-869-4121
Misty Gandy, prin. Fax 869-5023

**Edgewood, Van Zandt, Pop. 1,419**
Edgewood ISD 900/PK-12
804 E Pine St 75117 903-896-4332
Emmett Baker, supt. Fax 896-7056
www.edgewood-isd.net
Edgewood HS 300/9-12
804 E Pine St 75117 903-896-4856
Jerri Wehmeyer, prin. Fax 896-1050
Edgewood MS 200/6-8
804 E Pine St 75117 903-896-1530
Russell McDaniel, prin. Fax 896-7056

**Edinburg, Hidalgo, Pop. 76,876**
Edinburg Consolidated ISD 33,200/PK-12
PO Box 990 78540 956-289-2300
Dr. Rene Gutierrez, supt. Fax 383-3576
www.ecisd.us/
Barrientes MS 1,300/6-8
PO Box 990 78540 956-289-2430
Christina Esparza, prin. Fax 316-7749
Economedes HS 2,700/9-12
PO Box 990 78540 956-289-2450
Anthony Garza, prin. Fax 385-3050
Edinburg Alternative Education Academy Alt
PO Box 990 78540 956-289-2598
David Rivera, prin. Fax 316-7391
Edinburg HS 3,100/9-12
PO Box 990 78540 956-289-2400
Yesenia Molina, prin. Fax 386-1225
Edinburg North HS 2,800/9-12
PO Box 990 78540 956-289-2500
Mark Micallef, prin. Fax 316-7712
Edinburg South MS 1,400/6-8
PO Box 990 78540 956-289-2415
Dr. Mary Garza, prin. Fax 316-8817
Garza MS 1,100/6-8
PO Box 990 78540 956-289-2480
Anibal Gorena, prin. Fax 316-3109
Harwell MS 1,700/6-8
PO Box 990 78540 956-289-2440
Dr. Raul D'Lorm, prin. Fax 316-7303
Longoria MS 900/6-8
PO Box 990 78540 956-289-2486
Jorge Botello, prin. Fax 381-6442
Memorial MS 1,200/6-8
PO Box 990 78540 956-289-2470
Fermin Gonzalez, prin. Fax 316-7581
Vela HS 9-12
PO Box 990 78540 956-289-2650
Sylvia Ledesma, prin. Fax 383-3576
Vision Academy of Excellence Alt
PO Box 990 78540 956-289-2584
Ernestina Cano, prin. Fax 287-0812

South Texas ISD
Supt. — See Mercedes
South Texas Business Educ &Tech Academy 600/9-12
510 S Sugar Rd 78539 956-383-1684
Dr. Nora Casarez, prin. Fax 383-8544
South Texas Preparatory Academy 500/7-8
724 S Sugar Rd 78539 956-381-5522
Ana Castro, prin. Fax 381-1177

Rio Grande Bible Institute Post-Sec.
4300 S US Highway 281 78539 956-380-8100
University of Texas Pan American Post-Sec.
1201 W University Dr 78539 866-441-8812

**Edna, Jackson, Pop. 5,438**
Edna ISD 1,400/PK-12
601 N Wells 77957 361-782-3573
Robert O'Connor, supt. Fax 781-1002
www.ednaisd.org
Edna Alternative Center 50/Alt
112 W Ash 77957 361-782-9051
Edna HS 400/9-12
1303 W Gayle St 77957 361-782-5255
Demetric Wells, prin. Fax 781-1014
Edna JHS 300/6-8
505 W Gayle St 77957 361-782-2351
Paul Fleener, prin. Fax 781-1025

Edna Christian Academy 50/PK-12
PO Box 885 77957 361-782-2052

**El Campo, Wharton, Pop. 11,547**
El Campo ISD 3,500/PK-12
700 W Norris St 77437 979-543-6771
Kelly Waters M.Ed., supt. Fax 543-1670
www.ecisd.org
El Campo HS 1,000/9-12
600 W Norris St 77437 979-543-6341
Rich DuBroc, prin. Fax 543-2528
El Campo MS 700/6-8
4010 FM 2765 Rd 77437 979-543-6362
Mark Freeman, prin. Fax 541-5210

**Eldorado, Schleicher, Pop. 1,941**
Schleicher ISD 600/PK-12
PO Box W 76936 325-853-2514
Robert Gibson, supt. Fax 853-2695
www.scisd.net
Eldorado HS 100/9-12
PO Box W 76936 325-853-2514
Ernest Reynolds, prin. Fax 853-2710
Eldorado MS 200/5-8
PO Box W 76936 325-853-2514
Ezra Walling, prin. Fax 853-2895

**Electra, Wichita, Pop. 2,739**
Electra ISD 200/PK-12
PO Box 231 76360 940-495-3683
Scott Hogue, supt. Fax 495-3945
www.electraisd.net
Electra JSHS 100/7-12
400 E Roosevelt Ave 76360 940-495-2218
Michael Stevens, prin. Fax 495-3303

**Elgin, Bastrop, Pop. 7,996**
Elgin ISD 4,100/PK-12
PO Box 351 78621 512-281-3434
Dr. Jodi Duron, supt. Fax 285-5388
www.elginisd.net
Elgin HS 1,200/9-12
14000 County Line Rd 78621 512-281-3438
Cheryl Koury, prin. Fax 281-9804
Elgin MS 900/6-8
1351 N Avenue C 78621 512-281-3382
Riza Cooper, prin. Fax 281-9781
Phoenix HS 50/Alt
902 W 2nd St 78621 512-281-9774
Mike Adams, prin. Fax 281-9862

**Elkhart, Anderson, Pop. 1,338**
Elkhart ISD 1,300/PK-12
301 E Parker St 75839 903-764-2952
Dr. Ray DeSpain, supt. Fax 764-2466
www.elkhartisd.org/
Elkhart HS 300/9-12
301 E Parker St 75839 903-764-5161
Jason Ives, prin. Fax 764-8288
Elkhart MS 300/6-8
301 E Parker St 75839 903-764-2459
Ron Mays, prin. Fax 764-8287

Slocum ISD 400/PK-12
5765 E State Highway 294 75839 903-478-3624
Cliff Lasiter, supt. Fax 478-3030
www.slocumisd.org
Slocum HS 200/9-12
5765 E State Highway 294 75839 903-478-3624
Errin Deer, prin. Fax 478-3030

**Elmaton, Matagorda**
Tidehaven ISD, PO Box 129 77440 800/PK-12
Dr. Andrew Seigrist, supt. 979-843-4302
www.tidehavenisd.com
Tidehaven HS, PO Box 159 77440 200/9-12
Shane Wagner, prin. 979-843-4310
Tidehaven IS, PO Box 130 77440 200/6-8
Shane Wagner, prin. 979-843-4320

**Elm Mott, McLennan**
Connally ISD
Supt. — See Waco
Connally JHS 600/6-8
100 Hancock Dr 76640 254-296-7700
Vickie Dean, prin. Fax 829-2354

**El Paso, El Paso, Pop. 643,027**
Canutillo ISD 6,000/PK-12
7965 Artcraft Rd 79932 915-877-7400
Dr. Pedro Galaviz, supt. Fax 877-7414
www.canutillo-isd.org
Canutillo HS 1,600/9-12
6675 S Desert Blvd 79932 915-877-7800
Teresa Clapsaddle, prin. Fax 877-7807
Other Schools – See Canutillo

Clint ISD 11,100/PK-12
14521 Horizon Blvd 79928 915-926-4000
Juan Martinez, supt. Fax 926-4009
www.clintweb.net
East Montana MS 700/6-8
3490 Ascension Rd 79938 915-926-5200
Holly Garza, prin. Fax 855-0821
Estrada JHS 8-9
851 Darrington Rd 79928 915-926-4800
Mark Ayala, prin. Fax 852-2455
Horizon HS 1,000/10-12
14651 Horizon Blvd 79928 915-926-4200
Elena Acosta, prin. Fax 852-0357
Mountain View HS 900/9-12
14964 Greg Dr 79938 915-926-5000
Paul Harrington, prin. Fax 855-2503
Other Schools – See Clint

El Paso ISD 63,900/PK-12
PO Box 20100 79998 915-230-2000
Juan Cabrera, supt. Fax 887-5484
www.episd.org
Andress HS 1,900/9-12
5400 Sun Valley Dr 79924 915-236-4000
Lynn Gill, prin. Fax 757-6443
Armendariz MS 700/6-8
2231 Arizona Ave 79930 915-546-9012
Lorenzo Munoz, prin. Fax 577-0848
Austin HS 1,600/9-12
3500 Memphis Ave 79930 915-587-2500
Craig Kehrwald, prin. Fax 566-7360
Bassett MS 800/6-8
4400 Elm St 79930 915-231-2260
Michelle Kirkland, prin. Fax 565-1562
Bowie HS 1,200/9-12
801 S San Marcial St 79905 915-496-8200
Michael Warmack, prin. Fax 532-1918
Brown MS 900/6-8
7820 Helen Of Troy Dr 79912 915-774-4080
Carmen Solis-Rodriguez, prin. Fax 581-6424
Burges HS 1,500/9-12
7800 Edgemere Blvd 79925 915-780-1100
Randall Woods, prin. Fax 771-6914
Canyon Hills MS 900/6-8
8930 Eclipse St 79904 915-231-2240
Deborah Lunow, prin. Fax 757-8067
Center for Career & Technology Education Vo/Tech
1170 N Walnut St 79930 915-236-7900
Matthew Farley, prin. Fax 544-5976
Chapin HS 1,900/9-12
7000 Dyer St 79904 915-832-6730
Dr. Carla Gonzales, prin. Fax 565-9716

Charles MS 800/6-8
4909 Trojan Dr 79924 915-236-6550
Michael Mendoza, prin. Fax 821-0505
College Career and Technology Academy Alt
2851 Grant Ave 79930 915-236-7000
Adan Lopez, prin. Fax 585-4789
Coronado HS 2,800/9-12
100 Champions Pl 79912 915-236-2000
Angela Henderson, prin. Fax 587-6458
Delta Academy 100/Alt
6400 Delta Dr 79905 915-774-0447
Ernie Watts, admin. Fax 881-1245
El Paso HS 1,200/9-12
800 E Schuster Ave 79902 915-496-8300
Kristine Ferret, prin. Fax 532-2008
Franklin HS 3,000/9-12
900 N Resler Dr 79912 915-236-2200
Carla Gasway, prin. Fax 587-4094
Guillen MS 900/6-8
900 S Cotton St 79901 915-496-4620
Teresa Zamarripa, prin. Fax 532-1143
Henderson MS 800/6-8
5505 Robert Alva Ave 79905 915-887-3080
Elizabeth Maldonado, prin. Fax 772-3425
Hornedo MS 1,100/6-8
6101 High Ridge Dr 79912 915-881-2900
Micaela Varela, prin. Fax 581-7371
Irvin HS 1,700/9-12
9465 Roanoke Dr 79924 915-587-3500
Laron Sharp, prin. Fax 757-6450
Jefferson HS 1,100/9-12
4700 Alameda Ave 79905 915-496-8010
Federico Rojas, prin. Fax 532-2033
Lafarelle Alternative MS 50/Alt
4500 Lawrence Ave 79904 915-751-7186
Ernesto Pena, prin. Fax 751-1316
Lincoln MS 1,000/6-8
500 Mulberry Ave 79932 915-231-2180
Heidi Appel, prin. Fax 581-1371
Magoffin MS 900/6-8
4931 Hercules Ave 79904 915-774-4040
Rogelio Segovia, prin. Fax 757-7675
Morehead MS 900/6-8
5625 Confetti Dr 79912 915-231-2140
Armando Gallegos, prin. Fax 587-5355
Occupational Center Vo/Tech
5300 Warriors Dr 79932 915-230-2870
Fax 584-2940
Richardson MS 600/6-8
11350 Loma Franklin Dr 79934 915-822-8829
Joseph Manago, prin. Fax 822-8812
Ross MS 900/6-8
6101 Hughey Cir 79925 915-887-3060
Jason Yturralde, prin. Fax 771-6792
Silva Health Magnet HS 600/9-12
121 Val Verde St 79905 915-496-8100
Federico Rojas, prin. Fax 533-3695
Telles Academy 100/Alt
320 S Campbell St 79901 915-496-4600
Christian James, prin. Fax 532-0540
Terrace Hills MS 700/6-8
4835 Blossom Ave 79924 915-231-2120
Christopher Smith, prin. Fax 759-0615
Transmountain Early College HS 400/9-12
9570 Gateway Blvd N 79924 915-832-4270
Blanca Garcia, prin. Fax 751-2011
Wiggs MS 900/6-8
1300 Circle Dr 79902 915-231-2100
Timothy Luther, prin. Fax 533-2902
San Jacinto Adult Learning Center Adult
1216 Olive Ave 79901 915-230-3200
Gabriel Garcia, admin. Fax 544-7163

Socorro ISD 41,500/PK-12
12440 Rojas Dr 79928 915-937-0000
Jose Espinoza Ed.D., supt. Fax 851-7572
www.sisd.net
Americas HS 2,500/9-12
12101 Pellicano Dr 79936 915-937-2800
Patricia Cuevas, prin. Fax 855-6898
Clarke MS 1,100/6-8
1515 Bob Hope Dr 79936 915-937-5600
Thomas Redlinger, prin. Fax 857-3765
Eastlake HS 1,000/9-12
13000 Emerald Pass Ave 79928 915-937-3600
Gilbert Martinez, prin. Fax 937-3799
El Dorado HS 2,600/9-12
12401 Edgemere Blvd 79938 915-937-3200
Cynthia Retana, prin. Fax 851-7820
Ensor MS 900/6-8
13600 Ryderwood Dr 79928 915-937-6000
Naomi Esparza, prin. Fax 851-7590
Hernando MS 1,100/6-8
3451 Rich Beem 79938 915-937-9800
Venessa Betancourt, prin. Fax 937-9898
K.E.Y.S. Academy 100/Alt
12380 Pine Springs Dr 79928 915-937-4000
Dr. Magdalena Aguilar, prin. Fax 937-4006
Mission Early College HS 500/9-12
10700 Gateway Blvd E 79927 915-937-1200
Jason Long, prin. Fax 860-2935
Montwood HS 2,900/9-12
12000 Montwood Dr 79936 915-937-2400
Rosa Mireles-Menchaca, prin. Fax 937-2422
Montwood MS 800/6-8
11710 Pebble Hills Blvd 79936 915-937-5800
Sylvia Esparza, prin. Fax 856-9909
Options HS 200/Alt
12380 Pine Springs Dr 79928 915-937-1300
Dr. Magdalena Aguilar, prin. Fax 859-2603
Pebble Hills HS 100/9-12
14400 Pebble Hills Blvd 79938 915-937-9400
Troy Byrne, prin. Fax 851-7912
Puentes MS 6-8
3216 Tim Foster 79938 915-937-9200
Janie Tidwell, prin. Fax 851-7855
Sanchez MS 800/6-8
321 N Rio Vista Rd 79927 915-937-5200
Clarice Jones, prin. Fax 859-6636
Slider MS 900/6-8
11700 School Ln 79936 915-937-5400
Steve Troxel, prin. Fax 857-5804
Socorro HS 2,700/9-12
10150 Alameda Ave 79927 915-937-2000
Jesse Teran, prin. Fax 937-2394
Socorro MS 600/6-8
321 Bovee Rd 79927 915-937-5000
Jonathan Valdez, prin. Fax 859-6955
Sun Ridge MS 900/6-8
2210 Sun Country Dr 79938 915-937-6600
Ignacio Estorga, prin. Fax 851-7730

Ysleta ISD 43,900/PK-12
9600 Sims Dr 79925 915-434-0000
Dr. Xavier De La Torre, supt. Fax 591-4144
www.yisd.net
Bel Air HS 2,200/9-12
731 N Yarbrough Dr 79915 915-434-2000
Louis Martinez, prin. Fax 593-6110
Camino Real MS 700/6-8
9393 Alameda Ave 79907 915-434-8300
Charles Garcia, prin. Fax 858-3743
Chavez Academy 100/Alt
7814 Alameda Ave 79915 915-434-9600
Graciela Martinez, prin. Fax 779-2068
Del Valle HS 1,900/9-12
950 Bordeaux Dr 79907 915-434-3000
Antonio Acuna, prin. Fax 858-1427
Desert View MS 500/6-8
1641 Billie Marie Dr 79936 915-434-5300
Michelle Kehrwald, prin. Fax 591-9327
Eastwood HS 2,200/9-12
2430 Mcrae Blvd 79925 915-434-4000
Armenia Smith, prin. Fax 594-8014
Eastwood MS 1,000/7-8
2612 Chaswood St 79935 915-434-4300
James Boatright, prin. Fax 591-9426
Hanks HS 2,000/9-12
2001 N Lee Trevino Dr 79936 915-434-5000
Gloria Spencer, prin. Fax 598-4621
Hillcrest MS 600/7-8
8040 Yermoland Dr 79907 915-434-2200
Dana DeRouen, prin. Fax 591-9439
Indian Ridge MS 800/6-8
11201 Pebble Hills Blvd 79936 915-434-5400
Pauline Muela, prin. Fax 591-9447
Parkland HS 1,300/9-12
5932 Quail Ave 79924 915-434-6000
Dr. Darryl Hensen, prin. Fax 434-6291
Parkland MS 700/6-8
6045 Nova Way 79924 915-434-6300
Javier Selgado, prin. Fax 757-6608
Plato Academy 200/Alt
8441 Alameda Ave 79907 915-434-9000
Michael Martinez, prin. Fax 434-9080
Ranchland Hills MS 400/7-8
7615 Yuma Dr 79915 915-434-2300
Carmen Crawford, prin. Fax 592-0036
Rio Bravo MS 400/6-8
525 Greggerson Dr 79907 915-434-8400
Dr. Sandra Calzada, prin. Fax 872-0269
Riverside HS 1,300/9-12
301 Midway Dr 79915 915-434-7000
Daniel Gurany, prin. Fax 779-6983
Riverside MS 600/7-8
7615 Mimosa Ave 79915 915-434-7300
Marie Anaya, prin. Fax 772-7549
Tejas School of Choice 200/Alt
7500 Alpha Ave 79915 915-434-9900
Dr. Lucy Lozano-Lerma, prin. Fax 772-8366
Valle Verde Early College HS 400/9-12
919 Hunter Dr 79915 915-434-1500
Paul Covey, prin. Fax 594-7112
Valley View MS 600/6-8
8660 N Loop Dr 79907 915-434-3300
Penny Bankston, prin. Fax 858-3615
Ysleta HS 1,600/9-12
8600 Alameda Ave 79907 915-434-8000
Silvia Rendon, prin. Fax 858-3299
Ysleta MS 400/6-8
8691 Independence Dr 79907 915-434-8200
Homero Silva, prin. Fax 858-0261
Ysleta Community Learning Center Adult
121 Padres Dr 79907 915-434-9400
Fred Anaya, prin. Fax 858-6307

---

Anamarc College Post-Sec.
3210 Dyer St 79930 915-351-8100
Anamarc College Post-Sec.
8720 Gateway Blvd E Ste D 79907 915-351-8100
Cathedral HS 500/9-12
1309 N Stanton St 79902 915-532-3238
Aurora Lujan, prin. Fax 533-8248
El Paso Community College Post-Sec.
PO Box 20500 79998 915-831-2000
Faith Christian Academy 500/PK-12
8960 Escobar Dr 79907 915-594-3305
Shannon Nieman, supt. Fax 593-5474
Father Yermo HS 200/9-12
250 Washington St 79905 915-533-3185
Karina Tapia, prin. Fax 544-0738
Immanuel Christian S 600/PK-12
1201 Hawkins Blvd 79925 915-778-6160
J.D. Zubia, head sch Fax 772-8207
International Business College Post-Sec.
5700 Cromo Dr 79912 915-842-0422
International Business College Post-Sec.
1155 N Zaragoza Rd Ste 100 79907 915-859-0422
Jesus Chapel S 200/PK-12
10200 Album Ave 79925 915-593-1153
Alba Wilcox, prin. Fax 593-1113
Kaplan College Post-Sec.
8360 Burnham Rd Ste 100 79907 915-595-1935
Loretto Academy 700/PK-12
1300 Hardaway St 79903 915-566-8400
Abe Ramirez, prin. Fax 564-0563
North Loop Christian Academy 50/PK-12
8617 N Loop Dr 79907 915-872-9435
Valerie Devine, dir.
Patterson Institute 200/7-12
517 S Florence St 79901 915-533-8286
Pipo Academy of Hair Design Post-Sec.
3000 Pershing Dr 79903 915-565-3491
Radford S 100/PK-12
2001 Radford St 79903 915-565-2737
Southwest University at El Paso Post-Sec.
1414 Geronimo Dr 79925 915-778-4001
Tec de Monterrey Prep S 9-12
5450 Hurd Pl 79912 915-581-5600
Tri-State Cosmetology Institute Post-Sec.
601 N Cotton St Ste 5 79902 915-585-8777
Tri-State Cosmetology Institute Post-Sec.
6800 Gateway Blvd E Ste 4A 79915 915-778-1741
University of Texas at El Paso Post-Sec.
500 W University Ave 79968 915-747-5000
Vista College Post-Sec.
6101 Montana Ave 79925 866-442-4197
Western Technical College Post-Sec.
9624 Plaza Cir 79927 915-532-3737
Western Technical College Post-Sec.
9451 Diana Dr 79924 915-566-9621

**Elsa, Hidalgo, Pop. 5,655**
Edcouch-Elsa ISD
Supt. — See Edcouch
Edcouch-Elsa HS 1,300/9-12
401 N Yellowjacket Dr 78543 956-262-6944
Jaime Garcia, prin. Fax 262-9018
Truan JHS 800/7-8
E 9th St 78543 956-262-6082
Aldo Vidal, prin. Fax 262-6079

**Elysian Fields, Harrison**
Elysian Fields ISD 1,000/PK-12
PO Box 120 75642 903-633-2420
Maynard Chapman, supt. Fax 633-2498
www.efisd.net
Elysian Fields HS 300/9-12
PO Box 120 75642 903-633-2420
Jack Parker, prin. Fax 633-2498
Elysian Fields MS 300/6-8
PO Box 120 75642 903-633-2420
Brandon Goswick, prin. Fax 633-2326

**Emory, Rains, Pop. 1,215**
Rains ISD 1,500/PK-12
PO Box 247 75440 903-473-2222
John Rouse, supt. Fax 473-3053
www.rainsisd.org
Rains HS 500/9-12
PO Box 247 75440 903-473-2222
Randell Wellman, prin. Fax 473-5584
Rains JHS 400/6-8
PO Box 247 75440 903-473-2222
Gina Hildebrandt, prin. Fax 473-5162

**Ennis, Ellis, Pop. 18,329**
Ennis ISD 5,800/PK-12
PO Box 1420 75120 972-872-7000
Dr. John Chapman, supt. Fax 875-8667
www.ennis.k12.tx.us
Ennis HS 1,600/9-12
2301 Ensign Rd 75119 972-872-3500
David Averett, prin. Fax 875-6337
Ennis JHS 800/7-8
3101 Ensign Rd 75119 972-872-3850
Wade Bishop, prin. Fax 875-9044

**Era, Cooke**
Era ISD 400/K-12
108 Hargrove St 76238 940-665-5961
Jeremy Thompson, supt. Fax 665-5311
www.eraisd.net
Era JSHS 200/6-12
108 Hargrove St 76238 940-665-5961
Jereme Dietz, prin. Fax 665-5311

**Euless, Tarrant, Pop. 48,852**
Hurst-Euless-Bedford ISD
Supt. — See Bedford
Alternative Education Program 50/Alt
1100 Raider Dr Ste 100 76040 817-354-3398
Dr. William Westmoreland, prin. Fax 358-5001
Central JHS 1,000/7-9
3191 W Pipeline Rd 76040 817-354-3350
Randy Belcher, prin. Fax 354-3357
Euless JHS 900/7-9
306 Airport Fwy 76039 817-354-3340
Rita Wiles, prin. Fax 354-3345
KEYS HS 100/Alt
1100 Raider Dr Ste 100 76040 817-354-3580
Dr. June Jacoby, prin. Fax 354-3586
Trinity SHS 2,400/10-12
500 N Industrial Blvd 76039 817-571-0271
Micheal Harris, prin. Fax 354-3322

**Eustace, Henderson, Pop. 976**
Eustace ISD 1,400/PK-12
PO Box 188 75124 903-425-5151
Dr. Coy Holcombe, supt. Fax 425-5147
www.eustaceisd.net
Eustace HS 400/9-12
PO Box 188 75124 903-425-5161
Stan Sowers, prin. Fax 425-5227
Eustace MS 400/6-8
PO Box 188 75124 903-425-5171
Truman Oakley, prin. Fax 425-5146

**Evadale, Jasper, Pop. 1,471**
Evadale ISD 500/PK-12
PO Box 497 77615 409-276-1337
Gary Fairchild, supt. Fax 276-1908
www.evadalek12.net
Evadale HS 100/9-12
PO Box 497 77615 409-276-1337
Rusty Minyard, prin. Fax 276-1050

Evadale JHS 100/6-8
PO Box 497 77615 409-276-1337
Cheryl Jones, prin. Fax 276-1588

**Evant, Coryell, Pop. 421**
Evant ISD 200/PK-12
PO Box 339 76525 254-471-5536
James Slone, supt. Fax 471-5629
www.evantisd.org/
Evant HS 100/7-12
PO Box 339 76525 254-471-5536
Craig Taylor, prin. Fax 471-5629

**Everman, Tarrant, Pop. 6,051**
Everman ISD 6,600/PK-12
608 Townley Dr 76140 817-568-3500
Curtis Amos, supt. Fax 568-3508
www.eisd.org
Baxter JHS 800/7-8
3038 Shelby Rd 76140 817-568-3530
Kentrel Phillips, prin. Fax 568-3594
Everman Academy HS 1,300/9-12
300 Shelby Rd 76140 817-568-3520
Martin DeHoyos, prin. Fax 568-3516
Everman HS, 1000 S Race St 76140 1,300/9-12
Melvin Bedford, prin. 817-568-5200

**Fabens, El Paso, Pop. 8,249**
Fabens ISD 2,400/PK-12
PO Box 697 79838 915-765-2600
Poncho Garcia, supt. Fax 764-2968
www.fabensisd.net/
Fabens HS 700/9-12
PO Box 697 79838 915-765-2620
Ruben Carrillo, prin. Fax 764-4953
Fabens MS 600/6-8
PO Box 697 79838 915-765-2630
Dr. Joe Keith, prin. Fax 764-7263

**Fairfield, Freestone, Pop. 2,920**
Fairfield ISD 1,800/PK-12
615 Post Oak Rd 75840 903-389-2532
Rick Edwards, supt. Fax 389-7050
www.fairfieldisd.net
Fairfield HS 500/9-12
615 Post Oak Rd 75840 903-389-4177
Von Wade M.Ed., prin. Fax 389-5453
Fairfield JHS 400/6-8
615 Post Oak Rd 75840 903-389-4210
Bryan Gawryszewski M.Ed., prin. Fax 389-5454

**Falfurrias, Brooks, Pop. 4,970**
Brooks County ISD 1,500/PK-12
PO Box 589 78355 361-325-8000
David Perry, supt. Fax 325-1913
www.bcisdistrict.net
Falfurrias HS 400/9-12
PO Box 589 78355 361-325-8091
Dr. Cynthia Perez, prin. Fax 325-8158
Falfurrias JHS 300/6-8
PO Box 589 78355 361-325-8071
Maria Vidaurri, prin. Fax 325-2220

**Falls City, Karnes, Pop. 604**
Falls City ISD 400/K-12
PO Box 399 78113 830-254-3551
Tylor Chaplin, supt. Fax 254-3354
www.fcisd.net
Falls City JSHS 200/7-12
PO Box 399 78113 830-254-3551
Christy Blocker, prin. Fax 254-3354

**Farmers Branch, Dallas, Pop. 28,241**
Carrollton-Farmers Branch ISD
Supt. — See Carrollton
Field MS 900/6-8
13551 Dennis Ln 75234 972-968-3900
Stephanie Cherney, prin. Fax 968-3910

---

Brookhaven College Post-Sec.
3939 Valley View Ln 75244 972-860-4700

**Farmersville, Collin, Pop. 3,235**
Farmersville ISD 1,400/PK-12
501A State Highway 78 N 75442 972-782-6601
Jeff Adams, supt. Fax 784-7293
www.farmersvilleisd.net
Farmersville HS 400/9-12
499 State Highway 78 N 75442 972-782-7757
Wayne Callaway, prin. Fax 782-7245
Farmersville JHS 300/6-8
501 State Highway 78 N 75442 972-782-6202
Dr. Josh Martin, prin. Fax 782-7029

**Farwell, Parmer, Pop. 1,360**
Farwell ISD 600/PK-12
PO Box F 79325 806-481-3371
Kelly Lusk, supt. Fax 481-9275
www.farwellschools.org
Farwell HS 100/9-12
PO Box F 79325 806-481-3351
Coby Norman, prin. Fax 481-3531
Farwell JHS 100/6-8
PO Box F 79325 806-481-9260
Kristy White, prin. Fax 481-9258

**Fayetteville, Fayette, Pop. 257**
Fayetteville ISD 200/PK-12
PO Box 129 78940 979-378-4242
Jeff Harvey, supt. Fax 378-4246
www.fayettevilleisd.net
Fayetteville S 200/PK-12
PO Box 129 78940 979-378-4242
Janice Motal, prin. Fax 378-4246

**Ferris, Ellis, Pop. 2,412**
Ferris ISD 2,500/PK-12
PO Box 459 75125 972-544-3858
James Hartman, supt. Fax 544-2784
www.ferrisisd.org
Ferris HS 700/9-12
PO Box 461 75125 972-544-3737
Kevin Dixon, prin. Fax 544-2029

Ferris JHS 300/6-8
PO Box 459 75125 972-544-2279
Rhonda Renner, prin. Fax 544-2281

**Fischer, Comal**
Comal ISD
Supt. — See New Braunfels
Canyon Lake HS 900/9-12
8555 FM 32 78623 830-885-1700
Corbee Wunderlich, prin. Fax 885-1701

**Flatonia, Fayette, Pop. 1,376**
Flatonia ISD 600/PK-12
PO Box 189 78941 361-865-2941
Beverly Mikulenka, supt. Fax 865-2940
www.flatoniaisd.net
Flatonia HS 300/7-12
PO Box 189 78941 361-865-2941
Chris Sodek, prin. Fax 865-2944
Whispering Hills Achievement Center 50/Alt
PO Box 189 78941 361-865-2941
Robin Branecky, prin. Fax 865-2940

**Florence, Williamson, Pop. 1,128**
Florence ISD 1,000/PK-12
PO Box 489 76527 254-793-2850
Paul Michalewicz, supt. Fax 793-3055
florenceisd.net
Florence HS 300/9-12
PO Box 489 76527 254-793-2495
Steve Elder, prin. Fax 793-3784
Florence MS 200/6-8
PO Box 489 76527 254-793-2504
John Rueter Ed.D., prin. Fax 793-3054

**Floresville, Wilson, Pop. 6,407**
Floresville ISD 3,700/PK-12
1200 5th St 78114 830-393-5300
Sherri Bays Ed.D., supt. Fax 393-5399
www.fisd.us
Floresville Alternative S 50/Alt
335 Alternative Ln 78114 830-393-5368
Bud Box, prin. Fax 393-5706
Floresville HS 1,000/9-12
1813 Tiger Ln 78114 830-393-5370
Sandra Galinzoga, prin. Fax 393-5719
Floresville MS 900/6-8
2601 B St 78114 830-393-5350
Marcia Gonzales, prin. Fax 393-5339

**Flower Mound, Denton, Pop. 63,499**
Lewisville ISD 49,900/PK-12
1800 Timber Creek Rd 75028 469-713-5200
Kevin Rogers Ed.D., supt. Fax 350-9500
www.lisd.net
Downing MS 700/6-8
5555 Bridlewood Blvd 75028 469-713-5962
Lisa Lingren, prin. Fax 350-9176
Flower Mound 9th Grade Campus 9-9
3411 A Peters Colony Rd 75022 469-713-5999
Will Skelton, prin.
Flower Mound HS 3,200/10-12
3411 Peters Colony Rd 75022 469-713-5192
Sonya Lail, prin. Fax 350-9244
Forestwood MS 600/6-8
2810 Morriss Rd 75028 469-713-5972
Dave Tickner, prin. Fax 350-9184
Lamar MS 800/6-8
4000 Timber Creek Rd 75028 469-713-5966
Rebecca Clark, prin. Fax 350-9204
Marcus 9th Grade Campus 9-9
5707A Morriss Rd 75028 469-948-8900
Chantell Upshaw, prin.
Marcus HS 3,200/10-12
5707 Morriss Rd 75028 469-713-5196
Gary Shafferman, prin. Fax 350-9313
McKamy MS 1,100/6-8
2401 Old Settlers Rd 75022 469-713-5991
Peter Taggart, prin. Fax 350-9477
Shadow Ridge MS 800/6-8
2050 Aberdeen Dr 75028 469-713-5984
Gary Gibson, prin. Fax 350-9215
Other Schools – See Carrollton, Highland Village, Lewisville, The Colony

---

Coram Deo Academy 600/K-12
4900 Wichita Trl 75022 972-237-0232
Temple Christian Academy 200/K-12
2501 Northshore Blvd 75028 972-874-8700
Dr. Richard Wallace, admin. Fax 539-4649

**Floydada, Floyd, Pop. 3,029**
Floydada ISD 500/PK-12
226 W California St 79235 806-983-3498
Dr. Gilbert Trevino, supt. Fax 983-5739
www.floydadaisd.esc17.net
Floydada HS 200/9-12
618 Whirlwind Aly 79235 806-983-2340
Wayne Morren, prin.
Floydada JHS 100/7-8
618 Whirlwind Aly 79235 806-983-4961
Wayne Morren, prin. Fax 983-5739

**Follett, Lipscomb, Pop. 459**
Follett ISD 200/PK-12
PO Box 28 79034 806-653-2301
George Auld, supt. Fax 653-2036
www.follettisd.net
Follett S 200/PK-12
PO Box 28 79034 806-653-2301
Brianna Ethridge, prin. Fax 653-2036

**Forestburg, Montague**
Forestburg ISD 200/PK-12
PO Box 415 76239 940-964-2323
John Metzler, supt. Fax 964-2531
www.forestburgisd.net
Forestburg S 200/PK-12
PO Box 415 76239 940-964-2323
Randy Seeds, prin. Fax 964-2531

**Forney, Kaufman, Pop. 14,459**
Forney ISD 8,200/PK-12
600 S Bois d Arc St 75126 972-564-4055
Suzanne McWilliams, supt. Fax 552-3038
www.forneyisd.net
Brown MS 600/7-8
1050 Windmill Farms Blvd 75126 972-564-3967
Jody Fadely, prin. Fax 355-1099
Forney HS 1,300/9-12
800 FM 741 75126 972-564-3890
Stephen Whiffen, prin. Fax 564-5616
North Forney HS 1,000/9-12
6170 Falcon Way 75126 972-762-4159
Dr. Jason Johnston, prin. Fax 355-0311
Warren MS 700/7-8
811 S Bois D Arc St 75126 469-762-4156
Joseph Pouncy, prin. Fax 552-1693

**Forsan, Howard, Pop. 209**
Forsan ISD 700/PK-12
PO Box 689 79733 432-457-2223
Randy Johnson, supt. Fax 457-2225
forsan.esc18.net
Forsan JSHS 400/6-12
PO Box 689 79733 432-457-2223
Terry McDonald, prin. Fax 457-2225

**Fort Davis, Jeff Davis, Pop. 1,186**
Fort Davis ISD 200/PK-12
PO Box 1339 79734 432-426-4440
Graydon Hicks, supt. Fax 426-3841
www.fdisd.com
Fort Davis JSHS 100/6-12
PO Box 1339 79734 432-426-4444
Luane Porter, prin. Fax 426-4449

**Fort Hancock, Hudspeth, Pop. 1,741**
Fort Hancock ISD 500/PK-12
PO Box 98 79839 915-769-3811
Jose Franco, supt. Fax 769-3940
www.forthancockisd.net
Fort Hancock HS 200/9-12
PO Box 98 79839 915-769-3811
Lorena Molinar, prin. Fax 769-0044
Fort Hancock MS 100/6-8
PO Box 98 79839 915-769-3811
Lorena Molinar, prin. Fax 769-0045

**Fort Hood, Bell, Pop. 27,754**
Killeen ISD
Supt. — See Killeen
Murphy MS 500/6-8
53393 Sun Dance Dr 76544 254-336-6530
Mike Quinn, prin. Fax 336-6579
Smith MS 800/6-8
51000 Tank Destroyer Blvd 76544 254-336-1050
Chad Wolf, prin. Fax 336-1056

**Fort Stockton, Pecos, Pop. 8,231**
Fort Stockton ISD 2,400/PK-12
101 W Division St 79735 432-336-4000
Ralph Traynham, supt. Fax 336-4008
www.fsisd.net/
Fort Stockton HS 600/9-12
101 W Division St 79735 432-336-4101
Gil-Ray Madrid, prin. Fax 336-4113
Fort Stockton MS 500/6-8
101 W Division St 79735 432-336-4131
Roy Alvarado, prin. Fax 336-4136

**Fort Worth, Tarrant, Pop. 728,297**
Castleberry ISD 3,700/PK-12
5228 Ohio Garden Rd 76114 817-252-2000
John Ramos, supt. Fax 252-2097
www.castleberryisd.net
Castleberry HS 800/9-12
215 Churchill Rd 76114 817-252-2100
Dr. Amy Ellis, prin. Fax 252-2199
Marsh MS 900/6-8
415 Hagg Dr 76114 817-252-2200
Derrick Spurlock, prin. Fax 738-3454
TRUCE Learning Center Alt
1101 Merritt St 76114 817-252-2490
Chris McGrath, prin. Fax 252-2498
Other Schools – See River Oaks

Crowley ISD
Supt. — See Crowley
Crowley MS 600/7-8
3800 W Risinger Rd 76123 817-370-5650
Robert Gillies, prin. Fax 370-5656
North Crowley 9th Grade Campus 700/9-9
4630 McPherson Blvd 76123 817-297-5896
Daryle Moffett, prin. Fax 297-5878
North Crowley HS 1,700/10-12
9100 S Hulen St 76123 817-263-1250
Stefani Allen, prin. Fax 263-1282

Eagle Mtn.-Saginaw ISD 17,200/PK-12
1200 Old Decatur Rd 76179 817-232-0880
Jim Chadwell Ed.D., supt. Fax 847-6124
www.emsisd.com
Boswell HS 2,100/9-12
5805 W Bailey Boswell Rd 76179 817-237-3314
Nika Davis, prin. Fax 238-8706
Chisholm Trail HS 900/9-12
3100 NW College Dr 76179 817-232-7112
Dr. Dana Barnes, prin. Fax 232-7110
Creekview MS 700/6-8
6716 Bob Hanger St 76179 817-237-4261
Anthe Anagnostis, prin. Fax 237-2387
Highland MS 800/6-8
1001 E Bailey Boswell Rd 76131 817-847-5143
Karen Pressley, prin. Fax 847-1922
Hollenstein Career and Technology Center Vo/Tech
5501 Marine Creek Pkwy 76179 817-306-1925
Dana Eldredge, dir. Fax 306-1327
Prairie Vista MS 800/6-8
8000 Comanche Springs Dr 76131 817-847-9210
Anna King, prin. Fax 847-4255

Watson HS 100/Alt
5901 Hereford Dr 76179 817-238-7925
Melanie Stitt, prin. Fax 237-0753
Wayside MS 800/6-8
1300 Old Decatur Rd 76179 817-232-0541
Jason Sneed, prin. Fax 232-2391
Willkie MS 800/6-8
6129 Texas Shiner Dr 76179 817-237-9631
Elisha McDonald, prin. Fax 237-9643
Other Schools – See Saginaw

Fort Worth ISD 79,400/PK-12
100 N University Dr 76107 817-814-2000
Dr. Kent Scribner, supt. Fax 871-2112
www.fwisd.org
Applied Learning Academy 400/Alt
7060 Camp Bowie Blvd 76116 817-815-5500
Alice Buckley, prin. Fax 815-5550
Arlington Heights HS 1,700/9-12
4501 West Fwy 76107 817-815-1000
Sarah Weeks, prin. Fax 815-1050
Carter-Riverside HS 1,200/9-12
3301 Yucca Ave 76111 817-814-9000
Greg Ruthart, prin. Fax 814-9050
Daggett MS 400/6-8
1108 Carlock St 76110 817-814-5200
Cynthia Miles-Brown, prin. Fax 814-5250
Diamond Hill-Jarvis HS 900/9-12
1411 Maydell St 76106 817-815-0000
Yassmin Lee, prin. Fax 815-0050
Dunbar HS 800/9-12
5700 Ramey Ave 76112 817-815-3000
Sajade Miller, prin. Fax 815-3050
Eastern Hills HS 1,300/9-12
5701 Shelton St 76112 817-815-4000
Chad McCarty, prin. Fax 815-4050
Elder MS 1,200/6-8
709 NW 21st St 76164 817-814-4100
James Garcia, prin. Fax 814-4150
Forest Oak MS 800/6-8
3221 Pecos St 76119 817-815-8200
Paula Woods, prin. Fax 815-8250
Fort Worth ISD Collegiate HS 9-12
5301 Campus Dr 76119 817-815-4402
Lisa Castillo, prin. Fax 815-4208
Handley MS 500/6-8
2801 Patino Rd 76112 817-815-4200
Cheryl Johnson, prin. Fax 815-4250
International Newcomer Academy 300/Alt
7060 Camp Bowie Blvd 76116 817-815-5600
Rodrigo Durbin, prin. Fax 815-5650
Jacquet MS 500/7-8
2501 Stalcup Rd 76119 817-815-3500
Ricky Brown, prin. Fax 815-3550
James MS 1,100/6-8
1101 Nashville Ave 76105 817-814-0200
Joycelyn Barnett, prin. Fax 814-0250
Kirkpatrick MS 500/6-8
3201 Refugio Ave 76106 817-814-4200
Nick Torrez, prin. Fax 814-4250
Marine Creek Collegiate HS 9-12
4801 Marine Creek Pkwy 76179 817-515-7784
Tonni Grant, prin. Fax 515-7094
McClung MS 500/6-8
3000 Forest Ave 76112 817-815-5300
Norbert Whitaker, prin. Fax 815-5350
McLean MS 900/7-8
3816 Stadium Dr 76109 817-814-5300
Melissa Bryan, prin. Fax 814-8350
Meacham MS 700/6-8
3600 Weber St 76106 817-815-0200
Thomas Fraire, prin. Fax 815-0250
Meadowbrook MS 700/6-8
2001 Ederville Rd S 76103 817-815-4300
Katrina Smith, prin. Fax 815-4350
Metro Opportunity S Vo/Tech
2720 Cullen St 76107 817-814-6700
Gerald Magin, prin. Fax 814-6750
Monnig MS 600/6-8
3136 Bigham Blvd 76116 817-815-1200
Ron Rhone, prin. Fax 815-1250
Morningside MS 700/6-8
2751 Mississippi Ave 76104 817-815-8300
Angele Hodges, prin. Fax 815-8350
North Side HS 1,500/9-12
2211 Mckinley Ave 76164 817-814-4000
Antonio Martinez, prin. Fax 814-4050
Paschal HS 2,600/9-12
3001 Forest Park Blvd 76110 817-814-5000
Terri Mossige, prin. Fax 814-5050
Polytechnic HS Vo/Tech
1300 Conner Ave 76105 817-814-0000
Joshua Delich, prin. Fax 814-0050
Riverside MS 1,000/6-8
1600 Bolton St 76111 817-814-9200
Roberto Santana, prin. Fax 814-9250
Rosemont MS 900/7-8
1501 W Seminary Dr 76115 817-814-7200
Benjamin Leos, prin. Fax 814-7250
South Hills HS 1,500/9-12
6101 Mccart Ave 76133 817-814-7000
Dorothy Gomez, prin. Fax 814-7050
Southwest HS 1,400/9-12
4100 Altamesa Blvd 76133 817-814-8000
John Engel, prin. Fax 814-8050
Stripling MS 500/6-8
2100 Clover Ln 76107 817-815-1300
Keri Flores, prin. Fax 815-1350
Success HS 200/Alt
1003 W Cannon St 76104 817-815-2700
Ingrid Williams, prin. Fax 815-2750
Texas Academy of Biomedical Sciences 100/9-12
3813 Valentine St 76107 817-815-2300
Troy Langston, prin. Fax 815-2350
Trimble Technical HS Vo/Tech
1003 W Cannon St 76104 817-815-2500
Omar Ramos, prin. Fax 815-2550
Wedgwood MS 900/7-8
3909 Wilkie Way 76133 817-814-8200
Brian Rosatelli, prin. Fax 814-8250

World Languages Institute 6-8
1066 W Magnolia Ave 76104 817-815-2200
Guadalupe Barreto, prin. Fax 815-2250
Wyatt HS 1,200/9-12
2400 E Seminary Dr 76119 817-815-8000
Lewis Washington, prin. Fax 815-8050
Young Men's Leadership Academy 300/6-12
5100 Willie St 76105 817-815-3400
Rodney White, prin. Fax 815-3450
Other Schools – See Benbrook

Keller ISD
Supt. — See Keller
Central HS 2,500/9-12
9450 Ray White Rd, 817-744-2000
David Hinson, prin. Fax 744-2252
Fossil Hill MS 900/7-8
3821 Staghorn Cir S 76137 817-744-3050
Todd Lacey, prin. Fax 847-6990
Fossil Ridge HS 2,200/9-12
4101 Thompson Rd, 817-744-1700
David Hadley, prin. Fax 337-3407
Hillwood MS 1,200/7-8
8250 Parkwood Hill Blvd 76137 817-744-3350
Kathleen Eckert, prin. Fax 581-1810
Timber Creek HS 2,200/9-12
12350 Timberland Blvd, 817-744-2300
Todd Tunnell, prin. Fax 744-2338
Timberview MS 1,000/5-8
10300 Old Denton Rd, 817-744-2600
Carrie Jackson, prin. Fax 744-2638
Trinity Springs MS 1,000/7-8
3550 Keller Hicks Rd, 817-744-3500
Kimberly Burkhalton, prin. Fax 744-3538

Lake Worth ISD
Supt. — See Lake Worth
Collins MS 400/7-8
3651 Santos Dr 76106 817-306-4250
Kathy Harmon, prin. Fax 624-7058

Northwest ISD
Supt. — See Justin
Eaton HS, 1350 Eagle Blvd, 9-12
Dr. Carri Eddy, prin. 817-698-3955

White Settlement ISD 6,400/PK-12
401 S Cherry Ln 76108 817-367-1300
Frank Molinar, supt. Fax 367-1351
www.wsisd.com/
Brewer HS 1,700/9-12
1025 W Loop 820 N 76108 817-367-1200
Pam Turner, prin. Fax 367-1242
DAEP/Mesa HS 50/Alt
1000 S Cherry Ln Ste A 76108 817-367-1364
Jennifer Heddins, prin. Fax 367-1366
Other Schools – See White Settlement

---

All Saints' Episcopal S 900/PK-12
9700 Saints Cir 76108 817-560-5700
Dr. Thaddeus Bird, head sch Fax 560-9805
Anderson Private S 50/PK-12
14900 White Settlement Rd 76108 817-448-8484
Bethesda Christian S 400/K-12
4700 N Beach St 76137 817-281-6446
Vicki Vaughn, admin. Fax 581-5123
Brite Divinity School Post-Sec.
2925 Princeton St 76109 817-257-7575
Calvary Christian Academy 400/PK-12
1401 Oakhurst Scenic Dr 76111 817-332-3351
Sue Tidwell, admin. Fax 332-4621
Cassata HS 200/9-12
1400 Hemphill St 76104 817-926-1745
Trinette Robichaux, pres. Fax 926-3132
Christian Life Preparatory S 200/K-12
5253 Altamesa Blvd 76123 817-293-1500
Dr. Deborah Henry, admin. Fax 503-3092
College of Sts John Fisher & Thomas More Post-Sec.
801 W Shaw St 76110 817-923-8459
Covenant Classical S 200/K-12
1701 Wind Star Way 76108 817-820-0884
DeVry University Post-Sec.
301 Commerce St Ste 2000 76102 817-810-9114
Everest College Post-Sec.
5237 N Riverside Dr Ste 100 76137 817-838-3000
Everest College Post-Sec.
4200 South Fwy Ste 1940 76115 817-566-7700
Fort Worth Beauty School Post-Sec.
6785 Camp Bowie Blvd # 100 76116 817-924-4289
Fort Worth Country Day S 1,100/K-12
4200 Country Day Ln 76109 817-732-7718
Evan Peterson, head sch Fax 377-3425
Harris Hospital Post-Sec.
1301 Pennsylvania Ave 76104 817-878-2106
Harvest Christian Academy 300/PK-12
7200 Denton Hwy 76148 817-485-1660
Terry Caywood, hdmstr. Fax 514-6279
JPS Inst. for Health Career Development Post-Sec.
2400 Circle Dr 76119 817-920-7380
Kaplan College Post-Sec.
2001 Beach St Ste 201 76103 817-413-2000
Lake Country Christian S 400/PK-12
7050 Lake Country Dr 76179 817-236-8703
Nancy Purtell, admin. Fax 236-1103
Nolan HS 1,000/9-12
4501 Bridge St 76103 817-457-2920
Erin Vader, pres. Fax 496-9775
Ogle School of Hair Design Post-Sec.
6125 Interstate 20 Ste 128 76132 817-294-2950
Remington College Post-Sec.
300 E Loop 820 76112 817-451-0017
St. Peter's Classical S 100/PK-12
7601 Bellaire Dr S 76132 817-294-0124
Jeanette Johnson, head sch Fax 288-0180
Southwest Christian Prep S 400/7-12
6901 Altamesa Blvd 76123 817-294-9596
Dr. Penny Armstrong, pres. Fax 292-3644
Southwestern Baptist Theological Sem. Post-Sec.
PO Box 22000 76122 817-923-1921

Tarrant County College Post-Sec.
5301 Campus Dr 76119 817-515-8223
Tarrant County College Post-Sec.
4801 Marine Creek Pkwy 76179 817-515-8223
Temple Christian S 800/PK-12
6824 Randol Mill Rd 76120 817-457-0770
Dorothy Stringer, supt. Fax 457-0777
Texas Christian University Post-Sec.
2800 S University Dr 76129 817-257-7000
Texas Wesleyan University Post-Sec.
1201 Wesleyan St 76105 817-531-4444
Trinity Valley S 1,000/K-12
7500 Dutch Branch Rd 76132 817-321-0100
Gary Krahn Ph.D., head sch Fax 321-0105
University of N Texas Health Science Ctr Post-Sec.
3500 Camp Bowie Blvd 76107 817-735-2000

**Franklin, Robertson, Pop. 1,547**
Franklin ISD 1,100/PK-12
PO Box 909 77856 979-828-7000
Timothy Bret Lowry, supt. Fax 828-1910
www.franklinisd.net/
Franklin HS 300/9-12
PO Box 909 77856 979-828-7100
Timothy Luza, prin. Fax 828-3364
Franklin MS 300/5-8
PO Box 909 77856 979-828-7200
Susan Nelson, prin. Fax 828-7202

**Frankston, Anderson, Pop. 1,210**
Frankston ISD 700/PK-12
PO Box 428 75763 903-876-2556
Micah Lewis, supt. Fax 876-4558
www.frankstonisd.net
Frankston HS 200/9-12
PO Box 428 75763 903-876-3219
Donny Lee, prin. Fax 876-4558
Frankston MS 200/6-8
PO Box 428 75763 903-876-2215
Dr. Cindy Woody, prin. Fax 876-4558

**Fredericksburg, Gillespie, Pop. 10,449**
Fredericksburg ISD 2,900/PK-12
234 Friendship Ln 78624 830-997-9551
Dr. Eric Wright, supt. Fax 997-6164
www.fisd.org/
Fredericksburg HS 1,000/9-12
1107 S State Highway 16 78624 830-997-7551
Ralf Halderman, prin. Fax 997-8583
Fredericksburg MS 700/6-8
110 W Travis St 78624 830-997-7657
Missy Stevens, prin. Fax 997-1927
G.C.L.C. 50/Alt
1110 S Adams St 78624 830-997-9788
Blaine Hahn, prin. Fax 997-9788

---

Heritage S 200/K-12
310 Smokehouse Rd 78624 830-997-6597
Matthew Skinner, head sch Fax 997-4900

**Freeport, Brazoria, Pop. 11,851**
Brazosport ISD
Supt. — See Clute
Brazosport HS 1,000/9-12
PO Box Z 77542 979-730-7260
Rita Pintavalle, prin. Fax 730-7366
Freeport IS 500/7-8
PO Box Z 77542 979-730-7240
Brooke Merritt, prin. Fax 237-6329

**Freer, Duval, Pop. 2,808**
Freer ISD 900/PK-12
PO Box 240 78357 361-394-6025
Steve Van Matre, supt. Fax 394-5005
www.freerisd.org/
Freer HS 300/9-12
PO Box 240 78357 361-394-6717
Conrad Cantu, prin. Fax 394-5046
Freer JHS 200/6-8
PO Box 240 78357 361-394-7102
Rosalva Campos, prin. Fax 394-5016

**Friendswood, Galveston, Pop. 35,202**
Clear Creek ISD
Supt. — See League City
Brookside IS 800/6-8
3535 E FM 528 Rd 77546 281-284-3600
Lauren Ambeau, prin. Fax 284-3605
Clear Brook HS 2,500/9-12
4607 FM 2351 Rd 77546 281-284-2100
Michele Staley, prin. Fax 284-2105
Westbrook IS 1,300/6-8
302 W El Dorado Blvd 77546 281-284-3800
Stephanie McBride, prin. Fax 284-3805

Friendswood ISD 5,500/PK-12
302 Laurel Dr 77546 281-482-1267
Trish Hanks, supt. Fax 996-2513
www.fisdk12.net
Friendswood HS 2,000/9-12
702 Greenbriar Ave 77546 281-482-3413
Mark Griffon, prin. Fax 996-2523
Friendswood JHS 1,500/6-8
1000 Manison Pkwy 77546 281-996-6200
Dana Drew, prin. Fax 996-6262

---

Texas School of Business Post-Sec.
3208 E FM 528 Rd 77546 281-648-0880

**Friona, Parmer, Pop. 4,104**
Friona ISD 1,200/PK-12
909 E 11th St 79035 806-250-2747
Kenny Austin, supt. Fax 250-3805
www.frionaisd.com
Friona HS 300/9-12
909 E 11th St 79035 806-250-3951
Pam Ray, prin. Fax 259-2281
Friona JHS 300/6-8
909 E 11th St 79035 806-250-2788
Mark Sundre, prin. Fax 250-8155

**Frisco, Collin, Pop. 113,923**
Frisco ISD 35,300/PK-12
5515 Ohio Dr 75035 469-633-6000
Jeremy Lyon, supt. Fax 633-6050
www.friscoisd.org
Career Technology Education Center Vo/Tech
9889 Wade Blvd 75035 469-633-6780
Dianna Manuel, prin. Fax 633-6790
Clark MS 800/6-8
4600 Colby Dr 75035 469-633-4600
Joel Partin, prin. Fax 633-4650
Cobb MS 6-8
9400 Teel Pkwy, 469-633-4300
Phil Evans, prin. Fax 633-4310
Frisco Centennial HS 1,900/9-12
6901 Coit Rd 75035 469-633-5600
Randy Spain, prin. Fax 633-5650
Frisco HS 1,700/9-12
6401 Parkwood Blvd 75034 469-633-5500
Erin Miller, prin. Fax 633-5550
Griffin MS 600/6-8
3703 Eldorado Pkwy, 469-633-4900
Elizabeth Holcomb, prin. Fax 633-4950
Heritage HS 1,500/9-12
14040 Eldorado Pkwy 75035 469-633-5900
Mark Mimms, prin. Fax 633-5950
Hunt MS 600/6-8
4900 Legendary Dr 75034 469-633-5200
Danny Barrentine, prin. Fax 633-5210
Independence HS 9-12
10555 Independence Pkwy 75035 469-633-5400
Alan Waligura, prin. Fax 633-5450
Liberty HS 1,800/9-12
15250 Rolater Rd 75035 469-633-5800
Scott Warstler, prin. Fax 633-5850
Lone Star HS 9-12
2606 Panther Creek Pkwy, 469-633-5300
Karen Kraft, prin. Fax 633-5350
Maus MS 600/6-8
12175 Coit Rd 75035 469-633-5250
Chakosha Powell, prin. Fax 633-5260
Pearson MS 6-8
2323 Stonebrook Pkwy 75034 469-633-4450
Jamie Wisneski, prin. Fax 633-4460
Pioneer Heritage MS 700/6-8
1649 High Shoals Dr 75034 469-633-4700
Rocky Agan, prin. Fax 633-4750
Reedy HS 9-12
3003 Stonebrook Pkwy 75034 469-633-6400
Karen LeCocq, prin. Fax 633-6450
Roach MS 700/6-8
12499 Independence Pkwy 75035 469-633-5000
Terri Gladden, prin. Fax 633-5010
Stafford MS 800/6-8
2288 Little River Rd, 469-633-5100
Robin Scott, prin. Fax 633-5110
Staley MS 600/6-8
6927 Stadium Ln, 469-633-4500
Anita Lightfoot, prin. Fax 633-4550
Student Opportunity Center Alt
6928 Maple St, 469-633-6700
Sue Kirk, prin. Fax 633-6750
Trent MS 6-8
13131 Coleto Creek Dr, 469-633-4400
Shawn Perry, prin. Fax 633-4410
Vandeventer MS 6-8
6075 Independence Pkwy 75035 469-633-4350
Paige Hoes, prin. Fax 633-4360
Wakeland HS 1,600/9-12
10700 Legacy Dr, 469-633-5700
Chris Mogan, prin. Fax 633-5750
Wester MS 800/6-8
12293 Shepherds Hill Ln 75035 469-633-4800
Richard Manuel, prin. Fax 633-4850
Other Schools – See Mc Kinney, Plano

---

Collin College Post-Sec.
9700 Wade Blvd 75035 972-377-1790
Grace Covenant Academy 100/K-12
10633 John W Elliott Dr, 972-836-9422
Brian Smith, hdmstr.
Legacy Christian Academy 800/PK-12
5000 Academy Dr 75034 469-633-1330
Dr. Chris Harmon, hdmstr. Fax 633-1348

**Fritch, Hutchinson, Pop. 2,086**
Sanford-Fritch ISD 800/PK-12
PO Box 1290 79036 806-857-3122
Jim McClellan, supt. Fax 857-3795
www.sfisd.net
Sanford-Fritch HS 200/9-12
PO Box 1290 79036 806-857-3121
Jason Garrison, prin. Fax 857-9147
Sanford-Fritch JHS 200/6-8
PO Box 1290 79036 806-857-9268
Edith Allen, prin. Fax 857-9431

**Frost, Navarro, Pop. 641**
Frost ISD 400/PK-12
PO Box K 76641 903-682-2711
Duane Limbaugh, supt. Fax 682-2107
www.frostisd.org
Frost JSHS 200/6-12
PO Box K 76641 903-682-2541
Becky Melton, prin. Fax 682-2107

**Fruitvale, Van Zandt, Pop. 408**
Fruitvale ISD 400/PK-12
PO Box 77 75127 903-896-1191
Rebecca Bain, supt. Fax 896-1011
www.fruitvaleisd.com
Fruitvale HS 100/9-12
PO Box 77 75127 903-896-4363
Charles Harford, prin. Fax 896-1011
Fruitvale MS 100/6-8
PO Box 77 75127 903-896-4363
Charles Harford, prin. Fax 896-1011

**Fulshear, Fort Bend, Pop. 1,120**
Lamar Consolidated ISD
Supt. — See Rosenberg
Fulshear HS 9-12
9302 Bois D Arc Ln 77441 832-223-0000
Daniel Ward, prin.
Leaman JHS 7-8
9320 Bois D Arc Ln 77441 832-223-0000

**Gail, Borden, Pop. 230**
Borden County ISD 200/K-12
PO Box 95 79738 806-756-4313
Billy Collins, supt. Fax 756-4310
www.bcisd.net/
Borden S 200/K-12
PO Box 95 79738 806-756-4313
Bart McMeans, prin. Fax 756-4310

**Gainesville, Cooke, Pop. 15,668**
Gainesville ISD 2,800/PK-12
800 S Morris St 76240 940-665-4362
Jeffrey L. Brasher, supt. Fax 665-4473
www.gainesvilleisd.org
Gainesville HS 600/9-12
2201 S Interstate 35 76240 940-665-5528
Melissa Hutchison, prin. Fax 612-2795
Gainesville JHS 600/7-8
1201 S Lindsay St 76240 940-665-4062
Mary Patterson, prin. Fax 665-1432

---

North Central Texas College Post-Sec.
1525 W California St 76240 940-668-7731

**Galena Park, Harris, Pop. 10,842**
Galena Park ISD
Supt. — See Houston
Galena Park HS 1,900/9-12
1000 Keene St 77547 832-386-2800
Tony Gardea, prin. Fax 386-2802
Galena Park MS 1,000/6-8
400 Keene St 77547 832-386-1700
Shaunte Morris, prin. Fax 386-1738

**Galveston, Galveston, Pop. 47,004**
Galveston ISD 4,700/PK-12
PO Box 660 77553 409-766-5100
Larry Nichols, supt. Fax 762-8391
www.gisd.org/
Austin Magnet MS 500/5-8
1514 Avenue N 1/2 77550 409-761-3500
Cathy Vanness, prin. Fax 765-5946
Ball HS 1,700/9-12
4115 Avenue O 77550 409-766-5700
Joe Pillar, prin. Fax 766-5738
Central MS 400/7-8
3014 Sealy St 77550 409-761-6200
Cheryl Rutledge, dir. Fax 770-0649

---

Galveston College Post-Sec.
4015 Avenue Q 77550 409-944-4242
O'Connell College Preparatory HS 100/9-12
1320 Tremont St 77550 409-765-5534
Patti Abbott, prin. Fax 765-5536
Texas A&M University Galveston Post-Sec.
PO Box 1675 77553 409-740-4400
University of Texas Medical Branch Post-Sec.
301 University Blvd 77555 409-772-1011

**Ganado, Jackson, Pop. 1,997**
Ganado ISD 500/PK-12
PO Box 1200 77962 361-771-4200
John Hardwick Ed.D., supt. Fax 771-2280
www.ganadoisd.org
Ganado HS 200/9-12
PO Box 1200 77962 361-771-4300
Andy Bridges, prin. Fax 771-2280
Ganado JHS 6-8
PO Box 1200 77962 361-771-4309
Joey Rosalez, prin. Fax 771-4310

**Garden City, Glasscock, Pop. 334**
Glasscock County ISD 300/PK-12
PO Box 9 79739 432-354-2230
Tom Weeaks, supt. Fax 354-2503
www.gckats.net
Glasscock County JSHS 100/7-12
PO Box 9 79739 432-354-2244
Wayland Pierce, prin. Fax 354-2503

**Garland, Dallas, Pop. 223,158**
Garland ISD 57,500/PK-12
PO Box 469026 75046 972-494-8201
Dr. Bob Morrison, supt. Fax 485-4928
www.garlandisd.net
Austin Academy for Excellence MS 900/6-8
1125 Beverly Dr 75040 972-926-2620
Holly Muzzicato, prin. Fax 926-2633
Bussey MS 900/6-8
1204 Travis St 75040 972-494-8391
Mary Garcia, prin. Fax 494-8971
Classical Center at Brandenburg MS 1,200/6-8
626 Nickens Rd 75043 972-926-2630
Elise Mosty, prin. Fax 926-2633
Garland Alternative Education Center 100/Alt
2015 S Country Club Rd 75041 972-926-2691
Dr. Kim Lozada, prin. Fax 926-2692
Garland HS 2,700/9-12
310 S Garland Ave 75040 972-494-8492
Atticus Wisener, prin. Fax 494-8415
Houston MS 1,000/6-8
2232 Sussex Dr 75041 972-926-2640
Don Hernandez, prin. Fax 926-2647
Jackson Tech Center for Math & Science 1,200/6-8
1310 Bobbie Ln 75042 972-494-8362
David Dunphy, prin. Fax 494-8802
Lakeview Centennial HS 2,400/9-12
3505 Hayman Dr 75043 972-240-3740
Maresa Bailey, prin. Fax 240-3750
Lyles MS 900/6-8
4655 S Country Club Rd 75043 972-240-3720
Darrin Hemphill, prin. Fax 240-3723
Memorial Pathway Academy 100/Alt
2825 S 1st St 75041 972-926-2650
Jim Thomas, prin. Fax 926-2651
Naaman Forest HS 2,500/9-12
4843 Naaman Forest Blvd 75040 972-675-3091
Erika Crump, prin. Fax 675-3100
North Garland HS 2,100/9-12
2109 W Buckingham Rd 75042 972-675-3120
Glenda Williams, prin. Fax 675-3145
O'Banion MS 1,100/6-8
700 Birchwood Dr 75043 972-279-6103
John Tucci, prin. Fax 613-9532
Sellers MS 800/6-8
1009 Mars Dr 75040 972-494-8337
Vikki Mahagan, prin. Fax 494-8607
South Garland HS 2,000/9-12
600 Colonel Dr 75043 972-926-2700
Tracy Curtis, prin. Fax 926-2727
Webb MS 1,200/6-8
1610 Spring Creek Dr 75040 972-675-3080
Kenneth Washington, prin. Fax 675-3089
Other Schools – See Rowlett, Sachse

---

Amberton University Post-Sec.
1700 Eastgate Dr 75041 972-279-6511
Brighter Horizons Academy 700/PK-12
3145 Medical Plaza Dr 75044 972-675-2062
Dr. Iram Shaikh-Jilani, prin. Fax 675-2063
Garland Christian Academy 300/PK-12
1516 Lavon Dr 75040 972-487-0043
Brian Keith, admin. Fax 276-4079
International Beauty College #3 Post-Sec.
1225 Belt Line Rd Ste 7 75040 972-530-1103
National Beauty College Post-Sec.
354 E Interstate 30 Ste A 75043 972-226-6900
Remington College Post-Sec.
1800 Eastgate Dr 75041 972-686-7878

**Garrison, Nacogdoches, Pop. 884**
Garrison ISD 700/PK-12
459 N US Highway 59 75946 936-347-7000
Darren Webb, supt. Fax 347-2529
www.garrisonisd.com
Garrison HS 200/9-12
459 N US Highway 59 75946 936-347-7030
Reid Spivey, prin. Fax 347-7059
Garrison MS 200/6-8
459 N US Highway 59 75946 936-347-7020
William Travis Weeks, prin. Fax 347-7004

**Gary, Panola**
Gary ISD 400/PK-12
132 Bobcat Trl 75643 903-685-2291
Todd Greer, supt. Fax 685-2639
www.garyisd.org
Gary S 400/PK-12
132 Bobcat Trl 75643 903-685-2291
Tony Wood, prin. Fax 685-2639

**Gatesville, Coryell, Pop. 15,526**
Gatesville ISD 2,900/PK-12
311 S Lovers Ln 76528 254-865-7251
Eric Penrod, supt. Fax 865-2279
www.gatesvilleisd.org
Gatesville HS 800/9-12
311 S Lovers Ln 76528 254-865-8281
Shane Webb, prin. Fax 865-2293
Gatesville JHS 400/7-8
311 S Lovers Ln 76528 254-865-8271
Cindy Venable, prin. Fax 865-2252

**Georgetown, Williamson, Pop. 46,741**
Georgetown ISD 9,700/PK-12
603 Lakeway Dr 78628 512-943-5000
Dr. Fred Brent, supt. Fax 943-5004
www.georgetownisd.org
Benold MS 900/6-8
3407 Northwest Blvd 78628 512-943-5090
Leslie Michalik, prin. Fax 943-5099
Forbes MS 700/6-8
1911 NE Inner Loop 78626 512-943-5150
Leonard Rhoads, prin. Fax 943-5159
Georgetown Alternative Program 50/Alt
502 Patriot Way 78626 512-943-5196
Louis Garza, prin. Fax 943-5197
Georgetown East View HS 700/9-12
4490 E University Ave 78626 512-943-1800
Dr. Dave Denny, prin. Fax 943-1819
Georgetown HS 2,300/9-12
2211 N Austin Ave 78626 512-943-5100
Cade Smith, prin. Fax 943-5109
Richarte HS 100/Alt
2295 N Austin Ave 78626 512-943-5120
Marsha Winship, prin. Fax 943-5121
Tippit MS 800/6-8
1601 Leander Rd 78628 512-943-5040
Brian Dawson, prin. Fax 943-5049
Williamson County Academy 50/Alt
200 Wilco Way 78626 512-943-3260
Robert Fischer, prin. Fax 943-3288

---

Grace Academy 200/K-12
225 Grace Blvd, 512-864-9500
Jenny Courville, dir. Fax 868-5429
Southwestern University Post-Sec.
1001 E University Ave 78626 512-863-6511

**George West, Live Oak, Pop. 2,431**
George West ISD 1,100/PK-12
913 Houston St 78022 361-449-1914
Ty Sparks, supt. Fax 449-1426
www.gwisd.esc2.net/
George West HS 300/9-12
1013 Houston St 78022 361-449-1914
Richard Waterhouse, prin. Fax 449-3128
George West JHS 200/7-8
900 Houston St 78022 361-449-1914
Ashley Lowe, prin. Fax 449-3909

**Giddings, Lee, Pop. 4,822**
Giddings ISD 1,900/PK-12
PO Box 389 78942 979-542-2854
Roger Dees, supt. Fax 542-9264
www.giddings.txed.net
Giddings HS 700/9-12
PO Box 389 78942 979-542-3351
Chad Rood, prin. Fax 542-5312
Giddings MS 400/6-8
PO Box 389 78942 979-542-2057
Travis Grubbs, prin. Fax 542-3941

**Gilmer, Upshur, Pop. 4,805**
Gilmer ISD 2,400/PK-12
500 S Trinity St 75644 903-841-7400
Rick Albritton, supt. Fax 843-5279
www.gilmerisd.org
Bruce JHS 400/7-8
111 Bruce St 75645 903-841-7600
Bill Bradshaw, prin. Fax 843-6108
Gilmer HS 600/9-12
850 Buffalo St 75644 903-841-7500
Brian Bowman, prin. Fax 843-2171

Union Hill ISD 300/PK-12
2197 FM 2088 75644 903-762-2140
Dr. Troy Batts, supt. Fax 762-6845
www.uhisd.com
Union Hill HS 100/7-12
2197 FM 2088 75644 903-762-2138
Jason Crow, prin. Fax 762-6845

**Gladewater, Gregg, Pop. 6,285**
Gladewater ISD 2,000/PK-12
500 W Quitman Ave 75647 903-845-6991
Dr. Jerry Richardson, supt. Fax 845-6994
www.gladewaterisd.com
Gladewater HS 600/9-12
2201 W Gay Ave 75647 903-845-5591
Sandra King, prin. Fax 845-3694
Gladewater MS 400/6-8
700 Melba Ave 75647 903-845-2243
Chris Langford, prin. Fax 844-1738

Sabine ISD 1,300/PK-12
5424 FM 1252 W 75647 903-984-8564
Stacey Bryce, supt. Fax 984-6108
www.sabineisd.org
Sabine HS 300/9-12
5424 FM 1252 W 75647 903-984-8587
Eddie Shawn, prin. Fax 986-1103
Sabine MS 300/6-8
5424 FM 1252 W 75647 903-984-4767
Bill Middendorf, prin. Fax 984-8823

Union Grove ISD 600/PK-12
PO Box 1447 75647 903-845-5509
Brian Gray, supt. Fax 845-6178
www.ugisd.org
Union Grove JSHS 200/7-12
PO Box 1447 75647 903-845-5506
Kelly Moore, prin. Fax 845-3003

**Glenn Heights, Dallas, Pop. 11,061**
De Soto ISD
Supt. — See DeSoto
McCowan MS 900/6-8
1500 Majestic Meadows Dr 75154 972-274-8090
Sissy Lowe, prin. Fax 274-8099

---

Community Christian Academy 50/3-12
1810 S Hampton Rd 75154 972-274-0015
Dr. Nancie Rowe, admin. Fax 274-0078

**Glen Rose, Somervell, Pop. 2,402**
Glen Rose ISD 1,600/PK-12
PO Box 2129 76043 254-898-3900
Wayne Rotan, supt. Fax 897-3651
www.grisd.net
Glen Rose HS 500/9-12
PO Box 2129 76043 254-898-3800
Tommy Corcoran, prin. Fax 897-9871
Glen Rose JHS 400/6-8
PO Box 2129 76043 254-898-3700
Susan Wright, prin. Fax 897-4059

**Godley, Johnson, Pop. 999**
Godley ISD 1,400/PK-12
313 N Pearson St 76044 817-389-2536
Dr. Rich Dear, supt. Fax 389-2543
www.godleyisd.net/
Godley HS 400/9-12
9401 N Highway 171 76044 817-389-2265
Leigh Brown, prin. Fax 389-4455
Godley MS 300/7-8
409 N Pearson St 76044 817-389-2121
David Williams, prin. Fax 389-4357

**Goldthwaite, Mills, Pop. 1,857**
Goldthwaite ISD 600/PK-12
PO Box 608 76844 325-648-3531
Ronny Wright, supt. Fax 648-2456
www.goldisd.net/
Goldthwaite HS 200/9-12
PO Box 608 76844 325-648-3081
Stephanie Behrens, prin. Fax 648-2325
Goldthwaite MS 100/6-8
PO Box 608 76844 325-648-3630
Landon Sanderson, prin. Fax 648-3571

**Goliad, Goliad, Pop. 1,901**
Goliad ISD 1,400/PK-12
PO Box 830 77963 361-645-3259
Donald Egg, supt. Fax 645-3614
www.goliadisd.org
Goliad DAEP 50/Alt
PO Box 830 77963 361-645-3257
Russell Kowalik, prin. Fax 645-8039
Goliad HS 400/9-12
PO Box 830 77963 361-645-3257
Russell Kowalik, prin. Fax 645-8039
Goliad MS 200/7-8
PO Box 830 77963 361-645-3146
Mary Tippin, prin. Fax 645-8040

**Gonzales, Gonzales, Pop. 7,175**
Gonzales ISD 2,800/K-12
PO Box 157 78629 830-672-9551
Kimberly Strozier Ed.D., supt. Fax 672-7159
www.gonzalesisd.net
Gonzales HS 700/9-12
1801 N Sarah DeWitt Dr 78629 830-672-7535
Michael Garcia, prin. Fax 672-8273
Gonzales JHS 400/7-8
426 N College St 78629 830-672-8641
Wanda Fryer, prin. Fax 672-6466

**Goodrich, Polk, Pop. 267**
Goodrich ISD 200/PK-12
PO Box 789 77335 936-365-1100
Dr. Gary Bates, supt. Fax 365-3518
www.goodrichisd.net
Goodrich HS 100/9-12
PO Box 789 77335 936-365-1100
Lara Devillier, prin. Fax 365-2371
Goodrich MS 50/6-8
PO Box 789 77335 936-365-1100
Lara Devillier, prin. Fax 365-2371

**Gordon, Palo Pinto, Pop. 475**
Gordon ISD 200/PK-12
PO Box 47 76453 254-693-5582
Eric Hough, supt. Fax 693-5503
gordonisd.net
Gordon S 200/PK-12
PO Box 47 76453 254-693-5342
Holly Campbell, prin. Fax 693-5503

**Gorman, Eastland, Pop. 1,079**
Gorman ISD 300/PK-12
PO Box 8 76454 254-734-3171
Gary Speegle, supt. Fax 734-3393
www.gorman.esc14.net/
Gorman HS 100/9-12
PO Box 8 76454 254-734-3171
Brad Riker, prin. Fax 734-3425
Gorman MS 100/6-8
PO Box 8 76454 254-734-3171
Brad Riker, prin. Fax 734-4729

**Graford, Palo Pinto, Pop. 570**
Graford ISD 300/PK-12
400 W Division Ave 76449 940-664-3101
Dennis Holt, supt. Fax 664-2123
www.grafordisd.net
Graford JSHS 100/7-12
400 W Division Ave 76449 940-664-3101
Lori Henderson, prin. Fax 664-2026

**Graham, Young, Pop. 8,817**
Graham ISD 2,500/PK-12
400 3rd St 76450 940-549-0595
Sonny Cruse, supt. Fax 549-8656
www.grahamisd.com
Graham HS 700/9-12
1000 Brazos St 76450 940-549-1504
Joe Gordy, prin. Fax 549-4031
Graham JHS 600/6-8
1000 2nd St 76450 940-549-2002
Ginger Robbins, prin. Fax 549-6991
Graham Learning Center 50/Alt
701 Tennessee St 76450 940-549-1546
Amanda Townley, prin. Fax 549-4561

**Granbury, Hood, Pop. 7,903**
Granbury ISD 6,500/PK-12
600 W Pearl St 76048 817-408-4000
James Largent Ed.D., supt. Fax 408-4014
www.granburyisd.org
Acton MS 800/6-8
1300 James Rd 76049 817-408-4800
Jimmy Dawson, prin. Fax 408-4849
Crossland 9th Grade Ctr. 500/9-9
217 N Jones St 76048 817-408-4700
Ammie Hill, prin. Fax 408-4749
Granbury HS 1,300/10-12
2000 W Pearl St 76048 817-408-4600
Jeremy Ross, prin. Fax 408-4699
Granbury MS 800/6-8
2000 Crossland Rd 76048 817-408-4850
Pat Yelverton, prin. Fax 408-4899
STARS Accelerated HS 100/Alt
301 N Hannaford St 76048 817-408-4450
Ginna Marks, prin. Fax 408-4164

---

Cornerstone Christian Academy 100/PK-12
1905 W Pearl St Ste 105 76048 817-573-6485
Marci Martinez, admin. Fax 573-7604
North Central Texas Academy 200/PK-12
3846 N Highway 144 76048 254-897-4822
Todd Shipman, pres. Fax 897-7650

**Grandfalls, Ward, Pop. 353**
Grandfalls-Royalty ISD 100/PK-12
PO Box 10 79742 432-547-2266
Joe Helms, supt. Fax 547-2960
www.grisd.com
Grandfalls-Royalty S 100/PK-12
PO Box 10 79742 432-547-2266
Juan Rios, prin. Fax 547-2960

**Grand Prairie, Dallas, Pop. 172,425**
Grand Prairie ISD 24,500/PK-12
PO Box 531170 75053 972-264-6141
Dr. Susan Simpson-Hull, supt. Fax 237-5440
www.gpisd.org
Adams MS 800/6-8
833 W Tarrant Rd 75050 972-262-1934
Nneka Bernard, prin. Fax 522-3099
Crosswinds HS 300/Alt
1100 N Carrier Pkwy 75050 972-522-2950
Suzy Meyer, prin. Fax 522-2999
Dubiski Career HS Vo/Tech
2990 S State Highway 161 75052 972-343-7800
Apryl Baylor, prin. Fax 343-7899
Fannin MS 700/6-8
301 NE 28th St 75050 972-262-8668
Whitney Carlisle, prin. Fax 343-4799
Grand Prairie Early College HS 9-12
102 High School Dr 75050
Micah Taylor, chncllr.
Grand Prairie Fine Arts Academy 700/6-12
102 High School Dr 75050 972-237-5603
Maria Schell, prin. Fax 343-6399
Grand Prairie SHS 1,900/9-12
101 High School Dr 75050 972-809-5711
Lorimer Arendse, prin. Fax 809-5775
HOPE Academy 8-8
1502 College St 75050 972-522-3400
Suzy Meyer, prin. Fax 343-3499
Jackson MS 1,100/6-8
3504 Corn Valley Rd 75052 972-343-7500
Kristin Booth, prin. Fax 343-7599
Johnson DAEP Alt
650 Stonewall Dr 75052 972-262-7244
Kerry Rapier, prin. Fax 264-9479
Reagan MS 700/6-8
4616 Bardin Rd 75052 972-522-7300
Chris Bayer, prin. Fax 522-7399
South Grand Prairie Early College HS 9-12
305 W Warrior Trl 75052
Joanna Slaton, chncllr.
South Grand Prairie HS 9th Grade Campus 800/9-9
305 W Warrior Trl 75052 972-264-1769
Donnie Bartlett, prin. Fax 642-7902
South Grand Prairie SHS 2,300/10-12
301 W Warrior Trl 75052 972-343-1500
Donna Grant, prin. Fax 642-7902
Truman MS 600/6-8
1501 Coffeyville Trl 75052 972-641-7676
Letycia Fowler, prin. Fax 522-3999
Young Mens Leadership Academy 1,000/6-8
2205 SE 4th St 75051 972-264-8651
Chadd Johnson, prin. Fax 522-3699
Young Womens Leadership Academy 1,100/6-12
1204 E Marshall Dr 75051 972-343-7400
Jennifer Oliver, prin. Fax 343-7499

---

Arlington Career Institute Post-Sec.
901 E Avenue K 75050 972-647-1607
Jones Beauty College #2 Post-Sec.
311 W Pioneer Pkwy 75051 972-237-1988
Lincoln College of Technology Post-Sec.
2915 Alouette Dr 75052 972-660-5701

**Grand Saline, Van Zandt, Pop. 3,102**
Grand Saline ISD 1,100/PK-12
400 Stadium Dr 75140 903-962-7546
Trish Elliott, supt. Fax 962-7464
www.grandsalineisd.net
Grand Saline HS 300/9-12
500 Stadium Dr 75140 903-962-7533
Ricky LaPrade, prin. Fax 962-7482
Grand Saline MS 300/6-8
400 Stadium Dr 75140 903-962-7537
Brad Swain, prin. Fax 962-7474

**Grandview, Johnson, Pop. 1,542**
Grandview ISD 900/PK-12
PO Box 310 76050 817-866-2450
Joe Perrin, supt. Fax 866-3351
www.gvisd.org
Grandview HS 300/9-12
PO Box 310 76050 817-866-3320
Kirby Basham, prin. Fax 866-2645
Grandview JHS 300/6-8
PO Box 310 76050 817-866-2492
Jeff Hudson, prin. Fax 866-3912

**Granger, Williamson, Pop. 1,404**
Granger ISD 400/PK-12
PO Box 578 76530 512-859-2613
Randy Willis, supt. Fax 859-2446
www.grangerisd.net
Granger S 400/PK-12
PO Box 578 76530 512-859-2173
Mike Abbott, prin. Fax 859-2446

**Grapeland, Houston, Pop. 1,478**
Grapeland ISD 500/PK-12
PO Box 249 75844 936-687-4619
Gregg Spivey, supt. Fax 687-4624
www.grapelandisd.net
Grapeland HS 200/9-12
PO Box 249 75844 936-687-4661
Rick Frauenberger, prin. Fax 687-9739
Grapeland JHS 100/6-8
PO Box 249 75844 936-687-2351
Rick Frauenberger, admin. Fax 687-5285

**Grapevine, Tarrant, Pop. 45,499**
Grapevine-Colleyville ISD 13,500/PK-12
3051 Ira E Woods Ave 76051 817-251-5200
Dr. Robin Ryan, supt. Fax 251-5375
www.gcisd-k12.org
Cross Timbers MS 800/6-8
2301 Pool Rd 76051 817-251-5320
Lisa Dunn, prin. Fax 424-4296
Grapevine HS 2,100/9-12
3223 Mustang Dr 76051 817-251-5210
David Denning, prin. Fax 481-5957
Grapevine MS 800/6-8
301 Pony Pkwy 76051 817-251-5660
Linda Young, prin. Fax 424-1626
Other Schools – See Colleyville, Hurst

---

Grapevine Faith Christian S 800/PK-12
730 E Worth St 76051 817-442-9144
Ed Smith Ed.D., pres. Fax 442-9904
Novus Academy 100/1-12
204 N Dooley 76051 817-488-4555
Kathleen Edwards M.Ed., head sch Fax 488-4533

**Greenville, Hunt, Pop. 25,073**
Greenville ISD 4,700/PK-12
4004 Moulton St 75401 903-457-2500
Donald Jefferies, supt. Fax 457-2504
www.greenvilleisd.com
Greenville HS 1,000/9-12
3515 Lions Lair Rd 75402 903-457-2550
Heath Jarvis, prin. Fax 455-5158
Greenville MS 700/7-8
3611 Texas St 75401 903-457-2620
David Gish, prin. Fax 457-2628
Houston Education Center 100/Alt
3923 Henry St 75401 903-457-2688
Chip Gregory, prin. Fax 457-2689

Greenville Christian S 200/PK-12
8420 Jack Finney Blvd 75402 903-454-1111
Steven Bowers, hdmstr. Fax 455-8470

**Groesbeck, Limestone, Pop. 4,255**
Groesbeck ISD 1,700/PK-12
PO Box 559 76642 254-729-4100
Dr. Harold Ramm, supt. Fax 729-5167
www.groesbeckisd.net
Alternative Learning Center 50/Alt
PO Box 559 76642 254-729-4105
Jim Rosebrock, prin. Fax 729-3965
Groesbeck HS 500/9-12
1202 N Ellis St 76642 254-729-4101
Jim Rosebrock, prin. Fax 729-5458
Groesbeck MS 200/7-8
410 Elwood Enge Dr 76642 254-729-4102
Dayne Duncan, prin. Fax 729-8763

**Groom, Carson, Pop. 567**
Groom ISD 100/PK-12
PO Box 598 79039 806-248-7557
Jay Lamb, supt. Fax 248-7949
www.groomisd.net
Groom S 100/PK-12
PO Box 598 79039 806-248-7474
Jay Lamb, admin. Fax 248-7949

**Groves, Jefferson, Pop. 15,978**
Port Neches-Groves ISD
Supt. — See Port Neches
Groves MS 500/6-8
5201 Wilson St 77619 409-962-0225
James Arnett, prin. Fax 963-1898

**Groveton, Trinity, Pop. 1,043**
Centerville ISD 100/PK-12
10327 N State Highway 94 75845 936-642-1597
Mark Brown, supt. Fax 642-2810
www.centervilleisd.net
Centerville JSHS 50/7-12
10327 N State Highway 94 75845 936-642-1597
Andja Sailer, prin. Fax 642-2810

Groveton ISD 700/PK-12
PO Box 728 75845 936-642-1473
Don Hamilton, supt. Fax 642-1628
www.grovetonisd.net
Groveton JSHS 400/6-12
PO Box 700 75845 936-642-1128
Bryan Finch, prin. Fax 642-1616

**Grulla, Starr, Pop. 1,621**
Rio Grande City ISD
Supt. — See Rio Grande City
Grulla MS 800/6-8
PO Box 338 78548 956-487-5558
Clarissa Ibanez, prin. Fax 487-5633

**Gruver, Hansford, Pop. 1,190**
Gruver ISD 400/PK-12
PO Box 650 79040 806-733-2001
Troy Seagler, supt. Fax 733-5416
www.gruverisd.net
Gruver HS 100/9-12
PO Box 747 79040 806-733-2477
Nita Hudson, prin. Fax 733-2596
Gruver JHS 100/5-8
PO Box 709 79040 806-733-2081
Wade Callaway, prin. Fax 733-5523

**Gunter, Grayson, Pop. 1,485**
Gunter ISD 800/PK-12
PO Box 109 75058 903-433-4750
Dr. Jill Siler, supt. Fax 433-1053
www.gunterisd.org
Gunter HS 300/9-12
PO Box 109 75058 903-433-1542
Chris Dodd, prin. Fax 433-1492
Gunter MS 200/5-8
PO Box 109 75058 903-433-1545
Sara McCarty, prin. Fax 433-9306

**Gustine, Comanche, Pop. 473**
Gustine ISD 200/PK-12
503 W Main St 76455 325-667-7303
Ken Baugh, supt. Fax 667-7281
www.gustine.esc14.net/
Gustine S 200/PK-12
503 W Main St 76455 325-667-7303
Patti Blue, prin. Fax 667-0203

**Guthrie, King, Pop. 160**
Guthrie Common SD 100/PK-12
PO Box 70 79236 806-596-4466
Kevin Chisum, supt. Fax 596-4519
www.guthriejags.com
Guthrie S 100/PK-12
PO Box 70 79236 806-596-4466
Jodie Reel, prin. Fax 596-4519

**Hale Center, Hale, Pop. 2,231**
Hale Center ISD 700/PK-12
PO Box 1210 79041 806-839-2451
Carl Krug, supt. Fax 839-2195
www.hcisdowls.net
Carr MS 200/5-8
PO Box 1210 79041 806-839-2141
Mike Wiley, prin. Fax 839-4417
Hale Center HS 200/9-12
PO Box 1210 79041 806-839-2452
Alan Berry, prin. Fax 839-2059

**Hallettsville, Lavaca, Pop. 2,529**
Hallettsville ISD 900/PK-12
PO Box 368 77964 361-798-2242
Dr. JoAnn Bludau, supt. Fax 798-5902
www.hisdbrahmas.org
Hallettsville HS 300/9-12
PO Box 368 77964 361-798-2242
Darrin Bickham, prin. Fax 798-9297
Hallettsville JHS 300/5-8
PO Box 368 77964 361-798-2242
Sophie Teltschik, prin. Fax 798-3573

Sacred Heart S 300/PK-12
313 S Texana St 77964 361-798-4251
David Smolik, prin. Fax 798-4970

**Hallsville, Harrison, Pop. 3,526**
Hallsville ISD 3,700/PK-12
PO Box 810 75650 903-668-5990
Jim Dunlap, supt. Fax 668-5990
www.hisd.com
Hallsville DAEP Alt
PO Box 810 75650 903-668-5990
Jesse Casey, prin. Fax 668-5990
Hallsville HS 1,300/9-12
PO Box 810 75650 903-668-5990
John Martin, prin. Fax 668-5990
Hallsville JHS 700/6-8
PO Box 810 75650 903-668-5990
Lindsay Slaten, prin. Fax 668-5990

**Haltom City, Tarrant, Pop. 41,719**
Birdville ISD 23,700/PK-12
6125 E Belknap St 76117 817-847-5700
Darrell Brown Ph.D., supt. Fax 838-7261
www.birdvilleschools.net
Haltom HS 2,500/9-12
5501 Haltom Rd 76137 817-547-6000
David Hamilton, prin. Fax 547-6352
Haltom MS 800/6-8
5000 Hires Ln 76117 817-547-4000
Jill Belzer, prin. Fax 831-5778
North Oaks MS 600/6-8
4800 Jordan Park Dr 76117 817-547-4600
Bob Koerner Ed.D., prin. Fax 581-5352
Shannon HS 50/Alt
6010 Walker St 76117 817-547-5400
Silvia Ura Lugo, prin. Fax 831-5847
Other Schools – See North Richland Hills, Richland Hills, Watauga

**Hamilton, Hamilton, Pop. 3,076**
Hamilton ISD 800/PK-12
400 S College St 76531 254-386-3149
Clay Tarpley, supt. Fax 386-8885
hamiltonisd.org
Hamilton HS 200/9-12
611 S College St 76531 254-386-8167
Louis Lowe, prin. Fax 386-4677
Hamilton JHS 200/6-8
400 S College St 76531 254-386-8168
Mona Gloff, prin. Fax 386-8885

**Hamlin, Jones, Pop. 2,109**
Hamlin ISD 500/PK-12
PO Box 338 79520 325-576-2722
Brock Cartwright, supt. Fax 576-2152
www.hamlin.esc14.net
Hamlin JSHS 100/7-12
450 SW Avenue F 79520 325-576-3624
Nick McCollister, prin. Fax 576-3926

**Hamshire, Jefferson**
Hamshire-Fannett ISD 1,700/PK-12
PO Box 223 77622 409-243-2133
Pamela Lechler, supt. Fax 243-3437
www.hfisd.net
Hamshire-Fannett HS 500/9-12
PO Box 223 77622 409-243-2512
Jon Burris, prin. Fax 243-2518
Other Schools – See Beaumont

**Happy, Swisher, Pop. 670**
Happy ISD 200/PK-12
PO Box 458 79042 806-558-5331
Wade Wesley, supt. Fax 558-2070
www.happyisd.net
Happy HS 100/7-12
PO Box 458 79042 806-558-5311
Ray Keith, prin. Fax 558-4301

**Hardin, Liberty, Pop. 804**
Hardin ISD 1,200/PK-12
PO Box 330 77561 936-298-2112
Bob Parker, supt. Fax 298-9161
www.hardinisd.net/
Hardin HS 300/9-12
PO Box 330 77561 936-298-2118
Richard Ressler, prin. Fax 298-3612
Hardin JHS 200/7-8
PO Box 330 77561 936-298-2054
Julia Hall, prin. Fax 298-3264

**Harker Heights, Bell, Pop. 25,289**
Killeen ISD
Supt. — See Killeen
Eastern Hills MS 800/6-8
300 Indian Trl 76548 254-336-1100
Jeremy Key, prin. Fax 336-1115
Harker Heights HS 2,300/9-12
1001 E FM 2410 Rd 76548 254-336-0800
Larry Brazzil, prin. Fax 336-0829
Union Grove MS 800/6-8
101 E Iowa Dr 76548 254-336-6580
Dagmar Harris, prin. Fax 336-6593

**Harleton, Harrison**
Harleton ISD 700/PK-12
PO Box 510 75651 903-777-2372
Dr. Craig Coleman, supt. Fax 777-2406
www.harletonisd.net/
Harleton HS 200/9-12
PO Box 710 75651 903-777-2711
Tonya Knowlton, prin. Fax 777-2547
Harleton JHS 200/6-8
PO Box 610 75651 903-777-3010
Paul Davis, prin. Fax 777-3009

**Harlingen, Cameron, Pop. 64,588**
Harlingen Consolidated ISD 18,400/PK-12
407 N 77 Sunshine Strip 78550 956-430-9500
Dr. Arturo Cavazos, supt. Fax 430-9514
www.hcisd.org
Cano Freshman Academy 9-9
1701 W Lozano St 78550 956-430-4900
Vivian Bauer, prin. Fax 427-3772
Coakley MS 800/6-8
1402 S 6th St 78550 956-427-3000
Pedro Sanchez, prin. Fax 427-3006
Early College HS 300/9-12
2510 Pecan St Bldg R 78550 956-430-9690
Fax 430-9693
Gutierrez MS 800/6-8
3205 Wilson Rd 78552 956-430-4400
Mike Reyes, prin. Fax 430-4480
Harlingen HS 2,500/9-12
1201 Marshall St 78550 956-427-3600
Imelda Munivez, prin. Fax 427-3792
Harlingen HS South 2,000/9-12
1701 Dixieland Rd 78552 956-427-3800
Fernando Reyes, admin. Fax 427-3995
Harlingen S of Health Professions 8-9
2302 N 21st St 78550 956-430-4078
Tina Garza, prin. Fax 430-9717
Keys Academy 200/Alt
2809 N 7th St 78550 956-427-3220
Dr. Pamela Flores, prin. Fax 427-3223
Memorial MS 800/6-8
1901 Rio Hondo Rd 78550 956-427-3020
Alex Gonzalez, prin. Fax 427-3024
Secondary Education Alternative Center 50/Alt
1310 Sam Houston Dr 78550 956-427-3210
Daniel Araiza, prin. Fax 430-4487
Vela MS 800/6-8
801 S Palm Blvd 78552 956-427-3479
Tony Gonzales, prin. Fax 427-3549
Vernon MS 800/6-8
125 S 13th St 78550 956-427-3040
Gracie Gutierrez, prin. Fax 427-3046

Marine Military Academy 200/8-12
320 Iwo Jima Blvd 78550 956-423-6006
Col R. Glenn Hill, supt. Fax 421-9273
Texas State Technical College Post-Sec.
1902 Loop 499 N 78550 956-364-4000
University of Cosmetology Arts & Science Post-Sec.
913 N 13th St 78550 956-412-1212

**Harper, Gillespie, Pop. 1,183**
Harper ISD 600/PK-12
PO Box 68 78631 830-864-4044
Chris Stevenson, supt. Fax 864-4060
www.harper.txed.net/
Harper HS 200/9-12
PO Box 68 78631 830-864-4044
Dean Eckert, prin. Fax 864-4748
Harper MS 100/5-8
PO Box 68 78631 830-864-4044
Bonnie Stewart, prin. Fax 864-4748

**Harrold, Wilbarger**
Harrold ISD 100/K-12
18106 Stewart St 76364 940-886-2213
David Thweatt, supt. Fax 886-2215
www.harroldisd.net/
Harrold S 100/K-12
18106 Stewart St 76364 940-886-2213
Craig Templeton, prin. Fax 886-2215

**Hart, Castro, Pop. 1,112**
Hart ISD 300/PK-12
PO Box 490 79043 806-938-2143
Ken Rosser, supt. Fax 938-2610
www.hartisd.net
Hart JSHS 100/6-12
PO Box 490 79043 806-938-2141
Ramona Neudorf, prin. Fax 938-2610

**Hartley, Hartley, Pop. 536**
Hartley ISD 200/PK-12
PO Box 408 79044 806-365-4458
Scott Vincent, supt. Fax 365-4459
www.hartleyisd.net
Hartley S 200/PK-12
PO Box 408 79044 806-365-4458
Scott Vincent, supt. Fax 365-4459

**Haskell, Haskell, Pop. 3,278**
Haskell Consolidated ISD 700/PK-12
PO Box 937 79521 940-864-2602
Bill Alcorn, supt. Fax 864-8096
www.haskell.esc14.net/
Haskell HS 200/9-12
PO Box 937 79521 940-864-8535
Jeff York, prin. Fax 864-3977
Haskell JHS 100/6-8
PO Box 937 79521 940-864-5981
Kent Colley, prin. Fax 864-5982

Paint Creek ISD 200/PK-12
4485 FM 600 79521 940-864-2868
Rick Moeller, supt. Fax 863-4488
www.paintcreek.esc14.net
Paint Creek S 200/PK-12
4485 FM 600 79521 940-864-2868
Roy Gardner, prin. Fax 863-4488

**Haslet, Tarrant, Pop. 1,481**
Northwest ISD
Supt. — See Justin
Wilson MS 6-8
14250 Sendera Ranch Blvd 76052 817-698-7900
Mike Blankenship, prin. Fax 698-7970

**Hawkins, Wood, Pop. 1,237**
Hawkins ISD 800/PK-12
PO Box 1430 75765 903-769-2181
Dan Rose, supt. Fax 769-0505
www.hawkinsisd.org
Hawkins HS 200/9-12
PO Box 1430 75765 903-769-0571
Cindy Thatcher, prin. Fax 769-0573
Hawkins MS 200/6-8
PO Box 1430 75765 903-769-0552
David Ledkins, prin. Fax 769-0583

Jarvis Christian College Post-Sec.
Highway 80 E PR 7631 75765 903-730-4890

**Hawley, Jones, Pop. 626**
Hawley ISD 700/PK-12
PO Box 440 79525 325-537-2214
Jimmy J. Burns, supt. Fax 537-2265
www.hawley.esc14.net
Hawley HS 200/9-12
PO Box 440 79525 325-537-2722
Nikki Grisham, prin. Fax 537-2265
Hawley MS 200/6-8
PO Box 440 79525 325-537-2070
Chad Hoffman, prin. Fax 537-2265

**Hearne, Robertson, Pop. 4,418**
Hearne ISD 1,000/PK-12
900 Wheelock St 77859 979-279-3200
Henry Lind, supt. Fax 279-3631
www.hearneisd.com
Hearne HS 300/9-12
1201 W Brown St 77859 979-279-2332
Joslyn Pierce, prin. Fax 279-8006
Hearne JHS 100/7-8
1201B W Brown St 77859 979-279-2449
Jannie Mitchell, prin. Fax 279-8033

**Heath, Rockwall, Pop. 6,837**
Rockwall ISD
Supt. — See Rockwall
Rockwall-Heath HS 2,100/9-12
801 Laurence Dr 75032 972-772-2474
Dr. Tom Maglisceau, prin. Fax 698-2608

Fulton S 200/PK-12
1623 Laurence Dr 75032 972-772-4445

**Hebbronville, Jim Hogg, Pop. 4,553**
Jim Hogg County ISD 1,100/PK-12
PO Box 880 78361 361-527-3203
Pedro Lopez, supt. Fax 527-4928
www.jhcisdpk12.org
Hebbronville HS 300/9-12
PO Box 880 78361 361-527-3203
Eric Salinas, prin. Fax 527-5989
Hebbronville JHS 200/6-8
PO Box 880 78361 361-527-3203
Ray Garza, prin. Fax 527-5986

**Hedley, Donley, Pop. 328**
Hedley ISD 100/PK-12
PO Box 69 79237 806-856-5323
Colby Waldrop, supt. Fax 856-5372
www.hedleyisd.net
Hedley S 100/PK-12
PO Box 69 79237 806-856-5323
Reida Penman, prin. Fax 856-5372

**Helotes, Bexar, Pop. 7,218**
Northside ISD
Supt. — See San Antonio
O'Connor HS 3,100/9-12
12221 Leslie Rd 78023 210-397-4800
Jacqueline Horras, prin. Fax 695-4804

**Hemphill, Sabine, Pop. 1,176**
Hemphill ISD 900/PK-12
PO Box 1950 75948 409-787-3371
Reese Briggs, supt. Fax 787-4005
www.hemphill.esc7.net
Hemphill HS 300/9-12
PO Box 1950 75948 409-787-3371
Marc Griffin, prin. Fax 787-1259
Hemphill MS 300/5-8
PO Box 1950 75948 409-787-3371
Jeremy McDaniel, prin. Fax 787-4005

**Hempstead, Waller, Pop. 5,718**
Hempstead ISD 1,500/PK-12
PO Box 1007 77445 979-826-3304
Dr. Angela Gutsch, supt. Fax 826-5510
www.hempsteadisd.org
Hempstead HS 400/9-12
PO Box 1007 77445 979-826-5590
Eric Mullens, prin. Fax 826-4779
Hempstead MS 300/6-8
PO Box 1007 77445 979-826-5570
Lance Harjo, prin. Fax 826-5583

**Henderson, Rusk, Pop. 13,557**
Carlisle ISD 700/PK-12
8960 FM 13 W 75654 903-861-3801
Michael Payne, supt. Fax 861-3932
www.carl.sprnet.org/cisd2.htm
Carlisle HS 200/9-12
8960 FM 13 W 75654 903-861-3811
Sarah Baker, prin. Fax 861-0100
Carlisle JHS 200/6-8
8960 FM 13 W 75654 903-861-3811
Jennifer Gholson, prin. Fax 861-0100
Henderson ISD 3,400/PK-12
PO Box 728 75653 903-655-5000
Keith Boles, supt. Fax 657-9271
www.hendersonisd.org/
Henderson HS 900/9-12
PO Box 728 75653 903-655-5500
Terry Everitt, prin. Fax 657-7604
Henderson MS 800/6-8
PO Box 728 75653 903-655-5400
Hardy Dotson, prin. Fax 657-6499

Full Armor Christian Academy 100/K-12
PO Box 2035 75653 903-655-8489
Tricia Hall, head sch Fax 657-8267

**Henrietta, Clay, Pop. 3,103**
Henrietta ISD 900/PK-12
1801 E Crafton St 76365 940-720-7900
Jeff McClure, supt. Fax 538-7505
www.henrietta-isd.net
Henrietta HS 300/9-12
1700 E Crafton St 76365 940-720-7930
Gary Parrish, prin. Fax 538-7535
Henrietta JHS 200/6-8
308 E Gilbert St 76365 940-720-7920
Randy Zamzow, prin. Fax 538-7525
Midway ISD 100/PK-12
12142 State Highway 148 S 76365 940-476-2215
Alan Umholtz, supt. Fax 476-2226
www2.esc9.net/midway
Midway S 100/PK-12
12142 State Highway 148 S 76365 940-476-2222
Cherry Johnston, prin. Fax 476-2226

**Hereford, Deaf Smith, Pop. 15,284**
Hereford ISD 4,000/PK-12
601 N 25 Mile Ave 79045 806-363-7600
Dr. Kelli Moulton, supt. Fax 363-7647
www.herefordisd.net
Hereford Center for Accelerated Learning 50/Alt
239 Avenue H 79045 806-363-7720
Tony Barker, prin.
Hereford HS 1,200/9-12
200 Avenue F 79045 806-363-7620
Richard Sauceda, prin. Fax 363-7688
Hereford Preparatory Academy 300/8-8
704 La Plata St 79045 806-363-7740
Rene Cano, prin. Fax 363-7699

**Hermleigh, Scurry, Pop. 343**
Hermleigh ISD 200/PK-12
8010 Business 84 H 79526 325-863-2772
Ronnie Roemisch, supt. Fax 863-2713
www.hermleigh.esc14.net
Hermleigh S 200/PK-12
8010 Business 84 H 79526 325-863-2482
Eddie Richardson, prin. Fax 863-2713

**Hewitt, McLennan, Pop. 13,309**
Midway ISD
Supt. — See Woodway
Midway MS 1,100/7-8
800 N Hewitt Dr 76643 254-761-5680
Dr. Herbert Cox, prin. Fax 761-5775

**Hico, Hamilton, Pop. 1,369**
Hico ISD 400/PK-12
PO Box 218 76457 254-796-2181
Jon Hartgraves, supt. Fax 796-2446
www.hico-isd.net
Hico HS 200/6-12
PO Box 218 76457 254-796-2184
Shelli Stegall, prin. Fax 796-2446

**Hidalgo, Hidalgo, Pop. 11,192**
Hidalgo ISD 3,300/PK-12
PO Box 8220 78557 956-843-4401
Edward Blaha, supt. Fax 843-3343
www.hidalgo-isd.com
Diaz JHS 700/6-8
PO Box 8220 78557 956-843-4350
Sara Paz, prin. Fax 843-3198
Hidalgo Academy 50/Alt
PO Box 8220 78557 956-843-4390
Gregorio Solano, prin. Fax 843-3339
Hidalgo Early College HS 1,000/9-12
PO Box 8220 78557 956-843-4300
Judith Dimas, prin. Fax 843-3322

**Higgins, Lipscomb, Pop. 392**
Higgins ISD 100/PK-12
PO Box 218 79046 806-852-2631
Steve James, supt. Fax 852-3502
www.higginsisd.net
Higgins S 100/PK-12
PO Box 218 79046 806-852-2631
Steve James, supt. Fax 852-3502

**High Island, Galveston**
High Island ISD 200/PK-12
PO Box 246 77623 409-286-5317
D'Ann Cathriner-Vonderau Ed.D., supt. Fax 286-5351
www.highislandisd.com
High Island HS 100/9-12
PO Box 246 77623 409-286-5314
Kathy Smith, prin. Fax 286-2120
High Island MS 50/6-8
PO Box 246 77623 409-286-5314
Kathy Smith, prin. Fax 286-2120

**Highlands, Harris, Pop. 7,443**
Goose Creek Consolidated ISD
Supt. — See Baytown
Highlands JHS 1,100/6-8
1212 E Wallisville Rd 77562 281-420-4695
Gary Guy, prin. Fax 426-4301
POINT Alternative Center Alt
401 Jones Rd 77562 281-240-4630
Gary Allen, prin. Fax 426-2680

Chinquapin Preparatory S 200/6-12
2615 E Wallisville Rd 77562 281-426-5551

**Highland Village, Denton, Pop. 14,764**
Lewisville ISD
Supt. — See Flower Mound
Briarhill MS 1,000/6-8
2100 Briarhill Blvd 75077 469-713-5975
Chris Mattingly, prin. Fax 350-9167

**Hillsboro, Hill, Pop. 8,341**
Hillsboro ISD 2,000/PK-12
121 E Franklin St 76645 254-582-8585
Vicki Adams, supt. Fax 582-4165
www.hillsboroisd.org
Hillsboro HS 500/9-12
1600 Abbott Ave 76645 254-582-4100
Keith Hannah, prin. Fax 582-4108
Hillsboro JHS 300/7-8
210 E Walnut St 76645 254-582-4120
Cathryn Patterson, prin. Fax 582-4122

Hill College Post-Sec.
112 Lamar Dr 76645 254-659-7500

**Hitchcock, Galveston, Pop. 6,879**
Hitchcock ISD 800/PK-12
7801 Neville Ave 77563 409-316-6545
Carla Vickroy, supt. Fax 986-5141
www.hitchcockisd.org
Crosby MS 200/5-8
6625 FM 2004 Rd 77563 409-316-6542
Larry Allen, prin. Fax 986-9254
Hitchcock HS 300/9-12
6629 FM 2004 Rd 77563 409-316-6544
Kellie Edmundson, prin. Fax 986-9339

**Holland, Bell, Pop. 1,111**
Holland ISD 600/PK-12
PO Box 217 76534 254-657-0175
Cindy Gunn, supt. Fax 657-0172
www.hollandisd.org
Holland HS 200/9-12
PO Box 217 76534 254-657-2523
Britt Gordon, prin. Fax 657-2250
Holland MS 200/6-8
PO Box 217 76534 254-657-2224
Leah Smith, prin. Fax 657-2872

**Holliday, Archer, Pop. 1,747**
Holliday ISD 900/PK-12
PO Box 689 76366 940-586-1281
Dr. Kevin Dyes, supt. Fax 586-1492
www.hollidayisd.net
Holliday HS 300/9-12
PO Box 947 76366 940-586-1624
Shannon Owen, prin. Fax 586-9501
Holliday MS 200/6-8
PO Box 977 76366 940-586-1314
Kelly Carver, prin. Fax 586-4480

**Hondo, Medina, Pop. 8,749**
Hondo ISD 2,200/PK-12
PO Box 308 78861 830-426-3027
Dr. A'Lann Truelock, supt. Fax 426-7683
www.hondoisd.net
Hondo HS 600/9-12
2603 Avenue H 78861 830-426-3341
James Angst, prin. Fax 426-7690
McDowell MS 500/6-8
1602 27th St S 78861 830-426-2261
Steve Alvarado, prin. Fax 426-7624

**Honey Grove, Fannin, Pop. 1,640**
Honey Grove ISD 600/PK-12
1206 17th St 75446 903-378-2264
Todd Morrison, supt. Fax 378-2991
www.honeygroveisd.net/
Honey Grove HS 200/9-12
1206 17th St 75446 903-378-2264
Tammy Mariani, prin. Fax 378-3050
Honey Grove MS 100/6-8
1206 17th St 75446 903-378-2264
Lee Frost, prin. Fax 378-2095

**Hooks, Bowie, Pop. 2,693**
Hooks ISD 900/PK-12
100 E 5th St 75561 903-547-6077
Ronnie Thompson, supt. Fax 547-2943
www.hooksisd.net/
Hooks HS 300/9-12
401 E Avenue A 75561 903-547-2215
Shane Krueger, prin. Fax 547-6514
Hooks JHS 200/5-8
3921 FM 560 75561 903-547-2568
Craig Mahar, prin. Fax 547-2595

**Houston, Harris, Pop. 2,071,912**
Aldine ISD 63,600/PK-12
14910 Aldine Westfield Rd 77032 281-449-1011
Dr. Wanda Bamberg, supt. Fax 449-4911
www.aldineisd.org
Aldine MS 800/7-8
14908 Aldine Westfield Rd 77032 281-985-6580
Marcus Pruitt, prin. Fax 985-6480
Aldine Ninth Grade S 900/9-9
10650 North Fwy 77037 281-878-6800
Jennifer Merryman, prin. Fax 878-6824
Aldine SHS 2,100/10-12
11101 Airline Dr 77037 281-448-5231
Walter Stewart, prin. Fax 878-0641
Carver Magnet HS 900/9-12
2100 S Victory Dr 77088 281-878-0310
Anthony Watkins, prin. Fax 591-8579
COMPASS 200/Alt
1617 Lauder Rd 77039 281-985-6685
James Metcalf, prin. Fax 985-6688
Davis Ninth Grade S 9-9
12211 Ella Blvd 77067 281-873-1800
Heather Kirk, prin. Fax 539-4044

Davis SHS 10-12
12525 Ella Blvd 77067 281-539-4070
Thomas Colwell, prin. Fax 539-4075
Drew Academy 700/7-8
1910 W Little York Rd 77091 281-878-0360
Earnest Washington, prin. Fax 447-4694
Eisenhower Ninth Grade S 1,000/9-9
3550 W Gulf Bank Rd 77088 281-878-7700
LaTonia Amerson, prin. Fax 878-7736
Eisenhower SHS 2,200/10-12
7922 Antoine Dr 77088 281-878-0900
Benjamin Ibarra, prin. Fax 448-2936
Grantham Academy 1,000/7-8
13300 Chrisman Rd 77039 281-985-6590
Jessica Scott, prin. Fax 985-6595
Hall Center for Education 400/Alt
15014 Aldine Westfield Rd 77032 281-985-7446
Anthony Watkins, prin. Fax 985-7453
Hambrick MS 1,000/7-8
4600 Aldine Mail Rd 77039 281-985-6570
Rebecca Hoyt, prin. Fax 442-9036
Hoffman MS 700/7-8
6101 W Little York Rd 77091 713-613-7670
Rosalyn Sweat, prin. Fax 613-7675
Lewis MS 800/7-8
21255 W Hardy Rd 77073 281-209-8257
Cassandra Bell, prin. Fax 209-8267
MacArthur Ninth Grade S 1,000/9-9
12111 Gloger St 77039 281-985-7400
D'Ann Delgado, prin. Fax 985-7423
MacArthur SHS 2,400/10-12
4400 Aldine Mail Rd 77039 281-985-6330
Craig Mullenix, prin. Fax 985-6294
Nimitz Ninth Grade S 1,000/9-9
2425 WW Thorne Blvd 77073 281-209-8200
Tonya Landry, prin. Fax 209-8220
Nimitz SHS 2,400/10-12
2005 WW Thorne Blvd 77073 281-443-7480
Dr. Crystal Watson-Barrow, prin. Fax 233-4331
Plummer MS 900/7-8
11429 Spears Rd 77067 281-539-4000
Andrea Cain, prin. Fax 539-4017
Shotwell MS 1,000/7-8
6515 Trail Valley Way 77086 281-878-0960
Shirley Seals, prin. Fax 591-8564
Stovall MS 1,100/7-8
11201 Airline Dr 77037 281-878-0670
Elsa Wright, prin. Fax 448-0636
Victory Early College HS 400/9-12
4141 Victory Dr 77088 281-810-5675
Phyllis Cormier, prin. Fax 810-5698
Other Schools – See Humble

Alief ISD 45,100/PK-12
4250 Cook Rd 77072 281-498-8110
H.D. Chambers, supt. Fax 498-8730
www.aliefisd.net
Albright MS 1,200/7-8
6315 Winkleman Rd 77083 281-983-8411
Lori Wyatt, prin. Fax 983-8443
Alief Early College HS 300/9-12
2811 Hayes Rd Ste A 77082 281-988-3010
Beth Smith, prin. Fax 988-3066
Alief Learning Center Alt
4427 Belle Park Dr 77072 281-983-8000
Mary Wilson, prin. Fax 983-7701
Alief MS 900/6-8
4415 Cook Rd 77072 281-983-8422
Nancy Trent, prin. Fax 983-8053
Alief Taylor HS 2,800/9-12
7555 Howell Sugar Land Rd 77083 281-988-3500
Mary Williams, prin. Fax 561-7214
Crossroads Alternative Technology S Alt
12360 Bear Ram Rd 77072 281-988-3266
Tremayne Wickliffe, prin. Fax 988-3277
Elsik HS 2,800/10-12
12601 High Star Dr 77072 281-988-3150
Hilda Rodriguez, prin. Fax 530-7058
Elsik Ninth Grade Center 1,200/9-9
6767 S Dairy Ashford Rd 77072 281-988-3239
Vinson Lewis, prin. Fax 988-3319
Hastings HS 2,700/10-12
4410 Cook Rd 77072 281-498-8110
Patrick Cherry, prin. Fax 561-5763
Hastings Ninth Grade Center 1,200/9-9
6750 Cook Rd 77072 281-988-3139
Janie Saxton, prin. Fax 988-3419
Holub MS 900/7-8
9515 S Dairy Ashford Rd 77099 281-983-8433
Pauline Beckley, prin. Fax 983-8398
Kerr HS 800/9-12
8150 Howell Sugar Land Rd 77083 281-983-8484
Greg Freeman, prin. Fax 983-8014
Killough MS 1,000/7-8
7600 Synott Rd 77083 281-983-8444
Bryan Brown, prin. Fax 983-8067
O'Donnell MS 1,300/6-8
14041 Alief Clodine Rd 77082 281-495-6000
Amador Velasquez, prin. Fax 568-5029
Olle MS 1,000/7-8
9200 Boone Rd 77099 281-983-8455
Nelda Billescas, prin. Fax 983-8077
S.O.A.R. Adult
12360 Bear Ram Rd 77072 281-988-3266
Tremayne Wickliffe, prin. Fax 988-3277

Channelview ISD
Supt. — See Channelview
Aguirre JHS 6-8
15726 Wallisville Rd 77049 281-860-3300
Eric Lathan, prin. Fax 860-3320

Clear Creek ISD
Supt. — See League City
Clear Lake HS 2,700/9-12
2929 Bay Area Blvd 77058 281-284-1900
Karen Engle, prin. Fax 284-1905
Clear Lake IS 1,000/6-8
15545 El Camino Real 77062 281-284-3200
Michael Alvarez, prin. Fax 284-3205

Space Center IS 1,100/6-8
17400 Saturn Ln 77058 281-284-3300
Lonnie Leal, prin. Fax 284-3305

Cypress-Fairbanks ISD 104,200/PK-12
PO Box 692003 77269 281-897-4000
Dr. Mark Henry, supt. Fax 897-4125
www.cfisd.net
Adaptive Behavior Center Alt
12508 Windfern Rd 77064 281-897-4174
Chad Perry, dir. Fax 517-2884
Alternative Learning Center - East Alt
12508 Windfern Rd 77064 281-897-4171
Laurie Snyder, prin. Fax 897-4170
Aragon MS 1,700/6-8
16823 West Rd 77095 281-856-5100
Maria Mamaux, prin. Fax 856-5105
Bleyl MS 1,600/6-8
10800 Mills Rd 77070 281-897-4340
Stacia Carew, prin. Fax 897-4353
Campbell MS 1,300/6-8
11415 Bobcat Rd 77064 281-897-4300
Laura Perry, prin. Fax 807-8634
Cook MS 1,600/6-8
9111 Wheatland Dr 77064 281-897-4400
Sherma Duck, prin. Fax 897-3850
Cypress Creek HS 3,400/9-12
9815 Grant Rd 77070 281-897-4200
Sandy Trujillo, prin. Fax 807-8925
Cypress Falls HS 3,400/9-12
9811 Huffmeister Rd 77095 281-856-1000
Becky Denton, prin. Fax 856-1445
Cypress Ridge HS 3,000/9-12
7900 N Eldridge Pkwy 77041 713-807-8000
Stephanie Meshell, prin. Fax 807-8045
Dean MS 1,500/6-8
14104 Reo St 77040 713-460-6153
Chris Hecker, prin. Fax 460-6197
Jersey Village HS 3,300/9-12
7600 Solomon St 77040 713-896-3400
Ralph Funk, prin. Fax 896-3438
Kahla MS 1,400/6-8
16212 W Little York Rd 77084 281-345-3260
Ana Martin, prin. Fax 345-5275
Labay MS 1,600/6-8
15435 Willow River Dr 77095 281-463-5800
Patty Mooney, prin. Fax 463-5804
Langham Creek HS 3,000/9-12
17610 FM 529 Rd 77095 281-463-5400
David Hughes, prin. Fax 345-3153
Truitt MS 1,500/6-8
6600 Addicks Satsuma Rd 77084 281-856-1100
Teresa Baranowski, prin. Fax 856-1104
Watkins MS 1,300/6-8
4800 Cairnvillage St 77084 281-463-5850
Dr. Jose Martinez, prin. Fax 856-1565
Windfern HS of Choice 300/Alt
12630 Windfern Rd 77064 281-807-8684
Martha Strother, prin. Fax 807-8693
Other Schools – See Cypress, Katy

Fort Bend ISD
Supt. — See Sugar Land
Hodges Bend MS 1,300/6-8
16510 Bissonnet St 77083 281-634-3000
Deidra Lyons-Lewis, prin. Fax 634-3028
McAuliffe MS 500/6-8
16650 S Post Oak Rd 77053 281-634-3360
Mary Brewster, prin. Fax 634-3393
Willowridge HS 1,400/9-12
16301 Chimney Rock Rd 77053 281-634-2450
Joseph Chandler, prin. Fax 634-2513

Galena Park ISD 21,800/PK-12
14705 Woodforest Blvd 77015 832-386-1000
Dr. Angi Williams, supt. Fax 386-1298
www.galenaparkisd.com
Accelerated Center for Education Alt
13801 Hollypark Dr 77015 832-386-3670
Julien Guillory, prin. Fax 386-3671
Center for Success Alt
13801 Hollypark Dr 77015 832-386-3630
Julien Guillory, prin. Fax 386-3631
Cunningham MS 900/7-8
14110 Wallisville Rd 77049 832-386-4470
David Pierson, prin. Fax 386-4471
North Shore 9th Grade Center 1,200/9-9
13501 Hollypark Dr 77015 832-386-3400
Jason Bollich, prin. Fax 386-3401
North Shore MS 1,300/7-8
120 Castlegory Rd 77015 832-386-2600
Brett Lalor, prin. Fax 386-2643
North Shore SHS 3,400/10-12
353 N Castlegory Rd 77049 832-386-4100
Dr. Joe Coleman, prin. Fax 386-4101
Woodland Acres MS 500/6-8
12947 Myrtle Ln 77015 832-386-4700
Lee Ramirez, prin. Fax 386-4701
Other Schools – See Galena Park

Houston ISD 199,300/PK-12
4400 W 18th St 77092 713-556-6000
Terry Grier Ed.D., supt. Fax 556-6323
www.houstonisd.org
Attucks MS 400/6-8
4330 Bellfort St 77051 713-732-3670
Renita Perry, prin. Fax 732-3677
Austin HS 1,900/9-12
1700 Dumble St 77023 713-924-1600
Steve Guerrero, prin. Fax 923-3157
Baylor College of Medicine Academy 300/6-8
2610 Elgin St 77004 713-942-1932
Jyoti Malhan, prin. Fax 942-1943
Beechnut Academy 600/6-12
7055 Beechnut 77074 713-394-3500
Patrice Grovey, prin. Fax 777-4011
Black MS 500/6-8
1575 Chantilly Ln 77018 713-613-2505
Paolo Castagnoli, prin. Fax 613-2233

Burbank MS 1,400/6-8
315 Berry Rd 77022 713-696-2720
Rosa Hernandez, prin. Fax 696-2723
Carnegie-Vanguard HS 500/9-12
1501 Taft St 77019 713-732-3690
Ramon Moss, prin. Fax 732-3694
Chavez HS 2,900/9-12
8501 Howard Dr 77017 713-495-6950
Rene Sanchez, prin. Fax 495-6988
Clifton MS 1,000/6-8
6001 Golden Forest Dr 77092 713-613-2516
Rosa Cruz-Gaona, prin. Fax 613-2523
Community Services Alt
1102 Telephone Rd 77023 713-967-5285
Stephen MacLauchlan, prin. Fax 967-5223
Cullen MS 500/6-8
6900 Scott St 77021 713-746-8180
Clayton Crook, prin. Fax 746-8181
Davis HS 1,600/9-12
1101 Quitman St 77009 713-226-4900
Julissa Martinez, prin. Fax 226-4999
Deady MS 900/6-8
2500 Broadway St 77012 713-845-7411
Richard Smith, prin. Fax 649-5816
DeBakey Health Professions HS 900/9-12
3100 Shenandoah St 77021 713-741-2410
Agnes Perry, prin. Fax 746-5211
Dowling MS 1,300/6-8
14000 Stancliff St 77045 713-434-5600
Tynette Guinn, prin. Fax 434-5608
Edison MS 700/6-8
6901 Avenue I 77011 713-924-1800
Armando Lujan, prin. Fax 924-1316
Energy Institute 9-12
1808 Sampson St 77003 713-802-4620
Lori Lambropoulos, prin. Fax 556-9840
Fleming MS 600/6-8
4910 Collingsworth St 77026 713-671-4170
Sabrina Cuby-King, prin. Fax 671-4176
Fondren MS 700/6-8
6333 S Braeswood Blvd 77096 713-778-3360
Monique Lewis, prin. Fax 778-3362
Fonville MS 1,000/6-8
725 E Little York Rd 77076 713-696-2825
Roger Ibarra, prin. Fax 696-2829
Forest Brook MS 700/6-8
7525 Tidwell Rd 77016 713-631-7720
Tannisha Gentry, prin. Fax 636-4114
Furr HS 800/9-12
520 Mercury Dr 77013 713-675-1118
Dr. Bertie Simmons, prin. Fax 671-3612
Grady MS 500/6-8
5215 San Felipe St 77056 713-625-1411
Gretchen Kasper-Hoffman, prin. Fax 625-1415
Hamilton MS 1,300/6-8
139 E 20th St 77008 713-802-4725
Wendy Hampton, prin. Fax 802-4731
Harper Alternative S 100/Alt
4425 N Shepherd Dr 77018 713-802-4760
Raymond Glass, prin. Fax 802-4768
Hartman MS 1,400/6-8
7111 Westover St 77087 713-845-7435
Geovanny Ponce, prin. Fax 847-4706
HCC Life Skills 50/Alt
1301 Alabama St 77004 713-718-6882
Natalie Pruitt, prin. Fax 718-6815
Henry MS 1,000/6-8
10702 E Hardy Rd 77093 713-696-2650
Kenneth Brantley, prin. Fax 696-2657
High School Ahead Academy 400/6-8
5320 Yale St 77091 713-696-2643
Yolanda Jones, prin. Fax 696-2999
Hogg MS 700/6-8
1100 Merrill St 77009 713-802-4700
Angela Sugarek, prin. Fax 802-4708
Holland MS 700/6-8
1600 Gellhorn Dr 77029 713-671-3860
Lashonda Bilbo-Ervin, prin. Fax 671-3874
HS for Law Enforcement/Criminal Justice 500/9-12
4701 Dickson St 77007 713-867-5100
Carol Mosteit, prin. Fax 802-4600
HS for Performing & Visual Arts 700/9-12
4001 Stanford St 77006 713-942-1960
Robert Allen, prin. Fax 942-1968
Houston Math Science Tech Ctr 1,900/9-12
9400 Irvington Blvd 77076 713-696-0200
Rupak Gandhi, prin. Fax 696-8984
Jackson MS 1,000/6-8
5100 Polk St 77023 713-924-1760
Kelly Pichon, prin. Fax 924-1768
Johnston MS 1,500/6-8
10410 Manhattan Dr 77096 713-726-3616
Wenden Sanders, prin. Fax 726-3622
Jones Futures Academy 500/9-12
7414 St Lo Rd 77033 713-733-1111
Geovanny Ponce, prin. Fax 732-3450
Jordan HS for Careers Vo/Tech
5800 Eastex Fwy 77026 713-636-6900
John McAlpine, prin. Fax 636-6917
Kashmere HS 500/9-12
6900 Wileyvale Rd 77028 713-636-6400
Nancy Blackwell, prin. Fax 636-6433
Key MS 500/6-8
4000 Kelley St 77026 713-636-6000
Joseph Williams, prin. Fax 636-6008
Lamar HS 3,400/9-12
3325 Westheimer Rd 77098 713-522-5960
James McSwain, prin. Fax 535-3769
Las Americas MS 200/4-8
6501 Bellaire Blvd 77074 713-773-5300
Maria Moreno, prin. Fax 773-5303
Lee HS 1,600/9-12
6529 Beverlyhill St 77057 713-787-1700
Jonathan Trinh, prin. Fax 787-1723
Leland College Prep 300/6-12
1510 Jensen Dr 77020 713-226-2668
Dameion Crook, prin. Fax 226-4923

Long Academy 700/6-12
6501 Bellaire Blvd 77074 713-778-3380
Marcela Baez, prin. Fax 778-3387
Madison HS 2,000/9-12
13719 White Heather Dr 77045 713-433-9801
Orlando Reyna, prin. Fax 434-5242
Marshall MS 1,000/6-8
1115 Noble St 77009 713-226-2600
Michael Harrison, prin. Fax 226-2605
McReynolds MS 700/6-8
5910 Market St 77020 713-671-3650
Steven Stapleton, prin. Fax 671-3657
Middle College HS at Fraga 200/Alt
301 N Drennan 77003 713-718-6740
Angelica Vega, prin.
Middle College HS at Gulfton 200/Alt
5407 Gulfton St 77081 713-662-2551
Diana del Pilar, prin. Fax 662-2572
Milby HS 2,000/9-12
7414 St Lo Rd 77033 713-928-7401
Roy de la Garza, prin. Fax 928-7474
North Forest HS 1,300/9-12
10725 Mesa Dr 77078 713-636-4300
Richard Fernandez, prin. Fax 636-8116
North Houston Early College HS 400/9-12
99 Lyerly St 77022 713-696-6168
Angela Lundy-Jackson, prin. Fax 696-6172
Ortiz MS 1,000/6-8
6767 Telephone Rd 77061 713-845-5650
Noelia Longoria, prin. Fax 845-5646
Pershing MS 1,700/6-8
3838 Blue Bonnet Blvd 77025 713-295-5240
Kim Heckman, prin. Fax 295-5252
Reagan HS 2,000/9-12
413 E 13th St 77008 713-865-4400
Connie Berger, prin. Fax 802-4749
Revere MS 900/6-8
10502 Briar Forest Dr 77042 713-917-3500
Christian Delariva, prin. Fax 917-3505
Rogers S 800/K-12
5840 San Felipe St 77057 713-917-3565
David Muzyka, prin. Fax 917-3555
Scarborough HS 700/9-12
4141 Costa Rica Rd 77092 713-613-2200
Diego Linares, prin. Fax 613-2205
Sharpstown HS 1,300/9-12
7504 Bissonnet St 77074 713-771-7215
Rob Gasparello, prin. Fax 773-6103
Sharpstown International S 1,000/6-12
8330 Triola Ln 77036 713-778-3440
Thuy Le-Thai, prin. Fax 778-3444
Soar Center 200/Alt
4400 W 18th St 77092 713-556-7025
Sowmya Kumar, prin. Fax 556-7099
Sterling HS 1,000/9-12
11625 Martindale Rd 77048 713-991-0510
Justin Fuentes, prin. Fax 991-8111
Stevenson MS 1,400/6-8
9595 Winkler Dr 77017 713-943-5700
Ruth Ruiz, prin. Fax 943-5711
Sugar Grove MS 600/6-8
8405 Bonhomme Rd 77074 713-271-0214
Lynett Hookfin, prin. Fax 771-9342
Thomas MS 500/6-8
5655 Selinsky Rd 77048 713-732-3500
Khalilah Campbell-Rhone, prin. Fax 732-3511
Waltrip HS 1,700/9-12
1900 W 34th St 77018 713-688-1361
Edward Mitchell, prin. Fax 957-7743
Washington HS 800/9-12
119 E 39th St 77018 713-696-6600
Carlos Phillips, prin. Fax 696-6657
Welch MS 1,000/6-8
11544 S Gessner Rd 77071 713-778-3300
Inge Garibaldi, prin. Fax 995-6067
West Briar MS 1,400/6-8
13733 Brimhurst Dr 77077 281-368-2140
Keeley Simpson, prin. Fax 368-2194
Westbury HS 2,200/9-12
11911 Chimney Rock Rd 77035 713-723-6015
Susan Monaghan, prin. Fax 726-2165
Westside HS 3,000/9-12
14201 Briar Forest Dr 77077 281-920-8000
Marguerite Stewart, prin. Fax 920-8059
Wheatley HS 1,000/9-12
4801 Providence St 77020 713-671-3900
Shirley Rose, prin. Fax 671-3951
Worthing HS 800/9-12
9215 Scott St 77051 713-733-3433
Duane Clark, prin. Fax 731-5537
Yates HS 1,000/9-12
3703 Sampson St 77004 713-748-5400
Kenneth Davis, prin. Fax 746-8206
Young Womens College Preparatory Academy 6-12
1906 Cleburne St 77004 713-942-1441
Delesa O'Dell-Thomas, prin. Fax 942-1448
Other Schools – See Bellaire

Humble ISD
Supt. — See Humble
Quest Early College HS 200/9-12
15903 W Lake Houston Pkwy 77044 281-775-0866
Ginger Noyes, prin. Fax 641-6017
Summer Creek HS 2,000/9-12
14000 Weckford Blvd 77044 281-641-5400
Nolan Correa, prin. Fax 641-5417
Woodcreek MS 1,000/6-8
14600 Woodson Park Dr 77044 281-641-5200
Brent McDonald, prin. Fax 641-5217

Katy ISD
Supt. — See Katy
Mayde Creek HS 2,700/9-12
19202 Groschke Rd 77084 281-237-3000
Dr. Cazilda Steele, prin. Fax 644-1721
Mayde Creek JHS 1,200/6-8
2700 Greenhouse Rd 77084 281-237-3900
Dr. David Paz, prin. Fax 644-1650

Klein ISD
Supt. — See Klein
Klein Forest HS 3,500/9-12
11400 Misty Valley Dr 77066 832-484-4500
Patricia Crittendon, prin. Fax 484-7801
Klein IS 1,200/6-8
4710 W Mount Houston Rd 77088 832-249-4900
Bob Anderson, prin. Fax 249-4046
Ulrich IS 1,000/6-8
10103 Spring Cypress Rd 77070 832-375-7500
Dr. Jeff Bailey, prin. Fax 375-7599
Vistas HS Program Alt
12550 Bammel North Houston 77066 832-484-7650
Peggy Ekster, dir. Fax 484-7697
Wunderlich IS 1,500/6-8
11800 Misty Valley Dr 77066 832-249-5200
Dr. Chris Ruggerio, prin. Fax 249-4050

Pasadena ISD
Supt. — See Pasadena
Beverly Hills IS 1,000/6-8
11111 Beamer Rd 77089 713-740-0420
Stacy Barber, prin. Fax 740-4051
Dobie HS 3,600/9-12
10220 Blackhawk Blvd 77089 713-740-0370
Franklin Moses, prin. Fax 740-4158
Lewis Career and Technical HS Vo/Tech
1348 Genoa Red Bluff Rd 77034 713-740-5320
Steve Fleming, prin. Fax 740-5910
Queens IS 700/6-8
1452 Queens St 77017 713-740-0470
Troy Jones, prin. Fax 740-4102
Roberts MS, 13402 Conklin 77034 6-8
Jorly Thomas, prin. 713-740-5390
Thompson IS 1,000/6-8
11309 Sagedowne Ln 77089 713-740-0510
Melissa Allen, prin. Fax 740-4083

Sheldon ISD 7,100/PK-12
11411 C E King Pkwy 77044 281-727-2000
Fax 727-2085
www.sheldonisd.com
King HS 1,700/9-12
8540 C E King Pkwy 77044 281-727-3500
Demetrius McCall, prin. Fax 459-7346
King MS 800/6-8
8530 C E King Pkwy 77044 281-727-4300
Juan Melendez, prin. Fax 459-7452
Null MS 800/6-8
12117 Garrett Rd 77044 281-436-2800
Leroy Bradley, prin. Fax 436-2875
Sheldon Early College HS 300/9-12
8540 C E King Pkwy 77044 281-727-3043
Robert Hernandez, prin.

Spring Branch ISD 33,700/PK-12
955 Campbell Rd 77024 713-464-1511
Scott Muri Ed.D., supt. Fax 365-4664
www.springbranchisd.com
Guthrie Center for Excellence Vo/Tech
10660 Hammerly Blvd 77043 713-251-1300
Joe Kolenda, prin. Fax 251-1315
Landrum MS 800/6-8
2200 Ridgecrest Dr 77055 713-251-3700
Steven Speyrer, prin. Fax 251-3715
Memorial HS 2,500/9-12
935 Echo Ln 77024 713-251-2500
Lisa Weir, prin. Fax 251-2515
Memorial MS 1,300/6-8
12550 Vindon Dr 77024 713-251-3900
Dave Parker, prin. Fax 251-3915
Northbrook HS 2,000/9-12
1 Raider Cir 77080 713-251-2800
Randolph Adami, prin. Fax 251-2915
Northbrook MS 700/6-8
3030 Rosefield Dr 77080 713-251-4100
Sarah Guerrero, prin. Fax 251-4102
Spring Branch MS 1,100/6-8
1000 Piney Point Rd 77024 713-251-4400
Bryan Williams, prin. Fax 251-4415
Spring Forest MS 800/6-8
14240 Memorial Dr 77079 713-251-4600
Dr. Kaye Williams, prin. Fax 251-4615
Spring Oaks MS 800/6-8
2150 Shadowdale Dr 77043 713-251-4800
Paul Suess, prin. Fax 251-4815
Spring Woods HS 2,000/9-12
2045 Gessner Rd 77080 713-251-3100
Jennifer Parker, prin. Fax 251-3130
Spring Woods MS 800/6-8
9810 Neuens Rd 77080 713-251-5000
Deborah Silber, prin. Fax 251-5015
Stratford HS 2,000/9-12
14555 Fern Dr 77079 713-251-3400
Robert Gex, prin. Fax 251-3420

Spring ISD 36,500/PK-12
16717 Ella Blvd 77090 281-891-6000
Dr. Rodney Watson, supt. Fax 891-6006
www.springisd.org
Bammel MS 1,300/6-8
16711 Ella Blvd 77090 281-891-7900
Dr. H.P. Hyder, prin. Fax 891-7901
Claughton MS 1,300/6-8
3000 Spears Rd 77067 281-891-7950
Dr. David Baxter, prin. Fax 891-7951
DeKaney HS 2,800/9-12
22351 Imperial Valley Dr 77073 281-891-7260
Pamela Farinas, prin. Fax 891-7261
Early College Academy 100/9-12
1001 S Ridge Rd 77090 281-891-6880
Dr. Rene Garganta, prin. Fax 891-6881
Roberson MS 1,200/6-8
1500 S Ridge Rd 77090 281-891-7700
Tracey Walker-Daniels, prin. Fax 891-7701
Wells MS 1,300/6-8
4033 Gladeridge Dr 77068 281-891-7750
Henri Lewi, prin. Fax 891-7751
Westfield HS 3,300/9-12
16713 Ella Blvd 77090 281-891-7130
Alonzo Reynolds, prin. Fax 891-7131

Other Schools – See Spring

---

Aerosim Flight Academy Post-Sec.
12711 Blume Ave 77034 281-481-4700
Alexander-Smith Academy 100/9-12
10255 Richmond Ave Ste 100 77042 713-266-0920
Alfred G. Glassell School of Art Post-Sec.
PO Box 6826 77265 713-639-7500
Al-Hadi S of Accelerative Learning 300/PK-12
2313 S Voss Rd 77057 713-787-5000
American College of Acupuncture Post-Sec.
9100 Park West Dr 77063 713-780-9777
American InterContinental University Post-Sec.
9999 Richmond Ave 77042 832-201-3600
Anthem College Post-Sec.
70 FM 1960 Rd W 77090 888-852-7272
Art Institute of Houston Post-Sec.
4140 Southwest Fwy 77027 713-623-2040
Astrodome Career Center Post-Sec.
2656 S Loop W Ste 380 77054 713-664-5300
Aviation Institute of Maintenance Post-Sec.
7651 Airport Blvd 77061 713-644-7777
Awty International S 1,300/PK-12
7455 Awty School Ln 77055 713-686-4850
Lisa Darling, head sch Fax 686-4956
Banff S 100/PK-12
13726 Cutten Rd 77069 281-444-9326
Baylor College of Medicine Post-Sec.
1 Baylor Plz 77030 713-798-4951
Behold! Beauty Academy Post-Sec.
3823 Charleston St 77021 713-635-5252
Ben Taub Hospital Post-Sec.
2525 Holly Hall St 77054 713-746-6400
Beren Academy 300/PK-12
11333 Cliffwood Dr 77035 713-723-7170
Bridge S 300/6-12
3333 Bering Dr 77057 713-974-2066
Dr. Spyros Catechis, head sch Fax 825-8573
Center for Advanced Legal Studies Post-Sec.
3910 Kirby Dr Ste 200 77098 713-529-2778
Chamberlain College of Nursing Post-Sec.
11025 Equity Dr 77041 713-277-9800
Champion Beauty College Post-Sec.
3920 FM 1960 Ste 210 77068 281-583-9117
Clear Lake Christian S 300/K-12
14325 Crescent Landing Dr 77062 281-488-4883
Dr. Bruce Guillot M.S., prin. Fax 480-3287
College of Biblical Studies Post-Sec.
7000 Regency Square Blvd 77036 713-785-5995
Commonwealth Institute / Funeral Service Post-Sec.
415 Barren Springs Dr 77090 281-873-0262
Cristo Rey Jesuit HS 300/9-12
6700 Mount Carmel St 77087 281-501-1298
Katherine Cater, prin. Fax 501-3485
Culinary Institute LeNotre Post-Sec.
7070 Allensby St 77022 713-692-0077
Cypress Christian S 600/K-12
11123 Cypress N Houston Rd 77065 281-469-8829
Stephen Novotny, dir. Fax 469-6040
Darul Arqam North PK-12
11815 Adel Rd 77067 281-583-1984
DeVry University Post-Sec.
5051 Westheimer Rd Ste 500 77056 713-850-0888
DeVry University Post-Sec.
11125 Equity Dr 77041 713-973-3100
Duchesne Academy HS 300/9-12
10202 Memorial Dr 77024 713-468-8211
Don Cramp, prin. Fax 465-9809
Emery/Weiner S 500/6-12
9825 Stella Link Rd 77025 832-204-5900
Stuart Dow, head sch Fax 204-5910
Eternity Christian S 100/PK-12
1122 West Rd 77038 281-999-5107
Beth Bashinski, admin. Fax 999-0107
Everest Institute Post-Sec.
255 Northpoint Dr Ste 100 77060 281-447-7037
Everest Institute Post-Sec.
9700 Bissonnet St Ste 1400 77036 713-772-4200
Everest Institute Post-Sec.
7151 Office City Dr Ste 100 77087 713-645-7404
Family Christian Academy 300/PK-12
14718 Woodford Dr 77015 713-455-4483
John Bohacek, admin. Fax 450-3730
Fortis College Post-Sec.
6220 Westpark Dr Ste 180 77057 713-266-6594
Fortis College Post-Sec.
450 N Sam Houston Pkwy #200 77060
713-332-0062
Franklin Beauty School #2 Post-Sec.
4965 Martin Luther King 77021 713-645-9060
Gulf Coast Regional Blood Center Post-Sec.
1400 La Concha Ln 77054 713-790-1200
Holy Trinity Episcopal S 100/PK-12
11810 Lockwood Rd 77044 281-459-4323
Jeff Matthews, head sch Fax 459-4302
Houston Baptist University Post-Sec.
7502 Fondren Rd 77074 281-649-3000
Houston Christian HS 500/9-12
2700 W Sam Houston Pkwy N 77043 713-580-6000
Dr. Steve Livingston, hdmstr. Fax 580-6001
Houston Community College Post-Sec.
3100 Main St 77002 713-718-2000
Houston Graduate School of Theology Post-Sec.
2501 Central Pkwy Ste A19 77092 713-942-9505
Houston Quran Academy 200/PK-12
1902 Baker Rd 77094 281-717-4622
Houston Training School Post-Sec.
6630 Gulf Fwy 77087 713-649-5050
ICC Technical Institute Post-Sec.
3333 Fannin St Ste 203 77004 713-522-7799
Iman Academy Southwest 400/1-12
6240 Highway 6 S 77083
Incarnate Word Academy 300/9-12
609 Crawford St 77002 713-227-3637
Dr. Mary Aamodt, prin. Fax 227-1014
Institute of Cosmetology Post-Sec.
7011 Harwin Dr Ste 100 77036 713-783-9988
ITT Technical Institute Post-Sec.
2950 S Gessner Rd Ste 100 77063 713-952-2294

ITT Technical Institute Post-Sec.
15651 North Fwy 77090 281-873-0512
Jay's Technical Institute Post-Sec.
11910 Fondren Meadow Dr 77071 713-772-2410
Kinkaid S 1,400/PK-12
201 Kinkaid School Dr 77024 713-782-1640
Andrew Martire Ed.D., hdmstr. Fax 243-5055
Lone Star College - North Harris Post-Sec.
2700 WW Thorne Blvd 77073 281-618-5400
Lone Star College - University Park Post-Sec.
20515 State Highway 249 77070 281-290-2600
Lutheran HS North 300/9-12
1130 W 34th St 77018 713-880-3131
Dallas Lusk, head sch Fax 880-5447
Lutheran South Academy 800/PK-12
12555 Ryewater Dr 77089 281-464-8299
Sheila Psencik, hdmstr. Fax 464-6119
Mediatech Institute Post-Sec.
3324 Walnut Bend Ln 77042 832-242-3426
Memorial Hall S 50/4-12
2501 Central Pkwy A19 77092 713-688-5566
Dr. Kimberly Taylor, hdmstr. Fax 956-9751
Memorial Hospital System Post-Sec.
7737 Southwest Fwy 77074 713-776-5100
Memorial Private HS 50/7-12
14333 Fern Dr 77079 713-759-2288
Methodist Hospital Post-Sec.
6565 Fannin St 77030 713-441-2599
MIAT Institute of Technology Post-Sec.
533 Northpark Central Dr 77073 713-401-3399
North American College Post-Sec.
3203 N Sam Houston Pkwy W 77038 832-230-5555
Northland Christian S 600/PK-12
4363 Sylvanfield Dr 77014 281-440-1060
Daniel Woods, head sch Fax 440-7572
Northwest Educational Center Post-Sec.
2910 Antoine Dr Ste B100 77092 713-680-2929
Our Redeemer Lutheran North S 50/6-12
215 Rittenhouse St 77076 713-416-2640
Ladeina Brush, dir. Fax 699-1032
Page Parkes Center of Modeling & Acting Post-Sec.
1535 West Loop S Ste 100 77027 713-807-8200
Professional Career Training Institute Post-Sec.
227 Airtex Dr 77090 832-484-9100
Rainard S for Gifted Students 100/PK-12
11059 Timberline Rd 77043 713-647-7246
Remington College - Houston Post-Sec.
3110 Hayes Rd Ste 380 77082 281-899-1240
Remington College North Houston Post-Sec.
11310 Greens Crossing # 300 77067 281-885-4450
Rice University Post-Sec.
PO Box 1892 77251 713-348-0000
Royal Beauty Careers Post-Sec.
5020 FM 1960 Rd W Ste A12 77069 281-580-2554
St. Agnes Academy 900/9-12
9000 Bellaire Blvd 77036 713-219-5400
Sr. Jane Meyer, hdmstr. Fax 219-5499
St. John's S 1,300/K-12
2401 Claremont Ln 77019 713-850-0222
Mark Desjardins, hdmstr. Fax 622-2309
St. Pius X HS 700/9-12
811 W Donovan St 77091 713-692-3581
Sr. Donna Pollard, hdmstr. Fax 692-5725
St. Stephen's Episcopal School Houston 200/PK-12
1800 Sul Ross St 77098 713-821-9100
David Coe, head sch Fax 821-9156
St. Thomas' Episcopal S 600/PK-12
4900 Jackwood St 77096 713-666-3111
Michael Cusack, hdmstr. Fax 668-3887
St. Thomas HS 700/9-12
4500 Memorial Dr 77007 713-864-6348
Rev. Patrick Fulton, prin. Fax 864-5750
Sanford-Brown College Post-Sec.
9999 Richmond Ave 77042 713-779-1110
San Jacinto College Post-Sec.
5800 Uvalde Rd 77049 281-458-4050
San Jacinto College Post-Sec.
13735 Beamer Rd 77089 281-484-1900
School of Automotive Machinists Post-Sec.
1911 Antoine Dr 77055 713-683-3817
School of the Woods 400/PK-12
1321 Wirt Rd 77055 713-686-8811
Sherry Herron, hdmstr. Fax 686-1936
Second Baptist S 1,100/PK-12
6410 Woodway Dr 77057 713-365-2310
Dr. Jeff D. Williams, head sch Fax 365-2355
South Texas College of Law Post-Sec.
1303 San Jacinto St 77002 713-659-8040
Southwest Christian Academy 100/K-12
7400 Eldridge Pkwy 77083 281-561-7400
Paula Thurmond, prin. Fax 561-9823
Strake Jesuit College Prep S 900/9-12
8900 Bellaire Blvd 77036 713-774-7651
Ken Lojo, prin. Fax 774-6427
Tenney S 100/6-12
3500 S Gessner Rd 77063 713-783-6990
Texas Barber Colleges & Hairstyling Sch Post-Sec.
9275 Richmond Ave Ste 184 77063 713-953-0262
Texas Christian S 200/PK-12
17810 Kieth Harrow Blvd 77084 281-550-6060
Herc Palmquist, pres. Fax 550-2400
Texas Health School Post-Sec.
11211 Katy Fwy Ste 170 77079 713-932-9333
Texas Heart Institute Post-Sec.
PO Box 20345 77225 713-791-4026
Texas School of Business Post-Sec.
711 E Airtex Dr 77073 281-443-8900
Texas Southern University Post-Sec.
3100 Cleburne St 77004 713-313-7011
Texas Woman's University Post-Sec.
6700 Fannin St 77030 713-794-2000
The College of Health Care Professions Post-Sec.
240 Northwest Mall 77092 713-425-3100
The Ocean Corporation Post-Sec.
10840 Rockley Rd 77099 281-530-0202
Torah Girls Academy 50/9-12
10101 Fondren Rd Ste 136 77096 713-936-0644
Rabbi Yehoshua Wender, dean

Trend Barber College Post-Sec.
7725 W Bellfort St 77071 713-721-0000
Universal Technical Institute Post-Sec.
721 Lockhaven Dr 77073 800-510-5072
University of Houston Post-Sec.
4800 Calhoun Rd 77204 713-743-1000
University of Houston-Clear Lake Post-Sec.
2700 Bay Area Blvd 77058 281-283-7600
University of Houston-Downtown Post-Sec.
1 Main St 77002 713-221-8000
University of St. Thomas Post-Sec.
3800 Montrose Blvd 77006 713-522-7911
University of Texas Anderson Cancer Ctr. Post-Sec.
1515 Holcombe Blvd Unit 2 77030 713-792-6161
University of TX Health Science Center Post-Sec.
PO Box 20036 77225 713-500-4472
Veterans Affairs Medical Center Post-Sec.
2002 Holcombe Blvd 77030 713-794-7100
Vet Tech Institute Post-Sec.
4669 Southwest Fwy 77027 800-275-2736
Village S 900/PK-12
13077 Westella Dr 77077 281-496-7900
Gabriella Rowe M.A., head sch Fax 496-7799
Westbury Christian S 500/PK-12
10420 Hillcroft St 77096 713-551-8100
Western Academy 100/3-8
1511 Butlercrest 77080 713-461-7000
Xavier Educational Academy 100/5-12
3642 University Blvd # 101 77005 832-533-2652

**Howe, Grayson, Pop. 2,551**
Howe ISD 1,000/PK-12
105 W Tutt St 75459 903-532-3228
Kevin Wilson, supt. Fax 532-3205
www.howeisd.net
Howe HS 300/9-12
200 Ponderosa Rd 75459 903-532-3236
Michael Smiley, prin. Fax 532-3237
Howe MS 300/5-8
300 Beatrice St 75459 903-532-3286
Clay Wilson, prin. Fax 532-3287

**Hubbard, Hill, Pop. 1,406**
Hubbard ISD 400/PK-12
PO Box 218 76648 254-576-2564
Dr. Stu Musick, supt. Fax 576-5019
www.hubbardisd.com
Hubbard HS 100/9-12
PO Box 218 76648 254-576-2549
James Wright, prin. Fax 576-2477
Hubbard MS 100/6-8
PO Box 218 76648 254-576-2758
James Wright, prin. Fax 576-5017

**Huffman, Harris**
Huffman ISD 3,300/PK-12
PO Box 2390 77336 281-324-1871
Dr. Benny Soileau, supt. Fax 324-4319
www.huffmanisd.net
Hargrave HS 1,000/9-12
PO Box 2390 77336 281-324-1845
Brandon Perry, prin. Fax 324-3368
Huffman MS 800/6-8
PO Box 2390 77336 281-324-2598
Adam Skinner, prin. Fax 324-2710

**Hughes Springs, Cass, Pop. 1,726**
Hughes Springs ISD 1,200/PK-12
871 Taylor St 75656 903-639-3800
Sarah Dildine, supt. Fax 639-2624
www.hsisd.net
Hughes Springs HS 300/9-12
701 Russell 75656 903-639-3841
Heather McGregor, prin. Fax 639-3928
Hughes Springs JHS 300/6-8
609 Russell 75656 903-639-3812
Brian Nation, prin. Fax 639-3929

**Humble, Harris, Pop. 14,835**
Aldine ISD
Supt. — See Houston
Teague MS 800/7-8
21700 Rayford Rd 77338 281-233-4310
Sonya Hicks, prin. Fax 233-4318

Humble ISD 36,000/PK-12
PO Box 2000 77347 281-641-1000
Dr. Guy Sconzo, supt. Fax 641-1050
www.humble.k12.tx.us/
Atascocita HS 3,000/9-12
13300 Will Clayton Pkwy 77346 281-641-7500
Bill Daniels, prin. Fax 641-7713
Atascocita MS 1,100/6-8
18810 W Lake Houston Pkwy 77346 281-641-4600
Karl Koehler, prin. Fax 641-4617
Cambridge S Alt
18901 Timber Forest Dr 77346 281-641-7445
Tammey Harlan, prin. Fax 641-7399
Career & Technology Education Center Vo/Tech
9155 Will Clayton Pkwy 77338 281-641-7951
Dr. Marley Morris, dir. Fax 641-7967
Humble HS 1,500/9-12
1700 Wilson Rd 77338 281-641-6300
Charles Ned, prin. Fax 641-6517
Humble MS 1,100/6-8
11207 Will Clayton Pkwy 77346 281-641-4000
Henry Phipps, prin. Fax 641-4117
PACE Program 100/Alt
18901 Timber Forest Dr 77346 281-641-7400
Tammy Alexander, prin. Fax 641-7482
Sterling MS 800/6-8
1131 Wilson Rd 77338 281-641-6000
Damico Bartley, prin. Fax 641-6017
Timberwood MS 1,200/6-8
18450 Timber Forest Dr 77346 281-641-3800
Kenneth Buck, prin. Fax 641-3817
Other Schools – See Houston, Kingwood

---

Christian Life Center Academy 200/PK-12
6650 Rankin Rd 77396 281-319-0077
Rev. Richard Rodriguez, admin. Fax 319-4523

Humble Christian S 300/PK-12
16202 Old Humble Rd 77396 281-441-1313
Ted Howell, admin. Fax 441-1329

**Huntington, Angelina, Pop. 2,087**
Huntington ISD 1,800/PK-12
PO Box 328 75949 936-876-4287
David Flowers, supt. Fax 876-3212
www.huntingtonisd.com/
Huntington HS 500/9-12
PO Box 328 75949 936-876-4150
Jason Adams, prin. Fax 876-4009
Huntington MS 400/6-8
PO Box 328 75949 936-876-4722
Shane Stover, prin. Fax 876-4009
Pride Alternative S 50/Alt
PO Box 328 75949 936-876-4287
Matt Clifton, dir. Fax 876-4352

**Huntsville, Walker, Pop. 38,042**
Huntsville ISD 6,300/PK-12
441 FM 2821 Rd E 77320 936-435-6300
Dr. Howell Wright Ed.D., supt. Fax 435-6648
www.huntsville-isd.org
Huntsville HS 1,800/9-12
441 FM 2821 Rd E 77320 936-435-6100
Beth Burt, prin. Fax 293-2609
Mance Park MS 900/7-8
441 FM 2821 Rd E 77320 936-293-2755
Robert Bennett, prin. Fax 293-2759

---

Alpha Omega Academy 400/K-12
PO Box 8419 77340 936-438-8833
Paul Davidhizar, hdmstr. Fax 438-8844
Sam Houston State University Post-Sec.
1806 Avenue J 77340 936-294-1111
Summit Christian Academy 100/PK-12
PO Box 1590 77342 936-295-9601
Joyce Kumba, prin. Fax 295-9236

**Hurst, Tarrant, Pop. 36,447**
Grapevine-Colleyville ISD
Supt. — See Grapevine
GCISD Collegiate Academy 100/9-9
828 W Harwood Rd 76054
Bobbe Knutz, admin.

Hurst-Euless-Bedford ISD
Supt. — See Bedford
Bell SHS 2,100/10-12
1601 Brown Trl 76054 817-282-2551
Jim Bannister, prin. Fax 285-3200
Hurst JHS 1,000/7-9
500 Harmon Rd 76053 817-285-3220
Elizabeth Russo, prin. Fax 285-3225

---

Ogle School of Hair Design Post-Sec.
720 Arcadia St Apt B 76053 817-284-9231
Tarrant County College Post-Sec.
828 W Harwood Rd 76054 817-515-8223

**Hutto, Williamson, Pop. 14,315**
Hutto ISD 5,400/PK-12
200 College St 78634 512-759-3771
Dr. Douglas Killian, supt. Fax 759-4797
www.hipponation.org
Farley MS 600/6-8
303 County Road 137 78634 512-759-2050
Jorge Franco, prin. Fax 759-2033
Hutto HS 1,400/9-12
101 FM 685 78634 512-759-4700
Roy Christian, prin. Fax 759-4757
Hutto MS 900/6-8
1005 Exchange Blvd 78634 512-759-4541
Elizabeth Anderson, prin. Fax 759-4753

**Idalou, Lubbock, Pop. 2,236**
Idalou ISD 1,000/PK-12
PO Box 1338 79329 806-892-1900
Jim Waller, supt. Fax 892-3204
www.idalouisd.net/
Idalou HS 300/9-12
PO Box 1558 79329 806-892-1900
Janet Thornton, prin. Fax 892-2690
Idalou MS 300/5-8
PO Box 1343 79329 806-892-1900
Josh Damron, prin. Fax 892-2388

**Imperial, Pecos, Pop. 277**
Buena Vista ISD 100/PK-12
PO Box 310 79743 432-536-2225
Mark Dominguez, supt. Fax 536-2469
www.bvisd.net
Buena Vista S 100/PK-12
PO Box 310 79743 432-536-2225
Julian Castillo, prin. Fax 536-2469

**Ingleside, San Patricio, Pop. 9,243**
Ingleside ISD 2,200/PK-12
PO Box 1320 78362 361-776-7631
Troy Mircovich, supt. Fax 776-0267
www.inglesideisd.org
Ingleside HS 600/9-12
2807 Mustang Dr 78362 361-776-2712
Dawn Whidden, prin. Fax 776-5200
Taylor JHS 300/7-8
2739 Mustang Dr 78362 361-776-2232
Heather Waugh, prin. Fax 776-2192

**Ingram, Kerr, Pop. 1,786**
Ingram ISD 1,000/PK-12
510 College St 78025 830-367-5517
Dr. Robert Templeton, supt. Fax 367-5631
www.ingramisd.net
Ingram MS 200/6-8
510 College St 78025 830-367-4111
Mindy Merkel, prin. Fax 367-7335
Ingram-Tom Moore HS 500/9-12
510 College St 78025 830-367-4111
Justin Crittenden, prin. Fax 367-7332

**Iola, Grimes, Pop. 393**
Iola ISD 500/PK-12
PO Box 159 77861 936-394-2361
Chad Jones, supt. Fax 394-2132
www.iolaisd.net
Iola JSHS 200/7-12
PO Box 159 77861 936-394-2361
Scott Martindale, prin. Fax 394-4700

**Iowa Park, Wichita, Pop. 6,289**
Iowa Park Consolidated ISD 1,800/PK-12
PO Box 898 76367 940-592-4193
Steve Moody, supt. Fax 592-2136
www.ipcisd.net/
George MS 400/6-8
412 E Cash St 76367 940-592-2196
Darla Biddy, prin. Fax 592-2801
Iowa Park HS 500/9-12
1 Bob Dawson Dr 76367 940-592-2144
Tim Bartram, prin. Fax 592-2583

**Ira, Scurry**
Ira ISD 300/K-12
6143 W FM 1606 79527 325-573-2629
Jay Waller, supt. Fax 573-5825
www.ira.esc14.net/
Ira S 300/K-12
6123 W FM 1606 79527 325-573-2628
Dale Jones, prin. Fax 573-5825

**Iraan, Pecos, Pop. 1,225**
Iraan-Sheffield ISD 500/PK-12
PO Box 486 79744 432-639-2512
Kevin Allen, supt. Fax 639-2501
isisd.net
Iraan HS 100/9-12
PO Box 486 79744 432-639-2512
Jim Baum, prin. Fax 639-2501
Iraan JHS 100/6-8
PO Box 486 79744 432-639-2512
Michael Meek, prin. Fax 639-2501
Other Schools – See Sheffield

**Iredell, Bosque, Pop. 338**
Iredell ISD 100/PK-12
PO Box 39 76649 254-364-2411
Patrick Murphy, supt. Fax 364-2206
www.iredell-isd.com
Iredell S 100/PK-12
PO Box 39 76649 254-364-2411
Patrick Murphy, prin. Fax 364-2206

**Irving, Dallas, Pop. 212,044**
Carrollton-Farmers Branch ISD
Supt. — See Carrollton
Bush MS 700/6-8
515 Cowboys Pkwy 75063 972-968-3700
Matt Warnock, prin. Fax 968-3710
Ranchview HS 800/9-12
8401 Valley Ranch Pkwy E 75063 972-968-5000
Sherie Skruch, prin. Fax 968-5010

Irving ISD 33,700/PK-12
PO Box 152637 75015 972-600-5000
Dr. Jose L. Parra, supt. Fax 215-5201
www.irvingisd.net
Austin MS 900/6-8
825 E Union Bower Rd 75061 972-600-3100
Toscha Reeves, prin. Fax 721-3105
Bowie MS 900/6-8
600 E 6th St 75060 972-600-3000
Jennifer Anderson, prin. Fax 721-3044
Cardwell Career Preparatory Center 400/Alt
101 E Union Bower Rd 75061 972-600-6140
Maurice Evans, prin. Fax 273-6188
Crockett MS 600/6-8
2431 Hancock St 75061 972-600-4700
Francisco Miranda, prin. Fax 313-4770
de Zavala MS 900/6-8
707 W Pioneer Dr 75061 972-600-6000
Anika Horgan, prin. Fax 273-8924
Houston MS 1,000/6-8
3033 Country Club Dr W 75038 972-600-7500
Jeffrey Dorman, prin. Fax 261-2399
Irving HS 2,300/9-12
900 N O Connor Rd 75061 972-600-6300
Ahna Gomez, prin. Fax 273-8319
Johnson MS 900/6-8
3601 W Pioneer Dr 75061 972-600-0500
Isabel Salazar, prin. Fax 986-6830
Lamar MS 1,000/6-8
219 Crandall Rd 75060 972-600-4400
Joe Moreno, prin. Fax 313-4499
MacArthur HS 2,600/9-12
3700 N MacArthur Blvd 75062 972-600-7200
Daniel Cummings, prin. Fax 261-2298
Nimitz HS 2,400/9-12
100 W Oakdale Rd 75060 972-600-5700
Curtis Mauricio, prin. Fax 273-8610
Singley Academy 1,700/9-12
4601 N MacArthur Blvd 75038 972-600-5300
Dr. Andre Smith, prin. Fax 258-5301
Travis MS 1,000/6-8
1600 Finley Rd 75062 972-600-0100
Laurie Gilcrease, prin. Fax 261-2450
Wheeler Transitional Center 50/Alt
1600 E Shady Grove Rd 75060 972-600-3750
Mackenzie Casall, prin. Fax 554-3769

---

Anthem College Post-Sec.
4250 N Belt Line Rd 75038 888-852-7272
Aviation Institute of Maintenance Post-Sec.
400 E Airport Fwy 75062 214-333-9711
Cistercian Preparatory S 400/5-12
3660 Cistercian Rd 75039 469-499-5400
Fr. Paul McCormick, hdmstr. Fax 499-5440
DeVry University Post-Sec.
4800 Regent Blvd 75063 972-929-6777
Highlands S 400/PK-12
1451 E Northgate Dr 75062 972-554-1980
Gerard Doyle, prin. Fax 721-1691
Islamic S of Irving 500/PK-12
2555 Esters Rd 75062 972-812-2230
North Lake College Post-Sec.
5001 N MacArthur Blvd 75038 972-273-3000
StoneGate Christian Academy 100/PK-12
2833 W Shady Grove Rd 75060 972-790-0070
Virginia Wirth, prin. Fax 790-6560
Tint School of Makeup & Cosmetology Post-Sec.
2716 W Irving Blvd 75061 972-513-1176
Universal Technical Institute Post-Sec.
5151 Regent Blvd 75063 877-873-1080
University of Dallas Post-Sec.
1845 E Northgate Dr 75062 972-721-5000

**Italy, Ellis, Pop. 1,835**
Italy ISD 600/PK-12
300 College 76651 972-483-1815
Jaime Velasco, supt. Fax 483-6152
www.italyisd.info/
Italy JSHS 300/6-12
300 College 76651 972-483-7411
Lee Joffre, prin. Fax 483-1500

**Itasca, Hill, Pop. 1,623**
Itasca ISD 600/PK-12
123 N College St 76055 254-687-2922
Glenn Pittman, supt. Fax 687-2637
www.itascaisd.org
Itasca HS 200/9-12
123 N College St 76055 254-687-2922
Mark Parsons, prin. Fax 687-2637
Itasca MS 200/5-8
208 N Files St 76055 254-687-2922
Kristi Sargent, prin. Fax 687-2637

**Ivanhoe, Fannin, Pop. 869**
Sam Rayburn ISD 500/PK-12
9363 E FM 273 75447 903-664-2255
Jeff Irvin, supt. Fax 664-2406
www.srisd.org
Rayburn JSHS 200/7-12
9363 E FM 273 75447 903-664-2165
Wendy Keeton, prin. Fax 664-2407

**Jacksboro, Jack, Pop. 4,489**
Jacksboro ISD 1,000/PK-12
750 W Belknap St 76458 940-567-7203
Dennis Bennett, supt. Fax 567-2214
www.jacksboroisd.net/
Jacksboro HS 200/9-12
1400 N Main St 76458 940-567-7204
Brad Burnett, prin. Fax 567-6028
Jacksboro MS 200/6-8
812 W Belknap St 76458 940-567-7205
Sara Mathis, prin. Fax 567-2681

**Jacksonville, Cherokee, Pop. 14,356**
Jacksonville ISD 4,900/PK-12
PO Box 631 75766 903-586-6511
Dr. Chad Kelly, supt. Fax 586-3133
www.jisd.org
Compass Center 50/Alt
PO Box 631 75766 903-589-3926
David Adams, prin. Fax 586-7158
Jacksonville HS 1,200/9-12
PO Box 631 75766 903-586-3661
Karen Kubara, prin. Fax 586-8229
Jacksonville MS 700/7-8
PO Box 631 75766 903-586-3686
Holly Searcy, prin. Fax 586-8071

---

Baptist Missionary Theological Seminary Post-Sec.
PO Box 670 75766 903-586-2501
Jacksonville College Post-Sec.
105 B J Albritton Dr 75766 903-586-2518

**Jarrell, Williamson, Pop. 971**
Jarrell ISD 1,000/PK-12
PO Box 9 76537 512-746-2124
Dr. Bill Chapman, supt. Fax 746-2518
www.jarrellisd.org
Jarrell HS 300/9-12
PO Box 9 76537 512-746-2188
Michael Stovall, prin. Fax 746-2183
Jarrell MS 300/6-8
PO Box 9 76537 512-746-4180
Abbe Lester, prin. Fax 746-4280

**Jasper, Jasper, Pop. 7,490**
Jasper ISD 2,700/PK-12
128 Park Ln 75951 409-384-2401
Dr. Richard Skuza, supt. Fax 382-1084
www.jasperisd.net
Jasper HS 700/9-12
400 Bulldog Ave 75951 409-384-3242
Kevin Smith, prin. Fax 382-1310
Jasper JHS 400/6-8
211 2nd St 75951 409-384-3585
John Seybold, prin. Fax 382-1160

**Jayton, Kent, Pop. 530**
Jayton-Girard ISD 200/PK-12
PO Box 168 79528 806-237-2991
Trig Overbo, supt. Fax 237-2670
www.jaytonjaybirds.com
Jayton S 200/PK-12
PO Box 168 79528 806-237-2991
Lyle Lackey, prin. Fax 237-2670

**Jefferson, Marion, Pop. 2,067**
Jefferson ISD 1,200/PK-12
1600 Martin Luther King Dr 75657 903-665-2461
Rob Barnwell, supt. Fax 665-7367
jeffersonisd.org/
Jefferson HS 300/9-12
1 Bulldog Dr 75657 903-665-2461
Craig Evers, prin. Fax 665-2146
Jefferson JHS 400/5-8
804 N Alley St 75657 903-665-2461
Dr. Patrick Winters, prin. Fax 665-7149

**Jewett, Leon, Pop. 1,158**
Leon ISD 800/PK-12
12168 US Highway 79 75846 903-626-1400
Mike Baldree, supt. Fax 626-1420
www.leonisd.net/
Leon HS 200/9-12
12168 US Highway 79 75846 903-626-1475
Jay Winn, prin. Fax 626-1490
Leon JHS 200/6-8
12168 US Highway 79 75846 903-626-1450
J.D. Foley, prin. Fax 626-1455

**Joaquin, Shelby, Pop. 818**
Joaquin ISD 800/PK-12
11109 US Highway 84 E 75954 936-269-3128
Phil Worsham, supt. Fax 269-3615
www.joaquinisd.net/
Joaquin HS 200/9-12
11109 US Highway 84 E 75954 936-269-3128
James Jackson, prin. Fax 269-9123
Joaquin JHS 200/6-8
11109 US Highway 84 E 75954 936-269-3128
Terri Gray, prin. Fax 269-9123

**Johnson City, Blanco, Pop. 1,640**
Johnson City ISD 700/K-12
PO Box 498 78636 830-868-7410
David Shanley, supt. Fax 868-7375
johnsoncity.tx.schoolwebpages.com/
Johnson HS 200/9-12
PO Box 498 78636 830-868-4025
Julie Storer, prin. Fax 868-9244
Johnson MS 200/5-8
PO Box 498 78636 830-868-9025
Cammie Ockman, prin. Fax 868-7375

**Jonesboro, Coryell**
Jonesboro ISD 200/PK-12
PO Box 125 76538 254-463-2111
Matt Dossey, supt. Fax 463-4457
www.jonesboroisd.net
Jonesboro S 200/PK-12
PO Box 125 76538 254-463-2111
Kendra Gustin, admin. Fax 463-4457

**Joshua, Johnson, Pop. 5,826**
Joshua ISD 5,400/PK-12
PO Box 40 76058 817-202-2500
Fran Marek, supt. Fax 641-2738
www.joshuaisd.org
Joshua HS Ninth Grade Campus 400/9-9
1035 S Broadway St 76058 817-202-2500
Kenny Bodine, prin. Fax 556-4640
Joshua SHS 900/10-12
909 S Broadway St 76058 817-202-2500
Mick Cochran, prin. Fax 556-3404
Loflin MS 700/7-8
6801 FM 1902 76058 817-202-2500
Damon Patterson, prin. Fax 202-9140
New Horizon HS 100/Alt
603 Plum St 76058 817-202-2500
Kenny Bodine, prin. Fax 202-8948

---

Joshua Christian Academy 100/PK-12
PO Box 1379 76058 817-295-7377

**Jourdanton, Atascosa, Pop. 3,848**
Jourdanton ISD 1,400/PK-12
200 Zanderson Ave 78026 830-769-3548
Dr. Lana Collavo, supt. Fax 769-3272
www.jourdantonisd.net/
Jourdanton HS 400/9-12
200 Zanderson Ave 78026 830-769-2350
Keith Chapman, prin. Fax 769-3065
Jourdanton JHS 300/6-8
200 Zanderson Ave 78026 830-769-2234
Robert Rutkowski, prin. Fax 769-2998

**Junction, Kimble, Pop. 2,554**
Junction ISD 700/PK-12
1700 College St 76849 325-446-3510
Renee Schulze, supt. Fax 446-4413
www.junctionisd.net
Junction HS 200/9-12
1700 College St 76849 325-446-3326
Josh Limmer, prin. Fax 446-8206
Junction MS 100/6-8
1700 College St 76849 325-446-2464
Janda Castillo, prin. Fax 446-2255

**Justin, Denton, Pop. 3,207**
Northwest ISD 15,500/PK-12
2001 Texan Dr 76247 817-215-0000
Dr. Karen Rue, supt. Fax 215-0170
www.nisdtx.org
Northwest HS 2,300/9-12
2301 Texan Dr 76247 817-215-0200
Jason Childress, prin. Fax 215-0262
Pike MS 1,000/6-8
2200 Texan Dr 76247 817-215-0400
Christopher Jones, prin. Fax 215-0425
Other Schools – See Fort Worth, Haslet, Rhome, Roanoke, Trophy Club

**Karnack, Harrison**
Karnack ISD 200/PK-12
PO Box 259 75661 903-679-3117
Cozzetta Robinson, supt. Fax 679-4252
karnackisd.org/
Karnack HS 100/9-12
PO Box 259 75661 903-679-3113
Tony Thomas, prin. Fax 679-4264

**Karnes City, Karnes, Pop. 3,027**
Karnes City ISD 1,000/PK-12
314 N Highway 123 78118 830-780-2321
Jeanette Winn, supt. Fax 780-3823
www.kcisd.net
Karnes City HS 300/9-12
400 N Highway 123 78118 830-780-2321
Brian Uriegas, prin. Fax 780-4352

Karnes City JHS 200/6-8
410 N Highway 123 78118 830-780-2321
Theresa Molina, prin. Fax 780-4382

**Katy, Harris, Pop. 13,902**
Cypress-Fairbanks ISD
Supt. — See Houston
Alternative Learning Center - West Alt
19350 Rebel Yell Dr 77449 281-855-4310
Stacie Wicke, prin. Fax 855-4307
Cypress Lakes HS 3,400/9-12
5750 Greenhouse Rd 77449 281-856-3800
Sarah Harty, prin. Fax 856-3808
Thornton MS 1,300/6-8
19802 Kieth Harrow Blvd 77449 281-856-1500
Reginald Mitchell, prin. Fax 856-1548

Katy ISD 61,200/PK-12
PO Box 159 77492 281-396-6000
Alton Frailey, supt. Fax 644-1800
www.katyisd.org/
Beckendorff JHS 1,600/6-8
8200 S Fry Rd 77494 281-237-8800
Mindy Dickerson, prin. Fax 644-1635
Beck JHS 1,200/6-8
5200 S Fry Rd 77450 281-237-3300
Carra Flemming, prin. Fax 644-1630
Cardiff JHS 1,100/6-8
3900 Dayflower Dr 77449 281-234-0600
Richard Hull, prin. Fax 644-1855
Cinco Ranch HS 3,100/9-12
23440 Cinco Ranch Blvd 77494 281-237-7000
James Cross, prin. Fax 644-1735
Cinco Ranch JHS 1,100/6-8
23420 Cinco Ranch Blvd 77494 281-237-7300
Elizabeth Kuylen, prin. Fax 644-1640
Katy HS 2,800/9-12
6331 Highway Blvd 77494 281-237-6700
Dr. Rick Hull, prin. Fax 644-1702
Katy JHS 1,300/6-8
5350 Franz Rd 77493 281-237-6800
Dr. Jake Leblanc, prin. Fax 644-1645
McDonald JHS 900/6-8
3635 Lakes of Bridgewater 77449 281-237-5300
Dr. Kenneth Cummings, prin. Fax 644-1655
McMeans JHS 1,200/6-8
21000 Westheimer Pkwy 77450 281-237-8000
Dr. Susan Rice, prin. Fax 644-1660
Memorial Parkway JHS 900/6-8
21203 Highland Knolls Dr 77450 281-237-5800
Emily Craig, prin. Fax 644-1665
Miller Career and Technology Ctr Vo/Tech
1734 Katyland Dr 77493 281-237-6300
Dr. Anna Webb-Storey, prin. Fax 644-1775
Morton Ranch HS 3,200/9-12
21000 Franz Rd 77449 281-237-7800
Lee Crews, prin. Fax 644-1747
Morton Ranch JHS 1,200/6-8
2498 N Mason Rd 77449 281-237-7400
Mark McCord, prin. Fax 644-1670
Opportunity Awareness Center Alt
1732 Katyland Dr 77493 281-237-6350
Becky Bracewell-Tucker, prin. Fax 644-1780
Raines HS 50/Alt
1732 Katyland Dr 77493 281-237-1500
Becky Bracewell-Tucker, prin. Fax 644-1780
Seven Lake JHS 6-8
6026 Katy Gaston Rd 77494 281-234-2100
Dr. Imelda Medrano, prin. Fax 644-1885
Seven Lakes HS 3,700/9-12
9251 S Fry Rd 77494 281-237-2800
Ted Vierling, prin. Fax 644-1791
Taylor HS 2,800/9-12
20700 Kingsland Blvd 77450 281-237-3100
Jeff Stocks, prin. Fax 644-1760
Tompkins HS 9-12
4400 Falcon Landing Blvd 77494 281-234-1000
Mark Grisdale, prin. Fax 644-1910
West Memorial JHS 800/6-8
22311 Provincial Blvd 77450 281-237-6400
Gina Cobb, prin. Fax 644-1675
WoodCreek JHS 1,900/6-8
1801 WoodCreek Bend Ln 77494 281-234-0800
Kerri Finnesand, prin. Fax 644-1860
Other Schools – See Houston

Faith West Academy 600/PK-12
2225 Porter Rd 77493 281-391-5683
Mary Strickland, prin. Fax 391-2606
St. John XXIII HS 400/9-12
1800 W Grand Pkwy 77449 281-693-1000
Tim Jaureguito, prin. Fax 693-1001

**Kaufman, Kaufman, Pop. 6,619**
Kaufman ISD 3,800/PK-12
1000 S Houston St 75142 972-932-2622
Dr. Lori Blaylock, supt. Fax 932-3325
www.kaufmanisd.net
Campbell HS 100/Alt
4814 County Road 151 75142 972-932-8789
Gary Campbell, prin. Fax 932-2278
Kaufman HS 1,000/9-12
3205 S Houston St 75142 972-932-2811
Dr. Dan Crawford, prin. Fax 932-1948
Norman JHS 500/7-8
3701 S Houston St 75142 972-932-2410
Jeremy Melton, prin. Fax 932-7771

Kaufman Christian S 100/PK-12
401 N Shannon St 75142 972-932-6111
Christy Butler, admin. Fax 962-6111

**Keene, Johnson, Pop. 5,659**
Keene ISD 800/PK-12
PO Box 656 76059 817-774-5200
Ricky Stephens, supt. Fax 774-5400
www.keeneisd.org/
Keene Alternative Learning Center 50/Alt
PO Box 656 76059 817-774-5370
Ted O'Neil, prin. Fax 774-5405
Keene HS 300/9-12
PO Box 656 76059 817-774-5220
Sandra Denning, prin. Fax 774-5401
Keene JHS 200/6-8
PO Box 656 76059 817-774-5270
Billie Hopps, prin. Fax 774-5402

Chisholm Trail Academy 200/9-12
PO Box 717 76059 817-641-6626
Southwestern Adventist University Post-Sec.
PO Box 567 76059 817-645-3921

**Keller, Tarrant, Pop. 38,916**
Keller ISD 32,600/PK-12
350 Keller Pkwy 76248 817-744-1000
Randy Reid, supt. Fax 744-1263
www.kellerisd.net
Indian Springs MS 900/7-8
305 Bursey Rd 76248 817-744-3200
Sandy Troudt, prin. Fax 431-4432
Keller HS 2,600/9-12
601 Pate Orr Rd N 76248 817-744-1400
Dr. Michael Nasra, prin. Fax 337-3362
Keller Learning Center 100/Alt
250 College Ave 76248 817-744-4465
Christy Johnson, prin. Fax 744-4464
Keller MS 800/7-8
300 College Ave 76248 817-744-2900
Sandra Chapa, prin. Fax 377-3512
Other Schools – See Fort Worth

Messiah Lutheran Classical Academy 100/PK-10
1308 Whitley Rd 76248 817-431-5486
Erika Mildred, hdmstr. Fax 431-8536
Toni & Guy Hairdressing Academy Post-Sec.
1185 S Main St 76248 817-697-3037

**Kemp, Kaufman, Pop. 1,139**
Kemp ISD 1,500/PK-12
905 S Main St 75143 903-498-1314
Phil Edwards, supt. Fax 498-1315
kemp.ednet10.net
Kemp HS 400/9-12
220 State Highway 274 75143 903-498-9222
Marietta Maxwell, prin. Fax 498-9275
Kemp JHS 300/6-8
1000 Tolosa Rd 75143 903-498-1343
Clay Tracy, prin. Fax 498-1359

**Kenedy, Karnes, Pop. 3,282**
Kenedy ISD 700/PK-12
401 FM 719 78119 830-583-4100
Fax 583-9950
www.kenedy.isd.tenet.edu
Kenedy HS 200/9-12
401 FM 719 78119 830-583-4100
Randy Tiemann, prin. Fax 583-9126
Kenedy MS 100/6-8
401 FM 719 78119 830-583-4100
Timothy Richter, prin. Fax 583-9519

**Kennard, Houston, Pop. 331**
Kennard ISD 300/PK-12
304 State Highway 7 E 75847 936-655-2161
Richard Cooper, supt. Fax 655-2327
www.kennardisd.net
Kennard JSHS 100/6-12
304 State Highway 7 E 75847 936-655-2121
Stephen Tuggle, prin. Fax 655-2327

**Kennedale, Tarrant, Pop. 6,631**
Kennedale ISD 3,100/PK-12
PO Box 467 76060 817-563-8000
Gary Dugger, supt. Fax 483-3610
www.kennedaleisd.net
Kennedale HS 1,000/9-12
PO Box 1208 76060 817-563-8100
Justin Marchel, prin. Fax 563-3718
Kennedale JHS 500/7-8
PO Box 489 76060 817-563-8200
Michael Cagle, prin. Fax 483-3655

Fellowship Academy 200/PK-12
PO Box 738 76060 817-483-2400
Monica Collier, admin. Fax 483-2404

**Kerens, Navarro, Pop. 1,548**
Kerens ISD 600/PK-12
200 Bobcat Ln 75144 903-396-2924
Don Denbow, supt. Fax 396-2334
www.kerensisd.org
Kerens S 600/PK-12
200 Bobcat Ln 75144 903-396-2931
Gayle White, prin. Fax 396-2334

**Kermit, Winkler, Pop. 5,630**
Kermit ISD 1,300/PK-12
601 S Poplar St 79745 432-586-1000
Denise Shetter, supt. Fax 586-1016
www.kisd.esc18.net
Kermit HS 300/9-12
601 S Poplar St 79745 432-586-1050
Rocky Ford, prin. Fax 586-1055
Kermit JHS 300/5-8
601 S Poplar St 79745 432-586-1040
Gabe Espino, prin. Fax 586-1045

**Kerrville, Kerr, Pop. 22,087**
Kerrville ISD 4,600/PK-12
1009 Barnett St 78028 830-257-2200
Dan Troxell Ph.D., supt. Fax 257-2249
www.kerrvilleisd.net
Hill Country HS 50/Alt
1200 Sidney Baker St 78028 830-257-2232
Steve Schwarz, prin. Fax 792-5020
Peterson MS 700/7-8
1607 Sidney Baker St 78028 830-257-2204
Donna Jenschke, prin. Fax 257-1300
Tivy HS 1,300/9-12
3250 Loop 534 78028 830-257-2212
Jarrett Jachade, prin. Fax 895-3575

Conlee's College of Cosmetology Post-Sec.
320 W Water St Ste E 78028 830-896-2380
Our Lady of the Hills Catholic HS 100/9-12
235 Peterson Farm Rd 78028 830-895-0501
Therese Schwarz, prin. Fax 895-3470
Schreiner University Post-Sec.
2100 Memorial Blvd 78028 830-896-5411

**Kilgore, Gregg, Pop. 12,762**
Kilgore ISD 3,900/PK-12
301 N Kilgore St 75662 903-988-3900
Cara Cooke, supt. Fax 983-3212
www.kisd.org
Kilgore Alternative Education Center 50/Alt
301 N Kilgore St 75662 903-988-3921
Julie Hope, coord. Fax 984-0571
Kilgore HS 1,000/9-12
301 N Kilgore St 75662 903-988-3901
Greg Brown, prin. Fax 984-0571
Kilgore MS 900/6-8
301 N Kilgore St 75662 903-988-3902
April Cox, prin. Fax 984-6225

Kilgore College Post-Sec.
1100 Broadway Blvd 75662 903-984-8531

**Killeen, Bell, Pop. 120,349**
Killeen ISD 38,900/PK-12
PO Box 967 76540 254-336-0000
Dr. John Craft, supt. Fax 526-0010
www.killeenisd.org
Ellison HS 2,400/9-12
909 E Elms Rd 76542 254-336-0600
David Dominguez, prin. Fax 336-0606
Gateway Complex 100/Alt
4100 Zephyr Rd 76543 254-336-1700
Christopher Halpayne, prin. Fax 336-1711
Killeen Early College HS 9-12
6200 W Central Texas Exprwy 76549 254-336-0260
Kathleen Burke, prin. Fax 336-0271
Killeen HS 2,000/9-12
500 N 38th St 76543 254-336-7208
Susan Buckley, prin. Fax 336-0413
KISD Career Center Vo/Tech
1320 Stagecoach Rd 76542 254-336-3804
Scott Herald, dir. Fax 336-2303
Liberty Hill MS 900/6-8
4500 Kit Carson Trl 76542 254-336-1370
Kurt Hulett, prin. Fax 336-1403
Live Oak Ridge MS 800/6-8
2600 Robinett Rd 76549 254-336-2490
Wanda Stidom, prin. Fax 336-2498
Manor MS 700/6-8
1700 S W S Young Dr 76543 254-336-1310
Jennifer Washington, prin. Fax 336-1317
Nolan MS 700/6-8
505 E Jasper Dr 76541 254-336-1150
Lolly Garcia, prin. Fax 336-1162
Palo Alto MS 900/6-8
2301 W Elms Rd 76549 254-336-1200
Matt Widacki, prin. Fax 336-1217
Patterson MS 800/6-8
8383 W Trimmier Rd 76542 254-336-7100
Jill Balzer, prin. Fax 336-7136
Rancier MS 700/6-8
3301 Hilliard Ave 76543 254-336-1250
Micah Wells, prin. Fax 336-1254
Shoemaker HS 2,200/9-12
3302 S Clear Creek Rd 76549 254-336-0900
Sandra Forsythe, prin. Fax 336-0937
STEM Academy 9-12
3302 S Clear Creek Rd 76549 254-336-0900
Fax 520-1118
Other Schools – See Fort Hood, Harker Heights

Central Texas College Post-Sec.
PO Box 1800 76540 254-526-7161
Memorial Christian Academy 300/PK-12
PO Box 11269 76547 254-526-5403
Doyle Banks, admin. Fax 634-2030
Texas A&M University Central Texas Post-Sec.
1001 Leadership Pl 76549 254-519-5400

**Kingsville, Kleberg, Pop. 25,996**
Kingsville ISD 3,700/PK-12
PO Box 871 78364 361-592-3387
Carol G. Perez Ed.D., supt. Fax 595-7805
www.kingsvilleisd.com
King HS 1,000/9-12
PO Box 871 78364 361-595-8600
Jose Mireles, prin. Fax 595-9170
Memorial MS 500/7-8
PO Box 871 78364 361-595-8675
Dr. Alys Williams, prin. Fax 592-4198
Pogue Options Alternative Academy 9-12
PO Box 871 78364 361-595-9137
Diana Guerrero-Pena, prin.

Ricardo ISD 700/PK-8
138 W County Road 2160 78363 361-592-6465
Dr. Maria Canales, supt. Fax 592-3101
www.ricardoisd.us
Ricardo MS 300/5-8
138 W County Road 2160 78363 361-592-6465
Dr. Cynthia Flores, prin. Fax 593-0707

Santa Gertrudis ISD 400/PK-12
PO Box 592 78364 361-592-5087
Mary Springs, supt. Fax 592-5335
www.sgisd.net
Santa Gertrudis Academy 200/9-12
PO Box 592 78364 361-384-5041
Les Dragon, prin. Fax 592-5335

Presbyterian Pan American S 200/9-12
PO Box 1578 78364 361-592-4307
Texas A&M University Kingsville Post-Sec.
700 University Blvd 78363 361-593-2111

**Kingwood, Harris, Pop. 37,397**
Humble ISD
Supt. — See Humble
Creekwood MS 900/6-8
3603 W Lake Houston Pkwy 77339 281-641-4400
Walt Winicki, prin. Fax 641-4417
Kingwood HS 2,700/9-12
2701 Kingwood Dr 77339 281-641-6900
Ted Landry, prin. Fax 641-7217
Kingwood MS 1,000/6-8
2407 Pine Terrace Dr 77339 281-641-4200
Bob Atteberry, prin. Fax 641-4217
Kingwood Park HS 1,600/9-12
4015 Woodland Hills Dr 77339 281-641-6600
Lisa Drabing, prin. Fax 641-6617
Riverwood MS 1,100/6-8
2910 High Valley Dr 77345 281-641-4800
Donnie Bodron, prin. Fax 641-4817

---

Lone Star College - Kingwood Post-Sec.
20000 Kingwood Dr 77339 281-312-1600
Northeast Christian Academy 200/PK-12
1711 Hamblen Rd 77339 281-359-1090
Brad Baggett, head sch Fax 359-5560

**Kirbyville, Jasper, Pop. 2,112**
Kirbyville Consolidated ISD 1,500/PK-12
206 E Main St 75956 409-423-2284
Richard Hazlewood, supt. Fax 423-2367
www.kirbyvillecisd.org/
Kirbyville HS 400/9-12
100 E Wildcat Dr 75956 409-423-7500
Dennis Reeves, prin. Fax 423-5313
Kirbyville JHS 200/6-8
2200 S Margaret Ave 75956 409-420-0692
Eric Cormier, prin. Fax 423-6654

**Klein, Harris, Pop. 12,000**
Klein ISD 45,000/PK-12
7200 Spring Cypress Rd 77379 832-249-4000
Dr. Jim Cain, supt. Fax 249-4015
www.kleinisd.net
Doerre IS 1,200/6-8
18218 Theiss Mail Route Rd 77379 832-249-5700
Nicole Patin, prin. Fax 249-4054
Kleb IS 1,300/6-8
7425 Louetta Rd 77379 832-249-5500
Jessica Haddox, prin. Fax 249-4053
Klein Annex - Alternative Education 100/Alt
7302 Kleingreen Ln 77379 832-249-4800
Kim Kaufman, dir. Fax 249-4045
Klein HS 3,100/9-12
16715 Stuebner Airline Rd 77379 832-484-4000
Larry Whitehead, prin. Fax 484-7821
Krimmel IS 1,000/6-8
7070 FM 2920 Rd 77379 832-375-7200
Scott Crowe, prin. Fax 375-7150
Strack IS 1,100/6-8
18027 Kuykendahl Rd Ste S 77379 832-249-5400
Andrea Comer, prin. Fax 249-4051
Other Schools – See Houston, Spring

**Knippa, Uvalde, Pop. 688**
Knippa ISD 300/PK-12
PO Box 99 78870 830-934-2176
Jeff Cottrill, supt. Fax 934-2490
www.knippaisd.net
Knippa S 300/PK-12
PO Box 99 78870 830-934-2177
Jeff Cottrill, prin. Fax 934-2490

**Knox City, Knox, Pop. 1,121**
Knox City-O'Brien Consolidated ISD 300/PK-12
606 E Main St 79529 940-657-3521
Louis Baty, supt. Fax 657-3379
www.knoxcityschools.net
Knox City HS 100/9-12
606 E Main St 79529 940-657-3565
Colin Howeth, prin. Fax 657-3379
Other Schools – See O Brien

**Kopperl, Bosque**
Kopperl ISD 200/PK-12
PO Box 67 76652 254-889-3502
Kenneth Bateman, supt. Fax 889-3443
www.kopperlisd.org
Kopperl S 200/PK-12
PO Box 67 76652 254-889-3502
Katrina Adcock, prin. Fax 889-3443

**Kountze, Hardin, Pop. 2,103**
Kountze ISD 1,300/PK-12
PO Box 460 77625 409-246-3352
John Ferguson, supt. Fax 246-3217
kountzeisd.org
Kountze HS 400/9-12
PO Box 460 77625 409-246-3474
Chet Deaver, prin. Fax 246-8180
Kountze MS 200/7-8
PO Box 460 77625 409-246-3551
Patti Crouch, prin. Fax 246-8907

**Kress, Swisher, Pop. 707**
Kress ISD 200/PK-12
200 E 5th St 79052 806-684-2652
Doug Setliff, supt. Fax 684-2687
www.kressonline.net
Kress JSHS 100/7-12
200 E 5th St 79052 806-684-2651
Leah Zeigler, prin. Fax 684-2687

**Krum, Denton, Pop. 4,096**
Krum ISD 1,800/PK-12
1200 Bobcat Blvd 76249 940-482-6000
Cody Carroll, supt. Fax 482-3929
www.krumisd.net
Krum HS 500/9-12
1200 Bobcat Blvd 76249 940-482-2601
Michelle Pieniazek, prin. Fax 482-2997
Krum MS 400/6-8
1200 Bobcat Blvd 76249 940-482-2602
Shelly Enloe, prin. Fax 482-6299

**Kyle, Hays, Pop. 27,512**
Hays Consolidated ISD 15,300/PK-12
21003 Interstate 35 78640 512-268-2141
Michael McKie, supt. Fax 268-2147
www.hayscisd.net
Chapa MS 600/6-8
3311 Dacy Ln 78640 512-268-8500
Lisa Walls, prin. Fax 295-7824
Lehman HS 2,100/9-12
1700 Lehman Rd 78640 512-268-8454
Michelle Chae, prin. Fax 268-2146
Simon MS 600/6-8
3839 E FM 150 78640 512-268-8507
Dr. Jose Puga, prin. Fax 268-4146
Wallace MS 800/6-8
1500 W Center St 78640 512-268-2891
Brenda Agnew, prin. Fax 268-1853
Other Schools – See Buda

**Ladonia, Fannin, Pop. 606**
Fannindel ISD 200/PK-12
601 W Main St 75449 903-367-7251
H.L. Milton M.S., supt. Fax 367-7252
fannindel.esc8.net/
Fannindel HS 100/6-12
601 W Main St 75449 903-367-7251
Robert Milton M.S., prin. Fax 367-7252

**La Feria, Cameron, Pop. 7,287**
La Feria ISD 3,700/PK-12
PO Box 1159 78559 956-797-8300
Rey Villarreal, supt. Fax 797-3737
www.laferiaisd.org/
Green JHS 500/7-8
PO Box 1159 78559 956-797-8400
Michael Torres, prin. Fax 797-2157
La Feria Academy 100/Alt
PO Box 1159 78559 956-797-8360
Carlos Verduzco, prin. Fax 797-1583
La Feria HS 900/9-12
PO Box 1159 78559 956-797-8370
Isaac Rodriguez, prin. Fax 797-9374

**Lago Vista, Travis, Pop. 5,961**
Lago Vista ISD 1,300/PK-12
PO Box 4929 78645 512-267-8300
Darren Webb, supt. Fax 267-8304
www.lagovistaisd.net
Lago Vista HS 400/9-12
PO Box 4929 78645 512-267-8300
Heather Stoner, prin. Fax 267-8304
Lago Vista MS 300/5-8
PO Box 4929 78645 512-267-8300
Paul Thailing, prin. Fax 267-8329

**La Grange, Fayette, Pop. 4,573**
La Grange ISD 1,900/PK-12
PO Box 100 78945 979-968-7000
Dr. Randy Albers, supt. Fax 968-8155
www.lgisd.net/
La Grange HS 600/9-12
PO Box 100 78945 979-968-4800
John Pineda, prin. Fax 968-6744
La Grange MS 300/7-8
PO Box 100 78945 979-968-4747
Cliff Kinder, prin. Fax 968-6419

**La Joya, Hidalgo, Pop. 3,984**
La Joya ISD 29,000/PK-12
200 W Expressway 83 78560 956-323-2000
Dr. Alda T. Benavides, supt. Fax 323-2010
www.lajoyaisd.net/
Academy of Health Science Professionals 9-11
801 N Coyote Dr 78560
Le-Ann Alaniz, prin.
Carter Early College HS 200/9-12
603 N Coyote Dr 78560 956-584-4842
Sylvia Sepulveda, prin. Fax 584-4843
College and Career Center Alt
603 N College Dr 78560 956-519-4031
Ronny Cabrera, dir. Fax 519-4030
De Zavala MS 700/6-8
603 Tabasco Rd 78560 956-580-5472
Magda Villarreal, prin. Fax 580-5494
HOPE Academy 100/Alt
101 E Expressway 83 78560 956-580-6121
Lindolfo Zamora, prin. Fax 580-6125
La Joya Early College HS 9-12
801 N Coyote Dr 78560 956-323-2935
Domingo Villarreal, prin. Fax 519-4046
La Joya HS 2,500/9-12
604 N Coyote Dr 78560 956-580-5100
Antonio Cano, prin. Fax 580-5103
LaJoya ISD West Academy 200/Alt
801 N Coyote Dr 78560 956-580-5900
Norma Garcia, prin. Fax 580-5960
Salinas STEM Early College HS 9-12
801 N Coyote Dr 78560 956-580-5908
Diana Garcia, prin. Fax 580-5402
Other Schools – See Alton, Mission, Palmview, Penitas

**Lake Dallas, Denton, Pop. 6,973**
Lake Dallas ISD 4,100/PK-12
PO Box 548 75065 940-497-4039
Gayle Stinson, supt. Fax 497-3737
www.ldisd.net
Lake Dallas MS 1,000/6-8
PO Box 548 75065 940-497-4037
Jim Parker, prin. Fax 497-4028
Other Schools – See Corinth

**Lake Jackson, Brazoria, Pop. 26,471**
Brazosport ISD
Supt. — See Clute
Lake Jackson IS 900/7-8
100 Oyster Creek Dr 77566 979-730-7250
Susan Wood, prin. Fax 292-2804

---

Brazosport Christian S 200/PK-12
200 Willow Dr Ste B 77566 979-297-0563
Stephen Meier, head sch Fax 297-8455
Brazosport College Post-Sec.
500 College Dr 77566 979-230-3000

**Lake Worth, Tarrant, Pop. 4,497**
Lake Worth ISD 3,200/PK-12
6805 Telephone Rd 76135 817-306-4200
John Hebert, supt. Fax 237-2583
www.lwisd.org
Lake Worth HS 700/9-12
4210 Boat Club Rd 76135 817-306-4200
Mike Ellis, prin. Fax 237-0697
Other Schools – See Fort Worth

**La Marque, Galveston, Pop. 14,302**
La Marque ISD 1,700/PK-12
PO Box 7 77568 409-938-4251
Terri Watkins, supt. Fax 908-5012
www.lmisd.net
La Marque HS 700/9-12
PO Box 7 77568 409-938-4261
Andre Credit, prin. Fax 908-5036
La Marque JHS 400/7-8
PO Box 7 77568 409-938-7250
Krystal Harris, prin. Fax 908-5036
Renaissance STEM Academy 100/6-10
PO Box 7 77568 409-908-5100
Olatunji Oduwole, prin. Fax 908-5094

**Lamesa, Dawson, Pop. 9,364**
Klondike ISD 300/PK-12
2911 County Road H 79331 806-462-7334
Steve McLaren, supt. Fax 462-7333
klondike.esc17.net
Klondike S 300/PK-12
2911 County Road H 79331 806-462-7332
Tony Bushong, prin. Fax 462-7333

Lamesa ISD 1,900/PK-12
PO Box 261 79331 806-872-5461
Ron Miller, supt. Fax 872-6220
www.lamesa.esc17.net
Lamesa HS 400/9-12
PO Box 261 79331 806-872-8385
Chris Riggins, prin. Fax 872-6608
Lamesa MS 400/6-8
PO Box 261 79331 806-872-8301
Jesse Galdean, prin. Fax 872-2949
Lamesa Success Academy 50/Alt
PO Box 261 79331 806-872-5410
Brad Froman, admin. Fax 872-6220

**Lampasas, Lampasas, Pop. 6,551**
Lampasas ISD 3,400/PK-12
207 W 8th St 76550 512-556-6224
Randall J. Hoyer Ed.D., supt. Fax 556-8711
www.lampasas.k12.tx.us
Lampasas HS 1,000/9-12
207 W 8th St 76550 512-564-2310
Mark Kehoe, prin. Fax 564-2406
Lampasas MS 800/6-8
207 W 8th St 76550 512-556-3101
Dana Holcomb, prin. Fax 556-0245

**Lancaster, Dallas, Pop. 35,843**
Lancaster ISD 6,100/PK-12
422 S Centre Ave 75146 972-218-1400
Dr. Michael McFarland, supt. Fax 218-1401
www.lancasterisd.org
Hall Learning Center Alt
602 E 2nd St 75146 972-218-1441
Eleanor Webb, prin. Fax 218-1442
Lancaster HS 1,700/9-12
200 E Wintergreen Rd 75134 972-218-1800
Joseph Showell, prin. Fax 218-5797
Lancaster MS 800/7-8
822 W Pleasant Run Rd 75146 972-218-1660
Pamela Brown, prin. Fax 218-3080

---

Cedar Valley College Post-Sec.
3030 N Dallas Ave 75134 972-860-8201

**Laneville, Rusk**
Laneville ISD 200/PK-12
7415 FM 1798 W 75667 903-863-5353
Dr. Brian Nichols, supt. Fax 863-2736
www.lanevilleisd.org/
Laneville S 200/PK-12
7415 FM 1798 W 75667 903-863-5353
Teresa Shelton, prin. Fax 863-2376

**La Porte, Harris, Pop. 33,263**
La Porte ISD 7,700/PK-12
1002 San Jacinto St 77571 281-604-7000
Lloyd Graham, supt. Fax 604-7010
www.lpisd.org
Dewalt Alternative S 100/Alt
1002 San Jacinto St 77571 281-604-6900
Debbie Stewart, prin. Fax 604-6904
La Porte HS 2,100/9-12
1002 San Jacinto St 77571 281-604-7500
Todd Schoppe, prin. Fax 604-7516
La Porte JHS 600/7-8
1002 San Jacinto St 77571 281-604-6600
Cynthia Anderson, prin. Fax 604-6605
Lomax JHS 600/7-8
1002 San Jacinto St 77571 281-604-6700
Candace Pohl, prin. Fax 604-6730

**La Pryor, Zavala, Pop. 1,634**
La Pryor ISD 500/PK-12
PO Box 519 78872 830-365-4000
Ramon Abarca, supt. Fax 365-4006
www.lapryor.net
La Pryor HS 200/7-12
PO Box 519 78872 830-365-4007
Matthew McHazlett, prin. Fax 365-4026

**Laredo, Webb, Pop. 235,714**
Laredo ISD 24,800/PK-12
1702 Houston St 78040 956-273-1000
Dr. A. Marcus Nelson, supt. Fax 273-1403
www.laredoisd.org/

Cantu Health Science Magnet S 9-12
2002 San Bernardo Ave 78040 956-795-3874
Geraldina Arredondo, dir. Fax 795-3875
Christen MS 1,300/6-8
2001 Santa Maria Ave 78040 956-273-6400
Carlos Cruz, prin. Fax 795-3732
Cigarroa HS 1,400/9-12
2600 Zacatecas St 78046 956-273-6800
Laura Flores, prin. Fax 795-3814
Cigarroa MS 1,300/6-8
2600 Palo Blanco St 78046 956-273-6100
Jose Cerda, prin. Fax 718-2208
Lamar MS 1,400/6-8
1818 N Arkansas Ave 78043 956-273-6200
Margarita Taboada, prin. Fax 795-3766
Lara Academy 100/Alt
2901 E Travis St 78043 956-273-7900
Robert Chaney, prin. Fax 726-0350
Martin HS 1,900/9-12
2002 San Bernardo Ave 78040 956-273-7100
Guillermo Pro, prin. Fax 795-3860
Memorial MS 700/6-8
2002 Marcella Ave 78040 956-273-6600
Lizzy Newsome, prin. Fax 795-3780
Nixon HS 2,000/9-12
2000 E Plum St 78043 956-273-7400
Dr. Gerardo Cruz, prin. Fax 795-3844
Perez S for Engineering & Technology 9-12
2600 Zacatecas St 78046 956-795-3800
Alfredo Perez, prin. Fax 795-3814
Trevino S of Communications & Fine Arts 9-12
2102 E Lyon 78043 956-273-7800
Dr. Martha Villarreal, prin. Fax 273-7895
Valdez HS Alt
2502 Galveston St 78043 956-273-8000
Melissa Valdez, prin. Fax 795-3643

Texas A&M International University ISD 11-12
5201 University Blvd 78041 956-326-2860
Dr. Patricia Uribe, supt. Fax 326-2864
www.tamiu.edu/coas/theacademy
Texas Academy of International & STEM 11-12
5201 University Blvd 78041 956-326-2860
Dr. Patricia Uribe, dir. Fax 326-2863

United ISD 40,500/PK-12
201 Lindenwood Dr 78045 956-473-6201
Roberto J. Santos, supt. Fax 728-8691
www.uisd.net
Alexander HS 2,800/9-12
3600 E Del Mar Blvd 78041 956-473-5800
Ernesto Sandoval, prin. Fax 473-5999
Alexander Magnet HS 9-12
3600 E Del Mar Blvd 78041 956-473-5866
Elvira Gaona, dean Fax 473-5998
Bruni-Vergar MS 900/6-8
5910 Saint Luke 78046 956-473-6600
Clare G. Flores, prin. Fax 473-6699
Clark MS 800/6-8
500 W Hillside Rd 78041 956-473-7500
Rene Rodriguez, prin. Fax 473-7599
Garcia MS 500/6-8
499 Pena Dr 78046 956-473-5000
Clotilde Gamez, prin. Fax 473-5099
Gonzalez MS 1,100/6-8
5208 Santa Claudia 78043 956-473-7000
Patricia Perez, prin. Fax 473-7099
Johnson HS 2,500/9-12
5626 Cielito Lindo 78046 956-473-5100
Armando Salazar, prin. Fax 473-5281
Los Obispos MS 1,000/6-8
4801 S Ejido Ave 78046 956-473-7800
Jessica C. Salazar, prin. Fax 473-1899
Trautmann MS 1,100/6-8
8501 Curly Ln 78045 956-473-7400
Leticia Menchaca, prin. Fax 473-7499
United 9th Grade Campus 9-9
8800 McPherson Rd 78045 956-473-2400
Arlene Trevino, dean Fax 473-2499
United HS 2,900/10-12
2811 United Ave 78045 956-473-5600
Alberto Aleman, prin. Fax 473-1980
United Magnet HS 9-12
2811 United Ave 78045 956-473-5627
Angelica Sanchez, dean Fax 473-1981
United MS 1,100/6-8
700 E Del Mar Blvd 78041 956-473-7300
Rebecca Morales, prin. Fax 473-7399
United S.T.E.P. Academy 100/Alt
1600 Espejo-Molina Rd 78046 956-473-6500
Gerardo Rodriguez, dean Fax 473-6599
United South HS 2,800/9-12
4001 Los Presidentes Ave 78046 956-473-5400
Adriana P. Ramirez, prin. Fax 473-5599
United South Magnet HS 9-12
4001 Los Presidentes Ave 78046 956-473-5440
Priscilla Munoz, dean Fax 473-5598
United South MS 1,400/6-8
3707 Los Presidentes Ave 78046 956-473-7700
Martha Alvarez, prin. Fax 473-7799
Washington MS 1,300/6-8
10306 Riverbank Dr 78045 956-473-7600
Beth Porter, prin. Fax 473-7699

Kaplan College Post-Sec.
6410 McPherson Rd 78041 956-717-5909
Laredo Community College Post-Sec.
1 W End Washington St 78040 956-722-0521
St. Augustine HS 400/9-12
1300 Galveston St 78040 956-724-8131
Olga Gentry, prin. Fax 725-9241
Texas A&M International University Post-Sec.
5201 University Blvd 78041 956-326-2000

**LaRue, Henderson**
La Poynor ISD 500/PK-12
13155 US Highway 175 E 75770 903-876-4057
Sherry Douglas, supt. Fax 876-4541
www.lapoynorisd.net/
La Poynor HS 100/9-12
13155 US Highway 175 E 75770 903-876-2373
Eric Carpenter, prin. Fax 876-2374
La Poynor JHS 100/6-8
13155 US Highway 175 E 75770 903-876-2373
Eric Carpenter, prin. Fax 876-2374

**Lasara, Willacy, Pop. 1,039**
Lasara ISD 500/PK-12
PO Box 57 78561 956-642-3598
Sara Alvarado, supt. Fax 642-3546
www.lasaraisd.net/
Lasara HS 100/9-12
PO Box 57 78561 956-642-3271
Alejos Salazar, prin. Fax 642-3546

**Latexo, Houston, Pop. 319**
Latexo ISD 500/PK-12
PO Box 975 75849 936-544-5664
Don Elsom, supt. Fax 544-5332
www.latexoisd.net
Latexo JSHS 200/7-12
PO Box 975 75849 936-544-5664
Adam Ivy, prin. Fax 544-8456

**La Vernia, Wilson, Pop. 1,011**
La Vernia ISD 3,100/PK-12
13600 US Highway 87 W 78121 830-779-6600
Dr. Jose Moreno, supt. Fax 779-2304
www.lvisd.org
La Vernia HS 900/9-12
225 Bluebonnet Rd 78121 830-779-6630
Kimberley Martin, prin. Fax 779-3218
La Vernia JHS 800/6-8
195 Bluebonnet Rd 78121 830-779-6650
Anthony Kosub, prin. Fax 779-6651

**La Villa, Hidalgo, Pop. 1,955**
La Villa ISD 600/PK-12
PO Box 9 78562 956-262-4755
Dr. Judith M. Solis, supt. Fax 262-7323
www.lavillaisd.org
La Villa Early College HS 200/9-12
PO Box 9 78562 956-262-4715
Dr. Sandra Nieto, prin. Fax 262-9798
La Villa MS 100/6-8
PO Box 9 78562 956-262-4760
Dr. Alfredo Salinas, prin. Fax 262-5243

**Lazbuddie, Parmer**
Lazbuddie ISD 200/PK-12
PO Box 9 79053 806-965-2156
Joanna Martinez, supt. Fax 965-2892
www.lazbuddieisd.org
Lazbuddie S 200/PK-12
PO Box 9 79053 806-965-2152
Ken Hoskins, prin. Fax 965-2892

**League City, Galveston, Pop. 81,913**
Clear Creek ISD 36,600/PK-12
PO Box 799 77574 281-284-0000
Dr. Greg Smith, supt. Fax 284-0005
www.ccisd.net
Bayside IS 600/6-8
4430 Village Way 77573 281-284-3000
James Thomas, prin. Fax 284-3005
Clear Creek HS 2,100/9-12
2305 E Main St 77573 281-284-1700
James Majewski, prin. Fax 284-1705
Clear Creek IS 800/6-8
2451 E Main St 77573 281-284-2300
Jerry Herd, prin. Fax 284-2305
Clear Falls HS 1,700/9-12
4380 Village Way 77573 281-284-1100
Paul House, prin. Fax 284-1106
Clear Path Alternative S 200/Alt
400 S Kansas Ave 77573 281-284-1600
Sandra Davenport, prin. Fax 284-1605
Clear Springs HS 2,400/9-12
501 Palomino St 77573 281-284-1300
Gail Love, prin. Fax 284-1305
Creekside IS 800/6-8
4320 W Main St 77573 281-284-3500
Peter Caterina, prin. Fax 284-3505
League City IS 400/6-8
2588 Webster St 77573 281-284-3400
Kimberly Brouillard, prin. Fax 284-3405
Victory Lakes IS 900/6-8
2880 W Walker St 77573 281-284-3700
Adam Douglas, prin. Fax 284-3705
Other Schools – See Friendswood, Houston, Seabrook

Bay Area Christian S 700/PK-12
4800 W Main St 77573 281-332-4814
Jason Nave, head sch Fax 554-5495
Devereux-Texas Treatment Network Post-Sec.
1150 Devereux Dr 77573 800-373-0011

**Leakey, Real, Pop. 417**
Leakey ISD 200/K-12
PO Box 1129 78873 830-232-5595
Dr. Barbara Skipper, supt. Fax 232-5535
www.leakeyisd.org
Leakey S 200/K-12
PO Box 1129 78873 830-232-5595
Gerald Lugaresi, prin. Fax 232-5535

**Leander, Williamson, Pop. 25,831**
Leander ISD 32,600/PK-12
PO Box 218 78646 512-570-0000
Bret Champion Ed.D., supt. Fax 570-0054
www.leanderisd.org
Leander Extended Opportunity Center Alt
300 S West Dr 78641 512-570-2230
Teresa Hatcher, prin. Fax 570-2234
Leander HS 2,000/9-12
3301 S Bagdad Rd 78641 512-570-1000
Tiffany Spicer, prin. Fax 570-1005
Leander MS 800/6-8
410 S West Dr 78641 512-570-3200
Christine Simpson, prin. Fax 570-3205
New Hope HS 50/Alt
401 S West Dr 78641 512-570-2200
Barbara Spelman, prin. Fax 570-2204
Rouse HS 1,800/9-12
1222 Raider Way 78641 512-570-2000
John Graham, prin. Fax 570-2005
Stiles MS 6-8
3250 Barley Rd 78641 512-570-3800
Susan Cole, prin. Fax 570-3805
Wiley MS 1,300/6-8
1526 Raider Way 78641 512-570-3600
Chris Simpson, prin. Fax 570-3605
Other Schools – See Austin, Cedar Park

Sterling Classical S 200/PK-12
11880 Old 2243 W Ste 700 78641 512-259-2722

**Lefors, Gray, Pop. 490**
Lefors ISD 200/PK-12
PO Box 390 79054 806-835-2533
Joe Waldron, supt. Fax 835-2238
www.leforsisd.net
Lefors S 200/PK-12
PO Box 390 79054 806-835-2533
Kelley Porter, prin. Fax 835-2238

**Leggett, Polk**
Leggett ISD 200/PK-12
PO Box 68 77350 936-398-2804
Jana Lowe, supt. Fax 398-2078
www.leggettisd.net
Leggett JSHS 100/7-12
PO Box 68 77350 936-398-2412
Jana Lowe, prin. Fax 398-0889

**Lenorah, Martin**
Grady ISD 200/PK-12
3500 FM 829 79749 432-459-2444
Leandro Gonzales, supt. Fax 459-2729
grady.tx.schoolwebpages.com
Grady S 200/PK-12
3500 FM 829 79749 432-459-2445
Gary Jones, prin. Fax 459-2729

**Leonard, Fannin, Pop. 1,933**
Leonard ISD 900/PK-12
1 Tiger Aly 75452 903-587-2318
Larry LaFavers, supt. Fax 587-2845
www.leonardisd.net
Leonard HS 300/9-12
1 Tiger Aly 75452 903-587-3556
Brad Maxwell, prin. Fax 587-8011
Leonard JHS 200/6-8
1 Tiger Aly 75452 903-587-2315
Chris Mason, prin. Fax 587-2228

**Levelland, Hockley, Pop. 13,427**
Levelland ISD 2,100/PK-12
704 11th St 79336 806-894-9628
Jeff Northern, supt. Fax 894-2583
www.levellandisd.net
Levelland HS 700/9-12
704 11th St 79336 806-894-8515
Gary Bridges, prin. Fax 894-6029
Levelland MS 600/6-8
704 11th St 79336 806-894-6355
John Clanton, prin. Fax 894-8935

South Plains College Post-Sec.
1401 College Ave 79336 806-894-9611

**Lewisville, Denton, Pop. 93,105**
Lewisville ISD
Supt. — See Flower Mound
Career Center East Vo/Tech
2553 FM 544 75056 469-713-5211
Jeff Wagley, prin. Fax 626-1640
Delay MS 800/6-8
2103 Savage Ln 75057 469-713-5191
Jim Baker, prin. Fax 350-9174
Durham MS 800/6-8
2075 S Edmonds Ln 75067 469-713-5963
Brian McCoo, prin. Fax 350-9182
Hedrick MS 600/6-8
1526 Bellaire Blvd 75067 469-713-5188
Barbara Hamric, prin. Fax 350-9196
Huffines MS 900/6-8
1440 N Valley Pkwy 75077 469-713-5990
Estella Rupard, prin. Fax 350-9199
Jackson Career Center Vo/Tech
1597 S Edmonds Ln 75067 469-713-5186
Randall Holder, prin. Fax 350-9342
Killian MS 800/6-8
2561 FM 544 75056 469-713-5977
Deanne Angonia, prin. Fax 350-9200
Lewisville HS 1,600/11-12
1098 W Main St 75067 469-713-5190
Jeffrey Kajs, prin. Fax 350-9291
Lewisville HS Harmon Campus 500/9-10
1250 W Round Grove Rd 75067 469-713-5201
Tony Fontana, prin. Fax 626-1680
Lewisville HS Killough Campus 400/9-10
1301 Summit Ave 75077 469-713-5987
Pam Flores, prin. Fax 350-9304
Lewisville Learning Center 200/Alt
1601 S Edmonds Ln 75067 469-713-5185
Kecia Theodore, prin. Fax 350-9350
Night HS Adult
1601 S Edmonds Ln 75067 469-948-7665
Bronson Lewis, admin. Fax 350-9588

Lakeland Christian Academy 500/PK-12
397 S Stemmons Fwy 75067 972-219-3939
Tena Mitchell, dir. Fax 219-9601
Willow Bend Academy 100/5-12
101 E Southwest Pkwy # 101 75067 972-436-3839
Ed Pilkington, pres. Fax 436-3930

**Lexington, Lee, Pop. 1,158**
Lexington ISD 900/PK-12
8731 N Highway 77 78947 979-773-2254
Dr. Brad Schnautz, supt. Fax 773-4455
www.lexingtonisd.net
Lexington HS 300/9-12
8731 N Highway 77 78947 979-773-2255
Sarah Garrison, prin. Fax 773-4455
Lexington MS 200/6-8
8731 N Highway 77 78947 979-773-2255
William Paul, prin. Fax 773-4455

**Liberty, Liberty, Pop. 8,274**
Liberty ISD, 1600 Grand Ave 77575 2,200/PK-12
Dr. Cody Abshier, supt. 936-336-7213
www.libertyisd.net
Liberty HS 600/9-12
2615 Jefferson Dr 77575 936-336-6483
Dr. Chad Barrett, prin. Fax 336-3931
Liberty MS 500/6-8
2515 Jefferson Dr 77575 936-336-3582
Rhonda Smith, prin. Fax 336-1021

**Liberty Hill, Williamson, Pop. 951**
Liberty Hill ISD 2,700/PK-12
301 Forrest St 78642 512-260-5580
Dr. Rob Hart, supt. Fax 260-5581
www.libertyhill.txed.net
Liberty Hill HS 800/9-12
16500 W State Highway 29 78642 512-260-5500
Bobby Mabry, prin. Fax 260-5510
Liberty Hill JHS 500/7-8
13125 W State Highway 29 78642 512-379-3300
Annette Coe, prin. Fax 379-3310

**Lindale, Smith, Pop. 4,737**
Lindale ISD 3,800/PK-12
PO Box 370 75771 903-881-4000
Stan Surratt, supt. Fax 881-4004
www.lindaleeagles.org
Lindale HS 1,100/9-12
PO Box 370 75771 903-881-4050
Casey Neal, prin. Fax 882-2813
Lindale JHS 600/7-8
PO Box 370 75771 903-881-4150
Jeremy Chilek, prin. Fax 881-4049

**Linden, Cass, Pop. 1,960**
Linden-Kildare Consolidated ISD 800/PK-12
205 Kildare Rd 75563 903-756-5027
Trevor Rogers, supt. Fax 756-7242
www.lkcisd.net
Linden-Kildare HS 300/9-12
205 Kildare Rd 75563 903-756-7026
Keri Winters, prin. Fax 756-8512
Stephens JHS 200/6-8
205 Kildare Rd 75563 903-756-5381
Randall Wright, prin. Fax 756-8832

**Lindsay, Cooke, Pop. 1,000**
Lindsay ISD 500/K-12
PO Box 145 76250 940-668-8923
Nora Curry, supt. Fax 668-2662
www.lindsayisd.org/
Lindsay HS 300/7-12
PO Box 145 76250 940-668-8474
Steven Cope, prin. Fax 665-1637

**Lingleville, Erath**
Lingleville ISD 200/PK-12
PO Box 134 76461 254-968-2596
Curt Haley, supt. Fax 965-5821
www.lingleville.us
Lingleville S 200/PK-12
PO Box 134 76461 254-968-2596
Cheryl Hudson, prin. Fax 965-5821

**Lipan, Hood, Pop. 426**
Lipan ISD 200/PK-8
211 N Kickapoo St 76462 254-646-2266
Cindy Edwards, supt. Fax 646-3499
www.lipanindians.net/
Lipan JHS 50/7-8
211 N Kickapoo St 76462 254-646-2266
Steve Bryant, prin. Fax 646-3499

**Little Elm, Denton, Pop. 25,208**
Little Elm ISD 6,800/PK-12
PO Box 6000 75068 972-292-1847
Matthew Gutierrez, supt. Fax 294-1107
www.leisd.ws
Lakeside MS 1,400/7-8
400 Lobo Ln 75068 972-292-3200
Clint Miller, prin. Fax 292-3009
Little Elm HS 1,600/9-12
1900 Walker Ln 75068 972-292-1840
Renee Pentecost, prin. Fax 292-3505

**Littlefield, Lamb, Pop. 6,333**
Littlefield ISD 1,400/PK-12
1207 E 14th St 79339 806-385-4150
Robert Dillard, supt. Fax 385-6297
www.littlefield.k12.tx.us
Littlefield HS 400/9-12
1207 E 14th St 79339 806-385-5683
Ricky Hobbs, prin. Fax 385-3603
Littlefield JHS 300/6-8
1207 E 14th St 79339 806-385-3922
Trevor Edgemon, prin. Fax 385-5603

**Little River, Bell, Pop. 1,936**
Academy ISD 1,100/PK-12
704 E Main St 76554 254-982-4304
Kevin Sprinkles, supt. Fax 982-0023
www.academyisd.net
Academy HS 300/9-12
602 E Main St 76554 254-982-4201
Alex Remschel, prin. Fax 982-4420
Academy MS 400/6-8
501 E Main St 76554 254-982-4620
Stephen Ash, prin. Fax 982-4776

Bell County Alternative S Alt
706 E Rio Poco 76554 254-982-3505
Terry Day, prin. Fax 982-3506

**Live Oak, Bexar, Pop. 12,703**
Judson ISD 23,300/PK-12
8012 Shin Oak Dr 78233 210-945-5100
Dr. Carl Montoya, supt. Fax 945-6900
www.judsonisd.org
Judson Early College Academy 300/9-12
8230 Palisades Dr 78148 210-619-0200
Michael McFalls, prin. Fax 659-1990
Other Schools – See Converse, San Antonio, Universal City

**Livingston, Polk, Pop. 5,275**
Big Sandy ISD
Supt. — See Dallardsville
Big Sandy S 500/PK-12
FM 1276 77351 936-563-1000
Kevin Foster, prin. Fax 563-1010

Livingston ISD 4,000/PK-12
PO Box 1297 77351 936-328-2100
Dr. Brent Hawkins, supt. Fax 328-2109
www.livingstonisd.com
Alternative Education Program Alt
1 Lions Ave 77351 936-328-2353
Karen Maxey, prin. Fax 328-2352
Challenge Academy Alt
400 FM 350 S 77351 936-967-1600
Lana Smith, prin. Fax 967-8603
Livingston HS 1,100/9-12
400 FM 350 S 77351 936-967-1600
Bakewell Barron, prin. Fax 967-8603
Livingston JHS 900/6-8
1801 Highway 59 Loop N 77351 936-328-2120
Brandon Boyd, prin. Fax 328-2139

**Llano, Llano, Pop. 3,210**
Llano ISD 1,800/PK-12
1400 Oatman St 78643 325-247-4747
Casey Callahan, supt. Fax 247-5623
www.llanoisd.org
Llano HS 500/9-12
2509 S State Highway 16 78643 325-248-2200
David Wuest, prin. Fax 247-2122
Llano JHS 400/6-8
400 E State Highway 71 E 78643 325-247-4659
Todd Keele, prin. Fax 247-5821

Llano Christian Academy 100/PK-12
PO Box 728 78643 325-247-4942
Dr. Alice Smith, hdmstr.

**Lockhart, Caldwell, Pop. 12,574**
Lockhart ISD 4,800/PK-12
PO Box 120 78644 512-398-0000
Tina Knudsen, supt. Fax 398-0025
www.lockhartisd.org
Lockhart HS 1,000/10-12
1 Lion Country Dr 78644 512-398-0300
Deanna Juarez, prin. Fax 398-0302
Lockhart HS Freshman Campus 400/9-9
419 Bois DArc St 78644 512-398-0170
Denisha Jackson-Presley, prin. Fax 398-0226
Lockhart JHS 1,100/6-8
500 City Line Rd 78644 512-398-0770
Mark Estrada, prin. Fax 398-0772
Pride HS 50/Alt
1503 N Colorado St 78644 512-398-0130
Sam Lockhart, prin. Fax 398-0132

**Lockney, Floyd, Pop. 1,837**
Lockney ISD 500/PK-12
PO Box 428 79241 806-652-2115
Phil Cotham, supt. Fax 652-2729
www.lockneyisd.net
Lockney HS 200/9-12
PO Box 1058 79241 806-652-3325
Todd Hallmark, prin. Fax 652-4945
Lockney JHS 100/6-8
PO Box 550 79241 806-652-2236
Craig Setliff, prin. Fax 652-4920

**Lohn, McCulloch**
Lohn ISD 100/PK-12
PO Box 277 76852 325-344-5749
Leon Freeman, supt. Fax 344-5789
www.lohnisd.net
Lohn S 100/PK-12
PO Box 277 76852 325-344-5749
Steve Coston, prin. Fax 344-5790

**Lometa, Lampasas, Pop. 834**
Lometa ISD 300/PK-12
PO Box 250 76853 512-752-3384
David Rice, supt. Fax 752-3424
www.lometaisd.net
Lometa S 300/PK-12
PO Box 250 76853 512-752-3384
Robby Moore, prin. Fax 752-3424

**Lone Oak, Hunt, Pop. 584**
Lone Oak ISD 900/PK-12
8162 US Highway 69 S 75453 903-662-5427
Lance Campbell, supt. Fax 662-5290
www.loisd.net
Lone Oak HS 300/9-12
8204 US Highway 69 S 75453 903-662-0981
Jeff Hicks, prin. Fax 662-0984
Lone Oak MS 200/6-8
8160 US Highway 69 S 75453 903-662-5121
Dr. Shannon Wilhite, prin. Fax 662-5017

**Longview, Gregg, Pop. 79,235**
Longview ISD 7,800/PK-12
PO Box 3268 75606 903-381-2200
Dr. James Wilcox, supt. Fax 753-5389
www.lisd.org
Forest Park MS 500/6-8
PO Box 3268 75606 903-446-2510
Bill Bradshaw, prin. Fax 446-2501
Foster MS 700/6-8
PO Box 3268 75606 903-446-2710
John York, prin. Fax 758-2052
Judson MS 500/6-8
PO Box 3268 75606 903-446-2610
Dennis Mitchell, prin. Fax 663-0275
LEAD Academy, PO Box 3268 75606 8-12
Kimberly Shumaker, prin. 903-381-3921
Longview HS 2,000/9-12
PO Box 3268 75606 903-663-1301
James Brewer, prin. Fax 663-7180

Pine Tree ISD 5,000/PK-12
PO Box 5878 75608 903-295-5000
Dr. Teresa Farler, supt. Fax 295-5004
www.ptisd.org
ExCEL HS 9-12
PO Box 5878 75608 903-295-6753
Tyrance Barnett, prin. Fax 295-5145
PACE Alternative Discipline Center 300/Alt
PO Box 5878 75608 903-295-5130
Shalonda Adams, prin. Fax 295-5145
Pine Tree HS 1,200/9-12
PO Box 5878 75608 903-295-5031
Cindy Gabehart, prin. Fax 295-5029
Pine Tree JHS 700/7-8
PO Box 5878 75608 903-295-5081
Vanessa Robinson, prin. Fax 295-5082

Spring Hill ISD 1,900/PK-12
3101 Spring Hill Rd 75605 903-759-4404
Steven Snell, supt. Fax 297-0141
www.shisd.net
Spring Hill HS 500/9-12
3101 Spring Hill Rd 75605 903-446-3300
Denny Lind, prin. Fax 323-7766
Spring Hill JHS 500/6-8
3101 Spring Hill Rd 75605 903-323-7718
Michael Moore, prin. Fax 323-7765

Christian Heritage S 200/K-12
2715 FM 1844 75605 903-663-4151
Doug Carr, hdmstr. Fax 663-4587
East Texas Christian S 200/PK-12
PO Box 8053 75607 903-757-7891
Renee Sawyer, admin. Fax 619-0349
Le Tourneau University Post-Sec.
PO Box 7001 75607 903-233-3000
Longview Christian S 200/K-12
1236 Pegues Pl 75601 903-297-3501
Karen Williams, dir. Fax 758-1463
St. Mary's Catholic S 200/PK-12
405 Hollybrook Dr 75605 903-753-1657
Amy Allen, prin. Fax 758-7347
Trinity S of Texas 300/PK-12
215 N Teague St 75601 903-753-0612
Gary Whitwell, head sch Fax 753-4812
Vista College Post-Sec.
1905 W Loop 281 Ste 21 75604 866-442-4197

**Loop, Gaines, Pop. 223**
Loop ISD 100/PK-12
PO Box 917 79342 806-487-6411
Dick Van Hoose, supt. Fax 487-6416
www.loopisd.net/
Loop S 100/PK-12
PO Box 917 79342 806-487-6411
Dick Van Hoose, supt. Fax 487-6416

**Loraine, Mitchell, Pop. 595**
Loraine ISD 100/PK-12
PO Box 457 79532 325-737-2225
Dennis Hill, supt. Fax 737-2701
www.loraine.esc14.net
Loraine S 100/PK-12
PO Box 457 79532 325-737-2225
Steven Parker, prin. Fax 737-2019

**Lorena, McLennan, Pop. 1,682**
Lorena ISD 1,600/PK-12
PO Box 97 76655 254-857-3239
Dr. Sandra Talbert, supt. Fax 857-4533
www.lorenaisd.net
Lorena HS 500/9-12
PO Box 97 76655 254-857-4604
Kevin Johnson, prin. Fax 857-3883
Lorena MS 500/6-8
PO Box 97 76655 254-857-4621
Dr. Celia Drews, prin. Fax 857-3419

**Lorenzo, Crosby, Pop. 1,134**
Lorenzo ISD 300/PK-12
PO Box 520 79343 806-634-5591
Dr. Jerrod Pickering, supt. Fax 634-5928
www.lorenzoisd.net/
Lorenzo JSHS 100/7-12
PO Box 520 79343 806-634-5592
Matt Birdwell, prin. Fax 634-5788

**Los Fresnos, Cameron, Pop. 5,528**
Los Fresnos Consolidated ISD 10,200/PK-12
PO Box 309 78566 956-254-5010
Gonzalo Salazar, supt. Fax 233-4031
www.lfcisd.net
Los Cuates MS 800/6-8
PO Box 309 78566 956-254-5182
Alma Atkinson, prin. Fax 233-6265
Los Fresnos HS 1,900/10-12
PO Box 309 78566 956-254-5300
Ronnie Rodriguez, prin. Fax 233-3570
Reseca MS 900/6-8
PO Box 309 78566 956-254-5159
Elizabeth Swantner, prin. Fax 233-6209
Other Schools – See San Benito

**Lott, Falls, Pop. 750**
Rosebud-Lott ISD — 600/PK-12
1789 US Highway 77 76656 — 254-583-4510
Don Hancock Ed.D., supt. — Fax 583-4469
www.rlisd.org/
Rosebud-Lott HS — 200/9-12
1789 US Highway 77 76656 — 254-583-7967
Todd Williams, prin. — Fax 583-1130
Rosebud-Lott MS — 100/7-8
1789 US Highway 77 76656 — 254-583-7962
Todd Williams, prin. — Fax 583-2904
Other Schools – See Rosebud

**Louise, Wharton, Pop. 991**
Louise ISD — 500/PK-12
PO Box 97 77455 — 979-648-2982
Dr. Garth Oliver, supt. — Fax 648-2520
louiseisd.net
Louise HS — 100/9-12
PO Box 97 77455 — 979-648-2202
Donna Kutac, prin. — Fax 648-2142
Louise JHS — 100/6-8
PO Box 97 77455 — 979-648-2262
Donna Kutac, prin. — Fax 648-2520

**Lovelady, Houston, Pop. 635**
Lovelady ISD — 500/PK-12
PO Box 99 75851 — 936-636-7616
Dr. Micah Dyer, supt. — Fax 636-2212
www.loveladyisd.net
Lovelady JSHS — 200/7-12
PO Box 280 75851 — 936-636-7636
Michael King, prin. — Fax 636-2305

**Lubbock, Lubbock, Pop. 226,600**
Frenship ISD
Supt. — See Wolfforth
Heritage MS — 700/6-8
6110 73rd St 79424 — 806-794-9400
Greg Hernandez, prin. — Fax 793-8956
Reese Education Center — 100/Alt
9421 4th St 79416 — 806-885-4910
Farley Reeves, prin. — Fax 885-2442
Terra Vista MS — 600/6-8
1111 Upland Ave 79416 — 806-796-0076
Brent Lowrey, prin. — Fax 796-1540

Lubbock ISD — 25,800/PK-12
1628 19th St 79401 — 806-219-0000
Dr. Berhl Robertson, supt. — Fax 766-1210
www.lubbockisd.org
Atkins MS — 500/6-8
5401 Avenue U 79412 — 806-766-1522
Chris Huber, prin. — Fax 766-2226
Cavazos MS — 600/6-8
210 N University Ave 79415 — 806-219-3200
Mike Worth, prin. — Fax 766-6627
Coronado HS — 2,200/9-12
4910 29th St 79410 — 806-219-1100
Jerry Adams, prin. — Fax 766-0560
Dunbar College Preparatory Academy — 600/6-8
2010 E 26th St 79404 — 806-766-1300
Lori Alexander, prin. — Fax 766-1320
Estacado HS — 800/9-12
1504 E Itasca St 79403 — 806-219-1400
Jimmy Moore, prin. — Fax 766-1952
Evans MS — 800/6-8
4211 58th St 79413 — 806-219-3600
Flo Touchstone, prin. — Fax 766-0570
Hutchinson MS — 800/6-8
3102 Canton Ave 79410 — 806-219-3800
Heidi Dye, prin. — Fax 766-0538
Irons MS — 700/6-8
5214 79th St 79424 — 806-219-4000
Ken Casarez, prin. — Fax 766-2070
Lubbock HS — 2,000/9-12
2004 19th St 79401 — 806-219-1600
Doug Young, prin. — Fax 766-1469
MacKenzie MS — 600/6-8
5402 12th St 79416 — 806-219-4200
John Martinez, prin. — Fax 766-0510
Martin ATC — Vo/Tech
3201 Avenue Q 79411 — 806-219-2800
Charlotte Sessom, coord. — Fax 766-6675
Matthews Alternative HS — 200/Alt
417 N Akron Ave 79415 — 806-216-2600
Carolyn Thompson, prin. — Fax 766-1532
Monterey HS — 2,000/9-12
3211 47th St 79413 — 806-219-1900
Les Purkeypile, prin. — Fax 766-0509
Slaton MS — 700/6-8
1602 32nd St 79411 — 806-219-4400
Julio Aguilar, prin. — Fax 766-1571
Talkington S for Young Women Leaders — 300/6-12
415 N Ivory Ave 79403 — 806-219-2200
Berta Fogerson, prin. — Fax 766-1738
Wilson MS — 500/6-8
4402 31st St 79410 — 806-219-4600
Kelly Brownfield, prin. — Fax 766-0814

Lubbock-Cooper ISD — 3,400/PK-12
16302 Loop 493 79423 — 806-863-7100
Keith Bryant, supt. — Fax 863-3130
www.lcisd.net
Lubbock-Cooper Bush MS — 6-8
3425 118th St 79423 — 806-776-0750
Edna Parr, prin. — Fax 776-0751
Lubbock-Cooper HS — 900/9-12
16302 Loop 493 79423 — 806-863-7105
Angie Inklebarger, prin. — Fax 863-2877
Lubbock-Cooper MS — 500/6-8
16302 Loop 493 79423 — 806-863-7104
Tami Gunset, prin. — Fax 863-7163

Roosevelt ISD — 1,100/PK-12
1406 County Road 3300 79403 — 806-842-3282
Jimmy Parker, supt. — Fax 842-3266
www.roosevelt.k12.tx.us/
Roosevelt HS — 300/9-12
1406 County Road 3300 79403 — 806-842-3283
Michael Brooks, prin. — Fax 842-3931
Roosevelt JHS — 300/6-8
1406 County Road 3300 79403 — 806-842-3218
Damon McCall, prin. — Fax 842-3337

---

All Saints Episcopal S — 300/PK-11
3222 103rd St 79423 — 806-745-7701
American Commercial College — Post-Sec.
2007 34th St 79411 — 806-747-4339
Christ the King S — 300/PK-12
4011 54th St 79413 — 806-795-8283
Christine Wanjura, prin. — Fax 795-9715
Covenant Sch. of Nursing & Allied Health — Post-Sec.
2002 W Loop 289 Ste 120 79407 — 806-797-0955
Kaplan College — Post-Sec.
1421 9th St 79401 — 806-765-7051
Kingdom Preparatory Academy — 200/PK-12
PO Box 64028 79464 — 806-767-9334
Lubbock Christian S — 300/PK-12
2604 Dover Ave 79407 — 806-796-8700
Lubbock Christian University — Post-Sec.
5601 19th St 79407 — 806-796-8800
Lubbock Hair Academy — Post-Sec.
2844 34th St 79410 — 806-795-0806
Lubbock Junior Academy — 50/K-10
PO Box 6277 79493 — 806-795-4481
Methodist Hospital — Post-Sec.
3615 19th St 79410 — 806-792-1011
Southcrest Christian S — 300/PK-12
3801 S Loop 289 79423 — 806-797-7400
Linda Merriott M.Ed., supt. — Fax 776-0546
South Plains College — Post-Sec.
819 S Gilbert Dr 79416 — 806-885-3048
Texas Tech University — Post-Sec.
PO Box 45005 79409 — 806-742-2011
Texas Tech University Health Science Ctr — Post-Sec.
3601 4th St 79430 — 806-743-1000
Trinity Christian HS — 300/7-12
6701 University Ave 79413 — 806-791-6583
Moira Jacobson, prin. — Fax 745-8461
Vista College — Post-Sec.
4620 50th St 79414 — 866-442-4197

**Lucas, Collin, Pop. 5,074**
Lovejoy ISD
Supt. — See Allen
Lovejoy HS — 1,100/9-12
2350 Estates Pkwy, — 469-742-8700
Chris Mayfield, prin. — Fax 742-8701
Willow Springs MS — 7-8
1101 W Lucas Rd, — 469-702-8500
Kent Messer, prin. — Fax 702-8501

---

Lucas Christian Academy — 400/K-12
505 W Lucas Rd, — 972-429-4362
Julie Montgomery, admin. — Fax 429-5141

**Lueders, Jones, Pop. 342**
Lueders-Avoca ISD — 100/PK-12
334 Vandeventer St 79533 — 325-228-4211
Bob Spikes, supt. — Fax 228-4513
www.laisd.esc14.net
Other Schools – See Avoca

**Lufkin, Angelina, Pop. 34,621**
Hudson ISD — 2,700/PK-12
6735 Ted Trout Dr 75904 — 936-875-3351
Mary Ann Whiteker, supt. — Fax 875-9209
www.hudsonisd.org
Hudson HS — 700/9-12
6735 Ted Trout Dr 75904 — 936-875-9232
John Courtney, prin. — Fax 875-9307
Hudson MS — 600/6-8
6735 Ted Trout Dr 75904 — 936-875-9292
Richard Crenshaw, prin. — Fax 875-9317

Lufkin ISD — 8,400/PK-12
PO Box 1407 75902 — 936-634-6696
Dr. LaTonya Goffney, supt. — Fax 634-8864
www.lufkinisd.org
Alternative S — Alt
PO Box 1407 75902 — 936-632-7203
Drew Huffty, prin. — Fax 632-7209
Lufkin HS — 2,200/9-12
309 S Medford Dr 75901 — 936-632-7721
Kurt Stephens, prin. — Fax 632-8132
Lufkin MS — 1,800/6-8
900 E Denman Ave 75901 — 936-630-4444
Jesus Gomez, prin. — Fax 632-4444

Zavalla ISD
Supt. — See Zavalla
Stubblefield Learning Center — 50/Alt
208 N John Redditt Dr 75904 — 936-897-2271

---

Academy of Hair Design — Post-Sec.
512 S Chestnut St 75901 — 936-634-8440
Angelina College — Post-Sec.
PO Box 1768 75902 — 936-639-1301

**Luling, Caldwell, Pop. 5,365**
Luling ISD — 1,400/PK-12
212 E Bowie St 78648 — 830-875-3191
Tim Glover, supt. — Fax 875-3193
www.luling.txed.net
Gerdes JHS — 300/6-8
214 E Bowie St 78648 — 830-875-2121
Ernie Amaton, prin. — Fax 875-5482
Luling HS — 400/9-12
218 E Travis St 78648 — 830-875-2458
James Teafatiller, prin. — Fax 875-2751

**Lumberton, Hardin, Pop. 11,830**
Lumberton ISD — 3,600/PK-12
121 S Main St 77657 — 409-923-7580
John Valastro, supt. — Fax 755-7848
www.lumberton.k12.tx.us
Lumberton HS — 1,100/9-12
103 S LHS Dr 77657 — 409-923-7890
Darwin Davis, prin. — Fax 755-6576
Lumberton MS — 600/7-8
123 S Main St 77657 — 409-923-7581
Leanna Stringer, prin. — Fax 751-0641

**Lyford, Willacy, Pop. 2,606**
Lyford Consolidated ISD — 1,500/PK-12
PO Box 220 78569 — 956-347-3900
Eduardo Infante, supt. — Fax 347-5588
www.lyfordcisd.net
Lyford HS — 500/9-12
PO Box 220 78569 — 956-347-3909
Veronica Sanches, prin. — Fax 347-5034
Lyford MS — 300/6-8
PO Box 220 78569 — 956-347-3910
Jose Escamilla, prin. — Fax 347-2351

**Lytle, Atascosa, Pop. 2,470**
Lytle ISD — 1,700/PK-12
PO Box 745 78052 — 830-709-5100
Michelle Carroll Smith, supt. — Fax 709-5104
lytleisd.squarespace.com
Lytle HS — 500/9-12
PO Box 190 78052 — 830-709-5105
Amy Bibler, prin. — Fax 709-5107
Lytle JHS — 300/6-8
PO Box 825 78052 — 830-709-5115
Kenneth Dykes, prin. — Fax 709-5119

**Mabank, Kaufman, Pop. 2,981**
Mabank ISD — 3,400/PK-12
310 E Market St 75147 — 903-880-1300
Dr. Russell Marshall, supt. — Fax 880-1303
www.mabankisd.net
Mabank Academy — Alt
310 E Market St 75147 — 903-880-1600
Brad Koskelin, prin. — Fax 880-1603
Mabank DAEP — Alt
310 E Market St 75147 — 903-880-1600
Brad Koskelin, prin. — Fax 880-1603
Mabank HS — 1,000/9-12
310 E Market St 75147 — 903-880-1600
Brad Koskelin, prin. — Fax 880-1603
Mabank JHS — 500/7-8
310 E Market St 75147 — 903-880-1670
Barbie Conrad, prin. — Fax 880-1673

**Mc Allen, Hidalgo, Pop. 129,344**
McAllen ISD — 25,200/PK-12
2000 N 23rd St 78501 — 956-618-6000
James J. Ponce Ed.D., supt. — Fax 686-8362
www.mcallenisd.org/
Achieve Early College HS — 400/9-12
3200 Pecan Blvd 78501 — 956-872-1653
Rosalba Martinez, prin. — Fax 872-1650
Brown MS — 900/6-8
2700 S Ware Rd 78503 — 956-632-8700
Alfredo Gutierrez, prin. — Fax 632-8709
Cathey MS — 1,100/6-8
1800 N Cynthia St 78501 — 956-971-4300
Melvin L. Benford, prin. — Fax 632-2811
De Leon MS — 800/6-8
4201 N 29th Ln 78504 — 956-632-8800
Philip Grossweiler, prin. — Fax 632-8805
Fossum MS — 800/6-8
7800 N Ware Rd 78504 — 956-971-1105
Monica Kaufmann, prin. — Fax 618-9718
Instruction & Guidance Center — 50/Alt
2604 Galveston Ave 78501 — 956-971-4393
Efrain Amaya, prin. — Fax 971-4294
Lamar Academy — 100/Alt
1009 N 10th St 78501 — 956-632-3222
Cindy Pena, prin. — Fax 632-3662
Lincoln MS — 700/6-8
1601 N 27th St 78501 — 956-971-4200
Maribelle Elizondo, prin. — Fax 971-4273
McAllen HS — 2,100/9-12
2021 La Vista Ave 78501 — 956-632-3100
Albert Canales, prin. — Fax 632-3114
Memorial HS — 2,200/9-12
101 E Hackberry Ave 78501 — 956-632-5201
Pedro Alvarez, prin. — Fax 632-5226
Morris MS — 900/6-8
1400 Trenton Rd 78504 — 956-618-7300
Brian McClenny, prin. — Fax 632-3666
Rowe HS — 2,000/9-12
2101 N Ware Rd 78501 — 956-632-5100
Paz Elizondo, prin. — Fax 632-5121
Travis MS — 700/6-8
600 Houston Ave 78501 — 956-971-4242
Stanley F. Crounse, prin. — Fax 632-8454

Sharyland ISD
Supt. — See Mission
Sharyland North JHS — 800/7-8
5100 W Dove Ave 78504 — 956-686-1415
Leticia Leal, prin. — Fax 668-0425

---

Covenant Christian Academy — 500/PK-11
4201 N Ware Rd 78504 — 956-686-7886
Milton Gonzalez, prin. — Fax 686-9470
Kaplan College — Post-Sec.
1500 S Jackson Rd 78503 — 956-630-1499
South Texas Christian Academy — 300/PK-12
7001 N Ware Rd 78504 — 956-682-1117
South Texas College — Post-Sec.
3201 Pecan Blvd 78501 — 956-872-8311
South Texas Vocational-Technical Inst. — Post-Sec.
2400 Daffodil Ave 78501 — 956-631-1107
Taylor Christian S — 50/PK-12
2021 W Jackson Ave 78501 — 956-686-7574
Laura Vaca M.Ed., dir. — Fax 682-4945
University of Cosmetology Arts & Science — Post-Sec.
8401 N 10th St 78504 — 956-687-9444

**Mc Camey, Upton, Pop. 1,870**
Mc Camey ISD — 500/PK-12
PO Box 1069 79752 — 432-652-3666
Janet Hunt, supt. — Fax 652-4219
www.mcisd.esc18.net

Mc Camey HS | 100/9-12
PO Box 1069 79752 | 432-652-3666
Jay McWilliams, prin. | Fax 652-4245
Mc Camey MS | 100/5-8
PO Box 1069 79752 | 432-652-3666
Ronnie Golson, prin. | Fax 652-4246

**Mc Gregor, McLennan, Pop. 4,934**
Mc Gregor ISD | 1,400/PK-12
PO Box 356 76657 | 254-840-2828
Kevin Houchin, supt. | Fax 840-4077
www.mcgregor-isd.org
Isbill JHS | 400/6-8
PO Box 356 76657 | 254-840-3251
Paul Miller, prin. | Fax 840-3572
Mc Gregor HS | 400/9-12
PO Box 356 76657 | 254-840-2853
Robert White, prin. | Fax 840-2489

**Mc Kinney, Collin, Pop. 128,217**
Frisco ISD
Supt. — See Frisco
Scoggins MS | 900/6-8
7070 Stacy Rd 75070 | 469-633-5150
Barbara Warner, prin. | Fax 633-5160

Mc Kinney ISD | 24,600/PK-12
1 Duvall St 75069 | 469-302-4000
Dr. Rick McDaniel, supt. | Fax 302-4071
www.mckinneyisd.net
Cockrill MS | 1,200/6-8
1351 Hardin Rd 75071 | 469-302-7900
Dr. Amber Epperson, prin. | Fax 302-7901
Dowell MS | 1,200/6-8
301 Ridge Rd 75070 | 469-302-6700
Alan Arbabi, prin. | Fax 302-6701
Evans MS | 1,400/6-8
6998 Eldorado Pkwy 75070 | 469-302-7100
Todd Young, prin. | Fax 302-7101
Faubion MS | 1,000/6-8
2000 Rollins St 75069 | 469-302-6900
Jimmy Bowser, prin. | Fax 302-6901
Johnson MS | 900/6-8
3400 Community Ave 75071 | 469-302-4900
Mitch Curry, prin. | Fax 302-4901
Mc Kinney Boyd HS | 2,900/9-12
600 N Lake Forest Dr 75071 | 469-302-5400
Dr. Jennifer Peirson, prin. | Fax 302-5401
Mc Kinney HS | 2,100/9-12
1400 Wilson Creek Pkwy 75069 | 469-302-5700
Gordon Butler, prin. | Fax 302-5701
Mc Kinney North HS | 1,800/9-12
2550 Wilmeth Rd 75071 | 469-302-4300
Jimmy Spann, prin. | Fax 302-4301
Serenity HS | 50/Alt
2100 W White Ave 75069 | 469-302-7830
Juli Ferraro, prin. | Fax 302-7831

---

Collin College | Post-Sec.
2200 W University Dr 75071 | 972-548-6790
Cornerstone Christian Academy | 300/PK-12
PO Box 3143 75070 | 214-491-5700
Dr. Jeff Guleserian, hdmstr.
McKinney Christian Academy | 500/PK-12
3601 Bois D Arc Rd 75071 | 214-544-2658
Bob Lovelady, head sch | Fax 542-5056
North Texas Christian Academy | 100/PK-12
3201 N Central Expy 75071 | 214-544-1794

**Mc Lean, Gray, Pop. 771**
McLean ISD | 200/PK-12
PO Box 90 79057 | 806-779-2571
Pam Mitchell, supt. | Fax 779-2248
www.mcleanisd.com
McLean S | 100/PK-12
PO Box 90 79057 | 806-779-2671
Raymond Glass, prin. | Fax 779-2248

**Mc Leod, Cass**
Mc Leod ISD | 400/PK-12
PO Box 350 75565 | 903-796-7181
Cathy May, supt. | Fax 796-8443
www.mcleodisd.net
Mc Leod HS | 100/9-12
PO Box 350 75565 | 903-796-7181
Jim Spurlin, prin. | Fax 796-8443
Mc Leod MS | 100/6-8
PO Box 350 75565 | 903-796-7181
Jim Spurlin, prin. | Fax 796-8443

**Madisonville, Madison, Pop. 4,327**
Madisonville Consolidated ISD | 2,300/PK-12
PO Box 879 77864 | 936-348-2797
Keith Smith, supt. | Fax 348-2751
www.madisonvillecisd.org
Madisonville HS | 600/9-12
PO Box 879 77864 | 936-348-2721
Shaye Murphy, prin. | Fax 348-5753
Madisonville JHS | 500/6-8
PO Box 819 77864 | 936-348-3587
C. Keith Smith, prin. | Fax 348-5603

**Magnolia, Montgomery, Pop. 1,381**
Magnolia ISD | 11,900/PK-12
PO Box 88 77353 | 281-356-3571
Dr. Todd Stephens Ph.D., supt. | Fax 356-1328
www.magnoliaisd.org
Alpha Academy | 100/Alt
PO Box 329 77353 | 281-252-2265
Dean Frederick, prin. | Fax 252-2268
Bear Branch JHS | 900/7-8
PO Box 606 77353 | 281-356-6088
Ben King Ed.D., prin. | Fax 252-2060
Magnolia HS | 1,700/9-12
PO Box 428 77353 | 281-356-3572
Jeff Springer, prin. | Fax 252-2092
Magnolia JHS | 900/7-8
PO Box 476 77353 | 281-356-1327
Mike Metz, prin. | Fax 252-2125

Magnolia West HS | 1,700/9-12
PO Box 426 77353 | 281-252-2550
Brandon Garza Ed.D., prin. | Fax 252-2560

**Malakoff, Henderson, Pop. 2,275**
Cross Roads ISD | 600/PK-12
14434 FM 59 75148 | 903-489-2001
Leland Hand, supt. | Fax 489-2527
www.crossroadsisd.org
Cross Roads HS | 200/9-12
14434 FM 59 75148 | 903-489-1275
Mack Lowe, prin. | Fax 489-0054
Cross Roads JHS | 200/6-8
14434 FM 59 75148 | 903-489-2667
Julie West-Koepp, prin. | Fax 489-3840

Malakoff ISD | 1,300/PK-12
1308 FM 3062 75148 | 903-489-1152
Randy Perry, supt. | Fax 489-2566
www.malakoffisd.org/
Malakoff Alternative Program | 50/Alt
1209 W Royall Blvd 75148 | 903-489-4132
Danielle Copeland, prin. | Fax 489-3239
Malakoff HS | 300/9-12
15201 FM 3062 75148 | 903-489-1527
Martin Brumit, prin. | Fax 489-0971
Malakoff MS | 300/6-8
106 N Cedar St 75148 | 903-489-0264
Quintin Watkins, prin. | Fax 489-1812

**Manor, Travis, Pop. 4,931**
Manor ISD | 7,700/PK-12
10335 US Highway 290 E 78653 | 512-278-4000
Kevin Brackmeyer, supt. | Fax 278-4017
www.manorisd.net
Manor Excel Academy | 100/Alt
600 E Parsons St 78653 | 512-278-4075
Eduardo Lozano, prin. | Fax 278-4859
Manor HS | 1,200/9-12
12700 Gregg Manor Rd 78653 | 512-278-4800
Emilio Vargas, prin. | Fax 278-4803
Manor MS | 800/6-8
12900 Gregg Manor Rd 78653 | 512-278-4600
Davin Vogler, prin. | Fax 278-4285
Manor New Tech HS | 300/9-12
10323 US Highway 290 E 78653 | 512-278-4875
Steven Zipkes, prin. | Fax 278-4880
Other Schools – See Austin

**Mansfield, Tarrant, Pop. 55,102**
Mansfield ISD | 32,000/PK-12
605 E Broad St 76063 | 817-299-6300
Dr. Jim Vaszauskas, supt. | Fax 473-5465
www.mansfieldisd.org
Barber Career Tech Academy | Vo/Tech
1120 W Debbie Ln 76063 | 817-314-1600
Catherine Hudgins, prin. | Fax 453-6840
Jobe MS | 800/7-8
2491 Gertie Barrett Rd 76063 | 682-314-4400
Elizabeth Hostin, prin. | Fax 561-3899
Jones MS | 900/7-8
4500 E Broad St 76063 | 682-314-4600
Travis Moore, prin. | Fax 453-7380
Lake Ridge HS | 9-12
101 N Day Miar Rd 76063 | 682-314-0400
Dr. Vonda Nunley, prin. | Fax 548-2110
Legacy HS | 2,100/9-12
1263 N Main St 76063 | 682-314-0600
Dr. Shelly Butler, prin. | Fax 453-7653
Mansfield Frontier HS | 200/9-12
1120 W Debbie Ln 76063 | 682-314-1600
Catherine Hudgins, prin. | Fax 453-6840
Mansfield HS | 2,500/9-12
3001 E Broad St 76063 | 682-314-0100
Jennifer Young, prin. | Fax 473-5424
Phoenix Academy | 100/Alt
902 E Broad St 76063 | 682-314-1700
Regenia Crane, prin. | Fax 473-5477
Wester MS | 900/7-8
1520 N Walnut Creek Dr 76063 | 817-314-1800
Jennifer Powers, prin. | Fax 453-7213
Worley MS | 900/7-8
500 Pleasant Ridge Dr 76063 | 682-314-5100
Julia McMains, prin. | Fax 473-5623
Other Schools – See Arlington

**Manvel, Brazoria, Pop. 5,107**
Alvin ISD
Supt. — See Alvin
Manvel HS | 2,200/9-12
19601 Highway 6 77578 | 281-245-2232
Charlotte Liptack, prin. | Fax 245-2268
Manvel JHS | 6-8
7302 McCoy Rd 77578 | 281-245-3700
Raymond Root, prin. | Fax 692-9078
Rodeo Palms JHS | 800/6-8
101 Palm Desert Dr 77578 | 281-245-2078
Shawn Williams, prin. | Fax 489-8169

**Marathon, Brewster, Pop. 427**
Marathon ISD | 100/PK-12
PO Box 416 79842 | 432-386-4431
Ebby Loeffler, supt. | Fax 386-4395
www.marathonisd.com/
Marathon S | 100/PK-12
PO Box 416 79842 | 432-386-4431
Ebby Loeffler, supt. | Fax 386-4395

**Marble Falls, Burnet, Pop. 5,987**
Marble Falls ISD | 4,100/PK-12
1800 Colt Cir 78654 | 830-693-4357
Dr. Chris Allen, supt. | Fax 693-5685
www.marblefallsisd.org
Falls Career HS | Vo/Tech
1800 Colt Cir 78654 | 830-798-3621
Peggy Little, admin. | Fax 798-3636
Marble Falls HS | 1,100/9-12
2101 Mustang Dr 78654 | 830-693-4375
Manuel Lunoff, prin. | Fax 693-6079
Marble Falls MS | 900/6-8
1511 Pony Dr 78654 | 830-693-4439
Roger Barr, prin. | Fax 693-7788

---

Faith Academy of Marble Falls | 200/K-12
PO Box 1240 78654 | 830-798-1333
Joseph Rispoli, admin. | Fax 798-1332
Living Word Academy | 50/1-12
918 2nd St 78654 – Robert Hill, prin. | 830-693-3339

**Marfa, Presidio, Pop. 1,967**
Marfa ISD | 300/PK-12
PO Box T 79843 | 432-729-5500
Andrew Peters, supt. | Fax 729-4310
marfaisd.org
Marfa JSHS | 200/6-12
PO Box T 79843 | 432-729-5500
Mary Paul, prin. | Fax 729-4053

**Marion, Guadalupe, Pop. 1,060**
Marion ISD | 1,400/PK-12
PO Box 189 78124 | 830-914-2803
Kelly Walters, supt. | Fax 420-2300
www.marionisd.net
Marion HS | 400/9-12
PO Box 189 78124 | 830-914-2803
Elizardo Hernandez, prin. | Fax 420-3639
Marion MS | 300/6-8
PO Box 189 78124 | 830-914-2803
Jon Lindholm, prin. | Fax 420-3206

**Marlin, Falls, Pop. 5,913**
Marlin ISD | 1,100/PK-12
130 Coleman St 76661 | 254-883-3585
Michael Seabolt, supt. | Fax 883-6612
www.marlinisd.org
Marlin HS | 300/9-12
1400 Capps St 76661 | 254-883-2394
Stephanie Nuner, prin. | Fax 883-3470
Marlin MS | 200/6-8
678 Success Dr 76661 | 254-883-9241
Stephanie Nuner, prin. | Fax 883-2839

**Marshall, Harrison, Pop. 23,237**
Marshall ISD | 5,800/PK-12
1305 E Pinecrest Dr 75670 | 903-927-8700
Dr. Marcell Smith, supt. | Fax 935-0203
www.marshallisd.com
Marshall HS | 1,400/9-12
1900 Maverick Dr 75670 | 903-927-8800
Katina Brown, prin. | Fax 938-7052
Marshall JHS | 800/7-8
700 W Houston St 75670 | 903-927-8830
Linda Lister, prin. | Fax 927-8837

---

East Texas Baptist University | Post-Sec.
1 Tiger Dr 75670 | 903-935-7963
Texas State Technical College | Post-Sec.
2650 E End Blvd S 75672 | 903-935-1010
Wiley College | Post-Sec.
711 Wiley Ave 75670 | 903-927-3300

**Mart, McLennan, Pop. 2,183**
Mart ISD | 600/PK-12
700 E Navarro Ave 76664 | 254-876-2523
Todd Gooden, supt. | Fax 876-3028
www.martisd.org/
Mart HS | 200/9-12
700 E Navarro Ave 76664 | 254-876-2574
Betsy Burnett, prin. | Fax 876-2575
Mart MS | 200/5-8
700 E Navarro Ave 76664 | 254-876-2762
Dr. Tawnya Nail, prin. | Fax 876-2792

**Mason, Mason, Pop. 2,094**
Mason ISD | 700/PK-12
PO Box 410 76856 | 325-347-1144
Pam Kruse, supt. | Fax 294-4412
www.masonisd.net/
Mason HS | 200/9-12
PO Box 410 76856 | 325-347-1122
Chris Habecker, prin. | Fax 347-8247
Mason JHS | 200/5-8
PO Box 410 76856 | 325-347-1122
Mitchel Rasberry, prin. | Fax 347-5461

**Matador, Motley, Pop. 605**
Motley County ISD | 200/PK-12
PO Box 310 79244 | 806-347-2676
William Cochran, supt. | Fax 347-2871
www.motleyco.org
Motley County S | 200/PK-12
PO Box 310 79244 | 806-347-2676
Tim Hill, prin. | Fax 347-2871

**Mathis, San Patricio, Pop. 4,929**
Mathis ISD | 1,600/PK-12
PO Box 1179 78368 | 361-547-3378
Benny Hernandez, supt. | Fax 547-4198
www.mathisisd.org
Mathis HS | 400/9-12
PO Box 1179 78368 | 361-547-3322
Albert Arismendi, prin. | Fax 547-4139
Mathis MS | 300/6-8
PO Box 1179 78368 | 361-547-2381
Randy Tiemman, prin. | Fax 547-4156

**Maud, Bowie, Pop. 1,042**
Maud ISD | 500/PK-12
PO Box 1028 75567 | 903-585-2219
Charles Martin, supt. | Fax 585-5451
www.maudisd.net
Maud S | 500/PK-12
PO Box 1028 75567 | 903-585-2219
David Hedges, prin. | Fax 585-5451

**May, Brown**
May ISD | 200/PK-12
3400 E County Road 411 76857 | 254-259-2091
Donald Rhodes, supt. | Fax 259-3514
www.mayisd.com
May JSHS | 100/7-12
3400 E County Road 411 76857 | 254-259-2131
Steven Howard, prin. | Fax 259-2706

**Maypearl, Ellis, Pop. 920**
Maypearl ISD 1,000/PK-12
PO Box 40 76064 972-435-1000
Ritchie Bowling M.Ed., supt. Fax 435-1001
www.maypearlisd.org
Maypearl HS 300/9-12
PO Box 40 76064 972-435-1020
Debbie Griffin, prin. Fax 435-1021
Maypearl JHS 200/7-8
PO Box 40 76064 972-435-1015
Lesley Austin, prin. Fax 435-1016

**Meadow, Terry, Pop. 593**
Meadow ISD 300/PK-12
604 4th St 79345 806-539-2246
Darrian Dover, supt. Fax 539-2529
www.meadowisd.net
Meadow HS 100/6-12
604 4th St 79345 806-539-2222
Steve Reynolds, prin. Fax 539-2334

**Medina, Bandera, Pop. 3,931**
Medina ISD 300/PK-12
PO Box 1470 78055 830-589-2855
Penny White, supt. Fax 589-7150
www.medinaisd.org
Medina S 200/PK-12
PO Box 1470 78055 830-589-2851
John McNamara, prin. Fax 589-7150

**Melissa, Collin, Pop. 4,615**
Melissa ISD 1,600/PK-12
1904 Cooper St 75454 972-837-2411
Keith Murphy, supt. Fax 837-4233
www.melissaisd.org
Melissa HS 500/9-12
3150 Cardinal Dr 75454 972-837-4216
Mike Carter, prin. Fax 837-4381
Melissa MS 200/6-8
2950 Cardinal Dr 75454 972-837-4355
Jim Miller, prin. Fax 837-4497

**Memphis, Hall, Pop. 2,281**
Memphis ISD 600/PK-12
PO Box 460 79245 806-259-5900
Kent Lemons, supt. Fax 259-2515
www.memphisisd.net
Memphis HS 200/9-12
PO Box 460 79245 806-259-5910
Dick Hutcherson, prin. Fax 259-3026
Memphis MS 100/6-8
PO Box 460 79245 806-259-5920
Kennith Hardin, prin. Fax 259-2051

**Menard, Menard, Pop. 1,468**
Menard ISD 300/PK-12
PO Box 729 76859 325-396-2404
amy bannowsky, supt. Fax 396-2143
www.menardisd.net
Menard HS 100/9-12
PO Box 729 76859 325-396-2513
Joe Jones, prin. Fax 396-2053
Menard JHS 100/6-8
PO Box 729 76859 325-396-2348
Cordelia Kothmann, admin. Fax 396-2761

**Mercedes, Hidalgo, Pop. 15,537**
Mercedes ISD 5,400/PK-12
PO Box 419 78570 956-514-2000
Dr. Daniel Trevino, supt. Fax 514-2033
www.misdtx.net
Chacon MS 800/6-8
PO Box 419 78570 956-514-2200
Orlando Rodriguez, prin. Fax 514-2212
Mercedes Academic Academy 100/Alt
PO Box 419 78570 956-825-5076
Heather Garza, dir. Fax 514-2171
Mercedes Early College HS 300/9-12
PO Box 419 78570 956-825-5180
Jeanne Venecia, prin. Fax 514-2175
Mercedes HS 1,100/9-12
PO Box 419 78570 956-514-2100
Patricia Masso, prin. Fax 514-2111

South Texas ISD 3,200/7-12
100 Med High Dr 78570 956-565-2454
Marla Guerra Ed.D., supt. Fax 565-9129
www.stisd.net
Science Academy of South Texas 700/9-12
900 Med High Dr 78570 956-565-4620
Irma Castillo, prin. Fax 565-9112
South Texas HS for Health Professions 900/9-12
700 Med High Dr 78570 956-565-2237
Barbara Heater, prin. Fax 565-4039
Other Schools – See Edinburg, Olmito, San Benito

**Meridian, Bosque, Pop. 1,479**
Meridian ISD 500/PK-12
PO Box 349 76665 254-435-2081
Dr. John Horak, supt. Fax 435-2025
www.meridianisd.org
Meridian JSHS 200/6-12
PO Box 349 76665 254-435-2723
Paul Booth, prin. Fax 435-2199

**Merit, Hunt**
Bland ISD 600/PK-12
PO Box 216 75458 903-776-2239
Rick Tidwell, supt. Fax 776-2240
www.blandisd.net
Bland HS 200/9-12
PO Box 216 75458 903-776-2239
Dustin Evans, prin. Fax 776-2426
Bland MS 100/6-8
PO Box 216 75458 903-776-2239
Kevin Hamilton, prin. Fax 527-5491

**Merkel, Taylor, Pop. 2,564**
Merkel ISD 900/PK-12
PO Box 430 79536 325-928-5813
Bryan Allen, supt. Fax 928-3910
www.merkel.esc14.net
Merkel HS 300/9-12
PO Box 430 79536 325-928-4667
Joseph O'Malley, prin. Fax 928-4684
Merkel JHS 200/7-8
PO Box 430 79536 325-928-5511
Casey Hodges, prin. Fax 928-3138

**Mertzon, Irion, Pop. 768**
Irion County ISD 300/PK-12
PO Box 469 76941 325-835-6111
Billy Barnett, supt. Fax 835-2017
www.irion-isd.org
Irion County MSHS 200/7-12
PO Box 469 76941 325-835-2881
Shannon Chapman, prin. Fax 835-2298

**Mesquite, Dallas, Pop. 137,317**
Mesquite ISD 38,200/PK-12
405 E Davis St 75149 972-288-6411
Dr. David Vroonland, supt. Fax 882-7787
www.mesquiteisd.org
Agnew MS 800/7-8
729 Wilkinson Dr 75149 972-882-5750
Donna Gallegos, prin. Fax 882-5760
Berry MS 900/6-8
2675 Bear Dr 75181 972-882-5850
Sandra Bibb, prin. Fax 882-5888
Horn HS 2,200/9-12
3300 E Cartwright Rd 75181 972-882-5200
Bruce Perkins, prin. Fax 882-5291
Kimbrough MS 800/7-8
3900 N Galloway Ave 75150 972-882-5900
Chris Brott, prin. Fax 882-5942
McDonald MS 1,000/7-8
2930 N Town East Blvd 75150 972-882-5700
Debra Bassinger, prin. Fax 882-5710
Mesquite Academy 200/Alt
2704 Motley Dr 75150 972-882-7570
Connie Boone, prin. Fax 882-7579
Mesquite HS 2,800/9-12
300 E Davis St 75149 972-882-7800
Kevin Samples, prin. Fax 882-7876
New MS 1,000/7-8
3700 S Belt Line Rd 75181 972-882-5600
Stacy Carpenter, prin. Fax 882-5620
North Mesquite HS 2,500/9-12
18201 Lyndon B Johnson Fwy 75150 972-882-7900
Douglas Barber, prin. Fax 882-7908
Poteet HS 1,600/9-12
3300 Poteet Dr 75150 972-882-5300
Karyn Cummings, prin. Fax 882-5353
Terry MS 900/6-8
2351 Edwards Church Rd 75181 972-882-5650
Danny Taylor, prin. Fax 882-5660
Vanston MS 700/7-8
3230 Karla Dr 75150 972-882-5801
Emilio Duran, prin. Fax 882-5848
West Mesquite HS 1,800/9-12
2500 Memorial Blvd 75149 972-882-7600
Alisia Coday, prin. Fax 882-7611
Wilkinson MS 900/6-8
2100 Crest Park Dr 75149 972-882-5950
Leslie Feinglas, prin. Fax 882-5988

Carrington College Post-Sec.
3733 W Emporium Cir 75150 972-682-2800
Dallas Christian S 600/PK-12
1515 Republic Pkwy 75150 972-270-5495
Eastfield College Post-Sec.
3737 Motley Dr 75150 214-860-7100
Hands On Therapy School Post-Sec.
1804 N Galloway Ave 75149 972-285-6133
Metroplex Beauty School Post-Sec.
519 N Galloway Ave 75149 972-288-5485

**Mexia, Limestone, Pop. 7,378**
Mexia ISD 2,000/PK-12
PO Box 2000 76667 254-562-4000
Dr. Sharon Ross, supt. Fax 562-4007
mexia.schoolfusion.us
Mexia HS 500/9-12
PO Box 2000 76667 254-562-4010
Larry Adair, prin. Fax 562-2142
Mexia JHS 400/6-8
PO Box 2000 76667 254-562-4020
Thurman Brown, prin. Fax 562-5053
Mexia S of Choice 50/Alt
PO Box 2000 76667 254-562-4023
John Schaefer, prin. Fax 562-4024

**Miami, Roberts, Pop. 592**
Miami ISD 200/PK-12
PO Box 368 79059 806-868-3971
Donna Gill, supt. Fax 868-3171
www.miamiisd.net
Miami S 200/PK-12
PO Box 368 79059 806-868-3971
Randall Hall, prin. Fax 868-3171

**Midland, Midland, Pop. 109,776**
Greenwood ISD 1,600/PK-12
2700 FM 1379 79706 432-685-7800
Ariel Elliott, supt. Fax 685-7804
www.greenwood.esc18.net
Brooks MS 300/6-8
2700 FM 1379 79706 432-685-7837
John-Paul Huber, prin. Fax 685-7838
Greenwood HS 500/9-12
2700 FM 1379 79706 432-685-7805
Stacy Jones, prin. Fax 685-7814

Midland ISD 21,800/PK-12
615 W Missouri Ave 79701 432-240-1000
Dr. Ryder Warren, supt. Fax 689-1976
www.midlandisd.net/
Abell JHS 900/7-8
3201 Heritage Blvd 79707 432-689-6200
Jenifer Neatherlin, prin. Fax 689-6217
Advanced Technology Center Vo/Tech
3200 W Cuthbert Ave 79701 432-681-6312
Kim Evans, dir.
Alamo JHS 800/7-8
3800 Storey Ave 79703 432-689-1700
Leann Dumas, prin. Fax 689-1712
Coleman HS 100/Alt
1600 E Golf Course Rd 79701 432-689-5000
David Moore, prin. Fax 689-5016
Early College at Midland College 300/9-12
3600 N Garfield St 79705 432-685-4641
Renee Aldrin, prin. Fax 685-4669
Goddard JHS 900/7-8
2500 Haynes Dr 79705 432-689-1300
Shelly King, prin. Fax 689-1321
Lee Freshman HS 800/9-9
1400 E Oak Ave 79705 432-689-1250
Bobby Stults, prin. Fax 689-1253
Lee SHS 2,100/10-12
3500 Neely Ave 79707 432-689-1600
Stan VanHoozer, prin. Fax 689-1647
Midland Freshman HS 700/9-9
100 E Gist Ave 79701 432-689-1200
Robert Cedillo, prin. Fax 689-1209
Midland SHS 2,000/10-12
906 W Illinois Ave 79701 432-689-1100
Carlin Grammer, prin. Fax 689-1144
San Jacinto JHS 700/7-8
1400 N N St 79701 432-689-1350
Deborah Kendricks, prin. Fax 689-1385

Midland Christian S 1,200/PK-12
2001 Culver Dr 79705 432-694-1661
Midland College Post-Sec.
3600 N Garfield St 79705 432-685-4500
Trinity S of Midland 500/PK-12
3500 W Wadley Ave 79707 432-697-3281
Rev. Walter Prehn Ph.D., head sch Fax 697-7403

**Midlothian, Ellis, Pop. 17,760**
Midlothian ISD 7,500/PK-12
100 Walter Stephenson Rd 76065 972-775-8296
Dr. Lane Ledbetter, supt. Fax 775-1757
www.midlothian-isd.net
Midlothian Heritage HS 9-12
4000 FM 1387 76065 972-775-6509
Krista Tipton, prin. Fax 775-7841
Midlothian HS 2,300/9-12
923 S 9th St 76065 972-775-8237
Dr. Al Hemmle, prin. Fax 775-3178
Seale MS 800/6-8
700 George Hopper Rd 76065 972-775-6145
Coy Tipton, prin. Fax 775-1502
Walnut Grove MS 1,000/6-8
990 N Walnut Grove Rd 76065 972-775-5355
Brian Blackwell, prin. Fax 775-8127

**Milano, Milam, Pop. 425**
Milano ISD 400/PK-12
PO Box 145 76556 512-455-2533
Robert Westbrook, supt. Fax 455-9311
www.milanoisd.net
Milano HS 100/9-12
PO Box 145 76556 512-455-9333
Tracy Brewer, prin. Fax 455-9336
Milano JHS 100/6-8
PO Box 145 76556 512-455-6701
Tracy Brewer, prin. Fax 455-9186

**Miles, Runnels, Pop. 823**
Miles ISD 400/PK-12
PO Box 308 76861 325-468-2861
Robert Gibson, supt. Fax 468-2179
www.milesisd.net
Miles JSHS 200/7-12
PO Box 308 76861 325-468-2861
Robin Graves, prin. Fax 468-2179

**Milford, Ellis, Pop. 717**
Milford ISD 200/PK-12
PO Box 545 76670 972-493-2911
Don Clingenpeel, supt. Fax 493-2429
www.milfordisd.org
Milford S 200/PK-12
PO Box 545 76670 972-493-2921
Don Clingenpeel, prin. Fax 493-4600

**Millsap, Parker, Pop. 400**
Millsap ISD 800/PK-12
201 E Brazos St 76066 940-682-3100
Dr. David Belding, supt. Fax 682-4476
www.millsapisd.net
Millsap HS 300/9-12
600 Bulldog Dr 76066 940-682-4994
Tammy Addison, prin. Fax 682-4035
Millsap MS 200/6-8
301 E Brazos St 76066 940-682-4994
Jeff Clark, prin. Fax 682-4476

**Mineola, Wood, Pop. 4,457**
Mineola ISD 1,600/PK-12
1000 W Loop 564 75773 903-569-2448
Kim Tunnell, supt. Fax 569-5155
www.mineolaisd.net
Mineola HS 500/9-12
1000 W Loop 564 75773 903-569-3000
David Sauer, prin. Fax 569-1930
Mineola MS 300/6-8
1000 W Loop 564 75773 903-569-5338
Mike Sorenson, prin. Fax 569-5339

**Mineral Wells, Palo Pinto, Pop. 16,580**
Mineral Wells ISD 3,600/PK-12
906 SW 5th Ave 76067 940-325-6404
Dr. Gail G. Haterius, supt. Fax 325-6378
www.mwisd.net/
Mineral Wells Academy 50/Alt
3810 Ram Blvd 76067 940-325-3033
Jeff Smith, admin. Fax 325-6044
Mineral Wells HS 1,000/9-12
3801 Ram Blvd 76067 940-325-4408
Jon Almeida, prin. Fax 325-7623

Mineral Wells JHS 500/7-8
1301 SE 14th Ave 76067 940-325-0711
Wendell Barker, prin. Fax 328-0450

---

Community Christian S 100/PK-12
2501 Garrett Morris Pkwy 76067 940-328-1333
Doug Jefferson, admin. Fax 328-1277

**Mission, Hidalgo, Pop. 76,804**
La Joya ISD
Supt. — See La Joya
Chavez MS 800/6-8
78 Showers Rd 78572 956-580-6182
Daniel Villarreal, prin. Fax 580-6169
Garcia MS 800/6-8
933 Paula St, 956-584-0800
Santana Galven, prin. Fax 584-0817
Juarez-Lincoln HS 2,200/9-12
7801 W Mile 7 Rd, 956-519-4150
Eduardo Alaniz, prin. Fax 519-4160
LaJoya ISD East Academy Alt
2916 W Mile 3 Rd, 956-519-5746
Ricardo Estrada, prin. Fax 519-5752
Memorial MS 700/6-8
2610 N Moorefield Rd, 956-580-6087
Rolando Rios, prin. Fax 580-6084
Richards MS 800/6-8
7005 Ann Richards Rd 78572 956-519-5710
Thomas Ocana, prin. Fax 519-5726
Salinas MS 700/6-8
6101 N Bentsen Palm Dr, 956-584-6355
Dr. Antonio Uresti, prin. Fax 584-6356

Mission Consolidated ISD 15,600/PK-12
1201 Bryce Dr 78572 956-323-5505
Dr. Ricardo Lopez, supt. Fax 323-5634
www.mcisd.net/
Mission Collegiate HS 100/9-12
1201 Bryce Dr 78572 956-323-6120
Orlando Farias, prin.
Mission HS 2,000/9-12
1201 Bryce Dr 78572 956-323-5700
Edilberto Flores, prin. Fax 323-5890
Mission JHS 900/6-8
1201 Bryce Dr 78572 956-323-3300
Ada Castillo, prin. Fax 323-3338
Mission Options S 100/Alt
1201 Bryce Dr 78572 956-323-3960
Maria Aleman, prin. Fax 323-8223
Roosevelt Alternative S 100/Alt
1201 Bryce Dr 78572 956-323-3900
Eduardo Alaniz, prin. Fax 323-3925
Veterans Memorial HS 1,800/9-12
1201 Bryce Dr 78572 956-323-3000
Angie Garcia, prin. Fax 323-3280
White JHS 900/6-8
1201 Bryce Dr 78572 956-323-3600
Brenda Betancourt, prin. Fax 323-3632
Other Schools – See Alton, Palmhurst

Sharyland ISD 10,100/PK-12
1106 N Shary Rd 78572 956-580-5200
Dr. Robert O'Connor, supt. Fax 585-2972
www.sharylandisd.org
Gray JHS 800/7-8
1106 N Shary Rd 78572 956-580-5333
Lori Ann Garza, prin. Fax 580-5346
Sharyland Advanced Academic Academy 9-12
1106 N Shary Rd 78572 956-584-6467
Ivan Karr, prin.
Sharyland HS 3,000/9-12
1106 N Shary Rd 78572 956-580-5300
Carolyn Mendiola, prin. Fax 580-5311
Sharyland Pioneer HS 9-12
1106 N Shary Rd 78572 956-271-1600
James Heath, prin.
Other Schools – See Mc Allen

---

Juan Diego Academy 9-12
PO Box 3888 78573 956-583-2752
Bob Schmidt, prin. Fax 583-3782

**Missouri City, Fort Bend, Pop. 65,862**
Fort Bend ISD
Supt. — See Sugar Land
Baines MS 1,500/6-8
9000 Sienna Ranch Rd 77459 281-634-6870
Jennifer Roberts, prin. Fax 634-6880
Elkins HS 2,000/9-12
7007 Knights Ct 77459 281-634-2600
Barbara Whitaker, prin. Fax 634-2674
Hightower HS 2,300/9-12
3333 Hurricane Ln 77459 281-634-5240
Viretta West, prin. Fax 634-5333
Lake Olympia MS 1,200/6-8
3100 Lake Olympia Pkwy 77459 281-634-3520
Deirdre Holloway, prin. Fax 634-3549
Marshall HS 1,300/9-12
1220 Buffalo Run 77489 281-634-6630
Cozette Church-Gaston, prin. Fax 634-6650
Missouri City MS 800/6-8
202 Martin Ln 77489 281-634-3440
Jerrie Kammerman, prin. Fax 634-3473
Progressive HS Alt
1555 Independence Blvd 77489 281-634-2900
Dr. Cory Collins, prin. Fax 634-2913
Quail Valley MS 1,000/6-8
3019 FM 1092 Rd 77459 281-634-3600
Karissa Ogle, prin. Fax 634-3632
Ridge Point HS 1,100/9-12
500 Waters Lake Blvd 77459 281-327-5200
Tammy Edwards, prin. Fax 327-5201

**Monahans, Ward, Pop. 6,896**
Monahans-Wickett-Pyote ISD 2,000/PK-12
606 S Betty Ave 79756 432-943-6711
Kellye Riley, supt. Fax 943-2307
www.mwpisd.esc18.net
Monahans Education Center 50/Alt
813 S Alice Ave 79756 432-943-2019
Chad Smith, prin. Fax 943-2593
Monahans HS 500/9-12
809 S Betty Ave 79756 432-943-2519
Patty Dominguez, prin. Fax 943-3327
Walker JHS 300/7-8
800 S Faye Ave 79756 432-943-4622
Chad Branham, prin. Fax 943-3723

**Mont Belvieu, Chambers, Pop. 3,784**
Barbers Hill ISD 4,400/PK-12
PO Box 1108 77580 281-576-2221
Greg Poole, supt. Fax 576-3410
www.bhisd.net/
Barbers Hill HS 1,300/9-12
PO Box 1108 77580 281-576-2221
Rick Kana, prin. Fax 576-3356
Barbers Hill MS North 700/6-8
PO Box 1108 77580 281-576-2221
Lance Murphy, prin. Fax 576-3353
Eagle Positive Intervention Center Alt
PO Box 1108 77580 281-576-2221
Daniel Andrews, prin. Fax 576-3422
Other Schools – See Baytown

**Monte Alto, Hidalgo, Pop. 1,914**
Monte Alto ISD 1,100/PK-12
25149 1st St 78538 956-262-1381
Olivia Almanza, supt. Fax 262-5535
www.montealtoisd.org
Monte Alto HS 100/9-12
25149 1st St 78538 956-262-1381
Sabrina Franco, admin. Fax 262-5535
Monte Alto MS 300/6-8
25149 1st St 78538 956-262-1374
Jimmy Padilla, prin. Fax 262-1377

**Montgomery, Montgomery, Pop. 621**
Montgomery ISD 6,900/PK-12
PO Box 1475 77356 936-582-1333
Dr. Beau Rees, supt. Fax 582-6447
www.misd.org
Montgomery HS 2,000/9-12
22825 Highway 105 W 77356 936-597-6401
Phil Eaton, prin. Fax 597-6415
Montgomery JHS 1,100/7-8
19000 Stewart Creek Rd 77356 936-582-6400
Angie Chapman, prin. Fax 582-6329

**Moody, McLennan, Pop. 1,359**
Moody ISD 700/PK-12
12084A S Lone Star Pkwy 76557 254-853-2172
Chane Rascoe, supt. Fax 853-2886
www.moodyisd.org
Moody HS 200/9-12
11862 S Lone Star Pkwy 76557 254-853-3622
Joe Satterwhite, prin. Fax 853-3822
Moody MS 200/5-8
107 Coralee Ln 76557 254-853-2182
Andrew Miller, prin. Fax 853-2886

**Moran, Shackelford, Pop. 270**
Moran ISD 100/PK-12
PO Box 98 76464 325-945-3101
Danny Freeman, supt. Fax 945-2741
www.moran.esc14.net
Moran S 100/PK-12
PO Box 98 76464 325-945-3101
Michael Waggoner, prin. Fax 945-2741

**Morgan, Bosque, Pop. 480**
Morgan ISD 100/PK-12
PO Box 300 76671 254-635-2311
John Bryant, supt. Fax 635-2224
www.morganisd.org
Morgan S 100/PK-12
PO Box 300 76671 254-635-2311
Juan Ramirez, prin. Fax 635-2224

**Morton, Cochran, Pop. 1,996**
Morton ISD 400/PK-12
500 Champion Dr 79346 806-266-5505
Vicki Rice, supt. Fax 266-5449
www.mortonisd.net/
Morton HS 100/9-12
500 Champion Dr 79346 806-266-5505
John Albin, prin. Fax 266-5780
Morton JHS 100/6-8
500 Champion Dr 79346 806-266-5505
Glen Smith, prin. Fax 266-5739

**Moulton, Lavaca, Pop. 877**
Moulton ISD 300/K-12
PO Box C 77975 361-596-4609
Todd Grandjean, supt. Fax 596-7578
www.moultonisd.net
Moulton JSHS 100/7-12
PO Box C 77975 361-596-4691
Jamie Dornak, prin. Fax 596-7119

**Mount Calm, Hill, Pop. 312**
Mount Calm ISD 100/PK-12
PO Box 105 76673 254-993-2611
Barbara Lane, supt. Fax 993-1022
www.mcisd1.org
Mount Calm S 100/PK-12
PO Box 105 76673 254-993-2611
Pamela Taylor, prin. Fax 993-1022

**Mount Enterprise, Rusk, Pop. 445**
Mount Enterprise ISD 400/PK-12
301 NW 3rd St 75681 903-822-3721
Byron Jordan, supt. Fax 822-3633
www.meisd.esc7.net
Mount Enterprise JSHS 200/6-12
301 NW 3rd St 75681 903-822-3721
Chance Mays, prin. Fax 822-3633

**Mount Pleasant, Titus, Pop. 15,466**
Chapel Hill ISD 1,000/PK-12
1069 County Road 4660 75455 903-572-8096
Marc Levesque, supt. Fax 572-1086
www.chisddevils.com
Chapel Hill HS 300/9-12
1069 County Road 4660 75455 903-572-1086
Brandon Dennard, prin. Fax 572-3850
Chapel Hill JHS 200/6-8
1069 County Road 4660 75455 903-572-1086
Mike Clifton, prin. Fax 572-9747

Mount Pleasant ISD 5,500/PK-12
PO Box 1117 75456 903-575-2000
Judd Marshall, supt. Fax 575-2014
www.mpisd.net
Mount Pleasant HS 1,400/9-12
PO Box 1117 75456 903-575-2020
Dustin Cook, prin. Fax 575-2036
Mount Pleasant JHS 700/7-8
PO Box 1117 75456 903-575-2110
Kelli Glenn, prin. Fax 575-2117

---

Northeast Texas Community College Post-Sec.
PO Box 1307 75456 903-434-8100

**Mount Vernon, Franklin, Pop. 2,608**
Mount Vernon ISD 1,600/PK-12
PO Box 98 75457 903-537-2546
John Kaufman, supt. Fax 537-4784
www.mtvernonisd.net/pages/MVISD
Mount Vernon HS 400/9-12
PO Box 1139 75457 903-537-3700
Kelly Baird, prin. Fax 537-2536
Mount Vernon JHS 200/7-8
PO Box 1139 75457 903-537-2267
Craig Watson, prin. Fax 537-3601

**Muenster, Cooke, Pop. 1,534**
Muenster ISD 500/PK-12
PO Box 608 76252 940-759-2281
Steven Self, supt. Fax 759-5200
www.muensterisd.net
Muenster HS 200/7-12
PO Box 608 76252 940-759-2281
John York, prin. Fax 759-4614

---

Sacred Heart S 200/PK-12
PO Box 588 76252 940-759-2511
Dr. Rafael Rondon, prin. Fax 759-4422

**Muleshoe, Bailey, Pop. 5,137**
Muleshoe ISD 1,500/PK-12
514 W Avenue G 79347 806-272-7400
Dr. R.L. Richards, supt. Fax 272-4120
www.muleshoeisd.net
Muleshoe HS 300/9-12
514 W Avenue G 79347 806-272-7303
Steve Myatt, prin. Fax 272-7574
Watson JHS 300/6-8
514 W Avenue G 79347 806-272-7349
Erin Boatmun, prin. Fax 272-4983

**Mullin, Mills, Pop. 179**
Mullin ISD 100/PK-12
PO Box 128 76864 325-985-3374
Steven Mickelson, supt. Fax 985-3915
www.mullinisd.net
Mullin HS 100/7-12
PO Box 128 76864 325-985-3374
Steven Mickelson, admin. Fax 985-3372

**Mumford, Robertson**
Mumford ISD 600/PK-12
9755 FM 50, 979-279-3678
Pete Bienski, supt. Fax 279-5044
www.mumford.k12.tx.us
Mumford JSHS 200/7-12
9755 FM 50, 979-279-3678
Pete Bienski, prin. Fax 279-5044

**Munday, Knox, Pop. 1,285**
Munday Consolidated ISD 400/PK-12
PO Box 300 76371 940-422-4241
Dr. Skip Casey, supt. Fax 422-5331
www.esc9.net/munday
Munday Secondary S 200/7-12
PO Box 300 76371 940-422-4321
John Berry, prin. Fax 422-5331

**Murphy, Collin, Pop. 17,219**
Plano ISD
Supt. — See Plano
McMillen HS 9-10
750 N Murphy Rd 75094 469-752-8600
Brian Lyons, prin. Fax 752-8601
Murphy MS 1,000/6-8
620 N Murphy Rd 75094 469-752-7000
Brant Perry, prin. Fax 752-7001

**Nacogdoches, Nacogdoches, Pop. 32,466**
Central Heights ISD 1,100/PK-12
10317 US Highway 259 75965 936-564-2681
Bryan Lee, supt. Fax 569-6889
www.centralhts.org
Central Heights HS 300/9-12
10317 US Highway 259 75965 936-552-3408
David Russell, prin. Fax 560-2016
Central Heights MS 300/6-8
10317 US Highway 259 75965 936-552-3441
Andrew Binford, prin. Fax 564-0177

Martinsville ISD 400/PK-12
12952 E State Highway 7 75961 936-564-3455
Jay Ratcliff, supt. Fax 569-0498
www.martinsvilleisd.com
Martinsville S 400/PK-12
12952 E State Highway 7 75961 936-564-3455
Monty Pepper, prin. Fax 569-0498

Nacogdoches ISD 6,500/PK-12
PO Box 631521 75963 936-569-5000
Dr. Fred Hayes, supt. Fax 569-5797
www.nacisd.org
McMichael MS 800/6-8
PO Box 631521 75963 936-552-0519
Tim Mullican, prin. Fax 552-0523
Moses MS 600/6-8
PO Box 631521 75963 936-569-5001
Tammy Pankratz, prin. Fax 569-5031
Nacogdoches HS 1,700/9-12
PO Box 631521 75963 936-564-2466
Kenneth Wooten, prin. Fax 560-8162
Rector Technical HS 100/Alt
PO Box 631521 75963 936-569-3175
Jerry Winfield, prin. Fax 569-5775

Regents Academy 100/K-12
200 NE Stallings Dr 75961 936-559-7343
Stephen F. Austin State University Post-Sec.
1936 North St 75965 936-468-3401

**Natalia, Medina, Pop. 1,422**
Natalia ISD 1,100/PK-12
PO Box 548 78059 830-663-4416
Michael Steck, supt. Fax 663-4186
www.nataliaisd.net
Natalia HS 300/9-12
PO Box 548 78059 830-663-4417
Jesse Vela, prin. Fax 663-6410
Natalia JHS 200/6-8
PO Box 548 78059 830-663-4027
Fax 663-2347

**Navasota, Grimes, Pop. 6,996**
Navasota ISD 3,000/PK-12
PO Box 511 77868 936-825-4200
Rory Gesch, supt. Fax 825-4297
www.navasotaisd.org
Bizzell Academy, PO Box 511 77868 Alt
Kristi Jones, prin. 936-825-4296
Navasota HS 700/9-12
PO Box 511 77868 936-825-4250
Derek Bowman, prin. Fax 825-4293
Navasota JHS 600/6-8
PO Box 511 77868 936-825-4225
Charles Lester, prin. Fax 825-4260

**Nazareth, Castro, Pop. 311**
Nazareth ISD 200/PK-12
PO Box 189 79063 806-945-2231
Glen Waldo, supt. Fax 945-2431
www.nazarethisd.net/
Nazareth S 200/PK-12
PO Box 189 79063 806-945-2231
Jeanie Birkenfeld, prin. Fax 945-2431

**Neches, Anderson**
Neches ISD 400/PK-12
PO Box 310 75779 903-584-3311
Randy Snider, supt. Fax 584-3686
www.nechesisd.com
Other Schools – See Palestine

**Nederland, Jefferson, Pop. 17,344**
Nederland ISD 5,000/PK-12
220 N 17th St 77627 409-724-2391
Robert Madding, supt. Fax 724-4280
www.nederland.k12.tx.us
Alternative S Alt
220 N 17th St 77627 409-727-5241
Karen Bussell, prin. Fax 724-4236
Central MS 800/5-8
220 N 17th St 77627 409-727-5765
Charles Jehlen, prin. Fax 724-4275
Nederland HS 1,500/9-12
220 N 17th St 77627 409-727-2741
Dr. Steven Beagle, prin. Fax 726-2679
Wilson MS 800/5-8
220 N 17th St 77627 409-727-6224
Scott Clemmons, prin. Fax 726-2699

Faris Computer School Post-Sec.
1119 Kent Ave 77627 409-722-4072

**Needville, Fort Bend, Pop. 2,792**
Needville ISD 2,700/PK-12
PO Box 412 77461 979-793-4308
Curtis Rhodes, supt. Fax 793-3823
www.needvilleisd.com
Needville HS 800/9-12
PO Box 412 77461 979-793-4158
Richard Janacek, prin. Fax 793-5590
Needville JHS 400/7-8
PO Box 412 77461 979-793-4250
Karen Smart, prin. Fax 793-4575

**Nevada, Collin, Pop. 815**
Community ISD 1,600/PK-12
PO Box 400 75173 972-843-8400
Roosevelt Nivens, supt. Fax 843-8401
www.communityisd.org
Community HS 500/9-12
PO Box 400 75173 972-843-8414
Steve Morrow, prin. Fax 843-8415
Community MS 400/6-8
PO Box 400 75173 972-843-8411
Travis Taylor, prin. Fax 843-8412

**Newark, Wise, Pop. 987**

Victory in Christ Classical Luth Academy 50/PK-12
508 Main St 76071 817-489-5400
Ruth Rohloff, prin.

**New Boston, Bowie, Pop. 4,450**
New Boston ISD 1,400/PK-12
201 Rice St 75570 903-628-2521
Dr. Rose Mary Neshyba, supt. Fax 628-8990
www.nbschools.net
New Boston HS 400/9-12
1 W Lion Dr 75570 903-628-6551
Mark Schroeder, prin. Fax 628-3695
New Boston MS 300/6-8
1215 N State Highway 8 75570 903-628-6588
Denise Davis, prin. Fax 628-5132

**New Braunfels, Comal, Pop. 57,097**
Comal ISD 17,200/PK-12
1404 N Interstate 35 78130 830-221-2000
Andrew Kim, supt. Fax 221-2001
www.comalisd.org
Canyon HS 2,000/9-12
1510 N Interstate 35 78130 830-221-2400
Brad Brown, prin. Fax 221-2401
Canyon MS 900/6-8
2014 FM 1101 78130 830-221-2300
Fred Steubing, prin. Fax 221-2301
Church Hill MS 800/6-8
1275 N Business IH 35 78130 830-221-2800
Scott Hammond, prin. Fax 221-2801
Memorial Early College HS 100/9-12
1419 N Business 35 78130 830-221-2900
Chrysta Carlin, prin. Fax 221-2901
Mountain Valley MS 700/6-8
1165 Sattler Rd 78132 830-885-1300
Leslie Bonar, prin. Fax 885-1301
Other Schools – See Fischer, Spring Branch

New Braunfels ISD 7,600/PK-12
PO Box 311688 78131 830-643-5700
Randy Moczygemba, supt. Fax 643-5701
www.nbisd.org/
Learning Center 100/Alt
902 W San Antonio St 78130 830-627-6960
Jerry Clark, admin. Fax 627-6961
New Braunfels 9th Grade Center 700/9-9
659 S Guenther Ave 78130 830-643-5700
Christie Lawson, prin.
New Braunfels HS 1,600/10-12
2551 Loop 337 78130 830-627-6000
Kara Bock, prin. Fax 627-6001
New Braunfels MS 600/7-8
656 S Guenther Ave 78130 830-627-6270
Greg Hughes, prin. Fax 627-6271
Oakrun MS 900/6-8
415 Oak Run Pt 78132 830-627-6400
Shana Behling, prin. Fax 627-6401

New Braunfels Christian Academy 400/PK-12
220 FM 1863 78132 830-629-1821
H. Eric Pipkin M.A., head sch Fax 629-1880
St. John Paul II Catholic HS 100/9-12
6720 FM 482 78132 830-643-0802
Andrew Iliff, prin. Fax 643-0806

**New Caney, Montgomery, Pop. 3,000**
New Caney ISD 10,200/PK-12
21580 Loop 494 77357 281-577-8600
Kenn Franklin, supt. Fax 354-2639
www.newcaneyisd.org
Infinity Early College HS 9-12
22500 Eagle Dr 77357 281-577-8600
Rebecca Martin, prin.
Keefer Crossing MS 800/7-8
20350 FM 1485 Rd 77357 281-577-8840
Andy Pearson, prin. Fax 399-9859
Learning Center 50/Alt
20419 FM 1485 Rd 77357 281-577-2850
Jeremy Harris, prin. Fax 354-4137
New Caney HS 1,400/9-12
21650 Loop 494 77357 281-577-2800
David Loyacano, prin. Fax 354-0186
Other Schools – See Porter

**Newcastle, Young, Pop. 582**
Newcastle ISD 200/PK-12
PO Box 129 76372 940-846-3551
Ty Spitzer, supt. Fax 846-3452
www.newcastle-isd.net
Newcastle S 200/PK-12
PO Box 129 76372 940-846-3531
Ty Spitzer, admin. Fax 846-3452

**New Deal, Lubbock, Pop. 782**
New Deal ISD 700/PK-12
PO Box 280 79350 806-746-5833
Jimmy Noland, supt. Fax 746-5707
www.ndisd.net
New Deal HS 200/9-12
PO Box 250 79350 806-746-5933
Matt Reed, prin. Fax 746-5544
New Deal MS 200/5-8
PO Box 308 79350 806-746-6633
Matt Reed, prin. Fax 746-5244

**New Home, Lynn, Pop. 334**
New Home ISD 200/PK-12
225 N Main St, 806-924-7542
Leland Zant, supt. Fax 924-7520
www.newhomeisd.org/
New Home S 200/PK-12
225 N Main St, 806-924-7543
Shane Fiedler, prin. Fax 924-7520

**New London, Rusk, Pop. 978**
West Rusk ISD 1,000/PK-12
PO Box 168 75682 903-392-7850
Tommy Alexander, supt. Fax 895-2267
www.westrusk.esc7.net
West Rusk HS 200/9-12
PO Box 168 75682 903-392-7854
Jake Jackson, prin. Fax 895-4317
West Rusk JHS 200/6-8
PO Box 168 75682 903-392-7855
Leah Bobbitt, prin. Fax 392-7867

**New Summerfield, Cherokee, Pop. 1,102**
New Summerfield ISD 500/PK-12
PO Box 6 75780 903-726-3306
Gregg Weiss, supt. Fax 726-3405
www.nsisd.sprnet.org/
New Summerfield S 500/PK-12
PO Box 6 75780 903-726-3306
Gregg Weiss, supt. Fax 726-3405

**Newton, Newton, Pop. 2,458**
Newton ISD 1,100/PK-12
720 Rusk St 75966 409-420-6600
Michelle Barrow, supt. Fax 379-5130
www.newtonisd.net
Newton HS 300/9-12
720 Rusk St 75966 409-420-6600
Tim Kenebrew, prin. Fax 379-3321
Newton MS 300/6-8
720 Rusk St 75966 409-420-6600
Judy Holleman, prin. Fax 379-5082

**New Waverly, Walker, Pop. 1,019**
New Waverly ISD 900/PK-12
355 Front St 77358 936-344-6751
Dr. Darol Hail, supt. Fax 344-2438
www.new-waverly.k12.tx.us
New Waverly HS 300/9-12
355 Front St 77358 936-344-6451
Kris Drane, prin. Fax 344-6113
New Waverly JHS 200/6-8
355 Front St 77358 936-344-2246
Dudley Hawkes, prin. Fax 344-8313

**Nixon, Gonzales, Pop. 2,375**
Nixon-Smiley Consolidated ISD 1,000/PK-12
PO Box 400 78140 830-582-1536
Cathy L. Lauer Ph.D., supt. Fax 582-1920
www.nixonsmiley.net
Nixon-Smiley HS 300/9-12
PO Box 400 78140 830-582-1536
Trey Alexander, prin. Fax 582-2168
Nixon-Smiley MS 300/5-8
PO Box 400 78140 830-582-1536
Jane Dwyer, prin. Fax 582-2258

**Nocona, Montague, Pop. 3,004**
Nocona ISD 800/PK-12
220 Clay St 76255 940-825-3267
Dr. Vickie Gearheart, supt. Fax 825-4945
www.noconaisd.net/
Nocona HS 200/9-12
220 Clay St 76255 940-825-3264
Dr. Stacey Loyless, prin. Fax 825-7270
Nocona MS 200/6-8
220 Clay St 76255 940-825-3121
Dr. Laura Ice, prin. Fax 825-6151

Prairie Valley ISD 200/PK-12
12920 FM 103 76255 940-825-4425
W. Tucker, supt. Fax 825-4650
www.prairievalleyisd.net/
Prairie Valley JSHS 100/6-12
12920 FM 103 76255 940-825-4425
Lisa Sadler, prin. Fax 825-4650

**Nordheim, DeWitt, Pop. 305**
Nordheim ISD 100/PK-12
500 Broadway 78141 361-938-5211
Kevin Wilson, supt. Fax 938-5266
www.nordheimisd.org
Nordheim S 100/PK-12
500 Broadway 78141 361-938-5211
Lisa Karnei, prin. Fax 938-5266

**Normangee, Leon, Pop. 671**
Normangee ISD 500/PK-12
PO Box 219 77871 936-396-3111
Luke Allison, supt. Fax 396-3112
www.normangeeisd.org
Normangee HS 100/9-12
PO Box 219 77871 936-396-6111
Teddy Clevenger, prin. Fax 396-6879
Normangee MS 100/6-8
PO Box 219 77871 936-396-6111
Teddy Clevenger, prin. Fax 396-6879

**North Richland Hills, Tarrant, Pop. 62,179**
Birdville ISD
Supt. — See Haltom City
Birdville Center of Tech & Advanced Lrng Vo/Tech
7020 Mid Cities Blvd 76180 817-547-3800
Dr. Linda Anderson, dir. Fax 503-8965
Birdville HS 1,900/9-12
9100 Mid Cities Blvd 76180 817-547-8000
Jason Wells, prin. Fax 547-8009
North Richland MS 900/6-8
4800 Rufe Snow Dr 76180 817-547-4200
Ernie Valamides, prin. Fax 581-5372
North Ridge MS 800/6-8
7332 Douglas Ln 76182 817-547-5200
Steve Ellis, prin. Fax 581-5460
Richland HS 2,200/9-12
5201 Holiday Ln 76180 817-547-7000
Carla Rix, prin. Fax 581-5454
Smithfield MS 800/6-8
8400 Main St 76182 817-547-5000
Kyle Pekurney, prin. Fax 581-5480

Fort Worth Christian S 900/PK-12
6200 Holiday Ln 76180 817-520-6200

**North Zulch, Madison**
North Zulch ISD 400/PK-12
PO Box 158 77872 936-399-1000
Morris Lyon, supt. Fax 399-2025
www.nzisd.org
North Zulch JSHS 100/7-12
PO Box 158 77872 936-399-1030
Josh Smith, prin. Fax 399-2038

**Oak Ridge North, Montgomery, Pop. 3,010**

Oak Ridge Christian Academy 100/PK-12
27420 Robinson Rd, 281-298-5800
Jess Larson, hdmstr. Fax 292-2818

**Oakwood, Leon, Pop. 506**
Oakwood ISD 200/PK-12
631 N Holly St 75855 903-545-2600
Jackie Thomason, supt. Fax 545-2310
www.oakwoodisd.net
Oakwood JSHS 100/7-12
631 N Holly St 75855 903-545-2140
Stu Musick, prin. Fax 545-1820

**O Brien, Haskell, Pop. 105**
Knox City-O'Brien Consolidated ISD
Supt. — See Knox City
O'Brien MS 100/5-8
711 9th St 79539 940-657-3731
Mark Tucker, prin. Fax 657-3379

**Odem, San Patricio, Pop. 2,386**
Odem-Edroy ISD 1,100/PK-12
1 Owl Sq 78370 361-368-8121
Lisa Gonzales, supt. Fax 368-2879
www.oeisd.org/
Odem HS 300/9-12
1 Owl Sq 78370 361-368-3401
Ann Ewing, prin. Fax 368-3781
Odem JHS 200/6-8
1 Owl Sq 78370 361-368-8661
James Brannigan, prin. Fax 368-2033

**Odessa, Ector, Pop. 98,924**
Ector County ISD 28,400/PK-12
PO Box 3912 79760 432-456-0000
Tom Crowe, supt. Fax 456-9878
www.ectorcountyisd.org
Alternative Education Center 50/Alt
PO Box 3912 79760 432-456-0049
Charles Quintela, prin. Fax 456-0048
Bonham MS 1,000/6-8
PO Box 3912 79760 432-456-0429
David Steele, prin. Fax 456-0428
Bowie JHS 1,200/6-8
PO Box 3912 79760 432-456-0439
Mark Ferrer, prin. Fax 456-0438
Crockett MS 800/6-8
PO Box 3912 79760 432-456-0449
Mauricio Marquez, prin. Fax 456-0448
Ector MS 1,500/6-8
PO Box 3912 79760 432-456-0479
Kendra Herrera, prin. Fax 456-0478
Falcon Early College HS 100/9-12
PO Box 3912 79760 432-456-9879
Lindsey Lumpkin, prin. Fax 456-9878
New Tech Odessa HS 9-12
PO Box 3912 79760 432-456-6989
Betsabe Salcido, prin. Fax 456-6988
Nimitz MS 1,000/6-8
PO Box 3912 79760 432-456-0469
Robin Fawcett, prin. Fax 456-0468
Odessa Career & Tech Early College HS Vo/Tech
PO Box 3912 79760 432-456-6400
Linda Wilder, prin. Fax 456-6401
Odessa SHS 2,500/10-12
PO Box 3912 79760 432-456-0029
Gregory Nelson, prin. Fax 456-0028
Permian SHS 2,200/10-12
PO Box 3912 79760 432-456-0039
James Ramage, prin. Fax 456-0038
Wilson & Young Medal of Honor MS 600/6-8
PO Box 3912 79760 432-456-0459
Andrea Martin, prin. Fax 456-0458

UTPB STEM Academy K-12
4901 E University Blvd 79762 432-552-2580
Fax 552-2581
utpbstemacademy.org
UTPB STEM Academy K-12
4901 E University Blvd 79762 432-552-2580
Dr. Jennifer Seybert, prin. Fax 552-2581

---

American Commercial College Post-Sec.
5119 Twin Towers Blvd 79762 432-362-6768
Odessa College Post-Sec.
201 W University Blvd 79764 432-335-6400
University of Texas of the Permian Basin Post-Sec.
4901 E University Blvd 79762 432-552-2020

**O Donnell, Lynn, Pop. 817**
O'Donnell ISD 300/PK-12
PO Box 487 79351 806-428-3241
Cathy Amonett Ed.D., supt. Fax 428-3395
odonnell.esc17.net
O'Donnell HS 100/6-12
PO Box 487 79351 806-428-3247
Dusty Palmer M.Ed., prin. Fax 428-3759

**Oglesby, Coryell, Pop. 480**
Oglesby ISD 200/PK-12
125 College Ave 76561 254-456-2271
Jason Jones, supt. Fax 456-2522
www.oglesbyisd.net
Oglesby S 200/PK-12
125 College Ave 76561 254-456-2271
Jason Jones, supt. Fax 456-2916

**Olmito, Cameron**
South Texas ISD
Supt. — See Mercedes
South Texas Acad for Medical Professions 500/9-12
10650 N Expressway 77/83 78575 956-214-6100
Harry Goette, prin. Fax 214-8046

**Olney, Young, Pop. 3,242**
Olney ISD 800/PK-12
809 W Hamilton St 76374 940-564-3519
Dr. Greg Roach, supt. Fax 564-5205
www.olneyisd.net
Olney HS 200/9-12
704 W Grove St 76374 940-564-5637
Julie Johnson, prin. Fax 564-5733
Olney JHS 200/6-8
300 S Avenue H 76374 940-564-3517
Gunter Rodriguez, prin. Fax 564-8824

**Olton, Lamb, Pop. 2,197**
Olton ISD 700/PK-12
PO Box 388 79064 806-285-2641
Charles McIver, supt. Fax 285-2724
www.oltonisd.net
Olton HS 200/9-12
PO Box 667 79064 806-285-2691
Kenny Eudy, prin. Fax 285-3316
Olton JHS 100/6-8
PO Box 509 79064 806-285-2681
Brian Hunt, prin. Fax 285-3348

**Omaha, Morris, Pop. 1,001**
Pewitt Consolidated ISD 1,100/PK-12
PO Box 1106 75571 903-884-2804
Dr. Andy Reddock, supt. Fax 884-2866
www.pewittcisd.net
Pewitt HS 300/9-12
PO Box 1106 75571 903-884-2293
Scot Wright, prin. Fax 884-3111
Pewitt JHS 200/6-8
PO Box 1106 75571 903-884-2505
Meghan Alcorn, prin. Fax 884-2142

**Onalaska, Polk, Pop. 1,736**
Onalaska ISD 1,000/PK-12
PO Box 2289 77360 936-646-1000
Lynn Redden, supt. Fax 646-2605
www.onalaskaisd.net
Onalaska JSHS 400/7-12
PO Box 2289 77360 936-646-1020
Anthony Roberts, prin. Fax 646-1022

**Orange, Orange, Pop. 18,289**
Deweyville ISD
Supt. — See Deweyville
Deweyville JSHS 300/7-12
171 State Highway 12 W 77632 409-746-2685
Dr. Brad Haeggquist, prin. Fax 746-9343

Little Cypress-Mauriceville Cons ISD 3,600/PK-12
6586 FM 1130 77632 409-883-2232
Dr. Pauline Hargrove, supt. Fax 883-3509
www.lcmcisd.org/
Alternative Education Center Alt
7565 Highway 87 N 77632 409-670-4635
Steve Lisbony, admin.
Little Cypress JHS 500/6-8
6765 FM 1130 77632 409-883-2317
Ryan DuBose, prin. Fax 883-5044
Little Cypress-Mauriceville HS 1,100/9-12
7327 Highway 87 N 77632 409-886-5821
Dr. Terri Estes, prin. Fax 886-5762
Mauriceville MS 400/6-8
19952 FM 1130 77632 409-745-3970
Todd Loupe, prin. Fax 745-3383

West Orange-Cove Consolidated ISD 2,500/PK-12
PO Box 1107 77631 409-882-5600
Rickie R. Harris, supt. Fax 882-5467
www.woccisd.net
West Orange-Stark MS 500/6-8
PO Box 1107 77631 409-882-5520
Anthony Moten, prin. Fax 882-5545
Other Schools – See West Orange

---

Baptist Hospital Post-Sec.
608 Strickland Dr 77630 409-883-9361
Community Christian S 300/PK-12
3400 Martin Luther King Jr 77632 409-883-4531
Laurie Beard, prin. Fax 883-8855
Lamar State College Orange Post-Sec.
410 W Front St 77630 409-883-7750

**Orangefield, Orange**
Orangefield ISD 1,700/PK-12
PO Box 228 77639 409-735-5337
Dr. Stephen D. Patterson, supt. Fax 735-2080
www.orangefieldisd.net
Orangefield HS 500/9-12
PO Box 228 77639 409-735-3851
Dr. Benjamin Petty, prin. Fax 697-2301
Orangefield JHS 500/5-8
PO Box 228 77639 409-735-6737
Preston Clark, prin. Fax 792-9605

**Orange Grove, Jim Wells, Pop. 1,306**
Orange Grove ISD 1,800/PK-12
PO Box 534 78372 361-384-2495
Lynn Burton, supt. Fax 384-2148
www.ogisd.net
Orange Grove HS 500/9-12
PO Box 534 78372 361-384-2330
Arnold Diaz, prin. Fax 384-0206
Orange Grove JHS 400/6-8
PO Box 534 78372 361-384-2323
Gildardo Salazar, prin. Fax 384-9579

**Ore City, Upshur, Pop. 1,130**
Ore City ISD 900/PK-12
100 Rebel Rd N 75683 903-968-3300
Lynn Heflin, supt. Fax 968-3797
www.ocisd.net
Ore City HS 200/9-12
100 Rebel Rd N 75683 903-968-3300
Nathan Heflin, prin. Fax 968-8726
Ore City JHS 200/6-8
100 Rebel Rd N 75683 903-968-3300
Selenia Cato, prin. Fax 968-4913

**Overton, Rusk, Pop. 2,503**
Leveretts Chapel ISD 200/PK-12
8956 State Highway 42/135 N 75684 903-834-6675
Donna Johnson, supt. Fax 834-6602
www.leverettschapelisd.net
Leveretts Chapel HS 100/9-12
8956 State Highway 42/135 N 75684 903-834-3181
Joshua Johnson, prin. Fax 834-6602
Leveretts Chapel JHS 50/6-8
8956 State Highway 42/135 N 75684 903-834-3181
Matt Everett, prin. Fax 834-6602

Overton ISD 600/PK-12
PO Box 130 75684 903-834-6145
Stephen DuBose, supt. Fax 834-6755
www.overtonisd.net
Overton HS 200/9-12
PO Box 130 75684 903-834-6143
Kendall Smith, prin. Fax 834-3246
Overton MS 100/6-8
PO Box 130 75684 903-834-6146
Cindy Bundrick, prin. Fax 834-3256

**Ovilla, Ellis, Pop. 3,449**

---

Ovilla Christian S 400/PK-12
3251 Ovilla Rd 75154 972-617-1177
Dr. Derward Richardson, hdmstr. Fax 218-0135

**Ozona, Crockett, Pop. 3,206**
Crockett County Consolidated SD 800/PK-12
PO Box 400 76943 325-392-5501
Raul Chavarria, supt. Fax 392-5177
www.ozonaschools.net
Ozona HS 200/9-12
PO Box 400 76943 325-392-5501
Ronny Clayton, prin. Fax 392-5177
Ozona MS 200/6-8
PO Box 400 76943 325-392-5501
Tamara McWilliams, prin. Fax 392-5177

**Paducah, Cottle, Pop. 1,174**
Paducah ISD 200/PK-12
PO Box P 79248 806-492-3524
Jerry Baird, supt. Fax 492-2432
www.paducahisd.org
Paducah S 200/PK-12
810 Goodwin Ave 79248 806-492-2009
Will Flemons, prin. Fax 492-2193

**Paint Rock, Concho, Pop. 270**
Paint Rock ISD 200/PK-12
PO Box 277 76866 325-732-4314
Ron Cline, supt. Fax 732-4384
www.paintrockisd.net
Paint Rock S 200/PK-12
PO Box 277 76866 325-732-4314
Ron Cline, prin. Fax 732-4384

**Palacios, Matagorda, Pop. 4,670**
Palacios ISD 1,500/PK-12
1209 12th St 77465 361-972-5491
Paul Smith, supt. Fax 972-3567
www.palaciosisd.org
Palacios HS 400/9-12
100 Shark Dr 77465 361-972-2571
Stephanie Garcia, prin. Fax 972-6287
Palacios JHS 200/7-8
200 Shark Dr 77465 361-972-2417
Patrick Talbert, prin. Fax 972-6372

**Palestine, Anderson, Pop. 18,404**
Neches ISD
Supt. — See Neches
Neches HS 100/9-12
1509 County Road 346 75803 903-584-3443
Trent Cook, prin. Fax 584-3686

Palestine ISD 3,200/PK-12
1007 E Park Ave 75801 903-731-8000
Jason Marshall, supt. Fax 729-5588
www.palestineschools.org/
Palestine HS 800/9-12
1600 S Loop 256 75801 903-731-8005
William Stewart, prin. Fax 839-6489
Palestine JHS 400/7-8
233 Ben Milam Dr 75801 903-731-8008
Stephen Cooksey, prin. Fax 655-0731

Westwood ISD 1,700/PK-12
PO Box 260 75802 903-729-1776
Dr. Ed Lyman, supt. Fax 729-3696
www.westwoodisd.net
Westwood HS 400/9-12
PO Box 260 75802 903-729-1773
Kyle Lock, prin. Fax 729-8695
Westwood JHS 200/7-8
PO Box 260 75802 903-723-0423
Julana Harmon, prin. Fax 723-6765

**Palmer, Ellis, Pop. 1,973**
Palmer ISD 1,100/PK-12
PO Box 790 75152 972-449-3389
Kevin Noack, supt. Fax 845-2112
www.palmer-isd.org
Palmer HS 300/9-12
PO Box 790 75152 972-449-3487
Brian Warner, prin. Fax 845-3517
Palmer MS 400/4-8
PO Box 790 75152 972-449-3319
Kristin Middlebrooks, prin. Fax 845-3380

**Palmhurst, Hidalgo, Pop. 2,600**
Mission Consolidated ISD
Supt. — See Mission
Cantu JHS 700/6-8
5101 N Stewart Rd 78572 956-323-7800
Ana Lisa Flores, prin. Fax 323-7880

---

Faith Christian Academy 100/PK-12
4301 N Shary Rd, 956-581-7777
Robert Munne, prin. Fax 581-7786

**Palmview, Hidalgo, Pop. 5,455**
La Joya ISD
Supt. — See La Joya
Palmview HS 2,300/9-12
3901 N La Homa Rd, 956-519-5779
Yvonne Flores Ayala, prin. Fax 323-2775

**Pampa, Gray, Pop. 17,739**
Pampa ISD 3,600/PK-12
1233 N Hobart St 79065 806-669-4700
Dr. Larry Blair, supt. Fax 665-0506
www.pampaisd.net
Pampa HS 1,000/9-12
111 E Harvester Ave 79065 806-669-4800
Gene Suttle, prin. Fax 669-4826
Pampa JHS 700/6-8
4000 Bad Cattle Company Rd 79065 806-669-4901
Jill Faubion, prin. Fax 669-4742
Pampa Learning Center 50/Alt
400 N Faulkner St 79065 806-669-4750
Richard Steele, prin. Fax 669-4734

**Panhandle, Carson, Pop. 2,431**
Panhandle ISD 700/PK-12
PO Box 1030 79068 806-537-3568
Blair Brown, supt. Fax 537-5553
www.panhandleisd.net
Panhandle HS 200/9-12
PO Box 1030 79068 806-537-3897
Robin Fulce, prin. Fax 537-3476
Panhandle JHS 100/6-8
PO Box 1030 79068 806-537-3541
Gary Cates, prin. Fax 537-5725

**Paradise, Wise, Pop. 438**
Paradise ISD 1,100/PK-12
338 School House Rd 76073 940-969-5000
Mac Edwards, supt. Fax 969-5008
www.pisd.net
Paradise HS 300/9-12
338 School House Rd 76073 940-969-5010
Mark Mathis, prin. Fax 969-5009
Paradise MS 300/6-8
338 School House Rd 76073 940-969-5034
Greg Fletcher, prin. Fax 969-5025

**Paris, Lamar, Pop. 24,458**
Chisum ISD 800/PK-12
3250 S Church St 75462 903-737-2830
Tommy Chalaire, supt. Fax 737-2831
www.chisumisd.org
Chisum HS 300/9-12
3250 S Church St 75462 903-737-2800
Clint Miller, prin. Fax 737-2801
Chisum MS 200/6-8
3250 S Church St 75462 903-737-2806
Aaron Bridges, prin. Fax 737-2805

North Lamar ISD 2,900/PK-12
3201 Lewis Ln 75460 903-737-2000
John McCullough, supt. Fax 669-0129
www.northlamar.net
North Lamar HS 900/9-12
3201 Lewis Ln 75460 903-737-2011
Clint Hildreth, prin. Fax 669-0119
Stone MS 700/6-8
3201 Lewis Ln 75460 903-737-2041
Kelli Stewart, prin. Fax 669-0149

Paris ISD 3,200/PK-12
1920 Clarksville St 75460 903-737-7473
Paul Jones, supt. Fax 737-7484
www.parisisd.net
Paris HS 900/9-12
2255 S Collegiate Dr 75460 903-737-7400
Chris Vaughn, prin. Fax 737-7515
Paris JHS 500/7-8
2400 Jefferson Rd 75460 903-737-7434
Althea Dixon, prin. Fax 737-7534
Travis HS of Choice 50/Alt
3270 Graham St 75460 903-737-7560
Joan Moore, prin. Fax 737-7574

---

Paris Junior College Post-Sec.
2400 Clarksville St 75460 903-785-7661
Romeo Preparatory Academy for Boys 50/9-12
PO Box 1822 75461 214-454-3549
David Barker M.Ed., hdmstr.
Trinity Christian Academy 100/PK-12
2060 Farm Road 79 75460 903-785-9557

**Pasadena, Harris, Pop. 147,777**
Deer Park ISD
Supt. — See Deer Park
Deepwater JHS 700/6-8
501 Glenmore Dr 77503 832-668-7600
Scott Davis, prin. Fax 475-6138
Fairmont JHS 800/6-8
4911 Holly Bay Ct 77505 832-668-7800
Neil Munro, prin. Fax 998-4456

Pasadena ISD 50,200/PK-12
1515 Cherrybrook Ln 77502 713-740-0000
Kirk Lewis, supt. Fax 740-4042
www.pasadenaisd.org
Bondy IS 1,000/6-8
5101 Keith Ave 77505 713-740-0430
Dan Connolly, prin. Fax 740-4152
Card Career & Technical Center Vo/Tech
4320 Crenshaw Rd 77504 713-740-0802
Sarah Wrobleski, dir. Fax 740-4081
Guidance Center Alt
3010 Bayshore Blvd 77502 713-740-0792
Robert Sayavedra, prin. Fax 740-4108
Jackson IS 700/6-8
1020 Thomas Ave 77506 713-740-0440
Paula Sword, prin. Fax 740-4109
Kendrick MS, 3000 Watters 77504 6-8
Melissa Messenger, prin. 713-740-5380
Miller IS 800/6-8
1002 Fairmont Pkwy 77504 713-740-0450
Vanessa Reyes, prin. Fax 740-4106
Park View IS 900/6-8
3003 Dabney Dr 77502 713-740-0460
Rob Hasson, prin. Fax 740-4115
Pasadena HS 2,400/9-12
206 Shaver St 77506 713-740-0310
Joe Saavedra, prin. Fax 740-4085
Pasadena Memorial HS 2,700/9-12
4410 Crenshaw Rd 77504 713-740-0390
Angela Stallings, prin. Fax 740-4156
Rayburn HS 2,700/9-12
2121 Cherrybrook Ln 77502 713-740-0330
Robert Stock, prin. Fax 740-4157
San Jacinto IS 600/6-8
3600 Red Bluff Rd 77503 713-740-0480
Dianna Walker, prin. Fax 740-4153
Southmore IS 800/6-8
2000 Patricia Ln 77502 713-740-0500
Andrea Wenke, prin. Fax 740-4154
Sullivan MS, 1112 Queens Rd 77502 6-8
Kelly Cook, prin. 713-740-5420
Summit S 100/Alt
1838 E Sam Houston Pkwy S 77503 713-740-0290
Robert DeWolfe, prin. Fax 740-4049
Tegeler Career Center Vo/Tech
4949 Burke Rd 77504 713-740-0410
Jean Cain, prin. Fax 740-4077
Community S Adult
1838A E Sam Houston Pkwy S 77503 713-740-0298
Tom Swan, admin. Fax 740-4048
Other Schools – See Houston, South Houston

---

First Baptist Christian Academy 400/PK-12
7500 Fairmont Pkwy 77505 281-991-9191
Freddie Cullins, head sch Fax 991-7092
Interactive Learning Systems Post-Sec.
213 W Southmore Ave 77502 713-920-1120
San Jacinto College Post-Sec.
8060 Spencer Hwy 77505 281-476-1501
Texas Chiropractic College Post-Sec.
5912 Spencer Hwy 77505 281-487-1170

**Pattison, Waller, Pop. 462**
Royal ISD 2,100/PK-12
PO Box 489 77466 281-934-2248
Stacy Ackley, supt. Fax 934-2846
www.royal-isd.net
Other Schools – See Brookshire

**Pattonville, Lamar**
Prairiland ISD 1,200/PK-12
466 Farm Road 196 75468 903-652-6476
Jeff Ballard, supt. Fax 652-3738
www.prairiland.net
Prairiland HS 400/9-12
466 Farm Road 196 75468 903-652-5681
Jason Hostetler, prin. Fax 652-6400
Prairiland JHS 200/6-8
466 Farm Road 196 75468 903-652-5681
Leslie Watson, prin. Fax 652-3232

**Pearland, Brazoria, Pop. 89,386**
Alvin ISD
Supt. — See Alvin
Ryan JHS 1,000/6-8
11500 Shadow Creek Pkwy 77584 281-245-3210
Christina Lovette, prin. Fax 245-3221
Shadow Creek HS 9-12
11850 Broadway 77584 281-388-1130
Kelly Hestand, prin.

Pearland ISD, PO Box 7 77588 18,300/PK-12
John Kelly Ph.D., supt. 281-485-3203
www.pearlandisd.org
Dawson HS, 2050 Cullen Blvd 77581 2,000/9-12
Kelly Holt, prin. 281-412-8800
Miller JHS, 3301 Manvel Rd 77584 800/7-8
Kim Brooks, prin. 281-997-3900
PACE Center 100/Alt
2314 Old Alvin Rd 77581 281-412-1599
John Palombo, prin.
Pearland HS, 3775 S Main St 77581 2,400/9-12
Larry Berger, prin. 281-997-7445
Pearland JHS East 600/7-8
2315 Old Alvin Rd 77581 281-485-2481
Annette Chambliss, prin.
Pearland JHS South 700/7-8
4719 Bailey Rd 77584 281-727-1500
Jason Frerking, prin.
Pearland JHS West 700/7-8
2337 N Galveston Ave 77581 281-412-1222
Dana Miles, prin.
Turner HS, 4717 Bailey Rd 77584 9-12
Dr. Jennifer Morrow, prin. 281-727-1600

---

Eagle Heights Christian Academy 300/PK-12
3005 Pearland Pkwy 77581 281-485-6330
John Stahl, prin. Fax 485-8682
First Christian Academy PK-12
4205 W Broadway 77581 281-412-5182
Diane Duvall, prin. Fax 736-1460

**Pearsall, Frio, Pop. 9,098**
Pearsall ISD 2,100/PK-12
318 Berry Ranch Rd 78061 830-334-8001
Dr. Nobert Rodriguez, supt. Fax 334-8007
www.pearsallisd.org
Pearsall HS 600/9-12
1990 Maverick Dr 78061 830-334-8011
Dr. Garth Oliver, prin. Fax 334-5018
Pearsall JHS 500/6-8
607 E Alabama St 78061 830-334-8021
Sharon Neumann, prin. Fax 334-8025

**Pecos, Reeves, Pop. 8,754**
Pecos-Barstow-Toyah ISD 2,200/PK-12
PO Box 869 79772 432-447-7201
Fax 447-3076
pbtisd.esc18.net
Crockett MS 500/6-8
PO Box 869 79772 432-447-7461
Sam Martinez, prin. Fax 447-4853
Pecos HS 600/9-12
PO Box 869 79772 432-447-7400
Perry Putman, prin. Fax 447-9055

**Penelope, Hill, Pop. 198**
Penelope ISD 200/PK-12
PO Box 68 76676 254-533-2215
Scot Kelley, supt. Fax 533-2262
www.penelopeisd.org/
Penelope S 200/PK-12
PO Box 68 76676 254-533-2215
Scot Kelley, supt. Fax 533-2262

**Penitas, Hidalgo, Pop. 4,401**
La Joya ISD
Supt. — See La Joya
Saenz MS 600/6-8
39200 Mile 7 Rd 78576 956-519-4007
Servando Ramirez, prin. Fax 519-4016

**Pep, Hockley, Pop. 85**
Whiteface Consolidated ISD
Supt. — See Whiteface
P E P Alternative Co-op S 50/Alt
PO Box 394 79353 806-933-4499
Fredda Schooler, prin. Fax 933-4699

**Perrin, Jack, Pop. 396**
Perrin-Whitt Consolidated ISD 400/PK-12
216 N Benson St 76486 940-798-3718
John Kuhn, supt. Fax 798-3071
www.pwcisd.net
Perrin JSHS 200/7-12
216 N Benson St 76486 940-798-3845
David Tarver, prin. Fax 798-3071

**Perryton, Ochiltree, Pop. 8,746**
Perryton ISD 2,400/PK-12
PO Box 1048 79070 806-435-5478
Robert Hall, supt. Fax 435-4689
www.perrytonisd.com
Perryton HS 500/9-12
PO Box 1048 79070 806-435-3633
James Mireles, prin. Fax 435-2602
Perryton JHS 500/6-8
PO Box 1048 79070 806-435-3601
Janet Slaughter, prin. Fax 435-3624
Top-of-Texas Accelerated Education Ctr 50/Alt
PO Box 1048 79070 806-434-0389
Ludi Martin, prin. Fax 434-0402

**Petersburg, Hale, Pop. 1,201**
Petersburg ISD 300/PK-12
PO Box 160 79250 806-667-3585
David Foote, supt. Fax 667-3463
www.petersburgisd.net
Petersburg JSHS 100/7-12
PO Box 160 79250 806-667-3574
Ritchie Tarbet, prin. Fax 667-3463

**Petrolia, Clay, Pop. 676**
Petrolia ISD 500/PK-12
PO Box 176 76377 940-524-3555
Derrith Welch, supt. Fax 524-3370
www.petroliaisd.org/
Petrolia JSHS 200/7-12
PO Box 176 76377 940-524-3264
Wade Wesley, prin. Fax 524-3215

**Pettus, Bee, Pop. 551**
Pettus ISD 400/PK-12
PO Box D 78146 361-375-2296
Theresa Keel, supt. Fax 375-2295
www.pettusisd.com
Pettus HS 200/6-12
PO Box D 78146 361-375-2296
George Cromwell, prin. Fax 375-2565

**Pflugerville, Travis, Pop. 45,841**
Pflugerville ISD 22,700/PK-12
1401 Pecan St W 78660 512-594-0000
Alex Torrez Ph.D., supt. Fax 594-0005
www.pfisd.net
Cele MS 6-8
6000 Cele Rd 78660 512-594-3000
Brian Ernest, prin. Fax 594-3005
Hendrickson HS 2,300/9-12
2905 FM 685 78660 512-594-1100
Daniel Garcia, prin. Fax 594-1105
Kelly Lane MS 1,200/6-8
18900 Falcon Pointe Blvd 78660 512-594-2800
Dina Schaefer, prin. Fax 594-2805
PACE Alt
1401B Pecan St W 78660 512-594-1900
Mike Harvey, prin. Fax 594-1905
Park Crest MS 1,000/6-8
1500 N Railroad Ave 78660 512-594-2400
Paula Gamble, prin. Fax 594-2405
Pflugerville HS 2,300/9-12
1301 Pecan St W 78660 512-594-0500
Kirk Wrinkle, prin. Fax 594-0505
Pflugerville MS 1,000/6-8
1600 Settlers Valley Dr 78660 512-594-2000
Robert Stell, prin. Fax 594-2005
Provan Opportunity Center 200/Alt
1401 Pecan St W Ste A 78660 512-594-3600
Jeff Black, prin. Fax 594-3605
Other Schools – See Austin

**Pharr, Hidalgo, Pop. 70,290**
Pharr-San Juan-Alamo ISD 30,900/PK-12
PO Box 1150 78577 956-354-2000
Dr. Daniel King, supt. Fax 702-5648
www.psjaisd.us/
Buell Central Academy 200/Alt
218 E Juarez Ave 78577 956-354-2500
Mario Bracamontes, prin. Fax 354-3110
College Career & Technology Academy 200/Alt
1100 E US Highway 83 78577 956-784-8515
Yolanda Gomez, prin. Fax 354-3112
Escalante MS 600/6-8
6123 S Cage Blvd 78577 956-354-2670
Rafael Gonzalez, prin. Fax 354-3200
Johnson MS 900/6-8
500 E Sioux Rd 78577 956-354-2590
Linda Soto, prin. Fax 354-3212

Kennedy MS 700/6-8
600 W Hall Acres Rd 78577 956-354-2650
Norma Garza, prin. Fax 354-3206
Liberty MS 900/6-8
1212 Fir Rdg 78577 956-354-2610
Alfredo Carrillo, prin. Fax 354-3218
Pharr-San Juan-Alamo North Early Coll HS 2,200/9-12
500 E Nolana Loop 78577 956-354-2360
Linda Carrillo, prin. Fax 354-3140
Pharr-San Juan-Alamo Sonia Sotomayor HS 200/Alt
1200 E Polk Ave 78577 956-354-2510
Rosie Rakay, prin. Fax 354-3120
Pharr-San Juan-Alamo SW Early College HS 800/9-12
300 E Rancho Blanco Rd 78577 956-354-2480
Ranulfo Marquez, prin. Fax 354-3172
PSJA Thomas Jefferson Early College HS 400/9-12
714 E US Highway 83 78577 956-784-8525
Marisela Zepeda, prin. Fax 354-3100
Other Schools – See Alamo, San Juan

Valley View ISD 3,800/PK-12
9701 S Jackson Rd 78577 956-340-1000
Rolando Ramirez, supt. Fax 843-8688
www.vviewisd.net
Valley View Early College Campus 50/8-9
9701 S Jackson Rd 78577 956-340-1200
Tammie Garcia, prin. Fax 213-8438
Valley View HS 1,000/9-12
9701 S Jackson Rd 78577 956-340-1500
Jesus Garza, prin. Fax 843-8195
Valley View T-STEM Early College HS 9-12
9701 S Jackson Rd 78577 956-340-1500
Gustavo Guzman, prin. Fax 843-8195

---

Oratory Academy 700/PK-12
1407 W Moore Rd 78577 956-781-3056
Fr. Leo Daniels, head sch Fax 787-1516
Southern Careers Institute Post-Sec.
1500 N Jackson Rd 78577 956-687-1415

**Pilot Point, Denton, Pop. 3,793**
Pilot Point ISD 1,500/PK-12
829 S Harrison St 76258 940-686-8700
Dan Gist, supt. Fax 686-8705
www.pilotpointisd.com
Pilot Point HS 400/9-12
1300 N Washington St 76258 940-686-8740
Jason Southard, prin. Fax 686-8745
Pilot Point MS - J. Earl Selz Campus 200/7-8
828 S Harrison St 76258 940-686-8730
Dustin Toth, prin. Fax 686-8735

**Pineland, Sabine, Pop. 835**
West Sabine ISD 600/PK-12
PO Box 869 75968 409-584-2655
Mike Pate, supt. Fax 584-2139
www.westsabineisd.net
West Sabine JSHS 300/6-12
PO Box 869 75968 409-584-2525
Ryan Fuller, prin. Fax 584-2695

**Pittsburg, Camp, Pop. 4,399**
Pittsburg ISD 2,500/PK-12
PO Box 1189 75686 903-856-3628
Judy Pollan, supt. Fax 856-0269
pittsburgisd.net
Pittsburg HS 700/9-12
300 N Texas St 75686 903-856-3646
Jonathan Hill, prin. Fax 855-3325
Pittsburg JHS 400/7-8
313 Broach St 75686 903-856-6432
Terri Brown, prin. Fax 855-3357

**Plains, Yoakum, Pop. 1,468**
Plains ISD 500/PK-12
PO Box 479 79355 806-456-7401
Dr. Stephanie Howard, supt. Fax 456-4325
plainsisd.net/
Plains HS 100/9-12
PO Box 479 79355 806-456-7498
Benjamin Taylor, prin. Fax 456-4325
Plains MS 100/5-8
PO Box 479 79355 806-456-7490
Benjamin Taylor, prin. Fax 456-4325

**Plainview, Hale, Pop. 21,983**
Plainview ISD 4,900/PK-12
PO Box 1540 79073 806-293-6000
Dr. Rocky Kirk, supt. Fax 296-4014
www.plainviewisd.org
Ash S 100/Alt
908 Ash St 79072 806-293-6010
Rodney Wallace, dir. Fax 296-4183
Coronado MS 400/6-8
2501 Joliet St 79072 806-293-6020
Andrew Hannon, prin. Fax 296-4169
Estacado MS 400/6-8
2200 W 20th St 79072 806-293-6015
Ritchie Thornton, prin. Fax 290-4109
Plainview HS 1,300/9-12
1501 Quincy St 79072 806-293-6005
Tye Rogers, prin. Fax 296-4069

---

Plainview Christian Academy 200/PK-12
310 S Ennis St 79072 806-296-6034
Jennifer Hooper, prin. Fax 296-0074
Wayland Baptist University Post-Sec.
1900 W 7th St 79072 806-291-1000

**Plano, Collin, Pop. 253,492**
Frisco ISD
Supt. — See Frisco
Fowler MS 1,200/6-8
3801 McDermott Rd 75025 469-633-5050
Donnie Wiseman, prin. Fax 633-5060

Plano ISD 53,500/PK-12
2700 W 15th St 75075 469-752-8100
Dr. Brian Binggeli, supt. Fax 752-8096
www.pisd.edu
Academy HS 9-12
1701 Alma Dr 75075 972-905-8100
Lynn Ojeda, prin. Fax 752-8068
Armstrong MS 700/6-8
3805 Timberline Dr 75074 469-752-4600
Steven Ewing, prin. Fax 752-4601
Bowman MS 800/6-8
2501 Jupiter Rd 75074 469-752-4800
Kristopher Vernon, prin. Fax 752-4801
Carpenter MS 900/6-8
3905 Rainier Rd 75023 469-752-5000
Courtney Washington, prin. Fax 752-5001
Clark HS 1,500/9-10
523 W Spring Creek Pkwy 75023 469-752-7200
Janis Williams, prin. Fax 752-7201
Guinn Special Programs Center Alt
2221 Legacy Dr 75023 469-752-6900
Sharon Bradley, prin. Fax 752-6901
Haggard MS 900/6-8
2832 Parkhaven Dr 75075 469-752-5400
Julie-Anne Dean, prin. Fax 752-5401
Hendrick MS 900/6-8
7400 Red River Dr 75025 469-752-5600
Lisa Long, prin. Fax 752-5601
Jasper HS 1,800/9-10
6800 Archgate Dr 75024 469-752-7400
Dr. Matthew Endsley, prin. Fax 752-7401
Otto MS 900/6-8
504 N Star Rd 75074 469-752-8500
Antoine Spencer, prin. Fax 752-8501
Plano East SHS 3,000/11-12
3000 Los Rios Blvd 75074 469-752-9000
George King, prin. Fax 752-9001
Plano SHS 2,600/11-12
2200 Independence Pkwy 75075 469-752-9300
Sarah Watkins, prin. Fax 752-9301
Plano West SHS 2,200/11-12
5601 W Parker Rd 75093 469-752-9600
Kathy King, prin. Fax 752-9601
Renner MS 1,300/6-8
5701 W Parker Rd 75093 469-752-5800
Sonja Pegram, prin. Fax 752-5801
Rice MS 1,200/6-8
8500 Gifford Dr 75025 469-752-6000
Chris Glasscock, prin. Fax 752-6001
Robinson MS 1,000/6-8
6701 Preston Meadow Dr 75024 469-752-6200
Billie Jean Lee, prin. Fax 752-6201
Schimelpfenig MS 1,000/6-8
2400 Maumelle Dr 75023 469-752-6400
Jason Myatt, prin. Fax 752-6401
Shepton HS 1,600/9-10
5505 W Plano Pkwy 75093 469-752-7600
William McLaughlin, prin. Fax 752-7601
Vines HS 1,200/9-10
1401 Highedge Dr 75075 469-752-7800
Shauna Sanchez, prin. Fax 752-7801
Williams HS 1,100/9-10
1717 17th St 75074 469-752-8300
Gloria Martinez, prin. Fax 752-8301
Wilson MS 1,000/6-8
1001 Custer Rd 75075 469-752-6700
Selenda Sager, prin. Fax 752-6701
Other Schools – See Dallas, Murphy

---

Bethany Christian S 100/PK-12
3300 W Parker Rd 75075 972-596-5811
Dr. Marvin Effa, prin. Fax 596-5814
Collin College Post-Sec.
2800 E Spring Creek Pkwy 75074 972-881-5790
Coram Deo Academy 300/PK-12
9645 Independence Pkwy 75025 972-854-1300
Faith Lutheran S 100/PK-12
1701 E Park Blvd 75074 972-423-7448
Rev. Stephen Kieser, hdmstr. Fax 423-9618
John Paul II HS 600/9-12
900 Coit Rd 75075 972-867-0005
Thomas Poore, pres. Fax 867-7555
Prestonwood Christian Academy 1,400/PK-12
6801 W Park Blvd 75093 972-820-5300
Dr. Larry Taylor, head sch Fax 930-4008
St. Timothy Christian Academy 50/K-12
1501 H Ave 75074 972-509-7822
Margaret Whitaker, head sch Fax 509-7829
Spring Creek Academy 200/K-12
6000 Custer Rd 75023 972-517-6730
Willow Bend Academy 200/5-12
2220 Coit Rd Ste 500 75075 972-599-7882
Yorktown Education 100/K-12
5170 Village Creek Dr 75093 972-521-8610
Randall Reiners, head sch Fax 484-3696

**Pleasanton, Atascosa, Pop. 8,878**
Pleasanton ISD 3,200/PK-12
831 Stadium Dr 78064 830-569-1200
Matthew Mann, supt. Fax 569-2171
www.pisd.us
Pleasanton HS 900/9-12
831 Stadium Dr 78064 830-569-1250
Twila Guajardo, prin. Fax 569-4747
Pleasanton JHS 500/7-8
831 Stadium Dr 78064 830-569-1280
Jennifer Garcia, prin. Fax 569-1290

**Pollok, Angelina**
Central ISD 1,400/PK-12
7622 N US Highway 69 75969 936-853-2216
Dr. Allen Garner, supt. Fax 853-2215
www.centralisd.com
Central HS 400/9-12
7622 N US Highway 69 75969 936-853-2167
Justin Risner, prin. Fax 853-2208
Central JHS 400/5-8
7622 N US Highway 69 75969 936-853-2115
Kris Whisenant, prin. Fax 853-2348

**Ponder, Denton, Pop. 1,372**
Ponder ISD 1,300/PK-12
400 W Bailey St 76259 940-479-8200
Bruce Yeager, supt. Fax 479-8209
www.ponderisd.net
Ponder HS 400/9-12
400 W Bailey St 76259 940-479-8210
Shawn Simmons, prin. Fax 479-8219
Ponder JHS 300/6-8
400 W Bailey St 76259 940-479-8220
Ted Heers, prin. Fax 479-8229

**Poolville, Parker**
Poolville ISD 500/PK-12
PO Box 96 76487 817-594-4452
Jimmie Dobbs, supt. Fax 594-2651
www.poolville.net
Poolville HS 100/9-12
1001 Lone Star Rd 76487 817-599-5134
Shari John, prin. Fax 599-5171
Poolville JHS 100/6-8
PO Box 96 76487 817-594-4539
Matt Scott, prin. Fax 594-0081

**Port Aransas, Nueces, Pop. 3,435**
Port Aransas ISD 600/PK-12
100 S Station St 78373 361-749-1205
Wayne Johnson, supt. Fax 749-1215
www.paisd.net
Brundrett MS 100/6-8
100 S Station St 78373 361-749-1209
Chris Roche, prin. Fax 749-1218
Port Aransas HS 200/9-12
100 S Station St 78373 361-749-1206
Sharon McKinney, prin. Fax 749-1219

**Port Arthur, Jefferson, Pop. 53,210**
Port Arthur ISD 9,000/PK-12
PO Box 1388 77641 409-989-6100
Dr. Mark Porterie Ed.D., supt. Fax 989-6229
www.paisd.org
Career and Technical Education Vo/Tech
3501 Sgt Lucien Adams Blvd 77642 409-989-4750
Dr. Glenn Mitchell, prin. Fax 983-2204
Jefferson MS 1,000/6-8
2200 Jefferson Dr 77642 409-984-4860
Dr. Barbara Polk, prin. Fax 960-6057
Lincoln MS 700/6-8
1023 Abe Lincoln Ave 77640 409-984-8700
LaSonya Baptiste, prin. Fax 982-2847
Memorial 9th Grade Academy 600/9-9
2441 61st St 77640 409-736-1521
Gloria Dodson, prin. Fax 736-0267
Memorial HS 1,700/10-12
3501 Sgt Lucien Adams Blvd 77642 409-984-4000
Dr. Glenn Mitchell, prin. Fax 985-3376
Port Arthur Alternative Center Alt
PO Box 1388 77641 409-984-8650
Luther Thompson, prin. Fax 962-6013

---

Lamar State College Port Arthur Post-Sec.
1500 Procter St 77640 409-983-4921
Lighthouse Christian Academy 100/PK-12
2920 Lake Arthur Dr 77642 409-729-6000
Dwayne Oxner, hdmstr. Fax 724-2469

**Porter, Montgomery, Pop. 7,000**
New Caney ISD
Supt. — See New Caney
New Caney MS 900/6-8
22784 Highway 59 77365 281-577-8860
Bryan Applegate, prin. Fax 354-8725
Porter HS 1,400/9-12
22625 Sandy Ln 77365 281-577-5900
Dr. Ken Hodgkinson, prin. Fax 577-9175
White Oak MS 800/7-8
24161 Briar Berry Ln 77365 281-577-8800
Roger McAdoo, prin. Fax 354-5186
Woodridge Forest MS 6-8
4540 Woodridge Pkwy 77365 281-577-8800
Michelle Marable, admin.

**Port Isabel, Cameron, Pop. 4,982**
Point Isabel ISD 2,600/PK-12
101 Port Rd 78578 956-943-0000
Dr. Lisa Garcia, supt. Fax 943-0014
www.pi-isd.net/
Port Isabel HS 600/9-12
101 Port Rd 78578 956-943-0030
Dr. William Roach, prin. Fax 943-0648
Port Isabel JHS 500/6-8
101 Port Rd 78578 956-943-0060
Nancy Gonzalez, prin. Fax 943-0055

**Portland, San Patricio, Pop. 14,859**
Gregory-Portland ISD 4,400/PK-12
608 College St 78374 361-777-1091
Dr. Paul Clore, supt. Fax 777-1093
www.g-pisd.org
Gregory-Portland HS 1,300/9-12
4601 Wildcat Dr 78374 361-777-4251
Barbara Cade, prin. Fax 777-4272
Gregory-Portland JHS 700/7-8
4600 Wildcat Dr 78374 361-777-4042
Xavier Barrera, prin. Fax 643-3187

**Port Lavaca, Calhoun, Pop. 12,146**
Calhoun County ISD 4,200/PK-12
525 N Commerce St 77979 361-552-9728
Dr. James B. Cowley, supt. Fax 551-2648
www.calcoisd.org
Calhoun HS 1,100/9-12
201 Sandcrab Blvd 77979 361-552-3775
Nicole Amason, prin. Fax 551-2620
Hope HS 50/Alt
900 N Virginia St 77979 361-552-7084
Kelly Taylor, prin. Fax 551-2677
Travis MS 900/6-8
705 N Nueces St 77979 361-552-3784
Michael Torres, prin. Fax 551-2692

**Port Neches, Jefferson, Pop. 12,912**
Port Neches-Groves ISD 4,700/PK-12
620 Avenue C 77651 409-722-4244
Dr. Rodney Cavness, supt. Fax 724-7864
www.pngisd.org
Alternative Education Center Alt
1810 Port Neches Ave 77651 409-722-5924
Scott Ryan, prin. Fax 724-1448
Port Neches-Groves HS 1,400/9-12
1401 Merriman St 77651 409-729-7644
Marc Keith Ed.D., prin. Fax 722-7371
Port Neches MS 600/6-8
749 Central Dr 77651 409-722-8115
Kyle Hooper, prin. Fax 727-8342
Other Schools – See Groves

**Post, Garza, Pop. 5,351**
Post ISD 800/PK-12
501 S Avenue K 79356 806-495-3343
Mike Comeaux, supt. Fax 495-2945
www.postisd.net
Post HS 200/9-12
307 W 4th St 79356 806-495-2770
Marvin Self, prin. Fax 495-2792
Post MS 200/6-8
405 W 8th St 79356 806-495-2874
Robert Wilson, prin. Fax 495-2426

**Poteet, Atascosa, Pop. 3,241**
Poteet ISD 1,800/PK-12
PO Box 138 78065 830-742-3567
Andres Castillo, supt. Fax 742-3332
www.poteet.k12.tx.us
Poteet HS 500/9-12
PO Box 138 78065 830-742-3522
Debbie Akers, prin. Fax 742-8497
Poteet JHS 400/6-8
PO Box 138 78065 830-742-3571
Destiny Barrera, prin. Fax 742-8495

**Poth, Wilson, Pop. 1,900**
Poth ISD 800/PK-12
PO Box 250 78147 830-484-3330
Scott Caloss, supt. Fax 484-2961
www.pothisd.us
Poth HS 300/9-12
PO Box 250 78147 830-484-3322
Todd Pawelek, prin. Fax 484-3304
Poth JHS 200/6-8
PO Box 250 78147 830-484-3323
Todd Deaver, prin. Fax 484-3682

**Pottsboro, Grayson, Pop. 2,115**
Pottsboro ISD 1,300/PK-12
PO Box 555 75076 903-771-0083
Dr. Kevin Matthews, supt. Fax 786-9085
www.pottsboroisd.org/
Pottsboro HS 400/9-12
PO Box 555 75076 903-771-0085
Mark Youree, prin. Fax 786-6349
Pottsboro MS 300/5-8
PO Box 555 75076 903-771-2982
John Reves, prin. Fax 786-4902

**Prairie Lea, Caldwell**
Prairie Lea ISD 200/PK-12
PO Box 9 78661 512-488-2370
Larry Markert, supt. Fax 488-9006
www.plisd.net
Prairie Lea S 200/PK-12
PO Box 9 78661 512-488-2328
Darren Kesselus, prin. Fax 488-2425

**Prairie View, Waller, Pop. 5,483**

Prairie View A&M University Post-Sec.
PO Box 519 77446 936-261-3311

**Premont, Jim Wells, Pop. 2,649**
Premont ISD 600/PK-12
PO Box 530 78375 361-348-3915
Eric Ramos, supt. Fax 348-2882
www.premontisd.net
Premont HS 300/7-12
PO Box B 78375 361-348-3915
Michael Gonzalez, prin. Fax 348-2914

**Presidio, Presidio, Pop. 4,416**
Presidio ISD 1,500/PK-12
PO Box 1401 79845 432-229-3275
Dennis McEntire, supt. Fax 229-4228
www.presidio-isd.net
Franco MS 400/6-8
PO Box 1401 79845 432-229-3113
Dr. Edgar Tibayan, prin. Fax 229-4087
Presidio HS 300/9-12
PO Box 1401 79845 432-229-3365
Santos Lujan, prin. Fax 229-4625

**Priddy, Mills**
Priddy ISD 100/K-12
PO Box 40 76870 325-966-3323
Adrianne Burden, supt. Fax 966-3380
www.priddyisd.net
Priddy S 100/K-12
PO Box 40 76870 325-966-3323
Adrianne Burden, prin. Fax 966-3380

**Princeton, Collin, Pop. 6,693**
Princeton ISD 3,100/PK-12
321 Panther Pkwy 75407 469-952-5400
Philip Anthony, supt. Fax 736-3505
www.princetonisd.net
Clark JHS 500/7-8
301 Panther Pkwy 75407 469-952-5400
Anita Barch, prin. Fax 736-5903
Princeton HS 900/9-12
1000 E Princeton Dr 75407 469-952-5400
James Lovelady, prin. Fax 736-5902

**Progreso, Hidalgo, Pop. 5,505**
Progreso ISD 2,100/PK-12
PO Box 610 78579 956-565-3002
Martin Cuellar, supt. Fax 565-2128
progresoisd.wix.com/pisd
Progreso HS 500/9-12
PO Box 610 78579 956-565-4142
Diana Williams, prin. Fax 565-6029
Thompson MS 300/7-8
PO Box 610 78579 956-565-6539
Yulia Molina, prin. Fax 565-1718

**Prosper, Collin, Pop. 9,238**
Prosper ISD 4,800/PK-12
605 E 7th St 75078 469-219-2000
Drew Watkins Ed.D., supt. Fax 346-9247
www.prosper-isd.net
Prosper HS 1,300/9-12
301 Eagle Dr 75078 469-219-2180
Greg Wright, prin. Fax 346-9246
Reynolds MS 700/7-8
700 N Coleman St 75078 469-219-2165
Greg Bradley, prin. Fax 346-2455

Grace Academy of North Texas 100/K-10
4255 E Prosper Trl 75078 469-287-7111
Ann DeSantis, dir. Fax 632-1728

**Quanah, Hardeman, Pop. 2,586**
Quanah ISD 500/PK-12
PO Box 150 79252 940-663-2281
Ryan Turner, supt. Fax 663-2875
www.qisd.net
Quanah HS 200/9-12
PO Box 150 79252 940-663-2791
Rusty Brawley, prin. Fax 663-6447
Travis MS 100/6-8
PO Box 150 79252 940-663-2226
Gayle McKinley, prin. Fax 663-6361

**Queen City, Cass, Pop. 1,456**
Queen City ISD 1,100/PK-12
PO Box 128 75572 903-796-8256
Charlotte Williams, supt. Fax 796-0248
www.qcisd.net
Queen City HS 300/9-12
PO Box 128 75572 903-796-8259
Carla Dupree, prin. Fax 796-8258
Upchurch MS 300/5-8
PO Box 128 75572 903-796-6412
Steve Holmes, prin. Fax 796-0834

**Quinlan, Hunt, Pop. 1,373**
Boles ISD 500/PK-12
9777 FM 2101 75474 903-883-4464
Dr. Graham Sweeney, supt. Fax 883-4531
boles.ednet10.net
Boles HS 200/9-12
9777 FM 2101 75474 903-883-2918
Mikayle Moreland, prin. Fax 883-5109
Boles MS 200/5-8
9777 FM 2101 75474 903-883-4464
Sharon Roberts, prin. Fax 883-3097

Quinlan ISD 2,400/PK-12
401 E Richmond 75474 903-356-1200
Dr. Debra Crosby, supt. Fax 356-1201
www.quinlanisd.net
Ford HS 700/9-12
10064 Business Highway 34 S 75474 903-356-1600
Amy Griffin, prin. Fax 356-1699
Thompson MS 600/6-8
423 Panther Path 75474 903-356-1500
Brian Kinsworthy, prin. Fax 356-2414

**Quitman, Wood, Pop. 1,780**
Quitman ISD 1,100/PK-12
1201 E Goode St 75783 903-763-5000
Rhonda Turner, supt. Fax 763-2710
www.quitmanisd.net/
Quitman HS 400/9-12
1101 E Goode St 75783 903-763-5000
Cody Mize, prin. Fax 763-2589
Quitman JHS 200/6-8
1101 E Goode St 75783 903-763-5000
Angela Brown, prin. Fax 763-5526

**Ralls, Crosby, Pop. 1,930**
Ralls ISD 600/PK-12
810 Avenue I 79357 806-253-2509
Chris Wade, supt. Fax 253-2508
rallsisd.org
Ralls HS 100/9-12
1106 10th St 79357 806-253-2571
Migueal Salazar, prin. Fax 253-2609
Ralls MS 100/6-8
810 Avenue I 79357 806-253-2549
Jeremy Griffith, prin. Fax 253-4031
Recovery Educational Campus 50/Alt
1106 10th St 79357 806-253-2571
Miguel Salazar, prin. Fax 253-2609

**Randolph AFB, Bexar, Pop. 1,177**
Randolph Field ISD 1,200/PK-12
Building 1225 78148 210-357-2300
Lance Johnson, supt. Fax 357-2469
www.rfisd.net
Randolph HS 300/9-12
Building 1225 78148 210-357-2400
Mark Malone Ed.D., prin. Fax 357-2475
Randolph MS 300/6-8
Building 1225 78148 210-357-2400
Merrie Fox, prin. Fax 357-2475

**Ranger, Eastland, Pop. 2,441**
Ranger ISD 400/PK-12
1842 E Loop 254 76470 254-647-1187
Mike Thompson, supt. Fax 647-5215
www.ranger.esc14.net
Ranger JSHS 100/6-12
1842 E Loop 254 76470 254-647-3216
Karen Saunders, prin. Fax 647-1895

Ranger College Post-Sec.
1100 College Cir 76470 254-647-3234

**Rankin, Upton, Pop. 776**
Rankin ISD 200/PK-12
PO Box 90 79778 432-693-2461
Keith Richardson, supt. Fax 693-2353
www.rankinisd.net
Rankin JSHS 100/7-12
PO Box 90 79778 432-693-1161
Samuel Wyatt, prin. Fax 693-2453

**Raymondville, Willacy, Pop. 11,257**
Raymondville ISD 2,200/PK-12
419 FM 3168 78580 956-689-8176
Johnny Pineda, supt. Fax 689-0201
www.raymondvilleisd.org/
Green MS 500/6-8
419 FM 3168 78580 956-689-8171
Raul Valdez, prin. Fax 689-5330
Raymondville HS 600/9-12
419 FM 3168 78580 956-689-8170
Cris Flores, prin. Fax 689-8152
Raymondville Options Academic Academy Alt
419 FM 3168 78580 956-689-8185
Frank Garcia, prin.

**Red Oak, Ellis, Pop. 10,592**
Red Oak ISD 5,500/PK-12
PO Box 9000 75154 972-617-2941
Dr. J. Scott Niven, supt. Fax 617-4333
www.redoakisd.org
Red Oak HS 1,800/9-12
PO Box 9000 75154 972-617-3535
Dr. Doug Funk, prin. Fax 617-4796
Red Oak MS 900/6-8
PO Box 9000 75154 972-617-0066
Cristi Watts, prin. Fax 617-4786

**Redwater, Bowie, Pop. 1,037**
Redwater ISD 1,100/PK-12
PO Box 347 75573 903-671-3481
Dr. Kathy Allen, supt. Fax 671-2019
www.redwaterisd.org
Redwater HS 400/9-12
PO Box 347 75573 903-671-3421
Rhonda Roberts, prin. Fax 671-3259
Redwater JHS 200/7-8
PO Box 347 75573 903-671-3227
Lee Ann Corbin, prin. Fax 671-9921

**Refugio, Refugio, Pop. 2,860**
Refugio ISD 700/PK-12
212 W Vance St 78377 361-526-2325
Jack Gaskins, supt. Fax 526-2326
www.refugioisd.net/
Refugio HS 300/9-12
212 W Vance St 78377 361-526-2344
Melissa Gonzales, prin. Fax 526-1075
Refugio JHS, 212 W Vance St 78377 100/7-8
Ariel Aleman, prin. 361-526-2434

**Rhome, Wise, Pop. 1,498**
Northwest ISD
Supt. — See Justin
Chisholm Trail MS 1,200/6-8
583 FM 3433 76078 817-215-0600
Justin Vercher, prin. Fax 215-0648

**Rice, Ellis, Pop. 908**
Rice ISD 900/PK-12
1302 SW McKinney St 75155 903-326-4287
Lynn Jantzen, supt. Fax 326-4164
www.rice-isd.org
Rice HS 300/9-12
1400 SW McKinney St 75155 903-326-4502
Mike Richardson, prin. Fax 326-5042
Rice IS 400/3-8
1402 SW McKinney St 75155 903-326-4190
Robert Allen, prin. Fax 326-4620

**Richards, Grimes**
Richards ISD 100/PK-12
9477 Panther Dr 77873 936-851-2364
Martey Ainsworth, supt. Fax 851-2210
www.richardsisd.net
Richards JSHS 100/7-12
9477 Panther Dr 77873 936-851-2364
William Boyce, prin. Fax 851-2210

**Richardson, Dallas, Pop. 96,979**
Richardson ISD 34,700/PK-12
400 S Greenville Ave 75081 469-593-0000
Dr. Kay Waggoner, supt. Fax 593-0402
www.risd.org
Apollo JHS 700/7-9
1600 Apollo Rd 75081 469-593-7900
Yolanda Jackson, prin. Fax 593-7911
Berkner HS 1,900/10-12
1600 E Spring Valley Rd 75081 469-593-7000
Henry Hall, prin. Fax 593-7211
Berkner STEM Academy 9-12
1600 E Spring Valley Rd 75081 469-593-7006
Elizabeth Swaner, prin. Fax 593-7211
McAuliffe Learning Center 100/Alt
900 S Greenville Ave 75081 469-593-5800
Carmen Steward, prin. Fax 593-5805
Pearce HS 1,500/10-12
1600 N Coit Rd 75080 469-593-5000
Philip Bates, prin. Fax 593-5169
Richardson HS 1,800/10-12
1250 W Belt Line Rd 75080 469-593-3000
Charles Bruner, prin. Fax 593-3010
Richardson-North JHS 600/7-9
1820 N Floyd Rd 75080 469-593-5400
Josh Eason, prin. Fax 593-5434
Richardson-West JHS Tech Magnet 700/7-9
1309 Holly Dr 75080 469-593-3700
Fax 593-3666
Other Schools – See Dallas

Alexander S 50/7-12
409 International Pkwy 75081 972-690-9210
Canyon Creek Christian Academy 400/PK-12
2800 Custer Pkwy 75080 972-231-4890
Andy Wright, hdmstr. Fax 234-8414
DeVry University Post-Sec.
2201 N Central Expy Ste 200 75080 972-792-7450
IANT Quranic Academy 200/K-12
840 Abrams Rd 75081 972-231-8451
Sr. Shahnaz Chowdhury, prin.
ITT Technical Institute Post-Sec.
2101 Waterview Pkwy 75080 972-690-9100
North Dallas Adventist Academy 200/PK-12
302 Centennial Blvd 75081 972-234-6322
PCI Health Training Center Post-Sec.
1300 International Pkwy 75081 214-380-4322
Salam Academy PK-12
1515 Blake Dr 75081 972-704-4373
University of Texas at Dallas Post-Sec.
800 W Campbell Rd 75080 972-883-2111

**Richland Hills, Tarrant, Pop. 7,627**
Birdville ISD
Supt. — See Haltom City
Richland MS 600/6-8
7400 Hovenkamp Ave 76118 817-547-4400
James Whitfield, prin. Fax 595-5139

**Richland Springs, San Saba, Pop. 332**
Richland Springs ISD 100/PK-12
700 W Coyote Trl 76871 325-452-3524
Don Fowler, supt. Fax 452-3230
www.rscoyotes.net
Richland Springs S 100/PK-12
700 W Coyote Trl 76871 325-452-3427
Don Fowler, prin. Fax 452-3580

**Richmond, Fort Bend, Pop. 11,601**
Fort Bend ISD
Supt. — See Sugar Land
Bowie MS 700/6-8
700 Plantation Dr 77406 281-327-6200
Alfred Holland, prin. Fax 327-6201
Bush HS 2,100/9-12
6707 FM 1464 Rd, 281-634-6060
Dr. Cecilia Crear, prin. Fax 634-6066
Crockett MS 800/6-8
19001 Beechnut St, 281-634-6380
Thomas Graham, prin. Fax 327-6380
Travis HS 2,300/9-12
11111 Harlem Rd 77406 281-634-7000
Julie Diaz, prin. Fax 634-7010

Lamar Consolidated ISD
Supt. — See Rosenberg
Briscoe JHS 900/7-8
4300 FM 723 Rd 77406 832-223-4000
Mike Semmler, prin. Fax 223-4001
Foster HS 1,900/9-12
4400 FM 723 Rd 77406 832-223-3800
Fax 223-3801
George Ranch HS 1,300/9-12
8181 FM 762 Rd 77469 832-223-4200
Leslie Haack, prin. Fax 223-4201
Reading JHS 1,500/7-8
8101 FM 762 Rd 77469 832-223-4400
Juan Nava, prin. Fax 223-4401

Calvary Episcopal Preparatory 200/PK-12
1201 Austin St 77469 281-342-3161
Malcolm Smith, hdmstr. Fax 232-9449

**Riesel, McLennan, Pop. 994**
Riesel ISD 600/PK-12
600 E Frederick St 76682 254-896-5000
Brian Garner, supt. Fax 896-2981
www.rieselisd.org
Riesel JSHS 300/7-12
600 E Frederick St 76682 254-896-3171
Stephen English, prin. Fax 896-2981

**Rio Grande City, Starr, Pop. 13,814**
Rio Grande City ISD 10,800/PK-12
1 S Fort Ringgold St 78582 956-716-6700
Joel Trigo, supt. Fax 487-8506
www.rgccisd.org
Grulla HS 1,000/9-12
6884 E Highway 83 78582 956-487-7278
Guadalupe Garza, prin. Fax 487-4312
Preparatory for Early College HS 9-12
144 N FM 3167 78582 956-352-6349
Tina Gorena, prin. Fax 352-6387
Ringgold MS 700/6-8
1 S Fort Ringgold St 78582 956-716-6849
Jorge Pena, prin. Fax 716-6807
Rio Grande City HS 2,000/9-12
144 N FM 3167 78582 956-488-6000
Ricardo Saenz, prin. Fax 488-6050
Veterans MS 900/6-8
2700 W Eisenhower St 78582 956-488-0252
Maricela Garcia, prin. Fax 488-0261
Other Schools – See Grulla

Roma ISD
Supt. — See Roma
Barrera MS 700/6-8
258 N FM 649 78582 956-486-2670
Rodrigo Bazan, prin. Fax 486-2607

**Rio Hondo, Cameron, Pop. 2,354**
Rio Hondo ISD 2,200/PK-12
215 W Colorado St 78583 956-748-1000
Ismael Garcia, supt. Fax 748-1038
www.riohondoisd.net
Rio Hondo HS 600/9-12
215 W Colorado St 78583 956-748-1200
Deyanira Martinez-Garcia, prin. Fax 748-1204
Rio Hondo JHS 500/6-8
215 W Colorado St 78583 956-748-1150
Fidel Garza, prin. Fax 748-1154

**Rio Vista, Johnson, Pop. 866**
Rio Vista ISD 900/PK-12
PO Box 369 76093 817-373-2009
Tim Wright, supt. Fax 373-2076
www.rvisd.net
Rio Vista HS 200/9-12
PO Box 369 76093 817-373-2669
Tony Martin, prin. Fax 373-3047
Rio Vista MS 300/6-8
PO Box 369 76093 817-373-2009
Kathleen Kamphaus, prin. Fax 373-3046

**Rising Star, Eastland, Pop. 829**
Rising Star ISD 200/PK-12
PO Box 37 76471 254-643-1986
Mary Jane Atkins, supt. Fax 643-1922
www.risingstarisd.org
Rising Star JSHS 100/7-12
PO Box 37 76471 254-643-3521
Barbara Long, prin. Fax 643-5408

**River Oaks, Tarrant, Pop. 7,362**
Castleberry ISD
Supt. — See Fort Worth
REACH HS 50/Alt
1101 Merritt St 76114 817-252-2390
Wanda Mitchell, prin. Fax 252-2398

**Riviera, Kleberg, Pop. 688**
Riviera ISD 400/PK-12
203 Seahawk Dr 78379 361-296-3101
Karen Unterbrink, supt. Fax 296-3108
www.rivieraisd.us
Kaufer HS 300/7-12
203 Seahawk Dr 78379 361-296-3607
Cindy Pelagio, prin. Fax 296-3845

**Roanoke, Denton, Pop. 5,845**
Northwest ISD
Supt. — See Justin
Steele Accelerated HS 100/9-12
606 N Walnut St 76262 817-698-5800
Robin Ellis, prin. Fax 698-5840
Tidwell MS 900/6-8
3937 Haslet Roanoke Rd 76262 817-698-5900
Kim Barker, prin. Fax 698-5870

**Robert Lee, Coke, Pop. 1,034**
Robert Lee ISD 200/PK-12
1323 W Hamilton St 76945 325-453-4555
Dr. Aaron Hood, supt. Fax 453-2326
www.rlisd.net
Robert Lee HS 100/7-12
1323 W Hamilton St 76945 325-453-4557
David O'Dell, prin. Fax 453-2326

**Robinson, McLennan, Pop. 10,380**
Robinson ISD 2,200/PK-12
500 W Lyndale Ave 76706 254-662-0194
Dr. Michael Hope, supt. Fax 662-0215
www.risdweb.org
Robinson HS 700/9-12
500 W Lyndale Ave 76706 254-662-3840
Russ Meggs, prin. Fax 662-4007
Robinson JHS 500/6-8
500 W Lyndale Ave 76706 254-662-3843
David Wrzesinski, prin. Fax 662-1845

**Robstown, Nueces, Pop. 11,474**
Robstown ISD 2,500/PK-12
801 N 1st St 78380 361-767-6600
Dr. Maria Vidaurri, supt. Fax 387-6311
www.robstownisd.org/
Robstown HS 800/9-12
609 Highway 44 78380 361-387-5999
Pamela Kwiatkowski, prin. Fax 387-6702
Salazar Crossroads Academy Alt
400 W Ligustrum Blvd 78380 361-767-6600
Yolanda Reyna, prin.
Seale JHS 500/7-8
401 E Avenue G 78380 361-767-6631
Norma Castaneda, prin. Fax 387-6202

**Roby, Fisher, Pop. 640**
Roby Consolidated ISD 300/PK-12
PO Box 519 79543 325-776-2222
Heath Dickson, supt. Fax 776-2823
www.robycisd.org
Roby HS 100/9-12
PO Box 519 79543 325-776-2223
Jason Carter, prin. Fax 776-2823

**Rochelle, McCulloch**
Rochelle ISD 200/PK-12
PO Box 167 76872 325-243-5224
Steve Butler, supt. Fax 243-5283
www.rochelleisd.net
Rochelle S 200/PK-12
PO Box 167 76872 325-243-5224
Jym Dennis, prin. Fax 243-5283

**Rockdale, Milam, Pop. 5,537**
Rockdale ISD 1,600/PK-12
PO Box 632 76567 512-430-6000
Denise Monzingo, supt. Fax 446-3460
www.rockdaleisd.net
Rockdale HS 500/9-12
PO Box 632 76567 512-430-6140
Tiffany Commerford, prin. Fax 446-3512
Rockdale JHS 300/6-8
PO Box 632 76567 512-430-6100
April Eschberger, prin. Fax 446-2597

**Rockport, Aransas, Pop. 8,668**
Aransas County ISD 3,100/PK-12
PO Box 907 78381 361-790-2212
Joseph Patek, supt. Fax 790-2299
www.acisd.org
Rockport-Fulton HS 900/9-12
PO Box 907 78381 361-790-2220
Scott Rogers, prin. Fax 790-2206
Rockport-Fulton MS 700/6-8
PO Box 907 78381 361-790-2230
Michael Hannum, prin. Fax 790-2030

**Rocksprings, Edwards, Pop. 1,182**
Rocksprings ISD 300/PK-12
PO Box 157 78880 830-683-4137
David Velky, supt. Fax 683-4141
www.rockspringsisd.net
Rocksprings HS 100/9-12
PO Box 157 78880 830-683-4136
Sandra VanWinkle, prin. Fax 683-4141

**Rockwall, Rockwall, Pop. 36,881**
Rockwall ISD 14,100/PK-12
1050 Williams St 75087 972-771-0605
Jeff Bailey, supt. Fax 771-2637
www.rockwallisd.com
Cain MS 900/7-8
6620 FM 3097 75032 972-772-1170
Megan Gist, prin. Fax 772-2414
Rockwall HS 2,200/9-12
901 W Yellowjacket Ln 75087 972-771-7339
Dr. Courtney Gober, prin. Fax 772-2099
Rockwall Quest Academy 50/Alt
1050 Williams St 75087 972-772-2077
Brian Neely, prin. Fax 772-1055
Utley MS 700/7-8
1201 T L Townsend Dr 75087 972-771-5281
Todd Bradford, prin. Fax 772-1164
Williams MS 700/7-8
625 E FM 552 75087 972-771-8313
David Blake, prin. Fax 772-2033
Other Schools – See Heath

Heritage Christian Academy 300/PK-12
1408 S Goliad St 75087 972-772-3003
Dr. Ron Taylor, hdmstr. Fax 772-3770

**Rogers, Bell, Pop. 1,192**
Rogers ISD 900/PK-12
1 Eagle Dr 76569 254-642-3802
Jason Gilstrap, supt. Fax 642-3851
www.rogersisd.org
Rogers HS 300/9-12
1 Eagle Dr 76569 254-642-3224
Lee Vi Moses, prin. Fax 642-3037
Rogers MS 200/6-8
1 Eagle Dr 76569 254-642-3011
Lucinda Smith, prin. Fax 642-0033

**Roma, Starr, Pop. 9,764**
Roma ISD 6,600/PK-12
PO Box 187 78584 956-849-1377
Carlos Guzman, supt. Fax 849-3118
www.romaisd.com/
ALAS/I & G Center 50/Alt
PO Box 187 78584 956-849-2803
Maria Ramirez, prin. Fax 849-4421
Roma HS 1,800/9-12
PO Box 187 78584 956-849-1333
Marissa Belmontes, prin. Fax 849-2655
Roma MS 700/6-8
PO Box 187 78584 956-849-1434
Nicolasa Sarabia, prin. Fax 849-1895
Other Schools – See Rio Grande City

**Ropesville, Hockley, Pop. 433**
Ropes ISD 400/PK-12
304 Ranch Rd 79358 806-562-4031
Joel Willmon, supt. Fax 562-4059
www.ropesisd.us
Ropes JSHS 200/6-12
304 Ranch Rd 79358 806-562-4031
Tim Carter, prin. Fax 562-4059

**Roscoe, Nolan, Pop. 1,308**
Highland ISD 200/PK-12
6625 FM 608 79545 325-766-3652
Duane Hyde, supt. Fax 766-2281
www.highland.esc14.net/
Highland S 200/PK-12
6625 FM 608 79545 325-766-3652
Duane Hyde, supt. Fax 766-3869

Roscoe Collegiate ISD 400/PK-12
PO Box 579 79545 325-766-3629
Dr. Kim Alexander, supt. Fax 766-3138
www.roscoe.esc14.net
Roscoe JSHS 100/6-12
PO Box 10 79545 325-766-3327
Edward Morales, prin. Fax 766-3419

**Rosebud, Falls, Pop. 1,384**
Rosebud-Lott ISD
Supt. — See Lott
Rosebud-Lott Learning Center 50/Alt
PO Box 638 76570 254-583-7967
Fax 583-1130

**Rosenberg, Fort Bend, Pop. 30,297**
Lamar Consolidated ISD 25,800/PK-12
3911 Avenue I 77471 832-223-0000
Dr. Thomas Randle, supt. Fax 223-0002
www.lcisd.org
Alternative Learning Center 100/Alt
1708 Avenue M 77471 832-223-0900
Randall Donnell, admin. Fax 223-0901
George JHS 900/7-8
4601 Airport Ave 77471 832-223-3600
Eric Nicholie, prin. Fax 223-3601
Lamar Consolidated HS 1,700/9-12
4606 Mustang Ave 77471 832-223-3000
Dr. Michael Milstead, prin. Fax 223-3001
Lamar JHS 800/7-8
4814 Mustang Ave 77471 832-223-3200
Gerard Kipping, prin. Fax 223-3201
Terry HS 1,600/9-12
5500 Avenue N 77471 832-223-3400
Dr. Vera Wehring, prin. Fax 223-3401
Other Schools – See Fulshear, Richmond

**Rosharon, Brazoria, Pop. 1,128**
Fort Bend ISD
Supt. — See Sugar Land
Ferndell Henry Center for Learning 50/Alt
7447 FM 521 Rd 77583 281-327-6000
Michael Bolton, prin. Fax 327-6001

**Rotan, Fisher, Pop. 1,488**
Rotan ISD 300/PK-12
102 N McKinley Ave 79546 325-735-2332
Greg Decker, supt. Fax 735-2686
www.rotan.org
Rotan JSHS 100/9-12
102 N McKinley Ave 79546 325-735-3041
Scott Allen, prin. Fax 735-2520

**Round Rock, Williamson, Pop. 97,480**
Round Rock ISD 45,200/PK-12
1311 Round Rock Ave 78681 512-464-5000
Steve Flores Ph.D., supt. Fax 464-5090
www.roundrockisd.org
Cedar Ridge HS 2,300/9-12
2801 Gattis School Rd 78664 512-704-0100
Lynette Thomas, prin. Fax 704-0280
Chisholm Trail MS 1,000/6-8
500 Oakridge Dr 78681 512-428-2500
Robert Sormani, prin. Fax 428-2629
Fulkes MS 700/6-8
300 W Anderson Ave 78664 512-428-3100
Nancy Guererro, prin. Fax 428-3240
Hernandez MS 900/6-8
1901 Sunrise Rd 78664 512-424-8800
Mario Acosta, prin. Fax 424-8940
Hopewell MS 800/6-8
1535 Gulf Way, 512-464-5200
Karl Waggoner, prin. Fax 464-5349
Ridgeview MS 1,300/6-8
2000 Via Sonoma Dr, 512-424-8400
Travis Mutscher, prin. Fax 424-8540
Round Rock HS 2,600/9-12
201 Deepwood Dr 78681 512-464-6000
Natalie Nichols, prin. Fax 464-6190
Stony Point HS 2,500/9-12
1801 Tiger Trl 78664 512-428-7000
Anthony Watson, prin. Fax 428-7280
Success HS 100/Alt
500 Gattis School Rd 78664 512-428-7291
Thomasine Stewart, dir. Fax 428-7280
Walsh MS 1,100/6-8
3850 Walsh Ranch Blvd 78681 512-704-0800
Toni Hicks, prin. Fax 704-0940
Other Schools – See Austin

---

Concordia HS 100/9-12
1500 Royston Ln Ste A 78664 512-248-2547
Steve Glandorf, prin. Fax 252-3839
Round Rock Christian Academy 500/PK-12
301 N Lake Creek Dr Ste A 78681 512-255-4491
Rebecca Blauser, head sch Fax 255-6043

**Rowlett, Dallas, Pop. 55,115**
Garland ISD
Supt. — See Garland
Coyle MS 1,200/6-8
4500 Skyline Dr 75088 972-475-3711
Michael Bland, prin. Fax 412-7222
Rowlett HS 2,600/9-12
4700 President George Bush 75088 972-463-1712
Michelle Bounds, prin. Fax 412-2951
Schrade MS 1,300/6-8
6201 Danridge Rd 75089 972-463-8790
Rachael Brown, prin. Fax 463-8793

**Roxton, Lamar, Pop. 632**
Roxton ISD 200/PK-12
PO Box 307 75477 903-346-3213
Kelly R. Pickle, supt. Fax 346-3356
www.roxtonisd.org
Roxton S 200/PK-12
PO Box 307 75477 903-346-3213
Camesha Sanders, prin. Fax 346-3356

**Royse City, Rockwall, Pop. 9,169**
Royse City ISD 4,600/PK-12
PO Box 479 75189 972-636-2413
Kevin Worthy, supt. Fax 635-7037
www.rcisd.org
Brownling Academy Alt
PO Box 479 75189 972-635-5077
Lloyd Blaine, prin. Fax 635-2504
Royse City HS 1,200/9-12
PO Box 479 75189 972-636-9991
Sean Walker, prin. Fax 635-2906
Royse City MS 700/7-8
PO Box 479 75189 972-636-9544
Jere Craighead, prin. Fax 635-5093

**Rule, Haskell, Pop. 627**
Rule ISD 100/PK-12
1100 Union Ave 79547 940-997-2521
Barry McBroom, supt. Fax 997-2446
www.rule.esc14.net
Rule S 100/PK-12
1100 Union Ave 79547 940-997-2246
Jill Brown, prin. Fax 997-2446

**Runge, Karnes, Pop. 1,025**
Runge ISD 300/PK-12
PO Box 158 78151 830-239-4315
Pam Seipp, supt. Fax 239-4816
www.rungeisd.org
Runge JSHS 100/6-12
PO Box 158 78151 830-239-4315
Anna Gonzalez, prin. Fax 239-4816

**Rusk, Cherokee, Pop. 5,468**
Rusk ISD 2,200/PK-12
203 E 7th St 75785 903-683-5592
Scott Davis, supt. Fax 683-2104
www.ruskisd.net
Rusk HS 600/9-12
203 E 7th St 75785 903-683-5401
Scott Schwartz, prin. Fax 683-6090
Rusk JHS 500/6-8
203 E 7th St 75785 903-683-2502
John Burkhalter, prin. Fax 683-4363

**Sabinal, Uvalde, Pop. 1,672**
Sabinal ISD 500/PK-12
PO Box 338 78881 830-988-2472
Richard Grill, supt. Fax 988-7151
www.sabinalisd.net
Sabinal HS 100/9-12
PO Box 338 78881 830-988-2475
Luciano Castro, prin. Fax 988-7170
Sabinal JHS 100/6-8
PO Box 338 78881 830-988-2475
Luciano Castro, prin. Fax 988-7170

**Sabine Pass, Jefferson**
Sabine Pass ISD 300/PK-12
PO Box 1148 77655 409-971-2321
Kristi Heid, supt. Fax 971-2120
www.sabinepass.net
Sabine Pass S 300/PK-12
PO Box 1148 77655 409-971-2321
Andy Bates, prin. Fax 971-2120

**Sachse, Dallas, Pop. 19,902**
Garland ISD
Supt. — See Garland
Hudson MS 1,100/6-8
4405 Hudson Park 75048 972-675-3070
Jennifer Benavides, prin. Fax 675-3077
Sachse HS 2,600/9-12
3901 Miles Rd 75048 972-414-7450
Ray Merrill, prin. Fax 414-7458

**Sadler, Grayson, Pop. 336**
S & S Consolidated ISD 800/PK-12
PO Box 837 76264 903-564-6051
Tommy Hunter, supt. Fax 564-3492
www.sscisd.net/
S & S Consolidated HS 300/9-12
PO Box 837 76264 903-564-3768
Roger Reed, prin. Fax 564-7308
S & S Consolidated MS 200/6-8
PO Box 837 76264 903-564-7626
Lance Johnson, prin. Fax 564-7857

**Saginaw, Tarrant, Pop. 19,433**
Eagle Mtn.-Saginaw ISD
Supt. — See Fort Worth
Saginaw HS 2,200/9-12
800 N Blue Mound Rd 76131 817-306-0914
Patrick Torres, prin. Fax 306-1344

---

Trinity Baptist Temple Academy 100/PK-12
6045 WJ Boaz Rd 76179 817-237-4255
Gregg Jones, prin. Fax 237-5233

**Saint Jo, Montague, Pop. 1,027**
Saint Jo ISD 300/PK-12
PO Box L 76265 940-995-2668
Larry Smith, supt. Fax 995-2026
www.saintjoisd.net
Saint Jo JSHS 100/7-12
PO Box L 76265 940-995-2532
Katie Morman, prin. Fax 995-2087

**Salado, Bell, Pop. 2,113**
Salado ISD 1,400/PK-12
PO Box 98 76571 254-947-5479
Dr. Michael Novotny, supt. Fax 947-5605
www.saladoisd.org
Salado HS 400/9-12
PO Box 98 76571 254-947-5429
Ross Sproul, prin. Fax 947-6984
Salado JHS 200/7-8
PO Box 98 76571 254-947-6935
Paul Baird, prin. Fax 947-6934

**Saltillo, Hopkins**
Saltillo ISD 300/PK-12
PO Box 269 75478 903-537-2386
Kevin Woolley, supt. Fax 537-2191
www.saltilloisd.net
Saltillo S 300/PK-12
PO Box 269 75478 903-537-2386
Kevin Woolley, supt. Fax 537-2191

**San Angelo, Tom Green, Pop. 91,751**
Grape Creek ISD 1,100/PK-12
8207 US Highway 87 N 76901 325-658-7823
Barbie McMath, supt. Fax 658-8719
www.grapecreekisd.net/
Grape Creek HS 300/9-12
8207 US Highway 87 N 76901 325-653-1852
Roger Henderson, prin. Fax 653-3568
Grape Creek MS 200/6-8
8207 US Highway 87 N 76901 325-655-1735
Brad Behrendt, prin. Fax 657-2997

San Angelo ISD 14,200/PK-12
1621 University Ave 76904 325-947-3700
Dr. Carl Dethloff, supt. Fax 947-3771
www.saisd.org
Carver Learning Center 50/Alt
301 W 9th St 76903 325-659-3648
Sherie Loika, prin. Fax 657-4087
Central Freshman Campus 700/9-9
218 N Oakes St 76903 325-659-3576
Tim Reid, prin. Fax 659-3583
Central HS 2,000/10-12
655 Caddo St 76901 325-659-3400
Bill Waters, prin. Fax 659-3413
Glenn MS 1,200/6-8
2201 University Ave 76904 325-947-3841
Karen Clark, prin. Fax 947-3847
Lake View HS 1,200/9-12
900 E 43rd St 76903 325-659-3500
Monte Althaus, prin. Fax 653-8661
Lee MS 900/6-8
2500 Sherwood Way 76901 325-947-3871
Rikke Black, prin. Fax 947-3890
Lincoln MS 1,000/6-8
255 Lake View Heroes Dr 76903 325-659-3550
Ginger Luther, prin. Fax 659-3559

Wall ISD
Supt. — See Wall
Fairview Alternative Educational Coop 50/Alt
2405 Fairview School Rd 76904 325-651-7656
Albert Johnson, prin.

---

American Commercial College Post-Sec.
3177 Executive Dr 76904 325-942-6797
Angelo State University Post-Sec.
2601 W Avenue N 76909 800-946-8627
Cornerstone Christian S 200/PK-12
1502 N Jefferson St 76901 325-655-3439
Cynthia Robinson, admin. Fax 658-8998
San Angelo Christian Academy 100/PK-12
518 Country Club Rd 76904 325-651-8363
Shannon West Texas Memorial Hospital Post-Sec.
120 E Harris Ave 76903 325-653-6741

**San Antonio, Bexar, Pop. 1,308,790**
Alamo Heights ISD 4,800/PK-12
7101 Broadway St 78209 210-824-2483
Dr. Kevin Brown, supt. Fax 822-2221
www.ahisd.net
Alamo Heights HS 1,500/9-12
6900 Broadway St 78209 210-820-8850
Dr. Cordell Jones, prin. Fax 832-5777
Alamo Heights JHS 1,100/6-8
7607 N New Braunfels Ave 78209 210-824-3231
Laura Ancira, prin. Fax 832-5825

East Central ISD 9,400/PK-12
6634 New Sulphur Springs Rd 78263 210-648-7861
Roland Toscano, supt. Fax 648-0931
www.ecisd.net
Bexar County Learning Center 100/Alt
3621 Farm Rd 78223 210-335-1745
Meredith Rokas, prin. Fax 335-1746
East Central Heritage MS 1,100/6-8
8004 New Sulphur Springs Rd 78263 210-648-4546
Mary Alice McCulloch, prin. Fax 648-3501
East Central HS 2,700/9-12
7173 FM 1628 78263 210-649-2951
Shane McKay, prin. Fax 649-2752
Legacy MS 1,100/6-8
5903 SE Loop 410 78222 210-648-3118
Damon Trainer, prin. Fax 648-1068

Edgewood ISD 11,300/PK-12
5358 W Commerce St 78237 210-444-4500
Kenneth Jacobs, supt. Fax 444-4602
www.eisd.net
Brentwood MS 800/6-8
1626 Thompson Pl 78226 210-444-7675
Mary Inco, prin. Fax 444-7698
Edgewood Fine Arts Academy 100/9-12
607 SW 34th St 78237 210-444-7925
Jose DeHoyos, dir. Fax 444-7973
Frey Alternative Education Complex 50/Alt
900 S San Eduardo Ave 78237 210-444-8230
Gonzalo Ramirez, admin. Fax 444-8233
Garcia MS 800/6-8
3306 Ruiz St 78228 210-444-8075
Pamela Reece, prin. Fax 444-8098
Kennedy HS 1,400/9-12
1922 S General McMullen Dr 78226 210-444-8040
Cynthia Trevino, prin. Fax 444-8020
Memorial HS 1,200/9-12
1227 Memorial St 78228 210-444-8300
Michael Rodriguez, prin. Fax 444-8336
Wrenn MS 700/6-8
627 S Acme Rd 78237 210-444-8475
Nicole Cannon, prin. Fax 444-8498

Fort Sam Houston ISD 1,500/PK-12
4005 Winans Rd 78234 210-368-8701
Dr. Gail Siller, supt. Fax 368-8741
www.fshisd.net
Cole MSHS 700/6-12
4001 Winans Rd 78234 210-368-8730
Dr. Isabell Clayton, prin. Fax 368-8731

Harlandale ISD 14,800/PK-12
102 Genevieve Dr 78214 210-989-4300
Reynaldo Madrigal, supt. Fax 921-4356
www.harlandale.net
Harlandale HS 1,900/9-12
114 E Gerald Ave 78214 210-989-1000
Fred Anthony, prin. Fax 924-2335
Harlandale MS 900/6-8
300 W Huff Ave 78214 210-989-2000
Ricardo Marroquin, prin. Fax 977-8764
Kingsborough MS 700/6-8
422 E Ashley Rd 78221 210-989-2200
William Hall, prin. Fax 977-9463
Leal MS 800/6-8
743 W Southcross Blvd 78211 210-989-2400
Geraldine Balleza, prin. Fax 977-1459
McCollum HS 1,700/9-12
500 W Formosa Blvd 78221 210-989-1500
Aracelie Bunsen, prin. Fax 989-1580
STEM Early College HS 9-12
102 Genevieve Dr 78214 210-989-4557
Dr. Eddie Rodriguez, prin. Fax 921-4480
Tejeda Academy 200/Alt
12121 SE Loop 410 78221 210-989-4900
Jerry Soto, prin. Fax 977-1628
Wells MS 700/6-8
422 W Hutchins Pl 78221 210-989-2600
Jacob Garcia, prin. Fax 923-5126

Judson ISD
Supt. — See Live Oak
Judson Learning Academy 100/Alt
6909 N Loop 1604 E Ste 2010 78247 210-651-4080
Anthony Willard, prin. Fax 651-6834
Kirby MS 1,000/6-8
5441 Seguin Rd 78219 210-661-1140
Mary Duhart-Toppen, prin. Fax 662-9275
Metzger MS 900/6-8
7475 Binz Engleman Rd 78244 210-662-2210
Caroline Ross, prin. Fax 662-8390
Wagner HS 2,200/9-12
3000 N Foster Rd 78244 210-662-5000
Donald Stewart, prin. Fax 662-9896
Woodlake Hills MS 1,000/6-8
6625 Woodlake Pkwy 78244 210-661-1110
Daniel Brooks, prin. Fax 666-0169

Lackland ISD 1,100/PK-12
2460 Kenly Ave Bldg 8265 78236 210-357-5000
Dr. Burnie L. Roper, supt. Fax 357-5050
www.lacklandisd.net/
Stacey JSHS 300/7-12
2460 Kenly Ave Bldg 8265 78236 210-357-5100
Stephanie Mickey, prin. Fax 357-5109

North East ISD 66,700/PK-12
8961 Tesoro Dr 78217 210-407-0000
Dr. Brian Gottardy, supt. Fax 804-7017
www.neisd.net
Academy of Creative Education 100/Alt
3736 Perrin Central Bldg 2 78217 210-407-0740
Christopher Throm, prin. Fax 657-8976
Automotive Technology Academy Vo/Tech
3736 Perrin Central Blvd 78217 210-407-0742
David Bailey, dir. Fax 637-4992
Bradley MS 1,300/6-8
14819 Heimer Rd 78232 210-356-2600
Todd Bloomer, prin. Fax 491-8314
Bush MS 1,500/6-8
1500 Evans Rd 78258 210-356-2900
Gary Comalander, prin. Fax 491-8471
Churchill HS 3,000/9-12
12049 Blanco Rd 78216 210-356-0000
Justin Oxley, prin. Fax 442-0879
Design and Technology Academy 9-12
5110 Walzem Rd 78218 210-356-2233
Russ Claughton, dir. Fax 650-1285
Driscoll MS 1,100/6-8
17150 Jones Maltsberger Rd 78247 210-356-3200
Steven Zimmerman, prin. Fax 491-6467
Eisenhower MS 1,200/6-8
8231 Blanco Rd 78216 210-356-3500
John Smith, prin. Fax 442-0537
Electrical Systems Technology S Vo/Tech
2923 MacArthur Vw 78217 210-356-7697
Stephen Albert, prin. Fax 650-1195
Engineering & Technologies Academy 9-12
5110 Walzem Rd 78218 210-356-2317
Robert Lozano, dir. Fax 620-1227
Garner MS 900/6-8
4302 Harry Wurzbach Rd 78209 210-805-5100
David Crowe, prin. Fax 805-5138
Harris MS 1,400/6-8
5300 Knollcreek 78247 210-356-4100
Sean Maika, prin. Fax 657-8892
Hill MS 6-8
21314 Bulverde Rd 78259 210-356-8000
Rudy Jimenez, prin. Fax 494-2380
International HS of America 500/9-12
1400 Jackson Keller Rd 78213 210-356-0900
Kathy Bieser, dir. Fax 442-0409
Jackson MS 1,000/6-8
4538 Vance Jackson Rd 78230 210-356-4400
Erin Deason, prin. Fax 442-0580
Johnson HS 2,600/9-12
23203 Bulverde Rd 78259 210-356-0400
John Mehlbrech, prin. Fax 356-0430
Krueger MS, 438 Lanark Dr 78218 1,200/6-8
Cynthia Rubio, prin. 210-356-4700
Lee HS 2,400/9-12
1400 Jackson Keller Rd 78213 210-356-0800
Nicole Franco, prin. Fax 442-0325
Lopez MS 1,300/6-8
23103 Hardy Oak Blvd 78258 210-356-5000
Barry Lanford, prin. Fax 481-4072
MacArthur HS 2,600/9-12
2923 MacArthur Vw 78217 210-650-1100
Peter Martinez, prin. Fax 650-1195
Madison HS 3,300/9-12
5005 Stahl Rd 78247 210-356-1400
Debra Aceves-Torres, prin. Fax 637-4435
Nimitz MS 1,100/6-8
5426 Blanco Rd 78216 210-442-0450
Dana Stolhandske, prin. Fax 442-0489
North East Alternative Center 100/Alt
103 W Rampart Dr 78216 210-356-7400
Bill Fish, dir. Fax 442-0623
North East S of the Arts 9-12
1400 Jackson Keller Rd 78213 210-356-1033
Dena Mabry, dir. Fax 442-2507
Reagan HS 2,800/9-12
19000 Ronald Reagan 78258 210-356-1800
Brenda Shelton, prin. Fax 482-2222
Roosevelt HS 2,800/9-12
5110 Walzem Rd 78218 210-356-2200
Melvin Echard, prin. Fax 650-1291
STEM Academy Lee 9-12
1400 Jackson Keller Rd 78213 210-356-1001
Melissa Alcala, dir. Fax 442-0327
STEM Academy Nimitz 6-8
5426 Blanco Rd 78216 210-356-5501
Dr. Melissa Alcala, dir. Fax 442-0476
Tejeda MS 1,500/6-8
2909 E Evans Rd 78259 210-356-5600
John Bojescul, prin. Fax 482-2277
White MS 1,000/6-8
7800 Midcrown Dr 78218 210-650-1400
Cesar Uribe, prin. Fax 650-1443

Wood MS 1,000/6-8
14800 Judson Rd 78233 210-650-1300
Christine Lowak, prin. Fax 650-1309
Evening HS Adult
3736 Perrin Central Blvd #4 78217 210-407-0743
David Bailey, prin. Fax 637-4992

Northside ISD 91,100/PK-12
5900 Evers Rd 78238 210-397-8500
Dr. Brian Woods, supt. Fax 706-8772
nisd.net
Bernal MS 6-8
14045 Bella Vista Place 78253 210-398-1900
Glenda Munson, prin. Fax 679-8216
Brandeis HS 2,400/9-12
13011 Kyle Seale Pkwy 78249 210-397-8200
Dr. Geri Berger, prin. Fax 561-2000
Brennan HS 1,800/9-12
2400 Cottonwood Way 78253 210-398-1250
Gerardo Marquez, prin. Fax 645-3311
Briscoe MS 1,000/6-8
4265 Lone Star Pkwy 78253 210-398-1100
Javier Martinez, prin. Fax 674-0220
Business Careers HS 9-12
6500 Ingram Rd 78238 210-397-7070
Randy Neuenfeldt, prin. Fax 706-7076
Chavez Excel Academy 100/Alt
6500 Ingram Rd 78238 210-397-8120
Darren Calvert, prin. Fax 522-8953
Clark HS 2,700/9-12
5150 De Zavala Rd 78249 210-397-5150
Dr. Jerry Woods, prin. Fax 561-5250
Communications Arts HS 9-12
11600 W FM 471 78253 210-397-6043
Windy Barker, prin. Fax 688-6092
Connally MS 1,100/6-8
8661 Silent Sunrise 78250 210-397-1000
Cornelius Phelps, prin. Fax 257-1004
Construction Careers Academy Vo/Tech
9411 W Military Dr 78251 210-397-4294
Phillip Edge, prin.
Folks MS 6-8
9855 Swayback Rnch 78254 210-398-1600
Barry Perez, prin. Fax 257-3060
Garcia MS 1,400/6-8
14900 Kyle Seale Pkwy 78255 210-397-8400
Eric Tobias, prin. Fax 695-3830
Health Careers HS 800/9-12
4646 Hamilton Wolfe Rd 78229 210-397-5400
Linda Burk, prin. Fax 617-5423
Hobby MS 1,100/6-8
11843 Vance Jackson Rd 78230 210-397-6300
Lawrence Carranco, prin. Fax 690-6332
Holmes HS 2,600/9-12
6500 Ingram Rd 78238 210-397-7000
Ada Bohlken, prin. Fax 706-7030
Holmgreen Center 100/Alt
8580 Ewing Halsell Dr 78229 210-397-5460
Sharon Spencer, prin. Fax 617-5476
Jay HS 2,900/9-12
7611 Marbach Rd 78227 210-397-2700
Robert Harris, prin. Fax 678-2753
Jay Science and Engineering Academy 9-12
7611 Marbach Rd 78227 210-397-2773
Jay Sumpter, prin. Fax 678-2753
Jefferson MS 1,600/6-8
10900 Shaenfield Rd 78254 210-397-3700
Kevin Kearns, prin. Fax 257-4988
Jones MS 1,200/6-8
1256 Pinn Rd 78227 210-397-2100
Michella Wheat, prin. Fax 678-2113
Jordan MS 1,300/6-8
1725 Richland Hills Dr 78251 210-397-6150
Jennifer Alvarez, prin. Fax 523-4876
Luna MS 1,100/6-8
200 Grosenbacher Rd N 78253 210-397-5300
Lisa Richard, prin. Fax 645-5246
Marshall HS 2,500/9-12
8000 Lobo Ln 78240 210-397-7100
Susan Cleveland, prin. Fax 706-7175
Neff MS 1,300/6-8
5227 Evers Rd 78238 210-397-4100
Yvonne Correa, prin. Fax 523-4566
Northside Alternative HS 200/Alt
144 Hunt Ln 78245 210-397-7080
Dr. Darrell Rice, prin. Fax 706-7086
Northside Alternative MS North 50/Alt
11937 W Interstate 10 78230 210-397-2070
Dr. Karen Petersen, prin. Fax 561-2074
Northside Alternative MS South 50/Alt
5223 Blessing St 78228 210-397-6900
Dr. Karen Petersen, prin. Fax 431-6901
Pease MS 1,200/6-8
201 Hunt Ln 78245 210-397-2950
Katherine Lyssy, prin. Fax 678-2974
Rawlinson MS 1,100/6-8
14100 Vance Jackson Rd 78249 210-397-4900
Mark Rustan, prin. Fax 767-4055
Rayburn MS 1,000/6-8
1400 Cedarhurst Dr 78227 210-397-2150
Dr. Scott McKenzie, prin. Fax 678-2181
Ross MS 1,100/6-8
3630 Callaghan Rd 78228 210-397-6350
Lisa McConoghy, prin. Fax 431-6383
Rudder MS 1,100/6-8
6558 Horn Blvd 78240 210-397-5000
Dr. Mary Jewell, prin. Fax 561-5022
Stevens HS 2,600/9-12
600 N Ellison Dr 78251 210-397-6450
Harold Maldonado, prin. Fax 257-4304
Stevenson MS 1,500/6-8
8403 Tezel Rd 78254 210-397-7300
Chuck Baldridge, prin. Fax 706-7336
Stinson MS 1,300/6-8
13200 Skyhawk Dr 78249 210-397-3600
Lourdes Medina, prin. Fax 561-3609
Taft HS 2,500/9-12
11600 W FM 471 78253 210-397-6000
Tommy Garcia, prin. Fax 688-6072

Vale MS 1,300/6-8
2120 N Ellison Dr 78251 210-397-5700
Dana Gilbert-Perry, prin. Fax 257-1000
Warren HS 2,800/9-12
9411 W Military Dr 78251 210-397-4200
David Empson, prin. Fax 257-4246
Zachry MS 1,100/6-8
9410 Timber Path 78250 210-397-7400
Susan Allain, prin. Fax 706-7432
Other Schools – See Helotes

San Antonio ISD 53,900/PK-12
141 Lavaca St 78210 210-554-2200
Pedro Martinez, supt.
www.saisd.net
Brackenridge HS 1,800/9-12
400 Eagleland Dr 78210 210-228-1200
Yesenia Cordova, prin. Fax 534-9770
Burbank HS 1,300/9-12
1002 Edwards 78204 210-228-1210
Maribel Rodriguez, prin. Fax 533-4394
Connell MS 600/6-8
400 Hot Wells Blvd 78223 210-438-6835
Gregory Rivers, prin. Fax 534-6589
Cooper Academy 400/Alt
1700 Tampico St 78207 210-226-3042
Robert Loveland, prin. Fax 223-9031
Davis MS 700/6-8
4702 E Houston St 78220 210-978-7920
Julio Garcia, prin. Fax 662-8189
Edison HS 1,700/9-12
701 Santa Monica 78212 210-738-9720
Charles Munoz, prin. Fax 738-2408
Estrada Achievement Center 100/Alt
1112 S Zarzamora St 78207 210-438-6820
Donnie Whited, prin. Fax 227-8656
Fox Tech HS Vo/Tech
637 N Main Ave 78205 210-738-9730
Dr. Edward Garcia, prin. Fax 224-8792
Highlands HS 1,900/9-12
3118 Elgin Ave 78210 210-438-6800
Derrick Cade, prin. Fax 337-2567
Houston HS 900/9-12
4635 E Houston St 78220 210-978-7900
Darnell White, prin. Fax 666-2915
Jefferson HS 1,800/9-12
723 Donaldson Ave 78201 210-438-6570
Orlando Vera, prin. Fax 738-2406
Lanier HS 1,600/9-12
1514 W Cesar E Chavez Blvd 78207 210-978-7910
Michael Rodriguez, prin. Fax 224-9516
Longfellow MS 900/6-8
1130 E Sunshine Dr 78228 210-438-6520
Liz Solis, prin. Fax 433-0375
Navarro Academy 200/Alt
623 S Pecos La Trinidad 78207 210-438-6810
Annette Castillo, prin. Fax 226-5426
Page MS 500/6-8
401 Berkshire Ave 78210 210-228-1230
Patricia Ortiz, prin. Fax 533-7369
Pickett Academy 50/Alt
1931 E Houston St 78202 210-438-6825
Mary Alvarez-Garcia, prin. Fax 212-3997
Poe MS 700/6-8
814 Aransas Ave 78210 210-228-1235
Miriam Aguilar Guevara, prin. Fax 534-7299
Rogers MS 600/6-8
314 Galway St 78223 210-438-6840
Cynthia Ann Perez-Gomez, prin. Fax 333-7954
St. Phillips Early College HS 9-12
1801 Martin Luther King Dr 78203 210-486-2406
Dr. Derrick Thomas, prin. Fax 228-3094
Tafolla MS 900/6-8
1303 W Cesar E Chavez Blvd 78207 210-978-7930
Jeff Price, prin. Fax 227-7044
Twain MS 600/6-8
2411 San Pedro Ave 78212 210-738-9745
Ricky Flores, prin. Fax 738-0518
Wheatley MS 400/6-8
415 Gabriel 78202 210-738-9750
Carlos Flores, prin. Fax 227-9972
Young Mens Leadership Academy 4-8
545 S W W White Rd 78220 210-354-9652
Derrick Brown, prin. Fax 228-3070

South San Antonio ISD 9,700/PK-12
5622 Ray Ellison Blvd 78242 210-977-7000
Dr. Abelardo Saavedra, supt. Fax 977-7021
www.southsanisd.net
Alternative S, 324 Fenfield Ave 78211 50/Alt
Ruperto Becerra, prin. 210-977-7508
Career Education Center Vo/Tech
2615 Navajo St 78224 210-977-7350
Henry Yzaguirre, prin. Fax 977-7356
Dwight MS 500/6-8
2454 W Southcross Blvd 78211 210-977-7300
Yvonne Hernandez, prin. Fax 977-7316
Kazen MS 500/6-8
1520 Gillette Blvd 78224 210-977-7150
Patti Annunzio, prin. Fax 977-7155
Shepard MS 600/6-8
5558 Ray Ellison Blvd 78242 210-623-1875
Chriselda Bazaldua, prin. Fax 623-1894
South San Antonio HS 2,300/9-12
2515 Bobcat Ln 78224 210-977-7400
Lee Hernandez, prin. Fax 977-7430
Zamora MS 500/6-8
8638 Larkia St 78224 210-977-7278
Rosanna Carmona-Mercado, prin. Fax 977-7285

Southside ISD 5,200/PK-12
1460 Martinez Losoya Rd 78221 210-882-1600
Dr. Joe Gonzales, supt. Fax 626-0101
www.southsideisd.org/
Matthey MS 800/7-8
1460 Martinez Losoya Rd 78221 210-882-1601
Staci Weaver, prin. Fax 626-0113
Southside HS 1,300/9-12
1460 Martinez Losoya Rd 78221 210-882-1606
Maria Faqier, prin. Fax 626-0119

Southwest ISD 11,300/PK-12
11914 Dragon Ln 78252 210-622-4300
Dr. Lloyd Verstuyft, supt. Fax 622-4301
www.swisd.net/
McAuliffe MS 1,000/6-8
11914 Dragon Ln 78252 210-623-6260
Adrian Ramirez, prin. Fax 623-6261
Scobee MS 900/6-8
11914 Dragon Ln 78252 210-645-7500
Darin Kasper, prin. Fax 645-7501
Southwest Academy 100/Alt
11914 Dragon Ln 78252 210-622-4750
Juan Perez, prin. Fax 622-9502
Southwest HS 3,200/9-12
11914 Dragon Ln 78252 210-622-4500
Paul Black, prin. Fax 622-4501
Other Schools – See Atascosa

---

Achievers' Center for Education 50/5-12
5084 De Zavala Rd 78249 210-690-7359
Anne Zuber, admin. Fax 690-7307
Antonian College Preparatory HS 800/9-12
6425 West Ave 78213 210-344-9265
Tim Petersen, prin. Fax 344-9267
Atonement Academy 600/PK-12
15415 Red Robin Rd 78255 210-695-2240
Walter Spencer, hdmstr. Fax 695-9679
Baptist Health System-Sch of Health Prof Post-Sec.
8400 Datapoint Dr 78229 210-297-9636
Baptist University of the Americas Post-Sec.
8019 S Panam Expy 78224 210-924-4338
Brown Mackie College Post-Sec.
4715 Fredericksburg Rd #100 78229 210-425-2210
Cancer Therapy & Research Center Post-Sec.
7979 Wurzbach Rd 78229 210-450-5664
Career Point College Post-Sec.
4522 Fredericksburg Rd #A22 78201 210-732-3000
Castle Hills First Baptist S 400/PK-12
2220 NW Military Hwy 78213 210-377-8485
Michael Pinkston, supt. Fax 377-8473
Central Catholic HS 600/9-12
1403 N Saint Marys St 78215 210-225-6794
Paul Garro, prin. Fax 227-9353
Christian Academy of San Antonio 600/PK-12
325 Castroville Rd 78207 210-436-2277
Pamela Payne, supt. Fax 436-2210
Concorde Career College Post-Sec.
4803 NW Loop 410 Ste 200 78229 210-428-2000
Cornerstone Christian S 700/PK-12
4802 Vance Jackson Rd 78230 210-979-9203
Dr. Jerry Eshleman, supt. Fax 979-0310
Culinary Institute of America Post-Sec.
312 Pearl Pkwy Bldg 2 #2102 78215 210-554-6400
Everest Institute Post-Sec.
6550 1st Park Ten Blvd 78213 210-732-7800
Hallmark College Post-Sec.
10401 W Interstate 10 78230 210-690-9000
Hallmark College of Aeronautics Post-Sec.
8901 Wetmore Rd 78216 210-826-1000
Holy Cross of San Antonio 400/6-12
426 N San Felipe Ave 78228 210-433-9395
Henry Galindo, prin. Fax 433-2117
Incarnate Word HS 500/9-12
727 E Hildebrand Ave 78212 210-829-3100
Jennifer Salazar, prin. Fax 829-3120
ITT Technical Institute Post-Sec.
5700 Northwest Pkwy 78249 210-694-4612
ITT Technical Institute Post-Sec.
2895 NE Loop 410 78218 210-651-8500
Kaplan College Post-Sec.
7142 San Pedro Ave Ste 100 78216 210-733-0777
Kaplan College Post-Sec.
6441 NW Loop 410 78238 210-308-8584
Keystone S 400/PK-12
119 E Craig Pl 78212 210-735-4022
Brian Yager, head sch Fax 732-4905
Lamson Institute Post-Sec.
5819 NW Loop 410 Ste 160 78238 210-520-1800
Legacy Christian Academy 200/PK-12
2255 Horal St 78227 210-674-0490
Rev. Dennis Wall, chncllr. Fax 674-3615
Lutheran HS of San Antonio 100/9-12
18104 Babcock Rd 78255 210-694-4962
Patrick Maynard, prin. Fax 694-9150
Milan Institute Post-Sec.
6804 Ingram Rd 78238 210-647-5100
Milan Institute of Cosmetology Post-Sec.
605 SW Military Dr 78221 210-922-5900
Mims Classic Beauty College Post-Sec.
5121 Blanco Rd 78216 210-344-2041
New Life Christian Academy 200/PK-12
6601 W US Highway 90 78227 210-679-6001
Anthony Jackson, prin. Fax 679-6080
Northwest Vista College Post-Sec.
3535 N Ellison Dr 78251 210-486-4000
Oblate School of Theology Post-Sec.
285 Oblate Dr 78216 210-341-1366
Our Lady of the Lake University Post-Sec.
411 SW 24th St 78207 210-434-6711
Palo Alto College Post-Sec.
1400 W Villaret Blvd 78224 210-486-3000
Providence Catholic S 400/6-12
1215 N Saint Marys St 78215 210-224-6651
Alicia Garcia, prin. Fax 224-6214
Quest College Post-Sec.
5430 Fredericksburg Rd #310 78229 210-366-2701
River City Believers Academy 100/PK-12
16765 Lookout Rd 78233 210-656-2999
Shane Land M.Ed., prin. Fax 496-2888
St. Anthony Catholic HS 400/9-12
3200 McCullough Ave 78212 210-832-5600
Rene Escobedo, prin. Fax 832-5615
St. Gerard Catholic HS 100/9-12
521 S New Braunfels Ave 78203 210-533-8061
Michelle De Anda, prin. Fax 533-3697
St. Mary's Hall 500/PK-12
9401 Starcrest Dr 78217 210-483-9100
Jonathan Eades, head sch Fax 483-9299
St. Mary's University Post-Sec.
1 Camino Santa Maria St 78228 210-436-3011
St. Phillip's College Post-Sec.
1801 Martin Luther King Dr 78203 210-486-2000
San Antonio Beauty College #3 Post-Sec.
4130 Naco Perrin Blvd 78217 210-654-9734
San Antonio Beauty College #4 Post-Sec.
2423 Jamar St # 2 78226 210-433-7222
San Antonio Christian S 500/PK-12
19202 Redland Rd 78259 210-340-1864
Dr. William Walters, supt. Fax 340-0461
San Antonio College Post-Sec.
1300 San Pedro Ave 78212 210-486-0000
Sanford-Brown College Post-Sec.
4511 Horizon Hill Blvd 78229 210-246-7700
Scenic Hills Christian Academy 50/PK-10
11223 Bandera Rd 78250 210-523-2312
Southern Careers Institute Post-Sec.
238 SW Military Dr Ste 101 78221 210-271-0096
South Texas Vocational Technical Inst Post-Sec.
734 SE Military Dr 78214 888-822-4046
Southwest School Post-Sec.
602 W Southcross Blvd 78221 210-921-0951
Southwest School Post-Sec.
2402 San Pedro Ave 78212 210-225-7287
Texas A&M University San Antonio Post-Sec.
1 University Way 78224 210-784-1000
TMI - The Episcopal S of Texas 400/6-12
20955 W Tejas Trl 78257 210-698-7171
Dr. John W. Cooper, head sch Fax 698-0715
Trinity Christian Academy 200/K-12
5401 N Loop 1604 E 78247 210-653-2800
Dr. Susan Oldfield, prin. Fax 653-0303
Trinity University Post-Sec.
1 Trinity Pl 78212 210-999-7011
University Hospital Post-Sec.
4502 Medical Dr 78229 210-616-2000
University of Texas at San Antonio Post-Sec.
1 UTSA Cir 78249 210-458-4011
University of Texas Health Science Ctr. Post-Sec.
7703 Floyd Curl Dr 78229 210-567-7000
University of the Incarnate Word Post-Sec.
4301 Broadway St 78209 210-829-6000
Winston S San Antonio 100/K-12
8565 Ewing Halsell Dr 78229 210-615-6544
Dr. Charles Karulak, hdmstr. Fax 615-6627

**San Augustine, San Augustine, Pop. 2,090**
San Augustine ISD 800/PK-12
1002 Barrett St 75972 936-275-2306
Dr. Virginia Liepman, supt. Fax 275-9776
www.saisd.us
San Augustine HS 200/9-12
1002 Barrett St 75972 936-275-9603
Leasa Dunn, prin. Fax 275-9829
San Augustine MS 200/6-8
1002 Barrett St 75972 936-275-9603
Leasa Dunn, prin. Fax 275-9829

**San Benito, Cameron, Pop. 24,199**
Los Fresnos Consolidated ISD
Supt. — See Los Fresnos
Liberty Memorial MS 600/6-8
31579 FM 2893 78586 956-233-3900
Glafira Braga, prin. Fax 233-1074
Los Fresnos United HS 700/9-9
33790 FM 803 78586 956-254-5250
Jennifer Stumbaugh, prin. Fax 399-2047

San Benito Consolidated ISD 10,800/PK-12
240 N Crockett St 78586 956-361-6100
Dr. Filomena Leo, supt. Fax 361-6115
www.sbcisd.net
Cabaza MS 800/6-8
2901 Shafer Rd 78586 956-361-6600
Lupita Monsellaves, prin. Fax 361-6608
Callandret Positive Redirection Center 50/Alt
305 Doherty St 78586 956-361-6275
Ray Saldana, prin. Fax 361-6278
Gateway Academy 100/Alt
600 N Austin St 78586 956-361-6446
Rolando Guerra, prin. Fax 399-7985
Jordan MS 900/6-8
700 N McCullough St 78586 956-361-6650
Bobbie Jo Hushen, prin. Fax 361-6658
San Benito HS 2,000/10-12
450 S Williams Rd 78586 956-361-6500
Henry Sanchez, prin. Fax 361-6579
San Benito Riverside MS 700/6-8
35428 Padilla St 78586 956-361-6940
Marcus Ysasi, prin. Fax 361-6948
San Benito Veterans Memorial Academy 800/9-9
2115 N Williams Rd 78586 956-276-6000
Gilbert Galvan, prin. Fax 276-6008

South Texas ISD
Supt. — See Mercedes
Rising Scholars Academy of South Texas 7-8
151 S Helen Moore Rd 78586 956-399-4358
Carrie Sauceda, prin. Fax 399-3570

---

South Texas Training Center Post-Sec.
1901 W US Highway 77 78586 956-399-9698

**Sanderson, Terrell, Pop. 834**
Terrell County ISD 100/PK-12
PO Box 747 79848 432-345-2515
Kenn Norris, supt. Fax 345-2670
www.terrell.esc18.net
Sanderson HS 50/5-12
PO Box 747 79848 432-345-2515
Kenn Norris, prin. Fax 345-2670

**San Diego, Duval, Pop. 4,473**
San Diego ISD 1,300/PK-12
609 W Labbe St 78384 361-279-3382
Dr. Samuel Bueno, supt. Fax 279-1830
www.sdisd.esc2.net
Jaime JHS 300/6-8
609 W Labbe St 78384 361-279-3382
Carlos Trevino, prin. Fax 279-3139
San Diego HS 400/9-12
609 W Labbe St 78384 361-279-3382
Michael Gonzalez, prin. Fax 279-5098

**San Elizario, El Paso, Pop. 13,596**
San Elizario ISD 3,900/PK-12
PO Box 920 79849 915-872-3900
Sylvia Hopp, supt. Fax 872-3903
www.seisd.net
Garcia-Enriquez MS 600/7-8
PO Box 920 79849 915-872-3960
April Marioni, prin. Fax 872-3961
San Elizario HS 1,100/9-12
PO Box 920 79849 915-872-3970
Maribel Guillen, prin. Fax 872-3971

**Sanger, Denton, Pop. 6,799**
Sanger ISD 2,600/PK-12
601 Elm St 76266 940-458-7438
Kent Crutsinger, supt. Fax 458-5140
www.sangerisd.net/
Sanger HS 700/9-12
100 Indian Ln 76266 940-458-7497
Charlene Parham, prin. Fax 458-4637
Sanger MS 400/7-8
105 Berry St 76266 940-458-7916
Sally Herrell, prin. Fax 458-5111
Tutt HS 50/Alt
404 Hughes St 76266 940-458-5701
Dr. Ann Hughes, prin. Fax 458-5759

**San Isidro, Starr, Pop. 240**
San Isidro ISD 300/PK-12
PO Box 10 78588 956-481-3110
Mario Alvarado, supt. Fax 481-3930
www.sanisidroisd.org
San Isidro HS 100/9-12
PO Box 10 78588 956-481-3110
Anna Garcia, prin. Fax 481-3950

**San Juan, Hidalgo, Pop. 33,835**
Pharr-San Juan-Alamo ISD
Supt. — See Pharr
Austin MS 700/6-8
804 S Stewart Rd 78589 956-354-2570
Liza Navarro, prin. Fax 354-3194
Pharr-San Juan-Alamo Early College HS 2,000/9-12
805 Ridge Rd 78589 956-354-2300
Alejandro Elias, prin. Fax 354-3156
Pharr-San Juan-Alamo Elvis Ballew HS 200/Alt
715 S Standard Ave 78589 956-354-2520
Larissa Saenz, prin. Fax 354-3116
Yzaguirre MS 900/6-8
605 E FM 495 78589 956-354-2630
Rebecca Luna, prin. Fax 354-3230

**San Marcos, Hays, Pop. 44,109**
San Marcos Consolidated ISD 7,500/PK-12
PO Box 1087 78667 512-393-6700
Mark E. Eads, supt. Fax 393-6709
www.smcisd.net/
Goodnight MS 1,000/6-8
1301 N State Highway 123 78666 512-393-6550
Steve Dow, prin. Fax 393-6560
Miller MS 700/6-8
301 Foxtail Run 78666 512-393-6660
Richard Duvall, prin. Fax 393-6602
Phoenix Learning Center Alt
500 W Hutchison St 78666 512-393-6932
Judy Mitchell, prin. Fax 393-6999
San Marcos HS 2,200/9-12
2601 Rattler Rd 78666 512-393-6300
Kelli Lopez, prin. Fax 393-6893

---

Gary Job Corps Center Post-Sec.
PO Box 967 78667 512-396-6561
San Marcos Academy 300/7-12
2801 Ranch Road 12 78666 512-753-8000
Jimmie Scott, pres. Fax 753-8031
San Marcos Adventist Academy 100/PK-10
PO Box 801 78667 512-392-9475
Texas State University San Marcos Post-Sec.
601 University Dr 78666 512-245-2111

**San Perlita, Willacy, Pop. 573**
San Perlita ISD 300/PK-12
PO Box 37 78590 956-248-5563
Albert Pena, supt. Fax 248-5561
www.spisd.org
San Perlita HS 100/9-12
PO Box 37 78590 956-248-5250
Ramiro Moreno, prin. Fax 248-5103
San Perlita MS 100/6-8
PO Box 37 78590 956-248-5250
Ramiro Moreno, prin. Fax 248-5103

**San Saba, San Saba, Pop. 3,082**
San Saba ISD 700/PK-12
808 W Wallace St 76877 325-372-3771
Leigh Ann Glaze, supt. Fax 372-5977
www.san-saba.net
San Saba HS 200/9-12
808 W Wallace St 76877 325-372-3786
Dr. Scott Snyder, prin. Fax 372-3478
San Saba MS 200/5-8
808 W Wallace St 76877 325-372-3200
Dave Lewis, prin. Fax 372-5228

**Santa Anna, Coleman, Pop. 1,086**
Santa Anna ISD 300/PK-12
701 Bowie St 76878 325-348-3136
David Robinett, supt. Fax 348-3141
santaanna.netxv.net
Santa Anna HS 100/7-12
701 Bowie St 76878 325-348-3137
Laurie Hunter, prin. Fax 348-3149

**Santa Fe, Galveston, Pop. 12,112**
Santa Fe ISD 4,600/PK-12
PO Box 370 77510 409-925-9001
Dr. Leigh Wall, supt. Fax 925-4002
www.sfisd.org/

Santa Fe HS 1,400/9-12
PO Box 370 77510 409-925-2700
Colleen Dale, prin. Fax 925-2773
Santa Fe JHS 1,100/6-8
PO Box 370 77510 409-925-9300
Kimberly Ross, prin. Fax 927-4106

**Santa Maria, Cameron, Pop. 732**
Santa Maria ISD 700/PK-12
PO Box 448 78592 956-565-6308
Maria Chavez, supt. Fax 565-0598
www.smisd.net
Santa Maria HS 200/9-12
PO Box 448 78592 956-565-9144
Cindy Taylor, prin. Fax 514-1968
Santa Maria MS 200/6-8
PO Box 448 78592 956-565-6309
Maria Rodriguez, prin. Fax 565-6720

**Santa Rosa, Cameron, Pop. 2,866**
Santa Rosa ISD 1,200/PK-12
PO Box 368 78593 956-636-9800
Heriberto Villarreal, supt. Fax 636-1439
www.srtx.org
Nelson MS 300/6-8
PO Box 368 78593 956-636-9850
John Gray, prin. Fax 636-1519
Santa Rosa HS 300/9-12
PO Box 368 78593 956-636-9830
Rebecca Corpus, prin. Fax 636-1496

**Santo, Palo Pinto**
Santo ISD 500/PK-12
PO Box 67 76472 940-769-2835
Greg Gilbert, supt. Fax 769-3116
www.santoisd.net/
Santo JSHS 300/6-12
PO Box 67 76472 940-769-3847
Nick Heupel, prin. Fax 769-2796

**Saratoga, Hardin**
West Hardin County Consolidated ISD 600/PK-12
39227 Highway 105 77585 936-274-5061
John Andrus, supt. Fax 274-4321
westhardin.org
West Hardin MSHS 200/7-12
39227 Highway 105 77585 936-274-5061
Alan Andrus, prin. Fax 274-5671

**Savoy, Fannin, Pop. 820**
Savoy ISD 300/PK-12
302 W Hayes St 75479 903-965-5262
Brian Neal, supt. Fax 965-7282
www.savoyisd.org
Savoy JSHS 100/7-12
302 W Hayes St 75479 903-965-4024
Mike Smith, prin. Fax 965-5608

**Schertz, Guadalupe, Pop. 30,563**
Schertz-Cibolo-Universal City ISD 13,100/PK-12
1060 Elbel Rd 78154 210-945-6200
Greg Gibson Ed.D., supt. Fax 945-6292
www.scuc.txed.net
Clemens HS 1,800/9-12
1001 Elbel Rd 78154 210-945-6501
Melissa Sosa, prin. Fax 945-6590
Corbett JHS 1,000/7-8
12000 Ray Corbett Dr 78154 210-619-4150
David Knox, prin. Fax 619-4190
Steele Enhanced Learning Center 2,200/Alt
204 Wright Ave 78154 210-945-6401
David Berry, prin. Fax 945-6410
Other Schools – See Cibolo

**Schulenburg, Fayette, Pop. 2,828**
Schulenburg ISD 700/PK-12
521 North St 78956 979-743-3448
Lisa Meysembourg, supt. Fax 743-4721
www.schulenburg.txed.net
Schulenburg HS 300/6-12
150 College St 78956 979-743-3605
Brent Niemeier, prin. Fax 743-4721

**Scurry, Kaufman, Pop. 668**
Scurry-Rosser ISD 900/PK-12
10705 S State Highway 34 75158 972-452-8823
Rhonda Porter, supt. Fax 452-8586
www.scurry-rosser.com/
Scurry-Rosser HS 300/9-12
8321 S State Highway 34 75158 972-452-8823
Chad Collins, prin. Fax 452-3694
Scurry-Rosser MS 400/4-8
10729 S State Highway 34 75158 972-452-8823
Tara Bachtel, prin. Fax 452-8902

**Seabrook, Harris, Pop. 11,727**
Clear Creek ISD
Supt. — See League City
Seabrook IS 1,000/6-8
2401 Meyer Rd 77586 281-284-3100
David Williams, prin. Fax 284-3105

**Seagraves, Gaines, Pop. 2,405**
Seagraves ISD 600/PK-12
PO Box 577 79359 806-387-2035
Dr. Kevin Spiller, supt. Fax 387-2944
www.seagravesisd.net/
Seagraves HS 100/9-12
PO Box 1505 79359 806-387-2520
Artemio Ontiveros, prin. Fax 387-2944
Seagraves JHS 100/6-8
PO Box 938 79359 806-387-2646
Josh Goen, prin. Fax 387-2451

**Sealy, Austin, Pop. 5,953**
Sealy ISD 2,700/PK-12
939 Tiger Ln 77474 979-885-3516
Sheryl Moore, supt. Fax 885-6457
www.sealyisd.com
Sealy HS 800/9-12
2372 Championship Dr 77474 979-885-3515
Megan Oliver, prin. Fax 987-3398
Sealy JHS 600/6-8
939 Tiger Ln 77474 979-885-3292
Terri Kendrick, prin. Fax 877-0743

**Seguin, Guadalupe, Pop. 24,967**
Navarro ISD 1,600/PK-12
6450 N State Highway 123 78155 830-372-1930
Dee Carter, supt. Fax 372-1853
www.nisd.us
Navarro HS 500/9-12
6350 N State Highway 123 78155 830-372-1931
Gary Haass, prin. Fax 401-5570
Navarro JHS 300/7-8
6450 N State Highway 123 78155 830-401-5550
Luke Morales, prin. Fax 379-3135

Seguin ISD 7,300/PK-12
1221 E Kingsbury St 78155 830-401-8600
Stetson Roane, supt. Fax 379-0392
www.seguin.k12.tx.us
Barnes MS 500/6-8
1539 Joe Carrillo Blvd 78155 830-379-4717
Michael Garza, prin. Fax 379-4239
Briesemeister MS 500/6-8
1616 W Court St 78155 830-379-0600
Elisa Carter, prin. Fax 379-0615
Burges Alternative S Alt
225 N Saunders St 78155 830-401-1261
Wade Cherry, prin. Fax 379-0088
Mercer-Blumberg Learning Center 100/Alt
1205 E Kingsbury St 78155 830-401-8690
Jay Law, prin. Fax 379-1362
Seguin HS 1,900/9-12
815 Lamar 78155 830-372-5770
Hector Esquivel, prin. Fax 372-9851

---

Lifegate Christian S 200/K-12
395 Lifegate Ln 78155 830-372-0850
Kendra Thomas, prin. Fax 372-0895
Seguin Beauty College Post-Sec.
102 E Court St 78155 830-372-0935
Seguin Christian Academy 50/PK-10
PO Box 2647 78156 830-433-4131
Allison Haeussler, prin.
Texas Lutheran University Post-Sec.
1000 W Court St 78155 830-372-8000

**Seminole, Gaines, Pop. 6,373**
Seminole ISD 2,500/PK-12
207 SW 6th St 79360 432-758-3662
Gary Laramore, supt. Fax 758-9833
www.seminoleisd.net/
Seminole HS 600/9-12
2100 NW Avenue D 79360 432-758-5873
Robert Chappell, prin. Fax 758-8146
Seminole JHS 600/6-8
600 NW Avenue J 79360 432-758-9431
Daylan Sellers, prin. Fax 758-5795
Seminole Success Center 50/Alt
206 SW 3rd St 79360 432-758-2772
Seth Davis, prin. Fax 758-3625

**Seymour, Baylor, Pop. 2,715**
Seymour ISD 600/PK-12
409 W Idaho St 76380 940-889-3525
Dr. John Baker, supt. Fax 889-5340
www.seymour-isd.net
Seymour HS 200/9-12
409 W Idaho St 76380 940-889-2947
Brian Bibb, prin. Fax 889-1045
Seymour MS 200/5-8
409 W Idaho St 76380 940-889-4548
Morris Davis, prin. Fax 889-4962

**Shady Shores, Denton, Pop. 2,560**
Denton ISD
Supt. — See Denton
Myers MS 6-8
131 N Garza Rd 76208 940-369-1500
Angela Ricks, prin. Fax 498-0050

**Shallowater, Lubbock, Pop. 2,469**
Shallowater ISD 1,600/PK-12
1100 Avenue K 79363 806-832-4531
Dr. Kenny Border, supt. Fax 832-4350
www.shallowaterisd.net
Shallowater Early College HS Woodward 50/Alt
1100 Avenue K 79363 806-832-4531
Carol Johnson, prin. Fax 832-4350
Shallowater HS 400/9-12
1100 Avenue K 79363 806-832-4531
Tom Johnson, prin. Fax 832-4523
Shallowater MS 500/5-8
1100 Avenue K 79363 806-832-4531
Aron Strickland, prin. Fax 832-5543

**Shamrock, Wheeler, Pop. 1,874**
Shamrock ISD 300/PK-12
100 S Illinois St 79079 806-256-3492
Dr. Kenneth Shields, supt. Fax 256-3628
www.shamrockisd.net
Shamrock HS 100/9-12
100 S Illinois St 79079 806-256-2241
Brandon Mahler, prin. Fax 256-3628
Shamrock JHS 100/6-8
100 S Illinois St 79079 806-256-3492
Ed Berngen, admin. Fax 256-3628

**Sheffield, Pecos**
Iraan-Sheffield ISD
Supt. — See Iraan
Challenge HS 100/Alt
1 Schoolhouse Rd 79781 432-836-4572
Dr. Candra Cade, prin. Fax 836-4691

**Shelbyville, Shelby**
Shelbyville ISD 800/PK-12
PO Box 325 75973 936-598-2641
Dr. Ray West, supt. Fax 598-6842
www.shelbyville.k12.tx.us
Shelbyville S 800/PK-12
PO Box 325 75973 936-598-7323
Mario Osby, prin. Fax 598-6842

**Shenandoah, Montgomery, Pop. 2,111**

---

Aveda Institute Post-Sec.
19241 David Memorial Dr 77385 936-539-6770

**Shepherd, San Jacinto, Pop. 2,281**
Shepherd ISD 1,900/PK-12
1401 S Byrd Ave 77371 936-628-3396
Steve Pierce, supt. Fax 628-3841
www.shepherdisd.net/
Shepherd HS 500/9-12
1401 S Byrd Ave 77371 936-628-3371
Jimmy Meekins, prin. Fax 628-6986
Shepherd MS 400/6-8
1401 S Byrd Ave 77371 936-628-3377
Brenda Cronin, prin. Fax 628-6749

**Sherman, Grayson, Pop. 37,575**
Sherman ISD 6,800/PK-12
2701 N Loy Lake Rd 75090 903-891-6400
Lloyd Treadwell, supt. Fax 891-6407
www.shermanisd.net
Piner MS 900/7-8
402 W Pecan St 75090 903-891-6470
Clinton Petty, prin. Fax 891-6475
Sherman HS 1,600/9-12
2201 E Lamar St 75090 903-891-6440
Peggy VanMarter, prin. Fax 891-6446
Other Schools – See Denison

---

Austin College Post-Sec.
900 N Grand Ave 75090 903-813-2000
Diamonds Cosmetology College Post-Sec.
1950 N Grand Ave 75090 903-891-0758
Texoma Christian S 300/PK-12
3500 W Houston St 75092 903-893-7076
Jeff Burley, head sch Fax 891-8486

**Shiner, Lavaca, Pop. 2,046**
Shiner ISD 600/PK-12
PO Box 804 77984 361-594-3121
Trey Lawrence, supt. Fax 594-3925
www.shinerisd.net
Shiner JSHS 300/7-12
PO Box 804 77984 361-594-3131
Brad Oden, prin. Fax 594-4295

---

Shiner Catholic S 300/PK-12
PO Box 725 77984 361-594-2313
Neely Yackel, prin. Fax 594-8599

**Sidney, Comanche**
Sidney ISD 100/PK-12
PO Box 190 76474 254-842-5500
Doug Bowden, supt. Fax 842-5731
www.sidney.esc14.net/
Sidney S 100/PK-12
PO Box 190 76474 254-842-5500
James Rucker, prin. Fax 842-5731

**Sierra Blanca, Hudspeth, Pop. 550**
Sierra Blanca ISD 100/K-12
PO Box 308 79851 915-369-3741
Evelyn Loeffler, supt. Fax 369-2605
www.sierrablancaisd.net
Sierra Blanca S 100/K-12
PO Box 308 79851 915-369-2781
Evelyn Loeffler, prin. Fax 369-2605

**Silsbee, Hardin, Pop. 6,524**
Silsbee ISD 2,700/K-12
415 Highway 327 W 77656 409-980-7800
Richard Bain, supt. Fax 980-7897
www.silsbeeisd.org
Edwards-Johnson Memorial Silsbee MS 700/6-8
1140 Highway 327 E 77656 409-980-7800
Sunee Stephens, prin. Fax 980-7875
Silsbee HS 800/9-12
1575 US Highway 96 N 77656 409-980-7800
Don Muckleroy, prin. Fax 980-7881

---

Southeast Texas Career Institute Post-Sec.
975 Highway 327 E Ste 150 77656 409-386-2020

**Silverton, Briscoe, Pop. 724**
Silverton ISD 200/PK-12
PO Box 608 79257 806-823-2476
Michelle Francis, supt. Fax 823-2276
www.silvertonisd.net
Silverton S 200/PK-12
PO Box 608 79257 806-823-2476
Michelle Francis, supt. Fax 823-2276

**Simms, Bowie**
Simms ISD 500/PK-12
PO Box 9 75574 903-543-2219
Rex Burks, supt. Fax 543-2512
www.simmsisd.net/
Bowie HS 200/9-12
PO Box 9 75574 903-543-2219
Lisa Hudgeons, prin. Fax 543-2512
Bowie MS 100/6-8
PO Box 9 75574 903-543-2219
Lisa Hudgeons, prin. Fax 543-2512

**Sinton, San Patricio, Pop. 5,646**
Sinton ISD 2,200/PK-12
PO Box 1337 78387 361-364-6800
Pari Whitten, supt. Fax 364-6905
www.sintonisd.net/
Sinton HS 600/9-12
400 N Pirate Blvd 78387 361-364-6650
Daniel Smith, prin. Fax 364-6668
Smith MS 500/6-8
900 S San Patricio St 78387 361-364-6840
Jennifer Davis, prin. Fax 364-6856

**Skidmore, Bee, Pop. 917**
Skidmore-Tynan ISD 800/K-12
224 W Main St 78389 361-287-3426
Dr. Randy Hoyer, supt. Fax 287-3442
www.stisd.esc2.net
Skidmore-Tynan HS 300/9-12
224 W Main St 78389 361-287-3426
Hank Looney, prin. Fax 287-0146
Skidmore-Tynan JHS 200/6-8
224 W Main St 78389 361-287-3426
Dana Scott, prin. Fax 287-0714

**Slaton, Lubbock, Pop. 6,048**
Slaton ISD 1,300/PK-12
140 E Panhandle St 79364 806-828-6591
Julee Becker, supt. Fax 828-5506
www.slatonisd.net/
Slaton HS 300/9-12
105 N 20th St 79364 806-828-5833
Chris Kennedy, prin. Fax 828-1229
Slaton JHS 300/6-8
300 W Jean St 79364 806-828-6583
Jim Andrus, prin. Fax 828-2080

**Slidell, Wise**
Slidell ISD 200/PK-12
PO Box 69 76267 940-466-3118
Greg Enis, supt. Fax 466-3062
www.slidellisd.net/
Slidell JSHS 100/6-12
PO Box 69 76267 940-466-3118
Marty Hair, prin. Fax 466-3607

**Smithville, Bastrop, Pop. 3,753**
Smithville ISD 1,700/PK-12
PO Box 479 78957 512-237-2487
Dr. Rock McNulty, supt. Fax 237-2775
www.smithvilleisd.org
Smithville HS 500/9-12
PO Box 479 78957 512-237-2451
Kenneth Parker, prin. Fax 237-5643
Smithville JHS 400/6-8
PO Box 479 78957 512-237-2407
Dr. Bethany Logan, prin. Fax 237-5624

**Smyer, Hockley, Pop. 469**
Smyer ISD 400/PK-12
PO Box 206 79367 806-234-2935
Dane Kerns, supt. Fax 234-2411
www.smyer-isd.org
Smyer JSHS 200/7-12
PO Box 206 79367 806-234-2935
William Black, prin. Fax 234-2411

**Snook, Burleson, Pop. 502**
Snook ISD 600/PK-12
PO Box 87 77878 979-272-8307
Brenda Krchnak, supt. Fax 272-5041
www.snookisd.org
Snook Secondary S 100/6-12
PO Box 87 77878 979-272-8307
Dr. Kenzie Bond, prin. Fax 272-5041

**Snyder, Scurry, Pop. 11,101**
Snyder ISD 2,700/PK-12
2901 37th St 79549 325-574-8900
Jim Kirkland, supt. Fax 573-9025
www.snyderisd.net
Snyder HS 700/9-12
2901 37th St 79549 325-574-8800
Britenie Polk, prin. Fax 573-9500
Snyder JHS 500/6-8
2901 37th St 79549 325-574-8700
Jorge Mendez, prin. Fax 574-6024

---

Western Texas College Post-Sec.
6200 College Ave 79549 325-573-8511

**Somerset, Bexar, Pop. 1,624**
Somerset ISD 3,900/PK-12
PO Box 279 78069 866-852-9858
Dr. Saul Hinojosa, supt. Fax 852-9860
www.sisdk12.net
Early College Leadership Academy 9-12
PO Box 279 78069 855-999-4634
Brandon Van Vleck, prin.
Somerset HS 1,000/9-12
PO Box 279 78069 866-852-9861
Angela Dominguez, prin. Fax 667-2608
Other Schools – See Von Ormy

**Somerville, Burleson, Pop. 1,362**
Somerville ISD 500/PK-12
PO Box 997 77879 979-596-2153
Charles Camarillo, supt. Fax 596-1778
www.somervilleisd.org
Somerville Secondary S 200/7-12
PO Box 997 77879 979-596-1534
Dan Garza, prin. Fax 596-1778

**Sonora, Sutton, Pop. 3,018**
Sonora ISD 1,000/PK-12
807 S Concho Ave 76950 325-387-6940
Ross Aschenbeck, supt. Fax 387-5090
www.sonoraisd.net
Sonora HS 300/9-12
807 S Concho Ave 76950 325-387-6940
Ken Wimberley, prin. Fax 387-5348
Sonora JHS 200/6-8
807 S Concho Ave 76950 325-387-6940
Brandon Duncan, prin. Fax 387-2007

**Sour Lake, Hardin, Pop. 1,788**
Hardin-Jefferson ISD 2,000/PK-12
PO Box 490 77659 409-981-6400
Shannon Holmes Ed.D., supt. Fax 287-2283
www.hjisd.net/
Hardin-Jefferson HS 600/9-12
PO Box 639 77659 409-981-6430
Diana Valdez Ed.D., prin.
Henderson MS, PO Box 649 77659 500/6-8
Darrell Westfall, prin. 409-981-6420

**South Houston, Harris, Pop. 16,918**
Pasadena ISD
Supt. — See Pasadena
South Houston HS 2,600/9-12
3820 S Shaver St 77587 713-740-0350
Steve Fullen, prin. Fax 740-4155
South Houston IS 800/6-8
900 College Ave 77587 713-740-0490
Laura Gomez, prin. Fax 740-4097

**Southlake, Tarrant, Pop. 26,042**
Carroll ISD 7,700/PK-12
2400 N Carroll Ave 76092 817-949-8282
Dr. David Faltys, supt. Fax 949-8228
www.southlakecarroll.edu
Carroll HS 1,300/9-10
800 N White Chapel Blvd 76092 817-949-5600
Paul Giamanco, prin. Fax 949-5656
Carroll MS 600/7-8
1800 Kirkwood Blvd 76092 817-949-5400
Stephanie Mangels, prin. Fax 949-5454
Carroll SHS 1,300/11-12
1501 W Southlake Blvd 76092 817-949-5800
M. Shawn Duhon, prin. Fax 949-5858
Dawson MS 700/7-8
400 S Kimball Ave 76092 817-949-5500
Ryan Wilson, prin. Fax 949-5555

---

Clariden S 100/PK-12
100 Clariden Ranch Rd 76092 682-237-0400
Sallie Wells, hdmstr. Fax 831-0300

**Southland, Garza**
Southland ISD 200/PK-12
190 Eighth St 79364 806-996-5599
Craig Hamilton, supt. Fax 996-5342
www.southlandisd.net
Southland S 200/PK-12
190 Eighth St 79364 806-996-5339
Craig Hamilton, prin. Fax 996-5595

**Spearman, Hansford, Pop. 3,341**
Spearman ISD 800/PK-12
403 E 11th Ave 79081 806-659-3233
Wm. Clay Montgomery, supt. Fax 659-2079
www.spearmanisd.net
Spearman HS 200/9-12
403 E 11th Ave 79081 806-659-2584
Colynn Harrison, prin. Fax 659-3824
Spearman JHS 200/6-8
313 W 5th Ave 79081 806-659-2563
Shane Whiteley, prin. Fax 659-3933

**Spicewood, Burnet**
Lake Travis ISD
Supt. — See Austin
Lake Travis MS 800/6-8
4932 Bee Creek Rd 78669 512-533-6200
Jodie Villemaire, prin. Fax 533-6201

**Splendora, Montgomery, Pop. 1,597**
Splendora ISD 3,500/PK-12
23419 FM 2090 Rd 77372 281-689-3128
Dr. Genese Bell, supt. Fax 689-7509
www.splendoraisd.org/
Splendora HS 1,000/9-12
23747 FM 2090 Rd 77372 281-689-8008
Dr. Nate Session, prin. Fax 689-8675
Splendora JHS 500/6-8
23411 FM 2090 Rd 77372 281-689-6343
Kent Broussard, prin. Fax 689-8702

**Spring, Harris, Pop. 53,043**
Conroe ISD
Supt. — See Conroe
York JHS 1,800/7-8
3515 Waterbend Cv 77386 832-592-8600
James Kacur, prin. Fax 592-8684

Klein ISD
Supt. — See Klein
Hildebrandt IS 900/6-8
22800 Hildebrandt Rd 77389 832-249-5100
Joffrey Jones, prin. Fax 249-4068
Klein Collins HS 3,400/9-12
20811 Ella Blvd 77388 832-484-5500
Randy Kirk, prin. Fax 484-7811
Klein Oak HS 4,100/9-12
22603 Northcrest Dr 77389 832-484-5000
Dr. Brian Greeney, prin. Fax 484-7831
Schindewolf IS 1,300/6-8
20903 Ella Blvd 77388 832-249-5900
Curtis Simmons, prin. Fax 249-4072

Spring ISD
Supt. — See Houston
Bailey MS 1,200/6-8
3377 James Leo Dr 77373 281-891-8000
Tarrynce Robinson, prin. Fax 891-8001
Dueitt MS 1,000/6-8
1 Eagle Xing 77373 281-891-7800
Ben Bostick, prin. Fax 891-7801
Spring HS 3,500/9-12
19428 Interstate 45 77373 281-891-7000
Tia Simmons, prin. Fax 891-7001
Twin Creeks MS 900/6-8
27100 Cypresswood Dr 77373 281-891-7850
Dario Villota, prin. Fax 891-7851
Wunsche SHS Vo/Tech
900 Wunsche Loop 77373 281-891-7650
Bob Thompson, prin. Fax 891-7651

---

Cunae International S 100/PK-12
5655 Creekside Forest Dr 77389 281-516-3770
Anji Price, dir.
Frassati Catholic HS 9-12
22151 Frassati Way 77389 832-616-3217
Sr. John Paul Myers, prin. Fax 907-0675

**Spring Branch, Comal**
Comal ISD
Supt. — See New Braunfels
Smithson Valley HS 2,100/9-12
14001 State Highway 46 W 78070 830-885-1000
Michael Wahl, prin. Fax 885-1001
Smithson Valley MS 900/6-8
6101 FM 311 78070 830-885-1200
Michael Keranen, prin. Fax 885-1201
Spring Branch MS 900/6-8
21053 State Highway 46 W 78070 830-885-8800
Chris Smith, prin. Fax 885-8801

**Springtown, Parker, Pop. 2,624**
Springtown ISD 2,900/PK-12
301 E 5th St 76082 817-220-1700
Mike Kelley, supt. Fax 523-5766
www.springtownisd.net
Springtown HS 900/9-12
915 W Highway 199 76082 817-220-3888
Scott McPherson, prin. Fax 523-5290
Springtown MS 500/7-8
500 Pojo Dr 76082 817-220-7455
Mark Wilson, prin. Fax 220-2395

**Spur, Dickens, Pop. 1,312**
Spur ISD 300/PK-12
PO Box 250 79370 806-271-3272
Loretta Velez, supt. Fax 271-4575
www.spurbulldogs.com
Spur MSHS 100/6-12
PO Box 250 79370 806-271-3385
Brent Kirkland, prin. Fax 271-4575

**Spurger, Tyler**
Spurger ISD 400/PK-12
PO Box 38 77660 409-429-3464
Charles Zeller, supt. Fax 429-3770
www.spurgerisd.org
Spurger HS 200/7-12
PO Box 38 77660 409-429-3464
Ronald Ford, prin. Fax 429-3770

**Stafford, Fort Bend, Pop. 17,344**
Stafford Municipal SD 3,200/PK-12
1625 Staffordshire Rd 77477 281-261-9200
Dr. Robert Bostic, supt. Fax 261-9249
www.staffordmsd.org
Stafford Alternative Education Center Alt
1625 Staffordshire Rd 77477 281-261-9280
Carlotta Allen, admin. Fax 208-6118
Stafford HS 1,000/9-12
1625 Staffordshire Rd 77477 281-261-9239
Misti Morgan, prin. Fax 261-9347
Stafford MS 500/7-8
1625 Staffordshire Rd 77477 281-261-9215
Andre Roberson, prin. Fax 261-9349

**Stamford, Jones, Pop. 3,075**
Stamford ISD 600/PK-12
507 S Orient St 79553 325-773-2705
Shaun Barnett, supt. Fax 773-5684
www.stamford.esc14.net
Stamford HS 200/9-12
507 S Orient St 79553 325-773-2701
Casey Stone, prin. Fax 773-4015
Stamford MS 100/6-8
507 S Orient St 79553 325-773-2651
Kevin White, prin. Fax 773-4052

**Stanton, Martin, Pop. 2,466**
Stanton ISD 800/PK-12
PO Box 730 79782 432-756-2244
David Carr, supt. Fax 756-2052
www.stanton.esc18.net/
Stanton HS 200/9-12
PO Box 730 79782 432-756-3326
Mark Cotton, prin. Fax 756-2248
Stanton MS 200/6-8
PO Box 730 79782 432-756-2544
Albert Chavez, prin. Fax 756-2702

**Stephenville, Erath, Pop. 16,950**
Huckabay ISD 200/K-12
200 County Road 421 76401 254-968-8476
Dr. Cheryl Floyd, supt. Fax 965-3740
www.hisd.us
Huckabay S 200/K-12
200 County Road 421 76401 254-968-5274
Dr. Cheryl Floyd, prin. Fax 965-3740

Stephenville ISD 3,600/PK-12
2655 W Overhill Dr 76401 254-968-7990
Matt Underwood, supt. Fax 968-5942
www.sville.us
Henderson JHS 500/7-8
2798 W Frey St 76401 254-968-6967
Rene Goodwin, prin. Fax 965-7018
Stephenville HS 1,000/9-12
2650 W Overhill Dr 76401 254-968-4141
Stephanie Traweek, prin. Fax 968-4897

---

Stephenville Beauty College Post-Sec.
951 S Lillian St 76401 254-968-2111
Tarleton State University Post-Sec.
PO Box T0001 76402 254-968-9000

**Sterling City, Sterling, Pop. 875**
Sterling City ISD 200/K-12
PO Box 786 76951 325-378-4781
Bob Rauch, supt. Fax 378-2283
www.sterlingcityisd.net
Sterling City HS 100/6-12
PO Box 786 76951 325-378-5821
Ty Stevens, prin. Fax 378-2087

**Stinnett, Hutchinson, Pop. 1,860**
Plemons-Stinnett-Phillips Cons ISD 600/PK-12
PO Box 3440 79083 806-878-2858
Bill Wiggins, supt. Fax 878-3585
www.pspcisd.net

West Texas HS 200/9-12
PO Box 3440 79083 806-878-2456
Kent Torbert, prin. Fax 878-3585
West Texas MS 100/6-8
PO Box 3440 79083 806-878-2247
Kevin Freriks, prin. Fax 878-3585

**Stockdale, Wilson, Pop. 1,428**
Stockdale ISD 700/K-12
PO Box 7 78160 830-996-3551
Paul Darilek, supt. Fax 996-1071
www.stockdaleisd.net
Stockdale HS 200/9-12
PO Box 7 78160 830-996-3103
Sandy Lynn, prin. Fax 996-1046
Stockdale JHS 200/6-8
PO Box 7 78160 830-996-3153
Sharon Dunn, prin. Fax 996-3055

**Stratford, Sherman, Pop. 2,009**
Stratford ISD 600/PK-12
PO Box 108 79084 806-366-3300
Jerry Birdsong, supt. Fax 366-3304
www.stratfordisd.net
Stratford HS 200/9-12
PO Box 108 79084 806-366-3330
Phillip Hanna, prin. Fax 366-3304
Stratford JHS 200/5-8
PO Box 108 79084 806-366-3320
Clint Seward, prin. Fax 366-3307

**Strawn, Palo Pinto, Pop. 647**
Strawn ISD 200/PK-12
PO Box 428 76475 254-672-5313
Brent Dawson, supt. Fax 672-5662
www.strawnschool.net/
Strawn S 200/PK-12
PO Box 428 76475 254-672-5776
Richard Mitchell, prin. Fax 672-5662

**Sudan, Lamb, Pop. 949**
Sudan ISD 400/PK-12
PO Box 249 79371 806-227-2431
Scott Harrell, supt. Fax 227-2146
www.sudanisd.net
Sudan JSHS 200/8-12
PO Box 659 79371 806-227-2431
Gordon Martin, prin. Fax 227-2121

**Sugar Land, Fort Bend, Pop. 76,889**
Fort Bend ISD 67,700/PK-12
16431 Lexington Blvd 77479 281-634-1000
Charles Dupre Ed.D., supt. Fax 634-1700
www.fortbendisd.com
Austin HS 2,400/9-12
3434 Pheasant Creek Dr, 281-634-2000
Mary Ellen Edge, prin. Fax 634-2074
Clements HS 2,700/9-12
4200 Elkins Rd 77479 281-634-2150
David Yaffie, prin. Fax 634-2168
Dulles HS 2,100/9-12
550 Dulles Ave 77478 281-634-5600
Ronnie Edwards, prin. Fax 634-5681
Dulles MS 1,300/6-8
500 Dulles Ave 77478 281-634-5750
Dee Knox, prin. Fax 634-5781
First Colony MS 1,100/6-8
3225 Austin Pkwy 77479 281-634-3240
Scott Wagoner, prin. Fax 634-3267
Fort Settlement MS 1,100/6-8
5440 Elkins Rd 77479 281-634-6440
Michael Hejducek, prin. Fax 634-6456
Garcia MS 1,300/6-8
18550 Old Richmond Rd, 281-634-3160
Dr. Rizvan Quadri, prin. Fax 634-3166
Kempner HS 2,400/9-12
14777 Voss Rd, 281-634-2300
Chris Morgan, prin. Fax 634-2378
Sartartia MS 1,200/6-8
8125 Homeward Way 77479 281-634-6310
Dr. Jennifer Nichols, prin. Fax 634-6373
Sugar Land MS 1,300/6-8
321 7th St, 281-634-3080
Leonard Brogan, prin. Fax 634-3108
Technical Education Center Vo/Tech
540 Dulles Ave 77478 281-634-5671
Fax 634-5700
Wood Alternative Ctr for Learning 50/Alt
138 Avenue F, 281-634-3320
Trevor Lemon, admin. Fax 634-3331
Other Schools – See Houston, Missouri City, Richmond, Rosharon

---

Ft. Bend Christian Academy 800/PK-12
1250 7th St 77478 281-263-9175
Dr. John Lindsell, head sch Fax 263-9147
Trent Internationale S 200/PK-12
2553 Cordes Dr 77479 281-980-5800
Elaine Gaskamp, prin. Fax 980-6106

**Sulphur Bluff, Hopkins**
Sulphur Bluff ISD 200/PK-12
PO Box 30 75481 903-945-2460
Dustin Carr, supt. Fax 945-2459
www.sulphurbluffisd.net/
Sulphur Bluff S 200/PK-12
PO Box 30 75481 903-945-2460
Amy Northcutt, prin. Fax 945-2459

**Sulphur Springs, Hopkins, Pop. 15,115**
North Hopkins ISD 500/PK-12
1994 Farm Road 71 W 75482 903-945-2192
Donna George, supt. Fax 945-2531
www.northhopkins.net/
North Hopkins JSHS 200/6-12
1994 Farm Road 71 W 75482 903-945-2192
Rob Stanley, prin. Fax 945-2531

Sulphur Springs ISD 3,500/PK-12
631 Connally St 75482 903-885-2153
Michael Lamb, supt. Fax 439-6162
www.ssisd.net/
Sulphur Springs HS 1,200/9-12
1200 Connally St 75482 903-885-2158
Derek Driver, prin. Fax 439-6116
Sulphur Springs MS 900/6-8
832 Wildcat Way 75482 903-885-7741
Jena Williams, prin. Fax 439-6126

**Sundown, Hockley, Pop. 1,386**
Sundown ISD 700/PK-12
PO Box 1110 79372 806-229-3021
Scott Marshall, supt. Fax 229-2004
www.sundownisd.com
Sundown HS 200/9-12
PO Box 1110 79372 806-229-2511
Brent Evans, prin. Fax 229-2004
Sundown MS 200/6-8
PO Box 1110 79372 806-229-4691
Eddie Carter, prin. Fax 229-2004

**Sunnyvale, Dallas, Pop. 5,012**
Sunnyvale ISD 1,200/PK-12
417 E Tripp Rd 75182 972-226-5974
Doug Williams, supt. Fax 226-6882
www.sunnyvaleisd.com
Sunnyvale HS 400/9-12
222 N Collins Rd 75182 972-203-4600
Ron Sterling, prin. Fax 226-2854
Sunnyvale MS 400/5-8
216 N Collins Rd 75182 972-226-2922
Carmen Ayo, prin. Fax 226-0982

**Sunray, Moore, Pop. 1,899**
Sunray ISD 600/PK-12
PO Box 240 79086 806-948-4411
Brian Thompson, supt. Fax 948-5274
www.sunrayisd.net
Sunray HS 200/9-12
PO Box 240 79086 806-948-5515
Sid Whiteley, prin. Fax 948-5399
Sunray MS 200/5-8
PO Box 240 79086 806-948-4444
Pam Keisling, prin. Fax 948-4208

**Sweeny, Brazoria, Pop. 3,645**
Sweeny ISD 1,900/PK-12
1310 N Elm St 77480 979-491-8000
Randy Miksch, supt. Fax 491-8030
www.sweenyisd.org
Sweeny HS 600/9-12
1310 N Elm St 77480 979-491-8100
Robert Morrison, prin. Fax 491-8171
Sweeny JHS 500/6-8
1310 N Elm St 77480 979-491-8200
Michael Saul, prin. Fax 491-8274

**Sweetwater, Nolan, Pop. 10,784**
Sweetwater ISD 2,300/PK-12
207 Musgrove St 79556 325-235-8601
Terry Pittman, supt. Fax 235-5561
www.sweetwaterisd.net/
Sweetwater HS 500/9-12
1205 Ragland St 79556 325-235-4371
Dr. Ron Morris, prin. Fax 235-4861
Sweetwater MS 500/6-8
305 Lamar St 79556 325-236-6303
Jeff Withrow, prin. Fax 236-6941

---

Texas State Technical College Post-Sec.
300 Homer K Taylor Dr 79556 325-235-7300

**Taft, San Patricio, Pop. 3,018**
Taft ISD 1,100/PK-12
400 College St 78390 361-528-2636
Jose Lopez, supt. Fax 528-2223
www.taftisd.net
Taft HS 300/9-12
502 Rincon Rd 78390 361-528-2636
Angel Lopez, prin. Fax 528-3918
Taft JHS 300/6-8
727 McIntyre Ave 78390 361-528-2636
John Jones, prin. Fax 528-5477

**Tahoka, Lynn, Pop. 2,660**
Tahoka ISD 600/PK-12
PO Box 1230 79373 806-561-4105
Dr. George McFarland, supt. Fax 561-4160
www.tahokaisd.us
Tahoka HS 200/9-12
PO Box 1500 79373 806-561-4538
Jeffrey Perez, prin. Fax 561-6082
Tahoka MS 100/6-8
PO Box 1500 79373 806-561-4538
Jeffrey Fleenor, prin. Fax 561-6082

**Tatum, Rusk, Pop. 1,369**
Tatum ISD 1,500/PK-12
PO Box 808 75691 903-947-6482
Dr. Dee Hartt Ed.D., supt. Fax 947-3295
www.tatumisd.org
Tatum HS 500/9-12
PO Box 808 75691 903-947-6482
Allen Koch, prin. Fax 947-6206
Tatum MS 200/6-8
PO Box 808 75691 903-947-6482
Brandon Milam, prin. Fax 947-3295

**Taylor, Williamson, Pop. 14,982**
Taylor ISD 2,300/PK-12
3101 N Main St Ste 104 76574 512-365-1391
Jerry Vaughn, supt. Fax 365-3800
www.taylorisd.org
Taylor HS 900/9-12
355 FM 973 76574 512-365-1291
Andrew Maddox, prin. Fax 365-9334
Taylor MS 600/6-8
304 Carlos Parker Blvd NW 76574 512-365-8591
Hector Martinez, prin. Fax 365-8589

**Teague, Freestone, Pop. 3,527**
Teague ISD 1,200/PK-12
420 N 10th Ave 75860 254-739-1300
Dr. Nate Carman, supt. Fax 739-5223
www.teagueisd.org
Teague HS 300/9-12
420 N 10th Ave 75860 254-739-1500
Chris Skinner, prin. Fax 739-2724
Teague JHS 300/6-8
420 N 10th Ave 75860 254-739-1450
Drake Paris, prin. Fax 739-5896

**Temple, Bell, Pop. 64,746**
Belton ISD
Supt. — See Belton
Lake Belton MS 700/6-8
8818 Tarver Dr 76502 254-215-2900
Kris Hobson, prin. Fax 215-2901
North Belton MS 6-8
7907 Prairie View Rd 76502 254-316-5200
Joe Brown, prin. Fax 316-5201

Temple ISD 8,000/PK-12
PO Box 788 76503 254-215-8473
Dr. Robin Battershell, supt. Fax 215-6783
www.tisd.org
Bonham MS 600/6-8
4600 Midway Dr 76502 254-215-6600
Sandra Atmar, prin. Fax 215-6634
Edwards Academy 200/Alt
1414 W Barton Ave 76504 254-215-6944
Phillip Perry, prin. Fax 215-6946
Lamar MS 600/6-8
2120 N 1st St 76501 254-215-6444
Billy Madden, prin. Fax 215-6483
Temple HS 1,900/9-12
415 N 31st St 76504 254-215-7000
Dr. Jason Mayo, prin. Fax 899-6926
Travis Science Academy 500/6-8
1551 S 25th St 76504 254-215-6300
Kristina Carter, prin. Fax 215-6352
Wheatley Alternative Education Center 100/Alt
515 E Avenue D 76501 254-215-5665
Carl Pleasant, prin. Fax 215-5673

---

Central Texas Beauty College Post-Sec.
2010 S 57th St 76504 254-773-9911
Central Texas Christian S 600/PK-12
4141 W FM 93 76502 254-939-5700
Brian Littlefield, head sch Fax 939-5769
Holy Trinity Catholic HS 100/9-12
6608 W Adams Ave 76502 254-771-0787
Dr. Veronica Alonzo, prin. Fax 771-2285
Scott & White Memorial Hospital & Clinic Post-Sec.
2401 S 31st St 76508 254-724-5177
Temple College Post-Sec.
2600 S 1st St 76504 254-298-8282

**Tenaha, Shelby, Pop. 1,146**
Tenaha ISD 600/PK-12
PO Box 318 75974 936-248-5000
Scott Tyner, supt. Fax 248-3902
www.tenahaisd.com/
Tenaha HS 300/6-12
PO Box 318 75974 936-248-5000
Judy Monroe, prin. Fax 248-3626

**Terlingua, Brewster, Pop. 54**
Terlingua Common SD 100/K-12
PO Box 256 79852 432-371-2281
Bobbie Jones, supt. Fax 371-2245
www.terlinguacsd.com
Big Bend S 50/K-12
PO Box 256 79852 432-371-2281
Bobbie Jones, admin. Fax 371-2245

**Terrell, Kaufman, Pop. 15,583**
Terrell ISD 4,200/PK-12
700 N Catherine St 75160 972-563-7504
Kenn Norris, supt. Fax 563-1406
www.terrellisd.org
Alternative Education Center Alt
305 W College St 75160 972-563-6319
Charles Neal, prin. Fax 563-4786
Furlough MS 600/7-8
1351 Colquitt Rd 75160 972-563-7501
Jay Thompson, prin. Fax 563-5721
Phoenix Center, 204 W High St 75160 Alt
Charles Neal, prin. 972-551-5796
Terrell HS 1,000/9-12
400 Poetry Rd 75160 972-563-7525
Dr. Juan Solis, prin. Fax 563-6318

---

Poetry Community Christian S 200/K-12
18688 FM 986 75160 972-563-7227
Dr. Anne Horan, admin. Fax 563-0025
Southwestern Christian College Post-Sec.
PO Box 10 75160 972-524-3341

**Texarkana, Bowie, Pop. 35,750**
Liberty-Eylau ISD 2,800/PK-12
2901 Leopard Dr 75501 903-832-1535
Roger Hailey, supt. Fax 838-9444
www.leisd.net
Liberty-Eylau HS 700/9-12
2905 Leopard Dr 75501 903-832-1535
Kendrick Smith, prin. Fax 831-6113
Liberty-Eylau MS 800/5-8
5555 Leopard Dr 75501 903-838-5555
William Houff, prin. Fax 832-6700
Liberty-Eylau S of Success 50/Alt
766 Macedonia Rd 75501 903-831-5767
Barry Baker, prin. Fax 838-0493

Pleasant Grove ISD 1,800/PK-12
8500 N Kings Hwy 75503 903-831-4086
Todd Williams Ed.D., supt. Fax 831-4435
www.pgisd.net
Pleasant Grove HS 600/9-12
5406 McKnight Rd 75503 903-832-8005
Darren Williams, prin. Fax 832-5381

Pleasant Grove MS 400/6-8
5605 Cooks Ln 75503 903-831-4295
Linda Erie, prin. Fax 831-5501

Red Lick ISD 500/K-8
3511 N FM 2148 75503 903-838-8230
Nick Blain, supt. Fax 831-6134
www.redlickisd.com
Red Lick MS 200/5-8
3511 N FM 2148 75503 903-838-6006
Jason Dempsey, prin. Fax 831-6134

Texarkana ISD 6,900/PK-12
4241 Summerhill Rd 75503 903-794-3651
Paul Norton, supt. Fax 792-2632
www.txkisd.net
Options S 100/Alt
3201 Lincoln Ave 75503 903-793-5632
Marsha Burris, prin. Fax 792-2632
Texas HS 1,900/9-12
4001 Summerhill Rd 75503 903-794-3891
Brad Bailey, prin. Fax 792-8971
Texas MS 1,500/6-8
2100 College Dr 75503 903-793-5631
Tim Lambert, prin. Fax 792-2935

---

Texarkana College Post-Sec.
2500 N Robison Rd 75501 903-823-3456
Texas A&M University Texarkana Post-Sec.
7101 University Ave 75503 903-223-3000
Victory Connections Academy 50/3-8
7504 W 7th St 75501 903-791-6004
Carl Teel, supt.
Wadley Regional Medical Center Post-Sec.
1000 Pine St 75501 903-798-8000

**Texas City, Galveston, Pop. 44,454**
Texas City ISD 5,900/PK-12
PO Box 1150 77592 409-916-0100
Cynthia Lusignolo Ed.D., supt. Fax 942-2655
www.tcisd.org/
Blocker MS 900/7-8
1800 9th Ave N 77590 409-916-0700
Julie Southworth, prin. Fax 942-2755
Texas City HS 1,600/9-12
1431 9th Ave N 77590 409-916-0800
Holly LaRoe, prin. Fax 942-2672
Wilson Alternative S 50/Alt
1508 6th St N 77590 409-916-0280
Joy Toney, prin. Fax 942-2462

---

College of the Mainland Post-Sec.
1200 N Amburn Rd 77591 409-938-1211

**Texline, Dallam, Pop. 485**
Texline ISD 100/K-12
PO Box 60 79087 806-362-4667
Jody Johnson, supt. Fax 362-4538
www.texlineisd.net
Texline S 100/K-12
PO Box 60 79087 806-362-4284
Terrell Jones, prin. Fax 362-4938

**The Colony, Denton, Pop. 35,324**
Lewisville ISD
Supt. — See Flower Mound
Griffin MS 700/6-8
5105 N Colony Blvd 75056 469-713-5973
Michele Sandefur, prin. Fax 350-9187
Lakeview MS 800/6-8
4300 Keys Dr 75056 469-713-5974
Jeremy Turner, prin. Fax 350-9202
The Colony HS 1,900/9-12
4301 Blair Oaks Dr 75056 469-713-5178
Tim Baxter, prin. Fax 350-9336

**The Woodlands, Montgomery, Pop. 92,202**
Conroe ISD
Supt. — See Conroe
Academy of Science & Technology 9-12
3701 College Park Dr 77384 936-709-3250
Dr. Susan Caffery, hdmstr. Fax 709-3299
Knox JHS 1,200/7-8
12104 Sawmill Rd 77380 832-592-8400
Joe Daw, prin. Fax 592-8410
McCullough JHS 2,200/7-8
3800 S Panther Creek Dr 77381 832-592-5100
Chris McCord, prin. Fax 592-5116
The Woodlands College Park SHS 2,500/9-12
3701 College Park Dr 77384 936-709-3000
Dr. Mark Murrell, prin. Fax 709-3019
The Woodlands HS Ninth Grade Campus 1,000/9-9
10010 Branch Crossing Dr 77382 832-592-8200
Dr. Chris Povich, prin. Fax 592-8299
The Woodlands SHS 3,100/10-12
6101 Research Forest Dr 77381 936-709-1200
Gregg Colschen, prin. Fax 709-1299

---

Cooper S 1,000/PK-12
1 John Cooper Dr 77381 281-367-0900
Michael Maher, hdmstr. Fax 292-9201
Esprit International S 100/PK-12
4890 W Panther Creek Dr 77381 281-298-9200
Grace School of Theology Post-Sec.
PO Box 7477 77387 877-476-8674
Legacy Preparatory Christian Academy 200/PK-12
9768 Research Forest Dr, 936-337-2000
Audra May, admin. Fax 755-1797
Woodlands Christian Academy 400/PK-12
5800 Academy Way 77384 936-273-2555
Julie Ambler, head sch Fax 271-3115

**Thorndale, Milam, Pop. 1,329**
Thorndale ISD 600/PK-12
PO Box 870 76577 512-898-2538
Glenn Coles, supt. Fax 898-5356
www.thorndale.txed.net
Thorndale HS 200/9-12
PO Box 870 76577 512-898-2321
Dalton West, prin. Fax 898-5558
Thorndale MS 100/6-8
PO Box 870 76577 512-898-2670
Lee Hafley, prin. Fax 898-5505

**Thrall, Williamson, Pop. 832**
Thrall ISD 400/K-12
201 S Bounds St 76578 512-898-0062
Tommy Hooker, supt. Fax 898-5349
www.thrallisd.com
Thrall MSHS 200/6-12
201 S Bounds St 76578 512-898-5193
Travis Dube, prin. Fax 898-2132

**Three Rivers, Live Oak, Pop. 1,845**
Three Rivers ISD 500/PK-12
351 S School Rd 78071 361-786-3626
Kenneth Rohrbach, supt. Fax 786-2555
www.trisd.org
Three Rivers JSHS 200/7-12
351-A S School Rd 78071 361-786-3531
Charles Odom, prin. Fax 786-2555

**Throckmorton, Throckmorton, Pop. 823**
Throckmorton ISD 200/PK-12
210 College St 76483 940-849-2411
Ken Baugh, supt. Fax 849-3345
www.throck.org
Throckmorton S 100/PK-12
210 College St 76483 940-849-2421
David Farquhar, prin. Fax 849-3345

**Tilden, McMullen, Pop. 261**
McMullen County ISD 200/PK-12
PO Box 359 78072 361-274-2000
Dave Underwood, supt. Fax 274-3665
www.mcisd.us
McMullen County S 200/PK-12
PO Box 359 78072 361-274-2000
Joe Timms, prin. Fax 274-3580

**Timpson, Shelby, Pop. 1,144**
Timpson ISD 600/PK-12
PO Box 370 75975 936-254-2463
Mid Johnson, supt. Fax 254-3878
www.timpsonisd.com
Timpson HS 200/9-12
PO Box 370 75975 936-254-3125
Ronald Lindgren, prin. Fax 254-3263
Timpson MS 100/6-8
PO Box 370 75975 936-254-2078
Calvin Smith, prin. Fax 254-2355

**Tioga, Grayson, Pop. 788**
Tioga ISD 200/PK-12
PO Box 159 76271 940-437-2366
Dr. Charles Holloway, supt. Fax 437-9986
www.tiogaisd.net/
Tioga S 200/PK-12
PO Box 159 76271 940-437-2366
Josh Ballinger, prin. Fax 437-9986

**Tivoli, Refugio, Pop. 475**
Austwell-Tivoli ISD 200/K-12
207 Redfish St 77990 361-286-3212
Dr. Antonio Aguirre, supt. Fax 286-3637
www.atisd.net
Austwell-Tivoli JSHS 100/7-12
207 Redfish St 77990 361-286-3582
Stephen Maldonado, prin. Fax 286-3637

**Tolar, Hood, Pop. 677**
Tolar ISD 600/PK-12
PO Box 368 76476 254-835-4718
Travis Stilwell, supt. Fax 835-4704
www.tolarisd.org
Tolar HS 200/9-12
PO Box 368 76476 254-835-4316
Brad Morgan, prin. Fax 835-4237
Tolar JHS 100/6-8
PO Box 368 76476 254-835-5207
Lindsay Morgan, prin. Fax 835-5208

**Tomball, Harris, Pop. 10,569**
Tomball ISD 10,600/PK-12
310 S Cherry St 77375 281-357-3100
Huey Kinchen, supt. Fax 357-3128
www.tomballisd.net
Tomball Alternative Education Center Alt
1302 Keefer Rd 77375 281-357-3281
Becky Dale, prin. Fax 357-3291
Tomball HS 2,300/9-12
30330 Quinn Rd 77375 281-357-3220
Greg Quinn, prin. Fax 357-3248
Tomball JHS 700/7-8
30403 Quinn Rd 77375 281-357-3000
Chad Allman, prin. Fax 357-3027
Tomball Memorial HS 800/9-12
19100 Northpointe Ridge Ln 77377 281-357-3230
Carol Houston, prin. Fax 357-3240
Willow Wood JHS 900/7-8
11770 Gregson Rd 77377 281-357-3030
Robert Frost, prin. Fax 357-3045

---

Concordia Lutheran HS 400/9-12
700 E Main St 77375 281-351-2547
Joel Bode, head sch Fax 255-8806
Lone Star College - Tomball Post-Sec.
30555 State Highway 249 77375 281-351-3300
Rosehill Christian S 400/PK-12
19830 FM 2920 Rd 77377 281-351-8114
Dean Unsicker, head sch Fax 516-3418
Woodlands Preparatory S 300/PK-12
27440 Kuykendahl Rd 77375 281-516-0600
Jorge Lerdo, head sch Fax 516-1155

**Tom Bean, Grayson, Pop. 1,019**
Tom Bean ISD 700/K-12
PO Box 128 75489 903-546-6076
Troy Roberts, supt. Fax 546-6104
www.tbisd.org
Tom Bean HS 300/9-12
PO Box 128 75489 903-546-6319
Dr. Susan Foster, prin. Fax 546-6319
Tom Bean MS 200/6-8
PO Box 128 75489 903-546-6161
Julie Cummings, prin. Fax 546-6798

**Tornillo, El Paso, Pop. 1,568**
Tornillo ISD 1,400/PK-12
PO Box 170 79853 915-765-3000
Jeannie Meza-Chavez, supt. Fax 765-3099
www.tisd.us/
Tornillo HS 400/9-12
PO Box 170 79853 915-765-3500
Mauro Guerrero, prin. Fax 765-3599
Tornillo JHS 200/7-8
PO Box 170 79853 915-765-3400
Marco Tristan, prin. Fax 765-3499

**Trent, Taylor, Pop. 330**
Trent ISD 200/PK-12
PO Box 105 79561 325-862-6125
Leanna West, supt. Fax 862-6448
www.trent.esc14.net
Trent S 200/PK-12
PO Box 105 79561 325-862-6125
Leanna West, prin. Fax 862-6448

**Trenton, Fannin, Pop. 627**
Trenton ISD 500/PK-12
PO Box 5 75490 903-989-2245
Rick Foreman, supt. Fax 989-2767
www.trentonisd.com
Trenton HS 200/9-12
PO Box 5 75490 903-989-2242
Rick Foreman, prin. Fax 989-2767
Trenton MS 100/5-8
PO Box 5 75490 903-989-2243
Trent Hamilton, prin. Fax 989-5173

**Trinidad, Henderson, Pop. 863**
Trinidad ISD 200/PK-12
105 W Eaton St 75163 903-778-2673
Corey Jenkins, supt. Fax 778-4120
www.trinidadisd.com
Trinidad S 200/PK-12
105 W Eaton St 75163 903-778-2673
Corey Jenkins, admin. Fax 778-4120

**Trinity, Trinity, Pop. 2,644**
Trinity ISD 1,000/PK-12
PO Box 752 75862 936-594-3569
Dave Plymale, supt. Fax 594-8425
www.trinityisd.net/
Trinity HS 300/9-12
PO Box 752 75862 936-594-3560
Eric Kelley, prin. Fax 594-2162
Trinity MS 200/6-8
PO Box 752 75862 936-594-2321
Brittaney Cassidy, prin. Fax 594-3041

**Trophy Club, Denton, Pop. 7,926**
Northwest ISD
Supt. — See Justin
Medlin MS 800/6-8
601 Parkview Dr 76262 817-215-0500
Dr. Eric Drewery, prin. Fax 215-0548
Nelson HS 1,900/9-12
2775 Bobcat Blvd 76262 817-698-5600
Dr. Ron Myers, prin. Fax 698-5670

**Troup, Smith, Pop. 1,837**
Troup ISD 1,100/PK-12
PO Box 578 75789 903-842-3067
Stuart Bird, supt. Fax 842-4563
www.troupisd.org
Troup HS 300/9-12
PO Box 578 75789 903-842-3065
David Smith, prin. Fax 842-4563
Troup MS 300/6-8
PO Box 578 75789 903-842-3081
Ava Johnson, prin. Fax 842-4563

**Troy, Bell, Pop. 1,625**
Troy ISD 1,300/PK-12
PO Box 409 76579 254-938-2595
Neil Jeter, supt. Fax 938-7323
www.troyisd.org
Mays MS 300/6-8
PO Box 409 76579 254-938-2543
Michelle Jolliff, prin. Fax 938-2880
Troy HS 400/9-12
PO Box 409 76579 254-938-2561
Randy Hicks, prin. Fax 938-2328

**Tulia, Swisher, Pop. 4,912**
Tulia ISD 1,100/PK-12
702 NW 8th St 79088 806-995-4591
Steve Post, supt. Fax 995-3169
www.tuliaisd.net
Tulia HS 300/9-12
501 Hornet Pl 79088 806-995-2759
Mike Allison, prin. Fax 995-4413
Tulia JHS 200/6-8
421 NE 3rd St 79088 806-995-4842
Casey McBroom, prin. Fax 995-4498

**Turkey, Hall, Pop. 416**
Turkey-Quitaque ISD 200/PK-12
11826 Highway 86 79261 806-455-1411
Jon Davidson, supt. Fax 455-1718
www.valleypatriots.com/
Valley S 200/PK-12
11826 Highway 86 79261 806-455-1411
Jackie Jenkins, prin. Fax 455-1718

**Tuscola, Taylor, Pop. 734**
Jim Ned Consolidated ISD 1,000/PK-12
PO Box 9 79562 325-554-7500
Bobby Easterling, supt. Fax 554-7740
www.jimned.esc14.net

Jim Ned HS 300/9-12
PO Box 9 79562 325-554-7755
David Hogan, prin. Fax 554-7550
Jim Ned MS 300/6-8
PO Box 9 79562 325-554-7870
Jay Wise, prin. Fax 554-7750

**Tyler, Smith, Pop. 95,596**
Chapel Hill ISD 3,500/PK-12
11134 County Road 2249 75707 903-566-2441
Donni Cook Ed.D., supt. Fax 566-8469
www.chapelhillisd.org
Chapel Hill HS 1,000/9-12
13172 State Highway 64 E 75707 903-566-2311
Lamond Dean, prin. Fax 565-5155
Chapel Hill MS 800/6-8
13174 State Highway 64 E 75707 903-566-1491
Debbie Black, prin. Fax 565-5125

Tyler ISD 18,400/PK-12
PO Box 2035 75710 903-262-1000
Dr. Marty Crawford, supt. Fax 262-1178
www.tylerisd.org
Boulter Creative Arts Magnet S 500/6-8
2926 Garden Valley Rd 75702 903-262-1390
Rodney Curry, prin. Fax 262-1392
Dogan MS 500/6-8
2621 N Border Ave 75702 903-262-1450
Vanessa Holmes, prin. Fax 262-1451
Hogg MS 600/6-8
920 S Broadway Ave 75701 903-262-1500
Eddie Dunn, prin. Fax 262-1501
Hubbard MS 900/6-8
1300 Hubbard Dr 75703 903-262-1560
Kevin Blain, prin. Fax 262-1566
Lee HS 2,700/9-12
411 E Southeast Loop 323 75701 903-262-2625
Gary Brown, prin. Fax 262-2630
Moore MST Magnet MS 1,000/6-8
1200 S Tipton Ave 75701 903-262-1640
Claude Lane, prin. Fax 262-1648
Plyler Alternative S 100/Alt
807 W Glenwood Blvd 75701 903-262-3070
Vanessa Choice, dir. Fax 262-3138
Stewart MS 400/6-8
2800 W Shaw St 75701 903-262-1710
Theodore Timms, prin. Fax 262-1711
Three Lakes MS 6-8
2445 Three Lakes Pkwy 75703 903-952-4400
Forrest Kaiser, prin.
Tyler HS 1,900/9-12
1120 N Northwest Loop 323 75702 903-262-2850
Kenneth Gay, prin. Fax 262-2852

All Saints Episcopal S 700/PK-12
2695 S Southwest Loop 323 75701 903-579-6000
Randal Brown, head sch Fax 579-6002
Bishop Gorman Regional Catholic MSHS 400/6-12
1405 E Southeast Loop 323 75701 903-561-2424
Jim Franz, prin. Fax 561-2645
Christian Heritage S 100/K-12
961 County Road 1143 75704 903-593-2702
Calvin Todd, admin. Fax 531-2226
East Texas Christian Academy 300/PK-12
2448 Roy Rd 75707 903-561-8642
Jim Bell M.Ed., pres. Fax 561-9620
Good Shepherd S 100/PK-12
2525 Old Jacksonville Rd 75701 903-592-4045
Walter Banek, head sch Fax 596-7149
Grace Community S Upper Campus 600/6-12
3001 University Blvd 75701 903-566-5661
Jay Ferguson, hdmstr. Fax 566-1156
King's Academy Christian S 100/K-12
7330 S Broadway Ave 75703 903-534-9992
Michael Partain, head sch Fax 526-7929
Star College of Cosmetology Post-Sec.
520 E Front St 75702 903-596-7860
Texas College Post-Sec.
2404 N Grand Ave 75702 903-593-8311
Tyler Junior College Post-Sec.
PO Box 9020 75711 903-510-2200
University of Texas at Tyler Post-Sec.
3900 University Blvd 75701 903-566-7000

**Universal City, Bexar, Pop. 18,038**
Judson ISD
Supt. — See Live Oak
Kitty Hawk MS 1,300/6-8
840 Old Cimarron Trl 78148 210-945-1220
Rodney Vigil, prin. Fax 659-0687

First Baptist Academy 500/PK-12
1401 Pat Booker Rd 78148 210-658-5331
Teri Flynn, admin. Fax 658-7024

**Utopia, Uvalde, Pop. 224**
Utopia ISD 200/PK-12
PO Box 880 78884 830-966-1928
John Walts, supt. Fax 966-6162
www.utopiaisd.net
Utopia S 200/PK-12
PO Box 880 78884 830-966-3339
Ken Mueller, prin. Fax 966-6162

**Uvalde, Uvalde, Pop. 15,676**
Uvalde Consolidated ISD 4,000/PK-12
PO Box 1909 78802 830-278-6655
Jeanette Ball, supt. Fax 591-4909
www.ucisd.net
Morales JHS 400/8-8
PO Box 1909 78802 830-591-2980
Elizabeth Sandoval, prin. Fax 591-2975
Uvalde HS 1,200/9-12
PO Box 1909 78802 830-591-2950
Jose Hernandez, prin. Fax 591-2960

Southwest School Post-Sec.
122 W North St 78801 830-278-4103
Southwest Texas Junior College Post-Sec.
2401 Garner Field Rd 78801 830-278-4401

**Valentine, Jeff Davis, Pop. 134**
Valentine ISD 50/PK-12
PO Box 188 79854 432-467-2671
William Cook, supt. Fax 467-2004
www.valentineisd.com
Valentine S 50/PK-12
PO Box 188 79854 432-467-2671
William Cook, supt. Fax 467-2004

**Valera, Coleman**
Panther Creek Consolidated ISD 200/PK-12
129 Private Road 3421 76884 325-357-4506
Dwin Nanny, supt. Fax 357-4470
www.pcreek.net
Panther Creek S 200/PK-12
129 Private Road 3421 76884 325-357-4449
Dwin Nanny, admin. Fax 357-4470

**Valley Mills, Bosque, Pop. 1,193**
Valley Mills ISD 700/PK-12
PO Box 518 76689 254-932-5210
Dr. Judi Whitis, supt. Fax 932-6601
www.vmisd.net
Valley Mills HS 200/9-12
PO Box 518 76689 254-932-5251
Jason Sansom, prin. Fax 932-6601
Valley Mills JHS 100/7-8
PO Box 518 76689 254-932-5251
Jason Sansom, prin. Fax 932-6601

**Valley View, Cooke, Pop. 748**
Valley View ISD 700/PK-12
106 Newton St 76272 940-726-3659
William Stokes, supt. Fax 726-3614
www.vvisd.net
Valley View HS 200/9-12
106 Newton St 76272 940-726-3522
Chris Heskett, prin. Fax 726-3862
Valley View MS 200/5-8
106 Newton St 76272 940-726-3244
Matthew Chalmers, prin. Fax 726-3786

**Van, Van Zandt, Pop. 2,615**
Van ISD 2,100/PK-12
PO Box 697 75790 903-963-8328
Don Dunn, supt. Fax 963-3904
www.vanschools.org
Van HS 700/9-12
PO Box 697 75790 903-963-8623
Jeff Hutchins, prin. Fax 963-5591
Van JHS 300/7-8
PO Box 697 75790 903-963-8321
Jason Johnson, prin. Fax 963-3277

**Van Alstyne, Grayson, Pop. 2,993**
Van Alstyne ISD 1,300/PK-12
549 Miller Ln 75495 903-482-8802
Dr. John Spies, supt. Fax 482-6086
www.vanalstyneisd.org
Van Alstyne HS 400/9-12
1722 N Waco St 75495 903-482-8803
Jeremiah Johnson, prin. Fax 482-8887
Van Alstyne MS 400/5-8
1314 N Waco St 75495 903-482-8804
Ryan Coleman, prin. Fax 482-8890

**Vanderbilt, Jackson, Pop. 392**
Industrial ISD 1,200/PK-12
PO Box 369 77991 361-284-3226
Anthony Williams, supt. Fax 284-3349
www.iisd1.org
Industrial HS 300/9-12
PO Box 399 77991 361-284-3226
Jim Green, prin. Fax 284-3328
Industrial JHS 300/6-8
PO Box 367 77991 361-284-3226
Caleb McCain, prin. Fax 284-3049

**Van Horn, Culberson, Pop. 2,041**
Culberson County-Allamore ISD 300/PK-12
400 W 7th St 79855 432-283-2245
Dalia Benavides, supt. Fax 283-9062
www.ccaisd.net/
Van Horn S 100/PK-12
PO Box 899 79855 432-283-2245
Kittie Gibson, prin. Fax 283-9062

**Van Vleck, Matagorda, Pop. 1,828**
Van Vleck ISD 900/PK-12
142 4th St S 77482 979-245-8518
John O'Brien, supt. Fax 245-1214
www.vvisd.org
Herman MS 200/6-8
719 1st St 77482 979-245-6401
David Holubec, prin. Fax 245-8538
Van Vleck HS 300/9-12
133 S 4th St 77482 979-245-4664
Brandon Hood, prin. Fax 244-3485

**Vega, Oldham, Pop. 874**
Vega ISD 300/K-12
PO Box 190 79092 806-267-2123
Dr. Paul Uttley, supt. Fax 267-2146
www.vegalonghorn.com
Vega HS 200/7-12
PO Box 190 79092 806-267-2126
Micah Timmons, prin. Fax 267-2146

**Venus, Johnson, Pop. 2,914**
Venus ISD 1,900/PK-12
100 Student Dr 76084 972-366-3448
Dr. Renee Warner, supt. Fax 366-8742
www.venusisd.net
Venus HS 500/9-12
12 Bulldog Dr 76084 972-366-8815
Randall Buck, prin. Fax 366-8919
Venus MS 400/6-8
1 Bulldog Dr 76084 972-366-3358
Kimberly Buck, prin. Fax 366-1740

**Veribest, Tom Green**
Veribest ISD 300/PK-12
PO Box 490 76886 325-655-4912
Bobby Fryar, supt. Fax 655-3355
www.veribestisd.net
Veribest HS 100/7-12
PO Box 490 76886 325-655-2851
Jim Meredith, prin. Fax 653-0551

**Vernon, Wilbarger, Pop. 10,848**
Northside ISD 200/K-12
18040 US Highway 283 76384 940-552-2551
Jack Coody, supt. Fax 553-4919
www.northsideisd.us
Northside S 200/K-12
18040 US Highway 283 76384 940-552-2551
Mark Haught, prin. Fax 553-4913

Vernon ISD 2,200/PK-12
1713 Wilbarger St 76384 940-553-1900
Tom Woody, supt. Fax 553-3802
www.vernonisd.org
Vernon HS 600/9-12
2102 Yucca Ln 76384 940-553-3377
Dr. Chris Granger, prin. Fax 553-4531
Vernon MS 400/6-8
2200 Yamparika St 76384 940-552-6231
Michael Campos, prin. Fax 552-0504

Vernon College Post-Sec.
4400 College Dr 76384 940-552-6291

**Victoria, Victoria, Pop. 61,923**
Bloomington ISD 800/PK-12
2875 FM 616 77905 361-897-1652
Delores Warnell, supt. Fax 897-1214
www.bisd-tx.org/
Other Schools – See Bloomington

Victoria ISD 10,500/PK-12
PO Box 1759 77902 361-576-3131
Dr. Robert Jaklich Ed.D., supt. Fax 788-9643
www.visd.net/
Cade MS 6-8
PO Box 1759 77902 361-788-2840
Jill Lau, prin. Fax 788-2886
Career and Technology Institute Vo/Tech
PO Box 1759 77902 361-788-9288
Melissa Correll, prin. Fax 788-9656
Howell MS 700/6-8
PO Box 1759 77902 361-578-1561
Clark Motley, prin. Fax 788-9547
Liberty Academy 100/9-12
PO Box 1759 77902 361-788-9650
Sheila O'Briant, prin. Fax 788-9700
Mitchell Guidance Center 50/Alt
PO Box 1759 77902 361-788-9658
Tedrick Valentine, prin. Fax 788-9665
Stroman MS 900/6-8
PO Box 1759 77902 361-578-2711
Dawn Maroney, prin. Fax 788-9800
Victoria Area Ctr for Advanced Learning 9-12
PO Box 1759 77902 361-788-9650
Sheila Garcia, prin. Fax 788-9649
Victoria East HS 9-12
PO Box 1759 77902 361-788-2820
Lisa Blundell, prin. Fax 788-2826
Victoria West HS 9-12
PO Box 1759 77902 361-788-2830
Debbie Crick, prin. Fax 788-2836
Welder MS 700/6-8
PO Box 1759 77902 361-575-4553
Richard Wright, prin. Fax 788-9629

Citizens Medical Center Post-Sec.
2701 Hospital Dr 77901 361-573-9181
Devereux-Texas Treatment Network Post-Sec.
120 David Wade Dr 77902 800-383-5000
Faith Academy 400/PK-12
PO Box 4824 77903 361-572-4568
Dr. Chris Royael, supt. Fax 573-5058
St. Joseph HS 300/9-12
110 E Red River St 77901 361-573-2446
Bill McArdle, prin. Fax 573-4221
Texas Vocational School Post-Sec.
1921 E Red River St 77901 361-575-4768
University of Houston-Victoria Post-Sec.
3007 N Ben Wilson St 77901 361-570-4848
Victoria Beauty College Post-Sec.
1508 N Laurent St 77901 361-575-4526
Victoria College Post-Sec.
2200 E Red River St 77901 361-573-3291

**Vidor, Orange, Pop. 10,443**
Vidor ISD 4,900/PK-12
120 E Bolivar St 77662 409-951-8700
Dr. Jay Killgo, supt. Fax 769-0093
www.vidorisd.org/
AIM Center HS 100/Alt
500 Stadium St 77662 409-951-8780
Roxanne Manuel, prin. Fax 769-0443
Vidor HS 1,400/9-12
500 Orange St 77662 409-951-8902
Travis Maines, prin. Fax 769-6767
Vidor JHS 700/7-8
945 N Tram Rd 77662 409-951-8970
Dr. Debra Jordan, prin. Fax 769-6754

**Von Ormy, Bexar, Pop. 1,084**
Somerset ISD
Supt. — See Somerset
Somerset JHS 600/7-8
4730 W Loop 1604 78073 866-852-9862
Rose Chapa, prin. Fax 448-2738

**Waco, McLennan, Pop. 122,806**
Bosqueville ISD 600/PK-12
7636 Rock Creek Rd 76708 254-757-3113
James Skeeler, supt. Fax 752-4909
www.bosquevilleisd.org

Bosqueville HS 300/9-12
7636 Rock Creek Rd 76708 254-752-8513
Cliff Heath, prin. Fax 752-0326
Bosqueville MS 6-8
7636 Rock Creek Rd 76708 254-759-7077
Sara Mynarcik, prin. Fax 752-5459

Bruceville-Eddy ISD
Supt. — See Eddy
Axtell/Bruceville-Eddy Learning Center 50/Alt
2601 Franklin Ave 76710 254-753-3422
Fax 753-3602

China Spring ISD 2,400/PK-12
6301 Sylvia St 76708 254-836-1115
Marc Faulkner, supt. Fax 836-0559
www.chinaspringisd.net
Other Schools – See China Spring

Connally ISD 2,300/PK-12
200 Cadet Way 76705 254-296-6460
Wesley Holt, supt. Fax 412-5530
www.connally.org
Connally Early College HS 9-12
200 Cadet Way 76705 254-296-6460
Greg Kelly, prin. Fax 412-5530
Connally HS 600/9-12
900 N Lacy Dr 76705 254-296-6700
Jill Talamantez, prin. Fax 412-5549
Other Schools – See Elm Mott

Gholson ISD 100/PK-12
137 Hamilton Dr 76705 254-829-1528
Pamela Brown, supt. Fax 829-0054
www.gholsonisd.org
Gholson S 100/PK-12
137 Hamilton Dr 76705 254-829-1528
Heather McCartney, prin. Fax 829-0054

La Vega ISD 2,900/PK-12
400 E Loop 340 76705 254-799-4963
Dr. Sharon Shields, supt. Fax 799-8642
www.lavegaisd.org
La Vega HS 700/9-12
555 N Loop 340 76705 254-799-4951
Elicia Krumnow, prin. Fax 799-0720
La Vega JHS George Dixon Campus 400/7-8
4401 Orchard Ln 76705 254-799-2428
Chris Borland, prin. Fax 799-8943

Midway ISD
Supt. — See Woodway
Midway HS 2,100/9-12
8200 Mars Dr 76712 254-761-5650
Jeff Gasaway, prin. Fax 761-5770

Waco ISD 11,800/PK-12
PO Box 27 76703 254-755-9473
Bonny Cain Ed.D., supt. Fax 755-9690
www.wacoisd.org
ATLAS Academy 6-8
6100 Tennyson Dr 76710 254-754-5491
Sandra Gibson, dean Fax 750-3576
Brazos HS Credit Recovery 100/Alt
200 W Waco Dr 76701 254-754-6283
Larry Hawkins, prin. Fax 753-2975
Carver MS 500/6-8
1601 J J Flewellen Rd 76704 254-757-0787
Alonza McAdoo, prin. Fax 750-3442
Chavez MS 500/6-8
700 S 15th St 76706 254-750-3736
Dr. Bill Shepard, prin. Fax 750-3739
Greater Waco Advanced Health Care Acad Vo/Tech
Viking Dr 76710
Brandon Cope, dir.
Greater Waco Advanced Manufacturing Acad Vo/Tech
2401 J J Flewellen Rd 76704 254-412-7900
Brandon Cope, dir. Fax 755-9620
Tennyson MS 600/6-8
6100 Tennyson Dr 76710 254-772-1440
Lisa Hall, prin. Fax 741-4970
University HS 1,400/9-12
3201 S New Rd 76706 254-756-1843
Kendra Strange, prin. Fax 750-3709
Waco HS 1,400/9-12
2020 N 42nd St 76710 254-776-1150
Ed Love, prin. Fax 741-4815
Wiley Opportunity Center 100/Alt
1030 E Live Oak St 76704 254-757-3829
Fax 750-3772

---

Baylor University Post-Sec.
1 Bear Pl Unit 97056 76798 254-710-1011
ITT Technical Institute Post-Sec.
3700 S Jack Kultgen Ste 100 76706 254-523-3940
Live Oak Classical S 200/PK-12
PO Box 647 76703 254-714-1007
Alison Moffatt, head sch Fax 714-1150
McLennan Community College Post-Sec.
1400 College Dr 76708 254-299-8000
New Creation Adventist S 50/K-10
800 W State Highway 6 76712 254-772-8775
Reicher Catholic HS 200/9-12
2102 N 23rd St 76708 254-752-8349
Jeff Heiple, prin. Fax 752-8408
Texas Christian Academy 200/6-12
4600 Sanger Ave 76710 254-772-5474
Texas State Technical College Post-Sec.
3801 Campus Dr 76705 254-799-3611
Vanguard College Preparatory S 100/7-12
2517 Mount Carmel Dr 76710 254-772-8111
Bill Borg, head sch Fax 772-8263

**Waelder, Gonzales, Pop. 1,062**
Waelder ISD 300/K-12
PO Box 247 78959 830-788-7161
Mark Lanier, admin. Fax 788-7429
www.waelderisd.org
Waelder S 300/K-12
PO Box 247 78959 830-788-7151
Jeffrey Kirby, prin. Fax 788-7323

**Wall, Tom Green**
Wall ISD, PO Box 259 76957 1,000/K-12
Walter Holik, supt. 325-651-7790
www.wallisd.net
Wall HS, PO Box 259 76957 300/9-12
Russell Dacy, prin. 325-651-7790
Wall MS, PO Box 259 76957 300/6-8
Ryan Snowden, prin. 325-651-7790
Other Schools – See San Angelo

**Waller, Waller, Pop. 2,288**
Waller ISD 5,600/PK-12
2214 Waller St 77484 936-931-3685
Danny Twardowski, supt. Fax 372-5576
www.wallerisd.net
Schultz JHS 700/6-8
19010 Stokes Rd 77484 936-931-9103
Stephanie Fletcher, prin. Fax 372-9302
Waller HS 1,600/9-12
20950 Fields Store Rd 77484 936-372-3654
Dr. Brian Merrell, prin. Fax 372-4114
Waller JHS 600/6-8
2402 Waller St 77484 936-931-1353
Eric Meldahl, prin. Fax 931-4044

**Wallis, Austin, Pop. 1,240**
Brazos ISD 900/PK-12
PO Box 819 77485 979-478-6551
Earl Jarrett, supt. Fax 478-6413
www.brazosisd.net/
Brazos HS 200/9-12
PO Box 458 77485 979-478-6000
Mary McCarthy, prin. Fax 478-6002
Brazos MS 200/6-8
PO Box 879 77485 979-478-6411
Clay Hudgins, prin. Fax 478-6042
Prairie Harbor Alternative S Alt
PO Box 819 77485 979-217-1581
Glenda Hooper, prin. Fax 217-1607

**Walnut Springs, Bosque, Pop. 805**
Walnut Springs ISD 200/PK-12
PO Box 63 76690 254-797-2133
Pat Garrett, supt. Fax 797-2191
www.walnutspringsisd.net
Walnut Springs S 200/PK-12
PO Box 63 76690 254-797-2133
Michele Garza, prin. Fax 797-2191

**Warren, Tyler, Pop. 751**
Warren ISD 1,300/PK-12
PO Box 69 77664 409-547-2241
Brad McEachern, supt. Fax 547-3405
www.warrenisd.net
Warren HS 400/9-12
PO Box 190 77664 409-547-2243
James Swinney, prin. Fax 547-0214
Warren JHS 300/6-8
PO Box 205 77664 409-547-2241
Kristina Wiedman, prin. Fax 547-2740

**Waskom, Harrison, Pop. 2,131**
Waskom ISD 800/PK-12
PO Box 748 75692 903-687-3361
Jimmy Cox, supt. Fax 687-3253
www.waskomisd.net
Waskom HS 200/9-12
PO Box 748 75692 903-687-3361
Kassie Watson, prin. Fax 687-2897
Waskom MS 300/5-8
PO Box 748 75692 903-687-3361
Bonita Cherry, prin. Fax 687-3372

**Watauga, Tarrant, Pop. 22,948**
Birdville ISD
Supt. — See Haltom City
Watauga MS 700/6-8
6300 Maurie Dr 76148 817-547-4800
Shannon Houston, prin. Fax 581-5369

**Water Valley, Tom Green**
Water Valley ISD 300/PK-12
PO Box 250 76958 325-484-2478
Jimmy Hannon, supt. Fax 484-3359
www.wvisd.net/
Water Valley JSHS 200/7-12
PO Box 250 76958 325-484-2424
Jimmy Hannon, prin. Fax 484-3359

**Waxahachie, Ellis, Pop. 29,212**
Waxahachie ISD 7,000/PK-12
411 N Gibson St 75165 972-923-4631
Jeremy Glenn Ed.D., supt. Fax 923-4759
www.wisd.org
Finley JHS 900/6-8
2401 Brown St 75165 972-923-4680
Adan Casas, prin. Fax 923-4687
Howard JHS 700/6-8
265 Broadhead Rd 75165 972-923-4771
Jacob Perry, prin. Fax 923-3817
Waxahachie Challenge Academy Alt
614 N Getzendaner St 75165 972-923-4695
Robert Woodhouse, prin. Fax 923-4717
Waxahachie Global HS 400/9-12
600 W 2nd St 75165 972-923-4761
Ken Lynch, prin. Fax 923-4738
Waxahachie HS 1,300/9-12
1000 N Highway 77 75165 972-923-4600
Al Benskin, prin. Fax 923-4617
Waxahachie HS of Choice 50/Alt
614 N Getzendaner St 75165 972-923-4758
Robert Woodhouse, prin. Fax 923-4717

---

Southwestern Assemblies of God Univ. Post-Sec.
1200 Sycamore St 75165 972-937-4010
Waxahachie Preparatory Academy 100/K-12
PO Box P 75168 972-937-0440
Scott Marks, admin. Fax 937-5033

**Weatherford, Parker, Pop. 24,879**
Peaster ISD 1,000/PK-12
3602 Harwell Lake Rd 76088 817-341-5000
Matt Adams, supt. Fax 341-5003
www.peaster.net
Peaster HS 300/9-12
3600 Harwell Lake Rd 76088 817-341-5000
Darla Henry, prin. Fax 341-5027
Peaster MS 200/7-8
8512 FM Road 920 76088 817-341-5000
Darren Grudt, prin. Fax 341-5052

Weatherford ISD 7,600/PK-12
1100 Longhorn Dr 76086 817-598-2800
Dr. Jeffrey Hanks, supt. Fax 598-2955
www.weatherfordisd.com
Hall MS 600/7-8
902 Charles St 76086 817-598-2822
Jeanette McNeely, prin. Fax 598-2854
Tison MS 600/7-8
102 Meadowview Rd 76087 817-598-2960
Carolyn Harrison, prin. Fax 598-2963
Weatherford HS 1,600/10-12
2121 Bethel Rd 76087 817-598-2847
Kristy Dowd, prin. Fax 598-2881
Weatherford Ninth Grade Center 600/9-9
1007 S Main St 76086 817-598-2847
Eric Sams, prin. Fax 598-2928

---

Weatherford Christian S 200/PK-12
111 E Columbia St 76086 817-596-7807
Courtney McKeown, head sch Fax 596-0529
Weatherford College Post-Sec.
225 College Park Dr 76086 817-594-5471

**Webster, Harris, Pop. 10,170**

---

Iman Academy Southeast 300/1-12
825 Jetstream 77598
ITT Technical Institute Post-Sec.
1001 Magnolia St 77598 281-316-4700
Remington College Houston Southeast Post-Sec.
20985 Interstate 45 S 77598 800-560-6192

**Weimar, Colorado, Pop. 2,127**
Weimar ISD 500/PK-12
506 W Main St 78962 979-725-9504
Jon Wunderlich, supt. Fax 725-8737
www.weimarisd.org/
Weimar HS 200/9-12
506 W Main St 78962 979-725-9504
Darrin Bickham, prin. Fax 725-8737
Weimar JHS 100/5-8
101 N West St 78962 979-725-9515
Stacey Heger, prin. Fax 725-8383

**Welch, Dawson, Pop. 221**
Dawson ISD 100/PK-12
PO Box 180 79377 806-489-7568
Johnny Tubb, supt. Fax 489-7463
www.dawsonisd.us
Dawson S 100/PK-12
PO Box 180 79377 806-489-7461
Michelle Tijerina, prin. Fax 489-7463

**Wellington, Collingsworth, Pop. 2,160**
Wellington ISD 600/PK-12
609 15th St 79095 806-447-3102
Kurt Ashmore, supt. Fax 447-5124
www.wellingtonisd.net
Wellington HS 200/9-12
811 15th St 79095 806-447-3172
Jermaine Cantu, prin. Fax 447-9012
Wellington JHS 100/6-8
1504 Amarillo St 79095 806-447-3152
Tim Webb, prin. Fax 447-5089

**Wellman, Terry, Pop. 202**
Wellman-Union Consolidated ISD 200/PK-12
PO Box 69 79378 806-637-4910
Dwayne Chenault, supt. Fax 637-2585
wellman.esc17.net
Wellman-Union HS 100/6-12
PO Box 129 79378 806-637-4619
Michael Norman, prin. Fax 637-2585

**Wells, Cherokee, Pop. 772**
Wells ISD 300/PK-12
PO Box 469 75976 936-867-4466
Dale Morton, supt. Fax 867-4497
www.wells.esc7.net
Wells HS 100/7-12
PO Box 469 75976 936-867-4400
Gary Applewhite, prin. Fax 867-4497

**Weslaco, Hidalgo, Pop. 35,580**
Weslaco ISD 17,100/PK-12
PO Box 266 78599 956-969-6500
Ruben Alejandro Ph.D., supt. Fax 969-2664
www.wisd.us
Central MS 1,000/6-8
503 E 6th St 78596 956-969-6710
Patricia Munoz, prin. Fax 969-0779
CTE - Early College HS 100/9-9
PO Box 266 78599 956-969-6897
Sergio Garcia, prin. Fax 969-2664
Cuellar MS 700/6-8
1201 S Bridge Ave 78596 956-969-6720
Mario Hernandez, prin. Fax 973-9797
Garza MS 1,100/6-8
1111 W Sugar Cane Dr 78599 956-969-6774
John Garlic, prin. Fax 447-0484
Hoge MS 1,100/6-8
2302 N International Blvd 78596 956-969-6730
Pablo Vallejo, prin. Fax 514-0903
Horton Alternative Education Program Alt
PO Box 266 78599 956-969-6916
Jose Garcia, prin. Fax 969-6782
South Palms Garden HS 200/Alt
3907 Camino Real Viejo 78596 956-565-0404
Tina Wells, prin. Fax 565-5994

Weslaco East HS 2,100/9-12
810 S Pleasantview Dr 78596 956-969-6950
Dr. Raul Cantu, prin. Fax 968-8693
Weslaco HS 2,400/9-12
1005 W Pike Blvd 78596 956-969-6700
Yvett Morales, prin. Fax 968-8008

Advanced Barber College and Hair Design Post-Sec.
2818 S International Blvd 78596 956-969-0341
South Texas Vocational-Technical Inst. Post-Sec.
2419 Haggar St 78599 956-969-1564

**West, McLennan, Pop. 2,777**
West ISD 1,200/PK-12
801 N Reagan St 76691 254-826-7500
David Truitt, supt. Fax 826-7503
www.westisd.net/
West HS 500/9-12
801 N Reagan St 76691 254-981-2050
Don Snook, prin. Fax 826-7514
West MS 300/6-8
801 N Reagan St 76691 254-981-2120
Michele Scott, prin. Fax 826-7524

**Westbrook, Mitchell, Pop. 253**
Westbrook ISD 200/PK-12
PO Box 99 79565 325-644-2311
Todd Burleson, supt. Fax 644-5101
www.westbrookisd.com
Colorado City Alternative S Alt
PO Box 99 79565 325-644-2311
Cassie Petty, prin. Fax 644-5101
Westbrook S 200/PK-12
PO Box 99 79565 325-644-2311
Cassie Petty, prin. Fax 644-5101

**West Columbia, Brazoria, Pop. 3,841**
Columbia-Brazoria ISD 3,000/PK-12
PO Box 158 77486 979-345-5147
Steven Galloway, supt. Fax 345-4890
www.cbisd.com
Columbia HS 800/9-12
PO Box 158 77486 979-799-1720
Chris Miller, prin. Fax 345-6785
Other Schools – See Brazoria

**West Lake Hills, Travis, Pop. 3,003**
Eanes ISD
Supt. — See Austin
Westlake Alternative S Alt
601 Camp Craft Rd 78746 512-327-2203
Dr. John Carter, prin.

**West Orange, Orange, Pop. 3,387**
West Orange-Cove Consolidated ISD
Supt. — See Orange
West Orange-Stark HS 700/9-12
1400 Newton St 77630 409-882-5570
Rod Anderson, prin. Fax 882-5573

**Wharton, Wharton, Pop. 8,727**
Wharton ISD 2,000/PK-12
2100 N Fulton St 77488 979-532-6201
Tina Herrington, supt. Fax 532-6228
www.whartonisd.net
Wharton HS 600/9-12
1 Tiger Ave 77488 979-532-6800
Mark Anglin, prin. Fax 532-6807
Wharton JHS 500/7-8
1120 N Rusk St 77488 979-532-6840
Tod Nix, prin. Fax 532-6849

Wharton County Junior College Post-Sec.
911 E Boling Hwy 77488 979-532-4560

**Wheeler, Wheeler, Pop. 1,576**
Kelton ISD 100/PK-12
16703 FM 2697 79096 806-826-5795
Doug Rice, supt. Fax 826-3601
keltonisd.com
Kelton S 100/PK-12
16703 FM 2697 79096 806-826-5795
Johnny James, prin. Fax 826-3601

Wheeler ISD 500/PK-12
PO Box 1010 79096 806-826-5241
Bryan Markham, supt. Fax 826-3118
www.wheelerschools.net
Wheeler S 500/PK-12
PO Box 1010 79096 806-826-5534
Mike Bailey, prin. Fax 826-3118

**White Deer, Carson, Pop. 983**
White Deer ISD 400/PK-12
PO Box 517 79097 806-883-2311
Karl Vaughn, supt. Fax 883-2321
www.whitedeerisd.net/
White Deer JSHS 100/7-12
PO Box 248 79097 806-883-2311
Darla Forney, prin. Fax 883-5029

**Whiteface, Cochran, Pop. 442**
Whiteface Consolidated ISD 300/PK-12
PO Box 7 79379 806-287-1154
Dr. Cassidy McBrayer, supt. Fax 287-1131
www.whitefaceschool.net
Whiteface JSHS 100/6-12
PO Box 67 79379 806-287-1104
Chris Mendez, prin. Fax 287-1131
Other Schools – See Pep

**Whitehouse, Smith, Pop. 7,533**
Whitehouse ISD 4,700/PK-12
106 Wildcat Dr 75791 903-839-5500
Daniel DuPree, supt. Fax 839-5515
www.whitehouseisd.org
Whitehouse HS 1,400/9-12
901 E Main St 75791 903-839-5551
Jonathan Campbell, prin. Fax 839-5530
Whitehouse JHS 800/7-8
108 Wildcat Dr 75791 903-839-5590
Josh Garred, prin. Fax 839-5518

**White Oak, Gregg, Pop. 6,394**
White Oak ISD 1,400/PK-12
200 S White Oak Rd 75693 903-291-2000
Michael Gilbert, supt. Fax 291-2222
www.woisd.net
White Oak HS 400/9-12
200 S White Oak Rd 75693 903-291-2000
Don Noll, prin. Fax 291-2034
White Oak MS 400/6-8
200 S White Oak Rd 75693 903-291-2050
Ronnie Hinkle, prin. Fax 291-2035

**Whitesboro, Grayson, Pop. 3,755**
Whitesboro ISD 1,500/PK-12
115 4th St 76273 903-564-4200
Ryan Harper, supt. Fax 564-9303
www.whitesboroisd.org
Whitesboro HS 400/9-12
1 Bearcat Dr 76273 903-564-4208
Marlene Monk, prin. Fax 564-4288
Whitesboro MS 400/6-8
600 4th St 76273 903-564-4240
Ted Beal, prin. Fax 564-5939

**White Settlement, Tarrant, Pop. 15,816**
White Settlement ISD
Supt. — See Fort Worth
Brewer MS 900/7-8
1000 S Cherry Ln 76108 817-367-1267
Sherri Kottwitz, prin. Fax 367-1268

**Whitewright, Grayson, Pop. 1,571**
Whitewright ISD 800/PK-12
PO Box 888 75491 903-364-2155
Steve Arthur, supt. Fax 364-2839
whitewrightisd.com
Whitewright HS 200/9-12
PO Box 888 75491 903-364-2535
Kevin Weaver, prin. Fax 364-2579
Whitewright MS 200/6-8
PO Box 888 75491 903-364-2151
Bobby Worthy, prin. Fax 364-5263

**Whitharral, Hockley**
Whitharral ISD 200/K-12
PO Box 225 79380 806-299-1184
Ed Sharp, supt. Fax 299-1257
www.whitharralisd.org/
Whitharral S 200/K-12
PO Box 225 79380 806-299-1135
Carla Kristinek, prin. Fax 299-1257

**Whitney, Hill, Pop. 2,048**
Whitney ISD 1,600/PK-12
PO Box 518 76692 254-694-2254
Gene Solis, supt. Fax 694-4001
www.whitney.k12.tx.us
Whitney HS 400/9-12
PO Box 518 76692 254-694-3457
Chris Hestilow, prin. Fax 694-4206
Whitney MS 300/6-8
PO Box 518 76692 254-694-3446
Wayne Redding, prin. Fax 694-2064

**Wichita Falls, Wichita, Pop. 102,278**
City View ISD 900/PK-12
1025 City View Dr 76306 940-855-4042
Steve Harris, supt. Fax 851-8889
www.cityview-isd.net/
City View JSHS 400/7-12
1600 City View Dr 76306 940-855-7511
Raymond Weathersbee, prin. Fax 851-5027

Wichita Falls ISD 13,700/PK-12
PO Box 97533 76307 940-235-1000
Michael Kuhrt, supt. Fax 720-3228
www.wfisd.net
Barwise Leadership Academy 500/6-8
3807 Kemp Blvd 76308 940-235-1108
Omar Montemayor, prin. Fax 235-1109
Carrigan Vocational Center Vo/Tech
1609 Blonde St 76301 940-235-1091
Synthia Kirby, prin. Fax 235-1092
Denver Alternative Center Alt
1823 5th St 76301 940-235-1101
Linda Nichols, prin. Fax 235-1102
Harrell Accelerated Learning Center 100/Alt
3115 5th St 76301 940-235-1096
Gena Woodard, prin. Fax 235-1097
Hirschi HS 700/9-12
3106 Borton St 76306 940-235-1070
Doug Albus, prin. Fax 235-1300
Kirby JHS 400/7-8
1715 Loop 11 76306 940-235-1113
Fax 235-1114
McNiel JHS 600/7-8
4712 Barnett Rd 76310 940-235-1118
Tania Rushing, prin. Fax 235-1119
Rider HS 1,700/9-12
4611 Cypress Ave 76310 940-235-1077
Dee Palmore, prin. Fax 235-1301
Wichita Falls HS 1,400/9-12
2149 Avenue H 76309 940-235-1084
Debbie Dipprey, prin. Fax 235-1302

American Commercial College Post-Sec.
4317 Barnett Rd 76310 940-691-0454
Christ Academy 200/PK-12
5105 Stone Lake Dr 76310 940-692-2853
Dr. Jerry Meadows, hdmstr. Fax 692-2657
Midwestern State University Post-Sec.
3410 Taft Blvd 76308 940-397-4000
Notre Dame S 200/PK-12
2821 Lansing Blvd 76309 940-692-6041
Michael Edghill, prin. Fax 692-2811
United Regional Health Care System Post-Sec.
1600 11th St 76301 940-764-3187
Wichita Christian S 300/PK-12
1615 Midwestern Pkwy 76302 940-763-1347

**Willis, Montgomery, Pop. 5,574**
Willis ISD 6,500/PK-12
204 W Rogers St 77378 936-856-1200
Dr. Tim Harkrider, supt. Fax 856-5182
www.willisisd.org/
Brabham MS 700/6-8
10000 FM 830 Rd 77318 936-890-2312
Kimmie Devillier, prin. Fax 856-2910
Lucas MS 800/6-8
1304 N Campbell St 77378 936-856-1274
Ivan Velasco, prin. Fax 856-1065
Stubblefield Academy 50/Alt
207 Philpot St 77378 936-856-1288
Tanya Maddin, prin. Fax 890-0312
Willis HS 1,800/9-12
1201 FM 830 Rd 77378 936-856-1250
Travis Utecht, prin. Fax 856-3391

**Willow Park, Parker, Pop. 3,938**

Trinity Christian Academy 400/PK-12
4954 E IH-20 Service Rd S 76087 817-441-5897
Michael Skaggs, head sch Fax 441-9063

**Wills Point, Van Zandt, Pop. 3,473**
Wills Point ISD 2,600/PK-12
338 W North Commerce St 75169 903-873-5100
Randy Hancock, supt. Fax 873-2462
www.wpisd.com
Wills Point HS 800/9-12
1800 W South Commerce St 75169 903-873-2371
Jim Lamb, prin. Fax 873-6008
Wills Point JHS 400/7-8
200 Tiger Dr 75169 903-873-4924
Glenn Wilson, prin. Fax 873-4873

New Frontiers Christian Academy 50/K-12
24385 Interstate 20 75169 903-873-2440
Julann Goldsmith, admin. Fax 873-2440

**Wilson, Lynn, Pop. 487**
Wilson ISD 100/PK-12
PO Box 9 79381 806-628-6271
Jerry Burger, supt. Fax 628-6441
www.wilson.esc17.net
Wilson S 100/PK-12
PO Box 9 79381 806-628-6271
Brenda Prather, prin. Fax 628-6441

**Wimberley, Hays, Pop. 2,602**
Wimberley ISD 2,000/PK-12
951 FM 2325 78676 512-847-2414
Dwain York, supt. Fax 847-2142
www.wimberleyisd.net
Danforth JHS 500/6-8
200 Texan Blvd 78676 512-847-2181
Greg Howard, prin. Fax 847-7897
Wimberley HS 700/9-12
100 Carney Ln 78676 512-847-5729
Jason Valentine, prin. Fax 847-7269

**Windcrest, Bexar, Pop. 5,256**

Milan Institute of Cosmetology Post-Sec.
5403 Walzem Rd 78218 210-656-1991

**Windthorst, Archer, Pop. 398**
Windthorst ISD 500/PK-12
PO Box 190 76389 940-423-6688
Don Windham, supt. Fax 423-6505
www.windthorstisd.net
Windthorst JHS 100/6-8
PO Box 190 76389 940-423-6605
Darla Tackett, prin. Fax 423-6505
Windthorst HS 200/9-12
PO Box 190 76389 940-423-6680
Lonnie Hise, prin. Fax 423-6505

**Wink, Winkler, Pop. 931**
Wink-Loving ISD 400/PK-12
PO Box 637 79789 432-527-3880
Dr. Dewitt Smith, supt. Fax 527-3505
www.wlisd.net
Wink JSHS 100/7-12
PO Box 637 79789 432-527-3880
Scotty Carman, prin. Fax 527-3505

**Winnie, Chambers, Pop. 3,222**
East Chambers ISD 1,300/PK-12
1955 State Highway 124 77665 409-296-6100
Scott Campbell, supt. Fax 296-3528
www.eastchambers.net
East Chambers HS 400/9-12
234 E Buccaneer Dr 77665 409-296-6100
Steve Franzen, prin. Fax 296-9596
East Chambers JHS 200/7-8
1931 State Highway 124 77665 409-296-6100
Lou Ann Rainey, prin. Fax 296-2724

**Winnsboro, Wood, Pop. 3,395**
Winnsboro ISD 1,500/PK-12
207 E Pine St 75494 903-342-3737
Susan Morton, supt. Fax 342-3380
www.winnsboroisd.org
Memorial MS 400/5-8
505 S Chestnut St 75494 903-342-5711
Jeff Akin, prin. Fax 342-6689
Winnsboro HS 400/9-12
409 Newsome St 75494 903-342-3641
David Pinnell, prin. Fax 342-3645

**Winona, Smith, Pop. 574**
Winona ISD 1,000/PK-12
611 Wildcat Dr 75792 903-939-4001
Wiley E. Vonner, supt. Fax 877-9387
www.winonaisd.org
Winona HS 300/9-12
611 Wildcat Dr 75792 903-939-4100
Brian Lowe, prin. Fax 939-4199

Winona MS 200/6-8
611 Wildcat Dr 75792 903-939-4040
Missy Gimble, prin. Fax 877-9150

**Winters, Runnels, Pop. 2,547**
Winters ISD 600/PK-12
603 N Heights St 79567 325-754-5574
Bruce Davis, supt. Fax 754-5374
www.wintersisd.org
Winters HS 200/9-12
603 N Heights St 79567 325-754-5516
Sammy Edwards, prin. Fax 754-5085
Winters JHS 100/6-8
603 N Heights St 79567 325-754-5518
Terry Payne, prin. Fax 754-5085

**Woden, Nacogdoches**
Woden ISD 800/PK-12
PO Box 100 75978 936-564-2073
Brady Taylor, supt. Fax 564-1250
www.wodenisd.org/
Woden HS 200/9-12
PO Box 100 75978 936-564-7903
Dr. Jerry Meador, prin. Fax 462-4962
Woden JHS 200/6-8
PO Box 100 75978 936-564-2481
Dr. Jerry Meador, prin. Fax 462-4982

**Wolfe City, Hunt, Pop. 1,375**
Wolfe City ISD 600/PK-12
505 W Dallas St 75496 903-496-7333
Vernon Richardson, supt. Fax 496-7905
www.wcisd.net
Wolfe City HS 200/9-12
8353 State Highway 34 N 75496 903-496-2891
Chris Sheets, prin. Fax 496-7124
Wolfe City MS 100/6-8
PO Box L 75496 903-496-7333
Sean Martin, prin. Fax 496-2112

**Wolfforth, Lubbock, Pop. 3,636**
Frenship ISD 7,800/PK-12
PO Box 100 79382 806-866-9541
Dr. Michelle McCord, supt. Fax 866-4135
www.frenship.us
Frenship HS 1,900/9-12
PO Box 100 79382 806-866-4440
Kim Spicer, prin. Fax 866-9370
Frenship MS 600/6-8
PO Box 100 79382 806-866-4464
Jerry Jerabek, prin. Fax 866-2181
Other Schools – See Lubbock

**Woodsboro, Refugio, Pop. 1,498**
Woodsboro ISD 500/PK-12
PO Box 770 78393 361-543-4518
Jeff Dyer, supt. Fax 543-4856
www.wisd.net
Woodsboro Secondary S 200/7-12
PO Box 770 78393 361-543-4521
Linda Garza, prin. Fax 543-5140

**Woodson, Throckmorton, Pop. 262**
Woodson ISD 100/PK-12
PO Box 287 76491 940-345-6528
Gordon Thomas, supt. Fax 345-6549
www.woodsonisd.net
Woodson S 100/PK-12
PO Box 287 76491 940-345-6521
Casey Adams, prin. Fax 345-6549

**Woodville, Tyler, Pop. 2,545**
Woodville ISD 1,300/PK-12
505 N Charlton St 75979 409-283-3752
Glen Conner, supt. Fax 283-7962
www.woodvilleeagles.org
Woodville HS 300/9-12
505 N Charlton St 75979 409-283-3714
Morgan Wright, prin. Fax 331-3427
Woodville MS 300/6-8
505 N Charlton St 75979 409-283-7109
Eric Holton, prin. Fax 331-3418

**Woodway, McLennan, Pop. 8,360**
Midway ISD 7,200/PK-12
13885 Woodway Dr 76712 254-761-5610
George Kazanas Ed.D., supt. Fax 761-5789
www.midwayisd.org/
Other Schools – See Hewitt, Waco

**Wortham, Freestone, Pop. 1,060**
Wortham ISD 500/PK-12
PO Box 247 76693 254-765-3095
David Allen, supt. Fax 765-3473
www.worthamisd.org
Wortham HS 100/9-12
PO Box 247 76693 254-765-3094
David Hayes, prin. Fax 765-3085
Wortham MS 100/6-8
PO Box 247 76693 254-765-3523
David Hayes, prin. Fax 765-3512

**Wylie, Dallas, Pop. 40,460**
Wylie ISD 12,900/PK-12
PO Box 490 75098 972-429-3000
Dr. David Vinson, supt. Fax 442-5368
www.wylieisd.net
Achieve Academy Alt
PO Box 490 75098 972-429-2390
Melissa True, prin. Fax 941-9213
Burnett JHS 700/7-8
PO Box 490 75098 972-429-3200
Mike Evans, prin. Fax 442-1447
Cooper JHS 600/7-8
PO Box 490 75098 972-429-3250
Shawn Miller, prin. Fax 941-9175
McMillan JHS 600/7-8
PO Box 490 75098 972-429-3225
Jon Peters, prin. Fax 941-6372
Wylie East HS 1,600/9-12
PO Box 490 75098 972-429-3150
Mike Williams, prin. Fax 442-2874
Wylie HS 1,700/9-12
PO Box 490 75098 972-429-3100
Virdie Montgomery, prin. Fax 442-1879

---

Wylie Preparatory Academy 300/K-12
4110 Skyview Ct 75098 972-442-1388
Brenda Kirby, admin. Fax 429-3568

**Yantis, Wood, Pop. 386**
Yantis ISD 400/PK-12
105 W Oak St 75497 903-383-2463
Dr. Peter Running, supt. Fax 383-7620
www.yantisisd.net
Yantis HS 200/6-12
105 W Oak St 75497 903-383-2463
Jerry Brem, prin. Fax 383-3075

**Yoakum, Lavaca, Pop. 5,752**
Yoakum ISD 1,600/PK-12
315 E Gonzales St 77995 361-293-3162
Tom Kelley, supt. Fax 293-6678
www.yoakumisd.net/
Yoakum HS 500/9-12
100 Poth St 77995 361-293-3442
Chris Wegener, prin. Fax 293-2145
Yoakum JHS 300/6-8
103 McKinnon St 77995 361-293-3111
Patrick Frank, prin. Fax 293-5787

**Yorktown, DeWitt, Pop. 2,079**
Yorktown ISD 500/PK-12
PO Box 487 78164 361-564-2252
Linda Bettin, supt. Fax 564-2254
www.yisd.org
Yorktown HS 200/9-12
PO Box 487 78164 361-564-2252
Carlos Garza, prin. Fax 564-2274
Yorktown JHS 100/6-8
PO Box 487 78164 361-564-2252
Carlos Garza, prin. Fax 564-2289

**Zapata, Zapata, Pop. 5,080**
Zapata County ISD 3,500/PK-12
PO Box 158 78076 956-765-6546
Roberto Hein, supt. Fax 765-8350
www.zcisd.org
Zapata HS 900/9-12
PO Box 3750 78076 956-765-0280
Gerardo Garcia, prin. Fax 765-0274
Zapata MS 700/6-8
PO Box 3636 78076 956-765-6542
Elsa Martinez, prin. Fax 765-9204

**Zavalla, Angelina, Pop. 708**
Zavalla ISD 400/PK-12
431 E Main St 75980 936-897-2271
Michael Woodard, supt. Fax 897-2674
www.zavallaisd.org
Zavalla JSHS 200/6-12
431 E Main St 75980 936-897-2301
Ricky Oliver, prin. Fax 897-2674
Other Schools – See Lufkin

**Zephyr, Brown**
Zephyr ISD 200/PK-12
11625 County Road 281 76890 325-739-5331
Stanton Marwitz, supt. Fax 739-5906
zephyr.netxv.net
Zephyr S 200/PK-12
11625 County Road 281 76890 325-739-5331
DeeAnna Blanton, prin. Fax 739-2126

# UTAH

## UTAH OFFICE OF EDUCATION
**PO Box 144200, Salt Lake City 84114-4200**
**Telephone 801-538-7500**
**Fax 801-538-7768**
**Website http://www.schools.utah.gov/main/**

Superintendent of Public Instruction Martell Menlove

## UTAH BOARD OF EDUCATION
**250 E 500 S, Salt Lake City 84111-3284**

Chairperson Debra Roberts

## REGIONAL SERVICE CENTERS (RSC)

Central Utah Educational Services
Jason Strate, dir. 435-896-4469
195 E 500 N, Richfield 84701 Fax 896-4767
www.cues.k12.ut.us

Northeastern Utah Educational Services
Duke Mossman, dir. 435-654-1921
35 S Main St, Heber City 84032 Fax 654-2403
www.nucenter.org

Southeast Educational Service Center
J.J. Grant, dir. 435-637-1173
685 E 200 S, Price 84501 Fax 637-1178
seschools.org

Southwest Educational Development Ctr
Edna LaMarca, dir. 435-586-2865
520 W 800 S, Cedar City 84720 Fax 586-2868
www.sedc.k12.ut.us

## PUBLIC, PRIVATE AND CATHOLIC SECONDARY SCHOOLS

**Alpine, Utah, Pop. 9,390**
Alpine SD
Supt. — See American Fork
Timberline MS 1,300/7-9
500 W Canyon Crest Rd 84004 801-610-8765
Peter Glahn, prin. Fax 763-7045

**Altamont, Duchesne, Pop. 222**
Duchesne SD
Supt. — See Duchesne
Altamont JSHS 200/7-12
PO Box 130 84001 435-738-1345
Dean Wilson, prin. Fax 738-1370

**American Fork, Utah, Pop. 25,678**
Alpine SD 63,600/K-12
575 N 100 E 84003 801-610-8400
Sam Jarman, supt. Fax 610-8516
alpineschools.org
American Fork JHS 1,800/7-9
20 W 1120 N 84003 801-610-8750
Jeff Schoonover, prin. Fax 756-8407
American Fork SHS 2,000/10-12
510 N 600 E 84003 801-610-8800
Dan Weishar, prin. Fax 756-8575
Alpine Adult S Adult
759 E Pacific Dr 84003 801-610-8188
Kip Bromley, dir. Fax 492-3550
Other Schools – See Alpine, Eagle Mountain, Highland, Lehi, Lindon, Orem, Pleasant Grove, Saratoga Sprngs

---

American Heritage S 500/K-12
736 N 1100 E 84003 801-642-0055

**Beaver, Beaver, Pop. 3,076**
Beaver SD 1,500/K-12
PO Box 31 84713 435-438-2291
Dr. Ray Terry, supt. Fax 438-5898
www.beaver.k12.ut.us
Beaver HS 500/7-12
PO Box 71 84713 435-438-2301
Brady Fails, prin. Fax 438-1519
Other Schools – See Milford

**Bicknell, Wayne, Pop. 324**
Wayne SD 500/K-12
PO Box 127 84715 435-425-3813
Burke Torgerson, supt. Fax 425-3806
www.waynesd.org
Wayne HS 200/9-12
PO Box 217 84715 435-425-3411
Mary Bray, prin. Fax 425-3480
Wayne MS 100/6-8
PO Box 128 84715 435-425-3421
Lance Peterson, prin. Fax 425-3130

**Big Water, Kane, Pop. 468**
Kane SD
Supt. — See Kanab
Big Water HS 50/7-12
PO Box 410126 84741 435-675-5821
Andrew Roundy, prin. Fax 675-5821

**Blanding, San Juan, Pop. 3,283**
San Juan SD 2,700/K-12
200 N Main St 84511 435-678-1211
Dr. Douglas Wright, supt. Fax 678-1272
www.sjsd.org
Lyman MS 300/6-8
535 N 100 E 84511 435-678-1398
Aaron Brewer, prin. Fax 678-1399
San Juan HS 400/9-12
311 N Bronco Way 84511 435-678-1301
Bob Peterson, prin. Fax 678-1396
Other Schools – See Montezuma Creek, Monticello, Monument Valley

**Bountiful, Davis, Pop. 41,539**
Davis SD
Supt. — See Farmington
Bountiful JHS 600/7-9
30 W 400 N 84010 801-402-6000
Kathy Ashton, prin. Fax 402-6001
Bountiful SHS 1,400/10-12
695 Orchard Dr 84010 801-402-3900
Gregory Wilkey, prin. Fax 402-3901
Millcreek JHS 800/7-9
245 E 1000 S 84010 801-402-6200
Brock Jackman, prin. Fax 402-6201
Mueller Park JHS 600/7-9
955 Mueller Park Rd 84010 801-402-6300
Deanne Kapetanov, prin. Fax 402-6301
South Davis JHS 1,000/7-9
298 W 2600 S 84010 801-402-6400
Jeff Jorgensen, prin. Fax 402-6401
Viewmont SHS 1,700/10-12
120 W 1000 N 84010 801-402-4200
Dan Linford, prin. Fax 402-4201

**Brigham City, Box Elder, Pop. 17,553**
Box Elder SD 11,200/K-12
960 S Main St 84302 435-734-4800
Dr. Ronald Tolman, supt. Fax 734-4833
www.besd.net
Box Elder MS 1,000/8-9
18 S 500 E 84302 435-734-4880
Keith Mecham, prin. Fax 734-4885
Box Elder SHS 1,400/10-12
380 S 600 W 84302 435-734-4840
Gary Allen, prin. Fax 734-4846
Young Community HS 100/Alt
230 W 200 S 84302 435-734-4834
Matt Webb, prin. Fax 734-4860
Other Schools – See Garland, Grouse Creek, Park Valley

**Castle Dale, Emery, Pop. 1,623**
Emery County SD
Supt. — See Huntington
Emery SHS 400/10-12
PO Box 499 84513 435-381-2689
Larry Davis, prin. Fax 381-5370

**Castle Valley, Grand, Pop. 315**

---

Daystar Adventist Academy 50/K-12
HC 64 Box 2201 84532 435-259-7719
Alexa Hernandez, supt. Fax 259-5209

**Cedar City, Iron, Pop. 28,202**
Iron SD 7,300/K-12
2077 W Royal Hunte Dr 84720 435-586-2804
Dr. Shannon Dulaney, supt. Fax 586-2815
irondistrict.org
Adult HS/Southwest Education Academy 100/Alt
510 W 800 S 84720 435-586-2870
Steve Schofield, prin. Fax 586-2815
Canyon View HS 1,000/9-12
166 W 1925 N 84721 435-586-2813
Rich Nielsen, prin. Fax 586-2849
Canyon View MS 900/6-8
1865 N Main St 84721 435-586-2830
Conrad Aitken, prin. Fax 586-2837
Cedar HS 1,100/9-12
703 W 600 S 84720 435-586-2820
John Dodds, prin. Fax 586-2826
Cedar MS 1,000/6-8
2215 W Royal Hunte Dr 84720 435-586-2810
Bylynda Murray, prin. Fax 586-2829
Foothill HS 50/Alt
270 E 1600 N 84721 435-867-2513
Steve Schofield, prin. Fax 586-2815
Other Schools – See Parowan

---

Southern Utah University Post-Sec.
351 W Center St 84720 435-586-7700
Southwest Applied Technology College Post-Sec.
510 W 800 S 84720 435-586-2899

**Centerville, Davis, Pop. 15,086**
Davis SD
Supt. — See Farmington
Centerville JHS 1,000/7-9
625 S Main St 84014 801-402-6100
Spencer Hansen, prin. Fax 402-6101

**Clearfield, Davis, Pop. 28,950**
Davis SD
Supt. — See Farmington
Clearfield SHS 1,600/10-12
931 S 1000 E 84015 801-402-8200
Suzi Jensen, prin. Fax 402-8336
North Davis JHS 1,100/7-9
835 S State St 84015 801-402-6500
Brian Hunt, prin. Fax 402-6501

---

Vista College Post-Sec.
1785 E 1450 S Ste 300 84015 866-442-4197

**Coalville, Summit, Pop. 1,348**
North Summit SD 1,000/PK-12
PO Box 497 84017 435-336-5654
Jerre Holmes, supt. Fax 336-2401
www.nsummit.org
North Summit HS 300/9-12
PO Box 497 84017 435-336-5656
Russell Hendry, prin. Fax 336-0309
North Summit MS 300/5-8
PO Box 497 84017 435-336-5678
Brett Richins, prin. Fax 336-4474

**Cottonwood Heights, Salt Lake, Pop. 32,636**
Canyons SD
Supt. — See Sandy
Brighton HS 1,700/9-12
2220 E Bengal Blvd, 801-826-5800
Charisse Hilton, prin. Fax 826-5809
Butler MS 600/6-8
7530 S 2700 E, 801-826-6800
Paula Logan, prin. Fax 826-6809

**Delta, Millard, Pop. 3,399**
Millard SD 3,000/PK-12
285 E 450 N 84624 435-864-1000
David Styler, supt. Fax 864-5684
www.millardk12.org/
Delta HS 600/9-12
50 W 300 N 84624 435-864-5610
Teresa Thompson, prin. Fax 864-5619
Delta MS 600/6-8
251 E 300 N 84624 435-864-5660
Rebecca Callister, prin. Fax 864-5669
Delta Technical Center Vo/Tech
305 E 200 N 84624 435-864-5710
Dean Fowles, dir. Fax 864-5719
Other Schools – See Fillmore, Garrison

**Draper, Salt Lake, Pop. 41,208**
Canyons SD
Supt. — See Sandy
Corner Canyon HS 9-12
12943 S 700 E 84020 801-826-6400
Mary Bailey, prin. Fax 826-6409

Draper Park MS 1,000/6-8
13133 S 1300 E 84020 801-826-6900
Mary Anderson, prin. Fax 826-6909

---

Ameritech College Post-Sec.
12257 Business Park Dr #108 84020 801-816-1444
Argosy University / Salt Lake City Post-Sec.
121 W Election Rd Ste 300 84020 801-601-5000
Art Institute of Salt Lake City Post-Sec.
121 W Election Rd 84020 801-601-4700
Juan Diego Catholic HS 800/9-12
300 E 11800 S 84020 801-984-7602
Galey Colosimo, prin. Fax 984-7601
St. John the Baptist MS 400/6-8
300 E 11800 S 84020 801-984-7613
Jim Markosian, prin. Fax 984-7649

**Duchesne, Duchesne, Pop. 1,664**
Duchesne SD 4,600/K-12
PO Box 446 84021 435-738-1240
Dr. David Brotherson, supt. Fax 738-1254
www.dcsd.org
Duchesne JSHS 300/7-12
PO Box 330 84021 435-738-1260
Stan Young, prin. Fax 738-1261
Other Schools – See Altamont, Roosevelt, Tabiona

**Dugway, Tooele, Pop. 749**
Tooele County SD
Supt. — See Tooele
Dugway JSHS 100/7-12
5020 5th St 84022 435-831-4566
Jeff Wyatt, prin. Fax 831-4951

**Eagle Mountain, Utah, Pop. 20,745**
Alpine SD
Supt. — See American Fork
Frontier MS 7-9
1427 E Mid Valley Rd, 801-610-8777
Scott Sumner, prin. Fax 789-3800

**Eden, Weber, Pop. 593**
Weber SD
Supt. — See Ogden
Snowcrest JHS 300/7-9
2755 N Highway 162 84310 801-476-5360
Curtis VandenBosch, prin. Fax 476-5399

**Enterprise, Washington, Pop. 1,701**
Washington County SD
Supt. — See Saint George
Enterprise JSHS 400/7-12
PO Box 460 84725 435-878-2248
Rick Palmer, prin. Fax 878-2479

**Ephraim, Sanpete, Pop. 5,963**
South Sanpete SD
Supt. — See Manti
Ephraim MS 400/6-8
555 S 100 E 84627 435-283-4037
Timothy Miller, prin. Fax 283-4885

---

Snow College Post-Sec.
150 College Ave 84627 435-283-7000

**Escalante, Garfield, Pop. 794**
Garfield SD
Supt. — See Panguitch
Escalante HS 100/7-12
PO Box 228 84726 435-826-4205
Bert Steele, prin. Fax 826-4231

**Eureka, Juab, Pop. 666**
Tintic SD 200/PK-12
PO Box 210 84628 435-433-6363
Kodey Hughes, supt. Fax 433-6643
www.tintic.k12.ut.us
Tintic JSHS 100/7-12
PO Box 230 84628 435-433-6939
Greg Thornock, admin. Fax 433-6845
Other Schools – See Trout Creek

**Farmington, Davis, Pop. 17,985**
Davis SD 66,000/PK-12
PO Box 588 84025 801-402-5261
Dr. W. Bryan Bowles, supt. Fax 402-5249
www.davis.k12.ut.us
Farmington JHS 800/7-9
150 S 200 W 84025 801-402-6900
Brent Stephens, prin. Fax 402-6901
Other Schools – See Bountiful, Centerville, Clearfield, Kaysville, Layton, Sunset, Syracuse, West Point, Woods Cross

**Ferron, Emery, Pop. 1,614**
Emery County SD
Supt. — See Huntington
San Rafael JHS 300/7-9
PO Box 790 84523 435-384-2335
Doug Mecham, prin. Fax 384-3354

**Fillmore, Millard, Pop. 2,397**
Millard SD
Supt. — See Delta
Fillmore MS 300/5-8
435 S 500 W 84631 435-743-5660
Dennis Alldredge, prin. Fax 743-5669
Millard HS 300/9-12
200 W Eagle Ave 84631 435-743-5610
George Richardson, prin. Fax 743-5619

**Garland, Box Elder, Pop. 2,370**
Box Elder SD
Supt. — See Brigham City
Bear River MS 700/8-9
300 E 1500 S 84312 435-257-2540
Eldon Petersen, prin. Fax 257-3945
Bear River SHS 900/10-12
1450 S Main St 84312 435-257-2500
Kristi Capener, prin. Fax 257-3899

**Garrison, Millard**
Millard SD
Supt. — See Delta
EskDale HS 50/9-12
1000 Circle Dr 84728 435-855-2148
Nomi Sheppard, lead tchr. Fax 855-2148
Garrison 7th & 8th S 50/7-8
1000 Circle Dr 84728 435-855-2148
Nomi Sheppard, lead tchr. Fax 855-2148

**Grantsville, Tooele, Pop. 8,741**
Tooele County SD
Supt. — See Tooele
Grantsville HS 700/9-12
155 E Cherry Dr 84029 435-884-4500
Mark Ernst, prin. Fax 884-4519
Grantsville JHS 400/7-8
318 S Hale St 84029 435-884-4510
Charles Mohler, prin. Fax 884-4513

**Green River, Emery, Pop. 946**
Emery County SD
Supt. — See Huntington
Green River JSHS 100/7-12
PO Box 450 84525 435-564-3461
Nolan Johnson, prin. Fax 564-3508

**Grouse Creek, Box Elder**
Box Elder SD
Supt. — See Brigham City
Grouse Creek S 50/K-10
PO Box 16 84313 435-747-7321
Viola Foy, lead tchr. Fax 747-7182

**Gunnison, Sanpete, Pop. 3,235**
South Sanpete SD
Supt. — See Manti
Gunnison Valley HS 300/9-12
PO Box 460 84634 435-528-7256
Trevor Powell, prin. Fax 528-3556
Gunnison Valley MS 300/6-8
PO Box 1090 84634 435-528-5337
Alan Peterson, prin. Fax 528-5397

**Harrisville, Weber, Pop. 5,477**
Weber SD
Supt. — See Ogden
Orion JHS 1,000/7-9
370 W 2000 N, 801-452-4700
Nick Harris, prin. Fax 452-4777

**Heber City, Wasatch, Pop. 11,241**
Wasatch SD 5,200/K-12
101 E 200 N 84032 435-654-0280
Terry Shoemaker, supt. Fax 654-4714
www.wasatch.edu/
Rocky Mountain MS 800/7-8
800 School House Way 84032 435-654-9350
Justin Kelly, prin. Fax 654-9343
Wasatch HS 1,500/9-12
930 S 500 E 84032 435-654-0640
Shawn Kelly, prin. Fax 654-3011
Wasatch HS North Campus 50/Alt
180 E 600 S 84032 435-654-4231
Jacki Burnham, prin. Fax 654-9465

**Helper, Carbon, Pop. 2,166**
Carbon SD
Supt. — See Price
Helper MS 200/6-8
151 Uintah St 84526 435-472-5441
Mika Salas, prin. Fax 472-3502

**Herriman, Salt Lake, Pop. 21,297**
Jordan SD
Supt. — See West Jordan
Copper Mountain MS 7-9
12106 S Anthem Park Blvd, 801-412-1200
Kim Baker, prin. Fax 412-1230
Fort Herriman MS 1,300/7-9
14058 S Mirabella Dr, 801-412-2450
Rodney Shaw, prin. Fax 412-2454
Herriman HS 1,900/10-12
11917 S 6000 W, 801-567-8530
James Birch, prin. Fax 567-8545

**Highland, Utah, Pop. 15,197**
Alpine SD
Supt. — See American Fork
Lone Peak SHS 2,200/10-12
10189 N 4800 W 84003 801-610-8810
Rhonda Bromley, prin. Fax 763-7064
Mountain Ridge JHS 1,300/7-9
5525 W 10400 N 84003 801-610-8758
Mark Whitaker, prin. Fax 763-7018

**Hildale, Washington, Pop. 2,719**
Washington County SD
Supt. — See Saint George
Water Canyon S PK-12
250 W Newel Ave 84784 435-668-2847
Darin Thomas, prin.

**Holladay, Salt Lake**
Granite SD
Supt. — See Salt Lake City
Bonneville JHS 800/7-9
5330 S 1660 E 84117 385-646-5124
Rocky Lambourne, prin. Fax 646-5127
Olympus JHS 800/7-9
2217 E Murray Holladay Rd 84117 385-646-5224
Mark Grant, prin. Fax 646-5227

**Huntington, Emery, Pop. 2,105**
Emery County SD 2,400/PK-12
PO Box 120 84528 435-687-9846
Kirk Sitterud, supt. Fax 687-9849
emerycsd.org
Canyon View JHS 200/7-9
PO Box 250 84528 435-687-2265
James Jones, prin. Fax 687-9546
Other Schools – See Castle Dale, Ferron, Green River

**Hurricane, Washington, Pop. 13,404**
Washington County SD
Supt. — See Saint George
Hurricane HS 800/10-12
345 W Tiger Blvd 84737 435-635-3280
Jody Rich, prin. Fax 635-3719
Hurricane MS 600/8-9
395 N 200 W 84737 435-635-4634
Jan Goodwin, prin. Fax 635-4663

**Hyrum, Cache, Pop. 7,476**
Cache County SD
Supt. — See North Logan
Mountain Crest SHS 1,600/10-12
255 S 800 E 84319 435-245-6093
Teri Cutler, prin. Fax 245-3818
South Cache JHS 1,200/8-9
10 S 480 W 84319 435-245-6433
Lynn Archibald, prin. Fax 245-6662

**Junction, Piute, Pop. 190**
Piute County SD 300/PK-12
PO Box 69 84740 435-577-2912
Shane Erickson, supt. Fax 577-2561
www.piutek12.org
Piute JSHS 200/7-12
PO Box 9 84740 435-577-2912
Kennedy Sylvester, lead tchr. Fax 577-2512

**Kamas, Summit, Pop. 1,803**
South Summit SD 1,500/PK-12
285 E 400 S 84036 435-783-4301
Dr. Shad Sorenson, supt. Fax 783-4501
www.ssummit.org
South Summit HS 400/9-12
45 S 300 E 84036 435-783-4313
Wade Woolstenhulme, prin. Fax 783-4765
South Summit MS 400/5-8
355 E 300 S 84036 435-783-4341
Steve Camp, prin. Fax 783-2787

**Kanab, Kane, Pop. 4,263**
Kane SD 1,200/K-12
746 S 175 E 84741 435-644-2555
Robert Johnson, supt. Fax 644-2509
www.kane.k12.ut.us
Kanab HS 200/9-12
59 Cowboy Dr 84741 435-644-5821
Brenan Jackson, prin. Fax 644-5242
Kanab MS 100/7-8
690 Cowboy Way 84741 435-644-5800
Mandie Luce, prin. Fax 644-5121
Other Schools – See Big Water, Lake Powell, Orderville

**Kaysville, Davis, Pop. 26,897**
Davis SD
Supt. — See Farmington
Canyon Heights S 100/Alt
525 DATC Dr 84037 801-402-0720
Marci Flocken, prin. Fax 402-0551
Centennial JHS 7-9
740 Sunset Dr 84037 801-402-0100
Aaron Hogge, prin. Fax 402-0101
Davis Applied Technology College Vo/Tech
550 E 300 S 84037 801-593-2500
Mike Bouwhuis, dir. Fax 593-2400
Davis SHS 2,300/10-12
325 S Main St 84037 801-402-8800
Rich Swanson, prin. Fax 402-8801
Fairfield JHS 1,100/7-9
951 N Fairfield Rd 84037 801-402-7000
Bryon Nielsen, prin. Fax 402-7001
Kaysville JHS 1,000/7-9
100 E 350 S 84037 801-402-7200
Curtis Stromberg, prin. Fax 402-7201
Mountain HS 300/Alt
490 S 500 E 84037 801-402-0450
Kathleen Chronister, prin. Fax 402-0451

---

Davis Applied Technology College Post-Sec.
550 E 300 S 84037 801-593-2500

**Kearns, Salt Lake, Pop. 34,126**
Granite SD
Supt. — See Salt Lake City
Jefferson JHS 1,000/7-9
5850 S 5600 W 84118 385-646-5194
Jared Reynolds, prin. Fax 646-5195
Kearns JHS 800/7-9
4040 W Sams Blvd 84118 385-646-5204
Kandace Barber, prin. Fax 646-5206
Kearns SHS 1,600/10-12
5525 S Cougar Ln 84118 385-646-5380
Maile Loo, prin. Fax 646-5382

**Lake Powell, San Juan, Pop. 15**
Kane SD
Supt. — See Kanab
Lake Powell HS 50/7-12
1000 Ferry Rd 84533 435-684-2268
Gordon Miller, prin. Fax 684-3821

**Laketown, Rich, Pop. 240**
Rich SD
Supt. — See Randolph
Rich MS 100/6-8
PO Box 129 84038 435-946-3359
Kip Motta, prin. Fax 946-3366

**Layton, Davis, Pop. 65,397**
Davis SD
Supt. — See Farmington
Central Davis JHS 900/7-9
663 Church St 84041 801-402-7100
T.J. Barker, prin. Fax 402-7101
Layton SHS 1,700/10-12
440 Wasatch Dr 84041 801-402-4800
Ryck Astle, prin. Fax 402-4801
Legacy JHS 800/7-8
411 N 3200 W 84041 801-402-4700
Dr. Kenneth Hadlock, prin. Fax 402-4701
North Layton JHS 1,000/7-9
1100 W Antelope Dr 84041 801-402-6600
Ed Campbell, prin. Fax 402-6601

Northridge SHS 1,800/10-12
2430 N Hill Field Rd 84041 801-402-8500
Luke Rasmussen, prin. Fax 402-8501

---

Broadview University Post-Sec.
869 W Hill Field Rd 84041 801-660-6000
Eagle Gate College Post-Sec.
915 N 400 W 84041 801-546-7500
Fran Brown College of Beauty Post-Sec.
587 N Main St 84041 801-546-6166
Layton Christian Academy 500/PK-12
2352 E Highway 193 84040 801-771-7141
Northridge Learning Center 200/K-12
2405 N Hill Field Rd 84041 801-776-4532

**Lehi, Utah, Pop. 46,111**
Alpine SD
Supt. — See American Fork
Lehi JHS 1,300/7-9
700 Cedar Hollow Rd 84043 801-768-7010
Kevin Thomas, prin. Fax 768-7016
Lehi SHS 1,900/10-12
180 N 500 E 84043 801-610-8805
David Mower, prin. Fax 768-7007
Willowcreek MS 1,200/7-9
2275 W 300 N 84043 801-610-8766
Jarom Becar, prin. Fax 766-5168

---

Mountainland Applied Technology College Post-Sec.
2301 N Ashton Blvd 84043 801-753-6282

**Lindon, Utah, Pop. 9,825**
Alpine SD
Supt. — See American Fork
Oak Canyon JHS 1,100/7-9
111 S 725 E 84042 801-610-8138
Doug Webb, prin. Fax 785-8768

---

Evan's Hairstyling College Post-Sec.
284 W 200 N 84042 801-224-6034

**Logan, Cache, Pop. 47,175**
Cache County SD
Supt. — See North Logan
Cache HS 100/Alt
265 W 1400 N 84341 435-755-0716
Sheri Hansen, prin. Fax 755-0721

Logan CSD 6,100/PK-12
101 W Center St 84321 435-755-2300
Frank Schofield, supt. Fax 755-2311
www.loganschools.org
Logan HS 1,700/9-12
162 W 100 S 84321 435-755-2380
Shane Ogden, prin. Fax 755-2387
Logan South Campus 100/Alt
325 W 400 S 84321 435-755-2395
Larry Comadena, dean Fax 755-2396
Mt. Logan MS 1,300/6-8
875 N 200 E 84321 435-755-2370
Daryl Guymon, prin. Fax 755-2370

---

Bridgerland Applied Technology Center Post-Sec.
1301 N 600 W 84321 435-753-6780
New Horizons Beauty College Post-Sec.
550 N Main St Ste 115 84321 435-753-9779
Stevens Henager College Post-Sec.
755 S Main St 84321 435-752-0903
Utah State University Post-Sec.
1400 Old Main Hl 84322 435-797-1000

**Magna, Salt Lake, Pop. 25,413**
Granite SD
Supt. — See Salt Lake City
Brockbank JHS 1,000/7-9
2935 S 8560 W 84044 385-646-5134
Christine Straatman, prin. Fax 646-5135
Cyprus SHS 1,500/10-12
8623 W 3000 S 84044 385-646-5300
Rob McDaniel, prin. Fax 646-5303
Matheson JHS 1,200/7-9
3650 S Montclair St 84044 385-646-5290
Dawn Hauser, prin. Fax 646-5299

---

Stansbury Academy 100/8-12
8265 W 2700 S 84044 385-382-6604

**Manila, Daggett, Pop. 308**
Daggett SD 200/PK-12
PO Box 249 84046 435-784-3174
Bruce Northcott, supt. Fax 784-3920
www.dsdf.org
Manila JSHS 100/7-12
PO Box 249 84046 435-784-3174
Guy Gonder, prin. Fax 784-3271

**Manti, Sanpete, Pop. 3,220**
South Sanpete SD 3,100/PK-12
39 S Main St 84642 435-835-2261
Kent Larsen, supt. Fax 835-2265
www.ssanpete.org/
Manti HS 600/9-12
100 W 500 N 84642 435-835-2281
George Henrie, prin. Fax 835-2285
Other Schools – See Ephraim, Gunnison

**Mapleton, Utah, Pop. 7,784**
Nebo SD
Supt. — See Spanish Fork
Mapleton JHS 1,200/7-9
362 E 1200 N 84664 801-489-2892
RaShel Anderson, prin. Fax 489-2899

**Midvale, Salt Lake, Pop. 27,166**
Canyons SD
Supt. — See Sandy
Hillcrest HS 1,600/9-12
7350 S 900 E 84047 801-826-6000
Gregory Leavitt, prin. Fax 826-6009

Midvale MS 500/6-8
7852 S Pioneer St 84047 801-826-7300
Wendy Dau, prin. Fax 826-7309

---

Kendall's Academy of Beauty Arts/Science Post-Sec.
7353 S 900 E 84047 801-561-5610

**Milford, Beaver, Pop. 1,385**
Beaver SD
Supt. — See Beaver
Milford HS 200/7-12
PO Box 159 84751 435-387-2751
David Cluff, prin. Fax 387-2494

**Moab, Grand, Pop. 4,967**
Grand SD 1,500/PK-12
264 S 400 E 84532 435-259-5317
Dr. Scott Crane, supt. Fax 259-6212
www.grandschools.org
Grand County HS 500/9-12
608 S 400 E 84532 435-259-8931
Stephen Hren, prin. Fax 259-4191
Grand County MS 200/7-8
439 S 100 E 84532 435-259-7158
Melinda Snow, prin. Fax 259-6221
Arches Education Center Adult
608 S 400 E 84532 435-719-4840
Ron Dolphin, admin.

**Monroe, Sevier, Pop. 2,221**
Sevier SD
Supt. — See Richfield
South Sevier HS 400/9-12
430 W 100 S 84754 435-527-4651
Randy Madsen, prin. Fax 527-4653
South Sevier MS 300/6-8
300 E Center St 84754 435-527-4607
Michael Willes, prin. Fax 527-4636

**Montezuma Creek, San Juan, Pop. 332**
San Juan SD
Supt. — See Blanding, UT
Whitehorse HS, PO Box 660 84534 300/7-12
Brian Dixon, prin. 435-678-1854

**Monticello, San Juan, Pop. 1,935**
San Juan SD
Supt. — See Blanding, UT
Monticello JSHS, PO Box 69 84535 300/7-12
Lewis Whitaker, prin. 435-587-2465

**Monument Valley, San Juan**
San Juan SD
Supt. — See Blanding, UT
Monument Valley JSHS 200/7-12
PO Box 360008 84536 435-678-1208
Spencer Singer, prin. Fax 678-1258

**Morgan, Morgan, Pop. 3,652**
Morgan SD 2,400/PK-12
PO Box 530 84050 801-829-3411
Dr. Doug Jacobs, supt. Fax 829-3531
www.morgansd.org
Morgan HS 700/9-12
PO Box 917 84050 801-829-3418
Wade Murdock, prin. Fax 829-6553
Morgan MS 600/6-8
PO Box 470 84050 801-829-3467
Terry Allen, prin. Fax 829-0645

**Moroni, Sanpete, Pop. 1,398**
North Sanpete SD
Supt. — See Mount Pleasant
North Sanpete MS 400/7-8
PO Box 307 84646 435-436-8206
ODee Hansen, prin. Fax 436-8208

**Mount Pleasant, Sanpete, Pop. 3,193**
North Sanpete SD 2,500/PK-12
220 E 700 S 84647 435-462-2485
Dr. Sam Ray, supt. Fax 462-2480
www.nsanpete.org
North Sanpete HS 800/9-12
390 E 700 S 84647 435-462-2452
Nan Ault, prin. Fax 462-3112
Other Schools – See Moroni

---

Wasatch Academy 300/8-12
120 S 100 W 84647 435-462-1400
Joseph Loftin, hdmstr. Fax 462-1450

**Murray, Salt Lake, Pop. 45,548**
Granite SD
Supt. — See Salt Lake City
Cottonwood SHS 1,700/10-12
5715 S 1300 E 84121 385-646-5264
Alan Parrish, prin. Fax 646-5266

Murray CSD 6,400/K-12
147 E 5065 S 84107 801-264-7400
Dr. Steven Hirase, supt. Fax 264-7456
www.murrayschools.org/
Hillcrest JHS 800/7-9
126 E 5300 S 84107 801-264-7442
Jennifer Covington, prin. Fax 264-4820
Murray SHS 1,500/10-12
5440 S State St 84107 801-264-7460
John Goldhardt, prin. Fax 264-7461
Riverview JHS 700/7-9
751 W Tripp Ln 84123 801-264-7446
Jim Bouwman, prin. Fax 264-7458

---

Cameo College of Essential Beauty Post-Sec.
124 E 5770 S 84107 801-484-6173
Eagle Gate College Post-Sec.
5588 S Green St 84123 801-333-8100
ITT Technical Institute Post-Sec.
920 W Levoy Dr 84123 801-263-3313
Mt. Vernon Academy 100/K-12
184 E Vine St 84107 801-266-5521

**Nephi, Juab, Pop. 5,328**
Juab SD 2,300/K-12
346 E 600 N 84648 435-623-1940
Rick Robins, supt. Fax 623-1941
www.juab.k12.ut.us
Juab HS 700/9-12
802 N 650 E 84648 435-623-1764
Royd Darrington, prin. Fax 623-1772
Juab JHS 400/7-8
555 E 800 N 84648 435-623-1541
Ken Rowley, prin. Fax 623-4995

**North Logan, Cache, Pop. 8,096**
Cache County SD 14,700/K-12
2063 N 1200 E 84341 435-752-3925
Dr. Steven Norton, supt. Fax 753-2168
www.ccsdut.org
Other Schools – See Hyrum, Logan, Richmond, Smithfield

**North Ogden, Weber, Pop. 17,100**
Weber SD
Supt. — See Ogden
North Ogden JHS 700/7-9
575 E 2900 N 84414 801-452-4800
Wendy Long, prin. Fax 452-4839

**Ogden, Weber, Pop. 80,717**
Ogden CSD 12,200/K-12
1950 Monroe Blvd 84401 801-737-7300
Sandy Coroles, supt. Fax 627-7654
www.ogdensd.org
Highland JHS 900/7-9
325 Gramercy Ave 84404 801-737-7700
Shannon Wilcox, prin. Fax 737-7710
Lomond HS 1,100/10-12
1080 9th St 84404 801-737-7900
Dale Wilkinson, prin. Fax 737-8510
Mound Fort JHS 800/7-9
1396 Liberty Ave 84404 801-737-7800
Rebecca Ellis, prin. Fax 625-8993
Mt. Ogden JHS 900/7-9
3260 Harrison Blvd 84403 801-737-8600
Jessica Bennington, prin. Fax 627-7641
Ogden HS 1,200/10-12
2828 Harrison Blvd 84403 801-737-8700
Stacey Briggs, prin. Fax 737-8672
Washington Alternative HS 300/Alt
455 28th St 84401 801-737-7400
Benjamin Carrier, prin. Fax 737-7405

Weber SD 30,100/K-12
5320 Adams Ave Pkwy 84405 801-476-7800
Jeff Stephens, supt. Fax 476-7893
www.wsd.net
Bell JHS 700/7-9
165 W 5100 S 84405 801-452-4600
Lenn Ward, prin. Fax 452-4639
Bonneville SHS 1,400/10-12
251 E 4800 S 84405 801-452-4050
Larry Hadley, prin. Fax 476-1837
South Ogden JHS 800/7-9
650 E 5700 S 84405 801-452-4460
Michele Parry, prin. Fax 452-4499
Two Rivers HS 200/Alt
955 W 12th St 84404 801-476-3920
Jeff Marchant, prin. Fax 476-3940
Wahlquist JHS 1,000/7-9
2656 N 2400 W 84404 801-452-4640
Sue Sweet, prin. Fax 452-4679
Weber SHS 1,800/10-12
430 W Weber High Dr 84414 801-476-3700
Velden Wardle, prin. Fax 476-3799
Other Schools – See Eden, Harrisville, North Ogden, Plain City, Roy, West Haven

---

Marinello School of Beauty Post-Sec.
3721 S 250 W 84405 801-394-5718
Nightingale College Post-Sec.
4155 Harrison Blvd Ste 100 84403 801-689-2160
Ogden-Weber Applied Technology College Post-Sec.
200 N Washington Blvd 84404 801-627-8300
St. Joseph's HS 200/9-12
1790 Lake St 84401 801-394-1515
Clay Jones, prin. Fax 394-6428
Stevens Henager College Post-Sec.
PO Box 9428 84409 801-392-1471
Utah Schools for the Deaf and the Blind Post-Sec.
742 Harrison Blvd 84404 801-629-4700
Weber State University Post-Sec.
1001 University Cir 84408 801-626-6000

**Orderville, Kane, Pop. 575**
Kane SD
Supt. — See Kanab
Valley HS 100/7-12
PO Box 128 84758 435-648-2278
Jim Wood, prin. Fax 648-2366

**Orem, Utah, Pop. 85,397**
Alpine SD
Supt. — See American Fork
Alpine Summit 50/Alt
1581 W 1000 S 84058 801-610-8183
Lynn Gerratt, dir. Fax 227-7831
Canyon View JHS 1,100/7-9
655 E 950 N 84097 801-610-8130
Wade Lott, prin. Fax 227-8706
Lakeridge JHS 1,200/7-9
951 S 400 W 84058 801-610-8134
Kathy Knudsen, prin. Fax 227-2490
Mountain View SHS 1,300/10-12
665 W Center St 84057 801-610-8160
Taran Chun, prin. Fax 227-8764
Orem JHS 900/7-9
765 N 600 W 84057 801-610-8142
Joe Jensen, prin. Fax 227-8796
Orem SHS 1,100/10-12
175 S 400 E 84097 801-610-8165
Mike Browning, prin. Fax 227-8774

Polaris HS Alt
1551 W 1000 S 84058 801-610-8180
Lori Thorn, prin. Fax 227-2447

Timpanogos SHS 1,300/10-12
1450 N 200 E 84057 801-610-8175
Theron Murphy, prin. Fax 223-3134

---

Broadview University Post-Sec.
898 N 1200 W 84057 801-822-5800

Meridian S 200/PK-12
280 S 400 E 84097 801-374-5480

Stevens Henager College Post-Sec.
1476 Sandhill Rd 84058 801-373-0285

Utah College of Dental Hygiene Post-Sec.
1176 S 1480 W 84058 801-426-8234

Utah Valley University Post-Sec.
800 W University Pkwy 84058 801-863-8000

**Panguitch, Garfield, Pop. 1,509**

Garfield SD 900/K-12
PO Box 398 84759 435-676-8821
Ben Dalton, supt. Fax 676-8266
www.garfk12.org

Panguitch HS 100/9-12
PO Box 393 84759 435-676-8805
Rod Quarnberg, prin. Fax 676-8521

Panguitch MS 100/7-8
PO Box 393 84759 435-676-8225
Rod Quarnberg, prin. Fax 676-2518

Other Schools – See Escalante, Tropic

**Park City, Summit, Pop. 7,439**

Park City SD 4,300/K-12
2700 Kearns Blvd 84060 435-645-5600
Ember Conley, supt. Fax 645-5609
www.pcschools.us

Park City Learning Center 100/Alt
2400 Kearns Blvd 84060 435-645-5626
Lyndsay Anderson, prin. Fax 645-5627

Park City SHS 1,000/10-12
1750 Kearns Blvd 84060 435-645-5650
Bob O'Connor, prin. Fax 645-5659

Treasure Mountain International S 700/8-9
2530 Kearns Blvd 84060 435-645-5640
Emily Sutherland, prin. Fax 645-5649

**Park Valley, Box Elder**

Box Elder SD
Supt. — See Brigham City

Park Valley S 50/K-10
788 Education Dr 84329 435-871-4411
Melissa Morris, lead tchr. Fax 871-4444

**Parowan, Iron, Pop. 2,772**

Iron SD
Supt. — See Cedar City

Parowan HS 400/7-12
PO Box 337 84761 435-477-3366
Roy Mathews, prin. Fax 477-3743

**Payson, Utah, Pop. 18,014**

Nebo SD
Supt. — See Spanish Fork

Mt. Nebo JHS 900/7-9
851 W 450 S 84651 801-465-6040
Kaye Isakson, prin. Fax 465-6045

Payson JHS 1,100/7-9
1025 Highway 198 84651 801-465-6015
Carl Swenson, prin. Fax 465-6023

Payson SHS 1,100/10-12
1050 S Main St 84651 801-465-6025
Ben Ford, prin. Fax 465-6067

**Plain City, Weber, Pop. 5,416**

Weber SD
Supt. — See Ogden

Fremont SHS 1,800/10-12
1900 N 4700 W 84404 801-452-4000
Rod Belnap, prin. Fax 452-4049

**Pleasant Grove, Utah, Pop. 32,692**

Alpine SD
Supt. — See American Fork

Pleasant Grove JHS 1,400/7-9
810 N 100 E 84062 801-610-8146
Brian Jolley, prin. Fax 785-8743

Pleasant Grove SHS 1,900/10-12
700 E 200 S 84062 801-610-8170
Tim Brantley, prin. Fax 785-8744

---

Llahona Preparatory Academy 200/PK-12
2464 W 450 S 84062 801-785-7850

**Price, Carbon, Pop. 8,585**

Carbon SD 3,500/K-12
251 W 400 N 84501 435-637-1732
Steve Carlsen, supt. Fax 637-9417
www.carbonschools.org

Carbon HS 600/9-12
750 E 400 N 84501 435-637-2463
Bruce Bean, prin. Fax 637-4127

Lighthouse HS 100/Alt
251 W 400 N 84501 435-637-7540
Karlene Bianco, prin. Fax 637-4019

Mont Harmon MS 500/6-8
60 W 400 N 84501 435-637-0510
Seth Allred, prin. Fax 637-6074

Other Schools – See Helper

---

Utah State University Eastern Post-Sec.
451 E 400 N 84501 435-613-5000

**Provo, Utah, Pop. 108,411**

Provo CSD 13,100/PK-12
280 W 940 N 84604 801-374-4800
Keith C. Rittel, supt. Fax 374-4808
www.provo.edu

Centennial MS 1,000/7-8
305 E 2320 N 84604 801-374-4621
Gaye Gibbs, prin. Fax 374-4626

Dixon MS 800/7-8
750 W 200 N 84601 801-374-4980
Jarod Sites, prin. Fax 374-4884

Independence HS 300/Alt
636 Independence Ave 84601 801-374-4920
L. Quisenberry-Steadman, prin. Fax 370-4614

Oak Springs S Alt
1300 E Center St 84606 801-374-4858
Dennis Meyers, prin. Fax 374-4999

Provo HS 1,600/9-12
1125 N University Ave 84604 801-373-6550
Karen Brown, prin. Fax 374-4880

Timpview HS 2,000/9-12
3570 Timpview Dr 84604 801-221-9720
Dr. Todd McKee, prin. Fax 224-4210

East Bay Post HS Adult
515 E 1860 S 84606 801-374-4874
Bryce Vellinga, admin. Fax 374-4872

Provo Adult Education Adult
243 E 2320 N 84604 801-374-4840
Anita Craven, coord. Fax 374-4816

---

AmeriTech College Post-Sec.
2035 N 550 W 84604 801-377-2900

Brigham Young University 84602 Post-Sec.
801-422-4636

Dallas Roberts Academy of Hair Design Post-Sec.
1700 N State St Ste 18 84604 801-375-1501

Provo College Post-Sec.
1450 W 820 N 84601 801-818-8900

Rocky Mountain Univ of Health Profession Post-Sec.
561 E 1860 S 84606 801-375-5125

Utah Valley Regional Medical Center Post-Sec.
1034 N 500 W 84604 801-373-7850

Von Curtis Academy of Hair Design Post-Sec.
480 N 900 E 84606 801-374-5111

**Randolph, Rich, Pop. 458**

Rich SD 500/K-12
PO Box 67 84064 435-793-2135
Dale Lamborn, supt. Fax 793-2136
www.richschool.org

Rich HS 100/9-12
PO Box 278 84064 435-793-2365
Rick Larsen, prin. Fax 793-2375

Other Schools – See Laketown

**Richfield, Sevier, Pop. 7,458**

Sevier SD 4,700/PK-12
180 E 600 N 84701 435-896-8214
Cade Douglas, supt. Fax 896-8804
www.seviersd.org

Cedar Ridge HS 100/Alt
555 W 100 N 84701 435-896-9464
George Chappell, prin. Fax 896-9475

Red Hills MS 500/6-8
400 S 600 W 84701 435-896-6421
Selena Terry, prin. Fax 896-6423

Richfield HS 600/9-12
495 W Center 84701 435-896-8247
Brent Gubler, prin. Fax 896-8246

Other Schools – See Monroe, Salina

**Richmond, Cache, Pop. 2,447**

Cache County SD
Supt. — See North Logan

North Cache JHS 1,100/8-9
157 W 600 S 84333 435-258-2452
Terry Williams, prin. Fax 258-5437

**Riverton, Salt Lake, Pop. 37,974**

Jordan SD
Supt. — See West Jordan

Jordan Academy for Technology & Careers Vo/Tech
12723 S Park Ave 84065 801-412-1300
Nicole Plenert, admin.

Oquirrh Hills MS 1,200/7-9
12949 S 2700 W 84065 801-412-2350
Michael Glenn, prin. Fax 412-2370

Riverton HS 2,000/10-12
12476 S 2700 W 84065 801-256-5800
Carolyn Gough, prin. Fax 256-5880

South Hills MS 1,100/7-9
13508 S 4000 W 84065 801-412-2400
Ben Jameson, prin. Fax 412-2430

**Roosevelt, Duchesne, Pop. 5,853**

Duchesne SD
Supt. — See Duchesne

Roosevelt JHS 700/6-8
350 W 200 S 84066 435-725-4585
Mike Ross, prin. Fax 725-4622

Union HS 800/9-12
135 N Union St Ste 124-3 84066 435-725-4525
Rick Nielsen, prin. Fax 725-4576

---

Uintah Basin Applied Technology College Post-Sec.
1100 E Lagoon St 84066 435-722-6900

**Roy, Weber, Pop. 35,969**

Weber SD
Supt. — See Ogden

Roy JHS 900/7-9
5400 S 2100 W 84067 801-476-5260
Kirt Swalberg, prin. Fax 476-5299

Roy SHS 1,600/10-12
2150 W 4800 S 84067 801-476-3600
Gina Butters, prin. Fax 476-3699

Sand Ridge JHS 800/7-9
2075 W 4600 S 84067 801-476-5320
Scott Elliot, prin. Fax 476-5359

**Saint George, Washington, Pop. 70,848**

Washington County SD 24,900/PK-12
121 W Tabernacle St 84770 435-673-3553
Larry Bergeson, supt. Fax 673-3216
www.washk12.org

Desert Hills HS 1,000/10-12
828 Desert Hills Dr 84790 435-674-0885
Rusty Taylor, prin. Fax 674-2606

Desert Hills MS 800/8-9
936 Desert Hills Dr 84790 435-628-0001
Brian Stevenson, prin. Fax 674-6477

Dixie HS 1,000/10-12
350 E 700 S 84770 435-673-4682
Sharla Campbell, prin. Fax 673-2384

Dixie MS 700/7-9
825 S 100 E 84770 435-628-0441
Tim Lowe, prin. Fax 674-6467

Millcreek HS 200/10-12
2410 E Riverside Dr 84790 435-628-2462
Russell Holmes, prin. Fax 628-8206

Pine View HS 1,000/10-12
2850 E 750 N 84790 435-628-5255
Mike Mees, prin. Fax 628-0327

Pine View MS 800/8-9
2145 E 130 N 84790 435-628-7915
Mike Stephenson, prin. Fax 634-0470

Snow Canyon HS 1,000/10-12
1385 Lava Flow Dr 84770 435-634-1967
Warren Brooks, prin. Fax 634-1130

Snow Canyon MS 900/8-9
1215 Lava Flow Dr 84770 435-674-6474
Brad Bench, prin. Fax 628-3289

Other Schools – See Enterprise, Hildale, Hurricane

---

Dixie Applied Technology College Post-Sec.
1506 S Silicon Way 84770 435-674-8400

Dixie State College of Utah Post-Sec.
225 S 700 E 84770 435-652-7500

Evan's Hairstyling College Post-Sec.
955 E Tabernacle St 84770 435-673-6128

Hairitage Hair Academy Post-Sec.
900 S Bluff St Ste 9 84770 435-673-5233

Stevens-Henager College Post-Sec.
720 S River Rd Ste C130 84790 435-628-9150

**Salem, Utah, Pop. 6,343**

Nebo SD
Supt. — See Spanish Fork

Salem Hills SHS 1,100/10-12
150 Skyhawk Blvd 84653 801-423-3200
Bart Peery, prin. Fax 423-3206

Salem JHS 7-9
598 N Main St 84653 801-423-6550
Robert Fleming, prin. Fax 423-6558

**Salina, Sevier, Pop. 2,467**

Sevier SD
Supt. — See Richfield

North Sevier HS 300/9-12
350 W 400 N 84654 435-529-3717
Jade Shepherd, prin. Fax 529-7910

North Sevier MS 200/6-8
135 N 100 W 84654 435-529-3841
Rod Hinck, prin. Fax 529-7377

**Salt Lake City, Salt Lake, Pop. 178,350**

Granite SD 65,600/PK-12
2500 S State St 84115 385-646-5000
Dr. Martin Bates, supt. Fax 646-4207
www.graniteschools.org

Churchill JHS 600/7-9
3450 E Oakview Dr 84124 385-646-5144
Terri Roylance, prin. Fax 646-5147

Evergreen JHS 800/7-9
3401 S 2000 E 84109 385-646-5164
Wesley Cutler, prin. Fax 646-5165

Granite Park JHS 800/7-9
3031 S 200 E 84115 385-646-5174
Daniel Stirland, prin. Fax 646-5175

Granite Peaks Alternative HS 300/Alt
501 E 3900 S 84107 385-646-4666
Rick Anthony, dir. Fax 646-4667

Granite Technical Institute Vo/Tech
2500 S State St 84115 385-646-4350
Devon Hartley, prin. Fax 646-4347

Olympus SHS 1,500/10-12
4055 S 2300 E 84124 385-646-5400
Steve Perschon, prin. Fax 646-5405

Skyline SHS 1,400/10-12
3251 E 3760 S 84109 385-646-5420
Doug Bingham, prin. Fax 646-5422

Wasatch JHS 900/7-9
3750 S 3100 E 84109 385-646-5244
John Anderson, prin. Fax 646-5246

Other Schools – See Holladay, Kearns, Magna, Murray, Taylorsville, West Valley

Salt Lake City SD 25,200/PK-12
440 E 100 S 84111 801-578-8599
Dr. McKell Withers, supt. Fax 578-8248
www.slcschools.org

Bryant MS 500/7-8
40 S 800 E 84102 801-578-8118
James Yapias, prin. Fax 578-8125

Clayton MS 600/7-8
1470 S 1900 E 84108 801-481-4810
Linda Richins, prin. Fax 481-4884

East HS 2,000/9-12
840 S 1300 E 84102 801-583-1661
Greg Maughan, prin. Fax 584-2927

Glendale MS 800/6-8
1430 W Andrew Ave 84104 801-974-8319
Chris Gesteland, prin. Fax 974-8356

Highland HS 1,600/9-12
2166 S 1700 E 84106 801-484-4343
Chris Jensen, prin. Fax 481-4893

Hillside MS 500/7-8
1825 S Nevada St 84108 801-481-4828
Jane Bernston, prin. Fax 481-4831

Horizonte Instruction & Training Center 600/Alt
1234 S Main St 84101 801-578-8574
Mindi Holmdahl, prin. Fax 578-8577

Innovations Early College HS 9-12
1633 S Edison St 84115 801-481-4946
Kenneth Grover, prin. Fax 584-2927

Northwest MS 700/7-8
1730 W 1700 N 84116 801-578-8547
Rachel Nance, prin. Fax 578-8558

West HS 2,400/9-12
241 N 300 W 84103 801-578-8500
Paul Sagers, prin. Fax 578-8516

---

Broadview Entertainment Arts University Post-Sec.
240 Morris Ave 84115 801-300-4300
Fortis College Post-Sec.
3949 S 700 E Ste 150 84107 801-713-0915
Independence University Post-Sec.
4021 S 700 E Ste 400 84107 800-972-5149
Intermountain Christian S 300/PK-12
6515 S Lion Ln 84121 801-365-0370
Mitch Menning, head sch Fax 942-8813
Judge Memorial Catholic HS 700/9-12
650 S 1100 E 84102 801-363-8895
Patrick Lambert, prin. Fax 521-3920
Kendall's Academy of Beauty Arts/Science Post-Sec.
2230 S 700 E 84106 801-486-0101
Latter Day Saints Business College Post-Sec.
95 N 300 W Fl 8th 84101 801-524-8100
Midwives College of Utah Post-Sec.
1174 E Graystone Way Ste 2 84106 801-649-5230
Myotherapy College of Utah Post-Sec.
336 Bugatti Dr 84115 801-484-7624
Neumont University Post-Sec.
143 S Main St 84111 888-638-6668
Realms of Inquiry S 50/6-12
4998 S Galleria Dr 84123 801-467-5911
Rowland Hall HS 300/9-12
843 S Lincoln St 84102 801-355-7494
Alan Sparrow, head sch Fax 355-0474
Rowland Hall MS 200/6-8
970 E 800 S 84102 801-355-0272
Alan Sparrow, head sch Fax 355-0474
Salt Lake Community College Post-Sec.
4600 S Redwood Rd 84123 801-957-4111
Skin Works School of Advanced Skin Care Post-Sec.
2121 Nowell Cir 84115 801-530-0001
Stevens Henager College Post-Sec.
383 W Vine St 84123 801-531-1180
University of Utah Post-Sec.
201 S 1460 E 84112 801-581-7200
Veterans Affairs Medical Center Post-Sec.
500 Foothill Dr 84148 801-582-1565
Western Governors University Post-Sec.
4001 S 700 E Ste 700 84107 801-274-3280
Westminster College Post-Sec.
1840 S 1300 E 84105 801-484-7651

**Sandy, Salt Lake, Pop. 85,199**
Canyons SD 27,500/K-12
9150 S 500 W 84070 801-826-5000
Dr. James Briscoe, supt. Fax 826-5053
www.canyonsdistrict.org
Albion MS 500/6-8
2755 E Newcastle Dr 84093 801-826-6700
Darrell Jensen, prin. Fax 826-6709
Alta HS 2,500/9-12
11055 S 1000 E 84094 801-826-5600
Brian McGill, prin. Fax 826-5609
CTEC Vo/Tech
825 E 9085 S 84094 801-826-6600
Ken Spurlock, prin. Fax 826-6609
Eastmont MS 600/6-8
10100 S 1300 E 84094 801-826-7000
Stacy Kurtzhals, prin. Fax 826-7009
Indian Hills MS 800/6-8
1180 E Sanders Rd 84094 801-826-7100
Doug Graham, prin. Fax 826-7109
Jordan HS 1,700/9-12
95 E Beetdigger Blvd 84070 801-826-6200
Tom Sherwood, prin. Fax 826-6209
Mt. Jordan MS 700/6-8
9351 S Mountaineer Ln 84070 801-826-7400
Molly Hart, prin. Fax 826-7409
Union MS 900/6-8
615 E 8000 S 84070 801-826-7500
Kelly Tauteoli, prin. Fax 826-7509
Entrada HS Adult
825 E 9085 S 84094 801-826-6670
Amy Boettger, dir. Fax 826-6679
Other Schools – See Cottonwood Heights, Draper, Midvale

---

DeVry University Post-Sec.
9350 S 150 E Ste 420 84070 801-565-5110
Francois D. Hair Design Academy Post-Sec.
11339 S 700 E 84070 801-561-2244
Waterford S 900/PK-12
1480 E 9400 S 84093 801-816-2201
Brandon Bennett Ph.D., head sch Fax 523-6229

**Saratoga Sprngs, Utah, Pop. 17,223**
Alpine SD
Supt. — See American Fork
Vista Heights MS 1,500/7-9
484 W Pony Express Pkwy, 801-610-8770
Dr. Steve Stewart, prin. Fax 768-4226
Westlake HS 2,200/9-12
99 N 200 W, 801-610-8815
Gary Twitchell, prin. Fax 768-1068

**Smithfield, Cache, Pop. 9,375**
Cache County SD
Supt. — See North Logan
Sky View SHS 1,600/10-12
520 S 250 E 84335 435-563-6273
Dave Swenson, prin. Fax 563-9534

**South Jordan, Salt Lake, Pop. 49,075**
Jordan SD
Supt. — See West Jordan
Bingham HS 2,400/10-12
2160 W 10400 S 84095 801-256-5100
Christen Richards-Khong, prin. Fax 256-5151
Elk Ridge MS 1,400/7-9
3659 W 9800 S 84095 801-412-2800
Wyatt Bentley, prin. Fax 412-2830
South Jordan MS 1,600/7-9
10245 S 2700 W 84095 801-412-2900
Shawn McLeod, prin. Fax 412-2930
Valley HS 500/Alt
325 W 11000 S 84095 801-572-7035
Sharon Jensen, prin. Fax 572-7038

---

American Heritage of South Jordan 300/K-12
11100 S Redwood Rd 84095 801-254-3882

**Spanish Fork, Utah, Pop. 33,849**
Nebo SD 29,100/PK-12
350 S Main St 84660 801-354-7400
Rick Nielsen, supt. Fax 798-4010
www.nebo.edu
Diamond Fork JHS 1,400/7-9
50 N 900 E 84660 801-798-4052
Troy Peterson, prin. Fax 798-4098
Landmark/Cornerstone HS 300/Alt
612 S Main St 84660 801-798-4030
Lynn Mecham, prin. Fax 798-4044
Maple Mountain SHS 1,200/10-12
51 N 2550 E 84660 801-794-6740
John Penrod, prin. Fax 794-6744
Spanish Fork JHS 1,200/7-9
600 S 820 E 84660 801-798-4075
Dwight Liddiard, prin. Fax 798-4097
Spanish Fork SHS 1,100/10-12
99 N 300 W 84660 801-798-4060
David McKee, prin. Fax 798-4004
Other Schools – See Mapleton, Payson, Salem, Springville

**Springville, Utah, Pop. 28,786**
Nebo SD
Supt. — See Spanish Fork
Legacy S 50/Alt
165 S 700 E 84663 801-489-2840
Susan Boothe, prin. Fax 489-2808
Springville JHS 900/7-9
189 S 1470 E 84663 801-489-2880
Ryan McGuire, prin. Fax 489-2838
Springville SHS 1,200/10-12
1205 E 900 S 84663 801-489-2870
Everett Kelepolo, prin. Fax 489-2806

**Stansbury Park, Tooele, Pop. 5,041**
Tooele County SD
Supt. — See Tooele
Stansbury HS 50/9-12
5300 N Aberdeen Ln 84074 435-882-2479
Gailynn Warr, prin. Fax 882-4049

**Sunset, Davis, Pop. 4,981**
Davis SD
Supt. — See Farmington
Sunset JHS 900/7-9
1610 N 250 W 84015 801-402-6700
Jonathan Gochberg, prin. Fax 402-6701

**Syracuse, Davis, Pop. 23,777**
Davis SD
Supt. — See Farmington
Syracuse JHS 1,100/7-9
1450 S 2000 W 84075 801-402-6800
Chris Keime, prin. Fax 402-6801
Syracuse SHS 2,000/10-12
665 S 2000 W 84075 801-402-7900
Wendy Nelson, prin. Fax 402-7901

**Tabiona, Duchesne, Pop. 166**
Duchesne SD
Supt. — See Duchesne
Tabiona HS 100/7-12
PO Box 470 84072 435-738-1320
Darrin Jenkins, prin. Fax 738-1332

**Taylorsville, Salt Lake, Pop. 56,089**
Granite SD
Supt. — See Salt Lake City
Bennion JHS 1,000/7-9
6055 S 2700 W, 385-646-5114
Rod Horton, prin. Fax 646-5115
Eisenhower JHS 1,000/7-9
4351 S Redwood Rd 84123 385-646-5154
Mark Ellermeier, prin. Fax 646-5158
Hartvigsen S 200/Alt
1510 W 5400 S 84123 385-646-4585
Janice Wayman, prin. Fax 646-4256
Taylorsville SHS 1,800/10-12
5225 S Redwood Rd 84123 385-646-5455
Dr. Garett Muse, prin. Fax 646-5457

**Tooele, Tooele, Pop. 30,935**
Tooele County SD 10,800/K-12
92 Lodestone Way 84074 435-833-1900
Scott Rogers, supt. Fax 833-1912
tooeleschools.org/SitePages/Home.aspx
Blue Peak HS 100/Alt
211 Tooele Blvd 84074 435-833-8700
Bryce Eardley, prin. Fax 833-8785
Johnsen JHS 800/7-8
2152 N 400 W 84074 435-833-1939
Jared Small, prin. Fax 843-3816
Tooele HS 2,000/9-12
301 W Vine St 84074 435-833-1978
Jeff Hamm, prin. Fax 833-1984
Tooele JHS 800/7-8
411 W Vine St 84074 435-833-1921
Bill Gochis, prin. Fax 833-1923
Other Schools – See Dugway, Grantsville, Stansbury Park, Wendover

---

Tooele Applied Technology College Post-Sec.
66 W Vine St 84074 435-248-1800

**Tropic, Garfield, Pop. 524**
Garfield SD
Supt. — See Panguitch
Bryce Valley HS 100/7-12
PO Box 70 84776 435-679-8835
Jeff Brinkerhoff, prin. Fax 679-8539

**Trout Creek, Tooele**
Tintic SD
Supt. — See Eureka
West Desert JSHS 50/7-12
440 Pony Express Rd 84083 435-693-3112
Tony White, head sch Fax 693-3109

**Vernal, Uintah, Pop. 8,901**
Uintah SD 7,000/PK-12
635 W 200 S 84078 435-781-3100
Mark Dockins Ed.D., supt. Fax 781-3107
www.uintah.net/
Uintah HS 1,100/9-12
1880 W 500 N 84078 435-781-3110
Julie Wilde, prin. Fax 781-3117
Uintah MS 1,000/6-8
161 N 1000 W 84078 435-781-3130
Kathleen Hawkins, prin. Fax 781-3134
Vernal MS 900/6-8
721 W 100 S 84078 435-781-3140
Mistalyn Leis, prin. Fax 781-3143
Ashley Valley Education Center Adult
559 N 1700 W 84078 435-781-4675
Andrea McKea, admin. Fax 781-4679

**Wendover, Tooele, Pop. 1,381**
Tooele County SD
Supt. — See Tooele
Wendover JSHS 200/7-12
PO Box 610 84083 435-665-2343
Clint Spindler, prin. Fax 665-7706

**West Haven, Weber, Pop. 10,042**
Weber SD
Supt. — See Ogden
Rocky Mountain JHS 1,000/7-9
4350 W 4800 S 84401 801-476-5220
Nicole Meibos, prin. Fax 476-5259

**West Jordan, Salt Lake, Pop. 99,828**
Jordan SD 47,800/K-12
7387 S Campus View Dr 84084 801-567-8100
Dr. Patrice Johnson, supt. Fax 567-8064
www.jordandistrict.org
Copper Hills HS 2,400/10-12
5445 W New Bingham Hwy, 801-256-5300
Todd Quarnberg, prin. Fax 256-5393
Jensen MS 800/7-9
8105 S 3200 W 84088 801-412-2850
Bryan Leggat, prin. Fax 412-2875
Jordan Academy for Technology & Careers Vo/Tech
9301 S Wights Fort Rd 84088 801-256-5900
Chris Titus, prin. Fax 256-5930
Sunset Ridge MS 1,400/7-9
8292 S Skyline Arch Dr, 801-412-2475
Larry Urry, prin. Fax 412-2490
West Hills MS 1,300/7-9
8270 S Grizzly Way, 801-412-2300
Stacy Evans, prin. Fax 412-2327
West Jordan HS 1,800/10-12
8136 S 2700 W 84088 801-256-5600
Michael Kochevar, prin. Fax 256-5670
West Jordan MS 1,000/7-9
7550 S Redwood Rd 84084 801-412-2100
Dixie Crowther, prin. Fax 412-2140
Southpointe Adult HS Adult
9301 S Wights Fort Rd 84088 801-256-5954
Allen Arko, coord. Fax 256-5955
Other Schools – See Herriman, Riverton, South Jordan

---

Broadview University Post-Sec.
1902 W 7800 S 84088 801-304-4224

**West Point, Davis, Pop. 9,305**
Davis SD
Supt. — See Farmington
West Point JHS 1,200/7-9
2775 W 550 N 84015 801-402-8100
Jed Johansen, prin. Fax 402-8101

**West Valley, Salt Lake, Pop. 122,084**
Granite SD
Supt. — See Salt Lake City
Granger SHS 1,700/10-12
3580 S 3600 W 84119 385-646-5320
Dr. David Dunn, prin. Fax 646-5322
Hunter JHS 1,100/7-9
6131 W Wending Ln 84128 385-646-5184
Doug Wagstaff, prin. Fax 646-5185
Hunter SHS 2,100/10-12
4200 S 5600 W 84120 385-646-5360
Craig Stauffer, prin. Fax 646-5495
Kennedy JHS 1,000/7-9
4495 S 4800 W 84120 385-646-5214
Mary Anne Stevens, prin. Fax 646-5215
Valley JHS 900/7-9
4195 S 3200 W 84119 385-646-5234
David Holt, prin. Fax 646-5235
West Lake JHS 1,100/7-9
3400 S 3450 W 84119 385-646-5254
Ike Spencer, prin. Fax 646-5259

---

Everest College Post-Sec.
3280 W 3500 S 84119 801-840-4800
Premier Hair Academy Post-Sec.
4062 S 4000 W 84120 801-966-8414

**Woods Cross, Davis, Pop. 9,426**
Davis SD
Supt. — See Farmington
Woods Cross SHS 1,300/10-12
600 W 2200 S 84010 801-402-4500
John Haning, prin. Fax 402-4501

---

Benchmark S 100/8-12
592 W 1350 S 84010 801-299-5300

# VERMONT

## VERMONT DEPARTMENT OF EDUCATION
**120 State St, Montpelier 05620-0002**
**Telephone 802-828-3135**
**Fax 802-828-3140**
**Website http://www.state.vt.us/educ/**

Commissioner of Education Armando Vilaseca

## VERMONT BOARD OF EDUCATION
**120 State St, Montpelier 05620-0002**

Chairperson Stephan Morse

## PUBLIC, PRIVATE AND CATHOLIC SECONDARY SCHOOLS

**Arlington, Bennington, Pop. 1,195**
Battenkill Valley Supervisory Union 300/K-12
530A E Arlington Rd 05250 802-375-9744
Judith Pullinen, supt. Fax 375-2368
www.bvsu.org
Arlington Memorial HS 200/6-12
529 E Arlington Rd 05250 802-375-2589
Christopher Barnes, prin. Fax 375-1547

**Barre, Washington, Pop. 8,882**
Barre Supervisory Union 2,500/PK-12
120 Ayers St 05641 802-476-5011
John Pandolfo, supt. Fax 476-4944
www.bsuvt.org/
Spaulding HS 700/9-12
155 Ayers St 05641 802-476-4811
Tom Sedore, prin. Fax 479-4535

VT Technical Centers
Supt. — None
Barre Technical Center Vo/Tech
155 Ayers St 05641 802-476-6237
Penny Chamberlin, prin. Fax 476-4045

---

Central Vermont Academy 50/K-12
317 Vine St 05641 802-479-0868

**Barton, Orleans, Pop. 727**
Orleans Central Supervisory Union 1,100/PK-12
130 Kinsey Rd 05822 802-525-1204
Donald Van Nostrand, supt. Fax 525-1276
www.ocsu.org
Other Schools – See Orleans

**Bellows Falls, Windham, Pop. 3,056**
Windham Northeast Supervisory Union 1,200/K-12
25 Cherry St 05101 802-463-9958
Christopher Kibbe, supt. Fax 463-9705
www.wnesu.org
Bellows Falls MS 300/5-8
15 School St 05101 802-463-4366
Karen Bukowski, prin. Fax 463-9738
Bellows Falls Union HS 300/9-12
PO Box 429 05101 802-463-3944
Christopher Hodsden, prin. Fax 463-9322

**Bennington, Bennington, Pop. 8,960**
Southwest Vermont Supervisory Union 3,000/K-12
246 S Stream Rd 05201 802-447-7501
James Culkeen, supt. Fax 447-0475
www.svsu.org
Mt. Anthony Union HS 1,000/9-12
301 Park St 05201 802-447-7511
Suzanne Maguire, prin. Fax 442-1260
Mt. Anthony Union MS 600/6-8
747 East Rd 05201 802-447-7541
Tim Payne, prin. Fax 442-1262

VT Technical Centers
Supt. — None
SW VT Career Development Center Vo/Tech
321 Park St 05201 802-447-0220
Fax 442-1745

---

Bennington College Post-Sec.
1 College Dr 05201 802-442-5401
Grace Christian S 200/PK-12
104 Kocher Dr 05201 802-447-2233
Joyce Lloyd, admin. Fax 442-8403
Southern Vermont College Post-Sec.
982 Mansion Dr 05201 802-447-4000

**Bethel, Windsor, Pop. 558**
Windsor Northwest Supervisory Union 500/PK-12
PO Box 395 05032 802-234-0264
Meg Powden, supt. Fax 234-0261
www.wnwsu.org/
Whitcomb JSHS 100/7-12
273 Pleasant St 05032 802-234-9966
Owen Bradley, prin. Fax 234-5779
Other Schools – See Rochester

**Bradford, Orange, Pop. 774**
Orange East Supervisory Union 1,100/K-12
530 Waits River Rd 05033 802-222-5216
Beth Cobb, supt. Fax 222-4451
www.oesu.org

Oxbow HS 400/7-12
36 Oxbow Dr 05033 802-222-5214
Doug Harris, prin. Fax 222-5847

VT Technical Centers
Supt. — None
River Bend Career & Tech Center Vo/Tech
PO Box 618 05033 802-222-5212
Robert St. Pierre, admin. Fax 222-4621

**Brandon, Rutland, Pop. 1,631**
Rutland Northeast Supervisory Union 1,600/PK-12
49 Court Dr 05733 802-247-5757
Jeanne Collins, supt. Fax 247-5548
www.rnesu.org
Otter Valley Union JSHS 600/7-12
2997 Franklin St 05733 802-247-6833
James Avery, prin. Fax 247-4627

**Brattleboro, Windham, Pop. 7,206**
VT Technical Centers
Supt. — None
Windham Regional Career Center Vo/Tech
45 Career Cir 05301 802-451-3900
Michael Burnett, dir. Fax 451-3933

Windham Southeast Supervisory Union 2,500/K-12
53 Green St 05301 802-254-3730
Ron Stahley, supt. Fax 254-3733
www.wssu.k12.vt.us
Brattleboro Area MS 300/7-8
109 Sunny Acres St 05301 802-451-3500
Keith Lyman, prin. Fax 451-3502
Brattleboro Union HS 900/9-12
131 Fairground Rd 05301 802-451-3400
Steve Perrin, prin. Fax 451-3935

---

Austine School for the Deaf Post-Sec.
60 Austine Dr 05301 802-258-9522
SIT Post-Sec.
PO Box 676 05302 802-257-7751
The William Center Post-Sec.
209 Austine Dr 05301 802-258-9537
Union Institute & University Post-Sec.
3 University Way Ste 3 05301 800-871-8165

**Bristol, Addison, Pop. 1,992**
Addison Northeast Supervisory Union 1,600/PK-12
72 Munsill Ave Ste 601 05443 802-453-3657
David Adams, supt. Fax 453-2029
www.anesu.org
Mt. Abraham Union MSHS 28 800/7-12
220 Airport Dr 05443 802-453-2333
Carol Fenimore, prin. Fax 453-4359

**Burlington, Chittenden, Pop. 41,355**
Burlington SD 3,700/PK-12
150 Colchester Ave 05401 802-865-5332
Howard W. Smith, supt. Fax 864-8501
www.bsdvt.org/
Burlington HS 1,000/9-12
52 Institute Rd, 802-864-8411
Amy Mellencamp, prin. Fax 864-8408
Edmunds MS 400/6-8
275 Main St 05401 802-864-8486
Bonnie Johnson-Aten, prin. Fax 864-2218
Horizon S Alt
14 S Williams St 05401 802-864-8496
Lynn Kennedy, dir. Fax 864-2213
Hunt MS 400/6-8
1364 North Ave, 802-864-8469
Len Phelan, prin. Fax 864-8467

VT Technical Centers
Supt. — None
Burlington Technical Center Vo/Tech
52 Institute Rd, 802-864-8426
Mark Aliquo, dir. Fax 864-8521

---

Burlington College Post-Sec.
351 North Ave 05401 802-862-9616
Champlain College Post-Sec.
PO Box 670 05402 802-860-2700
Fletcher Allen Health Care Post-Sec.
111 Colchester Ave 05401 802-847-5133

Rock Point S 50/9-12
1 Rock Point Rd, 802-863-1104
C.J. Spirito, head sch Fax 863-6628
University of Vermont Post-Sec.
194 S Prospect St 05401 802-656-3131

**Cabot, Washington, Pop. 226**
Washington NE Supervisory Union
Supt. — See Plainfield
Cabot S 200/PK-12
PO Box 98 05647 802-563-2289
David Schilling, prin. Fax 563-2022

**Canaan, Essex, Pop. 390**
Essex North Supervisory Union 200/PK-12
PO Box 100 05903 802-266-3330
Christopher Masson, supt. Fax 266-7085
www.essexnorth.org
Canaan S 200/PK-12
99 School St 05903 802-266-8910
Deborah Lynch, prin. Fax 266-7068

**Castleton, Rutland, Pop. 1,470**
Addison-Rutland Supervisory Union
Supt. — See Fair Haven
Castleton Village S 100/6-8
PO Box 68 05735 802-468-2203
Linda Peltier, prin. Fax 468-5131

---

Castleton State College Post-Sec.
86 Seminary St 05735 802-468-5611

**Chelsea, Orange**
Orange-Windsor Supervisory Union
Supt. — See South Royalton
Chelsea S 200/K-12
6 School St 05038 802-685-4551
Mark Blount, prin. Fax 685-3310

**Chester, Windsor, Pop. 997**
Two Rivers Supervisory Union
Supt. — See Ludlow
Green Mountain Union MSHS 400/7-12
716 VT Route 103 S 05143 802-875-2146
Thomas Ferenc, prin. Fax 875-3183

**Colchester, Chittenden**
Colchester SD 2,100/PK-12
PO Box 27 05446 802-264-5999
Larry Waters, supt. Fax 863-4774
www.csdvt.org
Colchester HS 700/9-12
PO Box 900 05446 802-264-5700
Amy Minor, prin. Fax 264-5757
Colchester MS 500/6-8
PO Box 30 05446 802-264-5800
Michele Cote, prin. Fax 264-5858

---

St. Michael's College Post-Sec.
1 Winooski Park 05439 802-654-2000

**Concord, Essex, Pop. 268**
Essex-Caledonia Supervisory Union 500/PK-8
PO Box 255 05824 802-695-3373
Brian Rayburn, supt. Fax 695-1334
ecsuvt.org.p9.hostingprod.com
Other Schools – See Gilman

**Craftsbury Common, Orleans**
Orleans Southwest Supervisory Union
Supt. — See Hardwick
Craftsbury S 200/K-12
PO Box 73 05827 802-586-2541
Merri Greenia, prin. Fax 586-7524

---

Sterling College Post-Sec.
PO Box 72 05827 802-586-7711

**Danville, Caledonia, Pop. 378**
Caledonia Central Supervisory Union 600/PK-12
PO Box 216 05828 802-684-3801
Dr. Mathew Forest, supt. Fax 684-1190
www.ccsuonline.org
Danville S 300/PK-12
148 Peacham Rd 05828 802-684-3651
Kerin Hoffman, prin. Fax 684-1192

**Derby, Orleans, Pop. 595**
North Country Supervisory Union
Supt. — See Newport
North Country Union JHS 300/7-8
57 Jr High Dr 05829 802-766-2276
Nicole Corbett, prin. Fax 766-2287

**Dorset, Bennington, Pop. 249**

Long Trail S 200/6-12
1045 Kirby Hollow Rd 05251 802-867-5717
Steven Dear, head sch Fax 867-4525

**Duxbury, See Waterbury**
Washington West Supervisory Union
Supt. — See Waitsfield
Crossett Brook MS 300/5-8
5672 VT Route 100 05676 802-244-6100
Tom Drake, prin. Fax 244-6899

**East Burke, Caledonia, Pop. 132**

Burke Mountain Academy 50/9-12
PO Box 78 05832 802-626-5607

**Enosburg Falls, Franklin, Pop. 1,309**
Franklin Northeast Supervisory Union
Supt. — See Richford
Enosburg Falls HS 300/9-12
PO Box 417 05450 802-933-7777
Erik Remmers, prin. Fax 933-5375
Enosburg Falls MS 100/6-8
PO Box 417 05450 802-933-7777
Rachel Reynolds, prin. Fax 933-5013

VT Technical Centers
Supt. — None
Cold Hollow Career Center Vo/Tech
PO Box 530 05450 802-933-4003
Nathan Demar, dir. Fax 933-2431

**Essex Junction, Chittenden, Pop. 9,092**
Chittenden Central Supervisory Union 2,600/PK-12
51 Park St 05452 802-879-5579
Judith DeNova, supt. Fax 878-1370
www.ccsuvt.org
Essex HS 1,300/9-12
2 Educational Dr 05452 802-879-7121
Robert Reardon, prin. Fax 879-5503
Lawton MS 300/6-8
104 Maple St 05452 802-878-1388
Laurie Singer, prin. Fax 879-8175

Essex Town SD 1,300/PK-8
58 Founders Rd 05452 802-878-8168
Mark Andrews, supt. Fax 878-5190
www.etsdvt.org
Essex MS 400/6-8
60 Founders Rd 05452 802-879-7173
Kevin Briggs, prin. Fax 879-1363

VT Technical Centers
Supt. — None
Essex Technical Center Vo/Tech
2 Educational Dr Ste 200 05452 802-879-5558
Robert Travers, dir. Fax 879-5593

**Fairfax, Franklin**
Franklin West Supervisory Union 1,300/PK-12
4497 Highbridge Rd 05454 802-370-3113
Ned Kirsch, supt. Fax 370-3115
www.fwsu.org
Bellows Free Academy Fairfaz 600/PK-12
75 Hunt St 05454 802-849-6711
Thomas Walsh, prin. Fax 849-2611

**Fair Haven, Rutland, Pop. 2,236**
Addison-Rutland Supervisory Union 1,400/PK-12
49 Main St 05743 802-265-4905
Ronald Ryan, supt. Fax 265-2158
www.arsu.org
Fair Haven Union HS 400/9-12
33 Mechanic St 05743 802-265-4966
Brett Blanchard, prin. Fax 265-3602
Other Schools – See Castleton

**Gilman, Essex**
Essex-Caledonia Supervisory Union
Supt. — See Concord
Gilman MS 50/5-8
PO Box 97 05904 802-892-5969
Nancy Croteau, prin. Fax 892-9045

**Hardwick, Caledonia, Pop. 1,309**
Orleans Southwest Supervisory Union 1,000/K-12
PO Box 338 05843 802-472-6531
Joanne LeBlanc, supt. Fax 472-6250
www.ossu.org/
Hazen Union JSHS 400/7-12
PO Box 368 05843 802-472-6511
Mike Moriarty, prin. Fax 472-3327
Other Schools – See Craftsbury Common

**Hinesburg, Chittenden, Pop. 642**
Chittenden South Supervisory Union
Supt. — See Shelburne
Champlain Valley Union HS 15 1,300/9-12
369 CVU Rd 05461 802-482-7100
Jeff Evans, prin. Fax 482-7108

**Hyde Park, Lamoille, Pop. 449**
Lamoille North Supervisory Union 1,900/PK-12
95 Cricket Hill Rd 05655 802-888-3142
Dr. Edith Beatty, supt. Fax 888-7908
lnsu.cloudaccess.net
Lamoille Union HS 600/9-12
736 VT 15 W 05655 802-888-4261
Brian Schaffer, prin. Fax 888-2997
Lamoille Union MS 300/7-8
736 VT 15 W 05655 802-851-1300
Wendy Savery, prin. Fax 851-1397

VT Technical Centers
Supt. — None
Green Mountain Technology & Career Ctr Vo/Tech
PO Box 600 05655 802-888-4447
Joe Teegarden, dir. Fax 888-7368

**Jericho, Chittenden, Pop. 1,303**
Chittenden East Supervisory Union
Supt. — See Richmond
Browns River MS 400/5-8
20 River Rd 05465 802-899-3711
Kevin Hamilton, prin. Fax 899-4281
Mt. Mansfield Union HS 900/9-12
211 Browns Trace Rd 05465 802-899-4690
Michael Weston, prin. Fax 899-2904

**Johnson, Lamoille, Pop. 1,395**

Johnson State College Post-Sec.
337 College Hl 05656 802-635-2356

**Ludlow, Windsor, Pop. 795**
Two Rivers Supervisory Union 1,100/PK-12
609 Route 103 S 05149 802-875-3365
Bruce Williams, supt. Fax 875-6439
su.trsu.org/
Black River MSHS 200/7-12
43 Main St 05149 802-228-4721
Shannon Martin, prin. Fax 228-7233
Other Schools – See Chester

**Lyndon Center, Caledonia**
VT Technical Centers
Supt. — None
Lyndon Institute Technical Center Vo/Tech
PO Box 127 05850 802-626-3357
Daren Houck, head sch Fax 626-9345

**Lyndonville, Caledonia, Pop. 1,188**

Lyndon State College Post-Sec.
PO Box 919 05851 802-626-6200

**Manchester, Bennington, Pop. 746**

Burr and Burton Academy 700/9-12
PO Box 498 05254 802-362-1775
Mark Tashjian, hdmstr. Fax 362-0574

**Marlboro, Windham**

Marlboro College Post-Sec.
PO Box A 05344 802-257-4333

**Middlebury, Addison, Pop. 6,363**
Addison Central Supervisory Union 1,800/PK-12
49 Charles Ave 05753 802-382-1274
Dr. Peter Burrows, supt. Fax 388-0024
www.addisoncentralsu.org
Middlebury Union HS 600/9-12
73 Charles Ave 05753 802-382-1500
Fax 382-1101
Middlebury Union MS 300/7-8
48 Deerfield Ln 05753 802-382-1600
Patrick Reen, prin. Fax 382-1215

VT Technical Centers
Supt. — None
Hannaford Career Center Vo/Tech
51 Charles Ave 05753 802-382-1012
D. Lynn Coale, prin. Fax 388-2591

Middlebury College 05753 Post-Sec.
802-443-5000

**Milton, Chittenden, Pop. 1,843**
Milton Town SD 1,600/PK-12
42 Herrick Ave 05468 802-893-5400
Dr. John Barone, supt. Fax 893-3213
www.mtsd-vt.org
Milton HS 500/9-12
17 Rebecca Lander Dr 05468 802-893-5400
Anne Blake, prin. Fax 893-3247
Milton MS 300/6-8
42 Herrick Ave 05468 802-893-5400
Barbara Burrington, prin. Fax 893-3213

**Montpelier, Washington, Pop. 7,675**
Montpelier SD 900/K-12
5 High School Dr Unit 1 05602 802-223-9796
Dr. Brian Ricca, supt. Fax 223-9795
www.mpsvt.org/
Main Street MS 200/5-8
170 Main St 05602 802-223-3404
Pamela Arnold, prin. Fax 223-9225
Montpelier HS 300/9-12
5 High School Dr 05602 802-225-8000
Michael McRaith, prin. Fax 223-9227

Washington Central Supervisory Union 1,700/PK-12
1130 Gallison Hill Rd 05602 802-229-0553
William Kimball, supt. Fax 229-2761
www.wcsuonline.org
Union 32 JSHS 800/7-12
930 Gallison Hill Rd 05602 802-229-0321
Steven Dellinger-Pate, prin. Fax 223-7411

Community College of Vermont Post-Sec.
PO Box 489 05601 802-828-2800
New England Culinary Institute Post-Sec.
56 College St 05602 877-223-6324
Union Institute & University Post-Sec.
62 Ridge St Ste 2 05602 802-828-8500
Vermont College of Fine Arts Post-Sec.
36 College St 05602 802-828-8600

**Morrisville, Lamoille, Pop. 1,933**
Lamoille South Supervisory Union 1,600/K-12
46 Copley Ave 05661 802-888-4541
Tracy Wrend, supt. Fax 888-6710
www.lamoillesouthsu.org

Peoples Academy 300/9-12
202 Copley Ave 05661 802-888-4600
Phil Grant, prin. Fax 888-6726
Peoples Academy MS 300/5-8
202 Copley Ave 05661 802-888-1402
Karen Weeks, prin. Fax 888-6488
Other Schools – See Stowe

**Newport, Orleans, Pop. 4,495**
North Country Supervisory Union 2,600/PK-12
121 Duchess Ave Ste A 05855 802-334-5847
John A. Castle, supt. Fax 334-6528
www.ncsuvt.org
North Country Union HS 900/9-12
PO Box 725 05855 802-334-7921
William Rivard, prin. Fax 334-1618
Other Schools – See Derby

VT Technical Centers
Supt. — None
North Country Career Center Vo/Tech
PO Box 705 05855 802-334-5469
Eileen Illuzzi, prin. Fax 334-3492

United Christian Academy 100/K-12
65 School St 05855 802-334-3112
John Carpenter, head sch Fax 334-2305

**North Clarendon, Rutland**
Rutland South Supervisory Union 1,000/PK-12
64 Grange Hall Rd 05759 802-775-3264
Dave Younce, supt. Fax 775-8063
www.rssu.org/
Mill River Union JSHS 600/7-12
2321 Middle Rd 05759 802-775-1925
Andy Pomeroy, prin. Fax 775-6447

**Northfield, Washington, Pop. 2,049**
Washington South Supervisory Union 700/PK-12
37 Cross St Ste 1 05663 802-485-7755
Laurie Gossens, supt. Fax 485-3348
www.wssu.org
Northfield MSHS 300/6-12
37 Cross St Ste 1 05663 802-485-4500
Ryan Parkman, prin. Fax 485-4440

Norwich University Post-Sec.
158 Harmon Dr 05663 802-485-2000

**Orleans, Orleans, Pop. 796**
Orleans Central Supervisory Union
Supt. — See Barton
Lake Region Union HS 400/9-12
317 Lake Region Rd 05860 802-754-6521
Andre Messier, prin. Fax 754-2780

**Plainfield, Washington, Pop. 393**
Washington NE Supervisory Union 700/PK-12
PO Box 470 05667 802-454-9924
Nancy Thomas, supt. Fax 454-9934
Twinfield Union S 400/PK-12
106 Nasmith Brook Rd 05667 802-426-3213
Mark Mooney, prin. Fax 426-4085
Other Schools – See Cabot

Goddard College Post-Sec.
123 Pitkin Rd 05667 802-454-8311

**Poultney, Rutland, Pop. 1,589**
Rutland Southwest Supervisory Union 600/PK-12
168 York St 05764 802-287-5286
Joan Paustian Ed.D., supt. Fax 287-2284
www.rswsu.org
Poultney HS 200/7-12
154 E Main St 05764 802-287-5861
Jim Frail, prin. Fax 287-2304

Green Mountain College Post-Sec.
1 Brennan Cir 05764 802-287-8000

**Proctor, Rutland**
Rutland Central Supervisory Union
Supt. — See Rutland
Proctor JSHS 200/7-12
4 Park St 05765 802-459-3353
Adam Rosenberg, prin. Fax 459-6323

**Putney, Windham, Pop. 508**

Landmark College Post-Sec.
1 River Rd S 05346 802-387-4767
Putney S 200/9-12
418 Houghton Brook Rd 05346 802-387-5566
Emily Jones, head sch Fax 387-6278

**Randolph, Orange, Pop. 1,947**
Orange Southwest Supervisory Union 1,100/K-12
24 Central St 05060 802-728-5052
Dr. Brent Kay, supt. Fax 728-4844
www.orangesouthwest.org
Randolph Union JSHS 500/7-12
15 Forest St 05060 802-728-3397
David Barnett, prin. Fax 728-6703

VT Technical Centers
Supt. — None
Randolph Technical Career Center Vo/Tech
17 Forest St 05060 802-728-9595
Jason Gingold, dir. Fax 728-9596

**Randolph Center, Orange**

Vermont Technical College Post-Sec.
PO Box 500 05061 802-728-1000

**Richford, Franklin, Pop. 1,314**
Franklin Northeast Supervisory Union 1,700/PK-12
PO Box 130 05476 802-848-7661
Jay Nichols, supt. Fax 848-3531
fnesu.net

Richford JSHS 200/7-12
1 Corliss Hts 05476 802-848-7416
Beth O'Brien, prin. Fax 848-3210
Other Schools – See Enosburg Falls

**Richmond, Chittenden, Pop. 707**
Chittenden East Supervisory Union 2,700/PK-12
PO Box 282 05477 802-434-2128
John Alberghini, supt. Fax 434-2196
www.cesu.k12.vt.us
Camels Hump MS 400/5-8
173 School St 05477 802-434-2188
Mark Carbone, prin. Fax 434-2192
Other Schools – See Jericho

**Rochester, Windsor, Pop. 297**
Windsor Northwest Supervisory Union
Supt. — See Bethel
Rochester S 200/K-12
222 S Main St 05767 802-767-3161
Catherine Knight, prin. Fax 767-1130

**Rutland, Rutland, Pop. 16,220**
Rutland Central Supervisory Union 1,000/PK-12
16 Evelyn St 05701 802-775-4342
Dr. Debra Taylor, supt. Fax 775-7319
www.rcsu.org
Other Schools – See Proctor, West Rutland

Rutland City SD 2,300/K-12
6 Church St 05701 802-773-1900
Mary Moran, supt. Fax 773-1927
rutlandcitypublicschools.org/
Rutland HS, 22 Stratton Rd 05701 1,000/9-12
William Olsen, prin. 802-773-1955
Rutland MS 300/7-8
67 Library Ave 05701 802-773-1960
Wilfred Cunningham, prin. Fax 773-1914

VT Technical Centers
Supt. — None
Stafford Technical Center Vo/Tech
8 Stratton Rd 05701 802-770-1033
Ted Guilmette, dir. Fax 770-1066

---

College of Saint Joseph Post-Sec.
71 Clement Rd 05701 802-773-5900
Mt. St. Joseph Academy 100/9-12
127 Convent Ave 05701 802-775-0151
Sarah Fortier, prin. Fax 775-0424
Rutland Area Christian S 100/PK-12
112 Lincoln Ave 05701 802-775-0709
Dia Lind, prin. Fax 786-0111
Rutland Regional Medical Center Post-Sec.
160 Allen St 05701 802-775-7111

**Saint Albans, Franklin, Pop. 6,736**
Franklin Central Supervisory Union 2,700/PK-12
28 Catherine St 05478 802-524-2600
Dr. Kevin Dirth, supt. Fax 524-1540
www.fcsuvt.org
Bellows Free Academy 1,100/9-12
71 S Main St 05478 802-527-6555
Chris Mosca, prin. Fax 527-6402

VT Technical Centers
Supt. — None
Northwest Technical Center Vo/Tech
71 S Main St 05478 802-527-6517
Leann Wright, dir. Fax 527-6469

---

Direct Learning International Post-Sec.
PO Box 846 05478 800-489-4114

**Saint Johnsbury, Caledonia, Pop. 6,424**

---

St. Johnsbury Academy 900/9-12
PO Box 906 05819 802-748-8171
Tom Lovett, hdmstr. Fax 748-2358

**Saxtons River, Windham, Pop. 550**

---

Vermont Academy 200/9-12
PO Box 500 05154 802-869-6200
Sean Brennan, head sch Fax 869-6242

**Sharon, Windsor**

---

Sharon Academy 200/7-12
PO Box 207 05065 802-763-2500
Michael Livingston, prin. Fax 763-2502

**Shelburne, Chittenden, Pop. 581**
Chittenden South Supervisory Union 4,100/PK-12
5420 Shelburne Rd Ste 300 05482 802-383-1234
Elaine Pinckney, supt. Fax 383-1242
www.cssu.org/
Other Schools – See Hinesburg

---

Lake Champlain Waldorf HS 50/9-12
122 Bostwick Rd 05482 802-495-0834

**South Burlington, Chittenden, Pop. 17,544**
South Burlington SD 2,400/K-12
550 Dorset St 05403 802-652-7250
David Young, supt. Fax 652-7257
www.sbschools.net
South Burlington HS 900/9-12
550 Dorset St 05403 802-652-7000
Patrick Burke, prin. Fax 652-7006
Tuttle MS 500/6-8
500 Dorset St 05403 802-652-7100
Karsten Schlenter, prin. Fax 652-7152

---

Advanced Welding Institute Post-Sec.
2 Green Tree Dr Ste 3 05403 802-660-0600
O'Briens Training Center Post-Sec.
1233 Shelburne Rd Ste 200 05403 802-658-9591
Rice Memorial HS 400/9-12
99 Proctor Ave 05403 802-862-6521
Msgr. Bernard Bourgeois, prin. Fax 864-9931
Vermont Commons S 100/7-12
75 Green Mountain Dr 05403 802-865-8084
Dexter Mahaffey Ph.D., head sch Fax 865-2429

**South Duxbury, Washington**
Washington West Supervisory Union
Supt. — See Waitsfield
Harwood Union HS 600/7-12
458 VT Route 100 05660 802-244-5186
Lisa Atwood, prin. Fax 882-1199

**South Royalton, Windsor, Pop. 674**
Orange-Windsor Supervisory Union 900/PK-12
461 Waterman Rd 05068 802-763-8840
Bruce Labs, supt. Fax 763-3235
www.owsu.org
South Royalton S 400/PK-12
223 S Windsor St 05068 802-763-8844
Dean Stearns, prin. Fax 763-3233
Other Schools – See Chelsea

---

Vermont Law School Post-Sec.
PO Box 96 05068 802-831-1000

**Springfield, Windsor, Pop. 3,895**
Springfield SD 1,300/K-12
60 Park St 05156 802-885-5141
Zachary McLaughlin, supt. Fax 885-8169
www.ssdvt.org
Gateway S Alt
13 Fairground Rd 05156 802-885-3477
Nancy Wiese, coord. Fax 885-3473
Riverside MS 300/6-8
13 Fairground Rd 05156 802-885-8490
Becky Read, prin. Fax 885-8442
Springfield HS 500/9-12
303 South St 05156 802-885-7900
Bob Thibault, prin. Fax 885-4459

VT Technical Centers
Supt. — None
River Valley Technical Center Vo/Tech
307 South St 05156 802-885-8300
Scott Farr, dir. Fax 885-8454

**Stowe, Lamoille, Pop. 492**
Lamoille South Supervisory Union
Supt. — See Morrisville
Stowe HS 200/9-12
413 Barrows Rd 05672 802-253-7229
Jeff Maher, prin. Fax 253-6911
Stowe MS 200/6-8
413 Barrows Rd 05672 802-253-6913
Dan Morrison, prin. Fax 253-5314

**Stratton Mountain, Windham, Pop. 50**

---

Stratton Mountain S 100/7-12
7 World Cup Cir 05155 802-297-1886
Christopher Kaltsas, hdmstr. Fax 297-0020

**Swanton, Franklin, Pop. 2,303**
Franklin Northwest Supervisory Union 2,200/PK-12
100 Robin Hood Dr 05488 802-868-4967
Winton Goodrich, supt. Fax 868-4265
www.fnwsu.org
Missisquoi Valley Union MSHS 900/7-12
100 Thunderbird Dr 05488 802-868-7311
Dennis Hill, prin. Fax 868-3129

**Thetford, Orange**

---

Thetford Academy 300/7-12
PO Box 190 05074 802-785-4805

**Townshend, Windham**
Windham Central Supervisory Union 900/PK-12
1219 VT Route 30 05353 802-365-9510
Dr. Steven John, supt. Fax 365-7934
www.windhamcentral.org
Leland & Gray Union HS 400/7-12
PO Box 128 05353 802-365-7355
Dr. Dorinne Dorfman, prin. Fax 365-4126

**Vergennes, Addison, Pop. 2,536**
Addison Northwest Supervisory Union 1,100/K-12
11 Main St Ste B100 05491 802-877-3332
JoAn Canning, supt. Fax 877-3628
www.anwsu.org
Vergennes Union HS 600/7-12
50 Monkton Rd 05491 802-877-2938
Stephanie Taylor, prin. Fax 877-2558

**Waitsfield, Washington, Pop. 162**
Washington West Supervisory Union 1,800/PK-12
340 Mad River Park Ste 7 05673 802-496-2272
Brigid Nease, supt. Fax 496-6515
www.wwsu.org/
Other Schools – See Duxbury, South Duxbury

---

Green Mountain Valley S 100/8-12
271 Moulton Rd 05673 802-496-2150
David Gavett, prin. Fax 496-6819

**Websterville, Washington, Pop. 545**

---

Websterville Baptist Christian S 100/PK-12
PO Box 1 05678 802-479-0141

**Wells River, Orange, Pop. 387**
Blue Mountain SD 400/PK-12
2420 Route 302 05081 802-757-2766
Emilie Knisley, supt. Fax 757-2790
www.bmuschool.org
Blue Mountain Union S 21 400/PK-12
2420 Route 302 05081 802-757-2711
Scott Blood, prin. Fax 757-3894

**West Dover, Windham**

---

Mount Snow Academy 100/6-12
25 Mt Snow Rd 05356 802-464-1100

**West Rutland, Rutland, Pop. 2,007**
Rutland Central Supervisory Union
Supt. — See Rutland
West Rutland S 400/PK-12
713 Main St 05777 802-438-2288
Joseph Fleming, prin. Fax 438-5708

**White River Junction, Windsor, Pop. 2,238**
Hartford SD 1,600/PK-12
73 Highland Ave 05001 802-295-8600
Tom DeBalsi, supt. Fax 295-8602
www.hsdvt.com
Hartford HS 600/9-12
37 Highland Ave 05001 802-295-8610
Joseph Collea, prin. Fax 295-8611
Hartford Memorial MS 400/6-8
245 Highland Ave 05001 802-295-8640
John Grant, prin. Fax 295-8641

VT Technical Centers
Supt. — None
Hartford Area Career & Technology Center Vo/Tech
1 Gifford Rd 05001 802-295-8630
Doug Heavisides, prin. Fax 295-8631

---

Mid Vermont Christian S 100/PK-12
399 W Gilson Ave 05001 802-295-6800
Robert Bracy M.Ed., hdmstr. Fax 295-3748

**Whitingham, Windham**
Windham Southwest Supervisory Union
Supt. — See Wilmington
Twin Valley MSHS 200/6-12
4299 VT Route 100 05361 802-368-2880
Thomas Fitzgerald, prin. Fax 368-7382

**Williamstown, Orange**
Orange North Supervisory Union 700/PK-12
111B Brush Hill Rd 05679 802-433-5818
Susette Bollard, supt. Fax 433-5825
www.onsu.org/
Williamstown MSHS 300/6-12
120 Hebert Rd 05679 802-433-5350
Scott Lang, prin. Fax 433-1037

**Williston, Chittenden**
Williston SD 1,100/PK-8
195 Central School Dr 05495 802-878-2762
Walter Nardelli, supt. Fax 871-6101
www.wsdvt.org
Williston Central S 700/3-8
195 Central School Dr 05495 802-878-2762
Jackie Parks, admin. Fax 871-6101

---

Northern Vermont Regional Day Program Post-Sec.
195 Central School Dr 05495 802-879-4787
Vermont College of Cosmetology Post-Sec.
400 Cornerstone Dr Ste 220 05495 802-863-4666

**Wilmington, Windham, Pop. 457**
Windham Southwest Supervisory Union 500/PK-12
1 School St 05363 802-464-1300
Christopher Pratt Ed.D., supt. Fax 464-1303
www.windhamsw.k12.vt.us/
Other Schools – See Whitingham

**Windsor, Windsor, Pop. 2,011**
Windsor Southeast Supervisory Union 1,100/K-12
105 Main St Ste 200 05089 802-674-2144
David Baker, supt. Fax 674-6357
wsesu.net
Windsor HS 200/7-12
19 Ascutney St 05089 802-674-6344
Tiffany Cassano, prin. Fax 674-9802

**Winooski, Chittenden, Pop. 7,032**
Winooski SD 800/PK-12
60 Normand St 05404 802-655-0485
Sean McMannon, supt. Fax 655-7602
www.wsdschools.org
Winooski HS 300/9-12
80 Normand St 05404 802-655-3530
Leon Wheeler, prin. Fax 655-6538
Winooski MS 200/6-8
80 Normand St 05404 802-655-3530
Leon Wheeler, prin. Fax 655-6538

**Woodstock, Windsor, Pop. 897**
Windsor Central Supervisory Union 1,000/PK-12
70 Amsden Way 05091 802-457-1213
Alice Worth, supt. Fax 457-2989
www.wcsu.net/
Woodstock Union HS 400/9-12
100 Amsden Way 05091 802-457-1317
Garon Smail, prin. Fax 457-1850
Woodstock Union MS 200/7-8
100 Amsden Way 05091 802-457-1330
Dana Peterson, prin. Fax 457-5048

# VIRGINIA

## VIRGINIA DEPARTMENT OF EDUCATION
**PO Box 2120, Richmond 23218-2120**
**Telephone 804-225-2020**
**Fax 804-371-2099**
**Website http://www.pen.k12.va.us**

Superintendent of Public Instruction Dr. Patricia Wright

## VIRGINIA BOARD OF EDUCATION
**PO Box 2120, Richmond 23218-2120**

President David Foster

## PUBLIC, PRIVATE AND CATHOLIC SECONDARY SCHOOLS

**Abingdon, Washington, Pop. 8,107**
Regional Academic Governors SD
Supt. — See Richmond
Holton Governor's S 10-12
PO Box 1987 24212 276-619-4326
Danny Dixon, dir. Fax 619-4309

Washington County SD 7,400/PK-12
812 Thompson Dr 24210 276-739-3003
Dr. Brian Ratliff, supt. Fax 623-4137
www.wcs.k12.va.us
Abingdon HS 900/9-12
705 Thompson Dr 24210 276-739-3200
Jimmy King, prin. Fax 628-1897
Stanley MS 700/6-8
297 Stanley St 24210 276-739-3300
Scott Allen, prin. Fax 676-1945
Washington Co. Career & Tech Educ Ctr Vo/Tech
255 Stanley St 24210 276-739-3100
Brian Johnson, prin. Fax 623-4126
Other Schools – See Bristol, Damascus, Glade Spring

---

Cornerstone Christian Academy 100/PK-12
PO Box 2228 24212 276-623-7164
Dr. Clay Brinson, head sch
Virginia Highlands Community College Post-Sec.
PO Box 828 24212 276-739-2400
Washington County Adult Skill Center Post-Sec.
848 Thompson Dr 24210 276-676-1948

**Accomac, Accomack, Pop. 513**
Accomack County SD 5,100/PK-12
PO Box 330 23301 757-787-5754
Dr. Michael Glascoe, supt. Fax 787-2951
www.accomack.k12.va.us
Other Schools – See Chincoteague, Oak Hall, Onley, Tangier

**Afton, Nelson**

---

Afton Christian S 50/PK-12
9357 Critzers Shop Rd 22920 540-456-6853
Lori Knight, head sch Fax 456-6236

**Alberta, Brunswick, Pop. 294**

---

Southside Virginia Community College Post-Sec.
109 Campus Dr 23821 434-949-1000

**Aldie, Loudoun**
Loudoun County SD
Supt. — See Ashburn
Champe HS 9-12
41535 Sacred Mountain St 20105 703-722-2680
John Gabriel, prin. Fax 722-2681
Mercer MS 700/6-8
42149 Greenstone Dr 20105 703-957-4340
Robert Phillips, prin. Fax 444-8068

**Alexandria, Alexandria, Pop. 135,858**
Alexandria CSD 12,300/PK-12
1340 Braddock Pl 22314 703-619-8000
Alvin Crawley Ed.D., supt. Fax 619-8090
www.acps.k12.va.us
Hammond MS 400/6-8
4646 Seminary Rd 22304 703-461-4100
Meilin Jao, prin. Fax 461-4111
Washington MS 500/6-8
1005 Mount Vernon Ave 22301 703-706-4500
Jesse Mazur, prin. Fax 299-7597
Williams HS 2,200/10-12
3330 King St 22302 703-824-6800
Jesse Dingle Ed.D., prin. Fax 824-6826
Williams HS - Howard Campus 800/9-9
3801 W Braddock Rd 22302 703-824-6750
jesse.dingle Ed.D., prin. Fax 824-6781

Fairfax County SD
Supt. — See Falls Church
Bryant Alternative HS 300/Alt
2709 Popkins Ln 22306 703-660-2100
William Hunt, admin. Fax 660-2097
Edison HS 1,700/9-12
5801 Franconia Rd 22310 703-924-8000
Pamela Brumfield, prin. Fax 924-8097
Glasgow MS 1,400/6-8
4101 Fairfax Pkwy 22312 703-813-8700
Shawn DeRose, prin. Fax 813-8797
Hayfield JSHS 3,000/7-12
7630 Telegraph Rd 22315 703-924-7400
Tracey Phillips, prin. Fax 924-7497
Holmes MS 800/6-8
6525 Montrose St 22312 703-658-5900
Roberto Pamas, prin. Fax 658-5997
Jefferson HS 9-12
6560 Braddock Rd 22312 703-750-8300
Dr. Evan Glazer, prin. Fax 750-5010
Montrose Alternative Learning Center Alt
6525 Montrose St 22312 703-658-5800
Susan Lee, admin.
Mount Vernon HS 1,900/9-12
8515 Old Mount Vernon Rd 22309 703-619-3100
Nardos King, prin. Fax 619-3197
Sandburg MS 1,200/7-8
8428 Fort Hunt Rd 22308 703-799-6100
Terrence Yarborough, prin. Fax 799-6197
Twain MS 900/7-8
4700 Franconia Rd 22310 703-313-3700
Baek Chong, prin. Fax 313-3797
West Potomac HS 2,400/9-12
6500 Quander Rd 22307 703-718-2500
Alexander Case, prin. Fax 718-2597
Whitman MS 1,000/7-8
2500 Parkers Ln 22306 703-660-2400
Roger Vanderhye, prin. Fax 660-2497

Regional Academic Governors SD
Supt. — See Richmond
Jefferson Science & Tech HS 1,900/9-12
6560 Braddock Rd 22312 703-750-8300
Dr. Evan Glazer, prin. Fax 750-5036

---

Bishop Ireton HS 800/9-12
201 Cambridge Rd 22314 703-751-7606
Dr. Thomas Curry, head sch Fax 212-8173
Commonwealth Academy 100/3-12
1321 Leslie Ave 22301 703-548-6912
Dr. Susan Johnson, hdmstr. Fax 548-6914
Episcopal HS 400/9-12
1200 N Quaker Ln 22302 703-933-3000
F. Robertson Hershey, hdmstr. Fax 933-3017
Gardner S, 4913 Franconia Rd 22310 6-12
Erick Johnson, head sch 703-822-9300
Global Health College Post-Sec.
25 S Quaker Ln 22314 703-212-7410
Islamic Saudi Academy 600/K-12
8333 Richmond Hwy 22309 703-780-0606
Protestant Episcopal Theologcl. Seminary Post-Sec.
3737 Seminary Rd 22304 703-370-6600
St. Stephen's & St. Agnes S 1,100/PK-12
1000 Saint Stephens Rd 22304 703-751-2700
Kirsten Adams, head sch Fax 751-7142

**Altavista, Campbell, Pop. 3,366**
Campbell County SD
Supt. — See Rustburg
Altavista JSHS 700/6-12
904 Bedford Ave 24517 434-369-4768
Ty Gafford, prin. Fax 369-5191

**Amelia Court House, Amelia, Pop. 1,087**
Amelia County SD 1,800/PK-12
8701 Otterburn Rd Ste 101 23002 804-561-2621
Dr. Jack McKinley, supt. Fax 561-3057
www.amelia.k12.va.us
Amelia County HS 600/9-12
8500 Otterburn Rd 23002 804-561-2101
Tommy Moon, prin. Fax 561-4567
Amelia County MS 600/5-8
8740 Otterburn Rd 23002 804-561-4422
Dr. Sarah Tanner-Anderson, prin. Fax 561-6525

---

Amelia Academy 200/PK-12
PO Box 106 23002 804-561-2270

**Amherst, Amherst, Pop. 2,173**
Amherst County SD 4,500/PK-12
PO Box 1257 24521 434-946-9387
Dr. Steven Nichols, supt. Fax 946-9346
www.amherst.k12.va.us
Amherst County HS 1,400/9-12
139 Lancer Ln 24521 434-946-2898
William Wells, prin. Fax 946-2263
Amherst MS 400/6-8
165 Gordons Fairgrounds Rd 24521 434-946-0691
Christie Cundiff, prin. Fax 946-0258
Other Schools – See Madison Heights

**Annandale, Fairfax, Pop. 39,850**
Fairfax County SD
Supt. — See Falls Church
Annandale HS 2,500/9-12
4700 Medford Dr 22003 703-642-4100
Tim Thomas, prin. Fax 642-4197
Poe MS 1,100/6-8
7000 Cindy Ln 22003 703-813-3800
Maria Eck, prin. Fax 813-3897

---

iGlobal University Post-Sec.
7700 Little River Tpke #600 22003 703-941-2020
Northern Virginia Community College Post-Sec.
8333 Little River Tpke 22003 703-323-3000
Springfield Beauty Academy Post-Sec.
4223 Annandale Rd 22003 703-256-5662
University of Northern Virginia Post-Sec.
7601 Little River Tpke 22003 703-941-0949
Washington Baptist University Post-Sec.
4300 Evergreen Ln 22003 703-333-5904
Westwood College - Annandale Post-Sec.
7619 Little River Tpke #500 22003 703-642-3770

**Appomattox, Appomattox, Pop. 1,694**
Appomattox County SD 2,300/PK-12
PO Box 548 24522 434-352-8251
Dorinda Grasty Ed.D., supt. Fax 352-0883
www.appomattox.schoolfusion.us
Appomattox HS 700/9-12
198 Evergreen Ave 24522 434-352-7146
Dr. Francis Moreno, prin. Fax 352-0822
Appomattox MS 600/6-8
2020 Church St 24522 434-352-8257
Cheryl Servis, prin. Fax 352-5621

---

Cornerstone Christian Academy 100/PK-12
PO Box 897 24522 434-352-2345
Geoffrey Hubler Ph.D., prin. Fax 352-2345

**Arlington, Arlington, Pop. 201,587**
Arlington County SD 22,700/PK-12
1426 N Quincy St 22207 703-228-6000
Dr. Patrick Murphy, supt. Fax 228-6188
www.apsva.us
Arlington Career Center Vo/Tech
816 S Walter Reed Dr 22204 703-228-5800
Margaret Chung, prin. Fax 228-5815
Arlington Mill HS Alt
816 S Walter Reed Dr # 222 22204 703-228-5350
Dr. Barbara Thompson, prin. Fax 522-2437
Governors Career and Technical Academy Vo/Tech
816 South Walter Reed Dr 22204 703-323-2263
Gunston MS 800/6-8
2700 S Lang St 22206 703-228-6900
Dr. Lori Wiggins, prin. Fax 519-9183
Jefferson MS 700/6-8
125 S Old Glebe Rd 22204 703-228-5900
Keisha Boggan, prin. Fax 979-3744
Kenmore MS 800/6-8
200 S Carlin Springs Rd 22204 703-228-6800
Dr. John Word, prin. Fax 998-3069
Langston HS Continuation Alt
2121 N Culpeper St 22207 703-228-5295
Cleveland James, prin. Fax 807-0614
Swanson MS 900/6-8
5800 Washington Blvd 22205 703-228-5500
Bridget Loft, prin. Fax 536-2775
Wakefield HS 1,600/9-12
1325 S Dinwiddie St 22206 703-228-6700
Dr. Christian Willmore, prin. Fax 228-6760
Washington-Lee HS 2,200/9-12
1301 N Stafford St 22201 703-228-6200
Gregg Robertson, prin. Fax 524-9814
Williamsburg MS 1,000/6-8
3600 N Harrison St 22207 703-228-5450
Gordon Laurie, prin. Fax 536-2870

Woodland Secondary Program 600/Alt
4100 Vacation Ln 22207 703-228-6363
Casey Robinson, prin. Fax 558-0317
Yorktown HS 2,000/9-12
5200 Yorktown Blvd 22207 703-228-5400
Dr. Raymond Pasi, prin. Fax 228-5409

---

Argosy University/Washington DC Post-Sec.
1550 Wilson Blvd Ste 600 22209 703-526-5800
Art Institute of Washington Post-Sec.
1820 Fort Myer Dr 22209 703-358-9550
Bishop Denis J. O'Connell HS 1,200/9-12
6600 Little Falls Rd 22213 703-237-1400
Joseph Vorbach Ph.D., head sch Fax 237-1412
Chamberlain College of Nursing Post-Sec.
2450 Crystal Dr 22202 703-416-7300
Court Reporting Institute of Arlington Post-Sec.
4300 Wilson Blvd Ste 140 22203 703-875-1200
DeVry University Post-Sec.
2450 Crystal Dr 22202 703-414-4000
Graham Webb Intl. Academy of Hair Post-Sec.
1621 N Kent St # 1617LL 22209 703-243-9322
Institute for the Psychological Sciences Post-Sec.
2001 Jefferson Davis # 511 22202 703-416-1441
Keller Graduate School Post-Sec.
2450 Crystal Dr 22202 703-414-4000
Marymount University Post-Sec.
2807 N Glebe Rd 22207 703-522-5600
University of Management and Technology Post-Sec.
1901 Fort Myer Dr Ste 700 22209 703-516-0035
Westwood College - Ballston Post-Sec.
4420 Fairfax Dr 22203 703-243-3900

**Ashburn, Loudoun, Pop. 41,992**
Loudoun County SD 60,100/PK-12
21000 Education Ct 20148 571-252-1000
Dr. Eric Williams, supt. Fax 252-1003
www.lcps.org/
Briar Woods HS 1,800/9-12
22525 Belmont Ridge Rd 20148 703-957-4400
Edward Starzenski, prin. Fax 542-5923
Broad Run HS 1,800/9-12
21670 Ashburn Rd 20147 571-252-2300
David Spage, prin. Fax 252-2301
Eagle Ridge MS 1,100/6-8
42901 Waxpool Rd 20148 571-252-2140
Scott Phillips, prin. Fax 779-8977
Farmwell Station MS 1,200/6-8
44281 Gloucester Pkwy 20147 571-252-2320
Sherryl Loya, prin. Fax 771-6495
Rock Ridge HS 9-12
43460 Loudoun Reserve Dr 20148 571-996-2100
John Duellman, prin. Fax 996-2101
Stone Bridge HS 1,900/9-12
43100 Hay Rd 20147 571-252-2200
Matthew Wilburn, prin. Fax 252-2201
Stone Hill MS 1,100/6-8
23415 Evergreen Ridge Dr 20148 703-957-4420
Jodi Day, prin. Fax 223-0585
Trailside MS 6-8
20325 Claiborne Pkwy 20147 571-252-2280
Bridget Beichler, prin. Fax 724-1086
Other Schools – See Aldie, Chantilly, Hamilton, Leesburg, Potomac Falls, Purcellville, South Riding, Sterling

---

Loudoun S for the Gifted 50/6-12
PO Box 618 20146 703-956-5020
Susan Talbott, dir. Fax 858-0843
Strayer University Post-Sec.
45150 Russell Branch Pkwy 20147 703-729-8800
Virginia Academy 700/PK-12
19790 Ashburn Rd 20147 571-209-5500
Michael Taylor, prin. Fax 209-5845

**Ashland, Hanover, Pop. 7,029**
Hanover County SD 18,200/K-12
200 Berkley St 23005 804-365-4500
Dr. Michael Gill, supt. Fax 365-4680
www.hcps.us
Henry HS 1,500/9-12
12449 W Patrick Henry Rd 23005 804-365-8000
Dr. Wanda Bibb, prin. Fax 365-8027
Liberty MS 1,100/6-8
13496 Liberty School Rd 23005 804-365-8060
Donald Latham, prin. Fax 365-8061
Other Schools – See Mechanicsville

---

Randolph-Macon College Post-Sec.
PO Box 5005 23005 804-752-7200

**Axton, Henry**

---

Carlisle S 500/PK-12
300 Carlisle Rd 24054 276-632-7288
Thomas Hudgins, head sch Fax 632-9545

**Bassett, Henry, Pop. 1,078**
Henry County SD
Supt. — See Collinsville
Bassett HS 1,200/9-12
85 Riverside Dr 24055 276-629-1731
John Gibbs, prin. Fax 629-9329

**Bastian, Bland**
Bland County SD 900/PK-12
361 Bears Trl 24314 276-688-3361
Dr. Chris Stacy, supt. Fax 688-4659
www.bland.k12.va.us
Other Schools – See Rocky Gap

**Bealeton, Fauquier, Pop. 4,295**
Fauquier County SD
Supt. — See Warrenton
Cedar-Lee MS 700/6-8
11138 Marsh Rd 22712 540-422-7430
David Lee, prin. Fax 422-7449

Liberty HS 1,200/9-12
6300 Independence Ave 22712 540-422-7630
Sam Cox, prin. Fax 422-7389

**Bedford, Bedford, Pop. 6,098**
Bedford County SD 10,300/K-12
PO Box 748 24523 540-586-1045
Dr. Douglas Schuch, supt. Fax 586-7747
bedford.sharpschool.net
Alternative Education Center Alt
600 Edmund St 24523 540-586-3517
Tracy Piestrak, admin.
Bedford MS 600/6-8
503 Longwood Ave 24523 540-586-7735
Rhetta Watkins, prin. Fax 586-4957
Bedford Science and Technology Center Vo/Tech
600 Edmund St 24523 540-586-3933
Kim Halterman, admin. Fax 586-7711
Governors Health Science Academy Vo/Tech
600 Edmund St 24523 540-586-3933
Kim Halterman, prin. Fax 586-7711
Liberty HS 900/9-12
100 Minute Man Dr 24523 540-586-2541
Dr. Kathleen Dills, prin. Fax 586-7720
Other Schools – See Forest, Moneta

**Ben Hur, Lee**
Lee County SD
Supt. — See Jonesville
Lee County Career & Technical Center Vo/Tech
PO Box 100 24218 276-346-1960
James Graham, prin. Fax 346-2831

**Bent Mountain, Roanoke**

---

Bent Mountain Christian Academy 50/K-12
PO Box 66 24059 540-494-8356
Karen Scott, admin. Fax 929-9028

**Berryville, Clarke, Pop. 4,082**
Clarke County SD 2,100/PK-12
309 W Main St 22611 540-955-6100
Chuck Bishop, supt. Fax 955-6109
www.clarke.k12.va.us
Clarke County HS 700/9-12
627 Mosby Blvd 22611 540-955-6130
Dana Waring, prin. Fax 955-6139
Johnson-Williams MS 500/6-8
200 Swan Ave 22611 540-955-6160
Evan Robb, prin. Fax 955-6169

**Big Stone Gap, Wise, Pop. 5,523**
Wise County SD
Supt. — See Wise
Powell Valley MS 500/5-8
3137 2nd Ave E 24219 276-523-0195
Paul Clendenon, prin. Fax 523-4762
Union HS 700/9-12
322 Powell Valley Rd 24219 276-523-1290
Dan Roop, prin. Fax 523-6804

---

Mountain Empire Community College Post-Sec.
3441 Mountain Empire Rd 24219 276-523-2400

**Blacksburg, Montgomery, Pop. 41,455**
Montgomery County SD
Supt. — See Christiansburg
Blacksburg HS 1,100/9-12
3401 Bruin Ln 24060 540-951-5706
Brian Kitts, prin. Fax 951-5714
Blacksburg MS 800/6-8
3109 Prices Fork Rd 24060 540-951-5800
Amanda Weidner, prin. Fax 951-5808

---

Dayspring Christian Academy 300/K-12
PO Box 909 24063 540-552-7777
William Hampton, admin. Fax 552-7778
Edward Via College of Osteopathic Med. Post-Sec.
2265 Kraft Dr 24060 540-231-4000
Virginia Polytechnic Inst. & State Univ. Post-Sec.
24061 540-231-6000

**Blackstone, Nottoway, Pop. 3,575**

---

Kenston Forest S 300/PK-12
75 Ridge Rd 23824 434-292-7218

**Bluefield, Tazewell, Pop. 5,359**
Tazewell County SD
Supt. — See Tazewell
Graham HS 500/9-12
210 Valleydale St 24605 276-326-1235
John O'Neal, prin. Fax 326-1128
Graham MS 500/6-8
1 Academic Cir 24605 276-326-1101
Lee Salyers, prin. Fax 322-1409

---

Bluefield College Post-Sec.
3000 College Dr 24605 276-326-3682

**Bowling Green, Caroline, Pop. 1,090**
Caroline County SD 3,900/PK-12
16261 Richmond Tpke 22427 804-633-5088
Dr. George Parker, supt. Fax 633-5563
www.ccps.us
Other Schools – See Milford

**Boydton, Mecklenburg, Pop. 430**
Mecklenburg County SD 4,800/PK-12
PO Box 190 23917 434-738-6111
Dr. Janet Crawley, supt. Fax 738-6679
www.mcpsweb.org
Other Schools – See Skipwith, South Hill

**Bridgewater, Rockingham, Pop. 5,553**
Rockingham County SD
Supt. — See Harrisonburg
Ashby HS 1,000/9-12
800 N Main St 22812 540-828-2008
Phil Judd, prin. Fax 828-4764

---

Bridgewater College Post-Sec.
402 E College St 22812 540-828-8000

**Bristol, Bristol, Pop. 17,490**
Bristol CSD 2,400/PK-12
220 Lee St 24201 276-821-5600
Rex Gearheart, supt. Fax 821-5601
www.bvps.org/
Virginia HS 700/9-12
1200 Long Crescent Dr 24201 276-821-5858
Ronnie Collins, prin. Fax 821-5851
Virginia MS 500/6-8
501 Piedmont Ave 24201 276-821-5660
Bo Love, prin. Fax 821-5661

Washington County SD
Supt. — See Abingdon
Battle HS 600/9-12
21264 Battle Hill Dr 24202 276-642-5300
Randy Poole, prin. Fax 645-2386
Wallace MS 500/6-8
13077 Wallace Pike 24202 276-642-5400
David Lambert, prin. Fax 645-2365

---

Graham Bible College Post-Sec.
PO Box 1630 24203 423-968-4201
Southeast Culinary & Hospitality College Post-Sec.
100 Piedmont Ave 24201 276-591-5699
Virginia Intermont College Post-Sec.
1013 Moore St 24201 276-669-6101

**Bristow, Prince William**
Prince William County SD
Supt. — See Manassas
Marsteller MS 1,600/6-8
14000 Sudley Manor Dr 20136 703-393-7608
Roberta Knetter, prin. Fax 530-6327

**Broadway, Rockingham, Pop. 3,640**
Rockingham County SD
Supt. — See Harrisonburg
Broadway HS 1,000/9-12
269 Gobbler Dr 22815 540-896-7081
Donna Abernathy, prin. Fax 896-2640
Hillyard MS 800/6-8
226 Hawks Hill Dr 22815 540-896-8961
Dave Baker, prin. Fax 896-6641

**Buchanan, Botetourt, Pop. 1,142**
Botetourt County SD
Supt. — See Fincastle
James River HS 500/9-12
9906 Springwood Rd 24066 540-254-1121
James Talbott, prin. Fax 254-2765

**Buckingham, Buckingham, Pop. 370**
Buckingham County SD 1,600/PK-12
15595 W James Anderson Hwy 23921 434-969-6100
Dr. Cecil Snead, supt. Fax 969-1176
www.bcpschools.org
Buckingham County HS 600/9-12
78 Knights Rd 23921 434-969-6160
Rudy Roethel, prin. Fax 969-3209
Buckingham County MS 400/6-8
1184 High School Rd 23921 434-969-1044
J.B. Heslip, prin. Fax 969-4290

**Buena Vista, Buena Vista, Pop. 6,530**
Buena Vista CSD 900/K-12
2329 Chestnut Ave Ste A 24416 540-261-2129
Dr. Mary Holm, supt. Fax 261-2967
www.bvcps.net
McCluer HS 300/8-12
100 Bradford Dr 24416 540-261-2127
Anna Graham, prin. Fax 261-1828

---

Southern Virginia University Post-Sec.
1 University Hill Dr 24416 540-261-8400

**Bumpass, Louisa**

---

Piedmont Christian S 100/PK-12
2382 Bethany Church Rd 23024 540-872-3543
Marsha Badertscher, head sch Fax 872-3873

**Burke, Fairfax, Pop. 39,726**
Fairfax County SD
Supt. — See Falls Church
Lake Braddock JSHS 4,100/7-12
9200 Burke Lake Rd 22015 703-426-1000
David Thomas, prin. Fax 426-1093

**Carson, Prince George**
Jointly Operated Vo Tech SD
Supt. — None - Lolita Hall, dir.
Rowanty Technical Center Vo/Tech
20000 Rowanty Rd 23830 434-246-5741
Fax 246-5721

**Castlewood, Russell, Pop. 2,028**
Russell County SD
Supt. — See Lebanon
Castlewood HS 400/8-12
304 Blue Devil Cir 24224 276-762-9449
Nathan Breeding, prin. Fax 762-9418

---

Learning Center 50/PK-10
PO Box 133 24224 276-762-5700
Ken Johnson, admin. Fax 762-7116

**Centreville, Fairfax, Pop. 68,513**
Fairfax County SD
Supt. — See Falls Church
Mountain View Alternative HS 200/Alt
5775 Spindle Ct 20121 703-522-6840
Kimberly Thomas, admin.
Stone MS 900/7-8
5500 Sully Park Dr 20120 703-631-5500
Amielia Mitchell, prin. Fax 631-5598

---

Ad Fontes Academy 200/K-12
PO Box 916 20122 571-345-4755
Columbia College Post-Sec.
5940 Centreville Crest Ln 20121 703-266-0508

**Chantilly, Fairfax, Pop. 22,194**
Fairfax County SD
Supt. — See Falls Church
Chantilly Governor's STEM Academy 9-12
4201 Stringfellow Rd 20151 703-222-7460
Virginia Muller, prin. Fax 222-7497
Chantilly HS 2,600/9-12
4201 Stringfellow Rd 20151 703-222-8100
Teresa Johnson, prin. Fax 222-8197
Franklin MS 800/7-8
3300 Lees Corner Rd 20151 703-904-5100
Sharon Eisenberg, prin. Fax 904-5197
Rocky Run MS 1,000/7-8
4400 Stringfellow Rd 20151 703-802-7700
Anthony Terrell, prin. Fax 802-7797
Westfield HS 2,800/9-12
4700 Stonecroft Blvd 20151 703-488-6300
Anthony Copeland, prin. Fax 488-6397

Loudoun County SD
Supt. — See Ashburn
Lunsford MS 1,200/6-8
26020 Ticonderoga Rd 20152 703-722-2660
Carrie Simms, prin. Fax 327-2420

---

Auburn S 50/K-12
3800 Concorde Pkwy 20151 703-793-9353
Heather Hargrave M.Ed., head sch Fax 793-9355
ITT Technical Institute Post-Sec.
14420 Albemarle Point # 100 20151 703-263-2541

**Charles City, Charles City, Pop. 131**
Charles City County SD 800/PK-12
10910 Courthouse Rd 23030 804-652-4612
Dr. David Gaston, supt. Fax 829-6723
www.ccps.net
Charles City HS 200/7-12
10039 Courthouse Rd 23030 804-829-9249
Panagiotis Tsigaridas, prin. Fax 829-2644

**Charlotte Court House, Charlotte, Pop. 538**
Charlotte County SD 2,000/PK-12
PO Box 790 23923 434-542-5151
Nancy Leonard, supt. Fax 542-4261
www.ccpsk12.org
Central MS 500/6-8
PO Box 748 23923 434-542-4536
Michael Haskins, prin. Fax 542-4630
Randolph-Henry HS 700/9-12
PO Box 668 23923 434-542-4111
Robbie Mason, prin. Fax 542-4114

**Charlottesville, Charlottesville, Pop. 42,217**
Albemarle County SD 13,200/PK-12
401 McIntire Rd 22902 434-296-5826
Dr. Pamela Moran, supt. Fax 296-5869
www.k12albemarle.org/
Albemarle HS 1,800/9-12
2775 Hydraulic Rd 22901 434-975-9300
Jay Thomas, prin. Fax 974-4335
Burley MS 500/6-8
901 Rose Hill Dr 22903 434-295-5101
James Asher, prin. Fax 984-4975
Health and Medical Sciences Academy 9-12
1400 Independence Way 22902 434-244-3100
Kitina Dudley, dir.
Jouett MS 600/6-8
210 Lambs Ln 22901 434-975-9320
Kathryn Baylor, prin. Fax 975-9325
Math Engineering and Science Academy 9-12
2775 Hydraulic Rd 22901 434-975-9300
Tony Wayne, dir. Fax 974-4335
Monticello HS 1,100/9-12
1400 Independence Way 22902 434-244-3100
Dr. Jesse Turner, prin. Fax 244-3104
Murray HS 100/Alt
1200 Forest St 22903 434-296-3090
Ashby Kindler, prin. Fax 979-6479
Sutherland MS 600/6-8
2801 Powell Creek Dr 22911 434-975-0599
Rick Vrhovac, prin. Fax 975-0852
Walton MS 400/6-8
4217 Red Hill Rd 22903 434-977-5615
Alison Dwier-Selden, prin. Fax 296-6648
Other Schools – See Crozet

Charlottesville CSD 4,200/PK-12
1562 Dairy Rd 22903 434-245-2400
Dr. Rosa Atkins, supt. Fax 245-2603
www.ccs.k12.va.us
Buford MS 500/7-8
1000 Cherry Ave 22903 434-245-2411
Eric Johnson, prin. Fax 245-2611
Charlottesville HS 1,200/9-12
1400 Melbourne Rd 22901 434-245-2410
Jill Dahl, prin. Fax 245-2610
Lugo-McGinness Academy Alt
341 11th St NW 22903 434-245-2406
Stephanie Carter, admin.

Jointly Operated Vo Tech SD
Supt. — None – Lolita Hall, dir.
Charlottsville-Albemarle Tech Center Vo/Tech
1000 Rio Rd E 22901 434-973-4461
Bruce Bosselman, dir. Fax 973-4876

---

American National University Post-Sec.
3926 Seminole Trl 22911 434-220-7960
Covenant S 500/PK-12
175 Hickory St 22902 434-220-7329
Miller S of Albemarle 200/8-12
1000 Samuel Miller Loop 22903 434-823-4805
Sam Hale, admin. Fax 823-6617

Piedmont Virginia Community College Post-Sec.
501 College Dr 22902 434-977-3900
St. Anne's-Belfield S 900/PK-12
2132 Ivy Rd 22903 434-296-5106
David Lourie, hdmstr. Fax 979-1486
Tandem Friends S 200/5-12
279 Tandem Ln 22902 434-296-1303
Andy Jones-Wilkins, hdmstr. Fax 296-1886
University of Virginia Post-Sec.
PO Box 400160 22904 434-924-0311
Virginia School of Massage Post-Sec.
153 Zan Rd 22901 434-293-4031

**Chatham, Pittsylvania, Pop. 1,254**
Pittsylvania County SD 9,200/PK-12
PO Box 232 24531 434-432-2761
Lillian D. Holland, supt. Fax 432-9560
www.pcs.k12.va.us
Chatham HS 700/9-12
100 Chatham Cavalier Cir 24531 434-432-8305
Randy Foster, prin. Fax 432-8351
Chatham MS 500/6-8
11650 US Highway 29 24531 434-432-2169
Cedric Hairston, prin. Fax 432-2842
Pittsylvania Career Tech Vo/Tech
11700 US Highway 29 24531 434-432-9416
Angela Rigney, prin. Fax 432-0516
Regional Alternative Center Alt
956 Woodlawn Academy Rd 24531 434-432-8185
Deborah Powell, prin. Fax 432-8186
Other Schools – See Dry Fork, Gretna, Ringgold

---

Chatham Hall S 100/9-12
800 Chatham Hall Cir 24531 434-432-2941
Suzanne Buck, head sch Fax 432-1002
Hargrave Military Academy 200/7-12
200 Military Dr 24531 434-432-2481
Don Broome, pres. Fax 432-3129

**Chesapeake, Chesapeake, Pop. 216,170**
Chesapeake CSD 38,700/K-12
PO Box 16496 23328 757-547-0165
Dr. James Roberts, supt. Fax 547-0196
www.cpschools.com/
Chesapeake Alternative S Alt
605 Providence Rd 23325 757-578-7046
Dr. Penny Schultz, prin. Fax 578-7068
Chesapeake Center Science & Tech Vo/Tech
1617 Cedar Rd 23322 757-547-0134
Shonda Pittman-Windham, prin. Fax 547-2391
Crestwood MS 600/6-8
1420 Great Bridge Blvd 23320 757-494-7560
Michael Ward, prin. Fax 494-7599
Deep Creek HS 1,300/9-12
2900 Margaret Booker Dr 23323 757-558-5302
Page Bagley, prin. Fax 558-5305
Deep Creek MS 500/6-8
1955 Deal Dr 23323 757-558-5321
Dr. Muriel Barefield, prin. Fax 558-5320
Governors STEM Academy 9-12
2007 Grizzly Trl 23323 757-558-4493
Karen Black, coord.
Grassfield HS 2,100/9-12
2007 Grizzly Trl 23323 757-558-4749
Michael Perez, prin. Fax 558-9240
Great Bridge HS 1,600/9-12
301 Hanbury Rd W 23322 757-482-5191
Jeffrey Johnson, prin. Fax 482-5559
Great Bridge MS 1,300/6-8
441 Battlefield Blvd S 23322 757-482-5128
Craig Mills, prin. Fax 482-0210
Greenbrier MS 900/6-8
1016 Greenbrier Pkwy 23320 757-548-5309
Dr. Michael Mustain, prin. Fax 548-8921
Hickory HS 1,900/9-12
1996 Hawk Blvd 23322 757-421-4295
Alfredia Turner, prin. Fax 421-2190
Hickory MS 1,600/6-8
1997 Hawk Blvd 23322 757-421-0468
Dr. Deborah Hutchens, prin. Fax 421-0475
Indian River HS 1,600/9-12
1969 Braves Trl 23325 757-578-7000
Naomi Dunbar, prin. Fax 578-7004
Indian River MS 800/6-8
2300 Old Greenbrier Rd 23325 757-578-7030
Terre Werts, prin. Fax 578-7036
Jolliff MS 700/6-8
1021 Jolliff Rd 23321 757-465-5246
Quentin Hicks, prin. Fax 465-1646
Owens MS 1,100/6-8
1997 Horseback Run 23323 757-558-5382
Amber Dortch, prin. Fax 558-5386
Smith HS 2,200/9-12
1994 Tiger Dr 23320 757-548-0696
Paul Joseph, prin. Fax 548-0531
Smith MS 1,000/6-8
2500 Rodgers St 23324 757-494-7590
Judith Thurston, prin. Fax 494-7680
Western Branch HS 2,200/9-12
1968 Bruin Pl 23321 757-638-7900
Dr. Thomas Whitley, prin. Fax 638-7904
Western Branch MS 900/6-8
4201 Hawksley Dr 23321 757-638-7920
Dr. Samuel Khoshaba, prin. Fax 638-7926

---

Atlantic Shores Christian S 300/7-12
1217 Centerville Tpke N 23320 757-479-9598
Gary Carlson, head sch Fax 479-5311
Aviation Institute of Maintenance Post-Sec.
2211 S Military Hwy 23320 757-363-2121
Centura College Post-Sec.
932 Ventures Way 23320 757-549-2121
DeVry University Post-Sec.
1317 Executive Blvd Ste 100 23320 757-382-5680
Everest College Post-Sec.
825 Greenbrier Cir Ste 100 23320 757-361-3900

Greenbrier Christian Academy 600/PK-12
311 Kempsville Rd 23320 757-547-9595
Dr. Ron White, supt. Fax 547-9569
Sentara College of Health Sciences Post-Sec.
1441 Crossways Blvd Ste 105 23320 757-388-2900
StoneBridge S 300/PK-12
PO Box 9247 23321 757-488-2214
Kathy Rader, head sch Fax 465-7637
Strayer University Post-Sec.
676 Independence Pkwy # 300 23320 757-382-9900
Tidewater Community College Post-Sec.
1428 Cedar Rd 23322 757-822-5100

**Chester, Chesterfield, Pop. 20,491**
Chesterfield County SD
Supt. — See Chesterfield
Carver College & Career Academy 300/Alt
12400 Branders Bridge Rd 23831 804-768-6182
Dr. Ken Butta, prin. Fax 768-6171
Carver MS 1,100/6-8
3800 Cougar Trl 23831 804-524-3620
Dr. John Murray, prin. Fax 520-0189
Dale HS 2,400/9-12
3626 W Hundred Rd 23831 804-768-6245
Pamela Lunsden, prin. Fax 768-6256
Davis MS 1,200/6-8
601 Corvus Ct 23836 804-541-4700
Ed Maynes, prin. Fax 530-2717

---

John Tyler Community College Post-Sec.
13101 Jefferson Davis Hwy 23831 804-796-4000
Life Christian Academy 100/PK-12
16801 Harrowgate Rd 23831 804-526-5941

**Chesterfield, Chesterfield**
Chesterfield County SD 59,200/PK-12
PO Box 10 23832 804-748-1405
Dr. Marcus Newsome, supt. Fax 796-7178
mychesterfieldschools.com
Bird HS 1,700/9-12
10301 Courthouse Rd 23832 804-768-6110
Dr. Laura Hebert, prin. Fax 768-6117
Chesterfield Technical Center Vo/Tech
10101 Courthouse Rd 23832 804-768-6160
Dr. Colleen Bryant, prin. Fax 768-6164
Governor's Career and Technical Academy Vo/Tech
10301 Courthouse Rd 23832 804-768-6110
Dr. Laura Hebert, prin. Fax 768-6117
Matoaca HS 1,900/9-12
17700 Longhouse Ln 23838 804-590-3108
Belinda Merriman, prin. Fax 590-3022
Other Schools – See Chester, Matoaca, Midlothian, N Chesterfield

---

Guardian Christian Academy 300/PK-10
6851 Courthouse Rd 23832 804-715-3210
Glenda Paul, dir. Fax 715-3237
Richmond Christian S 300/PK-12
6511 Belmont Rd 23832 804-276-3193
Trevor Collazo, prin. Fax 276-9106

**Chilhowie, Smyth, Pop. 1,774**
Smyth County SD
Supt. — See Marion
Chilhowie HS 400/9-12
PO Box 2280 24319 276-646-8966
Mike Sturgill, prin. Fax 646-5951
Chilhowie MS 300/6-8
PO Box 5018 24319 276-646-3942
Sam Blevins, prin. Fax 646-0210

**Chincoteague, Accomack, Pop. 2,859**
Accomack County SD
Supt. — See Accomac
Chincoteague HS 300/6-12
4586 Main St 23336 757-336-6166
Warren Holland, prin. Fax 336-1902

**Christchurch, Middlesex**

---

Christchurch S 200/9-12
49 Seahorse Ln 23031 804-758-2306
John Byers, hdmstr. Fax 758-0721

**Christiansburg, Montgomery, Pop. 20,645**
Montgomery County SD 9,600/PK-12
750 Imperial St 24073 540-382-5100
Brenda Blackburn, supt. Fax 381-6127
www.mcps.org
Christiansburg HS 1,100/9-12
100 Independence Blvd 24073 540-382-5178
Dr. Kevin Siers, prin. Fax 381-6525
Christiansburg MS 800/6-8
1205 Buffalo Dr 24073 540-394-2180
Jason Garretson, prin. Fax 394-2197
Montgomery Central Alt
208 College St 24073 540-381-6100
Larry Lowe, prin. Fax 381-6185
Other Schools – See Blacksburg, Elliston, Riner, Shawsville

**Clifton, Fairfax, Pop. 280**
Fairfax County SD
Supt. — See Falls Church
Centreville HS 2,400/9-12
6001 Union Mill Rd 20124 703-802-5400
David Jagels, prin. Fax 802-5497
Liberty MS 1,100/7-8
6801 Union Mill Rd 20124 703-988-8100
Catherine Cipperly, prin. Fax 988-8197

**Clifton Forge, Alleghany, Pop. 3,785**
Regional Academic Governors SD
Supt. — See Richmond
Jackson River Governor's HS 11-12
PO Box 1000 24422 540-863-2872
Eddie Graham, dir. Fax 863-2915

---

Dabney S. Lancaster Community College Post-Sec.
PO Box 1000 24422 540-863-2800

**Clintwood, Dickenson, Pop. 1,403**
Dickenson County SD 1,900/PK-12
PO Box 1127 24228 276-926-4643
Haydee Robinson, supt. Fax 926-6374
www.dickenson.k12.va.us
Ridgeview HS 700/9-12
310 Wolfpack Way 24228 276-835-1600
Rodney Compton, prin.
Ridgeview MS, 320 Wolfpack 24228 500/6-8
John Whitner, prin. 276-835-1601

**Cloverdale, Botetourt, Pop. 3,095**
Botetourt County SD
Supt. — See Fincastle
Read Mountain MS 700/6-8
182 Orchard Hill Dr 24077 540-966-8655
Beth Mast, prin. Fax 966-8656

**Coeburn, Wise, Pop. 2,115**
Wise County SD
Supt. — See Wise
Coeburn MS 400/5-8
PO Box 670 24230 276-395-2135
Angie Clendenon, prin. Fax 395-5453
Eastside HS 400/9-12
PO Box 2036 24230 276-395-3389
Bryan Crutchfield, prin. Fax 395-5167

**Collinsville, Henry, Pop. 7,233**
Henry County SD 7,300/PK-12
PO Box 8958 24078 276-634-4700
Dr. Jared Cotton, supt. Fax 638-2925
www.henry.k12.va.us
Fieldale-Collinsville MS 900/6-8
645 Miles Rd 24078 276-647-3841
Corbin Campbell, prin. Fax 647-4090
Other Schools – See Bassett, Martinsville, Ridgeway

**Colonial Beach, Westmoreland, Pop. 3,440**
Colonial Beach SD 600/K-12
16 Irving Ave N 22443 804-224-0906
Dr. Kevin Newman, supt. Fax 224-8357
www.cbschools.net
Colonial Beach HS 200/8-12
100 1st St 22443 804-224-7166
Jennifer Grigsby, prin. Fax 224-7465

**Colonial Heights, Colonial Heights, Pop. 17,059**
Colonial Heights CSD 2,900/K-12
512 Boulevard, 804-524-3400
Dr. Joseph Cox, supt. Fax 526-4524
www.colonialhts.net
Colonial Heights HS 900/9-12
3600 Conduit Rd, 804-524-3405
Kristin Janssen, prin. Fax 520-7222
Colonial Heights MS 700/6-8
500 Conduit Rd, 804-524-3420
William Hortz, prin. Fax 526-9288

**Courtland, Southampton, Pop. 1,266**
Southhampton County SD 2,900/PK-12
PO Box 96 23837 757-653-2692
Dr. Alvera Parrish, supt. Fax 653-9422
www.southampton.k12.va.us/
Southampton HS 900/9-12
23350 Southampton Pkwy 23837 757-653-2751
Allene Atkinson, prin. Fax 653-0414
Southampton MS 600/6-8
23450 Southampton Pkwy 23837 757-653-9250
Darian Bell, prin. Fax 653-7251
Southampton Technical Career Center Vo/Tech
23450 Southampton Pkwy 23837 757-653-9170
Linda Adams, admin. Fax 653-9404

---

Southampton Academy 300/PK-12
26495 Old Plank Rd 23837 757-653-2512

**Covington, Covington, Pop. 5,839**
Alleghany County SD
Supt. — See Low Moor
Alleghany HS 900/9-12
210 Mountaineer Dr 24426 540-863-1700
Dwayne Ross, prin. Fax 863-1705
Clifton MS 700/6-8
1000 Riverview Farm Rd 24426 540-863-1726
Brenda Siple, prin. Fax 863-1731

Covington CSD 900/PK-12
340 E Walnut St 24426 540-965-1400
Thomas Long, supt. Fax 965-1404
www.covingtoncityschools.us
Covington HS 300/8-12
606 S Lexington Ave 24426 540-965-1410
Dr. Shannon Fuhrman, prin.

Jointly Operated Vo Tech SD
Supt. — None – Lolita Hall, dir.
Jackson River Tech Center Vo/Tech
105 E Country Club Ln 24426 540-862-1308
Glenn Spangler, dir. Fax 862-3592

**Crewe, Nottoway, Pop. 2,296**
Nottoway County SD
Supt. — See Nottoway
Nottoway HS 700/9-12
5267 Old Nottoway Rd 23930 434-292-5373
Dr. Daisy Hicks, prin. Fax 292-3021
Nottoway MS 400/7-8
5279 Old Nottoway Rd 23930 434-292-5375
Roger Coleman, prin. Fax 292-7479

**Crozet, Albemarle, Pop. 5,475**
Albemarle County SD
Supt. — See Charlottesville
Henley MS 800/6-8
5880 Rockfish Gap Tpke 22932 434-823-4393
Dr. Beth Costa, prin. Fax 823-2711
Western Albemarle HS 1,000/9-12
5941 Rockfish Gap Tpke 22932 434-823-8700
Dr. John Werner, prin. Fax 823-8711

**Crozier, Goochland**

---

Salem Christian S 100/PK-12
1700 Cardwell Rd 23039 804-784-4174
Todd Brooking, admin.

**Culpeper, Culpeper, Pop. 15,837**
Culpeper County SD 7,700/K-12
450 Radio Ln 22701 540-825-3677
Dr. Anthony S. Brads, supt. Fax 829-2111
www.culpeperschools.org
Binns MS 700/6-8
205 E Grandview Ave 22701 540-825-6894
Sherri Harkness, prin. Fax 829-9926
Culpeper County HS 1,000/9-12
14240 Achievement Dr 22701 540-825-8310
Jeff Dietz, prin. Fax 829-6615
Culpeper County MS 1,100/6-8
14300 Achievement Dr 22701 540-825-4140
Cathy Timmons, prin. Fax 825-7543
Eastern View HS 1,200/9-12
16332 Cyclone Way 22701 540-825-0621
E.G. Bradshaw, prin. Fax 825-9802

**Cumberland, Cumberland, Pop. 383**
Cumberland County SD 1,500/PK-12
PO Box 170 23040 804-492-4212
Dr. Amy Griffin Ed.D., supt. Fax 492-9869
www.cucps.k12.va.us
Cumberland HS 500/9-12
PO Box 140 23040 804-492-4212
Jeff Scales, prin. Fax 492-9871
Cumberland MS 300/5-8
PO Box 184 23040 804-492-4212
Jeff Dingeldein, prin. Fax 492-9868

**Daleville, Botetourt, Pop. 2,539**
Botetourt County SD
Supt. — See Fincastle
Lord Botetourt HS 1,100/9-12
1435 Roanoke Rd 24083 540-992-1261
Andy Dewease, prin. Fax 992-8381
STEM - Health Academy 9-12
57 S Center Dr 24083 540-992-3658
Stacey Jones, contact

**Damascus, Washington, Pop. 807**
Washington County SD
Supt. — See Abingdon
Damascus MS 200/6-8
32101 Government Rd 24236 276-739-4100
Scott Keith, prin. Fax 475-4032
Holston HS 300/9-12
21308 Monroe Rd 24236 276-739-4000
Kendra Honaker, prin. Fax 475-4024

**Danville, Danville, Pop. 42,537**
Danville CSD 5,200/PK-12
PO Box 9600 24543 434-799-6400
Stanley Jones, supt. Fax 799-5008
www.danvillepublicschools.org
Bonner MS 600/6-8
300 Apollo Ave 24540 434-799-6446
Daphne Wall, prin. Fax 797-8867
Galileo Magnet HS 200/9-12
230 S Ridge St 24541 434-773-8186
Jay Lancaster, prin. Fax 773-8188
Langston Focus S 100/Alt
228 Cleveland St 24541 434-799-5249
Jocelyn Fitzgerald, prin. Fax 797-8925
Washington HS 1,400/9-12
701 Broad St 24541 434-799-6410
Randall Stokes, prin. Fax 799-5251
Westwood MS 400/6-8
500 Apollo Ave 24540 434-797-8860
Joseph Baez, prin. Fax 797-8874
Adult & Continuing Education Center Adult
141 Goode St 24541 434-799-6471
Jackie Rochford, coord. Fax 797-8869

---

American National University Post-Sec.
336 Old Riverside Dr 24541 434-793-6822
Averett University Post-Sec.
420 W Main St 24541 434-791-5600
Danville Community College Post-Sec.
1008 S Main St 24541 434-797-2222
Danville Regional Medical Center Post-Sec.
142 S Main St 24541 434-799-4510
Westover Christian Academy 400/PK-12
5665 Riverside Dr 24541 434-822-0800
Shawn Weeks, admin. Fax 822-0441

**Dayton, Rockingham, Pop. 1,520**
Rockingham County SD
Supt. — See Harrisonburg
Dayton Learning Center Alt
PO Box 10 22821 540-879-2831
Emily Holloway, prin. Fax 879-2578
Pence MS 800/6-8
375 Bowman Rd 22821 540-879-2535
Camala Kite, prin. Fax 879-2179

**Dendron, Surry, Pop. 267**
Surry County SD
Supt. — See Surry
Jackson MS 300/5-8
4255 New Design Rd 23839 757-267-2810
Dr. Charlome Pierce, prin. Fax 267-0809
Surry County HS 300/9-12
1675 Hollybush Rd 23839 757-267-2211
Giron Wooden, prin. Fax 267-2978

**Dinwiddie, Dinwiddie**
Dinwiddie County SD 3,800/K-12
PO Box 7 23841 804-469-4190
William Clark, supt. Fax 469-4197
www.dinwiddie.k12.va.us
Dinwiddie County HS 1,100/9-12
PO Box 299 23841 804-469-4280
Randall Johnson, prin. Fax 469-4293
Dinwiddie County MS 700/6-8
PO Box 340 23841 804-469-5430
Alfred Cappellanti, prin. Fax 469-3389

**Disputanta, Prince George**
Prince George County SD
Supt. — See Prince George
Prince George Education Center Alt
11455 Prince George Dr 23842 804-733-2748
Mattie Thweatt, prin. Fax 733-2749

**Dry Fork, Pittsylvania**
Pittsylvania County SD
Supt. — See Chatham
Tunstall HS 900/9-12
100 Trojan Cir 24549 434-724-7111
Brian Boles, prin. Fax 724-4588
Tunstall MS 700/6-8
1160 Tunstall High Rd 24549 434-724-7086
Deborah Stowe, prin. Fax 724-7907

**Dublin, Pulaski, Pop. 2,500**
Pulaski County SD
Supt. — See Pulaski
Dublin MS 600/6-8
650 Giles Ave 24084 540-643-0367
Adam Joyce, prin. Fax 674-0813
Pulaski County HS 1,400/9-12
5414 Cougar Trail Rd 24084 540-643-0747
Michael Grim, prin. Fax 674-4722

---

New River Community College Post-Sec.
PO Box 1127 24084 540-674-3600

**Duffield, Scott, Pop. 90**
Scott County SD
Supt. — See Gate City
Rye Cove HS 300/8-12
164 Eagles Nest Ln 24244 276-940-2701
Reagan Mullins, prin. Fax 940-2277

**Dumfries, Prince William, Pop. 4,762**
Prince William County SD
Supt. — See Manassas
Potomac HS 1,600/9-12
3401 Panther Pride Dr 22026 703-441-4200
Michael Wright, prin. Fax 441-4497
Potomac MS 1,100/6-8
3130 Panther Pride Dr 22026 703-221-4996
Kevin Smith, prin. Fax 221-4998

---

St. John Paul the Great HS 500/9-12
17700 Dominican Dr 22026 703-445-0300
Sr. Mary Jordan Hoover, prin. Fax 445-0301

**Eastville, Northampton, Pop. 300**
Northampton County SD
Supt. — See Machipongo
Northampton HS 500/9-12
PO Box 38 23347 757-678-5151
Michael Myers, prin. Fax 678-5244
Northampton MS 300/7-8
PO Box 38 23347 757-678-5151
Fax 678-5244

**Elkton, Rockingham, Pop. 2,698**
Rockingham County SD
Supt. — See Harrisonburg
East Rockingham HS 700/9-12
250 Eagle Rock Rd 22827 540-298-7450
Eric Baylor, prin. Fax 298-7462
Elkton MS 500/6-8
21063 Blue and Gold Dr 22827 540-298-1228
Dr. Ramona Pence, prin. Fax 298-0029

**Elliston, Montgomery, Pop. 900**
Montgomery County SD
Supt. — See Christiansburg
Eastern Montgomery HS 300/9-12
4695 Crozier Rd 24087 540-268-3010
Daniel Knott, prin. Fax 268-3012

**Emory, Washington, Pop. 1,238**

---

Emory & Henry College Post-Sec.
PO Box 947 24327 276-944-4121

**Emporia, Emporia, Pop. 5,846**
Greensville County SD 2,600/PK-12
105 Ruffin St 23847 434-634-3748
Dr. Angela Wilson, supt. Fax 634-3495
www.gcps1.com
Greensville County HS 700/9-12
403 Harding St 23847 434-634-2195
Michelle Burton, prin.
Wyatt MS 600/6-8
206 Slagles Lake Rd 23847 434-634-5159
Medicus Riddick, prin. Fax 634-0442

**Ewing, Lee, Pop. 438**
Lee County SD
Supt. — See Jonesville
Walker HS 300/8-12
126 Blue Gray Rd 24248 276-445-4111
Ron Earley, prin. Fax 445-3046

**Exmore, Northampton, Pop. 1,433**

---

Broadwater Academy 300/PK-12
PO Box 546 23350 757-442-9041

**Fairfax, Fairfax, Pop. 21,900**
Fairfax County SD
Supt. — See Falls Church
Fairfax HS 2,700/9-12
3501 Rebel Run 22030 703-219-2200
David Goldfarb, prin. Fax 219-2297
Frost MS 1,000/7-8
4101 Pickett Rd 22032 703-426-5700
Eric McCann, prin. Fax 426-5797

Lanier MS 1,200/7-8
3801 Jermantown Rd 22030 703-934-2400
Erin Lenart, prin. Fax 934-2497
Robinson JSHS 3,900/7-12
5035 Sideburn Rd 22032 703-426-2100
Matthew Eline, prin. Fax 426-2197
Woodson HS 2,100/9-12
9525 Main St 22031 703-503-4600
Scott Poole, prin. Fax 503-4697
Fairfax County Adult HS Adult
4105 Whitacre Rd 22032 703-503-6407
Brad Rickel, prin.

---

Columbia College Post-Sec.
8300 Merrifield Ave 22031 703-206-0508
George Mason University Post-Sec.
4400 University Dr 22030 703-993-1000
New S of Northern VA 100/4-12
9431 Silver King Ct 22031 703-691-3040
John Potter M.S., hdmstr. Fax 691-3041
Paul VI HS 900/9-12
10675 Fairfax Blvd 22030 703-352-0925
Ginny Colwell, prin. Fax 273-9845
Trinity Christian S 700/K-12
11204 Braddock Rd 22030 703-273-8787
David Vanderpoel Ph.D., hdmstr. Fax 501-6744
Virginia International University Post-Sec.
11200 Waples Mill Rd # 360 22030 703-591-7042

**Falls Church, Falls Church, Pop. 11,898**
Fairfax County SD 172,900/PK-12
8115 Gatehouse Rd 22042 703-423-1000
Dr. Karen Garza, supt. Fax 423-1007
www.fcps.edu
Falls Church HS 1,600/9-12
7521 Jaguar Trl 22042 703-207-4000
Michael Yohe, prin. Fax 207-4097
Jackson MS 1,200/7-8
3020 Gallows Rd 22042 703-204-8100
Chad Lehman, prin. Fax 204-8197
Longfellow MS 1,300/7-8
2000 Westmoreland St 22043 703-533-2600
Carole Kihm, prin. Fax 533-2697
Marshall HS 1,700/9-12
7731 Leesburg Pike 22043 703-714-5400
Jeffrey Litz, prin. Fax 714-5497
Stuart HS 1,800/9-12
3301 Peace Valley Ln 22044 703-824-3900
Penny Gros, prin. Fax 824-3997
Fairfax County Adult HS Adult
7510 Lisle Ave 22043 703-506-2251
Robert Landon, admin.
Other Schools – See Alexandria, Annandale, Burke, Centreville, Chantilly, Clifton, Fairfax, Herndon, Lorton, Mc Lean, Reston, Springfield, Vienna

Falls Church CSD 1,800/K-12
800 W Broad St Ste 203 22046 703-248-5600
Dr. Toni Jones, supt. Fax 248-5613
www.fccps.org/
Henderson MS 300/6-8
7130 Leesburg Pike 22043 703-720-5700
Ty Harris, prin. Fax 720-5710
Mason HS 700/9-12
7124 Leesburg Pike 22043 703-248-5500
Tyrone Byrd, prin. Fax 248-5533

---

California University of Management/Sci Post-Sec.
400 N Washington St 22046 703-663-8088
Child Development Ctr. of Northern VA Post-Sec.
111 N Cherry St 22046
Fairfax Hospital Post-Sec.
3300 Gallows Rd 22042 703-698-3371
J Leland Center for Theological Studies Post-Sec.
1306 N Highland St 22201 703-812-4757
MedTech College Post-Sec.
6565 Arlington Blvd Ste 100 22042 703-237-6200
Standard Healthcare Services Coll of Nrg Post-Sec.
1073 W Broad St Ste 201 22046 703-891-1787
Stratford University Post-Sec.
7777 Leesburg Pike Ste 100S 22043 703-821-8570
Trinity S at Meadow View 200/7-12
2849 Meadow View Rd 22042 703-876-1920
Andrew Zwerneman, hdmstr. Fax 641-9220

**Falmouth, Stafford, Pop. 4,116**
Stafford County SD
Supt. — See Stafford
Drew MS 500/6-8
501 Cambridge St 22405 540-371-1415
Tammara Hanna, prin. Fax 371-1447

**Farmville, Prince Edward, Pop. 8,093**
Prince Edward County SD 2,300/K-12
35 Eagle Dr 23901 434-315-2100
Dr. K. David Smith, supt. Fax 392-1911
www.pecps.k12.va.us
Prince Edward County Career & Tech Ed Vo/Tech
35 Eagle Dr 23901 434-315-2140
Dr. Brad Bryant, prin. Fax 392-9018
Prince Edward County HS 700/9-12
35 Eagle Dr 23901 434-315-2130
Zoltan Kerestely, prin. Fax 392-1901
Prince Edward MS 700/5-8
35 Eagle Dr 23901 434-315-2120
Tammy Hurt, prin. Fax 392-4286

---

Fuqua S, PO Box 328 23901 400/PK-12
John Melton, head sch 434-392-4131
Longwood University Post-Sec.
201 High St 23909 434-395-2000

**Ferrum, Franklin, Pop. 1,932**

---

Ferrum College Post-Sec.
PO Box 1000 24088 540-365-2121

**Fincastle, Botetourt, Pop. 352**
Botetourt County SD 5,600/PK-12
143 Poor Farm Rd 24090 540-473-8263
John S. Busher, supt. Fax 473-8298
www.bcps.k12.va.us
Botetourt Technical Education Center Vo/Tech
253 Poor Farm Rd 24090 540-473-8216
James Bradshaw, prin. Fax 473-8376
Central Academy MS 500/6-8
367 Poor Farm Rd 24090 540-473-8333
Tim McClung, prin. Fax 473-8398
Other Schools – See Buchanan, Cloverdale, Daleville

**Fishersville, Augusta, Pop. 7,346**
Augusta County SD
Supt. — See Verona
Wilson Memorial HS 700/9-12
189 Hornet Rd 22939 540-886-4286
Dr. Kelly Troxell, prin. Fax 886-4611
Wilson MS 600/6-8
232 Hornet Rd 22939 540-245-5185
Donald Curtis, prin. Fax 245-5189

Jointly Operated Vo Tech SD
Supt. — None – Lolita Hall, dir.
Valley Vocational Tech Center Vo/Tech
49 Hornet Rd 22939 540-245-5002
Laura Tait, prin. Fax 885-0407

Regional Academic Governors SD
Supt. — See Richmond
Shenandoah Valley Governor's S 11-12
49 Hornet Rd 22939 540-245-5088
Lee Ann Whitesell, dir. Fax 886-6476

---

Augusta Health Post-Sec.
PO Box 1000 22939 540-332-4539

**Flint Hill, Rappahannock, Pop. 207**

---

Wakefield Country Day S 200/PK-12
PO Box 739 22627 540-635-8555

**Floyd, Floyd, Pop. 419**
Floyd County SD 2,000/PK-12
140 Harris Hart Rd NE 24091 540-745-9400
Dr. Kevin W. Harris Ed.D., supt. Fax 745-9496
www.floyd.k12.va.us
Floyd County HS 800/8-12
721 Baker St SE 24091 540-745-9450
Scott Watson, prin. Fax 745-9481

**Forest, Bedford, Pop. 9,010**
Bedford County SD
Supt. — See Bedford
Forest MS 1,000/6-8
100 Ashwood Dr 24551 434-525-6630
Scott Simmons, prin. Fax 525-1284
Jefferson Forest HS 1,300/9-12
1 Cavalier Cir 24551 434-525-2674
Dr. LeeAnn Calvert, prin. Fax 525-0106

---

Timberlake Christian S 400/PK-12
202 Horizon Dr 24551 434-237-5943
Jeff Abbett, admin. Fax 239-3319

**Fork Union, Fluvanna**

---

Fork Union Military Academy 400/6-12
PO Box 278 23055 434-842-3212
J. Scott Burhoe, pres. Fax 842-4300

**Fort Defiance, Augusta**
Augusta County SD
Supt. — See Verona
Fort Defiance HS 800/9-12
195 Fort Defiance Rd 24437 540-245-5050
Larry Landes, prin. Fax 245-5054
Stewart MS 600/6-8
118 Fort Defiance Rd 24437 540-245-5046
Brenda Walton, prin. Fax 245-5049

**Franklin, Southampton, Pop. 8,431**
Franklin CSD 1,300/PK-12
207 W 2nd Ave 23851 757-569-8111
Dr. Willie J. Bell, supt. Fax 516-1015
www.franklincity.k12.va.us
Franklin HS 300/9-12
310 Crescent Dr 23851 757-562-5187
Ronnie Watson, prin. Fax 562-3656
King MS 200/6-8
501 Charles St 23851 757-562-4631
Lisa B. Francis, prin. Fax 562-0231

---

Paul D. Camp Community College Post-Sec.
100 N College Dr 23851 757-569-6700

**Fredericksburg, Fredericksburg, Pop. 23,462**
Fredericksburg CSD 3,300/PK-12
817 Princess Anne St 22401 540-372-1130
Dr. David Melton, supt. Fax 372-1111
www.cityschools.com
Monroe HS 900/9-12
2300 Washington Ave 22401 540-372-1100
Dr. Taneshia Rachal, prin. Fax 373-8643
Walker-Grant MS 700/6-8
1 Learning Ln 22401 540-372-1145
Melanie Kay-Wyatt, prin. Fax 891-5449

Regional Academic Governors SD
Supt. — See Richmond
Commonwealth Governor's HS 9-12
12301 Spotswood Furnace Rd 22407 540-548-1278
Merri Kae Vanderploeg, dir. Fax 548-1736

Spotsylvania County SD 23,500/PK-12
8020 River Stone Dr 22407 540-834-2500
Scott Baker Ed.D., supt. Fax 834-2550
www.spotsylvania.k12.va.us
Battlefield MS 800/6-8
11120 Leavells Rd 22407 540-786-4400
Sheila Smith, prin. Fax 786-7109
Chancellor HS 1,400/9-12
6300 Harrison Rd 22407 540-786-2606
Jacqueline Bass-Fortune, prin. Fax 786-1176
Chancellor MS 800/6-8
6320 Harrison Rd 22407 540-786-8099
Cynthia Franzen, prin. Fax 785-9392
Freedom MS 900/6-8
7315 Smith Station Rd 22407 540-548-1030
Alan Jacobs, prin. Fax 786-0782
Massaponax HS 1,900/9-12
8201 Jefferson Davis Hwy 22407 540-710-0419
Dr. Joe Pisani, prin. Fax 710-1596
Riverbend HS 1,900/9-12
12301 Spotswood Furnace Rd 22407 540-548-4051
Dr. Troy Wright, prin. Fax 548-2964
Other Schools – See Spotsylvania

Stafford County SD
Supt. — See Stafford
Dixon-Smith MS 800/6-8
503 Deacon Rd 22405 540-899-0860
Lisa Besceglia, prin. Fax 899-0881
Gayle MS 900/6-8
100 Panther Dr 22406 540-373-0383
Robin Lloyd, prin. Fax 373-8856
Stafford HS 1,900/9-12
63 Stafford Indians Ln 22405 540-371-7200
Joe Lewis, prin. Fax 371-2389

---

Career Training Solutions Post-Sec.
10304 Spotsylvania Ave #400 22408 540-373-2200
Faith Baptist S 300/PK-12
4105 Plank Rd 22407 540-786-4953
Fredericksburg Academy 400/PK-12
10800 Academy Dr 22408 540-898-0020
Karen Moschetto, head sch Fax 898-0440
Fredericksburg Christian Upper S 500/6-12
9400 Thornton Rolling Rd 22408 540-371-3852
Cliff Williams M.Ed., prin. Fax 371-4121
Lighthouse Academy of Fredericksburg 100/PK-12
10713 Tidewater Trl 22408 540-372-9699
Mary Washington Hospital Post-Sec.
1001 Sam Perry Blvd 22401 540-899-1565
St. Michael the Archangel HS 9-12
6301 Campus Dr 22407 540-548-8748
Tim Hamer, prin.
University of Mary Washington Post-Sec.
1301 College Ave 22401 540-654-1000
Virginia Baptist College Post-Sec.
4105 Plank Rd 22407 540-785-5440

**Front Royal, Warren, Pop. 14,067**
Warren County SD 5,300/K-12
210 N Commerce Ave 22630 540-635-2171
L. Gregory Drescher, supt. Fax 636-4195
www.wcps.k12.va.us
Skyline HS 1,100/8-12
151 Skyline Vista Dr 22630 540-631-0366
Michael Smith, prin. Fax 635-4026
Warren County HS 1,000/8-12
155 Westminster Dr 22630 540-635-4144
Ernestine Jordan, prin. Fax 636-3244

---

Christendom College Post-Sec.
134 Christendom Dr 22630 540-636-2900
Front Royal Christian S 100/PK-12
80 N Lake Ave 22630 540-635-6799
Lorraine Hewitt, dir. Fax 635-6152
Randolph-Macon Academy 400/6-12
200 Academy Dr 22630 540-636-5200
David Wesley, pres. Fax 636-5344
Riverfront Christian S 200/PK-12
55 E Strasburg Rd 22630 540-635-8202
Cindy Martin, dir. Fax 636-4418

**Gainesville, Prince William, Pop. 11,049**
Prince William County SD
Supt. — See Manassas
Bull Run MS 1,800/6-8
6308 Catharpin Rd 20155 703-753-9969
Matthew Phythian, prin. Fax 753-9610
Gainesville MS 1,500/6-8
8001 Limestone Dr 20155 703-753-2997
Catherine Porter-Lucas, prin. Fax 753-4331

**Galax, Galax, Pop. 6,941**
Galax CSD 1,300/K-12
223 Long St 24333 276-236-2911
Bill Sturgill, supt. Fax 236-5776
www.gcps.k12.va.us/
Galax JSHS 500/8-12
200 Maroon Tide Dr 24333 276-236-2991
Justin Iroler, prin. Fax 236-8011

**Gate City, Scott, Pop. 2,016**
Scott County SD 3,700/PK-12
340 E Jackson St 24251 276-386-6118
John Ferguson, supt. Fax 386-2684
scott.k12.va.us
Gate City HS 500/10-12
178 Harry Fry Dr 24251 276-386-7522
Michael Lane, prin. Fax 386-2695
Gate City MS 500/7-9
170 Harry Fry Dr 24251 276-386-6065
Cindy Dorton, prin. Fax 386-2556
Scott County Career & Technical Center Vo/Tech
150 Broadwater Ave 24251 276-386-6515
Ralph Quesinberry, prin. Fax 386-2852
Other Schools – See Duffield, Nickelsville

**Glade Spring, Washington, Pop. 1,443**
Washington County SD
Supt. — See Abingdon

Glade Spring MS 300/6-8
33474 Stagecoach Rd 24340 276-739-3800
Kelly Holmes, prin. Fax 429-4211
Henry HS 400/9-12
31437 Hillman Hwy 24340 276-739-3700
Andrew Hockett, prin. Fax 944-2125

**Glen Allen, Henrico, Pop. 14,427**
Henrico County SD
Supt. — See Richmond
Academy at Virginia Randolph 300/Alt
2204 Mountain Rd 23060 804-261-5085
Jesse Casey, prin. Fax 261-5087
Center for Education & Human Development 9-12
10700 Staples Mill Rd 23060 804-501-3300
Ryan Conway, prin.
Center for Information Technology 9-12
4801 Twin Hickory Rd 23059 804-364-8000
Lynne Norris, prin.
Deep Run HS 1,700/9-12
4801 Twin Hickory Rd 23059 804-364-8000
Leonard Pritchard, prin. Fax 364-0887
Glen Allen HS 1,100/9-12
10700 Staples Mill Rd 23060 804-501-3300
Dr. Gwen Miller, prin. Fax 501-3309
Holman MS 800/6-8
600 Concourse Blvd 23059 804-346-1300
Brian Fellows Ph.D., prin. Fax 346-1309
Hungary Creek MS 900/6-8
4909 Francistown Rd 23060 804-527-2640
Robert Moose, prin. Fax 527-2642
Short Pump MS 800/6-8
4701 Pouncey Tract Rd 23059 804-360-0800
Thomas McAuley, prin. Fax 360-0808

---

ECPI University Post-Sec.
4305 Cox Rd 23060 804-934-0100
Stratford University Post-Sec.
11104 W Broad St 23060 804-290-4231

**Glenns, Middlesex**

---

Rappahannock Community College Post-Sec.
12745 College Dr 23149 804-758-6700

**Gloucester, Gloucester**
Gloucester County SD 5,500/PK-12
6099 T C Walker Rd 23061 804-693-5300
Dr. Walter Clemons, supt. Fax 693-6275
gets.gc.k12.va.us
Gloucester HS 1,900/9-12
6680 Short Ln 23061 804-693-2526
Nate Collins, prin. Fax 693-7685
Page MS 400/6-8
5198 T C Walker Rd 23061 804-693-2540
Ginny Wilburn, prin. Fax 693-2111
Peasley MS 900/6-8
2885 Hickory Fork Rd 23061 804-693-1499
Dr. Robert Parsons, prin. Fax 693-1497

**Gloucester Point, Gloucester, Pop. 9,193**

---

College of William and Mary Post-Sec.
PO Box 1346 23062 804-684-7000

**Goochland, Goochland, Pop. 840**
Goochland County SD 2,400/PK-12
PO Box 169 23063 804-556-5630
James Lane, supt. Fax 556-3847
www.glnd.k12.va.us
Goochland HS 800/9-12
3250 River Rd W Ste A 23063 804-556-5322
Mike Newman, prin. Fax 556-6485
Goochland MS 600/6-8
3250 River Rd W Ste B 23063 804-556-5320
Jennifer Rucker, prin. Fax 556-6223

**Great Falls, Fairfax, Pop. 14,902**

---

AVI Career Training Post-Sec.
10130 Colvin Run Rd Ste A 22066 703-759-2200

**Gretna, Pittsylvania, Pop. 1,254**
Pittsylvania County SD
Supt. — See Chatham
Gretna HS 600/9-12
PO Box 398 24557 434-656-2246
Kenyon Scott, prin. Fax 656-3045
Gretna MS 400/6-8
201 Coffey St 24557 434-656-2217
Vera Glass, prin. Fax 656-6122

**Grundy, Buchanan, Pop. 1,011**
Buchanan County SD 3,300/PK-12
PO Box 833 24614 276-935-4551
Tommy Justus, supt. Fax 935-7150
www.buc.k12.va.us
Buchanan County Tech & Career Center Vo/Tech
1124 Almarine Dr 24614 276-935-4541
Sue Cook, prin. Fax 935-4682
Grundy HS 500/9-12
1300 Golden Wave Dr 24614 276-935-2106
Leslie Horne, prin. Fax 935-8602
Other Schools – See Honaker, Hurley, Pilgrims Knob

---

Appalachian School of Law Post-Sec.
PO Box 2825 24614 800-895-7411

**Halifax, Halifax, Pop. 1,298**
Halifax County SD 5,500/PK-12
PO Box 1849 24558 434-476-2171
Dr. Merle Herndon, supt. Fax 476-1858
www.halifax.k12.va.us
Halifax County Career Center Vo/Tech
PO Box 1849 24558 434-476-5515
David Riddle, lead tchr. Fax 476-5527
Other Schools – See South Boston

**Hamilton, Loudoun, Pop. 498**
Loudoun County SD
Supt. — See Ashburn
Harmony MS 600/6-8
38174 W Colonial Hwy 20158 540-751-2500
Eric Stewart, prin. Fax 751-2501

---

The Catholic Distance University Post-Sec.
120 E Colonial Hwy 20158 888-254-4238

**Hampden Sydney, Prince Edward, Pop. 1,436**

---

Hampden-Sydney College Post-Sec.
1 College Rd 23943 434-223-6000

**Hampton, Hampton, Pop. 132,850**
Hampton CSD 21,600/PK-12
1 Franklin St 23669 757-727-2000
Jeffrey Smith, supt. Fax 727-2002
www.hampton.k12.va.us
Architecture & Applied Arts Academy 9-12
522 Woodland Rd 23669 757-850-5000
Bethel HS 1,900/9-12
1067 Big Bethel Rd 23666 757-825-4400
Ralph Saunders, prin. Fax 825-4465
Campus at Lee Alt
1646 Briarfield Rd 23669 757-727-1327
Myra Chambers, dir. Fax 268-3304
Davis MS 700/6-8
1435 Todds Ln 23666 757-825-4520
Violet Whiteman, prin. Fax 825-4533
Eaton MS 700/6-8
2108 Cunningham Dr 23666 757-825-4540
Sharon Slater, prin. Fax 825-4551
Governors Health Science Academy Vo/Tech
1067 Big Bethel Rd 23666 757-825-4400
Hampton HS 1,700/9-12
1491 W Queen St 23669 757-825-4430
Tiffany Hardy, prin. Fax 825-4711
Jones Magnet MS 700/6-8
1819 Nickerson Blvd 23663 757-850-7900
Dr. Daniel Bowling, prin. Fax 850-5395
Kecoughtan HS 1,900/9-12
522 Woodland Rd 23669 757-850-5000
Jeffrey Mordica, prin. Fax 850-5153
Lindsay MS 600/6-8
1636 Briarfield Rd 23661 757-825-4560
Angela Byrd-Wright, prin. Fax 825-4839
Phoebus HS 1,200/9-12
100 Ireland St 23663 757-727-1000
Mark Hudson, prin. Fax 727-0981
Spratley Gifted Center 600/3-8
339 Woodland Rd 23669 757-850-5032
Dr. Kenneth Crum, prin. Fax 850-5186
Syms MS 1,100/6-8
170 Fox Hill Rd 23669 757-850-5050
Michael Blount, prin. Fax 850-5413

Jointly Operated Vo Tech SD
Supt. — None – Lolita Hall, dir.
New Horizons Career & Tech-Butler Farm Vo/Tech
520 Butler Farm Rd 23666 757-766-1100
Dewey Ray, prin. Fax 766-3591

Newport News CSD
Supt. — See Newport News
New Horizons Alt
520 Butler Farm Rd 23666 757-766-1100
David Creamer, prin. Fax 766-3591

Regional Academic Governors SD
Supt. — See Richmond
New Horizons Governor's S Science/Tech. 11-12
520 Butler Farm Rd 23666 757-766-1100
Vikki Wismer, dir. Fax 224-5421

---

Bethel College Post-Sec.
1705 Todds Ln 23666 757-826-1883
Bryant & Stratton College Post-Sec.
4410 Claiborne Sq E Ste 233 23666 757-896-6001
Faith Outreach Education Center 100/PK-12
3105 W Mercury Blvd 23666 757-838-8949
Rev. Bobby Hartman, admin. Fax 838-4434
Hampton Christian MSHS 200/6-12
2419 N Armistead Ave 23666 757-838-7427
Tyler Ashworth, prin. Fax 827-8067
Hampton University 23669 Post-Sec.
757-727-5000
Riverside Academy Post-Sec.
2244 Executive Dr 23666 757-315-3683
Thomas Nelson Community College Post-Sec.
99 Thomas Nelson Dr 23666 757-825-2700
Virginia School of Hair Design Post-Sec.
101 W Queens Way 23669 757-722-0211

**Harrisonburg, Harrisonburg, Pop. 47,739**
Harrisonburg CSD 4,800/K-12
1 Court Sq 22802 540-434-9916
Scott Kizner, supt. Fax 434-5196
www.harrisonburg.k12.va.us
Harrisonburg HS 1,300/9-12
1001 Garbers Church Rd 22801 540-433-2651
Cynthia Prieto, prin. Fax 433-3595
Harrison MS 800/5-8
1311 W Market St 22801 540-434-1949
Don Vale, prin. Fax 434-4052
Skyline MS 500/5-8
470 Linda Ln 22802 540-434-6862
Daniel Kirwan, prin. Fax 434-6453

Jointly Operated Vo Tech SD
Supt. — None – Lolita Hall, dir.
Massanutten Tech Center Vo/Tech
325 Pleasant Valley Rd 22801 540-434-5961
Marshall Price, dir. Fax 434-1402

Rockingham County SD 11,100/PK-12
100 Mount Clinton Pike 22802 540-564-3200
Dr. Carol Fenn, supt. Fax 564-3241
www.rockingham.k12.va.us/
Other Schools – See Bridgewater, Broadway, Dayton, Elkton, Penn Laird

---

American National University Post-Sec.
1515 Country Club Rd 22802 540-432-0943
Eastern Mennonite S 400/K-12
801 Parkwood Dr 22802 540-236-6000
Eastern Mennonite University Post-Sec.
1200 Park Rd 22802 540-432-4000
James Madison University Post-Sec.
800 S Main St 22807 540-568-6211
Rockingham Memorial Hospital Post-Sec.
235 Cantrell Ave 22801 540-564-5407

**Haymarket, Prince William, Pop. 1,713**
Prince William County SD
Supt. — See Manassas
Battlefield HS 2,600/9-12
15000 Graduation Dr 20169 571-261-4400
Amy Ethridge-Conti, prin. Fax 261-4411
Reagan MS 6-8
15801 Tanning House Pl 20169 571-402-3500
Alfie Turner, prin. Fax 782-1638

**Heathsville, Northumberland, Pop. 142**
Northumberland County SD
Supt. — See Lottsburg
Northumberland HS 400/9-12
201 Academic Ln 22473 804-580-5192
Dr. Travis Burns, prin.
Northumberland MS 300/6-8
175 Academic Ln 22473 804-580-5753
Michael Ransome, prin.

**Herndon, Fairfax, Pop. 22,605**
Fairfax County SD
Supt. — See Falls Church
Carson MS 1,400/7-8
13618 McLearen Rd 20171 703-925-3600
Gordon Stokes, prin. Fax 925-3697
Herndon HS 2,300/9-12
700 Bennett St 20170 703-810-2200
William Bates, prin. Fax 810-2262
Herndon MS 900/7-8
901 Locust St 20170 703-904-4800
Justine Klena, prin. Fax 904-4897

---

Temple Baptist S 200/PK-12
1545 Dranesville Rd 20170 703-437-7400

**Highland Springs, Henrico, Pop. 15,359**
Henrico County SD
Supt. — See Richmond
Advance College Academy 9-12
15 S Oak Ave 23075 804-328-4000
Allen Riddle, prin.
Center for Engineering 9-12
15 S Oak Ave 23075 804-328-4000
Billy Batkins, prin.
Highland Springs HS 1,800/9-12
15 S Oak Ave 23075 804-328-4000
Pamela Bell, prin. Fax 328-4013
Highland Springs Technical Center Vo/Tech
100 Tech Dr 23075 804-328-4075
William Crowder, prin. Fax 328-4074
Highland Springs Adult Ed Center Adult
201 E Nine Mile Rd 23075 804-328-4095
Gregory Lawson, prin.

**Hillsville, Carroll, Pop. 2,663**
Carroll County SD 3,500/PK-12
605 Pine St Ste 9 24343 276-728-3191
Dr. Strader Blankenship, supt. Fax 728-3195
www.ccpsd.k12.va.us
Blue Ridge Crossroads Governor's Academy Vo/Tech
100 Cavs Ln 24343 276-728-2125
Roland Hall, coord.
Carroll County HS 900/9-12
100 Cavs Ln 24343 276-728-2125
Charles Thompson, prin. Fax 728-9067
Carroll County MS 300/6-8
1036 N Main St 24343 276-728-2382
Marc Quesenberry, prin. Fax 728-4089
Regional Alternative Education Center Alt
205 Oak St 24343 276-728-9055
Jessee Woods, prin.

**Honaker, Russell, Pop. 1,440**
Buchanan County SD
Supt. — See Grundy
Council HS 100/8-12
7802 Helen Henderson Hwy 24260 276-859-2627
Chris Hagerman, prin. Fax 859-6227

Russell County SD
Supt. — See Lebanon
Honaker HS 500/8-12
PO Box 764 24260 276-873-6363
Tony Bush, prin. Fax 873-7252

**Hopewell, Hopewell, Pop. 21,953**
Hopewell CSD 4,200/PK-12
103 N 12th Ave 23860 804-541-6400
Dr. Melody Hackney, supt. Fax 541-6401
www.hopewell.k12.va.us
Hopewell HS 1,100/9-12
400 S Mesa Dr 23860 804-541-6402
Thomas M. Pond, prin. Fax 541-6403
Woodlawn Learning Center 300/Alt
1100 Dinwiddie Ave 23860 804-541-6414
Joyce Jones, prin. Fax 458-2064
Woodson MS 900/6-8
1000 Winston Churchill Dr 23860 804-541-6404
Shannon Royster, prin. Fax 541-6405

---

West End Christian S 200/PK-12
1600 Atlantic St 23860 804-458-6142
Amy Griggs, prin. Fax 458-7183

**Hot Springs, Bath, Pop. 727**
Bath County SD
Supt. — See Warm Springs
Bath County HS 300/8-12
464 Charger Ln 24445 540-839-2431
Sarah Rowe, prin. Fax 839-3290

**Hurley, Buchanan**
Buchanan County SD
Supt. — See Grundy
Hurley HS 200/8-12
6339 Hurley Rd 24620 276-566-7642
Pam Dotson, prin. Fax 566-7127

**Hurt, Pittsylvania, Pop. 1,295**

---

Faith Christian Academy 200/PK-12
PO Box 670 24563 434-324-8276
Lisa Moore, admin. Fax 324-8279

**Independence, Grayson, Pop. 933**
Grayson County SD 1,700/PK-12
PO Box 888 24348 276-773-2832
Dr. Larry Massie, supt. Fax 773-2939
www.grayson.k12.va.us
Grayson County Career & Technical Center Vo/Tech
PO Box 707 24348 276-773-2951
Fax 773-2396
Grayson County HS 800/8-12
PO Box 828 24348 276-773-2131
Brandi Ray, prin. Fax 773-2682

**Isle of Wight, Isle of Wight**

---

Isle of Wight Academy 600/PK-12
PO Box 105 23397 757-357-3866

**Jetersville, Nottoway**
Jointly Operated Vo Tech SD
Supt. — None - Lolita Hall, dir.
Amelia-Nottoway Technical Center Vo/Tech
148 Votech Rd 23083 434-645-7854
Mary Tisdale, dir. Fax 645-1044

Nottoway County SD
Supt. — See Nottoway
Piedmont Alternative S Alt
148 Votech Rd 23083 434-645-7854
Mary Tisdale, dir. Fax 645-1044

**Jonesville, Lee, Pop. 1,025**
Lee County SD 3,200/PK-12
153 School Board Pl 24263 276-346-2107
Mark Carter, supt. Fax 346-0307
www.leectysch.com/
Jonesville MS 200/6-8
160 Bulldog Cir 24263 276-346-1011
Dr. Lynn Metcalfe, prin. Fax 346-1411
Lee HS 700/9-12
200 General Ln 24263 276-346-0173
Michelle Warner, prin. Fax 346-4032
Other Schools – See Ben Hur, Ewing, Pennington Gap

**Kenbridge, Lunenburg, Pop. 1,244**
Lunenburg County SD 1,600/PK-12
PO Box 710 23944 434-676-2467
Charles Berkley, supt. Fax 676-1000
www.lun.k12.va.us
Other Schools – See Victoria

**Keysville, Charlotte, Pop. 820**
Regional Academic Governors SD
Supt. — See Richmond
Governor's S of Southside VA 11-12
200 Daniel Rd 23947 434-736-2086
Karen Puckett, dir. Fax 736-2082

---

Southside Virginia Community College Post-Sec.
200 Daniel Rd 23947 434-736-2018

**Kilmarnock, Lancaster, Pop. 1,466**
Lancaster County SD
Supt. — See Weems
Lancaster MS 500/4-8
191 School St 22482 804-462-5100
Jessica Davis, prin. Fax 435-0589

**King and Queen Court House, King and Queen, Pop. 84**
King & Queen County SD 800/PK-12
PO Box 97 23085 804-785-5981
Dr. Carol Carter, supt. Fax 785-5686
www.kqps.net
Central HS 300/8-12
17024 The Trl 23085 804-785-6102
Antione Monroe, prin. Fax 785-5129

**King George, King George, Pop. 4,296**
King George County SD 4,100/K-12
PO Box 1239 22485 540-775-5833
Dr. Robert B. Benson, supt. Fax 775-2165
www.kgcs.k12.va.us
King George HS 1,300/9-12
10100 Foxes Way 22485 540-775-3535
Dr. Jesse Boyd, prin. Fax 775-8426
King George MS 700/7-8
8246 Dahlgren Rd 22485 540-775-2331
Jennifer Collins, prin. Fax 775-0263

**King William, King William, Pop. 228**
King William County SD 2,300/PK-12
PO Box 185 23086 804-769-3434
Dr. Mark Jones, supt. Fax 769-3312
www.kwcps.k12.va.us
Hamilton-Holmes MS 500/6-8
18444 King William Rd 23086 804-769-3434
Beverly Young, prin.
King William HS, 80 Cavalier Dr 23086 600/9-12
Dr. Stanley Waskiewicz, prin. 804-769-3434

**Lancaster, Lancaster**
Lancaster County SD
Supt. — See Weems
Lancaster HS 400/9-12
PO Box 790 22503 804-462-5177
Erskine Morgan, prin. Fax 462-5100

**Lawrenceville, Brunswick, Pop. 1,414**
Brunswick County SD 2,000/PK-12
1718 Farmers Field Rd 23868 434-848-3138
Dora Wynn M.Ed., supt. Fax 848-4001
www.brun.k12.va.us
Brunswick HS 600/9-12
2171 Lawrenceville Plank Rd 23868 434-848-2716
Christopher Coleman, prin. Fax 848-6303
Russell MS 400/6-8
19400 Christanna Hwy 23868 434-848-2132
Dr. Virginia Berry, prin. Fax 848-6201

---

Brunswick Academy 300/PK-12
2100 Planters Rd 23868 434-848-2220
Dave Newsom, head sch Fax 848-4729

**Lebanon, Russell, Pop. 3,395**
Russell County SD 4,300/PK-12
PO Box 8 24266 276-889-6500
Dr. Brenda Hess, supt. Fax 889-6508
www.russell.k12.va.us
Lebanon HS 700/8-12
PO Box 217 24266 276-889-6539
Joseph Long, prin. Fax 889-0622
Russell County Alternative Center Alt
PO Box 8 24266 276-889-6521
Michael Roberson, prin. Fax 889-6527
Russell County Career & Technology Ctr Vo/Tech
PO Box 849 24266 276-889-6550
Jenny Fields, prin. Fax 889-4470
Other Schools – See Castlewood, Honaker

**Leesburg, Loudoun, Pop. 41,241**
Loudoun County SD
Supt. — See Ashburn
Belmont Ridge MS 1,400/6-8
19045 Upper Belmont Pl 20176 571-252-2220
Ryan Hitchman, prin. Fax 669-1455
Douglass S Alt
407 E Market St 20176 571-252-2060
Dr. John Robinson, prin. Fax 771-6555
Harper Park MS 1,000/6-8
701 Potomac Station Dr NE 20176 571-252-2820
Elizabeth Robinson, prin. Fax 779-8867
Heritage HS 1,200/9-12
520 Evergreen Mill Rd SE 20175 571-252-2800
Jeffrey Adam, prin. Fax 252-2801
Loudoun County HS 1,400/9-12
415 Dry Mill Rd SW 20175 571-252-2000
Dr. Michelle Luttrell, prin. Fax 252-2001
Monroe Technology Center Vo/Tech
715 Childrens Center Rd SW 20175 571-252-2080
Wagner Grier, prin. Fax 771-6563
Riverside HS 9-12
19019 Upper Belmont Pl 20176 571-554-8900
Doug Anderson, prin.
Simpson MS 1,000/6-8
490 Evergreen Mill Rd SE 20175 571-252-2840
Chad Runfola, prin. Fax 771-6643
Smart's Mill MS 1,000/6-8
850 N King St 20176 571-252-2030
William Waldman, prin. Fax 252-2043
Tuscarora HS 9-12
801 N King St 20176 571-252-1900
Pamela Paul-Jacobs, prin. Fax 252-1901

**Lexington, Lexington, Pop. 6,907**
Lexington CSD 500/K-8
300 Diamond St 24450 540-463-7146
Scott Jefferies, supt. Fax 464-5230
www.lexedu.org
Lylburn-Downing MS 200/6-8
302 Diamond St 24450 540-463-3532
Steven Eckstrom, prin.

Rockbridge County SD 2,600/PK-12
2893 Collierstown Rd 24450 540-463-7386
John Reynolds, supt. Fax 463-7823
www.rockbridge.k12.va.us/
Maury River MS 300/6-8
600 Waddell St 24450 540-463-3129
Randy Walters, prin. Fax 464-4838
Rockbridge County HS 1,000/9-12
143 Greenhouse Rd 24450 540-463-5555
Haywood Hand, prin. Fax 463-6152

---

Rockbridge Christian Academy 100/PK-12
PO Box 570 24450 540-463-5456
Mary Phillips, admin. Fax 463-3485
Virginia Military Institute Post-Sec.
319 Letcher Ave 24450 540-464-7230
Washington and Lee University Post-Sec.
204 W Washington St 24450 540-458-8400

**Locust Grove, Orange**
Orange County SD
Supt. — See Orange
Locust Grove MS 700/6-8
6368 Flat Run Rd 22508 540-661-4480
Kimberly Crandall, prin. Fax 854-6430

---

Germanna Community College Post-Sec.
2130 Germanna Hwy 22508 540-423-9030

**Locust Hill, Middlesex**
Middlesex County SD
Supt. — See Saluda
St. Clare Walker MS 300/6-8
PO Box 9 23092 804-758-2561
Tracy Seitz, prin. Fax 758-0834

**Lorton, Fairfax, Pop. 17,779**
Fairfax County SD
Supt. — See Falls Church
South County HS 2,000/9-12
8501 Silverbrook Rd 22079 703-446-1600
Matt Ragone, prin. Fax 446-1697
South County MS 7-8
8700 Laurel Crest Dr 22079 703-690-5500
Marsha Manning, prin. Fax 690-5597

---

Metropolitan S of the Arts Academy 6-12
9601 Ox Rd 22079 703-399-0444
Cheryl Wilhoyte Ph.D., head sch Fax 373-2700

**Lottsburg, Northumberland**
Northumberland County SD 1,500/PK-12
2172 Northumberland Hwy 22511 804-529-6134
Dr. Rebecca Gates, supt. Fax 529-6449
www.nucps.net
Other Schools – See Heathsville

**Lovingston, Nelson, Pop. 495**
Nelson County SD 2,000/PK-12
PO Box 276 22949 434-260-7646
Dr. Jeff Comer, supt. Fax 263-7115
www.nelson.k12.va.us
Nelson County HS 600/9-12
6919 Thomas Nelson Hwy 22949 434-263-8317
Todd Weidow, prin. Fax 263-5987
Nelson MS 500/6-8
6925 Thomas Nelson Hwy 22949 434-263-4801
Dr. Roger Dunnick, prin. Fax 263-4483

**Low Moor, Alleghany, Pop. 252**
Alleghany County SD 2,400/K-12
PO Box 140 24457 540-863-1800
Eugene Kotulka, supt. Fax 863-1804
www.alleghany.k12.va.us/
Other Schools – See Covington

**Luray, Page, Pop. 4,837**
Page County SD 3,500/PK-12
735 W Main St 22835 540-743-6533
Donna Whitley-Smith, supt. Fax 743-7784
www.pagecounty.k12.va.us
Luray HS 500/9-12
243 Bulldog Dr 22835 540-743-3800
Clint Runyan, prin. Fax 743-5524
Luray MS 400/6-8
14 Luray Ave 22835 540-843-2660
Kelly Lawton, prin. Fax 743-1709
Page County Technical Ctr Vo/Tech
525 Middleburg Rd 22835 540-778-7282
Roger Mello, prin. Fax 778-4272
Other Schools – See Shenandoah

**Lynchburg, Lynchburg, Pop. 73,910**
Campbell County SD
Supt. — See Rustburg
Brookville HS 1,000/9-12
100 Laxton Rd 24502 434-239-2636
Tom Cole, prin. Fax 239-6706
Brookville MS 700/6-8
320 Bee Dr 24502 434-239-9267
Edwin Martin, prin. Fax 237-8974

Lynchburg CSD 8,700/PK-12
PO Box 2497 24505 434-515-5000
Dr. Scott S. Brabrand, supt. Fax 846-1500
www.lcsedu.net
Dunbar MS for Innovation 600/6-8
1200 Polk St 24504 434-515-5310
Kacey M. Crabbe, prin. Fax 522-3727
Fort Hill Community S Alt
1350 Liggates Rd 24502 434-515-5150
Cathy L. Viar, coord. Fax 522-2322
Glass HS 1,400/9-12
2111 Memorial Ave 24501 434-515-5370
Dr. Tracy S. Richardson, prin. Fax 522-3741
Heritage HS 1,100/9-12
3020 Wards Ferry Rd 24502 434-515-5400
Timothy T. Beatty, prin. Fax 582-1137
Linkhorne MS 600/6-8
2525 Linkhorne Dr 24503 434-515-5330
Nancy Claudio, prin. Fax 384-2810
Sandusky MS 600/6-8
805 Chinook Pl 24502 434-515-5350
Leverne L. Marshall, prin. Fax 582-1183
XLR8 STEM Academy 11-12
3506 Wards Rd 24502 434-832-7731
Susan W. Cash, dir.
Adult Learning Center Adult
1200 Polk St 24504 434-515-5160
Howard Brown, lead tchr. Fax 522-2320

Regional Academic Governors SD
Supt. — See Richmond
Central VA Governor's S Science & Tech 11-12
3020 Wards Ferry Rd 24502 434-477-5980
Dr. Steven Smith, dir. Fax 239-4140

---

American National University Post-Sec.
104 Candlewood Ct 24502 434-239-3500
Centra College of Nursing Post-Sec.
905 Lakeside Dr Ste A 24501 434-200-3070
Central Virginia Community College Post-Sec.
3506 Wards Rd 24502 434-832-7600
Doss Junior Academy 100/K-12
19 George St 24502 434-237-1899
Holy Cross Regional S 200/PK-12
2125 Langhorne Rd 24501 434-847-5436
Doug Washington, prin. Fax 847-4156
Liberty Christian Academy 2,000/PK-12
100 Mountain View Rd 24502 434-832-2000
John Patterson, prin. Fax 832-2027
Liberty University Post-Sec.
1971 University Blvd 24502 434-582-2000
Lynchburg College Post-Sec.
1501 Lakeside Dr 24501 434-544-8100

Lynchburg General Hosp School of Nursing Post-Sec.
1901 Tate Springs Rd 24501 434-947-3070
Miller-Motte Technical College Post-Sec.
1011 Creekside Ln 24502 434-239-5222
New Covenant S 400/K-12
122 Fleetwood Dr 24501 434-847-8313
Randolph College Post-Sec.
2500 Rivermont Ave 24503 434-947-8000
Virginia Episcopal S 200/9-12
400 V E S RD 24503 434-385-3600
Tommy Battle, hdmstr. Fax 385-3603
Virginia University of Lynchburg Post-Sec.
2058 Garfield Ave 24501 434-528-5276

**Machipongo, Northampton**
Northampton County SD 1,800/PK-12
7207 Young St 23405 757-678-5151
Charles E. Lawrence, supt. Fax 678-7267
www.ncpsk12.com
TECH Center Alt
7207 Young St 23405 757-678-5151
Melinda Phillips, prin. Fax 678-7267
Other Schools – See Eastville

**Mc Lean, Fairfax, Pop. 46,663**
Fairfax County SD
Supt. — See Falls Church
Cooper MS 800/7-8
977 Balls Hill Rd 22101 703-442-5800
Arlene Randall, prin. Fax 442-5897
Langley HS 2,000/9-12
6520 Georgetown Pike 22101 703-287-2700
Fred Amico, prin. Fax 287-2797
Mc Lean HS 2,000/9-12
1633 Davidson Rd 22101 703-714-5700
Ellen Reilly, prin. Fax 714-5797

---

Madeira S 300/9-12
8328 Georgetown Pike 22067 703-556-8200
Pilar Cabeza de Vaca, head sch Fax 893-3289
Oakcrest S 200/6-12
850 Balls Hill Rd 22101 703-790-5450
Mary Ortiz Ph.D., head sch Fax 790-5380
Potomac S 1,000/K-12
1301 Potomac School Rd 22101 703-356-4100
John Kowalik, hdmstr. Fax 883-9031
Reformed Theological Seminary Post-Sec.
1651 Old Meadow Rd Ste 300 22102 703-448-3393

**Madison, Madison, Pop. 214**
Madison County SD 1,800/PK-12
60 School Board Ct 22727 540-948-3780
Dr. Matthew Eberhardt, supt. Fax 948-6988
www2.madisonschools.k12.va.us
Madison County HS 600/9-12
68 Mountaineer Ln 22727 540-948-3785
Gary Wintersgill, prin. Fax 948-4425
Wetsel MS 400/6-8
186 Mountaineer Ln 22727 540-948-3783
Timothy Taylor, prin. Fax 948-4809

**Madison Heights, Amherst, Pop. 11,015**
Amherst County SD
Supt. — See Amherst
Monelison MS 600/6-8
257 Trojan Rd 24572 434-846-1307
Regina Phillips, prin. Fax 846-5318

---

Temple Christian S 300/PK-12
PO Box 970 24572 434-846-0024

**Manassas, Manassas, Pop. 36,735**
Manassas CSD 7,000/K-12
8700 Centreville Rd Ste 400 20110 571-377-6000
Dr. Catherine Magouyrk, supt. Fax 257-8801
Johnson Learning Center Alt
9051 Tudor Ln 20110 571-377-7250
Dr. Lukisa Barrera-Gibbs, prin. Fax 257-8844
Metz JHS 1,000/7-8
9700 Fairview Ave 20110 571-377-6800
Kimberly Buckheit, prin. Fax 257-8615
Osbourn HS 2,100/9-12
9005 Tudor Ln 20110 571-377-7000
Cathy Benner, prin. Fax 530-0937

Prince William County SD 79,400/PK-12
PO Box 389 20108 703-791-7200
Steven Walts Ed.D., supt. Fax 791-8033
www.pwcs.edu
Benton MS 1,300/6-8
7411 Hoadly Rd 20112 703-791-0727
Denise Huebner, prin. Fax 791-0977
Jackson HS 2,500/9-12
8820 Rixlew Ln 20109 703-365-2900
Richard Nichols, prin. Fax 365-6984
New Directions Alternative S Alt
8886 Rixlew Ln 20109 703-393-7261
Robert Eichorn, prin. Fax 393-3083
Osbourn Park HS 2,800/9-12
8909 Euclid Ave 20111 703-365-6500
Neil Beech, prin. Fax 365-6798
Parkside MS 1,200/6-8
8602 Mathis Ave 20110 703-361-3106
Mary Jane Boynton, prin. Fax 361-8993
Saunders MS 1,100/6-8
13557 Spriggs Rd 20112 703-670-9188
Sheila Huckestein, prin. Fax 670-3078
Stonewall MS 1,100/6-8
10100 Lomond Dr 20109 703-361-3185
John Miller, prin. Fax 368-1266
Other Schools – See Bristow, Dumfries, Gainesville, Haymarket, Manassas Park, Nokesville, Triangle, Woodbridge

Regional Academic Governors SD
Supt. — See Richmond
Governor's S @ Innovation Park 11-12
10910 University Blvd 20110 703-993-7027
Karen Dalfrey Ph.D., dir. Fax 993-7025

---

American Military University Post-Sec.
10110 Battleview Pkwy # 114 20109 703-330-5398
Aviation Institute of Maintenance Post-Sec.
10640 Davidson Pl 20109 703-257-5515
DeVry University Post-Sec.
10432 Balls Ford Rd Ste 130 20109 866-613-8662
ECPI University Post-Sec.
10021 Balls Ford Rd # 100 20109 703-330-5300
Seton S 400/7-12
9314 Maple St 20110 703-368-3220
Anne Carroll, prin. Fax 393-1199
Strayer University Post-Sec.
9990 Battleview Pkwy 20109 703-330-8400

**Manassas Park, Manassas Park, Pop. 13,791**
Manassas Park CSD 3,000/PK-12
1 Park Center Ct Ste A 20111 703-335-8850
Dr. C. Bruce McDade, supt. Fax 361-4583
www.mpark.net
Manassas Park HS 800/9-12
8200 Euclid Ave 20111 703-361-9131
Dr. Debbie Bergeron, prin. Fax 330-1218
Manassas Park MS 700/6-8
8202 Euclid Ave 20111 703-361-1510
Pam Kalso, prin. Fax 331-3538

Prince William County SD
Supt. — See Manassas
New Dominion Alternative S Alt
8220 Conner Dr 20111 703-361-9808
Michael Lint, prin. Fax 361-2864

**Marion, Smyth, Pop. 5,878**
Smyth County SD 4,400/PK-12
121 Bagley Cir Ste 300 24354 276-783-3791
Dr. Michael Robinson, supt. Fax 783-3291
www.scsb.org
Marion MS 500/6-8
134 Wilden St 24354 276-783-4466
Damon Mazoff, prin. Fax 783-4952
Marion SHS 700/9-12
848 Stage St 24354 276-783-4731
Mike Davidson, prin. Fax 783-4117
Smyth Career & Technology Center Vo/Tech
147 Fox Valley Rd 24354 276-646-8117
Songia Widener, prin. Fax 646-4009
Other Schools – See Chilhowie, Saltville

**Martinsville, Martinsville, Pop. 13,595**
Henry County SD
Supt. — See Collinsville
Laurel Park MS 800/6-8
280 Laurel Park Ave 24112 276-632-7216
Jo Ellen Hylton, prin. Fax 632-4865
Center for Community Learning Adult
340 Ridgedale Dr 24112 276-638-1668
Lynn Fitzgibbons, coord. Fax 638-3942

Martinsville CSD 2,300/PK-12
PO Box 5548 24115 276-403-5820
Pamela Heath, supt. Fax 403-5825
www.martinsville.k12.va.us
Martinsville HS 700/9-12
351 Commonwealth Blvd E 24112 276-403-5870
Angela Weinerth, prin. Fax 632-1516
Martinsville MS 500/5-8
201 Brown St 24112 276-403-5886
Cynthia Tarpley, prin. Fax 638-4140

Regional Academic Governors SD
Supt. — See Richmond
Piedmont Governor's S for Math/Sci/Tech 11-12
PO Box 984 24114 276-403-5624
Brian Pace, prin. Fax 403-5638

---

American National University Post-Sec.
905 Memorial Blvd N 24112 276-632-5621
Patrick Henry Community College Post-Sec.
645 Patriot Ave 24112 276-638-8777

**Mathews, Mathews, Pop. 530**
Mathews County SD 1,200/K-12
PO Box 369 23109 804-725-3909
Nancy Welch, supt. Fax 725-3951
www.mathews.k12.va.us
Hunter MS 400/5-8
PO Box 339 23109 804-725-2434
Laurel Byrd, prin. Fax 725-2337
Mathews HS 400/9-12
PO Box 38 23109 804-725-3702
Dr. Toni Childress, prin. Fax 725-5778

**Matoaca, Chesterfield, Pop. 2,359**
Chesterfield County SD
Supt. — See Chesterfield
Matoaca MS 1,100/6-8
6001 Hickory Rd 23803 804-590-3110
Dr. Gayle Hines, prin. Fax 590-9378

**Max Meadows, Wythe, Pop. 559**
Wythe County SD
Supt. — See Wytheville
Ft. Chiswell HS 500/9-12
1 Pioneer Trl 24360 276-637-3437
Robbie Patton, prin. Fax 637-6316
Ft. Chiswell MS 400/6-8
101 Pioneer Trl 24360 276-637-4400
Brett Booher, prin. Fax 637-4452

**Mechanicsville, Hanover, Pop. 35,793**
Hanover County SD
Supt. — See Ashland
Atlee HS 1,600/9-12
9414 Atlee Station Rd 23116 804-723-2100
Dr. John Wheeler, prin. Fax 723-2131
Chickahominy MS 1,200/6-8
9450 Atlee Station Rd 23116 804-723-2160
Mark Beckett, prin. Fax 723-2191
Georgetown S Alt
10000 Learning Ln 23116 804-723-3460
Brian Ford, admin. Fax 723-3470
Hanover Center for Trades and Technology Vo/Tech
10002 Learning Ln 23116 804-723-2020
Justin Roerink, admin. Fax 723-2039
Hanover HS 1,300/9-12
10307 Chamberlayne Rd 23116 804-723-3700
Kristina Reece, prin. Fax 723-3759
Jackson MS 1,200/6-8
8021 Lee Davis Rd 23111 804-723-2260
Nancy Disharoon, prin. Fax 723-2261
Lee-Davis HS 1,600/9-12
7052 Mechanicsville Tpke 23111 804-723-2200
Charles Stevens, prin. Fax 723-2202
Oak Knoll MS 900/6-8
10295 Chamberlayne Rd 23116 804-365-4740
Caroline Harris, prin. Fax 365-4741

**Melfa, Accomack, Pop. 396**

---

Eastern Shore Community College Post-Sec.
29300 Lankford Hwy 23410 757-789-1789

**Middleburg, Loudoun, Pop. 655**

---

Foxcroft S 100/9-12
PO Box 5555 20118 540-687-5555
Catherine McGehee, head sch Fax 687-8061
Middleburg Academy 200/9-12
35321 Notre Dame Ln 20117 540-687-5581
Colley Bell, head sch Fax 687-3103

**Middletown, Frederick, Pop. 1,237**

---

Lord Fairfax Community College Post-Sec.
173 Skirmisher Ln 22645 540-868-7000

**Midland, Fauquier, Pop. 218**
Fauquier County SD
Supt. — See Warrenton
Southeastern Alternative S Alt
4484 Catlett Rd 22728 540-422-7390
Dr. Shelly Neibauer, prin. Fax 422-7409

**Midlothian, Chesterfield**
Chesterfield County SD
Supt. — See Chesterfield
Bailey Bridge MS 1,500/6-8
12501 Bailey Bridge Rd 23112 804-739-6200
Kume Goranson, prin. Fax 739-6211
Career and Technical Center @ Hull Vo/Tech
13900 Hull St Rd 23112 804-639-8668
Brian Russell, prin. Fax 639-6394
Clover Hill HS 1,800/9-12
13301 Kelly Green Ln 23112 804-639-4940
Dr. Deborah Marks, prin. Fax 739-5000
Cosby HS 2,100/9-12
14300 Fox Club Pkwy 23112 804-639-8340
Dr. Brenda Mayo, prin. Fax 639-8357
James River HS 2,100/9-12
3700 James River Rd 23113 804-378-2420
Jeff Ellick, prin. Fax 379-2695
Manchester HS 1,900/9-12
12601 Bailey Bridge Rd 23112 804-739-6275
Pete Koste, prin. Fax 739-6340
Midlothian HS 1,500/9-12
401 Charter Colony Pkwy 23114 804-378-2440
Shawn Abel, prin. Fax 378-2450
Midlothian MS 1,200/6-8
13501 Midlothian Tpke 23113 804-378-2460
Dr. Patrick Stanfield, prin. Fax 378-7556
Robious MS 1,300/6-8
2701 Robious Crossing Dr 23113 804-378-2510
Dr. Patrick Held, prin. Fax 378-2519
Swift Creek MS 1,000/6-8
3700 Old Hundred Rd S 23112 804-739-6315
Dr. James Frye, prin. Fax 739-6322
Tomahawk Creek MS 1,200/6-8
1600 Learning Place Loop 23114 804-378-7120
Dr. David Ellena, prin. Fax 794-2672

---

Empire Beauty School Post-Sec.
10807 Hull Street Rd 23112 800-575-5983
Millwood S 200/PK-12
15100 Millwood School Ln 23112 804-639-3200

**Milford, Caroline**
Caroline County SD
Supt. — See Bowling Green
Caroline HS 1,200/9-12
19155 Rogers Clark Blvd 22514 804-633-9886
Jeff Wick, prin. Fax 633-2435
Caroline MS 1,000/6-8
13325 Devils Three Jump Rd 22514 804-633-6561
Angela Wright, prin. Fax 633-9014

**Mineral, Louisa, Pop. 464**
Louisa County SD 4,200/PK-12
953 Davis Hwy 23117 540-894-5115
Dr. Deborah Pettit Ed.D., supt. Fax 894-0252
www.lcps.k12.va.us
Louisa HS 1,400/9-12
757 Davis Hwy 23117 540-894-5436
Lee Downey, prin. Fax 894-0534
Louisa MS 1,100/6-8
1009 Davis Hwy 23117 540-894-5457
Dr. Lisa Chen, prin. Fax 894-5096

**Moneta, Bedford**
Bedford County SD
Supt. — See Bedford
Staunton River HS 1,100/9-12
1095 Golden Eagle Dr 24121 540-297-7151
Joshua Cornett, prin. Fax 297-4514
Staunton River MS 800/6-8
1293 Golden Eagle Dr 24121 540-297-4152
Dr. Karen Woodford, prin. Fax 297-4076

**Monterey, Highland, Pop. 147**
Highland County SD 200/PK-12
PO Box 250 24465 540-468-6300
Dr. Thomas Schott, supt. Fax 468-6306
www.highland.k12.va.us
Highland JSHS 100/6-12
PO Box 430 24465 540-468-6320
Tim Good, prin. Fax 468-6332

**Montross, Westmoreland, Pop. 382**
Westmoreland County SD 1,700/PK-12
141 Opal Ln 22520 804-493-8018
Rebecca Lowry, supt. Fax 493-9323
division.wmlcps.org
Montross MS 400/6-8
8884 Menokin Rd 22520 804-493-9818
Jane Geyer, prin. Fax 493-0918
Washington & Lee HS 500/9-12
16380 Kings Hwy 22520 804-493-8015
Dashan Turner, prin. Fax 493-0243

**Mount Jackson, Shenandoah, Pop. 1,975**
Regional Academic Governors SD
Supt. — See Richmond
Massanutten Regional Governor's S 11-12
6375 Main St 22842 540-477-3226
Susan Fream, dir. Fax 477-3523

Shenandoah County SD
Supt. — See Woodstock
Triplett Tech Vo/Tech
6375 Main St 22842 540-477-3161
Connie Pangle, prin. Fax 477-2402

**Mouth of Wilson, Grayson**

---

Oak Hill Academy 100/8-12
2635 Oak Hill Rd 24363 276-579-2619
Dr. Michael Groves, pres. Fax 579-4722

**Narrows, Giles, Pop. 2,019**
Giles County SD
Supt. — See Pearisburg
Narrows HS 300/8-12
1 Green Wave Ln 24124 540-726-2384
Mark Husband, prin. Fax 726-2775

**Naruna, Campbell**
Campbell County SD
Supt. — See Rustburg
Campbell JSHS 600/6-12
PO Box 7 24576 434-376-2015
Dabney Hanson, prin. Fax 376-5859

**New Castle, Craig, Pop. 151**
Craig County SD 700/PK-12
PO Box 245 24127 540-864-5191
Kelly Wilmore, supt. Fax 864-6885
www.craig.k12.va.us/
Craig County MSHS 400/6-12
25239 Craigs Creek Rd 24127 540-864-5185
Robert Stump, prin. Fax 864-5636

**New Kent, New Kent, Pop. 227**
Jointly Operated Vo Tech SD
Supt. — None - Lolita Hall, dir.
Bridging Comm Reg Career & Technical Ctr Vo/Tech
7930 New Chipping Ln 23124 804-966-8575
Dr. Stephen Trexler, prin. Fax 966-8769

New Kent County SD 2,900/PK-12
PO Box 110 23124 804-966-9650
Dr. David Myers, supt. Fax 966-8556
www.newkentschools.org
New Kent County HS 900/9-12
7365 Egypt Rd 23124 804-966-9671
Chris Valdrighi, prin. Fax 966-2773
New Kent County MS 700/6-8
7501 Egypt Rd 23124 804-966-9655
Sammy Fudge, prin. Fax 966-2703

**New Market, Shenandoah, Pop. 2,116**

---

Shenandoah Valley Academy 200/9-12
234 W Lee Hwy 22844 540-740-3161

**Newport News, Newport News, Pop. 174,010**
Jointly Operated Vo Tech SD
Supt. — None - Lolita Hall, dir.
New Horizons Career & Tech-Woodside Vo/Tech
13400 Woodside Ln 23608 757-874-4444
Bruce Schaffer, prin. Fax 872-8951

Newport News CSD 29,400/PK-12
12465 Warwick Blvd 23606 757-591-4500
Dr. Ashby Kilgore, supt.
www.sbo.nn.k12.va.us
Achievable Dream MSHS 500/6-12
5720 Marshall Ave 23605 757-283-7820
Marylin Sinclair-White, prin. Fax 283-7844
Aviation Academy Vo/Tech
902B Bland Blvd 23602 757-886-2745
Dr. Aaron Smith, dir. Fax 877-5647
Crittenden MS 800/6-8
6158 Jefferson Ave 23605 757-591-4900
Felicia Barnett, prin. Fax 838-8261
Denbigh HS 1,400/9-12
259 Denbigh Blvd 23608 757-886-7700
Dr. Eleanor Blowe, prin. Fax 872-6542
Dozier MS 1,100/6-8
432 Industrial Park Dr 23608 757-888-3300
Lisa Gatz, prin. Fax 887-3662
Enterprise Academy Alt
813 Diligence Dr Ste 110 23606 757-591-4971
Dr. Darwin Mills, prin. Fax 873-3507
Gildersleeve MS 1,100/6-8
1 Minton Dr 23606 757-591-4862
Courtney Mompoint, prin. Fax 596-2059
Governors STEM Academy 9-12
5800 Marshall Ave 23605 757-928-6100
Heritage HS 1,200/9-12
5800 Marshall Ave 23605 757-928-6100
Shameka Gerald, prin. Fax 247-9058
Hines MS 900/6-8
561 McLawhorne Dr 23601 757-591-4878
Dr. Amanda Corbin-Staton, prin. Fax 591-0119
Huntington MS 600/6-8
3401 Orcutt Ave 23607 757-928-6846
Cleo Holloway, prin. Fax 245-8451
Menchville HS 1,800/9-12
275 Menchville Rd 23602 757-886-7722
Robert Surry, prin. Fax 875-0648
New Horizons Alt
13400 Woodside Ln 23608 757-874-4444
Bruce Schaffer, prin. Fax 872-8951
Passage MS 1,000/6-8
400 Atkinson Way 23608 757-886-7600
Janelle Spitz, prin. Fax 886-7661
Point Option Alternative S Alt
813 Diligence Dr Ste 100 23606 757-591-7408
Michael Bonfiglio, dir. Fax 865-4508
Warwick HS 1,600/9-12
51 Copeland Ln 23601 757-591-4700
Dr. Rory Stapleton, prin. Fax 596-7415
Washington MS 400/6-8
3700 Chestnut Ave 23607 757-928-6860
Sean Callender, prin. Fax 247-1119
Woodside HS 2,100/9-12
13450 Woodside Ln 23608 757-886-7530
Sean Callender, prin. Fax 877-0480
Other Schools – See Hampton

---

Apprentice School Post-Sec.
4101 Washington Ave 23607 757-380-3809
Centura College Post-Sec.
616 Denbigh Blvd 23608 757-874-2121
Christopher Newport University Post-Sec.
1 Avenue of the Arts 23606 757-594-7000
Denbigh Baptist Christian S 300/PK-12
13010 Mitchell Point Rd 23602 757-249-2654
Robert Law, admin. Fax 249-9480
Everest College Post-Sec.
803 Diligence Dr 23606 757-873-1111
Hampton Roads Academy 600/PK-12
739 Academy Ln 23602 757-884-9100
Peter Mertz, hdmstr. Fax 884-9137
Medical Careers Institute Post-Sec.
1001 Omni Blvd Ste 305 23606 866-708-6174
Peninsula Catholic HS 300/8-12
600 Harpersville Rd 23601 757-596-7247
Janine Franklin, prin. Fax 591-9718
Riverside School of Health Careers Post-Sec.
316 Main St 23601 757-240-2200

**Nickelsville, Scott, Pop. 382**
Scott County SD
Supt. — See Gate City
Twin Springs HS 300/8-12
273 Titan Ln 24271 276-479-2185
Sammy Parks, prin. Fax 479-3103

**Nokesville, Prince William, Pop. 1,327**
Fauquier County SD
Supt. — See Warrenton
Kettle Run HS 1,100/9-12
7403 Academic Ave 20181 540-422-7330
Major Warner, prin. Fax 422-7359

Prince William County SD
Supt. — See Manassas
Brentsville District HS 1,000/9-12
12109 Aden Rd 20181 703-594-2161
Katherine Meints, prin. Fax 594-2365
Patriot HS 1,700/9-12
10504 Kettle Run Rd 20181 703-594-3020
Michael Bishop Ed.D., prin. Fax 594-3022

**Norfolk, Norfolk, Pop. 234,855**
Norfolk CSD 33,300/PK-12
PO Box 1357 23501 757-628-3830
Dr. Samuel King, supt. Fax 628-3820
www.nps.k12.va.us/
Academy of Discovery at Lakewood 3-8
1701 Alsace Ave 23509 757-628-2477
Thomas Smigiel, prin. Fax 628-2486
Academy of Intl Studies at Rosemont 100/6-8
1330 Branch Rd 23513 757-852-4610
Dr. Lynnell Gibson, prin. Fax 852-4615
Azalea Gardens MS 900/6-8
7721 Azalea Garden Rd 23518 757-531-3000
Dr. Reuthenia Clark, prin. Fax 531-3013
Blair MS 1,200/6-8
730 Spotswood Ave 23517 757-628-2400
Dr. Mark Makovec, prin. Fax 628-2422
Granby HS 2,100/9-12
7101 Granby St 23505 757-451-4110
Ted Daughtrey, prin. Fax 451-4118
Lake Taylor HS 1,300/9-12
1384 Kempsville Rd 23502 757-892-3200
Dr. Reba Miller, prin. Fax 892-3210
Lake Taylor MS 1,000/6-8
1380 Kempsville Rd 23502 757-892-3230
Craig Reed, prin. Fax 892-3240
Madison Alternative S Alt
3700 Bowdens Ferry Rd 23508 757-628-3417
Leesa Mundell, coord. Fax 628-3406
Maury HS 1,700/9-12
322 Shirley Ave 23517 757-628-3344
Karen Berg, prin. Fax 628-3359
Norfolk Technical Center Vo/Tech
1330 N Military Hwy 23502 757-892-3300
Kevin Monroe, coord. Fax 892-3305
Northside MS 800/6-8
8720 Granby St 23503 757-531-3150
Richard Fraley, prin. Fax 531-3144
Norview HS 1,800/9-12
6501 Chesapeake Blvd 23513 757-852-4500
Dr. Marjorie Stealey, prin. Fax 852-4511
Norview MS 1,200/6-8
6325 Sewells Point Rd 23513 757-852-4600
Walter Brower, prin. Fax 852-4590
Ruffner Academy 900/6-8
610 May Ave 23504 757-628-2466
Sallie Cooke, prin. Fax 628-2465
Washington HS 1,400/9-12
1111 Park Ave 23504 757-628-3575
Adrian Day, prin. Fax 628-3566
Granby Evening School Adult
7101 Granby St 23505 757-451-4110
Brandon Bell, prin. Fax 451-4049

Regional Academic Governors SD
Supt. — See Richmond
Governor's S for the Arts 400/9-12
254 Granby St # 2 23510 757-451-4711
Dr. Andrea Warren, dir. Fax 451-4715

---

Bina HS 50/9-12
425 Washington Park 23517 757-627-2462
Centura College Post-Sec.
7020 N Military Hwy 23518 757-853-2121
De Paul Medical Center Post-Sec.
150 Kingsley Ln 23505 757-489-5120
Eastern Virginia Medical School Post-Sec.
PO Box 1980 23501 757-446-5600
Faith Academy S of Excellence 100/PK-12
1010 E 26th St 23504 757-624-1724
Karen Reaves, admin. Fax 961-7369
Fortis College Post-Sec.
6300 Center Dr Ste 100 23502 757-499-5447
ITT Technical Institute Post-Sec.
5425 Robin Hood Rd Ste 100 23513 757-466-1260
Norfolk Academy 1,200/1-12
1585 Wesleyan Dr 23502 757-461-6236
Dennis Manning, hdmstr. Fax 455-3181
Norfolk Christian S 500/6-12
255 Thole St 23505 757-423-5770
Pat McCarty, head sch Fax 440-5388
Norfolk Collegiate S 400/6-12
7336 Granby St 23505 757-480-2885
Scott Kennedy, hdmstr. Fax 588-8655
Norfolk State University Post-Sec.
700 Park Ave 23504 757-823-8600
Old Dominion University Post-Sec.
5115 Hampton Blvd 23529 757-683-3000
Tidewater Community College Post-Sec.
121 College Pl 23510 757-822-1122
Tidewater Tech Post-Sec.
5301 E Princess Anne Rd 23502 757-858-8324
Virginia Wesleyan College Post-Sec.
1584 Wesleyan Dr 23502 757-455-3200
Wards Corner Beauty Academy Post-Sec.
7525 Tidewater Dr Ste 200 23505 757-583-3300
Yeshiva Aish Kodesh 50/9-12
612 Colonial Ave 23507 757-623-6070

**N Chesterfield, Chesterfield**
Chesterfield County SD
Supt. — See Chesterfield
Falling Creek MS 1,200/6-8
4724 Hopkins Rd, 804-743-3640
Melanie Knowles, prin. Fax 743-3644
Manchester MS 1,400/6-8
7401 Hull Street Rd, 804-674-1385
Sarah Fraher, prin. Fax 674-1394
Meadowbrook HS 1,700/9-12
4901 Cogbill Rd, 804-743-3675
Andrew Mey, prin. Fax 743-3686
Monacan HS 1,400/9-12
11501 Smoketree Dr, 804-378-2480
William Broyles, prin. Fax 378-2489
Providence MS 800/6-8
900 Starlight Ln, 804-674-1355
Dr. Derek Wasnock, prin. Fax 674-1361
Salem Church MS 800/6-8
9700 Salem Church Rd, 804-768-6225
Dr. Greg Ecroyd, prin. Fax 768-6230

---

Bryant & Stratton College Post-Sec.
8141 Hull Street Rd, 804-745-2444
Centura College Post-Sec.
7914 Midlothian Tpke, 804-330-0111
Virginia College Post-Sec.
7200 Midlothian Tpke, 804-977-5100

**Norton, Norton, Pop. 3,857**
Norton CSD 900/PK-12
PO Box 498 24273 276-679-2330
Dr. Keith Perrigan, supt. Fax 679-4315
www.nortoncityschools.org/
Burton HS 300/8-12
109 11th St SW 24273 276-679-2554
Aaron Williams, prin. Fax 679-2664

Wise County SD
Supt. — See Wise
Central HS 700/9-12
301 Industrial Park Rd 24273 276-328-8015
Charles Collins, prin. Fax 328-8316

**Nottoway, Nottoway**
Nottoway County SD 2,400/PK-12
10321 E Colonial Trail Hwy 23955 434-645-9596
Dr. Daniel Grounard, supt. Fax 645-1266
www.nottowayschools.org/
Other Schools – See Crewe, Jetersville

**Oak Hall, Accomack, Pop. 245**
Accomack County SD
Supt. — See Accomac
Arcadia HS 600/9-12
PO Box 69 23416 757-824-5613
Rose Taylor, prin. Fax 824-0767
Arcadia MS 500/6-8
PO Box 220 23416 757-824-4862
Brian Tupper, prin. Fax 824-6618

Badger Vocational Education Center North Vo/Tech
PO Box 69 23416 757-824-6386
Rose Taylor, dir. Fax 824-0767

**Oakton, Fairfax, Pop. 32,914**

---

Dominion Christian S 200/K-12
10922 Vale Rd 22124 703-758-1055
Matt Michell, head sch
Flint Hill S 1,100/PK-12
3320 Jermantown Rd 22124 703-584-2300
John Thomas, hdmstr. Fax 584-2369

**Oakwood, Buchanan**

---

Appalachian College of Pharmacy Post-Sec.
1060 Dragon Rd 24631 276-498-4190

**Onley, Accomack, Pop. 509**
Accomack County SD
Supt. — See Accomac
Badger Vocational Education Center South Vo/Tech
PO Box 302 23418 757-787-4522
Brian Patterson, dir. Fax 787-2194
Nandua HS 600/9-12
26350 Lankford Hwy 23418 757-787-4514
Brian Patterson, prin. Fax 787-2194
Nandua MS 500/6-8
20330 Warrior Dr 23418 757-787-7037
John Killmon, prin. Fax 787-8807

**Orange, Orange, Pop. 4,610**
Orange County SD 5,100/K-12
200 Dailey Dr 22960 540-661-4550
Dr. Brenda Tanner, supt. Fax 661-4599
www.ocss-va.org
Orange County HS 1,500/9-12
201 Selma Rd 22960 540-661-4300
Kelly Guemple, prin. Fax 661-4299
Prospect Heights MS 500/6-8
202 Dailey Dr 22960 540-661-4400
Renee Bourke, prin. Fax 661-4399
Other Schools – See Locust Grove

**Palmyra, Fluvanna, Pop. 102**
Fluvanna County SD 2,100/PK-12
14455 James Madison Hwy 22963 434-589-8208
Gena Keller, supt. Fax 589-5393
www.fluco.org
Fluvanna County HS 1,200/8-12
1918 Thomas Jefferson Pkwy 22963 434-589-3666
James Barlow, prin. Fax 591-2075

Regional Academic Governors SD
Supt. — See Richmond
Blue Ridge Virtual Governor's HS 9-12
14455 James Madison Hwy 22963 434-589-8208
Marc Carraway, dir. Fax 589-2248

**Pearisburg, Giles, Pop. 2,771**
Giles County SD 2,400/PK-12
151 School Rd 24134 540-921-1421
Dr. Terry Arbogast, supt. Fax 921-1424
sbo.gilesk12.org/
Giles County Technology Center Vo/Tech
1827 Wenonah Ave 24134 540-921-1166
Forest Fowler, prin. Fax 921-3906
Giles HS 700/8-12
1825 Wenonah Ave 24134 540-921-1711
Jason Mills, prin. Fax 921-3861
Other Schools – See Narrows

**Pennington Gap, Lee, Pop. 1,760**
Lee County SD
Supt. — See Jonesville
Pennington MS 400/6-8
201 Middle School Dr 24277 276-546-1453
Jerry Hounshell, prin. Fax 546-3515

**Penn Laird, Rockingham**
Rockingham County SD
Supt. — See Harrisonburg
Montevideo MS 700/6-8
7648 McGaheysville Rd 22846 540-289-3401
Drew Miller, prin. Fax 289-3601
Spotswood HS 800/9-12
368 Blazer Dr 22846 540-289-3100
Robert Dansey, prin. Fax 289-3301

**Petersburg, Petersburg, Pop. 31,887**
Petersburg CSD 4,800/PK-12
255 E South Blvd 23805 804-732-0510
Dr. Joseph Melvin, supt. Fax 732-0514
www.petersburg.k12.va.us
Blandford Program Mathematics Humanities 300/Alt
816 E Bank St 23803 804-862-7078
Wayne Carter, coord. Fax 862-7198
Johns JHS 600/8-9
3101 Homestead Dr 23805 804-862-7020
Shannon Washington, prin. Fax 862-5434
Petersburg HS 900/10-12
3101 Johnson Rd 23805 804-861-4884
Alicia Fields, prin. Fax 862-7188
Pittman Alternative S Alt
35 Pine St 23803 804-862-7207
Gloria Graves, coord.

Regional Academic Governors SD
Supt. — See Richmond
Appomattox Reg. Governor's S Arts/Tech 400/9-12
512 W Washington St 23803 804-722-0200
Dr. James Victory, dir. Fax 722-0201

---

Richard Bland College Post-Sec.
11301 Johnson Rd 23805 804-862-6100
Southside Regional Medical Center Post-Sec.
737 S Sycamore St 23803 804-765-5800
Virginia State University Post-Sec.
1 Hayden Dr 23806 804-524-5000

**Pilgrims Knob, Buchanan**
Buchanan County SD
Supt. — See Grundy
Twin Valley HS 300/8-12
PO Box 190 24634 276-259-7818
Rick Goodman, prin. Fax 259-6147

**Poquoson, Poquoson, Pop. 11,990**
Poquoson CSD 2,200/PK-12
500 City Hall Ave 23662 757-868-3055
Dr. Jennifer Parish, supt. Fax 868-3107
www.poquoson.k12.va.us
Poquoson HS 800/9-12
51 Odd Rd 23662 757-868-7123
Brandon Ratliff, prin. Fax 868-3141
Poquoson MS 600/6-8
985 Poquoson Ave 23662 757-868-6031
Todd Perelli, prin. Fax 868-4220

**Portsmouth, Portsmouth, Pop. 93,145**
Portsmouth CSD 14,200/PK-12
PO Box 998 23705 757-393-8751
Dr. Elie Bracy, supt. Fax 393-5236
pps.k12.va.us
Churchland HS 1,400/9-12
4301 Cedar Ln 23703 757-686-2500
Dr. Susan Bechtol, prin. Fax 686-2504
Churchland MS 900/7-8
4051 River Shore Rd 23703 757-686-2512
Barbara Kimzey, prin. Fax 686-2515
Cradock MS 600/7-8
21 Alden Ave 23702 757-393-8788
Angela Flowers, prin. Fax 393-5020
New Directions Center Alt
401 West Rd 23707 757-393-8728
Dr. Robert Sheppard, prin. Fax 393-5351
Norcom HS 1,300/9-12
1801 London Blvd 23704 757-393-5442
Shameka Pollard, prin. Fax 393-5449
Waters MS 600/7-8
600 Roosevelt Blvd 23701 757-558-2813
Alice Graham, prin. Fax 485-2829
Wilson HS 1,300/9-12
1401 Elmhurst Ln 23701 757-465-2907
Timothy Johnson, prin. Fax 405-1335
Adult Education Adult
2801 Turnpike Rd 23707 757-393-8822
Barbara Shears-Walker, coord. Fax 393-5246
EXCEL Campus Adult
1401 Elmhurst Ln 23701 757-465-2958
Timothy Johnson, prin. Fax 465-2913

---

Alliance Christian Academy 200/PK-12
5809 Portsmouth Blvd 23701 757-488-5552
Kimberley Johnson, admin. Fax 488-3192
Hicks Academy of Beauty Culture Post-Sec.
904 Loudoun Ave 23707 757-399-2400
Portsmouth Christian S 700/PK-12
3214 Elliott Ave 23702 757-393-0725
Nancy Stafford, admin. Fax 397-7487
Tidewater Community College Post-Sec.
120 Campus Dr 23701 757-822-2124

**Potomac Falls, Loudoun**
Loudoun County SD
Supt. — See Ashburn
Potomac Falls HS 1,500/9-12
46400 Algonkian Pkwy 20165 571-434-3200
Dr. Elizabeth Noto, prin. Fax 434-3201

**Powhatan, Powhatan**
Powhatan County SD 3,800/PK-12
2320 Skaggs Rd 23139 804-598-5700
Dr. Eric Jones, supt. Fax 598-5705
www.powhatan.k12.va.us
Powhatan HS 1,400/9-12
1800 Judes Ferry Rd 23139 804-598-5710
Tracie Omohundro, prin. Fax 598-0036
Powhatan JHS 700/7-8
4135 Old Buckingham Rd 23139 804-598-5782
Jason Tibbs, prin. Fax 403-3065

---

Blessed Sacrament S 300/PK-12
2501 Academy Rd 23139 804-598-4211
Paula Ledbetter, prin. Fax 598-1053

**Prince George, Prince George, Pop. 2,019**
Prince George County SD 6,400/PK-12
PO Box 400 23875 804-733-2700
Dr. Bobby Browder, supt. Fax 733-2737
pgs.k12.va.us
Clements JHS 1,100/8-9
7800 Laurel Spring Rd 23875 804-733-2730
Christine Romig, prin. Fax 733-3783
Prince George SHS 1,300/10-12
7801 Laurel Spring Rd 23875 804-733-2720
Michael Nelson, prin. Fax 861-4530
Other Schools – See Disputanta

**Pulaski, Pulaski, Pop. 8,916**
Pulaski County SD 4,600/PK-12
202 N Washington Ave 24301 540-994-2550
Dr. Thomas Brewster, supt. Fax 994-2552
www.pcva.us
Pulaski MS 500/6-8
500 Pico Ter 24301 540-643-0767
Mary Rash, prin. Fax 980-8571
Other Schools – See Dublin

Regional Academic Governors SD
Supt. — See Richmond
SW VA Governor's S Science Math & Tech 11-12
100 Northwood Dr 24301 540-440-5502
Rebecca Phillips, dir. Fax 994-5841

**Purcellville, Loudoun, Pop. 7,498**
Loudoun County SD
Supt. — See Ashburn
Blue Ridge MS 900/6-8
551 E A St 20132 540-751-2520
Brion Bell, prin. Fax 338-6823
Loudoun Valley HS 1,100/9-12
340 N Maple Ave 20132 540-751-2400
Susan Ross, prin. Fax 751-2401
Woodgrove HS 1,500/9-12
36811 Allder School Rd 20132 540-751-2600
William Shipp, prin. Fax 751-2601

---

Loudoun Christian HS 9-12
601 Yaxley Dr 20132 540-999-5272
Deborah Daniel, head sch
Patrick Henry College Post-Sec.
10 Patrick Henry Cir 20132 540-338-1776

**Quicksburg, Shenandoah**
Shenandoah County SD
Supt. — See Woodstock
Jackson HS 500/9-12
150 Stonewall Ln 22847 540-477-2732
Michael Dorman, prin. Fax 477-2098
North Fork MS 300/6-8
1018 Caverns Rd 22847 540-477-2953
Todd Lynn, prin. Fax 477-2562

**Radford, Radford, Pop. 16,003**
Radford CSD 1,600/PK-12
1612 Wadsworth St 24141 540-731-3647
Robert Graham, supt. Fax 731-4419
www.rcps.org/
Dalton IS 200/7-8
60 Dalton Dr 24141 540-731-3651
Greg Payne, prin. Fax 731-5033
Radford HS 500/9-12
50 Dalton Dr 24141 540-731-3649
W. Jeff Smith, prin. Fax 731-4427

---

Radford University Post-Sec.
801 E Main St 24142 540-831-5000

**Reston, Fairfax, Pop. 56,325**
Fairfax County SD
Supt. — See Falls Church
Hughes MS 900/7-8
11401 Ridge Heights Rd 20191 703-715-3600
Aimee Monticchio, prin. Fax 715-3697
South Lakes HS 2,300/9-12
11400 S Lakes Dr 20191 703-715-4500
Kimberly Retzer, prin. Fax 715-4597

---

AKS Massage School Post-Sec.
11793 Indian Ridge Rd 20191 703-304-1146

**Richlands, Tazewell, Pop. 5,766**
Tazewell County SD
Supt. — See Tazewell
Richlands HS 700/9-12
138 Tornado Aly 24641 276-964-4602
Kimberly Ringstaff, prin. Fax 963-1049
Richlands MS 600/6-8
185 Learning Ln 24641 276-963-5370
Glayde Brown, prin. Fax 963-0210

---

Southwest Virginia Community College Post-Sec.
PO Box SVCC 24641 276-964-2555

**Richmond, Richmond, Pop. 200,073**
Henrico County SD 47,100/PK-12
PO Box 23120 23223 804-652-3600
Dr. Patrick Kinlaw, supt. Fax 652-3856
henricoschools.us
Advance College Academy 9-12
2910 N Parham Rd 23294 804-527-4600
Sheralyne Tierseron, prin.
Brookland MS 1,000/6-8
9200 Lydell Dr 23228 804-261-5000
Nicholas Barlett, prin. Fax 261-5003
Byrd MS 1,000/6-8
9400 Quioccasin Rd 23238 804-750-2630
Cheri Guempel, prin. Fax 750-2629
Center for Communications 9-12
7053 Messer Rd 23231 804-226-8700
Beverly Lanier, prin.
Center for Medical Sciences 9-12
2101 Pump Rd 23238 804-750-2600
Todd Phillips, prin.
Center for the Arts 9-12
302 Azalea Ave 23227 804-228-2718
Dr. Stephanie Poxon, prin. Fax 228-2754
Center for the Humanities 9-12
8301 Hungary Spring Rd 23228 804-756-3000
Bruce Marr, prin.
Center for World Languages 9-12
2910 N Parham Rd 23294 804-527-4618
Dr. Anne Fano, prin. Fax 527-4611
Ctr for Leadrshp Govt & Global Economics 9-12
8701 Three Chopt Rd 23229 804-673-3700
Robert Peck, prin.
Fairfield MS 900/6-8
5121 Nine Mile Rd 23223 804-328-4020
Art Raymond, prin. Fax 328-4031
Freeman HS 1,700/9-12
8701 Three Chopt Rd 23229 804-673-3700
Anne Poates, prin. Fax 673-3713
Godwin HS 1,800/9-12
2101 Pump Rd 23238 804-750-2600
Elizabeth Armbruster, prin. Fax 750-2611
Henrico HS 1,700/9-12
302 Azalea Ave 23227 804-228-2700
Dr. Hebert Monroe, prin. Fax 228-2715
Hermitage HS 1,700/9-12
8301 Hungary Spring Rd 23228 804-756-3000
Andrew Armstrong, prin. Fax 672-1501
Hermitage Technical Center Vo/Tech
8301 Hungary Spring Rd 23228 804-756-3020
Terrie Allsbrooks, prin. Fax 756-3025

Moody MS 1,000/6-8
7800 Woodman Rd 23228 804-261-5015
Paul Llewellyn, prin. Fax 261-5024
Pocahontas MS 900/6-8
12000 Three Chopt Rd 23233 804-364-0830
Kimberly Sigler, prin. Fax 364-0847
Rolfe MS 1,000/6-8
6901 Messer Rd 23231 804-226-8730
Michael Jackson, prin. Fax 226-8739
Tuckahoe MS 1,100/6-8
9000 Three Chopt Rd 23229 804-673-3720
Ann Greene, prin. Fax 673-3731
Tucker HS 1,500/9-12
2910 N Parham Rd 23294 804-527-4600
Dr. Robert Lowerre, prin. Fax 527-4618
Varina HS 1,900/9-12
7053 Messer Rd 23231 804-226-8700
Ann Marie Seely, prin. Fax 226-8706
Wilder MS 900/6-8
6900 Wilkinson Rd 23227 804-515-1100
Solomon Jefferson, prin. Fax 515-1110
Mt. Vernon Adult Ed Complex Adult
7850 Carousel Ln 23294 804-527-4660
Gregory Lawson M.Ed., admin.
Other Schools – See Glen Allen, Highland Springs, Sandston

Regional Academic Governors SD 2,600/9-12
PO Box 2120 23218 804-225-2884
Dr. Donna Poland, admin. Fax 786-5466
www.doe.virginia.gov/instruction/governors_school_programs
Walker Governor's S for Gov & Int Study 9-12
1000 N Lombardy St 23220 804-354-6800
Jeff McGee Ph.D., dir. Fax 354-6939
Other Schools – See Abingdon, Alexandria, Clifton Forge, Fishersville, Fredericksburg, Hampton, Keysville, Lynchburg, Manassas, Martinsville, Mount Jackson, Norfolk, Palmyra, Petersburg, Pulaski, Roanoke, Tappahannock, Warrenton

Richmond CSD 21,600/PK-12
301 N 9th St 23219 804-780-7700
Dr. Dana Bedden, supt. Fax 780-4122
www.richmond.k12.va.us
Armstrong HS 1,000/9-12
2300 Cool Ln 23223 804-780-4449
April Hawkins, prin. Fax 780-4485
Binford MS 300/6-8
1701 Floyd Ave 23220 804-780-6231
Tyrus Lyles, prin. Fax 780-6057
Boushall MS 400/6-8
3400 Hopkins Rd 23234 804-780-5016
Widad Abed, prin. Fax 780-5396
Brown MS 800/6-8
6300 Jahnke Rd 23225 804-319-3013
Jonathan Morris, prin. Fax 319-3009
Elkhardt-Thompson MS. 600/6-8
7825 Forest Hill Ave 23225 804-272-7554
Joi Lowery, prin. Fax 560-5115
Franklin Military Academy 400/6-12
701 N 37th St 23223 804-780-8526
Sheron Carter-Gunter, prin. Fax 780-8054
Henderson MS 600/6-8
4319 Old Brook Rd 23227 804-780-8288
Deberry Goodwin, prin. Fax 228-5357
Hill MS 500/6-8
3400 Patterson Ave 23221 804-780-6107
LaShante Knight, prin. Fax 780-8754
Huguenot HS 1,100/9-12
7945 Forest Hill Ave 23225 804-320-7967
Jafar Barakat, prin. Fax 560-9103
Jefferson HS 900/9-12
4100 W Grace St 23230 804-780-6028
Candance Veney-Chaplin, prin. Fax 780-6295
King MS 700/6-8
1000 Mosby St 23223 804-780-8011
Dr. Valerie Harris, prin. Fax 780-5590
Marshall HS 900/9-12
4225 Old Brook Rd 23227 804-780-6052
Beverly Britt, prin. Fax 780-4991
MathScience Innovation Center K-12
2401 Hartman St 23223 804-343-6525
Julia Cothran Ed.D., prin. Fax 780-4454
Open HS 200/9-12
600 S Pine St 23220 804-780-4661
Pete Glessman, prin. Fax 780-4865
Richmond Alternative S Alt
119 W Leigh St 23220 804-780-4388
Dana Hawes, prin. Fax 780-8184
Richmond Career Educ & Employment Acad Alt
4314 Crutchfield St 23225 804-780-5037
Maurice Burton, prin.
Richmond Community HS 200/9-12
201 E Brookland Park Blvd 23222 804-285-1015
J. Austin Brown, prin. Fax 282-1303
Richmond Technical Center North Vo/Tech
2015 Seddon Way 23230 804-780-6272
Nancy Holmes, prin. Fax 780-6040
Richmond Technical Center South Vo/Tech
2020 Westwood Ave 23230 804-780-6237
Nancy Holmes, prin. Fax 780-6061
Wythe HS 900/9-12
4314 Crutchfield St 23225 804-780-5037
Reva Green, prin. Fax 780-5043

---

Banner Christian S 200/K-12
1501 S Providence Rd 23236 804-276-5200
Dr. Thomas Burkett, hdmstr. Fax 276-7620
Baptist Theological Seminary Post-Sec.
8040 Villa Park Dr Ste 250 23228 804-355-8135
Benedictine HS 300/9-12
12829 River Rd 23238 804-708-9500
Jesse Grapes, hdmstr.
Bon Secours Memorial College of Nursing Post-Sec.
8550 Magellan Pkwy Ste 1100 23227 804-627-5300
Collegiate S 1,600/PK-12
103 N Mooreland Rd 23229 804-741-7077
Stephen Hickman, hdmstr. Fax 741-9797
Cooper Episcopal S 100/6-8
2124 N 29th St 23223 804-822-6610
Mike Maruca, head sch
East End Christian Academy 50/PK-12
3294 Britton Rd 23231 804-795-9266
Suzanne Helland, dir. Fax 795-2222
ECPI University Post-Sec.
800 Moorefield Park Dr 23236 804-330-5533
Elijah House Academy 200/PK-12
6627 Jahnke Rd Ste B 23225 804-755-7051
Jesse Kell, head sch Fax 377-6800
Fortis College Post-Sec.
2000 Westmoreland St Ste A 23230 804-323-1020
Grove Christian S 200/PK-12
8701 Ridge Rd 23229 804-741-2860
Heidi Smith, admin. Fax 754-8534
ITT Technical Institute Post-Sec.
300 Gateway Centre Pkwy 23235 804-330-4992
J. Sargeant Reynolds Community College Post-Sec.
PO Box 85622 23285 804-371-3000
Medical Careers Institute Post-Sec.
2809 Emerywood Pkwy 23294 877-338-0006
Orchard House S 100/5-8
500 N Allen Ave 23220 804-228-2436
Nancy Davies, dir. Fax 228-1069
Precious Blessing Academy 100/PK-12
4823 Bryce Ln 23224 804-232-7180
Lois Bias, dean
Richmond Academy of SDA 100/PK-12
12285 Patterson Ave 23238 804-784-0036
St. Catherine's S 900/PK-12
6001 Grove Ave 23226 804-288-2804
Dr. Terrie Scheckelhoff Ph.D., head sch Fax 285-8169
St. Christopher's S 1,000/PK-12
711 Saint Christophers Rd 23226 804-282-3185
Charles Stillwell, hdmstr. Fax 285-3914
St. Gertrude HS 300/9-12
3215 Stuart Ave 23221 804-358-9114
Peggy Boon, prin. Fax 355-5682
St. Mary's Hospital Post-Sec.
5801 Bremo Rd 23226 804-285-2011
Southside Baptist Christian S 100/PK-12
5515 Bryce Ln 23224 804-745-8699
Rev. Reginald Stinson, head sch Fax 591-2833
Steward S 600/PK-12
11600 Gayton Rd 23238 804-740-3394
G. Daniel Frank, head sch Fax 740-1464
Tawheed Prep S 6-12
1202 Oak St 23220 804-344-3350
Trinity Episcopal S 400/8-12
3850 Pittaway Dr 23235 804-272-5864
Dr. Thomas Aycock, hdmstr. Fax 272-4652
Union Presbyterian Seminary Post-Sec.
3401 Brook Rd 23227 804-355-0671
University of Richmond Post-Sec.
28 Westhampton Way 23173 804-289-8000
Veritas S 300/PK-12
3400 Brook Rd 23227 804-272-9517
Keith Nix, head sch Fax 272-9518
Victory Christian Academy 200/PK-12
8491 Chamberlayne Rd 23227 804-262-8256
Andrea Cassidy M.Ed., prin. Fax 553-1905
Virginia Commonwealth University Post-Sec.
901 W Franklin St 23284 804-828-0100
Virginia Home for Boys & Girls Post-Sec.
8716 W Broad St 23294 804-270-6566
Virginia School for the Deaf and Blind Post-Sec.
PO Box 2120 23218 757-247-2058
Virginia Union University Post-Sec.
1500 N Lombardy St 23220 804-257-5600
Yeshiva of Virginia 50/9-12
6801 Patterson Ave 23226 804-288-7610

**Ridgeway, Henry, Pop. 734**
Henry County SD
Supt. — See Collinsville
Magna Vista HS 900/9-12
701 Magna Vista School Rd 24148 276-956-3147
JaMese Black, prin. Fax 956-1401

**Riner, Montgomery, Pop. 845**
Montgomery County SD
Supt. — See Christiansburg
Auburn HS 400/9-12
1650 Auburn School Dr 24149 540-382-5160
Carl Pauli, prin. Fax 381-6110
Auburn MS 300/6-8
4163 Riner Rd 24149 540-382-5165
Guylene Wood-Setzer, prin. Fax 381-6562

**Ringgold, Pittsylvania**
Pittsylvania County SD
Supt. — See Chatham
Dan River HS 700/9-12
100 Wildcat Circle 24586 434-822-7081
Steven D. Mayhew, prin. Fax 822-7347
Dan River MS 500/6-8
5875 Kentuck Rd 24586 434-822-6027
Emily Reynolds, prin. Fax 822-6548

**Roanoke, Roanoke, Pop. 94,517**
Regional Academic Governors SD
Supt. — See Richmond
Roanoke Valley Governor's S Science/Tech 9-12
2104 Grandin Rd SW 24015 540-853-2116
Dr. John Kowalski, dir. Fax 853-1056

Roanoke CSD 12,800/PK-12
PO Box 13145 24031 540-853-2502
Dr. Rita Bishop, supt. Fax 853-2951
www.rcps.info
Addison MS 500/6-8
1220 5th St NW 24016 540-853-2681
Robert Johnson, prin. Fax 853-1424
Breckinridge MS 600/6-8
3901 Williamson Rd NW 24012 540-853-2251
Tracey Anderson, prin. Fax 853-6505
Fleming HS 1,600/9-12
3649 Ferncliff Ave NW 24017 540-853-2781
Archie Freeman, admin.
Forest Park Academy Alt
2730 Melrose Ave NW 24017 540-853-2923
Eric Anderson, admin. Fax 853-1773
Henry HS 2,000/9-12
2102 Grandin Rd SW 24015 540-853-2255
Joseph Jablonski, prin. Fax 853-1575
Jackson MS 500/6-8
1004 Montrose Ave SE 24013 540-853-6040
Christian Kish, prin. Fax 853-6027
Madison MS 600/6-8
1160 Overland Rd SW 24015 540-853-2351
Whitney Johnson, prin. Fax 853-1050
Roanoke Technical Education Center Vo/Tech
2200 Grandin Rd SW 24015 540-853-2803
Kathleen Duncan, prin. Fax 853-1062
Taylor Learning Academy Alt
3229 Williamson Rd NW 24012 540-853-1461
Elizabeth Williams, prin. Fax 853-1216
Wilson MS 500/6-8
1813 Carter Rd SW 24015 540-853-2358
Rosalind Henderson, prin. Fax 853-2004

Roanoke County SD 14,100/K-12
5937 Cove Rd 24019 540-562-3700
Dr. Gregory Killough, supt. Fax 562-3994
www.rcs.k12.va.us
Cave Spring HS 900/9-12
3712 Chaparral Dr 24018 540-772-7550
Steve Spangler, prin. Fax 772-2107
Cave Spring MS 700/6-8
4880 Brambleton Ave 24018 540-772-7560
Fiona Hill, prin. Fax 772-2195
Hidden Valley HS 1,100/9-12
5000 Titan Trl 24018 540-776-7320
Rhonda Stegall, prin. Fax 776-7322
Hidden Valley MS 800/6-8
4902 Hidden Valley School 24018 540-772-7570
Mike Riley, prin. Fax 772-7519
Northside HS 1,000/9-12
6758 Northside High School 24019 540-561-8155
Frank Dent, prin. Fax 561-8160
Northside MS 700/6-8
6810 Northside High School 24019 540-561-8145
Lori Wimbush, prin. Fax 561-8152
Other Schools – See Salem, Vinton

---

BarPalma Beauty Careers Academy Post-Sec.
3535 Franklin Rd SW Ste D 24014 540-343-0153
Community HS 50/8-12
302 Campbell Ave SE 24013 540-345-1688
Josh Chapman, dir. Fax 400-0335
Faith Christian S 300/PK-12
3585 Buck Mountain Rd 24018 540-769-5200
Peter Baur, hdmstr. Fax 769-6030
Hollins University Post-Sec.
PO Box 9707 24020 540-362-6000
Jefferson College of Health Sciences Post-Sec.
101 Elm Ave SE 24013 540-985-8483
Miller-Motte Technical College Post-Sec.
4444 Electric Rd Ste A 24018 540-597-1010
North Cross S 500/PK-12
4254 Colonial Ave 24018 540-989-6641
Parkway Christian Academy 300/PK-12
3230 King St NE 24012 540-982-2400
Erica Dixon M.Ed., admin. Fax 982-2005
Roanoke Catholic S 500/PK-12
621 N Jefferson St 24016 540-982-3532
Patrick Patterson, prin. Fax 345-0785
Roanoke Valley Christian S 300/PK-12
PO Box 7010 24019 540-366-2432
Rick Brown, admin. Fax 366-9719
Skyline College Post-Sec.
5234 Airport Rd NW 24012 540-563-8000
University of Fairfax Post-Sec.
1818 Electric Rd 24018 888-980-9151
Virgina Tech Carilion School of Medicine Post-Sec.
2 Riverside Cir Ste M140 24016 540-526-2500
Virginia Western Community College Post-Sec.
PO Box 14007 24038 540-857-8922

**Rocky Gap, Bland**
Bland County SD
Supt. — See Bastian
Bland County HS 200/7-12
PO Box 9 24366 276-928-1100
Temple Musser, prin. Fax 928-1988

**Rocky Mount, Franklin, Pop. 4,700**
Franklin County SD 7,500/PK-12
25 Bernard Rd 24151 540-483-5138
W. Mark Church Ph.D., supt. Fax 483-5806
www.frco.k12.va.us
Franklin County HS 2,200/9-12
700 Tanyard Rd 24151 540-483-0221
Debora Decker, prin. Fax 483-5149
Franklin MS West 800/7-8
225 Middle School Rd 24151 540-483-5105
Dr. Bernice Cobbs, prin. Fax 483-5585
Gereau CATCE Vo/Tech
150 Technology Dr 24151 540-483-5446
Jerome Johnson, prin. Fax 483-5788
Adult Education Center Adult
50 Claiborne Ave 24151 540-483-0179
Debbie Hamrick, coord. Fax 483-1297

---

Christian Heritage Academy 100/PK-12
625 Glennwood Dr 24151 540-483-5855
Deke Andrews, hdmstr. Fax 483-9355

**Rural Retreat, Wythe, Pop. 1,472**
Wythe County SD
Supt. — See Wytheville
Rural Retreat HS 400/9-12
321 E Buck Ave 24368 276-686-4143
Dyer Jackson, prin. Fax 686-4601
Rural Retreat MS 300/6-8
325 E Buck Ave 24368 276-686-5200
Shannon Vaught, prin. Fax 686-4944

**Rustburg, Campbell, Pop. 1,389**
Campbell County SD 8,200/PK-12
PO Box 99 24588 434-332-3458
Dr. Robert Johnson, supt. Fax 528-1655
www.campbell.k12.va.us
Campbell Technical Center Vo/Tech
194 Dennis Riddle Dr 24588 434-821-6213
Jon Hardie, prin. Fax 821-2808
Cornerstone Learning Center Alt
194 Dennis Riddle Dr 24588 434-477-5583
Denton Sisk, dir. Fax 821-4512
Rustburg HS 900/9-12
PO Box 830 24588 434-332-5171
Clayton Stanley, prin. Fax 332-1187
Rustburg MS 700/6-8
PO Box 130 24588 434-332-5141
Katherine Bowles, prin. Fax 332-2058
Other Schools – See Altavista, Lynchburg, Naruna

**Ruther Glen, Caroline**

Carmel S 100/PK-12
PO Box 605 22546 804-448-3288
Brent Miller, hdmstr. Fax 448-3146

**Saint George, Greene**

Blue Ridge S 200/9-12
273 Mayo Dr, 434-985-2811
William Darrin, hdmstr. Fax 985-7215

**Salem, Salem, Pop. 24,439**
Roanoke County SD
Supt. — See Roanoke
Burton Center for Arts and Technology Vo/Tech
1760 Roanoke Blvd 24153 540-857-5000
Jason Suhr, prin. Fax 857-5061
Glenvar HS 600/9-12
4549 Malus Dr 24153 540-387-6536
Joseph Hafey, prin. Fax 387-6347
Glenvar MS 400/6-8
4555 Malus Dr 24153 540-387-6322
Jamie Soltis, prin. Fax 387-6283

Salem CSD 3,900/PK-12
510 S College Ave 24153 540-389-0130
Dr. H. Alan Seibert, supt. Fax 389-4135
www.salem.k12.va.us
Lewis MS 900/6-8
616 S College Ave 24153 540-387-2513
Dr. Forest Jones, prin. Fax 389-8914
Salem HS 1,300/9-12
400 Spartan Dr 24153 540-387-2437
Scott Habeeb, prin. Fax 387-2543

American National University Post-Sec.
1813 E Main St 24153 540-986-1800
ITT Technical Institute Post-Sec.
2159 Apperson Dr 24153 540-989-2500
Roanoke College Post-Sec.
221 College Ln 24153 540-375-2500

**Saltville, Smyth, Pop. 2,062**
Smyth County SD
Supt. — See Marion
Northwood HS 300/9-12
PO Box Y 24370 276-496-7751
Stan Dunham, prin. Fax 496-3216
Northwood MS 200/6-8
156 Long Hollow Rd 24370 276-624-3341
Marianne Blevins, prin. Fax 624-3535

**Saluda, Middlesex, Pop. 753**
Middlesex County SD 1,200/PK-12
PO Box 205 23149 804-758-2277
Thomas Taylor, supt. Fax 758-3727
www.mcps.k12.va.us/
Middlesex HS 400/9-12
PO Box 206 23149 804-758-2132
Jeannie Duke, prin. Fax 758-2786
Other Schools – See Locust Hill

**Sandston, Henrico, Pop. 7,426**
Henrico County SD
Supt. — See Richmond
Elko MS 900/6-8
5901 Elko Rd 23150 804-328-4110
Dominique Friend, prin. Fax 328-4115

New Bridge Academy 100/K-12
5701 Elko Rd 23150 804-737-7833
Rev. J.D. Sluss, admin. Fax 737-1181

**Shawsville, Montgomery, Pop. 1,291**
Montgomery County SD
Supt. — See Christiansburg
Shawsville MS 200/6-8
4179 Oldtown Rd 24162 540-268-2262
David Dickinson, prin. Fax 268-1868

**Shenandoah, Page, Pop. 2,351**
Page County SD
Supt. — See Luray
Page County HS 600/9-12
184 Panther Dr 22849 540-652-8712
David Cale, prin. Fax 652-8308
Page County MS 400/6-8
198 Panther Dr 22849 540-652-3400
Lance Moran, prin. Fax 652-8308

**Skipwith, Mecklenburg**
Mecklenburg County SD
Supt. — See Boydton
Bluestone HS 600/9-12
6825 Skipwith Rd 23968 434-372-5177
Pauline Keeton, prin. Fax 372-5217
Bluestone MS 500/6-8
250 Middle School Rd 23968 434-372-3266
Mary Shores, prin. Fax 372-3362

**Smithfield, Isle of Wight, Pop. 7,922**
Isle of Wight County SD 5,500/PK-12
820 W Main St 23430 757-357-4393
Dr. James Thornton M.Ed., supt. Fax 357-0849
www.iwcs.k12.va.us
Smithfield HS 1,300/9-12
14171 Turner Dr 23430 757-357-3108
Casey Roberts, prin. Fax 357-7253
Smithfield MS 600/7-8
14175 Turner Dr 23430 757-365-4100
Fred Eng, prin. Fax 365-4222
Other Schools – See Windsor

**South Boston, Halifax, Pop. 8,032**
Halifax County SD
Supt. — See Halifax
Halifax HS 1,700/9-12
PO Box 310 24592 434-572-4977
Michael Lewis, prin. Fax 572-2675
Halifax MS 1,300/6-8
1011 Middle School Cir 24592 434-572-4100
Faye Bruce, prin. Fax 572-4106

Carlbrook S 100/9-12
3046 Carlbrook Rd 24592 434-476-2406

**South Hill, Mecklenburg, Pop. 4,561**
Mecklenburg County SD
Supt. — See Boydton
Park View HS 800/9-12
205 Park View Cir 23970 434-447-3435
Paige Kindley, prin. Fax 447-7876
Park View MS 600/6-8
365 Dockery Rd 23970 434-447-3761
Mark Mabey, prin. Fax 447-4920

**South Riding, Loudoun, Pop. 23,365**
Loudoun County SD
Supt. — See Ashburn
Freedom HS 1,900/9-12
25450 Riding Center Dr 20152 703-957-4300
Michelle Luttrell, prin. Fax 542-2086

**Spotsylvania, Spotsylvania**
Spotsylvania County SD
Supt. — See Fredericksburg
Courtland HS 1,200/9-12
6701 Smith Station Rd 22553 540-898-4445
Clifton Conway, prin. Fax 898-4458
Ni River MS 700/6-8
11632 Catharpin Rd 22553 540-785-3990
Scott Belako, prin. Fax 785-0658
Post Oak MS 800/6-8
6959 Courthouse Rd, 540-582-7517
Karen Foster, prin. Fax 582-7510
Spotsylvania Career & Technical Center Vo/Tech
6713 Smith Station Rd 22553 540-898-2655
Meghan O'Connor, prin. Fax 891-1784
Spotsylvania HS 1,100/9-12
6975 Courthouse Rd, 540-582-3882
Rusty Davis, prin. Fax 582-3890
Spotsylvania MS 800/6-8
8801 Courthouse Rd 22553 540-582-6341
Lane Byrd, prin. Fax 582-3207
Thornburg MS 700/6-8
6929 N Roxbury Mill Rd, 540-582-7600
Kirk Tower, prin. Fax 582-7606

**Springfield, Fairfax, Pop. 29,504**
Fairfax County SD
Supt. — See Falls Church
Irving MS 1,000/7-8
8100 Old Keene Mill Rd 22152 703-912-4500
Danny Little, prin. Fax 912-4597
Key MS 800/7-8
6402 Franconia Rd 22150 703-313-3900
Christopher Larrick, prin. Fax 313-3997
Lee HS 1,800/9-12
6540 Franconia Rd 22150 703-924-8300
Deirdre Lavery, prin. Fax 924-8397
West Springfield HS 2,300/9-12
6100 Rolling Rd 22152 703-913-3800
Michael Mukai, prin. Fax 913-3897

Accotink Academy Post-Sec.
8519 Tuttle Rd 22152
GW Community S 50/9-12
9001 Braddock Rd Ste 111 22151 703-978-7208
ITT Technical Institute Post-Sec.
7300 Boston Blvd 22153 703-440-9535

**Stafford, Stafford**
Stafford County SD 27,000/PK-12
31 Stafford Ave 22554 540-658-6000
Dr. W. Bruce Benson, supt. Fax 658-5963
stafford.schoolfusion.us
Brooke Point HS 1,700/9-12
1700 Courthouse Rd 22554 540-658-6080
Scott McClellan, prin. Fax 658-6072
Colonial Forge HS 2,000/9-12
550 Courthouse Rd 22554 540-658-6115
Greg Daniel, prin. Fax 658-6120
Heim MS 800/6-8
320 Telegraph Rd 22554 540-658-5910
Mary McGraw, prin. Fax 658-0329
Mountain View HS 1,800/9-12
2135 Mountain View Rd, 540-658-6840
James Stemple, prin. Fax 658-6855
North Stafford HS 1,700/9-12
839 Garrisonville Rd 22554 540-658-6150
Thomas Nichols, prin. Fax 658-6158
Poole MS 900/6-8
800 Eustace Rd 22554 540-658-6190
Robert Bingham, prin. Fax 658-6176
Stafford MS 600/6-8
101 Spartan Dr 22554 540-658-6210
Mark Smith, prin. Fax 658-6204
Thompson MS 1,100/6-8
75 Walpole St 22554 540-658-6420
Andrew Grider, prin. Fax 658-6430

Wright MS 800/6-8
100 Wood Dr, 540-658-6240
William Boatwright, prin. Fax 658-6238
Other Schools – See Falmouth, Fredericksburg

Grace Preparatory S 100/PK-12
2202 Jefferson Davis Hwy 22554 540-657-4500
Ken Gross, admin. Fax 628-0323

**Stanardsville, Greene, Pop. 363**
Greene County SD 3,000/PK-12
PO Box 1140 22973 434-939-9000
Dr. Andrea Whitmarsh, supt. Fax 985-4686
www.greenecountyschools.com
Greene County Technical Education Center Vo/Tech
10415 Spotswood Trl 22973 434-939-9005
Scott Lucas, prin. Fax 985-2071
Monroe HS 800/9-12
254 Monroe Dr 22973 434-939-9004
Kyle Pursel, prin. Fax 985-1461
Monroe MS 700/6-8
148 Monroe Dr 22973 434-939-9003
Katie Brunelle, prin. Fax 985-1359

**Staunton, Staunton, Pop. 23,179**
Augusta County SD
Supt. — See Verona
Beverley Manor MS 700/6-8
58 Cedar Green Rd 24401 540-886-5806
Dr. Sarah Melton, prin. Fax 886-4019
Riverheads HS 500/9-12
19 Howardsville Rd 24401 540-337-1921
Max Lowe, prin. Fax 337-0258

Staunton CSD 2,600/K-12
116 W Beverley St 24401 540-332-3920
Dr. Linda Reviea, supt. Fax 332-3924
www.staunton.k12.va.us
Genesis Alternative Education Alt
1751 Shutterlee Mill Rd 24401 540-332-3934
Robert Craft, dir. Fax 332-3973
Lee HS 700/9-12
1200 N Coalter St 24401 540-332-3926
Dr. Mark Rowicki, prin. Fax 332-3994
Shelburne MS 600/6-8
300 Grubert Ave 24401 540-332-3930
Jennifer Morris, prin. Fax 332-3933

Grace Christian HS 100/9-12
19 S Market St 24401 540-886-9109
Brian Fitzgerald, prin. Fax 886-5958
Mary Baldwin College Post-Sec.
PO Box 1500 24402 540-887-7019
Staunton School of Cosmetology Post-Sec.
PO Box 2385 24402 540-885-0808
Stuart Hall S 200/6-12
PO Box 210 24402 540-885-0356
Mark Eastham, hdmstr. Fax 886-2275
Virginia School for the Deaf and Blind Post-Sec.
PO Box 2069 24402 540-332-9000

**Stephens City, Frederick, Pop. 1,772**
Frederick County SD
Supt. — See Winchester
Aylor MS 600/6-8
901 Aylor Rd 22655 540-869-3736
David Rudy, prin. Fax 867-2756
Sherando HS 1,500/9-12
185 S Warrior Dr 22655 540-869-0060
John Nelson, prin. Fax 869-5183

Shenandoah Valley Christian Academy 200/PK-12
PO Box 1360 22655 540-869-4600

**Sterling, Loudoun, Pop. 26,953**
Loudoun County SD
Supt. — See Ashburn
Dominion HS 1,300/9-12
21326 Augusta Dr 20164 571-434-4400
Dr. W. John Brewer, prin. Fax 434-4401
Park View HS 1,300/9-12
400 W Laurel Ave 20164 571-434-4500
Kirk Dolson, prin. Fax 434-4501
River Bend MS 1,100/6-8
46240 Algonkian Pkwy 20165 571-434-3220
David Shaffer, prin. Fax 444-7578
Seneca Ridge MS 1,000/6-8
98 Seneca Ridge Dr 20164 571-434-4420
Mark McDermott, prin. Fax 444-7567
Sterling MS 900/6-8
201 W Holly Ave 20164 571-434-4520
Gus Martinez, prin. Fax 444-7492

**Strasburg, Shenandoah, Pop. 6,272**
Shenandoah County SD
Supt. — See Woodstock
Signal Knob MS 500/6-8
687 Sandy Hook Rd 22657 540-465-3422
Christopher Cook, prin. Fax 465-5412
Strasburg HS 700/9-12
250 Ram Dr 22657 540-465-5195
Morgan Saeler, prin. Fax 465-5461

**Stuart, Patrick, Pop. 1,391**
Patrick County SD 2,500/PK-12
PO Box 346 24171 276-694-3163
William Sroufe Ed.D., supt. Fax 694-3170
www.patrick.k12.va.us
Patrick County HS 1,000/8-12
215 Cougar Ln 24171 276-694-7137
Trey Cox, prin. Fax 694-6997

**Stuarts Draft, Augusta, Pop. 9,108**
Augusta County SD
Supt. — See Verona
Stuarts Draft HS 800/9-12
1028 Augusta Farms Rd 24477 540-946-7600
James Nycum, prin. Fax 946-7605

Stuarts Draft MS — 500/6-8
1088 Augusta Farms Rd 24477 — 540-946-7611
Scott Musick, prin. — Fax 946-7613

---

Ridgeview Christian S — 100/PK-12
PO Box 477 24477 — 540-337-1025
Jeremy Woody, prin. — Fax 337-3718

**Suffolk, Suffolk, Pop. 82,776**
Jointly Operated Vo Tech SD
Supt. — None – Lolita Hall, dir.
Pruden Center for Industry/Technology — Vo/Tech
4169 Pruden Blvd 23434 — 757-925-5651
Andre Skinner, dir. — Fax 925-5639

Suffolk CSD — 14,400/PK-12
100 N Main St 23434 — 757-925-6750
Dr. Deran Whitney, supt. — Fax 925-6751
www.spsk12.net/
Forest Glen MS — 400/6-8
200 Forest Glen Dr 23434 — 757-925-5780
Melvin Bradshaw, prin. — Fax 925-5557
Kennedy MS — 600/6-8
2325 E Washington St 23434 — 757-934-6212
Vivian Covington, prin. — Fax 925-5594
King's Fork HS — 1,500/9-12
351 Kings Fork Rd 23434 — 757-923-5240
Ron Leigh Ed.D., prin. — Fax 923-5242
King's Fork MS — 1,100/6-8
350 Kings Fork Rd 23434 — 757-923-5246
Jennifer Presson, prin. — Fax 925-5754
Lakeland HS — 1,200/9-12
214 Kenyon Rd 23434 — 757-925-5790
Douglas Wagoner, prin. — Fax 925-5599
Nansemond River HS — 1,500/9-12
3301 Nansemond Pkwy 23434 — 757-923-4101
Thomas McLemore, prin. — Fax 538-5430
Turlington Woods S — Alt
629 Turlington Rd 23434 — 757-934-6215
Kinsey Bynum, prin. — Fax 925-5583
Yeates MS — 1,100/6-8
4901 Bennetts Pasture Rd 23435 — 757-923-4105
Daniel O'Leary, prin. — Fax 538-5416

---

Nansemond-Suffolk Academy — 800/PK-12
3373 Pruden Blvd 23434 — 757-539-8789
Deborah Russell, head sch — Fax 934-8363
Suffolk Beauty Academy — Post-Sec.
860 Portsmouth Blvd 23434 — 757-934-0656
Suffolk Christian Academy — 200/K-12
3488 Godwin Blvd 23434 — 757-925-4461
Tamra VanDorn, hdmstr. — Fax 924-1194

**Surry, Surry, Pop. 239**
Surry County SD — 900/PK-12
PO Box 317 23883 — 757-294-5229
Lloyd Hamlin, supt. — Fax 294-5263
www.surryschools.net/
Other Schools – See Dendron

**Sussex, Sussex, Pop. 256**
Sussex County SD — 500/K-12
PO Box 1368 23884 — 434-246-1099
Arthur Jarrett Ed.D., supt. — Fax 246-8214
www.sussex.k12.va.us
Sussex Central HS — 400/9-12
PO Box 1307 23884 — 434-246-6051
Alvina Matthews, prin. — Fax 246-5503
Sussex Central MS — 200/6-8
PO Box 1387 23884 — 434-246-2251
Morris Taylor, prin. — Fax 246-8912

**Sweet Briar, Amherst**

---

Sweet Briar College — Post-Sec.
134 Chapel Rd 24595 — 434-381-6100

**Swoope, Augusta**
Augusta County SD
Supt. — See Verona
Buffalo Gap HS — 600/9-12
1800 Buffalo Gap Hwy 24479 — 540-337-6021
Dr. Ian Marshall, prin. — Fax 337-6236

**Tangier, Accomack, Pop. 722**
Accomack County SD
Supt. — See Accomac
Tangier S — 100/K-12
PO Box 245 23440 — 757-891-2234
Dr. Nina Pruitt, prin. — Fax 891-2572

**Tappahannock, Essex, Pop. 2,335**
Essex County SD — 1,600/PK-12
PO Box 756 22560 — 804-443-4366
Dr. Scott Burckbuchler, supt. — Fax 443-4498
www.essex.k12.va.us
Essex HS — 500/9-12
PO Box 1006 22560 — 804-443-4301
Andrew Hipple, prin. — Fax 443-4272
Essex IS — 500/5-8
PO Box 609 22560 — 804-443-3040
Heather Gentry, prin. — Fax 445-1079

Regional Academic Governors SD
Supt. — See Richmond
Chesapeake Bay Governor's S — 10-12
PO Box 1410 22560 — 804-443-0267
Terri Perkins, dir. — Fax 443-4039

---

St. Margaret's S — 100/8-12
PO Box 158 22560 — 804-443-3357
Lindy Williams, head sch — Fax 443-1832

**Tazewell, Tazewell, Pop. 4,565**
Tazewell County SD — 6,600/PK-12
209 W Fincastle St 24651 — 276-988-5511
Christine Kinser, supt. — Fax 988-6765
tazewell.k12.va.us
Tazewell County Career Technical Center — Vo/Tech
260 Advantage Dr 24651 — 276-988-2529
Rodney Gillespie, prin. — Fax 988-5494
Tazewell HS — 600/9-12
167 Cosby Ln 24651 — 276-988-6502
Timothy Hollar, prin. — Fax 988-3263
Tazewell MS — 500/6-8
367 Hope St 24651 — 276-988-6513
Buffie Crabtree, prin. — Fax 988-2363
Other Schools – See Bluefield, Richlands

**The Plains, Fauquier, Pop. 213**
Fauquier County SD
Supt. — See Warrenton
Marshall MS — 500/6-8
4048 Zulla Rd 20198 — 540-422-7450
David Graham, prin. — Fax 422-7469

---

Wakefield S — 400/PK-12
PO Box 107 20198 — 540-253-7600
David Colon, hdmstr. — Fax 253-5492

**Toano, James City**
Williamsburg-James City County SD
Supt. — See Williamsburg
Toano MS — 700/6-8
7817 Richmond Rd 23168 — 757-566-4251
Tracey Jones, prin. — Fax 566-3006

**Triangle, Prince William, Pop. 7,762**
Prince William County SD
Supt. — See Manassas
Graham Park MS — 800/6-8
3613 Graham Park Rd 22172 — 703-221-2118
Maria Ramadane, prin. — Fax 221-1079

**Verona, Augusta, Pop. 4,194**
Augusta County SD — 10,200/K-12
PO Box 960 24482 — 540-245-5100
Dr. Eric Bond, supt. — Fax 245-5115
www.augusta.k12.va.us
Other Schools – See Fishersville, Fort Defiance, Staunton, Stuarts Draft, Swoope

**Victoria, Lunenburg, Pop. 1,693**
Lunenburg County SD
Supt. — See Kenbridge
Central HS — 500/9-12
131 K V Rd 23974 — 434-696-2137
John Long, prin. — Fax 696-1322
Lunenburg MS — 400/6-8
583 Tomlinson Rd 23974 — 434-696-2161
Dr. Sharon Stanislause, prin. — Fax 696-2162

**Vienna, Fairfax, Pop. 15,197**
Fairfax County SD
Supt. — See Falls Church
Kilmer MS — 1,100/7-8
8100 Wolftrap Rd 22182 — 703-846-8800
Ronald James, prin. — Fax 846-8897
Madison HS — 2,000/9-12
2500 James Madison Dr 22181 — 703-319-2300
Dan Meier, prin. — Fax 319-2397
Oakton HS — 2,200/9-12
2900 Sutton Rd 22181 — 703-319-2700
John Banbury, prin. — Fax 319-2797
Thoreau MS — 800/7-8
2505 Cedar Ln 22180 — 703-846-8000
Greg Hood, prin. — Fax 846-8097

---

Fairfax Christian S — 200/K-12
1624 Hunter Mill Rd 22182 — 703-759-5100
Jo Thoburn, pres. — Fax 759-2143
University of the Potomac — Post-Sec.
2070 Chain Bridge Rd # G100 22182 — 703-709-5875

**Vinton, Roanoke, Pop. 7,942**
Roanoke County SD
Supt. — See Roanoke
Byrd HS — 1,100/9-12
2902 E Washington Ave 24179 — 540-890-3090
Dr. Richard Turner, prin. — Fax 890-7568
Byrd MS — 900/6-8
2910 E Washington Ave 24179 — 540-890-1035
Tammy Newcomb, prin. — Fax 890-0703

**Virginia Beach, Virginia Beach, Pop. 422,328**
Virginia Beach CSD — 70,300/PK-12
PO Box 6038 23456 — 757-263-1000
Dr. Aaron Spence, supt. — Fax 263-1397
www.vbschools.com/
Advanced Technology Center — Vo/Tech
1800 College Cres, — 757-648-5800
Michael Taylor, dir. — Fax 468-4235
Bayside HS — 2,000/9-12
4960 Haygood Rd 23455 — 757-648-5200
James Miller, prin. — Fax 473-5123
Bayside MS — 1,100/7-8
965 Newtown Rd 23462 — 757-648-4400
Dr. Paula Johnson, prin. — Fax 473-5185
Brandon MS — 1,300/6-8
1700 Pope St 23464 — 757-648-4450
Dr. Christy McQueeney, prin. — Fax 366-4550
Corporate Landing MS — 1,400/6-8
1597 Corporate Landing Pkwy 23454 — 757-648-4500
Freddie Alarcon, prin. — Fax 437-6487
Cox HS — 2,000/9-12
2425 Shorehaven Dr 23454 — 757-648-5250
Dr. Randi Riesbeck, prin. — Fax 496-6731
First Colonial HS — 2,000/9-12
1272 Mill Dam Rd 23454 — 757-648-5300
Dr. Nancy Farrell, prin. — Fax 496-6719
Great Neck MS — 1,100/6-8
1848 N Great Neck Rd 23454 — 757-648-4550
Dr. Eugene Soltner, prin. — Fax 496-6774
Green Run HS — 1,700/9-12
1700 Dahlia Dr, — 757-648-5350
Todd Tarkenton, prin. — Fax 431-4153
Independence MS — 1,300/6-8
1370 Dunstan Ln 23455 — 757-648-4600
Carey Manugo, prin. — Fax 460-0508
Kellam HS — 1,800/9-12
2665 W Neck Rd 23456 — 757-648-5100
Bruce Biehl, prin. — Fax 648-5133
Kempsville HS — 1,800/9-12
5194 Chief Trl 23464 — 757-648-5450
William Harris, prin. — Fax 474-7919
Kempsville MS — 900/6-8
860 Churchill Dr 23464 — 757-648-4700
Dr. Patti Jenkins, prin. — Fax 474-8449
Landstown HS — 2,400/9-12
2001 Concert Dr 23456 — 757-648-5500
Dr. Brian Matney, prin. — Fax 468-1860
Landstown MS — 1,500/6-8
2204 Recreation Dr 23456 — 757-648-4750
John Parkman, prin. — Fax 430-3247
Larkspur MS — 1,600/6-8
4696 Princess Anne Rd 23462 — 757-648-4800
Melanie Hamblin, prin. — Fax 474-8598
Lynnhaven MS — 1,100/6-8
1250 Bayne Dr 23454 — 757-648-4850
Dr. Violet Hoyle, prin. — Fax 496-6793
Ocean Lakes HS — 2,300/9-12
885 Schumann Dr 23454 — 757-648-5550
Dr. Cheryl Askew, prin. — Fax 721-4309
Plaza MS — 1,100/6-8
3080 S Lynnhaven Rd 23452 — 757-648-4900
Rodney Burnsworth, prin. — Fax 431-5331
Princess Anne HS — 1,900/9-12
4400 Virginia Beach Blvd 23462 — 757-648-5600
Dr. Daniel Smith, prin. — Fax 473-5004
Princess Anne MS — 1,400/6-8
2323 Holland Rd, — 757-648-4950
Alex Bergren, prin. — Fax 430-0972
Renaissance Academy — Alt
5100 Cleveland St 23462 — 757-648-6000
Kay Thomas, prin. — Fax 473-5111
Salem HS — 1,900/9-12
1993 Sundevil Dr 23464 — 757-648-5650
Matthew Delaney, prin. — Fax 474-0100
Salem MS — 1,100/6-8
2380 Lynnhaven Pkwy 23464 — 757-648-5000
Dr. James Smith, prin. — Fax 474-8467
Tallwood HS — 2,100/9-12
1668 Kempsville Rd 23464 — 757-648-5700
Dr. James Avila, prin. — Fax 479-5534
Technical & Career Education Center — Vo/Tech
2925 N Landing Rd 23456 — 757-648-5850
David Swanger, dir. — Fax 427-5558
Virginia Beach MS — 800/6-8
600 25th St 23451 — 757-648-5050
Dr. Sandra Brown, prin. — Fax 437-4708
Adult Learning Center — Adult
4160 Virginia Beach Blvd 23452 — 757-648-6050
Paul Palonbo, dir. — Fax 306-0999

---

Advanced Technology Institute — Post-Sec.
5700 Southern Blvd # 100 23462 — 757-490-1241
Atlantic University — Post-Sec.
215 67th St 23451 — 757-631-8101
Bishop Sullivan Catholic HS — 400/9-12
4552 Princess Anne Rd 23462 — 757-467-2881
Dennis Price, prin. — Fax 467-0284
Bryant & Stratton College — Post-Sec.
301 Centre Pointe Dr 23462 — 757-499-7900
Cape Henry Collegiate S — 900/PK-12
1320 Mill Dam Rd 23454 — 757-481-2446
Dr. Christopher S. Garran, head sch — Fax 481-9194
Centura College — Post-Sec.
2697 Dean Dr Ste 100 23452 — 757-340-2121
Coastal Christian Academy — 50/K-12
640 Kempsville Rd 23464 — 757-217-2151
Rev. Mary Strickland, admin. — Fax 467-5298
ECPI University — Post-Sec.
5555 Greenwich Rd Ste 300 23462 — 757-671-7171
OakTree Academy — 200/PK-12
817 Kempsville Rd 23464 — 757-248-9560
Terri Turley, admin. — Fax 248-9594
Regent University — Post-Sec.
1000 Regent University Dr 23464 — 757-352-4127
Rudy & Kelly Academy of Hair & Nails — Post-Sec.
1920 Centerville Tpke # 114 23464 — 757-473-0994
Tidewater Community College — Post-Sec.
1700 College Cres, — 757-822-7100
Virginia Beach Friends S — 100/PK-12
1537 Laskin Rd 23451 — 757-428-7534
Linda Serrette, hdmstr. — Fax 428-7511
Virginia Beach Theological Seminary — Post-Sec.
2221 Centerville Tpke 23464 — 757-479-3706

**Wakefield, Sussex, Pop. 921**

---

Tidewater Academy — 200/PK-12
217 W Church St 23888 — 757-899-5401

**Warm Springs, Bath, Pop. 122**
Bath County SD — 600/PK-12
PO Box 67 24484 — 540-839-2722
Sue Hirsh, supt. — Fax 839-3040
www.bath.k12.va.us
Other Schools – See Hot Springs

**Warrenton, Fauquier, Pop. 9,361**
Fauquier County SD — 11,200/PK-12
320 Hospital Dr Ste 40 20186 — 540-422-7000
Dr. David Jeck, supt. — Fax 422-7057
www.fcps1.org
Auburn MS — 600/6-8
7270 Riley Rd 20187 — 540-422-7410
Steve Kadilak, prin. — Fax 422-7429
Fauquier HS — 1,200/9-12
705 Waterloo Rd 20186 — 540-422-7300
Clarence Burton, prin. — Fax 347-0089
Taylor MS — 400/6-8
350 E Shirley Ave 20186 — 540-422-7470
Ruth Nelson, prin. — Fax 422-7489

Warrenton MS 500/6-8
244 Waterloo St 20186 540-422-7490
Barbara Bannister, prin. Fax 422-7509
Other Schools – See Bealeton, Midland, Nokesville, The Plains

Regional Academic Governors SD
Supt. — See Richmond
Mountain Vista Governor's S 11-12
6480 College St 20187 540-347-6237
Dr. Rosanne Williamson, prin. Fax 266-3617

---

Highland S 500/PK-12
597 Broadview Ave 20186 540-878-2700
Henry Berg, head sch Fax 878-2731
Providence Christian Academy 100/PK-12
6872 Watson Ct 20187 540-349-4989
Rev. Young Shin Ph.D., hdmstr. Fax 349-3915

**Warsaw, Richmond, Pop. 1,495**
Jointly Operated Vo Tech SD
Supt. — None - Lolita Hall, dir.
Northern Neck Technical Center Vo/Tech
13946 History Land Hwy 22572 804-333-4940
Bernard Davis, prin. Fax 333-0538

Richmond County SD 1,200/K-12
PO Box 1507 22572 804-333-3681
James Smith Ed.D., supt. Fax 333-5586
www.richmond-county.k12.va.us
Rappahannock HS 300/8-12
6914 Richmond Rd 22572 804-333-3551
David Ferguson, prin. Fax 333-5186

**Washington, Rappahannock, Pop. 133**
Rappahannock County SD 900/K-12
6 School House Rd 22747 540-227-0023
Donna Matthews, supt. Fax 987-8896
www.rappahannockschools.us
Rappahannock County HS 300/8-12
12576 Lee Hwy 22747 540-227-0745
Michael Tupper, prin. Fax 987-9331

**Waynesboro, Waynesboro, Pop. 20,421**
Waynesboro CSD 3,100/PK-12
301 Pine Ave 22980 540-946-4600
Dr. Jeffrey Cassell, supt. Fax 946-4608
www.waynesboro.k12.va.us
Collins MS 700/6-8
1625 Ivy St 22980 540-946-4635
Janet Buchheit, prin. Fax 946-4642
Waynesboro HS 900/9-12
1200 W Main St 22980 540-946-4616
Tim Teachey, prin. Fax 946-4621

---

Fishburne Military S 100/7-12
225 S Wayne Ave 22980 540-946-7700
Dan Baranik, hdmstr. Fax 946-7738

**Weems, Lancaster**
Lancaster County SD 1,300/PK-12
2330 Irvington Rd 22576 804-462-5100
Steve Parker, supt. Fax 435-3309
www.lcs.k12.va.us
Other Schools – See Kilmarnock, Lancaster

**West Point, King William, Pop. 3,232**
West Point SD 800/PK-12
PO Box T 23181 804-843-4368
Dr. David Holleran, supt. Fax 843-4421
www.wpschools.net
West Point HS 300/9-12
2700 Mattaponi Ave 23181 804-843-3630
Mark Dorsey, prin. Fax 843-3406
West Point MS 200/6-8
1040 Thompson Ave 23181 804-843-9810
David Daniel, prin. Fax 843-9812

**Weyers Cave, Augusta, Pop. 2,429**

---

Blue Ridge Community College Post-Sec.
PO Box 80 24486 540-234-9261

**Williamsburg, Williamsburg, Pop. 13,648**
Williamsburg-James City County SD 10,700/K-12
PO Box 8783 23187 757-603-6400
Steven Constantino Ed.D., supt.
wjccschools.org/web/
Berkeley MS 900/6-8
1118 Ironbound Rd 23188 757-229-8051
Amour Mickel, prin. Fax 229-6133
Hornsby MS 900/6-8
850 Jolly Pond Rd 23188 757-565-9400
Jessica Ellison, prin. Fax 565-9401
Jamestown HS 1,200/9-12
3751 John Tyler Hwy 23185 757-259-3600
Dr. Cathy Worley, prin. Fax 259-3759
Lafayette HS 1,100/9-12
4460 Longhill Rd 23188 757-565-0373
Anita Swinton, prin. Fax 565-4268
Warhill HS 1,100/9-12
4615 Opportunity Way 23188 757-565-4615
Dr. Jeffrey Carroll, prin. Fax 565-9101
Other Schools – See Toano

York County SD
Supt. — See Yorktown
Bruton HS 600/9-12
185 E Rochambeau Dr 23188 757-220-4050
Arletha Dockery, prin. Fax 220-4090

Queens Lake MS 500/6-8
124 W Queens Dr 23185 757-220-4080
Kendra Crump Ed.D., prin. Fax 220-4074
School of the Arts 9-12
185 E Rochambeau Dr 23188 757-220-4050
Arletha Dockery, prin. Fax 369-2611

---

College of William and Mary Post-Sec.
PO Box 8795 23187 757-221-4000
Providence Classical S 200/K-12
6000 Easter Cir 23188 757-565-2900
Susan Oweis, head sch Fax 565-3720
Walsingham Academy Upper S 200/8-12
PO Box 8702 23187 757-229-6026
Sr. Mary Jeanne Osterle, prin. Fax 259-1401
Williamsburg Christian Academy 200/PK-12
101 School House Ln 23188 757-220-1978
Lawrence Vaught, head sch Fax 741-4009

**Winchester, Winchester, Pop. 25,545**
Frederick County SD 13,000/K-12
PO Box 3508 22604 540-662-3888
Dr. David Sovine, supt. Fax 722-2788
www.frederick.k12.va.us
Byrd MS 900/6-8
134 Rosa Ln 22602 540-662-0500
Teresa Ritenour, prin. Fax 662-7790
Frederick County MS 700/6-8
441 Linden Dr 22601 540-667-4233
Susan Brinkmeier, prin. Fax 667-2392
Howard Center Vo/Tech
156 Dowell J Cir 22602 540-662-8997
Janelle Ball-Brooks, dir. Fax 662-9112
Millbrook HS 1,300/9-12
251 First Woods Dr 22603 540-545-2800
Carolyn Butler, prin. Fax 545-7962
Wood HS 1,300/9-12
161 Apple Pie Ridge Rd 22603 540-667-5226
Joseph Salyer, prin. Fax 667-3154
Wood MS 900/6-8
1313 Amherst St 22601 540-667-7500
Grant Javersak, prin. Fax 667-7500
Other Schools – See Stephens City

Winchester CSD 4,100/PK-12
PO Box 551 22604 540-667-4253
Dr. Mark Lineburg, supt. Fax 722-6198
www.wps.k12.va.us
Handley HS 1,200/9-12
PO Box 910 22604 540-662-3471
Michael Dufrene, prin. Fax 722-6722
Morgan MS 1,200/5-8
48 S Purcell Ave 22601 540-667-7171
Jerry Putt, prin. Fax 723-8897

---

Grafton School Post-Sec.
PO Box 2500 22604 540-542-0200
Mountain View Christian Academy 100/K-12
153 Narrow Ln 22602 540-868-1231
Dr. Minta Hardman, admin. Fax 869-8976
Shenandoah University Post-Sec.
1460 University Dr 22601 540-665-4500
Winchester Memorial Hospital Post-Sec.
PO Box 3340 22604 540-722-8000

**Windsor, Isle of Wight, Pop. 2,598**
Isle of Wight County SD
Supt. — See Smithfield
Tyler MS 300/6-8
23320 N Court St 23487 757-242-3229
Dr. Steve Marable, prin. Fax 242-3405
Windsor HS 500/9-12
24 Church St 23487 757-242-6172
Daniel Soderholm, prin. Fax 242-4948

**Wirtz, Franklin**

---

Smith Mountain Lake Christian Academy 50/PK-12
2485 Lost Mountain Rd # B 24184 540-719-1192
Lincoln Bryan, admin. Fax 721-4627

**Wise, Wise, Pop. 3,248**
Wise County SD 6,200/PK-12
PO Box 1217 24293 276-328-8017
Greg Mullins-Int. Supt., dir. Fax 328-3350
www.wise.k12.va.us
Addington MS 500/5-8
PO Box 977 24293 276-328-8821
Greg Jessee, prin. Fax 328-2044
Wise County Career-Technical Center Vo/Tech
PO Box 1218 24293 276-328-6113
Larry Hamilton, prin. Fax 328-4443
Other Schools – See Big Stone Gap, Coeburn, Norton

---

University of Virginia College at Wise Post-Sec.
1 College Ave 24293 276-328-0100
Wise County Christian S 100/PK-12
PO Box 3297 24293 276-328-3297
James Bryant, prin. Fax 328-3248

**Woodberry Forest, Madison**

---

Woodberry Forest S 400/9-12
898 Woodberry Forest Rd 22989 540-672-3900
Dr. Byron Hulsey, hdmstr. Fax 672-0928

**Woodbridge, Prince William, Pop. 3,887**
Prince William County SD
Supt. — See Manassas

Beville MS 1,200/6-8
4901 Dale Blvd 22193 703-878-2593
Timothy Keenan, prin. Fax 730-1274
Forest Park HS 2,400/9-12
15721 Forest Park Dr 22193 703-583-3200
Richard Martinez, prin. Fax 583-6867
Freedom HS 1,900/9-12
15201 Neabsco Mills Rd 22191 703-583-1405
Inez Bryant, prin. Fax 583-8705
Gar-Field HS 2,500/9-12
14000 Smoketown Rd 22192 703-730-7000
Dr. Cherif Sadki, prin. Fax 730-7197
Godwin MS 1,100/6-8
14800 Darbydale Ave 22193 703-670-6166
Jehovanni Mitchell, prin. Fax 670-9888
Hylton HS 2,200/9-12
14051 Spriggs Rd 22193 703-580-4000
David Cassady, prin. Fax 580-4299
Lake Ridge MS 1,200/6-8
12350 Mohican Rd 22192 703-494-5154
Christie Taylor, prin. Fax 494-8246
Lynn MS 900/6-8
1650 Prince William Pkwy 22191 703-494-5157
Jorge Neves, prin. Fax 491-5141
Rippon MS 1,000/6-8
15101 Blackburn Rd 22191 703-491-2171
Gail Stone, prin. Fax 491-2487
Woodbridge HS 2,800/9-12
3001 Old Bridge Rd 22192 703-497-8000
David Huckestein, prin. Fax 497-8117
Woodbridge MS 1,100/6-8
2201 York Dr 22191 703-494-3181
Skyles Calhoun, prin. Fax 491-1441

---

Christ Chapel Academy 600/PK-12
13909 Smoketown Rd 22192 703-670-3822
Rev. Paul Miklich, admin. Fax 897-7905
Everest College Post-Sec.
14555 Potomac Mills Rd 22192 571-408-2100
Heritage Christian S 400/PK-12
14510 Spriggs Rd 22193 703-680-6629
Dr. Brian Kosa, prin.
Stratford University Post-Sec.
14349 Gideon Dr 22192 703-897-1982

**Woodstock, Shenandoah, Pop. 5,017**
Shenandoah County SD 6,200/PK-12
600 N Main St Ste 200 22664 540-459-6222
Dr. Jeremy Raley, supt. Fax 459-6707
www.shenandoah.k12.va.us
Central HS 800/9-12
1147 Susan Ave 22664 540-459-2161
Melissa Hensley, prin. Fax 459-5932
Muhlenberg MS 600/6-8
1251 Susan Ave 22664 540-459-2941
Mandy Roller, prin. Fax 459-5965
Other Schools – See Mount Jackson, Quicksburg, Strasburg

---

Massanutten Military Academy 100/7-12
614 S Main St 22664 540-459-2167
Dr. David Skipper, head sch Fax 459-5421

**Wytheville, Wythe, Pop. 8,065**
Wythe County SD 4,400/PK-12
1570 W Reservoir St 24382 276-228-5411
Dr. Jeff Perry, supt. Fax 228-9192
wcps.wythe.k12.va.us
Scott Memorial MS 300/6-8
950 S 7th St 24382 276-228-2851
Brad Haga, prin. Fax 228-8261
Wythe Co. Technical Center Vo/Tech
1505 W Spiller St 24382 276-228-5481
Anthony Sykes, prin. Fax 228-8254
Wythe HS 500/9-12
1 Maroon Way 24382 276-228-3157
Dante Lee, prin. Fax 228-4124
Other Schools – See Max Meadows, Rural Retreat

---

Wytheville Community College Post-Sec.
1000 E Main St 24382 276-223-4700

**Yorktown, York, Pop. 195**
York County SD 12,500/PK-12
302 Dare Rd 23692 757-898-0300
Dr. Victor Shandor, supt. Fax 890-0771
www.yorkcountyschools.org
Grafton HS 1,300/9-12
403 Grafton Dr 23692 757-898-0530
Royce Hart, prin. Fax 898-0533
Grafton MS 900/6-8
405 Grafton Dr 23692 757-898-0525
Karen Cagle, prin. Fax 898-0534
Tabb HS 1,100/9-12
4431 Big Bethel Rd 23693 757-867-7400
Angela Seiders, prin. Fax 867-7414
Tabb MS 800/6-8
300 Yorktown Rd 23693 757-898-0320
Antonia Fox, prin. Fax 867-7425
York HS 1,100/9-12
9300 George Washington Mem 23692 757-898-0354
Dr. Shannon Butler, prin. Fax 898-8235
Yorktown MS 800/6-8
11201 George Washington Mem 23690 757-898-0360
Susan Hutton, prin. Fax 898-0412
Other Schools – See Williamsburg

---

Summit Christian Academy 100/7-12
4209 Big Bethel Rd 23693 757-867-7005
Tim Grimes, hdmstr.

# WASHINGTON

## WASHINGTON DEPARTMENT OF EDUCATION
**PO Box 47200, Olympia 98504-7200**
**Telephone 360-725-6000**
**Fax 360-753-6712**
**Website http://www.k12.wa.us**

Superintendent of Public Instruction Randy Dorn

## WASHINGTON BOARD OF EDUCATION
**PO Box 47206, Olympia 98504-7206**

Executive Director

## EDUCATIONAL SERVICE DISTRICTS (ESD)

North Central ESD 171
Dr. Richard McBride, supt. 509-665-2610
PO Box 1847, Wenatchee 98807 Fax 662-9027
www.ncesd.org
Northeast Washington ESD 101
Dr. Michael Dunn, supt. 509-789-3800
4202 S Regal St, Spokane 99223 Fax 789-3780
www.esd101.net
Northwest ESD 189
Dr. Gerald Jenkins, supt. 360-299-4000
1601 R Ave, Anacortes 98221 Fax 299-4070
www.nwesd.org/

Olympic ESD 114
Greg Lynch, supt. 360-479-0993
105 National Ave N Fax 478-6869
Bremerton 98312
www.oesd.wednet.edu
ESD 123
Bruce Hawkins, supt. 509-547-8441
3918 W Court St, Pasco 99301 Fax 544-5795
www.esd123.org
Puget Sound ESD
John Welch, supt. 800-917-7600
800 Oakesdale Ave SW Fax 917-7777
Renton 98057
www.psesd.org

ESD 113
Dana Anderson, supt. 360-464-6700
6005 Tyee Dr SW, Tumwater 98512 Fax 464-6900
www.esd113.org
ESD 112
Dr. Tim Merlino, supt. 360-750-7500
2500 NE 65th Ave Fax 750-9706
Vancouver 98661
www.esd112.org
ESD 105
Steve Myers, supt. 509-575-2885
33 S 2nd Ave, Yakima 98902 Fax 575-2918
www.esd105.org/

## PUBLIC, PRIVATE AND CATHOLIC SECONDARY SCHOOLS

**Aberdeen, Grays Harbor, Pop. 16,223**
Aberdeen SD 5 3,300/PK-12
216 N G St 98520 360-538-2000
Dr. Thomas Opstad Ed.D., supt. Fax 538-2014
www.asd5.org
Aberdeen HS 1,000/9-12
410 N G St 98520 360-538-2040
Sherri Northington, prin. Fax 538-2046
Harbor HS 100/Alt
300 N Williams St 98520 360-538-2180
Derek Cook, prin. Fax 538-2183
Miller JHS 500/7-8
100 E Lindstrom St 98520 360-538-2100
Lisa Griebel, prin. Fax 538-2106
Twin Harbors Skills Center Vo/Tech
410 N G St 98520 360-538-2038
Lynn Green, dir. Fax 538-2057

Wishkah Valley SD 117 100/K-12
4640 Wishkah Rd 98520 360-532-3128
Dennis Johnson, supt. Fax 533-4638
www.wishkah.org
Wishkah Valley S 100/K-12
4640 Wishkah Rd 98520 360-532-3128
Dennis Johnson, supt. Fax 533-4638

---

Grays Harbor College Post-Sec.
1620 Edward P Smith Dr 98520 360-532-9020

**Amanda Park, Grays Harbor, Pop. 240**
Lake Quinault SD 97 200/K-12
PO Box 38 98526 360-288-2260
Rich DuBois, supt. Fax 288-2732
www.lakequinaultschools.org
Lake Quinault MSHS 100/6-12
PO Box 38 98526 360-288-2414
Keith Samplawski, prin. Fax 288-2209

**Amboy, Clark, Pop. 1,593**
Battle Ground SD 119
Supt. — See Brush Prairie
Amboy MS 600/5-8
22115 NE Chelatchie Rd 98601 360-885-6050
Michael Maloney, prin. Fax 885-6055

**Anacortes, Skagit, Pop. 15,315**
Anacortes SD 103 2,700/PK-12
2200 M Ave 98221 360-293-1200
Dr. Mark Wenzel, supt. Fax 293-1222
www.asd103.org
Anacortes HS 900/9-12
1600 20th St 98221 360-293-2166
Jon Ronngren, prin. Fax 293-0744
Anacortes MS 400/7-8
2202 M Ave 98221 360-293-1230
Patrick Harrington, prin. Fax 293-1231
Cap Sante HS 50/Alt
1717 J Ave 98221 360-293-1225
Jon Ronngren, admin. Fax 293-0744
Other Schools – See Mount Vernon

**Arlington, Snohomish, Pop. 17,235**
Arlington SD 16 5,800/PK-12
315 N French Ave 98223 360-618-6200
Kristine McDuffy Ed.D., supt. Fax 618-6221
www.asd.wednet.edu
Arlington HS 1,500/9-12
18821 Crown Ridge Blvd 98223 360-618-6300
Brian Beckley, prin. Fax 618-6310
Haller MS 600/6-8
600 E 1st St 98223 360-618-6400
Jeff Larson, prin. Fax 618-6411
Post MS 600/6-8
1220 E 5th St 98223 360-618-6450
Yvonne Walker, prin. Fax 618-6455
Weston HS 100/Alt
4407 172nd St NE 98223 360-618-6340
Will Nelson, prin. Fax 618-6341

**Asotin, Asotin, Pop. 1,220**
Asotin-Anatone SD 420 600/PK-12
PO Box 489 99402 509-243-1100
Dale Bonfield, supt. Fax 243-4251
www.aasd.wednet.edu
Asotin JSHS 300/6-12
PO Box 489 99402 509-243-4151
Jerry Uhling, prin. Fax 243-4090

**Auburn, King, Pop. 65,915**
Auburn SD 408 14,300/K-12
915 4th St NE 98002 253-931-4900
Dr. Alan Spicciati, supt. Fax 931-8006
www.auburn.wednet.edu
Auburn HS 1,600/9-12
711 E Main St 98002 253-931-4880
Richard Zimmerman, prin. Fax 931-4701
Auburn Mountainview HS 1,500/9-12
28900 124th Ave SE 98092 253-804-4539
Terri Herren, prin. Fax 876-2507
Auburn Riverside HS 1,700/9-12
501 Oravetz Rd SE 98092 253-804-5154
Dave Halford, prin. Fax 804-5168
Cascade MS 700/6-8
1015 24th St NE 98002 253-931-4995
Isaiah Johnson, prin. Fax 833-7580
Mt. Baker MS 900/6-8
620 37th St SE 98002 253-804-4555
Greg Brown, prin. Fax 931-0661
Olympic MS 700/6-8
1825 K St SE 98002 253-931-4966
Jason Hill, prin. Fax 939-2753
Rainier MS 800/6-8
30620 116th Ave SE 98092 253-931-4843
Ben Talbert, prin. Fax 939-4318
West Auburn HS 200/Alt
401 W Main St 98001 253-931-4990
Lenny Holloman, prin. Fax 931-4707

Federal Way SD 210
Supt. — See Federal Way
Jefferson HS 1,800/9-12
4248 S 288th St 98001 253-945-5600
Adrienne Chacon, prin. Fax 945-5656

Kilo MS 600/6-8
4400 S 308th St 98001 253-945-4700
Margaret Peterson, prin. Fax 945-4747
Sequoyah MS 600/6-8
3425 S 360th St 98001 253-945-3670
Springy Yamasaki, prin. Fax 945-3699

---

Auburn Adventist Academy 300/9-12
5000 Auburn Way S 98092 253-939-5000
Green River Community College Post-Sec.
12401 SE 320th St 98092 253-833-9111
Rainier Christian MS 100/7-8
20 49th St NE 98002 253-639-7715
Tess Johnson, prin. Fax 639-3184

**Bainbridge Island, Kitsap, Pop. 22,174**
Bainbridge Island SD 303 3,800/PK-12
8489 Madison Ave NE 98110 206-842-4714
Faith Chapel, supt. Fax 842-2928
www.bisd303.org
Bainbridge HS 1,300/9-12
9330 NE High School Rd 98110 206-842-2634
Duane Fish, prin. Fax 780-1260
Eagle Harbor HS 100/Alt
9530 NE High School Rd 98110 206-780-1646
David Shockley, prin. Fax 855-0511
Woodward MS 500/7-8
9125 Sportsman Club Rd NE 98110 206-842-4787
Mike Florian, prin. Fax 780-4525

**Battle Ground, Clark, Pop. 16,976**
Battle Ground SD 119
Supt. — See Brush Prairie
Agriculture Science & Environmental Ed Alt
PO Box 200 98604 360-885-5361
Richard Hogg, lead tchr. Fax 885-5365
Battle Ground HS 2,100/9-12
PO Box 200 98604 360-885-6500
Mike Hamilton, prin. Fax 687-6590
CAM Academy 500/Alt
PO Box 200 98604 360-885-6803
Ryan Cowl, prin. Fax 885-6808
Chief Umtuch MS 600/5-8
PO Box 200 98604 360-885-6350
Elizabeth Beattie, prin. Fax 885-6355
Daybreak MS 500/5-8
PO Box 200 98604 360-885-6900
Kevin Palena, prin. Fax 885-6948
River HomeLink 300/Alt
PO Box 200 98604 360-334-8200
Mark Clements, prin. Fax 334-8223
Tukes Valley MS 400/5-8
PO Box 200 98604 360-885-6250
Diana Harris, prin. Fax 885-6297

---

Columbia Adventist Academy 100/9-12
11100 NE 189th St 98604 360-687-3161
Firm Foundation Christian S 400/PK-12
1919 SW 25th Ave 98604 360-687-8382
Julie Olson, prin. Fax 687-8799

**Belfair, Mason, Pop. 3,769**
North Mason SD 403 — 2,100/PK-12
71 E Campus Dr 98528 — 360-277-2300
Dana Rosenbach, supt. — Fax 277-2320
www.northmasonschools.org
Hawkins MS — 400/6-8
300 E Campus Dr 98528 — 360-277-2302
Thomas Worlund, prin. — Fax 277-2324
North Mason HS — 700/9-12
200 E Campus Dr 98528 — 360-277-2303
Chad Collins, prin. — Fax 277-2323
PACE Academy — Alt
71 E Campus Dr 98528 — 360-277-2210
Anne Crosby, admin. — Fax 277-2320

**Bellevue, King, Pop. 117,650**
Bellevue SD 405 — 18,100/PK-12
PO Box 90010 98009 — 425-456-4000
J. Tim Mills Ed.D., supt. — Fax 456-4176
www.bsd405.org
Bellevue Big Picture S — 100/6-12
14844 SE 22nd St 98007 — 425-456-7800
Bethany Spinler, prin. — Fax 456-7805
Bellevue HS — 1,400/9-12
10416 Wolverine Way 98004 — 425-456-7000
Scott Powers, prin. — Fax 456-7005
Chinook MS — 1,000/6-8
2001 98th Ave NE 98004 — 425-456-6300
Dr. Vic Anderson, prin. — Fax 456-6304
Highland MS — 500/6-8
15027 Bel Red Rd 98007 — 425-456-6400
Katie Klug, prin. — Fax 456-6499
Interlake HS — 1,500/9-12
16245 NE 24th St 98008 — 425-456-7200
Maria Frieboes-Gee, prin. — Fax 456-7215
International S — 500/6-12
445 128th Ave SE 98005 — 425-456-6500
Jennifer Rose, prin. — Fax 456-6565
Newport HS — 1,700/9-12
4333 Factoria Blvd SE 98006 — 425-456-7400
Dion Yahoudy, prin. — Fax 456-7530
Odle MS — 700/6-8
11650 SE 60th St 98006 — 425-456-6600
Aaron Miller, prin. — Fax 456-6616
Sammamish HS — 1,100/9-12
100 140th Ave SE 98005 — 425-456-7600
Tom Duenwald, prin. — Fax 456-7665
Tillicum MS — 800/6-8
16020 SE 16th St 98008 — 425-456-6700
James Peterson, prin. — Fax 456-6770
Tyee MS — 800/6-8
13630 SE Allen Rd 98006 — 425-456-6800
Susan Thomas, prin. — Fax 456-6801

---

Academic Institute — 50/6-12
2495 140th Ave NE Ste D210 98005 — 425-401-6844
Jennifer Vice, dir. — Fax 556-6972
Bellevue College — Post-Sec.
3000 Landerholm Cir SE 98007 — 425-564-1000
Dartmoor S — 100/1-12
2340 130th Ave NE 98005 — 425-885-6296
Kimm Conroy M.Ed., head sch — Fax 885-1137
DeVry University — Post-Sec.
600 108th Ave NE Ste 230 98004 — 425-455-2242
Eastside Academy — 50/9-12
1717 Bellevue Way NE 98004 — 425-452-9920
Toni Esparza, dir. — Fax 452-5723
Evergreen Beauty School — Post-Sec.
14045 NE 20th St Ste B 98007 — 425-643-0270
Forest Ridge School of the Sacred Heart — 400/5-12
4800 139th Ave SE 98006 — 425-641-0700
Mark Pierotti, hdmstr. — Fax 643-3881

**Bellingham, Whatcom, Pop. 77,637**
Bellingham SD 501 — 10,500/PK-12
1306 Dupont St 98225 — 360-676-6400
Dr. Greg Baker, supt. — Fax 676-2793
bellinghamschools.org
Bellingham HS — 1,100/9-12
2020 Cornwall Ave 98225 — 360-676-6575
Jeff Vaughn, prin. — Fax 647-6803
Fairhaven MS — 500/6-8
110 Parkridge Rd 98225 — 360-676-6450
Robert Kalahan, prin. — Fax 647-6887
Kulshan MS — 600/6-8
1250 Kenoyer Dr, — 360-676-4886
Meagan Dawson, prin. — Fax 647-6892
Options HS — 100/Alt
2015 Franklin St 98225 — 360-647-6871
Byron Gerard, prin. — Fax 647-6872
Sehome HS — 1,100/9-12
2700 Bill McDonald Pkwy 98225 — 360-676-6481
Michelle Kuss-Cybula, prin. — Fax 647-6863
Shuksan MS — 700/6-8
2717 Alderwood Ave 98225 — 360-676-6454
Amy Carder, prin. — Fax 647-6879
Squalicum HS — 1,300/9-12
3773 E McLeod Rd 98226 — 360-676-6471
James Everett, prin. — Fax 676-6561
Whatcom MS — 600/6-8
810 Halleck St 98225 — 360-676-6460
Jeffrey Coulter, prin. — Fax 647-6899

Ferndale SD 502
Supt. — See Ferndale
Windward HS — 200/9-12
5275 Northwest Dr 98226 — 360-383-9289
Jill Iwasaki, prin. — Fax 383-9152

Meridian SD 505 — 1,100/PK-12
214 W Laurel Rd 98226 — 360-398-7111
Tom Churchill, supt. — Fax 398-8966
www.meridian.wednet.edu
Meridian HS — 500/9-12
194 W Laurel Rd 98226 — 360-398-8111
Derek Forbes, prin. — Fax 398-7720
Other Schools – See Lynden

---

Bellingham Beauty School — Post-Sec.
4192 Meridian St 98226 — 360-734-1090
Bellingham Technical College — Post-Sec.
3028 Lindbergh Ave 98225 — 360-752-7000
Charter College Bellingham — Post-Sec.
410 W Bakerview Rd 98226 — 360-647-5000
Explorations Academy — 50/8-12
PO Box 3014 98227 — 360-671-8085
Northwest Indian College — Post-Sec.
2522 Kwina Rd 98226 — 360-676-2772
St. Paul's Academy — 400/PK-12
1509 E Victor St 98225 — 360-733-1750
Toni & Guy Hairdressing Academy — Post-Sec.
1411 Railroad Ave 98225 — 360-676-8444
Western Washington University — Post-Sec.
516 High St 98225 — 360-650-3000
Whatcom Community College — Post-Sec.
237 W Kellogg Rd 98226 — 360-383-3000

**Benton City, Benton, Pop. 2,971**
Kiona-Benton City SD 52 — 1,300/PK-12
1105 Dale Ave 99320 — 509-588-2000
Wade Haun, supt. — Fax 588-5580
www.kibesd.org
Kiona-Benton City HS — 500/9-12
1105 Dale Ave 99320 — 509-588-2140
Clay Henry, prin. — Fax 588-2651
Kiona-Benton City MS — 400/6-8
1105 Dale Ave 99320 — 509-588-2040
Chuck Feth, prin. — Fax 588-2905

**Bickleton, Klickitat, Pop. 87**
Bickleton SD 203 — 100/K-12
PO Box 10 99322 — 509-896-5473
Ric Palmer, supt. — Fax 896-2071
www.bickletonschools.org
Bickleton S — 100/K-12
PO Box 10 99322 — 509-896-5473
Ric Palmer, prin. — Fax 896-2071

**Blaine, Whatcom, Pop. 4,469**
Blaine SD 503 — 2,100/PK-12
765 H St 98230 — 360-332-5881
Ron Spanjer Ed.D., supt. — Fax 332-7568
www.blaine.k12.wa.us
Blaine HS — 600/9-12
1055 H St 98230 — 360-332-6045
Scott Ellis, prin. — Fax 332-0333
Blaine MS — 500/6-8
975 H St 98230 — 360-332-8226
Darren Benson, prin. — Fax 332-0444

**Bonney Lake, Pierce, Pop. 16,669**
Sumner SD 320
Supt. — See Sumner
Bonney Lake HS — 1,400/9-12
10920 199th Avenue Ct E, — 253-891-5700
Cris Turner, prin. — Fax 891-5797
Lakeridge MS — 600/6-8
5909 Myers Rd E, — 253-891-5100
Toby Udager, prin. — Fax 891-5145
Mountain View MS — 600/6-8
10921 199th Avenue Ct E, — 253-891-5200
Curtis Hurst, prin. — Fax 891-5245

**Bothell, King, Pop. 32,149**
Edmonds SD 15
Supt. — See Lynnwood
Lynnwood HS — 1,700/9-12
18218 North Rd 98012 — 425-431-7520
David Golden, prin. — Fax 431-7527

Northshore SD 417 — 19,500/PK-12
3330 Monte Villa Pkwy 98021 — 425-408-7701
Larry Francois, supt. — Fax 408-7702
www.nsd.org
Bothell SHS — 1,600/10-12
9130 NE 180th St 98011 — 425-408-7000
Bob Stewart, prin. — Fax 408-7002
Canyon Park JHS — 800/7-9
23723 23rd Ave SE 98021 — 425-408-6300
Sebastian Ziz, prin. — Fax 408-6302
Northshore JHS — 700/7-9
12101 NE 160th St 98011 — 425-408-6700
Tiffany Rodriguez, prin. — Fax 408-6702
Secondary Academy for Success — 100/Alt
22107 23rd Dr SE 98021 — 425-408-6600
Donna Tyo, prin. — Fax 408-6602
Skyview JHS — 900/7-9
21404 35th Ave SE 98021 — 425-408-6800
Dawn Mark, prin. — Fax 408-6802
Other Schools – See Kenmore, Woodinville

---

Bastyr University — Post-Sec.
14500 Juanita Dr NE 98028 — 425-602-3000
Cascadia Community College — Post-Sec.
18345 Campus Way NE 98011 — 425-352-8000
Cedar Park Christian S — 1,100/PK-12
16300 112th Ave NE 98011 — 425-488-9778
Dr. Clint Behrends, supt. — Fax 483-5765

**Bremerton, Kitsap, Pop. 34,864**
Bremerton SD 100-C — 4,900/PK-12
134 Marion Ave N 98312 — 360-473-1000
Dr. Aaron Leavell, supt. — Fax 473-1040
www.bremertonschools.org
Bremerton HS — 1,300/9-12
1500 13th St 98337 — 360-473-0800
John Polm, prin. — Fax 473-0820
Mountain View MS — 900/6-8
2400 Perry Ave 98310 — 360-473-0600
Michaeleen Gelhaus, prin. — Fax 473-0620
Renaissance HS / Phoenix Academy — 100/Alt
3400 1st St 98312 — 360-473-4700
Kristen Morga, prin. — Fax 792-1350

West Sound Technical Skills Center — Vo/Tech
101 National Ave N 98312 — 360-473-0550
Shani Watkins, dir. — Fax 478-5090

Central Kitsap SD 401
Supt. — See Silverdale
Eastside Alternative HS — 100/Alt
7070 Tibardis Rd NW 98311 — 360-662-2870
Jeremy Monroe, prin. — Fax 662-2871
Fairview JHS — 700/7-9
8107 Central Valley Rd NW 98311 — 360-662-2600
Kathy Wales, prin. — Fax 662-2601
Olympic HS — 900/10-12
7070 Stampede Blvd NW 98311 — 360-662-2700
Rebecca Johnson, prin. — Fax 662-2701

---

Crosspoint Academy — 200/K-12
4012 Chico Way NW 98312 — 360-377-7700
Nick Sweeney, admin. — Fax 377-7795
Everest College — Post-Sec.
155 Washington Ave Ste 200 98337 — 360-473-1120
Olympic College — Post-Sec.
1600 Chester Ave 98337 — 360-792-6050

**Brewster, Okanogan, Pop. 2,353**
Brewster SD 111 — 800/PK-12
PO Box 97 98812 — 509-689-3418
Eric Driessen, supt. — Fax 689-0749
brewsterbears.org/
Brewster Alternative S — 50/Alt
PO Box 97 98812 — 509-689-8031
Linda Dezellum, admin. — Fax 689-0675
Brewster HS — 300/9-12
PO Box 97 98812 — 509-689-3449
Linda Dezellem, prin. — Fax 689-0675
Brewster MS — 6-8
PO Box 97 98812 — 509-689-3449
Greg Austin, admin. — Fax 689-0675

**Bridgeport, Douglas, Pop. 2,379**
Bridgeport SD 75 — 700/PK-12
PO Box 1060 98813 — 509-686-5656
Scott Sattler, supt. — Fax 686-2221
www.bridgeport.wednet.edu
Aurora HS — 50/Alt
PO Box 1060 98813 — 509-686-8770
Tamra Jackson, prin. — Fax 686-9622
Bridgeport HS — 200/9-12
PO Box 1060 98813 — 509-686-8770
Tamra Jackson, prin. — Fax 686-9622
Bridgeport MS — 200/5-8
PO Box 1060 98813 — 509-686-9501
Brian Ellis, admin. — Fax 686-4052

**Brier, Snohomish, Pop. 5,840**
Edmonds SD 15
Supt. — See Lynnwood
Brier Terrace MS — 700/7-8
22200 Brier Rd 98036 — 425-431-7834
Alex Alexander, prin. — Fax 431-7836

**Brush Prairie, Clark, Pop. 2,603**
Battle Ground SD 119 — 11,800/K-12
11104 NE 149th St 98606 — 360-885-5300
Mark Hottowe, supt. — Fax 885-5310
www.battlegroundps.org
Summit View HS — 300/Alt
11104 NE 149th St 98606 — 360-885-6350
Bill Penrose, prin. — Fax 885-5402
Other Schools – See Amboy, Battle Ground, Vancouver

Hockinson SD 98 — 1,500/K-12
17912 NE 159th St 98606 — 360-448-6400
Sandra Yager, supt. — Fax 448-6409
www.hocksd.org
Hockinson HS — 700/9-12
16819 NE 159th St 98606 — 360-448-6450
Brian Lehner, prin. — Fax 448-6459
Hockinson MS — 500/6-8
15916 NE 182nd Ave 98606 — 360-448-6440
Slade McSheehy, prin. — Fax 448-6449

**Buckley, Pierce, Pop. 4,221**
White River SD 416 — 3,600/PK-12
PO Box 2050 98321 — 360-829-0600
Janel Keating, supt. — Fax 829-3358
www.whiteriver.wednet.edu
Glacier MS — 800/6-8
PO Box 1976 98321 — 360-829-3395
Robin Cerato, prin. — Fax 829-3391
White River HS — 1,200/9-12
PO Box 1683 98321 — 360-829-3352
Elaine Mathews, prin. — Fax 829-3351

---

Rainier School, PO Box 600 98321 — Post-Sec.

**Burbank, Walla Walla, Pop. 3,235**
Columbia SD 400 — 900/PK-12
755 Maple St 99323 — 509-547-2136
Dr. Lou Gates, supt. — Fax 546-0603
www.csd400.org/
Columbia HS — 300/9-12
787 Maple St 99323 — 509-545-8573
Kyle Miller, prin. — Fax 545-6553
Columbia MS — 200/6-8
835 Maple St 99323 — 509-545-8571
Mike Taylor, prin. — Fax 547-4277

**Burien, King, Pop. 31,292**
Highline SD 401 — 18,700/PK-12
15675 Ambaum Blvd SW 98166 — 206-631-3000
Dr. Susan Enfield, supt. — Fax 631-3393
www.highlineschools.org
Big Picture MSHS — 200/7-12
440 S 186th St 98148 — 206-631-7700
Tim Schlosser, prin. — Fax 631-7749

Highline HS 1,400/9-12
225 S 152nd St 98148 206-631-6700
Vicki Fisher, prin. Fax 631-6758
Puget Sound Skills Center Vo/Tech
18010 8th Ave S 98148 206-631-7300
Dr. Thomas Mosby, prin. Fax 631-7337
Sylvester MS 600/7-8
16222 Sylvester Rd SW 98166 206-631-6000
Kyle Linman, prin. Fax 631-6064
Other Schools – See Des Moines, SeaTac, Seattle, Tukwila

Kennedy HS 900/9-12
140 S 140th St 98168 206-246-0500
Michael Prato, prin. Fax 242-0831

**Burlington, Skagit, Pop. 8,211**
Burlington-Edison SD 100 3,800/K-12
927 E Fairhaven Ave 98233 360-757-3311
Laurel Browning, supt. Fax 755-9198
www.be.wednet.edu/
Burlington-Edison HS 1,200/9-12
301 N Burlington Blvd 98233 360-757-4074
Todd Setterlund, prin. Fax 757-3350

Skagit Adventist Academy 100/PK-12
530 N Section St 98233 360-755-9261
Doug White, prin.

**Camas, Clark, Pop. 18,670**
Camas SD 117 6,200/K-12
841 NE 22nd Ave 98607 360-335-3000
Mike Nerland, supt. Fax 335-3001
www.camas.wednet.edu/
Camas HS 1,800/9-12
26900 SE 15th St 98607 360-833-5750
Steve Marshall, prin. Fax 833-5751
Hayes Freedom HS 100/9-12
1919 NE Ione St 98607 360-833-5602
Amy Holmes, prin. Fax 833-5601
Liberty MS 700/6-8
1612 NE Garfield St 98607 360-833-5850
Marilyn Boerke, prin. Fax 833-5851
Skyridge MS 800/6-8
5220 NW Parker St 98607 360-833-5800
Aaron Smith, prin. Fax 833-5801

Evergreen SD 114
Supt. — See Vancouver
Union HS 2,100/9-12
6201 NW Friberg Strunk St 98607 360-604-6250
Brian Grimsted, prin. Fax 604-6202

**Carnation, King, Pop. 1,754**
Riverview SD 407
Supt. — See Duvall
Riverview Learning Center 200/Alt
32302 NE 50th St 98014 425-844-4960
Christopher Mirecki, prin. Fax 844-4962
Tolt MS 700/6-8
3740 Tolt Ave 98014 425-844-4600
Christopher Lupo, prin. Fax 844-4602

**Carson, Skamania, Pop. 2,177**
Stevenson-Carson SD 303
Supt. — See Stevenson
Columbia Gorge S Alt
441 Hot Springs Ave 98610 509-427-4645
Brian Howe, prin. Fax 879-4320

**Cashmere, Chelan, Pop. 3,023**
Cashmere SD 222 1,500/PK-12
210 S Division St 98815 509-782-3355
Glenn Johnson, supt. Fax 782-4747
www.cashmere.wednet.edu
Cashmere HS 500/9-12
329 Tigner Rd 98815 509-782-2914
Tony Boyle, prin. Fax 782-2891
Cashmere MS 400/5-8
300 Tigner Rd 98815 509-782-2001
Sara Graves, prin. Fax 782-2547

**Castle Rock, Cowlitz, Pop. 1,912**
Castle Rock SD 401 1,400/PK-12
600 Huntington Ave S 98611 360-501-2940
Susan Barker, supt. Fax 501-3140
www.castlerockschools.org
Castle Rock HS 500/9-12
5180 Westside Hwy 98611 360-501-2930
Ryan Greene, prin. Fax 501-2999
Castle Rock MS 200/6-8
615 Front Ave SW 98611 360-501-2920
Tiffany Golden, prin. Fax 501-3125

**Cathlamet, Wahkiakum, Pop. 521**
Wahkiakum SD 200 500/K-12
PO Box 398 98612 360-795-3971
Bob Garrett, supt. Fax 795-0545
www.wahksd.k12.wa.us
Thomas MS 100/6-8
PO Box 398 98612 360-795-3261
Theresa Libby, prin. Fax 795-3205
Wahkiakum HS 200/9-12
PO Box 398 98612 360-795-3271
Stephanie Leitz, prin. Fax 795-0545

**Centralia, Lewis, Pop. 15,816**
Centralia SD 401 3,500/K-12
PO Box 610 98531 360-330-7600
Steve Warren, supt. Fax 330-7604
www.centralia.k12.wa.us
Centralia HS 1,100/9-12
813 Eshom Rd 98531 360-330-7605
Josue Lowe, prin. Fax 330-7616
Centralia MS 500/7-8
901 Johnson Rd 98531 360-330-7619
Greg Domingos, prin. Fax 330-7622
Other Schools – See Chehalis

Centralia College Post-Sec.
600 Centralia College Blvd 98531 360-736-9391

**Chattaroy, Spokane**
Riverside SD 416 1,500/PK-12
34515 N Newport Hwy 99003 509-464-8201
Roberta Kramer Ed.D., supt. Fax 464-8206
www.riversidesd.org
Riverside Achievement Center 50/Alt
34515 N Newport Hwy 99003 509-464-8478
Janet Kemp, prin. Fax 464-8479
Riverside HS 500/9-12
4120 E Deer Park Milan Rd 99003 509-464-8550
John McCoy, prin. Fax 464-8556
Riverside MS 300/6-8
3814 E Deer Park Milan Rd 99003 509-464-8450
Kristy Misiaszek, prin. Fax 464-8447

**Chehalis, Lewis, Pop. 7,074**
Adna SD 226 600/K-12
179 Dieckman Rd 98532 360-748-0362
Jim Forrest, supt. Fax 748-9217
www.adnaschools.org
Adna MSHS 400/6-12
121 Adna School Rd 98532 360-748-8552
Kevin Young, prin. Fax 748-1625

Centralia SD 401
Supt. — See Centralia
Centralia Alternative Program 50/Alt
2100 N National Ave 98532 360-748-2163
Faye Olason, lead tchr. Fax 748-2164

Chehalis SD 302 2,800/PK-12
310 SW 16th St 98532 360-807-7200
Ed Rothlin, supt. Fax 748-8899
www.chehalis.k12.wa.us
Chehalis MS 600/6-8
1060 SW 20th St 98532 360-807-7230
Chris Simpson, prin. Fax 740-1849
West HS 1,000/9-12
342 SW 16th St 98532 360-807-7235
Bob Walters, prin. Fax 748-3664

Lewis County Adventist S 100/PK-10
PO Box 1203 98532 360-748-3213

**Chelan, Chelan, Pop. 3,828**
Lake Chelan SD 129 1,500/K-12
PO Box 369 98816 509-682-3515
Robert Manahan Ed.D., supt. Fax 682-5842
www.chelanschools.org/
Chelan HS 400/9-12
PO Box 369 98816 509-682-4061
Barry DePaoli, prin. Fax 682-5001
Chelan MS 300/6-8
PO Box 369 98816 509-682-4073
Brad Wilson, prin. Fax 682-5001
Chelan S of Innovation Alt
PO Box 369 98816 509-682-3515
Crosby Carpenter, prin.
Holden Village Community S 50/K-12
PO Box 369 98816 509-682-3515
Karen Crowell, prin. Fax 682-5842

**Cheney, Spokane, Pop. 10,120**
Cheney SD 360 4,800/PK-12
12414 S Andrus Rd 99004 509-559-4599
Dr. Debra Clemens, supt. Fax 559-4508
www.cheneysd.org
Cheney HS 1,200/9-12
460 N 6th St 99004 509-559-4000
Troy Heuett, prin. Fax 559-4005
Cheney MS 900/6-8
740 W Betz Rd 99004 509-559-4400
Mike Stark, prin. Fax 559-4479
Three Springs HS 100/Alt
460 N 6th St 99004 509-559-4521
Ryan Fitzgerald, admin. Fax 559-4582
Other Schools – See Spokane

Eastern Washington University Post-Sec.
526 5th St 99004 509-359-6200

**Chewelah, Stevens, Pop. 2,514**
Chewelah SD 36 600/PK-12
PO Box 47 99109 509-685-6800
Richard Linehan, supt. Fax 935-8605
www.chewelah.k12.wa.us
Chewelah Alternative HS 50/Alt
PO Box 47 99109 509-685-6800
Jon Symonds, admin. Fax 935-0379
Jenkins JSHS 300/7-12
PO Box 138 99109 509-685-6800
Shawn Anderson, prin. Fax 935-9206

**Chimacum, Jefferson**
Chimacum SD 49 1,000/K-12
PO Box 278 98325 360-302-5890
Rick Thompson, supt. Fax 732-4336
www.csd49.org
Chimacum HS 300/9-12
PO Box 278 98325 360-302-5900
Whitney Meissner, prin. Fax 732-7359
Chimacum MS 300/6-8
PO Box 278 98325 360-302-5944
Stuart Prince, prin. Fax 732-6859

**Clarkston, Asotin, Pop. 7,028**
Clarkston SD J 250-185 2,600/K-12
PO Box 70 99403 509-758-2531
Tim Winter, supt. Fax 758-3326
www.csdk12.org
Adams HS 700/9-12
PO Box 370 99403 509-758-5591
Eric Anderson, prin. Fax 758-2831

Educational Opportunity Center 200/Alt
1284 Chestnut St 99403 509-758-4508
Elece Lockridge, prin. Fax 758-4509
Lincoln MS 400/7-8
1945 4th Ave 99403 509-758-5506
Mike Sperry, prin. Fax 758-7838

**Cle Elum, Kittitas, Pop. 1,804**
Cle Elum-Roslyn SD 404 900/PK-12
2690 State Route 903 98922 509-649-4850
Gary Wargo, supt. Fax 649-2404
www.cersd.org
Cle Elum-Roslyn HS 300/9-12
2692 State Route 903 98922 509-649-4900
Brett Simpson, prin. Fax 649-3563
Strom MS 200/6-8
2694 State Route 903 98922 509-649-4800
Lara Gregorich-Bennett, prin. Fax 649-3634
Other Schools – See Roslyn

**Clyde Hill, King, Pop. 2,918**

Bellevue Christian JSHS 500/7-12
1601 98th Ave NE 98004 425-454-4028
Blake DeYoung, prin. Fax 454-4418

**Colbert, Spokane**
Mead SD 354
Supt. — See Mead
Mountainside MS 700/7-8
4717 E Day Mount Spokane Rd 99005 509-465-7400
Craig Busch, prin. Fax 465-7420

Northwest Christian HS 200/9-12
5104 E Bernhill Rd 99005 509-238-4005

**Colfax, Whitman, Pop. 2,773**
Colfax SD 300 700/K-12
1207 N Morton St 99111 509-397-3042
Jerry Pugh, supt. Fax 397-5835
www.colfax.k12.wa.us
Colfax JSHS 300/7-12
1110 N Morton St 99111 509-397-4368
Nathan Whittle, prin. Fax 397-2414

**College Place, Walla Walla, Pop. 8,557**
College Place SD 250 500/K-10
1755 S College Ave 99324 509-525-4827
Timothy Payne, supt. Fax 525-3741
www.cpps.org
College Place HS 100/9-10
1755 S College Ave 99324 509-522-3312
Kirk Jameson, prin. Fax 522-3306
Sager MS 200/6-8
1755 S College Ave 99324 509-525-5300
Dale Stopperan, prin. Fax 525-6005

Walla Walla University Post-Sec.
204 S College Ave 99324 509-527-2615
Walla Walla Valley Academy 200/9-12
300 SW Academy Way 99324 509-525-1050

**Colton, Whitman, Pop. 412**
Colton SD 306 200/K-12
706 Union St 99113 509-229-3385
Nathan Smith, supt. Fax 229-3374
www.colton.k12.wa.us
Colton S 200/K-12
706 Union St 99113 509-229-3386
Nathan Smith, prin. Fax 229-3374

**Colville, Stevens, Pop. 4,534**
Colville SD 115 2,000/K-12
217 S Hofstetter St 99114 509-684-7850
Pete Lewis, supt. Fax 684-7855
www.colsd.org
Colville HS 600/9-12
154 Highway 20 E 99114 509-684-7800
Kevin Knight, prin. Fax 684-7809
Colville JHS 400/6-8
990 S Cedar St 99114 509-684-7820
Paul Dumas, prin. Fax 684-7825
Panorama S 200/Alt
225 S Hofstetter St 99114 509-684-7840
Ann McKern, prin. Fax 684-2819

**Concrete, Skagit, Pop. 682**
Concrete SD 11 600/K-12
45389 Airport Way Rm 103 98237 360-853-4000
Barbara Hawkings, supt. Fax 853-4004
www.concrete.k12.wa.us
Concrete MSHS 200/7-12
7830 S Superior Ave 98237 360-853-4015
Mike Holbrook, prin. Fax 853-4066
Twin Cedars HS 50/Alt
45389 Airport Way Rm 110 98237 360-853-4015
Mike Holbrook, dir. Fax 853-4066

**Connell, Franklin, Pop. 4,122**
North Franklin SD J 51-162 2,000/K-12
PO Box 829 99326 509-234-2021
Gregg Taylor, supt. Fax 234-9200
www.nfsd.org
Connell HS 600/9-12
PO Box 829 99326 509-234-2911
Tim Peterson, prin. Fax 234-2921
Olds JHS 300/7-8
PO Box 829 99326 509-234-3931
Jim Jacobs, prin. Fax 234-8171
Palouse Junction HS 50/Alt
PO Box 829 99326 509-234-1055
George Farrah, prin. Fax 234-9200

**Cosmopolis, Grays Harbor, Pop. 1,610**
North River SD 200 100/PK-12
2867 N River Rd 98537 360-532-3079
David Pickering, supt. Fax 532-1738
www.nr.k12.wa.us/

North River S — 100/PK-12
2867 N River Rd 98537 — 360-532-3079
Sean Pierson, prin. — Fax 532-1738

**Coulee City, Grant, Pop. 541**
Coulee-Hartline SD 151 — 200/K-12
PO Box 428 99115 — 509-632-5231
Dr. James Evans, supt. — Fax 632-5166
www.achsd.org/chsd.htm
Almira-Coulee-Hartline HS — 100/9-12
413 N 4th St 99115 — 509-632-5231
Dr. James Evans, prin. — Fax 632-5166

**Coulee Dam, Okanogan, Pop. 1,042**
Grand Coulee Dam SD 301J — 700/PK-12
110 Stevens Ave 99116 — 509-633-2143
Dr. Dennis Carlson, supt. — Fax 633-2530
www.gcdsd.org
Lake Roosevelt HS — 200/7-12
505 Crest Dr 99116 — 509-633-1442
Brandon Byers, prin. — Fax 633-0356

**Coupeville, Island, Pop. 1,760**
Coupeville SD 204 — 1,000/K-12
501 S Main St 98239 — 360-678-2400
Dr. Jim Shank, supt. — Fax 678-4834
www.coupeville.k12.wa.us
Coupeville HS — 300/9-12
501 S Main St 98239 — 360-678-2410
Dr. Jim Shank, prin. — Fax 678-0540
Coupeville MS — 300/6-8
501 S Main St 98239 — 360-678-2410
Dr. Jim Shank, prin. — Fax 678-0540

**Covington, King, Pop. 16,615**
Kent SD 415
Supt. — See Kent
Cedar Heights MS — 700/7-8
19640 SE 272nd St 98042 — 253-373-7620
Heidi Maurer, prin. — Fax 373-7628
Kentwood HS — 2,100/9-12
25800 164th Ave SE 98042 — 253-373-7680
John Kniseley, prin. — Fax 373-7326
Mattson MS — 600/7-8
16400 SE 251st St 98042 — 253-373-7670
James Schiechl, prin. — Fax 373-7673

Tahoma SD 409
Supt. — See Maple Valley
Tahoma SHS — 1,800/10-12
18200 SE 240th St 98042 — 425-413-6200
Terry Duty, prin. — Fax 413-6333

---

Rainier Christian HS — 200/9-12
26201 180th Ave SE 98042 — 253-735-1413
Justin Evans, admin. — Fax 887-8234

**Cowiche, Yakima, Pop. 418**
Highland SD 203 — 1,100/K-12
PO Box 38 98923 — 509-678-4173
Mark Anderson, supt. — Fax 678-4177
www.highland.wednet.edu/
Highland HS — 300/10-12
17000 Summitview Rd 98923 — 509-678-7268
Brandon Jensen, prin. — Fax 678-4140
Highland JHS — 200/7-9
17000 Summitview Rd 98923 — 509-678-7268
Kelly Thorson, prin. — Fax 678-4140

**Creston, Lincoln, Pop. 228**
Creston SD 73 — 100/PK-12
485 SE E St 99117 — 509-636-2721
William Wadlington, supt. — Fax 636-2910
www.creston.wednet.edu
Creston S — 100/PK-12
485 SE E St 99117 — 509-636-2721
William Wadlington, prin. — Fax 636-2910

**Curlew, Ferry, Pop. 114**
Curlew SD 50 — 200/PK-12
PO Box 370 99118 — 509-779-4931
Dr. John Glenewinkel, supt. — Fax 779-4938
www.curlew.wednet.edu
Curlew S — 200/PK-12
PO Box 370 99118 — 509-779-4931
Dr. John Glenewinkel, admin. — Fax 779-4938

**Cusick, Pend Oreille, Pop. 205**
Cusick SD 59 — 300/K-12
305 Monumental Rd 99119 — 509-445-1125
Don Hawpe, supt. — Fax 445-1598
www.cusick.wednet.edu/
Cusick JSHS — 100/6-12
305 Monumental Rd 99119 — 509-445-1125
Stephen Bollinger, admin. — Fax 445-1598

**Darrington, Snohomish, Pop. 1,303**
Darrington SD 330 — 400/K-12
PO Box 27 98241 — 360-436-1323
Dave Holmer, supt. — Fax 436-2045
www.dsd.k12.wa.us
Darrington HS — 200/9-12
PO Box 27 98241 — 360-436-1140
Dave Holmer, prin. — Fax 436-1089

**Davenport, Lincoln, Pop. 1,697**
Davenport SD 207 — 600/PK-12
801 7th St 99122 — 509-725-1481
Jim Kowalkowski, supt. — Fax 725-2260
www.davenport.wednet.edu/
Davenport JSHS — 300/7-12
801 7th St 99122 — 509-725-4021
Chad Prewitt, prin. — Fax 725-2260

**Dayton, Columbia, Pop. 2,459**
Dayton SD 2 — 500/PK-12
609 S 2nd St 99328 — 509-382-2543
Doug Johnson, supt. — Fax 382-2081
www.daytonsd.org
Dayton HS — 200/9-12
614 S 3rd St 99328 — 509-382-4775
Paul Shaber, prin. — Fax 382-2081
Dayton MS — 100/6-8
614 S 3rd St 99328 — 509-382-4775
Paul Shaber, prin. — Fax 382-2081

**Deer Park, Spokane, Pop. 3,505**
Deer Park SD 414 — 2,000/K-12
PO Box 490 99006 — 509-464-5500
Travis Hanson, supt. — Fax 464-5510
www.dpsd.org
Alternative S — Alt
PO Box 550 99006 — 509-468-3500
Joe Feist, prin. — Fax 468-3510
Deer Park HS — 700/9-12
PO Box 550 99006 — 509-468-3500
Joe Feist, prin. — Fax 468-3510
Deer Park MS — 400/6-8
PO Box 882 99006 — 509-464-5800
Tim Olietti, prin. — Fax 464-5810

**Deming, Whatcom, Pop. 349**
Mt. Baker SD 507 — 1,600/K-12
PO Box 95 98244 — 360-383-2000
Charles Burleigh, supt. — Fax 383-2009
www.mtbaker.wednet.edu
Mt. Baker JSHS — 700/7-12
PO Box 95 98244 — 360-383-2015
Matt Durand, prin. — Fax 383-2029

**Des Moines, King, Pop. 27,680**
Highline SD 401
Supt. — See Burien
Mount Rainier HS — 1,600/9-12
22450 19th Ave S 98198 — 206-631-7000
Julie Hunter, prin. — Fax 631-7099
Pacific MS — 700/7-8
22705 24th Ave S 98198 — 206-631-5800
Diana Garcia, prin. — Fax 631-5860

Kent SD 415
Supt. — See Kent
Kent Mountain View Academy — 400/Alt
22420 Military Rd S 98198 — 253-373-7488
Stephanie Knipp, prin. — Fax 373-7490

---

Highline Community College — Post-Sec.
PO Box 98000 98198 — 206-878-3710

**DuPont, Pierce, Pop. 7,501**
Steilacoom Historical SD 1
Supt. — See Steilacoom
Pioneer MS — 600/6-8
1750 Bobs Hollow Ln 98327 — 253-583-7200
Andre Stout, prin. — Fax 583-7292

**Duvall, King, Pop. 6,458**
Riverview SD 407 — 3,300/K-12
PO Box 519 98019 — 425-844-4500
Dr. Anthony L. Smith, supt. — Fax 844-4502
www.riverview.wednet.edu
Cedarcrest HS — 900/9-12
29000 NE 150th St 98019 — 425-844-4800
Clarence Lavarias, prin. — Fax 844-4802
Other Schools – See Carnation

**Easton, Kittitas, Pop. 472**
Easton SD 28 — 100/PK-12
PO Box 8 98925 — 509-656-2317
Dr. Patrick Dehuff, supt. — Fax 656-2585
www.easton.wednet.edu/
Easton S — 100/PK-12
PO Box 8 98925 — 509-656-2317
Dr. Patrick Dehuff, supt. — Fax 656-2585

**Eastsound, San Juan**
Orcas Island SD 137 — 400/K-12
557 School Rd 98245 — 360-376-2284
Eric Webb, supt. — Fax 376-2283
www.orcasislandschools.org
OASIS K-12, 557 School Rd 98245 — 300/Alt
Eric Webb, supt. — 360-376-1598
Orcas Island HS — 100/9-12
715 School Rd 98245 — 360-376-2287
Kyle Freeman, prin. — Fax 376-6078
Orcas Island MS — 100/7-8
611 School Rd 98245 — 360-376-2286
Kyle Freeman, prin. — Fax 376-5410

---

Orcas Christian Day S — 100/K-12
PO Box 669 98245 — 360-376-6683
Tom Roosma, prin. — Fax 376-7642

**East Wenatchee, Douglas, Pop. 12,915**
Eastmont SD 206 — 4,900/K-12
800 Eastmont Ave 98802 — 509-884-7169
Dr. Garn Christensen, supt. — Fax 884-4210
www.eastmont206.org
Eastmont JHS — 900/8-9
905 8th St NE 98802 — 509-884-2407
David Woods, prin. — Fax 884-1988
Eastmont SHS — 1,400/10-12
955 3rd St NE 98802 — 509-884-6665
Lance Noell, prin. — Fax 884-8805

**Eatonville, Pierce, Pop. 2,651**
Eatonville SD 404 — 1,900/K-12
PO Box 698 98328 — 360-879-1000
Krestin Bahr, supt. — Fax 879-1086
www.eatonville.wednet.edu/
Eatonville HS — 700/9-12
PO Box 699 98328 — 360-879-1200
John Paul Colgan, prin. — Fax 879-1284
Eatonville MS — 500/6-8
PO Box 910 98328 — 360-879-1400
Janna Rush, prin. — Fax 879-1480

**Edgewood, Pierce, Pop. 9,076**
Puyallup SD 3
Supt. — See Puyallup
Edgemont JHS — 400/7-9
2300 110th Ave E 98372 — 253-841-8727
Eric Molver, prin. — Fax 840-8883

---

Salvation Christian Academy — 100/PK-10
10622 8th St E 98372 — 253-952-7163
Rev. Vadim Hetman, prin. — Fax 952-7164

**Edmonds, Snohomish, Pop. 38,105**
Edmonds SD 15
Supt. — See Lynnwood
Edmonds Heights K-12 S — Alt
23200 100th Ave W 98020 — 425-431-7840
Scott Mauk, prin. — Fax 431-7849
Edmonds-Woodway HS — 1,600/9-12
7600 212th St SW 98026 — 425-431-7900
Terrance Mims, prin. — Fax 431-7929
Scriber Lake HS — 200/Alt
23200 100th Ave W 98020 — 425-431-7270
Andrea Hillman, prin. — Fax 431-7272

---

Solomon Christian S — 50/7-12
8021 230th St SW 98026 — 425-640-9000
Richard Lee, prin. — Fax 458-9327

**Edwall, Lincoln**

---

Christian Heritage S — 100/K-12
48009 Ida Ave E 99008 — 509-236-2224
Brad Cain M.Ed., admin. — Fax 236-2412

**Ellensburg, Kittitas, Pop. 17,598**
Ellensburg SD 401 — 2,900/K-12
1300 E 3rd Ave 98926 — 509-925-8000
Dr. Paul Farris, supt. — Fax 925-8025
ellensburg.schoolfusion.us
Ellensburg HS — 900/9-12
1203 E Capitol Ave 98926 — 509-925-8300
Jeff Ellersick, prin. — Fax 925-8305
Excel HS — Alt
CWU Michaelson Hall # 122 98926 — 509-963-2428
Jeff Ellersick, prin.
Morgan MS — 700/6-8
400 E 1st Ave 98926 — 509-925-8200
Michelle Bibich, prin. — Fax 925-8202

---

Central Washington University — Post-Sec.
400 E University Way 98926 — 509-963-1111

**Elma, Grays Harbor, Pop. 2,963**
Elma SD 68 — 1,600/K-12
1235 Monte Elma Rd 98541 — 360-482-2822
Howard King, supt. — Fax 482-2092
www.elma.wednet.edu
East Grays Harbor HS — 50/Alt
1235 Monte Elma Rd 98541 — 360-482-5086
Gina Franchini, prin. — Fax 482-2109
Elma HS — 600/9-12
1235 Monte Elma Rd 98541 — 360-482-3121
Kevin Acuff, prin. — Fax 482-1200
Elma MS — 300/6-8
1235 Monte Elma Rd 98541 — 360-482-2237
Sunshine Perry, prin. — Fax 482-4872

Mary M. Knight SD 311 — 200/PK-12
2987 W Matlock Brady Rd 98541 — 360-426-6767
Dr. Ellen Perconti, supt. — Fax 427-5516
www.marymknight.com
Knight JSHS — 100/6-12
2987 W Matlock Brady Rd 98541 — 360-426-6767
John Schultz, prin. — Fax 427-5516

**Endicott, Whitman, Pop. 289**
Endicott SD 308 — 100/PK-8
308 School Dr 99125 — 509-657-3523
Jim Baldwin, supt. — Fax 657-3521
www.endicott.wednet.edu
Other Schools – See Saint John

**Entiat, Chelan, Pop. 1,090**
Entiat SD 127 — 400/PK-12
2650 Entiat Way 98822 — 509-784-1800
Dr. Ismael Vivanco, supt. — Fax 784-2986
www.entiatschools.org
Entiat Middle & HS — 200/6-12
2650 Entiat Way 98822 — 509-784-1911
Miles Caples, prin. — Fax 784-2986

**Enumclaw, King, Pop. 10,407**
Enumclaw SD 216 — 4,100/K-12
2929 McDougall Ave 98022 — 360-802-7100
Michael Nelson, supt. — Fax 802-7140
www.enumclaw.wednet.edu/
Enumclaw HS — 1,400/9-12
226 Semanski St 98022 — 360-802-7669
Jill Burnes, prin. — Fax 802-7676
Enumclaw MS — 500/6-8
550 Semanski St 98022 — 360-802-7150
Steve Rabb, prin. — Fax 802-7224
Thunder Mountain MS — 500/6-8
42018 264th Ave SE 98022 — 360-802-7492
Virginia Callison, prin. — Fax 802-7500

**Ephrata, Grant, Pop. 7,502**
Ephrata SD 165 — 2,300/K-12
499 C St NW 98823 — 509-754-2474
Dr. Jerry Simon, supt. — Fax 754-4712
www.ephrataschools.org
Ephrata HS — 700/9-12
333 4th Ave NW 98823 — 509-754-5285
Dan Martell, prin. — Fax 754-4993
Ephrata MS — 300/7-8
384 A St SE 98823 — 509-754-4659
Ken Murray, prin. — Fax 754-5625

Sage Hills Alternative S 100/Alt
35 K St SE 98823 509-754-7547
Frank Cardwell, prin. Fax 754-7227

**Everett, Snohomish, Pop. 98,083**
Everett SD 2 18,500/PK-12
3900 Broadway 98201 425-385-4000
Dr. Gary Cohn, supt. Fax 385-4012
www.everettsd.org
Cascade HS 1,900/9-12
801 E Casino Rd 98203 425-385-6000
Cathy Woods, prin. Fax 385-6002
Eisenhower MS 900/6-8
10200 25th Ave SE 98208 425-385-7500
Stefani Koetje, prin. Fax 385-7502
Everett HS 1,400/9-12
2416 Colby Ave 98201 425-385-4400
Sally Lancaster, prin. Fax 385-4402
Evergreen MS 1,000/6-8
7621 Beverly Ln 98203 425-385-5700
Larry Fleckenstein, prin. Fax 385-5702
Gateway MS 700/6-8
15404 Silver Firs Dr 98208 425-385-6600
Shelley Petillo, prin. Fax 385-6602
North MS 700/6-8
2514 Rainier Ave 98201 425-385-4800
Mary O'Brien, prin. Fax 385-4802
Sequoia HS 300/Alt
3516 Rucker Ave 98201 425-385-5100
Kelly Shepherd, prin. Fax 385-5102
Other Schools – See Mill Creek

Mukilteo SD 6 14,700/K-12
9401 Sharon Dr 98204 425-356-1274
Dr. Marci Larsen, supt. Fax 356-1310
www.mukilteo.wednet.edu
ACES HS 200/Alt
9700 Holly Dr 98204 425-366-3900
Marcie Polin, prin. Fax 366-3902
Explorer MS 900/6-8
9600 Sharon Dr 98204 425-366-5000
Ali Williams, prin. Fax 366-5002
Mariner HS 2,100/9-12
200 120th St SW 98204 425-366-5700
Brent Kline, prin. Fax 366-5702
Sno-Isle Vo Skills Ctr Vo/Tech
9001 Airport Rd 98204 425-348-2220
Dave Rudy, prin. Fax 356-2201
Voyager MS 800/6-8
11711 4th Ave W 98204 425-366-5300
Wes Bailey, prin. Fax 366-5302
Other Schools – See Mukilteo

---

Archbishop Thomas Murphy HS 500/9-12
12911 39th Ave SE 98208 425-379-6363
Steve Schmutz, prin. Fax 385-2875
Everest College Post-Sec.
906 SE Evertt Mall Way #600 98208 425-789-7960
Everett Community College Post-Sec.
2000 Tower St 98201 425-388-9100
ITT Technical Institute Post-Sec.
1615 75th St SW Ste 220 98203 425-583-0200
Milan Institute of Cosmetology Post-Sec.
607 SE Everett Mall Way #5 98208 425-353-8193
Montessori S of Snohomish County 100/PK-12
1804 Puget Dr 98203 425-355-1311
Trinity Lutheran College Post-Sec.
2802 Wetmore Ave 98201 425-249-4800

**Everson, Whatcom, Pop. 2,414**
Nooksack Valley SD 506 1,600/PK-12
3326 E Badger Rd 98247 360-988-4754
Dr. Mark Johnson, supt. Fax 988-8983
www.nv.k12.wa.us/
Nooksack Valley HS 500/9-12
3326 E Badger Rd 98247 360-988-2641
Matt Galley, prin. Fax 988-7058
Other Schools – See Nooksack

**Fall City, King, Pop. 1,940**
Snoqualmie Valley SD 410
Supt. — See Snoqualmie
Chief Kanim MS 400/6-8
PO Box 639 98024 425-831-8225
Kirk Dunckel, prin. Fax 831-8290

**Federal Way, King, Pop. 82,130**
Federal Way SD 210 21,900/PK-12
33330 8th Ave S 98003 253-945-2000
Dr. Tammy Campbell, supt. Fax 945-2001
www.fwps.org
Beamer HS 1,900/9-12
35999 16th Ave S 98003 253-945-2570
Joni Hall, prin. Fax 945-2599
Career Academy Vo/Tech
31455 28th Ave S 98003 253-945-5800
Christine Corbley, prin. Fax 945-5858
Decatur HS 1,400/9-12
2800 SW 320th St 98023 253-945-5200
David Brower, prin. Fax 945-5252
Federal Way Acceleration Academy Alt
2104 S 314th St Ste 2104 98003 253-945-4590
Ashley Barker, prin.
Federal Way HS 1,500/9-12
30611 16th Ave S 98003 253-945-5400
Matt Oberst, prin. Fax 945-5454
Federal Way Public Academy 300/Alt
34620 9th Ave S 98003 253-945-3270
Kurt Lauer, prin. Fax 945-3399
Illahee MS 800/6-8
36001 1st Ave S 98003 253-945-4600
Jerry Warren, prin. Fax 945-4646
International Academy Alt
31455 28th Ave S 98003 253-945-5800
Mark Orr, prin. Fax 945-5858
Lakota MS 800/6-8
1415 SW 314th St 98023 253-945-4800
Craig Tutt, prin. Fax 945-4848
Sacajawea MS 700/6-8
1101 S Dash Point Rd 98003 253-945-4900
JoAnne Fernandes, prin. Fax 945-4949
Saghalie MS 500/6-8
33914 19th Ave SW 98023 253-945-5000
Marin Miller, prin. Fax 945-5050
Other Schools – See Auburn, Kent

---

Christian Faith S 300/PK-12
33645 20th Ave S 98003 253-943-2500
Debbie Schindler, head sch Fax 200-1335
Cortiva Institute - Federal Way Post-Sec.
2030 S 314th St 98003 253-237-5300
DeVry University Post-Sec.
3600 S 344th Way 98001 253-943-2800
Gene Juarez Academy of Beauty Post-Sec.
2222 S 314th St 98003 253-839-6483

**Ferndale, Whatcom, Pop. 10,997**
Ferndale SD 502 3,600/PK-12
PO Box 698 98248 360-383-9200
Dr. Linda Quinn Ed.D., supt. Fax 383-9201
www.ferndale.wednet.edu
Ferndale HS 1,400/9-12
PO Box 428 98248 360-383-9240
Jeff Gardner, prin. Fax 383-9242
Horizon MS 400/6-8
PO Box 1769 98248 360-383-9850
Faye Britt, prin. Fax 383-9852
Vista MS 400/6-8
PO Box 1328 98248 360-383-9370
Kim Hawes, prin. Fax 383-9372
Other Schools – See Bellingham

**Fife, Pierce, Pop. 8,348**
Fife SD 417
Supt. — See Tacoma
Columbia JHS 500/8-9
2901 54th Ave E 98424 253-517-1600
Mark Robinson, prin. Fax 517-1605

**Forks, Clallam, Pop. 3,383**
Quillayute Valley SD 402 3,100/PK-12
411 S Spartan Ave 98331 360-374-6262
Diana Reaume, supt. Fax 374-6990
www.qvschools.org
Forks Alternative S 50/Alt
411 S Spartan Ave 98331 360-374-6262
Cindy Feasel, prin. Fax 374-2360
Forks HS 300/9-12
261 S Spartan Ave 98331 360-374-6262
Cindy Feasel, prin. Fax 374-9657
Forks JHS, 191 S Spartan Ave 98331 7-8
Kevin Rawie, prin. 360-374-6262

**Freeland, Island, Pop. 1,970**

---

Northwest Institute of Literary Arts Post-Sec.
PO Box 639 98249 360-331-0307

**Friday Harbor, San Juan, Pop. 2,106**
San Juan Island SD 149 800/K-12
PO Box 458 98250 360-378-4133
Dr. Danna Diaz, supt. Fax 378-6276
www.sjisd.wednet.edu
Friday Harbor HS 300/9-12
PO Box 458 98250 360-378-5215
Fred Woods, prin. Fax 378-2647
Friday Harbor MS 100/7-8
PO Box 458 98250 360-378-5214
Fred Woods, prin. Fax 378-9750
Griffin Bay S 50/Alt
PO Box 458 98250 360-378-3292
Dr. Danna Diaz, admin. Fax 378-2211

---

Spring Street International S 100/5-12
505 Spring St 98250 360-378-6393
Louis Prussack, head sch Fax 378-4220

**Garfield, Whitman, Pop. 585**
Garfield SD 302 100/PK-8
PO Box 398 99130 509-635-1331
Zane Wells, supt. Fax 635-1332
www.garpal.net
Garfield-Palouse MS 50/6-8
PO Box 398 99130 509-635-1331
Zane Wells, prin. Fax 635-1332

**Gig Harbor, Pierce, Pop. 6,870**
Peninsula SD 401 9,200/PK-12
14015 62nd Ave NW 98332 253-530-1000
Charles Cuzzetto, supt. Fax 530-1010
www.psd401.net/
Gig Harbor HS 1,600/9-12
5101 Rosedale St NW 98335 253-530-1400
Tom Leacy, prin. Fax 530-1420
Goodman MS 600/6-8
3701 38th Ave NW 98335 253-530-1600
D.J. Sigurdson, prin. Fax 530-1620
Harbor Ridge MS 600/6-8
9010 Prentice Ave 98332 253-530-1900
Mike Benoit, prin. Fax 530-1920
Henderson Bay HS 100/Alt
8402 Skansie Ave 98332 253-530-1700
Brian Tovey, prin. Fax 530-1720
Kopachuck MS 700/6-8
10414 56th St NW 98335 253-530-4100
Heidi Fedore, prin. Fax 530-4120
Peninsula HS 1,400/9-12
14105 Purdy Dr NW 98332 253-530-4400
Dave Goodwin, prin. Fax 530-4420
Other Schools – See Lakebay

**Glenwood, Klickitat**
Glenwood SD 401 50/K-12
PO Box 12 98619 509-364-3438
Heather Gimlin, supt. Fax 364-3689
www.glenwood.k12.wa.us/
Glenwood S 50/K-12
PO Box 12 98619 509-364-3438
Heather Gimlin, supt. Fax 364-3689

**Goldendale, Klickitat, Pop. 3,344**
Goldendale SD 404 1,000/K-12
604 E Brooks St 98620 509-773-5177
Mark Heid, supt. Fax 773-6028
www.goldendaleschools.org
Goldendale HS 400/9-12
525 E Simcoe Dr 98620 509-773-5846
John Westerman, prin. Fax 773-6900
Goldendale MS 300/5-8
520 E Collins St 98620 509-773-4323
Dave Barta, prin. Fax 773-4579

**Graham, Pierce, Pop. 21,945**
Bethel SD 403
Supt. — See Spanaway
Cougar Mountain MS 400/6-8
5108 260th St E 98338 253-683-8000
Bethany Aoki, prin. Fax 683-8098
Frontier MS 500/6-8
22110 108th Ave E 98338 253-683-8300
Mark Barnes, prin. Fax 683-8398
Graham-Kapowsin HS 1,300/9-12
22100 108th Ave E 98338 253-683-6100
Matthew Yarkosky, prin. Fax 683-6198

**Grandview, Yakima, Pop. 10,766**
Grandview SD 200 3,500/K-12
913 W 2nd St 98930 509-882-8500
Kevin Chase, supt. Fax 882-2029
www.gsd200.org
Compass HS 100/Alt
913 W 2nd St 98930 509-882-8540
Kim Casey, prin. Fax 882-8739
Grandview HS 800/9-12
1601 W 5th St 98930 509-882-8750
Mike Closner, prin. Fax 882-8739
Grandview MS 800/6-8
1401 W 2nd St 98930 509-882-8600
Paul Voorhees, prin. Fax 882-3538

**Granger, Yakima, Pop. 3,222**
Granger SD 204 1,500/PK-12
701 E Ave 98932 509-854-1515
Margarita C. Lopez, supt. Fax 854-1126
www.gsd.wednet.edu
Granger HS 500/9-12
701 E Ave 98932 509-854-1115
Tricia Anderson, prin. Fax 854-2757
Granger MS 500/5-8
701 E Ave 98932 509-854-1003
Stephanie Funk, prin. Fax 854-1083

**Granite Falls, Snohomish, Pop. 3,190**
Granite Falls SD 332 2,100/K-12
205 N Alder St 98252 360-691-7717
Linda Hall, supt. Fax 691-4459
www.gfalls.wednet.edu
Crossroads Alternative HS 100/Alt
205 N Alder Ave 98252 360-283-4407
Bridgette Perrigoue, prin. Fax 283-4307
Granite Falls HS 700/9-12
1401 100th St NE 98252 360-691-7713
Kevin Davis, prin. Fax 283-4414
Granite Falls MS 500/6-8
405 N Alder Ave 98252 360-691-7710
Dave Bianchini, prin. Fax 283-4415

**Harrington, Lincoln, Pop. 416**
Harrington SD 204 100/PK-12
PO Box 204 99134 509-253-4331
Dr. Mike Perry, supt. Fax 456-6306
www.harrsd.k12.wa.us
Harrington HS 100/7-12
PO Box 204 99134 509-253-4331
Justin Bradford, prin. Fax 456-6306

**Hoquiam, Grays Harbor, Pop. 8,401**
Hoquiam SD 28 1,600/PK-12
305 Simpson Ave 98550 360-538-8200
Mike Parker, supt. Fax 538-8202
hoquiam.net
Hoquiam HS 500/9-12
501 W Emerson Ave 98550 360-538-8210
Brock Maxfield, prin. Fax 538-8212
Hoquiam MS 400/6-8
200 Spencer St 98550 360-538-8220
Traci Sandstrom, prin. Fax 538-8222

**Hunters, Stevens**
Columbia SD 206 200/PK-12
PO Box 7 99137 509-722-3311
Michael Young, supt. Fax 722-3310
www.columbia206.com
Columbia S 200/PK-12
PO Box 7 99137 509-722-3311
Matt McLain, prin. Fax 722-3310

**Ilwaco, Pacific, Pop. 906**
Ocean Beach SD 101
Supt. — See Long Beach
Hilltop S, PO Box F 98624 5-8
Dr. Chad Madsen, prin.
Ilwaco HS 400/9-12
PO Box F 98624 360-642-3731
Dave Tobin, prin. Fax 642-1224

**Inchelium, Ferry, Pop. 393**
Inchelium SD 70 100/K-12
PO Box 285 99138 509-722-6181
Kim Spacek, supt. Fax 722-6192
www.inchelium.wednet.edu
Inchelium S 100/K-12
PO Box 285 99138 509-722-6181
John Moddrell, prin. Fax 722-6192

**Ione, Pend Oreille, Pop. 442**
Selkirk SD 70
Supt. — See Metaline Falls
Selkirk MSHS 100/6-12
10372 Highway 31 99139 509-446-3505
Greg Goodnight, prin. Fax 446-2408

**Issaquah, King, Pop. 29,272**
Issaquah SD 411 17,600/PK-12
565 NW Holly St 98027 425-837-7000
Ron Thiele, supt. Fax 837-7005
www.issaquah.wednet.edu
Beaver Lake MS 900/6-8
25025 SE 32nd St 98029 425-837-4150
Stacy Cho, prin. Fax 837-4195
Issaquah HS 1,900/9-12
700 2nd Ave SE 98027 425-837-6000
Andrea McCormick, prin. Fax 837-6078
Issaquah MS 800/6-8
400 1st Ave SE 98027 425-837-6800
Corrine DeRosa, prin. Fax 837-6855
Pacific Cascade MS 800/6-8
24635 SE Issaquah Fall City 98029 425-837-5900
Dana Bailey, prin. Fax 837-5910
Pine Lake MS 800/6-8
3200 228th Ave SE 98075 425-837-5700
Michelle Caponigro, prin. Fax 837-5762
Skyline HS 2,000/9-12
1122 228th Ave SE 98075 425-837-7700
Donna Hood, prin. Fax 837-7705
Tiger Mountain Community HS 100/Alt
355 SE Evans St 98027 425-837-6200
Michael Schiehser, prin. Fax 837-6225
Other Schools – See Renton

**Joyce, Clallam**
Crescent SD 313 200/K-12
PO Box 20 98343 360-928-3311
Dr. Clayton Mork, supt. Fax 928-3066
www.crescentschooldistrict.org
Crescent MSHS 100/7-12
PO Box 20 98343 360-928-3311
Clayton Mork, prin. Fax 928-3066

**Kahlotus, Franklin, Pop. 189**
Kahlotus SD 56 100/PK-12
PO Box 69 99335 509-282-3338
Mark Bitzer, supt. Fax 282-3339
www.kahlotussd.org
Kahlotus S 100/PK-12
PO Box 69 99335 509-282-3338
Ron Hopkins, prin. Fax 282-3339

**Kalama, Cowlitz, Pop. 2,270**
Kalama SD 402 1,000/K-12
548 China Garden Rd 98625 360-673-5282
James Sutton, supt. Fax 673-5228
kalamaschools.org
Kalama JSHS 600/6-12
548 China Garden Rd 98625 360-673-5212
Mike Hamilton, prin. Fax 673-1280

**Kelso, Cowlitz, Pop. 11,473**
Kelso SD 458 4,900/PK-12
601 Crawford St 98626 360-501-1900
Glenn Gelbrich, supt. Fax 501-1944
www.kelso.wednet.edu
Coweeman MS 500/6-8
2000 Allen St 98626 360-501-1750
Greg Gardner, prin. Fax 501-1782
Huntington MS 600/6-8
500 Redpath St 98626 360-501-1700
Chris Clark, prin. Fax 501-1723
Kelso HS 1,600/9-12
1904 Allen St 98626 360-501-1800
John Gummel, prin. Fax 501-1843
Loowit HS 50/Alt
1904 Allen St 98626 360-501-1951
Lacey DeWeert, prin. Fax 501-1954

**Kenmore, King, Pop. 19,563**
Northshore SD 417
Supt. — See Bothell
Inglemoor SHS 1,600/10-12
15500 Simonds Rd NE 98028 425-408-7200
Vicki Sherwood, prin. Fax 408-7202
Kenmore JHS 700/7-9
20323 66th Ave NE 98028 425-408-6400
Joshua Sanchez, prin. Fax 408-6402

**Kennewick, Benton, Pop. 72,070**
Finley SD 53 1,000/PK-12
224606 E Game Farm Rd 99337 509-586-3217
Lance Hahn, supt. Fax 586-4408
www.finleysd.org
Finley MS 200/6-8
37208 S Finley Rd 99337 509-586-7561
Michael Harrington, prin. Fax 582-8452
River View HS 300/9-12
36509 S Lemon Dr 99337 509-582-2158
Chris Davis, prin. Fax 586-9297

Kennewick SD 17 15,900/K-12
1000 W 4th Ave 99336 509-222-5000
Dave Bond, supt. Fax 222-5050
www.ksd.org
Desert Hills MS 900/6-8
6011 W 10th Pl 99338 509-222-6600
Steve Jones, prin. Fax 222-6601
Highlands MS 900/6-8
425 S Tweedt St 99336 509-222-6700
Lori McCord, prin. Fax 222-6701
Horse Heaven Hills MS 900/6-8
3500 S Vancouver St 99337 509-222-6800
Diana Burns, prin. Fax 222-6801
Kamiakin HS 1,600/9-12
600 N Arthur St 99336 509-222-7000
Chris Chelin, prin. Fax 222-7001
Kennewick HS 1,500/9-12
500 S Dayton St 99336 509-222-7100
Ron King, prin. Fax 222-7101
Legacy HS Alt
202 S Dayton St 99336 509-222-6552
Dennis Boatman, prin. Fax 222-5059
Park MS 800/6-8
1011 W 10th Ave 99336 509-222-6900
Shaun Espe, prin. Fax 222-6901
Phoenix HS 100/9-12
1315 W 4th Ave 99336 509-222-7400
Jill Mulhousen, lead tchr. Fax 222-5153
Southridge HS 1,500/9-12
3520 Southridge Blvd 99338 509-222-7200
Steve Biehn, prin. Fax 222-7201
Tri-Tech Vocational Skills Center Vo/Tech
5929 W Metaline Ave 99336 509-222-7300
Paul Randall, prin. Fax 222-7301

**Kent, King, Pop. 85,961**
Federal Way SD 210
Supt. — See Federal Way
TAF Academy 200/Alt
26630 40th Ave S 98032 253-945-5187
Paul Tyler, prin. Fax 945-5191
Totem MS 600/6-8
26630 40th Ave S 98032 253-945-5100
Christine Baker, prin. Fax 945-5151

Kent SD 415 27,000/PK-12
12033 SE 256th St 98030 253-373-7000
Dr. Calvin Watts, supt. Fax 373-7231
www.kent.k12.wa.us
iGrad Alt
25668 104th Ave SE, 253-373-4723
Carol Cleveland, prin. Fax 373-7989
Kentlake HS 1,800/9-12
21401 SE Falcon Way 98042 253-373-4900
Dr. Joe Potts, prin. Fax 373-4908
Kent-Meridian HS 2,100/9-12
10020 SE 256th St, 253-373-7405
Dr. Wade Barringer, prin. Fax 373-7411
Kent Phoenix Academy 300/9-12
11000 SE 264th St, 253-373-7542
Merrilee Lyle, prin. Fax 373-7554
Kentridge HS 2,200/9-12
12430 SE 208th St 98031 253-373-7345
Mike Albrecht, prin. Fax 373-7363
Meridian MS 600/7-8
23480 120th Ave SE 98031 253-373-7383
Darice Johnson, prin. Fax 373-7395
Mill Creek MS 900/7-8
620 Central Ave N 98032 253-373-7446
Tammy Unruh, prin. Fax 373-7478
Other Schools – See Covington, Des Moines, Renton

**Kettle Falls, Stevens, Pop. 1,505**
Kettle Falls SD 212 700/K-12
PO Box 458 99141 509-738-6625
Thaynan Knowlton, supt. Fax 738-6375
www.kfschools.org
Kettle Falls HS 300/9-12
PO Box 458 99141 509-738-6388
James Hill, prin. Fax 738-2670
Kettle Falls MS 200/5-8
PO Box 458 99141 509-738-6014
Tracy Vining, prin. Fax 738-2401

**Kingston, Kitsap, Pop. 2,022**
North Kitsap SD 400
Supt. — See Poulsbo
Kingston HS 900/9-12
26201 Siyaya Ave NE 98346 360-396-3300
Christy Cole, prin. Fax 396-3941
Kingston MS 700/6-8
9000 NE West Kingston Rd 98346 360-396-3400
Craig Barry, prin. Fax 396-3945

**Kirkland, King, Pop. 46,527**
Lake Washington SD 414
Supt. — See Redmond
Emerson HS 100/9-12
10903 NE 53rd St 98033 425-936-2300
Nell Ballard-Jones, prin. Fax 936-2305
Environmental & Adventure S 100/6-8
8040 NE 132nd St 98034 425-936-2355
Victor Scarpelli, prin. Fax 825-0921
Finn Hill MS 300/6-8
8040 NE 132nd St 98034 425-936-2340
Victor Scarpelli, prin. Fax 814-2955
International Community S 400/7-12
11133 NE 65th St 98033 425-936-2380
Gregory Moncada, prin. Fax 889-6881
Juanita HS 1,000/9-12
10601 NE 132nd St 98034 425-936-1600
Gary Moed, prin. Fax 936-1637
Kamiakin MS 300/6-8
14111 132nd Ave NE 98034 425-936-2400
Joe Joss, prin. Fax 823-2921
Kirkland MS 400/6-8
430 18th Ave 98033 425-936-2420
Deborah McCarson, prin. Fax 889-1589
Lake Washington HS 1,000/9-12
12033 NE 80th St 98033 425-936-1700
Christina Thomas, prin. Fax 936-1751
Northstar MS 100/6-8
11822 NE 75th St 98033 425-936-1760
Nell Ballard-Jones, prin. Fax 828-3364

---

Eastside Preparatory S 200/5-12
10613 NE 38th Pl 98033 425-822-5668
Dr. Terry Macaluso, head sch Fax 822-5648
Lake Washington Institute of Technology Post-Sec.
11605 132nd Ave NE 98034 425-739-8100
Northwest University Post-Sec.
PO Box 579 98083 425-822-8266
Providence Classical Christian S 200/PK-12
11727 NE 118th St 98034 425-774-6622
Puget Sound Adventist Academy 100/9-12
5320 108th Ave NE 98033 425-822-7554

**Kittitas, Kittitas, Pop. 1,352**
Kittitas SD 403 600/K-12
PO Box 599 98934 509-968-3115
Monty Sabin, supt. Fax 968-4730
www.ksd403.org/
Kittitas HS 300/6-12
PO Box 599 98934 509-968-3902
Christopher Brauer, prin. Fax 968-3370

**Klickitat, Klickitat, Pop. 348**
Klickitat SD 402 100/K-12
PO Box 37 98628 509-369-4145
Jerry Lynch, supt. Fax 369-3422
www.klickitat.wednet.edu/
Klickitat S 100/K-12
PO Box 37 98628 509-369-4145
Kevin Davis, prin. Fax 369-3422

**La Center, Clark, Pop. 2,714**
La Center SD 101 1,600/K-12
PO Box 1840 98629 360-263-2131
Dr. Mark Mansell, supt. Fax 263-1140
www.lacenterschools.org/
La Center HS 500/9-12
PO Box 1780 98629 360-263-1700
Carol Patton, prin. Fax 263-1705
La Center MS 400/6-8
PO Box 1750 98629 360-263-2136
Lauri Landerholm, prin. Fax 263-5936

**Lacey, Thurston, Pop. 39,269**
North Thurston SD 3 13,600/PK-12
305 College St NE 98516 360-412-4400
Raj Manhas, supt. Fax 412-4410
www.nthurston.k12.wa.us
Aspire MS 300/6-8
5900 54th Ave SE 98513 360-412-4730
Courtney Crawford, prin. Fax 412-4739
Chinook MS 600/6-8
4301 6th Ave NE 98516 360-412-4760
Kirsten Rae, prin. Fax 412-4769
Komachin MS 800/7-8
3650 College St SE 98503 360-412-4740
Kimberly Mueller, prin. Fax 412-4749
Nisqually MS 600/6-8
8100 Steilacoom Rd SE 98503 360-412-4770
Karen Owen, prin. Fax 493-2756
North Thurston HS 1,400/9-12
600 Sleater Kinney Rd NE 98506 360-412-4800
Steve Rood, prin. Fax 412-4819
River Ridge HS 1,100/9-12
350 River Ridge Dr SE 98513 360-412-4820
Monica Sweet, prin. Fax 412-4839
South Sound HS 200/Alt
411 College St NE 98516 360-412-4880
Angela Grizzle, prin. Fax 412-4889
Timberline HS 1,600/9-12
6120 Mullen Rd SE 98503 360-412-4860
Paul Dean, prin. Fax 412-4879

---

Northwest Christian HS 200/9-12
4710 Park Center Ave NE 98516 360-491-2966
Dr. Terry Ketchum, prin. Fax 491-3086
Pope John Paul II HS 50/9-12
5608 Pacific Ave SE 98503 360-438-7600
Ronald Edwards, prin. Fax 438-7607
St. Martin's University Post-Sec.
5000 Abbey Way SE 98503 360-491-4700

**La Conner, Skagit, Pop. 873**
La Conner SD 311 600/K-12
PO Box 2103 98257 360-466-3171
Dr. Tim Bruce, supt. Fax 466-3523
www.lcsd.wednet.edu
La Conner HS 200/9-12
PO Box 2103 98257 360-466-3173
Cheryl Sullivan, prin. Fax 466-1062
La Conner MS 200/6-8
PO Box 2103 98257 360-466-4113
Cheryl Sullivan, prin. Fax 466-0153

**LaCrosse, Whitman, Pop. 304**
LaCrosse SD 126 100/K-12
111 Hill Ave 99143 509-549-3591
Doug Curtis, supt. Fax 549-3529
www.lacrossesd.k12.wa.us
LaCrosse JSHS 50/6-12
111 Hill Ave 99143 509-549-3592
Jeff Pietila, prin. Fax 549-3529

**Lakebay, Pierce**
Peninsula SD 401
Supt. — See Gig Harbor
Key Penninsula MS 400/6-8
5510 Key Peninsula Hwy N 98349 253-530-4200
Jeri Goebel, prin. Fax 530-4220

**Lake Stevens, Snohomish, Pop. 26,753**
Lake Stevens SD 4 7,900/PK-12
12309 22nd St NE 98258 425-335-1500
Dr. Amy Beth Cook, supt. Fax 335-1549
www.lkstevens.wednet.edu
Cavelero Mid HS 1,200/8-9
8220 24th St SE 98258 425-335-1630
Mike Snow, prin. Fax 397-9413

Lake Stevens HS 1,700/10-12
2908 113th Ave NE 98258 425-335-1515
Eric Cahan, prin. Fax 335-1524

**Lake Tapps, Pierce, Pop. 11,482**
Dieringer SD 343 1,400/K-8
1320 178th Ave E, 253-862-2537
Dr. Judy Neumeier-Martinson, supt. Fax 862-8472
www.dieringer.wednet.edu
North Tapps MS 500/6-8
20029 12th St E, 253-862-2776
Nate Salisbury, prin. Fax 862-2587

**Lakewood, Pierce, Pop. 52,506**
Clover Park SD 400 11,500/PK-12
10903 Gravelly Lake Dr SW 98499 253-583-5000
Debbie LeBeau, supt. Fax 583-5198
www.cloverpark.k12.wa.us
Clover Park HS 1,100/9-12
11023 Gravelly Lake Dr SW 98499 253-583-5500
Tim Stults, prin. Fax 583-5508
Harrison Preparatory S 500/6-12
9103 Lakewood Dr SW 98499 253-583-5418
Lisa Boyd, prin. Fax 583-5417
Hudtloff MS 600/6-8
8102 Phillips Rd SW 98498 253-583-5400
Greg Wilson, prin. Fax 583-5408
Lakes HS 1,400/9-12
10320 Farwest Dr SW 98498 253-583-5550
Karen Mauer-Smith, prin. Fax 583-5558
Lochburn MS 600/6-8
5431 Steilacoom Blvd SW 98499 253-583-5420
Josh Zarling, prin. Fax 583-5428
Mann MS 400/6-8
11509 Holden Rd SW 98498 253-583-5440
Steve Seberson, prin. Fax 583-5448
Woodbrook MS 500/6-8
14920 Spring St SW 98439 253-583-5460
Nancy LaChapelle, prin. Fax 583-5468

---

Clover Park Technical College Post-Sec.
4500 Steilacoom Blvd SW 98499 253-589-5800
Pierce College Post-Sec.
9401 Farwest Dr SW 98498 253-964-6500

**Lamont, Whitman, Pop. 66**
Lamont SD 264 50/5-8
602 Main St 99017 509-257-2463
Joseph Whipple, supt. Fax 257-2316
www.spraguelamont.org
Lamont MS 50/5-8
602 Main St 99017 509-257-2463
Joseph Whipple, admin. Fax 257-2316

**Langley, Island, Pop. 1,005**
South Whidbey SD 206 1,500/K-12
5520 Maxwelton Rd 98260 360-221-6100
Dr. Josephine Moccia, supt. Fax 221-3835
www.sw.wednet.edu
Langley MS 400/6-8
723 Camano Ave 98260 360-221-5100
Suzi Mach, prin. Fax 221-8545
South Whidbey Academy 100/Alt
5476 Maxwelton Rd 98260 360-221-7879
David Pfeiffer, dir.
South Whidbey HS 500/9-12
5675 Maxwelton Rd 98260 360-221-4300
John Paton, prin. Fax 221-5797

**Leavenworth, Chelan, Pop. 1,933**
Cascade SD 228 1,200/PK-12
330 Evans St 98826 509-548-5885
Bill Motsenbocker, supt. Fax 548-6149
www.cascadesd.org
Cascade HS 400/9-12
10190 Chumstick Hwy 98826 509-548-5277
Elia Daley, prin. Fax 548-7458
Icicle River MS 300/6-8
10195 Titus Rd 98826 509-548-4042
Fax 548-6646

**Lind, Adams, Pop. 553**
Lind-Ritzville SD 200/PK-12
PO Box 340 99341 509-677-3481
Robert Roettger, supt. Fax 677-3463
www.lrschools.org
Lind/Ritzville MS 100/6-8
507 N E St 99341 509-677-3408
Cindy Deska, prin. Fax 677-3420
Other Schools – See Ritzville

**Long Beach, Pacific, Pop. 1,362**
Ocean Beach SD 101 1,000/K-12
PO Box 778 98631 360-642-3739
Jenny Risner, supt. Fax 642-1298
www.ocean.k12.wa.us
Other Schools – See Ilwaco

**Longview, Cowlitz, Pop. 35,373**
Longview SD 122 6,800/PK-12
2715 Lilac St 98632 360-575-7000
Dr. Dan Zorn, supt. Fax 575-7022
www.longview.k12.wa.us
Cascade MS 500/6-8
2821 Parkview Dr 98632 360-577-2701
Noma Hudson, prin. Fax 577-2790
Discovery HS Alt
2742 Harding St 98632 360-575-2926
Jill Diehl, admin. Fax 575-7114
Long HS 1,000/9-12
2903 Nichols Blvd 98632 360-575-7110
Rich Reeves, prin. Fax 575-7112
Monticello MS 500/6-8
1225 28th Ave 98632 360-575-7050
Angela Allen, prin. Fax 575-7220
Morris HS 1,200/9-12
1602 Mark Morris Ct 98632 360-575-7770
Philip Suek, prin. Fax 575-7699

Mt. Solo MS 500/6-8
5300 Mt Solo Rd 98632 360-577-2800
Jay Opgrande, prin. Fax 577-2888

---

Lower Columbia College Post-Sec.
PO Box 3010 98632 360-442-2311
Stylemasters College of Hair Design Post-Sec.
1224 Commerce Ave 98632 360-636-2720
Three Rivers Christian S 100/7-12
2441 42nd Ave 98632 360-636-1600
Scott Grove, admin. Fax 577-5955

**Lopez Island, San Juan**
Lopez Island SD 144 200/K-12
86 School Rd 98261 360-468-2202
Brian Auckland, supt. Fax 468-2212
www.lopezislandschool.org
Lopez Island MSHS 100/6-12
86 School Rd 98261 360-468-2202
Dave Sather, prin. Fax 468-2212

**Lyle, Klickitat, Pop. 484**
Lyle SD 406 300/K-12
PO Box 368 98635 509-365-2191
Andrew Kelly, supt. Fax 365-5000
www.lyleschools.org
Lyle HS 100/9-12
PO Box 522 98635 509-365-2211
Andrew Kelly, prin. Fax 365-2665
Lyle MS 50/6-8
PO Box 522 98635 509-365-2211
Andrew Kelly, prin. Fax 365-2665

**Lynden, Whatcom, Pop. 11,746**
Lynden SD 504 2,700/K-12
1203 Bradley Rd 98264 360-354-4443
Jim Frey, supt. Fax 354-7662
www.lynden.wednet.edu
Lynden HS 900/9-12
1201 Bradley Rd 98264 360-354-4401
Todd Apple, prin. Fax 354-0991
Lynden MS 600/6-8
516 Main St 98264 360-354-2952
Molly Mitchell-Mumma, prin. Fax 354-6631

Meridian SD 505
Supt. — See Bellingham
Meridian MS 300/6-8
861 Ten Mile Rd 98264 360-398-2291
Gerald Sanderson, prin. Fax 398-8131

---

Cornerstone Christian S 100/1-12
8872 Northwood Rd 98264 360-318-0663
Lynden Christian HS 300/9-12
515 Drayton St 98264 360-354-3221
Dr. Kevin Kaemingk, prin. Fax 354-1047
Lynden Christian MS 300/5-8
503 Lyncs Dr 98264 360-354-3358
Aaron Bishop, prin. Fax 354-6690

**Lynnwood, Snohomish, Pop. 34,119**
Edmonds SD 15 19,100/PK-12
20420 68th Ave W 98036 425-431-7000
Nick Brossoit Ed.D., supt. Fax 431-7006
www.edmonds.wednet.edu
Alderwood MS 700/7-8
20000 28th Ave W 98036 425-431-7579
Erin Murphy, prin. Fax 431-7580
College Place MS 600/7-8
7501 208th St SW 98036 425-431-7451
Sam Yuhan, prin. Fax 431-7449
Meadowdale HS 1,500/9-12
6002 168th St SW 98037 425-431-7650
Kevin Allen, prin. Fax 431-7655
Meadowdale MS 700/7-8
6500 168th St SW 98037 425-431-7707
Jennifer Knisely, prin. Fax 431-7714
Other Schools – See Bothell, Brier, Edmonds, Mountlake Terrace

---

Edmonds Community College Post-Sec.
20000 68th Ave W 98036 425-640-1459

**Mabton, Yakima, Pop. 2,272**
Mabton SD 120 800/K-12
PO Box 37 98935 509-894-4852
Minerva Morales, supt. Fax 894-4769
www.msd120.org
Mabton JSHS 300/7-12
PO Box 38 98935 509-894-4951
Caleb Oten, prin. Fax 894-4761

**Mansfield, Douglas, Pop. 319**
Mansfield SD 207 100/PK-12
PO Box 188 98830 509-683-1012
Cora Nordby, supt. Fax 683-1281
www.mansfield.wednet.edu/
Mansfield S 100/PK-12
PO Box 188 98830 509-683-1012
Cora Nordby, prin. Fax 683-1281

**Manson, Chelan, Pop. 1,456**
Manson SD 19 700/PK-12
PO Box A 98831 509-687-3140
Matt Charlton, supt. Fax 687-9877
www.manson.org
Manson HS 300/9-12
PO Box A 98831 509-687-9585
Don Vanderholm, prin. Fax 687-6109
Manson MS 100/6-8
PO Box A 98831 509-687-9585
Todd Smith, prin. Fax 687-6109

**Maple Valley, King, Pop. 21,591**
Tahoma SD 409 7,500/PK-12
25720 Maple Valley Black Di 98038 425-413-3400
Rob Morrow, supt. Fax 413-3455
www.tahomasd.us

Other Schools – See Covington, Ravensdale

**Marysville, Snohomish, Pop. 56,950**
Lakewood SD 306 2,400/PK-12
17110 16th Dr NE 98271 360-652-4500
Dr. Michael Mack, supt. Fax 652-4502
www.lwsd.wednet.edu
Lakewood HS 800/9-12
17023 11th Ave NE 98271 360-652-4505
Mike Curl, prin. Fax 652-4507
Lakewood MS 600/6-8
16800 16th Dr NE 98271 360-652-4510
Bryan Toutant, prin. Fax 652-4512

Marysville SD 25 9,100/PK-12
4220 80th St NE 98270 360-653-7058
Dr. Becky Berg, supt. Fax 629-1993
www.msvl.k12.wa.us
Academy of Construction & Engineering 300/9-12
8301 84th St NE 98270 360-657-6374
Shawn Stevenson, prin. Fax 657-6288
Arts & Technology HS 400/9-12
7204 27th Ave NE 98271 360-653-0664
Terri Kaltenbach, prin. Fax 629-1940
Bio Med Academy 400/9-12
8301 84th St NE 98270 360-629-1891
Angela Delgado, prin. Fax 629-1887
Cedarcrest MS 800/6-8
6400 88th St NE 98270 360-653-0850
Dr. Sheila Gerrish, prin. Fax 657-6470
Heritage HS 100/9-12
7204 27th Ave NE 98271 360-653-0690
Shelly Lacy, prin. Fax 629-1960
International S of Communication 400/9-12
8301 84th St NE 98270 360-653-0695
Susan Hegeberg, prin. Fax 653-0655
Marysville MS 900/6-8
4923 67th St NE 98270 360-653-0615
Angela Hansen, prin. Fax 657-6396
Marysville Mountain View HS 200/9-12
4317 76th St NE 98270 360-653-0628
Dawn Bechtholdt, prin. Fax 629-1989
Marysville-Pilchuck HS 1,200/9-12
5611 108th St NE 98271 360-653-0600
Andrew Frost, prin. Fax 657-6184
School for the Entrepreneur 400/9-12
8301 84th St NE 98270 360-651-5702
David Rose, prin. Fax 651-5773
Tenth Street MS 200/6-8
7204 27th Ave NE 98271 360-653-0665
Terri Kaltenbach, prin. Fax 629-1950
Totem MS 700/6-8
1605 7th St 98270 360-653-0610
Tarra Patrick, prin. Fax 657-6297

---

Grace Academy 300/PK-12
8521 67th Ave NE 98270 360-659-8517
Timothy Lugg, prin. Fax 653-5899

**Mattawa, Grant, Pop. 4,417**
Wahluke SD 73 1,800/K-12
PO Box 907 99349 509-932-4565
Aaron Chavez, supt. Fax 932-4571
www.wsd73.wednet.edu
Sentinel Technical Alternative HS 50/Alt
PO Box 907 99349 509-932-3133
Mia Benjamin, prin. Fax 932-3320
Wahluke HS 500/9-12
PO Box 907 99349 509-932-4477
Mia Benjamin, prin. Fax 932-4241
Wahluke JHS 500/6-8
PO Box 907 99349 509-932-4455
Andrew Harlow, prin. Fax 932-4282

**Mead, Spokane, Pop. 7,091**
Mead SD 354 9,100/K-12
2323 E Farwell Rd 99021 509-465-6000
Thomas Rockefeller, supt. Fax 465-6020
www.mead354.org
Mount Spokane HS 1,500/9-12
6015 E Mt Spokane Park Dr 99021 509-465-7200
Darren Nelson, prin. Fax 465-7220
Other Schools – See Colbert, Spokane

**Medical Lake, Spokane, Pop. 4,877**
Medical Lake SD 326 1,900/PK-12
PO Box 128 99022 509-565-3100
Timothy Ames, supt. Fax 565-3102
www.mlsd.org/
Medical Lake Alternative HS 50/Alt
PO Box 128 99022 509-565-3141
Tricia Hensel-Smith, prin. Fax 565-3149
Medical Lake HS 500/9-12
PO Box 128 99022 509-565-3200
John McSmith, prin. Fax 565-3201
Medical Lake MS 400/6-8
PO Box 128 99022 509-565-3300
Sylvia Campbell, prin. Fax 565-3301

---

Lakeland Village School Post-Sec.
PO Box 200 99022

**Mercer Island, King, Pop. 21,809**
Mercer Island SD 400 4,300/K-12
4160 86th Ave SE 98040 206-236-3300
Dr. Gary Plano, supt. Fax 236-3333
www.mercerislandschools.org
Crest Learning Center 100/Alt
4150 86th Ave SE 98040 206-236-3390
Vicki Puckett, admin. Fax 236-3394
Islander MS 1,000/6-8
8225 SE 72nd St 98040 206-236-3400
MaryJo Budzius, prin. Fax 236-3408
Mercer Island HS 1,500/9-12
9100 SE 42nd St 98040 206-236-3350
Vicki Puckett, prin. Fax 236-3358

Northwest Yeshiva HS 100/9-12
5017 90th Ave SE 98040 206-232-5272
Privett Academy 100/6-12
PO Box 42 98040 206-232-0059

**Metaline Falls, Pend Oreille, Pop. 233**
Selkirk SD 70 200/PK-12
PO Box 129 99153 509-446-2951
Nancy Lotze, supt. Fax 446-2929
www.selkirk.k12.wa.us
Other Schools – See Ione

**Mill Creek, Snohomish, Pop. 17,443**
Everett SD 2
Supt. — See Everett
Heatherwood MS 900/6-8
1419 Trillium Blvd SE 98012 425-385-6300
Laura Phillips, prin. Fax 385-6302
Jackson HS 1,900/9-12
1508 136th St SE 98012 425-385-7000
Dave Peters, prin. Fax 385-7002

**Monroe, Snohomish, Pop. 16,699**
Monroe SD 103 7,200/K-12
200 E Fremont St 98272 360-804-2500
Dr. Fredrika Smith, supt. Fax 804-2529
www.monroe.wednet.edu
Leaders in Learning HS 100/Alt
639 W Main St 98272 360-804-2800
Blake Baird, coord. Fax 804-2819
Monroe HS 1,700/9-12
17001 Tester Rd 98272 360-804-4500
John Lombardi, prin. Fax 804-4699
Park Place MS 800/6-8
1408 W Main St 98272 360-804-4300
Terry Cheshire, prin. Fax 804-4399
Sky Valley Education Center 800/Alt
351 Short Columbia St 98272 360-804-2700
Karen Rosencrans, dir. Fax 804-2759
Other Schools – See Snohomish

**Montesano, Grays Harbor, Pop. 3,841**
Montesano SD 66 1,200/PK-12
302 N Church St 98563 360-249-3942
Dan Winter, supt. Fax 841-7198
www.monteschools.org
Montesano JSHS 600/7-12
303 N Church St 98563 360-249-4041
Alec Pugh, prin. Fax 841-7527

**Morton, Lewis, Pop. 1,107**
Morton SD 300/PK-12
PO Box 1219 98356 360-496-5300
John Hannah, supt. Fax 586-3208
www.morton.wednet.edu
Morton JSHS 100/7-12
PO Box 1169 98356 360-496-5137
John Hannah, prin. Fax 496-6035

**Moses Lake, Grant, Pop. 19,890**
Moses Lake SD 161 7,600/PK-12
920 W Ivy Ave 98837 509-766-2650
Dr. Michelle Price, supt. Fax 766-2678
www.moseslakeschools.org
Chief Moses MS 1,000/6-8
1111 E Nelson Rd 98837 509-766-2661
Kristi Hofheins, prin. Fax 766-2680
Endeavor MS 300/6-8
6527 Patton Blvd NE 98837 509-766-2667
Ryan Pike, admin. Fax 766-2690
Frontier MS 700/6-8
517 W 3rd Ave 98837 509-766-2662
Frank Atkinson, prin. Fax 766-2663
Moses Lake HS 2,100/9-12
803 Sharon Ave E 98837 509-766-2666
Mark Harris, prin. Fax 766-2682

Big Bend Community College Post-Sec.
7662 Chanute St NE 98837 509-793-2222
Moses Lake Christian Academy 200/PK-12
1475 Nelson Rd NE Ste A 98837 509-765-9704
Stephanie Voigt, dir. Fax 765-3698

**Mossyrock, Lewis, Pop. 745**
Mossyrock SD 206 600/K-12
PO Box 478 98564 360-983-3181
Dr. Karen Ernest, supt. Fax 983-8111
www.mossyrockschools.org
Mossyrock JSHS 200/7-12
PO Box 478 98564 360-983-3183
Lori Cournyer, prin. Fax 983-3188

**Mountlake Terrace, Snohomish, Pop. 18,701**
Edmonds SD 15
Supt. — See Lynnwood
Mountlake Terrace HS 1,300/9-12
21801 44th Ave W 98043 425-431-7776
Greg Schwab, prin. Fax 431-7771

Cedar Park Christian JSHS - Mountlake 100/7-12
23607 54th Ave W 98043 425-774-7773
Al Carpenter, admin. Fax 774-3218

**Mount Vernon, Skagit, Pop. 30,973**
Anacortes SD 103
Supt. — See Anacortes
Northwest Career & Technical Academy Vo/Tech
2205 W Campus Pl 98273 360-848-0706
Dr. Linda Miller, prin. Fax 848-7586

Mount Vernon SD 320 5,600/K-12
124 E Lawrence St 98273 360-428-6110
Carl Bruner, supt. Fax 428-6172
www.mountvernonschools.org/
LaVenture MS 400/6-8
1200 N Laventure Rd 98273 360-428-6116
Dave Riddle, prin. Fax 428-6189
Mount Baker MS 500/6-8
2310 E Section St 98274 360-428-6127
Tim Newall, prin. Fax 428-6155
Mount Vernon HS 1,900/9-12
314 N 9th St 98273 360-428-6100
Rod Merrell, prin. Fax 428-6152

Mt. Vernon Christian S 300/PK-12
820 W Blackburn Rd 98273 360-424-9157
Jeffrey Droog, supt. Fax 424-9256
Northwest Hair Academy Post-Sec.
615 S 1st St 98273 360-336-6553
Skagit Valley College Post-Sec.
2405 E College Way 98273 360-416-7600

**Mukilteo, Snohomish, Pop. 19,401**
Mukilteo SD 6
Supt. — See Everett
Harbour Pointe MS 800/6-8
5000 Harbour Pointe Blvd 98275 425-366-5100
Kevin Rohrich, prin. Fax 366-5102
Kamiak HS 2,100/9-12
10801 Harbour Pointe Blvd 98275 425-366-5400
Mike Gallagher, prin. Fax 366-5402
Olympic View MS 800/6-8
2602 Mukilteo Speedway 98275 425-366-5200
Devin McLane, prin. Fax 366-5202

**Naches, Yakima, Pop. 787**
Naches Valley SD JT3 1,400/K-12
PO Box 99 98937 509-653-2220
Duane Lyons, supt. Fax 653-1211
www.nvsd.org
Naches Valley HS 500/9-12
PO Box 159 98937 509-653-1732
Rich Rouleau, prin. Fax 653-2921
Naches Valley MS 500/5-8
PO Box 39 98937 509-653-1599
Todd Hilmes, prin. Fax 653-2729

**Napavine, Lewis, Pop. 1,693**
Napavine SD 14 800/PK-12
PO Box 840 98565 360-262-3303
Dr. Richard Jones, supt. Fax 262-9737
www.napa.k12.wa.us
Napavine JSHS 300/7-12
PO Box 357 98565 360-262-3301
Jason Prather, prin. Fax 262-9541

**Naselle, Pacific, Pop. 396**
Naselle-Grays River Valley SD 155 200/K-12
793 State Route 4 98638 360-484-7121
Dr. Lisa Nelson, supt. Fax 484-3191
www.naselle.wednet.edu
Naselle-Grays River Valley S 100/K-12
793 State Route 4 98638 360-484-7121
Karen Wirkkala, prin. Fax 484-3191
Naselle Youth Camp HS 100/Alt
11S Youth Camp Ln 98638 360-484-3269
Alan Bennett, prin. Fax 484-7109

**Neah Bay, Clallam, Pop. 795**
Cape Flattery SD 401
Supt. — See Sekiu
Neah Bay JSHS 7-12
PO Box 86 98357 360-645-2221
Matthew Vandeleur, prin. Fax 645-2574

**Newport, Pend Oreille, Pop. 2,055**
Newport SD 56-415 1,000/PK-12
PO Box 70 99156 509-447-3167
Dave Smith, supt. Fax 447-2553
www.newport.wednet.edu
Halstead MS 300/5-8
PO Box 70 99156 509-447-2426
Janet Burcham, prin. Fax 447-4914
Newport HS 400/9-12
PO Box 70 99156 509-447-2481
Troy Whittle, prin. Fax 447-4354

**Nine Mile Falls, Spokane**
Nine Mile Falls SD 325 1,600/PK-12
10110 W Charles Rd 99026 509-340-4300
Brian Talbott, supt. Fax 340-4301
www.9mile.org
Lakeside HS 600/9-12
5909 Highway 291 99026 509-340-4200
Brent Osborn, prin. Fax 340-4201
Lakeside MS 400/6-8
6169 Highway 291 99026 509-340-4100
Jeff Baerwald, prin. Fax 340-4101

**Nooksack, Whatcom, Pop. 1,290**
Nooksack Valley SD 506
Supt. — See Everson
Nooksack Valley MS 400/6-8
404 W Columbia St 98276 360-966-7561
Joel VanderYacht, prin. Fax 966-7805

**North Bend, King, Pop. 5,558**
Snoqualmie Valley SD 410
Supt. — See Snoqualmie
Twin Falls MS 600/6-8
46910 SE Middle Fork Rd 98045 425-831-4150
Fax 831-4140
Two Rivers S 100/Alt
330 Ballarat Ave N 98045 425-831-4200
Amy Montanye-Johnson, prin. Fax 831-4210

**Northport, Stevens, Pop. 287**
Northport SD 211 200/K-12
PO Box 1280 99157 509-732-4251
Wes Harris, supt. Fax 732-6606
www.northportschools.org
Northport HS 100/9-12
PO Box 1280 99157 509-732-4430
Don Baribault, prin. Fax 732-6606

**Oakesdale, Whitman, Pop. 413**
Oakesdale SD 324 100/PK-12
PO Box 228 99158 509-285-5296
Dr. Jake Dingman, supt. Fax 285-5121
www.gonighthawks.net
Oakesdale HS 50/7-12
PO Box 228 99158 509-285-5296
Dr. Jake Dingman, supt. Fax 285-5121

**Oak Harbor, Island, Pop. 20,413**
Oak Harbor SD 201 5,400/PK-12
350 S Oak Harbor St 98277 360-279-5000
Dr. Lance Gibbon, supt. Fax 279-5070
www.ohsd.net
Midway HS Alt
350 S Oak Harbor St 98277 360-279-5575
Jerrod Fleury, prin. Fax 279-5565
North Whidbey MS 600/6-8
67 NE Izett St 98277 360-279-5500
William Weinsheimer, prin. Fax 279-5516
Oak Harbor HS 1,700/9-12
1 Wildcat Way 98277 360-279-5800
Dwight Lundstrom, prin. Fax 279-5794
Oak Harbor MS 600/6-8
150 SW 6th Ave 98277 360-279-5300
Shane Evans, prin. Fax 279-5399

North Whidbey Christian HS 6-12
675 E Whidbey Ave 98277 360-675-5352
Rev. Doug Fakkema, admin.

**Oakville, Grays Harbor, Pop. 661**
Oakville SD 400 300/K-12
PO Box H 98568 360-273-0171
Kathy Lorton, supt. Fax 273-6724
oakvilleschools.org/
Oakville JSHS 100/7-12
PO Box H 98568 360-273-5947
Michael Auton, prin. Fax 273-8229

**Ocean Shores, Grays Harbor, Pop. 5,358**
North Beach SD 64 600/PK-12
PO Box 159 98569 360-289-2447
Stanley Pinnick, supt. Fax 289-2492
www.northbeachschools.org
North Beach HS 200/9-12
PO Box 969 98569 360-289-3888
Brett Mackey, prin. Fax 289-0996
North Beach JHS 100/7-8
PO Box 969 98569 360-289-3888
Brett Mackey, prin. Fax 289-0996

**Odessa, Lincoln, Pop. 895**
Odessa SD 105-157-166 J 200/PK-12
PO Box 248 99159 509-982-2668
Dan Read, supt. Fax 982-0163
www.odessa.wednet.edu
Odessa JSHS 100/7-12
PO Box 248 99159 509-982-2111
Jamie Nelson, prin. Fax 982-0163

**Okanogan, Okanogan, Pop. 2,464**
Okanogan SD 105 1,000/K-12
PO Box 592 98840 509-422-3629
Dr. Richard Johnson, supt. Fax 422-1525
www.oksd.wednet.edu
Okanogan HS 300/9-12
PO Box 592 98840 509-422-3770
Bob Shacklett, prin. Fax 422-3656
Okanogan MS 300/6-8
PO Box 592 98840 509-422-2680
Brett Baum, prin. Fax 422-0068

**Olympia, Thurston, Pop. 44,308**
Olympia SD 111 9,200/PK-12
1113 Legion Way SE 98501 360-596-6100
Dick Cvitanich, supt. Fax 596-6111
osd.wednet.edu
Avanti HS 200/9-12
1113 Legion Way SE 98501 360-596-7900
Michael Velasquez, prin. Fax 596-7901
Capital HS 1,300/9-12
2707 Conger Ave NW 98502 360-596-8000
Jennifer Hewitt, prin. Fax 596-8001
Jefferson MS 300/6-8
2200 Conger Ave NW 98502 360-596-3200
Michael Cimino, prin. Fax 596-3201
Marshall MS 400/6-8
3939 20th Ave NW 98502 360-596-7600
Condee Wood, prin. Fax 596-7601
Olympia HS 1,800/9-12
1302 North St SE 98501 360-596-7000
Matt Grant, prin. Fax 596-7001
Reeves MS 400/6-8
2200 Quince St NE 98506 360-596-3400
Geoff Parks, prin. Fax 596-3401
Washington MS 800/6-8
3100 Cain Rd SE 98501 360-596-3000
Paul Anders, prin. Fax 596-3001

Tumwater SD 33
Supt. — See Tumwater
Secondary Options HS 100/Alt
7741 Littlerock Rd SW 98512 360-709-7760
Jeanette Holocher, lead tchr. Fax 709-7762
West Black Hills HS 800/9-12
7741 Littlerock Rd SW 98512 360-709-7800
Dave Myers, prin. Fax 709-7802

Evergreen State College Post-Sec.
2700 Evergreen Pkwy NW 98505 360-867-6000
Gospel Outreach Christian S 50/1-12
1925 S Bay Rd NE 98506 360-786-0070
David Hill, prin. Fax 357-1417
NOVA S 100/6-8
2020 22nd Ave SE 98501 360-491-7097
Barbara Hutton, head sch Fax 491-0775

South Puget Sound Community College — Post-Sec.
2011 Mottman Rd SW 98512 — 360-754-7711

**Omak, Okanogan, Pop. 4,701**
Omak SD 19 — 1,500/PK-12
PO Box 833 98841 — 509-826-0320
Dr. Erik Swanson, supt. — Fax 826-7689
www.omaksd.org
Highlands HS of Omak — 50/Alt
PO Box 833 98841 — 509-826-8504
Wayne Barrett, prin. — Fax 826-8532
Omak HS — 400/9-12
PO Box 833 98841 — 509-826-5150
David Kirk, prin. — Fax 826-8515
Omak MS — 400/6-8
PO Box 833 98841 — 509-826-2320
Kathy Miller, prin. — Fax 826-7696

---

Wenatchee Valley College — Post-Sec.
116 W Apple Ave 98841 — 509-422-7800

**Onalaska, Lewis, Pop. 606**
Onalaska SD 300 — 900/PK-12
540 Carlisle Ave 98570 — 360-978-4111
Jeff Davis, supt. — Fax 978-4185
www.onysd.wednet.edu
Onalaska HS — 300/9-12
540 Carlisle Ave 98570 — 360-978-4111
Richard Rasanen, prin. — Fax 978-4185

**Oroville, Okanogan, Pop. 1,653**
Oroville SD 410 — 700/PK-12
816 Juniper St 98844 — 509-476-2281
Steve Quick, supt. — Fax 476-2190
www.oroville.wednet.edu/
Oroville JSHS — 300/7-12
816 Juniper St 98844 — 509-476-3612
Kristin Sarmiento, prin. — Fax 476-3224

**Orting, Pierce, Pop. 6,443**
Orting SD 344 — 2,300/K-12
121 Whitesell St NE 98360 — 360-893-6500
Dr. Marci Shepard, supt. — Fax 893-2300
www.orting.wednet.edu
Orting HS — 800/9-12
320 Washington Ave N 98360 — 360-893-2246
Diane Fox, prin. — Fax 893-5701
Orting MS — 500/6-8
111 Whitehawk Blvd NW 98360 — 360-893-3565
Aaron Lee, prin. — Fax 893-2919

**Othello, Adams, Pop. 7,325**
Othello SD 147-163-55 — 3,800/K-12
1025 S 1st Ave 99344 — 509-488-2659
George Juarez, supt. — Fax 488-5876
www.othelloschools.org
Desert Oasis HS — Alt
825 E Ash St 99344 — 509-488-4534
Russell Kovalenko, prin. — Fax 488-5876
McFarland MS — 800/6-8
790 S 10th Ave 99344 — 509-488-3326
Dennis Adams, prin. — Fax 488-6788
Othello HS — 1,000/9-12
340 S 7th Ave 99344 — 509-488-3351
Carlos Gonzalez, prin. — Fax 488-6779

**Palouse, Whitman, Pop. 974**
Palouse SD 301 — 100/PK-12
600 E Alder St 99161 — 509-878-1921
Calvin Johnson, supt. — Fax 878-1948
www.garpal.net
Garfield-Palouse HS — 100/9-12
600 E Alder St 99161 — 509-878-1921
Tim Coles, prin. — Fax 878-1675

**Pasco, Franklin, Pop. 58,798**
Pasco SD 1 — 15,600/K-12
1215 W Lewis St 99301 — 509-543-6700
Saundra Hill, supt. — Fax 546-6728
www.psd1.org
Chiawana HS — 2,100/9-12
8125 W Argent Rd 99301 — 509-543-6786
John Wallwork, prin. — Fax 543-6730
Delta HS — 9-12
5801 Broadmoor Blvd 99301 — 509-416-7860
Jenny Rodriguez, prin.
McLoughlin MS — 1,600/7-8
2803 N Road 88 99301 — 509-547-4542
Dominique Dennis, prin. — Fax 543-6797
New Horizons HS — 200/Alt
3110 W Argent Rd 99301 — 509-543-6796
Seth Johnson, prin. — Fax 546-2864
Ochoa MS — 1,000/7-8
1801 E Sheppard St 99301 — 509-543-6742
Jackie Ramirez, prin. — Fax 543-6744
Pasco HS — 1,900/9-12
1108 N 10th Ave 99301 — 509-547-5581
Raul Sital, prin. — Fax 546-2684
Stevens MS — 1,000/7-8
1120 N 22nd Ave 99301 — 509-543-6798
Charlotte Stingley, prin. — Fax 546-2854

---

Charter College Pasco — Post-Sec.
5278 Outlet Dr 99301 — 509-546-3900
Columbia Basin College — Post-Sec.
2600 N 20th Ave 99301 — 509-547-0511
Kingspoint Christian S — 200/PK-12
7900 W Court St 99301 — 509-547-6498
DeAnna Henning, admin. — Fax 547-6788
Tri Cities Preparatory S — 200/9-12
9612 Saint Thomas Dr 99301 — 509-546-2465
Arlene Jones, prin. — Fax 546-2490
Tri-City Adventist S — 200/PK-10
4115 W Henry St 99301 — 509-547-8092
Erma Lee, prin. — Fax 547-8516

**Pateros, Okanogan, Pop. 658**
Pateros SD 122 — 100/K-12
PO Box 98 98846 — 509-923-2751
Lois Davies, supt. — Fax 923-2283
www.pateros.org
Pateros S — 100/K-12
PO Box 98 98846 — 509-923-2343
Michael Hull, prin. — Fax 923-1931

**Pe Ell, Lewis, Pop. 610**
Pe Ell SD 301 — 300/PK-12
PO Box 368 98572 — 360-291-3244
Kyle MacDonald, supt. — Fax 291-3823
www.peell.k12.wa.us/
Pe Ell S — 300/PK-12
PO Box 368 98572 — 360-291-3244
Kyle MacDonald, supt. — Fax 291-3823

**Pomeroy, Garfield, Pop. 1,407**
Pomeroy SD 110 — 300/K-12
PO Box 950 99347 — 509-843-3393
Doug LaMunyan, supt. — Fax 843-3046
www.psd.wednet.edu
Pomeroy JSHS — 200/7-12
PO Box 950 99347 — 509-843-1331
Doug LaMunyan, admin. — Fax 843-8245

**Port Angeles, Clallam, Pop. 18,283**
Port Angeles SD 121 — 3,800/PK-12
216 E 4th St 98362 — 360-457-8575
Dr. Marc Jackson, supt. — Fax 457-4649
www.portangelesschools.org/
Lincoln HS — 100/Alt
924 W 9th St 98363 — 360-452-9502
Cindy Crumb, prin. — Fax 417-1993
North Olympic Peninsula Skill Center — Vo/Tech
905 W 9th St 98363 — 360-565-1533
Fax 417-9068
Port Angeles HS — 1,200/9-12
304 E Park Ave 98362 — 360-452-7602
Jeff Clark, prin. — Fax 452-0256
Stevens MS — 600/7-8
1139 W 14th St 98363 — 360-452-5590
Charles Lisk, prin. — Fax 457-5709

---

Peninsula College — Post-Sec.
1502 E Lauridsen Blvd 98362 — 360-452-9277

**Port Hadlock, Jefferson, Pop. 2,742**

---

Northwest School of Wooden Boatbuilding — Post-Sec.
42 N Water St 98339 — 360-385-4948

**Port Orchard, Kitsap, Pop. 10,384**
South Kitsap SD 402 — 9,700/K-12
2689 Hoover Ave SE 98366 — 360-874-7000
Michelle Reid, supt. — Fax 874-7068
www.skitsap.wednet.edu
Cedar Heights JHS — 700/7-9
2220 Pottery Ave 98366 — 360-874-6020
Andrew Cain, prin. — Fax 874-6420
Explorer Academy — 200/Alt
425 Mitchell Ave 98366 — 360-443-3605
Pat Oster, prin. — Fax 443-3624
Sedgewick JHS — 800/7-9
8995 SE Sedgwick Rd 98366 — 360-874-6090
Daniel Novick, prin. — Fax 874-6430
South Kitsap Discovery/Alternative HS — 200/Alt
2150 Fircrest Dr SE 98366 — 360-443-3680
Pat Oster, prin. — Fax 443-3704
South Kitsap SHS — 2,200/10-12
425 Mitchell Ave 98366 — 360-874-5600
Jerry Holsten, prin. — Fax 874-5892
Whitman JHS — 700/7-9
1887 Madrona Dr SE 98366 — 360-874-6160
Brian Carlson, prin. — Fax 874-6440

---

Burley Christian S — 100/PK-12
14687 Olympic Dr SE 98367 — 253-851-8619
Dennis Myers, admin.

**Port Townsend, Jefferson, Pop. 8,812**
Port Townsend SD 50 — 1,200/PK-12
1610 Blaine St 98368 — 360-379-4501
Dr. David Engle, supt. — Fax 385-3617
www.ptschools.org
Blue Heron MS — 400/4-8
3939 San Juan Ave 98368 — 360-379-4540
Diane Lashinsky, prin. — Fax 379-4548
Port Townsend HS — 500/9-12
1500 Van Ness St 98368 — 360-379-4520
Carrie Ehrhardt, prin. — Fax 379-4505

---

Jefferson Community S — 50/7-12
280 Quincy St Ste I 98368 — 360-385-0622

**Poulsbo, Kitsap, Pop. 8,738**
North Kitsap SD 400 — 6,100/PK-12
18360 Caldart Ave NE 98370 — 360-396-3000
Dr. Patrice Page, supt.
www.nkschools.org
North Kitsap HS — 1,300/9-12
1780 NE Hostmark St 98370 — 360-396-3100
Judson Miller, prin. — Fax 396-3927
Poulsbo MS — 700/6-8
2003 NE Hostmark St 98370 — 360-396-3200
Diane Otterby, prin. — Fax 396-3904
Other Schools – See Kingston

---

Northwest College of Art and Design — Post-Sec.
16301 Creative Dr NE 98370 — 360-779-9993
West Sound Academy — 100/6-12
PO Box 807 98370 — 360-598-5954

**Prescott, Walla Walla, Pop. 314**
Prescott SD 402-37 — 200/K-12
PO Box 65 99348 — 509-849-2215
Brett Cox, supt. — Fax 849-2800
www.prescott.k12.wa.us/
Prescott JSHS — 100/7-12
PO Box 65 99348 — 509-849-2215
Dr. Jodi Thew, prin. — Fax 849-2800

**Prosser, Benton, Pop. 5,618**
Prosser SD 116 — 2,800/K-12
1126 Meade Ave Ste A 99350 — 509-786-3323
Dr. Ray Tolcacher, supt. — Fax 786-2062
www.prosserschools.org/
Housel MS — 700/6-8
2001 Highland Dr 99350 — 509-786-1732
Michael Denny, prin. — Fax 786-2814
Prosser Falls HS — 50/Alt
1500 Grant Ave 99350 — 509-786-2527
Syndi Duehn, prin. — Fax 786-3427
Prosser HS — 800/9-12
1203 Prosser Ave 99350 — 509-786-1224
Kevin Lusk, prin. — Fax 786-4227

**Pullman, Whitman, Pop. 28,533**
Pullman SD 267 — 2,500/PK-12
240 SE Dexter St 99163 — 509-332-3581
Dr. Paul Sturm, supt. — Fax 336-7202
www.psd267.org
Lincoln MS — 500/6-8
315 SE Crestview St 99163 — 509-334-3411
Cameron Grow, prin. — Fax 336-7203
Pullman HS — 700/9-12
510 NW Greyhound Way 99163 — 509-332-1551
Joseph Thornton, prin. — Fax 332-6868

---

Pullman Christian S — 100/K-12
345 SW Kimball Dr 99163 — 509-332-3545
Sherri Goetze, prin.
Washington State University — Post-Sec.
PO Box 641067 99164 — 509-335-3564

**Puyallup, Pierce, Pop. 35,083**
Bethel SD 403
Supt. — See Spanaway
Pierce County Skills Center — Vo/Tech
16117 Canyon Rd E 98375 — 253-683-5950
Michelle Ledbetter, dir. — Fax 683-6079

Puyallup SD 3 — 20,500/K-12
PO Box 370 98371 — 253-841-1301
Dr. Timothy Yeomans, supt. — Fax 840-8959
www.puyallup.k12.wa.us
Aylen JHS — 700/7-9
101 15th St SW 98371 — 253-841-8723
Kevin Mensonides, prin. — Fax 840-8856
Ballou JHS — 700/7-9
9916 136th St E 98373 — 253-841-8725
Krista Bates, prin. — Fax 840-8819
Emerald Ridge SHS — 1,500/10-12
12405 184th St E 98374 — 253-435-6300
Kevin Hampton, prin. — Fax 435-6310
Ferrucci JHS — 800/7-9
3213 Wildwood Park Dr 98374 — 253-841-8756
Steve Leifsen, prin. — Fax 840-8855
Glacier View JHS — 800/7-9
12807 184th St E 98374 — 253-840-8922
Jack Widmann, prin. — Fax 435-6570
Kalles JHS — 700/7-9
501 7th Ave SE 98372 — 253-841-8729
Guy Kovacs, prin. — Fax 840-8984
Puyallup SHS — 1,600/10-12
105 7th St SW 98371 — 253-841-8711
David Sunich, prin. — Fax 841-8624
Rogers SHS — 1,700/10-12
12801 86th Ave E 98373 — 253-841-8717
Jason Smith, prin. — Fax 840-8802
Stahl JHS — 800/7-9
9610 168th Street Ct E 98375 — 253-840-8881
Troy Hodge, prin. — Fax 840-8992
Walker HS — 100/Alt
5715 Milwaukee Ave E 98372 — 253-841-8781
Alicia Nosworthy, prin. — Fax 840-8981
Other Schools – See Edgewood

---

BJ's Beauty & Barber College — Post-Sec.
12020 Meridian E Ste G 98373 — 253-848-1595
Cascade Christian JSHS — 500/7-12
811 21st St SE 98372 — 253-445-9706
Dr. Ken Friesen, prin. — Fax 445-0859
Pierce College — Post-Sec.
1601 39th Ave SE 98374 — 253-840-8470

**Quilcene, Jefferson, Pop. 571**
Quilcene SD 48 — 700/K-12
PO Box 40 98376 — 360-765-3363
Wally Lis, supt. — Fax 765-3015
www.quilcene.wednet.edu
Crossroads Community S — 50/Alt
PO Box 40 98376 — 360-765-3363
Jenelle Cleland, dir. — Fax 765-4183
Quilcene S — 200/K-12
PO Box 40 98376 — 360-765-3363
Dr. Gary Stebbins, prin. — Fax 765-4183

**Quincy, Grant, Pop. 6,701**
Quincy SD 144-101 — 2,600/K-12
119 J St SW 98848 — 509-787-4571
John Boyd, supt. — Fax 787-4336
www.qsd.wednet.edu
High Tech HS — Vo/Tech
404 1st Ave SW 98848 — 509-787-1678
Garry Stidman, prin. — Fax 787-1680
Quincy HS — 700/9-12
16 6th Ave SE 98848 — 509-787-3501
David Talley, prin. — Fax 787-8989

Quincy JHS 400/7-8
417 C St SE 98848 509-787-4435
Scott Ramsey, prin. Fax 787-8949

**Rainier, Thurston, Pop. 1,719**
Rainier SD 307 800/PK-12
PO Box 98 98576 360-446-2207
Tim Garchow, supt. Fax 446-2918
www.rainier.wednet.edu
Rainier HS 300/9-12
PO Box 98 98576 360-446-2205
Bryon Bahr, prin. Fax 446-2208
Rainier MS 200/6-8
PO Box 98 98576 360-446-2206
Bryon Bahr, prin. Fax 446-7414

**Randle, Lewis**
White Pass SD 303 400/PK-12
PO Box 188 98377 360-497-3791
Chuck Wyborney, supt. Fax 497-2560
www.whitepass.k12.wa.us
White Pass JSHS 200/7-12
516 Silverbrook Rd 98377 360-497-5816
Chris Schumaker, prin. Fax 497-7773

**Ravensdale, King, Pop. 1,086**
Tahoma SD 409
Supt. — See Maple Valley
Tahoma JHS 1,200/8-9
25600 SE Summit Landsburg 98051 425-413-5600
Rhonda Ham, prin. Fax 413-5500

**Raymond, Pacific, Pop. 2,787**
Raymond SD 116 900/PK-12
1016 Commercial St 98577 360-942-3415
Dr. Stephen Holland, supt. Fax 942-3416
www.raymondschooldistrict.org
Raymond JSHS 300/7-12
1016 Commercial St 98577 360-942-3415
Dave Vetter, prin. Fax 942-2504

Willapa Valley SD 160 300/K-12
22 Viking Way 98577 360-942-5855
Rob Friese, supt. Fax 942-3216
www.willapa.wednet.edu
Willapa Valley HS 100/9-12
22 Viking Way 98577 360-942-2006
Nancy Morris, prin. Fax 942-3216
Willapa Valley MS 100/6-8
22 Viking Way 98577 360-942-2006
Nancy Morris, prin. Fax 942-3216

**Reardan, Lincoln, Pop. 562**
Reardan-Edwall SD 9 600/PK-12
PO Box 225 99029 509-796-2701
Marcus Morgan, supt. Fax 796-4954
www.reardan.net
Reardan JSHS 300/7-12
PO Box 225 99029 509-796-2701
Debi Newsum, prin. Fax 796-4954

**Redmond, King, Pop. 51,981**
Lake Washington SD 414 21,100/K-12
PO Box 97039 98073 425-936-1200
Dr. Traci Pierce, supt. Fax 936-1213
www.lwsd.org
Evergreen MS 500/6-8
6900 208th Ave NE 98053 425-936-2320
Robert Johnson, prin. Fax 868-0105
Redmond HS 1,500/9-12
17272 NE 104th St 98052 425-936-1800
Jane Todd, prin. Fax 936-1839
Redmond MS 600/6-8
10055 166th Ave NE 98052 425-936-2440
Kelly Clapp, prin. Fax 556-9806
Rose Hill MS 300/6-8
13505 NE 75th St 98052 425-936-2460
Erin Bowser, prin. Fax 556-0629
Stella Schola MS 100/6-8
13505 NE 75th St 98052 425-936-2475
Erin Bowser, prin. Fax 936-2476
Other Schools – See Kirkland, Sammamish

---

Bear Creek S 800/PK-12
8905 208th Ave NE 98053 425-898-1720
Patrick Carruth, hdmstr. Fax 898-1430
DigiPen Institute of Technology Post-Sec.
9931 Willows Rd NE 98052 425-558-0299
Overlake S 500/5-12
20301 NE 108th St 98053 425-868-1000
Matthew Horvat, head sch Fax 868-5771

**Renton, King, Pop. 85,890**
Issaquah SD 411
Supt. — See Issaquah
Liberty HS 1,200/9-12
16655 SE 136th St 98059 425-837-4800
Josh Almy, prin. Fax 837-4905
Maywood MS 900/6-8
14490 168th Ave SE 98059 425-837-6900
Jason Morse, prin. Fax 837-6910

Kent SD 415
Supt. — See Kent
Meeker MS 700/7-8
12600 SE 192nd St 98058 253-373-7284
Shannon Nash, prin. Fax 373-7560
Northwood MS 600/7-8
17007 SE 184th St 98058 253-373-7780
Sherilyn Ulland, prin. Fax 373-7788

Renton SD 403 14,500/K-12
300 SW 7th St 98057 425-204-2300
Dr. Art Jarvis, supt. Fax 204-2456
www.rentonschools.us
Hazen HS 1,500/9-12
1101 Hoquiam Ave NE 98059 425-204-4200
Kate O'Brien, prin. Fax 204-4220
Lindbergh HS 1,300/9-12
16426 128th Ave SE 98058 425-204-3200
Tres Genger, prin. Fax 204-3220
McKnight MS 1,100/6-8
1200 Edmonds Ave NE 98056 425-204-3600
Debbie Belew-Nyquist, prin. Fax 204-3680
Nelsen MS 1,000/6-8
2403 Jones Ave S 98055 425-204-3000
Colin Falk, prin. Fax 204-3079
Renton HS 1,300/9-12
400 S 2nd St 98057 425-204-3400
Giovanna San Martin, prin. Fax 204-3412
Other Schools – See Seattle

---

Everest College Post-Sec.
981 Powell Ave SW Ste 200 98057 425-255-3281
Pima Medical Institute Post-Sec.
555 S Renton Village Pl 110 98057 425-228-9600
Renton Technical College Post-Sec.
3000 NE 4th St 98056 425-235-2352

**Republic, Ferry, Pop. 1,028**
Republic SD 309 300/K-12
30306 E Highway 20 99166 509-775-3173
Dr. John Glenewinkel, supt. Fax 775-3712
www.republic.wednet.edu
Republic HS 100/9-12
30306 E Highway 20 99166 509-775-3171
Michael Church, prin. Fax 775-1098
Republic JHS 50/7-8
30306 E Highway 20 99166 509-775-3171
Michael Church, prin. Fax 775-1098

**Richland, Benton, Pop. 46,846**
Richland SD 400 11,400/K-12
615 Snow Ave 99352 509-967-6000
Dr. Rick Schulte, supt. Fax 942-2401
www.rsd.edu
Carmichael MS 900/6-8
620 Thayer Dr 99352 509-967-6425
Brian Stadelman, prin. Fax 942-2471
Chief Joseph MS 700/6-8
504 Wilson St, 509-967-6400
Jon Lobdell, prin. Fax 942-2492
Hanford HS 1,500/9-12
450 Hanford St, 509-967-6500
Ken Gosney, prin. Fax 371-2601
Richland HS 1,900/9-12
930 Long Ave 99352 509-967-6535
Tim Praino, prin. Fax 942-2512
River's Edge HS 200/Alt
975 Gillespie St 99352 509-967-6450
Dan Chubb, prin. Fax 942-2598
Other Schools – See West Richland

---

Liberty Christian S of the Tri-Cities 400/PK-12
2200 Williams Blvd, 509-946-0602
Karen Bjur, prin. Fax 943-5623
Lucas Marc Academy Post-Sec.
71 Gage Blvd 99352 509-591-4979

**Ridgefield, Clark, Pop. 4,650**
Ridgefield SD 122 2,200/K-12
2724 S Hillhurst Rd 98642 360-619-1300
Dr. Nathan McCann, supt. Fax 619-1397
www.ridge.k12.wa.us
Ridgefield HS 700/9-12
2630 S Hillhurst Rd 98642 360-619-1320
Tony VanderMaas, prin. Fax 619-1395
View Ridge MS 300/7-8
510 Pioneer St 98642 360-619-1400
Chris Griffith, prin. Fax 619-1459

---

Cedar Tree Classical Christian S 200/K-12
20601 NE 29th Ave 98642 360-887-0190

**Ritzville, Adams, Pop. 1,650**
Lind-Ritzville SD
Supt. — See Lind
Lind-Ritzville HS 100/9-12
209 E Wellsandt Rd 99169 509-659-1720
Tom Arlt, prin. Fax 659-5140

**Rochester, Thurston, Pop. 2,337**
Rochester SD 401 2,100/K-12
10140 Highway 12 SW 98579 360-273-5536
Kimberly Fry, supt. Fax 273-5547
www.rochester.wednet.edu
HEART Alternative HS 50/Alt
10140 Highway 12 SW 98579 360-273-5017
Matt Ishler, prin. Fax 273-5017
Rochester HS 600/9-12
19800 Carper Rd SW 98579 360-273-5534
Matt Ishler, prin. Fax 273-2570
Rochester MS 500/6-8
PO Box 398 98579 360-273-5958
Will Maus, prin. Fax 273-2045

**Rockford, Spokane, Pop. 465**
Freeman SD 358 900/K-12
15001 S Jackson Rd 99030 509-291-3695
Randy Russell, supt. Fax 291-3636
www.freemansd.org
Freeman HS 300/9-12
14626 S Jackson Rd 99030 509-291-3721
Jim Straw, prin. Fax 291-7337
Freeman MS 200/6-8
15001 S Jackson Rd 99030 509-291-7301
Ben Ferney, prin. Fax 291-3636

**Rosalia, Whitman, Pop. 547**
Rosalia SD 320 200/PK-12
916 S Josephine Ave 99170 509-523-3061
Larry Keller, supt. Fax 523-3861
www.rosaliaschools.org
Rosalia S 200/PK-12
916 S Josephine Ave 99170 509-523-3061
Darrell Kuhn, prin. Fax 523-3861

**Roslyn, Kittitas, Pop. 872**
Cle Elum-Roslyn SD 404
Supt. — See Cle Elum
Swiftwater Alternative S 50/Alt
205 W Idaho St 98941 509-649-4990
Mel Blair, prin. Fax 649-2270

---

Mayflower Christian S PK-12
2nd & Idaho 98941 509-674-5022
Debbie Cernick, admin.

**Royal City, Grant, Pop. 2,135**
Royal SD 160 1,600/PK-12
PO Box 486 99357 509-346-2222
Rosemarie Search, supt. Fax 346-8746
www.royal.wednet.edu/
Royal HS 400/9-12
PO Box 486 99357 509-346-2256
Matt Ellis, prin. Fax 346-9739
Royal MS 400/7-8
PO Box 486 99357 509-346-2268
David Jaderlund, prin. Fax 346-2269

**Saint John, Whitman, Pop. 519**
Endicott SD 308
Supt. — See Endicott
Endicott-St. John MS 50/6-8
301 W Nob Hill 99171 509-657-3523
Mike Suhling, prin. Fax 657-3521

St. John SD 322 200/PK-12
301 W Nob Hill Rd 99171 509-648-3336
Suzanne Schmick, supt. Fax 648-3451
www.sje.wednet.edu
St. John-Endicott HS 100/9-12
301 W Nob Hill Rd 99171 509-648-3336
Mark Purvine, prin. Fax 648-3451

**Sammamish, King, Pop. 44,087**
Lake Washington SD 414
Supt. — See Redmond
Eastlake HS 1,300/9-12
400 228th Ave NE 98074 425-936-1500
Chris Bede, prin. Fax 836-6609
Inglewood MS 700/6-8
24120 NE 8th St 98074 425-936-2360
Tim Patterson, prin. Fax 868-0628
Renaissance S of Art & Reasoning 100/6-8
400 228th Ave NE 98074 425-936-1544
Chris Bede, prin. Fax 836-6609
STEM, 400 228th Ave SE 98074 9-12
Cindy Dueanas, prin. 425-936-2770

---

Eastside Catholic HS 800/6-12
232 228th Ave SE 98074 425-295-3000
Polly Skinner, prin. Fax 392-5160

**SeaTac, King, Pop. 24,721**
Highline SD 401
Supt. — See Burien
Academy of Citizenship & Empowerment HS 400/9-12
4424 S 188th St 98188 206-631-6500
Nicole Fitch, prin. Fax 631-6520
Chinook MS 600/7-8
18650 42nd Ave S 98188 206-631-5700
Karin Jones, prin. Fax 631-5770
Global Connections HS 400/9-12
4424 S 188th St Bldg 300 98188 206-631-6550
Nicole Fitch, prin. Fax 631-6522

---

Seattle Christian S 500/K-12
18301 Military Rd S 98188 206-246-8241
Gloria Hunter, supt. Fax 246-9066

**Seattle, King, Pop. 578,438**
Highline SD 401
Supt. — See Burien
Arts and Academics Academy 300/9-12
830 SW 116th St 98146 206-631-6250
Jacqueline Downey, prin. Fax 631-6162
Cascade MS 600/7-8
11212 10th Ave SW 98146 206-631-5500
Libby DeBell, prin. Fax 631-5568
Health Sciences & Human Services HS 400/9-12
830 SW 116th St 98146 206-631-6200
Jenni Maughan, prin. Fax 631-6160
New Start HS 100/Alt
814 SW 120th St 98146 206-631-7750
Michael Sita, prin. Fax 631-7780
Technology Engineering Communications HS 300/9-12
830 SW 116th St Bldg 500 98146 206-631-6300
Vanessa Banner, prin. Fax 631-6164

Renton SD 403
Supt. — See Renton
Dimmitt MS 1,000/6-8
12320 80th Ave S 98178 425-204-2800
Anna Horton, prin. Fax 204-2812
Secondary Learning Center 300/Alt
7800 S 132nd St 98178 425-204-2100
Ronald Mahan, prin. Fax 204-2111

Seattle SD 1 47,900/PK-12
PO Box 34165 98124 206-252-0000
Dr. Larry Nyland, supt. Fax 252-0102
www.seattleschools.org
Addams MS 6-8
11051 34th Ave NE 98125 206-252-4500
Paula Montgomery, prin.
Ballard HS 1,600/9-12
1418 NW 65th St 98117 206-252-1000
Keven Wynkoop, prin. Fax 252-1001

Center S 300/9-12
305 Harrison St 98109 206-252-9850
Oksana Britsova, prin. Fax 252-9851
Cleveland STEM HS 800/9-12
5511 15th Ave S 98108 206-252-7800
George Breland, prin. Fax 252-7801
Denny International MS 900/6-8
2601 SW Kenyon St 98126 206-252-9000
Jeff Clarke, prin. Fax 252-9001
Eckstein MS 1,300/6-8
3003 NE 75th St 98115 206-252-5010
Treena Sterk, prin. Fax 252-5011
Franklin HS 1,400/9-12
3013 S Mount Baker Blvd 98144 206-252-6150
Jennifer Wiley, prin. Fax 252-6151
Garfield HS 1,700/9-12
400 23rd Ave 98122 206-252-2270
Ted Howard, prin. Fax 252-2271
Hale HS 1,100/9-12
10750 30th Ave NE 98125 206-252-3680
Jill Hudson, prin. Fax 262-3681
Hamilton International MS 900/6-8
1610 N 41st St 98103 206-252-5810
Tip Blish, prin. Fax 252-5811
Ingraham HS 1,000/9-12
1819 N 135th St 98133 206-252-3880
Martin Floe, prin. Fax 252-3881
Interagency Academy 400/Alt
3528 S Ferdinand St 98118 206-743-3930
Kaaren Andrews, prin. Fax 743-3931
Kurose MS 700/6-8
3928 S Graham St 98118 206-252-7700
Mia Williams, prin. Fax 252-7701
Madison MS 800/6-8
3429 45th Ave SW 98116 206-252-9200
Robert Gary, prin. Fax 252-9201
McClure MS 500/6-8
1915 1st Ave W 98119 206-252-1900
Shannon Conner, prin. Fax 252-1901
Mercer MS 900/6-8
1600 S Columbian Way 98108 206-252-8000
Chris Carter, prin. Fax 252-8001
Middle College HS at Seattle University 9-12
901 12th Ave 98122 206-720-3078
Cindy Nash, prin.
Middle College HS at Univ of WA 9-12
PO Box 355845 98195 206-685-3476
Cindy Nash, prin. Fax 616-3664
Middle College HS Northgate Mall Academy 200/9-12
401 NE Northgate Way 98125 206-366-7940
Cindy Nash, prin. Fax 366-7941
NOVA HS 300/9-12
2410 E Cherry St 98122 206-252-3500
Mark Perry, prin. Fax 252-3501
Rainier Beach HS 400/9-12
8815 Seward Park Ave S 98118 206-252-6350
Dwane Chappelle, prin. Fax 252-6351
Roosevelt HS 1,700/9-12
1410 NE 66th St 98115 206-252-4810
Brian Vance, prin. Fax 252-4811
Sealth International HS 1,200/9-12
2600 SW Thistle St 98126 206-252-8550
Aida Fraser-Hammer, prin. Fax 252-8551
Seattle World S 200/Alt
301 21st Ave E 98112 206-252-2200
Concie Pedroza, prin. Fax 252-2201
South Lake Alternative HS 100/Alt
8601 Rainier Ave S 98118 206-252-6600
Keith Smith, prin. Fax 252-6601
Washington MS 1,100/6-8
2101 S Jackson St 98144 206-252-2600
Susan Follmer, prin. Fax 252-2601
West Seattle HS 1,000/9-12
3000 California Ave SW 98116 206-252-8800
Ruth Medsker, prin. Fax 252-8801
Whitman MS 1,000/6-8
9201 15th Ave NW 98117 206-252-1200
Susan Kleitsch, prin. Fax 252-1201

---

Academy Northwest / Family Academy 300/K-12
PO Box 66839 98166 206-246-9227
Amazing Grace Christian S 200/PK-10
10056 Renton Ave S 98178 206-723-5526
Dr. David-Paul Zimmerman, admin.
Antioch University Post-Sec.
2326 6th Ave 98121 206-441-5352
Argosy University/Seattle Post-Sec.
2601A Elliott Ave 98121 206-283-4500
Art Institute of Seattle Post-Sec.
2323 Elliott Ave 98121 206-448-0900
Bainbridge Graduate Institute Post-Sec.
220 2nd Ave S Ste 400 98104 206-855-9559
Bakke Graduate University Post-Sec.
1013 8th Ave Ste 401 98104 206-264-9100
Billings MS 100/6-8
7217 Woodlawn Ave NE 98115 206-547-4614
Ted Kalmus, head sch Fax 545-8505
Bishop Blanchet HS 1,000/9-12
8200 Wallingford Ave N 98103 206-527-7700
Sheila Kries, prin. Fax 527-7712
Bush S 600/K-12
3400 E Harrison St 98112 206-322-7978
Percy Abram Ph.D., head sch Fax 860-3876
City University of Seattle Post-Sec.
521 Wall St Ste 100 98121 206-239-4500
Cornish College of the Arts Post-Sec.
1000 Lenora St 98121 800-726-ARTS
Cortiva Institute - Seattle Post-Sec.
425 Pontius Ave N Ste 100 98109 206-282-1233
Divers Institute of Technology Post-Sec.
1341 N Northlake Way 98103 800-634-8377
Everest College Post-Sec.
2111 N Northgate Way 98133 206-440-3090

Explorer West MS 100/6-8
10015 28th Ave SW 98146 206-935-0495
Evan Hundley, head sch Fax 932-7113
Gene Juarez Academy of Beauty Post-Sec.
10715 8th Ave NE 98125 206-365-6900
Holy Names Academy 700/9-12
728 21st Ave E 98112 206-323-4272
Elizabeth Swift, prin. Fax 323-5254
ITT Technical Institute Post-Sec.
12720 Gateway Dr S Ste 100 98168 206-244-3300
King's HS 400/9-12
19303 Fremont Ave N 98133 206-546-7241
Bob Ruhlman, prin. Fax 546-7214
Lakeside MS 300/5-8
13510 1st Ave NE 98125 206-368-3630
Bernie Noe, hdmstr. Fax 368-3639
Lakeside Upper S 500/9-12
14050 1st Ave NE 98125 206-368-3600
Bernie Noe, hdmstr. Fax 368-3638
Lake Washington Girls MS 100/6-8
810 18th Ave 98122 206-709-3800
Patricia Hearn, head sch Fax 323-9860
Menachem Mendel Seattle Cheder 100/PK-12
8511 15th Ave NE 98115 206-523-9766
North Seattle Community College Post-Sec.
9600 College Way N 98103 206-934-3600
Northwest S 500/6-12
1415 Summit Ave 98122 206-682-7309
Mike McGill, head sch Fax 467-7353
O'Dea HS 400/9-12
802 Terry Ave 98104 206-622-6596
James Walker, prin. Fax 340-4110
Photographic Center Northwest Post-Sec.
900 12th Ave 98122 206-720-7222
Pima Medical Institute Post-Sec.
9709 3rd Ave NE Ste 400 98115 206-322-6100
Sanford-Brown College Post-Sec.
645 Andover Park W 98188 206-575-1865
Seattle Academy of Arts & Sciences 400/6-12
1201 E Union St 98122 206-323-6600
Joe Puggelli, head sch Fax 323-6618
Seattle Central Community College Post-Sec.
1701 Broadway 98122 206-587-3800
Seattle Girls' S 100/5-8
2706 S Jackson St 98144 206-709-2228
Rafael del Castillo, head sch Fax 329-1580
Seattle Institute of Oriental Medicine Post-Sec.
444 NE Ravenna Blvd Ste 101 98115 206-517-4541
Seattle Lutheran HS 100/9-12
4100 SW Genesee St 98116 206-937-7722
Dave Meyer, dir. Fax 937-6781
Seattle Nativity S 6-8
2800 S Massachusetts St 98144 206-270-7230
Rick McDougall, dir.
Seattle Pacific University Post-Sec.
3307 3rd Ave W 98119 206-281-2000
Seattle Preparatory S 700/9-12
2400 11th Ave E 98102 206-324-0400
Maureen Reid, prin. Fax 323-6509
Seattle School of Theology & Psychology Post-Sec.
2501 Elliott Ave 98121 206-876-6100
Seattle University Post-Sec.
901 12th Ave 98122 206-296-6000
Seattle Waldorf HS 100/9-12
7777 62nd Ave NE 98115 206-522-2644
Shorewood Christian S 200/PK-12
10300 28th Ave SW 98146 206-933-1056
Tim Lorenz, prin. Fax 932-9002
South Seattle Community College Post-Sec.
6000 16th Ave SW 98106 206-934-5300
University of Washington 98195 Post-Sec.
206-543-2100
University Preparatory Academy 500/6-12
8000 25th Ave NE 98115 206-525-2714
Matt Levinson, head sch Fax 525-9659

**Sedro Woolley, Skagit, Pop. 10,288**
Sedro-Woolley SD 101 4,200/K-12
801 Trail Rd 98284 360-855-3500
Phil Brockman, supt. Fax 855-3574
www.swsd.k12.wa.us
Cascade MS 600/7-8
905 McGarigle Rd 98284 360-855-3520
Scott McPhee, prin. Fax 855-3521
Sedro-Woolley HS 1,200/9-12
1235 3rd St 98284 360-855-3510
Kerri Carlton, prin. Fax 855-3517
State Street HS 300/Alt
800 State St 98284 360-855-3550
Mark Nilson, prin. Fax 855-3551

**Sekiu, Clallam, Pop. 27**
Cape Flattery SD 401 200/K-12
PO Box 109 98381 360-963-2329
Kandy Ritter, supt. Fax 963-2373
www.capeflattery.wednet.edu
Other Schools – See Neah Bay

**Selah, Yakima, Pop. 6,994**
Selah SD 119 3,400/PK-12
104 W Naches Ave Ste H 98942 509-698-8000
Shane Backlund, supt. Fax 698-8099
www.selah.k12.wa.us
Selah Academy 100/Alt
308 W Naches Ave 98942 509-698-8450
Joe Coscarart, admin. Fax 698-8451
Selah HS 700/9-12
801 N 1st St 98942 509-698-8500
Jennifer Kindle, prin. Fax 698-8508
Selah MS 500/6-8
411 N 1st St 98942 509-698-8400
Marc Gallaway, prin. Fax 698-8399

**Sequim, Clallam, Pop. 6,414**
Sequim SD 323 2,900/K-12
503 N Sequim Ave 98382 360-582-3260
Kelly Shea, supt. Fax 683-6303
www.sequim.k12.wa.us/
Olympic Peninsula Academy 100/Alt
221 W Fir St 98382 360-582-3400
Randy Hill, admin. Fax 582-9229
Sequim HS 1,000/9-12
601 N Sequim Ave 98382 360-582-3600
Shawn Langston, prin. Fax 681-8688
Sequim MS 700/6-8
301 W Hendrickson Rd 98382 360-582-3500
Vince Riccobene, prin. Fax 582-9486

**Shelton, Mason, Pop. 9,392**
Pioneer SD 402 800/PK-8
611 E Agate Rd 98584 360-426-9115
Martin A. Brewer, supt. Fax 426-1036
www.psd402.org
Pioneer MS 400/4-8
611 E Agate Rd 98584 360-426-8291
Bracken Budge, prin. Fax 426-1036

Shelton SD 309 4,200/PK-12
700 S 1st St 98584 360-426-1687
Dr. Alex Apostle, supt. Fax 427-8610
www.sheltonschools.org
Choice HS 200/Alt
807 W Pine St 98584 360-426-7664
Stacey Anderson, prin. Fax 462-1203
Oakland Bay JHS 700/8-9
3301 N Shelton Springs Rd 98584 360-426-7991
Bracken Budge, prin. Fax 427-2940
Shelton SHS 1,000/10-12
3737 N Shelton Springs Rd 98584 360-426-4471
Wanda Berndtson, prin. Fax 427-6141

**Shoreline, King, Pop. 50,457**
Shoreline SD 412 8,600/PK-12
18560 1st Ave NE 98155 206-393-4203
Rebecca Miner, supt. Fax 393-4204
www.shorelineschools.org
Einstein MS 700/7-8
19343 3rd Ave NW 98177 206-393-4730
Fax 393-4735
Kellogg MS 600/7-8
16045 25th Ave NE 98155 206-393-4783
Lisa Gonzalez, prin. Fax 393-4780
Shorecrest HS 1,400/9-12
15343 25th Ave NE 98155 206-393-4286
Lori Longo, prin. Fax 393-4284
Shorewood HS 1,500/9-12
17300 Fremont Ave N 98133 206-393-4372
Bill Dunbar, prin. Fax 393-4711

---

Greenwood Academy of Hair Design Post-Sec.
18336 Aurora Ave N Ste 103 98133 206-542-1111
King's JHS 200/7-8
19345 Crista Ln N 98133 206-546-7243
Jordana Halkett, prin. Fax 546-7250
Shoreline Christian S 200/PK-12
2400 NE 147th St 98155 206-364-7777
Timothy Visser, admin. Fax 364-0349
Shoreline Community College Post-Sec.
16101 Greenwood Ave N 98133 206-546-4101

**Silverdale, Kitsap, Pop. 17,925**
Central Kitsap SD 401 11,200/K-12
PO Box 8 98383 360-662-1610
David McVicker, supt. Fax 662-1611
www.cksd.wednet.edu
Central Kitsap HS 1,300/10-12
PO Box 8 98383 360-662-2400
Steve Coons, prin. Fax 662-2401
Central Kitsap JHS 800/7-9
PO Box 8 98383 360-662-2300
Scott McDaniel, prin. Fax 662-2301
Klahowya Secondary S 1,000/7-12
PO Box 8 98383 360-662-4000
Jodie Woolf, prin. Fax 662-4001
New Frontiers JHS 50/Alt
PO Box 8 98383 360-662-1570
Jeremy Monroe, prin. Fax 662-1571
Ridgetop MS 700/7-9
PO Box 8 98383 360-662-2900
Stuart Crisman, prin. Fax 662-2901
Westside Alternative HS 200/Alt
PO Box 8 98383 360-662-2570
Jeremy Monroe, prin. Fax 662-2571
Other Schools – See Bremerton

**Skykomish, King, Pop. 197**
Skykomish SD 404 50/K-12
PO Box 325 98288 360-677-2623
Martin Schmidt, supt. Fax 677-2418
www.skykomishschool.com
Skykomish JSHS 50/7-12
PO Box 325 98288 360-677-2623
Martin Schmidt, admin. Fax 677-2418

**Snohomish, Snohomish, Pop. 8,810**
Monroe SD 103
Supt. — See Monroe
Hidden River MS 400/6-8
9224 Paradise Lake Rd 98296 360-804-4100
Brett Wille, prin. Fax 804-4199

Snohomish SD 201 9,800/PK-12
1601 Avenue D 98290 360-563-7300
William Mester Ph.D., supt. Fax 563-7279
www.sno.wednet.edu
AIM HS 100/Alt
525 13th St 98290 360-563-3400
June Shirey, admin. Fax 862-9433
Centennial MS 900/7-8
3000 S Machias Rd 98290 360-563-4525
Dave Sage, prin. Fax 563-4585

Glacier Peak HS 1,600/9-12
7401 144th Pl SE 98296 360-563-7500
Jim Dean, prin. Fax 563-7631
Snohomish HS 1,700/9-12
1316 5th St 98290 360-563-4000
Beth Porter, prin. Fax 563-4183
Valley View MS 700/7-8
14308 Broadway Ave 98296 360-563-4225
Nancy Rhoades, prin. Fax 563-4236

**Snoqualmie, King, Pop. 10,237**
Snoqualmie Valley SD 410 5,700/PK-12
PO Box 400 98065 425-831-8000
Joel Aune, supt. Fax 831-8040
www.svsd410.org/
Mount Si HS 1,600/9-12
8651 Meadowbrook Way SE 98065 425-831-8100
John Belcher, prin. Fax 831-8222
Other Schools – See Fall City, North Bend

**Soap Lake, Grant, Pop. 1,484**
Soap Lake SD 156 400/K-12
410 Ginkgo St S 98851 509-246-1822
Dan McDonald, supt. Fax 246-0669
www.slschools.org
Smokiam Alternative HS 100/Alt
410 Ginkgo St S 98851 509-246-0572
Loris Blair, prin. Fax 246-0669
Soap Lake MSHS 200/6-12
410 Ginkgo St S 98851 509-246-1201
Jacob Bang, prin. Fax 246-1722

**South Bend, Pacific, Pop. 1,566**
South Bend SD 118 600/PK-12
PO Box 437 98586 360-875-6041
Join Tienhaara, supt. Fax 875-6062
www.southbend.wednet.edu
South Bend JSHS 200/7-12
PO Box 437 98586 360-875-5707
Jason Nelson, prin. Fax 875-6036

**Spanaway, Pierce, Pop. 24,048**
Bethel SD 403 14,400/PK-12
516 176th St E 98387 253-683-6000
Tom Seigel, supt. Fax 683-6019
www.bethelsd.org
Bethel HS 1,100/9-12
22215 38th Ave E 98387 253-683-7000
Cliff Anderson, prin. Fax 683-7098
Bethel MS 400/6-8
22001 38th Ave E 98387 253-683-7200
Julie Shultz-Bartlett, prin. Fax 683-7298
Cedarcrest MS 400/6-8
19120 13th Avenue Ct E 98387 253-683-7500
Scott Martin, prin. Fax 683-7598
Challenger HS 300/Alt
18020 B St E 98387 253-683-6800
Jeff Johnson, prin. Fax 847-2530
Liberty MS 6-8
7319 Eustis Hunt Rd 98387 253-683-6500
Tom Mitchell, prin. Fax 683-6598
Spanaway Lake HS 1,200/9-12
1305 168th St E 98387 253-683-5600
Julie Baublits, prin. Fax 683-5698
Other Schools – See Graham, Puyallup, Tacoma

**Spangle, Spokane, Pop. 277**
Liberty SD 362 400/PK-12
29818 S North Pine Creek Rd 99031 509-624-4415
Kyle Rydell, supt. Fax 245-3288
www.libertysd.us
Liberty HS 100/9-12
6404 E Spangle Waverly Rd 99031 509-245-3229
Aaron Fletcher, prin. Fax 245-3205

---

Upper Columbia Academy 300/9-12
3025 E Spangle Waverly Rd 99031 509-245-3600

**Spokane, Spokane, Pop. 199,521**
Cheney SD 360
Supt. — See Cheney
Westwood MS 500/6-8
6120 S Abbott Rd 99224 509-559-4150
Dr. Erika Burden, prin.

Mead SD 354
Supt. — See Mead
Five Mile Prairie S Alt
8621 N Five Mile Rd 99208 509-465-7700
Bruce Olgard, prin. Fax 465-7720
MEAD Alternative HS 100/Alt
529 W Hastings Rd 99218 509-465-6900
Bruce Olgard, prin. Fax 465-6920
Mead HS 1,600/9-12
302 W Hastings Rd 99218 509-465-7000
Teresa Laher, prin. Fax 465-7020
Northwood MS 800/7-8
13120 N Pittsburg St 99208 509-465-7500
Dave Stenersen, prin. Fax 465-7520
Riverpoint Academy 9-12
11008 N Newport Hwy 99218 509-465-7900
Moleena Harris, admin.

Spokane SD 81 28,900/PK-12
200 N Bernard St 99201 509-354-5900
Shelley Redinger Ph.D., supt. Fax 354-5965
www.spokaneschools.org
ACE Alt
3754 W Indian Trail Rd 99208 509-328-7041
Sandi Skok, prin. Fax 328-7582
Chase MS 800/7-8
4747 E 37th Ave 99223 509-354-5000
John Andes, prin. Fax 354-5100
Community S at Bancroft 100/Alt
1025 W Spofford Ave 99205 509-354-7100
Dr. Cindy McMahon, prin. Fax 354-7070
Daybreak S 50/Alt
628 S Cowley St 99202 509-624-3227
Richard Miles, prin. Fax 835-4272
Ferris HS 1,600/9-12
3020 E 37th Ave 99223 509-354-6000
Ken Schutz, prin. Fax 354-6161
Garry MS 600/7-8
725 E Joseph Ave 99208 509-354-5200
Rob Reavis, prin. Fax 354-5212
Glover MS 600/7-8
2404 W Longfellow Ave 99205 509-354-5400
Kim Halcro, prin. Fax 354-5399
Lewis & Clark HS 1,900/9-12
521 W 4th Ave 99204 509-354-7000
Jeremy Ochse, prin. Fax 354-6969
Medicine Wheel Academy Alt
1300 W Knox Ave 99205 509-354-5693
Pam Austin, prin. Fax 354-5914
NEWTECH Skills Center Vo/Tech
4141 N Regal St 99207 509-354-7470
Will Sarett, prin. Fax 354-7474
North Central HS 1,200/9-12
1600 N Howard St 99205 509-354-6300
Steve Fisk, prin. Fax 354-6303
Rogers HS 1,500/9-12
1622 E Wellesley Ave 99207 509-354-6600
Lori Wyborney, prin. Fax 354-6665
Sacajawea MS 800/7-8
401 E 33rd Ave 99203 509-354-5500
Adam Swinyard, prin. Fax 354-5505
Salk MS 700/7-8
6411 N Alberta St 99208 509-354-5600
Carole Meyer, prin. Fax 354-5542
Shadle Park HS 1,500/9-12
4327 N Ash St 99205 509-354-6700
Eric Sylling, prin. Fax 354-6710
Shaw MS 600/7-8
4106 N Cook St 99207 509-354-5800
Jon Swett, prin. Fax 354-5899
TEC at Bryant Alternative S 300/Alt
910 N Ash St 99201 509-354-7810
Suzanne Smith, prin. Fax 354-7816

West Valley SD 363
Supt. — See Spokane Valley
West Valley HS 900/9-12
8301 E Buckeye Ave 99212 509-922-5488
John Custer, prin. Fax 928-3676

---

All Saints MS 300/5-8
1428 E 33rd Ave 99203 509-624-5712
Katherine Hicks, prin. Fax 624-7752
Carrington College Post-Sec.
10102 E Knox Ave Ste 200 99206 509-532-8888
Glen Dow Academy of Hair Design Post-Sec.
309 W Riverside Ave 99201 509-624-3244
Gonzaga Preparatory S 900/9-12
1224 E Euclid Ave 99207 509-483-8511
Cindy Reopelle, prin. Fax 483-3124
Gonzaga University Post-Sec.
502 E Boone Ave 99258 800-986-9585
Holy Family Hospital Post-Sec.
5633 N Lidgerwood St 99208 509-482-2450
Interface College Post-Sec.
178 S Stevens St 99201 509-467-1727
Northwest HVAC Training Center Post-Sec.
204 E Nora Ave 99207 509-747-8810
Palisades Christian Academy 100/PK-10
1115 N Government Way 99224 509-325-1985
Dan Wister M.Ed., prin. Fax 324-8904
Sacred Heart Medical Center Post-Sec.
101 W 8th Ave 99204 509-455-3040
St. George's S 400/K-12
2929 W Waikiki Rd 99208 509-466-1636
Joe Kennedy, head sch Fax 467-3258
Spokane Community College Post-Sec.
1810 N Greene St 99217 509-533-7000
Spokane Falls Community College Post-Sec.
3410 W Fort George Wright 99224 509-533-3500
Summit Christian Academy - Spokane 400/K-12
8913 N Nettleton Ln 99208 509-924-4618
Elena Solodyankin M.Ed., admin. Fax 467-4942
Whitworth University Post-Sec.
300 W Hawthorne Rd 99251 509-777-1000

**Spokane Valley, Spokane, Pop. 87,059**
Central Valley SD 356 12,300/K-12
19307 E Cataldo Ave, 509-228-5400
Ben Small, supt. Fax 228-5439
www.cvsd.org
Barker HS 100/Alt
13313 E Broadway Ave, 509-228-4050
Kamiel Youseph, prin. Fax 228-4059
Bowdish MS 500/6-8
2109 S Skipworth Rd, 509-228-4700
Ty Larsen, prin. Fax 228-4714
Central Valley HS 1,900/9-12
821 S Sullivan Rd, 509-228-5100
Mike Hittle, prin. Fax 228-5109
Evergreen MS 600/6-8
14221 E 16th Ave, 509-228-4780
John Parker, prin. Fax 228-4789
Greenacres MS 800/6-8
17409 E Sprague Ave, 509-228-4860
Vern DiGiovanni, prin. Fax 228-4869
Horizon MS 400/6-8
3915 S Pines Rd, 509-228-4940
Jesse Hardt, prin. Fax 228-4983
North Pines MS 500/6-8
701 N Pines Rd, 509-228-5020
Lora Jackson, prin. Fax 228-5029
University HS 1,700/9-12
12420 E 32nd Ave, 509-228-5240
Keven Frandsen, prin. Fax 228-5249
East Valley SD 361 4,100/K-12
3830 N Sullivan Rd Bldg 1, 509-924-1830
Kelly Shea, supt. Fax 927-9500
www.evsd.org
East Valley HS 1,100/9-12
15711 E Wellesley Ave, 509-927-3200
Jim McAdam, prin. Fax 921-6830
East Valley MS 500/7-8
4920 N Progress Rd, 509-924-9383
Doug Kaplicky, admin. Fax 927-3214
Washington Academy of Arts & Technology 700/Alt
12325 E Grace Ave, 509-241-5001
Barbara Cruse, prin. Fax 921-5687

West Valley SD 363 3,600/PK-12
PO Box 11739 99211 509-924-2150
Dr. Gene Sementi, supt. Fax 922-5295
www.wvsd.org
Centennial MS 600/6-8
915 N Ella Rd, 509-922-5482
Karen Bromps, prin. Fax 891-9520
Dishman Hills HS 300/Alt
115 S University Rd Ste A, 509-927-1100
Julie Poage, prin. Fax 891-5052
Spokane Valley HS 100/9-12
2011 N Hutchinson Rd, 509-922-5475
Larry Bush, prin. Fax 922-5477
West Valley City MS 200/5-8
8920 E Valleyway Ave, 509-921-2836
Dusty Andres, prin. Fax 921-2849
Other Schools – See Spokane

---

ITT Technical Institute Post-Sec.
13518 E Indiana Ave, 509-926-2900
Valley Christian S 200/PK-12
10212 E 9th Ave, 509-924-9131
Derick Tabish, admin. Fax 924-2971

**Sprague, Lincoln, Pop. 438**
Sprague SD 8 100/K-12
PO Box 305 99032 509-257-2591
Patrick Whipple, supt. Fax 257-2539
www.spraguelamont.org
Sprague HS 50/9-12
PO Box 305 99032 509-257-2511
Bill Ressel, prin. Fax 257-2539

**Springdale, Stevens, Pop. 275**
Mary Walker SD 207 400/PK-12
PO Box 159 99173 509-258-4534
Kevin Jacka, supt. Fax 258-4707
www.marywalker.org/
Springdale MS 100/6-8
PO Box 159 99173 509-258-7357
Matthew Cobb, prin. Fax 258-7756
Walker Alternative HS 50/Alt
PO Box 159 99173 509-258-4533
Matthew Cobb, prin. Fax 258-4555
Walker HS 200/9-12
PO Box 159 99173 509-258-4533
Matthew Cobb, prin. Fax 258-4555
Other Schools – See Valley

**Stanwood, Snohomish, Pop. 6,009**
Stanwood-Camano SD 401 4,800/K-12
26920 Pioneer Hwy 98292 360-629-1200
Dr. Jean Shumate, supt. Fax 629-1242
www.stanwood.wednet.edu
Lincoln Hill Academy 50/Alt
7600 272nd St NW 98292 360-629-1340
Ryan Ovenell, prin. Fax 629-1341
Lincoln Hill HS 200/Alt
7600 272nd St NW 98292 360-629-1340
Ryan Ovenell, prin. Fax 629-1341
Port Susan MS 500/6-8
7506 267th St NW 98292 360-629-1360
Dan Johnston, prin. Fax 629-1365
Saratoga S 100/Alt
9307 271st St NW 98292 360-629-1372
Curt Chester, lead tchr. Fax 629-1256
Stanwood HS 1,500/9-12
7400 272nd St NW 98292 360-629-1300
Christine DelPozo, prin. Fax 629-1310
Stanwood MS 600/6-8
9405 271st St NW 98292 360-629-1350
Tod Klundt, prin. Fax 629-1354

**Steilacoom, Pierce, Pop. 5,521**
Steilacoom Historical SD 1 2,700/PK-12
511 Chambers St 98388 253-983-2200
Kathi Weight, supt. Fax 584-7198
www.steilacoom.k12.wa.us
Steilacoom HS 800/9-12
54 Sentinel Dr 98388 253-983-2300
Debra Hay, prin. Fax 983-2393
Other Schools – See DuPont

**Stevenson, Skamania, Pop. 1,431**
Stevenson-Carson SD 303 1,400/K-12
PO Box 850 98648 509-427-5674
Karen Douglass, supt. Fax 427-4028
www.scsd.k12.wa.us
Stevenson HS 300/9-12
PO Box 850 98648 509-427-5631
Sarah Marino, prin. Fax 427-5639
Wind River MS 100/7-8
PO Box 850 98648 509-427-5631
Brian Morris, prin. Fax 427-5639
Other Schools – See Carson

**Sultan, Snohomish, Pop. 4,514**
Sultan SD 311 1,900/K-12
514 4th St 98294 360-793-9800
Dan Chaplik, supt. Fax 793-9890
www.sultan.k12.wa.us
Sultan HS 600/9-12
13715 310th Ave SE 98294 360-793-9860
Tami Nesting, prin. Fax 793-9864

Sultan MS 400/6-8
301 High Ave 98294 360-793-9850
Nathan Plummer, prin. Fax 793-9859

**Sumner, Pierce, Pop. 9,086**
Sumner SD 320 8,300/K-12
1202 Wood Ave 98390 253-891-6000
Dr. Sara Johnson, supt. Fax 891-6097
www.sumnersd.org
Sumner HS 1,500/9-12
1707 Main St 98390 253-891-5500
Bill Gaines, prin. Fax 891-5585
Sumner MS 700/6-8
1508 Willow St 98390 253-891-5000
Jennifer Williams, prin. Fax 891-5045
Other Schools – See Bonney Lake

**Sunnyside, Yakima, Pop. 15,748**
Sunnyside SD 201 6,300/K-12
1110 S 6th St 98944 509-837-5851
Dr. Richard Cole, supt. Fax 837-0535
www.sunnysideschools.org
Harrison MS 700/6-8
810 S 16th St 98944 509-837-3601
Robert Bowman, prin. Fax 837-0450
Sierra Vista MS 700/6-8
916 N 16th St 98944 509-836-8500
Doug Rogers, prin. Fax 836-8515
Sunnyside HS 1,700/9-12
1801 E Edison Ave 98944 509-837-2601
Ryan Maxwell, prin. Fax 837-0494

---

Sunnyside Christian HS 100/9-12
1820 Sheller Rd 98944 509-837-8995
Dean Wagenaar, prin. Fax 837-8895

**Tacoma, Pierce, Pop. 182,594**
Bethel SD 403
Supt. — See Spanaway
Spanaway MS 500/6-8
15701 B St E 98445 253-683-5400
Tami Nelson, prin. Fax 683-5498

Fife SD 417 3,600/PK-12
5802 20th St E 98424 253-517-1000
Kevin Alfano, supt. Fax 517-1055
www.fifeschools.com
Fife HS 800/10-12
5616 20th St E 98424 253-517-1100
Ron Ness, prin. Fax 517-1105
Other Schools – See Fife

Franklin Pierce SD 402 7,400/PK-12
315 129th St S 98444 253-298-3000
Dr. Frank Hewins, supt. Fax 298-3015
www.fpschools.org
Ford MS 900/6-8
1602 104th St E 98445 253-298-3600
Heather Renner, prin. Fax 298-3615
GATES HS 300/Alt
813 132nd St S 98444 253-298-4000
Val Jones, prin. Fax 298-4015
Keithley MS 700/6-8
12324 12th Ave S 98444 253-298-4300
Tom Edwards, prin. Fax 298-4315
New Pathways Alt
813 132nd St S 98444 253-298-4000
Val Jones, prin. Fax 298-4015
Pierce HS 1,100/9-12
11002 18th Ave E 98445 253-298-3800
Ron Hartley, prin. Fax 298-3814
Washington HS 1,000/9-12
12420 Ainsworth Ave S 98444 253-298-4700
James Hester, prin. Fax 298-4715

Tacoma SD 10, PO Box 1357 98401 28,000/PK-12
Carla Santorno, supt. 253-571-1000
www.tacoma.k12.wa.us
Baker MS 600/6-8
8001 S J St 98408 253-571-5000
Scott Rich, prin. Fax 571-5091
First Creek MS 800/6-8
1801 E 56th St 98404 253-571-2700
Rebecca Owens, prin. Fax 571-2717
Foss HS 1,000/9-12
2112 S Tyler St 98405 253-571-7300
Lysandra Ness, prin. Fax 571-7466
Giaudrone MS 600/6-8
4902 S Alaska St 98408 253-571-5811
Billy Harris, prin. Fax 571-5812
Gray MS 600/6-8
6229 S Tyler St 98409 253-571-5200
Shaun Martin, prin. Fax 571-5201
Lee MS 500/6-8
602 N Sprague Ave 98403 253-571-7700
Christi Brandt, prin. Fax 571-7710
Lincoln HS 1,500/9-12
701 S 37th St 98418 253-571-6700
Patrick Erwin, prin. Fax 571-6789
Mason MS 800/6-8
3901 N 28th St 98407 253-571-7000
Patrice Sulkosky, prin. Fax 571-7091
Meeker MS 700/6-8
4402 Nassau Ave NE 98422 253-571-6500
Timothy Berndt, prin. Fax 571-6503
Mount Tahoma HS 1,500/9-12
4634 S 74th St 98409 253-571-3800
Kevin Kannier, prin. Fax 571-3801
Oakland HS 300/Alt
3319 S Adams St 98409 253-571-5100
John Jones, prin. Fax 571-5101
Science and Math Institute 300/9-12
5501 N Pearl St 98407 253-571-2300
Jon Ketler, prin. Fax 571-2310
Stadium HS 1,600/9-12
111 N E St 98403 253-571-3100
Kevin Ikeda, prin. Fax 571-3101
Stewart MS 600/6-8
6501 S 10th St 98465 253-571-4200
Zeek Edmond, prin. Fax 571-4244
Tacoma School of the Arts 500/9-12
1102 A St 98402 253-571-7900
Jon Ketler, dir. Fax 571-7901
Truman MS 800/6-8
5801 N 35th St 98407 253-571-5600
Justina Johnson, prin. Fax 571-5680
Wilson HS 1,500/9-12
1202 N Orchard St 98406 253-571-6000
Dan Besett, prin. Fax 571-6162

---

Bates Technical College Post-Sec.
1101 Yakima Ave 98405 253-680-7000
Bellarmine Prep S 1,000/9-12
2300 S Washington St 98405 253-752-7701
Cindy Davis, prin. Fax 756-3887
BJ's Beauty & Barber College Post-Sec.
5239 S Tacoma Way 98409 253-473-4320
Corban University School of Ministry Post-Sec.
4301 N Stevens St 98407 253-759-6104
Covenant HS 100/9-12
620 S Shirley St 98465 253-759-9570
Richard Hannula, prin. Fax 759-1377
Everest College Post-Sec.
2156 Pacific Ave 98402 253-207-4000
Evergreen Chinese Academy 100/PK-12
5025 N Pearl St 98407 253-376-3553
Evergreen Lutheran HS 100/9-12
7306 Waller Rd E 98443 253-946-4488
Rev. Nathan Seiltz, prin. Fax 529-9475
Faith Evangelical College & Seminary Post-Sec.
3504 N Pearl St 98407 253-752-2020
Life Christian Academy 600/PK-12
1717 S Union Ave 98405 253-756-5300
Mount Rainier Lutheran HS 100/9-12
12108 Pacific Ave S 98444 253-284-4433
Craig Neumiller, dean Fax 284-4435
Pacific Lutheran University Post-Sec.
12180 Park Ave S 98447 253-531-6900
Tacoma Baptist S 300/PK-12
2052 S 64th St 98409 253-475-7226
Brad McCain, prin. Fax 471-9949
Tacoma Christian Academy 100/PK-10
2014 S 15th St 98405 253-572-1742
Alex Slobodyanik, prin.
Tacoma Community College Post-Sec.
6501 S 19th St 98466 253-566-5000
University of Puget Sound Post-Sec.
1500 N Warner St 98416 253-879-3100
Wright Academy 700/PK-12
7723 Chambers Creek Rd W 98467 253-620-8300
Robert Camner, hdmstr. Fax 620-8431
Wright S 400/PK-12
827 N Tacoma Ave 98403 253-272-2216
Christian Sullivan, head sch Fax 572-3616

**Taholah, Grays Harbor, Pop. 818**
Taholah SD 77 100/PK-12
PO Box 249 98587 360-276-4780
David Tomlin, supt. Fax 276-4370
www.taholah.org
Taholah S 100/PK-12
PO Box 249 98587 360-276-4729
Curtis Cleveringa, prin. Fax 276-4370

**Tekoa, Whitman, Pop. 764**
Tekoa SD 265 200/PK-12
PO Box 869 99033 509-284-3281
Dr. Connie Kliewer, supt. Fax 284-2045
www.tekoa.wednet.edu
Tekoa JSHS 100/7-12
PO Box 869 99033 509-284-3401
Daniel Hutton, prin. Fax 284-5802

**Tenino, Thurston, Pop. 1,631**
Tenino SD 402 1,300/PK-12
PO Box 4024 98589 360-264-3400
Joe Belmonte, supt. Fax 264-3438
www.teninoschools.org
Tenino HS 400/9-12
PO Box 4024 98589 360-264-3500
David Chappell, prin. Fax 264-3538
Tenino MS 300/6-8
PO Box 4024 98589 360-264-3600
Sharon Connally, prin. Fax 264-3638

**Thorp, Kittitas, Pop. 235**
Thorp SD 400 100/PK-12
PO Box 150 98946 509-964-2107
Dr. Linda Martin, supt. Fax 964-2313
www.thorpschools.org/
Thorp S 100/PK-12
PO Box 150 98946 509-964-2107
Dr. Linda Martin, prin. Fax 964-2313

**Toledo, Lewis, Pop. 712**
Toledo SD 237 800/PK-12
PO Box 469 98591 360-864-6325
Chris Rust, supt. Fax 864-6326
www.toledoschools.us
Toledo HS 300/9-12
PO Box 820 98591 360-864-2391
Martin Huffman, prin. Fax 864-2396
Toledo MS 200/6-8
PO Box 668 98591 360-864-2395
Heather Ogden, prin. Fax 864-8147

**Tonasket, Okanogan, Pop. 1,010**
Tonasket SD 404 1,200/PK-12
35 Highway 20 98855 509-486-2126
Steve McCullough, supt. Fax 486-1263
www.tonasket.wednet.edu
Tonasket Choice HS 100/Alt
35 Highway 20 98855 509-486-1428
Chelsea Freeman, lead tchr.
Tonasket HS 400/9-12
35 Highway 20 98855 509-486-2161
Jeff Hardesty, prin. Fax 486-4382
Tonasket MS 200/6-8
35 Highway 20 98855 509-486-2147
Jay Tyus, prin. Fax 486-1576

**Toppenish, Yakima, Pop. 8,831**
Toppenish SD 202 3,600/PK-12
306 Bolin Dr 98948 509-865-4455
John M. Cerna, supt. Fax 865-2067
www.toppenish.wednet.edu/
EAGLE HS 300/Alt
143 Ward Rd 98948 509-865-3377
Frank Harris, prin. Fax 865-7327
Toppenish HS 700/9-12
141 Ward Rd 98948 509-865-3370
Brenda Mallonee, prin. Fax 865-3244
Toppenish MS 700/6-8
104 Goldendale Ave 98948 509-865-2730
Dawn Weddle, prin. Fax 865-7503

---

Heritage University Post-Sec.
3240 Fort Rd 98948 509-865-8500

**Touchet, Walla Walla, Pop. 415**
Touchet SD 300 300/K-12
PO Box 135 99360 509-394-2352
Susan Bell, supt. Fax 394-2952
www.touchet.k12.wa.us
Touchet JSHS 200/6-12
PO Box 135 99360 509-394-2352
Susan Bell, admin. Fax 394-2952

**Toutle, Cowlitz**
Toutle Lake SD 130 600/K-12
5050 Spirit Lake Hwy 98649 360-274-6182
Scott Grabenhorst, supt. Fax 274-7608
www.toutlesd.k12.wa.us
Toutle Lake JSHS 300/7-12
5050 Spirit Lake Hwy 98649 360-274-6132
Greg McDaniel, prin. Fax 274-7615

**Trout Lake, Klickitat, Pop. 545**
Trout Lake SD R-400 100/K-12
PO Box 488 98650 509-395-2571
Doug Dearden, supt. Fax 395-2399
www.troutlake.k12.wa.us/
Trout Lake S 100/K-12
PO Box 488 98650 509-395-2571
Crystal Lantz, prin. Fax 395-2399

**Tukwila, King, Pop. 17,643**
Highline SD 401
Supt. — See Burien
Raisbeck Aviation HS 400/9-12
9229 E Marginal Way S 98108 206-631-7200
Bruce Kelly, prin. Fax 716-0200

Tukwila SD 406 3,000/K-12
4640 S 144th St 98168 206-901-8000
Dr. Nancy Coogan, supt. Fax 901-8016
www.tukwila.wednet.edu
Foster HS 900/9-12
4242 S 144th St 98168 206-901-7900
Pat Larson, prin. Fax 901-7907
Showalter MS 600/6-8
4628 S 144th St 98168 206-901-7800
Brett Christopher, prin. Fax 901-7807

---

Le Cordon Bleu College of Culinary Arts Post-Sec.
360 Corporate Dr N 98188 407-888-4000

**Tumwater, Thurston, Pop. 16,544**
Tumwater SD 33 5,900/PK-12
621 Linwood Ave SW 98512 360-709-7000
John Bash, supt. Fax 709-7002
www.tumwater.k12.wa.us
Bush MS 500/7-8
2120 83rd Ave SW 98512 360-709-7400
Linda O'Shaughnessy, prin. Fax 709-7402
New Market Skills Center Vo/Tech
7299 New Market St SW 98501 360-570-4500
Kris Blum, dir. Fax 570-4502
Tumwater HS 1,100/9-12
700 Israel Rd SW 98501 360-709-7600
Jeff Broome, prin. Fax 709-7602
Tumwater MS 400/7-8
6335 Littlerock Rd SW 98512 360-709-7500
Jon Wilcox, prin. Fax 709-7502
Other Schools – See Olympia

**Twisp, Okanogan, Pop. 890**
Methow Valley SD 350
Supt. — See Winthrop
Methow Valley Independent Learning Ctr 50/Alt
220 Highway 20 98856 509-997-8006
Deborah Dekalb, prin. Fax 997-5980

**Union Gap, Yakima, Pop. 5,960**

---

La Salle HS 200/9-12
3000 Lightning Way 98903 509-225-2900
Ted Kanelopoulos, prin. Fax 225-2950

**University Place, Pierce, Pop. 28,698**
University Place SD 83 5,600/K-12
3717 Grandview Dr W 98466 253-566-5600
Patricia Banks, supt. Fax 566-5607
www.upsd.wednet.edu
Curtis JHS 1,000/8-9
3725 Grandview Dr W 98466 253-566-5670
Jayne Hofstrand, prin. Fax 566-5644
Curtis SHS 1,400/10-12
8425 40th St W 98466 253-566-5710
Eric Brubaker, prin. Fax 566-5626

**Valley, Stevens, Pop. 135**
Mary Walker SD 207
Supt. — See Springdale
Springdale Academy Alt
PO Box 158 99181 509-937-2224
John Axtell, coord.

Valley SD 070 1,100/PK-12
3030 Huffman Rd 99181 509-937-2791
Kevin Foster, supt. Fax 937-2691
www.valleysd.org/
Paideia HS 50/9-12
3043 Huffman Rd 99181 509-937-2655
Matthew Cox, prin. Fax 937-2656

**Vancouver, Clark, Pop. 153,919**
Battle Ground SD 119
Supt. — See Brush Prairie
Laurin MS 600/5-8
13601 NE 97th Ave 98662 360-885-5200
Nick Krause, prin. Fax 885-5205
Pleasant Valley MS 400/5-8
14320 NE 50th Ave 98686 360-885-5500
Tamarah Grigg, prin. Fax 885-5510
Prairie HS 1,400/9-12
11311 NE 119th St 98662 360-885-5000
Travis Drake, prin. Fax 885-5050

Evergreen SD 114 26,000/K-12
PO Box 8910 98668 360-604-4000
John Deeder, supt. Fax 892-5307
www.evergreenps.org/
Cascade MS 1,000/6-8
PO Box 8910 98668 360-604-3600
Lisa Wagner-Tschirgi, prin. Fax 604-3602
Clark County Skills Center Vo/Tech
PO Box 8910 98668 360-604-1050
Karene Duffy, dir. Fax 604-1052
Covington MS 1,000/6-8
PO Box 8910 98668 360-604-6300
Charbonneau Gourde, prin. Fax 604-6302
Evergreen HS 1,900/9-12
PO Box 8910 98668 360-604-3700
Lisa Emmerich, prin. Fax 604-3702
Frontier MS 1,000/6-8
PO Box 8910 98668 360-604-3200
Maria Stevens, prin. Fax 604-3202
Heritage HS 2,100/9-12
PO Box 8910 98668 360-604-3400
Derek Garrison, prin. Fax 604-3402
Lacks Health & Bioscience HS 9-12
PO Box 8910 98668 360-604-6340
Julie Tumelty, prin. Fax 604-6342
Legacy HS 200/Alt
PO Box 8910 98668 360-604-3900
Michele DeShaw, prin. Fax 604-3902
Mountain View HS 1,800/9-12
PO Box 8910 98668 360-604-6100
Matt Johnson, prin. Fax 604-6102
Pacific MS 1,100/6-8
PO Box 8910 98668 360-604-6500
Tracy Thompson, prin. Fax 604-6502
Shahala MS 1,100/6-8
PO Box 8910 98668 360-604-3800
Gregg Brown, prin. Fax 604-3802
Wy' East MS 800/6-8
PO Box 8910 98668 360-604-6400
Caroline Garrett, prin. Fax 604-6402
Other Schools – See Camas

Vancouver SD 37 22,100/K-12
PO Box 8937 98668 360-313-1000
Dr. Steven Webb, supt. Fax 313-1001
www.vansd.org
Alki MS 700/6-8
1800 NW Bliss Rd 98685 360-313-3200
Darci Fronk, prin. Fax 313-3201
Columbia River HS 1,400/9-12
800 NW 99th St 98665 360-313-3900
Alex Otoupal, prin. Fax 313-3901
Discovery MS 800/6-8
800 E 40th St 98663 360-313-3300
Mark Cain, prin. Fax 313-3301
Fir Grove Childrens Center 100/Alt
2920 Falk Rd 98661 360-313-1800
Daniel Bettis, prin. Fax 313-1801
Ft. Vancouver HS 1,400/9-12
5700 E 18th St 98661 360-313-4000
Scott Parker, prin. Fax 313-4001
Gaiser MS 900/6-8
3000 NE 99th St 98665 360-313-3400
Mike Lane, prin. Fax 313-3401
Hudson's Bay HS 1,400/9-12
1601 E McLoughlin Blvd 98663 360-313-4400
Val Seeley, prin. Fax 313-4401
Jefferson MS 800/6-8
3000 NW 119th St 98685 360-313-3700
Tom Adams, prin. Fax 313-3701
Lee MS 600/6-8
8500 NW 9th Ave 98665 360-313-3500
Curt Scheidel, prin. Fax 313-3501
Lewis and Clark HS 200/Alt
2901 General Anderson Rd 98661 360-313-4350
Jody ViDelco, prin. Fax 313-4351
McLoughlin MS 900/6-8
5802 MacArthur Blvd 98661 360-313-3600
Travis Boeh, prin. Fax 313-3601
School of Arts & Academics 600/6-12
3101 Main St 98663 360-313-4600
James O'Banion, prin. Fax 313-4601
Skyview HS 1,900/9-12
1300 NW 139th St 98685 360-313-4200
James Gray, prin. Fax 313-4201

---

Charter College Vancouver Post-Sec.
17200 SE Mill Plain Ste 100 98683 360-448-2000
Clark College Post-Sec.
1933 Fort Vancouver Way 98663 360-992-2000
Everest College Post-Sec.
120 NE 136th Ave Ste 130 98684 360-254-3282
Hosanna Christian S 100/PK-10
4120 NE St Johns Rd 98661 360-906-0941
Sue Bishoprick, prin. Fax 694-0224
International Air & Hospitality Academy Post-Sec.
2901 E Mill Plain Blvd 98661 360-695-2500
King's Way Christian S 700/PK-12
3300 NE 78th St 98665 360-574-1613
School of Piano Technology for the Blind Post-Sec.
2510 E Evergreen Blvd 98661 360-693-1511
Seton Catholic HS 100/9-12
811 NE 112th Ave Ste 200 98684 360-258-1932
Ed Little, prin. Fax 258-1936
Washington State School for the Blind Post-Sec.
2214 E 13th St 98661
Washington State School for the Deaf Post-Sec.
611 Grand Blvd 98661

**Vashon, King, Pop. 10,291**
Vashon Island SD 402 1,400/PK-12
PO Box 547 98070 206-463-2121
Michael Soltman, supt. Fax 463-6262
www.vashonsd.org
McMurray MS 400/6-8
9329 SW Cemetery Rd 98070 206-463-9168
Greg Allison, prin. Fax 463-9707
Vashon Island HS 500/9-12
9600 SW 204th St 98070 206-463-9171
Danny Rock, prin. Fax 463-1944

**Waitsburg, Walla Walla, Pop. 1,189**
Waitsburg SD 401-100 300/K-12
PO Box 217 99361 509-337-6301
Dr. Carol Clarke, supt. Fax 337-6042
www.waitsburgsd.org/
Preston Hall MS 100/7-8
PO Box 217 99361 509-337-9474
Stephanie Wooderchak, prin. Fax 337-6170
Waitsburg HS 100/9-12
PO Box 217 99361 509-337-6351
Stephanie Wooderchak, prin. Fax 337-6551

**Walla Walla, Walla Walla, Pop. 30,829**
Walla Walla SD 140 5,900/PK-12
364 S Park St 99362 509-527-3000
Dr. Bill Jordan, supt. Fax 529-7713
www.wwps.org
Garrison MS 600/6-8
906 Chase Ave 99362 509-527-3040
Robert Elizondo, prin. Fax 527-3048
Lincoln Alternative HS Alt
421 S 4th Ave 99362 509-527-3083
Marci Knauft, prin. Fax 527-3011
Pioneer MS 700/6-8
450 Bridge St 99362 509-527-3050
Mira Gobel, prin. Fax 526-5212
Walla Walla HS 1,900/9-12
800 Abbott Rd 99362 509-527-3020
Pete Peterson, prin. Fax 527-3034

---

DeSales HS 100/8-12
919 E Sumach St 99362 509-525-3030
Lynne Kuntz, prin. Fax 527-0361
Walla Walla Community College Post-Sec.
500 Tausick Way 99362 509-522-2500
Whitman College Post-Sec.
345 Boyer Ave 99362 509-527-5111

**Wapato, Yakima, Pop. 4,948**
Wapato SD 207 3,400/PK-12
PO Box 38 98951 509-877-4181
Becky Imler, supt. Fax 877-6077
www.wapatosd.org
PACE HS 100/Alt
310 S Wasco Ave 98951 509-877-6138
Gary Babcock, prin. Fax 877-6164
Wapato HS 900/9-12
1202 S Camas Ave 98951 509-877-3138
Eric Diener, prin. Fax 877-5079
Wapato MS 800/6-8
1309 Kateri Ln 98951 509-877-2173
Anna Keifer, prin. Fax 877-6232

**Warden, Grant, Pop. 2,646**
Warden SD 146-161 1,000/PK-12
101 W Beck Way 98857 509-349-2366
Dr. David LaBounty, supt. Fax 349-2367
www.warden.wednet.edu
Warden HS 300/9-12
101 W Beck Way 98857 509-349-2581
Courtney McCoy, prin. Fax 349-2531
Warden MS 300/6-8
101 W Beck Way 98857 509-349-2902
Trever Summers, prin. Fax 349-2531

**Washougal, Clark, Pop. 13,617**
Washougal SD 112-6 3,000/K-12
4855 Evergreen Way 98671 360-954-3000
Dawn Tarzian, supt. Fax 835-7776
www.washougal.k12.wa.us
Canyon Creek MS 300/6-8
9731 Washougal River Rd 98671 360-954-3500
Sandi Christensen, prin. Fax 837-1500
Excelsior HS 100/Alt
1401 39th St 98671 360-954-3300
Carol Boyden, prin. Fax 835-1182
Jemtegaard MS 400/6-8
35300 SE Evergreen Hwy 98671 360-954-3400
David Cooke, prin. Fax 835-9145
Washougal HS 900/9-12
1201 39th St 98671 360-954-3100
Aaron Hansen, prin. Fax 835-3968

**Washtucna, Adams, Pop. 206**
Washtucna SD 109-43 100/K-12
PO Box 688 99371 509-646-3237
Brent Seedall, supt. Fax 646-3249
www.tucna.wednet.edu
Washtucna S 100/K-12
PO Box 688 99371 509-646-3237
Brent Seedall, prin. Fax 646-3249

**Waterville, Douglas, Pop. 1,124**
Waterville SD 209 300/K-12
PO Box 490 98858 509-745-8584
Fax 745-9073
www.waterville.wednet.edu/
Waterville JSHS 200/6-12
PO Box 490 98858 509-745-8583
Tabatha Mires, prin. Fax 745-9073

**Wellpinit, Stevens**
Wellpinit SD 49 500/K-12
PO Box 390 99040 509-258-4535
John Adkins, supt. Fax 258-4065
www.wellpinit.org
Columbia Basin Alliance HS 50/Alt
PO Box 390 99040 509-258-4535
Terry Bartolino, prin. Fax 258-7857
Fort Simcoe Alliance HS 50/Alt
PO Box 390 99040 509-258-4535
Terry Bartolino, prin. Fax 258-7857
Wellpinit Alliance HS 50/Alt
PO Box 390 99040 509-258-4535
Terry Bartolino, dir. Fax 258-7378
Wellpinit HS 100/9-12
PO Box 390 99040 509-258-4535
Kristopher Herda, prin. Fax 258-7378
Wellpinit MS 100/6-8
PO Box 390 99040 509-258-4535
Kristopher Herda, prin. Fax 258-7378

**Wenatchee, Chelan, Pop. 31,295**
Wenatchee SD 246 7,400/K-12
PO Box 1767 98807 509-663-8161
Brian Flones, supt. Fax 663-3082
www.wenatcheeschools.org
Foothills MS 600/6-8
1410 Maple St 98801 509-664-8961
Mark Goveia, prin. Fax 663-6610
Orchard MS 500/6-8
1024 Orchard Ave 98801 509-662-7745
Taunya Brown, prin. Fax 663-8042
Pioneer MS 600/6-8
1620 Russell St 98801 509-663-7171
Rob Cline, prin. Fax 663-0453
Wenatchee HS 2,100/9-12
1101 Millerdale Ave 98801 509-663-8117
Eric Anderson, prin. Fax 663-2573
Wenatchee Valley Technical Skills Center Vo/Tech
327 E Penny Rd Ste D 98801 509-662-8827
Pete Jelsing, dir. Fax 662-5993
Westside HS 200/Alt
1510 9th St 98801 509-663-7947
Kory Kalahar, prin. Fax 664-3005

---

Academy of Hair Design Post-Sec.
208 S Wenatchee Ave 98801 509-662-9082
Cascade Christian Academy 200/PK-12
600 N Western Ave 98801 509-662-2723
River Academy 200/PK-12
PO Box 4485 98807 509-665-2415
Eric DeVries, hdmstr. Fax 662-9235
Wenatchee Valley College Post-Sec.
1300 5th St 98801 509-682-6800

**Westport, Grays Harbor, Pop. 2,036**
Ocosta SD 172 700/PK-12
2580 S Montesano St 98595 360-268-9125
Dr. Paula Akerlund, supt. Fax 268-2540
Ocosta JSHS 300/7-12
2580 S Montesano St 98595 360-268-9125
Brian Hunter, prin. Fax 268-0908

**West Richland, Benton, Pop. 11,498**
Richland SD 400
Supt. — See Richland
Enterprise MS 900/6-8
5200 Paradise Dr 99353 509-967-6200
Jennifer Klauss, prin. Fax 967-5685

**White Salmon, Klickitat, Pop. 2,180**
White Salmon Valley SD 405-17 1,200/K-12
PO Box 157 98672 509-493-1500
Dr. Jerry Lewis, supt. Fax 493-2275
www.whitesalmonschools.org/
Columbia HS 400/9-12
PO Box 1339 98672 509-493-1970
Craig McKee, prin. Fax 493-4182
Henkle MS 400/7-8
PO Box 1309 98672 509-493-1502
Haley Ortega, prin. Fax 493-3385
White Salmon Academy 50/Alt
1455 NW Bruin Country Rd 98672 509-493-1970
Craig McKee, prin. Fax 493-4182

**White Swan, Yakima, Pop. 779**
Mount Adams SD 209 1,000/PK-12
PO Box 578 98952 509-874-2611
Henry Strom, supt. Fax 874-2960
www.mtadams.wednet.edu
Mount Adams MS 100/7-8
PO Box 578 98952 509-874-8626
Joey Castilleja, prin. Fax 874-2646
White Swan HS 300/9-12
PO Box 578 98952 509-874-2324
Joey Castilleja, prin. Fax 874-2646

**Wilbur, Lincoln, Pop. 857**
Wilbur SD 200 300/K-12
PO Box 1090 99185 509-647-2221
Steve Gaub, supt. Fax 647-2509
www.wilbur.wednet.edu
Wilbur JSHS 100/7-12
PO Box 1090 99185 509-647-5602
Carla Hudson, prin. Fax 647-2509

**Wilson Creek, Grant, Pop. 198**
Wilson Creek SD 167-202 100/K-12
PO Box 46 98860 509-345-2541
Dr. Mike Riggs, supt. Fax 345-2288
www.wilsoncreek.org
Wilson Creek JSHS 100/7-12
PO Box 46 98860 509-345-2541
Sally Nelson, prin. Fax 345-2288

**Winlock, Lewis, Pop. 1,291**
Winlock SD 232 700/PK-12
311 NW Fir St 98596 360-785-3582
Shannon Criss, supt. Fax 864-3101
www.winlockschools.org
APOLO Alternative S 100/Alt
311 NW Fir St 98596 360-785-3537
Boyd Calder, prin.
Winlock HS 200/9-12
241 N Military Rd 98596 360-785-3537
Brian Maley, prin. Fax 864-3104
Winlock MS 200/6-8
241 N Military Rd 98596 360-785-3046
Brian Maley, prin. Fax 864-3105

**Winthrop, Okanogan, Pop. 390**
Methow Valley SD 350 500/PK-12
18 Twin Lakes Rd 98862 509-996-9205
Tom Venable, supt. Fax 996-9208
www.methow.org
Liberty Bell JSHS 300/7-12
18 Twin Lakes Rd 98862 509-996-2215
Deborah Dekalb, prin. Fax 996-3609
Other Schools – See Twisp

**Wishram, Klickitat, Pop. 339**
Wishram SD 94 100/PK-12
PO Box 8 98673 509-748-2551
Michael Roberts, supt. Fax 748-2127
www.wishramschool.org
Wishram S 100/PK-12
PO Box 8 98673 509-748-2551
Michael Roberts, supt. Fax 748-2127

**Woodinville, King, Pop. 10,516**
Northshore SD 417
Supt. — See Bothell
Leota JHS 600/7-9
19301 168th Ave NE 98072 425-408-6500
Obadiah Dunham, prin. Fax 408-6502
Timbercrest JHS 800/7-9
19115 215th Way NE, 425-408-6900
Joe Mismas, prin. Fax 408-6902
Woodinville SHS 1,300/10-12
19819 136th Ave NE 98072 425-408-7400
Kurt Criscione, prin. Fax 408-7402

---

Chrysalis S 200/K-12
14241 NE Woodinville Duvall 98072 425-481-2228

**Woodland, Cowlitz, Pop. 5,391**
Woodland SD 404 2,100/PK-12
800 2nd St 98674 360-841-2700
Michael Green, supt. Fax 841-2701
www.woodlandschools.org/
Woodland HS 600/9-12
1500 Dike Access Rd 98674 360-841-2800
John Shoup, prin. Fax 841-2801
Woodland MS 300/5-8
755 Park St 98674 360-841-2850
Jake Hall, prin. Fax 841-2851
Woodland TEAM HS 100/Alt
800 3rd St 98674 360-841-2800
Dan Uhlenkott, prin. Fax 841-2801

---

West Coast Training Post-Sec.
PO Box 970 98674 360-225-6787

**Yakima, Yakima, Pop. 89,018**
East Valley SD 90 2,900/K-12
2002 Beaudry Rd 98901 509-573-7300
John Schieche, supt. Fax 573-7340
www.evsd90.org
East Valley Central MS 700/6-8
2010 Beaudry Rd 98901 509-573-7500
Matt Toth, prin. Fax 573-7540
East Valley HS 800/9-12
1900 Beaudry Rd 98901 509-573-7400
Dorthea Say, prin. Fax 573-7440

West Valley SD 208 4,800/K-12
8902 Zier Rd 98908 509-972-6000
Dr. Michael Brophy, supt. Fax 972-6001
www.wvsd208.org
West Valley Freshman Campus 400/9-9
9206 Zier Rd 98908 509-972-5600
Bill Oppliger, prin. Fax 972-5601
West Valley HS 1,100/10-12
9800 Zier Rd 98908 509-972-5900
Bill Oppliger, prin. Fax 972-5901
West Valley JHS 800/7-8
7505 Zier Rd 98908 509-972-5800
Jim Fannin, prin. Fax 972-5801

Yakima SD 7 15,200/PK-12
104 N 4th Ave 98902 509-573-7000
Dr. Jack Irion, supt. Fax 573-7181
www.yakimaschools.org/
Davis HS 2,100/9-12
212 S 6th Ave 98902 509-573-2500
Ryan McDaniel, prin. Fax 573-2525
Eisenhower HS 2,000/9-12
611 S 44th Ave 98908 509-573-2600
Jewel Brumley, prin. Fax 573-2626
Franklin MS 800/6-8
410 S 19th Ave 98902 509-573-2100
Sherry Anderson, prin. Fax 573-2121
Lewis & Clark MS 700/6-8
1114 W Pierce St 98902 509-573-2200
Victor Nourani, prin. Fax 573-2222
Stanton Academy 300/Alt
802 River Rd 98902 509-573-1200
Dave Chaplin, prin. Fax 573-1212
Washington MS 700/6-8
510 S 9th St 98901 509-573-2300
Bill Hilton, prin. Fax 573-2323
Wilson MS 800/6-8
902 S 44th Ave 98908 509-573-2400
Ernesto Araiza, prin. Fax 573-2424
Yakima Valley Technical Skills Center Vo/Tech
1120 S 18th St 98901 509-573-5500
Craig Dwight, prin. Fax 834-2041

---

Pacific Northwest Univ of Health Science Post-Sec.
111 University Pkwy Ste 202 98901 509-452-5100
Perry Technical Institute Post-Sec.
2011 W Washington Ave 98903 509-453-0374
Professional Beauty School Post-Sec.
PO Box 9243 98909 509-877-6443
Riverside Christian S 400/PK-12
721 Keys Rd 98901 509-965-2602
Rick Van Beek, admin. Fax 966-7031
Yakima Adventist Christian S 100/PK-10
1200 City Reservoir Rd 98908 509-966-1933
Renae Young, prin.
Yakima Valley Community College Post-Sec.
PO Box 22520 98907 509-574-4600

**Yelm, Thurston, Pop. 6,363**
Yelm Community SD 2 5,500/PK-12
PO Box 476 98597 360-458-1900
Andy Wolf, supt. Fax 458-6178
www.ycs.wednet.edu
Ridgeline MS 700/7-9
PO Box 476 98597 360-400-1100
John Johnson, prin. Fax 400-1256
Yelm Extension S 200/Alt
PO Box 476 98597 360-458-2002
Brian Wharton, admin. Fax 458-6146
Yelm HS 1,200/10-12
PO Box 476 98597 360-458-7777
Brian Wharton, prin. Fax 458-6198
Yelm MS 700/7-9
PO Box 476 98597 360-458-3600
Heidi Bunker, prin. Fax 458-6122

---

Eagle View Christian S 100/PK-12
13036 Morris Rd SE 98597 360-458-3090
Barbara Ballou, prin. Fax 458-4990

**Zillah, Yakima, Pop. 2,907**
Zillah SD 205 1,400/PK-12
213 4th Ave 98953 509-829-5911
Kevin McKay, supt. Fax 829-6290
www.zillahschools.org/
Zillah HS 400/9-12
1602 2nd Ave 98953 509-829-5565
Mike Torres, prin. Fax 829-5285
Zillah MS 200/7-8
1301 Cutler Way 98953 509-829-5511
Justin Irion, prin. Fax 829-0754

# WEST VIRGINIA

**WEST VIRGINIA DEPARTMENT OF EDUCATION**
**1900 Kanawha Blvd E Rm 358, Charleston 25305-0330**
**Telephone 304-558-2681**
**Fax 304-558-0048**
**Website wvde.state.wv.us**

State Superintendent of Schools James Phares

**WEST VIRGINIA BOARD OF EDUCATION**
**1900 Kanawha Blvd E Rm 358, Charleston 25305-0330**

President L. Wade Linger

## REGIONAL EDUCATION SERVICE AGENCIES (RESA)

RESA I
Dr. Robin Lewis, dir. 304-256-4712
400 Neville St, Beckley 25801 Fax 256-4683
resa1.k12.wv.us/

RESA II
Dr. Dee Cockrille, dir. 304-529-6205
2001 McCoy Rd, Huntington 25701 Fax 529-6209
resa2.k12.wv.us/

RESA III
Kelly Watts, dir. 800-257-3723
501 22nd St, Dunbar 25064 Fax 766-7915
resa3.k12.wv.us

RESA IV
David Warvel, dir., 404 Old Main Dr 304-872-6440
Summersville 26651 Fax 872-6442
resa4.k12.wv.us/

RESA V
Joseph Oliverio, dir. 304-485-6513
2507 9th Ave, Parkersburg 26101 Fax 485-6515
resa5.k12.wv.us

RESA VII
Gabriel Devono, dir. 304-624-6554
1201 N 15th St, Clarksburg 26301 Fax 624-5223
resa7.k12.wv.us

RESA VIII
Jane Lynch, dir., 109 S College St 304-267-3595
Martinsburg 25401 Fax 267-3728
www.resa8.org

RESA VI
Nick Zervos, dir. 304-243-0440
30 G C and P Rd, Wheeling 26003 Fax 243-0443
resa6.k12.wv.us/

## PUBLIC, PRIVATE AND CATHOLIC SECONDARY SCHOOLS

**Ansted, Fayette, Pop. 1,400**
Fayette County SD
Supt. — See Fayetteville
Ansted MS 200/5-8
PO Box 766 25812 304-658-5170
Richard Petitt, prin. Fax 658-3059

**Ashton, Mason**
Mason County SD
Supt. — See Point Pleasant
Hannan JSHS 300/7-12
15638 Ashton Upland Rd 25503 304-743-2571
Karen Bare-Oldham, prin. Fax 743-4513

**Athens, Mercer, Pop. 1,039**

---

Concord University Post-Sec.
PO Box 1000 24712 800-344-6679

**Avondale, McDowell**
McDowell County SD
Supt. — See Welch
Sandy River MS 300/6-8
PO Box 419 24811 304-938-2407
Sara Garrett, prin. Fax 938-2418

**Baker, Hardy**
Hardy County SD
Supt. — See Moorefield
East Hardy HS 200/9-12
PO Box 120 26801 304-897-5948
Jennifer Strawderman, prin. Fax 897-6261

**Barboursville, Cabell, Pop. 3,916**
Cabell County SD
Supt. — See Huntington
Barboursville MS 800/6-8
1400 Central Ave 25504 304-733-3003
Brent Jarrell, prin. Fax 733-3009

**Beaver, Raleigh, Pop. 1,300**

---

Victory Baptist Academy 100/K-12
PO Box 549 25813 304-255-4535

**Beckley, Raleigh, Pop. 17,086**
Raleigh County SD 12,100/PK-12
105 Adair St 25801 304-256-4500
David Price, supt. Fax 256-4739
boe.rale.k12.wv.us
Academy of Careers and Technology Vo/Tech
390 Stanaford Rd 25801 304-256-4615
Charles Pack, dir. Fax 256-4674
Beckley-Stratton MS 700/6-8
401 Grey Flats Rd 25801 304-256-4616
Rachel Pauley, prin. Fax 256-4616
Park MS 400/6-8
212 Park Ave 25801 304-256-4586
Jacquelin McPeake, prin. Fax 256-4709
Wilson HS 1,400/9-12
400 Stanaford Rd 25801 304-256-4646
Ron Cantley, prin. Fax 256-4642
Other Schools – See Coal City, Glen Daniel, Shady Spring, Sophia

---

New River Community & Technical College Post-Sec.
221 George St Ste 2 25801 304-929-5450

St. Francis de Sales S 200/PK-10
622 S Oakwood Ave 25801 304-252-4087
Karen Wynne, prin. Fax 252-4087
Valley College Post-Sec.
120 New River Town Ctr #C 25801 304-252-9547
Veterans Administration Hospital Post-Sec.
200 Veterans Ave 25801 304-255-2121

**Belington, Barbour, Pop. 1,905**
Barbour County SD
Supt. — See Philippi
Belington MS 200/6-8
469 Morgantown Pike 26250 304-823-1281
Michael Ferguson, prin. Fax 823-2403

**Belle, Kanawha, Pop. 1,248**
Kanawha County SD
Supt. — See Charleston
DuPont MS 400/6-8
1 Panther Dr 25015 304-348-1978
Romie Canterbury, prin. Fax 949-1793
Riverside HS 1,200/9-12
1 Warrior Way 25015 304-348-1996
Valery Harper, prin. Fax 348-1921

**Belmont, Pleasants, Pop. 892**
Pleasants County SD
Supt. — See Saint Marys
Pleasants County MS 400/5-8
510 Riverview Dr 26134 304-299-5275
Lori Barnhart, prin. Fax 665-2451

**Berkeley Springs, Morgan, Pop. 614**
Morgan County SD 2,600/PK-12
247 Harrison Ave 25411 304-258-2430
David Banks, supt. Fax 258-9146
www.morganschools.net
Berkeley Springs HS 800/9-12
149 Concord Ave 25411 304-258-2871
Mitch Nida, prin. Fax 258-5058
Warm Springs MS 500/6-8
271 Warm Springs Way 25411 304-258-1500
Gene Brock, prin. Fax 258-4600
Other Schools – See Paw Paw

**Bethany, Brooke, Pop. 1,014**

---

Bethany College 26032 Post-Sec.
304-829-7000

**Blacksville, Monongalia, Pop. 166**
Monongalia County SD
Supt. — See Morgantown
Clay-Battelle MSHS 500/6-12
PO Box A 26521 304-432-8208
David Cottrell, prin. Fax 432-8189

**Bluefield, Mercer, Pop. 10,213**
Mercer County SD
Supt. — See Princeton
Bluefield HS 700/9-12
535 W Cumberland Rd 24701 304-325-9116
Michael Collins, prin. Fax 325-0529
Bluefield MS 500/6-8
2002 Stadium Dr 24701 304-325-2481
Kimberly Miller, prin. Fax 325-2156

---

Bluefield Regional Medical Center Post-Sec.
500 Cherry St 24701 304-327-1701
Bluefield State College Post-Sec.
219 Rock St 24701 304-327-4000
Valley View SDA S 50/K-12
PO Box 6312 24701 304-325-8679

**Bradshaw, McDowell, Pop. 335**
McDowell County SD
Supt. — See Welch
Riverview HS 500/9-12
512 Mountaineer Hwy 24817 304-967-7480
Michael Tye, prin. Fax 967-2502

**Branchland, Lincoln**
Lincoln County SD
Supt. — See Hamlin
Guyan Valley MS 300/6-8
5312 McLellan Hwy 25506 304-824-3235
Jonah Adkins, prin. Fax 824-3459

**Bridgeport, Harrison, Pop. 8,059**
Harrison County SD
Supt. — See Clarksburg
Bridgeport HS 800/9-12
515 Johnson Ave 26330 304-326-7137
Mark DeFazio, prin. Fax 842-6288
Bridgeport MS 500/6-8
413 Johnson Ave 26330 304-326-7142
Carole Crawford, prin. Fax 842-6275

---

Heritage Christian S 100/PK-12
225 Newton Ave 26330 304-842-1740
Linda Simms, admin. Fax 842-1750
West Virginia Junior College Post-Sec.
176 Thompson Dr 26330 304-842-4007

**Buckeye, Pocahontas**
Pocahontas County SD
Supt. — See Marlinton
Marlinton MS 200/5-8
1 Copperhead Way 24924 304-799-6773
Joseph Riley, prin. Fax 799-7278

**Buckhannon, Upshur, Pop. 5,544**
Upshur County SD 3,900/PK-12
102 Smithfield St 26201 304-472-5480
Roy Wager, supt. Fax 472-0258
www.upshurschools.com
Buckhannon-Upshur HS 1,100/9-12
270 BU Dr 26201 304-472-3720
Robert Wilmoth, prin. Fax 472-0772
Buckhannon-Upshur MS 800/6-8
553 Route 20 South Rd 26201 304-472-1520
Renee Warner, prin. Fax 472-6864
Eberle Technical Center Vo/Tech
RR 5 Box 2 26201 304-472-1259
Dr. Michael Cutright, dir. Fax 472-3418

---

West Virginia Wesleyan College Post-Sec.
59 College Ave 26201 304-473-8000

**Buffalo, Putnam, Pop. 1,223**
Putnam County SD
Supt. — See Winfield

Buffalo HS 300/9-12
3317 Buffalo Rd 25033 304-937-2661
Tawny Stilianoudakis, prin. Fax 937-3470

**Bunker Hill, Berkeley**
Berkeley County SD
Supt. — See Martinsburg
Musselman MS 1,100/6-8
105 Pride Ave 25413 304-229-1965
James Holland, prin. Fax 229-1967

**Cameron, Marshall, Pop. 941**
Marshall County SD
Supt. — See Moundsville
Cameron JSHS 400/7-12
2012 Blue and Gold Rd 26033 304-686-3336
Jack Cain, prin. Fax 686-3510

**Capon Bridge, Hampshire, Pop. 353**
Hampshire County SD
Supt. — See Romney
Capon Bridge MS 400/6-8
PO Box 147 26711 304-856-2534
Ann Downs, prin. Fax 856-3192

**Cedar Grove, Kanawha, Pop. 982**
Kanawha County SD
Supt. — See Charleston
Cedar Grove MS 6-8
PO Box K 25039 304-949-1642
Melissa Lawrence, prin. Fax 949-3418

**Ceredo, Wayne, Pop. 1,432**
Wayne County SD
Supt. — See Wayne
Ceredo-Kenova MS 200/6-8
PO Box 705 25507 304-453-3588
Tonji Bowen, prin. Fax 453-4420

**Chapmanville, Logan, Pop. 1,250**
Logan County SD
Supt. — See Logan
Chapmanville HS 700/9-12
200 Vance St 25508 304-855-4522
Katherine Moore, prin. Fax 855-1911
Chapmanville MS 600/5-8
300 Vance St 25508 304-855-8378
Jason Browning, prin. Fax 855-1307

**Charleston, Kanawha, Pop. 49,755**
Kanawha County SD 27,600/PK-12
200 Elizabeth St 25311 304-348-7770
Ronald Duerring Ed.D., supt. Fax 348-7735
kcs.kana.k12.wv.us
Adams MS 700/6-8
2002 Presidential Dr 25314 304-348-6652
John Moyers, prin. Fax 348-6592
Capital HS 1,300/9-12
1500 Greenbrier St 25311 304-348-6500
Larry Bailey, prin. Fax 348-6509
Carver Career Center Vo/Tech
4799 Midland Dr 25306 304-348-1965
Phil Calvert, prin. Fax 348-1938
Chandler Academy Alt
1900 School St 25387 304-348-6690
Wayman Wilson, prin.
Garnet Career Center Vo/Tech
422 Dickinson St 25301 304-348-6195
Wendy Bailey, prin. Fax 348-6198
Jackson MS 600/6-8
812 Park Ave 25302 304-348-6123
Jessica Austin, prin. Fax 348-1999
Mann MS 500/6-8
4300 MacCorkle Ave SE 25304 304-348-1971
Jon Anderson, prin. Fax 348-6591
Sissonville HS 600/9-12
6100 Sissonville Dr 25312 304-348-1954
Ron Reedy, prin. Fax 348-6565
Sissonville MS 500/5-8
100 Middle School Ln 25312 304-348-1993
Brian Eddy, prin. Fax 348-6594
Washington HS 1,100/9-12
1522 Tennis Club Rd 25314 304-348-7729
George Aulenbacher, prin. Fax 344-4947
Other Schools – See Belle, Cedar Grove, Clendenin, Cross Lanes, Dunbar, East Bank, Elkview, Nitro, Saint Albans, South Charleston

---

Carver Career and Tech Education Center Post-Sec.
4799 Midland Dr 25306 304-348-1965
Charleston Catholic HS 400/6-12
1033 Virginia St E 25301 304-342-8415
Colleen Hoyer, prin. Fax 342-1259
Charleston School of Beauty Culture Post-Sec.
210 Capitol St 25301 304-346-9603
Cross Lanes Christian S 300/K-12
5330 Floradale Dr 25313 304-776-5020
Garnet Career Center Post-Sec.
422 Dickinson St 25301 304-348-6195
Kanawha Vlly Community Technical College Post-Sec.
2001 Union Carbide Dr 25303 304-205-6700
University of Charleston Post-Sec.
2300 MacCorkle Ave SE 25304 304-357-4800
West Virginia Junior College Post-Sec.
1000 Virginia St E 25301 304-345-2820

**Charles Town, Jefferson, Pop. 5,074**
Jefferson County SD 8,700/PK-12
110 Mordington Ave 25414 304-725-9741
Susan Wall, supt. Fax 725-6487
boe.jeff.k12.wv.us
Charles Town MS 700/6-8
193 High St 25414 304-725-7821
Tim Sites, prin. Fax 728-7526
Washington HS 1,100/9-12
300 Washington Patriots Dr 25414 304-885-5110
Judy Marcus, prin. Fax 885-5108
Other Schools – See Harpers Ferry, Shenandoah Junction, Shepherdstown

---

American Public University Post-Sec.
111 W Congress St 25414 877-755-2787

**Charmco, Greenbrier**
Greenbrier County SD
Supt. — See Lewisburg
Greenbrier West HS 400/9-12
PO Box 325 25958 304-438-6191
Amy Robertson, prin. Fax 438-9189

**Clarksburg, Harrison, Pop. 16,197**
Harrison County SD 11,000/PK-12
PO Box 1370 26302 304-624-3325
Dr. Mark Manchin, supt. Fax 624-3361
www.harcoboe.net
Byrd HS 800/9-12
1 Eagle Way 26301 304-326-7200
Steven Gibson, prin. Fax 624-3211
Harrison County Alternative Learning Ctr Alt
1349 Shinnston Pike 26301 304-326-7560
Ed Propst, prin. Fax 624-3245
Irving MS 600/6-8
443 Lee Ave 26301 304-326-7420
Susan Ferrell, prin. Fax 624-3388
Liberty HS 600/9-12
1 Mountaineer Dr 26301 304-326-7470
Pamela Knight, prin. Fax 623-3159
Mountaineer MS 500/6-8
2 Mountaineer Dr 26301 304-326-7620
John Rogers, prin. Fax 326-7632
United Technical Center Vo/Tech
251 Marietta St 26301 304-326-7580
Matthew Call, dir. Fax 622-6138
Other Schools – See Bridgeport, Lost Creek, Lumberport, Shinnston

---

Clarksburg Beauty Academy Post-Sec.
120 S 3rd St 26301 304-624-6475
Emmanuel Christian S 100/PK-12
1318 N 16th St 26301 304-624-6125
Fax 624-5349
Notre Dame HS 200/7-12
127 E Pike St 26301 304-623-1026
Dr. Carroll Morrison, prin. Fax 623-1026

**Clay, Clay, Pop. 483**
Clay County SD 2,000/PK-12
PO Box 120 25043 304-587-4266
Kenneth Tanner, supt. Fax 587-4181
www.claycountyschools.org
Clay County HS 600/9-12
PO Box 729 25043 304-587-4226
Melinda Isaacs, prin. Fax 587-2723
Clay County MS 400/6-8
PO Box 489 25043 304-587-2343
Anita Stephenson, prin. Fax 587-2759

**Clear Fork, Wyoming**
Wyoming County SD
Supt. — See Pineville
Westside HS 600/9-12
HC 65 Box 275 24822 304-682-8965
Robin Hall, prin. Fax 682-6273

**Clendenin, Kanawha, Pop. 1,218**
Kanawha County SD
Supt. — See Charleston
Hoover HS 700/9-12
5856 Elk River Rd N 25045 304-965-3394
Michael Kelley, prin. Fax 965-1871

**Coal City, Raleigh, Pop. 1,761**
Raleigh County SD
Supt. — See Beckley
Independence HS 700/9-12
PO Box 1595 25823 304-683-3228
Johnathan Henry, prin. Fax 683-4393

**Craigsville, Nicholas, Pop. 2,184**
Nicholas County SD
Supt. — See Summersville
Nicholas County Career and Technical Ctr Vo/Tech
215 Milam Addition Rd 26205 304-742-5416
Thomas Bayless, prin. Fax 742-3953

**Crawley, Greenbrier**
Greenbrier County SD
Supt. — See Lewisburg
Western Greenbrier MS 300/6-8
315 Timberwolf Dr 24931 304-392-6446
Christy Bailey, prin. Fax 392-6785

**Cross Lanes, Kanawha, Pop. 9,816**
Kanawha County SD
Supt. — See Charleston
Jackson MS 600/6-8
5445 Big Tyler Rd 25313 304-776-3310
Rhonda Donohoe, prin. Fax 776-3305

**Crum, Wayne, Pop. 179**
Wayne County SD
Supt. — See Wayne
Crum MS 100/6-8
PO Box 9 25669 304-393-3200
Lorinda Newman, prin. Fax 393-4429

**Delbarton, Mingo, Pop. 564**
Mingo County SD
Supt. — See Williamson
Burch MS 100/5-8
275 Bulldog Blvd 25670 304-475-2700
Leah Wireman, prin. Fax 475-5106
Mingo Central HS 800/9-12
1000 King Cole Hwy 25670 304-426-6603
Theresa Jones, prin.
Mingo County Extended Learning Center Adult
165 Bulldog Blvd 25670 304-475-3347
Thomas Hoffman, prin. Fax 475-3797

**Dunbar, Kanawha, Pop. 7,684**
Kanawha County SD
Supt. — See Charleston
Dunbar MS 400/6-8
325 27th St 25064 304-766-0363
Donnell Gilliam, prin. Fax 766-0365
Franklin Career & Technical Center Vo/Tech
500 28th St 25064 304-766-0369
Dr. Paula Potter, prin. Fax 766-0371

**Dunmore, Pocahontas**
Pocahontas County SD
Supt. — See Marlinton
Pocahontas County HS 400/9-12
271 Warrior Way 24934 304-799-6565
Robert Miller, prin. Fax 799-6893

**East Bank, Kanawha, Pop. 953**
Kanawha County SD
Supt. — See Charleston
East Bank MS 400/6-8
PO Box 897 25067 304-595-2311
Michael Wilkinson, prin. Fax 595-4676

**Eleanor, Putnam, Pop. 1,501**
Putnam County SD
Supt. — See Winfield
Putnam Career & Technical Center Vo/Tech
PO Box 640 25070 304-586-3494
Fax 586-4467
Washington MS 300/6-8
PO Box 660 25070 304-586-2875
Valerie Stewart, prin. Fax 586-3037

**Elizabeth, Wirt, Pop. 816**
Wirt County SD 1,000/PK-12
PO Box 189 26143 304-275-4279
Mary Jane Pope-Albin, supt. Fax 275-4581
www.edline.net/pages/wirtboe
Wirt County HS 300/9-12
PO Box 219 26143 304-275-4241
Elizabeth Smith, prin. Fax 275-3271
Wirt County MS 300/5-8
PO Box 699 26143 304-275-3977
Jason Ward, prin. Fax 275-4257

**Elkins, Randolph, Pop. 7,020**
Randolph County SD 4,200/PK-12
40 11th St 26241 304-636-9150
Terry George, supt. Fax 636-9157
boe.rand.k12.wv.us
Elkins HS 900/9-12
100 Kennedy Dr 26241 304-636-9170
David Fincham, prin. Fax 636-9168
Elkins MS 700/6-8
308 Robert E Lee Ave 26241 304-636-9176
Rich Carr, prin. Fax 636-9178
Randolph Co. Alternative Learning Center 50/Alt
1425 S Davis Ave 26241 304-636-9156
Angela Wilson, prin. Fax 636-9157
Randolph County Technical Center Vo/Tech
200 Kennedy Dr 26241 304-636-9195
John Daniels, prin. Fax 636-9169
Other Schools – See Harman, Mill Creek, Pickens

---

Davis & Elkins College Post-Sec.
100 Campus Dr 26241 304-637-1900
Highland Adventist S 50/K-12
1 Old Leadsville Rd 26241 304-636-4274

**Elkview, Kanawha, Pop. 1,216**
Kanawha County SD
Supt. — See Charleston
Elkview MS 700/6-8
5090 Elk River Rd N 25071 304-348-1947
Melissa Lovejoy, prin. Fax 348-6590

---

Elk Valley Christian S 100/PK-12
58 Mount Pleasant Dr 25071 304-965-7063
Jack Suttle, prin. Fax 965-7064

**Ellenboro, Ritchie, Pop. 363**
Ritchie County SD
Supt. — See Harrisville
Ritchie County HS 400/9-12
201 Ritchie County School 26346 304-869-3526
Kelly Waggoner, prin. Fax 869-3031
Ritchie County MS 300/6-8
105 Ritchie County School 26346 304-869-3512
Michael Dotson, prin. Fax 869-3519

**Fairmont, Marion, Pop. 18,276**
Marion County SD 7,900/PK-12
200 Gaston Ave 26554 304-367-2100
Gary Price, supt. Fax 367-2111
www.marionboe.com/
Barnes Learning Center Alt
100 Naomi St 26554 304-367-2127
Travus Oates, prin. Fax 367-2174
East Fairmont HS 700/9-12
1993 Airport Rd 26554 304-367-2140
David Nuzum, prin. Fax 367-2180
East Fairmont MS 400/7-8
221 Mason St 26554 304-367-2123
Jay Michael, prin. Fax 367-2179
Fairmont HS 700/9-12
1 Loop Park Dr 26554 304-367-2150
Tyson Furgason, prin. Fax 366-5988
West Fairmont MS 600/5-8
110 10th St 26554 304-366-5631
Lisa Lister, prin. Fax 366-5636
Marion County Adult & Community Educ. Adult
601 Locust Ave 26554 304-363-7323
Donna Metz, prin. Fax 366-2483
Other Schools – See Fairview, Farmington, Mannington, Monongah

---

Fairmont State University Post-Sec.
1201 Locust Ave 26554 304-367-4892

Pierpont Community & Technical College Post-Sec.
1201 Locust Ave 26554 304-367-4692

**Fairview, Marion, Pop. 404**
Marion County SD
Supt. — See Fairmont
Fairview MS 100/5-8
17 Jesses Run Rd 26570 304-449-1312
Steve Rodriguez, prin. Fax 449-1305

**Farmington, Marion, Pop. 368**
Marion County SD
Supt. — See Fairmont
Marion County Technical Center Vo/Tech
2 N Marion Dr 26571 304-986-3590
Raymond Frazier, prin. Fax 986-3440
North Marion HS 800/9-12
1 N Marion Dr 26571 304-986-3063
Russelle DeVito, prin. Fax 986-3086

**Fayetteville, Fayette, Pop. 2,872**
Fayette County SD 6,400/PK-12
111 Fayette Ave 25840 304-574-1176
Serena Starcher, supt. Fax 574-3643
www.boe.faye.k12.wv.us
Fayetteville HS 500/7-12
515 W Maple Ave 25840 304-574-0560
Bryan Parsons, prin. Fax 574-0118
Other Schools – See Ansted, Hico, Meadow Bridge, Oak Hill, Smithers

**Follansbee, Brooke, Pop. 2,935**
Brooke County SD
Supt. — See Wellsburg
Follansbee MS 500/5-8
1400 Main St 26037 304-527-1942
Stephanie Brown, prin. Fax 527-1954

**Fort Gay, Wayne, Pop. 690**
Wayne County SD
Supt. — See Wayne
Tolsia HS 400/9-12
1 Rebel Dr 25514 304-648-5566
Reba Sanders-Wallace, prin. Fax 648-5447

**Foster, Boone**
Boone County SD
Supt. — See Madison
Boone County Career & Tech Ctr Vo/Tech
3505 Daniel Boone Pkwy # B 25081 304-369-4585
Jeffrey Nelson, prin. Fax 369-3692

---

Boone County Career Center Post-Sec.
3505 Daniel Boone Pkwy # B 25081 304-369-4585
Southern WV Community & Technical Coll. Post-Sec.
3505 Daniel Boone Pkwy # A 25081 304-369-2952

**Franklin, Pendleton, Pop. 713**
Pendleton County SD 1,000/PK-12
PO Box 888 26807 304-358-2207
Doug Lambert, supt. Fax 358-2936
pendletoncountyschools.com/
Pendleton County MSHS 500/7-12
PO Box 40 26807 304-358-2573
Lori Moore, prin. Fax 358-7701

---

Future Generations Graduate School Post-Sec.
400 Road Less Traveled Rd 26807 304-358-2000

**Gerrardstown, Berkeley**
Berkeley County SD
Supt. — See Martinsburg
Mountain Ridge MS 6-8
2771 Gerrardstown Rd 25420 304-229-8833
Dr. Ron Branch, admin. Fax 229-8830

**Gilbert, Mingo, Pop. 447**
Mingo County SD
Supt. — See Williamson
Gilbert MS 200/5-8
100 Lion Dr 25621 304-664-8197
Daniel Dean, prin. Fax 664-8249

**Glen Dale, Marshall, Pop. 1,510**
Marshall County SD
Supt. — See Moundsville
Marshall HS 1,200/9-12
1300 Wheeling Ave 26038 304-843-4444
Rick Jones, prin. Fax 843-4419

**Glen Daniel, Raleigh**
Raleigh County SD
Supt. — See Beckley
Liberty HS 600/9-12
PO Box 265 25844 304-934-5307
Lori Knight, prin. Fax 934-5307
Trap Hill MS 400/6-8
665 Coal River Rd 25844 304-934-5392
Jerry Bawgus, prin. Fax 934-5393

**Glenville, Gilmer, Pop. 1,501**
Gilmer County SD 900/PK-12
201 N Court St 26351 304-462-7386
Gabriel DeVono, supt. Fax 462-5103
www.edline.net/pages/Gilmer_County_SD
Gilmer County JSHS 400/7-12
300 Pine St 26351 304-462-7960
Athanasia Butcher, prin. Fax 462-7059

---

Glenville State College Post-Sec.
200 High St 26351 304-462-7361

**Grafton, Taylor, Pop. 5,091**
Taylor County SD 2,400/PK-12
71 Utt Dr 26354 304-265-2497
Kathleen Green, supt. Fax 265-2508
www.taylorcountyboe.net
Grafton HS 600/9-12
400 Riverside Dr 26354 304-265-3046
Joseph Findley, prin. Fax 265-2156
Taylor County MS 700/5-8
670 Spring Hills Rd 26354 304-265-0722
Matt Keener, prin. Fax 265-4623
Taylor County Vocational Center Vo/Tech
115 Luby St 26354 304-265-1050
Dr. Joseph Findley, prin. Fax 265-1058

**Grantsville, Calhoun, Pop. 561**
Calhoun County SD
Supt. — See Mount Zion
Calhoun Gilmer Career Center Vo/Tech
5260 E Little Kanawha Hwy 26147 304-354-6151
Bryan Sterns, dir. Fax 354-6154

**Hambleton, Tucker, Pop. 231**
Tucker County SD
Supt. — See Parsons
Tucker County HS 300/9-12
116 Mountain Lion Way 26269 304-478-3111
Jay Hamric, prin. Fax 478-3725

**Hamlin, Lincoln, Pop. 1,134**
Lincoln County SD 3,400/PK-12
10 Marland Ave 25523 304-824-3033
Patricia Lucas, supt. Fax 824-7947
boe.linc.k12.wv.us
Lincoln HS 900/9-12
81 Lincoln Panther Way 25523 304-824-6000
Dana Snyder, prin. Fax 824-6063
Other Schools – See Branchland

**Harman, Randolph, Pop. 143**
Randolph County SD
Supt. — See Elkins
Harman S 200/PK-12
PO Box 130 26270 304-227-4114
Tammie Daniels, prin. Fax 227-3610

**Harpers Ferry, Jefferson, Pop. 283**
Jefferson County SD
Supt. — See Charles Town
Harpers Ferry MS 400/6-8
1710 W Washington St 25425 304-535-6357
Eric Vandell, prin. Fax 535-6986

**Harrisville, Ritchie, Pop. 1,865**
Ritchie County SD 1,500/PK-12
134 S Penn Ave 26362 304-643-2991
Edward Toman, supt. Fax 643-2994
www.ritchieschools.com
Other Schools – See Ellenboro

**Hedgesville, Berkeley, Pop. 311**
Berkeley County SD
Supt. — See Martinsburg
Hedgesville HS 1,700/9-12
109 Ridge Rd N 25427 304-754-3354
Ron Lyons, prin. Fax 754-7445
Hedgesville MS 700/6-8
334 School House Dr 25427 304-754-3313
Elizabeth Adams, prin. Fax 754-6613

**Hico, Fayette, Pop. 272**
Fayette County SD
Supt. — See Fayetteville
Midland Trail HS 300/9-12
PO Box 89 25854 304-658-5184
Diane Blume, prin. Fax 658-5185

**Hilltop, Fayette, Pop. 613**

---

Mountainview Christian S 100/PK-12
2 Mountain View Rd 25855 304-465-0502
Rev. Rudell Bloomfield, hdmstr. Fax 465-5484

**Hinton, Summers, Pop. 2,623**
Summers County SD 1,500/PK-12
116 Main St 25951 304-466-6000
Vicki Hinerman, supt. Fax 466-6008
www.edline.net/pages/summerscountyschools
Summers County HS 400/9-12
1 Bobcat Dr 25951 304-466-6040
Kari Vicars, prin. Fax 466-6044
Summers MS 300/5-8
400 Temple St 25951 304-466-6030
M. Susie Hudson, prin. Fax 466-2271

**Hundred, Wetzel, Pop. 296**
Wetzel County SD
Supt. — See New Martinsville
Hundred HS 100/9-12
PO Box 830 26575 304-775-5221
Daniel Gottron, prin. Fax 775-2922

**Huntington, Cabell, Pop. 47,796**
Cabell County SD 12,600/PK-12
2850 5th Ave 25702 304-528-5000
William Smith, supt. Fax 528-5080
www.cabellcountyschools.com
Cabell County Alternative S 50/Alt
2850 5th Ave 25702 304-528-5060
Brenda Scott, prin. Fax 528-5134
Cabell County Career Technology Center Vo/Tech
1035 Norway Ave 25705 304-528-5106
Michael Baumann, prin. Fax 528-5110
Huntington East MS 500/6-8
1 Campbell Dr 25705 304-528-9508
Frank Barnett, prin. Fax 528-5197
Huntington HS 1,600/9-12
1 Highlander Way 25701 304-528-6400
Greg Webb, prin. Fax 528-6422
Huntington MS 600/6-8
925 3rd St 25701 304-528-5180
James Paxton, prin. Fax 528-5215
Other Schools – See Barboursville, Milton, Ona

Wayne County SD
Supt. — See Wayne
Spring Valley HS 1,000/9-12
1 Timberwolf Ln 25704 304-429-1699
Steve Morris, prin. Fax 429-7315
Vinson MS 300/6-8
3851 Piedmont Rd 25704 304-429-1641
Tammy Forbush, prin. Fax 429-6162

---

Cabell Huntington Hospital Post-Sec.
1340 Hal Greer Blvd 25701 304-526-2111
Covenant S 200/K-12
2400 Johnstown Rd 25701 304-781-6741
Shane Artrip, hdmstr. Fax 781-6742
Grace Christian S 200/PK-12
1111 Adams Ave 25704 304-522-8635
Huntington Junior College Post-Sec.
900 5th Ave 25701 304-697-7550
Huntington School of Beauty Culture Post-Sec.
5636 US Route 60 Ste 14 25705 304-736-6289
ITT Technical Institute Post-Sec.
5183 US Route 60 Bldg 1 25705 304-733-8700
Marshall University Post-Sec.
1 John Marshall Dr 25755 304-696-3170
Mountwest Community & Technical College Post-Sec.
1 Mountwest Way 25701 866-676-5533
St. Joseph Central HS 100/9-12
600 13th St 25701 304-525-5096
William Archer, prin. Fax 525-0781
St. Mary's Medical Center Post-Sec.
2900 1st Ave 25702 304-526-1270

**Hurricane, Putnam, Pop. 6,205**
Putnam County SD
Supt. — See Winfield
Hurricane HS 1,100/9-12
3350 Teays Valley Rd 25526 304-562-9851
Richard Campbell, prin. Fax 562-5460
Hurricane MS 900/6-8
518 Midland Trl 25526 304-562-5503
Carl Caldwell, prin. Fax 562-7163

---

Calvary Baptist Academy 200/K-12
3655 Teays Valley Rd 25526 304-757-6768
Milton Thompson, prin. Fax 757-6777

**Institute, Kanawha**

---

West Virginia State University Post-Sec.
PO Box 1000 25112 304-766-3000

**Inwood, Berkeley, Pop. 2,871**
Berkeley County SD
Supt. — See Martinsburg
Musselman HS 1,600/9-12
126 Excellence Way 25428 304-229-1950
Holly Kleppner, prin. Fax 229-1959

**Kenova, Wayne, Pop. 3,199**
Wayne County SD
Supt. — See Wayne
Buffalo MS 300/6-8
298 Buffalo Creek Rd 25530 304-429-6062
Elizabeth Ryder, prin. Fax 429-7245

**Keyser, Mineral, Pop. 5,316**
Mineral County SD 4,100/PK-12
1 Baker Pl 26726 304-788-4200
Shawn Dilly, supt. Fax 788-4204
boe.mine.k12.wv.us/
Keyser HS 700/9-12
1 Tornado Way 26726 304-788-4230
Michael Lewis, prin. Fax 788-4234
Keyser MS 700/5-8
700 Harley O Staggers Sr Dr 26726 304-788-4220
Julie McBee, prin. Fax 788-4225
Mineral County Alternative S 50/Alt
50 Clary St 26726 304-788-4213
Jenni Woy, prin. Fax 788-4623
Mineral County Technical Center Vo/Tech
600 Harley O Staggers Sr Dr 26726 304-788-4240
Joseph Keckley, prin. Fax 788-4243
Other Schools – See Ridgeley

---

Potomac State College of West Virginia U Post-Sec.
101 Fort Ave 26726 304-788-6820

**Kingwood, Preston, Pop. 2,912**
Preston County SD 4,600/PK-12
731 Preston Dr 26537 304-329-0580
Stephen Wotring, supt. Fax 329-0720
www.prestonboe.com
Central Preston MS 300/6-8
500 Knight Dr 26537 304-329-0033
Karen Ovesney, prin. Fax 329-2389
Preston HS 1,400/9-12
400 Knight Dr 26537 304-329-0400
Dr. David Pastrick, prin. Fax 329-3899
Other Schools – See Masontown, Tunnelton

**Le Roy, Jackson**
Jackson County SD
Supt. — See Ripley
Roane-Jackson Tech Ctr Vo/Tech
9450 Spencer Rd 25252 304-372-7335
Ben Cummings, dir. Fax 372-7336

**Lewisburg, Greenbrier, Pop. 3,773**
Greenbrier County SD 5,300/PK-12
202 Chestnut St 24901 304-647-6470
Sallie Dalton, supt. Fax 647-6490
www.greenbriercountyschools.org
Greenbrier East HS 1,100/9-12
1 Spartan Ln 24901 304-647-6464
Jeff Bryant, prin. Fax 645-2698
Other Schools – See Charmco, Crawley, Ronceverte

---

West Virginia Sch./Osteopathic Medicine Post-Sec.
400 N Lee St 24901 304-645-6270

**Lindside, Monroe**
Monroe County SD
Supt. — See Union

Monroe County Technical Center Vo/Tech
RR 1 Box 97 24951 304-753-9971
Tricia King, dir. Fax 753-9792
Monroe HS 500/9-12
RR 1 Box 97-1A 24951 304-753-5182
Lisa Mustain, prin. Fax 753-5184

**Logan, Logan, Pop. 1,749**
Logan County SD 6,300/PK-12
PO Box 477 25601 304-792-2060
Phyllis Doty, supt. Fax 752-3711
lc2.boe.loga.k12.wv.us
Logan HS 800/9-12
1 Wildcat Way 25601 304-752-6606
Kelly Stanley, prin. Fax 752-6614
Logan MS 800/5-8
14 Wildcat Way 25601 304-752-1804
Ernestine Sutherland, prin. Fax 752-0207
Willis Vo-Tech Center Vo/Tech
PO Box 1747 25601 304-752-4687
David Adkins, prin. Fax 752-2943
Other Schools – See Chapmanville, Mallory, Man

**Lost Creek, Harrison, Pop. 482**
Harrison County SD
Supt. — See Clarksburg
South Harrison HS 400/9-12
3073 Hawk Hwy 26385 304-326-7440
Dr. Greg Moore, prin. Fax 745-4292
South Harrison MS 300/6-8
2323 Hawk Hwy 26385 304-326-7460
Scott Hage, prin. Fax 745-5587

**Lumberport, Harrison, Pop. 868**
Harrison County SD
Supt. — See Clarksburg
Lumberport MS 400/6-8
314 Main St 26386 304-326-7540
Lori Scott, prin. Fax 584-4602

**Mc Mechen, Marshall, Pop. 1,914**

---

Bishop Donahue Memorial HS 100/9-12
325 Logan St, 304-233-3850
Thomas Wise, prin. Fax 233-8677

**Madison, Boone, Pop. 3,064**
Boone County SD 4,500/PK-12
69 Avenue B 25130 304-369-3131
John Hudson, supt. Fax 369-0855
www.boonecountyboe.org
Madison MS 600/6-8
404 Riverside Dr W 25130 304-369-4464
Shann Elkins, prin. Fax 369-5800
Scott HS 700/9-12
1 Skyhawk Pl 25130 304-369-3011
Allen Halley, prin. Fax 369-6564
Other Schools – See Foster, Seth, Van

**Mallory, Logan, Pop. 1,628**
Logan County SD
Supt. — See Logan
Man MS 500/5-8
PO Box 390 25634 304-583-8037
Cynthia Caldwell, prin. Fax 583-8253

**Man, Logan, Pop. 759**
Logan County SD
Supt. — See Logan
Man HS 400/9-12
800 E McDonald Ave 25635 304-583-6521
Patricia English, prin. Fax 583-6566

**Mannington, Marion, Pop. 2,054**
Marion County SD
Supt. — See Fairmont
Mannington MS 300/5-8
113 Clarksburg St 26582 304-986-1050
Richard Ott, prin. Fax 986-1747

**Marlinton, Pocahontas, Pop. 1,050**
Pocahontas County SD 1,100/PK-12
926 5th Ave 24954 304-799-4505
Dr. Donald Bechtel, supt. Fax 799-4499
sites.google.com/site/pocahontasboe
Other Schools – See Buckeye, Dunmore

**Martinsburg, Berkeley, Pop. 16,642**
Berkeley County SD 16,900/PK-12
401 S Queen St 25401 304-267-3500
Manny Arvon, supt. Fax 267-3506
berkeleycountyschools.org/
Martinsburg HS 1,800/9-12
701 S Queen St 25401 304-267-3530
Trent Sherman, prin. Fax 267-3536
Martinsburg North MS 600/6-8
250 East Rd, 304-267-3540
Rebekah Eyler, prin. Fax 264-5066
Martinsburg South MS 900/6-8
150 Bulldog Blvd 25401 304-267-3545
Rosa Clark, prin. Fax 264-5062
Rumsey Technical Institute Vo/Tech
3274 Hedgesville Rd, 304-754-7925
Donna VanMetre, dir. Fax 754-7933
Spring Mills HS 9-12
499 Campus Dr, 304-274-5141
Marc Arvon, prin. Fax 274-5144
Spring Mills MS 700/6-8
255 Campus Dr, 304-274-5030
Nancy White, prin. Fax 274-3598
Other Schools – See Bunker Hill, Gerrardstown, Hedgesville, Inwood

---

Blue Ridge Community & Technical College Post-Sec.
13650 Apple Harvest Dr, 304-260-4380
Faith Christian Academy 300/PK-12
138 Greensburg Rd, 304-263-0011
Eric Kerns, admin. Fax 267-0638
International Beauty School Post-Sec.
201 W King St 25401 304-263-4929
Martinsburg College Post-Sec.
341 Aikens Ctr, 304-263-6262
Valley College Post-Sec.
287 Aikens Ctr, 304-263-0979

**Mason, Mason, Pop. 951**
Mason County SD
Supt. — See Point Pleasant
Wahama JSHS 400/7-12
PO Box 348 25260 304-773-5539
John Bond, prin. Fax 773-5216

**Masontown, Preston, Pop. 539**
Preston County SD
Supt. — See Kingwood
West Preston MS 200/6-8
167 S Main St 26542 304-864-5221
Lee Livengood, prin. Fax 864-5298

**Meadow Bridge, Fayette, Pop. 378**
Fayette County SD
Supt. — See Fayetteville
Meadow Bridge JSHS 200/7-12
870 Main St 25976 304-484-7917
Cynthia Hedrick, prin. Fax 484-7921

**Middlebourne, Tyler, Pop. 809**
Tyler County SD 1,400/PK-12
PO Box 25 26149 304-758-2145
Robin Daquilante, supt. Fax 758-4566
www.tylercountypublicschools.com
Other Schools – See Sistersville

**Mill Creek, Randolph, Pop. 718**
Randolph County SD
Supt. — See Elkins
Tygarts Valley MSHS 400/7-12
RR 1 Box 290 26280 304-335-4575
Steve Wamsley, prin. Fax 335-6963

**Milton, Cabell, Pop. 2,401**
Cabell County SD
Supt. — See Huntington
Milton MS 600/6-8
1 Panther Trl 25541 304-743-7308
Joedy Cunningham, prin. Fax 743-7324

**Monongah, Marion, Pop. 1,032**
Marion County SD
Supt. — See Fairmont
Monongah MS 200/5-8
550 Camden Ave 26554 304-367-2164
Steve Malnick, prin. Fax 367-2190

**Montgomery, Fayette, Pop. 1,593**

---

Bridgemont Community & Technical College Post-Sec.
619 2nd Ave 25136 304-734-6600
West Virginia University Inst of Tech. Post-Sec.
405 Fayette Pike 25136 888-554-8324

**Moorefield, Hardy, Pop. 2,511**
Hardy County SD 2,100/PK-12
510 Ashby St 26836 304-530-2348
Barbara Whitecotton, supt. Fax 530-2340
www.hardycountyschools.com/
Moorefield HS 400/9-12
401 N Main St 26836 304-530-6034
Dwight Williams, prin. Fax 530-7569
Moorefield MS 300/6-8
303 Caledonia Heights Rd 26836 304-434-3000
Patrick McGregor, prin. Fax 434-3003
Other Schools – See Baker

---

Eastern WV Community & Technical College Post-Sec.
316 Eastern Dr 26836 304-434-8000

**Morgantown, Monongalia, Pop. 29,068**
Monongalia County SD 10,100/PK-12
13 S High St 26501 304-291-9210
Dr. Frank Devono, supt. Fax 291-3015
boe.mono.k12.wv.us
Alternative Learning Center Alt
500 Green Bag Rd Ste G1 26501 304-291-9210
Kim Greene, prin. Fax 296-1379
Monongalia County Tech Education Center Vo/Tech
1000 Mississippi St 26501 304-291-9240
Nancy Napolillo, prin. Fax 291-9247
Morgantown HS 1,600/9-12
109 Wilson Ave 26501 304-291-9260
Fax 291-9263
Mountaineer MS 500/6-8
991 Price St 26505 304-594-1165
Crystal Nantz, prin. Fax 594-1677
South MS 700/6-8
500 E Parkway Dr 26501 304-291-9340
Sandra Brown, prin. Fax 291-9306
Suncrest MS 500/6-8
360 Baldwin St 26505 304-291-9335
James Napolillo, prin. Fax 284-9362
University HS 1,300/9-12
131 Bakers Ridge Rd 26508 304-291-9270
Shari Burgess, prin. Fax 291-9248
Westwood MS 400/6-8
670 River Rd 26501 304-291-9300
Leonard Haney, prin. Fax 284-9368
Adult Basic Education Adult
1000 Mississippi St 26501 304-291-9243
Michael Johnston, prin. Fax 291-9247
Other Schools – See Blacksville

---

Monongalia County Tech Education Center Post-Sec.
1000 Mississippi St 26501 304-291-9240
Morgantown Beauty College Post-Sec.
276 Walnut St 26505 304-292-8475
Trinity Christian S 300/PK-12
200 Trinity Way 26505 304-291-4659
Ken Howard, supt. Fax 291-4660
West Virginia Junior College Post-Sec.
148 Willey St 26505 304-296-8282
West Virginia University Post-Sec.
PO Box 6201 26506 304-293-0111
West Virginia University Hospital Post-Sec.
PO Box 8150 26506 304-598-4000

**Moundsville, Marshall, Pop. 9,248**
Marshall County SD 4,600/PK-12
PO Box 578 26041 304-843-4400
Michael Hince, supt. Fax 843-4409
boe.mars.k12.wv.us
Moundsville MS 500/6-8
223 Tomlinson Ave 26041 304-843-4440
Sandy McAllister, prin. Fax 843-4446
Other Schools – See Cameron, Glen Dale, Wheeling

**Mount Gay Shamrock, Logan, Pop. 1,768**

---

Southern WV Community & Technical Coll. Post-Sec.
2900 Dempsey Branch Rd 25637 304-792-7098

**Mount Hope, Fayette, Pop. 1,370**

---

Appalachian Bible College Post-Sec.
161 College Dr 25880 304-877-6428

**Mount Zion, Calhoun**
Calhoun County SD 1,100/PK-12
540 Alan B Mollohan Dr 26151 304-354-7011
Timothy Woodward, supt. Fax 354-7420
www.edline.net/pages/Calhoun_CSD
Calhoun County MSHS 600/5-12
50 Underwood Cir 26151 304-354-6148
Fax 354-7382
Other Schools – See Grantsville

**Mullens, Wyoming, Pop. 1,540**
Wyoming County SD
Supt. — See Pineville
Mullens MS 200/5-8
801 Moran Ave 25882 304-294-5757
Terri Lea Smith, prin. Fax 294-5762

**New Cumberland, Hancock, Pop. 1,085**
Hancock County SD 4,300/PK-12
PO Box 1300 26047 304-564-3411
Suzan Smith, supt. Fax 564-3990
www.hancockschools.org
Oak Glen HS 600/9-12
195 Golden Bear Dr 26047 304-564-3500
David Smith, prin. Fax 387-2079
Oak Glen MS 600/5-8
39 Golden Bear Dr 26047 304-387-2363
Virginia Greene, prin. Fax 387-4624
Rockefeller Career Center Vo/Tech
80 Rockefeller Cir 26047 304-564-3337
Martin Hudek, dir. Fax 564-4058
Other Schools – See Weirton

**New Martinsville, Wetzel, Pop. 5,337**
Wetzel County SD 2,800/PK-12
333 Foundry St 26155 304-455-2441
Dennis Albright, supt. Fax 455-3446
www.wetzelcountyschools.com
Magnolia HS 400/9-12
601 Maple Ave 26155 304-455-1990
Kathi Schmalz, prin. Fax 455-5536
Other Schools – See Hundred, Paden City, Pine Grove

**New Richmond, Wyoming, Pop. 235**
Wyoming County SD
Supt. — See Pineville
Wyoming County East HS 500/9-12
PO Box 390 24867 304-294-5200
Barry Smith, prin. Fax 294-5400

**Nitro, Kanawha, Pop. 7,083**
Kanawha County SD
Supt. — See Charleston
Nitro HS 800/9-12
1300 Park Ave 25143 304-755-4321
Jason Redman, prin. Fax 755-4345

**Nutter Fort Stonewood, Harrison, Pop. 1,562**

---

West Virginia Business College Post-Sec.
116 Pennsylvania Ave 26301 304-624-7695

**Oak Hill, Fayette, Pop. 7,618**
Fayette County SD
Supt. — See Fayetteville
Collins MS 800/5-8
601 Jones Ave 25901 304-469-3711
Robert Keaton, prin. Fax 465-1352
Fayette Institute of Technology Vo/Tech
300 W Oyler Ave 25901 304-469-2911
Barry Crist, prin. Fax 469-6963
Oak Hill HS 900/9-12
350 W Oyler Ave 25901 304-469-3551
Tim Payton, prin. Fax 465-1769

**Oceana, Wyoming, Pop. 1,373**
Wyoming County SD
Supt. — See Pineville
Oceana MS 300/5-8
HC 65 Box 403 24870 304-682-6296
Shanda Lester, prin. Fax 682-6330

**Omar, Logan, Pop. 551**

---

Beth Haven Christian S 100/PK-12
PO Box 620 25638 304-946-4447

**Ona, Cabell**
Cabell County SD
Supt. — See Huntington
Cabell Midland HS 1,900/9-12
2300 US Route 60 25545 304-743-7400
Lloyd McGuffin, prin. Fax 743-7577

**Paden City, Wetzel, Pop. 2,615**
Wetzel County SD
Supt. — See New Martinsville
Paden City HS 200/7-12
201 N 4th Ave 26159 304-337-2266
Jason Salva, prin. Fax 337-2290

**Parkersburg, Wood, Pop. 30,848**
Wood County SD 13,400/PK-12
1210 13th St 26101 304-420-9663
John Flint, supt. Fax 420-9513
www.edline.net/pages/WCS
Blennerhassett MS 600/6-8
444 Jewell Rd 26101 304-863-3356
Clint Spencer, prin. Fax 863-3357
Caperton Center for Applied Tech Vo/Tech
300 Campus Dr 26104 304-424-8365
Pier Bocchini, coord. Fax 424-8366
Edison MS 600/6-8
1201 Hillcrest St 26101 304-420-9525
Jean Mewshaw, prin. Fax 420-9527
Hamilton MS 600/6-8
3501 Cadillac Dr 26104 304-420-9547
Kevin Campbell, prin. Fax 420-9567
Parkersburg HS 1,800/9-12
2101 Dudley Ave 26101 304-420-9595
Pam Goots, prin. Fax 420-9604
Parkersburg South HS 1,600/9-12
1511 Blizzard Dr 26101 304-420-9610
Tim McCartney, prin. Fax 420-9607
Van Devender MS 400/6-8
918 31st St 26104 304-420-9645
Darlene Murphy, prin. Fax 420-9647
Wood County Technical Center Vo/Tech
1515 Blizzard Dr 26101 304-420-9501
Doug Kiger, prin. Fax 485-1048
Other Schools – See Vienna, Williamstown

---

American National University Post-Sec.
110 Park Shopping Center Dr 26101 304-699-3005
Camden Clark Memorial Hospital Post-Sec.
800 Garfield Ave 26101 304-424-2204
Mountain State College Post-Sec.
1508 Spring St 26101 304-485-5487
Parkersburg Catholic HS 200/7-12
3201 Fairview Ave 26104 304-485-6341
Karen Robinson, prin. Fax 485-4697
West Virginia University at Parkersburg Post-Sec.
300 Campus Dr 26104 304-424-8000

**Parsons, Tucker, Pop. 1,472**
Tucker County SD 1,100/PK-12
100 Education Ln 26287 304-478-2771
Eddie Campbell Ed.D., supt. Fax 478-3422
www.tuckercountyschools.com
Other Schools – See Hambleton

**Paw Paw, Morgan, Pop. 498**
Morgan County SD
Supt. — See Berkeley Springs
Paw Paw JSHS 100/7-12
60 Pirate Cir 25434 304-947-7425
Melinda Kasekamp, prin. Fax 947-5913

**Petersburg, Grant, Pop. 2,438**
Grant County SD 1,800/PK-12
204 Jefferson Ave 26847 304-257-1011
Dr. DeEdra Bolton, supt. Fax 257-2453
grantcountyschools.org
Petersburg JSHS 700/7-12
207 Viking Dr 26847 304-257-1444
Randolph West, prin. Fax 257-5243
South Branch Career & Technical Center Vo/Tech
401 Pierpont St 26847 304-257-1331
Tracy Chenoweth, dir. Fax 257-2270

**Peterstown, Monroe, Pop. 646**
Monroe County SD
Supt. — See Union
Peterstown MS 300/5-8
36 College Dr 24963 304-753-4322
Angie Terry, prin. Fax 753-5376

**Philippi, Barbour, Pop. 2,882**
Barbour County SD 2,400/PK-12
45 School St 26416 304-457-3030
Dr. F. Joseph Super, supt. Fax 457-3559
www.wvschools.com/barbourcountyschools/
Barbour County Vocational Center Vo/Tech
25 Horseshoe Dr 26416 304-457-4807
Rebecca Nesbitt, dir. Fax 457-3009
Barbour HS 700/9-12
99 Horseshoe Dr 26416 304-457-1360
Mark Lamb, prin. Fax 457-2658
Philippi MS 300/6-8
611 Cherry Hill Rd 26416 304-457-2999
David Neff, prin. Fax 457-2561
Other Schools – See Belington

---

Alderson-Broaddus University Post-Sec.
101 College Hill Dr 26416 304-457-1700

**Pickens, Randolph, Pop. 66**
Randolph County SD
Supt. — See Elkins
Pickens S 50/K-12
PO Box 146 26230 304-924-5525
Christine Long, prin. Fax 924-6460

**Pine Grove, Wetzel, Pop. 551**
Wetzel County SD
Supt. — See New Martinsville
Valley HS 200/9-12
44 Lumberjack Ln 26419 304-889-3151
Jessica Stine, prin. Fax 889-2534

**Pineville, Wyoming, Pop. 659**
Wyoming County SD 4,100/PK-12
PO Box 69 24874 304-732-6262
Frank Blackwell, supt. Fax 732-7226
boe.wyom.k12.wv.us/
Pineville MS 300/5-8
PO Box 470 24874 304-732-6442
Terry Shumate, prin. Fax 732-6737
Wyoming County Career & Technical Center Vo/Tech
1207 Bearhole Rd 24874 304-732-8050
Sheila D. Mann, dir. Fax 732-8332
Other Schools – See Clear Fork, Mullens, New Richmond, Oceana

**Poca, Putnam, Pop. 970**
Putnam County SD
Supt. — See Winfield
Poca HS 500/9-12
97 School Rd 25159 304-755-5001
Victor Donalson, prin. Fax 755-5009
Poca MS 300/6-8
2884 Charleston Rd 25159 304-755-7343
Deborah Shrewsbury, prin. Fax 755-8930

**Point Pleasant, Mason, Pop. 4,266**
Mason County SD 4,300/PK-12
1200 Main St 25550 304-675-4540
Suzanne Dickens, supt. Fax 675-7226
www.edline.net/pages/mcboewv
Mason County Career Center Vo/Tech
281 Scenic Dr 25550 304-675-3039
Ruth Caplinger, dir. Fax 675-3413
Point Pleasant MSHS 1,200/7-12
280 Scenic Dr 25550 304-675-1350
William Cottrill, prin. Fax 675-7480
Other Schools – See Ashton, Mason

**Princeton, Mercer, Pop. 6,324**
Mercer County SD 9,200/PK-12
1403 Honaker Ave 24740 304-487-1551
Deborah Akers Ed.D., supt. Fax 425-5844
boe.merc.k12.wv.us
Mercer County Technical Education Ctr Vo/Tech
1397 Stafford Dr, 304-425-9551
Linda Cox, dir. Fax 425-0833
Pikeview HS 700/9-12
3566 Eads Mill Rd, 304-384-7586
Mark Godfrey, prin. Fax 384-7901
Pikeview MS 600/6-8
3550 Eads Mill Rd, 304-384-3600
J. Bryan Staten, prin. Fax 384-3605
Princeton HS 1,100/9-12
1321 Stafford Dr 24740 304-425-8101
Lori Comer, prin. Fax 425-2823
Princeton MS 600/6-8
300 N Johnston St 24740 304-425-7517
David Lee, prin. Fax 487-2250
Other Schools – See Bluefield, Rock

---

American National University Post-Sec.
421 Hilltop Dr, 304-431-1600
Mercer Christian Academy 200/PK-12
314 Oakvale Rd Ste A 24740 304-425-5671
Valley College Post-Sec.
616 Harrison St 24740 304-425-2323

**Prosperity, Raleigh, Pop. 1,474**

---

Greater Beckley Christian S 200/PK-12
PO Box 670 25909 304-255-1571
Dr. James Fritz, admin. Fax 582-0341

**Ravenswood, Jackson, Pop. 3,825**
Jackson County SD
Supt. — See Ripley
Ravenswood HS 500/9-12
100 Plaza Dr 26164 304-273-9301
Jaquetta Hendricks, prin. Fax 273-9556
Ravenswood MS 300/6-8
409 Sycamore St 26164 304-273-5480
Gary Higginbotham, prin. Fax 273-5746

**Richwood, Nicholas, Pop. 2,006**
Nicholas County SD
Supt. — See Summersville
Richwood HS 400/9-12
1 Valley Ave 26261 304-846-2591
James Weber, prin. Fax 846-2684
Richwood MS 300/6-8
2 Valley Ave 26261 304-846-2638
Gene Collins, prin. Fax 846-9632

**Ridgeley, Mineral, Pop. 658**
Mineral County SD
Supt. — See Keyser
Frankfort HS 500/9-12
393 Falcon Way 26753 304-726-4767
Joseph Riley, prin. Fax 726-8597
Frankfort MS 600/5-8
356 Golden Rd 26753 304-726-4339
Patricia Twigg, prin. Fax 726-4626

**Ripley, Jackson, Pop. 3,223**
Jackson County SD 5,000/PK-12
PO Box 770 25271 304-372-7300
Blaine Hess, supt. Fax 372-7312
jackson.wv.schoolwebpages.com
Ripley HS 1,000/9-12
2 School St 25271 304-372-7355
William Hosaflook, prin. Fax 372-7334
Ripley MS 700/6-8
1 W School St 25271 304-372-7350
Tim Brown, prin. Fax 372-7332
Other Schools – See Le Roy, Ravenswood

**Rock, Mercer**
Mercer County SD
Supt. — See Princeton

Montcalm HS 300/7-12
5366 Simmons River Rd 24747 304-589-3719
Craig Havens, prin. Fax 589-7140

**Romney, Hampshire, Pop. 1,832**
Hampshire County SD 3,600/PK-12
111 School St 26757 304-822-3528
Tilden Hackworth, supt. Fax 822-5382
boe.hamp.k12.wv.us/
Hampshire County HS Career Training Ctr Vo/Tech
HC 63 Box 1980 26757 304-822-5016
Tim Scalletta, admin. Fax 822-3220
Hampshire HS 1,100/9-12
157 Trojan Way 26757 304-822-5016
Camella Hardinger, prin. Fax 822-5760
Romney MS 400/6-8
296 Calvert Dr 26757 304-822-5014
John Watson, prin. Fax 822-5744
Other Schools – See Capon Bridge

---

West Virginia Schools/Deaf and Blind Post-Sec.
26757

**Ronceverte, Greenbrier, Pop. 1,742**
Greenbrier County SD
Supt. — See Lewisburg
Eastern Greenbrier MS 900/6-8
RR 1 Box 150 24970 304-647-6498
Preston Modlin, prin. Fax 647-3087

**Saint Albans, Kanawha, Pop. 10,870**
Kanawha County SD
Supt. — See Charleston
Hayes MS 500/6-8
830 Strawberry Rd 25177 304-722-0222
Scott Monty, prin. Fax 722-0247
McKinley MS 400/6-8
3000 Kanawha Ter 25177 304-722-0218
Amy Scott, prin. Fax 722-0246
Saint Albans HS 1,100/9-12
2100 Kanawha Ter 25177 304-722-0212
Jeff Kelley, prin. Fax 722-0211

---

Mountaineer Beauty College Post-Sec.
PO Box 547 25177 304-727-9999

**Saint Marys, Pleasants, Pop. 1,851**
Pleasants County SD 1,300/PK-12
202 Fairview Ave 26170 304-684-2215
George Wells, supt. Fax 684-3569
www.edline.net/pages/pleasantscountyschools
Mid-Ohio Valley Technical Institute Vo/Tech
2134 N Pleasants Hwy 26170 304-684-2464
Ryan Haught, prin. Fax 684-2544
Saint Marys HS 400/9-12
2330 N Pleasants Hwy 26170 304-684-2421
Jayne Tebay, prin. Fax 684-3859
Other Schools – See Belmont

**Salem, Harrison, Pop. 1,554**

---

Salem International University Post-Sec.
PO Box 500 26426 888-235-5024

**Scott Depot, Putnam**

---

Teays Valley Christian S 400/K-12
6562 Teays Valley Rd 25560 304-757-9550
Jack Davis, supt. Fax 757-2560

**Seth, Boone**
Boone County SD
Supt. — See Madison
Sherman HS 400/9-12
PO Box AB 25181 304-837-3301
Todd Barnette, prin. Fax 837-7529
Sherman JHS 200/7-8
PO Box AA 25181 304-837-3694
Matthew Riggs, prin. Fax 837-7603

**Shady Spring, Raleigh, Pop. 2,968**
Raleigh County SD
Supt. — See Beckley
Shady Spring HS 800/9-12
PO Box 2001 25918 304-256-4647
Deanna Massey, prin. Fax 256-4711
Shady Spring MS 700/6-8
500 Flat Top Rd 25918 304-256-4570
Matthew Bell, prin. Fax 256-4612

**Shenandoah Junction, Jefferson, Pop. 673**
Jefferson County SD
Supt. — See Charles Town
Jefferson HS 1,300/9-12
4141 Flowing Springs Rd 25442 304-725-8491
Kenneth Garvey, prin. Fax 728-6590
Wildwood MS 600/6-8
1209 Shenandoah Junction Rd 25442 304-728-4518
Patricia Brockway, prin. Fax 728-9521

**Shepherdstown, Jefferson, Pop. 1,690**
Jefferson County SD
Supt. — See Charles Town
Shepherdstown MS 300/6-8
54 Minden St 25443 304-876-6120
William Kerlina, prin. Fax 876-6428

---

Shepherd University Post-Sec.
PO Box 5000 25443 304-876-5000

**Shinnston, Harrison, Pop. 2,173**
Harrison County SD
Supt. — See Clarksburg
Lincoln HS 600/9-12
100 Jerry Toth Dr 26431 304-326-7400
James Lopez, prin. Fax 592-3415

**Sistersville, Tyler, Pop. 1,391**
Tyler County SD
Supt. — See Middlebourne

Tyler Consolidated HS 400/9-12
1993 Silver Knight Dr 26175 304-758-9000
Kent Yoho, prin. Fax 758-9006
Tyler Consolidated MS 300/6-8
1993 Silver Knight Dr 26175 304-758-9000
Suzette Miller, prin. Fax 758-9006

**Smithers, Fayette, Pop. 800**
Fayette County SD
Supt. — See Fayetteville
Valley MSHS 500/6-12
PO Box 459 25186 304-442-8284
Lee Loy, prin. Fax 442-5865

**Sophia, Raleigh, Pop. 1,330**
Raleigh County SD
Supt. — See Beckley
Independence MS 500/6-8
PO Box 1171 25921 304-683-4542
Teresa Lester, prin. Fax 683-4552

**South Charleston, Kanawha, Pop. 13,050**
Kanawha County SD
Supt. — See Charleston
South Charleston HS 1,000/9-12
1 Eagle Way 25309 304-766-0352
Michael Arbogast, prin. Fax 768-4663
South Charleston MS 400/6-8
400 3rd Ave 25303 304-348-1918
Henry Graves, prin. Fax 744-4869

**Spencer, Roane, Pop. 2,289**
Roane County SD 2,500/PK-12
PO Box 609 25276 304-927-6400
Jerry Garner, supt. Fax 927-6402
www.roanecountyschools.com/
Roane County HS 700/9-12
1 Raider Way 25276 304-927-6420
Mitchell Nida, prin. Fax 927-6404
Spencer MS 400/5-8
102 Chapman Ave 25276 304-927-6415
Jacqueline Durst, prin. Fax 927-6416

**Summersville, Nicholas, Pop. 3,550**
Nicholas County SD 4,000/PK-12
400 Old Main Dr 26651 304-872-3611
Keith Butcher, supt. Fax 872-4626
boe.nich.k12.wv.us
Nicholas County HS 800/9-12
30 Grizzley Ln 26651 304-872-2141
Kendra Rapp, prin. Fax 872-3026
Summersville MS 600/6-8
40 Grizzley Ln 26651 304-872-5092
Kristina Frame, prin. Fax 872-6314
Other Schools – See Craigsville, Richwood

---

New Life Christian Academy 100/PK-12
899 Broad St 26651 304-872-1148

**Sutton, Braxton, Pop. 987**
Braxton County SD 2,000/PK-12
98 Carter Braxton Dr 26601 304-765-7101
David Dilly, supt. Fax 765-7148
boe.brax.k12.wv.us/
Braxton County HS 600/9-12
200 Jerry Burton Dr 26601 304-765-7331
Tony Minney, prin. Fax 765-7976
Braxton County MS 300/7-8
100 Carter Braxton Dr 26601 304-765-2644
Denver Drake, prin. Fax 765-2696

**Tunnelton, Preston, Pop. 293**
Preston County SD
Supt. — See Kingwood
South Preston MS 200/6-8
48 Middle School Dr 26444 304-568-2331
Jim Hoit, prin. Fax 568-2759

**Union, Monroe, Pop. 551**
Monroe County SD 1,900/PK-12
PO Box 330 24983 304-772-3094
Joetta Basile, supt. Fax 772-5020
boe.monr.k12.wv.us
Other Schools – See Lindside, Peterstown

**Upperglade, Webster**
Webster County SD
Supt. — See Webster Springs
Webster County HS 500/7-12
1 Highlander Dr 26266 304-226-5772
Stacey Cutlip, prin. Fax 226-5792

**Van, Boone, Pop. 209**
Boone County SD
Supt. — See Madison
Van JSHS 300/6-12
PO Box 100 25206 304-245-8237
Garth Mock, prin. Fax 245-8695

---

Christian Faith Academy 50/K-12
PO Box 210 25206 304-245-5711
Melanie Harvey, prin. Fax 823-0573

**Vienna, Wood, Pop. 10,628**
Wood County SD
Supt. — See Parkersburg
Jackson MS 600/6-8
1601 34th St 26105 304-420-9551
Richard Summers, prin. Fax 295-9954

---

Ohio Valley University Post-Sec.
1 Campus View Dr 26105 304-865-6000

**Wayne, Wayne, Pop. 1,402**
Wayne County SD 7,100/PK-12
212 N Court St 25570 304-272-5116
Sandra Pertee, supt. Fax 272-6500
boe.wayn.k12.wv.us
Wayne HS 600/9-12
100 Pioneer Rd 25570 304-272-5639
Sara Stapleton, prin. Fax 272-6439
Wayne MS 600/6-8
200 Pioneer Rd 25570 304-272-3227
Beth Webb, prin. Fax 272-5811
Other Schools – See Ceredo, Crum, Fort Gay, Huntington, Kenova

**Webster Springs, Webster, Pop. 772**
Webster County SD 1,500/PK-12
315 S Main St 26288 304-847-5638
Dr. Martha Dean, supt. Fax 847-2538
boe.webs.k12.wv.us/
Other Schools – See Upperglade

**Weirton, Hancock, Pop. 19,434**
Hancock County SD
Supt. — See New Cumberland
Weir HS 600/9-12
100 Red Rider Rd 26062 304-748-7600
Dan Enich, prin. Fax 748-7602
Weir MS 700/5-8
125 Sinclair Ave 26062 304-748-6080
Sara Parsons, prin. Fax 748-0847

---

Madonna HS 200/9-12
150 Michael Way 26062 304-723-0545
Jamie Lesho, prin. Fax 723-0564
West Virginia Northern Community College Post-Sec.
150 Park Ave 26062 304-723-2210

**Welch, McDowell, Pop. 2,358**
McDowell County SD 3,500/PK-12
30 Central Ave 24801 304-436-8441
Nelson Spencer, supt. Fax 436-4008
boe.mcdo.k12.wv.us
McDowell County Vocational Tech Ctr Vo/Tech
PO Box V 24801 304-436-3488
Dennis Jarvis, prin. Fax 436-8063
Mount View MSHS 400/6-12
950 Mount View Rd 24801 304-436-2939
Debra Hall, prin. Fax 436-4714
Other Schools – See Avondale, Bradshaw

**Wellsburg, Brooke, Pop. 2,772**
Brooke County SD 3,200/PK-12
1201 Pleasant Ave 26070 304-737-3481
Toni Shute, supt. Fax 737-3480
www.edline.net/pages/brookecountyschools
Brooke County Alternative Learning Ctr Alt
29 Bruin Dr 26070 304-527-1410
Melissa Figlioli, admin. Fax 527-3604
Brooke HS 1,000/9-12
29 Bruin Dr 26070 304-527-1410
Tim Pannett, prin. Fax 527-3604
Wellsburg MS 500/5-8
1447 Main St 26070 304-737-2922
Jennifer Sisinni, prin. Fax 737-2976
Other Schools – See Follansbee

**West Liberty, Ohio, Pop. 1,514**

---

West Liberty University Post-Sec.
208 University Dr 26074 304-336-5000

**Weston, Lewis, Pop. 4,051**
Lewis County SD 2,600/PK-12
239 Court Ave 26452 304-269-8300
Dr. Joseph Mace, supt. Fax 269-8305
www.edline.net/pages/Lewis_County_School_District
Bland MS 800/5-8
358 Court Ave 26452 304-269-8325
Julie Smith, prin. Fax 269-8310
Lewis County HS 800/9-12
205 Minuteman Dr 26452 304-269-8315
Derek Lambert, prin. Fax 269-8319

**West Union, Doddridge, Pop. 823**
Doddridge County SD 1,200/PK-12
103 Sistersville Pike 26456 304-873-2300
Rick Coffman, supt. Fax 873-2210
boe.dodd.k12.wv.us
Doddridge County HS 400/9-12
79 Bulldog Dr 26456 304-873-2521
Dr. Gregory Kuhns, prin. Fax 873-1873
Doddridge County MS 300/5-8
65 Doddridge County School 26456 304-873-2332
Dr. Deborah Kuhns, prin. Fax 873-2541

**Wheeling, Ohio, Pop. 27,794**
Marshall County SD
Supt. — See Moundsville
Sherrard MS 400/6-8
1000 Fairmont Pike 26003 304-233-3331
Cassie Porter, prin. Fax 233-6418

Ohio County SD 5,400/PK-12
2203 National Rd 26003 304-243-0300
Dr. Dianna Vargo, supt. Fax 243-0328
wphs.ohio.k12.wv.us/ocbe/
Bridge Street MS 300/6-8
19 Junior Ave 26003 304-243-0381
Raquel Welch-McLeod, prin. Fax 243-0385
Triadelphia MS 400/6-8
1636 National Rd 26003 304-243-0387
Ann Coleman, prin. Fax 243-0392
Wheeling MS 200/6-8
3500 Chapline St 26003 304-243-0425
Richard McCardle, prin. Fax 243-0426
Wheeling Park HS 1,700/9-12
1976 Park View Rd 26003 304-243-0400
Amy Minch, prin. Fax 243-0449

---

Central Catholic HS 200/9-12
75 14th St 26003 304-233-1660
Rebecca Sancomb, prin. Fax 233-3187
Linsly S 500/5-12
60 Knox Ln 26003 304-233-3260
Justin Zimmerman, hdmstr. Fax 232-1975
Ohio Valley Medical Center Post-Sec.
2000 Eoff St 26003 304-234-8294
Scott College of Cosmetology Post-Sec.
1502 Market St 26003 304-232-7798
West Virginia Business College Post-Sec.
1052 Main St 26003 304-232-0361
West Virginia Northern Community College Post-Sec.
1704 Market St 26003 304-233-5900
Wheeling Hospital Post-Sec.
1 Medical Park 26003 304-243-3000
Wheeling Jesuit University Post-Sec.
316 Washington Ave 26003 304-243-2000

**Williamson, Mingo, Pop. 3,116**
Mingo County SD 3,300/PK-12
RR 2 Box 310 25661 304-235-3333
Randy Keathley, supt. Fax 235-3410
mingoboe.us/
Tug Valley HS 400/9-12
555 Panther Ave 25661 304-235-2266
Johnny Branch, prin. Fax 235-2636
Other Schools – See Delbarton, Gilbert

---

Ambassador Christian Academy 100/PK-12
701 Alderson St 25661 304-236-3501
Matthew Gilman, admin. Fax 236-3503
Nolan Christian Academy 50/K-12
30 Nolan St 25661 304-235-3914
Earl White, admin. Fax 235-2919
Southern WV Community & Technical Coll. Post-Sec.
1601 Armory Dr 25661 304-235-6046

**Williamstown, Wood, Pop. 2,880**
Wood County SD
Supt. — See Parkersburg
Williamstown HS 600/7-12
219 W 5th St 26187 304-375-6151
Pat Peters, prin. Fax 375-6194

---

Wood County Christian S 300/PK-12
113 W 9th St 26187 304-375-2000
Robert Smith, prin. Fax 375-2000

**Winfield, Putnam, Pop. 2,257**
Putnam County SD 9,800/PK-12
77 Courthouse Dr 25213 304-586-0500
Harold Hatfield, supt. Fax 586-0553
www.putnamschools.com
Winfield HS 800/9-12
3022 Winfield Rd 25213 304-586-3279
Bruce McGrew, prin. Fax 586-3601
Winfield MS 600/6-8
3280 Winfield Rd 25213 304-586-3072
Gary Cook, prin. Fax 586-0920
Other Schools – See Buffalo, Eleanor, Hurricane, Poca

# WISCONSIN

## WISCONSIN DEPARTMENT PUBLIC INSTRUCTION
**PO Box 7841, Madison 53707-7841**
**Telephone 608-266-3390**
**Fax 608-267-1052**
**Website dpi.wi.gov**

Superintendent of Public Instruction — Tony Evers PhD

## COOPERATIVE EDUCATIONAL SERVICE AGENCIES (CESA)

CESA 1
Jim Rickabaugh, admin. — 262-787-9500
N25W23131 Paul Rd Ste 100 — Fax 787-9501
Pewaukee 53072
www.cesa1.k12.wi.us

CESA 2
Gary Albrecht, admin. — 262-473-1473
1221 Innovation Dr — Fax 472-2269
Whitewater 53190
www.cesa2.org

CESA 3
Joe Price, admin., 1300 Industrial Dr — 608-822-3276
Fennimore 53809 — Fax 822-3860
www.cesa3.k12.wi.us

CESA 4
Guy Leavitt, admin. — 800-514-3075
923 Garland St E — Fax 786-4801
West Salem 54669
www.cesa4.k12.wi.us

CESA 5
Jeremy Biehl, admin. — 608-742-8811
626 E Slifer St, Portage 53901 — Fax 742-2384
www.cesa5.org/

CESA 6
Dr. Joan Wade, admin. — 920-233-2372
2935 Universal Ct, Oshkosh 54904 — Fax 236-0580
www.cesa6.org

CESA 7
Jeffery Dickert, admin. — 920-492-5960
595 Baeten Rd, Green Bay 54304 — Fax 492-5965
www.cesa7.k12.wi.us

CESA 8
Donald Viegut, admin. — 920-855-2114
PO Box 320, Gillett 54124 — Fax 855-2299
www.cesa8.k12.wi.us

CESA 9
Dr. Karen Wendorf-Heldt, admin. — 715-453-2141
PO Box 449, Tomahawk 54487 — Fax 453-7519
www.cesa9.org

CESA 10
Mike Haynes, admin. — 715-723-0341
725 W Park Ave — Fax 720-2070
Chippewa Falls 54729
www.cesa10.k12.wi.us

CESA 11
Jerry Walters, admin. — 715-986-2020
225 Ostermann Dr — Fax 986-2040
Turtle Lake 54889
www.cesa11.k12.wi.us

CESA 12
Kenneth Kasinski, admin. — 715-682-2363
618 Beaser Ave, Ashland 54806 — Fax 682-7244
www.cesa12.org

## PUBLIC, PRIVATE AND CATHOLIC SECONDARY SCHOOLS

**Abbotsford, Clark, Pop. 2,301**
Abbotsford SD — 700/PK-12
PO Box A 54405 — 715-223-6715
Reed Welsh, supt. — Fax 223-4239
www.abbotsford.k12.wi.us
Abbotsford MSHS — 300/6-12
PO Box 70 54405 — 715-223-2386
Ryan Bargender, prin. — Fax 223-4239
Falcon Enterprise Alternative HS — Alt
PO Box A 54405 — 715-223-0118
Ann Kleiber, prin. — Fax 223-0119

**Adams, Adams, Pop. 1,940**
Adams-Friendship Area SD
Supt. — See Friendship
Adams-Friendship HS — 500/9-12
1109 E North St 53910 — 608-339-3921
Tanya Kotlowski, prin. — Fax 339-2569
Adams-Friendship MS — 400/6-8
420 N Main St 53910 — 608-339-4064
Jeffrey Krull, prin. — Fax 339-2434

**Albany, Green, Pop. 1,005**
Albany SD — 400/PK-12
400 5th St 53502 — 608-862-3225
Stephen Guenther, supt. — Fax 862-3230
www.albany.k12.wi.us
Albany Community MS — 100/5-8
400 5th St 53502 — 608-862-3135
Connie Gregerson, prin. — Fax 862-3230
Albany HS — 100/9-12
400 5th St 53502 — 608-862-3135
Connie Gregerson, prin. — Fax 862-3230

**Algoma, Kewaunee, Pop. 3,136**
Algoma SD — 600/PK-12
1715 Division St 54201 — 920-487-7001
Nicholas Cochart, supt. — Fax 487-7016
www.algomaschools.org
Algoma MSHS — 300/7-12
1715 Division St 54201 — 920-487-7001
Nicholas Cochart, prin. — Fax 487-7005

**Alma, Buffalo, Pop. 776**
Alma SD — 300/PK-12
S1618 State Road 35 54610 — 608-685-4416
Steven Sedlmayr, supt. — Fax 685-4446
www.alma.k12.wi.us
Alma HS — 100/9-12
S1618 State Road 35 54610 — 608-685-4416
Steven Sedlmayr, prin. — Fax 685-4446

**Alma Center, Jackson, Pop. 492**
Alma Center-Humbird-Merrillan SD — 700/PK-12
PO Box 308 54611 — 715-964-8271
Paul Fischer, supt. — Fax 964-1005
www.achm.k12.wi.us
Lincoln HS — 200/9-12
PO Box 308 54611 — 715-964-5311
Paul Janson, prin. — Fax 964-1005
Lincoln JHS — 100/7-8
PO Box 308 54611 — 715-964-5311
Paul Janson, prin. — Fax 964-1005

**Almond, Portage, Pop. 447**
Almond-Bancroft SD — 200/PK-12
1336 Elm St 54909 — 715-366-2941
Dann Boxx, admin. — Fax 366-2940
www.abschools.k12.wi.us
Almond-Bancroft S — 200/PK-12
1336 Elm St 54909 — 715-366-2941
Jeff Rykal, prin. — Fax 366-2943

**Altoona, Eau Claire, Pop. 6,546**
Altoona SD — 1,300/PK-12
809 7th St W 54720 — 715-839-6032
Connie Biedron, supt. — Fax 839-6066
www.altoona.k12.wi.us
Altoona HS — 500/9-12
711 7th St W 54720 — 715-839-6031
Jeff Pepowski, prin. — Fax 839-6028
Altoona MS — 300/6-8
1903 Bartlett Ave 54720 — 715-839-6030
Gary Pszeniczny, prin. — Fax 839-6099

**Amery, Polk, Pop. 2,886**
Amery SD — 1,700/PK-12
543 Minneapolis Ave S 54001 — 715-268-9771
Stephen Schiell, supt. — Fax 268-7300
www.amerysd.k12.wi.us
Amery HS — 500/9-12
555 Minneapolis Ave S 54001 — 715-268-9771
Shawn Doerfler, prin. — Fax 268-7792
Amery MS — 300/6-8
501 Minneapolis Ave S 54001 — 715-268-9771
Thomas Bensen, prin. — Fax 268-4967

**Amherst, Portage, Pop. 1,031**
Tomorrow River SD — 1,000/PK-12
357 N Main St 54406 — 715-824-5521
Dennis Raabe, supt. — Fax 824-7177
www.amherst.k12.wi.us
Amherst HS — 300/9-12
357 N Main St 54406 — 715-824-5522
Mark Luetschwager, prin. — Fax 824-5454
Amherst MS — 200/5-8
357 N Main St 54406 — 715-824-5524
Phillip Tubbs, prin. — Fax 824-5454

**Antigo, Langlade, Pop. 8,127**
Antigo SD — 2,600/PK-12
120 S Dorr St 54409 — 715-627-4355
Donald Childs Ph.D., supt. — Fax 623-3279
www.antigo.k12.wi.us
Antigo HS — 900/9-12
1900 10th Ave 54409 — 715-623-7611
Thomas Zamzow, prin. — Fax 623-7624
Antigo MS — 500/6-8
815 7th Ave 54409 — 715-623-4173
Brian Misfeldt, prin. — Fax 627-4982

**Appleton, Outagamie, Pop. 71,375**
Appleton Area SD — 14,900/PK-12
PO Box 2019 54912 — 920-832-6161
Lee Allinger, supt. — Fax 832-1725
www.aasd.k12.wi.us
Appleton East HS — 1,400/9-12
2121 E Emmers Dr 54915 — 920-832-6212
Matt Mineau, prin. — Fax 832-4880
Appleton North HS — 1,400/9-12
5000 N Ballard Rd 54913 — 920-832-4300
James Huggins, prin. — Fax 832-4301
Appleton West HS — 1,200/9-12
610 N Badger Ave 54914 — 920-832-6219
Greg Hartjes, prin. — Fax 832-4198
Einstein MS — 400/7-8
324 E Florida Ave 54911 — 920-832-6240
Dave Mueller, prin. — Fax 832-6164
Madison MS — 600/7-8
2020 S Carpenter St 54915 — 920-832-6276
David Torrey, prin. — Fax 832-6337
Roosevelt MS — 300/7-8
318 E Brewster St 54911 — 920-832-6294
Al Brant, prin. — Fax 832-4605
Wilson MS — 400/7-8
225 N Badger Ave 54914 — 920-832-6226
Mark McQuade, prin. — Fax 832-4857

---

Fox Valley Lutheran HS — 600/9-12
5300 N Meade St 54913 — 920-739-4441
Steve Granberg, prin. — Fax 739-4418
Fox Valley Technical College — Post-Sec.
PO Box 2277 54912 — 920-735-5600
Gill-Tech Academy of Hair Design — Post-Sec.
230 S McCarthy Rd 54914 — 920-739-8684
Globe University — Post-Sec.
5045 W Grande Market Dr 54913 — 920-364-1100
Lawrence University — Post-Sec.
711 E Boldt Way 54911 — 920-832-7000
Rasmussen College — Post-Sec.
3500 E Destination Dr # 100 54915 — 920-750-5900
St. Elizabeth Hospital — Post-Sec.
1506 S Oneida St 54915 — 920-738-2015
St. Francis Xavier HS — 600/9-12
1600 W Prospect Ave 54914 — 920-733-6632
Mike Mauthe, prin. — Fax 733-5513
St. Francis Xavier MS — 400/6-8
2626 N Oneida St 54911 — 920-730-8849
Dave Callan, prin. — Fax 730-4147

**Arcadia, Trempealeau, Pop. 2,912**
Arcadia SD — 1,100/PK-12
756 Raider Dr 54612 — 608-323-3315
Louie Ferguson, supt. — Fax 323-2256
www.arcadia.k12.wi.us/
Arcadia HS — 300/9-12
756 Raider Dr 54612 — 608-323-3334
Michele Butler, prin. — Fax 323-2256
Arcadia MS — 200/6-8
358 E River St 54612 — 608-323-7500
Sam Ruud, prin. — Fax 323-7015

**Argyle, Lafayette, Pop. 857**
Argyle SD — 300/PK-12
PO Box 256 53504 — 608-543-3318
Dr. Robert Gilpatrick, supt. — Fax 543-3868
www.argyle.k12.wi.us
Argyle MSHS — 200/6-12
PO Box 256 53504 — 608-543-3318
Phillip Updike, prin. — Fax 543-3868

**Ashland, Ashland, Pop. 7,896**
Ashland SD — 2,100/PK-12
2000 Beaser Ave 54806 — 715-682-7080
Keith Hilts, supt. — Fax 682-7097
www.ashland.k12.wi.us
Ashland HS — 700/9-12
1900 Beaser Ave 54806 — 715-682-7089
Greg Posewitz, prin. — Fax 682-2075
Ashland MS — 500/6-8
203 11th St E 54806 — 715-682-7087
Paul Gilbertson, prin. — Fax 682-7944

---

Northland College — Post-Sec.
1411 Ellis Ave 54806 — 715-682-1699

Wisconsin Indianhead Technical College Post-Sec.
2100 Beaser Ave 54806 715-682-4591

**Athens, Marathon, Pop. 1,096**
Athens SD 500/PK-12
PO Box F 54411 715-257-7511
Timothy Micke, supt. Fax 257-7502
www.athens1.org
Athens HS 200/9-12
PO Box F 54411 715-257-7511
Juli Gauerke, prin. Fax 257-7651
Athens MS 100/6-8
PO Box F 54411 715-257-7511
Juli Gauerke, prin. Fax 257-7651

**Auburndale, Wood, Pop. 703**
Auburndale SD 900/PK-12
PO Box 139 54412 715-652-2117
Gerald Eichman, supt. Fax 652-2836
www.aubschools.com
Auburndale MSHS 400/6-12
PO Box 190 54412 715-652-2115
Aaron Engel, prin. Fax 652-6322

**Augusta, Eau Claire, Pop. 1,531**
Augusta SD 600/PK-12
E19320 Bartig Rd 54722 715-286-2291
Ryan Nelson, supt. Fax 286-3336
www.augusta.k12.wi.us
Augusta MSHS 200/6-12
E19320 Bartig Rd 54722 715-286-2291
Ken Abel, prin. Fax 286-3393

**Baldwin, Saint Croix, Pop. 3,900**
Baldwin-Woodville Area SD 1,600/PK-12
550 US Highway 12 54002 715-684-3411
Eric Russell, supt. Fax 684-3168
www.bwsd.k12.wi.us
Baldwin-Woodville HS 500/9-12
1000 13th Ave 54002 715-684-3321
Dave Brandvold, prin. Fax 684-5160
Other Schools – See Woodville

**Balsam Lake, Polk, Pop. 991**
Unity SD 1,000/PK-12
1908 150th St 54810 715-825-3515
Brandon Robinson, supt. Fax 825-3517
www.unity.k12.wi.us/
Unity HS 300/9-12
1908 150th St 54810 715-825-2131
Jason Cress, prin. Fax 825-4430
Unity MS 300/5-8
1908 150th St 54810 715-825-2101
Elizabeth Jorgensen, prin. Fax 825-4410

**Bangor, LaCrosse, Pop. 1,446**
Bangor SD 600/PK-12
PO Box 99 54614 608-486-2331
David Laehn, supt. Fax 486-4587
www.bangor.k12.wi.us
Bangor MSHS 300/6-12
PO Box 99 54614 608-486-2331
Don Addington, prin. Fax 486-4587

**Baraboo, Sauk, Pop. 11,882**
Baraboo SD 3,000/PK-12
101 2nd Ave 53913 608-355-4698
Lori Mueller, supt. Fax 355-3960
www.baraboo.k12.wi.us
Baraboo HS 1,000/9-12
1201 Draper St 53913 608-355-3940
Glenn Bildsten, prin. Fax 355-3962
Young MS 700/6-8
1531 Draper St 53913 608-355-3930
John Gunnell, prin. Fax 355-3998

University of Wisconsin Baraboo/Sauk Co. Post-Sec.
1006 Connie Rd 53913 608-355-5230

**Barneveld, Iowa, Pop. 1,221**
Barneveld SD 400/K-12
105 W Douglas St 53507 608-924-4711
Kevin Knudson, supt. Fax 924-1646
www.barneveld.k12.wi.us
Barneveld MSHS 200/6-12
105 W Douglas St 53507 608-924-4711
Ben Jones, prin. Fax 924-1646

**Barron, Barron, Pop. 3,378**
Barron Area SD 1,300/PK-12
100 W River Ave 54812 715-537-5612
Craig Broeren, supt. Fax 637-5161
www.barron.k12.wi.us
Barron HS 400/9-12
1050 E Woodland Ave 54812 715-537-5627
Kirk Haugestuen, prin. Fax 637-1603
Riverview MS 300/5-8
135 W River Ave 54812 715-537-5641
Scott Stralka, prin. Fax 637-5373

**Bayfield, Bayfield, Pop. 459**
Bayfield SD 400/PK-12
300 N 4th St 54814 715-779-3201
Dr. David Aslyn, supt. Fax 779-5268
www.bayfield.k12.wi.us
Bayfield HS 100/9-12
300 N 4th St 54814 715-779-3201
David Aslyn, prin. Fax 779-5226
Bayfield MS 100/6-8
300 N 4th St 54814 715-779-3201
Jeff Gordon, prin. Fax 779-5226

**Bayside, Milwaukee, Pop. 4,320**
Fox Point Bayside SD
Supt. — See Fox Point
Bayside MS 400/5-8
601 E Ellsworth Ln 53217 414-247-4167
Don Galster, prin. Fax 351-7164

**Beaver Dam, Dodge, Pop. 16,040**
Beaver Dam SD 3,300/PK-12
705 McKinley St 53916 920-885-7300
Stephen Vessey, supt. Fax 885-7306
www.bdusd.org
Beaver Dam HS 1,000/9-12
500 Gould St 53916 920-885-7313
Mark DiStefano, prin. Fax 885-7317
Beaver Dam MS 700/6-8
108 4th St 53916 920-885-7365
John Casper, prin. Fax 885-7415
Smith Learning Academy 100/Alt
400 E Burnett St 53916 920-885-7423
Mark DiStefano, prin. Fax 885-7429

Moraine Park Technical College Post-Sec.
700 Gould St 53916 920-887-1441
Wayland Academy 200/9-12
101 N University Ave 53916 920-356-2120
Joseph Lennertz, head sch Fax 887-3373

**Belleville, Dane, Pop. 2,367**
Belleville SD 1,000/PK-12
625 W Church St 53508 608-424-3315
Pam Yoder, supt. Fax 424-3486
www.belleville.k12.wi.us/
Belleville HS 300/9-12
635 W Church St 53508 608-424-1902
Nate Perry, prin. Fax 424-3692
Belleville MS 200/7-8
625 W Church St 53508 608-424-1902
Nate Perry, prin. Fax 424-3692

**Belmont, Lafayette, Pop. 980**
Belmont Community SD 300/PK-12
PO Box 348 53510 608-762-5131
Christy Larson, supt. Fax 762-5129
www.belmont.k12.wi.us
Belmont JSHS 100/6-12
PO Box 348 53510 608-762-5131
Mike Beranek, prin. Fax 762-5129

**Beloit, Rock, Pop. 35,780**
Beloit SD 6,400/K-12
1633 Keeler Ave 53511 608-361-4000
Thomas Johnson, supt. Fax 361-4122
www.sdb.k12.wi.us
Aldrich IS 700/4-8
1859 Northgate Dr 53511 608-361-3600
Mark Smullen, prin. Fax 361-4122
Beloit Learning Academy Alt
1033 Woodward Ave 53511 608-361-4310
Tina Goecks, prin. Fax 361-4122
Cunningham IS 300/4-8
910 Townline Ave 53511 608-361-2200
Jennifer Fanning, prin. Fax 361-4122
Fruzen IS 700/4-8
2600 Milwaukee Rd 53511 608-361-2000
Kevin Kitslaar, prin. Fax 361-4122
McNeel IS 800/4-8
1524 Frederick St 53511 608-361-3800
Anthony Bosco, prin. Fax 361-4122
Memorial HS 1,800/9-12
1225 4th St 53511 608-361-3000
Tina Salzman, prin. Fax 361-4122

School District of Beloit Turner 1,500/PK-12
1237 E Inman Pkwy 53511 608-364-6372
Dr. Dennis McCarthy, supt. Fax 364-6373
www.turnerschools.org/
Turner HS 400/9-12
1231 E Inman Pkwy 53511 608-364-6370
Ryan Bertelsen, prin. Fax 365-4768
Turner MS 400/6-8
1237 E Inman Pkwy 53511 608-364-6367
Cory Everson, prin. Fax 364-6369

Beloit College Post-Sec.
700 College St 53511 608-363-2000
Rock County Christian HS 100/6-12
916 Bushnell St 53511 608-365-7378
Bob Cerniglia, prin. Fax 365-7382

**Benton, Lafayette, Pop. 970**
Benton SD 200/PK-12
PO Box 7 53803 608-759-4002
Kyle Luedtke, admin. Fax 759-3805
www.benton.k12.wi.us
Benton HS 100/7-12
PO Box 7 53803 608-759-4002
Kyle Luedtke, prin. Fax 759-3805

**Berlin, Green Lake, Pop. 5,480**
Berlin Area SD 1,700/PK-12
295 E Marquette St 54923 920-361-2004
Dr. Robert Eidahl Ed.D., supt. Fax 361-2170
www.berlin.k12.wi.us
Berlin HS 600/9-12
222 Memorial Dr 54923 920-361-2000
Lynn Mork, prin. Fax 361-2005
Berlin MS 300/6-8
242 Memorial Dr 54923 920-361-2441
Mike Raether, prin. Fax 361-3379

**Birchwood, Washburn, Pop. 440**
Birchwood SD 300/PK-12
300 S Wilson St 54817 715-354-3471
Frank Helquist, supt. Fax 354-3469
www.birchwood.k12.wi.us/
Birchwood HS 100/9-12
300 S Wilson St 54817 715-354-3471
Jeff Stanley, prin. Fax 354-3469

**Black River Falls, Jackson, Pop. 3,539**
Black River Falls SD 1,800/PK-12
301 N 4th St 54615 715-284-4357
Dr. Shelly Severson, supt. Fax 284-7064
www.brf.org
Black River Falls HS 500/9-12
1200 Pierce St 54615 715-284-4324
Thomas Chambers, prin. Fax 284-7626
Black River Falls MS 400/6-8
1202 Pierce St 54615 715-284-5315
David Roou, prin. Fax 284-0364

**Blair, Trempealeau, Pop. 1,358**
Blair-Taylor SD 600/PK-12
PO Box 107 54616 608-989-2881
Jeff Eide, supt. Fax 989-2451
btsd.k12.wi.us
Blair-Taylor MSHS 300/7-12
PO Box 107 54616 608-989-2525
Dana Eide, prin. Fax 989-9161

**Blanchardville, Lafayette, Pop. 822**
Pecatonica Area SD 400/PK-12
PO Box 117 53516 608-523-4248
Jill Underly, supt. Fax 523-4286
www.pecatonica.k12.wi.us
Pecatonica JSHS 200/6-12
PO Box 117 53516 608-523-4285
Jill Underly, admin. Fax 523-4286

**Bloomer, Chippewa, Pop. 3,508**
Bloomer SD 1,200/PK-12
1310 17th Ave 54724 715-568-2800
Dr. Mary Randall, supt. Fax 568-5315
www.bloomer.k12.wi.us
Bloomer HS 400/9-12
1310 17th Ave 54724 715-568-5300
Chad Steinmetz, prin. Fax 568-5304
Bloomer MS 300/5-8
600 Jackson St 54724 715-568-1025
Luke Barth, prin. Fax 568-3687

**Bonduel, Shawano, Pop. 1,465**
Bonduel SD 900/PK-12
PO Box 310 54107 715-758-4860
Patrick Rau, supt. Fax 758-4869
www.bonduel.k12.wi.us
Bonduel HS 300/9-12
PO Box 310 54107 715-758-4850
Jane Wonderling, prin. Fax 758-4859
Bonduel MS 200/6-8
PO Box 310 54107 715-758-4840
Mark Margelofsky, prin. Fax 758-4849

**Boscobel, Grant, Pop. 3,210**
Boscobel Area SD 900/PK-12
1110 Park St 53805 608-375-4164
Fax 375-2378
www.boscobel.k12.wi.us
Boscobel HS 300/9-12
300 Brindley St 53805 608-375-4161
Fax 375-2640
Boscobel MS 100/7-8
300 Brindley St 53805 608-375-4161
Fax 375-2640

**Bowler, Shawano, Pop. 282**
Bowler SD 400/PK-12
500 S Almon St 54416 715-793-4101
Faith Gagnon, supt. Fax 793-1302
www.bowler.k12.wi.us
Bowler JSHS 200/7-12
500 S Almon St 54416 715-793-4101
Kim Ninabuck, prin. Fax 793-1302

**Boyceville, Dunn, Pop. 1,080**
Boyceville Community SD 800/PK-12
1003 Tiffany St 54725 715-643-3647
Kevin Sipple, supt. Fax 643-3127
www.boyceville.k12.wi.us
Boyceville HS 200/9-12
1003 Tiffany St 54725 715-643-3647
Steven Glocke, prin. Fax 643-2209
Boyceville MS 100/7-8
1003 Tiffany St 54725 715-643-3647
Steven Glocke, prin. Fax 643-2209

**Brillion, Calumet, Pop. 3,113**
Brillion SD 1,000/PK-12
315 S Main St 54110 920-756-2368
Dominick Madison Ph.D., supt. Fax 756-3705
www.brillion.k12.wi.us
Brillion HS 300/9-12
W1101 County Road HR 54110 920-756-9238
Peter Kittel, prin. Fax 756-9427
Brillion MS 200/6-8
315 S Main St 54110 920-756-2166
Bonnie Olson, prin. Fax 756-3705

**Brodhead, Green, Pop. 3,270**
Brodhead SD 1,100/PK-12
2501 W 5th Ave 53520 608-897-2141
Leonard Lueck, supt. Fax 897-2770
www.brodhead.k12.wi.us
Brodhead HS 300/9-12
2501 W 5th Ave 53520 608-897-2155
James Matthys, prin. Fax 897-3026
Brodhead MS 200/6-8
2100 W 9th Ave 53520 608-897-2184
Dr. Lisa Semrow, prin. Fax 897-2789

**Brookfield, Waukesha, Pop. 37,413**
Elmbrook SD 6,800/PK-12
PO Box 1830 53008 262-781-3030
Mark Hansen, supt. Fax 790-4095
www.elmbrookschools.org
Central HS 1,300/9-12
16900 Gebhardt Rd 53005 262-785-3910
Brett Gruetzmacher, prin. Fax 785-3993
East HS 1,300/9-12
3305 Lilly Rd 53005 262-781-3500
Andy Farley, prin. Fax 790-5445
Wisconsin Hills MS 900/6-8
18700 W Wisconsin Ave 53045 262-785-3960
Lisa Rettler, prin. Fax 785-3967
Other Schools – See Elm Grove

---

Anthem College Post-Sec.
440 S Executive Dr Ste 200 53005 888-852-7272
Brookfield Academy 900/PK-12
3462 N Brookfield Rd 53045 262-783-3200
Ottawa University Post-Sec.
245 S Executive Dr Ste 110 53005 262-879-0200

**Brown Deer, Milwaukee, Pop. 11,652**
Brown Deer SD 800/PK-12
8200 N 60th St 53223 414-371-6750
Dr. Deb Kerr, admin. Fax 371-6751
browndeer.schoolfusion.us
Brown Deer MSHS 600/7-12
8060 N 60th St 53223 414-371-7000
Tosha Womack, prin. Fax 371-7001

**Bruce, Rusk, Pop. 772**
Bruce SD 500/PK-12
104 W Washington Ave 54819 715-868-2533
Joni Weinert, supt. Fax 868-2534
www.bruce.k12.wi.us
Bruce HS 200/9-12
104 W Washington Ave 54819 715-868-2585
Larry Villiard, prin. Fax 868-2534
Bruce MS 100/6-8
104 W Washington Ave 54819 715-868-2585
Larry Villiard, prin. Fax 868-2534

**Brussels, Door**
Southern Door SD 1,100/PK-12
2073 County Road DK 54204 920-825-7311
Patricia Vickman, supt. Fax 825-7155
www.southerndoor.k12.wi.us
Southern Door HS 400/9-12
2073 County Road DK 54204 920-825-7333
Steve Bousley, prin. Fax 825-7081
Southern Door MS 300/6-8
2073 County Road DK 54204 920-825-7321
Gary Langenberg, prin. Fax 825-7692

**Burlington, Racine, Pop. 10,361**
Burlington Area SD 3,200/PK-12
100 N Kane St 53105 262-763-0210
Peter Smet, supt. Fax 763-0215
www.basd.k12.wi.us
Burlington HS 1,200/9-12
400 Mc Canna Pkwy 53105 262-763-0200
Eric Burling, prin. Fax 763-0216
Karcher MS 500/7-8
225 Robert St 53105 262-763-0190
Fax 767-5580

---

Catholic Central HS 200/9-12
148 McHenry St 53105 262-763-1510
Dave Wieters, prin. Fax 763-1509

**Butternut, Ashland, Pop. 367**
Butternut SD 100/PK-12
PO Box 247 54514 715-769-3434
Joseph Zirngibl, supt. Fax 769-3712
www.lightatorch.info
Butternut S 100/PK-12
PO Box 247 54514 715-769-3434
Joseph Zirngibl, admin. Fax 769-3712

**Cadott, Chippewa, Pop. 1,424**
Cadott Community SD 900/PK-12
426 Myrtle St 54727 715-289-3795
Damon Smith, supt. Fax 289-3748
www.cadott.k12.wi.us
Cadott HS 300/9-12
426 Myrtle St 54727 715-289-3795
Matthew McDonough, prin. Fax 289-3085
Cadott JHS 100/7-8
426 Myrtle St 54727 715-289-3795
Matthew McDonough, prin. Fax 289-3085

**Cambria, Columbia, Pop. 765**
Cambria-Friesland SD 400/PK-12
410 E Edgewater St 53923 920-348-5548
Timothy Raymond, supt. Fax 348-5119
www.cf.k12.wi.us
Cambria-Friesland MSHS 200/6-12
410 E Edgewater St 53923 920-348-5135
James Meyer, prin. Fax 348-5119

**Cambridge, Dane, Pop. 1,441**
Cambridge SD 900/PK-12
403 Blue Jay Way 53523 608-423-4345
Bernard Nikolay, supt. Fax 423-9869
www.cambridge.k12.wi.us
Cambridge HS 300/9-12
403 Blue Jay Way 53523 608-423-3261
Keith Schneider, prin. Fax 423-9598
Nikolay MS 200/6-8
211 South St 53523 608-423-7335
Krista Jones, prin. Fax 423-4499

**Cameron, Barron, Pop. 1,761**
Cameron SD 1,000/PK-12
PO Box 378 54822 715-458-4560
Joe Leschisin, admin. Fax 458-4822
www.cameron.k12.wi.us
Cameron HS 300/9-12
PO Box 378 54822 715-458-4560
John Meznarich, prin. Fax 458-4236
Cameron MS 200/5-8
PO Box 378 54822 715-458-4560
Hans Schmidt, prin. Fax 458-3436

**Campbellsport, Fond du Lac, Pop. 1,998**
Campbellsport SD 1,400/PK-12
114 W Sheboygan St 53010 920-533-8381
Paul A. Amundson, admin. Fax 533-5726
www.csd.k12.wi.us
Campbellsport HS 500/9-12
114 W Sheboygan St 53010 920-533-4811
Todd Hencsik, prin. Fax 533-3521
Campbellsport MS 200/6-8
114 W Sheboygan St 53010 920-533-4811
Todd Hencsik, prin. Fax 533-3521

**Casco, Kewaunee, Pop. 569**
Luxemburg-Casco SD
Supt. — See Luxemburg
Luxemburg-Casco MS 300/7-8
619 Church Ave 54205 920-837-2205
Mike Snowberry, prin. Fax 837-7517

**Cashton, Monroe, Pop. 1,094**
Cashton SD 600/PK-12
PO Box 129 54619 608-654-5131
David Bell, supt. Fax 654-5136
www.cashton.k12.wi.us
Cashton JSHS 300/6-12
PO Box 129 54619 608-654-5131
Jennifer Butzler, prin. Fax 654-5136

**Cassville, Grant, Pop. 939**
Cassville SD 200/PK-12
715 E Amelia St 53806 608-725-5116
John Luster, supt. Fax 725-2353
www.cassvillesd.k12.wi.us
Cassville JSHS 100/7-12
715 E Amelia St 53806 608-725-5116
John Luster, prin. Fax 725-2353

**Cazenovia, Sauk, Pop. 314**
Weston SD 300/PK-12
E2511A County Rd S 53924 608-986-2151
Emily Miller, supt. Fax 986-2205
www.weston.k12.wi.us
Weston HS 100/9-12
E2511A County Rd S 53924 608-986-2151
Michael Crneckiy, prin. Fax 986-2205
Weston MS 100/6-8
E2511A County Rd S 53924 608-986-2151
Michael Crneckiy, prin. Fax 986-2205

**Cecil, Shawano, Pop. 563**

---

Wolf River Lutheran HS 50/9-12
PO Box 77 54111 715-745-2400
Caroline Bedroske, dir. Fax 745-2496

**Cedarburg, Ozaukee, Pop. 11,308**
Cedarburg SD 3,000/K-12
W68N611 Evergreen Blvd 53012 262-376-6100
Todd Bugnacki, supt. Fax 376-6110
www.cedarburg.k12.wi.us
Cedarburg HS 1,100/9-12
W68N611 Evergreen Blvd 53012 262-376-6200
Jeff Nelson, prin. Fax 376-6210
Webster MS 700/6-8
W75N624 Wauwatosa Rd 53012 262-376-6500
Tony DeRosa, prin. Fax 376-6510

**Cedar Grove, Sheboygan, Pop. 2,097**
Cedar Grove-Belgium Area SD 1,200/PK-12
321 N 2nd St 53013 920-668-8686
Dr. Jeanne Courneene, supt. Fax 668-8605
www.cedargrovebelgium.k12.wi.us/
Cedar Grove-Belgium HS 300/9-12
321 N 2nd St 53013 920-668-8686
Josh Ketterhagen, prin. Fax 668-8605
Cedar Grove-Belgium MS 400/5-8
321 N 2nd St 53013 920-668-8518
Jodi Swagel, prin. Fax 668-8566

**Chetek, Barron, Pop. 2,205**
Chetek-Weyerhaeuser Area SD 800/PK-12
PO Box 6 54728 715-924-2226
Mark Johnson, supt. Fax 924-2376
www.cwasd.k12.wi.us
Chetek-Weyerhaeuser Area HS 300/9-12
PO Box 6 54728 715-924-3137
Larry Zeman, prin. Fax 924-2921
Chetek-Weyerhaeuser Area MS 200/6-8
PO Box 6 54728 715-924-3136
Larry Zeman, prin. Fax 924-1794

**Chilton, Calumet, Pop. 3,890**
Chilton SD 1,200/PK-12
530 W Main St 53014 920-849-8109
Claire Martin, supt. Fax 849-4539
www.chilton.k12.wi.us
Chilton HS 400/9-12
530 W Main St 53014 920-849-2358
Ty Breitlow, prin. Fax 849-3998
Chilton MS 300/5-8
530 W Main St 53014 920-849-9152
Richard Appel, prin. Fax 849-7210

**Chippewa Falls, Chippewa, Pop. 13,496**
Chippewa Falls Area USD 4,600/PK-12
1130 Miles St 54729 715-726-2417
Heidi Taylor-Eliopoulos, supt. Fax 726-2781
cfsd.chipfalls.k12.wi.us
Chippewa Falls HS 1,500/9-12
735 Terrill St 54729 715-726-2406
Becky Davis, prin. Fax 726-2792
Chippewa Falls MS 1,000/6-8
750 Tropicana Blvd 54729 715-726-2400
Susan Kern, prin. Fax 726-2789

---

McDonell Central HS 100/7-12
1316 Bel Air Blvd 54729 715-723-9126
Br. Roger Betzold, prin. Fax 723-1501
Notre Dame MS 100/6-8
1316 Bel Air Blvd 54729 715-723-4777
Br. Roger Betzold, prin. Fax 723-3353

**Clayton, Polk, Pop. 562**
Clayton SD 400/PK-12
PO Box 130 54004 715-948-2163
Cathleen Shimon, supt. Fax 948-2362
www.claytonschooldistrict.new.rschooltoday.com
Clayton HS 100/9-12
PO Box 130 54004 715-948-2163
Edward Cerney, prin. Fax 948-2362
Clayton MS 100/6-8
PO Box 130 54004 715-948-2163
Edward Cerney, prin. Fax 948-2362

**Clear Lake, Polk, Pop. 1,055**
Clear Lake SD 600/PK-12
1101 3rd St SW 54005 715-263-2114
Brad Ayer, supt. Fax 263-2933
www.clearlake.k12.wi.us
Clear Lake HS 200/9-12
1101 3rd St SW 54005 715-263-2113
George Smith, prin. Fax 263-3550
Clear Lake JHS 100/7-8
1101 3rd St SW 54005 715-263-2113
George Smith, prin. Fax 263-3550

**Cleveland, Manitowoc, Pop. 1,481**

---

Lakeshore Technical College Post-Sec.
1290 North Ave 53015 920-693-1000

**Clinton, Rock, Pop. 2,131**
Clinton Community SD 1,200/PK-12
PO Box 566 53525 608-676-5482
Dr. Randy Refsland, supt. Fax 676-4444
www.clinton.k12.wi.us
Clinton HS 400/9-12
PO Box 566 53525 608-676-2223
Phil Pape, prin. Fax 676-4444
Clinton MS 400/5-8
PO Box 559 53525 608-676-2275
Ben Simmons, prin. Fax 676-5176

**Clintonville, Waupaca, Pop. 4,497**
Clintonville SD 1,400/PK-12
45 W Green Tree Rd 54929 715-823-7215
Tom O'Toole, supt. Fax 823-1315
www.clintonville.k12.wi.us
Clintonville HS 400/9-12
64 W Green Tree Rd 54929 715-823-7215
Lance Bagstad, prin. Fax 823-1481
Clintonville MS 400/5-8
255 N Main St 54929 715-823-7215
Scott Werfal, prin. Fax 823-1443

**Colby, Clark, Pop. 1,841**
Colby SD 900/PK-12
PO Box 139 54421 715-223-2301
Steven Kolden, supt. Fax 223-4539
www.colby.k12.wi.us
Colby HS 300/9-12
PO Box 110 54421 715-223-2338
Marcia Diedrich, prin. Fax 223-4388
Colby MS 200/5-8
PO Box 110 54421 715-223-8869
Jim Hagen, prin. Fax 223-6754

**Coleman, Marinette, Pop. 713**
Coleman SD 600/PK-12
347 Business 141 N 54112 920-897-4011
Brian Walters, supt. Fax 897-4921
www.coleman.k12.wi.us
Coleman MSHS 200/6-12
343 Business 141 N 54112 920-897-3822
Doug Polomis, prin. Fax 897-2015

**Colfax, Dunn, Pop. 1,143**
Colfax SD 800/PK-12
601 University Ave 54730 715-962-3773
William Yingst, supt. Fax 962-4024
www.colfax.k12.wi.us/
Colfax MSHS 400/7-12
601 University Ave 54730 715-962-3155
John Dachel, prin. Fax 962-4024

**Columbus, Columbia, Pop. 4,934**
Columbus SD 1,200/PK-12
200 W School St 53925 920-623-5950
Dr. Bryan Davis, supt. Fax 623-5958
www.columbus.k12.wi.us
Columbus HS 400/9-12
1164 Farnham St 53925 920-623-5956
Jacob Ekern, prin. Fax 623-5959
Columbus MS 400/4-8
400 S Dickason Blvd 53925 920-623-5954
Paul Kurth, prin. Fax 623-5742

---

Wisconsin Academy 100/9-12
N2355 Du Borg Rd 53925 920-623-3300

**Combined Locks, Outagamie, Pop. 3,308**
Kimberly Area SD 5,000/PK-12
PO Box 159 54113 920-788-7900
Bob Mayfield Ed.D., supt. Fax 788-7919
www.kimberly.k12.wi.us
Other Schools – See Kimberly

**Cornell, Chippewa, Pop. 1,446**
Cornell SD 300/PK-12
PO Box 517 54732 715-861-6947
Dr. Paul Schley, supt. Fax 239-6587
www.cornell.k12.wi.us
Cornell JSHS 100/6-12
PO Box 517 54732 715-861-6947
David Elliott, prin. Fax 239-6587

**Cottage Grove, Dane, Pop. 6,069**
Monona Grove SD
Supt. — See Monona
Glacial Drumlin MS 800/5-8
801 Damascus Trl 53527 608-839-8437
Renee Tennant, prin. Fax 839-8984

**Crandon, Forest, Pop. 1,853**
Crandon SD 900/PK-12
9750 US Highway 8 W 54520 715-478-3339
Fax 478-5130
www.crandon.k12.wi.us

Crandon HS 200/9-12
9750 US Highway 8 W 54520 715-478-6125
Andy Space, prin. Fax 478-5570
Crandon MS 200/6-8
9750 US Highway 8 W 54520 715-478-6124
Andy Space, prin. Fax 478-5130

**Crivitz, Marinette, Pop. 971**
Crivitz SD 600/PK-12
400 South Ave 54114 715-854-2721
Patrick Mans, supt. Fax 854-3755
www.crivitz.k12.wi.us
Crivitz HS 200/9-12
400 South Ave 54114 715-854-2721
Jeff Baumann, prin. Fax 854-3755

**Cross Plains, Dane, Pop. 3,510**
Middleton-Cross Plains Area SD
Supt. — See Middleton
Glacier Creek MS 600/5-8
2800 N Military Rd 53528 608-829-9420
Tim Keeler, prin. Fax 798-5425

**Cuba City, Grant, Pop. 2,077**
Cuba City SD 600/PK-12
101 N School St 53807 608-744-2847
Roger Kordus, supt. Fax 744-2324
www.cubacity.us
Cuba City HS 300/9-12
101 N School St 53807 608-744-8888
James Boebel, prin. Fax 744-2324

**Cudahy, Milwaukee, Pop. 17,945**
Cudahy SD 2,600/PK-12
2915 E Ramsey Ave 53110 414-294-7400
Dr. James Heiden, supt. Fax 294-4083
www.cudahy.k12.wi.us/
Cudahy HS 800/9-12
4950 S Lake Dr 53110 414-294-2700
Christopher Haeger, prin. Fax 769-2379
Cudahy MS 400/6-8
5530 S Barland Ave 53110 414-294-2830
Kim Berner, prin. Fax 489-3010

**Cumberland, Barron, Pop. 2,141**
Cumberland SD 1,000/PK-12
1010 8th Ave 54829 715-822-5124
Barry Rose, supt. Fax 822-5136
www.csdmail.com
Cumberland HS 300/9-12
1000 8th Ave 54829 715-822-5121
Ritchie Narges, prin. Fax 822-5138
Cumberland MS 300/5-8
980 8th Ave 54829 715-822-5122
Colin Green, prin. Fax 822-5132

**Darlington, Lafayette, Pop. 2,431**
Darlington Community SD 800/PK-12
11630 Center Hill Rd 53530 608-776-2006
Dr. Denise Wellnitz, supt. Fax 776-3407
www.darlington.k12.wi.us
Darlington HS 200/9-12
11838 Center Hill Rd 53530 608-776-4001
Douglas McArthur, prin. Fax 776-2378

**Deerfield, Dane, Pop. 2,294**
Deerfield Community SD 800/PK-12
300 Simonson Blvd 53531 608-764-5431
Michelle Jensen, supt. Fax 764-2556
www.deerfield.k12.wi.us
Deerfield HS 200/9-12
300 Simonson Blvd 53531 608-764-5431
Brad Johnsrud, prin. Fax 764-5433
Deerfield MS 100/7-8
300 Simonson Blvd 53531 608-764-5431
Brad Johnsrud, prin. Fax 764-5433

**De Forest, Dane, Pop. 8,802**
De Forest Area SD 3,500/PK-12
520 E Holum St 53532 608-842-6500
Dr. Sue Bordon, supt. Fax 842-6576
www.deforest.k12.wi.us
De Forest Area HS 1,000/9-12
815 Jefferson St 53532 608-842-6600
Machell Schwarz, prin. Fax 842-6615
De Forest Area MS 1,000/5-8
404 Yorktown Rd 53532 608-842-6000
Fax 842-6015

**Delafield, Waukesha, Pop. 7,026**

---

St. John's Northwestern Military Academy 300/7-12
1101 Genesee St 53018 262-646-3311
Dr. Jack H. Albert, pres. Fax 646-7128

**Delavan, Walworth, Pop. 8,369**
Delavan-Darien SD 2,500/PK-12
324 Beloit St 53115 262-728-2642
Dr. Robert Crist, supt. Fax 728-5954
www.ddschools.org
Delavan-Darien HS 800/9-12
150 Cumming St 53115 262-728-2642
Mark Schmitt, prin. Fax 728-9713
Phoenix MS 500/6-8
414 Beloit St 53115 262-728-2642
Fax 728-0359

---

Wisconsin School for the Deaf Post-Sec.
309 W Walworth Ave 53115

**Denmark, Brown, Pop. 2,098**
Denmark SD 1,500/PK-12
450 N Wall St 54208 920-863-4000
Tony Klaubauf, supt. Fax 863-4015
www.denmark.k12.wi.us
Denmark HS 500/9-12
450 N Wall St 54208 920-863-4200
Oran Nehls, prin. Fax 863-8856
Denmark MS 300/6-8
450 N Wall St 54208 920-863-4100
Joe Koch, prin. Fax 863-3184

**De Pere, Brown, Pop. 23,399**
De Pere SD 3,900/K-12
1700 Chicago St 54115 920-337-1032
Benjamin Villarruel, supt. Fax 337-1033
www.depere.k12.wi.us
De Pere HS 1,300/9-12
1700 Chicago St 54115 920-337-1020
Annette Deuman, prin. Fax 337-1041
De Pere MS 700/7-8
700 Swan Rd 54115 920-337-1024
Betty Hartman, prin. Fax 337-1049

West De Pere SD 2,900/PK-12
400 Reid St Ste W 54115 920-337-1393
John Zegers, supt. Fax 337-1398
www.wdpsd.com
West De Pere HS 800/9-12
665 Grant St 54115 920-338-5200
Dr. Russell Gerke, prin. Fax 338-5310
West De Pere MS 600/6-8
1177 S 9th St 54115 920-337-1099
James Finley, prin. Fax 337-1380

---

St. Norbert College Post-Sec.
100 Grant St 54115 920-337-3181

**De Soto, Vernon, Pop. 286**
De Soto Area SD 600/PK-12
615 Main St 54624 608-648-0102
Fax 648-3959
www.desoto.k12.wi.us
De Soto HS 200/9-12
615 Main St 54624 608-648-0100
Linzi Gronning, prin. Fax 648-0117
De Soto MS 100/6-8
615 Main St 54624 608-648-0104
Linzi Gronning, prin. Fax 648-0117

**Dodgeville, Iowa, Pop. 4,656**
Dodgeville SD 1,300/PK-12
307 N Iowa St 53533 608-935-3307
Dr. Jeffrey Jacobson, supt. Fax 935-3021
www.dsd.k12.wi.us/
Dodgeville HS 400/9-12
912 W Chapel St 53533 608-935-3307
Laura Nyberg, prin. Fax 935-9540
Dodgeville MS 300/6-8
951 W Chapel St 53533 608-935-3307
Sally Baxter, prin. Fax 935-9643

**Dousman, Waukesha, Pop. 2,279**
Kettle Moraine SD
Supt. — See Wales
Kettle Moraine MS 900/6-8
301 E Ottawa Ave 53118 262-965-6500
Michael Comiskey, prin. Fax 965-6506

**Drummond, Bayfield, Pop. 153**
Drummond Area SD 400/PK-12
PO Box 40 54832 715-739-6669
John Knight, supt. Fax 739-6345
www.dasd.k12.wi.us
Drummond HS 100/9-12
PO Box 40 54832 715-739-6231
Kristine Lamb, prin. Fax 739-6345
Drummond MS 100/7-8
PO Box 40 54832 715-739-6231
Kristine Lamb, prin. Fax 739-6345

**Dunbar, Marinette, Pop. 48**

---

Northland International University Post-Sec.
W10085 Pike Plains Rd 54119 715-324-6900

**Durand, Pepin, Pop. 1,916**
Durand SD 900/PK-12
PO Box 190 54736 715-672-8919
Greg Doverspike, supt. Fax 672-8930
www.durand.k12.wi.us
Durand MSHS 500/6-12
PO Box 190 54736 715-672-8917
Bill Clouse, prin. Fax 672-8930

---

Assumption Catholic MS 100/4-8
901 W Prospect St 54736 715-672-5617
Mary Lansing, prin. Fax 672-3931

**Eagle River, Vilas, Pop. 1,377**
Northland Pines SD 1,400/PK-12
1800 Pleasure Island Rd 54521 715-479-6487
Mike Richie Ed.D., supt. Fax 479-7633
www.npsd.k12.wi.us/
Northland Pines HS 500/9-12
1800 Pleasure Island Rd 54521 715-479-4473
Jim Brewer, prin. Fax 479-5808
Northland Pines MS 300/6-8
1700 Pleasure Island Rd 54521 715-479-6479
Jacqueline Coghlan, prin. Fax 479-7303

**East Troy, Walworth, Pop. 4,231**
East Troy Community SD 1,700/PK-12
2043 Division St 53120 262-642-6710
Dr. Christopher Hibner, supt.
www.easttroy.k12.wi.us
East Troy HS 600/9-12
3128 Graydon Ave 53120 262-642-6760
Rick Penniston, prin. Fax 642-6776
East Troy MS 400/6-8
3143 Graydon Ave 53120 262-642-6740
Peter Synes, prin. Fax 642-6743

**Eau Claire, Eau Claire, Pop. 64,812**
Eau Claire Area SD 10,100/PK-12
500 Main St 54701 715-852-3000
Dr. Mary Ann Hardebeck, supt. Fax 852-3004
www.ecasd.us
Delong MS 900/6-8
2000 Vine St 54703 715-852-4900
Dr. Tim O'Reilly, prin. Fax 852-4904
Memorial HS 1,700/9-12
2225 Keith St 54701 715-852-6300
David Oldenberg, prin. Fax 852-6304
North HS 1,400/9-12
1801 Piedmont Rd 54703 715-852-6600
Dave Valk, prin. Fax 852-6604
Northstar MS 500/6-8
2711 Abbe Hill Dr 54703 715-852-5100
Tim Skutley, prin. Fax 852-5104
South MS 800/6-8
2115 Mitscher Ave 54701 715-852-5200
Dianna Zeegers, prin. Fax 852-5204

---

Chippewa Valley Technical College Post-Sec.
620 W Clairemont Ave 54701 715-833-6200
Globe University Post-Sec.
4955 Bullis Farm Rd 54701 715-855-6600
Immanuel Lutheran HS 100/9-12
501 Grover Rd 54701 715-836-6621
Joel Gullerud, prin. Fax 836-6634
Professional Hair Design Academy Post-Sec.
3408 Mall Dr 54701 715-835-2345
Regis HS 200/9-12
2100 Fenwick Ave 54701 715-830-2271
Paul Pedersen, prin. Fax 830-5461
Regis MS 100/7-8
2100 Fenwick Ave 54701 715-830-2272
Paul Pedersen, prin. Fax 830-5461
Sacred Heart Hospital Post-Sec.
900 W Clairemont Ave 54701 715-839-4131
University of Wisconsin Post-Sec.
PO Box 4004 54702 715-836-2637

**Edgar, Marathon, Pop. 1,476**
Edgar SD 700/PK-12
PO Box 196 54426 715-352-2351
Cari Guden, supt. Fax 352-3198
www.edgar.k12.wi.us
Edgar HS 200/9-12
PO Box 196 54426 715-352-2352
Jordan Sinz, prin. Fax 352-3198
Edgar MS 100/6-8
PO Box 198 54426 715-352-2727
Jordan Sinz, prin. Fax 352-3022

**Edgerton, Rock, Pop. 5,394**
Edgerton SD 1,800/PK-12
200 Elm High Dr 53534 608-561-6100
Dr. Dennis Pauli, supt. Fax 884-9327
www.edgerton.k12.wi.us
Edgerton HS 500/9-12
200 Elm High Dr 53534 608-561-6020
Dr. Mark Coombs, prin. Fax 884-7969
Edgerton MS 400/6-8
300 Elm High Dr 53534 608-561-6030
Clark Bretthauer, prin. Fax 884-2279

---

Oaklawn Academy 200/6-9
432 Liguori Rd 53534 608-884-3425

**Elcho, Langlade, Pop. 333**
Elcho SD 300/PK-12
PO Box 800 54428 715-275-3225
William Fisher, supt. Fax 275-4388
www.elcho.k12.wi.us
Elcho HS 100/6-12
PO Box 800 54428 715-275-3707
Shawn Rude, prin. Fax 275-4388

**Elkhart Lake, Sheboygan, Pop. 964**
Elkhart Lake - Glenbeulah SD 500/PK-12
PO Box 326 53020 920-876-3381
Dr. Ann Buechel-Haack, supt. Fax 876-3511
www.elgs.k12.wi.us/
Elkhart Lake - Glenbeulah HS 100/9-12
PO Box 326 53020 920-876-3381
Jim Brown, prin. Fax 876-3511

**Elkhorn, Walworth, Pop. 9,969**
Elkhorn Area SD 3,000/K-12
3 N Jackson St 53121 262-723-3160
Jason Tadlock, supt. Fax 723-4652
www.elkhorn.k12.wi.us
Elkhorn Area HS 900/9-12
482 E Geneva St 53121 262-723-4920
Chris Trottier, prin. Fax 723-8092
Elkhorn Area MS 700/6-8
627 E Court St 53121 262-723-6800
Bryan Frost, prin. Fax 723-4967

---

Gateway Technical College Post-Sec.
400 County Road H 53121 262-741-8200

**Elk Mound, Dunn, Pop. 858**
Elk Mound Area SD 1,100/PK-12
405 University St 54739 715-879-5066
Dr. Ronald Walsh, supt. Fax 879-5846
www.elkmound.k12.wi.us
Elk Mound HS 300/9-12
405 University St 54739 715-879-5521
Paul Weber, prin. Fax 879-5846
Elk Mound MS 300/5-8
302 University St 54739 715-879-5595
Eric Wright, prin. Fax 879-5886

**Ellsworth, Pierce, Pop. 3,234**
Ellsworth Community SD 1,700/PK-12
300 Hillcrest St 54011 715-273-3900
Barry Cain, supt. Fax 273-5775
www.ellsworth.k12.wi.us
Ellsworth HS 500/9-12
323 Hillcrest St 54011 715-273-3904
Mark Stoesz, prin. Fax 273-6824
Ellsworth MS 500/5-8
312 Panther Dr 54011 715-273-3908
Jon Dodge, prin. Fax 273-6834

**Elm Grove, Waukesha, Pop. 5,869**
Elmbrook SD
Supt. — See Brookfield
Pilgrim Park MS 800/6-8
1500 Pilgrim Pkwy 53122 262-785-3920
Mark Peperkorn, prin. Fax 785-3933

**Elmwood, Pierce, Pop. 815**
Elmwood SD 300/PK-12
213 S Scott St 54740 715-639-2711
Paul Blanford Ed.D., supt. Fax 639-3110
www.elmwood.k12.wi.us
Elmwood HS 100/9-12
213 S Scott St 54740 715-639-2721
Christopher Segerstrom, prin. Fax 639-3110
Elmwood MS 100/6-8
213 S Scott St 54740 715-639-2721
Christopher Segerstrom, prin. Fax 639-3110

**Elroy, Juneau, Pop. 1,424**
Royall SD 500/PK-12
1501 Academy St 53929 608-462-2600
Mark Gruen, supt. Fax 462-2618
www.royall.k12.wi.us
Royall MSHS 200/7-12
1501 Academy St 53929 608-462-2600
Scott Uppena, prin. Fax 462-2618

**Evansville, Rock, Pop. 4,947**
Evansville Community SD 1,800/PK-12
340 Fair St 53536 608-882-5224
Jerry Roth, supt. Fax 882-6564
www.evansville.k12.wi.us
Evansville HS 500/9-12
640 S 5th St 53536 608-882-4600
Scott Everson, prin. Fax 882-6157
McKenna MS 400/6-8
307 S 1st St 53536 608-882-4780
Jason Knott, prin. Fax 882-5744

**Fall Creek, Eau Claire, Pop. 1,306**
Fall Creek SD 800/PK-12
336 E Hoover Ave 54742 715-877-2123
Dr. Joseph Sanfelippo, supt. Fax 877-2911
www.fallcreek.k12.wi.us
Fall Creek HS 300/9-12
336 E Hoover Ave 54742 715-877-2809
Brian Schulner, prin. Fax 877-2911
Fall Creek MS 200/6-8
336 E Hoover Ave 54742 715-877-2511
Brad LaPoint, prin. Fax 877-2911

**Fall River, Columbia, Pop. 1,685**
Fall River SD 500/PK-12
PO Box 116 53932 920-484-3333
Kellie Manning, supt. Fax 484-3600
www.fallriver.k12.wi.us
Fall River HS 300/6-12
PO Box 116 53932 920-484-3333
Dan Dowden, prin. Fax 484-3600

**Fennimore, Grant, Pop. 2,489**
Fennimore Community SD 800/PK-12
1397 9th St 53809 608-822-3243
Jamie Nutter, supt. Fax 822-3250
www.fennimore.k12.wi.us
Fennimore JSHS 300/7-12
510 7th St 53809 608-822-3245
Dan Bredeson, prin. Fax 822-3247

---

Southwest Wisconsin Technical College Post-Sec.
1800 Bronson Blvd 53809 608-822-3262

**Fish Creek, Door**
Gibraltar Area SD 500/PK-12
3924 State Highway 42 54212 920-868-3284
Tina Van Meer, supt. Fax 868-2714
www.gibraltar.k12.wi.us
Gibraltar HS 200/9-12
3924 State Highway 42 54212 920-868-3284
Kirk Knutson, prin. Fax 868-2714
Gibraltar MS 100/7-8
3924 State Highway 42 54212 920-868-3284
Kirk Knutson, prin. Fax 868-2714

**Fitchburg, Dane, Pop. 24,633**
Verona Area SD
Supt. — See Verona
Savanna Oaks MS 500/6-8
5890 Lacy Rd 53711 608-845-4000
Sandy Eskrich, prin. Fax 845-4020

**Florence, Florence, Pop. 589**
Florence SD 400/PK-12
PO Box 440 54121 715-528-3217
Ben Niehaus, supt. Fax 528-5338
www.florence.k12.wi.us
Florence HS 200/9-12
PO Box 440 54121 715-528-3215
Brandon Jerue, admin. Fax 528-5330
Florence MS 100/7-8
PO Box 440 54121 715-528-3215
Brandon Jerue, admin. Fax 528-5338

**Fond du Lac, Fond du Lac, Pop. 42,372**
Fond du Lac SD 6,900/PK-12
72 W 9th St 54935 920-929-2900
James Sebert Ed.D., supt. Fax 929-6804
www.fonddulac.k12.wi.us
Fond du Lac HS 2,100/9-12
801 Campus Dr 54935 920-929-2740
Michelle Hagen, prin. Fax 929-6964
Sabish MS 600/6-8
100 N Peters Ave 54935 920-929-2800
Torrie Rochon-Luft, prin. Fax 929-2807
Theisen MS 500/6-8
525 E Pioneer Rd 54935 920-929-2850
Brad Nerat, prin. Fax 929-2854
Woodworth MS 500/6-8
101 Morningside Dr 54935 920-929-6900
Steven Hill, prin. Fax 929-6944

---

Fond du Lac Christian S 100/PK-12
720 Rienzi Rd 54935 920-924-2177
Dr. Wendy Lundberg, admin. Fax 322-9459
Marian University Post-Sec.
45 S National Ave 54935 920-923-7600
Moraine Park Technical College Post-Sec.
235 N National Ave 54935 920-922-8611
St. Mary's Springs Academy 500/3-8
63 E Merrill Ave 54935 920-921-9610
Erin Flood, prin. Fax 921-0457
St. Mary's Springs HS 200/9-12
255 County Road K 54937 920-921-4870
Doug Olig, pres. Fax 921-2786
University of Wisconsin Fond du Lac Post-Sec.
400 University Dr 54935 920-929-1100
Winnebago Lutheran Academy 400/9-12
475 E Merrill Ave 54935 920-921-4930
David Schroeder, prin. Fax 921-4280

**Fort Atkinson, Jefferson, Pop. 12,238**
Fort Atkinson SD 2,800/PK-12
201 Park St 53538 920-563-7800
Dr. Jeff Zaspel, supt. Fax 563-7809
www.fortschools.org
Fort Atkinson HS 1,000/9-12
925 Lexington Blvd 53538 920-563-7811
Dan Halvorsen, prin. Fax 563-7810
Fort Atkinson MS 600/6-8
310 S 4th St E 53538 920-563-7833
Robert Abbott, prin. Fax 563-7838

**Fountain City, Buffalo, Pop. 848**
Cochrane-Fountain City SD 700/PK-12
S2770 State Road 35 54629 608-687-7771
Thomas Hiebert, supt. Fax 687-3312
www.cfc.k12.wi.us
Cochrane-Fountain City JSHS 300/7-12
S2770 State Road 35 54629 608-687-4391
Steve Stoppelmoor, prin. Fax 687-6412

**Fox Point, Milwaukee, Pop. 6,600**
Fox Point Bayside SD 900/PK-8
7300 N Lombardy Rd 53217 414-247-4167
Dr. Vance Dalzin, admin. Fax 351-7164
www.foxbay.k12.wi.us
Other Schools – See Bayside

Maple Dale-Indian Hill SD 500/PK-8
8377 N Port Washington Rd 53217 414-351-7380
Jennifer Wimmer, supt.
www.mapledale.k12.wi.us
Maple Dale S 300/3-8
8377 N Port Washington Rd 53217 414-351-7380
Tim Reymer, prin.

**Franklin, Milwaukee, Pop. 34,981**
Franklin SD 4,300/PK-12
8255 W Forest Hill Ave 53132 414-529-8220
Steve Patz, supt. Fax 529-8230
www.franklin.k12.wi.us
Forest Park MS 700/7-8
8225 W Forest Hill Ave 53132 414-529-8250
Christopher Reuter, prin. Fax 529-8249
Franklin HS 1,400/9-12
8222 S 51st St 53132 414-423-4640
Michael Nowak, prin. Fax 421-0558

**Frederic, Polk, Pop. 1,124**
Frederic SD 500/PK-12
1437 Clam Falls Dr 54837 715-327-5630
Josh Robinson, admin. Fax 327-5609
www.frederic.k12.wi.us/
Frederic 6-12 S 300/6-12
1437 Clam Falls Dr 54837 715-327-4223
Ryan Fitzgerald, prin. Fax 327-8655

**Fredonia, Ozaukee, Pop. 2,138**
Northern Ozaukee SD 1,300/PK-12
401 Highland Dr 53021 262-692-2489
Dave Karrels, supt. Fax 692-6257
www.nosd.edu
Ozaukee HS 200/9-12
401 Highland Dr 53021 262-692-2453
Joseph Hastreiter, prin. Fax 692-6257
Ozaukee MS 100/6-8
401 Highland Dr 53021 262-692-2463
Charles Schwartz, prin. Fax 692-2313

**Freedom, Outagamie**
Freedom Area SD 1,600/PK-12
N4021 County Rd E, Kaukauna WI 54130
920-788-7944
Kevin Kilstofte, supt. Fax 788-7949
www.freedomschools.k12.wi.us
Freedom HS 500/9-12
N4021 County Rd E, Kaukauna WI 54130
920-788-7940
Kurt Erickson, prin. Fax 788-7700
Freedom MS 400/6-8
N4021 County Rd E, Kaukauna WI 54130
920-788-7945
Ken Fisher, prin. Fax 788-7701

**Friendship, Adams, Pop. 720**
Adams-Friendship Area SD 1,700/PK-12
201 W 6th St 53934 608-339-3213
Rick Waski, supt. Fax 339-6213
www.af.k12.wi.us
Other Schools – See Adams

**Galesville, Trempealeau, Pop. 1,463**
Galesville-Ettrick-Trempealeau SD 1,400/PK-12
PO Box 4000 54630 608-582-4657
Aaron Engel, supt. Fax 582-4961
www.getsd.org
Coulee Region HS Alt
16935 N Main St 54630 608-582-2200
Troy White, prin. Fax 582-4263

Gale-Ettrick-Tremp HS 400/9-12
PO Box 4000 54630 608-582-2291
Troy White, prin. Fax 582-4263
Gale-Ettrick-Tremp MS 300/6-8
19650 Prairie Ridge Ln 54630 608-582-3500
Matt Wenthe, prin. Fax 582-3501

**Genoa City, Walworth, Pop. 3,006**
Genoa City J2 SD 600/PK-8
PO Box 250 53128 262-279-1051
Kellie Bohn, supt. Fax 279-1052
Brookwood MS 300/4-8
PO Box 250 53128 262-279-1053
Pam Larson, prin. Fax 279-1052

**Germantown, Washington, Pop. 19,491**
Germantown SD 4,000/PK-12
N104W13840 Donges Bay Rd 53022 262-253-3900
Jeff Holmes, supt. Fax 251-6999
www.germantown.k12.wi.us
Germantown HS 1,400/9-12
W180N11501 River Ln 53022 262-253-3400
Joel Farren, prin. Fax 253-3494
Kennedy MS 900/6-8
W160N11836 Crusader Ct 53022 262-253-3450
Susan Climer, prin. Fax 253-3499

---

ITT Technical Institute Post-Sec.
W177N9886 Rivercrest # 200 53022 262-257-7100

**Gillett, Oconto, Pop. 1,370**
Gillett SD 600/PK-12
PO Box 227 54124 920-855-2137
Todd Carlson, supt. Fax 855-1557
www.gillett.k12.wi.us
Gillett HS 200/9-12
PO Box 227 54124 920-855-2137
Steve Linssen, prin. Fax 855-6600
Gillett MS 100/6-8
PO Box 227 54124 920-855-2137
Steve Linssen, prin. Fax 855-6600

**Gilman, Taylor, Pop. 409**
Gilman SD 400/PK-12
325 N 5th Ave 54433 715-447-8211
Georgia Kraus, supt. Fax 447-8731
www.gilman.k12.wi.us
Gilman JSHS 200/7-12
325 N 5th Ave 54433 715-447-8211
Daniel Peggs, prin. Fax 447-8731

**Gilmanton, Buffalo**
Gilmanton SD 200/PK-12
PO Box 28 54743 715-946-3158
Glen Denk, supt. Fax 946-3474
www.ghs.k12.wi.us
Gilmanton HS 50/9-12
PO Box 28 54743 715-946-3158
Kory Rud, prin. Fax 946-3474
Gilmanton MS 50/5-8
PO Box 28 54743 715-946-3158
Kory Rud, prin. Fax 946-3174

**Glendale, Milwaukee, Pop. 12,578**
Glendale-River Hills SD 1,000/PK-8
2600 W Mill Rd 53209 414-351-7170
Larry Smalley, supt. Fax 434-0109
www.glendale.k12.wi.us
Glen Hills MS 500/4-8
2600 W Mill Rd 53209 414-351-7160
Dr. Haydee Smith, prin. Fax 351-8100

Nicolet UNHSD 1,100/9-12
6701 N Jean Nicolet Rd 53217 414-351-7520
Robert Kobylski, supt. Fax 351-7526
nicolet.k12.wi.us/
Nicolet Union HS 1,100/9-12
6701 N Jean Nicolet Rd 53217 414-351-7524
Greg Kabara, prin. Fax 351-7526

---

Bryant & Stratton College Post-Sec.
500 W Silver Spring Dr K340 53217 414-961-9600
Columbia College of Nursing Post-Sec.
4425 N Port Washington Rd 53212 414-326-2330

**Glenwood City, Saint Croix, Pop. 1,234**
Glenwood City SD 700/PK-12
850 Maple St 54013 715-265-4757
Timothy Johnson, supt. Fax 265-4214
www.gcsd.k12.wi.us
Glenwood City HS 200/9-12
850 Maple St 54013 715-265-4266
Patrick Gretzlock, prin. Fax 265-7129
Glenwood City MS 200/6-8
850 Maple St 54013 715-265-4266
Patrick Gretzlock, prin. Fax 265-7129

**Glidden, Ashland, Pop. 505**
Chequamegon SD
Supt. — See Park Falls
Chequamegon MS 200/6-8
64 S Grant St 54527 715-264-2141
Diana Rein, prin. Fax 264-3413

**Goodman, Marinette, Pop. 271**
Goodman-Armstrong Creek SD 100/PK-12
PO Box 160 54125 715-336-2575
Ben Niehaus, supt. Fax 336-2576
www.goodman.k12.wi.us
Goodman JSHS 100/6-12
PO Box 160 54125 715-336-2575
Ben Niehaus, prin. Fax 336-2576

**Grafton, Ozaukee, Pop. 11,349**
Grafton SD 2,100/PK-12
1900 Washington St 53024 262-376-5400
Dr. Mel Lightner, supt. Fax 376-5599
www.grafton.k12.wi.us
Grafton HS 800/9-12
1950 Washington St 53024 262-376-5500
Scott Mantei, prin. Fax 376-5510

Long MS 500/6-8
700 Hickory St 53024 262-376-5800
Liz Kayzar, prin. Fax 376-5810

**Granton, Clark, Pop. 353**
Granton Area SD 200/K-12
217 N Main St 54436 715-238-7292
Charles Buckel, supt. Fax 238-7288
www.granton.k12.wi.us
Granton HS 100/6-12
217 N Main St 54436 715-238-7175
Rhonda Opelt, prin. Fax 238-7827

**Grantsburg, Burnett, Pop. 1,314**
Grantsburg SD 1,600/PK-12
480 E James Ave 54840 715-463-5499
Joni Burgin, supt. Fax 463-2534
www.gk12.net/
Grantsburg HS 300/9-12
480 E James Ave 54840 715-463-2531
Joshua Watt, prin. Fax 463-5068
Grantsburg MS 300/4-8
480 E James Ave 54840 715-463-2455
Bill Morrin, prin. Fax 463-3209

**Green Bay, Brown, Pop. 101,558**
Ashwaubenon SD 3,200/PK-12
1055 Griffiths Ln 54304 920-492-2900
Brian Hanes, supt. Fax 492-2911
www.ashwaubenon.k12.wi.us
Ashwaubenon HS 1,000/9-12
2391 S Ridge Rd 54304 920-492-2950
Brian Nelsen, prin. Fax 492-2912
Parkview MS 800/6-8
955 Willard Dr 54304 920-492-2940
Kris Hucek, prin. Fax 492-2944

Green Bay Area SD 20,300/PK-12
PO Box 23387 54305 920-448-2000
Dr. Michelle Langenfeld, supt. Fax 448-3562
www.greenbay.k12.wi.us
East HS 1,300/9-12
1415 E Walnut St 54301 920-448-2090
Lori Frerk, prin. Fax 448-2166
Edison MS 1,100/6-8
442 Alpine Dr 54302 920-391-2450
Jonathon Wiebel, prin. Fax 391-2531
Franklin MS 700/6-8
1233 Lore Ln 54303 920-492-2670
Jackie Hauser, prin. Fax 492-5563
Lombardi MS 900/6-8
1520 S Point Rd 54313 920-492-2625
Jim Van Abel, prin. Fax 492-5564
Minoka-Hill S Alt
325 N Roosevelt St 54301 920-448-2150
Vicki Bayer, prin. Fax 448-3562
Preble HS 2,200/9-12
2222 Deckner Ave 54302 920-391-2400
Natasha Rowell, prin. Fax 391-2530
Southwest HS 1,200/9-12
1331 Packerland Dr 54304 920-492-2650
Rod Bohm, prin. Fax 492-5561
Washington MS 900/6-8
314 S Baird St 54301 920-448-2095
Margaret Lardinois, prin. Fax 448-3551
West HS 1,000/9-12
966 Shawano Ave 54303 920-492-2600
Mark Flaten, prin. Fax 492-2641

Howard-Suamico SD 5,800/PK-12
2706 Lineville Rd 54313 920-662-7878
Damian LaCroix, supt. Fax 662-9777
www.hssd.k12.wi.us
Bay Port HS 1,700/9-12
2710 Lineville Rd 54313 920-662-7000
Michael Frieder, prin. Fax 662-7291
Bay View MS 900/7-8
1217 Cardinal Ln 54313 920-662-8196
Steve Meyers, prin. Fax 662-7979

---

Bellin College Post-Sec.
3201 Eaton Rd 54311 920-433-6699
Bellin Hospital Post-Sec.
PO Box 23400 54305 920-433-3497
Empire Beauty School Post-Sec.
2575 W Mason St 54303 920-494-1430
Globe University Post-Sec.
2620 Development Dr 54311 920-264-1600
Green Bay Adventist Junior Academy 50/K-10
1422 Shawano Ave 54303 920-494-2741
Kiana Binford, prin. Fax 494-6507
ITT Technical Institute Post-Sec.
470 Security Blvd 54313 920-662-9000
Northeastern Wisconsin Lutheran HS 100/9-12
1311 S Robinson Ave 54311 920-469-6810
Chris Nelson, dir. Fax 469-2200
Northeast Wisconsin Technical College Post-Sec.
PO Box 19042 54307 920-498-5444
Notre Dame De La Baie Academy 700/9-12
610 Maryhill Dr 54303 920-429-6100
John Ravizza, prin. Fax 429-6168
Rasmussen College Post-Sec.
904 S Taylor St Ste 100 54303 920-593-8400
St. Vincent Hospital Post-Sec.
PO Box 13508 54307 920-433-8155
University of Wisconsin Post-Sec.
2420 Nicolet Dr 54311 920-465-2000
Wisconsin College of Cosmetology Post-Sec.
PO Box 28257 54324 920-336-8888

**Greendale, Milwaukee, Pop. 13,859**
Greendale SD 2,600/PK-12
6815 Southway 53129 414-423-2700
Kim Amidzich Ed.D., admin. Fax 423-2723
www.greendale.k12.wi.us
Greendale HS 900/9-12
6801 Southway 53129 414-423-0110
Steven Lodes, prin. Fax 423-1667
Greendale MS 600/6-8
6800 Schoolway 53129 414-423-2800
John Weiss, prin. Fax 423-2806

---

Luther HS 300/9-12
5201 S 76th St 53129 414-421-4000
Dr. Wayne Jensen, prin. Fax 421-4071

**Greenfield, Milwaukee, Pop. 36,124**
Greenfield SD 3,800/PK-12
4850 S 60th St 53220 414-855-2050
Lisa Elliott, supt. Fax 855-2051
www.greenfield.k12.wi.us
Greenfield HS 1,300/9-12
4800 S 60th St 53220 414-281-6200
Paul Thusius, prin. Fax 281-8860
Greenfield MS 900/6-8
3200 W Barnard Ave 53221 414-282-4700
Brad Iding, prin. Fax 282-1017

Whitnall SD 2,300/PK-12
5000 S 116th St 53228 414-525-8400
Dr. Lowell Holtz, supt. Fax 525-8401
www.whitnall.com
Whitnall HS 800/9-12
5000 S 116th St 53228 414-525-8500
Jacquelyn Winter, prin. Fax 525-8501
Whitnall MS 500/6-8
5025 S 116th St 53228 414-525-8650
Lynn LeRoy, prin. Fax 525-8651

**Green Lake, Green Lake, Pop. 956**
Green Lake SD 300/PK-12
PO Box 369 54941 920-294-6411
Ken Bates, supt. Fax 294-6589
www.glsd.k12.wi.us
Green Lake JSHS 100/7-12
PO Box 369 54941 920-294-6411
Mary Allen, prin. Fax 294-6589

**Greenville, Outagamie**
Hortonville SD
Supt. — See Hortonville
Greenville MS 600/5-8
N1450 Fawn Ridge Dr 54942 920-757-7140
Travis Lawrence, prin. Fax 757-7141

**Greenwood, Clark, Pop. 1,021**
Greenwood SD 300/PK-12
PO Box 310 54437 715-267-6101
Todd Felhofer, supt. Fax 267-6113
www.greenwood.k12.wi.us/
Greenwood MSHS 100/7-12
PO Box 310 54437 715-267-6101
Todd C. Fischer, prin. Fax 267-6113

**Gresham, Shawano, Pop. 545**
Gresham SD 200/PK-12
501 Schabow St 54128 715-787-3211
Keary Mattson, supt. Fax 787-3951
www.gresham.k12.wi.us/
Gresham HS 100/9-12
501 Schabow St 54128 715-787-3211
Keary Mattson, prin. Fax 787-3951

**Hales Corners, Milwaukee, Pop. 7,616**

---

Sacred Heart School of Theology Post-Sec.
PO Box 429 53130 414-425-8300

**Hammond, Saint Croix, Pop. 1,895**
St. Croix Central SD 1,500/PK-12
PO Box 118 54015 715-796-2256
Tim Widiker, supt. Fax 796-2460
www.scc.k12.wi.us
St. Croix Central HS 400/9-12
1751 Broadway St 54015 715-796-5383
Dr. Glenn Webb, prin. Fax 796-5662
St. Croix Central MS 400/5-8
PO Box 118 54015 715-796-2256
Scott Woodington, prin. Fax 796-2460

**Hartford, Washington, Pop. 14,070**
Hartford J1 SD 1,700/PK-8
402 W Sumner St 53027 262-673-3155
Dr. Mark Smits, admin. Fax 673-3548
www.hartfordjt1.k12.wi.us
Central MS 500/6-8
1100 Cedar St 53027 262-673-8040
Joe Viste, prin. Fax 673-7596

Hartford UNHSD 1,500/9-12
805 Cedar St 53027 262-670-3200
Dr. Lisa Olson, supt. Fax 673-8943
www.huhs.org
Hartford Union HS 1,500/9-12
805 Cedar St 53027 262-670-3200
Chad Ellefson, prin. Fax 673-8943

**Hartland, Waukesha, Pop. 8,992**
Arrowhead UNHSD 2,300/9-12
700 North Ave 53029 262-369-3611
Craig Jefson, supt. Fax 367-7406
www.arrowheadschools.org
Arrowhead Union HS 2,300/9-12
700 North Ave 53029 262-369-3611
Gregg Wieczorek, prin. Fax 367-4693

Hartland-Lakeside J3 SD 1,200/PK-8
800 N Shore Dr 53029 262-369-6700
Dr. Glenn Schilling, supt. Fax 369-6755
www.hartlake.org
North Shore MS 400/6-8
800 N Shore Dr 53029 262-369-6767
Michele Schmidt, prin. Fax 369-6766

---

Lake Country Lutheran HS 200/9-12
401 Campus Dr 53029 262-367-8600
Dwayne Jobst, prin. Fax 367-0611
University Lake S 300/PK-12
PO Box 290 53029 262-367-6011
Ron Smyczek, head sch Fax 367-3146

**Hayward, Sawyer, Pop. 2,245**
Hayward Community SD 1,900/PK-12
15930 W 5th St 54843 715-634-2619
Craig Olson, supt. Fax 634-3560
www.hayward.k12.wi.us
Hayward HS 600/9-12
15930 W 5th St 54843 715-634-2619
Todd Johnson, prin. Fax 634-2761
Hayward MS 400/6-8
15930 W 5th St 54843 715-634-2619
Hugh Duffy, prin. Fax 634-9953

---

Lac Courte Oreilles Ojibwa Comm College Post-Sec.
13466 W Trepania Rd 54843 715-634-4790

**Hazel Green, Grant, Pop. 1,238**
Southwestern Wisconsin SD 600/PK-12
PO Box 368 53811 608-854-2261
John Costello, supt. Fax 854-2305
www.swsd.k12.wi.us
Southwestern Wisconsin HS 200/9-12
PO Box 368 53811 608-854-2261
Cynthia Lacey, prin. Fax 854-2315

**Hilbert, Calumet, Pop. 1,124**
Hilbert SD 400/PK-12
PO Box 390 54129 920-853-3558
Anthony Sweere, supt. Fax 853-7030
www.hilbert.k12.wi.us
Hilbert HS 200/9-12
PO Box 390 54129 920-853-3558
Anthony Sweere, prin. Fax 853-7030
Hilbert MS 100/5-8
PO Box 390 54129 920-853-3558
Anthony Sweere, prin. Fax 853-7030

**Hillsboro, Vernon, Pop. 1,405**
Hillsboro SD 500/PK-12
PO Box 526 54634 608-489-2221
Curt Bisarek, supt. Fax 489-2811
www.hillsboro.k12.wi.us
Hillsboro MSHS 200/6-12
PO Box 526 54634 608-489-2221
Greg Zimmerman, prin. Fax 489-2811

**Holcombe, Chippewa, Pop. 266**
Lake Holcombe SD 100/PK-12
27331 262nd Ave 54745 715-595-4241
Jeffrey Mastin, supt. Fax 595-6383
www.lakeholcombe.k12.wi.us
Lake Holcombe S 100/PK-12
27331 262nd Ave 54745 715-595-4241
Mark Porter, prin. Fax 595-6383

**Holmen, LaCrosse, Pop. 8,875**
Holmen SD 3,800/PK-12
1019 McHugh Rd 54636 608-526-6610
Dale Carlson, supt. Fax 526-1333
www.holmen.k12.wi.us
Holmen HS 1,100/9-12
1001 McHugh Rd 54636 608-526-3372
Robert Baer, prin. Fax 526-9446
Holmen MS 900/6-8
502 N Main St 54636 608-526-3391
Ryan Vogler, prin. Fax 526-6716

**Horicon, Dodge, Pop. 3,609**
Horicon SD 700/PK-12
611 Mill St 53032 920-485-2898
Gary Berger, supt. Fax 485-3601
www.horicon.k12.wi.us
Horicon JHS 100/7-8
841 Gray St 53032 920-485-4441
Teresa Graven, prin. Fax 485-3244
Horicon SHS 300/9-12
841 Gray St 53032 920-485-4441
Teresa Graven, prin. Fax 485-3244

**Hortonville, Outagamie, Pop. 2,685**
Hortonville SD 3,400/PK-12
PO Box 70 54944 920-779-7900
Dr. Heidi Schmidt, supt. Fax 779-7903
www.hasd.org
Hortonville HS 1,100/9-12
155 Warner St 54944 920-779-7933
Todd Timm, prin. Fax 779-7935
Hortonville MS 400/5-8
220 Warner St 54944 920-779-7922
Steven Gromala, prin. Fax 779-7923
Other Schools – See Greenville

**Howards Grove, Sheboygan, Pop. 3,170**
Howards Grove SD 800/K-12
403 Audubon Rd 53083 920-565-4454
Christopher Peterson, supt. Fax 565-4461
www.hgsd.k12.wi.us
Howards Grove HS 300/9-12
401 Audubon Rd 53083 920-565-4450
Scott Fritz, prin. Fax 565-4451
Howards Grove MS 300/5-8
506 Kennedy Ave 53083 920-565-4452
Andy Hansen, prin. Fax 565-4460

**Hudson, Saint Croix, Pop. 12,505**
Hudson SD 5,600/PK-12
644 Brakke Dr 54016 715-377-3700
Dr. Nick Ouellette, supt. Fax 377-3726
www.hudson.k12.wi.us
Hudson HS 1,700/9-12
1501 Vine St 54016 715-377-3800
Peg Shoemaker, prin. Fax 377-3801
Hudson MS 1,300/6-8
1300 Carmichael Rd 54016 715-377-3820
Ann Mitchell, prin. Fax 377-3821

**Hurley, Iron, Pop. 1,529**
Hurley SD 300/PK-12
5503 W Range View Dr 54534 715-561-4900
Christopher Patritto, supt. Fax 561-4953
www.hurley.k12.wi.us
Hurley S 300/PK-12
5503 W Range View Dr 54534 715-561-4900
Melissa Oja, dean Fax 561-4157

**Hustisford, Dodge, Pop. 1,121**
Hustisford SD 400/PK-12
PO Box 326 53034 920-349-8109
Douglas Keiser Ph.D., supt. Fax 349-3716
www.hustisford.k12.wi.us
Hustisford JSHS 200/6-12
PO Box 326 53034 920-349-3261
Meg Perron, prin. Fax 349-8495

**Independence, Trempealeau, Pop. 1,329**
Independence SD 400/PK-12
23786 Indee Blvd 54747 715-985-3172
Paul Vine, supt. Fax 985-2303
www.indps.k12.wi.us
Independence MSHS 100/6-12
23786 Indee Blvd 54747 715-985-3172
Barry Schmitt, prin. Fax 985-2303

**Iola, Waupaca, Pop. 1,297**
Iola-Scandinavia SD 700/PK-12
450 Division St 54945 715-445-2411
David C. Dyb Ed.D., supt. Fax 445-4468
www.iola.k12.wi.us
Iola-Scandinavia MSHS 300/7-12
540 S Jackson St 54945 715-445-2411
Sara Anderson, prin. Fax 445-5119

**Jackson, Washington, Pop. 6,685**

---

Kettle Moraine Lutheran HS 400/9-12
3399 Division Rd 53037 262-677-4051
David Bartelt, supt. Fax 677-4290
Living Word Lutheran HS 200/9-12
2230 Living Word Ln 53037 262-677-9353
Dave Miskimen, prin. Fax 677-8357

**Janesville, Rock, Pop. 62,455**
Janesville SD 9,800/PK-12
527 S Franklin St, 608-743-5000
Dr. Karen Schulte, supt. Fax 743-5110
www.janesville.k12.wi.us/sdj
Craig HS 1,600/9-12
401 S Randall Ave 53545 608-743-5200
Dr. Alison Bjoin, prin. Fax 743-5150
Edison MS 700/6-8
1649 S Chatham St 53546 608-743-5900
James Lemire, prin. Fax 743-5910
Franklin MS 600/6-8
450 N Crosby Ave, 608-743-6000
Charles Urness Ph.D., prin. Fax 743-6010
Marshall MS 900/6-8
25 S Pontiac Dr 53545 608-743-6200
Synthia Taylor, prin. Fax 743-6210
Parker HS 1,400/9-12
3125 Mineral Point Ave, 608-743-5600
Chris Laue, prin. Fax 743-5550

---

Blackhawk Technical College Post-Sec.
PO Box 5009 53547 608-758-6900
University of Wisconsin Rock County Post-Sec.
2909 Kellogg Ave 53546 608-758-6565
WI School for Visually Handicapped Post-Sec.
1700 W State St 53546 608-758-6100

**Jefferson, Jefferson, Pop. 7,891**
Jefferson SD 1,900/PK-12
206 S Taft Ave 53549 920-675-1000
Craig Gerlach, supt. Fax 675-1020
www.sdoj.org
Jefferson HS 600/9-12
700 W Milwaukee St 53549 920-675-1100
Mark Rollefson, prin. Fax 675-1120
Jefferson MS 400/6-8
501 S Taft Ave 53549 920-675-1300
David Wallace, prin. Fax 675-1320

---

St. Coletta School, RR 1 Box 43 53549 Post-Sec.

**Johnson Creek, Jefferson, Pop. 2,707**
Johnson Creek SD 600/PK-12
PO Box 39 53038 920-699-2811
Michael Garvey Ph.D., supt. Fax 699-2801
www.johnsoncreek.k12.wi.us/
Johnson Creek HS 300/6-12
PO Box 39 53038 920-699-3481
Cale Vogel, prin. Fax 699-3566

**Juda, Green, Pop. 357**
Juda SD 300/PK-12
N2385 Spring St 53550 608-934-5251
Traci Davis, supt. Fax 934-5254
www.judaschool.com
Juda HS 100/9-12
N2385 Spring St 53550 608-934-5251
Traci Davis, prin. Fax 934-5254

**Juneau, Dodge, Pop. 2,802**
Dodgeland SD 800/PK-12
401 S Western Ave 53039 920-386-4404
Annette Thompson, supt. Fax 386-4498
www.dodgeland.k12.wi.us
Dodgeland HS 300/9-12
401 S Western Ave 53039 920-386-4404
Jeffrey Sauer, prin. Fax 386-2601
Dodgeland MS 200/6-8
401 S Western Ave 53039 920-386-4404
Marcia Modaff, prin. Fax 386-0345

**Kaukauna, Outagamie, Pop. 15,244**
Kaukauna Area SD 3,300/PK-12
1701 County Road CE 54130 920-766-6100
Mark Duerwaechter, admin. Fax 766-6104
www.kaukauna.k12.wi.us
Kaukauna HS 1,100/9-12
1701 County Road CE 54130 920-766-6113
Mike Werbowsky, prin. Fax 766-6157
River View MS 500/5-8
101 Oak St 54130 920-766-6111
Dan Joseph, prin. Fax 766-6109

**Kenosha, Kenosha, Pop. 96,606**
Kenosha SD 21,500/PK-12
3600 52nd St 53144 262-359-6300
Dr. Sue Savaglio-Jarvis, supt. Fax 359-7672
www.kusd.edu
Bradford HS 1,700/9-12
3700 Washington Rd 53144 262-359-6200
Dr. Kurt Sinclair, prin. Fax 359-5948
Bullen MS 800/6-8
2804 39th Ave 53144 262-359-4460
Andy Baumgart, prin. Fax 359-4487
Hillcrest S 100/Alt
4616 24th St 53144 262-359-6118
Eitan Benzaquen, prin. Fax 359-7870
Indian Trail Academy 1,600/9-12
6800 60th St 53144 262-359-8700
Maria Kotz, prin. Fax 359-8756
Lance MS 900/6-8
4515 80th St 53142 262-359-2240
Chad Dahlk, prin. Fax 359-2184
Lincoln MS 700/6-8
6729 18th Ave 53143 262-359-6296
Star Daley, prin. Fax 359-5966
Mahone MS 1,100/6-8
6900 60th St 53144 262-359-8100
Terri Huck, prin. Fax 359-6851
Reuther Central HS 500/Alt
913 57th St 53140 262-359-6160
Karen Walters, prin. Fax 359-6281
Tremper HS 2,100/9-12
8560 26th Ave 53143 262-359-2200
Richard Aiello, prin. Fax 359-2187
Washington MS 600/6-8
811 Washington Rd 53140 262-359-6291
Curtiss Tolefree, prin. Fax 359-6056
Other Schools – See Pleasant Prairie

---

Carthage College Post-Sec.
2001 Alford Park Dr 53140 262-551-8500
Christian Life S 800/PK-12
10700 75th St 53142 262-694-3900
Rev. Susan Nelson, supt. Fax 694-3312
Gateway Technical College Post-Sec.
3520 30th Ave 53144 262-564-2200
St. Joseph Catholic Academy 500/6-12
2401 69th St 53143 262-654-8651
Robert Freund, pres. Fax 654-1615
University of Wisconsin Post-Sec.
PO Box 2000 53141 262-595-2345

**Keshena, Menominee, Pop. 1,238**
Menominee Indian SD 800/PK-12
PO Box 1330 54135 715-799-3824
Wendell Waukau, supt. Fax 799-4659
www.misd.k12.wi.us
Menominee Indian HS 200/9-12
PO Box 850 54135 715-799-3846
Leslie Shawanokasic, prin. Fax 799-5558
Other Schools – See Neopit

---

College of Menominee Nation Post-Sec.
PO Box 1179 54135 715-799-5600

**Kewaskum, Washington, Pop. 3,967**
Kewaskum SD 1,900/PK-12
PO Box 37 53040 262-626-8427
James Smasal, supt. Fax 626-2961
www.kewaskumschools.org
Kewaskum Career Academy Vo/Tech
PO Box 426 53040 262-626-8427
Scott Jornlin, prin. Fax 626-4702
Kewaskum HS 600/9-12
PO Box 426 53040 262-626-8427
William Loss, prin. Fax 626-4214
Kewaskum MS 400/6-8
PO Box 432 53040 262-626-8427
Julie Skelton, prin. Fax 626-4214

**Kewaunee, Kewaunee, Pop. 2,918**
Kewaunee SD 800/PK-12
915 2nd St 54216 920-388-3230
Karen Treml, supt. Fax 388-5174
www.kewaunee.k12.wi.us
Kewaunee HS 300/9-12
911 3rd St 54216 920-388-2951
Michael Holtz, prin. Fax 388-5165
Kewaunee MS 200/6-8
921 3rd St 54216 920-388-2458
Kacy Rohr, prin. Fax 388-5696
Lakeshore Alternative S 50/Alt
915 2nd St 54216 920-388-3230
Michael Holtz, prin. Fax 388-5174

**Kiel, Manitowoc, Pop. 3,708**
Kiel Area SD 1,400/PK-12
PO Box 201 53042 920-894-2266
Dr. Louise Blankenheim, supt. Fax 894-5100
www.kiel.k12.wi.us/
Kiel HS 400/9-12
PO Box 218 53042 920-894-2263
Corey Baumgartner, prin. Fax 894-5101
Kiel MS 400/5-8
PO Box 197 53042 920-894-2264
Dr. Deborah Sixel, prin. Fax 894-5100

**Kimberly, Outagamie, Pop. 6,394**
Kimberly Area SD
Supt. — See Combined Locks
Gerritts MS 600/7-8
545 S John St 54136 920-788-7905
Eric Brinkmann, prin. Fax 788-7914
Kimberly HS 1,400/9-12
1662 E Kennedy Ave 54136 920-687-3024
Michael Rietveld, prin. Fax 687-3029

**Kohler, Sheboygan, Pop. 2,103**
Kohler SD 600/PK-12
333 Upper Rd 53044 920-803-7200
Quynh Trueblood, supt. Fax 459-2930
www.kohlerpublicschools.org/
Kohler HS 100/9-12
333 Upper Rd 53044 920-803-7202
Timothy Brown, prin. Fax 459-2930
Kohler MS 6-8
333 Upper Rd 53044 920-803-7202
Timothy Brown, prin. Fax 459-2930

**La Crosse, LaCrosse, Pop. 50,284**
La Crosse SD 7,000/PK-12
807 East Ave S 54601 608-789-7600
Randy Nelson, supt. Fax 789-7960
www.lacrosseschools.org/
Central HS 1,100/9-12
1801 Losey Blvd S 54601 608-789-7900
Jeffrey Fleig, prin. Fax 789-7931
Lincoln MS 400/6-8
510 9th St S 54601 608-789-7780
Melissa Murray, prin. Fax 789-7181
Logan HS 900/9-12
1500 Ranger Dr 54603 608-789-7700
Dr. Deborah Markos, prin. Fax 789-7711
Logan MS 400/6-8
1450 Avon St 54603 608-789-7740
Jay Pica, prin. Fax 789-7754
Longfellow MS 500/6-8
1900 Denton St 54601 608-789-7670
Penny Reedy, prin. Fax 789-7975
7 Rivers Community HS Alt
807 East Ave S 54601 608-789-7600
Penny Reedy, prin.

---

Aquinas HS 400/9-12
315 11th St S 54601 608-784-0287
Ted Knutson, prin. Fax 782-8851
Aquinas MS South Campus 100/7-8
315 11th St S 54601 608-784-0156
Patricia Kosmatka, prin. Fax 784-0229
Gunderson Medical Foundation Post-Sec.
1836 South Ave 54601 608-782-7300
Providence Academy 100/PK-12
716 Windsor St 54603 608-784-6167
University of Wisconsin La Crosse Post-Sec.
1725 State St 54601 608-785-8000
Viterbo University Post-Sec.
900 Viterbo Dr 54601 608-796-3000
Western Technical College Post-Sec.
400 7th St N 54601 608-785-9200

**Ladysmith, Rusk, Pop. 3,376**
Ladysmith SD 900/PK-12
1700 Edgewood Ave E 54848 715-532-5277
Paul Uhren, supt. Fax 532-7445
ladysmith.k12.wi.us
Ladysmith HS 300/9-12
1700 Edgewood Ave E 54848 715-532-5531
Robert Lecheler, prin. Fax 532-5961
Ladysmith MS 200/6-8
115 E 6th St S 54848 715-532-5252
Andrew Grimm, prin. Fax 532-7455

**La Farge, Vernon, Pop. 740**
La Farge SD 200/PK-12
301 W Adams St 54639 608-625-0107
Shawn Donovan, supt. Fax 625-0118
www.lafarge.k12.wi.us/
La Farge HS 100/9-12
301 W Adams St 54639 608-625-2400
Angela Egge, prin. Fax 625-0152
La Farge MS 50/6-8
301 W Adams St 54639 608-625-2400
Angela Egge, prin. Fax 625-0152

**Lake Geneva, Walworth, Pop. 7,583**
Lake Geneva J1 SD 1,600/PK-8
208 E South St 53147 262-348-1000
James Gottinger, supt. Fax 248-9704
www.lakegenevaschools.com
Lake Geneva MS 700/6-8
600 N Bloomfield Rd 53147 262-348-3000
Drew Halbesma, prin. Fax 348-3092

Lake Geneva-Genoa City UHSD 1,500/9-12
208 E South St 53147 262-348-1000
Dr. James Gottinger, supt. Fax 248-9704
www.lakegenevaschools.com
Badger HS 1,500/9-12
220 E South St 53147 262-348-2000
Bob Kopydlowski, prin. Fax 248-6178

**Lake Mills, Jefferson, Pop. 5,657**
Lake Mills Area SD 1,300/PK-12
120 E Lake Park Pl 53551 920-648-2215
Dean Sanders, supt. Fax 648-5795
www.lakemills.k12.wi.us
Lake Mills HS 400/9-12
615 Catlin Dr 53551 920-648-2355
Pamela Streich, prin. Fax 648-2357
Lake Mills MS 400/5-8
318 College St 53551 920-648-2358
Jennifer Nicholson, prin. Fax 648-8928

---

Lakeside Lutheran HS 400/9-12
231 Woodland Beach Rd 53551 920-648-2321
James Grasby, prin. Fax 648-5625

**Lancaster, Grant, Pop. 3,854**
Lancaster Community SD 900/PK-12
925 W Maple St 53813 608-723-2175
Rob Wagner, supt. Fax 723-6397
www.lancastersd.k12.wi.us
Lancaster HS 300/9-12
806 E Elm St 53813 608-723-2173
Mark Uppena, prin. Fax 723-2441
Lancaster MS 200/6-8
802 E Elm St 53813 608-723-6425
Mark Uppena, prin. Fax 723-6731

**Land O Lakes, Vilas**

Conserve S 50/10-11
5400 N Black Oak Lake Rd 54540 715-547-1300
Stefan Anderson, hdmstr. Fax 547-1386

**Laona, Forest, Pop. 574**
Laona SD 200/PK-12
5216 Forest Ave 54541 715-674-2143
Laurie Asher, supt. Fax 674-5904
www.laona.k12.wi.us
Laona JSHS 100/7-12
5216 Forest Ave 54541 715-674-2143
Jim Bradley, prin. Fax 674-5904

**Lena, Oconto, Pop. 558**
Lena SD 400/PK-12
304 E Main St 54139 920-829-5703
David Honish, supt. Fax 829-5122
www.lena.k12.wi.us
Alternative S 50/Alt
304 E Main St 54139 920-829-5703
David Honish, prin. Fax 829-5122
Lena HS 100/9-12
304 E Main St 54139 920-829-5244
Ben Pytleski, prin. Fax 829-5122
Lena MS 100/6-8
304 E Main St 54139 920-829-5244
Ben Pytleski, prin. Fax 829-5122

**Little Chute, Outagamie, Pop. 10,339**
Little Chute Area SD 1,300/PK-12
325 Meulemans St Ste A 54140 920-788-7605
David Botz, supt. Fax 788-7603
www.littlechute.k12.wi.us
Little Chute HS 500/9-12
1402 Freedom Rd 54140 920-788-7600
Daniel Valentyn, prin. Fax 788-7841
Little Chute MS 200/7-8
325 Meulemans St Ste B 54140 920-788-7607
Lori Van Handel, prin. Fax 788-7615

**Livingston, Iowa, Pop. 663**
Iowa-Grant SD 800/PK-12
498 County Road IG 53554 608-943-6311
Linda Erickson, supt. Fax 943-8438
www.igs.k12.wi.us
Iowa-Grant HS 200/9-12
462 County Road IG 53554 608-943-6312
Chris Gotto, prin. Fax 943-8707

**Lodi, Columbia, Pop. 3,022**
Lodi SD 1,400/PK-12
115 School St 53555 608-592-3851
Charles Pursell, supt. Fax 592-3852
www.lodi.k12.wi.us
Lodi HS 500/9-12
1100 Sauk St 53555 608-592-3853
Vincent Breunig, prin. Fax 592-1045
Lodi MS 400/6-8
900 Sauk St 53555 608-592-3854
Joe Prosek, prin. Fax 592-1035

**Lomira, Dodge, Pop. 2,408**
Lomira SD 1,000/PK-12
PO Box 919 53048 920-269-4396
Robert Lloyd, admin. Fax 269-4996
www.lomira.k12.wi.us/
Lomira HS 400/9-12
PO Box 919 53048 920-269-4396
Debra Janke, prin. Fax 269-4128
Lomira MS 200/6-8
PO Box 919 53048 920-269-4396
Robert Lloyd, prin. Fax 269-4996

**Loyal, Clark, Pop. 1,258**
Loyal SD 600/PK-12
PO Box 10 54446 715-255-8552
Cale Jackson, supt. Fax 255-8553
www.loyal.k12.wi.us
Loyal HS 200/9-12
PO Box 10 54446 715-255-8511
Christopher Lindner, prin. Fax 255-8553
Loyal JHS 100/7-8
PO Box 10 54446 715-255-8511
Christopher Lindner, prin. Fax 255-8553

**Luck, Polk, Pop. 1,101**
Luck SD 500/PK-12
810 S 7th St 54853 715-472-2151
Rick Palmer, supt. Fax 472-2159
www.lucksd.k12.wi.us
Luck JSHS 200/7-12
810 S 7th St 54853 715-472-2152
Brad Werner, prin. Fax 472-2159

**Luxemburg, Kewaunee, Pop. 2,502**
Luxemburg-Casco SD 1,900/PK-12
PO Box 70 54217 920-845-2391
Glenn Schlender, supt. Fax 845-5871
www.luxcasco.k12.wi.us
Luxemburg-Casco HS 600/9-12
PO Box 410 54217 920-845-2336
Adam Kurth, prin. Fax 845-2280
Other Schools – See Casco

**Mc Farland, Dane, Pop. 7,692**
Mc Farland SD 3,300/PK-12
5101 Farwell St 53558 608-838-3169
Scott Brown, admin. Fax 838-3074
www.mcfarland.k12.wi.us
Indian Mound MS 500/6-8
6330 Exchange St 53558 608-838-8980
Erin Tarnutzer, prin. Fax 838-4588
Mc Farland HS 700/9-12
5103 Farwell St 53558 608-838-3166
James Hickey, prin. Fax 838-4562

**Madison, Dane, Pop. 226,807**
Madison Metro SD 25,500/PK-12
545 W Dayton St 53703 608-663-1879
Jennifer Cheatham, supt. Fax 204-0342
www.madison.k12.wi.us
Black Hawk MS 400/6-8
1402 Wyoming Way 53704 608-204-4360
Sean Storch, prin. Fax 204-0368
Cherokee Heights MS 500/6-8
4301 Cherokee Dr 53711 608-204-1240
Kevin Brown, prin. Fax 204-0378
East HS 1,600/9-12
2222 E Washington Ave 53704 608-204-1600
Mary Kelley, prin. Fax 204-0388
Hamilton MS 700/6-8
4801 Waukesha St 53705 608-204-4620
Henry Schmelz, prin. Fax 204-0417
Innovative & Alternative Education 50/Alt
1045 E Dayton St 53703 608-204-4220
Sally Schultz, prin. Fax 204-1580
Jefferson MS 600/6-8
101 S Gammon Rd 53717 608-663-6403
Anne Fischer, prin. Fax 442-2193
LaFollette HS 1,500/9-12
702 Pflaum Rd 53716 608-204-3600
Chad Wiese, prin. Fax 204-0435
Memorial HS 1,900/9-12
201 S Gammon Rd 53717 608-663-5990
Jay Affeldt, prin. Fax 442-2197
O'Keeffe MS 500/6-8
510 S Thornton Ave 53703 608-204-6820
Tony Dugas, prin. Fax 204-0561
Sennett MS 600/6-8
502 Pflaum Rd 53716 608-204-1920
Tremayne Clardy, prin. Fax 204-0495
Shabazz-City HS 100/Alt
1601 N Sherman Ave 53704 608-204-2440
Aric Soderbloom, prin. Fax 204-0503
Sherman MS 400/6-8
1610 Ruskin St 53704 608-204-2100
Michael Hernandez, prin. Fax 204-0501
Spring Harbor MS 300/6-8
1110 Spring Harbor Dr 53705 608-204-1100
Pam Waite, prin. Fax 204-0509
Toki MS 500/6-8
5606 Russett Rd 53711 608-204-4740
Nicole Schaefer, prin. Fax 204-0523
West HS 2,100/9-12
30 Ash St 53726 608-204-4100
Beth Thompson, prin. Fax 204-0529
Whitehorse MS 400/6-8
218 Schenk St 53714 608-204-4480
Deborah Ptak, prin. Fax 204-0538

Abundant Life Christian S 300/K-12
4901 E Buckeye Rd 53716 608-221-1520
Doug Butler, prin. Fax 221-8572
Edgewood College Post-Sec.
1000 Edgewood College Dr 53711 608-663-4861
Edgewood HS 600/9-12
2219 Monroe St 53711 608-257-1023
Robert Growney, prin. Fax 257-9133
Empire Beauty School Post-Sec.
6414 Odana Rd 53719 608-270-0188
Globe University Post-Sec.
4901 Eastpark Blvd 53718 608-216-9400
Herzing University Post-Sec.
5218 E Terrace Dr 53718 608-249-6611
ITT Technical Institute Post-Sec.
2450 Rimrock Rd Ste 100 53713 608-288-6301
Madison Area Technical College Post-Sec.
1701 Wright St 53704 608-246-6100
Madison Media Institute Post-Sec.
2702 Agriculture Dr 53718 608-663-2000
St. Ambose Academy 100/6-12
602 Everglade Dr 53717 608-827-5863
Scott Schmiesing, prin.
University of Wisconsin Post-Sec.
500 Lincoln Dr 53706 608-262-1234

**Manawa, Waupaca, Pop. 1,362**
Manawa SD 700/PK-12
800 Beech St 54949 920-596-2525
Dr. Melanie Oppor, supt. Fax 596-5308
www.manawa.k12.wi.us
Little Wolf JSHS 300/7-12
515 E 4th St 54949 920-596-5800
Daniel Wolfgram, prin. Fax 596-2655

**Manitowoc, Manitowoc, Pop. 33,258**
Manitowoc SD 5,300/PK-12
PO Box 1657 54221 920-686-4777
Marcia Flaherty, supt. Fax 686-4780
www.manitowocpublicschools.com
Lincoln SHS 1,200/10-12
1433 S 8th St 54220 920-683-4861
Luke Valitchka, prin. Fax 683-4845
Washington JHS 600/7-9
2101 Division St 54220 920-683-4857
Kathleen Lemberger, prin. Fax 683-7989
Wilson JHS 600/7-9
1201 N 11th St 54220 920-683-4859
Eric Johnson, prin. Fax 683-7988

Empire Beauty School Post-Sec.
1034 S 18th St 54220 920-684-3028
Manitowoc Lutheran HS 200/9-12
4045 Lancer Cir 54220 920-682-0215
Ryan Rathje, prin. Fax 682-2363
Roncalli HS 400/9-12
2000 Mirro Dr 54220 920-682-8801
Tim Olson, prin. Fax 686-8110
St. Francis of Assisi MS 200/6-8
2109 Marshall St 54220 920-683-6884
Steve Thiele, prin. Fax 683-6882
Silver Lake College of the Holy Family Post-Sec.
2406 S Alverno Rd 54220 920-684-6691
University of Wisconsin Manitowoc Post-Sec.
705 Viebahn St 54220 920-683-4700

**Maple, Douglas**
Maple SD 1,400/PK-12
PO Box 188 54854 715-363-2431
Dr. Sara Croney, supt. Fax 363-2191
www.nw-tigers.org
Northwestern HS 400/9-12
PO Box 218 54854 715-363-2434
Mark Carlson, prin. Fax 363-2523
Other Schools – See Poplar

**Marathon, Marathon, Pop. 1,520**
Marathon City SD 600/PK-12
PO Box 37 54448 715-443-2226
Richard Parks, supt. Fax 443-2611
www.marathon.k12.wi.us
Marathon HS 300/9-12
PO Box 37 54448 715-443-2226
David Beranek, prin. Fax 443-2611

**Marinette, Marinette, Pop. 10,850**
Marinette SD 2,100/PK-12
2139 Pierce Ave 54143 715-735-1400
Dr. Tim Baneck, supt. Fax 732-7930
www.marinette.k12.wi.us
Marinette HS 700/9-12
2135 Pierce Ave 54143 715-735-1300
Corry Lambie, prin. Fax 732-7929
Marinette MS 600/5-8
1011 Water St 54143 715-735-1500
Michael Whisler, prin. Fax 732-7939

Northeast Wisconsin Technical College Post-Sec.
1601 University Dr 54143 715-735-9361
St. Thomas Aquinas Academy 100/PK-12
1200 Main St 54143 715-735-7481
Peter Mayhew, admin. Fax 735-3375
University of Wisconsin Marinette Post-Sec.
750 W Bay Shore St 54143 715-735-4300

**Marion, Waupaca, Pop. 1,253**
Marion SD 500/PK-12
1001 N Main St 54950 715-754-2511
James Bena, supt. Fax 754-4508
www.marion.k12.wi.us
Marion JSHS 200/7-12
105 School St 54950 715-754-5273
Daniel Breitrick, prin. Fax 754-1350

**Markesan, Green Lake, Pop. 1,472**
Markesan SD 700/PK-12
PO Box 248 53946 920-398-2373
Duane Bark, supt. Fax 398-3281
www.markesan.k12.wi.us
Markesan HS 200/9-12
PO Box 248 53946 920-398-2373
John Koopman, prin. Fax 398-3281
Markesan MS 200/6-8
PO Box 248 53946 920-398-2373
John Koopman, prin. Fax 398-3281

**Marshall, Dane, Pop. 3,813**
Marshall SD 1,200/PK-12
PO Box 76 53559 608-655-3466
Dr. Barb Sramek, supt. Fax 655-4481
www.marshall.k12.wi.us
Marshall HS 400/9-12
PO Box 76 53559 608-655-1310
Brian Sniff, prin. Fax 655-3046
Marshall MS 200/7-8
PO Box 76 53559 608-655-1571
Lisa Blochwitz, prin. Fax 655-1591

**Marshfield, Wood, Pop. 18,924**
Marshfield SD 3,800/PK-12
1010 E 4th St 54449 715-387-1101
Deirdre Wells, supt. Fax 387-0133
www.marshfield.k12.wi.us
Marshfield HS 1,200/9-12
1401 E Becker Rd 54449 715-387-8464
Steve Sukawaty, prin. Fax 384-3589
Marshfield MS 600/7-8
900 E 4th St 54449 715-387-1249
David Schoepke, prin. Fax 384-9269

Columbus HS 100/9-12
710 S Columbus Ave 54449 715-387-1177
Steven VanWhye, prin. Fax 384-4535
Columbus MS 100/6-8
710 S Columbus Ave 54449 715-387-1177
Steven VanWyhe, prin. Fax 384-4535
Marshfield Clinic/St. Josephs Hospital Post-Sec.
1000 N Oak Ave 54449 715-221-6332
Mid-State Technical College Post-Sec.
2600 W 5th St 54449 715-387-2538
St. Joseph Hospital/Marshfield Clinic Post-Sec.
611 N Saint Joseph Ave 54449 715-387-1713
Univ. of Wisconsin - Marshfield/Wood Co. Post-Sec.
2000 W 5th St 54449 715-389-6530

**Mauston, Juneau, Pop. 4,366**
Mauston SD 1,500/PK-12
510 Grayside Ave 53948 608-847-5451
Dr. Christine M. Weymouth, supt. Fax 847-4635
www.maustonschools.org

Mauston HS 500/9-12
800 Grayside Ave 53948 608-847-4410
Jim Dillin, prin. Fax 847-4802
Olson MS 300/6-8
508 Grayside Ave 53948 608-847-6603
Michael Gonzalez, prin. Fax 847-4925

**Mayville, Dodge, Pop. 5,113**
Mayville SD 1,300/PK-12
N8210 State Road 28 53050 920-387-7963
Dr. Patricia Antony, supt. Fax 387-7979
www.mayvilleschools.com
Mayville HS 500/9-12
500 N Clark St 53050 920-387-7960
Robert Clark, prin. Fax 387-7977
Mayville MS 500/3-8
445 N Henninger St 53050 920-387-7970
John Schlender, prin. Fax 387-7974

**Mazomanie, Dane, Pop. 1,638**
Wisconsin Heights SD 800/PK-12
10173 US Highway 14 53560 608-767-2595
Mark Elworthy Ed.D., supt. Fax 767-3579
www.wisheights.k12.wi.us
Wisconsin Heights HS 200/9-12
10173 US Highway 14 53560 608-767-2586
Asta Sepetys, prin. Fax 767-2062
Wisconsin Heights MS 200/6-8
10173 US Highway 14 53560 608-767-2586
Asta Sepetys, prin. Fax 767-2062

**Medford, Taylor, Pop. 4,279**
Medford Area SD 2,200/PK-12
124 W State St 54451 715-748-4620
Patrick Sullivan, supt. Fax 748-6839
www.medford.k12.wi.us
Medford Alternative HS Alt
624 College St 54451 715-748-4620
Kellie Keene, lead tchr.
Medford HS 700/9-12
1015 W Broadway Ave 54451 715-748-5951
Jill Lybert, prin. Fax 748-6438
Medford MS 600/5-8
509 Clark St 54451 715-748-2516
Al Leonard, prin. Fax 748-1213

**Mellen, Ashland, Pop. 725**
Mellen SD 300/PK-12
PO Box 500 54546 715-274-3601
Michael Cox, supt. Fax 274-3715
www.mellendiggers.org
Mellen HS 100/9-12
PO Box 500 54546 715-274-3601
Kevin Buxton, prin. Fax 274-3715

**Melrose, Jackson, Pop. 499**
Melrose-Mindoro SD 700/PK-12
N181 State Hwy 108 54642 608-488-2201
Del DeBerg, supt. Fax 488-2805
www.mel-min.k12.wi.us
Melrose-Mindoro HS 200/9-12
N181 State Hwy 108 54642 608-488-2201
Jeff Arzt, prin. Fax 488-2805

**Menasha, Winnebago, Pop. 17,081**
Menasha JSD 3,600/PK-12
PO Box 360 54952 920-967-1400
Chris VanderHeyden, supt. Fax 751-5038
www.mjsd.k12.wi.us
Maplewood MS 800/6-8
1600 Midway Rd 54952 920-967-1600
Dr. Bev Sturke, prin. Fax 832-5837
Menasha HS 1,000/9-12
420 7th St 54952 920-967-1800
Dr. Lawrence Haase, prin. Fax 751-5223

---

University of Wisconsin Fox Valley Post-Sec.
1478 Midway Rd 54952 920-832-2600

**Menomonee Falls, Waukesha, Pop. 35,186**
Menomonee Falls SD 4,300/PK-12
W156N8480 Pilgrim Rd 53051 262-255-8440
Patricia Greco, supt. Fax 255-8461
www.sdmfschools.org
Menomonee Falls HS 1,500/9-12
W142N8101 Merrimac Dr 53051 262-255-8444
Corey Golla, prin. Fax 255-8377
North MS 900/6-8
N88W16750 Garfield Dr 53051 262-255-8450
Lynn Grimm, prin. Fax 255-8475

---

Bethlehem Lutheran S - South 100/5-8
N84W15252 Menomonee Ave 53051 262-251-3120
Daryl Weber, prin. Fax 251-4679
Calvary Baptist S 200/PK-12
N84W19049 Menomonee Ave 53051 262-251-0328
Jeff Chestnut, admin. Fax 250-0624

**Menomonie, Dunn, Pop. 15,977**
Menomonie Area SD 3,100/K-12
215 Pine Ave NE 54751 715-232-1642
Joe Zydowsky, supt. Fax 232-1317
msd.k12.wi.us
Menomonie HS 1,000/9-12
1715 5th St W 54751 715-232-2606
David Munoz, prin. Fax 232-2629
Menomonie MS 700/6-8
920 21st St SE 54751 715-232-1673
Stacey Everson, prin. Fax 232-5486

---

University of Wisconsin Post-Sec.
712 Broadway St S 54751 715-232-1122

**Mequon, Ozaukee, Pop. 22,848**
Mequon-Thiensville SD 3,600/PK-12
5000 W Mequon Rd 53092 262-238-8500
Demond Means, supt. Fax 238-8520
www.mtsd.k12.wi.us
Homestead HS 1,400/9-12
5000 W Mequon Rd 53092 262-238-5646
Brett Bowers, prin. Fax 238-5633
Lake Shore MS 400/6-8
11036 N Range Line Rd 53092 262-238-7613
Kate Dunning, prin. Fax 238-7650
Steffen MS 400/6-8
6633 W Steffen Dr 53092 262-238-4706
Deborah Anderson, prin. Fax 238-4740

---

Concordia University Post-Sec.
12800 N Lake Shore Dr 53097 262-243-5700
Lumen Christi MS 200/4-8
11300 N Saint James Ln 53092 262-242-7960
Kelly Fyfe, prin. Fax 512-8986
Milwaukee Area Technical College Post-Sec.
5555 W Highland Rd 53092 262-238-2200

**Mercer, Iron, Pop. 516**
Mercer SD 100/PK-12
2690 W Margaret St 54547 715-476-2154
Erik Torkelson, supt. Fax 476-2587
www.mercer.k12.wi.us
Mercer S 100/PK-12
2690 W Margaret St 54547 715-476-2154
Erik Torkelson, admin. Fax 476-2587

**Merrill, Lincoln, Pop. 9,553**
Merrill Area SD 2,800/PK-12
1111 N Sales St 54452 715-536-4581
Walter Leipart, supt. Fax 536-1788
www.maps.k12.wi.us
Merrill HS 1,100/9-12
1201 N Sales St 54452 715-536-4594
Shannon Murray, prin. Fax 536-5504
Prairie River MS 600/6-8
106 N Polk St 54452 715-536-9593
Gerald Beyer, prin. Fax 536-6378

**Merton, Waukesha, Pop. 3,309**
Merton Community SD 900/PK-8
PO Box 15 53056 262-538-2227
Ronald Russ, supt. Fax 538-3937
www.merton.k12.wi.us
Merton IS 500/5-8
PO Box 15 53056 262-538-1130
Jay Posick, prin. Fax 538-4978

**Middleton, Dane, Pop. 17,031**
Middleton-Cross Plains Area SD 6,100/PK-12
7106 South Ave 53562 608-829-9000
Dr. Donald Johnson, supt. Fax 836-1536
www.mcpasd.k12.wi.us
Kromrey MS 700/5-8
7009 Donna Dr 53562 608-829-9530
Steve Soeteber, prin. Fax 831-8388
Middleton HS 1,900/9-12
2100 Bristol St 53562 608-829-9660
Dr. Stephen Plank, prin. Fax 831-1995
Other Schools – See Cross Plains

---

Globe University Post-Sec.
1345 Deming Way 53562 608-830-6900

**Milton, Rock, Pop. 5,493**
Milton SD 3,400/PK-12
448 E High St 53563 608-868-9200
Timothy J. Schigur, supt. Fax 868-9215
www.milton.k12.wi.us
Milton HS 1,000/9-12
114 W High St 53563 608-868-9300
Jeremy Bilhorn, prin. Fax 868-9399
Milton MS 500/7-8
20 E Madison Ave 53563 608-868-9350
Laura Jennaro, prin. Fax 868-9269

**Milwaukee, Milwaukee, Pop. 580,512**
Milwaukee SD 73,200/PK-12
PO Box 2181 53201 414-475-8393
Dr. Darienne Driver, supt. Fax 475-8595
www.milwaukee.k12.wi.us
Achievement Center Alt
606 W Concordia Ave 53212 414-286-4100
Hayden Headley, dir.
ASSATA 100/Alt
3517 W Courtland Ave 53209 414-345-6113
Carlotta Pritchett, prin. Fax 345-9893
Audubon Technology & Communication Ctr 600/6-8
3300 S 39th St 53215 414-902-7800
Leon Groce, prin. Fax 902-7815
Audubon Technology & Communication HS 300/9-12
3300 S 39th St 53215 414-902-7806
Leon Groce, prin. Fax 902-7869
Banner Prep HS of Milwaukee 100/Alt
4610 W State St 53208 414-461-9561
Karen Huff, admin. Fax 461-9846
Bay View MSHS 1,400/7-12
2751 S Lenox St 53207 414-294-2400
Aaron Shapiro, prin. Fax 294-2415
Bradley Tech & Trade HS Vo/Tech
700 S 4th St 53204 414-212-2400
Tamara Hines, prin. Fax 212-2415
Career Youth Development S 50/Alt
3517 W Courtland Ave 53209 414-449-5960
Lawrence Roth, admin. Fax 449-5971
Groppi HS 500/Alt
1312 N 27th St 53208 414-934-8200
Joel Eul, prin. Fax 934-8215
Hamilton HS 1,700/9-12
6215 W Warnimont Ave 53220 414-327-9300
Rosana Mateo, prin. Fax 327-9315
King International HS 1,500/9-12
1801 W Olive St 53209 414-267-0700
Dr. Jennifer Smith, prin. Fax 267-0715
King International MS 500/6-8
4950 N 24th St 53209 414-616-5200
Tamara Ellis, prin.
Lad Lake Synergy MSHS 100/Alt
2820 W Grant St 53215 414-332-2675
Glen Stavens, admin.
Lincoln MS of the Arts 900/6-8
820 E Knapp St 53202 414-212-3300
Ramon Evans, prin. Fax 212-3315
MacDowell Montessori S 500/PK-12
6415 W Mount Vernon Ave 53213 414-935-1400
Andrea Corona, prin. Fax 935-1415
Madison Academic Campus 1,100/9-12
8135 W Florist Ave 53218 414-393-6100
Gregory Ogunbowale, prin. Fax 393-6222
Meir S 500/3-9
1555 N Martin Luther King 53212 414-212-3200
Michelle Morris Carter, prin. Fax 212-3215
Milwaukee HS of the Arts 800/9-12
2300 W Highland Ave 53233 414-934-7000
Barry Applewhite, prin. Fax 934-7015
Milwaukee S of Languages 1,100/6-12
8400 W Burleigh St 53222 414-393-5700
Jennifer Smith, admin. Fax 393-5715
Morse-Marshall S for Gifted and Talented 1,200/6-12
4141 N 64th St 53216 414-393-2300
Larry Farris, prin. Fax 393-2315
New School for Community Services 200/Alt
609 N 8th St 53233 414-298-9390
Hector Rosales, lead tchr. Fax 298-9395
NOVA MSHS 100/Alt
2320 W Burleigh St 53206 414-874-0283
Patricia Bridges, dir. Fax 874-0284
Obama S of Career & Tech Educ 200/K-12
5075 N Sherman Blvd 53209 414-393-4900
Dr. Mateva Harris, prin.
Project STAY 300/Alt
609 N 8th St 53233 414-298-9300
Diane Rosado, admin. Fax 298-9315
Pulaski HS 1,300/9-12
2500 W Oklahoma Ave 53215 414-902-8900
Darrell Williams, prin. Fax 902-8915
Reagan Preparatory HS 1,200/9-12
4965 S 20th St 53221 414-304-6100
Michael Roemer, prin. Fax 304-6115
Riverside University HS 1,600/9-12
1615 E Locust St 53211 414-906-4900
Michael Harris, prin. Fax 906-4915
Roosevelt Creative Arts MS 700/6-8
800 W Walnut St 53205 414-267-8800
Keushum Willingham, prin. Fax 267-8815
Shalom HS 100/Alt
1749 N 16th St 53205 414-933-5019
Gwendolyn Spencer, admin. Fax 933-5433
South Division HS 1,100/9-12
1515 W Lapham Blvd 53204 414-902-8300
Jesus Santos, prin. Fax 902-8315
Southeastern Education Center 50/Alt
4050 N 34th St 53216 414-875-9452
Darren Buckley, admin. Fax 875-9004
Vincent HS 1,300/9-12
7501 N Granville Rd 53224 262-236-1200
Matthew Boswell, prin. Fax 236-1254
Washington HS of Info Technology 800/9-12
2525 N Sherman Blvd 53210 414-875-5900
Tanya Adair, prin.
Wedgewood Park International S 700/6-8
6506 W Warnimont Ave 53220 414-604-7800
Suzanne Kirby, prin. Fax 604-7815
WI Consrv Lifelong Learning S 700/K-12
1017 N 12th St 53233 414-304-6800
Raymond Unanka, prin. Fax 304-6815

West Allis SD 9,100/PK-12
1205 S 70th St Ste 600 53214 414-604-3000
Fax 256-6314
www.wawm.k12.wi.us
Other Schools – See West Allis, West Milwaukee

---

Alverno College Post-Sec.
PO Box 343922 53234 414-382-6000
Atlas Preparatory Academy 900/PK-12
1039 E Russell Ave 53207 414-385-0771
Aurora Health Care Post-Sec.
3000 W Montana St 53215 414-647-3000
Believers in Christ Christian Academy 200/PK-12
4065 N 25th St 53209 414-444-1146
Blood Center of SE Wisconsin Post-Sec.
1701 W Wisconsin Ave 53233 414-937-6338
Bryant & Stratton College Post-Sec.
310 W Wisconsin Ave Ste 500 53203 414-276-5200
Bufkin Christian Academy 100/PK-12
827 N 34th St 53208 414-934-8885
Texas Bufkin, admin. Fax 934-8886
Cardinal Stritch University Post-Sec.
6801 N Yates Rd 53217 414-410-4000
Columbia Hospital Post-Sec.
2025 E Newport Ave 53211 414-961-3800
Cristo Rey Jesuit HS 9-12
1215 S 45th St 53214 414-436-4600
Luke Harrison, prin.
Destiny HS 300/9-12
7210 N 76th St 53223 414-353-4430
Kristen Reed, prin. Fax 353-0637
DeVry University Post-Sec.
411 E Wisconsin Ave Ste 300 53202 414-278-7677
Divine Savior-Holy Angels HS 700/9-12
4257 N 100th St 53222 414-462-3742
Dan Quesnell, prin. Fax 466-0590
Early View Academy of Excellence 400/PK-10
7132 W Good Hope Rd 53223 414-431-0001
Eastbrook Academy 400/PK-12
5375 N Green Bay Ave 53209 414-228-7905
Jay Wriedt, head sch Fax 228-9854
Everest College Post-Sec.
1311 N 6th St 53212 414-831-8400
Froedtert Memorial Lutheran Hospital Post-Sec.
PO Box 26099 53226 414-259-2606
Holy Redeemer Christian Academy 500/PK-12
3500 W Mother Daniels Way 53209 414-466-1800

Holy Wisdom Academy West Campus 100/4-8
3344 S 16th St 53215 414-383-3453
Julie Ann Robinson, prin. Fax 672-2645
Hope Christian HS 200/9-12
3215 N Dr Martin L King Dr 53212 414-264-4476
ITT Technical Institute Post-Sec.
6300 W Layton Ave 53220 414-282-9494
Kaplan College Post-Sec.
111 W Pleasant St Ste 101 53212 414-225-4610
Marquette University Post-Sec.
PO Box 1881 53201 414-288-7700
Marquette University HS 1,100/9-12
3401 W Wisconsin Ave 53208 414-933-7220
Jeff Monday, prin. Fax 937-8588
Medical College of Wisconsin Post-Sec.
8701 W Watertown Plank Rd 53226 414-955-8296
Messmer HS 700/9-12
742 W Capitol Dr 53206 414-264-5440
Jim Piatt, pres. Fax 264-6430
Milwaukee Area Technical College Post-Sec.
700 W State St 53233 414-297-6282
Milwaukee Career College Post-Sec.
3077 N Mayfair Rd Ste 300 53222 800-754-1009
Milwaukee Institute of Art & Design Post-Sec.
273 E Erie St 53202 414-847-3200
Milwaukee Lutheran HS 600/9-12
9700 W Grantosa Dr 53222 414-461-6000
Matthew Pankow, prin. Fax 461-2733
Milwaukee School of Engineering Post-Sec.
1025 N Broadway 53202 414-277-7300
Milwaukee SDA S 100/K-10
10900 W Mill Rd 53225 414-353-3520
Mohammed S 200/PK-12
317 W Wright St 53212 414-263-6772
Mt. Lebanon Lutheran S - Omega Campus 100/4-8
8444 W Melvina St 53222 414-463-5030
Jonathan Winkel, dir. Fax 463-5086
Mount Mary University Post-Sec.
2900 N Menomonee River Pkwy 53222
414-258-4810
Nativity Jesuit MS 100/4-8
1515 S 29th St 53215 414-645-1060
Melodie Wyttenbach, pres. Fax 645-0505
Northwest Catholic S - Upper Campus 200/4-8
8202 W Denver Ave 53223 414-352-6927
Diana Erlandson, prin. Fax 352-7258
Notre Dame MS 100/5-8
1420 W Scott St 53204 414-671-3000
Patrick Landry, prin. Fax 671-3170
Pius XI HS 800/9-12
135 N 76th St 53213 414-290-7000
Dr. Melinda Skrade, pres. Fax 290-7001
Prince of Peace MS 300/PK-K, 6-8
1646 S 22nd St 53204 414-645-4922
P. Blaszczyk, prin. Fax 645-4940
St. Anthony HS 9-12
4807 S 2nd St 53207 414-763-6352
Fax 384-1733
St. Anthony MS 6-8
2156 S 4th St 53207 414-810-3858
Fax 810-3938
St. Francis Hospital Post-Sec.
3237 S 16th St 53215 414-647-5106
St. Joan Antida HS 300/9-12
1341 N Cass St 53202 414-272-8423
Maria Schram, prin. Fax 272-3135
St. Luke's Medical Center Post-Sec.
2900 W Oklahoma Ave 53215 414-649-7500
St. Thomas More HS 400/9-12
2601 E Morgan Ave 53207 414-481-8370
Dr. Mark Joerres, prin. Fax 481-3382
Salam S 700/PK-12
4707 S 13th St 53221 414-282-0504
The Art Institute of Wisconsin Post-Sec.
320 E Buffalo St Ste 100 53202 414-978-5000
Torah Academy of Milwaukee 100/9-12
6800 N Green Bay Ave 53209 414-352-6789
Travis Academy 400/PK-12
8616 N Steven Rd 53223 414-342-4950
Thomas Lane, admin. Fax 342-4957
University of Wisconsin Post-Sec.
PO Box 413 53201 414-229-1122
University S 1,100/PK-12
2100 W Fairy Chasm Rd 53217 414-352-6000
Laura Fuller, admin. Fax 352-8076
Vici Beauty School Post-Sec.
11010 W Hampton Ave 53225 414-464-5002
Wisconsin Conservatory of Music Post-Sec.
1584 N Prospect Ave 53202 414-276-5760
Wisconsin Institute for Torah Study 100/9-12
3288 N Lake Dr 53211 414-963-9317
Earl Lebakken, prin. Fax 963-1519
Wisconsin Lutheran College Post-Sec.
8800 W Bluemound Rd 53226 414-443-8800
Wisconsin Lutheran HS 800/9-12
330 Glenview Ave 53213 414-453-4567
Msgr. Phil Leyrer, prin. Fax 453-3001
WI School of Professional Psychology Post-Sec.
9120 W Hampton Ave Ste 212 53225 414-464-9777
Zablocki VA Medical Center Post-Sec.
5000 W National Ave 53295 414-384-2000

**Mineral Point, Iowa, Pop. 2,475**
Mineral Point SD 700/PK-12
705 Ross St 53565 608-987-0740
Luke Francois, supt. Fax 987-3766
www.mineralpointschools.org
Mineral Point HS 200/9-12
705 Ross St 53565 608-987-0730
Mitch Wainwright, prin. Fax 987-3766
Mineral Point MS 100/6-8
705 Ross St 53565 608-987-0720
Vickie Dahl, prin. Fax 987-3766

**Minocqua, Oneida, Pop. 440**
Lakeland UNHSD 800/9-12
9573 State Highway 70 54548 715-356-5252
Todd Kleinhans, supt. Fax 356-1892
www.luhs.k12.wi.us
Lakeland HS 800/9-12
9573 State Highway 70 54548 715-356-5252
James Bouche, prin. Fax 356-1892

**Mishicot, Manitowoc, Pop. 1,424**
Mishicot SD 900/PK-12
PO Box 280 54228 920-755-4633
Colleen Timm, supt. Fax 755-4068
www.mishicot.k12.wi.us
Mishicot HS 300/9-12
PO Box 280 54228 920-755-2311
Thomas Ellenbecker, prin. Fax 755-2390
Mishicot MS 200/6-8
PO Box 280 54228 920-755-2808
Colleen Timm, prin. Fax 755-2390

**Mondovi, Buffalo, Pop. 2,751**
Mondovi SD, 337 N Jackson St 54755 1,200/PK-12
Greg Corning, supt. 715-926-3684
www.mondovi.k12.wi.us
Mondovi HS 300/9-12
337 N Jackson St 54755 715-926-3656
Mike Bruning, prin. Fax 926-3617
Mondovi MS, 337 N Jackson St 54755 200/6-8
Mike Bruning, prin. 715-926-3656

**Monona, Dane, Pop. 7,407**
Monona Grove SD 2,400/PK-12
5301 Monona Dr 53716 608-221-7660
Dr. Daniel Olson Ed.D., supt. Fax 221-7688
www.mononagrove.org
Monona Grove HS 900/9-12
4400 Monona Dr 53716 608-221-7666
Dr. Paul Brost, prin. Fax 221-7690
Other Schools – See Cottage Grove

**Monroe, Green, Pop. 10,726**
Monroe SD 2,600/PK-12
925 16th Ave Ste 3 53566 608-328-7171
Cory Hirsbrunner, supt. Fax 328-7214
www.monroeschools.com
Monroe HS 700/9-12
1600 26th St 53566 608-328-7117
Chris Medenwaldt, prin. Fax 328-7230
Monroe MS 500/6-8
1510 13th St 53566 608-328-7120
Brian Boehm, prin. Fax 328-7224

---

Paul Mitchell The School Post-Sec.
1015 18th Ave Ste 212 53566 608-329-7004

**Montello, Marquette, Pop. 1,476**
Montello SD 700/PK-12
222 Forest Ln 53949 608-297-7617
Dr. B. Lynn Brown, supt. Fax 297-7726
www.montello.k12.wi.us
Montello JSHS 300/7-12
222 Forest Ln 53949 608-297-2126
Chuck Harsh, prin. Fax 297-9390

**Monticello, Green, Pop. 1,208**
Monticello SD 400/PK-12
334 S Main St 53570 608-938-4194
Allen Brokopp, supt. Fax 938-1062
www.monticello.k12.wi.us/
Monticello HS 100/9-12
334 S Main St 53570 608-938-4194
Mark Gustafson, prin. Fax 938-1062
Monticello MS 100/6-8
334 S Main St 53570 608-938-4194
Mark Gustafson, prin. Fax 938-1062

**Mosinee, Marathon, Pop. 3,964**
Mosinee SD 2,100/PK-12
591 W State Highway 153 54455 715-693-2530
Dr. Ann Schultz, supt. Fax 693-7272
www.mosineeschools.org
Mosinee HS 700/9-12
1000 High St 54455 715-693-2550
Nathan Lehman, prin. Fax 693-1152
Mosinee MS 800/4-8
700 High St 54455 715-693-3660
Joshua Sween, prin. Fax 693-6655

---

Northland Lutheran HS 100/9-12
2107 Tower Rd 54455 715-359-3400
Ryan Wiechmann, prin. Fax 241-9203
WI Valley Lutheran HS 100/9-12
601 Maple Ridge Rd 54455 715-693-2693
Dave Beringer, admin. Fax 693-5962

**Mount Calvary, Fond du Lac, Pop. 757**

---

St. Lawrence Seminary HS 200/9-12
301 Church St 53057 920-753-7500
David Bartel, dean Fax 753-7507

**Mount Horeb, Dane, Pop. 6,889**
Mount Horeb Area SD 2,400/PK-12
1304 E Lincoln St 53572 608-437-2400
Debra Klein, supt. Fax 437-5597
www.mhasd.k12.wi.us
Mount Horeb HS 700/9-12
305 S 8th St 53572 608-437-2400
Stephanie Spoehr, prin. Fax 437-4926
Mount Horeb MS 500/6-8
900 E Garfield St 53572 608-437-2400
Jeff Rasmussen, prin. Fax 437-6227

**Mukwonago, Waukesha, Pop. 7,291**
Mukwonago SD 4,800/K-12
385 County Road NN E 53149 262-363-6300
Shawn McNulty, supt. Fax 363-6272
www.masd.k12.wi.us
Mukwonago HS 1,700/9-12
605 W School Rd 53149 262-363-6200
James Darin, prin. Fax 363-6239
Park View MS 700/7-8
930 N Rochester St 53149 262-363-6292
Mark Doome, prin. Fax 363-6320
Norris SD 100/6-12
W247S10395 Center Dr 53149 262-662-5911
Sara Trampf, supt. Fax 662-5502
www.norriscenter.org/
Norris JSHS 100/6-12
W247S10395 Center Dr 53149 262-662-5911
Christopher Fountain, prin. Fax 662-5502

**Muscoda, Grant, Pop. 1,294**
Riverdale SD 700/PK-12
PO Box 66 53573 608-739-3832
Bryce Bird, supt. Fax 739-3751
www.riverdale.k12.wi.us/
Riverdale HS 200/9-12
PO Box 66 53573 608-739-3116
Jonthan Schmidt, prin. Fax 739-4486
Riverdale MS 200/5-8
800 N 6th St 53573 608-739-3101
Shari Hougan, prin. Fax 739-9118

**Muskego, Waukesha, Pop. 23,915**
Muskego-Norway SD 4,800/PK-12
S87W18763 Woods Rd 53150 262-971-1800
Dr. Kelly Thompson, supt. Fax 679-5790
www.muskegonorway.org/
Bay Lane MS 700/5-8
S75W16399 Hilltop Dr 53150 262-971-1810
Dawn Zandt, prin. Fax 422-2204
Lake Denoon MS 800/5-8
W216S10586 Crowbar Dr 53150 262-971-1820
Linda O'Bryan, prin. Fax 662-1588
Muskego HS 1,700/9-12
W183S8750 Racine Ave 53150 262-971-1790
Todd Irvine, prin. Fax 679-3534

**Nashotah, Waukesha, Pop. 1,378**

---

Nashotah House Post-Sec.
2777 Mission Rd 53058 262-646-6500

**Necedah, Juneau, Pop. 904**
Necedah Area SD 700/PK-12
1801 S Main St 54646 608-565-2256
Larry Gierach, supt. Fax 565-3201
www.necedahschools.org
Necedah MSHS 400/6-12
1801 S Main St 54646 608-565-2256
Mark Becker, prin. Fax 565-7044

**Neenah, Winnebago, Pop. 25,158**
Neenah SD 6,200/PK-12
410 S Commercial St 54956 920-751-6800
Mary Pfeiffer Ph.D., supt. Fax 751-6809
www.neenah.k12.wi.us
Neenah HS 2,100/9-12
1275 Tullar Rd 54956 920-751-6900
Brian Wunderlich, prin. Fax 751-7001
Shattuck MS 900/7-8
600 Elm St 54956 920-751-6850
Stephanie Phernetton, prin. Fax 751-6899

---

St. Mary Catholic HS 200/9-12
1050 Zephyr Dr 54956 920-722-7796
Patrick Batey, prin. Fax 722-5940
St. Mary Catholic MS 200/6-8
1000 Zephyr Dr 54956 920-727-0279
Mike Zuleger, prin. Fax 727-1215
Theda Clark Regional Medical Center Post-Sec.
130 2nd St 54956 920-729-2004

**Neillsville, Clark, Pop. 2,446**
Neillsville SD 500/PK-12
614 E 5th St 54456 715-743-3323
John Gaier, supt. Fax 743-8718
www.neillsville.k12.wi.us
Neillsville MSHS 500/7-12
401 Center St 54456 715-743-8738
Craig Ruskin, prin. Fax 743-8714

**Nekoosa, Wood, Pop. 2,530**
Nekoosa SD 1,200/K-12
600 S Section St 54457 715-886-8000
Terry Whitmore, supt. Fax 886-8012
www.nekoosasd.net
Alexander MS 500/4-8
540 Birch St 54457 715-886-8040
Jon Sprehn, prin. Fax 886-8097
Nekoosa Academy Alt
310 1st St 54457 715-886-8190
Clint Rogers, prin. Fax 886-8191
Nekoosa HS 400/9-12
500 Cedar St 54457 715-886-8060
Michael Kumm, prin. Fax 886-8087

**Neopit, Menominee, Pop. 682**
Menominee Indian SD
Supt. — See Keshena
Menominee Indian MS 100/6-8
PO Box 9 54150 715-756-2324
Stephanie Feldner, prin. Fax 756-2496

**Neosho, Dodge, Pop. 566**

---

Victory Christian HS 50/9-12
PO Box 46 53059 920-625-3995
Katie Kluever, coord. Fax 625-3995

**New Auburn, Chippewa, Pop. 537**
New Auburn SD 300/PK-12
PO Box 110 54757 715-237-2202
Scott Johnson, supt. Fax 237-2350
www.newauburn.k12.wi.us

New Auburn JSHS 200/7-12
PO Box 110 54757 715-237-2505
Cory Martens, prin. Fax 237-2350

**New Berlin, Waukesha, Pop. 39,208**
New Berlin SD 4,400/K-12
4333 S Sunnyslope Rd 53151 262-789-6200
Joe Garza, supt. Fax 786-0512
www.nbexcellence.org/
Eisenhower MSHS 1,200/7-12
4333 S Sunnyslope Rd 53151 262-789-6300
Michael Fesenmaier, prin. Fax 789-6313
New Berlin West MSHS 1,200/7-12
18695 W Cleveland Ave 53146 262-789-6400
John Budish, prin. Fax 789-6442

---

Heritage Christian Schools 500/PK-12
3500 S West Ln 53151 262-432-0333
John Davis, pres. Fax 432-0542

**New Glarus, Green, Pop. 2,162**
New Glarus SD 800/PK-12
PO Box 7 53574 608-527-2410
Dr. Jennifer Thayer, supt. Fax 527-5101
www.ngsd.k12.wi.us
New Glarus HS 300/9-12
PO Box 7 53574 608-527-2410
Jeff Eichelkraut, prin. Fax 527-5101
New Glarus MS 100/5-8
PO Box 67 53574 608-527-2410
Mark Stateler, prin. Fax 527-5101

**New Holstein, Calumet, Pop. 3,214**
New Holstein SD 1,100/PK-12
1715 Plymouth St 53061 920-898-5115
Dan Nett, supt. Fax 898-4112
www.nhsd.k12.wi.us
New Holstein HS 400/9-12
1715 Plymouth St 53061 920-898-4256
Rodney Figuero, prin. Fax 898-4112
New Holstein MS 200/6-8
1717 Plymouth St 53061 920-898-4769
Richard Amundson, prin. Fax 898-4810

**New Lisbon, Juneau, Pop. 2,524**
New Lisbon SD 600/PK-12
500 S Forest St 53950 608-562-3700
Dennis Birr, supt. Fax 562-5333
www.newlisbon.k12.wi.us
New Lisbon JSHS 300/7-12
500 S Forest St 53950 608-562-3700
Gary Syftestad, prin. Fax 562-5333

**New London, Waupaca, Pop. 7,241**
New London SD 2,500/PK-12
901 W Washington St 54961 920-982-8530
Dr. Kathleen Gwidt, supt. Fax 982-8551
www.newlondon.k12.wi.us
New London HS 800/9-12
1700 Klatt Rd 54961 920-982-8420
Danielle Sievert, prin. Fax 982-8440
New London IS / MS 700/5-8
1000 W Washington St 54961 920-982-8532
Pete Schulz, prin. Fax 982-8605

**New Richmond, Saint Croix, Pop. 8,254**
New Richmond SD 3,100/PK-12
701 E 11th St 54017 715-243-7411
Patrick Olson, supt. Fax 246-3638
www.newrichmond.k12.wi.us
New Richmond HS 800/9-12
701 E 11th St 54017 715-243-7451
Tom Wissink, prin. Fax 243-7464
New Richmond MS 700/6-8
701 E 11th St 54017 715-243-7472
Doug Hatch, prin. Fax 246-0580

---

Wisconsin Indianhead Technical College Post-Sec.
1019 S Knowles Ave 54017 715-246-6561

**Niagara, Marinette, Pop. 1,609**
Niagara SD 500/PK-12
700 Jefferson Ave 54151 715-251-1330
Dan Nett, supt. Fax 251-4544
www.niagara.k12.wi.us
Niagara JSHS 200/7-12
700 Jefferson Ave 54151 715-251-4541
Kipp Beaudoin, prin. Fax 251-3715

**North Fond du Lac, Fond du Lac, Pop. 4,969**
North Fond Du Lac SD 1,200/PK-12
225 McKinley St 54937 920-929-3750
Aaron Sadoff, supt. Fax 929-3696
www.nfdl.k12.wi.us
Allen MS 300/6-8
305 Mckinley St 54937 920-929-3754
Adam Broten, prin. Fax 929-3747
Mann HS 400/9-12
325 Mckinley St 54937 920-929-3740
Samantha Freimund, prin. Fax 929-3664

**Oak Creek, Milwaukee, Pop. 33,834**
Oak Creek-Franklin SD 6,000/PK-12
7630 S 10th St 53154 414-768-5886
Sara Burmeister, supt. Fax 768-6172
ocfsd.org
Oak Creek East MS 900/6-8
9330 S Shepard Ave 53154 414-768-6260
Annalee Bennin, prin. Fax 768-6293
Oak Creek HS 2,000/9-12
340 E Puetz Rd 53154 414-768-6100
Michael Read, prin. Fax 768-6130
Oak Creek West MS 500/6-8
8401 S 13th St 53154 414-768-6250
Michael Maxson, prin. Fax 768-6296

---

Milwaukee Area Technical College Post-Sec.
6665 S Howell Ave 53154 414-571-4500

**Oakfield, Fond du Lac, Pop. 1,057**
Oakfield SD 500/PK-12
PO Box 99 53065 920-583-4117
Sue Green, supt. Fax 583-4033
www.oakfield.k12.wi.us/
Oakfield HS 200/9-12
PO Box 39 53065 920-583-3141
Carmen Klassy, prin. Fax 583-4673
Oakfield MS 100/6-8
PO Box 39 53065 920-583-3141
Carmen Klassy, prin. Fax 583-4673

**Oconomowoc, Waukesha, Pop. 15,586**
Oconomowoc Area SD 4,700/K-12
W360N7077 Brown St 53066 262-560-1115
Dr. Roger Rindo, supt.
www.oasd.k12.wi.us
Nature Hill IS 800/5-8
850 N Lake Rd 53066 262-569-4945
Jason Curtis, prin. Fax 569-4958
Oconomowoc HS 1,500/9-12
641 E Forest St 53066 262-560-3100
Joseph Moylan, prin. Fax 567-8960
Silver Lake IS 700/5-8
555 Oconomowoc Pkwy 53066 262-560-4305
Ellyn Helberg, prin. Fax 560-4318

**Oconto, Oconto, Pop. 4,472**
Oconto USD 1,000/PK-12
400 Michigan Ave 54153 920-834-7814
Aaron Malczewski, supt. Fax 834-9884
www.oconto.k12.wi.us
Oconto HS 300/9-12
1717 Superior Ave 54153 920-834-7812
Bill Slough, prin. Fax 834-7804
Oconto MS 300/5-8
400 Michigan Ave 54153 920-834-7806
Adam DeWitt, prin. Fax 834-9884

**Oconto Falls, Oconto, Pop. 2,850**
Oconto Falls SD 1,800/PK-12
200 N Farm Rd 54154 920-848-4471
Dr. Dean Hess, supt. Fax 848-4474
www.ocontofalls.k12.wi.us
Oconto Falls HS 600/9-12
PO Box 988 54154 920-848-4467
Bruce Russell, prin. Fax 846-4444
Washington MS 400/6-8
102 S Washington St 54154 920-846-4463
Lou Hobyan, prin. Fax 846-4453

**Omro, Winnebago, Pop. 3,492**
Omro SD 1,300/PK-12
455 Fox Trl 54963 920-685-5666
Fax 685-5757
www.omro.k12.wi.us
Omro HS 400/9-12
455 Fox Trl 54963 920-685-7405
Kelly Spors, prin. Fax 685-7040
Omro MS 300/6-8
455 Fox Trl 54963 920-685-7403
Paul Williams, prin. Fax 685-5757

**Onalaska, LaCrosse, Pop. 17,449**
Onalaska SD 3,000/PK-12
1821 E Main St 54650 608-781-9700
Dr. Francis Finco, supt. Fax 781-9712
www.onalaska.k12.wi.us
Onalaska HS 900/9-12
700 Hilltopper Pl 54650 608-783-4561
Jared Schaffner, prin. Fax 783-0102
Onalaska MS 600/6-8
711 Quincy St 54650 608-783-5366
Jed Kees, prin. Fax 781-8030

---

Globe University Post-Sec.
2651 Midwest Dr 54650 608-779-2600
Luther HS 300/9-12
1501 Wilson St 54650 608-783-5435
Paul Wichmann, prin. Fax 783-4758
The Salon Professional Academy Post-Sec.
566 Theater Rd 54650 608-781-8772

**Ontario, Vernon, Pop. 550**
Norwalk-Ontario-Wilton SD 700/PK-12
PO Box 130 54651 608-337-4403
Dr. Kelly Burhop, supt. Fax 337-4348
www.now.k12.wi.us/
Brookwood JSHS 300/7-12
PO Box 130 54651 608-337-4401
Brad Pettit, prin. Fax 337-4348

**Oostburg, Sheboygan, Pop. 2,866**
Oostburg SD 1,000/PK-12
PO Box 700100 53070 920-564-2346
Kevin Bruggink, supt. Fax 564-6138
oostburg.k12.wi.us
Oostburg HS 300/9-12
PO Box 700100 53070 920-564-2346
Scott Greupink, prin. Fax 564-6138
Oostburg MS 200/6-8
PO Box 700100 53070 920-564-2383
Sherri Stengel, prin. Fax 564-6138

**Oregon, Dane, Pop. 9,079**
Oregon SD 3,500/K-12
123 E Grove St 53575 608-835-4000
Brian Busler, supt. Fax 835-9509
www.oregonsd.org
Oregon HS 1,100/9-12
456 N Perry Pkwy 53575 608-835-4300
Kelly Meyers, prin. Fax 835-7894
Oregon MS 500/7-8
601 Pleasant Oak Dr 53575 608-835-4800
Shannon Anderson, prin. Fax 835-3849

**Orfordville, Rock, Pop. 1,432**
Parkview SD, PO Box 250 53576 700/PK-12
Dr. Steve Lutzke, supt. 608-879-2717
www.parkview.k12.wi.us
Parkview JSHS 300/7-12
408 W Beloit St 53576 608-879-2994
William Trow, prin. Fax 879-2732

**Osceola, Polk, Pop. 2,529**
Osceola SD 1,800/PK-12
PO Box 128 54020 715-294-4140
Mark Luebker, supt. Fax 294-2428
www.osceola.k12.wi.us
Osceola HS 600/9-12
PO Box 128 54020 715-294-2127
Adam Spiegel, prin. Fax 755-2068
Osceola MS 400/6-8
PO Box 128 54020 715-294-4180
Rebecca Styles, prin. Fax 294-2428

---

Valley Christian S 50/PK-12
933A 248th St 54020 715-294-3373
Ken Callahan, admin. Fax 294-3373

**Oshkosh, Winnebago, Pop. 65,117**
Oshkosh Area SD 9,500/PK-12
PO Box 3048 54903 920-424-0395
Stan Mack, supt. Fax 424-0466
www.oshkosh.k12.wi.us
Merrill MS 400/6-8
108 W New York Ave 54901 920-424-0177
Cindy Olson, prin. Fax 424-7512
Oshkosh North HS 1,300/9-12
1100 W Smith Ave 54901 920-424-7000
Jacqueline Schleicher, prin. Fax 424-4054
Oshkosh West HS 1,800/9-12
375 N Eagle St 54902 920-424-4090
Erin Kohl, prin. Fax 424-4950
South Park MS 400/6-8
1551 Delaware St 54902 920-424-0431
Lisa McLaughlin, prin. Fax 424-7513
Stanley MS 300/6-8
915 Hazel St 54901 920-424-0442
Philip Marshall, prin. Fax 424-7515
Tipler MS 400/6-8
325 S Eagle St 54902 920-424-0320
Jay Jones, prin. Fax 424-7514
Traeger MS 500/6-8
3000 W 20th Ave 54904 920-424-0065
Jill Pascarella, prin. Fax 424-7511

---

Fox Valley Technical College Post-Sec.
150 N Campbell Rd 54902 920-233-9191
Lourdes Academy HS 200/9-12
110 N Sawyer St 54902 920-235-5670
Fax 235-7453
Lourdes Academy MS 200/6-8
110 N Sawyer St 54902 920-235-5670
Fax 235-7453
Mercy Medical Center Post-Sec.
PO Box 3370 54903 920-233-5110
University of Wisconsin Post-Sec.
800 Algoma Blvd 54901 920-424-1234
Valley Christian S 200/PK-12
3450 Vinland St 54901 920-231-9704
Bradley Dunn, admin. Fax 231-9804

**Osseo, Trempealeau, Pop. 1,691**
Osseo-Fairchild SD 900/PK-12
50851 East St 54758 715-597-3141
William Tourdot Ed.D., supt. Fax 597-3606
www.ofsd.k12.wi.us
Osseo-Fairchild HS 300/9-12
50900 Francis St 54758 715-597-3141
Drew Semingson, prin. Fax 597-3647
Osseo MS 200/6-8
50900 Francis St 54758 715-597-3141
Drew Semingson, prin. Fax 597-3647

**Owen, Clark, Pop. 936**
Owen-Withee SD 500/PK-12
PO Box 417 54460 715-229-2151
Robert Houts, supt. Fax 229-4322
www.owen-withee.k12.wi.us
Owen-Withee HS 200/9-12
PO Box 417 54460 715-229-2151
Julie Van Ark, prin. Fax 229-4322
Owen-Withee JHS 100/7-8
PO Box 417 54460 715-229-2151
Julie Van Ark, prin. Fax 229-4322

**Palmyra, Jefferson, Pop. 1,774**
Palmyra-Eagle Area SD 1,100/PK-12
PO Box 901 53156 262-495-7101
Steven Bloom, supt. Fax 495-7151
www.palmyra.k12.wi.us
Palmyra-Eagle HS 300/9-12
PO Box 901 53156 262-495-7101
Nicholas Schultek, prin. Fax 495-7146
Palmyra-Eagle MS 200/7-8
PO Box 901 53156 262-495-7101
Nicholas Schultek, prin. Fax 495-7146

**Pardeeville, Columbia, Pop. 2,095**
Pardeeville Area SD 800/PK-12
PO Box 130 53954 608-429-2153
Earl Knitt, supt. Fax 429-2277
www.pardeeville.k12.wi.us
Pardeeville HS 300/9-12
PO Box 130 53954 608-429-2153
Jason Lemay, prin. Fax 429-2277
Pardeeville MS 200/5-8
PO Box 130 53954 608-429-2153
Ted Lenz, prin. Fax 429-2277

**Park Falls, Price, Pop. 2,367**
Chequamegon SD 800/PK-12
420 9th St N 54552 715-762-2474
David Anderson, admin. Fax 762-5469
www.csdk12.net
Chequamegon HS 300/9-12
400 9th St N 54552 715-762-2474
Timothy Kief, prin. Fax 762-5674

Other Schools – See Glidden

**Patch Grove, Grant, Pop. 198**
River Ridge SD 400/PK-12
PO Box 78 53817 608-994-2715
Dr. Lee Pritzl, supt. Fax 994-2891
www.rrsd.k12.wi.us
River Ridge MSHS 200/7-12
PO Box 78 53817 608-994-2715
Rodney Lewis, prin. Fax 994-2891

**Pembine, Marinette, Pop. 189**
Beecher-Dunbar-Pembine SD 300/PK-12
PO Box 247 54156 715-324-5314
Chris Metras, supt. Fax 324-5282
www.pembine.k12.wi.us/
Pembine JSHS 100/6-12
PO Box 247 54156 715-324-5314
Chris Metras, admin. Fax 324-5282

**Pepin, Pepin, Pop. 835**
Pepin Area SD 200/PK-12
PO Box 128 54759 715-442-2391
Bruce Quinton, supt. Fax 442-3607
pepin.k12.wi.us
Pepin HS 100/9-12
PO Box 128 54759 715-442-2391
Bruce Quinton, prin. Fax 442-3607

**Peshtigo, Marinette, Pop. 3,466**
Peshtigo SD 1,200/PK-12
341 N Emery Ave 54157 715-582-3677
Kim Eparvier, supt. Fax 582-3850
www.peshtigo.k12.wi.us
Peshtigo MSHS 600/7-12
380 Green St 54157 715-582-3711
Chad Sodini, prin. Fax 582-0740

**Pewaukee, Waukesha, Pop. 8,065**
Pewaukee SD 2,600/PK-12
404 Lake St 53072 262-691-2100
Dr. JoAnn Sternke, supt. Fax 691-1052
pewaukeeschools.schoolfusion.us
Clark MS 400/7-8
472 Lake St 53072 262-691-2100
Randy Daul, prin. Fax 695-5004
Pewaukee HS 800/9-12
510 Lake St 53072 262-691-2100
Marty Van Hulle, prin. Fax 695-5006

---

Trinity Academy 100/PK-12
W225N3131 Duplainville Rd 53072 262-695-2933
Waukesha County Technical College Post-Sec.
800 Main St 53072 262-691-5566

**Phelps, Vilas**
Phelps SD 100/K-12
4451 Old School Rd 54554 715-545-2724
Delnice Hill, supt. Fax 545-3728
www.phelps.k12.wi.us
Phelps HS 50/9-12
4451 Old School Rd 54554 715-545-2724
Jason Pertile, dean Fax 545-3728

**Phillips, Price, Pop. 1,454**
Phillips SD 800/PK-12
PO Box 70 54555 715-339-2419
Rick Morgan, supt. Fax 339-2416
www.phillips.k12.wi.us/
Phillips HS 300/9-12
PO Box 70 54555 715-339-2141
Colin Hoogland, prin. Fax 339-2144
Phillips MS 200/6-8
PO Box 70 54555 715-339-2141
Colin Hoogland, prin. Fax 339-2144

**Pittsville, Wood, Pop. 868**
Pittsville SD 600/PK-12
5459 Elementary Ave Ste 2 54466 715-884-6694
Paul Vine, supt. Fax 884-5218
www.pittsville.k12.wi.us
Pittsville HS 200/9-12
5407 1st Ave 54466 715-884-6412
Mark Weddig, prin. Fax 884-2870

**Plainfield, Waushara, Pop. 852**
Tri-County Area SD 500/PK-12
409 S West St 54966 715-335-6366
Tony Marinack, supt. Fax 335-6365
www.tricounty.k12.wi.us
Tri-County HS 200/7-12
409 S West St 54966 715-335-6366
Nicholas Marti, prin. Fax 335-6322

**Platteville, Grant, Pop. 11,124**
Platteville SD 1,500/PK-12
780 N 2nd St 53818 608-342-4000
Connie Valenza, supt. Fax 342-4412
www.platteville.k12.wi.us
Platteville HS 500/9-12
710 E Madison St 53818 608-342-4020
Timothy Engh, prin. Fax 342-4427
Platteville MS 500/4-8
40 E Madison St 53818 608-342-4010
Jason Julius, prin. Fax 342-4497

---

University of Wisconsin Post-Sec.
1 University Plz 53818 608-342-1491

**Pleasant Prairie, Kenosha, Pop. 19,418**
Kenosha SD
Supt. — See Kenosha
Lakeview Technology Academy Vo/Tech
9449 88th Ave 53158 262-359-8155
William Hittman, prin. Fax 359-8159

**Plum City, Pierce, Pop. 598**
Plum City SD 300/PK-12
907 Main St 54761 715-647-2591
Mary Baier, supt. Fax 647-3015
www.plumcity.k12.wi.us
Plum City JSHS 100/6-12
907 Main St 54761 715-647-2591
Paul Churchill, prin. Fax 647-3015

**Plymouth, Sheboygan, Pop. 8,357**
Plymouth SD 2,100/PK-12
125 S Highland Ave 53073 920-892-2661
Carrie Dassow Ph.D., supt. Fax 892-6366
www.plymouth.k12.wi.us
Plymouth HS 800/9-12
125 S Highland Ave 53073 920-893-6911
Jennifer Rauscher, prin. Fax 892-6366
Riverview MS 500/6-8
300 Riverside Cir 53073 920-892-4353
Chris Scudella, prin. Fax 892-5072

**Poplar, Douglas, Pop. 589**
Maple SD
Supt. — See Maple
Northwestern MS 300/6-8
PO Box 46 54864 715-364-2218
T. Krieg, prin. Fax 364-2540

**Portage, Columbia, Pop. 10,179**
Portage Community SD 2,300/PK-12
305 E Slifer St 53901 608-742-4879
Charles Poches, supt. Fax 742-4950
www.portage.k12.wi.us
Bartels MS 300/6-8
2505 New Pinery Rd 53901 608-742-2165
Robert Meicher, prin. Fax 745-4884
Portage HS 800/9-12
301 E Collins St 53901 608-742-8545
Robin Kvalo, prin. Fax 742-0617

**Port Edwards, Wood, Pop. 1,802**
Port Edwards SD 400/K-12
801 2nd St 54469 715-887-9000
Kyle Cronan, supt. Fax 887-9040
www.pesd.k12.wi.us
Edwards HS 200/9-12
801 2nd St 54469 715-887-9000
Kyle Cronan, prin. Fax 887-9040
Edwards MS 100/6-8
801 2nd St 54469 715-887-9000
Cara Christy, prin. Fax 887-9040

**Port Washington, Ozaukee, Pop. 11,098**
Port Washington-Saukville SD 2,700/PK-12
100 W Monroe St 53074 262-268-6000
Michael Weber Ph.D., supt. Fax 268-6020
www.pwssd.k12.wi.us
Jefferson MS 800/5-8
1403 N Holden St 53074 262-268-6100
Arlan Galarowicz, prin. Fax 268-6120
Port Washington HS 900/9-12
427 W Jackson St 53074 262-268-5500
Eric Burke, prin. Fax 268-5520

---

Port Washington Catholic MS 100/5-8
1802 N Wisconsin St 53074 262-284-2682
Rick Goeden, prin. Fax 284-4168

**Port Wing, Bayfield, Pop. 160**
South Shore SD 100/PK-12
PO Box 40 54865 715-774-3500
Clendon Gustafson, supt. Fax 774-3569
www.sshore.k12.wi.us
South Shore JSHS 100/7-12
PO Box 40 54865 715-774-3500
Clendon Gustafson, prin. Fax 774-3569

**Potosi, Grant, Pop. 686**
Potosi SD 300/PK-12
128 US Highway 61 N 53820 608-763-2162
Ronald Saari, supt. Fax 763-2035
www.potosisd.k12.wi.us
Potosi HS 100/9-12
128 US Highway 61 N 53820 608-763-2161
Mike Uppena, prin. Fax 763-2035
Potosi MS 100/6-8
128 US Highway 61 N 53820 608-763-2162
Mike Uppena, prin. Fax 763-2035

**Poynette, Columbia, Pop. 2,497**
Poynette SD 1,100/PK-12
PO Box 10 53955 608-635-4347
Matt Shappell, supt. Fax 635-9200
www.poynette.k12.wi.us
Poynette HS 300/9-12
PO Box 10 53955 608-635-4347
Mark Hoernke, prin. Fax 635-9201
Poynette MS 300/6-8
PO Box 10 53955 608-635-4347
Brian Sutton, prin. Fax 635-9233

**Prairie du Chien, Crawford, Pop. 5,867**
Prairie du Chien Area SD 1,100/PK-12
800 E Crawford St 53821 608-326-3700
Drew Johnson, supt. Fax 326-0000
www.pdc.k12.wi.us
Prairie du Chien HS 400/9-12
800 E Crawford St 53821 608-326-3700
Andy Banasik, prin. Fax 326-3709

---

St. John Nepomucene MS 100/6-8
720 S Wacouta Ave 53821 608-326-4400
Wade Marlow, prin. Fax 326-4876

**Prairie du Sac, Sauk, Pop. 3,923**
Sauk Prairie SD 2,700/PK-12
440 13th St 53578 608-643-5990
Cliff Thompson, supt. Fax 643-6216
www.saukprairieschools.org
Sauk Prairie HS 800/9-12
105 9th St 53578 608-643-5900
Chad Harnisch, prin. Fax 643-5419
Other Schools – See Sauk City

**Prairie Farm, Barron, Pop. 472**
Prairie Farm SD 300/PK-12
630 River Ave S 54762 715-455-1683
Patrick Olson, supt. Fax 455-1056
www.prairiefarm.k12.wi.us
Prairie Farm HS 100/9-12
630 River Ave S 54762 715-455-1861
Casey Fossum, prin. Fax 455-1869
Prairie Farm MS 100/6-8
630 River Ave S 54762 715-455-1841
Casey Fossum, prin. Fax 455-1869

**Prentice, Price, Pop. 653**
Prentice SD 300/PK-12
PO Box 110 54556 715-428-2811
Randall Bergman, supt. Fax 428-2815
www.prentice.k12.wi.us
Prentice MSHS 100/5-12
PO Box 110 54556 715-428-2811
Melissa Pilgrim, prin. Fax 428-2815

**Prescott, Pierce, Pop. 4,176**
Prescott SD 1,200/PK-12
1220 Saint Croix St 54021 715-262-5782
Dr. Rick Spicuzza, supt. Fax 262-5091
www.prescott.k12.wi.us
Prescott HS 400/9-12
1220 Saint Croix St 54021 715-262-5010
David Vortherms, prin. Fax 262-4888
Prescott MS 300/6-8
125 Elm St N 54021 715-262-5054
Jim Dalluhn, prin. Fax 262-3965

**Princeton, Green Lake, Pop. 1,208**
Princeton SD 400/PK-12
PO Box 147 54968 920-295-6571
Sam Santacroce, supt. Fax 295-4778
www.princeton.k12.wi.us
Princeton S 400/PK-12
PO Box 147 54968 920-295-6571
Sam Santacroce, prin. Fax 295-4778

**Pulaski, Brown, Pop. 3,500**
Pulaski Community SD 3,800/PK-12
PO Box 36 54162 920-822-6000
Bec Kurzynske, supt. Fax 822-6005
www.pulaskischools.org
Pulaski Community MS 800/6-8
911 S Saint Augustine St 54162 920-822-6500
Patrick Fullerton, prin. Fax 822-6505
Pulaski HS 1,200/9-12
1040 S Saint Augustine St 54162 920-822-6700
John Matczak, prin. Fax 822-6707

**Racine, Racine, Pop. 76,696**
Racine USD 20,000/PK-12
3109 Mount Pleasant St 53404 262-635-5600
Dr. Lolli Haws, supt. Fax 631-7121
www.rusd.org
Case HS 1,900/9-12
7345 Washington Ave 53406 262-619-4200
Jody Bloyer, prin. Fax 619-4259
Gilmore MS 800/6-8
2330 Northwestern Ave 53404 262-619-4260
Bryan Wright, prin. Fax 619-4272
Horlick HS 2,100/9-12
2119 Rapids Dr 53404 262-619-4300
Angela Apmann, prin. Fax 619-4390
Jerstad-Agerholm MS 700/6-8
3601 Lasalle St 53402 262-664-6075
Doug Clum, prin. Fax 664-6120
McKinley MS 900/6-8
2340 Mohr Ave 53405 262-664-6150
Cheri Kulland, prin. Fax 664-6196
Mitchell MS 800/6-8
2701 Drexel Ave 53403 262-664-6400
Soren Gajewski, prin. Fax 664-6444
Park HS 1,800/9-12
1901 12th St 53403 262-619-4400
Dennis Christensen, prin. Fax 619-4490
Racine Alternative Education 100/Alt
2405 Northwestern Ave 53404 262-664-6600
Eliot Underhill, dir. Fax 664-6644
Starbuck MS 800/6-8
1516 Ohio St 53405 262-664-6500
Andre Bennett, prin. Fax 664-6510
Walden III MSHS 300/6-12
1012 Center St 53403 262-664-6250
Rob Kreil, dir. Fax 664-6255

---

All Saints Healthcare System Post-Sec.
1320 Wisconsin Ave 53403 262-636-2846
Gateway Technical College Post-Sec.
1001 Main St 53403 262-619-6200
Midwest College of Oriental Medicine Post-Sec.
6232 Bankers Rd 53403 262-554-2010
Racine Lutheran HS 200/9-12
251 Luedtke Ave 53405 262-637-6538
Dave Burgess, prin. Fax 637-6601
St. Catherine HS 400/6-12
1200 Park Ave 53403 262-632-2785
Christopher Olley, pres. Fax 632-5144

**Randolph, Columbia, Pop. 1,798**
Randolph SD 600/PK-12
110 Meadowood Dr 53956 920-326-2427
Kevin Knudson, supt. Fax 326-2439
www.rsdwi.org
Randolph HS 200/9-12
110 Meadowood Dr 53956 920-326-2425
Debra Torrison, prin. Fax 326-2430

**Random Lake, Sheboygan, Pop. 1,574**
Random Lake SD 900/PK-12
605 Random Lake Rd 53075 920-994-4342
Thomas Malmstadt, supt. Fax 994-4820
www.randomlake.k12.wi.us
Random Lake HS 300/9-12
605 Random Lake Rd 53075 920-994-9193
Scott Schultz, prin. Fax 994-4820

Random Lake MS 300/5-8
605 Random Lake Rd 53075 920-994-2498
Amanda Jacobson, prin. Fax 994-4820

**Reedsburg, Sauk, Pop. 9,120**
Reedsburg SD 2,600/PK-12
501 K St 53959 608-524-2016
Thomas Benson, supt. Fax 524-6818
www.rsd.k12.wi.us
Reedsburg Area HS 900/9-12
1100 S Albert Ave 53959 608-524-4327
Rob Taylor, prin. Fax 524-1373
Webb MS 500/6-8
707 N Webb Ave 53959 608-524-2328
Casey Campbell, prin. Fax 524-1161

**Reedsville, Manitowoc, Pop. 1,195**
Reedsville SD 600/PK-12
340 Manitowoc St 54230 920-754-4341
Tony Butturini, supt. Fax 754-4344
www.reedsville.k12.wi.us
Reedsville HS 200/9-12
340 Manitowoc St 54230 920-754-4341
Tony Butturini, prin. Fax 754-4344

**Rhinelander, Oneida, Pop. 7,686**
Rhinelander SD 2,300/K-12
665 Coolidge Ave Ste B 54501 715-365-9700
Kelli Jacobi, supt. Fax 365-9713
www.rhinelander.k12.wi.us
Rhinelander HS 900/9-12
665 Coolidge Ave Ste B 54501 715-365-9500
David Ditzler, prin. Fax 365-9568
Williams MS 500/6-8
915 Acacia Ln 54501 715-365-9220
Paul Johnson, prin. Fax 365-9296

---

Nicolet Area Technical College Post-Sec.
PO Box 518 54501 715-365-4410

**Rib Lake, Taylor, Pop. 905**
Rib Lake SD 500/PK-12
PO Box 278 54470 715-427-3222
Lori Manion, supt. Fax 427-3221
www.riblake.k12.wi.us
Rib Lake HS 100/9-12
PO Box 278 54470 715-427-3220
Rick Cardey, prin. Fax 427-5022
Rib Lake MS 100/6-8
PO Box 278 54470 715-427-5446
Rick Cardey, prin. Fax 427-3221

**Rice Lake, Barron, Pop. 8,342**
Rice Lake Area SD 2,300/PK-12
700 Augusta St 54868 715-234-9007
Larry Brown, supt. Fax 234-4552
www.ricelake.k12.wi.us
Rice Lake HS 800/9-12
30 S Wisconsin Ave 54868 715-234-2181
Curt Pacholke, prin. Fax 234-6679
Rice Lake MS 600/5-8
204 Cameron Rd 54868 715-234-8156
Josh Tomesh, prin. Fax 234-9439

---

Univ. of Wisconsin Center-Barron County Post-Sec.
1800 College Dr 54868 715-234-8176
Wisconsin Indianhead Technical College Post-Sec.
1900 College Dr 54868 715-234-7082

**Richfield, Washington, Pop. 11,239**
Richfield J1 SD 400/PK-8
PO Box 127 53076 262-628-1032
Tara Villalobos, admin. Fax 628-3013
www.richfield.k12.wi.us
Richfield ES 200/3-8
PO Box 127 53076 262-628-1032
Tara Villalobos, admin. Fax 628-3013

**Richland Center, Richland, Pop. 5,137**
Ithaca SD 400/PK-12
24615 State Hwy 58 53581 608-585-2512
Robert Smudde, admin. Fax 585-2505
www.ithaca.k12.wi.us/
Ithaca HS 100/9-12
24615 State Hwy 58 53581 608-585-2311
Robert Smudde, admin. Fax 585-2505
Ithaca MS 100/6-8
24615 State Hwy 58 53581 608-585-2311
Robert Smudde, admin. Fax 585-2505

Richland SD 1,400/PK-12
1996 US Hwy 14 W 53581 608-647-6106
Jarred Burke, admin. Fax 647-8454
www.richland.k12.wi.us
Richland Center HS 400/9-12
1996 US Hwy 14 W 53581 608-647-6131
Jon Bosworth, prin. Fax 647-8734
Richland MS 300/6-8
1801 State Hwy 80 S 53581 608-647-6381
David Guy, prin. Fax 647-4735

---

University of Wisconsin Richland Post-Sec.
1200 US Hwy 14 W 53581 608-647-6186

**Rio, Columbia, Pop. 1,045**
Rio Community SD 500/PK-12
411 Church St 53960 920-992-3141
Mark McGuire, supt. Fax 992-3157
www.rio.k12.wi.us
Rio MSHS 300/6-12
411 Church St 53960 920-992-3141
Cory Hinkel, prin. Fax 992-3157

**Ripon, Fond du Lac, Pop. 7,674**
Ripon Area SD 1,600/PK-12
PO Box 991 54971 920-748-4600
Dr. Mary Whitrock, supt. Fax 748-2715
www.ripon.k12.wi.us
Crossroads Alternative Education 50/Alt
PO Box 991 54971 920-748-4616
Anne Lang, prin. Fax 748-4805
Ripon HS 500/9-12
PO Box 991 54971 920-748-4616
Seth Meinel, prin. Fax 748-4622
Ripon MS 400/6-8
PO Box 991 54971 920-748-4638
Thomas Hoh, prin. Fax 748-4653

---

Ripon College Post-Sec.
PO Box 248 54971 920-748-8115

**River Falls, Pierce, Pop. 14,778**
River Falls SD 3,000/PK-12
852 E Division St 54022 715-425-1800
Jamie Benson, supt. Fax 425-1804
www.rfsd.k12.wi.us
Meyer MS 600/6-8
230 N 9th St 54022 715-425-1820
Mark Chapin, prin. Fax 425-1823
River Falls HS 1,000/9-12
818 Cemetery Rd 54022 715-425-1830
Kit Luedtke, prin. Fax 425-1827

---

University of Wisconsin Post-Sec.
410 S 3rd St 54022 715-425-3911

**Rosendale, Fond du Lac, Pop. 1,054**
Rosendale-Brandon SD 900/PK-12
300 W Wisconsin St 54974 920-872-2851
Gary Hansen, supt. Fax 872-2647
www.rbsd.k12.wi.us
Laconia HS 300/9-12
301 W Division St 54974 920-872-2161
Wayne Weber, prin. Fax 872-2777
Rosendale IS 200/4-8
200 S Main St 54974 920-872-2126
John Hokenson, prin. Fax 872-2061

**Rosholt, Portage, Pop. 506**
Rosholt SD 600/PK-12
PO Box 310 54473 715-677-4542
Marc Christianson, supt. Fax 677-3543
www.rosholt.k12.wi.us
Rosholt HS 200/9-12
PO Box 310 54473 715-677-4541
James Grygleski, prin. Fax 677-6767
Rosholt MS 100/6-8
PO Box 310 54473 715-677-4541
James Grygleski, prin. Fax 677-6767

**Rothschild, Marathon, Pop. 5,209**

---

Globe University Post-Sec.
1480 County Road XX 54474 715-301-1300

**Saint Croix Falls, Polk, Pop. 2,110**
St. Croix Falls SD 1,100/PK-12
PO Box 130 54024 715-483-2507
Mark Burandt, supt. Fax 483-3695
www.scf.k12.wi.us
St. Croix Falls HS 400/9-12
PO Box 130 54024 715-483-2507
Peggy Ryan, prin. Fax 483-3695
St. Croix Falls MS 300/5-8
PO Box 130 54024 715-483-2507
Joe Connors, prin. Fax 483-3695

**Saint Francis, Milwaukee, Pop. 9,213**
St. Francis SD 1,300/PK-12
4225 S Lake Dr 53235 414-747-3900
Blake Peuse, supt. Fax 482-7198
www.sfsd.k12.wi.us
Deer Creek IS 400/4-8
3680 S Kinnickinnic Ave 53235 414-482-8400
Guy Powell, prin. Fax 482-8406
Saint Francis HS 600/9-12
4225 S Lake Dr 53235 414-747-3600
Andrew Muszytowski, prin. Fax 747-3605

---

St. Francis Seminary Post-Sec.
3257 S Lake Dr 53235 414-747-6400

**Salem, Kenosha**
Central HSD of Westosha 1,200/9-12
PO Box 38 53168 262-843-2321
Dr. Scott Pierce, admin. Fax 843-4069
www.westosha.k12.wi.us
Central-Westosha HS 1,200/9-12
PO Box 38 53168 262-843-2321
Lisa Albrecht, prin. Fax 843-4069

**Sauk City, Sauk, Pop. 3,378**
Sauk Prairie SD
Supt. — See Prairie du Sac
Sauk Prairie MS 600/6-8
207 Maple St 53583 608-643-5500
Ted Harter, prin. Fax 643-5503

**Seneca, Crawford**
Seneca SD 300/PK-12
PO Box 34 54654 608-734-3411
David Boland, supt. Fax 734-3430
www.seneca.k12.wi.us
Seneca HS 100/9-12
PO Box 34 54654 608-734-3411
David Boland, prin. Fax 734-3430
Seneca JHS 100/5-8
PO Box 34 54654 608-734-3411
David Boland, prin. Fax 734-3430

**Seymour, Outagamie, Pop. 3,392**
Seymour Community SD 2,400/PK-12
10 Circle Dr 54165 920-833-2304
Peter Ross, supt. Fax 833-6037
www.seymour.k12.wi.us/
Seymour Community HS 700/9-12
10 Circle Dr 54165 920-833-2306
Tom Mueller, prin. Fax 833-7608
Seymour MS 400/6-8
10 Circle Dr 54165 920-833-7199
Judy Schenk, prin. Fax 833-9376

**Shawano, Shawano, Pop. 9,050**
Shawano SD 2,600/PK-12
218 County Road B 54166 715-526-3194
Gary Cumberland, supt. Fax 526-6072
www.shawanoschools.com
Shawano Community HS 800/9-12
220 County Road B 54166 715-526-2175
Scott Zwirschitz, prin. Fax 524-8414
Shawano Community MS 500/6-8
1050 S Union St 54166 715-526-2192
Mary Kramer, prin. Fax 526-5037

**Sheboygan, Sheboygan, Pop. 48,427**
Sheboygan Area SD 9,200/PK-12
830 Virginia Ave 53081 920-459-3500
Joseph Sheehan Ph.D., supt. Fax 459-6487
www.sheboygan.k12.wi.us
Farnsworth MS 600/6-8
1017 Union Ave 53081 920-459-3655
Todd DeBruin, prin. Fax 459-3660
Mann MS 600/6-8
2820 Union Ave 53081 920-459-3666
Vicki Ritchie, prin. Fax 459-3669
North HS 1,500/9-12
1042 School Ave 53083 920-459-3600
Jason Bull, prin. Fax 459-3601
South HS 1,200/9-12
3128 S 12th St 53081 920-459-3637
Mike Trimberger, prin. Fax 459-6733
Urban MS 700/6-8
1226 North Ave 53083 920-459-3680
Ted Distefano, prin. Fax 459-4065

---

Lakeland College Post-Sec.
PO Box 359 53082 920-565-1000
Sheboygan Area Lutheran HS 200/9-12
3323 University Dr 53081 920-452-3323
Allen Holzheimer, prin. Fax 452-1310
Sheboygan County Christian HS 100/9-12
929 Greenfield Ave 53081 920-458-9981
Rhonda Anderson B.S., prin. Fax 458-9957
University of Wisconsin Sheboygan Post-Sec.
1 University Dr 53081 920-459-6600

**Sheboygan Falls, Sheboygan, Pop. 7,719**
Sheboygan Falls SD 1,800/PK-12
220 Amherst Ave 53085 920-467-7893
Jean Born, supt. Fax 467-7899
www.sheboyganfalls.k12.wi.us
Sheboygan Falls HS 600/9-12
220 Amherst Ave 53085 920-467-7890
Luke Goral, prin. Fax 467-7825
Sheboygan Falls MS 500/5-8
101 School St 53085 920-467-7880
Meloney Markofski, prin. Fax 467-7885

**Shell Lake, Washburn, Pop. 1,340**
Shell Lake SD 600/PK-12
271 Highway 63 S 54871 715-468-7816
David Bridenhagen, supt. Fax 468-7812
www.shelllake.k12.wi.us
Shell Lake JSHS 300/7-12
271 Highway 63 S 54871 715-468-7814
Heather Cox, prin. Fax 468-7989

---

Wisconsin Indianhead Technical College Post-Sec.
505 Pine Ridge Dr 54871 715-468-2815

**Shiocton, Outagamie, Pop. 910**
Shiocton SD 700/PK-12
PO Box 68 54170 920-986-3351
Nichole Schweitzer, supt. Fax 986-3291
www.shiocton.k12.wi.us
Shiocton HS 200/7-12
PO Box 68 54170 920-986-3351
Kelly Zeinert, prin. Fax 986-3291

**Shorewood, Milwaukee, Pop. 12,886**
Shorewood SD 2,000/PK-12
1701 E Capitol Dr 53211 414-963-6901
Martin Lexmond Ph.D., supt. Fax 963-6904
www.shorewoodschools.org
Shorewood HS 600/9-12
1701 E Capitol Dr 53211 414-963-6921
Tim Kenney, prin. Fax 961-2819
Shorewood IS 300/7-8
3830 N Morris Blvd 53211 414-963-6951
Mark Harris, prin. Fax 963-6946

**Shullsburg, Lafayette, Pop. 1,223**
Shullsburg SD 400/PK-12
444 N Judgement St 53586 608-965-4427
Loras Kruser, admin. Fax 965-3794
www.shullsburg.k12.wi.us
Shullsburg HS 100/9-12
444 N Judgement St 53586 608-965-4427
Joseph Diedrich, prin. Fax 965-3794
Shullsburg JHS 100/6-8
444 N Judgement St 53586 608-965-4427
Joseph Diedrich, prin. Fax 965-3794

**Siren, Burnett, Pop. 776**
Siren SD 500/PK-12
24022 4th Ave 54872 715-349-2290
Scott Johnson, supt. Fax 349-7476
www.siren.k12.wi.us
Siren HS 200/6-12
24022 4th Ave 54872 715-349-2277
Sarah Johnson, prin. Fax 349-7476

**Slinger, Washington, Pop. 5,014**
Slinger SD 3,000/PK-12
207 Polk St 53086 262-644-9615
Daren Sievers, supt. Fax 644-7514
www.slinger.k12.wi.us
Slinger HS 900/9-12
209 Polk St 53086 262-644-5261
Philip Ourada, prin. Fax 644-0479
Slinger MS 600/6-8
521 Olympic Dr 53086 262-644-5226
Dean Goneau, prin. Fax 644-7353

**Soldiers Grove, Crawford, Pop. 590**
North Crawford SD 500/PK-12
47050 County Road X 54655 608-735-4318
Dr. Daniel Davies, supt. Fax 735-4317
www.northcrawford.com
North Crawford HS 100/9-12
47050 County Road X 54655 608-735-4311
Brandon Munson, prin. Fax 624-6269

**Solon Springs, Douglas, Pop. 597**
Solon Springs SD 300/PK-12
8993 E Baldwin Ave 54873 715-378-2263
Michael Cox, supt. Fax 378-2073
www.solonk12.net
Solon Springs S 300/PK-12
8993 E Baldwin Ave 54873 715-378-2263
Geraldine Muller, prin. Fax 378-2073

**Somers, Kenosha**

---

Shoreland Lutheran HS 300/9-12
PO Box 295 53171 262-859-2595
Paul Scriver M.Ed., prin. Fax 859-2783

**Somerset, Saint Croix, Pop. 2,588**
Somerset SD 1,600/PK-12
PO Box 100 54025 715-247-3313
Randal Rosburg, supt. Fax 247-5588
www.somerset.k12.wi.us
Somerset HS 500/9-12
PO Box 100 54025 715-247-3355
Chris Moore, prin. Fax 247-3864
Somerset MS 500/5-8
PO Box 100 54025 715-247-4400
Sara Eichten, prin. Fax 247-4437

**South Milwaukee, Milwaukee, Pop. 20,823**
South Milwaukee SD 3,300/PK-12
901 15th Ave 53172 414-766-5000
Dr. Rita Olson, supt. Fax 766-5005
www.sdsm.k12.wi.us/
South Milwaukee HS 1,200/9-12
801 15th Ave 53172 414-766-5100
Beth Kaminski, prin. Fax 766-5131
South Milwaukee MS 700/6-8
1001 15th Ave 53172 414-766-5800
James Hendrickson, prin. Fax 766-5803

**South Wayne, Lafayette, Pop. 489**
Black Hawk SD 300/PK-12
PO Box 303 53587 608-439-5400
Dr. William Chambers, supt. Fax 439-1022
www.blackhawk.k12.wi.us
Black Hawk HS 100/6-12
PO Box 303 53587 608-439-5371
Cory Milz, prin. Fax 439-1022

**Sparta, Monroe, Pop. 9,396**
Sparta Area SD 2,600/PK-12
201 E Franklin St 54656 608-269-3151
John Hendricks, supt. Fax 366-3526
www.spartan.org
Sparta HS 700/9-12
506 N Black River St 54656 608-366-3504
Samuel Russ, prin. Fax 366-3506
Sparta Meadowview MS 500/6-8
1225 N Water St 54656 608-366-3497
Jeffery Krull, prin. Fax 366-3500

**Spencer, Marathon, Pop. 1,903**
Spencer SD 800/PK-12
PO Box 418 54479 715-659-5347
Michael Endreas, supt. Fax 659-5470
www.spencer.k12.wi.us
Spencer JSHS 400/6-12
PO Box 418 54479 715-659-4211
Jerry Zanotelli, prin. Fax 659-5470

**Spooner, Washburn, Pop. 2,637**
Spooner Area SD 1,200/PK-12
801 County Highway A 54801 715-635-2171
Michelle Schwab, supt. Fax 635-7174
www.spooner.k12.wi.us
Spooner HS 400/9-12
801 County Highway A 54801 715-635-2172
Sarah Johnson, prin. Fax 635-7074
Spooner MS 300/5-8
750 Oak St 54801 715-635-2173
Bradley Larrabee, prin. Fax 635-7074

**Spring Green, Sauk, Pop. 1,601**
River Valley SD 1,300/PK-12
660 W Daley St 53588 608-588-2551
Tom Wermuth, supt. Fax 588-2558
www.rvschools.org
River Valley HS 500/9-12
660 Varsity Blvd 53588 608-588-2554
Kim Kaukl, prin. Fax 588-2827
River Valley MS 300/6-8
660 W Daley St 53588 608-588-2556
James Radtke, prin. Fax 588-2026

**Spring Valley, Pierce, Pop. 1,346**
Spring Valley SD 600/PK-12
PO Box 249 54767 715-778-5551
Dr. Donald Haack, supt. Fax 778-4761
www.springvalley.k12.wi.us
Spring Valley MSHS 200/6-12
PO Box 249 54767 715-778-5554
Gretchen Cipriano, prin. Fax 778-5556

**Stanley, Chippewa, Pop. 3,592**
Stanley-Boyd Area SD 900/PK-12
507 E 1st Ave 54768 715-644-5534
James Jones, supt. Fax 644-5584
www.stanleyboyd.k12.wi.us
Stanley-Boyd HS 300/9-12
507 E 1st Ave 54768 715-644-5534
Dave Ludy, prin. Fax 644-6701
Stanley-Boyd MS 100/6-8
507 E 1st Ave 54768 715-644-5715
Dave Ludy, prin. Fax 644-5584

**Stevens Point, Portage, Pop. 26,351**
Stevens Point Area SD 6,900/PK-12
1900 Polk St 54481 715-345-5456
Lee Bush Ed.D., supt. Fax 345-7302
www.pointschools.net
Fernandez Ctr for Alternative Learning 100/Alt
1025 Clark St 54481 715-345-5592
Jesse Jackson, prin. Fax 345-7374
Franklin JHS 800/7-9
2000 Polk St 54481 715-345-5413
Connie Negaard, prin. Fax 345-5696
Jacobs JHS 700/7-9
2400 Main St 54481 715-345-5422
Jeff Gulan, prin. Fax 345-7340
Stevens Point Area SHS 1,600/10-12
1201 Northpoint Dr 54481 715-345-5400
Jon Vollendorf, prin. Fax 345-5408

---

Mid-State Technical College Post-Sec.
1001 Centerpoint Dr 54481 715-344-3063
Pacelli HS 200/9-12
1301 Maria Dr 54481 715-341-2442
Jeffrey Brengman, prin. Fax 341-6779
St. Peter MS 200/6-8
708 1st St 54481 715-344-1890
Ellen Lopas, prin. Fax 342-2005
Stevens Point Christian Academy 50/K-12
801 County Road HH 54481 715-341-3275
Heidi Uitenbroek, admin. Fax 341-3023
University of Wisconsin Post-Sec.
2100 Main St 54481 715-346-0123

**Stockbridge, Calumet, Pop. 630**
Stockbridge SD 200/PK-12
PO Box 188 53088 920-439-1782
David Moscinski, supt. Fax 439-1150
www.stockbridge.k12.wi.us/
Stockbridge HS 100/9-12
PO Box 188 53088 920-439-1158
Chad Marx, prin. Fax 439-1150
Stockbridge MS 50/6-8
PO Box 188 53088 920-439-1158
Chad Marx, prin. Fax 439-1150

**Stoughton, Dane, Pop. 12,430**
Stoughton Area SD 3,100/PK-12
320 North St 53589 608-877-5000
Tim Onsager, admin. Fax 877-5028
www.stoughton.k12.wi.us
River Bluff MS 800/6-8
235 N Forrest St 53589 608-877-5503
Fred Potter, prin. Fax 877-5508
Stoughton HS 1,100/9-12
600 Lincoln Ave 53589 608-877-5601
Mike Kruse, prin. Fax 877-5619

**Stratford, Marathon, Pop. 1,570**
Stratford SD 900/PK-12
PO Box 7 54484 715-687-3130
Scott Winch, supt. Fax 687-4074
www.stratford.k12.wi.us
Stratford HS 9-12
PO Box 7 54484 715-687-4311
Janeen LaBorde, prin. Fax 687-4652
Stratford MS 200/6-8
PO Box 7 54484 715-687-4311
Janeen LaBorde, prin. Fax 687-4652

**Strum, Trempealeau, Pop. 1,111**
Eleva-Strum SD 600/PK-12
W23597 US Highway 10 54770 715-695-2696
Craig Semingson, admin. Fax 695-3519
www.esschools.k12.wi.us/
Eleva-Strum MSHS 300/7-12
W23597 US Highway 10 54770 715-695-2696
Cory Kulig, prin. Fax 695-3938

**Sturgeon Bay, Door, Pop. 9,041**
Sevastopol SD 400/PK-12
4550 State Highway 57 54235 920-743-6282
Dr. Linda Underwood, supt. Fax 743-4009
www.sevastopol.k12.wi.us
Sevastopol HS 200/9-12
4550 State Highway 57 54235 920-743-6282
Adam Baier, prin. Fax 743-4009
Sevastopol MS 100/6-8
4550 State Highway 57 54235 920-743-6282
Adam Baier, prin. Fax 743-4009
Sturgeon Bay SD 1,200/PK-12
1230 Michigan St 54235 920-746-2800
Daniel Tjernagel, supt. Fax 746-3888
www.sturbay.k12.wi.us
Sturgeon Bay HS 400/9-12
1230 Michigan St 54235 920-746-2800
Robert Nickel, prin. Fax 746-3888
Walker MS 200/6-8
19 N 14th Ave 54235 920-746-2810
Randy Watermolen, prin. Fax 746-3885

---

Northeast Wisconsin Technical College Post-Sec.
229 N 14th Ave 54235 920-746-4900

**Sun Prairie, Dane, Pop. 28,546**
Sun Prairie Area SD 5,600/PK-12
501 S Bird St 53590 608-834-6500
Tim Culver, supt. Fax 834-6555
www.spasd.k12.wi.us
Cardinal Heights Upper MS 1,000/8-9
220 Kroncke Dr 53590 608-318-8000
Ryan Ruggles, prin. Fax 318-8192
Prairie Phoenix Academy 100/Alt
160 South St 53590 608-834-6900
Wendi Tavs, prin. Fax 834-6992
Sun Prairie HS 1,400/10-12
888 Grove St 53590 608-834-6700
Lisa Heipp, prin. Fax 834-6792

---

Diesel Truck Driver Training School Post-Sec.
7190 Elder Ln 53590 608-837-7800

**Superior, Douglas, Pop. 26,443**
Superior SD 4,600/PK-12
3025 Tower Ave 54880 715-394-8700
Janna Stevens, supt. Fax 394-8708
www.superior.k12.wi.us
Superior HS 1,400/9-12
2600 Catlin Ave 54880 715-394-8720
Kent Bergum, prin. Fax 394-8760
Superior MS 1,000/6-8
3626 Hammond Ave 54880 715-394-8740
Richard Flaherty, prin. Fax 395-8483

---

Maranatha Academy 100/PK-12
4916 S State Road 35 54880 715-399-8757
Keith Russell, admin. Fax 399-8758
University of Wisconsin Post-Sec.
PO Box 2000 54880 715-394-8101
Wisconsin Indianhead Technical College Post-Sec.
600 N 21st St 54880 715-394-6677

**Suring, Oconto, Pop. 532**
Suring SD 400/PK-12
PO Box 158 54174 920-842-2178
Kelly Casper, supt. Fax 842-4570
www.suring.k12.wi.us
Suring HS 100/9-12
PO Box 158 54174 920-842-2182
Steven Huisman, prin. Fax 842-4570

**Sussex, Waukesha, Pop. 10,416**
Hamilton SD 4,700/PK-12
W220N6151 Town Line Rd 53089 262-246-1973
Dr. Kathleen Cooke, supt. Fax 246-6552
www.hamilton.k12.wi.us/
Hamilton HS 1,400/9-12
W220N6151 Town Line Rd 53089 262-246-6471
Candis Mongan, prin. Fax 246-1885
Templeton MS 1,000/6-8
N59W22490 Silver Spring Dr 53089 262-246-6477
Dr. Paul Mielke, prin. Fax 246-0465

**Thorp, Clark, Pop. 1,612**
Thorp SD 500/PK-12
PO Box 429 54771 715-669-5548
James Montgomery, admin. Fax 669-5403
www.thorp.k12.wi.us/
Thorp HS 200/7-12
PO Box 449 54771 715-669-5401
Brad Ceranski, prin. Fax 669-5403

**Three Lakes, Oneida, Pop. 604**
Three Lakes SD 600/PK-12
6930 W School St 54562 715-546-3496
Dr. George Karling, supt. Fax 546-8125
www.threelakessd.k12.wi.us
Three Lakes HS 300/7-12
6930 W School St 54562 715-546-3321
Dr. William Greb, prin. Fax 546-2828

**Tigerton, Shawano, Pop. 725**
Tigerton SD 300/PK-12
PO Box 10 54486 715-535-4000
Dr. Wayne Johnson, admin. Fax 535-4010
www.tigerton.k12.wi.us
Tigerton MSHS 200/6-12
PO Box 40 54486 715-535-4001
David Battenberg, prin. Fax 535-1355

**Tomah, Monroe, Pop. 8,916**
Tomah Area SD 3,100/PK-12
129 W Clifton St 54660 608-374-7004
Cindy Zahrte, supt. Fax 372-5087
www.tomah.k12.wi.us
Kupper Learning Center 100/Alt
1310 Townline Rd 54660 608-374-7020
Paul Skofronick, admin. Fax 374-8710
Tomah HS 900/9-12
901 Lincoln Ave 54660 608-374-7358
Bill Paris, prin. Fax 374-7290
Tomah MS 700/6-8
612 Hollister Ave 54660 608-374-7882
Steven Buss, prin. Fax 374-7303

**Tomahawk, Lincoln, Pop. 3,356**
Tomahawk SD 1,400/PK-12
1048 E King Rd 54487 715-453-5551
Cheryl Baker, supt. Fax 453-6736
www.tomahawk.k12.wi.us
Tomahawk HS 500/9-12
1048 E King Rd 54487 715-453-2106
Scott Swenty, prin. Fax 453-1437
Tomahawk MS 300/6-8
1048 E King Rd 54487 715-453-5371
Trisha Detert, prin. Fax 453-9630

**Tony, Rusk, Pop. 113**
Flambeau SD 300/PK-12
PO Box 86 54563 715-532-3183
Matthew Spets, supt. Fax 532-5405
www.flambeau.k12.wi.us

Flambeau S 300/PK-12
PO Box 86 54563 715-532-3183
Erica Schley, prin. Fax 532-5405

**Turtle Lake, Barron, Pop. 1,031**
Turtle Lake SD 500/PK-12
205 Oak St 54889 715-986-2597
Kent Kindschy, admin. Fax 986-2444
www.turtlelake.k12.wi.us
Turtle Lake HS 100/9-12
205 Oak St 54889 715-986-4470
Brian Buck, prin. Fax 986-2444

**Two Rivers, Manitowoc, Pop. 11,594**
Two Rivers SD 1,600/PK-12
4521 Lincoln Ave 54241 920-793-4560
Lisa Quistorf, supt. Fax 793-4014
www.trschools.k12.wi.us
Clarke MS 500/5-8
4608 Bellevue Pl 54241 920-794-1614
Tim Wester, prin. Fax 793-1819
Two Rivers HS 500/9-12
4519 Lincoln Ave 54241 920-793-2291
Larry Schlosser, prin. Fax 793-5068

**Union Grove, Racine, Pop. 4,851**
Union Grove UNHSD 1,000/9-12
3433 S Colony Ave 53182 262-878-4427
Alan Mollerskov, supt. Fax 878-3291
www.ug.k12.wi.us
Union Grove HS 1,000/9-12
3433 S Colony Ave 53182 262-878-2434
Thomas Hermann, prin. Fax 878-4056

---

Union Grove Christian S 100/PK-12
417 15th Ave 53182 262-878-1264
James Elkins, prin. Fax 878-2085

**Valders, Manitowoc, Pop. 958**
Valders Area SD 1,000/K-12
138 E Wilson St 54245 920-775-9500
Debra Hunt, supt. Fax 775-9509
www.valders.k12.wi.us
Valders HS 400/9-12
201 E Wilson St 54245 920-775-9530
Julie Laabs, prin. Fax 775-9509
Valders MS 300/5-8
138 Jefferson St 54245 920-775-9520
Kelly Isselmann, prin. Fax 775-9509

**Verona, Dane, Pop. 10,419**
Verona Area SD 4,900/PK-12
700 N Main St 53593 608-845-4300
Dean Gorrell, supt. Fax 845-4321
www.verona.k12.wi.us
Badger Ridge MS 500/6-8
740 N Main St 53593 608-845-4100
Michael Murphy, prin. Fax 845-4120
Verona Area HS 1,500/9-12
300 Richard St 53593 608-845-4400
Pam Hammen, prin. Fax 845-4420
Other Schools – See Fitchburg

**Viola, Vernon, Pop. 694**
Kickapoo Area SD 500/PK-12
S6520 State Highway 131 54664 608-627-0101
Douglas Olsen, supt. Fax 627-0118
www.kickapoo.k12.wi.us
Kickapoo MSHS 200/6-12
S6520 State Highway 131 54664 608-627-0100
Aaron Mithum, prin. Fax 627-0132

**Viroqua, Vernon, Pop. 4,314**
Viroqua Area SD 1,100/PK-12
115 N Education Ave 54665 608-637-1186
Dr. Robert Knadle, supt. Fax 637-8554
www.viroqua.k12.wi.us
Viroqua HS 300/9-12
100 Blackhawk Dr 54665 608-637-3191
Katherine Klos, prin. Fax 637-8034
Viroqua MS 300/5-8
100 Blackhawk Dr 54665 608-637-3171
John Schneider, prin. Fax 637-8034

---

Cornerstone Christian Academy 50/PK-12
S3655 Duncan Ln 54665 608-634-4102
Jim Schweitzer, admin. Fax 634-4162
Youth Initiative HS 50/9-12
500 E Jefferson St Ste 302 54665 608-637-6445
Matthew Voz, admin. Fax 637-6445

**Wabeno, Forest, Pop. 550**
Wabeno Area SD 500/PK-12
PO Box 460 54566 715-473-2592
Kimberly Odekirk Ph.D., supt. Fax 473-5201
www.wabeno.k12.wi.us
Wabeno JSHS 200/7-12
PO Box 460 54566 715-473-5122
Matthew Paulsen, prin. Fax 473-3406

**Wales, Waukesha, Pop. 2,532**
Kettle Moraine SD 4,100/PK-12
563 A J Allen Cir 53183 262-968-6300
Patricia Deklotz, supt. Fax 968-6390
www.kmsd.edu/
Kettle Moraine HS 1,400/9-12
349 N Oak Crest Dr 53183 262-968-6200
Jeffrey Walters, prin. Fax 968-6217
Other Schools – See Dousman

**Walworth, Walworth, Pop. 2,799**
Big Foot UNHSD 500/9-12
PO Box 99 53184 262-275-2116
Dorothy Kaufmann, admin. Fax 275-5117
www.bigfoot.k12.wi.us
Big Foot Union HS 500/9-12
PO Box 99 53184 262-275-2116
Dorothy J. Kaufmann, admin. Fax 275-5117

**Washburn, Bayfield, Pop. 2,031**
Washburn SD 500/PK-12
PO Box 730 54891 715-373-6188
Dr. Thomas Wiatr, supt. Fax 373-5877
www.washburn.k12.wi.us
Washburn HS 200/9-12
PO Box 730 54891 715-373-6188
Dr. Thomas Wiatr, prin. Fax 373-5877
Washburn MS 100/6-8
PO Box 730 54891 715-373-6199
Al Krause, prin. Fax 373-0586

**Washington Island, Door**
Washington SD 100/K-12
888 Main Rd 54246 920-847-2507
Tammy Kielbasa, supt. Fax 847-2865
www.island.k12.wi.us
Washington Island HS 50/9-12
888 Main Rd 54246 920-847-2507
Tammy Kielbasa, prin. Fax 847-2865

**Waterford, Racine, Pop. 5,327**
Waterford Graded JSD 1 1,600/K-8
819 W Main St 53185 262-514-8250
Christopher Joch, supt. Fax 514-8251
www.waterford.k12.wi.us
Fox River MS 400/7-8
921 W Main St 53185 262-514-8240
Darlene Markle, prin. Fax 514-8241

Waterford UNHSD 1,100/9-12
507 W Main St 53185 262-534-9059
Keith Brandstetter, supt. Fax 534-6871
www.waterforduhs.k12.wi.us
Waterford Union HS 1,100/9-12
100 Field Dr 53185 262-534-3189
Daniel Foster, prin. Fax 534-4971

**Waterloo, Jefferson, Pop. 3,304**
Waterloo SD 700/PK-12
813 N Monroe St 53594 920-478-3633
Brian Henning, admin. Fax 478-3821
www.waterloo.k12.wi.us
Waterloo HS 300/9-12
813 N Monroe St 53594 920-478-2171
Brad Donner, prin. Fax 478-9539
Waterloo MS 100/5-8
813 N Monroe St 53594 920-478-2696
Shannon Karcher, prin. Fax 478-3987

**Watertown, Jefferson, Pop. 23,579**
Watertown Unified SD 3,900/PK-12
111 Dodge St 53094 920-262-1460
Cassandra Schug, supt. Fax 262-1469
www.watertown.k12.wi.us
Riverside MS 800/6-8
131 Hall St 53094 920-262-1480
Daniela Stuckey, prin. Fax 262-1468
Watertown HS 1,300/9-12
825 Endevour Dr 53098 920-262-7500
Scott Mantei, prin. Fax 262-7545

---

Luther Preparatory S 400/9-12
1300 Western Ave 53094 920-261-4352
Matthew Crass, pres. Fax 262-8118
Maranatha Baptist Bible Coll & Seminary Post-Sec.
745 W Main St 53094 920-261-9300
Trinity-St. Luke's Lutheran S 100/5-8
303 Clark St 53094 920-206-1844
James Moeller, prin. Fax 206-1750

**Waukesha, Waukesha, Pop. 69,639**
Waukesha SD 12,400/PK-12
222 Maple Ave 53186 262-970-1000
Todd Gray, supt. Fax 970-1021
www.waukesha.k12.wi.us
Butler MS 1,000/6-8
310 N Hine Ave 53188 262-970-2900
Jason Sadowski, prin. Fax 970-2920
Horning MS 800/6-8
2000 Wolf Rd 53186 262-970-3300
Mark Wegner, prin. Fax 970-3320
North HS 1,200/9-12
2222 Michigan Ave 53188 262-970-3500
Rebecca Newcomer, prin. Fax 970-3520
Paul MS 600/6-8
400 N Grand Ave 53186 262-970-3100
Rob Bennett, prin. Fax 970-3120
South HS 1,100/9-12
401 E Roberta Ave 53186 262-970-3705
Timothy Joynt, prin. Fax 970-3720
West HS 1,300/9-12
3301 Saylesville Rd 53189 262-970-3900
David LaBorde, prin. Fax 970-3920

---

Carroll University Post-Sec.
100 N East Ave 53186 262-547-1211
Catholic Memorial HS 700/9-12
601 E College Ave 53186 262-542-7101
Robert Hall, prin. Fax 542-1633
DeVry University Post-Sec.
N14W23833 Stone Ridge Dr 53188 262-347-2911
St. Joseph MS 200/6-8
818 N East Ave 53186 262-896-2930
Joseph Heinecke, prin. Fax 896-2935
University of Wisconsin Waukesha Post-Sec.
1500 N University Dr 53188 262-521-5200

**Waunakee, Dane, Pop. 11,963**
Waunakee Community SD 3,700/PK-12
905 Bethel Cir 53597 608-849-2000
Randy Guttenberg, supt. Fax 849-2350
www.waunakee.k12.wi.us
Waunakee HS 1,100/9-12
301 Community Dr 53597 608-849-2100
Brian Kersten, prin. Fax 849-2164
Waunakee MS 600/7-8
1001 South St 53597 608-849-2060
Marcy Peters-Felice, prin. Fax 849-2088

---

Madison Country Day S 300/PK-12
5606 River Rd 53597 608-850-6000
Luke Felker, hdmstr. Fax 850-6006

**Waupaca, Waupaca, Pop. 6,011**
Waupaca SD 2,100/PK-12
515 School St 54981 715-258-4121
David Poeschl, supt. Fax 258-4125
www.waupaca.k12.wi.us/
Waupaca HS 800/9-12
E2325 King Rd 54981 715-258-4131
Robert Becker, prin. Fax 258-4135
Waupaca MS 500/5-8
1149 Shoemaker Rd 54981 715-258-4140
Ben Rayome, prin. Fax 256-5681

**Waupun, Dodge, Pop. 11,240**
Waupun Area SD 1,700/PK-12
950 Wilcox St 53963 920-324-9341
Tonya Gubin, supt. Fax 324-2630
www.waupun.k12.wi.us
Waupun Area JSHS 600/7-12
801 E Lincoln St 53963 920-324-5591
Jeff Finstad, prin. Fax 324-6980

---

Central Wisconsin Christian S 300/PK-12
301 Fox Lake Rd 53963 920-324-4233
Mark Buteyn, admin. Fax 324-5036

**Wausau, Marathon, Pop. 38,312**
Wausau SD 8,400/PK-12
PO Box 359 54402 715-261-0500
Dr. Kathleen Williams, supt. Fax 261-2503
www.wausauschools.org/
Mann MS 800/6-8
3101 N 13th St 54403 715-261-0725
Julie Sprague, prin. Fax 261-2035
Muir MS 900/6-8
1400 Stewart Ave 54401 715-261-0100
Larry Mancl, prin. Fax 261-2461
Wausau East HS 1,200/9-12
2607 N 18th St 54403 715-261-0650
Bradley Peck, prin. Fax 845-2913
Wausau West HS 1,400/9-12
1200 W Wausau Ave 54401 715-261-0850
Jeb Steckbauer, prin. Fax 261-3260

---

Faith Christian Academy 100/PK-12
225 S 28th Ave 54401 715-842-0797
Dave Wysong, admin. Fax 842-1042
Newman Catholic MSHS 300/6-12
1130 W Bridge St 54401 715-845-8274
James Delikowski, prin. Fax 842-1302
Northcentral Technical College Post-Sec.
1000 W Campus Dr 54401 715-675-3331
Rasmussen College Post-Sec.
1101 Westwood Dr 54401 715-841-8000
State College of Beauty Culture Post-Sec.
1930 Grand Ave 54403 715-849-5368
University of Wisconsin Marathon County Post-Sec.
518 S 7th Ave 54401 715-261-6235
Wausau Hospital Center Post-Sec.
333 Pine Ridge Blvd 54401 715-847-2117

**Wausaukee, Marinette, Pop. 563**
Wausaukee SD 500/PK-12
PO Box 258 54177 715-856-5153
Ann Kox, supt. Fax 856-6592
www.wausaukee.k12.wi.us
Wausaukee HS 200/9-12
PO Box 258 54177 715-856-5151
Jared Deschane, prin. Fax 856-6592
Wausaukee JHS 100/7-8
PO Box 258 54177 715-856-5151
Jared Deschane, prin. Fax 856-6592

**Wautoma, Waushara, Pop. 2,182**
Wautoma Area SD 1,500/PK-12
PO Box 870 54982 920-787-7112
Jeff Kasuboski, supt. Fax 787-1389
www.wautomasd.org
Parkside MS 500/4-8
PO Box 870 54982 920-787-4577
Deb Premo, prin. Fax 787-7336
Wautoma HS 400/9-12
PO Box 870 54982 920-787-3354
Tom Rheinheimer, prin. Fax 787-1513

**Wauwatosa, Milwaukee, Pop. 45,454**
Wauwatosa SD 7,200/PK-12
12121 W North Ave 53226 414-773-1000
Phil Ertl, supt. Fax 773-1019
www.wauwatosaschools.org
East HS 1,200/9-12
7500 Milwaukee Ave 53213 414-773-2000
Nick Hughes, prin. Fax 773-2020
Longfellow MS 900/6-8
7600 W North Ave 53213 414-773-2400
Jason Galien, prin. Fax 773-2420
Plank Road S 100/Alt
9501 W Watertown Plank Rd 53226 414-257-7128
Tom Seidl, prin. Fax 257-6620
West HS 1,000/9-12
11400 W Center St 53222 414-773-3000
Frank Calarco, prin. Fax 773-3020
Whitman MS 700/6-8
11100 W Center St 53222 414-773-2600
Jeff Keranen, prin. Fax 773-2620

---

Bryant & Stratton College Post-Sec.
10950 W Potter Rd 53226 414-302-7000

**Wauzeka, Crawford, Pop. 697**
Wauzeka-Steuben SD 200/PK-12
301 E Main St 53826 608-875-5311
Dr. Michael S. Garrow, supt. Fax 875-5100
www.wauzeka.k12.wi.us

Wauzeka-Steuben S 200/PK-12
301 E Main St 53826 608-875-5311
Robert Sailer, prin. Fax 875-5100

**Webster, Burnett, Pop. 634**
Webster SD 700/PK-12
PO Box 9 54893 715-866-4391
Jim Erickson, supt. Fax 866-4283
www.webster.k12.wi.us
Webster HS 200/9-12
PO Box 9 54893 715-866-4281
Josh Hetfeld, prin. Fax 866-4377
Webster MS 200/5-8
PO Box 9 54893 715-866-4282
Diana Lesneski, prin. Fax 866-4377

**West Allis, Milwaukee, Pop. 59,182**
West Allis SD
Supt. — See Milwaukee
Central HS 1,400/9-12
8516 W Lincoln Ave 53227 414-604-3110
Dr. Amy VanDeuren, prin. Fax 546-5536
Hale HS 1,700/9-12
11601 W Lincoln Ave 53227 414-604-3210
Matthew Lesar, prin. Fax 546-5734
Lane IS 6-8
1300 S 109th St 53214 414-329-6610
Delshon Henry, prin. Fax 259-0306
Lincoln IS 400/6-8
7815 W Lapham St 53214 414-604-4210
Adam Hengel, prin. Fax 777-7256
West Allis West Milwaukee Learning Ctr Alt
1135 S 70th St 53214 414-604-3510
Greg Goelz, prin. Fax 454-0293
Wright IS 1,000/6-8
9501 W Cleveland Ave 53227 414-604-3410
Jeff Thomson, prin. Fax 546-5785

---

Grace Christian Academy 200/PK-12
8420 W Beloit Rd 53227 414-327-4200
Cynthia Hummitzsch, admin. Fax 327-4386
Milwaukee Area Technical College Post-Sec.
1200 S 71st St 53214 414-456-5500

**West Bend, Washington, Pop. 30,669**
West Bend SD 6,500/PK-12
735 S Main St 53095 262-335-5435
Ted Neitzke, supt. Fax 335-5470
www.west-bend.k12.wi.us
Badger MS 900/7-8
727 S 6th Ave 53095 262-335-5456
Kurt Becker, prin. Fax 306-4380
East HS 1,200/9-12
1305 E Decorah Rd 53095 262-335-5532
James Curler, prin. Fax 335-8242
Spartan Sun Alternative S Alt
1305 S Main St 53095 262-335-5587
Dave Uelman, prin. Fax 335-8251
West HS 1,200/9-12
1305 E Decorah Rd 53095 262-335-5587
James Curler, prin. Fax 335-8251

---

Moraine Park Technical College Post-Sec.
2151 N Main St 53090 262-335-5706
University of Wisconsin Washington Co Post-Sec.
400 S University Dr 53095 262-335-5200

**Westby, Vernon, Pop. 2,182**
Westby Area SD 1,100/PK-12
206 West Ave S 54667 608-634-0101
Charles Norton, supt. Fax 634-0118
www.westby.k12.wi.us
Westby Area HS 300/9-12
206 West Ave S 54667 608-634-3101
Karl Stoker, prin. Fax 634-0123
Westby Area MS 300/5-8
206 West Ave S 54667 608-634-0200
Mike Weninger, prin. Fax 634-0218

**Westfield, Marquette, Pop. 1,241**
Westfield SD 1,100/PK-12
N7046 County Road M 53964 608-296-2107
John Eyerly, supt. Fax 296-2938
www.westfield.k12.wi.us
Westfield Area HS 400/9-12
N7046 County Road M 53964 608-296-2141
David Moody, prin. Fax 296-2293
Westfield Area MS 200/7-8
N7046 County Road M 53964 608-296-2141
David Moody, prin. Fax 296-2293

**West Milwaukee, Milwaukee, Pop. 4,109**
West Allis SD
Supt. — See Milwaukee
West Milwaukee IS 500/6-8
5104 W Greenfield Ave 53214 414-604-3310
Jeffery Taylor, prin. Fax 389-3815

**Weston, Marathon, Pop. 12,921**
D.C. Everest Area SD 5,600/PK-12
6300 Alderson St 54476 715-359-4221
Kristine Gilmore, supt. Fax 359-2056
www.dce.k12.wi.us
D.C. Everest HS 1,400/10-12
6500 Alderson St 54476 715-359-6561
Thomas Johansen, prin. Fax 355-7220
D.C. Everest JHS 900/8-9
1000 Machmueller St 54476 715-359-0511
Jason McFarlane, prin. Fax 359-9395

**West Salem, LaCrosse, Pop. 4,740**
West Salem SD 1,800/PK-12
405 Hamlin St E 54669 608-786-0700
Troy Gunderson, supt. Fax 786-2960
www.wsalem.k12.wi.us
West Salem HS 500/9-12
490 Mark St N 54669 608-786-1220
Mark Carlson, prin. Fax 786-1273
West Salem MS 400/6-8
450 Mark St N 54669 608-786-2090
Dean Buchanan, prin. Fax 786-1081

---

Coulee Christian S 200/PK-12
230 Garland St W 54669 608-786-3004
Dr. Tammy Chandler, admin. Fax 786-3005

**Weyauwega, Waupaca, Pop. 1,882**
Weyauwega-Fremont SD 900/PK-12
PO Box 580 54983 920-867-8800
Scott Bleck, supt. Fax 867-8815
www.wegafremont.k12.wi.us
Weyauwega-Fremont HS 300/9-12
PO Box 580 54983 920-867-8950
Jeremy Schroeder, prin. Fax 867-8975
Weyauwega-Fremont MS 200/6-8
PO Box 580 54983 920-867-8850
Jeremy Schroeder, prin. Fax 867-8875

**Whitefish Bay, Milwaukee, Pop. 13,847**
Whitefish Bay SD 3,000/PK-12
1200 E Fairmount Ave 53217 414-963-3921
John Thomsen, supt. Fax 963-3959
www.wfbschools.com
Whitefish Bay HS 1,000/9-12
1200 E Fairmount Ave 53217 414-963-3928
Amy Levek, prin. Fax 963-3870
Whitefish Bay MS 700/6-8
1144 E Henry Clay St 53217 414-963-6800
Mike O'Connor, prin. Fax 963-6808

---

Dominican HS 300/9-12
120 E Silver Spring Dr 53217 414-332-1170
Edward Foy, prin. Fax 332-4101

**Whitehall, Trempealeau, Pop. 1,550**
Whitehall SD 700/PK-12
PO Box 37 54773 715-538-4374
Michael Beighley, supt. Fax 538-4639
www.whitehallsd.k12.wi.us
Whitehall Memorial MSHS 200/7-12
PO Box 37 54773 715-538-4364
Mike Beighley, prin. Fax 538-4639

**White Lake, Langlade, Pop. 352**
White Lake SD 200/PK-12
PO Box 67 54491 715-882-8421
William Fisher, supt. Fax 882-2914
www.whitelake.k12.wi.us
White Lake JSHS 100/7-12
PO Box 67 54491 715-882-2361
Glenda Boldig, prin. Fax 882-2914

**Whitewater, Walworth, Pop. 14,180**
Whitewater USD 1,900/PK-12
419 S Elizabeth St 53190 262-472-8700
Eric Runez, supt. Fax 472-8710
www.wwusd.org
Whitewater HS 600/9-12
534 S Elizabeth St 53190 262-472-8100
Doug Parker, prin. Fax 472-8181
Whitewater MS 400/6-8
401 S Elizabeth St 53190 262-472-8300
Dr. Tanya Wojciechowicz, prin. Fax 472-8310

---

University of Wisconsin Post-Sec.
800 W Main St 53190 262-472-1234

**Wild Rose, Waushara, Pop. 719**
Wild Rose SD 600/PK-12
PO Box 276 54984 920-622-4203
Craig Hayes, supt. Fax 622-4604
www.wildrose.k12.wi.us
Wild Rose MSHS 300/6-12
PO Box 276 54984 920-622-4201
Chris Nelson, prin. Fax 622-4801

**Williams Bay, Walworth, Pop. 2,540**
Williams Bay SD 600/PK-12
PO Box 1410 53191 262-245-1575
Dr. Wayne Anderson, supt. Fax 245-5877
www.williamsbayschool.org
Williams Bay HS 200/9-12
PO Box 1410 53191 262-245-6224
William White, prin. Fax 245-5877
Williams Bay JHS 100/7-8
PO Box 1410 53191 262-245-6224
William White, prin. Fax 245-5877

---

Faith Christian S 200/PK-12
PO Box 1230 53191 262-245-9404
Craig Skrede, admin. Fax 245-0128
G Williams College of Aurora University Post-Sec.
PO Box 210 53191 262-245-5531

**Wilmot, Kenosha, Pop. 442**
Wilmot UNHSD 1,100/9-12
PO Box 8 53192 262-862-9005
Daniel S. Kopp, admin. Fax 862-6413
www.wilmothighschool.com
Wilmot HS 1,100/9-12
PO Box 8 53192 262-862-2351
Dr. John LaFleur, prin. Fax 862-6929

**Wind Point, Racine, Pop. 1,708**

---

Prairie S 700/PK-12
4050 Lighthouse Dr, 262-752-2500
Dr. Nat Coffman, head sch Fax 752-2517

**Winneconne, Winnebago, Pop. 2,364**
Winneconne Community SD 1,500/PK-12
PO Box 5000 54986 920-582-5802
Margaret Larson, supt. Fax 582-5816
www.winneconne.k12.wi.us
Winneconne HS 500/9-12
PO Box 5000 54986 920-582-5810
Leah Michaud, prin. Fax 582-5813
Winneconne MS 400/6-8
PO Box 5000 54986 920-582-5800
Todd Schroeder, prin. Fax 582-5812

**Winter, Sawyer, Pop. 305**
Winter SD 300/PK-12
PO Box 310 54896 715-266-3301
Kurt Lindau, admin. Fax 266-2216
www.winter.k12.wi.us/
Winter HS 100/9-12
PO Box 310 54896 715-266-3301
Kurt Lindau, admin. Fax 266-9221
Winter MS 100/6-8
PO Box 310 54896 715-266-6701
Kurt Lindau, admin. Fax 266-2216

**Wisconsin Dells, Columbia, Pop. 2,648**
Wisconsin Dells SD 1,700/PK-12
811 County Road H 53965 608-254-7769
Terrance Slack, supt. Fax 254-8058
www.sdwd.k12.wi.us
Spring Hill MS 300/6-8
300 Vine St 53965 608-253-2468
Hugh Gaston, prin. Fax 254-6397
Wisconsin Dells HS 600/9-12
520 Race St 53965 608-253-1461
Fax 254-6288

**Wisconsin Rapids, Wood, Pop. 18,141**
Wisconsin Rapids SD 5,400/PK-12
510 Peach St 54494 715-424-6700
Colleen Dickmann, supt. Fax 422-6070
www.wrps.org
East JHS 800/8-9
311 Lincoln St 54494 715-424-6730
Kevin Yeske, prin. Fax 422-6270
Lincoln SHS 1,200/10-12
1801 16th St S 54494 715-424-6750
Ronald Rasmussen, prin. Fax 422-6097
River Cities HS 100/Alt
2390 48th St S 54494 715-424-6798
Kathi Stebbins Hintz, prin. Fax 422-6370

---

Assumption HS 200/9-12
445 Chestnut St 54494 715-422-0910
Paul Klinkhammer, prin. Fax 422-0912
Assumption MS 100/7-8
440 Mead St 54494 715-422-0950
Joan Bond, prin. Fax 422-0955
Mid-State Technical College Post-Sec.
500 32nd St N 54494 715-422-5300

**Wittenberg, Shawano, Pop. 1,064**
Wittenberg-Birnamwood SD 1,200/PK-12
400 W Grand Ave 54499 715-253-2213
Garrett Rogowski, supt. Fax 253-3588
www.wittbirn.k12.wi.us/
Wittenberg-Birnamwood HS 400/9-12
400 W Grand Ave 54499 715-253-2211
Jill Sharp, prin. Fax 253-3588

**Wonewoc, Juneau, Pop. 810**
Wonewoc-Union Center SD 400/PK-12
101 School Rd 53968 608-464-3165
Steven Lozeau, supt. Fax 464-3325
www.wc.k12.wi.us
Wonewoc HS 100/9-12
101 School Rd 53968 608-464-3165
Michelle Noll, prin. Fax 464-3325
Wonewoc JHS 50/6-8
101 School Rd 53968 608-464-3165
Michelle Noll, prin. Fax 464-3325

**Woodville, Saint Croix, Pop. 1,320**
Baldwin-Woodville Area SD
Supt. — See Baldwin
Viking MS 500/5-8
500 Southside Dr 54028 715-698-2456
Scott Benoy, prin. Fax 698-3315

**Wrightstown, Brown, Pop. 2,803**
Wrightstown Community SD 1,300/PK-12
PO Box 128 54180 920-532-5551
Carla Buboltz, supt. Fax 532-4664
www.wrightstown.k12.wi.us
Wrightstown HS 500/9-12
PO Box 128 54180 920-532-0525
Scott Thompson, prin. Fax 532-0860
Wrightstown MS 400/5-8
PO Box 128 54180 920-532-5553
Lee Mierow, prin. Fax 532-3869

# WYOMING

## WYOMING DEPARTMENT OF EDUCATION

**2300 Capitol Ave, Cheyenne 82001-3644**
**Telephone 307-777-7673**
**Fax 307-777-6234**
**Website edu.wyoming.gov**

Superintendent of Public Instruction — Richard Crandall

## WYOMING BOARD OF EDUCATION

**2300 Capitol Ave, Cheyenne 82001-3644**

Chairperson — Gerald "Joe" Reichardt

## BOARDS OF COOPERATIVE EDUCATIONAL SERVICES (BOCES)

Carbon Co. Higher Education Center BOCES
David Throgmorton Ph.D., dir. — 307-328-9274
812 E Murray St, Rawlins 82301 — Fax 324-3338
www.cchec.org

Central Wyoming BOCES
Jeana Lam-Pickett, admin. — 307-268-3309
125 College Dr, Casper 82601 — Fax 268-2731
www.caspercollege.edu/boces/index.html

Fremont County BOCES
Sandy Barton, dir. — 307-856-2028
320 W Main St, Riverton 82501 — Fax 856-4058
www.fcboces.org

Northeast Wyoming BOCES
Julie Cudmore, dir. — 307-682-0231
410 N Miller Ave, Gillette 82716 — Fax 686-7628
www.newboces.com/

Northwest Wyoming BOCES
Carolyn Conner, dir. — 307-864-2171
PO Box 112, Thermopolis 82443 — Fax 864-9463
www.nwboces.com/

Oyster Ridge BOCES
Heidi Currutt, dir. — 307-877-6958
20 Adaville Dr, Diamondville 83116 — Fax 828-9040
www.kemmereroutreach.com

Region V BOCES
Doris Woodbury, dir. — 307-733-8210
PO Box 899, Wilson 83014 — Fax 733-8462
boces5.org

Sublette BOCES
Ward Wise, dir. — 307-367-6873
PO Box 977, Pinedale 82941 — Fax 367-6634
www.subletteboces.com

Sweetwater BOCES
Bernadine Craft Ph.D., dir. — 307-382-1607
PO Box 428, Rock Springs 82902 — Fax 382-1875
www.westernwyoming.edu/services/boces/

Uinta BOCES
Michael Williams, dir. — 307-789-5742
1013 W Cheyenne Dr Unit A — Fax 789-7975
Evanston 82930
www.uintaeducation.org

Uinta County SD #4 & #6 BOCES
Karla Behunin, dir. — 307-782-6401
PO Box 130, Mountain View 82939 — Fax 782-7410
www.westernwyoming.edu/distance/vlc/

Western Sublette 9 BOCES
Angie Clifford, dir. — 307-276-5522
PO Box 706, Big Piney 83113 — Fax 276-3480
www.sublette9boces.org

## PUBLIC, PRIVATE AND CATHOLIC SECONDARY SCHOOLS

**Afton, Lincoln, Pop. 1,881**
Lincoln County SD 2 — 2,600/K-12
PO Box 219 83110 — 307-885-3811
Allan Allred, supt. — Fax 885-9562
www.lcsd2.org
Star Valley HS — 700/9-12
444 W Swift Creek Ln 83110 — 307-885-7847
Homer Bennett, prin. — Fax 885-3299
Star Valley MS — 400/7-8
999 Warrior Way 83110 — 307-885-5208
Kem Cazier, prin. — Fax 885-0472
Swift Creek HS — 50/Alt
PO Box 219 83110 — 307-885-7139
McKay Young, prin. — Fax 885-9562
Other Schools – See Cokeville

**Baggs, Carbon, Pop. 438**
Carbon County SD 1
Supt. — See Rawlins
Little Snake River Valley S — 200/K-12
PO Box 9 82321 — 307-383-2185
Joel Thomas, prin. — Fax 383-2184

**Basin, Big Horn, Pop. 1,274**
Big Horn County SD 4 — 300/K-12
PO Box 151 82410 — 307-568-2684
Mary Fisher, supt. — Fax 568-2654
www.bgh4.k12.wy.us/
Riverside HS — 100/9-12
PO Box 151 82410 — 307-568-2416
Tony Anson, prin. — Fax 568-2415
Other Schools – See Manderson

**Big Horn, Sheridan, Pop. 487**
Sheridan County SD 1
Supt. — See Ranchester
Big Horn HS — 100/9-12
PO Box 490 82833 — 307-674-8190
Ben Smith, prin. — Fax 672-5306
Big Horn MS — 100/6-8
PO Box 490 82833 — 307-674-8190
Richard Welch, prin. — Fax 672-5306

**Big Piney, Sublette, Pop. 550**
Sublette County SD 9 — 600/K-12
PO Box 769 83113 — 307-276-3322
Kevin Garvey, supt. — Fax 276-3731
www.sublette9.org
Big Piney HS — 200/9-12
PO Box 769 83113 — 307-276-3324
Jeff Makelky, prin. — Fax 276-3480
Big Piney MS — 200/6-8
PO Box 769 83113 — 307-276-3315
Stanley Dodds, prin. — Fax 276-5209

**Buffalo, Johnson, Pop. 4,536**
Johnson County SD 1 — 1,200/K-12
601 W Lott St 82834 — 307-684-9571
Gerry Chase, supt. — Fax 684-5182
www.jcsd1.k12.wy.us
Buffalo HS — 400/9-12
29891 Old Highway 87 82834 — 307-684-2269
Chad Bourgeois, prin. — Fax 684-9481
Clear Creek MS — 200/6-8
361 W Gatchell St 82834 — 307-684-5594
Darren Schmidt, prin. — Fax 684-9096
Other Schools – See Kaycee

**Burlington, Big Horn, Pop. 287**
Big Horn County SD 1
Supt. — See Cowley
Burlington HS — 100/9-12
PO Box 9 82411 — 307-762-3334
Matt Davidson, prin. — Fax 762-3604
Burlington MS — 50/7-8
PO Box 9 82411 — 307-762-3334
Matt Davidson, prin. — Fax 762-3604

**Burns, Laramie, Pop. 295**
Laramie County SD 2
Supt. — See Pine Bluffs
Burns JSHS — 300/7-12
PO Box 160 82053 — 307-245-4100
Jerry Becking, prin. — Fax 547-3583

**Casper, Natrona, Pop. 54,284**
Natrona County SD 1 — 12,200/PK-12
970 N Glenn Rd 82601 — 307-253-5200
Steve Hopkins, supt. — Fax 253-5333
www.natronaschools.org/
Casper Classical Academy — 200/6-9
900 S Beverly St 82609 — 307-253-3160
Marie Puryear, prin. — Fax 253-2286
Centennial JHS — 500/6-8
1421 Waterford 82609 — 307-253-2900
Mike Britt, prin. — Fax 253-2891
CY MS — 700/6-9
2900 Cyclone Blvd 82604 — 307-253-2700
Valerie Braughton, prin. — Fax 253-2683
Frontier MS — 200/6-8
900 S Beverly St 82609 — 307-253-2300
Casey Cloninger, prin. — Fax 253-2286
Morgan JHS — 800/6-8
1440 S Elm St 82601 — 307-253-2500
Steve Ellbogen, prin. — Fax 253-2411
Natrona County SHS — 1,800/9-12
930 S Elm St 82601 — 307-253-1700
Shannon Harris, prin. — Fax 253-1507
ProStart, 500 S Wolcott St 82601 — Vo/Tech
Calvin Colling, prin. — 307-234-9612
Roosevelt HS — 200/Alt
140 E K St 82601 — 307-253-1400
Shawna Trujillo, prin. — Fax 253-1450
Star Lane Center — Alt
1400 S Fairdale Ave 82601 — 307-253-3100
Chad Sharpe, prin. — Fax 253-3117
Transitions Learning Center — Alt
2000 Casper St 82604 — 307-253-4350
Chris Bolender, prin. — Fax 253-4321
Walsh HS — 1,500/9-12
3500 E 12th St 82609 — 307-253-2000
Brad Diller, prin. — Fax 253-2066
Other Schools – See Midwest

---

Casper College — Post-Sec.
125 College Dr 82601 — 307-268-2110
SAGE Technical Service Truck Driving Sch — Post-Sec.
2368 Oil Dr 82604 — 800-307-0242
Wyoming School for the Deaf — Post-Sec.
539 Payne Ave 82609

**Cheyenne, Laramie, Pop. 58,048**
Laramie County SD 1 — 13,100/K-12
2810 House Ave 82001 — 307-771-2100
Mark Stock, supt. — Fax 771-2364
www.laramie1.org/
Carey JHS — 700/7-8
1780 E Pershing Blvd 82001 — 307-771-2580
Derek Nissen, prin. — Fax 771-2578
Central HS — 1,300/9-12
5500 Education Dr 82009 — 307-771-2680
Steve Newton, prin. — Fax 771-2699
East HS — 1,300/9-12
2800 E Pershing Blvd 82001 — 307-771-2663
Samuel Mirich, prin. — Fax 771-2679
Johnson JHS — 600/7-8
1236 W Allison Rd 82007 — 307-771-2640
John Balow, prin. — Fax 771-2660
McCormick JHS — 700/7-8
6000 Education Dr 82009 — 307-771-2650
Jeff Conine, prin. — Fax 771-2661
South HS — 700/9-12
1213 W Allison Rd 82007 — 307-771-2410
Philip Thompson, prin. — Fax 771-2420
Triumph HS — 200/Alt
1250 W College Dr 82007 — 307-771-2500
Michael Helenbolt, prin. — Fax 771-2508

---

Cheeks Intl Academy of Beauty Culture — Post-Sec.
207 W 18th St 82001 — 307-637-8700
CollegeAmerica — Post-Sec.
6101 Yellowstone Rd Ste 101 82009 — 307-632-7048
Institute of Business & Medical Careers — Post-Sec.
1854 Dell Range Blvd 82009 — 307-433-8363
Laramie County Community College — Post-Sec.
1400 E College Dr 82007 — 307-778-5222
Webster Christian S — 100/PK-12
PO Box 21239 82003 — 307-635-2175
DeAnn Gomez, admin. — Fax 773-8523

**Chugwater, Platte, Pop. 210**
Platte County SD 1
Supt. — See Wheatland
Chugwater HS — 50/9-12
406 5th St 82210 — 307-422-3501
Tom Waring, prin. — Fax 422-3433
Chugwater JHS — 50/7-8
406 5th St 82210 — 307-422-3501
Tom Waring, prin. — Fax 422-3433

**Clearmont, Sheridan, Pop. 141**
Sheridan County SD 3 — 100/K-12
PO Box 125 82835 — 307-758-4412
Charles Auzqui, supt. — Fax 758-4444
www.sheridan3.com
Arvada-Clearmont HS — 50/9-12
PO Box 125 82835 — 307-758-4412
Christy Wright, prin. — Fax 758-4444
Arvada-Clearmont JHS — 50/7-8
PO Box 125 82835 — 307-758-4412
Christy Wright, prin. — Fax 758-4444

**Cody, Park, Pop. 9,367**
Park County SD 6 — 2,200/K-12
919 Cody Ave 82414 — 307-587-4253
Ray Schulte, supt. — Fax 527-5762
www.park6.org
Cody HS — 700/9-12
919 Cody Ave 82414 — 307-587-4251
Barton Bailey, prin. — Fax 587-9369
Cody MS — 500/6-8
919 Cody Ave 82414 — 307-587-4273
Tim Foley, prin. — Fax 587-3547

---

West Park Hospital — Post-Sec.
707 Sheridan Ave 82414 — 307-527-7501

**Cokeville, Lincoln, Pop. 533**
Lincoln County SD 2
Supt. — See Afton
Cokeville JSHS — 100/7-12
PO Box 220 83114 — 307-279-3273
Keith Harris, prin. — Fax 279-3221

**Cowley, Big Horn, Pop. 654**
Big Horn County SD 1 — 800/PK-12
PO Box 688 82420 — 307-548-2254
Shon Hocker, supt. — Fax 548-7610
bighorn1.com
Rocky Mountain HS — 200/9-12
PO Box 280 82420 — 307-548-2723
Tim Winland, prin. — Fax 548-6452
Rocky Mountain MS — 100/6-8
PO Box 280 82420 — 307-548-2723
Tim Winland, prin. — Fax 548-6452
Other Schools – See Burlington

**Dayton, Sheridan, Pop. 749**
Sheridan County SD 1
Supt. — See Ranchester
Tongue River HS — 100/9-12
PO Box 408 82836 — 307-655-2236
Mark Fritz, prin. — Fax 655-9798

**Diamondville, Lincoln, Pop. 720**
Lincoln County SD 1 — 600/K-12
PO Box 335 83116 — 307-877-9095
Teresa Chaulk, supt. — Fax 877-9638
www.lcsd1.k12.wy.us
Other Schools – See Kemmerer

**Douglas, Converse, Pop. 6,039**
Converse County SD 1 — 1,400/K-12
615 Hamilton St 82633 — 307-358-2942
Dr. Dan Espeland, supt. — Fax 358-3934
converse1schools.org
Douglas HS — 500/9-12
615 Hamilton St 82633 — 307-358-2940
Dan Edwards, prin. — Fax 358-2737
Douglas MS — 400/6-8
615 Hamilton St 82633 — 307-358-9771
Eric Pingrey, prin. — Fax 358-5315

**Dubois, Fremont, Pop. 957**
Fremont County SD 2 — 200/K-12
PO Box 188 82513 — 307-455-5545
Martha Gale, supt. — Fax 455-2178
www.fremont2.org/
Dubois HS — 100/9-12
PO Box 188 82513 — 307-455-5524
Brandon Farris, prin. — Fax 455-2654
Dubois MS — 50/6-8
PO Box 188 82513 — 307-455-5524
Brandon Farris, prin. — Fax 455-2654

**Encampment, Carbon, Pop. 445**
Carbon County SD 2
Supt. — See Saratoga
Encampment S — 100/K-12
PO Box 277 82325 — 307-327-5442
Michael Erickson, prin. — Fax 327-5142

**Ethete, Fremont, Pop. 1,530**
Fremont County SD 14 — 600/PK-12
638 Blue Sky Hwy 82520 — 307-332-3904
Terry Smith, supt. — Fax 332-7567
www.fremont14.k12.wy.us
Wyoming Indian HS — 100/9-12
638 Blue Sky Hwy 82520 — 307-332-9765
Phil Garhart, prin. — Fax 335-7739
Wyoming Indian MS — 100/6-8
638 Blue Sky Hwy 82520 — 307-332-2992
Pamela Gambler, prin. — Fax 335-7318

**Evanston, Uinta, Pop. 12,128**
Uinta County SD 1 — 2,900/K-12
PO Box 6002 82931 — 307-789-7571
Dr. James Bailey, supt. — Fax 789-6225
www.uinta1.com
Davis MS — 300/6-8
PO Box 6002 82931 — 307-789-8096
Jim Harrell, prin. — Fax 789-3386
Evanston HS — 800/9-12
PO Box 6002 82931 — 307-789-0757
Doug Rigby, prin. — Fax 789-7447
Evanston MS — 300/6-8
PO Box 6002 82931 — 307-789-5499
Eric Christenot, prin. — Fax 789-7972
Horizon Alternative S — 100/Alt
PO Box 6002 82931 — 307-789-0122
Doug Rigby, prin. — Fax 789-2522

**Farson, Sweetwater, Pop. 309**
Sweetwater County SD 1
Supt. — See Rock Springs
Farson-Eden HS — 100/9-12
PO Box 400 82932 — 307-273-9301
Michael Estes, prin. — Fax 273-9313
Farson-Eden MS — 50/6-8
PO Box 400 82932 — 307-273-9301
Michael Estes, prin. — Fax 273-9313

**Fort Washakie, Fremont, Pop. 1,730**
Fremont County SD 21 — 500/PK-12
90 Ethete Rd 82514 — 307-332-5983
H. Terry Ebert, supt. — Fax 332-7267
www.fortwashakieschool.com
Fort Washakie HS — 50/9-12
90 Ethete Rd 82514 — 307-332-0142
Shad Hamilton, prin. — Fax 332-7267
Fort Washakie MS — 100/7-8
90 Ethete Rd 82514 — 307-332-2380
Elberta Monroe, prin. — Fax 332-3597

**Gillette, Campbell, Pop. 28,659**
Campbell County SD 1 — 7,900/K-12
PO Box 3033 82717 — 307-682-5171
Dr. Boyd Brown, supt. — Fax 682-6619
www.campbellcountyschools.net/
Campbell County HS — 1,400/10-12
1000 Camel Dr 82716 — 307-682-7247
Troy Zickefoose, prin. — Fax 682-3914
Sage Valley JHS — 900/7-9
1000 W Lakeway Rd 82718 — 307-682-2225
Terry Quinn, prin. — Fax 687-7614
Twin Spruce JHS — 800/7-9
100 E 7th St 82716 — 307-682-3144
Dana Lyman, prin. — Fax 686-1969
Westwood HS — 100/Alt
7 Opportunity Spur 82718 — 307-682-9809
Kelly Morehead, prin. — Fax 686-7566
Other Schools – See Wright

---

Gillette College — Post-Sec.
300 W Sinclair St 82718 — 307-686-0254

**Glendo, Platte, Pop. 203**
Platte County SD 1
Supt. — See Wheatland
Glendo HS — 50/9-12
305 N Paige Ave 82213 — 307-735-4471
Stanetta Twiford, prin. — Fax 735-4220
Glendo JHS — 50/7-8
305 N Paige Ave 82213 — 307-735-4471
Stanetta Twiford, prin. — Fax 735-4220

**Glenrock, Converse, Pop. 2,551**
Converse County SD 2 — 600/K-12
PO Box 1300 82637 — 307-436-5331
Kirk Hughes, supt. — Fax 436-8235
www.cnv2.k12.wy.us/
Glenrock HS — 200/9-12
PO Box 1300 82637 — 307-436-9201
Christopher Gray, prin. — Fax 436-8517
Glenrock Intermediate MS — 100/5-8
PO Box 1300 82637 — 307-436-9258
Coley Shadrick, prin. — Fax 436-7507

**Green River, Sweetwater, Pop. 12,356**
Sweetwater County SD 2 — 2,600/K-12
320 Monroe Ave 82935 — 307-872-5500
Donna Little-Kaumo, supt. — Fax 872-5518
www.sw2.k12.wy.us
Expedition Academy — 100/10-12
351 Monroe Ave 82935 — 307-872-4800
Ralph Obray, prin. — Fax 872-4797
Green River HS — 700/9-12
1615 Hitching Post Dr 82935 — 307-872-4747
Darren Howard, prin. — Fax 872-4758
Lincoln MS — 400/7-8
350 Monroe Ave 82935 — 307-872-4400
Matt Mikkelsen, prin. — Fax 872-4477

**Greybull, Big Horn, Pop. 1,834**
Big Horn County SD 3 — 500/K-12
640 8th Ave N 82426 — 307-765-4756
Barry Bryant, supt. — Fax 765-4617
gps.bgh3.k12.wy.us
Greybull HS — 200/9-12
640 8th Ave N 82426 — 307-765-2537
Ty Flock, prin. — Fax 765-2870
Greybull MS — 100/6-8
640 8th Ave N 82426 — 307-765-4492
Scott McBride, prin. — Fax 765-2586

**Guernsey, Platte, Pop. 1,136**
Platte County SD 2 — 200/K-12
PO Box 189 82214 — 307-836-2735
Dave Barker, supt. — Fax 836-2450
www.guernseysunrise.org
Guernsey-Sunrise HS — 100/9-12
PO Box 189 82214 — 307-836-2745
Kyle Gunderson, prin. — Fax 836-2450
Guernsey-Sunrise JHS — 50/7-8
PO Box 189 82214 — 307-836-2745
Kyle Gunderson, prin. — Fax 836-2450

**Hanna, Carbon, Pop. 829**
Carbon County SD 2
Supt. — See Saratoga
Hanna-Elk Mountain-Medicine Bow JSHS — 100/7-12
PO Box 810 82327 — 307-325-6545
Steven Priest, prin. — Fax 325-9223

**Hulett, Crook, Pop. 375**
Crook County SD 1
Supt. — See Sundance
Hulett S — 200/K-12
PO Box 127 82720 — 307-467-5231
Linda Wolfskill, prin. — Fax 467-5280

**Jackson, Teton, Pop. 9,432**
Teton County SD 1 — 2,400/K-12
PO Box 568 83001 — 307-733-2704
Gillian Chapman Ed.D., supt. — Fax 734-1219
www.tcsd.org
Jackson Hole HS — 600/9-12
PO Box 568 83001 — 307-732-3700
Dr. Scott Crisp, prin. — Fax 732-3720
Jackson Hole MS — 500/6-8
PO Box 568 83001 — 307-733-4234
Debbie Pfortmiller, prin. — Fax 733-4254
Summit HS — 100/9-12
PO Box 568 83001 — 307-733-9116
Beth Auge, prin. — Fax 739-8922

---

Journeys S — 200/PK-12
700 Coyote Canyon Rd 83001 — 307-733-1313
Nate McClennen, head sch — Fax 733-7560

**Kaycee, Johnson, Pop. 260**
Johnson County SD 1
Supt. — See Buffalo
Kaycee K-12 S — 200/K-12
PO Box 6 82639 — 307-738-2573
Andrea Gilbert, prin. — Fax 738-2495

**Kemmerer, Lincoln, Pop. 2,635**
Lincoln County SD 1
Supt. — See Diamondville
Kemmerer JSHS — 200/7-12
1525 3rd West Ave 83101 — 307-877-6991
Orlen Zempel, prin. — Fax 877-4117
New Frontier HS — 50/Alt
1004 Elk St 83101 — 307-877-5819
David Gardner, prin. — Fax 877-5644

**Lander, Fremont, Pop. 7,311**
Fremont County SD 1 — 1,300/K-12
863 Sweetwater St 82520 — 307-332-4711
Dave Barker, supt. — Fax 332-6671
www.landerschools.org
Lander MS — 400/6-8
755 Jefferson St 82520 — 307-332-4040
Julie Shanley, prin. — Fax 332-0435
Lander Valley HS — 500/9-12
350 Baldwin Creek Rd 82520 — 307-332-4433
Lisa Hafer, prin. — Fax 332-2861
Pathfinder HS — 50/Alt
626 Washington St 82520 — 307-335-7050
Jannette Van Patten, prin. — Fax 335-8695

---

Wyoming State Training School — Post-Sec.
8204 State Highway 789 82520 — 307-332-5302

**Laramie, Albany, Pop. 30,183**
Albany County SD 1 — 3,300/PK-12
1948 E Grand Ave 82070 — 307-721-4400
Dr. Jubal C. Yennie, supt. — Fax 721-4408
www.acsd1.org
Laramie HS — 800/9-12
1275 N 11th St 82072 — 307-721-4420
Stacy Bush, prin. — Fax 721-4419
Laramie JHS — 600/6-9
1355 N 22nd St 82072 — 307-721-4430
Debra Fisher, prin. — Fax 721-4435
Whiting HS — 50/Alt
801 S 24th St 82070 — 307-721-4449
Jeff Lewis, prin. — Fax 721-4519
Other Schools – See Rock River

---

University of Wyoming — Post-Sec.
1000 E University Ave 82071 — 307-766-1121
WyoTech — Post-Sec.
4373 N 3rd St 82072 — 307-742-3776

**Lingle, Goshen, Pop. 467**
Goshen County SD 1
Supt. — See Torrington
Lingle-Ft. Laramie HS — 100/9-12
PO Box 379 82223 — 307-837-2296
Jerry Vandersloot, prin. — Fax 837-3025
Lingle-Ft. Laramie MS — 100/6-8
PO Box 379 82223 — 307-837-2283
Jerry Vandersloot, prin. — Fax 837-2057

**Lovell, Big Horn, Pop. 2,347**
Big Horn County SD 2 — 700/K-12
502 Hampshire Ave 82431 — 307-548-2259
Dr. Rick Woodford, supt. — Fax 548-7555
www.bgh2.k12.wy.us/
Lovell HS — 200/9-12
502 Hampshire Ave 82431 — 307-548-2256
Scott O'Tremba, prin. — Fax 548-9452
Lovell MS — 200/6-8
325 W 9th St 82431 — 307-548-6553
Douglas Hazen, prin. — Fax 548-6136

**Lusk, Niobrara, Pop. 1,541**
Niobrara County SD 1 — 600/PK-12
PO Box 629 82225 — 307-334-3793
Aaron Carr, supt. — Fax 334-0126
www.lusk.k12.wy.us
Niobrara County HS — 300/9-12
PO Box 1050 82225 — 307-334-3320
Marty Wood, prin. — Fax 334-2331

**Lyman, Uinta, Pop. 2,090**
Uinta County SD 6 — 800/K-12
PO Box 1090 82937 — 307-786-4100
Colby Gull, supt. — Fax 787-3241
www.uinta6.k12.wy.us/
Lyman HS — 200/9-12
PO Box 1090 82937 — 307-786-4100
Todd Limoges, prin. — Fax 787-3241
Lyman IS — 200/5-8
PO Box 1090 82937 — 307-786-4100
Christy Campbell, prin. — Fax 787-3241

**Manderson, Big Horn, Pop. 112**
Big Horn County SD 4
Supt. — See Basin
Cloud Peak MS 100/5-8
PO Box 97 82432 307-568-2846
Shane Schaffner, prin. Fax 568-3885

**Meeteetse, Park, Pop. 325**
Park County SD 16 100/K-12
PO Box 218 82433 307-868-2501
Jay Curtis, supt. Fax 868-9264
www.park16.org
Meeteetse S 100/K-12
PO Box 218 82433 307-868-2501
Cory Dziowgo, prin. Fax 868-9264

**Midwest, Natrona, Pop. 395**
Natrona County SD 1
Supt. — See Casper
Midwest S 200/PK-12
256 Lewis 82643 307-253-3500
Chris Tobin, prin. Fax 253-3520

**Moorcroft, Crook, Pop. 998**
Crook County SD 1
Supt. — See Sundance
Moorcroft HS 200/9-12
PO Box 129 82721 307-756-3446
Becky Waters, prin. Fax 756-3724

**Mountain View, Uinta, Pop. 1,273**
Uinta County SD 4 800/K-12
PO Box 130 82939 307-782-3377
Jeff Newton, supt. Fax 782-6879
www.uinta4.com
Mountain View HS 200/9-12
PO Box 130 82939 307-782-6340
Ben Carr, prin. Fax 782-6967
Mountain View MS 200/6-8
PO Box 130 82939 307-782-6338
Lane Stratton, prin. Fax 782-6876

**Newcastle, Weston, Pop. 3,468**
Weston County SD 1 800/K-12
116 Casper Ave 82701 307-746-4451
Brad LaCroix, supt. Fax 746-3289
www.weston1.k12.wy.us
Newcastle HS 200/9-12
116 Casper Ave 82701 307-746-2713
Tracy Ragland, prin. Fax 746-2350
Newcastle MS 200/6-8
116 Casper Ave 82701 307-746-2746
Todd Quigley, prin. Fax 746-4983

**Pavillion, Fremont, Pop. 225**
Fremont County SD 6 300/PK-12
PO Box 10 82523 307-856-7970
Diana Clapp, supt. Fax 856-3385
www.fre6.k12.wy.us/
Wind River HS 100/9-12
PO Box 10 82523 307-856-7970
Ceatriss Wall, prin. Fax 856-8641
Wind River MS 6-8
PO Box 10 82523 307-856-7970
Ceatriss Wall, prin. Fax 856-8641

**Pine Bluffs, Laramie, Pop. 1,114**
Laramie County SD 2 900/K-12
PO Box 489 82082 307-245-4050
Jon Abrams, supt. Fax 245-3561
laramie2.org
Pine Bluffs JSHS 200/7-12
PO Box 520 82082 307-245-4000
Todd Sweeter, prin. Fax 245-3144
Other Schools – See Burns

**Pinedale, Sublette, Pop. 1,999**
Sublette County SD 1 1,000/K-12
PO Box 549 82941 307-367-2139
Jay Harnack, supt. Fax 367-4626
www.sub1.org
Pinedale HS 300/9-12
PO Box 549 82941 307-367-2137
Benjamin Smith, prin. Fax 367-2611
Pinedale MS 200/6-8
PO Box 549 82941 307-367-2821
Jeryl Fluckiger, prin. Fax 367-4217
Skyline HS Alt
PO Box 549 82941 307-367-2137
Benjamin Smith, prin. Fax 367-2611

**Powell, Park, Pop. 6,232**
Park County SD 1 1,700/K-12
160 N Evarts St 82435 307-764-6186
Kevin Mitchell, supt. Fax 764-6156
www.park1.net
Powell HS 500/9-12
160 N Evarts St 82435 307-764-6181
Jim Kuhn, prin. Fax 764-6151
Powell MS 400/6-8
160 N Evarts St 82435 307-764-6185
Jason Sleep, prin. Fax 764-6155
Shoshone Learning Center 50/Alt
160 N Evarts St 82435 307-764-6187
Ginger Sleep, prin. Fax 764-6157

---

Northwest College Post-Sec.
231 W 6th St 82435 307-754-6000

**Ranchester, Sheridan, Pop. 853**
Sheridan County SD 1 900/K-12
PO Box 819 82839 307-655-9541
Marty Kobza, supt. Fax 655-9477
www.sheridan.k12.wy.us/
Tongue River MS 100/6-8
PO Box 879 82839 307-655-9533
Pete Kilbride, prin. Fax 655-9894
Other Schools – See Big Horn, Dayton

**Rawlins, Carbon, Pop. 9,144**
Carbon Co. Higher Education Center BOCES
812 E Murray St 82301 307-328-9274
David Throgmorton Ph.D., dir. Fax 324-3338
www.cchec.org
Vocational Campus Vo/Tech
1650 N Higley Blvd 82301 307-328-9204
Fax 328-9273

Carbon County SD 1 1,300/K-12
615 Rodeo St 82301 307-328-9200
Fletcher Turcato, supt. Fax 328-9258
www.crb1.net
Cooperative HS 50/Alt
615 Rodeo St 82301 307-328-9250
Mark Gaines, prin. Fax 328-9258
Rawlins HS 400/9-12
1401 Colorado St 82301 307-328-9280
Tom Weed, prin. Fax 328-9286
Rawlins MS 400/6-8
1001 Brooks St 82301 307-328-9201
Kevin O'Dea, prin. Fax 328-9226
Other Schools – See Baggs

**Riverton, Fremont, Pop. 10,330**
Fremont County SD 25 2,400/K-12
121 N 5th St W 82501 307-856-9407
Terry Snyder, supt. Fax 856-3390
www.fremont25.k12.wy.us
Riverton HS 700/9-12
121 N 5th St W 82501 307-856-9491
John Griffith, prin. Fax 856-2333
Riverton MS 600/6-8
121 N 5th St W 82501 307-856-9443
Cheryl Mowry, prin. Fax 857-1695

---

Central Wyoming College Post-Sec.
2660 Peck Ave 82501 307-855-2000

**Rock River, Albany, Pop. 236**
Albany County SD 1
Supt. — See Laramie
Rock River S 50/K-12
PO Box 128 82083 307-378-2271
Wade Fiscus, prin. Fax 378-2505

**Rock Springs, Sweetwater, Pop. 22,670**
Sweetwater County SD 1 5,300/K-12
PO Box 1089 82902 307-352-3400
Kelly McGovern, supt. Fax 352-3411
www.sweetwater1.org
Black Butte HS Alt
PO Box 1089 82902 307-352-3290
Michael Maloney, prin. Fax 503-3192
Rock Springs HS 1,300/9-12
PO Box 1089 82902 307-352-3440
Darrin Peppard, prin. Fax 315-2632
Rock Springs JHS 800/7-8
PO Box 1089 82902 307-352-3474
Tina Johnson, prin. Fax 316-5634
Other Schools – See Farson, Wamsutter

---

Western Wyoming Community College Post-Sec.
2500 College Dr 82901 307-382-1600

**Saratoga, Carbon, Pop. 1,658**
Carbon County SD 2 600/K-12
PO Box 1530 82331 307-326-5271
Dr. Jim Copeland, supt. Fax 326-8089
www.crb2.k12.wy.us
Saratoga MSHS 200/7-12
PO Box 1710 82331 307-326-5246
Linda Butler, prin. Fax 326-9607
Other Schools – See Encampment, Hanna

**Sheridan, Sheridan, Pop. 17,182**
Sheridan County SD 2 3,200/K-12
PO Box 919 82801 307-674-7405
Craig Dougherty, supt. Fax 674-5041
www.scsd2.com/
Fort Mackenzie HS 50/Alt
1301 Avon St 82801 307-673-8730
Troy Lake, prin. Fax 673-8732
Sheridan HS 900/9-12
1056 Long Dr 82801 307-672-2495
Brent Leibach, prin. Fax 672-8071
Sheridan JHS 700/6-8
500 Lewis St 82801 307-672-9745
Mitch Craft, prin. Fax 672-5311
Wright Place 50/Alt
1301 Avon St 82801 307-673-8730
Troy Lake, prin. Fax 673-8732

---

Sheridan College Post-Sec.
PO Box 1500 82801 307-674-6446

**Shoshoni, Fremont, Pop. 645**
Fremont County SD 24 400/PK-12
112 W 3rd St 82649 307-876-2583
Bruce Thoren, supt. Fax 876-2469
www.fremont24.com/
Shoshoni HS 100/9-12
112 W 3rd St 82649 307-876-2576
Carl Rice, prin. Fax 876-9325
Shoshoni JHS 100/7-8
112 W 3rd St 82649 307-876-2576
Carl Rice, prin. Fax 876-9325

**Sundance, Crook, Pop. 1,174**
Crook County SD 1 1,100/K-12
PO Box 830 82729 307-283-2299
Byron Stutzman, supt. Fax 283-1810
www.crook1.com
Bear Lodge HS, PO Box 1160 82729 50/Alt
Darlene Hartman-Hallman, prin. 307-283-2144
Sundance JSHS 200/7-12
PO Box 850 82729 307-283-1007
Mark Broderson, prin. Fax 283-2300
Other Schools – See Hulett, Moorcroft

**Ten Sleep, Washakie, Pop. 257**
Washakie County SD 2 100/K-12
PO Box 105 82442 307-366-2223
Jimmy Phelps, supt. Fax 366-2304
www.wsh2.k12.wy.us
Ten Sleep HS 50/9-12
PO Box 105 82442 307-366-2233
Russell Budmayr, prin. Fax 366-2304
Ten Sleep MS 50/7-8
PO Box 105 82442 307-366-2233
Russell Budmayr, prin. Fax 366-2304

**Thermopolis, Hot Springs, Pop. 2,973**
Hot Springs County SD 1 700/K-12
415 Springview St 82443 307-864-6515
Dustin Hunt, supt. Fax 864-6615
www.hotsprings1.org
Hot Springs County HS 200/9-12
415 Springview St 82443 307-864-6511
Scott Shoop, prin. Fax 864-3970
Thermopolis MS 200/5-8
415 Springview St 82443 307-864-6551
Breez Daniels, prin. Fax 864-6608

**Torrington, Goshen, Pop. 6,432**
Goshen County SD 1 1,800/K-12
626 W 25th Ave 82240 307-532-2171
Jean Chrostoski, supt. Fax 532-7085
www.goshen1.org
Torrington HS 400/9-12
2400 W C St 82240 307-532-7101
Jim English, prin. Fax 532-2696
Torrington MS 300/6-8
2742 W E St 82240 307-532-7014
Marvin Haiman, prin. Fax 532-8402
Other Schools – See Lingle, Yoder

---

Eastern Wyoming College Post-Sec.
3200 W C St 82240 307-532-8200

**Upton, Weston, Pop. 1,090**
Weston County SD 7 200/K-12
PO Box 470 82730 307-468-2461
Dr. Summer Stephens, supt. Fax 468-2797
bobcat.weston7.k12.wy.us
Upton HS 100/9-12
PO Box 470 82730 307-468-2361
Peter Wilson, prin. Fax 468-2459
Upton MS 100/6-8
PO Box 470 82730 307-468-9331
Clark Coberly, prin. Fax 468-2832

**Wamsutter, Sweetwater, Pop. 442**
Sweetwater County SD 1
Supt. — See Rock Springs
Desert MS 50/6-8
PO Box 10 82336 307-324-7811
Jared Hardman, prin. Fax 589-1164

**Wheatland, Platte, Pop. 3,590**
Platte County SD 1 1,100/K-12
1350 Oak St 82201 307-322-3175
Dennis Fischer, supt. Fax 322-2084
platte1.org
Wheatland HS 300/9-12
1350 Oak St 82201 307-322-2075
Frank Jesse, prin. Fax 322-9739
Wheatland MS 200/6-8
1350 Oak St 82201 307-322-1518
Steven Loyd, prin. Fax 322-1560
Other Schools – See Chugwater, Glendo

**Worland, Washakie, Pop. 5,424**
Washakie County SD 1 1,400/K-12
1900 Howell Ave 82401 307-347-9286
David Nicholas, supt. Fax 347-8116
www.wsh1.k12.wy.us
Worland HS 400/9-12
801 S 17th St 82401 307-347-2412
Kevin Smith, prin. Fax 347-8549
Worland MS 300/6-8
2150 Howell Ave 82401 307-347-3233
Ryan Clark, prin. Fax 347-3710

**Wright, Campbell, Pop. 1,786**
Campbell County SD 1
Supt. — See Gillette
Wright JSHS 200/7-12
PO Box 490 82732 307-464-0140
Hal Johnson, prin. Fax 464-0154

**Yoder, Goshen, Pop. 151**
Goshen County SD 1
Supt. — See Torrington
Southeast HS 100/9-12
PO Box 160 82244 307-532-7176
Randy Epler, prin. Fax 532-5771
Southeast JHS 100/7-8
PO Box 160 82244 307-532-7176
Randy Epler, prin. Fax 532-5771

# CHARTER SCHOOLS

| School | Address | City,State | Zip code | Telephone | Fax | Grade | Contact |
|---|---|---|---|---|---|---|---|
| **Alaska** | | | | | | | |
| Academy Charter S | 801 E Arctic Ave | Palmer, AK | 99645-6179 | 907-746-2358 | 746-2368 | K-8 | Barbara Gerard |
| Alaska Native Cultural Charter S | 550 Bragaw St | Anchorage, AK | 99508 | 907-742-1370 | 742-1373 | K-8 | Sibongile Agerter |
| American Charter Academy | 244 S Sylvan Rd Ste 110 | Wasilla, AK | 99623 | 907-352-0150 | 352-0180 | 2-12 | Becky Huggins |
| Anvil City Science Academy | PO Box 131 | Nome, AK | 99762-0131 | 907-443-6207 | 443-5144 | 5-8 | Todd Hindman |
| Aquarian Charter S | 1705 W 32nd Ave | Anchorage, AK | 99517-2002 | 907-742-4900 | 742-4919 | K-6 | Lucas Saltzman |
| Aurora Borealis Charter S | 705 Frontage Rd Ste A | Kenai, AK | 99611-7740 | 907-283-0292 | 283-0293 | K-8 | Larry Nauta |
| Birchtree Charter S | 7107 E Palmer Wasilla Hwy | Palmer, AK | 99645-7763 | 907-745-1831 | 745-1843 | K-8 | Cathey Busbey |
| Chinook Charter S | 3002 International St | Fairbanks, AK | 99701-7391 | 907-452-5020 | 452-5048 | K-8 | Wendy Demers |
| Eagle Academy Charter S | 10901 Mausel St | Eagle River, AK | 99577 | 907-742-3025 | 742-3035 | K-6 | Kitty Logan |
| Family Partnership Charter S | 401 E Fireweed Ln Ste 100 | Anchorage, AK | 99503 | 907-742-3700 | 742-3710 | K-12 | Deanne Carroll |
| Fireweed Academy | 995 Soundview Ave Ste 2 | Homer, AK | 99603 | 907-235-9728 | 235-8561 | K-6 | Kiki Abrahamson |
| Fronteras Spanish Immersion S | PO Box 871433 | Wasilla, AK | 99687-1433 | 907-745-2223 | 745-6132 | K-8 | Jennifer Schmidt |
| Frontier Charter S | 400 W Northern Lights Blvd | Anchorage, AK | 99503 | 907-742-1180 | 742-1188 | K-12 | Gerald Finkler |
| Highland Tech Charter S | 5530 E Northern Lights Blvd | Anchorage, AK | 99504 | 907-742-1700 | 742-1711 | 6-12 | Michael Shapiro |
| Juneau Community Charter S | 10014 Crazy Horse Dr | Juneau, AK | 99801-8529 | 907-586-2526 | 586-3543 | K-8 | |
| Kaleidoscope S | 549 N Forest Dr | Kenai, AK | 99611-7410 | 907-283-0804 | 283-3786 | K-6 | Robin Dahlman |
| Ketchikan Charter S | 410 Schoenbar Rd | Ketchikan, AK | 99901-6218 | 907-225-8568 | 247-8568 | K-8 | Robert Marshall |
| Kokrine Charter S | 601 Loftus Rd | Fairbanks, AK | 99709-3430 | 907-474-0958 | 479-2104 | 7-12 | Josh Snow |
| Midnight Sun Family Learning Center | 7362 W Parks Hwy # 714 | Wasilla, AK | 99623 | 907-357-6786 | 373-6786 | K-8 | Jeannie Troshynski |
| P.A.I.D.E.I.A. Cooperative S | 7801 E 32nd Ave | Anchorage, AK | 99503 | 907-742-4164 | 742-4165 | K-12 | Monte Thacker |
| Rilke Schule German Schl of Arts & Sci | 2511 Sentry Dr Ste 100 | Anchorage, AK | 99507-4469 | 907-742-7455 | 742-7456 | K-8 | Dean Ball |
| Soldotna Montessori Charter S | 162 E Park Ave | Soldotna, AK | 99669-7552 | 907-260-9221 | 260-9032 | K-6 | Mary Jo Sanders |
| Star of the North Secondary S | 2945 Monk Ct | North Pole, AK | 99705-6129 | 907-490-9025 | 490-9021 | 7-12 | Bao Do |
| Tongass S of Arts & Sciences | 410 Schoenbar Rd Ste 202 | Ketchikan, AK | 99901 | 907-225-5720 | 225-8822 | PK-6 | Marion Gonzales |
| Twindly Bridge Charter S | 141 E Seldon Rd Ste C | Wasilla, AK | 99654-3358 | 907-376-6680 | 746-6683 | K-12 | John Weetman |
| Watershed S | 4975 Decathlon Ave | Fairbanks, AK | 99709 | 907-374-9350 | 374-9360 | K-8 | Jarrod Decker |
| Winterberry Charter S | 4802 Bryn Mawr Ct | Anchorage, AK | 99508-4720 | 907-742-0139 | 742-4985 | K-8 | Shanna Mall |
| **Arizona** | | | | | | | |
| AAEC - Estrella Mountain HS | 3400 N Dysart Rd | Avondale, AZ | 85392 | 623-535-0754 | 535-1210 | 9-12 | Dr. Mona Ramirez Ed.D. |
| AAEC - Paradise Valley | 3775 E Union Hills Dr | Phoenix, AZ | 85050 | 602-569-1101 | 569-6372 | 9-12 | Dr. Martha Braly |
| AAEC - Prescott Valley | 7500 E Civic Cir | Prescott Valley, AZ | 86314 | 928-775-3200 | 775-3201 | 9-12 | Patrick Welert |
| AAEC - Red Mountain Early College HS | 2165 N Power Rd | Mesa, AZ | 85215-2971 | 480-854-1504 | 854-3564 | 9-12 | Brian Snoddy M.Ed. |
| AAEC - South Mountain | 2002 E Baseline Rd | Phoenix, AZ | 85042-6906 | 602-323-9890 | 323-9869 | 9-12 | Linda LaFontain |
| Acacia ES | 12955 E Colossal Cave Rd | Vail, AZ | 85641-9091 | 520-879-2200 | 879-2201 | K-5 | Terri Brooks |
| Academy Adventures Midtown ES | 3025 N Winstel Blvd | Tucson, AZ | 85716 | 520-777-3757 | 207-6489 | K-5 | |
| Academy Adventures PS | 3902 N Flowing Wells Rd | Tucson, AZ | 85705-2403 | 520-407-1200 | 407-1201 | K-5 | MaryAnn Penczar |
| Academy Del Sol - Hope | 6740 S Santa Clara Ave | Tucson, AZ | 85706 | 520-325-2800 | 325-2811 | K-8 | |
| Academy Del Sol - Midtown | 4525 E Broadway Blvd | Tucson, AZ | 85711 | 520-325-2800 | 325-2812 | K-8 | Jason Riegert |
| Academy Del Sol - Star Valley | 7102 W Valley Crest Pl | Tucson, AZ | 85757 | 520-789-7733 | | K-8 | Jason Reigert |
| Academy of Building Industries | 1547 E Lipan Blvd | Fort Mohave, AZ | 86426-6031 | 928-788-2601 | 788-2610 | 9-12 | Jean Thomas |
| Academy of Excellence | 425 N 36th St | Phoenix, AZ | 85008-6303 | 602-389-4271 | 389-4278 | K-8 | Dr. Eula Dean |
| Academy of Excellence Central AZ | 1530 S Arizona Blvd | Coolidge, AZ | 85228 | 520-723-4773 | | K-8 | |
| Academy of Math & Science | 1557 W Prince Rd | Tucson, AZ | 85705-3023 | 520-293-2676 | 888-1732 | K-12 | Tatyana Chayka |
| Academy of Mathematics and Science South | 3335 W Flower St | Phoenix, AZ | 85017 | 520-887-5392 | | K-8 | |
| Academy of Tucson ES | 9209 E Wrightstown Rd | Tucson, AZ | 85715-5514 | 520-886-6076 | 886-6575 | K-4 | Carole Rostash |
| Academy of Tucson HS | 10720 E 22nd St | Tucson, AZ | 85748-7029 | 520-733-0096 | 733-0097 | 9-12 | Jose Garcia |
| Academy of Tucson MS | 7310 E 22nd St | Tucson, AZ | 85710 | 520-749-1413 | 749-2824 | 5-8 | Larry Speta |
| Academy With Community Partners | 433 N Hall | Mesa, AZ | 85203-7407 | 480-833-0068 | 833-8966 | 9-12 | Margaret Williamson |
| Accelerated Learning Center | 4105 E Shea Blvd | Phoenix, AZ | 85028 | 602-485-0309 | 485-9356 | 9-12 | Frank Canady Ed.D. |
| Accelerated Schools | 5245 N Camino De Oeste | Tucson, AZ | 85745-8925 | 520-743-2256 | 743-2417 | PK-12 | David Jones |
| ACCLAIM Academy | 7624 W Indian School Rd | Phoenix, AZ | 85033-3009 | 623-691-0919 | 691-6091 | K-8 | Jose Martinez |
| ACE Charter HS - North | 1929 N Stone Ave | Tucson, AZ | 85705-5642 | 520-623-5843 | 791-9893 | 9-12 | Jay Slauter |
| Acorn Montessori Charter S | 8556 E Loos Dr | Prescott Valley, AZ | 86314-6455 | 928-772-5778 | 775-8654 | 2-8 | Cynthia Johnson |
| Acorn Montessori Charter S - West | 7555 E Long Look Dr | Prescott Valley, AZ | 86314-5507 | 928-775-0238 | 775-8654 | PK-1 | Dawn Grantham |
| Adams Traditional Academy | 2323 W Parkside Ln | Phoenix, AZ | 85027 | 602-938-5517 | 938-1179 | PK-8 | Sharon Malone |
| Adventure S | 5757 E Pima St | Tucson, AZ | 85712-5609 | 520-296-0656 | 721-4472 | K-5 | Brian Henderson |
| All Aboard Charter S | 5827 N 35th Ave | Phoenix, AZ | 85017-1915 | 602-433-0500 | 973-8208 | K-5 | Rhonda Newton |
| Alta Vista Charter HS | 5040 S Campbell Ave | Tucson, AZ | 85706-1510 | 520-294-4922 | 294-4933 | 9-12 | Alicia Alvarez |
| Ambassador Academy | 3820 E Ray Rd Ste 8 | Phoenix, AZ | 85044 | 480-961-2214 | 993-3222 | K-5 | Dr. Elba Reyes |
| American Heritage Academy | 2030 E Cherry St | Cottonwood, AZ | 86326-6963 | 928-634-2144 | 634-9053 | K-12 | Tony Rhinehart |
| American Heritage Academy | 132 W General Crook Trl | Camp Verde, AZ | 86322 | 928-567-0462 | 567-0464 | K-8 | Darrell White |
| American Leadership Academy | 4507 S Mountain Rd | Mesa, AZ | 85212 | 480-420-2110 | 420-2109 | K-6 | Paul Sinclair |
| American Leadership Academy | 23908 S Hawes Rd | Queen Creek, AZ | 85142 | 480-987-4500 | 882-1330 | 7-12 | Tommy Roberts |
| American Leadership Academy | 19843 E Chandler Hts Rd | Queen Creek, AZ | 85142 | 480-420-2150 | 888-8595 | K-6 | Maureen Poirer |
| American Leadership Academy | 34696 N Village Ln | San Tan Valley, AZ | 85142 | 480-420-2100 | 729-6003 | K-6 | Kimberley Saffell |
| American Leadership Academy | 4380 N Hunt Hwy | Florence, AZ | 85132 | 480-344-9800 | 518-5245 | K-6 | Stuart Enkey |
| American Leadership Academy | 3155 S San Tan Village Pkwy | Gilbert, AZ | 85295 | 480-988-3204 | 988-3280 | K-6 | Robert Brown |
| Amerischools Academy - Camelback | 1333 W Camelback Rd | Phoenix, AZ | 85013-2106 | 602-532-0100 | 532-9964 | K-8 | Jennifer Gordievsky |
| Amerischools Academy - Country Club | 1150 N Country Club Rd | Tucson, AZ | 85716-3942 | 520-620-1100 | 624-4376 | K-8 | Jordan Krause |
| Amerischools Academy - Yuma North | 1220 S 4th Ave | Yuma, AZ | 85364 | 928-919-7203 | 919-7205 | K-6 | Bill Wachunas |
| Amerischools Academy - Yuma South | 2098 S 3rd Ave | Yuma, AZ | 85364-6425 | 928-329-1100 | 329-9177 | K-6 | Ashley Fox |
| Anthem Preparatory Academy | 39808 N Gavilan Peak Pkwy | Anthem, AZ | 85086-2523 | 623-465-4776 | 465-4832 | K-12 | Bryan Smith |
| Apache Trail HS | 945 W Apache Trl | Apache Junction, AZ | 85120 | 480-288-0337 | 288-0340 | 9-12 | Greg Garland |
| Archway Academy - Glendale | 23276 N 83rd Ave | Peoria, AZ | 85383 | 623-866-4710 | | K-5 | Jack Kersting |
| Archway Classical Academy - Arete | 4525 E Baseline Rd | Gilbert, AZ | 85234 | 480-422-4233 | | K-5 | Neil Gillingham |
| Archway Classical Academy - Chandler | 1951 N Alma School Rd | Chandler, AZ | 85224-2840 | 480-855-6474 | 855-7475 | K-5 | Leanne Fawcett |
| Archway Classical Academy Cicero | 7205 N Pima Rd | Scottsdale, AZ | 85250 | 480-424-1790 | | K-7 | Dr. Mark Discher |
| Archway Classical Academy - N Phoenix | 13613 N Cave Creek Rd Ste C | Phoenix, AZ | 85022 | 602-996-4355 | 889-0187 | K-5 | David Denton |
| Archway Classical Academy - Scottsdale | 7496 E Tierra Buena Ln | Scottsdale, AZ | 85260 | 480-776-0413 | 889-7014 | K-4 | Lisa Armstrong |
| Archway Classical Academy - Trivium | 14130 W McDowell Rd | Goodyear, AZ | 85395 | 623-414-4883 | 889-6286 | K-5 | Theresa Krueger |
| Archway Classical Academy - Veritas | 3102 N 56th St Ste 100 | Phoenix, AZ | 85018 | 602-489-7341 | 263-7997 | K-5 | William Haley |
| Arete Preparatory Academy | 4525 E Baseline Rd | Gilbert, AZ | 85234 | 480-222-4233 | 222-4234 | 6-12 | Robert Wagner |
| Arizona Academy of Science | 1875 N Central Ave | Phoenix, AZ | 85004-1507 | 602-253-1199 | 595-8693 | K-8 | |
| AZ Call-A-Teen Center of Excellence | 649 N 6th Ave | Phoenix, AZ | 85003-1659 | 602-252-6721 | 252-2952 | 9-12 | Kelly Sheick |
| Arizona Charter Academy | 16025 N Dysart Rd | Surprise, AZ | 85374 | 623-974-4959 | 974-4840 | K-12 | Heather Henderson |
| Arizona City ES | 12115 W Benito Dr | Arizona City, AZ | 85231 | 520-466-2450 | | PK-8 | |
| Arizona College Prep Academy | 7444 E Broadway Blvd | Tucson, AZ | 85710-1411 | 520-722-1200 | 722-0052 | K-8 | Charlene Mendoza |
| Arizona Collegiate HS | 3161 N 33rd Ave | Phoenix, AZ | 85017 | 623-498-8200 | 269-2970 | 9-12 | Michael Dunbar |
| AZ Compass Prep S | 2020 N Arizona Ave | Chandler, AZ | 85225 | 480-779-2000 | 779-2100 | 7-12 | Bryant Robinson |
| AZ Connections Academy | 335 E Germann Rd Ste 140 | Gilbert, AZ | 85297 | 480-782-5842 | 323-2905 | K-12 | Kerri Wright |
| AZ Conservatory for Arts & Academics | 16454 N 28th Ave | Phoenix, AZ | 85053 | 623-878-0986 | 776-7956 | K-5 | Christopher Lalley |
| AZ Conservatory for Arts & Academics | 2820 W Kelton Ln | Phoenix, AZ | 85053-3028 | 602-266-4278 | 978-2764 | 6-12 | Holly Foged |
| Arizona Language Preparatory | 751 E Union Hills Dr | Phoenix, AZ | 85024 | 602-996-1595 | | K-4 | Sara Hecht |
| Arizona School for the Arts | 1410 N 3rd St | Phoenix, AZ | 85004 | 602-257-1444 | 252-7795 | 5-12 | Dr. Leah Roberts |
| Arizona Virtual Academy | 99 E Virginia Ave Ste 200 | Phoenix, AZ | 85004 | 866-476-1320 | 595-6874 | K-12 | Kelly Van Sande |
| Arroyo ES | 4535 W Cholla St | Glendale, AZ | 85304-3599 | 602-896-5100 | 896-5120 | K-8 | Philip Liles |
| Arts Academy at Estrella Mountain | 2504 S 91st Ave | Tolleson, AZ | 85353-8921 | 623-227-0769 | 936-5337 | PK-8 | Kimberly Steele-Haynes |
| Arts Academy at Scottsdale | 6140 E Thunderbird Rd | Scottsdale, AZ | 85254 | 480-376-3190 | 998-4029 | K-6 | Charles Boebinger |
| ASU Preparatory Academy | 735 E Fillmore St | Phoenix, AZ | 85006-3324 | 602-257-4843 | 257-4852 | K-8 | David Lujan |
| ASU Prep Polytechnic HS | 7350 E Unity Ave | Mesa, AZ | 85212 | 480-727-5750 | | 9-12 | |
| Athlos Traditional Academy | 3201 S Gilbert Rd | Chandler, AZ | 85286 | 480-270-5422 | 237-5780 | K-8 | Nicole McMillian |
| Avalon Charter School | 1045 S San Marcos Dr | Apache Junction, AZ | 85120 | 480-671-4584 | 671-4586 | K-8 | |
| AZTEC HS | 2330 W 28th St | Yuma, AZ | 85364-6954 | 928-314-1900 | 726-2826 | 9-12 | Molly Kelly |
| BASIS Ahwatukee | 10210 S 50th Pl | Phoenix, AZ | 85044 | 480-659-2294 | 696-3607 | 4-12 | Kristen Jordison |
| Basis Chandler | 1800 E Chandler Blvd | Chandler, AZ | 85225 | 480-907-6072 | 907-6624 | 5-12 | Stephanie Terrell |
| BASIS Flagstaff | 1700 N Gemini Dr | Flagstaff, AZ | 86001 | 928-774-5502 | 774-5503 | 5-12 | Kara Kelty |
| BASIS Mesa | 5010 S Eastmark Pkwy | Mesa, AZ | 85212 | 602-239-4807 | 822-1259 | 4-12 | David Hubalik |
| BASIS Oro Valley | 11155 N Oracle Rd | Oro Valley, AZ | 85737 | 520-308-5220 | 308-5078 | 6-12 | Sean Aiken |
| BASIS Peoria | 25950 N Lake Pleasant Pkwy | Peoria, AZ | 85383 | 623-215-4920 | 566-9109 | 5-12 | Ashley Brown |
| BASIS Phoenix | 11850 N 32nd St | Phoenix, AZ | 85028 | 602-595-9870 | 595-9820 | 5-12 | Petra Pajtas |
| BASIS Phoenix Central PS | 201 E Indianola Ave | Phoenix, AZ | 85012 | 602-559-5399 | 283-7500 | K-4 | |

| School | Address | City,State | Zip code | Telephone | Fax | Grade | Contact |
|---|---|---|---|---|---|---|---|
| BASIS Prescott | 1901 Prescott Lakes Pkwy | Prescott, AZ | 86301 | 928-277-0334 | 458-5562 | 5-12 | |
| BASIS Scottsdale | 11440 N 136th St | Scottsdale, AZ | 85259-3812 | 480-451-7500 | 451-4555 | 5-12 | Hadley Ruggles M.A. |
| BASIS - Tucson | 3825 E 2nd St | Tucson, AZ | 85716-4368 | 520-326-6367 | 326-6359 | K-6 | Jason Shorbe |
| BASIS Tucson North | 5740 E River Rd | Tucson, AZ | 85750 | 520-326-3444 | | 5-12 | Julia Toews |
| Benchmark S | 4120 E Acoma Dr | Phoenix, AZ | 85032-4753 | 602-765-3582 | 765-1932 | K-6 | Barbara Darroch |
| Bennett Academy | 2930 W Bethany Home Rd | Phoenix, AZ | 85017-1615 | 602-943-1317 | 943-0280 | K-8 | Dr. Nancy Bennett |
| Bennett Academy - Venture | 1535 W Dunlap Ave | Phoenix, AZ | 85020 | 602-242-4220 | | K-5 | Shawn Lane |
| Berean Academy | 1169 Colombo Ave | Sierra Vista, AZ | 85635 | 520-459-4113 | 459-4121 | K-12 | Mark Bennett |
| Blueprint HS | 670 N Arizona Ave Ste 1 | Chandler, AZ | 85225 | 480-892-0235 | 892-0236 | 9-12 | Robert Rodenbaugh |
| Bradley Academy of Excellence | PO Box 6060 | Goodyear, AZ | 85338 | 800-993-1458 | 932-9904 | PK-8 | |
| Bright Beginnings S | 400 N Andersen Blvd | Chandler, AZ | 85224-8273 | 480-821-1404 | 821-1463 | K-6 | Karen Edris |
| Burke Basic S | 131 E Southern Ave | Mesa, AZ | 85210-5355 | 480-964-4602 | 964-6566 | K-6 | Glen Gaddie |
| Butterfield ES | 44150 W Maricopa Casa Grand | Maricopa, AZ | 85138 | 520-568-6100 | 568-6109 | K-6 | Janel Hildick |
| Calibre Academy Surprise | 15688 W Acoma Dr | Surprise, AZ | 85379-5652 | 623-556-2179 | 547-2806 | K-8 | Deborah Boehm |
| Cambridge Academy - Mesa Campus | 9412 E Brown Rd | Mesa, AZ | 85207-4338 | 480-641-2828 | 325-2365 | K-6 | Amy Monarrez |
| Cambridge Academy - Queen Creek | 20365 E Ocotillo Rd | Queen Creek, AZ | 85142 | 480-987-3577 | 987-4281 | K-8 | Kaylee Gonzalez |
| Cambridge Preparatory Academy | 12115 W Benito Dr | Arizona City, AZ | 85231 | 520-466-2450 | | K-12 | |
| Camelback Academy | 7634 W Camelback Rd | Glendale, AZ | 85303-5627 | 623-247-2204 | 247-1113 | K-8 | Karen Kordon |
| Candeo Schools | 9965 W Calle Lejos | Peoria, AZ | 85383-1117 | 623-979-6500 | 979-6510 | K-8 | Dr. Stephanie Musser Ed.D. |
| Canyon Pointe Academy | 4941 W Union Hills Dr | Glendale, AZ | 85308-1486 | 602-896-1166 | 896-1164 | K-6 | Suzanne Smailagic |
| Canyon Rose Academy | 3686 W Orange Grove Rd #192 | Tucson, AZ | 85741 | 520-797-4884 | 797-8868 | 9-12 | Christopher Golston |
| Canyon View Prep Academy | 9030 E Florentine Rd | Prescott Valley, AZ | 86314 | 928-775-5115 | 775-6253 | 9-12 | Debra Slagle |
| Carden of Tucson S | 5260 N Royal Palm Dr | Tucson, AZ | 85705-1148 | 520-293-6661 | 408-7366 | K-8 | Bette Jeppson |
| Career Success HS - Duffy Campus | 2550 E Jefferson St | Phoenix, AZ | 85034 | 602-393-4200 | 393-4205 | 9-12 | Jason Lobik |
| Career Success HS - Main Campus | 3816 N 27th Ave | Phoenix, AZ | 85017-4703 | 602-285-5525 | 285-0026 | 9-12 | Renee Gayden |
| Career Success JSHS - North Phoenix | 2325 E Bell Rd | Phoenix, AZ | 85022 | 602-687-8282 | 687-8283 | 7-12 | Eric Pawlak |
| Career Success S - Sage Campus | 3120 N 32nd St | Phoenix, AZ | 85018-6202 | 602-955-0355 | 955-4805 | K-8 | Kurt Walker |
| Carpe Diem E-Learning Community S | 3777 W 22nd Ln | Yuma, AZ | 85364-5905 | 928-317-3113 | 317-0828 | 7-12 | Jon Larson |
| CASA Academy | 1500 W Maryland Ave | Phoenix, AZ | 85015 | 602-892-5022 | 892-5023 | K-3 | Tacey Clayton |
| Caurus Academy | 41900 N 42nd Ave | Anthem, AZ | 85086-1595 | 623-551-5083 | 551-5679 | K-8 | Dameon Blair M.S. |
| Center for Academic Success ES | 900 Carmelita Dr | Sierra Vista, AZ | 85635 | 520-458-4200 | 458-1409 | K-8 | Stephen Huff |
| Center for Academic Success ES | 1415 F Ave | Douglas, AZ | 85607-1655 | 520-805-1558 | 458-1409 | K-8 | Marcela Munguia |
| Center for Academic Success HS | 900 Carmelita Dr | Sierra Vista, AZ | 85635 | 520-458-4200 | 458-6396 | 9-12 | Stephen Huff |
| Center for Academic Success HS | 510 N G Ave | Douglas, AZ | 85607-2822 | 520-364-2616 | 417-0973 | 9-12 | Marcela Munguia |
| Center for Educational Excellence | 1700 E Elliot Rd Ste 9 | Tempe, AZ | 85284-1631 | 480-632-1940 | 632-1398 | K-8 | Stacey Cochran |
| Challenge Charter S | 5801 W Greenbriar Dr | Glendale, AZ | 85308-3847 | 602-938-5411 | 938-5393 | K-6 | Gregory Miller |
| Challenger Basic S | 1315 N Greenfield Rd | Gilbert, AZ | 85234-2813 | 480-830-1750 | 830-1763 | K-6 | |
| Champion Schools | 7900 S Jesse Owens Pkwy | Phoenix, AZ | 85042 | 602-341-6527 | 341-6529 | K-8 | Carolyn Sawyer |
| Chandler Preparatory Academy | 1951 N Alma School Rd | Chandler, AZ | 85224-2840 | 480-855-5410 | 855-7789 | 6-12 | Daniel Sullivan |
| Children First Academy - Phoenix | 1648 S 16th St | Phoenix, AZ | 85034 | 602-712-0500 | 712-0506 | K-10 | Rachael Lay |
| Children First Academy - Tempe | 1938 E Apache Blvd | Tempe, AZ | 85281 | 480-557-6211 | 557-6249 | K-8 | Jevon Lewis |
| Children Reaching for the Sky Prep | 1844 S Alvernon Way | Tucson, AZ | 85711-5607 | 520-790-8400 | 620-6570 | K-5 | Lee Griffin |
| Childrens Success Academy | PO Box 11368 | Tucson, AZ | 85734-1368 | 520-799-8403 | 799-8427 | K-5 | |
| City HS | 48 E Pennington St | Tucson, AZ | 85701-1535 | 520-623-7223 | 547-0680 | 9-12 | Carrie Brennan |
| Civano Community S | 10625 E Drexel Rd | Tucson, AZ | 85747-6120 | 520-879-1700 | 879-1701 | K-5 | Connie Erickson |
| Compass HS | PO Box 17810 | Tucson, AZ | 85731-7810 | 520-296-4070 | 296-4103 | 9-12 | John Ferguson |
| Concordia Charter S | 142 N Date | Mesa, AZ | 85201-6419 | 480-461-0555 | 461-0556 | K-6 | Mike McCarthy |
| Concordia Charter S - Navajo Mission | 1/4 Mile E of Highway 191 | Round Rock, AZ | 86547 | 928-787-2869 | 787-2867 | K-3 | Esther Davis |
| Cooley MS | 1100 S Recker Rd | Gilbert, AZ | 85296 | 480-279-8300 | 279-8305 | 7-8 | Dr. Randy Mahlerwein |
| Copper Canyon Academy | 7785 W Peoria Ave | Peoria, AZ | 85345-5922 | 623-930-1734 | 930-8709 | K-8 | Ed MacDonald |
| Copper Point HS | 732 W Roger Rd | Tucson, AZ | 85705 | 520-624-7169 | | 6-12 | Joseph McKnight |
| Cornerstone Charter S | 7107 N Black Canyon Hwy | Phoenix, AZ | 85021-7619 | 602-595-2198 | 242-2398 | 9-12 | Casey Weiss |
| Country Gardens Charter S | 6313 W Southern Ave | Laveen, AZ | 85339 | 602-237-3741 | 237-3892 | K-12 | Goldie Burge |
| Coyote Springs ES | 6625 N Cattletrack Rd | Prescott Valley, AZ | 86314 | 928-759-4300 | 759-4320 | K-6 | Candice Blakely Stump |
| Crestview College Prep HS | 2616 E Greenway Rd | Phoenix, AZ | 85032-4320 | 602-765-8470 | 765-8471 | 9-12 | Kristin Schaefer |
| Crown Charter S | PO Box 363 | Litchfield Park, AZ | 85340-0363 | 623-535-9300 | 535-5410 | K-6 | James Shade |
| Crown Point HS | 4802 N 59th Ave | Phoenix, AZ | 85033 | 623-845-0781 | 849-2840 | 9-12 | Claudia Ramirez |
| Deer Valley Academy | 18424 N 51st Ave | Glendale, AZ | 85308-1443 | 602-467-6874 | 467-6955 | 9-12 | Barbara Dalicandro |
| Desert Cove ES | 11020 N 28th St | Phoenix, AZ | 85028-2500 | 602-449-3400 | 449-3405 | K-6 | Chad Lanese |
| Desert Heights Charter S | 5821 W Beverly Ln | Glendale, AZ | 85306-1801 | 602-896-2900 | 467-9540 | K-8 | Katherine Miller |
| Desert Heights Preparatory Academy | 3540 W Union Hills Dr | Glendale, AZ | 85308 | 602-896-2900 | 467-9540 | 5-12 | Chelsey Peitz |
| Desert Hills HS | 1515 S Val Vista Dr | Gilbert, AZ | 85296-3854 | 480-813-1151 | 813-1161 | 9-12 | Michael Olguin |
| Desert Marigold S | 6210 S 28th St | Phoenix, AZ | 85042-4715 | 602-243-6909 | 243-6933 | PK-12 | Charles Burkum |
| Desert Pointe Academy | 7785 W Peoria Ave | Peoria, AZ | 85345-5922 | 623-930-1734 | 930-8709 | 9-12 | Ed McDonald |
| Desert Rose Academy | 326 W Fort Lowell Rd | Tucson, AZ | 85705-3816 | 520-797-4884 | 797-8868 | 9-12 | Michael Lee |
| Desert Sky Community S | 1350 N Arcadia Ave | Tucson, AZ | 85712 | 520-745-3888 | 745-5110 | K-5 | Shelly Adrian |
| Desert Springs Academy | 10129 E Speedway Blvd | Tucson, AZ | 85748 | 520-321-1709 | 321-9316 | K-8 | Mary Spatola |
| Desert Springs Preparatory ES | 6010 E Acoma Dr | Scottsdale, AZ | 85254-2599 | 602-449-7100 | 449-7105 | PK-6 | Derek Hummert |
| Desert Star Community S | 1240 S Recycler Rd | Cornville, AZ | 86325-5224 | 928-282-0171 | 284-9565 | K-8 | Cheryl LeBlanc |
| Desert View Academy | 2363 S Kennedy Ln | Yuma, AZ | 85365-2416 | 928-314-1102 | 314-1086 | K-6 | Deb Wiegel |
| Destiny S | 798 E Prickly Pear Dr | Globe, AZ | 85501-2395 | 928-425-0925 | 425-0927 | K-8 | Scott Williamson |
| Digital Technology Academy | 1250 W Continental Rd | Green Valley, AZ | 85614 | 520-219-4383 | | K-8 | |
| DINE Southwest HS | HC 63 Box 303 | Winslow, AZ | 86047-9424 | 928-657-3272 | 657-3272 | 9-12 | Leah Claw |
| Discovery Plus Academy | PO Box 1089 | Pima, AZ | 85543 | 928-485-2498 | 485-2508 | K-5 | Dee Ann Williams |
| Dobson Academy | PO Box 6070 | Chandler, AZ | 85246-6070 | 480-855-6325 | 855-6323 | K-8 | Dr. Taime Bengochea |
| EAGLE College Prep: Maryvale | 3950 N 53rd Ave | Phoenix, AZ | 85031 | 602-638-0820 | 638-0821 | K-8 | Yesenia Fitzhugh |
| EAGLE College Prep: Mesa | 1619 E Main St | Mesa, AZ | 85203 | 602-638-0802 | 638-0806 | K-8 | Tracy Allen |
| EAGLE College Prep S | 2450 W South Mountain Ave | Phoenix, AZ | 85041 | 602-323-5400 | 323-5401 | K-8 | |
| EAGLE Harmony S | 2435 E Pecan Rd | Phoenix, AZ | 85040 | 602-268-1212 | 237-5140 | K-8 | |
| Eastpointe HS | 8495 E Broadway Blvd | Tucson, AZ | 85710-4009 | 520-731-8180 | 731-8179 | 9-12 | |
| East Valley Academy | 855 W 8th Ave | Mesa, AZ | 85210 | 480-981-2008 | 641-4473 | 9-12 | Pat Goolsby |
| Edge Charter S - Himmel Park | 2555 E 1st St | Tucson, AZ | 85716-4152 | 520-881-1389 | 881-0852 | 9-12 | Rob Pecharich |
| Edge Charter S - Northwest | 231 W Giaconda Way | Tucson, AZ | 85704-4341 | 520-877-9179 | 881-0852 | 9-12 | Rob Pecharich |
| EdOptions HS | 2150 E Southern Ave | Tempe, AZ | 85282 | 480-621-3365 | | 9-12 | |
| Educational Opportunity Center | 3818 W 16th St | Yuma, AZ | 85364 | 928-329-0990 | 783-0886 | 9-12 | |
| EduPreneurship Student Center | 7801 N 27th Ave | Phoenix, AZ | 85051-6675 | 602-973-8998 | 973-5510 | K-8 | Deborah Salas |
| Edu-Prize S | 4567 W Roberts Rd | Queen Creek, AZ | 85142 | 480-888-1610 | | 1-6 | |
| Edu-Prize S | 580 W Melody Ave | Gilbert, AZ | 85233-1418 | 480-813-9537 | 813-6742 | K-8 | Dr. Robbie McCamman |
| E-Institute at Avondale | 1035 E Van Buren St | Avondale, AZ | 85323 | 623-760-9061 | 760-9068 | 9-12 | Curtis Gardner |
| E-Institute at Metro | 9201 N 29th Ave | Phoenix, AZ | 85051 | 602-439-5026 | 889-0351 | 9-12 | Eric Luthi |
| E-Institute at Surprise | 16578 W Greenway Rd Ste 204 | Surprise, AZ | 85388-2184 | 623-544-9285 | 546-9540 | 9-12 | Casey Robertson |
| E-Institute at Union Hills | 3515 W Union Hills Dr | Glendale, AZ | 85308-2429 | 602-843-3891 | 843-4375 | 9-12 | Rick Wolff |
| E-Institute Charter HS at Grovers | 4744 W Grovers Ave | Glendale, AZ | 85308 | 602-621-4398 | 889-0351 | 9-12 | Charlene Shores M.Ed. |
| E-Institute HS at Buckeye | 6213 S Miller Rd | Buckeye, AZ | 85326 | 623-505-7118 | 505-3594 | 9-12 | Kathy Wenzlau |
| El Dorado HS | 2200 N Arizona Ave Ste 17 | Chandler, AZ | 85225-3452 | 480-726-9536 | 726-9543 | 9-12 | Dave Miller |
| Empower College Prep | 5757 N Central Ave | Phoenix, AZ | 85012 | 602-283-5720 | | 9-12 | Brian Holman |
| Encore Arts Academy | 7618 E University Dr | Mesa, AZ | 85207-6601 | 480-981-1500 | 641-4473 | K-8 | Joyce Bulger |
| Esperanza Community Collegial Academy | 2507 E Bell Rd | Phoenix, AZ | 85032-2413 | 602-996-1125 | 996-4238 | 9-12 | |
| Esperanza Montessori Academy | 4848 S 2nd St | Phoenix, AZ | 85040 | 602-243-7788 | 243-7799 | K-3 | Adrian Ruiz |
| Estrella HS | 510 N Central Ave | Avondale, AZ | 85323-1909 | 623-932-6561 | 932-1263 | 9-12 | J.D. Corey |
| Estrella Mountain S | 10301 S San Miguel Ave | Goodyear, AZ | 85338-9696 | 623-327-2820 | 327-2829 | K-8 | Sharon Marine |
| Fireside ES | 3725 E Lone Cactus Dr | Phoenix, AZ | 85050 | 602-449-4700 | 449-4705 | K-6 | Wendy Allen |
| Flagstaff Arts and Leadership Academy | 3401 N Fort Valley Rd | Flagstaff, AZ | 86001 | 928-779-7223 | 779-7041 | 7-12 | Laura Kelly |
| Flagstaff Junior Academy | 306 W Cedar Ave | Flagstaff, AZ | 86001-1413 | 928-774-6007 | 774-7268 | PK-8 | Thomas Drumm |
| Foothills Academy | 7191 E Ashler Hills Dr | Scottsdale, AZ | 85266-9300 | 480-488-5583 | 488-6902 | K-12 | Dr. Donald Senneville |
| Fort Mojave ES | 1760 E Joy Ln | Fort Mohave, AZ | 86426 | 928-768-3986 | 768-8075 | K-6 | Shanon Ferguson |
| Fountain Hills Charter S | PO Box 18419 | Fountain Hills, AZ | 85269 | 480-837-0046 | 837-0024 | K-8 | Lynda Rice |
| Franklin Charter S - Crismon | 22120 E Queen Creek Rd | Queen Creek, AZ | 85142 | 480-987-0722 | 987-3517 | K-6 | Shalisa Arnold |
| Franklin Charter S - Gilbert | 1475 S Val Vista Dr | Gilbert, AZ | 85296 | 480-632-0722 | 632-8716 | K-6 | Diana Dana |
| Franklin Charter S - Power | 22951 S Power Rd | Queen Creek, AZ | 85142 | 480-677-8400 | 677-8555 | K-6 | Bryce Solberg |
| Franklin HS | 18864 E Germann Rd | Queen Creek, AZ | 85142 | 480-558-1197 | 659-5354 | 7-12 | Mark McAfee |
| Franklin Phonetic PS Sunnyslope | 9317 N 2nd St | Phoenix, AZ | 85020 | 602-870-6674 | | K-5 | Debra Denette |
| Franklin Phonetic S | 6116 E State Route 69 | Prescott Valley, AZ | 86314-2806 | 928-775-6747 | 775-6740 | K-8 | Christina Gabaldon M.A. |
| Freedom Academy North | 28700 N Pima Rd | Scottsdale, AZ | 85266 | 602-424-0771 | 424-0773 | K-6 | Veronica Gatling |
| Freedom Academy South | 3916 E Paradise Ln | Phoenix, AZ | 85032 | 602-424-0771 | 424-0773 | K-8 | Linda Hoffman |
| Freire Freedom S | 47 E Pennington St | Tucson, AZ | 85701 | 520-352-0057 | 352-0058 | 6-8 | Joann Groh |
| Freire Freedom S | 300 E University Blvd | Tucson, AZ | 85705-7899 | 520-906-7552 | 624-7518 | 6-8 | JoAnn Groh |
| Friendly House Academia Del Pueblo S | 201 E Durango St | Phoenix, AZ | 85004-2913 | 602-258-4353 | 416-7375 | K-8 | Mark Mazon |
| Future Investment MS | 1854 S Alvernon Way | Tucson, AZ | 85711 | 520-747-3733 | 745-2848 | 6-8 | Lee Griffin |
| GateWay Early College HS | 108 N 40th St | Phoenix, AZ | 85034-1795 | 602-286-8762 | 286-8752 | 9-12 | |
| GEM Charter S | 1704 N Center St | Mesa, AZ | 85201-2223 | 480-833-2622 | 833-2655 | K-6 | Nelleke van Savooyen |
| Genesis Academy | 525 E McDowell Rd | Phoenix, AZ | 85004-1537 | 602-254-8090 | 254-8094 | 9-12 | Karen Callahan |
| Gervin Prep Academy | 2801 E Southern Ave | Phoenix, AZ | 85042 | 480-219-2121 | 633-6787 | 6-8 | Dr. Manuel Madrid |
| Gilbert Arts Academy | 862 E Elliot Rd | Gilbert, AZ | 85234-6912 | 480-325-6100 | 632-2077 | K-6 | Lisa Figueroa |
| Gilbert Early College HS | 717 W Ray Rd # 101 | Gilbert, AZ | 85233 | 480-545-8011 | 558-7038 | 7-12 | |
| Girls Leadership Academy | 715 W Mariposa St | Phoenix, AZ | 85013-2449 | 602-274-7318 | 274-7549 | 6-12 | Debra Skinner |
| Glassford Hill MS | 6901 Panther Path | Prescott Valley, AZ | 86314-2252 | 928-759-4600 | 759-4620 | 7-8 | Dr. Theresa Matteson |

| School | Address | City,State | Zip code | Telephone | Fax | Grade | Contact |
|---|---|---|---|---|---|---|---|
| Glendale Preparatory Academy | 23276 N 83rd Ave Ste 1 | Peoria, AZ | 85383 | 623-889-0822 | 889-0825 | 6-12 | Brandon Crowe |
| Glendale Preparatory Academy | 7201 W Beardsley Rd | Glendale, AZ | 85308-5673 | 602-889-0822 | 889-0825 | 6-12 | Brandon Crowe |
| Glenview College Prep HS | 3802 W Maryland Ave | Phoenix, AZ | 85019 | 602-841-1221 | 841-1364 | 9-12 | Chris Ecton |
| Gowan Science Academy | 1590 S Avenue C | Yuma, AZ | 85364-4118 | 928-539-1200 | 539-1299 | 1-5 | Jamie Haines |
| Grand Canyon College Prep Charter S | 5301 S McClintock Dr | Tempe, AZ | 85283 | 480-233-3622 | 491-7096 | 6-12 | David Gordon |
| Great Expectations Academy | 1466 W Camino Antigua | Sahuarita, AZ | 85629-9720 | 520-399-2121 | 399-2123 | K-8 | Mark Phillips |
| Ha:San Prep & Leadership Charter S | 1333 E 10th St | Tucson, AZ | 85719-5808 | 520-882-8826 | 882-8651 | 9-12 | Robin Kauakahi |
| Happy Valley S | 7140 W Happy Valley Rd | Peoria, AZ | 85383-3255 | 623-376-2900 | 376-9030 | K-6 | James Born |
| Happy Valley S East | 266 E Westbrooke Rd | San Tan Valley, AZ | 85140 | 480-560-5540 | | K-6 | Jareed Palmer |
| Harvest Preparatory Academy | 350 E 18th St | Yuma, AZ | 85364-5723 | 928-782-2052 | 819-5976 | K-12 | Dr. Deborah Ybarra |
| Harvest Preparatory Academy Goodyear | 14900 W Van Buren St | Goodyear, AZ | 85395 | 602-708-2334 | 236-3248 | K-8 | Tara Walters |
| Harvest Preparatory Academy - San Luis | 1044 N 10th Ave | San Luis, AZ | 85349 | 928-782-2052 | 819-5976 | K-5 | Alicia Schroeder |
| Havasu Preparatory Academy | 3155 Maricopa Ave | Lk Havasu Cty, AZ | 86406 | 928-854-4011 | | K-8 | Amy Hanon |
| Haven Montessori S | 621 W Clay Ave | Flagstaff, AZ | 86001 | 928-522-0985 | 774-7412 | K-K | Elisa McKnight |
| Hayes HS | PO Box 10899 | Bapchule, AZ | 85121 | 520-315-5100 | 315-5115 | 9-12 | Crispin Zamudio |
| Hearn Academy | 17606 N 7th Ave | Phoenix, AZ | 85023-1567 | 602-896-9160 | 896-1997 | K-8 | Gaye Leo |
| Heritage Academy | 32 S Center St | Mesa, AZ | 85210-1306 | 480-969-5641 | 969-6972 | 7-12 | Earl Taylor |
| Heritage Academy - Laveen | 4275 W Baseline Rd | Laveen, AZ | 85339 | 602-290-8546 | 926-2656 | 9-12 | Kim Ellsworth |
| Heritage Academy - Queen Creek | 19630 Germann Rd | Queen Creek, AZ | 85242 | 480-461-4400 | 452-0833 | 9-12 | Spencer Bowers |
| Heritage ES | 6805 N 125th Ave | Glendale, AZ | 85307 | 623-935-1931 | 935-1931 | K-8 | Justin Dye |
| Heritage ES - Williams Campus | 790 E Rodeo Rd | Williams, AZ | 86046-9653 | 928-635-3998 | 635-3999 | K-5 | Kaytie Thies |
| Hermosa Montessori Charter S | 12051 E Fort Lowell Rd | Tucson, AZ | 85749-9702 | 520-749-5518 | 749-6087 | K-8 | Sheila Stolov |
| Hiaki HS | 4747 W Calle Vicam | Tucson, AZ | 85757-8860 | 520-883-5051 | | 9-12 | |
| Highland Free S | 510 S Highland Ave | Tucson, AZ | 85719-6427 | 520-623-0104 | 903-1318 | K-6 | Nicholas Sofka |
| Hillcrest Academy | 3761 S Power Rd | Mesa, AZ | 85212 | 480-325-8950 | 353-2832 | K-12 | Jerad Hunsaker |
| Hirsch Academy | 6535 E Osborn Rd | Scottsdale, AZ | 85251 | | | K-4 | |
| Holsteiner Agricultural S | 44400 W Honeycutt Rd | Maricopa, AZ | 85138 | 520-568-8620 | | K-6 | Tanya Graysmark |
| Hope HS | 7620 W Lower Buckeye Rd | Phoenix, AZ | 85043 | 623-772-8013 | 772-8021 | 9-12 | Krissyn Sumare |
| Hope HS Online | 5651 W Talavi Blvd Ste 170 | Glendale, AZ | 85306 | 602-674-8344 | 943-9700 | 7-12 | Erin Horn |
| Horizon Community Learning Center | 16233 S 48th St | Phoenix, AZ | 85048-0801 | 480-659-3000 | 659-3022 | K-12 | Betsy Fera |
| Huachuca Mountain ES | 3555 E Fry Blvd | Sierra Vista, AZ | 85635-2972 | 520-515-2960 | 515-2966 | K-6 | Karen Kukuchka |
| Humanities & Sciences Academy | 1105 E Broadway Rd | Tempe, AZ | 85282-1505 | 480-317-5900 | 829-4999 | 9-12 | Sue Durkin |
| Humanities & Sciences Institute | 5201 N 7th St | Phoenix, AZ | 85014-2802 | 602-650-1333 | 650-1881 | 9-12 | |
| Humboldt ES | PO Box 8 | Humboldt, AZ | 86329-0008 | 928-759-4400 | 759-4420 | K-6 | Lisa Uvila |
| Imagine Avondale ES | 950 N Eliseo Felix Jr Way | Avondale, AZ | 85323 | 602-344-1730 | 344-1740 | PK-8 | Kim Agnew |
| Imagine Charter S at Bell Canyon | 18052 N Black Canyon Hwy | Phoenix, AZ | 85053-1715 | 602-547-7920 | 547-7923 | K-8 | Joshua Jordan |
| Imagine Charter S at Camelback | 5050 N 19th Ave | Phoenix, AZ | 85015-3205 | 602-344-4620 | 344-4630 | K-8 | Debbie Yarbrough |
| Imagine Charter S at Cortez Park | 3535 W Dunlap Ave | Phoenix, AZ | 85051-5303 | 602-589-9840 | 589-9841 | K-8 | Jason Whitaker |
| Imagine Charter S at Desert West | 6738 W McDowell Rd | Phoenix, AZ | 85035-4642 | 602-344-7150 | 344-7160 | K-8 | Bill Heintz |
| Imagine Charter S at East Mesa | 9701 E Southern Ave | Mesa, AZ | 85209-3769 | 480-355-6830 | 355-6840 | K-9 | Melynda Hache |
| Imagine Charter S at Rosefield | 12050 N Bullard Ave | Surprise, AZ | 85379-6325 | 623-344-4300 | 344-4310 | K-8 | James Mecca |
| Imagine Charter S at Tempe | 1538 E Southern Ave | Tempe, AZ | 85282-5687 | 480-355-1640 | 355-1650 | K-6 | Selethia Benn |
| Imagine Charter S at West Gilbert | 2061 S Gilbert Rd | Gilbert, AZ | 85295-4620 | 480-855-2700 | 855-2701 | K-8 | Matt Rowley |
| Imagine Coolidge ES | 1290 W Vah Ki Inn Rd | Coolidge, AZ | 85128 | 520-723-5391 | 723-5491 | K-8 | Freddie Villalon |
| Imagine Prep at Surprise | 14850 N 156th Ave | Surprise, AZ | 85379-5653 | 623-344-1770 | 214-1083 | 7-12 | Chris McComb |
| Imagine Prep - Superstition | 1843 W 16th Ave | Apache Junction, AZ | 85120 | 480-355-0530 | 355-0540 | 6-12 | Frank Stirpe |
| Incito S | 877 N Sarival Rd | Goodyear, AZ | 85338 | 623-398-6868 | | K-8 | April Black |
| Intelli School - Glendale | 13806 N 51st Ave | Glendale, AZ | 85306-4834 | 602-564-7210 | 564-7301 | 9-12 | |
| Intelli School - Main | 1727 N Arizona Ave Ste 5 | Chandler, AZ | 85225 | 480-855-5318 | 855-5904 | 9-12 | |
| Intelli School - Metro Center | 3327 W Peoria Ave | Phoenix, AZ | 85029 | 602-564-7240 | 564-7241 | 9-12 | |
| Intelli School - Paradise Valley | 1427 E Bell Rd Ste 102 | Phoenix, AZ | 85022 | 602-564-7280 | 564-7281 | 9-12 | |
| International Charter S of AZ | 1973 E Maryland Ave | Phoenix, AZ | 85016 | 602-241-1111 | | 5-12 | |
| International Commerce Institute | 5201 N 7th St | Phoenix, AZ | 85014-2802 | 602-650-1116 | 650-1881 | 9-12 | |
| International Commerce Institute - Tempe | 1105 E Broadway Rd | Tempe, AZ | 85282-1505 | 480-317-5900 | 829-4999 | 9-12 | |
| iSchool 2020 | 3777 W 22nd Ln | Yuma, AZ | 85364 | 928-317-3113 | 783-3473 | 9-12 | Ryan Hackmann |
| Jefferson Academy of Advanced Learning | 40 S 11th St | Show Low, AZ | 85901-6001 | 928-537-5432 | 537-0440 | K-12 | Sandy Stewart |
| Jefferson Preparatory HS | 16635 N 51st Ave | Glendale, AZ | 85306 | 602-595-2990 | 595-2440 | 9-12 | Tawnya Mecham |
| Keystone Montessori Charter S | 1025 E Liberty Ln | Phoenix, AZ | 85048-8462 | 480-460-7312 | 283-8402 | K-9 | Cindy Maschoff |
| Khalsa Montessori S | 2536 N 3rd St | Phoenix, AZ | 85004-1308 | 602-252-3759 | 252-1890 | K-6 | Keerat Giordano |
| Khalsa Montessori S | 3701 E River Rd | Tucson, AZ | 85718-6633 | 520-529-3611 | 615-0625 | K-8 | Nirvair Khalsa |
| Kingman Academy of Learning HS | 3420 N Burbank St | Kingman, AZ | 86409-3105 | 928-681-2900 | 681-2424 | 9-12 | Jeff Martin |
| Kingman Academy of Learning IS | 3419 Harrison St | Kingman, AZ | 86409-3604 | 928-681-3200 | 681-2424 | 3-5 | Stacy Matthews |
| Kingman Academy of Learning MS | 3269 Harrison St | Kingman, AZ | 86409-3679 | 928-692-5265 | 681-2424 | 6-8 | Dawn Day |
| Kingman Academy of Learning PS | 3400 N Burbank St | Kingman, AZ | 86409-3105 | 928-692-2500 | 692-2505 | K-2 | Trudi Bradley |
| Lake Valley ES | 3900 N Starlight Dr | Prescott Valley, AZ | 86314-2493 | 928-759-4200 | 759-4220 | K-6 | Tusanne Cordes |
| La Paloma Academy | 2050 N Wilmot Rd | Tucson, AZ | 85712-3039 | 520-721-4205 | 721-4263 | K-8 | Brendan Ewald |
| La Paloma Academy - Lakeside | 8140 E Golf Links Rd | Tucson, AZ | 85730 | 520-733-7373 | 733-7392 | K-8 | Sean Watins |
| La Paloma Academy South | 5660 S 12th Ave | Tucson, AZ | 85706 | 520-807-9668 | | K-8 | Paul Bummer |
| Larkspur ES | 2430 E Larkspur Dr | Phoenix, AZ | 85032-7022 | 602-449-3300 | 449-3305 | K-6 | Marian Ouellette |
| Las Puertas Community S | 4560 S Coach Rd | Tucson, AZ | 85714 | 520-546-9296 | | 6-9 | |
| La Tierra Community S | 124 N Virginia St | Prescott Valley, AZ | 86314 | 928-445-5100 | | K-6 | Jennifer Roderick |
| Leading Edge Academy at East Mesa | 10115 E University Dr | Mesa, AZ | 85207 | 480-984-5645 | 627-3634 | K-6 | Derrick Jamerson |
| Leading Edge Academy -ES | 717 W Ray Rd | Gilbert, AZ | 85233 | 480-545-6646 | | K-6 | Lori Anderson |
| Leading Edge Academy - Maricopa | 18700 N Porter Rd | Maricopa, AZ | 85138 | 520-568-7800 | | K-6 | Mathew Reese |
| Leading Edge Academy - Queen Creek | 4815 W Hunt Hwy | Queen Creek, AZ | 85142 | 480-655-6787 | 655-6788 | K-12 | Steve Butcher |
| Leading Edge Academy San Tan | 7377 W Hunt Hwy | Queen Creek, AZ | 85142 | 480-882-1631 | | 6-12 | Nick Schuerman |
| Learning Foundation & Performing Arts | 5761 E Brown Rd | Mesa, AZ | 85205-4400 | 480-807-1100 | 807-1190 | K-12 | Nikki Triggs |
| Learning Foundation & Performing Arts S | 3939 E Warner Rd | Gilbert, AZ | 85296 | 480-240-8025 | | K-6 | |
| Learning Foundation & Performing Arts S | 1120 S Gilbert Rd | Gilbert, AZ | 85296-3465 | 480-635-9400 | 635-1907 | K-12 | Robert Villa |
| Learning Foundation Performing Arts S | 851 N Stapley Dr | Mesa, AZ | 85203-5644 | 480-834-6202 | 834-3991 | K-12 | Jeannine Rucker |
| Legacy Traditional Charter S | 2747 S Recker Rd | Gilbert, AZ | 85295 | 480-397-9260 | 223-6453 | K-8 | |
| Legacy Traditional S - Avondale Campus | 12320 W Van Buren St | Avondale, AZ | 85323 | 623-344-0330 | 932-7848 | K-8 | |
| Legacy Traditional S - Casa Grande | 1274 E ONeil Dr | Casa Grande, AZ | 85122 | 520-421-2323 | 421-4443 | K-8 | Jennifer Hackett M.Ed. |
| Legacy Traditional S - Laveen Campus | 7900 S 43rd Ave | Laveen, AZ | 85339 | 623-344-0472 | 237-0477 | K-8 | |
| Legacy Traditional S - Maricopa | 17760 Regent Dr | Maricopa, AZ | 85138 | 520-423-9999 | 423-9997 | K-8 | Nicole Mangum M.Ed. |
| Legacy Traditional S - Northwest Tucson | 3500 W Cortaro Farms Rd | Tucson, AZ | 85742 | 520-505-3640 | 579-6833 | K-8 | Christine Fitzsimmons |
| Legacy Traditional S - Queen Creek | 41800 N Barnes Pkwy | San Tan Valley, AZ | 85140 | 480-655-5553 | 655-5558 | K-8 | Marie Wilson M.Ed. |
| Legacy Traditional S - Surprise | 14506 W Sweetwater Ave | Surprise, AZ | 85379 | 623-299-9820 | 299-9821 | K-8 | |
| Liberty Arts Academy | 3015 S Power Rd | Mesa, AZ | 85212-3000 | 480-830-3444 | 830-4335 | K-6 | Julia Angel |
| Liberty HS | 1300 E Cedar St | Globe, AZ | 85501 | 928-402-8024 | 402-8358 | 9-12 | |
| Liberty Traditional Charter S | 4027 N 45th Ave | Phoenix, AZ | 85031-2840 | 602-442-8791 | 353-9270 | K-8 | Jeremy Parker |
| Liberty Traditonal S - Saddleback | 3715 N Washington Ave | Douglas, AZ | 85607 | 520-364-6311 | | K-4 | Edward Mealy |
| Lifelong Learning Academy | 3295 W Orange Grove Rd | Tucson, AZ | 85741-2937 | 520-219-4383 | 544-0220 | K-8 | |
| Life Skills Center of Arizona | 8123 N 35th Ave Ste 2 | Phoenix, AZ | 85051 | 602-242-6400 | 242-6823 | 9-12 | |
| Lincoln Traditional S | 10444 N 39th Ave | Phoenix, AZ | 85051-1179 | 602-896-6300 | 896-6320 | K-8 | Tara Mayole |
| Luke ES | 7300 N Dysart Rd | Glendale, AZ | 85307-2218 | 623-876-7300 | 876-7305 | K-8 | Amalia Garcia |
| Madison Highland Prep S | 1431 E Campbell Ave | Phoenix, AZ | 85014 | 602-745-3800 | 745-3899 | 9-11 | |
| Madison Preparatory S | 5815 S Mcclintock Dr | Tempe, AZ | 85283-3227 | 480-345-2306 | 345-0059 | 7-12 | Paul Grant |
| Maricopa ES | 44150 W Maricopa Casa Grand | Maricopa, AZ | 85138 | 520-568-5160 | 568-5166 | K-6 | Dr. Jennifer Robinson |
| Maricopa Wells MS | 44150 W Maricopa Casa Grand | Maricopa, AZ | 85138 | 520-568-7100 | 568-7104 | 7-8 | Rick Abel |
| Maryvale Preparatory Academy | 6301 W Indian School Rd | Phoenix, AZ | 85033-3326 | 602-247-6095 | 889-6282 | K-5 | Mac Esau |
| Masada Charter S | PO Box 2277 | Colorado City, AZ | 86021-2277 | 928-875-2525 | 875-2526 | K-9 | Leanne Timpson |
| Math & Science Success Academy | 434 W Lerdo Rd | Tucson, AZ | 85756 | 520-751-2783 | 888-1732 | K-12 | Adriana Rodriguez |
| Maya HS | 3660 W Glendale Ave | Phoenix, AZ | 85051-8335 | 602-242-3442 | 242-5255 | 9-12 | John Anderson |
| Mesa Arts Academy | 221 W 6th Ave | Mesa, AZ | 85210-2446 | 480-844-3965 | 844-0205 | K-8 | Sue Douglas |
| Mesquite ES | 9455 E Rita Rd | Tucson, AZ | 85747-6300 | 520-879-2100 | 879-2101 | K-5 | Diane Samorano |
| Metropolitan Arts Institute | 1700 N 7th Ave Ste 100 | Phoenix, AZ | 85007 | 602-258-9500 | 258-9504 | 9-12 | Matthew Baker |
| Mexicayotl Charter S | 338 N Morley Ave | Nogales, AZ | 85621-2801 | 520-287-6790 | 287-0037 | K-8 | Corina Aguirre |
| Midtown HS | 7318 W Lynwood St | Phoenix, AZ | 85035-4542 | 623-936-8682 | 936-8559 | 9-12 | |
| Midtown PS | 4735 N 19th Ave | Phoenix, AZ | 85015-3725 | 602-265-5133 | 604-2337 | K-5 | Judy White |
| Milestones Charter S | 4707 E Robert E Lee St | Phoenix, AZ | 85032-9529 | 602-404-1009 | 404-5456 | K-8 | Tara Cabardo |
| Mingus Springs Charter S | 3600 Sunset Dr | Chino Valley, AZ | 86323-5054 | 928-636-4766 | 636-5149 | K-8 | Dawn Gonzales |
| Mission Heights Prep HS | 1376 E Cottonwood Ln | Casa Grande, AZ | 85122 | 520-836-9383 | | 9-12 | Drew Goodson |
| Mission Montessori Academy | 4530 E Gold Dust Ave | Phoenix, AZ | 85028 | 602-466-1153 | | 7-8 | Joslyn Maike |
| Mission Montessori del Cielo | 5550 E Mercer Ln | Scottsdale, AZ | 85254 | 480-284-8000 | 284-8875 | PK-K | |
| Mission Montessori del Jardin | 5550 E Mercer Ln | Scottsdale, AZ | 85254 | 480-699-4950 | 314-3346 | 1-3 | |
| Mission Montessori del Norte | 5550 E Mercer Ln | Scottsdale, AZ | 85254 | 480-840-1609 | 840-1676 | 4-6 | |
| Mission Montessori on the Desert | 5550 E Mercer Ln | Scottsdale, AZ | 85254 | 480-860-4330 | 657-3715 | PK-K | |
| Mohave Accelerated ES | 625 Marina Blvd | Bullhead City, AZ | 86442 | 928-704-9345 | 704-4977 | K-5 | Jeremy Klingensmith |
| Mohave Accelerated ES East | 2850 Silver Creek Rd | Bullhead City, AZ | 86442 | 928-704-9345 | 704-4977 | K-5 | Sandra Smith |
| Mohave Accelerated Learning Center | PO Box 21288 | Bullhead City, AZ | 86439-1288 | 928-704-9345 | 704-4977 | 6-12 | Vickie Christensen |
| Montessori Academy | 6050 N Invergordon Rd | Paradise Valley, AZ | 85253 | 480-945-1121 | 874-2928 | K-8 | Juli Newman |
| Montessori Charter S of Flagstaff | 850 N Locust St | Flagstaff, AZ | 86001 | 928-226-1212 | 774-0337 | K-8 | Kim Loaiza |
| Montessori Charter S of Flagstaff-Cedar | 2212 E Cedar Ave | Flagstaff, AZ | 86004-1922 | 928-774-1600 | 774-0424 | 7-8 | Marlane Spencer |
| Montessori Childrens House | 2400 W Datsi St | Camp Verde, AZ | 86322-8412 | 928-567-1878 | 567-2107 | K-K | Janet Taylor |
| Montessori Day Charter S - Mountainside | 9215 N 14th St | Phoenix, AZ | 85020-2713 | 602-943-7672 | 395-0271 | K-8 | Pat Freeman |
| Montessori Day S - Chandler Lakeshore | 1700 W Warner Rd | Chandler, AZ | 85224-2676 | 480-730-8886 | 730-9072 | PK-7 | Theresa Averill |

| School | Address | City,State | Zip code | Telephone | Fax | Grade | Contact |
|---|---|---|---|---|---|---|---|
| Montessori de Santa Cruz Charter S | PO Box 4706 | Tubac, AZ | 85646-4706 | 520-398-0536 | 398-0776 | K-8 | |
| Montessori Education Centre Charter S | 2834 E Southern Ave | Mesa, AZ | 85204-5517 | 480-926-8375 | 503-0515 | PK-6 | Tammy Whiting |
| Montessori Education Ctr - Charter S N | 815 N Gilbert Rd | Mesa, AZ | 85203-5805 | 480-964-1381 | 668-5457 | PK-6 | Rachel Lichtenbergher |
| Montessori House Charter S | 2415 N Terrace Cir | Mesa, AZ | 85203-1220 | 480-464-2800 | 464-2836 | K-6 | Sherie Richardson |
| Montessori Schoolhouse | 1301 E Fort Lowell Rd | Tucson, AZ | 85719-2239 | 520-319-8668 | 881-4096 | K-5 | Michael Ebner |
| Mosaica Online HS | 3738 N 16th St | Phoenix, AZ | 85016 | 602-282-0240 | | 9-12 | |
| Mountain Oak Charter S | 1455 Willow Creek Rd | Prescott, AZ | 86301 | 928-541-7700 | 445-1301 | K-8 | |
| Mountain Rose Academy | 3686 W Orange Grove Rd #192 | Tucson, AZ | 85741 | 520-797-4884 | 797-8868 | 9-12 | Jennifer Haley |
| Mountain S | 311 W Cattle Drive Trl | Flagstaff, AZ | 86005 | 928-779-2392 | 773-3246 | PK-5 | Renee Fauset |
| Mountain View ES | 8601 E Loos Dr | Prescott Valley, AZ | 86314-6476 | 928-759-4700 | 759-4720 | K-6 | JoAnne Bindell |
| Mountain View Preparatory S | 1 N Willard St | Cottonwood, AZ | 86326 | 928-649-8144 | 649-8145 | K-8 | Stephanie Jones |
| Mt. Turnbull Academy | PO Box 129 | Bylas, AZ | 85530 | 928-475-3050 | 475-3051 | 9-12 | Jayson Stanley |
| New Horizon S for the Performing Arts | 446 E Broadway Rd | Mesa, AZ | 85204-2020 | 480-655-7444 | 655-8220 | K-6 | Jim Wyler |
| New School for the Arts | 1216 E Apache Blvd | Tempe, AZ | 85281-6005 | 480-481-9235 | 970-6625 | 6-12 | Katy Cardenas |
| New Visions Academy | 125 S 6th St | Cottonwood, AZ | 86326-4239 | 928-634-7320 | 634-7494 | 9-12 | Ann Shaw |
| New Visions Academy - St. John's Campus | PO Box 791 | Saint Johns, AZ | 85936-0791 | 928-337-3268 | 337-3383 | 9-12 | Leisa Crosby |
| New World Educational Center Charter S | 5818 N 7th St | Phoenix, AZ | 85014 | 602-238-9577 | 238-9210 | K-12 | Jesus Armenta |
| NFL YET College Prep Academy | 4848 S 2nd St | Phoenix, AZ | 85040-2122 | 602-243-7788 | 243-7799 | 7-12 | |
| Northern AZ Academy for Career Dev. | PO Box 125 | Taylor, AZ | 85939-0125 | 928-536-4222 | 536-4441 | 9-12 | Cindy Johnson |
| Northern AZ Academy for Career Dev. | 502 Airport Rd | Winslow, AZ | 86047-5400 | 928-289-3329 | 289-4485 | 9-12 | Joe Garguil |
| Northland Preparatory Academy | 3300 E Sparrow Ave | Flagstaff, AZ | 86004-6703 | 928-214-8776 | 214-8778 | 7-12 | Toni Keberlein |
| North Phoenix Preparatory Academy | 13613 N Cave Creek Rd Ste F | Phoenix, AZ | 85022-5137 | 602-996-4355 | 889-0161 | 6-12 | Kevin Topper |
| North Pointe Preparatory S | 10215 N 43rd Ave | Phoenix, AZ | 85051-1025 | 623-209-0017 | 209-0021 | 7-12 | Richard Gow |
| Northpoint Expeditionary Learning Acad | 551 1st St | Prescott, AZ | 86301-2599 | 928-717-3272 | 717-2316 | 9-12 | Charles Mentken |
| North Star Charter S | 10720 W Indian School Rd | Phoenix, AZ | 85037-5721 | 623-907-2661 | 907-2501 | 9-12 | Kurt Huzar |
| Nosotros Academy | 440 N Grande Ave | Tucson, AZ | 85745-2703 | 520-624-1023 | 624-7999 | 3-12 | Paul Felix |
| Odyssey Institute | 1495 Verrado Way | Buckeye, AZ | 85326 | 623-402-4090 | | 6-9 | Bryan Pratt |
| Odyssey Preparatory Academy | 6500 S Apache Rd | Buckeye, AZ | 85326 | 623-327-3111 | 327-0554 | K-6 | Kenneth Olson |
| Odyssey Preparatory Academy | 17532 W Harrison St | Goodyear, AZ | 85338 | 623-882-1140 | 882-1196 | K-6 | Liz Douglass |
| Odyssey Preparatory Academy | 950 N Peart Rd | Casa Grande, AZ | 85122 | 520-381-2360 | 876-0492 | K-5 | Patty Messer |
| Old Vail MS | 13299 E Colossal Cave Rd | Vail, AZ | 85641-9090 | 520-879-2400 | 879-2401 | 6-8 | Dr. Laurie Emery |
| Ombudsman Charter S - Central | 1525 N Oracle Rd | Tucson, AZ | 85705 | 520-624-2260 | 882-2160 | 6-12 | Emily Langfeldt |
| Ombudsman Charter S - East | 3943 E Thomas Rd | Phoenix, AZ | 85018-7511 | 602-840-2997 | 840-1402 | 6-12 | Emily Langfeldt |
| Ombudsman Charter S - East II | 4041 E Thomas Rd Ste 106 | Phoenix, AZ | 85018 | 602-667-7759 | 667-7793 | 9-12 | |
| Ombudsman Charter S - Metro | 4220 W Northern Ave | Phoenix, AZ | 85051-5753 | 602-840-2997 | 842-6157 | 6-12 | |
| Ombudsman Charter S - Northeast | 3242 E Bell Rd | Phoenix, AZ | 85032-2727 | 602-485-9872 | 367-0367 | 6-12 | |
| Ombudsman Charter S - Northwest | 9516 W Peoria Ave | Peoria, AZ | 85345-6100 | 602-840-2997 | 840-1402 | 6-12 | Emily Langfeldt |
| Ombudsman Charter S - Valencia | 1686 W Valencia Rd Ste 100 | Tucson, AZ | 85746 | 520-573-5858 | 807-9333 | 6-12 | Emily Langfeldt |
| Ombudsman Charter S - West | 3618 W Bell Rd | Glendale, AZ | 85308-4338 | 602-840-2997 | 840-1402 | 6-12 | Emily Langfeldt |
| Omega Alpha Academy | 1402 N San Antonio Ave | Douglas, AZ | 85607-2434 | 520-805-1261 | 805-1272 | K-12 | Jose Frisby |
| Open Doors Community S | 13644 N Sandario Rd | Marana, AZ | 85653 | 520-744-2484 | | K-8 | |
| Orangewood S | 7337 N 19th Ave | Phoenix, AZ | 85021-7998 | 602-347-2900 | 347-2920 | K-8 | Andree Charlson |
| PACE Preparatory Academy | 6711 E 2nd St | Prescott Valley, AZ | 86314 | 928-775-0719 | 649-9570 | 9-12 | Bill Sakelarios |
| Paideia Academy of South Phoenix | 7777 S 15th Ter | Phoenix, AZ | 85042-6754 | 602-343-3040 | 381-9029 | PK-6 | Dr. Brian Winsor |
| Painted Rock Academy | 14800 N 25th Dr | Phoenix, AZ | 85023 | 602-466-8855 | | K-8 | Britainy McMillan |
| Palm Valley ES | 2801 N 135th Ave | Goodyear, AZ | 85395 | 623-535-6400 | 935-0058 | PK-8 | Jennifer Benjamin |
| Pan-American Charter ES | 3001 W Indian School Rd | Phoenix, AZ | 85017-4168 | 602-266-3989 | 266-3979 | K-8 | Marta Pasos |
| Paradise Education Center | 15533 W Paradise Ln | Surprise, AZ | 85374-5851 | 623-975-2646 | 975-2841 | K-8 | Allison Gonzales |
| Paradise Honors HS | 12775 N 175th Ave | Surprise, AZ | 85388 | 623-546-7215 | 975-4380 | 9-12 | Mike Sears |
| Paragon Science Academy | 2975 W Linda Ln | Chandler, AZ | 85224 | 480-814-1600 | 814-1661 | K-12 | Selim Tanyeri |
| Paramount Academy | 11039 W Olive Ave | Peoria, AZ | 85345-9200 | 623-977-0614 | 977-0615 | K-8 | Kurt DeRuyter |
| Park View MS | 9030 E Florentine Rd | Prescott Valley, AZ | 86314 | 928-775-5115 | 775-6253 | 6-8 | James Herrera |
| Patagonia Montessori S | PO Box 628 | Patagonia, AZ | 85624 | 520-394-9530 | 394-2864 | PK-8 | Jessi Beebe |
| Pathfinder Academy | 2906 N Boulder Cyn | Mesa, AZ | 85207 | 480-986-7071 | 986-9858 | K-8 | Susan Stradling |
| Patriot Academy | 19023 E San Tan Blvd | Queen Creek, AZ | 85142 | 480-279-4780 | 807-1209 | K-8 | Jay Brown |
| Paulden Community S | 24850 N Naples St | Paulden, AZ | 86334 | 928-636-1430 | 636-3087 | K-8 | James Sexton |
| Peak S | 2016 N 1st St Ste A | Flagstaff, AZ | 86004-4241 | 928-779-0771 | 779-0774 | K-8 | Paula Drossman |
| Peoria Accelerated HS | 8885 W Peoria Ave | Peoria, AZ | 85345-6442 | 623-979-0031 | 979-0113 | 9-12 | Marcus Englund |
| Phoenix Advantage Charter S | 3738 N 16th St | Phoenix, AZ | 85016-5915 | 602-263-8777 | 263-8822 | K-8 | Isaac Perez |
| Phoenix College Prep Academy | 1202 W Thomas Rd | Phoenix, AZ | 85013 | 602-285-7998 | 285-7697 | 9-12 | |
| Phoenix Collegiate Academy | 5610 S Central Ave | Phoenix, AZ | 85040 | 602-268-9900 | 268-9911 | 2-12 | Rachel Bennett Yanof |
| Phoenix School of Academic Excellence | 5310 N 12th St | Phoenix, AZ | 85014 | 602-241-7876 | 424-0281 | 7-12 | |
| Pillar Academy of Business & Finance | 1589 E Plantation Rd | Mohave Valley, AZ | 86440 | 928-346-3925 | 346-3930 | 9-12 | |
| Pima Partnership S | 1346 N Stone Ave | Tucson, AZ | 85705-7338 | 520-326-2528 | 326-2527 | 7-12 | |
| Pima Rose Academy | 3686 W Orange Grove Rd #192 | Tucson, AZ | 85741 | 520-797-4884 | 797-8868 | 9-12 | Joanne Vigilant |
| Pima Vocational HS - Downtown | 97 E Congress St | Tucson, AZ | 85701 | 520-243-1745 | | 9-12 | |
| Pima Vocational HS - Main | 1550 S 6th Ave | Tucson, AZ | 85713 | 520-243-1740 | 903-0753 | 9-12 | Gloria Proo |
| Pima Vocational HS Northwest | 5025 W Ina Rd | Tucson, AZ | 85743 | 520-443-6469 | | 9-12 | Gloria Proo |
| Pine Forest Charter S | 1120 W Kaibab Ln | Flagstaff, AZ | 86001-6217 | 928-779-9880 | 779-9792 | K-8 | Michael Heffernan |
| Pinnacle HS - Casa Grande | 409 W McMurray Blvd | Casa Grande, AZ | 85122 | 520-423-2380 | 423-2383 | 9-12 | |
| Pinnacle HS - Mesa | 151 N Centennial Way | Mesa, AZ | 85201-6734 | 480-668-5003 | 668-5005 | 9-12 | |
| Pinnacle HS - Nogales | 2055 N Grand Ave | Nogales, AZ | 85621-1038 | 520-281-5109 | 281-5132 | 9-12 | |
| Pinnacle HS - Tempe E | 1712 E Guadalupe Rd Ste 101 | Tempe, AZ | 85283-3983 | 480-785-7776 | 785-7778 | 9-12 | |
| Pinnacle HS - Tempe W | 2224 W Southern Ave Ste 2 | Tempe, AZ | 85282-4345 | 602-414-0950 | 414-0927 | 9-12 | |
| Pinnacle Peak ES | 7690 E Williams Dr | Scottsdale, AZ | 85255-4801 | 602-449-6700 | 449-6705 | K-6 | Lora Herbein |
| Pinnacle Pointe Academy | 6753 W Pinnacle Peak Rd | Glendale, AZ | 85310-5301 | 623-537-3535 | 537-4433 | K-6 | |
| Pinnacle Virtual HS | 3225 S Hardy Dr | Tempe, AZ | 85282 | 480-755-8222 | 755-8111 | 7-12 | |
| Pioneer Preparatory S | 6510 W Clarendon Ave | Phoenix, AZ | 85033 | 623-933-3733 | 252-0022 | K-6 | Tony Best |
| Polytechnic ES | 6950 E Williams Field Rd | Mesa, AZ | 85212 | 480-727-5700 | 727-5701 | K-6 | Claudia Mendoza |
| PPEP TEC - Chavez Learning Center | 1233 N Main St Ste B | San Luis, AZ | 85349 | 928-627-8550 | 627-8980 | 9-12 | Angelica Sanchez |
| PPEP TEC - Fernandez Learning Center | 1840 E Benson Hwy | Tucson, AZ | 85714-1770 | 520-889-8276 | 741-4369 | 9-12 | |
| PPEP TEC - Paul Learning Center | 220 E Florence Blvd | Casa Grande, AZ | 85122 | 520-836-6549 | 836-0290 | 9-12 | Leticia Lujan |
| PPEP TEC - Powell Learning Center | 4116 Avenida Cochise Ste F | Sierra Vista, AZ | 85635-5843 | 520-458-8205 | 458-8293 | 9-12 | |
| PPEP TEC - Raul H. Castro Learning Ctr | 1122 G Ave | Douglas, AZ | 85607 | 520-364-4405 | 364-1405 | 9-12 | Raul Torrez |
| PPEP TEC - Soltero Learning Center | 8677 E Golf Links Rd | Tucson, AZ | 85730-1315 | 520-290-9167 | 290-9220 | 9-12 | Randy Kempton |
| PPEP TEC - Yepez Learning Center | 115 N Columbia Ave | Somerton, AZ | 85350 | 928-627-9648 | 627-9197 | 9-12 | Gloria Rodriguez |
| Precision Academy | 7318 W Lynwood St | Phoenix, AZ | 85035-4542 | 623-936-8682 | 936-8559 | 9-12 | Dr. Caroline White |
| Precision Academy System Charter S | 3906 E Broadway Rd | Phoenix, AZ | 85040-2996 | 602-453-3661 | 453-3667 | 9-12 | Steven Isham |
| Premier Charter HS | 7544 W Indian School Rd | Phoenix, AZ | 85033-3030 | 623-245-1500 | 245-1506 | 9-12 | Debbie Petersen |
| Prescott Prep S | 325 N Washington Ave | Prescott, AZ | 86301-2639 | 928-541-1090 | 541-9939 | 9-12 | Jennifer Womack |
| Prescott Valley S | PO Box 27348 | Prescott Valley, AZ | 86312 | 928-772-8744 | 775-4457 | K-12 | Monika Fuller |
| Presidio S | 1695 E Fort Lowell Rd | Tucson, AZ | 85719-2319 | 520-881-5222 | 881-5522 | K-12 | Mindy White |
| Primavera Online HS | 2471 N Arizona Ave Ste 1 | Chandler, AZ | 85225 | 480-456-6678 | 355-2100 | 7-12 | George Barnes |
| Pueblo Del Sol ES | 3555 E Fry Blvd | Sierra Vista, AZ | 85635-2972 | 520-515-2970 | 515-2973 | K-6 | Tom Yarborough |
| Quail Run ES | 3303 E Utopia Rd | Phoenix, AZ | 85050-3900 | 602-449-4400 | 449-4405 | K-6 | Marta Maynard |
| Quest HS | 217 E Olympic Dr | Phoenix, AZ | 85042 | 480-831-6057 | 831-6095 | 9-12 | Melissa Barnett |
| RCB Medical Arts Academy | 6049 N 43rd Ave | Phoenix, AZ | 85019-1641 | 602-973-6018 | 589-1349 | 9-12 | Steven Durand |
| Reyes Maria Ruiz Leadership Academy | 4848 S 2nd St | Phoenix, AZ | 85040 | 602-243-7788 | 243-7799 | 4-6 | Armando Ruiz |
| Ridgeline Academy | 33625 N North Valley Pkwy | Phoenix, AZ | 85085 | 623-223-1335 | | K-6 | Keven Barker |
| Rimrock Public HS | PO Box 248 | Rimrock, AZ | 86335-0248 | 928-567-9213 | 567-9304 | 9-12 | Kathleen McCabe |
| Rincon Vista MS | 10770 E Bilby Rd | Tucson, AZ | 85747 | 520-879-3200 | 879-3201 | 6-8 | Lydia Crain |
| Rising S | 7444 E Broadway Blvd | Tucson, AZ | 85710 | 520-730-2657 | | 6-12 | George Rising Ph.D. |
| Riverbend Preparatory S | 5625 S 51st Ave | Laveen, AZ | 85339 | 602-285-3003 | 285-5560 | K-6 | Joseph Hattrick |
| Royal Palm MS | 8520 N 19th Ave | Phoenix, AZ | 85021-4293 | 602-347-3200 | 347-3220 | 6-8 | Heidi Keefer |
| RSD HS - Blended Learning Academy | 13615 N 35th Ave | Phoenix, AZ | 85029 | 602-993-5225 | 993-0506 | 9-12 | Red Davis |
| SABIS International | 1903 E Roeser Rd | Phoenix, AZ | 85040-3341 | 602-305-8865 | 323-5526 | K-8 | Goldie LaPorte |
| Saddleback ES | 44150 W Maricopa Casa Grand | Maricopa, AZ | 85138 | 520-568-6110 | 568-6119 | PK-6 | Felicia Williams |
| Sage Academy | 1055 E Hearn Rd | Scottsdale, AZ | 85254 | 602-485-3402 | 485-7874 | K-8 | |
| Sandpiper ES | 6724 E Hearn Rd | Scottsdale, AZ | 85254-3316 | 602-449-6300 | 449-6305 | K-6 | Steve Jeras |
| San Pedro Valley HS | 360 S Patagonia St | Benson, AZ | 85602-6533 | 520-720-6726 | 720-6702 | 9-12 | Richard Connet |
| Santa Cruz ES | 44150 W Maricopa Casa Grand | Maricopa, AZ | 85138 | 520-568-5170 | 568-5176 | K-6 | Dr. Loraine Conley |
| San Tan Charter S | 3959 E Elliot Rd | Gilbert, AZ | 85234 | 480-222-0811 | 539-1028 | PK-12 | Kristofer Sippel |
| Santa Rosa ES | 44150 W Maricopa Casa Grand | Maricopa, AZ | 85138 | 520-568-6152 | 568-6155 | PK-6 | Eva Safranek |
| Satori Charter S | 3727 N 1st Ave | Tucson, AZ | 85719-1609 | 520-293-7555 | 293-7020 | 2-8 | Jesse Ramos |
| School for Integrated Academics & Tech | 1145 E Washington St | Phoenix, AZ | 85034 | 602-258-3912 | 340-1965 | 9-12 | Nicole Biggs |
| Scottsdale Country Day S | 10460 N 56th St | Scottsdale, AZ | 85253 | 480-452-5777 | | K-6 | Steve Prahcharov |
| Scottsdale Preparatory Academy | 16537 N 92nd St | Scottsdale, AZ | 85260-1528 | 480-776-1970 | 776-1975 | 5-12 | Alison Chaney |
| Sedona Charter S | 165 Kachina Dr | Sedona, AZ | 86336-4303 | 928-204-6464 | 204-6486 | K-8 | Alice Madar |
| Self Development Charter S | 1515 E Indian School Rd | Phoenix, AZ | 85014 | 480-830-8006 | | K-5 | |
| Self Development Charter S | 1709 N Greenfield Rd | Mesa, AZ | 85205-3103 | 480-641-2640 | 641-2678 | K-8 | Anjie Majeed |
| Sequoia Charter ES | 1460 S Horne | Mesa, AZ | 85204-5760 | 480-890-4002 | | K-6 | Donna Driggers |
| Sequoia Charter Secondary S | 1460 S Horne | Mesa, AZ | 85204-5760 | 480-649-7737 | 649-0711 | 9-12 | Amy Fraser |
| Sequoia Choice S - AZ Distance Learning | 323 N Gilbert Rd Ste 104 | Mesa, AZ | 85203 | 480-461-3222 | 461-3222 | K-12 | Cindy Chleborad |
| Sequoia Choice - Star Academy | 323 N Gilbert Rd Ste 108 | Mesa, AZ | 85203 | 480-834-7400 | 834-7402 | K-12 | Cindy Chleborad |
| Sequoia ES | 1460 S Horne | Mesa, AZ | 85204 | 480-890-4002 | 890-4107 | K-6 | Amy Fraser |
| Sequoia Lehi ES | 2331 N Horne | Mesa, AZ | 85203 | 480-397-9890 | 397-4003 | PK-6 | Jennifer Young |
| Sequoia Pathfinder Academy | 4816 S Eastmark Pkwy | Mesa, AZ | 85212 | 480-351-8070 | 351-8407 | K-6 | Juliane Hillock |

| School | Address | City,State | Zip code | Telephone | Fax | Grade | Contact |
|---|---|---|---|---|---|---|---|
| Sequoia Pathway Academy | 19265 N Porter Rd | Maricopa, AZ | 85138-4053 | 520-568-9333 | 568-9444 | K-12 | Jonathan Gentile |
| Sequoia S for the Deaf & Hard of Hearing | 1460 S Horne | Mesa, AZ | 85204-5760 | 480-890-4001 | 890-4113 | K-12 | Heather Laine |
| Sequoia School - Sequoia Village S | 982 Full House Ln | Show Low, AZ | 85901-4042 | 928-537-1208 | 537-4275 | K-12 | Mindy Savoia |
| Sequoia STAR Academy | 323 N Gilbert Rd | Mesa, AZ | 85203 | 480-834-7400 | 834-7402 | 7-12 | Lynn McConnell |
| Shelby S | 249 W Standage Dr | Payson, AZ | 85541 | 928-478-4706 | 478-0681 | K-10 | Ezra Stuyvesant |
| Sky Islands S | 6000 E 14th St | Tucson, AZ | 85711-4601 | 520-382-9210 | 382-5888 | 9-12 | Dr. Shari Popen |
| Skyline District 5 S | PO Box 10858 | Bapchule, AZ | 85121 | 520-315-3236 | 315-3233 | 5-12 | Vaughn Flannigan |
| Skyline Prep HS | 7500 S 40th St | Phoenix, AZ | 85042 | 602-343-4980 | 343-4996 | 9-12 | Muhammad Sumare |
| Skyview S | 125 S Rush St | Prescott, AZ | 86303-4432 | 928-776-1730 | 776-1742 | K-8 | Scott McCreery |
| Sonoran Desert S | 6724 S Kings Ranch Rd | Gold Canyon, AZ | 85118 | 480-396-5463 | 396-4980 | 5-12 | Patricia Dalman |
| Sonoran Science Academy - Broadway | 6880 E Broadway Blvd | Tucson, AZ | 85710 | 520-751-2401 | 751-2451 | K-8 | Erdal Kocak |
| Sonoran Science Academy - Davis Monthan | 5741 E Ironwood St | Tucson, AZ | 85708 | 520-300-5699 | 207-7698 | 6-12 | Peggy Fontenot M.Ed. |
| Sonoran Science Academy - Peoria | 17667 N 91st Ave | Peoria, AZ | 85382 | 623-776-9344 | 933-8001 | K-8 | Barbara Bagwill |
| Sonoran Science Academy - Phoenix | 4837 E McDowell Rd | Phoenix, AZ | 85008-4225 | 602-244-9855 | 244-9856 | K-12 | Jim Satterlee |
| Sonoran Science Academy - Tucson | 2325 W Sunset Rd | Tucson, AZ | 85741-3809 | 520-665-3430 | 665-3440 | K-12 | Dr. Adnan Doyuran Ph.D. |
| Sonoran Sky ES | 12990 N 75th St | Scottsdale, AZ | 85260-4746 | 602-449-6500 | 449-6505 | PK-6 | Robert Dawson |
| Sossaman MS | 18655 E Jacaranda Blvd | Queen Creek, AZ | 85142 | 480-279-8500 | 279-8505 | 7-8 | Nancy Diab |
| Southern Arizona Community Academy | 2470 N Tucson Blvd | Tucson, AZ | 85716-2469 | 520-319-6113 | 319-6115 | 9-12 | Abelardo Cubillas |
| Southgate Academy | 850 W Valencia Rd | Tucson, AZ | 85706-7619 | 520-741-7900 | 741-7901 | K-12 | Sherry Matyjasik |
| South Phoenix Prep and Arts School | 7450 S 40th St | Phoenix, AZ | 85025 | 877-225-8711 | | PK-4 | Tanya Brown M.Ed. |
| South Pointe Charter ES | 2033 E Southern Ave | Phoenix, AZ | 85040 | 602-276-1943 | 276-2726 | K-6 | Nadine Taylor |
| South Pointe HS | 8325 S Central Ave | Phoenix, AZ | 85042-6576 | 602-243-0600 | 243-0800 | 9-12 | Larry McGill |
| South Pointe JHS | 217 E Olympic Dr | Phoenix, AZ | 85042 | 602-268-3782 | 268-4863 | 7-8 | Gayle Taylor |
| South Ridge HS | 1122 S 67th Ave | Phoenix, AZ | 85043-4417 | 623-247-0106 | 247-0527 | 9-12 | Melissa Rivers |
| Southside Community S | 2701 S Campbell Ave | Tucson, AZ | 85713-5080 | 520-623-7102 | 623-7125 | 6-12 | |
| South Valley Prep & Arts Academy | 7500 S 40th St | Phoenix, AZ | 85042 | 877-225-2118 | 437-2901 | 5-8 | Sara Bartling |
| South Verde Technology Magnet S | 410 Camp Lincoln Rd | Camp Verde, AZ | 86322 | 928-567-8076 | 567-8093 | 9-12 | Steve King |
| Southwest Leadership Academy | 4301 W Fillmore St | Phoenix, AZ | 85043 | 602-265-2000 | | 9-12 | Gregory Fowler |
| STAR S | 145 Leupp Rd | Flagstaff, AZ | 86004-8501 | 928-415-4157 | 225-2179 | K-8 | Dr. Mark Sorenson |
| StarShine Academy Creative Community | 3535 E McDowell Rd | Phoenix, AZ | 85008 | 602-957-9557 | 956-0065 | K-12 | |
| Starshine Fay Landrum Academy | 1902 W Roeser Rd | Phoenix, AZ | 85041 | 602-237-6030 | | K-12 | |
| STEM Academy Polytechnic | 6110 S Sagewood St | Mesa, AZ | 85212 | 480-727-5750 | | 5-8 | |
| Stepping Stones Academy | 35812 N 7th St | Phoenix, AZ | 85086-7410 | 623-465-4910 | 587-8514 | K-8 | Dedre Alliger |
| Step Up S | 44 E 5th St | Mesa, AZ | 85201 | 480-344-2600 | 850-0004 | K-8 | |
| Student Choice HS | 1833 N Scottsdale Rd | Tempe, AZ | 85281-1563 | 480-947-9511 | 947-9624 | 9-12 | Catherine McAllister |
| Student Choice HS - Paradise Valley | 4645 E Marilyn Rd | Phoenix, AZ | 85032 | 602-334-4101 | 493-0033 | 9-12 | Sherry Jones |
| Student Choice HS - Peoria | 8194 W Deer Valley Rd | Peoria, AZ | 85382-2127 | 623-242-2722 | 566-1634 | 9-12 | Jaime Claros |
| Summit HS | 728 E Mcdowell Rd | Phoenix, AZ | 85006-2592 | 602-258-8959 | 258-8953 | 9-12 | James Sigman |
| Sun Valley Charter S | 5806 S 35th Pl | Phoenix, AZ | 85040 | 602-692-4914 | 612-2196 | K-6 | Tanae Morrison M.Ed. |
| Sun Valley HS | 1143 S Lindsay Rd | Mesa, AZ | 85204-6298 | 480-497-4800 | 497-1314 | 9-12 | Joe Procopio |
| Sweetwater S | 4602 W Sweetwater Ave | Glendale, AZ | 85304-1505 | 602-896-6500 | 896-6520 | K-8 | Luanne Herman |
| SySTEM Phoenix | 1301 E Almeria Rd | Phoenix, AZ | 85006 | 602-710-1873 | | 6-12 | Angelica Cruz |
| Tanque Verde ES | 2600 N Fennimore Ave | Tucson, AZ | 85749-8194 | 520-749-4244 | 749-4292 | K-6 | Susan Centers |
| Tartesso ES | 29677 W Indianola Ave | Buckeye, AZ | 85396 | 623-474-5403 | 474-5441 | K-8 | Liz Burton |
| Taylion Virtual Academy | 4744 W Grovers Ave | Glendale, AZ | 85308-3453 | 855-297-2466 | 889-7806 | 9-12 | Charlene Shores |
| Teleos Preparatory Academy | 1401 E Jefferson St | Phoenix, AZ | 85034-2315 | 602-275-5455 | 275-5954 | K-8 | Brian Taylor |
| Telesis Preparatory Academy | 2598 Starlite Ln | Lk Havasu Cty, AZ | 86403-4946 | 928-855-8661 | 855-9302 | K-12 | Sandra Breece Ed.D. |
| Tempe Preparatory Academy | 1251 E Southern Ave | Tempe, AZ | 85282-5605 | 480-839-3402 | 755-0546 | 6-12 | David Baum |
| Thoman Air and Space Academy | 730 W Calle Arroyo Sur | Green Valley, AZ | 85614 | 520-219-4383 | | K-8 | Mary Lou Klem |
| Toltecali Academy | 251 W Irvington Rd | Tucson, AZ | 85714 | 520-882-3029 | 882-3041 | 9-12 | |
| Tri-City College Prep HS | 5522 Side Rd | Prescott, AZ | 86301-8483 | 928-777-0403 | 777-0402 | 9-12 | Keri Milliken |
| Triumphant Learning Center | 201 E Main St | Safford, AZ | 85546-2051 | 928-348-8422 | 348-8423 | K-8 | Robin Dutt |
| Trivium Preparatory Academy | 925 N Sarival Ave | Goodyear, AZ | 85338-2318 | 623-414-4883 | 889-6286 | 6-12 | Dave Beskar |
| Tucson Collegiate Prep | 40 W Fort Lowell | Tucson, AZ | 85706 | 520-870-1670 | | 6-8 | Steve Campbell |
| Tucson Country Day S | 9239 E Wrightstown Rd | Tucson, AZ | 85715-5514 | 520-296-0883 | 290-1521 | K-8 | Dr. Deborah Anders |
| Tucson International Academy | 2700 W Broadway Blvd | Tucson, AZ | 85745 | 520-792-3255 | 792-3245 | K-12 | Jennifer Herrera |
| Tucson International Academy East Campus | 2700 W Broadway Blvd | Tucson, AZ | 85745 | 520-792-3255 | 792-3245 | K-10 | Peter Meehan |
| Tucson International Academy - Midvale | 2700 W Broadway Blvd | Tucson, AZ | 85745 | 520-792-3255 | 792-3245 | K-12 | Valarie Verdugo |
| Tucson International Academy West Campus | 2700 W Broadway Blvd | Tucson, AZ | 85745 | 520-792-3255 | 792-3245 | K-12 | Lin Wu |
| Tucson Preparatory S | 104 E Prince Rd | Tucson, AZ | 85705 | 520-622-4185 | 622-4755 | 9-12 | Jody Sullivan |
| Vail Academy and HS | 7762 E Science Park Dr | Tucson, AZ | 85747 | 520-879-1900 | 879-1901 | K-12 | Dennis Barger |
| Valley Academy - Charter S | 1520 W Rose Garden Ln | Phoenix, AZ | 85027-3529 | 623-516-7747 | 516-2703 | PK-8 | Victoria Wilber M.Ed. |
| Val Vista Academy | 4120 S Val Vista Dr | Gilbert, AZ | 85297 | 480-656-5555 | 689-5952 | K-8 | Teresa Buri |
| Vechij Himdag Mashchamakud | 168 S Skill Center Rd | Sacaton, AZ | 85147 | 520-562-3286 | | 9-12 | |
| Vector Prep and Arts Academy | 2020 N Arizona Ave | Chandler, AZ | 85225 | 480-779-2000 | 779-2100 | K-6 | Deborah Coleman |
| Verde Valley Montessori Charter S | PO Box 2678 | Cottonwood, AZ | 86326 | 928-634-3288 | 634-9781 | PK-8 | Maryann Green |
| Veritas Preparatory Academy | 3102 N 56th St Ste 200 | Phoenix, AZ | 85018-6606 | 602-263-1128 | 263-7997 | 6-12 | Douglas Minson |
| Victory HS | PO Box 8374 | Phoenix, AZ | 85066-8374 | 602-243-7583 | 243-7563 | 9-12 | Dr. Shirley Branham |
| Villa Montessori - Phoenix | 2802 E Meadowbrook Ave | Phoenix, AZ | 85016 | 602-955-2210 | 381-4017 | K-8 | Margo O'Neill |
| Vision Charter S | 5901 S Santa Cruz Calle | Tucson, AZ | 85709-6000 | 520-444-0241 | 741-8123 | 9-12 | |
| Visions Unlimited Academy | 1275 E Barney Ln | Benson, AZ | 85602-7955 | 520-586-8691 | 586-3074 | K-8 | Richard Valentine |
| Vista College Preparatory S | 812 S 6th Ave | Phoenix, AZ | 85003 | 602-374-7159 | 374-8201 | K-5 | Julia Meyerson |
| Vista Grove Preparatory Academy | 2929 E McKellips Rd | Mesa, AZ | 85213 | 480-924-1500 | 924-0552 | PK-9 | Abelardo Batista |
| Webster Basic S | 5399 N Pima Rd | Scottsdale, AZ | 85250 | 480-291-6900 | 291-6901 | K-6 | Vicki Dry |
| Webster Basic S | 7301 E Baseline Rd | Mesa, AZ | 85209-4907 | 480-986-2335 | 373-9176 | PK-6 | Kelly Wade |
| Western Institute Leadership Development | 1300 S Belvedere Ave | Tucson, AZ | 85711 | 520-615-2200 | 615-2112 | 9-12 | Judith Anderson |
| Western S of Science and Technology | 6515 W Indian School Rd | Phoenix, AZ | 85033 | 623-249-3900 | 243-9030 | 7-9 | Peter Boyle |
| Westland S | 4141 N 67th Ave | Phoenix, AZ | 85033-3314 | 623-247-6456 | 247-6520 | K-12 | |
| West Phoenix HS | 3835 W Thomas Rd | Phoenix, AZ | 85019-4434 | 602-269-1110 | 269-1112 | 9-12 | Alex Horton |
| Westwind Preparatory Academy | 2045 W Northern Ave | Phoenix, AZ | 85021-5157 | 602-864-7731 | 864-7720 | 6-12 | Debra Slagle |
| Whispering Wind Academy | 15844 N 43rd St | Phoenix, AZ | 85032-4124 | 602-449-7300 | 449-7305 | K-6 | Johnny Brownlie |
| Willow Creek Charter S | 2100 Willow Creek Rd | Prescott, AZ | 86301-5391 | 928-776-1212 | 776-0009 | K-8 | Terese Soto |
| Youngker HS | 3000 S Apache Rd | Buckeye, AZ | 85326-3998 | 623-474-0200 | 474-0141 | 9-12 | Randy Stillman |
| Young Scholars Academy | 1501 E Valencia Rd | Bullhead City, AZ | 86426 | 928-704-1100 | 704-1177 | K-8 | Tonnie Smith |
| Youth Works Charter HS | 1915 E 36th St | Tucson, AZ | 85713 | 520-623-5843 | | 9-12 | Scott Cordier |
| YouthWorks Charter HS - South | 1915 E 36th St | Tucson, AZ | 85713 | 520-495-4113 | 628-2820 | 9-12 | Jay Slauter |

## Arkansas

| School | Address | City,State | Zip code | Telephone | Fax | Grade | Contact |
|---|---|---|---|---|---|---|---|
| Academic Center of Excellence | 21 Funtastic Dr | Cabot, AR | 72023-6005 | 501-743-3520 | 843-0283 | 7-12 | Michele Evans |
| Academics Plus Charter ES | 900 Edgewood Dr | Maumelle, AR | 72113-6275 | 501-803-0666 | 803-9748 | K-6 | Diane Gross |
| Academics Plus Charter HS | 900 Edgewood Dr | Maumelle, AR | 72113-6275 | 501-851-3333 | 851-2599 | K-12 | Rob McGill |
| Arkansas Virtual Academy | 4702 W Commercial Dr Ste B3 | No Little Rock, AR | 72116 | 866-339-4951 | 664-4226 | K-10 | Dr. Scott Sides |
| Benton County HS of the Arts | 1110 W Poplar St | Rogers, AR | 72756 | 479-631-2787 | 899-6479 | 9-12 | Barbara Padgett |
| Benton County School of the Arts | 1110 W Poplar St | Rogers, AR | 72756 | 479-636-2272 | 636-5447 | K-8 | Dr. Renee Deshommes |
| Brunson New Vision Charter S | PO Box 1210 | Warren, AR | 71671-1210 | 870-226-2351 | 226-8541 | 4-5 | Regina Scroggins |
| Cloverdale Magnet MS | 6300 Hinkson Rd | Little Rock, AR | 72209-4712 | 501-447-2500 | 447-2501 | 6-8 | Wanda Ruffins |
| Covenant Keepers Charter S | 5615 Geyer Springs Rd | Little Rock, AR | 72209 | 501-682-7550 | 682-7577 | 6-8 | Dr. Valerie Tatum |
| Cross County Elementary Technology Acad | 2622 Highway 42 | Cherry Valley, AR | 72324-8674 | 870-588-3337 | 588-4454 | K-6 | Mindy Searcy |
| Cross County HS A New Tech S | 21 County Road 215 | Cherry Valley, AR | 72324-8957 | 870-588-3337 | 588-4606 | 7-12 | Stephen Prince |
| Eastside New Vision Charter S | PO Box 1210 | Warren, AR | 71671-1210 | 870-226-6761 | 226-8538 | K-3 | Sara Weaver |
| eStem Public Charter ES | 112 W 3rd St | Little Rock, AR | 72201-2702 | 501-748-9200 | 975-4092 | K-4 | Dr. Cindy Barton |
| eStem Public Charter HS | 123 W 3rd St | Little Rock, AR | 72201-2701 | 501-748-9335 | 748-9370 | 9-12 | Ruthie Walls |
| eStem Public Charter MS | 112 W 3rd St | Little Rock, AR | 72201-2702 | 501-748-9200 | 975-4092 | 5-8 | Dr. Cindy Barton |
| Exalt Academy Of Southwest Little Rock | 6111 W 83rd St | Little Rock, AR | 72209 | 501-568-3279 | 568-3286 | K-2 | Tina Long |
| Farmington Career Academy | 278 W Main St | Farmington, AR | 72730-2920 | 479-266-1860 | 267-6065 | 10-12 | Jon Purifoy |
| Flightline Upper Academy | 1030 Cannon Dr | No Little Rock, AR | 72114 | 501-988-1085 | 988-1090 | 5-8 | Evan McGrew |
| Haas Hall Academy | 3880 N Front St | Fayetteville, AR | 72703 | 479-966-4930 | 966-4932 | 8-12 | Dr. Martin Schoppmeyer |
| Imboden Area Charter S | PO Box 297 | Imboden, AR | 72434-0297 | 870-869-3015 | 869-3016 | K-8 | Judy Warren |
| Jacksonville Lighthouse Charter S | 251 N 1st St | Jacksonville, AR | 72076 | 501-985-1200 | 985-1201 | K-6 | Norman Whitfield |
| Jacksonville Lighthouse Coll Prep Acad | 251 N 1st St | Jacksonville, AR | 72076 | 501-985-1228 | 985-1233 | 7-12 | Will Felton |
| Jacksonville Lighthouse Flightline S | Bldg 1030 Cannon Dr | Jacksonville, AR | 72099 | 501-988-1085 | 988-1090 | 5-8 | Evan McGrew |
| KIPP Blytheville College Preparatory S | 1200 Byrum Rd | Blytheville, AR | 72315-8119 | 870-780-6333 | 780-6310 | 5-8 | Maisie Wright |
| KIPP Delta College Preparatory S | 514 Missouri | Helena, AR | 72342-3751 | 870-753-9444 | 753-9450 | 5-8 | Heather Saunders |
| KIPP Delta Collegiate High School | 320 Missouri | Helena, AR | 72342-3709 | 870-338-8138 | 338-8623 | 9-12 | Todd Dixon |
| KIPP Delta Elementary Literacy Academy | 215 Cherry St | Helena, AR | 72342 | 870-753-9800 | 753-9801 | K-4 | John Bennetts |
| Lisa Academy | 21 Corporate Hill Dr | Little Rock, AR | 72205-4537 | 501-227-4942 | 227-4952 | 6-12 | Ilker Fidan |
| Lisa Academy-North Little Rock | 5410 Landers Rd | No Little Rock, AR | 72117-1935 | 501-945-2727 | 945-2728 | K-12 | |
| Little Rock Prep Academy | 4520 S University Ave | Little Rock, AR | 72204-7739 | 501-683-1855 | 683-1847 | K-8 | Jennifer McMahan |
| Miner Academy | 800 School St | Bauxite, AR | 72011-9143 | 501-557-5453 | 557-2235 | 6-12 | Tyler Tarver |
| Northwest Arkansas Classical Academy | 1302 Melissa Dr Ste 100 | Bentonville, AR | 72712-7942 | 479-715-6662 | 821-7365 | K-8 | Timm Petersen |
| Osceola STEM Academy | 112 N School St | Osceola, AR | 72370-2413 | 870-563-2150 | 622-1025 | 5-8 | Christel Smith |
| Pea Ridge Manufacturing & Business Acad | 781 W Pickens | Pea Ridge, AR | 72751 | 479-451-0490 | | 11-12 | Charley Clark |
| Pine Bluff Lighthouse S | 708 W 2nd Ave | Pine Bluff, AR | 71601 | 870-534-0277 | 534-0263 | K-7 | Brent Mitchell |
| Premier HS of Little Rock | 1621 Dr Martin Luther King | Little Rock, AR | 72206 | 501-246-3161 | 677-0271 | 9-12 | Mia Meadows |
| Quest MS of Pine Bluff | 308 S Blake St | Pine Bluff, AR | 71601-3622 | 870-536-1063 | 676-0271 | 5-8 | Kasey Porchia |
| Quest MS of West Little Rock | 1815 Rahling Rd | Little Rock, AR | 72223 | 501-821-0382 | | 6-8 | Chris Stevens |

| School | Address | City,State | Zip code | Telephone | Fax | Grade | Contact |
|---|---|---|---|---|---|---|---|
| SIATech Little Rock | 6724 Interstate 30 | Little Rock, AR | 72209 | 501-562-0039 | 562-7671 | 9-12 | Katie Tatum |
| Washington Academy Charter S | 3512 Grand Ave | Texarkana, AR | 71854 | 870-772-4792 | 774-2185 | 7-12 | Terry Taylor |
| **California** | | | | | | | |
| Abraxis Charter HS | PO Box 2587 | Santa Rosa, CA | 95405-0587 | 707-539-2897 | 539-2778 | 9-12 | Martin Wilkes |
| Acacia Charter ES | 1016 E Bianchi Rd | Stockton, CA | 95210 | 209-477-7013 | 477-7015 | K-5 | Patricia Lingerfelt |
| Acacia Charter MS | 1605 E March Ln | Stockton, CA | 95210 | 209-477-7014 | 956-2182 | 6-8 | Theresa Johnson |
| Academia Avance Charter S | PO Box 42095 | Los Angeles, CA | 90042-0095 | 323-230-7270 | 652-0994 | 6-12 | Ricardo Mireles |
| Academia Moderna | 2410 Broadway | Walnut Park, CA | 90255-6342 | 323-923-0383 | 923-0380 | K-5 | Carrie Checca |
| Academies of the Antelope Valley | 6300 W Avenue L | Lancaster, CA | 93536-4540 | | | 7-12 | Chris Grado |
| Academy for Academic Excellence | 17500 Mana Rd | Apple Valley, CA | 92307-2181 | 760-946-5414 | 242-6398 | K-12 | Lisa Lamb |
| Academy of Alameda ES | 401 Pacific Ave | Alameda, CA | 94501 | 510-748-4017 | 523-5304 | K-5 | Nora Bullock |
| Academy of Alameda MS | 401 Pacific Ave | Alameda, CA | 94501 | 510-214-2460 | 523-5801 | 6-8 | Matt Huxley |
| Academy of Arts and Sciences | 1865 Herndon Ave | Clovis, CA | 93611 | 559-937-4227 | 329-4227 | K-12 | J.J. Lewis |
| Academy of Arts and Sciences | 4560 Alvarado Canyon Rd | San Diego, CA | 92120 | 619-937-4227 | 329-4227 | K-12 | JJ Lewis |
| Academy of Arts and Sciences | 900 Hampshire Rd Suite A | Westlake Vlg, CA | 91361 | 805-937-4227 | 329-4227 | K-12 | Elizabeth Oberreiter |
| Academy of Arts and Sciences: Sonoma | 7165 Burton Ave | Rohnert Park, CA | 94928 | 707-937-4227 | 329-4227 | K-12 | J.J. Lewis |
| Academy of Business Law & Education | 6515 Inglewood Ave | Stockton, CA | 95207-3871 | 209-478-1600 | 235-2986 | 9-12 | Matthew George |
| Academy of Careers & Exploration | PO Box 249 | Helendale, CA | 92342-0249 | 760-952-2396 | 952-1178 | K-12 | William Brown |
| Academy of Personalized Learning | 2195 Larkspur Ln | Redding, CA | 96002-0629 | 530-945-2892 | | K-12 | Patricia Dougherty |
| Academy of Science and Engineering | 5753 Rodeo Rd | Los Angeles, CA | 90016 | 323-545-1100 | 545-1102 | 9-11 | Teresa Henderson-Johnson |
| Accelerated Achievement Academy | 1059 N State St | Ukiah, CA | 95482-3413 | 707-463-7080 | 463-7085 | 4-12 | Selah Sawyer |
| Accelerated Charter ES | 119 E 37th St | Los Angeles, CA | 90011-2603 | 323-846-6694 | 846-0686 | K-6 | Susan Raudry |
| Accelerated S | 4000 S Main St | Los Angeles, CA | 90037-1022 | 323-235-6343 | 235-6346 | K-8 | Francis Reading |
| ACE Charter HS | 1776 Educational Park Dr | San Jose, CA | 95133 | 408-251-1362 | 251-1366 | 9-12 | Jahsve Worthy |
| ACE Charter HS | 570 Airport Way | Camarillo, CA | 93010-8500 | 805-437-1410 | 437-1491 | 9-12 | Ron Fisher |
| ACE Franklin McKinley MS | 1665 Santee Dr | San Jose, CA | 95122 | 408-426-6361 | | 5-7 | Cesar Torrico |
| ACE I Empower Academy | 625 S Sunset Ave | San Jose, CA | 95116 | 408-729-3920 | | 5-8 | Lorena Chavez |
| Achieve Academy | 303 Hegenberger Rd Ste 301 | Oakland, CA | 94621-1419 | 510-904-6440 | 904-6761 | 4-5 | Lucy Schmidt |
| Achieve Charter S of Paradise | 771 Elliott Rd | Paradise, CA | 95969-3913 | 530-872-4100 | 872-4105 | K-8 | Casey Taylor |
| Adelante Charter S of Santa Barbara | 1102 E Yanonali St | Santa Barbara, CA | 93103 | 805-966-7392 | 966-7243 | K-6 | Juanita Hernandez |
| Advanced Learning Academy | 335 E Walnut St | Santa Ana, CA | 92701 | 714-480-4300 | 480-4399 | K-8 | Kim Garcia |
| Alameda Community Learning Center | 1900 3rd St | Alameda, CA | 94501 | 510-521-7123 | 521-7350 | 6-12 | Patti Wilczek |
| Alder Grove Charter S | 714 F St | Eureka, CA | 95501-1036 | 707-268-0854 | 268-0813 | K-12 | J. Allen-San Giovanni |
| Alexander Science Center | 3737 S Figueroa St | Los Angeles, CA | 90007-4366 | 213-746-1995 | 746-7443 | K-5 | Norma Spencer |
| Alianza Charter S | 115 Casserly Rd | Watsonville, CA | 95076-9740 | 831-728-6333 | 728-6947 | K-8 | Rafael Ramirez |
| Alliance 6-12 College Ready Academy | 8926 Sunland Blvd | Sun Valley, CA | 91352 | 213-220-0451 | 943-4931 | 6-12 | Jonathan Tiongco |
| Alliance Alice Baxter College-Ready HS | 461 W 9th St | San Pedro, CA | 90731 | 310-221-0430 | | 9-12 | Robert Canosa-Carr |
| Alliance Bloomfield Technology HS | 7907 Santa Fe Ave | Huntington Park, CA | 90255 | 323-537-2060 | 537-2044 | 9-12 | Ani Meymerian |
| Alliance College-Ready Academy 16 | 1552 W Rockwood St | Los Angeles, CA | 90026 | 213-241-8533 | 943-4931 | 9-12 | Carmen Vazquez-Mancini |
| Alliance College-Ready Middle Academy 12 | 100 E 49th St | Los Angeles, CA | 90011 | 323-238-7270 | | 6-8 | Robin Manly |
| Alliance College-Ready Middle Academy 8 | 3651 E First St | Los Angeles, CA | 90063 | 323-269-2156 | | 6-8 | Melissa Chew |
| Alliance College-Ready Middle Academy 9 | 5886 Compton Ave | Los Angeles, CA | 90001 | 323-484-0450 | | 6-8 | Sandra Mejia |
| Alliance Collins Family College-Ready HS | 2071 Saturn Ave | Huntington Park, CA | 90255-3635 | 323-923-1588 | 923-1589 | 9-12 | Robert Delfino |
| Alliance Gertz-Ressler HS | 2023 S Union Ave | Los Angeles, CA | 90007-1326 | 213-745-8141 | 745-8142 | 6-12 | James Waller |
| Alliance Health Services Academy HS | 12226 S Western Ave | Los Angeles, CA | 90047-5240 | 323-972-9010 | 905-1578 | 9-12 | Carla McCullough |
| Alliance Leadership Middle Academy | 2941 W 70th St | Los Angeles, CA | 90043 | 323-920-4388 | | 6-8 | Sheri Johnson |
| Alliance Morgan McKinzie HS | 113 S Rowan Ave | Los Angeles, CA | 90063 | 323-859-0750 | 859-0758 | 9-12 | Arthur Sanchez |
| Alliance Neuwirth Leadership Academy | 4610 S Main St | Los Angeles, CA | 90037 | 323-342-2874 | 342-2875 | 9-12 | Miguel Gamboa |
| Alliance Ouchi-O'Donovan 6-12 Complex | 5356 5th Ave | Los Angeles, CA | 90043-2622 | 323-596-2290 | 596-2295 | 6-12 | Dea Tramble |
| All Tribes American Indian Charter S | PO Box 1432 | Valley Center, CA | 92082-1432 | 760-749-5982 | 749-4153 | PK-12 | Mary Ann Donohue |
| Almond Acres Charter Academy | 1601 L St | San Miguel, CA | 93451 | 805-467-2095 | 467-2098 | K-8 | Bob Bourgault |
| Alpha: Cindy Avitia HS | 1881 Cunningham Ave | San Jose, CA | 95122 | 408-758-1195 | 791-1558 | 9-10 | Will Eden |
| Alpha: Jose Hernandez MS | 1601 Cunningham Ave | San Jose, CA | 95122 | 408-780-0831 | | 6-8 | Hope Evans |
| Alpha Charter S | 7900 Eloise Ave | Elverta, CA | 95626 | 916-991-2244 | 991-0271 | 9-12 | Michael Borgaard |
| Alpha I Blanca Alvarado MS | 1601 Cunningham Ave | San Jose, CA | 95122 | 408-455-1223 | | 6-7 | John Glover |
| Alta Vista Charter S | 11988 Hesperia Rd Ste B | Hesperia, CA | 92345-1426 | 760-947-0006 | | K-12 | Ken Larson |
| Alta Vista Community Charter S | 173 Oak St | Auburn, CA | 95603 | 530-745-1220 | 885-7066 | K-5 | Patricia Leftridge |
| Alternative Coop Education Charter S | 400 Hemlock St | Vacaville, CA | 95688-2616 | 707-453-6245 | 448-7933 | K-6 | Gricelda Rodriguez |
| Alvarado Academy | 26247 Ellis St | Madera, CA | 93638-0813 | 559-675-2070 | 675-2074 | K-8 | Dr. Nicolas Retana |
| Alvina Charter ES | 295 W Saginaw Ave | Caruthers, CA | 93609-9710 | 559-864-9411 | 864-1808 | K-8 | Mike Iribarren |
| Ambassador Sanchez Charter S | 5659 E Kings Canyon Rd | Fresno, CA | 93727 | 559-470-8222 | | 9-12 | David Petropulos |
| American Indian Charter HS | PO Box 12063 | Oakland, CA | 94604-2363 | 510-482-6000 | 482-6002 | 9-12 | Maya Woods-Cadiz |
| American Indian Charter S | 3637 Magee Ave | Oakland, CA | 94619-1427 | 510-482-6000 | 482-6002 | 5-8 | Maya Woods-Cadiz |
| American Indian Charter S II | 171 12th St | Oakland, CA | 94607-4900 | 510-893-8701 | 893-0345 | 5-8 | Maya Woods-Cadiz |
| American River Charter S | 6620 Wentworth Springs Rd | Georgetown, CA | 95634-9701 | 530-333-8340 | 333-8346 | K-12 | Susan Whittington |
| Americas Finest Charter S | 730 45th St | San Diego, CA | 92102 | 619-694-4790 | 794-2762 | K-8 | Jan Perry |
| Anahuacalmecac Intl University Prep S | 4736 Huntington Dr S | Los Angeles, CA | 90032 | 323-352-3148 | 352-8758 | K-12 | |
| Anderson New Technology HS | 2098 North St | Anderson, CA | 96007-3477 | 530-365-3100 | 365-2957 | 9-12 | Carol Germano |
| Animo College Preparatory Academy | 2265 E 103rd St | Los Angeles, CA | 90002-3132 | 323-568-4136 | 568-4190 | 9-12 | Melodie West |
| Animo Ellen Ochoa Charter MS | 5156 Whittier Blvd | Los Angeles, CA | 90022 | 323-565-3245 | | 6-8 | Marco Duran |
| Animo Inglewood Charter HS | 3425 W Manchester Blvd | Inglewood, CA | 90305-2101 | 323-565-2100 | 565-2109 | 9-12 | Leilani Abulon |
| Animo Jackie Robinson Charter HS | 3500 S Hill St | Los Angeles, CA | 90007-4333 | 323-846-5800 | 846-8760 | 9-12 | Kristine Botello |
| Animo James B. Taylor Charter MS | 810 E 111th Place | Los Angeles, CA | 90059 | 323-568-8613 | 568-8617 | 6-8 | Cristina De Jesus |
| Animo Jefferson Charter MS | 1655 E 27th St | Los Angeles, CA | 90011-2202 | 323-232-1857 | 232-6505 | 6-8 | Cristina De Jesus |
| Animo Leadership Charter HS | 11044 S Freeman Ave | Inglewood, CA | 90304-2418 | 323-565-4420 | 565-4421 | 9-12 | Julio Murcia |
| Animo Mae Jemison Charter MS | 12700 Avalon Blvd | Los Angeles, CA | 90061 | 323-565-4450 | 754-1382 | 6-8 | Meghan Schooler |
| Animo Pat Brown Charter HS | 8255 Beach St | Los Angeles, CA | 90001-4014 | 323-585-3312 | 585-8985 | 9-12 | Joshua Hartford |
| Animo Phillis Wheatley Charter MS | 12226 S Western Ave | Los Angeles, CA | 90047 | 323-600-6099 | | 6-8 | Meghan Maguire |
| Animo Ralph Bunche Charter HS | 1655 E 27th St | Los Angeles, CA | 90011-2202 | 323-232-9436 | 232-9440 | 9-12 | Nancy Padilla-Flores |
| Animo South Los Angeles HS | 11100 S Western Ave | Los Angeles, CA | 90047-4845 | 323-779-0544 | 779-0565 | 9-12 | Taiala Carvalho |
| Animo Venice HS | 820 Broadway St | Venice, CA | 90291-3408 | 310-392-8751 | 392-8752 | 9-12 | Julio Murcia |
| Animo Watts Charter HS | 12628 Avalon Blvd | Los Angeles, CA | 90061-2728 | 323-756-3930 | 756-3947 | 9-12 | Abraham Devilliers |
| Animo Western Charter MS | 12226 S Western Ave | Los Angeles, CA | 90047-5240 | 323-600-6000 | 652-1849 | 6-8 | Antonio Garcia |
| Animo Westside Charter MS | 5456 McConnell Ave | Los Angeles, CA | 90066 | 323-565-3251 | 227-9739 | 6-8 | Lemuel Mosset |
| Annenberg HS | 4000 S Main St | Los Angeles, CA | 90037-1022 | 323-235-6343 | 235-6346 | 9-12 | Marcus Whilhite |
| Antelope Valley Learning Academy | 1240 Commerce Center Dr | Lancaster, CA | 93534 | 661-952-5520 | 940-9908 | K-12 | Erin Wade |
| Antioch Charter Academy | 3325 Hacienda Way | Antioch, CA | 94509-5407 | 925-755-7311 | 755-7313 | K-8 | Todd Heller |
| Antioch Charter Academy II | 1201 W 10th St | Antioch, CA | 94509-1406 | 925-755-1252 | 755-7527 | K-8 | Jeannie Dubitsky |
| Apple Academy Charter S | 4920 S Western Ave | Los Angeles, CA | 90062 | 323-348-4276 | | K-5 | Laurie Inman |
| Aptitud Community Academy at Goss | 2475 Van Winkle Ln | San Jose, CA | 95116-3758 | 408-928-7650 | 928-7651 | PK-7 | Natasha Wexler |
| Ararat Charter S | 6555 Sylmar Ave | Van Nuys, CA | 91401-6202 | 818-994-2904 | 994-8096 | K-5 | Eduardo Villela |
| ARISE HS | 3301 E 12th St Ste 205 | Oakland, CA | 94601-2940 | 510-436-5487 | 436-5493 | 9-12 | Mahru Elahi |
| Arroyo Paseo Charter HS | 3773 El Cajon Blvd | San Diego, CA | 92105 | 619-677-3017 | 677-3018 | 9-12 | Joe Bennett |
| Arroyo Vista Charter S | 2491 School House Rd | Chula Vista, CA | 91915-2534 | 619-656-9676 | 656-1858 | K-8 | Patricia Roth |
| Arts in Action Community Charter S | 1241 S Soto St | Los Angeles, CA | 90023-2652 | 323-266-4371 | 266-4371 | K-5 | Elysa Vargas |
| Arundel ES | 200 Arundel Rd | San Carlos, CA | 94070-1999 | 650-508-7311 | 508-7314 | K-4 | Ray Dawley |
| ASA Charter S | 3512 N E St | San Bernardino, CA | 92405-2110 | 909-475-3322 | 883-2708 | K-12 | Melissa Campbell |
| Aspire Alexander Twilight College Prep S | 2360 El Camino Ave | Sacramento, CA | 95821-5611 | 916-979-1788 | 979-1796 | K-5 | Jamie Wallen |
| Aspire Alexander Twilight Secondary Acad | 2360 El Camino Ave | Sacramento, CA | 95821-5611 | 916-979-1788 | 979-1796 | 6-12 | Robert Spencer |
| Aspire APEX Academy | 444 N American St | Stockton, CA | 95202 | 209-466-3861 | 466-4290 | K-5 | Melissa Brookens |
| Aspire Capitol Heights Academy | 2520 33rd St | Sacramento, CA | 95817-1943 | 916-739-8520 | 739-8529 | K-8 | Stephan Sanders |
| Aspire College Academy | 8030 Atherton St | Oakland, CA | 94605-3430 | 510-562-8030 | 562-8013 | K-5 | Jessica Newburn |
| Aspire Eres Academy | 1936 Courtland Ave | Oakland, CA | 94601-4614 | 510-436-9760 | 436-9765 | K-8 | Courtney Walker |
| Aspire Firestone Academy | 8929 Kauffman Ave | South Gate, CA | 90280-3422 | 323-249-5740 | 568-2017 | K-5 | Dustin Katch |
| Aspire Gateway Academy | 8929 Kauffman Ave | South Gate, CA | 90280-3422 | 323-249-5750 | 249-5759 | K-5 | Stefan Bean |
| Aspire Golden State College Prep Academy | 1009 66th Ave | Oakland, CA | 94621-3535 | 510-567-9631 | 632-1569 | 6-12 | Thomas Kadelbach |
| Aspire Inskeep Academy | 123 W 59th St | Los Angeles, CA | 90003-1103 | 323-235-8400 | 232-8030 | K-6 | Amy Coventry |
| Aspire Junior Collegiate Academy | 6724 S Alameda St | Huntington Park, CA | 90255-3617 | 323-583-5421 | | K-5 | Mallory Barnes |
| Aspire Langston Hughes Academy | 2050 West Ln | Stockton, CA | 95205-3358 | 209-943-2389 | 943-2901 | 6-12 | Anthony Solina |
| Aspire Lugo Academy | 6100 Carmelita Ave | Huntington Park, CA | 90255 | 323-585-1153 | 585-1283 | K-5 | Sandra Kim |
| Aspire Ollin University Prep Academy | 2540 E 58th St | Huntington Park, CA | 90255 | 323-277-2901 | | 6-12 | Jennifer Garcia |
| Aspire Pacific College Prep Academy | 2565 E 58th St | Huntington Park, CA | 90255-2606 | 323-589-2800 | 589-2802 | 10-12 | John Zapata |
| Aspire Port City Academy | 2040 West Ln | Stockton, CA | 95205-3358 | 209-943-2389 | 943-2901 | K-5 | Shelby Scheideman |
| Aspire Richmond CA College Prep Academy | 3040 Hilltop Mall Rd | Richmond, CA | 94806 | 510-646-1696 | | 8-12 | Javier Walteros |
| Aspire Richmond Technology Academy | 3040 Hilltop Mall Rd | Richmond, CA | 94806 | 510-480-0660 | | K-5 | Arlena Ford |
| Aspire River Oaks Charter S | 1801 Pyrenees Ave | Stockton, CA | 95210-5207 | 209-956-8100 | 956-8102 | K-5 | Kris Jamison |
| Aspire Slauson Academy | 123 W 59th St | Los Angeles, CA | 90003-1103 | 323-235-8400 | 232-8030 | K-6 | Paul Delgado |
| Aspire Tate Academy | 123 W 59th St | Los Angeles, CA | 90003-1103 | 323-235-8400 | 583-7271 | K-6 | Ana Martinez |
| Aspire Titan Academy | 6720 S Alameda St | Huntington Park, CA | 90255-3617 | 323-583-5421 | 588-7342 | K-5 | Kim Benaraw |
| Aspire Triumph Technology Academy | 3200 62nd Ave | Oakland, CA | 94605 | 510-638-9445 | 638-0744 | K-5 | Jessica Chacon |
| Aspire University Charter S | 3313 Coffee Rd | Modesto, CA | 95355-1534 | 209-544-8722 | 544-8864 | K-5 | Laura Thompson |
| Aspire Vanguard College Prep Acad | 5255 1st St | Empire, CA | 95319 | 209-269-9977 | 538-1620 | 6-12 | Salvador Padilla |
| Aspire Vincent Shalvey Academy | 10038 N Highway 99 | Stockton, CA | 95212-2127 | 209-931-5399 | 931-5185 | K-5 | Karla Fachner |
| Assurance Learning Academy | 5701 S Western Ave | Los Angeles, CA | 90062 | 323-272-1225 | 945-2430 | K-12 | Jeffrey Martineau |
| Audeo Charter S | 10170 Huennekens St | San Diego, CA | 92121-2964 | 858-678-2050 | 552-9394 | 6-12 | Tim Tuter |

| School | Address | City,State | Zip code | Telephone | Fax | Grade | Contact |
|---|---|---|---|---|---|---|---|
| Aveson Global Leadership Acadmey | 1919 Pinecrest Dr | Altadena, CA | 91001-2116 | 626-797-1440 | 797-1918 | 6-12 | Kate Bean |
| Aveson School of Leaders | 1919 Pinecrest Dr | Altadena, CA | 91001-2116 | 626-797-1440 | 797-1918 | K-5 | Kate Bean |
| Bachrodt Charter Academy | 102 Sonora Ave | San Jose, CA | 95110-1499 | 408-535-6211 | 535-6588 | K-5 | Rigo Palacios |
| Ballington Academy for the Arts/Sciences | 1525 W Main St | El Centro, CA | 92243-2211 | 760-353-0140 | 353-0745 | K-6 | Doreen Mulz |
| Banks Charter S | PO Box 80 | Pala, CA | 92059-0080 | 760-742-3300 | 742-3102 | K-5 | Eric Kosch |
| Barona Indian Charter S | 1095 Barona Rd | Lakeside, CA | 92040-1516 | 619-443-0948 | 443-7280 | K-8 | Josh Stepner |
| Bay Area Technology S | 8251 Fontaine St | Oakland, CA | 94605-4109 | 510-382-9932 | 382-9934 | 6-12 | Hayri Hatipoglu |
| Baypoint Preparatory Academy | 26089 Girard St | Hemet, CA | 95244 | 951-658-1700 | 658-0723 | K-12 | Nancy Spencer |
| Bayshore Prep Charter S | 1175 Linda Vista Dr | San Marcos, CA | 92078-3811 | 760-471-0847 | 736-0275 | K-12 | Nancy Spencer |
| Bayside Community Day S | 24521 Cactus Ave | Moreno Valley, CA | 92553 | 951-571-7890 | 571-7891 | 6-12 | Dr. Henry Herreras |
| Bay View Academy | 222 Casa Verde Way | Monterey, CA | 93940 | 831-751-3142 | | K-5 | Catherine Glick |
| Beacon Classical Academy | 2400 Euclid Ave | National City, CA | 91950 | 619-267-5500 | | K-8 | Alma Van Nice |
| Beckford Charter S for Enriched Studies | 19130 Tulsa St | Northridge, CA | 91326-2698 | 818-360-1924 | 832-9831 | K-5 | Shelly Brower |
| Bella Mente Montessori Academy | 1737 W Vista Way | Vista, CA | 92083 | 760-621-8948 | 639-0611 | K-8 | Erin Feeley |
| Bellevue-Sante Fe Charter S | 1401 San Luis Bay Dr | San Luis Obispo, CA | 93405-8007 | 805-595-7169 | 595-9013 | K-6 | Brian Getz |
| Berkley Maynard Academy | 6200 San Pablo Ave | Oakland, CA | 94608-2228 | 510-658-2900 | 658-1013 | K-8 | Jay Stack |
| Big Picture HS - Fresno | 1207 S Trinity St | Fresno, CA | 93706-2611 | 559-420-1234 | | 7-12 | Pasquale Catanzarite |
| Big Sur Charter S | PO Box 138 | Big Sur, CA | 93920-0138 | 831-667-0203 | 884-5454 | K-12 | Shawna Garritson |
| Binkley ES | 4965 Canyon Dr | Santa Rosa, CA | 95409-3204 | 707-539-6060 | 539-4862 | PK-6 | Kelly Lister |
| Birmingham Community HS | 17000 Haynes St | Van Nuys, CA | 91406-5499 | 818-758-5200 | 342-5877 | 9-12 | Bill Parks |
| Bitney College Prep HS | 135 Joerschke Dr | Grass Valley, CA | 95945-5249 | 530-477-1235 | 272-1091 | 9-12 | Russ Jones |
| Blue Oak Charter S | 450 W East Ave | Chico, CA | 95926 | 530-879-7483 | 879-7490 | K-8 | Nathan Rose |
| Bowling Green Chacon Language & Science | 6807 Franklin Blvd | Sacramento, CA | 95823 | 916-433-7321 | 433-7388 | PK-6 | Sylvia Silva-Torres |
| Bowling Green McCoy Academy | 4211 Turnbridge Dr | Sacramento, CA | 95823-1929 | 916-433-5426 | 433-5429 | K-6 | Susan Gibson |
| Bowman Charter S | 13777 Bowman Rd | Auburn, CA | 95603-3196 | 530-885-1974 | 888-8175 | K-8 | Kelly Graham |
| Bridges Academy | 1702 McLaughlin Ave | San Jose, CA | 95122-2936 | 408-283-6400 | 283-6419 | 7-8 | Alex Frontini |
| BRIDGES Charter S | 1335 Calle Bouganvilla | Thousand Oaks, CA | 91360-6604 | 805-492-3560 | | K-8 | Jay Guidetti |
| Bright Star Secondary Academy | 2636 S Mansfield Ave | Los Angeles, CA | 90016-3512 | 424-789-8337 | | 9-12 | Monique Bonilla |
| Brittan Acres ES | 2000 Belle Ave | San Carlos, CA | 94070-3798 | 650-508-7307 | 508-7310 | K-4 | John Triska |
| Buckingham Charter Magnet HS | 188 Bella Vista Rd Ste B | Vacaville, CA | 95687-5413 | 707-453-7300 | 453-7303 | 9-12 | |
| Bullis Charter S | 102 W Portola Ave | Los Altos, CA | 94022-1210 | 650-947-4939 | 947-4989 | K-8 | Wanny Hersey |
| Burton Pathways Charter Academy | 1414 W Olive Ave | Porterville, CA | 93257 | 559-782-4748 | 782-4708 | 9-12 | Jan Mekeel |
| Burton Technology Academy HS | 10101 S Broadway | Los Angeles, CA | 90003-4534 | 323-920-6125 | 920-6950 | 9-12 | Rogelio Sanchez |
| Butterfield Charter HS | 600 W Grand Ave | Porterville, CA | 93257-2029 | 559-782-7057 | 782-7090 | 9-12 | Staci Phipps |
| Cain MS | 150 Palm Ave | Auburn, CA | 95603-3712 | 530-823-6106 | 823-0943 | 6-8 | Scott Bentley |
| Calahan Community Charter S | 18722 Knapp St | Northridge, CA | 91324-3099 | 818-886-4612 | 886-0760 | K-5 | Michelle Wells |
| Caliber: Beta Academy | 4301 Berk Ave | Richmond, CA | 94804 | 510-685-1768 | | K-6 | Natalie Walchuk |
| Cali Calmecac Language Academy | 9491 Starr Rd | Windsor, CA | 95492-9460 | 707-837-7747 | 837-7752 | K-8 | Jeanne Acuna |
| California Academy for Liberal Studies | 7350 N Figueroa St | Los Angeles, CA | 90041 | 213-239-0063 | 254-4099 | 9-12 | Connie Rivas |
| California Academy for Liberal Studies | 7350 N Figueroa St | Los Angeles, CA | 90041 | 323-254-4427 | 254-4099 | 6-8 | Nancy Villagomez |
| CA Connections Academy @ North Bay | 20932 Big Canyon Rd | Middletown, CA | 95461 | 949-306-8498 | | K-12 | Richard Savage |
| California Connections Academy @ Ripon | 580 N Wilma Ave | Ripon, CA | 95366 | 209-253-1208 | 253-0406 | PK-12 | Amy Hunt |
| California Heritage Youthbuild Academy | 8544 Airport Rd | Redding, CA | 96002-9210 | 530-378-5254 | 378-5256 | 9-12 | Cathy Taylor |
| California Military Institute | 755 N A St | Perris, CA | 92570 | 951-443-2731 | 943-0473 | 6-12 | Michael Rhodes |
| California Montessori Project-Amer River | 6838 Kermit Ln | Fair Oaks, CA | 95628-3048 | 916-864-0081 | 864-0084 | K-8 | Radene Girola |
| California Montessori Project-Capitol | 2635 Chestnut Hill Dr | Sacramento, CA | 95826-2912 | 916-325-0910 | 325-0912 | K-8 | Bernie Evangelista |
| California Montessori Project-Elk Grove | 8828 Elk Grove Blvd Ste 4 | Elk Grove, CA | 95624-1875 | 916-714-9699 | 714-9703 | K-8 | Kathleen Merz |
| California Montessori Project-Orangevale | 6545 Beech Ave | Orangevale, CA | 95662 | 916-673-9389 | 673-9396 | K-6 | Kim Aldridge |
| California Montessori Project-Shingl Spr | 4645 Buckeye Rd | Shingle Springs, CA | 95682-9505 | 530-672-3095 | 672-3097 | K-8 | Kim Zawilski |
| California Pacific Charter S | PO Box 8 | Warner Springs, CA | 92086 | 855-225-7227 | | K-12 | Lisa Newhall |
| California Prep Sutter 8-12 | 15898 Central St | Meridian, CA | 95957 | | | 8-12 | Chiara Hilborn |
| California Prep Sutter K-7 | 15898 Central St | Meridian, CA | 95957 | | | K-7 | Anne Haney |
| California Virtual Academies | 2360 Shasta Way Ste A | Simi Valley, CA | 93065-1800 | 805-581-0202 | 581-0330 | K-12 | Katrina Abston |
| Camarillo Academy of Progressive Educ | 777 Aileen St | Camarillo, CA | 93010 | 805-384-1415 | 385-1473 | K-8 | MaryEllen Lang |
| Camino Nuevo Academy #2 | 1575 W 2nd St | Los Angeles, CA | 90026 | 213-736-5542 | 736-5664 | K-8 | Heather McManus |
| Camino Nuevo Academy - Cisneros | 1018 Mohawk St | Los Angeles, CA | 90026-3131 | 213-353-5300 | 596-3878 | K-8 | Shannon Leonard |
| Camino Nuevo Charter Academy | 697 S Burlington Ave | Los Angeles, CA | 90057 | 213-736-5542 | 736-5664 | PK-8 | Mark Healy |
| Camino Nuevo Charter HS | 1215 Miramar St | Los Angeles, CA | 90026 | 213-240-8700 | | 9-12 | Marisol Pineda-Conde |
| Camino Nuevo Charter HS 2 | 3500 W Temple St | Los Angeles, CA | 90004-3620 | 213-736-5566 | 736-5066 | 9-12 | Julie Jhun |
| Camino Nuevo Charter S Burlington Campus | 697 S Burlington Ave | Los Angeles, CA | 90057-3743 | 213-413-4245 | 413-8553 | K-8 | Mark Healy |
| Camino Nuevo ES - Jose Castellanos | 1723 Cordova St | Los Angeles, CA | 90007 | 323-730-7160 | 737-5626 | K-5 | Yvonne Carrillo |
| Camino Science & Natural Rsrcs Charter S | 3060 Snows Rd | Camino, CA | 95709-9578 | 530-644-2204 | 644-5412 | K-8 | Boyd Holler |
| Camptonville Academy | 321 16th St | Marysville, CA | 95901-4223 | 530-742-2786 | 742-6067 | K-12 | Christopher Mahurin |
| Canyon ES | 421 Entrada Dr | Santa Monica, CA | 90402-1303 | 310-454-7510 | 454-7543 | K-5 | Nicole Sheard |
| Capistrano Connections Academy | 33272 Valle Rd | San Juan Capo, CA | 92675 | 949-461-1667 | | K-12 | Richard Savage |
| Capitol Collegiate Academy | 2118 Meadowview Rd | Sacramento, CA | 95832-1212 | 916-476-5796 | | K-8 | Penny Schwinn |
| Capitol Heights Academy | 2520 33rd St | Sacramento, CA | 95817 | 916-739-8520 | 739-8529 | K-5 | Stephan Sanders |
| Carpenter Community Charter S | 3909 Carpenter Ave | Studio City, CA | 91604-3793 | 818-761-4363 | 508-6724 | K-5 | Joseph Martinez |
| Carver S of Arts & Sciences | 10101 Systems Pkwy | Sacramento, CA | 95827-3007 | 916-228-5751 | 228-5760 | 9-12 | Allegra Alessandri |
| Casa Ramona Academy for Technology | 1524 W 7th St | San Bernardino, CA | 92411-2508 | 909-888-3132 | | K-12 | Esther Ramos Estrada |
| Castlemont Junior Academy | 8601 MacArthur Blvd Ste 300 | Oakland, CA | 94605 | 510-775-0900 | 277-9089 | 6-8 | Lisa Haynes |
| Castlemont Primary Academy | 8601 MacArthur Blvd Ste 300 | Oakland, CA | 94605 | 510-775-0900 | 277-9089 | K-5 | Lisa Haynes |
| Castle Rock Charter S | 1260 Glenn St | Crescent City, CA | 95531-2113 | 707-464-0390 | 464-9606 | K-12 | Jeff Slayton |
| Cecil Avenue Math & Science Academy | 1430 Cecil Ave | Delano, CA | 93215-1444 | 661-721-5030 | 721-5097 | 6-8 | Darrell Hennessee |
| Ceiba College Preparatory Academy | 260 W Riverside Dr | Watsonville, CA | 95076 | 831-345-6056 | 464-3213 | 6-12 | Tom Brown |
| Celerity Cardinal Charter S | 7330 Bakman Ave | Sun Valley, CA | 91352 | 323-223-9184 | 688-3835 | K-5 | Wilbur Estrada |
| Celerity Dyad Charter S | 4501 Wadsworth Ave | Los Angeles, CA | 90011-3637 | 323-231-1202 | 231-1255 | K-8 | Patrick Stickley |
| Celerity Nascent Charter S | 3417 W Jefferson Blvd | Los Angeles, CA | 90018-3235 | 323-732-6613 | 733-2977 | K-8 | Sergio Alvarez Ruiz |
| Celerity Octavia Charter S | 3010 Estara Ave | Los Angeles, CA | 90065-2205 | 310-904-2012 | 843-9912 | K-8 | Daniela Gapezzani |
| Celerity Palmati Charter S | 6501 Laurel Canyon Blvd | North Hollywood, CA | 91606-1520 | 818-753-2712 | 301-2278 | K-6 | Titchamroeun Son |
| Celerity Sirius Charter S | 310 E El Segundo Blvd | Compton, CA | 90222-2315 | 310-764-1234 | 868-2517 | K-5 | Jason Rios |
| Celerity Troika Charter S | 1495 Colorado Blvd | Los Angeles, CA | 90041-2366 | 323-344-0160 | 344-0165 | K-8 | Karina Solis |
| Centennial College Preparatory Academy | 2079 Saturn Ave | Huntington Park, CA | 90255-3635 | 323-826-9616 | 588-7342 | 6-7 | Jesicah Rolapp |
| Center for Advanced Learning | 4016 S Central Ave | Los Angeles, CA | 90011-2708 | 323-232-0245 | 233-3675 | K-5 | Brooke Jackson |
| Center for Advanced Research Technology | 2555 Clovis Ave | Clovis, CA | 93612-3901 | 559-248-7400 | 248-7423 | 11-12 | Rick Watson |
| Central California Connections Academy | 4020 S Demaree St Ste B | Visalia, CA | 93277 | 559-713-1324 | 713-1330 | K-12 | Richard Savage |
| Central City Value S | 221 N Westmoreland Ave | Los Angeles, CA | 90004-4815 | 213-471-4686 | 471-4693 | 9-12 | Joaquin Arroyo |
| Century Academy for Excellence | 2400 W 85th St | Inglewood, CA | 90305-1816 | 323-752-8834 | 752-8874 | 6-8 | Giselle Edman |
| Century Community Charter S | 901 Maple St | Inglewood, CA | 90301-3823 | 310-412-2286 | 412-4085 | 6-8 | Dana Means |
| Cesar Chavez Language Academy | 2750 W Steele Ln | Santa Rosa, CA | 95403 | 707-528-5011 | 528-5012 | K-8 | Francisco Gonzalez |
| Charter Alternatives Academy | 28050 Road 148 | Visalia, CA | 93292 | 559-730-7491 | 730-7490 | 7-12 | Carlos Peralta |
| Charter Alternative S | 6520 Oak Dell Rd | El Dorado, CA | 95623-4322 | 530-622-6984 | 621-2543 | K-8 | David Publicover |
| Charter Community S and Home Study Acad | 6767 Green Valley Rd | Placerville, CA | 95667-8984 | 530-295-2259 | 642-0492 | 7-12 | David Publicover |
| Charter HS of Arts Multimedia/Performing | 6842 Van Nuys Blvd | Van Nuys, CA | 91405 | 818-994-7614 | 994-0099 | 9-12 | Christopher Bright Ph.D. |
| Charter Home School Academy | 211 W Tulare Ave | Visalia, CA | 93277 | 559-730-7916 | 735-8060 | K-8 | Steve Rodriguez |
| Charter Montessori ES Blue Oak Campus | 2391 Merrychase Dr | Cameron Park, CA | 95682-9094 | 530-676-0164 | 676-0758 | K-5 | Paul Stewart |
| Charter S of Morgan Hill | 9530 Monterey Rd | Morgan Hill, CA | 95037-9356 | 408-463-0618 | 463-0267 | K-8 | Paige Cisewski |
| Charter S of San Diego | 10170 Huennekens St | San Diego, CA | 92121-2964 | 858-678-2020 | 552-6660 | 7-12 | Ginese Quann |
| Chatsworth Charter HS | 10027 Lurline Ave | Chatsworth, CA | 91311-3199 | 818-678-3400 | 709-6952 | 9-12 | Dr. Timothy Guy Ed.D. |
| Chawanakee Academy | PO Box 210 | O Neals, CA | 93645 | 559-868-4200 | 868-4222 | K-12 | Gary Talley |
| Chicago Park Community Charter S | 15725 Mount Olive Rd | Grass Valley, CA | 95945-7906 | 530-346-2153 | 346-8559 | K-8 | Dan Zeisler |
| Chico Country Day S | 102 W 11th St | Chico, CA | 95928-6006 | 530-895-2650 | 895-9159 | K-8 | Megan Neely |
| Children of Promise Preparatory Academy | 3130 W 111th Pl | Inglewood, CA | 90303-2315 | 310-677-3014 | 677-1599 | K-3 | Carleton Lincoln |
| Children's Community Charter S | 6830 Pentz Rd | Paradise, CA | 95969-2902 | 530-877-2227 | 872-1396 | K-8 | Emily Mullins |
| CHIME Institute's Schwarzenegger Cmnty S | 19722 Collier St | Woodland Hills, CA | 91364-3618 | 818-346-5100 | 346-5120 | K-8 | Jennifer Hill |
| Chrysalis Charter S | PO Box 709 | Palo Cedro, CA | 96073-0709 | 530-547-9726 | 547-9734 | K-8 | Irene Salter |
| Chula Vista Learning Community Charter S | 590 K St | Chula Vista, CA | 91911-1118 | 619-426-2885 | 426-3048 | PK-12 | Dr. Jorge Ramirez |
| Cielo Vista Charter S | 650 S Paseo Dorotea | Palm Springs, CA | 92264-1499 | 760-416-8250 | 416-8253 | K-6 | Devlin Clinton |
| Circle of Independent Learning | 4700 Calaveras Ave | Fremont, CA | 94538-1124 | 510-797-0100 | 797-0118 | K-12 | Stephanie Lytle |
| Citizens of the World 2 Charter S | 5620 De Longpre Ave | Los Angeles, CA | 90028 | 323-464-4063 | 372-3847 | K-4 | Dr. Ramona Patrick |
| Citizens of the World 3 Charter S | 11561 Gateway Blvd | Los Angeles, CA | 90064 | 310-391-6611 | 775-4122 | K-5 | Alison Kerr |
| Citizens of the World Charter S | 1316 N Bronson Ave | Hollywood, CA | 90028 | 323-464-4292 | 464-8292 | K-4 | Marissa Berman |
| City Arts & Technology HS | 325 La Grande Ave | San Francisco, CA | 94112-2866 | 415-841-2200 | 695-5326 | 9-12 | Brianna Winn |
| City Heights Preparatory Academy | 3770 Altadena Ave | San Diego, CA | 92105-3007 | 619-795-3137 | | 6-12 | Dr. Marnie Nair |
| City HS | 11625 W Pico Blvd | Los Angeles, CA | 90064 | 310-273-2489 | 273-2499 | 9-12 | Sherri Werner |
| City Honors Charter HS | 120 W Regent St | Inglewood, CA | 90301 | 310-680-4880 | 680-5144 | 9-12 | Thelma Brown |
| City Language Immersion Charter S | 4041 Hilcrest Dr | Los Angeles, CA | 90008 | 323-294-4937 | 294-4938 | K-5 | Raul Alarcon |
| City S | 11625 W Pico Blvd | Los Angeles, CA | 90064-2908 | 310-273-2489 | 273-2499 | 6-8 | Sheri Werner |
| Civicorps Academy | 101 Myrtle St | Oakland, CA | 94607-2543 | 510-992-7800 | 992-7950 | 9-12 | Tessa Nicholas |
| Classical Academy | 2950 Bear Valley Pkwy S | Escondido, CA | 92025-7446 | 760-546-0101 | 739-8289 | K-8 | Cameron Curry |
| Classical Academy HS | 207 E Pennsylvania Ave | Escondido, CA | 92025 | 760-480-9845 | 739-8289 | 9-12 | Dana Moen |
| Clayton Valley Charter HS | 1101 Alberta Way | Concord, CA | 94521-3747 | 925-682-7474 | 825-7859 | 9-12 | Jeff Eben |
| Clear Passage Educational Center | 1471 Martin Luther King Jr | Long Beach, CA | 90813 | 888-502-1116 | | 9-12 | Vivianna Trujillo |
| Clemente Charter S | 5701 Fishburn Ave | Maywood, CA | 90270 | 323-984-9008 | | PK-5 | Norma Moreno |
| Cleveland HS | 8140 Vanalden Ave | Reseda, CA | 91335-1199 | 818-885-2300 | 727-0964 | 9-12 | Cindy Duong |
| Clovis Online S / Enterprise | 1655 David E Cook Way | Clovis, CA | 93611 | 559-327-4400 | 327-4490 | K-12 | Kevin Cookingham |
| Coastal Academy Charter | 4096 Calle Platino | Oceanside, CA | 92056 | 760-631-4020 | 631-4027 | K-8 | Marcy Cashin |

| School | Address | City,State | Zip code | Telephone | Fax | Grade | Contact |
|---|---|---|---|---|---|---|---|
| Coastal Grove Charter S | PO Box 510 | Arcata, CA | 95518-0510 | 707-825-8804 | 825-1761 | K-8 | Bettina Eipper |
| Cole Academy | 333 E Walnut St | Santa Ana, CA | 92701-5928 | 714-836-9023 | 836-9041 | K-5 | Jon Norton |
| Coleman Tech HS | 3540 Aero Ct | San Diego, CA | 92123 | 858-874-4338 | 874-5645 | 9-12 | Dr. Neil McCurdy |
| Colfax Charter ES | 11724 Addison St | North Hollywood, CA | 91607-3202 | 818-761-5115 | 985-6017 | K-5 | Robyn Friedman |
| College and Career Preparatory Academy | 1669 E Wilshire Ave Ste 603 | Santa Ana, CA | 92705 | 714-547-9986 | | 9-12 | Byron Fairchild |
| College Bridge Academy | 2824 S Main St | Los Angeles, CA | 90007 | 323-249-7845 | 249-1170 | 9-12 | Noel Trout |
| College Connection Academy | 1855 Lucretia Ave | San Jose, CA | 95122 | 408-347-4827 | | 7-8 | Amber Andrade |
| College Preparatory MS | 5150 Jackson Dr | La Mesa, CA | 91942-9001 | 619-303-2782 | 303-3759 | 5-8 | Christina Callaway |
| College Prep HS | 26400 Dartmouth St | Hemet, CA | 92544-6302 | 951-925-5155 | | 9-12 | Frank Green |
| College Ready Middle Academy #4 | 9719 S Main St | Los Angeles, CA | 90003-4135 | 323-451-3009 | 455-1655 | 6-8 | Darron Evans |
| College Ready Middle Academy #5 | 211 S Avenue 20 | Los Angeles, CA | 90031-2508 | 323-352-8034 | 352-8980 | 6-8 | Suzette Torres |
| Collegiate Charter HS | 312 N Record Ave | Los Angeles, CA | 90063 | 213-304-7077 | | 9-12 | Vanessa Jackson |
| Collins School at Cherry Valley | 1001 Cherry St | Petaluma, CA | 94952-2065 | 707-778-4740 | 778-4839 | K-8 | Fran Hansell |
| Come Back Kids Charter S | 3939 13th St | Riverside, CA | 92501 | 951-826-6454 | | 9-12 | Debra Sacks |
| Community Charter Early College HS | 11500 Eldridge Ave | Lake View Ter, CA | 91342-6522 | 818-485-0951 | 485-0952 | 9-12 | Jennifer Reyes |
| Community Charter MS | 11500 Eldridge Ave | Lake View Ter, CA | 91342-6522 | 818-485-0933 | 485-0940 | 6-8 | Dr. Ron Alatorre |
| Community Collaborative Charter S | 32248 Crown Valley Rd | Acton, CA | 93510 | 760-494-9646 | 897-7558 | K-12 | Ryan Woodard |
| Community Collaborative Charter S | 5715 Skvarla Ave | McClellan, CA | 95652 | 916-286-5161 | 643-2031 | K-12 | Jon Campbell |
| Community Magnet ES | 11301 Bellagio Rd | Los Angeles, CA | 90049-1705 | 310-476-2281 | 472-6391 | K-5 | Carla Cretaro |
| Community Outreach Academy | 5640 Dudley Blvd | McClellan, CA | 95652 | 916-286-1950 | 640-0227 | K-6 | Larissa Gonchar |
| Community Outreach Academy | 3800 Bolivar Ave | North Highlands, CA | 95660 | 916-286-1908 | 286-1992 | 7-8 | Yuliya Hall |
| Community Preparatory Academy | 7511 Raymond Ave | Los Angeles, CA | 90044 | 323-751-1460 | 704-3045 | K-5 | Janis Bucknor |
| Community Preparatory Academy | 3717 S La Brea Ave # 106 | Los Angeles, CA | 90016 | 323-487-9227 | 704-3045 | 6-8 | |
| Community Roots Academy | 23431 Knollwood | Aliso Viejo, CA | 92656 | 949-831-4272 | | K-8 | Jeremy Cavallaro |
| Community S for Creative Education | 2111 International Blvd | Oakland, CA | 94606 | 510-517-0331 | | K-8 | Kathryn Wilson |
| Competitive Edge Charter Academy | 34450 Stonewood Dr | Yucaipa, CA | 92399-6852 | 909-790-3207 | 790-8364 | K-8 | Joe Mead |
| Connect Community Charter S | 635 Oakside Ave | Redwood City, CA | 94063 | 650-562-7190 | 562-7191 | K-8 | Alicia Yamashita |
| Connecting Waters Charter S | 12420 Bentley St | Waterford, CA | 95386-9158 | 209-874-9463 | 874-9531 | K-12 | Sherri Nelson |
| Connections VPA Academy | 17555 Tuolumne Rd | Tuolumne, CA | 95379-9701 | 209-928-4228 | 928-1422 | 7-12 | Diana Harford |
| Conservatory of Vocal/Instrumental Arts | 3800 Mountain Blvd | Oakland, CA | 94619 | 510-285-7511 | | K-8 | Carolynn Jennings |
| Conservatory Vocal Instrumental Arts HS | 3637 Magee Ave | Oakland, CA | 94619 | 510-328-1119 | | 9-12 | Valerie Abad |
| CORE Butte Charter S | 260 Cohasset Rd Ste 120 | Chico, CA | 95926-2282 | 530-894-3952 | 566-9819 | K-12 | Jonelle Pena |
| CORE Placer Charter S | 1033 S Auburn St | Colfax, CA | 95713 | 530-346-8340 | 346-2446 | K-12 | Julie Haycock |
| Cornerstone Academy Preparatory | 1598 Lucretia Ave | San Jose, CA | 95122-3817 | 408-361-3876 | | K-6 | Shara Hegde |
| Corona Charter S | 9400 Remick Ave | Pacoima, CA | 91331-4223 | 818-834-5805 | 834-8075 | 6-8 | Diana Gamez |
| Cottonwood Creek Charter S | 3425 Brush St | Cottonwood, CA | 96022 | 530-347-7200 | 347-9375 | K-8 | Mark Boyle |
| County Collaborative Charter S | 3291 Buckman Springs Rd | Pine Valley, CA | 91962 | 858-472-5222 | | K-12 | Ryan Woodard |
| Cox Academy | 9860 Sunnyside St | Oakland, CA | 94603-2750 | 510-904-6300 | 904-6730 | K-5 | Kevin King |
| Creative Arts Charter S | 1601 Turk St | San Francisco, CA | 94115-4527 | 415-749-3509 | 749-3437 | K-8 | Paul Greenwood |
| Creative Connections Arts Academy | 7201 Arutas Dr | North Highlands, CA | 95660-2809 | 916-566-1870 | 566-1871 | K-6 | Rue Avant |
| Creative Connections Arts Academy | 6444 Walerga Rd | North Highlands, CA | 95660-3945 | 916-566-3470 | 566-3505 | 7-12 | Rue Avant |
| Credo HS | 1290 Southwest Blvd | Rohnert Park, CA | 94928 | 707-664-0600 | | 9-12 | Chip Romer |
| Creekside Charter S | PO Box 2891 | Olympic Valley, CA | 96146 | 530-581-1036 | 581-2012 | K-8 | Jeff Kraunz |
| Crenshaw Arts-Technology Charter HS | 4120 11th Ave | Los Angeles, CA | 90008-3712 | 323-778-7700 | 778-7712 | 9-12 | Patricia Smith |
| Crescent Valley Public Charter S | 309 W Main St Ste 110 | Visalia, CA | 93291-6257 | 559-970-5894 | 243-9102 | K-12 | Shellie Escobedo |
| Crescent View Charter West HS | 1901 E Shields Ave | Fresno, CA | 93726 | 559-470-8822 | 225-1205 | 9-12 | Abby Sipes |
| Crescent View South Charter S | 1901 E Shields Ave | Fresno, CA | 93726-5313 | 559-222-8439 | 222-8430 | K-12 | Rafael Aguilar |
| Crossroads Charter S | 418 W 8th St | Hanford, CA | 93230-4536 | 559-583-5060 | 585-7298 | K-12 | Laurie Blue |
| Crown Preparatory Academy | 2055 W 24th St | Los Angeles, CA | 90018-1925 | 213-448-9747 | 410-2271 | 5-8 | Matthew DeFord |
| Cruz Leadership Academy | 14265 Story Rd | San Jose, CA | 95127 | 408-729-2281 | | 9-12 | Jesus Rios |
| Cypress Charter HS | 2039 Merrill St | Santa Cruz, CA | 95062-4176 | 831-477-0302 | 477-7659 | 9-12 | Les Forster |
| Dailey Charter ES | 3135 N Harrison Ave | Fresno, CA | 93704-5299 | 559-248-7060 | 227-5530 | K-5 | Gia Shirley |
| Dantzler Preparatory Charter ES | 5940 S Budlong Ave | Los Angeles, CA | 90044 | 323-290-6968 | | K-5 | Akeysha Allen-Goods |
| Dantzler Preparatory Charter MS | 5029 S Vermont Ave | Los Angeles, CA | 90037-2907 | 323-290-6930 | 460-9606 | 6-8 | Candice Waters |
| Darby Avenue Charter S | 10818 Darby Ave | Northridge, CA | 91326-3199 | 818-360-1824 | 832-9761 | K-5 | Lucy Lee |
| Darnall Charter S | 6020 Hughes St | San Diego, CA | 92115-6520 | 619-582-1822 | 287-4732 | K-8 | Leslie Dahab |
| DaVinci Academy JSHS | 1400 E 8th St | Davis, CA | 95616-2404 | 530-757-7154 | 759-2178 | 7-12 | Troy Allen |
| DaVinci Communications S | 12495 Isis Ave | Hawthorne, CA | 90250 | 310-725-5800 | 643-7659 | 9-12 | Nathan Barrymore |
| DaVinci Design S | 12501 Isis Ave | Hawthorne, CA | 90250 | 310-725-5800 | 643-7659 | 9-12 | Kate Parsons |
| DaVinci Health Sciences Charter S | PO Box 8830 | Chula Vista, CA | 91912-8830 | 619-420-0066 | 420-0677 | K-8 | Amber Goslee |
| DaVinci Innovation Academy | 13500 Aviation Blvd | Hawthorne, CA | 90250 | 310-725-5800 | 643-7659 | K-8 | Michelle Rainey |
| DaVinci Science S | 13500 Aviation Blvd | Hawthorne, CA | 90250 | 310-725-5800 | 643-3013 | K-12 | Steve Wallis |
| Dearborn Elementary Charter Academy | 9240 Wish Ave | Northridge, CA | 91325-2533 | 818-349-4381 | 886-2149 | K-5 | Kimberly Estrada |
| Dehesa Charter S | 1441 Montiel Rd Ste 143 | Escondido, CA | 92026-2242 | 760-743-7880 | 743-7919 | K-12 | Terri Novacek |
| De La Hoya Animo Charter HS | 1114 S Lorena St | Los Angeles, CA | 90023-2915 | 323-780-1259 | 780-4862 | 9-12 | Cynthia Ybarra |
| Delta Bridges Charter S | 703 E Swain Rd | Stockton, CA | 95207 | 209-477-4001 | | K-5 | Bill Redford |
| Delta Charter ES | PO Box 127 | Clarksburg, CA | 95612-0127 | 916-744-1200 | 744-1246 | K-6 | Steve Lewis |
| Delta Charter S | 343 Soquel Ave | Santa Cruz, CA | 95062-2355 | 831-477-5213 | 479-6173 | 9-12 | Mary Gaukel Forster |
| Delta Charter S | 31400 S Koster Rd | Tracy, CA | 95304-8824 | 209-830-6363 | 830-9707 | K-12 | Jeffery Tilton |
| Delta Home Charter S | 804 N Hunter St | Stockton, CA | 95202 | 209-937-4227 | 329-4227 | K-12 | Jeffery Tilton |
| Delta Keys Charter S | 722 W March Ln | Stockton, CA | 95207 | 209-830-6363 | | K-12 | Russell Irwin |
| Delta Launch Charter S | 722 W March Ln | Stockton, CA | 95207 | 209-830-6363 | | K-12 | Gary Pogue |
| Del Vista Math & Science Academy | 710 Quincy St | Delano, CA | 93215-3044 | 661-721-5040 | 721-5087 | PK-5 | Ana Ruiz |
| Denair Charter Academy | 3460 Lester Rd | Denair, CA | 95316-9502 | 209-634-0917 | 669-9282 | K-12 | Dawn Allen |
| Denair Elementary Charter Academy | 3460 Lester Rd | Denair, CA | 95316 | 209-632-8887 | | K-5 | Sara Michelena |
| Desert Sands Charter HS | 44130 20th St W | Lancaster, CA | 93534 | 661-942-3357 | 944-4857 | 9-12 | Jessica Sherlock |
| Design Tech HS | 1800 Rollins Rd | Burlingame, CA | 94010 | 650-394-5157 | | 9-12 | Ken Montgomery |
| Diamond Technology Institute | 112 Diamond Dr | Watsonville, CA | 95076-3184 | 831-728-6225 | 728-6233 | 11-12 | Marci Keller |
| Diego Hills Charter S | 4585 College Ave | San Diego, CA | 92115 | 619-286-0312 | 286-0791 | 8-12 | Armando Martinez |
| Diego Valley Charter S | 511 N 2nd St | El Cajon, CA | 92021 | 619-286-0312 | 286-0791 | K-12 | Craig Beswick |
| Discovery Charter Preparatory S | 12550 Van Nuys Blvd | Pacoima, CA | 91331-1354 | 818-897-1187 | 897-1295 | 9-12 | Karen Smith |
| Discovery Charter S | 1100 Camino Biscay | Chula Vista, CA | 91910-7737 | 619-656-0797 | 656-3899 | K-8 | Sandy Du-Song |
| Discovery Charter S | 51 E Beverly Pl | Tracy, CA | 95376-3191 | 209-831-5240 | 831-5243 | 5-8 | Virginia Stewart |
| Discovery Charter S | 4021 Teale Ave | San Jose, CA | 95117-3433 | 408-243-9800 | 243-9812 | K-8 | Dale Jones |
| Discovery Charter S II | 762 Sunset Glen Dr | San Jose, CA | 95123 | 408-300-3158 | 972-9114 | PK-8 | Dale Jones |
| Dixie Canyon Community Charter S | 4220 Dixie Canyon Ave | Sherman Oaks, CA | 91423-3904 | 818-784-6283 | 788-3340 | K-5 | Lea Moche |
| Dixon Montessori Charter S | 355 N Almond St | Dixon, CA | 95620-2702 | 707-678-8953 | 676-5215 | K-8 | Joanne Green |
| Downtown Charter Academy | 301 12th St | Oakland, CA | 94607 | 510-444-1702 | 444-1703 | 6-8 | Angela Ortega |
| Downtown College Preparatory | 1460 The Alameda | San Jose, CA | 95126-2652 | 408-271-1730 | 271-1734 | 9-12 | Ruth Schriver |
| Downtown College Preparatory MS | 1155 E Julian St | San Jose, CA | 95116 | 408-271-8120 | 271-8855 | 6-8 | Pedro Cuevas |
| Downtown College Prep MS | 2800 Ocala Ave | San Jose, CA | 95148 | 408-942-7000 | 942-7007 | 6-8 | Brandon Jones |
| Downtown College Prep S | 2888 Ocala Ave | San Jose, CA | 95148 | 408-942-7000 | 742-9000 | 6-8 | Terri Furton |
| Downtown Value S | 950 W Washington Blvd | Los Angeles, CA | 90015-3312 | 213-748-8062 | 748-8868 | K-8 | Ana Chavez |
| Dunham Charter S | 4111 Roblar Rd | Petaluma, CA | 94952-9202 | 707-795-5050 | 795-5166 | PK-6 | Adam Schaible |
| Dunlap Leadership Academy | 39500 Dunlap Rd | Dunlap, CA | 93621 | 559-305-7320 | 338-2026 | 9-12 | Judi Szpor |
| e3 Civic HS | 395 11th Ave 6th Floor | San Diego, CA | 92101 | 619-241-4306 | | 9-12 | Helen Griffith |
| Eagle Peak Montessori S | 800 Hutchinson Rd | Walnut Creek, CA | 94598-4505 | 925-946-0994 | 946-9409 | 1-8 | Michelle Hammons |
| Early College Acad for Leaders/Scholars | 2050 N San Fernando Rd | Los Angeles, CA | 90065-1267 | 323-276-5525 | 276-5534 | 9-12 | Ricardo Esquivel |
| East Bay Innovation Academy | 3400 Malcolm Ave | Oakland, CA | 94605 | 510-577-9557 | | 6-12 | Devin Krugman |
| East Oakland Leadership Academy | 2614 Seminary Ave | Oakland, CA | 94605-1570 | 510-562-5238 | 562-5239 | K-8 | Dr. Laura Armstrong |
| East Palo Alto Academy | 1050 Myrtle St | East Palo Alto, CA | 94303 | 650-839-8900 | 839-8902 | 9-12 | Amika Guillaume |
| East Palo Alto Charter S | 1286 Runnymede St | East Palo Alto, CA | 94303-1332 | 650-614-9100 | 614-9183 | K-8 | Sharon Johnson |
| eCademy Charter S | 1100 Cahill Ave | Turlock, CA | 95380-4102 | 209-669-3410 | 669-0180 | K-12 | Robin Swartz |
| Edison-Bethune Charter Academy | 1616 S Fruit Ave | Fresno, CA | 93706-2819 | 559-457-2530 | 498-0711 | K-6 | Rodolfo Garcia |
| Edison Charter Academy | 3531 22nd St | San Francisco, CA | 94114-3405 | 415-970-3330 | 285-0527 | K-8 | Adrienne Morrell |
| Eel River Charter S | PO Box 218 | Covelo, CA | 95428-0218 | 707-983-6946 | 983-6197 | K-6 | Betty Tuttle |
| Einstein Academy | 3035 Ash St | San Diego, CA | 92102-1718 | 619-795-1190 | 795-1180 | K-5 | Greta Bouterse |
| Einstein Academy MS | 458 26th St | San Diego, CA | 92102 | 619-795-1190 | 795-1180 | 6-8 | David Sciarretta |
| Einstein Acad for Letters Art & Sciences | 8844 Burton Way | Beverly Hills, CA | 90211 | 310-409-2940 | | K-12 | Michael Fishler |
| Einstein Acad for Letters Art & Sciences | 25443 Orchard Village Rd | Valencia, CA | 91355 | 661-666-3677 | | K-6 | Scott Cusack |
| Einstein Acad Letters Arts Sci | 28141 Kelly Johnson Pkwy | Santa Clarita, CA | 91355 | 661-702-0755 | 775-0321 | 7-12 | Edward Gika |
| EJE Academy Charter ES | 851 S Johnson Ave | El Cajon, CA | 92020-5811 | 619-401-4150 | 401-4151 | K-8 | Delia Pacheco |
| El Camino Real Charter HS | 5440 Valley Circle Blvd | Woodland Hills, CA | 91367-5996 | 818-595-7500 | 710-9023 | 9-12 | David Fehte |
| Elevate ES | 6845 University Ave | San Diego, CA | 92115 | 858-751-4774 | 839-3700 | K-5 | Robert Elliott |
| Elk Grove Charter S | 10065 Atkins Dr | Elk Grove, CA | 95757-4309 | 916-714-1653 | 714-1721 | K-12 | Marc Levine |
| El Oro Way Charter S | 12230 El Oro Way | Granada Hills, CA | 91344-1600 | 818-360-2288 | 360-3264 | K-5 | SooJoon Choi |
| El Rancho Charter S | 181 S Del Giorgio Rd | Anaheim, CA | 92808-1307 | 714-997-6238 | 281-8791 | 7-8 | John Besta |
| El Sol Santa Ana Science & Arts Academy | 1010 N Broadway | Santa Ana, CA | 92701-3408 | 714-543-0023 | 543-0026 | K-8 | Monique Daviss |
| Emelita Academy Charter S | 17931 Hatteras St | Encino, CA | 91316-1099 | 818-342-6353 | 774-9352 | K-5 | Elizabeth Mayorga |
| Emerson MS | 1650 Selby Ave | Los Angeles, CA | 90024-5716 | 310-234-3100 | 474-6517 | 6-8 | Dimone Watson |
| Emerson Parkside Academy | 2625 Josie Ave | Long Beach, CA | 90815-1511 | 562-420-2631 | 420-7642 | K-5 | Adilis Vitetta |
| Empire Springs Charter S | 15350 Riverview Rd | Helendale, CA | 92342 | 951-242-8800 | 252-8801 | K-12 | Kathleen Hermsmeyer |
| Empower Charter S | 2230 E Jewett St | San Diego, CA | 92111 | 858-292-1304 | 292-1358 | K-6 | Demetria Brown |
| Enadia ES | 22944 Enadia Way | West Hills, CA | 91307-2206 | 818-595-3900 | 716-7738 | K-5 | Heather Jeanne |
| Encino Charter ES | 16941 Addison St | Encino, CA | 91316-3433 | 818-784-1762 | 995-7110 | K-5 | Marcia Koff |
| Encore HS for Performing & Visual Arts | 16955 Lemon St | Hesperia, CA | 92345-5139 | 760-956-2632 | 956-7052 | 7-12 | Denise Griffin |
| Encore HS for the Arts - Riverside | 3800 Main St | Riverside, CA | 92501 | 951-824-1358 | | 7-12 | Denise Griffin |

| School | Address | City,State | Zip code | Telephone | Fax | Grade | Contact |
|---|---|---|---|---|---|---|---|
| Endeavor College Prep Charter S | 126 Bloom St | Los Angeles, CA | 90012-1902 | 323-947-7311 | 843-9502 | K-8 | Edward Morris |
| Environmental Charter HS | 16315 Grevillea Ave | Lawndale, CA | 90260-2858 | 310-214-3400 | 214-3410 | 9-12 | Alison Diaz |
| Environmental Charter MS | 3600 W Imperial Hwy | Inglewood, CA | 90303-2714 | 310-793-0157 | 680-9843 | 6-8 | Beth Bernstein-Yamashiro |
| Environmental Charter MS | 812 W 165th Pl | Gardena, CA | 90247-5105 | 310-425-1605 | 217-1096 | 6-8 | Robert Gloria |
| Environmental Science & Technology HS | 2930 Fletcher Dr | Los Angeles, CA | 90065-1407 | 323-739-0560 | 739-0565 | 9-12 | Andres Versage |
| Envision Academy for Arts & Technology | 1515 Webster St | Oakland, CA | 94612-3355 | 510-596-8901 | 596-8905 | 9-12 | Laura Robell |
| Epic Charter S | 1112 29th Ave | Oakland, CA | 94601 | 510-689-2035 | 904-6751 | 6-8 | Michael Hatcher |
| EPIC de Cesar Chavez | 410 W J St | Tehachapi, CA | 93561 | 661-822-4381 | 822-4703 | 9-12 | David Villarino |
| EPIC S | 2945 Ramco St | West Sacramento, CA | 95691 | 916-286-1960 | | K-8 | Toolie Younger |
| Epiphany Prep Charter S | 6134 Benson Ave | San Diego, CA | 92114 | 619-677-2180 | | K-7 | Jose Villarreal Ed.D. |
| Equitas Academy 3 | 2723 W 8th St | Los Angeles, CA | 90005 | 213-201-0440 | | K-K | Malka Borrego |
| Equitas Academy Charter S | 2723 W 8th St | Los Angeles, CA | 90005 | 213-201-0440 | 652-4444 | 5-8 | Malka Borrego |
| Equitas Academy Charter S | 1700 W Pico Blvd | Los Angeles, CA | 90015 | 213-201-0440 | | K-5 | Kelli Kilty |
| Escondido Charter HS | 1868 E Valley Pkwy | Escondido, CA | 92027-2525 | 760-737-3154 | 738-8996 | 9-12 | Denny Snyder |
| Escuela Popular Accelerated Family Lrng | 467 N White Rd | San Jose, CA | 95127-1441 | 408-275-7190 | 275-7192 | K-12 | Patricia Reguerin |
| Escuela Popular HS Academy | 149 N White Rd | San Jose, CA | 95127 | 408-275-7191 | 259-1595 | 9-12 | Gricelda Gonzalez |
| Everest Public HS | 455 5th Ave | Redwood City, CA | 94063 | 650-366-1050 | 366-1892 | 9-12 | Christopher Lewine |
| Everest Value S | 668 S Catalina St | Los Angeles, CA | 90010 | 213-487-7736 | | K-8 | Christopher Medinger |
| Evergreen Institute of Excellence | 19500 Learning Way | Cottonwood, CA | 96022 | 530-347-3411 | 347-7954 | K-12 | Leila Dumore |
| Excel Charter Academy | 1855 N Main St | Los Angeles, CA | 90031-3227 | 323-222-5010 | 222-5148 | 6-8 | Gloria Gasca |
| Excel Prep Charter S | 25560 Alessandro Blvd | Moreno Valley, CA | 92553 | 909-864-6000 | 864-6100 | K-8 | Alex Lucero |
| Excel Prep Charter S - IE | 25560 Alessandro Blvd | Moreno Valley, CA | 92553 | 800-940-3918 | | K-8 | Jacquet Dumas |
| Excelsior Education Center Charter S | 18422 Bear Valley Rd # 11 | Victorville, CA | 92395-5850 | 760-245-4262 | 245-4009 | 7-12 | William Flynn |
| Executive Preparatory Academy of Finance | 2506 W Imperial Hwy | Hawthorne, CA | 90250 | 310-467-4175 | | 9-12 | Monique Woodley |
| Extera Public School | 2226 E 3rd St | Los Angeles, CA | 90033 | 323-780-8300 | 780-8301 | K-6 | Jim Kennedy Ed.D. |
| Extera Public S # 2 | 1015 S Lorena St | Los Angeles, CA | 90023 | 323-263-3600 | 263-3633 | K-5 | Jim Kennedy |
| Fairmont Charter ES | 1355 Marshall Rd | Vacaville, CA | 95687-5519 | 707-453-6240 | 447-0759 | K-6 | Deanna Brownlee |
| Family First Charter S | 4953 Marine Ave | Lawndale, CA | 90260-1250 | 310-263-3204 | | 9-12 | Paul Guzman |
| Family Partnership Home Study Charter S | 625 S McClelland | Santa Maria, CA | 93454 | 805-686-5339 | 686-4658 | K-12 | Todd Mitchell |
| Fammatre Charter ES | 2800 New Jersey Ave | San Jose, CA | 95124-1556 | 408-377-5480 | 377-8751 | K-5 | Lisa MacFarland |
| Farnham Charter S | 15711 Woodard Rd | San Jose, CA | 95124-2697 | 408-377-3321 | 377-7237 | K-5 | Jocelyn Garcia-Thome |
| Feaster Charter S | 670 Flower St | Chula Vista, CA | 91910-1399 | 619-422-8397 | 422-4780 | K-8 | Francisco Velasco |
| Fenton Avenue Charter S | 11828 Gain St | Sylmar, CA | 91342-7132 | 818-896-7482 | 890-9986 | 2-5 | Stacy Hutter |
| Fenton Leadership Academy | 8926 Sunland Blvd | Sun Valley, CA | 91352 | 818-962-3636 | | K-2 | Jennifer Miller |
| Fenton Primary Center | 11351 Dronfield Ave | Pacoima, CA | 91331 | 818-896-7482 | 890-9986 | K-1 | Richard Parra |
| Fenton STEM Academy | 8926 Sunland Blvd | Sun Valley, CA | 91352 | 818-962-3636 | | 3-5 | Jennifer Miller |
| Finch S | PO Box 428 | Orland, CA | 95963-0428 | 530-865-1683 | 865-1688 | K-12 | Lisa Morgan |
| Folsom Cordova Community Charter S | 715 Riley St | Folsom, CA | 95630-3053 | 916-985-2239 | 985-3665 | K-8 | Wayne Edney |
| Foothill Leadership Academy | 19401 Susan Way | Sonora, CA | 95370 | 209-606-2213 | | K-8 | Ian McVey |
| Forest Charter S | 470 Searls Ave | Nevada City, CA | 95959-3030 | 530-265-4823 | 265-5037 | K-12 | Peter Sagebiel |
| Forest Ranch Charter S | 15815 Cedar Creek Rd | Forest Ranch, CA | 95942 | 530-891-3154 | 891-3155 | K-6 | Christia Marasco |
| Forestville Academy | 6321 Hwy 116 | Forestville, CA | 95436-9606 | 707-887-2279 | 887-2185 | 2-8 | Phyllis Parisi |
| Fortune S | 6829 Stockton Blvd Ste 380 | Sacramento, CA | 95823-2396 | 916-287-4470 | 287-4477 | K-8 | Odisa Nyong |
| Francophone Charter S of Oakland | 9736 Lawlor St | Oakland, CA | 94605 | 510-394-4110 | | K-8 | Ben Daoudi |
| Fremont Charter S | 1120 W 22nd St | Merced, CA | 95340-3540 | 209-385-6627 | 385-6301 | K-6 | Dawn Walker |
| Freshwater Charter MS | 75 Greenwood Heights Dr | Eureka, CA | 95503-9441 | 707-442-2969 | 442-9527 | 7-8 | Si Talty |
| Frontier ES | 1854 Mustang Dr | Hanford, CA | 93230 | 559-585-2430 | 585-2440 | K-5 | John Raven |
| Fuenta Nueva Charter S | 1730 Janes Rd | Arcata, CA | 95521-9623 | 707-822-3348 | 822-5862 | K-5 | Beth Wylie |
| Fusion Charter S | 2217 Geer Rd | Turlock, CA | 95382 | 209-667-0327 | | 7-12 | Siobhan Hanna |
| Futures HS | 3701 Stephen Dr | North Highlands, CA | 95660-4532 | 916-286-1902 | 263-6059 | 7-12 | Nataliya Burko |
| Gabriella Charter S | 1435 Logan St | Los Angeles, CA | 90026-3307 | 213-413-5741 | 413-5874 | K-8 | Rhonda Sivaraman |
| Gardner Charter S | 647 E St | Chula Vista, CA | 91910 | 619-934-0300 | | K-6 | Shannon Richardson |
| Garfield ES | 3600 Middlefield Rd | Menlo Park, CA | 94025-3010 | 650-369-3759 | 367-4358 | K-8 | Michelle Griffith |
| GARR Academy of Math & Entrepreneurial | 1724 W 53rd St | Los Angeles, CA | 90062 | 323-294-2008 | 295-3936 | K-5 | Annitra Edmond |
| Gates ES | 23882 Landisview Ave | Lake Forest, CA | 92630-5199 | 949-837-2260 | 837-5013 | K-6 | Yvonne Estling |
| Gateway Academy | 1520 Yosemite Ave | Escalon, CA | 95320 | 209-838-7177 | 838-6703 | K-8 | Jennifer Klopatek-Drisco |
| Gateway College and Career Academy | 4800 Magnolia Ave | Riverside, CA | 92506 | 951-222-8934 | | 9-12 | Miguel Contreras |
| Gateway HS | 1430 Scott St | San Francisco, CA | 94115-3510 | 415-749-3600 | 749-2716 | 9-12 | Michael Fuller |
| Gateway International S | 900 Morse Ave | Sacramento, CA | 95864-7710 | 916-286-1985 | | K-8 | Joi Tikoi |
| Gateway MS | 1512 Golden Gate Ave | San Francisco, CA | 94115-4515 | 415-922-1001 | 922-1055 | 6-8 | Aaron Watson |
| Germain Charter Academy | 20730 Germain St | Chatsworth, CA | 91311-2418 | 818-341-5821 | 882-3599 | K-5 | Sonia Ugarte |
| Glacier Charter HS | 41267 Highway 41 | Oakhurst, CA | 93644-9403 | 559-642-1422 | 642-1592 | 9-12 | Michael Cox |
| Global College Prep Charter HS | 3243 Center Court Ln | Antelope, CA | 95843-9111 | 916-339-4680 | 339-4684 | 6-12 | Doug Hughey |
| Global Education Academy | 4141 S Figueroa St | Los Angeles, CA | 90037-2038 | 323-232-9588 | 232-9587 | K-5 | Craig Merrill |
| Global Education Academy 2 | 2020 Oak St | Los Angeles, CA | 90007 | 323-537-7225 | 232-9587 | K-5 | David Warken |
| Global Education Academy MS | 1374 W 35th St | Los Angeles, CA | 90007 | 323-641-7283 | 641-7314 | 6-8 | Rosalind Mickels-Miller |
| GOALS Academy | 412 W Carl Karcher Way | Anaheim, CA | 92801 | 714-563-2390 | 563-2401 | PK-6 | Debra Schroeder |
| Goethe International Charter S | 12500 Braddock Dr | Los Angeles, CA | 90066-6808 | 310-306-3484 | 306-3245 | K-8 | Gwenis Laura |
| Golden Eagle Charter S | 2226 S Mount Shasta Blvd #C | Mount Shasta, CA | 96067 | 530-926-5800 | 926-5826 | K-12 | Shelly Adams |
| Golden Oak Montessori S of Hayward | 2652 Vergil Ct | Castro Valley, CA | 94546 | 510-931-7868 | | 1-8 | Maria Omari |
| Golden Valley Charter S | 3585 Maple St Ste 101 | Ventura, CA | 93003-3507 | 805-642-3435 | 642-3468 | K-12 | Terri Adams |
| Golden Valley Orchard S | 6550 Filbert Ave | Orangevale, CA | 95662 | 916-987-1490 | 987-1102 | K-8 | John Baker |
| Golden Valley River S | 9601 Lake Natoma Dr | Orangevale, CA | 95662-5099 | 916-987-6141 | 987-6741 | K-8 | Deborah Lenny |
| Gold Rush Charter S | 16331 Hidden Valley Rd | Sonora, CA | 95370 | 209-532-9781 | 532-9234 | K-12 | Ron Hamilton |
| Gompers Preparatory Academy | 1005 47th St | San Diego, CA | 92102-3626 | 619-263-2171 | 264-4342 | 6-12 | Vince Riveroll |
| Gorman Learning Center | 1826 Orange Tree Ln | Redlands, CA | 92374-2821 | 909-307-6312 | 793-5964 | K-12 | Denice Burchett |
| Granada Hills Charter HS | 10535 Zelzah Ave | Granada Hills, CA | 91344-5999 | 818-360-2361 | 363-9504 | 9-12 | Brian Bauer |
| Grass Valley Charter S | 225 S Auburn St | Grass Valley, CA | 95945 | 530-273-8723 | 271-0557 | PK-8 | Brian Martinez |
| Gratton ES | 4500 S Gratton Rd | Denair, CA | 95316-9762 | 209-632-0505 | 632-7810 | K-8 | Shannon Sanford |
| Grayson Charter S | PO Box 7 | Westley, CA | 95387-0007 | 209-892-4725 | 894-3393 | K-5 | Arturo Duran |
| Greater San Diego Academy | 13881 Campo Rd Ste A-5 | Jamul, CA | 91935-3208 | 619-669-3050 | 669-3066 | K-12 | Gail Levine |
| Great Valley Academy | 486 Button Ave | Manteca, CA | 95336-8596 | 209-824-5400 | 239-3436 | K-8 | Russell Howell |
| Great Valley Academy | 3200 Tully Rd | Modesto, CA | 95350 | 209-576-2283 | 576-2838 | K-8 | Michael Ruehle |
| Greene Academy | 2950 W River Dr | Sacramento, CA | 95833-3767 | 916-567-5560 | | 7-10 | Leslie Sargent |
| Green Valley Charter S | 947 6th St | Los Banos, CA | 93635 | 209-675-7699 | | K-5 | Tisha Blackwood-Freitas |
| Grimmway Academy | 901 Nectarine Ct | Arvin, CA | 93203 | 661-855-8200 | | K-6 | Joanna Kendrick |
| Grizzly ChalleNGe Charter S | PO Box 3209 | San Luis Obispo, CA | 93403-3209 | 805-782-6882 | 594-6341 | 10-12 | Paul Piette |
| Grove S | 200 Nevada St | Redlands, CA | 92373-5385 | 909-798-7831 | 307-6464 | 7-12 | Ben Moudry |
| Guajome Park Academy | 2000 N Santa Fe Ave | Vista, CA | 92083-1534 | 760-631-8500 | 631-8504 | K-12 | Bob Hampton |
| Guidance Charter HS | 37230 37th St E | Palmdale, CA | 93550 | 661-285-1600 | 285-1601 | 7-12 | Kamal Al-Khatib |
| Guidance Charter S | 1125 E Palmdale Blvd Ste B | Palmdale, CA | 93550-4867 | 661-272-1701 | 272-1728 | K-6 | Kamal Al-Khatib |
| Hale Charter Academy | 23830 Califa St | Woodland Hills, CA | 91367-2922 | 818-313-7400 | 346-7517 | 6-8 | Christopher Perdigao |
| Hallmark Charter S | 2445 9th St | Sanger, CA | 93657-2780 | 559-524-7170 | 875-3573 | K-12 | Alfred Sanchez |
| Hamlin Charter Academy | 22627 Hamlin St | West Hills, CA | 91307-3603 | 818-348-4741 | 348-3506 | K-5 | Bette Kaplan |
| Harbor Springs Charter S | 43466 Business Park Dr | Temecula, CA | 92590 | 866-252-8800 | 252-8801 | K-12 | Kathleen Hermsmeyer |
| Hardy Brown College Prep | 190 Carousel Mall | San Bernardino, CA | 92401-1536 | 909-884-1410 | 889-5002 | K-8 | Toiya Allen |
| Harmony Magnet Academy | 19429 Road 228 | Strathmore, CA | 93267 | 559-568-0347 | 568-1929 | 9-12 | Jeff Brown |
| Hart-Ransom Academic Charter S | 3920 Shoemake Ave | Modesto, CA | 95358-8577 | 209-523-0401 | 523-1064 | K-12 | David Cline |
| Harvest Ridge Cooperative Charter S | 9050 Old State Hwy | Newcastle, CA | 95658-9515 | 916-259-1425 | 259-1428 | K-8 | Janet Sutton |
| Hawking STEAM Charter S | 1355 2nd Ave | Chula Vista, CA | 91911 | 619-498-8830 | | K-12 | Carmen Diaz |
| Hawthorne Math & Science Academy | 4467 W Broadway | Hawthorne, CA | 90250-3819 | 310-973-8184 | 973-8167 | 9-12 | Esau Berumen M.Ed. |
| Haynes Charter for Enriched Studies | 6624 Lockhurst Dr | West Hills, CA | 91307-3135 | 818-716-7310 | 716-7249 | K-5 | Barbara Meade |
| Healdsburg Charter S @ Healdsburg ES | 400 1st St | Healdsburg, CA | 95448-3939 | 707-431-3440 | 431-3592 | K-2 | Stephanie Feith |
| Healdsburg Charter S - Fitch Mountain | 520 Monte Vista Ave | Healdsburg, CA | 95448 | 707-473-4449 | 473-4483 | 3-5 | Amber Stringfellow |
| Health Careers Academy | 931 E Magnolia St | Stockton, CA | 95202 | 209-933-7360 | | 9-12 | Traci Miller |
| Health Sciences HS & Middle College | 3910 University Ave Ste 100 | San Diego, CA | 92105-7302 | 619-528-9070 | 528-9084 | 10-12 | Dr. Sheri Johnson |
| Health Sciences MS | 3910 University Ave Ste 100 | San Diego, CA | 92105-7302 | 619-528-9070 | | 6-9 | Jeff Bonine |
| Hearthstone S | 2280 6th St | Oroville, CA | 95965 | 530-532-5644 | 532-5794 | K-12 | Kim Guzzetti |
| Heather ES | 2757 Melendy Dr | San Carlos, CA | 94070-3604 | 650-508-7303 | 508-7306 | K-4 | Pam Jasso |
| Heights Charter S | 2710 Alpine Blvd | Alpine, CA | 91901 | 619-792-9000 | | K-8 | Diana Whyte |
| Helix Charter HS | 7323 University Ave | La Mesa, CA | 91942 | 619-644-1940 | 462-9266 | 9-12 | Mike Lewis Ed.D. |
| Henry HS | 251 S 12th St | Richmond, CA | 94804 | 510-235-2439 | 235-2487 | 9-12 | Evelia Villa |
| Heritage Charter S | 1855 E Valley Pkwy | Escondido, CA | 92027-2517 | 760-737-3111 | 737-9322 | K-8 | Dennis Snyder |
| Heritage Digital Academy Charter MS | 2255 E Valley Pkwy | Escondido, CA | 92027 | 760-294-5599 | | 6-8 | Shawn Roner |
| Heritage Peak Charter S | 6450 20th St | North Highlands, CA | 95660 | 866-992-9033 | 348-4325 | K-12 | Dr. Paul Keefer |
| Hesby Oaks Leadership Charter S | 15530 Hesby St | Encino, CA | 91436-1519 | 818-528-7000 | 907-0788 | K-8 | Movses Tarakhchyan |
| Hickman Charter S | 13306 4th St | Hickman, CA | 95323-9634 | 209-874-9070 | 874-1457 | K-8 | Paul Gardner |
| Hickman ES | 13306 4th St | Hickman, CA | 95323-9634 | 209-874-1816 | 874-3721 | K-5 | Candetta Holdren |
| Hickman MS | 13306 4th St | Hickman, CA | 95323-9634 | 209-556-6540 | 874-3721 | 6-8 | Candetta Holdren |
| Higher Learning Academy | 2625 Plover St | Sacramento, CA | 95815 | 916-286-5183 | 643-9893 | K-8 | Anjam Khan |
| Highlands Community Charter S | 1333 Grand Ave | Sacramento, CA | 95838 | 916-844-2283 | 471-0552 | 1-12 | Kirk Williams |
| High Tech ES | 2150 Cushing Rd | San Diego, CA | 92106 | 619-564-6700 | | K-5 | Anne Worrall |
| High Tech ES Chula Vista | 1949 Discovery Falls Dr | Chula Vista, CA | 91915-2037 | 619-591-2550 | 591-2553 | K-5 | Stacey Lopaz |
| High Tech ES North County | 1460 W San Marcos Blvd | San Marcos, CA | 92078-4017 | 760-759-2785 | 759-2788 | K-2 | Amanda Massey |
| High Tech Explorer ES | 2230 Truxtun Rd Ste A | San Diego, CA | 92106 | 619-795-3600 | 795-3090 | K-5 | Briony Chown |
| High Tech High Media Arts | 2230 Truxtun Rd Ste B | San Diego, CA | 92106 | 619-398-8620 | 758-9568 | 9-12 | Robert Kuhl |
| High Tech HS Chula Vista | 1945 Discovery Falls Dr | Chula Vista, CA | 91915-2037 | 619-591-2500 | 591-2503 | 9-12 | Lillian Hsu |

| School | Address | City,State | Zip code | Telephone | Fax | Grade | Contact |
|---|---|---|---|---|---|---|---|
| High Tech HS North County | 1420 W San Marcos Blvd | San Marcos, CA | 92078-4017 | 760-759-2700 | 759-2799 | 9-12 | Isaac Jones |
| High Tech International HS | 2855 Farragut Rd | San Diego, CA | 92106-6029 | 619-398-4900 | 758-1960 | 9-12 | Abe Correa |
| HighTech LA | 17111 Victory Blvd | Van Nuys, CA | 91406-5455 | 818-609-2640 | 881-1754 | 9-12 | Marsha Rybin |
| High Tech Middle Media Arts | 2230 Truxtun Rd Ste B | San Diego, CA | 92106 | 619-398-8640 | 758-9568 | 6-8 | Steve Elizondo |
| High Tech MS | 2359 Truxtun Rd | San Diego, CA | 92106 | 619-814-5060 | 243-5050 | 6-8 | Nicole Hinostro |
| High Tech MS Chula Vista | 1949 Discovery Falls Dr | Chula Vista, CA | 91915 | 619-591-2530 | 591-2533 | 6-8 | Melissa Daniels |
| High Tech MS North County | 1460 W San Marcos Blvd | San Marcos, CA | 92078-4017 | 760-759-2750 | 759-2779 | 6-8 | Emilio Torres |
| Holly Drive Leadership Academy | 4801 Elm St | San Diego, CA | 92102-1354 | 619-266-7333 | 266-7330 | K-8 | Alysia Smith |
| Holt College Prep Academy | 3201 Morada Ln | Stockton, CA | 95212-3110 | 209-955-1477 | 955-1472 | 6-12 | Jeff Palmquist |
| HomeTech Charter S | 7126 Skyway | Paradise, CA | 95969-3271 | 530-872-1171 | 872-1172 | K-12 | Michael Ervin |
| Hope Academy Charter S | 57725 29 Palms Hwy Ste 403 | Yucca Valley, CA | 92284 | 760-820-4725 | 365-5880 | K-12 | R. Helmadollar |
| Hopper STEM Academy | 601 Grace Ave | Inglewood, CA | 90301 | 310-910-0230 | | 6-8 | Adell Walker |
| Horizon Charter S | PO Box 489000 | Lincoln, CA | 95648-9000 | 916-408-5200 | 408-5223 | K-12 | Cynthia Wood Ph.D. |
| Hume Lake Charter S | 64144 Hume Lake Rd | Hume, CA | 93628-9600 | 559-305-7565 | 305-7707 | K-12 | Michael Stockdale |
| ICEF Inglewood Elementary Charter Acad | 434 S Grevillea Ave | Inglewood, CA | 90301-2300 | 323-298-6420 | 293-9092 | K-5 | Shuron Owens-Lincoln |
| ICEF Inglewood Middle Charter Academy | 304 E Spruce Ave | Inglewood, CA | 90301-2711 | 323-298-6425 | 293-9092 | 6-8 | Shuron Owens-Lincoln |
| ICEF Vista Academy | 4471 Inglewood Blvd | Los Angeles, CA | 90066-6209 | 323-298-6400 | 317-2839 | K-5 | Kristen Buczek |
| ICEF Vista Middle Academy | 4471 Inglewood Blvd | Los Angeles, CA | 90066-6209 | 323-298-6400 | 317-2839 | 6-8 | Kristen Buczek |
| IFTIN Charter S | 5465 El Cajon Blvd | San Diego, CA | 92115-3620 | 619-265-2411 | 265-2484 | K-8 | Amal Hersi |
| iLEAD Innovation Studios | 28050 Hasley Canyon Rd | Castaic, CA | 91384 | 800-925-1502 | | K-12 | Dawn Evenson |
| iLEAD Lancaster Charter S | 254 E Ave K-4 | Lancaster, CA | 93535 | 661-722-4287 | | K-8 | Lynn Boop |
| Imagine School at Imperial Valley | 1150 N Imperial Ave | El Centro, CA | 92243 | 760-592-7250 | 592-7251 | K-7 | Grace Jiminez |
| Imagine S Coachella Valley | 84-090 Ave 50 | Coachella, CA | 92236 | 760-391-9200 | | K-2 | Dustin Kerns |
| Impact Academy of Arts & Technology | 2560 Darwin St | Hayward, CA | 94545-3451 | 510-300-1560 | 300-1565 | 9-12 | Sean McClung |
| Imperial Beach Charter S | 650 Imperial Beach Blvd | Imperial Beach, CA | 91932-2794 | 619-628-5600 | 628-5680 | 1-8 | Pamela Reichert-Montiel |
| Imperial Beach Charter School West | 525 3rd St | Imperial Beach, CA | 91932-1101 | 619-628-8900 | 628-8980 | PK-K | Melissa Griffith |
| Incubator S | 7400 West Manchester | Los Angeles, CA | 90045 | 310-338-2490 | 338-2496 | 6-8 | Woochan Park |
| Independence Charter Academy | PO Box 249 | Helendale, CA | 92342 | 760-952-1760 | 245-1034 | K-12 | Michael Hayhurst |
| Independence Charter S | 3920 Blue Bird Dr | Modesto, CA | 95356-0254 | 209-545-4415 | 545-2682 | K-8 | Julie Villanueba |
| Ingenium Charter S | 22250 Elkwood St | Canoga Park, CA | 91304-5501 | 818-456-4590 | | K-6 | Michael Kinnaman |
| Ingenuity Charter S | 6130 Skyline Dr | San Diego, CA | 92114 | 619-487-1163 | 487-9682 | 6-12 | Dr. Jonathan Dean |
| Inland Leaders Charter S | 13456 Bryant St | Yucaipa, CA | 92399-5441 | 909-446-1100 | 446-1125 | K-8 | Michael Gordon |
| Innovations Academy | 10380 Spring Canyon Rd | San Diego, CA | 92131-3699 | 619-271-1414 | 271-1418 | K-8 | Christine Kuglen |
| Innovative Horizons Charter S | 1461 N A St | Perris, CA | 92570-1968 | 951-657-0728 | 940-5103 | K-8 | Jason Archard |
| Insight S of California | 2360 Shasta Way Ste B | Simi Valley, CA | 93065-1876 | 800-670-5391 | 884-9671 | 9-12 | Jose Salas |
| Inspire Charter S | 33323 Santiago Rd | Acton, CA | 93510 | 760-269-2214 | 269-2216 | K-12 | Cris Alcala |
| Inspire Charter S - South | 4612 Dehesa Rd | El Cajon, CA | 92019 | 619-784-7481 | 784-7482 | K-12 | Herbert Nichols |
| Inspire School of Arts and Sciences | 901 Esplanade | Chico, CA | 95926 | 530-891-3090 | 891-3089 | 9-12 | Jerry Crosby |
| Integrity Charter S | 701 National City Blvd | National City, CA | 91950-1123 | 619-336-0808 | 336-1526 | K-8 | |
| Intellectual Virtues Acad of Long Beach | 3601 Linden Ave | Long Beach, CA | 90807 | 562-912-7017 | | 6-8 | Jacquie Bryant |
| Intermountain STEM Academy Charter S | 13412 Bottle Rock Rd | Cobb, CA | 95426 | 707-928-4873 | 928-4653 | 5-8 | Tim Gill |
| International S of Monterey | 1720 Yosemite St | Seaside, CA | 93955-3914 | 831-583-2165 | 899-7653 | K-5 | Sean Madden |
| Ipakanni Early College Charter S | 1459 Downer St | Oroville, CA | 95965 | 530-532-1165 | | 6-12 | Walter Gramps |
| IQ Academy California Los Angeles | 1830 Nogales St | Rowland Heights, CA | 91748-2945 | 888-997-4722 | 398-5515 | K-12 | Carol Henson |
| Island Community Day S | 1776 6th Avenue Dr | Kingsburg, CA | 93631-1701 | 559-897-1046 | 897-1265 | 4-8 | Misti Jennings |
| Island S | 7799 21st Ave | Lemoore, CA | 93245-9694 | 559-924-6424 | 924-0247 | K-8 | Charlotte Hines |
| Ivy Academia De Soto Campus | 5461 Winnetka Ave | Winnetka, CA | 91364 | 818-348-8190 | 348-8339 | 3-7 | Kathy Pino |
| Ivy Academia Entrepreneurial Charter S | 7353 Valley Circle Blvd | West Hills, CA | 91304-6706 | 818-716-0771 | 914-3674 | 7-12 | Kathy Pino |
| Ivy Bound Academy | 15355 Morrison St | Sherman Oaks, CA | 91403-1514 | 818-808-0158 | 808-0157 | 5-8 | Kiumars Arzani |
| Ivy Bound Academy MST Charter MS | 20040 Parthenia St | Northridge, CA | 91324 | 818-646-4992 | 646-4993 | 5-8 | Michelle Pacifici |
| IvyTech Charter S | 6591 Collins Dr | Moorpark, CA | 93021 | 805-222-5188 | 426-8245 | 7-12 | Jacqueline Gardner |
| Jacobs High Tech HS | 2861 Womble Rd | San Diego, CA | 92106-6025 | 619-243-5000 | 243-5050 | 9-12 | Brett Peterson |
| Jacoby Creek Charter S | 1617 Old Arcata Rd | Bayside, CA | 95524-9324 | 707-822-4896 | 822-4898 | K-8 | Catherine Stone |
| Jardin De la Infancia | 307 E 7th St | Los Angeles, CA | 90014-2209 | 213-614-1745 | 614-2047 | K-1 | Zuzy Chavez |
| Jew Academies | 1944 Flint Ave | San Jose, CA | 95148 | 408-223-3750 | 223-7346 | K-8 | Laura Alvarez |
| Johnson JHS | 1300 Stroud Ave | Kingsburg, CA | 93631-1000 | 559-897-1091 | 897-6867 | 7-8 | Laura North |
| Jordan MS | 7911 Winnetka Ave | Winnetka, CA | 91306 | 818-882-2496 | 882-1798 | 6-8 | Dr. Maria Alvarado |
| Journey S | 27102 Foxborough | Aliso Viejo, CA | 92656-3377 | 949-448-7232 | 448-7256 | K-5 | Gavin Keller |
| Juan Bautista de Anza Charter S | 2101 S Marina Dr | Salton City, CA | 92274 | 760-767-5850 | 759-1221 | 1-12 | Dr. Sandra Thorpe |
| Juarez ES | 1450 Marina Way S | Richmond, CA | 94804 | 510-215-7009 | 215-7016 | K-5 | |
| Julian Charter S | PO Box 1780 | Julian, CA | 92036-1780 | 866-853-0003 | 765-3849 | K-12 | Jennifer Cauzza |
| Justice Street Academy Charter | 23350 Justice St | West Hills, CA | 91304-4402 | 818-346-4388 | 346-4649 | K-5 | Cynthia Hernandez |
| Kairos Public School Vacaville Academy | 129 Elm St | Vacaville, CA | 95688 | 707-356-9210 | | K-8 | Jared Austin |
| Kavod Charter ES | 3201 Marathon Dr | San Diego, CA | 92123 | 858-386-0887 | | K-5 | Alexa Greenland |
| Kawana Academy of Arts and Sciences | 2121 Moraga Dr | Santa Rosa, CA | 95404-6114 | 707-545-4283 | 573-9065 | PK-6 | Carolina Castro |
| Keiller Leadership Academy MS | 7270 Lisbon St | San Diego, CA | 92114-3007 | 619-263-9266 | 262-2217 | K-8 | Joel Christman |
| Kenny Charter S | 3525 M L King Blvd | Sacramento, CA | 95817 | 916-277-6500 | 277-6507 | K-8 | Gail Johnson |
| Kenter Canyon ES | 645 N Kenter Ave | Los Angeles, CA | 90049-1999 | 310-472-5918 | 472-9738 | K-5 | Dr. Terry Moren |
| Kern Workforce 2000 Academy | 5801 Sundale Ave | Bakersfield, CA | 93309-2924 | 661-827-3158 | 396-2987 | 10-12 | Roman Aguilar |
| Keyes To Learning Charter S | PO Box 519 | Keyes, CA | 95328-0519 | 209-634-6467 | 669-7121 | PK-12 | Rusty Wynn |
| Kid Street Learning Center | PO Box 6784 | Santa Rosa, CA | 95406-0784 | 707-525-9223 | 525-9432 | K-6 | Linda Conklin |
| King-Chavez Academy of Excellence | 2850 Logan Ave | San Diego, CA | 92113-2412 | 619-232-2825 | 232-2943 | K-8 | Jorge Collins |
| King/Chavez Arts Academy | 415 31st St | San Diego, CA | 92102-4236 | 619-525-7320 | 696-7459 | 3-5 | Shelley Baca |
| King/Chavez Athletics Academy | 415 31st St | San Diego, CA | 92102-4236 | 619-525-7320 | 744-3817 | 3-5 | Shelley Baca |
| King-Chavez Community HS | 201 A St | San Diego, CA | 92101 | 619-704-1020 | 704-1021 | 9-12 | Dr. Kevin Bradshaw |
| King/Chavez Preparatory Academy | 500 30th St | San Diego, CA | 92102 | 619-744-3828 | 744-3829 | 6-8 | Scott Worthing |
| King/Chavez Primary Academy | 415 31st St | San Diego, CA | 92102-4236 | 619-525-7320 | 696-7459 | K-2 | Gerry Guevara |
| King City Arts Magnet S | 415 Pearl St | King City, CA | 93930-2919 | 831-385-5473 | 385-1016 | K-5 | Brad Smith |
| Kings River-Hardwick S | 10300 Excelsior Ave | Hanford, CA | 93230-9794 | 559-584-4475 | 585-1422 | K-8 | Cathlene Anderson |
| KIPP Academy of Innovation | 4800 E Cesar Chavez Ave | Los Angeles, CA | 90022 | 323-406-8000 | 406-8002 | 5-8 | Alice Lai |
| KIPP Academy of Opportunity | 7019 S Van Ness Ave | Los Angeles, CA | 90047-1659 | 323-778-0125 | 778-0162 | 5-8 | Tanya Piyaratanaphipat |
| KIPP Adelante Preparatory Academy | 1475 6th Ave Ste 100 | San Diego, CA | 92101-3245 | 619-233-3242 | 233-3212 | 5-8 | Christa Coleman |
| KIPP Bayview Academy | 1060 Key Ave | San Francisco, CA | 94124-3563 | 415-467-2522 | 467-9522 | 5-8 | Sherrye Hubbard |
| KIPP Bridge Charter S | 991 14th St | Oakland, CA | 94607-3230 | 510-874-7255 | 874-6796 | 5-8 | Elizabeth Raji-Greig |
| KIPP Comienza Community Prep S | 6410 Rita Ave | Huntington Park, CA | 90255-4126 | 323-589-1450 | 589-1716 | K-4 | Shirley Appleman |
| KIPP Empower Academy | 8466 S Figueroa St | Los Angeles, CA | 90003-2729 | 323-750-2279 | 750-7902 | K-4 | Neela Parasnis |
| KIPP Heritage Academy | 2545 Sherlock Dr | San Jose, CA | 95121 | 408-318-7256 | | 5-8 | |
| KIPP Ignite Academy | 9110 S Central Ave | Los Angeles, CA | 90002 | 323-486-6402 | 486-6403 | K-4 | Cassandra Cope |
| KIPP I Heartwood Academy | 1250 S King Rd | San Jose, CA | 95122-2146 | 408-926-5477 | 926-5478 | 5-8 | Judy Tang |
| Kipp II Prize Preparatory Academy | 1250 S King Road | San Jose, CA | 95122 | 408-251-5600 | 251-5602 | 5-8 | Autumn Zangrilli |
| KIPP Iluminar Academy | 4800 E Cesar Chavez Ave | Los Angeles, CA | 90022 | 323-800-5218 | 489-4471 | K-4 | Mara Bond |
| KIPP King Collegiate HS | 2005 Via Barrett | San Lorenzo, CA | 94580-1315 | 510-828-9509 | 317-2333 | 9-12 | Kate Belden |
| KIPP Los Angeles College Preparatory | 2810 Whittier Blvd | Los Angeles, CA | 90023-1527 | 323-264-7737 | 264-7730 | 5-8 | Carlos Lanuza |
| KIPP Philosophers Academy | 8300 S Central Ave | Los Angeles, CA | 90001-3707 | 323-584-6664 | 584-6666 | 5-8 | Heidi Kunkel |
| KIPP Promesa Prep S | 207 S Dacotah St | Los Angeles, CA | 90063 | 323-486-6400 | 486-6401 | K-4 | Adriana Rodriguez |
| KIPP Raices Academy | 668 S Atlantic Blvd | Los Angeles, CA | 90022-3212 | 323-780-3900 | 780-3939 | K-4 | Chelsea Zegarski |
| KIPP San Francisco Bay Academy | 1430 Scott St | San Francisco, CA | 94115-3510 | 415-440-4306 | 440-4308 | 5-8 | Ellen Bray |
| KIPP San Francisco College Preparatory | 1195 Hudson Ave | San Francisco, CA | 94124 | 415-643-6951 | 826-9182 | 9-12 | Caroline Gifford |
| KIPP San Jose Collegiate Charter S | 1790 Educational Park Dr | San Jose, CA | 95133-1703 | 408-937-3752 | 937-3755 | 9-12 | Tom Ryan |
| KIPP Scholar Academy | 1729 W MLK Jr Blvd | Los Angeles, CA | 90062 | 323-292-2272 | 292-2555 | 5-8 | Tiffany Moore |
| KIPP Sol Academy | 4800 E Cesar Chavez Ave | Los Angeles, CA | 90022 | 323-800-5220 | 800-5221 | 5-5 | |
| KIPP Summit Academy | 2005 Via Barrett | San Lorenzo, CA | 94580-1315 | 510-258-0106 | 258-0097 | 5-8 | Salome Portugal |
| KIPP Vida Preparatory Academy | 5101 S Western Ave | Los Angeles, CA | 90062 | 323-406-8007 | 406-8008 | K-4 | Erendira Flores |
| Knowledge Enlightens You (KEY) Academy | 1570 Ward St | Hayward, CA | 94541 | 510-543-4124 | 862-0209 | K-8 | Krista Kastriotis |
| Lake County International Charter S | PO Box 984 | Middletown, CA | 95461-0984 | 707-987-3063 | 825-9344 | K-8 | Gwendolyn Maupin-Ahern |
| Lakeview Charter Academy | 11465 Kagel Canyon St | Lake View Ter, CA | 91342-6505 | 818-485-0340 | 485-0342 | 6-8 | Danny Herrera |
| Lakeview Charter HS | 13361 Glenoaks Blvd | Sylmar, CA | 91342 | 818-356-2591 | 356-2581 | 9-12 | Adam Almeida |
| Language Academy | 2850 49th St | Sacramento, CA | 95817-2303 | 916-277-7137 | 277-7141 | K-8 | Eduardo De Leon |
| Larchmont Charter ES | 1265 N Fairfax Ave | West Hollywood, CA | 90046 | 323-656-6418 | 656-6407 | K-10 | Mersedeh Emrani |
| Lashon Academy | 7477 Kester Ave | Van Nuys, CA | 91405 | 818-514-4566 | 337-0102 | K-6 | Sara Garcia |
| La Sierra Academy | 1735 E Houston Ave | Visalia, CA | 93292-2349 | 559-733-6963 | 733-6845 | 7-12 | Anjelica Zermeno |
| La Tijera S | 1415 N La Tijera Blvd | Inglewood, CA | 90302-1078 | 310-680-5260 | 419-2537 | K-8 | Ugema James |
| Latino College Preparatory Academy | 14271 Story Rd | San Jose, CA | 95127 | 408-729-2281 | 285-5324 | 9-12 | Raul Lomeli |
| Laurel Preparatory Academy | 10170 Huennekens St | San Diego, CA | 92121 | 858-678-4812 | | 6-12 | Lynne Alipio |
| Laurel Tree Charter S | 4555 Valley West Blvd | Arcata, CA | 95521 | 707-822-5626 | 822-5654 | K-12 | Brenda Sutter |
| Laverne Elementary Preparatory Academy | PO Box 400880 | Hesperia, CA | 92340-0880 | 760-948-4333 | 948-9333 | K-8 | Debbie Tarver |
| LaVerne Science & Technology Charter S | 250 W La Verne Ave | Pomona, CA | 91767-2375 | 909-397-4684 | 392-0191 | K-6 | Dolores Lobaina |
| La Vida Charter S | 16201 N Highway 101 | Willits, CA | 95490-8724 | 707-459-6344 | 459-6377 | K-12 | Ann Kelly |
| Lazear Charter Academy | 824 29th Ave | Oakland, CA | 94601-2205 | 510-689-2000 | | K-8 | Sarah Morrill |
| Leadership HS | 350 Seneca Ave | San Francisco, CA | 94112 | 415-841-8910 | 841-8925 | 9-12 | Beth Silbergeld |
| Leadership Public S - Hayward | 28000 Calaroga Ave | Hayward, CA | 94545-4600 | 510-300-1340 | 372-0396 | 9-12 | Michael DeSousa |
| Leadership Public S - Richmond | 880 Bissell Ave | Richmond, CA | 94801 | 510-235-4522 | 588-4593 | 9-12 | Shawn Benjamin |
| Leadership Public S - San Jose | 1881 Cunningham Ave | San Jose, CA | 95122-1712 | 408-937-2700 | 937-2705 | 9-12 | Jessica Diaz |
| Learning Choice Academy | 9950 Scripps Lake Dr | San Diego, CA | 92131 | 619-463-8811 | 463-8339 | K-12 | Debi Gooding |
| Learning for Life Charter S | 330 Reservation Rd Ste F | Marina, CA | 93933-3286 | 831-582-9820 | 582-9825 | 7-12 | Cindy Dotson |
| Learning Works! | 88 N Daisy Ave | Pasadena, CA | 91107-3704 | 626-564-2871 | 564-2870 | 7-12 | Mikala Rahn |
| Lemoore Middle College HS | 555 College Dr | Lemoore, CA | 93245-9248 | 559-925-3552 | 925-6059 | 9-12 | Charles Gent |

| School | Address | City,State | Zip code | Telephone | Fax | Grade | Contact |
|---|---|---|---|---|---|---|---|
| Lemoore University Charter S | 100 Vine St | Lemoore, CA | 93245-3418 | 559-924-6890 | 924-6839 | 5-8 | Crescenciano Camarena |
| Lennox Math Science & Technology Academy | 10319 Firmona Ave | Lennox, CA | 90304-1419 | 310-680-5600 | 671-5029 | 9-12 | Armando Mena |
| Libertas College Preparatory Charter S | 3875 Dublin Ave | Los Angeles, CA | 90008 | 310-902-6808 | | 4-8 | Anna Carlstone-Hurst |
| Liberty Charter HS | 8425 Palm St | Lemon Grove, CA | 91945 | 619-668-2131 | 668-2133 | 9-12 | Debbie Beyer |
| Liberty ES | 170 Liberty School Rd | Petaluma, CA | 94952 | 707-795-4380 | 795-6468 | PK-6 | Chris Rafanelli |
| Life Learning Academy | 651 8th St | San Francisco, CA | 94130-1901 | 415-397-8957 | 397-9274 | 9-12 | Teri Delane |
| Lifeline Education Charter S | 357 E Palmer St | Compton, CA | 90221-2610 | 310-605-2510 | 764-4890 | 6-12 | Paula DeGroat |
| Life Source International Charter S | 44339 Beech Ave | Lancaster, CA | 93534 | 661-579-2970 | 579-2977 | K-7 | Deberae Culpepper |
| Lighthouse Community Charter S | 444 Hegenberger Rd | Oakland, CA | 94621-1418 | 510-271-8801 | 271-8803 | K-12 | Paul Koh |
| Lincoln ES | 1900 Mariposa St | Kingsburg, CA | 93631-2044 | 559-897-5141 | 897-3537 | 2-3 | Matt Stovall |
| Lincoln Street S | 1135 Lincoln St | Red Bluff, CA | 96080 | 530-528-7301 | 529-4120 | K-8 | Rich DuVarney |
| Linscott Charter S | 220 Elm St | Watsonville, CA | 95076-5025 | 831-728-6301 | 761-5478 | K-8 | Julie Wiley |
| Literacy First Charter S | 799 E Washington Ave | El Cajon, CA | 92020-5327 | 619-579-7232 | 579-5730 | K-12 | Debbie Beyer |
| Live Oak Charter S | PO Box 2054 | Petaluma, CA | 94953-2054 | 707-762-9020 | 762-9019 | K-8 | Matthew Morgan |
| Livermore Valley Charter HS | 2451 Portola Ave | Livermore, CA | 94551 | 925-456-9000 | 456-9009 | 9-12 | Eric Dillie |
| Livermore Valley Charter S | 3252 Constitution Dr | Livermore, CA | 94551 | 925-443-1690 | 443-1692 | K-8 | Tara Aderman |
| Locke College Prep Acad Blue | 325 E 111th St | Los Angeles, CA | 90061 | 323-420-2067 | | 10-12 | Dr. Peggy Gutierrez |
| Locke College Prep Academy | 325 E 111th St | Los Angeles, CA | 90061 | 323-420-2170 | | 9-9 | Nyesha Philpot |
| Locke College Prep Acad Gold | 325 E 111th St | Los Angeles, CA | 90061 | 323-420-2110 | | 10-12 | Dr. James Martin |
| Lockhurst Drive ES | 6170 Lockhurst Dr | Woodland Hills, CA | 91367-1299 | 818-888-5280 | 346-0283 | K-5 | Aleta Johnson |
| Loma Vista Charter S | 467 E Honolulu St | Lindsay, CA | 93247-2116 | 559-562-5111 | 562-4637 | K-12 | Dennis Doane |
| Loma Vista Immersion Academy | 207 Maria Dr | Petaluma, CA | 94954-2301 | 707-765-4302 | 765-4343 | K-6 | Jorge Arvizu |
| Long Valley Charter S | PO Box 7 | Doyle, CA | 96109-0007 | 530-827-2395 | 827-3562 | K-12 | Sheri Morgan |
| Loomis Basin Charter S | 5438 Laird Rd | Loomis, CA | 95650-8916 | 916-652-2642 | 652-1809 | K-8 | Erika Sloane |
| Los Angeles Academy of Arts & Enterprise | 600 S La Fayette Park Pl | Los Angeles, CA | 90057-3243 | 213-487-0600 | 487-0500 | 6-12 | David Calvo |
| Los Angeles International Charter S | 625 Coleman Ave | Los Angeles, CA | 90042-4903 | 323-257-1499 | 257-1497 | 9-12 | Clifford Moseley |
| Los Angeles Leadership Academy | 2670 Griffin Ave | Los Angeles, CA | 90031 | 323-381-8484 | 381-8489 | K-8 | Roger Lowenstein |
| Los Angeles Leadership Academy - HS | 234 E Avenue 33 | Los Angeles, CA | 90031 | 323-227-7719 | 227-7721 | 9-12 | Roger Lowenstein |
| Los Feliz Charter S for the Arts | 2709 Media Center Dr | Los Angeles, CA | 90065-1700 | 323-539-2810 | 539-2815 | K-6 | Linda Lee |
| LPS College Park Charter S | 8601 MacArthur Blvd | Oakland, CA | 94605 | 510-633-0750 | 291-9783 | 9-12 | Alexandrea Creer |
| Luskin Academy | 2941 W 70th St | Los Angeles, CA | 90043-4420 | 213-905-1210 | 905-1215 | 9-12 | Rosalio Medrano |
| MAAC Community Charter S | 1385 3rd Ave | Chula Vista, CA | 91911-4302 | 619-476-0749 | 476-0913 | 9-12 | Debbie VanEnkevort |
| Madera County Independent Academy | 1105 S Madera Ave | Madera, CA | 93637 | 559-662-4636 | 675-8313 | K-12 | Brett Salinas |
| Magnolia Science Academy | 18238 Sherman Way | Reseda, CA | 91335-4550 | 818-609-0507 | 609-0534 | 6-12 | Mustafa Sahin M.Ed. |
| Magnolia Science Academy | 102 Baker St E | Costa Mesa, CA | 92626 | 714-557-7002 | 242-1449 | 6-12 | Laura Schlottman |
| Magnolia Science Academy 2 | 17125 Victory Blvd | Van Nuys, CA | 91406 | 818-758-0300 | 758-0333 | 6-12 | Suat Acar M.Ed. |
| Magnolia Science Academy 3 | 1254 E Helmick St | Carson, CA | 90746 | 310-637-3806 | 933-4767 | 6-12 | Steven Selcuk Keskinturk |
| Magnolia Science Academy 4 | 11330 Graham Pl | Los Angeles, CA | 90064 | 310-473-2464 | 473-2416 | 6-12 | Lisa Ross |
| Magnolia Science Academy 5 | 18230 Kittridge St | Reseda, CA | 91335 | 818-219-0676 | 609-0534 | 6-12 | Brad Plonka |
| Magnolia Science Academy 6 | 3754 Dunn Dr | Los Angeles, CA | 90034 | 310-842-8555 | 842-8558 | 6-8 | John G. Terzi |
| Magnolia Science Academy 7 | 18355 Roscoe Blvd | Northridge, CA | 91325 | 818-886-0585 | 975-5215 | K-5 | Fatih Metin |
| Magnolia Science Academy 8 | 6411 Orchard Ave | Bell, CA | 90201 | 310-826-3925 | 826-3926 | 6-8 | Jason Hernandez |
| Magnolia Science Academy - San Diego | 6365 Lake Atlin Ave | San Diego, CA | 92119-3206 | 619-644-1300 | 644-1600 | 6-8 | Gokhan Serce |
| Magnolia Science Academy Santa Clara | 14271 Story Rd | San Jose, CA | 95127 | 408-258-1427 | 516-5555 | 6-12 | Michele Ryan |
| Making Waves Academy | 4123 Lakeside Dr | Richmond, CA | 94806-1942 | 510-262-1511 | 262-1518 | 5-12 | Alton Nelson |
| Manzanita Charter MS | 2925 Technology Ct | Richmond, CA | 94806-1952 | 510-222-3500 | 222-3555 | 6-8 | Jim Trombley |
| Manzanita Public Charter S | 991 Mountain View Blvd | Vandenberg AFB, CA | 93437 | 805-734-5600 | 734-3572 | K-6 | Suzanne Nicastro |
| Mare Island Technology Academy HS | 2 Positive Pl | Vallejo, CA | 94589-1825 | 707-552-6482 | 552-0288 | 6-12 | Matt Smith |
| Maria Montessori Charter Academy | 1850 Wildcat Blvd | Rocklin, CA | 95765-5471 | 916-630-1510 | 624-7305 | K-8 | Brent Boothby |
| Marquez Charter S | 16821 Marquez Ave | Pacific Plsds, CA | 90272-3294 | 310-454-4019 | 573-1532 | K-5 | Alberto Hananel |
| Marysville Charter Academy for the Arts | 1917 B St | Marysville, CA | 95901-3731 | 530-749-6157 | 741-7892 | 7-12 | Tim Malone |
| Math and Science College Preparatory | 3200 W Adams Blvd | Los Angeles, CA | 90018 | 323-821-1393 | 607-1453 | 9-9 | Janette Rodriguez |
| Mattole Valley Charter S | PO Box 211 | Petrolia, CA | 95558 | 707-629-3634 | 629-3649 | PK-12 | Richard Graey |
| McGill School of Success | 3025 Fir St | San Diego, CA | 92102-1123 | 619-239-0632 | 239-1318 | K-3 | Sobeida Fuentes |
| Meadows Arts & Technology ES | 2000 La Granada Dr | Thousand Oaks, CA | 91362-2016 | 805-495-7037 | 374-1160 | K-5 | Brenda Priske |
| Merced Scholars Charter S | 1850 Wardrobe Ave | Merced, CA | 95341 | 209-381-5165 | 381-5166 | 6-12 | Mark Pintor |
| Merkin MS | 2023 S Union Ave | Los Angeles, CA | 90007-1326 | 213-748-0141 | 748-0142 | 6-8 | Meghan Van Pelt |
| Method Charter S | 24620 Jefferson St | Murrieta, CA | 92562 | 951-461-4620 | | K-12 | Jessica Venezia |
| Method S | 317 E Foothill Blvd | Arcadia, CA | 91006 | 626-408-5882 | | K-12 | Jessica Venezia |
| Metro Charter S | 320 W 15th St | Los Angeles, CA | 90015 | 213-377-5708 | 943-1502 | K-5 | Kim Clerx |
| MET Sacramento Charter HS | 810 V St | Sacramento, CA | 95818-1330 | 916-264-4700 | 264-4701 | 9-12 | Vince Wolfe |
| Mid Valley Alternative Charter S | 9895 7th Ave | Hanford, CA | 93230-8802 | 559-583-1149 | 582-7565 | K-8 | Todd Barlow |
| Milagro Charter S | 1855 N Main St | Los Angeles, CA | 90031-3227 | 323-223-1786 | 223-8593 | K-5 | Sascha Robinett |
| Millennium Charter HS | 51 E Beverly Pl | Tracy, CA | 95376-3191 | 209-831-5240 | 831-5243 | 9-12 | Virginia Stewart |
| Millennium Charter HS | 901 Blanco Circle | Salinas, CA | 93901 | 831-755-0830 | | 9-12 | Peter Gray |
| Minarets Charter HS | PO Box 208 | O Neals, CA | 93645-0208 | 559-868-8659 | 868-8686 | 9-12 | Daniel Ching |
| Mirus Secondary S | 14073 Main St Ste 103 | Hesperia, CA | 92345-4675 | 760-947-7100 | 947-7135 | 7-12 | Mary Bixby |
| Mission Preparatory S | 75 Francis St | San Francisco, CA | 94112 | 415-508-9626 | | K-8 | Jane Henzerling |
| Mission View Charter S | 20655 Soledad Canyon Rd #12 | Santa Clarita, CA | 91351 | 661-272-1225 | 945-2430 | 7-12 | Bill Toomey |
| Miwok Valley Language Academy | 1010 Saint Francis Dr | Petaluma, CA | 94954-5322 | 707-765-4304 | 765-4380 | K-6 | Brett Wilson |
| Mohan High School | 644 W 17th St | Los Angeles, CA | 90015-3400 | 213-342-2870 | 342-2871 | 9-12 | Loreen Riley |
| Mojave River Academy | 16519 Victor St | Victorville, CA | 92395 | 760-245-3222 | 245-3774 | K-12 | Nancy Lewis |
| Monarch Academy | 1445 101st Ave | Oakland, CA | 94603-3207 | 510-568-3101 | 655-1222 | K-5 | Jen Green |
| Monarch Learning Center | PO Box 992418 | Redding, CA | 96099-2418 | 530-247-7307 | 243-4819 | K-8 | |
| Montague Charter Academy | 13000 Montague St | Pacoima, CA | 91331-4146 | 818-899-0215 | 834-9782 | K-5 | Dr. Mario Martinez |
| Monterey Bay Charter S | 1004B David Ave | Pacific Grove, CA | 93950-5443 | 831-655-4638 | 655-4815 | K-8 | Cassandra Bridge |
| Monterey County Home Charter S | PO Box 80851 | Salinas, CA | 93912-0851 | 831-755-0331 | 755-0837 | K-12 | Justin McCollum |
| Mountain Home Charter S | 41267 Highway 41 | Oakhurst, CA | 93644-9403 | 559-642-1422 | 642-1592 | K-8 | Michael Cox |
| Mountain Oaks S | PO Box 1209 | San Andreas, CA | 95249-1209 | 209-754-0532 | 754-3556 | K-12 | Anne Colman |
| Mountain View Montessori Charter S | 12219 2nd Ave | Victorville, CA | 92395 | 760-843-3303 | 843-1074 | K-6 | Laurien Spiller |
| Mt Lassen Charter S | 100 David S Hall St | Herlong, CA | 96113 | 530-252-4313 | 252-4314 | K-6 | Patrick Condon |
| Mueller Charter S | 715 I St | Chula Vista, CA | 91910-5199 | 619-422-6192 | 422-0356 | K-9 | Dr. Kevin Riley |
| Muir Charter S | 12338 McCourtney Rd | Grass Valley, CA | 95949 | 530-272-4008 | 366-7349 | 9-12 | Richard Guess |
| Multicultural Learning Center | 7510 De Soto Ave | Canoga Park, CA | 91303-1430 | 818-716-5783 | 716-1085 | K-8 | Gayle Nadler |
| Museum S | 211 Maple St | San Diego, CA | 92103-6527 | 619-236-8712 | 236-8906 | K-8 | Phil Beaumont |
| Napa Valley Language Academy | 2700 Kilburn Ave | Napa, CA | 94558-5623 | 707-253-3678 | 259-8427 | K-6 | Alejandra Uribe |
| National University Academy | 2030 University Dr | Vista, CA | 92083 | 760-631-5842 | 631-6201 | 6-12 | Kimberleigh Marro |
| National University Academy | 11355 N Torrey Pines Rd | La Jolla, CA | 92037 | 760-630-4080 | 631-6201 | K-12 | Kimberleigh Marro |
| National University Academy | 1101 National Dr Ste C | Sacramento, CA | 95834 | 760-630-4080 | | K-12 | Kimberleigh Marro |
| Natomas Charter S | 4600 Blackrock Dr | Sacramento, CA | 95835-1250 | 916-928-5353 | 928-5333 | PK-12 | Ting Sun Ph.D. |
| Natomas-Pacific Pathways Prep | 3700 Del Paso Rd | Sacramento, CA | 95834-9606 | 916-567-5740 | 567-5749 | 9-12 | Tom Rutten |
| Natomas Pacific Pathways Prep MS | 3700 Del Paso Rd | Sacramento, CA | 95834 | 916-567-5741 | 567-5749 | 6-8 | David Hunt |
| NAVA College Preparatory Academy | 1319 E 41st St | Los Angeles, CA | 90010 | 213-846-2203 | 521-1668 | 9-12 | Luis Rodiguez |
| Nea Community Learning Center | 1900 3rd St | Alameda, CA | 94501 | 510-748-4008 | 864-4281 | K-12 | Annalisa Moore |
| Nestle Avenue ES | 5060 Nestle Ave | Tarzana, CA | 91356-4399 | 818-342-6148 | 609-9864 | K-5 | Cheryl Gray-Sortino |
| Nestor Language Academy Charter S | 1455 Hollister St | San Diego, CA | 92154-4003 | 619-628-0900 | 628-0980 | K-8 | Guadalupe Avilez |
| Nevada City Charter S | 750 Hoover Ln | Nevada City, CA | 95959-2910 | 530-265-1885 | 265-1889 | K-8 | Brynn Bourke |
| Nevada City S for the Arts | 13032 Bitney Springs Rd # 8 | Nevada City, CA | 95959-9017 | 530-273-7736 | 273-1378 | K-8 | Holly Pettitt |
| NEW Academy Canoga Park | 21425 Cohasset St | Canoga Park, CA | 91303-1450 | 818-710-2640 | 710-2654 | PK-5 | Patricia Gould |
| NEW Academy of Science & Arts | 379 Loma Dr | Los Angeles, CA | 90017-1149 | 213-413-9183 | 413-9187 | PK-5 | Dr. Eric Todd Ed.D. |
| Newcastle Charter S | 8951 Valley View Dr | Newcastle, CA | 95658-9723 | 916-663-3307 | 663-3524 | PK-8 | Liz Staton |
| New Day Academy | 214 W 1st St | Alturas, CA | 96101-3903 | 530-233-3861 | 233-3864 | K-12 | Laura Van Acker |
| New Designs Charter S | 2303 Figueroa Way | Los Angeles, CA | 90007-2504 | 213-765-9084 | 765-0214 | 6-12 | Stephen Gyesaw |
| New Designs Charter S - Watts | 12714 Avalon Blvd | Los Angeles, CA | 90061 | 323-418-0600 | 418-1600 | 6-12 | Joseph Ntung |
| New Heights Charter S | 2202 W Martin Luther King | Los Angeles, CA | 90008 | 323-508-0155 | 508-0156 | K-8 | Amy Berfield |
| New Horizons Charter Academy | 5955 Lankershim Blvd | North Hollywood, CA | 91601 | 818-655-9602 | 655-9607 | K-8 | Richard Thomas |
| New Jerusalem ES | 31400 S Koster Rd | Tracy, CA | 95304-9543 | 209-835-2597 | 835-2613 | K-8 | Donald Patzer |
| New Joseph Bonnheim Community Charter S | 7300 Marin Ave | Sacramento, CA | 95820 | 916-643-7400 | 691-9858 | K-6 | Christie Wells-Artman |
| New Los Angeles Charter S | 1919 S Burnside Ave | Los Angeles, CA | 90016-1114 | 323-939-6400 | 939-6411 | 6-8 | Brooke Rios |
| Newman Leadership Academy | 1314 E Date St | San Bernardino, CA | 92404-4234 | 909-522-4461 | | K-6 | Joyce Payne |
| New Millenium Secondary S | 1301 W 182nd St Ste B | Gardena, CA | 90248-3322 | 310-999-6162 | 999-6163 | 9-12 | Samantha Navarro |
| New S of San Francisco | 2929 19th St | San Francisco, CA | 94110 | 415-401-8489 | | K-5 | Ryan Chapman |
| New Spirit Charter Academy | 4147 E Dakota Ave | Fresno, CA | 93726 | 559-221-6300 | | PK-5 | Kathy Brown |
| New Technology HS | 1400 Dickson St | Sacramento, CA | 95822-3437 | 916-433-2839 | 433-2840 | 9-12 | Kenneth Durham |
| New Village Charter HS | 147 N Occidental Blvd | Los Angeles, CA | 90026-4601 | 213-385-4015 | 385-4020 | 9-12 | Andrea Purcell |
| New Vision MS | 2050 Pacific St | San Bernardino, CA | 92404-6179 | 909-888-8390 | 888-8470 | 6-8 | Alex Lucero |
| New West Charter S | 1905 Armacost Ave | Los Angeles, CA | 90025 | 310-943-5444 | 231-3399 | 6-12 | Dr. Sharon Weir |
| NextGeneration STEAM Academy | 18001 Commercial St | Lathrop, CA | 95330 | 209-229-4736 | | K-8 | Leslie Pombo |
| Nightingale S | 1721 Carpenter Rd | Stockton, CA | 95206-3809 | 209-933-7260 | 234-1850 | K-8 | Myra Machuca |
| Nobel MS | 9950 Tampa Ave | Northridge, CA | 91324-1142 | 818-773-4700 | 701-9480 | 6-8 | Derek Horowitz |
| Nord Country Charter S | 5554 California St | Chico, CA | 95973-9795 | 530-891-3138 | 891-3273 | K-6 | Kathleen Dahlgren |
| Northcoast Prep and Performing Arts Acad | PO Box 276 | Arcata, CA | 95518-0276 | 707-822-0861 | 822-0878 | 9-12 | Michael Bazemore |
| North County Trade Tech HS | 1126 N Melrose Dr | Vista, CA | 92083-3467 | 760-598-0782 | 598-0895 | 9-12 | Doreen Quinn |
| Northern Summit Academy | PO Box 1156 | Cottonwood, CA | 96022 | 530-949-0154 | 472-1127 | K-12 | Julia Knight |
| North Oakland Community Charter S | 1000 42nd St | Oakland, CA | 94608-3621 | 510-655-0540 | 655-1222 | K-8 | Stephen Ajani |
| North Valley Military Institute | 12105 Allegheny St | Sun Valley, CA | 91352 | 818-368-1557 | 368-1935 | 6-12 | Mark Ryan |
| North Valley Pivot Charter School | 2550 Lakewest Dr | Chico, CA | 95928-8419 | 877-544-1423 | | 6-12 | Jayna Gaskill |

| School | Address | City,State | Zip code | Telephone | Fax | Grade | Contact |
|---|---|---|---|---|---|---|---|
| Northwest Prep Charter S | 2590 Piner Rd | Santa Rosa, CA | 95401 | 707-522-3320 | 522-3101 | 7-12 | Joyce Hamilton |
| Norton Space and Aeronautics Academy | 503 E Central Ave | San Bernardino, CA | 92408-2313 | 909-386-2300 | 386-7855 | K-12 | Guadalupe Girard |
| Nova Academy Early College HS | 1010 W 17th St | Santa Ana, CA | 92706 | 714-569-0948 | 569-1693 | 9-12 | Doreen Fioretto |
| Novato Charter S | 940 C St | Novato, CA | 94949-5060 | 415-883-4254 | 883-1859 | K-8 | Nikki Lloyd |
| Nueva Esperanza Charter Academy | 1218 4th St | San Fernando, CA | 91340 | 818-256-1951 | 256-2397 | 6-12 | Kristi Duenas |
| Nueva Vista Language Academy | 120 Garces Hwy | Delano, CA | 93215-3328 | 661-721-5070 | 721-3638 | PK-5 | Anamarie Sanchez |
| Nuview Bridge Early College HS | 30401 Reservoir Ave | Nuevo, CA | 92567-9361 | 951-928-8498 | 928-0186 | 9-12 | Dr. Jason Fowler Ed.D. |
| Oakdale Charter HS | 1235 E D St | Oakdale, CA | 95361-3223 | 209-848-4361 | 848-4363 | 9-12 | Dennis Hitch |
| Oak Grove ES | 8760 Bower St | Sebastopol, CA | 95472-2450 | 707-823-5225 | 829-2614 | K-5 | Paige Gardner |
| Oakland Charter Academy | 4215 Foothill Blvd | Oakland, CA | 94601 | 510-532-6751 | 532-6753 | 6-8 | David Camarena |
| Oakland Charter HS | 345 12th St | Oakland, CA | 94607-4217 | 510-893-8700 | 893-8705 | 9-12 | Raquel Olivia-Gomez |
| Oakland Military Institute College Prep | 3877 Lusk St | Oakland, CA | 94608 | 510-594-3900 | 597-9886 | 6-12 | Rick Wallis |
| Oakland S for the Arts | 530 18th St | Oakland, CA | 94612 | 510-873-8800 | 873-8816 | 6-12 | Donn Harris |
| Oakland Unity HS | 6038 Brann St | Oakland, CA | 94605-1544 | 510-635-7170 | 635-3830 | 9-12 | Sam Brewer |
| Oakland Unity MS | 6038 Brann St | Oakland, CA | 94605 | 510-635-7170 | | 6-8 | Damon Grant |
| Oak Park Prep S | 2315 34th St | Sacramento, CA | 95817 | 916-533-4861 | | 7-8 | Annie Cervenka |
| Oasis Charter S | 1135 Westridge Pkwy | Salinas, CA | 93907-2529 | 831-424-9003 | 424-9005 | K-8 | Dr. Juanita Perea |
| Obama Charter S | PO Box 72028 | Los Angeles, CA | 90002 | 323-566-1965 | 566-1418 | K-5 | Chaleese Norman |
| Ocean Charter S | 12606 Culver Blvd | Los Angeles, CA | 90066-6506 | 310-827-5511 | 827-2012 | K-3 | Stephanie Edwards |
| Ocean Charter S | 7400 W Manchester Ave | Los Angeles, CA | 90045 | 310-348-9050 | 348-9085 | 4-8 | Stephanie Edwards |
| Ocean Grove Charter S | 1166 Broadway Ste Q | Placerville, CA | 95667-5745 | 800-979-4436 | 295-3583 | K-12 | Randy Gaschler |
| O'Donovan Middle Academy | 5355 S 4th Ave | Los Angeles, CA | 90043 | 323-294-3172 | 596-2698 | 6-8 | Edith Funes |
| Odyssey Charter S | 725 W Altadena Dr | Altadena, CA | 91001-4103 | 626-229-0993 | 229-0586 | K-8 | Lauren O'Neill |
| O'Farrell Charter S | 6130 Skyline Dr | San Diego, CA | 92114-5620 | 619-263-3009 | 263-4339 | PK-12 | Dr. Jonathan Dean |
| Old Adobe ES | 2856 Old Adobe Rd | Petaluma, CA | 94954-9546 | 707-765-4301 | 765-4334 | K-6 | Jeff Williamson |
| Old Town Academy | 2120 San Diego Ave | San Diego, CA | 92110 | 619-574-6225 | 683-2096 | K-8 | Jon Centofranchi |
| Olive Grove Charter S | PO Box 370 | New Cuyama, CA | 93254 | 805-623-1111 | 623-8512 | K-12 | Laura Mudge |
| Olivet Elementary Charter S | 1825 Willowside Rd | Santa Rosa, CA | 95401-3923 | 707-522-3045 | 522-3047 | K-6 | Mary Reynolds |
| one.Charter | 800 Douglas Rd | Stockton, CA | 95207-3607 | 209-468-9079 | 468-4651 | 7-12 | Janine Cuaresma |
| OnePurpose S | 948 Hollister Ave | San Francisco, CA | 94124 | 415-657-0277 | | K-5 | Antonio Tapia |
| Open Charter Magnet S | 5540 W 77th St | Los Angeles, CA | 90045-3214 | 310-568-0735 | 568-0904 | K-5 | Antoinette Cass |
| Opportunities for Learning Charter S | 18523 Soledad Canyon Rd | Canyon Country, CA | 91351 | 661-424-1337 | 424-1129 | 7-12 | Jesus Franco |
| Opportunities for Learning S | 33621 Del Obispo St Ste E | Dana Point, CA | 92629 | 949-248-1282 | 248-2450 | K-12 | Jesus Franco |
| Optimist Charter S | 6957 N Figueroa St | Los Angeles, CA | 90042-1245 | 323-443-3100 | | 7-12 | Lynn DeYoung |
| Options for Youth - Apple Valley | 13675 Niabi Rd | Apple Valley, CA | 92308 | 760-247-6078 | 961-1723 | 7-12 | Kathy Lento |
| Options for Youth - Arden | 2125 Fulton Ave | Sacramento, CA | 95825 | 916-971-3175 | 971-3186 | 7-12 | Jocelyn Baldwin |
| Options for Youth Burbank 1 | 1610 W Burbank Blvd | Burbank, CA | 91506 | 818-566-7525 | 566-7712 | K-12 | Jesus Franco |
| Options for Youth Burbank 2 | 401 S Glenoaks Blvd | Burbank, CA | 91502 | 818-566-9809 | 566-9819 | 7-12 | Bill Tynan |
| Options for Youth Carmichael | 5825 Windmill Way | Carmichael, CA | 95608 | 916-485-5155 | 485-5484 | 7-12 | Jesus Franco |
| Options for Youth Charter S | 405 S San Gabriel Blvd | San Gabriel, CA | 91776 | 626-282-0390 | 282-0391 | 7-12 | Maricela Frymark |
| Options for Youth - Chino 1 | 7011 Schaefer Ave Ste E | Chino, CA | 91710 | 909-465-9529 | 465-9809 | 7-12 | Wendy Gillespie |
| Options for Youth - Chino 2 | 5475 Philadelphia St Ste B | Chino, CA | 91710 | 909-591-6559 | 591-8438 | 7-12 | Maricela Frymark |
| Options for Youth - Fontana 1 | 16981 Foothill Blvd | Fontana, CA | 92335 | 909-357-3168 | 357-2875 | 7-12 | Wendy Gillespie |
| Options for Youth - Fontana 2 | 17216 Slover Ave | Fontana, CA | 92337 | 909-429-0482 | 429-9212 | 7-12 | Wendy Gillespie |
| Options for Youth - Hesperia 1 | 15461 Main St | Hesperia, CA | 92345 | 760-948-3355 | | 7-12 | |
| Options for Youth Irwindale | 16023 Arrow Hwy Ste C | Baldwin Park, CA | 91706 | 626-337-9352 | 337-4503 | 7-12 | Maricela Frymark |
| Options for Youth La Crescenta | 3115 Foothill Blvd Ste K | La Crescenta, CA | 91214-4244 | 626-236-2060 | 236-2062 | 7-12 | Maricela Frymark |
| Options for Youth North Highlands | 3542 A St | North Highlands, CA | 95660 | 916-338-2375 | 338-2417 | 7-12 | Jocelyn Baldwin |
| Options for Youth Northridge | 8415 Reseda Blvd | Northridge, CA | 91324 | 818-886-8392 | 886-8393 | 7-12 | Bill Tynan |
| Options for Youth - Ontario | 3130 Inland Empire Blvd | Ontario, CA | 91764 | 909-476-5959 | 476-3636 | 7-12 | Maricela Frymark |
| Options for Youth Orangevale | 9470 Madison Ave | Orangevale, CA | 95662 | 916-988-4138 | 988-4176 | 7-12 | Jocelyn Baldwin |
| Options for Youth Pomona | 695 E Foothill Blvd | Pomona, CA | 91767 | 909-593-2163 | 596-5627 | 7-12 | Maricela Frymark |
| Options for Youth - Rancho | 9849 Foothill Blvd | Rch Cucamonga, CA | 91730 | 909-466-9082 | 466-9083 | 7-12 | Maricela Frymark |
| Options for Youth Rancho Cordova | 11088 Olson Dr | Rancho Cordova, CA | 95670-5650 | 916-631-8113 | 631-8121 | 7-12 | Jocelyn Baldwin |
| Options for Youth San Bernardino I | 985 S E St Ste A | San Bernardino, CA | 92408-1941 | 909-381-6260 | 381-6230 | 7-12 | Jocelyn Baldwin |
| Options for Youth San Bernardino II | 1181 E Highland Ave | San Bernardino, CA | 92404 | 909-882-8500 | 882-8315 | 7-12 | Raquel Velasco |
| Options for Youth Sylmar | 13752 Foothill Blvd | Sylmar, CA | 91342 | 818-698-4168 | | 7-12 | Bryan Gillespie |
| Options for Youth - Upland | 310 N Mountain Ave | Upland, CA | 91786-5115 | 909-946-0500 | 946-0506 | 7-12 | Bill Tynan |
| Options for Youth Van Nuys | 6628 Van Nuys Blvd | Van Nuys, CA | 91405 | 818-781-9059 | 781-9067 | 7-12 | Wendy Gillespie |
| Options for Youth Victorville - 1 | 14725 7th St | Victorville, CA | 92395 | 760-955-5525 | 955-1107 | 7-12 | Bill Tynan |
| Options for Youth Victorville - 2 | 11975 Hesperia Rd | Hesperia, CA | 92345 | 760-955-5900 | 955-5919 | 7-12 | Kathy Lento |
| Options for Youth Victorville - 3 | 15378 Ramona Ave | Victorville, CA | 92392 | 760-245-9086 | | 7-12 | Kathy Lento |
| Options for Youth Victorville - 4 | 15048 Bear Valley Rd Ste E | Victorville, CA | 92395 | 760-241-8300 | 241-8879 | 7-12 | Kathy Lento |
| Orange County Educational Arts Academy | 825 N Broadway | Santa Ana, CA | 92701-3423 | 714-558-2787 | 558-2775 | K-8 | Kathy Lento |
| Orange County HS of the Arts | 1010 N Main St | Santa Ana, CA | 92701-3602 | 714-560-0900 | 664-0463 | 7-12 | Kristin Collins |
| Orchard View Charter S | 700 Watertrough Rd | Sebastopol, CA | 95472-3917 | 707-823-4709 | 823-6187 | K-12 | Steven Wagner |
| Orcutt Academy | PO Box 161 | Los Alamos, CA | 93440 | 805-937-6515 | 937-9108 | K-8 | Cathy Stroud |
| Orcutt Academy | 610 Pinal Ave | Orcutt, CA | 93455 | 805-938-8550 | 938-8995 | 9-12 | Joe Dana |
| Our Community Charter S | 10045 Jumilla Ave | Chatsworth, CA | 91311-3507 | 818-350-5000 | 350-5007 | K-8 | Rhett Carter |
| Oxford Preparatory Academy | 23000 Via Santa Maria | Mission Viejo, CA | 92691 | 949-305-6111 | 297-4747 | K-8 | Jude Stabiler |
| Oxford Preparatory Academy | 5862 C St | Chino, CA | 91710 | 909-464-2672 | 248-0459 | K-8 | Jeff Rich |
| Pacific Coast Charter S | 294 Green Valley Rd | Watsonville, CA | 95076-1300 | 831-786-2180 | 786-2192 | K-12 | Andrew Crowe |
| Pacific Collegiate Charter S | PO Box 1701 | Santa Cruz, CA | 95061-1701 | 831-479-7785 | 427-5254 | 7-12 | Suzanne Smith |
| Pacific Community Charter S | PO Box 984 | Point Arena, CA | 95468-0984 | 707-882-4131 | 882-4132 | K-12 | Archie Douglas |
| Pacific Law Academy | 1621 Brookside Rd | Stockton, CA | 95207 | 209-933-7445 | | 9-12 | Sigrid Hillscan |
| Pacific View Charter S | 3670 Ocean Ranch Blvd | Oceanside, CA | 92056-2669 | 760-757-0161 | 435-2666 | K-12 | Carol Sanderson |
| Pacific View Charter S | 2937 Moore Ave | Eureka, CA | 95501-3316 | 707-269-9490 | 269-9491 | K-12 | Gina Campbell |
| Pacoima Charter S | 11016 Norris Ave | Pacoima, CA | 91331-2598 | 818-899-0201 | 890-3812 | K-5 | James Malloy |
| Pajaro Valley HS | 500 Harkins Slough Rd | Watsonville, CA | 95076 | 831-728-8102 | 728-6944 | 9-12 | Sylvia Fajardo |
| Palisades Charter ES | 800 Via De La Paz | Pacific Plsds, CA | 90272-3617 | 310-454-3700 | 459-5627 | K-5 | Alison Niizawa |
| Palisades Charter HS | 15777 Bowdoin St | Pacific Plsds, CA | 90272-3586 | 310-230-6623 | 454-6076 | 9-12 | Joan Ingle |
| Palmdale Aerospace Academy | 38060 20th St E | Palmdale, CA | 93550 | 661-273-3680 | 266-7201 | 7-12 | Dr. Pamela Magee |
| Palm Desert Charter MS | 74200 Rutledge Way | Palm Desert, CA | 92260-2646 | 760-862-4320 | 862-4327 | 6-8 | Dr. Laura Herman |
| Paradise Charter MS | 6473 Clark Rd | Paradise, CA | 95969-3501 | 530-872-7277 | 872-2924 | 6-8 | Sallie Fraser |
| Paradise Charter S | 3361 California Ave | Modesto, CA | 95358-9213 | 209-524-0184 | 524-0363 | K-8 | Chris Reid |
| Paradise eLearning Academy | 5911 Maxwell Dr | Paradise, CA | 95969-4023 | 530-872-6425 | 872-6418 | 9-12 | Heath Thomason |
| Paragon Collegiate Academy | 1608 Sampson St | Marysville, CA | 95901 | 530-742-2505 | 763-5772 | K-8 | Kathleen Blacklock |
| Para Los Ninos Charter S | 1617 E 7th St | Los Angeles, CA | 90021-1207 | 213-239-6605 | | K-5 | Laura Cotney |
| Para Los Ninos - Gratts ECC | 474 Hartford Ave | Los Angeles, CA | 90017-1306 | 213-481-3200 | 977-5449 | PK-2 | Santa Acuna |
| Para Los Ninos MS | 835 Stanford Ave | Los Angeles, CA | 90021-1847 | 213-896-2640 | 896-2660 | 6-8 | Dr. Juan Ramirez |
| Paramount Collegiate Academy | 3510 Hazeltine Ln | Roseville, CA | 95747 | 916-757-1479 | | 6-12 | Sandra Mejia |
| Pasadena Rosebud Academy | 3544 Canon Blvd | Altadena, CA | 91001-4008 | 626-797-7704 | | K-1 | Dawn Douglas |
| Paseo Grande Charter S | 2444 Marconi Ave | Sacramento, CA | 95821 | 661-272-1225 | | K-8 | Shawn Brumfield Ed.D. |
| Pathways Academy Charter | 5256 South Mission Rd | Bonsall, CA | 92003 | 858-610-1102 | | K-12 | Dave Petropulos |
| Pathways Charter S | 150 Professional Center Dr | Rohnert Park, CA | 94928 | 707-585-6510 | 585-6515 | K-12 | Ryan Woodard |
| Pathways Community S | 8800 S San Pedro St | Los Angeles, CA | 90003 | 323-481-2334 | | 9-12 | Dr. Robert Tavonatti |
| Pathways ICare Charter S | 1020 Sundown Way | Roseville, CA | 95661-4473 | 916-784-6107 | 771-0893 | K-8 | Erica Hamilton |
| Pathways to College Charter S | PO Box 402672 | Hesperia, CA | 92340-2672 | 760-949-8002 | 947-9648 | K-8 | Christina Smith |
| Peabody Charter S | 3018 Calle Noguera | Santa Barbara, CA | 93105-2899 | 805-563-1172 | 569-7042 | K-6 | Joe Williams |
| Peak to Peak Mountain Charter S | 19009 Cerro Noroeste Rd | Pine Mountain C, CA | 93222 | 661-242-3811 | | K-8 | Demian Barnett |
| Penngrove ES | 365 Adobe Rd | Penngrove, CA | 94951 | 707-778-4755 | 778-4831 | K-6 | Mindy Moffatt |
| Petaluma Accelerated Charter S | 110 Ellis St | Petaluma, CA | 94952 | 707-778-4750 | 778-4789 | 7-8 | Amy Fadeji |
| Petaluma Accelerated Charter S | 110 Ellis St | Petaluma, CA | 94952 | 707-778-4750 | | 7-8 | Matthew Harris |
| Phoenix Academy | PO Box 4925 | San Rafael, CA | 94913-4925 | 415-491-0581 | 491-0981 | 9-12 | Matthew Harris |
| Piner-Olivet Charter S | 2707 Francisco Ave | Santa Rosa, CA | 95403-1869 | 707-522-3310 | 522-3317 | 7-8 | Raquel Rose |
| Pioneer ES | 1888 Mustang Dr | Hanford, CA | 93230 | 559-584-8831 | 584-7049 | PK-5 | Kim Kern |
| Pioneer MS | 101 W Pioneer Way | Hanford, CA | 93230-9489 | 559-584-0112 | 584-0118 | 6-8 | Sharon Cronk |
| Pioneer Technical Center | 1105 S Madera Ave | Madera, CA | 93637-5576 | 559-664-1600 | 673-5569 | 9-12 | Nichole Walsh |
| Pittman S | 701 E Park St | Stockton, CA | 95202-2207 | 209-933-7496 | 942-2769 | K-8 | Leslie Neumeier |
| Pivot Online Charter - North Bay | 2999 Cleveland Ave Ste D | Santa Rosa, CA | 95403 | 707-843-4676 | 544-2908 | K-12 | Adrienne Machado |
| Pivot Online Charter S | 1030 La Bonita Dr | San Marcos, CA | 92078 | 760-591-0217 | | 6-12 | Jayna Gaskell |
| Plainview Academic Charter Academy | 10819 Plainview Ave | Tujunga, CA | 91042-1633 | 818-353-1730 | 353-6658 | K-5 | Jayna Gaskell |
| Plumas Charter S | 175 N Mill Creek Rd | Quincy, CA | 95971-9678 | 530-283-3851 | 283-3841 | K-12 | Kenneth Johnson |
| Pomelo Community Charter S | 7633 March Ave | West Hills, CA | 91304-5233 | 818-887-9700 | 887-1744 | K-5 | Taletha Washburn |
| Port of Los Angeles HS | 250 W 5th St | San Pedro, CA | 90731-3304 | 310-832-9201 | 832-1605 | 9-12 | Andrea Ferber |
| PREPA TEC - Los Angeles | 2410 Broadway | Walnut Park, CA | 90255-6342 | 323-923-0383 | 923-0380 | 6-8 | Gaetano Scotti |
| Preuss S | 9500 Gilman Dr | La Jolla, CA | 92093-5004 | 858-822-3000 | 822-1620 | 6-12 | Xavier Reyes |
| Price Charter MS | 2650 New Jersey Ave | San Jose, CA | 95124-1520 | 408-377-2532 | 377-7406 | 6-8 | Scott Barton |
| Primary Charter S | 51 E Beverly Pl | Tracy, CA | 95376-3191 | 209-831-5240 | 831-5243 | K-4 | Denee Signorelli |
| Primary Years Academy | 1540 N Lincoln St | Stockton, CA | 95204 | 209-933-7355 | 941-4580 | K-5 | Virginia Stewart |
| Provisional Accelerated Learning Academy | PO Box 7100 | San Bernardino, CA | 92411-0100 | 909-887-7002 | 887-8942 | 9-12 | Jean Segura |
| Public Policy Charter S | 1701 Browning Blvd | Los Angeles, CA | 90062 | 323-205-7920 | | 5-8 | Lynette Forte |
| Public Safety Academy | 1482 E Enterprise Dr | San Bernardino, CA | 92408-0161 | 909-382-4574 | | 6-12 | Donna Jacobson |
| PUC Community Charter ES | 14019 Sayre St | Sylmar, CA | 91342 | 818-492-1890 | 492-1881 | K-5 | Kathy Toy |
| PUC Inspire Charter Academy | 919 Eighth St | San Fernando, CA | 91340 | 818-492-1880 | | 6-8 | Jocelyn Velez |
| Puente Charter S | 10000 S Western Ave | Los Angeles, CA | 90047 | 323-756-4921 | 754-8464 | K-K | Megan McGarry |
| Puente Charter S | 501 S Boyle Ave | Los Angeles, CA | 90033-3816 | 323-780-8900 | | K-K | Karen Castro |

| School | Address | City,State | Zip code | Telephone | Fax | Grade | Contact |
|---|---|---|---|---|---|---|---|
| Quail Lake Charter S | 4087 N Quail Lake Dr | Clovis, CA | 93619-4646 | 559-524-6720 | 292-1276 | K-8 | Kim Labosky |
| REACH | 708 Gravenstein Hwy N | Sebastopol, CA | 95472-2808 | 707-823-8618 | 829-6285 | K-8 | Julie Heinsen |
| Reagan ES | 1180 Diane Ave | Kingsburg, CA | 93631-2830 | 559-897-6986 | 897-6987 | 4-6 | Bobby Rodriguez |
| REALM Charter HS | 1222 University Ave | Berkeley, CA | 94702-1766 | 510-665-8300 | 809-9899 | 9-12 | Victor Diaz |
| REALM Charter MS | 2023 8th St | Berkeley, CA | 94710-2026 | 510-809-9800 | 809-9899 | 6-8 | Victor Diaz |
| Redding School of the Arts II | 955 Inspiration Pl | Redding, CA | 96003-8297 | 530-243-7145 | 243-4318 | K-8 | Margaret Johnson |
| Redding STEM Academy | 3711 Oasis Rd | Redding, CA | 96003 | 530-275-5480 | 275-5416 | K-8 | John Husome |
| Redwood Academy of Ukiah | PO Box 1383 | Ukiah, CA | 95482-1383 | 707-467-0500 | 467-4942 | 7-12 | Rod Logan |
| Redwood Coast Montessori | 1611 Peninsula Dr | Arcata, CA | 95521 | 707-832-4194 | 832-4194 | K-8 | Bryan Little |
| Redwood Preparatory Charter S | 1355 Ross Hill Rd | Fortuna, CA | 95540 | 707-682-6149 | | K-8 | Lisa Jager |
| Renaissance Arts Academy | 1800 Colorado Blvd | Los Angeles, CA | 90041-1340 | 323-259-5700 | 259-5718 | K-12 | Sidnie Myrick |
| Resolute Academy Charter | 1265 E 112th St | Los Angeles, CA | 90059 | 323-559-6284 | | 5-8 | Natasha Barriga-Sperstei |
| Revere Charter MS | 1450 Allenford Ave | Los Angeles, CA | 90049-3614 | 310-917-4800 | 576-7957 | 6-8 | Thomas Iannucci |
| Richmond Charter Academy | 251 S 12th St | Richmond, CA | 94804 | 510-899-4806 | 235-2469 | 6-8 | Jorge Lopez |
| Richmond College Prep S | PO Box 2814 | Richmond, CA | 94802-2814 | 510-235-2066 | | K-6 | Allie Welch |
| Ridgecrest Charter S | 325 S Downs St | Ridgecrest, CA | 93555-4531 | 760-375-1010 | 375-7766 | K-8 | Tina Ellingsworth |
| Riebli ES | 315 Mark West Springs Rd | Santa Rosa, CA | 95404-1101 | 707-524-2980 | 524-2986 | K-6 | Patty Dineen |
| Rincon Valley Charter S | 5305 Dupont Dr | Santa Rosa, CA | 95409-3843 | 707-539-3410 | 537-1791 | 7-8 | Matt Reno |
| Rio Valley Charter S | 1530 W Kettleman Ln Ste A | Lodi, CA | 95242 | 209-368-4934 | 368-4953 | K-12 | Marcie Grill |
| Rise Ko Hyang MS | 3020 Wilshire Blve Ste 2 | Los Angeles, CA | 90010 | 424-789-8338 | 256-3974 | 6-8 | Eliza Kim |
| Rising Sun Montessori S | 7006 Rossmore | El Dorado Hills, CA | 95762 | 916-936-2333 | | PK-8 | Karl Zierhut |
| Riverbank Language Academy Charter S | 2400 Stanislaus St | Riverbank, CA | 95367-2233 | 209-869-8093 | 869-0430 | K-8 | Vanessa Rojas |
| River Charter S Lighthouse Charter | 1500 Park Blvd | West Sacramento, CA | 95691 | 916-744-1212 | | K-8 | Steve Lewis |
| River Islands Technology Academy | 1175 Marina Dr | Lathrop, CA | 95330 | 209-229-4700 | | K-7 | Brenda Scholl |
| River MS | 2447 Old Sonoma Rd | Napa, CA | 94558-6006 | 707-253-6813 | 258-2800 | 6-8 | Celeste Akiu |
| River Montessori Charter S | 3880 Cypress Dr | Petaluma, CA | 94954 | 707-778-6414 | 773-5800 | 1-6 | Kelly Mannion |
| River Oak Charter S | 555 Leslie St | Ukiah, CA | 95482-5507 | 707-467-1855 | 467-1857 | K-8 | Rima Meechan |
| River Oaks Academy Charter S | 920 Hampshire Rd Ste X | Westlake Vlg, CA | 91361 | 805-777-7999 | 777-7998 | K-12 | Claudia Weintraub |
| Riverside County Education Academy | 13730 Perris Blvd | Moreno Valley, CA | 92553 | 951-826-4905 | | 9-12 | Santos Campos |
| Riverside Drive ES | 13061 Riverside Dr | Sherman Oaks, CA | 91423-2199 | 818-990-4525 | 789-4835 | K-5 | Kesia Doucette |
| Riverside Preparatory S | PO Box 455 | Oro Grande, CA | 92368-0455 | 760-243-5884 | 843-3766 | K-12 | Eugene Titus |
| River Springs Charter S | 43466 Business Park Dr | Temecula, CA | 92590-5526 | 951-252-8800 | 252-8801 | K-12 | Amy Podratz |
| River Valley Charter S | 9707 1/2 Marilla Dr | Lakeside, CA | 92040-2868 | 619-390-2579 | 390-2581 | 7-12 | Travis Wall |
| Roberts Institute of Learning Charter S | 6785 Imperial Ave | San Diego, CA | 92114-4317 | 619-674-6019 | 546-0274 | K-6 | Shelia Malveaux |
| Rocketship Academy Brilliant Minds | 2960 Story Road | San Jose, CA | 95127 | 408-708-5650 | 618-8637 | PK-4 | Amy Filsinger |
| Rocketship Alma Academy | 198 W Alma Ave | San Jose, CA | 95110 | 877-931-6838 | 982-3691 | K-5 | Hana Martinez |
| Rocketship Discovery Prep S | 370 Wooster Ave | San Jose, CA | 95116-1095 | 408-217-8951 | 217-9251 | K-6 | Eesir Kaur |
| Rocketship Fuerza Community Prep | 70 S Jackson Ave | San Jose, CA | 95116 | 408-708-5744 | | K-4 | Maricela Guerrero |
| Rocketship Los Suenos Academy | 331 S 34th St | San Jose, CA | 95116 | 877-684-4028 | 935-6084 | K-5 | Judy Lavi |
| Rocketship Mateo Sheedy ES | 788 Locust St | San Jose, CA | 95110 | 408-286-3330 | 286-3331 | K-5 | Jason Fromoltz |
| Rocketship Mosaic ES | 950 Owsley Ave | San Jose, CA | 95122 | 408-899-2607 | 899-2613 | K-5 | Danny Etcheverry |
| Rocketship Si Se Puede Academy | 2249 Dobern Ave | San Jose, CA | 95116-3405 | 408-286-3344 | 286-3331 | K-12 | Heidy Shinn |
| Rocketship Spark Academy | 683 Sylvandale Ave | San Jose, CA | 95111 | 408-622-6651 | 622-5748 | K-5 | Jaclyn O'Brien |
| Rocklin Academy | 6532 Turnstone Way | Rocklin, CA | 95765-5865 | 916-632-6580 | 784-3034 | K-6 | Laura Regan |
| Rocklin Academy at Meyers Street | 5035 Meyers St | Rocklin, CA | 95677-2811 | 916-632-6580 | 784-3034 | K-6 | Wendy Mitchell |
| Rocklin Academy Gateway | 6550 Lonetree Blvd | Rocklin, CA | 95765 | 916-632-6580 | 784-3034 | PK-8 | Jillyane Antoon |
| Rocklin Independent Charter Academy | 3250 Victory Dr | Rocklin, CA | 95765 | 916-632-3195 | | K-12 | Mark Williams |
| Rocky Point Charter S | 3500 Tamarack Dr | Redding, CA | 96003-1747 | 530-225-0456 | 225-0499 | K-8 | Deborah Stierli |
| Romero Charter S | 1157 S Berendo St | Los Angeles, CA | 90006 | 213-413-9600 | 413-9699 | 6-8 | Jose Castillo |
| Roosevelt Community Learning Center | 31191 Road 180 | Visalia, CA | 93292-9585 | 559-592-9160 | 592-2927 | K-12 | Daniel Huecker |
| Roosevelt ES | 1185 10th Ave | Kingsburg, CA | 93631-2100 | 559-897-5193 | 897-6865 | 1-1 | Lori Willson |
| Rosa Parks Academy | 1930 S D St | Stockton, CA | 95206-2489 | 209-944-5590 | 465-2690 | K-5 | Natalie June |
| Roseland Accelerated MS | 1777 West Ave | Santa Rosa, CA | 95407-7449 | 707-546-7089 | 546-0434 | 7-8 | Haley Piazza |
| Roseland Collegiate Prep | 80 Ursuline Rd | Santa Rosa, CA | 95403 | 707-528-1764 | 528-8605 | 7-10 | Danielle Yount |
| Roseland University Preparatory S | 100 Sebastopol Rd | Santa Rosa, CA | 95407-6928 | 707-566-9990 | 566-9992 | 9-12 | Sue Reese |
| Roses in Concrete Community S | 4551 Steele St | Oakland, CA | 94619 | 510-698-3794 | | K-8 | Jeff Duncan-Andrade |
| Sacramento HS | 2315 34th St | Sacramento, CA | 95817-1299 | 916-277-6200 | 277-6370 | 9-12 | Michelle Seijas |
| Sacramento Valley Charter S | 2301 Evergreen Ave | West Sacramento, CA | 95691 | 916-596-6422 | 564-5764 | K-8 | Sheila Gibson |
| St. Hope Public School 7 | 5201 Strawberry Ln | Sacramento, CA | 95820-4815 | 916-649-7850 | 277-7039 | K-8 | Erin Marston |
| Salmon Creek S | 1935 Bohemian Hwy | Occidental, CA | 95465-9100 | 707-874-1205 | 874-1226 | 2-8 | Rene McBride |
| Samueli Academy | 1901 N Fairview St | Santa Ana, CA | 92706 | 714-619-0245 | 619-0252 | 9-12 | Anthony Saba |
| San Carlos Charter Learning Center | 750 Dartmouth Ave | San Carlos, CA | 94070 | 650-508-7343 | 508-7341 | K-8 | Stacy Emory |
| San Diego Cooperative Charter S | 7260 Linda Vista Rd | San Diego, CA | 92111-6128 | 858-496-1613 | 467-9741 | K-8 | Dr. Sarah Saluta |
| San Diego Cooperative Charter S 2 | PO Box 13926 | San Diego, CA | 92170 | 619-840-6993 | | K-8 | Anthony Villasenor |
| San Diego Cooperative Charter S 2 | 3550 Logan Ave | San Diego, CA | 92113 | 619-840-6993 | | K-8 | Anthony Vissasenor |
| San Diego Global Vision Academy | 3430 School St | San Diego, CA | 92116-3423 | 619-600-5321 | 550-3637 | K-5 | Dena Harris |
| San Diego Neighborhood Homeschools | 3548 Seagate Way Ste 140 | Oceanside, CA | 92056-2676 | 760-295-1117 | 509-4691 | K-12 | Salvador Leon |
| San Diego Virtual Charter S | 7950 University Ave | La Mesa, CA | 91942 | 619-713-7271 | 308-6007 | 7-12 | Brennan McLaughlin |
| San Francisco Flex Academy | 1350 7th Ave | San Francisco, CA | 94122 | 415-762-8800 | 366-2637 | 6-12 | Charleston Brown |
| Sanger Academy Charter S | 2207 9th St | Sanger, CA | 93657-2711 | 559-524-6840 | 875-8045 | K-8 | Christy Platt |
| San Jacinto Valley Academy | 480 N San Jacinto Ave | San Jacinto, CA | 92583-2729 | 951-654-6113 | 644-5083 | K-12 | Penny Harrison |
| San Joaquin Building Futures Academy | PO Box 213030 | Stockton, CA | 95213-9030 | 209-468-8140 | 468-4951 | 9-12 | Janine Cuaresma |
| San Jose Charter Academy | 2021 W Alwood St | West Covina, CA | 91790-3259 | 626-856-1693 | 480-7125 | K-8 | Dr. Denise Patton |
| San Jose Conservation Corps Charter S | 1560 Berger Dr | San Jose, CA | 95112-2703 | 408-283-7171 | | 12-12 | Stephanie Ogden |
| San Juan Choices Charter S | 4425 Laurelwood Way | Sacramento, CA | 95864-0881 | 916-979-8378 | | 7-12 | Anthony Oddo |
| San Lorenzo Valley USD Charter S | 325 Marion Ave | Ben Lomond, CA | 95005 | 831-335-0932 | 336-0131 | K-12 | Rhonda Schlosser |
| San Miguel ES | 5350 Faught Rd | Santa Rosa, CA | 95403-1205 | 707-524-2960 | 524-2968 | K-6 | Nicole Lamare |
| Santa Barbara Charter S | 6100 Stow Canyon Rd | Goleta, CA | 93117-1705 | 805-967-6522 | 967-6382 | K-8 | |
| Santa Clarita Valley International S | 28060 Hasley Canyon Rd | Castaic, CA | 91384 | 661-705-4820 | 607-0295 | K-12 | Kimberlee Shaw |
| Santa Monica Blvd Community Charter S | 1022 N Van Ness Ave | Los Angeles, CA | 90038-3252 | 323-469-0971 | 462-4093 | K-6 | David Riddick |
| Santa Rosa Academy | 28237 La Piedra Rd | Menifee, CA | 92584-8947 | 951-672-2400 | 672-6060 | K-12 | Midge James |
| Santa Rosa Accelerated Charter | 4650 Badger Rd | Santa Rosa, CA | 95409-2633 | 707-528-5319 | 528-5644 | 5-6 | Matt Marshall |
| Santa Rosa Charter Academy | 3838 Eagle Rock Blvd | Los Angeles, CA | 90065-3638 | 323-254-1703 | 254-0958 | 6-8 | Shirley Aragon |
| Santa Rosa Charter S | PO Box 2508 | Santa Rosa, CA | 95405 | 707-547-2480 | 547-2482 | PK-8 | LaDonna Moore |
| Santa Rosa Charter S for the Arts | 2230 Lomitas Ave | Santa Rosa, CA | 95404 | 707-522-3170 | 522-3172 | K-8 | Paul Gaudreau |
| Santa Rosa French-American Charter S | 1350 Sonoma Ave | Santa Rosa, CA | 95405-6623 | 707-522-3161 | | K-6 | Pascal Stricher |
| Santa Ynez Valley Charter S | PO Box 59 | Santa Ynez, CA | 93460-0059 | 805-686-7360 | 686-7383 | K-8 | Mark Palmerston |
| Santiago Charter MS | 515 N Rancho Santiago Blvd | Orange, CA | 92869-2724 | 714-997-6366 | 532-4758 | 7-8 | James D'Agostino |
| Sartorette Charter S | 3850 Woodford Dr | San Jose, CA | 95124-3736 | 408-264-4380 | 264-1758 | K-5 | Scott Johnson |
| SAVA: Sacramento Academic and Vocational | 3141 Dwight Rd Ste 400 | Elk Grove, CA | 95758-6473 | 916-428-3200 | 428-3232 | 7-12 | Morri Elliott |
| SAVA: Sacramento Academic and Vocational | 5330 Power Inn Rd Ste D | Sacramento, CA | 95820-6757 | 916-387-8063 | 387-0139 | 7-12 | Morri Elliott |
| SCALE Leadership Academy | 13089 Peyton Dr | Chino Hills, CA | 91709 | 888-315-4660 | | 6-8 | Lawrence Wynder |
| Schaefer Charter S | 1370 San Miguel Rd | Santa Rosa, CA | 95403-1986 | 707-522-3015 | 522-3017 | K-6 | Joe Hamp |
| School of Arts and Enterprise | 295 N Garey Ave | Pomona, CA | 91767-5429 | 909-622-0699 | 620-1018 | 6-12 | Lucille Berger |
| School of Extended Educational Options | 1460 E Holt Ave Ste 100 | Pomona, CA | 91767 | 909-397-4900 | 622-2496 | 7-12 | Tom Sweeney |
| School of Unlimited Learning | 2336 Calaveras St | Fresno, CA | 93721-1104 | 559-498-8543 | 237-0956 | 9-12 | Dr. Mark Wilson |
| Science and Technology Charter S | PO Box 458 | Knights Landing, CA | 95645-0458 | 530-735-6435 | 735-6155 | K-6 | Barbara Herms |
| Sebastopol Independent Charter S | PO Box 1170 | Sebastopol, CA | 95473-1170 | 707-824-9700 | 824-1432 | K-8 | Dr. Chris Topham |
| Serna Charter S | 19 S Central Ave | Lodi, CA | 95240-2901 | 209-331-7809 | 331-7997 | K-6 | Maria Cervantes |
| Serrania Charter for Enriched Studies | 5014 Serrania Ave | Woodland Hills, CA | 91364-3350 | 818-340-6700 | 592-0565 | K-5 | Luis Alvarado |
| Shasta Charter Academy | 1401 Gold St | Redding, CA | 96001-1937 | 530-245-2600 | 245-2611 | 8-12 | Ben Claassen M.A. |
| Shasta Charter Academy | 1401 Gold St | Redding, CA | 96001 | 530-245-2600 | 245-2611 | 9-12 | Benjamin Claassen |
| Shenandoah HS | 6540 Koki Ln | El Dorado, CA | 95623-4328 | 530-622-6212 | 622-1071 | 9-12 | Debby Hanson |
| Shenandoah Valley MS | 10010 Shenandoah Rd | Plymouth, CA | 95669 | 209-257-5334 | | 5-8 | |
| Sherman Oaks Charter S | 14755 Greenleaf St | Sherman Oaks, CA | 91403-4199 | 818-784-8283 | 981-8258 | K-5 | Michelle Gorsuch |
| Sherwood Montessori S | 746 Moss Ave | Chico, CA | 95926-2900 | 530-513-2296 | | K-8 | Michelle Yezbick |
| SIATech Charter S | 1949 Avenida del Oro | Oceanside, CA | 92056 | 760-945-1227 | 631-3411 | 9-12 | Dr. Linda Dawson |
| Sierra Academy of Expeditionary Learning | 340 Buena Vista St | Grass Valley, CA | 95945 | 530-268-2200 | | 9-12 | Erica Crane |
| Sierra Charter S | 1931 N Fine Ave | Fresno, CA | 93727-1534 | 559-490-4290 | 490-4292 | K-12 | Lisa Marasco |
| Sierra Expeditionary Learning | 11603 Donner Pass Rd | Truckee, CA | 96161-4953 | 530-414-5326 | 448-8115 | K-8 | David Manahan |
| Sierra Foothill Charter S | 4952 School House Rd | Catheys Valley, CA | 95306-9710 | 209-742-6222 | 742-6922 | K-8 | Alfonso Garagarza |
| Sierra Montessori Academy | 16229 Duggans Rd | Grass Valley, CA | 95949 | 530-268-9990 | 268-0613 | K-8 | Henry Bietz |
| Sierra Vista Charter HS | 351 N K St | Tulare, CA | 93274 | 559-687-7384 | 687-7388 | 9-12 | Larriann Torrez |
| Silicon Valley Flex Academy | 305 W Main Ave | Morgan Hill, CA | 95037-4530 | 408-659-0088 | | 9-12 | Caroline Wood |
| Silver Oak HS | 951 Palisade St | Hayward, CA | 94542 | 510-370-3334 | | 9-12 | Elaine Blasi |
| Simon Technology Acad HS | 10720 Wilmington Ave | Los Angeles, CA | 90059-1236 | 323-744-2122 | 744-2123 | 9-12 | Dr. Clarence Miller |
| Six Rivers Charter HS | 1720 M St | Arcata, CA | 95521-5741 | 707-825-2428 | 825-2034 | 9-12 | Nic Collart |
| Sixth Grade Academy | 700 Bantam Way | Petaluma, CA | 94952-1709 | 707-778-4724 | | 6-6 | Renee Semik |
| Sixth Street Prep-STREAM S | 12219 2nd Ave | Victorville, CA | 92395 | 760-241-0962 | 241-2497 | K-6 | Linda Rueter |
| Skirball MS | 603 E 115th St | Los Angeles, CA | 90059-2322 | 323-905-1377 | 905-1378 | 6-8 | Joy May-Harris |
| Sky Mountain Charter S | 4535 Missouri Flat Rd | Placerville, CA | 95667-6846 | 530-295-3566 | 295-3583 | K-12 | Susan Clark |
| Smidt Technology HS | 211 S Avenue 20 | Los Angeles, CA | 90031-2508 | 323-352-3206 | | 9-12 | Dr. Dean Marolla-Turner |
| Smythe Academy of Arts & Sciences | 2781 Northgate Blvd | Sacramento, CA | 95833-2208 | 916-566-2740 | 566-3584 | PK-6 | Ken Dandurand |
| Smythe Academy of Arts & Sciences | 700 Dos Rios St | Sacramento, CA | 95811-0434 | 916-566-3430 | 566-3531 | 7-8 | Melissa Jewell |
| SOAR Charter Academy | 198 W Mill St | San Bernardino, CA | 92408 | 909-888-3300 | 888-3310 | K-8 | Trisha Lancaster |
| Sol Aureus College Prep Charter S | 6620 Gloria Dr | Sacramento, CA | 95831-1655 | 916-421-0600 | 421-0601 | K-8 | Norman Hernandez |
| Soledad Enrichment Action Charter S | 222 N Virgil Ave | Los Angeles, CA | 90004-3622 | 213-480-4200 | 480-4199 | 9-12 | Margaret Godinez |

| School | Address | City,State | Zip code | Telephone | Fax | Grade | Contact |
|---|---|---|---|---|---|---|---|
| Sonoma Charter S | 17202 Highway 12 | Sonoma, CA | 95476 | 707-935-4232 | 935-4207 | K-8 | Kevin Kassebaum |
| Sonoma Mountain ES | 1900 Rainier Cir | Petaluma, CA | 94954-2543 | 707-765-4305 | 765-4385 | K-6 | Michele Gochberg |
| South Bay Charter S | 6077 Loma Ave | Eureka, CA | 95503 | 707-443-4828 | 444-3690 | K-8 | Gary Storts |
| South Sutter Charter S | 4535 Missouri Flat Rd Ste1A | Placerville, CA | 95667 | 800-979-4436 | 295-3583 | K-12 | Jason Jones |
| Spark Charter S | 739 Morse Ave | Sunnyvale, CA | 94085 | 408-752-2631 | | K-8 | Bill Overton Ed.D. |
| Spring Creek Matanzas Charter S | 1687 Yulupa Ave | Santa Rosa, CA | 95405-7778 | 707-546-6183 | 528-8027 | 4-6 | Kate Westrich |
| Spring Creek Matanzas Charter S | 4675 Mayette Ave | Santa Rosa, CA | 95405-7399 | 707-545-1771 | 545-6926 | PK-3 | Jay Dowd |
| Squaw Valley Preparatory | PO Box 2891 | Olympic Valley, CA | 96146 | 530-581-1036 | 581-2012 | 6-12 | Jeff Kraunz |
| Stallworth Charter S | 1610 E Main St | Stockton, CA | 95205 | 209-948-4511 | 943-5218 | PK-8 | Robin Mooreziad |
| Stanislaus Alternative Charter S | 1120 13th St | Modesto, CA | 95354 | 209-238-6801 | 238-4216 | 9-12 | Julie Moore |
| Steele Canyon Charter HS | 12440 Campo Rd | Spring Valley, CA | 91978-2331 | 619-660-3500 | 660-7198 | 9-12 | Don Hohimer |
| Stella Middle Charter Academy | 2636 S Mansfield Ave | Los Angeles, CA | 90016-3512 | 323-406-7155 | 954-6415 | 5-6 | Darryl Garris |
| Stellar Charter School | 5885 E Bonnyview Rd | Redding, CA | 96001-4535 | 530-245-7730 | 245-7731 | K-12 | Patti Furnari |
| Stern Math and Science S | 5151 State Univ Dr Lot 7 | Los Angeles, CA | 90032 | 323-987-2144 | 987-2149 | 9-12 | Kirsten Woo Ph.D. |
| Stockton Collegiate International ES | PO Box 2286 | Stockton, CA | 95201-2286 | 209-390-9861 | 390-9862 | K-5 | Scott Luhn |
| Stockton Collegiate International S | PO Box 2286 | Stockton, CA | 95201 | 209-390-9861 | 390-9862 | 6-12 | Scott Luhn |
| Stockton Early College Academy | 349 E Vine St | Stockton, CA | 95202 | 209-933-7370 | 939-9504 | 9-12 | Joshaua Thom |
| Stockton HS | 22 S Van Buren St | Stockton, CA | 95203-3118 | 209-933-7365 | 469-3740 | 9-12 | Maryann Santella |
| Stone Bridge S | 1680 Los Carneros Ave | Napa, CA | 94559 | 707-252-5522 | 251-9767 | K-8 | Bill Bindewald |
| Stony Point Academy | 3223 Primrose Ave | Santa Rosa, CA | 95407 | 707-568-7504 | | K-9 | Lisa Katimbang |
| STREAM Charter S | 479 Oro Dam Blvd | Oroville, CA | 95965 | 530-534-1633 | | K-8 | Donald Phillips |
| Success One Charter S | 451 S Villa Ave | Willows, CA | 95988 | 530-934-6575 | | K-5 | Susan Domenighini |
| Summit Charter Academy | 2036 E Hatch Rd | Modesto, CA | 95351-5142 | 209-538-8082 | 538-1620 | K-5 | Jamey Olney |
| Summit Charter Academy - Lombardi Campus | 1509 Lombardi St | Porterville, CA | 93257-9293 | 559-788-6445 | | K-6 | Treasure Weisenberger |
| Summit Charter Academy - Mathew Campus | 175 S Mathew St | Porterville, CA | 93257-2710 | 559-782-5902 | 782-5907 | K-6 | Lily Shimer |
| Summit Charter Collegiate Academy | 15550 Redwood St | Porterville, CA | 93257 | 559-788-6440 | 788-6444 | 6-12 | Krista Gaines-Herrera |
| Summit K2 Charter S | 1800 Elm St | El Cerrito, CA | 94530 | 510-697-2843 | | 7-12 | Kelly Garcia |
| Summit Leadership Academy High Desert | 12850 Muscatel St | Hesperia, CA | 92344-5566 | 760-949-9202 | 949-9257 | 9-12 | Shannon Brandner |
| Summit Preparatory Charter HS | 890 Broadway St | Redwood City, CA | 94063-3105 | 650-556-1110 | 556-1121 | 9-12 | Penelope Pak |
| Summit Preparatory Charter S | 5100 S Broadway Ave | Los Angeles, CA | 90037 | 323-642-8806 | | 4-8 | Arianna Haut |
| Summit Public S: Rainier | 1750 S White Rd | San Jose, CA | 95127 | 408-831-3104 | 831-3105 | 9-12 | Kevin Bock |
| Summit Public S: Shasta | 699 Serramonte Blvd | Daly City, CA | 94015 | 650-799-4719 | 799-4721 | 9-12 | Caitlyn Herman |
| Summit Public S: Tahoma | 285 Blossom Hill Rd | San Jose, CA | 95123 | 408-729-1981 | 729-3853 | 9-12 | Nicholas Kim |
| Summit Public School: Denali | 495 Mercury Dr | Sunnyvale, CA | 94085-4707 | 669-600-5697 | | 6-12 | Joe Bielecki |
| SunRidge Charter S | 7285 Hayden Ave | Sebastopol, CA | 95472-4359 | 707-824-2844 | 824-2861 | K-8 | Kalen Wood |
| Sunrise MS | 1149 E Julian St | San Jose, CA | 95116 | 877-659-4785 | | 6-8 | Teresa Robinson |
| Sunset Charter S | 1755 S Crystal Ave | Fresno, CA | 93706-2797 | 559-457-3310 | 495-1334 | K-8 | Juan Silva |
| Sutter Peak Charter Academy | 6450 20th St | Rio Linda, CA | 95673 | 866-992-9033 | | K-12 | Heather Marshall |
| Sycamore Academy Science & Cultural Arts | 23151 Palomar St | Wildomar, CA | 92595 | 951-678-5217 | 678-5932 | K-6 | Barbara Hale |
| Sycamore Valley Academy | 4230 W Tulare Ave | Visalia, CA | 93277 | 559-622-3236 | 622-3237 | K-8 | Ruth Dutton |
| Synergy Charter Academy | PO Box 78999 | Los Angeles, CA | 90016-0999 | 323-235-7960 | 235-7970 | K-5 | Kristine Miklos |
| Synergy Kinetic Academy | PO Box 78999 | Los Angeles, CA | 90016-0999 | 323-846-2225 | 846-2234 | 6-8 | Christine Mayhill |
| Synergy Quantum Academy | PO Box 78999 | Los Angeles, CA | 90016-0999 | 323-846-4716 | 846-4729 | 9-12 | Dr. Phillip Gedeon |
| Synergy S | 355 E Leland Rd | Pittsburg, CA | 94565 | 925-252-1900 | 252-1933 | 6-12 | Cheryl Townsend |
| Taft Charter HS | 5461 Winnetka Ave | Woodland Hills, CA | 91364-2592 | 818-227-3600 | 592-0877 | 9-12 | Daniel Steiner |
| Taylion Academy | 1184 W 2nd St Ste 101 | San Bernardino, CA | 92410 | 909-889-5152 | 889-5154 | K-12 | |
| Taylion High Desert Academy | 11336 Bartlett Ave Ste 9 | Adelanto, CA | 92301 | 855-246-0088 | | K-12 | Timothy Smith |
| Taylion San Diego Academy | 100 N Rancho Santa Fe Rd | San Marcos, CA | 92069-1279 | 760-295-5564 | 295-5614 | K-12 | Timothy Smith |
| TEACH Academy of Technologies | 10045 S Western Ave | Los Angeles, CA | 90047 | 323-777-2068 | 777-7143 | 5-8 | Dr. Greg Perez |
| TEACH Tech Charter HS | 10000 S Western Ave | Los Angeles, CA | 90047 | 323-750-8471 | 750-8477 | 9-12 | Raul Carranza |
| TEAM Charter S | 600 E Main St | Stockton, CA | 95202 | 209-462-2282 | | PK-5 | Marlesse Cavazos |
| Tehama eLearning Academy | 715 Jackson St Ste B | Red Bluff, CA | 96080-3771 | 530-527-0188 | 527-0273 | 6-12 | Rich DuVarney |
| Temecula Preparatory S | 35777 Abelia St | Winchester, CA | 92596-8450 | 951-926-6776 | 926-6797 | K-12 | Michael Tracy |
| Temecula Valley Charter S | 35755 Abelia St | Winchester, CA | 92596-8450 | 951-294-6775 | 294-6780 | K-8 | Lois Hastings |
| Tennenbaum Family Technology HS | 2050 N San Fernando Rd | Los Angeles, CA | 90065-1267 | 323-276-5545 | | 9-12 | Dr. Abigail Nunez |
| Thomas Charter HS | 101 W Adell St | Madera, CA | 93638-0877 | 559-675-6626 | 675-6612 | 9-12 | Tera Napier |
| Thomas Charter S | 101 W Adell St | Madera, CA | 93638-0877 | 559-674-1192 | 674-8955 | K-8 | Tera Napier |
| Three Rivers Charter S | 1211 Del Mar Dr | Fort Bragg, CA | 95437 | 707-964-1128 | 964-1003 | K-12 | Roger Coy |
| Thrive Public Charter S | 4260 54th St | San Diego, CA | 92115 | 619-839-9543 | | K-8 | Nicole Assisi |
| Tierra Linda MS | 750 Dartmouth Ave | San Carlos, CA | 94070-1769 | 650-508-7370 | 508-7341 | 5-8 | John Nazar |
| Tierra Pacifica Charter S | 986 Bostwick Ln | Santa Cruz, CA | 95062 | 831-462-9404 | 477-0936 | K-8 | Linda Lambdin |
| Today's Fresh Start Charter S | 2301 E Rosencrans Ave | Compton, CA | 90221 | 310-631-1502 | | K-8 | Tanya Goff |
| Today's Fresh Start Charter S | 6422 Crenshaw Blvd | Los Angeles, CA | 90043 | | | K-8 | |
| Today's Fresh Start Charter S | 2255 W Adams Blvd | Los Angeles, CA | 90018 | 323-732-6636 | | K-8 | |
| Today's Fresh Start Charter S | 4476 Crenshaw Blvd | Los Angeles, CA | 90043 | 323-299-2105 | | K-8 | |
| Today's Fresh Start Charter S | 3405 W Imperial Hwy | Inglewood, CA | 90303 | 310-680-7599 | | K-8 | Jeanette Parker |
| Topanga Charter ES | 22075 Topanga School Rd | Topanga, CA | 90290-3835 | 310-455-3711 | 455-3517 | K-6 | Steven Gediman |
| Topeka Charter S for Advanced Studies | 9815 Topeka Dr | Northridge, CA | 91324-1800 | 818-886-2266 | 885-7682 | K-5 | Temika Dixon |
| Tree of Life Montessori Charter S | PO Box 966 | Ukiah, CA | 95482-0966 | 707-462-0913 | 462-0914 | PK-8 | Celeste Beck |
| Trillium Charter S | 1464 Spear Ave | Arcata, CA | 95521-4882 | 707-822-4721 | 822-7054 | PK-5 | Marianne Keller |
| Triumph Center for Early Childhood Ed | 4104 Martin Luther King Jr | Sacramento, CA | 95820 | 916-731-8200 | | PK-PK | Allison Ferry |
| Triumph Charter S | 13361 Glenoaks Blvd | Sylmar, CA | 91342 | 818-356-2795 | 979-6579 | 6-12 | Christine Graves |
| Trivium Charter S | 1600 Berkeley | Lompoc, CA | 93436 | 805-291-1303 | | K-12 | Trisha Vais |
| Tubman Village Charter S | 6880 Mohawk St | San Diego, CA | 92115-1728 | 619-668-8635 | 668-2480 | K-8 | Aimee Nimtz |
| Twin Hills Charter MS | 1685 Watertrough Rd | Sebastopol, CA | 95472-4647 | 707-823-7446 | 823-6470 | 6-8 | Catherine Bosch |
| Twin Ridges Home Study Charter S | 111 New Mohawk Rd | Nevada City, CA | 95959-3270 | 530-478-1815 | 478-0266 | K-8 | Jenny Travers |
| Twin Rivers Charter S | 840 Cooper Ave | Yuba City, CA | 95991-3849 | 530-755-2872 | 673-1847 | K-8 | Stephen Montana |
| Uncharted Shores Academy | 330 E St | Crescent City, CA | 95531-3945 | 707-464-9828 | 464-1428 | PK-8 | Margie Rouge |
| Union Street Charter S | 470 Union St | Arcata, CA | 95521-6429 | 707-822-4845 | 825-9025 | K-5 | John Schmidt |
| University Charter MS | 700 Temple Ave | Camarillo, CA | 93010 | 805-484-1872 | 388-5814 | 6-8 | Gayle Hughes |
| University HS | 2611 E Matoian Way MS/UH134 | Fresno, CA | 93740-0001 | 559-278-8263 | 278-0447 | 9-12 | Dr. James Bushman |
| University Preparation S | 550 Temple Ave | Camarillo, CA | 93010-4833 | 805-482-4608 | 388-5814 | PK-5 | Charmon Evans |
| University Preparatory Academy | 2315 Canoas Garden Ave | San Jose, CA | 95125-2005 | 408-723-1839 | 779-0519 | 7-12 | Daniel Ordaz |
| University Preparatory HS | 915 S Mooney Blvd | Visalia, CA | 93277-2214 | 559-730-2529 | 737-4378 | 9-12 | Eric Thiessen |
| University Preparatory S | 2200 Eureka Way | Redding, CA | 96001-0337 | 530-245-2790 | 245-2791 | 6-12 | Shelle Peterson |
| University Preparatory Value HS | 700 Wilshire Blvd 4th Flr | Los Angeles, CA | 90017 | 213-335-3730 | | 9-12 | David Doyle |
| Urban Discovery Academy | 730 45th St | San Diego, CA | 92102 | 619-788-4668 | 688-9796 | K-8 | Mike Seal |
| Urban Montessori Charter S | 5328 Brann St | Oakland, CA | 94619 | 510-842-1181 | 535-3841 | K-8 | David Castillo |
| USC East College Prep | 3825 N Mission Rd | Los Angeles, CA | 90031 | 323-285-1441 | | 9-12 | Andrew Goltermann |
| Valdez Leadership Academy | 1855 Lucretia Ave | San Jose, CA | 95122 | 408-384-4015 | 936-3095 | 9-12 | Jeffrey Camarillo |
| Vallejo Charter S | 2833 Tennessee St | Vallejo, CA | 94591 | 707-556-8620 | 556-8624 | K-8 | Marilyn Abelon |
| Valley Arts & Science Academy | 735 N Glenn Ave | Fresno, CA | 93728-3714 | 559-497-8272 | 497-5621 | K-6 | Sandy Fuerte |
| Valley Charter ES | 16514 Nordhoff St | North Hills, CA | 91343-3724 | 818-810-6713 | 810-9667 | K-5 | Leslie Lainer |
| Valley Charter HS | 108 Campus Way | Modesto, CA | 95350-5803 | 209-238-6800 | 238-6897 | 9-12 | Susan Nisan |
| Valley Charter MS | 9229 Haskell Ave | North Hills, CA | 91343 | 818-830-7562 | 830-7672 | 6-8 | Matthew Rubin |
| Valley Life Charter S | 3737 W Walnut Ave | Visalia, CA | 93277 | 559-761-1299 | | K-12 | Lori Lackey |
| Valley Oak Charter S | PO Box 878 | Ojai, CA | 93024-0878 | 805-640-4421 | 646-4700 | K-12 | Laura Fulmer |
| Valley Oaks Charter S | 1300 17th St | Bakersfield, CA | 93301-4504 | 661-852-6750 | 633-5287 | K-12 | Deanna Downs |
| Valley Preparatory Academy | 4221 N Hughes Ave | Fresno, CA | 93705-1611 | 559-225-7737 | 225-0976 | K-8 | Shelly Lether |
| Valley View Charter Prep | 2453 Grand Canal Blvd | Stockton, CA | 95207 | 916-866-9033 | 991-5770 | K-12 | John Mittan |
| Valor Academy Charter HS | 8015 Van Nuys Blvd | Panorama City, CA | 91402 | 323-934-8910 | 934-8916 | 9-12 | Evelyn Licea |
| Valor Academy Charter S | 9034 Burnet Ave | North Hills, CA | 91343 | 818-830-1700 | 830-1799 | 5-8 | Maurice Regalado |
| Van Gogh Charter S | 17160 Van Gogh St | Granada Hills, CA | 91344-1299 | 818-360-2141 | 831-9081 | K-5 | Pamela Merloni |
| Vantage Point Charter S | 10862 Spenceville Rd | Penn Valley, CA | 95946-9625 | 530-432-5312 | 432-8744 | K-12 | Thomas Bivens |
| Vaughn Next Century Learning Center | 13330 Vaughn St | San Fernando, CA | 91340 | 818-896-7461 | 834-9036 | PK-12 | Anita Zepeda |
| Ventura S of Arts & Global Education | PO Box 392 | Ventura, CA | 93002-0392 | 805-648-5503 | 648-5539 | K-8 | Mary Galvin |
| Venture Academy | PO Box 213030 | Stockton, CA | 95213-9030 | 209-468-5940 | 468-9000 | K-12 | Kathleen Focacci |
| View Park Accelerated MS | 5010 11th Ave | Los Angeles, CA | 90043-4816 | 323-290-6970 | 290-9271 | 6-8 | Leslie Shaw-Mcgee |
| View Park Prep Accelerated Charter ES | 3751 W 54th St | Los Angeles, CA | 90043-2356 | 323-290-6950 | 298-4935 | K-5 | Kenneth Wheeler |
| View Park Prep Accelerated HS | 5701 Crenshaw Blvd | Los Angeles, CA | 90043-2409 | 323-290-6975 | 881-4924 | 9-12 | Dr. Hurshel Williams |
| Village Charter Academy | 7357 Jordan Ave | Canoga Park, CA | 91303 | 818-716-2887 | | K-5 | Jennifer Clark |
| Village Charter S | 2590 Piner Rd | Santa Rosa, CA | 95401 | 707-524-2848 | | K-8 | Rebecca Ivanoff |
| Village ES | 900 Yulupa Ave | Santa Rosa, CA | 95405-7099 | 707-545-5754 | 573-0951 | K-6 | Maria McCormick |
| Vincent Academy | 2501 Chestnut St | Oakland, CA | 94607 | 510-452-2100 | 452-2101 | K-5 | Kate Nicol |
| Visalia Charter Independent Study | 1821 W Meadow Ave | Visalia, CA | 93277 | 559-735-8055 | 622-3170 | 9-12 | Michele Reid |
| Visions in Education Charter S | 5030 El Camino Ave | Carmichael, CA | 95608 | 916-971-5331 | 971-5590 | K-12 | Dr. Jody Graf |
| Vista Charter MS | 2900 W Temple St | Los Angeles, CA | 90026 | 213-201-4000 | 201-5861 | 6-8 | Jose Kubes |
| Vista Heritage Charter MS | 2609 W Fifth St | Santa Ana, CA | 92703 | 714-988-2720 | 201-5861 | 6-8 | Lauri Martin |
| Vista Oaks Charter S | 14301 Byron Hwy | Byron, CA | 94514 | 925-420-6616 | | K-8 | Joy Groen |
| Vista Real Charter HS | 401 S A St Ste 3 | Oxnard, CA | 93030-5278 | 805-486-5449 | 486-5455 | 9-12 | Corrine Manley |
| Voices Academy at Morgan Hill | 16870 Murphy Ave | Morgan Hill, CA | 95037 | 408-763-5770 | | K-8 | Juan Carlos Villasenor |
| Voices Academy at Mt. Pleasant | 14271 Story Rd | San Jose, CA | 95127 | 408-684-3503 | | K-8 | Maria Madrigal |
| Voices College-Bound Language Academy | 715 Hellyer Ave | San Jose, CA | 95111 | 408-361-1960 | | K-8 | Frances Teso |
| Walden Academy | 1149 W Wood St | Willows, CA | 95988 | 530-361-6480 | | PK-5 | |
| Washington Charter S | 45768 Portola Ave | Palm Desert, CA | 92260-4861 | 760-862-4350 | 862-4356 | K-5 | Allan Lehmann |
| Washington ES | 1501 Ellis St | Kingsburg, CA | 93631-1896 | 559-897-2955 | 897-6863 | PK-K | Jennifer DuPras M.Ed. |
| Watsonville Charter S of the Arts | 75 Whiting Rd | Watsonville, CA | 95076 | 831-728-8123 | 728-6286 | K-8 | Amy Thomas |

| School | Address | City,State | Zip code | Telephone | Fax | Grade | Contact |
|---|---|---|---|---|---|---|---|
| Watts Learning Center | 310 W 95th St | Los Angeles, CA | 90003-4012 | 323-754-9900 | 754-0935 | K-5 | Kelly Baptiste |
| Watts Learning Ctr Charter MS | 8800 S San Pedro St | Los Angeles, CA | 90003 | 323-565-4800 | 750-5051 | 6-8 | Gayle Windom |
| W.E.B. DuBois Charter S | 2604 Martin Luther King Blv | Fresno, CA | 93706 | 559-486-1166 | 486-1199 | K-12 | Linda Washington |
| Weimar Hills Charter S | PO Box 255 | Weimar, CA | 95736-0255 | 530-637-4121 | 637-4054 | 6-8 | Marge Sigenfuse |
| Welby Way Charter ES & Gifted Magnet Ctr | 23456 Welby Way | West Hills, CA | 91307-3328 | 818-348-1975 | 704-8726 | K-5 | Jennifer Yoo |
| West Charter S | 5350 Faught Rd | Santa Rosa, CA | 95403-1205 | 707-524-2741 | 524-2782 | K-8 | Pam Carpenter |
| Westchester Secondary Charter S | 8540 La Tijera Blvd | Los Angeles, CA | 90045 | 310-216-6800 | | 6-10 | Janet Landon |
| Western Center Academy | 2345 Searl Pkwy | Hemet, CA | 92543 | 951-791-0033 | 791-0032 | 6-12 | Paul Bailey |
| Western Sierra Collegiate Academy | 660 Menlo Dr | Rocklin, CA | 95765 | 916-778-4544 | 626-5540 | 7-12 | Gregg Moses |
| Westlake Charter MS | 1985 Pebblewood Dr | Sacramento, CA | 95834 | 916-567-5760 | 567-5769 | 6-8 | John Eick |
| Westlake Charter S | 3800 Del Paso Rd | Sacramento, CA | 95834 | 916-567-5760 | 567-5769 | K-4 | John Eick |
| West Park Charter Academy | 2695 S Valentine Ave | Fresno, CA | 93706-9042 | 559-485-0727 | 497-1944 | K-12 | Ralph Vigil |
| West Sacramento Early College Prep S | 1504 Fallbrook St | West Sacramento, CA | 95691 | 916-375-7680 | | 6-12 | Jessica Anderson |
| Westside Innovative School House | 6550 W 80th St | Los Angeles, CA | 90045 | 310-642-9474 | 642-9475 | K-7 | Dr. Shawna Draxton |
| Westside Prep Charter S - Eastside | 6469 Guthrie St | North Highlands, CA | 95660-3944 | 916-566-1860 | 566-1861 | 7-8 | Renee Scott-Femenella |
| Westside Prep Charter S - Frontier | 6691 Silverthorne Cir | Sacramento, CA | 95842-2654 | 916-566-1840 | 344-8932 | 7-8 | Ellen Giffin |
| Westside Prep Charter S - Westside | 6537 W 2nd St | Rio Linda, CA | 95673 | 916-566-1990 | 566-1991 | 7-8 | Laura Lofgren |
| Westwood Charter ES | 2050 Selby Ave | Los Angeles, CA | 90025-6397 | 310-474-7788 | 475-1295 | K-5 | Kathy Flores |
| Westwood Charter S | PO Box 56 | Westwood, CA | 96137-0056 | 877-256-2994 | 256-2964 | K-12 | Marty Growdon |
| Wheatland Charter Academy | 123 Beale Hwy | Beale AFB, CA | 95903 | 530-788-0248 | 788-0518 | K-5 | Jodie Jacklett |
| White Oaks ES | 1901 White Oak Way | San Carlos, CA | 94070-4799 | 650-508-7317 | 508-7320 | K-4 | Allison Liner |
| Whitmore Charter HS | PO Box 307 | Ceres, CA | 95307-0307 | 209-556-1617 | 538-7931 | 9-12 | David Viss |
| Whitmore Charter S | PO Box 307 | Ceres, CA | 95307-0307 | 209-556-1610 | 538-7931 | K-8 | David Viss |
| Wilbur Charter S for Enriched Academics | 5213 Crebs Ave | Tarzana, CA | 91356-4010 | 818-345-1090 | 881-8128 | K-5 | Deborah Plat |
| Wilder's Preparatory Academy Charter S | 830 N La Brea Ave | Inglewood, CA | 90302-2206 | 310-671-5578 | 671-2424 | K-8 | Rosalyn S. Robinson |
| Willits Charter ES | 405 E Commercial St | Willits, CA | 95490 | 707-459-1400 | 455-6650 | K-5 | Kara McClellan |
| Willits Charter S | 1431 S Main St | Willits, CA | 95490 | 707-459-5506 | 459-5576 | 6-12 | Jennifer Lockwood |
| Willow Creek Academy | 636 Nevada St | Sausalito, CA | 94965-1654 | 415-331-7530 | 331-1622 | K-8 | Carol Cooper |
| Willowside MS | 5285 Hall Rd | Santa Rosa, CA | 95401-7304 | 707-542-3322 | 525-4439 | 6-8 | Brian Howard |
| Wilson College Prep S | 400 105th Ave | Oakland, CA | 94603-2968 | 510-635-7737 | 635-7727 | 6-12 | Michelle Cortez |
| Wisdom Academy for Young Scientists | 706 E Manchester Ave | Los Angeles, CA | 90001 | 323-752-6655 | 752-6344 | K-5 | Edward Cabil |
| Wonderful College Prep Academy | 1942 Randolph St | Delano, CA | 93215 | 661-454-3000 | 454-3099 | 6-12 | Ricardo Esquivel |
| Woodlake ES | 23231 Hatteras St | Woodland Hills, CA | 91367-3199 | 818-347-7097 | 883-3953 | K-5 | Mario Thompson |
| Woodland Hills Charter S | 22201 San Miguel St | Woodland Hills, CA | 91364-3039 | 818-347-9220 | 347-2365 | K-5 | Antoinette Brusca |
| Woodland Star Charter S | 17811 Arnold Dr | Sonoma, CA | 95476-4019 | 707-996-3849 | 996-4369 | K-8 | Sheila Reilly |
| Woodson Charter S | 3333 N Bond Ave | Fresno, CA | 93726-5712 | 559-229-3529 | 229-0459 | 7-12 | Victor Martinez |
| Woodward Leadership Academy | 1777 W Base Line St | San Bernardino, CA | 92410 | 909-266-1762 | | K-6 | Jaqueline Johnson |
| Wright Charter S | 4389 Price Ave | Santa Rosa, CA | 95407-6500 | 707-542-0556 | 542-0418 | K-8 | Terrena Rodebaugh |
| Yav Pem Suab Academy | 7555 S Land Park Dr | Sacramento, CA | 95831-3863 | 916-433-5057 | 433-5289 | K-6 | Vince Xiong |
| Yosemite-Wawona Elementary Charter | 7925 Chilnualna Falls Rd | Yosemite NtPk, CA | 95389 | 209-375-6383 | 375-1029 | 1-5 | Esme McCarthy |
| Youth Opportunities Unlimited S | 915 W Manchester Ave | Los Angeles, CA | 90044 | 323-789-4731 | 778-4612 | 9-12 | Maisha James-McIntosh |
| Yuba City Charter S | 256 Wilbur Ave | Yuba City, CA | 95991-5536 | 530-822-9667 | 822-9629 | K-12 | James Ferreira |
| Yuba County Career Prep Charter S | 1104 E St | Marysville, CA | 95901-4825 | 530-741-6025 | 741-6032 | K-12 | Rocco Greco |
| Yuba Environmental Science Charter Acad | PO Box 430 | Oregon House, CA | 95962 | 530-692-2210 | 692-3241 | PK-8 | Katheryn Smith |
| Yuba River Charter S | 505 Main St | Nevada City, CA | 95959 | 530-265-6060 | 265-6070 | K-8 | Ron Charles |
| Yu Ming Charter S | 1086 Alcatraz Ave | Emeryville, CA | 94608 | 415-452-2063 | 452-2095 | K-8 | Sue Park |

**Colorado**

| School | Address | City,State | Zip code | Telephone | Fax | Grade | Contact |
|---|---|---|---|---|---|---|---|
| Academy 360 | 12000 E 47th Ave | Denver, CO | 80239 | 303-574-1360 | | K-4 | Eric Brucz |
| Academy Charter S | 1551 Prairie Hawk Dr | Castle Rock, CO | 80109-7900 | 303-660-4881 | 660-6385 | K-8 | Yvette Brown |
| Academy for Advanced & Creative Learning | 2510 N Chestnut St | Colorado Spgs, CO | 80907-5912 | 719-434-6566 | 434-9696 | K-8 | Nikki Myers |
| Academy of Urban Learning Charter S | 2417 W 29th Ave | Denver, CO | 80211 | 303-282-0900 | 282-0902 | 9-12 | Michelle Kennard |
| Academy | 11800 Lowell Blvd | Westminster, CO | 80031-5097 | 303-289-8088 | 289-8087 | K-12 | David Floodeen |
| ACE Community Challenge Charter S | 948 Santa Fe Dr | Denver, CO | 80204-3937 | 303-436-9588 | 436-0919 | 8-10 | Rachel Ramirez |
| Addenbrooke Classical Academy | 3940 S Teller St | Lakewood, CO | 80235 | 303-989-1336 | 986-5509 | K-12 | Charles Wright |
| Alta Vista Charter ES | PO Box 449 | Lamar, CO | 81052-0449 | 719-336-2154 | 336-0170 | K-6 | Talara Coen |
| American Academy Charter S | 6971 Mira Vista Ln | Castle Pines, CO | 80108 | 720-292-5200 | 733-2641 | K-8 | Erin Kane |
| American Academy Charter S - Parker | 11155 Motsenbocker Rd | Parker, CO | 80134 | 720-292-5600 | 644-3792 | K-8 | Erin Kane |
| Animas HS | PO Box 4414 | Durango, CO | 81302 | 970-247-2474 | 247-2483 | 9-12 | Jake Lauer |
| Aspen Community Charter S | PO Box 336 | Woody Creek, CO | 81656-0336 | 970-923-4080 | 923-6207 | K-8 | Jim Gilchrist |
| Aspen Ridge Prep S | 705 Austin Ave | Erie, CO | 80516 | 720-242-6225 | 294-0573 | K-5 | Kera Pratt |
| Aspen View Academy | 2131 Low Meadow Blvd | Castle Rock, CO | 80109 | 720-733-3436 | 660-5959 | PK-8 | Jason Edwards |
| Atlas Preparatory S | 1602 S Murray Blvd | Colorado Spgs, CO | 80916 | 719-358-7196 | 355-1819 | 5-12 | Zachary McComsey |
| Aurora Academy Charter S | 10251 E 1st Ave | Aurora, CO | 80010-4308 | 303-367-5983 | 367-5820 | K-8 | Pat Leger |
| Axl Academy | 14100 E Jewell Ave | Aurora, CO | 80012 | 303-377-0758 | 597-1547 | PK-8 | Brent Reckman |
| Banning Lewis Ranch Academy | 7094 Cottonwood Tree Dr | Colorado Spgs, CO | 80927-5000 | 719-570-0075 | 522-2900 | K-8 | Andrew Franko |
| Battle Rock Charter S | 11351 Road G | Cortez, CO | 81321-9569 | 970-565-3237 | 564-1140 | K-6 | Karen Casgrain |
| Belle Creek Charter S | 9290 E 107th Ave | Henderson, CO | 80640-8964 | 303-468-0160 | 468-0164 | K-8 | Irene German |
| Blair Edison Charter S | 4905 Cathay St | Denver, CO | 80249-8376 | 303-371-9570 | 371-8348 | K-8 | Vernon Jones |
| Boulder Prep Charter HS | 5075 Chaparral Ct | Boulder, CO | 80301-3589 | 303-545-6186 | 545-6187 | 9-12 | Lili Adeli |
| Bromley East Charter S | 356 Longspur Dr | Brighton, CO | 80601-8700 | 720-685-3297 | 685-9513 | K-8 | Lori Sheldon |
| Caprock Academy | 714 24 1/2 Rd | Grand Junction, CO | 81505 | 970-243-1771 | 243-3612 | K-12 | Kristin Trezise |
| Carbondale Community Charter S | PO Box 365 | Carbondale, CO | 81623-0365 | 970-963-9647 | 704-0501 | K-8 | Tom Penzel |
| Carbon Valley Charter S | 4040 Coriolis Way | Frederick, CO | 80504-5449 | 303-774-9555 | 774-9592 | PK-8 | Julie Johnson |
| Cardinal Community Academy | 3101 County Road 65 | Keenesburg, CO | 80643-8604 | 303-732-9312 | 732-9314 | K-8 | April Dowdy |
| Challenge to Excellence Charter S | 16995 Carlson Dr | Parker, CO | 80134-8000 | 303-841-9816 | 840-3246 | K-8 | Linda Parker |
| Chavez Academy | 2500 W 18th St | Pueblo, CO | 81003-1152 | 719-295-1623 | 295-1625 | K-8 | Lori Montanez |
| Chavez Academy | 3752 Tennyson St | Denver, CO | 80212-1914 | 303-455-0848 | 855-7252 | K-8 | Kamini Patel |
| Cherry Creek Academy Charter | 6260 S Dayton St | Englewood, CO | 80111-5203 | 303-779-8988 | 779-8817 | K-8 | Jay Cerny |
| Cheyenne Mountain Charter Academy | 1832 S Wahsatch Ave | Colorado Spgs, CO | 80905-2341 | 719-471-1999 | 799-6149 | K-6 | Ward Barr |
| Children's Kiva Montessori S | 510 N Beech St | Cortez, CO | 81321 | 970-564-4850 | | K-8 | Josh Warinner |
| CIVA Charter S | 4635 Northpark Dr | Colorado Spgs, CO | 80918-3813 | 719-633-1306 | 633-1691 | 9-12 | Randy Zimmerman |
| Classical Academy Central | 1655 Springcrest Rd | Colorado Spgs, CO | 80920-1545 | 719-265-9766 | 265-1751 | K-6 | Rebecca DeMeyer |
| Classical Academy East | 12201 Cross Peak Vw | Colorado Spgs, CO | 80921-3438 | 719-282-1181 | 260-9743 | K-6 | Amy Nelson |
| Classical Academy HS | 975 Stout Rd | Colorado Spgs, CO | 80921-3801 | 719-484-0091 | 484-0085 | 9-12 | Sean Shields |
| Classical Academy JHS | 975 Stout Rd | Colorado Spgs, CO | 80921-3801 | 719-484-0091 | 487-2339 | 7-8 | Hugh DiPretore |
| Classical Academy North | 975 Stout Rd | Colorado Spgs, CO | 80921-3801 | 719-484-0081 | 484-0078 | K-6 | Don Stump |
| Collegiate Academy of Colorado | 8420 Sangre De Cristo Rd | Littleton, CO | 80127-4201 | 303-972-7433 | 932-0695 | K-12 | Christian Becker |
| Colorado Calvert Academy | 155 Boardwalk Dr Ste 547 | Fort Collins, CO | 80525 | 970-232-3317 | 258-1591 | K-8 | Elizabeth Davis |
| Colorado Charter HS | 1175 Osage St Ste 100 | Denver, CO | 80204-3445 | 303-892-8475 | 825-3011 | 10-12 | Clark Callahan |
| Colorado Early Colleges Douglas County | 10235 Parkglenn Way | Parker, CO | 80138 | 720-638-6824 | | 9-12 | John Etzell |
| Colorado Early Colleges Fort Collins | 4800 Wheaton Dr | Fort Collins, CO | 80525 | 970-377-0044 | 377-1144 | 9-12 | Sandi Brown |
| Colorado Springs Charter Academy | 2577 N Chelton Rd | Colorado Spgs, CO | 80909-1345 | 719-636-2722 | 636-2726 | K-8 | Jacob Murphy |
| Colorado Springs Early Colleges | 4405 N Chestnut St # E | Colorado Spgs, CO | 80907 | 719-955-4675 | 260-1253 | 9-12 | Jason Dilger |
| Colorado Virtual Academy | 1526 Cole Blvd Ste 200 | Lakewood, CO | 80401 | 866-220-2027 | | 9-12 | Melissa Lambrecht |
| Community Leadership Academy | 6880 Holly St | Commerce City, CO | 80022-2536 | 303-288-2711 | 288-2714 | PK-8 | Ron Jajdelski |
| Community Prep Charter S | 332 E Willamette Ave | Colorado Spgs, CO | 80903-1116 | 719-227-8836 | 227-8897 | 9-12 | Marty Schneider |
| Compass Montessori Charter S | 10399 W 44th Ave | Wheat Ridge, CO | 80033-2701 | 303-420-8288 | 420-0139 | PK-6 | Bill Kottenstette |
| Compass Montessori Charter S | 4441 Salvia St | Golden, CO | 80403-1698 | 303-271-1977 | 271-1984 | PK-12 | Bill Kottenstette |
| Connect Charter S | 104 W 7th St | Pueblo, CO | 81003 | 719-542-0224 | 583-9799 | 6-8 | Jeff Hawkins |
| Crest Academy | 220 W 12th St | Salida, CO | 81201 | 719-539-2977 | 530-5234 | 5-8 | Karen Lundberg |
| Crestone Charter S | PO Box 400 | Crestone, CO | 81131-0400 | 719-256-4907 | 256-4908 | K-12 | Michael Hayes |
| Crown Pointe Academy | 2900 W 86th Ave | Westminster, CO | 80031-3849 | 303-428-1882 | 428-1938 | K-8 | Keith Ouweneel |
| DCS Montessori Charter S | 311 E Castle Pines Pkwy | Castle Rock, CO | 80108 | 303-387-5625 | 387-5626 | PK-8 | Jeromy Johnson |
| Denver Justice HS | 300 E 9th Ave | Denver, CO | 80203 | 303-480-5610 | 995-5546 | 9-12 | Gary Losh |
| Denver Language S | 451 Newport St | Denver, CO | 80220 | 303-557-0852 | 393-6805 | K-8 | Kathy Benzel |
| Denver S of Science and Technology | 2000 Valentia St | Denver, CO | 80238 | 303-320-5570 | | 6-12 | Jeff Desserich |
| Denver S of Science & Technology-Byers | 150 S Pearl St | Denver, CO | 80209 | 303-524-6350 | 524-6355 | 6-8 | Brad White |
| Denver S of Science and Technology - CG | 8499 E Stoll Pl | Denver, CO | 80238 | 303-802-4120 | | 6-8 | John Clark |
| Denver S of Science & Technology-Cole HS | 3240 Humboldt St | Denver, CO | 80205 | 303-524-6354 | | 9-12 | Ben Cairns |
| Denver S of Science & Technology-Cole MS | 1350 E 33rd Ave | Denver, CO | 80207 | 303-524-6354 | 524-6309 | 6-8 | Shawn Smith |
| Denver S of Science & Technology CV HS | 3111 W Dartmouth Ave | Denver, CO | 80236 | 303-524-6320 | | 9-12 | Rebecca Meyer |
| Denver S of Science & Technology CV MS | 3001 S Federal Blvd | Denver, CO | 80236 | 720-524-6374 | | 6-8 | Jennifer Leupold |
| Denver S of Science and Technology - GVR | 4800 Telluride St | Denver, CO | 80249-6803 | 303-524-6300 | 389-7398 | 6-12 | Jenna Kalin |
| Downtown Denver Expeditionary S | 1860 Lincoln St | Denver, CO | 80203 | 720-424-2350 | | K-5 | Erin Sciscione |
| Eagle County Charter Academy | 1105 Miller Ranch Rd | Edwards, CO | 81632-6425 | 970-926-0656 | 926-0786 | K-8 | Kim Walter |
| Eagle Ridge Academy | 3551 E Southern St | Brighton, CO | 80601-0015 | 303-655-0773 | 655-9155 | 9-12 | Ben Ploeger |
| Early College of Arvada | 4905 W 60th Ave | Arvada, CO | 80003 | 720-473-4400 | 308-4701 | 6-12 | Eric Covington |
| Excel Academy | 11500 W 84th Ave | Arvada, CO | 80005-5272 | 303-467-2295 | 467-2291 | K-8 | Nancy Hall |
| Flagstaff Academy | 2040 Miller Dr | Longmont, CO | 80501 | 303-651-7900 | 651-7922 | PK-8 | Robin Lowe |
| Fort Collins Montessori S | 1900 S Taft Hill Rd | Fort Collins, CO | 80526 | 970-631-8612 | | PK-3 | Frank Vincent |
| Foundations Academy | 340 S 45th Ave | Brighton, CO | 80601-4652 | 303-659-9519 | 835-7151 | K-8 | Peg Kastberg |
| Franklin Academy | 2270 Plaza Dr | Highlands Ranch, CO | 80129-1501 | 720-383-4519 | 974-1738 | PK-8 | Bob Barber |
| Free Horizon Montessori S | 581 Conference Pl | Golden, CO | 80401-5615 | 303-231-9801 | 231-9983 | PK-8 | Kresta Vuolo |
| Frontier Academy Charter S | 2560 W 29th St | Greeley, CO | 80631-8507 | 970-330-1780 | 330-4334 | K-5 | Dr. Bradford Every |
| Frontier Academy Charter S | 6530 W 16th St | Greeley, CO | 80634-8675 | 970-339-9153 | 339-5631 | 6-12 | Dr. Stephen Seedorf |

| School | Address | City,State | Zip code | Telephone | Fax | Grade | Contact |
|---|---|---|---|---|---|---|---|
| Frontier Charter Academy | 418 Yoder St | Calhan, CO | 80808 | 719-347-3156 | 347-3054 | K-8 | Karin Gurokovich |
| Georgetown Community S | PO Box 74 | Georgetown, CO | 80444-0074 | 303-569-3277 | 569-2761 | PK-6 | Sharon Warren |
| Girls Athletic Leadership S | 750 Galapago St | Denver, CO | 80204 | 303-282-6437 | | 6-12 | Carrie Donovan |
| Global Village Academy | 403 S Airport Blvd Unit A | Aurora, CO | 80017 | 303-309-6657 | 317-6538 | K-8 | Courtney Black |
| Global Village Academy | 555 W 112th Ave | Northglenn, CO | 80234 | 303-446-7100 | 446-7101 | K-8 | Lisa Pond |
| Global Village Academy Colorado Springs | 1702 N Murray Blvd | Colorado Spgs, CO | 80915 | 719-645-8063 | 591-6784 | K-4 | Alicia Welch |
| Global Village Academy Fort Collins | 2130 W Horsetooth Rd | Fort Collins, CO | 80526 | 970-282-3767 | 282-3766 | K-4 | Dianne Houghtaling |
| GLOBE Charter S | 3302 Alpine Pl | Colorado Spgs, CO | 80909-2100 | 719-630-0577 | 630-0395 | K-6 | Heidi Breakey |
| Gloval Village Academy | 18451 Ponderosa Dr | Parker, CO | 80134 | 720-476-8044 | | K-8 | Lance Howard |
| GOAL Academy | 107 W 11th St | Pueblo, CO | 81003 | 877-776-4625 | 746-2874 | 9-12 | Ken Crowell |
| Golden View Classical Academy | 601 Corporate Cir | Golden, CO | 80401 | 303-598-6700 | 598-6698 | K-12 | Robert Garrow |
| Great Plains Academy | 444 E Front St | Byers, CO | 80103 | 720-360-0706 | 489-3857 | K-12 | Justin Schmidt |
| Guffey Community Charter S | PO Box 147 | Guffey, CO | 80820-0147 | 719-689-2093 | 689-3407 | PK-8 | Pam Moore |
| Highline Academy Northeast | 19451 E Maxwell Pl | Denver, CO | 80249 | 303-454-2706 | | K-8 | Sara Alesandrini |
| Highline Academy Southeast | 2170 S Dahlia St | Denver, CO | 80222 | 303-759-7808 | 759-7809 | K-8 | Kali Garofoli |
| High Point Academy | 6750 N Dunkirk St | Aurora, CO | 80019 | 303-217-5152 | 217-5153 | PK-8 | Keri Melmed |
| Hope Online Learning Academy | 373 Inverness Pkwy Ste 205 | Englewood, CO | 80112-5898 | 720-402-3000 | 675-3013 | K-12 | Heather O'Mara |
| Horizons K-8 School | 4545 Sioux Dr | Boulder, CO | 80303-3732 | 720-561-5580 | 561-5580 | K-8 | John McCluskey |
| Huerta Preparatory HS | 2727 W 18th St | Pueblo, CO | 81003 | 719-583-1030 | 545-2389 | 9-12 | Crystal Gallegos |
| Imagine Charter S at Firestone | 5753 Twilight Ave | Firestone, CO | 80504-6481 | 303-772-3711 | 772-3977 | PK-8 | Nancy Box |
| Imagine Classical Academy - Indigo Ranch | 6464 Peterson Rd | Colorado Spgs, CO | 80923 | 719-495-7360 | 495-4239 | PK-8 | Frank Fowler |
| Independence Academy | 651 29 Rd | Grand Junction, CO | 81504 | 970-254-6850 | 241-2064 | K-8 | Damon Lockhart |
| Indian Peaks Charter S | PO Box 1819 | Granby, CO | 80446-1819 | 970-887-3805 | 887-3829 | K-8 | Sue Thurston |
| Irwin Charter Academy | 1801 Howard Ave | Colorado Spgs, CO | 80909 | 719-302-9100 | 632-4178 | K-5 | Cindee Will |
| Irwin Charter ES | 5525 Astrozon Blvd | Colorado Spgs, CO | 80916 | 719-302-9107 | 884-0992 | K-5 | Elizabeth Berg |
| Irwin Charter HS | 5525 Astrozon Blvd | Colorado Spgs, CO | 80916-4226 | 719-302-9109 | 576-8071 | 9-12 | Alex Marquez |
| Irwin Charter MS | 5525 Astrozon Blvd | Colorado Spgs, CO | 80916-4226 | 719-302-9108 | 591-9993 | 6-8 | Holly Varnum |
| Jefferson Academy | 11251 Reed Way | Broomfield, CO | 80020 | 303-887-1992 | 887-2435 | 7-12 | Heather Grantham |
| Jefferson Academy | 9955 Yarrow St | Broomfield, CO | 80021-4048 | 303-438-1011 | 438-1046 | K-6 | Michael Nolan |
| Juniper Ridge Charter S | 640 24 1/2 Rd | Grand Junction, CO | 81505-1245 | 970-639-0884 | | K-6 | Patrick Ebel |
| Justice HS | 805 Excalibur St | Lafayette, CO | 80026-1909 | 720-328-4864 | 328-4865 | 9-12 | Tijani Cole |
| KIPP Denver Collegiate HS | 451 S Tejon St | Denver, CO | 80223 | 303-922-5324 | 922-9910 | 9-12 | Kurt Pusch |
| KIPP Montbello College Prep | 5290 Kittredge St | Denver, CO | 80239-5628 | 303-307-1970 | | 5-8 | Danielle D'Ascenzo |
| KIPP Montbello Collegiate HS | 11200 E 45th Ave | Denver, CO | 80239 | 720-452-2570 | | 9-12 | Grant Erwin |
| KIPP Montbello ES | 19451 E Maxwell Pl | Denver, CO | 80249 | 720-452-2551 | 570-2066 | K-2 | Lindsey Lorehn |
| KIPP Sunshine Peak Academy | 375 S Tejon St | Denver, CO | 80223-1961 | 303-623-5772 | 623-0410 | 5-8 | Emily Yates |
| Knowledge Quest Academy | 705 School House Dr | Milliken, CO | 80543-3154 | 970-587-5742 | 587-5750 | K-8 | Linda Spreitzer |
| Lake George Charter S | PO Box 420 | Lake George, CO | 80827-0420 | 719-748-3911 | 748-8151 | PK-8 | Bill Fredenburg |
| Landmark Academy at Reunion | 10566 Memphis St | Commerce City, CO | 80022-6236 | 303-287-2901 | 287-4196 | K-8 | Matt Carlton |
| Legacy Academy | 1975 Legacy Cir | Elizabeth, CO | 80107 | 303-646-2636 | 646-2635 | K-8 | Kurt Naber |
| Liberty Common ES | 1725 Sharp Point Dr | Fort Collins, CO | 80525-4424 | 970-482-9800 | 482-8007 | K-6 | Keith Churchill |
| Liberty Common HS | 2745 Minnesota Dr | Fort Collins, CO | 80525 | 970-672-5500 | 672-5499 | 7-12 | Bob Shaffer |
| Life Skills Center of Colorado Springs | 1810 Eastlake Blvd | Colorado Spgs, CO | 80910-3422 | 719-471-0684 | 471-4392 | 9-12 | Mary Ruben-Clapper |
| Lincoln Academy | 7180 Oak St | Arvada, CO | 80004-1416 | 303-467-5363 | 467-5367 | PK-8 | Janelle Johnson |
| Littleton Academy Charter S | 1200 W Mineral Ave | Littleton, CO | 80120-4536 | 303-798-5252 | 798-0298 | K-8 | Shelly Russell |
| Littleton Preparatory Charter S | 5301 S Bannock St | Littleton, CO | 80120-1742 | 303-734-1995 | 734-3620 | K-8 | Kimberly Ash |
| Lotus S for Excellence | 11001 E Alameda Ave Ste A | Aurora, CO | 80012 | 303-360-0052 | 360-0071 | K-12 | Eray Idil |
| Loveland Classical Charter S | 3835 14th St SW | Loveland, CO | 80537 | 970-541-1507 | 776-9227 | K-12 | Ian Stout |
| Maclaren Charter S | 303 Austin Bluffs Pkwy | Colorado Spgs, CO | 80918 | 719-313-4488 | 313-4491 | 6-12 | Mary Faith Hall |
| Madison Charter Academy | 660 Syracuse St | Colorado Spgs, CO | 80911-2546 | 719-391-3977 | 391-1744 | K-6 | Dr. Anne |
| Shearer-Shineman | | | | | | | |
| Magon Academy | 5301 Lowell Blvd | Denver, CO | 80221 | 303-412-7610 | 412-7658 | K-8 | Kaye Taavialma |
| Marble Charter S | 418 W Main St | Marble, CO | 81623 | 970-963-9550 | 963-8435 | K-10 | Amy Rusby |
| Mesa Valley Community S | 2387 Patterson Rd | Grand Junction, CO | 81505 | 970-254-7202 | 243-3075 | K-12 | Laurajean Downs |
| Monarch Montessori of Denver | 4895 Peoria St | Denver, CO | 80239 | 303-712-2001 | 500-0646 | K-5 | Rob Clemens |
| Montessori del Mundo | 15503 E Mississippi Ave # B | Aurora, CO | 80017 | 720-863-8629 | | PK-2 | Karen Farquharson |
| Montessori Peaks Academy | 9904 W Capri Ave | Littleton, CO | 80123-3535 | 303-972-2627 | 933-4182 | PK-6 | Char Weaver |
| Monument Academy | 1150 Village Ridge Pt | Monument, CO | 80132-8992 | 719-481-1950 | 481-1948 | PK-8 | Dr. Don Griffin |
| Mountain MS | 108 W 31st St | Durango, CO | 81301 | 970-828-5600 | | 6-8 | Shane Voss |
| Mountain Phoenix Community S | 4725 Miller St | Wheat Ridge, CO | 80033 | 303-728-9100 | 728-9801 | PK-8 | Dirk Angevine |
| Mountain Sage Community S | 2310 E Prospect Rd Ste A | Fort Collins, CO | 80525 | 970-568-5456 | 482-1803 | K-8 | Liv Helmericks |
| Mountain Song Community S | 2904 W Kiowa St | Colorado Spgs, CO | 80904 | 719-203-6364 | 375-0180 | K-7 | Dr. Evelyn Cortez-Ford |
| Mountain View Core Knowledge S | 890 Field Ave | Canon City, CO | 81212-9250 | 719-275-1980 | 275-1998 | K-8 | Karen Sartori |
| New America S - Jeffco | 5806 W Alameda Ave | Lakewood, CO | 80226-3533 | 303-894-3171 | 237-4119 | 9-12 | Jon Berninzoni |
| New America S - Lowry | 9125 E 7th Pl | Denver, CO | 80230-7111 | 303-320-9854 | 363-8083 | 9-12 | Annie Trujillo |
| New Vision Charter S | 2366 E 1st St | Loveland, CO | 80537-5906 | 970-593-6827 | 461-1947 | K-8 | Phil Borchelt |
| North Routt Charter S | 26990 Eagle Ln | Clark, CO | 80428 | 970-871-6062 | 871-6067 | K-8 | Brandon LaChance |
| North Star Academy | 16700 Keystone Blvd | Parker, CO | 80134-3544 | 720-851-7827 | 851-0976 | K-8 | Kendra Hossfeld |
| Odyssey S of Denver | 6550 E 21st Ave | Denver, CO | 80207 | 303-316-3944 | 316-4016 | K-8 | Marcia Fulton |
| Paradox Valley Charter S | PO Box 420 | Paradox, CO | 81429-0420 | 970-859-7236 | 859-7235 | PK-8 | Jon Orris |
| Parker Core Knowledge Charter S | 11661 N Pine Dr | Parker, CO | 80138-8022 | 303-840-7070 | 840-9785 | PK-8 | Teri Aplin |
| Passage Charter S | 703 S 9th St | Montrose, CO | 81401-4409 | 970-249-8066 | 249-3497 | 9-12 | Corinne Vogenthaler |
| Paul Academy of Arts & Knowledge | 4512 McMurry Ave | Fort Collins, CO | 80525-3400 | 970-226-2800 | 226-2806 | PK-5 | Phyllis Nakagawa |
| Peak to Peak Charter S | 800 Merlin Dr | Lafayette, CO | 80026-2146 | 303-453-4600 | 453-4613 | K-12 | Kyle Mathews |
| Pikes Peak Prep S | 525 E Costilla St | Colorado Spgs, CO | 80903-3764 | 719-570-7575 | 475-0831 | K-12 | Stephanie Atencio |
| Pikes Peak S of Expeditionary Learning | 11925 Antlers Ridge Dr | Falcon, CO | 80831 | 719-522-2580 | | PK-8 | Don Knapp |
| Pinnacle Charter S | 1001 W 84th Ave | Federal Heights, CO | 80260-4717 | 303-450-3985 | 255-6305 | K-12 | Dr. William Wiener |
| Pioneer Charter S | 3230 E 38th Ave | Denver, CO | 80205-3726 | 303-329-8412 | 468-1133 | PK-8 | Richard Barrett |
| Platte River Academy | 4085 Lark Sparrow St | Highlands Ranch, CO | 80126-5209 | 303-221-1070 | 221-1069 | K-8 | Mike Munier |
| Prairie Creeks Charter S | 56729 Colorado Ave | Strasburg, CO | 80136 | 303-622-6328 | 622-6327 | 9-12 | Thomas Winter |
| Prospect Ridge Academy | 2555 Preble Creek Pkwy | Broomfield, CO | 80023-8096 | 720-399-0300 | 545-2163 | K-12 | April Wilkin |
| Provost Academy | 7730 E Belleview Ave # AG9 | Greenwood Vlg, CO | 80111 | 303-770-1240 | 771-1210 | 9-12 | Jennifer Wiebesiek |
| Pueblo S for the Arts & Sciences | 2415 Jones Ave | Pueblo, CO | 81004 | 719-404-2680 | 404-2681 | K-8 | Brian Repola |
| Ridge View Academy | 28101 E Quincy Ave | Watkins, CO | 80137-9502 | 303-766-3000 | 766-2151 | 9-12 | Ed Cope |
| Ridgeview Classical S | 1800 S Lemay Ave | Fort Collins, CO | 80525-1240 | 970-494-4620 | 494-4625 | K-12 | Derek Anderson |
| Rocky Mountain Academy of Evergreen | 2959 Royale Elk Way | Evergreen, CO | 80439 | 303-670-1070 | 670-1253 | PK-8 | Dr. Roberta Harrell |
| Rocky Mountain Classical Academy | 4620 Antelope Ridge Dr | Colorado Spgs, CO | 80922 | 719-622-8000 | 622-8004 | K-8 | Christianna Fogler |
| Rocky Mountain Deaf S | 10300 W Nassau St | Denver, CO | 80235 | 303-984-5749 | 984-7290 | PK-12 | Amy Novotny |
| Rocky Mountain Prep | 7808 Cherry Creek South Dr | Denver, CO | 80231 | 720-863-8920 | 863-8940 | PK-5 | Jen Heller |
| Roosevelt-Edison Charter S | 205 Byron Dr | Colorado Spgs, CO | 80910-2599 | 719-637-0311 | 380-0176 | K-5 | Steve Tompkins |
| Ross Montessori Charter S | 407 Merrill Ave | Carbondale, CO | 81623-1643 | 970-963-7199 | 963-7342 | K-8 | Sonya Hemmen M.A. |
| St. Vrain Montessori Charter S | 1055 Delaware Ave | Longmont, CO | 80501 | 303-682-4339 | 682-8925 | PK-6 | Katie Torres |
| Salida Del Sol Academy | 111 E 26th St | Greeley, CO | 80634 | 970-347-8223 | | K-8 | Joe Melendez |
| SkyView Academy | 6161 Business Center Dr | Highlands Ranch, CO | 80130 | 303-471-8439 | 470-1903 | PK-12 | Richard Barrett |
| SOAR | 4800 Telluride St | Denver, CO | 80249 | 720-287-5100 | 287-5119 | K-5 | Marc Waxman |
| Southwest Early College Charter S | 3001 S Federal Blvd | Denver, CO | 80236-2711 | 303-935-5473 | 935-5591 | 9-12 | Halley Joseph |
| Southwest Open Charter S | 410 N Dolores Rd | Cortez, CO | 81321 | 970-565-1150 | 565-8770 | 9-12 | Jennifer Carter |
| Stargate Charter S | 3951 Cottonwood Lakes Blvd | Thornton, CO | 80241-2187 | 303-450-3936 | 450-3941 | K-8 | Josh Cochran |
| Stone Creek Charter S | 33520 Highway 6 | Edwards, CO | 81632 | 970-569-3327 | 569-3492 | K-8 | John Brendza |
| STRIVE Prep - Excel | 2960 N Speer Blvd | Denver, CO | 80211-3795 | 303-630-0360 | | 9-12 | Kate Schrepfer |
| STRIVE Prep - GVR | 4800 Telluride St | Denver, CO | 80249-6803 | 303-999-2893 | | 6-8 | Ken Greenbaum |
| STRIVE Prep - Lake Campus | 1820 Lowell Blvd | Denver, CO | 80204-1549 | 303-551-7200 | | 6-8 | Rebecca Utton |
| STRIVE Prep - Montbello | 5000 Crown Blvd | Denver, CO | 80239 | 303-999-3825 | | 6-8 | Jennifer Troy |
| STRIVE Prep - Ruby Hill | 2626 W Evans Ave | Denver, CO | 80219 | 720-460-2800 | | 6-8 | Alexa Mason |
| STRIVE Prep - SMART | 3201 W Arizona Ave | Denver, CO | 80219-3941 | 303-962-9880 | | 9-12 | Antonio Vigil |
| STRIVE Prep - Sunnyside | 4735 Pecos St | Denver, CO | 80211 | 720-723-2000 | | 6-8 | Betsy Peterson |
| STRIVE Prep - Westwood | 3201 W Arizona Ave | Denver, CO | 80219-3941 | 303-962-9880 | 962-9886 | 6-8 | Shana deVaca |
| Summit MS | 4655 Hanover Ave | Boulder, CO | 80305-6036 | 720-561-3900 | 561-3901 | 6-8 | Adam Galvin |
| Swallows Charter Academy | 278 S McCulloch Blvd | Pueblo West, CO | 81007-2844 | 719-547-1627 | 547-2509 | K-12 | Dr. Cindy Compton |
| TCA College Pathways | 12201 Cross Peak Vw | Colorado Spgs, CO | 80921-3438 | 719-494-0631 | 484-0087 | 7-12 | Steve Wright |
| Twin Peaks Charter Academy | 340 S Sunset St | Longmont, CO | 80501 | 303-772-7286 | 485-0394 | K-12 | Mic Finn |
| Two Roads Charter S | 6980 Pierce St | Arvada, CO | 80003 | 303-423-3377 | 467-6955 | K-12 | Wendy Noel |
| Union Colony Prep ES | 1051 29th Street Rd | Evans, CO | 80620 | 970-673-4997 | 353-2271 | K-6 | Angela Keedy |
| Union Colony Prep S | 2000 Clubhouse Dr | Greeley, CO | 80634-3643 | 970-673-4546 | 330-7604 | 7-12 | Lance Mosness |
| University Preparatory S | 2409 Arapahoe St | Denver, CO | 80205 | 303-292-0463 | 296-2844 | K-3 | David Singer |
| University Schools | 6525 W 18th St | Greeley, CO | 80634-8674 | 970-506-7000 | 506-7070 | K-12 | Dr. Sherry Gerner |
| Valiant Academy | 6915 Palmer Park Blvd | Colorado Spgs, CO | 80915 | 719-495-1100 | | K-8 | |
| Vanguard Classical S | 801 Yosemite St | Denver, CO | 80230 | 303-691-2384 | 226-5529 | K-8 | Robert Miller |
| Vanguard Classical S | 17101 E Ohio Dr | Aurora, CO | 80017 | 303-338-4110 | 338-4129 | K-12 | Robert Miller |
| Vanguard S | 1605 S Corona Ave | Colorado Spgs, CO | 80905 | 719-471-1999 | 634-4180 | 7-12 | Colin Mullaney |
| Venture Prep Charter S | 2540 Holly St | Denver, CO | 80207 | 303-893-0805 | 320-7665 | 9-12 | Ken Burdette |
| Vision Charter Academy | 1080 Pioneer Rd | Delta, CO | 81416 | 970-874-8226 | 874-8336 | K-8 | Caryn Braddy |
| Vista Charter S | PO Box 10000 | Montrose, CO | 81402-9701 | 970-249-4470 | 252-3354 | 9-12 | Beth Sass |
| Westgate Community S | 12500 Washington St | Thornton, CO | 80241 | 303-425-0967 | 452-4519 | K-8 | Sharon Collins |
| West Ridge Academy | 6200 W 20th St | Greeley, CO | 80634 | 970-330-3671 | 330-3679 | K-9 | Russ Spicer |
| Wilson Academy | 8300 W 94th Ave | Westminster, CO | 80021-4590 | 303-431-3694 | 423-4388 | PK-8 | Carole Bartusiak |
| Windsor Charter Academy | 680 Academy Ct | Windsor, CO | 80550-3101 | 970-674-5020 | 674-5017 | K-12 | Rebecca Teeples |

| School | Address | City,State | Zip code | Telephone | Fax | Grade | Contact |
|---|---|---|---|---|---|---|---|
| World Compass Academy | 2490 S Perry St | Castle Rock, CO | 80104 | 303-814-5200 | | PK-5 | Jim McDevitt |
| Wyatt Academy | 3620 Franklin St | Denver, CO | 80205-3325 | 303-292-5515 | 292-5111 | K-8 | Joe Taylor |
| Youth & Family Academy Charter S | 1920 Valley Dr | Pueblo, CO | 81008-1764 | 719-546-1740 | 542-1335 | 7-12 | Alan Nelms |

## Connecticut

| School | Address | City,State | Zip code | Telephone | Fax | Grade | Contact |
|---|---|---|---|---|---|---|---|
| Achievement First Bridgeport Academy | 529 Noble Ave | Bridgeport, CT | 06608 | 203-333-9128 | 333-9142 | 5-8 | Challa Flemming |
| Achievement First Bridgeport Academy | 655 Stillman St | Bridgeport, CT | 06608 | 203-338-0593 | 338-0714 | K-4 | Heather Wachter |
| Achievement First Hartford Academy ES | 305 Greenfield St | Hartford, CT | 06112 | 860-695-6560 | 242-6457 | K-4 | Ernest Peterson |
| Achievement First Hartford Academy HS | 305 Greenfield St | Hartford, CT | 06112 | 860-695-6680 | 722-8138 | 9-12 | Emily Banks |
| Achievement First Hartford Academy MS | 305 Greenfield St | Hartford, CT | 06112 | 860-695-6760 | 242-6457 | 5-8 | Sorby Grant |
| Achievement First Summit S | 85 Edwards St | Hartford, CT | 06120 | 860-695-6200 | 722-8805 | K-8 | Benjamin Cruse |
| Amistad Academy ES | 130 Edgewood Ave | New Haven, CT | 06511 | 203-772-7000 | 772-2520 | K-4 | Amanda Alonzy |
| Amistad Academy MS | 130 Edgewood Ave | New Haven, CT | 06511 | 203-772-7000 | 776-0229 | 5-8 | Katie Poynter |
| Bridge Academy | 401 Kossuth St | Bridgeport, CT | 06608 | 203-336-9999 | 336-9852 | 7-12 | Timothy Dutton |
| Common Ground HS | 358 Springside Ave | New Haven, CT | 06515-1024 | 203-389-4333 | 389-7458 | 9-12 | Lizanne Cox |
| Elm City College Preparatory ES | 407 James St | New Haven, CT | 06513 | 203-772-7010 | 498-0712 | K-4 | Andrew Poole |
| Elm City College Preparatory MS | 794 Dixwell Ave | New Haven, CT | 06511 | 203-772-5332 | 772-3641 | 5-8 | Rebecca Good |
| Elm City HS | 49 Prince St | New Haven, CT | 06519 | 203-772-1092 | 772-1784 | 9-9 | Jeff Sudmeyer |
| Elm City Montessori S | 375 Quinnipiac Ave | New Haven, CT | 06513 | 203-903-4031 | 490-2316 | PK-5 | Dr. Alissa Levy |
| Explorations Charter S | 71 Spencer St | Winsted, CT | 06098-1128 | 860-738-9070 | 738-9092 | 9-12 | Jill Johnson |
| Great Oaks Charter S | 510 Barnum Ave | Bridgeport, CT | 06608 | 203-870-8188 | 870-8189 | 6-12 | Monica Filppu |
| Highville Charter S | 1 Science Park | Hamden, CT | 06517 | 203-287-0528 | 287-0693 | PK-10 | Craig Drazek |
| Integrated Day Charter S | 68 Thermos Ave | Norwich, CT | 06360-6943 | 860-892-1900 | 892-1902 | PK-8 | Anna James |
| Interdistrict S for Arts & Communication | 190 Governor Winthrop Blvd | New London, CT | 06320-6633 | 860-447-1003 | 447-0470 | 6-8 | David Howes |
| Jumoke Academy | 339 Blue Hills Ave | Hartford, CT | 06112 | 860-527-0575 | 525-7758 | PK-12 | Dr. Michael Sharpe |
| Milner S | 104 Vine St | Hartford, CT | 06112-2295 | 860-695-4380 | 278-4694 | PK-8 | Karen Lott |
| Museum Academy | 10 Targeting Centre | Windsor, CT | 06095 | 860-231-7800 | 231-7236 | PK-5 | Shandra Brown M.Ed. |
| New Beginnings Family Academy | 184 Garden St | Bridgeport, CT | 06605-1213 | 203-384-2897 | 384-2898 | K-8 | Ronelle Swagerty |
| Odyssey Community S | 579 Middle Tpke W | Manchester, CT | 06040-2728 | 860-645-1234 | 533-0324 | K-8 | Elaine Stancliffe |
| Park City Prep Charter S | 510 Barnum Ave | Bridgeport, CT | 06608 | 203-953-3766 | 953-3771 | 6-8 | Bruce Ravage |
| Side by Side Charter S | 10 Chestnut St | Norwalk, CT | 06854-2928 | 203-857-0306 | 838-2666 | PK-8 | Matthew Nittoly |
| Stamford Academy | 229 North St | Stamford, CT | 06901-1112 | 203-324-6300 | 324-6310 | 9-12 | David Williams |
| Trailblazers Academy | 83 Lockwood Ave | Stamford, CT | 06902 | 203-977-5690 | 977-5688 | 6-8 | Michael McGuire |
| Washington Academy | 246 Dixwell Ave | New Haven, CT | 06511 | 203-691-6535 | | K-1 | John Taylor |

## Delaware

| School | Address | City,State | Zip code | Telephone | Fax | Grade | Contact |
|---|---|---|---|---|---|---|---|
| Academia Antonia Alonso | 1200 N French St | Wilmington, DE | 19884 | 302-660-3746 | | K-5 | Jesus Urdiales |
| Academy of Dover Charter S | 104 Saulsbury Rd | Dover, DE | 19904-2705 | 302-674-0684 | 674-3894 | K-5 | |
| Campus Community S | 350 Pear St | Dover, DE | 19904-3016 | 302-736-0403 | 736-5330 | K-8 | Catherine Balsley Ed.D. |
| Charter S of Wilmington | 100 N DuPont Rd | Wilmington, DE | 19807-3199 | 302-651-2727 | 652-1246 | 9-12 | Samuel Paoli |
| Delaware Acad of Pub Safety & Security | 801 N DuPont Hwy | New Castle, DE | 19720-2544 | 302-322-6050 | 322-4029 | 9-12 | Chuck Hughes |
| Delaware College Preparatory Academy | 501 W 28th St | Wilmington, DE | 19802 | 302-762-7424 | 762-7426 | K-5 | Angela Dennis |
| Delaware Design-Lab HS | 179 Stanton Christiana Rd | Newark, DE | 19702 | 215-820-7547 | | 9-12 | Dr. Cristina C. Alvarez |
| Delaware MET | 300 E 8th St | Wilmington, DE | 19801-3606 | 302-660-3938 | | 9-12 | Amy Cantymagli |
| Delaware Military Academy | 112 Middleboro Rd | Wilmington, DE | 19804-1621 | 302-998-0745 | 998-3521 | 9-12 | Anthony Pullella |
| Early College HS at DE State University | 1200 N DuPont Hwy | Dover, DE | 19901 | 302-857-6739 | 535-7526 | 9-12 | Dr. Evelyn Edney |
| East Side Charter S | 3000 N Claymont St | Wilmington, DE | 19802-2807 | 302-762-5834 | 762-3864 | PK-8 | Dr. Lamont Browne |
| Edison Charter S | 2200 N Locust St | Wilmington, DE | 19802-4429 | 302-778-1101 | 778-2232 | K-8 | Salome Thomas-El |
| Family Foundations Academy | 1101 Delaware St | New Castle, DE | 19720-6033 | 302-324-8901 | 324-8908 | K-8 | Dr. Tennell Brewington |
| First State Montessori Academy | 1000 N French St | Wilmington, DE | 19801 | 302-576-1500 | 576-1501 | K-6 | Courtney Fox |
| Gateway Lab S | 2501 Centerville Rd | Wilmington, DE | 19808-1603 | 302-633-4091 | 633-5680 | 1-8 | Catherine Dolan |
| Kuumba Academy Charter S | 1200 N French St | Wilmington, DE | 19884 | 302-472-6450 | 472-6452 | K-8 | Sally Maldonado |
| Las Americas Aspira Academy | 326 Ruthar Dr | Newark, DE | 19711-8017 | 302-292-1463 | 292-1291 | K-8 | Margaret Lopez Waite |
| MOT Charter S | 1156 Levels Rd | Middletown, DE | 19709-7700 | 302-376-5125 | 376-5120 | K-8 | Linda Jennings |
| Moyer Academy | 610 E 17th St | Wilmington, DE | 19802 | 302-428-9501 | 428-9506 | 6-12 | Alana Walls |
| Newark Charter S | 200 McIntire Dr | Newark, DE | 19711 | 302-369-2001 | 368-3460 | K-12 | Gregory Meece |
| Odyssey Charter S Lower Campus | 4319 Lancaster Pike | Wilmington, DE | 19805 | 302-994-6490 | 994-6915 | K-5 | Dr. Nick Manolakos |
| Odyssey Charter S Upper Campus | 201 Bayard Ave | Wilmington, DE | 19805-3331 | 302-655-5760 | 655-5761 | 6-8 | Dr. Nick Manolakos |
| Positive Outcomes Charter S | 3337 S Dupont Hwy | Camden, DE | 19934-1378 | 302-697-8805 | 697-8813 | 7-12 | Edward Emmett |
| Prestige Academy | 1121 Thatcher St | Wilmington, DE | 19802 | 302-762-3240 | 762-4782 | 5-8 | Cordie Greenlea |
| Providence Creek Academy Charter S | PO Box 265 | Clayton, DE | 19938-0265 | 302-653-6276 | 653-7850 | K-8 | Audrey Erschen |
| Reach Academy for Girls | 170 Lukens Dr | New Castle, DE | 19720-2727 | 302-654-3720 | 654-3724 | K-8 | Tara Allen |
| Sussex Academy of Arts and Sciences | 21150 Airport Rd | Georgetown, DE | 19947-5573 | 302-856-3636 | 856-3376 | 6-12 | Patricia Oliphant Ed.D. |

## District Of Columbia

| School | Address | City,State | Zip code | Telephone | Fax | Grade | Contact |
|---|---|---|---|---|---|---|---|
| Academy of Hope Public Charter S | 421 Alabama Ave SE | Washington, DC | 20032 | 202-269-6623 | | Adult | Lecester Johnson |
| Academy of Hope Public Charter S | 601 Edgewood St NE | Washington, DC | 20032 | 202-269-6623 | | K-3 | |
| Achievement Prep Academy ES | 1500 Mississippi Ave SE | Washington, DC | 20032 | 202-562-1214 | 645-4811 | K-3 | Susan Cannon |
| Achievement Preparatory Academy | 908 Wahler Pl SE | Washington, DC | 20032-4098 | 202-562-1214 | 562-1219 | 4-8 | Janice Lewis |
| Angelou Charter HS | 5600 E Capitol St NE | Washington, DC | 20019-6732 | 202-379-4335 | 315-3995 | 9-12 | Corey Carter |
| Angelou Charter S - Young Adult | 5600 E Capitol St NE | Washington, DC | 20019 | 202-289-8898 | 315-3995 | Adult | Sarah Navarro |
| AppleTree Early Learning - Columbia Hts | 2750 14th St NW | Washington, DC | 20009 | 202-667-9490 | | PK-PK | Ryan Tauriainen |
| AppleTree Early Learning-Douglass Knoll | 2017 Savannah Ter SE | Washington, DC | 20020 | 202-629-2545 | 629-2548 | PK-PK | Rebecca Kimport |
| AppleTree Early Learning - Lincoln Park | 138 12th St NE | Washington, DC | 20002-6471 | 202-621-6581 | 621-6584 | PK-PK | Karen Lamonth M.A. |
| AppleTree Early Learning - Oklahoma Ave | 330 21st St NE | Washington, DC | 20002 | 202-629-2179 | 629-2189 | PK-PK | Ntaka Wellington |
| AppleTree Early Learning - Parklands | 2011 Savannah St SE | Washington, DC | 20020 | 202-889-0643 | 506-1894 | PK-PK | Shelton Lee |
| AppleTree Early Learning - Southwest | 801 7th St SW | Washington, DC | 20024 | 202-506-9190 | 646-0510 | PK-PK | Jevonna Willis |
| Basis DC Charter S | 410 8th St NW | Washington, DC | 20004 | 202-393-5437 | 803-5764 | 5-12 | Tim Eyerman |
| Bethune Day Academy | 5412 16th St NW | Washington, DC | 20011 | 202-459-4710 | 536-2670 | PK-8 | Jubria Lewis |
| Bridges Public Charter S | 1250 Taylor St NW | Washington, DC | 20011-5600 | 202-545-0515 | 545-0517 | PK-3 | Olivia Smith |
| Bridges Public Charter S - Sharpe | 4300 13th St NW | Washington, DC | 20011 | 202-545-0515 | | PK-3 | |
| Briya Charter S | 1755 Newton St NW | Washington, DC | 20010 | 202-797-7337 | | PK-12 | Christie McKay |
| Briya Charter S | 3912 Georgia Ave NW | Washington, DC | 20011-5861 | 202-545-2020 | 797-8470 | PK-12 | Christie McKay |
| Briya Charter S | 2333 Ontario Rd NW | Washington, DC | 20009 | 202-232-7777 | | PK-12 | Christie McKay |
| Capital City Public Charter S | 100 Peabody St NW | Washington, DC | 20011 | 202-808-9800 | 387-7074 | PK-12 | Belicia Reaves |
| Cedar Tree Academy | 701 Howard Rd SE | Washington, DC | 20020 | 202-610-4193 | 610-2845 | PK-K | Dr. Latonya Henderson |
| Center City Pub Charter S - Brightwood | 6008 Georgia Ave NW | Washington, DC | 20011-5104 | 202-723-3322 | 291-0219 | PK-8 | Shavone Gibson |
| Center City Pub Charter S - Capitol Hill | 1503 E Capitol St SE | Washington, DC | 20003-1508 | 202-547-7556 | 547-5686 | PK-8 | Sharise Whitfield |
| Center City Pub Charter S - Congress Hts | 220 Highview Pl SE | Washington, DC | 20032-1581 | 202-562-7070 | 547-5829 | PK-8 | Niya White |
| Center City Public Charter S - Petworth | 510 Webster St NW | Washington, DC | 20011-4758 | 202-726-9212 | 726-3378 | PK-8 | Nazo Burgy |
| Center City Public Charter S - Shaw | 711 N St NW | Washington, DC | 20001 | 202-234-1093 | 462-6875 | PK-8 | Ralph Boyd |
| Center City Public Charter S - Trinidad | 1217 W Virginia Ave NE | Washington, DC | 20002 | 202-723-3322 | 398-4832 | PK-8 | Vernetta Christian |
| Chavez - Capitol Hill HS | 709 12th St SE | Washington, DC | 20003 | 202-547-3424 | 547-2507 | 9-12 | Zenada Mahon |
| Chavez - Parkside MSHS | 3701 Hayes St NE | Washington, DC | 20019-1702 | 202-398-2230 | 398-2535 | 6-12 | DeWan Jordan |
| Chavez Prep MS | 770 Kenyon St NW | Washington, DC | 20010 | 202-723-3975 | 723-3976 | 6-8 | Robert McCarty |
| Children's Guild DC | 2146 24th Pl NE | Washington, DC | 20018 | 202-774-5442 | | K-8 | |
| Community Academy Pub Charter - Amos 1 | 1300 Allison St NW | Washington, DC | 20011-4441 | 202-723-4100 | 723-6867 | PK-5 | Masi Preston |
| Community Academy Pub Charter - Amos 2 | 33 Riggs Rd NE | Washington, DC | 20011 | 202-723-5136 | 723-5139 | PK-2 | Tanya Clark-Morgan |
| Community Academy Pub Charter - Amos 5 | 1400 1st St NW | Washington, DC | 20001 | 202-332-6565 | | PK-5 | Sharise Whitfield |
| Community Academy Pub Charter - Butler | 1400 1st St NW | Washington, DC | 20001-1763 | 202-234-2122 | 234-2166 | PK-5 | William Thomas |
| Community Academy Pub Charter - Online | 1351 Nicholson St NW | Washington, DC | 20011 | 540-788-1492 | 843-5881 | K-8 | John Sloane |
| Community College Prep Academy | 2405 Martin L King Ave SE | Washington, DC | 20020 | 202-610-5780 | | Adult | C. Vanessa Spinner |
| Creative Minds International Charter S | 3700 N Capitol St NW | Washington, DC | 20011 | 202-588-0370 | 588-0263 | PK-5 | Dr. Golnar Abedin |
| Democracy Prep Congress Hts Charter S | 3100 Martin L King Ave SE | Washington, DC | 20032 | 202-561-0860 | 561-0864 | PK-7 | Sean Riedy |
| DC Bilingual Public Charter S | 33 Riggs Rd NE | Washington, DC | 20011 | 202-332-4200 | 745-2562 | PK-5 | Daniela Anello |
| District of Columbia International S | PO Box 43250 | Washington, DC | 20010 | 202-459-4790 | 787-3995 | 6-8 | Simon Rodberg |
| DC Prep Charter ES - Anacostia | 1102 W St SE | Washington, DC | 20020 | 202-729-3500 | 889-2785 | PK-3 | Maria-Teresa Duvall |
| DC Prep Charter ES - Benning | 100 41st St NE | Washington, DC | 20019-3310 | 202-398-2838 | 398-2839 | PK-6 | Raymond Weeden |
| DC Prep Charter MS - Edgewood | 707 Edgewood St NE | Washington, DC | 20017-3341 | 202-832-5700 | 635-4412 | 4-8 | Shaunte Edmonds |
| DC Scholars Charter S | 5601 E Capitol St SE | Washington, DC | 20019 | 202-559-6138 | 618-9396 | PK-5 | Rebecca Crouch |
| Doar Charter S for Performing Arts | 705 Edgewood St NE Fl 2 | Washington, DC | 20017-3341 | 202-269-4646 | 403-3222 | PK-8 | John Goldman |
| Eagle Academy Charter S | 1017 New Jersey Ave SE | Washington, DC | 20003 | 202-459-6825 | 479-6796 | PK-3 | Nicole Walker |
| Eagle Academy Charter S - Congress Hts. | 3400 Wheeler Rd SE | Washington, DC | 20032 | 202-544-2646 | 544-0187 | PK-3 | Jeffrey Cline |
| Early Childhood Academy | 4025 9th St SE | Washington, DC | 20032-6051 | 202-373-0035 | 373-5586 | PK-3 | Wendy Edwards |
| Excel Academy Public Charter S | 2501 M L K Jr SE | Washington, DC | 20020 | 202-373-0097 | 373-0477 | PK-8 | Lela Johnson |
| Friendship Charter MS - Woodridge | 2959 Carlton Ave NE | Washington, DC | 20018-2615 | 202-635-6500 | 635-6481 | 4-8 | Rictor Craig |
| Friendship Charter S - Blow-Pierce | 725 19th St NE | Washington, DC | 20002-4713 | 202-572-1070 | 399-6157 | PK-8 | Dr. Jeffrey Grant |
| Friendship Charter S - Chamberlain | 1345 Potomac Ave SE | Washington, DC | 20003-4411 | 202-547-5800 | 547-4554 | PK-8 | Morrise Harbour |
| Friendship Charter S - Online | 120 Q St NE | Washington, DC | 20002 | 202-281-1700 | 281-1799 | K-12 | |
| Friendship Charter S - Southeast Academy | 645 Milwaukee Pl SE | Washington, DC | 20032-2606 | 202-562-1980 | 562-0726 | PK-5 | Joseph Speight |
| Friendship Charter S - Technology Prep | 645 Milwaukee Pl SE | Washington, DC | 20032 | 202-562-1980 | 562-1817 | 6-12 | Doranna Tindle-Mason |
| Friendship Collegiate Academy | 4095 Minnesota Ave NE | Washington, DC | 20019-3541 | 202-396-5500 | 396-8229 | 9-12 | Peggy Jones |
| Harmony DC Public Charter S | 62 T St NE | Washington, DC | 20002 | 202-529-7500 | 529-7501 | K-6 | Fatih Oner |
| Haynes Public Charter S | 4501 Kansas Ave NW | Washington, DC | 20011 | 202-706-5838 | 706-5832 | PK-12 | Phyllis Hedlund |
| Haynes Public Charter S | 3600 Georgia Ave NW | Washington, DC | 20010 | 202-667-4446 | 667-8811 | 5-8 | Myron Long |

| School | Address | City,State | Zip code | Telephone | Fax | Grade | Contact |
|---|---|---|---|---|---|---|---|
| Hospitality Public Charter HS | 1851 9th St NW | Washington, DC | 20001 | 202-737-4150 | 737-4151 | 9-12 | Jacqueline Hayden |
| Howard University MS of Math & Science | 405 Howard Pl NW | Washington, DC | 20059-0001 | 202-806-7725 | 865-0271 | 6-8 | Yohance Maqubela |
| Ideal Academy | 6130 N Capitol St NW | Washington, DC | 20011-1405 | 202-729-6660 | 729-6677 | PK-8 | George Rutherford Ph.D. |
| IDEA Public Charter HS | 1027 45th St NE | Washington, DC | 20019-3802 | 202-399-4750 | 399-4387 | 9-12 | Justin Rydstrom |
| Imagine Hope Community Charter - Lamond | 6200 Kansas Ave NE | Washington, DC | 20011 | 202-722-4421 | 722-4431 | PK-6 | Camille Tharpe |
| Imagine Hope Community Charter - Tolson | 2917 8th St NE | Washington, DC | 20017-1669 | 202-832-7370 | 832-7644 | PK-8 | Dr. Chloe Marshall |
| Ingenuity Prep Charter S | 4600 Livingston Rd SE | Washington, DC | 20032 | 202-374-8458 | | PK-2 | Aaron Cuny |
| Inspired Teaching S | 200 Douglas St NE | Washington, DC | 20002 | 202-248-6825 | 248-6939 | PK-8 | Zoe Duskin |
| KIPP DC: AIM Academy | 2600 Douglass Pl SE | Washington, DC | 20020-4419 | 202-678-5477 | 678-4383 | 5-8 | Kristy Ochs |
| KIPP DC: College Preparatory | 1401 Brentwood Pkwy NE | Washington, DC | 20002 | 202-678-2527 | 678-0082 | 9-12 | Jessica Cunningham |
| KIPP DC: Connect Academy | 1375 Mount Olivet Rd NE | Washington, DC | 20002 | 202-396-5477 | 223-4504 | PK-K | Donny Tiengtum |
| KIPP DC: Discover Academy | 2600 Douglass Pl SE | Washington, DC | 20020-4419 | 202-678-7735 | 678-0085 | PK-K | Philonda Johnson |
| KIPP DC: Grow Academy | 421 P St NW | Washington, DC | 20001 | 202-986-4769 | 986-1625 | PK-K | Lauren Ellis |
| KIPP DC: Heights Academy | 2600 Douglass Pl SE | Washington, DC | 20020 | 202-610-5323 | 610-6555 | 1-4 | Cherese Brauer |
| KIPP DC: KEY Academy | 4801 Benning Rd SE | Washington, DC | 20019-6145 | 202-582-5477 | 582-0152 | 5-8 | David Ayala |
| KIPP DC: LEAD Academy | 421 P St NW | Washington, DC | 20001 | 202-223-4505 | 223-4504 | 1-3 | Mekia Love |
| KIPP DC: LEAP Academy | 4801 Benning Rd SE | Washington, DC | 20019-6145 | 202-582-5327 | 582-4680 | PK-K | Abraham Clayman |
| KIPP DC: Promise Academy | 4801 Benning Rd SE | Washington, DC | 20019 | 202-265-7766 | 582-4686 | 1-4 | Casey McNabb |
| KIPP DC: Spring Academy | 1375 Mount Olivet Rd NE | Washington, DC | 20002-2509 | 202-397-5477 | 223-4504 | K-4 | Lindsey Hoy |
| KIPP DC: Valor Academy | 5300 Blaine St NE | Washington, DC | 20019 | | | 5-8 | Gillian Connor |
| KIPP DC: WILL Academy | 421 P St NW | Washington, DC | 20001-2417 | 202-328-9455 | 328-9457 | 4-8 | Kate Finley |
| KIPP DC Arts & Technology Academy | 5300 Blaine St NE | Washington, DC | 20019 | 202-398-6811 | | PK-K | Allison Artis |
| KIPP DC Northeast Academy | 1375 Mount Olivet Rd NE | Washington, DC | 20002 | 202-398-5477 | | 5-7 | John Barnhardt |
| KIPP DC Quest Academy | 5300 Blaine St NE | Washington, DC | 20019 | 202-397-5477 | | 1-4 | Cherese Brauer |
| Latin American Montessori Bilingual S | 1375 Missouri Ave NW | Washington, DC | 20011-1807 | 202-525-5105 | 722-4125 | PK-5 | Cristina Encinas |
| Latin American Montessori Bilingual S | 1800 Perry St NE | Washington, DC | 20018 | 202-525-5105 | 621-8621 | PK-5 | Cristina Encinas |
| LAYC Career Academy | 3047 15th St NW | Washington, DC | 20009 | 202-319-2228 | 462-5696 | Adult | Nicole Hanrahan |
| Lee Montessori Public Charter S | 200 Douglas St NE | Washington, DC | 20002 | 202-779-9740 | 318-0763 | PK-2 | Megan Hubbard |
| Marshall Academy | 2427 M L K Jr Ave SE | Washington, DC | 20020 | 202-563-6862 | 563-6946 | 9-12 | Alexandra Pardo |
| Meridian Public Charter S | 3031 14th St NW | Washington, DC | 20009 | 202-387-9830 | 387-7605 | PK-8 | Tamara Cooper |
| Monument Academy | 500 19th St NE | Washington, DC | 20002 | 202-545-3180 | | 5-8 | Marlene Magrino |
| Mundo Verde Bilingual Charter S | 30 P St NW | Washington, DC | 20001 | 202-630-8373 | 667-4811 | PK-4 | Kristin Scotchmer |
| National Collegiate Prep Charter HS | 4600 Livingston Rd SE | Washington, DC | 20032 | 202-832-7737 | 832-7736 | 9-12 | Dianne Brown Ed.D. |
| Next Step Public Charter S | 3047 15th St NW | Washington, DC | 20009 | 202-319-2249 | 234-0001 | Adult | Susan Evans-Espinoza |
| Options Public Charter S | 1375 E St NE | Washington, DC | 20002-5429 | 202-547-1028 | 547-1272 | 6-12 | Amos Pierre |
| Paul - International HS | 5800 8th St NW | Washington, DC | 20011-1900 | 202-291-7499 | 291-7495 | 6-12 | Kenya Wilson |
| Perry Street Preparatory S | 1800 Perry St NE | Washington, DC | 20018 | 202-529-4400 | 526-2214 | PK-12 | Rachel Crouch |
| Potomac Prep Charter S | 4401 8th St NE | Washington, DC | 20017 | 202-526-6003 | 526-6005 | PK-8 | Dr. Marian White-Hood |
| Rocketship Public Charter S | 2335 Raynolds Pl SE | Washington, DC | 20020 | 877-806-0920 | | PK-3 | |
| Roots Public Charter S | 15 Kennedy St NW | Washington, DC | 20011 | 202-882-8073 | 882-8075 | PK-8 | Dr. Bernida Thompson |
| Rosario International Public Charter S | 1100 Harvard St NW | Washington, DC | 20009-5356 | 202-797-4700 | 232-6442 | Adult | Holly-Ann Fresco |
| Rosario International Public Charter S | 514 V St NE | Washington, DC | 20002 | 202-734-4900 | | 6-8 | Dr. Jorge Delgado |
| St. Coletta Special Education Charter S | 1901 Independence Ave SE | Washington, DC | 20003-1733 | 202-350-8680 | 350-8699 | PK-12 | Janice Corazza |
| SEED Public Charter S | 4300 C St SE | Washington, DC | 20019-4100 | 202-248-7773 | 248-3021 | 6-12 | Dr. Adrian Manuel |
| Sela Charter S | 6015 Chillum Pl NE | Washington, DC | 20011 | 202-670-7352 | | PK-3 | Natalie Arthurs |
| Shining Stars Montessori Academy | 6015 Chillum Pl NE | Washington, DC | 20011 | 202-723-1467 | 319-2309 | PK-3 | Regina Rodriguez |
| Somerset Prep Academy | 3301 Wheeler Rd SE | Washington, DC | 20032 | 202-562-9104 | 457-1980 | 6-10 | James Griffin |
| Stokes Charter S | 3700 Oakview Ter NE | Washington, DC | 20017 | 202-265-7237 | 265-4656 | PK-5 | Maura Varley-Gutierrez |
| Tree of Life Charter S | 2315 18th Pl NE | Washington, DC | 20018-3610 | 202-832-1108 | 832-1113 | PK-8 | Patricia Williams |
| Two Rivers Public Charter S | 1234 4th St NE | Washington, DC | 20002-3432 | 202-543-8477 | 543-8479 | 6-8 | Elaine Hou |
| Two Rivers Public Charter S | 1227 4th St NE | Washington, DC | 20002-3431 | 202-546-4477 | 546-0869 | PK-8 | Maggie Bello |
| Two Rivers Public Charter S - Young | 820 26th St NE | Washington, DC | 20002 | 202-388-1360 | | PK-1 | Maggie Bello |
| Washington Latin Public Charter S | 5200 2nd St NW | Washington, DC | 20011 | 202-223-1111 | 723-1171 | 5-12 | Diana Smith |
| Washington MST Public Charter HS | 1920 Bladensburg Rd NE | Washington, DC | 20002-1812 | 202-636-8011 | 636-3495 | 9-12 | N'Deye Diagne |
| Washington Yu Ying Public Charter S | 220 Taylor St NE | Washington, DC | 20017 | 202-635-1950 | 635-1960 | PK-5 | Maquita Alexander |
| Wright Charter S | 770 M St SE | Washington, DC | 20003 | 202-388-1011 | 388-5197 | 8-12 | Dr. Marco Clark |
| YouthBuild Public Charter S | 3014 14th St NW | Washington, DC | 20009-6819 | 202-319-0141 | 518-0618 | Adult | Andrea Henson |
| | | **Florida** | | | | | |
| Academic Solutions Academy | 4099 N Pine Island Rd | Sunrise, FL | 33351 | 954-572-6600 | 572-6444 | 9-12 | Andrew Kinlock |
| AcadeMir Charter MS | 10601 SW 48th St | Miami, FL | 33165 | 305-967-8492 | 392-1928 | 6-8 | Dr. Carolina Claro |
| AcadeMir Charter S West | 14880 SW 26th St | Miami, FL | 33185 | 305-485-9911 | 485-9944 | K-5 | Dr. Carolina Claro |
| AcadeMir Prep Academy | 10870 SW 113th Pl | Miami, FL | 33176 | 305-596-4149 | 596-4151 | K-5 | Dr. Carolina Claro |
| Academy at the Farm | 9500 Alex Lange Way | Dade City, FL | 33525-8213 | 352-588-9737 | 588-0508 | K-8 | Ray Polk |
| Academy Da Vinci | 1060 Keene Rd | Dunedin, FL | 34698 | 727-298-2778 | 502-6065 | K-5 | Lucy Foran |
| Academy for Positive Learning Charter S | 1200 N Dixie Hwy | Lake Worth, FL | 33460 | 561-585-6104 | 585-7849 | K-8 | Renatta Adan-Espinoza |
| Academy of Arts & Minds | 3138 Commodore Plz | Miami, FL | 33133-5814 | 305-448-1100 | 448-9737 | 9-12 | Antonietta DiGirolamo |
| Academy of Business & Leadership Educ | 7 Williams St | Saint Augustine, FL | 32084 | 904-826-1606 | 794-4119 | 5-8 | Scott Beebe |
| Academy of Environmental Science | 12695 W Fort Island Trl | Crystal River, FL | 34429-5290 | 352-795-8793 | 249-2100 | 9-12 | Ben Stofcheck |
| Academy of International Education | 1080 La Baron Dr | Miami Springs, FL | 33166 | 305-883-3900 | 883-3901 | K-8 | Vera Hirsh |
| Acceleration MS | 3365 Seminole Ave | Fort Myers, FL | 33916 | 239-400-1818 | 689-8511 | 6-8 | George Coats |
| Access Charter S | 600 E Colonial Dr | Orlando, FL | 32807 | 321-319-0640 | 319-0643 | 6-12 | Roger Watkins |
| Achievement Academy - Bartow | 695 E Summerlin St | Bartow, FL | 33830-4848 | 863-533-0690 | 534-0798 | PK-PK | Cindi Parker-Pearson |
| Achievement Academy - Lakeland | 716 E Bella Vista St | Lakeland, FL | 33805-3009 | 863-683-6504 | 688-9292 | PK-PK | Cindi Parker-Pearson |
| Achievement Academy - Winter Haven | 2211 28th St NW | Winter Haven, FL | 33881 | 863-965-7586 | 968-5016 | PK-PK | Cindi Parker-Pearson |
| Adler ES | 4515 38th Ave N | St Petersburg, FL | 33713 | 727-329-9545 | 522-2854 | K-6 | Greg Decosmo |
| Advantage Academy | 304 W Prosser Dr | Plant City, FL | 33563 | 813-567-0801 | 441-0272 | K-8 | Keith Miller |
| Advantage Academy at Waterstone | 855 Waterstone Way | Homestead, FL | 33033-5941 | 305-248-6206 | 248-6208 | K-8 | Nancy Roque |
| Advantage Academy Santa Fe | 9790 SW 107th Ct | Miami, FL | 33176 | 786-228-5309 | 718-1921 | K-5 | Yesenia Cantillo |
| Alachua Learning Center | PO Box 1389 | Alachua, FL | 32616 | 386-418-2080 | 418-4116 | K-8 | Krishna Rivera |
| Alee Academy Charter S | 1705 E County Road 44 | Eustis, FL | 32736 | 352-357-9426 | 357-8426 | 9-12 | Jennings Neeld |
| Allen Leadership Academy | 940 Caliph St | Opa Locka, FL | 33054 | 305-615-2977 | 615-3032 | K-5 | Latoya Robinson |
| Aloma Charter HS | 495 N Semoran Blvd Ste 8 | Winter Park, FL | 32792-3802 | 407-657-4343 | 657-4317 | 9-12 | Daniel Mullins |
| Alpha Charter S of Excellence | 1217 SW 4th St | Miami, FL | 33135 | 305-643-2132 | 642-3717 | K-5 | Isabel Navas |
| Alpha International Academy | 121 S 24th Ave | Hollywood, FL | 33020-4901 | 954-505-7974 | 505-7976 | K-5 | Raquel Lipscomb |
| Altoona S | 42630 State Road 19 | Altoona, FL | 32702 | 352-669-3444 | 669-3407 | K-5 | Walter Schmidt |
| AMI Kids Emerald Coast | 207 4th St SE | Ft Walton Bch, FL | 32548-5636 | 850-244-2711 | 244-2171 | 6-12 | Audra Ray |
| Apalachicola Bay Charter S | 98 12th St | Apalachicola, FL | 32320 | 850-653-1222 | 653-1857 | K-8 | Chimene Johnson |
| Archimedean Academy | 12425 SW 72nd St | Miami, FL | 33183-2513 | 305-279-6572 | 675-8448 | K-5 | Susan Simpson |
| Archimedean Middle Conservatory | 12425 SW 72nd St | Miami, FL | 33183-2513 | 305-279-6572 | 675-8448 | 6-8 | Vasiliki Moysidis |
| Archimedean Upper Conservatory | 12425 SW 72nd St | Miami, FL | 33183 | 305-279-6572 | 675-8448 | 9-12 | Demetrios Demopoulos |
| Ascend Career Academy | 5251 Coconut Creek Pkwy | Margate, FL | 33063 | 954-978-4555 | | 9-12 | Vincent Alessi |
| ASPIRA Arts DECO | 1 NE 19th St | Miami, FL | 33132-1030 | 305-576-1512 | 576-0810 | 6-8 | Maria Caceres |
| Aspira Leadership and College Prep | 13330 SW 288th St | Homestead, FL | 33033 | 305-246-1111 | 246-1433 | K-8 | Garrick Keidan |
| ASPIRA Raul Martinez Charter S | 13300 Memorial Hwy | North Miami, FL | 33161-3940 | 305-893-8050 | 891-6055 | 6-9 | Kenneth Feria |
| Aspire Charter Academy | 928 Malone Dr | Orlando, FL | 32810 | 407-297-9955 | | K-5 | Pamela Schenkel |
| Athenian Academy of Pasco | 3118 Seven Springs Blvd | New Port Richey, FL | 34655-3340 | 727-372-0200 | 376-1916 | K-8 | Christy Messer |
| Athenian Academy | 2289 N Hercules Ave | Clearwater, FL | 33763 | 727-298-2718 | 298-2719 | K-8 | Kathy Hershelman |
| Atlantic Montessori Charter S | 9893 Pines Blvd | Pembroke Pines, FL | 33024 | 754-263-2700 | 263-2596 | K-3 | Juana Garcia |
| Atlantic Montessori Charter S | 9069 Taft St | Pembroke Pines, FL | 33024 | 954-790-8943 | | K-5 | Juana Garcia |
| Avant Garde Academy | 1100 Hillcrest Dr | Hollywood, FL | 33021 | 954-924-8006 | 924-8044 | 6-10 | Gustavo Prats |
| Avant Garde Academy | 2025 McKinley St | Hollywood, FL | 33020 | 954-816-6153 | | K-8 | Dr. Steven Blinder |
| Aventura City of Excellence Charter S | 3333 NE 188th St | Aventura, FL | 33180-2933 | 305-466-1499 | 466-1339 | K-8 | Julie Alm |
| Bay Haven Charter Academy | 2501 Hawks Landing Blvd | Panama City, FL | 32405-6658 | 850-248-3500 | 248-3514 | PK-8 | Larry Bolinger |
| Beacon College Preparatory | 13400 NW 28th Ave | Opa Locka, FL | 33054 | 786-353-6109 | | PK-5 | Patrick Evans |
| Believers Academy | 5840 Corporate Way Ste 100 | West Palm Beach, FL | 33407-2040 | 561-340-2507 | 340-2510 | 9-12 | Lori Dyer |
| Bellalago Charter Academy | 3651 Pleasant Hill Rd | Kissimmee, FL | 34746-2935 | 407-933-1690 | 933-2143 | K-8 | Wendy Honeycutt |
| Bell Creek Academy | 13221 Boyette Rd | Riverview, FL | 33569 | 813-793-6075 | 413-2985 | 6-12 | Dr. Margaret Fahringer |
| Belle Glade Excel | 555 SW 16th St | Belle Glade, FL | 33430 | 561-257-5210 | 983-8020 | K-5 | Shikira Williams |
| Belmont Academy | 496 SW Ring Ct | Lake City, FL | 32025 | 386-487-0487 | 755-7989 | PK-12 | Michael Cady |
| Berkley Accelerated MS | 5316 Berkley Rd | Auburndale, FL | 33823-8493 | 863-984-2400 | 984-2411 | 6-8 | Jill Bolender |
| Berkley ES | 5240 Berkley Rd | Auburndale, FL | 33823-8491 | 863-968-5024 | 968-5026 | PK-5 | Gayle Thomas |
| Beulah Academy of Science | 8633 Beulah Rd | Pensacola, FL | 32526-5203 | 850-944-2822 | 941-0702 | 6-8 | Sherry Bailey |
| Big Pine Academy | 30220 Overseas Hwy | Big Pine Key, FL | 33043-3357 | 305-872-1266 | 872-1265 | PK-7 | Cathy Hoffman |
| Biscayne HS | 1680 Dunn Ave Ste 8 | Jacksonville, FL | 32218 | 904-423-8855 | | 9-12 | Erica Williams |
| Boca Raton Charter S | 269 NE 14th St | Boca Raton, FL | 33432 | 561-750-0437 | 750-7880 | K-5 | Louise Nelson |
| Bok Academy | 13901 Highway 27 | Lake Wales, FL | 33859 | 863-638-1010 | 638-1212 | 6-8 | Damien Moses |
| Bonita Springs Charter S | 25380 Bernwood Dr | Bonita Springs, FL | 34135-7850 | 239-992-6932 | 992-7359 | K-8 | Carissa Carroll |
| Bonita Springs Preparatory\Fitness Acad | 28011 Performance Ln | Bonita Springs, FL | 34135 | 239-498-6864 | 495-7178 | K-8 | William Moore |
| Boulware Springs Charter S | 1303 NE 23rd Ave | Gainesville, FL | 32609 | 352-215-2175 | | K-5 | Kay Abbitt |
| Bridgeprep Academy Greater Miami | 137 NE 19th St | Miami, FL | 33132 | 786-477-4372 | 446-8714 | K-8 | Ana Natali |
| Bridgeprep Academy Interamerican | 621 Beacom Blvd | Miami, FL | 33135 | 305-643-4833 | 643-4832 | K-8 | Mitzie Ortiz |
| BridgePrep Academy of Hollywood Hills | 1400 N 46th Ave | Hollywood, FL | 33021 | 954-362-8268 | 362-8271 | K-5 | Melissa Devlin |
| Bridgeprep Academy of Tampa | 2418 W Swann Ave | Tampa, FL | 33609 | 813-258-5652 | 258-5654 | K-8 | Christine Harris |
| Bridgeprep Academy of Village Green | 4707 SW 127th Ave | Miami, FL | 33175 | 305-290-4246 | 554-7611 | K-8 | Paricia Garcia |
| Bridgeprep Academy South | 10700 SW 56th St | Miami, FL | 33165 | 305-271-3109 | 271-5315 | K-8 | Patricia Perez |

| School | Address | City,State | Zip code | Telephone | Fax | Grade | Contact |
|---|---|---|---|---|---|---|---|
| Bright Futures Academy | 10350 Riverside Dr | Palm Bch Gdns, FL | 33410 | 561-253-7504 | 658-0565 | K-8 | Kendall Artusi |
| Brooks-DeBartolo Collegiate HS | 10948 N Central Ave | Tampa, FL | 33612 | 813-971-5600 | 971-5656 | 9-12 | Kristine Bennett |
| Brooksville Engineering Science Tech. | 835 School St | Brooksville, FL | 34601 | 352-544-2373 | | 9-12 | Andre Buford |
| Broward Community Charter S West | 11421 NW 56th Dr | Coral Springs, FL | 33076 | 954-345-6500 | 345-1199 | K-5 | Michael Astalos |
| Broward Math and Science S | 6101 NW 31st St | Margate, FL | 33063 | 954-969-8488 | 756-8053 | K-12 | |
| Burns Science & Technology Charter S | 160 Ridge Rd | Oak Hill, FL | 32759-9773 | 386-210-4915 | 210-4922 | K-8 | Dr. Janet McGee |
| Byrneville Charter S | 1600 Byrneville Rd | Century, FL | 32535-3640 | 850-256-6350 | 256-6357 | K-5 | Dee Wolfe-Sullivan |
| Canoe Creek Charter S | 3600 Canoe Creek Rd | Saint Cloud, FL | 34772-9132 | 407-891-7320 | 891-7330 | PK-8 | Julie Ramirez |
| Cape Coral Charter S | 76 Mid Cape Ter | Cape Coral, FL | 33991-2008 | 239-995-0904 | 995-0369 | K-8 | Bonnie Brett |
| Cape Coral Preparatory & Fitness Academy | 2107 Santa Barbara Blvd | Cape Coral, FL | 33991 | 239-829-5134 | 242-0477 | K-8 | Jennifer Fowler |
| Capstone Academy | 4901 W Fairfield Dr | Pensacola, FL | 32506-4111 | 850-458-7735 | 455-7754 | PK-K | Charles Thomas |
| Capstone Academy Milton Charter S | 5308 Stewart St | Milton, FL | 32570 | 850-626-3091 | 626-3093 | PK-PK | Claire Errington |
| Caring & Sharing Charter S | PO Box 5936 | Gainesville, FL | 32627-5936 | 352-372-1004 | 372-0894 | PK-6 | Curtis Peterson |
| Central Charter S | 4515 N State Road 7 | Laud Lakes, FL | 33319 | 954-735-6295 | 735-6232 | K-8 | Tonya Dix |
| Central Florida Leadership Academy | 427 N Primrose Dr | Orlando, FL | 32803 | 407-480-2352 | 289-5204 | 6-11 | Tiffany Ward |
| Central HS | 700 W 23rd St Bldg H | Panama City, FL | 32405 | 850-215-0770 | 763-7613 | 9-12 | Jeremy Knapp |
| Chain of Lakes Collegiate HS | 999 Avenue H NE | Winter Haven, FL | 33881 | 863-298-6800 | 298-6801 | 11-12 | Bridget Fetter |
| Championship Academy | 3367 N University Dr | Davie, FL | 33328 | 954-362-3415 | 640-9678 | K-8 | Gustavo Prats |
| Championship Academy | 1100 Hillcrest Dr | Hollywood, FL | 33021 | 954-924-8006 | 924-8044 | K-8 | Gustavo Prats |
| Chancery High Charter | 7001 S Orange Blossom Trl | Orlando, FL | 32809 | 407-850-9791 | 850-9856 | 9-12 | Amy Wright |
| Channelside Academy of Math & Science | 1029 E Twiggs St | Tampa, FL | 33602 | 813-579-9649 | 463-2439 | K-8 | Suzanne Elder |
| Charter HS of the Americas | 970 W Flagler St | Miami, FL | 33130 | 305-325-1001 | 324-9934 | 9-12 | Barbara Sanchez |
| Charter S of Excellence - Davie | 2801 N University Dr | Pembroke Pines, FL | 33024 | 954-433-8838 | 433-8636 | K-5 | Jennifer Jaynes |
| Charter S of Excellence - Ft Lauderdale | 1217 SE 3rd Ave | Fort Lauderdale, FL | 33316-1905 | 954-522-2997 | 522-3159 | K-5 | Lisa Castro |
| Charter S of Excellence Riverland | 3550 Davie Blvd | Fort Lauderdale, FL | 33312-3438 | 954-581-0167 | 581-0195 | K-5 | Fiona Johnson |
| Charter School of Excellence Tamarac 1 | 7595 NW 61st St | Tamarac, FL | 33321 | 954-721-8902 | 721-8908 | K-5 | Fiona Johnson |
| Chataqua Learn and Serve | PO Box 813 | Defuniak Spgs, FL | 32435 | 850-892-5013 | 892-7895 | Adult | Kim Lonas |
| Chautauqua Learn & Serve Charter S | 1118 Magnolia Ave | Panama City, FL | 32401-2815 | 850-785-5056 | 785-5071 | 9-Adu | Cynthia McCauley |
| Children's Reading Center | 7901 Saint Johns Ave | Palatka, FL | 32177 | 386-328-9990 | 328-9949 | K-5 | Dr. Geri Melosh |
| Chiles Academy | 868 George W Engram Blvd | Daytona Beach, FL | 32114-1859 | 386-322-6102 | 258-4681 | 6-12 | Anne Ferguson |
| Choices in Learning Charter S | 1100 E State Road 434 | Winter Springs, FL | 32708-2715 | 407-302-1005 | 542-5553 | K-5 | Janet Kearney |
| City of Hialeah Education Academy | 2590 W 76th St | Hialeah, FL | 33016-6888 | 305-362-4006 | 362-7006 | 6-12 | Carlos Alvarez |
| City of Palms Charter HS | 2830 Winkler Ave Ste 201 | Fort Myers, FL | 33916 | 239-561-6611 | 561-6230 | 9-12 | Sarah White |
| City of Pembroke Pines Central ES | 12350 Sheridan St | Pembroke Pines, FL | 33026-3813 | 954-322-3330 | 322-3389 | K-5 | Sean Chance |
| City of Pembroke Pines Central MS | 12350 Sheridan St | Pembroke Pines, FL | 33026-3813 | 954-322-3300 | 322-3383 | 6-8 | Sean Chance |
| City of Pembroke Pines Charter HS | 17189 Sheridan St | Pembroke Pines, FL | 33331-1934 | 954-538-3700 | 538-3715 | 9-12 | Peter Bayer |
| City of Pembroke Pines East ES | 10801 Pembroke Rd | Pembroke Pines, FL | 33025-1707 | 954-443-4800 | 443-4811 | K-5 | Kenneth Bass |
| City of Pembroke Pines West ES | 1680 SW 184th Ave | Pembroke Pines, FL | 33029-6120 | 954-450-6990 | 443-4820 | K-5 | Michael Castellano |
| City of Pembroke Pines West MS | 18500 Pembroke Rd | Pembroke Pines, FL | 33029 | 954-443-4847 | 447-1691 | 6-8 | Michael Castellano |
| Clark Advanced Learning Center | 2400 SE Salerno Rd | Stuart, FL | 34997 | 772-419-5750 | 419-5760 | 10-12 | Debra Kohuth |
| Classical Preparatory Charter S | 16500 Lyceum Way | Spring Hill, FL | 34610 | 727-803-7903 | | K-8 | Ben Davis |
| Clay Charter Academy | 1417 Red Apple Rd | Middleburg, FL | 32068 | 904-406-1607 | 406-1608 | K-8 | Angela Galyan |
| C.O.A.S.T. Charter S | PO Box 338 | Saint Marks, FL | 32355 | 850-925-6344 | 925-6396 | PK-8 | Alyssa Higgins |
| Collegiate HS at NW FL State College | 100 College Blvd E | Niceville, FL | 32578-1347 | 850-729-4949 | 729-4950 | 10-12 | Anthony Boyer |
| Community Charter S of Excellence | 11604 N 15th St | Tampa, FL | 33612 | 813-931-5500 | 971-5232 | K-5 | Matthew Torano M.Ed. |
| Compass Middle Charter S | 550 E Clower St | Bartow, FL | 33830-6403 | 863-519-8701 | 519-8704 | 5-8 | Anita Fine |
| Coral Reef Montessori Academy | 10853 SW 216th St | Cutler Ridge, FL | 33170 | 305-255-0064 | 255-4085 | K-8 | Lucy Canzoneri-Golden |
| Coral Springs Charter S | 3205 N University Dr | Coral Springs, FL | 33065-4115 | 954-340-4100 | 340-4111 | 6-12 | Gary Springer |
| Cornerstone Academy Charter S | 5903 Randolph Ave | Orlando, FL | 32809 | 407-608-7171 | | K-8 | Renee Pancoast |
| Cornerstone Academy HS | 5903 Randolph Ave | Orlando, FL | 32809 | 407-608-7171 | 608-7172 | 9-12 | Renee Pancoast Ed.D. |
| Coronado HS | 3057 Cleveland Ave | Fort Myers, FL | 33901 | 239-337-9140 | 337-9141 | 9-12 | Charley Pease |
| Countryside Montessori Charter S | 5852 Ehren Cutoff | Land O Lakes, FL | 34639 | 813-996-0991 | 996-0993 | 1-8 | Dr. Michael Rom |
| Crossroad Academy Charter S | 470 Strong Rd | Quincy, FL | 32351 | 850-875-9626 | 875-1403 | PK-9 | Kevin Forehand |
| Dayspring Academy ES | 8911 Timber Oaks Ave | Port Richey, FL | 34668-2426 | 727-862-8600 | 868-5175 | K-5 | Brenda Garcia |
| Dayspring Academy MS | 9509 Palm Ave | Port Richey, FL | 34668-4647 | 727-847-9003 | 848-8774 | 6-10 | Sara Capwell |
| Discovery Academy at Lake Alfred | 1000 N Buena Vista Dr | Lake Alfred, FL | 33850-2031 | 863-295-5955 | 295-5978 | 6-8 | Kevin Warren |
| Discovery Academy of Science | 1380 Pinehurst Rd | Dunedin, FL | 34698 | 727-330-2424 | 499-6828 | K-12 | Emre Akbaba |
| Discovery MS | 11421 NW 56th Dr | Coral Springs, FL | 33076 | 954-345-6500 | 345-1199 | 6-8 | Michael Astalos |
| DJB Technical Academy | 13830 Jetport Commerce Pkwy | Fort Myers, FL | 33913 | 239-476-9100 | 561-9864 | 9-12 | Dr. Joseph Torregrasso |
| Doctors Charter S of Miami Shores | 11301 NW 5th Ave | Miami Shores, FL | 33168-3343 | 305-754-2381 | 751-5833 | 6-12 | Nicholas Dorn |
| Dolphin Park HS | 3206 S University Dr | Miramar, FL | 33025 | 954-433-1573 | 433-1589 | 9-12 | Vanessia Blackshire |
| Doral Academy | 2450 NW 97th Ave | Doral, FL | 33172-2308 | 305-597-9999 | 591-2669 | K-5 | Eleonora Cuesta |
| Doral Academy HS | 11100 NW 27th St | Doral, FL | 33172 | 305-597-9950 | 477-6762 | 9-12 | Carlos Ferrals |
| Doral Academy Preparatory MS | 2601 NW 112th Ave | Doral, FL | 33172-1804 | 305-591-0020 | 591-9251 | 6-8 | Carlos Ferrals |
| Doral Performing Arts\Entertainment Acad | 11100 NW 27th St | Doral, FL | 33172 | 305-597-9950 | 591-9251 | 9-12 | Carlos Ferralls |
| Downtown Doral Charter ES | 8390 NW 53rd St | Doral, FL | 33166 | 305-569-2223 | 569-2226 | K-3 | Jeanette Acevedo |
| Downtown Miami Charter S | 305 NW 3rd Ave | Miami, FL | 33128-1606 | 305-579-2112 | 579-2115 | K-6 | Dr. Rebecca Dinda |
| Duval Charter S at Arlington | 100 Bell Tel Way | Jacksonville, FL | 32216 | 904-724-1536 | 721-5381 | K-8 | Michelle Thompson |
| Duval Charter S at Baymeadows | 7510 Baymeadows Way | Jacksonville, FL | 32256 | 904-638-7947 | 466-4101 | K-12 | Kim Stidham |
| Duval Charter S at Flagler Center | 12755 Flagler Center Blvd | Jacksonville, FL | 32258 | 904-899-1010 | 899-1011 | K-8 | Adam Cross |
| Duval Charter S at Mandarin | 5209 Shad Rd | Jacksonville, FL | 32257 | 904-440-2901 | 440-2902 | K-8 | Dawn Lamb |
| Duval Charter S at Southside | 8680 AC Skinner Pkwy | Jacksonville, FL | 32256 | 904-423-5348 | 423-5349 | K-8 | Ashley Doty |
| Duval Charter S at Westside | 9238 103rd St | Jacksonville, FL | 32210 | 904-421-0250 | 423-2601 | K-8 | Tania Woods |
| Eagle Arts Academy | 1000 Wellington Trace | Wellington, FL | 33414 | 561-412-4087 | | K-6 | Ann Simone |
| Eagles Nest Charter Academy | 3698 NW 15th St | Lauderhill, FL | 33311 | 954-635-2308 | 990-6921 | K-8 | Christine Mentis |
| Eagles Nest MS | 3698 NW 15th St | Lauderhill, FL | 33311 | 954-635-2308 | 990-6921 | 6-8 | Christine Mentis |
| Early Beginnings Academy | 1411 NW 14th Ave | Miami, FL | 33125-1616 | 305-325-1080 | 325-1044 | PK-2 | Makeesha Coleman |
| Early Career Academy | 4809 Memorial Hwy | Tampa, FL | 33634 | 813-434-1389 | 888-8451 | 11-12 | |
| Easter Seals Charter S | 1219 Dunn Ave | Daytona Beach, FL | 32114-2405 | 386-255-4568 | 258-7677 | PK-PK | April Leopold |
| Educational Horizons Charter S | 1281 S Wickham Rd | West Melbourne, FL | 32904-2450 | 321-729-0786 | 802-6823 | K-6 | Cynthia Thomas |
| EdVenture Charter S | 115 E Coast Ave | Hypoluxo, FL | 33462 | 561-582-1454 | 547-9682 | 9-12 | Patricia Ryan |
| Einstein Montessori S | 5910 SW Archer Rd | Gainesville, FL | 32608 | 352-335-4321 | 335-1575 | 2-8 | Christine Aurelio |
| Enterprise HS | 2461 N McMullen Booth Rd | Clearwater, FL | 33759 | 727-474-1237 | 725-3470 | 9-12 | Donna Hulbert |
| Escambia Charter S | 391 90 9 Ranch Rd | Cantonment, FL | 32533-9098 | 850-937-0500 | 968-5605 | 9-12 | Jerome Chisholm |
| Everest Charter S | 10054 W McNab Rd | Tamarac, FL | 33321 | 954-532-3015 | 876-1696 | K-8 | Raul Baez |
| Everglades Preparatory Academy | 360 E Main St Bldg C | Pahokee, FL | 33476 | 561-924-3002 | 924-3013 | 9-12 | Edna Stevens |
| Everglades Preparatory Academy | 2251 E Mowry Dr | Homestead, FL | 33033 | 786-601-1969 | 377-5759 | 6-12 | Aimee Leyva |
| Excelsior Charter Academy | 3520 NW 191st St | Miami Gardens, FL | 33056 | 786-565-9188 | 623-0900 | K-9 | Janell Wyartt |
| Excelsior Charter S of Broward | 10046 W McNab Rd | Tamarac, FL | 33321-1894 | 954-726-5227 | 722-2451 | K-5 | Cristina Reynolds |
| Excelsior Language Academy of Hialeah | 369 E 10th St | Hialeah, FL | 33010 | 305-897-9004 | 883-5279 | PK-8 | Clint Duvo |
| Expressions Learning Arts Academy | 5408 SW 13th St | Gainesville, FL | 32608-5038 | 352-373-5223 | 373-6327 | K-5 | Juniper Digiovanni |
| Fair Babson Park ES | 815 N Scenic Hwy | Babson Park, FL | 33827-9795 | 863-678-4664 | 678-4669 | PK-5 | Elizabeth Tyler |
| Flagler HS | 1951 W Copans Rd | Pompano Beach, FL | 33064 | 754-220-7899 | 973-3199 | 9-12 | Bernard Bell |
| Florida Autism Center of Excellence | 6310 E Sligh Ave | Tampa, FL | 33617 | 813-985-3223 | 985-3199 | PK-12 | Annie Russell |
| Florida Futures Academy | 1760 N Congress Ave | West Palm Beach, FL | 33409 | 561-215-0933 | | 9-12 | Carolyn Taylor |
| Florida International Academy | 13400 NW 28th Ave | Opa Locka, FL | 33054 | 305-685-8190 | 688-1745 | K-8 | Sonia Mitchell |
| Florida SIA Tech at Gainesville | 7022 NW 10th Pl | Gainesville, FL | 32605 | 352-333-7952 | 333-7953 | 9-12 | Christal Blue |
| Florida Southwestern Collegiate HS | 8099 College Pkwy | Fort Myers, FL | 33919 | 239-432-6767 | 433-6912 | 9-12 | Dr. Brian Botts |
| Florida State University School | 3000 School House Rd | Tallahassee, FL | 32311 | 850-245-3700 | 245-3997 | K-12 | Lynn Wicker |
| Florida Virtual @ Palm Beach County | 9143 Philips Hwy Ste 590 | Jacksonville, FL | 32259 | 904-287-3268 | 330-1116 | K-12 | Karen Parker |
| Focus Academy | 304 Druid Hills Rd | Temple Terrace, FL | 33617 | 813-443-5558 | 443-5630 | 9-12 | Fran McCrimmon M.Ed. |
| Fort Myers Preparatory & Fitness Academy | 4740 S Cleveland Ave | Fort Myers, FL | 33907 | 239-333-0766 | 333-0768 | K-8 | Stephan Terebieniec |
| Four Corners Charter S | 9100 Teacher Ln | Davenport, FL | 33897-6212 | 407-787-4300 | 787-4331 | K-8 | Denise Thompson |
| Franklin Academy | 7882 S Military Trl | Boynton Beach, FL | 33436 | 561-767-4700 | 952-6925 | K-8 | Christopher Glinton |
| Franklin Academy | 4500 NW 103 Ave | Sunrise, FL | 33351 | 954-206-0850 | 497-3296 | K-8 | Dr. Daniel Sandberg |
| Franklin Academy | 18800 Pines Blvd | Pembroke Pines, FL | 33029 | 954-703-2294 | 436-2861 | K-8 | Elena Diaz |
| Franklin Academy | 5651 Hood Rd | Palm Bch Gdns, FL | 33418 | 561-348-2525 | | K-8 | Ivy Bernardo |
| Franklin Academy | 6301 S Flamingo Rd | Cooper City, FL | 33330 | 954-780-5533 | 252-8147 | K-8 | Doug Piper |
| Galileo S for Gifted Learning | 2251 Jitway Ave | Sanford, FL | 32771 | 321-249-9221 | | K-6 | Michelle Nunez |
| Gamla Charter S | 8600 Jog Rd | Boynton Beach, FL | 33472 | 561-742-8017 | 742-8018 | K-8 | Elanit Weizman |
| Gamla Charter S | 11155 SW 112th Ave | Miami, FL | 33176 | 305-596-6266 | 596-6964 | K-8 | Jose Baca |
| Gamla Charter S North Broward | 2620 Hollywood Blvd | Hollywood, FL | 33020-4807 | 954-342-4064 | 342-4107 | K-8 | Sharon Miller |
| Gamla Charter School South Broward | 6511 W Sunrise Blvd | Plantation, FL | 33313 | 954-587-8348 | 587-8347 | K-8 | Stephanie Washofsky |
| Gamla Preparatory Academy | 2650 Van Buren St | Hollywood, FL | 33020 | 954-924-6495 | 924-6496 | 6-12 | Orli Goldstein |
| Gardens S of Technology Arts | 9153 Roan Ln | Palm Bch Gdns, FL | 33403 | 561-290-7661 | 449-3470 | K-8 | Dr. Kevin Kovacs |
| Gateway Charter ES | 12850 Commonwealth Dr | Fort Myers, FL | 33913-8039 | 239-768-5048 | 768-5710 | K-4 | Sara Abraham M.Ed. |
| Gateway Charter HS | 12770 Gateway Blvd | Fort Myers, FL | 33913-8654 | 239-768-3350 | 768-3874 | 5-12 | Sara Abraham |
| Genesis Preparatory S | 207 NW 23rd Ave | Gainesville, FL | 32609-3604 | 352-379-1188 | 379-1142 | K-3 | Charmaine Henry |
| Gibson Charter S | 1682 NW 4th Ave | Miami, FL | 33136 | 305-438-0895 | 438-0896 | K-8 | Fareed Khan |
| Glades Academy | 7368 State Road 15 | Pahokee, FL | 33476 | 561-924-9402 | 924-9279 | K-8 | Dr. Don Zumpano |
| Global Outreach Charter Academy | 9570 Regency Square Blvd | Jacksonville, FL | 32225 | 904-551-7104 | 551-7120 | K-8 | Tangia Anderson |
| Goodwill L.I.F.E. Academy | 5100 Tice St Ste D | Fort Myers, FL | 33905-5203 | 239-334-4434 | 334-4439 | 6-12 | Lynn Pottorf |
| Governors Charter Academy | 4351 Mahan Dr | Tallahassee, FL | 32308-5724 | 850-391-5259 | 391-5260 | K-6 | Dr. Adriane Peters |
| Green Springs HS | 3555 NW 7th St | Miami, FL | 33125 | 305-720-2996 | 541-5559 | 9-12 | Enrique Palma |
| Greentree Preparatory Charter S | 750 NW 180th Ter | Pembroke Pines, FL | 33029 | 954-780-8733 | 430-7706 | K-5 | Rosa Pou |
| G-STAR School of the Arts | 2065 Prairie Rd Bldg J | Palm Springs, FL | 33406-7700 | 561-967-2023 | 963-8975 | 9-12 | Kim Collins M.Ed. |
| Gulf Coast Acad of Science & Technology | 10444 Tillery Rd | Spring Hill, FL | 34608-3706 | 352-688-5092 | 688-5095 | 6-8 | Nevin Siefert |

| School | Address | City,State | Zip code | Telephone | Fax | Grade | Contact |
|---|---|---|---|---|---|---|---|
| Gulf Coast Charter Academy South | 215 Airport Pulling Rd N | Naples, FL | 34104 | 239-784-1539 | 263-4443 | K-6 | Gwen DaPore |
| Gulf Coast MS | 2139 Deborah Dr | Spring Hill, FL | 34608 | 352-666-5790 | 666-5792 | 6-8 | Dave Schoelles |
| Gulfstream Goodwill LIFE Academy | 3800 S Congress Ave | Boynton Beach, FL | 33426 | 561-259-1000 | 259-1011 | 9-12 | Cindy Maunder |
| Harris Preparatory Academy | 1408 E Blount St | Pensacola, FL | 32503-5620 | 850-432-2273 | 432-4624 | K-5 | Celestine Lewis |
| Hartridge Academy | 1400 US Highway 92 | Winter Haven, FL | 33881-8137 | 863-956-4434 | 956-3267 | K-5 | Debra Richards |
| Hawn Charter School of the Arts | 565 S Lakeview Dr Unit 110 | Lake Helen, FL | 32744-3520 | 386-228-3900 | 228-3901 | K-8 | Dr. Carol Kelley |
| Healthy Learning Academy | 13505 W Newberry Rd | Newberry, FL | 32669 | 352-372-2279 | 372-1665 | K-5 | Anni Egan |
| Henderson Hammock Charter S | 10322 Henderson Rd | Tampa, FL | 33625 | 813-739-6633 | 739-6681 | K-8 | Kristen Taylor |
| Highly Inquisitive & Versatile Ed | 5855 NW 171st St | Miami, FL | 33015 | 305-231-4888 | 231-4881 | K-8 | Carlos Gonzalez |
| Hillcrest ES | 1051 State Road 60 E | Lake Wales, FL | 33853-4258 | 863-678-4216 | 678-4086 | PK-5 | Jennifer Barrow |
| Hillsborough Academy of Math & Science | 9659 W Waters Ave | Tampa, FL | 33635 | 813-793-6085 | 413-2984 | K-8 | Cristina Fuentes |
| Hollywood Academy of Arts & Science | 1705 Van Buren St | Hollywood, FL | 33020 | 954-925-6404 | 925-8123 | K-8 | Mark Hage |
| Hope Center for Autism Charter S | 1695 SE Indian St | Stuart, FL | 34997-4962 | 772-334-3288 | 334-2203 | PK-2 | Staci Routt |
| Hope Charter S | 1550 E Crown Point Rd | Ocoee, FL | 34761-3722 | 407-656-4673 | 264-6960 | K-8 | Veronica Rickles |
| Horizon Charter S of Tampa | 5429 Beaumont Center # 800 | Tampa, FL | 33634 | 813-887-3800 | 885-9626 | K-8 | Sheila Thomley |
| iGeneration Empowerment Acad of Broward | 6101 NW 31st St | Margate, FL | 33063 | 954-582-7245 | 317-4004 | 6-12 | Marjorie Waldo |
| Imagine Charter S at Broward | 9001 Westview Dr | Coral Springs, FL | 33067 | 954-255-0020 | 255-1336 | K-8 | Maria Tracy |
| Imagine Charter S at Lakewood Ranch | 10535 Portal Xing | Bradenton, FL | 34211 | 941-750-0900 | 750-0966 | PK-8 | Selenia Quinones |
| Imagine Charter S at Land O' Lakes | 2940 Sunlake Blvd | Land O Lakes, FL | 34638 | 813-428-7444 | 428-7445 | K-8 | Aimee Williams |
| Imagine Charter S at North Lauderdale | 1395 S State Road 7 | N Lauderdale, FL | 33068-4023 | 954-973-8900 | 974-5588 | K-5 | Erin Kelly |
| Imagine Charter S at North Manatee | 9275 49th Ave E | Palmetto, FL | 34221 | 941-981-5345 | 981-5349 | K-8 | Matthew Loge |
| Imagine Charter S at Town Center | 775 Town Center Blvd | Palm Coast, FL | 32164 | 386-586-0100 | 586-2784 | PK-8 | James Menard |
| Imagine Charter S at West Melbourne | 3355 Imagine Way | West Melbourne, FL | 32904 | 321-768-6200 | 768-6300 | PK-6 | Brian DeGonzague |
| Imagine Charter S at Weston | 2500 Glades Cir | Weston, FL | 33327-2253 | 954-659-3600 | 659-3620 | K-5 | Nadine Laham |
| Imagine Charter S Nau Campus | 4402 SW Yamada Dr | Port St Lucie, FL | 34953 | 772-237-8600 | 237-8620 | K-8 | Melissa Adams |
| Imagine MS West | 2500 Glades Cir | Weston, FL | 33327 | 954-659-3600 | 659-3620 | 6-8 | Nadine Laham |
| Imagine MSHS at North Port | 2757 Sycamore St | North Port, FL | 34289 | 941-426-2050 | 423-8252 | 6-12 | Dr. Steve Black |
| Imagine S at Evening Rose | 3611 Austin Davis Ave | Tallahassee, FL | 32308 | 850-877-5187 | 877-6463 | K-6 | Linda John |
| Imagine S at North Port | 1000 Innovation Ave | North Port, FL | 34289 | 941-426-2050 | 423-8252 | K-5 | Aleischa Coover |
| Imagine S at Palmer Ranch | 6220 McIntosh Rd | Sarasota, FL | 34238 | 941-257-1125 | 923-1124 | K-8 | Alisa Wright |
| Imagine S - Chancellor Campus | 3333 High Ridge Rd | Boynton Beach, FL | 33426 | 561-585-1189 | 585-1166 | K-8 | Susan Onori |
| Imagine S Plantation Campus | 8200 Peters Rd | Plantation, FL | 33324 | 954-358-4200 | 472-1994 | K-8 | Ethiel Calvo |
| Imagine South Lake Charter S | 2750 Hartwood Marsh Rd | Clermont, FL | 34711 | 352-243-2960 | 243-2967 | K-8 | Jennifer Fornes |
| Imagine South Vero Charter S | 6000 4th St | Vero Beach, FL | 32968 | 772-567-2728 | 410-0329 | PK-8 | Chris Rock |
| IMater Academy | 600 W 20th St | Hialeah, FL | 33010 | 305-884-6320 | 884-6321 | PK-5 | Brenda Cruz |
| iMater Academy MSHS | 651 W 20th St | Hialeah, FL | 33010 | 305-805-5722 | 805-5723 | 6-12 | Teresa Santalo |
| Immokalee Community S | 123 N 4th St | Immokalee, FL | 34142 | 239-867-3223 | 867-3224 | K-5 | Dr. Betty Kotowski |
| Independence Academy | 12902 E US Highway 92 | Dover, FL | 33527 | 813-707-1060 | 707-8060 | K-8 | Shane Clark |
| Indian River Charter HS | 6055 College Ln | Vero Beach, FL | 32966-1285 | 772-567-6600 | 567-6338 | 9-12 | Cynthia Trevino-Aversa |
| Inlet Grove Community HS | 600 W 28th St | Riviera Beach, FL | 33404 | 561-881-4600 | 881-4668 | 9-12 | Emma Banks |
| Innovation Charter S | 600 SW 3rd St | Pompano Beach, FL | 33060 | 754-715-1777 | | K-5 | Tiffanie Holm |
| Innovations MS | 2768 N Hiawassee Rd | Orlando, FL | 32818-3319 | 407-429-7901 | | 6-8 | Dr. Patricia Lightner |
| Integrated Science and Asian Culture | 301 Westward DR | Miami Springs, FL | 33166 | 305-863-8030 | 863-8031 | K-8 | Ofelia Alvarez |
| International S of Broward | 3100 NW 75th Ave | Hollywood, FL | 33024-2355 | 954-987-2026 | 987-7261 | 6-12 | Michelle Garay |
| International Studies Charter S | 2480 SW 8th St | Miami, FL | 33135 | 305-643-2955 | 643-2956 | 6-12 | Victoriano Rodriguez |
| International Studies Virtual Academy | 11100 NW 27th St | Doral, FL | 33172 | 305-592-5744 | 477-6762 | 6-12 | Jorge Nunez |
| Island Park HS | 16520 S Tamiami Trl Ste 190 | Fort Myers, FL | 33908 | 239-204-5965 | 243-0043 | 9-12 | A.J. Nauss |
| Island S | PO Box 1090 | Boca Grande, FL | 33921-1090 | 941-964-8016 | 964-8017 | K-5 | Jean Thompson |
| Island Village Montessori S | 11011 Clark Rd | Sarasota, FL | 34241 | 941-954-4999 | 484-2150 | K-8 | Alison Rini |
| Island Village Montessori S Sarasota | 11011 Clark Rd | Sarasota, FL | 34241 | 941-954-4999 | 342-6502 | K-6 | Alison Rini |
| Island Village Montessori S Venice | 2001 Pinebrook Rd | Venice, FL | 34292-1560 | 941-484-4999 | 484-2150 | K-12 | Jennifer Ocana |
| Jackson Preparatory S | 546 Mary Esther Blvd | Ft Walton Bch, FL | 32548 | 850-833-3321 | 833-3292 | K-8 | Kaye McKinley |
| Jewel Charter Academy | 705 Blake Ave | Cocoa, FL | 32922 | 321-634-5462 | 634-5465 | K-8 | Thomas Cole |
| JFK Charter S | 4696 Davis Rd | Lake Worth, FL | 33461-5204 | 561-868-6100 | 963-4697 | K-7 | Sharon Hench |
| Just Arts and Management Charter MS | 2450 NW 97th Ave | Doral, FL | 33172 | 305-597-9999 | 591-2669 | 6-8 | Eleonara Cuesta |
| Just for Girls Academy | 1011 21st St E | Bradenton, FL | 34208 | 941-243-3954 | 243-3963 | K-5 | Deanna Smith |
| Keys Gate Charter HS | 2325 SE 28th Ave | Homestead, FL | 33035-2280 | 305-230-5630 | 230-1347 | 9-12 | Corinne Baez |
| Keys Gate Charter S | 2000 SE 28th Ave | Homestead, FL | 33035-2102 | 305-230-1616 | 230-1347 | K-8 | Corinne Baez |
| Key West Collegiate Charter S | 5901 College Rd | Key West, FL | 33040-4315 | 305-296-5927 | 809-3191 | 9-12 | Cory Oliver |
| Key West Montessori Charter S | 1400 United St | Key West, FL | 33040 | 305-293-1400 | | 1-6 | Lynn Barras |
| Kids Community College Charter S -Orange | 1475 E Silver Star Rd | Ocoee, FL | 34761 | 407-982-2421 | 203-3867 | K-5 | Dr. Andy Westerman |
| Kids Community College - Riverview South | 10030 Mathog Rd | Riverview, FL | 33578 | 813-671-1440 | 354-3614 | K-8 | Karen Seder |
| Kids Community College SE Charter S | 11519 McMullen Rd | Riverview, FL | 33569 | 813-699-4600 | 671-1245 | K-5 | Martha Caballero |
| Kidz Choice Charter S | 1800 N Douglas Rd | Pembroke Pines, FL | 33024 | 954-251-2419 | 260-5935 | K-5 | Lilly Swanson |
| Kings Kids Academy of Health Sciences | 3000 N 34th St | Tampa, FL | 33605 | 813-238-4900 | 238-6700 | K-5 | Lillia Stroud |
| KIPP Impact MS | 1440 McDuff Ave N | Jacksonville, FL | 32254 | 904-683-6643 | 683-9895 | 5-8 | Warren Buck |
| KIPP VOICE ES | 1440 McDuff Ave N | Jacksonville, FL | 32254 | 904-683-6643 | 683-9895 | K-4 | Kimberly Davidson |
| Kissimmee Charter Academy | 2850 Bill Beck Blvd | Kissimmee, FL | 34744-4073 | 407-847-1400 | 847-1401 | PK-8 | Lori McCarley |
| Lake Eola Charter S | 135 N Magnolia Ave | Orlando, FL | 32801-2301 | 407-246-0900 | 246-6334 | K-8 | Veronica Denoia |
| Lakeland Montessori MS | 800 E Palmetto St | Lakeland, FL | 33801-5529 | 863-413-0003 | 812-4689 | 7-8 | Heather Manrow |
| Lakeland Montessori Schoolhouse | 1124 N Lake Parker Ave | Lakeland, FL | 33805 | 863-413-0003 | 413-0006 | PK-6 | Heather Manrow |
| Lakeside Academy | 716 S Main St | Belle Glade, FL | 33430-4202 | 561-993-5000 | 993-5001 | K-6 | Vinnisha Jones |
| Lake Wales HS | 1 Highlander Way | Lake Wales, FL | 33853-8517 | 863-678-4222 | 678-4064 | 9-12 | Donna Dunson |
| Lauderhill HS | 4131 NW 16th St | Lauderhill, FL | 33313 | 954-731-2585 | 731-2587 | 9-12 | Sharard Walker |
| LBA Academy | 13835 NW 97th Ave | Hialeah, FL | 33018 | 305-827-3022 | 827-3023 | 9-12 | Chayma Gomez |
| Learning Gate Community S | 16215 Hanna Rd | Lutz, FL | 33549-5701 | 813-948-4190 | 948-7587 | K-8 | Michelle Mason |
| Learning Lodge Academy | 5844 Pine Hill Rd | Port Richey, FL | 34668 | 727-389-0067 | | K-5 | Kerrie Cuffe |
| Learning Path Academy | 1340 Kenwood Rd | West Palm Beach, FL | 33401 | 561-832-0232 | 370-6869 | PK-5 | Isis Rosso |
| Legacy Charter HS | 1550 E Crown Point Rd | Ocoee, FL | 34761 | 407-656-4673 | 264-6960 | 9-12 | Roberta VanHouten |
| Legacy Preparatory Academy | 302 E Linebaugh Ave | Tampa, FL | 33612 | 813-253-0053 | 253-0182 | 6-8 | Yolanda Capers |
| Legends Academy Charter S | 3032 Monte Carlo Tr | Orlando, FL | 32805 | 407-985-5195 | 650-8355 | K-12 | |
| Lincoln-Marti Charter S | 3500 W 84th St | Hialeah, FL | 33018 | 305-827-8080 | 827-8004 | K-8 | Yaimy Fernandez |
| Lincoln-Marti Charter S | 970 W Flagler St | Miami, FL | 33130 | 305-325-1001 | 324-9934 | K-12 | Nataly Parra |
| Lincoln-Marti Charter S - International | 103 E Lucy St | Florida City, FL | 33034 | 305-242-3330 | 242-3331 | K-8 | Barbara Sanchez |
| Literacy Leadership Technology Academy | 6771 Madison Ave | Tampa, FL | 33619-6836 | 813-234-0940 | 234-0946 | K-8 | Lesley Logan |
| Lone Star HS | 8050 Lone Star Rd Ste 1 | Jacksonville, FL | 32211-6227 | 904-725-5998 | 724-3172 | 9-12 | LaShanda Roberts |
| Lutz Preparatory S | 17951 N US Highway 41 | Lutz, FL | 33549 | 813-428-7100 | 428-7061 | K-8 | Bonnie Guertin |
| Magnolia Montessori Academy | 1540 New Jersey Rd | Lakeland, FL | 33803 | 863-797-4991 | | K-5 | Aurielle Hollinger |
| Manatee Charter S | 4550 30th St E | Bradenton, FL | 34203 | 941-465-4296 | 465-4297 | K-8 | Quantas Simmons |
| Manatee S for the Arts | 700 Haben Blvd | Palmetto, FL | 34221-4173 | 941-721-6800 | 721-6805 | 6-12 | Dr. Bill Jones |
| Manatee S of Arts and Sciences | 3700 32nd St W | Bradenton, FL | 34205-2708 | 941-755-5012 | 755-7934 | PK-6 | Paul Galloway |
| Marco Island Academy | 2255 San Marco Rd | Marco Island, FL | 34145 | 239-393-5133 | 393-5143 | 9-12 | Melissa Scott |
| Marco Island Charter MS | 1401 Trinidad Ave | Marco Island, FL | 34145-3949 | 239-377-3200 | 377-3201 | 6-8 | George Abounader |
| Marion Charter MS | 3233 SE Maricamp Rd | Ocala, FL | 34471 | 352-812-7960 | | 6-8 | Mary Pinson |
| Marion Charter S | 39 Cedar Rd | Ocala, FL | 34472-8331 | 352-687-2100 | 687-2700 | K-5 | Michelle Axson |
| Marion Military Academy | 3443 SW 20th St | Ocala, FL | 34474 | 352-291-6600 | 291-6601 | 9-12 | Tom Adair |
| Mascotte Conversion Charter ES | 460 Midway Ave | Mascotte, FL | 34753-8800 | 352-429-2294 | 429-4836 | PK-5 | Wayne Cockcroft |
| Mason Classical Academy | 3073 Horseshoe Dr Ste 104 | Naples, FL | 34104 | 239-227-2838 | 201-2056 | K-12 | David Hull |
| Mater Academy | 8003 NW 103rd St | Hialeah Gardens, FL | 33016 | 305-698-9900 | 698-3822 | K-5 | Cecilia Bermeosolo |
| Mater Academy | 8625 Byron Ave | Miami Beach, FL | 33141 | 305-864-2889 | 864-2890 | K-12 | Marisol Gomez |
| Mater Academy at Mount Sinai | 4300 Alton Rd | Miami Beach, FL | 33140 | 305-604-1453 | 604-1454 | K-8 | Eileen Hernandez |
| Mater Academy Charter MSHS | 7901 NW 103rd St | Hialeah Gardens, FL | 33016-2419 | 305-828-1886 | 828-6175 | 6-12 | Judith Marty |
| Mater Academy East Charter HS | 998 SW 1st St | Miami, FL | 33130-1112 | 305-324-6963 | 324-6966 | 6-12 | Alex Tamargo |
| Mater Academy East Charter S | 450 SW 4th St | Miami, FL | 33130-1410 | 305-324-4667 | 324-6580 | K-5 | Beatrice Riera |
| Mater Academy HS International Studies | 795 NW 32nd St | Miami, FL | 33127 | 305-634-0445 | 634-0446 | 9-12 | Ileana Melian |
| Mater Academy Lakes HS | 17300 NW 87th Ave | Hialeah, FL | 33015 | 305-698-8000 | 698-1800 | 6-12 | Rene Rovirosa |
| Mater Academy of International Studies | 795 NW 32nd St | Miami, FL | 33127 | 305-634-0445 | 634-0446 | K-8 | Ileana Melian |
| Mater Gardens Academy | 9010 NW 178th Ln | Hialeah, FL | 33018-6548 | 305-512-9775 | 512-3708 | K-8 | Lourdes Isla-Marrero |
| Mater Grove Academy | 2805 SW 32nd Ave | Miami, FL | 33133 | 305-442-4992 | 442-4993 | K-8 | Sheila Caleo-Gonzalez |
| Mater International Academy | 3405 NW 27th Ave | Miami, FL | 33142 | 305-638-8016 | 638-8017 | K-1 | Ileana Melian |
| Mater Performing Arts Academy | 7901 NW 103rd St | Hialeah Gardens, FL | 33016-2419 | 305-828-1886 | 828-6175 | 9-12 | Judith Marty |
| Mater Virtual Academy | 17300 NW 87th Ave | Hialeah, FL | 33015 | 305-512-3917 | 512-3912 | 6-12 | Ofelia Alvarez |
| Mavericks HS | 1100 N Main St | Kissimmee, FL | 34744 | 321-250-1871 | 846-0816 | 9-12 | Carl Martin |
| Mavericks HS at Palm Springs | 3525 S Congress Ave | Palm Springs, FL | 33461 | 561-623-6935 | 641-6370 | 9-12 | Chykimberly Bullard |
| Mavericks HS of Central Broward | 424 W Sunrise Blvd | Fort Lauderdale, FL | 33311 | 954-446-9234 | 522-1539 | 9-12 | Nadine Leblanc |
| Mavericks HS of North Broward County | 3500 North Andrews Ave | Pompano Beach, FL | 33064 | 954-944-4123 | 784-3681 | 9-12 | Deanna Allen |
| Mavericks HS of North Miami-Dade County | 16150 NE 17th Ave | N Miami Beach, FL | 33162-4744 | 786-629-7053 | 949-5604 | 9-12 | Alejandro Madrigal |
| Mavericks HS of South Miami-Dade County | 698 N Homestead Blvd | Homestead, FL | 33030-6207 | 305-909-6307 | 248-2913 | 9-12 | Daniel Walke |
| McAuliffe Charter ES | 2817 SW 3rd Ln | Cape Coral, FL | 33991-1151 | 239-283-4511 | 282-0376 | PK-5 | Jacquelin Collins |
| Mc Intosh Area Charter S | PO Box 769 | Mc Intosh, FL | 32664-0769 | 352-591-9797 | 591-9747 | K-5 | Jolene Vining |
| McKeel Academy of Technology | 1810 W Parker St | Lakeland, FL | 33815-1243 | 863-499-2818 | 603-6339 | 6-12 | Joyce Powell |
| McKeel Central Academy | 411 N Florida Ave | Lakeland, FL | 33801-4803 | 863-499-1287 | 688-1607 | K-5 | Michele Spurgeon |
| Melrose HS | 2744 Davie Blvd | Fort Lauderdale, FL | 33312 | 954-681-4096 | 797-4446 | 9-12 | Ismael Villafane |
| Miami Arts Charter S | 3900 Biscayne Blvd | Miami, FL | 33137 | 305-763-6257 | 740-5670 | 6-12 | Alfredo de la Rosa |
| Miami Childrens Museum Charter S | 980 MacArthur Cswy | Miami, FL | 33132-1604 | 305-329-3758 | 329-3767 | K-2 | Nina Cortina |
| Miami Community Charter HS | 18720 SW 352nd St | Florida City, FL | 33034 | 786-243-9981 | 217-6804 | 9-12 | Dr. Jila Rezaie |
| Miami Community Charter MS | 18720 SW 352nd St | Florida City, FL | 33034 | 786-243-9981 | 217-6804 | 6-8 | Jacqueline Sera-Sirven |

| School | Address | City,State | Zip code | Telephone | Fax | Grade | Contact |
|---|---|---|---|---|---|---|---|
| Miami Community Charter S | 101 S Redland Rd | Florida City, FL | 33034-4630 | 305-245-2552 | 245-2527 | K-5 | Dr. Jila Rezaie |
| Micanopy Area Cooperative S | 802 NW Seminary Ave | Micanopy, FL | 32667-8500 | 352-466-0990 | 466-4090 | PK-5 | Brenda Maynard |
| Micanopy MS | PO Box 109 | Micanopy, FL | 32667-0109 | 352-466-1090 | 466-1030 | 6-8 | Tara Lowe-Phillips |
| Milburn Academy - Deland | 913 E New York Ave | DeLand, FL | 32724 | 386-738-9150 | 738-9151 | 6-12 | Art Sands |
| Milburn Academy | 1031 Mason Ave | Daytona Beach, FL | 32117 | 386-304-0086 | 304-0087 | 6-12 | Art Sands |
| Minneola Conversion Charter ES | 320 E Pearl St | Minneola, FL | 34715 | 352-394-2600 | 394-2079 | K-5 | Sherry Watts |
| Montessori Academy of Early Enrichment | 6300 Lake Worth Rd | Greenacres, FL | 33463 | 561-649-0004 | 649-0964 | PK-5 | Jean Ranck |
| Montessori of Winter Garden Charter S | 855 E Plant St Ste 600 | Winter Garden, FL | 34787 | 407-654-2045 | 654-2046 | PK-6 | |
| Murray Hill HS | 929 McDuff Ave S | Jacksonville, FL | 32205 | 904-866-4516 | 388-8297 | 9-12 | Erica Williams |
| MYcroSchool Gainesville | 2209 NW 13th St | Gainesville, FL | 32609 | 352-379-2902 | 379-2956 | 9-12 | Randy Starling |
| MYcroSchool Jacksonville | 1584 Normandy Village Pkwy | Jacksonville, FL | 32221 | 904-783-3611 | 783-3703 | 9-12 | Rachel Maldonado |
| MYcroSchool Pinellas HS | 840 3rd Ave S | St Petersburg, FL | 33701 | 727-825-3710 | 825-3751 | 9-12 | Michael Warren |
| Nap Ford Community Charter S | 325 N Parramore Ave | Orlando, FL | 32801 | 407-245-8711 | 245-8712 | PK-5 | Jennifer Porter-Smith |
| Nature Coast MS | 6830 NW 140th St | Chiefland, FL | 32626-8271 | 352-490-0700 | 490-0702 | 6-8 | Charles Bowe |
| New Beginnings HS | 3425 Lake Alfred Rd | Winter Haven, FL | 33881 | 863-298-5666 | 298-5675 | 6-12 | Ashlee Wright |
| New Dimensions HS | 4900 Old Pleasant Hill Rd | Kissimmee, FL | 34759-3430 | 407-870-9949 | 870-8976 | 9-12 | Dr. Jacqueline Grimm |
| NEW Generation Prep HS of Perfroming Art | 2890 W Cypress Creek Rd | Fort Lauderdale, FL | 33309 | 754-222-7772 | 970-9933 | 9-12 | Kionnie Maura |
| New Life Charter Academy | 3260 Stirling Rd | Hollywood, FL | 33021 | 954-381-5199 | 734-6408 | K-5 | Shirley Brunache |
| Newpoint Pinellas Academy & HS | 21810 US Highway 19 N | Clearwater, FL | 33765 | 727-475-1256 | 725-3395 | 6-12 | Chris Wiand |
| New Springs S | 2410 E Busch Blvd | Tampa, FL | 33612 | 813-933-5025 | 527-9982 | K-8 | Yanus Aksu |
| North Bay Haven Charter Academy | 1104A Balboa Ave | Panama City, FL | 32401 | 850-248-0205 | 215-0644 | K-5 | Michael McLaughlin |
| North Bay Haven Charter MSHS | 1 Buccaneer Dr | Panama City, FL | 32404 | 850-248-0801 | 248-1201 | 6-12 | Michelle Gainer |
| North Broward Academy of Excellence | 8200 SW 17th St | N Lauderdale, FL | 33068 | 954-718-2211 | 718-2215 | K-5 | Staci Valbrun |
| North Broward Academy of Excellence MS | 8200 SW 17th St | N Lauderdale, FL | 33068-4101 | 954-718-2211 | 718-2215 | 6-8 | Staci Valbrun |
| North County Charter S | 6640 Old Dixie Hwy | Vero Beach, FL | 32967 | 772-794-1941 | 794-1945 | K-5 | Beth Miller |
| North Gardens HS | 4692 NW 183rd St | Miami Gardens, FL | 33055 | 786-528-6308 | 621-1611 | 9-12 | Neisha Mack-Freeman |
| North Nicholas HS | 428 SW Pine Island Rd | Cape Coral, FL | 33991 | 239-242-4230 | 242-4231 | 9-12 | Janet Morris |
| North Park HS | 3400 NW 135th St | Opa Locka, FL | 33054-4708 | 305-720-2995 | 953-3289 | 9-12 | Michael Rivera |
| North University HS | 4800 N University Dr | Sunrise, FL | 33351 | 954-746-4483 | 741-8113 | 9-12 | Byron Foster |
| Oakland Avenue Charter S | 456 E Oakland Ave | Oakland, FL | 34760 | 407-877-2039 | 877-6222 | K-5 | Pamela Wolfcale |
| Oasis Charter ES | 3415 Oasis Blvd | Cape Coral, FL | 33914-4924 | 239-542-1577 | 549-7662 | K-5 | Steven Hook |
| Oasis Charter HS | 3519 Oasis Blvd | Cape Coral, FL | 33914 | 239-541-1167 | 541-1590 | 9-12 | Shannon Treece |
| Oasis Charter MS | 3507 Oasis Blvd | Cape Coral, FL | 33914 | 239-945-1999 | 540-7677 | 6-8 | Keith Graham |
| Oasis MS | 4304 32nd St W | Bradenton, FL | 34205 | 941-749-1979 | 714-7333 | 6-8 | Edna Bailey |
| Oasis Preparatory Academy | 5200 W South St | Orlando, FL | 32811 | 407-930-2581 | | K-5 | Tabitha Woods-Jackson |
| Ocean Studies Charter S | 92295 Overseas Hwy | Tavernier, FL | 33070 | 305-852-7700 | | K-3 | Jennifer Flores |
| Odyssey Charter ES | 1755 Eldron Blvd SE | Palm Bay, FL | 32909-6832 | 321-733-0442 | 733-1178 | K-6 | Wendi Nolder |
| Odyssey Charter JSHS | 1350 Wyoming Dr SE | Palm Bay, FL | 32909 | 321-345-4117 | 327-7261 | 7-12 | Dr. Monica Knight |
| Odyssey Preparatory Academy | 1350 Wyoming Dr SE | Palm Bay, FL | 32909 | 321-345-4117 | | PK-6 | Constance Ortiz |
| Okaloosa Academy | 720 Lovejoy Rd NW | Ft Walton Bch, FL | 32548 | 850-864-3133 | 834-4305 | 6-12 | Ray Sansom |
| One Room S House Project | 4180 NE 15th St | Gainesville, FL | 32609-2011 | 352-376-4014 | 376-3345 | K-8 | Eric Torres |
| Orange County Preparatory Academy | 10250 University Blvd | Orlando, FL | 32817 | 407-414-5767 | 748-5717 | K-7 | Nicole Duslak |
| Orlando Science Charter ES | 2611 Technology Dr | Orlando, FL | 32804 | 407-253-7304 | 253-7305 | PK-5 | Michael Singleton |
| Orlando Science Charter MSHS | 2427 Lynx Ln | Orlando, FL | 32804 | 407-253-7304 | 253-7305 | 6-12 | Necati Sahin |
| Our Children's Academy | 555 Burns Ave | Lake Wales, FL | 33853-3335 | 863-679-3338 | 679-3944 | PK-9 | Debra Johnson |
| Palm Acres Charter HS | 507 Sunshine Blvd | Lehigh Acres, FL | 33971 | 239-333-3300 | 333-3301 | 9-12 | Leila Pineiro |
| Palm Bay Academy | 2112 Palm Bay Rd NE | Palm Bay, FL | 32905 | 321-984-2710 | 984-0799 | K-5 | Madhu Longani |
| Palm Bay Charter MS | 635 Community College SE | Palm Bay, FL | 32909 | 321-726-9005 | 726-3938 | 6-8 | Jerry RunnerSmith |
| Palm Bay Language Immersion S | 1465 Troutman Blvd NE | Palm Bay, FL | 32905 | 321-723-4218 | 953-5160 | K-3 | Madhu Longani |
| Palm Bay Preparatory Academy | 700 W 23rd St | Panama City, FL | 32405 | 850-215-0770 | 763-7613 | 6-12 | Kathy Fontaine |
| Palm Beach Maritime Academy | 600 S East Coast Ave | Lantana, FL | 33462 | 561-578-5700 | 337-3400 | K-8 | Marie Turchiaro |
| Palm Beach Maritime Academy HS | 1518 Lantana Rd | Lantana, FL | 33462 | 561-547-3775 | 540-5177 | 9-12 | Marie Turchiaro |
| Palm Beach S for Autism | 8480 Lantana Rd | Lake Worth, FL | 33467 | 561-533-9917 | 533-9918 | PK-9 | Olive Balbosa |
| Palmetto Charter S | 1601 17th St W | Palmetto, FL | 34221-6151 | 941-723-3711 | 729-5805 | K-8 | Brian Bustle |
| Palm Glades Preparatory Academy | 22655 SW 112th Ave | Miami, FL | 33170 | 786-272-2269 | 446-8956 | 6-12 | Archalena Coats |
| Palm Harbor Academy | 95 Old Kings Rd N | Palm Coast, FL | 32137 | 386-447-9692 | | K-5 | Esther Hamilton |
| Palm Pointe Educ Research S at Tradition | 10680 SW Academic Way | Port St Lucie, FL | 34987 | 772-345-3245 | 345-3244 | K-8 | Debra Snyder |
| Panacea Preparatory Charter S | 201 N University Dr | Coral Springs, FL | 33071 | 954-341-5550 | 341-5557 | K-5 | Christine Mentis |
| Paragon Academy of Technology | 502 N 28th Ave | Hollywood, FL | 33020 | 954-925-0155 | 925-0209 | 6-8 | Dr. Steven Montes |
| Paramount Charter S | 7100 W Oakland Park Blvd | Sunrise, FL | 33313 | 954-372-6325 | 944-5903 | K-8 | Jillian Wilson |
| Passport S | 5221 Curry Ford Rd | Orlando, FL | 32812-8741 | 407-658-9900 | 658-9911 | K-8 | Dr. Osvaldo Garcia |
| Pathways Academy | 101 State St W | Jacksonville, FL | 32202-3099 | 904-633-8125 | 633-8364 | 9-12 | Erica Trent |
| Pathways Academy | 4850 N State Road 7 | Laud Lakes, FL | 33319 | 954-739-6166 | 333-3853 | K-8 | Yudit Silva |
| Patriot Oaks Academy | 475 Longleaf Pine Pkwy | Saint Johns, FL | 32259 | 904-547-4050 | | K-8 | Emily Harrison |
| Pemayetv Emahakv Charter S | 100 E Harney Pond Rd NE | Okeechobee, FL | 34974 | 863-467-2501 | 467-8610 | PK-8 | Brian Greseth |
| Pembroke Pines FSU Charter ES | 601 SW 172nd Ave | Pembroke Pines, FL | 33029 | 954-499-4244 | 499-3016 | K-5 | |
| Pensacola Beach ES | 900 Via De Luna Dr | Pensacola Beach, FL | 32561-2262 | 850-934-4020 | 934-4040 | K-5 | Jeff Castleberry |
| Pepin Academies | 10530 Lake Saint Charles Bl | Riverview, FL | 33578 | 813-677-6700 | 677-6755 | 3-12 | Dr. Craig Butz |
| Pepin Academies | 3916 E Hillsborough Ave | Tampa, FL | 33610-4542 | 813-236-1755 | 236-1195 | 3-12 | Dr. Craig Butz |
| Pepin Academies - Pasco | 9804 Little Rd | New Port Richey, FL | 34654 | 727-233-2961 | 233-2963 | 3-11 | Celeste Kellar |
| Performing Arts Academy | 1324 Kingsley Ave | Orange Park, FL | 32073 | 904-269-0039 | 269-0487 | K-5 | Trisha Leitem |
| Pineapple Cove Classical Academy | 3355 Imagine Way | West Melbourne, FL | 32904 | 321-317-5766 | | K-6 | Dr. Kelly Gunter |
| Pinecrest Academy - North Campus | 10207 W Flagler St | Miami, FL | 33174-1743 | 305-553-9762 | 553-9763 | PK-8 | Victoria Larrauri |
| Pinecrest Academy - South Campus | 15130 SW 80th St | Miami, FL | 33193-1302 | 305-386-0800 | 386-6298 | K-5 | Eleine Clemente |
| Pinecrest Cove Academy | 4101 SW 107th Ave | Miami, FL | 33165 | 305-480-2097 | 207-1897 | K-8 | Susie Dopico |
| Pinecrest Creek Charter S | 1100 Lee Rd | Orlando, FL | 32810 | 407-757-2706 | 757-2711 | K-5 | |
| Pinecrest Preparatory Academy | 14301 SW 42nd St | Miami, FL | 33175-7832 | 305-207-1027 | 207-1897 | K-5 | Ana Diaz |
| Pinecrest Preparatory Academy HS | 14901 SW 42nd St | Miami, FL | 33185 | 305-559-8583 | 559-8584 | 6-12 | Maria Nunez |
| Pinecrest Preparatory S Orlando | 8503 Daetwyler Dr | Orlando, FL | 32827 | 407-856-8359 | 856-8361 | K-8 | Yasmeen Khan |
| Pinellas Academy of Math and Science | 1775 S Highland Ave | Largo, FL | 33756 | 727-330-9449 | 581-9205 | K-8 | Linda Schwerer |
| Pinellas Preparatory Academy | 2300 Belcher Rd S Ste 100 | Largo, FL | 33771 | 727-536-3600 | 536-3661 | 4-8 | Amanda Matsumoto |
| Pinellas Primary Academy | 2300 Belcher Rd S | Largo, FL | 33771 | 727-536-3600 | 536-3661 | PK-3 | Nancy Walker |
| Pivot Charter HS | 2675 Winkler Ave Ste 200 | Fort Myers, FL | 33901 | 239-243-8266 | 689-5474 | 6-12 | Joy Moore |
| Pivot Charter S | 3020 S Falkenburg Rd | Riverview, FL | 33578 | 813-626-6724 | 626-6712 | 6-12 | Elizabeth Bretz |
| Pivot Charter S | 8129 N Pine Island Rd | Tamarac, FL | 33321 | 954-720-3001 | 722-5578 | 6-12 | David Heeb |
| Plato Academy Clearwater | 2045 Palmetto St | Clearwater, FL | 33765 | 727-793-2400 | 793-2405 | PK-8 | Dawn Parker |
| Plato Academy Largo | 7100 142nd Ave | Largo, FL | 33771 | 727-286-6244 | 286-6247 | K-8 | Veronica Deakins |
| Plato Academy Palm Harbor | 1601 Curlew Rd | Palm Harbor, FL | 34683 | 727-286-6249 | 286-6253 | K-8 | Stephen Donnelly |
| Plato Academy Pinellas Park | 9200 49th St N | Pinellas Park, FL | 33783 | 727-521-7260 | 521-7261 | K-2 | Carrie Roberts |
| Plato Academy St. Petersburg | 3901 Park St N | St Petersburg, FL | 33709 | 727-623-9987 | 827-2879 | K-8 | Jennifer Perez |
| Plato Academy Seminole | 10888 126th Ave | Largo, FL | 33778 | 727-400-6885 | 400-6890 | K-8 | Karen Staab |
| Plato Academy Tarpon Springs | 2795 Keystone Rd | Tarpon Springs, FL | 34688 | 727-940-5232 | 940-5247 | K-8 | Danielle Turro |
| Polk Avenue ES | 110 E Polk Ave | Lake Wales, FL | 33853-4199 | 863-678-4244 | 678-4680 | PK-5 | Gail Quam |
| Polk Pre-Collegiate Academy | 5316 Berkley Rd | Auburndale, FL | 33823 | 863-984-2400 | 984-2411 | 9-10 | Cathy Carver |
| Polk State College Collegiate HS | 3425 Winter Lake Rd | Lakeland, FL | 33803 | 863-669-2322 | 669-2944 | 11-12 | Sallie Brisbane |
| Polk State Lakeland Gateway to Coll HS | 3425 Winter Lake Rd | Lakeland, FL | 33803 | 863-669-2322 | 669-2330 | 11-12 | Sallie Brisbane |
| Potentials Charter S | 1201 Australian Ave | Riviera Beach, FL | 33404-6635 | 561-842-3213 | 863-4352 | PK-5 | Bairbre Flood |
| Princeton House Charter S | 1166 Lee Rd | Orlando, FL | 32810-5847 | 407-523-7121 | 523-7187 | PK-5 | Kim Gelalia |
| Prosperitas Leadership Academy Charter | 4526 S Orange Blossom Trl | Orlando, FL | 32839 | 407-854-3945 | 854-3955 | 9-12 | Nadia Pierre |
| Putnam Academy of Arts and Sciences | 113 Putnam County Blvd | East Palatka, FL | 32131-4020 | 386-326-4212 | 326-6235 | 6-8 | Carla Aycock |
| Putnam EDGE HS | PO Box 1258 | Palatka, FL | 32178 | 386-385-7292 | | 9-12 | Lisa Parsons |
| Quantum HS | 1275 Gateway Blvd | Boynton Beach, FL | 33426 | 561-293-2971 | 277-0590 | 9-12 | Dr. Joy Hicks-Gomez |
| RAMZ Academy Miami | 2609 NW 7th St | Miami, FL | 33125 | 786-445-5697 | 642-8624 | K-5 | Dr. Maybelline Truesdell |
| RCMA Leadership Academy | 18236 S US Highway 301 | Wimauma, FL | 33598 | 813-672-5159 | 633-6119 | 6-8 | Mark Haggett |
| RCMA Wimauma Academy | 18240 S US Highway 301 | Wimauma, FL | 33598 | 813-672-5159 | 633-6119 | K-5 | Mark Haggett |
| Reading Edge Academy | 2975 Enterprise Rd | DeBary, FL | 32713-2708 | 386-668-8911 | 668-8443 | K-5 | Margaret Comardo |
| Renaissance Charter S | 300 NW Cashmere Blvd | Port St Lucie, FL | 34986 | 772-344-5982 | 344-5985 | K-8 | Dr. Chandra Glenn-Phillips |
| Renaissance Charter S at Central Palm | 6696 S Military Tr | Lake Worth, FL | 33463 | 561-209-7106 | 209-7107 | K-8 | Jackson Self |
| Renaissance Charter S at Chickasaw Trail | 8203 Valencia College Ln | Orlando, FL | 32825 | 321-206-0662 | 206-0664 | K-8 | Cindy Townsend |
| Renaissance Charter S at Cooper City | 2800 N Palm Ave | Cooper City, FL | 33026 | 954-668-2500 | 668-2980 | K-8 | Amanda Delgado |
| Renaissance Charter S at Coral Springs | 6250 W Sample Rd | Coral Springs, FL | 33067 | 954-369-1179 | 780-5411 | K-8 | Diana Sierra-Krumrie |
| Renaissance Charter S at Cypress | 8151 Okeechobee Blvd | West Palm Beach, FL | 33411 | 561-282-5860 | | K-8 | Rachel Mellion |
| Renaissance Charter S at Goldenrod | 6004 S Goldenrod Rd | Orlando, FL | 32822 | 321-536-2952 | | K-8 | Marilyn Rivera |
| Renaissance Charter S at Hunter's Creek | 4140 Town Center Blvd | Orlando, FL | 32837 | 407-206-3103 | 206-3104 | K-8 | Vanessa Suarez |
| Renaissance Charter S at Palms West | 12031 Southern Blvd | Loxahatchee, FL | 33470 | 561-214-6782 | 214-6783 | K-8 | Steve Epstein |
| Renaissance Charter S at Pines | 10501 Pines Blvd | Pembroke Pines, FL | 33026 | 954-862-1283 | 862-1284 | K-8 | Daniel Verdier |
| Renaissance Charter S at Plantation | 6701 W Sunrise Blvd | Plantation, FL | 33313 | 954-556-9700 | 556-9701 | K-8 | Lori Butler |
| Renaissance Charter S at Summit | 2001 Summit Blvd | West Palm Beach, FL | 33406 | 561-228-5240 | 228-5241 | K-8 | Heather Czeskleba |
| Renaissance Charter S at Tradition | 10900 SW Tradition Pkwy | Fort Pierce, FL | 34987 | 772-236-2180 | | K-8 | Stacy Schmidt |
| Renaissance Charter S at University | 8399 N University Dr | Tamarac, FL | 33321-1711 | 954-414-0996 | 414-0998 | K-8 | LaShonda White |
| Renaissance Charter S at Wellington | 3220 S State Rd 7 | Wellington, FL | 33449 | 561-228-5242 | | K-8 | Andrea Reilly |
| Renaissance Charter S at West Palm Beach | 1889 Palm Beach Lakes Blvd | West Palm Beach, FL | 33409 | 561-839-1994 | 839-1995 | K-8 | Michael Lupton |
| Renaissance Elementary Charter S | 10651 NW 19th St | Doral, FL | 33172 | 305-591-2225 | 591-2984 | K-5 | Maria Torres |
| Renaissance Learning Academy | 1310 N Congress Ave | West Palm Beach, FL | 33409 | 561-296-1776 | 296-1791 | 9-12 | Toby Honsberger |
| Renaissance Learning Center | 18370 Limestone Creek Rd | Jupiter, FL | 33458 | 561-640-0270 | | PK-8 | Dr. Manny Abreu |
| Renaissance Middle Charter S | 8360 NW 33rd St | Miami, FL | 33132 | 305-728-4622 | 401-1978 | 6-8 | Maria Torres |
| Richardson Montessori S | 9390 N Florida Ave | Tampa, FL | 33612 | 813-930-2988 | 930-2929 | K-6 | Tommie Brumfield |

| School | Address | City,State | Zip code | Telephone | Fax | Grade | Contact |
|---|---|---|---|---|---|---|---|
| Ridgeview Global Studies Academy | 1000 Dunson Rd | Davenport, FL | 33896-8383 | 863-419-3171 | 419-3172 | PK-5 | Ralph Frier |
| RISE Academy S of Science and Technology | 6101 NW 31st St | Margate, FL | 33063 | 954-968-7977 | 968-8386 | K-8 | Sharon Smith |
| Rising Leaders Academy | 1527 Lincoln Ave | Panama City, FL | 32405 | 850-215-0844 | 215-1711 | K-12 | Suha Jaber |
| River City Science Academy | 7565 Beach Blvd | Jacksonville, FL | 32216 | 904-855-8010 | 855-8014 | 6-12 | Ozan Sipahioglu |
| River City Science Academy Elementary | 7555 Beach Blvd | Jacksonville, FL | 32216 | 904-855-8010 | 727-9245 | K-5 | Michael Steinhardt |
| River City Science Academy - Innovations | 8313 Baycenter Rd | Jacksonville, FL | 32256 | 904-647-5110 | 551-0821 | K-8 | Mesut Erdogan |
| Riviera Beach Maritime Academy | 251 W 11th St | Riviera Beach, FL | 33404-7534 | 561-841-7600 | 841-7626 | 9-12 | Tonya Hicks |
| Round Lake Conversion Charter ES | 31333 Round Lake Rd | Mount Dora, FL | 32757-9599 | 352-385-4399 | 735-1860 | PK-5 | Linda Bartberger |
| Rowlett Academy for Arts & Communication | 3500 9th St E | Bradenton, FL | 34208-4516 | 941-708-6100 | 708-6109 | K-5 | Brian Flynn |
| Royal Palm Charter S | 7135 Babcock St SE | Palm Bay, FL | 32909 | 321-723-0650 | 722-1117 | K-8 | Shannon Shupe |
| St. Augustine Public Montessori S | 7 Williams St | Saint Augustine, FL | 32084 | 904-342-5350 | 342-5354 | 1-6 | Judi Dunlap |
| St. Johns Community Campus | 62 Cuna St | Saint Augustine, FL | 32084 | 904-209-6842 | | 9-12 | Lynne Funcheon |
| St. Paul S of Excellence | 85 M L King Ave | Saint Augustine, FL | 32084 | 904-829-9910 | | K-5 | Brian Barrett |
| Saint Peter's Academy | 4250 38th Ave | Vero Beach, FL | 32967-1711 | 772-562-1963 | 567-8361 | PK-6 | Ruth Jefferson |
| St. Petersburg Collegiate HS | PO Box 13489 | St Petersburg, FL | 33733-3489 | 727-341-4610 | 341-7166 | 10-12 | Starla Metz |
| Samsula Academy | 248 N Samsula Dr | New Smyrna, FL | 32168-8762 | 386-423-6650 | 423-6651 | K-5 | Peggy Comardo |
| San Jose Academy | 4072 Sunbeam Rd | Jacksonville, FL | 32257 | 904-425-1725 | 683-9101 | 6-12 | Amy Printy |
| Sarasota Academy of the Arts | 4466 Fruitville Rd | Sarasota, FL | 34232 | 941-377-2278 | 404-4492 | K-8 | Cecilia Blankenship |
| Sarasota Military Academy | 801 Orange Ave | Sarasota, FL | 34236-4116 | 941-926-1700 | 926-1701 | 9-12 | Robin Livingston |
| Sarasota Military Academy Prep | 3101 Bethel Ln | Sarasota, FL | 34240 | 941-877-7737 | 877-7738 | 6-8 | Thomas Vara |
| Sarasota S of Arts & Sciences | 645 Central Ave | Sarasota, FL | 34236-4016 | 941-330-1855 | 330-1835 | 6-8 | Tara Tahmosh |
| Sarasota Suncoast Academy | 8084 Hawkins Rd | Sarasota, FL | 34241 | 941-924-4242 | 924-8282 | K-5 | Steve Crump |
| S for Accelerated Lrng & Technologies | 4811 Payne Stewart Dr | Jacksonville, FL | 32209-9208 | 904-328-5003 | 768-8618 | 9-12 | Michael LaRoche |
| School of Arts & Sciences | 3208 Thomasville Rd | Tallahassee, FL | 32308-7904 | 850-386-6566 | 386-8183 | K-8 | Julie Fredrickson |
| School of Success Academy | 6974 Wilson Blvd | Jacksonville, FL | 32210-3663 | 904-573-0880 | 573-0889 | 6-8 | G. Mills |
| Sculptor Charter S | 1301 Armstrong Dr | Titusville, FL | 32780-7907 | 321-264-4000 | 264-4011 | K-8 | Patricia O'Sullivan |
| Seacoast Collegiate HS | 109 Greenway Trl | Santa Rsa Bch, FL | 32459 | 850-200-4170 | | 9-11 | Jonathan Davignon |
| Seacost Charter Academy | 9100 Regency Square Blvd N | Jacksonville, FL | 32211-8103 | 904-562-4780 | 726-0249 | K-5 | Marla Stremmel |
| Seagull Academy for Independent Living | 6250 N Military Trl | Riviera Beach, FL | 33407 | 561-540-8110 | 540-8331 | 6-12 | Linda Moore |
| Seaside Community Charter S | 2630 State Road A1A | Jacksonville, FL | 32233 | 904-853-6287 | 485-8448 | K-4 | Sharon Sanders |
| Seaside Neighborhood S | PO Box 4610 | Santa Rsa Bch, FL | 32459-4610 | 850-231-0396 | 231-4725 | 5-8 | Kim Mixon |
| Sebastian Charter JHS | 782 Wave St | Sebastian, FL | 32958-5049 | 772-388-8838 | 388-8815 | 5-8 | Dr. Martha McAdams |
| Seed S of Miami | 15800 NW 42nd Ave | Miami Gardens, FL | 33054 | 855-818-7333 | 503-7033 | 6-12 | Kara Locke |
| Seminole Heights Charter HS | 4006 N Florida Ave | Tampa, FL | 33603 | 813-234-0809 | 236-2406 | 9-12 | Dr. Bobby Smith |
| Seminole Science Charter S | 3580 N US Higvhway 17/92 | Lake Mary, FL | 32746 | 407-864-8296 | 253-7305 | K-8 | |
| Sheeler Charter HS | 871 E Semoran Blvd | Apopka, FL | 32703 | 407-886-1825 | 886-7482 | 9-12 | Tona Coley |
| Sigsbee Charter S | 939 Felton Rd | Key West, FL | 33040-6798 | 305-294-1861 | 292-6869 | PK-5 | Elisa Jannes |
| Six Mile Charter Academy | 6851 Lancer Ave | Fort Myers, FL | 33912-4334 | 239-768-9375 | 225-2477 | K-8 | Eric Lewis |
| Sky Academy Englewood | 881 S River Rd | Englewood, FL | 34223 | 941-999-4775 | 999-4796 | 6-7 | John Bailey |
| Sky Academy Venice | 705 Center Rd | Venice, FL | 34285 | 941-244-2626 | 244-2319 | 6-8 | Steve Smith |
| Somerset Academy | 20801 Johnson St | Pembroke Pines, FL | 33029-1916 | 954-442-0233 | 442-0813 | K-5 | Bernardo Montero |
| Somerset Academy | 18491 SW 134th Ave | Miami, FL | 33177-2923 | 305-969-6074 | 969-6077 | K-8 | Suzette Ruiz |
| Somerset Academy Bay | 9500 SW 97th Ave | Miami, FL | 33176 | 305-274-0682 | 274-0683 | K-8 | Salli Hernandez |
| Somerset Academy Boca | 333 SW 4th Ave | Boca Raton, FL | 33432 | 561-393-1091 | 393-1092 | K-8 | Bonnie May |
| Somerset Academy Canyons HS | 9385 Boynton Beach Blvd | Boynton Beach, FL | 33472 | 561-732-8252 | 732-8253 | 6-12 | Daniel Fernandez |
| Somerset Academy Central Miramar Campus | 9300 Pembroke Rd | Miramar, FL | 33025 | 954-435-1570 | 435-1571 | K-12 | Athena Guillen |
| Somerset Academy Charter Conservatory HS | 20807 Johnson St | Pembroke Pines, FL | 33029 | 954-442-0233 | 442-0813 | 9-12 | Bernardo Montero |
| Somerset Academy - Davie | 3788 Davie Rd | Davie, FL | 33312 | 954-584-5528 | 584-5598 | K-5 | Dina Miller |
| Somerset Academy Eagle Campus | 8711 Lone Star Rd | Jacksonville, FL | 32211 | 904-551-3292 | 854-0917 | K-12 | LaTatia Ray |
| Somerset Academy East Preparatory | 2000 S State Road 7 | Miramar, FL | 33023 | 954-987-7890 | 987-7891 | K-6 | Dr. Mary Stuart |
| Somerset Academy HS | 20805 Johnson St | Pembroke Pines, FL | 33029 | 954-442-0233 | 442-0813 | 9-12 | Bernardo Montero |
| Somerset Academy Hollywood | 2000 S State Road 7 | Hollywood, FL | 33023 | 954-987-7890 | 987-7891 | K-8 | Dr. Mary Stuart |
| Somerset Academy MS | 18491 SW 134th Ave | Miami, FL | 33177 | 305-969-6074 | 969-6077 | 6-8 | Suzette Ruiz |
| Somerset Academy MS | 20803 Johnson St | Pembroke Pines, FL | 33029-1916 | 954-442-0233 | 442-0813 | 6-8 | Bernardo Montero |
| Somerset Academy Miramar | 12601 Somerset Blvd | Miramar, FL | 33027 | 305-829-2406 | 829-4477 | PK-8 | Alexandra Prieto |
| Somerset Academy Pompano | 3311 NW 9th Ave | Pompano Beach, FL | 33064-2036 | 954-946-4144 | 946-4005 | K-8 | Dr. Donna Kaye |
| Somerset Academy Silver Palms | 23255 SW 115th Ave | Homestead, FL | 33032-4505 | 305-257-3737 | 257-3751 | K-12 | Kerri O'Sullivan |
| Somerset Academy South Homestead | 300 SE 1st Dr | Homestead, FL | 33030 | 305-245-6108 | 245-6109 | K-12 | Layda Morales |
| Somerset Academy South Miami | 5876 SW 68th St | South Miami, FL | 33143 | 305-740-0509 | 740-0510 | K-8 | Kim Guilarte |
| Somerset City Arts Conservatory | 47 NW 16 St | Homestead, FL | 33030 | 305-246-4949 | 249-4919 | K-6 | Idalia Suarez |
| Somerset Gables Academy | 624 Anastasia Ave | Coral Gables, FL | 33134 | 305-442-8626 | 442-8627 | K-8 | Suzette Ruiz |
| Somerset Miramar South S | 12425 SW 53rd St | Miramar, FL | 33027-5493 | 305-829-2406 | 829-4477 | K-5 | Alexandra Prieto |
| Somerset Oaks Academy | 1000 Old Dixie Hwy | Homestead, FL | 33030 | 305-247-3993 | 247-3994 | K-8 | Idalia Suarez |
| Somerset Pines Academy | 901 NE 33rd St | Pompano Beach, FL | 33064-5231 | 954-786-5980 | 786-5981 | K-8 | Dr. Donna Kaye |
| Somerset Preparatory Academy | 1429 Broward Rd | Jacksonville, FL | 32218 | 904-503-0661 | 379-5936 | PK-10 | David Cook |
| Somerset Prep North Lauderdale | 7101 Kimberly Blvd | N Lauderdale, FL | 33068 | 954-718-5065 | 718-5066 | K-12 | Donyale McGhee |
| Somerset Village Academy | 225 NW 29th St | Wilton Manors, FL | 33311 | 954-390-0971 | 390-0972 | K-8 | Shannine Sadesky |
| South Broward Montessori Charter S | 520 NW 5th St | Hallandale Bch, FL | 33009 | 954-251-1443 | 251-1820 | K-5 | Elaine Padron |
| South Florida Autism Charter S | 18305 NW 75 Pl | Hialeah, FL | 33015 | 305-823-2700 | 823-2705 | K-11 | Dr. Tamara Moodie-Ramdeen |
| South McKeel Academy | 2222 Edgewood Dr S | Lakeland, FL | 33803-3631 | 863-510-0044 | 510-0021 | K-7 | Kim Benson |
| South Tech Academy | 1300 SW 30th Ave | Boynton Beach, FL | 33426-9099 | 561-369-7004 | 369-7024 | 9-12 | Ellen Gray |
| South Tech Preparatory Academy | 1325 Gateway Blvd | Boynton Beach, FL | 33426 | 561-318-8087 | 369-7024 | 6-8 | Nicole Handy |
| Sports Leadership Academy of Miami | 604 NW 12th Ave | Miami, FL | 33136 | 305-326-0003 | 326-0004 | 6-12 | Alex Tamargo |
| Spring Creek Conversion Charter ES | 44440 Spring Creek Rd | Paisley, FL | 32767-9063 | 352-669-3275 | 669-3762 | PK-6 | Wesley Locke |
| State College of Florida Collegiate S | 5840 26th St W | Bradenton, FL | 34207 | 941-752-5491 | 758-4801 | 6-12 | Kelly Monod |
| Stellar Leadership Academy | 7900 NW 27th Ave Ste F-1 | Miami, FL | 33147-4909 | 305-693-2273 | 693-8016 | 9-12 | Dr. Angel Chaisson |
| Student Leadership Academy | 200 Field Ave E | Venice, FL | 34285-3936 | 941-485-5551 | 485-2694 | 6-8 | Vickie Marble |
| Summerville Advantage Academy | 11575 SW 243rd St | Homestead, FL | 33032-7163 | 305-253-2123 | 253-4304 | K-8 | Victoria Ramos |
| Suncoast S for Innovative Studies | 845 S School Ave | Sarasota, FL | 34237 | 941-953-4433 | 953-4435 | PK-8 | Stephen Evans |
| SunEd HS | 2360 W Oakland Park Blvd | Oakland Park, FL | 33311 | 954-678-3939 | 485-6243 | 9-12 | DeeEtte Naukana |
| SunEd HS of North Broward | 1121 Banks Rd | Margate, FL | 33063 | 954-246-4004 | 379-2722 | 9-12 | Tammy Lara |
| Sunshine ES | 502 N 28th Ave | Hollywood, FL | 33020 | 954-925-0155 | 925-0209 | K-5 | Dr. Steven Montes |
| Sunshine High Charter | 6600 Old Winter Garden Rd | Orlando, FL | 32835 | 407-641-4156 | 886-7482 | 9-12 | Margaret Olmo |
| Tallahassee S of Math & Science | 3434 N Monroe St | Tallahassee, FL | 32303 | 850-681-7827 | 325-6706 | K-8 | Ahmet Temel |
| Team Success S of Excellence | 202 13th Ave E | Bradenton, FL | 34208-3246 | 941-714-7260 | 714-7333 | K-8 | Fredrick Spence |
| Terrace Community MS | 11734 Jefferson Rd | Thonotosassa, FL | 33592-2101 | 813-987-6555 | 324-8974 | 6-8 | Tahvia Shaw |
| Therapeutic Learning Center | 2109 ARC Dr | Saint Augustine, FL | 32084 | 904-824-8932 | 824-8063 | PK-PK | Paulette Hudson |
| Tiger Academy | 6079 Bagley Rd | Jacksonville, FL | 32209-1805 | 904-309-6840 | 309-6867 | PK-5 | Charles McWhite |
| Toussaint L'Ouverture HS | 301 SW 14th Ave | Delray Beach, FL | 33444-1455 | 561-266-1200 | 266-1286 | 9-12 | Mandy Freeman |
| Town and Country Charter HS | 7555 W Waters Ave | Tampa, FL | 33615 | 813-902-2858 | 884-7817 | 9-12 | Cloty Davis |
| Treasure Village Montessori Charter S | 86731 Overseas Hwy | Islamorada, FL | 33036 | 305-852-3482 | 852-2432 | PK-8 | Kelly Mangel |
| Trinity S for Children | 2402 W Osborne Ave | Tampa, FL | 33603-1434 | 813-874-2402 | 874-2412 | K-8 | Dr. Madeline O'Dea |
| Turner Learning Academy | 2201 SW 42nd Ave | West Park, FL | 33023-3456 | 954-463-8404 | 463-3566 | K-5 | Maxine Spence |
| UCP Charter S Downtown Campus | 3305 S Orange Ave | Orlando, FL | 32806-6125 | 407-852-3333 | 852-3301 | PK-2 | Lillian Flores |
| UCP East Campus | 12702 Science Dr | Orlando, FL | 32826 | 407-281-0441 | 281-0442 | PK-5 | |
| UCP Kissimmee/Osceola Campus | 1820 Armstrong Blvd | Kissimmee, FL | 34741 | 407-852-3300 | 932-3480 | PK-2 | Ana Useche |
| UCP Lake Mary/Seminole Campus | 756 N Sun Dr | Lake Mary, FL | 32746 | 407-852-3300 | 852-3301 | PK-K | Marife Gomez |
| UCP Pine Hills Charter S | 5800 Golf Club Pkwy | Orlando, FL | 32808-4800 | 407-299-5553 | 299-5520 | PK-2 | Marcelle Healy |
| UCP Transitional Learning Academy | 8291 Curry Ford Rd | Orlando, FL | 32822 | 407-852-3300 | 852-3301 | 6-12 | Stacey Ricketts |
| UCP West Orange Charter S | 1297 Winter Garden Vineland | Winter Garden, FL | 34787 | 407-852-3300 | 905-0532 | K-5 | |
| University Academy | 1980 Discovery Loop | Panama City, FL | 32405 | 850-481-4410 | | K-5 | Elizabeth Crowe Ph.D. |
| University Preparatory Academy | 1701 10th St S | St Petersburg, FL | 33705 | 727-498-3379 | 498-3377 | K-12 | Darius Adamson |
| University Preparatory Academy | 2101 N Australian Ave | West Palm Beach, FL | 33407 | 561-670-1138 | | K-8 | Richard Ledgister |
| Valor Academy of Leadership | 4819 Soutel Dr | Jacksonville, FL | 32208 | 904-469-8195 | 524-8440 | 6-12 | John Taylor |
| Valrico Lake Advantage Academy | 13306 Boyette Rd | Riverview, FL | 33569 | 813-699-5049 | 413-5191 | K-5 | Lauren Herbert |
| Viera Charter S | 6206 Breslay Dr | Viera, FL | 32940 | 321-541-1434 | 608-2322 | K-8 | Dr. Julie Cady |
| Village of Excellence Academy | 8718 N 46th St | Temple Terrace, FL | 33617-6002 | 813-988-8632 | 983-0683 | K-5 | Dr. Cametra Edwards |
| Village of Excellence Academy MS | 4600 E Busch Blvd | Tampa, FL | 33617 | 813-374-9972 | 304-2202 | 6-8 | Dr. Cametra Edwards |
| Villages Charter HS | 251 Buffalo Trl | The Villages, FL | 32162 | 352-259-3777 | 259-3850 | 9-12 | Dr. Bill Zwick |
| Villages Charter Intermediate Center | 521 Old School Rd | The Villages, FL | 32162 | 352-259-2300 | 259-2056 | 2-3 | LeAnne Yerk |
| Villages Charter MS | 450 Village Campus Cir | The Villages, FL | 32162 | 352-259-0044 | 753-1113 | 6-8 | Dr. Peggy Irwin |
| Villages Charter Primary Center | 420 Village Campus Cir | The Villages, FL | 32162 | 352-259-7700 | 259-7707 | K-1 | LeAnne Yerk |
| Visible Men Academy Charter S | 921 63rd Ave E | Bradenton, FL | 34203 | 941-758-7588 | 893-4028 | K-8 | Neil Phillips |
| Walton Academy & Pathways Charter S | 389 Dorsey Ave | Defuniak Spgs, FL | 32435-3013 | 850-892-3999 | 892-7854 | 6-12 | Steve Ruder |
| Walton Academy for the Performing Arts | 4817 N Florida Ave | Tampa, FL | 33603-2117 | 813-231-9272 | 231-9271 | K-5 | Tanika Walton |
| Waverly Academy | PO Box 440624 | Jacksonville, FL | 32222 | 904-647-8552 | 515-5353 | 6-8 | Tumika Mondy |
| Wayman Academy of the Arts | 1176 Labelle St | Jacksonville, FL | 32205-6487 | 904-695-9995 | 693-1127 | K-5 | Simaran Bakshi |
| Wells Charter S | 2426 Remington Blvd | Kissimmee, FL | 34744-8467 | 407-697-1020 | 697-1021 | K-8 | Bonnie Brett |
| West Broward Academy | 10066 W McNab Rd | Tamarac, FL | 33321 | 754-702-2320 | 263-5900 | K-8 | Raul Baez |
| Western Academy Charter S | 650 Royal Palm Blvd Ste 300 | Ryl Palm Bch, FL | 33411 | 561-792-4123 | 422-0674 | K-8 | Linda Terranova |
| West University Charter HS | 11602 N 15th St | Tampa, FL | 33612 | 813-774-4396 | 971-5011 | 9-12 | Leon Wilson |
| Whispering Winds Charter S | PO Box 506 | Chiefland, FL | 32644-0506 | 352-490-5799 | 490-7242 | K-8 | Dr. J. Suzann Cornell |
| Wilson ES | 306 Florida Ave | Lake Wales, FL | 33853-3121 | 863-678-4211 | 678-4217 | PK-5 | Barbara Jones |
| Windsor Preparatory Academy | 5175 45th St N | St Petersburg, FL | 33714 | 727-475-1297 | 527-7637 | K-8 | Veronica Fly |
| Winthrop Charter S | 6204 Scholars Hill Ln | Riverview, FL | 33578 | 813-235-4811 | 315-4403 | K-8 | Terry Johnson |
| Woodmont Charter S | 10402 N 56th St | Temple Terrace, FL | 33617 | 813-708-1596 | 739-7301 | K-8 | Latasha Scurry |

| School | Address | City,State | Zip code | Telephone | Fax | Grade | Contact |
|---|---|---|---|---|---|---|---|
| Woodville MS | 1900 Natural Bridge Rd | Tallahassee, FL | 32305 | 850-487-7043 | 921-4281 | 6-8 | Nancy Stokely |
| Workforce Advantage Academy | 2113 E South St | Orlando, FL | 32803-6502 | 407-898-7228 | 898-6448 | 11-12 | Belinda Jones |
| Worthington HS | 1711 Worthington Rd | West Palm Beach, FL | 33409 | 561-537-5696 | 697-4366 | 9-12 | Eric Paul |
| Youth Co-Op Preparatory Charter S | 7700 W 20th Ave | Hialeah Gardens, FL | 33016 | 305-819-8855 | 819-8455 | K-12 | Maritza Aragon |
| **Georgia** | | | | | | | |
| Amana Academy | 285 S Main St | Alpharetta, GA | 30009-1937 | 678-624-0989 | 624-0892 | K-8 | Cherisse Campbell |
| Athens Community Career Academy | 240 Mitchell Bridge Rd | Athens, GA | 30606 | 706-357-5244 | 353-3877 | 9-12 | Katy Arrowood |
| Atlanta Classical Academy | 3260 Northside Dr NW | Atlanta, GA | 30305 | 404-369-3500 | 795-1049 | K-9 | Dr. Terrance Moore |
| Atlanta Heights Charter S | 3712 Martin Luther King Jr | Atlanta, GA | 30331 | 404-472-3003 | 264-2132 | K-8 | Noletha High |
| Atlanta Neighborhood Charter MS | 820 Essie Ave SE | Atlanta, GA | 30316-2425 | 678-904-0051 | 904-0052 | 6-8 | Cathey Goodgame |
| Atlanta Neighborhood Charter S | 688 Grant St SE | Atlanta, GA | 30315-1420 | 404-624-6226 | 624-9093 | K-5 | Lara Zelski |
| Baconton Community Charter S | 260 E Walton St | Baconton, GA | 31716-7782 | 229-787-9999 | 787-0077 | PK-12 | Lynn Pinson |
| Baldwin College and Career Academy | 155 GA Highway 49 W | Milledgeville, GA | 31061 | 478-453-6429 | 453-5060 | 7-12 | Dr. Cloise Williams |
| Berrien Academy Performance Learning Ctr | 1015 Exum Rd | Nashville, GA | 31639-2730 | 229-686-6576 | 686-6580 | 9-12 | Michele Garner |
| Bishop Hall Charter S | 220 N Pinetree Blvd | Thomasville, GA | 31792 | 229-227-1397 | 558-9420 | 9-12 | Chris Huckans |
| Brighten Academy | 3264 Brookmont Pkwy | Douglasville, GA | 30135 | 770-615-3680 | 575-3614 | K-8 | Lisa McDonald |
| Carroll County College and Career Acad | 1075 Newnan Rd | Carrollton, GA | 30116-6435 | 770-832-8380 | 830-5037 | 9-12 | Cindy Clanton |
| Centennial Place Academy | 531 Luckie St NW | Atlanta, GA | 30313-2401 | 404-802-8550 | 853-4089 | K-8 | Alison Shelton |
| Central Educational Center | 160 Martin Luther King Dr | Newnan, GA | 30263-2331 | 678-423-2000 | 423-2008 | 8-12 | Mark Ballou |
| Chamblee Charter HS | 3688 Chamblee Dunwoody Rd | Chamblee, GA | 30341-2185 | 678-676-6902 | 676-6910 | 9-12 | Norman Sauce |
| Charter Conservatory Liberal Arts/Tech. | 149 Northside Dr E | Statesboro, GA | 30458-1089 | 912-764-5888 | 489-8493 | 5-12 | Corliss Reese |
| Chattahoochie Hills Charter S | 9670 Rivertown Rd | Fairburn, GA | 30213 | 678-466-7300 | 466-7305 | K-5 | Walt Butler |
| Cherokee Charter Academy | 2126 Sixes Rd | Canton, GA | 30114 | 678-385-7322 | 385-7323 | K-8 | Dr. Scott O'Prey |
| Chesnut ES Charter | 4576 N Peachtree Rd | Dunwoody, GA | 30338-5892 | 678-676-7102 | 676-7110 | PK-5 | Veronica Williams |
| Chestatee Academy | 2740 Fran Mar Dr | Gainesville, GA | 30506-1136 | 770-297-6270 | 297-6275 | 6-8 | Dr. David Robles |
| Chestnut Mountain Creative S of Inquiry | 4841 Union Church Rd | Flowery Branch, GA | 30542-5202 | 770-967-3121 | 967-4891 | K-5 | Wade Pearce |
| Clear Creek MS | 1020 Clear Creek Rd | Ellijay, GA | 30536-7898 | 706-276-5150 | 276-5151 | 7-8 | David Mashburn |
| Clubview ES | 2836 Edgewood Rd | Columbus, GA | 31906-1298 | 706-565-3017 | 565-3022 | PK-5 | Teresa Lawson |
| Coastal Empire Montessori Charter S | 301 Buckhalter Rd | Savannah, GA | 31405 | 912-395-4070 | 201-5051 | PK-5 | Stephanie Babcock-Wright |
| Coweta Charter Academy | 6675 Highway 16 | Senoia, GA | 30276 | 770-599-0228 | 599-0556 | K-6 | Tiffany Pollock |
| Dekalb Academy of Tech & Environment | 1492 Kelton Dr | Stone Mountain, GA | 30083 | 678-999-9290 | 999-9294 | K-8 | Dr. Maury Wills |
| DeKalb PATH Academy | 3007 Hermance Dr NE | Atlanta, GA | 30319-2627 | 404-846-3242 | 846-3243 | 5-8 | Suttiwan Cox |
| DeKalb Prepatory Academy | 1402 Austin Dr | Decatur, GA | 30032-3838 | 404-937-2000 | 937-2020 | K-4 | Michael Daly |
| Destiny Achievers Academy of Excellence | 3595 Linecrest Rd | Ellenwood, GA | 30294-1839 | 404-328-0898 | 328-1294 | 9-12 | Dr. Charles Maxwell |
| Douglas Co. College & Career Institute | 4600 Timber Ridge Dr | Douglasville, GA | 30135-1225 | 770-947-7690 | 947-3896 | 9-12 | Mandy Johnson |
| Drew Charter S | 301 E Lake Blvd SE | Atlanta, GA | 30317-3152 | 404-687-0001 | 687-0480 | PK-12 | Peter McKnight |
| Effingham College & Career Academy | 2940 GA Highway 21 S | Rincon, GA | 31326 | 912-754-5610 | 754-5611 | 10-12 | Travis Nesmith |
| Elite Scholars Academy | 5968 Maddox Rd | Morrow, GA | 30260 | 404-362-3811 | 362-3850 | 6-12 | Dr. Shonda Shaw |
| Ellijay ES | 32 McCutchen St | Ellijay, GA | 30540-3302 | 706-276-5020 | 276-5022 | 2-4 | Lauree Pierce |
| Ellijay PS | 196 McCutchen St | Ellijay, GA | 30540-3393 | 706-276-5010 | 276-5013 | PK-1 | Stephanie Burnette |
| Flowery Branch HS | 6603 Spout Springs Rd | Flowery Branch, GA | 30542-5529 | 770-967-8000 | 967-1218 | 9-12 | Dr. Jason Carter |
| Floyd County College and Career Academy | 100 Tom Poe Dr SW | Rome, GA | 30161-6776 | 706-236-1860 | 236-1862 | 9-12 | Eric Waters |
| Forsyth County Academy | 1130 Dahlonega Hwy | Cumming, GA | 30040 | 770-781-3141 | 888-1193 | 9-12 | Betty Pope |
| Fulton Leadership Academy | 1706 Washington Ave | Atlanta, GA | 30344 | 404-472-3529 | 472-3520 | 6-12 | Douglas Ward |
| Futral Road ES | 180 Futral Rd | Griffin, GA | 30224-7454 | 770-229-3735 | 233-6001 | PK-5 | Ben Steele |
| Gateway to College Academy | 555 N Indian Creek Dr | Clarkston, GA | 30021-2361 | 678-891-3220 | 891-3610 | 9-12 | Robert Wigfall |
| Gilmer HS | 408 Bobcat Trl | Ellijay, GA | 30540-5406 | 706-276-5080 | 276-5088 | 9-12 | Eric McFee |
| Gilmer MS | 1860 S Main St | Ellijay, GA | 30540-5407 | 706-276-5030 | 276-5035 | 5-6 | Larry Walker |
| Glascock County Consolidated S | 1230 Panther Way | Gibson, GA | 30810-4238 | 706-598-2121 | 598-2611 | PK-12 | Danny Lovering |
| GLOBE Academy | 2225 Heritage Dr NE | Atlanta, GA | 30345 | 404-464-7040 | | K-4 | Christi Elliott-Earby |
| Golden Isles Career Academy | 4404 Glynco Pkwy | Brunswick, GA | 31525-6852 | 912-280-4000 | 261-2285 | 9-12 | Dr. Rick Townsend |
| Gwinnett Online Campus | 713 Hi Hope Rd | Lawrenceville, GA | 30043 | 770-326-8082 | 326-8064 | 4-12 | Dr. Christopher Ray |
| Gwinnett S of Math Science and Tech | 970 McElvaney Ln | Lawrenceville, GA | 30044 | 678-518-6700 | 518-6702 | 9-12 | I.V. Bray |
| Hapeville Charter Career Academy | 6045 Buffington Rd | College Park, GA | 30349 | 404-766-0101 | 941-1102 | 9-12 | Jannard Rainey |
| Hapeville Charter MS | 3535 S Fulton Ave | Hapeville, GA | 30354-1701 | 404-767-7730 | 767-7706 | 6-8 | Marcia Lowe |
| Harris Elementary Charter S | 2300 Danielsville Rd | Athens, GA | 30601-1038 | 706-357-5203 | 357-5209 | PK-5 | Xernona Thomas |
| Heart of Georgia College & Career Acad | 720 Industrial Blvd | Dublin, GA | 31021 | 478-689-4774 | 689-6593 | 9-12 | Tiffany Lofton |
| Heritage Preparatory Academy | 569 M L King Jr Dr NW | Atlanta, GA | 30314 | 678-399-2810 | | 6-8 | Dr. Natilee Brown-Van |
| Hillcrest ES | 1100 Edgewood Dr | Dublin, GA | 31021-5599 | 478-277-9833 | 277-9809 | K-5 | Demme McManus |
| Houston County Career Academy | 1311 Corder Rd | Warner Robins, GA | 31088-7117 | 478-322-3280 | 322-3294 | 9-12 | Sabrina Phelps |
| International Academy of Smyrna | 2144 S Cobb Dr SE Ste A | Smyrna, GA | 30080 | 678-370-0980 | 370-0981 | K-8 | Kari Schrock |
| International Community S | 2418 Wood Trail Ln | Decatur, GA | 30033 | 404-499-8969 | 499-8968 | K-5 | Marcy Criner |
| International Studies Magnet ES | 2237 Cutts Dr | Albany, GA | 31705-3899 | 229-431-3384 | 431-3381 | K-5 | Dr. Zeda George |
| Ivy Preparatory Academy | 3705 Engineering Dr | Norcross, GA | 30092 | 770-342-0089 | 342-0088 | 6-12 | Victoria Hudson |
| Ivy Preparatory Academy at Kirkwood | 1807 Memorial Dr SE | Atlanta, GA | 30317 | 404-622-2727 | 622-2725 | 6-12 | Kendra Shipmon |
| Jenkins-White Charter ES | 800 15th Ave | Augusta, GA | 30901-4145 | 706-737-7320 | 731-7651 | PK-5 | Lori Johnson |
| Kennesaw Charter Science & Math Academy | 3010 Cobb Pkwy NW | Kennesaw, GA | 30152-2502 | 678-290-9628 | 290-9638 | K-6 | Kay Frey |
| Kindezi S - Old 4th Ward | 386 Pine St | Atlanta, GA | 30308 | 404-719-4005 | | K-5 | Gilberte Pascal |
| Kindezi S | 1890 Detroit Ave NW | Atlanta, GA | 30314 | 404-671-4910 | 671-4901 | K-6 | Hyla Hardrick |
| Kingsley ES | 2051 Brendon Dr | Dunwoody, GA | 30338-4599 | 678-874-8902 | 874-8910 | PK-5 | Brent McBride |
| KIPP Atlanta Collegiate S | 98 Anderson Ave NW | Atlanta, GA | 30314 | 404-574-5126 | 574-5129 | 9-12 | David Howland |
| KIPP South Fulton Academy | 1286 Washington Ave | East Point, GA | 30344-3537 | 678-278-0160 | 278-0165 | 5-8 | Jondre Pryor |
| KIPP STRIVE Academy | 1444 Lucile Ave SW | Atlanta, GA | 30310 | 404-753-1530 | 753-1532 | 5-8 | Christy Harris |
| KIPP STRIVE Primary Academy | 1444 Lucile Ave SW | Atlanta, GA | 30310 | 404-753-1530 | 753-1532 | K-4 | Mini'imah Shaheed |
| KIPP Vision Academy | 660 McWilliams Rd SE | Atlanta, GA | 30315 | 404-537-5252 | 671-4882 | 5-8 | Tasha Davis |
| KIPP Vision PS | 660 McWilliams Rd SE | Atlanta, GA | 30315 | 404-537-5252 | 671-4882 | K-2 | Dr. Wheda Carletos |
| KIPP WAYS Academy | 350 Temple St NW | Atlanta, GA | 30314 | 404-475-1941 | 475-1946 | 5-8 | Dwight Ho-Sang |
| KIPP WAYS PS | 350 Temple St | Atlanta, GA | 30314 | 404-475-1941 | 475-1946 | K-2 | Tandi Prillerman |
| Lake Oconee Academy | 1021 Titan Cir | Greensboro, GA | 30642 | 706-454-1562 | 453-1773 | K-8 | Otho Tucker Ph.D. |
| Lamar County College and Career Academy | 1 Trojan Way | Barnesville, GA | 30204 | 770-358-8641 | 358-8649 | 9-12 | Matt Adams |
| Lanier Charter Career Academy | 2719 Tumbling Creek Rd | Gainesville, GA | 30504 | 770-532-3161 | 532-3156 | 9-12 | Dr. Cindy Blakley |
| Latin Academy | 1442 Metropolitan Pkwy SW | Atlanta, GA | 30310 | 404-753-4050 | 753-0290 | 6-8 | Aja Kweliona |
| Latin College Prep | 2626 Hogan Rd | East Point, GA | 30344 | 404-753-4050 | 753-0290 | 6-8 | Andre Mitchell |
| Latin Grammar S | 1442 Metropolitan Pkwy SW | Atlanta, GA | 30310 | 404-753-4050 | 753-0290 | K-5 | Alka Franceschi |
| Leadership Preparatory Academy | 6400 Woodrow Rd | Lithonia, GA | 30038 | 678-526-2531 | | K-8 | Lonnie Hall |
| Liberty College and Career Academy | 245 Darsey Rd | Hinesville, GA | 31313 | 912-876-4904 | | 9-12 | Tom Alexander |
| Main Street Academy | 2861 Lakeshore Dr | College Park, GA | 30337 | 404-768-0081 | 767-2491 | K-8 | Jeff Homan |
| Martin Technology Acad of Math & Science | 4216 Martin Rd | Flowery Branch, GA | 30542-3509 | 770-965-1578 | 965-1668 | K-5 | Tamara Etterling |
| McEver Arts Academy | 3265 Montgomery Dr | Gainesville, GA | 30504-5515 | 770-534-7473 | 531-3055 | K-5 | Pam Doig |
| Morgan County ES | 1640 Buckhead Rd | Madison, GA | 30650 | 706-752-4750 | 752-4751 | 3-5 | Ty Snyder |
| Morgan County HS | 1231 College Dr | Madison, GA | 30650-1499 | 706-752-4900 | 752-4901 | 9-12 | Dr. Jim Malanowski |
| Morgan County MS | 920 Pearl St | Madison, GA | 30650-1021 | 706-752-4800 | 752-4801 | 6-8 | Dr. Darrell Stephens |
| Morgan County PS | 993 East Ave | Madison, GA | 30650-1498 | 706-752-4700 | 752-4701 | PK-2 | Lisa Daniel |
| Mountain Education Charter HS | 901 Fairview School Rd | Demorest, GA | 30535 | 706-754-4461 | 754-5181 | 9-12 | Sherrie Witten |
| Mountain Education Charter HS | 218 School St | Blairsville, GA | 30512 | 706-745-9575 | 745-3588 | 9-12 | Roy Perrin |
| Mountain Education Charter HS | 4560 Old Highway 76 | Blue Ridge, GA | 30513 | 706-632-6100 | 632-0461 | 9-12 | Lori Chastain |
| Mountain Education Charter HS | 175 Primary School Rd | Ellijay, GA | 30540 | 706-276-5002 | 276-5008 | 9-12 | Timothy Mount |
| Mountain Education Charter HS | 123 Mountain View Dr | Dahlonega, GA | 30533 | 706-219-4664 | 219-4665 | 9-12 | Tracy Sanford |
| Mountain Education Charter HS | 191 Old Big A School Rd | Toccoa, GA | 30577 | 706-886-3114 | 886-3127 | 9-12 | Debbie Gurley |
| Mountain Education Charter HS | 328 Old Blairsville Rd | Cleveland, GA | 30528 | 706-865-0727 | 348-4498 | 9-12 | Joe Cash |
| Mountain Education Charter HS | 121 D B Carrol | Jasper, GA | 30143 | 706-253-1750 | 253-1755 | 9-12 | Ron Hunter |
| Mountain View ES | 350 Calvin Jackson Dr | Ellijay, GA | 30540-5589 | 706-276-5100 | 276-5102 | K-4 | Charles Walker |
| Mount Vernon Exploratory S | 4844 Jim Hood Rd | Gainesville, GA | 30506-2834 | 770-983-1759 | 983-1663 | K-5 | Connie Daniels |
| Murphey MS | 2216 Bungalow Rd | Augusta, GA | 30906 | 706-737-7350 | 737-7353 | 6-8 | Sean Middleton |
| Museum S of Avondale Estates | 923 Forrest Blvd | Decatur, GA | 30030-4730 | 404-289-0320 | | PK-6 | Katherine Kelbaugh |
| New Life Academy of Excellence | 4725 River Green Pkwy | Duluth, GA | 30096 | 678-720-9870 | 720-9875 | K-8 | Alphonsa Foward |
| Newton College & Career Academy | 144 Ram Dr | Covington, GA | 30014-1956 | 678-625-6769 | 625-6041 | 10-12 | Chad Walker |
| North Metro Academy of Performing Arts | 182 Hunter St | Norcross, GA | 30071 | 770-903-3400 | 903-2950 | K-8 | Dr. Burrell Pope |
| Northwest Georgia College & Career Acad | 2300 Maddox Chapel Rd NE | Dalton, GA | 30721-6645 | 706-876-3600 | 876-3602 | 9-12 | Jay Williams |
| Odyssey Charter S | 14 Saint John Cir | Newnan, GA | 30265 | 770-251-6111 | 251-6606 | K-8 | Andy Geeter |
| Oglethorpe Charter S | 7202 Central Ave | Savannah, GA | 31406 | 912-395-5075 | 201-7626 | 6-8 | Dr. Kevin Wall |
| Pataula Charter Academy | PO Box 332 | Edison, GA | 39846 | 229-835-3322 | 835-2233 | K-8 | Kylie Holley |
| Peachtree Charter MS | 4664 N Peachtree Rd | Atlanta, GA | 30338-5898 | 678-676-7702 | 676-7710 | 6-8 | Scott Heptinstall |
| Provost Academy of Georgia | 100 Edgewood Ave NE Ste 915 | Atlanta, GA | 30303 | 404-577-8593 | 669-2303 | 9-12 | Monica Henson |
| Putnam County ES | 314 S Washington Ave | Eatonton, GA | 31024-1126 | 706-485-5312 | 923-2808 | 3-5 | Scott Sauls |
| Putnam County HS | 300 War Eagle Rd | Eatonton, GA | 31024-2304 | 706-485-9971 | 485-3128 | 9-12 | Barry Lollis |
| Putnam County MS | 140 Sparta Hwy | Eatonton, GA | 31024-8493 | 706-485-8547 | 485-7090 | 6-8 | Dr. Susan Usry |
| Putnam County PS | 162 Old Glenwood Springs Rd | Eatonton, GA | 31024-6525 | 706-485-5141 | 485-4147 | PK-2 | Fernando Aker |
| Rockdale Career Academy | 1064 Culpepper Dr SW | Conyers, GA | 30094-5985 | 770-388-5677 | 388-5678 | 9-12 | Dr. Miki Edwards |
| Sardis Enrichment School | 2805 Sardis Rd | Gainesville, GA | 30506-2228 | 770-532-0104 | 531-3057 | PK-5 | Neil Yarrington |
| Savannah Classical Academy | 705 E Anderson St | Savannah, GA | 31401 | 912-395-4040 | | K-8 | |
| Sawyer Road ES | 840 Sawyer Rd | Marietta, GA | 30062-2263 | 770-429-9923 | 429-9936 | K-5 | Susan Graves |
| Scholars Academy Charter S | 6630 Camp St | Riverdale, GA | 30274 | 770-756-9710 | 629-4755 | K-5 | |
| Sedalia Park ES | 2230 Lower Roswell Rd | Marietta, GA | 30068-3359 | 770-509-5162 | 509-5342 | K-5 | Karen Wacker |
| Smoke Rise ES | 1991 Silver Hill Rd | Stone Mountain, GA | 30087-1699 | 678-874-3602 | 874-3610 | PK-5 | Pamela McCloud |

| School | Address | City,State | Zip code | Telephone | Fax | Grade | Contact |
|---|---|---|---|---|---|---|---|
| South Eastern Early College & Career Acd | 413 Pete Phillips Dr | Vidalia, GA | 30474 | 912-293-1318 | | 9-12 | Shelly Smith |
| Spout Springs S of Enrichment | 6640 Spout Springs Rd | Flowery Branch, GA | 30542-5575 | 770-967-4860 | 967-4883 | K-5 | Arlene Thomas |
| Taliaferro County S | 557 Broad St NW | Crawfordville, GA | 30631-2918 | 706-456-2575 | 456-2689 | PK-12 | Jemessyn Foster |
| Tapestry Charter Public S | PO Box 48082 | Atlanta, GA | 30362 | 678-268-6403 | | 6-9 | Barbara Boone |
| THINC Academy | 1 College Cir | LaGrange, GA | 30240 | 706-443-5826 | 523-0266 | 11-12 | Dr. Chris Williams |
| Tybee Island Maritime Academy | PO Box 1519 | Tybee Island, GA | 31328 | 912-395-4060 | | K-5 | Patrick Rossiter |
| Unidos Dual Language Charter S | 4475 Hendrix Dr | Forest Park, GA | 30297-1244 | 404-361-3494 | 362-8898 | PK-4 | Nancy Said |
| Walton HS | 1590 Bill Murdock Rd | Marietta, GA | 30062-5999 | 770-578-3225 | 578-3227 | 9-12 | Judith McNeill |
| Wauka Mtn Multiple Intelligences Academy | 5850 Brookton Lula Rd | Gainesville, GA | 30506-2909 | 770-983-3221 | 983-1019 | PK-5 | Dr. Jo Dinnan |
| Webster County HS | 7168 Washington St | Preston, GA | 31824-5232 | 229-828-3315 | 828-3206 | 9-12 | Janie Downer |
| Wesley International Academy | 211 Memorial Dr SE | Atlanta, GA | 30312 | 678-904-9137 | 904-9138 | K-8 | Dr. Keisha Hancock |
| Westside Atlanta Charter S | 1903 Drew Dr NW | Atlanta, GA | 30318 | 404-228-9678 | | K-4 | Delana Reeves |
| World Language Academy | 4670 Winder Hwy | Flowery Branch, GA | 30542-3611 | 770-967-5854 | 967-3496 | PK-4 | Britney Bennett |
| World Language Academy | 3215 Poplar Springs Rd | Gainesville, GA | 30507 | 770-533-4004 | 533-4018 | 5-8 | Brittney Bennett |
| Wynnton Arts Academy | 2303 Wynnton Rd | Columbus, GA | 31906-2540 | 706-748-3147 | 748-3151 | K-5 | Carolyn Mull |

## Hawaii

| School | Address | City,State | Zip code | Telephone | Fax | Grade | Contact |
|---|---|---|---|---|---|---|---|
| Connections New Century Charter S | 174 Kamehameha Ave | Hilo, HI | 96720-2865 | 808-961-3664 | 961-2665 | K-12 | John Thatcher |
| Hakipu'u Learning Center | PO Box 1159 | Kaneohe, HI | 96744 | 808-235-9155 | 235-9160 | 4-12 | Charlene Hoe |
| Halau Ku Mana Charter S | 2101 Makiki Heights Dr | Honolulu, HI | 96822 | 808-945-1600 | 945-1604 | 4-12 | Mahina Duarte |
| Hawaii Academy of Arts & Science | PO Box 1494 | Pahoa, HI | 96778-1494 | 808-965-3730 | 965-3733 | K-12 | Steve Hirakami |
| Hawaii Technology Academy | 94-810 Moloalo St | Waipahu, HI | 96797 | 808-676-5444 | 676-5470 | K-12 | Leigh Fitzgerald M.Ed. |
| Innovations Public Charter S | 75-5815 Queen Kaahumanu Hwy | Kailua Kona, HI | 96740 | 808-327-6205 | 327-6209 | K-8 | Jennifer Hiro |
| Kamaile Academy | 85-180 Ala Akau St | Waianae, HI | 96792-2323 | 808-697-7110 | 697-7115 | PK-12 | Anna Winslow |
| Kanuikapono Charter S | 4333 Kukuihale Rd | Anahola, HI | 96703 | 808-822-9032 | 482-3055 | K-12 | Ku'uipo Torio |
| Kanu 'o Ka 'Aina Charter S | PO Box 398 | Kamuela, HI | 96743 | 808-887-8144 | 887-8146 | K-12 | Allyson Tamura |
| Ka'u Learning Academy | PO Box 89 | Naalehu, HI | 96772 | 808-498-0761 | | 3-6 | Kathryn Tydlacka M.Ed. |
| Ka 'Umeke Ka'eo Public Charter S | 222 Desha Ave | Hilo, HI | 96720-4815 | 808-933-3482 | 933-3488 | K-10 | Huihui Kanahele-Mossman |
| Ka Waihona O Ka Na'auao Charter S | 89-195 Farrington Hwy | Waianae, HI | 96792-4102 | 808-620-9030 | 620-9036 | K-8 | Alvin Parker |
| Kawaikini Charter S | 3-1821 Kaumualii Hwy Ste J | Lihue, HI | 96766 | 808-632-2032 | 246-4635 | K-12 | Kaleimakamae Ka'auwai |
| Ke Ana La'ahana Public Charter S | 1500 Kalanianaole Ave | Hilo, HI | 96720-4914 | 808-961-6228 | 961-6229 | 7-12 | Mapuana Waipa |
| Ke Kula Ni'ihau Kekaha Public Charter S | 8135 Kekaha Rd | Kekaha, HI | 96752 | 808-337-0481 | 337-1289 | PK-12 | Haunani Seward |
| Ke Kula 'O Nawahiokalani'opu'u Charter S | 16-120 Opukahaia St | Keaau, HI | 96749-8135 | 808-982-4260 | 966-7821 | K-8 | Dr. Kauanoe Kamana |
| Ke Kula 'O Samuel Kamakau Lab S | 46-500 Kuneki St | Kaneohe, HI | 96744 | 808-235-9175 | 235-9173 | PK-12 | Dr. Meahilahila Kelling |
| Kihei Charter S | PO Box 1098 | Kihei, HI | 96753 | 808-875-0700 | 874-6745 | K-12 | Dan Kuhar |
| Kona Pacific Public Charter S | PO Box 115 | Kealakekua, HI | 96750 | 808-322-4900 | 322-4906 | K-8 | Usha Kotner |
| Kualapu'u Charter ES | PO Box 260 | Kualapuu, HI | 96757-0260 | 808-567-6900 | 567-6906 | K-6 | Lydia Trinidad |
| Kua 'O Ka La Public Charter S | 14-5322 Kalapana Kapoho Rd | Pahoa, HI | 96778 | 808-965-5098 | 965-9618 | K-12 | Susan Osborne |
| Kula Aupuni Niihau A Kahelelani Aloha | 8315 Kekaha Rd | Kekaha, HI | 96752 | 808-337-2022 | 337-2033 | K-12 | Hedy Sullivan |
| Lanikai ES | 140 Alala Rd | Kailua, HI | 96734-3199 | 808-266-7844 | 266-7848 | PK-6 | Ed Noh |
| Malama Honua Charter S | 41-054 Ehukai St | Waimanalo, HI | 96795 | 808-259-5522 | | K-2 | Denise Espania |
| Na Wai Ola Public Charter S | 181355 Volcano Rd | Mountain View, HI | 96771 | 808-968-2318 | 968-0778 | K-6 | Daniel Caluya M.Ed. |
| SEEQS Charter S | 845 22nd Ave | Honolulu, HI | 96816-4521 | 808-677-3377 | | 6-12 | Buffy Cushman-Patz |
| Thompson Academy | 1040 Richards St Ste 220 | Honolulu, HI | 96813 | 808-441-8000 | 683-7062 | K-12 | Diana Oshiro |
| University Laboratory S | 1776 University Ave | Honolulu, HI | 96822-2447 | 808-956-7833 | 956-7260 | K-12 | Keoni Jeremiah |
| Volcano S of Arts & Sciences | PO Box 845 | Volcano, HI | 96785-0845 | 808-985-9800 | 985-9898 | K-8 | Ardith Renteria |
| Voyager Charter S | 2428 Wilder Ave | Honolulu, HI | 96822-2418 | 808-521-9770 | 521-9772 | K-8 | Marybeth Barr |
| Wai'alae ES | 1045 19th Ave | Honolulu, HI | 96816-4699 | 808-733-4880 | 733-4886 | K-5 | Wendy Lagareta |
| Waimea Charter MS | 67-1229 Mamalahoa Hwy | Kamuela, HI | 96743-8429 | 808-887-6090 | 887-6087 | 6-8 | Amy Kendziorski M.Ed. |
| West Hawaii Explorations Academy | 73-4460 Queen Kaahumanu Hwy | Kailua Kona, HI | 96740-2632 | 808-327-4751 | 327-4750 | 6-12 | Curtis Muraoka |

## Idaho

| School | Address | City,State | Zip code | Telephone | Fax | Grade | Contact |
|---|---|---|---|---|---|---|---|
| Academy | 1295 Alpine Ave | Pocatello, ID | 83202 | 208-232-1447 | 232-1448 | K-8 | Joel Lovstedt |
| American Heritage Charter S | 1736 S 35th W | Idaho Falls, ID | 83402 | 208-529-6570 | 529-3344 | K-9 | Tiffnee Hurst |
| Another Choice Virtual Charter S | 1014 W Hemingway Blvd | Nampa, ID | 83651-1733 | 208-475-4255 | 475-4274 | K-12 | Dr. Kelsey Williams |
| ANSER Charter S | 202 E 42nd St | Garden City, ID | 83714-6315 | 208-426-9840 | 426-9863 | K-8 | Dr. Suzanne Gregg |
| ARTEC Charter S | 1070 Elkhorn Cir N | Twin Falls, ID | 83301-8355 | 208-732-6346 | 736-4770 | 9-12 | Michael Gibson |
| Bird Charter S | 614 S Madison Ave | Sandpoint, ID | 83864-8724 | 208-255-7771 | 263-9441 | 6-12 | Alan Millar |
| Blackfoot Charter Community Learning Ctr | 2801 Hunters Loop | Blackfoot, ID | 83221-6206 | 208-782-0744 | 782-1330 | K-5 | Dr. Fred Ball |
| Chief Tahgee Elementary Academy | PO Box 2717 | Fort Hall, ID | 83203-0217 | 208-237-2710 | 237-1734 | K-6 | Joel Weaver |
| Coeur D'Alene Charter Academy | 4904 N Duncan Dr | Coeur d Alene, ID | 83815-8329 | 208-676-1667 | 676-8667 | 6-12 | Dan Nicklay |
| Compass Charter S | 2511 W Cherry Ln | Meridian, ID | 83642-1135 | 208-855-2802 | 895-0197 | K-12 | Kelly Trudeau |
| Falcon Ridge Charter S | 278 S Ten Mile Rd | Kuna, ID | 83634-1768 | 208-922-9228 | 922-4198 | K-8 | Mark Green |
| Heritage Academy | 500 S Lincoln Ave | Jerome, ID | 83338-3027 | 208-595-1617 | | K-8 | Dr. Christine Ivie |
| Heritage Community Charter S | 1803 E Ustick Rd | Caldwell, ID | 83605-6607 | 208-453-8070 | 453-8077 | K-8 | Javier Castaneda |
| Idaho Arts Charter S | 1220 5th St N | Nampa, ID | 83687-3416 | 208-463-4324 | 468-0572 | K-12 | Jackie Collins |
| Idaho College & Career Readiness Academy | 1965 S Eagle Rd Suite 150 | Meridian, ID | 83642 | 866-917-2420 | 917-2416 | 9-12 | Monte Pittman |
| Idaho Connects Online S | 12639 W Explorer Dr Ste 185 | Boise, ID | 83713-1889 | 208-287-3668 | 287-3671 | 6-12 | Vickie McCullough |
| Idaho Digital Learning Academy | PO Box 10017 | Boise, ID | 83707 | 208-342-0207 | 577-4034 | K-12 | Dr. Cheryl Charlton |
| Idaho Distance Education Academy | PO Box 338 | Deary, ID | 83823-0338 | 208-877-1513 | 877-1713 | K-12 | Jason Bransford |
| Idaho Science and Technology Charter S | 21 N 550 W | Blackfoot, ID | 83221-5562 | 208-785-7827 | 785-9913 | 6-8 | Tami Dortch |
| Idaho Virtual Academy | 1965 S Eagle Rd Ste 190 | Meridian, ID | 83642-9246 | 208-322-3559 | 322-3688 | K-12 | Kelly Edginton |
| Inspire Virtual Charter S | 600 N Steelhead Way Ste 164 | Boise, ID | 83704-9620 | 208-322-4002 | 322-4008 | K-12 | Karen Glassman |
| iSucceed Virtual HS | 6148 N Discovery Way # 120 | Boise, ID | 83713 | 208-375-3116 | 375-3117 | 9-12 | Aaron Ritter |
| Jefferson Charter S | 1209 Adam Smith Ave | Caldwell, ID | 83605-5487 | 208-455-8772 | 455-8713 | K-12 | Chuck Ward |
| Kootenai Bridge Academy | 606 River Ave | Coeur D Alene, ID | 83814 | 208-930-4515 | 930-4791 | 11-12 | Charles Kenna |
| Legacy Charter S | 4015 Legacy Way | Nampa, ID | 83686-5801 | 208-467-0947 | 467-0948 | K-6 | Seth Stallcop |
| Liberty Charter S | 9955 Kris Jensen Ln | Nampa, ID | 83686-4742 | 208-466-7952 | 466-7961 | K-12 | Mark Wachsmuth |
| McKenna Charter HS | 675 S Haskett St | Mountain Home, ID | 83647-3375 | 208-580-2449 | 580-2450 | 9-12 | Larry Slade |
| Meridian Medical Arts Charter HS | 1789 E Heritage Park Ln | Meridian, ID | 83646-4855 | 208-855-4075 | 855-4081 | 9-12 | Scott Hill |
| Meridian Technical Charter HS | 3800 N Locust Grove Rd | Meridian, ID | 83646-5510 | 208-288-2928 | 288-5685 | 9-12 | Randy Yadon |
| Monticello Montessori Charter S | 4707 Sweetwater | Ammon, ID | 83406-7546 | 208-419-0742 | 419-0765 | K-6 | Randy Crisler |
| Moscow Charter S | 1723 E F St | Moscow, ID | 83843-9571 | 208-883-3195 | 892-3855 | K-8 | Tony Bonuccelli |
| North Idaho STEM Charter Academy | PO Box 434 | Rathdrum, ID | 83858 | 208-687-8002 | | K-9 | Scott Thomson |
| North Star Charter S | 839 N Linder Rd | Eagle, ID | 83616-4427 | 208-939-9600 | 939-6090 | K-12 | Melissa Andersen |
| North Valley Academy | 906 Main St | Gooding, ID | 83330 | 208-934-4567 | 934-4522 | K-12 | Gayle DeSmet |
| Odyssey Charter S | 1235 Jones St | Idaho Falls, ID | 83401 | 208-557-3627 | | 6-12 | Karl Peterson |
| Palouse Prairie S | PO Box 9511 | Moscow, ID | 83843-0120 | 208-882-3684 | 882-3689 | K-8 | Jacob Ellsworth |
| Payette River Technical Academy | 721 W 12th St Ste A | Emmett, ID | 83617-3827 | 208-365-0985 | 365-7800 | 9-12 | William Knickrehm |
| Pocatello Community Charter S | 995 S Arthur Ave | Pocatello, ID | 83204-3400 | 208-478-2522 | 478-2622 | K-8 | Michael Mendive |
| Rolling Hills Charter S | 8900 Horseshoe Bend Rd | Boise, ID | 83714-3859 | 208-939-5400 | 939-5401 | K-8 | Shane Pratt M.Ed. |
| Sage International S of Boise | 457 E Parkcenter Blvd | Boise, ID | 83706 | 208-343-7243 | 287-0829 | K-12 | Don Keller |
| Taylors Crossing Charter S | 1445 Wood River Rd | Idaho Falls, ID | 83401-5095 | 208-552-0397 | 904-3814 | K-12 | Daniel Wendt |
| Upper Carmen Charter S | PO Box 33 | Carmen, ID | 83462 | 208-756-4590 | 756-6695 | K-6 | Sue Smith |
| Victory Charter S | 9779 Kris Jensen Ln | Nampa, ID | 83686-4741 | 208-442-9400 | 442-9401 | K-12 | Dr. Marianne Saunders |
| Village Charter S | 219 N Roosevelt St | Boise, ID | 83706-1850 | 208-336-2000 | 367-1234 | K-8 | Tony Richard |
| Vision Charter S | 19291 Ward Ln | Caldwell, ID | 83605-7936 | 208-455-9220 | 455-9121 | K-12 | Wendy Oldenkamp |
| White Pine Charter S | 2959 John Adams Pkwy | Ammon, ID | 83406-4508 | 208-522-4432 | 522-4452 | K-8 | Jeremy Clarke |
| Xavier Charter S | 1218 N College Rd W | Twin Falls, ID | 83301 | 208-734-3947 | 733-1348 | K-12 | Gary Moon |

## Illinois

| School | Address | City,State | Zip code | Telephone | Fax | Grade | Contact |
|---|---|---|---|---|---|---|---|
| Academy for Global Citizenship | 4647 W 47th St | Chicago, IL | 60632 | 773-582-1100 | 582-1101 | K-7 | Anne Gillespie |
| Academy of Scholastic Achievement S | 4651 W Madison St | Chicago, IL | 60644-3646 | 773-921-1315 | 921-8324 | 10-12 | Nicole Simpson Ed.D. |
| ACE Technical Charter HS | 5410 S State St | Chicago, IL | 60609-6382 | 773-548-8705 | 548-8706 | 9-12 | Marvin Talley |
| Addams HS | 1814 S Union Ave | Chicago, IL | 60616-1045 | 312-563-1746 | 563-1756 | 9-12 | Theresa Comparini |
| Albizu Campos HS | 2739 W Division St | Chicago, IL | 60622-2854 | 773-342-8022 | 342-6609 | 10-12 | Matthew Rodrguez |
| Amandla Charter S | 6800 S Stewart Ave | Chicago, IL | 60621 | 773-535-7150 | 535-7151 | 5-11 | Jennifer Kirmes |
| Asian Human Services - Passages Charter | 1643 W Bryn Mawr Ave | Chicago, IL | 60660 | 773-433-3530 | 769-3229 | PK-8 | Ken Johnson |
| Aspira - Antonia Pantoja Alternative HS | 3121 N Pulaski Rd | Chicago, IL | 60641-5447 | 773-252-0970 | 427-0872 | 10-12 | Dr. Martha Zurita |
| ASPIRA Business and Finance HS | 2989 N Milwaukee Ave | Chicago, IL | 60618 | 773-252-0970 | | 9-12 | |
| ASPIRA Haugan MS | 3729 W Leland Ave | Chicago, IL | 60625-5706 | 773-252-0970 | 427-0872 | 6-8 | Pablo Ortega |
| ASPIRA - Mirta Ramirez Computer Science | 1711 N California Ave | Chicago, IL | 60647 | 773-252-0970 | 252-0094 | 12-12 | Jefferson Lim |
| Austin Business & Entrepreneurship S | 231 N Pine Ave | Chicago, IL | 60644-2333 | 773-534-6316 | 534-6267 | 9-12 | Wayne Issa |
| Austin Career Education Center | 5352 W Chicago Ave | Chicago, IL | 60651-2857 | 773-626-6988 | 626-2641 | 10-12 | Debra Williams |
| Baker College Prep | 2710 E 89th St | Chicago, IL | 60617 | 773-535-6340 | 913-0346 | 9-Adu | Vincent Gay |
| Bronzeville Lighthouse Charter S | 8 W Root St | Chicago, IL | 60609-2931 | 773-535-1460 | 285-1564 | K-8 | Christina Page |
| Butler College Prep | 821 E 103rd St | Chicago, IL | 60628 | 773-535-5490 | 442-0343 | 9-12 | Christopher Goins |
| Cambridge Lakes S | 900 Wester Blvd | Pingree Grove, IL | 60140-2050 | 847-464-4300 | 464-0318 | PK-8 | Kathleen Poole |
| Catalyst Charter - Maria | 6727 S California Ave | Chicago, IL | 60629 | 773-993-1770 | 993-1771 | K-12 | Dawn Sandoval |
| Catalyst Charter S - Circle Rock | 5608 W Washington Blvd | Chicago, IL | 60644 | 773-945-5025 | 626-2345 | K-8 | Ayanna Mitchell |
| CCA Academy | 1231 S Pulaski Rd | Chicago, IL | 60623 | 773-762-2272 | 762-2065 | 10-12 | Myra Sampson |
| Chatham Academy | 9035 S Langley Ave | Chicago, IL | 60619 | 773-651-1500 | 651-1523 | 10-12 | Lisa Williams |
| Chicago Bulls College Prep S | 2040 W Adams St | Chicago, IL | 60612 | 773-534-7599 | 850-0192 | 9-12 | Wendy Erskine |
| Chicago Collegiate Charter S | 11816 S Indiana Ave | Chicago, IL | 60628 | 773-536-9098 | | 4-7 | Beth Napleton |
| Chicago International Charter S - Avalon | 1501 E 83rd Pl | Chicago, IL | 60619-6501 | 773-721-0858 | 731-0142 | K-8 | Brandon Kimble |

| School | Address | City,State | Zip code | Telephone | Fax | Grade | Contact |
|---|---|---|---|---|---|---|---|
| Chicago International Charter S - Basil | 1816 W Garfield Blvd | Chicago, IL | 60609-5606 | 773-778-9455 | 778-9456 | K-8 | Elizabeth Tieche |
| Chicago International Charter S - Bond | 13300 S Langley Ave | Chicago, IL | 60827 | 773-468-1300 | 253-0988 | K-6 | Lloyd Knight |
| Chicago International Charter S Bucktown | 2235 N Hamilton Ave | Chicago, IL | 60647-3360 | 773-645-3321 | 645-3327 | K-8 | Christy Krier |
| Chicago International Charter S Hawkins | 801 E 133rd Pl | Chicago, IL | 60827 | 773-264-0505 | | 7-12 | Rodney Hull |
| Chicago International Charter S Jackson | 315 Summit St | Rockford, IL | 61107 | 815-316-0093 | 316-0170 | K-8 | Angelique Watson |
| Chicago International Charter S Longwood | 1309 W 95th St | Chicago, IL | 60643-1496 | 773-238-5330 | 238-5350 | 3-12 | Kenyatta Stansberry |
| Chicago International Charter S - Loomis | 9535 S Loomis St | Chicago, IL | 60643 | 773-429-8955 | 429-8441 | K-2 | Lindsey Girard |
| Chicago International Charter S Prairie | 11530 S Prairie Ave | Chicago, IL | 60628-5691 | 773-928-0480 | 928-6971 | K-8 | April Shaw |
| Chicago International Charter S - Quest | 1443 N Ogden Ave | Chicago, IL | 60610 | 773-565-2100 | 951-2906 | 6-12 | Joyce Pae |
| Chicago International Charter S W Belden | 2245 N McVicker Ave | Chicago, IL | 60639-2766 | 773-637-9430 | 637-9791 | K-8 | Scott Frauenheim |
| Chicago Intl Charter S - Irving Park | 3820 N Spaulding Ave | Chicago, IL | 60618-4413 | 773-433-5000 | 433-5009 | K-8 | Karin Breo M.Ed. |
| Chicago Intl Charter S Northtown | 3900 W Peterson Ave Ste 1 | Chicago, IL | 60659-3162 | 773-478-3655 | 478-6029 | 9-12 | Dr. Josh Emmett |
| Chicago Intl Charter S Ralph Ellison | 1817 W 80th St | Chicago, IL | 60620 | 773-478-4434 | 224-2594 | 9-12 | Kimberly Hinton |
| Chicago Intl Charter S Washington Park | 110 E 61st St | Chicago, IL | 60637 | 773-347-0200 | 324-3300 | K-8 | Shaymora Blanks |
| Chicago Intl Charter S Wrightwood | 8130 S California Ave | Chicago, IL | 60652-2716 | 773-434-4575 | 434-2026 | K-8 | Ashley Gibson |
| Chicago Math and Science Academy | 7212 N Clark St | Chicago, IL | 60626-2416 | 773-761-8960 | 761-8961 | 6-12 | Aydin Kara |
| Chicago Virtual Charter S | 38 S Peoria St | Chicago, IL | 60607-2628 | 312-267-4486 | 676-3689 | K-12 | Amy Biasbas |
| Christopher House Charter ES | 5235 W Belden St | Chicago, IL | 60639 | 773-922-7542 | | K-2 | Kristin Novy |
| Comer College Prep S | 7131 S South Chicago Ave | Chicago, IL | 60619 | 773-729-3969 | 729-3960 | 9-12 | Kelly Estee |
| Community Youth Development Institute | 7836 S Union Ave | Chicago, IL | 60620-2409 | 773-224-2273 | 224-2214 | 10-12 | Aaron Royster |
| DRW College Prep | 931 S Homan Ave | Chicago, IL | 60624 | 773-893-4500 | 893-4501 | 9-12 | Matthew Kelley |
| DuSable Leadership Academy | 4934 S Wabash Ave | Chicago, IL | 60615-2115 | 773-535-1170 | 535-1912 | 12-12 | Frank Davis |
| 8 Points Charter S | 352 Franklin Dr | Jacksonville, IL | 62650 | 217-271-1000 | 271-1001 | 5-8 | Bridget English |
| El Cuarto Ano - Association House | 1116 N Kedzie Ave | Chicago, IL | 60651-4152 | 773-772-7170 | 772-8617 | 10-12 | Anthony Rodriguez |
| EPIC Academy | 8255 S Houston Ave | Chicago, IL | 60617-2191 | 773-535-7930 | 535-7934 | 9-12 | Matthew King |
| Erie Charter S | 1405 N Washtenaw Ave | Chicago, IL | 60622 | 773-486-7161 | 486-7234 | K-8 | Velia Soto |
| Excel Academy - Woodlawn | 7530 S South Shore Dr | Chicago, IL | 60649 | 773-902-7800 | 902-7615 | 9-9 | Anthony Haley |
| Foundations College Prep S | 1233 W 109th Pl | Chicago, IL | 60643 | 773-298-5800 | | 6-7 | Sarah Hunko-Baker |
| Frazier Preparatory Academy | 3711 W Douglas Blvd | Chicago, IL | 60623 | 773-521-1303 | 521-1365 | PK-8 | Donn Tignanelli |
| Galapagos Charter ES | 3814 W Iowa St | Chicago, IL | 60651-3708 | 773-384-9400 | 384-4866 | K-8 | Amy Jackson |
| Galapagos Charter S | 2605 School St | Rockford, IL | 61101 | 815-708-7946 | 708-7966 | K-8 | Michael Lane |
| Golder College Prep S | 1454 W Superior St | Chicago, IL | 60642 | 312-265-9925 | 243-8402 | 9-12 | Rosa Alanis |
| Great Lakes Academy Charter S | 8401 S Saginaw Ave | Chicago, IL | 60617 | 773-530-3040 | 530-3039 | K-2 | Katherin Myers |
| Hansberry College Prep | 8748 S Aberdeen St | Chicago, IL | 60620 | 773-729-3400 | 304-1995 | 9-12 | Lauryn Fullerton |
| Harvey Middle College S | 10001 S Woodlawn Ave | Chicago, IL | 60628-1696 | 773-291-6517 | 291-6199 | 10-12 | Devon Morales |
| Horizon Sci Academy - Southwest Charter | 5401 S Western Blvd | Chicago, IL | 60609 | 773-498-3355 | 498-4984 | K-10 | Matt Yildiz |
| Houston HS | 7847 S Jeffery Blvd | Chicago, IL | 60649 | 773-723-9630 | 723-9022 | 10-12 | Kim Ellison |
| HSA Belmont Charter S | 5035 W North Ave | Chicago, IL | 60639 | 773-237-2702 | 237-2726 | K-7 | Serdar Kartal |
| HSA McKinley Park Charter S | 2245 W Pershing Rd | Chicago, IL | 60609 | 773-247-8400 | 247-8401 | K-12 | Cafer Cengiz |
| Innovation HS | 17 N State St Fl 3 | Chicago, IL | 60602 | 312-999-9360 | 999-9361 | 10-12 | LaShaun Jackson |
| Instituto Health Sciences Career Academy | 2520 S Western Ave | Chicago, IL | 60608 | 773-890-8020 | 376-8573 | 9-12 | Hillyn Sennholtz |
| Instituto Justice - Lozano | 2570 S Blue Island Ave | Chicago, IL | 60608-4817 | 773-696-3610 | 890-1537 | 10-12 | Cynthia Nambo |
| Instituto Justice - Lozano Mastery | 2520 S Western Ave | Chicago, IL | 60608 | 773-890-0055 | 890-1537 | 9-12 | Cynthia Nambo |
| Intrinsic Charter HS | 4540 W Belmont Ave | Chicago, IL | 60641 | 708-887-2735 | 887-2812 | 7-12 | Melissa Zaikos |
| Johnson College Prep HS | 6350 S Stewart Ave | Chicago, IL | 60621 | 312-348-1888 | 278-0449 | 9-12 | Matthew Brown |
| KIPP Ascend MS | 1616 S Avers Ave | Chicago, IL | 60623 | 773-521-4399 | 521-4766 | 6-8 | Lauren Henley |
| KIPP Ascend PS | 1440 S Christiana | Chicago, IL | 60623 | 773-522-1261 | 522-1185 | K-5 | Ellen Bhattacharyya |
| KIPP Bloom College Prep S | 5515 S Lowe Ave | Chicago, IL | 60621 | 773-938-8565 | 783-6910 | 5-8 | Ellen Sale |
| KIPP Create College Prep S | 4818 W Ohio St | Chicago, IL | 60644-1702 | 773-938-8553 | 287-4548 | 5-8 | Kate Mazurek |
| Latino Youth HS | 2001 S California Ave | Chicago, IL | 60608-2486 | 773-648-2130 | 648-2098 | 10-12 | Jose Martinez |
| LEARN 6 in North Chicago | 3131 Sheridan Rd | Great Lakes, IL | 60088 | 847-473-3845 | 473-2988 | K-8 | Kelly Tyson |
| LEARN 7 Charter ES | 3021 W Carroll Ave | Chicago, IL | 60612 | 773-584-4350 | 826-7918 | K-5 | TaMikka Sykes |
| LEARN 8 Charter MS | 3021 W Carroll Ave | Chicago, IL | 60612 | 773-584-4300 | 826-7933 | 6-8 | Jessica Beasley |
| LEARN 9 Campus in Waukegan | 540 S McAlister Ave | Waukegan, IL | 60085 | 773-850-9646 | | K-3 | Dr. CasSandra Brooks |
| LEARN Charter S Campbell Campus | 212 S Francisco Ave | Chicago, IL | 60612 | 773-826-0370 | 826-0109 | K-5 | Karin McGuire |
| LEARN Charter S Excel Campus | 3021 W Carroll Ave | Chicago, IL | 60612 | 312-243-7001 | 243-7160 | K-5 | Sekou Robertson |
| LEARN Charter S Hunter Perkins Campus | 1700 W 83rd St | Chicago, IL | 60620 | 773-488-1634 | 488-1753 | K-7 | Jon Bennett |
| LEARN Charter S - Romano Butler Campus | 1132 S Homan Ave | Chicago, IL | 60624-4344 | 773-722-0200 | 826-0015 | PK-8 | Robin Johnson |
| LEARN Charter S - South Chicago Campus | 8914 S Buffalo Ave | Chicago, IL | 60617 | 773-722-8577 | | K-8 | Tina Walker |
| Legacy Academy for Excellence Charter S | 4029 Prairie Rd | Rockford, IL | 61102 | 815-961-1100 | | K-12 | Barbara Forte |
| Legacy Charter ES | 4217 W 18th St | Chicago, IL | 60623-2325 | 773-542-1640 | 542-1699 | PK-8 | Lisa Kenner |
| Legal Prep Academy Charter HS | 4319 W Washington Blvd | Chicago, IL | 60624 | 773-922-7800 | | 9-12 | Ashley Gibson |
| Little Black Pearl Arts Academy HS | 1060 E 47th St | Chicago, IL | 60653 | 773-285-1211 | 285-1633 | 9-12 | Monica Haslip |
| Locke Charter Academy | 3141 W Jackson Blvd | Chicago, IL | 60612-2729 | 773-265-7232 | 265-7258 | PK-8 | Patrick Love |
| McKinley Lakeside HS | 2920 S Wabash Ave | Chicago, IL | 60616 | 312-949-5010 | 949-5015 | 10-12 | Irma Plaxico |
| Montessori S of Englewood | 6550 S Seeley Ave | Chicago, IL | 60636 | 773-535-9255 | 535-9590 | K-5 | Rita Nolan |
| Moving Everest Charter S | 416 N Laramie Ave | Chicago, IL | 60644 | 502-791-6327 | | K-1 | Mika Krause |
| Muchin College Prep S | 1 N State St Ste 700 | Chicago, IL | 60602 | 312-445-4680 | 332-0058 | 9-12 | Kimberly Neal |
| Namaste ES | 3737 S Paulina St | Chicago, IL | 60609-2047 | 773-715-9558 | 376-6495 | K-8 | Rickie Yudin |
| Noble Academy | 1443 N Ogden Ave | Chicago, IL | 60610 | 312-574-1527 | 575-4217 | 9-9 | Pablo Sierra |
| Noble Street College Prep | 1010 N Noble St | Chicago, IL | 60642 | 773-862-1449 | 278-0421 | 9-12 | Ellen Metz |
| North Lawndale College Prep at Collins | 1313 S Sacramento Dr | Chicago, IL | 60623-2297 | 773-542-6766 | 542-6995 | 8-12 | Tim Bouman |
| North Lawndale College Prep - Christiana | 1615 S Christiana Ave | Chicago, IL | 60623 | 773-542-1490 | 542-1492 | 9-12 | Tim Bouman |
| Perspectives Charter MS | 8131 S May St | Chicago, IL | 60620 | 773-358-6300 | 358-6399 | 6-8 | Sauda Porter |
| Perspectives Charter S - Joslin Campus | 1930 S Archer Ave | Chicago, IL | 60616-6505 | 312-225-7400 | 225-7411 | 6-12 | Stephen Todd |
| Perspectives HS of Technology | 8131 S May St | Chicago, IL | 60620 | 773-358-6120 | 358-6129 | 9-12 | Stephanie Kristovic |
| Perspectives/IIT Math & Science Academy | 3663 S Wabash Ave | Chicago, IL | 60653 | 773-358-6800 | 358-6055 | 6-12 | Julie Puzon |
| Perspectives Leadership Academy | 8131 S May St | Chicago, IL | 60620-3007 | 773-358-6100 | 358-6199 | 6-12 | Sarah Severson |
| Plato Learning Academy | 5545 W Harrison St | Chicago, IL | 60644 | 773-413-3090 | 413-3095 | K-8 | Christopher Austria |
| Polaris Charter Academy | 620 N Sawyer Ave | Chicago, IL | 60624-1598 | 773-534-0820 | 534-6645 | K-8 | Michelle Navarre |
| Prairie Crossing Charter S | 1571 Jones Point Rd | Grayslake, IL | 60030-3536 | 847-543-9722 | 543-9744 | K-8 | Geoff Deigan |
| Pritzker College Prep Campus | 4131 W Cortland St | Chicago, IL | 60639-4923 | 773-394-2848 | 394-2931 | 9-12 | Pablo Sierra |
| Prologue Early College HS | 1135 N Cleaver St | Chicago, IL | 60642 | 773-935-9925 | 935-8357 | 9-12 | Walter Perkins |
| Prologue-Johnston S of Art & Design | 1549 W 95th St | Chicago, IL | 60643 | 773-341-2260 | 341-2922 | 9-12 | Joyce Bowen |
| Providence Englewood Charter S | 6515 S Ashland Ave | Chicago, IL | 60636-3003 | 773-434-0202 | 434-0196 | K-8 | Angela Johnson-Williams |
| Quest Charter Academy | 2503 N University St | Peoria, IL | 61604 | 309-402-0030 | 685-3001 | 5-12 | Dr. Nicole Woods |
| Rauner College Prep Campus | 1337 W Ohio St | Chicago, IL | 60642-6430 | 312-226-5345 | 226-3552 | 9-12 | Jennifer Reid |
| Robertson Charter S | 2240 E Geddes Ave | Decatur, IL | 62526-5127 | 217-428-7072 | 428-9214 | K-8 | Cordell Ingram |
| Rowe - Clark Math & Science Academy | 3645 W Chicago Ave | Chicago, IL | 60651-3934 | 773-242-2212 | 826-6936 | 9-12 | Brenda Cora |
| Rowe ES | 1424 N Cleaver St | Chicago, IL | 60642 | 312-445-5870 | 445-5875 | K-7 | Ana Martinez |
| Shabazz International Charter S | 7823 S Ellis Ave | Chicago, IL | 60619-3213 | 773-651-1221 | 651-0302 | K-12 | Shannon Mason |
| SIU East St. Louis Charter S | 601 James R Thompson Blvd | E Saint Louis, IL | 62201-1129 | 618-482-8370 | 482-8372 | 9-12 | Veronica Washington |
| Sizemore Academy of B Shabazz | 6936 S Hermitage Ave | Chicago, IL | 60636 | 773-535-9144 | 535-9499 | K-8 | Danielle Robinson |
| Southland College Prep | 4601 Sauk Trl | Richton Park, IL | 60471 | 708-748-8105 | | 9-12 | Dr. Blondean Davis |
| Springfield Ball Charter S | 2530 E Ash St | Springfield, IL | 62703-5600 | 217-525-3275 | 525-3316 | PK-8 | Matthew Fraas |
| Sullivan House Alternative HS | 8164 S South Chicago Ave | Chicago, IL | 60617-1041 | 773-978-8680 | 375-1482 | 10-12 | Dr. Thomas Gattuso |
| Truman Middle College HS | 1145 W Wilson Ave | Chicago, IL | 60640-5691 | 773-907-4840 | 907-4844 | 10-12 | MaryAnn Soley |
| UCCS - Carter Woodson Campus | 4444 S Evans Ave | Chicago, IL | 60653 | 773-624-0700 | 624-0707 | 6-8 | Jared Washington |
| UCCS - Donoghue Campus | 707 E 37th St | Chicago, IL | 60653-1406 | 773-285-5301 | 285-5389 | PK-5 | Errika Baker |
| UCCS - North Kenwood/Oakland Campus | 1119 E 46th St | Chicago, IL | 60653-4403 | 773-536-2399 | 536-2435 | PK-5 | Tonya Howell |
| UCCS - Woodlawn Campus | 6420 S University Ave | Chicago, IL | 60637-3608 | 773-752-8101 | 324-0653 | 6-12 | Michael Lackenbach |
| UIC College Prep S | 1231 S Damen Ave | Chicago, IL | 60608 | 312-768-4858 | 496-7149 | 9-12 | Tressie McDonough |
| UNO Charter Garcia Campus HS | 4248 W 47th St | Chicago, IL | 60632 | 773-579-3480 | 376-5785 | 9-12 | Alex Rock |
| UNO Charter S - Bartolome De Las Casas | 1641 W 16th St | Chicago, IL | 60608-2039 | 312-432-3224 | 432-1066 | K-8 | Courtney Mix-Binish |
| UNO Charter S - Brighton Park | 4420 S Fairfield Ave | Chicago, IL | 60632 | 773-455-5434 | 455-5435 | K-8 | Laura Castle |
| UNO Charter S - Carlos Fuentes Campus | 2845 W Barry Ave | Chicago, IL | 60618-7015 | 312-279-9826 | 279-9852 | K-8 | Joann Tanner |
| UNO Charter S - Octavio Paz Campus | 2651 W 23rd St | Chicago, IL | 60608-3609 | 773-890-1054 | 890-1069 | K-8 | Martin Masterson |
| UNO Charter S - Officer Donald Marquez | 2916 W 47th St | Chicago, IL | 60632-1907 | 773-321-2200 | 321-2250 | K-8 | Stephanie Medina |
| UNO Charter S - Omar Torres | 4248 W 47th St | Chicago, IL | 60632 | 773-579-3475 | 376-5645 | K-8 | Christopher Allen |
| UNO Charter S - Roberto Clemente | 2050 N Natchez Ave | Chicago, IL | 60707 | 312-455-5425 | 455-5456 | K-8 | Erin Neubert |
| UNO Charter S - Rogers Park | 7416 N Ridge Blvd | Chicago, IL | 60645 | 312-455-5440 | 455-5443 | K-12 | John Keith |
| UNO Charter S - Rufino Tamayo Campus | 5135 S California Ave | Chicago, IL | 60632-2124 | 773-434-6355 | 434-5036 | K-8 | Erasmo Montalvan |
| UNO Charter S - Sandra Cisneros | 2744 W Pershing Rd | Chicago, IL | 60632 | 773-376-8830 | 376-8825 | K-8 | Molly Robinson |
| UNO Charter S - Santiago | 2510 W Cortez St | Chicago, IL | 60622 | 312-455-5410 | 455-5411 | K-8 | Melissa Sweazy |
| UNO Charter School - Soccer Academy HS | 5025 S St. Louis Ave | Chicago, IL | 60632 | 312-455-5446 | 455-5447 | 9-12 | Angelina Bua |
| UNO Charter S - SPC Daniel Zizumbo | 4248 W 47th St | Chicago, IL | 60632 | 773-579-3470 | 376-5605 | K-8 | Christopher Allen |
| UNO Soccer Academy | 5050 S Homan Ave | Chicago, IL | 60632 | 312-455-5450 | 455-5451 | PK-8 | Thomas Denneen |
| Urban Prep Academy Charter S - Englewood | 6201 S Stewart Ave | Chicago, IL | 60621-3247 | 773-535-9724 | 535-0012 | 9-12 | Dennis Lacewell |
| Urban Prep Academy Charter S - West | 1326 W 14th Pl | Chicago, IL | 60608 | 773-534-8860 | 534-8914 | 9-12 | Ron Bryant |
| Urban Prep - Bronzeville | 521 E 35th St | Chicago, IL | 60616 | 773-624-3444 | 624-3405 | 9-12 | Richard Glass |
| Westside Holistic Leadership Academy | 4909 W Division St | Chicago, IL | 60651-3161 | 773-261-0994 | 261-1029 | 10-12 | Daisy Lopez |
| West Town Academy | 534 N Sacramento Blvd | Chicago, IL | 60612 | 312-563-9044 | 563-9672 | 10-12 | Robert Meyer |
| YCCS Virtual HS | 1900 W Van Buren St Rm 2417 | Chicago, IL | 60612 | 312-429-0027 | 243-5733 | 10-12 | Elizabeth Roth |
| Young Womens Leadership S | 2641 S Calumet Ave | Chicago, IL | 60616-2901 | 312-949-9400 | 949-9142 | 8-12 | Dr. Ruanda McCullough |
| YouthBuild McLean County Charter S | 360 Wylie Dr Ste 305 | Normal, IL | 61761-5500 | 309-454-3898 | 454-3913 | 10-12 | Suzanne Fitzgerald |
| Youth Connection Leadership Academy | 3424 S State St Fl 2 | Chicago, IL | 60616-5000 | 312-225-4668 | 225-4862 | 10-12 | Keisha Davis-Johnson |

## Indiana

| School | Address | City,State | Zip code | Telephone | Fax | Grade | Contact |
|---|---|---|---|---|---|---|---|
| Anderson Preparatory Academy | 101 W 29th St | Anderson, IN | 46016 | 765-649-8472 | | K-12 | Jill Barker |
| Aspire Charter Academy | 4900 W 15th Ave | Gary, IN | 46406-2308 | 219-944-7400 | 944-7474 | K-8 | Rasheeda Green |
| Avondale Meadows Academy | 3980 Meadows Dr | Indianapolis, IN | 46205-3114 | 317-803-3182 | 803-2367 | K-5 | Kelly Herron |
| Beacon Academy | 620 Cumberland Ave | West Lafayette, IN | 47906-1522 | 765-838-2045 | 838-2034 | 7-12 | Dr. Deb Lukens |
| Bloomington Project S | 349 S Walnut St | Bloomington, IN | 47401-3568 | 812-558-0041 | 334-5873 | K-9 | Catherine Diersing |
| Bowman Leadership Academy | 975 W 6th Ave | Gary, IN | 46402-1708 | 219-883-4826 | 883-1331 | K-12 | Sarita Stevens |
| Brown Charter Academy | 3600 N German Church Rd | Indianapolis, IN | 46235-8504 | 317-891-0730 | 891-0908 | K-8 | James Hill |
| Campagna Academy Charter S | 7403 Cline Ave | Schererville, IN | 46375-2645 | 219-322-8614 | 322-8436 | 9-12 | Elena Dwyre |
| Canaan Community Academy | 8775 N Canaan Main St | Canaan, IN | 47224 | 812-839-0003 | | K-6 | Donna Taylor |
| Career Academy South Bend | 3801 Crescent Cir | South Bend, IN | 46628 | 574-299-9800 | 288-6125 | 5-12 | Paul Schlottman |
| Carpe Diem - Meridian | 2240 N Meridian St | Indianapolis, IN | 46208 | 317-921-7497 | 921-7299 | 6-12 | LaNier Echols |
| Carpe Diem - Northwest | 5435 West Pike Plaza Rd | Indianapolis, IN | 46254 | 317-808-8749 | | 9-12 | Rosalie Pettigrew |
| Carpe Diem - Shadeland | 4410 N Shadeland Ave | Indianapolis, IN | 46226 | 317-677-1950 | | K-5 | Byron Brown |
| Charter School of the Dunes | 7300 Melton Rd | Gary, IN | 46403 | 219-939-9690 | 939-9031 | K-12 | Dr. Joi Patterson |
| Christel House Academy South | 2717 S East St | Indianapolis, IN | 46225-2104 | 317-783-4690 | 783-4693 | K-12 | William Lance |
| Christel House Academy West | 55 N Tibbs Ave | Indianapolis, IN | 46222 | 317-783-4690 | 783-4693 | K-3 | Richard Hunt |
| Community Montessori S | 4102 Saint Joseph Rd | New Albany, IN | 47150-9750 | 812-948-1000 | 948-0441 | PK-12 | Barbara Burke-Fondren |
| Damar Charter Academy | 5125 Decatur Blvd | Indianapolis, IN | 46241 | 317-455-2400 | 455-2447 | K-12 | Aimee Brown |
| Decatur Township S for Excellence | 5106 S High School Rd | Indianapolis, IN | 46221 | 317-856-0900 | 856-0143 | 7-12 | Tim VanWanzeele |
| Discovery Charter S | 800 Canonie Dr | Chesterton, IN | 46304 | 219-983-9800 | 929-5723 | K-8 | Ernesto Martinez |
| Donnan MS | 1202 E Troy Ave | Indianapolis, IN | 46203 | 317-217-1979 | | K-8 | Michael Dunagan |
| Early Career Academy | 9511 Angola Ct | Indianapolis, IN | 46268 | 317-688-1272 | | 9-12 | |
| East Chicago Lighthouse Charter S | 3916 Pulaski St | East Chicago, IN | 46312 | 219-378-7450 | 378-9070 | K-7 | Krysten Ivy Wendell |
| East Chicago Urban Enterprise Academy | 1402 E Chicago Ave | East Chicago, IN | 46312-3587 | 219-392-3650 | 392-3652 | K-8 | Charlotte Jackson |
| Enlace Academy | 3725 Kiel Ave | Indianapolis, IN | 46224 | 317-383-0607 | 383-0605 | K-8 | Kevin Kubacki |
| Excel Center | 630 Nichol Ave | Anderson, IN | 46016 | 317-524-3930 | 374-0047 | 9-12 | Brandy Bast |
| Excel Center | 300 N 17 St | Noblesville, IN | 46060 | 317-524-4501 | 524-4003 | K-8 | Shatoya Jordan |
| Excel Center | 2721 Kenwood Ave | South Bend, IN | 46628 | 574-472-7330 | 472-7301 | 9-12 | Randy Beachy |
| Excel Center | 3919 Madison Ave | Indianapolis, IN | 46227 | 317-607-7635 | | K-8 | Patrick Fassnacht |
| Excel Center | 1635 W Michigan St | Indianapolis, IN | 46205 | 317-524-4141 | 524-4337 | 9-12 | Patrick Fassnacht |
| Excel Center | 101 W Superior St | Kokomo, IN | 46901 | 317-524-3642 | 457-3367 | 9-12 | Nick Parks |
| Excel Center | 615 N 18th St | Lafayette, IN | 47904 | 317-524-3641 | 420-7916 | 9-12 | Jeff Hoover |
| Excel Center | 1215 S J St | Richmond, IN | 47374 | 317-524-3734 | 935-7511 | 9-12 | Markous Jewett |
| Faulkner Academy | 1111 W 2nd St | Marion, IN | 46952-3674 | 765-662-9910 | 662-9918 | K-6 | Janice Adams |
| Gary Lighthouse Charter S | 3201 Pierce St | Gary, IN | 46408 | 219-880-1762 | 884-4858 | K-7 | Rachid Kharchaf |
| Gary Middle College | 556 Washington St | Gary, IN | 46402-1915 | 219-888-7120 | | 9-12 | Timothy Pivarnik |
| Geist Montessori S | 13942 E 96th St | Mc Cordsville, IN | 46055 | 317-335-1158 | 335-1265 | K-8 | Susan Fries |
| Hammond Academy of Science & Tech | 33 Muenich Ct | Hammond, IN | 46320-1706 | 219-852-0500 | 852-4153 | 6-12 | Dr. Sean Egan |
| Herron Charter HS | 110 E 16th St | Indianapolis, IN | 46202-2404 | 317-231-0010 | 231-3759 | 9-12 | Janet McNeal |
| Hoosier Academy | 2855 N Franklin Rd | Indianapolis, IN | 46219 | 317-547-1400 | 547-1500 | K-6 | Dr. Byron Ernest |
| Hoosier Academy HS | 2855 N Franklin Rd | Indianapolis, IN | 46219 | 317-495-6494 | 454-0670 | 7-12 | Dr. Dominique Franklin |
| Hope Academy | 8102 Clearvista Pkwy | Indianapolis, IN | 46256-1661 | 317-572-9356 | 849-1455 | 9-12 | Linda Gagyi |
| Howe Community HS | 4900 Julian Ave | Indianapolis, IN | 46201-3755 | 317-693-1980 | | 7-12 | Tyler Small |
| Imagine Indiana Life Sciences Academy W | 4950 W 34th St | Indianapolis, IN | 46224-1646 | 317-297-9100 | 297-9460 | K-8 | Bianca Rivers |
| Indiana College Preparatory S | 4050 E 38th St | Indianapolis, IN | 46218 | 317-914-5868 | | K-8 | Yvonne Adkins |
| Indiana Connections Academy | 6640 Intech Blvd Ste 250 | Indianapolis, IN | 46278 | 317-818-5590 | 818-6000 | K-12 | Melissa Brown |
| Indiana Math and Science Academy | 4575 W 38th St | Indianapolis, IN | 46254-3313 | 317-298-0025 | 282-0505 | K-8 | Murat Atlihan |
| Indiana Math and Science Academy North | 7435 N Keystone Ave | Indianapolis, IN | 46240 | 317-259-7300 | 259-7363 | K-12 | Abdulkadir Parlar |
| Indiana Math and Science Academy South | 2710 Bethel Ave | Indianapolis, IN | 46203 | 317-780-1200 | 780-0400 | K-8 | Cathy Sparks |
| Indianapolis Academy of Excellence | 1145 E 22nd St | Indianapolis, IN | 46202 | 317-653-4009 | 653-4008 | K-3 | Tara Gustin |
| Indianapolis Lighthouse Charter S | 1780 Sloan Ave | Indianapolis, IN | 46203-3640 | 317-351-1534 | 351-1804 | PK-12 | Kim Randall |
| Indianapolis Lighthouse Charter S East | 4002 N Franklin Rd | Indianapolis, IN | 46226-5297 | 317-897-2472 | 897-0302 | 6-8 | Steven Pelych |
| Indianapolis Metropolitan HS | 1635 W Michigan St | Indianapolis, IN | 46222-3852 | 317-524-4638 | 524-4114 | 9-12 | Mark Forner |
| Indiana Virtual S | 1111 E 54th St Ste 144 | Indianapolis, IN | 46220 | 317-581-5355 | 581-5399 | 6-12 | Graham Clark |
| Inspire Academy - A S of Inquiry | 1620 S Madison St | Muncie, IN | 47302 | 765-216-7980 | 216-7798 | K-7 | Leslie Draper |
| Irvington Community S | 6705 Julian Ave | Indianapolis, IN | 46219-6642 | 317-357-5359 | 357-9752 | K-12 | David Nidiffer |
| Johnson Academy | 4625 Werling Dr | Fort Wayne, IN | 46806 | 260-441-8727 | 441-9357 | K-5 | Dawn Starks |
| Joshua Academy | 1230 E Illinois St | Evansville, IN | 47711-5745 | 812-401-6300 | 401-6307 | K-6 | Pamela Decker |
| KIPP Indianapolis College Prep | 1740 E 30th St | Indianapolis, IN | 46218 | 317-547-5477 | 547-5499 | 5-8 | Aleesia Johnson |
| KIPP Indianapolis Unite ES | 1740 E 30th St | Indianapolis, IN | 46218-2605 | 317-547-5477 | 547-5499 | K-4 | Ellen Reuter |
| Lighthouse College Preparatory Academy | 725 Clark Rd | Gary, IN | 46406-1822 | 219-977-9583 | 977-9725 | 8-12 | Angela West |
| Manual HS | 2405 Madison Ave | Indianapolis, IN | 46225-2196 | 317-217-1983 | 396-5399 | 9-12 | Hanno Becker |
| Marion Academy | 2107 N Riley | Indianapolis, IN | 46218 | 317-983-1300 | 225-4174 | 6-12 | Emmitt Carney |
| Marshall Leadership Academy | 2310 Weisser Park Ave | Fort Wayne, IN | 46803-3462 | 260-755-0193 | | K-8 | Tameka Wilson |
| Mays Community Academy | 929 E South St | Mays, IN | 46155 | 765-645-5577 | | K-8 | Nansi Custer |
| Neighbors New Vistas HS | 5391 Central Ave | Portage, IN | 46368 | 219-850-4448 | 850-4445 | 9-12 | Anna Swope |
| New Community S | 1904 Elmwood Ave | Lafayette, IN | 47904-2224 | 765-420-9617 | 420-9672 | K-8 | Misty Ndiritu |
| Nexus Academy of Indianapolis | 6101 N Keystone Ave Ste 302 | Indianapolis, IN | 46220 | 317-252-5919 | 252-5917 | 9-12 | Jamie Brady |
| Options Charter S | 530 W Carmel Dr | Carmel, IN | 46032-2566 | 317-815-2098 | 846-3806 | 9-12 | Michael Hirsch |
| Options Charter S - Noblesville | 9945 Cumberland Pointe Blvd | Noblesville, IN | 46060-4905 | 317-773-8659 | 773-9017 | 9-12 | Michelle Walden |
| Padua Academy | 349 N Warman Ave | Indianapolis, IN | 46222-4079 | 317-636-3739 | 636-3740 | K-8 | Cindy Greer |
| Paramount S of Excellence | 3020 Nowland Ave | Indianapolis, IN | 46201 | 317-775-6660 | 423-0569 | K-8 | Tommy Reddicks |
| Phalen @ Francis Scott Key S | 3920 Baker Dr | Indianapolis, IN | 46235-1619 | 317-226-4103 | 226-3730 | PK-6 | Sheila Burlock |
| Phalen Leadership Academy | 2323 N Illinois St | Indianapolis, IN | 46208 | 317-333-6980 | 924-8383 | K-3 | Kris Walker-Guess |
| Renaissance Academy | 4093 W US Highway 20 | La Porte, IN | 46350-8269 | 219-878-8711 | 311-8321 | PK-8 | Kieran McHugh |
| Rock Creek Community Academy | 11525 Highway 31 | Sellersburg, IN | 47172 | 812-246-9271 | 246-0722 | K-12 | Sara Hauselman |
| Rural Community Academy | 2385 N State Road 63 | Sullivan, IN | 47882-7152 | 812-382-4500 | 382-4055 | K-8 | Susie Pierce |
| Signature S | 610 Main St | Evansville, IN | 47708-1618 | 812-421-1820 | 421-9189 | 9-12 | Jean Hitchcock |
| Smith Academy for Excellence | 725 W Washington Blvd | Fort Wayne, IN | 46802 | 260-579-6939 | 424-3846 | 2-12 | Thomas Smith |
| Southeast Neighborhood S of Excellence | 1601 Barth Ave | Indianapolis, IN | 46203-2743 | 317-423-0204 | 631-4401 | K-8 | Dr. Kristie Sweeney |
| Success Academy | 3408 Ardmore Trl | South Bend, IN | 46628 | 574-288-5333 | | PK-4 | Dean Fecher |
| Tindley Accelerated S | 3960 Meadows Dr | Indianapolis, IN | 46205-3114 | 317-545-1745 | 547-4415 | 9-12 | Marcus Robinson |
| Tindley Collegiate Academy | 4020 Meadows Pkwy | Indianapolis, IN | 46205 | 317-777-7740 | 377-1435 | 5-8 | Kelli Marshall |
| Tindley Genesis Academy | 2540 N Capitol Ave | Indianapolis, IN | 46208 | 317-777-6832 | 547-4323 | K-3 | Todd Hawks |
| Tindley Preparatory Academy | 4010 Sherman Dr | Indianapolis, IN | 46205 | 317-777-6290 | 546-7198 | 5-8 | Patrick Jones |
| Tindley Renaissance Academy | 4020 Sherman Dr | Indianapolis, IN | 46226 | 317-777-7290 | 377-1808 | K-4 | Clarisse Mendoza |
| Tindley Summit Academy | 4002 N Franklin Rd | Indianapolis, IN | 46218 | 317-777-6830 | 534-3566 | K-3 | Shy-Quon Ely |
| 21st Century Charter S | 556 Washington St | Gary, IN | 46402 | 219-886-9339 | 886-9333 | PK-12 | Christopher Evans |
| Veritas Academy | 530 E Ireland Rd | South Bend, IN | 46614-2660 | 574-287-3230 | 287-2643 | K-8 | Germaine Smith |
| Vision Academy | 1751 E Riverside Dr | Indianapolis, IN | 46202 | 317-632-2006 | 662-3792 | K-7 | Ian Yearwood |
| Xavier S of Excellence | 3423 S Michigan St | South Bend, IN | 46614 | 574-231-6600 | 231-6640 | K-8 | Tania Grimes Ed.D. |

## Iowa

| School | Address | City,State | Zip code | Telephone | Fax | Grade | Contact |
|---|---|---|---|---|---|---|---|
| Prescott ES | 1151 White St | Dubuque, IA | 52001-5005 | 563-552-4200 | 552-4201 | PK-5 | Christine McCarron |
| Vista Early College S | 621 Tornado Dr | Storm Lake, IA | 50588-2277 | 712-732-8065 | 732-8068 | 9-12 | Beau Ruleaux |
| West Central Charter HS | PO Box 54 | Maynard, IA | 50655-0054 | 563-637-2283 | 637-2294 | 11-12 | Stuart Fuhs |

## Kansas

| School | Address | City,State | Zip code | Telephone | Fax | Grade | Contact |
|---|---|---|---|---|---|---|---|
| Abilene Virtual S | 213 N Broadway St | Abilene, KS | 67410-2648 | 785-263-2630 | | 6-12 | B. Roth |
| Caney Valley Charter Academy | 601 E Bullpup Blvd | Caney, KS | 67333-2543 | 620-879-9232 | 879-9232 | 10-12 | Ron Oyler |
| Erie HS | 1400 N Main St | Erie, KS | 66733-5006 | 620-244-3287 | 244-3290 | 9-12 | Noah Francis |
| Greeley County JSHS | 400 W Lawrence St | Tribune, KS | 67879-9636 | 620-376-4265 | 376-2465 | 6-12 | Kenneth Huff |
| Hope Street Charter Academy | 1900 SW Hope St | Topeka, KS | 66604 | 785-438-4280 | 271-3684 | 9-12 | Dale Noll |
| Hugoton Learning Academy | 529 S Main St | Hugoton, KS | 67951-2432 | 620-428-6374 | 428-6378 | 7-12 | Jan Kilbourne |
| Insight S of Kansas | 16740 W 175th St | Olathe, KS | 66062 | 913-592-4600 | 664-2796 | K-12 | Heather Appleby |
| Kinsley-Offerle JSHS | 716 Colony Ave | Kinsley, KS | 67547-1155 | 620-659-2126 | 659-2180 | 7-12 | William King |
| Lawrence Virtual HS | 1104 E 1000 Rd | Lawrence, KS | 66047-9409 | 785-832-5620 | 832-5621 | 9-12 | Keith Wilson |
| Lawrence Virtual S | 1104 E 1000 Rd | Lawrence, KS | 66047-9409 | 785-832-5620 | 832-5621 | K-8 | Keith Wilson |
| Service Valley Charter Academy | PO Box 129 | Oswego, KS | 67356-0129 | 620-421-3449 | 421-3640 | K-8 | Ray Huff |
| Smoky Valley Virtual Charter S | 121 S Main St | Lindsborg, KS | 67456 | 785-227-4292 | 227-3610 | K-12 | Cody Whetstone |
| 21st Century Learning Academy | PO Box 7 | Mullinville, KS | 67109 | 620-548-2289 | 548-2389 | 6-12 | Brian Deterding |
| Walton Rural Life ES | PO Box 140 | Walton, KS | 67151-0140 | 620-837-3161 | 837-5669 | K-4 | Jason Chalashtari |
| West Franklin Learning Center | PO Box 407 | Williamsburg, KS | 66095 | 785-746-5766 | | 9-12 | Braden Anshutz |
| Yoder Charter S | PO Box 78 | Yoder, KS | 67585-0078 | 620-465-2605 | 465-2307 | K-8 | Delon Martens |

## Kentucky

| School | Address | City,State | Zip code | Telephone | Fax | Grade | Contact |
|---|---|---|---|---|---|---|---|
| Taylor County Virtual Charter Academy | 300 Ingram Ave | Campbellsville, KY | 42718-1625 | 270-465-4431 | 465-5731 | 5-12 | Dr. Bill Mattingly |

## Louisiana

| School | Address | City,State | Zip code | Telephone | Fax | Grade | Contact |
|---|---|---|---|---|---|---|---|
| Akili Academy of New Orleans | 3811 N Galvez St | New Orleans, LA | 70117 | 504-355-4172 | 355-4176 | K-7 | Allison Lowe |
| Algiers Technology Academy | 6501 Berkley Dr | New Orleans, LA | 70131-5513 | 504-302-7071 | 324-6998 | 9-12 | Nia Mitchell |
| ARISE Academy | 3819 Saint Claude Ave | New Orleans, LA | 70117 | 504-615-6354 | 456-2087 | PK-6 | Rachel Wong |

| School | Address | City,State | Zip code | Telephone | Fax | Grade | Contact |
|---|---|---|---|---|---|---|---|
| Ashe Charter S | 1456 Gardena Dr | New Orleans, LA | 70122 | 504-373-6267 | 896-4003 | K-8 | Ryan Bennett |
| Audubon Charter S | 428 Broadway St | New Orleans, LA | 70118 | 504-324-7100 | 866-1691 | PK-3 | Latoye Brown |
| Audubon Charter S | 1111 Milan St | New Orleans, LA | 70115 | 504-324-7110 | 866-1691 | 4-8 | Latoye Brown |
| Avoyelles Charter S | 201 Longfellow Rd | Mansura, LA | 71350-4292 | 318-240-9991 | 253-4198 | K-12 | Julie Roy |
| Baton Rouge Charter Academy at Mid-City | 1900 N Lobdell Blvd | Baton Rouge, LA | 70806 | 225-663-1057 | 610-1831 | K-8 | Dr. Tiffanye McCoy-Thomas |
| Baton Rouge University Prep ES | 5300 Monarch Ave | Baton Rouge, LA | 70811 | 225-364-9805 | | K-K | Meghan Turner |
| Bayou Community Academy | 800 E 7th St | Thibodaux, LA | 70301 | 985-446-3011 | | PK-8 | Dr. Melanie Becnel |
| Beekman Charter S | 15190 A M Baker Rd | Bastrop, LA | 71220-6408 | 318-281-1743 | 283-5100 | PK-9 | Roy McCoy |
| Behrman S | 715 Opelousas Ave | New Orleans, LA | 70114-2499 | 504-302-7090 | 309-8042 | PK-8 | Rene Lewis-Carter |
| Belle Chase Academy | 100 5th St | Belle Chasse, LA | 70037-1002 | 504-433-5850 | 433-5590 | K-8 | Jane Dye |
| Bricolage Academy | 3368 Esplanade Ave | New Orleans, LA | 70119 | 504-539-4505 | | K-1 | Josh Densen |
| Capdau Charter S | 4621 Canal St | New Orleans, LA | 70119 | 504-872-9257 | 280-2312 | PK-8 | Rulonda Green |
| Capitol HS | 1000 N 23rd St | Baton Rouge, LA | 70802-3398 | 225-239-7506 | 227-2420 | 9-12 | Keisha Netterville |
| Carver Collegiate Academy | 5552 Read Blvd | New Orleans, LA | 70126 | 504-308-3660 | 754-7980 | 9-12 | Jerel Bryant |
| Celerity Crestworth Charter S | 10650 Avenue F | Baton Rouge, LA | 70807-2501 | 225-239-7508 | | 6-8 | Teryn Bryant |
| Celerity Dalton Charter S | 3605 Ontario St | Baton Rouge, LA | 70805 | 225-239-7502 | 357-1171 | PK-5 | Arneisha Brisco |
| Celerity Lanier Charter S | 4705 Lanier Dr | Baton Rouge, LA | 70812-4020 | 225-239-7503 | 663-2950 | PK-5 | Alicia Franklin |
| Clark Prep HS | 1301 N Derbigny St | New Orleans, LA | 70116-2213 | 504-373-6202 | 827-4538 | 9-12 | Reginald Coleman |
| Coghill Accelerated Academy | 4617 Mirabeau Ave | New Orleans, LA | 70126 | 504-373-6237 | 308-3661 | PK-8 | Aisha Jones |
| Cohen College Prep MSHS | 3520 Dryades St | New Orleans, LA | 70115 | 504-335-0400 | 617-7200 | 6-12 | Rahel Wondwossen |
| Community S for Apprenticeship Learning | 1555 Madison Ave | Baton Rouge, LA | 70802-3460 | 225-336-1410 | 336-1414 | 6-8 | LaMont Cole |
| Craig Charter S | 1423 Saint Philip St | New Orleans, LA | 70116 | 504-373-6298 | | PK-8 | Ora Wiley |
| Crescent Leadership Academy | 2701 Lawrence St | New Orleans, LA | 70114 | 504-702-5790 | 948-1804 | 7-12 | Nick Dean |
| Crocker College Prep | 2301 Marengo St | New Orleans, LA | 70115 | 504-335-0404 | 285-9980 | PK-5 | Amanda Aiken |
| D'Arbonne Woods Charter S | 1002 Sterlington Hwy | Farmerville, LA | 71241 | 318-368-8051 | 368-8053 | K-12 | Pam Schooler |
| Delhi Charter S | 6940 Highway 17 | Delhi, LA | 71232-7021 | 318-878-0433 | 878-0434 | K-12 | Brett Raley |
| Dibert S | 4217 Orleans Ave | New Orleans, LA | 70119-4605 | 504-373-6205 | 488-4091 | PK-8 | Diana Archuleta |
| Downsville Charter S | PO Box 8 | Downsville, LA | 71234-0008 | 318-982-5318 | 982-5737 | PK-12 | Tony Cane |
| Easton Charter HS | 3019 Canal St | New Orleans, LA | 70119-6305 | 504-324-7400 | 324-7946 | 9-12 | Alexina Medley |
| Einstein Charter S | 5100 Cannes St | New Orleans, LA | 70129-1203 | 504-324-7450 | 254-4121 | PK-8 | Shawn Toranto |
| Einstein Charter S | 5316 Michoud Blvd | New Orleans, LA | 70129 | 504-503-0110 | | PK-8 | Shawn Toranto |
| Eisenhower ES | 3700 Tall Pines Dr | New Orleans, LA | 70131-8499 | 504-302-7109 | 398-7129 | PK-8 | Deanna Rogers |
| Encore Academy | 4217 Orleans Ave | New Orleans, LA | 70119 | 504-444-2224 | | PK-6 | Terri Smith |
| Esperanza Charter S | 4407 S Carrollton Ave | New Orleans, LA | 70119-6823 | 504-373-6272 | 488-1813 | K-8 | Nicole Saulny |
| Excellence Academy Charter S for Arts | 811 Washington St | Monroe, LA | 71201 | 318-350-6855 | 410-1625 | 6-8 | Shandra Naylor-Smith |
| Fischer Academy | 1801 L B Landry Ave | New Orleans, LA | 70114-6166 | 504-302-7111 | 363-1013 | PK-8 | Dahme Bolden |
| Franklin HS | 2001 Leon C Simon Dr | New Orleans, LA | 70122-3525 | 504-286-2600 | 286-2642 | 9-12 | Dr. Daniel Casey |
| Gentilly Terrace S | 4720 Painters St | New Orleans, LA | 70122-5099 | 504-708-2053 | 284-5847 | PK-8 | Edward Brown |
| Glencoe Charter S | 4491 Highway 83 | Franklin, LA | 70538-7500 | 337-923-6900 | 923-0982 | K-8 | Michael Parrie |
| Green Charter S | 2319 Valence St | New Orleans, LA | 70115-5959 | 504-304-3532 | 896-4147 | K-8 | Ava Lee |
| Habans Charter ES | 3819 Herschel St | New Orleans, LA | 70114-6898 | 504-941-1810 | | PK-6 | Litouri Smith |
| Harney Spirit of Excellence Acad | 2503 Willow St | New Orleans, LA | 70113-3234 | 504-373-6230 | 891-6919 | PK-8 | Eileen Williams |
| Harte Charter S | 5300 Berkley Dr | New Orleans, LA | 70131 | 504-373-6281 | 304-1817 | K-8 | Jamar McKneely |
| Haynes Charter ES | 8600 Elm Grove Garden Dr | Baton Rouge, LA | 70807 | 225-774-1311 | 774-1323 | PK-5 | Diana Haynes |
| Hughes Academy | 3519 Trafalgar St | New Orleans, LA | 70119-2041 | 504-373-6251 | 267-9760 | PK-8 | Franchesca Cain |
| Hynes Charter S | 990 Harrison Ave | New Orleans, LA | 70124-3800 | 504-324-7160 | 488-0213 | PK-8 | Michelle Douglas |
| Inspire Charter Academy | 5454 N Foster Dr | Baton Rouge, LA | 70805 | 225-356-3936 | | K-8 | Lorna Davis |
| International HS | 727 Carondelet St | New Orleans, LA | 70130 | 504-613-5703 | 566-1142 | 9-12 | Sean Wilson |
| International S of Louisiana | 1400 Camp St | New Orleans, LA | 70130-4208 | 504-654-1088 | 654-1086 | K-8 | Melanie Tennyson |
| International S of Louisiana | 8101 Simon St | Metairie, LA | 70003 | 504-934-4875 | 754-7875 | K-8 | Melanie Tennyson |
| Jeff Community S | PO Box 19227 | New Orleans, LA | 70179 | 504-373-6258 | 308-3620 | PK-5 | Patricia Perkins |
| Jefferson Chamber Foundation Academy | 475 Manhattan Blvd | Harvey, LA | 70058-4441 | 504-410-3121 | 410-3120 | 9-12 | Millie Harris |
| Jefferson RISE Charter S | 501B Lapalco Blvd | Gretna, LA | 70056 | 504-410-5905 | | 6-6 | Kathleen Sullivan |
| Karr Charter HS | 3332 Huntlee Dr | New Orleans, LA | 70131 | 504-302-7135 | 301-2721 | 9-12 | Harold Clay |
| Kenilworth Science & Technology Charter | 7600 Boone Ave | Baton Rouge, LA | 70808 | 225-766-8111 | 767-9061 | 6-8 | Hasan Suzuk |
| Kenner Discovery Health Sciences Academy | 2504 Maine Ave | Metairie, LA | 70003 | 504-233-4720 | | PK-8 | Patty Glaser Ph.D. |
| King Charter S for Science & Tech | 1617 Caffin Ave | New Orleans, LA | 70117-2909 | 504-940-2243 | 940-2276 | PK-12 | Dr. Doris Hicks Ed.D. |
| KIPP: East Community PS | 5500 Piety Dr | New Orleans, LA | 70126 | 504-301-2964 | | K-4 | Jennifer Carey |
| KIPP Believe College Prep S | 9330 Forshey St | New Orleans, LA | 70118 | 504-304-8857 | 304-8862 | 5-8 | Luke Naegele |
| KIPP Believe PS | 421 Burdette St | New Orleans, LA | 70118 | 504-266-2050 | 264-9363 | K-4 | Sarah Beth Greenberg |
| KIPP Central City Academy | 2514 3rd St | New Orleans, LA | 70113 | 504-609-2283 | 708-5334 | 5-8 | Alex Jarrell |
| KIPP Central City PS | 2625 Thalia St | New Orleans, LA | 70113 | 504-373-6290 | 302-9737 | K-4 | Korbin Johnson |
| KIPP McDonogh 15 MS | 5500 Piety Dr | New Orleans, LA | 70126-2308 | 504-609-2280 | 264-5598 | 5-8 | Deanna Reddick |
| KIPP McDonogh 15 PS | 721 Saint Philip St | New Orleans, LA | 70116-2795 | 504-592-8520 | 592-8515 | PK-4 | Mark Burton |
| KIPP New Orleans Leadership Academy | 2300 Saint Claude Ave | New Orleans, LA | 70117 | 504-373-6256 | 322-3924 | K-7 | Jonny Bartlett |
| KIPP Renaissance HS | 5316 Michoud Blvd | New Orleans, LA | 70129 | 504-373-6255 | 322-3924 | 9-12 | Joey LaRoche |
| Lafayette Academy | 2727 S Carrollton Ave | New Orleans, LA | 70118-4387 | 504-861-8370 | 861-8369 | PK-8 | Monica Boudouin |
| Lake Area New Tech Early College HS | 6026 Paris Ave | New Orleans, LA | 70122-2726 | 504-267-8811 | 267-8833 | 9-12 | Darren Lewis |
| Lake Forest Charter ES | 12000 Hayne Blvd | New Orleans, LA | 70128-1127 | 504-826-7140 | 248-7020 | PK-8 | Mardele Early |
| Landry - O.P. Walker HS | 1200 L B Landry Ave | New Orleans, LA | 70114 | 504-302-7170 | 309-2960 | 9-12 | Mary Laurie |
| Laureate Academy Charter S | 3400 6th St | Harvey, LA | 70058 | 504-503-0170 | | K-1 | Claire Heckerman |
| Linwood Public Charter S | 401 W 70th St | Shreveport, LA | 71106 | 318-865-4800 | 865-0542 | 6-8 | Vickie Carroll |
| Louisiana Connections Academy | 4664 Jamestown Ave | Baton Rouge, LA | 70808 | 225-372-8389 | 448-2798 | K-12 | Glenda Jones |
| Louisiana Key Academy | 3172 Government St | Baton Rouge, LA | 70806 | 225-298-1223 | | 1-3 | Evelyn Gauthreaux |
| Louisiana S for Agricultural Sciences | 5303 Highway 115 | Bunkie, LA | 71322-4301 | 318-346-8029 | 346-4479 | 8-12 | Blaine Dauzat |
| Louisiana Virtual Charter Academy | 4962 Florida Blvd | Baton Rouge, LA | 70806 | 877-490-3596 | | K-12 | |
| Lusher Charter Lower S | 7315 Willow St | New Orleans, LA | 70118-5232 | 504-862-5110 | 866-4292 | K-5 | Kathleen Riedlinger |
| Lusher Charter MSHS | 5624 Freret St | New Orleans, LA | 70115-6598 | 504-304-3960 | 861-1839 | 6-12 | Kathleen Riedlinger |
| Lycee Francais de la Nouvelle Orleans | 5951 Patton St | New Orleans, LA | 70115 | 504-620-5500 | 875-2441 | K-4 | Keith Bartlett |
| Madison Preparatory Academy | 1555 Madison Ave | Baton Rouge, LA | 70802 | 225-636-5863 | 336-1414 | 9-12 | Alisa Welsh |
| MAX Charter S | PO Box 2072 | Thibodaux, LA | 70310 | 985-227-9500 | 227-9515 | 1-8 | Linda Musson Ed.D. |
| McDonogh 32 S | 800 De Armas St | New Orleans, LA | 70114-4414 | 504-302-7144 | 363-1058 | PK-8 | Andre Duvoisin |
| McDonogh 42 S | 1651 N Tonti St | New Orleans, LA | 70119 | 504-942-3660 | 942-0731 | PK-8 | Annafaye Caminita |
| McDonogh City Park Academy | 2733 Esplanade Ave | New Orleans, LA | 70119-3332 | 504-940-1740 | 940-1780 | K-8 | Christine Mitchell |
| Mentorship Academy | 339 Florida St | Baton Rouge, LA | 70801 | 225-346-5180 | | 9-12 | Robert Webb |
| Moton Charter S | 4040 Eagle St | New Orleans, LA | 70118 | 504-245-4400 | 248-7300 | PK-7 | Paulette Bruno |
| Nelson Charter S | 3121 Saint Bernard Ave | New Orleans, LA | 70119-1916 | 504-943-1311 | 943-9824 | PK-8 | Chancey Nash Ed.D. |
| NET Charter HS | 1614 Oretha Castle Haley Bl | New Orleans, LA | 70113 | 504-267-9060 | 267-9059 | 9-12 | Elizabeth Ostberg |
| New Orleans Charter Science and Math HS | 5625 Loyola Ave | New Orleans, LA | 70115-5014 | 504-324-7061 | 309-4178 | 9-12 | Chana Benenson |
| New Orleans Military & Maritime Academy | 425 OBannon St | New Orleans, LA | 70114 | 504-227-3810 | 875-4326 | 9-12 | Cecilia Garcia |
| New Vision Learning Academy | 507 Swayze St | Monroe, LA | 71201-8130 | 318-338-9995 | 338-9987 | PK-12 | Rev. Andrew Mansfield |
| Osborne ES | 6701 Curran Blvd | New Orleans, LA | 70126 | 504-400-0614 | 711-0754 | PK-6 | Traci-Amanda Washington |
| Plessy Community S | 2021 Pauger St | New Orleans, LA | 70116 | 504-503-0055 | | PK-2 | Joan Reilly |
| ReNEW Aaron ES | 10200 Curran Blvd | New Orleans, LA | 70127 | 504-717-6543 | 644-4183 | PK-8 | Heather Gilchrist |
| ReNEW Accelerated HS | 3649 Laurel St | New Orleans, LA | 70115 | 504-267-3882 | | 9-12 | Vasy McCoy |
| ReNEW Cultural Arts Academy | 3128 Constance St | New Orleans, LA | 70115-2337 | 504-367-3307 | 315-2672 | PK-8 | Ron Gubitz |
| ReNEW Schaumburg ES | 9501 Grant St | New Orleans, LA | 70127-4256 | 504-304-1532 | | PK-8 | Laci Blondell |
| ReNEW SciTech Academy | 820 Jackson Ave | New Orleans, LA | 70130 | 504-267-4574 | 267-0572 | PK-8 | Tim Hearin |
| Sci Academy | 5552 Read Blvd | New Orleans, LA | 70127 | 504-373-6264 | 324-0171 | 9-12 | Rhonda Dale-Hart |
| Singleton Charter S | 2220 Oretha C Haley Blvd | New Orleans, LA | 70113-1508 | 504-568-3466 | 569-3378 | PK-8 | Debra J. Williams |
| Success Preparatory Academy | 2011 Bienville St | New Orleans, LA | 70112 | 504-909-6275 | 571-6317 | K-7 | Niloy Gangopadhyay |
| Tubman ES | 2013 General Meyer Ave | New Orleans, LA | 70114-1533 | 504-227-3800 | 227-3801 | PK-8 | Julie Lause |
| Virtual Academy of Lafourche | 639 Harrison St | Thibodaux, LA | 70301-2739 | 985-446-2877 | 446-2993 | K-12 | Julie Bourgeois |
| Williams ES | 11755 Dwyer Rd | New Orleans, LA | 70128-3454 | 504-373-6288 | 245-2796 | PK-8 | Kelly Batiste |
| Williams ES | 3127 Martin Luther King Jr | New Orleans, LA | 70125 | 504-522-0100 | 910-1045 | K-5 | Krystal Hardy |
| Wilson Charter S | 3617 General Pershing St | New Orleans, LA | 70125-4530 | 504-373-6274 | 308-3615 | PK-8 | Logan Crowe |
| Wright Charter S | 1426 Napoleon Ave | New Orleans, LA | 70115-3958 | 504-304-3916 | 896-4095 | 6-12 | Sharon Clark |
| Young Audiences Charter S | 1407 Virgil St | Gretna, LA | 70053 | 504-304-6332 | 267-4667 | PK-5 | Brandon House |
| **Maine** | | | | | | | |
| Cornville Regional Charter S | 1192 W Ridge Rd | Cornville, ME | 04976-6214 | 207-474-3944 | 474-0665 | K-6 | Travis Works |
| Maine Academy of Natural Sciences | PO Box 159 | Hinckley, ME | 04944-0159 | 207-238-4200 | 238-4207 | 9-12 | Troy Frost |
| **Maryland** | | | | | | | |
| Academy for College & Career Exploration | 1300 W 36th St | Baltimore, MD | 21211-2303 | 410-396-7607 | 396-0432 | 6-12 | Peter Jurovich |
| AFYA Charter MS | 2800 Brendan Ave | Baltimore, MD | 21213-1213 | 410-485-2102 | | 6-8 | Katie Marts |
| Baltimore Collegiate S for Boys | 1101 Winston Ave | Baltimore, MD | 21212 | 443-929-1899 | | 4-6 | John Snowdy |
| Baltimore International Academy | 4410 Frankford Ave | Baltimore, MD | 21206 | 410-426-3650 | 426-3651 | K-8 | John Enkiri |
| Baltimore IT Academy | 900 Woodbourne Ave | Baltimore, MD | 21212 | 443-642-2067 | | 6-8 | Sandy Mason |
| Baltimore Leadership S for Young Women | 128 W Franklin St | Baltimore, MD | 21201 | 443-642-2048 | 338-2684 | 6-12 | Chevonne Hall |
| Baltimore Montessori Charter S | 1600 Guilford Ave | Baltimore, MD | 21202-2823 | 410-528-5393 | 528-8126 | PK-8 | Allison Shecter |
| Banneker Blake Academy Arts & Sciences | PO Box 11311 | Baltimore, MD | 21239 | 443-499-8007 | | 6-8 | Patrick McDonald |
| Carroll Creek Montessori Charter S | 7215 Corporate Ct | Frederick, MD | 21703 | 301-663-7970 | 663-6107 | PK-5 | Marilyn Horan |
| Chesapeake Charter S | 20945 Great Mills Rd | Lexington Park, MD | 20653-4370 | 301-863-9585 | 863-9586 | K-8 | Angela Funya |
| Chesapeake Math & IT Academy | 6100 Frost Pl | Laurel, MD | 20707 | 301-350-6052 | 350-6029 | 6-12 | Mehmet Gunes |

| School | Address | City,State | Zip code | Telephone | Fax | Grade | Contact |
|---|---|---|---|---|---|---|---|
| Chesapeake Math & IT Academy South | 9822 Fallard Ct | Upper Marlboro, MD | 20772 | 240-573-7250 | 823-9326 | 6-12 | Ali Gurbuz |
| Chesapeake Math & IT ES | 6151 Chevy Chase Dr | Laurel, MD | 20707 | 240-573-7240 | 776-2322 | K-5 | Treesa Elam-Respass |
| Chesapeake Science Point Charter S | 7321 Parkway Dr | Hanover, MD | 21076-1159 | 410-757-5277 | 757-5280 | 6-12 | Mehmet Gurbuz |
| City Neighbors Charter S | 4301 Raspe Ave | Baltimore, MD | 21206-1913 | 410-325-2627 | 325-2489 | K-8 | Nicholas Brown |
| City Neighbors Hamilton S | 5609 Sefton Ave | Baltimore, MD | 21214-2300 | 443-642-2052 | 426-0190 | K-8 | Obidimma Okobi |
| City Neighbors HS | 5609 Sefton Ave | Baltimore, MD | 21214 | 443-642-2119 | | 9-12 | Danique Dolly |
| City Springs ES | 100 S Caroline St | Baltimore, MD | 21231-1798 | 410-396-9165 | 396-9113 | PK-8 | Rhonda Richetta |
| College Park Academy | 7501 Adelphi Rd | Hyattsville, MD | 20783 | 240-696-3206 | 422-0510 | 6-9 | Bernadette Brewster |
| Collington Square ES | 1409 N Collington Ave | Baltimore, MD | 21213-3418 | 410-396-9198 | 396-8632 | PK-8 | Melvin Holmes |
| ConneXions: A Community Based Arts S | 2801 N Dukeland St | Baltimore, MD | 21216 | 410-984-1418 | 669-4418 | 6-12 | Kia Harper |
| Coppin Academy | 2500 W North Ave | Baltimore, MD | 21216-3633 | 410-951-2602 | 951-2610 | 9-12 | Aisha Almond |
| Creative City Charter S | 2810 Shirley Ave | Baltimore, MD | 21215 | 443-642-3600 | | K-4 | Traci Mathena |
| Crossroads S | 1601 E Lombard St | Baltimore, MD | 21231 | 443-984-2737 | | 6-8 | Matthew Ebert |
| Empowerment Academy | 851 Braddish Ave | Baltimore, MD | 21216-4723 | 443-984-2381 | 362-2454 | PK-8 | Marie Parfait-Davis |
| Excel Academy | 7910 Scott Rd | Landover, MD | 20785 | 301-925-2320 | | K-8 | Diane Kanu |
| Frederick Classical Charter S | 8455 Spires Way Ste CC | Frederick, MD | 21701 | 240-236-1200 | | K-7 | Erica Cummins |
| Green S | 2851 Kentucky Ave | Baltimore, MD | 21213-1215 | 410-488-5312 | 488-5314 | K-5 | Kate Primm |
| Hampstead Hill Academy | 500 S Linwood Ave | Baltimore, MD | 21224-3800 | 410-396-9146 | 396-3637 | PK-8 | Matthew Hornbeck |
| Imagine Andrews Charter S | 4701 San Antonio Blvd | Andrews AFB, MD | 20762 | 301-350-6002 | 599-5620 | K-8 | H. Douglas Rice |
| Imagine - Foundations at Leeland | 14111 Oak Grove Rd | Upper Marlboro, MD | 20774 | 301-383-1899 | 218-1454 | K-8 | Lance Pace |
| Imagine Foundations at Morningside | 6900 Ames St | Morningside, MD | 20746-3504 | 301-817-0544 | 817-0956 | K-6 | Dr. Peter Thompson |
| Imagine - Lincoln Public Charter S | 4207 Norcross St | Temple Hills, MD | 20748 | 301-808-5600 | 808-5611 | K-8 | Danielle Goddard |
| Independence S Local I HS | 1250 W 36th St | Baltimore, MD | 21211-2301 | 410-642-2504 | 467-1091 | 9-12 | Dimitric Roseboro |
| Jackson Charter S | 900 Woodbourne Ave | Baltimore, MD | 21216 | 443-320-9499 | | 5-8 | Damia Thomas |
| Jemison STEM Academy West | 2000 Edgewood St | Baltimore, MD | 21216 | 443-642-2110 | 984-2774 | 6-12 | Audrey Freeman |
| KIPP Harmony Academy | 4701 Greenspring Ave | Baltimore, MD | 21209 | 443-642-2027 | | K-8 | Natalia Walter |
| Maryland Acad of Technology & Health Sci | 2801 N Dukeland St | Baltimore, MD | 21216 | 410-545-0955 | 396-0338 | 6-12 | Charles Spain |
| Midtown Academy | 1398 W Mount Royal Ave | Baltimore, MD | 21217-4134 | 410-225-3257 | 225-3514 | K-8 | Suzanne Penny |
| Monarch Academy | 2525 Kirk Ave | Baltimore, MD | 21218 | 443-642-2402 | 254-0201 | K-8 | Cera Rebello |
| Monarch Academy Charter S | 6730 Baymeadow Dr | Glen Burnie, MD | 21060-6412 | 410-760-2072 | 760-1321 | K-8 | Maurine Larkin |
| Monarch Global Academy Contract S | 430 Brock Bridge Rd | Laurel, MD | 20724 | 301-886-8648 | | K-8 | Donna O'Shea |
| Monocacy Valley Montessori S | 217 Dill Ave | Frederick, MD | 21701-4905 | 301-668-5013 | 668-5015 | K-8 | Nancy Radkiewicz |
| New Era Academy | 2700 Seamon Ave | Baltimore, MD | 21225-1117 | 443-984-2415 | 355-1130 | 6-12 | Sandra Simmons |
| Northwood Appold Community Academy | 4417 Loch Raven Blvd | Baltimore, MD | 21218-1554 | 410-323-9546 | 323-1836 | K-5 | |
| Patterson Park ES | 27 N Lakewood Ave | Baltimore, MD | 21224-1155 | 410-558-1230 | 558-1003 | PK-8 | Dr. Charles Kramer |
| REACH Partnership S | 2801 Saint Lo Dr | Baltimore, MD | 21213 | 443-642-2291 | | 8-12 | Michael Frederick |
| Renaissance Academy | 1301 McCulloh St | Baltimore, MD | 21217-3044 | 443-984-3164 | 947-2968 | 9-12 | Nikkia Rowe |
| Roots and Branches S | 1807 Harlem Ave | Baltimore, MD | 21217-1411 | 443-642-2320 | | K-5 | Anne Rossi |
| Rosemont ES | 2777 Presstman St | Baltimore, MD | 21216-4025 | 410-396-0574 | 545-3298 | PK-8 | Dwayne Wheeler |
| Southwest Baltimore Charter S | 1300 Herkimer St | Baltimore, MD | 21223 | 443-984-3385 | 685-3492 | K-8 | Brandon Pinkney |
| Tunbridge ES | 5504 York Rd | Baltimore, MD | 21212 | 410-323-8692 | | PK-8 | Sheila Adams |
| Turning Point Academy | 7800 Good Luck Rd | Lanham Seabrook, MD | 20706-3505 | 301-552-0164 | 552-7307 | K-8 | Rhonda Clomax |
| Wolfe Street Academy | 245 S Wolfe St | Baltimore, MD | 21231-2622 | 410-396-9140 | 396-8064 | PK-5 | Mark Gaither |

## Massachusetts

| School | Address | City,State | Zip code | Telephone | Fax | Grade | Contact |
|---|---|---|---|---|---|---|---|
| Academy of Pacific Rim Charter S | 1 Westinghouse Plz | Hyde Park, MA | 02136-2075 | 617-361-0050 | 361-0045 | 5-12 | Chris Collins |
| Advanced Math & Science Academy | 201 Forest St | Marlborough, MA | 01752-3012 | 508-597-2400 | 597-2499 | 6-12 | Dr. Michael Curry |
| Alma del Mar Charter S | 26 Madeira Ave | New Bedford, MA | 02746 | 774-206-6827 | 206-6833 | K-5 | Emily Stainer |
| Amesbury: Amesbury Innovation HS | 71 Friend St | Amesbury, MA | 01913 | 978-388-8037 | 388-8073 | 9-12 | Eryn Maguire |
| Argosy Collegiate Charter S | 263 Hamlet St | Fall River, MA | 02724 | 508-567-4725 | | 6-12 | Kristen Pavao |
| Atlantis Charter S | 37 Park St | Fall River, MA | 02721-1712 | 508-672-3537 | 672-2474 | K-8 | Robert Beatty |
| Banneker Charter Public S | 21 Notre Dame Ave | Cambridge, MA | 02140-2505 | 617-497-7771 | 497-4223 | K-6 | Sherley Bretous-Carre |
| Barnstable Comm Horace Mann Charter S | 165 Bearses Way | Hyannis, MA | 02601 | 508-790-6485 | 790-6432 | K-3 | Kathleen Podesky |
| Baystate Academy | 2001 Roosevelt Ave | Springfield, MA | 01104 | 413-366-5100 | 366-5101 | 6-12 | Tim Sneed |
| Bentley Academy Charter S | 25 Memorial Dr | Salem, MA | 01970-5295 | 978-740-1260 | 740-1164 | K-5 | Justin Vernon |
| Berkshire Arts & Technology Charter S | PO Box 267 | Adams, MA | 01220-0267 | 413-743-7311 | 743-7327 | 6-12 | April West |
| Boston Collegiate Charter S | 11 Mayhew St | Dorchester, MA | 02125-1628 | 617-265-1172 | 265-1176 | 5-12 | Sarah Morland |
| Boston Day & Evening Academy | 20 Kearsarge Ave | Roxbury, MA | 02119-2318 | 617-635-6789 | 635-6380 | 9-12 | Alison Hramiec |
| Boston Green Academy | 20 Warren St | Brighton, MA | 02135 | 617-635-9860 | 635-9858 | 9-12 | Matthew Holzer |
| Boston Preparatory Charter S | 1286 Hyde Park Ave | Hyde Park, MA | 02136-2714 | 617-333-6688 | 333-6689 | 6-12 | Sharon Liszanckie |
| Boston Renaissance Charter S | 1415 Hyde Park Ave | Hyde Park, MA | 02136 | 617-357-0900 | 357-0949 | K-6 | Roger Harris |
| Bridge Boston Charter S | 2 McLellan St | Dorchester, MA | 02121 | 857-229-1601 | 674-0861 | PK-3 | Jennifer Daly |
| Brooke East Boston Charter S | 94 Horace St | East Boston, MA | 02128 | 617-268-1006 | 569-6417 | K-8 | Mary C. Cole |
| Brooke Mattapan Charter S | 150 American Legion Hwy | Dorchester, MA | 02124 | 617-268-1006 | 474-4612 | K-8 | Kathryn Megrian |
| Brooke Roslindale Charter S | 190 Cummins Hwy | Roslindale, MA | 02131-3722 | 617-325-7977 | 325-2260 | K-8 | Meghan Parquette |
| Cape Cod Lighthouse Charter S | 195 Route 137 | Harwich, MA | 02645 | 774-408-7994 | 237-9041 | 6-8 | Paul Niles |
| City on a Hill Charter S | 58 Circuit St | Roxbury, MA | 02119-1925 | 617-445-1515 | 445-9153 | 9-12 | Cristin Berry |
| City on a Hill Charter S | 777 Church St | New Bedford, MA | 02745 | 508-985-6402 | | 9-12 | Kimberly Wall |
| City on a Hill Charter S | 2181 Washington St | Roxbury, MA | 02119 | 617-516-5888 | 533-9420 | 9-12 | Sonya Pratt |
| Codman Academy | 637 Washington St | Dorchester, MA | 02124-3510 | 617-287-0700 | 287-9064 | K-12 | Thabiti Brown |
| Community Charter S of Cambridge | 245 Bent St | Cambridge, MA | 02141-2001 | 617-354-0047 | 354-3624 | 6-12 | Caleb Hurst-Hiller |
| Community Day Arlington ES | 150 Arlington St | Lawrence, MA | 01841 | 978-722-8311 | 722-8514 | PK-4 | Brent Merten |
| Community Day Charter S | 190 Hampshire St | Lawrence, MA | 01840-1251 | 978-722-2583 | 682-1013 | PK-8 | Mary Chance |
| Community Day Charter S Gateway | 9 Ballard Way | Lawrence, MA | 01843 | 978-688-4283 | 688-4370 | K-8 | |
| Community Day S R. Kingman Webster | 50 Pleasant St | Lawrence, MA | 01841 | 978-686-9327 | | K-8 | |
| Conservatory Lab Charter S | 2120 Dorchester Ave | Dorchester, MA | 02124 | 617-254-8904 | 254-8909 | PK-8 | Diana Lam |
| Davis Leadership Academy Charter S | 23 Leonard St | Dorchester, MA | 02122-2718 | 617-474-7950 | 474-7957 | 6-8 | Karmala Sherwood |
| Dorchester Collegiate Academy | 131 Hancock St | Dorchester, MA | 02125-2136 | 617-379-3029 | | 4-8 | Robert Flynn |
| Dudley Street Neighborhood S | 6 Shirley St | Roxbury, MA | 02119 | 617-227-8055 | | K-5 | Dawn Lewis |
| Excel Academy Charter S | 1150 Saratoga St | East Boston, MA | 02128-1228 | 617-561-1371 | 963-7162 | 5-8 | Nina Cronan |
| Excel Academy - Chelsea | 180 2nd St | Chelsea, MA | 02150 | 617-336-9970 | 516-1676 | 5-8 | Katherine Pereira |
| Excel Academy - East Boston | 58 Moore St | East Boston, MA | 02128 | 617-874-4080 | 516-1603 | 5-8 | Jocelyn Foulke |
| Foster Charter S | 10 New Bond St | Worcester, MA | 01606-2699 | 508-854-8400 | 854-8484 | K-12 | Brian Haas |
| Four Rivers Charter S | 248 Colrain Rd | Greenfield, MA | 01301-9701 | 413-775-4577 | 775-4578 | 7-12 | Peter Garbus |
| Foxborough Regional Charter S | 131 Central St | Foxboro, MA | 02035-2458 | 508-543-2508 | 543-7982 | K-12 | Ronald Griffin |
| Franklin Classical Charter S | 201 Main St | Franklin, MA | 02038-1933 | 508-541-3434 | 541-5396 | K-8 | Heather Zolnowski |
| Freire Social Justice Charter S | PO Box 1009 | Holyoke, MA | 01041 | 413-536-3201 | 536-3206 | 9-12 | Ljuba Marsh |
| Global Learning Charter S | 190 Ashley Blvd | New Bedford, MA | 02746-1752 | 508-991-4105 | 991-4110 | 5-12 | Dr. Stephen Furtado |
| Hampden Charter S of Science | 20 Johnson Rd | Chicopee, MA | 01022-1065 | 413-593-9090 | 294-2648 | 6-12 | Harun Celik |
| Hilltown Cooperative Charter S | 1 Industrial Pkwy | Easthampton, MA | 01027 | 413-529-7178 | 527-1530 | K-8 | Daniel Klatz |
| Hill View Montessori Charter S | 75 Foundation Ave | Haverhill, MA | 01835-6926 | 978-521-2616 | 521-2656 | K-8 | Debra Diggins |
| Holyoke Community Charter S | 2200 Northampton St | Holyoke, MA | 01040-3430 | 413-533-0111 | 536-5444 | K-8 | Sonia Pope |
| Innovation Academy Charter S | 72 Tyng Rd | Tyngsboro, MA | 01879-2044 | 978-649-0432 | 649-6337 | 5-12 | Gregory Orpen |
| Kennedy Academy for Health Careers | 360 Huntington Ave | Boston, MA | 02115 | 617-373-8576 | 373-7850 | 9-12 | Dr. Caren Walker-Gregory |
| King Charter S of Excellence | 285 Dorset St | Springfield, MA | 01108 | 413-214-7806 | 214-7838 | K-5 | Juraye Pierson |
| KIPP Academy Boston Charter S | 384 Warren St | Roxbury, MA | 02119 | 617-238-7300 | 652-7461 | 5-8 | Nikki Barnes |
| KIPP Academy Lynn Charter S | 90 High Rock St | Lynn, MA | 01902 | 781-598-1609 | 598-1639 | 5-12 | Drea DeAngelo |
| Lawrence Family Development Charter S | 34 West St | Lawrence, MA | 01841-3426 | 978-689-9863 | 689-8133 | K-8 | Ralph Carrero |
| Lowell Collegiate Charter S | 25 Father John Sarantos Way | Lowell, MA | 01854 | 978-458-1399 | 458-1366 | K-5 | Frederick Randall |
| Lowell Community Charter S | 206 Jackson St | Lowell, MA | 01852-2106 | 978-323-0800 | 323-4600 | K-7 | Kathy Egmont |
| Lowell Middlesex Academy Charter S | 67 Middle St | Lowell, MA | 01852-1868 | 978-656-3165 | 459-0456 | 9-12 | Margaret McDevitt |
| Marblehead Community Charter S | 17 Lime St | Marblehead, MA | 01945-2530 | 781-631-0777 | 631-0500 | 4-8 | Helena Cullen-Hamzeh |
| Martha's Vineyard Charter S | PO Box 1150 | West Tisbury, MA | 02575-1150 | 508-693-9900 | 696-9008 | K-12 | Robert Moore |
| MATCH Charter S | 1001 Commonwealth Ave | Boston, MA | 02215-1308 | 617-232-0300 | 232-2838 | K-12 | Hannah Larkin |
| McAuliffe Regional Charter S | 139 Newbury St Ste 1 | Framingham, MA | 01701 | 508-879-9000 | 879-1066 | 6-8 | Kristin Harrison |
| Mystic Valley Regional Charter S | 770 Salem St | Malden, MA | 02148-4415 | 781-388-0222 | 321-5688 | K-12 | Martin Trice |
| Neighborhood House Charter S | 21 Queen St | Dorchester, MA | 02122-2509 | 617-825-0703 | 825-1829 | PK-8 | Kate Scott |
| Parker Charter Essential S | 49 Antietam St | Ayer, MA | 01434-5230 | 978-772-3293 | 772-3295 | 7-12 | Todd Sumner |
| Phoenix Academy | 15 Union St | Lawrence, MA | 01840 | 978-722-8410 | 686-3613 | 9-12 | Sarah Caney |
| Phoenix Charter Academy | 59 Nichols St | Chelsea, MA | 02150-1225 | 617-889-3100 | 889-3144 | 9-12 | Sarah Miller |
| Phoenix Charter Academy Springfield | 1 Federal St Building 104 | Springfield, MA | 01109 | 413-233-4412 | | 9-12 | Mickey Buhl |
| Pioneer Charter S of Science | 51 Summer St | Everett, MA | 02149-3741 | 617-389-7277 | 389-7278 | 7-12 | Sanela Jonuz |
| Pioneer Charter S of Science II | 97 Main St | Saugus, MA | 01906 | 781-666-3907 | 666-3910 | 7-10 | Shayne Turkolu |
| Pioneer Valley Chinese Immrsn Charter S | 317 Russell St | Hadley, MA | 01035 | 413-582-7040 | 582-7068 | K-12 | Kathleen Wang |
| Pioneer Valley Performing Arts Charter S | 15 Mulligan Dr | South Hadley, MA | 01075-7511 | 413-552-1580 | 552-1594 | 7-12 | Scott Goldman |
| Prospect Hill Academy Charter S | 50 Essex St | Cambridge, MA | 02139 | 617-284-7800 | 284-7980 | K-12 | Angela Allen Ph.D. |
| Rising Tide Charter S | 6 Resnik Rd | Plymouth, MA | 02360-4873 | 508-747-2620 | 830-9441 | 5-12 | Jill Crafts |
| River Valley Charter S | 2 Perry Way | Newburyport, MA | 01950-4001 | 978-465-0065 | 465-0119 | K-8 | Andrew Willemsen |
| Roxbury Prep HS | 86 Wachusett St | Jamaica Plain, MA | 02130 | 617-858-2288 | | 9-12 | Shradha Patel |
| Roxbury Prep Mission Hill Campus | 120 Fisher Ave | Roxbury, MA | 02120-3320 | 617-566-2361 | 566-2373 | 5-8 | Ryan Kelly |
| Roxbury Prep S Dorchester Campus | 206 Magnolia St | Dorchester, MA | 02121 | 617-858-2300 | 275-5760 | 5-8 | Dan Cosgrove |
| Roxbury Prep S Lucy Stone Campus | 22 Regina Rd | Dorchester, MA | 02124 | 617-979-0115 | 822-7527 | 5-8 | Amy Zaffuto |
| SABIS International Charter S | 160 Joan St | Springfield, MA | 01129-1530 | 413-783-2600 | 783-2555 | K-12 | Karen Reuter |
| Salem Academy Charter S | 45 Congress St | Salem, MA | 01970-5579 | 978-744-2105 | 744-7246 | 6-12 | Stephanie Callahan |
| Salem Community Charter S | 1 Museum Pl | Salem, MA | 01970 | 978-825-3470 | 825-3475 | 9-12 | Jessica Yurwitz |
| Seven Hills Charter S | 51 Gage St | Worcester, MA | 01605-3014 | 508-799-7500 | 713-0956 | K-8 | Michael Barth |

| School | Address | City,State | Zip code | Telephone | Fax | Grade | Contact |
|---|---|---|---|---|---|---|---|
| Silver Hill Horace Mann Charter S | 675 Washington St | Haverhill, MA | 01832-4500 | 978-374-3448 | 374-3461 | K-5 | Margaret Shepherd |
| Sizer S | 500 Rindge Rd | Fitchburg, MA | 01420 | 978-345-2701 | 345-9127 | 7-12 | David Perrigo |
| South Shore Charter S | 100 Longwater Cir | Norwell, MA | 02061-1650 | 781-982-4202 | 982-4201 | K-12 | Alicia Savage |
| Springfield Prep Charter S | 370 Pine St | Springfield, MA | 01105 | 413-231-2722 | 215-0004 | K-1 | Bill Spirer |
| Sturgis Charter Public S | 427 Main St | Hyannis, MA | 02601-3905 | 508-778-1782 | 771-6785 | 9-12 | Eric Hieser |
| UP Academy | 215 Dorchester St | South Boston, MA | 02127 | 617-635-8819 | 635-8820 | 6-8 | Katy Buckland |
| UP Academy | 60 Allen St | Lawrence, MA | 01840 | 978-722-8159 | 722-8533 | 6-8 | Komal Bhasin |
| UP Academy Dorchester | 35 Westville St | Dorchester, MA | 02124 | 617-635-8810 | 635-8815 | PK-8 | Lana Ewing |
| UP Academy Holland | 85 Olney St | Dorchester, MA | 02121-3535 | 617-635-8832 | 220-3023 | PK-5 | Jabari Peddie |
| UP Academy Oliver MS | 233 Haverhill St | Lawrence, MA | 01840 | 978-242-7446 | 722-8527 | 6-8 | Dr. Katy Abdelahad |
| Veritas Preparatory Charter S | 370 Pine St | Springfield, MA | 01105 | 413-539-0055 | | 5-8 | Rachel Romano |
| **Michigan** | | | | | | | |
| Abney Academy - ES | 1435 Fulton St E | Grand Rapids, MI | 49503-3853 | 616-454-5541 | 454-5598 | K-5 | Damon Pitt |
| Abney Academy - MS | 256 Alger St SE | Grand Rapids, MI | 49507 | 616-301-2810 | 301-2814 | 6-8 | Damon Pitt |
| Academic and Career Education Academy | 884 E Isabella Rd | Midland, MI | 48640-8326 | 989-631-5202 | 631-4541 | 9-12 | Michelle Zielinski |
| Academy of Business and Technology | 19625 Wood St | Melvindale, MI | 48122-2201 | 313-382-3422 | 382-3906 | 6-12 | Delores Jones-Bell |
| Academy of Business and Technology ES | 5277 Calhoun St | Dearborn, MI | 48126-3203 | 313-581-2223 | 581-2247 | K-5 | Dr. Paul Merritt |
| Academy of International Studies | 3056 Hanley St | Hamtramck, MI | 48212 | 313-873-9900 | 873-9201 | K-8 | Dawn Lynk-Jones |
| Academy of Warren | 13943 E 8 Mile Rd | Warren, MI | 48089-3351 | 586-552-8010 | 552-8014 | K-8 | Jim Perry |
| Academy of Waterford | 3000 Sashabaw Rd | Waterford, MI | 48329-4040 | 248-674-1649 | 674-3173 | K-8 | Ahmed Saber |
| Achieve Charter Acadmey | 3250 Denton Rd | Canton, MI | 48188-2110 | 734-397-0960 | 397-0968 | K-7 | Jen Conley |
| Advanced Technology Academy | 4801 Oakman Blvd | Dearborn, MI | 48126-3755 | 313-625-4700 | 582-9407 | K-12 | Cynthia Anderson |
| A.G.B.U. Alex & Marie Manoogian S | 22001 Northwestern Hwy | Southfield, MI | 48075-4081 | 248-569-2988 | 569-1346 | K-12 | Dyana Kezelian |
| Allen Academy | 8666 Quincy St | Detroit, MI | 48204-2306 | 313-898-6444 | 898-6555 | K-12 | Georgia Burrell |
| Alternative Educational Acad Ogemaw Co. | 2389 S M 76 | West Branch, MI | 48661 | 989-362-3006 | 362-9076 | 6-12 | Dana McGrew |
| American Montessori Academy | 14800 Middlebelt Rd | Livonia, MI | 48154-4031 | 734-525-7100 | 525-8952 | K-2 | David Poirier |
| American Montessori Academy Upper ES | 17175 Olympia | Redford, MI | 48240 | 313-533-0000 | 533-0005 | 3-6 | Renee Arnot |
| Ann Arbor Learning Community | 3980 Research Park Dr | Ann Arbor, MI | 48108-2220 | 734-477-0340 | 929-6505 | K-8 | Abby Kuhn |
| Arbor Academy | 55 Arbor St | Battle Creek, MI | 49015-2903 | 269-963-5851 | 964-2643 | K-6 | Allison Gumper |
| Arbor Preparatory HS | 6800 Hitchingham Rd | Ypsilanti, MI | 48197 | 734-961-9700 | 961-9701 | 9-12 | Ana Salazar |
| Arts Academy in the Woods | 32101 Caroline | Fraser, MI | 48026-3209 | 586-294-0391 | 294-0617 | 9-12 | Michael Mitchell |
| Arts & Technology Academy of Pontiac | 888 Enterprise Dr | Pontiac, MI | 48341 | 248-452-9309 | 452-9312 | PK-12 | Septembra Williams |
| Augusta Academy | 600 W Michigan Ave | Augusta, MI | 49012 | 269-731-5454 | 964-2643 | K-6 | Brandy Resman |
| Bahweting Charter S | 1301 Marquette Ave | Sault S Marie, MI | 49783-9533 | 906-635-5055 | 635-3805 | K-8 | Dr. Theresa Kallstrom |
| Battle Creek Area Learning Center | 15 Arbor St | Battle Creek, MI | 49015-2903 | 269-565-4782 | 565-4784 | 9-12 | Timothy Allard |
| Battle Creek Montessori Academy | 399 20th St N | Springfield, MI | 49037 | 269-339-3308 | 339-3309 | PK-8 | Jessica Eldridge |
| Bay-Arenac Community HS | 805 Langstaff St | Essexville, MI | 48732-1367 | 989-893-8811 | 895-7749 | 9-12 | Ryan Donlan |
| Bay City Academy - Farragut Campus | 301 N Farragut St | Bay City, MI | 48708 | 989-414-8250 | | K-4 | Jill Plant |
| Bay City Academy - Madison Arts Campus | 400 N Madison Ave | Bay City, MI | 48708 | 989-414-5480 | | 5-8 | Amber Johnson |
| Benton Harbor Charter S | 455 Riverview Dr | Benton Harbor, MI | 49022-5080 | 269-925-3807 | 927-3673 | PK-8 | Tim Harris |
| Black River Public S | 491 Columbia Ave | Holland, MI | 49423-4838 | 616-355-0055 | 355-0057 | K-12 | Shannon Brunink |
| Blended Lrng Acad Credit Recovery HS | 1754 E Clark Rd | Lansing, MI | 48906 | 517-574-4667 | | 9-12 | Dr. Tim Brannan |
| Blue Water Middle College Academy | 323 Erie St | Port Huron, MI | 48060 | 810-989-5805 | 989-5848 | 9-12 | Pete Spencer |
| Boggs S | 4141 Mitchell St | Detroit, MI | 48207 | 313-923-2301 | 923-2300 | K-6 | Julia Putnam |
| Bradford Academy | 24218 Garner St | Southfield, MI | 48033-2900 | 248-351-0000 | 356-4770 | K-12 | Cheryl Paull |
| Branch Line S | 16360 Hubbard St | Livonia, MI | 48154 | 734-335-0663 | | K-8 | Jennifer Wilkins |
| Bridge Academy East and West | 9600 Buffalo St | Hamtramck, MI | 48212-3323 | 313-624-6100 | 624-6200 | K-8 | Dr. Mohamad Issa |
| Burton Glen Charter Academy | 4171 E Atherton Rd | Burton, MI | 48519-1435 | 810-744-2300 | 744-2400 | K-8 | Denesha Rawls-Smith |
| Byron Center Charter S | 9930 Burlingame Ave SW | Byron Center, MI | 49315-8631 | 616-878-4852 | 878-7196 | K-12 | Thomas Berriman |
| Caniff Liberty Academy | 2650 Caniff St | Hamtramck, MI | 48212 | 313-872-2000 | 338-3344 | K-8 | Rebecca Snoblin |
| Canton Charter Academy | 49100 Ford Rd | Canton, MI | 48187-5415 | 734-453-9517 | 453-9551 | K-8 | Kelie Fuller |
| Canton Preparatory HS | 46610 Cherry Hill Rd | Canton, MI | 48187 | 734-656-0003 | 656-0009 | 9-10 | Matthew Chesney |
| Capstone Academy | 3500 John R St | Detroit, MI | 48201 | 313-202-6082 | 831-3510 | 4-12 | Brian Serafino |
| Carleton Academy | 2001 W Hallett Rd | Hillsdale, MI | 49242-1959 | 517-437-2000 | 437-2919 | K-12 | Colleen Gadwood |
| Carver Academy | 14510 2nd Ave | Highland Park, MI | 48203-5715 | 313-865-6024 | 865-6658 | K-8 | Dez'arae Adams |
| CASMAN Alternative Academy | 225 9th St | Manistee, MI | 49660-3109 | 231-723-4981 | 723-1555 | 7-12 | Michelle VanVoorst |
| Central Academy | 2459 S Industrial Hwy | Ann Arbor, MI | 48104-6129 | 734-822-1100 | 822-1101 | PK-12 | Dr. Luay Shalabi |
| Cesar Chavez Academy - Elementary East | 4130 Maxwell St | Detroit, MI | 48214 | 313-924-0317 | 924-0425 | K-5 | Adasina Philyaw |
| Chandler Park Academy ES | 20200 Kelly Rd | Harper Woods, MI | 48225-1203 | 313-884-8830 | 884-9130 | K-5 | Marian Flaggs |
| Chandler Park Academy HS | 20234 Kelly Rd | Harper Woods, MI | 48225 | 313-499-3010 | 499-3052 | 9-12 | Shaun Black |
| Chandler Park Academy MS | 20100 Kelly Rd | Harper Woods, MI | 48225-1201 | 313-839-9886 | 839-3221 | 6-8 | Kenneth Williams |
| Chandler Woods Charter Academy | 6895 Samrick Ave NE | Belmont, MI | 49306-8844 | 616-866-6000 | 866-6001 | PK-8 | Joe Hammond |
| Charlevoix Montessori Academy for Arts | 115 W Hurlbut St | Charlevoix, MI | 49720-1510 | 231-547-9000 | 547-9464 | K-12 | Phoebe Gohs |
| Chatfield S | 231 Lake Dr | Lapeer, MI | 48446-1661 | 810-667-8970 | 667-8983 | K-8 | Matt Young |
| Chavez HS | 1761 Waterman St | Detroit, MI | 48209-2194 | 313-551-0611 | 552-0552 | 9-12 | Juan Martinez |
| Chavez Lower Academy | 8126 W Vernor Hwy | Detroit, MI | 48209-1524 | 313-843-9440 | 297-6948 | K-2 | Gabriela Jaime |
| Chavez MS | 6782 Goldsmith St | Detroit, MI | 48209-2089 | 313-842-0006 | 842-0167 | 6-8 | April Jenkins |
| Chavez Upper ES | 4100 Martin St | Detroit, MI | 48210-2806 | 313-361-1083 | 361-1095 | 3-5 | Thomas Goodley |
| Cole Academy | 1915 W Mount Hope Ave | Lansing, MI | 48910-2434 | 517-372-0038 | 372-1446 | K-6 | Brian Shaughnessy |
| Commonwealth Community Development Acad | 13477 Eureka St | Hamtramck, MI | 48212-1754 | 313-366-9470 | 366-9471 | K-8 | Angela Moore |
| Concord Academy - Boyne | 401 E Dietz Rd | Boyne City, MI | 49712-9653 | 231-582-0194 | 582-4214 | K-12 | Rebekah Leist |
| Concord Academy-Petoskey | 2468 Atkins Rd | Petoskey, MI | 49770-9003 | 231-439-6800 | 439-6803 | K-12 | Robert Ollar |
| Conner Creek Academy East | 16911 Eastland St | Roseville, MI | 48066-2078 | 586-779-8055 | 498-8734 | K-6 | Karen Smith |
| Consortium College Preparatory HS | 4366 Military St | Detroit, MI | 48210 | 313-964-2339 | 964-3922 | 5-12 | Jeffrey Maxwell |
| Countryside Academy | 4800 Meadowbrook Rd | Benton Harbor, MI | 49022-9629 | 269-944-3319 | 944-0242 | K-12 | Lyn Sperry |
| Covenant House Academy Central | 2959 Martin Luther King Jr | Detroit, MI | 48208 | 313-899-6900 | 899-6910 | 9-12 | Anna West |
| Covenant House Academy East | 7600 Goethe St | Detroit, MI | 48214-1762 | 313-267-4315 | 267-4320 | 9-12 | Nathaniel King |
| Covenant House Academy - Grand Rapids | 50 Antoine St SW | Grand Rapids, MI | 49507 | 616-364-2000 | | 9-12 | Doreen Mangrum |
| Covenant House Academy SW | 1450 25th St | Detroit, MI | 48216 | 313-297-8720 | 297-8730 | 9-12 | Jennifer Joubert |
| Creative Montessori Academy | 15100 Northline Rd | Southgate, MI | 48195-2408 | 734-284-5600 | 281-2637 | PK-8 | Carol Hutton |
| Creative Technologies Academy | 350 Pine St | Cedar Springs, MI | 49319-8680 | 616-696-4905 | 696-4920 | K-12 | Daniel George |
| Crescent Academy | 17570 W 12 Mile Rd | Southfield, MI | 48076-1905 | 248-423-4581 | 423-1027 | PK-12 | Cherise Cupidore M.Ed. |
| Crockett Academy | 4851 14th St | Detroit, MI | 48208-2204 | 313-896-6078 | 896-1363 | K-12 | Michael Jackson |
| Cross Creek Charter Academy | 7701 Kalamazoo Ave SE | Byron Center, MI | 49315-9534 | 616-656-4000 | 656-4001 | PK-8 | Joe Nieuwkoop |
| Crossroads Charter Academy | 215 N State St | Big Rapids, MI | 49307-1444 | 231-796-6589 | 796-9874 | K-6 | Ross Meads |
| Crossroads Charter Academy | 215 Spruce St W | Big Rapids, MI | 49307-1471 | 231-796-9041 | 796-9790 | 7-12 | Ross Meads |
| da Vinci Institute | 559 Murphy St | Jackson, MI | 49202 | 517-780-9980 | 780-9747 | K-8 | Kristi Neelis |
| da Vinci Institute | 2255 Emmons Rd | Jackson, MI | 49201-8335 | 517-796-0031 | 796-0320 | 9-12 | Sandy Maxson |
| Dearborn Academy | 19310 Ford Rd Ste 2 | Dearborn, MI | 48128-2403 | 313-982-1300 | 982-9087 | K-8 | Afrin Alavi |
| DeTour Arts & Technology Academy | 202 Division St | De Tour Village, MI | 49725 | 906-297-2011 | 297-3403 | K-12 | Brooke Maciag |
| Detroit Academy of Arts & Sciences | 2985 E Jefferson Ave | Detroit, MI | 48207-4288 | 313-259-1744 | 393-0460 | K-6 | Turquoise Neal |
| Detroit Academy of Arts & Sciences | 3100 E Jefferson Ave | Detroit, MI | 48207 | 313-259-1704 | | 6-8 | Turquoise Neal |
| Detroit Achievement Academy | 7000 W Outer Dr | Detroit, MI | 48235 | 313-468-9518 | | K-3 | Sharon Yaecker-Roesser |
| Detroit Community ES | 12675 Burt Rd | Detroit, MI | 48223-3314 | 313-537-3570 | 537-6904 | K-8 | Sharon McPhail |
| Detroit Community HS | 12675 Burt Rd | Detroit, MI | 48223-3314 | 313-537-3570 | 537-6904 | 9-12 | Sharon McPhail |
| Detroit Delta Prep Acad Social Justice | 3550 John C Lodge Fwy | Detroit, MI | 48201 | 313-638-1444 | | 9-12 | Meagan Brown |
| Detroit Edison Academy | 1903 Wilkins St | Detroit, MI | 48207-2112 | 313-833-1100 | 833-8653 | K-12 | Ralph Bland |
| Detroit Enterprise Academy | 11224 Kercheval St | Detroit, MI | 48214-3323 | 313-823-5799 | 823-0342 | K-8 | Chanavia Patterson |
| Detroit Leadership Academy | 13550 Virgil St | Detroit, MI | 48223-3051 | 313-242-1500 | 241-1527 | K-9 | Pauline Nagle |
| Detroit Merit Academy | 1091 Alter Rd | Detroit, MI | 48215-2861 | 313-331-3328 | 331-3278 | PK-8 | Sandra Terry-Martin |
| Detroit Premier Academy | 7781 Asbury Park | Detroit, MI | 48228-3685 | 313-945-1472 | 945-1744 | K-8 | James Kinsey |
| Detroit Public Safety Academy | 1250 Rosa Parks Blvd | Detroit, MI | 48216 | 313-965-6916 | 965-6938 | 7-12 | Isaiah Pettway |
| Detroit Service Learning Academy | 21605 W 7 Mile Rd | Detroit, MI | 48219-1810 | 313-541-7619 | 541-7656 | K-8 | Shannon Smith |
| Douglass International Acad | 21700 Marlow St | Oak Park, MI | 48237 | 248-953-2003 | | PK-6 | Rashid Faisal |
| Dove Academy of Detroit | 20001 Wexford St | Detroit, MI | 48234 | 313-366-9110 | 366-9130 | PK-8 | Brandon Slone M.Ed. |
| Dream Academy | 248 9th St | Benton Harbor, MI | 49022-4723 | 269-926-1587 | 926-2371 | 9-12 | Lacey James |
| Eagle Crest Charter Academy | 11950 Riley St | Holland, MI | 49424-8553 | 616-786-2400 | 786-4692 | K-8 | Jack DeLeeuw Ed.D. |
| Eagle's Nest Academy | 5005 Cloverlawn Dr | Flint, MI | 48504 | 810-965-1514 | 787-9160 | K-4 | Dr. Reginald Flynn |
| Early Career Academy | 1522 E Big Beaver Rd | Troy, MI | 48083 | 248-509-2022 | | 11-12 | Dr. Amy Boyles |
| East Arbor Charter Academy | 6885 Merritt Rd | Ypsilanti, MI | 48197 | 734-484-5506 | 547-3078 | K-8 | Tanesha Newby |
| East Shore Leadership Academy | 1403 7th St | Port Huron, MI | 48060 | 810-247-0687 | | K-5 | Nancy Gardner |
| Eaton Academy | 21450 Universal Ave | Eastpointe, MI | 48021-2969 | 586-777-1519 | 777-1527 | K-8 | Kenis Wallevand |
| El-Hajj Malik El-Shabazz Academy | 1028 W Barnes Ave | Lansing, MI | 48910-1377 | 517-267-8474 | 484-0095 | PK-6 | Vincent Price |
| Ellis Academy | 18977 Schaefer Hwy | Detroit, MI | 48235-1762 | 313-927-5395 | 927-5376 | K-8 | Michael Johnson |
| Ellis Academy West | 19800 Beech Daly Rd | Redford, MI | 48240-1348 | 313-450-0300 | 450-0305 | K-8 | Dr. Ticheal Jones |
| Endeavor Charter Academy | 380 Helmer Rd N | Springfield, MI | 49037-7776 | 269-962-9300 | 962-9393 | K-8 | Angela Wyckoff |
| Excel Charter Academy | 4201 Breton Rd SE | Grand Rapids, MI | 49512-3857 | 616-281-9339 | 281-6707 | K-8 | Daniel Bartels |
| Experiencia Preparatory Academy | 950 Selden St | Detroit, MI | 48201 | 313-262-6861 | | K-12 | Dr. Risha Ring |
| Faxon Language Immersion Academy | 28555 Middlebelt Rd | Farmingtn Hls, MI | 48334 | 248-702-6272 | 702-6376 | K-8 | Rosalie Cohen |
| Flagship Charter Academy | 13661 Wisconsin St | Detroit, MI | 48238-2356 | 313-933-7933 | 933-9061 | K-8 | Faren D'Abell |
| FlexTech HS | 7707 Conference Center Dr | Brighton, MI | 48114 | 810-844-3366 | 229-2331 | 9-12 | Melanie Laber |
| Ford Academy: S for Creative Studies | 10225 3rd St | Detroit, MI | 48202 | 313-826-1159 | 731-0400 | K-5 | Felicia Brimage |
| Ford Academy | PO Box 1148 | Dearborn, MI | 48121-1148 | 313-982-6200 | 982-6195 | 9-12 | Cora Christmas |
| Ford Academy/Schl for Creative Studies | 485 W Milwaukee St | Detroit, MI | 48202 | 313-481-4000 | 481-4001 | 6-12 | Dr. Curtis Lewis |
| Forest Academy | 5196 Comstock Ave | Kalamazoo, MI | 49048 | 269-488-2315 | 488-2317 | K-6 | Amanda Brown |

| School | Address | City,State | Zip code | Telephone | Fax | Grade | Contact |
|---|---|---|---|---|---|---|---|
| Fortis Academy | 3875 Golfside Rd | Ypsilanti, MI | 48197-3726 | 734-572-3623 | 572-5792 | K-8 | Ira Kleiman |
| Four Corners Montessori Academy | 1075 E Gardenia Ave | Madison Heights, MI | 48071-3433 | 248-542-7001 | 542-7901 | PK-8 | Chris Schoenherr |
| Frontier International Academy | 13200 Conant St | Hamtramck, MI | 48212 | 313-462-6300 | 316-4554 | 6-12 | Dr. Mohamad Issa |
| GEE Edmonson Academy | 1300 W Canfield St | Detroit, MI | 48201-1097 | 313-228-0910 | 447-2533 | PK-8 | Domini Nailer |
| GEE White Academy | 5161 Charles St | Detroit, MI | 48212-2462 | 313-866-3595 | 866-3476 | PK-8 | Felicia Jones M.Ed. |
| Genesee STEM Academy | 310 W Oakley St | Flint, MI | 48503 | 810-600-6466 | 600-6445 | K-7 | Rita Cheek |
| Global Heights Academy | 23713 Joy Rd | Dearborn Hts, MI | 48127-1408 | 313-624-3400 | 624-3401 | PK-5 | Shawn Robson |
| Global Preparatory Academy | 26200 Ridgemont St | Roseville, MI | 48066-3270 | 586-575-9500 | 491-2556 | PK-8 | Nicole Woods |
| Global Tech Academy | 1715 E Forest Ave | Ypsilanti, MI | 48198 | 734-390-9625 | | K-5 | Mohamad Issa |
| Grand Blanc Academy | 5135 E Hill Rd | Grand Blanc, MI | 48439-7637 | 810-953-3140 | 953-3165 | K-8 | Patty Wood |
| Grand Rapids Child Discovery Center | 409 Lafayette Ave SE | Grand Rapids, MI | 49503-5329 | 616-459-0330 | 732-4437 | K-5 | John Robinson |
| Grand Rapids Ellington Acad Arts & Tech | 600 Burton St SE | Grand Rapids, MI | 49507 | 616-241-6300 | 635-2803 | K-12 | Cynthia Springer |
| Grand River Academy | 28111 8 Mile Rd | Livonia, MI | 48152 | 248-893-6100 | 479-1996 | K-8 | Alan Harper |
| Grand River Prep HS | 650 52nd St SE | Kentwood, MI | 49548-5837 | 616-261-1800 | 261-1853 | 9-12 | Koree Woodward |
| Grand Traverse Academy | 1245 Hammond Rd E | Traverse City, MI | 49686-9000 | 231-995-0665 | 995-0880 | K-12 | Susan Dameron |
| Grattan Academy ES | 12047 Old Belding Rd NE | Belding, MI | 48809-9367 | 616-691-8999 | 691-9857 | K-5 | Elizabeth Kreiner |
| Grattan Academy HS | 9481 Jordan Rd | Greenville, MI | 48838-9437 | 616-754-9360 | 754-9363 | 6-12 | Tom Kreiner |
| Greater Heights Academy | 3196 W Pasadena Ave | Flint, MI | 48504 | 810-768-3860 | 768-3865 | K-5 | Lisa Leimeister |
| Great Lakes Academy | 46312 Woodward Ave | Pontiac, MI | 48342-5006 | 248-334-6434 | 334-6457 | K-8 | Aaron Williams |
| Great Lakes Cyber Academy | 2140 University Park # 270 | Okemos, MI | 48864 | 517-381-5062 | 381-5090 | 9-12 | Heather Ballien |
| Great Lakes Explorations Academy | 6200 W KL Ave | Kalamazoo, MI | 49009 | 844-492-4532 | | K-8 | |
| Great Oaks Academy | 4257 Bart Ave | Warren, MI | 48091-1977 | 586-427-4540 | 427-4541 | K-8 | Damon Williams |
| Greenspire S | 1026 Red Dr | Traverse City, MI | 49684 | 231-421-5905 | 805-1327 | 6-8 | Kevin Kelly |
| Hamilton Academy | 14223 Southampton St | Detroit, MI | 48213-3744 | 313-866-4505 | 344-7981 | K-8 | Dr. P. Bilbrew |
| Hamtramck Academy | 11420 Conant St | Hamtramck, MI | 48212-3134 | 313-368-7312 | 368-7376 | K-8 | Michael Griffie |
| Hanley International Academy | 2400 Denton St | Hamtramck, MI | 48212 | 313-875-8888 | 875-8889 | PK-8 | Shameka McPherson |
| Heston Academy | 1350 N Saint Helen Rd | Saint Helen, MI | 48656 | 989-632-3390 | 632-3393 | PK-12 | David Patterson |
| Highland Park Renaissance Academy | 45 E Buena Vista St | Highland Park, MI | 48203-3392 | 313-957-3005 | 868-0345 | PK-12 | Carmen Willingham |
| Hillsdale Preparatory S | 160 Mechanic Rd | Hillsdale, MI | 49242-1053 | 517-437-4625 | 437-3830 | K-8 | Stephen Philipp |
| Holly Academy | 820 Academy Rd | Holly, MI | 48442-1546 | 248-634-5554 | 634-5564 | K-8 | Julie Kildee |
| Honey Creek Community S | PO Box 1406 | Ann Arbor, MI | 48106-1406 | 734-994-2636 | 994-2341 | K-8 | Al Waters |
| Hope Academy | 12121 Broadstreet Ave | Detroit, MI | 48204 | 313-934-0054 | 934-0074 | K-8 | Dr. Ronald E. Williams |
| Hope Academy of West Michigan | 240 Brown St SE | Grand Rapids, MI | 49507 | 616-301-8458 | 264-3346 | K-12 | Phil Haack |
| Hope of Detroit Academy | 4443 N Campbell St | Detroit, MI | 48210-2520 | 313-897-8720 | 897-5142 | K-8 | Ali Abdel |
| Huron Academy | 11401 Metropolitan Pkwy | Sterling Hts, MI | 48312-2937 | 586-446-9170 | 446-9173 | K-6 | Mark Talbot |
| ICademy Global | 8485 Homestead Dr | Zeeland, MI | 49464 | 616-748-5637 | 772-0373 | K-12 | Brook Drooger |
| Innocademy | 8485 Homestead Dr | Zeeland, MI | 49464 | 616-748-5637 | 772-0373 | K-12 | Brook Drooger |
| Innocademy Allegan Campus | 2611 56th St | Fennville, MI | 49408 | 269-561-4050 | 772-0373 | K-5 | Chad Zuber |
| Insight S of Michigan | 6512 Centurion Dr Ste 320 | Lansing, MI | 48917 | 877-842-3793 | | 6-12 | Marcus Moore |
| International Academy of Flint | 2820 S Saginaw St | Flint, MI | 48503-5708 | 810-600-5000 | 600-5300 | K-12 | Kendra Giles |
| International Academy of Saginaw | 1944 Iowa Ave | Saginaw, MI | 48601-5213 | 989-921-1000 | 921-1001 | K-8 | Christopher Matheson |
| International Prep Academy | 4201 W Outer Dr | Detroit, MI | 48221 | 313-457-6400 | 494-8142 | PK-7 | Dr. Christopher Lindsay |
| Island City Academy | 6421 S Clinton Trl | Eaton Rapids, MI | 48827-9698 | 517-663-0111 | 663-0167 | PK-8 | William Aaron Warren |
| Jackson Preparatory & Early College S | 2111 Emmons Rd | Jackson, MI | 49201 | 517-768-7093 | 795-2735 | 6-12 | Shane Malmquist |
| Jefferson International Academy | 60 S Lynn Ave | Waterford, MI | 48328 | 248-682-5000 | 481-2053 | PK-7 | Dr. Elizabeth Herron-Ruff |
| Joy Preparatory Academy | 1129 Oakman Blvd | Detroit, MI | 48238-2950 | 313-867-7828 | 867-7831 | K-2 | Fran Gardulescu |
| Joy Preparatory Academy | 15055 Dexter Ave | Detroit, MI | 48238-2124 | 313-340-0023 | 340-0678 | 3-8 | Frances Gardulescu |
| Kalamazoo Covenant Academy | 400 W Crosstown Pkwy | Kalamazoo, MI | 49001 | | | 9-12 | Gretchen LaHaie |
| Kensington Woods HS | PO Box 206 | Lakeland, MI | 48143 | 517-545-0828 | 545-7588 | 6-12 | Markus Muennix |
| Keys Grace Academy | 27321 Hampden St | Madison Heights, MI | 48071 | 248-629-7700 | 629-7708 | K-12 | Lisa Mansour |
| Keystone Academy | 47925 Bemis Rd | Belleville, MI | 48111-9760 | 734-697-9470 | 697-9471 | K-8 | Keturah Godfrey |
| King Education Center | 16827 Appoline St | Detroit, MI | 48235-4205 | 313-341-4944 | 341-7014 | K-8 | Dr. Constance Price |
| Kingsbury Country Day S | 5000 Hosner Rd | Oxford, MI | 48370-1000 | 248-628-2571 | 628-3612 | PK-8 | Tom Mecsey |
| Knapp Charter Academy | 1759 Leffingwell Ave NE | Grand Rapids, MI | 49525-4531 | 616-364-1100 | 364-9780 | PK-8 | Dave Turcotte |
| Lakeside Charter S | 3921 Oakland Dr | Kalamazoo, MI | 49008 | 269-202-5536 | 381-5332 | 4-12 | Steven Laidacker |
| Landmark Academy | 4800 Lapeer Rd | Kimball, MI | 48074-1517 | 810-982-7210 | 982-0679 | K-12 | Debby Wilton |
| Lansing Charter Academy | 3300 Express Ct | Lansing, MI | 48910-4370 | 517-882-9585 | 882-9587 | K-6 | Alvin Ward |
| Laurus Academy | 24590 Lahser Rd | Southfield, MI | 48033-6040 | 248-799-8401 | 799-8404 | K-8 | Dr. Raul Calderon |
| Leelanau Montessori Academy | PO Box 838 | Suttons Bay, MI | 49682-0838 | 231-271-8609 | 271-8689 | PK-6 | Rebecca Creighton |
| Legacy Charter Academy | 4900 E Hildale St | Detroit, MI | 48234-2225 | 313-368-2215 | 432-2807 | K-8 | Letoskey Carey |
| Life Skills Center of Pontiac | 142 Auburn Ave | Pontiac, MI | 48342-3008 | 248-322-1163 | 322-1164 | 9-12 | Keisha Palmer |
| Life Tech Academy | 3101 Technology Blvd Ste A | Lansing, MI | 48910 | 517-325-5469 | 325-5468 | 7-12 | Thomas Ackerson |
| Lighthouse Academy | 3330 36th St SE | Grand Rapids, MI | 49512 | 616-949-2287 | 949-2379 | K-12 | Jamie San Miguel |
| Lighthouse Academy - North Campus | 1260 Ekhart St NE | Grand Rapids, MI | 49503 | 616-965-9700 | 965-9701 | 3-12 | Todd Penning |
| Light of the World Academy | 550 E Hamburg St | Pinckney, MI | 48169 | 734-720-9760 | 720-9763 | PK-6 | Kathy Moorehouse |
| Lincoln-King Academy | 13436 Grove St | Detroit, MI | 48235 | 313-862-2352 | 862-2462 | PK-8 | Carolyn Brown |
| Linden Charter Academy | 3244 N Linden Rd | Flint, MI | 48504-1753 | 810-720-0515 | 720-0626 | K-8 | Deonna Washington |
| Mackinac Preparatory Academy | 888 Enterprise Dr | Pontiac, MI | 48341 | 866-339-6818 | 913-6100 | K-12 | Hope Curtin |
| Macomb Academy | 39092 Garfield Rd | Clinton Twp, MI | 48038-2790 | 586-228-2201 | 228-2210 | 12-12 | Andrew Wise |
| Macomb Montessori Academy | 14057 E 9 Mile Rd | Warren, MI | 48089 | 586-359-2138 | 533-2812 | K-8 | Ashley Ogonowski |
| Madison Academy | 6170 Torrey Rd | Flint, MI | 48507 | 810-655-2949 | 655-2931 | K-6 | Tricai Osborne |
| Madison Academy - HS | 3266 S Genesee Rd | Burton, MI | 48519 | 810-875-9050 | 877-6255 | 7-12 | Joddi Mills |
| Madison-Carver Academy | 19900 McIntyre St | Detroit, MI | 48219 | 313-486-4626 | | K-8 | Pamela Farris |
| Marshall Academy | 18203 Homer Rd | Marshall, MI | 49068-8718 | 269-781-6330 | 781-8749 | K-12 | Brent Swan |
| Merritt Academy | 59900 Havenridge Rd | New Haven, MI | 48048-1915 | 586-749-6000 | 749-8582 | PK-12 | Nathan Seiferlein |
| Metro Charter Academy | 34800 Ecorse Rd | Romulus, MI | 48174-1642 | 734-641-3200 | 641-6530 | K-8 | Shelli Wildfong |
| Michigan Collegiate MSHS | 31300 Ryan Rd | Warren, MI | 48092-1354 | 586-777-5792 | 698-0392 | 7-12 | Russel Woodruff |
| Michigan Connections Academy | 3950 Heritage Ave Ste 100 | Okemos, MI | 48864-3389 | 517-507-5390 | 507-5389 | K-12 | Bryan Klochack |
| Michigan Great Lakes Virtual Academy | 50 Filer St Ste F | Manistee, MI | 49660 | 855-380-2480 | 794-6416 | K-12 | Kendall Schroeder |
| Michigan Math & Science Academy | 8155 Ritter | Center Line, MI | 48015-1452 | 586-920-2163 | 920-2164 | K-12 | Oguzhan Yildiz M.Ed. |
| Michigan S for the Arts | 825 Golf Dr | Pontiac, MI | 48341 | 248-338-2787 | 499-8843 | K-9 | Dr. Carl Byerly |
| Michigan Technical Academy | 19940 Mansfield St | Detroit, MI | 48235-2332 | 313-272-1649 | 272-1849 | PK-4 | Phillip Price |
| Michigan Technical Academy | 23750 Elmira St | Redford, MI | 48239 | 313-537-9311 | 537-9312 | 5-8 | James Spruill |
| Michigan Virtual Academy | 678 Front Ave NW | Grand Rapids, MI | 49504-5325 | 877-794-9427 | 843-5871 | K-12 | Andrei Nichols |
| Midland Acad Advanced & Creative Studies | 4653 E Bailey Bridge Rd | Midland, MI | 48640-8542 | 989-496-2404 | 496-2466 | K-12 | Dr. Kathryn Shick |
| Mid-Michigan Leadership Academy | 730 W Maple St | Lansing, MI | 48906-5086 | 517-485-5379 | 485-5892 | K-8 | Dr. Sephira Shuttlesworth |
| Momentum Academy | 99 E Woodward Heights Blvd | Hazel Park, MI | 48030 | 248-336-5600 | 808-6478 | PK-8 | Kevelin Jones |
| Morey Montessori Public School Academy | 418 W Blanchard Rd | Shepherd, MI | 48883 | 989-866-6741 | 866-6737 | PK-8 | Eric Johnson |
| Mt. Clemens Montessori Academy | 1070 Hampton Rd | Mount Clemens, MI | 48043-2955 | 586-465-5545 | 465-2283 | PK-5 | Stelgene P'sachoulias |
| Multicultural Academy | 5550 Platt Rd | Ann Arbor, MI | 48108-9762 | 734-677-0732 | 677-0740 | PK-8 | Patricia Eggleston M.S. |
| Murphy Performance Academy | 23901 Fenkell St | Detroit, MI | 48223-1431 | 313-494-7585 | 494-7550 | K-8 | Malon Harris |
| Muskegon Covenant Academy | 125 Catherine Ave | Muskegon, MI | 49442 | 231-720-3100 | | 9-12 | Jim VanBergen |
| Muskegon Montessori Academy | 2950 McCracken St | Norton Shores, MI | 49441 | 231-766-7500 | 766-7215 | K-6 | Ali DuBois |
| Nataki Talibah Schoolhouse of Detroit | 19176 Northrop St | Detroit, MI | 48219-1857 | 313-531-3720 | 531-3779 | K-8 | Samara Etheridge |
| New Bedford Academy | 6315 Secor Rd | Lambertville, MI | 48144-9411 | 734-854-5437 | 854-1573 | K-8 | Greg Sauter |
| New Beginnings Academy | 211 E Michigan Ave | Ypsilanti, MI | 48198-5677 | 734-481-9001 | 544-2706 | K-6 | Kenya Crockett |
| New Branches Charter Academy | 3662 Poinsettia Ave SE | Grand Rapids, MI | 49508 | 616-243-6221 | 243-0305 | K-8 | Terry Larkin |
| New Paradigm College Prep S | 2450 S Beatrice St | Detroit, MI | 48217 | 313-406-7060 | | K-5 | Tamara Collins |
| New Paradigm Glazer Academy | 2001 La Belle St | Detroit, MI | 48238-2941 | 313-852-1500 | 852-1499 | PK-6 | Eddie Thomas |
| New Paradigm Loving Academy | 1000 Lynn St | Detroit, MI | 48211-1081 | 313-252-3028 | 866-0989 | PK-8 | Ronald Newton |
| New School High | 46250 Ann Arbor Rd | Plymouth, MI | 48170 | 734-386-6601 | | 9-10 | Cyndi Burnstein |
| New Standard Academy | 2040 W Carpenter Rd | Flint, MI | 48505 | 810-787-3330 | | PK-8 | Calvin Sims |
| Nexus Academy of Grand Rapids | 801 Broadway Ave NW Ste 225 | Grand Rapids, MI | 49504 | 616-458-4992 | 458-6088 | 9-12 | Daniel McMinn |
| Nexus Academy of Lansing | 2175 University Park Dr | Okemos, MI | 48864 | 517-347-7793 | 347-7864 | 9-12 | Charles Carver |
| Nexus Academy of Royal Oak | 31333 Southfield Rd Ste 200 | Beverly Hills, MI | 48025 | 248-593-8440 | 593-8264 | 9-12 | Michael Foley |
| Noor International Academy | 37412 Dequindre Rd | Sterling Hts, MI | 48310 | 586-365-5000 | 365-5001 | PK-8 | Nawal Hamadeh |
| North Central Academy | 5055 Corey Rd | Mancelona, MI | 49659-9467 | 231-584-2080 | 584-2082 | K-12 | Patrick Cleland |
| Northridge Academy | 530 W Pierson Rd | Flint, MI | 48505-3114 | 810-785-8811 | 785-9844 | K-8 | Latricia Brown-Coates |
| North Saginaw Charter Academy | 2332 Trautner Dr | Saginaw, MI | 48604-9593 | 989-249-5400 | 249-5800 | K-8 | Sarah Simpson |
| North Star Academy | 3030 Wright St | Marquette, MI | 49855-9649 | 906-226-0156 | 226-0167 | K-12 | Joseph Kukulski |
| Oakland Academy | 6325 Oakland Dr | Portage, MI | 49024-2589 | 269-324-8951 | 324-8974 | PK-6 | Henry Winter |
| Oakland FlexTech Academy | 24245 Karim Blvd | Novi, MI | 48375 | 248-426-8530 | 426-8557 | 9-12 | Sarah Pazur |
| Oakland International Academy | 6111 Miller St | Detroit, MI | 48211 | 313-925-1000 | 925-1133 | 2-4 | Ahmed Saber |
| Oakland International Academy | 4001 Miller St | Detroit, MI | 48211-1554 | 313-923-0790 | 923-0927 | PK-1 | Ahmed Saber |
| Oakland International Academy - HS | 2619 Florian St | Hamtramck, MI | 48212 | 313-285-8990 | 784-9438 | 9-12 | Ahmed Saber |
| Oakland International Academy Middle | 8228 Conant St | Detroit, MI | 48211 | 313-347-0246 | 347-0250 | 5-8 | Ahmed Saber |
| Oakside Scholars Charter Academy | 355 Summit Dr | Waterford, MI | 48328 | 248-706-2000 | 920-0351 | K-8 | Kathleen Grinwis |
| Ojibwe Charter S | 11507 W Industrial Dr | Brimley, MI | 49715-9087 | 906-248-2530 | 248-2532 | K-12 | Stephanie Vittitow |
| Old Redford Academy ES | 17195 Redford St | Detroit, MI | 48219-3259 | 313-532-7510 | 543-2055 | PK-5 | Tomeka Dixon |
| Old Redford Academy MS | 22122 W McNichols Rd | Detroit, MI | 48219-3245 | 313-653-3888 | 412-2162 | 6-8 | Chavonne McGowan |
| Old Redford Academy Prep HS | 8001 W Outer Dr | Detroit, MI | 48235-3293 | 313-543-3080 | 543-3129 | 9-12 | Charles Davis |
| Outlook Academy | 2879 116th Ave | Allegan, MI | 49010 | 269-673-2161 | 673-2361 | 5-12 | Rick Cain |
| Pansophia Academy | 52 Abbott Ave | Coldwater, MI | 49036-1430 | 517-279-4686 | 279-0089 | K-12 | Jamie Mueller |
| Paragon Charter Academy | 3750 McCain Rd | Jackson, MI | 49201-7675 | 517-750-9500 | 750-9501 | K-8 | Ben Kriesch |
| Paramount Charter Academy | 3624 S Westnedge Ave | Kalamazoo, MI | 49008-2969 | 269-553-6400 | 553-6401 | PK-8 | Jodi Donkin |
| Pathways Academy | 11340 E Jefferson Ave | Detroit, MI | 48214 | 734-221-0977 | | 7-12 | Nathaniel King |
| Plymouth Educational Center | 1460 E Forest Ave | Detroit, MI | 48207-1000 | 313-831-3280 | 831-5766 | PK-8 | Mark Rankin |

| School | Address | City,State | Zip code | Telephone | Fax | Grade | Contact |
|---|---|---|---|---|---|---|---|
| Plymouth Scholars Charter Academy | 48484 N Territorial Rd | Plymouth, MI | 48170 | 734-459-6149 | 864-0341 | K-8 | Walter Reese |
| Pollack Academic Center of Excellence | 23777 Southfield Rd | Southfield, MI | 48075-3458 | 248-569-1060 | 569-1403 | K-8 | Dr. Damian Perry |
| Pontiac Academy for Excellence | 196 Cesar E Chavez Ave | Pontiac, MI | 48342 | 248-745-9420 | 745-1275 | K-12 | Roslyn Braitwaite |
| Presque Isle Academy | 20830 Cedar St | Onaway, MI | 49765 | 989-733-6708 | 733-6701 | 9-12 | Earl Bassett |
| Prevail Academy | 353 Cass Ave | Mount Clemens, MI | 48043-2112 | 586-783-0173 | 783-0179 | K-8 | Colleen Furman |
| Quest Charter Academy | 24745 Van Born Rd | Taylor, MI | 48180-1221 | 734-299-0534 | 299-0577 | K-8 | Ralph Garza |
| Reach Academy | 25275 Chippendale St | Roseville, MI | 48066 | 586-498-9171 | 498-9173 | K-8 | Nicole Young |
| Redford Service Learning Academy | 25940 Grand River Ave | Redford, MI | 48240 | 313-539-4115 | 539-4660 | K-8 | Robert Warmack |
| Regent Park Scholars Charter Academy | 15865 E 7 Mile Rd | Detroit, MI | 48205 | 313-371-1300 | 221-9942 | K-8 | Crystal Byse |
| Reh Academy | 2201 Owen St | Saginaw, MI | 48601-3466 | 989-753-2349 | 753-1819 | PK-9 | Kate Scheid |
| Renaissance Public S Academy | 2797 S Isabella Rd | Mount Pleasant, MI | 48858-2067 | 989-773-9889 | 772-4503 | K-8 | Lisa Bergman |
| Richfield Public School Academy | 3807 N Center Rd | Flint, MI | 48506-2642 | 810-736-1281 | 736-2326 | 3-8 | Pamela Haldy |
| Ridge Park Charter Academy | 4120 Camelot Ridge Dr SE | Grand Rapids, MI | 49546-2432 | 616-222-0093 | 222-0138 | K-8 | Emory Wyckoff |
| Rising Stars Academy | 23855 Lawrence | Center Line, MI | 48015 | 586-806-6455 | 806-6967 | 12-12 | Deborah Prentiss |
| Riverside Academy East | 7124 Miller Rd | Dearborn, MI | 48126-1918 | 313-624-3200 | 624-3201 | K-5 | Eman Radha |
| Riverside Academy West | 6409 Schaefer Rd | Dearborn, MI | 48126-2212 | 313-624-3600 | 624-3601 | 6-12 | Ramzi Saab |
| Rose Leadership Academy | 15000 Trojan St | Detroit, MI | 48235 | 313-397-3333 | 397-4155 | 9-12 | Russell Harris |
| Ross-Hill Academy ES | 3111 Elmwood St | Detroit, MI | 48207-2418 | 313-922-8088 | 922-2015 | K-8 | Phyllis Ross |
| Rutherford Winans Academy | 16411 Curtis St | Detroit, MI | 48235-3202 | 313-852-0709 | 852-0702 | PK-5 | Karen Abbott |
| Saginaw Learn to Earn Academy | 1000 Tuscola St | Saginaw, MI | 48607-1421 | 989-399-8775 | | 9-12 | Brad Gomoluch |
| Saginaw Preparatory Academy | 5173 Lodge St | Saginaw, MI | 48601-6829 | 989-752-9600 | 752-9618 | PK-8 | Molly Rundell |
| St. Clair County Intervention Academy | 1170 Michigan Rd | Port Huron, MI | 48060-4658 | 810-966-1649 | 966-4312 | 6-12 | Troy Peyerk |
| Schools for the Future Detroit | 3550 John C Lodge Fwy | Detroit, MI | 48201 | 248-809-2288 | 809-2093 | 9-12 | Stephanie Hall |
| South Arbor Charter Academy | 8200 Carpenter Rd | Ypsilanti, MI | 48197-9800 | 734-528-2821 | 528-2829 | K-8 | Kim Bondy |
| South Canton Scholars Charter Academy | 3085 S Canton Center Rd | Canton, MI | 48188 | 734-398-5658 | 547-3077 | K-8 | Sabrina Terenzi |
| South Pointe Scholars Charter Academy | 10550 Geddes Rd | Ypsilanti, MI | 48198 | 734-484-0118 | 864-0353 | K-8 | Nancy Kouba |
| Star International Academy | 24425 Hass St | Dearborn Hts, MI | 48127-3275 | 313-724-8990 | 724-8994 | PK-12 | Ali Bazzi |
| Starr Detroit Academy | 19360 Harper Ave | Harper Woods, MI | 48225 | 313-649-2200 | 924-5490 | K-8 | Sharon Karpinski |
| State Street Academy | 1110 State St | Bay City, MI | 48706-3699 | 989-684-6484 | 684-6202 | K-6 | Joy Wagner |
| Stewart Perfomance Academy | 13120 Wildemere St | Detroit, MI | 48238-3336 | 313-327-0058 | | K-8 | Detra Coleman |
| Stockwell Academy | 9758 E Highland Rd | Howell, MI | 48843-9098 | 810-632-2200 | 632-2201 | K-8 | Jessica Moceri |
| Stockwell Preparatory Academy | 1032 Karl Greimel Dr | Brighton, MI | 48116-9471 | 810-225-9940 | 225-9941 | 9-12 | Steven Beyer |
| Success Mile Academy | 27300 Dequindre Rd | Warren, MI | 48092 | 586-353-2108 | 353-2109 | K-8 | Thomas Gladieux |
| Summit Academy | PO Box 310 | Flat Rock, MI | 48134-0310 | 734-379-6810 | 379-6745 | K-8 | Leann Hedke |
| Summit Academy HS | 18601 Middlebelt Rd | Romulus, MI | 48174-9290 | 734-955-1730 | 955-1737 | 9-12 | Erin Avery |
| Summit Academy MS | 18601 Middlebelt Rd | Romulus, MI | 48174-9290 | 734-955-1712 | 955-1729 | 6-8 | Leann Hedke |
| Summit Academy North ES | 28697 Sibley Rd | Romulus, MI | 48174-9736 | 734-789-1428 | 789-1431 | K-5 | Michael Bravo |
| SW Detroit Lighthouse Charter Academy | 4001 29th St | Detroit, MI | 48210 | 313-782-4422 | 782-4469 | K-7 | Sherrie Buchzeiger |
| Taylor Exemplar Academy | 26727 Goddard Rd | Taylor, MI | 48180-3912 | 734-941-7742 | 941-9641 | K-8 | Julie Zirille |
| Taylor International Academy | 26555 Franklin Rd | Southfield, MI | 48033 | 248-354-1500 | 354-1501 | PK-8 | Robert Davis |
| Taylor Preparatory HS | 9540 Telegraph Rd | Taylor, MI | 48180 | 734-668-2100 | 668-2101 | 9-12 | Aquan Miles |
| Three Lakes Academy | W17352 Main St | Curtis, MI | 49820 | 906-586-6631 | 586-6573 | K-7 | Susan Pann |
| Three Oaks Public School Academy | 1212 Kingsley St | Muskegon, MI | 49442-4025 | 231-767-3365 | 777-9815 | K-6 | Monecia Vasbinder |
| Timberland Charter Academy | 2574 McLaughlin Ave | Muskegon, MI | 49442-4439 | 231-767-9700 | 767-9710 | K-8 | Angelia Coleman |
| Timbuktu Academy of Science & Technology | 10800 E Canfield St | Detroit, MI | 48214-1601 | 313-823-6000 | 823-9748 | K-6 | ChaRhonda Edgerson |
| Tipton Academy | 1615 Belton St | Garden City, MI | 48135 | 734-261-0500 | | PK-6 | Suzanne March |
| Trillium Academy | 15740 Racho Blvd | Taylor, MI | 48180-5211 | 734-374-8222 | 374-5025 | K-12 | Angela Romanowski |
| Triumph Academy | 3000 Vivian Rd | Monroe, MI | 48162-8600 | 734-240-2610 | 240-2785 | K-8 | Amy Tansel |
| Trix Performance Academy | 13700 Bringard Dr | Detroit, MI | 48205-1156 | 313-852-8644 | 866-8655 | K-8 | Emily Piccoli |
| Universal Academy | 4833 Ogden | Detroit, MI | 48210 | 313-581-5006 | 581-5514 | PK-12 | Uzma Anjum |
| Universal Learning Academy | 28015 Joy Rd | Westland, MI | 48185 | 734-402-5900 | 402-5901 | PK-12 | Michelle Hadous |
| University Prep Academy Murray ES | 435 Amsterdam St | Detroit, MI | 48202-3407 | 313-309-0552 | 309-0487 | PK-5 | Kimberly Llorens |
| University Preparatory Academy HS | 600 Antoinette St | Detroit, MI | 48202-3457 | 313-874-4340 | 874-4510 | 9-12 | Dannon Holley |
| University Preparatory Academy MS | 5310 Saint Antoine St | Detroit, MI | 48202-4131 | 313-831-0100 | 831-4197 | 6-8 | Aisha Scott |
| University Preparatory Acad Thompson ES | 957 Holden St | Detroit, MI | 48202-3443 | 313-874-9800 | 874-9822 | K-5 | Tamara Johnson |
| University Prep Science & Math ES | 2251 Antietam Ave | Detroit, MI | 48207 | 313-782-4400 | | K-5 | Kimberly Phillips |
| University Prep Science & Math HS | 2664 Franklin St | Detroit, MI | 48207 | 313-393-9166 | 393-9165 | 9-12 | Zetia Hogan |
| University Prep Science & Math MS | 5100 John R St | Detroit, MI | 48202 | 313-832-8400 | 833-4816 | 6-8 | Jennifer Spencer |
| University Yes Academy | PO Box 2716 | Detroit, MI | 48202 | 313-270-2556 | 646-6887 | K-12 | Joe Kotarski |
| Vanderbilt Charter Academy | 301 W 16th St | Holland, MI | 49423-3417 | 616-820-5050 | 820-5051 | PK-8 | Holly Hillary |
| Vanguard Charter Academy | 1620 52nd St SW | Wyoming, MI | 49519-9629 | 616-538-3630 | 538-3646 | K-8 | Mark DeJong |
| Virtual Learning Academy of St. Clair | 499 Range Rd | Marysville, MI | 48040-2220 | 810-364-8990 | 364-7474 | 9-12 | Denice Lapish |
| Vista Charter Academy | 711 32nd St SE | Grand Rapids, MI | 49548-2307 | 616-246-6920 | 246-6930 | K-8 | Heather Guerra |
| Vista Meadows Academy | 20651 W Warren St | Dearborn Hts, MI | 48127-2698 | 313-240-4347 | 441-9169 | 9-12 | Darrlyn Harrison |
| Voyageur Academy | 4321 Military St | Detroit, MI | 48210-2451 | 313-361-4180 | 361-4770 | K-6 | Aundrea Johnson |
| Walden Green Montessori S | 17339 Roosevelt Rd | Spring Lake, MI | 49456 | 616-842-4523 | 842-4522 | K-8 | Mark Neidlinger |
| Walker Charter Academy | 1801 3 Mile Rd NW | Grand Rapids, MI | 49544-1445 | 616-785-2700 | 785-0894 | K-8 | Steve Bagley |
| Walton Charter Academy | 744 E Walton Blvd | Pontiac, MI | 48340-1361 | 248-371-9300 | 371-1642 | K-8 | Mona Boersma |
| Warrendale Charter Academy | 19400 Sawyer St | Detroit, MI | 48228-3330 | 313-240-4200 | 240-4203 | K-8 | Vondra Glass |
| Washington-Parks Academy | 11685 Appleton | Redford, MI | 48239 | 313-592-6061 | 242-5156 | K-8 | Kalyani Bhatt |
| Washtenaw Technical Middle College | 4800 E Huron River Dr | Ann Arbor, MI | 48105-4800 | 734-973-3410 | 973-3464 | 10-12 | Dr. Karl Covert |
| Waterford Montessori Academy | 4860 Midland Ave | Waterford, MI | 48329 | 248-674-2400 | 674-2424 | PK-5 | Theo Papatheodoropoulos |
| W-A-Y Academy | 555 Briarwood Cir | Ann Arbor, MI | 48108 | 734-249-9929 | | 7-12 | Rachel Sarkody |
| WAY Academy-Flint | 817 E Kearsley St | Flint, MI | 48503 | 810-412-8655 | 820-2642 | 7-12 | |
| W-A-Y Academy West Campus | 19321 W Chicago St | Detroit, MI | 48228 | 313-444-9398 | | 7-11 | |
| WAY Michigan | 407 E Fort St | Detroit, MI | 48226 | 313-444-9292 | | 6-12 | Michelle Sarkody |
| Wells Academy | 281 S Fair Ave | Benton Harbor, MI | 49022-7219 | 269-926-2885 | 926-2923 | K-7 | Charlie Lovelady |
| Wellspring Preparatory HS | 1031 Page St NE | Grand Rapids, MI | 49505-5544 | 616-235-9500 | 235-2526 | 9-12 | Jessica Knoth |
| West MI Academy Environmental Science | 4463 Leonard St NW | Grand Rapids, MI | 49534-2138 | 616-791-7454 | 791-7453 | PK-12 | Scott Morgan |
| West Michigan Acad of Arts & Academics | 17350 Hazel St | Spring Lake, MI | 49456-1222 | 616-844-9961 | 844-9941 | PK-8 | Cathy Cantu |
| West Michigan Aviation Academy | 5363 44th St SE | Grand Rapids, MI | 49512 | 616-446-8886 | 957-0491 | 9-12 | Patrick Cwayna |
| Weston Preparatory Academy | 22930 Chippewa St | Detroit, MI | 48219-1161 | 313-387-6038 | 387-6180 | K-8 | Philip Yaccick |
| West Village Academy - South Campus | 3530 Westwood St | Dearborn, MI | 48124-3100 | 313-274-9200 | 274-0062 | K-8 | Coletta Counts |
| White Pine Academy | 510 Russell St | Leslie, MI | 49251-9478 | 517-589-8961 | 589-9194 | K-8 | Keven Numinen |
| Winans Academy of Performing Arts ES | 9740 McKinney St | Detroit, MI | 48224-2503 | 313-640-4610 | 640-4611 | K-5 | Tomi Ingram |
| Winans Academy Performing Arts HS | 7616 E Nevada St | Detroit, MI | 48234-3284 | 313-365-5578 | 365-5684 | 6-12 | Lindsberg Pettway M.A. |
| Windemere Park Charter Academy | 3100 W Saginaw St | Lansing, MI | 48917-2307 | 517-327-0700 | 327-0800 | PK-8 | Yvonne Thomas |
| Windover HS | 919 Smith Rd | Midland, MI | 48640-4164 | 989-832-0852 | 839-7699 | 9-12 | Gina Wilson |
| Woodland Park Academy | 2083 E Grand Blanc Rd | Grand Blanc, MI | 48439-2700 | 810-695-4710 | 695-1658 | K-8 | Jeremy Brown |
| Woodland S | 7224 Supply Rd | Traverse City, MI | 49696-9416 | 231-947-7474 | 947-7667 | K-8 | Nathan Tarsa |
| Woodward Academy | 951 E Lafayette St | Detroit, MI | 48207-2999 | 313-961-2108 | 963-3501 | PK-8 | Jeremaine Kyles |
| WSC Academy | 855 Jefferson St | Ypsilanti, MI | 48197 | 734-794-0218 | 794-0216 | 9-12 | Portia Davis-Mann |
| Youth Advancement Academy | 6750 Chime St | Kalamazoo, MI | 49009 | 269-353-4193 | 353-4214 | 9-12 | Amber Long |

**Minnesota**

| School | Address | City,State | Zip code | Telephone | Fax | Grade | Contact |
|---|---|---|---|---|---|---|---|
| Academia Cesar Chavez | 1800 Ames Ave | Saint Paul, MN | 55119-4898 | 651-778-2940 | 778-2942 | K-6 | Ramona de Rosales |
| Academic Arts HS | 60 Marie Ave E | West Saint Paul, MN | 55118-5910 | 651-457-7427 | 554-7611 | 9-12 | Krissy Wright |
| Achieve Language Academy | 2169 Stillwater Ave E | Saint Paul, MN | 55119-3508 | 651-738-4875 | 738-8268 | PK-8 | Mary Apuli |
| AFSA HS | 100 Vadnais Blvd | Vadnais Heights, MN | 55127 | 651-209-3910 | 209-3911 | 9-12 | Becky Meyer |
| AFSA MS | 1435 Midway Pkwy | Saint Paul, MN | 55108 | 612-260-2662 | 493-2088 | 6-8 | Becky Meyer |
| Arcadia Charter S | 1719 Cannon Rd | Northfield, MN | 55057 | 507-663-8806 | 663-8802 | 6-12 | Ryan Krominga |
| Art and Science Academy | 903 6th Avenue Ct NE | Isanti, MN | 55040 | 763-568-4091 | | K-5 | Carlo Galeazzi |
| Aspen Academy | 14825 Zinran Ave | Savage, MN | 55378-4557 | 952-226-5940 | 226-5949 | K-8 | Cynthia Sherar |
| Athlos Leadership Academy | 10100 Noble Parkway N | Brooklyn Park, MN | 55443 | 763-777-8942 | 315-0601 | PK-8 | Jennifer Geraghty |
| Augsburg Fairview Academy /Health Career | 2504 Columbus Ave | Minneapolis, MN | 55404-4432 | 612-333-1614 | 339-2229 | 9-12 | Ricky White |
| Aurora Charter S | 2101 E 26th St | Minneapolis, MN | 55404-4102 | 612-870-3891 | 870-4287 | K-8 | Matthew Cisewski |
| Avalon Charter S | 700 Glendale St | Saint Paul, MN | 55114 | 651-649-5495 | 649-5462 | 6-12 | Carrie Bakken |
| Bdote Learning Center | 3216 E 29th St | Minneapolis, MN | 55406 | 612-279-6380 | | K-3 | Michael Huerth |
| Beacon Academy | 9060 Zanzibar Ln N | Maple Grove, MN | 55311 | 763-546-9999 | 416-3682 | K-8 | Sean Koster |
| Best Academy | 1300 Olson Memorial Hwy | Minneapolis, MN | 55411 | 612-221-8901 | | K-6 | Ellen Stewart |
| Best Academy-Lincoln | 2131 12th Ave N | Minneapolis, MN | 55411 | 612-381-9743 | | 6-8 | Ellen Stewart |
| Birch Grove Community S | PO Box 2242 | Tofte, MN | 55615-2242 | 218-663-0170 | 663-7904 | PK-5 | Diane Blanchette |
| Bluesky Online Charter S | 33 Wentworth Ave E Ste 100 | West Saint Paul, MN | 55118-3432 | 651-642-0888 | 642-0435 | 7-12 | Amy Larsen |
| Bluffview Montessori S | 1321 Gilmore Ave | Winona, MN | 55987-2459 | 507-452-2807 | 452-6869 | K-8 | Stephanie Wehman |
| Bright Water ES | 5140 Fremont Ave N | Minneapolis, MN | 55430-3419 | 612-302-3410 | 302-5911 | K-6 | Angela Wroblewski |
| Cannon River STEM S | 1800 14th St NE | Faribault, MN | 55021-2508 | 507-331-7836 | | K-8 | Nalani McCutcheon |
| Cedar Riverside Community Charter S | 1610 S 6th St Ste 100 | Minneapolis, MN | 55454-1102 | 612-339-5767 | 339-2951 | K-8 | Walt Stull |
| City Academy | 958 Jessie St | Saint Paul, MN | 55130-4058 | 651-298-4624 | 292-6511 | 9-12 | Milo Cutter |
| Clarkfield Charter S | 301 13th St | Clarkfield, MN | 56223 | 320-669-1995 | 669-1997 | PK-6 | Kathy Koetter |
| College Prep Elementary S | 355 Randolph Ave | Saint Paul, MN | 55102 | 651-605-2360 | 605-2369 | K-6 | Michael Raimondi |
| Cologne Academy | 1221 Village Pkwy | Cologne, MN | 55322-9248 | 952-466-2276 | 466-4030 | K-8 | Lynn Gluck-Peterson |
| Community of Peace Academy | 471 Magnolia Ave E | Saint Paul, MN | 55130-3849 | 651-776-5151 | 771-4841 | K-12 | Cara Quinn |
| Community School of Excellence | 170 Rose Ave W | Saint Paul, MN | 55117-4437 | 651-917-0073 | 917-3717 | K-8 | Mo Chang |
| Cornerstone Montessori ES | 1611 Ames Ave | Saint Paul, MN | 55106 | 651-774-5000 | | K-6 | Liesl Taylor |
| Crosslake Community Charter S | 36974 County Road 66 | Crosslake, MN | 56442-2527 | 218-692-5437 | 692-5437 | K-8 | Todd Lyscio |
| Crosslake Community Online HS | 36974 County Road 66 | Crosslake, MN | 56442 | 218-692-5437 | 692-5437 | 9-12 | Todd Lyscio |

| School | Address | City,State | Zip code | Telephone | Fax | Grade | Contact |
|---|---|---|---|---|---|---|---|
| Cyber Village Academy | 768 Hamline Ave S | Saint Paul, MN | 55116-2224 | 651-523-7170 | 523-7113 | 2-12 | Dave Glick |
| Dakota Area Community Charter S | 220 Golden Rule Rd | Dakota, MN | 55925-7103 | 507-643-6869 | 643-6953 | K-5 | Lisa Kent |
| DaVinci Academy of Arts and Science | 13001 Central Ave NE | Blaine, MN | 55434 | 763-754-6577 | 754-6578 | K-8 | Debra Lach |
| Discovery Public S | 126 8th St NW | Faribault, MN | 55021-4241 | 507-331-5423 | 331-2618 | 6-12 | Jim Severson |
| Discovery Woods Montessori Charter S | 604 N 7th St | Brainerd, MN | 56401 | 218-828-8200 | | K-6 | Stephanie Dess |
| DREAM Technical Academy | 1705 16th Street NE | Willmar, MN | 56201 | 320-262-5640 | | 7-12 | Doug Knick |
| Dugsi Academy | 1091 Snelling Ave N | Saint Paul, MN | 55108-2705 | 651-642-0667 | 642-0668 | K-8 | Abdulkadir Osman |
| Eagle Ridge Academy Charter S | 7255 Flying Cloud Dr | Eden Prairie, MN | 55344-3549 | 952-746-7760 | 746-7765 | K-12 | Jason Ulbrich |
| East Range Academy of Tech & Science | 2000 Siegel Blvd | Eveleth, MN | 55734-8642 | 218-744-7965 | 744-2349 | 10-12 | Judy Youso |
| E.C.H.O. Charter S | PO Box 158 | Echo, MN | 56237-0158 | 507-925-4143 | 925-4165 | K-8 | Kenneth Alexander |
| Edvisions Off Campus S | PO Box 307 | Henderson, MN | 56044-0307 | 507-248-3101 | 665-2752 | 9-12 | Gigi Dobosenski |
| El Colegio Charter S | 4137 Bloomington Ave | Minneapolis, MN | 55407-3332 | 612-728-5728 | 728-5790 | 9-12 | Norma C. Garces |
| Excell Academy for Higher Learning | 6510 Zane Ave N | Brooklyn Park, MN | 55429-1559 | 763-533-0500 | 533-0508 | PK-3 | Sabrina Williams |
| Face to Face Academy | 1165 Arcade St | Saint Paul, MN | 55106-2615 | 651-772-5621 | 772-5566 | 8-12 | Jennifer Plum |
| Fraser Academy | 1534 6th St NE | Minneapolis, MN | 55413-1319 | 612-465-8600 | 465-8603 | K-5 | Linda Silrum |
| Friendship Acad of Fine Arts Charter S | 2600 E 38th St | Minneapolis, MN | 55406-3022 | 612-879-6703 | 879-6707 | K-4 | Nell Collier |
| Glacial Hills ES | PO Box 189 | Starbuck, MN | 56381-0189 | 320-239-3840 | 239-2803 | K-6 | Deb Mathias |
| Global Academy | 4065 Central Ave NE | Columbia Hts, MN | 55421 | 763-404-8200 | 781-5260 | K-8 | Helen Fisk |
| Great Expectations S | PO Box 310 | Grand Marais, MN | 55604-0310 | 218-387-9322 | 387-9344 | K-8 | Peter James |
| Great River S | 1326 Energy Park Dr | Saint Paul, MN | 55108-5202 | 651-305-2780 | 305-2781 | 1-12 | Samuel O'Brien |
| Green Isle Community S | PO Box 277 | Green Isle, MN | 55338-0277 | 507-326-7144 | 326-5434 | PK-6 | Mary Menne |
| Harbor City International S | 332 W Michigan St Ste 300 | Duluth, MN | 55802-1644 | 218-722-7574 | 625-6068 | 9-12 | Paul McGlynn |
| Harvest Prep S - Seed Academy | 1300 Olson Memorial Hwy | Minneapolis, MN | 55411-3968 | 612-381-9743 | 381-0748 | PK-6 | Eric Mahmoud |
| Hennepin ES | 2123 Clinton Ave | Minneapolis, MN | 55404 | 612-237-3430 | 871-2406 | K-6 | Dr. Julie Henderson |
| Hiawatha College Prep | 3800 Pleasant Ave | Minneapolis, MN | 55409 | 612-353-4324 | | 5-8 | John Kaczorek |
| Hiawatha Collegiate HS | 1611 E 46th St | Minneapolis, MN | 55407 | 612-547-9056 | | 9-9 | Nicole Cooley |
| Hiawatha Leadership Academy | 1611 E 46th St | Minneapolis, MN | 55407 | 612-455-4004 | | K-4 | Daniela Vasan |
| Hiawatha Leadership Academy | 3810 E 56th St | Minneapolis, MN | 55417 | 612-987-5688 | 825-4777 | PK-4 | Jess Hayes |
| Higher Ground Academy | 1381 Marshall Ave | Saint Paul, MN | 55104-6353 | 651-645-1000 | 645-2100 | K-12 | Bill Wilson |
| High School for Recording Arts | 1166 University Ave W | Saint Paul, MN | 55104-4169 | 651-287-0890 | 287-0891 | 9-12 | Anthony Simmons |
| Hmong College Prep Academy | 1515 Brewster St | Saint Paul, MN | 55108 | 651-209-8002 | 289-1802 | K-8 | Dr. Christianna Hang |
| Hmong College Prep Academy HS | 1515 Brewster St | Saint Paul, MN | 55108-2612 | 612-209-8002 | 209-8003 | 9-12 | Dr. Christianna Hang |
| Hope Community Academy | 720 Payne Ave | Saint Paul, MN | 55130-4127 | 651-796-4500 | 796-4599 | K-8 | MayChy Vu |
| International Spanish Language Academy | 5959 Shady Oak Rd S | Minnetonka, MN | 55343-8969 | 952-746-6020 | 746-6023 | K-4 | Karen Terhaar |
| Jeffrey Academy | 1550 Summit Ave | Saint Paul, MN | 55105-2274 | 651-414-6000 | 414-6006 | 5-8 | Brenda Natala |
| Jennings Community Learning Center | 2455 University Ave W | Saint Paul, MN | 55114-1507 | 651-649-5403 | 649-5490 | 9-12 | Bill Zimneiwicz |
| Kaleidoscope Charter S | 7525 Kalland Ave NE | Otsego, MN | 55301 | 763-428-1890 | 428-1691 | K-8 | Dr. Brett Wedlund |
| Kato Public Carter S | 110 N 6th St | Mankato, MN | 56001-4443 | 507-387-5524 | 387-5680 | 7-12 | Lisa Dudley |
| KIPP North Star Academy | 5034 Oliver Ave N | Minneapolis, MN | 55430 | 612-287-9700 | 287-9702 | 5-8 | Luwam Arefe |
| La Crescent Montessori & STEM S | 1116 S Oak St | La Crescent, MN | 55947-1560 | 507-895-4054 | 895-4064 | PK-12 | Tammy Stremcha |
| Lafayette Public Charter S | PO Box 125 | Lafayette, MN | 56054-0125 | 507-228-8943 | 228-8288 | K-8 | Andrea Harder |
| Lakes International Language Academy | 246 11th Ave SE | Forest Lake, MN | 55025 | 651-464-0771 | 464-4429 | PK-6 | Cam Hedlund |
| Lakes International Language Academy | 19850 Fenway Ave N | Forest Lake, MN | 55025 | 651-464-8989 | 464-8990 | 4-6 | Cam Hedlund |
| Leadership Academy | 2872 26th Ave S | Minneapolis, MN | 55406 | 612-728-8915 | 724-4719 | 5-12 | Shawn Fondow |
| Learning for Leadership Charter | 3300 5th St NE | Minneapolis, MN | 55418-1117 | 612-789-9598 | 789-0547 | K-12 | Matthew Jarolimek |
| LIFE Prep | 930 Geranium Ave E | Saint Paul, MN | 55106-2610 | 651-793-6624 | 793-6633 | PK-6 | Bart Johnson |
| Lighthouse Academy of Nations | 2600 E 26th St | Minneapolis, MN | 55406-1201 | 612-722-2555 | 729-2274 | 9-12 | Farhan Hussein |
| Lincoln International S | 2520 Minnehaha Ave | Minneapolis, MN | 55404-4118 | 612-872-8690 | 879-9557 | 9-12 | Brad Tipka |
| Lionsgate Academy | 3420 Nevada Ave N | Crystal, MN | 55427 | 763-486-5359 | 390-0012 | 7-12 | Diane Halpin Ph.D. |
| Lionsgate Academy AIM | 2342 Helen St N | North St Paul, MN | 55109 | 651-486-5359 | | K-12 | Diane Halpin |
| Loveworks Academy for Arts | 2225 Zenith Ave N | Golden Valley, MN | 55422-3852 | 952-522-6830 | 522-6840 | K-8 | April Harrison |
| Main Street S of Performing Arts | 1320 Mainstreet | Hopkins, MN | 55343-7497 | 952-224-1340 | 224-2955 | 9-12 | Matt McFarlane |
| Mastery S | 1300 Olson Memorial Hwy | Minneapolis, MN | 55411 | 612-381-9743 | 381-0748 | K-8 | Denise Smith |
| Math & Science Academy | 8430 Woodbury Xing | Woodbury, MN | 55125-9433 | 651-578-8061 | 578-7532 | 6-12 | Bob Kreischer |
| Metro Deaf S | 1471 Brewster St | Saint Paul, MN | 55108-2612 | 651-224-3995 | 222-0939 | PK-12 | Melissa Sweetmilk |
| Milroy Area Charter S | PO Box 129 | Milroy, MN | 56263-0129 | 507-336-2563 | 336-2568 | PK-6 | Heidi Sachariason |
| Minisinaakwaang Leadership Academy | 20930 367th Ln | McGregor, MN | 55760 | 218-768-5301 | 768-3357 | K-12 | Todd Lee |
| Minneapolis Academy Charter S | 5011 31st Ave S | Minneapolis, MN | 55417-1405 | 612-455-1340 | 455-1345 | 5-8 | Leon Cooper |
| Minneapolis College Prep Charter S | 2131 12th Ave N | Minneapolis, MN | 55411 | 612-200-2274 | 529-2710 | 9-12 | James Barnett |
| Minnesota International MS | 277 12th Ave N | Minneapolis, MN | 55401-1026 | 612-465-8465 | 465-8411 | 5-8 | Faysal Ali |
| Minnesota Internship Center | 1821 University Ave W # 271 | Saint Paul, MN | 55104 | 651-387-7489 | 280-4908 | 9-12 | Janet White |
| Minnesota Internship Center Charter | 2507 Fremont Ave N | Minneapolis, MN | 55411 | 612-238-3020 | | 9-12 | Robert Heise |
| Minnesota Internship Center Charter | 2507 Fremont Ave N | Minneapolis, MN | 55411 | 612-238-0750 | | 9-12 | Kristin Quinn |
| Minnesota Internship Center Charter | 2507 Fremont Ave N | Minneapolis, MN | 55411 | 612-588-1449 | | 9-12 | Nicole Hollins |
| Minnesota Math and Science Academy | 169 Jenks Avenue | Saint Paul, MN | 55117 | 651-246-0845 | | K-6 | Ozer Asdemir |
| Minnesota New Country S | PO Box 488 | Henderson, MN | 56044-0488 | 507-248-3353 | 248-3604 | 7-12 | Nancy Pfarr |
| Minnesota Online HS | 2314 University Ave W | Saint Paul, MN | 55114 | 800-764-8166 | 586-2870 | 9-12 | Elissa Raffa |
| Minnesota Virtual HS | 180 5th St E # M10A | Saint Paul, MN | 55101 | 612-746-7977 | 928-2802 | 6-12 | Bill Glenz |
| MTCS Connections Academy | 1336 Energy Park Dr | Saint Paul, MN | 55108 | 651-523-0888 | | K-10 | Melissa Gould |
| MTS HS | 2872 26th Ave S | Minneapolis, MN | 55406 | 612-722-9013 | 722-0013 | 9-12 | Dr. Ronald Salazar |
| MTS MS | 2526 27th Ave S | Minneapolis, MN | 55406 | 612-724-4680 | 729-0536 | 6-8 | Justin Birchem |
| MTS P.E.A.S.E. Academy | 601 13th Ave SE | Minneapolis, MN | 55414 | 612-378-1377 | 378-4886 | 9-12 | Michael Durchslag |
| Nasha Shkola Charter S | 3500 Williston Rd | Minnetonka, MN | 55345 | 952-746-1880 | 452-8672 | K-12 | Jake Nelson |
| Natural Science Academy | 920 Holley Ave Ste 3 | Saint Paul Park, MN | 55071 | 651-925-5050 | 925-5051 | K-5 | Kendra Hunding |
| Naytahwaush Community S | PO Box 8 | Naytahwaush, MN | 56566-0008 | 218-936-2112 | | K-6 | Terri Anderson |
| Nerstrand Charter S | PO Box 156 | Nerstrand, MN | 55053-0156 | 507-333-6850 | 333-6870 | K-5 | Bonnie Jean Flom |
| New Century Academy | 1000 5th Ave SE | Hutchinson, MN | 55350 | 320-234-3660 | 234-3668 | 7-12 | |
| New City S | 229 13th Ave NE | Minneapolis, MN | 55413-1117 | 612-623-3309 | 623-3319 | K-8 | Jitendrapal Kundan |
| New Discoveries Montessori Academy | 1000 5th Ave SE | Hutchinson, MN | 55350-7028 | 320-234-6362 | 234-6300 | K-6 | Dave Conrad |
| New Heights Charter S | 614 Mulberry St W | Stillwater, MN | 55082-4858 | 651-439-1962 | 439-0716 | K-12 | Thomas Kearney |
| New Millenium Academy | 2620 Russell Ave N | Minneapolis, MN | 55411-1725 | 612-377-6260 | 377-6261 | K-8 | Yee Yang |
| Noble Academy | 9477 Decatur Dr N | Minneapolis, MN | 55445 | 763-592-7706 | 592-7707 | K-5 | Neal Thao |
| Northeast College Prep Charter S | 2511 Taylor St NE | Minneapolis, MN | 55418 | 612-248-8240 | | K-3 | Carl Phillips |
| Northern Lights Community S | PO Box 2829 | Warba, MN | 55793-2829 | 218-492-4400 | 492-4402 | 6-12 | David Hagman |
| North Lakes Academy | 308 15th St SW | Forest Lake, MN | 55025 | 651-982-2688 | 464-6409 | 9-12 | Jackie Saunders |
| North Lakes Academy | 255 7th Ave NW Ste B | Forest Lake, MN | 55025-1177 | 651-982-2773 | 464-6409 | 5-8 | Caroline Little |
| North Shore Community S | 5926 Ryan Rd | Duluth, MN | 55804-9672 | 218-525-0663 | 525-0024 | K-6 | Barry Wolff |
| North Star Academy | 3301 Technology Dr | Duluth, MN | 55811-4115 | 218-728-9556 | 728-2075 | K-8 | Bonnie Jorgenson |
| Northwest Passage HS | 11345 Robinson Dr NW | Coon Rapids, MN | 55433-4061 | 763-862-9223 | 862-9250 | 9-12 | Peter Wieczorek |
| Nova Classical Academy | 1455 Victoria Way | Saint Paul, MN | 55102 | 651-209-6320 | 209-6325 | K-12 | Bruce Watkins |
| Odyssey Academy | 6201 Noble Ave N | Brooklyn Center, MN | 55429-2483 | 763-971-8200 | 549-2380 | K-9 | John Sedey |
| Oshki Ogimaag Charter S | PO Box 320 | Grand Portage, MN | 55605-0320 | 218-475-2112 | 475-2119 | K-6 | Anna Deschampe |
| PACT Charter S | 7250 E Ramsey Pkwy | Ramsey, MN | 55303-6902 | 763-712-4200 | 712-4201 | K-12 | Josh Nyquist |
| Paideia Academy Charter S | 7200 147th St W | Apple Valley, MN | 55124-9008 | 952-953-6200 | 432-2130 | K-8 | Marci Levy Maguire |
| Paladin Academy | 308 Northtown Dr NE | Blaine, MN | 55434-1039 | 763-786-4799 | 786-4798 | 9-12 | Leisa Irwin |
| Parnassus Preparatory S | 11201 96th Ave N | Maple Grove, MN | 55369 | 763-496-1416 | 898-3977 | K-12 | Constance Ford |
| Partnership Academy | 305 E 77th St | Richfield, MN | 55423-4312 | 612-866-3630 | 866-3640 | K-5 | Lisa Hendricks |
| Pillager Area Charter S | PO Box 130 | Pillager, MN | 56473-0130 | 218-746-3875 | 746-3876 | 9-12 | Mark Wolhart |
| Prairie Creek Community S | 27695 Denmark Ave | Northfield, MN | 55057-5333 | 507-645-9640 | 645-8234 | K-5 | Simon Tyler |
| Prairie Seeds Academy | 6200 W Broadway Ave | Minneapolis, MN | 55428-2826 | 763-450-1388 | 450-1389 | K-8 | Choua Yang |
| Prodeo Academy | 1555 40th Ave NE | Columbia Hts, MN | 55421 | 612-559-4881 | | K-8 | Richard Campion |
| Raleigh Academy | 5905 Raleigh St | Duluth, MN | 55807-2343 | 218-628-0697 | 628-2264 | K-5 | Danielle Perich |
| Ridgeway Community S | 35564 County Road 12 | Houston, MN | 55943-4006 | 507-454-9566 | 454-9567 | PK-5 | Jodi Dansingburg |
| River's Edge Academy | 188 Plato Blvd W | Saint Paul, MN | 55107-2021 | 651-234-0150 | 234-0159 | 9-12 | Meghan Cavalier |
| Riverway Learning Community Charter S | 1733 W Service Dr Ste 18 | Winona, MN | 55987-2286 | 507-474-6120 | 474-6190 | PK-12 | Katey Wadewitz |
| Rochester Math and Science Academy | 415 16th St SW | Rochester, MN | 55902-2125 | 507-252-5995 | | K-8 | Abdulkadir Abdulle |
| Rochester Off Campus Charter HS | 2364 Valleyhigh Dr NW | Rochester, MN | 55901-7641 | 507-282-3325 | 282-0976 | 9-12 | Jay Martini |
| Rochester STEM Academy | 415 16th St SW | Rochester, MN | 55902 | 507-281-2381 | | 9-12 | Bryan Rossi Ph.D. |
| Sage Academy Charter S | 3900 85th Ave N | Brooklyn Park, MN | 55443-1908 | 763-315-4020 | 315-4028 | 9-12 | Diane Scholten |
| Saint Cloud Math and Science Academy | 136 Division St | Waite Park, MN | 56387 | 320-249-0069 | | K-4 | Tammy Bengtson |
| St. Croix Preparatory Academy | 4260 Stagecoach Trl N | Stillwater, MN | 55082-1197 | 651-395-5900 | 395-5901 | K-12 | Jon Gutierrez |
| Saint Paul City S | 260 Edmund Ave | Saint Paul, MN | 55103-1783 | 651-225-9177 | 487-7551 | K-8 | Nancy Dana |
| Saint Paul Conservatory Performing Art | 16 5th St W | Saint Paul, MN | 55102-1403 | 651-290-2225 | 290-9000 | 9-12 | Callie Jacobs |
| Schoolcraft Learning Community S | PO Box 1685 | Bemidji, MN | 56619-1685 | 218-586-3284 | 586-3285 | K-8 | Scott Anderson |
| Sejong Academy of Minnesota | 1330 Blair Ave N | Saint Paul, MN | 55104 | 651-330-6944 | 330-7011 | K-8 | Dr. Jill Watson |
| Seven Hills Classical Academy Upper S | 8600 Bloomington Ave S | Bloomington, MN | 55425 | 952-426-6000 | | 6-8 | Carl Schlueter |
| Seven Hills Preparatory Academy | 8600 Bloomington Ave | Bloomington, MN | 55425-1920 | 952-426-6000 | 426-6020 | K-8 | Dr. Alice Woog |
| Sojourner Truth Academy | 3820 Emerson Ave N | Minneapolis, MN | 55412-2039 | 612-588-3599 | 588-0217 | K-8 | Julie Guy |
| Southside Family Charter S | 4500 Clinton Ave | Minneapolis, MN | 55419 | 612-872-8322 | 872-0612 | K-8 | Stan Hacker |
| Spectrum 6th Grade Center | 11044 Industrial Circle NW | Elk River, MN | 55330 | 763-241-8703 | | 6-6 | Vanessta Spark |
| Spectrum HS | 17796 Industrial Cir NW | Elk River, MN | 55330 | 763-241-8703 | 633-1380 | 6-12 | Vanessta Spark |
| Star of the North Academy Charter S | 1562 Viking Blvd | East Bethel, MN | 55011 | 763-812-1367 | | K-6 | Lulzim Axhijaj |
| STEP Academy | 4100 66th St E | Inver Grove, MN | 55076 | 651-289-6120 | 457-4692 | 6-12 | Mustafa Ibrahim |
| Stonebridge World S | 4530 Lyndale Ave S | Minneapolis, MN | 55419 | 612-877-7400 | 877-7444 | K-6 | Barbara Novy |
| Stride Academy | 1025 18th St N | Saint Cloud, MN | 56303-1205 | 320-230-5340 | 253-0006 | K-3 | Larry Peterson |
| Stride Academy South Campus | 3241 Oakham Ln | Saint Cloud, MN | 56301 | 320-217-6940 | 217-6318 | 4-8 | Donna Nordstrom |
| Swan River Montessori Charter S | 500 Maple St | Monticello, MN | 55362 | 763-271-7926 | 295-0075 | PK-6 | Katie Curtis |

| School | Address | City,State | Zip code | Telephone | Fax | Grade | Contact |
|---|---|---|---|---|---|---|---|
| TEAM Academy | 220 17th Ave NE | Waseca, MN | 56093-2753 | 507-833-8326 | 833-8327 | K-6 | Jill Courtney |
| Treknorth HS | 2400 Pine Ridge Ave NW | Bemidji, MN | 56601 | 218-444-1888 | 444-1893 | 6-12 | Dan McKeon |
| Trio Wolf Creek Distance Learning | 10363 Liberty Ln | Chisago City, MN | 55013-5418 | 651-213-2017 | 257-0576 | 4-12 | Tracy Quarnstrom |
| Twin Cities Academy | 835 5th St E | Saint Paul, MN | 55106-5260 | 651-205-4797 | 205-4799 | 6-8 | Betsy Lueth |
| Twin Cities Academy HS | 835 5th St E | Saint Paul, MN | 55106-5260 | 651-284-4797 | 205-4799 | 9-12 | Betsy Lueth |
| Twin Cities German Immersion S | 1031 Como Ave | Saint Paul, MN | 55103-1021 | 651-492-7106 | 330-2270 | K-8 | Ann Jurewicz |
| Twin Cities International ES | 277 12th Ave N | Minneapolis, MN | 55401-1026 | 612-821-6470 | 821-6477 | K-4 | Abdirashid Warsame |
| Ubah Medical Academy Charter S | 1600 Mainstreet | Hopkins, MN | 55343-7409 | 952-540-2942 | 540-2950 | 9-12 | Musa Farah |
| Universal Academy Charter S | 1745 University Ave W | Saint Paul, MN | 55104 | 651-442-3124 | | K-8 | Farhiya Einte |
| Upper Mississippi Academy | 426 Osceola Ave S | Saint Paul, MN | 55102 | 651-528-8091 | 683-2042 | 6-12 | Brad Blue |
| Urban Academy Charter S | 1668 Montreal Ave | Saint Paul, MN | 55116 | 651-215-9419 | 215-9571 | K-6 | Mongsher Ly |
| Venture Academy | 315 27th Ave SE | Minneapolis, MN | 55414-3234 | 612-345-9040 | 294-6737 | 6-7 | Jon Bacal |
| Vermilion Country S | PO Box 629 | Tower, MN | 55790 | 218-753-1246 | | 7-12 | Kevin Fitton |
| Voyageurs Expeditionary HS | 3724 Bemidji Ave N | Bemidji, MN | 56601-4335 | 218-444-3130 | 444-3126 | 6-12 | Julie Johnson-Willborg |
| Watershed HS | 6541 16th Ave S | Minneapolis, MN | 55423-1751 | 612-871-4363 | 871-1004 | 9-12 | Destiny Sparks |
| West Concord Charter School | PO Box 318 | West Concord, MN | 55985 | 507-527-2791 | | K-6 | Nicole Musolf |
| West Side Summit Charter S | 497 Humboldt Ave | Saint Paul, MN | 55107 | 651-200-4543 | | K-8 | |
| Woodbury Leadership Academy | 600 Weir Dr | Woodbury, MN | 55125 | 651-379-2681 | | K-8 | Dan Hurley |
| Woodson Institute for Excellence | 300 Industrial Blvd NE | Minneapolis, MN | 55413-4507 | 612-522-4022 | 522-4012 | K-8 | LaTanya Washington |
| World Learner Charter S | 112050 Hundertmark Rd | Chaska, MN | 55318-2817 | 952-368-7398 | 368-6094 | K-6 | Deana Siekmann |
| Yinghua Academy | 1616 Buchanan St NE | Minneapolis, MN | 55413-1609 | 612-788-9095 | 788-9079 | K-8 | Susan Berg |

## Mississippi

| School | Address | City,State | Zip code | Telephone | Fax | Grade | Contact |
|---|---|---|---|---|---|---|---|
| Hayes Cooper Center for Math & Science | 500 N Martin Luther King | Merigold, MS | 38759-9632 | 662-748-2734 | 748-2735 | PK-6 | Renee Lamastus |

## Missouri

| School | Address | City,State | Zip code | Telephone | Fax | Grade | Contact |
|---|---|---|---|---|---|---|---|
| Academia Los Ninos ES | 5123 E Truman Rd | Kansas City, MO | 64127 | 816-994-0396 | 472-1471 | K-5 | Angela Haywood-Gaskin |
| Academie Lafayette S | 3421 Cherry St | Kansas City, MO | 64109 | 816-888-7400 | 888-7410 | K-3 | Heather Royce |
| Academie Lafayette S | 6903 Oak St | Kansas City, MO | 64113-2530 | 816-361-7735 | 361-5788 | 4-8 | Elimane Mbengue |
| Academy for Integrated Arts | 5604 Troost Ave | Kansas City, MO | 64110 | 816-444-1720 | 444-1721 | K-4 | Tricia DeGraff |
| Academy of Envrnmntl Sci & Math ES | 3325 Bell | Saint Louis, MO | 63106 | 314-932-1464 | | K-5 | Anna Westlund |
| Academy of Envrnmntl Sci & Math MS | 3021 Hickory St | Saint Louis, MO | 63104 | 314-345-5673 | | 6-8 | CeAndre Perry |
| Allen Village HS | 4251 Bridger Rd | Kansas City, MO | 64111 | 816-931-0177 | 561-4640 | 9-12 | Amy Washington |
| Allen Village S | 706 W 42nd St | Kansas City, MO | 64111-3120 | 816-931-0177 | 561-4640 | K-12 | Amy Washington |
| Alta Vista Charter HS | 1524 Paseo Blvd | Kansas City, MO | 64127 | 816-471-2582 | 221-0012 | 9-12 | Eduardo Mendez |
| Alta Vista Charter MS | 2640 Belleview | Kansas City, MO | 64108 | 816-471-2139 | 960-4913 | 6-8 | Melody Stutzman |
| Banneker Charter Academy Technology | 6401 Rockhill Rd | Kansas City, MO | 64131-1122 | 816-926-9110 | 363-8721 | PK-8 | Dr. Marian Brown |
| Better Learning Communities Academy | 2153 Salisbury St Ste C | Saint Louis, MO | 63107 | 314-436-2603 | 436-2602 | K-3 | Angela Haywood-Gaskin |
| Biome S | 4471 Olive St | Saint Louis, MO | 63108 | 314-531-0982 | 737-7187 | K-1 | Debi Weaver |
| Brookside Charter Academy | 1815 E 63rd St | Kansas City, MO | 64130 | 816-531-2192 | 756-3055 | K-8 | Roger Offield |
| Carondelet Leadership Academy | 7604 Michigan Ave | Saint Louis, MO | 63111-3332 | 314-802-8744 | 802-8721 | K-8 | Patrice Coffin |
| Chinese S | 3740 Marine Ave | Saint Louis, MO | 63118 | 314-533-0975 | | K-4 | Dr. Lydia Chen |
| City Garden Montessori Charter S | 1618 Tower Grove Ave | Saint Louis, MO | 63110 | 314-664-7646 | 664-4997 | PK-8 | Dr. Nicole Evans Ed.D. |
| Confluence Academy-Old North St. Louis | 3017 N 13th St | Saint Louis, MO | 63107-3924 | 314-241-1110 | 241-1115 | K-8 | Sonya Murray |
| Confluence Academy-South City Campus | 4235 S Compton Ave | Saint Louis, MO | 63111 | 314-481-4700 | 351-0240 | K-8 | Pam Davenport |
| Confluence Academy-Walnut Park Campus | 5421 Thekla Ave | Saint Louis, MO | 63120-2513 | 314-383-8900 | 383-8925 | K-8 | Sheldon McAfee |
| Confluence Prep Academy | 310 N 15th St | Saint Louis, MO | 63103 | 314-588-1247 | 588-1296 | 9-12 | Mike Powers |
| Crossroads Academy of Kansas City | 1015 Central St | Kansas City, MO | 64105-1619 | 816-221-2600 | 221-2601 | K-8 | Tysie McDowell-Ray |
| DeLaSalle Charter S | 3737 Troost Ave | Kansas City, MO | 64109-2658 | 816-561-4445 | 561-6106 | 9-12 | Mark Williamson |
| EAGLE College Preparatory S | 2617 Shenandoah Ave | Saint Louis, MO | 63104 | 314-450-7651 | 735-4471 | K-2 | |
| EAGLE College Preparatory S | 3716 Morganford Rd | Saint Louis, MO | 63116 | 314-664-7627 | 664-6250 | K-8 | TarynAnn Barry |
| French S | 3740 Marine Ave | Saint Louis, MO | 63118 | 314-533-0975 | | K-5 | Conrad Wildsmith |
| Frontier S of Innovation | 6700 Corporate Dr Ste 150 | Kansas City, MO | 64120 | 816-363-1907 | 363-1165 | K-10 | Ugur Demircan |
| Gateway Science Academy | 6576 Smiley Ave | Saint Louis, MO | 63139 | 314-932-7513 | 932-7514 | K-5 | Nuh Celik |
| Gateway Science Academy | 5049 Fyler Ave | Saint Louis, MO | 63139 | 314-261-4361 | 261-4364 | 6-12 | Matt Sagnak |
| Gateway Science Academy | 6651 Gravois Ave | Saint Louis, MO | 63116 | 314-669-9000 | 669-9944 | K-5 | Wendy Gilliam |
| Genesis Promise Academy | 3800 E 44th St | Kansas City, MO | 64130-2183 | 816-921-0775 | 921-4268 | K-8 | Kevin Foster |
| Grand Center Arts Academy | 711 N Grand Blvd | Saint Louis, MO | 63103 | 314-533-1791 | 371-4630 | 6-12 | Matt Frederickson |
| Hawthorn Leadership S for Girls | 1901 N Kingshighway Blvd | Saint Louis, MO | 63113 | 314-361-5323 | | 6-8 | Dr. Robyn Wiens |
| Hogan Preparatory Academy | 6409 Agnes Ave | Kansas City, MO | 64132 | 816-444-4479 | 444-4268 | 6-8 | William Mcdowell |
| Hogan Preparatory Academy | 1221 E Meyer Blvd | Kansas City, MO | 64131-1207 | 816-444-3464 | 363-0473 | 9-12 | Dr. Jason Beavers |
| Hogan Preparatory Academy | 5809 Michigan Ave | Kansas City, MO | 64130 | 816-444-5010 | 361-2410 | K-5 | Heidi Mackey |
| Hope Leadership Academy | 2800 E Linwood Blvd | Kansas City, MO | 64128-1544 | 816-921-1213 | 931-6142 | K-3 | Sean Saunders |
| International S | 3740 Marine Ave | Saint Louis, MO | 63118 | 314-533-0975 | | 6-7 | Dr. Lydia Chen |
| Jamaa Learning Center | 7220 N Lindbergh Blvd # 13 | Saint Louis, MO | 63042 | 314-329-8507 | 721-8980 | K-8 | Gales Nicole |
| Kauffman S | 6401 Paseo Blvd | Kansas City, MO | 64131 | 816-268-5660 | 268-5645 | 5-12 | Hannah Lofthus |
| KIPP Endeavor Academy | PO Box 22624 | Kansas City, MO | 64113-0624 | 816-241-3994 | 241-3339 | 5-8 | Jake Schmitz |
| KIPP Inspire S | 1212 N 22nd St | Saint Louis, MO | 63106 | 314-296-3502 | | 5-8 | Jeremy Esposito |
| KIPP Triumph Academy | 955 Arcade Ave | Saint Louis, MO | 63112 | 314-454-9255 | 249-4328 | 5-8 | Elizabeth Valerio |
| KIPP Victory Academy | 955 Arcade Ave | Saint Louis, MO | 63112 | 314-454-9255 | | K-2 | Tiara Abu |
| KIPP Wisdom Academy | 2647 Ohio Ave | Saint Louis, MO | 63118 | 314-384-9561 | 975-0072 | K-1 | Jacob Shiffrin |
| Lafayette Preparatory Academy | 1881 Pine St | Saint Louis, MO | 63103 | 314-880-4458 | 880-4459 | K-4 | Susan Marino |
| Lamb ES | 1000 Charlotte St | Kansas City, MO | 64106-3051 | 816-842-8040 | 842-2727 | K-8 | Judy Akers |
| La Salle Charter S | 4145 Kennerly Ave | Saint Louis, MO | 63113-2942 | 314-531-9820 | 531-4820 | 5-8 | Phillip Pusateri |
| Lift for Life Academy | 1731 S Broadway | Saint Louis, MO | 63104-4050 | 314-436-2337 | 231-1299 | 6-12 | Cathy McGrath |
| New Hope Academy | 1001 Bennington Ave | Kansas City, MO | 64126 | 816-595-0800 | 595-0801 | 9-12 | Laquanda Carpenter |
| North Side Community S | 3033 N Euclid Ave | Saint Louis, MO | 63115 | 314-385-4500 | 385-9538 | PK-5 | John Grote |
| Parks ES | 3715 Wyoming St | Kansas City, MO | 64111-3945 | 816-753-6700 | 753-3436 | K-3 | Fleming Steve |
| Pathway Academy | 2015 E 72nd St | Kansas City, MO | 64132-1756 | 816-631-7100 | 621-7101 | K-6 | Jennifer Fleming |
| Preclarus Mastery Academy | 620 N Grand Blvd | Saint Louis, MO | 63103 | 314-454-0815 | 338-7435 | 5-8 | Marshall Peeples |
| Premier Charter S | 5279 Fyler Ave | Saint Louis, MO | 63139-1300 | 314-645-9600 | 645-9700 | K-8 | Julie Frugo |
| St. Louis College Prep HS | 1224 Grattan St | Saint Louis, MO | 63104 | 314-561-3440 | 667-3477 | 9-12 | Mike Malone |
| Scuola Vita Nuova | 535 Garfield Ave | Kansas City, MO | 64124 | 816-231-5788 | 231-5181 | K-8 | Nicole Goodman |
| South City Preparatory Academy | 1224 Grattan St | Saint Louis, MO | 63104 | 314-561-3440 | 667-3477 | 5-7 | Mike Malone |
| Spanish S | 4011 Papin St | Saint Louis, MO | 63110 | 314-533-0597 | | K-5 | Arlene Galve-Salgado |
| Tolbert Community Academy | 3400 Paseo Blvd | Kansas City, MO | 64109-2429 | 816-561-0114 | 561-1015 | K-8 | Trasi Ashley |
| University Academy | 6801 Holmes Rd | Kansas City, MO | 64131-1382 | 816-412-5900 | 410-0322 | K-12 | Tony Kline |

## Nevada

| School | Address | City,State | Zip code | Telephone | Fax | Grade | Contact |
|---|---|---|---|---|---|---|---|
| Academy for Career Education | 2800 Vassar St | Reno, NV | 89502-3214 | 775-324-3900 | 324-3901 | 9-12 | Bob DeRuse |
| Agassi Academy | 1201 W Lake Mead Blvd | Las Vegas, NV | 89106-2411 | 702-948-6000 | 948-6002 | K-8 | Chris Smith |
| Alpine Academy | 605 Boxington Way Ste 112 | Sparks, NV | 89434 | 775-356-1166 | 356-1168 | 9-12 | Jill Ross |
| American Preparatory Academy | 6000 W Oakey Blvd | Las Vegas, NV | 89146 | 702-266-7889 | 802-3142 | K-10 | Stacie Schwartz |
| Bailey Charter ES | 210 Gentry Way | Reno, NV | 89502-4209 | 775-323-6767 | 323-6799 | K-6 | Michelle Engebretson |
| Beacon Academy of Nevada | 7360 W Flamingo Rd | Las Vegas, NV | 89147 | 702-726-8600 | 538-9500 | 9-12 | Tambre Tondryk |
| Carson Montessori S | 2263 Mouton Dr | Carson City, NV | 89706-0446 | 775-887-9500 | 887-9502 | K-6 | Jessica Daniels |
| Coral Academy of Science Charter S | 1701 Valley Rd | Reno, NV | 89512 | 775-322-0274 | 322-1378 | K-5 | Seyzi Tandogan |
| Coral Academy of Science Charter S | 1350 E 9th St | Reno, NV | 89512-2904 | 775-323-2332 | 323-2366 | 5-12 | Seyzi Tandogan |
| Coral Academy of Science - Las Vegas | 8185 Tamarus St | Las Vegas, NV | 89123-2464 | 702-269-8512 | 269-3258 | K-2 | Ercan Aydogdu |
| Coral Academy of Science - Las Vegas | 2150 Windmill Pkwy | Henderson, NV | 89074 | 702-485-3510 | 722-2718 | 3-5 | Ercan Aydogdu |
| Coral Academy of Science - Las Vegas | 1051 Sandy Ridge Ave | Henderson, NV | 89052 | 702-776-8800 | 776-8803 | 6-12 | Ercan Aydogdu |
| Delta Academy | 4075 N Rancho Dr | Las Vegas, NV | 89130 | 702-396-2252 | 396-0848 | 7-12 | Dr. Kyle Konold |
| Discovery Charter S | 3883 E Mesa Vista Ave | Las Vegas, NV | 89120 | 702-547-5682 | 547-5685 | K-8 | Dr. David Price |
| Doral Academy | 9625 W Saddle Ave | Las Vegas, NV | 89147-8089 | 702-776-6491 | 802-2638 | K-8 | Bridget Bilbray-Phillips |
| Doral Academy Cactus Campus | 9025 W Cactus Ave | Las Vegas, NV | 89178 | 702-960-7500 | 960-7960 | K-7 | Danielle Marshall |
| Elko Institute for Academic Achievement | 1031 Railroad St Ste 107 | Elko, NV | 89801 | 775-738-3422 | 738-3488 | K-8 | Connie Zeller |
| Explore Knowledge Academy | 5871 Mountain Vista St | Las Vegas, NV | 89120 | 702-870-5032 | 871-5032 | K-12 | Abbe Mattson |
| Founders Academy | 4025 N Rancho Dr | Las Vegas, NV | 89130 | 702-998-8368 | 998-1328 | K-10 | Timm Petersen |
| High Desert Montessori Charter S | 2590 Orovada St | Reno, NV | 89512-2119 | 775-624-2800 | 624-2801 | PK-9 | Tammie Stockton |
| Honors Academy of Literature | 195 N Arlington Ave | Reno, NV | 89501 | 775-737-4084 | 737-4533 | 1-8 | J-Lynn Van Pelt |
| I Can Do Anything Charter HS | 1195 Corporate Blvd Ste C | Reno, NV | 89502-2363 | 775-857-1544 | 857-6825 | 9-12 | Dawn Gilmore |
| Imagine S at Mountain View | 6610 Grand Montecito Pkwy | Las Vegas, NV | 89149 | 702-253-0251 | 253-0254 | K-5 | Dr. Eve Breier |
| Innovations International Charter S | 1600 E Oakey Blvd | Las Vegas, NV | 89104-3334 | 702-216-4337 | 216-4353 | K-6 | Dr. Connie Malin |
| Innovations International Charter S | 950 E Sahara Ave | Las Vegas, NV | 89104-3022 | 702-216-4337 | 216-4353 | 7-12 | Dr. Connie Malin |
| Leadership Academy | 7495 W Azure Dr | Las Vegas, NV | 89130 | 702-350-1472 | 825-2684 | 6-12 | Byron Richardson |
| Learning Bridge | 505 S Pioche Hwy | Ely, NV | 89301 | 775-289-3500 | 289-3511 | K-8 | Mary Flanagan |
| Mariposa Dual Language Academy | 3875 Glen St | Reno, NV | 89502 | 775-826-4040 | 826-4030 | K-5 | Chris McBride |
| Mater Academy of Nevada | 3445 Mountain Vista St | Las Vegas, NV | 89121 | 702-485-2400 | 485-3322 | K-8 | Renee Fairless |
| Nevada Connections Academy | 555 Double Eagle Ct | Reno, NV | 89521 | 775-826-4200 | 826-4288 | K-12 | Steve Werlein |
| Nevada State HS | 233 N Stephanie St | Henderson, NV | 89074 | 702-953-2600 | 953-2608 | 11-12 | Dr. John Hawk |
| Nevada Virtual Academy | 8965 S Eastern Ave Ste 330 | Las Vegas, NV | 89123 | 702-407-1825 | 407-5055 | K-12 | Caroline McIntosh |
| Oasis Academy | PO Box 6322 | Fallon, NV | 89407 | 775-423-5437 | 423-5433 | K-8 | Melissa Mackedon |
| Odyssey Charter S | 2251 S Jones Blvd | Las Vegas, NV | 89146-3161 | 702-257-0578 | 259-7793 | K-12 | Tim Lorenz |
| One Hundred Academy of Excellence | 2341 Comstock Dr | North Las Vegas, NV | 89032-3512 | 702-636-2551 | 636-9475 | K-5 | Peggy M Selma |
| Pinecrest Academy | 1360 S Boulder Hwy | Henderson, NV | 89015 | 702-749-3500 | 749-9995 | K-8 | Carrie Buck |

| School | Address | City,State | Zip code | Telephone | Fax | Grade | Contact |
|---|---|---|---|---|---|---|---|
| Quest Preparatory Academy | 7495 W Azure Dr | Las Vegas, NV | 89130 | 702-631-4751 | 586-0836 | K-12 | Deb Roberson |
| Rainbow Dreams Academy | 950 W Lake Mead Blvd | Las Vegas, NV | 89106-2339 | 702-638-0222 | 638-0220 | K-5 | Brenda McKinney |
| Rainshadow Community Charter HS | 121 Vesta St | Reno, NV | 89502-2913 | 775-322-5566 | 322-5509 | 9-12 | Steve West Ph.D. |
| Sierra Nevada Academy | 13880 Stead Blvd | Reno, NV | 89506-1579 | 775-677-4500 | 677-4441 | K-8 | Kim Regan |
| Silver Sands Montessori Charter S | 1841 Whitney Mesa Dr | Henderson, NV | 89014 | 702-522-6220 | 522-6218 | K-8 | Marlo Tsuchiyama |
| Silver State Charter S | 788 Fairview Dr | Carson City, NV | 89701 | 775-883-7900 | 883-9130 | 7-12 | Steve Knight |
| Somerset Academy of Las Vegas | 385 W Centennial Pkwy | North Las Vegas, NV | 89084 | 702-633-5616 | 633-5628 | K-8 | Dr. Francine Mayfield |
| Somerset Academy of Las Vegas | 50 N Stephanie | Henderson, NV | 89074 | 702-998-0500 | 998-0503 | K-8 | Reggie Farmer |
| Somerset Academy of Las Vegas | 4650 Losee Rd | North Las Vegas, NV | 89030 | 702-902-5466 | 902-5444 | K-10 | Dan Phillips |
| Somerset Academy of Las Vegas | 7038 Sky Pointe Dr | Las Vegas, NV | 89131 | 702-478-8888 | 478-8844 | K-10 | Gayle Jefferson |

## New Hampshire

| School | Address | City,State | Zip code | Telephone | Fax | Grade | Contact |
|---|---|---|---|---|---|---|---|
| Academy for Science & Design | 486 Amherst St Unit 1 | Nashua, NH | 03063 | 603-595-4705 | 262-9163 | 6-12 | Jennifer Cava |
| Birches Academy of Academics and Art | 419 S Broadway | Salem, NH | 03079 | 603-458-6399 | | 1-8 | Dr. Dael Angelico-Hart |
| Cocheco Arts and Technology Academy | 40 Hampshire Cir | Dover, NH | 03820-2961 | 603-742-0700 | 742-7207 | 9-12 | James Friel M.Ed. |
| Compass Classical Academy | 15 Elkins St | Franklin, NH | 03235 | 603-729-3370 | | K-5 | Judy Tilton |
| CSI Charter S | 26 Washington St | Penacook, NH | 03303-1519 | 603-753-0194 | 753-6429 | 9-12 | James Gorman |
| Founders Academy | 5 Perimeter Rd | Manchester, NH | 03103 | 603-952-4705 | 624-0057 | 6-12 | Maureen Mooney |
| Frost Charter S | PO Box 967 | North Conway, NH | 03860 | 603-356-6332 | | K-5 | |
| Gate City Charter S for the Arts | 7 Henry Clay Dr | Merrimack, NH | 03054 | 603-943-5273 | | K-8 | Karin Cevasco |
| Granite State Arts Academy | 16 Route 111 | Derry, NH | 03038 | 603-912-4944 | | 9-12 | Mark Bograd |
| Great Bay eLearning Charter S | 30 Linden St | Exeter, NH | 03833-2622 | 603-775-8638 | 775-8528 | 7-12 | Peter Stackhouse |
| Ledyard Charter Academy | PO Box 327 | Lebanon, NH | 03766 | 603-727-4772 | | 9-12 | John Higgins |
| Making Community Connections | 60 Rogers St | Manchester, NH | 03103 | 603-935-7488 | | 6-12 | Edmond Marceau |
| Making Community Connections Charter S | 149 Emerald St Ste UP3 | Keene, NH | 03431 | 603-283-0844 | | 9-12 | Elizabeth Cardine |
| MicroSociety Academy Charter S | 500 W Hollis St | Nashua, NH | 03062 | 603-595-7877 | | K-5 | Amy Bottomley |
| Mill Falls Charter S | 100 William Loeb Dr | Manchester, NH | 03109 | 603-232-5176 | 518-7489 | K-6 | Laura Wrubleski |
| Mountain Village Charter S | 13 NH Route 25 | Plymouth, NH | 03264 | 603-536-3900 | 947-0189 | K-8 | Matt Thornton |
| Next Charter S | 5 Hood Rd | Derry, NH | 03038 | 603-437-6398 | 437-6398 | 9-12 | Joseph Crawford |
| North Country Charter Academy | 260 Cottage St Ste A | Littleton, NH | 03561-4137 | 603-444-1535 | 444-9843 | 7-12 | Lisa Lavoie |
| PACE Career Academy | 65 Pinewood Rd | Allenstown, NH | 03275 | 603-210-1882 | 210-2341 | 9-12 | Martin Castle |
| Polaris Charter S | 100 Coolidge Ave | Manchester, NH | 03102 | 603-634-0034 | 634-0041 | K-6 | Jennifer Murdock - Smith |
| Seacoast Charter S | 171 Watson Rd | Dover, NH | 03820 | 603-842-5764 | 842-5415 | K-8 | Peter Sweet |
| Strong Foundations Charter S | 715 Riverwood Dr | Pembroke, NH | 03275-3701 | 603-225-2715 | 225-2738 | K-8 | Beth McClure |
| Surry Village Charter S | 449 Route 12A | Surry, NH | 03431 | 603-357-9700 | 357-9701 | K-8 | Dr. Matora Fiorey |
| TEAMS Charter S | 26 Washington St | Penacook, NH | 03303-1519 | 603-753-4022 | 753-6429 | 9-12 | George Rogers |
| Virtual Learning Academy | 30 Linden St | Exeter, NH | 03833-2622 | 603-778-2500 | 651-5038 | 6-12 | Stephen Kossakoski |

## New Jersey

| School | Address | City,State | Zip code | Telephone | Fax | Grade | Contact |
|---|---|---|---|---|---|---|---|
| Academy Charter HS | 1725 Main St | South Belmar, NJ | 07719-3051 | 732-681-8377 | 681-8375 | 9-12 | Dr. Mary Jo McKinley |
| Academy for Urban Leadership HS | 612 Amboy Ave | Perth Amboy, NJ | 08861 | 848-203-3742 | 203-3948 | 9-12 | Dr. Nestor Collazo |
| Atlantic City Community Charter S | 200 N Texas Ave | Atlantic City, NJ | 08401 | 609-541-3149 | | K-8 | Jessica Richard |
| Banneker Preparatory Charter S | PO Box 128 | Willingboro, NJ | 08046 | 609-531-0158 | | 6-8 | Richard Wilson M.A. |
| BelovED Community Charter S | 508 Grand St | Jersey City, NJ | 07302 | 201-630-4700 | 918-6137 | K-5 | Kelly Convery |
| Bergen Arts and Science Charter ES | 30 Madonna Pl | Garfield, NJ | 07026 | 862-247-8510 | 247-8511 | K-3 | |
| Bergen Arts and Science Charter HS | 43 Maple Ave | Hackensack, NJ | 07601 | 201-968-5039 | 968-5044 | 8-12 | |
| Bergen Arts and Science Charter MS | 200 MacArthur Ave | Garfield, NJ | 07026-1214 | 973-253-0002 | 253-0110 | 4-8 | Nihat Guvercin |
| Bridgeton Charter S | 790 E Commerce Ave | Bridgeton, NJ | 08302 | 856-497-8202 | | K-1 | Yvonne Cribbs |
| Burch Charter S of Excellence | 100 Linden Ave | Irvington, NJ | 07111-2560 | 973-373-3223 | 373-3228 | PK-5 | Dr. Dorian Dorsey |
| Camden Academy Charter HS | 879 Beideman Ave | Camden, NJ | 08105-4227 | 856-365-1000 | 365-8179 | 9-12 | Dr. Marvin Jones |
| Camden Community Charter S | 415 N 9th St | Camden, NJ | 08102 | 856-635-0310 | | K-7 | Andrea Surratt |
| Camden Prep Charter S | 1500 S 8th St | Camden, NJ | 08104 | 856-379-4488 | | K-K | Michael Ambriz |
| Camden's Pride Charter S | 879 Beideman Ave | Camden, NJ | 08105-4227 | 856-365-1000 | 965-5358 | K-4 | Dr. Richelle Baughn |
| Camden's Promise Charter S | 879 Beideman Ave | Camden, NJ | 08105-4227 | 856-365-1000 | 365-1005 | 5-8 | Dr. Joseph Conway |
| Central Jersey College Prep Charter S | 17 Schoolhouse Rd | Somerset, NJ | 08873-4245 | 732-302-9991 | 302-9992 | K-12 | Tarkan Topcuoglu |
| ChARTer-TECHnical HS for Performing Arts | 413 New Rd | Somers Point, NJ | 08244-2143 | 609-926-7694 | 926-8472 | 9-12 | Dr. Brian McGuire |
| Classical Academy Charter S of Clifton | 20 Valley Rd | Clifton, NJ | 07013-1030 | 973-278-7707 | 277-7720 | 6-8 | Vincent DeRosa |
| College Achieve Charter S | 365 Emerson Ave | Plainfield, NJ | 07062 | 908-625-1879 | 441-9877 | K-8 | Mike Piscal |
| Community Charter S of Paterson | 75 Spruce St | Paterson, NJ | 07501-1720 | 973-413-2057 | 345-7623 | K-7 | Mark Valli |
| Compass Academy Charter School | 23 W Chestnut Ave | Vineland, NJ | 08360 | 856-899-5570 | 431-7971 | K-5 | Sue Little |
| Cramer Hill ES | 1033 Cambridge Ave | Camden, NJ | 08105 | 856-726-0027 | | K-3 | |
| Discovery Charter S | 240 Halsey St | Newark, NJ | 07102 | 973-623-0222 | 623-0024 | 4-8 | Barbara Weiland |
| East Orange Community Charter S | 99 Washington St | East Orange, NJ | 07017-1006 | 973-996-0400 | 996-0398 | K-4 | Harvin Dash |
| Edison Energysmart Charter S | 92 Cortelyou Ln | Somerset, NJ | 08873 | 732-412-7643 | 412-7645 | K-7 | Oguz Yildiz |
| Edwards Academic Charter S | 509 Bramhall Ave | Jersey City, NJ | 07304-2730 | 201-433-5300 | | K-8 | Mona Lisa Kalina |
| Elysian Charter S | 301 Garden St Ste 5 | Hoboken, NJ | 07030-5895 | 201-876-0102 | 876-9576 | K-8 | Harry Laub Ph.D. |
| Empowerment Academy Charter S | 508 Grand St | Jersey City, NJ | 07302 | 201-630-4700 | | K-5 | Rhema Stradford |
| Englewood on the Palisades Charter S | 65 W Demarest Ave | Englewood, NJ | 07631-2316 | 201-569-9765 | 568-9576 | K-5 | Shirl Burns M.Ed. |
| Environment Comm Opportunity Charter S | 817 Carpenter St | Camden, NJ | 08102-1132 | 856-963-2627 | 963-2628 | K-5 | Dr. Antoinette Dendtler |
| Ethical Community Charter S | 95 Broadway | Jersey City, NJ | 07306 | 201-984-4151 | 200-9931 | K-7 | Marta Bergamini |
| Foundation Academy Charter IS | 363 W State St | Trenton, NJ | 08618 | 609-920-9200 | 920-9205 | 3-8 | Graig Weiss |
| Foundation Collegiate Academy | 22 Grand St | Trenton, NJ | 08611 | 609-920-9200 | 920-9205 | 9-12 | Shavonne McMillan |
| Freedom Prep Charter S | 1000 Atlantic Ave | Camden, NJ | 08104 | 856-962-0766 | 962-0769 | 6-8 | Ron Brady |
| Freire Charter S | PO Box 120 | Newark, NJ | 07101 | 973-733-9393 | 733-9377 | 9-11 | Tauheedah Baker-Jones |
| Golden Door Charter S | 3044 John F Kennedy Blvd | Jersey City, NJ | 07306-3604 | 201-795-4400 | 795-3308 | K-8 | Brian Stiles |
| Gray Charter S | 55 Liberty St | Newark, NJ | 07102-4815 | 973-824-6661 | 824-2296 | K-8 | Verna Gray |
| Greater Brunswick Charter S | 429 Joyce Kilmer Ave | New Brunswick, NJ | 08901-3322 | 732-448-1052 | 448-1055 | K-8 | Donna Medea |
| Great Futures Charter HS | 225 Morris Blvd | Jersey City, NJ | 07302 | 201-716-1520 | 716-1530 | 9-12 | John Gonzalez |
| Great Oaks Charter MSHS | 24 Maiden Ln | Newark, NJ | 07102-5801 | 973-565-9170 | | 6-12 | Jared Taillefer |
| Hatikvah International Academy Charter S | 7 Lexington Ave | East Brunswick, NJ | 08816-5033 | 732-254-8300 | 254-8380 | K-5 | Dr. Marcia Grayson |
| Hoboken Charter S | 4 Garden St | Hoboken, NJ | 07030-3502 | 201-963-3280 | 963-0695 | PK-12 | Deirdra Grode |
| Hoboken Dual Language Charter S | 123 Jefferson St | Hoboken, NJ | 07030 | 201-427-1458 | 706-4491 | K-6 | Jennifer Sargent |
| Holland Charter S | 190 Oliver St | Paterson, NJ | 07501 | 973-345-2212 | 345-2233 | K-8 | Christina Scano |
| Hope Academy Charter S | 601 Grand Ave | Asbury Park, NJ | 07712 | 732-988-4227 | 988-9125 | K-8 | DaVisha Pratt |
| Hope Community Charter S | 836 S 4th St | Camden, NJ | 08103 | 856-379-3448 | | K-4 | Robin Ruiz |
| International Academy of Atlantic City | 729 Cardinal Way | Galloway, NJ | 08205 | 609-498-6350 | | K-12 | Peter Caporilli |
| International Academy of Trenton | 720 Bellevue Ave | Trenton, NJ | 08618 | 609-759-2005 | 337-7933 | K-5 | Dr. Taneisha Spall |
| International Charter S of Trenton | 105 Grand St | Trenton, NJ | 08611-2417 | 609-394-3111 | 394-3116 | K-4 | Melissa Benford |
| Jersey City Community Charter S | 128 Danforth Ave | Jersey City, NJ | 07305-2626 | 201-433-2288 | 433-5803 | K-8 | Eugene Brown |
| Jersey City Global Charter S | 255 Congress St | Jersey City, NJ | 07307-3420 | 201-636-8540 | 636-8543 | K-3 | Nadira Raghunandan |
| Kingdom Charter S of Leadership | 121 W Church St | Blackwood, NJ | 08012-3971 | 856-232-0100 | | K-6 | Riscee Langhorne |
| KIPP Cooper Norcross | 525 Clinton St | Camden, NJ | 08103 | 856-966-9600 | | K-1 | Anne Kadowaki |
| Knowledge A to Z Charter S | 1725 Park Blvd | Camden, NJ | 08103 | 856-375-1140 | | K-4 | Tishara Landi |
| Lady Liberty Academy Charter S | 746 Sandford Ave | Newark, NJ | 07106 | 973-623-9005 | 483-0807 | K-8 | Lynette Dortrait |
| LEAP Academy University Charter S | 549 Cooper St | Camden, NJ | 08102-1210 | 856-614-0400 | 342-7900 | K-12 | Janice Strigh |
| Learning Community Charter S | 2495 John F Kennedy Blvd | Jersey City, NJ | 07304-2007 | 201-332-0900 | 332-4981 | K-8 | Colin Hogan |
| Link Community Charter S | 23 Pennsylvania Ave | Newark, NJ | 07114 | 973-642-0529 | 642-1978 | 5-8 | Kathleen Hester J.D. |
| Mastery S of Camden North Camden ES | 800 Erie St | Camden, NJ | 08102 | 856-371-3513 | | K-5 | |
| Merit Preparatory Charter S | 909 Broad St | Newark, NJ | 07102 | 973-642-4400 | 367-7706 | 6-8 | Kimberly White |
| M.E.T.S. Charter S | 211 Sherman Ave | Jersey City, NJ | 07307 | 201-526-8500 | 526-7630 | 6-12 | Ian Fallstich |
| Millville Public Charter S | 1101 Wheaton Ave Ste 220 | Millville, NJ | 08332-2003 | 856-506-8143 | | K-5 | Colleen McLaughlin |
| Newark Educators Community Charter S | 9-11 Hill St | Newark, NJ | 07102 | 973-732-3848 | 732-3847 | PK-5 | Dina Velez |
| Newark Legacy Charter S | 823 S 16th St | Newark, NJ | 07108 | 973-642-7000 | 556-1250 | K-6 | Paula White Bradley |
| Newark Prep Charter S | 570 Broad St | Newark, NJ | 07102 | 862-307-7010 | 307-7107 | 9-12 | Tora Townsend |
| New Horizons Community Charter S | 45 Hayes St | Newark, NJ | 07103-3019 | 973-848-0400 | 596-0984 | K-5 | Andre Hollis |
| North Star Academy Charter S | 10 Washington Pl | Newark, NJ | 07102-3106 | 973-642-0101 | 642-5800 | K-12 | Michael Ambriz |
| Obama Green Charter HS | 35 Watchung Ave | Plainfield, NJ | 07060-1207 | 877-643-4064 | | 9-12 | Steven King |
| PACE Charter School of Hamilton | 1949 Hamilton Ave | Hamilton, NJ | 08619-3736 | 609-587-2288 | 587-8483 | K-5 | Debbie Pontoriero |
| Passaic Arts and Science Charter S | 7 Saint Francis Way | Passaic, NJ | 07055 | 973-928-5544 | 928-5545 | 4-8 | Vahit Sevinc |
| Paterson Arts and Science Charter S | 764 11th Ave | Paterson, NJ | 07514 | 862-336-1550 | 336-1551 | K-6 | Nihat Guvercin |
| Paterson Charter S for Science and Tech | 276 Wabash Ave | Paterson, NJ | 07503 | 973-345-4400 | 345-4636 | K-6 | Riza Gurcanli M.Ed. |
| Paterson Charter S for Science and Tech | 196 W Railway Ave | Paterson, NJ | 07503 | 973-247-0600 | 247-9924 | 7-12 | Riza Gurcanli |
| People's Preparatory HS | 321 Bergen St | Newark, NJ | 07103-2639 | 973-622-1790 | 622-1453 | 9-12 | Jess Rooney |
| Phillip's Academy Charter S | 342 Central Ave | Newark, NJ | 07103-2808 | 973-624-0644 | 624-0102 | K-8 | Mark Shultz |
| Pride Academy Charter S | 117 Elmwood Ave | East Orange, NJ | 07018 | 973-672-3200 | 672-3207 | 5-8 | Fiona Thomas |
| Princeton Charter S | 100 Bunn Dr | Princeton, NJ | 08540-2821 | 609-924-0575 | 924-0282 | K-8 | Lawrence Patton |
| Queen City Academy Charter S | 815 W 7th St | Plainfield, NJ | 07063-1449 | 908-753-4700 | 753-4816 | K-8 | Danielle West |
| Red Bank Charter S | 58 Oakland St | Red Bank, NJ | 07701-1104 | 732-450-2092 | 936-1923 | PK-8 | Meredith Pennotti |
| Ridge & Valley Charter S | 1234 State Route 94 | Blairstown, NJ | 07825-4115 | 908-362-1114 | 362-6680 | K-8 | Nanci Dvorsky |
| Riverbank Charter S of Excellence | 1300 Hornberger Ave | Roebling, NJ | 08554-1313 | 609-499-4321 | 447-0350 | K-3 | Beth Kelley |
| Robeson Charter S for the Humanities | 643 Indiana Ave | Trenton, NJ | 08638-3821 | 609-394-7721 | 394-7720 | 4-8 | Candace Kenyatta |
| Roseville Community Charter S | 11 Gray St | Newark, NJ | 07107-1529 | 973-908-8057 | 733-9555 | K-1 | |
| Soaring Heights Charter S | 1 Romar Ave | Jersey City, NJ | 07305-1713 | 201-434-4800 | 434-7474 | K-8 | Claudia Zuorick |
| Sussex Co. Charter S for Technology | 385 N Church Rd | Sparta, NJ | 07871-3307 | 973-383-3250 | 383-2901 | 6-8 | Jill Eckel |
| TEAM Academy Charter S | 60 Park Pl Ste 802 | Newark, NJ | 07102-5508 | 973-705-8326 | 556-1238 | K-12 | Joanna Belcher |

| School | Address | City,State | Zip code | Telephone | Fax | Grade | Contact |
|---|---|---|---|---|---|---|---|
| Teaneck Community Charter S | 563 Chestnut Ave | Teaneck, NJ | 07666 | 201-833-9600 | 833-9225 | K-8 | Anthony Calandrillo |
| Thomas Charter MS | 308 S 9th St | Newark, NJ | 07103 | 973-621-0060 | 792-0066 | 5-8 | John Gamble |
| Thomas Charter S | 370 S 7th St | Newark, NJ | 07103-2047 | 973-621-0060 | 621-0061 | PK-4 | Dr. Karen Young-Thomas |
| Treat Academy Charter S - North | 443 Clifton Ave | Newark, NJ | 07104-1339 | 973-482-8811 | 482-7681 | K-8 | Theresa Adubato |
| Treat Academy Chartr S - Central | 180 William St | Newark, NJ | 07103 | 973-286-1020 | 286-1050 | K-8 | Theresa Adubato |
| Trenton Stem-to-Civics Charter S | 1555 Pennington Rd | Ewing, NJ | 08618 | 609-503-1103 | | 9-12 | Dr. Leigh Byron |
| Union County TEAMS Charter S | 515 W 4th St | Plainfield, NJ | 07060-4225 | 908-754-9043 | 754-7790 | K-12 | Sheila Thorpe |
| Unity Charter S | 1 Evergreen Pl | Morristown, NJ | 07960 | 973-292-1808 | 267-9288 | K-8 | Dr. Karen Lake |
| University Academy Charter HS | 275 W Side Ave | Jersey City, NJ | 07305-1130 | 201-200-3200 | 200-3262 | 9-12 | Erie Lugo |
| University Heights Charter S | 74 Hartford St | Newark, NJ | 07103-2832 | 973-623-1965 | 623-8511 | K-8 | Misha Simmonds B.A. |
| Varisco-Rogers Charter S | 233 Woodside Ave | Newark, NJ | 07104-3113 | 973-481-9001 | 481-9009 | K-8 | Teressa Segarra |
| Village Charter S | 101 Sullivan Way | Trenton, NJ | 08628-3425 | 609-695-0110 | 695-1880 | K-8 | Keoke Wooten-Johnson |
| Vineland Public Charter S | 2724 S Main Rd | Vineland, NJ | 08360 | 856-691-1004 | 691-1005 | K-7 | Kimberly Hutchinson |

## New Mexico

| School | Address | City,State | Zip code | Telephone | Fax | Grade | Contact |
|---|---|---|---|---|---|---|---|
| ABQ Charter Academy | 405 Dr Martin Luther King | Albuquerque, NM | 87102 | 505-242-6640 | 242-6872 | 9-12 | Amy Roble |
| Academy for Technology and the Classics | 74 A Van NU PO | Santa Fe, NM | 87508 | 505-473-4282 | 467-6513 | 7-12 | Susan Lumley |
| Academy of Trades & Technology | 2551 Karsten Ct SE | Albuquerque, NM | 87102-5083 | 505-765-5517 | 765-5898 | 9-12 | Christopher Hotchkiss |
| ACE Leadership HS | 1240 Bellamah Ave NW | Albuquerque, NM | 87104 | 505-242-4733 | 242-2220 | 9-12 | Tori Stephens-Shauger |
| Albuquerque Institute of Math & Science | 933 Bradbury Dr SE | Albuquerque, NM | 87106-4374 | 505-559-4249 | 243-9235 | 6-12 | Kathy Sandoval-Snider |
| Albuquerque School of Excellence | 13201 Lomas Blvd NE | Albuquerque, NM | 87112-7001 | 505-312-7711 | 312-7712 | 1-12 | Salih Aykac |
| Albuquerque Sign Language Academy | 620 Lomas Blvd NW | Albuquerque, NM | 87102 | 505-247-1701 | 247-1704 | K-9 | Raphael Martinez M.A. |
| Albuquerque Talent Development Academy | 1800 Atrisco Dr NW | Albuquerque, NM | 87120 | 505-503-2465 | 831-7031 | 9-12 | Rommie Compher |
| Alma D Arte Charter HS | 402 W Court Ave | Las Cruces, NM | 88005 | 575-541-0145 | 527-5329 | 9-12 | Mark Harshorne |
| Anansi Charter S | PO Box 1709 | El Prado, NM | 87529-1709 | 575-776-2256 | 776-5561 | K-6 | Michele Hunt |
| Anthony Charter S | 780 Landers Rd | Anthony, NM | 88021 | 575-882-0600 | 882-0603 | 7-12 | Colleen Adolph |
| ASK Academy | 1380 Rio Rancho Dr SE # 361 | Rio Rancho, NM | 87124 | 505-891-0757 | 891-2115 | 7-12 | Paul Reeves |
| Bataan Military Academy | 5555 McLeod Rd NE | Albuquerque, NM | 87109 | 505-292-5588 | 232-3230 | 9-12 | Jan Zink |
| Biehl Charter HS | 123 4th St SW | Albuquerque, NM | 87102-3201 | 505-299-9409 | 299-9493 | 9-12 | Frank McCulloch |
| Carinos De Los Ninos S | PO Box 130 | Cordova, NM | 87523 | 505-351-4721 | 351-1366 | K-8 | Vernon Jaramillo |
| Chavez Community S | 1325 Palomas Dr SE | Albuquerque, NM | 87108 | 505-877-0558 | 242-1466 | 9-12 | Tani Arness |
| Cien Aguas International S | 2000 Randolph Rd SE | Albuquerque, NM | 87106 | 505-255-0001 | 255-0400 | K-8 | Michael Rodriguez |
| Coral Community Charter S | 4401 Silver Ave SE | Albuquerque, NM | 87108 | 505-292-6725 | | K-4 | Donna Eldredge |
| Corrales International S | 5500 Wilshire Ave NE | Albuquerque, NM | 87113 | 505-344-9733 | 338-1409 | K-12 | Dr. Elsy Fierro Diaz |
| Cottonwood Classical Preparatory S | 7801 Jefferson St NE | Albuquerque, NM | 87109 | 505-998-1021 | 341-9510 | 6-12 | Sam Obenshain |
| Cottonwood Valley Charter S | PO Box 1829 | Socorro, NM | 87801-1829 | 575-838-2026 | 838-2420 | K-8 | Kim Schaffer |
| Creative Education Preparatory Institute | 4801 Montano Rd NW | Albuquerque, NM | 87120-2428 | 505-314-2374 | 314-2377 | 9-12 | Elisa Bohannon |
| Deming Cesar Chavez Charter HS | 315 E 1st St | Deming, NM | 88030 | 575-544-8404 | 544-8755 | 9-12 | Ray Trejo |
| Digital Arts and Technology Academy | 1011 Lamberton Pl NE | Albuquerque, NM | 87107-1641 | 505-341-0888 | 341-0749 | 9-12 | Lisa Myhre |
| Dorn Community Charter S | 1119 Edith Blvd SE | Albuquerque, NM | 87102 | 505-243-1434 | 243-6943 | K-2 | Ellen Esquibel-Bellamy |
| Duncan Heritage Academy | 816 Broadway Blvd SE | Albuquerque, NM | 87102 | 505-839-4971 | 831-9027 | K-8 | J. Moncada |
| East Mountain HS | PO Box 340 | Sandia Park, NM | 87047-0340 | 505-281-7400 | 281-4173 | 9-12 | Monique Siedschlag |
| El Camino Real Charter S | 3713 Isleta Blvd SW | Albuquerque, NM | 87105-5990 | 505-314-2212 | 314-2216 | K-12 | Paym Greene |
| Estancia Valley Classical Academy | PO Box 2340 | Moriarty, NM | 87035 | 505-832-2223 | 832-5006 | K-12 | |
| Explore Academy | 3831 Midway Place NE | Albuquerque, NM | 87109 | 505-468-1092 | 468-1098 | 9-12 | |
| GREAT Academy | 6001A San Mateo Blvd NE | Albuquerque, NM | 87109 | 505-792-0306 | 792-0225 | 9-12 | |
| Gutierrez MS | 69 Gail Harris Blvd | Roswell, NM | 88203 | 575-347-9703 | 347-9707 | 6-8 | Joe Andreis |
| Health Leadership HS | 1900 Randolph Rd SE | Albuquerque, NM | 87106 | 505-750-4547 | | 9-12 | Blanca Lopez |
| Health Sciences Academy | PO Box 80001 | Albuquerque, NM | 87198 | 505-362-6115 | | 7-12 | Lorna Sanraj |
| Horizon Academy - West | 3021 Todos Santos St NW | Albuquerque, NM | 87120 | 505-998-0459 | 998-0463 | PK-5 | Cynthia Carter |
| International S at Mesa del Sol | 2660 Eastman Ave SE | Albuquerque, NM | 87106 | 505-508-3295 | 508-3328 | K-8 | Dr. Sean Joyce |
| Jefferson Montessori Academy | 500 W Church St | Carlsbad, NM | 88220 | 575-234-1703 | 887-9391 | K-12 | Cindy Holguin |
| Kennedy HS | 4300 Blake Rd SW | Albuquerque, NM | 87121 | 505-873-1165 | 242-7444 | 9-12 | Robert Baade |
| King Community S | 1905 Mountain Rd NW | Albuquerque, NM | 87104 | 505-344-0746 | 344-0789 | K-6 | Tamara Henderson |
| La Academia de Esperanza | 5200 Sequoia Rd NW | Albuquerque, NM | 87120 | 505-764-5500 | 764-5501 | 6-12 | Steve Woods |
| La Academia Dolores Huerta | 1480 N Main St | Las Cruces, NM | 88001 | 575-526-2984 | 523-5407 | 6-8 | Octavio Casillas |
| La Jicarita Community S | PO Box 552 | Penasco, NM | 87553 | 915-496-7933 | | K-6 | Dr. Deborah Anglada |
| La Promesa Early Learning Center | 7500 La Morada NW | Albuquerque, NM | 87120 | 505-268-3274 | 268-3276 | PK-8 | Dr. Analee Maestas |
| La Resolana Leadership Academy | 230 Truman St NE | Albuquerque, NM | 87108 | 505-243-8114 | 243-8385 | 6-8 | Justina Montoya |
| Las Montanas Charter S | 201 E Lohman Ave | Las Cruces, NM | 88001-3686 | 575-636-2100 | 527-7686 | 9-12 | Richard Robinson |
| La Tierra Montessori S of the Arts & Sci | State Road 68 Building 854 | Alcalde, NM | 87511 | 505-852-0200 | 852-0326 | K-8 | Suzanne Lynne |
| Learning Community Charter S | 5555 McLeod Rd NE | Albuquerque, NM | 87109 | 505-332-3200 | 332-8780 | 6-12 | Viola Martinez |
| Leopold Charter S | 1422 Highway 180 E | Silver City, NM | 88061-7837 | 575-538-2547 | 388-4970 | 6-12 | Eric Ahner |
| Lindrith Area Heritage Charter S | PO Box 119 | Lindrith, NM | 87029 | 575-774-6669 | | K-8 | Rebecca Gibson M.A. |
| Los Puentes Charter S | 4012 4th St NW | Albuquerque, NM | 87107 | 505-342-5959 | 341-0836 | 7-12 | Micaela Smith |
| MASTERS Program | 6401 S Richards Ave | Santa Fe, NM | 87508 | 505-428-7320 | 428-7322 | 10-12 | Anne Salzmann |
| McCurdy Charter S | PO Box 2250 | Espanola, NM | 87532 | 505-692-6090 | 692-6095 | K-12 | Janette Archuleta |
| Media Arts Collaborative Charter S | 4401 Central Ave NE | Albuquerque, NM | 87108 | 505-243-1957 | 268-1651 | 6-12 | Glenna Voigt M.A. |
| Middle College HS | 200 College Rd Ste 9 | Gallup, NM | 87301-5603 | 505-722-9945 | 722-9946 | 10-12 | Connie Torres |
| Mission Achievement & Success Charter S | 1718 Yale Blvd SE | Albuquerque, NM | 87106 | 505-242-3118 | 243-3062 | 6-9 | JoAnn Myers |
| Monte Del Sol Charter S | PO Box 4068 | Santa Fe, NM | 87502-4068 | 505-982-5225 | 982-5321 | 7-12 | Dr. Robert Jessen |
| Montessori ES | 1730 Montano Rd NW | Albuquerque, NM | 87107 | 505-796-0149 | 796-0147 | K-8 | Mary Jane Besante |
| Montessori of the Rio Grande Charter S | 1650 Gabaldon Dr NW | Albuquerque, NM | 87104-2761 | 505-842-5993 | 242-2907 | PK-6 | Bonnie Dodge |
| Moreno Valley HS | PO Box 1037 | Angel Fire, NM | 87710-1037 | 575-377-3100 | 377-7263 | 9-12 | Douglas Wine |
| Mosaic Academy | 450 Llano St | Aztec, NM | 87410 | 505-334-6364 | 334-6364 | K-8 | Diane Mittler |
| Mountain Mahogany Community S | 5014 4th St NW | Albuquerque, NM | 87107-3908 | 505-341-1424 | 341-1428 | K-8 | Baylor DelRosario |
| Native American Community Academy | 1000 Indian School Rd NW | Albuquerque, NM | 87104 | 505-266-0992 | 266-2905 | 6-12 | Kara Bobroff |
| New America S - Las Cruces | PO Box 16680 | Las Cruces, NM | 88004 | 505-527-9085 | 527-9153 | 9-12 | Margarita Porter |
| New America School | 1734 Isleta Blvd SW | Albuquerque, NM | 87105 | 505-222-4360 | 873-2602 | 9-12 | LaTricia Mathis |
| New Mexico Connections Academy | 4001 Office Ct 201-204 | Santa Fe, NM | 87507 | 505-428-2131 | 424-9092 | 4-12 | Athena Trujillo |
| New Mexico International School | 8650 Alameda Blvd NE | Albuquerque, NM | 87122 | 505-503-7670 | | K-5 | Todd Knouse |
| New Mexico School for the Arts | 275 E Alameda St | Santa Fe, NM | 87501 | 505-310-4194 | 629-4108 | 9-12 | Cindy Montoya |
| New Mexico Virtual Academy | 845 Sullivan Ave | Farmington, NM | 87401 | 505-436-2383 | 258-4080 | 6-12 | Deborah Jackson |
| North Valley Academy | 7939 4th St NW | Los Ranchos, NM | 87114 | 505-998-0501 | 998-0505 | K-8 | Susan McConnell |
| Nuestros Valores Charter S | 6800 Gonzales Rd SW | Albuquerque, NM | 87121 | 505-873-7758 | 873-3567 | 9-12 | Monica Aguilar |
| Public Academy for Performing Arts | 3000 Adams St NE | Albuquerque, NM | 87110 | 505-830-3128 | 830-9930 | 6-12 | Doreen Winn |
| Red River Valley Charter S | PO Box 742 | Red River, NM | 87558-0742 | 575-754-6117 | 754-3258 | PK-8 | Karen Phillips |
| Rio Gallinas S for Ecology and the Arts | 1107 Montezuma St | Las Vegas, NM | 87701 | 505-454-8687 | 454-8688 | K-8 | Gerald Garcia |
| Roots & Wings Community S | HC 81 Box 22 | Questa, NM | 87556 | 575-586-2076 | 586-2087 | K-8 | |
| Sage Montessori Charter S | 3821 Singer Blvd NE | Albuquerque, NM | 87109 | 505-797-4305 | 797-4294 | K-8 | Felix Garcia |
| SAMS Academy | 4100 Aerospace Pkwy NW | Albuquerque, NM | 87120 | 505-338-8601 | 296-0510 | 7-12 | Coreen Carrillo |
| San Diego Riverside Charter S | PO Box 99 | Jemez Pueblo, NM | 87024-0099 | 575-834-7419 | 834-9167 | K-8 | Karen Mayhew |
| School of Dreams Academy | 1800 Main St NE | Los Lunas, NM | 87031 | 505-866-7632 | 866-0780 | 7-12 | Michael Ogas |
| Sena Charter HS | 69 Hotel Cir NE | Albuquerque, NM | 87123-1202 | 505-237-2373 | 237-2380 | 9-12 | Nadine Torres |
| South Valley Academy | 3426 Blake Rd SW | Albuquerque, NM | 87105-5009 | 505-452-3132 | 452-3133 | 9-12 | Julie Radoslovich |
| South Valley Preparatory S | 2813 Gun Club Rd SW | Albuquerque, NM | 87105 | 505-222-5642 | 222-5647 | 6-8 | Charlotte Trujillo |
| Southwest Intermediate Learning Center | 10301 Candelaria Rd NE | Albuquerque, NM | 87112-1504 | 505-296-7677 | 296-0510 | 7-8 | Al Baysinger M.A. |
| Southwest Primary Learning Center | 10301 Candelaria Rd NE | Albuquerque, NM | 87112-1504 | 505-296-7677 | 296-0510 | 4-6 | Al Baysinger M.A. |
| Southwest Secondary Learning Center | 10301 Candelaria Rd NE | Albuquerque, NM | 87112-1504 | 505-296-7677 | 296-0510 | 7-12 | Robert Pasztor |
| Taos Academy | 110 Paseo Del Canon W | Taos, NM | 87571 | 575-751-3109 | 751-3394 | 5-12 | Traci Filiss |
| Taos Charter S | 1303 Paseo Del Canon | Taos, NM | 87571-6738 | 575-751-7222 | 751-7546 | K-8 | Dr. Deidre McAdam |
| Taos Integrated School of the Arts | PO Box 668 | Taos, NM | 87571 | 575-758-7755 | 758-7766 | K-8 | Susan Germann |
| Taylor Academy | 3900 Del Rey Blvd | Las Cruces, NM | 88012 | 575-652-4006 | 652-4621 | K-8 | Cynthia Risner |
| Tierra Adentro - NM Sch Acedemics/Art | 1511 Central Ave NE | Albuquerque, NM | 87106 | 505-967-4720 | 967-4721 | 6-12 | Veronica Torres |
| Tierra Encantada Charter S | 551 Alarid St | Santa Fe, NM | 87501-3733 | 505-983-3337 | 983-6637 | 7-12 | Daniel Benavidez |
| Turqoise Trail ES | 13A San Marcos Loop | Santa Fe, NM | 87508-7083 | 505-986-4000 | 474-7862 | PK-6 | Dr. Ray Griffin |
| 21st Century Public Academy | 6805 Academy Pkwy West NE | Albuquerque, NM | 87109 | 505-254-0280 | 254-8507 | 5-8 | Mary Tarango |
| Uplift Community S | 406 Highway 564 | Gallup, NM | 87301 | 505-863-4333 | 863-4885 | K-6 | James Cammon |
| Vista Grande HS | 213 Paseo Del Canon E | Taos, NM | 87571-6239 | 575-758-5100 | 758-5102 | 9-12 | Isabelle St. Onge |
| Walatowa Charter HS | PO Box 669 | Jemez Pueblo, NM | 87024-0669 | 575-834-0443 | 834-0449 | 9-12 | Arrow Wilkinson |

## New York

| School | Address | City,State | Zip code | Telephone | Fax | Grade | Contact |
|---|---|---|---|---|---|---|---|
| Academic Leadership Charter S | 677 E 141st St | Bronx, NY | 10454-2410 | 718-585-4215 | 585-4837 | K-5 | Norma Figueroa-Hurwitz |
| Academy Charter S | 117 N Franklin St | Hempstead, NY | 11550-1314 | 516-408-2200 | 292-2329 | K-6 | Clarence Williams |
| Academy of the City Charter S | 3614 12th St | Astoria, NY | 11106 | 718-487-9857 | 785-9592 | K-2 | Richard Lee |
| Achievement First Apollo Charter S | 350 Linwood St | Brooklyn, NY | 11208-2116 | 718-235-2647 | 235-2649 | K-4 | Jabari Sims |
| Achievement First Aspire Charter S | 982 Hegeman Ave | Brooklyn, NY | 11208-4434 | 718-838-0205 | 228-8839 | K-5 | Sarah Kasok |
| Achievement First Brooklyn HS | 1485 Pacific St | Brooklyn, NY | 11216 | 718-363-2260 | 363-2262 | 9-12 | |
| Achievement First Brownsville Charter S | 2021 Bergen St | Brooklyn, NY | 11233-4801 | 718-471-2600 | 342-3458 | K-5 | Michelle Kagan |
| Achievement First Bushwick Charter S | 1300 Greene Ave | Brooklyn, NY | 11237-4502 | 718-471-2560 | 453-0428 | K-12 | Michael Rosskamm |
| Achievement First Crown Heights Charter | 790 E New York Ave | Brooklyn, NY | 11203-1212 | 718-774-0762 | 774-0830 | K-12 | Camilla Lopez |
| Achievement First East New York ES | 557 Pennsylvania Ave | Brooklyn, NY | 11207-5727 | 718-485-4924 | 342-5194 | K-8 | Injy Carpenter |
| Achievement First Endeavor S | 510 Waverly Ave | Brooklyn, NY | 11238-2702 | 718-622-4786 | 789-1649 | K-12 | Tom Kaiser |
| Achievement First North Brooklyn Prep S | 200 Woodbine St | Brooklyn, NY | 11221 | 718-471-2690 | 402-1818 | K-8 | Elena Knappen |
| Albany Community Charter S | 65 Krank St | Albany, NY | 12202-1150 | 518-433-1500 | 433-1501 | K-5 | S. Neal Currie |

| School | Address | City,State | Zip code | Telephone | Fax | Grade | Contact |
|---|---|---|---|---|---|---|---|
| Albany Leadership Charter HS for Girls | 19 Hackett Blvd | Albany, NY | 12208-3407 | 518-694-5300 | 694-5307 | 9-12 | Christina Roberts |
| Amani Charter S | PO Box 3022 | Mount Vernon, NY | 10553-3022 | 914-668-6450 | 699-0839 | 5-8 | Debra Stern |
| Amber Charter S | 220 E 106th St | New York, NY | 10029-4020 | 212-534-9667 | 534-6225 | K-5 | Dr. Vasthi Acosta |
| American Dream Charter S | 510 E 141st St | Bronx, NY | 10454 | 212-437-8318 | 227-2760 | 6-8 | Melissa Melkonian |
| Bedford Stuyvesant Collegiate Charter S | 800 Gates Ave | Brooklyn, NY | 11221-2203 | 718-669-7460 | 669-7771 | 5-12 | Mabel Lajes-Guiteras |
| Bed-Stuy New Beginnings Charter S | 82 Lewis Ave | Brooklyn, NY | 11206-7013 | 718-453-1001 | 452-2090 | K-5 | Joshua Morales |
| Beginning With Children Charter S | 850 Kent Ave | Brooklyn, NY | 11205 | 718-388-8847 | 388-8936 | K-8 | Valerie Davis-Fells |
| Beginning With Children Charter S II | 215 Heyward St | Brooklyn, NY | 11206 | 718-302-7700 | 302-7701 | PK-3 | Esosa Ogbahon |
| Believe Northside Charter HS | 424 Leonard St | Brooklyn, NY | 11222-3908 | 347-390-1273 | 390-1274 | 9-12 | Reshma Baig |
| Boys Prep Charter S of New York | 1695 Seward Ave | Bronx, NY | 10473 | 646-783-3589 | 346-9096 | K-5 | Peter Herzberg |
| Brighter Choice Charter MS for Boys | 395 Elk St | Albany, NY | 12206-2707 | 518-703-6100 | 694-5551 | 5-8 | Derick Brown |
| Brighter Choice Charter MS for Girls | 395 Elk St | Albany, NY | 12206-2707 | 518-694-5550 | 694-5551 | 5-8 | Kimberly Arrington |
| Brighter Choice Charter S for Boys | 116 N Lake Ave | Albany, NY | 12206-2710 | 518-694-8200 | 694-8201 | K-4 | Karen McLean |
| Brighter Choice Charter S for Girls | 250 Central Ave | Albany, NY | 12206-2639 | 518-694-4100 | 694-4123 | K-4 | Marcus Puccioni |
| Brilla College Preparatory Charter S | 413 E 144th St | Bronx, NY | 10454 | 347-273-8439 | | K-5 | Kelsey Kopro |
| Bronx Academy of Promise Charter S | 1349 Inwood Ave | Bronx, NY | 10452-3222 | 718-293-6950 | 681-8225 | K-8 | Catherine Jackvony |
| Bronx Charter S for Better Learning | 3740 Baychester Ave | Bronx, NY | 10466-5031 | 718-655-6660 | 655-5555 | K-5 | Shubert Jacobs |
| Bronx Charter S for Children | 388 Willis Ave | Bronx, NY | 10454-1303 | 718-402-3300 | 402-3258 | K-5 | Doreen Land |
| Bronx Charter S for Excellence | 1960 Benedict Ave | Bronx, NY | 10462-4402 | 718-828-7301 | 828-7302 | K-8 | Charlene Reid |
| Bronx Charter S for the Arts | 950 Longfellow Ave | Bronx, NY | 10474-4809 | 718-893-1042 | 893-7910 | K-5 | Dr. Nicholas Stapleton |
| Bronx Community Charter S | 3170 Webster Ave | Bronx, NY | 10467-4902 | 718-584-1400 | 944-1405 | K-5 | Martha Andrews |
| Bronx Global Learning Institute | 750 Concourse Vlg W | Bronx, NY | 10451-3865 | 718-993-1740 | 993-1965 | K-5 | Celia Domenich |
| Bronx Lighthouse Charter S | 1001 Intervale Ave | Bronx, NY | 10459-3151 | 646-915-0025 | 915-0037 | K-12 | Stacy Winitt |
| Bronx Preparatory Charter S | 3872 3rd Ave | Bronx, NY | 10457-8222 | 718-294-0841 | 294-2381 | 5-12 | Jacqueline King-Robinson |
| Brooklyn Ascend Lower S | 205 Rockaway Pkwy | Brooklyn, NY | 11212-3444 | 718-907-9147 | 240-9140 | K-6 | Brandon Sorlie |
| Brooklyn Charter S | 545 Willoughby Ave | Brooklyn, NY | 11206-6815 | 718-302-2085 | 302-2426 | K-5 | Omigbade Escayg |
| Brooklyn Dreams Charter S | 259 Parkville Ave | Brooklyn, NY | 11230-1310 | 718-859-8400 | 586-0347 | K-6 | Yvette Wilds |
| Brooklyn East Collegiate Charter S | 80 Underhill Ave | Brooklyn, NY | 11238-3509 | 718-250-5760 | 250-5761 | 5-8 | Eric Green |
| Brooklyn Excelsior Charter S | 856 Quincy St | Brooklyn, NY | 11221-3612 | 718-246-5681 | 246-5864 | K-8 | Adam Stevens |
| Brooklyn LAB Charter S | PO Box 25734 | Brooklyn, NY | 11202 | 347-429-8439 | 612-9127 | 6-8 | Eric Tucker Ph.D. |
| Brooklyn Prospect Charter S | 3002 Fort Hamilton Pkwy | Brooklyn, NY | 11218-1608 | 347-889-7041 | 889-7038 | 6-12 | LaNolia Omowanile |
| Brooklyn Scholars Charter S | 2635 Linden Blvd | Brooklyn, NY | 11208-4907 | 718-348-9360 | 348-9362 | K-8 | Desiree Kirton |
| Brooklyn S of Inquiry | 50 Avenue P | Brooklyn, NY | 11204-6105 | 718-621-5730 | 621-5735 | K-8 | Donna Taylor |
| Brooklyn Urban Garden Charter S | 500 19th St | Brooklyn, NY | 11215-6204 | 212-437-8318 | | 6-8 | Linda Rosenbury |
| Broome Street Academy | 121 Avenue of the Americas | New York, NY | 10013-1510 | 212-453-0295 | 966-7253 | 9-12 | Jeremy Kaplan |
| Brownsville Ascend Charter S | 1501 Pitkin Ave | Brooklyn, NY | 11212 | 347-390-2773 | 342-1082 | K-6 | Erica Murphy |
| Brownsville Collegiate Charter S | 364 Sackman St | Brooklyn, NY | 11212-7614 | 718-636-0370 | 296-8321 | 5-9 | Jessica Simmons |
| Buffalo Academy of Science Charter S | 190 Franklin St | Buffalo, NY | 14202 | 716-854-2490 | 854-5039 | 7-12 | Mustafa Ersoy |
| Buffalo United Charter S | 325 Manhattan Ave | Buffalo, NY | 14214-1809 | 716-835-9862 | 835-6272 | K-8 | Tammy Messmer |
| Bushwick Ascend Charter S | 751 Knickerbocker Ave | Brooklyn, NY | 11221-5336 | 718-240-9162 | 484-0498 | K-3 | Dellianna Burrows |
| Canarsie Ascend Charter S | 9719 Flatlands Ave | Brooklyn, NY | 11236-3729 | 718-907-0153 | | K-1 | Brenda Daniels |
| Central Queens Academy Charter S | 5530 Junction Blvd | Elmhurst, NY | 11373-4622 | 718-271-6200 | 271-6900 | 5-5 | Jesse Tang |
| Challenge Preparatory Charter S | 710 Hartman Ln | Far Rockaway, NY | 11691 | 718-327-1352 | 327-1361 | K-3 | Latoiya Tolliver-Revell |
| Charter S for Applied Technologies | 2303 Kenmore Ave | Buffalo, NY | 14207-1311 | 716-876-7505 | 876-9758 | K-12 | Efrain Martinez |
| Charter S of Educational Excellence | 260 Warburton Ave | Yonkers, NY | 10701-2226 | 914-476-5070 | 476-2858 | K-8 | Cindy Lopez |
| Charter S of Inquiry | 15 Ashland Ave | Buffalo, NY | 14222 | | | K-8 | |
| Child Development Center of the Hamptons | 110 Stephen Hands Path | East Hampton, NY | 11937 | 631-324-0207 | 324-4112 | K-5 | Robert Budd |
| Children's Aid Society Charter S | 1919 Prospect Ave | Bronx, NY | 10457-6506 | 347-871-9002 | 583-6238 | K-5 | Ife Lenard |
| Citizens of the World Charter S | 424 Leonard St | Brooklyn, NY | 11222-3908 | 718-384-1386 | | K-5 | Meredith Cronk |
| Citizens of the World Charter S | 791 Empire Blvd | Brooklyn, NY | 11213-5653 | 718-221-5095 | | K-5 | Martine King |
| City Polytechnic HS | 105 Johnson St | Brooklyn, NY | 11201 | 718-875-1473 | 875-1947 | 9-12 | Yusuf Muhammad |
| Community Partnership Charter S | 241 Emerson Pl | Brooklyn, NY | 11205-3808 | 718-399-3824 | 399-1495 | K-7 | Melanie Bryon |
| Community Roots Charter S | 51 Saint Edwards St | Brooklyn, NY | 11205-2932 | 718-858-1629 | 858-1754 | K-6 | Allison Keil |
| Compass Charter S | 300 Adelphi St | Brooklyn, NY | 11205 | 718-310-3588 | 852-4682 | K-5 | Brooke Peters |
| Coney Island Prep Public Charter S | 501 West Ave | Brooklyn, NY | 11224-4220 | 718-513-6951 | 513-6955 | 5-8 | Jacob Mnookin |
| Cultural Arts Academy at Spring Creek | 1400 Linden Blvd | Brooklyn, NY | 11212-5149 | 718-683-3300 | 272-1330 | K-3 | Laurie Midgette |
| de Hostos Charter S | 938 Clifford Ave | Rochester, NY | 14621-4808 | 585-544-6170 | 544-3848 | K-8 | Jeffrey Halsdorfer |
| Democracy Preparatory Harlem HS | 212 W 120th St | New York, NY | 10027 | 212-932-7791 | 666-3706 | 9-12 | Steve Popper |
| Democracy Prep Charter HS | 222 W 134th St | New York, NY | 10030 | 212-281-3061 | 281-3064 | 9-12 | Natasha Trivers |
| Democracy Prep Endurance Charter S | 250 W 127th St | New York, NY | 10027-2957 | 212-316-7602 | 316-7022 | 6-8 | Margaret Marrer |
| Discovery Charter S | 133 Hoover Dr | Rochester, NY | 14615 | 585-342-4032 | 342-4003 | K-2 | Joseph Saia |
| DREAM Charter S | 232 E 103rd St | New York, NY | 10029 | 212-722-0232 | 348-5979 | K-7 | Eve Colavito |
| Eagle Academy for Young Men III | 17110 Linden Blvd | Jamaica, NY | 11434-1327 | 718-723-4703 | 723-4709 | 6-8 | Kenyatte Reid |
| East Harlem Scholars Academy | 1573 Madison Ave | New York, NY | 10029-3819 | 212-348-2518 | 348-2848 | K-8 | Cheyenne Sao Roque |
| East Harlem Scholars Academy II | 2050 2nd Ave | New York, NY | 10029 | 212-831-0650 | 289-7967 | K-8 | |
| Elmwood Village Charter S | 40 Days Park | Buffalo, NY | 14201-2008 | 716-886-4581 | 348-3707 | K-8 | John Sheffield |
| Enterprise Charter S | 275 Oak St | Buffalo, NY | 14203-1638 | 716-855-2114 | 855-2967 | K-8 | Dr. Heather Lyon |
| Equality Charter S | 4140 Hutchinson River Pkwy | Bronx, NY | 10475 | 718-320-3032 | 320-3721 | 6-8 | Caitlin Franco |
| Equity Project Charter S | 549 Audubon Ave | New York, NY | 10040-3401 | 646-254-6451 | 202-3584 | 5-8 | Zeke Vanderhoek |
| Ethical Community Charter S | 700 Park Ave | Brooklyn, NY | 11206-5269 | 718-599-2176 | 599-2814 | K-4 | Annette Keane |
| Evergreen Charter S | 605 Peninsula Blvd | Hempstead, NY | 11550 | 516-292-2060 | | K-5 | Maritza Meyers |
| Excellence Boys Charter S | 225 Patchen Ave | Brooklyn, NY | 11233-1529 | 718-638-1830 | 638-2548 | K-9 | Kevin Hall |
| Excellence Girls Charter S | 794 Monroe St | Brooklyn, NY | 11221-3501 | 718-638-1875 | 228-6670 | K-4 | Celestina De La Garza |
| Explore Charter S | 655 Parkside Ave | Brooklyn, NY | 11226-1505 | 718-703-4484 | 703-8550 | K-8 | Rod Bowen |
| Explore Empower Charter S | 188 Rochester Ave | Brooklyn, NY | 11213-3102 | 718-771-2090 | 771-2128 | K-5 | Beth Doyle |
| Explore Exceed Charter S | 443 Saint Marks Ave | Brooklyn, NY | 11238-3707 | 718-989-6702 | 701-8328 | K-8 | Curtis Palmore |
| Explore Excel Charter S | 1077 Remsen Ave | Brooklyn, NY | 11236-3451 | 347-303-3245 | 272-1827 | K-4 | Dana Bogle |
| Fahari Academy Charter S | 72 Veronica Pl | Brooklyn, NY | 11226-4122 | 718-215-3185 | 282-5397 | 5-9 | Dirk Tillotson |
| Family Life Academy Charter S | 14 W 170th St | Bronx, NY | 10452-3227 | 718-410-8100 | 410-8800 | K-8 | Angel Rodriguez |
| Family Life Academy Charter S II | 296 E 140th St | Bronx, NY | 10454 | 718-410-8100 | | K-3 | Lourdes Arroyo |
| Family Life Academy Charter S III | 296 E 140th St | Bronx, NY | 10454 | 718-410-8100 | | K-5 | Andrea Hernandez |
| Future Leaders Institute | 134 W 122nd St | New York, NY | 10027-5501 | 212-678-2868 | 866-2367 | K-8 | Ismael Colon |
| Genesee Community Charter S | 657 East Ave | Rochester, NY | 14607-2101 | 585-697-1960 | 271-5904 | K-6 | Lisa Wing |
| Girls Preparatory Charter S | 442 E Houston St | New York, NY | 10002-1122 | 212-388-0241 | 388-1086 | K-8 | Anne Lackritz |
| Girls Preparatory Charter S of the Bronx | 681 Kelly St Rm 205 | Bronx, NY | 10455-3410 | 718-292-2113 | 292-5586 | K-4 | Josie Carbone |
| Global Community Charter S | 2350 5th Ave | New York, NY | 10037 | 646-360-2363 | 390-6036 | K-1 | Phyllis Siwiec |
| Global Concepts Charter S | 1001 Ridge Rd | Lackawanna, NY | 14218-1755 | 716-821-1903 | 821-9563 | K-12 | Jeanne Tribuzzi |
| Grand Concourse Academy Charter S | 925 Hutchinson River Pkwy | Bronx, NY | 10465 | 718-684-6505 | 684-6514 | K-5 | Ira Victor |
| Great Oaks Charter S | 38 Delancey St | New York, NY | 10002 | 212-233-5152 | 267-4357 | 6-7 | Kristin Levine |
| Green Tech High Charter S | 321 Northern Blvd | Albany, NY | 12210-2635 | 518-694-3400 | 694-3401 | 9-12 | Dr. Paul Miller |
| Growing Up Green Charter S | 3927 28th St | Long Is City, NY | 11101-3728 | 347-642-4306 | 642-4310 | K-4 | Matthew Greenberg |
| Hahn Expeditionary Learning S | 5800 Tilden Ave | Brooklyn, NY | 11203 | 718-629-1204 | 629-1076 | 9-12 | Veronica Coleman |
| Harbor Science & Arts Charter S | 132 E 111th St | New York, NY | 10029-2602 | 917-261-2700 | 360-7429 | K-8 | Joanne Hunt |
| Harlem Childrens Zone Promise Academy I | 245 W 129th St | New York, NY | 10027-1953 | 646-556-6290 | 368-3621 | K-12 | Tonya White |
| Harlem Childrens Zone Promise Academy II | 2005 Madison Ave | New York, NY | 10035-1215 | 646-556-6285 | 492-1542 | K-5 | Sheryl Ragland |
| Harlem Childrens Zone Promise Acad II MS | 35 E 125th St | New York, NY | 10035 | 646-437-1481 | | 6-8 | Kevin Dougherty |
| Harlem Hebrew Language Academy Charter S | 147 Saint Nicholas Ave | New York, NY | 10026 | 212-866-4608 | 537-0280 | K-2 | Robin Natman |
| Harlem Link Charter S | 20 W 112th St | New York, NY | 10026-3902 | 212-289-3249 | 289-3686 | K-5 | Steven Evangelista |
| Harlem Prep Charter S | 240 E 123rd St Frnt 1 | New York, NY | 10035-2068 | 212-876-9953 | 876-9926 | K-6 | Lindsay Malanga |
| Harlem Village Academy Charter HS | 35 W 124th St | New York, NY | 10027 | 646-812-9200 | | 9-12 | Cari Winterich |
| Harlem Village Academy Charter S | 244 W 144th St | New York, NY | 10030 | 646-812-9300 | 548-9576 | 5-8 | Jason Epting |
| Harlem Village Acad Ldrshp Charter S | 2351 1st Ave | New York, NY | 10035 | 646-812-9400 | 996-1626 | 5-8 | Lisa Fromelt |
| Health Sciences Charter S | 1140 Ellicott St | Buffalo, NY | 14209-1934 | 716-888-4080 | 464-7623 | 9-12 | Dr. Hank Stopinski |
| Hebrew Language Academy Charter S | 2186 Mill Ave | Brooklyn, NY | 11234 | 718-377-7200 | 377-7220 | K-4 | Laura Silver |
| Heketi Community Charter S | 423 E 138th St | Bronx, NY | 10454-3041 | 718-260-6002 | 292-7154 | K-5 | Cynthia Rosario |
| Hellenic Classical Charter S | 646 5th Ave | Brooklyn, NY | 11215-5401 | 718-499-0957 | 499-0959 | K-8 | Christine Tettonis |
| Hyde Leadership Charter S | 730 Bryant Ave | Bronx, NY | 10474-6006 | 718-991-5500 | 842-8616 | K-12 | Betsy Olney |
| Hyde Leadership Charter S | 330 Alabama Ave | Brooklyn, NY | 11207-4005 | 718-495-5620 | 495-5827 | K-2 | Sandra DuPree |
| Icahn Charter S 1 | 1525 Brook Ave | Bronx, NY | 10457-8005 | 718-716-8105 | 214-6596 | K-8 | Sandra Lugo |
| Icahn Charter S 2 | 1640 Bronxdale Ave | Bronx, NY | 10462-3302 | 212-828-6107 | 828-7308 | K-7 | Brenda Carrasquillo |
| Icahn Charter S 3 | 1500 Pelham Pkwy S | Bronx, NY | 10461-1100 | 718-828-0034 | 794-2357 | K-6 | Midga Agosto |
| Icahn Charter S 4 | 1500 Pelham Pkwy S | Bronx, NY | 10461-1100 | 718-828-0034 | 828-0664 | K-5 | Michelle Allen |
| Icahn Charter S 5 | 1500 Pelham Pkwy S | Bronx, NY | 10461-1100 | 718-828-0034 | 794-2359 | K-3 | Lawford Cunningham |
| Icahn Charter S 6 | 1701 Fulton Ave | Bronx, NY | 10457-7546 | 718-294-1706 | 583-6194 | K-2 | Brian Geelan |
| Icahn Charter S 7 | 1535 Story Ave | Bronx, NY | 10473-4555 | 718-828-0034 | 828-0664 | K-6 | Laura Longobardo |
| Imagine Me Leadership Charter S | 818 Schenck Ave | Brooklyn, NY | 11207-7904 | 347-985-2140 | 985-2145 | K-3 | Bevon Thompson |
| International Leadership Charter HS | 2900 Exterior St | Bronx, NY | 10463-7103 | 718-562-2300 | 562-2235 | 9-12 | Dr. Elaine Lopez |
| Invictus Preparatory Charter S | 370 Fountain Ave | Brooklyn, NY | 11208-4304 | 718-235-1682 | 235-1685 | 5-8 | Cliff Thomas |
| Inwood Academy for Leadership Charter S | 93 Nagle Ave | New York, NY | 10040-1438 | 212-942-1450 | 942-2740 | 5-7 | Christina Reyes |
| Izquierdo Health & Science Charter S | 800 Home St | Bronx, NY | 10456 | 718-378-0490 | 378-0492 | 6-10 | Richard Burke |
| Johnson Charter S | 15 Jewett Pkwy | Buffalo, NY | 14214 | 716-856-4390 | | K-4 | David Bouie |
| Johnson Charter S | 30 Watervliet Ave | Albany, NY | 12206-1983 | 518-432-4300 | 432-4311 | K-4 | Dr. Jerome Watts |
| Johnson Fruit Belt Community Charter S | 15 Jewett Pkwy | Buffalo, NY | 14214 | 716-856-4390 | 856-4391 | K-4 | Michael Sullivan |
| King Center Charter S | 156 Newburgh Ave | Buffalo, NY | 14211 | 716-891-7912 | 895-2058 | K-8 | Antoinette Rhodes |
| King's Collegiate Charter S | 1084 Lenox Rd | Brooklyn, NY | 11212-1930 | 718-342-6047 | 342-6727 | 5-8 | Scott Schuster |
| KIPP Academy Charter HS | 625 W 133rd St | New York, NY | 10027-7303 | 212-991-2626 | 862-9679 | 9-12 | Natalie Webb |
| KIPP Academy Charter MS | 250 E 156th St | Bronx, NY | 10451-4796 | 718-665-3555 | 585-7982 | 5-8 | Frank Corcoran |

| School | Address | City,State | Zip code | Telephone | Fax | Grade | Contact |
|---|---|---|---|---|---|---|---|
| Kipp Academy ES | 730 Concourse Vlg W | Bronx, NY | 10451 | 718-943-3737 | 292-7199 | K-4 | William Cardenas |
| KIPP A.M.P. Charter S | 1224 Park Pl | Brooklyn, NY | 11213-2703 | 718-943-3740 | 774-3673 | 5-12 | Emily Carroll |
| KIPP STAR College Prep Charter S | 433 W 123rd St | New York, NY | 10027-5002 | 212-991-2650 | 666-4723 | K-12 | Stacy Johnson |
| KIPP Tech Valley Charter S | 1 Dudley Hts | Albany, NY | 12210-2601 | 518-694-9494 | 694-9411 | 5-8 | Don Applyrs |
| KIPP Washington Heights MS | 21 Jumel Pl | New York, NY | 10032-4316 | 212-991-2620 | 342-2521 | 5-5 | Danny Swersky |
| La Cima Charter S | 800 Gates Ave | Brooklyn, NY | 11221-2203 | 718-443-2136 | 443-7291 | K-5 | Andrea Zayas |
| Launch Expeditionary Learning Charter S | 1580 Dean St | Brooklyn, NY | 11213-1713 | 718-221-1064 | 604-6915 | 6-8 | Geoffrey Roehm |
| Lavelle Preparatory Charter S | 1 Teleport Dr | Staten Island, NY | 10311 | 347-630-1760 | 466-5746 | 6-8 | Christopher Zilinski |
| Leadership Preparatory Charter S 4 | 1001 E 100th St | Brooklyn, NY | 11236 | 347-390-0570 | 534-3881 | K-8 | Emily Crouch |
| Leadership Preparatory Ocean Hill S | 51 Christopher Ave | Brooklyn, NY | 11212-8014 | 718-250-5767 | 881-9666 | K-3 | Nikeya Bridges |
| Leadership Prep Bedford Stuy Charter S | 141 Macon St | Brooklyn, NY | 11216-2206 | 718-636-0360 | 636-0747 | K-7 | Sultana Noormuhammad |
| Leadership Prep Brownsville Charter S | 985 Rockaway Ave | Brooklyn, NY | 11212-5152 | 718-669-7461 | 228-6496 | K-4 | Katie Newton |
| Lefferts Gardens Charter S | 601 Parkside Ave | Brooklyn, NY | 11226-1509 | 718-284-1480 | 284-2162 | K-5 | Wendy Ramos |
| Lindsay Wildcat Academy Charter S | 17 Battery Pl | New York, NY | 10004-1207 | 212-209-6006 | 635-3874 | 9-12 | Ronald Tabano |
| Manhattan Charter S | 100 Attorney St | New York, NY | 10002-3405 | 212-533-2743 | 533-2820 | K-5 | Genie DePolo |
| Manhattan Charter S II | 220 Henry St | New York, NY | 10002-4815 | 212-964-3792 | 964-3795 | K-1 | Joanne Mejias |
| Merrick Academy-Queens Public Charter S | 20701 Jamaica Ave | Queens Village, NY | 11428-1544 | 718-479-3753 | 479-8108 | K-6 | Tonya Johnson |
| MESA Charter HS | 231 Palmetto St | Brooklyn, NY | 11221-4712 | 917-257-6876 | 227-2763 | 9-12 | Arthur Samuels |
| Metropolitan Lighthouse Charter S | 500 Courtlandt Ave | Bronx, NY | 10451-5032 | 718-893-0640 | 893-0675 | K-5 | Courtney Russell |
| Middle Village Prep Charter S | 6802 Metropolitan Ave | Middle Village, NY | 11379 | 718-869-2933 | 821-2498 | 6-8 | Ronald Rivera |
| Mott Hall Charter S | 1260 Franklin Ave | Bronx, NY | 10456-3502 | 718-991-9139 | 991-9150 | 6-6 | Geovanti Steward |
| Mott Haven Academy Charter S | 170 Brown Pl | Bronx, NY | 10454-4141 | 718-292-7015 | 292-7823 | K-5 | Jessica Nauiokas |
| Neighborhood Charter S of Harlem | 132 W 124th St | New York, NY | 10027 | 646-701-7117 | 484-6652 | K-3 | Brett Gallini |
| New American Academy Charter S | 5800 Tilden Ave | Brooklyn, NY | 11203-4824 | 718-968-6520 | 968-6521 | K-1 | |
| Newburgh Preparatory Charter HS | 471 Broadway | Newburgh, NY | 12550-5332 | 845-565-4040 | 565-4033 | 9-12 | Thomas Fitzgerald |
| New Dawn Charter HS | 242 Hoyt St | Brooklyn, NY | 11217-2913 | 347-505-9103 | 505-2516 | 9-12 | Dr. Sarah Asmussen |
| New Heights Academy Charter S | 1818 Amsterdam Ave | New York, NY | 10031-1715 | 212-283-5400 | 507-9314 | 5-12 | Robert Parkes |
| New Hope Academy Charter S | 475 E 57th St | Brooklyn, NY | 11203-6010 | 718-337-8303 | 504-3883 | K-5 | Keishea Allen |
| New Roots Charter S | PO Box 936 | Ithaca, NY | 14851 | 607-882-9220 | 882-9230 | 9-12 | Tina Nilsen-Hodges |
| New Visions Charter HS for Humanities | 99 Terrace View Ave | Bronx, NY | 10463-5079 | 718-817-7686 | 817-7688 | 9-12 | Seth Levin |
| New Visions Charter HS Humanities III | 3000 Avenue X | Brooklyn, NY | 11235 | 718-368-4145 | | 9-12 | Ivan Cohen |
| New Visions Charter HS Humanities II | 455 Southern Blvd | Bronx, NY | 10455-4911 | 718-665-5380 | 665-5383 | 9-12 | Richard Gonzlez |
| New Visions Charter HS II | 900 Tinton Ave | Bronx, NY | 10456-7411 | 718-665-3671 | 645-7409 | 9-12 | Stacey King |
| New Visions Charter HS Math & Sci III | 3000 Avenue X | Brooklyn, NY | 11235 | 718-934-9240 | 934-9171 | 9-12 | Nissi Jonathan |
| New Visions Charter HS Math & Science | 99 Terrace View Ave | Bronx, NY | 10463-5079 | 718-817-7683 | 817-7685 | 9-12 | Julia Chun |
| New World Preparatory Charter S | 26 Sharpe Ave | Staten Island, NY | 10302 | 718-705-8990 | 442-1583 | 6-8 | Jamie Esperon |
| New York City Montessori Charter S | 423 E 138th St | Bronx, NY | 10454 | 347-226-9094 | 226-9097 | PK-4 | Gina Sardi |
| New York French American Charter S | 311 W 120th St | New York, NY | 10027 | 212-666-4134 | | K-5 | Edith Boncompain |
| Niagara Charter S | 2077 Lockport Rd | Niagara Falls, NY | 14304-1109 | 716-297-4520 | 297-4617 | K-6 | Darci Novak |
| North Side S | 1650 Utopia Pkwy | Whitestone, NY | 11357 | 718-229-5050 | 402-2028 | PK-3 | Irene Kouba |
| NYC Autism Charter S | 433 E 100th St | New York, NY | 10029-6606 | 212-860-2580 | 860-2960 | K-12 | Julie Fisher |
| NYC Charter HS for AECI | 838 Brook Ave | Bronx, NY | 10451-4620 | 646-400-5566 | 585-4780 | 9-12 | Eugene Foley |
| Ocean Hill Collegiate Charter S | 1137 Herkimer St | Brooklyn, NY | 11233-3109 | 718-250-5765 | 250-5766 | 5-6 | Hannah Solomon |
| Opportunity Charter S | 240 W 113th St | New York, NY | 10026-3306 | 212-866-6137 | 665-7436 | 6-12 | Marya Baker |
| Oracle Charter S | 888 Delaware Ave | Buffalo, NY | 14209-2008 | 716-362-3188 | 362-3187 | 9-12 | John Ashwood |
| Our World Neighborhood Charter S | 3612 35th Ave | Astoria, NY | 11106-1227 | 718-392-3405 | 392-2840 | K-8 | Brian Ferguson |
| PAVE Academy | 732 Henry St | Brooklyn, NY | 11231-3229 | 718-858-7813 | 858-7814 | K-5 | Spencer Robertson |
| Peninsula Prep Academy Charter S | 611 Beach 19th St | Far Rockaway, NY | 11691 | 347-403-9231 | 327-2580 | K-5 | Ruth Peets-Butcher |
| Professional Preparatory Charter S | 616 Quincy St | Brooklyn, NY | 11221-1812 | 718-285-3787 | 919-0486 | K-5 | Rafiq Kalam Id-Din |
| PUC Achieve Charter S | 14 Mark St | Rochester, NY | 14605-1331 | 585-730-5899 | | 5-5 | Heather Donnelly |
| Renaissance Charter HS for Innovation | 410 E 100th St | New York, NY | 10029-6604 | 212-722-5871 | 430-8555 | 9-12 | Nicholas Tishuk |
| Renaissance Charter S | 3559 81st St | Jackson Heights, NY | 11372-5033 | 718-803-0060 | 803-3785 | K-12 | Stacey Gauthier |
| Riverhead Charter S | 3685 Middle Country Rd | Calverton, NY | 11933-1807 | 631-369-5800 | | K-8 | Raymond Ankrum |
| Riverton Street Charter S | 11834 Riverton St | Saint Albans, NY | 11412-4024 | 718-481-8200 | 923-3315 | K-5 | Verone Kennedy |
| ROADS Charter S I | 1495 Herkimer St | Brooklyn, NY | 11233 | 718-280-9819 | 498-0604 | 9-12 | Abeku Hayes |
| ROADS Charter S II | 1010 Rev James A Polite Ave | Bronx, NY | 10459-3053 | 718-861-7515 | 861-7518 | 9-12 | Seth Litt |
| Rochdale Early Advantage Charter S | 12205 Smith St | Jamaica, NY | 11434-2522 | 718-978-0075 | 978-0110 | K-3 | Lena Richarson |
| Rochester Academy Charter S | 901 Portland Ave | Rochester, NY | 14621 | 585-467-9201 | 467-9250 | 7-12 | Mehmet Demirtas |
| Rochester Academy Charter S of the Arts | 299 Kirk Rd | Rochester, NY | 14612 | 845-826-4586 | | K-2 | Donna Cozine |
| Rochester Career Mentoring Charter S | 30 Hart St Ste 3 | Rochester, NY | 14605-1100 | 585-232-1045 | | 9-12 | Daniel McFarlane |
| Rochester Prep ES | 899 Jay St | Rochester, NY | 14611 | 585-235-0008 | 235-0014 | K-4 | Jaimie Brillante |
| Rochester Prep ES - West Campus | 1020 Maple St | Rochester, NY | 14611 | 585-368-5090 | 368-5091 | K-1 | Kaitlin Driscoll |
| Rochester Prep MS - Brooks Campus | 630 Brooks Ave | Rochester, NY | 14619-2255 | 585-436-8629 | 436-5985 | 5-8 | Patrick Pastore |
| Rochester Prep MS - West Campus | 1020 Maple St | Rochester, NY | 14611-1614 | 585-368-5090 | 368-5091 | 5-7 | Kelli Ragin |
| Roosevelt Childrens Academy Charter S | 105 Pleasant Ave | Roosevelt, NY | 11575-2126 | 516-867-6202 | 867-6206 | K-8 | Dr. Ron Boykins |
| St. Hope Leadership Academy | 222 W 134th St | New York, NY | 10030-3002 | 212-283-1204 | 283-1207 | 5-8 | Constance Bond |
| Sisulu-Walker Charter S | 125 W 115th St | New York, NY | 10026-2908 | 212-663-8216 | 866-5793 | K-5 | Michelle Haynes |
| South Bronx Charter S Intl Culture/Arts | 383 E139th St | Bronx, NY | 10454 | 718-292-5737 | 292-1205 | K-5 | Evelyn Hey |
| South Bronx Classical Charter S | 977 Fox St | Bronx, NY | 10459-3320 | 718-860-4340 | 860-4125 | K-5 | Lester Long |
| South Bronx Classical Charter S II | 333 E 135th St | Bronx, NY | 10454 | 718-860-4340 | 860-4125 | K-5 | Leena Gyftopoulos |
| South Buffalo Charter S | 154 S Ogden St | Buffalo, NY | 14210 | 716-826-7213 | 826-7168 | K-8 | Carrie Dzierba |
| Southside Academy Charter S | 2200 Onondaga Creek Blvd | Syracuse, NY | 13207-2300 | 315-476-3019 | 476-6639 | K-8 | Delvin Vick |
| Staten Island Community Charter S | 309 Saint Pauls Ave | Staten Island, NY | 10304-2217 | 347-857-6981 | 861-0601 | K-3 | Dr. Michael Courtney |
| Success Academy Charter Harlem 1 | 34 W 118th St | New York, NY | 10026-1937 | 646-747-7170 | 457-5659 | K-7 | Danique Loving |
| Success Academy Charter Harlem 2 | 144 E 128th St Ste 3 | New York, NY | 10035-1329 | 646-442-6600 | 281-4638 | K-5 | Noah Green |
| Success Academy Charter Harlem 3 | 141 E 111th St | New York, NY | 10029-2641 | 646-747-6700 | 478-9492 | K-5 | Richard Seigler |
| Success Academy Charter Harlem 4 | 240 W 113th St | New York, NY | 10026-3306 | 646-442-6500 | 478-9493 | K-5 | William Loskoch |
| Success Academy Charter Harlem 5 | 301 W 140th St | New York, NY | 10030-1406 | 646-380-2590 | 961-4731 | K-3 | Khari Shabazz |
| Success Academy Charter S Bed-Stuy 2 | 211 Throop Ave | Brooklyn, NY | 11206-5701 | 718-704-1439 | | K-1 | Beth Davis-Dillard |
| Success Academy Charter S Bed-Stuy 1 | 70 Tompkins Ave | Brooklyn, NY | 11206-5616 | 718-635-3294 | 964-6598 | K-2 | Monica Burris |
| Success Academy Charter S Bensonhurst | 99 Avenue P | Brooklyn, NY | 11204 | 347-514-7082 | | K-4 | Jonathan Dant |
| Success Academy Charter S Bergen Beach | 1420 E 68th St | Brooklyn, NY | 11234 | 347-817-2017 | | K-4 | Jessica Johnson |
| Success Academy Charter S Bronx 3 | 968 Cauldwell Ave | Bronx, NY | 10456-6804 | 646-790-2145 | | K-2 | Colleen Stewart |
| Success Academy Charter S Bronx 4 | 885 Bolton Ave | Bronx, NY | 10473 | 646-558-0043 | | K-12 | Shea Reeder |
| Success Academy Charter S Bronx 1 | 339 Morris Ave | Bronx, NY | 10451-6122 | 347-286-7950 | 479-1192 | K-5 | Elizabeth Vandlik |
| Success Academy Charter S Bronx 2 | 450 Saint Pauls Pl | Bronx, NY | 10456-1938 | 347-286-7966 | 479-1194 | K-8 | Vanessa Bangser |
| Success Academy Charter S Cobble Hill | 284 Baltic St | Brooklyn, NY | 11201-6402 | 718-704-1460 | | K-1 | Kerri Tabarcea |
| Success Academy Charter S Crown Hts | 1025 Eastern Pkwy | Brooklyn, NY | 11213 | 646-790-2129 | | K-4 | Kristen Cipriano |
| Success Academy Charter S Fort Greene | 101 Park Ave | Brooklyn, NY | 11205 | 646-790-2137 | | K-12 | Nina Fink |
| Success Academy Charter S Harlem Central | 461 W 131st St | New York, NY | 10027 | 646-569-5900 | | 5-8 | Andrew Malone |
| Success Academy Charter S Harlem West | 215 W 114th St Fl 5 | New York, NY | 10026 | 646-569-5920 | | 5-8 | Andrea Klein |
| Success Academy Charter S Hell's Kitchen | 439 W 49th St | New York, NY | 10019 | 646-790-2153 | | K-5 | Jenny Obiaya |
| Success Academy Charter S Prospect Hts | 760 Prospect Pl | Brooklyn, NY | 11216 | 646-790-2121 | | K-12 | Monica Komery |
| Success Academy Charter S - Rosedale | 14765 249th St | Laurelton, NY | 11413 | 347-514-7060 | | K-4 | Christina Danielsen |
| Success Academy Charter S Springfield Gd | 13255 Ridgedale St | Laurelton, NY | 11413 | 347-602-4335 | | K-4 | Sumera Ansari |
| Success Academy Charter S Upper West | 145 W 84th St Fl 2 | New York, NY | 10024-4614 | 646-274-1580 | | K-2 | Carrie Roby |
| Success Academy Charter S Williamsburg | 183 S 3rd St Fl 4 | Brooklyn, NY | 11211 | 718-704-1419 | | K-3 | Abigail Johnson |
| Success Academy Charter Washington Hts | 701 Fort Washington Ave | New York, NY | 10040 | 646-558-0027 | | K-4 | Kelsey DePalo |
| Success Academy Union Square | 40 Irving Pl | New York, NY | 10003 | 646-790-2161 | | K-5 | Paola Zalkind |
| Summit Academy Charter S | 27 Huntington St | Brooklyn, NY | 11231-1824 | 718-875-1403 | 875-1891 | 6-9 | Natasha Campbell |
| Syracuse Academy of Science Charter S | 1001 Park Ave | Syracuse, NY | 13204-2125 | 315-428-8997 | 428-9109 | K-12 | Tolga Hayali Ed.D. |
| Tapestry Charter S | 65 Great Arrow Ave | Buffalo, NY | 14216-3203 | 716-204-5883 | 204-5887 | K-12 | Lynn Bass |
| Tech International Charter S | 3120 Corlear Ave | Bronx, NY | 10463-3976 | 718-549-1908 | 240-0363 | 6-6 | Adjowah K. Scott |
| True North Troy Preparatory S | 2 Polk St | Troy, NY | 12180-5512 | 518-445-3100 | 445-3101 | K-8 | Paul Powell |
| Tubman Charter S | 3565 3rd Ave | Bronx, NY | 10456-3403 | 718-537-9912 | 537-9858 | K-8 | Cleveland Person |
| UFT Charter S | 800 Van Siclen Ave | Brooklyn, NY | 11207 | 718-927-5540 | | K-12 | Michelle White |
| Unity Prep S of Brooklyn | 432 Monroe St | Brooklyn, NY | 11221-1111 | 212-437-8372 | | 6-12 | Joshua Beauregard |
| University Preparatory Charter HS | 1290 Lake Ave | Rochester, NY | 14613 | 585-672-1280 | 458-2732 | 7-12 | Dr. Connie Lucchese |
| University Prep Charter HS | 600 Saint Anns Ave | Bronx, NY | 10455-2800 | 718-585-0560 | 585-0563 | 9-12 | Ashish Kapadia |
| Urban Choice Charter S | 545 Humboldt St | Rochester, NY | 14610-1221 | 585-288-5702 | 654-9882 | K-8 | Christina Schermerhorn |
| Urban Dove Charter S | 600 Lafayette Ave | Brooklyn, NY | 11216-1020 | 718-783-8232 | 783-8239 | 9-10 | Lewis Thomas |
| Utica Academy of Science Charter S | 1214 Lincoln Ave | Utica, NY | 13502 | 315-266-1072 | 266-1073 | 6-12 | Fehmi Damkaci |
| Vertus Charter S | 2 Austin St | Rochester, NY | 14606 | 585-747-8911 | | 9-12 | Dr. Leigh McGuigan |
| VOICE Charter S of NY | 3715 13th St | Long Is City, NY | 11101-6024 | 718-361-1694 | 537-1703 | K-5 | Frank Headley |
| West Buffalo Charter S | 113 Lafayette Ave | Buffalo, NY | 14213 | 716-923-1534 | 768-0980 | K-4 | Andrea Todoro |
| Western NY Maritime Charter S | 266 Genesee St | Buffalo, NY | 14204-1453 | 716-842-6289 | 842-4241 | 9-12 | Lawrence Astyk |
| Westminster Community Charter S | 24 Westminster Ave | Buffalo, NY | 14215-1614 | 716-816-3450 | 838-7468 | K-8 | Dr. Ayinde Rudolph |
| Williamsburg Charter S | 198 Varet St | Brooklyn, NY | 11206-3703 | 718-782-9830 | 782-9834 | 9-12 | Marsha Spampinato |
| Williamsburg Collegiate Charter S | 157 Wilson St | Brooklyn, NY | 11211-7706 | 718-302-4018 | 302-4641 | 5-12 | J. T. Leaird |
| Young Women's College Prep Charter S | 311 Flower City Park | Rochester, NY | 14615-3614 | 585-254-0320 | | 7-12 | Jennifer Gkourlias Ed.D. |

## North Carolina

| School | Address | City,State | Zip code | Telephone | Fax | Grade | Contact |
|---|---|---|---|---|---|---|---|
| Academy of Moore County | 12588 US Highway 15 501 | Aberdeen, NC | 28315 | 910-757-0401 | 757-0403 | K-5 | Allyson Schoen |
| A.C.E. Academy | 7807 Caldwell Rd | Harrisburg, NC | 28075 | 704-456-7153 | 626-2655 | K-5 | Laila Minott |
| Alpha Academy | PO Box 35476 | Fayetteville, NC | 28303-0476 | 910-223-7711 | 678-9011 | K-8 | Eugene Slocum |
| American Renaissance ES | 132 E Broad St | Statesville, NC | 28677 | 704-924-8870 | 873-1398 | K-8 | Tony Hall |

| School | Address | City,State | Zip code | Telephone | Fax | Grade | Contact |
|---|---|---|---|---|---|---|---|
| Anderson Creek Club Charter S | 4940 Ray Rd | Spring Lake, NC | 28390 | 910-814-9001 | 814-9002 | K-5 | Ozie Lee Hall |
| Arapahoe Charter S | 9005 NC Highway 306 S | Arapahoe, NC | 28510-9699 | 252-249-2599 | 249-1316 | K-10 | Thomas McCarthy |
| Aristotle Preparatory Academy | 2461 Arty Ave | Charlotte, NC | 28208 | 704-215-4550 | | K-4 | Lauren Tucker |
| Arts Based S | 1380 N Martin Luther King | Winston Salem, NC | 27101 | 336-748-4116 | 748-4117 | K-8 | Robin Hollis |
| ArtSpace Charter S | 2030 US 70 Hwy | Swannanoa, NC | 28778-8211 | 828-298-2787 | 298-6221 | K-8 | Lori Cozzi |
| Bear Grass Charter S | 6344 E Bear Grass Rd | Williamston, NC | 27892 | 252-789-1010 | 789-1014 | 6-12 | Donna Moore |
| Bethany Community MS | 181 Bethany Rd | Reidsville, NC | 27320-7464 | 336-951-2500 | 951-0087 | 6-8 | Vicky Bethel |
| Bethel Hill Charter S | 401 Bethel Hill School Rd | Roxboro, NC | 27574-7503 | 336-599-2823 | 599-9299 | K-6 | Stephen Hester |
| Bradford Preparatory S | 2502 Salome Church Rd | Charlotte, NC | 28262 | 704-549-0080 | 549-0085 | K-8 | Kelly Painter |
| Brevard Academy | 299 Andante Ln | Brevard, NC | 28712-9125 | 828-885-2665 | 862-3497 | K-8 | Barbara Grimm |
| Bridges Academy | 2587 Pleasant Ridge Rd | State Road, NC | 28676-9318 | 336-874-2721 | 874-3804 | K-8 | Merry Lowe |
| Brown Leadership Academy | PO Box 1433 | Elizabethtown, NC | 28337 | 910-862-2965 | 862-3054 | 6-12 | Roland McKoy |
| Cabarrus Charter Academy | 355 Poplar Crossing Dr NW | Concord, NC | 28027 | 704-789-2500 | 789-2501 | K-7 | Kevin Senter |
| Cape Fear Center for Inquiry | 2525 Wonder Way | Wilmington, NC | 28401 | 910-362-0000 | 362-0048 | K-8 | Lori Roy |
| Capitol Encore Academy | 126 Hay St | Fayetteville, NC | 28301 | 910-849-0888 | 491-6786 | K-5 | Sylvia Adamczyk |
| Cardinal Charter S | 1020 St Charles Pl | Cary, NC | 27513 | 919-653-5000 | 653-6000 | K-6 | Crystal Scillitani |
| Carolina International S | 9545 Poplar Tent Rd | Concord, NC | 28027 | 704-455-3847 | 455-4672 | K-12 | David Kukielski |
| Caroline STEM Academy | 8310 McAlpine Park Dr | Charlotte, NC | 28211 | 704-780-4677 | | 9-12 | Caroline Upchurch |
| Carter Community Charter S | 1955 W Cornwallis Rd | Durham, NC | 27705 | 919-797-2340 | 797-2343 | K-8 | Gail Taylor |
| Casa Esperanza Montessori Charter S | 2600 Sumner Blvd Ste 130 | Raleigh, NC | 27616-5146 | 919-855-9811 | 855-9813 | K-8 | Diana Bush |
| Central Park S for Children | 724 Foster St | Durham, NC | 27701-2111 | 919-682-1200 | 683-1261 | K-6 | John Heffernan |
| Charlotte Choice Charter S | 1000 Anderson St | Charlotte, NC | 28205 | 704-272-8308 | 455-6368 | K-6 | Lorenzo Johnson |
| Charlotte Lab S | PO Box 30034 | Charlotte, NC | 28230 | 980-277-4522 | | K-4 | Mary Moss-Brown |
| Charlotte Learning Academy | 701 Scaleybark Rd | Charlotte, NC | 28209 | 980-355-2077 | | 6-10 | Stacey Rose |
| Charlotte Secondary S | 8601 McAlpine Park Dr | Charlotte, NC | 28211 | 704-295-0137 | 295-0156 | 6-12 | Donna Rogers |
| Charter Day S | 7055 Bacons Way NE | Leland, NC | 28451-7960 | 910-655-1214 | 655-1549 | K-8 | Mike Frank |
| Chatham Charter S | PO Box 245 | Siler City, NC | 27344-0245 | 919-742-4550 | 742-2518 | K-12 | Dr. John Eldridge |
| Children's Village Academy | PO Box 2206 | Kinston, NC | 28502-2206 | 252-939-1958 | 939-1242 | K-8 | Gloria Battle |
| CIS Academy | 818 W 3rd St | Pembroke, NC | 28372-7307 | 910-521-1669 | 521-1670 | 6-8 | Billy Haggans |
| Clover Garden S | 2454 Altamahaw Union Ridge | Burlington, NC | 27217 | 336-586-9440 | 586-9477 | K-12 | Walter Finnigan |
| College Preparatory & Leadership Academy | 5700 Riverdale Dr | Jamestown, NC | 27282 | 336-884-0131 | 883-0109 | K-7 | Dr. Michelle Johnson |
| Columbus Charter S | 35 Bacons Way | Whiteville, NC | 28472-6225 | 910-641-4042 | 641-4043 | K-8 | Steven Smith |
| Commonwealth HS | 5112 Central Ave | Charlotte, NC | 28205 | 704-899-4998 | 469-4661 | 9-12 | Tom Hanley |
| Community Charter S | 510 S Torrence St | Charlotte, NC | 28204-3160 | 704-377-3180 | 377-3182 | K-5 | Anissa Miller |
| Community S of Davidson | 404 Armour St | Davidson, NC | 28036 | 704-896-6262 | 896-2025 | K-12 | Joy Warner |
| Cornerstone Charter Academy | 2535 New Garden Rd E | Greensboro, NC | 27455 | 336-482-3855 | 482-3857 | K-8 | Brent Smith |
| Corvian Community School | 9501 David Taylor Dr | Charlotte, NC | 28262 | 704-717-7550 | 717-7558 | K-5 | Stacey Haskell |
| Crosscreek Charter S | 306 Sandalwood Ave | Louisburg, NC | 27549-2650 | 919-497-3198 | 497-0232 | K-8 | Robin Jackson |
| Crossroads Charter HS | 5500 N Tryon St | Charlotte, NC | 28213-7120 | 704-597-5100 | 597-3941 | 9-12 | Gentry Campbell |
| Delany New S for Children | 119 Brevard Rd | Asheville, NC | 28806-2922 | 828-236-9441 | 236-9442 | K-8 | Buffy Fowler |
| Dillard Academy | PO Box 1188 | Goldsboro, NC | 27533-1188 | 919-581-0166 | 581-0122 | K-5 | Hilda Hicks |
| Douglass Academy | 507 N 6th St | Wilmington, NC | 28401 | 910-763-1976 | 763-1974 | K-3 | Barbra Jones |
| Dynamic Community Charter S | 5510 Munford Rd | Raleigh, NC | 27612 | 919-787-7388 | | 6-10 | Terri Zobel |
| East Wake Academy | 400 NMC Dr | Zebulon, NC | 27597-2759 | 919-404-0444 | 404-2377 | K-12 | Stephen Gay |
| Endeavor Charter S | 4879 One World Way | Wake Forest, NC | 27587 | 919-848-0333 | 848-8716 | K-8 | Steve McAdams |
| Envision Science Academy | 9400 Forum Dr | Raleigh, NC | 27615 | 919-435-4002 | | K-6 | Steve Pond |
| Evergreen Community Charter S | 50 Bell Rd | Asheville, NC | 28805-1538 | 828-298-2173 | 298-2269 | K-8 | Dr. Susan Gottfried |
| Excelsior Classical Academy | 4100 N Roxboro St | Durham, NC | 27704 | 919-907-0410 | | K-8 | Cynthia Gadol |
| Expedition S | 437 Dimmocks Mill Rd #33 | Hillsborough, NC | 27278 | 919-960-1748 | | K-6 | Tammy Finch |
| Exploris S: K-8 Learning Community | 401 Hillsborough St | Raleigh, NC | 27603 | 919-715-3690 | 715-2042 | K-8 | Summer Clayton |
| Falls Lake Academy | 1701 E Lyon Station Rd | Creedmoor, NC | 27522 | 919-964-9003 | 964-9008 | K-9 | Dr. Robert Daniel |
| Flemington Academy | PO Box 300 | Lake Waccamaw, NC | 28450 | 910-646-2237 | 356-0028 | 6-12 | Dr. Tom Simmons |
| Forsyth Academy | 5426 Shattalon Dr | Winston Salem, NC | 27106-1919 | 336-922-1121 | 922-1033 | K-8 | Wendy Barajas |
| Franklin Academy | 1127 Chalks Rd | Wake Forest, NC | 27587 | 919-570-8262 | 570-8241 | K-12 | Denise Kent |
| Franklin S of Innovation | 21 Innovation Dr | Asheville, NC | 28806 | 828-237-4860 | 318-8125 | 6-9 | Michelle Vruwink |
| Gaston College Preparatory S | 320 Pleasant Hill Rd | Gaston, NC | 27832-9511 | 252-308-6932 | 308-6936 | K-12 | Kevika Amar |
| Global Scholars Academy | 311 Dowd St | Durham, NC | 27701 | 919-682-5903 | 956-8535 | K-7 | Agatha Brown |
| Grandfather Academy | PO Box 98 | Banner Elk, NC | 28604 | 828-898-5465 | 898-8513 | K-12 | Frank Rosato |
| Gray Stone Day S | PO Box 650 | Misenheimer, NC | 28109 | 704-463-0567 | 463-0569 | 9-12 | Helen Nance |
| Greensboro Academy | 4049 Battleground Ave | Greensboro, NC | 27410 | 336-286-8404 | 286-8403 | K-8 | Rudy Swofford |
| Guilford Preparatory Academy | 2210 E Cone Blvd | Greensboro, NC | 27405 | 336-954-1344 | 954-1965 | K-8 | Robin Buckrham |
| Haliwa-Saponi Tribal S | 130 Haliwa Saponi Trl | Hollister, NC | 27844-9390 | 252-257-5853 | 257-1093 | K-12 | Michelle Barian |
| Hawbridge S | PO Box 40 | Saxapahaw, NC | 27340 | 336-376-1122 | 376-6996 | 6-12 | Dr. Robert P.Kreiner |
| Healthy Start Academy | 807 W Chapel Hill St | Durham, NC | 27701-3112 | 919-956-5599 | 688-9027 | K-8 | James McCormick |
| Henderson Collegiate | 906 Health Center Rd | Henderson, NC | 27536 | 252-598-1038 | 598-1037 | 4-8 | Eric Sanchez |
| Heritage Collegiate Leadership Academy | PO Box 1170 | Windsor, NC | 27983 | 252-794-0597 | 794-0598 | K-3 | Kashi Bazemore-Hall |
| Hope Elementary Charter S | 1116 N Blount St | Raleigh, NC | 27604-1302 | 919-834-0941 | 834-9338 | K-5 | Clarissa Fleming |
| Howard S for the Arts & Educ | 1004 Herring Ave E | Wilson, NC | 27893-3311 | 252-293-4150 | 293-4151 | K-8 | Dr. JoAnne Woodard |
| Institute for Development Young Leaders | 1305 W Club Blvd | Durham, NC | 27705 | 919-973-4178 | 401-8005 | K-6 | Yvette Munroe |
| Invest Collegiate | 2045 Suttle Ave | Charlotte, NC | 28208 | 704-370-4000 | 973-7876 | K-7 | Dr. Antoinette Ellison |
| Invest Collegiate-Imagine | 1000 Brevard Rd #175 | Asheville, NC | 28806 | 828-633-6491 | 633-6494 | K-10 | Laura Townley |
| Island Montessori Charter S | 6339 Carolina Beach Rd | Wilmington, NC | 28412 | 910-795-4860 | 707-1201 | 1-6 | Brian Corrigan |
| Jefferson Classical Academy | 2527 US 221A Hwy | Mooresboro, NC | 28114-7698 | 828-657-9998 | 657-9012 | K-12 | Joseph Maimone |
| Joy Charter S | 107 S Driver St | Durham, NC | 27703 | 919-908-1600 | 402-4263 | K-8 | Alex Quigley |
| Kennedy Charter S | 617 N Summit Ave | Charlotte, NC | 28216 | 704-688-2939 | 688-2962 | K-12 | Dr. Elva Cooper |
| Kestrel Heights S | 4700 S Alston Ave | Durham, NC | 27713-4419 | 919-484-1300 | 484-1355 | K-12 | Dr. Mark Tracy |
| KIPP Academy Charlotte | 931 Wilann Dr | Charlotte, NC | 28215-2147 | 704-537-2044 | 537-2855 | 5-8 | Tiffany Flowers |
| KIPP Halifax College Prep | 515 Becker Dr | Roanoke Rapids, NC | 27870 | 252-410-0277 | 308-9656 | 5-8 | Marlow Wilkins |
| Lake Lure Classical Academy | PO Box 6 | Lake Lure, NC | 28746 | 828-625-9292 | 625-9298 | K-12 | Jessica Boland |
| Lake Norman Charter S | 12435 S Old Statesville Rd | Huntersville, NC | 28078 | 704-948-8600 | 948-8778 | 5-12 | Shannon Stein |
| Langtree Charter Academy | 154 Foundation Ct | Mooresville, NC | 28117 | 704-705-1698 | 360-3026 | K-8 | Joan Roman |
| Learning Center | 945 Connahetta St | Murphy, NC | 28906-3524 | 828-835-7240 | 835-9471 | K-8 | Mary Jo Dyre |
| Lincoln Charter S Denver | 7834 Galway Ln | Denver, NC | 28037 | 704-483-6611 | 483-1039 | K-12 | Dave Machado |
| Lincoln Charter S Lincolnton | 133 Eagle Nest Rd | Lincolnton, NC | 28092-7383 | 704-736-9888 | 736-1166 | K-8 | Rachel Greer |
| Longleaf School of the Arts | 207 E Hargett St | Raleigh, NC | 27601 | 919-896-8164 | 516-0923 | 9-12 | Rachel Davis |
| Magellan Charter S | 9324 Baileywick Rd | Raleigh, NC | 27615-1909 | 919-844-0277 | 844-3882 | 3-8 | Mary Griffin |
| Metrolina Regional Scholars Academy | 5225 77 Center Dr | Charlotte, NC | 28217 | 704-503-1112 | 503-1183 | K-8 | Anthony Yodice |
| Millennium Charter Academy | 500 Old Springs Rd | Mount Airy, NC | 27030-3034 | 336-789-7570 | 789-8445 | K-8 | Kirby McCrary |
| Mountain Community S | 613 Glover St | Hendersonville, NC | 28792-5451 | 828-696-8480 | 696-8451 | K-8 | Denise Pesce |
| Mountain Discovery Charter S | 890 Jenkins Branch Rd N | Bryson City, NC | 28713-4514 | 828-488-1222 | 488-0526 | K-8 | Carter Petty |
| Mountain Island Charter S | 13440 Lucia Riverbend Hwy | Mount Holly, NC | 28120 | 704-827-8840 | 827-8675 | K-12 | Justin Matthews |
| Neuse Charter S | 909 E Booker Dairy Rd | Smithfield, NC | 27577 | 919-938-1077 | 938-1079 | K-12 | Julie Jailall |
| New Dimensions S | 550 Lenoir Rd | Morganton, NC | 28655 | 828-437-5753 | 437-2980 | K-8 | Larry Wilkerson |
| NC Connections Academy | 2700 Meridian Pkwy | Durham, NC | 27713 | 800-382-6010 | | K-9 | |
| North Carolina Leadership Academy | PO Box 1728 | Kernersville, NC | 27285 | 336-992-2710 | 992-2714 | K-10 | Dottie Heath |
| Northeast Academy of Aerospace Tech | PO Box 2889 | Elizabeth City, NC | 27906 | 252-562-0653 | | 8-9 | |
| North East Carolina Prep S | 274 Husky Trl | Tarboro, NC | 27886 | 252-641-0464 | 641-1816 | K-10 | Myles Brite |
| Notheast Regional S of Biotech Ag | 1215 St Andrews St | Jamesville, NC | 27846 | 252-792-0241 | 792-0245 | 9-12 | Hallet Davis |
| Orange Charter S | 920 Corporate Dr | Hillsborough, NC | 27278-8557 | 919-644-6272 | 644-6275 | K-8 | Jonathan Corcoran |
| Oxford Preparatory S | 6041 Landis Rd | Oxford, NC | 27565 | 919-690-0360 | 690-0230 | 8-12 | Andrew Swanner |
| PACE Academy | 308 NC 54 | Carrboro, NC | 27510 | 919-933-7699 | 967-9905 | 9-12 | Rhonda Franklin |
| PAVE SE Raliegh Charter S | 2801 S Wilmington St | Raleigh, NC | 27603 | 804-480-9905 | | K-1 | Ariana Kanwit |
| Phoenix Academy | 4191 Mendenhall Oaks Pkwy | High Point, NC | 27265 | 336-869-0079 | 869-3399 | K-10 | Kimberly Norcross |
| Piedmont Classical HS | 1515 W Cornwallis Dr | Greensboro, NC | 27408 | 336-423-6614 | | 9-12 | Mary Sauer |
| Piedmont Community Charter S | PO Box 3706 | Gastonia, NC | 28054-0038 | 704-853-2428 | 853-3689 | K-12 | Jennifer Purdee |
| Pine Lake Preparatory S | 104 Yellow Wood Cir | Mooresville, NC | 28115 | 704-237-5300 | 237-5398 | K-12 | Christopher Terrill |
| Pinnacle Classical Academy | 900 S Post Rd | Shelby, NC | 28152 | 704-740-4040 | 482-5527 | K-7 | Robert Brown |
| Pioneer Springs Community S | 9200 Bob Beatty Rd | Charlotte, NC | 28269 | 704-494-0777 | | K-3 | Laura Mock |
| PreEminent Charter S | 3815 Rock Quarry Rd | Raleigh, NC | 27610-5123 | 919-235-0511 | 235-0514 | K-8 | Melanie Butler-Williams |
| Quality Education Academy | 5012 Lansing Dr Ste D | Winston Salem, NC | 27105 | 336-744-0804 | 293-0617 | K-12 | Simon Johnson |
| Queen City STEM S | PO Box 480064 | Charlotte, NC | 28269 | 704-802-2080 | | K-6 | |
| Queen's Grant Community S | 6400 Matthews Mint Hill Rd | Mint Hill, NC | 28227-9323 | 704-573-6611 | 573-0995 | K-12 | Christy Morrin |
| Quest Academy | 10908 Strickland Rd | Raleigh, NC | 27615 | 919-841-0441 | 841-0443 | K-8 | Elizabeth Readmond |
| Raleigh Charter HS | 1307 Glenwood Ave | Raleigh, NC | 27605 | 919-715-1155 | 715-1176 | 9-12 | Dr. Thomas Humble |
| Reaching All Minds Academy | 2703 Holloway St | Durham, NC | 27703 | 919-596-1899 | 882-8339 | K-3 | Thomas McKoy |
| Research Triangle Charter Academy | 2418 Ellis Rd | Durham, NC | 27703 | 919-957-7108 | 957-9698 | K-8 | Dr. Devon Carson |
| Research Triangle HS | PO Box 13453 | Durham, NC | 27709 | 919-998-6757 | 998-3402 | 9-12 | Eric Grunden |
| River Mill Academy | 1242 S Main St | Graham, NC | 27253-4537 | 336-229-0909 | 229-9975 | K-12 | Jeffrey Dishmon |
| Rocky Mount Prep S | 3334 Bishop Rd | Rocky Mount, NC | 27804 | 252-443-9923 | 443-9932 | K-12 | Douglas Haynes |
| Roxboro Community S | 115 Lake Dr | Roxboro, NC | 27573-5672 | 336-597-0020 | 597-3152 | 6-12 | Natalie Brozy |
| Sandhills Theatre Arts Renaissance S | 140 Southern Dunes Dr | Vass, NC | 28394-9218 | 910-695-1004 | 695-7322 | K-8 | Wesley Graner |
| Shining Rock Classical Academy | PO Box 561 | Waynesville, NC | 28786 | 828-738-2665 | | K-6 | Ben Butler |
| Socrates Academy | 3909 Weddington Rd | Matthews, NC | 28105 | 704-321-1711 | 321-1714 | K-8 | Kristen Prigano |
| South Brunswick Charter S | 4128 Vanessa Dr | Southport, NC | 28461 | 910-622-5322 | | K-3 | Michelle Mena |
| Southeastern Academy | 12251 NC Highway 41 N | Lumberton, NC | 28358-6892 | 910-738-7828 | 671-8067 | PK-8 | Kristen Stone |
| Southern Wake Academy | 5108 Old Powell Rd | Holly Springs, NC | 27540 | 919-567-9955 | 567-9956 | 6-12 | David Thomas |
| Sterling Montessori Academy | 202 Treybrooke Dr | Morrisville, NC | 27560-9300 | 919-462-8889 | 462-8890 | PK-8 | Bill Zajic |

| School | Address | City,State | Zip code | Telephone | Fax | Grade | Contact |
|---|---|---|---|---|---|---|---|
| Stewart Creek HS | 2701-F Freedom Dr | Charlotte, NC | 28208 | 888-437-9353 | | 9-12 | |
| Success Institute Charter S | PO Box 1332 | Statesville, NC | 28687 | 704-881-0441 | 881-0870 | K-8 | Tenna Williams |
| Sugar Creek Charter S | 4101 N Tryon St | Charlotte, NC | 28206-2066 | 704-509-5470 | 921-1004 | K-9 | Cheryl Turner |
| Summerfield Charter Academy | 5300 N US 220 | Summerfield, NC | 27358 | 336-643-1974 | 217-8367 | K-6 | Rudy Swofford |
| Summit Charter S | 370 Mitten Ln | Cashiers, NC | 28717 | 828-743-5755 | 743-9157 | K-8 | Dr. Jack Talmadge |
| Tiller S | 1950 US Highway 70 E | Beaufort, NC | 28516-7836 | 252-728-1995 | 728-3711 | K-5 | Virginia Jones |
| Torchlight Academy | 3211 Bramer Dr | Raleigh, NC | 27604-1603 | 919-850-9960 | 850-9961 | K-5 | Dr. Cynthia McQueen |
| Triad Math and Science Academy | 700 Creek Ridge Rd | Greensboro, NC | 27406 | 336-621-0061 | 621-0072 | K-12 | Fatih Kandil |
| Triangle Math and Science Academy | 312 Gregson Dr | Cary, NC | 27511 | 919-388-0077 | 651-1418 | K-12 | Alper Tekten |
| Two Rivers Community S | 1018 Archie Carroll Rd | Boone, NC | 28607 | 828-262-5411 | 262-5412 | K-8 | Jessica Gilway |
| Union Academy | 675 N M L King Jr Blvd | Monroe, NC | 28110 | 704-283-8883 | 283-8823 | K-12 | Dr. Ann Walters |
| United Community S | 5309 Idlewild Rd N | Charlotte, NC | 28227 | 980-819-0555 | 819-0663 | K-2 | Erika Hedgepeth |
| Uwharrie Charter Academy | PO Box 1282 | Asheboro, NC | 27204 | 336-610-0813 | 610-0815 | 9-12 | Heather Soja |
| Vance Charter S | 1227 Dabney Dr | Henderson, NC | 27536-3558 | 252-431-0440 | 436-0688 | K-8 | Sean Connolly |
| Veritas Community S | 4301 Shamrock Dr | Charlotte, NC | 28215 | 980-333-1939 | | K-3 | |
| Voyager Academy | 101 Hock Parc | Durham, NC | 27704 | 919-433-3301 | 433-3305 | K-12 | Jennifer Lucas |
| Wake Forest Charter Academy | 1851 Friendship Chapel Rd | Wake Forest, NC | 27587 | 919-263-8673 | 882-9038 | K-6 | Zachary Perfitt |
| Washington Montessori S | 2330 Old Bath Hwy | Washington, NC | 27889 | 252-946-1977 | 946-5938 | K-8 | Austin Smigel |
| Water's Edge Village S | PO Box 215 | Corolla, NC | 27927 | 252-453-4502 | 453-3154 | K-6 | Meghan Agresto |
| Wayne Preparatory Academy | 600 Tommys Rd | Goldsboro, NC | 27530 | 919-734-8085 | | K-4 | Dr. Todd Forgette |
| Williams Academy | PO Box 309 | Crossnore, NC | 28616-0309 | 828-733-5241 | 737-7915 | K-12 | Cyndi Austin Ed.D. |
| Willow Oak Montessori S | 50101 Governors Dr | Chapel Hill, NC | 27517 | 919-240-7787 | | 1-4 | Peter Rubinas |
| Wilmington Preparatory Academy | 134 Cinema Dr | Wilmington, NC | 28403 | 910-799-6776 | 338-1834 | K-8 | Kevin Johnson |
| Wilson Preparatory Academy | 2755 Tilghman Rd N | Wilson, NC | 27896 | 252-294-2533 | 294-2534 | K-8 | Daryl Woodard |
| Winterville Charter Academy | 4160 Bays Water Rd | Winterville, NC | 28590 | 866-642-3676 | 575-6801 | K-8 | |
| Woods Charter S | 160 Woodland Grove Ln | Chapel Hill, NC | 27516-4085 | 919-960-8353 | 960-0133 | K-12 | Cotton Bryan |
| Woodson S | 437 Goldfloss St | Winston Salem, NC | 27127-3125 | 336-723-6838 | 723-6425 | K-12 | Ruth Hopkins |
| Youngsville Academy | PO Box 250 | Youngsville, NC | 27596 | 919-307-5933 | | K-5 | |
| Z.E.C.A. School of Arts & Technology | 110 Branchwood Dr Ste C | Jacksonville, NC | 28546 | 910-219-8603 | 219-8604 | K-6 | Stacey Owens-Howard |
| **Ohio** | | | | | | | |
| A+ Arts Academy | 1395 Fair Ave | Columbus, OH | 43205 | 614-725-1186 | 725-2305 | PK-8 | David Fant |
| A+ Children's Academy | 100 Obetz Rd | Columbus, OH | 43207-4031 | 614-491-3270 | 492-0035 | PK-2 | Melinda Hardgrow |
| Academy For Urban Scholars HS | 1808 E Broad St | Columbus, OH | 43203 | 614-545-9890 | 545-9889 | 9-12 | Aaron Butler |
| Academy of Arts & Sciences | 201 W Erie Ave | Lorain, OH | 44052-1651 | 440-244-0156 | 244-3935 | K-12 | James Sinclair |
| Academy of Educational Excellence | 4747 Heatherdowns Blvd | Toledo, OH | 43614 | 330-382-2280 | | K-3 | |
| Academy of Urban Scholars | 1350 5th Ave Ste 100 | Youngstown, OH | 44504 | 330-774-9070 | 776-9636 | 9-12 | Kevin Ellerbre |
| Accelerated Achievement Academy East | 415 W Court St | Cincinnati, OH | 45203 | 513-246-4102 | | 9-12 | Gamal Brown |
| Achieve Career Preparatory Academy | 301 Collingwood Blvd | Toledo, OH | 43604-8600 | 419-243-8559 | 243-8583 | 9-12 | Kerry Gordon-Keese |
| Akron Digital Academy | 133 Merriman Rd | Akron, OH | 44303 | 330-237-2200 | 237-2207 | K-12 | David Bowlin Ed.D. |
| Akron Preparatory S | 1200 E Market St Ste 3360 | Akron, OH | 44305 | 330-247-6232 | 299-7173 | K-8 | |
| Akros MS | 265 Park St | Akron, OH | 44304 | 330-374-6704 | 374-6713 | 6-8 | Holly Piskula |
| Allen Academy III | 1206 Shuler Ave | Hamilton, OH | 45011-4566 | 513-868-2900 | 868-0498 | K-6 | Aleta Benson |
| Allen Academy II | 184 Salem Ave | Dayton, OH | 45406-5804 | 937-586-9756 | 586-9764 | 2-6 | Michelle Thomas |
| Allen Academy | 700 Heck Ave | Dayton, OH | 45417-4641 | 937-586-9815 | 586-0271 | 7-9 | Aundray Brooks |
| Allen Preparatory S | 627 Salem Ave | Dayton, OH | 45406-5822 | 937-278-4201 | 278-4229 | K-1 | Yolanda Clark |
| Alliance Academy of Cincinnati | 1712 Duck Creek Rd | Cincinnati, OH | 45207-1644 | 513-751-5555 | 751-5072 | K-8 | Dr. Christopher Petty |
| Alternative Education Academy | 1830 Adams St | Toledo, OH | 43604-4428 | 330-253-8680 | 514-8227 | K-12 | Margaret Ford |
| Apex Academy | 16005 Terrace Rd | East Cleveland, OH | 44112-2001 | 216-451-1725 | 451-1765 | K-8 | Michael Bean |
| Arch Academy | 727 E Jenkins Ave | Columbus, OH | 43207 | 614-299-9802 | | 9-12 | |
| Arts & College Preparatory Academy | 4401 Hilton Corporate Dr | Columbus, OH | 43232-4161 | 614-986-9974 | 986-9976 | 9-12 | Anthony Gatto |
| Ashland County Community Academy | 716 Union St | Ashland, OH | 44805-1823 | 419-903-0295 | 903-0341 | 9-12 | Donne Copenhaver |
| Auglaize County Educational Academy | 1130 E Albert St | Lima, OH | 45804-1614 | 419-738-4572 | 738-4591 | K-12 | Deborah Munis |
| Aurora Academy | 824 6th St | Toledo, OH | 43605 | 419-693-6841 | 693-4799 | K-8 | Cindy Wilson |
| Autism Academy of Learning | 110 Arco Dr Ste 1 | Toledo, OH | 43607 | 419-865-7487 | 865-8360 | K-12 | Mark Lafferty |
| Autism Model S | 3020 Tremainsville Rd | Toledo, OH | 43613-1901 | 419-897-4400 | 897-4403 | K-12 | Mary Walters |
| Beacon Hill Academy | PO Box 285 | Mount Eaton, OH | 44659-0285 | 330-359-5600 | | 6-12 | Bradley Herman |
| Bella Academy of Excellence | 19114 Bella Dr | Cleveland, OH | 44119 | 216-481-1500 | 481-4515 | K-6 | Arun Dutt |
| Bennett Venture Academy | 5130 Bennett Rd | Toledo, OH | 43612-3422 | 419-269-2247 | 269-2257 | K-8 | Xavier Owens |
| Berwyn East Academy | 1850 Bostwick Rd | Columbus, OH | 43227 | 614-564-9548 | | PK-3 | Shannan Jones |
| Bridges Community Academy | 190 Saint Francis Ave | Tiffin, OH | 44883-3475 | 419-455-9295 | 455-9296 | K-12 | Dona Kaufman |
| Broadway Academy | 3398 E 55th St | Cleveland, OH | 44127-1691 | 216-271-7747 | 271-6438 | PK-8 | Nathan Richards |
| Brookwood Academy | 2685 E Livingston Ave | Columbus, OH | 43209 | 614-231-1199 | 235-2280 | 9-12 | Ellen Wristen |
| Buckeye On-Line School for Success | 119 E 5th St | East Liverpool, OH | 43920-3030 | 866-642-9237 | 385-4535 | K-12 | Rick Sheppard |
| Buckeye Preparatory Academy | 1414 Gault St | Columbus, OH | 43205 | 614-300-3685 | 252-7083 | K-8 | Renee Dunn |
| Canton College Preparatory S | 110 Cleveland St | Canton, OH | 44707 | 330-455-0498 | | K-8 | Michael Tatonetti |
| Canton Harbor HS | 1731 Grace Ave NE | Canton, OH | 44705 | 330-452-8414 | 452-8452 | 9-12 | Joseph Cole |
| Capital HS | 640 Harrisburg Pike | Columbus, OH | 43223 | 614-228-2854 | 228-4679 | 9-12 | Monica Scott |
| Carpe Diem Charter S | 5641 Belmont Ave | Cincinnati, OH | 45224-3101 | 513-363-6600 | 363-6620 | 7-12 | Tyree Gaines |
| CASTLE HS | 3950 Prospect Ave E | Cleveland, OH | 44115 | 216-443-5400 | 443-9017 | 9-12 | Kamal Chatman |
| Celerity Tenacia Charter S | 4605 Hilton Corporate Dr | Columbus, OH | 43232 | 614-863-1604 | 388-1887 | K-2 | Craig Knotts |
| Center for Student Achievement | 21 Tropic St | Jackson, OH | 45640-1966 | 740-286-7839 | 286-7837 | 9-12 | Don Jenkins |
| Central Academy of Ohio | 2727 Kenwood Blvd | Toledo, OH | 43606-3216 | 419-205-9800 | 205-9899 | K-6 | Mohamad Issa |
| Chapelside Cleveland Academy | 3845 E 131st St | Cleveland, OH | 44120-4661 | 216-283-6589 | 283-3087 | K-8 | April Hart |
| Charles S at Ohio Dominican | 1270 Brentnell Ave | Columbus, OH | 43219-2017 | 614-258-8588 | 258-8584 | 9-12 | Gregory Brown |
| Chavez College Prep ES | 2400 Mock Rd | Columbus, OH | 43219 | 614-296-2718 | | K-5 | Jameica Shoultz |
| Cincinnati College Prep Academy | 1425 Linn St | Cincinnati, OH | 45214-2605 | 513-684-0777 | 684-8888 | K-12 | Guyton Mathews |
| Cincinnati Generation Academy | 7243 Eastlawn Dr | Cincinnati, OH | 45237 | 513-389-0968 | 389-0964 | K-6 | |
| Cincinnati Leadership Academy | 7243 Eastlawn Dr | Cincinnati, OH | 45237-3515 | 513-351-5737 | 351-5740 | K-8 | Kimberly Euler |
| Cincinnati State STEM Academy | 3520 Central Pkwy Ste 143 | Cincinnati, OH | 45223 | 513-569-1820 | 569-1824 | 9-12 | Yzvetta Macon |
| Cincinnati Technology Academy | 3800 Glenway Ave | Cincinnati, OH | 45205 | 513-471-7323 | 386-7931 | 9-12 | Roger Conners |
| Citizens Academy | 10118 Hampden Ave | Cleveland, OH | 44108 | 216-791-4195 | 791-3013 | K-5 | Jennifer Taylor |
| Citizens Academy East | 12523 Woodside Ave | Cleveland, OH | 44108-2422 | 216-367-9392 | 761-7398 | K-3 | Alicia Levy |
| Citizens Leadership Academy | 9711 Lamont Ave | Cleveland, OH | 44106-4124 | 216-229-8185 | 229-8516 | 6-8 | Shelly Saltzman |
| City Day Community S | 318 S Main St | Dayton, OH | 45402-2716 | 937-223-8130 | 223-8136 | K-8 | Paula Graham |
| City Prep Academy | 2800 S Hamilton Rd | Columbus, OH | 43232 | 614-322-7970 | | 6-8 | Kerry Hill |
| Clay Avenue Community S | 1030 Clay Ave | Toledo, OH | 43608-2167 | 419-727-9900 | 727-9902 | K-6 | Julie McLaughlin |
| Cleveland Art & Social Science Academy | 10701 Shaker Blvd | Cleveland, OH | 44104-3752 | 216-229-3000 | 229-3182 | K-8 | Deborah Mays |
| Cleveland College Preparatory S | 4906 Fleet Ave | Cleveland, OH | 44105 | 216-341-1347 | 341-4466 | K-8 | Phillip Penn |
| Cliff Park HS | 821 N Limestone St | Springfield, OH | 45503-3609 | 937-342-3006 | | 9-12 | John Stack |
| Collinwood Village Academy | 716 E 156th St | Cleveland, OH | 44110 | 216-451-4022 | 451-4040 | 9-12 | Bethany Scott |
| Colonial Preparatory Academy | 2199 5th St SW | Akron, OH | 44314-2405 | 330-752-2792 | | K-8 | David Stiles |
| Columbus Arts & Tech Academy | 2255 Kimberly Pkwy E | Columbus, OH | 43232-7210 | 614-577-0900 | 866-0300 | K-9 | Derrick Shelton |
| Columbus Bilingual Academy | 35 Midland Ave | Columbus, OH | 43223 | 614-324-1492 | 324-1060 | K-7 | Jermaine Kennedy |
| Columbus Bilingual Academy - North | 3360 Kohr Blvd | Columbus, OH | 43224 | 614-525-0309 | | K-7 | Erik Barbon |
| Columbus Collegiate Academy | 1469 E Main St | Columbus, OH | 43205-2152 | 614-299-5284 | 299-5303 | 6-8 | Celeste Ferguson |
| Columbus Collegiate Academy - West | 300 Dana Ave | Columbus, OH | 43223-1310 | 614-545-9570 | 545-9571 | K-5 | Celeste Ferguson |
| Columbus Humanities Arts & Tech Academy | 1333 Morse Rd | Columbus, OH | 43229-6322 | 614-261-1200 | 261-1201 | K-8 | Latasha Morgan M.Ed. |
| Columbus Performance & Fitness Academy | 2 Easton Oval Ste 525 | Columbus, OH | 43219-7008 | 614-318-0720 | 238-3184 | K-8 | Joan Pammer |
| Columbus Prep & Fitness Academy | 1258 Demorest Rd | Columbus, OH | 43204 | 614-318-0606 | 351-9804 | K-8 | Sandra Santos |
| Columbus Preparatory Academy | 3330 Chippewa St | Columbus, OH | 43204-1653 | 614-275-3600 | 275-3601 | K-8 | Chad Carr |
| Cornerstone Academy | 6015 E Walnut St | Westerville, OH | 43081-9620 | 614-775-0615 | 775-0633 | K-8 | Natalee Long |
| Coshocton Opportunity S | 1205 Cambridge Rd | Coshocton, OH | 43812-2741 | 740-622-3600 | 623-6860 | 9-12 | Roger Moore |
| Cruiser Academy | 2747 Winchester Pike | Columbus, OH | 43232 | 614-237-8756 | 237-9308 | 9-12 | Bill Young |
| CSR Academy | 1812 Central Pkwy | Cincinnati, OH | 45214-2304 | 513-651-9624 | 618-0272 | K-8 | Brandon Godzik |
| Dayton Business Technology HS | 348 W 1st St | Dayton, OH | 45402 | 937-225-3989 | 225-3998 | 9-12 | Karl Perkins |
| Dayton Early College Academy | 300 College Park Ave | Dayton, OH | 45469-0001 | 937-229-5780 | 229-5786 | 7-12 | David Taylor |
| Dayton Liberty Campus | 4401 Dayton Liberty Rd | Dayton, OH | 45417-5903 | 937-262-4080 | 262-4091 | K-8 | Dr. Theodore Wallace |
| Dayton SMART Bilingual Academy | 601 S Keowee St | Dayton, OH | 45410 | 937-222-2812 | 264-8683 | K-4 | Douglas Mangen |
| Dayton View Academy | 1416 W Riverview Ave | Dayton, OH | 45402-6217 | 937-567-9426 | 567-9446 | K-8 | Dr. Theodore Wallace |
| DECA PREP | 200 Homewood Ave | Dayton, OH | 45405-4328 | 937-610-0110 | 260-4478 | K-6 | Judy Hennessey Ph.D. |
| Discovery Academy | 3835 Secor Rd | Toledo, OH | 43623-4402 | 419-214-3266 | | K-6 | Noah Campbell |
| Dohn Community HS | 608 E McMillan St | Cincinnati, OH | 45206-1926 | 513-281-6100 | 281-6103 | 9-12 | Leando Davenport |
| Douglass Reclamation Academy | 3167 Fulton Rd | Cleveland, OH | 44109 | 216-961-5631 | 961-5637 | 9-12 | Iteisha Jefferson M.Ed. |
| Eagle Academy | 2014 Consaul St | Toledo, OH | 43605-1412 | 419-691-4876 | 691-5184 | K-12 | Mitchel Bean |
| Eagle Learning Center HS | 2665 Navarre Ave | Oregon, OH | 43616-3245 | 419-720-2003 | 720-2007 | 9-12 | Loren Dirr |
| Early College Academy | 345 E 5th Ave | Columbus, OH | 43201-2819 | 614-298-4742 | 298-9107 | 9-12 | Pete Maneff |
| East Academy | 15720 Kipling Ave | Cleveland, OH | 44110-3105 | 216-383-1214 | | K-8 | |
| East Preparatory Academy | 4129 Superior Ave | Cleveland, OH | 44103 | 216-539-0595 | | K-8 | Joy Beasley |
| Eastside Arts Academy | 6700 Lansing Ave | Cleveland, OH | 44105 | 216-441-9830 | 441-9834 | K-5 | Katherine Rybak |
| Edge Academy | 92 N Union St | Akron, OH | 44304-1347 | 330-535-4581 | 535-5074 | K-5 | Chris Burchfield |
| Educational Academy at Linden | 720 Mount Vernon Ave | Columbus, OH | 43203 | 614-252-7611 | 299-3680 | K-5 | Barbra Bowers |
| Educational Academy for Boys & Girls | 1500 W 3rd Ave | Columbus, OH | 43212 | 614-294-3020 | | K-5 | Estella Stephens |
| Einstein Academy | 3550 Crocker Rd | Westlake, OH | 44145 | 440-471-4982 | 617-6809 | 9-12 | Bruce Thomas |
| Electronic Classroom of Tomorrow | 3700 S High St Ste 95 | Columbus, OH | 43207-4083 | 614-492-8884 | 492-8894 | K-12 | Ricky Teeters |
| Elyria Community MS | 336 S Logan St | Elyria, OH | 44035 | 440-365-0390 | 365-0397 | 6-8 | Eric Fortuna |

| School | Address | City,State | Zip code | Telephone | Fax | Grade | Contact |
|---|---|---|---|---|---|---|---|
| Elyria Community S | 300 Abbe Rd N | Elyria, OH | 44035-3724 | 440-366-5225 | 366-6280 | K-5 | Eric Fortuna |
| Emerson Academy of Dayton | 501 Hickory St | Dayton, OH | 45410-1232 | 937-223-2889 | 660-6386 | K-8 | Ronald Albino M.Ed. |
| E Prep & Village Prep Charter S | 1417 E 36th St | Cleveland, OH | 44114 | 216-456-2070 | 361-9717 | K-8 | John McBride |
| E Prep & Village Prep Charter S | 9201 Crane Ave | Cleveland, OH | 44105-1627 | 216-298-1164 | 341-0106 | K-8 | Chris O'Brien |
| Everest HS | 1555 Graham Rd | Reynoldsburg, OH | 43068 | 614-367-1980 | | 9-12 | Doug Gillum |
| Fairborn Digital Academy | 700 Black Ln | Fairborn, OH | 45324-5844 | 937-879-0511 | 879-8160 | 9-12 | Erik Tritsch |
| FCI Academy | 2177 Mock Rd | Columbus, OH | 43219-1258 | 614-471-4527 | 471-4943 | K-12 | |
| Findlay Digital Academy | 1219 W Main Cross St # 101 | Findlay, OH | 45840 | 419-425-3598 | 425-3588 | 9-12 | Sandra White |
| Focus Learning Academy East | 4480 Refugee Rd | Columbus, OH | 43232-4459 | 614-269-0150 | 269-0151 | 9-12 | Jason Morton |
| Focus Learning Academy North | 4807 Evanswood Dr | Columbus, OH | 43229-6285 | 614-310-0430 | 310-0469 | 9-12 | Tiffany DeLong-Kocher |
| Focus Learning Academy Southwest | 190 Southwood Ave | Columbus, OH | 43207-1133 | 614-545-2000 | 545-1995 | 9-12 | Kerry Hill |
| Focus Learning Acad of Northern Columbus | 1880 E Dublin Granville Rd | Columbus, OH | 43229 | 614-547-0920 | 547-0924 | K-8 | Travis Budd |
| Foundation Academy | 1050 Wyandotte Ave | Mansfield, OH | 44906-1939 | 419-526-9540 | 526-9542 | K-10 | Joann Hipsher |
| Fox Academy | 1505 Jefferson Ave | Toledo, OH | 43604 | 419-720-4500 | 720-4502 | 7-12 | |
| Foxfire ES | 2805 Pinkerton Ln | Zanesville, OH | 43701 | 740-453-4509 | | K-4 | Amanda Matthews |
| Foxfire HS | PO Box 1818 | Zanesville, OH | 43702-1818 | 740-453-4509 | 455-4084 | 9-12 | Todd Whiteman |
| Foxfire IS | 2805 Pinkerton Ln | Zanesville, OH | 43701 | 740-453-4509 | | 5-8 | Amanda Matthews |
| Franklin Local Community S | PO Box 95 | Roseville, OH | 43777-0095 | 740-697-7317 | 697-0793 | 7-12 | Frank VanKirk |
| Franklinton Preparatory Academy | 40 Chicago Ave | Columbus, OH | 43222-1132 | 614-636-3721 | | 9-12 | Martin Griffith |
| Garfield Academy | 1379 Garfield Ave SW | Canton, OH | 44706 | 330-454-3128 | | 9-12 | |
| Gateway Academy of Ohio | 2323 Lake Club Dr | Columbus, OH | 43232 | 614-856-1149 | 856-1366 | 7-12 | Hydia Green |
| Glass City Academy | 1000 Monroe St | Toledo, OH | 43604 | 419-720-6311 | 720-6315 | 11-12 | Stewart Jesse |
| Global Village Academy | 5720 State Rd | Parma, OH | 44134 | 216-767-5956 | 767-5653 | K-6 | Oleh Holowatyj |
| Goal Digital Academy | 890 W 4th St Ste 400 | Mansfield, OH | 44906-2561 | 419-521-9008 | 529-2976 | K-12 | Patricia Jenkins |
| Graham Expeditionary MS | 140 E 16th Ave | Columbus, OH | 43201-1617 | 614-253-4000 | 253-4002 | 5-8 | Gregory Brown |
| Graham PS | 140 E 16th Ave | Columbus, OH | 43201 | 614-253-4001 | 643-5146 | K-5 | Eileen Meers |
| Graham S | 3950 Indianola Ave | Columbus, OH | 43214-3167 | 614-262-1111 | 262-5878 | 9-12 | Gregory Brown |
| Grant Leadership Academy | 2440 Dawnlight Ave | Columbus, OH | 43211 | 614-252-2087 | 252-2311 | K-6 | Jennifer Szallai |
| Greater Ohio Virtual S | 1879 Deerfield Rd | Lebanon, OH | 45036 | 513-695-2924 | 695-2588 | 9-12 | Patrick Pare |
| Greater Summit County Early Learning Ctr | 2141 Pickle Rd | Akron, OH | 44312-4221 | 330-945-5600 | | PK-4 | Teresa Graves |
| Great Expectations ES | 20 Arco Dr | Toledo, OH | 43607 | 419-490-6252 | | K-6 | David Mangen |
| Great Western Academy | 310 N Wilson Rd | Columbus, OH | 43204-6221 | 614-276-1028 | 276-1049 | K-8 | Jason Knight |
| Green Inspiration Academy | 4265 Northfield Rd | Highland Hills, OH | 44128-2811 | 216-378-9573 | 882-0554 | K-8 | Donna Kolb |
| Groveport Community S | 4485 S Hamilton Rd | Groveport, OH | 43125-9334 | 614-574-4100 | 574-4107 | K-8 | Dair Foster |
| Haley S | 4901 Galaxy Pkwy | Cleveland, OH | 44128 | 216-581-4259 | 510-5732 | K-6 | Richard Hronek |
| Hamilton Alternative Academy | 775 Rathmell Rd | Columbus, OH | 43207-4737 | 614-491-8044 | 491-5564 | K-12 | Allyson Price |
| Hamilton County Math & Science S | 2675 Civic Center Dr | Cincinnati, OH | 45231-1311 | 513-728-8620 | 728-8623 | K-8 | Dwan Moore M.Ed. |
| Hardin Community S | 400 Decatur St | Kenton, OH | 43326 | 419-673-3210 | | 6-12 | Wade Melton |
| Harrisburg Pike Community S | 680 Harrisburg Pike | Columbus, OH | 43223-2100 | 614-223-1510 | 223-1584 | K-5 | Lori Thayer |
| Harvard Avenue Community S | 12000 Harvard Ave | Cleveland, OH | 44105-5444 | 216-283-5100 | 283-5762 | K-8 | Pharon Holtrey |
| HBCU Preparatory School 1 | 12601 Shaker Blvd | Cleveland, OH | 44120 | 216-812-0244 | 812-0234 | K-12 | |
| HBCU Preparatory School 2 | 12601 Shaker Blvd | Cleveland, OH | 44120 | 216-426-8601 | 426-9528 | 3-5 | |
| Heir Force Community S | 150 W Grand Ave | Lima, OH | 45801-4006 | 419-228-9241 | 228-1555 | K-8 | Darwin Lofton |
| Hollingworth S for Talented & Gifted | 653 Miami St | Toledo, OH | 43605 | 419-705-3411 | 720-4923 | K-9 | Terrence Franklin |
| Hope Academy for Autism | 1628 Niles Rd SE | Warren, OH | 44484-5111 | 330-369-2454 | 369-2455 | K-12 | Kimberly Clinkscale |
| Hope Academy Northcoast Campus | 4310 E 71st St | Cleveland, OH | 44105-5759 | 216-429-0232 | 429-0249 | K-8 | |
| Hope Academy Northwest | 1441 W 116th St | Cleveland, OH | 44102-2301 | 216-226-6800 | 226-6805 | K-12 | |
| Hope Academy University Campus | 107 S Arlington St | Akron, OH | 44306-1328 | 330-535-7728 | 535-7864 | K-8 | |
| Hope Learning Academy of Toledo | 4234 Monroe St | Toledo, OH | 43606 | 419-297-6313 | 725-9184 | K-8 | Justin Bryson |
| Horizon Science Academy Cincinnati | 1055 Laidlaw Ave | Cincinnati, OH | 45237-5005 | 513-242-0099 | 242-2467 | K-8 | Ergun Sevilmis |
| Horizon Science Academy Cleveland HS | 6000 S Marginal Rd | Cleveland, OH | 44103 | 216-432-3660 | 432-3670 | 9-12 | Mustafa Ada |
| Horizon Science Academy Cleveland MS | 6100 S Marginal Rd | Cleveland, OH | 44103-1043 | 216-432-9940 | 432-9941 | 6-8 | |
| Horizon Science Academy Columbus ES | 2835 Morse Rd | Columbus, OH | 43231-6033 | 614-475-4585 | 475-4587 | K-5 | Jessica Lindskog |
| Horizon Science Academy Columbus HS | 1070 Morse Rd | Columbus, OH | 43229-6290 | 614-846-7616 | 846-7696 | 9-12 | |
| Horizon Science Academy Columbus MS | 2350 Morse Rd | Columbus, OH | 43229-5801 | 614-428-6564 | 428-6574 | 6-8 | Okan Celiker |
| Horizon Science Academy Dayton | 4751 Sue Anne Blvd | Dayton, OH | 45405 | 937-277-1177 | 277-3090 | K-4 | Jaime Lierly |
| Horizon Science Academy Dayton Downtown | 121 S Monmouth St | Dayton, OH | 45403 | 937-281-1980 | 281-1979 | K-8 | Ali Ozer |
| Horizon Science Academy Dayton HS | 250 Shoup Mill Rd | Dayton, OH | 45415-3517 | 937-281-1480 | 281-1481 | 5-12 | Ali Kucuker |
| Horizon Science Academy - Denison | 1700 Denison Ave | Cleveland, OH | 44109-2945 | 216-739-9911 | 739-9913 | K-8 | Bulent Akben M.Ed. |
| Horizon Science Academy Denison ES | 2261 Columbus Rd | Cleveland, OH | 44113-4230 | 216-661-8840 | 661-8850 | K-5 | Nicole Kratz |
| Horizon Science Academy of Lorain | 760 Tower Blvd | Lorain, OH | 44052 | 440-282-4277 | 282-4278 | K-12 | Fatih Sumer |
| Horizon Science Academy Springfield | 630 S Reynolds Rd | Toledo, OH | 43615-6314 | 419-535-0524 | 535-0525 | K-8 | Erin Schreiner |
| Horizon Science Academy Youngstown | 3403 Southern Blvd | Youngstown, OH | 44507-2044 | 330-782-3003 | 782-3356 | K-8 | Ferhat Kapki |
| Hughes High School | 10450 Superior Ave | Cleveland, OH | 44106 | 216-721-0845 | | 9-12 | Gamal Brown |
| IMAC HS | 445 Bowman St | Mansfield, OH | 44903 | 419-247-4475 | 247-3392 | 9-12 | Harold Dean |
| Imagine Akron Academy | 1585 Frederick Blvd | Akron, OH | 44320 | 330-379-1034 | 379-0489 | K-K | Julie Lewis |
| Imagine Cleveland Academy | 3443 E 93rd St | Cleveland, OH | 44104 | 216-641-1500 | 862-7168 | K-5 | Lisa Lyons |
| Imagine Columbus Primary Academy | 4656 Heaton Rd | Columbus, OH | 43229-6612 | 614-433-7510 | 433-7515 | K-8 | Renee Dunn |
| Imagine Hill Academy | 6145 Hill Ave | Toledo, OH | 43615 | 419-867-8167 | | K-5 | Zacharias Kantouros |
| Imagine Integrity Academy | 1565 Integrity Dr E | Columbus, OH | 43209 | 614-464-1500 | | K-5 | Michelle Brown |
| Imagine Leadership Academy | 2405 Romig Rd | Akron, OH | 44320-3826 | 330-753-1000 | 753-1005 | 1-6 | Erica Lucas |
| Imagine Woodbury Academy | 100 E Woodbury Dr | Dayton, OH | 45415 | 937-277-1710 | | K-5 | Kathryn Kountz |
| Impact Academy Cincinnati | 3060 Durrell Ave | Cincinnati, OH | 45207 | 513-751-2000 | | K-5 | Brandon Godzik |
| Insight School of Ohio | 2760 Airport Dr Ste 135 | Columbus, OH | 43219 | 614-300-2766 | 448-2739 | 9-12 | Amanda Conley |
| Intergenerational S | 11327 Shaker Blvd Ste 200 | Cleveland, OH | 44104-3805 | 216-721-0120 | 721-0126 | K-8 | Dr. Cathy Whitehouse |
| International Academy of Columbus | 1201 Schrock Rd | Columbus, OH | 43229-1117 | 614-844-5539 | 844-5857 | K-8 | Dr. Mouhamed Tarazi |
| Invictus HS | 3122 Euclid Ave | Cleveland, OH | 44115-2508 | 216-539-7200 | 361-3090 | 9-12 | Dean Manke |
| King Academy Community S | 224 W Liberty St | Cincinnati, OH | 45202 | 513-421-7519 | 421-1770 | K-8 | Andrea Martinez |
| KIPP Columbus | 2750 Agler Rd | Columbus, OH | 43224 | 614-263-6137 | 263-6207 | 5-8 | Hannah Powell |
| Klepinger Road Community S | 3650 Klepinger Rd | Dayton, OH | 45416-1919 | 937-610-1710 | 610-1730 | K-8 | Melissa McManaway |
| Lake Erie College Preparatory S | 14405 Saint Clair Ave | Cleveland, OH | 44110 | 216-453-4556 | 268-4951 | K-8 | Dr. Samuel Lockhart |
| Lake Erie International HS | 11650 Detroit Ave | Cleveland, OH | 44102 | 216-539-7229 | 651-6174 | 9-12 | John Stack |
| Lakeland Academy Community S | 101 Main St | Freeport, OH | 43973 | 740-658-1042 | 658-1062 | K-12 | Mindy Pittis |
| Lakeshore Intergenerational S | 18025 Marcella Rd | Cleveland, OH | 44119 | 216-586-3872 | | K-3 | Robin Bartley |
| Lakewood City Academy | 1470 Warren Rd | Lakewood, OH | 44107-3918 | 216-529-4037 | 227-5975 | 6-12 | Terrilynn Bornino-Elwell |
| Lakewood Digital Academy | PO Box 70 | Hebron, OH | 43025-0070 | 740-928-1915 | 928-3152 | K-12 | Dr. Eva Pound-Bickle |
| Lancaster Fairfield Community S | 320 E Locust St | Lancaster, OH | 43130-4437 | 740-652-7200 | 687-7178 | 9-12 | Jeffrey Graf |
| Lawrence County Academy | 11627 State Route 243 | Chesapeake, OH | 45619 | 740-867-6641 | 867-1371 | 7-12 | Robert Wilds |
| Liberty Preparatory S | PO Box 374 | Smithville, OH | 44677 | 330-669-0055 | 669-0055 | 9-12 | Brian Hessey |
| LifeLinks Community S | 205 W Crawford St | Van Wert, OH | 45891-1903 | 419-623-5380 | 238-3974 | 6-12 | Gordon Stemen |
| LifeSkills Center Columbus North | 1900 E Dublin Granville Rd | Columbus, OH | 43229-3553 | 614-891-9041 | 891-8571 | 9-12 | Abdirizak Farah |
| Life Skills Center Middleton | 631 S Breiel Blvd | Middletown, OH | 45044 | 513-423-1800 | 423-1818 | 9-12 | |
| Life Skills Center of Canton | 1100 Cleveland Ave NW | Canton, OH | 44702 | 330-456-4490 | | 9-12 | |
| Life Skills Center of Cincinnati | 2612 Gilbert Ave | Cincinnati, OH | 45206-1205 | 513-475-0222 | 475-0444 | 9-12 | |
| Life Skills Center of Dayton | 1721 N Main St | Dayton, OH | 45405-4143 | 937-274-2841 | 274-2873 | 9-12 | |
| Life Skills Center of Elyria | 2015 W River Rd N | Elyria, OH | 44035-2309 | 440-324-1755 | 324-1723 | 9-12 | |
| Life Skills Center of Hamilton County | 7710 Reading Rd | Cincinnati, OH | 45237-6800 | 513-821-6695 | 821-8755 | 9-12 | |
| Life Skills Center of North Akron | 1458 Brittain Rd | Akron, OH | 44310-3641 | 330-633-5990 | 633-7005 | 9-12 | |
| Life Skills Center of Northeast OH | 12201 Larchmere Blvd | Shaker Heights, OH | 44120-1101 | 216-421-7587 | 421-8189 | 9-12 | |
| Life Skills Center of Summit County | 2168 Romig Rd | Akron, OH | 44320-3879 | 330-745-3678 | 753-1506 | 9-12 | |
| Life Skills Center of Toledo | 1830 Adams St | Toledo, OH | 43604-4428 | 419-241-5504 | 241-9176 | 9-12 | |
| Life Skills Center of Trumbull County | 458 Franklin St SE | Warren, OH | 44483-5715 | 330-392-0231 | 392-0253 | 9-12 | |
| Life Skills Center of Youngstown | 3405 Market St | Youngstown, OH | 44507-2009 | 330-743-6698 | 743-6702 | 9-12 | |
| LifeSkills Columbus Southeast | 2400 S Hamilton Rd | Columbus, OH | 43232-4963 | 614-863-9175 | 863-9185 | 9-12 | |
| Life Skills HS of Cleveland | 4600 Carnegie Ave | Cleveland, OH | 44103 | 216-431-7571 | | 9-12 | |
| Lighthouse Community S | 6100 Desmond St | Cincinnati, OH | 45227-1897 | 513-561-7888 | 561-7818 | 6-12 | Amy Shrock |
| Lincoln Park Academy | 3185 W 41st St | Cleveland, OH | 44109 | 216-263-7008 | 263-7007 | K-8 | |
| Lincoln Preparatory S | 4215 Robert Ave | Cleveland, OH | 44109 | 216-772-1336 | 961-5378 | K-8 | Maureen Businger |
| London Academy | 40 S Walnut St | London, OH | 43140 | 740-852-5703 | 852-4609 | 9-12 | Pauline Swan |
| Lorain Community ES | 1110 W 4th St | Lorain, OH | 44052-1408 | 440-204-2130 | 204-2134 | K-4 | Melisa Shady |
| Lorain Community MS | 1110 W 4th St | Lorain, OH | 44052-1408 | 440-242-2023 | 204-2134 | 5-8 | Melisa Shady |
| Lorain Preparatory Academy | 4125 Leavitt Rd # 2 | Lorain, OH | 44053 | 440-282-3127 | 282-3179 | 3-8 | James Sinclair |
| Madison Ave School of the Arts | 1511 Madison Ave | Toledo, OH | 43604-4433 | 419-259-4000 | 243-1513 | K-5 | Daphne Williams |
| Madison Community S | 2015 W 95th St | Cleveland, OH | 44102-3791 | 216-651-5212 | 651-9040 | K-8 | Melissa Rice |
| Madisonville SMART ES | 4324 Homer Ave | Cincinnati, OH | 45227 | 513-241-1101 | | K-6 | Joe Calloway |
| Mahoning County HS | 100 Debartolo Pl Ste 220 | Youngstown, OH | 44512 | 330-965-2860 | | 9-12 | Jennifer Whittemore |
| Mahoning Unlimited Classroom | 7401 Market St Ste 519 | Youngstown, OH | 44512 | 330-965-7828 | 729-9349 | 4-12 | Brad Justice |
| Mahoning Valley Opportunity S | 496 Glenwood Ave | Youngstown, OH | 44502-1509 | 330-744-7656 | 743-9757 | 9-12 | David Macali |
| Main Street Preparatory Academy | 388 S Main St | Akron, OH | 44311 | 234-738-1925 | | 6-8 | |
| Mansfield Elective Academy | 445 Bowman St | Mansfield, OH | 44903-1201 | 567-247-4475 | 247-3392 | K-9 | Deborah Franklin |
| Mansfield Enhancement Academy | 445 Bowman St | Mansfield, OH | 44903 | 419-525-0105 | 525-0106 | 9-12 | Harold Dean |
| Marion City Digital Academy | 360 Presidential Dr | Marion, OH | 43302 | 740-223-3882 | 223-3878 | K-12 | Richard Fogle |
| Maritime Academy of Toledo | 803 Water St | Toledo, OH | 43604 | 419-244-9999 | 244-9898 | 5-12 | Jodi Johns |
| Marshall HS | 4720 Roosevelt Blvd | Middletown, OH | 45044 | 513-318-7078 | 425-6951 | 9-12 | Chuck Hall |
| Marshall HS | 13540 Lorain Ave | Cleveland, OH | 44111 | 216-961-9813 | | 9-12 | |
| Massillon Digital Academy | 930 17th St NE | Massillon, OH | 44646 | 330-830-3900 | 830-0953 | K-12 | Nicki Howard |
| Menlo Park Academy | 14440 Triskett Rd | Cleveland, OH | 44111 | 440-925-6365 | 925-0698 | K-8 | Denise Hieronymus |

| School | Address | City,State | Zip code | Telephone | Fax | Grade | Contact |
|---|---|---|---|---|---|---|---|
| Miamisburg Secondary Academy | 540 Park Ave | Miamisburg, OH | 45342-2854 | 937-866-3381 | 865-5250 | 7-12 | Greg Whitehead |
| Miami Valley Academies | 5656 Springboro Pike | Dayton, OH | 45449-2806 | 937-294-4522 | 294-4545 | K-12 | Robin Solazzo |
| Middlebury Academy | 88 Kent St | Akron, OH | 44305 | 330-752-2766 | 940-1339 | K-5 | Maureen Businger |
| Middletown Prep & Fitness Academy | 816 2nd Ave | Middletown, OH | 45044 | 513-424-6110 | 424-6121 | K-8 | Elizabeth Kelliher |
| Midnimo Cross Cultural Community S | 1567 Loretta Ave | Columbus, OH | 43211 | 614-261-7480 | 261-7481 | 6-9 | Marvis McGowan |
| Millenium Community ES | 3500 Refugee Rd | Columbus, OH | 43232-4862 | 614-255-5585 | 255-5580 | K-8 | Tijuana Russell |
| Mound Street Health Careers Academy | 354 Mound St | Dayton, OH | 45402-8325 | 937-223-3041 | 223-5867 | 9-12 | Ron Cothran |
| Mound Street IT Careers Academy | 354 Mound St | Dayton, OH | 45402-8325 | 937-223-3041 | 223-5867 | 9-12 | Ron Cothran |
| Mound Street Military Careers Academy | 354 Mound St | Dayton, OH | 45402-8325 | 937-223-3041 | 223-5867 | 9-12 | Ron Cothran |
| Mt. Auburn International Academy | 244 Southern Ave | Cincinnati, OH | 45219-3023 | 513-241-5500 | 241-5501 | K-12 | Wissam Sabbagh |
| Mt. Healthy Prep & Fitness Academy | 7601 Harrison Ave | Mount Healthy, OH | 45231 | 513-587-6280 | 521-4509 | K-8 | Timothy Baggs |
| Near West Intergenerational S | 3805 Terrett Ave | Cleveland, OH | 44113 | 216-961-4308 | | K-6 | Brooke King |
| Newark Digital Academy | 255 Woods Ave | Newark, OH | 43055-4436 | 740-328-2022 | 328-2270 | K-12 | John Lutz |
| New Beginnings Academy | 4707 Hilton Corporate Dr | Columbus, OH | 43232 | 614-367-0589 | 367-0921 | 8-12 | Gamal Brown |
| New Day Academy | 291 E 222nd St Ste 205 | Euclid, OH | 44123-1718 | 216-797-1602 | 797-1604 | K-12 | Terrance Walton |
| Next Frontier Academy | 1127 Copley Rd | Akron, OH | 44320 | 330-835-9755 | | 7-9 | |
| Nexus Academy of Cleveland | 3615 Superior Ave E | Cleveland, OH | 44114 | 216-361-1314 | | 9-12 | Brittiany Sanford |
| Nexus Academy of Columbus | 4689 Hilton Corporate Dr | Columbus, OH | 43232 | 614-866-4761 | | 9-12 | Jessica Hursey |
| Nexus Academy of Toledo | 600 Jefferson Ave | Toledo, OH | 43604 | 419-244-8875 | | 9-12 | Andrea Weilacher |
| Noble Academy - Cleveland | 1200 E 200th St | Euclid, OH | 44117-1172 | 216-486-8866 | 486-2846 | K-8 | |
| Noble Academy - Columbus | 1329 Bethel Rd | Columbus, OH | 43220-2611 | 614-326-0687 | 326-0691 | K-8 | Ali Kucuker |
| North Central Academy | 928 W Market St Ste B | Tiffin, OH | 44883 | 419-448-5786 | 448-5789 | 6-12 | Adam Pittis |
| North Dayton S of Discovery | 3901 Turner Rd | Dayton, OH | 45415-3654 | 937-278-6671 | 278-6964 | K-8 | Jacqueline Robbeloth |
| Northeast Ohio College Preparatory S | 2357 Tremont Ave | Cleveland, OH | 44113-4633 | 216-965-0580 | 394-0364 | K-12 | |
| Northland Prep & Fitness ES | 1875 Morse Rd | Columbus, OH | 43229-6603 | 614-318-0600 | 262-9111 | K-8 | Ashley Graver |
| Northmont Secondary Academy | 4916 National Rd | Clayton, OH | 45315 | | | 9-12 | George Caras |
| Northpointe Academy | 3648 Victory Ave | Toledo, OH | 43607-2564 | 419-535-1997 | 244-4205 | K-8 | Andre Fox |
| Norwood Conversion Community S | 2132 Williams Ave | Norwood, OH | 45212 | | | 9-12 | John Stacy |
| OAK Leadership Institute | 8610 Hough Ave | Cleveland, OH | 44106 | 216-229-7178 | | K-5 | Angela Bennett |
| Oakstone Community S | 5747 Cleveland Ave | Columbus, OH | 43231-2831 | 614-865-9643 | 865-9649 | PK-12 | Heather Kronewetter |
| Ohio College Preparatory S | 21100 Southgate Park Blvd | Maple Heights, OH | 44137 | 216-453-4550 | | K-8 | Christopher Terec |
| Ohio Connections Academy | 5181 Natorp Blvd Ste 150 | Mason, OH | 45040 | 513-234-4900 | | K-12 | Marie Hanna |
| Ohio Construction Academy | 1725 Jetway Blvd | Columbus, OH | 43219 | 614-226-4217 | | 9-12 | Barton Hacker |
| Ohio Virtual Academy | 1690 Woodlands Dr | Toledo, OH | 43607 | 866-339-9071 | 482-0955 | K-12 | Dr. Kristin Stewart |
| Old Brooklyn Community ES | 4430 State Rd | Cleveland, OH | 44109 | 216-661-7888 | 661-5975 | K-4 | Cherie Kaiser |
| Old Brooklyn Community MS | 4430 State Rd | Cleveland, OH | 44109-4705 | 216-351-0280 | 661-5975 | 5-8 | Karil Stohlman |
| Orion Academy | 1798 Queen City Ave | Cincinnati, OH | 45214-1427 | 513-251-6000 | 251-3851 | K-8 | Bryan Cannon |
| Outreach Academy-Students w/Disabilities | 9772 Diagonal Rd | Mantua, OH | 44255 | 330-274-2272 | 732-2575 | K-12 | Mary Wideman |
| Par - Excellence Academy | 96 Maholm St | Newark, OH | 43055-3994 | 740-344-7279 | 344-7272 | PK-6 | Gisele James |
| Parma Community ES | 7667 Day Dr | Parma, OH | 44129 | 440-888-5490 | 888-5890 | K-3 | Brian Belmont |
| Parma Community HS | 5983 W 54th St | Parma, OH | 44129 | 440-887-0319 | 845-2834 | 9-12 | Linda Geyer |
| Parma Community MS | 5983 W 54th St | Parma, OH | 44129 | 440-845-2587 | 845-2834 | 4-8 | Linda Geyer |
| Pathway S of Discovery | 173 Avondale Dr | Dayton, OH | 45404-2123 | 937-235-5498 | 235-5569 | K-8 | Keith Colbert |
| Patriot Preparatory Academy | 4938 Beatrice Dr | Columbus, OH | 43227-2113 | 614-864-5332 | 864-5381 | K-12 | H. David McIlrath |
| Pearl Academy | 4850 Pearl Rd | Cleveland, OH | 44109 | 216-741-2991 | | K-5 | Margaret Ford |
| Performance Academy of Eastland | 2220 S Hamilton Rd | Columbus, OH | 43232 | 614-314-6401 | 577-1933 | K-8 | |
| Phoenix Academy Community S | 1505 Jefferson Ave | Toledo, OH | 43604 | 419-720-4500 | | 7-12 | Craig Cotner |
| Phoenix Community Learning Center | 3595 Washington Ave | Cincinnati, OH | 45229-2617 | 513-351-5801 | 351-5809 | K-8 | Glenda Brown |
| Pickerington Community S | 7800 Refugee Rd | Pickerington, OH | 43147 | 614-830-2797 | | 9-12 | Bobby Blackburn |
| Pinnacle Academy | 860 E 222nd St | Euclid, OH | 44123 | 216-731-0127 | 731-0688 | K-8 | Jennifer Littlefield |
| Pleasant Community Digital S | 1105 Owens Rd W | Marion, OH | 43302 | 740-389-4815 | 389-6985 | K-K | Dr. Shelly Dason |
| Pleasant Education Academy | 1107 Owens Rd W | Marion, OH | 43302 | 740-389-4476 | | 9-12 | Lane Warner |
| Promise Academy | 1701 E 13th St | Cleveland, OH | 44114 | 216-443-0500 | 443-0506 | 9-12 | Dr. Cordelia Harris |
| Provost Academy Ohio | 1335 Dublin Rd | Columbus, OH | 43215 | 614-866-7570 | | 9-12 | Naim Sanders |
| Puritas Community ES | 15204 Puritas Ave | Cleveland, OH | 44135-2716 | 216-688-0680 | 688-0609 | K-4 | Margaret Colwell |
| Puritas Community MS | 5730 Broadview Rd | Parma, OH | 44134 | 216-688-0680 | | 6-8 | Rebecca Keeney |
| Puritas Community MS | 15204 Puritas Ave | Cleveland, OH | 44135 | 216-251-1596 | 251-3540 | 4-8 | Meg Colwell |
| QDA HS | 400 Mill Ave SE Ste 901 | New Phila, OH | 44663-3878 | 330-364-0618 | 364-0618 | K-12 | Steve Eckert |
| Quest Community S | 12000 Snow Rd | Parma, OH | 44130 | 216-220-4412 | | 9-12 | Dewey Chapman |
| REACH Academy | 2014 Consaul St | Toledo, OH | 43605 | 419-691-4876 | 691-5184 | K-5 | Shannon Kane |
| Renaissance Academy | 4300 Kimberly Pkwy N | Columbus, OH | 43232 | 614-866-7277 | | 9-12 | Sharice Martin |
| Richland Academy S of Excellence | 75 N Walnut St | Mansfield, OH | 44902-1211 | 419-522-8224 | | K-8 | Sandra Sutherland |
| Ridgedale Community S | 3103 Hillman Ford Rd | Morral, OH | 43337-9302 | 740-382-6065 | 383-6538 | K-12 | |
| Rise & Shine Academy | 3248 Warsaw St | Toledo, OH | 43608 | 419-244-9900 | 244-9906 | K-6 | Dr. Pat McKinstry |
| Rittman Academy | 100 Saurer St | Rittman, OH | 44270 | 330-927-7162 | 927-7405 | 9-12 | Kent Smith |
| River Gate HS | 458 Franklin St SE | Warren, OH | 44483 | 330-392-0231 | | 9-12 | Karen Wachter |
| Riverside Academy | 3280 River Rd | Cincinnati, OH | 45204-1214 | 513-921-7777 | 921-7704 | K-12 | |
| Road to Success Academy | 1555 Bryden Rd | Columbus, OH | 43205 | 614-252-4645 | | 9-12 | Alicia Henry |
| Rushmore Academy | 2222 Marion-Mount Gilead Rd | Marion, OH | 43302 | 740-387-2043 | 387-2169 | 9-12 | Steve Vanderhoff |
| Schnee Learning Center | 2222 Issaquah St | Cuyahoga Falls, OH | 44221-3704 | 330-922-1966 | 945-4059 | 9-12 | Dona Cardone |
| Sciotoville Elementary Academy | 5523 3rd St | Sciotoville, OH | 45662-5401 | 740-776-2920 | 776-2916 | K-4 | Rick Bowman |
| Sciotoville HS | 224 Marshall St | Sciotoville, OH | 45662-5549 | 740-776-6777 | 776-6812 | 5-12 | Michael Yeagle |
| Southern Ohio Academy | 522 Glenwood Ave | Sciotoville, OH | 45662 | 740-259-6843 | | 9-12 | Patricia Ciraso |
| South Scioto Academy | 707 E Jenkins Ave | Columbus, OH | 43207-1318 | 614-445-7684 | 445-7688 | K-8 | Courtney Watters |
| Southside Academy | 1400 Oak Hill Ave | Youngstown, OH | 44507 | 330-742-9090 | 743-1998 | K-8 | |
| Southwest Licking Digital Academy | 927 South St Unit A | Pataskala, OH | 43062-6014 | 740-927-3941 | 927-4648 | K-12 | Jeffrey Severino |
| Springfield Academy of Excellence | PO Box 1566 | Springfield, OH | 45501-1566 | 937-325-0933 | 325-0962 | K-6 | Edna Chapman |
| Springfield Prep & Fitness Academy | 1615 Selma Rd | Springfield, OH | 45505-4245 | 937-323-6250 | 323-6252 | K-8 | Darren Fansler |
| Stambaugh Charter Academy | 2420 Donald Ave | Youngstown, OH | 44509-1306 | 330-792-4806 | 787-0278 | K-8 | Landon Brown |
| Star Academy of Toledo | 5025 Glendale Ave | Toledo, OH | 43614-1855 | 419-720-6330 | 720-7372 | K-8 | Julieta Dinkins |
| STEAM Academy of Akron | 1338 Virginia Ave | Akron, OH | 44306 | 330-773-1100 | | K-5 | Nova O'Callaghan |
| STEAM Academy of Cincinnati | 6000 Murray Rd | Cincinnati, OH | 45229 | 513-221-1810 | | 9-12 | Anna Trachsel |
| STEAM Academy of Dayton | 545 Odlin Ave | Dayton, OH | 45405 | 937-262-7063 | | 9-12 | Corey Stroud |
| STEAM Academy of Warren | 261 Elm Rd NE | Warren, OH | 44483 | 330-394-3200 | 394-3600 | K-8 | Timothy Freeman |
| STEAM Academy of Warrensville Heights | 4700 Richmond Rd | Warrensvl Hts, OH | 44128 | 216-595-2866 | 595-3180 | K-6 | Gary Lane |
| Steel Academy | 1570 Creighton Ave | Akron, OH | 44310 | 330-687-0834 | | 6-12 | Angeline Lawrie |
| Stepstone Academy | 2121 E 32nd St | Cleveland, OH | 44115 | 440-260-6400 | 431-7897 | K-5 | |
| Stockyard Community ES | 3200 W 65th St | Cleveland, OH | 44102-5510 | 216-651-5143 | 651-9515 | K-6 | Amber Steele |
| Stockyard Community MS | 3224 W 65th St | Cleveland, OH | 44102 | 216-961-5052 | 651-9227 | 7-8 | Gregory Cek |
| Sullivant Avenue Community S | 3435 Sullivant Ave | Columbus, OH | 43204-1103 | 614-308-5991 | 308-5622 | K-6 | Jamie Lama |
| Summit Academy Akron ES | 2503 Leland Ave | Akron, OH | 44312 | 330-253-7441 | 253-7457 | K-6 | Dawn Presley |
| Summit Academy Akron HS | 464 S Hawkins Ave | Akron, OH | 44320 | 330-434-2343 | 434-5295 | 9-12 | Shelly Curcic |
| Summit Academy Akron MS | 2791 Mogadore Rd | Akron, OH | 44312 | 330-252-1510 | 784-8347 | 7-8 | |
| Summit Academy - Canton HS | 2400 Cleveland Ave NW | Canton, OH | 44709-3613 | 330-453-8547 | 453-8924 | 9-12 | John Fullerman |
| Summit Academy - Canton S | 1620 Market Ave S | Canton, OH | 44707 | 330-458-0393 | 458-0518 | K-8 | |
| Summit Academy Columbus | 2521 Fairwood Ave Ste 100 | Columbus, OH | 43207 | 614-237-5497 | 237-6519 | K-5 | |
| Summit Academy Community S Cincinnati | 1660 Sternblock Ln | Cincinnati, OH | 45237 | 513-321-0561 | 321-0795 | K-8 | Megan Fagan |
| Summit Academy Community S Dayton | 4128 Ceder Ridge Rd | Dayton, OH | 45414 | 937-278-4298 | 278-4613 | K-8 | Eric Marthaler |
| Summit Academy Community S for Alt Lrnrs | 2140 E 36th St | Lorain, OH | 44055-2756 | 440-277-4110 | 277-4112 | K-5 | A.J. Charpentier |
| Summit Academy Community S - Toledo | 1853 South Ave | Toledo, OH | 43609-2086 | 419-385-5730 | 385-5781 | K-8 | |
| Summit Academy Community S Warren | 2106 Arbor Ave SE | Warren, OH | 44484-5296 | 330-369-4233 | 369-4299 | K-6 | |
| Summit Academy Community S Xenia | 1694 Pawnee Dr | Xenia, OH | 45385 | 937-372-5210 | 372-5250 | K-8 | Cassy Stidham |
| Summit Academy Lorain - Secondary S | 1051 E St | Lorain, OH | 44052 | 440-288-0448 | 288-0997 | 9-12 | Joshua Preece M.Ed. |
| Summit Academy MS Columbus | 2521 Fairwood Ave Ste 200 | Columbus, OH | 43207 | 614-237-5497 | 237-6519 | 6-8 | Jennifer Hunter |
| Summit Academy MS - Lorain | 346 Illinois Ave | Lorain, OH | 44052 | 440-288-0448 | 288-0997 | 6-8 | Diane Soloman |
| Summit Academy - Middletown | 4700 Central Ave | Middletown, OH | 45044 | 513-422-8540 | 423-6352 | K-6 | Megan Bockelman |
| Summit Academy Middletown HS | 7 S Marshall Rd | Middletown, OH | 45044 | 513-420-9767 | 727-1520 | 7-12 | Beth Varley |
| Summit Academy Painesville | 268 N State St | Painesville, OH | 44077 | 440-358-0877 | 358-0397 | K-9 | Frank Cheraso |
| Summit Academy Parma | 5868 Stumph Rd | Parma, OH | 44130-1736 | 440-888-5407 | 888-5417 | K-12 | Eric Johnson |
| Summit Academy S for Alt Learners | 1461 Moncrest Dr NW | Warren, OH | 44485 | 330-399-1692 | 399-1768 | 7-12 | |
| Summit Academy Secondary S Toledo | 2913 S Republic Blvd | Toledo, OH | 43615 | 419-476-7859 | 476-7763 | 9-12 | Joseph Carone |
| Summit Academy Toledo Learning Center | 5115 Glendale Ave Ste N | Toledo, OH | 43614 | 419-476-0784 | 476-0763 | K-8 | Kurt Aey |
| Summit Academy Transition HS - Cinci | 5800 Salvia Ave | Cincinnati, OH | 45224 | 513-541-4000 | 541-4075 | 9-12 | Christy Brewer |
| Summit Academy Transition HS Columbus | 1855 E Dublin Granville Rd | Columbus, OH | 43229-3516 | 614-880-0714 | 880-0732 | 9-12 | Trina Moore |
| Summit Academy Transition HS Dayton | 251 Erdiel Dr | Dayton, OH | 45415 | 937-813-8952 | 813-8596 | 9-12 | Gary Miller |
| Summit Academy - Youngstown | 1400 Oak Hill Ave | Youngstown, OH | 44507-1018 | 330-747-0950 | 747-0957 | 8-12 | |
| Summit Academy Youngstown | 144 N Schenley Ave | Youngstown, OH | 44509 | 330-259-0421 | 259-0424 | K-7 | |
| Sunbridge S | 2151 N McCord Rd | Toledo, OH | 43615 | 419-725-5437 | | 9-12 | Erica Pharis |
| T2 Honors Academy | 18450 S Miles Rd | Warrensvl Hts, OH | 44128 | 216-510-5458 | | 6-8 | India Ford |
| T.C.P. World Academy | 6000 Ridge Ave | Cincinnati, OH | 45213-1624 | 513-531-9500 | 531-2406 | K-6 | Karen French |
| Toledo Prep & Fitness Academy | 3001 Hill Ave | Toledo, OH | 43607 | 419-535-3700 | 535-3701 | K-8 | Valerie Sandy |
| Toledo S for the Arts | 333 14th St | Toledo, OH | 43604-5459 | 419-246-8732 | 244-3979 | 6-12 | Martin Porter |
| Toledo SMART ES | 1850 Airport Hwy | Toledo, OH | 43609 | 419-214-3290 | 214-3294 | K-3 | Maria Gonzalez |
| Tomorrow Center | PO Box 216 | Edison, OH | 43320-0216 | 419-946-1900 | 947-9551 | 6-12 | Karen Seckel |
| Tooba Academy | 1950 Morse Rd | Columbus, OH | 43229 | 614-888-8536 | 888-8496 | K-8 | Nikia Camara |
| Townsend North Community S | 305 S Washington St | Castalia, OH | 44824 | 419-684-5402 | | 9-12 | Peter Bartkowiak |
| Towpath Trail HS | 275 W Market St | Akron, OH | 44303 | 234-542-0102 | | 9-12 | John Stack |

| School | Address | City,State | Zip code | Telephone | Fax | Grade | Contact |
|---|---|---|---|---|---|---|---|
| TRECA Digital Academy | 100 Executive Dr | Marion, OH | 43302-6306 | 740-389-4798 | 389-4517 | K-12 | Adam Clark |
| Trotwood Preparatory & Fitness Academy | 3100 Shiloh Springs Rd | Trotwood, OH | 45426-2247 | 937-854-4100 | 837-9759 | K-8 | Alison Foreman |
| UBAH Math & Reading Academy | 3850 Sullivant Ave | Columbus, OH | 43228 | 614-279-6000 | | K-5 | Lance Weber |
| University Academy | 107 S Arlington St | Akron, OH | 44306 | 330-535-7728 | | K-8 | |
| University of Cleveland Preparatory S | 1906 E 40th St | Cleveland, OH | 44103 | 216-361-9720 | 431-3375 | K-8 | Deirdra Shobe |
| Urbana Community S | 711 Wood St | Urbana, OH | 43078-1498 | 937-653-1478 | 652-3845 | K-12 | |
| Utica Shale Academy of Ohio | 38095 State Route 39 | Salineville, OH | 43945 | 330-679-8162 | | 9-12 | Eric Sampson |
| Virtual Community S of Ohio | 340 Waggoner Rd | Reynoldsburg, OH | 43068-9707 | 614-501-2002 | 386-1560 | K-12 | Jeff Nelson |
| Virtual Schoolhouse | 736 Lakeview Rd | Cleveland, OH | 44108-2608 | 216-541-2048 | 541-2018 | K-12 | Cindy Johnson |
| Voinovich Reclamation Academy | 11801 Buckeye Rd | Cleveland, OH | 44120-2620 | 216-295-1493 | | 9-12 | Jennifer Morison |
| Washington Park Community S | 4000 Washington Park Blvd | Newburgh Hts, OH | 44105-3211 | 216-271-6055 | 271-6099 | K-8 | Helene Jasinski |
| Watkins Academy | 24 N Jefferson St | Dayton, OH | 45402 | 937-220-9100 | | K-8 | |
| West Academy | 12913 Bennington Ave | Cleveland, OH | 44135-3761 | 216-251-5450 | 251-6410 | K-8 | |
| West Carrollton Secondary Academy | 3400 W Alex Bell Rd | West Carrollton, OH | 45449 | 937-859-5121 | | 11-12 | Candice Haffner |
| West Central Learning Academy | 522 W North St | Lima, OH | 45801-4215 | 419-227-9252 | 227-2511 | 7-12 | Connie Houser |
| Westpark Community ES | 16210 Lorain Ave | Cleveland, OH | 44111-5521 | 216-688-0271 | 688-0273 | K-4 | Sheila Delzani |
| Westpark Community MS | 16210 Lorain Ave | Cleveland, OH | 44111 | 216-251-7200 | 251-0355 | 5-8 | Mindy Kidd |
| West Preparatory Academy | 13111 Crossburn Ave | Cleveland, OH | 44135 | 216-772-1340 | 898-5894 | K-5 | Jennifer Heyman |
| Westside Academy | 4330 Clime Rd N | Columbus, OH | 43228-3439 | 614-272-9392 | 272-8940 | K-8 | |
| Westside Community S of the Arts | 3727 Bosworth Rd | Cleveland, OH | 44111-6037 | 216-688-1900 | 688-1902 | K-8 | Deborah Rotolo |
| Whitehall Prep & Fitness S | 3474 E Livingston Ave | Columbus, OH | 43227-2219 | 614-324-4585 | 238-3184 | K-8 | William Connick |
| Wildwood Environmental Academy | 1546 Dartford Rd | Maumee, OH | 43537-1374 | 419-868-9885 | 868-9981 | K-8 | Elizabeth Lewin |
| Winterfield Venture Academy | 305 Wenz Rd | Toledo, OH | 43615-6244 | 419-531-3285 | 531-3637 | K-8 | Nate Preston |
| Winton Preparatory Academy | 4750 Winton Rd | Cincinnati, OH | 45232 | 513-276-4166 | | K-8 | Lisa Davis |
| Youngstown Academy of Excellence | 1408 Rigby St | Youngstown, OH | 44506-1617 | 330-746-3970 | 746-3965 | K-8 | Lawrence Reeves |
| Youngstown Community ES | 50 Essex St | Youngstown, OH | 44502-1838 | 330-746-2240 | 746-6618 | K-6 | Dennis L. Rice |
| YouthBuild Columbus Comm S | 1183 Essex Ave | Columbus, OH | 43201-2925 | 614-291-0805 | 291-0890 | 9-12 | Nkenge Jacobs |
| Zanesville Community S | 920 Moxahala Ave | Zanesville, OH | 43701 | 740-588-5685 | 455-4331 | 9-12 | |
| Zenith Academy | 4606 Heaton Rd | Columbus, OH | 43229-6612 | 614-888-9943 | 888-6689 | K-9 | |
| Zenith Academy East | 2261 S Hamilton Rd | Columbus, OH | 43232-4301 | 614-577-0997 | 577-0995 | K-8 | |

## Oklahoma

| School | Address | City,State | Zip code | Telephone | Fax | Grade | Contact |
|---|---|---|---|---|---|---|---|
| Alexis Rainbow Arts Academy | 2401 NW 23rd St Ste 14 | Oklahoma City, OK | 73107 | 405-604-8727 | | PK-1 | Brian Prince |
| ASTEC Charter S | 2401 NW 23rd St Ste 39A | Oklahoma City, OK | 73107 | 405-947-6274 | 947-0035 | 6-12 | Dr. Freda Deskin |
| Brown Community S | 2 S Elgin Ave | Tulsa, OK | 74120-1808 | 918-425-1407 | 425-6693 | K-5 | Deborah Brown |
| Discovery School of Tulsa | 4821 S 72nd East Ave | Tulsa, OK | 74145-6502 | 918-960-3131 | 960-3130 | K-8 | Maureen Brown |
| Dove Science Academy | 919 NW 23rd St | Oklahoma City, OK | 73106-5691 | 405-524-9762 | 524-9471 | 6-12 | |
| Dove Science Academy | 280 S Memorial Dr | Tulsa, OK | 74112-2202 | 918-834-3936 | 834-3352 | 6-12 | Abidin Erez |
| Dove Science Academy | 4901 N Lincoln Blvd | Oklahoma City, OK | 73105-3322 | 405-605-5566 | 605-5578 | K-5 | |
| Epic One on One S | 4101 NW 122nd St Ste B | Oklahoma City, OK | 73120 | 405-749-4550 | 749-4540 | PK-12 | David Chaney |
| Harding Charter Preparatory HS | 3333 N Shartel Ave | Oklahoma City, OK | 73118-7277 | 405-606-8742 | 609-1677 | 9-12 | Dr. Mylo Miller |
| Harding Fine Arts Center | PO Box 18895 | Oklahoma City, OK | 73154-0895 | 405-702-4322 | 601-0904 | 9-12 | Barry Schmelzenbach |
| Harper Academy Charter S | 1215 NE 34th St | Oklahoma City, OK | 73111-4501 | 405-605-2600 | 605-2644 | 9-12 | Melvin Perry |
| Hupfeld Academy at Western Village | 1508 NW 106th St | Oklahoma City, OK | 73114-5214 | 405-751-1774 | 752-6833 | PK-5 | Ruthie Rayner |
| Independence Charter MS | 3232 NW 65th St | Oklahoma City, OK | 73116-3512 | 405-767-3000 | 767-3007 | 6-8 | Vana Baker |
| Insight S of Oklahoma | PO Box 490 | Nicoma Park, OK | 73066 | 405-835-2133 | | 7-12 | Kimberly Kelly |
| KIPP Reach College Preparatory | PO Box 776 | Oklahoma City, OK | 73101-0776 | 405-425-4622 | 425-4624 | 5-8 | Tracy McDaniel |
| KIPP Tulsa Academy | 1661 E Virgin St | Tulsa, OK | 74106-5552 | 918-794-8652 | 794-8712 | 5-8 | John Wolfkill |
| Oklahoma Connections Academy | 2425 Nowata Pl | Bartlesville, OK | 74006 | 918-977-3285 | 331-3629 | K-12 | Tammy Shepherd |
| Oklahoma Virtual Charter Academy | 7508 Dripping Springs Ln | Oklahoma City, OK | 73150 | 866-467-0848 | 259-8332 | K-12 | Sheryl Tatum |
| Rex Charter ES | 500 W Sheridan Ave | Oklahoma City, OK | 73102 | 405-587-8100 | | PK-3 | Joe Pierce Ed.D. |
| Sankofa Charter S | 111 E 1st St | Tulsa, OK | 74103-2816 | 918-425-1407 | | 6-8 | Richard Patterson |
| Santa Fe South ES | 301 SE 38th St | Oklahoma City, OK | 73129-3099 | 405-681-7480 | 681-7484 | K-5 | Chris Brewster |
| Santa Fe South HS | 301 SE 38th St | Oklahoma City, OK | 73129-3099 | 405-631-6100 | 681-6993 | 9-12 | Lance Seeright |
| Santa Fe South MS | 4712 S Santa Fe Ave | Oklahoma City, OK | 73109-7545 | 405-635-1053 | 635-0423 | 6-8 | Michael Figueroa |
| SeeWorth Academy | 12600 N Kelley Ave | Oklahoma City, OK | 73131-1869 | 405-475-6400 | 475-8566 | 3-12 | Stacey Golden |
| Tsunadeloquasdi Cherokee Immersion S | PO Box 520 | Tahlequah, OK | 74465 | 918-453-5400 | 467-4746 | PK-8 | |
| Tulsa Lighthouse Charter S | 105 E 63rd St N | Tulsa, OK | 74126 | 918-794-1442 | 794-1480 | PK-6 | Jamila Macarthur |
| Tulsa S of Arts and Sciences | 3441 E Archer St | Tulsa, OK | 74115 | 918-828-7727 | 828-7747 | 9-12 | Liesa Smith |

## Oregon

| School | Address | City,State | Zip code | Telephone | Fax | Grade | Contact |
|---|---|---|---|---|---|---|---|
| Academy for Character Education | PO Box 1652 | Cottage Grove, OR | 97424-0067 | 541-942-9707 | 942-7884 | K-12 | Ranell Curl |
| Academy of Arts and Academics | 615 Main St | Springfield, OR | 97477 | 541-744-6728 | 744-6713 | 9-12 | Mike Fisher |
| ACE Academy | 4222 NE 158th Ave | Portland, OR | 97230 | 503-546-9928 | 546-9708 | 11-12 | Mark Clifford |
| Alliance Charter Academy | 16075 Front St | Oregon City, OR | 97045 | 503-785-8556 | 722-4113 | 1-12 | Lara Fabrycki |
| Annex Charter S | 402 Annex Rd | Ontario, OR | 97914-8010 | 541-262-3280 | 262-3578 | K-8 | Steve Bishop |
| Arco Iris Spanish Immersion S | 13600 SW Allen Blvd | Beaverton, OR | 97005 | 503-473-0416 | | 1-6 | Jan Smith |
| Arlington ES | PO Box 10 | Arlington, OR | 97812-0010 | 541-454-2727 | 454-2335 | K-8 | Kevin Hunking |
| Arlington HS | PO Box 10 | Arlington, OR | 97812-0010 | 541-454-2632 | 454-2137 | 9-12 | Kevin Hunking |
| Armadillo Technical Institute | PO Box 1560 | Phoenix, OR | 97535-1560 | 541-535-3287 | | 4-12 | Kim DeCosta |
| Arthur Academy | 13717 SE Division St | Portland, OR | 97236-2841 | 503-252-3753 | 760-1204 | K-5 | John Luebke |
| Bethany Charter S | 11824 Hazelgreen Rd NE | Silverton, OR | 97381-9611 | 503-873-4300 | 873-0143 | K-8 | Kathy Frank |
| Burnt River S | PO Box 9 | Unity, OR | 97884 | 541-446-3336 | 446-3581 | K-12 | Lorrie Andrews |
| Butte Falls Charter S | PO Box 228 | Butte Falls, OR | 97522-0228 | 541-865-3563 | 865-3217 | K-12 | Dianne Gorman |
| Camas Valley S | PO Box 57 | Camas Valley, OR | 97416-0057 | 541-445-2131 | 445-2041 | K-12 | Patrick Lee |
| Career Technical HS | 801 SW Highway 101 Ste 404 | Lincoln City, OR | 97367-2752 | 541-351-8551 | 994-7592 | 9-12 | Sean Larson |
| Cascade Heights Charter S | 15301 SE 92nd Ave | Clackamas, OR | 97015 | 503-653-3996 | 653-1026 | K-8 | Holly Denman |
| Center for Advanced Learning | 1484 NW Civic Dr | Gresham, OR | 97030-5564 | 503-667-4978 | 492-1572 | 11-12 | Carol Eagan |
| Childs Way Charter S | 37895 Row River Rd | Culp Creek, OR | 97434-9610 | 541-946-1821 | 946-2007 | 5-12 | Michael Kerns |
| City View Charter S | PO Box 1808 | Hillsboro, OR | 97123 | 503-844-9424 | 844-9425 | K-8 | Jeffrey Hays |
| Clackamas Academy of Industrial Science | 995 S End Rd | Oregon City, OR | 97045 | 503-785-7860 | 785-8396 | 8-12 | Kyle Laier |
| Clackamas Middle College HS | 12021 SE 82nd Ave | Happy Valley, OR | 97086-7713 | 503-518-5925 | 518-5928 | 9-12 | Brian Sien |
| Clackamas Web Academy | 8740 SE Sunnybrook Blvd | Clackamas, OR | 97015-5737 | 503-659-4664 | 659-4994 | 1-12 | Brad Linn |
| Coburg Community Family Charter S | 91274 N Coburg Rd | Coburg, OR | 97408 | 541-790-3408 | 790-3532 | K-5 | Terry Hoagland |
| Community Roots S | 330 N James St | Silverton, OR | 97381 | 503-874-4107 | 874-4108 | K-6 | Miranda Traegar |
| Cove S | PO Box 68 | Cove, OR | 97824-0068 | 541-568-4424 | 568-4231 | K-12 | Bruce Neil |
| Dallas Community S | 788 SW Birch St | Dallas, OR | 97338 | | | K-8 | Dennis Schultz |
| Days Creek Charter S | PO Box 10 | Days Creek, OR | 97429-0010 | 541-825-3296 | 825-3052 | K-12 | Mark Angle |
| EAGLE Charter S | 999A Locust St NE | Salem, OR | 97301 | 503-339-7114 | 990-6909 | K-5 | Cliff Monroe |
| EagleRidge Charter HS | 677 S 7th St | Klamath Falls, OR | 97601 | 541-884-7627 | 871-7054 | 9-12 | Donald Peterson |
| Eddyville Charter S | 1 Eddyville School Rd | Eddyville, OR | 97343 | 541-875-2942 | 875-2491 | K-12 | Jennifer Johnson |
| Elkton Grade S | PO Box 390 | Elkton, OR | 97436-0390 | 541-584-2115 | 584-2113 | K-8 | Andy Boe |
| Elkton S | PO Box 390 | Elkton, OR | 97436-0390 | 541-584-2228 | 584-2227 | K-12 | Mike Hughes |
| Emerson Charter S | 105 NW Park Ave | Portland, OR | 97209-3315 | 503-525-6124 | 223-4875 | K-5 | Tara O'Neil |
| Estacada Early College | PO Box 2631 | Estacada, OR | 97023 | 503-630-5001 | 630-5206 | 10-12 | Joni Tabler |
| Estacada Web Academy | PO Box 2631 | Estacada, OR | 97023 | 503-630-5001 | 630-5206 | K-12 | Sean Gallagher |
| Forest Grove Community S | 1914 Pacific Ave | Forest Grove, OR | 97116-2326 | 503-359-4600 | 359-4622 | 1-8 | Vanessa Gray |
| Fossil Charter S | PO Box 206 | Fossil, OR | 97830 | 541-763-4384 | 763-4010 | K-12 | Brad Sperry |
| Four Rivers Community S | 2449 SW 4th Ave | Ontario, OR | 97914 | 541-889-3715 | 889-3718 | K-8 | Chelle Robins |
| Glendale Community Charter S | PO Box E | Glendale, OR | 97442-0605 | 541-832-1801 | 832-2486 | 9-12 | Brenyl Swanson |
| Goodall Environmental MS | 999B Locust St NE | Salem, OR | 97301 | 503-391-7030 | 391-4070 | 6-8 | Annie Morton |
| Gresham Arthur Academy | 1890 NE Cleveland Ave | Gresham, OR | 97030-4210 | 503-667-4900 | 667-4933 | K-5 | Amber Sparks |
| Harper Charter S | 2987 Harper Westfall Rd | Harper, OR | 97906-2008 | 541-358-2473 | 358-2488 | K-12 | Ron Talbot |
| Hope Chinese Charter S | PO Box 91602 | Portland, OR | 97291-0016 | 971-226-7500 | | K-2 | Julie Rickman |
| Howard Street Charter S | 710 Howard St SE | Salem, OR | 97302-3098 | 503-399-3408 | 375-7861 | 6-8 | Christina Tracy |
| Imbler Charter S | PO Box 164 | Imbler, OR | 97841-0164 | 541-534-2311 | 534-9560 | K-12 | Mike Mills |
| Ione Community Charter S | PO Box 167 | Ione, OR | 97843-0167 | 541-422-7131 | 422-7555 | K-12 | Henry Ramirez |
| Ivy S | 4212 NE Prescott St | Portland, OR | 97218 | 503-288-8820 | 288-8894 | 1-8 | Mary Zigman |
| Joseph Charter S | PO Box 787 | Joseph, OR | 97846-2023 | 541-432-7311 | 432-1100 | K-12 | Sherri Kilgore |
| KairosPDX Learning Academy Charter S | PO Box 12190 | Portland, OR | 97212 | 503-567-9820 | | K-5 | Zalika Gardner |
| Kids Unlimited Academy | 821 N Riverside Ave | Medford, OR | 97501 | 541-774-3900 | 772-3443 | K-5 | Lynn Eccleston |
| Kings Valley Charter S | 38840 Kings Valley Hwy | Philomath, OR | 97370-9750 | 541-929-2134 | 929-8179 | K-12 | Jamon Ellingson |
| KNOVA Learning Oregon | 18201 SE Stark St | Portland, OR | 97233 | 503-907-1023 | 907-1024 | K-8 | Raffi Martinian |
| Leadership & Entrepreneurship Charter HS | 2044 E Burnside St | Portland, OR | 97214-1674 | 503-254-2537 | 236-6783 | 9-12 | Carl Reinhold |
| Le Monde French Immersion ES | 2044 E Burnside St | Portland, OR | 97214 | 503-208-3198 | 233-8752 | K-4 | Chantal Martel |
| Lewis & Clark Montessori Charter S | 15600 SE 232nd Dr | Damascus, OR | 97089 | 503-427-0803 | 855-3017 | PK-3 | Melissa Harbert |
| Lighthouse S | 1500 16th St | North Bend, OR | 97459 | 541-751-1649 | | K-8 | Wade Lester |
| Logos Public Charter S | 400 Earhart St | Medford, OR | 97501-7828 | 541-842-3658 | 842-1927 | K-12 | Joe VonDoloski |
| Lourdes Charter S | 39059 Jordan Rd | Scio, OR | 97374-9330 | 503-394-3340 | | 1-8 | Linda Duman |
| Luckiamute Valley Charter S | 17475 Bridgeport Rd | Dallas, OR | 97338-9458 | 503-838-1933 | 606-9879 | K-8 | Dan Austin |
| Madrone Trail Charter S | 3070 Ross Ln | Central Point, OR | 97502 | 541-842-3657 | 715-0309 | K-8 | Joe Frodsham |
| Metro East Web Academy | 1394 NW Civic Dr | Gresham, OR | 97030-5569 | 503-258-4790 | 258-4791 | 6-12 | David Gray |
| Milwaukie Academy of the Arts | 11300 SE 23rd Ave | Milwaukie, OR | 97222-7753 | 503-353-5834 | 353-5845 | 9-12 | Tim Taylor |
| M.I.T.C.H. Charter S | 19550 SW 90th Ct | Tualatin, OR | 97062-7505 | 503-639-5757 | | K-8 | Melissa Meyer |
| Mosier Community S | PO Box 307 | Mosier, OR | 97040-0307 | 541-478-3321 | 478-2536 | K-8 | Brian Schimel |

| School | Address | City,State | Zip code | Telephone | Fax | Grade | Contact |
|---|---|---|---|---|---|---|---|
| Mountain View Academy | 65 S Pioneer St | Lowell, OR | 97452 | 541-937-8405 | | K-8 | Laurie Cardwell |
| Muddy Creek Charter S | 30252 Bellfountain Rd | Corvallis, OR | 97333-9524 | 541-752-0377 | 752-9481 | K-5 | Dan Hays |
| Multisensory Learning Academy | 22565 NE Halsey St | Fairview, OR | 97024-2642 | 503-405-7868 | 405-7869 | K-6 | Sheri Fitzsimmons |
| Network Charter S | 2550 Portland St | Eugene, OR | 97405 | 541-344-1229 | 344-5118 | 7-12 | Ame Beard |
| Nixyaawi Community S | PO Box 638 | Pendleton, OR | 97801-0638 | 541-429-7900 | 966-2671 | 9-12 | Ryan Heinrich |
| North Columbia Academy | 28168 Old Rainier Rd | Rainier, OR | 97048-3017 | 503-556-3777 | 556-3778 | 9-12 | Anne Montgomery |
| North Powder Charter S | PO Box 10 | North Powder, OR | 97867-0010 | 541-898-2244 | 898-2046 | PK-12 | Lance Dixon |
| Opal Charter S | 4015 SW Canyon Rd | Portland, OR | 97221-2759 | 503-471-9917 | 223-6600 | K-5 | Karen Belsey |
| Optimum Learning Environments Charter S | 7905 June Reid Pl NE | Keizer, OR | 97303-2559 | 503-399-5548 | 399-2647 | 1-5 | Marya Kalugin |
| Oregon City Service Learning Academy | 995 S End Rd | Oregon City, OR | 97045 | 503-785-8445 | 650-5483 | 7-12 | Tim Graham |
| Oregon Coast Technology S | 1500 16th St | North Bend, OR | 97459 | 541-756-8341 | 756-1313 | 7-12 | Bill Lucero |
| Oregon Connections Academy | 833 NW Santiam Blvd | Mill City, OR | 97360 | 503-897-2272 | | K-12 | Candyce Farthing |
| Oregon Trail Academy | 36225 SE Proctor Rd | Boring, OR | 97009 | 503-668-5521 | 668-6250 | K-9 | Ginger Redlinger |
| Oregon Virtual Academy | 400 Virginia Ave Ste 210 | North Bend, OR | 97459 | 541-751-8060 | 751-8016 | K-12 | Brandy Osborn |
| Paisley S | PO Box 97 | Paisley, OR | 97636-0097 | 541-943-3111 | 943-3129 | K-12 | William Wurtz |
| Phoenix S of Roseburg | 3131 NE Diamond Lake Blvd | Roseburg, OR | 97470-3632 | 541-673-3036 | 957-5906 | 8-12 | Ron Breyne |
| Pine Eagle Charter S | 375 N Main St | Halfway, OR | 97834-8153 | 541-742-2811 | 742-2810 | K-12 | Morgan Gover |
| Portland Arthur Academy | 7507 SE Yamhill St | Portland, OR | 97215-2284 | 503-257-3936 | 257-3929 | K-5 | Susan McCool |
| Portland Village ES | 7654 N Delaware Ave | Portland, OR | 97217-6417 | 503-445-0056 | 445-0058 | K-8 | Paul Berg |
| Powell Butte Community Charter S | 13650 SW Highway 126 | Powell Butte, OR | 97753-1604 | 541-548-1166 | 548-7635 | K-8 | Jackie LaFrenz |
| Prospect Charter S | PO Box 40 | Prospect, OR | 97536-0040 | 541-560-3653 | 560-3644 | K-12 | Tim Dexter |
| REALMS | 63175 O B Riley Rd | Bend, OR | 97701-9003 | 541-322-5323 | 322-5473 | 6-8 | Roger White |
| Redmond Proficiency Academy | 657 SW Glacier Ave | Redmond, OR | 97756-2710 | 541-526-0882 | 516-1160 | 6-12 | Dr. Jon Bullock |
| Reedsport Community Charter S | 2260 Longwood Dr | Reedsport, OR | 97467-1195 | 541-271-2141 | 271-2143 | 7-12 | Vincent Swagerty |
| Renaissance Public Academy | PO Box 208 | Molalla, OR | 97038 | 503-759-7002 | 759-7004 | 4-12 | Darrel Camp |
| Resource Link Charter S | 1255 Hemlock Ave | Coos Bay, OR | 97420-1298 | 541-267-1499 | 266-7314 | K-12 | Shelly McKnight |
| Reynolds Arthur Academy | 123 SW 21st St | Troutdale, OR | 97060 | 503-252-3753 | 761-4143 | K-6 | Chris Arnold |
| Ridgeline Montessori Public Charter S | 4500 W Amazon Dr | Eugene, OR | 97405 | 541-681-9662 | 681-4394 | K-8 | |
| Sage Community S | PO Box 655 | Chiloquin, OR | 97624-0655 | 541-783-2533 | 783-2544 | K-8 | Anna Fowler |
| Saint Helens Arthur Academy | 33035 Pittsburg Rd | Saint Helens, OR | 97051-3305 | 503-366-7030 | | K-8 | Michael Arthur |
| Sand Ridge Charter S | 30581 Sodaville Mtn Home Rd | Lebanon, OR | 97355-9008 | 541-258-2416 | 258-1898 | K-12 | Audrey Cota |
| Sauvie Island Academy | 14445 NW Charlton Rd | Portland, OR | 97231-1402 | 503-621-3426 | 621-3384 | K-8 | Darla Meeuwsen |
| SEI Academy Charter S | 3920 N Kerby Ave | Portland, OR | 97227-1255 | 503-249-1721 | 284-4456 | 6-8 | Timothy Rodgers |
| Sheridan Allprep Online Academy | PO Box 583 | Sheridan, OR | 97378 | 503-843-9330 | 758-1982 | K-12 | Jesse Eisenschmidt |
| Sheridan Japanese S | PO Box 446 | Sheridan, OR | 97378-0446 | 503-843-3400 | 843-7438 | 4-12 | Andrew Scott |
| Sherwood Charter S | PO Box 1342 | Sherwood, OR | 97140-1342 | 503-925-8007 | 925-8172 | K-8 | Joy Raboli |
| Siletz Valley S | PO Box 247 | Siletz, OR | 97380-0247 | 541-444-1100 | 444-2368 | K-12 | Sam Tupou |
| Silvies River Charter S | 39235 Highway 205 | Frenchglen, OR | 97736 | 541-589-2401 | 493-2660 | K-12 | Shawn Farrens |
| South Columbia Family S | 33589 High School Way | Warren, OR | 97053 | 503-366-9009 | 366-9010 | K-12 | Lori Bogen |
| Southwest Charter S | 0640 SW Bancroft St | Portland, OR | 97239 | 503-244-1697 | 244-1709 | K-8 | Anne Gurnee |
| Springwater Environmental Sciences S | PO Box 3010 | Oregon City, OR | 97045 | 503-631-7700 | 631-7720 | K-8 | Dawn Bolotow |
| Sunny Wolf Charter S | PO Box 438 | Wolf Creek, OR | 97497 | 541-866-2735 | 866-2738 | K-5 | Penelope DiGennaro |
| Sweet Home Charter S | 28721 Liberty Rd | Sweet Home, OR | 97386-9776 | 541-367-1833 | 367-1839 | K-6 | Scott Richards |
| Three Rivers Charter S | 4975 Willamette Falls Dr | West Linn, OR | 97068-3348 | 503-723-6019 | 723-6407 | 4-8 | Katherine Holtgraves |
| Triangle Lake Charter S | 20264 Blachly Grange Rd | Blachly, OR | 97412-9714 | 541-925-3262 | 925-3062 | K-12 | James Brookins |
| Trillium Charter S | 5420 N Interstate Ave | Portland, OR | 97217-4569 | 503-285-3833 | 249-0348 | K-12 | Kieran Connolly |
| Valley Inquiry Charter S | 5774 Hazelgreen Rd NE | Salem, OR | 97305 | 503-399-3150 | 391-4091 | K-5 | Manuel Palacio |
| Village S | 2855 Lincoln St | Eugene, OR | 97405-2737 | 541-345-7285 | 242-6874 | K-8 | Bob Kaminski |
| West Lane Technology Learning Center | 24936 Fir Grove Ln | Elmira, OR | 97437-9751 | 541-935-2101 | 935-8345 | 9-12 | Ken Woody |
| Woodburn Arthur Academy | 575 Gatch St | Woodburn, OR | 97071-4927 | 503-981-5746 | 981-5742 | K-5 | Glenn Izer |
| Woodland Charter S | PO Box 740 | Murphy, OR | 97533 | 541-846-4246 | | 1-8 | Lois Horan |

## Pennsylvania

| School | Address | City,State | Zip code | Telephone | Fax | Grade | Contact |
|---|---|---|---|---|---|---|---|
| Achievement House Charter S | 600 Eagleview Blvd Ste 1 | Exton, PA | 19341 | 484-615-6200 | 458-1204 | 7-12 | Don Asplen |
| ACT Academy Cyber Charter HS | 2111 Eastburn Ave | Philadelphia, PA | 19138-2630 | 267-297-6231 | | 9-12 | |
| Ad Prima Charter S | 3556 Frankford Ave | Philadelphia, PA | 19134 | 215-288-7062 | 288-8673 | K-6 | Meghan Allhouse |
| Ad Prima Charter S | 1922 N 63rd St | Philadelphia, PA | 19151 | 215-403-2953 | 292-4058 | K-8 | Aldo Cavalli |
| Agora Cyber Charter S | 590 N Gulph Rd | King of Prussia, PA | 19406 | 844-402-4672 | 254-8939 | K-12 | Kevin Corcoran |
| Allen Preparatory Charter S | 2601 S 58th St | Philadelphia, PA | 19143-6146 | 215-878-1544 | 727-0711 | 5-8 | Lawrence Jones |
| Alliance for Progress Charter S | 1630 N 16th St | Philadelphia, PA | 19121 | 215-232-4892 | 232-4894 | 4-8 | Joanna Hightower |
| Alliance for Progress Charter S | 1821 Cecil B Moore Ave | Philadelphia, PA | 19121-3135 | 215-232-4892 | 232-4893 | K-3 | Joanna Hightower |
| Architecture & Design Charter HS | 105 S 7th St | Philadelphia, PA | 19106 | 215-351-2900 | 351-9458 | 9-12 | Gregory Wright |
| ARISE Academy Charter HS | 2116 E Haines St | Philadelphia, PA | 19138-2600 | 215-563-1656 | | 9-12 | Gabriel Kuriloff |
| Arts Academy Charter ES | 601 W Union St | Allentown, PA | 18101 | 610-657-5388 | | K-5 | Jacqueline Vogel |
| Arts Academy Charter S | 1610 E Emmaus Ave | Allentown, PA | 18103 | 610-351-0234 | 351-0307 | 5-8 | Jan Labellarte |
| ASPIRA Bilingual Cyber Charter S | 4332 N 5th St | Philadelphia, PA | 19140 | 215-455-1300 | 455-1300 | K-12 | Cynthia Cruz-Vega |
| ASPIRA Olney HS | 100 W Duncannon Ave | Philadelphia, PA | 19120 | 215-456-3014 | 456-3064 | 9-12 | James Thompson |
| ASPIRA Stetson Charter S | 3200 B St | Philadelphia, PA | 19134-2202 | 215-291-4720 | 291-4168 | 5-8 | Thomas Mullin |
| Attucks Youth Build Charter S | 605 S Duke St | York, PA | 17401-3111 | 717-848-3610 | 843-3914 | 9-12 | Jacquie Martino-Miller |
| Avon Grove Charter S | 110 State Rd | West Grove, PA | 19390-8908 | 484-667-5000 | | K-12 | Kristen Bishop |
| Baden Academy Charter S | 1016 W State St | Baden, PA | 15005-1338 | 855-590-2227 | 869-4269 | K-5 | |
| Bear Creek Community Charter S | 2000 Bear Creek Blvd | Wilkes Barre, PA | 18702-9684 | 570-820-4070 | 270-6149 | K-8 | Brian Dugas |
| Beaver Area Academic Charter S | Gypsy Glen Rd | Beaver, PA | 15009 | 724-774-4022 | | 7-12 | Carrie Rowe |
| Belmont Academy Charter S | 907 N 41st St | Philadelphia, PA | 19104-1278 | 215-386-5768 | 386-5769 | K-K | Claire Cohen |
| Belmont Charter S | 4030 Brown St | Philadelphia, PA | 19104-4899 | 215-823-8208 | 823-8209 | 1-8 | Claire Cohen |
| Birney Charter S | 900 Lindley Ave | Philadelphia, PA | 19141-3999 | 215-456-3000 | 456-3113 | K-8 | Kareem Thomas |
| Boys Latin of Philadelphia Charter S | 5501 Cedar Ave | Philadelphia, PA | 19143 | 215-387-5149 | 387-5159 | 6-12 | Dr. Noah Tennant |
| Bracetti Academy Charter S | 1840 Torresdale Ave | Philadelphia, PA | 19124 | 215-291-4436 | 291-4985 | K-12 | Jana Somma |
| Bucks County Montessori Charter S | 219 Tyburn Rd | Fairless Hills, PA | 19030-4403 | 215-428-6700 | 428-6702 | K-6 | Brian Long |
| Byers Charter S | 1911 Arch St | Philadelphia, PA | 19103-1403 | 215-972-1700 | 972-1701 | PK-6 | Jesse Bean |
| Capital Area School for the Arts | 150 Strawberry Sq | Harrisburg, PA | 17101-1815 | 717-732-8450 | 732-8451 | 9-12 | Timothy Wendling |
| Center for Student Learning Charter S | 345 Lakeside Dr | Levittown, PA | 19054-3933 | 215-269-7390 | 269-7395 | 6-12 | Dr. Charles Bonner |
| Central Pennsylvania Digital Charter S | 721 N Juniata St Ste 3 | Hollidaysburg, PA | 16648 | 814-682-5258 | 946-8526 | K-12 | Angela Boutiller |
| Centre Learning Community Charter S | 2643 W College Ave | State College, PA | 16801-2604 | 814-861-7980 | 861-8030 | 5-8 | Kosta Dussias |
| Chester Charter S for the Arts | 200 Commerce Dr | Aston, PA | 19014 | 610-859-3010 | | K-8 | Akosua Watts |
| Chester Community Charter S | 214 E 5th St | Chester, PA | 19013-4510 | 610-447-0400 | 876-5716 | K-6 | Dr. David Clark |
| Chester County Family Academy | 530 E Union St | West Chester, PA | 19382 | 610-696-5910 | 696-6324 | K-2 | Susan Flynn |
| Circle of Seasons Charter S | 8380 Mohr Ln | Fogelsville, PA | 18051-1918 | 610-285-6267 | | K-5 | |
| City Charter HS | 201 Stanwix St | Pittsburgh, PA | 15222-1350 | 412-690-2489 | 690-2316 | 9-12 | Dr. Ron Sofo |
| Clemente Charter S | 136 S 4th St | Allentown, PA | 18102-5445 | 610-439-5181 | 435-4731 | 6-12 | Damian Romero |
| Clemente ES - Charter | 462 Walnut St | Allentown, PA | 18102 | 610-435-5334 | | K-6 | Samuel Polanco |
| Collegium Charter S | 535 James Hance Ct | Exton, PA | 19341-2560 | 610-903-1300 | 903-1317 | K-12 | Antoinette Rath |
| Columbus Charter S | 1242 S 13th St | Philadelphia, PA | 19147 | 215-389-6000 | 389-3374 | 6-8 | Rosemary Dougherty |
| Columbus Charter S | 916 Christian St | Philadelphia, PA | 19147-3808 | 215-925-7400 | 925-7491 | K-5 | Rosemary Dougherty |
| Commonwealth Connections Charter S | 4050 Crums Mill Rd | Harrisburg, PA | 17112-2827 | 717-651-7200 | 651-0670 | K-12 | Dr. Maurice Flurie |
| Community Academy of Philadelphia | 1100 E Erie Ave | Philadelphia, PA | 19124-5424 | 215-533-6700 | 533-6722 | K-12 | Joe Proietta |
| DeHostos Charter S | 6301 N 2nd St | Philadelphia, PA | 19120 | 215-455-2300 | 455-6312 | K-8 | |
| Delaware Valley Charter HS | 5201 Old York Rd | Philadelphia, PA | 19141-2985 | 215-455-2550 | 455-5701 | 9-12 | Dr. Harold Kurtz |
| Discovery Charter S | 4700 Parkside Ave | Philadelphia, PA | 19131-4712 | 215-879-8182 | 879-9510 | K-8 | Nina Brevard |
| Douglass Mastery Charter S | 2118 W Norris St | Philadelphia, PA | 19121-2100 | 215-684-5063 | 684-8916 | K-8 | Tom Weishaupt |
| Eastern University Academy Charter S | 3300 Henry Ave Ste 2 | Philadelphia, PA | 19129-1121 | 215-769-3131 | 769-3112 | 7-12 | Omar Barlow |
| Education Plus Academy Cyber Charter S | 487 Devon Park Dr | Wayne, PA | 19087 | 215-600-2709 | 600-3609 | K-8 | Lydia Jerchau |
| Environmental Charter S at Frick Park | 829 Milton St | Pittsburgh, PA | 15218-1005 | 412-247-7970 | 247-7971 | K-6 | Jon McCann |
| Erie Rise Leadership Academy Charter S | 2501 Plum St | Erie, PA | 16502 | 814-520-6468 | | K-6 | Terry Lang |
| Esperanza Academy Charter HS | 301 W Hunting Park Ave | Philadelphia, PA | 19140-2625 | 215-457-3667 | 457-4381 | 6-12 | David Rossi |
| Esperanza Cyber Charter S | 4261 N 5th St | Philadelphia, PA | 19140-2615 | 215-967-9703 | | 6-12 | |
| Evergreen Community Charter S | PO Box 523 | Mountainhome, PA | 18342-0523 | 570-595-6355 | 595-6038 | 6-12 | Jill Shoesmith |
| Executive Education Academy Charter S | 555 Union Blvd | Allentown, PA | 18109 | 484-841-7044 | | K-8 | Robert Lysek |
| Fell Charter S | 777 Main St | Simpson, PA | 18407-1236 | 570-282-5199 | 282-0930 | K-8 | Mary Jo Walsh |
| First Philadelphia Charter S | 4300 Tacony St | Philadelphia, PA | 19124-4134 | 215-743-3100 | 743-9877 | K-12 | Myra Mezei |
| Folk Arts-Cultural Treasures Charter S | 1023 Callowhill St | Philadelphia, PA | 19123-3704 | 215-569-2600 | 569-3985 | K-8 | Pheng Lim |
| Franklin Towne Charter ES | 4259 Richmond St | Philadelphia, PA | 19137-1930 | 215-289-3389 | 288-4041 | K-8 | Patrick Field |
| Franklin Towne Charter HS | PO Box 310 | Philadelphia, PA | 19105-0310 | 215-289-5000 | 535-8910 | 9-12 | Dr. Joseph Venditti Esq. |
| Freire Charter HS | 2027 Chestnut St | Philadelphia, PA | 19103-3301 | 215-592-4252 | 557-9051 | 9-12 | Dr. Kelly Davenport |
| Freire Charter S | 1026 Market St | Philadelphia, PA | 19107-4205 | 267-670-7499 | 670-7740 | 5-8 | Dr. Kelly Davenport |
| Gardner Charter S | 1615 E Elm St | Scranton, PA | 18505 | 570-941-4100 | 941-7699 | PK-8 | Maria Rozaieski |
| Gettysburg Montessori Charter S | 120 E Broadway | Gettysburg, PA | 17325 | 717-334-1120 | | K-6 | Faye Pleso |
| Gillingham Charter S | 915 Howard Ave | Pottsville, PA | 17901 | 570-955-3830 | | K-12 | |
| Global Leadership Academy | 4601 W Girard Ave | Philadelphia, PA | 19131-4615 | 267-295-5700 | 295-5701 | K-8 | Dr. Naomi Johnson-Booker |
| Graystone Academy Charter S | 139 Modena Rd | Coatesville, PA | 19320-4036 | 610-383-4311 | | K-6 | Marita Barber |
| Green Woods Charter S | 468 Domino Ln | Philadelphia, PA | 19128-4363 | 215-482-6337 | | K-8 | Jean Wallace |
| Harambee Institute of Science Technology | 640 N 66th St | Philadelphia, PA | 19151-3606 | 215-472-8770 | 472-9611 | K-8 | Damond Warren |
| Hill House Passport Academy Charter S | 510 Heldman St | Pittsburgh, PA | 15219 | 412-376-3724 | | 9-12 | Dwayne Homa |
| HOPE for Hyndman Charter S | 130 School Dr | Hyndman, PA | 15545 | 814-842-3918 | 842-6246 | K-12 | Dr. Thomas Otis |
| I-Lead Charter S | 401 Penn St | Reading, PA | 19601 | 855-453-2327 | | 9-12 | Angel Figueroa |
| Imagine Penn Hills Charter S | 200 Penn School Dr | Verona, PA | 15147 | 412-793-6471 | 793-6473 | K-6 | Tamara Allen |

| School | Address | City,State | Zip code | Telephone | Fax | Grade | Contact |
|---|---|---|---|---|---|---|---|
| Imani Education Circle Charter S | 5612 Greene St | Philadelphia, PA | 19144-2808 | 215-713-9240 | 713-9243 | K-8 | Adrienne Davis |
| Imhotep Institute Charter HS | 6201 N 21st St | Philadelphia, PA | 19138 | 215-438-4140 | 438-4160 | 9-12 | Cicely Peterson-Mangum |
| Independence Charter S | 1600 Lombard St | Philadelphia, PA | 19146-1507 | 215-238-8000 | 545-2924 | K-8 | Ramzy Andrawos |
| Infinity Charter S | 51 Banks St Ste 1 | Penbrook, PA | 17103-2067 | 717-238-1880 | | K-8 | Suzanne Gausman |
| Ketterer Charter S | 1133 Village Way | Latrobe, PA | 15650-5201 | 724-537-9110 | 537-9114 | 1-12 | Eric Guldin |
| Keystone Academy Charter S | 6649 Tulip St | Philadelphia, PA | 19135 | 215-332-2111 | 332-2840 | K-8 | John Goulding |
| Keystone Education Center Charter S | 425 S Good Hope Rd | Greenville, PA | 16125-8629 | 724-588-2511 | 588-2545 | 6-12 | Mike Gentile |
| Khepera Charter S | 926 W Sedgley Ave | Philadelphia, PA | 19140 | 215-843-1700 | 843-3530 | 6-8 | Verna Holmes |
| Khepera Charter S | 926 W Sedgley Ave | Philadelphia, PA | 19140 | 215-843-1700 | 843-3530 | K-5 | Mukasa Afrika |
| KIPP Dubois Collegiate Academy | 5070 Parkside Ave | Philadelphia, PA | 19131 | 215-307-3465 | 307-3271 | 9-12 | Aaron Bass |
| KIPP Philadelphia Charter S | 2709 N Broad St | Philadelphia, PA | 19132-2722 | 215-227-1728 | 827-5942 | 5-8 | Ryane Burke |
| KIPP Philadelphia ES | 2409 W Westmoreland St | Philadelphia, PA | 19129 | 267-687-7283 | 687-7295 | K-4 | Ben Speicher |
| KIPP West Philadelphia Prep Charter S | 5900 Baltimore Ave | Philadelphia, PA | 19143 | 215-294-2973 | 294-8707 | 5-8 | Cheshonna Miles |
| La Academia Charter S | 30 N Ann St | Lancaster, PA | 17602-3063 | 717-295-7763 | 399-6456 | 6-12 | Guillermo Barroso |
| Laboratory Charter S | 5339 Lebanon Ave | Philadelphia, PA | 19131 | 215-877-9881 | 877-9882 | 2-8 | |
| Laboratory Charter S | 800 N Orianna St | Philadelphia, PA | 19123 | 215-574-1680 | 574-0622 | K-8 | Elizabeth Bonner |
| Lancaster County Academy | 1202 Park City Ctr | Lancaster, PA | 17601 | 717-295-2499 | 392-8603 | 9-12 | Gerald Huesken |
| Lehigh Valley Academy | 1560 Valley Center Pkwy | Bethlehem, PA | 18017 | 610-866-9660 | | K-12 | Susan Mauser |
| Lehigh Valley Charter HS for the Arts | 321 E 3rd St | Bethlehem, PA | 18015 | 610-868-2971 | 868-1446 | 9-12 | Diane LaBelle |
| Lehigh Valley Dual Language Charter S | 551 Thomas St | Bethlehem, PA | 18015-3447 | 610-419-3120 | 419-3968 | K-6 | Lisa Pluchinsky |
| Lincoln Charter S | 559 W King St | York, PA | 17401-3776 | 717-699-1573 | 846-4031 | K-5 | Leonard Hart |
| Lincoln Leadership Academy Charter S | 1414 E Cedar St | Allentown, PA | 18109 | 484-860-3300 | | K-12 | Sandra Figueroa-Torres |
| Lincoln Park Performing Arts Charter S | 1 Lincoln Park | Midland, PA | 15059-1535 | 724-643-9004 | 643-0769 | K-12 | Patrick Poling |
| Manchester Academic Charter S | 1214 Liverpool St | Pittsburgh, PA | 15233-1309 | 412-322-0585 | 322-2176 | K-8 | Vasilios Scoumis |
| Maritime Academy Charter S | 2275 Bridge St | Philadelphia, PA | 19137-2307 | 215-535-4555 | 535-4398 | 4-12 | Edward Poznek |
| MaST Community Charter S | 1800 Byberry Rd | Philadelphia, PA | 19116-3012 | 215-348-1100 | 348-1217 | K-12 | John Swoyer |
| Mastery Charter HS Hardy Williams Campus | 5400 Warrington Ave | Philadelphia, PA | 19143-4810 | 267-499-2100 | 729-1892 | 7-10 | Lisa Bellamy |
| Mastery Charter HS - Lenfest Campus | 35 S 4th St | Philadelphia, PA | 19106-2710 | 215-922-1902 | 922-1903 | 7-12 | Steven Kollar |
| Mastery Charter HS - Pickett Campus | 5700 Wayne Ave | Philadelphia, PA | 19144-3314 | 215-866-9000 | 866-9001 | 6-12 | Jason Kegel |
| Mastery Charter HS - Shoemaker Campus | 5301 Media St | Philadelphia, PA | 19131-4035 | 267-296-7111 | 296-7112 | 7-12 | Sharif El-Mekki |
| Mastery Charter HS - Thomas Campus | 927 Johnston St | Philadelphia, PA | 19148-5016 | 267-236-0036 | 236-0030 | 7-12 | Kristy Fruit |
| Mastery Charter S Clymer Campus | 1201 W Rush St | Philadelphia, PA | 19133 | 215-223-2243 | 227-3697 | K-8 | Tiffany Holmes |
| Mastery Charter S Grover Cleveland Cmps | 3701 N 19th St | Philadelphia, PA | 19140 | 215-227-5042 | 893-5290 | K-8 | Charmaine Collins |
| Mastery Charter S -Hardy Williams Campus | 1712 S 56th St | Philadelphia, PA | 19143-5308 | 215-724-2343 | 724-2374 | K-8 | Sarah Elder |
| Mastery Charter S Harrity Campus | 5601 Christian St | Philadelphia, PA | 19143-2899 | 215-471-2908 | 471-3807 | PK-8 | Stuart Warshawer |
| Mastery Charter S Mann Campus | 5376 W Berks St | Philadelphia, PA | 19131-3198 | 215-581-5616 | 581-5610 | K-6 | Stan Bobowski |
| Mastery Charter S Pastorius | 5650 Sprague St | Philadelphia, PA | 19138-1744 | 215-951-5689 | | K-8 | David McDonough |
| Mastery Charter S Prep MS | 1798 W Hunting Park Ave | Philadelphia, PA | 19140 | 215-227-4408 | 227-3694 | 6-8 | Raymond Fields |
| Mastery Charter S Simon Gratz Campus | 1798 W Hunting Park Ave | Philadelphia, PA | 19140-3408 | 215-227-4408 | 227-3694 | 9-12 | Rickia Reid |
| Mastery Charter S Smedley Campus | 1790 Bridge St | Philadelphia, PA | 19124-1395 | 215-537-2523 | 537-3694 | K-6 | Brian McLaughlin |
| Mastery Charter S - Thomas Campus | 814 Bigler St | Philadelphia, PA | 19148-5023 | 267-296-7000 | 236-0030 | K-6 | Michael Farrell |
| Math Civics & Sciences Charter S | 447 N Broad St | Philadelphia, PA | 19123-3643 | 215-923-4880 | 923-4859 | 1-12 | Frank Devine |
| Medical Academy Charter S | 330 Howertown Rd | Catasauqua, PA | 18032 | 610-403-1150 | 403-1151 | 9-12 | Joanna Hughes |
| Memphis Street Academy Charter S | 2950 Memphis St | Philadelphia, PA | 19134-4314 | 215-291-4709 | 291-4754 | 5-8 | Aqueelah Ellzy |
| Montessori Regional Charter S | 3750 W 26th St | Erie, PA | 16506 | 814-833-7771 | 833-1838 | K-6 | Anthony Pirrello |
| Multi-Cultural Academy Charter S | 3821 N Broad St | Philadelphia, PA | 19140-3609 | 215-227-0513 | 227-0415 | 9-12 | James Higgins |
| New Day Charter S | 256 S 5th St | Huntingdon, PA | 16652 | 814-643-7112 | 643-7116 | 7-12 | Steven Fleck |
| New Foundations Charter S | 8001 Torresdale Ave | Philadelphia, PA | 19136-2917 | 215-624-8100 | 624-0600 | K-8 | Paul Stadelberger |
| New Foundations Charter S | 4850 Rhawn St | Philadelphia, PA | 19136-2935 | 215-344-6410 | 624-6817 | 9-12 | Paul Stadelberger |
| New Media Technology Charter S | 8034 Thouron Ave | Philadelphia, PA | 19150-2423 | 267-286-6900 | 286-6904 | 6-12 | Justin Pascale |
| Nittany Valley Charter S | 1612 Norma St | State College, PA | 16801-6228 | 814-867-3842 | 231-0795 | K-8 | Kara Martin |
| Northwood Academy | 4621 Castor Ave | Philadelphia, PA | 19124-3097 | 215-289-5606 | 289-5464 | K-8 | Amy Hollister |
| Pan American Academy Charter S | 2830 N American St | Philadelphia, PA | 19133-3517 | 215-425-1212 | 423-0871 | K-8 | Dr. Darcy Russotto |
| Pantoja Community Charter S | 4101 N American St | Philadelphia, PA | 19140-2606 | 215-329-2733 | 329-2433 | K-8 | Sandra Gonzalez |
| Pennsylvania Cyber Charter S | 652 Midland Ave | Midland, PA | 15059 | 724-643-1180 | 643-1963 | K-12 | Dr. Michael Conti |
| Pennsylvania Distance Learning Charter S | 2100 Corporate Dr Ste 500 | Wexford, PA | 15090-7647 | 724-933-7300 | 933-7655 | K-12 | Dr. Ed Mandell |
| Pennsylvania Leadership Charter S | 1332 Enterprise Dr | West Chester, PA | 19380-5970 | 610-701-3333 | | K-12 | Dr. James Hanak |
| PA Learners Online Cyber Charter S | 475 E Waterfront Dr | Homestead, PA | 15120-1144 | 412-394-5733 | | 9-12 | Dr. David Martin |
| Pennsylvania Virtual Charter S | 630 Park Ave | King of Prussia, PA | 19406-1408 | 610-275-8501 | 275-1719 | K-12 | Joanne Jones Barnett |
| People for People Charter S | 800 N Broad St | Philadelphia, PA | 19130-2202 | 215-763-7060 | 763-6210 | K-8 | Pri Seebadri |
| Perseus House Charter S of Excellence | 1511 Peach St | Erie, PA | 16501 | 814-480-5914 | 454-9859 | 7-12 | Dana LaFata |
| Philadelphia Academy Charter S | 1700 Tomlinson Rd | Philadelphia, PA | 19116 | 215-673-3990 | 673-3341 | 9-12 | Megan Simmons |
| Philadelphia Academy Charter S | 11000 Roosevelt Blvd | Philadelphia, PA | 19116-3961 | 215-676-8320 | 676-8340 | K-8 | Allyssa Schmitt |
| Philadelphia Charter S for the Arts/Sci | 1197 Haworth St | Philadelphia, PA | 19124-2505 | 215-537-2520 | 537-2861 | K-8 | Michael Rocco |
| Philadelphia Electrical & Tech Charter S | 1420 Chestnut St | Philadelphia, PA | 19102-2505 | 267-514-1823 | 514-1834 | 9-12 | Erin Dougherty |
| Philadelphia Montessori Charter S | 2227 Island Rd | Philadelphia, PA | 19142-1009 | 215-365-4011 | 365-4367 | K-6 | Carrie Kries |
| Philadelphia Performing Arts Charter S | 2600 S Broad St | Philadelphia, PA | 19145-4616 | 215-551-4000 | 551-1113 | K-5 | Angela Puleio |
| Philadelphia Performing Arts Charter S | 2407 S Broad St | Philadelphia, PA | 19148 | 215-551-4000 | 551-1113 | K-1 | Angela Puleio |
| Premier Arts and Science Charter S | 500 N 17th St | Harrisburg, PA | 17103-1423 | 717-234-3200 | | K-5 | Steven Rayzer |
| Preparatory Charter S | 1928 Point Breeze Ave | Philadelphia, PA | 19145-2612 | 215-334-6144 | 334-6147 | 9-12 | Patricia Sack |
| Propel Charter HS - Andrew Street | 605 E 10th Ave | Munhall, PA | 15120 | 412-462-4625 | 462-6980 | 9-12 | Angela Allie |
| Propel Charter HS - Braddock Hills | 1500 Yost Blvd | Pittsburgh, PA | 15221 | 412-271-4929 | 271-4905 | 9-12 | Bob Bischoff |
| Propel Charter S - Braddock Hills | 1500 Yost Blvd | Braddock Hills, PA | 15221 | 412-271-3061 | 271-0865 | K-8 | Jocelyn Artinger |
| Propel Charter S - East | 1611 Monroeville Ave | Turtle Creek, PA | 15145-1652 | 412-823-0347 | | K-8 | Sandra Gough |
| Propel Charter S - Hazelwood | 5401 Glenwood Ave | Pittsburgh, PA | 15208 | 412-325-7105 | | K-6 | Tina Chekan |
| Propel Charter S - Homestead | 129 E 10th Ave | Homestead, PA | 15120-1608 | 412-464-2604 | | K-8 | Carrie Miller |
| Propel Charter S - Mc Keesport | 2412 Versailles Ave | McKeesport, PA | 15132-2037 | 412-678-7215 | | K-8 | Mike Evans |
| Propel Charter S - Montour | 340 Bilmar Dr | Pittsburgh, PA | 15205-4620 | 412-539-0100 | 539-0109 | K-8 | Matt Strine |
| Propel Charter S - Northside | 1805 Buena Vista St | Pittsburgh, PA | 15212-3914 | 412-325-1412 | 325-1428 | K-8 | Ariane Watson |
| Propel Charter S - Pitcairn | 435 Agatha St | Pitcairn, PA | 15140-1310 | 412-457-0020 | | K-8 | Robert Bischoff |
| Renaissance Academy | 413 Fairview St | Phoenixville, PA | 19460 | 610-983-4080 | 983-4096 | K-12 | Gina Guarino-Buli |
| Sankofa Academy | 446 W Gay St | West Chester, PA | 19380-2851 | 610-696-0333 | 696-0620 | 5-12 | Dr. LaMont McKim |
| Sankofa Freedom Academy | 2501 Kensington Ave | Philadelphia, PA | 19125 | 215-228-2001 | 228-2099 | K-12 | Dr. Ayesha Imani |
| School Lane Charter S | 2400 Bristol Pike | Bensalem, PA | 19020-5293 | 215-245-6055 | 245-6058 | K-10 | Karen Schade |
| Seven Generations Charter S | 154 E Minor St | Emmaus, PA | 18049 | 610-421-8844 | | K-8 | Paul Hunter |
| Souderton Charter S Collaborative | 110 E Broad St | Souderton, PA | 18964-1276 | 215-721-4560 | 721-4071 | K-8 | Jennifer Arevalo |
| Southwest Leadership Academy | 7101 Paschall Ave | Philadelphia, PA | 19142-1031 | 215-729-1939 | 729-1976 | K-8 | Alphonso Evans |
| Spectrum Charter S | 4369 Northern Pike | Monroeville, PA | 15146-2807 | 412-374-8130 | 374-9629 | 9-12 | Michelle Johnson |
| Stone Valley Community Charter S | 13006 Greenwood Rd | Huntingdon, PA | 16652 | 814-667-2705 | 667-2231 | K-5 | Dr. Kim Connelly |
| Sugar Valley Rural Charter S | 236 E Main St | Loganton, PA | 17747-9502 | 570-725-7822 | 725-7825 | K-12 | Logan Coney |
| SusQ-Cyber Charter S | 240 Market St Box 1A | Bloomsburg, PA | 17815 | 866-370-1226 | 245-0246 | 9-12 | Patricia Leighow |
| Sylvan Heights Science Charter S | 915 S 13th St | Harrisburg, PA | 17104-3402 | 717-232-9220 | 232-9221 | K-4 | Timothy Hess M.Ed. |
| Tacony Academy Charter S | 1330 Rhawn St | Philadelphia, PA | 19111 | 215-742-5100 | 742-5200 | K-8 | Ashley Redfearn-Neswick |
| Tacony Academy Charter S | 6201 Keystone St | Philadelphia, PA | 19111 | 267-388-8656 | 388-8666 | 9-12 | Naimah Holliday |
| Thackston Charter MS | 625 E Philadelphia St | York, PA | 17403 | 717-846-6160 | 848-2856 | 5-8 | Denise Butts |
| Tidioute Community Charter S | 241 Main St | Tidioute, PA | 16351-1299 | 814-484-3550 | 484-3977 | K-12 | Dr. Doug Allen |
| 21st Century Cyber Charter S | 126 Wallace Ave | Downingtown, PA | 19335 | 484-875-5400 | 875-5404 | 6-12 | Kim McCully |
| Universal Alcorn Charter S | 3200 Dickinson St | Philadelphia, PA | 19146-3316 | 215-952-6219 | 952-0853 | K-8 | Sheila Mallory |
| Universal Audenried Charter HS | 3301 Tasker St | Philadelphia, PA | 19145 | 215-952-4801 | 952-4805 | 9-12 | Blanchard Diavua |
| Universal Bluford Charter S | 5801 Media St | Philadelphia, PA | 19131-3824 | 215-581-5502 | 581-5725 | K-6 | Crystal Gary-Nelson |
| Universal Creighton Charter S | 5401 Tabor Ave | Philadelphia, PA | 19120-2130 | 215-537-2531 | 537-8398 | K-8 | Wendy Baldwin |
| Universal Daroff Charter S | 5630 Vine St | Philadelphia, PA | 19139-1301 | 215-471-2905 | 471-3159 | K-8 | Anna Smith |
| Universal Institute Charter S | 801 S 15th St | Philadelphia, PA | 19146-2215 | 215-732-2876 | 732-8066 | K-8 | Jeffrey Williams |
| Universal Vare Charter MS | 2100 S 24th St | Philadelphia, PA | 19145-3222 | 215-952-8611 | 952-8520 | 5-8 | Craig Metcalfe |
| Urban Academy Greater Pittsburgh Charter | 327 N Negley Ave | Pittsburgh, PA | 15206-2851 | 412-361-1008 | 361-1042 | K-5 | Dr. Gail Edwards |
| Urban Pathways Charter S | 925 Penn Ave | Pittsburgh, PA | 15222 | 412-392-4601 | 392-4602 | K-5 | Kimberly Fitzgerald |
| Vida Charter S | 120 E Broadway | Gettysburg, PA | 17325 | 717-334-3643 | 334-9806 | K-6 | Cynthia Maldonado |
| Vision Academy Charter S | 41 E Baltimore Ave | Lansdowne, PA | 19050 | 484-466-6341 | 466-2124 | K-4 | Adem Oksuz |
| West Oak Lane Charter S | 7115 Stenton Ave | Philadelphia, PA | 19138-1136 | 215-927-7995 | 927-7980 | K-8 | Dr. Debbera Peoples-Lee |
| West Philadelphia Achievement Charter S | 6701 Callowhill St | Philadelphia, PA | 19151-3603 | 215-476-6471 | 476-6481 | K-5 | Christine Godfrey |
| Widener Partnership Charter S | 1450 Edgmont Ave | Chester, PA | 19013 | 610-872-1358 | 872-1794 | K-7 | Dr. Darlene Davis |
| Wiley Community Charter S | 1446 E Lake Rd | Erie, PA | 16507-1936 | 814-461-9600 | 461-0226 | K-8 | Peter Russo |
| Wissahickon Charter S | 4700 Wissahickon Ave | Philadelphia, PA | 19144 | 267-338-1020 | 338-1030 | K-8 | Kristi Littell |
| Wonderland Charter S | 2112 Sandy Dr | State College, PA | 16803-2282 | 814-234-5886 | | K-K | Harold Ohnmeis |
| World Communications Charter S | 512 S Broad St | Philadelphia, PA | 19146-1695 | 215-735-3198 | 735-3824 | 6-12 | Gamal Sherif Ed.D. |
| York Academy Regional Charter S | 32 W North St | York, PA | 17401 | 717-801-3900 | 718-1092 | K-6 | |
| Young Scholars Charter S | 900 N Marshall St | Philadelphia, PA | 19123-1307 | 215-232-9727 | 232-4542 | 6-8 | Jessika Rao |
| Young Scholars Kenderton Charter S | 1500 W Ontario St | Philadelphia, PA | 19140 | 215-227-4412 | | K-8 | Shakira Smith |
| Young Scholars of Central PA Charter S | 1530 Westerly Pkwy | State College, PA | 16801-2848 | 814-237-9727 | 237-1517 | K-8 | Levent Kaya |
| Young Scholars of Western PA | 600 Newport Dr | Pittsburgh, PA | 15234-2653 | 412-668-2064 | 668-2068 | K-6 | |
| YouthBuild Charter S | 1231 N Broad St Fl 3 | Philadelphia, PA | 19122-4023 | 215-627-8671 | 763-5774 | 12-12 | Simran Sidhu |

## Rhode Island

| School | Address | City,State | Zip code | Telephone | Fax | Grade | Contact |
|---|---|---|---|---|---|---|---|
| Academy for Career Exploration | 155 Harrison St | Providence, RI | 02907 | 401-456-1738 | 521-0653 | 9-12 | Mario Cirillo Ph.D. |
| Achievement 1st Providence Mayoral Acad | 370 Hartford Ave | Providence, RI | 02909 | 401-347-1106 | 633-6677 | K-2 | Morgan Carter |
| BEACON Charter S | 320 Main St | Woonsocket, RI | 02895-3138 | 401-671-6261 | 671-6264 | 9-12 | Michael Skeldon |

| School | Address | City,State | Zip code | Telephone | Fax | Grade | Contact |
|---|---|---|---|---|---|---|---|
| Blackstone Academy | 334 Pleasant St | Pawtucket, RI | 02860-5288 | 401-726-1750 | 726-1753 | 9-12 | Kyleen Carpenter |
| Blackstone Valley ES 1 | 291 Broad St | Cumberland, RI | 02864 | 401-335-3133 | 303-3185 | K-4 | Kyle Quadros |
| Blackstone Valley Prep ES 3 | 3 Fairlawn Way | Lincoln, RI | 02865 | 401-475-2680 | 475-2415 | K-4 | Josh Falk |
| Blackstone Valley Prep ES 2 | 52 Broad St | Cumberland, RI | 02864 | 401-305-6860 | 305-6866 | K-4 | Colleen Colarusso |
| Blackstone Valley Prep Mayoral Acad HS | 3357 Mendon Rd | Cumberland, RI | 02864 | 401-405-0320 | 405-0440 | 9-12 | Jonathon Santos Silva |
| Blackstone Valley Prep Mayoral Acad MS | 3 Fairlawn Way | Lincoln, RI | 02865 | 401-475-8829 | 475-8931 | 5-8 | Joy Souza |
| Compass S | 537 Old North Rd | Kingston, RI | 02881-1220 | 401-788-8322 | 788-8326 | K-8 | Michael Obel-Omia |
| Cuffee S | 459 Promenade St | Providence, RI | 02908-5601 | 401-453-2711 | 453-4964 | K-12 | Becky Coustan |
| Greene S | 94 John Potter Rd | West Greenwich, RI | 02817-2099 | 401-397-8601 | 397-8700 | 9-12 | Deanna Duncan |
| Highlander Charter S | 42 Lexington Ave | Providence, RI | 02907 | 401-277-2600 | 277-2603 | PK-12 | Rose Grant |
| Hope Academy | 1000 Eddy St | Providence, RI | 02905 | 401-280-5698 | | K-K | |
| International Charter S | 334 Pleasant St | Pawtucket, RI | 02860-5288 | 401-721-0824 | 721-0976 | K-5 | Darlene Pugnali Ph.D. |
| Kingston Hill Academy | 850 Stony Fort Rd | Saunderstown, RI | 02874-1003 | 401-783-8282 | 783-5656 | K-5 | Linda Paolillo |
| Learning Community S | 21 Lincoln Ave | Central Falls, RI | 02863-2012 | 401-722-9998 | 722-0990 | K-8 | Sarah Friedman |
| NEL/CPS Construction Career Academy | 4 Sharpe Dr | Cranston, RI | 02920-4410 | 401-270-8692 | 270-8697 | 9-12 | Dennis Curran |
| Nowell Leadership Academy II | 133 Delaine St | Providence, RI | 02909-2728 | 401-751-0405 | 751-0020 | 9-12 | Jodi Timpani |
| Nowell Leadership Academy I | 43 Hawes St | Central Falls, RI | 02863-3007 | | | 9-12 | Jodi Timpani |
| RI Nurses Institute Charter HS | 150 Washington St | Providence, RI | 02903 | 401-680-4900 | 331-5646 | 10-12 | Brian Butler |
| Segue Institute for Learning | 325 Cowden St | Central Falls, RI | 02863 | 401-721-0964 | 721-0984 | 6-8 | Melissa Lourenco |
| SouthSide Elementary Charter S | 126 Somerset St | Providence, RI | 02907-1034 | 401-921-5656 | | K-5 | |
| Times2 STEM Academy | 50 Fillmore St | Providence, RI | 02908-3105 | 401-272-5094 | 272-0555 | K-12 | Jerry Kowalczyk |
| Trinity Academy for the Performing Arts | 158 Messer St | Providence, RI | 02909-1741 | 401-524-7968 | 432-7882 | 7-10 | Nanci DeRobbio |
| Village Green Virtual Charter S | 135 Weybosset St | Providence, RI | 02903-3803 | 401-831-2878 | | 9-11 | Dr. Robert Pilkington |
| **South Carolina** | | | | | | | |
| Academy for Teaching and Learning | 109 Hinton St | Chester, SC | 29706-2022 | 803-385-6334 | 385-6335 | PK-8 | Robyn Brakefield |
| Academy of Hope Charter S | 3521 Juniper Bay Rd | Conway, SC | 29527-4227 | 843-397-5719 | 397-5712 | K-8 | Melissa McCloud |
| Aiken Performing Arts Academy | 130 Avery Ln | Aiken, SC | 29801-1902 | 803-644-4824 | 641-1155 | 9-12 | Keisha Lloyd-Kennedy |
| Anderson V Charter S | 1225 S McDuffie St | Anderson, SC | 29624-2746 | 864-260-5538 | 260-5911 | 9-12 | Katie Brown |
| Brashier Middle College HS | 1830 W Georgia Rd | Simpsonville, SC | 29680-7212 | 864-757-1800 | 757-1850 | 9-12 | Michael Sinclair |
| Bridges Preparatory S | PO Box 120 | Beaufort, SC | 29901 | 843-982-7732 | 982-7707 | K-7 | Bernie Schein |
| Bridgewater Academy | 191 River Landing Blvd | Myrtle Beach, SC | 29579 | 843-236-3689 | 236-4921 | K-8 | Steve Wilson |
| Calhoun Falls Charter S | 205 Edgefield St | Calhoun Falls, SC | 29628-1018 | 864-418-8014 | 418-9379 | 6-12 | Deirdre McCullough |
| Cape Romain Environmental Educ Charter S | 1011 Old Cemetery Rd | Mc Clellanville, SC | 29458-9735 | 843-887-3323 | 887-3525 | PK-7 | Margaret Crouch M.Ed. |
| Carolina School for Inquiry | PO Box 2484 | Columbia, SC | 29202-2484 | 803-691-1250 | 691-1247 | K-6 | LaQuisha Chester |
| Carolina Voyager Charter S | 30 Race St | Charleston, SC | 29403 | 843-203-3891 | 718-2913 | K-8 | Dr. Harry Walker |
| Charleston Charter S for Math & Science | 1002 King St | Charleston, SC | 29403 | 843-720-3085 | 720-3196 | 6-12 | Henry Walding |
| Charleston Development Academy | 233 Line St | Charleston, SC | 29403-5145 | 843-722-2689 | 722-2694 | PK-8 | Cecelia Gordon Rogers |
| Coastal Leadership Academy | 3710 Palmetto Pointe Blvd | Myrtle Beach, SC | 29588 | 843-504-8193 | 410-4826 | 9-12 | Melinda Tavernier |
| Coastal Montessori Charter S | 247 Wildcat Way | Pawleys Island, SC | 29585-5342 | 843-235-0413 | 235-0418 | 1-6 | Dr. Nathalie Hunt |
| Cooper Charter S | 4568 Seaboard Rd | Salters, SC | 29590-3365 | 843-387-5426 | 387-5444 | PK-7 | Dr. Kerry Singleton |
| Discovery S | 302 W Dunlap St | Lancaster, SC | 29720-2405 | 803-285-8430 | 416-8907 | K-5 | Tom McDuffie |
| East Cooper Montessori Charter S | 1120 Rifle Range Rd | Mount Pleasant, SC | 29464 | 843-216-2883 | 216-8880 | 1-8 | Jody Swanigan |
| East Point Academy | 1340 Knox Abbott Dr | Cayce, SC | 29033 | 803-739-4992 | 739-4977 | PK-5 | Renee Mathews |
| Felton Laboratory Charter S | PO Box 2349 | Orangeburg, SC | 29116 | 803-536-7034 | 533-3635 | K-8 | Dr. Gloria Winkler |
| Fox Creek HS | 165 Shortcut Rd | North Augusta, SC | 29860 | 803-613-9435 | 613-1533 | 9-12 | Josh Trahan |
| Garden City Preparatory Academy for Boys | 1195 Saint Matthews Rd | Orangeburg, SC | 29115 | 888-448-7641 | | 6-12 | Kevin Rasberry |
| Gray Collegiate Academy | 3833 Leaphart Rd | Orangeburg, SC | 29118 | 888-951-3321 | 569-1425 | 9-12 | Joedy Moots |
| GREEN Charter S | 1440 Pelham Rd Ste C | Greenville, SC | 29615 | 864-288-4134 | 288-0826 | K-7 | Adem Dokmeci |
| Greenville Technical Charter HS | PO Box 5616 | Greenville, SC | 29606-5616 | 864-250-8845 | 250-8846 | 9-12 | Dr. J. Brodie Bricker |
| Greer Middle College Charter HS | 138 W McElhaney Rd | Taylors, SC | 29687-5843 | 864-469-7571 | 469-7573 | 9-12 | Jimmy Armstrong Ph.D. |
| High Point Academy | 6655 Pottery Rd | Spartanburg, SC | 29303 | 864-316-9788 | 249-1516 | K-12 | Lori Manning |
| Horse Creek Academy | 1200 Toolebeck Rd | Aiken, SC | 29803 | 803-226-0160 | 226-0202 | PK-8 | Patti Strom |
| Imagine Columbia Leadership Academy | 3810 N Main St | Columbia, SC | 29203-6443 | 803-929-1140 | 929-1145 | K-5 | Suezan Turknett |
| James Island Charter HS | 1000 Fort Johnson Rd | Charleston, SC | 29412-8898 | 843-762-2754 | 762-5228 | 9-12 | Richard Gordon |
| Kennedy Charter S | 130 Avery Ln | Aiken, SC | 29801-1902 | 803-644-4824 | 641-1155 | 5-8 | Keisha Lloyd-Kennedy |
| Lake City College Preparatory Academy | 1310 N Matthews Rd | Lake City, SC | 29560-7015 | 843-374-0128 | 374-9029 | K-12 | Dr. Deloris Brown |
| Langston Charter MS | 1950 Woodruff Rd | Greenville, SC | 29607-5937 | 864-286-9700 | 286-9699 | 6-8 | Gregory Abel |
| Lead Academy | 29 Ridgeway Dr | Greenville, SC | 29605 | 864-770-1790 | 302-1278 | 5-8 | Rodney Johnson |
| Legacy Charter S Fuller Campus | 1613 W Washington St | Greenville, SC | 29601 | 864-214-1600 | 451-7023 | K-4 | Virginia Burrows |
| Legacy Charter S Parker Campus | 900 Woodside Ave | Greenville, SC | 29611-4221 | 864-248-0646 | 283-6444 | 5-12 | Frank Powell |
| Lowcountry Leadership Academy | 5139 Gibson Rd | Hollywood, SC | 29449 | 843-889-5527 | 889-5529 | K-10 | Mache Larkin |
| Lowcountry Montessori S | 749 Broad River Dr | Beaufort, SC | 29906 | 843-322-0577 | 322-0925 | K-12 | Amy Horn |
| Mathis HS | 2872 Azalea Dr | N Charleston, SC | 29405-8216 | 843-557-1611 | 747-5810 | 9-12 | Eleanor Hardy |
| Midlands Middle College | 1260 Lexington Dr | West Columbia, SC | 29170 | 803-822-3333 | 822-7039 | 11-12 | Carole Fearrington |
| Midlands STEM Academy | PO Box 1214 | Winnsboro, SC | 29180 | 864-684-7520 | | K-12 | Marie Milam |
| OCSD5 HS for Health Professions | 770 Stilton Rd | Orangeburg, SC | 29115 | 803-535-1693 | | 9-12 | Kimberly Broughton |
| Orange Grove Charter S | 1225 Orange Branch Rd | Charleston, SC | 29407-3336 | 843-763-1520 | 769-2245 | K-5 | John Clendaniel |
| PALM Charter HS | 136 Rodeo Dr | Myrtle Beach, SC | 29579-9400 | 843-903-6600 | 903-6602 | 9-12 | Mack Sarvis |
| Palmetto Academy of Learning and Success | PO Box 15432 | Myrtle Beach, SC | 29587-5432 | 843-839-1725 | 839-1726 | K-8 | Courtney Fancher |
| Palmetto Scholar's Academy | 2415 Avenue F | N Charleston, SC | 29405-1941 | 843-300-4118 | 300-4123 | 6-12 | Dr. Tim Gott |
| Palmetto S at Children's Attention Home | PO Box 2892 | Rock Hill, SC | 29732-4892 | 803-328-6555 | 327-8618 | K-8 | Dr. Hugh Wilson |
| Palmetto Youth Academy | 1209 N Douglas St | Florence, SC | 29501-0600 | 843-679-7070 | 679-7046 | 1-6 | Yvonne Burgess |
| Pattison's Academy for Comprehensive Ed. | 2014 Bees Ferry Rd | Charleston, SC | 29414-6603 | 843-556-1070 | 556-6742 | K-12 | Steve Kiernan |
| Pee Dee Math Science Technology Academy | 101 Docs Dr | Bishopville, SC | 29010 | 803-692-1814 | 883-8736 | K-5 | E. Keith Bailey |
| Phoenix Charter HS | PO Box 170 | Alcolu, SC | 29001-0170 | 803-505-6800 | 505-6801 | 9-12 | Elease Fulton |
| Provost Academy of South Carolina | 200 Arbor Lake Dr Ste 301 | Columbia, SC | 29223 | 803-735-9110 | 801-8040 | 9-12 | Stephanie Cagle |
| Quest Leadership Academy | 29 Ridgeway Dr | Greenville, SC | 29605 | 864-275-0465 | | PK-8 | Calandra Davis |
| Richland One Middle College S | 316 Beltline Blvd | Columbia, SC | 29205-3624 | 803-738-7114 | 738-7117 | 11-12 | Dr. Tiniece Javis |
| Richland Two Charter HS | 750 Old Clemson Rd | Columbia, SC | 29229 | 803-419-1348 | 738-7539 | 9-12 | Bobby Cunningham |
| Riverview Charter S | 81 Savannah Hwy | Beaufort, SC | 29906-6284 | 843-379-0123 | 379-0133 | K-5 | Alison Thomas |
| Riverwalk Academy | 2800 Faith Blvd | Rock Hill, SC | 29730 | 803-873-9295 | 827-8400 | K-12 | Naomi French |
| Royal Live Oaks Academy Arts & Sciences | PO Box 528 | Hardeeville, SC | 29927 | 843-784-2630 | 784-2623 | K-10 | Karen Wicks |
| South Carolina Calvert Academy | 100 Summit Pkwy | Columbia, SC | 29229-9000 | 803-462-0254 | 462-0326 | K-8 | Alexandria Gillicrese |
| SC Connections Academy | 220 Stoneridge Dr Ste 403 | Columbia, SC | 29210-8018 | 803-212-4712 | 212-4946 | K-12 | Amanda Ebel |
| SC Science Academy | 2015 Marion St | Columbia, SC | 29201 | 803-540-3421 | | 6-12 | |
| SC Virtual Charter School | 140 Stoneridge Dr Ste 420 | Columbia, SC | 29210-8200 | 803-253-6222 | 253-6279 | K-12 | Dr. Cherry Daniel |
| South Carolina Whitmore S | 510 Lexington Ave | Chapin, SC | 29036 | 866-476-6416 | 476-1646 | 9-12 | Ellen Ray |
| Spartanburg Preparatory S | PO Box 3343 | Spartanburg, SC | 29304 | 864-621-3882 | 804-6404 | K-9 | Dr. John Von Rohr |
| York Preparatory Academy | 1047 Golden Gate Ct | Rock Hill, SC | 29732 | 803-324-4400 | 496-2083 | K-12 | Diane Neville |
| Youth Academy Charter S | 711 Tomlinson St | Kingstree, SC | 29556-3723 | 843-355-5424 | 355-5425 | K-12 | Ja Ganna Kinloch |
| Youth Leadership Academy | 698 Concord Church Rd | Pickens, SC | 29671-9167 | 864-878-1103 | 878-5985 | 6-8 | Patsy Wood Smith |
| **Tennessee** | | | | | | | |
| Arrow Academy of Excellence | 645 Semmes St | Memphis, TN | 38111 | 901-207-1891 | | K-2 | Raychellet Williamson |
| Aspire Coleman ES | 3210 Raleigh Millington Rd | Memphis, TN | 38128-3398 | 901-416-4306 | | K-5 | Owen Ricciardi |
| Aspire Hanley ES #1 | 680 Hanley St | Memphis, TN | 38114-2534 | 901-416-5958 | | PK-6 | Megan McGrail |
| Aspire Hanley ES #2 | 680 Hanley St | Memphis, TN | 38114-2534 | 901-416-5958 | | PK-6 | Nickalous Manning |
| Aurora Collegiate Academy | 3804 Given Ave | Memphis, TN | 38122-3535 | 901-249-4615 | 249-4915 | K-5 | Rita Chan |
| Brick Church College Prep S | 2835 Brick Church Pike | Nashville, TN | 37207 | 615-806-6317 | | 5-8 | Dennis Wolff |
| Cameron College Prep S | 1034 1st Ave S | Nashville, TN | 37210 | 615-806-6320 | | 5-8 | Tait Danhausen |
| Chattanooga Charter School of Excellence | 5600 Brainerd Rd | Chattanooga, TN | 37411 | 423-402-8012 | | K-5 | Jennifer Huskins |
| Chattanooga Girls Leadership Academy | 1802 Bailey Ave | Chattanooga, TN | 37404-3005 | 423-702-7230 | | 6-12 | Elaine Swofford Ed.D. |
| Circles of Success Learning Academy | 867 S Parkway E | Memphis, TN | 38106-5605 | 901-322-7978 | 322-7993 | K-5 | Sheri Catron-Cooper |
| City University S Boys Preparatory | 1475 E Shelby Dr | Memphis, TN | 38116 | 901-775-2219 | 775-2044 | 6-8 | Tracie Greer |
| City University S Girls Preparatory | 1475 E Shelby Dr | Memphis, TN | 38116 | 901-775-2219 | | 6-8 | Tracie Greer |
| City University S of Liberal Arts | 1475 E Shelby Dr | Memphis, TN | 38116 | 901-775-2219 | 775-2044 | 9-12 | |
| Cornerstone Prep - Lester Campus | 320 Carpenter St | Memphis, TN | 38112 | 901-416-5969 | 416-5971 | PK-6 | Lisa Settle |
| DuBois S of Arts & Technology | 4475 S Germantown Rd | Memphis, TN | 38125 | 901-331-3346 | | K-12 | Audrey Hudson |
| DuBois S of Arts & Technology | 4184 Graceland Dr | Memphis, TN | 38116 | 901-331-3436 | | K-12 | Dalton Blackwell |
| East End Preparatory S | 1460 McGavock Pike | Nashville, TN | 37216 | 615-630-7470 | | K-4 | Jim Leckrone |
| Fairley HS | 4950 Fairley Rd | Memphis, TN | 38109-7375 | 213-220-1429 | | 9-12 | Marcus Jones |
| Frayser Achievement ES | 1602 Dellwood Ave | Memphis, TN | 38127-1399 | 901-416-3840 | 416-4836 | PK-5 | James Dennis |
| Freedom Preparatory Academy | 5132 Jonetta St | Memphis, TN | 38109-7061 | 901-259-5959 | 259-5950 | 6-12 | Sundiata Salaam |
| Freedom Prep ES - Westwood | 778 Parkrose Rd | Memphis, TN | 38109 | 901-259-5959 | | K-1 | Donique Nobles |
| GRAD Academy | 1880 Prospect St | Memphis, TN | 38106 | 901-206-8848 | | 9-12 | Keyundah Coleman |
| Humes Preparatory Academy - Upper S | 659 N Manassas St | Memphis, TN | 38107-3902 | 901-310-1332 | | 6-8 | Julia Callaway |
| Intrepid Preparatory S | 5432 Bell Forge Ln E | Antioch, TN | 37013 | 615-810-8443 | | 5-7 | Mia Howard |
| Ivy Academy Chattanooga | 8520 Dayton Pike | Soddy Daisy, TN | 37379 | 423-305-7494 | 305-7496 | 6-12 | Angie Markum |
| King Preparatory HS | 1530 Dellwood Ave | Memphis, TN | 38127 | 901-416-3880 | | 9-12 | Kimberly Hopkins-Clark |
| KIPP Academy Nashville ES | 1000 Sevier St | Nashville, TN | 37206 | 615-226-4484 | | K-1 | Amy Galloway |
| KIPP Academy Nashville MS | 123 Douglas Ave | Nashville, TN | 37207 | 615-226-4484 | | 5-8 | Laura Howarth |
| KIPP Memphis Academy ES | 2248 Shannon Ave | Memphis, TN | 38108 | 901-452-2682 | | K-1 | Jenna Molinski |
| KIPP Memphis Academy MS | 2110 Howell Ave | Memphis, TN | 38108 | 901-791-9793 | | 5-8 | Andy Bobowski |
| KIPP Memphis Collegiate ES | 230 Henry Ave | Memphis, TN | 38107 | 901-791-9391 | 791-9394 | K-4 | Grace Williams |

| School | Address | City,State | Zip code | Telephone | Fax | Grade | Contact |
|---|---|---|---|---|---|---|---|
| KIPP Memphis Collegiate HS | 2110 Howell Ave | Memphis, TN | 38108 | 901-791-9792 | 791-9796 | 9-10 | Richard Bailey |
| KIPP Memphis Collegiate MS | 230 Henry Ave | Memphis, TN | 38107 | 901-791-9390 | 791-9394 | 5-8 | Grace Williams |
| KIPP Memphis Preparatory MS | 2230 Corry Rd | Memphis, TN | 38106 | 901-881-5128 | | 5-6 | Crystal Windless |
| KIPP Memphis University MS | 3966 Sewannee Rd | Memphis, TN | 38109 | 901-577-3300 | | 6-6 | Mitch Bartkiewicz |
| KIPP Nashville College Prep MS | 3410 Knight Dr | Nashville, TN | 37207 | 615-226-4484 | 226-4401 | 5-7 | Nikki Miller |
| KIPP Nashville Collegiate HS | 123 Douglas Ave | Nashville, TN | 37207 | 615-226-4484 | | 9-12 | Jake Ramsey |
| Klondike Preparatory Academy | 1250 Vollintine Ave | Memphis, TN | 38107 | 901-310-1999 | | K-3 | Precious Boyle |
| Knowledge Academies | 5320 Hickory Hollow Pkwy | Antioch, TN | 37013 | 615-810-8370 | 877-0502 | 5-9 | Arielle McCallum |
| LEAD Academy | 2835 Brick Church Pike | Nashville, TN | 37205 | 615-352-1253 | 327-5425 | 5-8 | Nicolas Frank |
| LEAD Academy HS | 1704 Heiman St | Nashville, TN | 37208 | 615-327-5422 | | 9-12 | LaVoe Mulgrew |
| LEAD Preparatory Southeast | 531 Metroplex Dr | Nashville, TN | 37211 | 615-584-6649 | | 5-8 | Chris Elliott |
| Lester Prep | 320 Carpenter St | Memphis, TN | 38112 | 901-416-3640 | | 6-6 | |
| Libertas S at Brookmeade | 3777 Edenburg Dr | Memphis, TN | 38127 | 901-609-3611 | | PK-1 | Bob Nardo |
| Liberty Collegiate Academy | 3515 Gallatin Pike | Nashville, TN | 37216 | 615-564-1965 | 650-0912 | 5-8 | Annie Robison |
| Memphis Academy of Health Sciences | 3925 Chelsea Avenue Ext | Memphis, TN | 38108-2612 | 901-382-1441 | 382-1944 | 6-12 | Derrick Joyce |
| Memphis Academy of Science & Engineering | 1254 Jefferson Ave | Memphis, TN | 38104 | 901-333-1580 | 333-1582 | 6-12 | Ketia Francis |
| Memphis Business Academy | 2450 Frayser Blvd | Memphis, TN | 38127 | 901-353-1475 | 308-1430 | K-5 | Marsharee Shaw |
| Memphis Business Academy HS | 3306 Overton Crossing St | Memphis, TN | 38127 | 901-357-8680 | 357-8681 | 9-12 | Dr. Menthia Clark |
| Memphis Business Academy MS | 3306 Overton Crossing St | Memphis, TN | 38127 | 901-357-2711 | 357-2442 | 6-8 | Nina Nash |
| Memphis College Prep S | 278 Greenlaw Ave | Memphis, TN | 38105 | 901-620-6475 | 620-6476 | K-5 | Ashley Foxx |
| Memphis Grizzlies Prep Charter S | 168 Jefferson Ave | Memphis, TN | 38103-2219 | 901-474-0955 | 474-9049 | 9-12 | Elizabeth Simpson |
| Memphis Rise Academy | 2248 Shannon Ave | Memphis, TN | 38108 | 901-379-5750 | | 6-12 | Jack Vuylsteke |
| Memphis School of Excellence | 4450 S Mendenhall Rd | Memphis, TN | 38141 | 901-367-7814 | 367-7816 | 6-9 | Muhammet Turkay |
| Nashville Academy of Computer Science | 3307 Brick Church Pike | Nashville, TN | 37207 | 615-921-5000 | | 5-6 | Ali Deissler |
| Nashville Classical Charter S | 1310 Ordway Pl | Nashville, TN | 37206 | 615-538-5841 | | K-2 | Charlie Friedman |
| Nashville Prep Academy | 1300 56th Ave N | Nashville, TN | 37209 | 615-921-8440 | | 5-8 | Arlyn Ilgenfritz |
| New Vision Academy | 297 Plus Park Blvd | Nashville, TN | 37217-1003 | 615-360-1115 | | 5-8 | Tim Malone |
| Omni Prep North Pointe Lower S | 3333 Old Brownsville Rd | Memphis, TN | 38134 | 866-828-4912 | 828-4902 | K-1 | Mary Mitchell |
| Omni Prep North Pointe MS | 3333 Old Brownsville Rd | Memphis, TN | 38134 | 901-828-4912 | 828-4902 | 5-6 | Mary Mitchell |
| Pathways in Education | 4701 Elvis Presley Blvd | Memphis, TN | 38116 | | | 7-12 | |
| Power Center Academy HS | 6120 Winchester Rd | Memphis, TN | 38115 | 901-333-6874 | 922-6028 | 9-12 | Dr. Steevon Hunter |
| Power Center Academy MS | 6120 Winchester Rd | Memphis, TN | 38115 | 901-333-6874 | 922-6028 | 6-8 | Antonio Ryan |
| Promise Academy | 1346 Bryan St | Memphis, TN | 38108-2401 | 901-324-4456 | 324-4457 | K-4 | Thomas Beazley |
| Promise Academy Spring Hill | 3796 Frayser Raleigh Rd | Memphis, TN | 38128 | 901-410-0284 | | PK-1 | Patrick Washington |
| Purpose Preparatory S | 220 Venture Cir | Nashville, TN | 37228 | 615-724-0705 | | K-3 | Lagra Newman |
| RePublic HS | 3307 Brick Church Pike | Nashville, TN | 37207 | 615-921-6620 | | 9-9 | Kait Troy |
| Rocketship Nashville | 2526 Dickerson Pike | Nashville, TN | 37207 | 615-818-0209 | | K-4 | Christa Thomas |
| Rocketship United Academy | 320 Plus Park Blvd | Nashville, TN | 37217 | 585-957-6278 | | K-4 | James Robinson |
| Smithson-Craighead Academy | 730 Neelys Bend Rd | Madison, TN | 37115 | 615-228-9886 | 228-9799 | K-4 | Janelle Glover |
| Soulsville Charter S | 1115 College St | Memphis, TN | 38106 | 901-261-6366 | 261-6398 | 6-12 | NeShante Brown |
| Southern Avenue Charter S | 2221 Democrat Rd | Memphis, TN | 38132 | 901-743-7335 | 743-7677 | K-5 | |
| Southern Avenue MS | 2185 Democrat Rd | Memphis, TN | 38132 | 901-744-6644 | 744-6645 | 6-8 | Lytania Black |
| STAR Academy Charter S | 3260 James Rd | Memphis, TN | 38128-5351 | 901-387-5050 | 387-0798 | K-5 | Angela Holloway |
| STEM Prep Academy | 1162 Foster Ave | Nashville, TN | 37210 | 615-921-2200 | | 5-8 | Dr. Kristen McGraner |
| Strive Collegiate Academy | 3055 Lebanon Rd | Nashville, TN | 37214 | 615-208-5039 | | 5-5 | Lakendra Butler |
| Valor Collegiate Academy | 4527 Nolensville Pike | Nashville, TN | 37211 | 615-823-7982 | | 5-6 | Dr. Travis Commons |
| Veritas College Preparatory Charter S | 690 Mississippi Blvd | Memphis, TN | 38126 | 901-526-1900 | 526-1988 | 6-8 | Nick Getschman |
| Vision Preparatory Charter S | 260 Joubert Ave | Memphis, TN | 38109 | 901-651-7832 | | K-5 | Tom Benton |
| Whitney Achievement ES | 1219 Whitney Ave | Memphis, TN | 38127-7755 | 901-416-3949 | 416-3953 | PK-5 | Debra Broughton |
| **Texas** | | | | | | | |
| A+ Academy | 10327 Rylie Rd | Dallas, TX | 75217-8240 | 972-557-5578 | 557-5807 | PK-12 | Dr. Shala Flowers |
| Academy of Accelerated Learning | 6025 Chimney Rock Rd | Houston, TX | 77081-4011 | 713-773-4766 | 666-2532 | PK-5 | Doris Robins |
| Academy of Accelerated Learning | 6711 Bellfort St | Houston, TX | 77087-6456 | 713-645-0336 | 640-2435 | PK-5 | Doris Robins |
| Academy of Careers & Technologies | PO Box 681866 | San Antonio, TX | 78268-1866 | 210-226-7568 | 226-8548 | 9-12 | Akenese Iosefo |
| Academy of Dallas | 1030 Oak Park Dr | Dallas, TX | 75232-1238 | 214-371-9600 | 371-1053 | PK-8 | Conrad Hargest |
| Accelerated Learning Center | 721 Omaha Dr | Corpus Christi, TX | 78408-2839 | 361-887-7766 | 887-6035 | PK-12 | Maria Garza |
| Advantage Academy - Grand Prairie East | 300 W Pioneer Pkwy | Grand Prairie, TX | 75051 | 214-276-5800 | 276-5890 | 9-12 | Eureka Devers M.Ed. |
| Advantage Academy - Grand Prairie West | 955 Freetown Rd | Grand Prairie, TX | 75051 | 214-451-2120 | 602-2212 | PK-8 | Asusena Rios M.Ed. |
| Advantage Academy - North Duncanville | 4009 Joseph Hardin Dr | Dallas, TX | 75236-1507 | 214-276-5880 | 467-9131 | PK-8 | Darketsha Williams |
| Advantage Academy - Waxahachie | 701 W Highway 287 Byp | Waxahachie, TX | 75165-5163 | 972-451-2107 | 937-9876 | PK-8 | Aimee Barnes M.Ed. |
| AIA Houston ES | PO Box 20589 | Houston, TX | 77225-0589 | 713-728-9330 | 283-6190 | PK-6 | LaShawn Hoskins |
| AIA Lancaster ES | 901 E Belt Line Rd | Lancaster, TX | 75146 | 972-227-2105 | 283-6190 | PK-6 | LaShawn Hoskins |
| AIM College & Career Prep | 5200 Avenue N 1/2 | Galveston, TX | 77551 | 409-761-6302 | 770-0918 | 6-12 | Jean Fullen |
| Alamo Leadership Academy | 535 New Laredo Hwy | San Antonio, TX | 78211 | 210-922-1687 | 922-1630 | PK-12 | Cheryl Stewart |
| Alief Montessori Community S | 4215 H St | Houston, TX | 77072-5380 | 281-530-9406 | 530-2233 | PK-5 | Nancy Chieu |
| Allen Charter S | 5220 Nomas St | Dallas, TX | 75212-3229 | 972-794-5100 | 794-5101 | PK-5 | Sheila Ortiz |
| Alpha Charter S | 701 W State St | Garland, TX | 75040-6310 | 972-272-2173 | 205-9050 | PK-12 | Roberto Ayala |
| Altamira Academy | 220 Foremost Dr | Austin, TX | 78745 | 512-953-8301 | | PK-2 | Dan Horn |
| Ambassadors Preparatory Academy | 5001 Avenue U | Galveston, TX | 77551-6007 | 409-762-1115 | 762-1114 | PK-8 | Dr. Patricia Williams |
| Amigos Por Vida-Friends for Life Charter | 5503 El Camino Del Rey St | Houston, TX | 77081 | 713-349-9945 | 349-0671 | PK-8 | Freddy Delgado |
| Annunciation Home | 3610 Shell Rd | Georgetown, TX | 78628-9246 | 512-864-7755 | | K-12 | Holly Engleman |
| Aristoi Classical Academy | 5618 11th St | Katy, TX | 77493-1971 | 281-391-5003 | 391-5010 | K-10 | Brenda Davidson |
| Arlington Classics Academy | 2800 W Arkansas Ln | Arlington, TX | 76016-5819 | 817-274-2008 | 274-8768 | K-2 | Janna Allen |
| Arlington Classics Academy Intermediate | 5200 S Bowen Rd | Arlington, TX | 76017-3756 | 817-303-1553 | 549-0246 | 3-5 | Aaron Daffern |
| Arlington Classics Academy Middle | 5200 S Bowen Rd | Arlington, TX | 76017-3756 | 817-987-1819 | 549-0246 | 6-8 | Kurtis Flood |
| Athlos Leadership Academy | 4427 Chandler | San Antonio, TX | 78222 | 210-278-3883 | 278-3929 | PK-12 | Cheryl Stewart |
| Austin Academy | 621 W Euclid Ave | San Antonio, TX | 78212-5128 | 210-226-5441 | 226-6192 | K-8 | Yolanda Mendoza |
| Austin Achieve Public S | 5908 Manor Rd | Austin, TX | 78723-3631 | 512-522-4190 | 727-3788 | 6-12 | John Armbrust |
| Austin Can Academy Charter S | 2406 Rosewood Ave | Austin, TX | 78702-2408 | 512-477-4226 | 931-8034 | 9-12 | Frank Oakes |
| Austin Discovery S | 8509 FM 969 Ste 200 | Austin, TX | 78724-5771 | 512-674-0700 | 674-3133 | K-8 | Leigh Moss |
| Austin State University Charter S | PO Box 6072 | Nacogdoches, TX | 75962-0001 | 936-468-5899 | 468-7015 | K-5 | Lysa Hagan |
| Baker-Ripley Charter S | 6500 Rookin St | Houston, TX | 77074 | 713-273-3731 | | K-5 | Raquel Sosa-Gonzalez |
| Barkley/Ruiz ES | 1111 S Navidad St | San Antonio, TX | 78207-5813 | 210-978-7940 | 227-4029 | PK-5 | Jackie Ibarra-Lanford |
| BASIS San Antonio Medical Center | 8519 Floyd Curl Dr | San Antonio, TX | 78240 | 210-319-5525 | 877-9214 | 5-12 | Tiffany O'Neill |
| BASIS San Antonio North Central | 318 E Ramsey Rd | San Antonio, TX | 78216 | 210-775-4125 | | 5-9 | Abigail Hasberry |
| Bay Area Charter ES | 2600 Humble Dr | El Lago, TX | 77586-5900 | 281-326-4555 | 326-4888 | PK-5 | Aimee Felchak |
| Bay Area Charter MS | PO Box 2126 | League City, TX | 77574-2126 | 281-332-7788 | 316-8866 | 6-8 | Alton Robinson |
| Beta Academy | 9701 Almeda Genoa Rd | Houston, TX | 77075 | 832-331-2460 | | K-6 | Latisha Andrews |
| Bexar County Academy | 1485 Hillcrest Dr | San Antonio, TX | 78228-3900 | 210-432-8600 | 432-8667 | PK-8 | Linda Sleeper |
| Bonham Academy | 925 S Saint Marys St | San Antonio, TX | 78205-3410 | 210-228-3300 | 223-3899 | K-8 | Will Webber |
| Brazos River Charter S | PO Box 949 | Nemo, TX | 76070-0949 | 254-898-9226 | 898-2297 | K-12 | Bengie Laning |
| Brazos S for Inquiry & Creativity | 1055 W Tidwell | Houston, TX | 77091 | 713-681-1960 | 681-1979 | PK-6 | Tiffany Rock |
| Brazos S for Inquiry & Creativity | 6400 Southwest Fwy Ste S | Houston, TX | 77074 | 713-952-4300 | 952-4305 | PK-8 | Tiffany Rock |
| Brazos S for Inquiry & Creativity | 410 Bethel Ln | Bryan, TX | 77802-1005 | 979-774-5032 | 774-5039 | PK-8 | Christopher Osgood |
| Briarmeadow Charter S | 3601 Dunvale Rd | Houston, TX | 77063-5707 | 713-458-5500 | 458-5506 | PK-8 | Peter Heinze |
| Bright Ideas Charter S | 2507 Central Fwy E | Wichita Falls, TX | 76302-5802 | 940-767-1561 | 767-1904 | K-12 | Lynda Plummer |
| Briscoe ES | 2015 S Flores St | San Antonio, TX | 78204-1990 | 210-228-3305 | 222-0822 | PK-6 | Michelle Hickman |
| Brooks Academy at St. Philip of Jesus | 134 E Lambert St | San Antonio, TX | 78204 | 210-998-4452 | | K-6 | Susan Herrera |
| Brooks Academy of Science & Engineering | 3803 Lyster Rd | San Antonio, TX | 78235-5152 | 210-633-9006 | 633-9990 | 6-12 | Ixchell Gonzalez |
| Brooks Estrella Academy | 8005 Outer Circle Rd | San Antonio, TX | 78235 | 210-257-5175 | | K-6 | Nora Mozingo |
| Brown-Fellowship Leadership Academy | 5701 Red Bird Center Dr | Dallas, TX | 75237-1917 | 972-709-4700 | 635-6635 | 3-8 | Paula Brown |
| Brown-Fellowship Leadership S | 6901 S Westmoreland Rd | Dallas, TX | 75237 | 972-709-4700 | 709-6605 | PK-2 | Paula Brown |
| Brune Charter S | PO Box 399 | Leakey, TX | 78873-0399 | 830-232-7101 | 232-4279 | 1-12 | Albert Hernandez |
| Burch Charter S | 5703 Blanco Rd | San Antonio, TX | 78216-6616 | 210-431-9881 | 432-8467 | 4-6 | Laura Neitzel |
| Burnham ES | 7310 Bishop Flores Dr | El Paso, TX | 79912-1429 | 915-584-9499 | 585-8814 | K-5 | Audrey Shetty |
| Cage ES | 4528 Leeland St | Houston, TX | 77023-3095 | 713-924-1700 | 924-1704 | PK-5 | Jose Covarrubia |
| Cailloux-Najim S | PO Box 609 | Ingram, TX | 78025-0609 | 830-367-6100 | 367-2611 | 1-12 | Maria De La Cruz |
| Calallen Charter HS | 46 Cornett Dr | Corpus Christi, TX | 78410 | 361-242-5980 | 242-5682 | 10-12 | Dr. Janet Cunningham |
| Carpe Deim Charter S | 517 Soledad St | San Antonio, TX | 78205 | 210-718-4172 | | 6-12 | Nick Fleege |
| Carrollton Classical Academy | 2400 N Josey Ln | Carrollton, TX | 75006 | 972-245-2900 | 245-2999 | K-5 | Stephanie Scott |
| Cedar Hill Collegiate HS | 1515 W Belt Line Rd | Cedar Hill, TX | 75104 | 469-272-2021 | 293-2652 | 9-12 | Corey Seymour |
| Cedar Park Charter Academy | 1407 Raider Way | Leander, TX | 78641 | 512-259-2577 | 590-8717 | PK-12 | Michele Kelsay |
| Cedars International Academy | 8416 N Interstate 35 | Austin, TX | 78753-6438 | 512-419-1551 | 419-1581 | PK-8 | Heather Rauls |
| Challenge Early College HS | 5601 West Loop S | Houston, TX | 77081-2221 | 713-664-9712 | 664-9780 | 9-12 | Tonya Miller |
| Champions Academy | 2113 Cypress Landing Dr | Houston, TX | 77090 | 832-446-6762 | | K-5 | Kesha Fomby |
| Chaparral Star Academy | 14046 Summit Dr | Austin, TX | 78728 | 512-989-2672 | 251-9799 | K-12 | Marsha Hagin |
| Chapel Hill Academy | 4640 Sycamore School Rd | Fort Worth, TX | 76133-7356 | 817-289-0242 | 289-3657 | PK-5 | Victoria Sendejo M.Ed. |
| Chavez Academy | 4613 S Padre Island Dr | Corpus Christi, TX | 78411-4413 | 361-561-5651 | 561-5654 | 9-12 | Sandra Valencia |
| Children First Academy of Dallas | 315 E Wheatland Rd | Dallas, TX | 75241-5314 | 214-371-2545 | 371-0283 | PK-7 | Tiffani Mohammad |
| Children First Academy of Houston | 7803 Little York Rd | Houston, TX | 77016-2436 | 713-491-9030 | 491-9032 | PK-7 | |
| City Center Health Careers | 1114 Willow | San Antonio, TX | 78208-1343 | 210-255-8265 | 255-8270 | 6-12 | Michael Moretta |
| Cityscape S | 6211 E Grand Ave | Dallas, TX | 75223 | 214-824-4747 | 824-4447 | PK-5 | Carol Thorne |
| Clay Academy | 3303 Potters House Way | Dallas, TX | 75236-3037 | 214-467-4143 | 467-4143 | K-8 | Ericka Johnson-Allen |
| Clear Horizons Early College HS | 13735 Beamer Rd Box 913 | Houston, TX | 77089 | 281-929-4657 | 284-9960 | 9-12 | Dr. Brett Lemley |
| Clear View Education Center | 400 S Walnut St | Webster, TX | 77598-5120 | 281-284-1500 | 284-1505 | 9-12 | Michael Houston |

| School | Address | City,State | Zip code | Telephone | Fax | Grade | Contact |
|---|---|---|---|---|---|---|---|
| Collegiate HS | 101 Baldwin Blvd | Corpus Christi, TX | 78404-3805 | 361-698-2425 | 698-2427 | 9-12 | Tracie Rodriguez |
| Compass Academy Charter S | 1111 Pagewood Ave | Odessa, TX | 79761 | 432-366-2667 | 332-8667 | PK-12 | Ann Moore |
| Comquest Academy | 207 Peach St | Tomball, TX | 77375-4733 | 281-516-0611 | 516-9807 | 7-12 | Tanis Stanfield |
| C.O.R.E. Academy | 12707 Cullen Blvd | Houston, TX | 77047 | 713-457-2858 | | 3-9 | Nolan Jeffery |
| Corinth Classical Academy | 3600 Meadowview Dr | Corinth, TX | 76210 | 940-497-0148 | | K-7 | Amie Giacumakis |
| Cornerstone Academy | 8655 Emnora | Houston, TX | 77080 | 713-251-1600 | 251-1615 | 6-8 | Jill Wright |
| Corpus Christi College Prep HS | 3501 S Padre Island Dr | Corpus Christi, TX | 78415-2908 | 361-225-4240 | 561-5654 | 9-12 | Stephen Mora |
| Corpus Christi Montessori Charter S | 822 Ayers St | Corpus Christi, TX | 78404 | 361-852-0707 | 653-2340 | PK-8 | Cerise Weeks |
| Cove Charter Academy | 2205 FM 3046 | Copperas Cove, TX | 76522 | 254-238-8231 | 247-3931 | PK-12 | Mark Kelsay |
| Crockett ES | 2112 Crockett St | Houston, TX | 77007 | 713-802-4780 | 802-4783 | PK-5 | Claudia Chavez-Pinto |
| Crosstimbers Academy | PO Box 1327 | Weatherford, TX | 76086-1327 | 817-594-6220 | 594-6227 | 9-12 | Jay Lewis |
| Cumberland Academy | 1340 Shiloh Rd | Tyler, TX | 75703 | 903-581-2890 | 581-1476 | K-5 | Bobby Markle |
| Cumberland Academy HS | 7200 Paluxy Dr | Tyler, TX | 75703 | 903-504-5393 | | 9-12 | Kathy Parker |
| Cumberland Academy MS | 1040 Shiloh Rd | Tyler, TX | 75703 | 903-581-2890 | 581-1476 | 6-8 | Sherrill Echols |
| Dallas Can Academy Carrollton/Farmers | 2720 Hollandale Ln | Farmers Branch, TX | 75234-2035 | 972-243-2178 | 243-2669 | 9-12 | Amparo Hakemack |
| Dallas Can Academy - Grant East | 2901 Morgan Dr | Dallas, TX | 75241 | 972-228-4226 | | 9-12 | Rodney Milliner |
| Dallas Can Academy - Oak Cliff | 325 W 12th St | Dallas, TX | 75208 | 214-943-2244 | 946-4427 | 9-12 | Faustino Rivas |
| Dallas Can Academy - Pleasant Grove | 1227 N Masters Dr | Dallas, TX | 75217-3722 | 972-225-1194 | 225-1164 | 9-12 | Mene Khepera |
| Dallas Can Academy Ross Avenue | 4621 Ross Ave | Dallas, TX | 75204-4994 | 214-824-4226 | 841-7951 | 9-12 | Fernando Vadillo |
| Da Vinci S for Science and the Arts | 785 Southwestern Dr | El Paso, TX | 79912-1240 | 915-584-4024 | 581-9840 | 6-12 | Adeliz Stiles |
| DePelchin - Richmond Campus | 710 S 7th St | Richmond, TX | 77469-3445 | 281-342-4906 | | K-12 | Michael McKenzie |
| Draw Academy | 3920 Stoney Brook Dr | Houston, TX | 77063-6406 | 713-706-3729 | 706-3711 | PK-8 | Patricia Beistegui |
| Early College HS | 3939 Valley View Ln | Farmers Branch, TX | 75244-4906 | 972-968-6200 | 968-6210 | 9-12 | Michael Arreola |
| East Austin College Prep Academy | 6002 Jain Ln | Austin, TX | 78721 | 512-287-5000 | 928-1440 | 2-6 | Francisco Ramirez |
| East Austin College Prep - MLK Campus | 5800 E MLK Blvd | Austin, TX | 78721 | 512-287-5050 | | 7-12 | Dr. Ruben Pena |
| East Early College HS | 220 N Milby St | Houston, TX | 77003-1933 | 713-847-4809 | 847-4813 | 9-12 | Tamera Bolden |
| East Fort Worth Montessori Academy | 501 Oakland Blvd | Fort Worth, TX | 76103-1014 | 817-496-3003 | 496-3004 | PK-5 | Shello Tabb |
| East Texas Charter S Chadwick Campus | 2402 Alpine Rd | Longview, TX | 75601-3407 | 903-753-9400 | 753-0285 | 9-12 | Terry Lapic |
| East Texas Charter S - Nelms Campus | 2402 Alpine Rd | Longview, TX | 75601-3407 | 903-753-9400 | 753-0285 | 7-12 | Terry Lapic |
| Eastwood Academy | 1315 Dumble St | Houston, TX | 77023-1902 | 713-924-1697 | 924-1715 | 9-12 | Paula Fendley |
| Eden Park Academy | 6215 Manchaca Rd Bldg D | Austin, TX | 78745-4927 | 512-383-0613 | 383-0665 | K-6 | Johnnie Smith |
| Education Center International Academy | 302 N Town East Blvd | Sunnyvale, TX | 75182 | 214-628-9152 | 628-9124 | K-8 | Bob Densmore |
| Education Center International Academy | 8200 Schrade Rd | Rowlett, TX | 75088 | 972-412-8080 | 628-9124 | K-8 | Lisa Hiatt |
| Ehrhart S | PO Box 7733 | Beaumont, TX | 77726-7733 | 409-839-8200 | 839-8242 | PK-8 | Dr. Larry Haynes |
| El Paso Academy East | 11000 Argal Ct | El Paso, TX | 79935-3712 | 915-590-8589 | 590-0052 | 9-12 | Lionel Rubio |
| El Paso Academy West | 201 W Redd Rd | El Paso, TX | 79932 | 915-845-7997 | 845-7522 | 9-12 | Toni Kreye |
| El Paso Leadership Academy | 1918 Texas Ave | El Paso, TX | 79901 | 915-298-3900 | | 6-8 | Omar Yanar |
| Energized For Excellence ECC | 7419 Ashcroft Ave | Houston, TX | 77081 | 713-773-3600 | 773-3630 | PK-PK | Ada Cooper |
| Energized For Excellence ES | 6107 Bissonnet St | Houston, TX | 77081 | 713-773-3600 | 773-3630 | K-5 | Jose Cintron |
| Energized for STEM Academy Central | 9220 Jutland Rd | Houston, TX | 77073 | 713-773-3600 | 773-3630 | 9-12 | Dr. Shavon Clark |
| Energized For STEM Academy HS West | 7419 Ashcroft Dr | Houston, TX | 77081 | 713-773-3600 | 773-3630 | 9-12 | Shavon Clark |
| Energized for STEM Academy MS Central | 9220 Jutland Rd | Houston, TX | 77073 | 713-773-3600 | 773-3630 | 6-8 | Adrienne Henderson |
| Energized for STEM Academy West | 6107 Bissonnet | Houston, TX | 77081 | 713-773-3600 | 773-3630 | 6-8 | Ranier Perez |
| Evolution Academy Charter S | 1101 S Sherman St | Richardson, TX | 75081-4852 | 972-907-3755 | 907-3765 | 9-12 | Cynthia Jones Trigg |
| Excel Center | 1015 Norwood Park Blvd | Austin, TX | 78753 | 512-531-5500 | 339-5299 | 9-12 | Dr. Billy Harden |
| Excellence Academy MS | 6107 Bissonnet St | Houston, TX | 77081 | 713-773-3600 | 773-3630 | 6-8 | Arlene Kho |
| Excellence in Leadership Academy | 915 W Expressway 83 | Mission, TX | 78572 | 956-424-9504 | 585-4673 | PK-6 | Elizabeth B. Lopez |
| Fallbrook College Preparatory Academy | 12512 Walters Rd | Houston, TX | 77014-2784 | 281-880-1360 | 880-1362 | K-12 | Tarla Crumb |
| Focus Learning Academy | 2524 W Ledbetter Dr | Dallas, TX | 75233-4018 | 214-467-7751 | 572-9610 | PK-10 | Linus Walton |
| Ford Academy Alameda S for Art & Design | 318 W Houston St | San Antonio, TX | 78205-2427 | 210-226-4031 | 271-0125 | 9-12 | Wayne Boggs |
| Fort Worth Academy of Fine Arts | 3901 S Hulen St | Fort Worth, TX | 76109-3321 | 817-924-1482 | 926-9932 | 3-12 | Craig Schreckengast |
| Fort Worth Can Academy | 4301 Campus Dr | Fort Worth, TX | 76119-5535 | 817-431-4226 | 531-0443 | 9-12 | Ku-Masi Lewis |
| Fort Worth Can Academy South Campus | 1316 E Lancaster Ave | Fort Worth, TX | 76102 | 817-735-1515 | 735-1465 | 9-12 | William Arevelo |
| Founders Classical Academy | 500 Parker Sq | Flower Mound, TX | 75028 | 972-899-2521 | | K-5 | Sam Vanderplas |
| Founders Classical Academy | 790 Windbell Cir | Mesquite, TX | 75149 | 214-444-7255 | | K-8 | Dr. Shannon Nason |
| Founders Classical Academy in Dallas | 8510 Military Pkwy | Dallas, TX | 75227 | 214-238-8948 | | K-12 | John Heitzenrater |
| Founders Classical Academy in Lewisville | 1010 Bellaire Blvd | Lewisville, TX | 75067-5650 | 469-464-3415 | 524-9980 | K-12 | Jason Caros |
| Founders Classical Academy of Leander | 1303 Leander Dr | Leander, TX | 78641 | 512-259-0103 | 532-6503 | K-12 | Kathleen Arnn |
| Frank Inspire Academy | 11216 Bandera Rd | San Antonio, TX | 78249 | 210-638-5900 | | K-8 | Christopher Duke |
| Garza-Gonzales Charter S | 4129 Greenwood Dr | Corpus Christi, TX | 78416-1841 | 361-881-9988 | 881-9994 | PK-12 | Adolfo Chapa |
| Gateway Academy Sierra Vista | 4620 S Lucy | Laredo, TX | 78046 | 956-723-0345 | 712-1112 | 9-12 | Martha Delgado |
| Gateway Academy Townlake | 1230 Townlake Dr | Laredo, TX | 78041-3796 | 956-722-0747 | 722-0767 | 9-12 | Raymundo Gonzalez |
| Gateway Charter Academy | 6103 Houston School Rd | Dallas, TX | 75241-2516 | 214-375-2039 | 375-1842 | PK-12 | Robbie Moore |
| Gateway College Prep S | 3360 Westinghouse Rd | Georgetown, TX | 78626 | 512-868-4947 | 868-4946 | K-12 | Annette Stevenson |
| Gateway Tech HS | 2951 Williams Dr | Georgetown, TX | 78628-2701 | 512-868-5299 | 868-3744 | 9-12 | Annette Stevenson |
| GCCLR Institute of Technology | 4125 Greenwood Dr | Corpus Christi, TX | 78416 | 361-881-9988 | 814-1687 | PK-12 | Adolfo Chapa |
| Georgetown Charter Academy | 302 Serenada Dr | Georgetown, TX | 78628 | 512-863-9236 | 863-9290 | PK-12 | Josiah Perkins |
| Gervin Academy | 6944 S Sunbelt Dr | San Antonio, TX | 78218-3335 | 210-568-8800 | 568-8897 | PK-12 | Jesse Villanueva M.Ed. |
| Gervin Technology Center | 3030 E Commerce St | San Antonio, TX | 78220-1013 | 210-587-3576 | 587-3587 | 10-12 | Dorothy Wendorf |
| Golden Rule Charter S Cockrell Hill | 2602 W Illinois Ave | Dallas, TX | 75233-1002 | 214-333-9330 | 333-9325 | PK-8 | Irma Pizarro |
| Golden Rule Charter S DeSoto | 135 W Wintergreen Rd | DeSoto, TX | 75115 | 469-248-4463 | 248-4471 | PK-5 | Patricia Fergerson |
| Golden Rule Charter S Grand Prairie | 1729 Avenue B | Grand Prairie, TX | 75051-3416 | 214-333-9330 | 333-9325 | PK-6 | |
| Golden Rule Charter S Oak Cliff | 2602 W Illinois Ave | Dallas, TX | 75233-1002 | 214-333-9330 | 333-9325 | PK-12 | Vicente Delgado |
| Golden Rule Charter S Pleasant Grove | 2602 W Illinois Ave | Dallas, TX | 75233 | 214-333-9330 | 333-9325 | PK-4 | Vashti Gonzalez |
| GPISD Uplift at Lee ES | 401 E Grand Prairie Rd | Grand Prairie, TX | 75051 | 972-262-6785 | | K-2 | Dani Erbert |
| Grand Prairie Collegiate Institute | 401 E Grand Prairie Rd | Grand Prairie, TX | 75051 | 972-343-3120 | 343-3159 | 6-12 | Jennifer Ellison |
| Grand Preparatory S | 122 NE 2nd St | Grand Prairie, TX | 75050 | 972-854-0600 | | K-7 | Karen Salerno |
| Great Hearts Irving | 3350 W Story Rd | Irving, TX | 75038 | 469-759-3030 | | K-7 | Bryan Smith |
| Great Hearts Monte Vista | 319 E Mulberry Ave | San Antonio, TX | 78212 | 210-888-9485 | | 6-9 | Peter Crawford |
| Great Hearts Monte Vista South | 211 Belknap Pl | San Antonio, TX | 78212 | 210-888-9485 | | K-5 | Peter Crawford |
| Great Hearts Northern Oaks | 17223 Jones Maltsberger Rd | San Antonio, TX | 78247 | 210-888-9843 | | K-7 | Andrew Shivone |
| Hampton Preparatory S | 8915 S Hampton Rd | Dallas, TX | 75232-6002 | 972-421-1982 | 421-1986 | K-12 | Karen Salerno |
| Harlingen Leadership Academy | 4501 W Expressway 83 | Harlingen, TX | 78552-3604 | 956-364-2456 | 364-2453 | PK-5 | Cindy Sadler |
| Harmony S of Achievement | 16209 Kieth Harrow Blvd | Houston, TX | 77084 | 281-855-2500 | 656-8525 | K-5 | Melissa Knight |
| Harmony S of Advancement | 3171 N Sam Houston Pkwy W | Houston, TX | 77038-1219 | 281-741-8899 | 741-8006 | 9-12 | |
| Harmony S of Business-Dallas | 8080 President George Bush | Dallas, TX | 75252 | 214-321-0100 | 919-4352 | K-12 | |
| Harmony S of Discovery | 6270 Barker Cypress Rd | Houston, TX | 77084 | 281-861-5105 | 656-8525 | K-10 | Adnan Karanci |
| Harmony S of Excellence | 2015 SW Loop 410 | San Antonio, TX | 78227 | 210-645-7166 | 645-7178 | K-12 | Bambi Teaff |
| Harmony School of Excellence | 7340 Gessner Rd | Houston, TX | 77040-3144 | 713-983-8668 | 983-8667 | K-12 | Hasan Sazci |
| Harmony S of Excellence - Austin | 2100 E Saint Elmo Rd | Austin, TX | 78744-1050 | 512-693-0000 | 693-0008 | K-12 | Halit Eerogku |
| Harmony S of Excellence - Dallas | 1024 W Rosemeade Pkwy | Carrollton, TX | 75007 | 469-892-5556 | 892-5667 | 6-12 | |
| Harmony S of Excellence-Endeavor | 5668 W Little York Rd | Houston, TX | 77091 | 281-999-8400 | 999-8404 | K-12 | Kamil Yilmaz |
| Harmony S of Exploration | 9305 W Sam Houston Pkwy S | Houston, TX | 77099-5204 | 713-831-7406 | 831-7408 | K-3 | Ilker Fidan |
| Harmony S of Fine Arts and Technology | 9115 Kirby Dr | Houston, TX | 77054-2505 | 832-433-7001 | 433-7083 | K-9 | Bulent Coban |
| Harmony S of Ingenuity | 10555 Stella Link Rd | Houston, TX | 77025-5631 | 713-664-1020 | 664-1025 | K-12 | Edib Ercetin |
| Harmony S of Innovation | 9421 W Sam Houston Pkwy S | Houston, TX | 77099-1898 | 713-541-3030 | 541-3032 | PK-8 | |
| Harmony S of Innovation - Austin | 2124 E St Elmo Rd | Austin, TX | 78744 | 512-300-0895 | 330-4225 | K-5 | Talitha Alexander |
| Harmony S of Innovation - Dallas | 1024 W Rosemeade Pkwy | Carrollton, TX | 75007-6250 | 469-892-5556 | 892-5667 | K-12 | Eljasa Jasar |
| Harmony S of Innovation - El Paso | 5210 Fairbanks Dr | El Paso, TX | 79924-3907 | 915-757-2929 | 757-2202 | K-12 | Guvanch Atamyradov |
| Harmony S of Innovation - Euless | 701 S Industrial Blvd # 115 | Euless, TX | 76040 | 817-354-3000 | 354-3008 | K-4 | Serena Jackson |
| Harmony S of Innovation-Fort Worth | 8100 S Hulen St | Fort Worth, TX | 76123-2764 | 817-386-5505 | 977-1727 | 6-12 | Serkan Kilic |
| Harmony S of Innovation - Garland | 2302 Firewheel Pkwy | Garland, TX | 75040 | 972-212-4777 | 212-4778 | 6-12 | |
| Harmony S of Innovation-Laredo | 4608 Daugherty Ave | Laredo, TX | 78041 | 956-568-9495 | 568-9490 | K-12 | |
| Harmony S of Innovation - San Antonio | 8125 Glen Mont | San Antonio, TX | 78239-3499 | 210-265-1715 | 265-5364 | K-8 | |
| Harmony S of Nature & Athletics | 8120 W Camp Wisdom Rd | Dallas, TX | 75249 | 972-296-1000 | 296-2125 | K-12 | Bilal Ozen |
| Harmony S of Political Science | 13415 Ranch Road 620 N | Austin, TX | 78717-1020 | 512-284-9880 | 284-9632 | K-8 | Ednan Karanci |
| Harmony S of Science | 13415 W Bellfort Ave | Sugar Land, TX | 77478-3184 | 713-265-2525 | 265-2565 | PK-6 | |
| Harmony S of Science HS | 13522 W Airport Blvd | Sugar Land, TX | 77498-6313 | 281-302-6445 | 302-6745 | 9-12 | Huseyin Sari |
| Harmony Science Academy | 5435 S Braeswood Blvd | Houston, TX | 77096-4001 | 713-729-4400 | 729-6600 | K-8 | Emrullah Eraslan |
| Harmony Science Academy - Austin | 930 E Rundberg Ln | Austin, TX | 78753-4826 | 512-835-7900 | 835-7901 | 6-12 | Gina Gregory |
| Harmony Science Academy - Austin | 11800 Stonehollow Dr # 100 | Austin, TX | 78758 | 512-821-1700 | 821-1702 | K-8 | Celal Keskin |
| Harmony Science Academy - Beaumont | 4055 Calder Ave | Beaumont, TX | 77706-4925 | 409-838-4000 | 838-4009 | PK-12 | |
| Harmony Science Academy - Brownsville | 1124 Central Blvd | Brownsville, TX | 78520 | 956-574-9555 | 574-9558 | PK-12 | |
| Harmony Science Academy - Bryan | 2031 S Texas Ave | Bryan, TX | 77802-1834 | 979-779-2100 | 779-2110 | PK-8 | Mehmet Uguz |
| Harmony Science Academy - Dallas | 12005 Forestgate Dr | Dallas, TX | 75243-5442 | 214-954-7277 | 954-7993 | PK-12 | Fatih Ay |
| Harmony Science Academy - El Paso | 9405 Betel Dr | El Paso, TX | 79907-3457 | 915-859-4620 | 859-4630 | K-12 | Selcuk Bakir |
| Harmony Science Academy - Euless | 701 S Industrial Blvd # 115 | Euless, TX | 76040 | 817-354-3000 | 354-3008 | 5-12 | Mert Aykanat M.Ed. |
| Harmony Science Academy - Fort Worth | 5651 Westcreek Dr | Fort Worth, TX | 76133-2248 | 817-263-0700 | 263-0705 | K-12 | Angela Knapp |
| Harmony Science Academy - Garland | 2302 Firewheel Pkwy | Garland, TX | 75040 | 972-212-4777 | 212-4778 | K-5 | Christy Drekaj |
| Harmony Science Academy - Grand Prairie | 1102 NW 7th St | Grand Prairie, TX | 75050 | 972-642-9911 | 642-9922 | K-12 | Agil Sharifov |
| Harmony Science Academy HS | 9431 W Sam Houston Pkwy S | Houston, TX | 77099 | 713-492-0214 | 640-5581 | 9-12 | |
| Harmony Science Academy - Houston NW | 16200 State Highway 249 | Houston, TX | 77086-1014 | 281-444-1555 | 444-1015 | K-8 | Sezgin Aydi |
| Harmony Science Academy - Laredo | 4401 San Francisco Ave | Laredo, TX | 78041-4663 | 956-712-1177 | 712-1188 | K-12 | Mustafa Ayik |
| Harmony Science Academy - Lubbock | 1516 53rd St | Lubbock, TX | 79412-2916 | 806-747-1000 | 747-1005 | K-12 | Mehmet Bayar |
| Harmony Science Academy - North Austin | 1421 Wells Branch Pkwy #200 | Pflugerville, TX | 78660 | 512-251-5000 | 251-5001 | 6-12 | Fr. Bunyamin Bozdogan |
| Harmony Science Academy - Odessa | 2755 N Grandview Ave | Odessa, TX | 79762 | 432-363-6000 | 363-6001 | K-12 | Cetin Demir |
| Harmony Science Academy - San Antonio | 8505 Lakeside Pkwy | San Antonio, TX | 78245-2481 | 210-674-7788 | 674-7766 | K-12 | Irfan Turk |

| School | Address | City,State | Zip code | Telephone | Fax | Grade | Contact |
|---|---|---|---|---|---|---|---|
| Harmony Science Academy - Waco | 1900 N Valley Mills Dr | Waco, TX | 76710-2559 | 254-751-7878 | 751-7877 | K-12 | Serkan Beyhan |
| Harmony Science Academy - West Houston | 22400 Grand Corner Dr | Katy, TX | 77494-5718 | 832-437-3926 | 437-3927 | K-12 | |
| Harris MS | 325 Pruitt Ave | San Antonio, TX | 78204-2598 | 210-228-1220 | 226-9448 | 6-8 | Dr. Carol Velazquez |
| Harvest Preparatory Academy | 17770 Imperial Valley Dr | Houston, TX | 77060 | 832-446-3138 | 446-6362 | K-6 | Darlene Breaux |
| Hawthorne Academy | 115 W Josephine St | San Antonio, TX | 78212-4125 | 210-738-9795 | 733-1495 | PK-8 | Guadalupe Rodriguez |
| Heights Preparatory Charter S | 2650 Canada Dr | Dallas, TX | 75212 | 214-442-7094 | 442-7099 | K-12 | Andrew Baca |
| Helping Hands Charter S | 2200 E 6th St | Austin, TX | 78702 | 512-538-0177 | 232-9177 | K-7 | Holly Engleman |
| Higgs Carter King Gifted & Talented S | 511 Fredericksburg Rd | San Antonio, TX | 78201-6344 | 210-735-2341 | 733-6434 | PK-12 | Claudette Yarbrough |
| Highland Heights ES | 865 Paul Quinn St | Houston, TX | 77091-4154 | 713-696-2920 | 696-2922 | PK-5 | Geraldine Cox |
| Highland Park ES | 635 Rigsby Ave | San Antonio, TX | 78210-3099 | 210-228-3335 | 533-8132 | PK-5 | Joseph Cerna |
| Highland Park Gifted & Talented Academy | 901 E Drexel Ave | San Antonio, TX | 78210 | 210-293-4206 | 532-3810 | PK-6 | Martha Kizer |
| High Point Academy | 1256 Jim Wright Fwy | Wht Settlemt, TX | 76108 | 817-600-6401 | | K-8 | Katie Stellar |
| Hope Academy Charter S | 3015 N MacGregor Way | Houston, TX | 77004 | 832-217-3240 | 349-2054 | 9-12 | Jerome Washington |
| Hope S | 2849 9th Ave | Port Arthur, TX | 77642-3961 | 409-983-3244 | 983-6408 | 6-12 | Bobby Lopez |
| Horizon Montessori III - Harlingen | 801 N 13th St Ste 5 | Harlingen, TX | 78550 | 956-423-8200 | 423-8207 | PK-7 | Dr. Ronaldo Chavez |
| Horizon Montessori II - Weslaco | 1222 W Sugar Cane Dr | Weslaco, TX | 78599 | 956-969-0044 | 969-0065 | PK-8 | Valerie Uresti-Reyes |
| Horizon Montessori I - Mc Allen | 221 N Main St | McAllen, TX | 78501 | 956-668-1400 | 668-1404 | PK-8 | Dr. Esperanza Zendejas |
| Houston Acad for International Studies | 1810 Stuart St | Houston, TX | 77004-3043 | 713-942-1430 | 942-1433 | 9-12 | Melissa Jacobs |
| Houston Can Academy - Hobby | 9020 Gulf Fwy | Houston, TX | 77017-7007 | 832-379-4226 | 944-6736 | 9-12 | Dr. James Troutman |
| Houston Can Academy - North | 3401 Hardy St | Houston, TX | 77009 | 713-659-4226 | 651-1493 | 9-12 | Roslyn Philpott |
| Houston Gateway Acad - Elite Coll Prep | 7310 Bowie St | Houston, TX | 77012 | 832-649-2700 | 649-3092 | PK-8 | Tiffany Wright |
| Houston Gateway Academy - Coral Campus | 1020 Coral St | Houston, TX | 77012 | 832-649-2700 | 649-3092 | PK-12 | Ignacio Arroyo |
| Houston Gateway Academy - Evergreen | 3400 Evergreen Dr | Houston, TX | 77087-3715 | 713-644-8292 | 649-3092 | PK-8 | Yuridia Lubiano |
| Houston Heights HS | 1125 Lawrence St | Houston, TX | 77008-6651 | 713-868-9797 | 868-9750 | 9-12 | Richard Mik |
| Houston Heights Learning Academy | 902 W 8th St | Houston, TX | 77007-1408 | 713-869-9453 | 869-0785 | PK-5 | Yvette East |
| Huston Academy | 680 Peach Orchard Rd | Stephenville, TX | 76401 | 254-965-8883 | 965-8654 | 7-12 | Carol Taylor |
| IDEA Academy Alamo | 325 State Highway 495 | Alamo, TX | 78516 | 956-588-4005 | 588-4006 | K-5 | Ana Garza |
| IDEA Academy Allan | 1701 Vargas Rd | Austin, TX | 78741 | 512-646-2800 | 646-2801 | PK-9 | Robert Acosta |
| IDEA Academy Brownsville | 4395 Paredes Line Rd | Brownsville, TX | 78526-1296 | 956-832-5150 | 832-5716 | K-5 | Erica Matamoros |
| IDEA Academy Carver | 217 Robinson Pl | San Antonio, TX | 78202 | 210-223-8885 | 223-8970 | K-5 | Guadalupe Diaz |
| IDEA Academy Donna | 401 S 1st St | Donna, TX | 78537-3055 | 956-464-0203 | 464-8532 | PK-5 | Rebecca Saldana |
| IDEA Academy Eastside | 2519 Martin Luther King Dr | San Antonio, TX | 78220 | 210-239-4800 | 239-4801 | K-6 | Myrla Feria |
| IDEA Academy Edinburg | 2553 N Roegiers Rd | Edinburg, TX | 78541-8602 | 956-287-6100 | 287-6101 | PK-5 | Nora Perez |
| IDEA Academy Frontier | 2800 S Dakota Ave | Brownsville, TX | 78521-6133 | 956-541-2002 | 541-5561 | K-5 | Dora Villegas |
| IDEA Academy McAllen | 201 N Bentsen Rd | McAllen, TX | 78501-8297 | 956-429-4100 | 429-4126 | K-5 | Cassandra Flores |
| IDEA Academy Mission | 1600 S Schuerbach Rd | Mission, TX | 78572-1217 | 956-583-8315 | 424-3248 | K-5 | Marissa Falcon |
| IDEA Academy Monterrey Park | 222 SW 39th St | San Antonio, TX | 78237 | 210-239-4200 | | K-3 | Martha Short |
| IDEA Academy North Mission | 201 N Bentsen Rd | McAllen, TX | 78501 | 956-424-4300 | | K-6 | Adriana Villarreal |
| IDEA Academy Pharr | 600 E Las Milpas Rd | Pharr, TX | 78577 | 956-283-1515 | 783-1557 | PK-5 | Sonia Aguilar |
| IDEA Academy Riverview | 30 Palm Blvd | Brownsville, TX | 78537 | 956-832-5900 | | PK-6 | Radha Guajardo |
| IDEA Academy Rundberg | 9504 N IH 35 | Austin, TX | 78753 | 512-822-4800 | | K-6 | Karen Weissinger |
| IDEA Academy San Benito | 2151 Russell Ln | San Benito, TX | 78586 | 956-399-5252 | 361-9478 | K-5 | Tricia Noyola |
| IDEA Academy San Juan | 200 N Nebraska Ave | San Juan, TX | 78589 | 956-702-5150 | 702-4497 | K-5 | Michael Wagner |
| IDEA Academy South Flores | 6919 S Flores St | San Antonio, TX | 78221 | 210-239-4150 | | K-5 | Hailey McCarthy |
| IDEA Academy Walzem | 6445 Walzem Rd | San Antonio, TX | 78239 | 210-239-4600 | | K-3 | Evan Yates |
| IDEA Academy Weslaco | 2931 E Sugar Cane Dr | Weslaco, TX | 78599-2723 | 956-351-4100 | 351-4101 | K-5 | Jayne Pocquette |
| IDEA Academy Weslaco Pike | 1000 E Pike Blvd | Weslaco, TX | 78596 | 956-351-4850 | 351-4851 | K-3 | Silvia Martinez |
| IDEA College Prep Alamo | 325 State Highway 495 | Alamo, TX | 78516-6877 | 956-588-4005 | 588-4006 | 6-12 | Israel Ybarra |
| IDEA College Prep Allan | 220 Foremost Dr | Austin, TX | 78745-7324 | 512-646-2800 | 646-2801 | 6-12 | Steve Mudd |
| IDEA College Prep Brownsville | 4395 Paredes Line Rd | Brownsville, TX | 78526 | 956-832-5150 | 832-5716 | 6-12 | Erica Matamoros |
| IDEA College Prep Carver | 217 Robinson Pl | San Antonio, TX | 78202 | 210-223-8885 | 223-8970 | 6-12 | Chang John Yu |
| IDEA College Prep Donna | 401 S 1st St | Donna, TX | 78537-3055 | 956-464-0203 | 464-8532 | 6-12 | Christina Escamilla |
| IDEA College Prep Edinburg | 2553 N Roegiers Rd | Edinburg, TX | 78541 | 956-287-6100 | 287-6101 | 6-12 | Ramiro Gomez |
| IDEA College Prep Frontier | 2800 S Dakota Ave | Brownsville, TX | 78521 | 956-541-2002 | 541-5561 | 6-12 | Alex Anzaldua |
| IDEA College Prep McAllen | 201 N Bentsen Rd | McAllen, TX | 78501-8297 | 956-429-4100 | 429-4126 | 6-12 | Jon Alvarez |
| IDEA College Prep Mission | 1600 S Schuerbach Rd | Mission, TX | 78572-1217 | 956-583-8315 | 424-3248 | 6-12 | Yvonne Anglada |
| IDEA College Prep Monterrey Park | 222 SW 39th St | San Antonio, TX | 78237 | 210-239-4200 | | 6-6 | Curtis Lawrence |
| IDEA College Prep Pharr | 600 E Las Milpas Rd | Pharr, TX | 78577 | 956-283-1515 | 783-1557 | 6-12 | Claudia Ash |
| IDEA College Prep San Benito | 2151 Russell Ln | San Benito, TX | 78586-8969 | 956-399-5252 | 361-9478 | 6-12 | Joel Garcia |
| IDEA College Prep San Juan | 600 E Sioux Rd | San Juan, TX | 78589-3491 | 956-588-4021 | 588-4030 | 6-12 | Andrea Lopez |
| IDEA College Prep South Flores | 6919 S Flores St | San Antonio, TX | 78221 | 210-239-4150 | | 6-8 | Constantine Polites |
| IDEA College Prep Walzem | 8750 Fourwinds Dr | San Antonio, TX | 78239 | 210-239-4600 | | 6-6 | Dr. Khalil Graham |
| IDEA College Prep Weslaco | 2931 E Sugar Cane Dr | Weslaco, TX | 78599 | 956-351-4100 | 351-4101 | 6-12 | Diana Wagner |
| IDEA College Prep Weslaco Pike | 1000 E Pike Blvd | Weslaco, TX | 78596 | 956-351-4850 | 351-4851 | 6-6 | Nate Lowry |
| IDEA Quest Academy | 14001 N Rooth Rd | Edinburg, TX | 78541-4194 | 956-287-1003 | 287-2737 | K-5 | Rosa Chapa |
| IDEA Quest College Prep S | 14001 N Rooth Rd | Edinburg, TX | 78541-4194 | 956-287-1003 | 287-2737 | 6-12 | Jose De Leon |
| Ignite Charter S | 1205 S 7th St | Raymondville, TX | 78580 | 956-689-3300 | 292-0371 | PK-12 | Daniel Flores |
| Ignite Charter S | 1352 E 1st St | Mission, TX | 78572 | 956-519-2227 | 687-6062 | PK-12 | Alicia Garza |
| Ignite Charter S | 4737 S Sugar Rd | Edinburg, TX | 78539 | 956-380-6616 | 292-0371 | PK-12 | Manuel Ochoa |
| Ignite Charter S | 615 S International Blvd | Weslaco, TX | 78596 | 956-969-2600 | 969-1191 | PK-12 | Fernando Hinojosa |
| Ignite Charter S | 508 E Elizabeth St | Brownsville, TX | 78520 | 956-542-3363 | 542-3139 | PK-12 | Carrie Nance |
| Ignite Charter S | 5324 E US Highway 83 | Rio Grande City, TX | 78582 | 956-488-8883 | 292-0371 | PK-12 | Daniel Vasquez |
| Imagine International Academy | 2860 Virginia Pkwy | Mc Kinney, TX | 75071-3444 | 214-491-1500 | 491-1504 | K-12 | Julia Brady |
| Infinity Preparatory S | 1401 S MacArthur Blvd | Irving, TX | 75060-5848 | 469-621-9200 | | K-8 | Priscilla Pharms |
| Innovation Academy | 3900 University Blvd | Tyler, TX | 75799 | 903-730-3988 | | 3-9 | Aimee Dennis |
| Innovation Academy | 3201 N Eastman Rd | Longview, TX | 75605 | 903-686-0018 | 617-6814 | 3-8 | Angela Ladine |
| Innovation Academy | 1820 W Spring St | Palestine, TX | 75803 | 903-480-4070 | 480-4070 | 3-8 | Becky Rutledge |
| Inspired for Excellence Academy West | 9220 Jutland Rd | Houston, TX | 77033 | 713-641-1630 | 641-1669 | 5-8 | Leatha Gilmore |
| Inspired Vision Academy MSHS | 8501 Bruton Rd | Dallas, TX | 75217-1909 | 972-285-5758 | 285-0061 | 6-10 | Lucy Simpkins |
| Inspired Vision Charter ES | 8421 Bohannon Dr | Dallas, TX | 75217-1917 | 214-391-7964 | 391-7954 | PK-6 | Lana Sprayberry-King |
| International Leadership of Texas ES | 3301 N Shiloh Rd | Garland, TX | 75044 | 972-414-8000 | | K-5 | Irene Aguilar |
| International Leadership of Texas ES | 4950 S Bowen Rd | Arlington, TX | 76017 | 817-496-0400 | | K-5 | Antonio Verduzco |
| International Leadership of Texas HS | 4413 N Shiloh Rd | Garland, TX | 75044 | 972-414-3414 | | 9-12 | Anthony Palagonia |
| International Leadership of Texas HS | 2350 E Mayfield Rd | Arlington, TX | 76014 | 817-414-3414 | | 9-12 | Daniel Mendoza |
| International Leadership of Texas-Keller | 4201 Heritage Trace Pkwy | Fort Worth, TX | 76244 | 817-431-5135 | | 9-12 | Rodney Cooksy |
| International Leadership of Texas-Keller | 2301 Heritage Trace Pkwy | Fort Worth, TX | 76177 | 817-665-0646 | 232-8220 | K-8 | Pete Chapasko |
| International Leadership of Texas MS | 3301 N Shiloh Rd | Garland, TX | 75044 | 972-414-8000 | | 6-8 | Irene Aguilar |
| International Leadership of Texas MS | 4950 S Bowen Rd | Arlington, TX | 76017 | 817-419-9281 | | 6-8 | Antonio Verduzco |
| Irving MS | 1300 Delgado St | San Antonio, TX | 78207-1467 | 210-738-9740 | 734-0941 | 6-8 | Lanor Cantu |
| iSchoolHigh Amarillo | 6000 S Georgia St | Amarillo, TX | 79118 | 806-352-0171 | 397-5456 | 9-12 | |
| iSchool High at the Woodlands | 3232 College Park Dr | The Woodlands, TX | 77384 | 936-231-8594 | 861-3810 | 9-12 | |
| iSchoolHigh Hickory Creek | 800 Point Vista Rd Ste 518 | Hickory Creek, TX | 75065 | 940-247-2777 | | 9-12 | Aaron Wimberly |
| iSchool STEM | 1800 Lakeway Dr Ste 100 | Lewisville, TX | 75057-6438 | 972-317-2470 | 397-1633 | 9-12 | Stephanie Scott |
| iSchool University Park | 20515 State Highway 249 | Houston, TX | 77070-2764 | 281-251-5770 | 643-9673 | 9-12 | Mike Laird |
| Kandy Stripe Academy | 8701 Delilah St | Houston, TX | 77033 | 713-734-4909 | 731-7890 | PK-8 | Cassandra Anderson |
| Kelley Charter S | 802 Oblate Dr | San Antonio, TX | 78216-7330 | 210-431-9881 | 432-8467 | PK-3 | Ian Grice M.Ed. |
| KI Charter Academy | 120 Bert Brown St | San Marcos, TX | 78666 | 512-396-8500 | 754-3894 | 1-12 | Jerry Lager |
| Killeen Charter Academy | 3209 Atkinson | Killeen, TX | 76543 | 254-245-9787 | 213-5196 | PK-12 | Berkiesha Scott |
| King Academy | 3501 Martin Luther King Dr | San Antonio, TX | 78220-2325 | 210-978-7935 | 223-6907 | K-8 | Natasha Pinnix |
| Kingsway Leadership Academy | 1727 Senator Carlos Truan | Kingsville, TX | 78363 | 210-221-2591 | 221-2594 | PK-8 | Noemy Garcia |
| KIPP 3D Academy | 500 Tidwell Rd | Houston, TX | 77022 | 832-230-0566 | | 5-8 | Alison Cumbley |
| KIPP Academy MS | 10711 Kipp Way Dr | Houston, TX | 77099-2675 | 832-328-1051 | 328-0178 | 5-8 | Andrew Rubin |
| KIPP Academy MS West | 8500 Highway 6 S | Houston, TX | 77083 | 832-840-4693 | | 5-8 | Steven Khadam-Hir |
| KIPP Aspire Academy | 735 Fredericksburg Rd | San Antonio, TX | 78201-6348 | 210-735-7300 | 735-7305 | 5-8 | Roy Feliciano |
| KIPP Austin Academy of Arts & Letters | 8509 FM 969 Ste A | Austin, TX | 78724-5702 | 512-501-3640 | 501-3641 | 5-8 | Kevin Newman |
| KIPP Austin Beacon Prep | 5107 I-35 S Ste A | Austin, TX | 78744 | 512-651-1918 | 924-2872 | 5-8 | Katie Hayes |
| KIPP Austin College Prep S | 8509 FM 969 Ste 627 | Austin, TX | 78724 | 512-637-6870 | 637-6899 | 5-8 | Katie Shapiro |
| KIPP Austin Collegiate | 8509 FM 969 Ste 676 | Austin, TX | 78724-5701 | 512-501-3586 | 501-3587 | 9-12 | Carrie Donovan |
| KIPP Austin Comunidad | 8509 FM 969 Ste 628 | Austin, TX | 78724 | 512-501-3911 | 870-9224 | K-4 | Justin Scott |
| KIPP Austin Connections | 8509 FM 969 Ste 629 | Austin, TX | 78724 | 512-651-5537 | 870-9537 | K-4 | Bethany Blevins |
| KIPP Austin Leadership Elementary | 5107 I-35 S Ste A | Austin, TX | 78744 | 512-651-2168 | | K-4 | |
| KIPP Austin Obras | 5107 I-35 S Ste A | Austin, TX | 78744 | 512-651-2069 | | K-4 | |
| KIPP Austin Vista MS | 5107 I-35 S Ste A | Austin, TX | 78744 | 512-651-1921 | 461-8086 | 5-8 | Laura Farber |
| KIPP Camino Academy | 4343 W Commerce St | San Antonio, TX | 78237 | 210-829-4200 | | 5-8 | Bradley Tarrance |
| KIPP Coastal Village ES | 721 10th St | Galveston, TX | 77550 | 409-761-6800 | 765-5674 | PK-4 | Cherie Spencer |
| KIPP Coastal Village MS | 1110 21st St | Galveston, TX | 77550 | 409-761-6900 | | 5-8 | Robert Balshaw |
| KIPP CONNECT PS | 6700 Bellaire Blvd | Houston, TX | 77074 | 281-879-3023 | | PK-4 | Adam Kutac |
| KIPP Destiny ES | 3663 W Camp Wisdom Rd | Dallas, TX | 75237 | 972-708-8500 | | K-4 | Katie Gilleland |
| KIPP Destiny MS | 3663 W Camp Wisdom Rd | Dallas, TX | 75237 | 972-708-8500 | | 5-8 | Esmeralda Cardoso |
| KIPP DREAM Prep | 500 Tidwell Rd | Houston, TX | 77022 | 832-230-6082 | | PK-4 | Celeste Barretto |
| KIPP Esperanza Dual Language Academy | 103 Tuleta Dr | San Antonio, TX | 78212 | 210-317-2731 | | K-K | Michael Shay |
| KIPP Explore Academy | 5402 Lawndale St | Houston, TX | 77023 | 832-230-0547 | 924-5046 | PK-5 | Frank Cush |
| KIPP Generations Collegiate | 500 Tidwell Rd | Houston, TX | 77022 | 832-230-0566 | 328-0178 | 9-12 | Nancy Flores |
| KIPP Houston HS | 10711 Kipp Way Dr | Houston, TX | 77099-2675 | 832-328-1082 | 838-4293 | 9-12 | Lara Wheatley |
| KIPP Intrepid Preparatory S | 5402 Lawndale St | Houston, TX | 77023 | 281-879-3100 | 463-7318 | 6-8 | Susan Shenker |
| KIPP Legacy Preparatory S | 9606 Mesa Dr | Houston, TX | 77078 | 832-230-0567 | 491-7311 | PK-3 | Monique Payton |
| KIPP Liberation College Preparatory S | 5400 Martin Luther King Jr | Houston, TX | 77021 | 832-230-0565 | 842-6689 | 5-8 | Tai Ingram |

| School | Address | City,State | Zip code | Telephone | Fax | Grade | Contact |
|---|---|---|---|---|---|---|---|
| KIPP Northeast College Preparatory | 9680 Mesa Dr | Houston, TX | 77078 | 832-230-0567 | | 9-12 | Gillian Quinn-Pineda |
| KIPP PEACE ES | 5400 Martin Luther King Jr | Houston, TX | 77021 | 832-230-0564 | | PK-4 | Lisa Williams |
| KIPP Poder Academy | 128 S Audobon | San Antonio, TX | 78212 | 210-888-6513 | 888-6515 | 5-5 | Rachel Obermeier |
| KIPP Polaris Academy for Boys | 9636 Mesa Dr | Houston, TX | 77078 | 832-230-0567 | 633-4783 | 5-8 | Aaron Green |
| KIPP SHARP College Preparatory Lower S | 8430 Westglen Dr | Houston, TX | 77063 | 281-879-3000 | 915-0074 | PK-4 | Michelle Bennett |
| KIPP Sharpstown College Prep | 8440 Westpark Dr | Houston, TX | 77063-5808 | 281-879-3005 | 915-0074 | 5-8 | Karima Wilson |
| KIPP Shine Prep | 10711 Kipp Way Dr | Houston, TX | 77099-2675 | 832-328-1051 | 328-0178 | PK-5 | Deborah Shifrine |
| KIPP Spirit College Preparatory S | 11000 Scott St | Houston, TX | 77047 | 832-230-0562 | 731-1644 | 5-8 | Shequelle Foster-Gims |
| KIPP Sunnyside HS | 11000 Scott St | Houston, TX | 77047 | 832-230-0562 | 230-0570 | 9-12 | Lisa McClinton |
| KIPP Truth Academy | 3200 S Lancaster Rd # 230A | Dallas, TX | 75216 | 214-375-8326 | 375-2990 | 4-8 | Michael Horne |
| KIPP Truth ES | 3663 W Camp Wisdom Rd | Dallas, TX | 75237 | 214-893-4377 | | K-4 | Katie Hill |
| KIPP Unity PS | 8500 Highway 6 S | Houston, TX | 77083 | 832-230-0572 | | PK-4 | Kaleena Rosenbauer |
| KIPP University Prep HS | 4343 W Commerce St | San Antonio, TX | 78237 | 210-290-8720 | 290-9427 | 9-12 | Abbey Morton-Garland |
| KIPP Un Mundo Dual Language Academy | 4343 W Commerce St | San Antonio, TX | 78237 | 210-824-1905 | 485-1393 | K-2 | Nancy Ocasio |
| KIPP Voyage Academy for Girls | 9616 Mesa Dr | Houston, TX | 77078 | 832-230-0567 | 491-7311 | 5-8 | Tasha Ginn |
| KIPP ZENITH Academy | 11000 Scott St | Houston, TX | 77047 | 832-230-0562 | | PK-4 | Tiffany George Prados |
| Kolitz Academy | 12500 NW Military Hwy | San Antonio, TX | 78231 | 210-302-6900 | 302-6913 | K-8 | Kathryn Davis |
| Kometzky S | 1515A Grove Blvd | Austin, TX | 78741 | 512-471-5280 | 232-9177 | PK-12 | Christee Jackson |
| La Academia de Estrellas | 111 S Beckley Ave | Dallas, TX | 75203-2610 | 214-946-8908 | 946-8777 | PK-8 | Lorraine Mantei M.Ed. |
| La Amistad Love & Learning Academy | 10860 Rockley Rd | Houston, TX | 77099 | 281-988-9201 | 988-9201 | PK-1 | Syeda Alam |
| La Amistad Love & Learning Academy | 10860 Rockley Rd | Houston, TX | 77099 | 281-988-9201 | 988-9201 | PK-1 | Syeda Alam |
| La Amistad Love & Learning Academy | 10860 Rockley Rd | Houston, TX | 77099 | 281-988-9201 | 988-9201 | PK-5 | Syeda Alam |
| La Fe Preparatory S | 616 E Father Rahm Ave | El Paso, TX | 79901 | 915-533-4560 | 533-4175 | PK-8 | Amy O'Rourke |
| Lanier MS | 2600 Woodhead St | Houston, TX | 77098-1615 | 713-942-1900 | 942-1907 | 6-8 | Felicia Adams |
| Laredo Early College HS | 5241 University Blvd | Laredo, TX | 78041 | 956-273-7700 | 795-8185 | 9-12 | Israel Castilla |
| Las Americas Learning Center | 5808 Renwick Dr | Houston, TX | 77081 | 832-582-7327 | 582-7325 | K-6 | Lillian Alvarez |
| Laurel Ridge | 17720 Corporate Woods Dr | San Antonio, TX | 78259-3509 | 210-491-9400 | | PK-12 | Sally Arnold |
| Leadership Prep S | 8500 Teel Pkwy | Frisco, TX | 75034 | 972-294-6921 | 294-3416 | K-8 | Michelle Holland |
| Lee Academy | 1826 Basse Rd | San Antonio, TX | 78213 | 210-431-9881 | 582-2547 | 9-12 | Fernando Mesa M.Ed. |
| Legacy Preparatory Academy | 8510 Military Pkwy | Dallas, TX | 75227 | 469-287-8530 | 461-0794 | K-12 | Mary Davis |
| Legacy Preparatory Academy | 601 Accent Dr | Plano, TX | 75075 | 469-206-2250 | 461-0794 | K-12 | Rosa Reyes |
| Liberation Academy | 401 Present St | Missouri City, TX | 77489-1109 | 281-969-7766 | 969-7762 | K-6 | Audrey Sanders |
| Liberty HS | 6400 Southwest Fwy Ste A | Houston, TX | 77074-2213 | 713-458-5555 | 458-5567 | 9-12 | Monico Rivas |
| Life S - Cedar Hill ES | 129 W Wintergreen Rd | Cedar Hill, TX | 75104 | 972-293-2825 | 291-2877 | K-6 | Joy Shepherd |
| Life S - Lancaster ES | 950 S Interstate 35 E | Lancaster, TX | 75146 | 972-274-7950 | 274-7991 | K-6 | DeWayne Parker |
| Life S - Mountain Creek ES | 5525 W Illinois Ave | Dallas, TX | 75211 | 214-623-0012 | 467-2857 | K-3 | Kim Riepe |
| Life S - Oak Cliff ES | 4400 S R L Thornton Fwy | Dallas, TX | 75224-5110 | 214-376-8200 | 371-0297 | K-6 | Vince Dawes |
| Life S - Oak Cliff HS | 4400 S R L Thornton Fwy | Dallas, TX | 75224 | 214-413-1612 | 371-0193 | 7-12 | Elmer Avellaneda |
| Life S - Red Oak ES | 777 S Interstate 35 Rd | Red Oak, TX | 75154 | 469-552-9200 | 617-5767 | K-6 | Stephanie Colwell |
| Life S - Waxahachie HS | 170 W Butcher Rd | Waxahachie, TX | 75165 | 469-708-4444 | 708-4445 | 9-12 | Patrick Harvell |
| Life S - Waxahachie MS | 3295 Highway 77 | Waxahachie, TX | 75165 | 972-937-0715 | 937-0503 | 7-8 | Anne Beckman |
| Lighthouse Charter S | 2718 Frontier Dr | San Antonio, TX | 78227-4069 | 210-674-4100 | 674-4108 | PK-8 | Mary Salinas |
| Lindsley Park Community S | 7130 Lindsley Ave | Dallas, TX | 75223 | 214-321-9155 | 321-0702 | PK-3 | Tom Loew |
| LivingWay Leadership Academy | 350 Ruben M Torres Blvd | Brownsville, TX | 78520 | 956-554-0999 | 554-9701 | PK-12 | Cecilia Septimo |
| Lowell MS | 919 Thompson Pl | San Antonio, TX | 78226-1494 | 210-228-1225 | 223-6248 | 6-8 | Claudio Garcia |
| Luna Preparatory PS | 2020 N Lamar St | Dallas, TX | 75202 | 214-442-7882 | | K-5 | Karen Aikman |
| Luna Preparatory Secondary S | 2625 Elm St | Dallas, TX | 75226 | 214-445-3300 | | 6-12 | Candice Dagnino |
| Madla Early College HS | 1400 Villaret Blvd | San Antonio, TX | 78224 | 210-486-3686 | | 9-12 | Jeff Flores |
| Magnolia Montessori For All | 5100 Pecan Brook | Austin, TX | 78724 | 512-522-2429 | | PK-8 | Sara Cotner |
| Mainland Preparatory Academy | 319 Newman Rd | La Marque, TX | 77568-3440 | 409-934-9100 | 934-9130 | PK-8 | Wilma Green |
| Mainland Preparatory Academy | 319 Newman Rd | La Marque, TX | 77568 | 409-934-9100 | 934-9130 | K-8 | Wilma Green |
| Manara Academy | 8201 Tristar Dr | Irving, TX | 75063 | 972-304-1155 | 304-1150 | K-8 | Len Stevens |
| Mangum ES | 4315 Mangum Rd | Houston, TX | 77092 | 713-688-0505 | 688-3286 | PK-5 | Josefa Olivares |
| Massieu Academy | 823 N Center St | Arlington, TX | 76011-5859 | 817-460-0396 | 460-9867 | PK-12 | Karina Boyles |
| Mayes Institute | 5807 Calhoun Rd | Houston, TX | 77021-3301 | 713-747-5629 | 747-5683 | K-8 | Beatrice Mayes |
| Meadowland Charter S | 121 Old San Antonio Rd | Boerne, TX | 78006 | 830-331-4094 | 331-4096 | 7-12 | Geoff Knitt |
| Medical Center Charter S | 10420 Mullins Dr | Houston, TX | 77096 | 713-726-0223 | 726-0225 | PK-8 | Suparna Vashisht |
| Meridian Preparatory S | 1801 S Beach St | Fort Worth, TX | 76105-2122 | | | K-5 | Ginger Cole-Leffel |
| Meridian S | 2555 N Interstate 35 | Round Rock, TX | 78664 | 512-660-5230 | 660-5231 | K-12 | Rick Fernandez |
| Methodist Children's Home | 1111 Herring Ave | Waco, TX | 76708-3696 | 254-750-1298 | 750-1307 | 6-12 | Cristy Cunningham |
| Meyer HS | 1020 Elm St Bldg 100 | Waco, TX | 76704-2277 | 254-754-2288 | 754-8002 | 9-12 | Jared Gould |
| Meyerpark Charter S | PO Box 35616 | Houston, TX | 77235-5616 | 713-729-9712 | 729-9720 | K-5 | Julia Hutcherson |
| Midland Academy Charter S | 500 N Baird St | Midland, TX | 79701-4704 | 432-686-0003 | 686-0845 | K-12 | Janet Wallace |
| Mid-Valley Academy | 1785 W US Highway 77 | San Benito, TX | 78586 | 956-276-9930 | 276-9943 | 9-12 | Nancy Ramirez |
| Mid-Valley Academy | 200 N 17th St | McAllen, TX | 78501 | 956-618-2303 | 618-2323 | 9-12 | Ramiro Vela |
| Mid-Valley Academy | 103 E 2nd St | Mercedes, TX | 78570-2701 | 956-565-5417 | 565-8439 | 9-12 | Rogelio Hinojosa |
| Mighty Preparatory S | 3700 Wichita St | Fort Worth, TX | 76119 | 817-288-3800 | 288-3799 | K-8 | April Knox |
| Milburn Academy - Amarillo | 4106 SW 51st Ave | Amarillo, TX | 79109-6132 | 806-463-2284 | 463-2231 | 9-12 | Becky Pinson |
| Milburn Academy -Corpus Christi | 5333 Everhart Rd Bldg C | Corpus Christi, TX | 78411 | 361-225-4424 | 225-4945 | 9-12 | Ronald Medrano |
| Milburn Academy - Fort Worth | 6785 Camp Bowie Blvd | Fort Worth, TX | 76116 | 817-731-7627 | 731-7628 | 9-12 | Susan Richey |
| Milburn Academy - Houston | 713 E Airtex Dr | Houston, TX | 77073 | 281-209-3505 | 209-9475 | 9-12 | Dr. Loria Ewing |
| Milburn Academy - Killeen | 802 N 2nd St Bldg G | Killeen, TX | 76541 | 254-634-4444 | 634-4044 | 9-12 | Jerrod Barton |
| Milburn Academy - Lubbock | 2333 50th St | Lubbock, TX | 79412 | 806-740-0811 | 740-0804 | 9-12 | Lindsey Rambo |
| Milburn Academy - Midland | 3303 W Illinois Ave Ste 14 | Midland, TX | 79703 | 432-522-7200 | 522-5201 | 9-12 | Teffanie White |
| Milburn Academy - Odessa | 2419 N County Rd W | Odessa, TX | 79763 | 432-550-7833 | 550-7884 | 9-12 | Mary Janssen |
| Monticello Academy | 4618 San Pedro Ave | San Antonio, TX | 78212 | 210-738-0020 | 738-0033 | K-12 | Debbie Deleon |
| Mount Carmel Academy | 7155 Ashburn St | Houston, TX | 77061-2611 | 713-643-2008 | 645-0078 | 9-12 | Maureen Giacchino |
| Nelms Charter HS | 20625 Clay Rd | Katy, TX | 77449-5593 | 281-398-8031 | 398-8032 | 9-12 | Michael Dean |
| Nelms Charter MS | 20625 Clay Rd | Katy, TX | 77449-5593 | 281-398-8031 | 398-8032 | 5-8 | Michael Dean |
| New Frontiers Charter S | 4018 S Presa St | San Antonio, TX | 78223 | 210-533-3655 | 533-5077 | K-8 | Ruben Pesina |
| New Horizons S | 850 Highway 574 W | Goldthwaite, TX | 76844 | 325-938-5513 | 938-5512 | 1-12 | Suzanne Rush |
| Newman International Academy Arlington | 2011 S Fielder Rd | Arlington, TX | 76013 | 817-459-8555 | 394-6155 | PK-12 | Donna Hart |
| Newman International Academy Cedar Hill | 4603 Enchanted Bay Blvd | Arlington, TX | 76016 | 817-459-8555 | 394-6155 | PK-12 | David Slight |
| New Neighbor Campus | 6500 Rookin St | Houston, TX | 77074 | 713-273-3731 | | K-5 | Raquel Sosa-Gonzalez |
| North Hills S | 606 E Royal Ln | Irving, TX | 75039-3503 | 972-501-0645 | 501-9439 | K-12 | Heather Periera |
| Northwest Early College HS | 6701 S Desert Blvd | El Paso, TX | 79932-8501 | 915-877-1700 | 877-7033 | 9-12 | Tracy Speaker |
| Northwest Preparatory S | 4705 Lyons Ave | Houston, TX | 77020-4306 | 713-674-2105 | 676-1940 | PK-8 | Wiley Johnson |
| Northwest Preparatory S | 600 Charles St | Humble, TX | 77338-3847 | 713-672-1959 | 446-0077 | PK-8 | Wiley Johnson |
| Nova Academy | PO Box 170127 | Dallas, TX | 75217-0127 | 214-381-3422 | 381-3499 | PK-3 | Donna Houston-Woods |
| Nova Academy Southeast - Bruton | PO Box 170127 | Dallas, TX | 75217-0127 | 214-309-9030 | 398-6363 | PK-6 | Donna Houston-Woods |
| Nova Academy Southeast - Prichard | PO Box 170127 | Dallas, TX | 75217 | 972-808-7470 | 808-7471 | K-8 | Donna Houston-Woods |
| NYOS Charter S | 1605 Kramer Ln | Austin, TX | 78758-4284 | 512-275-1593 | 287-5258 | PK-3 | Terry Berkenhoff |
| NYOS Charter S | 12301 N Lamar Blvd | Austin, TX | 78753-1320 | 512-583-6967 | 583-6973 | 4-12 | Curtis Wilson |
| Oak Cliff Faith Family Academy | 300 W Kiest Blvd | Dallas, TX | 75224 | 214-375-7682 | 375-7681 | PK-12 | Mollie Purcell-Savage |
| Odyssey Academy | 2412 61st St | Galveston, TX | 77551 | 409-750-9289 | 740-3735 | PK-12 | Jennifer Goodman |
| Odyssey Preparatory S | 8787 N Houston Rosslyn Rd | Houston, TX | 77088-6430 | 713-983-0165 | 983-0294 | K-6 | Venora Goodie |
| Olive Tree Montessori Academy | 614 Hiett Ave | Arlington, TX | 76010 | 817-460-5000 | 460-5003 | PK-5 | Sadia Haq |
| Olympic Hills Charter S | 2200 E 6th St | Austin, TX | 78702 | 512-444-4835 | 232-9177 | K-12 | Dottie Goodman |
| Osborne ES | 800 Ringold St | Houston, TX | 77088-6337 | 281-405-2525 | 405-2528 | PK-5 | Jacqueline Parnell |
| Panola Charter S | PO Box 610 | Carthage, TX | 75633-0610 | 903-693-6355 | 693-6391 | 8-12 | Keith Koonce |
| Panola Early College HS | 1109 W Panola St | Carthage, TX | 75633-2397 | 903-694-4028 | 694-4030 | 8-12 | Keith Koonce |
| Paseo Del Norte Academy | 1599 George Dieter Dr | El Paso, TX | 79936 | 915-298-3637 | 298-3644 | 9-12 | Maria Maquera |
| Paso Del Norte Academy - Ysleta | 711 N Mesa St | El Paso, TX | 79902-3925 | 915-532-7216 | 532-2251 | 9-12 | Luis Liano |
| Pathfinder Camp | 20800 FM 150 W | Driftwood, TX | 78619-9202 | 512-858-4258 | 858-4960 | K-12 | Melissa Ruffin |
| Pathways 3H Ranch | 110 Youth Ranch Rd # 3H | Mountain Home, TX | 78058 | 830-866-3761 | 866-3705 | 6-12 | Sally Arnold |
| Pegasus Charter HS | 601 N Akard St Ste 203 | Dallas, TX | 75201-3303 | 214-740-9991 | 740-9799 | K-12 | Virginia Hart |
| Phoenix Charter S | 8501 Jack Finney Blvd | Greenville, TX | 75402-3018 | 903-454-7153 | 455-0604 | PK-12 | Mary Kahama |
| Phoenix S | 3333 Bering Dr | Houston, TX | 77057 | 713-784-6345 | | K-12 | Brett Schriewer |
| Pineywoods Community Academy | 602 S Raguet St | Lufkin, TX | 75904-3936 | 936-634-5515 | 634-5518 | PK-6 | Bruce Marchand |
| Pineywoods Community Academy | 602 S Raguet St | Lufkin, TX | 75904-3936 | 936-634-5515 | 634-5518 | 7-12 | Monica Gunter |
| Pinnacle Preparatory S | 2510 S Vernon Ave | Dallas, TX | 75224 | 214-442-6100 | 442-6181 | K-3 | Katie Leinenkugel |
| Porter S | PO Box 2053 | Wimberley, TX | 78676-6953 | 512-847-6867 | 847-0737 | 9-12 | Kenn Peters |
| Por Vida Academy | 1135 Mission Rd | San Antonio, TX | 78210-4505 | 210-532-9161 | 533-5612 | 9-12 | Joseph Rendon |
| Positive Solutions Charter S | 1325 N Flores St | San Antonio, TX | 78212-4900 | 210-299-1025 | 299-1052 | 9-12 | Steven Langseth |
| Premier HS of Abilene | 3161 S 23rd St | Abilene, TX | 79605 | 325-698-8111 | 695-5620 | 9-12 | Sue Pond |
| Premier HS of Amarillo | 3242 Hobbs Rd | Amarillo, TX | 79109 | 806-367-5447 | 315-9506 | 9-12 | Michael Griffin |
| Premier HS of Austin | 1701 W Ben White Blvd #100A | Austin, TX | 78704 | 512-444-8442 | 673-0058 | 9-12 | Jennifer Kasapi |
| Premier HS of Beaumont | 209 N 11th St | Beaumont, TX | 77702-2213 | 409-835-4303 | 835-2882 | 9-12 | Bonnie Whitehead |
| Premier HS of Brownsville | 955 Paredes Line Rd | Brownsville, TX | 78521-2659 | 956-550-0084 | 554-0890 | 9-12 | Norma Sorola |
| Premier HS of Brownwood/Early | 819 Early Blvd | Early, TX | 76802 | 325-643-3735 | 363-4987 | 6-12 | |
| Premier HS of Comanche | 1008 S Austin St | Comanche, TX | 76442 | 325-356-9673 | 794-8319 | 9-12 | |
| Premier HS of Dayton | 1709 County Road 611 | Dayton, TX | 77535-8561 | 936-257-8017 | 449-6775 | 9-12 | Ray Moore |
| Premier HS of Del Rio | 1503 Veterans Blvd | Del Rio, TX | 78840 | 830-298-2100 | 573-0849 | 9-12 | Berta Martinez |
| Premier HS of Dublin | 112 S Grafton St | Dublin, TX | 76446-2318 | 254-445-4844 | 857-6678 | 9-12 | Dan McIntosh |
| Premier HS of East El Paso | 8720 Gateway Blvd E Ste E | El Paso, TX | 79907 | 915-633-1598 | | 6-12 | Dr. Eduardo Servin |
| Premier HS of El Paso | 1035 Belvidere St Ste 116 | El Paso, TX | 79912 | 915-581-4300 | 581-4378 | 9-12 | Dr. Eduardo Servin |
| Premier HS of Fort Worth | 6411 Camp Bowie Blvd Ste B | Fort Worth, TX | 76116-5449 | 817-731-2028 | 728-0824 | 9-12 | Tawilhua Mitchell |

| School | Address | City,State | Zip code | Telephone | Fax | Grade | Contact |
|---|---|---|---|---|---|---|---|
| Premier HS of Granbury | 919 E US Highway 377 Ste 1 | Granbury, TX | 76048-1436 | 817-573-0435 | 895-9616 | 9-12 | Marsha Grissom |
| Premier HS of Huntsville | 2407 Sam Houston Ave Ste C | Huntsville, TX | 77340-5862 | 936-439-5204 | 622-9113 | 9-12 | Kevin Nichols |
| Premier HS of Irving South | 1081 W Shady Grove Rd | Irving, TX | 75060-5868 | 972-254-1016 | 565-1157 | 9-12 | Tiffini Miller |
| Premier HS of Laredo | 2201 Chihuahua St | Laredo, TX | 78043 | 956-723-7788 | 284-0175 | 9-12 | |
| Premier HS of Lewisville | 1800 Lakeway Dr | Lewisville, TX | 75057 | 972-316-4160 | | 9-12 | Debbie Foster |
| Premier HS of Lindale | 17141 State Highway 110 N | Lindale, TX | 75771-5933 | 903-881-9940 | 882-0183 | 6-12 | |
| Premier HS of Lubbock | 2002 W Loop 289 Ste 121 | Lubbock, TX | 79407-7701 | 806-763-1518 | 763-9310 | 9-12 | Thomas Martin |
| Premier HS of Midland | 4320 W Illinois Ave Ste A | Midland, TX | 79703-5591 | 432-682-0384 | 682-0897 | 9-12 | Holli Stockstill |
| Premier HS of Mission | 1203 St Claire Blvd | Mission, TX | 78572-8465 | 956-424-9290 | 859-0140 | 9-12 | Laura Thatcher |
| Premier HS of New Braunfels | 1928 S Seguin Ave Unit 100A | New Braunfels, TX | 78130-3911 | 512-832-0965 | 319-4382 | 9-12 | Richard Ramirez |
| Premier HS of North Austin | 1835 Kramer Ln Ste A600 | Austin, TX | 78758-4259 | 512-832-0965 | 563-6438 | 9-12 | Manuela Allen |
| Premier HS of Palmview | 406 W Veterans Blvd | Palmview, TX | 78572-8327 | 956-584-8458 | 584-9807 | 9-12 | Selma Femat |
| Premier HS of Pflugerville | 616 FM 685 Ste 204B | Pflugerville, TX | 78660 | 512-969-5100 | | 6-12 | Paulita Zuniga |
| Premier HS of Pharr | 200 E Expressway 83 Ste E | Pharr, TX | 78577-6506 | 956-781-8800 | 781-7464 | 9-12 | Rosie Zamora |
| Premier HS of Richardson | 1111 Digital Dr Ste 101 | Richardson, TX | 75081-1948 | 972-479-9602 | 885-9621 | 9-12 | Shaina Tackett-Cox |
| Premier HS of San Antonio | 502 E Ramsey Rd | San Antonio, TX | 78216-4639 | 210-524-8103 | 434-7578 | 9-12 | Berta Martinez |
| Premier HS of San Juan | 1200 E Business 83 | San Juan, TX | 78589-4758 | 956-961-4721 | 961-4724 | 9-12 | Alma Prado |
| Premier HS of Tyler | 1106 N Glenwood Blvd | Tyler, TX | 75702-5059 | 903-592-5222 | 592-0324 | 9-12 | Tabatha Ervin |
| Premier HS of Waco | 4720 N 19th St | Waco, TX | 76708-1213 | 254-752-0441 | 752-0445 | 9-12 | Lisa Linton |
| Premier Leadership Academy | 1630 Goliad Rd | San Antonio, TX | 78223 | 210-551-9608 | | PK-6 | Trina Cardenas |
| Premier Learning Academy | 5130 Casey St | La Marque, TX | 77568-2707 | 409-935-8369 | 935-3337 | K-12 | Cynthia Hallam |
| Project Chrysalis MS | 4528 Leeland St | Houston, TX | 77023-3047 | 713-924-1700 | 924-1704 | 6-8 | Jose Covarrubia |
| Pro-Vision S | 4590 Wilmington St | Houston, TX | 77051 | 713-748-0030 | 748-0037 | 5-12 | |
| Quest MS | 1301 Waters Ridge Dr | Lewisville, TX | 75057-6022 | 972-316-6700 | 316-6705 | 6-8 | Marci Stapp |
| Quest MS of Coppell | 1615 W Belt Line Rd | Carrollton, TX | 75006-6633 | 972-242-5864 | 523-8342 | 6-8 | Michelle Sanchez-Drain |
| Quinn Campus MS | 1020 Elm St Bldg 100 | Waco, TX | 76704-2277 | 254-754-8000 | 754-8009 | 5-8 | Deb Garton |
| Radiance Academy of Learning - Abndnt Lf | 8308 Fredericksburg Rd | San Antonio, TX | 78229 | 210-593-0111 | 615-3954 | PK-8 | Lois Chapa |
| Radiance Academy of Learning - Del Rio | 709 Kings Way | Del Rio, TX | 78840-2029 | 830-774-6230 | 774-6235 | 6-12 | Dot Steed |
| Ramirez Charter S | 702 Avenue T | Lubbock, TX | 79401-2303 | 806-219-6500 | 766-1825 | K-5 | Nancy Parker |
| Ranch Academy | 3120 VZ County Road 2318 | Canton, TX | 75103-4671 | 903-939-8000 | 479-1161 | 6-12 | Melissa Pardue |
| Ranch Academy - Tyler Campus | 14023 State Highway 155 S | Tyler, TX | 75703 | 903-479-3601 | 479-1161 | 1-12 | Timothy Rucker |
| Rapoport Academy East | 2000 J J Flewellen Rd | Waco, TX | 76704-1642 | 254-799-4191 | 799-4525 | PK-4 | Cindy Kubacak |
| Rapoport Academy North | 2200 MacArthur Dr | Waco, TX | 76708 | 254-313-1313 | | PK-4 | Heather Franks |
| Raven S | 143 Forest Service Road 233 | New Waverly, TX | 77358 | 936-344-7235 | 344-6396 | 9-12 | Will Gollihar |
| Reach Charter S | 520 Mercury Dr | Houston, TX | 77013-5217 | 713-671-4515 | 675-1118 | 9-12 | Bertie Simmons |
| Real Learning Academy | 6405 S IH 35 | Austin, TX | 78745 | 512-438-7325 | 383-0665 | PK-4 | Michelle Stahl |
| Rhodes MS | 3000 Tampico St | San Antonio, TX | 78207-6498 | 210-978-7925 | 433-7299 | 6-8 | Christopher Castro |
| Rhodes S - Lee | 12822 Robert E Lee Rd | Houston, TX | 77044-2411 | 281-458-4334 | 458-7595 | PK-6 | Joesette Simeon |
| Rhodes S - Southeast | 5874 Bellfort St | Houston, TX | 77033 | 832-962-8181 | 962-8171 | K-5 | Dr. Tammi Mitchell |
| Rhodes S - Tidwell | 12818 Tidwell Rd | Houston, TX | 77044 | 281-459-9797 | | PK-5 | Rosalyn Thierry |
| Richland Collegiate HS | 12800 Abrams Rd | Dallas, TX | 75243-2199 | 972-761-6888 | 761-6890 | 11-12 | Donna Walker |
| Ripley House Charter S | 4410 Navigation Blvd | Houston, TX | 77011-1036 | 713-315-6429 | 547-8201 | K-5 | Angela Wedlick |
| Ripley House MS | 4414 Navigation Blvd | Houston, TX | 77011 | 713-315-6430 | | 6-8 | Angela Wedlick |
| Rise Academy | PO Box 2837 | Lubbock, TX | 79408 | 806-744-0438 | 201-7088 | PK-8 | Richard Baumgartner |
| Riverside Park ES | 202 School St | San Antonio, TX | 78210-3940 | 210-228-3355 | 534-6987 | PK-5 | Homer Rivera |
| Saenz JHS | 1830 Basse Rd | San Antonio, TX | 78213-4606 | 210-431-9881 | 582-2587 | 7-8 | Fernando Mesa |
| St. Anthony S | 3732 Myrtle St | Dallas, TX | 75215-3849 | 214-421-3645 | 421-7416 | K-8 | David Ray |
| St. Mary's Academy Charter S | 507 N Filmore St | Beeville, TX | 78102 | 361-358-5601 | 358-5704 | K-8 | Hirma Elizondo |
| San Antonio Can Academy | 1807 Centennial Blvd | San Antonio, TX | 78211-1205 | 210-923-1226 | 928-3366 | 9-12 | Mark Peters |
| San Antonio S for Inquiry & Creativity | 4618 San Pedro Ave | San Antonio, TX | 78212-1411 | 210-738-0020 | 738-0033 | K-12 | Dr. Debbie De Leon |
| San Antonio Technology Academy | 2507 Fredericksburg Rd | San Antonio, TX | 78201 | 210-527-9250 | 225-7282 | 9-12 | Ben Johnson |
| Sanchez HS | 6001 Gulf Fwy | Houston, TX | 77023-5423 | 713-926-1112 | 926-8129 | 6-12 | John DeLaCruz |
| Save Our Streets Learning Center | 1700 Groesbeck St | Bryan, TX | 77803 | 979-703-1810 | 703-1834 | K-5 | Michael Blackshire |
| School for the Highly Gifted | 2990 S Highway 161 | Grand Prairie, TX | 75052 | 972-343-7864 | | 1-3 | Holly Mohler |
| School of Science and Technology | 4737 Saratoga Blvd | Corpus Christi, TX | 78413-2117 | 361-851-2450 | 851-2475 | K-12 | Ekrem Demirci |
| School of Science and Technology Alamo | 12200 Crownpoint Dr | San Antonio, TX | 78233-5371 | 210-657-6400 | 657-6401 | K-8 | Mehmet Nalcaci |
| School of Science & Technology Discovery | 5707 Bandera Rd | Leon Valley, TX | 78238-1918 | 210-543-1111 | 543-1112 | K-8 | Mustafa Kililioglu |
| School of Science and Technology HS | 1450 NE Loop 410 | San Antonio, TX | 78209-1513 | 210-804-0222 | 822-3422 | 6-12 | Celal Keskin |
| Sci-Tech Preparatory | 6405 S IH-35 | Austin, TX | 78744 | 512-220-9120 | 383-0665 | 6-12 | Mary Brinkman M.Ed. |
| Scott Collegiate Academy | 4116 Avenue N 1/2 | Galveston, TX | 77550-6957 | 409-761-6100 | 765-5946 | 5-8 | Debra Owens |
| Seashore Learning Center | 14493 S Padre Isl PMB 307A | Corpus Christi, TX | 78418 | 361-949-1222 | 949-6762 | PK-4 | Genger Holt |
| Seashore Middle Academy | 14493 S Padre Isl PMB 307A | Corpus Christi, TX | 78418 | 361-654-1134 | 654-1139 | 5-8 | Barbara Beeler |
| SER-Ninos Charter S | 5815 Alder Dr | Houston, TX | 77081-2708 | 713-667-6145 | 667-0645 | PK-8 | Charmaine Constantine |
| Settlement Home | 1600 Payton Gin Rd | Austin, TX | 78758-6506 | 512-836-2150 | 836-2159 | K-12 | Mayola Toliver |
| Shekinah Radiance Academy - Dallas Ctr | 201 N Erby Campbell Blvd | Royse City, TX | 75189 | 972-636-0055 | 636-0055 | K-8 | Deborah Vyborney |
| Shekinah Radiance Academy - Garland | 10715 Garland Rd Ste 100 | Dallas, TX | 75218 | 214-320-2500 | 320-2502 | PK-8 | Trina Garnes |
| Shekinah Radiance Academy - Walzem | 6663 Walzem Rd | San Antonio, TX | 78239-3612 | 210-967-6933 | 967-6280 | PK-12 | Emma Alexander |
| Shekinah Radiance Academy - W Columbia | 719 W Brazos Ave | West Columbia, TX | 77486 | 210-658-6848 | 658-7820 | K-12 | Shirley Johnson |
| Shoreline Academy | 1220 Gregory St | Taft, TX | 78390 | 361-528-3959 | 528-2143 | 7-12 | DeAnn Phillips |
| South Early College HS | 7414 St Lo Rd | Houston, TX | 77033-2732 | 713-732-3623 | 732-3425 | 10-12 | Steven Gourrier |
| South Plains Academy | 4008 Avenue R | Lubbock, TX | 79412-1603 | 806-744-0330 | 741-1089 | 9-12 | Michael Carothers |
| Southwest ES | 8440 Bissonnet St | Houston, TX | 77074-3908 | 713-988-5839 | 270-0076 | PK-5 | Pamela Sailors |
| Southwest HS | 6400 Westpark Dr Ste 200 | Houston, TX | 77057 | 713-954-9528 | 953-0119 | 9-12 | Cynthia Iyamu |
| Southwest MS | 6400 Westpark Dr Ste 200 | Houston, TX | 77057 | 713-954-9528 | 953-0119 | 6-8 | Cynthia Iyamu |
| Southwest Preparatory ES NW Campus | 4151 Culebra Rd | San Antonio, TX | 78228 | 210-819-7860 | 438-8253 | PK-6 | Cheryl Wills-Pacheco |
| Southwest Preparatory HS NW Campus | 6535 Culebra Rd | San Antonio, TX | 78238 | 210-432-2634 | 432-5482 | 7-12 | Sherry Head |
| Southwest Preparatory S NE Campus | 1258 Austin Hwy Ste 220 | San Antonio, TX | 78209-4820 | 210-829-8017 | 829-8514 | PK-8 | Veronica Champion |
| Southwest Preparatory S SE Campus | 735 S WW White Rd | San Antonio, TX | 78220-2524 | 210-333-1403 | 333-3024 | 6-12 | Javier Garcia |
| Southwest Prep S New Directions Campus | 1258 Austin Hwy Bldg 2 | San Antonio, TX | 78209-4891 | 210-828-2161 | 826-9962 | 9-12 | Veronica Champion |
| Storm ES | 435 Brady Blvd | San Antonio, TX | 78207-8099 | 210-978-8005 | 224-1998 | PK-5 | Claudia Ramos |
| Summit International Preparatory S | 1305 N Center St | Arlington, TX | 76011-4820 | 817-287-5121 | 287-5132 | K-12 | Priscilla Parhms |
| Tekoa Academy of Accelerated Studies | 1408 W Park Ave | Orange, TX | 77630 | 409-886-9864 | | PK-5 | Rhonda Orebo |
| Tekoa Academy of Accelerated Studies | 326 Thomas Blvd | Port Arthur, TX | 77640-5242 | 409-982-5400 | 982-8498 | K-6 | Dr. Paula Richardson |
| Tekoa Academy of Accelerated Studies | 327 Thomas Blvd | Port Arthur, TX | 77640 | 409-985-4738 | | 7-12 | Dr. Paula Richardson |
| Tekoa Academy of Accelerated Studies | 3119 Gulway Dr | Port Arthur, TX | 77642 | 409-982-5400 | | PK-PK | Dr. Paula Richardson |
| Temple Charter Academy | 7177 Airport Rd | Temple, TX | 76502 | 254-778-8682 | 853-4144 | PK-12 | Jason Osburn |
| Texas Connections Academy at Houston | 10550 Richmond Ave Ste 140 | Houston, TX | 77042 | 281-661-8293 | 780-2487 | 3-12 | Lea Ann Lockard |
| Texas Early College HS | 2400 E End Blvd S | Marshall, TX | 75672-7402 | 903-935-4109 | 935-4067 | 8-12 | Robert Bruce |
| Texas Education Centers at Aubrey | 1851 Oak Grove Pkwy | Little Elm, TX | 75068 | 972-292-3562 | 292-3563 | K-8 | Debbie Foster |
| Texas Education Centers at Denton | 4420 Country Club Rd | Denton, TX | 76210-3222 | 940-383-1972 | 383-7655 | K-8 | James Gandy |
| Texas Education Centers at Little Elm | 5901 Crestwood Pl | Little Elm, TX | 75068-3754 | 972-292-3562 | 292-2373 | K-8 | Chantelle Tarver |
| Texas Education Centers in Lewisville | 968 Raldon St | Lewisville, TX | 75067-5229 | 972-221-3564 | 221-3576 | K-8 | Donica Hill |
| Texas Empowerment Academy | 6414 N Hampton Dr | Austin, TX | 78723-2043 | 512-494-1076 | 494-1009 | K-5 | David Nowlin |
| Texas Empowerment Academy | 3613 Bluestein Dr | Austin, TX | 78721-2900 | 512-494-1076 | 494-0199 | 5-12 | David Nowlin |
| Texas Leadership Charter Acad Arlington | 2001 Brown Blvd | Arlington, TX | 76006 | 817-385-9338 | 861-1242 | K-6 | Ron Carroll |
| Texas Leadership Charter Academy Abilene | 1840 N 8th St | Abilene, TX | 79603 | 325-480-3500 | | K-5 | Melinda McCarty |
| Texas Leadership Charter Academy Midland | 3300 Thomas Ave | Midland, TX | 79703 | 432-242-7117 | 262-0994 | PK-12 | Desiree Parker |
| Texas NeuroRehabilitation Center | 1106 W Dittmar Rd | Austin, TX | 78745-6328 | 512-444-4835 | 462-6665 | K-12 | Dottie Goodman |
| Texas Preparatory S | PO Box 1643 | San Marcos, TX | 78667-1643 | 512-805-3000 | 805-7739 | K-6 | Daphne McDole |
| Texas S of the Arts | 6025 Village Pkwy | Fort Worth, TX | 76134 | 817-732-8372 | 732-8373 | K-8 | Natalie Texada |
| Texas Serenity Academy | 8500 Sweetwater Ln | Houston, TX | 77037 | 281-820-9540 | 820-6204 | K-8 | Michelle Foreman |
| Texas Virtual Academy | 1955 Lakeway Dr Ste 250B | Lewisville, TX | 75057 | 866-360-0161 | 506-6777 | 3-12 | Sara Baker |
| TLC Academy | PO Box 61726 | San Angelo, TX | 76906 | 325-652-3200 | 942-6795 | K-12 | Dr. Christopher Morrow |
| Travis Early College HS | 1915 N Main Ave | San Antonio, TX | 78212 | 210-738-9830 | 733-5486 | 9-12 | Miguel Elizondo |
| Treetops School International | 12500 S Pipeline Rd | Euless, TX | 76040-5853 | 817-283-1771 | 684-0892 | PK-12 | Lou Blanchard |
| Trinity Basin S - 10th St Campus | 831 W 10th St | Dallas, TX | 75208 | 214-296-9302 | 296-9306 | PK-4 | Matt Whitaker |
| Trinity Basin S - Ewing Campus | 808 N Ewing Ave | Dallas, TX | 75203-1524 | 214-942-8846 | 942-8864 | PK-4 | Lacy Zachary |
| Trinity Basin S - Jefferson Campus | 855 E 8th St | Dallas, TX | 75203 | 214-941-4881 | 941-4866 | 5-8 | Jennifer Masten |
| Trinity Basin S - Pafford Campus | 101 E Pafford St | Fort Worth, TX | 76110 | 817-840-7501 | 840-7502 | PK-6 | Jodi Rebarchek |
| Trinity Basin S - Panola Campus | 4400 Panola Ave | Fort Worth, TX | 76103 | 817-458-4222 | 946-9194 | PK-2 | Natasha Forge |
| Trinity Charter S - Big Sandy Campus | 15892 County Road 26 | Tyler, TX | 75707 | 512-459-1000 | 705-2447 | 6-12 | Nicki Cornejo |
| Trinity Charter S - Bokenkamp Campus | 5517 S Alameda St | Corpus Christi, TX | 78412 | 361-992-1412 | | K-12 | Hilda Vega |
| Trinity Charter S - Chapel Hill Campus | 15892 County Road 26 | Tyler, TX | 75707-2728 | 903-459-1000 | 705-2447 | K-12 | Nicki Cornejo |
| Trinity Charter S - Krause Center Campus | 25752 Kingsland Blvd | Katy, TX | 77494 | 281-392-7505 | 392-6887 | 6-12 | Sandra Flores |
| Trinity Charter S - New Life Campus | 650 Scarbourough | Canyon Lake, TX | 78133-4529 | 830-964-4390 | 964-4376 | 4-12 | Kellie Ragland |
| Trinity Charter S - Pegasus Campus | 896 Robin Ranch Rd | Lockhart, TX | 78644 | 512-432-1652 | 705-2447 | 3-12 | Keely Reynolds |
| Trinity Charter S - Willow Bend Campus | 2902 Highway 31 E | Tyler, TX | 75702 | | | K-12 | Nicki Cornejo |
| Trinity Environmental Academy | PO Box 570975 | Dallas, TX | 75357 | 972-920-6558 | 767-0494 | PK-12 | Michael Hooten |
| TSU Charter Lab S | 3100 Cleburne St | Houston, TX | 77004 | 713-741-1222 | 741-1220 | K-5 | Debbra Collins |
| Two Dimensions Preparatory Academy | 12121 Veterans Memorial Dr | Houston, TX | 77067-5237 | 281-227-4708 | 232-0032 | PK-5 | DeAteria Akan |
| Two Dimensions Preparatory Academy | 901 E 10th Ave | Corsicana, TX | 75110-6726 | 281-227-4700 | 872-2858 | PK-K | Shirley Harris |
| Two Dimensions Preparatory Academy | 12330 Vickery St | Houston, TX | 77039-3608 | 281-227-4700 | 987-7306 | PK-4 | Jamal Adams |
| UME Preparatory Academy | 3838 Spur 408 | Dallas, TX | 75236 | 214-545-6243 | 709-7951 | K-12 | Mike Spurlock |
| Universal Academy | 2616 N MacArthur Blvd | Irving, TX | 75062-5401 | 972-255-1800 | 255-6122 | PK-12 | Sheraton Duffey |
| Universal Academy - Flower Mound | 1001 E Sandy Lake Rd | Coppell, TX | 75019-3112 | 972-393-5834 | 255-6122 | PK-12 | Diane Moshier |
| University Charter S | 2200 E 6th St | Austin, TX | 78702-3457 | 512-495-9705 | 495-9631 | PK-5 | Tanya King |
| University HS | 2007 University Dr | Austin, TX | 78705 | 512-382-0072 | 232-9177 | 9-12 | Julie McElrath Ray |

| School | Address | City,State | Zip code | Telephone | Fax | Grade | Contact |
|---|---|---|---|---|---|---|---|
| University of Houston Charter S of Tech | 3855 Holman St | Houston, TX | 77204-6056 | 713-743-9111 | 743-9121 | K-5 | Dr. Carolyn Black |
| Uplift Peak Academy | 4600 Bryan St | Dallas, TX | 75204 | 214-821-7325 | 370-3972 | PK-12 | Priscilla Collins-Parhms |
| Uplift Triumph Preparatory S | 9411 Hargrove Dr | Dallas, TX | 75220 | 972-590-5100 | | K-5 | Christine Denison |
| Vanguard Academy Charter School | 1200 E Kelly Ave | Pharr, TX | 78577-5033 | 956-781-1701 | 781-8055 | PK-12 | Robert Olivarez |
| Vanguard Academy II | 901 S Athol St | Pharr, TX | 78577 | 956-702-0134 | 702-0166 | PK-5 | Patricia Cardoza |
| Vanguard Academy III | 155 E Business Highway 83 | Alamo, TX | 78516 | 956-702-2548 | 702-2731 | PK-5 | Myrna Ramirez |
| Varnett S - East | PO Box 1457 | Houston, TX | 77251-1457 | 713-637-6574 | 637-8319 | PK-5 | Gayle Voltz |
| Varnett S - Northeast | PO Box 1457 | Houston, TX | 77251-1457 | 713-631-4396 | 491-3597 | PK-5 | Toni Fisher |
| Varnett S - Southwest | PO Box 1457 | Houston, TX | 77251-1457 | 713-723-4699 | 283-1728 | PK-5 | Twilet Alexander |
| Victory Preparatory Academy | 6011 W Orem Dr | Houston, TX | 77085 | 713-729-6963 | 721-1665 | 9-12 | Letha Gilmore |
| Victory Preparatory Academy | 2903 Jensen Dr | Houston, TX | 77026-6019 | 713-229-0560 | 250-7074 | PK-12 | David Edgerson |
| Village Tech S | 535 S Clark Rd | Cedar Hill, TX | 75104 | 972-827-7843 | 291-1531 | PK-12 | Robert Johansen |
| Vista Academy of Amarillo | 6000 S Georgia St | Amarillo, TX | 79118-8804 | 806-352-0171 | 367-5449 | K-12 | Michael Griffin |
| Vista Academy of Austin | 1504 E 51st St | Austin, TX | 78723-3012 | 512-371-8933 | 433-9225 | K-5 | Miriam Spiller-Troilo |
| Vista Academy of Beaumont | 10255 Eastex Fwy Ste 100 | Beaumont, TX | 77708 | 409-434-4549 | 316-2728 | K-5 | Sherry Hanson |
| Vista Academy of Crockett | 1303 E Houston Ave | Crockett, TX | 75835 | 936-546-0493 | 546-0034 | K-5 | Deborah Kelly M.S. |
| Vista Academy of Dallas | 7300 Bruton Rd | Dallas, TX | 75217-1447 | 214-792-9331 | 792-9334 | K-6 | |
| Vista Academy of Denton | 4420 Country Club Rd | Denton, TX | 76210 | 940-565-8333 | 919-5316 | K-1 | Susan Thomas |
| Vista Academy of DeSoto | 1121 E Pleasant Run Rd | DeSoto, TX | 75115-4201 | 214-954-7075 | 725-8765 | K-4 | Misty Cole |
| Vista Academy of Edinburg | 2110 S McColl Rd | Edinburg, TX | 78539-8831 | 956-720-4361 | 595-1525 | K-5 | Norma McDaniel |
| Vista Academy of Elgin | 2418 FM 1704 | Elgin, TX | 78621-5565 | 512-285-2710 | 679-2521 | K-6 | Jenness LaPage |
| Vista Academy of Garland | 3024 Anita Dr | Garland, TX | 75041-2708 | 972-840-1100 | 840-1105 | K-8 | Campbell Gillis |
| Vista Academy of Hickory Creek | 800 Point Vista Dr Ste 518 | Hickory Creek, TX | 75065-7639 | 940-321-1144 | 231-9437 | K-5 | Kimberly Powell |
| Vista Academy of Humble | 901 Wilson Rd | Humble, TX | 77338 | 281-913-5107 | 655-1476 | K-5 | Sandra Gonzales |
| Vista Academy of Huntsville | 2407 Sam Houston Ave | Huntsville, TX | 77340-5862 | 936-291-0203 | 293-8096 | K-6 | Robbie Harris |
| Vista Academy of Jasper | 1501B S Wheeler St | Jasper, TX | 75951-5103 | 409-489-9222 | 489-9272 | K-8 | Laura McMillon |
| Vista Academy of North Garland | 1600 W Campbell Rd | Garland, TX | 75044-2300 | 972-530-7373 | 679-0860 | K-5 | Emily Mason |
| Vista Academy of Pasadena Beta Academy | 6109 Fairmont Pkwy | Pasadena, TX | 77505-4024 | 281-372-8999 | 345-6895 | K-4 | Latisha Andrews |
| Vista Academy of Richardson | 2101 E Renner Rd | Richardson, TX | 75082 | 972-530-7373 | | 3-6 | Emily Mason |
| Vista Academy of The Woodlands | 6565 Research Forest Dr | The Woodlands, TX | 77381-6030 | 936-242-1541 | 688-8037 | K-8 | Ferrell Yeokum |
| Vista Academy of Tyler | 3105 University Blvd Ste B | Tyler, TX | 75701-6614 | 903-504-5690 | 567-2247 | K-5 | Keith Garcia |
| Vista Academy of Willis | 202 S Thomason St | Willis, TX | 77378-8987 | 936-890-0100 | 890-0110 | K-8 | Kurt Goedrich |
| Vista del Futuro Charter S | 7310 Bishop Flores Dr | El Paso, TX | 79912 | 915-855-8143 | 855-8179 | K-6 | Yvonne Whitman |
| Waco Charter S | 615 N 25th St | Waco, TX | 76707-3443 | 254-754-8169 | 754-7389 | PK-5 | Sabrina Gray |
| WALIPP-TSU Academy | 5220 Scott St | Houston, TX | 77004 | 713-741-3600 | 741-3603 | 6-8 | Cheryl Lawson |
| Walker IS | 6500 N Interstate 35 | San Antonio, TX | 78218-3702 | 210-654-4411 | 599-3546 | 4-6 | Cristen Darden M.Ed. |
| Wallace Accelerated HS | 149 S State Highway 208 | Colorado City, TX | 79512-6603 | 325-728-2392 | 728-1025 | 8-12 | Stephen Reese |
| Washington Tyrannus S of the Arts | 8410 E FM 1518 N | Schertz, TX | 78154 | 210-659-0329 | 566-7195 | 6-12 | Angela Pennington |
| Waxahachie Faith Family Academy | 701 Ovilla Rd | Waxahachie, TX | 75167-9430 | 972-937-3704 | 937-5806 | PK-12 | Andy Cellars |
| Wells Branch Leadership Academy | 15201 Burnet Rd | Austin, TX | 78728 | 512-872-8440 | | PK-12 | Verlean West |
| Wesley ES | 800 Dillard St | Houston, TX | 77091-2301 | 713-696-2860 | 696-2866 | PK-5 | Rhonda LeDuff |
| Westchester Acad International Studies | 901 Yorkchester Dr | Houston, TX | 77079-3446 | 713-251-1800 | 251-1815 | 6-12 | Jennifer Collier |
| Westlake Academy | 2600 J T Ottinger Rd | Westlake, TX | 76262-8012 | 817-490-5757 | 490-5758 | K-12 | Rod Harding |
| White Memorial HS | PO Box 2126 | League City, TX | 77574-2126 | 281-316-0001 | 316-0018 | 9-12 | Jessica Gagewanamaker |
| Whittier MS | 2101 Edison Dr | San Antonio, TX | 78201-3499 | 210-738-9755 | 735-0704 | 6-8 | Janet Perez |
| Williams Charter MS | 6100 Knox St | Houston, TX | 77091-4143 | 713-696-2600 | 696-2604 | 6-8 | Corey Seymour |
| Williams Preparatory S | 1750 Viceroy Dr | Dallas, TX | 75235-2308 | 214-276-0352 | 637-6393 | K-12 | Priscilla Pharms |
| Winfree Academy Charter S | 2985 S State Highway 360 | Grand Prairie, TX | 75052-7615 | 214-204-2030 | 204-2034 | 9-12 | Corrine Johnson |
| Winfree Academy Charter S | 2550 Beckleymeade Ave # 150 | Dallas, TX | 75237 | 469-930-5199 | 930-5206 | 9-12 | |
| Winfree Academy Charter S | 1661 Gateway Blvd | Richardson, TX | 75080-3530 | 972-234-9855 | 234-9975 | 9-12 | David Stubblefield |
| Winfree Academy Charter S | 3110 Skyway Cir S | Irving, TX | 75038-4207 | 972-251-2010 | 251-4301 | 9-12 | Ridwan Williams |
| Winfree Academy Charter S | 341 Bennett Ln | Lewisville, TX | 75057-4801 | 214-222-2200 | 222-0201 | 9-12 | Madge Ennis |
| Winfree Academy Charter S | 6311 Boulevard 26 Ste 300 | N Richlnd Hls, TX | 76180-1595 | 817-590-2240 | 590-8724 | 9-12 | Heather Nichols |
| Wood Charter S at Afton Oaks | 620 E Afton Oaks Blvd | San Antonio, TX | 78232-1236 | 210-638-5000 | 638-5575 | 5-12 | Chris Skipper |
| Wood Charter S at Granbury | 1300 Crossland Rd | Granbury, TX | 76048-5208 | 210-638-5600 | 638-5675 | 4-12 | Marc Malloy |
| Wood Charter S at Hays County | 2250 Clovis R Barker Rd | San Marcos, TX | 78666-4002 | 210-638-5400 | 638-5475 | 5-12 | Jessica Raney |
| Wood Charter S at Meridell | 12550 W State Highway 29 | Liberty Hill, TX | 78642 | 512-528-2462 | | K-12 | Wendy Rollins |
| Wood Charter S at Rockdale | 696 N FM 487 | Rockdale, TX | 76567-6005 | 210-638-5700 | 638-5775 | 4-12 | Raymon Puente |
| Yes Prep S - Brays Oaks | 9000 W Bellfort St | Houston, TX | 77031-2410 | 713-967-8400 | 778-0917 | 6-12 | Chris Claflin |
| Yes Prep S - East End | 8329 Lawndale St | Houston, TX | 77012-3707 | 713-967-7800 | 921-2305 | 6-12 | Leah Peters |
| Yes Prep S - Fifth Ward | 1305 Benson St | Houston, TX | 77020-4044 | 713-924-0602 | 670-0032 | 6-12 | Barbara Campbell |
| Yes Prep S - Gulfton | 6565 De Moss Dr | Houston, TX | 77074-5099 | 713-967-9800 | 774-1808 | 6-12 | Hugh Guill |
| Yes Prep S - Northbrook | 3030 Rosefield Dr | Houston, TX | 77080 | 713-251-4200 | 251-4209 | 6-8 | Jermy Jones |
| Yes Prep S - North Central | 13703 Aldine Westfield Rd | Houston, TX | 77039-2001 | 281-227-2044 | 227-2090 | 6-12 | Bryan Reed |
| Yes Prep S - North Forest | 6602 Winfield Rd | Houston, TX | 77050-4704 | 713-967-8600 | 636-7895 | 6-12 | Eldridge Gilbert |
| Yes Prep S - Northside | 5215 Jensen Dr | Houston, TX | 77026-2514 | 713-924-0400 | 589-2502 | 6-8 | Maureen Israel |
| Yes Prep S - Southeast | 353 Crenshaw Rd | Houston, TX | 77034-1543 | 713-967-9400 | 910-2350 | 6-12 | Charles Schmidt |
| Yes Prep S - Southside | 5515 S Loop E | Houston, TX | 77033 | 713-924-5500 | | 6-6 | Chris Claflin |
| Yes Prep S - Southwest | 4411 Anderson Rd | Houston, TX | 77053-2307 | 713-967-9200 | 413-0003 | 6-12 | Eric Newcomer |
| Yes Prep S - West | 10535 Harwin Dr | Houston, TX | 77036-1505 | 713-967-8200 | 541-8518 | 6-12 | Ashleigh Fritz |
| Yes Prep S - White Oak | 5620 W Tidwell | Houston, TX | 77091 | 713-924-5200 | 589-2502 | 6-12 | |
| Young Learners Charter S | 3333 Bering Dr | Houston, TX | 77057 | 713-784-1215 | 780-2338 | PK-K | Lillian Conway |
| Young Learners S | 8432 Bissonnet St | Houston, TX | 77074 | 713-772-7100 | 772-7104 | PK-2 | Kristina Troutman |
| Young Scholars Academy of Excellence | 1809 Louisiana St | Houston, TX | 77002-8013 | 713-654-1404 | 654-1401 | PK-8 | Anella Coleman |
| Young Womens Leadership Academy | 2123 W Huisache Ave | San Antonio, TX | 78201-4809 | 210-438-6525 | 732-7999 | 6-12 | Delia McLerran |
| Young Women's Leadership Academy | 401 E 8th St | Fort Worth, TX | 76102 | 817-815-2400 | 815-2450 | 6-12 | Mia Hall |
| Yzaguirre S for Success | 2950 Broadway St | Houston, TX | 77017-1706 | 713-640-3753 | 454-0893 | 6-8 | Philip Cano |
| Yzaguirre S for Success | 2950 Broadway St | Houston, TX | 77017-1706 | 713-640-3734 | 454-0893 | PK-5 | Maria Barrientos |
| Yzaguirre S for Success | 2950 Broadway St | Houston, TX | 77017-1706 | 713-649-6201 | 641-1853 | 9-12 | Philip Cano |
| Yzaguirre S for Success | 2255 N Coria St | Brownsville, TX | 78520-8731 | 956-544-7103 | 542-2667 | PK-8 | Raul Yzaguirre |
| Zoe Learning Academy | 3229 Hadley St Ste A | Houston, TX | 77004 | 713-659-5252 | 724-8255 | PK-7 | Stonie Arbuckle |
| Zoe Learning Academy | 202 W Center St | Duncanville, TX | 75116 | 972-296-3335 | 296-3335 | PK-6 | Dr. Richard Rose |
| Zoe Learning Academy | 6701 Cullen Blvd | Houston, TX | 77021 | 713-748-4228 | 748-7833 | PK-6 | Lonnie Reynolds |
| **Utah** | | | | | | | |
| Academy for Math Engineering & Science | 5715 S 1300 E | Salt Lake City, UT | 84121-1023 | 801-278-9460 | 277-3527 | 9-12 | Brett Wilson |
| Alianza Academy-Columbus Center | 2530 S 500 E | Salt Lake City, UT | 84106 | 801-953-1157 | 953-1196 | K-8 | Steven Merrell |
| Alianza Academy-West Valley | 2440 S 1070 W | West Valley, UT | 84119 | 801-953-1157 | 953-1196 | K-8 | Mary Ann Petela |
| American Leadership Academy | 898 W 1100 S | Spanish Fork, UT | 84660-5654 | 801-794-2226 | 794-2130 | K-12 | Richard Morley |
| American Prep Academy - Accelerated S | 3636 W 3100 S | West Valley, UT | 84120 | 385-351-3090 | 351-3089 | K-12 | Carolyn Sharette |
| American Preparatory Academy Draper 2 | 11938 S Lone Peak Pkwy | Draper, UT | 84020 | 801-810-3590 | 810-3589 | K-12 | Carolyn Sharette |
| American Preparatory Academy Draper 1 | 12892 S Pony Express Rd | Draper, UT | 84020 | 801-553-8500 | 576-9300 | K-6 | Carolyn Sharette |
| American Preparatory Academy - Salem | 1195 Elk Ridge Dr | Salem, UT | 84653-5521 | 801-465-4434 | 465-7808 | K-9 | Carolyn Sharette |
| American Preparatory Academy - W Valley | 1255 W Crystal Ave | West Valley, UT | 84119 | 801-839-3613 | 839-3626 | K-9 | Carolyn Sharette |
| Aristotle Academy | 704 S 600 E | American Fork, UT | 84003 | 801-763-7286 | 756-7037 | K-8 | Warren Shenk |
| Bear River Charter S | 75 S 400 W | Logan, UT | 84321 | 435-753-8811 | 661-6118 | K-8 | Janet Adams |
| Beehive Science & Technology Academy | 830 E 9400 S | Sandy, UT | 84094 | 801-576-0070 | 618-4115 | 6-12 | Hanifi Oguz |
| Bowen Laboratory ES | 6700 Old Main Hl | Logan, UT | 84322-6700 | 435-797-3085 | 797-3668 | K-5 | Dan Johnson |
| Canyon Grove Academy | 588 W 3300 N | Pleasant Grove, UT | 84062 | 801-785-9300 | 785-8997 | K-9 | Julie Adamic |
| Canyon Rim Academy | 3005 S 2900 E | Salt Lake City, UT | 84109 | 801-474-2066 | 474-2085 | K-6 | Merry Fusselman |
| Channing Hall Charter S | 13515 S 150 E | Draper, UT | 84020-8602 | 801-572-2709 | 571-8786 | K-8 | Heather Shepherd |
| City Academy | 555 E 200 S | Salt Lake City, UT | 84102-2007 | 801-596-8489 | 521-4181 | 7-12 | Sonja Woodbury |
| DaVinci Academy of Science and the Arts | 2033 Grant Ave | Ogden, UT | 84401-0409 | 801-409-0700 | 334-8533 | K-12 | Fred Donaldson |
| Dual Immersion Academy | 1155 S Glendale Dr | Salt Lake City, UT | 84104 | 801-972-1425 | 972-9482 | PK-8 | Angela Fanjul |
| Early Light Academy | 11709 S Vadania Dr | South Jordan, UT | 84009 | 801-302-5988 | 727-0773 | K-9 | Sydney Young |
| East Hollywood HS | 2185 S 3600 W | West Valley, UT | 84119-1121 | 801-886-8181 | 972-9585 | 9-12 | Eric Lindsey |
| Edison Charter S - North | 180 E 2600 N | North Logan, UT | 84341-1551 | 435-787-2820 | 787-0299 | K-9 | Scott Jackson |
| Edison Charter S - South | 1275 W 2350 S | Nibley, UT | 84321-6181 | 435-752-0123 | 787-4350 | K-9 | Melani Kirk |
| Endeavor Hall Charter S | 2610 S Decker Lake Ln | West Valley, UT | 84119 | 801-972-1153 | 972-1163 | K-8 | Trudy Jack |
| Entheos Academy-Kearns | 4710 W 6200 S | Kearns, UT | 84118 | 801-417-5444 | 417-5448 | K-9 | Eric Robins |
| Entheos Academy-Magna | 2606 S 7200 W | Magna, UT | 84044 | 801-250-5233 | 250-5240 | K-9 | Jesse Meeks |
| Esperanza ES | 4956 W 3500 S | West Valley, UT | 84120 | 801-305-1450 | 722-8252 | K-6 | Eulogio Alejandre |
| Excelsior Academy | 124 E Erda Way | Tooele, UT | 84074-9735 | 435-882-3062 | 882-4997 | K-8 | Stephanie Eccles |
| Fast Forward Charter HS | 875 W 1400 N | Logan, UT | 84321-6804 | 435-713-4255 | 753-9615 | 9-12 | Stephanie Sorenson |
| Freedom Preparatory Academy | 1190 W 900 N | Provo, UT | 84604-3171 | 801-437-3100 | 437-3149 | K-12 | Lynne Herring |
| Gateway Preparatory Academy | 201 E Thoroughbred Way | Enoch, UT | 84721 | 866-867-5558 | 867-5497 | K-8 | Andrew Burt |
| Good Foundations Academy | 5101 S 1050 W | Riverdale, UT | 84405-3732 | 801-393-2950 | 393-2953 | K-6 | Brent Petersen |
| Guadalupe S | 1385 N 1200 W | Salt Lake City, UT | 84116 | 801-531-6100 | 531-6106 | K-4 | Richard Pater |
| Hancock Charter S | 125 N 100 E | Pleasant Grove, UT | 84062-2355 | 801-796-5646 | 785-4934 | K-8 | Julie Adamic |
| Hawthorn Academy - South Jordan Campus | 1437 W 11400 S | South Jordan, UT | 84095 | 801-260-3040 | 254-6677 | K-6 | Dr. Deborah Swensen |
| Hawthorn Academy - West Jordan Campus | 9062 S 2200 W | West Jordan, UT | 84088 | 801-282-9066 | 727-0836 | K-9 | Dr. Debra Swenson |
| HighMark Charter S | 2467 E South Weber Dr | South Weber, UT | 84405 | 801-476-4627 | 475-5803 | K-9 | Mary Johnston |
| Intech Collegiate HS | 1787 Research Park Way | North Logan, UT | 84341-5600 | 435-753-7377 | 753-3775 | 9-12 | Jason Stanger |
| Itineris Early College HS | 9301 S Wights Fort Rd | West Jordan, UT | 84088 | 801-256-5970 | 256-5992 | 10-12 | Stephen Jolley |
| Jefferson Academy | 1425 S Angel St | Kaysville, UT | 84037 | 801-593-8200 | 660-6996 | K-6 | Nicole Jones |
| Lakeview Academy | 527 W 400 N | Saratoga Spgs, UT | 84045 | 801-331-6788 | 331-6792 | K-9 | Rick Veasey |

| School | Address | City,State | Zip code | Telephone | Fax | Grade | Contact |
|---|---|---|---|---|---|---|---|
| Leadership Learning Academy | 100 W 2675 N | Layton, UT | 84041 | 801-593-9552 | 784-5174 | K-6 | Heidi Bauerle |
| Legacy Preparatory Academy | 1375 W Center St | North Salt Lake, UT | 84054-2952 | 801-936-0555 | 936-1038 | K-12 | Erin Taylor |
| Lewis Academy | 364 N State Road 198 | Santaquin, UT | 84655 | 801-754-3376 | 754-3102 | K-6 | Vickie Peterson |
| Lincoln Academy | 1582 W 3300 N | Pleasant Grove, UT | 84062-9041 | 801-756-2039 | 785-2109 | K-9 | Jake Hunt |
| Maeser Prep Academy | 320 W 600 S | Lindon, UT | 84042 | 801-235-9000 | 235-9010 | 7-12 | Robyn Ellis |
| Mana Aademy Charter S | 2355 S Technology Dr | West Valley, UT | 84119 | 801-972-6262 | 401-7135 | K-12 | Anapesi Kaili |
| Maria Montessori Academy | 2505 N 200 E | Ogden, UT | 84414 | 801-827-0150 | 827-0145 | K-7 | Stephanie Speicher |
| Merit College Prep Academy | 1440 W Center St | Springville, UT | 84663 | 801-491-7600 | 491-7650 | 7-12 | Kim Mitchell |
| Moab Charter S | 358 E 300 S | Moab, UT | 84532-2624 | 435-259-2277 | 259-6652 | K-6 | Emma Weiss |
| Monticello Academy | 2782 S Corporate Park Dr | West Valley, UT | 84120 | 801-417-8040 | 417-8041 | K-9 | Dr. Gregory Cox |
| Mountain Heights Academy | 9067 S 1300 W Ste 204 | West Jordan, UT | 84088 | 801-721-6329 | 670-0032 | 7-12 | DeLaina Tonks |
| Mountainville Academy | 195 S Main St | Alpine, UT | 84004-1630 | 801-756-9805 | 763-9823 | K-9 | Janese Vance |
| Navigator Pointe Academy | 6844 S Navigator Dr | West Jordan, UT | 84084 | 801-840-1210 | 840-1236 | K-9 | Judy Farris |
| North Davis Preparatory Academy | 1765 W Hill Field Rd | Layton, UT | 84041-7323 | 801-547-1809 | 547-1649 | K-9 | Ryan Robinson |
| Northern Utah Acad for Math Engnrg & Sci | 2750 University Park Blvd | Layton, UT | 84041-9099 | 801-395-3350 | 395-3351 | 10-12 | Alan Stokes |
| North Star Academy | 2920 W 14010 S | Bluffdale, UT | 84065-5331 | 801-302-9579 | 302-9578 | K-9 | Tana Archer |
| Odyssey Charter S | 738 Quality Dr | American Fork, UT | 84003-3309 | 801-492-8105 | 763-8743 | K-6 | Russell Schellhous |
| Ogden Preparatory Academy | 1415 Lincoln Ave | Ogden, UT | 84404 | 801-627-2066 | 394-2267 | K-6 | Amie Campbell |
| Ogden Preparatory Academy | 1435 Lincoln Ave | Ogden, UT | 84404 | 801-627-3066 | 395-2267 | 7-9 | Amie Campbell |
| Open Classroom | 134 D St | Salt Lake City, UT | 84103-2640 | 801-578-8144 | 578-8218 | PK-8 | Martin Yablonovsky |
| Pacific Heritage Academy | 1755 W 1100 N | Salt Lake City, UT | 84116 | 801-363-1892 | 364-4735 | K-8 | Dirk Matthias |
| Paradigm HS | 11577 S 3600 W | South Jordan, UT | 84095 | 801-676-1018 | 676-1036 | 9-12 | Fernando Seminario |
| Pinnacle Canyon Academy | 210 N 600 E | Price, UT | 84501-2613 | 435-613-8102 | 613-8105 | K-12 | Roberta Hardy |
| Pioneer HS for the Performing Arts | 555 E Main St | American Fork, UT | 84003 | 801-768-8787 | | 9-12 | Shari Badley |
| Promontory S of Expeditionary Learning | 1051 W 2700 S | Perry, UT | 84302 | 435-919-1900 | 919-1902 | K-8 | Jamie McKay |
| Providence Hall | 4795 W Mount Ogden Peak Dr | Herriman, UT | 84096 | 801-727-8260 | 253-4997 | K-12 | Nathan Marshall |
| Quest Academy | 4862 W 4000 S | West Haven, UT | 84401 | 801-731-9859 | 731-9860 | K-9 | Dr. David Bullock |
| Ranches Academy | 7789 N Tawny Owl Cir | Eagle Mountain, UT | 84005 | 801-789-4000 | 789-4001 | K-6 | Susie Scherer |
| Reagan Academy | 1143 W Center St | Springville, UT | 84663-3028 | 801-489-7828 | 491-2829 | K-8 | Brian Myrup |
| Renaissance Academy | 3435 N 1120 E | Lehi, UT | 84043-6538 | 801-768-4202 | 768-4295 | K-9 | Mark Ursic |
| Rockwell Charter HS | 3435 Stonebridge Ln | Eagle Mountain, UT | 84005 | 801-789-7625 | 789-7628 | 7-12 | Darren Beck |
| Salt Lake Arts Academy | 844 S 200 E | Salt Lake City, UT | 84111-4203 | 801-531-1173 | 531-7726 | 5-8 | Amy Wadsworth |
| Salt Lake Center for Science Education | 1400 W Goodwin Ave | Salt Lake City, UT | 84116 | 801-578-8226 | 578-8677 | 6-12 | Gina Sanzenbacher |
| Salt Lake School for the Performing Arts | 2291 S 2000 E | Salt Lake City, UT | 84106 | 801-466-6700 | 485-1707 | 9-12 | Susan Brady |
| Soldier Hollow Charter S | 2002 Olympic Dr | Midway, UT | 84049-6216 | 435-654-1347 | 654-1349 | K-6 | Brenda Hedden |
| Spectrum Academy | 665 Cutler Dr | North Salt Lake, UT | 84054 | 801-936-0318 | 936-0209 | 7-12 | Christina Guevera |
| Spectrum Academy | 575 Cutler Dr | North Salt Lake, UT | 84054 | 801-936-0318 | 936-0568 | K-6 | Ashley Pamp |
| Success Academy at SUU | 351 W University Blvd | Cedar City, UT | 84720 | 435-865-8790 | 865-8795 | 9-12 | John Tripp |
| Summit Academy | 1285 E 13200 S | Draper, UT | 84020-9000 | 801-572-4166 | 572-4169 | K-8 | Steve Crandall |
| Summit Academy - Bluffdale | 15327 S Noell Nelson Dr | Bluffdale, UT | 84065 | 801-987-8755 | 987-8733 | K-8 | Steve Crandall |
| Summit Academy HS | 14942 S 560 W | Bluffdale, UT | 84065 | 801-495-3272 | 495-3275 | 9-12 | Steve Crandall |
| Syracuse Arts Academy | 2893 W 1700 S | Syracuse, UT | 84075-9838 | 801-779-2066 | 779-2087 | K-9 | Jan Whimpey |
| Syracuse Arts Academy - North | 357 S 1550 W | Syracuse, UT | 84075 | 801-827-0540 | 774-9270 | K-6 | Judy Nixon |
| Timpanogos Academy | 70 S 100 E | Lindon, UT | 84042 | 801-785-4979 | 785-9690 | K-6 | Errol Porter |
| Tuacahn HS for the Performing Arts | 1100 Tuacahn | Ivins, UT | 84738-4700 | 435-652-3201 | 652-3306 | 9-12 | Rosanna Weeks |
| Uintah River HS | PO Box 235 | Fort Duchesne, UT | 84026-0235 | 435-725-4088 | 722-0811 | 9-12 | Ben Pugh |
| Utah Career Path HS | 450 S Simmons Way | Kaysville, UT | 84037 | 801-593-2440 | 593-2140 | 9-12 | Robyn Bagley |
| Utah Connections Academy | 687 W 700 S Ste E | Woods Cross, UT | 84087 | 801-298-6660 | 298-6670 | K-12 | Matthew Bryant |
| Utah County Academy of Science | 940 W 800 S | Orem, UT | 84058-5915 | 801-863-2222 | 225-2214 | 10-12 | Dr. Anna Trevino |
| Utah International Charter S | 350 E Baird Cir | Salt Lake City, UT | 84115 | 385-290-1306 | | 7-12 | Angela Rowland |
| Utah Virtual Academy | 310 E 4500 S Ste 620 | Murray, UT | 84107 | 801-262-4922 | 262-5086 | K-12 | Stacey Hutchings |
| Valley Academy Charter S | 539 N 870 W | Hurricane, UT | 84737 | 435-635-0772 | | K-8 | Kevin Dunkley |
| Venture Academy | 495 N 1500 W | Ogden, UT | 84404 | 801-393-3900 | 393-2006 | K-12 | Dr. Mark Child |
| Vista at Entrada S | 585 E Center St | Ivins, UT | 84738 | 435-673-4110 | 256-6433 | K-8 | Samuel Gibbs |
| Voyage Academy | 1891 N 1500 W | Clinton, UT | 84015 | 801-776-4900 | 776-1966 | K-6 | Stacee Phillips |
| Walden S of Liberal Arts | 4230 N University Ave | Provo, UT | 84604 | 801-374-1545 | 374-3397 | K-12 | Lois Bobo |
| Wasatch Peak Academy | 414 Cutler Dr | North Salt Lake, UT | 84054-2951 | 801-936-3066 | 936-0887 | K-6 | Emily Swan |
| Washington Academy | 2277 S 3000 E | Saint George, UT | 84790-8510 | 435-673-2232 | 673-0142 | K-8 | Anya Yeager M.S. |
| Weber State University Charter Academy | 1351 Edvalson St | Ogden, UT | 84408 | 801-626-6271 | 626-7427 | K-K | Camie Bearden M.Ed. |
| Webster Academy | 205 E 400 S | Orem, UT | 84058-6311 | 801-426-6624 | 426-6645 | K-6 | Rick Kempton |
| Weilenmann S of Discovery | 4199 Kilby Rd | Park City, UT | 84098 | 435-575-5411 | 575-5412 | K-8 | Cindy Phillips |
| **Virginia** | | | | | | | |
| Community Public Charter S | 901 Rose Hill Dr | Charlottesville, VA | 22903-5239 | 434-972-1607 | 984-4975 | 6-8 | Ashby Kindler |
| Green Run Collegiate Charter S | 1700 Dahlia Dr | Virginia Beach, VA | 23453-2199 | 757-648-5393 | | 9-12 | Barbara Winn |
| Henry S of Science and Arts | 611 W 31st St | Richmond, VA | 23225 | 804-888-7061 | | K-5 | Eileen Atkinson |
| Middleburg Community Charter S | 101 N Madison St | Middleburg, VA | 20117-2645 | 540-687-5048 | 527-1257 | PK-5 | David Larson |
| Murray Charter HS | 1200 Forest St | Charlottesville, VA | 22903-5264 | 434-296-3090 | 979-6479 | 9-12 | Ashby Kindler |
| York River Academy | 11201 George Washington Mem | Yorktown, VA | 23690 | 757-898-0516 | 890-1045 | 9-12 | Walter Cross |
| **Wisconsin** | | | | | | | |
| Advanced Learning Academy of WI | 100 W River Ave | Barron, WI | 54812-1052 | 715-537-5612 | 637-5161 | K-12 | Craig Broeren |
| A L B A | 1712 S 32nd St | Milwaukee, WI | 53215-2104 | 414-902-7525 | 902-7526 | PK-5 | Brenda Martinez |
| Alliance Charter ES | 215 E Forest Ave | Neenah, WI | 54956-2765 | 920-751-6970 | 751-6861 | K-5 | Melissa Chrisman |
| Alliance HS | 850 W Walnut St | Milwaukee, WI | 53205 | 414-267-5400 | 267-5415 | 9-12 | Tina Owen |
| ALPS Charter S | 325 S Eagle St | Oshkosh, WI | 54902 | 920-424-0320 | 424-7514 | 5-8 | Jay Jones |
| Andrews Academy | 1033 Woodward Ave | Beloit, WI | 53511 | 608-361-4300 | 361-4122 | 6-12 | Tina Goecks |
| Appleton Bilingual S | 913 N Oneida St | Appleton, WI | 54911 | 920-832-6232 | 832-6355 | K-5 | Joel Canon |
| Appleton Career Academy | 5000 N Ballard Rd | Appleton, WI | 54913-8942 | 920-832-4309 | 832-4301 | 9-12 | Patrick Lee |
| Appleton Central HS | PO Box 2019 | Appleton, WI | 54912-2019 | 920-832-6136 | 993-7074 | 6-12 | Justin Heitl |
| Appleton eSchool | 2121 E Emmers Dr | Appleton, WI | 54915-3802 | 920-832-6212 | 832-4880 | 7-12 | Matt Mineau |
| Appleton Public Montessori S | 1545 E Broadway Dr | Grand Chute, WI | 54915 | 920-832-6325 | 832-6322 | K-6 | Dom Ferrito |
| Appleton Technical Academy | 610 N Badger Ave | Appleton, WI | 54914 | 920-832-6234 | 832-4198 | 9-12 | Greg Hartjes |
| Ashland Elementary Charter S | 1101 Binsfield Rd | Ashland, WI | 54806 | 715-682-7823 | | 3-5 | Mary Zoesch |
| Badger Rock MS | 501 E Badger Rd | Madison, WI | 53713-2120 | 608-663-1633 | | 6-8 | Timothy Bubon |
| Banner S of Milwaukee | 7171 W Brown Deer Rd | Milwaukee, WI | 53223 | 414-375-1510 | 375-1511 | 6-8 | Darlynn Terry |
| Barron Area Montessori S | 808 E Woodland Ave | Barron, WI | 54812-1759 | 715-537-5621 | 637-9353 | PK-4 | Nancy Weise |
| Bayshore Community Academy | 400 Michigan Ave | Oconto, WI | 54153-1764 | 920-834-7406 | | 5-8 | Adam DeWitt |
| Birchwood Blue Hills Charter HS | 201 E Birch Ave | Birchwood, WI | 54817-8800 | 715-354-9809 | 354-3469 | 7-12 | Jeffrey Stanley |
| Birchwood Public Montessori S | 201 E Birch Ave | Birchwood, WI | 54817-8800 | 715-354-9809 | 354-3469 | K-6 | Jeffrey Stanley |
| Black River Area Green S | 333 S 7th St | Blk River Fls, WI | 54615-1678 | 715-284-4324 | 284-4081 | 11-12 | Thomas Chambers |
| Bobcat Virtual Academy | 300 S Wilson St | Birchwood, WI | 54817 | 715-354-3471 | | PK-12 | Jeffrey Stanley |
| Bridges Virtual S | 1201 N Sales St | Merrill, WI | 54452-3171 | 866-537-2743 | | K-12 | John Hagemeister |
| Brompton S | 7951 36th Ave | Kenosha, WI | 53142-2119 | 262-359-2191 | 359-2194 | K-8 | Suzanne Loewen |
| Bruce - Guadalupe Community S | 1028 S 9th St | Milwaukee, WI | 53204-1335 | 414-643-6441 | 649-9022 | K-8 | Pascual Rodriguez |
| Business & Economics Acad of Milwaukee | 3620 N 18th St | Milwaukee, WI | 53206-2362 | 414-615-3915 | 988-6704 | PK-8 | Alisha Birtha |
| Capitol West Academy | 3939 N 88th St | Milwaukee, WI | 53222-2748 | 414-465-1302 | 465-1319 | PK-8 | Donna Niccolai-Weber |
| C.A.R.E. Charter S | 2000 Polk St | Stevens Point, WI | 54481-5876 | 715-345-5260 | 345-5696 | 7-9 | Connie Negaard |
| Carmen HS of Science & Tech - Northwest | 5496 N 72nd St | Milwaukee, WI | 53218-2820 | 414-837-4000 | | 6-12 | Dr. Patricia Hoben |
| Carmen HS of Science and Tech - South | 1712 S 32nd St | Milwaukee, WI | 53215-2104 | 414-384-4444 | 384-4455 | 9-12 | Dr. Patricia Hoben |
| Catalyst Academy | 709 S Shawano St | New London, WI | 54961 | 920-982-8686 | | 7-12 | Jo Collar |
| Catalyst Charter MS | PO Box 991 | Ripon, WI | 54971 | 920-748-4638 | 748-4653 | 6-8 | Thomas Hoh |
| CAVE | PO Box 378 | Cameron, WI | 54822 | 715-458-4560 | 458-4236 | K-12 | Jon Griffith |
| Central City Cyberschool | 4301 N 44th St | Milwaukee, WI | 53216-1473 | 414-444-2330 | 444-2435 | K-8 | Christine Faltz |
| Central HS | 621 S Water St | Sheboygan, WI | 53081 | 920-459-6746 | 803-7756 | 9-12 | Duane Simmons |
| Central Wisconsin STEM Academy | 540 Birch St | Nekoosa, WI | 54457 | 715-886-8040 | | 4-7 | Clint Rogers |
| Central Wisconsin Virtual S | 357 N Main St | Amherst, WI | 54406 | 715-824-5522 | | 6-12 | Mark Luetschwager |
| Chippewa Valley Montessori Charter S | 400 Cameron St | Eau Claire, WI | 54703-5101 | 715-852-6950 | 852-6995 | PK-5 | Todd Johnson |
| Cirrus Charter HS | 301 W Division St | Rosendale, WI | 54974 | 920-872-2161 | | 9-12 | Wayne Weber |
| Clark Street Community S | 2429 Clark St | Middleton, WI | 53562-2619 | 608-829-9640 | | 9-12 | Jill Gurtner |
| Class ACT Charter S | 400 9th St N | Park Falls, WI | 54552 | 715-762-2474 | 762-5674 | 9-12 | Timothy Kief |
| Classical Charter S | 3310 N Durkee St | Appleton, WI | 54911-1215 | 920-832-4968 | 997-1390 | K-8 | Nancy Fischer |
| Community HS | 6700 N 80th St | Milwaukee, WI | 53223-5506 | 414-256-8200 | 256-8215 | 9-12 | Roxane Mayeur |
| Connects Learning Center | 6201 S Barland Ave | Cudahy, WI | 53110-2951 | 414-766-5090 | 766-5095 | 9-12 | Stacey Adamczyk |
| CORE 4-Edgerton ES | 5145 S 116th St | Hales Corners, WI | 53130-1001 | 414-525-8900 | 525-8901 | PK-PK | Lori Komas |
| CORE 4-Hales Corners ES | 11319 W Godsell Ave | Hales Corners, WI | 53130-1899 | 414-525-8800 | 525-8801 | PK-PK | Lori Komas |
| Coulee Montessori Charter S | 1611 Kane St | La Crosse, WI | 54601 | 608-789-7760 | 789-7080 | PK-8 | Laura Huber |
| CRE8 Charter S | PO Box 227 | Gillett, WI | 54124-0227 | 920-855-2137 | 855-6600 | K-5 | Steve Linssen |
| Creative Minds Charter S | 7450 Titus Dr | Minocqua, WI | 54548-9139 | 715-356-5206 | 356-1626 | 3-5 | Brent Johnson |
| Daniels University Preparatory Academy | 4834 N Mother Daniels Way | Milwaukee, WI | 53209 | 414-466-1650 | | K-8 | Theresa Adams |
| Denmark Community Charter S | 450 N Wall St | Denmark, WI | 54208-8000 | 920-863-4153 | 863-4036 | 7-12 | Melissa Dupke |
| De Soto Virtual S | 615 Main St | De Soto, WI | 54624 | 608-648-0102 | | K-12 | Scott Kelly |
| Dewey Academy of Learning | 1420 Harvey St | Green Bay, WI | 54302 | 920-272-7074 | 448-3560 | 9-12 | Molly O'Neill |
| Dimensions of Learning Academy | 6218 25th Ave | Kenosha, WI | 53143-4370 | 262-359-6849 | 359-3134 | K-8 | Diana Pearson |
| Discovery Charter S | 200 Fuller St | Columbus, WI | 53925-1647 | 920-623-5952 | 623-6026 | K-3 | Sue Sewell |

| School | Address | City,State | Zip code | Telephone | Fax | Grade | Contact |
|---|---|---|---|---|---|---|---|
| Downtown Montessori Academy | 2507 S Graham St | Milwaukee, WI | 53207-1609 | 414-744-6005 | 744-6007 | K-8 | Virginia Flynn |
| eAchieve Academy of Wisconsin | 222 Maple Ave | Waukesha, WI | 53186-4725 | 262-970-1074 | 970-1148 | 6-12 | Rick Nettesheim |
| Eagleville Elementary Charter S | S101W34511 County Road LO | Eagle, WI | 53119-1860 | 262-363-6258 | 594-5495 | 1-6 | Ron Schlicht |
| Early Learning Academy | 3871 E Bluestem Dr | Oak Creek, WI | 53154-6640 | 414-768-6220 | | PK-PK | Christopher Gabrhel |
| ES for the Arts and Academics | 3508 N 21st St | Sheboygan, WI | 53083 | 920-459-0947 | | K-5 | Ted Hamm |
| Elkhorn Options Virtual Charter S | 3 N Jackson St | Elkhorn, WI | 53121 | 262-723-3160 | 723-4652 | K-12 | Sara Tanner |
| Endeavor Charter S | 825 Endeavour Dr | Watertown, WI | 53098 | 920-262-7525 | | 9-12 | Bob Logan |
| Enrich Excel Achieve Learning Academy | 2607 N 18th St | Wausau, WI | 54403-3176 | 715-261-0636 | 845-2913 | 6-12 | Dr. Shannon Young |
| Escuela Verde | 3628 W Pierce St | Milwaukee, WI | 53215 | 414-988-7960 | 988-7961 | 7-12 | Joella Zocher |
| Exploration Academy | 400 N Main St | Verona, WI | 53593 | 608-845-4550 | | 9-12 | Pheng Lee |
| Fairview S | 6500 W Kinnickinnic River | Milwaukee, WI | 53219 | 414-546-7700 | 546-7715 | PK-8 | Joseph Hartlaub |
| Flambeau Charter S | PO Box 86 | Tony, WI | 54563-0086 | 715-532-5559 | 532-9040 | 7-12 | Dan Lathrop |
| Fond du Lac STEM Academy | 401 S Military Rd | Fond du Lac, WI | 54935 | 920-906-6722 | | 3-5 | Donald Smith |
| Fond du Lac STEM Institute | 401 S Military Rd | Fond du Lac, WI | 54935 | 920-906-6722 | | 6-8 | Donald Smith |
| Forest Lane Community S | 222 Forest Ln | Montello, WI | 53949-9390 | 608-297-2128 | 297-8075 | PK-6 | John Graf |
| Foster ES | 305 W Foster St | Appleton, WI | 54915-1515 | 920-832-6288 | 832-4831 | K-6 | Matt Zimmerman |
| Fox River Academy | 1000 S Mason St | Appleton, WI | 54914-5457 | 920-832-6260 | 993-7060 | 1-8 | Lori Leschisin |
| Fox West Academy | 220 Warner St | Hortonville, WI | 54944-8559 | 920-779-7929 | 779-7923 | 6-8 | Steven Gromala |
| GOAL Academy | PO Box 227 | Gillett, WI | 54124-0227 | 920-855-2137 | 855-6600 | 6-12 | Steve Linssen |
| Grandview HS | 2745 S 13th st | Milwaukee, WI | 53215 | 414-672-1168 | 672-1273 | 9-12 | Debi Harry |
| HACIL | 15930 W 5th St | Hayward, WI | 54843 | 715-934-2112 | 934-8080 | PK-12 | Crystal Hexum |
| Harborside Academy | 714 49th St | Kenosha, WI | 53140-3353 | 262-359-8400 | 359-8450 | 6-12 | William Haithcock |
| Hartland Fine Arts Leadership Academy | 232 Church St | Hartland, WI | 53029-1704 | 262-369-6710 | 369-6711 | K-2 | Heather Grindatti |
| Hawley Environmental S | 5610 W Wisconsin Ave | Milwaukee, WI | 53213-4200 | 414-256-8500 | 256-8515 | PK-5 | Patricia Cifax |
| Health Care Academy | 115 E 6th St S | Ladysmith, WI | 54848 | 715-532-5531 | 532-7899 | 9-12 | Robert Lecheler |
| Highland Community ES | 1030 Cardinal Dr | Highland, WI | 53543-9791 | 608-929-4525 | 929-4527 | PK-5 | Josh Tarrell |
| Highland Community HS | 1030 Cardinal Dr | Highland, WI | 53543-9791 | 608-929-4525 | 929-4527 | 9-12 | Josh Tarrell |
| Highland Community MS | 1030 Cardinal Dr | Highland, WI | 53543-9791 | 608-929-4525 | 929-4527 | 6-8 | Josh Tarrell |
| Highland Community S | 1706 W Highland Ave | Milwaukee, WI | 53233-1132 | 414-342-1412 | 342-1408 | PK-8 | Kathy Ronco |
| High Marq Environmental Charter S | 222 Forest Ln | Montello, WI | 53949 | 608-297-2126 | 297-7726 | 7-12 | Chuck Harsh |
| HS of Health Sciences | 349 N Oak Crest Dr | Wales, WI | 53183 | 262-968-6273 | | 9-11 | Stephen Plum |
| Hines Academy | 7151 N 86th St | Milwaukee, WI | 53224-4861 | 414-358-3542 | 760-4364 | PK-8 | Precious Washington |
| Hmong American Peace Academy | 4601 N 84th St | Milwaukee, WI | 53225 | 414-383-4944 | 383-4950 | PK-12 | Chris Her-Xiong |
| Honey Creek Continuous Progess Charter S | 6701 W Eden Pl | Milwaukee, WI | 53220-1335 | 414-604-7900 | 604-7915 | PK-5 | Gitanjali Chawla |
| Humboldt Park ES | 3230 S Adams Ave | Milwaukee, WI | 53207-2700 | 414-294-1700 | 294-1715 | PK-8 | Georgia Becker |
| IDEA Charter S | 4704 Camp Phillips Rd | Weston, WI | 54476-1573 | 715-359-6561 | | 6-12 | Steven Pophal |
| IDEAL Charter S | 1420 W Goldcrest Ave | Milwaukee, WI | 53221-5013 | 414-267-1600 | | K-8 | Jennifer Carter |
| IDEAS Academy | 830 Virginia Ave | Sheboygan, WI | 53081-4427 | 920-459-0950 | | 9-12 | Ted Hamm |
| IForward: Wisconsin's Online Charter S | 480 E James Ave | Grantsburg, WI | 54840-7959 | 855-447-4723 | 463-2534 | 6-12 | Billy Beesley |
| iLEAD Charter S | 510 Grayside Ave | Mauston, WI | 53948-1921 | 608-847-5451 | 847-4635 | 7-12 | Gil Saylor |
| Innovations STEM Academy | 1225 N Water St | Sparta, WI | 54656 | 608-366-3497 | | 6-8 | Toby Oswald |
| Island City Academy | 980 8th Ave | Cumberland, WI | 54829-9188 | 715-822-5122 | 822-5132 | 7-12 | Colin Green |
| Island City Virtual Academy | 1010 8th Ave | Cumberland, WI | 54829-9174 | 715-822-5124 | 822-5136 | K-12 | Barry Rose |
| Janesville Virtual Academy | 1831 Mount Zion Ave | Janesville, WI | 53545-1236 | 608-743-5146 | 743-5130 | 9-12 | Mary Ann Kahl |
| JEDI Virtual HS | 1221 Innovation Dr | Whitewater, WI | 53190 | 262-473-1469 | 472-2269 | 9-12 | Leslie Steinhaus |
| Journey Charter S | PO Box 991 | Ripon, WI | 54971-0991 | 920-748-1550 | | K-2 | Myra Misles-Krhin |
| Juneau County Charter S | N11003 17th Ave | Necedah, WI | 54646-7618 | 608-565-7494 | 565-7559 | 7-12 | Amy McMillen |
| Kaleidoscope Academy | 318 E Brewster St | Appleton, WI | 54911-3702 | 920-832-6294 | 832-4605 | 6-8 | Al Brant |
| Kenosha e-School | 1808 41st Pl | Kenosha, WI | 53140 | 262-359-7715 | 359-5933 | K-12 | Dan Tenuta |
| Kenosha Schl of Enhanced Tech/Curriculum | 6811 18th Ave | Kenosha, WI | 53143-4932 | 262-359-3800 | 359-3850 | K-8 | Angela Andersson |
| Kiel eSchool | PO Box 201 | Kiel, WI | 53042-0201 | 920-894-2266 | 894-5100 | 7-12 | Heidi Dorner |
| Kings Academy | 7798 N 60th St | Milwaukee, WI | 53223-4153 | 414-371-9100 | 371-9200 | PK-8 | Erika Lynn Whitehead |
| KM Explore Charter S | 219 N Oak Crest Dr | Wales, WI | 53183-9705 | 262-968-6300 | | PK-5 | Laura Dahm |
| KM Global S | 349 N Oak Crest Dr | Wales, WI | 53183-9711 | 262-968-6273 | 968-6390 | 9-12 | Michele Koper |
| La Casa de Esperanza Charter S | 410 Arcadian Ave | Waukesha, WI | 53186 | 262-547-0887 | 547-0735 | K-K | Kristy Casey |
| La Causa Charter S | PO Box 4188 | Milwaukee, WI | 53204-0188 | 414-902-1660 | 902-1676 | K-8 | Maria Ayala-Smith |
| La Crosse Design Institute | 1900 Denton St | La Crosse, WI | 54601-5816 | 608-789-7670 | 789-7975 | 6-8 | Penny Reedy |
| LaCrossroads Charter HS | 1801 Losey Blvd S | La Crosse, WI | 54601 | 608-789-7700 | 789-7711 | 9-12 | Troy McDonald |
| Lake Country Academy | 4101 Technology Pkwy | Sheboygan, WI | 53083-6049 | 920-208-3020 | 208-3022 | PK-8 | Carla Koepp |
| Laker Online Virtual Charter S | 205 Oak St | Turtle Lake, WI | 54889 | 715-986-4470 | 986-2444 | K-12 | Kent Kindschy |
| Lakeview Montessori S | 711 Pine St | Sparta, WI | 54656 | 608-366-3468 | 366-3473 | PK-6 | Patrick Olbert |
| Laurel HS | 100 Blackhawk Dr | Viroqua, WI | 54665-1399 | 608-637-3191 | 637-8034 | 9-12 | Katherine Klos |
| LEADS Primary Charter S | 1410 Waukechon Rd | Shawano, WI | 54166-3168 | 715-524-2134 | 526-4372 | PK-2 | Troy Edwards |
| LIFE Entrepreneurial S | 800 N Shore Dr | Hartland, WI | 53029 | 262-369-6767 | 369-3766 | 6-8 | Michele Schmidt |
| Lincoln Inquiry Charter S | 242 S Prince St | Whitewater, WI | 53190-1777 | 262-472-8500 | 472-8510 | PK-5 | Mary Kilar |
| Link2Learn Virtual Charter S | PO Box 6 | Chetek, WI | 54728-0006 | 715-924-2226 | 924-2376 | PK-12 | Cali Kohlmeyer |
| Little Chute Career Pathways | 325 Meulemans St Ste A | Little Chute, WI | 54140-3300 | 920-788-7600 | 788-7841 | 9-12 | Dan Valentyn |
| Little Chute FLEX Academy | 325 Meulemans St Ste B | Little Chute, WI | 54140 | 920-380-9250 | 788-7603 | K-7 | David Botz |
| Lumen Charter HS | PO Box 991 | Ripon, WI | 54971 | 920-748-4616 | 748-4622 | 9-12 | Seth Meinel |
| Magellan Charter MS | 225 N Badger Ave | Appleton, WI | 54914-3832 | 920-832-6226 | 832-4857 | 7-8 | Debra Moreland |
| Manitowoc County Comprehensive Charter S | 1010 Huron St | Manitowoc, WI | 54220-3314 | 920-683-4780 | 683-4782 | 1-8 | Kristen Lee |
| Maple Grove Charter S | 290 County Road F | Hamburg, WI | 54411-9141 | 715-536-7684 | 536-4221 | K-5 | Heidi Siebert Preul |
| Marathon Venture Academy | 100 Spring Valley Dr | Marathon, WI | 54448-3400 | 715-443-2538 | | 6-8 | Jeffrey Reiche |
| Marshall Charter S | PO Box 76 | Marshall, WI | 53559-0076 | 608-655-1310 | 655-3046 | 11-12 | Brian Sniff |
| Mauston Montessori Charter S | 708 Loomis Dr | Mauston, WI | 53948 | 608-847-5616 | | K-K | Lynda Oleinik |
| McKinley Academy | 1010 Huron St | Manitowoc, WI | 54220-3314 | 920-683-4780 | 683-4782 | 9-12 | Kristin Lee |
| McKinley Charter S | 1266 McKinley Rd | Eau Claire, WI | 54703-2220 | 715-852-6900 | 852-6904 | 6-12 | Peter Riley |
| Mead Charter S | 241 17th Ave S | Wisc Rapids, WI | 54495-2401 | 715-424-6777 | 422-6333 | PK-6 | Margie Dorshorst |
| Merrill Adult Diploma Academy | 1101A N Mill St | Merrill, WI | 54452-1179 | 715-536-1431 | 539-2769 | 10-12 | Shannon Murray |
| Merrimac Community Charter S | 360 School St | Merrimac, WI | 53561-9584 | 608-493-2217 | 493-2895 | PK-5 | Sid Malek |
| Mighty River Acad of Virtual Education | 800 E Crawford St | Pr du Chien, WI | 53821 | 608-326-3703 | | K-12 | |
| Milwaukee Academy of Science | 2000 W Kilbourn Ave | Milwaukee, WI | 53233-1625 | 414-933-0302 | 933-1426 | PK-12 | Judy Merryfield |
| Milwaukee College Prep - 38th St | 2623 N 38th St | Milwaukee, WI | 53210-2502 | 414-445-1000 | 445-1005 | K-7 | Maggy Olson |
| Milwaukee College Prep - Lloyd St | 1228 W Lloyd St | Milwaukee, WI | 53205-1243 | 414-264-6000 | 264-2004 | K-8 | Andy Vitrano |
| Milwaukee College Prep S - 36th St | 2449 N 36th St | Milwaukee, WI | 53210-3040 | 414-445-8020 | 445-8167 | K-8 | Kristen Foster |
| Milwaukee College Prep S North Campus | 1350 W North Ave | Milwaukee, WI | 53205-1264 | 414-264-6600 | 264-6607 | K-8 | Michael Morgan |
| Milwaukee Collegiate Academy | 4030 N 29th St | Milwaukee, WI | 53216-1816 | 414-873-4014 | 873-4344 | 9-12 | Rashida Evans |
| Milwaukee Community Cyber HS | 131 S 1st St | Milwaukee, WI | 53204 | 414-308-1230 | 308-1231 | 9-12 | Jan Dahlman |
| Milwaukee Environmental Sciences Charter | 6600 W Melvina St | Milwaukee, WI | 53216 | 414-353-3830 | | PK-5 | Roseann Lococo |
| Milwaukee Math & Science Academy | 110 W Burleigh St | Milwaukee, WI | 53212 | 414-263-6400 | 263-6403 | PK-8 | David Chief |
| Milwaukee Scholars Charter S | 7000 W Florist Ave | Milwaukee, WI | 53218-1855 | 414-393-0197 | | K-8 | Taneka Smith |
| Monona Grove Liberal Arts Charter S | 5301 Monona Dr | Monona, WI | 53716 | 608-316-1924 | 221-7688 | 9-12 | Kristen Langer |
| Montello Virtual S | 222 Forest Ln | Montello, WI | 53949 | 608-297-2128 | 297-8075 | K-12 | John Graf |
| Montessori ES | 211 N Fremont St | River Falls, WI | 54022 | 715-425-7645 | 425-5380 | PK-6 | Nate Schurman |
| Mosaic S | 830 Virginia Ave | Sheboygan, WI | 53081-4427 | 920-459-0946 | | 6-8 | Ted Hamm |
| New Century Charter S | 401 W Verona Ave | Verona, WI | 53593-1318 | 608-845-4900 | 845-4920 | K-5 | |
| New Directions Learning Community | 2601 Sullivan Ave | Kaukauna, WI | 54130-3564 | 920-766-6116 | 766-6122 | K-5 | Kim Benson |
| New Horizons for Learning | 1701 E Capitol Dr | Shorewood, WI | 53211-1911 | 414-963-6921 | 961-2819 | 9-12 | Tim Kenney |
| New Path Charter S | 512 Caldwell Ave | Oconto Falls, WI | 54154-1138 | 920-848-4455 | 848-3899 | 7-12 | Michael Kurzynske |
| Next Door Charter S | 2545 N 29th St | Milwaukee, WI | 53210-3155 | 414-562-2929 | 562-1979 | PK-K | Kate Linscott |
| Next Generation Academy | 1700 Klatt Rd | New London, WI | 54961 | 920-982-8420 | 982-8440 | 6-12 | Anne Ferge |
| Niikuusara Community S | 540 Birch St | Nekoosa, WI | 54457 | 715-886-8040 | 886-8097 | 4-8 | Jon Sprehn |
| North Division Charter HS | 1011 W Center St | Milwaukee, WI | 53206-3299 | 414-267-4900 | 267-5015 | 9-12 | Stanley McWilliams |
| Northeast Wisconsin Montessori S | 411 E Washington Ave | Cleveland, WI | 53015-1517 | 920-693-8241 | 693-8357 | 1-6 | Bill Klein |
| Northern Lakes Regional Academy | 33 Ann St | Rice Lake, WI | 54868-2265 | 715-234-9007 | | 9-12 | Curt Pacholke |
| Northern Waters Environmental S | 15930 W 5th St | Hayward, WI | 54843 | 715-634-2619 | 634-9953 | 6-10 | Brittany Roberts |
| Northland Pines Montessori Learning Ctr | 8234 Highway 70 W | Saint Germain, WI | 54558 | 715-542-3632 | | PK-4 | Tony Duffek |
| North Point Lighthouse Charter S | 4200 W Douglas Ave | Milwaukee, WI | 53209 | 414-461-5339 | 461-5482 | K-6 | Rachel Wagner |
| North Star Academy | 207 N 1st St | Cameron, WI | 54822-9703 | 715-537-5612 | 637-5161 | 9-12 | Craig Broeren |
| NorthStar Community Charter S | N14463 Highway 53 | Minong, WI | 54859-9483 | 715-466-2297 | 466-5149 | 4-8 | Curt Zamzow |
| Northwood ES | N14463 Highway 53 | Minong, WI | 54859 | 715-466-2297 | | PK-5 | Curt Zamzow |
| Northwood MSHS | N14463 Highway 53 | Minong, WI | 54859-9483 | 715-466-2297 | 466-5149 | 6-12 | Curt Zamzow |
| Northwoods Community ES | 9086 County K | Harshaw, WI | 54529-9731 | 715-282-8200 | 282-8218 | K-5 | Will Losch |
| Northwoods Community Secondary S | 665 Coolidge Ave | Rhinelander, WI | 54501-2898 | 715-365-9660 | 365-9687 | 6-12 | Will Losch |
| NR4Kids Charter S | 701 E 11th St | New Richmond, WI | 54017-2399 | 715-243-7403 | 246-4278 | PK-PK | Mike Ballard |
| Nuestro Mundo Community S | 902 Nichols Rd | Monona, WI | 53716-2565 | 608-663-1079 | 204-0364 | K-5 | Josh Forehand |
| Oakwood Environmental Educ Charter S | 1225 N Oakwood Rd | Oshkosh, WI | 54904-8456 | 920-424-0315 | 424-7591 | PK-5 | Kirby Schultz |
| Oconto Falls Alternative Learning Site | 320 E Central Ave | Oconto Falls, WI | 54154-1456 | 920-848-4455 | 848-3899 | 10-12 | Mark Trepanier |
| Oconto Literacy Charter S | 810 Scherer Ave | Oconto, WI | 54153-1110 | 920-834-7808 | 834-9883 | K-2 | Becky Spengler |
| Odyssey Charter S | 2037 N Elinor St | Appleton, WI | 54914-2255 | 920-832-6250 | 832-4389 | 3-6 | Kristin Comerford |
| Oredocker Project S | 203 11th St E | Ashland, WI | 54806 | 715-682-7087 | | 6-8 | Laura Comer |
| Osceola Charter Preschool | PO Box 128 | Osceola, WI | 54020-0128 | 715-294-3457 | 294-2428 | PK-PK | Peggy Weber |
| Ouisconsing S of Collaboration | 103 Pleasant St | Lodi, WI | 53555-1137 | 608-592-3855 | 592-1025 | 3-5 | Sherri Endress-Lovell |
| Park Community Charter S | 509 Lawe St | Kaukauna, WI | 54130-2099 | 920-766-6129 | 766-6544 | K-4 | Kenneth Kortens |
| Pathways Charter S | 1043 S Main St | West Bend, WI | 53095 | 262-306-7125 | | 7-9 | Tim Harder |
| Phantom Knight S of Opportunity | 400 Reid St Ste W | De Pere, WI | 54115-2164 | 920-425-1915 | 429-1919 | 7-12 | Dr. Jason Lau |
| Point of Discovery S | 1900 W Zinda Dr | Stevens Point, WI | 54481 | 715-345-5566 | | 6-8 | Dan Lathrop |

| School | Address | City,State | Zip code | Telephone | Fax | Grade | Contact |
|---|---|---|---|---|---|---|---|
| Portage Academy of Achievement | 117 W Franklin St | Portage, WI | 53901-1755 | 608-742-8545 | 745-0887 | 9-12 | Seth Meinel |
| Promethean Charter S | PO Box 247 | Butternut, WI | 54514 | 715-769-3434 | 769-3712 | 9-12 | Joseph Zirngibl |
| Quest ES | PO Box 991 | Ripon, WI | 54971-0991 | 920-748-4695 | 748-4698 | 3-5 | Randy Hatlen |
| Racine Civil Leaders Academy | 1325 Park Ave | Racine, WI | 53403 | 262-664-8500 | 664-8524 | PK-5 | Danielle Dekker |
| REAL Charter S | 5915 Erie St | Racine, WI | 53402-1925 | 262-664-8100 | 664-8110 | 6-12 | Curt Shircel |
| Renaissance Charter Alternative Academy | 1107 S Wasson Ln | River Falls, WI | 54022 | 715-425-7687 | 425-7693 | 9-12 | Kit Luedtke |
| Renaissance S for the Arts | 610 N Badger Ave | Appleton, WI | 54914-3405 | 920-832-5708 | 832-4198 | 9-12 | Greg Hartjes |
| Richland Online Academy | 1996 US Hwy 14 W | Richland Center, WI | 53581 | 608-647-6106 | | 6-12 | Rachel Schultz |
| River Falls eSchool | 852 E Division St | River Falls, WI | 54022 | 715-425-1800 | 425-1804 | 7-12 | Jennifer Peterson |
| River Valley Studio S | 830 W Daley St | Spring Green, WI | 53588-8813 | 608-588-2559 | 588-2550 | K-5 | Jaime Hegland |
| Rocketship Southside Community Prep | 3003 W Cleveland Ave | Milwaukee, WI | 53215 | 414-455-3539 | | K-4 | Brittany Kinser |
| Rock River Charter S | 31 W Milwaukee St | Janesville, WI | 53548-2911 | 608-743-5070 | 752-8430 | 9-12 | Dr. Lisa Peterson |
| Rock University HS | 2909 Kellogg Ave | Janesville, WI | 53546 | 608-758-6512 | | 10-12 | Jane Thompson |
| Rural Virtual Academy | 624 College St | Medford, WI | 54451 | 715-748-4620 | | PK-10 | Charlie Heckel |
| St. Croix Academy of Virtual Education | PO Box 118 | Hammond, WI | 54015 | 715-796-2256 | | K-12 | Stephani Owens |
| S.A.V.E. Academy | 801 County Highway A | Spooner, WI | 54801 | 715-635-0215 | 635-7074 | PK-12 | Kate McKinney |
| S for AGricultural & Environmental Study | 200 S Depot St | Fox Lake, WI | 53933 | 920-928-3136 | | PK-7 | Nicholas Vertz |
| School for Arts and Performance | 349 N Oak Crest Dr | Wales, WI | 53183 | 262-968-6273 | 968-6217 | 9-12 | Kevin Erickson |
| School for Early Developmnt & Achievment | 2020 W Wells St | Milwaukee, WI | 53233-2720 | 414-937-2024 | 937-2021 | PK-2 | Nicola Ciurro |
| School of Sci Engineering & Technology | PO Box 125 | Blair, WI | 54616-0125 | 608-989-9835 | 989-2451 | K-6 | Mike Thomley |
| School of Technology & Arts I | 1111 7th St S | La Crosse, WI | 54601-5474 | 608-789-7695 | 789-7030 | K-5 | Steve Michaels |
| School of Technology & Arts II | 510 9th St S | La Crosse, WI | 54601-4703 | 608-789-7780 | 789-7181 | 6-8 | Melissa Murray |
| Shapiro ES | 1050 W 18th Ave | Oshkosh, WI | 54902-6688 | 920-424-0164 | 424-7594 | PK-5 | Trina Anderson |
| Shared Journeys Charter S | 9004 W Lincoln Ave | West Allis, WI | 53227 | 414-328-6535 | 545-6230 | 7-12 | Lisa Colla |
| Sheboygan Leadership Academy | 1305 Saint Clair Ave | Sheboygan, WI | 53081 | 920-208-5930 | | PK-8 | Peggy Henseler |
| SOAR Charter HS | 1800 Pleasure Island Rd | Eagle River, WI | 54521 | 715-479-4473 | | 9-12 | Scott Foster |
| SOAR Charter S | 6485 Town Hall Rd | Land O Lakes, WI | 54540-9659 | 715-547-3619 | | 5-8 | Scott Foster |
| Sparta Area Independent Learning S | 201 E Franklin St | Sparta, WI | 54656 | 608-366-3430 | 366-3526 | 9-12 | Bob Sanders |
| Sparta Charter Preschool | 201 E Franklin St | Sparta, WI | 54656-1803 | 608-269-3151 | 366-3529 | PK-PK | Diane Everson-Riley |
| Sparta High Point Charter S | 201 E Franklin St | Sparta, WI | 54656-1803 | 608-366-3151 | 366-3529 | 6-12 | Peggy Jadack |
| Spooner Area Virtual Academy | 801 County Highway A | Spooner, WI | 54801 | 715-635-2171 | 635-7174 | K-12 | Kurt Kunkel |
| TAGOS Leadership Academy | 1350 N Parker Dr | Janesville, WI | 53545-0720 | 608-743-5071 | 743-5095 | 7-12 | Dr. Kim Ehrhardt |
| Tenor High S | 840 N Jackson St | Milwaukee, WI | 53202-3807 | 414-431-4371 | 431-4376 | 9-12 | Tyson Tlachac |
| Tesla Engineering Charter S | 2121 E Emmers Dr | Appleton, WI | 54915-3802 | 920-997-1399 | 832-4880 | 9-12 | Paul Weisse |
| THINK Academy | 6950 Knowledge Ave | Rudolph, WI | 54475-9729 | 715-424-6784 | 435-2070 | K-5 | Roxanne Filtz |
| Time 4 Learning Charter S | 5900 S 51st St | Greendale, WI | 53129-2634 | 414-423-2750 | | PK-PK | Tracy Flater |
| Tomah Area Montessori S | 26232 County CA | Tomah, WI | 54660 | 608-374-7019 | 372-5087 | PK-3 | Tim Gnewikow |
| Tomorrow River Community Charter S | 10186 County Road MM | Amherst Jct, WI | 54407-9053 | 715-281-4776 | 346-2730 | PK-6 | |
| Transitional Skills Center | 850 Maple St | Glenwood City, WI | 54013-4346 | 715-265-4266 | 265-7129 | 10-12 | Patrick Gretzlock |
| 21st Century eSchool | 2429 Clark St | Middleton, WI | 53562-2619 | 608-829-9027 | 831-5160 | K-12 | Jill Gurtner |
| 21st Century Prep S | 1220 Mound Ave | Racine, WI | 53404-3350 | 262-598-0026 | 598-0031 | PK-8 | Arletta Tucker |
| Universal Academy for the College Bound | 3872 N 8th St | Milwaukee, WI | 53206-3303 | 414-914-9220 | | K-5 | LaShawnda Holland |
| Universal Academy for the College Bound | 6850 N 53rd St | Milwaukee, WI | 53223 | 414-716-5858 | | 6-8 | Junius Yates |
| Urban Day S | 1441 N 24th St | Milwaukee, WI | 53205-1899 | 414-937-8400 | 937-8406 | PK-8 | S. Hendricks-Williams |
| Ed.D. | | | | | | | |
| Valley New S | 10 E College Ave Ste 228 | Appleton, WI | 54911 | 920-993-7037 | 832-1725 | 7-12 | Ben Vogel |
| Veritas HS | 3025 W Oklahoma Ave | Milwaukee, WI | 53215-4347 | 414-389-5575 | 389-5576 | 9-12 | Sherry Tolkan |
| Vernon County Area Better Futures HS | 100 Blackhawk Dr | Viroqua, WI | 54665-1399 | 608-637-3191 | 637-8034 | 10-12 | Katherine Klos |
| Verona Area Core Knowledge Charter S | 740 N Main St | Verona, WI | 53593-1153 | 608-845-4130 | 845-4961 | K-8 | Brett Stousland |
| Verona Area International S | 5890 Devoro Rd | Fitchburg, WI | 53711 | 608-845-4224 | 845-4220 | K-5 | Barbara Drake |
| Viroqua Area Montessori S | 115 N Education Ave | Viroqua, WI | 54665 | 608-637-7071 | 637-1211 | PK-4 | Ryan Rieber |
| Walworth County Education Alternative HS | 400 County Road H | Elkhorn, WI | 53121-2035 | 262-741-8138 | 741-8131 | 9-12 | Kelly Demerath |
| Warriner MSHS for Personalized Learning | 712 Riverfront Dr Ste 101 | Sheboygan, WI | 53081 | 920-459-0945 | 459-0950 | 6-12 | Duane Simmons |
| Waukesha Academy of Health Professions | 401 E Roberta Ave | Waukesha, WI | 53186-6637 | 262-970-3710 | 970-3720 | 9-12 | Richard Lehman |
| Waukesha East Alternative S | 1150 Whiterock Ave | Waukesha, WI | 53186 | 262-970-4355 | 970-4380 | 9-12 | Ryan Galante |
| Waukesha Engineering Preparatory Academy | 401 E Roberta Ave | Waukesha, WI | 53186-6637 | 262-970-3880 | 970-3720 | 9-12 | Timothy Joynt |
| Waukesha STEM Academy | 114 S Charles St | Waukesha, WI | 53186 | 262-970-2300 | 970-2320 | K-5 | James Murray |
| Waukesha STEM Academy | 130 Walton Ave | Waukesha, WI | 53186-5904 | 262-970-2500 | 970-2520 | 6-8 | James Murray |
| Waupaca County Charter S | PO Box 457 | Weyauwega, WI | 54983-0457 | 920-867-4744 | | 6-12 | Wendy Cartledge |
| Wausau Area Montessori Charter S | 3101 N 13th St | Wausau, WI | 54403-2317 | 715-261-0795 | 261-2035 | K-6 | Michael Wridt |
| Wausau EGL Academy | 2607 N 18th St | Wausau, WI | 54403-3176 | 715-261-0625 | 845-5341 | 9-12 | Tim Fetting |
| Wauwatosa STEM | 1060 Glenview Ave | Wauwatosa, WI | 53213-3034 | 414-773-1900 | 773-1920 | K-5 | Mike Heun |
| Westside Academy | 1940 N 36th St | Milwaukee, WI | 53208-1927 | 414-934-4400 | 934-4415 | K-8 | Zannetta Walker |
| Whitetail Academy Charter S | PO Box 86 | Tony, WI | 54563 | 715-532-5559 | 532-9040 | 9-12 | Dan Lathrop |
| Whittier ES | 4382 S 3rd St | Milwaukee, WI | 53207-4999 | 414-294-1400 | 294-1415 | PK-5 | Peggy Mystrow |
| Wildlands Research Charter S | E19320 Bartig Rd | Augusta, WI | 54722-7501 | 715-286-4400 | 877-2234 | 7-12 | Paul Tweed |
| Windlake Academy | 1445 S 32nd St | Milwaukee, WI | 53215 | 414-672-0726 | 672-2019 | 4-8 | Theresa Yurk |
| Windlake ES | 2433 S 15th St | Milwaukee, WI | 53215-3132 | 414-643-9052 | 643-0162 | K-3 | Jim Kotsonis |
| Wisconsin Connections Academy | PO Box 2019 | Appleton, WI | 54912-2019 | 920-832-4800 | 832-6284 | K-12 | Michelle Mueller |
| Wisconsin Virtual Learning | 401 Highland Dr | Fredonia, WI | 53021-9491 | 262-692-3988 | 692-3952 | PK-12 | Melissa Horn |
| WIVA | 4709 Dale Curtin Dr | Mc Farland, WI | 53558-8958 | 608-838-9482 | 838-9483 | K-12 | Dr. Leslye Moraski Erickson |
| Woodland Progressive Charter S | 7450 Titus Dr | Minocqua, WI | 54548-9139 | 715-356-5206 | 358-2649 | 6-8 | Brent Johnson |
| Woodlands S | 5510 W Blue Mound Rd | Milwaukee, WI | 53208-3012 | 414-475-1600 | 475-9575 | PK-8 | Patty Rogers |
| Woodlands S East | 3121 W State St | Milwaukee, WI | 53208-3494 | 414-937-2000 | | PK-K | Maureen Sullivan |
| Wright Charter MS | 1717 Fish Hatchery Rd | Madison, WI | 53713-1244 | 608-204-1340 | 204-0547 | 6-8 | Angela Crawford |
| **Wyoming** | | | | | | | |
| Arapahoe Charter HS | 189 Lefthand Ditch Rd | Riverton, WY | 82501 | 307-856-3862 | 856-3946 | 9-12 | Nick Campagna |
| Laramie Montessori Charter School | 365 W Grand Ave | Laramie, WY | 82072 | 307-742-2554 | 742-2858 | K-6 | Elizabeth Coffey |
| Poder Academy | 2201 Morrie Ave | Cheyenne, WY | 82001 | 307-632-2248 | | K-12 | Dr. Jayne Smith |
| Snowy Range Academy | 4037 E Grand Ave Ste A | Laramie, WY | 82070-5128 | 307-745-9930 | 745-9931 | K-9 | Dawn Wilson |

# BUREAU OF INDIAN AFFAIRS SCHOOLS

## BUREAU OF INDIAN AFFAIRS
## 1849 C St NW, Washington, DC 20240-0001
## Telephone 202-208-6123
## Fax 208-3312
## Website http://www.bie.edu/Schools/index.htm

| Agency/School | Address | City,State | Zip code | Telephone | Fax | Grade | Enr | Superintendent/Principal |
|---|---|---|---|---|---|---|---|---|
| **Arizona Navajo Central Agency** | **PO Box 6003** | **Chinle, AZ** | **86503-6003** | **928-674-5130** | **674-5134** | **K-12** | 50 | **Gloria Hale-Showalter** |
| Black Mesa Community S | PO Box 97 | Pinon, AZ | 86510-0097 | 928-674-3632 | 659-8187 | K-8 | 50 | Marie Rose |
| Cottonwood Day S | Navajo Route 4 | Chinle, AZ | 86503 | 928-725-3256 | 725-3243 | K-8 | | Ronald Thompson |
| Jeehdeez'a ES | PO Box 1073 | Pinon, AZ | 86510-1073 | 928-725-3308 | 725-3306 | K-5 | | Fonda Charley |
| Lukachukai Community S | PO Box 230 | Lukachukai, AZ | 86507 | 928-787-4418 | 787-4435 | K-8 | | Arthur Ben |
| Many Farms Community S | PO Box 70 | Many Farms, AZ | 86538-3070 | 928-781-6221 | 781-6376 | K-8 | | Jacqueline Benally |
| Many Farms HS | PO Box 307 | Many Farms, AZ | 86538 | 928-781-6226 | 781-6355 | 9-12 | | Dr. Carmelia Becenti |
| Nazlini Community S | HC 58 Box 35 | Ganado, AZ | 86505-9704 | 928-755-6125 | 755-3729 | K-6 | 50 | Helena Botone |
| Pinon Community S | PO Box 159 | Pinon, AZ | 86510-0159 | 928-725-3234 | 725-3232 | K-12 | | Jospeh Benally |
| Rock Point Community S | PO Box 560 | Rock Point, AZ | 86545 | 928-659-4221 | 659-4235 | K-12 | | Deanna Dougi |
| Rough Rock Community S | HC 61 Box 5050PTT | Chinle, AZ | 86503 | 928-728-3550 | 728-3502 | K-12 | | Frank White |
| **BIE-Arizona Navajo North Agency** | **PO Box 746** | **Tuba City, AZ** | **86045-0746** | **928-283-2218** | **283-2286** | **K-12** | 100 | **Donald Coffland** |
| Chilchinbeto Community S | PO Box 740 | Kayenta, AZ | 86033-0740 | 928-697-3800 | 697-3448 | K-8 | | Dr. Connie Williams |
| Dennehotso Boarding S | PO Box 2570 | Dennehotso, AZ | 86535-2570 | 928-658-3201 | 658-3221 | K-8 | | James Brown |
| Greyhills Academy HS | PO Box 160 | Tuba City, AZ | 86045-0160 | 928-283-6271 | 283-6604 | 9-12 | | Dr. Loren Hudson |
| Kaibeto Boarding S | PO Box 1420 | Kaibeto, AZ | 86053 | 928-673-3480 | 673-3489 | K-8 | | Phyllis N. Yazzie |
| Kayenta Community S | PO Box 188 | Kayenta, AZ | 86033-0188 | 928-697-3637 | 697-3490 | K-8 | | Carena Begay |

| Agency/School | Address | City,State | Zip code | Telephone | Fax | Grade | Enr | Superintendent/Principal |
|---|---|---|---|---|---|---|---|---|
| KinLani Bordertown Dormitory | 901 N Kinlani Dr | Flagstaff, AZ | 86001-1585 | 928-774-5270 | 556-9683 | 9-12 | | Desi Yazzie |
| Leupp S | Highway 99 | Leupp, AZ | 86035 | 928-686-6211 | 686-6216 | K-12 | | James Rollison |
| Little Singer Community S | PO Box AQ | Winslow, AZ | 86047 | 928-686-6108 | 686-6439 | K-6 | | Etta Shirley |
| Naa Tsis 'Aan Community S | PO Box 10010 | Tonalea, AZ | 86044-5010 | 928-672-2335 | 672-2609 | K-8 | | Lolita Paddock |
| Richfield Residential Hall | 765 W 1st Ave | Richfield, UT | 84701-2436 | 435-896-5101 | 896-6157 | 9-12 | | Cody Workman |
| Rocky Ridge Boarding S | PO Box 299 | Kykotsmovi, AZ | 86039-0299 | 928-725-3650 | 725-3655 | K-8 | | Dr. Elizabeth McAuley |
| Shonto Preparatory S | PO Box 7900 | Shonto, AZ | 86054-7900 | 928-672-3528 | 672-3505 | K-12 | 100 | Lemual Adson |
| Tonalea Day S | PO Box 39 | Tonalea, AZ | 86044-0039 | 928-283-6325 | 283-5158 | K-8 | | Veronica Klain |
| Tuba City Boarding S | PO Box 187 | Tuba City, AZ | 86045-0187 | 928-283-2330 | 283-2362 | K-8 | | Donald Coffland |
| **Billings Area Office** | **2021 4th Ave N** | **Billings, MT** | **59101-1405** | **406-247-7953** | **247-7965** | **K-12** | **100** | **Barbara Parisian** |
| Blackfeet Dormitory | PO Box 627 | Browning, MT | 59417-0627 | 406-338-7441 | 338-5725 | 1-12 | | Renee Tatsey |
| Northern Cheyenne Tribal S of Busby | PO Box 150 | Busby, MT | 59016-0150 | 406-592-3646 | 592-3645 | K-12 | | Frank No Runner |
| St. Stephens Indian S | PO Box 345 | Saint Stephens, WY | 82524-0345 | 307-856-4147 | 856-3742 | K-12 | | Mike Hejtmanek |
| Shoshone Bannock S | PO Box 790 | Pocatello, ID | 83204-0790 | 208-238-4200 | 238-2628 | 7-12 | 100 | Eric Lords |
| Two Eagle River S | PO Box 160 | Pablo, MT | 59855-0160 | 406-675-0292 | 675-0294 | 7-12 | | Dr. Michael Bandy |
| **Bureau of Indian Education Arizona South** | **2600 N Central Ave Ste 800** | **Phoenix, AZ** | **85004** | **602-265-1592** | **265-0293** | **K-12** | **300** | |
| Blackwater Community S | 3652 E Blackwater School Rd | Coolidge, AZ | 85128 | 520-215-5859 | 215-5862 | K-2 | | Jack Sharma |
| Casa Blanca Community S | PO Box 10940 | Bapchule, AZ | 85121 | 520-315-3489 | 315-3505 | K-4 | | Jacque Bradley |
| Dishchii'bikoh Community S | PO Box 80068 | Cibecue, AZ | 85911-0068 | 928-332-2480 | 332-2341 | K-12 | | Juan Aragon |
| Gila Crossing S | 4665 W Pecos Rd | Laveen, AZ | 85339 | 520-550-4834 | 550-4252 | K-8 | | Ruben Gonzalez |
| Kennedy S, John F. | PO Box 130 | Whiteriver, AZ | 85941-0130 | 928-338-4593 | 338-4592 | K-8 | | Dr. Rea Goklish |
| Roosevelt S, Theodore | PO Box 567 | Fort Apache, AZ | 85926-0567 | 928-338-4464 | 338-1009 | 6-8 | | |
| Salt River ES | 10005 E Osborn Rd | Scottsdale, AZ | 85256 | 480-362-2400 | 362-2401 | K-6 | | Cheryl Parker |
| San Simon S | HC 1 Box 8292 | Sells, AZ | 85634-9711 | 520-362-2231 | 362-2405 | K-8 | | Frank Rogers |
| Santa Rosa Day S | HC 1 Box 8400 | Sells, AZ | 85634-9713 | 520-361-2276 | 361-2511 | K-8 | | Maxine Roanhorse-Dineyaz |
| Santa Rosa Ranch S | HC 2 Box 7570 | Sells, AZ | 85634-9741 | 520-383-2359 | 383-3960 | K-8 | | Delbert Ortiz |
| Tohono O'Odham HS | HC 1 Box 8513 | Sells, AZ | 85634-9735 | 520-362-2400 | 362-2265 | 9-12 | 100 | Michael Krug |
| **Cheyenne River Agency** | **PO Box 2020** | **Eagle Butte, SD** | **57625-2020** | **605-964-8722** | **964-1155** | **K-12** | | |
| Cheyenne-Eagle Butte S | PO Box 672 | Eagle Butte, SD | 57625-0672 | 605-964-8777 | 964-8776 | K-12 | | Francine Hall |
| Pierre Indian Learning Center | 3001 E Sully Ave | Pierre, SD | 57501-4403 | 605-224-8661 | 224-8465 | 1-8 | | Darrell Jeanotte |
| Takini S | HC 77 Box 537 | Howes, SD | 57748-9511 | 605-538-4399 | 538-4315 | K-12 | | Barry Mann |
| Tiospaye Topa S | PO Box 300 | Ridgeview, SD | 57652-0300 | 605-733-2290 | 733-2299 | K-12 | | Gorgeous Paul Hamus |
| **Crow Creek/Lower Brule Educ Line Office** | **PO Box 245** | **Lower Brule, SD** | **57548-0245** | **605-473-0216** | **473-0217** | **K-12** | | |
| Crow Creek Sioux Tribal S | 101 Crow Creek Loop | Stephan, SD | 57346-6120 | 605-852-2455 | 852-2140 | K-12 | | Silas Blaine |
| Enemy Swim S | 13525 446th Ave | Waubay, SD | 57273-5715 | 605-947-4605 | 947-4188 | PK-8 | 200 | Virginia Dolney |
| Lower Brule Day S | PO Box 245 | Lower Brule, SD | 57548-0245 | 605-473-0216 | 473-0217 | PK-6 | | Theresa Young |
| Lower Brule HS | PO Box 245 | Lower Brule, SD | 57548-0245 | 605-473-5510 | 473-5207 | 7-12 | | Marice Ashley |
| Tiospa Zina Tribal S | PO Box 719 | Agency Village, SD | 57262-0719 | 605-698-3953 | 698-7686 | K-12 | 500 | Dr. Nadine Eastman |
| **Fort Defiance Agency** | **PO Box 110** | **Fort Defiance, AZ** | **86504-0110** | **928-729-7255** | **729-7286** | **K-12** | | **Jacqueline Wade** |
| Crystal Boarding S | Navajo Route 12 | Navajo, NM | 87328 | 505-777-2385 | 777-2648 | K-6 | | Lorraine Dodge |
| Dilcon Community S | HC 63 Box G | Winslow, AZ | 86047-9414 | 928-657-3485 | 657-3213 | K-8 | | Dr. Tommy Lewis |
| Greasewood Springs Community S | HC 58 Box 60 | Ganado, AZ | 86505-9706 | 928-654-3331 | 654-3384 | PK-8 | 200 | Lucinda Godinez |
| Hunters Point Boarding S | PO Box 99 | Saint Michaels, AZ | 86511-0099 | 928-871-4439 | 871-4435 | K-5 | 100 | GloJean Todacheene |
| Kin Dah Lichi'i Olta | PO Box 800 | Ganado, AZ | 86505-0800 | 928-755-3439 | 755-3448 | 1-8 | 200 | Ora James |
| Pine Springs Day S | 1001 Pine Springs Rd | Houck, AZ | 86506 | 928-871-4311 | 871-4341 | K-4 | 100 | Lou Ann Jones |
| Seba Dalkai Boarding S | HC 63 Box H | Winslow, AZ | 86047-9415 | 928-657-3208 | 657-3224 | K-8 | 100 | Maye Bigboy |
| Tiiyaatin Residential Hall | 1100 W Buffalo St | Holbrook, AZ | 86025-2330 | 928-524-6222 | 524-2231 | 9-12 | | Maye Bigboy |
| Wide Ruins Community S | PO Box 309 | Chambers, AZ | 86502-0309 | 928-652-3251 | 652-3252 | K-6 | 100 | Dr. Elvira Largie |
| Winslow Residential Hall | 600 N Alfred Ave | Winslow, AZ | 86047-3130 | 928-289-4483 | 289-2821 | 7-12 | | Helena Botone |
| **Hopi Agency** | **PO Box 568** | **Keams Canyon, AZ** | **86034-0519** | **928-738-2262** | **738-5139** | **K-12** | **500** | **John McIntosh** |
| First Mesa ES | PO Box 750 | Polacca, AZ | 86042-0750 | 928-737-2581 | 737-2323 | K-6 | | Lorrie Harding |
| Havasupai S | PO Box 40 | Supai, AZ | 86435-0040 | 928-448-2901 | 448-2108 | K-8 | | Gregory Mooring |
| Hopi Day S | PO Box 42 | Kykotsmovi, AZ | 86039-0042 | 928-734-2468 | 734-2470 | K-6 | | Dr. John Thomas |
| Hopi JSHS | PO Box 337 | Keams Canyon, AZ | 86034-0356 | 928-738-5111 | 738-5333 | 7-12 | 500 | Dr. Paul Reynolds |
| Hotevilla-Bacavi Community S | PO Box 48 | Hotevilla, AZ | 86030-0048 | 928-734-2462 | 734-2225 | K-8 | | Margarito Uranga |
| Keams Canyon ES | PO Box 397 | Keams Canyon, AZ | 86034-0385 | 928-738-2385 | 738-5519 | K-6 | 100 | Gary Polacca |
| Moencopi Day S | PO Box 185 | Tuba City, AZ | 86045-0185 | 928-283-5361 | 283-4662 | K-6 | | Donald Harvey |
| Second Mesa Day S | PO Box 98 | Second Mesa, AZ | 86043-0098 | 928-737-2571 | 737-2565 | K-6 | 300 | Alma Sinquah |
| **Minneapolis Agency** | **5600 American Blvd W** | **Minneapolis, MN** | **55437-1274** | **612-725-4591** | **713-4438** | **K-12** | **600** | **Lynn Lafferty** |
| Bug-O-Nay-Ge-Shig S | 15353 Silver Eagle Dr NW | Bena, MN | 56626-1012 | 218-665-3000 | 665-3024 | K-12 | 300 | Crystal Redgrave |
| Circle of Life S | PO Box 447 | White Earth, MN | 56591-0447 | 218-983-4180 | 983-3767 | K-12 | | Ann Wothe |
| Circle of Nations Indian Boarding S | 832 8th St N | Wahpeton, ND | 58075-3642 | 701-642-3796 | 642-1984 | 1-8 | | Brad Zachow |
| Flandreau Indian S | 1132 N Crescent St | Flandreau, SD | 57028-1288 | 605-997-3773 | 997-2601 | 9-12 | | Everall Fox |
| Fond du Lac Ojibwe S | 49 University Rd | Cloquet, MN | 55720 | 218-878-7571 | 878-7573 | K-12 | | Mike Rabideaux |
| Lac Courte Oreilles Ojibwa S | 8575 N Trepania Rd | Hayward, WI | 54843 | 715-634-8924 | 634-6058 | K-12 | | Mike Leahy |
| Lumsden Bahweting Anishinabe S, J.K. | 1301 Marquette Ave | Sault S Marie, MI | 49783-9533 | 906-635-5055 | 635-3805 | K-8 | 500 | Susan Palmer |
| Menominee Tribal S | PO Box 39 | Neopit, WI | 54150-0039 | 715-756-2354 | 756-2364 | K-8 | | Shannon Chapman |
| Meskwaki Settlement S | 1610 310th St | Tama, IA | 52339 | 641-484-4990 | 484-3264 | K-12 | | Jill Herink |
| Nah Tah Wahsh Public S Academy | N14911 Hannahville Road B 1 | Wilson, MI | 49896-9612 | 906-466-2952 | 466-2556 | K-12 | 200 | Tom Miller |
| Nay Ah Shing S | 43651 Oodena Dr | Onamia, MN | 56359-2320 | 320-532-4695 | 532-4675 | K-12 | | Christina Howard |
| Oneida Nation ES | PO Box 365 | Oneida, WI | 54155-0365 | 920-869-1676 | 869-1684 | PK-12 | 300 | Sharon Mousseau |
| **New Mexico Navajo Central Agency** | **PO Box 328** | **Crownpoint, NM** | **87313-0328** | **505-786-6152** | **786-6112** | **K-12** | **4,500** | **Charlotte Garcia** |
| Borrego Pass S | PO Box 679 | Crownpoint, NM | 87313-0679 | 505-786-5237 | 786-7078 | K-8 | 1,200 | John Bach |
| Dzilth-Na-O-Dith-Hle Comm S | 35 Road 7585 Ste 5003 | Bloomfield, NM | 87413-4936 | 505-632-1697 | 632-8563 | K-8 | 200 | Mike Walker |
| Lake Valley Navajo S | PO Box 748 | Crownpoint, NM | 87313-0748 | 505-786-5392 | 786-5956 | K-8 | 100 | Donald Pine |
| Mariano Lake Community S | PO Box 787 | Crownpoint, NM | 87313-0787 | 505-786-5265 | 786-5203 | PK-6 | 100 | Bernice Nakai |
| NaNeel Zhiin Ji'olta S | HC 79 Box 9 | Cuba, NM | 87013-9701 | 575-731-2272 | 731-2252 | K-8 | | Kenneth Toledo |
| Ojo Encino S | HC 79 Box 7 | Cuba, NM | 87013-9701 | 505-731-2333 | 731-2361 | K-8 | 100 | Vickie Blackwater |
| Pueblo Pintado Community S | HC 79 Box 80 | Cuba, NM | 87013-9600 | 575-655-3341 | 655-3342 | PK-8 | 300 | Christina Mescal |
| T'iists'oozi Bi'olta S | PO Box 178 | Crownpoint, NM | 87313-0178 | 505-786-6159 | 786-6163 | K-8 | | Virginia Jumbo |
| Tse'ii'ahi' Community S | PO Box 828 | Crownpoint, NM | 87313-0828 | 505-786-5389 | 726-5635 | K-4 | 100 | Charlotte Begay |
| **New Mexico Navajo South Educ Line Office** | **301 W Hill Ave Rm 118** | **Gallup, NM** | **87301-6310** | **505-863-8395** | **863-8363** | **K-12** | | **John McIntosh** |
| Alamo S | PO Box 5907 | Alamo, NM | 87825 | 575-854-2635 | 854-2545 | K-12 | 300 | Dr. Tamarah Pfeiffer |
| Baca Community S | PO Box 509 | Prewitt, NM | 87045-0509 | 505-972-2769 | 972-2310 | K-6 | 300 | Timothy Nelson |
| Bread Springs Day S | PO Box 1117 | Gallup, NM | 87305-1117 | 505-778-5665 | 778-5692 | K-3 | 100 | |
| Chi-Chil Tah/Jones Ranch S | PO Box 278 | Vanderwagen, NM | 87326-0278 | 505-778-5574 | 778-5575 | K-8 | 100 | Marlene Tsosie |
| Ch'ooshgai Community S | PO Box 321 | Tohatchi, NM | 87325-0321 | 505-733-2707 | 733-2703 | K-8 | 400 | Ethel Manuelito |
| Tohaali' Community S | PO Box 9857 | Newcomb, NM | 87455-9857 | 505-789-3201 | 789-3202 | K-8 | 200 | Delores Bitsilly |
| To'Hajiilee'He S | PO Box 3438 | Canoncito, NM | 87026-3438 | 505-908-2426 | 908-2914 | PK-12 | 300 | Dr. Karen Sanchez-Griego |
| Wingate ES | PO Box 1 | Fort Wingate, NM | 87316-0001 | 505-488-6300 | 488-6312 | K-8 | | Dr. Edie Morris |
| Wingate HS | PO Box 2 | Fort Wingate, NM | 87316-0002 | 505-488-6400 | 488-6444 | 9-12 | 500 | Gloria Arviso |
| **New Mexico North Agency** | **661 Roadrunner Dr** | **San Juan Pueblo, NM** | **87566-3700** | **505-753-1465** | **753-1475** | **K-12** | **200** | **Dr. Benjamin Atencio** |
| Jicarilla Dormitory | PO Box 1009 | Dulce, NM | 87528-1009 | 575-759-3101 | 759-3338 | 1-12 | | David Montoya |
| Ohkay Owingeh Community S | PO Box 1077 | San Juan Pueblo, NM | 87566-1077 | 505-852-2154 | 852-4305 | K-6 | 100 | Maxine Ortiz |
| San Ildefonso Day S | 36 Tunyo Po | Santa Fe, NM | 87506-7258 | 505-455-2366 | 455-2155 | K-6 | 50 | Julianna Trujillo |
| Santa Clara Day S | 2 Kee St | Espanola, NM | 87532 | 505-753-4406 | 753-8866 | K-6 | 100 | David Nez |
| Santa Fe Indian S | PO Box 5340 | Santa Fe, NM | 87502-5340 | 505-989-6300 | 989-6317 | 7-12 | | Roy Herrera |
| Taos Day S | PO Box 1850 | Taos, NM | 87571 | 575-758-3652 | 758-1566 | K-8 | 200 | Andrew Haimowitz |
| Te Tsu Geh Oweenge S | RR 42 Box 2 | Santa Fe, NM | 87506-8368 | 505-982-1516 | 982-2090 | K-6 | 50 | Veronica Martinez |
| **New Mexico South Education Line Office** | **1001 Indian School NW # 149** | **Albuquerque, NM** | **87104** | **505-563-3690** | **563-3078** | **K-12** | **2,800** | **Casey Sovo** |
| Isleta ES | 1000 Moonlight Dr SW | Albuquerque, NM | 87105 | 505-869-2321 | 869-1625 | K-6 | 200 | Victoria Johnson |
| Jemez Day S | PO Box 139 | Jemez Pueblo, NM | 87024-0139 | 575-834-7304 | 834-7081 | K-6 | 100 | Freddie Cardenas |
| Laguna ES | PO Box 191 | Laguna, NM | 87026-0191 | 505-552-9200 | 552-7294 | K-5 | 200 | Dr. Kay Morris |
| Laguna MS | PO Box 268 | Laguna, NM | 87026-0268 | 505-552-9091 | 552-6466 | 6-8 | 100 | Dr. Natalie Martinez |
| Mescalero Apache S | PO Box 230 | Mescalero, NM | 88340-0230 | 575-464-4431 | 464-4822 | PK-12 | 500 | Sergio Castanon |
| Pine Hill S | PO Box 220 | Pinehill, NM | 87357-0220 | 505-775-3242 | 775-3241 | K-12 | 300 | Grant Clawson |
| San Felipe Pueblo S | PO Box 4343 | San Felipe Pb, NM | 87001-4343 | 505-867-3365 | 867-6253 | K-8 | 400 | Maxine Ortiz-Abeyta |
| Sky City Community S | PO Box 349 | Pueblo of Acoma, NM | 87034-0349 | 505-552-6671 | 552-6672 | K-8 | 200 | Yvonne Haven |
| T'siya S, Zia | 1000 Borrego Canyon Rd | Zia Pueblo, NM | 87053-6104 | 505-867-3553 | 867-5079 | K-8 | | Robin Rodar |
| **Northern Navajo Agency** | **PO Box 3239** | **Shiprock, NM** | **87420-3239** | **505-368-3400** | **368-3409** | **K-12** | | **Dr. Joel Longie** |
| Aneth Community S | PO Box 600 | Montezuma Creek, UT | 84534-0600 | 435-651-3271 | 651-3272 | K-6 | 200 | Brenda Whitehorse |
| Atsa'biya'a'zh Community S | PO Box 1809 | Shiprock, NM | 87420-1809 | 505-368-2100 | 368-2076 | K-6 | | |
| Beclabito Day S | PO Box 1200 | Shiprock, NM | 87420-1200 | 928-656-3555 | 656-3557 | K-4 | | Tanya Amrine |
| Cove Day S | PO Box 2000 | Red Valley, AZ | 86544 | 928-653-4457 | 653-4415 | K-5 | 50 | Deborah Belone |
| Navajo Prep S | 1220 W Apache St | Farmington, NM | 87401-3886 | 505-326-6571 | 564-8099 | 9-12 | 300 | Betty Ojaye |
| Nenahnezad Community S | PO Box 337 | Fruitland, NM | 87416-0337 | 505-598-6922 | 960-0970 | K-6 | 200 | Dean Cunningham |
| Red Rock Day S | PO Box 2007 | Red Valley, AZ | 86544-2007 | 928-653-4456 | 653-5711 | K-8 | 200 | Deborah Belone |
| Sanostee Day S | PO Box 159 | Sanostee, NM | 87461-0159 | 505-723-2476 | 723-2425 | K-3 | 100 | David Smith |
| Shiprock Schools | PO Box 1809 | Shiprock, NM | 87420-1809 | 505-368-2100 | 368-2076 | PK-12 | 600 | Julia Donald |
| T'iis Nazbas Community S | PO Box 2002 | Teec Nos Pos, AZ | 86514 | 928-656-3252 | 656-3486 | K-8 | 200 | George Waybenais |
| **Oklahoma Education Office** | **200 NW 4th St Ste 4049** | **Oklahoma City, OK** | **73102-3072** | **405-605-6051** | **605-6057** | **K-12** | **100** | **Joy Martin** |
| Chickasaw Children's Village | 1185 Village Rd | Kingston, OK | 73439-1017 | 580-564-3060 | 564-3605 | 1-12 | | Sallie Wallace |
| Eufaula Dormitory | 716 Swadley Dr | Eufaula, OK | 74432-2201 | 918-689-2522 | 689-2438 | 1-12 | | Greg Anderson |

| Agency/School | Address | City,State | Zip code | Telephone | Fax | Grade | Enr | Superintendent/Principal |
|---|---|---|---|---|---|---|---|---|
| Jones Academy | 909 Jones Academy Rd | Hartshorne, OK | 74547-5119 | 918-297-2518 | 297-2364 | 1-12 | 100 | Brad Spears |
| Kickapoo Nation S | PO Box 106 | Powhattan, KS | 66527-0106 | 785-474-3550 | 474-3530 | K-12 | 100 | Elaine Schilling |
| Riverside Indian S | 101 Riverside Dr | Anadarko, OK | 73005 | 405-247-6670 | 247-5529 | 4-12 | | Tony Dearman |
| Sequoyah HS | PO Box 520 | Tahlequah, OK | 74465 | 918-453-5400 | 456-0634 | 7-12 | | Rita Bunch |
| Pacific Regional Office | 2800 Cottage Way Ste W2820 | Sacramento, CA | 95825-1886 | 916-978-6057 | 978-6056 | K-12 | 1,100 | |
| Duckwater Shoshone S | PO Box 140068 | Duckwater, NV | 89314-0068 | 775-863-0180 | 863-0199 | K-8 | 50 | Keith Honaker |
| Noli S | PO Box 700 | San Jacinto, CA | 92581-0700 | 951-654-5596 | 654-7198 | 6-12 | 100 | Donovan Post |
| Pyramid Lake HS | 711 State St | Nixon, NV | 89424 | 775-574-1016 | 574-1037 | 7-12 | | Jake Chapin |
| Sherman Indian HS | 9010 Magnolia Ave | Riverside, CA | 92503-3972 | 951-276-6332 | 276-6336 | 9-12 | | Roland Doepner |
| Pine Ridge Agency | PO Box 333 | Pine Ridge, SD | 57770-0333 | 605-867-1306 | 867-5610 | K-12 | | Norma Tibbitts |
| American Horse S | PO Box 660 | Allen, SD | 57714-0660 | 605-455-1209 | 455-2249 | PK-8 | 300 | Dr. Gloria Kitsopoulas |
| Crazy Horse S | PO Box 260 | Wanblee, SD | 57577-0260 | 605-462-6804 | 462-6510 | K-12 | 300 | Lynn Lawson |
| Isna Wica Owayawa-Loneman S | PO Box 50 | Oglala, SD | 57764-0050 | 605-867-6875 | 867-5109 | K-8 | 200 | Charles Cuny |
| Little Wound S | PO Box 500 | Kyle, SD | 57752-0500 | 605-455-6150 | 455-2703 | PK-12 | 900 | Dr. Anthony Fairbanks |
| Pine Ridge S | PO Box 1202 | Pine Ridge, SD | 57770-1202 | 605-867-5193 | 867-5482 | K-12 | 400 | Mona Miyasato |
| Porcupine S | PO Box 180 | Porcupine, SD | 57772-0180 | 605-455-6450 | 867-5480 | K-8 | | Lori Enright |
| Wounded Knee S | PO Box 350 | Manderson, SD | 57756-0350 | 605-867-4350 | 867-5156 | K-8 | | Alice Phelps |
| Portland Area Office | 911 NE 11th Ave | Portland, OR | 97232-4128 | 503-872-2743 | 231-6219 | PK-12 | 200 | |
| Chemawa Indian S | 3700 Chemawa Rd NE | Salem, OR | 97305-1199 | 503-399-5721 | 399-5870 | 9-12 | | Donald Tomin |
| Chief Leschi S | 5625 52nd St E | Puyallup, WA | 98371-3610 | 253-445-6000 | 445-2350 | K-12 | | Raymond Lorton |
| Couer D'Alene Tribal S | PO Box 338 | Desmet, ID | 83824-0338 | 208-686-5808 | 686-5080 | K-8 | 100 | Eric Kendra |
| Lummi HS | 2334 Lummi View Dr | Bellingham, WA | 98226-9277 | 360-758-4330 | 758-3152 | 9-12 | | Heather Leighton |
| Lummi Tribal S | 2334 Lummi View Dr | Bellingham, WA | 98226-9277 | 360-758-4300 | 758-3160 | K-8 | | Heather Leighton |
| Muckleshoot Tribal S | 15209 SE 376th St | Auburn, WA | 98092 | 253-931-6709 | 939-5568 | K-12 | 300 | Richard Torralba |
| Paschal Sherman Indian S | 169 N End Omak Lake Rd | Omak, WA | 98841 | 509-422-7590 | 422-7538 | K-9 | 200 | Raymond Leaver |
| Quileute Tribal S | PO Box 39 | La Push, WA | 98350 | 360-374-5702 | | K-12 | | Mark Jacobson |
| Wa He Lut Indian S | 11110 Conine Ave SE | Olympia, WA | 98513-9603 | 360-456-1311 | 456-1319 | K-8 | 100 | Harvey Whitford |
| Yakima Tribal S | PO Box 151 | Toppenish, WA | 98948 | 509-865-4478 | | 8-12 | 100 | Relyn Storm |
| Rosebud Agency | PO Box 669 | Mission, SD | 57555-0669 | 605-856-4478 | 856-4487 | K-12 | | Neva Sherwood |
| Marty Indian S | PO Box 187 | Marty, SD | 57361-0187 | 605-384-2212 | 384-5933 | K-12 | | Everdell Wright |
| St. Francis Indian S | PO Box 379 | Saint Francis, SD | 57572-0379 | 605-747-2299 | 747-2379 | K-12 | | Richard Bad Milk |
| South & Eastern States Agency | 545 Marriott Dr Ste 720 | Nashville, TN | 37214-5081 | 615-564-6630 | 564-6631 | PK-12 | 400 | |
| Ahafachkee S | HC 61 Box 40 | Clewiston, FL | 33440 | 863-983-6348 | 983-6535 | K-12 | | Jillian Wilson |
| Bogue Chitto S | 13241 Highway 491 N | Philadelphia, MS | 39350-5463 | 601-389-1000 | 389-1002 | K-8 | | Linda Dick |
| Cherokee Central ES | 1582 Ravensford Dr | Cherokee, NC | 28719 | 828-554-5020 | 554-5035 | K-5 | | Paula Coker |
| Cherokee Central HS | 1582 Ravensford Dr | Cherokee, NC | 28719 | 828-554-5030 | 554-5033 | 9-12 | | Woodreen Caldwell |
| Cherokee Central MS | 1582 Ravensford Dr | Cherokee, NC | 28719 | 828-554-5026 | 554-5029 | 6-8 | | Cance Carnes |
| Chitimacha Day S | 3613 Chitimacha Trl | Jeanerette, LA | 70544-8317 | 337-923-9960 | 923-7346 | K-8 | 100 | Tanya Rosamond |
| Choctaw Central HS | 150 Recreation Rd | Choctaw, MS | 39350-7180 | 601-663-7777 | 656-7077 | 9-12 | 400 | Fredrick Hickmon |
| Choctaw Central MS | 150 Recreation Rd | Choctaw, MS | 39350-7180 | 601-656-8938 | 656-1558 | 7-8 | 200 | Jackie Harpole |
| Conehatta S | 851 Tushka Rd | Conehatta, MS | 39057-2804 | 601-775-8254 | 775-9229 | K-8 | | Brian Parkman |
| Indian Island S | 10 Wabanaki Way | Indian Island, ME | 04468-1254 | 207-827-4285 | 827-3599 | PK-8 | 100 | Linda McLeod |
| Indian Township S | 13 School Dr | Princeton, ME | 04668-5000 | 207-796-2362 | 796-2726 | PK-8 | 100 | Maryanne Spearin |
| Miccosukee Indian S | PO Box 440021 | Miami, FL | 33144-0021 | 305-894-2364 | 894-2365 | K-12 | | Manuel Varela |
| Pearl River ES | 470 Industrial Rd | Choctaw, MS | 39350-4256 | 601-656-9051 | 656-9054 | K-6 | | Suzanne Hyatt |
| Rafferty S, Beatrice | 22 Bayview Dr | Pleasant Point, ME | 04667-4111 | 207-853-6085 | 853-2483 | PK-8 | 100 | Mike Chadwick |
| Red Water S | 106 Braves Blvd | Carthage, MS | 39051 | 601-267-8500 | 267-5193 | K-8 | | Terri Rhea |
| Standing Pine ES | 538 Highway 487 E | Carthage, MS | 39051-6031 | 601-267-9225 | 267-9129 | K-6 | | Jason Roberson |
| Tucker S | 126 E Tucker Cir | Philadelphia, MS | 39350-8351 | 601-656-8775 | 656-9341 | K-8 | | Joe Wood |
| Standing Rock Agency | PO Box E | Fort Yates, ND | 58538-0523 | 701-854-3497 | 854-7280 | K-12 | 200 | Linda Lawrence |
| Jamerson S, Theodore | 3315 University Dr | Bismarck, ND | 58504-7565 | 701-530-0677 | 530-0601 | K-8 | | Francis Azure |
| Rock Creek Grant S | PO Box 127 | Bullhead, SD | 57621-0127 | 605-823-4971 | 823-4350 | K-8 | | Clyde Naasz |
| Sitting Bull Day S | PO Box 26 | Little Eagle, SD | 57639-0026 | 605-823-4235 | 823-2292 | K-8 | | Lisa Bielawski |
| Standing Rock Community S | PO Box 377 | Fort Yates, ND | 58538-0377 | 701-854-3461 | 854-2078 | K-12 | 200 | Robert Taken Alive |
| Tate Topa Tribal S | PO Box 199 | Fort Totten, ND | 58335-0199 | 701-766-1400 | 766-1457 | K-8 | | Mark Mindt |
| Turtle Mountain Education Line Office | PO Box 30 | Belcourt, ND | 58316-0030 | 701-477-3463 | 477-9364 | PK-12 | 100 | Rose-Marie Davis |
| Dunseith Day S | PO Box 759 | Dunseith, ND | 58329-0759 | 701-263-4636 | 263-4200 | K-8 | | Michelle Thomas |
| Ojibwa Indian S | PO Box 600 | Belcourt, ND | 58316-0600 | 701-477-3108 | 477-6039 | K-8 | | Michael Blue |
| Twin Buttes S | 7997 7A St NW | Halliday, ND | 58636-4004 | 701-938-4396 | 938-4398 | K-8 | 50 | Chad Dahlen |
| White Shield S | 2 2nd Ave W | Roseglen, ND | 58775-6009 | 701-743-4350 | 743-4501 | K-12 | 100 | Gaillord Peltier |

# DEPARTMENT OF DEFENSE DEPENDENT SCHOOLS

## DEPT. OF DEFENSE DEPENDENT SCHOOLS
## 4040 Fairfax Dr Fl 9, Arlington, VA 22203-1613
## Telephone 703-588-3104
## Website http://www.dodea.edu

| District/School | Address | City,State | Zip code | Telephone | Fax | Grade | Enr | Superintendent/Principal |
|---|---|---|---|---|---|---|---|---|
| Fort Campbell Dependent SD | 77 Texas Ave | Fort Campbell, KY | 42223-5127 | 270-439-1927 | 439-6992 | PK-12 | 4,900 | Dr. Frank Calvano |
| Barkley ES | 4720 Polk Rd | Fort Campbell, KY | 42223-1900 | 270-439-1951 | 439-1901 | PK-5 | 600 | Rhonda Pawlawski |
| Barsanti ES | 7409 McAuliffe Loop | Fort Campbell, KY | 42223 | 270-640-1213 | 431-0519 | PK-5 | 600 | Dr. David Martin |
| Fort Campbell HS | 1101 Bastogne Ave | Fort Campbell, KY | 42223-5133 | 270-640-1219 | 431-9386 | 9-12 | 600 | Hugh McKinnon |
| Jackson ES | 675 Mississippi Ave | Fort Campbell, KY | 42223-5353 | 931-431-6211 | 431-4453 | PK-5 | 700 | Linda Shelton |
| Lincoln ES | 4718 Polk Rd | Fort Campbell, KY | 42223-1400 | 270-640-1212 | 439-2335 | PK-5 | 600 | Linda Haberman |
| Lucas ES, Andre | 2115 Airborne St | Fort Campbell, KY | 42223-5333 | 270-640-1208 | 431-5842 | PK-5 | 500 | Ted Turnipseed |
| Mahaffey MS | 585 S Carolina Ave | Fort Campbell, KY | 42223-5134 | 270-640-1215 | 439-3472 | 6-8 | 400 | Steve Gardner |
| Marshall ES | 75 Texas Ave | Fort Campbell, KY | 42223-5135 | 270-640-1214 | 439-4382 | PK-5 | 500 | Dr. Suzanne Jones |
| Wassom MS | 3066 Forest Rd | Fort Campbell, KY | 42223-5272 | 270-640-1218 | 439-0249 | 6-8 | 300 | Kimberly Butts |
| Fort Knox Community SD | 281 Fayette Ave | Fort Knox, KY | 40121-6201 | 502-624-2345 | 624-3969 | PK-12 | 2,300 | Frank Calvano Ed.D. |
| Fort Knox HS | 266 Maine St | Fort Knox, KY | 40121 | 502-624-6647 | 624-6171 | 9-12 | 400 | Gregg Mowen Ed.D. |
| Macdonald ES | 128 McCracken St | Fort Knox, KY | 40121-2706 | 502-624-5650 | 624-2108 | 1-5 | 200 | Laura Gibson M.A. |
| Scott MS | 266 Mississippi St | Fort Knox, KY | 40121-6814 | 502-624-2236 | 624-5433 | 6-8 | 300 | Youlanda Washington |
| Ph.D. | | | | | | | | |
| Van Voorhis ES | 120 Folger St | Fort Knox, KY | 40121-6086 | 502-624-5854 | 624-7267 | PK-5 | 500 | Sharon McGourty Perkins |
| Georgia / Alabama Dependent SD | 7441 Custer Rd Bldg 2670 | Fort Benning, GA | 31905-9647 | 706-545-7276 | 545-8227 | PK-8 | 2,600 | Dr. Christy Huddleston |
| Dexter ES, Herbert J. | 99 Yeager Ave | Fort Benning, GA | 31905-9699 | 706-545-3424 | 545-9106 | PK-5 | | Edwina Smith |
| Faith MS, Don C. | 1375 Ingersoll St | Fort Benning, GA | 31905-7200 | 706-545-0310 | 545-7800 | 6-8 | | Darrell Mood |
| Fort Rucker ES | PO Box 620279 | Fort Rucker, AL | 36362-0279 | 334-255-1607 | 268-7482 | 2-6 | | Dr. Vicki Gilmer |
| Fort Rucker PS | PO Box 620279 | Fort Rucker, AL | 36362-0279 | 334-255-2822 | 268-7483 | PK-1 | | Dr. Deborah Deas |
| Loyd ES, Frank R. | 5701 Santa Fe Rd | Fort Benning, GA | 31905-2724 | 706-544-8961 | 544-8972 | PK-5 | | Julita Martinez |
| Maxwell AFB ES | 800 Magnolia Blvd | Maxwell AFB, AL | 36112-5922 | 334-953-7804 | 953-4339 | PK-8 | 400 | Paul Hernandez |
| McBride ES, Morris R. | 700 Custer Rd | Fort Benning, GA | 31905-7402 | 706-544-9411 | 544-9299 | PK-5 | | Phyllis Parker |
| Stowers ES, Freddie | 7791 Stowers Dr | Fort Benning, GA | 31905-3130 | 706-544-2312 | 544-2349 | PK-5 | | Debbie Parks |
| White ES, Edward A. | 300 1st Division Rd | Fort Benning, GA | 31905-6627 | 706-545-4623 | 545-5469 | PK-5 | | Dr. Renee Mallory |
| Wilson ES, Richard G. | 112 Lavoie Ave | Fort Benning, GA | 31905-7523 | 706-545-5723 | 545-9505 | PK-5 | | Michelle Allen |
| NY/VA Domestic Dependent School System | 3308 John Quick Rd Ste 201 | Quantico, VA | 22134-1752 | 703-630-7012 | 784-3100 | PK-12 | 1,200 | Michael Gould |
| Crossroads ES | 3315 Purvis Rd | Quantico, VA | 22134 | 703-630-7065 | | PK-5 | 700 | Donna Kacmarski |
| Dahlgren S | 6117 Sampson Rd Ste 206 | Dahlgren, VA | 22448-5121 | 540-653-8822 | 653-4591 | PK-8 | | Dr. Jeffrey Duncan |
| Quantico MSHS | 3307 Purvis Rd | Quantico, VA | 22134-2198 | 703-630-7055 | 784-4851 | 6-12 | | Michael Johnson |
| West Point ES | 705A Barry Rd | West Point, NY | 10996-1196 | 845-938-2313 | 938-3352 | PK-4 | | Denise Webster-Cochenour |
| West Point MS | 705 Barry Rd | West Point, NY | 10996-1110 | 845-938-2923 | 938-2568 | 5-8 | | David Rudy |
| North Carolina Dependent SD | PO Box 70089 | Fort Bragg, NC | 28307-0089 | 910-907-0228 | 907-1405 | PK-9 | 4,600 | Dr. Emily Marsh |
| Albritton MS | PO Box 70089 | Fort Bragg, NC | 28307-0089 | 910-907-0201 | 432-4072 | 6-8 | 600 | Pat Schob |
| Bitz IS | 2028 Bevin St | Camp Lejeune, NC | 28547-1436 | 910-451-2575 | 451-1475 | 3-5 | 400 | Dewanda Sholar |
| Bowley ES | PO Box 70089 | Fort Bragg, NC | 28307-0089 | 910-907-0202 | 907-3513 | PK-5 | 300 | Mike Thornburg |
| Brewster MS | 883 Stone St | Camp Lejeune, NC | 28547-2501 | 910-451-2561 | 451-2600 | 6-8 | | Emilio Garza |

| District/School | Address | City,State | Zip code | Telephone | Fax | Grade | Enr | Superintendent/Principal |
|---|---|---|---|---|---|---|---|---|
| Butner PS | PO Box 70089 | Fort Bragg, NC | 28307-0089 | 910-907-0203 | 432-8400 | PK-2 | 500 | Kim McBroom |
| Delalio ES | 1500 Curtis Rd | Jacksonville, NC | 28540-3406 | 910-449-0601 | 449-0677 | PK-5 | | Wyonia Chevis |
| Devers ES | PO Box 70089 | Fort Bragg, NC | 28307-0089 | 910-907-0204 | 396-7374 | PK-5 | 500 | Cassandra White |
| Gordon ES | 4200 Percy Blvd | Cameron, NC | 28326-9832 | 910-907-1300 | 908-3504 | PK-5 | 500 | Joel Grim |
| Hampton PS | PO Box 70089 | Fort Bragg, NC | 28307 | 910-907-0205 | 908-1190 | PK-2 | | Priscilla Joiner |
| Heroes ES | 100 Barnett Way | Camp Lejeune, NC | 28547 | 910-449-8000 | | PK-5 | | Kendra White |
| Irwin IS | PO Box 70089 | Fort Bragg, NC | 28307-0089 | 910-907-0206 | 907-1247 | 2-5 | 500 | Miriam Breece |
| Johnson PS | 2027 Stone St | Camp Lejeune, NC | 28547-2506 | 910-451-2431 | 451-2433 | PK-2 | | Andrea Mial |
| Lejeune HS | 835 Stone St | Camp Lejeune, NC | 28547-2520 | 910-451-2451 | 451-3130 | 9-12 | | Eric Steimel |
| Shughart ES | 4800 Camel Rd | Cameron, NC | 28326-5056 | 910-907-0210 | | PK-5 | 600 | Dr. Carolyn Carr |
| Shughart MS | 4800 Camel Rd | Cameron, NC | 28326 | 910-907-0211 | 907-2150 | 6-8 | 500 | Karen Jones |
| Tarawa Terrace ES | 84 Iwo Jima Blvd | Tarawa Terrace, NC | 28543-1231 | 910-450-1635 | 450-1637 | PK-5 | | Leigh Anne Faulkner |
| South Carolina / Fort Stewart SD | 376 Davis Ave | Fort Stewart, GA | 31315-1033 | 912-369-6691 | 876-4339 | PK-6 | 5,900 | Dr. Samantha Ingram |
| Bolden S, Charles Frank | 2 Albacore St | Beaufort, SC | 29906 | 843-846-6112 | 846-9283 | 3-8 | 4,000 | Vicky Parr |
| Brittin ES | 2772 Hero Rd | Fort Stewart, GA | 31315-1713 | 912-368-3324 | 368-3412 | PK-6 | 600 | Dr. Theresa Davis |
| Diamond ES | 482 Davis Ave | Fort Stewart, GA | 31315-1015 | 912-876-5797 | 876-8350 | PK-6 | | Marva Tutt |
| Elliott ES, Middleton Stuart | 345 Elliott Dr | Beaufort, SC | 29906 | 843-846-6982 | 846-6720 | PK-2 | 300 | Latonya Leeks |
| Galer ES, Robert Edward | 221 E Cardinal Ln | Beaufort, SC | 29906 | 843-846-6100 | 846-1860 | PK-2 | 300 | Carol Kipp-Caldwell |
| Kessler ES, Patrick | 1127 Austin Rd | Fort Stewart, GA | 31315 | 912-368-3958 | 368-5048 | PK-6 | 100 | Dr. Djuna Crowder |
| Murray ES, Charles P. | 24 Murray Ave | Fort Stewart, GA | 31315 | 912-369-1576 | 767-3600 | PK-6 | 200 | Talisha Thompson |
| Pierce Terrace ES | 5715 Adams Ct | Columbia, SC | 29206-5379 | 803-782-1772 | 738-8895 | PK-2 | 300 | Taminika Shadd |
| Pinckney ES, Charles C. | 5900 Chesnut Rd | Columbia, SC | 29206-5365 | 803-787-6815 | 790-2169 | 3-6 | 200 | Annie Crandle |

# CATHOLIC SCHOOL SUPERINTENDENTS

## NATIONAL CATHOLIC EDUCATIONAL ASSOC.
**1005 N Glebe Rd Ste 525, Arlington, VA 22201-5792**
**Telephone 800-711-6232**
**Fax 243-0025**
**Website ncea.org**

| Archdiocese/Diocese | Address | City,State | Zip code | Telephone | Fax | Grade | Enr | Superintendent |
|---|---|---|---|---|---|---|---|---|
| Diocese of Albany | 40 N Main Ave | Albany, NY | 12203-1481 | 518-453-6602 | 453-6667 | PK-12 | 6,900 | Michael Pizzingrillo |
| Diocese of Alexandria | PO Box 7417 | Alexandria, LA | 71306-0417 | 318-445-6424 | 448-6121 | PK-12 | 2,800 | Thomas Roque |
| Diocese of Allentown | 1425 Mountain Dr N | Bethlehem, PA | 18015 | 610-866-0581 | 867-8702 | PK-12 | 12,500 | Philip Fromuth |
| Diocese of Altoona-Johnstown | 933 S Logan Blvd | Hollidaysburg, PA | 16648-3035 | 814-693-1401 | 696-6725 | PK-12 | 4,400 | Sr. Donna Leiden |
| Diocese of Amarillo | 1800 N Spring St | Amarillo, TX | 79107-7252 | 806-383-2243 | 383-8452 | PK-12 | 600 | Fr. Robert Busch Ph.D. |
| Archdiocese of Anchorage | 225 Cordova St | Anchorage, AK | 99501-2409 | 907-297-7790 | 297-7758 | PK-12 | 500 | |
| Diocese of Arlington | 200 N Glebe Rd Ste 503 | Arlington, VA | 22203 | 703-841-2519 | 524-8670 | PK-12 | 16,500 | Sr. Bernadette McManigal |
| Archdiocese of Atlanta | 2401 Lake Park Dr SE | Smyrna, GA | 30080 | 404-920-7700 | 920-7701 | PK-12 | 11,700 | Dr. Diane Starkovich Ph.D. |
| Diocese of Austin | 6225 E Highway 290 | Austin, TX | 78723 | 512-949-2400 | 949-2520 | PK-12 | 5,000 | Dr. Ned Vanders |
| Diocese of Baker | 2450 NE 27th St | Bend, OR | 97701 | 541-382-4701 | | PK-8 | 500 | Dr. Dennis Dempsey |
| Archdiocese of Baltimore | 320 Cathedral St | Baltimore, MD | 21201-4421 | 410-547-5515 | 539-5566 | PK-12 | 28,700 | Dr. Barbara Edmondson |
| Diocese of Baton Rouge | PO Box 2028 | Baton Rouge, LA | 70821-2028 | 225-336-8735 | 336-8711 | PK-12 | 16,000 | Dr. Melanie Verges |
| Diocese of Beaumont | PO Box 3948 | Beaumont, TX | 77704-3948 | 409-924-4328 | 838-4511 | PK-12 | 1,600 | Marcia Stevens |
| Diocese of Belleville | 2620 Lebanon Ave | Belleville, IL | 62221-3002 | 618-235-9601 | 235-7115 | PK-12 | 6,100 | Thomas Posnanski |
| Diocese of Biloxi | 1790 Popps Ferry Rd | Biloxi, MS | 39532-2118 | 228-702-2130 | 702-2178 | PK-12 | 3,500 | Dr. Mike Ladner |
| Diocese of Birmingham | PO Box 12047 | Birmingham, AL | 35202-2047 | 205-838-8303 | 838-8330 | PK-12 | 6,200 | Frances Lawlor |
| Diocese of Bismarck | 218 1st St SE | Minot, ND | 58701 | 701-838-1026 | | PK-12 | 2,500 | Fr. Justin Waltz |
| Diocese of Boise | 1501 S Federal Way Ste 400 | Boise, ID | 83705-2591 | 208-342-1311 | 342-0224 | PK-12 | 2,800 | |
| Archdiocese of Boston | 66 Brooks Dr | Braintree, MA | 02184 | 617-254-0100 | 783-4564 | PK-12 | 40,400 | Kathleen Mears |
| Diocese of Bridgeport | 238 Jewett Ave | Bridgeport, CT | 06606-2892 | 203-416-1375 | 372-1961 | PK-12 | 11,100 | Sr. Mary Walsh |
| Diocese of Brooklyn | 310 Prospect Park W | Brooklyn, NY | 11215 | 718-965-7300 | 965-7353 | PK-12 | 44,200 | Dr. Thomas Chadzutko |
| Diocese of Brownsville | 700 Virgen de San Juan | San Juan, TX | 78589-3030 | 956-784-5051 | 784-5081 | PK-12 | 3,900 | Sr. Cynthia A. Mello M.A. |
| Diocese of Buffalo | 795 Main St | Buffalo, NY | 14203-1250 | 716-847-5520 | 847-5593 | PK-12 | 16,500 | Sr. Carol Cimino Ed.D. |
| Diocese of Burlington | PO Box 2226 | S Burlington, VT | 05407 | 802-658-6110 | 658-6112 | PK-12 | 2,200 | Sr. Laura Della Santa |
| Diocese of Camden | 631 Market St | Camden, NJ | 08102 | 856-583-6103 | 756-0225 | PK-12 | 14,400 | Mary Boyle M.Ed. |
| Diocese of Charleston | 1662 Ingram Rd | Charleston, SC | 29407-4242 | 843-261-4096 | | PK-12 | 7,000 | Sandra Leatherwood |
| Diocese of Charlotte | 1123 S Church St | Charlotte, NC | 28203-4003 | 704-370-3244 | 370-3380 | PK-12 | 7,600 | Rev. Roger Arnsparger |
| Diocese of Cheyenne | PO Box 1468 | Cheyenne, WY | 82003 | 307-638-1530 | 637-7936 | PK-12 | 1,000 | Vernon Dobelmann |
| Archdiocese of Chicago | PO Box 1979 | Chicago, IL | 60690-1979 | 312-534-5200 | 534-5295 | PK-12 | 87,500 | Jim Rigg Ph.D. |
| Archdiocese of Cincinnati | 100 E 8th St | Cincinnati, OH | 45202 | 513-421-3131 | 421-6271 | PK-12 | 45,200 | Jim Rigg Ph.D. |
| Diocese of Cleveland | 1404 E 9th St | Cleveland, OH | 44114-1740 | 216-696-6525 | 579-9655 | PK-12 | 47,300 | Margaret Lyons |
| Diocese of Colorado Springs | 228 N Cascade Ave | Colorado Spgs, CO | 80903-1324 | 719-636-2345 | 866-6453 | PK-12 | 1,800 | Holly Goodwin |
| Diocese of Columbus | 197 E Gay St | Columbus, OH | 43215 | 614-221-5829 | 241-2563 | PK-12 | 17,400 | Dr. Joe Brettnacher Ph.D. |
| Diocese of Corpus Christi | PO Box 2620 | Corpus Christi, TX | 78403-2620 | 361-882-6191 | 693-6798 | PK-12 | 3,500 | Nannette Hatch |
| Diocese of Covington | 1125 Madison Ave | Covington, KY | 41011 | 859-392-1500 | 392-1500 | K-12 | 10,800 | Michael Clines |
| Diocese of Crookston | PO Box 610 | Crookston, MN | 56716 | 218-444-4262 | 444-1381 | PK-12 | 1,400 | Tina Stanger |
| Diocese of Dallas | PO Box 190507 | Dallas, TX | 75219-0507 | 214-379-2830 | 522-1753 | PK-12 | 14,900 | |
| Diocese of Davenport | 780 W Central Park Ave | Davenport, IA | 52804-1901 | 563-324-1911 | 324-5811 | PK-12 | 4,900 | Lee Morrison |
| Archdiocese of Denver | 1300 S Steele St | Denver, CO | 80210-2599 | 303-715-3200 | 715-2042 | PK-12 | 14,800 | Kevin Kijewski J.D. |
| Diocese of Des Moines | 601 Grand Ave | Des Moines, IA | 50309-2501 | 515-237-5013 | 237-5070 | PK-12 | 6,400 | Dr. Tracy Bonday |
| Archdiocese of Detroit | 305 Michigan Ave | Detroit, MI | 48226 | 313-237-4661 | 237-5857 | PK-12 | 33,000 | Dr. Brian Dougherty |
| Diocese of Dodge City | PO Box 137 | Dodge City, KS | 67801 | 620-227-1513 | 227-1570 | PK-8 | 1,100 | Trina Delgado |
| Archdiocese of Dubuque | 1229 Mount Loretta Ave | Dubuque, IA | 52003-8787 | 563-556-2580 | 556-5464 | PK-12 | 11,800 | Kimberly Hermsen |
| Diocese of Duluth | 2830 E 4th St | Duluth, MN | 55812-1501 | 218-724-9111 | 724-1056 | PK-8 | 1,600 | Cynthia Zook |
| Diocese of El Paso | 499 Saint Matthews St | El Paso, TX | 79907-4214 | 915-872-8426 | 872-8434 | PK-12 | 4,300 | Sr. Elizabeth Swartz |
| Diocese of Erie | PO Box 10397 | Erie, PA | 16514-0397 | 814-824-1241 | 824-1239 | PK-12 | 9,000 | Dr. Samuel Signorino |
| Diocese of Evansville | PO Box 4169 | Evansville, IN | 47724-0169 | 812-424-5536 | 424-0973 | PK-12 | 7,100 | Dr. Daryl Hagan |
| Diocese of Fairbanks | 615 Monroe St | Fairbanks, AK | 99701 | 907-456-4574 | 452-5978 | K-12 | 500 | Nancy Hanson |
| Diocese of Fall River | 423 Highland Ave | Fall River, MA | 02720-3718 | 508-678-2828 | 674-4218 | PK-12 | 7,100 | Michael Griffin Ph.D. |
| Diocese of Fargo | 5201 Bishops Blvd S Ste A | Fargo, ND | 58104 | 701-356-7907 | 356-7994 | PK-12 | 2,000 | Fr. Andrew Jasinski |
| Diocese of Fort Worth | 800 W Loop 820 S | Fort Worth, TX | 76108-2936 | 817-560-3300 | 244-8839 | PK-12 | 6,300 | Jennifer Pelletier |
| Diocese of Fresno | 1510 N Fresno St | Fresno, CA | 93703-3711 | 559-488-7420 | 488-7422 | PK-12 | 6,400 | Mona Faulkner |
| Diocese of Ft. Wayne-South Bend | PO Box 390 | Fort Wayne, IN | 46801-0390 | 260-422-4611 | 426-3077 | PK-12 | 12,300 | Marsha Jordan |
| Diocese of Gallup | PO Box 1338 | Gallup, NM | 87305-1338 | 505-863-4406 | 863-5555 | PK-12 | 1,400 | Jeanette Suter |
| Archdiocese of Galveston-Houston | 2403 Holcombe Blvd | Houston, TX | 77021-2023 | 713-741-8704 | 741-7379 | PK-12 | 17,900 | Dr. Julie Vogel |
| Diocese of Gary | 9292 Broadway | Merrillville, IN | 46410-7088 | 219-769-9292 | 738-9034 | PK-12 | 6,500 | Dr. Barbara O'Block Ed.D. |
| Diocese of Gaylord | 611 W North St | Gaylord, MI | 49735-8349 | 989-732-5147 | 705-3589 | PK-12 | 3,000 | Frank Sander |
| Diocese of Grand Island | PO Box 996 | Grand Island, NE | 68802-0996 | 308-382-6565 | 382-6569 | PK-12 | 1,400 | Gregory Logsdon |
| Diocese of Grand Rapids | 360 Division Ave S Ste 3A | Grand Rapids, MI | 49503 | 616-246-0590 | 551-5650 | PK-12 | 6,300 | David Faber |
| Diocese of Great Falls-Billings | PO Box 1708 | Helena, MT | 59601 | 406-442-5761 | 442-9047 | PK-12 | 2,500 | Dr. Timothy Uhl |
| Diocese of Green Bay | PO Box 23825 | Green Bay, WI | 54305-3825 | 920-272-8309 | 272-8273 | PK-12 | 10,700 | Sr. Kay Klackner |
| Diocese of Greensburg | 723 E Pittsburgh St | Greensburg, PA | 15601-2697 | 724-837-0901 | 837-0857 | PK-12 | 3,600 | Maureen Marsteller |
| Diocese of Harrisburg | 4800 Union Deposit Rd | Harrisburg, PA | 17111-3710 | 717-657-4804 | 657-3790 | PK-12 | 12,000 | Livia Riley |
| Archdiocese of Hartford | 467 Bloomfield Ave | Bloomfield, CT | 06002-2903 | 860-242-5573 | | PK-12 | 16,300 | Dr. Dale Hoyt Ed.D. |
| Diocese of Helena | 1313 11th Ave | Helena, MT | 59601 | 406-442-5761 | 442-9047 | PK-12 | 1,400 | Dr. Timothy Uhl |
| Diocese of Honolulu | 6301 Pali Hwy | Kaneohe, HI | 96744-5224 | 808-263-8844 | 262-6126 | PK-12 | 10,200 | Michael Rockers Ed.D. |
| Diocese of Houma-Thibodaux | PO Box 505 | Schriever, LA | 70395-0505 | 985-850-3114 | 850-3225 | PK-12 | 5,900 | Marian Fertitta |
| Archdiocese of Indianapolis | 1400 N Meridian St | Indianapolis, IN | 46202-2305 | 317-236-1430 | 261-3364 | PK-12 | 21,400 | Gina Kuntz Fleming |
| Diocese of Jackson | PO Box 2248 | Jackson, MS | 39225-2248 | 601-960-8470 | 960-8469 | PK-12 | 4,300 | Catherine Cook |
| Diocese of Jefferson City | PO Box 104900 | Jefferson City, MO | 65110-4900 | 573-635-9127 | 635-2286 | PK-12 | 7,100 | Rev. Joseph Corel |
| Diocese of Joliet | 16555 Weber Rd | Crest Hill, IL | 60403 | 815-838-2181 | 838-2182 | PK-12 | 22,200 | Rev. John Belmonte Ph.D. |
| Diocese of Juneau | 415 6th St Ste 300 | Juneau, AK | 99801-1091 | 907-586-2227 | 463-3237 | PK-6 | 100 | |
| Diocese of Kalamazoo | 215 N Westnedge Ave | Kalamazoo, MI | 49007-3760 | 269-903-0165 | 349-6440 | PK-12 | 3,400 | Margaret Erich |
| Archdiocese of Kansas City | 12615 Parallel Pkwy | Kansas City, KS | 66109-3748 | 913-721-1570 | 721-5598 | PK-12 | 15,400 | Dr. Kathleen O'Hara |
| Diocese of Kansas City-Saint Joseph | PO Box 419037 | Kansas City, MO | 64141-6037 | 816-756-1850 | 756-1571 | PK-12 | 11,600 | Dr. Dan Peters |
| Diocese of Knoxville | 805 S Northshore Dr | Knoxville, TN | 37919 | 865-584-3307 | 584-4319 | PK-12 | 3,400 | Sr. Mary Marta Abbott |
| Diocese of La Crosse | PO Box 4004 | La Crosse, WI | 54602 | 608-788-7707 | 788-7709 | PK-12 | 7,600 | Dr. Susan Holman |

| Archdiocese/Diocese | Address | City,State | Zip code | Telephone | Fax | Grade | Enr | Superintendent |
|---|---|---|---|---|---|---|---|---|
| Diocese of Lafayette | PO Box 3387 | Lafayette, LA | 70501 | 337-261-5529 | 261-5572 | PK-12 | 15,100 | Anna Larriviere |
| Diocese of Lafayette-in-Indiana | 2300 S 9th St | Lafayette, IN | 47909-2400 | 765-269-4670 | 269-4671 | PK-12 | 5,100 | Anne Marie Williams Ph.D. |
| Diocese of Lake Charles | 1112 Bilbo St | Lake Charles, LA | 70601-5226 | 337-433-9640 | 433-9685 | PK-12 | 2,500 | Kimberlee Gazzolo |
| Diocese of Lansing | 228 N Walnut St | Lansing, MI | 48933 | 517-342-2482 | 342-2515 | PK-12 | 9,600 | Sean Costello |
| Diocese of Laredo | 1201 Corpus Christi St | Laredo, TX | 78040-5354 | 956-753-5208 | 753-5203 | K-12 | 2,100 | Dr. Rosa Maria Vida |
| Diocese of Las Cruces | 1280 Med Park Dr | Las Cruces, NM | 88005-3239 | 575-523-7577 | 524-3874 | PK-8 | 600 | Ben Trujillo |
| Diocese of Las Vegas | PO Box 18316 | Las Vegas, NV | 89114-8316 | 702-697-3903 | 735-8941 | K-12 | 3,700 | Catherine Thompson |
| Diocese of Lexington | 1310 W Main St | Lexington, KY | 40508-2048 | 859-253-1993 | 253-0939 | PK-12 | 4,000 | Dr. Timothy Weaver Ph.D. |
| Diocese of Lincoln | PO Box 80328 | Lincoln, NE | 68501-0328 | 402-488-2040 | 488-6525 | K-12 | 7,000 | Rev. John Perkinton |
| Diocese of Little Rock | PO Box 7565 | Little Rock, AR | 72217-7565 | 501-664-0340 | 603-0518 | K-12 | 7,100 | Vernell Bowen M.Ed. |
| Archdiocese of Los Angeles | 3424 Wilshire Blvd | Los Angeles, CA | 90010-2241 | 213-637-7300 | 637-6140 | PK-12 | 81,500 | Dr. Kevin Baxter |
| Archdiocese of Louisville | 1935 Lewiston Dr | Louisville, KY | 40216-2523 | 502-448-8581 | 448-5518 | PK-12 | 20,800 | Leisa Schulz |
| Diocese of Lubbock | PO Box 98700 | Lubbock, TX | 79499-8700 | 806-792-3943 | 792-8109 | PK-12 | 400 | Christine Wanjura |
| Diocese of Madison | PO Box 44983 | Madison, WI | 53744-4983 | 608-821-3180 | 821-3181 | PK-12 | 7,600 | Michael Lancaster |
| Diocese of Manchester | PO Box 310 | Manchester, NH | 03105-0310 | 603-669-3100 | 669-0377 | PK-12 | 7,400 | Rev. John Fortin Ph.D. |
| Diocese of Marquette | 1004 Harbor Hills Dr | Marquette, MI | 49855 | 906-227-9127 | 225-0437 | PK-8 | 1,300 | Mark Salisbury |
| Diocese of Memphis | 5825 Shelby Oaks Dr | Memphis, TN | 38134-7316 | 901-373-1219 | 373-1223 | PK-12 | 6,900 | Janet M. Donato |
| Diocese of Metuchen | 146 Metlars Ln | Piscataway, NJ | 08854-4303 | 732-562-2446 | 562-1016 | PK-12 | 11,400 | Ellen Ayoub |
| Archdiocese of Miami | 9401 Biscayne Blvd | Miami Shores, FL | 33138-2970 | 305-762-1076 | 762-1115 | PK-12 | 34,200 | Kim Pryzbylski Ph.D. |
| Archdiocese of Milwaukee | PO Box 070912 | Milwaukee, WI | 53207 | 414-758-2256 | 769-3408 | PK-12 | 30,500 | Dr. Kathleen Cepelka |
| Archdiocese of Mobile | 352 Government St | Mobile, AL | 36602 | 251-438-4611 | 438-4612 | PK-12 | 6,300 | Gwen Byrd |
| Diocese of Monterey | 485 Church St | Monterey, CA | 93940-3207 | 831-373-1608 | 373-0173 | PK-12 | 5,000 | Kathleen Radecke |
| Diocese of Nashville | 30 White Bridge Rd | Nashville, TN | 37205-1401 | 615-352-7218 | 353-7972 | PK-12 | 6,200 | Dr. Therese Williams |
| Archdiocese of Newark | PO Box 9500 | Newark, NJ | 07104-0500 | 973-497-4260 | 497-4249 | PK-12 | 32,200 | Dr. Margaret Dames |
| Archdiocese of New Orleans | 7887 Walmsley Ave | New Orleans, LA | 70125-3496 | 504-866-7916 | 861-6260 | PK-12 | 39,700 | Dr. Jan Lancaster |
| Diocese of New Ulm | 1421 6th St N | New Ulm, MN | 56073 | 507-359-2966 | 354-0268 | PK-12 | 2,300 | Karla Cross |
| Archdiocese of New York | 1011 1st Ave Fl 6 | New York, NY | 10022 | 212-371-1000 | 758-3018 | PK-12 | 72,000 | Dr. Timothy McNiff |
| Diocese of Norwich | 43 Perkins Ave | Norwich, CT | 06360-3643 | 860-887-4086 | 887-9371 | PK-12 | 4,400 | Dr. John Shine |
| Diocese of Oakland | 2121 Harrison St | Oakland, CA | 94612 | 510-628-2154 | 451-5331 | PK-12 | 17,600 | Sr. Barbara Bray |
| Diocese of Ogdensburg | PO Box 369 | Ogdensburg, NY | 13669-0369 | 315-393-2920 | 314-7296 | PK-12 | 2,300 | Sr. Ellen Coughlin |
| Archdiocese of Oklahoma City | PO Box 32180 | Oklahoma City, OK | 73123-0380 | 405-721-5651 | 709-2811 | PK-12 | 4,900 | Dr. Cristiana Carter |
| Archdiocese of Omaha | 3300 N 60th St | Omaha, NE | 68104 | 402-557-5600 | 827-3792 | PK-12 | 19,000 | Patrick Slattery |
| Diocese of Orange | 13280 Chapman Ave | Garden Grove, CA | 92840 | 714-282-3000 | 282-5059 | PK-12 | 19,700 | Gregory Dhuyvetter |
| Diocese of Orlando | PO Box 1800 | Orlando, FL | 32802-1800 | 407-246-4900 | 246-4940 | PK-12 | 14,100 | Henry Fortier |
| Diocese of Owensboro | 600 Locust St | Owensboro, KY | 42301-2130 | 270-683-1545 | 683-6883 | PK-12 | 3,900 | Jim Mattingly |
| Diocese of Palm Beach | 9995 N Military Trl | West Palm Beach, FL | 33410-5497 | 561-775-9500 | 775-9556 | PK-12 | 6,400 | Gary Gelo |
| Diocese of Paterson | 777 Valley Rd | Clifton, NJ | 07013-2297 | 973-777-8818 | 779-0083 | PK-12 | 11,900 | Mary Baier |
| Diocese of Pensacola-Tallahassee | PO Box 13284 | Pensacola, FL | 32591 | 850-435-3540 | 436-6424 | PK-12 | 2,800 | Michael P. Juhas |
| Diocese of Peoria | 419 NE Madison Ave | Peoria, IL | 61603 | 309-671-1550 | 671-1579 | PK-12 | 11,200 | Sharon Weiss Ed.D. |
| Archdiocese of Philadelphia | 222 N 17th St | Philadelphia, PA | 19103-1295 | 215-587-3700 | 587-5644 | PK-12 | 71,100 | Mary Rochford |
| Diocese of Phoenix | 400 E Monroe St | Phoenix, AZ | 85004-2336 | 602-354-2345 | 354-2436 | PK-12 | 14,300 | MaryBeth Mueller |
| Diocese of Pittsburgh | 111 Blvd of the Allies | Pittsburgh, PA | 15222-1618 | 412-456-3090 | 456-3098 | PK-12 | 19,800 | Michael Latusek Ed.D. |
| Archdiocese of Portland | 2838 E Burnside St | Portland, OR | 97214-1895 | 503-233-8300 | 236-3683 | PK-12 | 13,800 | Br. William Dygert |
| Diocese of Portland | 510 Ocean Ave | Portland, ME | 04103-4900 | 207-773-6471 | 773-0182 | PK-12 | 3,300 | Rev. Louis Phillips Ph.D. |
| Diocese of Providence | 1 Cathedral Sq | Providence, RI | 02903-3695 | 401-278-4550 | 278-4596 | PK-12 | 14,400 | Daniel Ferris |
| Diocese of Pueblo | 101 N Greenwood St | Pueblo, CO | 81003 | 719-561-1121 | 561-2251 | PK-12 | 900 | John Brainard M.Ed. |
| Diocese of Raleigh | 7200 Stonehenge Dr | Raleigh, NC | 27613 | 919-821-9749 | 522-1695 | PK-12 | 8,800 | Dr. Michael Fedewa |
| Rapid City Catholic School System | 300 Fairmont Blvd | Rapid City, SD | 57701-5423 | 605-343-8484 | 343-1315 | K-12 | 700 | Barb Honeycutt |
| Diocese of Reno | 290 S Arlington Ave Ste 200 | Reno, NV | 89501-1713 | 775-326-9430 | 348-8619 | PK-12 | 1,700 | Karen Barreras |
| Diocese of Richmond | 7800 Carousel Ln | Richmond, VA | 23294-4201 | 804-359-5661 | 358-9159 | PK-12 | 9,100 | Annette Parsons |
| Diocese of Rochester | 1150 Buffalo Rd | Rochester, NY | 14624-1890 | 585-328-3228 | 328-3149 | PK-12 | 8,000 | Anthony Cook |
| Diocese of Rockford | PO Box 7044 | Rockford, IL | 61125-7044 | 815-399-4300 | 399-6278 | PK-12 | 14,400 | Michael Kagan |
| Diocese of Rockville Centre | PO Box 9023 | Rockville Ctr, NY | 11571-9023 | 516-678-5800 | 678-7362 | PK-12 | 30,300 | Sr. Joanne Callahan |
| Diocese of Sacramento | 2110 Broadway | Sacramento, CA | 95818-2518 | 916-733-0110 | 733-0120 | PK-12 | 13,700 | Lincoln Snyder |
| Diocese of Saginaw | 5800 Weiss St | Saginaw, MI | 48603-2762 | 989-799-7910 | 399-2257 | PK-12 | 3,100 | Mary Ann Deschaine |
| Diocese of St. Augustine | 11625 Old St Augustine Rd | Jacksonville, FL | 32258 | 904-262-3200 | 596-1042 | PK-12 | 10,500 | Rev. Scott Conway |
| Diocese of St. Cloud | 305 7th Ave N Ste 201 | Saint Cloud, MN | 56303-3633 | 320-251-0111 | 251-0259 | PK-12 | 4,900 | Linda Kaiser |
| Archdiocese of St. Louis | 4445 Lindell Blvd | Saint Louis, MO | 63108 | 314-792-7300 | 792-7350 | PK-12 | 44,000 | Kurt Nelson |
| Archdiocese of St. Paul | 328 Kellogg Blvd W | Saint Paul, MN | 55102-1900 | 651-291-4500 | 290-1628 | PK-12 | 32,800 | Dr. Jill Reilly |
| Diocese of St. Petersburg | PO Box 40200 | St Petersburg, FL | 33743-0200 | 727-347-5539 | 341-6848 | PK-12 | 12,900 | Elizabeth Agresta |
| Diocese of Salina | PO Box 825 | Salina, KS | 67402-0825 | 785-827-8746 | 827-6133 | PK-12 | 2,300 | Dr. Nick Compagnone |
| Diocese of Salt Lake City | 27 C St | Salt Lake City, UT | 84103-2302 | 801-328-8641 | 328-8643 | PK-12 | 5,500 | Sr. Mark Longe |
| Diocese of San Angelo | 499 Saint Matthews St | El Paso, TX | 79907-4214 | 915-872-8426 | 872-8423 | PK-8 | 700 | Sr. Elizabeth Ann Swartz |
| Archdiocese of San Antonio | 2718 W Woodlawn Ave | San Antonio, TX | 78228-5195 | 210-734-2620 | 734-9112 | PK-12 | 12,700 | Marti West |
| Diocese of San Bernardino | 1201 E Highland Ave | San Bernardino, CA | 92404-4641 | 909-475-5437 | 475-5477 | PK-12 | 7,300 | Patricia Vesely |
| Diocese of San Diego | PO Box 85728 | San Diego, CA | 92186-5728 | 858-490-8240 | 490-8272 | PK-12 | 14,400 | John Galvan |
| Archdiocese of San Francisco | 1 Peter Yorke Way | San Francisco, CA | 94109-6602 | 415-614-5660 | 614-5664 | PK-12 | 24,900 | Dr. Nina K. Russo |
| Diocese of San Jose | 1150 N 1st St Ste 100 | San Jose, CA | 95112 | 408-983-0185 | 983-0192 | PK-12 | 16,100 | Kathy Almazol |
| Archdiocese of Santa Fe | 4000 Saint Josephs Pl NW | Albuquerque, NM | 87120-1714 | 505-831-8173 | 831-8107 | PK-12 | 5,100 | Susan Murphy |
| Diocese of Santa Rosa | PO Box 1297 | Santa Rosa, CA | 95402 | 707-566-3311 | 566-3382 | PK-12 | 4,300 | Dr. John Collins |
| Diocese of Savannah | 2170 E Victory Dr | Savannah, GA | 31404 | 912-201-4121 | 201-4101 | K-12 | 5,400 | Michelle Kroll |
| Diocese of Scranton | 300 Wyoming Ave | Scranton, PA | 18503-1243 | 570-207-2251 | 207-2261 | PK-12 | 5,900 | Msgr. David L. Tressler |
| Archdiocese of Seattle | 710 9th Ave | Seattle, WA | 98104-2017 | 206-382-4861 | 654-4651 | PK-12 | 23,100 | Dr. Patrick Haggarty |
| Diocese of Shreveport | 3500 Fairfield Ave | Shreveport, LA | 71104-4108 | 318-219-7253 | 868-5057 | PK-12 | 1,800 | Sr. Carol Shively |
| Diocese of Sioux City | PO Box 3379 | Sioux City, IA | 51102-3379 | 712-255-7933 | 233-7598 | PK-12 | 6,100 | Dr. Dan Ryan |
| Diocese of Sioux Falls | 523 N Duluth Ave | Sioux Falls, SD | 57104-2714 | 605-988-3766 | 988-3795 | PK-12 | 5,100 | Katie Mellor |
| Diocese of Spokane | PO Box 1453 | Spokane, WA | 99210-1453 | 509-358-7330 | 358-7302 | PK-12 | 4,600 | Duane Schafer Ph.D. |
| Diocese of Springfield-Cape Girardeau | 601 S Jefferson Ave | Springfield, MO | 65806-3107 | 417-866-0841 | 866-1140 | PK-12 | 4,400 | Leon Witt |
| Diocese of Springfield | 1615 W Washington St | Springfield, IL | 62702-4757 | 217-698-8500 | 698-8620 | PK-12 | 10,800 | Jean Johnson |
| Diocese of Springfield | PO Box 1730 | Springfield, MA | 01102-1730 | 413-452-0830 | 452-0555 | PK-12 | 4,700 | Sr. M. Andrea Ciszewski |
| Diocese of Steubenville | PO Box 969 | Steubenville, OH | 43952-5969 | 740-282-3631 | 282-3327 | PK-12 | 1,800 | Paul Ward |
| Diocese of Stockton | 212 N San Joaquin St | Stockton, CA | 95202 | 209-466-0636 | 463-5937 | PK-12 | 4,200 | Carla Donaldson |
| Diocese of Superior | PO Box 969 | Superior, WI | 54880 | 715-392-2937 | 392-2015 | PK-8 | 2,400 | Peggy Schoenfuss |
| Diocese of Syracuse | 240 E Onondaga St | Syracuse, NY | 13202-2668 | 315-470-1450 | 470-1470 | PK-12 | 5,900 | William Crist |
| Diocese of Toledo | 1933 Spielbusch Ave | Toledo, OH | 43604-5360 | 419-244-6711 | 255-8269 | PK-12 | 19,900 | Christopher Knight |
| Diocese of Trenton | PO Box 5147 | Trenton, NJ | 08638-0147 | 609-406-7400 | 406-7429 | PK-12 | 20,900 | JoAnn Tier |
| Diocese of Tucson | PO Box 31 | Tucson, AZ | 85702-0031 | 520-838-2547 | 838-2589 | PK-12 | 7,300 | Sheri Dahl |
| Diocese of Tulsa | 820 S Boulder Ave | Tulsa, OK | 74119-1624 | 918-582-9177 | 582-1851 | PK-12 | 4,500 | Jim Pohlman |
| Diocese of Tyler | 1015 E Southeast Loop 323 | Tyler, TX | 75701-9656 | 903-534-1077 | 534-1370 | PK-12 | 1,000 | Dr. James Klassen |
| Diocese of Venice in Florida | 1000 Pinebrook Rd | Venice, FL | 34285-6426 | 941-484-9543 | 484-1121 | PK-12 | 4,400 | Dr. Kristy Swol |
| Diocese of Victoria | PO Box 4070 | Victoria, TX | 77903-4070 | 361-573-0828 | 573-5725 | PK-12 | 3,100 | John Quary |
| Archdiocese of Washington DC | 5001 Eastern Ave | Hyattsville, MD | 20782-3447 | 301-853-4500 | 853-7672 | PK-12 | 27,500 | Kelly Branaman |
| Diocese of Wheeling-Charleston | PO Box 230 | Wheeling, WV | 26003-0010 | 304-232-0444 | 233-8551 | PK-12 | 5,700 | Vincent de Paul Schmidt |
| Diocese of Wichita | 424 N Broadway St | Wichita, KS | 67202-2310 | 316-269-3950 | 269-2486 | PK-12 | 10,500 | Bob Voboril |
| Diocese of Wilmington | 1626 N Union St | Wilmington, DE | 19806-2540 | 302-573-3133 | 573-6945 | PK-12 | 12,200 | Louis De Angelo Ed.D. |
| Diocese of Winona | PO Box 588 | Winona, MN | 55987-0588 | 507-858-1269 | 454-8106 | PK-12 | 5,500 | Marsha Stenzel |
| Diocese of Worcester | 49 Elm St | Worcester, MA | 01609-2514 | 508-929-4317 | 929-4386 | PK-12 | 7,900 | Delma Josephson Ph.D. |
| Diocese of Yakima | 5301 Tieton Dr Ste B | Yakima, WA | 98908-3479 | 509-965-7117 | 966-8334 | PK-12 | 1,800 | Rev. Thomas Kuykendall |
| Diocese of Youngstown | 144 W Wood St | Youngstown, OH | 44503-1081 | 330-744-8451 | 744-5099 | K-12 | 8,400 | Mary Fiala |

# LUTHERAN SCHOOL SUPERINTENDENTS

## LUTHERAN CHURCH MISSOURI SYNOD
## 1333 S Kirkwood Rd, Saint Louis, MO 63122-7295
## Telephone 800-248-1930

Website http://www.lcms.org

### LUTHERAN SCHOOL SUPERINTENDENTS

| Region | Address | City,State | Zip code | Telephone | Fax | Superintendent |
|---|---|---|---|---|---|---|
| Atlantic | 171 White Plains Rd | Bronxville, NY | 10708-1923 | 914-894-4858 | | Jessica Hinsch Raba |
| California-Nevada-Hawaii | 2772 Constitution Dr Ste A | Livermore, CA | 94551-7571 | 925-245-4000 | 245-1107 | Dr. Robert Newton |
| Central Illinois | 1850 N Grand Ave W | Springfield, IL | 62702-1626 | 217-793-1802 | 793-1822 | Glenn Goeres |
| Eastern | 5111 Main St | Williamsville, NY | 14221-5203 | 716-634-5111 | 634-5452 | Dr. Chris Wicher |
| English | 33100 Freedom Rd | Farmington, MI | 48336-4030 | 248-476-0039 | 476-0188 | Rev. David Stechholz |
| Florida-Georgia | 5850 T G Lee Blvd Ste 500 | Orlando, FL | 32822 | 407-857-5556 | 857-5665 | Mark Brink |
| Indiana | 1145 Barr St | Fort Wayne, IN | 46802-3135 | 260-423-1511 | 423-1514 | Dr. Jon Mielke |
| Iowa East | 1100 Blairs Ferry Rd | Marion, IA | 52302-3093 | 319-373-2112 | 373-9827 | Jeff Pool |
| Iowa West | 409 Kenyon Rd Ste B | Fort Dodge, IA | 50501 | 515-576-7666 | 576-2323 | Sally Kraayenbrink |
| Kansas | 1000 SW 10th Ave | Topeka, KS | 66604-1104 | 785-357-4441 | 357-5071 | Keith Kohlmeier |
| Michigan | 3773 Geddes Rd | Ann Arbor, MI | 48105-3028 | 734-665-3791 | 665-0255 | Bruce Braun |
| Mid-South | 1675 Wynne Rd | Cordova, TN | 38016-4905 | 901-373-1343 | 373-4826 | Dr. Roger Paavola |
| Minnesota North | PO Box 604 | Brainerd, MN | 56401-0604 | 218-829-1781 | 829-0037 | Rev. Donald Fondow |
| Minnesota South | 14301 Grand Ave | Burnsville, MN | 55306-5790 | 952-435-2550 | 435-2581 | Sean Martens |
| Missouri | 660 Mason Ridge Center Dr | Saint Louis, MO | 63141-8557 | 314-590-6200 | 590-6201 | Dennis Gehrke |
| Montana | 30 Broadwater Ave | Billings, MT | 59101-1826 | 406-259-2908 | 259-1305 | Rev. Terry Forke |
| Nebraska | PO Box 407 | Seward, NE | 68434-0407 | 888-643-2961 | 643-2990 | Don Weber |
| New England | 400 Wilbraham Rd | Springfield, MA | 01109-2723 | 413-783-0131 | 783-0909 | Rev. Tim Yeadon |
| New Jersey | 1168 Springfield Ave | Mountainside, NJ | 07092-2906 | 908-233-8111 | 233-3883 | Caren Vogt |
| North Dakota | 413 E Ave D | Bismarck, ND | 58501 | 701-751-3424 | | Dr. James Baneck |
| Northern Illinois | 2301 S Wolf Rd | Hillside, IL | 60162-2211 | 708-449-3020 | 449-3026 | Mike Zimmer |
| Northwest | 1700 NE Knott St | Portland, OR | 97212-3301 | 503-288-8383 | 284-2785 | Paul Linnemann |
| North Wisconsin | 3103 Seymour Ln | Wausau, WI | 54401-4049 | 715-845-8241 | 845-3836 | Rev. Dwayne Lueck |
| Ohio | PO Box 38277 | Olmsted Falls, OH | 44138-0277 | 440-235-2297 | 235-1970 | Travis Grulke |
| Oklahoma | 308 NW 164th St | Edmond, OK | 73013 | 405-348-7600 | 384-7601 | Rev. Barrie Henke |
| Pacific Southwest | 1540 Concordia | Irvine, CA | 92612-3203 | 949-854-3232 | 854-8140 | Rachel Klitzing |
| Rocky Mountain | 14334 E Evans Ave | Aurora, CO | 80014-1408 | 303-695-8001 | 695-4047 | Rev. Allen Anderson |
| SELC | 559 Raritan Rd | Clark, NJ | 07066 | 732-382-7320 | 382-7512 | Rev. Andrew Dzurovcik |
| South Dakota | PO Box 89110 | Sioux Falls, SD | 57109-9110 | 605-361-1514 | 361-7959 | Rev. Dale Sattgast |
| Southeastern | 6315 Grovedale Dr | Alexandria, VA | 22310-2501 | 703-971-9371 | 922-6047 | Rev. John Denninger |
| Southern | 100 Mission Dr | Slidell, LA | 70460 | 504-282-2632 | 871-9696 | Glenn Gerber |
| Southern Illinois | 2408 Lebanon Ave | Belleville, IL | 62221-2529 | 618-234-4767 | 234-4830 | Roger Sprengel |
| South Wisconsin | 8100 W Capitol Dr | Milwaukee, WI | 53222-1981 | 414-464-8100 | 464-0602 | Mark L'Heureux |
| Texas | 7900 E Highway 290 | Austin, TX | 78724-2402 | 512-926-4272 | 926-1006 | Dr. William Hinz |
| Wyoming | 2400 S Hickory St | Casper, WY | 82604-3471 | 307-265-9000 | 234-6629 | John Hill |

# GENERAL CONFERENCE OF SEVENTH-DAY ADVENTISTS SUPERINTENDENTS

## NORTH AMERICAN DIV. OFFICE OF EDUCATION
## 12501 Old Columbia Pike, Silver Spring, MD 20904-6601
## Telephone 301-680-6400
## Fax 680-6464
## Website http://www.nadadventist.org

### GENERAL CONFERENCE OF SEVENTH-DAY ADVENTISTS SUPERINTENDENTS

| Conference | Address | City,State | Zip code | Telephone | Fax | Superintendent |
|---|---|---|---|---|---|---|
| **Atlantic Union** | **PO Box 1189** | **South Lancaster, MA** | **01561-1189** | **978-368-8333** | **368-7948** | **Astrid Thomassian** |
| Greater New York Conference | PO Box 5029 | Manhasset, NY | 11030-5029 | 516-627-9350 | 627-9272 | David Cadavero |
| New York Conference | 4930 W Seneca Tpke | Syracuse, NY | 13215-2225 | 315-469-6921 | 469-6924 | Kim Kaiser |
| Northeastern Conference | 11550 Merrick Blvd | Jamaica, NY | 11434-1852 | 718-291-8006 | 739-5133 | Viola Chapman |
| Northern New England Conference | 479 Main St | Westbrook, ME | 04092-4330 | 207-797-3760 | 797-2851 | Trudy Wright M.A. |
| Southern New England Conference | PO Box 1169 | South Lancaster, MA | 01561-1169 | 978-365-4551 | 365-3838 | Pat Giese |
| **Columbia Union Conference** | **5427 Twin Knolls Rd** | **Columbia, MD** | **21045-3200** | **301-596-0800** | **596-6758** | **Hamlet Canosa** |
| Allegheny East Conference | 767 Douglass Dr | Boyertown, PA | 19512 | 610-326-4610 | 326-3946 | Judy Dent |
| Allegheny West Conference | 1339 E Broad St | Columbus, OH | 43205-1588 | 614-252-5271 | 252-3246 | Dr. William Cox |
| Chesapeake Conference | 6600 Martin Rd | Columbia, MD | 21044-3999 | 410-995-1910 | 995-1434 | Jacqueline Messenger |
| Mountain View Conference | 1400 Liberty St | Parkersburg, WV | 26101-4124 | 304-422-4581 | 422-4582 | Larry Boggess |
| New Jersey Conference | 2303 Brunswick Ave | Lawrenceville, NJ | 08648 | 609-802-0840 | 396-9273 | Sadrail Saint-Ulysse |
| Ohio Conference | PO Box 1230 | Mount Vernon, OH | 43050-8230 | 740-397-4665 | 397-1648 | Ken Knudsen |
| Pennsylvania Conference | 720 Museum Rd | Reading, PA | 19611-1429 | 610-374-8331 | 374-9331 | Ray Hartwell |
| Potomac Conference | 606 Greenville Ave | Staunton, VA | 24401-4881 | 540-886-0771 | 886-5734 | Keith Hallam |
| **Lake Union Conference** | **PO Box 287** | **Berrien Springs, MI** | **49103** | **269-473-8200** | **471-7920** | **Garry Sudds** |
| Illinois Conference | 619 Plainfield Rd | Willowbrook, IL | 60527 | 630-856-2890 | 734-0929 | Ruth Horton Ed.D. |
| Indiana Conference | 15205 Westfield Blvd | Carmel, IN | 46032 | 317-844-6201 | 571-9281 | Herb Wrate |
| Lake Region Conference | 8517 S State St | Chicago, IL | 60619-5697 | 773-846-2661 | 846-5309 | Renee Humphreys |
| Michigan Conference | PO Box 24187 | Lansing, MI | 48909 | 517-316-1550 | 316-1501 | Diane Barlow |
| Wisconsin Conference | PO Box 100 | Fall River, WI | 53932 | 920-484-6555 | 484-6550 | Linda Rosen |
| **Mid-America Union Conference** | **PO Box 6128** | **Lincoln, NE** | **68506-0128** | **402-484-3000** | **483-4453** | **John Kriegelstein** |
| Central States Conference | 3301 Parallel Pkwy | Kansas City, KS | 66104-4354 | 913-371-1071 | 371-1609 | Judith Mason |
| Dakota Conference | 7200 N Washington St | Bismarck, ND | 58503 | 701-751-6177 | 751-6178 | Gerard Ban |
| Iowa-Missouri Conference | PO Box 65665 | West Des Moines, IA | 50265-0665 | 515-223-1197 | 223-5692 | Dr. Joseph Allison |
| Kansas-Nebraska Conference | 3440 SW Urish Rd | Topeka, KS | 66614-4601 | 785-478-4726 | 478-1000 | Gary Kruger |
| Minnesota Conference | 7384 Kirkwood Ct | Maple Grove, MN | 55369-5200 | 763-424-8923 | 424-9576 | Connie McCormick |
| Rocky Mountain Conference | 2520 S Downing St | Denver, CO | 80210-5818 | 303-282-3650 | 733-1843 | Lonnie Hetterle |
| **North Pacific Union Conference** | **5709 N 20th St** | **Ridgefield, WA** | **98642-7724** | **360-857-7000** | **857-7001** | **Dennis Plubell** |
| Alaska Conference | 6100 OMalley Rd | Anchorage, AK | 99507-6958 | 907-346-1004 | 346-3279 | Laurie Hosey |
| Idaho Conference | 7777 W Fairview Ave | Boise, ID | 83704-8418 | 208-375-7524 | 375-7526 | Patrick Frey |
| Montana Conference | 175 Canyon View Rd | Bozeman, MT | 59715-0607 | 406-587-3101 | 587-1598 | Phil Hudema |
| Oregon Conference | 19800 Oatfield Rd | Gladstone, OR | 97027 | 503-850-3500 | 654-5657 | Gale Crosby |
| Upper Columbia Conference | 3715 S Grove Rd | Spokane, WA | 99224 | 509-838-2761 | 838-4882 | Larry Marsh |
| Washington Conference | 32229 Weyerhaeuser Way S | Federal Way, WA | 98001 | 253-681-6008 | 681-6009 | Archie Harris |
| **Pacific Union Conference** | **PO Box 5005** | **Westlake Vlg, CA** | **91359-5005** | **805-413-7314** | **413-7319** | **Berit von Pohle** |
| Arizona Conference | PO Box 12340 | Scottsdale, AZ | 85267-2340 | 480-991-6777 | 991-4833 | Gus Martin |

| Conference | Address | City,State | Zip code | Telephone | Fax | Superintendent |
|---|---|---|---|---|---|---|
| Central California Conference | PO Box 770 | Clovis, CA | 93613-0770 | 559-347-3059 | 347-3054 | David Gillham |
| Hawaii Conference | 2728 Pali Hwy | Honolulu, HI | 96817-1485 | 808-595-7591 | 595-2345 | Miki Akeo Nelson |
| Nevada-Utah Conference | 10475 Double R Blvd | Reno, NV | 89521 | 775-322-6929 | 322-9371 | Arlyn Sundsted |
| Northern California Conference | PO Box 23165 | Pleasant Hill, CA | 94523-0165 | 925-603-5061 | 599-1304 | Bill Keresoma |
| Southeastern California Conference | PO Box 79990 | Riverside, CA | 92513 | 951-509-2307 | 509-2392 | Donald Dudley |
| Southern California Conference | PO Box 969 | Glendale, CA | 91209-0969 | 818-546-8400 | 546-8454 | Dr. Harold Crook |
| **Southern Union Conference** | **PO Box 923868** | **Norcross, GA** | **30010** | **770-408-1800** | **408-1801** | **Debra Fryson** |
| Carolina Conference | PO Box 44270 | Charlotte, NC | 28215 | 704-596-3200 | 596-5775 | Gary Rouse |
| Florida Conference | PO Box 2626 | Winter Park, FL | 32790-2626 | 407-644-5000 | 644-7550 | Frank Runnels Ed.D. |
| Georgia-Cumberland Conference | PO Box 12000 | Calhoun, GA | 30703-7001 | 706-629-7951 | 625-3684 | Kevin Kossick |
| Gulf States Conference | PO Box 240249 | Montgomery, AL | 36124-0249 | 334-272-7493 | 272-7987 | Stan Hobbs |
| Kentucky-Tennessee Conference | PO Box 1088 | Goodlettsville, TN | 37070-1088 | 615-859-1391 | 859-2120 | Chris Juhl |
| South Atlantic Conference | 3978 Memorial Dr | Decatur, GA | 30032 | 404-792-0535 | 792-7817 | Dr. James Lamb |
| South Central Conference | PO Box 78767 | Nashville, TN | 37207 | 615-226-6500 | 262-9141 | Dr. Eunice Warfield |
| Southeastern Conference | 1701 Robie Ave | Mount Dora, FL | 32757-6339 | 352-735-3142 | 735-3562 | Hubert Moril |
| **Southwestern Union Conference** | **PO Box 4000** | **Burleson, TX** | **76097-1630** | **817-295-0476** | **447-2443** | **Randy Gilliam** |
| Arkansas-Louisiana Conference | PO Box 31000 | Shreveport, LA | 71130-1000 | 318-631-6240 | 631-7611 | Steve Burton |
| Oklahoma Conference | PO Box 32098 | Oklahoma City, OK | 73123-0298 | 405-721-6110 | 721-7594 | Jack Francisco |
| Southwest Region Conference | PO Box 226289 | Dallas, TX | 75222-6289 | 214-943-4491 | 946-2528 | Samuel Green |
| Texas Conference | PO Box 800 | Alvarado, TX | 76009-0800 | 817-790-2255 | 783-5266 | John Hopps |
| Texico Conference | PO Box 1366 | Corrales, NM | 87048-1366 | 505-244-1611 | 244-1811 | Derral Reeve |